# The Lutheran Annual 2001

## of The Lutheran Church—Missouri Synod



*Compiled by*

Department of General Services
Office of Rosters and Statistics

*Published by*

1333 S. Kirkwood Road
St. Louis, MO 63122-7295

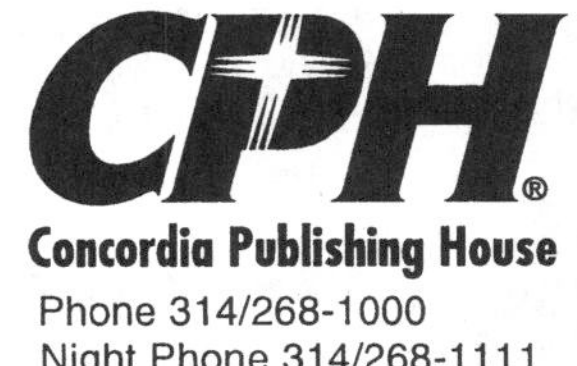


Phone 314/268-1000
Night Phone 314/268-1111

During the LWML's 60 years, they have funded more than 255 mission grants from over 14.5 million dollars.

---



For updates, corrections, or other changes regarding the roster and certified lay sections of the Lutheran Annual, notification must be sent in writing to the Office of Rosters and Statistics, The Lutheran Church—Missouri Synod, 1333 S. Kirkwood Rd., St. Louis, MO 63122-7295.

Advertising Policy: Concordia Publishing House reviews each ad for propriety and consistency with its mission. Acceptance of advertising does not constitute endorsement of the product or service and Concordia Publishing House cannot be held responsible for merchandise or claims made by its advertisers. Information on advertising placement is available through Concordia Publishing House, Attn: Lutheran Annual Advertising, 3558 S. Jefferson Ave., St. Louis, MO 63118. Phone (314) 268-1108.

# CONTENTS

## 2000 Church Festivals and Civil Holidays

New Year's Day . . . . . . . . . . . . . . . . . . January 1
Epiphany . . . . . . . . . . . . . . . . . . . . . . . . January 6
Martin Luther King Day . . . . . . . . . . . . January 15
Lincoln's Birthday . . . . . . . . . . . . . . . February 12
Washington's Birthday . . . . . . . . . . . . February 22
Ash Wednesday . . . . . . . . . . . . . . . . February 28
Palm Sunday . . . . . . . . . . . . . . . . . . . . . . . April 8
Good Friday . . . . . . . . . . . . . . . . . . . . . . . April 13
Easter . . . . . . . . . . . . . . . . . . . . . . . . . . . April 15
Easter Monday (Canada) . . . . . . . . . . . . . April 16
National Day of Prayer . . . . . . . . . . . . . . . . May 3

Mother's Day . . . . . . . . . . . . . . . . . . . . . . May 13
Armed Forces Day . . . . . . . . . . . . . . . . . May 19
Victoria Day (Canada) . . . . . . . . . . . . . . . May 21
Ascension Day . . . . . . . . . . . . . . . . . . . . May 24
Memorial Day . . . . . . . . . . . . . . . . . . . . . May 28
Pentecost (Whitsunday) . . . . . . . . . . . . . . . June 3
Trinity Sunday . . . . . . . . . . . . . . . . . . . . June 10
Flag Day . . . . . . . . . . . . . . . . . . . . . . . . . June 14
Father's Day . . . . . . . . . . . . . . . . . . . . . . June 17
Canada Day . . . . . . . . . . . . . . . . . . . . . . . . July 1
U.S. Independence Day . . . . . . . . . . . . . . . July 4

Labor Day . . . . . . . . . . . . . . . . . . . . . September 3
Citizenship Day . . . . . . . . . . . . . . . . September 17
Columbus Day . . . . . . . . . . . . . . . . . . . . October 8
Thanksgiving Day (Canada) . . . . . . . . . . October 8
United Nations Day . . . . . . . . . . . . . . . October 24
Reformation Day . . . . . . . . . . . . . . . . . October 31
Veterans Day . . . . . . . . . . . . . . . . . . November 11
Remembrance Day (Canada) . . . . . . November 11
Thanksgiving Day (U.S.) . . . . . . . . . . November 22
Advent Sunday . . . . . . . . . . . . . . . . . December 2
Christmas Day . . . . . . . . . . . . . . . . . December 25

Certain other days are fixed by proclamation. Only church days are noted in the daily calendar.

### • CALENDAR FOR 2000 •

**JANUARY**

| S | M | T | W | T | F | S |
|---|---|---|---|---|---|---|
| | | | | | | 1 |
| 2 | 3 | 4 | 5 | 6 | 7 | 8 |
| 9 | 10 | 11 | 12 | 13 | 14 | 15 |
| 16 | 17 | 18 | 19 | 20 | 21 | 22 |
| 23 | 24 | 25 | 26 | 27 | 28 | 29 |
| 30 | 31 | | | | | |

**FEBRUARY**

| S | M | T | W | T | F | S |
|---|---|---|---|---|---|---|
| | | 1 | 2 | 3 | 4 | 5 |
| 6 | 7 | 8 | 9 | 10 | 11 | 12 |
| 13 | 14 | 15 | 16 | 17 | 18 | 19 |
| 20 | 21 | 22 | 23 | 24 | 25 | 26 |
| 27 | 28 | 29 | | | | |

**MARCH**

| S | M | T | W | T | F | S |
|---|---|---|---|---|---|---|
| | | | 1 | 2 | 3 | 4 |
| 5 | 6 | 7 | 8 | 9 | 10 | 11 |
| 12 | 13 | 14 | 15 | 16 | 17 | 18 |
| 19 | 20 | 21 | 22 | 23 | 24 | 25 |
| 26 | 27 | 28 | 29 | 30 | 31 | |

**APRIL**

| S | M | T | W | T | F | S |
|---|---|---|---|---|---|---|
| | | | | | | 1 |
| 2 | 3 | 4 | 5 | 6 | 7 | 8 |
| 9 | 10 | 11 | 12 | 13 | 14 | 15 |
| 16 | 17 | 18 | 19 | 20 | 21 | 22 |
| 23 | 24 | 25 | 26 | 27 | 28 | 29 |
| 30 | | | | | | |

**MAY**

| S | M | T | W | T | F | S |
|---|---|---|---|---|---|---|
| | 1 | 2 | 3 | 4 | 5 | 6 |
| 7 | 8 | 9 | 10 | 11 | 12 | 13 |
| 14 | 15 | 16 | 17 | 18 | 19 | 20 |
| 21 | 22 | 23 | 24 | 25 | 26 | 27 |
| 28 | 29 | 30 | 31 | | | |

**JUNE**

| S | M | T | W | T | F | S |
|---|---|---|---|---|---|---|
| | | | | 1 | 2 | 3 |
| 4 | 5 | 6 | 7 | 8 | 9 | 10 |
| 11 | 12 | 13 | 14 | 15 | 16 | 17 |
| 18 | 19 | 20 | 21 | 22 | 23 | 24 |
| 25 | 26 | 27 | 28 | 29 | 30 | |

**JULY**

| S | M | T | W | T | F | S |
|---|---|---|---|---|---|---|
| | | | | | | 1 |
| 2 | 3 | 4 | 5 | 6 | 7 | 8 |
| 9 | 10 | 11 | 12 | 13 | 14 | 15 |
| 16 | 17 | 18 | 19 | 20 | 21 | 22 |
| 23 | 24 | 25 | 26 | 27 | 28 | 29 |
| 30 | 31 | | | | | |

**AUGUST**

| S | M | T | W | T | F | S |
|---|---|---|---|---|---|---|
| | | 1 | 2 | 3 | 4 | 5 |
| 6 | 7 | 8 | 9 | 10 | 11 | 12 |
| 13 | 14 | 15 | 16 | 17 | 18 | 19 |
| 20 | 21 | 22 | 23 | 24 | 25 | 26 |
| 27 | 28 | 29 | 30 | 31 | | |

**SEPTEMBER**

| S | M | T | W | T | F | S |
|---|---|---|---|---|---|---|
| | | | | | 1 | 2 |
| 3 | 4 | 5 | 6 | 7 | 8 | 9 |
| 10 | 11 | 12 | 13 | 14 | 15 | 16 |
| 17 | 18 | 19 | 20 | 21 | 22 | 23 |
| 24 | 25 | 26 | 27 | 28 | 29 | 30 |

**OCTOBER**

| S | M | T | W | T | F | S |
|---|---|---|---|---|---|---|
| 1 | 2 | 3 | 4 | 5 | 6 | 7 |
| 8 | 9 | 10 | 11 | 12 | 13 | 14 |
| 15 | 16 | 17 | 18 | 19 | 20 | 21 |
| 22 | 23 | 24 | 25 | 26 | 27 | 28 |
| 29 | 30 | 31 | | | | |

**NOVEMBER**

| S | M | T | W | T | F | S |
|---|---|---|---|---|---|---|
| | | | 1 | 2 | 3 | 4 |
| 5 | 6 | 7 | 8 | 9 | 10 | 11 |
| 12 | 13 | 14 | 15 | 16 | 17 | 18 |
| 19 | 20 | 21 | 22 | 23 | 24 | 25 |
| 26 | 27 | 28 | 29 | 30 | | |

**DECEMBER**

| S | M | T | W | T | F | S |
|---|---|---|---|---|---|---|
| | | | | | 1 | 2 |
| 3 | 4 | 5 | 6 | 7 | 8 | 9 |
| 10 | 11 | 12 | 13 | 14 | 15 | 16 |
| 17 | 18 | 19 | 20 | 21 | 22 | 23 |
| 24 | 25 | 26 | 27 | 28 | 29 | 30 |
| 31 | | | | | | |

### • CALENDAR FOR 2001 •

**JANUARY**

| S | M | T | W | T | F | S |
|---|---|---|---|---|---|---|
| | 1 | 2 | 3 | 4 | 5 | 6 |
| 7 | 8 | 9 | 10 | 11 | 12 | 13 |
| 14 | 15 | 16 | 17 | 18 | 19 | 20 |
| 21 | 22 | 23 | 24 | 25 | 26 | 27 |
| 28 | 29 | 30 | 31 | | | |

**FEBRUARY**

| S | M | T | W | T | F | S |
|---|---|---|---|---|---|---|
| | | | | 1 | 2 | 3 |
| 4 | 5 | 6 | 7 | 8 | 9 | 10 |
| 11 | 12 | 13 | 14 | 15 | 16 | 17 |
| 18 | 19 | 20 | 21 | 22 | 23 | 24 |
| 25 | 26 | 27 | 28 | | | |

**MARCH**

| S | M | T | W | T | F | S |
|---|---|---|---|---|---|---|
| | | | | 1 | 2 | 3 |
| 4 | 5 | 6 | 7 | 8 | 9 | 10 |
| 11 | 12 | 13 | 14 | 15 | 16 | 17 |
| 18 | 19 | 20 | 21 | 22 | 23 | 24 |
| 25 | 26 | 27 | 28 | 29 | 30 | 31 |

**APRIL**

| S | M | T | W | T | F | S |
|---|---|---|---|---|---|---|
| 1 | 2 | 3 | 4 | 5 | 6 | 7 |
| 8 | 9 | 10 | 11 | 12 | 13 | 14 |
| 15 | 16 | 17 | 18 | 19 | 20 | 21 |
| 22 | 23 | 24 | 25 | 26 | 27 | 28 |
| 29 | 30 | | | | | |

**MAY**

| S | M | T | W | T | F | S |
|---|---|---|---|---|---|---|
| | | 1 | 2 | 3 | 4 | 5 |
| 6 | 7 | 8 | 9 | 10 | 11 | 12 |
| 13 | 14 | 15 | 16 | 17 | 18 | 19 |
| 20 | 21 | 22 | 23 | 24 | 25 | 26 |
| 27 | 28 | 29 | 30 | 31 | | |

**JUNE**

| S | M | T | W | T | F | S |
|---|---|---|---|---|---|---|
| | | | | | 1 | 2 |
| 3 | 4 | 5 | 6 | 7 | 8 | 9 |
| 10 | 11 | 12 | 13 | 14 | 15 | 16 |
| 17 | 18 | 19 | 20 | 21 | 22 | 23 |
| 24 | 25 | 26 | 27 | 28 | 29 | 30 |

**JULY**

| S | M | T | W | T | F | S |
|---|---|---|---|---|---|---|
| 1 | 2 | 3 | 4 | 5 | 6 | 7 |
| 8 | 9 | 10 | 11 | 12 | 13 | 14 |
| 15 | 16 | 17 | 18 | 19 | 20 | 21 |
| 22 | 23 | 24 | 25 | 26 | 27 | 28 |
| 29 | 30 | 31 | | | | |

**AUGUST**

| S | M | T | W | T | F | S |
|---|---|---|---|---|---|---|
| | | | 1 | 2 | 3 | 4 |
| 5 | 6 | 7 | 8 | 9 | 10 | 11 |
| 12 | 13 | 14 | 15 | 16 | 17 | 18 |
| 19 | 20 | 21 | 22 | 23 | 24 | 25 |
| 26 | 27 | 28 | 29 | 30 | 31 | |

**SEPTEMBER**

| S | M | T | W | T | F | S |
|---|---|---|---|---|---|---|
| | | | | | | 1 |
| 2 | 3 | 4 | 5 | 6 | 7 | 8 |
| 9 | 10 | 11 | 12 | 13 | 14 | 15 |
| 16 | 17 | 18 | 19 | 20 | 21 | 22 |
| 23 | 24 | 25 | 26 | 27 | 28 | 29 |
| 30 | | | | | | |

**OCTOBER**

| S | M | T | W | T | F | S |
|---|---|---|---|---|---|---|
| | 1 | 2 | 3 | 4 | 5 | 6 |
| 7 | 8 | 9 | 10 | 11 | 12 | 13 |
| 14 | 15 | 16 | 17 | 18 | 19 | 20 |
| 21 | 22 | 23 | 24 | 25 | 26 | 27 |
| 28 | 29 | 30 | 31 | | | |

**NOVEMBER**

| S | M | T | W | T | F | S |
|---|---|---|---|---|---|---|
| | | | | 1 | 2 | 3 |
| 4 | 5 | 6 | 7 | 8 | 9 | 10 |
| 11 | 12 | 13 | 14 | 15 | 16 | 17 |
| 18 | 19 | 20 | 21 | 22 | 23 | 24 |
| 25 | 26 | 27 | 28 | 29 | 30 | |

**DECEMBER**

| S | M | T | W | T | F | S |
|---|---|---|---|---|---|---|
| | | | | | | 1 |
| 2 | 3 | 4 | 5 | 6 | 7 | 8 |
| 9 | 10 | 11 | 12 | 13 | 14 | 15 |
| 16 | 17 | 18 | 19 | 20 | 21 | 22 |
| 23 | 24 | 25 | 26 | 27 | 28 | 29 |
| 30 | 31 | | | | | |

### • CALENDAR FOR 2002 •

**JANUARY**

| S | M | T | W | T | F | S |
|---|---|---|---|---|---|---|
| | | 1 | 2 | 3 | 4 | 5 |
| 6 | 7 | 8 | 9 | 10 | 11 | 12 |
| 13 | 14 | 15 | 16 | 17 | 18 | 19 |
| 20 | 21 | 22 | 23 | 24 | 25 | 26 |
| 27 | 28 | 29 | 30 | 31 | | |

**FEBRUARY**

| S | M | T | W | T | F | S |
|---|---|---|---|---|---|---|
| | | | | | 1 | 2 |
| 3 | 4 | 5 | 6 | 7 | 8 | 9 |
| 10 | 11 | 12 | 13 | 14 | 15 | 16 |
| 17 | 18 | 19 | 20 | 21 | 22 | 23 |
| 24 | 25 | 26 | 27 | 28 | | |

**MARCH**

| S | M | T | W | T | F | S |
|---|---|---|---|---|---|---|
| | | | | | 1 | 2 |
| 3 | 4 | 5 | 6 | 7 | 8 | 9 |
| 10 | 11 | 12 | 13 | 14 | 15 | 16 |
| 17 | 18 | 19 | 20 | 21 | 22 | 23 |
| 24 | 25 | 26 | 27 | 28 | 29 | 30 |
| 31 | | | | | | |

**APRIL**

| S | M | T | W | T | F | S |
|---|---|---|---|---|---|---|
| | 1 | 2 | 3 | 4 | 5 | 6 |
| 7 | 8 | 9 | 10 | 11 | 12 | 13 |
| 14 | 15 | 16 | 17 | 18 | 19 | 20 |
| 21 | 22 | 23 | 24 | 25 | 26 | 27 |
| 28 | 29 | 30 | | | | |

**MAY**

| S | M | T | W | T | F | S |
|---|---|---|---|---|---|---|
| | | | 1 | 2 | 3 | 4 |
| 5 | 6 | 7 | 8 | 9 | 10 | 11 |
| 12 | 13 | 14 | 15 | 16 | 17 | 18 |
| 19 | 20 | 21 | 22 | 23 | 24 | 25 |
| 26 | 27 | 28 | 29 | 30 | 31 | |

**JUNE**

| S | M | T | W | T | F | S |
|---|---|---|---|---|---|---|
| | | | | | | 1 |
| 2 | 3 | 4 | 5 | 6 | 7 | 8 |
| 9 | 10 | 11 | 12 | 13 | 14 | 15 |
| 16 | 17 | 18 | 19 | 20 | 21 | 22 |
| 23 | 24 | 25 | 26 | 27 | 28 | 29 |
| 30 | | | | | | |

**JULY**

| S | M | T | W | T | F | S |
|---|---|---|---|---|---|---|
| | 1 | 2 | 3 | 4 | 5 | 6 |
| 7 | 8 | 9 | 10 | 11 | 12 | 13 |
| 14 | 15 | 16 | 17 | 18 | 19 | 20 |
| 21 | 22 | 23 | 24 | 25 | 26 | 27 |
| 28 | 29 | 30 | 31 | | | |

**AUGUST**

| S | M | T | W | T | F | S |
|---|---|---|---|---|---|---|
| | | | | 1 | 2 | 3 |
| 4 | 5 | 6 | 7 | 8 | 9 | 10 |
| 11 | 12 | 13 | 14 | 15 | 16 | 17 |
| 18 | 19 | 20 | 21 | 22 | 23 | 24 |
| 25 | 26 | 27 | 28 | 29 | 30 | 31 |

**SEPTEMBER**

| S | M | T | W | T | F | S |
|---|---|---|---|---|---|---|
| 1 | 2 | 3 | 4 | 5 | 6 | 7 |
| 8 | 9 | 10 | 11 | 12 | 13 | 14 |
| 15 | 16 | 17 | 18 | 19 | 20 | 21 |
| 22 | 23 | 24 | 25 | 26 | 27 | 28 |
| 29 | 30 | | | | | |

**OCTOBER**

| S | M | T | W | T | F | S |
|---|---|---|---|---|---|---|
| | | 1 | 2 | 3 | 4 | 5 |
| 6 | 7 | 8 | 9 | 10 | 11 | 12 |
| 13 | 14 | 15 | 16 | 17 | 18 | 19 |
| 20 | 21 | 22 | 23 | 24 | 25 | 26 |
| 27 | 28 | 29 | 30 | 31 | | |

**NOVEMBER**

| S | M | T | W | T | F | S |
|---|---|---|---|---|---|---|
| | | | | | 1 | 2 |
| 3 | 4 | 5 | 6 | 7 | 8 | 9 |
| 10 | 11 | 12 | 13 | 14 | 15 | 16 |
| 17 | 18 | 19 | 20 | 21 | 22 | 23 |
| 24 | 25 | 26 | 27 | 28 | 29 | 30 |

**DECEMBER**

| S | M | T | W | T | F | S |
|---|---|---|---|---|---|---|
| 1 | 2 | 3 | 4 | 5 | 6 | 7 |
| 8 | 9 | 10 | 11 | 12 | 13 | 14 |
| 15 | 16 | 17 | 18 | 19 | 20 | 21 |
| 22 | 23 | 24 | 25 | 26 | 27 | 28 |
| 29 | 30 | 31 | | | | |

## The Movable Festivals of the Church Year

The date of Easter determines the dates of all the movable festivals and days of the church year except those in Advent. *Advent 1* is always the Sunday nearest November 30, whether before or after. When the date of Easter has been determined, the church year will be arranged as follows:

*Ash Wednesday*, the beginning of Lent, is the Wednesday before the sixth Sunday before Easter (the 40th weekday before Easter). *Ascension* is on the Thursday after the sixth Sunday of Easter. *Pentecost* is seven weeks after Easter.

### Movable Dates in the Church Year, 1997–2017

| Year | Sundays after Epiphany | Ash Wednesday | Easter | Ascension | Pentecost | Sundays after Pentecost | First Advent Sunday |
|---|---|---|---|---|---|---|---|
| 1997 | 5 | Feb. 12 | March 30 | May 8 | May 18 | 27 | Nov. 30 |
| 1998 | 7 | Feb. 25 | April 12 | May 21 | May 31 | 25 | Nov. 29 |
| 1999 | 6 | Feb. 17 | April 4 | May 13 | May 23 | 26 | Nov. 28 |
| 2000 | 9 | March 8 | April 23 | June 1 | June 11 | 24 | Dec. 3 |
| 2001 | 8 | Feb. 28 | April 15 | May 24 | June 3 | 25 | Dec. 2 |
| 2002 | 5 | Feb. 13 | March 31 | May 9 | May 19 | 27 | Dec. 1 |
| 2003 | 8 | March 5 | April 20 | May 29 | June 8 | 24 | Nov. 30 |
| 2004 | 7 | Feb. 25 | April 11 | May 20 | May 30 | 25 | Nov. 28 |
| 2005 | 5 | Feb. 9 | March 27 | May 5 | May 15 | 27 | Nov. 27 |
| 2006 | 8 | March 1 | April 16 | May 25 | June 4 | 25 | Dec. 3 |
| 2007 | 7 | Feb. 21 | April 8 | May 17 | May 27 | 26 | Dec. 2 |
| 2008 | 4 | Feb. 6 | March 23 | May 1 | May 11 | 28 | Nov. 30 |
| 2009 | 7 | Feb. 25 | April 12 | May 21 | May 31 | 25 | Nov. 29 |
| 2010 | 6 | Feb. 17 | April 4 | May 13 | May 23 | 26 | Nov. 28 |
| 2011 | 9 | March 9 | April 24 | June 2 | June 12 | 23 | Nov. 27 |
| 2012 | 7 | Feb. 22 | April 8 | May 17 | May 27 | 26 | Dec. 2 |
| 2013 | 5 | Feb. 13 | March 31 | May 9 | May 19 | 27 | Dec. 1 |
| 2014 | 8 | March 5 | April 20 | May 29 | June 8 | 24 | Nov. 30 |
| 2015 | 6 | Feb. 18 | April 5 | May 14 | May 24 | 26 | Nov. 29 |
| 2016 | 5 | Feb. 10 | March 27 | May 5 | May 15 | 27 | Nov. 27 |
| 2017 | 8 | March 1 | April 16 | May 25 | June 4 | 25 | Dec. 3 |

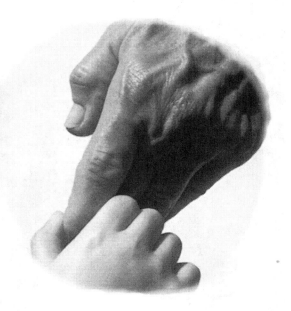

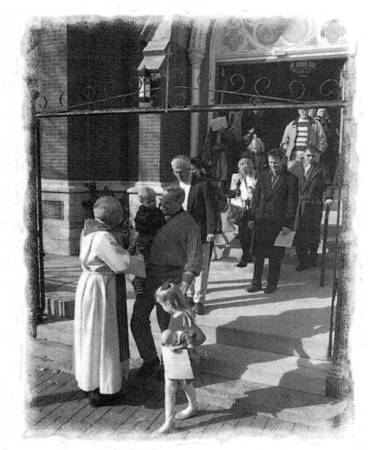

# JANUARY 2001

| Daily Lectionary | Dates of Historical Significance | Readings and Hymn of the Day | | Liturgical Color |
|---|---|---|---|---|
| 1 Mon Luke 1:68–79 & Mark 2 | **New Year's Day, *The Circumcision of Our Lord*** | | | White |
| 2 Tue Ps. 30 & Mark 3 | J. K. Wilhelm Loehe, d. 1872 | | | |
| 3 Wed Ps. 31 & Mark 4 | | | | |
| 4 Thu Ps. 32 & Mark 5 | Concordia Theological Seminary, Springfield, Ill., ded. 1874 | | | |
| 5 Fri Ps. 33 & Mark 6 | C. F. W. Walther arrived at New Orleans, 1839 | | | |
| **6 THE EPIPHANY OF OUR LORD** | ***R:*** Is. 60:1–6<br>***H:*** *LW* 73—O Morning Star, How Fair and Bright | ***E:*** Eph. 3:2–12 | ***G:*** Matt. 2:1–12 | White |
| 6 Sat Ps. 34 & Mark 7 | | | | |
| **7 THE BAPTISM OF OUR LORD**<br>**First Sunday after the Epiphany** | ***R:*** Is. 42:1–7<br>***H:*** *LW* 223—To Jordan Came the Christ, Our Lord | ***E:*** Acts 10:34–38 | ***G:*** Luke 3:15–17, 21–22 | White |
| 7 Sun Ps. 35 & Mark 8 | | | | |
| 8 Mon Ps. 36 & Mark 9 | J. A. O. Preus, 8th LCMS pres., b. 1920 | | | |
| 9 Tue Ps. 37 & Mark 10 | | | | |
| 10 Wed Ps. 38 & Mark 11 | | | | |
| 11 Thu Ps. 39 & Mark 12 | Walter A. Maier, Luth. Hour speaker, d. 1950 | | | |
| 12 Fri Ps. 40 & Mark 13 | | | | |
| 13 Sat Ps. 41 & Mark 14 | | | | |
| **14 SECOND SUNDAY**<br>**AFTER THE EPIPHANY** | ***R:*** Is. 62:1–5<br>***H:*** *LW* 270—Jesus, Priceless Treasure | ***E:*** 1 Cor. 12:1–11 | ***G:*** John 2:1–11 | Green |
| 14 Sun Ps. 42 & Mark 15–16 | | | | |
| 15 Mon Ps. 43 & Gen. 1–3 | | | | |
| 16 Tue Ps. 44 & Gen. 4–6 | | | | |
| 17 Wed Ps. 45 & Gen. 7–9 | | | | |
| 18 Thu Ps. 46 & Gen. 10–12 | **The Confession of St. Peter** | | | White |
| 19 Fri Ps. 47 & Gen. 13–15 | | | | |
| 20 Sat Ps. 48 & Gen. 16–18 | | | | |
| **21 THIRD SUNDAY**<br>**AFTER THE EPIPHANY** | ***R:*** Is. 61:1–6<br>***H:*** *LW* 314—O Christ, Our Light, O Radiance True | ***E:*** 1 Cor. 12:12–21, 26–27 | ***G:*** Luke 4:14–21 | Green |
| 21 Sun Ps. 49 & Gen. 19–21 | | | | |
| 22 Mon Ps. 50 & Gen. 22–24 | | | | |
| 23 Tue Ps. 51 & Gen. 25–27 | | | | |
| 24 Wed Ps. 52 & Gen. 28–30 | **St. Timothy, Pastor and Confessor** | | | White |
| 25 Thu Ps. 53 & Gen. 31–33 | **The Conversion of St. Paul** | | | White |
| 26 Fri Ps. 54 & Gen. 34–36 | **St. Titus, Pastor and Confessor** | | | White |
| 27 Sat Ps. 55 & Gen. 37–39 | | | | |
| **28 FOURTH SUNDAY**<br>**AFTER THE EPIPHANY** | ***R:*** Jer. 1:4–10<br>***H:*** *LW* 358—Seek Where You May to Find a Way | ***E:*** 1 Cor. 12:27–13:13 | ***G:*** Luke 4:21–32 | Green |
| 28 Sun Ps. 56 & Gen. 40–42 | | | | |
| 29 Mon Ps. 57 & Gen. 43–45 | | | | |
| 30 Tue Ps. 58 & Gen. 46–48 | | | | |
| 31 Wed Luke 1:68–79 & Gen. 49–50 | | | | |

# FEBRUARY 2001

| Daily Lectionary | Dates of Historical Significance | Readings and Hymn of the Day | | Liturgical Color |
|---|---|---|---|---|
| 1 Thu Luke 2:29–32 & Ex. 1–3 | | | | |
| 2 Fri Ps. 59 & Ex. 4–6 | **The Presentation of Our Lord** | | | White |
| 3 Sat Ps. 60 & Ex. 7–9 | | | | |
| **4 FIFTH SUNDAY**<br>**AFTER THE EPIPHANY** | ***R:*** Is. 6:1–8 (9–13)<br>***H:*** *LW* 82—Hail to the Lord's Anointed | ***E:*** 1 Cor. 14:12b–20 | ***G:*** Luke 5:1–11 | Green |
| 4 Sun Ps. 61 & Ex. 10–12 | | | | |
| 5 Mon Ps. 62 & Ex. 13–15 | | | | |
| 6 Tue Ps. 63 & Ex. 16–18 | | | | |
| 7 Wed Ps. 64 & Ex. 19–21 | | | | |
| 8 Thu Ps. 65 & Ex. 22–24 | | | | |
| 9 Fri Ps. 66 & Ex. 25–27 | | | | |
| 10 Sat Ps. 67 & Ex. 28–30 | | | | |
| **11 SIXTH SUNDAY**<br>**AFTER THE EPIPHANY** | ***R:*** Jer. 17:5–8<br>***H:*** *LW* 151—O Christ, Our Hope | ***E:*** 1 Cor. 15:12, 16–20 | ***G:*** Luke 6:17–26 | Green |
| 11 Sun Ps. 68 & Ex. 31–33 | | | | |
| 12 Mon Ps. 69 & Ex. 34–36 | | | | |
| 13 Tue Ps. 70 & Ex. 37–38 | | | | |
| 14 Wed Ps. 71 & Ex. 39–40 | | | | |
| 15 Thu Ps. 72 & Lev. 1–3 | | | | |
| 16 Fri Ps. 73 & Lev. 4–6 | | | | |
| 17 Sat Ps. 74 & Lev. 7–9 | | | | |
| **18 SEVENTH SUNDAY**<br>**AFTER THE EPIPHANY** | ***R:*** Gen. 45:3–8a, 15<br>***H:*** *LW* 453—My Soul, Now Praise Your Maker | ***E:*** 1 Cor. 15:35–38a, 42–50 | ***G:*** Luke 6:27–38 | Green |
| 18 Sun Ps. 75 & Lev. 10–12 | **Martin Luther, Doctor and Confessor,** d. 1546 | | | White |
| 19 Mon Ps. 76 & Lev. 13–15 | | | | |
| 20 Tue Ps. 77 & Lev. 16–18 | Ralph A. Bohlmann, 9th LCMS pres., b. 1932 | | | |
| 21 Wed Ps. 78 & Lev. 19–21 | J. K. Wilhelm Loehe, b. 1808 | | | |
| 22 Thu Ps. 79 & Lev. 22–24 | | | | |
| 23 Fri Ps. 80 & Lev. 25–27 | John W. Behnken, 6th LCMS pres., d. 1968 | | | |
| 24 Sat Ps. 81 & Num. 1–3 | **St. Matthias, Apostle** | | | Red |
| **25 THE TRANSFIGURATION OF OUR LORD**<br>**Last Sunday after the Epiphany** | ***R:*** Deut. 34:1–12<br>***H:*** *LW* 87—Oh, Wondrous Type! Oh, Vision Fair | ***E:*** 2 Cor. 4:3–6 | ***G:*** Luke 9:28–36 | White |

25 Sun Ps. 82 & Num. 4–6
26 Mon Ps. 83 & Num. 7–9
27 Tue Ps. 84 & Num. 10–12

**28 ASH WEDNESDAY** — ***R:*** Joel 2:12–19 ***E:*** 2 Cor. 5:20b–6:2 ***G:*** Matt. 6:1–6, 16–21 — Black/Purple
***H:*** *LW* 230—From Depths of Woe I Cry to You

28 Wed Luke 2:29–32 & Num. 13–15 — Concordia Publishing House ded. 1870

## MARCH 2001

1 Thu Is. 64:1–9 & Num. 16–18
2 Fri Ps. 85 & Num. 19–21
3 Sat Ps. 86 & Num. 22–24

**4 FIRST SUNDAY IN LENT** — ***R:*** Duet. 26:5–10 ***E:*** Rom. 10:8b–13 ***G:*** Luke 4:1–13 — Purple
***H:*** *LW* 297, 298—A Mighty Fortress Is Our God

4 Sun Ps. 87 & Num. 25–27
5 Mon Ps. 88 & Num. 28–30
6 Tue Ps. 89 & Num. 31–33
7 Wed Ps. 90 & Num. 34–36
8 Thu Ps. 91 & Deut. 1–3
9 Fri Ps. 92 & Deut. 4–6
10 Sat Ps. 93 & Deut. 7–9

**11 SECOND SUNDAY IN LENT** — ***R:*** Jer. 26:8–15 ***E:*** Phil. 3:17–4:1 ***G:*** Luke 13:31–35 — Purple
***H:*** *LW* 413—Lord, You I Love with All My Heart

11 Sun Ps. 94 & Deut. 10–12
12 Mon Ps. 95 & Deut. 13–15
13 Tue Ps. 96 & Deut. 16–18
14 Wed Ps. 97 & Deut. 19–21
15 Thu Ps. 98 & Deut. 22–24
16 Fri Ps. 99 & Deut. 25–27
17 Sat Ps. 100 & Deut. 28–30

**18 THIRD SUNDAY IN LENT** — ***R:*** Ex. 3:1–8a, 10–15 ***E:*** 1 Cor. 10:1–13 ***G:*** Luke 13:1–9 — Purple
***H:*** *LW* 288—May God Embrace Us with His Grace

18 Sun Ps. 101 & Deut. 31–34
19 Mon Ps. 102 & Luke 1
20 Tue Ps. 103 & Luke 2–3
21 Wed Ps. 104 & Luke 4–5 — Johann Sebastian Bach, b. 1685
22 Thu Ps. 105 & Luke 6–7
23 Fri Ps. 106 & Luke 8–9
24 Sat Ps. 107 & Luke 10–11

**25 FOURTH SUNDAY IN LENT** — ***R:*** Is. 12:1–6 ***E:*** 1 Cor. 1:18–31 or 1 Cor. 1:18, 22–25 ***G:*** Luke 15:1–3, 11–32 — Purple
***H:*** *LW* 357—I Trust, O Christ, in You Alone

25 Sun Ps. 108 & Luke 12–13 — **The Annunciation of Our Lord** — White
26 Mon Ps. 109 & Luke 14–15
27 Tue Ps. 110 & Luke 16–17
28 Wed Ps. 111 & Luke 18–19
29 Thu Ps. 112 & Luke 20–21
30 Fri Ps. 113 & Luke 22
31 Sat Is. 64:1–9 & Luke 23–24 — Concordia Historical Institute incorporated 1927

## APRIL 2001

**1 FIFTH SUNDAY IN LENT** — ***R:*** Is. 43:16–21 ***E:*** Phil. 3:8–14 ***G:*** Luke 20:9–19 — Purple
***H:*** *LW* 91—My Song Is Love Unknown

1 Sun Is. 25:1–9 & Rom 1–3
2 Mon Ps. 114 & Rom. 4–6
3 Tue Ps. 115 & Rom. 7–9
4 Wed Ps. 116 & Rom. 10–13
5 Thu Ps. 117 & Rom. 14–16 — H. C. Schwan, 3d LCMS pres., b. 1819
6 Fri Ps. 118 & 1 Cor. 1–3
7 Sat Ps. 119:1–8 & 1 Cor. 4–6

**8 PALM SUNDAY**
**Sunday of the Passion** — ***R:*** Deut. 32:36–39 ***E:*** Phil. 2:5–11 — Scarlet/Purple
***G:*** Luke 22:1–23:56 or Luke 23:1–49
***H:*** *LW* 105—Ride On, Ride On in Majesty

8 Sun Ps. 119:9–16 & 1 Cor. 7–9
9 Mon Ps. 119:17–24 & 1 Cor. 10–11
10 Tue Ps. 119:25–32 & 1 Cor. 12–14
11 Wed Ps. 119:33–40 & 1 Cor. 15–16

**12 MAUNDY THURSDAY** — ***R:*** Jer. 31:31–34 ***E:*** Heb. 10:15–39 ***G:*** Luke 22:7–20 — Scarlet/White
***H:*** *LW* 236, 237—Jesus Christ, Our Blessed Savior

12 Thu Ps. 119:41–48 & 2 Cor. 1–4

**13 GOOD FRIDAY** — ***R:*** Is. 52:13–53:12 or Hos. 6:1–6 ***E:*** Heb. 4:14–16; 5:7–9 — Black
***G:*** John 18:1–19:42 or John 19:17–30
***H:*** *LW* 111—A Lamb Alone Bears Willingly

13 Fri Ps. 119:49–56 & 2 Cor. 5–7
14 Sat Ps. 119:57–64 & 2 Cor. 8–10

**15 THE RESURRECTION OF OUR LORD**
**Easter Day** — ***R:*** Ex. 15:1–11 or Ps. 118:14–24 ***E:*** 1 Cor. 15:1–11 — White/Gold
***G:*** Luke 24:1–11 or John 20:1–9 (10–18)
***H:*** *LW* 123—Christ Jesus Lay in Death's Strong Bands

| | | |
|---|---|---|
| 15 Sun Ps. 119:65–72 & 2 Cor. 11–13 | Walther–Marbach Debate, Altenburg, Mo., 1841 | |
| 16 Mon Ps. 119:73–80 & Gal. 1–3 | | |
| 17 Tue Ps. 119:81–88 & Gal. 4–6 | | |
| 18 Wed Ps. 119:89–96 & Eph. 1–3 | | |
| 19 Thu Ps. 119:97–104 & Eph. 4–6 | | |
| 20 Fri Ps. 119:105–12 & Phil. 1–2 | | |
| 21 Sat Ps. 119:113–20 & Phil. 3–4 | | |

**22 SECOND SUNDAY OF EASTER** — ***R:*** Acts 5:12, 17–32 ***E:*** Rev. 1:4–18 ***G:*** John 20:19–31 — White
***H:*** *LW* 130—O Sons and Daughters of the King

| | | |
|---|---|---|
| 22 Sun Ps. 119:121–28 & Col. 1–2 | Fr. Pfotenhauer, 5th LCMS pres., b. 1859 | |
| 23 Mon Ps. 119:129–36 & Col. 3–4 | | |
| 24 Tue Ps. 119:137–44 & 1 Thess. 1–3 | | |
| 25 Wed Ps. 119:145–52 & 1 Thess. 4–5 | **St. Mark, Evangelist** | Red |
| 26 Thu Ps. 119:153–60 & 2 Thess. 1–3 | Missouri Synod organized, Chicago, 1847 | |
| 27 Fri Ps. 119:161–68 & 1 Tim. 1–3 | | |
| 28 Sat Ps. 119:169–76 & 1 Tim. 4–6 | | |

**29 THIRD SUNDAY OF EASTER** — ***R:*** Acts 9:1–20 ***E:*** Rev. 5:11–14 ***G:*** John 21:1–14 — White
***H:*** *LW* 134—With High Delight Let Us Unite

29 Sun Ps. 120 & 2 Tim. 1–2
30 Mon Is. 25:1–9 & 2 Tim. 3–4

## MAY 2001

| | | |
|---|---|---|
| 1 Tue 1 Sam. 2:1–10 & Titus, Philemon | **St. Philip and St. James, Apostles** | Red |
| 2 Wed Ps. 121 & Heb 1–4 | | |
| 3 Thu Ps. 122 & Heb. 5–7 | | |
| 4 Fri Ps. 123 & Heb 8–10 | Friedrich Konrad Dietrich Wyneken, 2nd LCMS pres., d. 1876 | |
| F. W. Husmann,1st sec. of LCMS, d. 1881 | | |
| 5 Sat Ps. 124 & Heb 11–13 | | |

**6 FOURTH SUNDAY OF EASTER** — ***R:*** Acts 13:15–16a, 26–33 ***E:*** Rev. 7:9–17 ***G:*** John 10:22–30 — White
***H:*** *LW* 412—The King of Love My Shepherd Is

| | | |
|---|---|---|
| 6 Sun Ps. 125 & James 1–3 | | |
| 7 Mon Ps. 126 & James 4–5 | **C. F. W. Walther, Doctor,** d. 1887 | White |
| 8 Tue Ps. 127 & 1 Peter 1–2 | | |
| 9 Wed Ps. 128 & 1 Peter 3–5 | | |
| 10 Thu Ps. 129 & 2 Peter | | |
| 11 Fri Ps. 130 & 1 John 1–3 | | |
| 12 Sat Ps. 131 & 1 John 4–5 | | |

**13 FIFTH SUNDAY OF EASTER** — ***R:*** Acts 13:44–52 ***E:*** Rev. 21:1–5 ***G:*** John 13:31–35 — White
***H:*** *LW* 126—At the Lamb's High Feast We Sing

| | | |
|---|---|---|
| 13 Sun Ps. 132 & 2 John, 3, John, Jude | Friedrich Konrad Dietrich Wyneken, LCMS pres., b. 1810 | |
| 14 Mon Ps. 133 & John 1–2 | Rosa Young, pioneer Alabama African American teacher, b. 1890 | |
| 15 Tue Ps. 134 & John 3–4 | English Synod joined LCMS 1911 | |
| 16 Wed Ps. 135 & John 5–6 | | |
| 17 Thu Ps. 136 & John 7–8 | | |
| 18 Fri Ps. 137 & John 9–10 | | |
| 19 Sat Ps. 138 & John 11–12 | | |

**20 SIXTH SUNDAY OF EASTER** — ***R:*** Acts 14:8–18 ***E:*** Rev. 21:10–14, 22–23 ***G:*** John 14:23–29 — White
***H:*** *LW* 353—Dear Christians, One and All, Rejoice

20 Sun Ps. 139 & John 13–14
21 Mon Ps. 140 & John 15–16
22 Tue Ps. 141 & John 17–18
23 Wed Ps. 142 & John 19

**24 THE ASCENSION OF OUR LORD** — ***R:*** Acts 1:1–11 ***E:*** Eph 1:16–23 ***G:*** Luke 24:44–53 — White
***H:*** *LW* 152—Up Through Endless Ranks of Angels

24 Thu Ps. 143 & John 20–21
25 Fri Ps. 144 & Acts 1–2
26 Sat Ps. 145 & Acts 3–4

**27 SEVENTH SUNDAY OF EASTER** — ***R:*** Acts 16:6–10 ***E:*** Rev. 22:12–17, 20 ***G:*** John 17:20–26 — White
***H:*** *LW* 271—Christ Is the World's Redeemer

| | | |
|---|---|---|
| 27 Sun Ps. 146 & Acts 5–6 | | |
| 28 Mon Ps. 147 & Acts 7–8 | | |
| 29 Tue Ps. 148 & Acts 9–10 | LCMS International Center ded. 1983 | |
| 30 Wed Ps. 149 & Acts 11–12 | | |
| 31 Thu 1 Sam. 2:1–10 & Acts 13–14 | **The Visitation** | White |

## JUNE 2001

1 Fri Is. 12:1–6 & Acts 15–16
2 Sat Ps. 150 & Acts 17–18

**3 PENTECOST** — ***R:*** Gen. 11:1–9 ***E:*** Acts 2:37–47 ***G:*** John 15:26–27; 16:4b–11 — Red
***H:*** *LW* 154—Come, Holy Ghost, God and Lord

| | | |
|---|---|---|
| 3 Sun Ps. 1 & Acts 19–20 | Franz A. O. Pieper, 4th LCMS pres., d. 1931<br>Oliver Harms, 7th LCMS pres., d. 1980 | |
| 4 Mon Ps. 2 & Acts 21–22 | | |
| 5 Tue Ps. 3 & Acts 23–24 | | |
| 6 Wed Ps. 4 & Acts 25–26 | | |
| 7 Thu Ps. 5 & Acts 27–28 | | |
| 8 Fri Ps. 6 & Joshua 1–5 | | |

9 Sat Ps. 7 & Joshua 6–8

| | | | | |
|---|---|---|---|---|
| 10 **THE HOLY TRINITY**<br>**First Sunday after Pentecost** | ***R:*** Prov. 8:22–31<br>***H:*** *LW* 156—Creator Spirit, Heavenly Dove | ***E:*** Rom. 5:1–5 | ***G:*** John 16:12–15 | White |

10 Sun Ps. 8 & Joshua 9–11
11 Mon Ps. 9 & Joshua 12–16 — **St. Barnabas, Apostle** — Red
First Concordia Seminary bldg., St. Louis, ded. 1850
12 Tue Ps. 10 & Joshua 17–21 — Walther Mausoleum, St. Louis, ded. 1892
13 Wed Ps. 11 & Joshua 22–24
14 Thu Ps. 12 & Judg. 1–3
15 Fri Ps. 13 & Judg. 4–6
16 Sat Ps. 14 & Judg. 7–9

| | | | | |
|---|---|---|---|---|
| 17 **SECOND SUNDAY**<br>**AFTER PENTECOST** | ***R:*** 1 Kings 8:(22–23, 27–30) 41–43<br>***H:*** *LW* 265—In the Very Midst of Life | ***E:*** Gal. 1:1–10 | ***G:*** Luke 7:1–10 | Green |

17 Sun Ps. 15 & Judg. 10–12
18 Mon Ps. 16 & Judg. 13–15
19 Tue Ps. 17 & Judg. 16–18
20 Wed Ps. 18 & Judg. 19–21
21 Thu Ps. 19 & Ruth
22 Fri Ps. 20 & 1 Sam. 1–3 — Lutheran Laymen's League org. 1917
23 Sat Ps. 21 & 1 Sam. 4–6

| | | | | |
|---|---|---|---|---|
| 24 **THE NATIVITY OF ST. JOHN THE BAPTIST**<br>**Third Sunday after Pentecost** | ***R:*** Malachi 3:1–4<br>***H:*** *LW* 187—When All the World Was Cursed | ***E:*** Acts 13:13–26 | ***G:*** Luke 1:57–67 (68–80) | White |

24 Sun Ps. 22 & 1 Sam. 7–9 — **The Nativity of St. John the Baptist**
25 Mon Ps. 23 & 1 Sam. 10–12 — **Presentation of the Augsburg Confession**
26 Tue Ps. 24 & 1 Sam. 13–15
27 Wed Ps. 25 & 1 Sam. 16–18 — Franz A. O. Pieper, 4th LCMS pres., b. 1852
28 Thu Ps. 26 & 1 Sam. 19–21
29 Fri Ps. 27 & 1 Sam.22–24 — **St. Peter and St. Paul, Apostles**
30 Sat Is. 12:1–6 & 1 Sam. 25–27 — Rosa Young, pioneer Alabama African American teacher, d. 1971

## JULY 2001

| | | | | |
|---|---|---|---|---|
| 1 **FOURTH SUNDAY**<br>**AFTER PENTECOST** | ***R:*** 2 Sam. 11:26–12:10, 13–15<br>***H:*** *LW* 352—God Loved the World So that He Gave | ***E:*** Gal. 2:11–21 | ***G:*** Luke 7:36–50 | Green |

1 Sun Deut. 32:1–4 & 1 Sam. 28–31
2 Mon Ps. 28 & 2 Sam. 1–3
3 Tue Ps. 29 & 2 Sam. 4–6
4 Wed Ps. 30 & 2 Sam. 7–9
5 Thu Ps. 31 & 2 Sam. 10–12
6 Fri Ps. 32 & 2 Sam 13–15
7 Sat Ps. 33 & 2 Sam.16–18

| | | | | |
|---|---|---|---|---|
| 8 **FIFTH SUNDAY**<br>**AFTER PENTECOST** | ***R:*** Zech. 12:7–10<br>***H:*** *LW* 381—Let Us Ever Walk with Jesus | ***E:*** Gal. 3:23–29 | ***G:*** Luke 9:18–24 | Green |

8 Sun Ps. 34 & 2 Sam. 19–21 — Lutheran Women's Missionary League org. 1942
9 Mon Ps. 35 & 2 Sam. 22–24
10 Tue Ps. 36 & 1 Kings 1–2 — Synodical Conference organized 1872
11 Wed Ps. 37 & 1 Kings 3–6
12 Thu Ps. 38 & 1 Kings 7–8
13 Fri Ps. 39 & 1 Kings 9–11
14 Sat Ps. 40 & 1 Kings 12–14

| | | | | |
|---|---|---|---|---|
| 15 **SIXTH SUNDAY**<br>**AFTER PENTECOST** | ***R:*** 1 Kings 19:14–21<br>***H:*** *LW* 382—"Take Up Your Cross," the Savior Said | ***E:*** Gal. 5:1, 13–25 | ***G:*** Luke 9:51–62 | Green |

15 Sun Ps. 41 & 1 Kings 15–17
16 Mon Ps. 42 & 1 Kings 18–20
17 Tue Ps. 43 & 1 Kings 21–22
18 Wed Ps. 44 & 2 Kings 1–3
19 Thu Ps. 45 & 2 Kings 4–6
20 Fri Ps. 46 & 2 Kings 7–9
21 Sat Ps. 47 & 2 Kings 10–12

| | | | | |
|---|---|---|---|---|
| 22 **ST. MARY MAGDALENE**<br>**Seventh Sunday after Pentecost** | ***R:*** Ruth 1:6–18 or Ex. 2:1–10<br>***H:*** *HS98* 880—For All the Faithful Women (st. 12, Mary Magdalene) | ***E:*** Acts 13:26–33a | ***G:*** John 20:1–2, 11–18 | White |

22 Sun Ps. 48 & 2 Kings 13–15 — **St. Mary Magdalene** — White
23 Mon Ps. 49 & 2 Kings 16–18
24 Tue Ps. 50 & 2 Kings 19–22
25 Wed Ps. 51 & 2 Kings 23–25 — **St. James the Elder, Apostle** — Red
26 Thu Ps. 52 & 1 Chron. 1–5
27 Fri Ps. 53 & 1 Chron. 6–10
28 Sat Ps. 54 & 1 Chron. 11–15 — Johann Sebastian Bach, d. 1750

| | | | | |
|---|---|---|---|---|
| 29 **EIGHTH SUNDAY**<br>**AFTER PENTECOST** | ***R:*** Deut. 30:9–14<br>***H:*** *LW* 402—Lord of Glory, You Have Bought Us | ***E:*** Col. 1:1–14 | ***G:*** Luke 10:25–37 | Green |

29 Sun Ps. 55 & 1 Chron. 16–20
30 Mon Ps. 56 & 1 Chron. 21–25
31 Tue Deut. 32:1–4 & 1 Chron. 26–29

## AUGUST 2001

1 Wed Hab. 3:2–19 & 2 Chron. 1–3
2 Thu Ps. 57 & 2 Chron. 4–6
3 Fri Ps. 58 & 2 Chron. 7–9
4 Sat Ps. 59 & 2 Chron. 10–12 — A. L. Barry, 10th LCMS pres., b. 1931

| | | | | |
|---|---|---|---|---|
| **5 NINTH SUNDAY AFTER PENTECOST** | ***R:*** Gen. 18:1–10a (10b–14)<br>***H:*** *LW* 277—One Thing's Needful | ***E:*** Col. 1:21–28 | ***G:*** Luke 10:38–42 | Green |
| 5 Sun Ps. 60 & 2 Chron. 13–15 | Third Lutheran Free Conference, Cleveland, 1858 | | | |
| 6 Mon Ps. 61 & 2 Chron. 16–18 | | | | |
| 7 Tue Ps. 62 & 2 Chron. 19–21 | | | | |
| 8 Wed Ps. 63 & 2 Chron. 22–24 | | | | |
| 9 Thu Ps. 64 & 2 Chron. 25–27 | | | | |
| 10 Fri Ps. 65 & 2 Chron. 28–30 | **St. Laurence, Martyr** | | | Red |
| 11 Sat Ps. 66 & 2 Chron. 31–33 | | | | |
| **12 TENTH SUNDAY AFTER PENTECOST** | ***R:*** Gen. 18:20–32<br>***H:*** *LW* 430, 431—Our Father, Who from Heaven Above | ***E:*** Col. 2:6–15 | ***G:*** Luke 11:1–13 | Green |
| 12 Sun Ps. 67 & 2 Chron. 34–36 | | | | |
| 13 Mon Ps. 68 & Ezra 1–5 | J. A. O. Preus, 8th LCMS pres., d. 1994 | | | |
| 14 Tue Ps. 69 & Ezra 6–10 | | | | |
| 15 Wed Ps. 70 & Neh. 1–3 | **St. Mary, Mother of Our Lord** | | | White |
| 16 Thu Ps. 71 & Neh. 4–6 | | | | |
| 17 Fri Ps. 72 & Neh. 7–9 | | | | |
| 18 Sat Ps. 73 & Neh. 10–13 | | | | |
| **19 ELEVENTH SUNDAY AFTER PENTECOST** | ***R:*** Eccl. 1:2; 2:18–26<br>***H:*** *LW* 445—Praise the Almighty | ***E:*** Col. 3:1–11 | ***G:*** Luke 12:13–21 | Green |
| 19 Sun Ps. 74 & Esther 1–3 | Gotthold Heinrich Löber, d. 1849 | | | |
| 20 Mon Ps. 75 & Esther 4–6 | | | | |
| 21 Tue Ps. 76 & Esther 7–10 | Formula of Concord signed at Gotha 1577 | | | |
| 22 Wed Ps. 77 & Job 1–3 | | | | |
| 23 Thu Ps. 78 & Job 4–6 | | | | |
| 24 Fri Ps. 79 & Job 7–9 | **St. Bartholomew, Apostle** | | | Red |
| 25 Sat Ps. 80 & Job 10–12 | | | | |
| **26 TWELFTH SUNDAY AFTER PENTECOST** | ***R:*** Gen. 15:1–6<br>***H:*** *LW* 300—Do Not Despair, O Little Flock | ***E:*** Heb. 11:1–3, 8–16 | ***G:*** Luke 12:32–40 | Green |
| 26 Sun Ps. 81 & Job 13–15 | | | | |
| 27 Mon Ps. 82 & Job 16–18 | | | | |
| 28 Tue Ps. 83 & Job 19–21 | | | | |
| 29 Wed Ps. 84 & Job 22–24 | | | | |
| 30 Thu Ps. 85 & Job 25–27 | | | | |
| 31 Fri Hab. 3:2–19 & Job 28–30 | | | | |

## SEPTEMBER 2001

| | | | | |
|---|---|---|---|---|
| 1 Sat 1 Chron. 29:10–13 & Job 31–33 | | | | |
| **2 THIRTEENTH SUNDAY AFTER PENTECOST** | ***R:*** Jer. 23:23–29<br>***H:*** *LW* 170—Triune God, Oh, Be Our Stay | ***E:*** Heb. 12:1–13 | ***G:*** Luke 12:49–53 | Green |
| 2 Sun Ps. 86 & Job 34–36 | | | | |
| 3 Mon Ps. 87 & Job 37–39 | | | | |
| 4 Tue Ps. 88 & Job 40–42 | | | | |
| 5 Wed Ps. 89 & Prov. 1–3 | | | | |
| 6 Thu Ps. 90 & Prov.4–7 | | | | |
| 7 Fri Ps. 91 & Prov. 8–10 | First Issue of *Der Lutheraner,* 1844 | | | |
| 8 Sat Ps. 92 & Prov. 11–13 | | | | |
| **9 FOURTEENTH SUNDAY AFTER PENTECOST** | ***R:*** Is. 66:18–23<br>***H:*** *LW* 300—A Multitude Comes | ***E:*** Heb. 12:18–24 | ***G:*** Luke 13:22–30 | Green |
| 9 Sun Ps. 93 & Prov. 14–16 | Second Concordia Seminary bldg., St. Louis, ded. 1883 | | | |
| 10 Mon Ps. 94 & Prov. 17–19 | | | | |
| 11 Tue Ps. 95 & Prov. 20–22 | | | | |
| 12 Wed Ps. 96 & Prov. 23–25 | | | | |
| 13 Thu Ps. 97 & Prov.26–28 | | | | |
| 14 Fri Ps. 98 & Prov. 29–31 | **Holy Cross Day** | | | Red |
| 15 Sat Ps. 99 & Eccl. 1–3 | | | | |
| **16 FIFTEENTH SUNDAY AFTER PENTECOST** | ***R:*** Prov. 25:6–7<br>***H:*** *LW* 394—Son of God, Eternal Savior | ***E:*** Heb. 13:1–8 | ***G:*** Luke 14:1, 7–14 | Green |
| 16 Sun Ps. 100 & Eccl. 4–6 | | | | |
| 17 Mon Ps. 101 & Eccl. 7–9 | | | | |
| 18 Tue Ps. 102 & Eccl. 10–12 | | | | |
| 19 Wed Ps. 103 & Song of Sol. 1–4 | | | | |
| 20 Thu Ps. 104 & Song of Sol. 5–3 | Concordia Publishing House founded 1869 | | | |
| 21 Fri Ps. 105 & Jer. 1–3 | **St. Matthew, Apostle and Evangelist** | | | Red |
| 22 Sat Ps. 106 & Jer. 4–6 | | | | |
| **23 SIXTEENTH SUNDAY AFTER PENTECOST** | ***R:*** Prov. 9:8–12<br>***H:*** *LW* 357—I Trust, O Christ, in You Alone | ***E:*** Philemon 1 (2–9) 10–21 | ***G:*** Luke 14:25–33 | Green |
| 23 Sun Ps. 107 & Jer. 7–9 | | | | |
| 24 Mon Ps. 108 & Jer. 10–12 | | | | |
| 25 Tue Ps. 109 & Jer. 13–15 | | | | |
| 26 Wed Ps. 110 & Jer. 16–18 | | | | |
| 27 Thu Ps. 111 & Jer. 19–22 | | | | |
| 28 Fri Ps. 112 & Jer. 23–25 | | | | |
| 29 Sat Ps. 113 & Jer. 26–28 | **St. Michael and All Angels** | | | White |
| **30 SEVENTEENTH SUNDAY AFTER PENTECOST** | ***R:*** Ex. 32:7–14<br>***H:*** *LW* 229—Jesus Sinners Will Receive | ***E:*** 1 Tim. 1:12–17 | ***G:*** Luke 15:1–10 | Green |
| 30 Sun 1 Chron. 29:10–13 & Jer. 29–31 | | | | |

## OCTOBER 2001

1 Mon Jonah 2:2–9 & Jer. 32–34
2 Tue Ps. 114 & Jer. 35–37 — Lutheran Hour started by LLL, 1930
3 Wed Ps. 115 & Jer. 38–40
4 Thu Ps. 116 & Jer. 41–43
5 Fri Ps. 117 & Jer. 44–47
6 Sat Ps. 118 & Jer. 48–50

**7 EIGHTEENTH SUNDAY AFTER PENTECOST**
*R:* Amos 8:4–7 *E:* 1 Tim. 2:1–8 *G:* Luke 16:1–13 — Green
*H:* *LW* 358—Seek Where You May to Find a Way

7 Sun Ps. 119:1–8 & Jer. 51–52
8 Mon Ps. 119:9–16 & Lam. 1–2
9 Tue Ps. 119:17–24 & Lam. 3–5 — Friedrich Pfotenhauer, 5th LCMS pres., d. 1939
10 Wed Ps. 119:25–32 & Ezek. 1–3
11 Thu Ps. 119:33–40 & Ezek. 4–6
12 Fri Ps. 119:41–48 & Ezek. 7–9
13 Sat Ps. 119:49–56 & Ezek. 10–12

**14 NINETEENTH SUNDAY AFTER PENTECOST**
*R:* Amos 6:1–7 *E:* 1 Tim. 6:6–16 *G:* Luke 16:19–31 — Green
*H:* *LW* 155—To God the Holy Spirit Let Us Pray

14 Sun Ps. 119:57–64 & Ezek. 13–15
15 Mon Ps. 119:65–72 & Ezek. 16–18
16 Tue Ps. 119:73–80 & Ezek. 19–21
17 Wed Ps. 119:81–88 & Ezek. 22–24
18 Thu Ps. 119:89–96 & Ezek. 25–27 — **St. Luke, Evangelist** — Red
19 Fri Ps. 119:97–104 & Ezek. 28–30
20 Sat Ps. 119:105–12 & Ezek. 31–33

**21 TWENTIETH SUNDAY AFTER PENTECOST**
*R:* Hab. 1:1–3; 2:1–4 *E:* 2 Tim. 1:3–14 *G:* Luke 17:1–10 — Green
*H:* *LW* 354—I Know My Faith Is Founded

21 Sun Ps. 119:113–20 & Ezek. 34–36
22 Mon Ps. 119:121–28 & Ezek. 37–39
23 Tue Ps. 119:129–36 & Ezek. 40–42
24 Wed Ps. 119:137–44 & Ezek. 43–45
25 Thu Ps. 119:145–52 & Ezek. 46–48 — C. F. W. Walther, 1st LCMS pres., b. 1811
26 Fri Ps. 119:153–60 & Dan. 1–3
27 Sat Ps. 119:161–68 & Dan. 4–6

**28 REFORMATION DAY** (observed)
Twenty-First Sunday after Pentecost
*R:* Jer. 31:31–34 *E:* Rom. 3:19–28 *G:* John 8:31–36 — Red
*H:* *LW* 355—Salvation unto Us Has Come

28 Sun. Ps. 119:169–76 & Dan. 7–9 — **St. Simon and St. Jude, Apostles** — Red
29 Mon Ps. 120 & Dan. 10–12
30 Tue Ps. 121 & Hos. 1–4
31 Wed Jonah 2:2–9 & Hos. 5–7 — **Reformation Day** — Red

## NOVEMBER 2001

1 Thu Ex. 15:1–18 & Hos. 8–10 — **All Saints' Day** — White
2 Fri Ps. 122 & Hos. 11–14 — **Commemoration of the Faithful Departed** — White
3 Sat Ps. 123 & Joel

**4 ALL SAINTS' DAY** (observed)
Twenty-Second Sunday after Pentecost
*R:* Is. 26:1–4, 8–9, 12–13, 19–21 *E:* Rev. 21:9–11, 22–27 (22:1–5) *G:* Matt. 5:1–12 — White
*H:* *LW* 191—For All the Saints

4 Sun Ps. 124 & Amos 1–5
5 Mon Ps. 125 & Amos 6–9
6 Tue Ps. 126 & Obad., Jonah
7 Wed Ps. 127 & Micah 1–3 — Synodical Conference Black Mission begun 1877
8 Thu Ps. 128 & Micah 4–7
9 Fri Ps. 129 & Nah.
10 Sat Ps. 130 & Hab. — Martin Luther, b. 1483

**11 THIRD-LAST SUNDAY IN THE CHURCH YEAR**
*R:* Ex. 32:15–20 or Mal. 4:1–2a *E:* 2 Thess. 3:1–5 or 2 Thess. 3:6–13
*G:* Luke 17:20–30 or Luke 21:5–19 — Green
*H:* *LW* 462—The Day Is Surely Drawing Near

11 Sun Ps. 131 & Zeph.
12 Mon Ps. 132 & Hag.
13 Tue Ps. 133 & Zech. 1–5 — Concordia College, Selma, Ala., opened 1922
14 Wed Ps. 134 & Zech. 6–10
15 Thu Ps. 135 & Zech.11–14
16 Fri Ps. 136 & Mal.
17 Sat Ps. 137 & Matt. 1–2

**18 SECOND-LAST SUNDAY IN THE CHURCH YEAR**
*R:* Jer. 8:4–7 or Is. 52:1–6 *E:* 2 Cor. 5:1–10 or 1 Cor. 15:54–58
*G:* Luke 19:11–27 — Green
*H:* *LW* 380—Forth in Your Name, O Lord, I Go

18 Sun Ps. 138 & Matt. 3–4
19 Mon Ps. 139 & Matt. 5–6
20 Tue Ps. 140 & Matt. 7–8
21 Wed Ps. 141 & Matt. 9–10

**22 THANKSGIVING DAY (U.S.)**
*R:* Deut. 8:1–10 *E:* Phil. 4:6–20 or 1 Tim. 2:1–4 *G:* Luke 17:11–19 — White
*H:* *LW* 443—Now Thank We All Our God

22 Thu Ps. 142 & Matt. 11–12
23 Fri Ps. 143 & Matt. 13–14
24 Sat Ps. 144 & Matt. 15–16

**25 LAST SUNDAY IN THE CHURCH YEAR**
**Sunday of the Fulfillment**
***R:*** Mal. 3:14–18 or Jer. 23:2–6 ***E:*** Rev. 22:6–13 or Col. 1:13–20
***G:*** Luke 12:42–48 or Luke 23:35–43
***H:*** *LW* 177—Wake, Awake, for Night Is Flying
Green

25 Sun Ps. 145 & Matt. 17–18
26 Mon Ps. 146 & Matt. 19–20
27 Tue Ps. 147 & Matt.21–22
28 Wed Ps. 148 & Matt. 23–24
29 Thu Ps. 149–150 & Matt. 25–26
30 Fri Ex. 15:1–18 & Matt. 27–28 — **St. Andrew, Apostle** — Red

# DECEMBER 2001

1 Sat Luke 1:46–55 & Rev. 1–2

**2 FIRST SUNDAY IN ADVENT**
***R:*** Is. 2:1–5 ***E:*** Rom. 13:11–14 ***G:*** Matt. 24:37–44 or Matt. 21:1–11
***H:*** *LW* 13—Savior of the Nations, Come
Purple/Blue

2 Sun Ps. 1 & Rev. 3–5
3 Mon Ps. 2 & Rev. 6–8
4 Tue Ps. 3 & Rev. 9–11
5 Wed Ps. 4 & Rev. 12–14
6 Thu Ps. 5 & Rev. 15–17
7 Fri Ps. 6 & Rev. 18–20
8 Sat Ps. 7 & Rev. 21–22

**9 SECOND SUNDAY IN ADVENT**
***R:*** Is. 11:1–10 ***E:*** Rom. 15:4–13 ***G:*** Matt. 3:1–12
***H:*** *LW* 14—On Jordan's Bank the Baptist's Cry
Purple/Blue

9 Sun Ps. 8 & Is. 1–3 — Log Cabin College, Perry Co, Mo., ded. 1839
10 Mon Ps. 9 & Is. 4–6
11 Tue Ps. 10 & Is. 7–9 — Oliver Harms, 7th LCMS pres., b. 1901
12 Wed Ps. 11 & Is. 10–12
13 Thu Ps. 12 & Is. 13–15
14 Fri Ps. 13 & Is. 16–18
15 Sat Ps. 14 & Is. 19–21

**16 THIRD SUNDAY IN ADVENT**
***R:*** Is. 35:1–10 ***E:*** James 5:7–10 ***G:*** Matt. 11:2–11
***H:*** *LW* 25—O People, Rise and Labor
Purple/Blue

16 Sun Ps. 15 & Is. 22–24
17 Mon Ps. 16 & Is. 25–27
18 Tue Ps. 17 & Is. 28–30
19 Wed Ps. 18 & Is. 31–33
20 Thu Ps. 19 & Is. 34–36
21 Fri Ps. 20 & Is. 37–39 — **St. Thomas, Apostle** — Red
22 Sat Ps. 21 & Is. 40–42

**23 FOURTH SUNDAY IN ADVENT**
***R:*** Is. 7:10–14 (15–17) ***E:*** Rom. 1:1–7 ***G:*** Matt. 1:18–25
***H:*** *LW* 31—Oh, Come, Oh, Come, Emmanuel
Purple/Blue

23 Sun Ps. 22 & Is.43–45

**24 THE NATIVITY OF OUR LORD**
**Christmas Eve**
***R:*** Is. 9:2–7 ***E:*** Titus 2:11–14 ***G:*** Luke 2:1–20
***H:*** *LW* 37, 38—From Heaven Above to Earth I Come
White

24 Mon Ps. 23 & Is. 46–48

**25 THE NATIVITY OF OUR LORD**
**Christmas Day**
***R:*** Is. 62:10–12 ***E:*** Titus 3:4–7 ***G:*** Luke 2:1–20
***H:*** *LW* 35—We Praise, O Christ, Your Holy Name
White

25 Tue Ps. 24 & Is. 49–51
26 Wed Ps. 25 & Is. 52–54 — **St. Stephen, First Martyr** — Red
27 Thu Ps. 26 & Is.55–57 — **St. John, Apostle and Evangelist** — White
28 Fri Ps. 27 & Is. 58–60 — **The Holy Innocents, Martyrs** — Red
29 Sat Ps. 28 & Is. 61–63

**30 FIRST SUNDAY**
**AFTER CHRISTMAS**
***R:*** Is. 63:7–9 ***E:*** Gal. 4:4–7 ***G:*** Matt. 2:13–15, 19–23
***H:*** *LW* 44—Let All Together Praise Our God
White

30 Sun Ps. 29 & Is. 64–6
31 Mon Luke 1:46–55 & Mark 1 — **New Year's Eve, *Eve of the Name of Jesus*** — White

**Investment Solutions Designed to Work for Your Lutheran Organization...**

**Today and Tomorrow.**

**Our Goal? To build a lasting relationship with your Lutheran organization and the people you serve by providing high-quality investment management services.**

**For a complimentary portfolio consultation, simply contact Lori Richardson, Vice President, Institutional Sales and Relationships at (800) 227-8602, extension 3131. She can provide you with more information, as well as show you how you can make your organization's resources work harder for you...and the people you serve.**

AAL CAPITAL MANAGEMENT CORPORATION

*A Subsidiary of Aid Association for Lutherans*
222 W. College Avenue, Appleton, WI 54919-0007

C-50825AD 9-00

# Christian HealthCare Network ‡ (CHN)

"Employee Benefit Plans created by Churches, Schools and Auxiliaries for the exclusive benefit of the professional and lay church worker."

**Employee Benefits**

• Health • Dental • Vision •
• Employee Assistance Plan •
• Ear Care Plan • Life Plan •

For more information
please contact:

P.O. Box 2057
Cathedral City, CA 92235-2057
(800) 871-7056 Extension 3

**‡ Formerly known as**
**The Lutheran Ministries Benefit Plans**

## MOVING DAY

Here are three startling facts!
- 17% of Americans move annually
- The U.S. citizen moves an average of seven times in a lifetime
- 50% of Lutherans who move more than 40 miles from their previous address never request a transfer

It's obvious we need to do a better job of both sending and receiving Lutherans on the move.
Here are three suggestions.

1. When a member is moving away:
   - Recognize this is a stressful time and probably a time of grieving.
   - Make an intentional contact when you hear of a move and ask how you can support.
   - Alert congregation members of the need to keep church office informed.
   - Provide support on moving day (Babysitting, meals, cleaning, etc.)
   - Put reminders about moving in a newsletter and bulletin.
   - Send for and provide information about churches in their new area (Location, Time of services, Staff names, Bulletins, Newsletters, Pictorial Directories, other helpful information.)
   - Encourage potential new pastors to make contact before the move.
   - Appoint or elect someone to oversee an intentional ministry for those who move.
   - Keep in touch with them and keep them in your prayers.
2. When a member is moving into the area:
   - Make a personal contact quickly; ask how you can help, keep them in your prayers.
   - Send a letter welcoming them to the community. Give helpful information like:
     Where and how to get a drivers license
     Where and how to get new plates for the car
     How to sign up for phone, utilities, etc.
     Options for Cable TV
     Options for newspaper subscriptions
     Local hospitals
     Location and phone number of school district, administration building
     Information on how to enroll children in Little league, community teams, etc.
     A brochure about your congregation
3. Use the synod's resources:
   - Use the Lutheran Annual for information on congregations.
   - Call the Church Information Center at 1-888-THE-LCMS to get more information on those congregations.
   - Order "Sent With God's Blessing" from CPH (800-325-3040). The stock number is SO1727. Cost is $5.50. This is an important resource for Boards of Elders; it gives specific strategies in membership referral.

Department of Evangelism Ministry
Board for Congregational Services

# THE LUTHERAN CHURCH—MISSOURI SYNOD

**International Center**
**1333 S Kirkwood Road**
**St Louis, MO 63122-7295**
**314/965-9000, or 314/965-9917 + EXT # (Touch Phone Only)**
**FAX 314/822-8307**
**LCMS Home Page http://www.lcms.org**
**Office Hours: 7:45—4:15**

The year following each name indicates when the present term expires.

## OFFICERS OF THE SYNOD

President: Rev Alvin L Barry, MTh, DD, 1333 S Kirkwood Rd, St Louis, MO 63122—314/965-9000 (2001)
First Vice President: Rev Robert T Kuhn, DD, 1333 S Kirkwood Rd, St Louis, MO 63122—314/965-9000 (2001)
Second Vice President: Rev Robert King, PhD, 902 Roland Court, Jefferson City, MO 65101—573/635-6538 (2001)
Third Vice President: Rev William C Weinrich, ThD, 6600 N Clinton St, Ft Wayne IN 46825—219/452-2100 (2001)
Fourth Vice President: Dr Roger Pittelko, MDiv, 6600 N Clinton St, Ft Wayne, IN—219/452-2100 (2001)
Fifth Vice President: Dr Wallace Schulz, LLD, 4751 Chateau Lane, Pacific, MO 63069-2942—314/271-2030 (2001)
Secretary: Dr Raymond Hartwig, DD, 1333 S Kirkwood Rd, St Louis, MO, 63122-7295—314/965-9000 (2001)
Vice President Finance-Treasurer: Mr Paul W Middeke, 1333 S Kirkwood Rd, St Louis, MO 63122—314/965-9000 (2001)
President Emeritus: Rev Ralph A Bohlmann, STM, PhD, DD, 12836 Stump Rd, Des Peres, MO 63131—314/821-7781

## BOARD OF DIRECTORS

*Officers:*

Chairman: Dr Donald K Muchow
Secretary: Dr Raymond L Hartwig (2001)

*Clergy Members:*

Dr Alvin L Barry, 1333 S Kirkwood Rd, St Louis, MO 63122-7295—314/965-9000 (2001)
Dr Karl L Barth, 13330 W Bluemound Rd #3, Elm Grove, WI 53122—262/789-5184 (2001)
Rev Roosevelt Gray, Jr, 25205 Waycross, Southfield, MI 48034—248/948-7929 (2004)
Dr Raymond L Hartwig, 1333 S Kirkwood Rd, St Louis, MO 63122-7295—314/965-9000 (2001)
Rev Ulmer Marshall, Jr, 6405 St Thomas Court, Mobile, AL 36618-3242—334/343-7273 (2001)
Dr Donald K Muchow, 5725 Galsworthy Ct, Austin, TX 78739—512/301-0431 (2001)

*Teacher Member:*

Mr Clifford A Dietrich, 6014 Andro Run, Ft Wayne, IN 46815—219/486-8881 (2001)

*Lay Members:*

Dr Betty Duda, 2450 Mikler, Oviedo, FL 32765—407/365-3203 (2004)
Mr Ernest E Garbe, 1661 N 2200 St, Dieterich, IL 62424—217/739-2243 (2004)
Dr Jean Garton, 2005 Fox Trail, Benton, AR 72015—501/776-0879 (2001)
Mr Oscar H Hanson, PO Box 16852, So Lake Tahoe CA 96151-6852—530/544-1889 (2004)
Mr Ted Kober, 1537 Avenue D, Suite 352, Billings MT 59102—406/256-1583 (2004)
Mr Richard D Peters, 873 White Pines Trail, Amery, WI 54001-5360—715/268-8782 (2001)
Mr Christian Preus, 16205 5th Ave N, Plymouth, MN 55447—612/475-0561 (2001)
Dr Edwin A Trapp, Jr, 7624 Glenn Albens Circle, Dallas, TX 75225—214/368-2876 (2001)

*Non-Voting Members:*

Dr Robert T Kuhn, First Vice President, 1333 S Kirkwood Rd, St Louis, MO 63122-7295—314/965-9000 (2001)
Mr Paul W Middeke, Vice President Finance/Treasurer, 1333 S Kirkwood Rd, St Louis, MO 63122-7295—314/965-9000 (2001)

*Staff Officer:*

Mr Brad Hewitt, Chief Administrative Officer

*International Center Chaplain:*

Dr Otto C Hintze, Ext 1429

### Legal Counsel

Pranschke and Holderle, L.C., 1610 Des Peres Rd, Suite 300, St Louis, MO 63131-1813—314/965-6455 FAX 314/966-2144 e-mail lpranschke@phlclaw.com

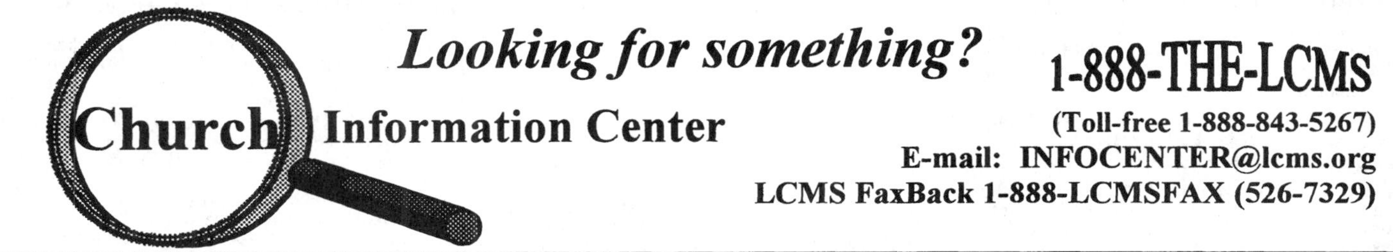

# ELECTED PROGRAM BOARDS

## Board for Mission Services

*Chairman:* Rev James P Johnson (2001) (see Ordained Section for Address)

*Board:* Revs Warren H Davis (2001), Matthew C Harrison (2004), James P Johnson (2001), Larry D LaDassor (2004); *Teacher:* Laurence Meissner (2001); *Laypersons:* Kermit Almstedt (2001), Robert Jennings (2004), Herman W Jensen (2001), John Lautenschlager (2004)

*Staff:* Dr Glenn O'Shoney, Executive Director; Rev Dave Andrus, Counselor for Blind Mission; Rev Thomas Benedum, Associate Director for Ministry to the Armed Forces; Mr Rudy Blank, Manager for Creative Media Services; Dr Allan Buckman, Director for World Services; Mr Curt Connolly, Counselor for Laborers For Christ; Dr Robert Gonzalez, Counselor for Hispanic Mission Field Development; Rev Kenneth Greinke, Director for World Team Support; Rev Paul M Heerboth, Editorial Assistant (part-time); Rev B Steve Hughey, Director for Partnerships; Ms Mary Jackson, Manager of World Services Support; Dr Velma Lubbert, Director for World Health Ministries; Rev Richard Manus, Counselor for Campus Ministry; Dr Daniel Mattson, Director for Theological Studies; Mr Wayne Meyer, Manager for Media Resource Production; Rev John Mueller, Director for Missionary Services; Mr Neal Rabe, Project Facilitator (part-time); Rev Harold Rau, Research Consultant (part-time); Mr Kenneth Reiner, Counselor for Logistic Services; Mr Les Schmidt, Counselor for Missionary Services; Mrs Karen Schrader, Assistant to the Executive Director; Rev Mark Schroeder, Missionary Training Program Coordinator; Dr Robert Scudieri, Director for North America; Mrs Karin Semler, Director for Information Services; Ms Dawn Smith, Counselor for Missionary Services; Mr Ross A Stroh, Director for Budget and Finance; Mr Sean Harlow, Counselor for Recruitment; Rev Rodger Venzke, Director for Ministry to the Armed Forces; Dr Kari Vo, Counselor for Mission Interpretation; Mrs Debra Williams, Manager for North America and Administrative Services Support.

*Area Directors:* Rev David Birner, *Taiwan, Japan, Korea, Philippines;* Mr Thomas Brinkley, *Togo, Cote d'Ivoire, Guinea;* Rev John Duitsman, *Kenya, Ethiopia, Eritrea, Sudan, Uganda*; Rev Jeff Ehlers, *Thailand, Myanmar, Laos, Cambodia, Vietnam, Indonesia, Papua New Guinea;* Rev Robert Hartfield, *Central Europe and the Baltics;* Dr Herbert Hoefer, *India and Sri Lanka;* Rev John Mehl, *Commonwealth of Independent States (former Soviet Union);* Mr Delano Meyer, *Ghana, Liberia, Nigeria, Sierra Leone, Botswana, South Africa*; Rev Craig Molitoris, *China, Hong Kong, Macau;* Dr Douglas Rutt, *Brazil, Argentina, Chile, Paraguay, Uruguay;* Rev James Tino, *Venezuela and the Caribbean, Puerto Rico, Jamaica, Haiti, Cuba;* Rev Michael Wakeland, *Mexico, Central America, Panama*

### Committees and Task Forces

**African Immigrant Ministry Task Force**

*Revs* Isaac Gyampadu, Yohannes Mengsteab, Terry Tieman; *Layperson:* Dereje Fantaye

**American Indian Ministry Task Force**

*Revs* Dennis Bauer, Clark Gies, Ricky Jacob, Harley Kopitski; *Laypersons:* William Huber, Marilu Johnsen, Bill Mason, Louise Slim, Helen Price

**Asian Indian Ministry Task Force**

*Revs* Jaya Bijjiga, Shadrak Katari, Ed Lang, Victor Raj; *Laypersons:* Franklin Sadhanand, Sagar Pilli, Valli Nagelli

**Black Ministry Task Force**

*Revs* Philip Saywrayne, S T Williams, CJ Wright; *Laypersons:* Charles Dorsey, Kaye Dumas, Carolyn White

**Blind Ministry Task Force**

*Rev* Robert Wahl; *Laypersons:* Marjorie Groth, Sheryl Hunt, Harvey Lauer, Terry Rogers

**Campus Ministry Task Force**

*Revs* Dan Decker, Norbert Firnhaber, Timothy Seals, Michael Thurau; *Laypersons:* Elizabeth Gonzalez, Marcia Mittwede, Lena Yamasaki Sievers

**Chinese Ministry Task Force**

*Revs* Terry Chan, Robert Fitzpatrick, Richard Law, Tich Luu

**Deaf Mission Task Force**

*Revs* David Carstens, Jerry Munz; *Laypersons:* Don Peterson, James Swalley, Paula Willig

**Hispanic Ministry Task Force**

*Revs* Benito Perez, Wilfredo Rivera; *Laypersons:* Leticia Godoy, Samuel Gomez, Aurora Ortiz, Lucy Wilke

**Hmong Ministry Task Force**

*Revs* Dwayne Lueck, Jeff Miller, Yia Vang, Zong Houa Yang

**Jewish Ministry Task Force**

*Revs* David Born, Bruce Lieske, John Perling; *Laypersons:* David Garrett, Paul Krentz, Jennifer Krupp

**Korean Ministry Task Force**

*Revs* Young Hwan Hong, Chang Soo Kim, Dong Joon Kim, Soo Min Lee, Shang Ik Moon

**Laborers For Christ Task Force**

Del Carman, John Corkhill Jr, Annetta Dellinger, Gil Heine, Ed Holderle, Dale Vogt

**Ministry to the Armed Forces Committee**

*Revs* Dr Jacob A O Preus III, Max W Wilk; *Layperson:* Gen John Shaud

**Muslim Ministry Task Force**

*Revs* Gary Rohwer; *Laypersons:* Salim Dil, Emile Homsi, Asaph James, Amer Khan, Cynthia Khan, Farrukh Mehdi Khan, Khurram Mehdi Khan, Cornelius Walters

**Vietnamese Ministry Task Force**

*Revs* Dung Do, Ninh Nguyen, Minh Chau Vo, Kinh Vu; *Laypersons:* Nam Tran

### Mission Societies with Service Agreements

**African Immigrant Lutheran Mission Society (AILMS)**

3799 East West Hwy, Hyattsville MD 20782 (301) 277-2302 FAX (301) 595-3028 Rev Yohannes Mengsteab Email: Ymengsert@aol.com Web www.aim-lutheran.org

**Compassion Vietnam Association**

550 N Parkcenter Dr Suite 204, Santa Ana, CA 92705-3529 (714) 560-8850 FAX (714) 560-8852 Dr Norbert C Oesch, Chairman

**Concordia Mission Society**

Dr Eugene Krentz *Executive Director* 36395 N Tara Ct Ingleside IL 60041-8576 (847) 587-4442 Dr JAO Preus III, President; Rev Tom Baker, Corresponding Secretary

**International Student Ministry, Inc. (ISM, Inc.)**

1605 Littleton Ct Fenton, MO 63026 (636) 349-8024 FAX (636) 349-7817 Rev Robert E Lange *Director* Email: robertelan@aol.com Web www.isminc.org

**Jamaica Lutheran Mission Society**

PO Box 99 Sterling NE 68443 Contact: Darrel Rathe (402) 866-5821 FAX (402) 866-5821 Email: DR30411@NAVIX.NET

**MOST Ministries**

PO Box 130678 Ann Arbor MI 48113 Contact: Gayle Sommerfeld (734) 994-7909 FAX (734) 994-7974 Email: mostmin@juno.com

**Tian Shan Mission Society**

1020 E Ramon Rd Palm Springs CA 92264 (760) 327-5611 FAX: (760) 322-6531 Contact: Hank Hohenstein (760) 329-1514 FAX: (760) 329-5313 Email: histone@gateway.net

## Board for Higher Education

**Concordia University System**

*Chairman:* Dr Ralph Reinke LiitD (2004)

*Revs* Richard Allsing (2004), Steve Briel (2001), Paul Maier, PhD (2001); Rev Raymond Mueller (2004), Rev Eugene Oesch (2004); *Teachers:* William Ludwig (2001); *Laypersons:* John Behrendt (2004), James C Holste, PhD (2004), Dr Elmer Gooding (2001), Mr Paul Hegland (2004), Gerhard Mundinger, MD (2004), Mr Don Prevallet (2004), Dr Lowell Schoer (2001), Mr Berne Schepman (2001), Dr Beverly Yahnke (2004); *Advisory:* Paul Middeke, Treasurer, Rev Robert Holst, PhD (2001), Rev Dr John Johnson, Rev Dr Dean Wenthe, Dr David Zersen (2002).

*Staff:* Rev William F Meyer, PhD, Executive Director/ President; Rev Alan Borcherding, PhD, Director of University Education; Dr L Dean Hempelmann, Director of Pastoral Education, Linda Lehr, Administrative Assistant.

## Standing Committees

**Colloquy for the Pastoral Ministry**

Rev Dr John Johnson; Rev Dr Dean Wenthe; Rev Dr Robert Kuhn. *Advisory:* Rev Dr William F Meyer, Rev Herbert Mueller.

**Colloquy for the Teaching Ministry**

Rev Dr Orville Walz, Rev Dr Robert Kuhn, Rev Dr Patrick Ferry. *Advisory:* Rev Dr William F Meyer.

## Boards of Regents

### Seminaries (US), Colleges/Universities

### Seminaries

**Concordia Theological Seminary—Fort Wayne, IN:**

*Chairman:* Rev David L. Anderson (2001)

*Revs* Mark Grunst (2001), Robert Kuhn (ex officio), Howard Patten (COP Rep); Jack Baumgarn (2004); *Teacher:* Louis Herring (2001); *Laypersons:* Johnny Buck (2004), Walter C Dissen (2001), Dr Clifford Meints (2004).

**Concordia Seminary—St Louis, MO:**

*Chairman:* Dr Conrad Kercher (2001)

*Revs* Dr Wallace Schulz (ex officio), Rev Dr John Nordling (2004), Rev Dr Arleigh Lutz (COP Rep), Rev Dr Edward Westcott, Jr (2001), Rev Dr Richard Schlecht (2001); *Teacher:* Allen H Loesel (2001); *Laypersons:* James Ralls (2004), John Wittenmeyer (2004). *Advisory:* Rev Dr James Kalthoff.

### Colleges/Universities

**Concordia College—Ann Arbor, MI:**

*Chairman:* To be elected

*Revs* C William Hoesman DP; Thomas Ahlersmeyer (2001); Rev Ronald Young (2006); *Teachers:* Jeanne Ollhoff (2001), Elaine Bickel (2006) *Laypersons:* Donald Bennett (2002), Leslie Fyans (2002), David Tuttle (2001), Beth Young (2001), Gerald Kluck (2001), Karl Kreft (2002), Dr Dale Gust (2006), Mrs Janice Wendorf (2002).

**Concordia University—Austin, TX:**

*Chairman:* Herbert Nelson (2002)

*Revs* Stephen Wagner (2001), Gerald Kieschnick (ex officio), Rev Dr Richard Noack (2003); *Teachers:* Curtis Riske (2006), Wayne Kramer (2001); *Laypersons:* Dr Henry Boehm (2001), Donald Graf (2001), David Howard (2002), Curtis Mickan (2002), Jim Burghard (2001), Dr Clarence Dockweiler(2006), Mrs Melissa Knippa (2002).

**Concordia College—Bronxville, NY:**

*Chairman:* Rev Dr David Benke

*Revs* Dr Gregory Wismar (2001), Rev Dr Thomas Green (2006); *Teachers:* Stanley Kramer (2006), Herbert Meissner (2001); *Laypersons:* Wesley Tervo (2001), Judy Barnes (2001), Joel Wilson (2001), Mrs Judith Wiegand (2006), John Pietruski, Jr (2002), Donald Krenz (2002), Paul Grandpre (2002), Gary Muller (2002).

**Concordia University—Irvine, CA:**

*Chairman:* Daniel Krueger (2001)

*Revs* Larry Stoterau (ex officio), Arthur Puls (2001), Thomas Meyer (2006); *Teachers:* Paul Hillmann (2001), Dr Marion Baden (2006); *Laypersons:* Dr Audrey Williams (2002), Eleanor Kruse (2001), Delbert Glanz (2002), Barbara Grimm (2002), Mr Donald Tietjen (2006), Peter Lee (2002), Melvin Olsen (2001).

**Concordia University Wisconsin—Mequon, WI:**

*Chairman:* Rev Dr Ronald Meyer

*Revs* James Herbolsheimer (2001), William Otto (2006); *Teachers:* Frank Wegner (2001), Donald Rohde (T) (2006); *Laypersons:* Warren Twietmeyer (2001), Dr Gordon Lofgren (2002), Chris Schmidt (2002), Donna Streufert (2001), John Ficken (2006), Ted Batterman (2002), Mr Robert Whipkey (Advisory), Robert Gehrt (2001), Eugene Groth (2002).

**Concordia University—Portland, OR:**

*Chairman:* Dr Charles Brondos (2004)

*Revs* James Wilson (2004), Warren Schumacher (ex officio), Philip Streufert (2006); *Teachers:* Gary Gable (2004), Robert Christian (2006); *Laypersons:* Mrs Gloria Edwards (2002), Mr Robert Boyer (2002), Matt Crawford (2002), Kathy Hone (2002), Char

Kroemer (2004), Marilyn Ludke (L) (2006), Thomas Muhly (2004).

**Concordia University—River Forest, IL:**
*Chairman:* William Ameiss (2003)
*Revs* Philip Kaufmann (2001), Thomas Nierman (2006) (ex officio); *Teachers:* Mr Richard Blatt (2006), Theodore Lams (2001); *Laypersons:* Dr Martha Dawkins (2006), John Duda (2002), Ronald Dietrich (2002), Dorothy Hildebrandt (2001), Dr Ann Horton (2002), Kathy Schulz (2001), Paula Trimpey (2001), Fred Wittinger (2002).

**Concordia University—St. Paul, MN:**
*Chairman:* To be elected
*Revs* Gerald Coleman (2006), Byron Northwick (2004), Lane Seitz (ex officio); *Teachers:* Dr Loma Meyer (2003), Paul Crisler (2004); *Laypersons:* Orrin Rinke (2002), Elizabeth Duda (2002), Mary Wise (2002), Dennis Bauer (2004), Lyla Hirsch (2004), Blake Rickbeil (2004), Gary Reinke (2002), Monica Eden (2006).

**Concordia College—Selma, AL:**
*Chairman:* Victor Dankis (2002)
*Revs* Orval Mueller (ex officio), Jimmy McCants (2004), Mark Griffin (2006); *Teachers:* Betty Knapp (2004), Donna Behnken (2006); *Laypersons:* Dr Joyce Verrett (2004), Archie Bourret (2002), Dr. Sam Givhan (2006), Jean King (2004), Alvin Foster (2004), Dr Robert Cade (2002), Cleveland Lewis (2002).

**Concordia University—Seward, NE:**
*Chairman:* Rev Eugene Gierke (ex officio)
*Revs* Wayne Schroeder (2001), Gerald Roggow (2006), Stanley Wehling (2006); *Teacher:* Dennis Hintz (2001); *Laypersons:* Susan Dumke (2001), William Kernen (2002), Del Toebben (2002), Raymond Joeckel (2002), Julia McCourt (2002), Virginia Hughes (2001), Roger Glawatz (2001), Larry Rathe (2006).

**Lutheran Lay Ministry Program**: (See Concordia University, Wisconsin, Mequon, WI).

# APPOINTED PROGRAM BOARDS

## Board for Black Ministry Services

*Chairman:* Rev James Brown (2001) (see Ordained Section for Address)
Frank K Marshall, Vice President (2001), Mary Smith, Secretary (2001), Naomi Dobson, Asst Secretary (2001), Revs Glenn Lucas (2001), James Wiggins (2001), Teachers, Jeffrey Howell (2001); *Laypersons:* Marvin Collins (2001), Linda Kennley (2001); President, Clergy Caucus, Rev Samuel Crosby.
*Staff:* Dr Bryant E Clancy Jr, Executive Director; Dr Phillip A Campbell, Director, Mission Networking; Willie Stallworth, Director, Family/Educational Resources.

## Board for Communication Services

*Chairman:* Charles Winterstein
*Board:* Revs David Albertin (2001), Bertram Lewis (2001); Charles Manske (2001); *Laypersons:* Todd Boettcher (2001), Jocelyn King (2001), Michael Smith (2001); *Teacher:* Charles Winterstein (2001).
*Staff:* Rev David Mahsman, Interim Executive Director; Kathy Miels, Administrative Assistant; Nancy Olson, Assistant for Special Projects; David Strand, Assistant to the Executive Director for Public Relations; Rev David Mahsman, Director, News and Information, and Executive Editor, *The Lutheran Witness* and *Reporter;* Rev James Rassbach, Director, Synod Relations; Lee Hagan, Interim Director, Broadcast; Joseph Isenhower, Manager, News Bureau; Paula Ross, Manager, Editorial Services for News and Information; Don Folkemer, Manager, Periodical Services, and Managing Editor, *The Lutheran Witness;* Carla Dubbelde, Editorial Manager, *The Lutheran Witness* district editions; Bruce Kueck, Assistant Director, News and Information, and Managing Editor, *Reporter*, Rick Steenbock, Assistant Director of Video; Mary Mantia, Customer Service Manager Video.

## KFUO/JUBILEE NETWORK

**85 Founders Lane**
**St Louis MO 63105**
**KFUO Phone # (314) 725-3030**

*Radio:* Rev David L Mahsman, Interim Executive Director; Dennis Stortz, Assistant Director of Broadcast, Radio; Chuck Rathert, General Manager and AM Program Director; John Fischer, Chief Engineer; Paula Zika, Director of Business and Support Services; James Connett, FM Program Director; Ronald Klemm, Director of Operations; William Kniesly, General Sales Manager; Tricia Oates, Educational Initiatives Manager.

### Advisory Councils

### Broadcast

Dr Bryant Clancy, Roland Eggerding, Joel Fletcher, Lee Hagen, Dr Jonathan Laabs, William Lindenberg, Dorothy Mansholt, Rev Roberto Rojas, Dr Martin Schramm.

### News and Information

Dr Thomas Ahlersmeyer, Jean Beres, Rev Juan Gonzalez, Rev Todd Jenks, Dr Alan Klaas, Ida Mall, Dr Jacob Preus, Alan Zacharias.

## Board for Congregational Services

*Chairman:* Rev Darwin Karsten
*Board:* Revs Victor Belton (2001), Darwin Karsten (2001), John Pless (2004); *Commissioned Ministers:* Dr David Held (2004), Debra Herman (2001), Dr Patricia Hoffman (2001); *Laypersons:* Arleen Keyne (2004), Kay McCreery (2001), Donald Pegosh (2001); *At Large:* Rev Naomichi Masaki (2004), Rev Stephen A Wiggins Sr (2004).
*Staff:* Dr LeRoy Wilke, Executive Director; Judith Christian, Director, Child Ministry; Lori Aadsen, Associate Director, Child Ministry; Jane Haas, Publications (part-time deployed), Child Ministry; Rev Dr David P Mulder, Director, Evangelism Ministry; Ralph Geisler, Associate Director, Evangelism Ministry; Rev Al Tormoehlen, Tell the Good News Grant Coordinator, Evangelism Ministry; Rev Jeffery S Schubert, Director, Family Ministry; Vacant, Director, School Ministry; Dr Ross Stueber, Associate Director, School Ministry; Ed Grube, Director of Publications (part-time deployed), School Ministry; Vacant, Director, Youth Ministry; Rev Terry K Dittmer, Associate Director, Youth Ministry; David Weidner, Associate Director/Youth Gathering Director, Youth Ministry; Julie Johnston, Associate Director, Youth Ministry; Krista Miller, Youth Gathering Registrar/Operations Manager, Youth Ministry.

## Board for Human Care Ministries

*Chairman:* Rev Thomas R Marcis Jr.
*Revs* Juan A Gonzalez (2001), Thomas R Marcis Jr (2001), Stephen B Wenk (2001); *Laypersons:* Mr Lowell Bartels (2001); Mrs Debra L Grime (2001), Dr Kurt Senske (2001); Mrs Dianne L Thompson (2001).
*Staff:* Deaconess Dorothy Prybylski, Interim Executive Director; Mrs Gale M Carr, Administrative Assistant; Ms Elaine R Bryant, Director, LCMS World Relief; Rev Jarold D Rux, Manager, Program Support, LCMS World Relief; Gregory Koenig, Manager, Communications, LCMS World Relief; Mrs. Barbara Hoffmann, Manager, Grant Administration, LCMS World Relief; Rev Carlos Hernandez, Director, Districts/Congregations; Rev Carl H Toelke Jr, PhD, DMin, Director, Social Ministry Organizations; George P Sears, Director, Operations and Financial Management; Deaconess Dorothy Prybylski, Director, Specialized Pastoral Care and Clinical Education (Chaplaincy); Rev Bruce M Hartung, PhD, Director, LCMS Health Ministries; Mrs Tera Liescheidt, RD, Manager, Health Promotions, LCMS Health Ministries; Mrs Marie Kienker, Manager, Housing Ministries (PT); Rev Roy Brockopp, Manager, Older Adult Ministries (PT); Mr Duane E Hingst, Manager, Older Adult Ministries (PT); Mrs Kim Krull, Manager, Communications (PT); Mr Ken Braun, Editor, Speak-Up (PT).

# COMMISSIONS

## Constitutional Matters

*Chairman:* Walter Tesch (2004) 1674 North 117th St, Milwaukee, WI 53226
*Revs* Albert M Marcis (2004), Alan J Barber (2001), Gerhard H Bode (2001), Raymond L Hartwig, DD, Secretary, non-voting (2001); *Laypersons:* David A Piehler (2001), Walter Tesch (2004).

## Doctrinal Review

*Chairman:* Dr Cameron MacKenzie (2001) (see Ordained Section for Address),
*Revs* Rev Larry Rast (2001), Rev Robert Dargatz (2001), Dr Thomas Manteufel (2001), Rev Larry Rockeman (2001)

## Ministerial Growth and Support

*Chairperson:* Bruce Schuchard, MDiv, STM, PhD (2001)
*Vice Chairperson:* Roger Gallup, MDiv, MA (2001)
*Corresponding Secretary:* Daniel Jastram, MDiv, MA, PhD (2001); *Members:* William Dunk, MSEd (2001); James Fandrey, MDiv, MTh, (2001); Robert Rodefeld, BSBA, MBA (2001); Richard Wenz, MA (2001); Herbert Mueller, MDiv (2001); Daniel Gard, MDiv (2001); *Advisory Members:* William F Meyer, MDiv, MA, PhD; Leroy Wilke, LittD; Barbara Ryan, BA; Edwin Suelflow, DD; *Staff:* Bruce M Hartung, MDiv, STM, PhD, Executive Director.

## Organizations

*Chairperson:* Rev Larry Nichols, MDiv (2001)
*Rev* Victor Raj, STM, ThD (2001); *Teacher:* Andrew Novy (2001); *Laypersons:* Bud Newberry (2001).
*Staff:* Staff Services, Staff of the Commission on Theology and Church Relations.

## Theology and Church Relations

*Chairman:* Gerald Kieschnick JD (2001)
*Revs* George Dolak (2001), Jeffrey Gibbs, STM, PhD (2001), Nathan Jastram, PhD (2001), David Lumpp, ThD (2001), Kurt Marquart, MA (2001), Scott Murray, PhD (2001), David Scaer, ThD (2001), Harold Senkbeil (2004), James W. Voelz, PhD (2001), William C Weinrich, ThD (2001), *Teacher:* Kenneth R Palmreuter, MA, LLD (2001); *Laypersons:* Shirley Bergman, PhD (2004), Donald Brosz (2001), Raymond Moldenhauer (2001), Gene Schnelz, LLB, JD (2001); *Advisory Members:* Revs Alvin L Barry, DD, John Johnson, ThD, PhD, Robert Kuhn, DD, Dean O Wenthe, ThM, PhD.
*Staff:* Rev Samuel H Nafzger, ThD, Executive Director; Rev Jerald C Joersz, STM, LLD, Associate Executive Director; Rev Joel Lehenbauer, STM, Assistant Executive Director.

## Worship

*Chairman:* Rev Richard C Resch (2001)
*Revs* Stephen Everette (2001), Ronald Feuerhahn (2001), Daniel Q Johnson (2001); *Teachers:* Mark Bender (2001), Janet Muth (2001); *Layperson:* Elizabeth Werner (2001).
*Staff:* Rev Paul J Grime, PhD, Executive Director; Rev Jon Vieker, Assistant Director.

# OTHER SYNODICAL ENTITIES

## Concordia Historical Institute

### Department of Archives and History

801 DeMun Ave, St Louis, MO 63105
314/505-7900
E-Mail: Chi@chi.lcms.org
Web address: http://chi.lcms.org/

*President:* Dr Jerzy Hauptmann (2001) 6526 NW Melody Ln, Parkville MO 64152
*Revs* James Bauer (2001), Raymond Hartwig (2001), Lawrence Rast Jr (2001); *Laypersons:* Barbara L Cooke (2004), Eunice Hausler (2004), Fred Luetkemeier (2004), Larry Lumpe (2004), Scott J Meyer, (2001); Al Mueller (2004), Marlin W Roos (2001); *Advisory:* Dr Gerald P Birkmann.
*Staff:* Rev Daniel Preus, STM, Director; Rev Marvin Huggins, Associate Director for Archives and Library; Rev Mark Loest, STM, Assistant Director for Reference and Museum.

## Concordia Publishing House

3558 S Jefferson Ave, St Louis, MO 63118
314/268-1000 FAX 314/268-1329

*Board:* Rev Mark Sell (2004); *Teacher:* Dr Gene Veith (2004); *Laypersons:* John Brickler (2004), Ruth Brighton (2001), Delores Bruncke (2004); Jack

Fleischli (2001), Norman Kleinschmidt (2001), Robert Knox (2004); Robert Rodefeld (2001); Rev Ray Hartwig, Representative of Synodical President; *Advisory Member:* Paul Middeke, Vice President Finance/Treasurer/Chief Financial Officer.

*Staff:* Rev Dr Stephen J Carter, President and Chief Executive Officer; Susan Turner, Assistant to the President; Dr Barry L Bobb, Vice President of Editorial; Donald Kampmeinert, Vice President of Operations; Paul Mertens, Vice President of Finance; George Oehlert, Vice President of Corporate Development; John Schiller, Vice President of Marketing.

### Christian Education Specialists

Mr James Lohman, Director; Dr David Ebeling, Facilitator to the Church-at-Large; Ms Gloria Lessmann, Iowa/KS/Neb/Western MO; Rev Ronald and Betty Brusius, Florida; Mr Jason Scheler, Michigan/Ohio; Mr Duane Twetten, WI/No IL; Mr Paul Berg, Minnesota; Mrs Sarah Sailer, North Dakota and South Dakota.

### Educational Development

Ms Jane L Fryar, Director; Dr Rodney Rathmann, Senior Editor, Day/Midweek School Materials; Ms Carolyn Bergt, Editor, Day/Midweek School Materials; Mr Clarence Berndt, Editor, Day/Midweek School Materials; Rev Edward Engelbrecht, Editor, Confirmation and Adult Materials; Ms Cynthia Wheeler, Senior Editor, Vacation Bible School Materials; Rev James Gimbel, Senior Editor, Sunday School and Youth Materials; Mr Tom Nummela, Editor, *Teachers Interaction*, Sunday School Materials; Ms Gail Paulitz, Editor, Sunday School Materials; Mr Mark Sengele, Editor, Youth Materials; Ms Cory Poole, Coordinator, Multimedia Components; Dr Thomas J Doyle, Adult/Family Life Editor-at-Large; Rev Roger Sonnenberg, Adult/Family Life Writer/Editor-at-Large.

### Church Resource Development

Rev Dr Frederic W Baue, Senior Editor, Church Resource Development; Ms Dawn Weinstock, Managing Editor, Book Team; Jane P Wilke, Acquisitions Editor, Children's and Teaching Resources; Rev Dr Christopher W Mitchell, Editor, Concordia Commentary Series; Rev Kenneth C Wagener, Senior Editor, Professional and Academic Books; Rev Hector Hoppe, Director, Multiethnic Resources; Rev Steven H Albers, Editor, *Concordia Pulpit Resources* and tracts; Rev Dr Philip H Lochhaas, Editor, *Portals of Prayer;* Rev Stephen Wenk, Editor, *Strength for the Day.*

### Music and Worship

Rev David Johnson, Director; Mr Gregory Gastler, Field Services Representative

### Products and services includes:

Sunday school, vacation Bible school, weekday and day school curriculum; youth and adult Bible studies; bulletins; offering envelopes; Bibles; professional and academic books; church supplies; music; videos; adult and children's books; computer products.

## Concordia University System

(See Board for Higher Education)

## KFUO

(See Board for Communication Services)

## Lutheran Church Extension Fund—Missouri Synod

1-800/843-5233 (The LCEF)

*Chairman:* Jon Schumacher (2000), 2020 Burnwood Ct, Brookfield, WI 53045

*Board:* Janet Johnson, Vice Chairman, (2001); *Revs* Dave Buegler (2001), Merlin Sepmeyer, (2001); *Laypersons:* Hans Tews, Secretary (2000), Marvin Thompson (2001), Duane Helm (1999), F Michael Maish (2001), Sandy Thompson, (2000), John Daniel, (2002), Luther Goehring, (2002), Paul Middeke, Treasurer, (2000), Dr Rober Kuhn, (2001).

*Staff:* Merle Freitag, President; Brenda Vickers, Executive Assistant; Victor W Bryant, Senior Vice President, Marketing; Gerald E Wendt, Senior Vice President, Loans & Real Estate; Carolyn Schlimpert, Vice President, Loans; Jeff J Miller, Senior Vice President, District and National Ministry Resources; Debbie Borawski, Demographic Services; Dave Meyer, Senior Vice President, Investor Services; Judy Hampton, Assistant Vice President, Investor Services; Mary Byrd, Kent Wilson, Loan Officers; Sandra Copley, Mary Schlosser, Asst Loan Officers; Karen Drier, Assistant Vice President, Information Center; Virgie Everett, Barb Siebenmorgen, Carol Wallace, Sharon Bollinger, Julie Webb, Information Representatives; Beverly Gregory, Assistant Vice President, Technology & Research; Brad Bucher, Assistant Vice President Regulatory Compliance; Thomas R Helfrich, Senior Vice President, Finance & Administration; Jane Absheer, Assistant Vice President, Administration; Kevin Bremer, Assistant Vice President, Finance; Ken Weber, Assistant Vice President, Accounting & Financial Reporting.

### Standing Committee

### Architecture

Gary Landhauser, Chairman; Donn Bohde, Secretary; Greg Beste, Ken Hirsch, Byron Perdue; *Architectural Advisors:* John Corkill, Frank Kohl, Norman Sessing, Richard Brumfield, Elmer Wind, Keith Myhre, James Mayer, John Mundinger, Ernest Verges, Craig Melde, Deon Bahr, *Liturgical and Artist Consultants:* Paul Grime, Richard W Wiegmann.

## The Lutheran Church—Missouri Synod Foundation

P. O. Box 229008, St. Louis, MO 63122-9008
314/965-9000 or 800/325-7912

*Chairman:* Mr Fred Bernthal (2002), 26 Sunrise Dr, Morris Plains, NJ 07950

*Board: Revs* George Black (2000), Ron Miller (2001), Roger Pittelko (Synodical President's representative) (2001); Laypersons: Kermit Almstedt (2001), Glenn Coats (2000), William Engel (2000), John Kuddes (2000), Leon Langemeier (2001), Donald Pegosh (stewardship representative), Robert Weber (2002), Paul Wiedenmann (2002); non-voting: Paul Middeke, LCMS CFO (2001).

*Staff:* Mark Stuenkel, President

*Administration*: Catherine Whitcomb, Vice President.

*Customer Support:* Tom Angus, Vice President; Linda Batterson, Vice President, Trust Services; Donald Horn, Ministry Support; Robert Knehans, Individual Ministry Support; Scott Radden, Individual Ministry Support; Wayne Sell, Individual Ministry Support; Tina Clasquin, Organizational Ministry Support; Elizabeth Trost, Organizational Ministry Support; Paul Geidel, Vice President, Gift Processing; Alan Butterworth, Technical Support; Glenn Levin, Gift Reporting.

*Finance:* Wayne Price, Vice President; Cathy Hederman, Controller; Steve Schneider, Accountant; Robert Vance, Accountant; Richard Christenson, Vice President, Investments; (Vacant), Account Manager/Analyst; (Vacant), Investment Administrator; Clemencia Penilla, Operations Supervisor; Mary Boyer, Operations Analyst/Coordinator.

*Individual Ministry:* Eugene Kuebler, Vice President; Wade Janssen, Principal Gifts; Becca Jones, Communication and Project Coordinator; Terry Gerdts (Missouri), Unit Mentor; Pam Moksnes (Minnesota), Unit Mentor; Paul Wills (Maryland), Unit Mentor; Rev. Dennis Bohren (Arizona); Carol Daudt (Arizona); Mark Davis (Arizona); Michael Fischer (Arizona); Stuart Craig (California); Dan Bacon (Colorado); Alvin Macke (Connecticut); Jon Baermann (Illinois); Robert Bewersdorf (Illinois); Martha Eggert (Illinois); Jeffrey Miller (Illinois); Terry Breininger (Indiana); Timothy Imler (Indiana); Richard "Red" Finch (Iowa); James Schroeder (Iowa); Susan Slater (Maryland); John Kidwell (Michigan); Thomas Mueller (Michigan); Deborah Torbet (Michigan); David Rohe (Missouri); Donnie Schnakenberg (Missouri); Harry "Ed" Weber (Montana) (PT); Sheri Janssen (Nebraska); Neal Koch (Nebraska); David Hildebrandt (New Jersey); Richard Paul (New York); John Hass (North Carolina); Edward Bean (North Dakota); Patricia Bilow (Ohio); Steven Schoenherr (Tennesee) Bervin Mirtsching (Texas); John Meyer (Wisconsin); Ronald Smith (Wisconsin).

*Information Technology:* Dorothy Kaestner, Vice President; Jason Perotka, Internal Customer Support; Jason Todd, Electronic Media Specialist.

*Marketing:* John Schoedel, Vice President.

*Organizational Ministry:* Lloyd Probasco, Vice President; Glenn Thiel, Coordinator, CUS and Seminaries; (Vacant), Coordinator, LCMS Ministries Support; Alex Pavlenko, Coordinator, High Schools, Early Childhood, RSO's.

## Worker Benefit Plans

1333 S Kirkwood Rd, St Louis, MO 63122-7295
314/965-7580 or 888/WBP-PLAN (927-7526)
FAX 314/996-1127
E-mail WBP-INFO@WBP.ORG

**Concordia Retirement Plan**
**Concordia Disability & Survivor Plan**
**Concordia Health Plan**
**Accident Insurance Programs**
**Pension Plan for Pastors & Teachers**

*Chairperson:* Guy E Miller Jr (2001), 1333 S Kirkwood Rd, St Louis, MO 63122-7295

*Board: Revs* Philip J Esala (2001), Fred C Gersch (2004); *Teacher:* LuJuana R Butts (2001); *Laypersons:* Howard F Crumb (2004), Lyle L Meyer (2001), Roland R Strickert (2004), Harvey W Wilkening (2001), Kenneth R Willis (2001), Joel R Wilson (2001), Paul W Middeke (ex officio).

*Staff:* Dan A Leeman, Executive Director; Ann Schmidt, Executive Assistant to Executive Director; Thomas J Neely, Director of Finance; Robert W Cushman, Director of Systems; Mark J Dunlop, Director of Member Services; Linda A Olsen, Director of Communications; James F Sanft, Director of Actuarial Services; Anita C Arnold, CPA/Investment; Darcie D Ball, Sr Systems Project Leader, Robert A List, Senior Benefits Consultant, Nanette Rasmussen, Assistant Actuary, Health, Eustolio Gomez, Coordinator for Retirement Planning & Financial Education, Connie J Ledbetter, Field Representative; Paul M Snyder, Field Representative.

# COUNCILS

## Council of Presidents

Dr Arleigh L Lutz, Chairman (2000) (see Ordained Section for Address)

## Placement Committee

*For Pastors/Vicars:* William Diekelman (2000), Eugene Gierke (2000), Rev Orval D Mueller (2000), David Callies (2000), Timothy Sims (2000).
*For Commissioned Ministers and certified Layworker Committee:* Ronald Meyer (2000).

# OTHER SERVICE UNITS

## Committee for Convention Nominations

(Members were elected at 2000 District Conventions)

| | |
|---|---|
| Eastern | Mr James Brese |
| English | Rev Larry Vogel |
| Iowa East | Mr Ray Lavrenz |
| Kansas | Rev Keith Kohlmeier |
| Michigan | Mr James Garber |
| Mid-South | Rev Paul Donner |
| Minnesota North | Mr Darold Krenz |
| Montana | Rev Mark Grunst |
| New England | Mr Robert Giger |
| New Jersey | Rev Robert Roegner |
| North Dakota | Mr Donald Brandenburg |
| Ohio | Dr David Buegler |
| Pacific Southwest | Dr Loren T Kramer |
| Rocky Mountain | Mr Daniel M Krueger |
| South Wisconsin | Dr Edwin Suelflow |
| Southeastern | Mrs Janis McDaniels |
| Southern Illinois | Mr Roger Etter |
| Texas | Rev Allen F Doering |

## Accounting Department

*Synodical Accounting:* Charles Rhodes, Executive Director; Kimberly Merten, Administrative Assistant; Karen Rehm, Director, Tax Reporting. Synod—Rosalito Silva, Director; Peter Krege, Manager; Jim Ehlers, Supervisor; Tina Hayes, Staff Accountant; Daryl Haake, Program Accountant; Alice Huff, Supervisor, Receipts; Bonnie Pearce, Budget and Systems Specialist; William Goetz, Financial Analyst. OIS—Gary Callies, Manager. CUS/BHE—Jim Winston, Manager. Payroll and Accounts Payable—Kenneth Pranschke, Manager; Gerry Alimagno, Supervisor, A/P; Sherry Tullman, Supervisor, Payroll.

## Electronic Media/Church Information Center

**1-888-THE-LCMS**
**infocenter@lcms.org**

David G Berner, Executive Director; Diane Grimm, Administrative Assistant; Linda Hoops, Manager, Church Information Center; Donna Cole, Caller Representative; Keven Ficken, Electronic Media Specialist; David Twillmann, Manager, Electronic Information Resources.

## General Services Department

**lcms_gen_services@lcms.org**

Ronald P Schultz, Executive Director; Barbara Knehans, Operations Manager; Michael Magee, Manager, Purchasing Services; Lynne Marvin, Director, Travel and Meeting Planning; Wendi Adams, Manager of Library Services; Gene Weeke, Director, Rosters and Statistics; Karen Eggemeyer, Manager, Editorial Services.

## Human Resources, Department of

Barbara Ryan, Executive Director; Dave Fiedler, Manager; Vencine Bush, Manager.

## Internal Audit Department

Joann P Spotanski, Executive Director; Michael A Louis, Manager; Laurie M Barnett, Christopher P Wood, Lisa M Bastin, Jaime F Ryberg, Senior Auditors; Chad J Cattoor, Sherry L McIlvaine, Jennifer N Bierman, Andrew C Rabe, Staff Auditors; Mary T Hummert, Administrative Assistant.

## Office of Information Systems

1333 S Kirkwood Rd, St Louis, MO 63122-7295
314/996-1900

*Board:* Stephen J Carter, Paul Middeke, Merle Freitag, Rodger W Hebermehl, Bradford L Hewitt, Dan A Leeman, William F Meyer, Mark Stuenkel, John H Whaley.

*Staff:* Alan Meyer, Executive Director; Tim Francisco, Director of Operations; Doug Traxler, Director of Technology; Myron Koehn, Director of Applications.

## LCMS Ministries Support

James Miller, Executive Director, Jeannie Kovacs, Administrative Assistant; K. Mark Weinrich, Senior Director; Hans Springer, Senior Director; Linda Sanders, Senior Director; Rev Ed Bertram, C.U.S. National Endowment Director; Harold Melser, Director of Development, World Mission; Terry Whittle, Creative Director; Rick Holtz, Assistant Director, Field Support; Janelle Brakhane, Assistant Director, Emerging Ministries; Beth Gower, Assistant Director, Information Services; Jeff Craig-Meyer, Assistant Director, C.U.S. National Endowment Campaign; Linda Watkins, Manager, Gift Processing; Rev Earl Feddersen, Copy Manager; Stacy Peck, Production Coordinator; Tammy Songer, Communications Coordinator, C.U.S. Campaign; Debra Feenstra, Manager, Missionary Support; Kathy Wakeman, Manager, Donor Care; Charlotte Danback, Telecare Coordinator; Sally Aschinger, Manager LWML/Group Programs; Jane Cauchon, Deployed Staff Support; Linda Buck, Telecare; Sandra Tochtrap, Telecare; Caroline Dressler, Donor Care; Nancy Rowley, Donor Care; Brian Forrester, Gift Processing; Carolyn Williams, Gift Processing; Marvin Kohlmeier, Mission and Ministry Representative, Kansas; Gary Thies, Mission and Ministry Representative, Iowa West/Nebraska; Don Cousens, Mission and Ministry Representative, New Jersey/Northeast; Peter Newman, Mission and Ministry Representative, Missouri.

## Planning and Research, Department of

Dr John O'Hara, Research Analyst.

## Office of the Treasurer

Mr Paul W Middeke, Vice President—Finance/Treasurer; Sandra L Bossman, Executive Assistant.

# EDUCATIONAL INSTITUTIONS OF SYNOD

## Faculties and Staff

## Seminaries

### CONCORDIA THEOLOGICAL SEMINARY

6600 N Clinton St, Fort Wayne IN 46825-4996
219/452-2100
Year Founded 1846

FAX Numbers
219/452-2121 President/Academic Dean/Business Office/Continuing Education
219/452-2227 Admissions/Seminary Relations
219/452-2285 Registrar/Dean of Students
219/452-2246 Development
219/452-2126 Library
219/452-2189 Placement/Vicarage/Field Education/Graduate Studies/Chapel
219/452-2270 DELTO/*CTQ*/Faculty
219/452-2253 Bookstore
219/452-2255 Russian Project

***President:*** Wenthe Dean O ThM MA PhD

***Professors Emeriti***
Houser William G MDiv PhD
Klug Eugene F MA DTheol
Luebke Martin F PhD
Mueller Norbert H STM DMin
Reuning Daniel G BA SMM
Surburg Raymond F ThD PhD

***Professors***
Bollhagen James G ThD Dean of Pastoral Education and Placement
Bunkowske Eugene W MDiv PhD Supervisor of DMiss Program
Judisch Douglas McC L MDiv PhD Faculty Secretary and Supervisor of Hispanic Ministries and Associate Editor of *Concordia Theological Quarterly*
Just Arthur A Jr STM PhD Dean of the Chapel
MacKenzie Cameron A STM PhD Chairman Department of Historical Theology
Scaer David P ThD Chairman Department of Systematic Theology and Editor of *Concordia Theological Quarterly* and Faculty Marshal
Weinrich William C MDiv DTheol Academic Dean
Zilz Melvin L PhD

***Associate Professors***
Gard Daniel L MDiv PhD Dean of Graduate Studies
Gieschen Charles A MTh PhD Chairman Department of Exegetical Theology
Maier Walter A III MDiv PhD Dean of Distance Learning
Marquart Kurt E MA
Nuffer Richard T BA JD MDiv Acting Dean of Pastoral Education and Placement
Rutt Douglas L MDiv DMiss Acting Supervisor of DMiss Program
Saleska John W BA MEd
Schulz K Detlev ThD Chairman Department of Pastoral Ministry/Missions

***Assistant Professors***
Fickenscher Carl C II MBA MDiv PhD Supervisor of Continuing Education
Pless John T MDiv Supervisor of Field Education
Quill Timothy CJ MPhil STM Coordinator of Russian Project
Rast Lawrence R Jr STM Assistant Academic Dean and Associate Editor of *Concordia Theological Quarterly*
Resch Richard C MM MDiv Kantor
Roethemeyer Robert V BA MDiv MALS Director of Library and Information Services
Scaer Peter J MDiv MA
Schroeder Randall A MEd MDiv PhD
Ziegler Roland F MDiv

***Professors—Modified Service***
Maier Walter A MA ThD
Muller Richard E MA MDiv
Zietlow Harold H BD PhD

***Visiting Professors***
Dretke James P MA MDiv DMiss
Pittelko Roger D STM DMin Supervisor of Vicarage

***Executive Staff***
Wingfield Albert B MA Vice President of Business Affairs

***Ordained Staff***
Bush David S MDiv Supervisor of Handicap Ministry
Evanson Charles J BA BD Deployed to Russian Project
Kind David A MDiv Admission Counselor
Klemsz Scott C MDiv Director of Admission and Public Relations
Lammert Richard A BA BS MLS MDiv Public Services Librarian
Lange George H BTh Director of Financial Aid
Ludwig Alan G STM Deployed to Russian Project
Powers Gregory J MDiv Accountant
Puls Timothy R MDiv Dean of Students
Scudder Michael R MDiv Admission Counselor
Smith Robert E MLS MDiv Electronic Resources Librarian
Wachholz Dean C MDiv Director of Development
Wesemann Kenneth R MS MDiv PhD Advisor on Personal Growth

***Deaconess Staff***
Nielsen, Pamela J MA Director of Community Services
Ostermann Joyce A BA Financial Aid Assistant
Watt Natalie J MAR Acquisitions Assistant

***Professional Staff***
Bascom Judith J Administrative Assistant Russian Project
Behning Trudy E BA Executive Assistant to President
Braden Patricia A BS MILS Technical Services Librarian
Caudill Michael D AA Controller
Feldkamp Judy M Administrative Assistant Graduate Studies
Gard Annette K BS Administrative Assistant DELTO Program
Gruber Margaret L BA Manager Telecommunications Manager
Hall Cynthia A Director of Food and Clothing Co-ops
Havekotte Alan W MDiv Development Counselor
Johnson Dan C BS Director of Major Gifts
Klinger John A MS Director of Information Technology
Luchnenko Candis L BS Director of Bookstore Services
Mueller Heidi D BA Chapel Administrative Assistant
Payne M Jane Administrative Assistant to Academic Dean
Robins Monica R BA Public Relations Officer
Rogers-Funk Mary C Administrative Assistant to Vice President of Business Affairs
Rutt Deborah L BA MS Associate Director of Development
Shoemaker Cheryl L BS Coordinator of International Students
Wachholz Betty M BA Relocation Coordinator
Wegman Barbara A AS Registrar

### CONCORDIA SEMINARY

801 DeMun Ave St Louis MO 63105
314/505-7000, FAX 314/505-7001
Year Founded 1839

***President:*** Johnson John F MA ThD PhD
***President Emeritus:*** Barth Karl L MDiv DD

***Professors Emeriti***
Berndt Juan Dipl DD
Brighton Louis A STM PhD
Fremder Alfred PhD
Graudin Arthur F MDiv DRel
Harm Rudolph H STM PhD
Hopmann Roland A BA
Hummel Horace D STM PhD
Ji Won Yong ThD
Kiehl Erich H ThD
Klann Richard MDiv PhD DD
Knippel Charles T STM PhD
Kopitske Harley L MDiv
Matthias Elmer W DMin
Pederson Eldon E MEd LHD
Robbert George S STM PhD
Rossow Francis C MA MDiv LittD
Schmelder William J STM
Schultz Richard J MEd MDiv DD
Vogel Leroy E STM

***Professors***
Bartelt Andrew H MA MDiv PhD Vice President for Academic Affairs and Executive Assistant to the President
Brauer James L SMM STM PhD Dean of Chapel
Kolb Robert A STM PhD Director of the Institute for Mission Studies and Mission Professor of Systematic Theology
Nagel Norman E MDiv PhD Graduate Professor of Systematic Theology
Raabe Paul R MA MDiv PhD Chairman of Department of Exegetical Theology
Raj A R Victor ThD Assistant Director of Institute for Mission Studies and Mission Professor of Exegetical Theology
Rosin Robert L MDiv PhD Chairman of the Department of Historical Theology
Rowold Henry ThD Mission Professor of Practical Theology
Voelz James W MDiv PhD Director of Graduate Studies
Wesselschmidt Quentin F MDiv PhD Chairman *Concordia Journal* Editorial Committee

***Associate Professors***
Adams David L MDiv PhD Director of Educational Technology
Arand Charles P ThD Assistant Dean of Faculty and Chairman Department of Systematic Theology

Berger David O MA MLS Director of Library Services
Eickmann Jerrold A MDiv Registrar and Academic Advisor
Feuerhahn Ronald R MPhil MDiv PhD
Gibbs Jeffrey A STM PhD Assistant Academic Advisor
Manteufel Thomas STM PhD Coordinator of the Correspondence School
Nielsen Glenn A STM PhD Director of Vicarage
Oberdeck John W MS MDiv PhD Director of Continuing Education
Salminen Bryan R PhD Coordinator of Specialized Testing and Counseling Services
Schrieber Paul L ThD
Warneck Richard H STM PhD Chairman of the Department of Practical Theology
Weise Robert W MS MDiv PhD Professor of Pastoral Ministry and the Life Sciences

***Assistant Professors***
Kloha Jeffrey J BA MDiv STM
Lessing Robert R MDiv STM Assistant Professor in Exegetical Theology
Okamoto Joel P BS MDiv STM ThD Assistant Professor in Systematic Theology
Peter David J BA MDiv DMin Director of the DMin Program
Rockemann Larry MDiv Vice President of Student Life and Director of Placement
Robinson Paul W STM
Saleska Timothy E MDiv MPhil PhD
Schmitt David R MA MDiv
Schuchard Bruce G STM PhD
Schumacher William W BA MDiv STM Assistant to the Director of Resident Field Education for Cross-cultural Experiences
Utech William G STM Director of Resident Field Education

### Hispanic Institute of Theology

501 W North Ave Suite 407
Melrose Park IL 60160
708/343-1395 FAX 708/343-1466

***Affiliated Faculty Members***
Dominguez Ruben LicTh MA Assistant Professor
Groll Douglas R MDiv DD Director Coordinator

***Executive Staff***
Brenner Dorothy Emerita
Dollase Edward A Vice President for Administrative Services
Fiedler Leonard V MEd Vice President for Development
Knackstedt Betty Ann RN Seminary Nurse
Mirly Joann MA in LS Assistant Director of Library Services
Thomas Glen D STM Vice President for Seminary Relations

***Professional Staff***
Bliese Mark J BA Coordinator of Technical Services Library
Bohlmann Gerard J BSE Information Systems Manager
Engfehr Lois M AA Director of Communications
Hoffmann Jan M BA Director of Campus Activities
Hofman Mark D BSE Director of Development
Horman Cindy A BA Information Systems Technical Assistant
Jackson Earlyn J Housing Officer
Kamps Adam M BA Development Officer
Lindvedt Marty C MS Assistant Coordinator of Specialized Testing and Counseling Services
Meyer John E STM Director of Alumni Activities
Moore Jeffery C BS MDiv STM Director of Ministerial Recruitment
Poellet Gretchen K BA Manager of Media Services
Redeker Michael J MDiv Admissions Counselor
Robinson Fred K MBA Accounting Manager/Food Service Coordinator
Schaper Gary G DMin Advisor on Personal Growth Toward Ministry
Sommer Valerie J Annual Fund Manager and Financial Information Coordinator

***Special Assistants***
Bergt Robert R MST MDiv Artist in Residence
Carr William W BS MDiv STM Assistant Registrar
Gerike Henry MA MDiv Director of Musical Activities
Maxwell Lee A MA ThD Director of the Concordia Archaeology Society

## Colleges/Universities

### CONCORDIA COLLEGE

**4090 Geddes Rd, Ann Arbor MI 48105**
**734/995-7300, FAX 734/995-4610 or 734/995-7455**
**Year Founded 1962**

***President:*** Koerschen James M PhD

***Professors Emeriti***
Aufdemberge Theodore P PhD
Beyer Marilyn A MA
Foelber Paul F PhD
Garske Herbert E MMus MA
Harting Walter F MEd
Heckert Jakob ThD
Kenney Donald EdD
Marino Quentin M MMus
Schmaltz Norman J PhD
Stelzer Wilbert W MA
Sturmfels John H MA SpA
von Fange Erich A PhD
Wilbert Warren N EdD

***Professors***
Adler Barbara J PhD
Allen Ronald M PhD
Grotjan Gayle PhD Dean School of Education
Joyce Mark L EdD
Looker Mark S PhD
Mahler William PhD Registrar and Director of Institutional Assessment
Marschke Paul O PhD
Mossman Donald J PhD
Sernett Gilbert SpA PhD
Shuta Richard J DB PhD
Skov Neil M MST MS EDD
Twietmeyer T Alan PhD
Wilke Wayne W STM PhD Executive Vice President-Academics

***Associate Professors***
Blersch Jeffrey MMT MUD
Carlson David PhD
Cedel Tom PhD Dean Arts and Sciences
Kalmes Michael W MEd
Klintworth Kathryn DA Coordinator of Academic Development
Lipp Carolyn E MMus
Pies Timothy N PhD Assessment Director—Degree Completion Programs
Sprik Jeanette PhD Dean of Adult Continuing Education
Steinkellner Beth MFA

***Assistant Professors***
Anderson David BA PhD
Ankerberg Erik BA MA
Behrendt Linda MS
Bird Laura MA PhD
Brandon Kevin MLS Director of the Library
Buesing Richard MLS Technical Librarian
Campbell Robert C MA
Frusti Timothy MA
Giese Curtis STM
Heinemann Brian W MEd Dean of Information Technology
Knotts Richard MEd
Lin Yi-Li DMA
Parrish Stephen AA BS AMLS MA PhD Librarian
Rowe Kathleen MA Director of Admissions
Schultz Andrew M MA

***Professional Staff***
De Boer Stephen BA MPA
Carlson Krissa Assistant Director of Alumni Affairs
Fliehman Dennis Admission Counselor
Flynn Daniel MEd Director of Counseling
Flynn Gail Advising Coordinator
Hardin Julie Director of Student Activities/RD
Houle David Director of Communication
Iverson Kim Director of Housing/RD
Kasten Robert BA Director of Athletics
Kennedy Kori Coach/Athletic Administrator
McDowell Karen Financial Aid Counselor
McMillan Linda BA Payroll Administrator/Accountant
Meyer Rob Admission Counselor
O'Brien Kevin MA Faculty Development/Technology
Piasecki Amy Financial Aid Counselor
Priskorn David Admission Counselor
Reilly Richelle Coach/Athletic Administrator
Reoma Joet MA Director of Computer Services
Seegert Lois Assistant Registrar
Shields Randall W ThD Campus Pastor/Coordinator of Pre-Sem Program
Shultz Beth Admission Counselor
Talcott Jane Director School of Continuing Education
Tanner Kevin Director of Security
Taylor Timothy Assessment Counselor
Tippery Alice Admissions Counselor
Trapp Philip BA Coach/Athletic Administrator
Valente Jason Vice President of Finance
Verseman Kathryn Director of Financial Aid
Vogt Don MS Vice President of Student Services
Wilde Daniel MS

***Part-Time/Visiting Faculty***
Bloom Wendy MFA
Czartoski Heather MS
Frost Juliana MA
Hile Claudia
Sleator Emma MA
Valaskova Anna MA
Wentzel Mark MFA
Zielke Ruth MA

### CONCORDIA UNIVERSITY AT AUSTIN

**3400 Interstate 35 North, Austin TX 78705-2799**
**512/486-2000, FAX 512/459-8517**
**Internet: http://www.concordia.edu**
**Year Founded 1926**

***President:*** Zersen David J MDiv MA DMin EdD

***Presidents Emeriti:*** Goltermann Samuel I DD
Martens Ray F MDiv STM STD

***Professors Emeriti***
Dinda Richard J MA MLS MALAS DLitt
Frahm John H MDiv PhD
Gastler Bernard MMus PhD
Riemer Milton H MDiv MA PhD JD
Rutz Harold A MMus
Tschatschula M Leroy MEd PhD
Vorwerk E Glenn MBA PhD

***Professors***
Doering Sandra K MEd EdD Dean School of Education
Duder Clyburn MA MDiv PhD
Heck Joel D MDiv ThM ThD Vice President of Academic Services
Jungemann John D MEd PhD Dean School of Liberal Arts and Sciences, Director of Institutional Research
Lacey Howard A MBA DBA Dean School of Business
Meissner Laurence L MS PhD
Stayton Susan MA PhD
Zielke Donald H PhD

***Associate Professors***
Allen Debra J MA PhD
Daley Jeffrey D MAEd PhD
Diaz-Alemany Daisy MEd PhD Dean School of Non-Traditional Studies
Driskill William C MA PhD Vice President of Student Services
Goddard Bartley E MS PhD
Haneke Dianne M MSEd PhD
Keiper Gertrude M MA EdD
Kroft David MFA
Lowery Linda C MEd Athletic Director, Golf Coach
Middendorf Michael P MDiv STM ThD
Muench Paul E MDiv THm PhD
Orton Thomas H MA
Pate Thomas R MS PhD
Rosenberger Michal L BS MS PhD
Scrogin Betty MAT EdD
Septowski Charles D MBA JD LLM
Stahlke Leonard E MDiv STM
Stevenson James N MS PhD
Zoch Theodore F MEd

***Assistant Professors***
Achterberg Robert A MChM
Dunsmoir Beryl A MA PhD
Figur Nilo L MA
Freese Faythe R MM DM
Haneke Dianne M MSEd PhD
Hilgendorf Thomas C MEd PhD
Kluth David L MDiv MA Vice President of Information and Technology Services
Krause Jay A MS PhD Vice President of Enrollment Services
Moyer Michael A PhD
Pierson Burton E MA PhD
Puffe Paul J MDiv MA ABD Director of Pre-Seminary Program
Schwartz Ann MA
Springstube Woodard MBA MA PhD
Trittin Brian L MS DMA
Trovall Carl C MDiv ABD Campus Pastor
Utzinger Jeffrey C MFA
Van Andel Roger MS
Voges Linda K BS MS EdD

***Faculty Without Rank***
Holmes Norman MLS MBA CAS Director of Library Services

***Adjunct Faculty***
Gardner James Michael MEd Baseball Coach

McConnell James H MA
McGehee Richard V MS PhD
Van Damme Deborah S MS
White David N MS
Yankowski Janice G BS MA

***Part-Time Faculty***
Adkins Lisa M MEd
Asif Tajuddin BA MA
Atwood Bill MBA
Beck Hubert F BA MDiv
Burnham Patricia A MM MME
Cooper Caren C BA MA PhD
Daniels Glenn P BSBA MS MBA
Dobson Nicholas P BA MA
Dixon C Lynn BAAS MS
Emmert Mark D BA CTEFLA
Essbaum Jill A BA MA
Firnhaber Norbert A MDiv MA DMin
Fitch LaVerne J MA PhD Director of Institutional Effectiveness
Fletcher Ronald W MSSM
Franco Robert BBA MBA
French Kerry M BA MM
Gohring Thomas R BA
Hefner David R MFA
Hinkle Jeffrey G BA Drama Director
King John A JD
Krabbenhoft Eloiese MA
Krebs Alfred N MA MDiv
Lawrie Jim B
Liebenow Mark R BS MS
McKelvey Michael E BM MM
Midkiff Ina J MBA
Montet Ellis J BA MA
Owens Philip J BS MS PhD
Rundell Bob R MA
Seeger Mark W MDiv
Strecker Richard A BBA JD
Suker Amy L BA MA
Wilburn Kathleen M BA MA EdD
Wilburn H Ralph BA MA PhD

***Administrative Staff***
Arldt Laura BA Director of Facility Scheduling
Benne Deborah G BS Cash Disbursements Manager
Bohot Lois BA Director of Research and Records
Bonnar Kathy M BA MA Career Planning
Braun Gregg MS Director of the Annual Fund
Broyles Mike BA Senior TV Producer
Butterfield Michael MS Vice President for Resource Development
Cantu Edward Softball Coach
Carey Shirley BBA Campaign Manager
Davis Sarah Resident Hall Director
Doering Martin E MDiv Coordinator of PELT and Colloquy
English Pamela MA Director of University Relations
Fein Lowell BTE MSEd Registrar
Fry Marcus X MLIS Technical Services Librarian
Goetz Philip BA Assistant TV Producer
Holobaugh Sherrah BA Admissions Counselor
Horn Cathy BA Assistant Director of Financial Assistance
Huey-Frenkel Sandra BA Director of Business Services
Johnson Ben Resident Hall Director
Johnson Shawn BA Assistant Director of Admissions-Freshmen
Jost James BS Men's Basketball Coach, Sports Information Director
Jost Patricia M MEd Director of Financial Assistance
Kasper Kristi BA Assistant Director of Admissions-Transfers
Kull Donna MA Director of Grants Coordinator
Lee Pamela BA CPA Vice President of Business and Finance
Liedtke Julie BA Associate Director of Admissions
Liedtke Richard BA Assistant Director of Admissions, Women's Basketball Coach
Lowrey Kathryn BA Employee Benefits Manager
Matetzschk Nancy BA Registrar's Office Manager
Mueller Suzanne BS Director of Alumni Services
Nunes Monique C MA Director Adult Degree Program Dallas Center
Officer Tracey BA Registrar's Office Special Projects Coordinator
Palmer Mark BA MA Administrative Computer Services
Perry LaTonya BS Volleyball Coach
Peterson Craig BS Intramural Director, Director of Security, Resident Hall Director
Shao Rodrick MBA Network Administrator
Siegrist Pamela Student Accounts Manager
Stephens Edward CPA Director of Accounting
Welton John BS Director of Major Gifts
Winkler Chris C MEd Director of Student Activities, NCAA Compliance Officer

## CONCORDIA COLLEGE

**171 White Plains Rd, Bronxville NY 10708-3101**
**914/337-9300, FAX 914/395-4500**
**Year Founded 1881**

***President:*** George Viji D EdD

***President Emeriti:*** Meyer Albert E MDiv LLD
Schultz Ralph C SMD

***Professors Emeriti***
Bayer Lester R EdD
Dorre Ralph O MA
Halter E Florence MA
Just Constance L MA

***Professors***
Borgen Wally D EdD
Burger Jane R PhD Director of Secondary Education Program Director of Placement
Franco Anne K EdD
Fraser Sherry J MSW ACSW Associate Dean for Residence Life and Faculty Marshal
Heschke Richard J DMA Dean of Academic Services
Jacobson David C MDiv PhD Provost
Lee E Yong PhD
Meier Robert J MS EdD Director of Computer Services
Miesner Donald R MDiv MA ThD Director Pre-Seminary Program
Peterson Clifford H MDiv STM EdD
Rehm Merlin D ThD Director of International Studies
Schultz Timothy P DMA
Sluberski Thomas R MDiv MA ThD

***Associate Professors***
Arat Serdar MFA
Bodling Kurt A MDiv STM MS Director of Library Services
Bucher Karen J PhD
Fuhrmann Gerald W MS
Gatz Yvonne K MSW
Maida Lori PhD Director of Assessment
Nakhai Mandana PhD Director of Writing Center
Peters Ralph E PhD
Reimann Andrew K MA MS
Roy George M BBA

***Assistant Professors***
Adams Joan Roper MSW
Bahr John MDiv Dean of Students
Dalgish Lynda MEd MSE
Klibonoff Jon D MMus
Russert David J MA
Zwernemann Bonnie MAT Coordinator of Student Teaching

***Instructor***
Burkee James MA
Galchutt Kathryn MA

***Staff***
Alessy Al Manager of Public Safety/Security
Blanco Mark E BA Registrar
Bolles Dan BA Manager of Schoenfeld Hall
Cook Kevin T MS Director of Advancement
DeLisio Gina MSWQ Assistant Director of Admission
Edwards Jenifer BA Assistant Director of Admission
Elwell Joy RN MS FNP Nurse Practitioner
Fick Kenneth T BA Director of Student Financial Aid
Folwaczny Carl BA Business Manager
Folwaczny Wendy BS Director of Career Development
Geiling Elizabeth MS Coordinator of Freshmen Advising
Greiner Robert BA Admission Counselor and Baseball Coach
Groth George PsyD Director of Concordia Connection
Hendricks Rebecca BA Assistant Director of Admissions
Hromulak Virginia MA Director of Accelerated Degree Program
Joerz Henry M MA Manager of Instructional Technology
Kremer Robert Director of Fitness Center
Laoutaris Kathy BA Assistant Athletic Director
Lonergan Dennis CPA BBA Chief Financial Officer
Luekens Katie Lynn MM Assistant to Dean of Students
Mahood Miki BA Director of Community Relations
Marquez Ivan BS Athletic Director
McQuade Francis MA Associate Director Accelerated Degree Program
Nagel Christopher MIM Vice President of Institutional Advancement Instructor in International Business
O'Connell Susan A BA Director of Marketing and Public Relations
O'Connor Ann B BA Business Office Manager
Padovano-Gulack Daniel S BA Bursar
Palmiere Paul MS Network Administrator
Pfeister Susan PhD Associate Director of Library Services
Sanger Amy BA Assistant Manager of College Services
Schulz Paul A BA Diector of Support Services
Springer John PC Administrator
Taylor Deric A MDiv Campus Chaplain
Tiso Gail Assistant Director of Student Financial Aid
Warnken Kevin W Manager of College Services

## CONCORDIA UNIVERSITY

**1530 Concordia West, Irvine CA 92612-3299**
**949/854-8002, FAX 949/854-6854**
**Year Founded 1976**

***President:*** Preus Jacob A O MDiv STM ThD

***President Emeritus:*** Halm D Ray MA EdD DD

***Professors Emeriti***
Baden Marian J MEd PhD
Baden Robert C MA PhD
Barnes Robert D MBA
Holtmeier Ronald G MST
Manske Charles L MDiv MA PhD
Marxhausen Benjamin W MA LLD
Mueller Roland M MA PhD
Nauss Allen H MDiv MEd PhD
Schulz Marlin W MSEd PhDEd

***Professors***
Bachman James V MA MDiv PhD Dean of School of Theology, Director of Lutheran Bereavement Ministry
Doyle Thomas J MS EdD Dean of Christ College Director of Graduate Program in Education Director of Placement
Ebel Kenneth K MST DA Acting Dean of School of Arts and Sciences (Fall) Director of Pre-Medical Professions Program
Geisler Herbert G Jr MAEd PhD Director of Music Activities
Harms Richard H MS PhD Chair of Business Division, Director of MBA and Business Administration Programs
Holl Mary K MA EdD Vice President for Administration
Mangels Kenneth E MAT PhD Dean of School of Arts and Sciences (Spring)
Moon Shang Ik MDiv MA PhD Executive Vice President
Morton Barbara MA PhD Dean of School of Education Director of Early Childhood Education Program
Rahn James E MA MS EdD
Rosenbladt W Rod BD MA PhD
Schlichtemeier Kent A MA EdD Associate Director of Major and Planned Gifts
Schramm Martin G MA MA PhD
Vieselmeyer Dean M MDiv MS PhD Vice President Student Services
Whelply Hal H Jr MA EdD Vice President Information Services

***Associate Professors***
Bachman Susan H MA PhD
Busch Michael L MA DMA Director of Choral Activities
Cosgrove Jennifer L MS PhD
Hartmann Dale W MA Archivist
Hoffman Patricia A MA PhD
Krueger Kurt J MAT MA PhD Provost
Mueller Steven P MDiv STM PhD Director of Pre-Seminary Program
Peters Timothy C EdD Director of Professional Studies Project Colloquy Program
Schultz Jack M MA PhD

***Assistant Professors***
Beck Gretchen J MAA MFA Director of Art Activities
Borst Katharine F MA PhD Cand
Brighton Mark A MDiv MA Chair of Theology Division
Browne Scott E MBA
Cattau Curt W MS Athletic Director Chair of Exercise and Sport Science Division Director of Sport Management Program (Spring)
Doering Dwight R MA PhD
Fleischli M Sue MA Academic Advisor
Jimenez-Silva Margarita EdM EdD Cand
Kemp Robert MA PhD Director of Pre-Law Program
Massmann Janice C MA
Mendez Edward W MA PhD Chair of Social Science Division

Mercier Deborah S MS Director of Undergraduate Elementary Education Program
Okubo Mason K MS MA PhD Chair of National Science Division (Fall)
Peters Rebecca R MA Director of Learning Center
Pfotenhauer Patra S MS Director of DCE Program
Schmidt Kristen A MA Director of Writing Center
Seltz Gregory P MDiv STM Director of Ethnic Pastor Certification Program
Senkbeil Peter L MA PhD Chair of Humanities Division Director of Theatre Activities
Soper Roderick B MS
Taylor Bret A MA Director Secondary Undergraduate Program
Thomsen Kerri L MS PhD
Vieselmeyer Dian K MA Academic Advisor
Williams Cheryl E PhD
Wise Jody L MS Athletic Director, Chair of Exercise and Sport Science Division, Director of Sport Management Program (Fall), Assistant Athletic Director (Spring)

***Instructor***
Maas Korey D STM

***Resident Faculty***
Brown Jacqueline Y MA
Brunell Richard P MBA
Gavin Thea L MA
Lyman Jennifer A PhD
Richter Matthew M DC
Rooney John L PhD

***Graduate Assistant***
Schulteis Melinda S MS

***Staff***
Aschbrenner Henry J MA Vice President Executive Director of Foundation
Borst Steven B MDiv Campus Pastor
Clavir Kenneth R MA Registrar
Gaylor Diane MS Librarian
Kempe Gladys V MA Director of English Language School
McDonald Lori L Director of Financial Aid
McDaniel Gary R MA EdD Vice President Enrollment Services
Rudi Alan K MBA MSTM Vice President Business Operations

## CONCORDIA UNIVERSITY WISCONSIN

**12800 N Lake Shore Dr, Mequon WI 53097-2402**
**262/243-5700, FAX 262/243-4351**
**Year Founded 1881**

***President:*** Ferry Patrick T MDiv PhD
***President Emeritus:*** Stuenkel Walter PhD DD

***Professors Emeriti***
Hake Rogers MDiv PhD
Hilgendorf M D DMin PhD
Jennrich Walter A MDiv PhD
Leonard Thomas PhD
Wangerin Norman P STM DD

***Professors***
Arnholt Philip J PhD
Baum Jon E PhD Chair Faculty Senate
Behnke John A DMus
Duchow Martin PhD Registrar
Eggebrecht David W PhD Vice President of Academics
Ellis William EdD Dean School of Business and Legal Studies
Ferry Patrick T MDiv PhD President
Garcia Albert L MDiv PhD Director of Lay Ministry and Colloquy Programs
Gresley Ruth S PhD Dean School of Human Services
Juergensen James PhD Dean School of Education
Konz Marsha PhD Director of Student Teaching
Korte Don PhD Chair Dept of Sciences
Kosche Kenneth MS DMA
Luptak Andrew MS PhD Vice President of Student Life
Maschke Timothy DMin PhD Chair Division of Theology
Meitler Carolyn PhD Chair Department of Mathematics
Mueller Lois MS EdD Chair Dept of Health and Human Performance
Sohn Lawrence EdD Executive Vice President
Veith Gene Edward PhD Director of Cranach Institute
Walther John F EdD Dean School of Graduate Studies

***Associate Professors***
Andritzky Joseph PhD
Beck John PhD Director of Freshman Year Experience
Beineke Thomas PhD
Canapa Sally PhD
Cario William PhD Assistant Vice President of Academics
Condie Brad PhD
Cope Steven MOT PhD
Denton Peggy PhD Chair Division of Occupational Therapy
Docheff Dennis PhD
Dvorak Leah PhD Chair Division of Science and Mathematics
Ferguson Randall MDiv PhD Chair Dept of Communication
He Peng PhD
Heinitz Jan PhD
Hilgendorf Mary PhD Chair Dept of Elementary Education
Jarratt David JD Chair Division of Legal Studies
Jastram Nathan MDiv PhD
Johnson Robert L PhD
Keiper Val PhD
Krenz David PhD Chair Division of Humanities
Lotegeluaki Samuel MDiv PhD
Lueders Bolwerk Carol PhD Director of Parish Nursing/BSN Completion
Menchaca Louis PhD Chair Division of Performing & Visual Arts
Menuge Angus PhD
Peterson Grace PhD Director of Nursing
Ratcliffe Kermit DMin
Rompelman Lynne PhD Chair Division of Social Science
Steffen Teresa PhD Chair Division of Physical Therapy
Stelmachowicz Cary EdD Chair Department of Secondary Education
Stone Gaylund PhD Dean School of Arts and Sciences
Tomesch Harald MDiv ThD
Wilmeth Thomas PhD Chair Department of English
Yahnke, David MD
Zietlow Paul MA PhD

***Assistant Professors***
Albinger Heather MS
Ambelang Joel MS Chair Division of Social Work
Bell Marjorie MS
Besch Michael PhD Vice President of Adult and Continuing Education
Blodgett Margaret MS
Bolender Joan MSN
Borst David MBA Director of MBA and Distance Learning
Braun Wayne DMin Campus Pastor
DeLap Russell MBA
Eyer Richard DMin Director of Christian Center for Bioethics, Morality, and Culture
Franz Ann PhD
Heikkinen E Kay PhD Madison, WI, Adult Ed Center Director
Hobus Mary MSN
Jones Louise Conley PhD Ft Wayne, iN, Adult Ed Center Director
Kaul Teresa MSN
Krueger Doreen MA
Leffin-Hedrick Tracey MA Chair Dept of Foreign Language
Locklair Gary MS Chair Dept of Computer Science
Makstenieks Santa MD
McDonald Ann PhD
Mino Lizabeth PhD
Mobley Susan PhD
Mollinger Louise MS
Montreal Steven PhD Program Director of Criminal Justice (Adult Ed)
Moser Christine MS OTR
Paavola Daniel ThM
Picus Karen MS
Piepenbrink Allen MA
Puffe Shiela MSEd
Rinker Craig PhD New Orleans, LA, Adult Ed Center Director
Saleska Thomas MSEd
Samuel Linda MS
Scheel Carrie MS
Schoedel Victoria EdD St. Louis, MO, Adult Ed Center Director
Schroeder R Edward MA Director of Financial Aid
Seider Candyce MS Chair Department of Early Childhood Education
Shawhan Jeff MFA
Stephens Carolyn MBA Program Director of Liberal Arts (Adult Ed)
Stolt Wendy MSW
Tews Rebecca PhD
Uden Michael MS
Valentino Theresa MFA
Walz Jeffery PhD
Weber Thomas PhD
Wolf Mark PhD
Zalewski Kathryn MA
Zimmermann Chris PhD

***Instructors***
Campanelli Janice MSN
Carlson Alexandra MS
Clason Marmy MA
Ehike Roland MDiv STM MA
Evans Elizabeth MA Sherman Park, WI, Adult Ed Center Director
Freese James MCM
Halloran Kari MSN
Korte Mary MS
Little Lynn MMus
Polubinsky Renee MS
Rathsack Fern MEd Mequon, WI Adult Ed Center Director
Reimer-Becker Donna MS
Rice Ann MA Green Bay/Appleton, WI, Adult Ed Center Director
Scheppa Timothy MS
Schwenke Mary MSN
Sisney Ned BS
Skony Suzanne MS
Slota Roseann MS CMA Program Director of Health Care Administration (Adult Ed)
Timpel Jean MA Director Learning Resource Center
Trotter John Indianapolis, IN, Adult Ed Center Director
Wanbaugh Teresa MBA Indianapolis, IN, Adult Ed Center Assistant Director

***Adjunct/Visiting Instructors***
Esselmann Jesse MILR
Hall Jocelyn MLH
Horgan John PhD
Mobley Van PhD
Pokorski Thomas MBA
Smith Carol MSW PhD
Wandschneider John PhD
Weedman Gail MSN

***Staff Officers***
Austin Jean MS Placement Counselor
Bandurski Jeffrey BA Director of Public Relations
Banner Barbara MBA Director of Human Resources
Boeck Richard Sr EE Executive Director Friends of Concordia
Benedum Charles Advancement Executive
Burns Patrice Milwaukee South Center Director
Capiak Noelle Admission Counselor
Crook Steve Assistant Dean of Student Life
Dolan Jill Admission Counselor/Visit Coordinator
Eberhardt Mary MA Director of Graduate & Adult Education Admission
Eichelberger James Director of Administrative Computing
Enters David MS Director of Wellness
Ferry Tamara PhD Director of Institutional Research
Freer Robert Food Service Manager
Frosch Jeffrey BA Admission Counselor
Gabrielsen Jeffrey MEd Head Football Coach
Gaschk Jill Assistant Registrar
Gaschk Ken MS Vice President of Enrollment Services
Genson Susan BA Director of Continuing Education
Gnan Peter MS Assistant Director of Admission
Grapatin Wendy MS Director of Multicultural Services
Heidtke Janice BA Assistant Director of Financial Aid
Hibbard Stephen Superintendent of Buildings and Grounds
Hilgendorf Duane MEd Vice President of Advancement
Jasper Joann Graduate Admission Counselor
Jiang Shaojie MS Director of International Student Recruitment
Kentopp Herm Director of Auxiliary Services
Kloepping Barry Admission Counselor
Knorr Karl Director for Student Success
Kosanke Jan BSRD Director of Food Service
Krenzke Thomas MLS Reference Librarian
Luedtke Jessica Director of Campus Safety
Martinsen Mike Director of Teacher Certification CUW Madison
McCoy Kathy Bookstore Manager
Meinzen Philip MS CFRE Assistant to the President
Mosel Kris Director of Resident Life
Newhouse Mark AS Network Administrator
Nimz Karen MS Serials Reference & Interlibrary Loan
Oliver Charles SID
Paulus Rita MSEd Director of Student Advising

Paynter Paul MA Assistant Athletic Director
Phillip Thomas BBS Vice President of Information Technology
Prochnow Allen Vice President of Finance & Administration
Reineck Robert Controller
Rohrer Sarah Off-Campus Centers Librarian
Smith Gene MLS Manager of Educational Technology
Stenson Mark Computer User Services Manager
Swingen Enid Admission Counselor, Milwaukee South Center (Adult Ed)
Thompson Dennis Admission Counselor
Tuffey Tracey MSW Counselor
VandeVrede Richard Manager of Network Operations
Vogts Kevin MDiv Director of Communications & Church Relations
Weaver Sarah MBA Distance Learning Coordinator
Williams Scott BA Director Instructional Technology
Witte Kenneth MAT Athletic Director
Wohlers Richard MDiv MALS Director of Library Services
Worzalla Jolene Admission Counselor

## CONCORDIA UNIVERSITY

**2811 NE Holman St, Portland OR 97211-6099**
**503/288-9371 FAX 503/280-8518**
**Internet: http://www.cu-portand.edu**
**Year Founded 1905**

***President:*** Schlimpert Charles E MEd PhD

***Professors Emeriti***
Brandt Dwaine MA PhD
Burgess John MBA MPA
Christian Carl MSEd EdD
Jacke Robert MEd
Kramer Frederick MA PhD Assistant to the President
Reinisch Richard O MA MDiv PhD
Scheck John F MDiv PhD
Spalteholz Hans R G MDiv MA MA
Wahlers Arthur G MA EdD Assistant to the President
Weber Erhardt P STD

***Professors***
Albrecht Jan MA EdD
Costi Robert Leland MA MBA PhD
Dockter DuWayne EdD
Driessner John EdD
Hanson Gary MA PhD
Hill Richard A MA PhD Chair Eng/Hum
Jager Mark MPA PhD Chair HCA/SCW
Kunert Charles J MS PhD Dean College of Arts and Sciences
Mannion Joseph MEd EdD Dean College of Education Director Secondary Education
Metzler Norman Paul Jacob STM MDiv ThD Chair Religion Pre-Theology/Classical Languages, Director of Continuing Education for Pastors
Schmidt Robert F STM MDiv PhD
Steffens Stephen F MA MPhil PhD
Wahlers Mark MS PhD Provost, Vice President Student Services/Enrollment Management
Widmer Ann MA EdD Dean School of Management
Wismar Richard MEd MEd Director of Church Worker Placement
Wright Daniel MA MDiv PhD

***Associate Professors***
Balke William H MS EdD(ABD) Executive Assistant to the President
Becker Matthew MDiv MA PhD (ABD) Director of Pastoral Studies Program
Bier Jeffrey A MBA MMIS
Braun Stephen B MBA
Bremer Nolan MDiv MSLS Librarian and Director of Library Services
DeRemer Mark PhD Director of MCL Program
Dunbar Kathy MEd
Edwards Lynnell MA PhD Director of Writing Center
Gebhard Frank MAT
Hoeffer Herb MDiv STM EdD
Horten Gerd J PhD
Keyne Lisa MPA PhD Assistant Provost for Academic Services
Krause Stephen BS MS EdD
Leonard Jonathan MS PhD
Munson Thomas BA MS PhD
Schuldheisz Joel M MEd PhD Athletic Director
Vegdahl Sonja MA
Voss Sharon L MAT EdD

***Assistant Professors***
Birkey Daniel MS Men's Soccer Coach
Eggert Jeanette G MA
Gross Larry MST Chair PAVA
Hicks Karen BS MALS Public Services Librarian
Keyne-Michaels Lynn MS Placement Administrator
Politte Paula MS
Reinisch Sheryl BA MEd
Rowland Julie MA
Ruff Mark BA MA PhD
Ruhnke Frederick BA MAT MA Colloquy
Simpson Kevin E PhD
Smith Jane MA Chair Social Science

***Faculty Without Rank***
Aufderheide Stan M Director, For the Sake of the Church/Planned & Major Gifts
Kiessling Richard Director of Church Relations
Yung Allan MDiv Assistant Chaplain for Chinese Students
Stoecklin Dennis BA CPA Vice President of Administration

***Part-Time Instructors***
Albrecht David Dir Emp
Anderson Barry PhD
Anderson Eric MA
Archer Barbara MBA
Artz Philip MA
Barbarick Brad MS
Bayless John JD
Benton-Wichman Dennis
Bevers Jerry PhD
Bohrer Elizabeth M Sc
Bolen Delores MA
Carlough Leslie JD
Carlson Dvenna MS PhD
Coyle Bernard PhD
DeWitz Patti MS
Dorrell Darrell MBA CPA
Forman Barbara MA
Gilbarg Paul MA
Hawthorne Jeralynne MS MS
Hermanson Carl MA
Hollenbeck Helen BA
Hope Bruce PhD
Houck Joe BS
Johnson Sidney MA
Kirkpatrick Maureen MA
Kleber Sharleen MS
Knowles Joanne PhD
Koepke Frank MDiv
Kohl Dave MA
Landy Grant BA
Lewis Greg BS
Long Bonnie MA
Macon Samuel MS
Maier Don BAE
Morris Karen MA
Nirschl Paula BS
Price D'Norgia MBA
Richards Bruce MEd
Roth Al PhD
Rountree Linda MA Dir ESL
Rumsch Bruce MDiv
Schlachter James MAT
Schuldheisz Mary MST
Tuchardt Paul BS BTh
Watters Georgeanne MA
Weihe Kathleen BS BS
Weniger Richard MEd

***Staff Officers***
Aboujaoude Emad Athletic Trainer
Barbarick Brad MS Head Men's Basketball Coach
Beaman Jay PhD Dir of Institutional Research
Bjorngrebe Robert AA CWC Director of Dining Services
Bush Mickie BS Registrar
Cullen James BA Director of Financial Aid
Fonger Ron Interim Director of Institutional Information and Technology Services
Hasibar Madeline Personnel Director
Holly John Director of Safety and Security
Houck Joe Intramural Director, Women's Volleyball Coach
Johnson Cynthia BS Career Center Director, Non-Traditional Services
Johnson Peter BA Director of Admissions
Landy Grant BA Women's Soccer Coach Sports Information Director
Lanza-Weil Carmella Dir Theater for Youth Program
McPheeters Andrew Asst Director International Student Services
Meyer Doug Director of Physical Plant Services
Nirschl Paula Women's Basketball Coach
Ruhnke Linda College Nurse
Sage Jacque Women's Fastpitch Coach
Schlimpert Patricia BS Director of Alumni Relations
Schuldheisz Joel Athletic Director
Seki Sumihiko Director of Pacific Rim Operations
Smith Glenn MA Dean of Students
Vance Rob Men's Baseball Coach
Witt Harry BS Director of Media Services

## CONCORDIA UNIVERSITY

**7400 Augusta St, River Forest IL 60305-1499**
**708/771-8300, FAX 708/209-3176**
**TDD 708/209-3000**
**Year Founded 1864**

***President:*** Heider George C MDiv PhD

***Presidents Emeriti***
Krentz Eugene L MDiv PhD LLD
Zimmerman Paul A MDiv PhD DD

***Provost Emeritus***
Young Norman E MS EdD

***Faculty Emeriti***
Aumann Conrad J MEd
Brockberg Harold F EdD
Busse Robert L MMus
Domroese Kenneth A PhD
Dumler Marvin J EdD
Faszholz Thomas O MDiv MA
Froehlich Charles D MDiv STM Professor of Classical Languages (Emeritus)
Gieschen Thomas E DMus
Grotelueschen Paul G MA Assistant University Archivist
Heinitz Kenneth L MA MDiv PhD STM
Hennig Julia A DMA
Heyne Eunice R MSW
Hildner Victor G MMus
Hillert Richard W DMus
Isenberg Wesley W MDiv PhD
Janzow F Samuel MA PhD
Jenne Natalie R DMA
Kreiss Paul T PhD Associate Dean of the School of Graduate Studies (Emeritus)
Kurth Lyle J MS EdD
Kusmik Cornell J MSLS
Laabs Charles W EdD
Latzke Henry R EdD
Lehmann William H Jr MDiv PhD
Lucht Wayne E PhD
Martin Walter W MA
Mueller Delbert W PhD
Nielsen George R PhD
Pieper Robert W MA
Radke Merle L PhD LLD
Rimbach Evangeline L PhD
Roberts Audrey V MALS MAEd MS
Roberts James O PhD
Schalk Carl F MMus LLD LHD
Schoepp Leonard H PhD
Sims Herbert A MA PhD
Sorenson Karl E MA
Spurgat Frederick A MBA PhD Special Assistant to the President
Zimmer R Allan EdD

***Professors***
Bartell Marvin H PhD Dean of the College of Arts and Sciences
Bertels Gary L MAR MA EdD Theology/Philosophy/Foreign Languages Department Chair
Bondavalli Bonnie J PhD JD Sociology/Social Work Chair
Boos Manfred B PhD Provost and Strategic Planning Committee Chair
Briedis Anita V PhD
Butts LuJuana R EdD Teacher Education Department Chair
Champagne Ruth I PhD
Calhoun Richard C PhD Assistant University Marshal
Eifert Eunice R PhD Art/Communication/Theatre Department Chair
Fahrenkrog Darlene M MAE
Fischer Richard R MMusEd DMA
Flandermeyer Roger H PhD
Gnewuch Donald E MDiv PhD Dean of the School of Graduate Studies
Hayes H Robert MAEd MA PhD Vice President for Student Services and Affirmative Action Officer
Kammrath William H PhD
Kirchenberg Ralph J MS Natural Science/Earth Science/Geography Department Chair
Klatt Lois A PED
Kuck Cynthia L MA PhD Dean of the College of Education

Kurth Lila M MA PhD English Department Chair
Kurth Ruth J PhD
Moehlenkamp Marilyn E PhD University Marshal
Morgenthaler Shirley K PhD
Rietschel William C EdD
Septeowski Dale J EdD
Sipe D Elaine EdD Dean of the University College and Director of Teacher Colloquy
Toepper Robert M PhD CURES Associate for Student Assessment/CURES Associate for Program Evaluation
Wente Steven F DMus Music Department Chair/Organist—Chapel of Our Lord
Wenzel Gary E PhD Registrar
Witte Dennis E PhD Vice President for Information Services

***Associate Professors***

Andritzky Frank W PhD
Dubois Alton Clark MA PhD
Duey William J BS MS PhD Human Performance Department Chair
Ewald William M MA MBA Business/Economics Department Chair/University Archivist
Helmke Richard A MS CAIS Systems Administrator
Hermann Alfred L MEd
Jabs Carol A MA PhD
Johnson Winston MS MEd PhD
Klotz Verner H Jr MSEd MS
Knutson Lora L MA PhD
Kretzschmar Judith C MPE
Palmer Rachel M EdD
Rogner David W MA PhD
Rose Patricia K PhD
Serra Deborah L PhD
Smith Curtis A EdD Associate Dean of the School of Graduate Studies
Smith Michael C PhD
Stadtwald Kurt W PhD History and Political Science Department Chair
Steinmann Andrew E MDiv PhD
Todd Mary L PhD Director of Honors Program
Tolson Carol A PhD Educational Leadership Department Chair
Tomal Daniel R PhD
Venzke Beth A PhD
Wilkie Wesley H MDiv
Zillman O John PhD Director of Educational and Synodical Placement and Psychology Department Chair

***Assistant Professors***

Baker Verna L MA Assistant Director of Field Experiences
Barz Jonathan M MA PhD Editor Lutheran Education Journal
Brown Charles P BMus MMus
Corsino Alison T MSEd
Cullen William G ThD Coordinator DCE Program
Eberle Chris J PhD
Eschelbach Michael A MDiv PhD
Harrison Jean E MMus
Hart Zachary P MS Assistant University Marshal
Hurless Bonnie R MA PhD
Klaustermeier Del R MA Curator of Art
Moe Aaron J PhD
Moeller Eric J MA MDiv PhD
Mosemann Brian M MDiv STM Director of the Pre-Seminary Program
O'Leary Michael L PhD
Raabe David L MS Director of Concordia University Research and Evaluation Services (CURES) and Mathematics/Computer Science Department Chair
Rahn Julia M BS PhD
Ranum Ingrid K MA
Rippstein Timothy A BA
Roberson Katherine A PhD CAIS Product Services Manager
Rohlwing Ruth L MA
Rowedder Laura J MS
Rundman Dawn L MS
Siekmann Lori C MA
Stahlke Jonathan E PhD
Venzke Randell C MA
Wassilak Kristin R MAR Coordinator of Deaconess Program
Wellen Lauren A MA
Wertz Richard P MDiv MBA
Wetzel Thomas A MA PhD
Wilkinson Cathryn MFA PhD Coordinator of International Study

***Staff***

Allmon Richard L MS MEd Director of Alumni and Foundation Relations
Baker-Watson Brian BS Head Football Coach
Bassett Lisa BA Coordinator of Campus Events
Becker Brian BA MMus Senior Director of Advancement
Becker Elizabeth BS Assistant Director of Concordia University Research and Evaluation Services (CURES)
Becker Peter D BA Director of Auxiliary Services
Berry Linda BA Manager of Administrative Information Systems
Brutlag Tammy BA ConTACT Manager
Buchanan Anne L BS MLS MS Reference/Instruction Librarian
Carter Christy BA MEd MA Director of Graduate Admission
Cesar Mary BA Director of Housekeeping
Chrusciel Pamalie BA Director of Human Resources
Crowley Jeff BA Undergraduate Admission Counselor
Dahms Sara E MA Career Services Counselor
Diefenbacher Victoria BMus BA Instructor Prepatory and Community Piano Program
Dinkel B Dianne BS MBA Senior Vice President for Administration
Doleski John (Wayne) BS MS Academic Advisor
Duey Reneé J Director of Business Services
Egan James BA Sports Information Director
Feagans Scott BA BS Information Technology Services Specialist
Fisher Janet L MS Director of Intercollegiate Athletics
Forrest Lee BA MA Director of Technical Services
Fort Terri J BS Director of Aquatics
Gilbert Carol MEd Assistant Dean of Students/ Director of Multicultural Affairs/Director of Learning Assistance
Gillespie Anne Assistant Director of Housekeeping
Goodwin Gail MA Academic Advisor/Learning Assistance Counselor
Goudy James BA Information Technology Services Specialist
Graudin Kathy BA MA Financial Aid Counselor
Gutenkunst Gary BS MA Residence Director/ Learning Assistance Advisor
Hampton David T BS Assistant Football Coach/Assistant Track and Field Coach
Herbert Susan Assistant Director of Student Financial Planning
Hess Mary E BS MEd Assistant Dean for Suburban Programs
Hubbuch Marsha BS MEd Assistant Director of Undergraduate Admission
Jeffers Marisa MA Director of Student Activities/Director of Residence Life/Assistant Dean of Students
Johnson Ada Director of Foundation Operations
Jones Jennifer A BA Freshmen Admission Counselor
Jones Jennifer L BA Director of Marketing Communications
Kincaid Melaine BA Director of Transfer Articulation and Commuter Services
King Christine BA MA Women's Head Softball Coach
Kirchoff Dan BS Assistant Volleyball Coach
Kline Katherine Student Financial Planning Counselor
Knepper Eric J BA MBA Financial Analyst
Kolbusz Marilyn BA MAdEd Director of Adult Admission (COMP)
Kosinsky James BA Director of Media Production Services
Law John W BA MLS Director of Library Services
Lempesis Spiro BA Head Basketball Coach
Ludwig Judy Assistant Registrar
Lueck Bonnie BS MA Satellite Coordinator for the West Suburban Satellite of Childcare Resource and Referral
Luu Aingoc (Anna) Ly BA Director of Accounting
Margis Tim AA Lieutenant Campus Security
McKenna Mary Manager of Print Services
McNally Patricia B MSM PhD Director of the Concordia Organizational Management Program/Associate Dean of the University College
Miller Brian BA MEd Head Men's Basketball Coach/Assistant Athletic Director
Montgomery Mary (Susan) BA Associate Director of Marketing Communications/Director of Public Relations
Moritz Joel W BA Resident Director/Assistant Football Coach
Nepomuceno Ellen Cristina O BS Accountant
Ness Deborah A MA Dean of Enrollment Services/ Director of Student Financial Planning
Nickerson Holly BMus Academic Advisor
Novak Sarah BS MS Head Women's Basketball Coach/Assistant Men's and Women's Track and Field Coach
Odom Tamela BA Transfer Admission Counselor
Olthoff Gary MA Manager of LutherNet Services
Pajer Katherine A BA MS Associate Director Graduate Admission
Peterson Barbara Manager of Media Services
Peterson Keith BA MS Director of Special and Planned Gifts
Peterson Luanne BS Adult Student Advisor (COMP)
Pierce Anthony L BA Head Men's and Women's Soccer Coach
Pruett Rick BA Head Women's Volleyball Coach/Assistant Softball Coach
Renggli Catherine MM Instructor Preparatory and Community Piano Program
Risch David BA Head Men's and Women's Cross Country Coach/Head Men's and Women's Track and Field Coach
Roggow Gloria BS Residence Hall Director
Sale Craig MM Director of the Preparatory and Community Piano Program
Scafidi Joseph BS Junior Accountant
Schuth Scott MS Director of Information Technology Services
Smith Stephen BA MDiv STM Campus Pastor
Sonntag Beth A BS MAdEd Director of Academic Advising
Steiner Glen BA MA Director of Operations
Steiner John Lieutenant Campus Security
Therwanger Harold L BA MDiv Director fo Church Relations
Thurbee Joshuah BA Admission Counselor
Waldron Mark BA MEd Assistant Director of Development/Kapelle and Wind Symphony Coordinator
Walther Daniel MA Director of Career Planning and Placement Services
Wangerow Joan Director of Purchasing
Wellen Lauren A MA Spirit Group Advisor
Wendt Amy M BA Undergraduate Admission Counselor
Wilharm Keith A BA MA Assistant to the Dean of the School of Graduate Studies
Winkelman Andrew BA Chief of Security
Wittman Tony BA Head Men's and Women's Tennis Coach
Woods Terri J BSE MS Head Athletic Trainer
Zacharias Alan BS CFRE Senior Vice President for University Advancement

***Adjunct Faculty***

Allmon, Richard L MS MEd
Ameiss David MS
Archibald Julie MSEd
Arroyo John MA
Arthur Curtis PhD
Beverly Weldon PhD
Bitoy Earl EdS
Blenz Marilyn
Bloch Marguerite EdD
Bloye Brian MMus
Brady Mark MA
Brassel Roosevelt EdD
Brutlag J Dale MA MS
Bryant Preston EdD
Carter Christy BA MEd MA
Catrambone Lois MS
Chekel Tom C
Chiles Harvey
Cillick Martin JD
Cochran Lisa Ann MA
Corsino Louis PhD
Costello Lisa MFA
Delfosse Dennis M MA
Dinkha Juliet
Dorjath David
Drake Tom MA
Estrada Ricardo A EdD
Everson Robert MM
Fair Lee BA
Fasetti James MBA
Fourté Leonard EdD
French Winifred
Gaytan Eddy H PhD
Gilbert Carol MEd
Gilfillan Ray BA
Girardi Marilyn MA
Gloppen Robert E
Grayson Dave
Gross Catherine
Groteluesschen Paul G MA

Gude George
Heckmon C Mark
Hedegaard Kristen
Heimsoth James M
Herts George
Hickman Joel
Hinz Julie BA
Hitzke Jeannine MA
Hoffhines Robert W
Hoffman Joan Bentley
Hopper Charles CAS
Hoskins Sarah C
Howard Gabrielle
Jastram Nathan R MDiv PhD
Jeffers Marisa MA
Katonah Janine
Keleher Patrick
Kellerman James PhD
Kirchoff Dan
Knapp Stephen A MDiv ThM
Kolbusz Marilyn MAdEd
Krapauskas Virgil
Lindeman Marilyn K
Lusthoff Craig JD
Machione Nancy MA
Manning Maura Elizabeth
McDonald Glena MEd CAS
McGovern Julie Ann
McGuire Dorothy C
McNall Miles
McNally Patty MSM PhD
McNamee Gwen MA
Midkiff Jeffrey
Millar Kenneth R MEd EdD
Miller Brian
Moe Gale
Monegain Louise
Mytys Alberta L BA MEd
Niekamp Mary MCM
Noddings Alicia
North Anita
Novak Sarah BS MS
Offermann Donald A MA PhD
O'Rourke Joseph
Phillips Abigail MA
Pietrantoni Joseph M Jr
Pietrusiak Jerome MSW MA
Popp Bruce
Prange Sherry
Prinz Andrew
Rand Gary
Richy John MDiv DMIN
Riggins Judith EdD
Rinaldi Gene MAdEd
Ross Elaine J
Sadek Nancy
Sale Craig MM
Schipull Douglas W PhD
Schreiner Judith MA
Schuman Miriam C BA MA
Schuth Scott MA
Silver Eugene MS
Simon Kathleen
Smith Janet
Smith Steve MDiv
Sonntag Beth A BS MAdEd
Spengler Kenneth J
Spice Michael BA
Stanger John G
Stoub Sandra
Studt Larry
Tanzer Gail MA
Taylor Ernest EdD
Tenges-Koepele Laura
Teske Inge MA
Venturi Hale Deniz
Walther Ruth PhD
Weith Wendy MS
White Linden
Wilborn Jack L

RIVER FOREST
Concordia Early Childhood Education Center
7400 Augusta St, River Forest IL 60305-1499
708/771-8300
Bartell Judith MAEd Teacher
Christian Elizabeth BS MA Teacher
Keller Jennifer M BS Assistant Director of the Early Childhood Education Center/Teacher
Knuth Doris M BA MEd Director of the Early Childhood Education Center
Neumann Amy BA MA Teacher
Vezner Heather BA MA Coordinator of Campus Child Care
Concordia Administrative Information System
7400 Augusta St, River Forest IL 60305-1499
708/209-3200 Fax 708/209-3177
Babchak Daniel BA Programmer/Analyst
Brutlag J Dale MS Technical Services Manager
Chu Chong Xian (David) MS Programmer/Analyst
Craig Clark BA Programmer/Analyst
Edmondson Corinne BA System/Analyst
Faga Matt BA Programmer/Analyst
Gillfillan Marianne BA MA System/Analyst
Gillfillan Ray BA Programmer/Analyst
Gouskos Nick AA Client Services Manager
Hadler Mike BA Programmer/Analyst
Hahn David BS Assistant Product Services Manager
Helmke Richard MS Systems Administrator
Hermansen Kari BA Billing Manager
Hermansen Scott MA Director of CAIS
McCarthy Tom System/Analyst
Roberson Kathy PhD Product Services Manager
Simpson Ruth Administrative Assistant
Smith Janet BA System Analyst
Spice Mike BS Networking Administrator

## CONCORDIA UNIVERSITY

**275 N Syndicate St, St Paul MN 55104-5494**
**651/641-8278 FAX 651/659-0207**
**Year Founded 1893**

***President:*** Holst Robert A MDiv STM PhD

***Professors Emeriti***
Barnes Robert E MEd
Bartling Fredrick A DAT
Brauer Friedrich E MMus
Carlstrom David E PhD
Engelhardt Walter H MA
Hagman Joan L MA
Heinicke Theodore G MA
Holtz Robert E EdD
Horn Margaret H BS BSLS
Kaden Kenneth P MA LittD
Kramer Roy E MA
Leininger Robert W MMus
Meyer Gerhardt V EdD
Meyer Loma R EdD PhD LLD
Middendorf Marvin L ThD
Niebergall William A EdD
Offermann Glenn W PhD
Peter Carroll E PhD
Rickels Robert E MA
Rutz Karl W ThD
Sohn Walter G STM
Solensten John M PhD
Titus Leon G MA MMus LittD
Treichel Herbert W MS LLD
Wenger John W MA
Wentzel Herman K EdD
Werling Henry F PhD

***Professors***
Bredehoft David J PhD
Buegel John E MA
Burkart Jeffrey E PhD Associate Dean for Christian Ministry
Carter Richard E ThD
Corrie Bruce P PhD
Eggert John R DMA
Hackett Nancy A PhD Director of Faculty Scholarship Center
Hanson Thomas R JD Associate Concordia School of Accelerated Learning
Lumpp David A ThD
Madson Kay H PhD Executive Vice President
Mennicke David L DMA
Reineck Marilyn F PhD
Schenk Kathryn E PhD
Schoenbeck Barbara F PhD Chair of Early Childhood Education Program
Schoenbeck Carl J PhD Vice President for Academic Affairs and Dean of the Faculty
Stellwagen Carol E PhD
Stohlmann Stephen C PhD
Streufert Eunice C PhD
Trapp Dale M PhD
Trapp Thomas H ThD
Winegarden Alan D PhD Dean of College of Arts and Sciences

***Associate Professors***
Arnold Steven F PhD Chair of Parish Education and Administration Program/DCE (sabbatical-fall)
Brynteson Richard D PhD
Charron Lori J N PhD
Charron Michael J MFA
DeWerff Robert E EdD Dean of College of Graduate and Continuing Studies (sabbatical-fall)
Heginbotham Eleanor E PhD
Kaufman Roberta C EdD Dean of College Education
LaMott Eric E PhD Vice President Information and Technology
Luebke Miriam E PsyD Associate Dean for Assessment, Counseling, and Academic Support
Mennicke Sheryll A PhD
Mueller Paul W DMiss Director of Oswald Hoffmann School of Christian Outreach
Potter Alisa M PhD
Pratt Susan L PhD
Schuler Mark T ThD
Sellke Donald H EdD Chair of Elementary and Secondary Education
Tesch Philip C JD Vice President for Student Affairs
Thomas Wilbur W III JD
Williams Keith J MFA

***Assistant Professors***
Beilke Debra J PhD
Clarkson Lesa M MAEd
Ford William L DMA
Guidera George A EdD Director of Placement (Professional Program Students) and Colloquy Program
Hancock Frances M EdD
Hunder Stephanie MFA
Jastram Daniel N PhD
Johnson Katryna M PhD
Knoche Charlotte PhD
Lien Craig MBS Co-Director, Information Technology in Management Major
Maly Lonn D MSEd
Morgan Stephen T PhD
Ness Karla F MFA
Nuckles Charles R PhD Director of the MA in Organizational Management
Ollhoff James MA Associate Dean, Concordia School of Human Services
Ollhoff Laurie PhD
Pickel Michele L PhD
Saylor Thomas PhD
Schuessler Joel N MS
Staley William E PhD Director of Southeast Asian Teacher Education Program
Stueber David J MA
Walcheski Michael PhD
Wenger Jonathan P MA
Zimmerman Dennis K MBA CPA

***Instructor***
Friedrich Thomas MA
Wood, Marjory Johnson MS

***Staff Officers***
Ahler Cynthia RN BSN Nurse/Director of Health and Wellness Center
Arnold Mary M Director of Human Resources
Benke Robert J MDiv Campus Pastor
Borchardt Diane H BA Director of Financial Aid
Braun Pamela MA Director of Career Development
Braun Rosemary A BA Director fo Academic Advising
Coleman Elizabeth A MEd Registrar
Connor Michael Director of Plant and Operations
Diekman Sue R MBC Director of Public Relations
Dorner Michael H MDiv Controller
Flynn Michael D BA Vice President for Special Gifts
Hartford Douglas B EdD Vice President for University Advancement
Krueger Sharon R MSE Associate Dean for Residential Life
McLemore-Sklar Maria R BA Director of Research and Grants
Morrell Scott T BA Associate Dean of Enrollment Services
O'Brien Daniel C MA Director of Athletics
Ries Thomas K MDiv MBA Vice President of Finance and Operations
Sachs James E JD Associate Dean for Judicial Affairs
Seying Laokouxang DMiss Director of Hmong Institute
Spiess Kristine A BA Director of Hand in Hand Day Care Center
Taylor Daniel J BA Director of Facilities Management
Utter Timothy P MA Director of Admissions
Walther Gretchen BA Director of Orientation Programs
Xiong Lee Pao MA Director of Community and Government Relations (on leave-full year)

**The Oswald Hoffmann School**
**Of Christian Outreach (OHSCO)**
**Center of Evangelism and Mission Studies**
USA 275 North Syndicate Street
St. Paul, MN 55104-5494
Office: 651-641-8701, FAX 651-603-6202
WWW:www.CSP.edu/OHSCO
E-Mail: OHSCO@CSP.edu

Paul Mueller, Director; Roger Ernst, Coordinator: Director of Christian Outreach Program; James Found, Outreach Professor; Ronald Harrington, Assistant to Director. Ministries: Director of Christian Outreach program (DCO), Lay leadership outreach training. Publications: OHSCO Newsletter, published semi annually, semi-annual letter to financial supporters.

## CONCORDIA COLLEGE
**1804 Green St, Selma AL 36701**
**334/874-5700**
**Year Founded 1922**

***President:*** Jenkins Julius PhD

***Professors Emeriti***
Droege Ralph EdD
Rivers Ronnie PhD

***Professors***
Adalikwu Chris PhD
Berry Geraldine PhD
Onyeaso Godwin DBA
Ramsey McNair EdD Dean of Development

***Associate Professors***
Holbird Doyle PhD
Orsborn Ruthie MA Dean of Research & Planning
Pegues Agnes MS Interim Dean of Student Services
Rauls Albert EdD
Richardson Phyllis MEd Dean of Academic Affairs
Weiss Joyce EdD

***Assistant Professors***
McKenzie Bobby MEd
Ngirailab Moses MA
Okoye Sheila MSC
Owens Joe MEd

***Staff Officers***
Bridges Tharsteen MBA Financial Aid Administrator
Brown Raymond BS Admissions Counselor
Daniel Jo Ann MS Librarian
DeRamus David BD Chaplain
Grayson Chinester Registrar
Harrison Ronnie BS Director of Regular Upward Bound Program
Hollins Gracie MA Director of Upward Bound Math and Science Program
Jarrett Sadie EdS Director of Counseling and Testing
McMillan Minnie MEd Assistant to Librarian
Moore Gwendolyn BS Acting Director of Admissions
Ncube Zibusico MBA Computer Technician
Pickens Evelyn BA Director of Enrollment Management/Placement Officer
Robinson Anthony BS Activity Director
Robinson Patricia BS Assistant to Financial Aid Administrator and Director of Counseling and Testing
Shelton Haddie MEd Counselor Regular Upward Bound Program
Shoals Steve MEd Coordinator Enrichment Lab
Smiley Arzelia BA Business Manager
Stephens David Admissions Counselor
Weerts Luke MA Director of Information Technology Development
Younce Loring MA Assistant Librarian

## CONCORDIA UNIVERSITY
**800 N Columbia Avenue, Seward NE 68434**
**402/643-3651, 800/535-5494**
**FAX 402/643-4073**
**Year Founded 1894**

***President:*** Walz Orville C EdD

***President Emeritus***
Reinke Ralph L MA LittD
Janzow W. Theophil DD PhD

***Professors Emeriti***
Beck Theodore MMus PhD
Becker E George MDiv PhD
Bergman Marvin MDiv MEd EdD PhD
Blomenberg Gilbert MSEd
Brott Eugene MA EdD
Daenzer Gilbert MAEd
Duensing Widen PhD
Dynneson Donald MFA
Einspahr Glenn MA EdD
Etzold Herman MDiv MS STM
Everts Carl MAEd PhD
Glaess Herman MEd EdD
Grothaus Larry MA PhD
Held David MAEd DMA
Holtzen LeeRoy MEd PhD
Klammer Werner MSEd
Krause Roy MS PhD
Krutz Charles MM
Langefeld Wilfred MDiv MA EdD
Martens Edmund MMus
Marxhausen Reinhold MFA LittD
Matthews Larry MS PhD
Oetting Eugene MAR MA EdD
Pflieger Robert MA
Seevers John EdD
Stobs Reuben MA PhD
Stork Martin MA EdD
Streufert Victor MS PhD
Zwick Richard MA PhD

***Professors***
Bassett Leonard MS PhD Dean College of Graduate Studies
Dolak E David MS MA EdD Executive Vice President Academic Services
Einspahr Kent MS PhD Chair Natural Sciences and Mathematics
Einspahr Kregg MS PhD
Fiala Robert MA PhD
Goldgrabe Eunice MA DA Chair Health and PE
Kinworthy John MA PhD
Lawin Priscilla MEd EdD Director Elementary Education
Meyer David MDiv STM PhD Chair Theology
Obermueller Stanley MSEd PhD Chair Business Administration
Ore Charles MM DMA Chair Music
Pfabe Jerrald MA PhD University Archivist/Chair Social Sciences
Preuss Judith MEd PhD Dean College of HPE and Education
Preuss William MEd EdD Director Teacher Lab/Clinical Experiences
Roebke Jenny MEd PhD Chair English, Languages, Communication, Theater Arts, General Studies
Schluckebier Lee EdD Director Colloquy & Special Programs
Schmidt Kenneth MFA PhD Professor of Art
Serck Leah MA EdD
Suhr John MS PhD Faculty Marshal
Thurber Daniel MA AD Dean College of Arts and Sciences
Vasconcellos A Paul MDiv MEd PhD
Weinhold John MA EdD Coordinator of Assessment
Wiegmann Richard MFA
Wolfram William MA MFA Chair Art

***Associate Professors***
Ashby Lisa MA PhD
Block Kenneth MDiv STM Director Pre-Seminary Program
Boye Vicki MEd PhD
Gernant Renea MA PhD
Huebschman Raymond MSEd EdD Dean of Information Technology
Langewisch Andrew MBA PhD
Lemke Mark MEd DEd
Meehl Mark BSEd MAR PhD Faculty Marshal
Reinke Edward MS PhD
Soloway Lynn MFA
Sylwester Don BA BSEd MS Director Computing Center
Wiegmann Mira MA PhD

***Assistant Professors***
Blanke Mark MS MA Director DCE Program
Bockelman James BSEd MFA
Creed Bruce MA
Deeter Christopher MEd Director Secondary Education
Dolak Grace-Ann MSEd PhD Director Academic Support Services
Fisher Rebecca MSEd Director Middle Level Education
Gubanyi Joseph MS
Herl Joseph PhD
Hermann Robert PhD
Holtorf Paul MDiv PhD
Homp Michelle Reeb MS PhD
Kuhn William MM
Mosemann Russell BA BSEd MS PhD
Moulds Russell MS PhD
Nelson Roberta MA PhD Director Early Childhood Education
Parker Micah MEd PhD
Preuss Timothy BSEd MS PhD
Royuk Brent BSEd MS
Sanatullova-Allison Elvira PhD
Schoepp Paul MA Assistant Director DCE Program
Schwehm Jeffery PhD
Snow John PhD
Uffelman Janell MEd
von Kampen Kurt MM

***Visiting Assistant Professor***
Miller Kathy PhD

***Instructor***
Ohlman Timothy BA

***Graduate Assistants***
Ernstmeyer Rebecca
Geidel Amanda
Jalas Darin
Voss Todd
Waterman Kristy

***Professional/Technical Staff***
Anderson Jennifer BSEd Assistant Director of Admission
Bergman Shirley PhD Director Lutheran Institute on Aging and Family
Block Marlene BA Managing Editor
Boettcher Myron MSLS Director Library Services
Brehmer Marcile Computer Operations
Brinkmeyer Carol BSEd Activities Coordinator
Brooks D Gene BSEd Director Student Life
Butler Connie Assistant Budget Officer
Chaffee Michelle JD Dean of Student Services
Ebel Thomas BSEd Athletic Trainer
Elwell Nancy MA Director Student Employment Program
Friedrich Brian MDiv VP for Institutional Advancement/Assistant to the President
Geidel Jeremy BSEd Admission Counselor/Head Baseball Coach
Greene Frank MAT Head Softball Coach and Instructor
Harre Fay MBA Vice President for Administrative Services
Hennig Gloria BA Director of Financial Aid
Hofman William BSEd Admission Counselor
Jalas Deanna BA Programmer/Analyst
Janssen Norman BS Major Gifts/Gift Planning Officer
Jungemann Lon MS Senior Systems Analyst/Programmer
Kenow Peter BSEd Director of Admission
Klenke Luther BSEd Director Campus Center
Koenig Donna Assistant Registrar
Kohlwey Martin Assistant Director Student Life
Lauer Mystique BA Curriculum/Children's Collections Specialist
Liesener Shirley BA Director Development and Advancement Operations
McAllister William MA Asst Head Football Coach
McCollum Jerris EdD Director Department of Lifelong Learning
Meyer Courtney MA Head Football Coach
Murray Rachel MA Assistant Director of Counseling
Nickolite Lisa BA Graphic Designer
Novak Dale Maintenance Supervisor
Ohlmann Glenn MA Technical Services Librarian
Plamann Marvin MA Admission Counselor
Poortinga Candyce Assistant Custodial Supervisor
Potratz Kevin MA Computer Programmer/Analyst
Probasco Ruth BA Director Alumni & University Relations
Richter Ronald MEd EdD Director International Education
Reinke Suzanne BA Accountant
Rosendahl Darla MA Director Placement/Career Planning
Schlueter Stanley Athletic Equipment Manager
Schmidt Grant BSEd MA Director Athletics
Schmidt Ralph MDiv Director Planned Gifts/Church Relations
Schnell Helen BA Admission Counselor
Schranz William MAT Head Men and Women's Soccer Coach
Simpson Jane BS Director Marketing Communication
Tiefel Ted BSEd Admission Office Manager
Varner Mel Director Operations
Vos Donald BSEd Dean of Enrollment Management
Wachholz William MDiv MA DMin Director Counseling
Werner Mathew MPA Assistant Director of Lifelong Learning
Woods Tymmi MILS Reference Librarian

## DISTRICTS OF THE SYNOD

| | |
|---|---|
| NORTHWEST | Washington, Oregon, Idaho, and Alaska |
| MONTANA | the State |
| NORTH DAKOTA | the State |
| SOUTH DAKOTA | the State |
| WYOMING | the State and western "Panhandle" of Nebraska |
| NEBRASKA | the State except western "Panhandle" |
| CALIFORNIA-NEVADA-HAWAII | California (except southern counties), Nevada (except southern tip), and Hawaii |
| KANSAS | the State |
| PACIFIC SOUTHWEST | Arizona, southern counties of California, and southern tip of Nevada |
| OKLAHOMA | the State |
| TEXAS | the State (except El Paso County) |
| ROCKY MOUNTAIN | Colorado, Utah, New Mexico, El Paso County, Texas |
| S.E.L.C. | represented in the following twelve states: Connecticut, Florida, Illinois, Indiana, Minnesota, Missouri, New Jersey, New York, Ohio, Pennsylvania, Virginia, Wisconsin, and in the provinces of Ontario and Quebec, Canada |
| MINNESOTA NORTH | Northern counties and Douglas County, Wisconsin |
| MINNESOTA SOUTH | Southern counties |
| NORTH WISCONSIN | including western part of Upper Peninsula of Michigan |
| SOUTH WISCONSIN | southern half |
| MICHIGAN | Lower Peninsula and eastern part of Upper Peninsula |
| EASTERN | western half of New York State, Pennsylvania (except York County), and Garrett County, Maryland |
| ATLANTIC | eastern half of New York State |
| NEW ENGLAND | Maine, Vermont, New Hampshire, Massachusetts, Connecticut, and Rhode Island |
| NEW JERSEY | the State |
| IOWA WEST | |
| IOWA EAST | vertical division approximately in the center |
| NORTHERN ILLINOIS | |
| CENTRAL ILLINOIS | Illinois |
| SOUTHERN ILLINOIS | |
| INDIANA | the State and north-central counties of Kentucky |
| OHIO | the State, West Virginia, and northeastern counties of Kentucky |
| SOUTHEASTERN | Maryland (except Garrett County), District of Columbia, Delaware, Virginia, North Carolina, South Carolina, and York County, Pennsylvania |
| MISSOURI | the State |
| MID-SOUTH | Arkansas, Tennessee, and southern counties of Kentucky |
| SOUTHERN | Louisiana, Mississippi, Alabama, and western tip of Florida |
| FLORIDA-GEORGIA | Florida (except western tip), Georgia, and Bahamas |
| ENGLISH | represented in the following fifteen states: Arizona, California, Florida, Georgia, Illinois, Indiana, Michigan, Minnesota, Missouri, Nebraska, New Jersey, New York, Ohio, Pennsylvania, Wisconsin, and in the provinces of Ontario and Quebec, Canada |

# OFFICERS OF THE 35 SYNODICAL DISTRICTS

NOTE: Officers serving *full-time* are indicated by the symbol (FT) following their name.

* Corrected to October 4, 2000

## U. S. DISTRICTS

### Atlantic District

Rev Dr David H Benke MDiv DMin (FT) President
Concordia College 171 White Plains Rd
Bronxville NY 10708 914/337-5700 X 1
FAX 914/337-7471
E-Mail: DaveBenke@aol.com
Web: AD-LCMS.ORG
Rev Charles Froehlich First Vice President
E-Mail: cwkjf@aol.com
Rev Warren Winterhoff Second Vice President
E-Mail: winterhoff@prodigy.net
Rev Peter Dorn Third Vice President
E-Mail: pbdorn@aol.com
Rev Deric Taylor Fourth Vice President
E-Mail: DAT@Concordia-ny.edu
Rev Robert Hartwell, Secretary
E-Mail: RevHartwell@aol.com
John Mesloh Treasurer
**At District Office Concordia College, 171 White Plains Rd Bronxville NY 10708 914/337-5700**
Rev. David Born (PT) *Mission*
E-Mail: DJBORN@aol.com
Paul Crumb (FT) *Mission Developer & Growth*
E-Mail: PaulHC@Bestweb.net
Janet George (PT) *Task Force Coordinator*
E-Mail: AD_JG@Concordia-NY.edu
Kristen Schultz (PT) *Lutheran School*
E-Mail: Gradu929@aol.com
William B Kletecka (FT) *Staff Executive Finance Stewardship and Church Extension Fund*
E-Mail: AD_WK@Concordia-NY.edu

**Counselors ***

1. S Dugan
2. V Nelson
3. D Nuss
4. G Carstens
5. K Meritt
6. M Bergbower
7. J Stoudt
8. R Lehenbauer
9. L Hendricks
10. W Puls
11. D Wackenhuth
12. H Koepchen

### California-Nevada-Hawaii District

Rev Walter C Tietjen DD (FT) President
465 Woolsey St San Francisco CA 94134-1999
Office 415/468-2336 Home 510/489-4611
FAX 415/468-5399
Rev Orval M Oswald DD President Emeritus
Rev Theodore B Zimmerman First Vice President
Rev Jeffrey D Dorth Regional Vice President
Rev Mark W Haas Regional Vice President
Rev Joe E Schruhl Regional Vice President
Rev Donald D Schneider Secretary
Arthur M Kroeger Treasurer
1987 Bonifacio St Ste 100
Concord CA 94520 925-686-1600
**At District Office 465 Woolsey St San Francisco CA 94134-1999 415/468-2336**
Rev Theo A Iverson (FT) *CEF President*
Rev Ed A Krueger (FT) *Assistant to the President Missions and Evangelism*
John H Whaley (FT) *Assistant to the President Business Administration*
Joel H Koerschen MA (FT) *Assistant to the President, Education*
Frank H Spiva (FT) *Assistant to the President Mission Development and Education*
4501 O'Hara Ave Ste C
Brentwood CA 94513 925/516-1558

**Counselors ***

1. R R Rice
2. D M Sauer
3. J E Glover
4. G J Matranga
5. C A Brehmer
6. L R Haack
7. S S Koberg
8. H S Draeger
9. R R Kringel
10. L A Miller
11. M W Gowen
12. D D Dubke
13. D K Claasen
14. J D Beyer
15. S A Quebe
16. A A Prange
17. N V Olson
18. D E Bestul
19. K E Degner

### Central Illinois District

Rev David J Bueltmann (FT) President
1850 N Grand Ave W
PO Box 7003
Springfield IL 62791-7003
Office 217/793-1802
FAX 217/793-1822
E-Mail: cidlcms@eosin.com
Rev Mark Miller First Vice President
Rev Michael Strong Second Vice President
Rev Geoffrey Robinson Secretary
Rev Michael Kettner, Assistant Secretary
Herbert Krueger Treasurer
1901 Byrne Brook Champaign IL 61821
Dr W Ronald YaDeau Financial Secretary
111 White Pines Decatur IL 62521
**At District Office 1850 N Grand Ave W PO Box 7003 Springfield IL 62791-7003 217/793-1802**
David Bernhardt (FT) *Administrative Assistant for Education*
David L Goldhammer (FT) *Business Manager and Church Extension Fund*
Rev Wesley Reimnitz (FT) *Administrative Assistant for Stewardship and Congregational Life*
Rev Joel Cluver (FT) *Administrative Assistant for Evangelism and Missions*
Jeffry Miller (FT) *Gift Planning Counselor*

**Counselors ***

1. D Meyer
2. B Lakamp
3. T Daly
4. D Ehlers
5. D Krueger
6. M Damery
7. G Renken
8. D Bishop
9. P Droegemueller
10. M Liese
11. M Eddy
12. P Pett
13. M Mohr
14. T Radtke
15. R Barth
16. D Likeness

### Eastern District

Rev John G Brunner DMin (FT) President
5111 Main St Williamsville NY 14221-5295
716/634-5111 FAX 716/634-5452
Rev Herman Frincke DD Honorary President
Rev Arnold E Kromphardt LLD Honorary President
Rev William Kay First Vice President
Rev Roger Nuerge Second Vice President
Rev Albert Zoller Third Vice President
Rev David Goodine Fourth Vice President
Rev Paul Doellinger Secretary
**At District Office 5111 Main St Williamsville NY 14221-5295 716/634-5111**
James Brese *Treasurer*
Richard Porter *LCEF Vice President*
Robert Foerster *Assistant to the President: Education & Schools*
David Weeks *Assistant to the President: Mission Facilitator*
Richard Paul *Gift Planning Counselor*

**Counselors ***

1. D Brammer
2. R Knepel
3. W Carney
4. K Curry
5. H Kitzmann
6. T Dallmann
7. T Block
8. G Pera
9. C Klug
10. H Grieves
11. A Litke
12. J Pingel
13. E Knoche
14. S Niermann
15. P. Anderson
16. K Blom
17. C Prostka

### English District

Rev David H Ritt DD (FT) President
33100 Freedom Rd Farmington MI 48336-4030
Office 248/476-0039 FAX 248/476-0188
Rev Roger D Pittelko DD President Emeritus
Rev Paul E Bacon DMin First Vice President
Rev David A Dressel Second Vice President
Rev Larry M Vogel Third Vice President
Rev Arnold W Frank Fourth Vice President
Rev David P Stechholz Secretary
**At District Office 33100 Freedom Rd Farmington MI 48336 248/476-0039**
Rev Robert L Fitzpatrick (FT) *Executive Assistant to the President-Missions*
Theodore O Geheb (FT) *Executive Assistant to the President-Parish Services*
Ronald Chewning (PT) *Executive Assistant to the President-Stewardship/Advancement*
Dale Lewis (FT) *LCEF Area Vice President*
Mrs Beth Kavasch Miles (FT) *Executive Assistant to the President-Business Finance and Treasurer*

**Counselors ***

1. M Rehm
2. R Tauscher
3. W Douthwaite
4. K Elseroad
5. B Eder
6. N Mirtschin
7. D Mathers
8. R Voelker
9. C Lentner
10. M Hackbardt
11. R Boelter
12. D Fitzpatrick
13. D Gruenwald
14. W Berkesch
15. L Schneekloth
16. M Matthews
17. C Aufdenkampe
18. R Natzke
19. M Bangert
20. N Schwartz
21. R Glock
22. L Esala
23. W Kimari
24. A Koch
25. T Chan

### Florida-Georgia District

Rev Gerhard C Michael Jr (FT) President
7207 Monetary Drive Orlando FL 32809-5724
407/857-5556
Rev James R Guelzow First Vice President
Rev T Kent Fuqua Second Vice President
Rev Erich H Heintzen DED Secretary
Thomas J Hanus Treasurer
Rev Dr August Bernthal President Emeritus
Rev. Edgar A Trinklein President Emeritus
Rev Dr Thomas R Zehnder President Emeritus
**At District Office 7207 Monetary Dr Orlando FL 32809-5724**
407/857-5556 FAX 407/857-5665
http://www.fla-lcms.org
Rev Gerald W Seaman (FT) *Executive Director Division for Outreach*
Mark A Brink (FT) *Executive Director Division for Parish Services*
Richard G Neubauer (FT) *Executive Director Division for Administration (LCEF)*
Paul Kralovanec (FT) *Planned Giving Counselor*

**Counselors ***

1. R A Strickert
2. F T Marshall
3. B N Kneser
4. R G Frahm
5. J V Glamann
6. J J Vehling
7. C S Gress
8. H J Glienke
9. R H Schuette
10. K A Koenig
11. M T Frith
12. R C Elsner
13. T E Dohrman
14. M P Ave-Lallemant
15. H F Jones
16. R C Jacobs
17. K J Dunker
18. W P Schmidt

### *Indiana District*

Rev Timothy E Sims (FT) President
1145 S Barr St Fort Wayne IN 46802-3180
219/423-1511 800/837-1145
Rev E H Zimmermann Honorary President
Rev Richard Radtke First Vice President
Rev Daniel P May Second Vice President
Rev Ralph Blomenberg Third Vice President
Rev Mark Pflughocht Fourth Vice President
Rev Gregory Fiechtner Secretary
Paul North Treasurer
103 Nansue Tipton IN 46072
**At District Office 1145 S Barr St Fort Wayne IN 46802-3180 219/423-1511 FAX 219/423-1514 800-837-1145**
Rev David V Dubbelde (FT) *Executive for Congregational Outreach*
Rev Eugene W Brunow (FT) *Executive for Congregational Services*
Lawrence L Jung (FT) *Executive for Congregational Resources & LCEF*
Rev Luther Strasen (PT) *Stewardship*
**At LCMS Foundation 2819 Maplecrest Fort Wayne IN 46815 219/485-4438 FAX 219/486-7519 800/795-5267**
Terry Breininger (FT) *Gift Planning Counselor*
Timothy Imler (FT) *Gift Planning Counselor*

**Counselors ***

1. A Burkman
2. G Nagy
3. K Wartick
4. C Fitchett
5. R Rohde
6. D Rauhut
7. O Lehenbauer
8. A Piering
9. S Zeckzer
10. D Brege
11. S Koenig
12. K Gremel
13. J Herfurth
14. A Hellert
15. A Wehrmeister
16. L Mitchell
17. F Mildenburger
18. M Flory
19. L Johnson
20. R Wurst, Jr
21. M Keller
22. B Kischnick
23. H Loppnow

### Iowa District East

Rev Gary M Arp DMin (FT) President
1100 Blairs Ferry Rd Marion IA 52302
319/373-2112
Rev Jerry Doellinger First Vice President
Rev Matthew Rueger Second Vice President
Rev Chris Gugel, Secretary
Bruce Tarbox Treasurer
**At District Office**
**1100 Blairs Ferry Rd Marion IA 52302 319/373-2112 FAX 319/373-9827**
Rev Wayne Knolhoff (FT) *Executive for Evangelism, Missions, Stewardship and Finance*
Rev Norman Rehmer (FT) *Executive for Education, Human Care, Youth and Communications*

Vacant (FT) *Business Manager*

**Counselors ***

1. D Rempfer
2A. T Hedtke
2B. B Eckhardt
3. D Arndt
4. C Pannier
5. K Kincaid
6. K Krueger
7. C Lauders
8. B Saunders
9. D Korth
10. T Wegener
11. M Beesley
12. A Hafner

## Iowa District West

Rev Paul G Sieveking (FT) President
PO Box 1155 1317 Tower Drive
Fort Dodge IA 50501-1155
515/576-7666 FAX 515/576-2323
E Mail iowawest@aol.com
E Mail paul.sieveking@iowawest.org
Web: iowawest.org
Rev Richard G Kapfer, President Emeritus
Rev John Schauer First Vice President
Rev Steven Turner Second Vice President
Rev Albert Buelow Secretary
James Christensen Treasurer
234 North 12th
Denison, IA 51442
**At District Office PO Box 1155 1317 Tower Drive Fort Dodge IA 50501 515/576-7666 E-Mail: iowawest@aol.com**
Rev Earl Pierce (FT) *Executive Assistant for Missions and Stewardship*
Rev Robert Riggert (FT) *Executive Assistant for Education and Youth*
Rev Erland Asmus (PT) *Executive Assistant for Human Care Ministry*
103 Circle Dr Lake City IA 51449
Rev David Fechner (PT) *Executive Assistant for Evangelism*
3110 Norman Dr Sioux City, IA 51104
Roger Curtis (FT) *Business Manager*
James Schroeder *Gift Planning Counselor*
302 E 2nd Box 337 Laurel NE 68745
877-913-2221 402-256-9410
FAX 402/256-9409
Gary Thies *Mission Development Counselor*
40718 Hwy E-16 Mapleton, IA 51034
712/882-1029
Carole White (FT) *LCEF Vice President*
6428 160th Ave Storm Lake IA 50588
712/732-4398

**Counselors ***

1. D Glawatz
2. L W Watkins
3. D Vogel
4. L Riemer
5. D Kuhnle
6. M Mahnken
7. T P Braun
8. R Burcham
9. D Angland
10. P Helmer
11. J Raether
12. L Fett
13. S Fiege
14. B. Boyce
15. D Ericksen
16. H Kramer
17. L Schmidt
18. J Wagoner
19. R Shorey
20. H Kuhn

## Kansas District

Rev Howard Patten (FT) President
1000 SW 10th Ave Topeka KS 66604
Rev Eugene Schmidt LLD Honorary President
Rev George Bruening DD Honorary President
Rev Arlen Bruns DD Honorary President
Rev Roland Boehnke First Vice President
Rev Robert Schaedel Second Vice President
Rev Joel HiestermanThird Vice President
Rev Keith Kohlmeier Fourth Vice President
Rev David Meier Secretary
**At District Office 1000 SW 10th Ave Topeka KS 66604 785/357-4441 FAX 785/357-5071 785/357-4451 Office of District President 785/357-4443 Accounting**
Rob Peterson *Treasurer*
Alan Gunderman (FT) *Executive Director of Parish Education*
Rev Gary Rueter (FT) *Executive Director of Missions and Stewardship*
Elmer Karstensen (FT) *Business Manager & Church Extension Fund Administrator*
Garry Niehoff *Planned Giving Counselor*
Vacant District Chaplain

**Counselors ***

1. M Eichler
2. M May
3. E Trost
4. N Tegtmeier
5. T Brooks
6. J Rath
7. D Gruoner
8. L Brakenhoff
9. J Ryding
10. T Harmon
11. M Boxman
12. D Adolf
13. G Bender
14. H Niermann
15. A Hoger
16. R Roberts

## Michigan District

Rev C William Hoesman (FT) President
3773 Geddes Rd Ann Arbor MI 48105-3098
Office 734/665-4248 (direct line)
FAX 734/665-0255
Rev Wayne H Wentzel First Vice President
Rev Arnold H Brammeier Second Vice President
Rev David P E Amier Third Vice President
Rev K Frank Graves Fourth Vice President
Rev Paul D Theiss Secretary
Ralph H Ferber Treasurer
**At District Office 3773 Geddes Rd Ann Arbor MI 48105-3098 734/665-3791 or 888/225-2111 FAX 734/665-0255**
Rev Michael Ruhl (FT) *Congregation Ministry Facilitator*
Rev Peter E Larsen (FT) *Congregation Ministry Facilitator*
Rev Richard J Wolfram (FT) *Congregation Ministry Facilitator*
Rev Galan D Walther (FT) *Congregation Ministry Facilitator*
Vacant (FT) *Congregation Ministry Facilitator*
George Locke (FT) *Superintendent of Schools*
Bruce Braun (FT) *Assistant Superintendent of Schools*
Chad Woltemath (FT) *Business Manager*
Vacant (FT) *Director of Development-Michigan District*

**Church Extension Fund Staff**
**800/242-3944 FAX 734/332-7811**

Ronald Steinke (FT) *CEF President/CEO*
Marshall Gibbs (FT) *CEF V P for Marketing*
John Bates (FT) *CEF V P for Business*

**LCMS Foundation Staff**

Deborah Torbet (FT) *Ministry Support Coordinator at Ann Arbor*
Jack Kidwell (FT) *Gift Planning Counselor at Saginaw* 800/726-7362
Tom Mueller (FT) *Gift Planning Counselor at Saginaw*

**Counselors ***

1. K C Jones
2. D M Nickel
3. V T Bening
4. W C Winter
5. L I Koke
6. W H Allwardt
7. K D Lueke
8. G A Meyer
9. D C Ahlschwede
10. W W Hessler
11. R R Kilponen
12. G L Sawyer
13. M W Ramthun
14. G A Doroh
15. B L Mueller
16. L F Witt
17. M P Schulz
18. P S Nickel
19. J E Merrill
20. R P Hillenbrand
21. D O Geary
22. H A Avers
23. C E Reinke
24. W L Morris
25. D G Huber
26. T A Nelson
27. T M Lubeck
28. D K Gerke
29. P G Frederick
30. D R Gadbaw
31. W D Kreger
32. L K Matro
33. J E Schroeder
34. R R Pollatz
35. R M Rohlfs
36. J E Heimsoth
37. F C Krause
38. D L Lassanske
39. P A Baerwolf
40. T R Brazinsky
41. R A Gerke
42. P R Naumann
43. R M Zagore
44. L D Johnson

## Mid-South District

Rev David W Callies (FT) President
823 Exocet Suite 102 Cordova TN 38018
901/737-3933
Rev Wilbert E Griesse President Emeritus
Rev Norman L Groteluschen President Emeritus
Rev Daniel Otto First Vice President
Rev Kenneth Lampe Second Vice President and Secretary
Rev Paul H Jilg Vice President
Rev Clifford L Herd Jr Vice President
Mr Allen Helms Teasurer
**At District Office 823 Exocet Suite 102 Cordova TN 38018 901/737-3933 FAX 901/737-3929**
Rev Terry Tieman (FT) *Executive Assistant to President for Missions and Outreach*
James Sorgatz (FT) *Executive Assistant to District President for Lutheran Schools and Congregational Services*
Steven Schoenherr (FT) *Gift Planning Counselor*
Paul Reaves (FT) *Executive Secretary, Business and Finance and LCEF Vice President*

**Counselors ***

1. B Hildebrandt
2. R Schoolcraft
3. C R Wenck
5. R Shewmaker
6. D P Glass
7. J Beyer
8. J Burns
9. P Schmidt
10. H C Powell
11. J C Redmann
12. P J Albers

## Minnesota North District

Rev David A Bode (FT) President
PO Box 604 Brainerd MN 56401-0604
Office 218/829-1781 Home 218/346-6409
800-482-5022 — FAX 218/829-0037
Rev David Strohschein First Vice President
Rev Kirk Lee Second Vice President
Rev Dan Abrahams Third Vice President
Rev Walter Brill Secretary
Orrin Rinke Treasurer
**At District Office**
**PO Box 604 Brainerd MN 56401-0604 218/829-1781 FAX 218/829-0037—800/482-5022**
Vacant (FT) *Mission and Ministry Facilitator Missions/Evangelism*
Rev Richard Hans (FT) *Mission and Ministry Facilitator Education/Youth/Stewardship*
George Miller (FT) *LCEF Vice President, Office Manager, Gift Planning Counselor*

**Counselors ***

1. D Bell
2. A Wierschke
3. J Neubauer
4. D Meyer
5. T Vaughan
6. D Becker
7. W Zeige
8. R Franck
9. M Vrudny
10. J Beck
11. S Tischer
12. D Kirsch
13. W Meyer
14. D Wagner
15. R Bloemker
16. P Warnier
17. R Boehnke
18. L Deitemeyer

## Minnesota South District

Rev Dr Lane R Seitz DMin (FT) President
14301 Grand Ave S Burnsville MN 55306-5790
952/435-2550 ext 12 FAX 952/435-2581
Rev Peter Meier First Vice President
Rev Dr Benjamin Buck Second Vice President
Rev Gerald Menk Third Vice President
Rev Randolph Sherren Fourth Vice President
Rev Daryl Gehlbach Secretary
Rev Dr. James Pragman *Executive Asst. to President*, ext 16
Mr David Roth (FT) *Asst. to Pres. Schools/Comm. Min.*, ext 11
Rev Daniel Decker (FT) *Asst to President in Missions*, ext 25
Vacant, *Assistant to Pres., Ministerial Health/Cong. Services*
Mr Kurt Fuhr (FT) *VP LCEF*, ext 14
Ms Lu Clemmensen, *Treasurer/Business Manager*, ext 20
Ms Pam Moksnes *Gift Planning Counselor* ext 21
Mr Glenn Thiel *Gift Planning Counselor*
651/641-8256

**Counselors ***

1. J Lee
2. J D Wende
3. J Marxhausen
4. J Markworth
5. J Dreyer
6. D Wippich
7. M Johnson
8. R Nowak
9. T Evans
10. T Braun
11. V Becker
12. G Schwanke
13. M Nirva
14. D Frederickson
15. W Mueller
16. L Kath
17. G Zimmer
18. P Aldrich
19. E Chase
20. K Hollibaugh
21. G Coop
22. L Rusert
23. R Reimers
24. I Possehl
25. K Werner
26. R Gardner

## Missouri District

Rev James W Kalthoff *DD* (FT) President
660 Mason Ridge Center Dr Suite 100
St Louis MO 63141-8557
Office 314/317-4550 FAX 314/317-4574
E Mail: presmodist@aol.com
Rev Peter Kurowski DMin First Vice President
Rev Alan Bachert DMin Second Vice President
Rev Gary Clayton Third Vice President
Rev Andrew Spallek Fourth Vice President
Rev David Hintz Secretary
Gary Fanger Treasurer
**At District Office 660 Mason Ridge Center Dr Suite 100 St Louis MO 63141-8557 314/317-4550 FAX 314/317-4575 http://mo.lcms.org**

Rev Edward Lang (FT) *Mission and Ministry Facilitator*
*Special and Cross Cultural Missions*
*Staff Advisor to Bd for Mission Services*
Dennis A Klussman (FT) *Vice President LCEF*
Rev Stuart Brassie DMin (FT) *Mission and Ministry Facilitator Staff Advisor to Bd for Congregational Services*
David Waterman MA (FT) *Director of Lutheran Schools Staff Advisor to Bd for Educational Services*
Roger Mailand MEd (FT) *Mission and Ministry Facilitator Staff Advisor to Bd for Family Life and Youth Services*
Vacant *Mission and Ministry Facilitator*
Michael Earickson (FT) *Director of Financial Planning and Control*
**Deployed Director of Pastoral Care**
Rev Allen Schenk (PT) 1-800/346-1201
**Deployed LCMS Foundation Staff**
Terry Gerdts (FT) *Gift Planning Counselor* 660/463-2892
Don Schnakenberg (FT) *Gift Planning Counselor* 660/463-2892
David Rohe (FT) *Gift Planning Counselor* 314/822-7033
**Deployed LCMS Mission/Ministry Representative**
Peter Newman (FT) 636/938-1442

**Counselors ***

1. R Schneider
2. P Short
3. W Kassulke
4. K Gerike
5. F Hertwig
6. R Beese
7. D Schmidt
8. D Johnson
9. M Hoyer
10. G Stolle
11. D Newman
12. K Ratcliffe
13. K Schamber
14. D Kettner
15. D Gaunt
16. T Larson
17. W Peckman
18. D Boisclair
19. D Marth
20. C Spomer
21. Vacant
22. L Eatherton
23. G Schack
24. P Rueckert
25. V Constien
26. R Hoehne
27. G Griffin
28. M Lavrenz
29. W Zastrow

## Montana District

Rev George F Wollenburg DD (FT) President
30 Broadwater Ave Billings MT 59101
Office 406/259-2908 Home 406/252-4232
FAX 406/259-1305
Rev David L Poovey First Vice President
Rev Terry Forke Second Vice President
Rev Howard Schreibeis Secretary
Linda Weber Treasurer
**District Office Address: 30 Broadwater Avenue Billings MT 59101**

**Counselors ***

1. A W Pullmann
2. M G Warmbier
3. J A Hageman
4. H E Drummond
5. G R Everson
6. E M Nelson

## Nebraska District

Rev Eugene V Gierke (FT) President
152 S Columbia PO Box 407 Seward NE 68434
Office 402/643-2961 FAX 402/643-2990
Rev Russell Sommerfeld First Vice President
Rev James Moll Second Vice President
Rev Roger Schepmann Third Vice President
Rev Norman Friedmeyer Fourth Vice President
Rev Arthur Brinkmeyer Secretary
Paul Pettit (FT) Treasurer and Vice President Lutheran Church Extension Fund
**At District Office 152 S Columbia PO Box 407 Seward NE 68434 402/643-2961**
Neil Sandfort (FT) *Administrative Assistant to the President, Education and Youth*
Neal Koch (FT) *Gift Planning Counselor LCMS Foundation*
Gary Lewien (FT) *Lutheran Church Extension Fund Promotion Director and Administrative Assistant to the President, District Communications*
Dr William Preuss (PT) *Administrative Assistant to the President, Evangelism*
Rev Leon Zimmerman (PT) *Administrative Assistant to the President, District Ministries*
*Gary Thies* Mission Development Counselor

**Counselors ***

1. D Miesner
2. D Irmer
3. P Rowoldt
4. P Albrecht
5. R Schermbeck
6. V Schramm
7. W Voelker
8. D Boeschen
9. R Boring
10. D Hanson
11. M Chaffee
12. L Rodencal
13. G Bruce
14. R Jank Jr
15. P Houser
16. D Linkugel
17. P Hannemann
18. D Palomaki
19. B Schut
20. T Booth
21. F Simon
22. A Schauer

## New England District

Rev James Keurulainen (FT) President
400 Wilbraham Rd Springfield MA 01109
Office 413/783-0131 FAX 413/783-0909
Home 781/329-5263
Rev Larry Nichols First Vice President
Rev Timothy Yeadon Second Vice President
Rev Timothy Knapp Third Vice President
Rev James Butler Secretary
Brenda Bacon (PT) Business Manager
Mr Ed Cebry Treasurer
159 Turnpike Rd Somers CT 06071
Home 860/749-8540
Rev Ingo Dutzmann (PT) *LCEF Vice President*
24 Laneway St Taunton MA 02780
Office 888/828-4546 FAX 508/828-4545
Mr Alvin Macke (FT) *Gift Planning Counselor*
263 Clubhouse Rd Lebanon CT 06249
Office 860/450-0943 FAX 860/450-1064

**Counselors ***

1. R Piller
2. W Reuning
3. C Kemp
4. D Tegeler
5. M Gruel
6. S Schuett
7. L Neuchterlien
8. J Schettenhelm
9. R Klauck

## New Jersey District

Rev William R Klettke (FT) President
1168 Springfield Ave Mountainside NJ 07092
Office 908/233-8111 FAX 908/233-3883
Rev Dr Donald W Sandmann President Emeritus
Rev Paul R Huneke First Vice President
Rev Dennis J Krueger Second Vice President
Rev Evan W Haener Third Vice President
Rev Stephen Vogt Secretary
Fred Bernthal Treasurer
**At District Office 1168 Springfield Ave Mountainside NJ 07092 908/233-8111**
Edward W Fanslau *Assistant Treasurer/Business Manager*
Anthony C Bracco *LCEF Vice President/ Congregation Resource Counselor*

**Counselors ***

1. R Holsten
2. R Palkewick
3. L R Vossler
4. R Smith
5. S Gewecke
6. J Pierce

## North Dakota District

Rev Larry Harvala (FT) President
Mailing Address PO Box 9029
Fargo ND 58106-9029
Location 2601 23rd Ave SW Fargo ND 58103-5018 701/293-9001 FAX 701/293-9022
Dr A Reimnitz DD President Emeritus
Rev Patrick O'Brien First Vice President
Rev Carlyle Roth Second Vice President
Rev Todd Smelser Secretary
Mr Robert Wurl Treasurer
**At District Office—Mailing Address PO Box 9029 Fargo ND 58106-9029**
**Location 2601 23rd Ave SW Fargo ND 58103-5018 701/293-9001 FAX 701/293-9022**
William L Sharpe MEd (FT) *Executive Director*
Ed Bean (FT) *Gift Planning Counselor*

**Counselors ***

1. D Rothchild
2. D Kirklen
3. A Scheblein
4. B Worral
5. C Johnson
6. A Eppen
7. R Carnicom
8. A Bertsch
9. L Wolfgram

## North Wisconsin District

Rev Arleigh L Lutz DD (FT) President
3103 Seymour Lane
PO Box 8064 Wausau WI 54402-8064
Office 715/845-8241
Rev Paul A Weber First Vice President
Rev Stephen K Wipperman Second Vice President
Rev Steven A Hulke Third Vice President
Rev Joel A. Hoelter Secretary
Harold Telschow Treasurer
**At District Office 3103 Seymour Lane PO Box 8064 Wausau WI 54402-8064 715/845-8241 FAX 715/845-3836**
Lee Belmas (FT) *Youth/Care Ministry*
Dennis Johnson (FT) *LCEF*
Rev Dwayne Lueck (FT) *Missions/Stewardship/ Evangelism*
George Swanson (FT) *Business Administrator*
Robert Whipkey (FT) *Education/Communications*

**Counselors ***

1. M C Kaarre
2. K E Griebel
3. G A Creighton
4. G D Lodholz
5. W J Trosien
6. K L Albers
7. C F Kramer
8. P H Wiegert
9. W C Plautz
10. J A Freimuth Jr
11. R R Connor
12. C Kessen
13. R R Buhrke
14. R J Kampfer
15. C W Kangas
16. D A Schalow
17. D P Albers
18. P L Shackel
19. V F Heim
20. D M Pfaffe

## Northern Illinois District

Rev William H Ameiss (FT) President
2301 S Wolf Rd Hillside IL 60162
Office 708/449-3020 FAX 708/449-3026
Home 630/668-7866 FAX 630/668-7868
Rev Dan Gilbert First Vice President
Rev Roger Gallup Second Vice President
Rev Matthew Troester Third Vice President
Rev Danny Tutwiler Secretary
Dale Kuhfahl Treasurer
**At District Office 2301 S Wolf Rd Hillside IL 60162 708/449-3020 FAX 708/449-3026**
Dr W James Kirchhoff (FT) *Executive for Christian Education, Schools*
Dale Kuhfahl (FT) *Business Manager*
Jon Baermann *Planned Giving Counselor*
Rev Reuben Baerwald (PT) *Assistant to President*
*Executives for Congregational Services*
*North Region:* Dr Jack Giles 801 Kimberly Way Lisle IL 60532 (630) 271-0173 FAX 630-271-0178
*West Region:* Rev Scott Snow 4555 Trail Ridge Road Rockford IL 61101 (815) 962-9073 FAX 815-962-9078
*East Region:* Rev Donald Gourlay 413 Division Oak Park IL 60302 (708) 386-2219 FAX 708-386-2109
*South Region:* Rev Martin Haeger 1055 South Myrtle Avenue Kankakee IL 60901-5457 815/929-0396 FAX 815/929-0397

**Counselors ***

1. D Brummer
2. L Jones
3. R Gotsch
4. J Lindemann
5. D Walker
6. S Kass
7. M Schultz
8. D Balgeman
9. P Schuth
10. S Cornwell
11. W Otten
12. J Prohl
13. P Boomhower
14. D Kretzschmar
15. R Weidler
16. K Krause
17. S Prech
18. L Frazier
19. R Collins
20. L Albrecht
21. W Barthel
22. D Speerbrecker
23. M Heggen
24. K Mehrl
25. K Wellnitz
26. D Ognoskie

## Northwest District

Rev Warren Schumacher (FT) President
1700 NE Knott Portland OR 97212
503/288-8383 FAX 503/284-2785
Rev Erhart L Bauer LLD Honorary President Emeritus
Rev Emil G Jaech DD Honorary President Emeritus
Rev Clemens Pera First Vice President
Rev Keith Eilers Second Vice President
Rev Tyrus Miles Third Vice President
Rev Jonathan Rockey Fourth Vice President
Rev Leonard Mietzner Fifth Vice President
Rev Laurence Meyer Sixth Vice President
Rev D Matthew Becker District Secretary
**At District Office 1700 NE Knott St Portland OR 97212 503/288-8383**
Rev Jerry Scansen (PT) *Pastoral Assistant to the President*
Dr Denny Langston *Director of Congregational Services*
Richard Weniger *Director Educational & Congregational Services*

Rev David Hoover *Director Expanding Ministries*
Jack Schulze *LCEF Promotions/Investments*
Larry Solberg *Business Manager & LCEF Area Vice President*

**Counselors ***

1. A Schultz
2. W Gehrke
3. P Schoenherr
4. D Chamberlain
5. D Schomburg
6. D Parshall
7. M Bertermann
8. M Hoelter
9. E Wichner
10. P Bohlken
11. J M Donnan
12. W Shimkus
13. V Lillich
14. A Werfelmann
15. M Hewitt
16. L Gutz
17. T Scharr
18. D Wildermuth
19. J Pulse
20. M Lieske
21. R Dallman
22. G Burza
23. J Markus
24. T Werfelmann
25. K Schauer

## Ohio District

Rev Ronald L Bergen (FT) President
6451 Columbia Rd PO Box 38277
Olmsted Falls OH 44138
Office 440/235-2297 FAX 440/235-1970
Rev Kenton G Wendorf First Vice President
Rev Gilbert J Duchow Second Vice President
Rev Terry L Cripe Third Vice President
Rev Paul Hoffman Secretary
**At District Office 6451 Columbia Rd PO Box 38277 Olmsted Falls OH 44138 440/235-2297**
Rev Richard Gahl (FT) *Executive Director*
Vacant (FT) *Director of Education Services*
Robert F Myers (FT) *Director of Ministerial Health*
David Bowers (FT) *Church Extension Fund Director*
Bonnie Mann (FT) *Chief Financial Officer*
Karen Dutton (PT) *Youth Coordinator*
Vacant (PT) *Gift Planning Counselor*

**Counselors ***

1. L Genter
2. R Behnke
3. D Meilander
4. D Riley
5. B Lewis
6. G Miller
7. E Van Scyoc
8. M Viets
9. R Reinhardt
10. E Linthicom
11. M Korte
12. P Reetz
13. A Wolka
14. T Bohlmann
15. C Johnson

## Oklahoma District

Rev William R Diekelman President
9222 N Garnett Road Owasso OK 74055-4424
Office 918/272-9858 Home 918/272-3639
FAX 918/272-4629 E Mail ok pres@aol.com
Rev Paul Hartman First Vice President
Rev Reed Lessing Second Vice President
Rev Gerhard Bode President Emeritus
**At District Office 9222 Garnett Rd Owasso OK 74055 912/272-9858 FAX 918/272-4629**
Brent England Treasurer
Janice Hedrick Public Relations
Leonard Busch Secretary of Education
8730 E Skelly Dr Tulsa OK 74129-3422
Office 918/622-2905
Home 918/252-1565
Rev John Walther Secretary of Stewardship
PO Box 66 Okarche OK 73762-0066
Office 405/263-7311
Home 405/263-7656 E Mail johnwalther@sprintmail.com
Rev William Geis Secretary of Missions
PO Box 368 Lone Wolf OK 73655
Office 405/846-5459 Home 405/846-9928
FAX 405/846-5672 E Mail wsgeis@aol.com
Myron Harms Secretary of Youth
3600 NW Expressway Oklahoma City OK 73112 Office 405/946-0605
Home 405/728-1858 FAX 405/946-0682
Rev Joseph Myers Human Care Secretary
PO Box 59 Garber OK 73738-0059 Office 405/863-2722
Home 405/863-2728
Rev David Reese Secretary of Evangelism
1008 W Plato Rd Duncan OK 73533
Office 405/255-3267 Home 405/255-0941
FAX 405/255-3001 E Mail gslc@texhoma.net
Elmer Wilkening Church Extension Secretary
6723 E 67 St Tulsa OK 74133 Office 918/584-3581 X230
Home 918/492-6283

**Counselors ***

1. M Wescoatt
2. V Goebel
3. D Krepel
4. R Mayer
5. C Reimer
6. H Klawitter
7. M Schultz
8. B Henke
9. G Brandt

## Pacific Southwest District

*(formerly Southern California)*

Rev Larry Stoterau (FT) President
1540 Concordia East Irvine CA 92612
949/854-3232
Rev Beryl Droegemueller First Vice President
Rev Roger Sonnenberg Second Vice President
Rev Tim Seals Third Vice President
Rev Kevin Wyssmann Fourth Vice President
Rev Richard Dannenbring Secretary
**At District Office 1540 Concordia East Drive Irvine CA 92612-3203 949/854-3232 FAX 949/854-8140**
John Nelson *Treasurer*
Rev Calvin R Fiege (PT) *Vice President of LCEF*
Mrs Rachel Klitzing (FT) *School Ministries*
Mrs Jean Beres (FT) *Director of Communication*
Thomas C Butz (FT) *Vice President of LCEF-Loan and Real Estate*

**Counselors ***

1. To be determined
2. G Barth
3. C Pearson
4. J Perling
5. J Gross
6. D Schleef
7. P Terhune
8. R Schroeder
9. N Stoppenhagen
10. J Zeile
11. P Terhune
12. J Lareva
13. R Juengel
14. W L Duerr Jr
15. W Smith
16. D Stueve
17. R Rebensal
18. R Smith
19. S Barckholtz
20. W Vogelsang Jr
21. R Schmidt
22. R Gredvig
23. L Busch
24. M Harding
25. A K Byars
26. H Teuscher
27. L Meyer
28. S Cluver

## Rocky Mountain District

(formerly Colorado)

Rev Roger L Krause (FT) President
14334 E Evans Ave Aurora CO 80014-1408
Office 303/695-8001 Home 303/840-8942
Rev Randy Walquist First Vice President
Rev Allen Anderson Second Vice President
Rev Norman Raedeke Third Vice President
Rev Bryan Cary Fourth Vice President
Rev Charles Blanco Secretary
**At District Office 14334 E Evans Ave Aurora CO 80014-1408 303/695-8001 FAX 303/695-4047**
Mr Paul Brill *Treasurer*
Rev Mark Larson (FT) *Executive—Missions*
Mr Paul Albers (FT) *Executive—Congregational Services*
Bernard Braunschweig (FT) *Executive Administration/LCEF Vice President*
Mr Gary Johnson *LCEF Promotion Director*
Mr Dan Bacon *Gift Planning Counselor*

**Counselors ***

1. P Neuberger
2. J Larson
3. M Goldhammer
4. R Nickel
5. E Maas
6. C Kellogg
7. G Rahe
8. R Saatkamp
9. R Sterle
10. D Bergman
11. J Elmshauser
12. G Bickner
13. R Baker
14. H Corcoran
15. D Boernke
16. K Schnegelberger
17. D Neidigk

## SELC District

Rev Carl H Krueger Jr President
4850 S Lake Dr Cudahy WI 53110
Office 414/481-0520 FAX 414/481-0736
Home 414/481-1000
Rev Andrew J Dzurovcik First Vice President
Rev Christopher Cahill Second Vice President
Rev Chris Ongstad Secretary
Rev Todd Biermann Evangelism
Paul Jurkovich Financial Secretary
17378 Bennett Rd North Royalton OH 44133
Keith Balla Treasurer
45 Shawnee Watchung NJ 07060
Rev Gerald L Kovac Missions

**Counselors ***

1. J Skopak
2. J Schonkaes
3. K Bergmann

## South Dakota District

Rev Vernon Schindler (FT) President
Mailing Address PO Box 89110
Sioux Falls SD 57109-9110
Location 3501 Gateway Blvd
Sioux Falls SD 57106 605/361-1514
Rev Dale Sattgast First Vice President
Rev Gene Bauman Second Vice President
Rev John Farden Secretary
Jerald Wulf Treasurer
1714 East Erskine Pierre SD 57501
**At District Office Mailing Address PO Box 89110 Sioux Falls SD 57109-9110 Location 3501 Gateway Blvd Sioux Falls SD 57106 605/361-1514 FAX 605/361-7959**
Howard O Shane (FT) *Executive Secretary*
Randall L Gayken (FT) *Business Manager*

**Counselors ***

1. R Reed
2. R Westad
3. J Urbach
4. D Tompkins
5. W Uecker
6. R Bailey
7. L Geyer
8. P Sparling
9. C Gies
10. S Sailer
11. J Werner

## South Wisconsin District

*Rev Ronald E Meyer* (FT) President
E Mail meyer@swd.lcms.org
8100 W Capitol Dr Milwaukee WI 53222-1981
Office 414/464-8100 Home 414/784-5232
FAX 414/464-0602
Rev John M Struve First Vice President
Rev James T Cumming Second Vice President
Rev Randolph Raasch Third Vice President
Rev Paul Borgman Fourth Vice President
Robert Lindau Jr Secretary
Rev Wayne K Huebner Assistant Secretary
Mrs Helen Snyder Treasurer
**At District Office 8100 West Capitol Drive Milwaukee WI 53222-1981 414/464-8100**
Robert C Freymark (FT) *Administrative Assistant Lutheran Schools*
E Mail freymark@swd.lcms.org
Rev Robert P Hoehner (FT) *Administrative Assistant Youth and Family*
EMail hoehner@swd/lcms.org
Vacant *Director of Communications*
Rev Wayne Schraeder (FT) *Administrative Support Stewardship/Evangelism/Human Care*
James Farrelly (PT) *Administrative Support Human Care/Older Adult*
Vacant (FT) *Administrative Assistant Missions*
Rev Ronald W Meier (PT) *Mission Support Associate*
Rev James F Laatsch (PT) *Mission Support Associate*
John E Meyer (FT) *Planned Giving Counselor*
E Mail 112223,2321@compuserve.com
Timothy Dittoff *Vice President LCEF*
E Mail dittoff@swd.lcms.org
William Hoeg *Business Manager*
E Mail hoeg@swd.lcms.org

**Counselors ***

1. A A Koch
2. G Richter
3. P Schmidt
4. P Peckman
5. T Eggebrecht
6. W Granke
7. G Meyer
8. W Reichmann
9. E Blonski
10. R Zick
11. M Sander
12. J Hartman
13. D Bergelin
14. M Krueger
15. D Lieske
16. J Brogaard
17. D Totsky
18. J Wille
19. D Schueler
20. M Hendrickson
21. L Thies
22. R Krug
23. T Feiertag
24. D Stein
25. W Wagner
26. J Keuch
27. T Gundlach

## Southeastern District

Rev Dr Arthur W Scherer (FT) President
6315 Grovedale Drive PO Box 10415
Alexandria VA 22310-0415
703/971-9371 ext 202 FAX (703) 922-6047
Rev Dr Jon Diefenthaler First Vice President
Rev Dr William Seaman Second Vice President
Rev James Wiggins Jr Third Vice President
Rev John Denninger Secretary
Mr Ralph Harrison Treasurer
11501 Burberry Dr Raleigh NC 27614-9020
**At District Office 6315 Grovedale Drive PO Box 10415 Alexandria VA 22310-0415 703/971-9371 FAX 703/922-6047**
Deaconess Sally J Hiller (FT) *Executive—Mission and Ministry*
Rev Lloyd Gaines (FT) *Executive - Black Urban Multi-Ethnic Ministries*

Mr Stephen Heemann (FT) *Executive—Chief Financial Officer and Vice President - LCEF*
*(FT) Deployed Mission and Ministry Facilitators:*
Rev Timothy Fangmeier (Southern Region)
PO Box 1877 Davidson NC 28036
(704) 641-5811
Rev Arthur M Umbach (Central Region)
2711 Valley Springs Rd Powhatan VA 23139
(804) 897-0161
Rev Kenneth G Carlson (Northern Region)
11501 Brandy Hall Lane
Gaithersburg MD 20878
(301) 279-2051

**Counselors ***

1. M Hagebusch
2. J. Banach
3. E Robertson
4. R Hinz
5. J Stoltenberg
6. L Stano
7. S Mentz
8. K Schnepp
9. R Wiechmann
10. T Naumann
11. J Kleinfelter
12. T Becker
13. J Costello
14. J McDaniels
15. T Baldinger
16. E F Meyer
17. D Roth
18. P Sizemore
19. J Greene

## Southern District

Rev Orval D Mueller (FT) President
PO Box 8396 New Orleans LA 70182
504/282-2632 FAX 504/283-4885
Rev Bernard H Ansorge First Vice President
Rev James P Brown Second Vice President
Rev Robert G Rupp Secretary
Mrs Connie Arbogast Treasurer
**At District Office The Lutheran Center 2240 Lake Shore Drive PO Box 8396 New Orleans LA 70122 (For POB use 70182) 504/282-2632 FAX 504/283-4885**
Charles J Kellison (FT) *Executive Assistant for Finance*
Eugene W Menzel (FT) *Executive Assistant for Parish Services*
Dr Jan C Case (FT) *Executive Assistant for Parish Ministries*

**Counselors ***

1. J Ertl
2. M Hayman
3. D Lofthus
4. M Muenchow
5. W Toncre
6. C Miller
7C. M Griffin
7N. W Brinkley
8. R Reinhardt
9. T Noon
10. R Lohmeyer
11. R St. Pierre
12. D DeRamus
13. E Hornig
14. G Weier
15. P Kummer

## Southern Illinois District

Rev Herbert C Mueller Jr (FT) President
2408 Lebanon Ave Belleville IL 62221
618/234-4767 FAX 618/234-4830
Rev John Lukomski First Vice President
Rev Mark Love Second Vice President
Rev George Gude Secretary
Mr Robert Streuter Treasurer 8 Buena Vista Murphysboro IL 62966-3005
**At District Office 2408 Lebanon Ave Belleville IL 62221 618/234-4767 FAX 618/234-4830**
Daniel C Roth (FT) *Executive Assistant/Mission Services*
Rev Paul Bramstedt *LCEF Area Vice President*

**Counselors ***

1. C Adair
2. R Ankney
3. W Weedon
4. S Theiss
5. M. Schuessler
6. D Schultz
7. M Henson

## Texas District

*Rev Gerald B Kieschnick* (FT) President
7900 E Highway 290 Austin TX 78724-2499
800/951-3478 512/926-4272
FAX 512/926-1006
Rev James Linderman First Vice President
Rev Donald Black Second Vice President
Rev David Rohde Third Vice President
Dr Robert Preece Fourth Vice President
Rev Ralph Hobratschk Secretary
Rev John Davenport Assistant Secretary
**At District Office 7900 E Highway 290 Austin TX 78724 800/951-3478 512/926-4272 FAX 512/926-1006**
Stephen C Block (FT) *Executive Directior Church Extension Fund*
Mrs Marlys Erickson (FT) *Treasurer*
John A Goeke (FT) *Director of Development for Missions*
Rev Kenneth Hennings (FT) *Mission and Ministry Coordinator*
Dr William V Hinz (PT) *Director of School Ministry*
Dr John M Hirsch (FT) *Director of Congregational and Worker Care*
Paul A Krentz (FT) *Mission and Ministry Facilitator Area B*
Rev Gary Pohl (FT) *Executive Director Lutheran Foundation of Texas*
Ron Scherch (FT) *Director of CAN-DO Missions*
William C Siegrist (FT) *Director of Development Church Extension Fund*
Lawrence R Winkler (FT) *Office Manager/Administrative Services*
Vacant (FT) *Director of Public Relations & Events*
Vacant (FT) *Director of Construction Church Extension Fund*
**At Deployed District Office - Amarillo**
Jon Braunersreuther (FT) *Mission and Ministry Facilitator—Area A*
7699 Canyon Drive Amarillo TX 79110
806/467-2439 FAX 806/467-2440
**At Deployed District Office - Houston**
Louis Jander (FT) *Mission and Ministry Facilitator—Area D*
10810 Glenora Drive Houston TX 77065
281/970-5308 FAX 281/970-5309
**At Deployed District Office - San Antonio**
Rev William Reagan (FT) *Mission and Ministry Facilitator—Area C*
1826 Basse Road San Antonio TX 78213
210/731-8257 FAX 210/731-8957

**Counselors ***

1. M Cattau
3. J Schneider
4. P Konz
5. R Boyce
6. D Loeschen
7. K Bersche
8. R Tieken
9. K Watson
11. D Little
12. R Mayerhoff
13. J Conley
14. R Pase
15. C Schinnerer
16. D Bahn
17. M Ramming
18. D Olson
19. M Doering
20. B Knippa
21. K Westergren
22. W Schumpe
23. B Schey
24. W Shupe
25. H Biar
26. J Feierabend
27. G Franke
28. W Pohland
31. W Schwertlich
32. M Hafer
33. H Graf
34. T Dinger
35. R Turner
36. D Tessmann
37. T Van Duzer
38. M Ramey
39. C Campbell Jr
41. H Fleischhauer
42. M Snow
43. B Bestian

## Wyoming District

Rev Ron M Garwood DD(FT) President
2400 Hickory Casper WY 82604
307/265-9000 FAX 307/234-6629
Rev Marvin L Temme First Vice President
Rev Richard O Boche Second Vice President
Rev Shawn L Kumm Secretary
Mr Walter Brantz Treasurer
**At District Office Lutheran Ministries Center 2400 Hickory Casper WY 82604 307/265-9000**
Rev Bradley D Heinecke *Mission Services*
Rev Lee E Rupert *Congregational Services*
Rev William C Heine *Education Executive*
Mr Jeffery Snyder *Business manager/LCEF Vice President*

**Counselors ***

1. P Found
2. R Neugebauer
3. P Bertram
4. R Asburry
5. J Christensen
6. L Wisroth
7. M Maas

# CHAIRMEN OF DISTRICT BOARDS AND COMMITTEES

Addresses Not Listed for Ordained and Commissioned Ministers

## Archivists

*Atlantic District* Rev Kurt Bodling
*California-Nevada-Hawaii District* Rev Karl H Wyneken
*Central Illinois District* Rev Marvin Lorenz
*Eastern District* Eunice Foote 10 Ellicott Ct Tonawanda NY 14150
*English District* Rev Victor F Halboth Jr
*Florida-Georgia District* Paul Wehr 1613 Druid Isle Rd Maitland FL 32751
*Indiana District*
*Iowa District East* Judy Westergren 1240 F Ave Marion IA 52302
*Iowa District West* Rev Albert H Buelow
*Kansas District* Rev George Bruening
*Michigan District* Vacant
*Mid-South District* Robert Prince 3209 Joslyn Memphis TN 38128
*Minnesota North District* Rev Gunard Heikkila
*Minnesota South District* Glenn Offermann
*Missouri District* Rev Marvin A Huggins
*Montana District* Rev Eugene Juergensen
*Nebraska District* Rev David Palomaki
*New England District* Rev Gregory Wismar
*New Jersey District* Rev Jack Wangerin
*North Dakota District* District Office
*North Wisconsin District* Rev Roger Moldenhauer
*Northern Illinois District*
*Northwest District* Rev Dwain Brandt
*Ohio District* Rev Manfred Rembold
*Oklahoma District* Mike Bradley 9832 N 147th E Ave Owasso OK 74055
*Pacific Southwest District (formerly Southern California)* Rev Dr Alfred J Freitag, Michael Doyle
*Rocky Mountain District* Lyle Schaefer 4680 Inca St Englewood CO 80110
*SELC District*
*South Dakota District* Rev Orlett D Brack
*South Wisconsin District* Rev Robert Schmidt
*Southeastern District* Judy Koucky 2712 Hickory St Alexandria VA 22305
*Southern District* Rev Dr Richard H Meyer
*Southern Illinois District* Helen Perschbacher 8643 Flamingo Rd Okawville IL 62271-9750
*Texas District* Vacant
*Wyoming District* Ruth Kucera 4500 So Poplar #307 Casper WY 82604

## Church Extension

*Atlantic District* William B Kletecka (District Office)
*California-Nevada-Hawaii District* Rev Robert F Fickenscher
*Central Illinois District* Mr Walt Karlowski 47 Gray Ln Decator IL 62526
*Eastern District* Paul Fromm 41 Rockdale Dr West Amherst NY 14228
*English District* Dale Lewis
*Florida-Georgia District* Richard H Neubauer
*Indiana District*
*Iowa District East* Rev Frederick Wood
*Iowa District West*
*Kansas District* Elmer Karstensen (District Office)
*Michigan District* Rev Daniel E Lochner
*Mid-South District* Rev John Reimold
*Minnesota North District* George Miller (District Office)
*Minnesota South District* Kurt Fuhr
*Missouri District* Mr Dennis Klussmann (District Office)
*Montana District* Leon Langemeier PO Box 187 Bridger MT 59104
*Nebraska District* Paul Pettit PO Box 407 Seward NE 68434
*New England District* Rev Ingo Dutzmann
*New Jersey District* Anthony Bracco 38 Markwood Drive Howell NJ 07731
*North Dakota District* Wm L Sharpe
*North Wisconsin District* Dennis Johnson (District Office)
*Northern Illinois District*
*Northwest District* Larry Solberg
*Ohio District* David Bowers
*Oklahoma District* Elmer Wilkening
*Pacific Southwest District (formerly Southern California)* Rev Cal Fiege
*Rocky Mountain District* Bernard Braunschweig (District Office)
*SELC District* Robert C Lange 3242 Edginton St Franklin Park IL 60131-2129
*South Dakota District* Randall L Gayken (District Office)
*South Wisconsin District* Ralph W Klevenow (District Office)
*Southeastern District* Stephen Heemann (District Office)
*Southern District* Harvey Wilkening 9460 Garfield Dr Shreveport LA 71118
*Southern Illinois District* Rev Paul Bramstedt 2408 Lebanon Ave Belleville IL 62221-2597
*Texas District* Chris Bannwolf 25 Courtside Cir San Antonio TX 78216
*Wyoming District* Jeffrey Snyder (District Office)

### Congregational Constitutions

*Atlantic District* Rev Warren Winterhoff
*California-Nevada-Hawaii District* Rebecca Calloway 1083 Palomino Rd Cloverdale CA 95425-1009
*Central Illinois District* Rev Karl Weber
*Eastern District*
*English District* Rev Philip Kraft
*Florida-Georgia District* Rev Richard Drankwalter
*Indiana District* Rev Jack Belk
*Iowa District East* Rev Leon Hodges
*Iowa District West*
*Kansas District* Jerry Larson 111 E 8th St Larned KS 67550
*Michigan District* Rev Lawrence Witto
*Mid-South District* Rev Mark Burger
*Minnesota North District* Rev William Stockman EM
*Minnesota South District* Rev David Winter
*Missouri District* Rev Walter Strickert
*Montana District* Rev David L Poovey
*Nebraska District* Rev Richard Gudgel
*New England District* Vernon Koch
*New Jersey District* Rev Stephen Vogt
*North Dakota District* Rev Todd Smelser
*North Wisconsin District* Rev Joel Hoelter
*Northern Illinois District*
*Northwest District* Rev Oscar Marquardt
*Ohio District* vacant
*Oklahoma District* Rev Harold Brockhoff
*Pacific Southwest District (formerly Southern California)* Rev David Schilling
*Rocky Mountain District* Gerland Klein 40951 Cty Rd D Yuma CO 80759
*SELC District* Rev Luther Bajus
*South Dakota District* Rev David Schwan
*South Wisconsin District* E John Raasch 253 S St Waukesha WI 53186
*Southeastern District* vacant
*Southern District* Rev Richard E Kuehnert
*Southern Illinois District* Rev Michael Hart 2305 Grand Ave Granite City IL 62040-4722
*Texas District* Rev Jerome Teichmiller
*Wyoming District* Rev Richard Boche

### Continuing Education

*Atlantic District* Rev Kenneth Hessel
*California-Nevada-Hawaii District* Rev Fred Stennfeld
*Central Illinois District* Rev Wayne Hoffman
*Eastern District*
*English District*
*Florida-Georgia District* Rev Thomas E Dohrman
*Indiana District*
*Iowa District East* Rev Harold Block
*Iowa District West* Rev Dr Richard Osslund
*Kansas District* DCE Ken Lueders
*Michigan District* Rev Gary Beck
*Mid-South District* Rev Harlan Heiserman
*Minnesota North District* Rev Richard Hans
*Minnesota South District* David Roth
*Missouri District* David Waterman
*Montana District* Rev Mark Grunst
*Nebraska District*
*New England District* Rev Robert Beinke
*New Jersey District*
*North Dakota District* Rev Clark Jahnke
*North Wisconsin District* Robert Whipkey (District Office)
*Northern Illinois District* Rev Dr Ronald Kolar
*Northwest District* Rev Dr Norman Metzler
*Ohio District* Vacant
*Oklahoma District* Mark Carter
*Pacific Southwest District (formerly Southern California)* Rev Alvin Young
*Rocky Mountain District* Rev Gary Rahe
*SELC District* Rev Edgar Anthony
*South Dakota District* Rev Paul Wenz
*South Wisconsin District* Rev Robert Zick
*Southeastern District* Deaconess Sally J Hiller
*Southern District* Eugene W Menzel (District Office)
*Southern Illinois District* Rev Charles Ramsey
*Texas District* Rev James Mann
*Wyoming District* Rev Marvin Temme
Concordia Seminary - St Louis Prof John Oberdeck 801 DeMun Ave St Louis MO 63105
Concordia Seminary - Fort Wayne Rev Richard C Resch
Concordia College - Ann Arbor Ms Jane Talcott 4090 Geddes Road Ann Arbor MI 48105
Concordia University - Austin Rev Dr Joel Heck Rehbein 3400 N Interstate 35 Austin Tx 78705
Concordia College - Bronxville Dr Wally Borgen 171 White Plains Rd Bronxville NY 10708-1923
Concordia University - Irvine Prof Timothy Peters 1530 Concordia West Irvine CA 92715-3299
Concordia University - Mequon Cheryl Carter 12800 N Lake Shore Dr Mequon WI 53092
Concorida University - Portland Rev Dr Norm Metzler
Concordia University - River Forest Dr Elaine Sipe 7400 Augusta St River Forest IL 60305-1499
Concordia University - St Paul Rev Robert De Werff
Concordia College - Selma Dr Julius Jenkins 1804 Green St Selma AL 36701
Concordia College - Seward Dr Lee Schluckebier 800 N Columbia Ave Seward NE 68434
Eastern Region Representative Rev Dr Harold Kitzmann
Midwest I Region Representative Rev John Rauh
Midwest II Region Representative Rev Dr Ben Buck
South and Southwest Region Representative - Open
Western Region Representative Rev Sergei Koberg

### Evangelism

*Atlantic District* DCE Dan Rath
*California-Nevada-Hawaii District* Rev Clinton Lutz
*Central Illinois District* Rev William Abbott
*Eastern District*
*English District* Rev Robert Fitzpatrick
*Florida-Georgia District* Rev Gerald W Seaman
*Indiana District*
*Iowa District East* Rev Parker Knoll
*Iowa District West* Rev Russell Senstad
*Kansas District* Rev Kevin Wilson
*Michigan District* Rev Michael Lutz
*Mid-South District* Rev Richard Elseroad
*Minnesota North District* Rev Richard Hans
*Minnesota South District*
*Missouri District* Rev Edward Lang
*Montana District* Rev Darold Reiner
*Nebraska District* Bill Preuss
*New England District* Rev John Hohe
*New Jersey District* Rev Phillip Grovenstein
*North Dakota District* Wm L Sharpe
*North Wisconsin District* Rev Dwayne Lueck
*Northern Illinois District* Rev Jock Ficken
*Northwest District* Glenn Herbold
*Ohio District* Vacant
*Oklahoma District* Rev David Reese
*Pacific Southwest District (formerly Southern California)* Vacant
*Rocky Mountain District* Vacant
*SELC District* Rev Todd Biermann
*South Dakota District* Rev Aaron Asmus
*South Wisconsin District* Vacant
*Southeastern District* Rev Timothy Fangmeier
*Southern District* Sub-committee of Mission Committee Rev Warren H Davis
*Southern Illinois District* Ron Friedrich 654 W Alton St Nashville IL 62263-1338
*Texas District* Rev Steve Sohns
*Wyoming District* Rev Larry Veland

### Legal Counselors

*Atlantic District* Capell & Visnic 3000 Marcus Ave Suite 1E9 Lake Success NY 11042
*California-Nevada-Hawaii District* William Morris 1771 Woodside Rd Redwood City CA 94061
*Central Illinois District* Mr Mark Steen 607 E Adams Springfield IL 62703
*Eastern District*
*English District* Douglas C Abraham 19500 Victor Pky #290 Livonia MI 48152
*Florida-Georgia District* John Gierach Esq PO Box 6027 Orlando FL 32803
*Indiana District* Ronald K Gehring 202 W Berry Suite 321 Ft Wayne IN 46802
*Iowa District East* Dean Spina 2001 1st Ave E Cedar Rapids IA 52402
*Iowa District West*
*Kansas District* Henry Schulties 1400 SW Topeka Ave Topeka KS 66612
*Michigan District* Dana Dever Dever & Dew PC 301 E Liberty Street Suite 585 Ann Arbor MI 48104-2251
*Mid-South District* Len Pranschke
*Minnesota North District* Rev Richard Hans
*Minnesota South District* Paul Melchert 121 W Main St Waconia MN 55387
*Missouri District* R Lynn Beckemeier 12813 Flushing Meadows Dr St Louis MO 63131
*Montana District* Lance Pedersen 1026 Blue Sage Ct Hardin MT 59034
*Nebraska District* Kermit Brashear Brashear & Ginn North Old Mill 711 N 108th Crt Omaha NE 68154-1714
*New England District* Robert Beer Maltbie Rd Box 332 Newton CT 06470 and Dean Radke 100 Great Meadow Rd Wethersfield CT 06109
*New Jersey District* Gary Algeier 4 Sandy Ln Randolph NJ 07869
*North Dakota District*
*North Wisconsin District* Att David Piehler PO Box, 1287 Wausau WI 54402
*Northern Illinois District* Boerger, Heerwagen, Lustoff, Brendemuhl, P.C. 2914 S Harlem Ave Riverside IL 60546
*Northwest District* Dan Lorenz 521 SW Clay Portland OR 97201
*Ohio District*
*Oklahoma District*
*Pacific Southwest District (formerly Southern California)*
*Rocky Mountain District* Kim Seter 5959 DTC Blvd Suite 300 Greenwood Village CO 80111
*SELC District* Ronald H Roby 1141 Orange Ave PO Box 2855 Winter Park FL 32790-2855
*South Dakota District* Vacant
*South Wisconsin District* Walter Tesch 933 N Mayfair Rd Wauwatosa WI 53226
*Southeastern District*
*Southern District* John Rochelle (Securities) Baldwin & Haspel 1100 Poydras New Orleans LA 70112
*Southern Illinois District* David O Hesi 3517 College Ave Alton IL 62002
*Texas District*
*Wyoming District* Larry Harrington PO Box 51214 Casper WY 82605-1214

### Ministerial Growth and Support

*Atlantic District* Mrs Lillian Biddle 22 Reede Ln Westbury NY 11590
*California-Nevada-Hawaii District* Rev Dr Harold S Draeger
*Central Illinois District* Rev Wayne Hoffman
*Eastern District*
*English District* Rev Alan Steinke
*Florida-Georgia District* Rev R Richard Armstrong
*Indiana District*
*Iowa District East*
*Iowa District West* Rev Ed Brandt
*Kansas District*
*Michigan District* Rev K Frank Graves
*Mid-South District* Len Pranschke
*Minnesota North District* Rev Donald Wilke
*Minnesota South District* Mrs Connie Marquart 690 60th St Dunnell MN 56127
*Missouri District* Rev James Kalthoff
*Montana District*
*Nebraska District* Rev Mark Rosenau
*New England District* Margaret Boger 2 Belmore Road N Providence RI 02904
*New Jersey District* Rev Paul Huneke
*North Dakota District* Rev Irv Bruenjes
*North Wisconsin District* Rev Arleigh L Lutz
*Northern Illinois District*
*Northwest District* Dan Lorenz
*Ohio District* Vacant
*Oklahoma District* Rev John Raddatz
*Pacific Southwest District (formerly Southern California)* Rev Harold Teuscher
*Rocky Mountain District* Rev Gary Rahe
*SELC District* Rev Albert Marcis
*South Dakota District* Rev Vernon Schindler DP
*South Wisconsin District* Rev Warren Granke
*Southeastern District* Rev Arthur Umbach
*Southern District* Rev Robert L Richter
*Southern Illinois District* Rev Charles Ramsey
*Texas District* Dr Gerald Brunworth
*Wyoming District* Rev Ronald Garwood DP
Concordia Seminary - St Louis Prof John Oberdeck 801 DeMun Ave St Louis MO 63105
Concordia Seminary - Fort Wayne Rev Richard C Resch
Concordia College - Ann Arbor Ms Jane Talcott 4090 Geddes Road Ann Arbor MI 48105
Concordia University - Austin Rev Dr Joel Heck Rehbein 3400 N Interstate 35 Austin Tx 78705
Concordia College - Bronxville Dr Wally Borgen 171 White Plains Rd Bronxville NY 10708-1923
Concordia University - Irvine Prof Timothy Peters 1530 Concordia West Irvine CA 92715-3299

Concordia University - Mequon Cheryl Carter 12800 N Lake Shore Dr Mequon WI 53092
Concorida University - Portland Rev Dr Norm Metzler
Concordia University - River Forest Dr Elaine Sipe 7400 Augusta St River Forest IL 60305-1499
Concordia University - St Paul Rev Robert DeWerff
Concordia College - Selma Dr Julius Jenkins 1804 Green St Selma AL 36701
Concordia College - Seward Dr Lee Schluckebier 800 N Columbia Ave Seward NE 68434
Eastern Region Representative Rev Dr Harold Kitzmann
Midwest I Region Representative Rev John Rauh
Midwest II Region Representative Rev Dr Ben Buck
South and Southwest Region Representative - Open
Western Region Representative Rev Sergei Koberg

## Missions

*Atlantic District* Rev David Born
*California-Nevada-Hawaii District* John Schaller PO Box 844 Tahoe City, CA 94061
*Central Illinois District* Rev Melvin Weseloh
*Eastern District*
*English District* Rev Robert Fitzpatrick
*Florida-Georgia District* Rev Gerald W Seaman
*Indiana District*
*Iowa District East* Richard Wenz
*Iowa District West* Rev Carl Droegemueller
*Kansas District* Don Hanson 1016 Ave J Ellsworth KS 67439
*Michigan District* Rev Michael Ruhl
*Mid-South District* Rev Douglas Kallesen
*Minnesota North District* Rev Richard Hans
*Minnesota South District*
*Missouri District* Rev Edward Lang
*Montana District* Vacant
*Nebraska District* Rev Leon Zimmerman
*New England District* Ken Fischer 80 Echo Drive Vernon CT 06066
*New Jersey District* Rev Robert Roegner
*North Dakota District* Wm L Sharpe
*North Wisconsin District* Rev Dwayne Lueck
*Northern Illinois District* Rev Mark Larson, Dave Tremain 219 Kendall Drive Yorkville, IL 60560-1040
*Northwest District* Rev David Hoover
*Ohio District* Vacant
*Oklahoma District* Rev Bill Geis
*Pacific Southwest District (formerly Southern California)* Rev Mike Brewer
*Rocky Mountain District* Vacant
*SELC District* Rev Paul Hoyer
*South Dakota District* Rev David Gunderson
*South Wisconsin District* Duane Graf
*Southeastern District* Deaconess Sally Hiller
*Southern District* Rev Warren H Davis
*Southern Illinois District* Rev Leroy Eckert
*Texas District* Vacant
*Wyoming District* Rev Bradley Heinecke

## Parish Education

*Atlantic District* Thomas Roemke
*California-Nevada-Hawaii District* Dee Christopher
*Central Illinois District* Rev Paul Droegemueller
*Eastern District*
*English District* Theodore O Geheb
*Florida-Georgia District* Mark A Brink
*Indiana District*
*Iowa District East* Rev Steven Rempfer
*Iowa District West* Rev Phill Andreasen
*Kansas District* Mark Schotte
*Michigan District* Bruce Braun
*Mid-South District* Mary Ann Schmand
*Minnesota North District* Rev Richard Hans
*Minnesota South District*
*Missouri District* David Waterman
*Montana District*
*Nebraska District*
*New England District* Lois Frerking
*New Jersey District* Shirley Carpenter 601 Graceland Pl Westfield NJ 07090
*North Dakota District* Wm L Sharpe
*North Wisconsin District* Robert Whipkey (District Office)
*Northern Illinois District* Barbara Johnson 906 West Villa Drive Des Plaines, IL 60016
*Northwest District* Richard Weniger
*Ohio District* Vacant
*Oklahoma District* Rev Leonard Busch
*Pacific Southwest District (formerly Southern California)* Vacant
*Rocky Mountain District* Marv Oestmann 17812 Eleigh Pl Aurora CO 80013
*SELC District*
*South Dakota District* Rev Ray Greenseth
*South Wisconsin District* Bryan Seider 2175 S Woodshire Dr New Berlin WI 53151
*Southeastern District* Deaconess Sally Hiller
*Southern District* Charles Schiller
*Southern Illinois District* Ron Friedrich
*Texas District*
*Wyoming District* Rev Lee Rupert

## Communications and/or Public Relations Directors

*Atlantic District* Kathy Jagow (District Office)
*California-Nevada-Hawaii District* Rev Ronald Youngdale
*Central Illinois District* Rev Rodger Abatie
*Eastern District*
*English District* Betty Mueller
*Florida-Georgia District* John List and Eileen Bishop 1181 S Rogers Cir Ste 20 Boca Raton FL 33487-2726
*Indiana District*
*Iowa District East* Rev Norman Rehmer
*Iowa District West* Rev Ed W Lichtsinn
*Kansas District*
*Michigan District* Debby Fall
*Mid-South District* Rev Ronald J Wiese
*Minnesota North District* Rev Richard Hans
*Minnesota South* Rev David Anderson
*Missouri District* Rev Harold Rau
*Montana District* Rev Henry Drummond
*Nebraska District* Gary Lewien (District Office)
*New England District* Wanda Weissbach (District Office)
*New Jersey District* Marion Monskie 12 Daniel St Dover NJ 07801
*North Dakota District* Wm L Sharpe
*North Wisconsin District* Robert Whipkey (District Office)
*Northern Illinois District* Jackie Bussert 121 Willow Road Elmhurst, IL 60126
*Northwest District*
*Ohio District* Rev Jeffrey Stephens and Rev Robert Hullinger
*Oklahoma District* Janet Hedrick (PR) (District Office)
*Pacific Southwest District (formerly Southern California)* Jean Beres Director
*Rocky Mountain District* Rev Harold Reiss
*SELC District Rev Robert Mataj*
*South Dakota District* Rev Howard O Shane
*South Wisconsin District* Rev Galan Walther
*Southeastern District* Deaconess Sally Hiller
*Southern District Cheryl Pitts PO Box 8396 New Orleans LA 70182*
*Southern Illinois District* Ron Friedrich
*Texas District* Rev Dennis Bragdon
*Wyoming District* Rev Nathan Brandt

## Human Care

*Atlantic District* Mrs Kathleen Funfgeld 31 Caumsett Woods Ln Woodbury NY 11797
*California-Nevada-Hawaii District* Jack Adolphson 460 35th Street Sacramento CA 95816
*Central Illinois District* Ed Schoenbaum 1108 S Grand Ave W Springfield IL 62704
*Eastern District* Rev David Weeks
*English District* Theodore O Geheb
*Florida-Georgia District* Mark A Brink
*Indiana District*
*Iowa District East* Vacant
*Iowa District West* Robert Wilcke 605 7th St Box 136 Battle Creek IA 51005
*Kansas District* Barb McComas
*Michigan District* Rev Warren Paulson
*Mid-South District* Rev Ronald Halamka
*Minnesota North District*
*Minnesota South District* Curtis Stoltenow
*Missouri District* Rev Allen Schenk
*Montana District* Vacant
*Nebraska District*
*New England District* Rev Robert Schipul
*New Jersey District*
*North Dakota District* Rev L Jay Reinke
*North Wisconsin District* DCE Lee Belmas
*Northern Illinois District* Rev Martin Balzer
*Northwest District* Glenn Herbold
*Ohio District* Vacant
*Oklahoma District* Rev Joseph Myers
*Pacific Southwest District (formerly Southern California)* Vacant
*Rocky Mountain District* Rev Douglas Escue
*SELC District* Rev Richard Schauer
*South Dakota District* Rev Timothy Heupel
*South Wisconsin District* Rev Bryan Osladil
*Southeastern District* Deaconess Sally Hiller
*Southern District* Sub-committee of Mission Committee Rev Warren H Davis
*Southern Illinois District* Ron Friedrich
*Texas District* Dr Keith Loomans
*Wyoming District* Bret Schroeder

## Stewardship

*Atlantic District* Michael Meese 225A Barnard Loop West Point NY 10996, Rev Victor Nelson
*California-Nevada-Hawaii District* Bill Wagner 1306 Bittern Way Suison CA 94585
*Central Illinois District* Rev Theodore Gall
*Eastern District*
*English District* Ronald Chewning
*Florida-Georgia District* Richard Neubauer 7207 Monetary Dr Orlando FL 32809-5724
*Indiana District*
*Iowa District East* Rev Tim Zimmermann
*Iowa District West* Rev Allen Hellwege
*Kansas District* Marilyn Greathouse 4101 Harvard Rd Lawrence KS 66049
*Michigan District* Rev Richard Wolfram
*Mid-South District* Jim Sorgatz
*Minnesota North District* Rev Richard Hans
*Minnesota South District*
*Missouri District* Rev Stuart Brassie
*Montana District* Rev Kent Stenzel
*Nebraska District* Rev Charles Gierke
*New England District* Rev H Lane Bridges
*New Jersey District* Rev Otto Baker
*North Dakota District* Ed Bean
*North Wisconsin District* Rev Dwayne Lueck
*Northern Illinois District*
*Northwest District* Rev David Hoover
*Ohio District* Vacant
*Oklahoma District* Rev John Walther
*Pacific Southwest District (formerly Southern California)*
*Rocky Mountain District* Rev Randy Bolt
*SELC District* Rev Thomas Soltis
*South Dakota District* Rev Peter Utecht
*South Wisconsin District* Rev Thomas Wink
*Southeastern District* Rev Arthur Umbach
*Southern District* Bob Beer 80 Skyline Trail Pell City AL 35128
*Southern Illinois District* Ron Friedrich
*Texas District* Rev Vic Kollmann
*Wyoming District* Walter Brantz 169A Sage Creek Rd Cody WY 82414

## Student Recruitment and/or Student Aid

NOTE: One committee serves both functions unless otherwise indicated (SR) (SA)
*Atlantic District* Stanley Kramer
*California-Nevada-Hawaii District* Rev Don Schneider
*Central Illinois District* Mr David Goldhammer
*Eastern District*
*English District* Theodore O Geheb
*Florida-Georgia District* Rev Peter Kolb
*Indiana District*
*Iowa District East* Rev Keith Piotter
*Iowa District West* Rev David Loeschen (SA) Dennis Andreasen 1432 City View Dr Denison IA 51442
*Kansas District* Rev John Duran
*Michigan District* Carl Middeldorf (SA)
*Mid-South District* Dr. Donald Ross
*Minnesota North District* Rev Richard Hans
*Minnesota South District*
*Missouri District* David Waterman
*Montana District* Rev Henry Drummond
*Nebraska District*
*New England District* Rev Charles Gustafson
*New Jersey District* Rev Stephen Vogt
*North Dakota District* Wm L Sharpe
*North Wisconsin District* DCE Lee Belmas (SR) Rev David Karolus (SA)
*Northern Illinois District*
*Northwest District* Rev Sidney Johnson
*Ohio District* Vacant
*Oklahoma District*
*Pacific Southwest District (formerly Southern California)* Jason Neben
*Rocky Mountain District* Rev Dwight Hellmers (SA)

*SELC District* Rev John Telloni
*South Dakota District* Rev Scott Sailer (SR)
Rev Howard O Shane (SA)
*South Wisconsin District* Rev Wayne Huebner
*Southeastern District* Stephen Heeman
*Southern District* Sandra Koester
*Southern Illinois District* Rev Timothy Mueller
*Texas District*
*Wyoming District* Gene Schreibeis PO Box 696 Worland WY 82401-0696

### Youth Ministry

*Atlantic District* Paul Marks SonRise PO Box 51 Pottersville NY 12860
*California-Nevada-Hawaii District* John Scheuermann
*Central Illinois District* DCE Dan Hauser
*Eastern District*
*English District* Theodore O Geheb
*Florida-Georgia District* Rev Ronald P Engel
*Indiana District*
*Iowa District East* Rev Tom Phillips
*Iowa District West* Rev Steve Schulz
*Kansas District* DCE Rebecca Brockman
*Michigan District* Rev Galan Walther
*Mid-South District* Ms Brenda Zesch
*Minnesota North District* Rev Richard Hans
*Minnesota South District* Tom Fuxa 23290 Hwy 7 Excelsior MN 55331
*Missouri District* Roger Mailand
*Montana District* Vacant
*Nebraska District*
*New England District* Ms Mary Ann Weyer PO Box 662 Danbury CT 06813-0662
*New Jersey District* DCE Dennis Meyers
*North Dakota District* Rev Bradley Stoltenow
*North Wisconsin District* DCE Lee Belmas
*Northern Illinois District* Betty McAdams 2908 Old Kent Drive Joliet IL 60435
*Northwest District* Richard Weniger
*Ohio District* Vacant
*Oklahoma District* Myron Harms
*Pacific Southwest District (formerly Southern California)* Dean Dammann
*Rocky Mountain District* Vacant
*SELC District* Tom Bailey 12200 S Nagle Palos Hgts IL 60463
*South Dakota District* Rev Timothy Rynearson
*South Wisconsin District* Duane Tweeten 8121 W Hope Ave Milwaukee WI 53222
*Southeastern District* Deaconess Sally Hiller
*Southern District* Rev David A Lewis
*Southern Illinois* Ron Friedrich
*Texas District* Rev Keith Speaks
*Wyoming District* Rev Marcus Zill

## PUBLISHING HOUSE

*Concordia Publishing House,* 3558 S Jefferson Ave, St Louis, MO 63118-3968. 314/268-1000 FAX 314/268-1329. Orders: 1-800-325-3040. Permissions: 1-800-325-0191. President Stephen J Carter.

## PUBLICATIONS

*The Lutheran Witness,* published monthly by the Board for Communication Services, 1333 S Kirkwood Rd, St. Louis, MO 63122-7295. Individual subscriptions $18.00 per year.

Districts not included in the first list below publish periodicals that are not distributed as part of *The Lutheran Witness.*

### EDITORS OF DISTRICT LUTHERAN WITNESS EDITIONS

**Armed Forces Edition**
Chaplain Thomas Benedum 1333 S Kirkwood Rd St Louis MO 63122-7295
E-Mail: thomas.benedum@lcms.org

**Indiana**
Rev E H Zimmermann 1145 S Barr St Ft Wayne IN 46802-3180

**Iowa West**
Rev E W Lichtsinn 905 Pierce Dr Storm Lake IA 50588
E-Mail: edluwit@ncn.net

**Kansas**
Linda Meyer 2318 W 10th Topeka KS 66604
E-Mail: lindam@kslcms.org

**Mid-South**
Dr Ron Wiese Trinity Lutheran Church 210 Washington Memphis TN 38103
E-Mail: rjwiese@aol.com

**Minnesota North**
Rev Tim Vaughan R R 2 Box 674 Ottertail MN 56571-9606
E-Mail: revtv@digitaljam.com

**Minnesota South**
Rev David P Anderson Immanuel Lutheran Church 1200 N North Ave Fairmont MN 56031
E-Mail: pastoranderson@yahoo.com

**North Dakota**
Rev Howard Jording Box 440 Hankinson ND 58041
E-Mail: hjjordin@hankinson.means.net

**Northwest**
Nikki Goettle 1700 N E Knott St Portland OR 97212
E-Mail: NikkiG@nowlcms.org

**North Wisconsin**
Sonja Baumeister 596 M 35 Negaunee MI 49866
E-Mail: luthwitnwd@aol.com

**Oklahoma**
Janice Hedrick 9222 N Garnett Road Owasso OK 74055-4424
E-Mail: OKPres@aol.com

**Rocky Mountain**
Rev Harold Reiss 420 S 40th Boulder CO 80303
E-Mail: Revreiss@aol.com

**SELC**
Rev Phil Miksad 705 Rhine Blvd Raritan NJ 08869
E-Mail: PTMIKSAD@aol.com

**South Dakota**
Holly A Shane 3809 E 28th St Sioux Falls SD 57103
E-Mail: holly_shane@hotmail.com

**Southern Illinois**
Lois Engfehr 19 Ramsgate Collinsville IL 62234

**Texas**
William Wagner 11768 Mission Trace San Antonio TX 78230

**Wyoming**
Melissa Wiley Lutheran Ministries Center 2400 S Hickory Casper WY 82604
E-Mail: WYODist@aol.com

### EDITORS OF OTHER DISTRICT PERIODICALS

**Atlantic**
Kelli Westfall District Editor 133 Lawrence Street New Hyde Park NY 11040

**California-Nevada-Hawaii**
Terri Hunter-Davis CNH District Office 465 Woolsey St San Francisco CA 94134-1999

**Central Illinois**
Rev Robert Low PO Box 315 Petersburg IL 62675

**Eastern**
Margaret Talboys 5111 Main St Williamsville NY 14221

**English**
Betty Mueller 6336 Donaldson Ave Troy MI 48098-1532

**Florida-Georgia**
Eileen Bishop c/o Bishop & List Interests 1181 S Rogers Cir Ste 20 Boca Raton FL 33487-2726

**Iowa East**
Mitchell Otto Prince of Peace Lutheran Church 1701 8th Street Coralville IA 52241-1601

**Michigan**
Walter Rummel PO Box 683 Sebewaing MI 48759

**Missouri**
Lynda Gosney-Smith Missouri District Office 3558 S Jefferson Ave St Louis MO 63118

**Montana**
Rev Henry Drummond c/o Christ For the Deaf Lutheran Church 1226 1st Avenue N Great Falls MT 59401

**Nebraska**
Lee Warneke Box 9 Plainview NE 68769

**New England**
Patricia Connery 38A Warren Woburn MA 01801

**New Jersey**
Marion Monskie 12 Daniel St Dover, NJ 07801-2004

**Northern Illinois**
Jackie Bussert 121 Willow Rd Elmhurst IL 60126

**Ohio**
Rev Robert Hullinger The District News 1739 Bella Vista Cincinnati OH 45237

**Pacific Southwest**
Jean Beres In Focus 1540 Concordia East Irvine CA 92715

**Southeastern**
Karen Smith Hupp 10150 Cross Creek Pl La Plata MD 20646

**Southern**
Cheryl A Pitts Spirit of Southern PO Box 8396 New Orleans LA 70182

**South Wisconsin**
Barbara Balwinski 8100 W Capitol Dr Milwaukee WI 53222

*Teachers Interaction* is published quarterly (September, December, March, June) by Concordia Publishing House, 3558 S Jefferson Ave, St Louis, MO 63118-3968. Editor: Tom Nummela. Single subscription, $10.75 per year. Bulk rates available. This magazine is designed for all volunteer teachers in a congregation.

*Happy Times* is published monthly by Concordia Publishing House, 3558 S Jefferson Ave, St Louis, MO 63118-3968. Editor: Earl Gaulke. Subscription rate $7.90 a year. Bulk rates available. This magazine is designed for use by children ages 3–5 and their parents.

*Concordia Pulpit Resources* is published quarterly by Concordia Publishing House, 3558 S Jefferson Ave, St Louis, MO 63118-3968. Subscription rate $43.95 per year. Editor: Rev Steven Albers. This publication is a lectionary-based journal designed to assist in sermon preparation.

*Concordia Theological Quarterly* (*CTQ*) is published quarterly in January, April, July, and October by the faculty of Concordia Theological Seminary, Fort Wayne, IN. Editor: David P Scaer; Associate Editor: Douglas McC L Judisch; Assistant Editor: Lawrence Rast; Editorial Committee: Richard Nuffer, Charles Gieschen, Timothy Quill, Dean Wenthe; Book Review Editor: William Weinrich; Editorial Assistant: Kim Hosier. Mail subscriptions to *Concordia Theological Quarterly,* Concordia Theological Seminary, 6600 N Clinton St, Fort Wayne, IN 46825. Subscription rate annually: USA - $15.00; Canada - $20.00; International - $35.00.

*Lutheran Education* is published quarterly—October, December, April, and June—by the faculty of Concordia University, River Forest, IL 60305-1499. Publisher: George C. Heider; Editor: Jonathan Barz; Associate Editors: Gary Bertels, LuJuana Butts, and William Rietschel; Editorial Assistant: Jo Ann Kiefer. Subscription rate: $10 per year. Add 3.25 per year for Canada and foreign surface mail. Add $15.25 per year for Canada and foreign air mail.

*Concordia Journal* is published quarterly in January, April, July, and October by Concordia Seminary, St Louis, MO. Editorial Committee: Dr Quentin F Wesselschmidt, Chairman, Dr Charles P Arand, Dr Andrew H Bartelt, Dr Jeffrey A Gibbs, Dr Paul R Raabe, Dr Robert L Rosin, Dr James L Brauer. Single subscription $12.00 (USA), $13.00 (Canada), $16.00 (foreign) per year. Mail subscriptions to *Concordia Journal,* Concordia Seminary, 801 DeMun Ave, St Louis, MO 63105.

*REPORTER,* a monthly newspaper that includes news for church leaders, and ideas and resources for the parish, is published 12 times a year by the Board for Communication Services. It is sent at synodical expense to "Ministers of Religion, Ordained and Commissioned"; lay members of District boards of directors; vicars; and to congregational chairmen, and head elders in LCMS congregations. Paid subscriptions to *REPORTER* are available to others for $18 per year. Checks should be payable to *"REPORTER"* and should be sent to *REPORTER* Subscriptions, PO Box 771669, St Louis, MO 63177-9902. Correspondence should be sent to *REPORTER* Editor, The Lutheran Church—Missouri Synod, 1333 S Kirkwood Road, St Louis, MO 63122-7295. E-Mail: Reporter@lcms.org.

*Portals of Prayer* is published quarterly by *Concordia Publishing House,* 3558 S Jefferson Ave, St Louis, MO 63118-3968. Subscription rate $5.60 a year. Bulk rates on request.

*Large Print Portals of Prayer* is published quarterly by Concordia Publishing House, 3558 S Jefferson Ave, St Louis, MO 63118-3968. Subscription rate $8.15 a year. Bulk rates on request.

*Strength for the Day* is published monthly by Concordia Publishing House, 3558 S Jefferson Ave, St Louis, MO 63118-3968. Subscription rate $9.45 a year. Bulk rates on request.

*My Devotions* is published monthly by Concordia Publishing House, 3558 S Jefferson Ave, St Louis, MO 63118-3968. Editor: Don Hoeferkamp. Subscription rate $7.00 a year. Bulk rates on request. This magazine is a daily devotional reading for children ages 8–12.

*Today's Light* is published monthly by Concordia Publishing House, 3558 S Jefferson Ave, St Louis, MO 63118-3968. Subscription rate is $18.90 a year. Bulk rates on request. Editor: Kenneth Wagener. This daily Bible reading guide takes the reader through the entire Bible in two years.

*Concordia Historical Institute Quarterly.* Editor: Dale E Griffin; Managing Editor: Rev Daniel Preus; Associate Editors: Ronald Feuerhahn, George Gude, Cameron A MacKenzie. Editorial Committee: Albert Buelow, Ronald Feuerhahn, Jerzy Hauptmann, Marvin Huggins, Glenn Offermann, Timothy Quill. Book Review Editor: Cameron MacKenzie. Single issues $7.50 ea. plus postage, $35.00 per year for active membership in Concordia Historical Institute, 801 DeMun Ave, St Louis, MO 63105.

*Issues in Christian Education* is published three times a year by the faculty of Concordia University, Seward, NE 68434. Editor: Dr Marvin Bergman; Editorial Committee: Profs Russell Moulds, Rebecca Rohm, Daniel Thurber, Orville C Walz, William Wolfram. Managing Editor: Marlene Block. Subscription $6.00; single copies $2.00 each.

### SELC Publications

*The Courier* (Luther League). Editor: Philip Lee, 5225 Lakewood, St Louis, MO 63123. Business Manager Thomas Bailey, 12200 S Nagie, Palos Heights, IL 60463

### Publications for the Blind

*The Lutheran Messenger.* Monthly braille and cassette tape.

*My Devotions,* braille and large print.

*Portals of Prayer,* braille and cassette tape.

*Lutheran Witness,* braille, large print, and cassette tape.

*Family Connection,* braille and large print.

*The Lutheran Digest,* braille and large print.

*Happy Times,* braille.

*Interaction,* cassette tape.

*LWML Quarterly,* braille, large type, and cassette tape.

Our Life in Christ Sunday school lessons. All grade levels, teacher and student. Braille, and large type.

Adult and High School Bible study guides, braille and large type (upon request—12 week advance notice).

Vacation Bible school materials, braille and large type (upon request—12 week advance notice).

*Teen Time,* (8 issues October–May) for teenage youth, braille and large type.

*Today's Light,* braille and large type

*Strength for the Day,* braille and large type.

*Lutheran Worship,* braille.

*The Lutheran Hymnal,* braille and large type.

*The Lutheran Layman,* cassette tape.

Address all requests for materials to Lutheran Library for the Blind, 1333 S Kirkwood Rd, St Louis, MO 63122-7295.

*Lutheran Library for the Blind* serves the blind/visually impaired people of all denominations throughout the world. Free lending library in braille, cassette tapes, and large print. Write for catalogs to Library for the Blind, 1333 S Kirkwood Rd, St Louis, MO 63122-7295.

*Volunteer Transcriber:* Anyone willing to assist in transcribing for the blind (or learning to transcribe braille) and helping in other phases of this ministry please contact the Lutheran Library for the Blind (toll free at 800-433-3954).

### Other Publications

*The Evangelgram.* A quarterly tabloid that shares examples of congregational evangelism programs, new materials, and general information about evangelism activities. Sold on a subscription basis. Evangelism Department, 1333 S Kirkwood Rd, St Louis, MO 63122-7295 or phone (314) 965-9000.

*Cross and Caduceus.* Periodical in support of the health and healing ministries of the Gospel. Published by LCMS Health Ministries staff within the Board for Human Care Ministries. Free on request. LCMS Health Ministries, 1333 S Kirkwood Rd, St Louis, MO 63122-7295.

*The Deaf Lutheran.* Bimonthly publication for the deaf. Editor: David Brown, 3434 Klusner Ave, Parma, OH 44134-5030. Business manager: Larry Ginter, 4134 Sarasota Dr, Parma, OH 44134. Individual subscriptions $6.00 per year. LCMS World Mission, International Lutheran Deaf Assn, 1333 S Kirkwood Rd, St Louis, MO 63122-7295.

*Worship Insert.* A quarterly supplement to the Reporter providing timely articles on worship, hymnody and the church year. Bulk copies may be obtained by contacting: Commission on Worship, LCMS, 1333 S Kirkwood Rd, St Louis, MO 63122-7295 or calling 314/965-9000

*LCMS Foundation News.* Quarterly newsletter of the LCMS Foundation. Available in quantity to congregations or individuals free of charge. Published by The Lutheran Church—Missouri Synod Foundation, 1333 S Kirkwood Rd, St Louis, MO 63122-7295.

*Ministry Report which is the Foundation's Annual Report.* Annual summary of the activity and financial status of the LCMS Foundation. Available in quantity to congregations or individuals free of charge. Published by The Lutheran Church—Missouri Synod Foundation, 1333 S Kirkwood Rd, St Louis, MO 63122-7295

*Sharing.* Newsletter published six issues a year. Individual and bulk subscriptions free on request. Newsletter also available on internet: http://worldrelief.lcms.org Includes descriptions of domestic and international activities of LCMS World Relief. Published by LCMS World Relief, Sharing, 1333 S Kirkwood Rd, St Louis, MO 63122-7295. 1-800/248-1930 Ext 1389.

# SYNODICAL INFORMATION

## Synodical Officers, Past and Present

### A. Presidents

C. F. W. Walther, 1847–50; 1864–78
  Residence: St. Louis
F. C. D. Wyneken, 1850–64
  Residence: St. Louis, 1850–59;
  Friedheim, IN, 1859–64
H. C. Schwan, 1878–99
  Residence: Cleveland, OH
Franz Pieper, 1899–1911
  Residence: St. Louis
F. Pfotenhauer, 1911–35
  Residence: Chicago
J. W. Behnken, 1935–62
  Residence: Oak Park, 1935–51;
  St. Louis, 1951–62
Oliver R. Harms, 1962–69
  Residence: St. Louis
J. A. O. Preus, 1969–81
  Residence: St. Louis
Ralph A. Bohlmann, 1981–1992
  Residence: St. Louis
Alvin Barry, 1992–
  Residence: St. Louis

### B. Vice-Presidents

Wm. Sihler, 1847–54; 1864–69; 1874–1878
Th. Brohm, 1851–57; 1860–64; 1869–74
H. C. Schwan, 1857–60
C. J. H. Fick, 1874–78
C. H. R. Lange, 1878–81
Carl Gross, 1878–99
Otto Hanser, 1881–84
C. H. Loeber, 1884–87
Henry Succop, 1887–90; 1905–08
H. C. Sauer, 1890–93
J. P. Beyer, 1893–99
C. C. Schmidt, 1899–1908
P. Brand, 1899–1917
F. Pfotenhauer, 1908–11
J. W. Miller, 1908–29
J. C. Strasen, 1908–14
John Hilgendorf, 1911–20
H. Speckhard, 1914–17
Fred Brand, 1917–29
H. P. Eckhardt, 1917–26
G. A. Bernthal, 1920–26
Wm. Dallmann, 1926–32
F. J. Lankenau, 1926–39
J. W. Behnken, 1929–35
Fred Randt, 1929–37
Henry Grueber, 1932–47
Karl Kretzschmar, 1935–38
Hermann Harms, 1938–59
A. J. Brunn, 1941–49
G. Chr. Barth, 1941–47
F. A. Hertwig, 1947–56
W. F. Lichtsinn, 1947–59
E. J. Friedrich, 1949–50
A. H. Grumm, 1950–59
Oliver R. Harms, 1956–62
R. P. Wiederaenders, 1959–73
George W. Wittmer, 1959–69
Arthur C. Nitz, 1959–65
Theo. F. Nickel, 1962–77
W. Harry Krieger, 1965–69;1972–74
Paul W. Streufert, 1965–72
Victor L. Behnken, 1969–71
Edwin C. Weber, 1969–81
Guido A. Merkens, 1971–83; 1986–89
Walter A. Maier Jr, 1973–95
August Bernthal, 1974–77
Robert C. Sauer, 1977–86; 1989–95
George Wollenburg, 1977–81; 1983–89
Gerhardt W. Hyatt, 1981–85
Joseph G. Lavalais, 1981–83
Robert H. King, 1986–
August Mennicke, 1986–95
Eugene W. Bunkowske, 1989–1998
Robert Kuhn, 1995–
Dale A. Meyer, 1995–1998
Wallace Schulz, 1995–
Roger Pittelko, 1998–
William Weinrich, 1998–

### C. Secretaries

F. W. Husmann, 1847–50; 1854–60
L. W. Habel, 1850–54
J. A. F. W. Mueller, 1860–66
Geo. Kuechle, 1866–74
Aug. Rohrlack, 1874–1905
R. D. Biedermann, 1905–20
M. F. Kretzmann, 1920–56
Walter C. Birkner, 1956–65
Herbert A. Mueller, 1965–83
Walter L. Rosin, 1983–98
Raymond L Hartwig, 1998–

### D. Treasurers

F. W. Barthel, 1847–57
Ferd. Boehlau, 1857–63
J. F. Schuricht Sr., 1863–81
C. F. W. Meier, 1881–1902
J. F. Schuricht Jr., 1902–14
Edmund Seuel, 1914–42
W. H. Schlueter, 1942–58
Martin E. Strieter, 1958–62
Milton Carpenter, 1962–77
Norman Sell, 1977–1999
Paul W. Middeke 1999–

### Congregations Received into Synodical Membership

#### 1997

| | |
|---|---|
| AT | Glory Korean, Bayside, NY |
| IW | Beautiful Savior, Polk City, IA |
| MNN | Faith Community Zimmerman, MN |
| PSW | Prince of Peace, Sant Clarita, CA |

#### 1998

| | |
|---|---|
| SW | Living Word, Jackson, WI |

#### 1999

| | |
|---|---|
| AT | Saint Mark, Hudson, NY |
| AT | Christ Assembly, Staten Island, NY |
| FG | University, Tallahassee, FL |
| IN | Lord Of Life, Westfield, IN |
| MDS | St Matthew, Conway, AR |
| MI | Living Hope, Fremont, MI |
| MI | Living Water, Mio, MI |
| MNN | Grace, Becker, MN |
| MO | St Paul, Branson, MO |
| NEB | Bingham, Bingham, NE |
| NI | Fellowship Of Faith, Mc Henry, IL |
| NI | Community Faith, Spring Grove, IL |
| NJ | Christ Assembly, Newark, NJ |
| NOW | Messiah, Post Falls, ID |
| NOW | Faith, Kingston, WA |
| PSW | Santisima Trindad, Chula Vista, CA |
| PSW | Celebration, Sylmar, CA |
| PSW | Mesquite, Mesquite, NV |
| PSW | Lamb Of God, Lake Havasu City, AZ |
| PSW | Faith Community, Las Vegas, NV |
| RM | Christ Triumphant, Denver, CO |
| RM | Epiphany, Littleton, CO |
| RM | Holy Cross, Walsenburg, CO |
| SD | Our Redeemer, Rapid City, SD |
| SO | Good Shepherd, Baton Rouge, LA |
| TX | Vietnamese, Houston, TX |
| TX | Good Shepherd, Borger, TX |

## General and Delegate Conventions of the Synod

| General Convs. | Delegate Convs | Year | Place |
|---|---|---|---|
| 1 | — | 1847 | Chicago |
| 2 | — | 1848 | St. Louis |
| 3 | — | 1849 | Fort Wayne |
| 4 | — | 1850 | St. Louis |
| 5 | — | 1851 | Milwaukee |
| 6 | — | 1852 | Fort Wayne |
| 7 | — | 1853 | Cleveland |
| 8 | — | 1854 | St. Louis |
| 9 | — | 1857 | Fort Wayne |
| 10 | — | 1860 | St. Louis |
| 11 | — | 1863 | Fort Wayne |
| 12 | — | 1864 | Fort Wayne |
| 13 | — | 1866 | St. Louis |
| 14 | — | 1869 | Fort Wayne |
| 15 | — | 1872 | St. Louis |
| 16 | 1 | 1874 | Fort Wayne |
| 17 | 2 | 1878 | St. Louis |
| 18 | 3 | 1881 | Fort Wayne |
| 19 | 4 | 1884 | St. Louis |
| 20 | 5 | 1887 | Fort Wayne |
| 21 | 6 | 1890 | Milwaukee |
| 22 | 7 | 1893 | St. Louis |
| 23 | 8 | 1896 | Fort Wayne |
| 24 | 9 | 1899 | St. Louis |
| 25 | 10 | 1902 | Milwaukee |
| 26 | 11 | 1905 | Detroit |
| 27 | 12 | 1908 | Fort Wayne |
| 28 | 13 | 1911 | St. Louis |
| 29 | 14 | 1914 | Chicago |
| 30 | 15 | 1917 | Milwaukee |
| 31 | 16 | 1920 | Detroit |
| 32 | 17 | 1923 | Fort Wayne |
| 33 | 18 | 1926 | St. Louis |
| 34 | 19 | 1929 | River Forest |
| 35 | 20 | 1932 | Milwaukee |
| 36 | 21 | 1935 | Cleveland |
| 37 | 22 | 1938 | St. Louis |
| 38 | 23 | 1941 | Fort Wayne |
| 39 | 24 | 1944 | Saginaw |
| 40 | 25 | 1947 | Chicago |
| 41 | 26 | 1950 | Milwaukee |
| 42 | 27 | 1953 | Houston |
| 43 | 28 | 1956 | St. Paul |
| 44 | 29 | 1959 | S. Francisco |
| 45 | 30 | 1962 | Cleveland |
| 46 | 31 | 1965 | Detroit |
| 47 | 32 | 1967 | New York |
| 48 | 33 | 1969 | Denver |
| 49 | 34 | 1971 | Milwaukee |
| 50 | 35 | 1973 | New Orleans |
| 51 | 36 | 1975 | Anaheim |
| 52 | 37 | 1977 | Dallas |
| 53 | 38 | 1979 | St. Louis |
| 54 | 39 | 1981 | St. Louis |
| 55 | 40 | 1983 | St. Louis |
| 56 | 41 | 1986 | Indianapolis |
| 57 | 42 | 1989 | Wichita |
| 58 | 43 | 1992 | Pittsburgh |
| 59 | 44 | 1995 | St. Louis |
| 60 | 45 | 1998 | St. Louis |

| Place | Number |
|---|---|
| St. Louis | 18 |
| Fort Wayne | 13 |
| Milwaukee | 7 |
| Chicago | 4 |
| Cleveland | 3 |
| Denver | 1 |
| Detroit | 3 |
| Houston | 1 |
| New Orleans | 1 |
| New York | 1 |
| Saginaw | 1 |
| St. Paul | 1 |
| San Francisco | 1 |
| Anaheim | 1 |
| Dallas | 1 |
| Indianapolis | 1 |
| Wichita | 1 |
| Pittsburgh | 1 |
| | 60 |

## Origin of Synodical Districts

| Name | First Meeting | Branched Off from (Division of) | Districts that Have Branched Off |
|---|---|---|---|
| Alberta-British Columbia°°° | 1921 | Minnesota | — |
| Argentine°° | 1927 | Brazil | — |
| Atlantic | 1907 | Eastern | New England, 1971<br>New Jersey, 1971 |
| Brazil° | 1904 | — | Argentine, 1927 |
| California-Oregon† | 1887 | Western | Oregon-Washington, 1899<br>California-Nevada,1899 |
| Calif-Nev-Hawaii* | 1899 | California-Oregon | Southern Calif,1930 |
| Central† | 1855 | — | Indiana, 1963<br>Ohio, 1963 |
| Central Illinois | 1909 | Illinois | — |
| Eastern | 1855 | — | Atlantic, 1907 |
| English | 1911 | — | Southeastern, 1939 |
| Florida-Georgia | 1948 | Southern | — |
| Illinois† | 1875 | Western | Tripartition, 1909 |
| Indiana | 1963 | Central | — |
| Iowa† | 1879 | Western | Division, 1936 |
| Iowa East | 1936 | Iowa | — |
| Iowa West | 1936 | Iowa | — |
| Kansas | 1888 | Western | Colorado, 1921<br>Oklahoma, 1924 |
| Manitoba-Saskatchewan°°° | 1922 | Minnesota | |
| Michigan<br>("Northern" prior to 1881) | 1882 | Northern | |
| Mid-South | 1966 | Western | — |
| Minnesota-Dakota<br>("Minnesota" since 1910)† | 1882 | Northwestern | South Dakota, 1906<br>N. Dakota-Montana, 1910 |
| Minnesota North | 1963 | Minnesota | — |
| Minnesota South | 1963 | Minnesota | — |
| Missouri | 1966 | Western | — |
| Montana | 1945 | N. Dak.-Montana | — |
| Nebraska† | 1882 | Western | Division, 1922 |
| Nebraska | 1970 | N. and S. Nebr. Merged | Wyoming, 1970 |
| New England | 1971 | Atlantic | — |
| New Jersey | 1971 | Atlantic | — |
| North Dakota-Montana† | 1910 | Minnesota-Dakota | Division, 1945 |
| North Dakota | 1945 | N. Dak.-Montana | — |
| North Wisconsin | 1918 | Wisconsin | — |
| Northern† | 1855 | — | Northwestern,1875<br>Canada,1879<br>Michigan, 1882 |
| Northern Illinois | 1909 | Illinois | — |
| Northern Nebraska† | 1922 | Nebraska | — |
| Northwest ("Oregon-Washington" before 1948) | 1899 | California-Oregon | — |
| Northwestern† | 1874 | Northern | Minnesota-Dakota, 1882<br>Wisconsin, 1882 |
| Ohio | 1963 | Central | — |
| Oklahoma | 1924 | Kansas | — |
| Ontario°°°<br>("Canada" before 1923) | 1879 | Northern | |
| Pacific Southwest*** | 1930 | California-Nevada | — |
| South Dakota | 1906 | Minnesota-Dakota | — |
| South Wisconsin | 1918 | Wisconsin | — |
| Southeastern | 1939 | Eastern & English | — |
| Southern | 1882 | Western | Texas, 1906<br>Florida-Georgia, 1948 |
| Southern Illinois | 1909 | Illinois | — |
| Southern Nebraska† | 1922 | Nebraska | — |
| SELC | 1971 | — | — |
| Texas | 1906 | Southern | — |
| The Rocky Mountain** | 1921 | Kansas | — |
| Western† | 1855 | — | Illinois, 1875<br>Iowa, 1879<br>Nebraska, 1882<br>Southern, 1882<br>California-Oregon, 1887<br>Kansas, 1888<br>Mid-South, 1966<br>Missouri, 1966 |
| Wisconsin† | 1882 | Northwestern | Division in 1918 |
| Wyoming | 1970 | Nebraska | — |

†=no longer in existence
*-name changed from California-Nevada in 1977
**=name changed from Colorado in 1983
***=name changed from Southern California in 1989
°=partner church status, Jan. 1, 1980
°°=partner church status, July, 1986
°°°=district of LCC partner church, 1989

# ROSTER OF CONGREGATIONS

Corrected to October 18, 2000

The following list includes all congregations of The Lutheran Church–Missouri Synod. The legal or corporate name of the congregation is not listed. Only a form of the name is used that briefly identifies a congregation in a locality (example: St. John, not St. John's Lutheran Church).

Congregations are listed according to the physical, town, village, or city in which the church building is located.

Congregation records are formatted in the following order:

*Physical City*, Congregation Name, non-member designation (*), telephone number

*Pastors.* If there is no pastor serving, "Vacant" will appear. (DM) after the name of a pastor indicates that he is a district missionary; (#) after the name of a minister serving that congregation indicates that he is a lay minister; (X) indicates that the minister is not certified by the Synod but is serving in a ministerial capacity.

*Commissioned Ministers*: These are Directors of Christian Education (DCE), Deaconesses (DEAC), Directors of Christian Outreach (DCO), Parish Assistant (PAST), serving a congregation. The church worker's classification abbreviation will appear after his/her name.

*Sunday Service Times:* The Time of Sunday Services; WS=Worship Service; SS=Sunday School; BC=Bible Class. An asterisk (*) after the times of services, indicates there are other seasonal or weekday services available. Call the number listed for more information.

*H=Handicapped.* All or some of the buildings are handicapped accessible.

*School Type:* EC=Early Childhood, EL=Elementary, and HS=High School are used to indicate the congregation has some relationship to a Lutheran School.

*District Abbreviation*: (See list below)

*Address*: If the congregation has both a physical and a mailing address, then the physical address lines and zip code are printed first, followed by the mailing address, city, and zip code

*FAX Number*

*E-mail Address*

## KEY TO OTHER ABBREVIATIONS

### Missouri Synod Districts

| | | | | | |
|---|---|---|---|---|---|
| AT | = Atlantic | MNN | = Minnesota North | OK | = Oklahoma |
| CNH | = Calif.-Nev.-Hawaii | MNS | = Minnesota South | PSW | = Pacific Southwest |
| CI | = Central Illinois | MO | = Missouri | RM | = Rocky Mountain |
| EA | = Eastern | MT | = Montana | S | = SELC District |
| EN | = English | NE | = New England | SD | = South Dakota |
| FG | = Florida-Georgia | NEB | = Nebraska | SE | = Southeastern |
| IN | = Indiana | ND | = North Dakota | SI | = Southern Illinois |
| IE | = Iowa East | NJ | = New Jersey | SO | = Southern |
| IW | = Iowa West | NW | = North Wisconsin | SW | = South Wisconsin |
| KS | = Kansas | NI | = Northern Illinois | TX | = Texas |
| MI | = Michigan | NOW | = Northwest | WY | = Wyoming |
| MDS | = Mid-South | OH | = Ohio | | |

### ALABAMA

**ALBERTVILLE—*CHRIST*** (256)891-0608
Kirk A Mc Quillan • WS 1030; SS 915;* • H • SO • 9363 US Highway 431 Albertville AL 35950-5504 • kirk@airnet.net

**ANDALUSIA—*EPIPHANY*** (334)385-2435
William H Marsh • EC/EL • SO • Hwy #5 36420 PO Box 309 Arlington AL 36722-0309

***NEW HOPE*** (334)427-1584
Merlin S Pohl • SO • 504 Montgomery St Andalusia AL 36420

**ATHENS—*OUR SAVIOR*** (256)230-6391
Reuben L Garber(EM) • WS 1030; SS 9 • H • SO • 550 US Highway 72 W Athens AL 35611-4210 • oslc@huntsvilleal.com

**ATMORE—*EBENEZER*** (334)446-3664
Moses J Clark(EM) • H • SO • 108 Harris St 36502-1807 PO Box 369 Atmore AL 36504-0369

**ATTALLA—*IMMANUEL*** (256)538-2598
Vacant • WS 130; SS 1230 • SO • 101 Hughes Ave Attalla AL 35954-2406

**AUBURN—*TRINITY*** (334)887-3901
Edward R Hornig • WS 8 1030; SS 915; BC 6 • H • SO • 446 S Gay St Auburn AL 36830-5937 • trinity@tlcauburn.org

**BESSEMER—*ZION*** (205)425-2091
Vacant • H • EC/EL • SO • 1201 24th St N Bessemer AL 35020-3339

**BIRMINGHAM—*FIRST*** (205)933-0380
Kurtis D Schultz • WS 8 1045; SS 915; BC 915 • H • SO • 2507 Highland Ave S Birmingham AL 35205-2497 • FAX(205)933-8879

***HOPE*** (205)956-1930
Norman L Schulz • WS 10; SS 9; BC 9 • H • SO • 4800 Montevallo Rd Birmingham AL 35210-3204

***PILGRIM*** (205)251-3451
Michael A Johnson Sr. • WS 1130; SS 10;* • H • EC/EL • SO • 447 1st St N Birmingham AL 35204-4323 • FAX(205)251-3451

***PRINCE PEACE*** (205)592-4432
Michael A Johnson Sr. • WS 930; SS 845;* • H • SO • 4413 R Arrington Jr Blvd N PO Box 320816 Birmingham AL 35232-0816

***REDEEMER*** (205)853-5739
Terry L Grund • H • SO • 1339 Springville Rd Birmingham AL 35215-6517

***ST PAUL*** (205)324-2063
Thomas R Noon • WS 11; SS 930;* • SO • 132 6th Ave S Birmingham AL 35205-4227 • FAX(205)324-2063

***TRINITY*** (205)923-6494
Vacant • WS 1030; SS 930; BC 930 • H • SO • 1730 Saint Charles Ave SW Birmingham AL 35211-2121

***VESTAVIA HILLS***
See Vestavia Hills

**CAMDEN—*HOLY CROSS*** (334)682-9552
John M Brown • H • SO • 4 Brown St Camden AL 36726-2006

**CULLMAN—*ST PAUL*** (256)734-3575
David A Last Harold G Hermetz • WS 8 1030; SS 915; BC 915 • H • EC/EL • SO • 513 4th Ave SE Cullman AL 35055-4322 • FAX(256)734-3540

**DAPHNE—*ASCENSION*** (334)626-7500
Thomas A Tews • H • SO • 6937 Highway 90 Daphne AL 36526-9501

***CONCORDIA***
See Montrose 1 NE

**DECATUR—*ST PAUL*** (256)353-8759
David A Lewis Duane N Maas • WS 815 1045; SS 930; BC 930 • H • EC • SO • 1700 Carridale St SW Decatur AL 35601-4638 • FAX(256)353-7496 • stpaulsdec@aol.com

**DOTHAN—*TRINITY*** (334)792-9745
Theodore M Richter • WS 1030; SS 9;* • H • EC • SO • 1440 S Park Ave Dothan AL 36301-3438 • FAX(334)792-9745 • trich716@ala.net

**ELBERTA—*ST MARK*** (334)986-8133
Keith J Ringers • H • SO • 13220 Main St 36530 PO Box 250 Elberta AL 36530-0250 • FAX(334)986-8134 • stmarks@gulftel.com

**ENTERPRISE—*CHRIST KING*** (205)347-6716
James E Endrihs • H • SO • 208 E Watts St Enterprise AL 36330-1813

**FAIRHOPE—*REDEEMER*** (334)928-8397
John P Jackson • H • SO • 200 S Section St 36532-1834 PO Box 411 Fairhope AL 36533-0411

**FLORALA—*FIRST*** (334)858-3515
Vacant • WS 9; SS 1045; BC 1045 • H • SO • 311 E 5th Ave 36442-1643 PO Box 212 Florala AL 36442-0212

**FLORENCE—*OUR REDEEMER*** (256)764-3902
David A Doroh • WS 9; SS 1015; BC 1015 • H • SO • 630 N Poplar St Florence AL 35630-4634

**FOLEY—*ST PAUL*** (334)943-6931
Michael S Taylor • H • EC • SO • 400 N Alston St 36535-3502 PO Box 759 Foley AL 36536-0759 • stpaul@gulftel.com

**FORT PAYNE—*PRINCE PEACE*** (205)845-4842
Vacant • H • SO • 114 First St SW Fort Payne AL 35967

**GADSDEN—*ST PETER*** (205)492-6941
Charles E Reichel • H • SO • 104 Gordon St Gadsden AL 35903-3106

***TRINITY*** (256)546-1712
Gary J Faith • WS 1045; SS 930;* • EC • SO • 1885 Rainbow Dr Gadsden AL 35901-5500 • FAX(256)546-7516 • tlc@cybrtyme.com

**GARDENDALE—*GOOD SHEPHERD*** (205)631-2355
Vacant • H • SO • 2456 Decatur Hwy Gardendale AL 35071-2335

**GULF SHORES—*ST JUDE BY SEA*** (334)968-JUDE
Deral E Rollings • H • SO • 312 E 16th Ave At Hwy 180 36547 PO Box 1263 Gulf Shores AL 36547-1263

**HANCEVILLE—*TRINITY*** (256)352-6442
Vacant • WS 10; SS 845; BC 845;* • H • SO • 505 Commercial St SE Hanceville AL 35077-5520 • FAX(256)352-5660 • davidr@airnet.net

**HARTSELLE—*CHRIST OUR***
Vacant • SO • Suite 701G Nance Ford Rd Hartselle AL 35640

**HUNTSVILLE—*ASCENSION*** (256)536-9987
Bernard H Ansorge • Susann M Gehring DCE • WS 8 1030 1140; SS 915; BC 915 • H • EC • SO • 3801 Oakwood Ave NW Huntsville AL 35810-4061 • FAX(256)536-8104 • aschval@hiwaay.net

***GRACE*** (256)881-0552
Richard P Lessmann R Paul Counts(EM) • T K Brandon DCE • WS 8 1030 11; SS 915; BC 920 • H • EC/EL • SO • 3321 S Memorial Pkwy Huntsville AL 35801-5342 • FAX(256)881-0563 • glc1@hiwaay.net

**KINGS LANDING—*HOPE***
Vacant • SO • 104 County Road 128 Sardis AL 36775-3123

**LILLIAN—*SHEP OF BAY*** (334)962-7682
Bruce C Donley • WS 8 10; SS 9;* • H • EC • SO • 12851 Perdido St Lillian AL 36549-4015

**MADISON—*FAITH*** (256)830-5600
James M Edge • WS 8 1045; SS 915 • H • SO • 660 Gillespie Rd Madison AL 35758 • FAX(256)830-5660 • faith³madison@juno.com

**MOBILE—*FAITH*** (205)471-1629
James B Marshall • H • EC/EL • SO • 1703 Martin Luther King Ave Mobile AL 36617

***GRACE*** (334)433-2749
Arlyn L Sturtz • WS 1030; SS 9; BC 9 • H • SO • 1356 Government St Mobile AL 36604-2008 • FAX(334)433-2197 • jwaite6265@aol.com

***HOLY CROSS*** (334)342-8755
William J Meyer • WS 815; SS 915; BC 915 • H • SO • 3900 Airport Blvd Mobile AL 36608-1622 • FAX(334)342-6934 • holycrossmobile@aol.com

***MOUNT CALVARY*** (205)471-4200
Lorenzo Mc Bride • H • EC/EL • SO • 1660 Limerick St 36605-4858 PO Box 6010 Mobile AL 36660-0010

***OUR SAVIOR*** (334)661-4524
Bruce C Hanson • BC 915;* • H • EC • SO • 5101 Government Blvd Mobile AL 36693-5077 • FAX(334)661-3369 • bp.hanson@prodigy.net

***TRINITY*** (334)456-7929
Ulmer Marshall • WS 10; SS 9;* • H • EC/EL • SO • 2668 Berkley Ave Mobile AL 36617-1704 • FAX(334)456-7909 • sdortch@bellsouth.net

**MONTGOMERY—*EPIPHANY*** (334)288-9465
Vacant • H • SO • 810 E South Blvd Montgomery AL 36116-2308

***GRACE*** (205)269-4465
Vacant • SO • 1066 Washington Ave Montgomery AL 36104-3849

***ST PAUL*** (334)272-6214
Carey P Elam • SO • 4475 Atlanta Hwy Montgomery AL 36109-3102 • cpelam@aol.com

***TRINITY*** (334)262-4326
Ferry L Nye • H • SO • 1104 Rosa L Parks Ave Montgomery AL 36108-3002 • FAX(334)263-3183

**MONTROSE 1 NE—*CONCORDIA*** (334)928-7536
Vacant • H • SO • 36559 PO Box 605 Daphne AL 36526-0605

**MUSCLE SHOALS—*CHRIST KING*** (205)381-3560
Glenn E Fischer • H • SO • Hwy 43 And Alt 72 35661 PO Box 2013 Muscle Shoals AL 35662-2013

**OAK HILL 1 S—*ST PAUL***
Vacant • SO • 36766 One mile S on Hwy 21 Oak Hill AL 36766-9999

**OZARK—*PRINCE PEACE*** (334)774-6758
Kirk D Miller • WS 8 1045; SS 940; BC 940 • SO • 1500 E Andrews Ave Ozark AL 36360-2743 • pop@snowhill.com

**PINSON—*HAVEN OF HOPE*** (205)856-1151
Vacant • H • SO • 5348 Old Springville Rd Pinson AL 35126-3630

**POINT CLEAR 1 E—*BETHEL*** (205)928-8327
Ulmer Marshall • H • SO • 6725 Co Rd 32 36564 PO Box 337 Point Clear AL 36564-0337

**PRATTVILLE—*BETHLEHEM*** (205)365-2088
Vacant • WS 930; SS 830; BC 5 • H • SO • 2738 Highway 82 W Prattville AL 36067-7126

**SARDIS—*HOPE***
See Kings Landing

**SCOTTSBORO—*TRINITY*** (256)574-4927
Vacant • H • SO • 3512 S Broad St Scottsboro AL 35769-7409

**SELMA—*TRINITY*** (205)874-8404
Steven Washington • WS 11; SS 945;* • H • SO • 36703 1900 Marie Foster St Selma AL 36703-2933

**SPANISH FORT—*ASCENSION***
See Daphne

**THOMASVILLE—*MESSIAH*** (334)636-2650
William H Marsh • SO • 1220 Martin Luther King Dr 36784 PO Box 286 Thomasville AL 36784-0286

**TUSCALOOSA—*CHRIST*** (205)752-0108
Ivory C Cameron(EM) • H • EC • SO • 2913 18th St Tuscaloosa AL 35401-4215

***HOLY CROSS*** (205)553-8004
Timothy W Killion • H • SO • 1401 University Blvd E Tuscaloosa AL 35404-2918

***UNIVERSITY*** (205)752-8784
Christopher D Hall • WS 1045; BC 945;* • H • SO • 911 5th Ave Tuscaloosa AL 35401-1207 • uniluchap@juno.com

**VESTAVIA HILLS—*VESTAVIA HILLS*** (205)823-1883
Clifford N Hellmers Jr. • Anna M Owens DCE • WS 8 1030; SS 9; BC 9 • H • EC • SO • 201 Montgomery Hwy S Birmingham AL 35216-1801 • FAX(205)823-4549 • vestluth@juno.com

**VREDENBURGH—*IMMANUEL*** (205)875-1551
Vacant • SO • PO Box 195 Vredenburgh AL 36481-0195

## ALASKA

**ANCHORAGE—*ANCHORAGE*** (907)272-5323
William Warren • WS 830;* • H • EC/EL • NOW • 1420 N St Anchorage AK 99501-4961 • FAX(907)274-8703 • alc@micronet.net

***BEAUT SAVIOR*** (907)522-3899
Chris J Reinke • WS 830 945 11; SS 945; BC 945 • H • EC/EL • NOW • 8100 Arctic Blvd Anchorage AK 99518-3003 • FAX(907)522-3359 • chrisjrein@aol.com

***ZION*** (907)338-3838
Richard W Rist • WS 9;* • H • EC/EL • NOW • 2100 Boniface Pkwy Anchorage AK 99504-3002 • FAX(907)333-4014 • zionpastor@gci.net

**CHUGIAK—*DENALI*** (907)688-5395
Kenneth E Schauer(DM) • H • EC • NOW • 18444 Old Glenn Hwy 99567-6840 PO Box 671792 Chugiak AK 99567-1792 • FAX(907)688-2158 • kenschau@aol.com

***OUR REDEEMER*** (907)688-2157
Thomas A Frizelle • WS 930; SS 11; BC 11;* • H • NOW • 18444 Old Glenn Hwy 99567 PO Box 670150 Chugiak AK 99567-0150 • FAX(907)688-2158 • orlc@mtaonline.net

**FAIRBANKS—*ZION*** (907)456-7660
Philip R Kuehnert Frederick J Schramm • H • EC • NOW • 2136 Mc Cullam Ave Fairbanks AK 99701-5714 • FAX(907)452-8752 • zion@polarnet.com

**HOMER—*FAITH*** (907)235-7600
Dennis J Neels • WS 930;* • H • EC • NOW • 3634 Soundview Ave Homer AK 99603-8332 • FAX(907)235-7660 • dneels@xyz.net

**JUNEAU—*FAITH*** (907)789-7568
James A Brubaker • H • EC/EL • NOW • 2500 Sunset Dr Juneau AK 99801-9371 • FAX(907)789-7568 • faithjno@alaska.net

**KENAI—*STAR OF NORTH*** (907)283-4153
Robert E Deardoff • NOW • 216 N Forest Dr Kenai AK 99611-7403 • FAX(907)283-4153 • sonlc@ptialaska.net

**PALMER—*ST JOHN*** (907)745-3338
Jonathan Rockey • WS 8 11;* • H • NOW • 440 E Elmwood Ave 99645-6670 PO Box 774 Palmer AK 99645-0774 • FAX(907)746-6117 • jonrock@pobox.alaska.net

**STERLING—*STERLING*** (907)262-9259
James Pearson(X) • H • NOW • 35070 Mc Call Rd 99672 PO Box 187 Sterling AK 99672-0187 • FAX(907)262-5359 • jpearson@gci.net

**WASILLA—*LAMB OF GOD*** (907)357-8077
Randall K Benscoter • H • NOW • 2101 Lucille St 99654-3803 PO Box 871093 Wasilla AK 99654 • randyben@mtaonline.net

## ARIZONA

**APACHE JUNCTION—*MOUNTAIN VIEW*** (480)982-8266
Roger F Hedstrom • H • EC • PSW • 2122 S Goldfield Rd 85219-4502 PO Box 868 Apache Junction AZ 85217-0868 • FAX(480)982-3374 • stev.reno@worldnet.att.net

**BENSON—*PEACE VALLEY*** (520)586-3171
Arlo T Janssen • * • H • EN • 306 S Gila St 85602-6670 PO Box 2467 Benson AZ 85602-2467

**BISBEE—*HOPE*** (530)432-5504
Emil L Dinkel • WS 1030 • H • PSW • 2134 S Bowers St 85603-6432 PO Box 4129 Bisbee AZ 85603-4129

**BLACK CANYON CITY—*GRACE*** (602)374-5225
Vacant • H • PSW • 18994 Vladimir St 85324 PO Box 1178 Black Canyon City AZ 85324-1178

**BULLHEAD CITY—*ST JOHN*** (520)758-2301
Vacant • * • H • PSW • 1664 Central Ave Bullhead City AZ 86442-8009 • FAX(520)758-2370

**CASA GRANDE—*TRINITY*** (520)836-2451
Frederick G Hazel III • Kevin M Foley DCE • * • H • EC • PSW • 1428 N Pueblo Dr Casa Grande AZ 85222-2914 • trinity3lutheran3church@yahoo.com

**CHANDLER—*EPIPHANY*** (480)963-6105
Larry A Stoterau • Joy E Schubert DCE • H • EC • PSW • 800 W Ray Rd Chandler AZ 85225-3120 • FAX(480)963-6170 • pastor1@telesouth1.com

**COOLIDGE—*CHRIST*** (602)836-1889
Vacant • H • PSW • PO Box 632 Coolidge AZ 85228-0632

**CORDES LAKES—*MOUNTAIN OF*** (602)632-8785
James N Harris(DM) • H • PSW • UKNWN 20135 E Stagecoach Trl Mayer AZ 86333-1032

**CORTARO—*MESSIAH***
See Tucson

**COTTONWOOD—*FAITH*** (520)634-7876
Michael T Vahle • H • EC • PSW • 2021 E Fir St Cottonwood AZ 86326-4558

**FLAGSTAFF—*PEACE*** (520)526-9578
Warren C Ueckert • WS 1015; SS 9; BC 9 • H • EC • PSW • 3430 N 4th St Flagstaff AZ 86004-1793

**FOUNTAIN HILLS—*TRINITY*** (602)837-0130
Donald K Schrage • H • PSW • 13770 N Fountain Hills Blvd 85268-3727 PO Box 17270 Fountain Hills AZ 85269-7270 • FAX(602)837-7453 • tlcfhaz@msn.com

**GILBERT—*CHRIST GREENFLD*** (480)892-8314
Kevin L Wyssmann • WS 730 9 1030; SS 9; BC 9;* • H • EC/EL • PSW • 425 N Greenfield Rd Gilbert AZ 85234-5053 • FAX(480)503-0437

**GLENDALE—*ATONEMENT***
See Phoenix

**GREEN VALLEY—*RISEN SAVIOR*** (520)625-2612
John W Stieve • * • H • EN • 555 S La Canada Dr Green Valley AZ 85614-2538 • FAX(520)625-2635 • risensavior@gci-net.com

**KINGMAN—*GOOD SHEPHERD*** (520)757-3525
John E Jaster • WS 10; SS 845; BC 845 • H • PSW • 3958 N Bank St Kingman AZ 86401-2727 • luther7@ctaz.com

**LAKE HAVASU CITY—*LAMB OF GOD*** (520)505-7220
Vacant • H • PSW • 111 Bunker Dr 86403-6856 PO Box 3343 Lake Havasu City AZ 86405-3343 • FAX(520)505-6424

**LAKE MONTEZUMA—*GRACE***
See Rimrock

**LAKESIDE—*SHEP MOUNTAINS***
See Pinetop

**LITCHFIELD PARK—*TRINITY*** (623)935-4665
David J Bolte • H • EC/EL • PSW • 830 E Plaza Cir Litchfield Park AZ 85340-4915 • FAX(623)935-5540 • drbolte@aol.com

**MAYER—*MOUNTAIN OF FAITH***
See Cordes Lakes

**MESA—*ETERNAL LIFE*** (602)985-0224
Burton F Giese • WS 8 930;* • H • PSW • 7000 E Arbor Ave Mesa AZ 85208-1001

***HOSANNA*** (480)984-1414
Joseph M Meyer • * • H • PSW • 9601 E Brown Rd Mesa AZ 85207-4400 • FAX(480)984-7839

***ST LUKE*** (480)969-4414
Robert J Flohrs • John E Hollmann DCE • H • EC • PSW • 807 N Stapley Dr Mesa AZ 85203-5698 • FAX(480)969-4801

**OVERGAARD—*FAITH*** (520)535-4555
Vacant • * • H • EN • 2750 Mogollon Dr 85933 PO Box 683 Overgaard AZ 85933-0683

**PAGE—*SHEPHERD DESER*** (520)645-9398
Marc D Spaeth • H • EC • RM • 331 S Lake Powell Blvd 86040 PO Box 343 Page AZ 86040-0343

**PARADISE VALLEY—*ST MARK***
See Phoenix

**PARKER—*MESSIAH*** (520)669-8964
Alan D Scott • * • H • EN • Eighth And Mohave 85344 PO Box 1576 Parker AZ 85344-1576

**PAYSON—*SHEPHERD PINES*** (520)474-5440
Todd W Arnold • WS 10; SS 9; BC 830;* • H • EN • 507 W Wade Ln Payson AZ 85541-4761

**PEORIA—*APOSTLES*** (623)979-3497
Daryl B Robarge Norman E Walter(EM) • WS 8 1045; SS 915; BC 930 • H • EC/EL • PSW • 7020 W Cactus Rd Peoria AZ 85381-5318 • FAX(623)979-5778 • revdbr@pop.phnx.uswest.net

***MOUNT ZION**** (623)825-9221
James S Swinford • WS 9; SS 1015; BC 1015 • H • PSW • 8902 W Deer Valley Rd Peoria AZ 85382-2449 • FAX(623)825-9221

**PHOENIX—*ATONEMENT*** (623)582-8785
John B Erickson • H • EC/EL/HS • PSW • 85026 4001 W Beardsley Rd Glendale AZ 85308-4713 • FAX(623)587-8512 • atonementlc@juno.com

***CHRIST*** (602)955-4830
Jeffery T Schrank Vernon F Ermeling Arnold W Frank • H • EC/EL/HS • EN • 3901 E Indian School Rd Phoenix AZ 85018-5236 • FAX(602)955-8073 • bhodgson@cclphoenix.org

***CHRIST REDEEMER*** (623)934-3286
Loel G Haak Vernon T Trahms(EM) • Kenneth J Hansen DCE • WS 8 830 1045; SS 930; BC 930 • H • EC/EL/HS • PSW • 8801 N 43rd Ave Phoenix AZ 85051-3641 • FAX(623)934-3298 • ctrlutheran@ctrlutheran.com

***FAMILY OF CHRIST*** (480)759-4047
Perry A Kopatz • H • EC • EN • 3501 E Chandler Blvd Phoenix AZ 85048 • FAX(480)759-9004 • family-of-christ.com

***KING OF KINGS*** (602)973-0500
Kenneth G Piepenbrink • WS 9;* • H • PSW • 3314 W Rose Ln Phoenix AZ 85017-1989

***MOUNT CALVARY*** (602)263-0402
Dann J Ettner • Stanley G Smidt DCE • WS 830 11; SS 945; BC 945;* • H • EC/EL/HS • PSW • 5105 N 7th Ave Phoenix AZ 85013-2286 • FAX(602)263-0403 • mtcalvary@azlutheran.org

***OUR SAVIOR DF**** (602)944-1911
Vacant • PSW • 6802 N 10th Ave Phoenix AZ 85013-1010

***SANTO TOMAS**** (602)276-5078
Cristiano Artigas(DM) • WS 9; SS 930;* • H • PSW • 8041 S 7th Ave Phoenix AZ 85041-7904 • FAX(602)276-5518

***ST MARK*** (602)992-1980
Herman W Jonas Daniel T Moriarity • Inger Koppenhauer DCE • H • EC/HS • PSW • 3030 E Thunderbird Rd Phoenix AZ 85032-5685 • FAX(602)992-7125 • StMarkAz@aol.com

***ST PAUL*** (623)846-2228
Merlin L Reith • WS 1030; SS 915; BC 915;* • H • EC/EL • PSW • 6301 W Indian School Rd Phoenix AZ 85033-3326 • FAX(623)846-1851 • stpaulphx@aol.com

***THE MASTER*** (602)997-7439
Michael S Harding • WS 8 • H • EC/EL/HS • PSW • 2340 W Cactus Rd Phoenix AZ 85029-2799 • FAX(602)674-0232 • lcompmsh@aol.com

**PINETOP—*SHEP MOUNTAINS*** (520)367-1183
R Wayne Morton • H • EN • 2035 S Penrod At Nadean 85935 HC 66 Box 19200 Pinetop AZ 85935-9451 • shepherdpt@juno.com

**PRESCOTT—*SHEPHERD HILLS*** (520)778-9122
Andrew K Byars • WS 830; SS 945; BC 9 • H • PSW • 1202 Green Ln Prescott AZ 86305-5231 • FAX(502)778-6952 • sothlcms@futureone.com

**PRESCOTT VALLEY—*TRINITY*** (520)772-8845
Dennis D Morner • WS 815 1030 9; SS 920; BC 930 • H • EC • PSW • 3950 N Valorie Dr Prescott Valley AZ 86314-8234 • dmorner@northlink.com

**RIMROCK—*GRACE COMMUNITY**** (520)567-4608
Vacant • WS 11;* • H • PSW • 5100 Stevenson Dr 86335 PO Box 1078 Rimrock AZ 86335-1078

**RIO RICO—*CHRISTUS REX*** (520)281-8048
Ted Schubkegel(X) • WS 9; BC 1015 • H • EN • 282 Rio Rico Dr Rio Rico AZ 85648-3242

**SCOTTSDALE—*DESERT FOOTHILLS*** (480)585-8007
Michael J Schmidt • H • EC • PSW • 29305 N Scottsdale Scottsdale AZ 85262-2197 • FAX(480)502-9427 • dflc29305@aol.com

***HOLY CROSS*** (602)994-4848
Vacant • H • PSW • 3110 N Hayden Rd Scottsdale AZ 85251-6619 • FAX(602)994-4848 • chcluth@aztec.asu.edu

***SHEPHERD DESERT*** (480)860-1188
Stephen L Theil Alan P Rosnau • Charles E Gerken DCE • WS 8 915 1030;* • H • EC/EL/HS • PSW • 9590 E Shea Blvd Scottsdale AZ 85260-6724

**SEDONA—*ROCK OF AGES*** (520)282-4091
Dana Wilhelmsen • H • PSW • 390 Dry Creek Rd Sedona AZ 86336-4332

**SHOW LOW—*SHEP MOUNTAINS***
See Pinetop

**SIERRA VISTA—*IMMANUEL*** (520)458-3883
Russell H Dineen • H • PSW • 2145 S Coronado Dr Sierra Vista AZ 85635-5540

**SUN CITY—*FOUNTAIN OF LIFE*** (623)933-8246
Keith B Lonsberry • * • H • PSW • 15630 N Del Webb Blvd Sun City AZ 85351-1602 • FAX(623)876-0190 • fol@azlutheran.org

**SUN LAKES—*RISEN SAVIOR*** (480)895-6782
Harold J Teuscher • H • PSW • 85248 9220 E Fairway Blvd Apt E-101 Sun Lakes AZ 85248-6579 • FAX(480)895-6782 • jcrisen@aol.com

**TEMPE—*ALLELUIA*** (480)894-2610
Lealand L Meyer • WS 11;* • H • PSW • 1034 S Mill Ave Tempe AZ 85281-5606 • FAX(480)894-4626 • alleluia@asu.edu

***BEAUTIFUL SAVIOR*** (480)967-2660
Earl A Bielefeld • WS 10; SS 10; BC 845 • H • PSW • 1337 W 11th St Tempe AZ 85281-5329 • FAX(480)967-1202 • bslc3@juno.com

***GETHSEMANE*** (480)839-0906
John W Krueger • WS 8 930 1045; SS 920; BC 920 • H • EC/EL • PSW • 1035 E Guadalupe Rd Tempe AZ 85283-3043 • FAX(480)839-8876 • glc@primenet.com

**TUCSON—*ASCENSION*** (520)297-3095
Ricky C Mensing Mark E Schumm • Aaron L Lytle DCE • WS 8 930 11; SS 930; BC 1045;* • H • EC • EN • 1220 W Magee Rd Tucson AZ 85704-3325 • FAX(520)742-4781 • rccm@azstarnet.com

***CATALINA*** (520)825-9255
Michael A Morehouse • WS 9; BC 1030;* • H • EC • EN • 15855 N Twin Lakes Dr Tucson AZ 85739-8895 • FAX(520)825-9788 • catalinalutheran@juno.com

***COMM OF CHRIST**** (602)623-7575
John D Kautz(X) • H • EN • 715 N Park Ave Tucson AZ 85719-5037

***FAITH*** (520)326-2262
Donald R Haase Brian R Dill Grant A Knepper • WS 8 1030; SS 930; BC 930;* • H • EL • EN • 3925 E 5th St Tucson AZ 85711-1953 • FAX(520)325-5625

***FOUNTAIN LIFE*** (520)747-1213
Kevin L Kritzer Craig A Michaelson • Ellen L Kunze DCE • WS 8 915 1030; SS 915; BC 915;* • H • EC/EL • PSW • 710 S Kolb Rd Tucson AZ 85710-4941 • FAX(520)747-9444

***HOLY TRINITY*** (520)294-8851
David G Poedel • WS 9;* • H • EN • 5951 S 12th Ave Tucson AZ 85706-3904 • padredave@juno.com

***MESSIAH*** (520)744-6984
Luther P Esala • H • EC • EN • 7701 N Silverbell Rd Tucson AZ 85743

***MOUNT OLIVE*** (520)298-0996
Patrick D Henry • H • EN • 2005 S Houghton Rd Tucson AZ 85748-7635

**WICKENBURG—*REDEEMER*** (520)684-2729
Randolph C Wahl • WS 10; BC 9 • H • PSW • 450 Rose Ln Wickenburg AZ 85390-1445 • FAX(520)684-2729

**YUMA—*CALVARY*** (520)783-3024
Stephen C Sanderson • WS 11;* • H • PSW • 711 S 7th Ave Yuma AZ 85364-2966 • FAX(561)325-0310 • pastor@calvary3lutheran.com

***CHRIST*** (520)726-0773
Vincent R Harman Roy E Thayer(#) • WS 8 1045; SS 930; BC 930 • H • EC/EL • PSW • 2555 S Engler Ave Yuma AZ 85365-3216 • FAX(520)726-6674 • christyuma@aol.com

## ARKANSAS

**ALEXANDER—*IMMANUEL*** (501)455-0464
Kenneth W Burton III • WS 11; SS 930; BC 930 • H • MDS • 15224 S Alexander Rd 72002-2300 PO Box 119 Alexander AR 72002-0119 • FAX(501)455-0464 • kwburton3@juno.com

***ZION***
See Avilla

**ALMA—*OUR SAVIOR*** (501)632-5428
Vacant • WS 230; SS 330; BC 330 • H • MDS • Highway 71 North 72921 PO Box 208 Alma AR 72921-0208

**AUGSBURG—*ZION*** (501)331-3277
Vacant • H • MDS • UKNWN 93 Augsburg Rd London AR 72847-8777

**AVILLA—*ZION*** (501)316-1100
Andrew W Toopes Horace W Garton Henry M Schaefer • Paula C Weiss DCE • WS 830; SS 10; BC 10 • H • EC/HS • MDS • UKNWN 300 Avilla E Alexander AR 72002-8876 • FAX(501)316-1101 • avillazionl@juno.com

**BATESVILLE—*HOPE*** (870)793-3078
Paul M Mehl • H • EL • MDS • 2415 E Main St Batesville AR 72501-7371 • FAX(870)793-3078 • hopeluth@juno.com

**BELLA VISTA—*BELLA VISTA*** (501)855-0272
Ronald M Pfluger • H • MDS • 1990 Forest Hills Blvd Bella Vista AR 72715 • FAX(501)876-6097 • bvlutheran@mc2k.com

**BENTON—*FIRST*** (501)315-4311
David L Oberdieck • MDS • 18181 Hwy I-30 72015 PO Box 1249 Benton AR 72018-1249 • pastoro@juno.com

**BENTONVILLE—*FAITH*** (501)273-9419
Todd A Jones • WS 830 11; SS 935; BC 935 • H • MDS • 1602 NW 12th St Bentonville AR 72712-4113 • FAX(501)271-7532 • office@faithbentonville.com

**BERRYVILLE—*OUR REDEEMER*** (870)423-4463
Kenneth C Haydon • WS 830;* • H • MDS • Hwy 221 N 72616 PO Box 777 Berryville AR 72616-0777

**BLYTHEVILLE—*FIRST*** (870)763-6339
Terry J Coday • WS 1030;* • H • MDS • 108 N 6th St 72315-3315 PO Box 573 Blytheville AR 72316

**BRINKLEY—*OUR SAVIOR*** (870)734-2016
Vacant • WS 1015; SS 915; BC 915 • H • MDS • 11935 Hwy 495 72021 RR 1 Box 246A Brinkley AR 72021-9636

**BRYANT—*FRIENDS IN CHRIST**** (501)847-5553
Vacant • WS 1015; SS 9; BC 9 • H • MDS • 4500 Highway 5 N Suite 3 Bryant AR 72022 • revschaefer@juno.com

**CAMDEN—*REDEEMER*** (870)836-5527
Vacant • H • MDS • Stjohnepiscopal 117 Harrisonnw 71701 537 Carson Ave Camden AR 71701-3325

**CHEROKEE VILLAGE—*PEACE*** (870)257-3957
Brian L Pummill • H • EC • MDS • 12 Choctaw Ctr 72529-7430 PO Box 960 Cherokee Village AR 72525-0960

**CLARKSVILLE—*GRACE*** (501)754-2769
Vacant • WS 1045; SS 1045;* • H • MDS • Brown And Buchanan Sts 72830 PO Box 406 Clarksville AR 72830-0406

**CONWAY—*PEACE*** (501)329-3854
Carl W Groh • WS 830 11; SS 945 • H • MDS • 800 S Donaghey Ave Conway AR 72032-6735 • plc@cyberback.com

***SAINT MATTHEW*** (501)329-2227
Ric L Mc Millian • WS 1015; SS 9; BC 9 • H • MDS • 1050 Morningside Dr Conway AR 72032-3644 • FAX(501)329-7895 • mcmillian@conwaycorp.net

**CORNING—*ST MATTHEW*** (870)857-3633
Vacant • WS 845; SS 10 • H • MDS • 501 N Missouri Ave 72422-1615 PO Box 248 Corning AR 72422-0248

**CROSSETT—*ST JOHN*** (870)364-6172
Vacant • WS 930 • H • MDS • 1505 Main St 71635-4125 PO Box 581 Crossett AR 71635-0581

**DE WITT—*ST LUKE*** (870)946-2312
Jeffrey M Kuddes • H • MDS • 903 E 2nd St De Witt AR 72042-3458

**EL DORADO—*OUR SAVIOR*** (870)862-1443
Wayne T Pick • WS 11; SS 945 • H • MDS • 900 W Faulkner St El Dorado AR 71730-5456 • oslceldo@ipa.net

**FAIRFIELD BAY—*FAITH*** (501)884-3375
David W Krause(EM) • WS 930; SS 830; BC 830 • H • MDS • 310 Snead Dr Fairfield Bay AR 72088-3906 • flcffb@juno.com

**FAYETTEVILLE—*ST JOHN*** (501)443-3609
Roger P Schoolcraft • WS 1015; SS 9; BC 9 • H • EC • MDS • 2730 E Township St Fayetteville AR 72703-4362

**FORREST CITY—*FAITH*** (870)633-8312
Leland E Bush • WS 1045; SS 930; BC 930 • H • MDS • 4525 N Washington St Forrest City AR 72335-7639

**FORT SMITH—*BETHEL*** (501)452-1521
Robert G Herring • WS 8 1030; SS 915; BC 915 • H • EC • MDS • 5400 Euper Ln Fort Smith AR 72903-3232 • arkpreacher@mail.com

***FIRST*** (501)785-2886
Allen D Stuckwisch • WS 8 1030; SS 915; BC 915;* • H • EC/EL • MDS • 419 N 12th St Fort Smith AR 72901-2802 • FAX(501)785-2902

***OUR REDEEMER*** (501)646-7611
Vacant • WS 1015; SS 9; BC 9 • H • EC • MDS • 2100 Cavanaugh Rd Fort Smith AR 72908-7844

**GILLETT—*ST PAUL*** (870)548-2554
Jeffrey M Kuddes • H • EC • MDS • 206 Rose Ave 72055 PO Box 419 Gillett AR 72055-0419

**GREENWOOD—*GRACE*** (501)996-7747
Mark M Burger • WS 1015; SS 9; BC 9 • H • MDS • 502 W Denver St 72936-4014 PO Box 425 Greenwood AR 72936-0425 • mmbrgr@juno.com

**HARDY 3W—*PEACE***
See Cherokee Village

**HARRISON—*FIRST*** (870)741-9777
Vacant • WS 1030; SS 9;* • H • MDS • 1001 Gipson Rd Harrison AR 72601-8893

**HEBER SPRINGS—*TRINITY*** (501)362-7156
Vacant • H • MDS • 300 Trailwood Dr Heber Springs AR 72543-9221

**HOLIDAY ISLAND—*GRACE*** (501)253-9040
Kenneth C Haydon • WS 1045; BC 930 • H • MDS • 179 Holiday Island Dr Holiday Island AR 72631-4821

**HORSESHOE BEND—*SHEPHERD*** (870)670-5482
David E Tews • WS 9; SS 1015; BC 1015 • H • MDS • 3rd And Profession 72512 PO Box 205 Horseshoe Bend AR 72512-0205 • shepherdofthehillscen30201@centurytel.net

**HOT SPRINGS—*FIRST*** (501)525-0322
Jonathan M Beyer Lyle D Muller(EM) • WS 830 11; SS 945; BC 945;* • H • EC • MDS • 105 Village Rd Hot Springs AR 71913-6715 • FAX(501)525-0142 • flchs@yahoo.com

**HOT SPRINGS VILLAGE—*FAITH*** (501)922-5700
Leslie A Weerts • WS 10; BC 9 • H • MDS • 71909 191 Andorra Dr Hot Springs Village AR 71909-7403

**JACKSONVILLE—*HOPE*** (501)982-1333
James D Burns • H • EC/EL/HS • MDS • 1904 Mc Arthur Dr Jacksonville AR 72076-3728 • jburns@aristotle.net

**JONESBORO—*PILGRIM*** (870)935-2001
Russell L Shewmaker • WS 10; SS 845; BC 845 • MDS • 1812 Rains St Jonesboro AR 72401-5046 • FAX(870)935-4717 • pilgrim@bscn.com

**LAFE—*ST JOHN*** (870)586-0319
Vacant • WS 1030; SS 915; BC 915 • H • MDS • Hwy 135 72436 PO Box 235 Lafe AR 72436-0235

**LITTLE ROCK—*CELEBRATION**** (501)455-0440
Vacant • H • MDS • 9300 S Chicot Rd Little Rock AR 72209

***CHRIST*** (501)663-5232
Russell C Hildebrandt Daniel W Schepmann • Brenda L Zesch DCE • H • HS • MDS • 315 S Hughes St Little Rock AR 72205-5128 • FAX(501)663-9542

***FIRST*** (501)372-1023
Richard H Rickus • H • HS • MDS • 314 E 8th St Little Rock AR 72202-3904 • dkwy@alltel.net

***GRACE*** (501)663-3631
James C Walter • WS 815 1045; SS 930; BC 930;* • H • EC/HS • MDS • 5124 Hillcrest Ave 72205-1802 PO Box 250769 Little Rock AR 72225-0769 • FAX(501)663-0625 • walter@aristotle.net

***LORD OF LIFE*** (501)223-2292
Martin L Marks • WS 1030; SS 915;* • H • EC/HS • MDS • 800 Kirby Rd Little Rock AR 72211-3018 • FAX(501)223-3606 • lollr@aol.com

**LONDON—*ZION***
See Augsburg

**LOWELL—*LIVING SAVIOR*** (501)770-2124
Donaldo Sonntag(DM) • WS 930; SS 1045;* • H • MDS • 106 N Bloomington Suite O 72745 PO Box 519 Lowell AR 72745-0519 • livingsaviorlcms@netzero.net

**MAGNOLIA—*FAITH*** (870)234-2040
Vacant • H • MDS • 1700 N Jackson St Magnolia AR 71753-2052 • FAX(870)234-5319

**MALVERN—*ST LUKE*** (501)337-9616
Kenneth W Burton III • WS 930; SS 1030; BC 1030 • H • MDS • 820 Sulphur Springs Rd Malvern AR 72104-5938

**MAUMELLE—*SHEPHERD PEACE*** (501)851-4546
Paul D Mayerhoff • H • HS • MDS • 449 Millwood Cir 72113-6321 PO Box 13143 Maumelle AR 72113-0143 • FAX(501)851-9030 • shepeace@cei.net

**MENA—*TRINITY*** (501)394-1290
Donley D Hesse(EM) • H • MDS • 1010 De Queen St Mena AR 71953-4128

**MOUNTAIN HOME—*REDEEMER*** (870)425-6071
Kenneth E Lampe Kenneth C Taglauer • H • MDS • 312 W North St Mountain Home AR 72653-3022 • FAX(870)425-2844 • redeemer@mtnhome.com

**NORTH LITTLE ROCK—*TRINITY*** (501)753-6824
Larry G Seiferth • WS 1030; SS 9; BC 9 • H • EC/HS • MDS • 3802 N Olive St N Little Rock AR 72116-8748 • FAX(501)753-6833 • pastrmoe@aol.com

**PARAGOULD—*REDEEMER*** (870)236-2162
Vacant • H • MDS • 829 W Kingshighway Paragould AR 72450-5940

**PINE BLUFF—*TRINITY*** (870)534-4316
Dean F Clausing • H • MDS • 4200 Old Warren Rd Pine Bluff AR 71603-6114 • FAX(870)534-5494 • clausing@ipa.net

**POCAHONTAS—*THE CROSS***
Warren W Schmidt(EM) • WS 1030; SS 930;* • H • MDS • 202 Jordan St 72455-3350 PO Box 573 Pocahontas AR 72455-0573

**PRAIRIE GROVE—*PEACE*** (501)846-3100
Roy W Bingenheimer(EM) • WS 9; SS 1030; BC 1030 • H • MDS • 1261 Black Nursery St 72753 PO Box 292 Prairie Grove AR 72753-0292

**ROGERS—*HOLY TRINITY*** (501)636-1135
Gordon W Besel • WS 8 1045; SS 915; BC 915;* • H • MDS • 1101 W Hudson Rd 72756-2328 PO Box 219 Rogers AR 72757-0219 • FAX(501)636-1188 • holytrin@arkansas.net

**RUSSELLVILLE—*ST JOHN*** (501)968-1309
Darrell C Kobs • Jerome A Wachter DCE • WS 9; SS 1015; BC 1015;* • H • MDS • 500 N Cumberland Ave Russellville AR 72801-2514 • stjohnschurch@cox-internet.com

**SEARCY—*OUR SHEPHERD*** (501)268-1613
Daniel G Jones • WS 830; SS 945; BC 945 • H • MDS • 2610 S Main St Searcy AR 72143-8314 • FAX(501)268-5254 • oslc@steward-net.com

**SPRINGDALE—*LIVING SAVIOR***
See Lowell

***SALEM*** (501)751-9359
Gerald L Renken • WS 8 1030; SS 915; BC 915 • H • EC/EL • MDS • 1800 W Emma Ave Springdale AR 72762-3905 • FAX(501)750-2028 • salem-lcms@juno.com

**STUTTGART—*ST JOHN*** (870)673-2858
Dwight D Riley • WS 8; SS 915; BC 915 • H • EC/EL • MDS • 205 E 5th St Stuttgart AR 72160-4319 • FAX(870)673-2936 • stjohnslc@future.net

**ULM—*ZION*** (870)241-3778
Thomas E Lakso • WS 10; SS 9;* • H • MDS • PO Box 158 Ulm AR 72170-0158

**WALDENBURG—*ZION*** (870)579-2276
Paul A Leigeber • H • MDS • 5612 Hwy 14 E 72475 PO Box 40 Waldenburg AR 72475-0040 • leigeber@inet³direct.com

**WEST MEMPHIS—*ST PAUL*** (870)735-0729
Vacant • H • MDS • Broadway At Rick Rd 72301 810 W Broadway St West Memphis AR 72301-2912

## CALIFORNIA

**AGOURA HILLS—*ST PAUL*** (818)889-1620
James D Henkell Mark A Schaefer • WS 830 10; SS 10; BC 10 • H • PSW • 30600 Thousand Oaks Blvd Agoura Hills CA 91301-1434 • FAX(818)889-1649 • RevJH@aol.com

**ALHAMBRA—*EMMAUS*** (626)289-3664
Ray F Kibler Patrick Jow Dale G Federwitz • WS 830 945 11; SS 945; BC 945 • H • EC/EL • PSW • 840 S Almansor St Alhambra CA 91801-4538 • FAX(626)576-0476 • emmauslutheran@earthlink.net

**ALMADEN—*SHEP OF VALLEY***
See San Jose

**ALTO LOMA—*SHEPHERD HILLS***
See Rancho Cucamonga

**ANAHEIM—*HEPHATHA*** (714)637-0887
Nathan R Riley • H • EC/EL/HS • PSW • 5900 E Santa Ana Canyon Rd Anaheim CA 92807-3201 • FAX(714)637-6088 • hephathalc@aol.com

***MT CALVARY DF*** (714)689-8380
Gerhard A Gehrs • H • PSW • 92803 C/O Rev G A Gehrs Jr 6262 Soledad Dr Riverside CA 92504-1523

***PRINCE PEACE*** (714)774-0993
Kerwin L Duerr • WS 8 915 1030; SS 915 • H • EC/EL/HS • PSW • 1421 W Ball Rd Anaheim CA 92802-1711 • FAX(714)774-0183 • princeofpeacelutheran@yahoo.com

***ST MARK*** (714)535-9742
Daniel C Mack • WS 9; SS 1030; BC 1030 • H • PSW • 10418 Katella Ave Anaheim CA 92804-6527 • FAX(714)535-9894 • missions11@aol.com

***ZION*** (714)535-1169
Thomas F Meyer Mark W Rossington • Dawn M Ruelle DCE Roger P Frick DCE • WS 8 11 930 630; SS 945; BC 1045 • H • EC/EL/HS • PSW • 222 N East St Anaheim CA 92805-3317 • FAX(714)254-7173

**ANTIOCH—*SAINT ANDREW*** (925)757-1672
Roger R Kuehn • H • CNH • 2507 San Jose Dr Antioch CA 94509-4172 • FAX(925)757-5709 • AndrewLuth@aol.com

**ANZA—*SHEP OF VALLEY*** (909)763-4226
Lloyd Strelow • WS 9; SS 1030; BC 1030;* • H • PSW • 56095 Pena Rd 92539-9690 PO Box 390668 Anza CA 92539-0668 • svls@msn.com

**APPLE VALLEY—*ASCENSION*** (760)247-7392
Vacant • WS 9 7; SS 1030; BC 1030 • H • PSW • 22130 Ottawa Rd Apple Valley CA 92308-6538 • FAX(760)247-7392 • alcms@mscomm.com

**ARCADIA—*OUR SAVIOR*** (626)447-7690
Roger R Sonnenberg Richard A Foss • WS 8 1045 7 • H • HS • PSW • 512 W Duarte Rd Arcadia CA 91007-7323 • FAX(626)447-9301

**ARCATA—*ARCATA*** (707)822-5117
James A Kabel • WS 930; SS 1045; BC 1045 • H • CNH • 151 E 16th St Arcata CA 95521-6004 • lcarcata@northcoast.com

**ARROYO GRANDE—*PEACE*** (805)489-2708
George A Lepper • WS 10 6; SS 830; BC 830 • H • EC • CNH • 244 N Oak Park Blvd Arroyo Grande CA 93420-2436 • FAX(805)474-1823

**ARTOIS—*ST PAUL*** (916)934-7470
Philip W Zabell • CNH • 565 Main St 95913 PO Box 229 Artois CA 95913-0229 • pzcard@hotmail.com

**ATASCADERO—*OF THE REDEEMER*** (805)466-9350
Thomas H Mueller • WS 10; SS 9; BC 9 • H • CNH • 4500 El Camino Real Atascadero CA 93422-2761 • lcr-atascadero@juno.cm

**ATWATER—*HOLY CROSS*** (209)358-3471
Robert L Rotnem • WS 1015; SS 9 • H • CNH • 1495 Underwood Ave Atwater CA 95301-2745

**AUBURN—*ST PAUL*** (530)885-5378
David F Poganski • H • HS • CNH • 275 Nation Dr Auburn CA 95603-3629 • dfpogostpaul@neworld.net

**BAKERSFIELD—*ALL NATIONS*** (661)397-4322
Vacant • WS 1030; SS 915; BC 930 • H • CNH • C/O Richard Hilgendorf 3913 Marsha St Bakersfield CA 93309

***BETHANY*** (661)399-3532
James W Tyler • WS 11; SS 930;* • H • CNH • 900 Day Ave Bakersfield CA 93308-1402

***GRACE*** (661)324-4315
James F Larsen • WS 1030; SS 915; BC 930 • H • CNH • 2530 Drake St Bakersfield CA 93301-2718

***PRAYER*** (661)871-1289
Vacant • WS 9; SS 1015; BC 1015 • H • EC • CNH • 8001 Panorama Dr Bakersfield CA 93306-7302 • martinscousin@aol.com

***ST JOHN*** (661)834-1412
Vacant • Paul D Hammontree DCE • WS 8 930 11; SS 930; BC 930;* • H • EC/EL • CNH • 912 New Stine Rd Bakersfield CA 93309-2999 • FAX(661)834-8972 • sjlc@kern.com

**BANNING—*GRACE*** (909)849-3232
John D Bucka • H • PSW • 1000 W Wilson St Banning CA 92220 • FAX(909)922-8244 • GLOMS@JUNO.COM

**BARSTOW—*CONCORDIA*** (760)256-2036
Wayne A Anderson • H • EC • PSW • 420 Avenue E Barstow CA 92311-2613 • FAX(760)256-5455

**BELL GARDENS—*SS PEDRO/PABLO*** (323)773-3056
Frank N Brundige(DM) • PSW • 6430 Colmar Ave Bell Gardens CA 90201-1718

**BELLFLOWER—*OUR SAVIOR*** (562)804-2187
J A Lossner(X) • H • PSW • 15700 Woodruff Ave Bellflower CA 90706-4018 • FAX(562)804-2187

**BENICIA—*BENICIA*** (707)746-0201
Gary A Bell • WS 8 930; BC 1045;* • H • EC • CNH • 201 Raymond Dr Benicia CA 94510-2747 • FAX(707)751-0873 • benicialutheran@aol.com

**BERKELEY—*BETHLEHEM*** (510)848-8821
Robert H O Sullivan • H • CNH • 3100 Telegraph Ave Berkeley CA 94705-1920

**BEVERLY HILLS—*MOUNT CALVARY*** (310)277-1164
R J Perling • WS 1030 • EL/HS • PSW • 436 S Beverly Dr Beverly Hills CA 90212-4402 • FAX(310)274-0923 • rjohn@perling.com

**BIG BEAR LAKE—*SHEPHERD PINES*** (909)866-8718
Vacant • WS 9; SS 1015; BC 1030;* • H • PSW • 42450 N Shore 92315 PO Box 1606 Big Bear Lake CA 92315-1606 • FAX(909)866-8718

**BISHOP—*GRACE*** (760)872-9791
Kenton A Puls • WS 1030;* • H • EC • PSW • 711 N Fowler St Bishop CA 93514-2617

**BLYTHE—*ZION*** (760)922-7321
Gerald L Hoemann • * • H • EC/EL • PSW • 721 E Chanslor Way Blythe CA 92225-1250 • FAX(760)922-7456 • zionblythe@juno.com

**BORON—*RESURRECTION*** (760)762-6889
Vacant • H • PSW • 27177 Twenty Mule Team Rd 93516-1643 PO Box 448 Boron CA 93596-0448

**BORREGO SPRINGS—*BORREGO*** (619)767-3119
Vacant • WS 10; BC 9 • H • EN • 601 Diamond Bar Rd 92004 PO Box 1122 Borrego Springs CA 92004-1122

**BRAWLEY—*TRINITY*** (760)344-1635
Vacant • H • PSW • 275 N First St Brawley CA 92227-1841 • FAX(760)344-8778 • trinityl@brawleyonline.com

**BREA—*CHRIST*** (714)529-2984
Richard A Dannenbring • WS 8 1030 6; SS 915; BC 915 • H • EC/EL/HS • PSW • 820 W Imperial Hwy Brea CA 92821-3808 • FAX(714)529-2157 • rdannenbring@clcs-brea.com

**BRENTWOOD—*RESURRECTION**** (925)634-5180
Michael R Lange • WS 830 1030; SS 930; BC 930 • H • CNH • 4501 Ohara Ave Brentwood CA 94513-2219 • FAX(925)634-1780 • resmin@prodigy.net

**BROWNSVILLE—*BROWNSVILLE**** (916)675-3463
Vacant • H • CNH • La Porte And Nero Rd 95919 PO Box 443 Brownsville CA 95919-0443 • oakholow@aol.com

**BUENA PARK—*BETHEL*** (714)527-4776
Theodore P Schaefer • WS 9; BC 8 • HS • PSW • 6441 Lincoln Ave Buena Park CA 90620-3644 • FAX(714)527-4788 • Bethelluth@aol.com

***MESSIAH*** (714)521-7705
Timothy B Muller • H • PSW • 6625 Dale St Buena Park CA 90621-3523 • FAX(714)521-7555

**BURBANK—*CHRIST*** (818)846-4415
Vacant • WS 10;* • H • PSW • 2400 W Burbank Blvd Burbank CA 91506-1238

***FIRST*** (818)848-7432
William L Brunold • Jonathan B Ruehs DCE • WS 8 1030; SS 915;* • H • EL/HS • PSW • 1001 S Glenoaks Blvd Burbank CA 91502-1585 • FAX(818)848-3801 • flcb@aol.com

**BURLINGAME—*TRINITY*** (650)347-6661
Harlan L Limmer • H • CNH • 1245 El Camino Real Burlingame CA 94010-4815 • tlc94010@aol.com

**BURNEY—*FAITH*** (530)335-3723
Vacant • H • CNH • 20400 Timber Dr Burney CA 96013-4113

**CALIFORNIA CITY—*TRINITY**** (760)373-4068
Neal R Blanke(DM) • WS 11; SS 10; BC 10 • H • PSW • 9124 Catalpa Ave 93505-2781 PO Box 2337 California City CA 93504-0337

**CAMARILLO—*FIRST***
Vacant • EC/EL • PSW • 380 Arneill Rd Camarillo CA 93010-6406

***PEACE*** (805)482-3313
Vacant • WS 8;* • H • EC • PSW • 71 Loma Dr Camarillo CA 93010-2315 • FAX(805)482-6044 • peace@vcnet.com

**CAMERON PARK—*LIGHT OF HILLS*** (530)677-9536
Alan J Sommer • WS 815; SS 945; BC 945 • H • HS • CNH • 3100 Rodeo Rd Cameron Park CA 95682 • FAX(530)677-4376 • 10th@loth.org

**CANOGA PARK—*CANOGA PARK*** (818)348-5714
Kenneth C Jenks • Janet L Just DCE • H • EL/HS • PSW • 7357 Jordan Ave Canoga Park CA 91303-1238 • FAX(818)348-1516

***OUR REDEEMER***
See Winnetka

**CANYON COUNTRY—*BETHLEHEM***
See Santa Clarita

**CAPISTRANO BEACH—*FAITH*** (949)496-1901
Ronald K Hodel • WS 8 1030 623; SS 915; BC 915 • H • PSW • 34381 Calle Portola Capistrano Beach CA 92624-1076 • FAX(949)496-1992 • faithlutheranl@juno.com

**CARLSBAD—*REDEEMER BY THE SEA*** (760)431-8990
Robert A Mc Donald(DM) • WS 830; SS 10; BC 10;* • H • PSW • 6355 Corte Del Abeto Ste 100 Carlsbad CA 92009-1443 • FAX(760)431-8990 • revrmcdrbtslc@juno.com

**CARPINTERIA—*FAITH*** (805)684-4707
David L Bloedel • WS 9;* • H • PSW • 1335 Vallecito Pl Carpinteria CA 93013-1431 • FAX(805)566-0073 • faithlc@juno.com

**CARSON—*ARK NOAH KOREAN****
See Culver City

**CARUTHERS—*OUR SAVIOR*** (559)864-3008
Mark J Wikstrom • H • CNH • 13441 S Quince St 93609 PO Box 215 Caruthers CA 93609-0215

**CASTAIC—*PRINCE OF PEACE**** (661)298-5706
Thomas J Lapacka • WS 1030; SS 930;* • H • PSW • Castaic Elementary School 30455 Park Vista Dr 91310 PO Box 592 Castaic CA 91384-0592 • FAX(661)298-5706 • lapackajt@aol.com

***PRINCE OF PEACE*** (661)298-5706
Vacant • PSW • PO Box 592 Castaic CA 91384

**CERRITOS—*CONCORDIA*** (562)926-7416
James K Pflueger Will C Hsu(DM) • H • EC/EL • PSW • 13633 183rd St Cerritos CA 90703-8940 • FAX(562)407-0610

**CHESTER—*OUR SAVIOR*** (530)258-2347
Vernon R Kettner • WS 9 • CNH • 161 Aspen St 96020 PO Box 706 Chester CA 96020-0706

**CHICO—*REDEEMER*** (530)342-6085
Vacant • WS 10; SS 9; BC 9 • H • EC/EL • CNH • 1355 Hawthorne Ave Chico CA 95926-2971 • FAX(530)342-6347 • redeemerch@juno.com

**CHINO—*IMMANUEL*** (909)628-2823
Robert P Den Ouden • WS 9; SS 10;* • H • HS • PSW • 5648 Jefferson Ave Chino CA 91710-3602

**CHINO HILLS—*LOVING SAVIOR*** (909)597-4668
Charles A Rauschek • WS 8 1030; SS 915; BC 915 • H • EC/EL • PSW • 14816 Peyton Dr Chino Hills CA 91709-2073 • FAX(909)597-5739 • lsothlc@aviastar.net

***LOVING SAVIOR CHINES**** (909)597-5771
Charles A Fox(DM) • HS • PSW • 14816 Peyton Dr Chino Hills CA 91709-2073 • FAX(909)597-5771 • pastorchip@aol.com

**CHULA VISTA—*CONCORDIA*** (619)422-6606
Richard W Schmidt • WS 9; SS 1045;* • H • HS • PSW • 267 E Oxford St Chula Vista CA 91911-3646 • FAX(619)422-6606 • pastorrschmidt@juno.com

***OF JOY*** (619)482-1214
Michael R Beyer • H • PSW • 810 Buena Vista Way Chula Vista CA 91910-6853 • FAX(619)482-1214 • chofjoy@juno.com

***PILGRIM*** (619)422-0492
Alan A Wyneken • WS 745; SS 9; BC 9 • H • EC/EL/HS • PSW • 497 E St Chula Vista CA 91910-2445 • FAX(619)422-2740

***SANTISIMA TRINIDAD*** (619)422-4278
Vacant • PSW • 267 E Oxford St Chula Vista CA 91911-3699

**CITRUS HEIGHTS—*MESSIAH*** (916)725-4550
Vacant • WS 9; SS 1030; BC 1030 • H • HS • CNH • 7801 Rosswood Dr 95621-1244 PO Box 7190 Citrus Heights CA 95621-7190 • FAX(916)723-4596 • messiahl@jps.net

**CLAREMONT—*ST LUKE*** (909)624-8898
John E Fibelkorn • WS 10; SS 845; BC 845 • H • HS • PSW • 2050 N Indian Hill Blvd Claremont CA 91711-2722

**CLEARLAKE—*ST JOHN*** (707)994-2829
David R Rose • WS 9; SS 10 • H • CNH • 14310 Memory Ln PO Box 338 Clearlake CA 95422-0338 • drrose@jps.net

**CLOVERDALE—*GRACE*** (707)894-2330
Curtis A Binz • WS 10; SS 845; BC 845 • H • CNH • 890 N Cloverdale Blvd 95425-3011 PO Box 455 Cloverdale CA 95425-0455

**COLTON—*ST JOHN*** (909)825-2395
Don C Wiley • WS 930; SS 11; BC 11;* • H • EC • PSW • 820 N La Cadena Dr Colton CA 92324-2774 • stjohnlcms@prodigy.net

**COLUSA—*BETHLEHEM*** (530)458-4943
David L Bunting • WS 9;* • CNH • 1600 Wescott Rd Colusa CA 95932-3228 • FAX(530)458-4943

**COMPTON—*ST PHILIP*** (310)635-8632
Richard H Snyder • SS 930;* • H • PSW • 1110 N Dwight Ave Compton CA 90222-3833 • FAX(310)635-0436

**CONCORD—*FIRST*** (925)671-9942
James W Mueller • H • EC/EL • CNH • 4000 Concord Blvd Concord CA 94519-1515 • FAX(925)671-9943

***HOLY CROSS*** (925)686-2000
Vacant • H • CNH • 1092 Alberta Way Concord CA 94521-3864 • FAX(925)686-6894

**CORNING—*MOUNT OLIVE*** (530)824-5530
Dallas D Dubke • H • CNH • 341 Solano St Corning CA 96021-3453

**CORONA—*GRACE*** (909)737-3217
James W Page • WS 8 1030; SS 915; BC 915;* • H • EL/HS • PSW • 1811 S Lincoln Ave Corona CA 92882-5813 • FAX(909)737-1750 • graceluthchurch@juno.com

**CORONADO—*RESURRECTION*** (619)435-1000
James W Hallerberg • WS 1015; SS 9; BC 9 • H • EC • PSW • 1111 5th St Coronado CA 92118-1807 • FAX(619)435-2638 • rlcluth@san.rr.com

**COSTA MESA—*CHRIST*** (949)631-1611
William B Hemenway Joseph H Strubbe Steven Hayes(#) • WS 8 10 1130; SS 910; BC 910;* • H • EC/EL/HS • PSW • 760 Victoria St Costa Mesa CA 92627-2968 • FAX(949)631-6224 • clccm@aol.com

**COVINA—*ST JOHN*** (626)332-3142
Patrick W Curley • WS 9; SS 1045;* • H • EC/EL/HS • PSW • 304 E Covina Blvd Covina CA 91722-2826 • FAX(626)332-1783 • stjohncovina@earthlink.net

***TRINITY*** (626)337-2971
Matthew A Payne • H • EC/HS • PSW • 16050 E San Bernardino Rd Covina CA 91722-3941 • trinitycovina@earthlink.net

**CRESCENT CITY—*GRACE*** (707)464-4712
David I Lewis • WS 830; SS 945; BC 945 • H • EC • CNH • 188 E Cooper Ave Crescent City CA 95531-2741 • FAX(707)464-4070 • grace95531@peoplepc.com

**CULVER CITY—*ARK NOAH KOREAN**** (310)834-5337
Kyung J Cha(DM) • PSW • 3735 Hughes Ave 90230 48 Camelback Ave N Carson CA 90745-5613 • FAX(310)834-5337

**CUPERTINO—*FAITH CHINESE*** (408)252-0552
Timothy K Ling • WS 930 • H • CNH • 5825 Bollinger Rd Cupertino CA 95014-3536 • FAX(408)252-0348 • revrevling@aol.com

***OUR SAVIOR*** (408)252-0345
Dennis E Bestul Walter J Schedler • WS 8 11; SS 930; BC 930 • H • EC/EL • CNH • 5825 Bollinger Rd Cupertino CA 95014-3536 • FAX(408)252-0558 • lcos.org

**CYPRESS—*HOLY CROSS*** (714)527-7225
Weldon H Leimer William D Lindenmeyer • * • H • EC/EL/HS • PSW • 4321 Cerritos Ave Cypress CA 90630-4216 • FAX(714)527-8472

**DALY CITY—*HOPE*** (650)991-4673
Daniel K Woo • WS 830 945 11; SS 945; BC 945 • H • EC/EL • CNH • 55 San Fernando Way Daly City CA 94015-2065 • FAX(650)991-9723

**DANVILLE—*MESSIAH*** (925)736-2270
Peter Ledic • H • EN • 2305 Camino Tassajara Danville CA 94526-4402 • FAX(925)736-0435 • mlclcms@pacbell.net

**DAVIS—*OUR FAITH*** (530)758-4546
Daniel A Schlensker • WS 10; SS 845 • H • CNH • 1801 Oak Ave Davis CA 95616-1005 • FAX(530)758-4546 • ourfaith@cwia.com

**DELANO—*OUR SAVIOUR*** (661)725-2225
Erwin L Lueker • SS 1030; BC 1030;* • H • CNH • 1017 Princeton St Delano CA 93215-2447

**DIAMOND BAR—*GRACE CHINESE**** (909)860-2865
Vacant • PSW • 23300 E Golden Springs Dr Diamond Bar CA 91765-2001 • FAX(909)860-8550

***MOUNT CALVARY*** (909)861-2740
Dennis W Stueve • Daniel Santamarina DCE Noel M Fairchild DCE • WS 8 1030; SS 915; BC 915 • H • EC/EL/HS • PSW • 23300 Golden Springs Dr Diamond Bar CA 91765-2001 • FAX(909)861-5481 • mtcal@juno.com

**DINUBA—*FIRST*** (559)591-0375
Frederick M Hoover • WS 1030; SS 845; BC 845 • H • CNH • 961 E Elizabeth Way Dinuba CA 93618-2014 • revfhoov@lightspeed.net

**DOWNEY—*GOOD SHEPHERD*** (562)803-4459
Dennis W Bottoms • H • EL • PSW • 13200 Clark Ave Downey CA 90242-4723 • FAX(562)803-4450

***MESSIAH*** (562)923-1215
Norman W Stoppenhagen • WS 8 930 11; SS 930; BC 930 • H • PSW • 10711 Paramount Blvd Downey CA 90241-3305 • FAX(562)923-9211 • luthmess@aol.com

**DSRT HOT SPGS—*CHRIST*** (760)329-9292
Paul E Miller • * • H • PSW • 66290 Estrella Ave 92240-4526 PO Box 669 Dsrt Hot Spgs CA 92240-0669 • dhs.christ@lutheran.com

**DUBLIN—*ST PHILIP*** (925)828-2117
Sergei S Koberg • WS 815 11; SS 945; BC 10 • H • EC/EL • CNH • 8850 Davona Dr Dublin CA 94568-1132 • FAX(925)829-6672

**EL CAJON—*CHRIST KING*** (619)448-5515
Wallace J Kimari • H • EC/HS • EN • 92020 9225 Carlton Hills Blvd #30 Santee CA 92071 • FAX(619)448-4497

***FIRST*** (619)444-7444
Scott F Rische • H • EC/HS • EN • 867 S Lincoln Ave El Cajon CA 92020-6424 • FAX(619)444-9892 • flc@ecflc.org

**EL CENTRO—*GRACE*** (760)352-5715
Lewis M Busch • WS 9; SS 1015; BC 1015 • H • EL • PSW • 768 W Holt Ave El Centro CA 92243-3228 • FAX(760)352-5389 • gracelutheranec@juno.com

**EL CERRITO—*GRACE*** (510)525-9004
N V Olson • WS 10; SS 10; BC 9 • H • CNH • 15 Santa Fe Ave El Cerrito CA 94530-4152 • FAX(510)525-9087 • revnvern@aol.com

**EL MONTE—*FIRST*** (626)448-0767
Kenneth D Christensen • H • EC/HS • PSW • 4900 Kings Row El Monte CA 91731-1483

***FIRST CHINESE****
Vacant • PSW • C/O First Lutheran Church 4900 Kings Row El Monte CA 91731-1483

**EL SEGUNDO—*ST JOHN*** (310)615-1072
Timothy W Schepman • WS 10 • H • EC • PSW • 1611 E Sycamore Ave El Segundo CA 90245-3331 • FAX(310)615-0640 • sjlcesca@aol.com

**EL TORO—*ABIDING SAVIOR***
See Lake Forest

**ELK GROVE—*LIGHT OF VALLEY**** (916)686-2728
Vacant • WS 10; SS 1115;* • CNH • 8990 Grove St Elk Grove CA 95624-2316

**ENCINITAS—*ST MARK*** (760)753-4776
Ralph H Buchhorn • H • PSW • 300 Santa Fe Dr Encinitas CA 92024-5131

**ESCONDIDO—*COMMUNITY*** (760)739-1650
William R Vogelsang • Kevin R Kersten DCE Chris D Deknatel DCE • H • EC • PSW • 3575 E Valley Pkwy Escondido CA 92027-5227 • FAX(760)739-8655

***GLORIA DEI*** (760)743-2478
Michael A L Eckelkamp • WS 8; SS 925; BC 925 • H • EC • PSW • 1087 W Country Club Ln Escondido CA 92026-1101 • FAX(760)746-4463 • info@gloriadeilc.com

***GRACE*** (760)745-0831
James P Young James P Miller • WS 8 11; SS 930; BC 11 • H • EC/EL • PSW • 643 W 13th Ave Escondido CA 92025-5620 • FAX(760)745-1612 • pastorjimy@home.com

**EUREKA—*TRINITY*** (707)442-4939
Thomas K Slater • H • CNH • 1008 Henderson St 1032 Henderson St Eureka CA 95501-4503 • FAX(707)442-4226 • trinuwaz@humboldt1.com

**EXETER—*TRINITY*** (559)592-4070
Michael S Franckowiak • WS 9; SS 1030; BC 1030 • H • EC • CNH • 420 Sequoia Dr Exeter CA 93221-1232

**FAIR OAKS—*FAITH*** (916)961-4252
Vacant • WS 815; SS 945 • H • EC/EL/HS • CNH • 4000 San Juan Ave Fair Oaks CA 95628-6829 • FAX(916)961-2604

**FAIRFIELD—*TRINITY*** (707)425-2944
Martin E Bergstrom • SS 845; BC 845 • H • EC/EL • CNH • 2075 Dover Ave Fairfield CA 94533-2346 • FAX(707)435-1122 • church@trinitylutheranchurch.net

**FALLBROOK—*ZION*** (760)728-8288
Mark W Demel • Steven H Mattoon DCE • WS 8; SS 915; BC 915 • H • EC/EL • PSW • 1405 E Fallbrook St Fallbrook CA 92028-2427 • FAX(760)451-0273 • zion1405@aol.com

**FERNDALE—*ST MARK*** (707)786-9353
L A Hubbard • WS 10; SS 9; BC UNKNOWN • H • CNH • 795 Berding St 95536 PO Box 1016 Ferndale CA 95536-1016 • stmarks@humboldtl.com

**FOLSOM—*MOUNT OLIVE*** (916)985-2984
Russell I Hess • Hilary Musselman DCE • WS 8; SS 915; BC 915 • H • EC/HS • CNH • 320 Montrose Dr Folsom CA 95630-2720 • FAX(916)985-2998

**FONTANA—*FIRST*** (909)823-3457
Donald G Dannenberg Harold A Boeche • WS 9 • H • EC/EL • PSW • 9315 Citrus Ave Fontana CA 92335-5563 • FAX(909)823-3499

**FORTUNA—*HOPE*** (707)725-4705
Vacant • H • CNH • 1480 Ross Hill Rd Fortuna CA 95540-3433

**FREMONT—*MEMORIAL-DEAF*** (510)656-0694
Roy L Dahmann • H • CNH • 874 Washington Blvd Fremont CA 94539-5222

***OUR SAVIOR*** (510)657-3191
Gregory S Stringer • H • EC • CNH • 858 Washington Blvd Fremont CA 94539-5222 • FAX(510)657-3174 • osl.fremont@juno.com

***PRINCE PEACE*** (510)793-3366
Thomas J Zelt • Gloria J Zupfer DEAC • WS 8 1015 1030; SS 915; BC 915 • H • EL • CNH • 38451 Fremont Blvd Fremont CA 94536-6030 • FAX(510)793-6993

**FRESNO—*EMMANUEL*** (559)485-5780
Bruce Neff • WS 9; SS 1030; BC 1030;* • H • CNH • 2822 E Floradora Ave Fresno CA 93703-3906 • FAX(559)485-5784

***PEACE*** (559)222-2320
Gregory S Young • WS 8 1030; SS 915; BC 915 • H • CNH • 4672 N Cedar Ave Fresno CA 93726-1001

***REDEEMER*** (209)439-8500
Vacant • H • CNH • 1084 W Bullard Ave Fresno CA 93711-2410

**FULLERTON—*OUR SAVIOR*** (714)525-5584
Timothy B Muller • H • PSW • 1521 W Orangethorpe Ave Fullerton CA 92833-4533

***ST STEPHEN*** (714)871-1711
Vacant • H • EC • PSW • 2311 E Chapman Ave Fullerton CA 92831-4203 • FAX(714)871-3132

***TRUE LOVE KOREAN*** (714)992-5008
Man S Kang(DM) • WS 930;* • PSW • 1521 W Orangethorpe Ave Fullerton CA 92833-4533 • FAX(714)827-9424

**GARDEN GROVE—*ST PAUL*** (714)537-4243
Vacant • H • EC/EL/HS • PSW • 13082 Bowen St Garden Grove CA 92843-1001 • FAX(714)741-8353

***TRUE LOVE KOREAN**** (714)537-4244
Vacant • H • PSW • 13082 Bowen St Garden Grove CA 92843-1001

***VIETNAMESE*** (714)537-4245
Kinh (Kenneth) T Vu • HS • PSW • 13082 Bowen St Garden Grove CA 92843-1001

**GEORGETOWN—*THE DIVIDE*** (530)333-2633
John A Westhafer • * • CNH • 6417 Main St 95634 PO Box 1293 Georgetown CA 95634-1293 • FAX(530)333-2633

**GILROY—*GOOD SHEPHERD*** (408)842-2713
Ronald E Koch • WS 930; SS 11; BC 11 • H • EC • CNH • 1735 Hecker Pass Rd Gilroy CA 95020-8837 • goodshep@hotcity.com

**GLENDALE—*ZION*** (818)243-3119
John F Hodde • WS 10; SS 1020; BC 845;* • H • EC/EL/HS • PSW • 301 N Isabel St Glendale CA 91206-3626 • FAX(818)243-9640 • zlcs@zionglendale.org

***ZION KOREAN**** (818)244-9315
Paul Y Park(DM) • PSW • 301 N Isabel St Glendale CA 91206-3626

**GLENDORA—*HOPE*** (626)335-5315
Paul C Terhune • Shelli Haynes DCE • WS 745; SS 9; BC 9 • H • EC/EL/HS • PSW • 1041 E Foothill Blvd Glendora CA 91741-3673 • FAX(626)852-0836 • lutherans@hopeglendora.org

**GOLETA—*GOOD SHEPHERD*** (805)967-1416
James P Johnson James A Schmidt • WS 8 1015; SS 910; BC 910;* • H • EC • PSW • 380 N Fairview Ave Goleta CA 93117-2207 • FAX(805)967-1416 • gslc2@juno.com

**GRANADA HILLS—*OUR SAVIOR FIRST*** (818)363-9505
James H Hahn • John H Mertes DCE • WS 830 11; SS 945; BC 10;* • H • EC/EL/HS • PSW • 16603 San Fernando Mission Granada Hills CA 91344-4223 • FAX(818)831-9222

**GRASS VALLEY—*GRACE*** (530)273-7043
Kurt E Degner • H • CNH • 1979 Ridge Rd 95945 PO Box 924 Grass Valley CA 95945-0924 • FAX(530)273-4206

**GREENVILLE—*FIRST*** (916)258-2347
Vernon R Kettner • H • CNH • Main And Bush 95947 PO Box 598 Greenville CA 95947-0598

**GRIDLEY—*GRACE*** (530)846-4736
Benseslado C Padilla • WS 8 1045; SS 930; BC 930;* • CNH • 585 Magnolia St Gridley CA 95948-2524 • GraceLutheran@manznet.com

**HACIENDA HEIGHTS—*HOLY TRINITY*** (626)333-9017
William M Cwirla • H • EC • PSW • 15710 Newton St Hacienda Heights CA 91745-4143 • FAX(626)333-6468 • wcwirla@earthlink.net

**HANFORD—*FIRST*** (559)582-2463
Michael N Vernava • WS 10; SS 845;* • EC • CNH • 9075 12th Ave Hanford CA 93230-2407

**HARBOR CITY—*ST MATTHEW*** (310)326-1958
Howard C Barth • WS 830 11; BC 10;* • H • PSW • 25000 Normandie Ave Harbor City CA 90710-2406

**HAYWARD—*GOOD SHEPHERD*** (510)782-0872
Gary W Mohr • WS 9;* • H • CNH • 166 W Harder Rd Hayward CA 94544-2742 • FAX(510)781-0317 • goodshepherdluth@juno.com

***GRACE*** (510)581-6620
Ricky L Adams • H • CNH • 1836 B St Hayward CA 94541-3140

**HEALDSBURG—*GOOD SHEPHERD*** (707)433-3835
James R Bothwell • Brady D Gurganious DCE • H • CNH • 1402 University St Healdsburg CA 95448-3019 • FAX(707)433-3835 • goodshepherd@metro.net

**HEMET—*PRINCE PEACE*** (909)925-6121
James A Hallmann Dale L Lashley • WS 8 1045; SS 930; BC 930 • H • PSW • 701 N Sanderson Ave Hemet CA 92545-1523 • FAX(909)766-6779 • peej@lasercom.net

***ST JOHN*** (909)925-7756
William A Ferguson • WS 815; SS 930 • H • EC/EL • PSW • 26410 Columbia St Hemet CA 92544-6248 • FAX(909)925-6136 • jesus@koan.com

**HESPERIA—*FAITH*** (760)244-5943
Ronald S Luedemann • WS 8 1030; SS 915; BC 925 • H • PSW • 9600 7th Ave Hesperia CA 92345-3462 • FAX(760)244-5943

**HIGHLAND—*MESSIAH*** (909)862-2923
John P Juedes • H • PSW • 7070 Palm Ave Highland CA 92346-3259 • messiah7@empirenet.com

**HOLLYWOOD—*BETHANY*** (323)662-4176
Dennis R Gano • EL • PSW • 90052 4975 W Sunset Blvd Los Angeles CA 90027-5813

**HOLTVILLE—*ST PAUL*** (760)356-4315
Allen R Deinert • WS 9; SS 1015; BC 1030 • H • PSW • 562 Chestnut Ave 92250-1408 548 Chestnut Ave Holtville CA 92250 • FAX(760)356-4315 • deinert@aol.com

**HUNTINGTON BEACH—*FAITH*** (714)962-5571
Timothy O Krieger • David L Rueter DCE • WS 830; SS 955;* • H • EC • PSW • 8200 Ellis Ave Huntington Beach CA 92646-1839 • FAX(714)378-4537 • tkrieger@faithhb.org

***REDEEMER*** (714)846-6330
William L Duerr Daniel N Harmelink • WS 8 11 930; SS 930; BC 930;* • H • EC • PSW • 16351 Springdale St Huntington Beach CA 92649-2773 • FAX(714)840-2679 • missio@earthlink.net

**IMPERIAL BEACH—*ST JAMES*** (619)424-6166
Bruce E Jeske • WS 8 11 3 6; SS 930; BC 930;* • H • EC/HS • PSW • 866 Imperial Beach Blvd Imperial Beach CA 91932-2703 • FAX(619)424-5129 • sjameslutheranchurch@home.com

**INDIO—*PRIMERA IGLESIA***
Vacant • PSW • PO Box 1743 Indio CA 91911-3699

***TRINITY*** (760)347-3971
Robert E Smith • * • H • EC • PSW • 81 500 Miles Ave 92201 PO Box W Indio CA 92202-2522 • revs455@aol.com

**INGLEWOOD—*CONCORDIA*** (323)672-8447
Vacant • WS 930; SS 11; BC 11 • H • HS • PSW • 3600 W Imperial Hwy Inglewood CA 90303-2714 • shenkel777@aol.com

***FAITH*** (323)750-3552
Dietrich N Schleef • WS 9 • H • HS • PSW • 3320 W 85th St 90305-1912 8517 S 11th Ave Inglewood CA 90305-1946 • FAX(323)750-4136 • faith-ing@luther95.net

***GOOD SHEPHERD*** (310)671-7644
Paul L Graff • WS 10; SS 845; BC 845 • H • EC/EL/HS • PSW • 901 Maple St Inglewood CA 90301-3823 • FAX(310)673-7488 • gslc1@flash.net

**IRVINE—*SHEPHERD PEACE*** (949)786-3326
Vacant • Barbara M Manske DEAC • H • EC • PSW • 18182 Culver Dr Irvine CA 92612-2702 • FAX(949)786-7186 • np0622@irvinecalutherlcms.com

**LA CRESCENTA—*GETHSEMANE*** (818)248-3738
Charles W Pearson Jr. • H • EL/HS • PSW • 2723 Orange Ave La Crescenta CA 91214-2124 • FAX(818)248-3487 • cpearl@aol.com

**LA JOLLA—*UNIVERSITY*** (858)453-0561
Brian W Hooper • H • PSW • 9595 La Jolla Shores Dr La Jolla CA 92037-1140 • FAX(858)453-9932

**LA MESA—*CHRIST*** (619)462-5211
Richard D Burkey • Cheri L Selander DCE • WS 8 1030 1045; SS 920; BC 930;* • H • EC/EL/HS • PSW • 7929 La Mesa Blvd La Mesa CA 91941-5029 • FAX(619)462-5275

**LA MIRADA—*MOUNT OLIVE*** (562)941-4610
Vacant • WS 945; BC 830 • H • PSW • 13518 Biola Ave La Mirada CA 90638-2955

**LA PUENTE—*HOLY CROSS*** (818)917-6033
Vacant • H • PSW • 14921 Amar Rd La Puente CA 91744-1961

**LAGUNA BEACH—*ST PAUL*** (949)494-7998
Alfonso O Espinosa • WS 8 1030; SS 930; BC 930;* • H • PSW • 1190 Morningside Dr Laguna Beach CA 92651-3038 • FAX(949)494-5961 • chirhoae@aol.com

**LAKE ARROWHEAD—*MOUNT*** (909)337-1412
Randall A Buecheler • Robert W Scholz DCE • H • EC • PSW • 27415 School Rd 92352 PO Box 250 Lake Arrowhead CA 92352-0250 • FAX(909)337-2003 • randybuecheler@mtcalvarylutheranchurch.com

**LAKE ELSINORE—*FIRST*** (909)674-2757
Kevin L Kolander • WS 1030; SS 9;* • H • PSW • 600 W Sumner Lake Elsinore CA 92530 • firstluth@kelp.net

**LAKE FOREST—*ABIDING SAVIOR*** (949)830-1460
Thomas J Rogers Timothy J Marshall • WS 745 1015 1130; SS 9; BC 9;* • H • EC/EL/HS • PSW • 23262 El Toro Rd Lake Forest CA 92630-4805 • FAX(949)830-6783 • abidingsavior@hotmail.com

**LAKE ISABELLA—*SHEPHERD HILLS*** (760)379-2343
Vacant • WS 1030; SS 9; BC 9 • H • CNH • 377 Hwy 155 PO Box S Lake Isabella CA 93240-8944

**LAKE VIEW TERRACE—*PEACE*** (213)899-3950
Jon Imme(DM) • PSW • 91392 11690 Fenton Ave Lake View Ter CA 91342-7180

**LAKESIDE—*MORNING STAR*** (619)443-6032
Arthur F Maynard • H • HS • EN • 12821 Ha Hana Rd Lakeside CA 92040-5061

**LANCASTER—*GRACE*** (661)948-1018
Vacant • Heidi A Cross DCE • H • EC/EL • PSW • 856 W Newgrove St Lancaster CA 93534-3010 • FAX(661)948-2731

**LAYTONVILLE—*SHEP OF VALLEY*** (707)984-8805
Carvel V Plitt(EM) • WS 10;* • H • CNH • Foster Rd 95454 PO Box 34 Laytonville CA 95454-0034

**LINDSAY—*MOUNT OLIVE*** (209)562-4879
John D Baumgartner • H • CNH • 1044 Parkside Ave Lindsay CA 93247-1501 • jbaumj@ocsnet.net

**LIVERMORE—*OUR SAVIOR*** (925)447-1246
Theodore E Hartman • Steven L Christopher DCE • WS 8 1045 930; SS 930; BC 930 • H • EC/EL • CNH • 3820 East Ave 94550-4829 1385 S Livermore Ave Livermore CA 94550-9532 • FAX(925)447-0201 • OSLC@pacbell.net

**LODI—*REDEEMER*** (209)368-2288
Vacant • WS 9; SS 1030; BC 1030 • H • CNH • 1845 S Ham Ln Lodi CA 95242-4579 • FAX(209)368-2288 • pastrdon@jps.net

***ST PETER*** (209)333-2223
Paul S Zimmermann • WS 8 1045; SS 930; BC 930 • H • EL • CNH • 2400 Oxford Way Lodi CA 95242-2854 • FAX(209)333-2224 • stpete@jps.net

**LOMITA—*ARK NOAH KOREAN****
See Culver City

**LOMPOC—*BETHANY*** (805)736-8615
Marvin D Moon • H • CNH • 135 S E St Lompoc CA 93436-6810

**LONG BEACH—*BETHANY*** (562)421-4711
John M Simon • WS 8 1045; SS 930; BC 930;* • H • EL • PSW • 4644 Clark Ave Long Beach CA 90808-1203 • FAX(562)429-1693

***FIRST*** (562)437-8532
Ronald J Kusel • WS 830 11; SS 10; BC 10 • H • EC • PSW • 905 Atlantic Ave 90813-4514 946 Linden Ave Long Beach CA 90813-4519 • FAX(562)437-5194 • firstlutheran@juno.com

***FIRST CAMBODIAN**** (562)437-8532
Chandara A Lee(#) • PSW • 905 Atlantic Ave 90813-4514 946 Linden Ave Long Beach CA 90813-4519 • FAX(562)437-5194

***GRACE*** (562)427-1706
Vacant • H • EC • PSW • 245 W Wardlow Rd Long Beach CA 90807-4428

***ST JOHN*** (323)423-3547
Dino F Tumbuan • PSW • 6698 Orange Ave Long Beach CA 90805-1537

***ST PAUL*** (562)596-4409
Brandon S Jones • WS 9 7; SS 1030; BC 1030;* • H • PSW • 2283 Palo Verde Ave Long Beach CA 90815-2362

**LOS ANGELES—*ARK NOAH KOREAN****
See Culver City

***ARK OF NOAH***
Vacant • PSW • 3735 Hughes Ave Los Angeles CA 90034-5103

***BRAZILIAN**** (213)732-4444
Dong J Kim(DM) • H • PSW • 987 S Gramercy Pl Los Angeles CA 90019-2199

***CHRIST*** (323)292-2344
Vacant • H • PSW • 1966 Concordia Walk Los Angeles CA 90062-2505 • padreviejo@aol.com

***EAGLE ROCK*** (323)255-4622
George E Milner Jr. • WS 11 • EN • 5032 N Maywood Ave Los Angeles CA 90041-2054 • FAX(323)255-8947 • gnedmilner@cs.com

***FAITH*** (323)755-2541
Allan P Baumgartel(DM) • H • PSW • PO Box 73658 Los Angeles CA 90003

***FIRST*** (310)838-6076
R J Perling • H • PSW • 3735 Hughes Ave Los Angeles CA 90034-5103 • 74467.1573@compuserv.com

***GRACE*** (323)234-9722
Vacant • H • PSW • 936 W Vernon Ave Los Angeles CA 90037-3039

***HIGHLAND PARK*** (323)255-0309
Nicholas D Wirtz • WS 9 1115; BC 1015 • H • EN • 6310 Aldama St Los Angeles CA 90042 • FAX(323)258-3562 • RevNWirtz@CS.com

***HOPE MEMORIAL*** (213)731-1721
Vacant • H • PSW • 3401 Somerset Dr Los Angeles CA 90016-4805

***LA SANTA CRUZ*** (323)269-7989
Jesus Martinez(#) • H • PSW • 2747 Whittier Blvd 90023-1469 PO Box 23570 Los Angeles CA 90023

***OUR SAVIOR*** (310)670-7272
Vacant • H • PSW • 90052 6705 W 77th St Westchester CA 90045-1101 • FAX(310)649-5440 • oursav@netzero.net

***PILGRIM DEAF*** (213)389-9940
Brian K Smith • H • PSW • 1233 S Vermont Ave Los Angeles CA 90006-2714 • brian.smith@deaftek.sprint.com

***ST PAUL*** (323)731-8384
Glenn A Lucas • WS 11; SS 930; BC 930 • H • EC • PSW • 3901 W Adams Blvd Los Angeles CA 90018-1756 • FAX(323)731-8372 • pastorg@pacificnet.net

***TRINITY CENTRAL*** (323)732-4444
Young-Hwan Hong • H • PSW • 987 S Gramercy Pl Los Angeles CA 90019-2155 • FAX(323)732-4444

***UNIV CHAPEL*** (310)208-4579
Timothy L Seals • H • PSW • 10915 Strathmore Dr Los Angeles CA 90024-2411

***YOUNG KWANG**** (213)387-3499
Kwang Man Lee(DM) Soo M Lee(DM) • PSW • 1233 S Vermont Ave Los Angeles CA 90006-2714

**LOS GATOS—*HOLY CROSS*** (408)356-3525
Paul G Hoffmann Michael R Abram • Douglas Weinrich DCE • H • EC • CNH • 15885 Los Gatos Almaden Rd Los Gatos CA 95032-3803 • FAX(408)358-4982 • holycross@holycrosslosgatos.org

**LUCERNE—*FIRST*** (707)274-5572
David R Rose • WS 11; SS 945; BC 945 • H • CNH • 3863 Country Club Dr PO Box 458 Lucerne CA 95458-0458 • drrose@jps.net

**MAMMOTH LAKES—*MAMMOTH*** (760)934-4051
Steven A Barckholtz • WS 10; SS 9; BC 9 • EC • PSW • 379 Old Mammoth Rd 93546 PO Box 7218 Mammoth Lakes CA 93546-7218 • mllutheran@qnet.com

**MANHATTAN BEACH—*FIRST*** (310)545-5653
Steven C Carlson • Scott A Corum DCE • WS 9; SS 1030; BC 1030 • H • EC • PSW • 1100 N Poinsettia Ave Manhattan Beach CA 90266-4918 • FAX(310)546-2318 • firstluth@earthlink.net

**MARTINEZ—*CHRIST*** (925)228-5120
Robert D Seible • H • CNH • 2370 Harbor View Dr Martinez CA 94553-3313

**MAYWOOD—*PALABRA DE DIOS**** (323)560-0089
Vacant • EC • PSW • 4421 E 61st St Maywood CA 90270

**MENIFEE—*GOOD SHEPHERD*** (909)672-6675
Scott W Lawson • WS 830 1045; SS 945; BC 945 • H • EC • PSW • 26800 Newport Rd Menifee CA 92584-9218 • FAX(909)672-6680 • gslcsc@yahoo.com

**MENLO PARK—*BETHANY*** (650)854-5897
Jonathan J Coyne • WS 930 2; SS 945; BC 830 • H • EC • CNH • 1095 Cloud Ave Menlo Park CA 94025-6203 • FAX(650)854-5910 • bethany1@flash.net

**MERCED—*ST PAUL*** (209)383-3301
Clarence H Eisberg • H • EC/EL • CNH • 2916 N Mc Kee Rd Merced CA 95340-2721 • FAX(209)383-3642 • stpaul-merced@cyberlynk.com

**MILL VALLEY—*PEACE*** (415)388-2065
David E Wobrock • WS 930; SS 11;* • H • CNH • 205 Tennessee Valley Rd Mill Valley CA 94941-3601 • FAX(415)381-7290

**MILPITAS—*MOUNT OLIVE*** (408)262-0506
Michael E Gibson • H • CNH • 1989 E Calaveras Blvd Milpitas CA 95035-6041 • FAX(408)262-9359 • mt-olive.org

**MISSION HILLS—*CHAPEL CROSS*** (818)892-8490
Vacant • WS 9 • H • EC/EL/HS • EN • 10000 Sepulveda Blvd Mission Hills CA 91345-2918 • cotl@juno.co

**MODESTO—*GRACE*** (209)522-8890
John H Mueller • Janice L Lee DCE • WS 815 • H • EC/EL • CNH • 617 W Orangeburg Ave Modesto CA 95350-4246 • FAX(209)529-7721 • ltietmeyer@aol.com

**MONROVIA—*FIRST*** (626)357-3543
Larry L Hintz • Steven R Hinman DCE • WS 830 10 6; SS 10 • H • EC/EL/HS • PSW • 1323 S Magnolia Ave Monrovia CA 91016-4021 • FAX(626)357-8296

**MONTCLAIR—*TRINITY*** (909)626-6552
Martin L Schroeder • WS 9; SS 1020;* • H • PSW • 91762-3845 5080 Kingsley St Montclair CA 91763-3845 • FAX(909)626-6552

**MONTEBELLO—*ST JOHN*** (323)728-8410
Douglas D Jones • WS 1030 9; SS 930; BC 9 • H • EC/EL/HS • PSW • 433 N 18th St Montebello CA 90640-3940 • FAX(323)728-3914 • stjohn@kaiwan.com

**MONTEREY—*BETHLEHEM*** (831)373-1523
Arnold G Steinbeck • WS 8 1030; SS 915; BC 915 • H • CNH • 800 Cass St Monterey CA 93940-2905 • FAX(831)373-1563 • steinarn@aol.com

**MOORPARK—*FAITH*** (805)532-1049
James H Nelesen • WS 930; SS 930; BC 815 • H • PSW • 123 Park Ln 93021 PO Box 377 Moorpark CA 93020-0377 • FAX(805)532-1049

**MORENO VALLEY—*GRACE KOREAN**** (909)924-4688
Du P Lee(DM) • H • PSW • 11650 Perris Blvd Moreno Valley CA 92557-6536

***SHEP OF VALLEY*** (909)924-4688
David E Schilling Ronald A Kraft • H • EC/EL • PSW • 11650 Perris Blvd Moreno Valley CA 92557-6536 • FAX(909)243-1834 • svlc@juno.com

**MOUNT SHASTA—*CHRIST*** (530)926-6395
Vacant • H • CNH • 1124 Pine Grove Dr Mount Shasta CA 96067-9712

**MOUNTAIN VIEW—*ST PAUL*** (650)967-0666
Donald D Schneider • WS 830 1030;* • H • EC • CNH • 1075 El Monte Ave Mountain View CA 94040-2320 • FAX(650)967-0667 • pastor@st-paul.org

**NAPA—*FAITH*** (707)224-4214
Stanley R Peterson • H • CNH • 2790 Kilburn Ave Napa CA 94558-5623

***ST JOHN*** (707)255-0119
Michael A Schmid • Stephen T Dierker DCE • WS 8 1045; SS 930; BC 930 • H • EC/EL • CNH • 3521 Linda Vista Ave Napa CA 94558-2703 • FAX(707)255-3041 • stjohns@fcs.net

**NEEDLES—*GRACE*** (760)326-3128
Vacant • SS 845; BC 845 • H • PSW • 1605 Washington St Needles CA 92363-2841 • DavidDeP@aol.com

**NEWBURY PARK—*CHRIST KING*** (805)498-2217
Vacant • Bonnie Hicks DCE • WS 8; SS 910; BC 910 • H • EC • PSW • 3947 Kimber Dr Newbury Park CA 91320-4829 • FAX(805)498-9798

**NEWMAN—*ST JAMES*** (209)862-3438
Robert L Junkin • H • CNH • 1102 P St 95360-1230 PO Box 816 Newman CA 95360-0816

**NORTH HIGHLANDS—*ZION*** (916)332-4001
William F Ellis Jr. • Richard C Barklage DCE • WS 8 11; SS 930; BC 930 • H • HS • CNH • 3644 Bolivar Ave North Highlands CA 95660-4350 • FAX(916)332-4030 • chlnejen@aol.com

**NORWALK—*KOREAN AMERICAN**** (562)651-1086
Vacant • PSW • 14134 Clarkdale Ave Norwalk CA 90650

***ST PAUL*** (562)864-5654
Vacant • WS 9; SS 1015; BC 1015 • H • EC • PSW • 11909 Rosecrans Ave 90650-4117 14134 Clarkdale Ave Norwalk CA 90650-4104 • FAX(562)864-5654 • cspucci@hotmail.com

***TRUE LOVE KOREAN***
See Fullerton

**OAKDALE—*ST JOHN***
See Valley Home

***ST LUKE*** (209)847-0607
C E Schack • H • CNH • 120 West Ave Oakdale CA 95361-3840

**OAKLAND—*FIRST TRINITY*** (510)534-1630
Henry H S Lai • WS 1030; SS 915; BC 915 • CNH • 1431 17th Ave Oakland CA 94606-4546

***MEMORIAL-DEAF***
See Fremont

***OUR REDEEMER*** (510)632-4841
Monte W Gusewelle • WS 1030; SS 915; BC 930 • H • CNH • 6038 Brann St Oakland CA 94605-1544

***PILGRIM*** (510)531-3715
Paul V Holt • H • EC • CNH • 3900 35th Ave Oakland CA 94619-1435 • llholt@concentric.net

**OCEANSIDE—*IMMANUEL*** (760)433-2770
Duane P Behnken • H • EC/HS • PSW • 1900 S Nevada St Oceanside CA 92054-6418 • FAX(760)433-1147

***SHEP OF VALLEY*** (760)433-9250
Allen Kolkman • WS 8 1030 915; SS 915; BC 915 • H • EL • PSW • 4510 N River Rd Oceanside CA 92057-5116 • FAX(760)433-9757 • lcmspastor@aol.com

**OJAI—*OUR REDEEMER*** (805)646-2064
Richard E Malmstrom • H • PSW • 1290 Grand Ave 93023 PO Box 1450 Ojai CA 93024-1450

**ONTARIO—*REDEEMER*** (909)986-2615
Norwood M Blanke Elmer W Matthias(EM) • Dorothy L Krans DEAC • WS 630;* • H • EC/EL/HS • PSW • 920 W 6th St Ontario CA 91762-1299 • FAX(909)986-0757 • redeemeron@aol.com

**ORANGE—*IGL CRISTO REY**** (714)633-8891
Johnny J Lopez(DM) • H • PSW • 802 E Chapman Ave 92866-1623 137 S Pine St Orange CA 92866-1600 • FAX(714)633-8269 • pastorjohnny@juno.com

***IMMANUEL*** (714)538-2373
Robert A Dargatz • WS 8 1045; SS 930; BC 930 • H • EC/EL/HS • PSW • 802 E Chapman Ave Orange CA 92866-1623 • FAX(714)538-7952 • immanuel.lutheran@juno.com

***ST JOHN*** (714)288-4400
Timothy M Klinkenberg Phillip L Sipes • Max J Murphy DCE • H • EC/EL/HS • PSW • 185 S Center St 92866-1527 154 S Shaffer St Orange CA 92866-1609 • FAX(714)288-4411

***ST PAUL*** (714)637-2640
Ronald L Martin Norman N Franzen Mark L Manning • Brian C Inouye DCE • H • EC/EL/HS • PSW • 1250 E Heim Ave Orange CA 92865-2920 • FAX(714)637-1963

***TAIWANESE****
Vacant • PSW • 6500 E Santiago Canyon Rd Orange CA 92869-1533

**ORANGE PARK ACRES—*SALEM*** (714)633-2366
Paul W Meyer Timothy A Blau • H • EC/EL • PSW • UKNWN 6500 E Santiago Canyon Rd Orange CA 92869-1533 • FAX(714)633-6937 • salemcas@pacbell.net

**ORANGEVALE—*GRACE*** (916)988-2471
Vacant • WS 10; SS 9; BC 9 • CNH • 5948 Pecan Ave 95662-4624 PO Box 1553 Orangevale CA 95662-1553 • FAX(916)988-2471 • grace@safenetonline.com

**OROVILLE—*CALVARY*** (530)533-5017
Vacant • Joan M Ross • WS 10; SS 9; BC 9 • H • EC • CNH • Foothill Blvd And Edgewood Dr 95966 10 Concordia Ln Oroville CA 95966-6300 • FAX(530)533-5203 • celc@2xtreme.net

**OXNARD—*CENTRO CRISTIANO*** (805)240-0074
Dennis N Bradshaw(DM) • WS 11;* • H • PSW • 905 Redwood St Oxnard CA 93033-5009

***ST JOHN*** (805)983-0330
Mark E Beyer Kenneth S Hahn • H • EL • PSW • 1500 N C St Oxnard CA 93030-3502 • FAX(805)983-2171 • khahn@stjohnspvt.k12.ca.us

**PACIFIC PALISADES—*PALISADES*** (310)459-2358
Vacant • WS 9 1115; SS 1020 • H • EC • PSW • 15905 Sunset Blvd Pacific Palisades CA 90272-3407 • FAX(310)230-9488 • pallu@earthlink.net

**PACIFICA—*OUR SAVIOR*** (650)359-1550
Daniel L Kistler • WS 10; SS 9; BC 845 • H • CNH • 4400 Cabrillo Hwy Pacifica CA 94044

**PALM DESERT—*PEACE/DESERT*** (760)776-7100
Vacant • H • EN • 74200 Country Club Dr Palm Desert CA 92260-1660

**PALM SPRINGS—*OUR SAVIOR*** (760)327-5611
Michael J Coppersmith • Christina A Keller DCE • WS 8;* • H • PSW • 1020 E Ramon Rd Palm Springs CA 92264-7702 • FAX(760)322-6531

**PALMDALE—*FIRST*** (661)947-6230
Wayne B Anderson • H • PSW • 38343 15th St E Palmdale CA 93550-4836 • FAX(661947-6230

**PALO ALTO—*TRINITY*** (650)853-1295
Stewart D Crown • WS 815 11; SS 945; BC 945 • H • CNH • 1295 Middlefield Rd Palo Alto CA 94301-3347 • FAX(650)328-1982 • pastorcrown@juno.com

**PANORAMA CITY—*EL REDENTOR*** (818)891-1038
Alfonso Conrado • H • PSW • 14445 Terra Bella St Panorama City CA 91402-1498

**PARADISE—*OUR SAVIOR*** (530)877-7321
Mark C Stenbeck • H • EC • CNH • 6404 Pentz Rd Paradise CA 95969-3626 • FAX(530)877-4447 • mstenbeck@aol.com

**PASADENA—*FAITH*** (626)351-5413
Barry C Foerster • WS 1030; SS 915; BC 915 • H • EC • PSW • 835 Hastings Ranch Dr Pasadena CA 91107-2245 • FAX(626)351-5414

***FIRST*** (626)793-1139
Christopher G Schaar • WS 10; SS 845; BC 9;* • H • PSW • 808 N Los Robles Ave Pasadena CA 91104-4317 • FAX(626)793-6642 • firstpasa@aol.com

***MOUNT OLIVE*** (626)794-2294
Jeffrey P Horn • H • PSW • 1118 N Allen Ave Pasadena CA 91104-3206 • refjeffhorn@juno.com

**PASO ROBLES—*TRINITY*** (805)238-3702
Daniel Rowe • WS 8 1030; SS 915; BC 915 • H • EC/EL • CNH • 940 Creston Rd Paso Robles CA 93446-3002 • FAX(805)238-7501 • churchoffice@tcsn.net

**PERRIS—*REDEEMER*** (909)657-3662
Robert F Rebensal • H • EC/EL • PSW • 555 N Perris Blvd Perris CA 92571-2811 • FAX(909)940-4668

**PETALUMA—*ST JOHN*** (707)762-4466
Larry L Gotfredson • WS 8 1030; SS 915; BC 915 • H • CNH • 455 Mc Near Ave Petaluma CA 94952-5210 • FAX(707)766-6043 • stjohn11@juno.com

**PICO RIVERA—*PEACE*** (562)949-5203
Wilfred W Glade • WS 9; SS 1030; BC 1030 • H • EC • PSW • 9412 Shade Ln Pico Rivera CA 90660-5340 • FAX(562)947-1154 • arrie44@aol.com

**PIEDMONT—*ZION*** (510)530-4213
Joe E Schruhl Waldemar R Vinovskis • H • EL • CNH • 5201 Park Blvd Piedmont CA 94611-3328 • FAX(510)530-2635

**PINE VALLEY—*INTER MOUNTAIN*** (619)473-8604
Arthur F Maynard • WS 1030; SS 915; BC 915 • H • EN • 28870 Oak Ln 91962 PO Box 255 Pine Valley CA 91962-0255

**PINOLE—*OUR SAVIOR*** (510)758-1961
Bill S Chu • WS 1030; SS 915;* • H • CNH • 3110 Avis Way Pinole CA 94564-1830 • oslcms@juno.com

**PITTSBURG—*GRACE*** (510)439-5857
Vacant • H • CNH • 195 Alvarado Ave Pittsburg CA 94565-4862 • FAX(510)439-0563 • gracelutheran@california.com

**PLACERVILLE—*FIRST*** (530)622-3022
Rodney A Hilpert Richard L Riggert • WS 8 930 11; SS 930; BC 930 • H • EC • CNH • 1200 Pinecrest Ct Placerville CA 95667-4728 • FAX(530)622-1326 • flc2@lps.net

**PLEASANT HILL—*FAITH*** (925)685-7353
Thomas G Norris • * • H • CNH • 50 Woodsworth Ln Pleasant Hill CA 94523-3314 • FAX(925)685-2403 • faithlcph@juno.com

**PLEASANTON—*CHRIST*** (510)351-4628
Wm P Grunow • SS 930; BC 930 • H • EN • 148 Ray St Ste G 94566-6649 1334 Devonshire Ave San Leandro CA 94579-1348

**POMONA—*ST PAUL*** (909)623-6368
Joel A Shaltanis • WS 9; SS 1030; BC 1030 • H • HS • PSW • 610 N San Antonio Ave Pomona CA 91767-4908 • stpauls@eee.org

**PORTOLA—*ST LUKE*** (530)832-1805
Emil P Leising(EM) • CNH • 496 W Sierra St Portola CA 96122

**POWAY—*MOUNT OLIVE*** (858)748-3871
Kenneth H Roberts • WS 9;* • H • EC/HS • PSW • 14280 Poway Rd Poway CA 92064-4929 • FAX(858)748-0693 • pastorkenr@juno.com

**QUARTZ HILL—*RESURRECTION*** (661)943-8433
Shawn O Stamm • H • PSW • 42217 55th St W Quartz Hill CA 93536-3669 • FAX(661)722-0166

**RAMONA—*RAMONA*** (760)789-1367
Vacant • WS 9; SS 1030; BC 1030 • H • EC/EL/HS • PSW • 520 16th St Ramona CA 92065-2622 • FAX(760)789-7372

**RANCHO CORDOVA—*CORDOVA*** (916)363-5687
John M Standley • SS 1030;* • H • HS • CNH • 10400 Coloma Rd Rancho Cordova CA 95670-2100 • Rjcorluth@aol.com

**RANCHO CUCAMONGA—*SHEPHERD*** (909)989-6500
Michael K Brewer Jason M Haynes Oswald A Waech(EM) • Jonathan Loesch DCE • WS 745; SS 1015 9; BC 1015 9;* • H • HS • PSW • 6080 Haven Ave Alta Loma CA 91737-3004 • FAX(909)989-4905 • soth@linkline.com

**RANCHO PALOS VERDES—*CHRIST*** (310)831-0848
John C Zeile • WS 8; SS 935; BC 935 • H • EC/EL • PSW • 90731 28850 S Western Ave Rancho Palos Verdes CA 90275-0803 • FAX(310)831-0090

***CHRIST***
See San Pedro

***MOUNT OLIVE*** (310)377-8541
James P Poerschke • WS 10; SS 845; BC 845 • H • EC • PSW • 5975 Armaga Spring Rd Rancho Palos Verdes CA 90275-4801 • FAX(310)377-9903

**RANCHO SANTA MARGAR—*MOUNT*** (949)459-1463
Philip J Beyer(DM) • PSW • 92688 1 Paulownia Rancho St Margarita CA 92688-1328

**RED BLUFF—*ST PAUL*** (530)527-3414
Dallas D Dubke • H • CNH • 455 Jefferson St 96080-3405 PO Box 726 Red Bluff CA 96080-0726

**REDDING—*TRINITY*** (530)221-6686
Stacy D Rollefson • WS 815 11; SS 945; BC 945;* • H • EC • CNH • 2440 Hilltop Dr Redding CA 96002-0506 • FAX(530)221-6695 • trinitylc@juno.com

**REDLANDS—*CHRIST KING*** (909)793-5703
Wiley J Smith • H • EC • PSW • 1505 Ford St Redlands CA 92373-7128

**REDONDO BEACH—*IMMANUEL*** (310)540-4435
Jess M Knauft • John L Hanke DCE • H • EC/HS • PSW • 706 Knob Hill Ave Redondo Beach CA 90277-4345 • FAX(310)316-7732

**REDWOOD CITY—*REDEEMER*** (650)366-5892
Harold S Draeger • WS 8 930 11; SS 930; BC 930 • H • EC/EL • CNH • 468 Grand St Redwood City CA 94062-2062 • FAX(650)366-5898 • redeemer@best.com

**RESEDA—*TRINITY*** (818)342-1633
Robert D Claiborne • * • H • PSW • 18425 Kittridge St Reseda CA 91335-6138 • FAX(707)215-7369 • tlcreseda@juno.com

**RIALTO—*GRACE*** (909)875-3163
Eric V Kaelberer • WS 9; SS 1030; BC 1030 • H • PSW • 539 N Acacia Ave Rialto CA 92376-5242 • FAX(909)875-5232

**RICHMOND—*MOUNT ZION*** (510)233-2299
Mario E Ancira • WS 10; SS 845; BC 9 • H • CNH • 5714 Solano Ave Richmond CA 94805-1535 • FAX(510)215-6233

***TRINITY*** (510)223-8822
Wayne R Brockman • WS 8 10; SS 845; BC 845 • H • CNH • 3301 Morningside Dr Richmond CA 94803-2516 • wrbrockman@earthlink.net

**RIDGECREST—*OUR SAVIOR*** (760)375-7921
Robert A Hoffman • H • EL • PSW • 735 N Fairview St 725 N Fairview St Ridgecrest CA 93555-3516 • FAX(760)375-7921

**RIVERSIDE—*FAITH*** (909)689-2626
Vacant • WS 8 930 11; SS 930; BC 930 • H • PSW • 4785 Jackson St Riverside CA 92503-8011 • FAX(909)689-3829 • CometoFaith@mindspring.com

***GETHSEMANE*** (909)684-6446
Paul M Stark • H • PSW • 891 W Blaine St Riverside CA 92507-3927 • FAX(909)684-6448 • gethsem2@earthlink.net

***IMMANUEL*** (909)682-7613
Lowell L Siebrass Mark A Jurkowski • WS 8 930; SS 930;* • H • EC/EL • PSW • 5545 Alessandro Blvd Riverside CA 92506-3576 • FAX(909)682-9403

**ROCKLIN—*HOLY CROSS*** (916)624-8185
John-Paul Meyer • WS 8 1030; SS 915; BC 915 • H • HS • CNH • 4701 Grove St Rocklin CA 95677-2425 • FAX(916)624-0813 • jpmeyer@pacbell.net

**ROSEMEAD—*ZION*** (818)280-5965
Alfred J Freitag(EM) • H • PSW • 3366 Gladys Ave Rosemead CA 91770-2518

**ROSEVILLE—*ST MATTHEW*** (916)773-5771
John P Gross • WS 830 11; SS 945; BC 945 • H • CNH • 699 Washington Blvd Ste A1 Roseville CA 95678-1567 • stmattrosv@jps.net

**SACRAMENTO—*GREENHAVEN*** (916)428-8449
William H Plath • WS 8 1030; SS 915; BC 915 • H • HS • CNH • 475 Florin Rd Sacramento CA 95831-2097 • FAX(916)428-3213 • glc-lcms@msn.com

***OUR SAVIOR*** (916)451-2855
George J Matranga • WS 9; SS 1045; BC 1045 • H • HS • CNH • 5461 44th St Sacramento CA 95820-5137 • OurSavior@Lanset.com

***PEACE*** (916)927-5934
Mark W Haas • Daniel K Mc Clure DCO • WS 8 930 1045; SS 930; BC 930;* • H • EC/HS • CNH • 924 San Juan Rd Sacramento CA 95834-2211 • FAX(916)927-5418 • plcsacto4u@juno.com

***TOWN & COUNTRY*** (916)481-2542
Vacant • WS 815 11; SS 945; BC 945 • H • EC/EL/HS • CNH • 4049 Marconi Ave Sacramento CA 95821-3940 • FAX(916)481-0648

***TRINITY*** (916)456-8701
Les H Self • WS 9 11; SS 10; BC 10 • H • HS • CNH • 1500 27th St Sacramento CA 95816-6307 • FAX(916)736-2369 • revles@jps.net

**SACRAMENTO/STOCKTON—*VALLEY*** (916)391-3463
Robert C Rowland • H • CNH • 95813 6425 Greenhaven Dr Sacramento CA 95831-1613

**SALINAS—*OUR SAVIOR*** (831)422-6352
James H Sorenson • WS 830 1030; SS 930; BC 930;* • H • EC • CNH • 1230 Luther Way Salinas CA 93901-1725 • FAX(831)422-5320 • lutherancos@redshift.com

**SAN BERNARDINO—*LA SANTISMA*** (909)882-5952
Mark L Mc Kenzie • WS 9 6;* • H • PSW • 2900 N E St San Bernardino CA 92405-3440 • FAX(909)882-5952 • stpmark@aol.com

***TRINITY*** (909)882-2989
Eugene L Fenton • H • PSW • 2900 N E St San Bernardino CA 92405-3440 • FAX(909)882-2989 • nfen2000@juno.com

**SAN DIEGO—*BETHANY*** (619)222-7295
Vacant • SS 915; BC 915;* • H • HS • PSW • Ocean Beach 92199 2051 Sunset Cliffs Blvd San Diego CA 92107-2535 • FAX(619)222-7295 • bethanylutheranob@juno.com

***CHRIST CNRSTNE*** (619)566-1860
Stewart N Reimnitz Chang S Kim(DM) Rodney R Scheer • WS 10; SS 10; BC 9 • H • EC/EL • PSW • Mira Mesa 92126 9028 Westmore Rd San Diego CA 92126-2406 • FAX(619)566-1965

***FAITH*** (619)582-1068
Donald J Brenner • WS 9 • H • HS • PSW • 5310 Orange Ave San Diego CA 92115-6015 • FAX(619)582-0354 • faithlcsd@juno.com

***GRACE*** (619)299-2890
Thomas T Bunnett(EM) • H • EC/EL/HS • PSW • 3993 Park Blvd San Diego CA 92103-3501 • FAX(619)295-4472

***GRACE STREET MISSION*** (619)299-2890
Vacant • * • H • PSW • 3993 Park Blvd San Diego CA 92103-3501

***HOLY CROSS*** (858)273-2886
Daniel C Hauschild • WS 9; SS 9; BC 1030 • H • HS • PSW • 3450 Clairemont Dr San Diego CA 92117-5937

***LIVING WATER*** (858)792-7691
Steven J Duescher • H • EN • Hampton Inn Motel 11920 El Camino Real 92130-1316 PMB 254 3525 Del Mar Heights Rd San Diego CA 92130-2122 • livingwatersd@juno.com

***OUR REDEEMER*** (619)262-0757
Herman W Mitschke • WS 830; SS 945; BC 945 • H • HS • PSW • 1370 Euclid Ave San Diego CA 92105-5424 • FAX(619)262-0403

***PEACE*** (858)268-4688
Rodger J Gredvig • WS 10; SS 845;* • H • HS • PSW • 6749 Tait St San Diego CA 92111-6531 • pgredvig@access1.net

***PRINCE PEACE*** (619)583-1436
Paul L Willweber • H • HS • PSW • 6801 Easton Ct San Diego CA 92120-2909 • FAX(619)583-1436 • willweber3@aol.com

***SHIELD FAITH**** (619)286-6440
George Gunter(DM) • H • PSW • 5310 Orange Ave San Diego CA 92115-6015 • FAX(619)593-7549 • geeogun@worldnet.att.net

***ST PAUL*** (619)272-6363
Richard C Allsing • Steven P Schedler DCE Scott E Jonas DCE • WS 8 940 11; SS 940; BC 940 • H • EC/EL/HS • PSW • 1376 Felspar St San Diego CA 92109-3001 • FAX(619)272-4397

***TRINITY*** (619)262-1089
Vacant • WS 1030; SS 9; BC 9;* • H • EC/EL/HS • PSW • 7210 Lisbon St San Diego CA 92114-3007 • FAX(619)262-8971

**SAN FERNANDO—*FIRST*** (818)361-1638
Vacant • WS 10; SS 9; BC 9 • H • EL • PSW • 777 N Maclay Ave San Fernando CA 91340-2138 • FAX(818)361-5509 • first.lcms.sanfernando@juno.com

**SAN FRANCISCO—*BETHEL*** (415)587-2525
John S Cassidy Jr. • Beverly Lipscomb DEAC • WS 1015;* • H • CNH • 2525 Alemany Blvd San Francisco CA 94112-3610 • FAX(415)585-7320

***CANAAN*** (415)221-0250
Vacant • CNH • 495 9th Ave San Francisco CA 94118

***GRACE*** (415)468-2937
Vacant • H • CNH • 465 Woolsey St San Francisco CA 94134-1962 • FAX(415)468-5399 • glc94134@aol.com

***HOLY SPIRIT*** (415)771-6658
David T Chan • Allan K Tong DCE • WS 930 3; SS 11 930; BC 930 • CNH • 1725 Washington St San Francisco CA 94109-3610 • FAX(415)771-6693

***NEW LIFE CHINESE*** (415)681-5433
Terrence C Chan(DM) • WS 930; SS 11; BC 11 • H • EN • 1608 Noriega St 94122-4254 PO Box 16648 San Francisco CA 94116-0646 • FAX(415)681-3262 • ptcnewlife@aol.com

***SHEPHERD HILLS*** (415)586-3424
Fred H Stennfeld • H • CNH • 395 Addison St San Francisco CA 94131-2626 • soth@hooked.net

***WEST PORTAL*** (415)661-0242
David P Stechholz • Karen L Jacob DCE • WS 830 11; SS 945; BC 945;* • EL • EN • 200 Sloat Blvd San Francisco CA 94132-1621 • FAX(415)661-8402 • richh@slip.net

***ZION*** (415)221-7500
Theodore B Zimmerman Richard R Rice • WS 8 11; SS 930; BC 930 • H • EL • CNH • 495 9th Ave San Francisco CA 94118-2912 • FAX(415)221-7141 • revtbz@aol.com

**SAN JACINTO—*FUENTE DE VIDA***
Vacant • PSW • 158 W 55th St San Jacinto CA 92583

**SAN JOSE—*CHRIST THE LIFE*** (408)259-1670
Theodore L Laesch Jr. • WS 1015; SS 9; BC 9 • H • CNH • 3412 Sierra Rd San Jose CA 95132-3032 • FAX(408)259-0574

***FIRST IMMANUEL*** (408)292-5404
Robert D Newton Gabriel E Vallejo Timothy A Gerdes Isidro Sandate • H • CNH • 374 S 3rd St San Jose CA 95112-3648 • FAX(408)297-8748

***OUR SAVIOR***
See Cupertino

***SHEP OF VALLEY*** (408)997-4848
Robert D Weller Jr. • WS 10; BC 845;* • H • EC • CNH • 1281 Redmond Ave San Jose CA 95120-2747 • FAX(408)997-4842 • svalleylut@aol.com

***TRINITY*** (408)377-4411
James F Kramer • WS 9; BC 1030;* • H • CNH • 1500 Leigh Ave San Jose CA 95125-5301 • FAX(408)377-4414 • trinity3sj@yahoo.com

**SAN LEANDRO—*CHRIST***
See Pleasanton

***HOPE*** (510)351-7410
Michael R Totten • H • CNH • 1801 Manor Blvd San Leandro CA 94579-1510

***ST PETER*** (510)638-7017
David M Sauer • WS 8 1030; BC 930;* • H • CNH • 172 Breed Ave San Leandro CA 94577-1812 • splcdave@juno.com

**SAN LORENZO—*CALVARY*** (510)278-2556
Vacant • WS 8 1045; SS 930; BC 930 • H • EC/EL • CNH • 17200 Via Magdalena San Lorenzo CA 94580-2928 • FAX(510)278-2557

***MEMORIAL-DEAF***
See Fremont

**SAN LUIS OBISPO—*ZION*** (805)543-8327
S C Molnar • H • CNH • 1010 Foothill Blvd San Luis Obispo CA 93405-1816 • FAX(805)543-8331 • zion@fix.net

**SAN MATEO—*GRACE*** (650)345-9068
Charles E Froh • WS 9; SS 1015; BC 1030 • H • EL • CNH • 2825 Alameda De Las Pulgas San Mateo CA 94403-3262 • FAX(650)377-4831

**SAN PABLO—*ROLLINGWOOD*** (510)223-1932
Donald A Jordan • WS 10; SS 845; BC 845 • H • CNH • 2393 Greenwood Dr San Pablo CA 94806-3116 • FAX(510)223-1932 • rollingwood@juno.com

**SAN RAFAEL—*RESURRECTION*** (415)479-1334
Lon R Haack • * • H • CNH • 1100 Las Gallinas Ave San Rafael CA 94903-1804 • FAX(415)479-1334 • lrhaack@aol.com

***TRINITY*** (415)454-4135
Myron W Ista • WS 830 11; SS 945; BC 10 • H • EC • CNH • 94901-5007 333 Woodland Ave San Rafael CA 94901 • FAX(415)454-6230

**SANTA ANA—*PEACE***
See Tustin

***TRINITY*** (714)542-0784
John G Durkovic • John J Chapman DCE • WS 9; SS 1030; BC 1030;* • H • EL/HS • PSW • 902 S Broadway Santa Ana CA 92701-5647 • FAX(714)543-0388

**SANTA BARBARA—*EMANUEL*** (805)687-3734
Stephen E Skov • WS 830 1015; SS 1015;* • H • PSW • 3721 Modoc Rd Santa Barbara CA 93105-4444 • FAX(805)687-9673 • stall5@aol.com

**SANTA CLARA—*RESURRECTION*** (408)241-2728
William K Schultz • WS 10; SS 845; BC 9 • H • CNH • 2495 Cabrillo Ave Santa Clara CA 95051-1801 • FAX(408)241-3197 • revwkschultz@juno.com

**SANTA CLARITA—*BETHLEHEM*** (661)252-0622
Martin J Brauer • Mark D Buchholz DCE • H • EC/EL/HS • PSW • 27265 Luther Dr Santa Clarita CA 91351-3711 • FAX(661)252-5043 • blcs@thegrid.net

**SANTA CRUZ—*MESSIAH*** (831)423-8330
Vacant • H • EC • CNH • 801 High St Santa Cruz CA 95060-2528 • FAX(831)423-6677 • messiah@gloryworks.com

**SANTA MARIA—*GRACE*** (805)925-3818
Ray R Kringel • Paul Marting DCE • H • EC • CNH • 423 E Fesler St Santa Maria CA 93454-4509

***OUR SAVIOR*** (805)937-1116
Stephen A Eckert • WS 815 1045; SS 930; BC 930 • H • CNH • 4725 S Bradley Rd Santa Maria CA 93455-5051 • FAX(805)937-2107 • lcos@lightspeed.net

**SANTA MONICA—*PILGRIM*** (310)829-4113
Ardon D Albrecht • WS 9; SS 1010; BC 1010 • H • EC/EL • PSW • 1730 Wilshire Blvd Santa Monica CA 90403-5510 • FAX(310)829-4970 • amenmail@aol.com

**SANTA PAULA—*TRINITY*** (805)525-5911
Richard E Malmstrom • H • PSW • 505 W Harvard Blvd 93060-3227 PO Box 952 Santa Paula CA 93061-0952

**SANTA ROSA—*ST LUKE*** (707)545-6772
Theodore C Mueller Clinton J Lutz • Fred W Karlen DCE • WS 830 10 1115;* • H • EC/EL • CNH • 905 Mendocino Ave Santa Rosa CA 95401-4812 • FAX(707)544-2112

***ST MARK*** (707)545-1230
James D Beyer Dennis J Durham • WS 8 11; SS 945;* • H • CNH • 4325 Mayette Ave 95405-7329 PO Box 2387 Santa Rosa CA 95405-0387 • FAX(707)545-5007 • stmark@stmarklc.org

**SANTA YNEZ—*SHEP OF VALLEY*** (805)688-8938
Lowell B Kindschy • H • EC • PSW • 3550 Baseline Ave Santa Ynez CA 93460-9744 • FAX(805)688-8938 • sotv@cwo.com

**SANTEE—*CELEBRATION**** (619)447-3290
Vacant • WS 1030; SS 930; BC 730;* • H • PSW • 8516 N Magnolia Ave Ste 203 Santee CA 92071

**SEASIDE—*FAITH*** (831)394-1312
Anton A Prange • WS 1030;* • H • CNH • 1460 Hilby Ave Seaside CA 93955-6034 • faith3seaside@juno.co

**SEBASTOPOL—*MOUNT OLIVE*** (707)823-6316
David H Stohlmann • H • EC • CNH • 460 Murphy Ave Sebastopol CA 95472-3611 • FAX(707)823-6316

**SELMA—*ST PAUL*** (209)896-5670
Vacant • WS 8;* • H • CNH • 2131 Stillman St 93662-3025 PO Box 409 Selma CA 93662-0409

**SHERMAN OAKS—*SHERMAN OAKS*** (818)789-0215
Alan R Koch • WS 10; SS 9; BC 9;* • H • EC • EN • 14847 Dickens St Sherman Oaks CA 91403-3627 • FAX(818)784-5736 • shermanoakslc@freensafe.com

**SIMI VALLEY—*TRINITY*** (805)526-2429
Alvin P Young • Susan M Wilschetz DCE Robert Mc Kinney DCE • WS 9 1030; SS 9; BC 745;* • H • EC/EL • PSW • 2949 Alamo St Simi Valley CA 93063-2185 • FAX(805)526-4857 • trinity@cnmnetwork.com

**SONOMA—*FAITH*** (707)996-7365
Alan G Piotter • * • H • EC • CNH • 19355 Arnold Dr Sonoma CA 95476-6301 • FAX(707)996-7365 • faith@vom.com

**SONORA—*ST MATTHEW*** (209)532-4639
John V Herrmann • H • CNH • 29 Hope Ln Sonora CA 95370-5824 • FAX(209)532-4932 • johnh@sonnet.com

**SOQUEL—*MOUNT CALVARY*** (831)475-6962
Stanley R Abraham • WS 1015; BC 9;* • H • CNH • 2601 Park Ave Soquel CA 95073-2818 • mtcal@cruzio.com

**SOUTH GATE—*PEACE*** (323)569-8185
C Philip Collier • H • PSW • 4513 Tweedy Blvd South Gate CA 90280

***REDEEMER*** (323)588-0934
Charles N Brady Boanerges Parrales(#) • WS 9;* • H • EL • PSW • 2626 Liberty Blvd South Gate CA 90280-2004 • FAX(323)588-0701 • theoldranger1@aol.com

**SOUTH SAN FRANCISCO—*FIRST*** (415)583-5131
Jeffrey L Schufreider • H • CNH • 94080 350 Dolores Way S San Francisco CA 94080-1414

**SPRING VALLEY—*ATONEMENT*** (619)670-7174
John W Ehlke • H • HS • PSW • 10245 Loma Rancho Dr Spring Valley CA 91978-1024

**STOCKTON—*IMMANUEL*** (209)465-8383
Stephen K Willweber • WS 10; SS 1015; BC 9 • H • EC • CNH • 2343 Country Club Blvd Stockton CA 95204-4704 • FAX(209)465-4583 • immanuellu@netzero.net

***ST ANDREW*** (209)957-8750
John E Glover • Ann M Rehbein DEAC • H • EC • CNH • 4910 Claremont Ave Stockton CA 95207-5708

***TRINITY*** (209)464-1936
James R Russow Peter R Sok(#) • Paul A Mieger DCE • WS 830 11 945; SS 945; BC 945 • H • EC/EL • CNH • 444 N American St Stockton CA 95202-2129 • FAX(209)464-0965 • Trinitystockton@aol.com

**SUNNYVALE—*ST MARK*** (408)736-6605
Rodney N Hall • H • CNH • 125 E Arques Ave Sunnyvale CA 94086-4300 • FAX(408)736-7015 • rodhall196@aol.com

**SUSANVILLE—*ST PAUL*** (530)257-2223
Ethan C Gebauer • H • CNH • 105 Ash St Susanville CA 96130-4539
**SYLMAR—*CELEBRATION*** (818)367-4699
Thomas J Cizmar • PSW • 15910 Joseph Ct Sylmar CA 91342-1123
**TAFT—*PEACE*** (661)765-2488
Vacant • WS 10; SS 9;* • H • CNH • 26 Emmons Park Dr Taft CA 93268-2318
**TEHACHAPI—*GOOD SHEPHERD*** (661)822-6817
Daniel T Alsop • H • EC • PSW • 329 S Mill St Tehachapi CA 93561-1623 • FAX(661)823-1554 • goodshepherd@bnis.net
**TEMECULA—*NEW COMMUNITY*** (909)676-1492
Steven J Leinhos • WS 830; SS 10; BC 10 • H • EC • PSW • 30470 Pauba Rd Temecula CA 92592-6214 • FAX(909)695-1520 • nclc@temecula.com
**TEMPLE CITY—*FIRST*** (626)287-0968
David R Brinkley Wen-Fu Chen(DM) • WS 830 11; SS 945; BC 945;* • H • EC/EL/HS • PSW • 9123 Broadway Temple City CA 91780-2301 • FAX(626)285-8648 • firstlut@postoffice.pacbell.net
**TERRA BELLA 4 NE—*ZION*** (559)535-4952
Marty E Reed • H • EL • CNH • 93270 10341 Road 256 Terra Bella CA 93270-9722 • FAX(559)535-2719 • zionevchur@jps.net
**THOUSAND OAKS—*REDEEMER*** (805)498-4813
Elroi Reimnitz • H • PSW • 667 Camino Dos Rios Thousand Oaks CA 91360-2354 • FAX(805)498-7847
**TORRANCE—*ASCENSION*** (310)793-0071
David A Boyd • Lisa F Murdock DCE • WS 815 11 • H • EC/EL/HS • PSW • 17910 Prairie Ave Torrance CA 90504-3713 • FAX(310)214-4657 • ascoffice2@aol.com
**TRACY—*ST PAUL*** (209)835-7438
Jeffrey D Dorth • Bruce Kleinert DCE James D Bush DCO • H • EC • CNH • 1635 Chester Dr Tracy CA 95376-2927 • FAX(209)835-7951
**TUJUNGA—*FAITH*** (818)352-4444
Claude H Baker • * • H • EL/HS • PSW • 7749 Apperson St 91042-2110 PO Box 577 Tujunga CA 91043-0577
**TURLOCK—*GOOD SHEPHERD*** (209)667-7712
Ronald A Youngdale • WS 8 1030; SS 915 • H • CNH • 640 Minaret Ave Turlock CA 95380-4199 • prayou@thevision.net
**TUSTIN—*PEACE*** (714)731-2226
Vacant • Mary E Dahlia DCE • WS 830 10; SS 10; BC 10 • H • PSW • 92781 18542 Vanderlip Ave Santa Ana CA 92705-3244 • FAX(714)731-3669 • ljstrelow@att.net
**TWENTYNINE PALMS—*IMMANUEL*** (760)367-9269
Vacant • WS 1030;* • H • PSW • 6450 Stardune Rd 92277 PO Box 1028 Twentynine Palms CA 92277-0960 • FAX(760)367-9269 • ipop@thegrid.com
**UKIAH—*FAITH*** (707)462-2618
M L Schulz • H • CNH • 560 Park Blvd Ukiah CA 95482-3701 • FAX(707)462-5546
**VACAVILLE—*BETHANY*** (707)451-6675
Lester T Seto • Brian L Wright DCE • WS 715 830 10 1115; SS 10 • H • EC/EL • CNH • 621 S Orchard Ave Vacaville CA 95688-4335 • FAX(707)451-1740 • lesterseto@aol.com
**VALLEJO—*FIRST*** (707)644-6260
David C Prinz • H • CNH • 912 Florida St Vallejo CA 94590-5512
**VALLEY CENTER—*LIGHT VALLEY*** (760)749-9733
Robert J Stevens • WS 9; BC 1015 • H • PSW • 28330 Lilac Rd Valley Center CA 92082-5415 • FAX(760)749-9733
**VALLEY HOME—*ST JOHN*** (209)847-0607
C E Schack • CNH • 4606 Michigan Ave 95361 C/O Rev C Schack 120 West Ave Oakdale CA 95361-3840
**VALLEY SPRINGS—*FOOTHILL*** (209)772-0940
Vacant • H • CNH • 225 E Highway 12 95252-9493 PO Box 541 Valley Springs CA 95252-0541
**VAN NUYS—*FIRST*** (818)989-5844
John A Sauer Kun W Hong(DM) • WS 830 11;* • H • EL/HS • PSW • 6952 Van Nuys Blvd Van Nuys CA 91405-3984 • FAX(818)989-0337
***ZION KOREAN**** 
See Glendale
**VENICE—*FIRST*** (310)821-2740
Kenneth W Frese • Thomas G Edelen DCE • H • EL • PSW • 815 Venice Blvd Venice CA 90291-4903 • FAX(310)823-4822 • frstluthrn@aol.com
**VENTURA—*FIRST*** (805)643-5586
Larry D Bogardus • WS 1030; SS 9; BC 9;* • H • PSW • 78 Chrisman Ave Ventura CA 93001-3236 • FAX(805)643-6732
***GRACE*** (805)642-2267
Benedict B Yaspelkis Jr. • WS 8 1030; SS 915; BC 915 • H • EL • PSW • 6190 Telephone Rd Ventura CA 93003-5334 • tommydee@jetlink.net
**VICTORVILLE—*ZION*** (760)245-9725
Norman W Schmoock • WS 8 11; SS 930; BC 930;* • H • EC/EL • PSW • 15342 Jeraldo Dr Victorville CA 92394-5580 • FAX(760)245-5945 • lori.knapp@eudoramail.com
**VISALIA—*GRACE*** (559)734-7694
John D Roth David J Kummer • Sandra F Eitel DCE • WS 8 930 11; SS 930;* • H • EL • CNH • 1111 S Conyer St Visalia CA 93277-2537 • FAX(559)734-0146
**VISTA—*FAITH*** (760)724-7700
Beryl D Droegemueller • WS 8 1030; SS 915;* • H • EL • PSW • 700 E Bobier Dr Vista CA 92084-3804 • FAX(760)724-6151 • bdrags@aol.com
**WALNUT—*CHRIST KING*** (909)595-3819
Vacant • HS • PSW • 555 Gartel Dr Walnut CA 91789-2009 • FAX(909)613-1620 • christtheking2@juno.com
***GRACE CHINESE****
See Diamond Bar
**WALNUT CREEK—*TRINITY*** (925)935-3360
Robert F Meyer • WS 9; SS 920; BC 1020 • H • EC • CNH • 2317 Buena Vista Ave Walnut Creek CA 94596-3017 • FAX(925)935-7902 • trinitylcs@tlcchurch.org
**WASCO—*TRINITY*** (661)758-5582
Erwin L Lueker • SS 1120;* • H • CNH • 1643 Palm Ave 93280-2431 PO Box 717 Wasco CA 93280-0717
**WATSONVILLE—*TRINITY*** (408)724-0176
Vacant • H • EC/EL • CNH • 175 Lawrence Ave Watsonville CA 95076-2916
**WEST COVINA—*IMMANUEL FIRST*** (818)919-1530
Fred L Page • EC/EL/HS • PSW • 512 S Valinda Ave West Covina CA 91790-3007 • FAX(818)919-5979
**WEST LOS ANGELE—*FIRST***
See Los Angeles
**WESTCHESTER—*OUR SAVIOR***
See Los Angeles
**WESTMINSTER—*ST LUKE*** (714)893-8074
Vacant • WS 10; SS 9;* • H • EL • PSW • 13552 Goldenwest St Westminster CA 92683-3119 • FAX(714)897-1569
**WHITTIER—*FAITH*** (562)941-0245
Thomas St Jean • H • EC/EL/HS • PSW • 9920 Mills Ave Whittier CA 90604-1032 • FAX(562)941-4451
***FAITH ARABIC**** (562)941-0245
Vacant • PSW • 14006 Mc Gee Dr Whittier CA 90605-2639 • FAX(562)941-4451
***HOPE*** (562)943-3888
Timothy P Beyer • EC/HS • PSW • 10327 Valley Home Ave Whittier CA 90603-2657 • FAX(562)943-5308 • hopelcms@aol.com
***TRINITY*** (562)699-7431
Robert J Schroeder • Phillip C Gaylor DCE Lola Denow • WS 8 1015; SS 915; BC 915 • H • EC/EL • PSW • 11716 Floral Dr Whittier CA 90601-2834 • FAX(562)699-7341 • 3nllcms@gte.net
**WILLITS—*ST JOHN*** (707)459-2988
Vacant • WS 11; SS 930 • CNH • 24 Mill Creek Dr Willits CA 95490-3015
**WILLOWS—*FIRST*** (916)934-2140
Philip W Zabell • H • CNH • 333 Vine St 95988-2444 PO Box 125 Willows CA 95988-0125 • pzcard@hotmail.com
**WINDSOR—*VINEYARD OF FAITH*** (707)837-8712
Jeffrey E Mueller Christopher Benson • R J Burnham DCE • WS 9 1045; SS 1045 9; BC 1045;* • H • CNH • 167 Arata Ln Windsor CA 95492-7514 • FAX(707)838-6214 • vof@vof.org
**WINNETKA—*OUR REDEEMER*** (818)341-3460
Gregory J Barth • H • EC/EL/HS • PSW • 8520 Winnetka Ave Winnetka CA 91306-1142 • church@our-redeemer.org
**WOODLAND—*ST PAUL*** (530)662-1935
Henry A Scherer • H • EC/EL • CNH • 625 W Gibson Rd Woodland CA 95695-5143 • FAX(530)662-1999
**YUBA CITY—*FIRST*** (530)673-8894
J M Elrod • Susan J Westrup DCE • H • EC/EL • CNH • 850 Cooper Ave Yuba City CA 95991-3849
**YUCAIPA—*GOOD SHEPHERD*** (909)790-1863
Phillip M Pledger • Ronald S Du Pree Jr. DCE • WS 8 1030 815; SS 915; BC 915;* • H • PSW • 34215 Avenue E Yucaipa CA 92399-2577 • FAX(909)790-5882
**YUCCA VALLEY—*GOOD SHEPHERD*** (760)365-2548
Thomas E Hendry • * • H • PSW • 59077 Yucca Trl Yucca Valley CA 92284-4736 • FAX(760)365-4472 • thendry@telis.org

## COLORADO

**AKRON—*TRINITY*** (303)345-2303
Gregg A Reiser • H • RM • 202 Birch Akron CO 80720-1533 • gareiser@iguana.ruralnet.net
**ALAMOSA—*TRINITY*** (719)589-4611
Karl F Wright • H • EC/EL • RM • 52 El Rio Dr 81101-2117 PO Box 1323 Alamosa CO 81101-1323 • tlcalmco@fone.net
**AMHERST—*ST PAUL*** (970)854-4310
Vacant • RM • 300 Monmouth Ave Amherst CO 80721 • hrathjen@hpdc.com
**ARRIBA—*IMMANUEL*** (719)768-3358
James M Elmshauser • H • RM • PO Box 178 Arriba CO 80804-0178
**ARVADA—*KING OF KINGS*** (303)425-7096
Thomas W Teske • WS 8 1045; BC 920;* • H • HS • RM • 8300 Pomona Dr Arvada CO 80005-2578 • FAX(303)425-5608 • rrevtom@aol.com
***PEACE*** (303)424-4454
David J Ahlman John R Larson • Paulette E Wegner DCE Timothy J Lindeman DCE Phillip L Johnson DCO • H • HS • RM • 5675 Field St Arvada CO 80002-2227 • FAX(303)940-7683 • peace@peacelutheran.net
***RISEN CHRIST*** (303)421-5872
James Winsor • WS 1015; SS 915; BC 915 • H • RM • 14850 W 72nd Ave Arvada CO 80007 • orthoprax@juno.com
**ASPEN—*MESSIAH*** (970)925-7725
Eric M Ahlemeyer • H • RM • 1235 Mountain View Dr Aspen CO 81611-1027
**AURORA—*HOPE*** (303)364-7416
Vacant • WS 815; SS 945; BC 945 • H • EC/EL/HS • RM • 1345 Macon St Aurora CO 80010-3516 • FAX(303)364-5320 • hopelcms@juno.com
***MOUNT OLIVE*** (303)755-9123
Jeffrey E Shearier • WS 8 930 11; SS 930; BC 930;* • H • EC/HS • RM • 11500 E Iliff Ave Aurora CO 80014-1177 • FAX(303)745-5912
***PEACE W CHRIST*** (303)693-5618
Michael J Hiller • Susan D Von Fange DCE John Paulus DCE John Elmshauser DCE • H • EL/HS • RM • 3290 S Tower Rd Aurora CO 80013-2367 • FAX(303)699-2777 • pwc.office@pwclc.org
**BAILEY—*SHEP ROCKIES*** (303)838-2161
Gary H Fricke • WS 9; SS 1045; BC 1045;* • H • RM • 106 Rosalie Rd 80421-2060 PO Box 505 Bailey CO 80421-0505 • FAX(303)838-2161 • sheporock@gateway.net
**BENNETT—*CHRIST REDEEMER*** (303)644-3044
Vacant • H • RM • 275 S Ash St 80102-8405 PO Box 537 Bennett CO 80102-0537
**BOULDER—*MOUNT HOPE*** (303)499-9800
Dennis E Brech • WS 9; SS 1015; BC 1015 • H • EC • RM • 1345 S Broadway St Boulder CO 80303-6722
***MOUNT ZION*** (303)443-4151
Neal F Mac Lachlan • WS 9;* • H • EC/EL • RM • 1680 Balsam Ave Boulder CO 80304-3539 • FAX(303)448-9547 • mtzion@indra.com
***UNIVERSITY*** (303)443-8720
Robert E Stuenkel • H • RM • 1202 Folsom St Boulder CO 80302-6810 • FAX(303)443-4847 • ulc@spot.colorado.edu
**BRIGHTON—*SUMMIT PEACE***
See Thornton
***ZION*** (303)659-2339
Dean H Boernke • Susan A Hart DCE • H • EC/EL • RM • 1400 Skeel St Brighton CO 80601-2336 • FAX(303)659-2342
**BROOMFIELD—*BEAUT SAVIOR*** (303)469-1785
Gregory N Thompson Joseph M Brennan Craig B Thomas • WS 8 1030; SS 915; BC 915;* • H • EC/EL/HS • RM • 6995 W 120th Ave 80020-2365 PO Box 8 Broomfield CO 80038-0008 • FAX(303)469-6999
***CHRIST THE ROCK***
See Superior
***RISEN SAVIOR*** (303)469-3521
Philip J Cameron • Kevin Hischke DCE • WS 8 1030; SS 915; BC 915 • H • HS • RM • 3031 W 144th Ave Broomfield CO 80020-9453 • FAX(303)635-0201 • office@rslc.org
**BUENA VISTA—*FAITH*** (719)395-2039
John E Maynard(#) • * • H • RM • 1617 W Main 81211 PO Box 1448 Buena Vista CO 81211-1448 • jmaynard@chaffee.net
**BURLINGTON—*TRINITY*** (719)346-7401
William H Viergutz • H • RM • 338 7th St Burlington CO 80807-1971 • trinity@rmi.net
**CANON CITY—*ST JOHN*** (719)275-0111
Harold R Baldwin • WS 9; SS 1030; BC 1030 • H • RM • 790 Greydene Ave Canon City CO 81212-2662 • revhrbaldy@aol.com
**CASTLE ROCK—*EPIPHANY*** (303)798-6859
Robert L Tasler • H • RM • Castle Rock High School 2842 Front St 80104 C/O Reverend Robert Tasler 8187 S Pennsylvania Ct Littleton CO 80122 • pbt45@ecentral.com
***MOUNT ZION*** (303)688-9550
Larry E Ziegler • H • RM • 750 Cantril St Castle Rock CO 80104-1818 • ZLCKEM@aol.com
**CHEYENNE WELLS—*GRACE*** (719)767-5862
Vacant • RM • PO Box 728 Cheyenne Wells CO 80810-0728
**COLORADO SPRINGS—*HOLY CROSS*** (719)596-0661
Michael L Flannery Douglas P Brauner John I Bernstein • Stacey L Tasler DCE Stephen G Fehl DCE • WS 8 930 11; SS 11 930; BC 11 930;* • H • EC • RM • 4125 Constitution Ave Colorado Springs CO 80909-1662 • FAX(719)596-0699
***IMMANUEL*** (719)636-5011
Timothy L Grassinger Robert J Swearer Lawrence J Dye • WS 8 930 1045; BC 930;* • H • EC/EL • RM • 846 E Pikes Peak Ave Colorado Springs CO 80903-3636 • FAX(719)636-5292
***KOREAN FIRST*** (719)393-1940
Michael E Lim • WS 12; SS 12;* • RM • 2728 Casden Circle 80909-6143 4444 Moonbeam Dr Colorado Springs CO 80916-3210
***REDEEMER*** (719)633-7661
Duwayne D Kirkeide David P Baese • Timothy J Moses DCE • EC/EL • RM • 2226 N Corona St 80907-7013 2215 N Wahsatch Ave Colorado Springs CO 80907-6939 • FAX(719)633-2127
***RESURRECTION*** (719)392-7045
Vincent S Larson • WS 10; SS 830; BC 830;* • H • EC • RM • 4444 Moonbeam Dr Colorado Springs CO 80916-3210
***ROCK OF AGES*** (719)632-9394
Ronald M Baker • H • EC • RM • 120 N 31st St 80904-2009 PO Box 6941 Colorado Springs CO 80934-6941 • FAX(719)632-0772 • rockofages@kktv.com
***SHEP SPRINGS*** (719)598-7446
Robert W Schaibley • H • RM • 9550 Otero Ave Colorado Springs CO 80920-1514 • FAX(719)598-8920 • lutheran@ix.netcom.com
**COMMERCE CITY—*OUR SAVIOUR*** (303)288-9577
Kevin M Peterson • WS 1015; SS 9; BC 9;* • H • HS • RM • 6770 Monaco St Commerce City CO 80022-2875 • oslc1@juno.com
**CORTEZ—*TRINITY*** (303)565-9346
David C Dahl • WS 8 1015;* • H • EC • RM • 208 N Dolores Rd 81321-4210 PO Box 989 Cortez CO 81321-0989 • dcdahl@frontier.net
**CRAIG—*FAITH*** (970)824-3043
Vacant • WS 9; SS 1015; BC 1015 • H • RM • PO Box 428 Craig CO 81626-0428
**CROOK—*FAITH ENGLISH*** (970)886-2335
David R Loeschke • H • RM • 319 6th St 80726 PO Box 123 Crook CO 80726-0123
**DELTA—*REDEEMER*** (970)874-3052
Marion C Hofman • WS 1030; SS 915; BC 915 • H • RM • 1000 Pioneer Rd Delta CO 81416-2613
**DENVER—*CHRIST*** (303)722-1424
William G Kohlmeier • H • EC • RM • 2695 S Franklin St Denver CO 80210-5924 • FAX(303)722-0933

***CHRIST TRIUMPHANT*** (303)758-3375
Henry A Corcoran • WS 830; SS 945; BC 945 • H • HS • RM • 1700 S Grant St 80210-3120 2811 E Colorado Ave Denver CO 80210 • FAX(303)758-3375 • hcorky@juno.com
***CORDERO DE DIOS*** (303)480-5262
Vacant • WS 11; SS 10; BC 10 • H • RM • 5200 Tejon St Denver CO 80221 • cordero@juno.com
***EMMAUS*** (303)433-3303
Roger E Schlechte • WS 10; SS 11; BC 11 • H • EC/EL/HS • RM • 3120 Irving St Denver CO 80211-3632 • FAX(303)433-2280
***FAITH*** (303)455-5878
Kurt A Van Fossan • WS 830 11; SS 945 • H • HS • RM • 4785 Elm Ct Denver CO 80211-1146 • FAX(303)455-8249 • faithlutheran@intelunk.net
***MOUNT CALVARY*** (303)297-3987
Vacant • H • HS • RM • 3560 York St Denver CO 80205-4159
***MOUNT ZION*** (303)429-0165
Bradley G Cusson • WS 830 11; BC 10;* • H • EC/HS • RM • 500 Drake St Denver CO 80221-4128 • FAX(303)429-0165 • mtzion80221@netzero.net
***REDEEMER*** (303)934-5447
Maurice W Goldhammer • * • H • HS • RM • 3300 W Nevada Pl Denver CO 80219-2740 • FAX(303)935-9256 • redeemerdenver@juno.com
***ST ANDREW*** (303)371-7014
Gary P Boye • H • EC/EL/HS • RM • 12150 Andrews Dr Denver CO 80239-4441 • FAX(303)371-7014
***ST JOHN*** (303)733-3777
Vacant • Darcy A Schipporeit DCE • H • HS • RM • 700 S Franklin St Denver CO 80209-4505 • FAX(303)778-6070 • st³johns@juno.com
***SUMMIT PEACE***
See Thornton
***TRINITY*** (303)934-2103
James D Bauer • WS 8 1045; SS 915; BC 930 • H • EC/HS • RM • 4225 W Yale Ave Denver CO 80219-5710 • FAX(303)934-6672 • pastorbauer@uswest.net
***UNIV HILLS*** (303)759-0161
Thomas M Fields • * • H • EC/EL/HS • RM • 4949 E Eastman Ave Denver CO 80222-7309 • FAX(303)757-7110 • church.uhills@qadas.com
**DURANGO—*ST PAUL*** (970)247-0357
Timothy C Evers • * • H • RM • 2611 Junction St 81301-4168 PO Box 2282 Durango CO 81302-2282
**EDWARDS—*GRACIOUS SAVIOR*** (970)926-3550
Daniel E Rohlwing • H • HS • RM • 33520 Hwy 6 81632 PO Box 250 Edwards CO 81632-9999 • FAX(970)926-5682 • gslc@vchs.org
**ELIZABETH—*CHRIST OUR SAVIOR*** (303)646-1378
Larry E Ziegler • H • RM • PO Box 738 Elizabeth CO 80107-0738
**ENGLEWOOD—*IMMANUEL*** (303)781-5887
Craig A Patterson • WS 10; SS 845; BC 845;* • H • HS • RM • 3695 S Acoma St Englewood CO 80110-3655 • immanuel@polnow.net
**ESTES PARK—*MOUNT CALVARY*** (970)586-4646
Henry R Rische • H • RM • 950 N Saint Vrain Ave 80517-6346 PO Box 1724 Estes Park CO 80517-1724
**EVERGREEN—*MOUNT HOPE*** (303)670-1387
Vacant • WS 9; SS 1030; BC 1030 • H • HS • RM • 30571 Chestnut Dr Evergreen CO 80439-8646 • FAX(303)670-5978
**FLAGLER—*ZION*** (719)765-4460
James M Elmshauser • RM • 722 Main Ave 80815-9200 PO Box 187 Flagler CO 80815-0187
**FORT COLLINS—*PEACE W CHRIST*** (970)226-4721
Frank E Winter • Mary C Hoppenrath DCE • H • EC/HS • RM • 1412 W Swallow Rd Fort Collins CO 80526-2413 • FAX(970)226-1857 • pwclc@info2000.net
***REDEEMER*** (970)225-9020
Timothy D Runtsch • Maria P Brovick DCE • H • EC/HS • RM • 6630 Brittany Dr Fort Collins CO 80525-5823 • FAX(970)225-9870 • redeemer@redeemer-lutheran.org
***ST JOHN*** (970)482-5316
Ronald P Nickel • Mark K Gabbert DCE • WS 8; SS 930;* • H • EC • RM • 305 E Elizabeth St Fort Collins CO 80524-3705 • FAX(970)482-5028 • stjohnslc@msn.com
**FORT LUPTON—*MOUNT CALVARY*** (303)857-6827
Charles W Blanco • WS 8 1030; SS 915; BC 915 • H • RM • 650 S Park Ave Fort Lupton CO 80621-1231 • cwblanco@worldnet.att.net
**FORT MORGAN—*TRINITY*** (970)867-5721
Vacant • WS 8 1030; SS 915; BC 915 • H • EC/EL • RM • 800 Sherman St Fort Morgan CO 80701-3542 • FAX(603)415-7705 • trinityc@twol.com
**FRANKTOWN/PARKER—*TRINITY*** (303)841-8620
Paul H Schneider • Thaddeus P Warren DCE • WS 8 1045; BC 930 • H • EC/EL/HS • RM • 80116 4740 N Highway 83 Franktown CO 80116-9661 • FAX(303)841-2761 • trinityfranktown@juno.com
**FRISCO—*CHRIST*** (970)453-8019
Donald W Ehrke • WS 1030; SS 930; BC 930 • H • RM • 14072 Hwy 9 80443 PO Box 4118 Breckenridge CO 80424-4118
**GENOA—*TRINITY*** (719)763-2289
Vacant • RM • 214 Second St 80818 PO Box 126 Genoa CO 80818-0126
**GLENWOOD SPRINGS—*HOLY CROSS*** (970)945-6871
Allen D Anderson • H • EC • RM • 0062 Rd 135 Glenwood Springs CO 81601 • FAX(970)945-2744 • aanderson5@juno.com
**GOLDEN—*NEW HOPE*** (303)279-2070
Vacant • HS • RM • 16600 W 50th Ave Golden CO 80403-1612
***ST LUKE*** (303)233-5658
Dwight D Hellmers • WS 9; SS 1030; BC 1030 • H • HS • RM • 13119 W 20th Ave Golden CO 80401-2201 • FAX(303)233-5706 • stlukesgoldenco@juno.com
**GRAND JUNCTION—*MESSIAH*** (970)245-2838
Gary L Buss Bruce A Skelton • WS 8 1030; SS 915; BC 915 • H • EL • RM • 81501 840 N 11th St Grand Junction CO 81501-3218 • FAX(970)245-8145 • messiahgj@juno.com
**GREELEY—*GLORIA CHRISTI*** (970)353-2554
Darrin L Kohrt • WS 8 1030; SS 915; BC 915 • H • EC/HS • RM • 1322 31st Ave Greeley CO 80634-6328 • gchristi@netzero.net
***TRINITY*** (970)330-1203
William H Keller • WS 8 1030; SS 920; BC 920;* • H • EL/HS • RM • 3000 35th Ave Greeley CO 80634-9418 • FAX(970)330-2844 • tlcgreeley@ctos.com
**GROVER 10 E—*ZION*** (307)245-3390
Bradley D Heinecke • WS 8;* • WY • 8 Mile Ne Of Grover 80729 C/O Grace English Luth PO Box 670 Pine Bluffs WY 82082
**GUNNISON—*MOUNT CALVARY*** (970)641-1860
Charles R Rafferty • H • RM • 711 N Main St 81230-2411 PO Box 662 Gunnison CO 81230-0662 • mtcalvary@westelk.com
**HAXTUN—*IMMANUEL*** (970)774-6236
David R Loeschke • H • RM • 400 N Colorado Ave 80731-2576 PO Box 116 Haxtun CO 80731-0116
**HIGHLANDS RANCH—*HOLY CROSS*** (303)683-1300
Marc Vander Werf • WS 8 1030; SS 915; BC 930 • H • EC/HS • RM • 9770 S Foothills Canyon Blvd Highlands Ranch CO 80129 • FAX(303)470-0165
**HOLYOKE—*ZION*** (970)854-2615
Gary A Rahe • WS 10; SS 830; BC 830 • H • RM • 240 S High School Ave Holyoke CO 80734-1727 • FAX(970)854-2314 • garahe@henge.com
**HUDSON—*GRACE*** (303)536-4734
Vacant • WS 1030;* • H • RM • 400 Cherry St PO Box 409 Hudson CO 80642-0409
**HUGO—*HOLY CROSS*** (719)763-2289
Vacant • H • RM • PO Box 425 Hugo CO 80821-0425
**JOHNSTOWN—*FAITH*** (970)587-9859
Clare B Skov • RM • 1011 W South 1st St 80534-8422 PO Box 70 Johnstown CO 80534-0070
**JULESBURG—*ST PAUL*** (970)474-2592
Vacant • WS 4;* • H • RM • Seventh And Maple Sts 80737 PO Box 72 Julesburg CO 80737-0072
**KIT CARSON—*TRINITY*** (719)767-5862
Vacant • H • RM • PO Box 306 Kit Carson CO 80825-0306
**LA JUNTA—*TRINITY*** (719)384-6555
Robert T Kunz • H • RM • 1601 Raton Ave La Junta CO 81050-3420
**LAFAYETTE—*ETERNAL SAVIOR*** (303)665-6105
Paul G Rhode • WS 9; SS 1015 • H • RM • 1241 Ceres Dr Lafayette CO 80026-1227
**LAKEWOOD—*BETHLEHEM*** (303)238-7676
David J Langewisch Steven J Wheeler • Sandra M Wendelin DCE Heidi N Fingerlin DCE • H • EC/EL/HS • RM • 2100 Wadsworth Blvd Lakewood CO 80215-2007 • FAX(303)238-7691
***CONCORDIA*** (303)989-5260
Kelly J Crabbe • Gregg A Mc Caslin DCE • H • EC/HS • RM • 13371 W Alameda Pkwy Lakewood CO 80228-3431 • FAX(303)989-3746 • Concordia@concordialcms.org
**LAMAR—*GRACE*** (719)336-5500
Vacant • H • RM • 1 Memorial Dr Lamar CO 81052-3998
**LEADVILLE—*GOOD SHEPHERD*** (719)486-0280
Donald W Ehrke • H • RM • PO Box 303 Leadville CO 80461-0303
**LITTLETON—*ASCENSION*** (303)794-4636
Arnold J Voigt • H • HS • RM • 1701 W Caley Ave Littleton CO 80120-3109 • FAX(303)794-1169 • alutheran@aol.com
***HOLY CROSS***
See Highlands Ranch
***HOSANNA*** (303)973-1706
Greg Peters • SS 915;* • H • EC/HS • RM • 10304 W Belleview Ave Littleton CO 80127-1732 • FAX(303)973-1422 • hosanna.lutheran@worldnet.att.net
***OUR FATHER*** (303)779-1332
Donald F Hinchey Werner K Boos Adrian E Hanft • Linda L Olsen DCE Margaret R Hinchey DCE • WS 8; SS 930;* • H • EC/HS • RM • 6335 S Holly St Littleton CO 80121-3555 • FAX(303)779-1668
***SHEPHERD HILLS*** (303)798-0711
Craig W Henningfield Richard W Holz Stephen C Lee • WS 8 930 1050; SS 930;* • H • EL/HS • RM • 7691 S University Blvd Littleton CO 80122-3144 • FAX(303)798-0718 • chenning1@aol.com
**LONGMONT—*CHRIST OUR SAVIOR*** (303)776-1789
John A Thieme • WS 830 11; SS 945; BC 945 • H • RM • 640 Alpine St Longmont CO 80501-4637 • FAX(303)776-8182 • info@coslongmont.org
***MESSIAH*** (303)776-2573
Kent E Schnegelberger • Melinda D Schluckebier DCE • WS 8 1030; SS 915; BC 915 • H • EC/EL • RM • 1335 Francis St Longmont CO 80501-2511 • FAX(303)776-2599 • kschnege@concentric.net
**LOUISVILLE—*CHRIST THE ROCK*** (303)438-5569
Keith L Besel • WS 1030; SS 915; BC 915 • H • RM • 263 Campus Dr 80027 3220 S Princess Cir Broomfield CO 80020-5413 • FAX(303)438-5569 • kbesel@ctrlc.org
**LOVELAND—*IMMANUEL*** (970)667-4506
Glen A Schlecht Albert H Schroeder • Eric R Smith DCE Debra J Arfsten DCE • WS 8 1045; SS 930; BC 930;* • H • EC/EL/HS • RM • 1101 Hilltop Dr Loveland CO 80537-4446 • FAX(970)667-0120 • immloveland@juno.com
***MOUNT OLIVE*** (970)669-7350
David W Feeder • WS 9; SS 1030; BC 1030 • H • RM • 80537 3411 S Taft Ave Loveland CO 80537-7405 • FAX(970)669-4715 • mountoliveloveland@juno.com
**MONTE VISTA—*ST PETER*** (719)852-3424
Bryan S Cary • WS 1015; BC 9;* • H • EC/EL • RM • 1821 Grande Ave Monte Vista CO 81144-1622 • stpeters@amigo.net
**MONTROSE—*HOPE*** (970)249-8811
Darryl S Hannenberg • H • RM • 600 N 2nd St Montrose CO 81401-3725
**MONUMENT—*FAMILY CHRIST*** (719)481-2255
Vacant • WS 9; SS 1030; BC 1030 • H • EC • RM • 675 Baptist Rd 80132 PO Box 1010 Monument CO 80132-1010 • FAX(719)481-2255 • hslavens@tri-lakesonline.net
**NIWOT—*DIVINE SAVIOR*** (303)652-2419
Bruce E Russell • H • RM • 80544 7070 N 83rd St Longmont CO 80503-8535
**NORTHGLENN—*GETHSEMANE*** (303)451-6895
Norman L Raedeke Bruce R Matzke • H • EC/EL/HS • RM • 10675 Washington St Northglenn CO 80233-4101 • FAX(303)451-1067 • glcco@juno.com
**PAGOSA SPRINGS—*OUR SAVIOR*** (970)731-4668
Richard A Bolland • WS 8 1045; SS 930; BC 930 • H • EC/EL • RM • Us 160 W And Meadows Dr 81147 56 Meadows Dr Pagosa Springs CO 81147-7662 • FAX(970)731-4668 • strshootcv@pagosa.net
**PAONIA—*IMMANUEL*** (970)527-3232
Otto H Hattstaedt • H • RM • PO Box 727 Paonia CO 81428-0727
**PUEBLO—*BETHANY*** (719)544-5269
Christopher E Kellogg • RM • 1802 Sheridan Rd 81001-1617 1726 Sheridan Rd Pueblo CO 81001-1615 • papak@bemail.com
***TRINITY*** (719)544-3016
Randy G Bolt • WS 8 1030; SS 915; BC 915;* • H • EC/EL • RM • 701 W Evans Ave Pueblo CO 81004-1523 • trinitypueblo@juno.com
**PUEBLO WEST—*OUR SAVIOR*** (719)547-2300
Donald A Barber • WS 1015; BC 9;* • H • RM • 275 W John Powell Blvd Pueblo West CO 81007 • oursaviorspw@juno.com
**RANGELY—*TRINITY*** (970)675-8138
Roger D Sterle • H • RM • 736 E Main St Rangely CO 81648-3225
**RIFLE 1 W—*EMMANUEL*** (970)625-2369
Dale V Heinlein • H • EC • RM • 81650 652 E 5th St Rifle CO 81650-2908
**ROCKY FORD—*ST PETER*** (719)254-6064
Vacant • H • RM • 952 Washington Ave Rocky Ford CO 81067-2433
**SALIDA—*FIRST*** (719)539-4311
Steven L Dreher • WS 9; SS 1015; BC 1015 • H • RM • 1237 F St Salida CO 81201-2509 • firstlutheranchurch@juno.com
**SILVERTHORNE—*CHRIST***
See Frisco
**STEAMBOAT SPRINGS—*CONCORDIA*** (970)879-0175
Vacant • WS 8 1030; SS 915; BC 915;* • H • RM • 755 Concordia Ln 80477 PO Box 770428 Steamboat Spr CO 80477-0428 • FAX(970)871-0190 • clc@snowcap.net
**STERLING—*FIRST ENGLISH*** (970)522-5142
Andrew W Dimit • H • RM • 701 Fairhurst St Sterling CO 80751-4525
***TRINITY*** (970)522-5942
Michael E Paulison • WS 8 1045 • H • EC • RM • 732 Clark St Sterling CO 80751-2944 • FAX(970)521-7763 • trinity@trinitysterling.org
**SUGAR CITY—*GRACE*** (719)267-3754
Vacant • RM • 403 Iowa St 81076 PO Box 214 Sugar City CO 81076-0214
**THORNTON—*SUMMIT PEACE*** (303)452-0448
William N Allshouse Darold F Boettcher(EM) • WS 8 1030; SS 915; BC 915 • H • RM • 80601202 4661 E 136th Ave Brighton CO 80601-7701 • summitofpeace@uswest.net
**VAIL—*GRACIOUS SAVIOR***
See Edwards
**WALSENBURG—*HOLY CROSS*** (719)742-3805
Vacant • * • H • RM • Walsenburg Mennonite Church 603 S Leon Ave 81089-2350 PO Box 761 123 CO 81089-0761 • flhill@rmi.net
**WELLINGTON—*ZION*** (303)568-9301
Vacant • WS 1030; SS 930; BC 930 • H • RM • 8322 2nd St 80549 PO Box 417 Wellington CO 80549-0417
**WESTCLIFFE—*HOPE*** (719)783-9773
Wayne W Riddering • WS 1030; SS 9; BC 9 • H • RM • 312 S 3rd St 81252-9502 308 3rd St Westcliffe CO 81252 • dedept1@ris.net
**WESTMINISTER—*MOUNT ZION***
See Denver
**WHEAT RIDGE—*WHEAT RIDGE*** (303)424-3161
James D Knapp • H • EC/HS • RM • 8600 W 38th Ave Wheat Ridge CO 80033-4366 • FAX(303)424-4378 • wrlutheran@cs.com
**WINDSOR—*HOLY CROSS*** (970)686-5599
Clare B Skov • WS 1045; SS 930;* • H • RM • 1450 Westwood Dr 80550-5918 PO Box 307 Windsor CO 80550 • c.t.skov@juno.com
**WOODLAND PARK—*FAITH*** (719)687-2303
Kevin C Kosberg • WS 8 1030; SS 915; BC 915;* • H • RM • 1310 Evergreen Heights Dr Woodland Park CO 80863-3304 • FAX(719)687-2303 • faithwp@rmi.net
**WRAY—*CALVARY*** (970)332-4630
Richard A Pierson • WS 9; SS 1015; BC 1015 • H • RM • 518 Dexter St Wray CO 80758-1630 • FAX(970)332-4023 • calvary@plains.net
**YUMA—*ST JOHN*** (970)848-2210
Vacant • H • RM • 405 S Albany St 80759-2505 PO Box 436 Yuma CO 80759-0436 • FAX(970)848-2210 • stjohns@rmi.net

## CONNECTICUT

**BANTAM—*SHEPHERD/HILLS*** (860)567-1433
Gregory Dwyer • WS 930;* • H • NE • 890 Bantam Rd 06750-1608 PO Box 47 Bantam CT 06750-0047 • gregory[3]dwyer@hotmail.com

**BRIDGEPORT—*ZION*** (203)367-4521
Vacant • EC/EL • NE • 612 Grand St Bridgeport CT 06604-3218 • FAX(203)335-6143 • zionschool@aol.com

**BRISTOL—*IMMANUEL*** (860)583-5649
H L Bridges Steven R Schumacher • WS 8 915; SS 920; BC 920;* • H • EC/EL • NE • 154 Meadow St Bristol CT 06010-5730 • FAX(860)585-4785 • il.church@snet.net

**CHESHIRE—*CHESHIRE*** (203)272-5106
Charles Gustafson • * • H • EC • NE • 660 W Main St 06410-3923 PO Box 157 Cheshire CT 06410-0157 • FAX(203)272-3523

**COVENTRY—*PRINCE OF PEACE*** (860)742-7548
Vacant • WS 9;* • EC • NE • 10 N River Rd Coventry CT 06238-1633 • psecker@snet.net

**DANBURY—*IMMANUEL*** (203)748-3320
Daniel L Wehmeier Walter J Harper • H • EC/EL • NE • 32 West St 26 West St Danbury CT 06810-7842 • FAX(203)744-3446 • immanueldnby@juno.com

**ENFIELD—*OUR REDEEMER*** (860)749-3167
Vacant • * • H • EC • NE • 20 North St 06082-3921 PO Box 887 Enfield CT 06083-0887 • lcor@portone.com

**GREENWICH—*FIRST*** (203)869-0032
Jimmy B Coffey Jr. • H • NE • 38 Field Point Rd Greenwich CT 06830-5338

***ST PAUL*** (203)531-8466
Kenneth M Ballas • EC • S • 286 Delavan Ave Greenwich CT 06830-5946 • FAX(203)531-6450

**GROTON—*FAITH*** (860)445-0483
Paul R Wagner • * • H • EC • NE • 625 Poquonnock Rd Groton CT 06340-4567 • FAX(860)445-0483 • flcgroton@aol.com

**HEBRON—*CHRIST*** (860)228-1152
Ralph A Sackschewsky • WS 9;* • H • NE • 330 Church St (Rt 85) 06248 PO Box 62 Hebron CT 06248-0062 • FAX(860)228-3230 • ralphs@connix.com

**LEBANON—*REDEEMER*** (860)423-4320
Scott R Schuett • * • NE • 328 Village Hill Rd 06249-1026 361 Beaumont Hwy Lebanon CT 06249-1103 • FAX(860)450-1064 • redeemer[3]lutheran@juno.com

**MADISON—*MADISON*** (203)245-4145
Volker S Heide • EC • NE • 9 Britton Ln Madison CT 06443

**MANCHESTER—*ZION*** (860)649-4243
Henry C Lubben • WS 930;* • NE • 112 Cooper St 120 Cooper St Manchester CT 06040-5837

**MERIDEN—*ST JOHN*** (203)238-2331
Vacant • H • EC • NE • 520 Paddock Ave Meriden CT 06450-6999 • FAX(203)237-9590 • St.john.lc@snet.net

**MIDDLETOWN—*GRACE*** (860)346-2641
Vacant • H • EC • NE • 1055 Randolph Rd Middletown CT 06457-5190 • FAX(860)344-0611 • grace.evan.lutheran@snet.net

**NAUGATUCK—*ST PAUL*** (203)729-8610
Andrew Green • NE • 350 Millville Ave Naugatuck CT 06770-3711

**NEW BRITAIN—*ST MATTHEW*** (860)223-3503
Donald R Neiswender(EM) • H • EC/EL • NE • 99 Franklin Square New Britain CT 06051-2606 • FAX(860)223-3503

**NEW FAIRFIELD—*GOOD SHEPHERD*** (203)746-9022
Roland M Klauck • * • H • NE • 2 Colonial Rd New Fairfield CT 06812-5023 • FAX(203)746-9022 • jk931@aol.com

**NEW HARTFORD—*ST PAUL*** (860)379-3172
Timothy R Yeadon • WS 8; SS 915; BC 915;* • H • EC • NE • 30 Prospect St New Hartford CT 06057-2221 • popetim@compsol.net

**NEW LONDON—*OUR REDEEMER*** (860)444-6529
Craig J Donofrio • NE • 31 Cedar Grove Ave New London CT 06320-5243 • redeemernl@aol.com

**NEW MILFORD—*TRINITY*** (860)354-3450
Frederick J Bunzel • H • NE • 107 Kent Rd 06776-3407 PO Box 388 New Milford CT 06776-0388 • FAX(860)354-3450

**NEWTOWN—*CHRIST KING*** (203)426-6300
Gregory J Wismar • * • H • NE • 85 Mount Pleasant Rd 06470-1535 PO Box 721 Newtown CT 06470-0721 • FAX(203)426-6300 • ctkingchrch@snet.net

**NIANTIC—*CHRIST*** (860)739-6849
Vacant • Tiffany A Silva DCE • H • EC • NE • 24 Society Rd Niantic CT 06357-1108 • FAX(860)739-6849 • clcms@uconect.net

**NORWALK—*ST PETER*** (203)847-1252
Robert D Beinke • * • H • NE • 208 Newtown Ave Norwalk CT 06851-2316 • FAX(203)846-4415 • mail@stpeterlc.norwalk.ct.us

**ORANGE—*ZION*** (203)795-3916
John G Schettenhelm • NE • 780 Grassy Hill Rd Orange CT 06477-1653

**SOUTH WINDSOR—*OUR SAVIOR*** (860)644-3350
Rolf A Buchmann Randall L Pekari Donald R Rau(#) • WS 9;* • H • EC • NE • 239 Graham Rd South Windsor CT 06074-1422 • FAX(860)644-9068 • our.savior.lutheran@snet.net

**STAMFORD—*TRINITY*** (203)966-3070
Jack Breznen • S • 265 Seaside Ave Stamford CT 06902-5418

**STORRS—*HOPE*** (860)429-5409
Philip J Secker • * • NE • 06268 62 Dog Ln Storrs Mansfield CT 06268-2220 • psecker@snet.net

**SUFFIELD—*GOOD SHEPHERD*** (860)668-2790
James L Kerner • * • NE • 585 South St 06078-2211 PO Box 155 Suffield CT 06078-0155 • gslc@usa.net

**TERRYVILLE—*HOLY TRINITY*** (860)582-0723
Richard L Neagley • H • NE • 8 Maple St Terryville CT 06786-5220 • FAX(860)583-1981 • htchurch@snet.net

***SHEPHERD/HILLS***
See Bantam

**TRUMBULL—*HOLY CROSS*** (203)268-7555
Emil A Witschy • * • H • EC • NE • 5995 Main St Trumbull CT 06611 • FAX(203)268-5499 • holycrss@connix.com

**WALLINGFORD—*ZION*** (203)269-6847
Robert C Hass • H • EC • NE • 235 Pond Hill Rd Wallingford CT 06492-5205

**WATERBURY—*ST JOHN*** (203)754-7618
Martin E Kiesel • H • NE • 503 Chase Pkwy Waterbury CT 06708-3303

**WEST HARTFORD—*BETHANY*** (860)521-5076
Carl J Anton Robert J Mikulastik • * • H • EC • NE • 1655 Boulevard West Hartford CT 06107-2502 • FAX(860)521-7066 • blcwhtfd@aol.com

***CHURCH OF THE DEAF*** (203)523-0345
Vacant • NE • 06091 400 Wilbraham Rd Springfield MA 01109

**WESTPORT—*ST PAUL*** (203)227-7441
Paul N E Teske • * • H • EC • S • 41 Easton Rd Westport CT 06880-2213 • FAX(203)222-9205 • info@stpaulwestport.org

## DELAWARE

**BEAR—*FAITH*** (302)834-1214
Vacant • * • H • EC • SE • 19701 2265 Red Lion Rd Bear DE 19701-1849 • FAX(302)834-3417 • faithc2@juno.com

**DOVER—*ST JOHN*** (302)734-7078
Arthur D Kringel • H • EC • SE • 113 Lotus St Dover DE 19901-4435 • artk770@aol.com

**NEW CASTLE—*FAITH***
See Bear

**NEWARK—*OUR REDEEMER*** (302)737-6176
Carl H Kruelle • * • H • EC • SE • 10 Johnson Rd Newark DE 19713-1808

**REHOBOTH BEACH—*OUR SAVIOR*** (302)227-3066
Vacant • WS 815 11; SS 930; BC 930 • H • SE • 7 Bay Vista Rd Rehoboth Beach DE 19971-1421 • FAX(302)227-0105

**SEAFORD—*CHRIST*** (302)629-9755
Donald G Meyer • Amy E Nerger DCE • H • SE • 315 N Shipley St Seaford DE 19973-2315

**SMYRNA—*PEACE*** (302)653-4312
Donald H Krompart • H • SE • 5048 Wheatleys Pond Rd Smyrna DE 19977-3723

**WILMINGTON—*CONCORDIA*** (302)478-3004
David E Mueller • H • EC • SE • 3003 Silverside Rd Wilmington DE 19810-3441 • FAX(302)478-7403

## DISTRICT OF COLUMBIA

**SILVER SPRING—*CAMPUS DEAF****
See Washington DC

**WASHINGTON—*CAMPUS DEAF**** (202)651-5102
Vacant • * • H • SE • 20090 C/O Gallaudet University 800 Florida Ave NW Washington DC 20002-3695 • FAX(301)589-0931 • george.natonick@gallandet.edu

**WASHINGTON DC—*MOUNT OLIVET*** (202)667-5357
John F Johnson • WS 11; SS 945; BC 945 • H • SE • 20005 1306 Vermont Ave NW Washington DC 20005-3607 • FAX(202)234-6631

***PEACE*** (202)398-5503
James Wiggins Jr. • H • SE • 20090 15 49th Pl NE Washington DC 20019-5302 • FAX(202)398-8552 • peacelutherandc@erols.com

## FLORIDA

**APOPKA—*ST PAUL*** (407)889-2634
Donald A Moore • WS 10; SS 9; BC 9 • H • FG • 261 S Mc Gee Ave Apopka FL 32703-4479 • FAX(407)889-2634 • stpaullcms@netzero.net

**ARCADIA—*GRACE*** (863)494-7008
Theodore R Hanus • WS 10; SS 830; BC 830;* • H • FG • 1004 W Oak St 34266-3369 PO Box 1753 Arcadia FL 34265-1753 • FAX(863)494-7008

**AVON PARK—*AVON PARK*** (863)784-0106
Vacant • WS 1130; SS 10;* • H • FG • 2523 US 27 S Suite 120 Avon Park FL 33825

**BARTOW—*REDEEMER*** (863)533-6054
Anthony J Douches • WS 1015; BC 9 • H • EC • FG • 390 E Parker St Bartow FL 33830-4721 • tonycaro@gateway.net

**BELLE GLADE—*ST PETER*** (407)996-2205
Richard L Arndt • H • FG • 125 E Canal St N Belle Glade FL 33430-3564

**BOCA RATON—*ST PAUL*** (561)395-0433
Dennis W Glick Stephen E Miguet August D Brown(#) • WS 8 930 11; SS 930; BC 930;* • H • EC/EL • FG • 701 W Palmetto Park Rd Boca Raton FL 33486-3561 • FAX(561)395-5348 • dglick@cyberfalcon.som

**BONIFAY—*GRACE**** (850)547-9898
Vacant • WS 830 • H • SO • East Hwy 90 32425 PO Box 972 Bonifay FL 32425-0972

**BONITA SPRINGS—*HOPE*** (941)992-6952
Rick C Carlton • WS 8 11; SS 930; BC 930;* • H • FG • 25999 Old 41 Rd Bonita Springs FL 34135-7824 • FAX(941)992-3254 • rccarlton@aol.com

**BOYNTON BEACH—*SON LIFE*** (561)738-5433
John D Johnson • WS 10; SS 9 • H • FG • 9301 Jog Rd Boynton Beach FL 33437-3653 • FAX(561)364-7884 • pastorjohnd@juno.com

**BRADENTON—*HOPE*** (941)755-3256
David G Hinman • WS 1030; SS 915; BC 915;* • H • EC • FG • 4635 26th St W Bradenton FL 34207-1702 • FAX(941)755-0586 • hopelutheran@juno.com

**BRANDON—*IMMANUEL*** (813)689-1787
Kenneth W Farnsworth Mark A Wood • WS 830; SS 945; BC 945 • H • EL • FG • 2913 John Moore Rd Brandon FL 33511-7139 • FAX(813)681-1526 • IMLC@ij.net

**BROOKSVILLE—*CHRIST*** (352)796-8331
Richard H Drankwalter • WS 830 11;* • H • FG • 475 North Ave W Brooksville FL 34601-1031 • FAX(352)754-4380 • clc@innet.com

**BROOKVILLE—*HOLY TRINITY***
See Masaryktown

**CALLAWAY—*GOOD SHEPHERD*** (850)871-6311
Gary E Hill • WS 8 1030; SS 915; BC 915 • H • EC/EL • SO • UKNWN 929 S Tyndall Pkwy Panama City FL 32404-7242 • FAX(850)871-3077 • goodshepherdlc@aol.com

**CANTONMENT—*TRINITY*** (904)968-0078
Sanford D Stanton • H • SO • 2385 Highway 297A Cantonment FL 32533-7686

**CAPE CANAVERAL—*CHRIST*** (321)783-3303
David G Mennicke • * • H • FG • 7511 N Atlantic Ave Cape Canaveral FL 32920-3701 • clccc@earthlink.net

**CAPE CORAL—*TRINITY*** (941)772-0172
Vacant • H • EC/EL • FG • 706 SW 6th Ave Cape Coral FL 33991-2490 • FAX(941)772-4691

**CARROLLWOOD—*MESSIAH*** (813)961-2182
James R Guelzow • WS 830; SS 945; BC 945 • H • EC/EL • FG • 33688 14920 Hutchison Rd Tampa FL 33625-5507 • FAX(813)961-0592

**CASSELBERRY—*ASCENSION*** (407)831-7788
Victor D Willmann James M Daub • WS 8 1030 1045; SS 915; BC 915;* • H • EC • FG • 351 Ascension Dr Casselberry FL 32707-3801 • FAX(407)831-2350 • ascension@ascensionlcms.org

**CHIEFLAND—*GOOD SHEPHERD*** (352)493-4597
Larry F Davis • WS 1030; SS 915; BC 915;* • H • FG • 14303 Nw 143rd Place 32626 PO Box 2090 Chiefland FL 32644-2090

**CLEARWATER—*BETHEL*** (727)799-3010
Timothy J Parsch • H • FG • 3166 Mc Mullen Booth Rd Clearwater FL 33761-2025 • FAX(727)796-4889

***FIRST*** (727)447-4504
Pat F A O Brien Keith G Less • WS 8 1030; SS 915; BC 915;* • H • EC/EL • FG • 1644 Nursery Rd Clearwater FL 33756-2437 • FAX(727)442-7473

***ROGATE DEAF***
See Largo

**CLEWISTON—*FAITH*** (813)983-7302
Vacant • WS 10;* • H • FG • 810 Cedar St 33440-2405 PO Box 338 Clewiston FL 33440-0338

**CRAWFORDVILLE—*TRINITY*** (904)926-7808
Vacant • WS 1030; BC 915;* • H • EC • FG • 3254 Coastal Hwy Crawfordville FL 32327-4200

**CRESTVIEW—*OUR SAVIOR*** (850)682-3154
Andrew C Watkins • WS 8 1045; SS 915;* • H • SO • 225 Bracewell St 32536-2456 178 W North Ave Crestview FL 32536-2356 • FAX(850)682-6008 • pastoroslc@cfi.net

**DAVIE—*GLORIA DEI*** (954)475-0683
Darrell Stuehrenberg • Michael R Stapleton DCE • WS 8 930 11; SS 930;* • H • EC/EL • FG • 7601 SW 39th St Davie FL 33328-2716 • FAX(954)474-2313 • gloriadei@juno.com

**DAYTONA BEACH—*HOLY CROSS***
See South Daytona

***TRINITY***
See Holly Hill

**DELRAY BEACH—*EMMANUEL*** (651)276-0205
Edouane Jean • FG • 400 N Swinton Ave Delray Beach FL 33444-3954

***TRINITY*** (561)278-1737
C S Gress Kenneth D Green II • H • EC/EL • FG • 400 N Swinton Ave Delray Beach FL 33444-3954 • FAX(561)272-3215 • trinity@trinitydelray.org

**DELTONA—*PROVIDENCE*** (904)789-3300
Paul N Rauscher • WS 8 1030; SS 915; BC 915 • H • FG • 1696 Providence Blvd Deltona FL 32725-4961 • FAX(904)789-0132 • lcp@mpinet.net

**DESTIN—*GRACE*** (904)654-1679
Paul W Kummer • WS 8 1030; SS 915; BC 915 • H • SO • 4100 Two Trees Rd Destin FL 32541-3319 • FAX(904)654-9588 • gracelutheran@destin.net

**DUNEDIN—*FAITH*** (727)733-2657
Herbert D Mitchell • WS 10; SS 9; BC 9 • H • FG • 1620 Pinehurst Rd Dunedin FL 34698-3842 • FAX(727)733-2637 • faithlutheran@ij.net

**DUNNELLON—*PEACE*** (352)489-5881
Kennard O Mueller • WS 930; SS 815; BC 815 • H • FG • 7201 S Hwy 41 Dunnellon FL 34432-2264

**ELLENTON 2 E—*FAITH*** (941)776-1395
Duane K Albers • H • FG • 34222 9608 US Highway 301 N Parrish FL 34219-8655

**ENGLEWOOD—*REDEEMER*** (941)475-2410
Warren J Thomason • SS 915;* • H • EC • FG • 6965 Mayport 34295 6970 Mineola Rd Englewood FL 34224-8035 • FAX(941)475-9726 • redeemer@ewol.com

**EUSTIS—*FAITH*** (352)589-5433
William P Schmidt • WS 8 11; SS 930; BC 930;* • H • EC/EL • FG • 2727 S Grove St Eustis FL 32726-7302 • FAX(352)589-1886 • faithmail@aol.com

**FORT LAUDERDALE—*FAITH*** (954)583-0360
Vacant • WS 9; SS 1015; BC 1015 • H • EC/EL • FG • Sw 31st Ave 11th Ct 33310 1161 SW 30th Ave Fort Lauderdale FL 33312-2856 • FAX(954)581-2918 • FaithLutheran2@juno.com

***GLORIA DEI***
See Davie

***GOOD SHEPHERD*** (305)583-7911
Vacant • H • FG • 1201 NW 27th Ave Fort Lauderdale FL 33311-5204

***PEACE*** (954)772-8010
Daniel P Czaplewski • H • EC/EL • FG • 1901 E Commercial Blvd Fort Lauderdale FL 33308-3726 • FAX(954)772-2232 • beachpew@aol.com

***ST PAUL***
See Weston

***TRINITY*** (954)463-2450
Louis H Abel • Troy A De la Motte DCE • WS 10; SS 845; BC 845 • H • EL • FG • 11 SW 11th St Fort Lauderdale FL 33315-1225 • FAX(954)767-4776 • trinityv@juno.com

**FORT MYERS—*GOOD SHEPHERD***
See North Fort Myers

***GRACE*** (941)694-3878
Vacant • WS 1030; SS 915; BC 915;* • H • FG • 14531 Old Olga Rd Fort Myers FL 33905-2300 • praylbor@peganet.com

***ST MICHAEL*** (941)939-4711
Jon H Zehnder • Lori A Lanning DCE • WS 815 1045; SS 930; BC 930;* • H • EC/EL • FG • 3595 Broadway Fort Myers FL 33901-8021 • FAX(941)939-1839 • rclinger@sml.org

***ZION*** (941)481-4040
Richard P Miller Steven J Hess • * • H • FG • 7401 Winkler Rd Fort Myers FL 33919-7155 • FAX(941)481-4102 • pastorhess@earthlink.net

**FORT PIERCE—*TRINITY*** (561)461-7272
Ronald P Engel • WS 8 1030; SS 915; BC 915 • H • FG • 2011 S 13th St Fort Pierce FL 34950-5238 • FAX(561)461-5999 • ftpierctle@aol.com

**FORT WALTON BEA—*GOOD***
See Shalimar

**FT LAUDERDALE—*GRACE*** (954)763-6286
George R Earhart • Troy A De la Motte DCE • WS 10;* • H • EC • FG • 1801 NE 13th St Fort Lauderdale FL 33304-1819 • FAX(954)764-6763 • earhartsflorida@juno.com

**GAINESVILLE—*ABIDING SAVIOR*** (352)331-4409
Charles T Reich • WS 830 11;* • H • EC • FG • 9700 W Newberry Rd Gainesville FL 32606-5545 • FAX(352)331-7777 • abidingsavior@juno.com

***FIRST*** (352)376-2062
Timothy M Hinz Kenneth L Babin • WS 830 11 1045; SS 945; BC 945;* • H • FG • 1801 NW 5th Ave Gainesville FL 32603-1624 • FAX(352)377-0408 • staff@flcgainesville.org

**GOLDEN GATE—*MESSIAH***
See Naples

**GULF BREEZE—*GOOD SHEPHERD*** (850)932-3263
Richard G Lohmeyer • Aaron V Pierce DCE • WS 8 1030; SS 915; BC 915;* • H • EC • SO • 4257 Gulf Breeze Pkwy Gulf Breeze FL 32561-3510 • FAX(850)934-6372 • goodshepherd@freent.com

**HIALEAH—*FAITH*** (305)888-6706
Mark Wessling • H • EC/EL • FG • 293 Hialeah Dr Hialeah FL 33010-5218

***ST ANDREW*** (305)821-3622
Christian G Burg • WS 930 • H • FG • 575 W 68th St Hialeah FL 33014-4902 • standrewsluthmia@juno.com

**HOBE SOUND—*BETHEL*** (561)546-5399
Henry C Abram • * • H • EC • FG • 7905 SE Federal Hwy Hobe Sound FL 33455-7012 • FAX(561)546-9847 • bethelluthchurch@aol.com

**HOLLY HILL—*TRINITY*** (904)255-7580
Frederick W Schultz • Mark E Wetherell DCE • H • EC/EL • FG • 1205 Ridgewood Ave Holly Hill FL 32117-2721 • FAX(904)255-7589

**HOLLYWOOD—*PRINCE PEACE*** (305)983-8599
Juan M Martin • H • FG • 3100 NW 75th Ave Hollywood FL 33024-2355

***ST MARK*** (954)922-7568
James J Vehling • Martha L Rupprecht Janine R Blair DCE • WS 9; SS 1015; BC 1015;* • H • EC/EL • FG • 502 N 28th Ave Hollywood FL 33020-3811 • FAX(954)925-5388

**HOMESTEAD—*HOSPITAL DE ALMA*** (305)247-0459
Benito Perez-Lopez(DM) • FG • 1955 N Krome Ave Homestead FL 33030 • FAX(305)228-0866 • BPerez6950@aol.com

**HOMOSASSA SPRIN—*FAITH***
See Lecanto

**HUDSON—*HOPE*** (727)863-6446
Douglas A Rosenvinge • WS 830 11; BC 945;* • H • EC • FG • 12321 Canton Ave Hudson FL 34669-1929 • FAX(727)861-1820 • hope³hudson@juno.com

**INVERNESS—*FIRST*** (352)726-1637
John G Fischer • WS 10 745; BC 845;* • H • FG • 1900 Highway 44 W Inverness FL 34453-3802 • jjfisch@citrus.infi.net

**JACKSONVILLE—*CELEBRATION*** (904)928-9901
Dale W Kaster • WS 9 • EN • 11265 Alumni Way Jacksonville FL 32246-6685 • FAX(904)641-0760 • jaxdale@aol.com

***GRACE*** (904)928-9136
Richard S Engel • Jason W Taylor DCE Heidi L Bierlein DCE • WS 830 11; SS 10; BC 10 • H • EC • FG • 12200 Mc Cormick Rd Jacksonville FL 32225-5563 • FAX(904)928-0181 • grace5@bellsouth.net

***GUARDIAN*** (904)268-5816
Kristopher R Whitby • WS 1030; SS 915;* • H • FG • 10113 Haley Rd Jacksonville FL 32257-5823 • FAX(904)268-5816 • guardluth@aol.com

***HOLY CROSS*** (904)724-3210
Alec E Pueschel • WS 10; SS 845; BC 845 • H • EC • FG • 6620 Arlington Expy Jacksonville FL 32211-7233 • FAX(904)724-9632 • holycrosslc@cxp.com

***OUR REDEEMER*** (904)766-4728
William P Reister • H • EC • FG • 5401 Dunn Ave Jacksonville FL 32218-4329 • FAX(904)766-4728 • wmreister@aol.com

***ST PAUL*** (904)765-4219
Frank T Marshall • H • FG • 2730 Edgewood Ave W Jacksonville FL 32209-2315 • FAX(904)765-7737 • FMarsh8925@aol.com

**JACKSONVILLE BEACH—*BETHLEHEM*** (904)249-5418
John R Buchheimer Dana A Brones • WS 8; SS 930; BC 930 • H • EC • FG • 1423 8th Ave N Jacksonville Beach FL 32250-3555 • FAX(904)249-7572

**KENDALL—*CONCORDIA*** (305)235-6123
Robert J Maulella • Jessie Perez DEAC • WS 8 10; SS 9; BC 9 • H • EC • FG • 33256 8701 SW 124th St Miami FL 33176-5215 • FAX(305)235-6525 • concordiakendallfl@juno.com

**KEY WEST—*GRACE*** (305)296-5161
Vacant • H • EC/EL • FG • 2713 Flagler Ave Key West FL 33040-3981 • FAX(305)296-0622

**LABELLE—*CHRIST KING*** (941)675-2733
Vacant • WS 830 • H • FG • 1362 Thigpen Rd 33935-6169 PO Box 2925 Labelle FL 33975-2925 • melkarau@aol.com

**LADY LAKE—*TRINITY*** (352)307-4500
Richard C Markworth • WS 9; SS 1030; BC 1030 • H • FG • 17330 S Us Hwy 441 32159 17330 South Hwy 441 Summerfield FL 34491 • FAX(352)307-4502 • trinity@webcombo.net

**LAKE CITY—*OUR REDEEMER*** (904)755-4299
Vacant • H • FG • State Rd 47 S 32055 RR 9 Box 560 Lake City FL 32024-8932 • FAX(904)755-3507

**LAKE MARY—*HOLY CROSS*** (407)333-0797
Paul M Hoyer Nathan J Guelzow • WS 8 930 11;* • H • EC • S • 760 N Sun Dr Lake Mary FL 32746-2507 • FAX(407)333-9977 • dennis@holycross-lakemary.org

**LAKE PLACID—*TRINITY*** (863)465-5253
Richard A Norris • Susan C Norris DCE • * • H • EC • FG • 25 Lakeview Ave 33852-9687 PO Box 1082 Lake Placid FL 33862-1082 • FAX(863)465-1074 • trinity@htn.net

**LAKE WALES—*LAKE WALES*** (863)676-4715
John V Glamann • * • H • EC/EL • FG • 640 S Scenic Hwy Lake Wales FL 33853-4832 • FAX(863)676-5578

**LAKE WORTH—*EPIPHANY*** (407)968-3627
Douglas E Fountain • WS 10; SS 845;* • H • EC • FG • 4460 Lyons Rd Lake Worth FL 33467-3614 • FAX(407)968-3627

***OUR SAVIOR*** (561)582-4430
Clarence F Reinke Jr. Donald D Kasischke • WS 815 1030; SS 930; BC 930;* • H • EC/EL • FG • 1615 Lake Ave Lake Worth FL 33460-3670 • FAX(561)582-1074 • osl@flinet.com

***SALEM HAITIAN*** (407)586-5691
Elie Louissaint • H • FG • 1020 S Dixie Hwy Lake Worth FL 33460-3697 • FAX(561)582-4319 • elie1020@yahoo.com

**LAKELAND—*CHRIST*** (863)682-7802
Vacant • H • EC • FG • 2715 Lakeland Hills Blvd Lakeland FL 33805-2219 • FAX(863)616-1040

***ST PAUL*** (863)644-7710
Dennison J Goff Stephen J Constien • James G Hahn DCE • WS 830 11; SS 945; BC 945;* • H • EC/EL • FG • 4450 Harden Blvd Lakeland FL 33813-1433 • FAX(863)644-7491

**LAND O LAKES—*HOLY TRINITY*** (813)949-7173
Gilbert A Kuehn • WS 8 10; BC 9;* • H • EC/EL • FG • 34639 20735 Leonard Rd Lutz FL 33549-8355 • FAX(813)949-7173 • holytrinitylutheranlol@juno.com

**LARGO—*CHRIST THE KING*** (727)595-2117
Vacant • WS 815 11; SS 930; BC 930;* • H • FG • 11220 Oakhurst Rd Largo FL 33774-4447 • FAX(727)593-3477 • ctklc@ctklc.org

***ROGATE*** (727)531-2761
Richard E Bradley • WS 10 • H • EC • FG • 33770 4825 E Bay Dr Clearwater FL 33764-6802

***ROGATE DEAF*** (813)536-3862
Larry J Larsen • H • FG • 33770 4825 E Bay Dr Clearwater FL 34624-6800

**LECANTO—*FAITH*** (352)527-3325
Vacant • WS 830; SS 10; BC 10 • H • FG • 935 S Crystal Glen Dr Lecanto FL 34461-8364 • FAX(352)527-7043

**LEESBURG—*BETHANY*** (352)787-7275
Gary C Genzen • * • H • FG • 1334 Griffin Rd Leesburg FL 34748 • FAX(352)787-0727

**LEHIGH ACRES—*BEAUTIFUL SAVIOR*** (941)368-7897
Vacant • WS 10; BC 9;* • H • FG • 215 Richmond Ave N Lehigh Acres FL 33972-5012

**LITTLE RIVER—*OUR SAVIOUR*** (305)691-1672
Vacant • H • FG • UKNWN 2362 NW 95th St Miami FL 33147-2416

**LUTZ—*HOLY TRINITY***
See Land O Lakes

**MARATHON—*MARTIN LUTHER*** (305)289-0700
Donald S Roberts • H • EL • FG • 325 122nd Street Gulf Marathon FL 33050-3503 • FAX(305)289-0700 • 105166

**MARCO ISLAND—*MARCO*** (941)394-0332
Ronald D Biel • * • H • EL • FG • 525 N Collier Blvd Marco Island FL 34145-1949 • FAX(941)394-9073 • marcoluth@aol.com

**MARIANNA—*ASCENSION*** (850)482-4691
Edmund E Schafer • WS 1030; SS 915 • H • SO • 3975 Hwy 90 Marianna FL 32446-8922

***GRACE****
See Bonifay

**MASARYKTOWN—*HOLY TRINITY*** (352)796-4066
Vacant • H • FG • 34609 1214 Broad St Spring Hill FL 34609-6812

**MELBOURNE—*REDEEMER*** (321)723-4152
Harlan R Schoenrock • WS 8 1030; SS 9; BC 9;* • H • FG • 12 E Avenue A Melbourne FL 32901-1354 • FAX(321)723-4152 • officel@digital.net

**MERRITT ISLAND—*FAITH*** (321)452-4080
Russell G Frahm L W Myers(EM) • WS 8; SS 930; BC 930 • H • EC • FG • 280 E Merritt Ave Merritt Island FL 32953-3415 • FAX(321)452-9147 • faithmi@faithcaring.org

**MIAMI—*BAY SHORE*** (305)758-1344
Erwin Perez-Arche • H • FG • 5051 Biscayne Blvd Miami FL 33137-3217 • epereza@aol.com

***CONCORDIA***
See Kendall

***HOSPITAL DE ALMA***
See Homestead

***OUR SAVIOUR***
See Little River

***REDEEMER*** (305)895-1647
Vacant • H • FG • 11101 NE 2nd Ave Miami FL 33161-7028

***SAN PABLO APOSTOL*** (305)271-6127
Vacant • H • FG • 10700 SW 56th St Miami FL 33165-7044

***ST MATTHEW*** (305)642-2860
Luis M Santana • WS 9 11; SS 1015;* • H • EC/EL • FG • 621 Beacom Blvd Miami FL 33135-2931 • FAX(305)642-3477

***ST PAUL*** (305)271-3171
Ronald H Schuette • H • EC/EL • FG • 10700 SW 56th St Miami FL 33165-7044 • FAX(305)271-3148

***TRINITY*** (305)216-0030
George E Poulos Jr. • WS 1030; SS 915; BC 915 • H • FG • 8601 SW 212th St 33189-3301 21721 SW 97th Ct Miami FL 33190-1176

***TRINITY***
See Cutler Ridge

**MIDDLEBURG—*ST PETER***
See Orange Park-Middleburg

**MILTON—*ETERNAL TRIN*** (850)623-5780
Daniel E Thies • H • SO • 6076 Old Bagdad Hwy Milton FL 32583-8943

**MIRAMAR—*MIRAMAR*** (305)987-1234
Juan M Martin • H • EC • FG • 7790 Lasalle Blvd Miramar FL 33023-4612

**MONTVERDE—*WOODLANDS*** (407)469-2525
Brian N Kneser Garrett L Knudson(DM) • David G Everson DCE • WS 8 1030; SS 915;* • H • EC • FG • 15333 County Rd 455 Montverde FL 34756-3775 • FAX(407)469-4742

**NAPLES—*FAITH*** (941)434-5811
Vacant • H • EC/EL • EN • 4150 Goodlette Rd N Naples FL 34103-3363 • FAX(941)434-5410 • faithnaple@aol.com

***GRACE*** (941)261-7421
James K Honig • * • H • EC/EL • FG • 860 Banyan Blvd Naples FL 34102-5112 • FAX(941)261-9337

***MESSIAH*** (941)455-2520
Robert C Jacobs • WS 8 1030; SS 915;* • H • EL • FG • 5800 Golden Gate Pkwy Naples FL 34116-7459 • FAX(941)455-0581 • messiahlutheran@worldnet.att.net

**NEW PORT RICHEY—*FAITH*** (727)849-4418
Roy A Lidbom Robert C Steinke • WS 8 11; SS 930; BC 930;* • H • FG • 5443 Sunset Rd New Port Richey FL 34652-1737 • FAX(727)844-3541 • faithnpr@gte.net

**NORTH FORT MYERS—*GOOD*** (941)995-7711
Martin Renner • H • EC/EL • FG • 33918 4770 Orange Grove Blvd Fort Myers FL 33903-4556 • FAX(941)995-0473

**NORTH MIAMI—*HOLY CROSS*** (305)893-0371
Dennis L Bartels • * • H • EC/EL • FG • 650 NE 135th St North Miami FL 33161-7519 • FAX(305)893-1845 • dbartels@holycrossministries.com

**NORTH PALM BEACH—*FAITH*** (561)848-4737
John L Frerking Daniel P Mc Pherson • Kathleen S Mc Coy DEAC • H • EC • FG • 555 US Highway 1 North Palm Beach FL 33408-4901 • FAX(561)881-1613 • faithnpbj@aol.com

**OCALA—*OUR REDEEMER*** (352)237-2233
Ronald R Mueller • WS 8; SS 930; BC 930 • H • FG • 5200 SW Highway 200 Ocala FL 34474-5737 • FAX(352)237-2233

***ST JOHN*** (352)629-1794
Richard W Lineberger Paul S Burtzlaff • WS 830 11; SS 945; BC 945;* • H • EC/EL • FG • 1915 SE Lake Weir Rd Ocala FL 34471-5424 • FAX(352)622-5564 • stjohnlc@digital.net

***TRINITY*** (352)840-0711
Vacant • EN • 4001 NE 25th Ave Ocala FL 34479 • FAX(352)854-2670

**OKEECHOBEE—*PEACE*** (863)763-5042
John C Hirst • WS 8; SS 915; BC 915 • H • EC • FG • 750 NW 23rd Ln Okeechobee FL 34972-4315 • FAX(863)763-0143 • hirst@okeechobee.com

**ORANGE PARK-MIDDLEBE—*ST*** (904)282-8876
Marc A Kappel • H • FG • 1614 S Blanding Blvd 32073 PO Box 898 Orange Park FL 32067-0898 • readdrj@medianoe.net

**ORLANDO—*ASCENSION***
See Casselberry

***CHRIST KING*** (407)876-2771
Gerald N Schultz • H • EC • FG • 4962 S Apopka Vineland Rd Orlando FL 32819-3104

***HOPE*** (407)657-4556
Paul W von Werder • WS 8 1030; SS 915; BC 915 • H • EC • FG • 2600 N Dean Rd Orlando FL 32817-2735 • FAX(407)657-8806 • paul@hopeoforlando.org

***OUR SAVIOR*** (407)295-0261
Christopher R Bodley • FG • 1750 Bruton Blvd Orlando FL 32805-5132

***PRINCE OF PEACE*** (407)277-3945
James R Wiebel John C Rallison • WS 8 915 1030 1130; SS 915; BC 1030 • H • EC • FG • 1515 S Semoran Blvd Orlando FL 32807-2997 • FAX(407)380-1802 • churchpop@aol.com

***RESURRECTION*** (407)855-1393
David H Parsch • H • FG • 200 W Lancaster Rd Orlando FL 32809-4955

***TRINITY*** (407)422-5704
Scott E Heitshusen • WS 8 930 11; SS 930; BC 930;* • H • EC/EL • FG • 123 E Livingston St Orlando FL 32801-1598 • FAX(407)423-2085 • tlcs@trinitydowntown.org

***ZION*** (407)293-5616
Paul M Foust • WS 930 1045; SS 815; BC 815;* • H • FG • 6330 Moore St Orlando FL 32818-5952

**OVIEDO—*ST LUKE*** (407)365-3408
Wally M Arp Brian D Roberts Gary S Schuschke • WS 8 11 930; SS 930; BC 930;* • H • EL • S • 2021 W State Road 426 Oviedo FL 32765-8524 • FAX(407)366-9346 • wmarp@stlukes-oviedo.org

**PALM COAST—*SHEPHERD COAST*** (904)446-2481
William Douthwaite III • WS 8 1030; SS 915; BC 915 • H • EC • EN • 101 Pine Lakes Pkwy N Palm Coast FL 32164-3636 • sotcms@pcfl.net

**PANAMA CITY—*GOOD SHEPHERD***
See Callaway

***REDEMPTION*** (850)763-0201
Vacant • SO • 1700 E 11th St Panama City FL 32401-4439

***TRINITY*** (850)763-2412
Edward A Meyer • WS 830 11; SS 10;* • H • SO • 1001 W 11th S Panama City FL 32401-2041 • FAX(850)913-9997 • Trinityluth@mindspring.com

**PANAMA CITY BEACH—*CHRIST OUR*** 888-298-9048
Robert R Lydick • WS 1030; SS 930; BC 930 • H • SO • 300 Clara Ave Panama City Beach FL 32407 • FAX(850)233-9900 • christoursavior1@juno.com

**PARRISH—*FAITH***
See Ellenton 2 E

**PEMBROKE PINES—*NEW LIFE*** (954)473-4353
Paul L Hasselbring • H • FG • PO Box 82311 Pembroke Pines FL 33082

**PENSACOLA—*GRACE*** (850)476-5667
Craig L Bickel Robert L Richter • WS 8 1030; SS 915; BC 915 • H • SO • 6601 N 9th Ave Pensacola FL 32504-7345 • FAX(850)476-1772

***IMMANUEL*** (850)438-8138
Stephen P Kamprath • WS 8 1030; SS 915; BC 915 • H • SO • 24 W Wright St 32501-4856 PO Box 12912 Pensacola FL 32576-2912 • FAX(850)438-8139 • ilcpen@aol.com

***JEHOVAH*** (850)433-2091
Warren H Davis • H • EC • SO • 2801 N 9th Ave Pensacola FL 32503-3603 • FAX(850)433-9767 • wdavis0919.aol.com

***REDEEMER***
See Warrington

***RESURRECTION*** (850)456-5340
David A Robatzen • WS 8 1030; SS 915; BC 915 • H • EC • SO • 4524 W Fairfield Dr 32506-4104 PO Box 3099 Pensacola FL 32516-3099 • FAX(850)455-8384 • resluth@bellsouth.net

***ST MATTHEW*** (850)477-0567
James P Brown • WS 11; SS 945;* • H • SO • 7049 Pensacola Blvd Pensacola FL 32505-1223

***TRINITY***
See Cantonment

**PLANT CITY—*HOPE*** (813)752-4622
Dean R Pfeffer • * • H • EC/EL • FG • 2001 N Park Rd Plant City FL 33566-2038 • FAX(813)707-1244 • pastorpfeffer@juno.com

**PLANTATION—*OUR SAVIOR*** (954)473-6888
Walter D Volz • WS 830 11;* • H • EC/EL • FG • 8001 NW 5th St Plantation FL 33324-1914 • FAX(954)473-6895 • oslc@gate.net

**PLANTATION KEY—*IMMANUEL*** (305)852-8711
Richard Y Roseman • H • FG • 33036 108 Ocean Dr Tavernier FL 33070-2340

**POMPANO BEACH—*HOPE*** (954)942-2570
Robert C Weikart • H • EC/EL • FG • 1840 NE 41st St Pompano Beach FL 33064-6071 • FAX(954)782-4673

**PORT CHARLOTTE—*OF THE CROSS*** (941)627-6060
Vacant • H • FG • 33952 2300 Luther Rd Punta Gorda FL 33983-2611 • FAX(941)627-5807

**PORT SAINT LUCIE—*GRACE*** (561)871-6599
Vacant • WS 8 1045; SS 930 • H • EC • FG • 710 SW Port Saint Lucie Blvd Port Saint Lucie FL 34953-2617 • FAX(561)871-7991 • gracepsl@juno.com

**PUNTA GORDA—*FAITH*** (941)639-6309
Barr T Chittick • * • H • FG • 4005 Palm Dr Punta Gorda FL 33950-7329 • FAX(941)639-3263

**RAINBOW LAKES E—*PEACE***
See Dunnellon

**RIVERVIEW—*CHRIST KING*** (813)677-1332
Brian J Hamer • H • FG • 11421 Big Bend Rd Riverview FL 33569 • FAX(813)671-3915

**ROCKLEDGE—*FAITH*** (321)636-5504
Ronald K Meyr • WS 830 1045; SS 945; BC 945 • H • S • 5550 Faith Dr Rockledge FL 32955-6338 • FAX(321)636-2030 • rmeyr04@aol.com

***FAITH***
See Rockledge

***TRINITY*** (407)636-5431
Jeffrey D Marquardt • WS 10; SS 9; BC 9 • H • EC/EL • FG • 1330 Fiske Blvd S Rockledge FL 32955-2318 • FAX(407)638-4498 • tlcschurch@iol15.com

**SAINT AUGUSTINE—*OUR SAVIOR*** (904)829-6823
Vacant • WS 1030; BC 9;* • H • FG • 21 Milton St St Augustine FL 32084

**SAINT CLOUD—*GRACE*** (407)892-4653
Peter L Kolb • WS 11 830; SS 945; BC 945;* • H • EC • FG • 1123 Louisiana Ave Saint Cloud FL 34769-3573 • FAX(407)892-9814

**SAINT PETERSBURG—*GRACE*** (727)527-1168
R Richard Armstrong • Randall Smith DCE • WS 830 11; SS 945; BC 945;* • H • EC/EL • FG • 4301 16th St N Saint Petersburg FL 33703-4425 • FAX(727)522-4535 • rrarms@aol.com

***OUR SAVIOR*** (727)344-2684
Mark T Couch • WS 815; SS 10; BC 10;* • H • EC/EL • FG • 301 58th St S Saint Petersburg FL 33707-1714 • FAX(727)381-3980

**SANFORD—*REDEEMER*** (407)322-3552
Elmer A Reuscher • WS 1030; SS 1030 • H • FG • 2525 S Oak Ave Sanford FL 32773-5155 • reuschere@worldnet.att.net

**SARASOTA—*BEAUT SAVIOR*** (941)355-2798
Wayman L Still • WS 8 1015; SS 915; BC 915 • H • FG • 7461 Prospect Rd Sarasota FL 34243-3348 • beautifulsavior@email.msn.com

***CONCORDIA*** (941)365-0844
Edward J De Witt Dana A Narring • WS 10; SS 845;* • H • EC/EL • FG • 2185 Wood St Sarasota FL 34237-7915 • FAX(941)365-6725 • concordia5@juno.com

***GOOD SHEPHERD*** (941)921-3673
Kevin A Koenig • WS 8 1030;* • H • FG • 5659 Honore Ave Sarasota FL 34233-3248 • FAX(941)923-3659 • goodshep@gte.com

**SATELLITE BEACH—*OUR SAVIOR*** (321)777-0232
Daniel M Hackney • WS 10; SS 9;* • H • FG • 1001 S Patrick Dr Satellite Beach FL 32937-3901 • FAX(321)777-3109 • rsavior@oslcms.org

**SEBRING—*FAITH*** (941)385-7848
Bruce R Sommerfield • SS 845 • H • EC/EL • FG • 2230 NE Lakeview Dr Sebring FL 33870-2300 • FAX(941)385-9439 • fls@strato.net

***FAMILY CHRIST*** (863)385-7848
Dale A Bond Sr. • WS 8 1030; BC 915;* • H • EL • MO • 2230 NE Lakeview Dr 911 W Mt Vernon Nixa MO 33870-2399 • FAX(863)385-9439

**SHALIMAR—*GOOD SHEPHERD*** (850)651-1022
Brian E Runge • M R Angerman DCE • WS 8 1045; SS 930; BC 930 • H • SO • 1 Meigs Dr Shalimar FL 32579-1286 • FAX(850)651-3663 • infoatgslc@aol.com

**SILVER SPRINGS—*FOREST*** (352)625-8700
Paul A Wheelhouse • H • EN • 1663 SE 183 Ave Rd Silver Springs FL 34488-6464 • forestluth@aol.com

**SOUTH DAYTONA—*HOLY CROSS*** (904)767-6542
David R Schillinger • H • EC • FG • 724 Big Tree Rd South Daytona FL 32119-2754 • FAX(904)788-3754

**SPRING HILL—*FOREST OAKS*** (352)683-9731
Milton O Lehr • * • H • FG • 8555 Forest Oaks Blvd Spring Hill FL 34606-6849 • FAX(352)683-1641

**STUART—*REDEEMER*** (561)286-0911
Vacant • WS 830 11; SS 945; BC 945 • H • EC/EL • FG • 2450 SE Ocean Blvd Stuart FL 34996-3312 • FAX(561)286-5645 • redeemer-lutheran@yahoo.com

**TALLAHASSEE—*EPIPHANY*** (904)385-7373
Charles T Kosberg • H • EC/EL • FG • 8300 Deer Lake Rd West Tallahassee FL 32312 • FAX(904)422-0984 • epipstar@aol.com

***UNIVERSITY*** (850)224-6059
Thomas E Dohrman • H • FG • 925 W Jefferson St Tallahassee FL 32304-8019 • ulc@nettally.com

**TAMPA—*FAMILY OF CHRIST**** (813)558-9343
David M Haara(DM) • WS 1030 9; SS 1030; BC 9 • H • EC • S • 16190 Bruce B Downs Blvd Tampa FL 33647

***HOLY TRINITY*** (813)839-6847
Lee H Stisser • WS 1030; SS 9; BC 9 • H • EC/EL • FG • 3712 W El Prado Blvd Tampa FL 33629-8722 • FAX(813)839-2706 • holytrinity5@juno.com

***MESSIAH***
See Carrollwood

***ST JOHN*** (813)935-5648
Donald R Hefta • WS 8 1030; SS 915; BC 915 • H • EL • FG • 10401 N Florida Ave Tampa FL 33612-6708 • FAX(813)935-6938 • stjohnl@usinternet.com

***ST MATTHEW*** (813)884-3097
Robert C Elsner • WS 8 1030; SS 915; BC 915 • H • EL • FG • 5601 Hanley Rd Tampa FL 33634-4905 • FAX(813)886-4155

***ZION*** (813)228-8272
Vacant • EL • FG • 2901 N Highland Ave Tampa FL 33602

**TAVERNIER—*IMMANUEL***
See Plantation Key

**TITUSVILLE—*GOOD SHEPHERD*** (321)267-4323
Todd A Jenks • H • EC • FG • 2073 Garden St Titusville FL 32796-3243 • FAX(321)267-1702

**VENICE—*LAKESIDE*** (941)493-5102
Randy Winkel • H • EC • FG • 2401 Tamiami Trl S Venice FL 34293-5000 • FAX(941)493-5102

**VERO BEACH—*OF THE REDEEMER*** (561)567-8193
Robert C Baker • WS 8 1030; SS 915; BC 915 • H • EC • FG • 900 27th Ave Vero Beach FL 32960-4011 • FAX(561)567-8109

**VIERA—*FAITH***
See Rockledge

**WARRINGTON—*REDEEMER*** (850)455-0330
Robert G Rupp Timothy M Seabaugh • WS 8; SS 915; BC 915 • H • SO • 333 Commerce St Pensacola FL 32507-3498 • FAX(850)455-3083 • tchpaul@pcola.gulf.net

**WAUCHULA—*PEACE VALLEY*** (813)773-2858
Vacant • H • FG • 1643 Stenstrom Rd 33873-9462 PO Box 667 Wauchula FL 33873-0667

**WEST PALM BEACH—*REDEEMER*** (561)832-8705
Kenneth E Larson • WS 10; BC 845;* • H • FG • 2300 S Dixie Hwy West Palm Beach FL 33401-7914

**WESTON—*ST PAUL*** (954)384-9096
Timothy J Hartner • David E Gieseking DCE • WS 830 11; SS 945; BC 945 • H • EC • FG • 580 Indian Trace Weston FL 33326-3366 • FAX(954)384-1037 • timothy@stpaulweston.org

**WINTER HAVEN—*GRACE*** (863)293-8447
Vacant • Judith E Meyer • WS 8 1030; SS 915; BC 915;* • H • EC/EL • FG • 327 Avenue C SE Winter Haven FL 33880-3245 • FAX(863)291-0935 • waqgrace@gte.net

**ZEPHYRHILLS—*OUR SAVIOR*** (813)782-1369
Norman R Springer • WS 10;* • H • FG • 5625 21st St Zephyrhills FL 33540-4556

## GEORGIA

**ALBANY—*TRINITY*** (912)436-5272
Michael G Zwemke • H • FG • 1508 Whispering Pines Rd Albany GA 31707-3558 • trinluth@planttel.net

**ALPHARETTA—*CHRIST SHEPHERD*** (770)475-0640
Kevin P Elseroad • Randy L Potts DCE • H • EC • EN • 4655 Webb Bridge Rd Alpharetta GA 30005 • FAX(770)442-1043 • kelseroad@mindspring.com

**ATHENS—*CHRISTUS VICTOR*** (706)543-3801
Vacant • H • FG • 1010 S Lumpkin Street Athens GA 30605-5121

***TRINITY*** (706)546-1280
David H Bernthal • WS 830; SS 945;* • H • EC • FG • 2535 Jefferson Rd Athens GA 30607-1204 • FAX(706)546-0150 • trinity@athens.net

**ATLANTA—*ASCENSION*** (404)255-0224
Vacant • H • EC • EN • 4000 Roswell Rd NE Atlanta GA 30342-4195 • FAX(404)256-0037

***CHRIST***
See East Point

***GRACE*** (404)875-5411
Vacant • WS 11; SS 1115; BC 930 • H • FG • 1155 N Highland Ave NE Atlanta GA 30306-3453

***RIVERCLIFF***
See Dunwoody

**AUGUSTA—*OUR REDEEMER*** (706)733-6076
Karl J Dunker Stephen P Roehrs • WS 815 11; SS 940; BC 940;* • H • EC • FG • 402 Aumond Rd Augusta GA 30909-3502 • kjdunker@aol.com

**BLAIRSVILLE—*ALL SAINTS*** (706)745-7777
Charles L Houska • H • FG • 2050 Earl Shelton Rd 30512 PO Box 2626 Blairsville GA 30514-2626 • rev1@whitelion.net

**BUFORD—*LIVING SAVIOR***
See Lawrenceville

**CARTERSVILLE—*SAVIOR OF ALL*** (770)387-0379
Frank H Martin • WS 815 1030; SS 930; BC 930 • H • FG • 58 Pine Grove Rd Cartersville GA 30120-4067 • saviorofall@mindspring.com

**COLUMBUS—*BETHLEHEM*** (705)327-8756
Vacant • H • FG • 621 17th Ave Columbus GA 31906-4007

***REDEEMER*** (706)322-5026
Carl L Peterson • H • EC/EL • FG • 4700 Armour Rd Columbus GA 31904-5229 • FAX(706)322-4408 • cllap@earthlink.net

**DECATUR—*PEACE*** (404)289-1474
Victor J Belton • H • FG • 1679 Columbia Dr Decatur GA 30032-4615 • FAX(404)289-1494 • pasbeltonvj@crf.cuis.edu

**DOUGLASVILLE—*PRINCE PEACE*** (770)942-4681
Langdon J Reinke • H • FG • 3988 Highway 5 Douglasville GA 30135-3365 • FAX(770)942-4681 • poplcmsga@juno.com

**DUNWOODY—*RIVERCLIFF*** (770)993-4316
Larry W Tieman • H • EC • FG • 30338 8750 Roswell Rd NW Atlanta GA 30350-1828 • FAX(770)518-6027 • rivercliff@mindspring.com

**EAST POINT—*CHRIST*** (404)767-2892
M P Ave-Lallemant • William L Gomez DCE • H • EC/EL • FG • 2719 Delowe Dr East Point GA 30344-2303 • FAX(404)767-0516 • peteave@aol.com

**GAINESVILLE—*GOOD SHEPHERD*** (770)532-2428
William B Womer • H • EC • FG • 600 S Enota Dr NE Gainesville GA 30501-2470 • FAX(770)532-2428

**HIRAM—*LOVING SHEPHERD*** (770)439-0800
Russel P Johnson Jr. • H • EN • 315 Main St 30141-3207 PO Box 1402 Hiram GA 30141-1402

**KENNESAW—*LIVING HOPE*** (770)425-6726
Jerry F Mc Namara • WS 9 1045; SS 1045 9 • H • EC • FG • 3450 Stilesboro Rd NW Kennesaw GA 30152-3208 • FAX(770)425-1142 • livnghope@aol.com

***LIVING HOPE***
See Marietta

**KINGSLAND—*HOLY TRINITY*** (912)729-6085
Philip H Young • WS 1030; SS 915; BC 915 • H • FG • 165 Camden Woods Pkwy Kingsland GA 31548

**LAWRENCEVILLE—*LIVING SAVIOR*** (770)237-3232
James F Richter • FG • 50 Taylor Rd Suwanee 30045 2159 Azalea Dr Lawrenceville GA 30043-2635 • FAX(770)237-2911 • livingsavior@mindspring.com

**LILBURN—*OAK ROAD*** (770)979-6391
George E Murdaugh • David A Probst DCE • WS 8 1030; SS 915; BC 915 • H • FG • 1004 Oak Rd SW Lilburn GA 30047-1827 • FAX(770)979-9619 • orlc@bellsouth.net

**MACON—*HOLY TRINITY*** (912)474-8393
Steven R Geske • H • FG • 1899 Tucker Rd Macon GA 31220-5399 • FAX(912)474-8951 • htrinity@mylink.net

**MARIETTA—*FAITH*** (770)973-8877
Gregory S Walton • * • H • EC/EL • FG • 2111 Lower Roswell Rd Marietta GA 30068-3355 • FAX(770)971-7796 • faithls@bellsouth.net

**MILLEDGEVILLE—*HOPE*** (912)452-3696
Vacant • WS 11; SS 945; BC 945 • H • FG • 214 Ga Highway 49 W Milledgeville GA 31061-3641 • hopeluth@accucom.net

**NEWNAN—*ZION*** (770)253-2884
Marlin A Mentz(EM) • FG • 53 Country Club Rd Newnan GA 30263-4727

**RIVERDALE—*HOLY CROSS*** (770)478-9324
David D Hansen • WS 11 830; SS 10; BC 10 • H • EC • FG • 377 Valley Hill Rd SW Riverdale GA 30274-2757 • FAX(770)478-9324

**ROME—*HOLY TRINITY*** (706)232-7257
John D Karch • WS 1030; BC 930;* • H • FG • 3000 Garden Lakes Blvd Rome GA 30165-1778 • FAX(706)232-7257 • pastorj16@aol.com

**ROSWELL—*RIVERCLIFF***
See Dunwoody

**SAVANNAH—*TRINITY*** (912)925-4839
Stephen E Schroeder • H • FG • 12391 Mercy Blvd Savannah GA 31419-3436

**STATESBORO—*ST PAUL*** (912)681-2481
Mark Q Louderback • H • FG • 18098 Ga Highway 67 Statesboro GA 30458-3800 • FAX(912)681-2481 • stpaul@bulloch.com

**STOCKBRIDGE—*LORD OF LIFE*** (770)474-3668
Thomas K Fuqua • WS 830 1030; SS 915; BC 6 • H • FG • 3250 Mount Zion Rd Stockbridge GA 30281-4124 • FAX(770)474-9410 • kf6634@mindspring.com

**STONE MOUNTAIN—*FIRST*** (770)413-2375
John D Reynolds • EN • 2546 Rockbridge Rd Stone Mountain GA 30087-3613 • stnemtluth@aol.com

**TIFTON—*PEACE*** (912)382-7344
Earl L Steffens • WS 11; BC 945;* • H • EC • FG • 604 Tennessee Dr 31794 PO Box 812 Tifton GA 31793-0812 • peace@csunet.net

**TOCCOA—*TRINITY*** (706)886-6723
Roger A Schwartz • H • FG • S Hwy 17 Alt 30577 PO Box 1154 Toccoa GA 30577-1419 • FAX(706)886-6723

**TUCKER—*ST MARK*** (404)938-4541
Ray L Borchelt • WS 8 1030; SS 915; BC 915 • H • FG • 2110 Brockett Rd Tucker GA 30084-4501

**VALDOSTA—*MESSIAH*** (912)244-0143
Richard E Pieplow • * • H • FG • 500 Baytree Rd Valdosta GA 31602-2810 • messiah@planttel.net

**WARNER ROBINS—*MOUNT CALVARY*** (912)922-1418
David C Brighton • WS 8 1045; SS 930; BC 930;* • H • FG • 336 Carl Vinson Pkwy Warner Robins GA 31088-3502 • FAX(912)922-7215 • Mt-Cal@mylink.net

**WOODSTOCK—*TIMOTHY*** (770)928-2812
Joseph M Polzin • WS 830 11; SS 945; BC 945 • H • EC • FG • 556 Arnold Mill Rd Woodstock GA 30188-2905 • FAX(678)445-7151

## HAWAII

**AIEA-OAHU—*OUR SAVIOR*** (808)488-3654
Mitchell W Gowen • Jacob Youmans DCE • WS 815 11 630; SS 945;* • H • EC/EL/HS • CNH • 98-1098 Moanalua Rd 96701 98-325 Koauka St Aiea HI 96701-4617 • FAX(808)488-0664 • oslc@aloha.net

**EWA BEACH-OAHU—*MESSIAH*** (808)689-6649
Vacant • H • EL/HS • CNH • 96706 91-679 Fort Weaver Rd Ewa Beach HI 96706-2533 • FAX(808)689-3337

**HILO-HAWAII—*CHRIST*** (808)935-8612
Eugene D Davidenas • H • CNH • 96720 595 Kapiolani St Hilo HI 96720-3936 • FAX(808)933-9236 • christhilo@juno.com

**HONOLULU-OAHU—*GOOD SHEPHERD*** (808)523-2927
Donald W Baron • WS 830 1030; SS 830; BC 830 • H • EC • CNH • 96817 638 N Kuakini St Honolulu HI 96817-2204 • FAX(808)536-1923

***OUR REDEEMER*** (808)946-4223
Thomas J Windsor James C Butt • WS 8 1045; SS 930;* • EL/HS • CNH • 96820 1404 University Ave Honolulu HI 96822-2414 • FAX(808)943-1027

**KAHULUI—*LAHAINA MISSION****
See Lahaina-Maui

**KAHULUI-MAUI—*EMMANUEL*** (808)877-3037
Milton E Fricke • Zachery C Brewer DCE • WS 8 1045; SS 930; BC 930 • H • EC/EL • CNH • 96732 520 W One St Kahului HI 96732-1352 • FAX(808)877-7413 • emmanmaui@aol.com

**KANEOHE-OAHU—*ST MARK*** (808)247-4565
Bruce R Betker • Joel C Oesch DCE • WS 830 11;* • H • EL/HS • CNH • 96744 45-725 Kamehameha Hwy Kaneohe HI 96744-2955 • FAX(808)247-4565 • btbetker@worldnet.att.net

**LAHAINA-MAUI—*LAHAINA MISSION**** (808)877-3037
Milton E Fricke • WS 5 • H • CNH • 655 Wainee St 96761 C/O Emmanuel Luth 520 W One St Kahului HI 96732-1352 • FAX(808)877-7413 • emmanmaui@aol.com

**WAHIAWA-OAHU—*TRINITY*** (808)621-6033
Darren M Pflughoeft • H • EC/EL • CNH • 96786 1611 California Ave Wahiawa HI 96786-2511 • FAX(808)621-6029 • tlcohana@aol.com

**WAIKOLOA—*WAIKOLOA**** (808)883-9255
Arthur F Wright • WS 10; SS 10; BC 9 • H • CNH • Waikoloa Community Center 68 1792 Melia St 68-1823 Hooko St PO Box 384629 Waikoloa HI 96738 • FAX(801)459-5376 • arthurfwright@aol.com

## IDAHO

**ABERDEEN—*ST PAUL*** (208)397-4967
Robert W Hemsath • WS 1130 • H • NOW • 552 S 2nd W St 83210 PO Box 506 Aberdeen ID 83210-0506

**ASHTON—*ZION*** (208)652-7438
Bruce W Kolasch • WS 815 11; SS 930; BC 930 • H • EC • NOW • Ninth And Main 83420 PO Box 387 Ashton ID 83420-0387 • FAX(208)652-7438 • zionashton@juno.com

**BOISE—*BEAU SAVIOR*** (208)336-3616
Vacant • * • H • EC • NOW • 2981 E Boise Ave Boise ID 83706-5717 • FAX(208)385-0137 • tkrieger@micron.net

***GOOD SHEPHERD*** (208)343-7212
David A Hrachovina Timothy J Pauls • H • EC/EL • NOW • 5009 Cassia St Boise ID 83705-1950

**BUHL—*ST JOHN*** (208)543-4282
Mark E Latham • H • EC/EL • NOW • 1128 Poplar St Buhl ID 83316-1636

**BUHL 9 SE/FILER 7 S—*CLOVER*** (208)326-4950
Mark E Christ • WS 930; SS 11; BC 11 • EC/EL • NOW • 83316 3552 N 1825 E Buhl ID 83316-6357 • FAX(208)326-5105 • cloverlc@filertel.com

**BURLEY—*ZION*** (208)678-9621
Vacant • H • EC • NOW • 2410 Miller Ave Burley ID 83318-2919 • zion@cyberhighway.net

**CALDWELL—*GRACE*** (208)459-4191
Philip J Bohlken • WS 1030 730; SS 915; BC 915 • H • EC • NOW • 2700 S Kimball Ave Caldwell ID 83605-5622 • amazing2700@juno.com

**CASCADE—*COUNCIL****
See Council

***SHEP MOUNTAINS*** (208)382-4422
Philip W Sievers • H • NOW • 212 N Hwy 55 83611 PO Box 37 Cascade ID 83611-0037 • FAX(208)382-4205 • siemtmin@cyberhighway.net

**COEUR D ALENE—*CHRIST KING*** (208)664-9231
John L Schmidt Dennis L Lorenz • Amy Upchurch DCE • WS 845 11; SS 10; BC 10 • H • EC • NOW • 1700 E Pennsylvania Ave Coeur D Alene ID 83814-5563 • FAX(208)664-9233 • ctk@ctkcda.org

**COUNCIL—*COUNCIL**** (208)253-4486
Vacant • H • NOW • St Judes N Us 95 83612 PO Box 37 Cascade ID 83611-0037 • siemtmin@cyberhighway.net

**EAGLE—*FRIENDSHIP*** (208)288-2404
Thomas J Hausch • WS 9; SS 1015; BC 1015;* • H • EC • NOW • Eagle Hs-State St @ Park Ln 83616 765 E Chinden Meridian ID 83642 • FAX(208)288-2402

**EDEN 3 S—*TRINITY*** (208)825-5277
Jeffrey R Potter • WS 1030; SS 9; BC 9 • H • EC • NOW • 83325 1602 E 1100 S Eden ID 83325-5216 • FAX(208)825-5277

**EMMETT—*OUR REDEEMER*** (208)365-5231
Michael L Mc Coy • H • EC • NOW • 407 S Hayes Ave Emmett ID 83617-2971 • mmccoy@micron.net

**FILER—*PEACE*** (208)326-5450
Gary S Benedix • WS 9; SS 1015; BC 1015 • H • EC/EL • NOW • 6th And Stevens 83328 PO Box 33 Filer ID 83328-0033 • FAX(208)326-5451 • peace@filertel.com

**GOODING—*CALVARY*** (208)934-5355
John M Donnan • WS 10; SS 9; BC 9 • H • NOW • 21st And California 83330 PO Box 525 Gooding ID 83330-0525 • mdonnan@northrim.net

**GRANGEVILLE—*TRINITY*** (208)983-0562
Robert A Korytkowski • H • NOW • 210 N Mill St Grangeville ID 83530-1873

**HAILEY—*VALLEY OF PEACE*** (208)788-3066
Vacant • WS 5;* • H • NOW • 704 Wintergreen 83333 PO Box 218 Hailey ID 83333-0218

**HOMEDALE—*MOUNT CALVARY*** (208)337-4248
Vacant • * • H • NOW • 621 W Idaho Ave PO Box 817 Homedale ID 83628-0817

**IDAHO FALLS—*HOPE*** (208)529-8080
William E Shimkus • WS 830 11; SS 940; BC 940 • H • EC/EL • NOW • 2071 12th St Idaho Falls ID 83404-5728 • FAX(208)529-8880 • pastorl@srv.net

***ST JOHN*** (208)522-5650
Richard W Collin • Carolyn M Grohn DCE • WS 830 11; SS 945; BC 945 • H • NOW • 290 7th St Idaho Falls ID 83401-4757 • FAX(208)522-8195 • stjluth@srv.net

**JEROME—*ST PAUL*** (208)324-2842
Baldwin A Camin • WS 1030; SS 9;* • H • NOW • 1301 N Davis St 83338-1617 PO Box 502 Jerome ID 83338-0502 • FAX(208)324-2842 • stpauls@magiclink.com

**KIMBERLY—*REDEEMER*** (208)423-5139
Vacant • H • NOW • 312 Irene St 83341-2066 400 Irene St Kimberly ID 83341-2068

**LEWISTON—*GOOD SHEPHERD*** (208)743-8331
Vacant • WS 1030;* • H • NOW • 3707 14th St Lewiston ID 83501-5709

**MC CALL—*OUR SAVIOR*** (208)634-5905
Philip J Di Gregorio • H • NOW • 100 W Forest St 83638 PO Box 912 Mc Call ID 83638-0912

**MERIDIAN—*CHRIST*** (208)888-1622
Robert E Cutler • * • H • NOW • 1406 W Cherry Ln Meridian ID 83642-1517 • christlc@usurf.com

**MOUNTAIN HOME—*FAITH*** (208)587-4127
Jerome V Wohlfeil • WS 1030; SS 915 • H • EL • NOW • 1190 N 6th E Mountain Home ID 83647-2032 • FAX(208)587-6172

**MULLAN—*EMMANUEL*** (208)744-1324
David P Haught • WS 9 • NOW • 120 Earle St 83846 PO Box 434 Mullan ID 83846-0434

**NAMPA—*ZION*** (208)466-6746
Michael D Schumacher • WS 8 1030; SS 915; BC 915 • H • EC/EL • NOW • 404 Nectarine St Nampa ID 83686-5041 • FAX(208)466-8826 • rev0466@aol.com

**NEW PLYMOUTH—*IMMANUEL*** (208)278-3080
Steven C Thomas • WS 11; SS 10; BC 10 • H • NOW • Elm And W Blvd 83655 PO Box 552 New Plymouth ID 83655-0552 • thomas.s.c@worldnet.att.net

**OSBURN—*BETHANY*** (208)752-8095
David P Haught • NOW • 1100 E Mullan Ave 83849 PO Box 805 Osburn ID 83849-0805

**POCATELLO—*FAITH*** (208)237-2391
Robert W Hemsath • H • EC • NOW • 856 W Eldredge Rd Pocatello ID 83201-5525 • faithlc@nicoh.com

***GRACE*** (208)237-0467
Manfred H Berndt • WS 830 11; SS 945; BC 945;* • H • EC/EL • NOW • 1350 Baldy Ave Pocatello ID 83201-7104 • FAX(208)237-4406

**POST FALLS—*MESSIAH*** (208)777-2887
Steven P Johnson • WS 9; SS 1030; BC 1030 • H • NOW • 608 N Spokane St Post Falls ID 83854

**RATHDRUM—*SHEPHERD HILLS*** (208)687-1809
Neil D Bloom • H • EC • NOW • 7255 W Hwy 53 Rathdrum ID 83858-9165

**RIGBY—*CROWN OF LIFE*** (208)745-7191
Vacant • H • NOW • 3856 E 300 N Rigby ID 83442-5422

**RUPERT—*TRINITY*** (208)436-3413
Leonard G Mietzner • H • NOW • 909 8th St Rupert ID 83350-1305 • FAX(208)436-1731

**SALMON—*SHEP OF VALLEY*** (208)756-4429
Michael G Warmbier • * • H • MT • Us Hwy 28 2 Miles E Of Town 83467 RR 1 Box 100AB Salmon ID 83467-9701 • FAX(208)756-4429 • warmbier@salmoninternet.com

**SANDPOINT—*CHRIST OUR REDE*** (208)263-7516
Stephen Nickodemus • WS 9; SS 930; BC 1045 • H • EC • NOW • 1900 W Pine St Sandpoint ID 83864-9328 • FAX(208)255-1326 • corlc@micron.net

**SODA SPRINGS—*HOPE***
Vacant • WS 9 • H • NOW • 211 E 4th S 83276-1617 PO Box 85 Soda Springs ID 83276-0085

**SPIRIT LAKE—*FIRST*** (208)623-5252
Karl G Petzke(EM) • * • NOW • Jefferson And Sixth 83869 PO Box 100 Spirit Lake ID 83869-0100

**TWIN FALLS—*IMMANUEL*** (208)733-7820
Lawrence M Vedder • WS 830 1030; SS 930; BC 930 • H • EC/EL • NOW • 2055 Filer Ave E Twin Falls ID 83301-4342 • FAX(208)735-9770 • immanuel@ltlink.com

**WEISER—*CONCORDIA*** (208)549-2563
Steven C Thomas • H • NOW • 402 E Court St Weiser ID 83672-2213

**WENDELL—*CHRIST*** (208)536-2588
Vacant • WS 7 • H • NOW • 175 2nd Ave W 83335-5312 PO Box 161 Wendell ID 83355-0161

## ILLINOIS

**ADDISON—*ST PAUL*** (630)543-6909
Ernest H Brooks • WS 8; BC 915;* • H • EC/EL/HS • NI • 37 W Army Trail Blvd Addison IL 60101-3501 • FAX(630)543-5768

**ALGONQUIN—*ST JOHN*** (847)658-9300
Rollin F Kuznik • * • H • EC/EL/HS • NI • Washington And Jefferson Sts 60102 300 Jefferson St Algonquin IL 60102-2693 • FAX(847)658-9331 • saintj³alg@worldnet.att.net

**ALSIP—*HOLY CROSS*** (708)597-5209
Chris D Ongstad • H • S • 4041 W 120th St Alsip IL 60803-2178

**ALTAMONT—*IMMANUEL*** (618)483-6395
Fred A Muenchow • WS 845;* • H • EL • CI • 203 E Division St Altamont IL 62411-1220 • FAX(618)483-6760

**ALTAMONT 3 SW—*BETHLEHEM*** (618)483-6756
Geoffrey L Robinson • WS 10 745; SS 9; BC 9 • H • EL • CI • 6351 N 200th St 62411 PO Box 187 Altamont IL 62411-0187

**ALTAMONT 6 NE—*ST PAUL*** (618)483-6993
David R Speers • H • EL • CI • 62411 5088 E 1400th Ave Altamont IL 62411-9652 • FAX(618)483-6993

**ALTAMONT 6 SE—*ZION*** (618)483-5571
Roland K Feickert • SS 815 • H • EL • CI • 5534 E 600th Ave Altamont IL 62411

**ALTON—*MESSIAH*** (618)465-5343
Randy J Fischer • WS 9; SS 1030; BC 1030 • H • SI • 920 Milton Rd Alton IL 62002-3172

**ANNA—*TRINITY*** (618)833-2475
Paul M Weber • SS 915; BC 930;* • H • SI • 205 W Jefferson Anna IL 62906

**ANTIOCH—*BEAUTIFUL SAVIOR*** (847)265-2450
Vacant • NI • 554 Parkway 60002 2312 Sand Lake Rd Lindenhurst IL 60046 • 9gruens@concentric.net

**ARENZVILLE—*TRINITY*** (217)997-5534
Daniel J Bishop • WS 10; SS 9; BC 9 • EC/EL • CI • Frederick St 62611 PO Box 49 Arenzville IL 62611-0049

**ARENZVILLE 8 W—*IMMANUEL*** (217)584-1701
Glenn R Niemann • WS 8;* • H • CI • 3781 Honey Point Rd Arenzville IL 62611

**ARLINGTON HEIGHTS—*FAITH*** (847)253-4839
C D Stuckmeyer William J Majer • WS 830;* • H • EN • 60005 431 S Arlington Heights Rd Arlington Hts IL 60005-1932 • FAX(847)398-5010

***LIVING CHRIST*** (847)577-7133
Paul J Klopke • H • NI • 60005 625 E Dundee Rd Arlington Heights IL 60004-1541 • lclcpastor@aol.com

***ST PETER*** (847)259-4114
Karl W Schmidt • Kevin L Borchers DCE • WS 8 930 11;* • H • EC/EL/HS • NI • 111 W Olive St Arlington Heights IL 60004-4766 • FAX(847)259-4185 • stpeter@concentric.net

**ATHENS—*IMMANUEL*** (217)636-8469
Richard A Becker • WS 10; SS 9; BC 9 • H • HS • CI • 302 W Washington St 62613 PO Box 377 Athens IL 62613-9042

**AUBURN—*TRINITY*** (217)438-6820
Richard R Harre • WS 8 1015; SS 915; BC 915 • H • CI • 1201 W Jackson St Auburn IL 62615-9372 • trinitylcms@auburnctnet.com

**AURORA—*EMMANUEL*** (630)851-2200
Burneal Fick Alex L Merlo • EL/HS • NI • Fourth Ave And Jackson St 60505 550 4th Ave Aurora IL 60505-4860 • FAX(630)851-7269

***HOPE*** (630)898-6754
John A Fritz • WS 9;* • H • NI • 1575 Reckinger Rd Aurora IL 60505-1625

***ST LUKE***
See Boulder Hill

***ST PAUL*** (630)820-3450
Jock E Ficken Alex L Merlo • WS 8 1030; SS 1030 915; BC 1030 915 • H • EC/EL • NI • 855 Constitution Dr 60506 555 E Benton St Aurora IL 60505-4440 • FAX(630)820-3452 • stpauls6@juno.com

**BALDWIN—*ST JOHN*** (618)785-2344
Leroy J Eckert • * • H • HS • SI • 304 S 5th St 62217-1304 PO Box 162 Baldwin IL 62217-0162 • FAX(801)749-9513 • leenlois@egyptian.net
**BARRINGTON—*ST MATTHEW*** (847)382-7002
Robert L Moll Gerald Schalk • WS 8;* • H • NI • 720 Dundee Ave Barrington IL 60010-4255 • FAX(847)382-7017 • stmatthewbarrington@ameritech.net
**BARRINGTON HILL—*FAITH***
See Carpentersville
**BARTLETT—*IMMANUEL*** (630)837-1166
Harold I Wahl • H • EC/EL/HS • NI • 1116 E Devon Ave Bartlett IL 60103-4760 • hiwahl@aol.com
**BARTONVILLE—*HOLY CROSS***
See Peoria
**BATAVIA—*IMMANUEL*** (630)879-7163
Ronald W Weidler • WS 8;* • H • EC/EL • NI • 950 Hart Rd Batavia IL 60510-9346 • FAX(630)879-7614
**BATH 4 NE—*ST JOHN*** (309)546-2434
Brian A Lesemann • H • CI • 62617 13961 CRE 1100 N Bath IL 62617-9715
**BEARDSTOWN—*SAINT JOHN*** (217)323-1288
Richard A Bremer • WS 9; SS 1015; BC 1015;* • EC/EL • CI • 601 Jefferson St 62618-1843 220 E 6th St Beardstown IL 62618-1868
**BEECHER—*ST PAUL*** (708)946-2050
Karl A Wellnitz • WS 9;* • H • NI • 1407 W Church Rd Beecher IL 60401-3425
***ZION*** (708)946-2271
Vacant • Linda A Meyer DEAC • WS 8 1030; SS 915; BC 915;* • H • EC/EL • NI • 540 Oak Park Ave PO Box 369 Beecher IL 60401-0369 • FAX(708)946-2611 • zionlutheranbeecher@hotmail.com
**BEECHER 7 NE—*ST JOHN*** (708)946-2561
Maynard L Toensing • HS • NI • 60401 28054 S Yates Ave Beecher IL 60401-3316 • Stjohnluthbchr@netzero.net
**BELLEVILLE—*SIGNAL HILL*** (618)397-1407
Henry A Simon Thomas G Volker • WS 8 920; SS 920; BC 920;* • H • SI • 8100 W Main St Belleville IL 62223-2018 • FAX(618)397-9220 • welcome@signalhillchurch.org
***ZION*** (618)233-2299
Gary W Byers Hyo Jong Kim • Jill A Hasstedt DCE • WS 8 1045 11; SS 930; BC 930;* • H • EC/EL • SI • 1810 Mc Clintock Ave Belleville IL 62221-6460 • FAX(618)233-2324 • officezion@aol.com
**BELVIDERE—*IMMANUEL*** (815)544-8058
Eugene E Wille • WS 8 1045; SS 915;* • H • EC/EL/HS • NI • 1045 Belvidere Rd 61008-6502 1225 E 2nd St Belvidere IL 61008-4598 • FAX(815)544-8059 • immanuel@sltic.com
**BENSENVILLE—*ZION*** (630)766-1039
Vacant • * • EC/EL/HS • NI • 865 S Church Rd Bensenville IL 60106-2904 • FAX(630)766-3902 • zionsec@juno.com
**BERWYN—*CONCORDIA*** (708)484-9784
Mark A Matthews • WS 830 11; SS 945; BC 10;* • H • EC • EN • 3144 Home Ave Berwyn IL 60402-2910 • FAX(708)484-9832 • THEOLDREV@HOTMAIL.COM
***GOOD SHEPHERD*** (708)788-9054
Robert A Sorensen • WS 1030;* • H • HS • NI • 6717 19th St Berwyn IL 60402-1802 • robtsorens@aol.com
**BETHALTO—*ZION*** (618)377-8314
Willard V Meyer Mark J Hofferber • H • SI • 625 Church Dr Bethalto IL 62010-1830 • FAX(618)377-8740 • zionchurch@ezl.com
**BLOOMINGTON—*GOOD SHEPHERD*** (309)662-8905
Chad D Lueck • WS 8 1030; SS 915; BC 915 • H • EC • CI • 3516 White Eagle Dr Bloomington IL 61704-9103 • gslcbn@dave-world.net
***OUR REDEEMER*** (309)662-3935
Thomas R Daly • WS 8 1030; SS 915; BC 915 • H • CI • 1822 E Lincoln St Bloomington IL 61701-7066 • FAX(309)662-5338 • orlc@gte.net
***TRINITY*** (309)828-6265
Thomas C Wirsing Allen L Steinbeck • Charles A Bahn DCE • WS 8 930 11; SS 815 930;* • H • CI • 801 S Madison St Bloomington IL 61701-6464 • FAX(309)828-0831 • info@trinluth.org
**BLUE ISLAND—*SALEM*** (708)388-1830
Vacant • EC/EL/HS • NI • 12951 S Maple Ave Blue Island IL 60406 • FAX(708)388-5176
**BLUFFS 3 E—*TRINITY*** (217)754-3517
Erik J Rottmann • H • CI • 1585 Trinity Rd Bluffs IL 62621
**BOLINGBROOK—*DIVINE SHEPHERD*** (708)759-5300
Vacant • H • EC • NI • 985 Lily Cache Ln Bolingbrook IL 60440-3131
**BONFIELD 4 SW—*ZION*** (815)426-2650
John M Kiefer • H • NI • 4478 Rt 17 W 60913 11478 W State Route 17 Bonfield IL 60913-7290
**BOURBONNAIS—*GOOD SHEPHERD*** (815)935-2663
Robert W Demchuk • WS 915; SS 1030; BC 1030 • H • NI • 3115 N 1000W Rd Bourbonnais IL 60914-4236
**BOWEN—*ST PAUL*** (217)696-2642
Vacant • * • CI • PO Box 65 Bowen IL 62316-0065
**BRAIDWOOD—*SHEP OF PEACE**** (815)458-9445
Jason W Zobel(DM) • WS 9; SS 1015; BC 1015 • H • NI • 307 Comet Dr 60408-2204 242 E Main St Braidwood IL 60408 • FAX(815)458-9446 • shepherd@shepherdofpeace.com
**BRIMFIELD—*ST PAUL*** (309)446-3233
Michael D Liese • H • CI • 204 W Clay St 61517 PO Box 297 Brimfield IL 61517-0297
**BROADLANDS 3 NW—*IMMANUEL*** (217)834-3289
Lynn A Podoll • WS 9;* • H • HS • CI • 2401 Cty Rd 400 N 61816 PO Box 229 Broadlands IL 61816-0229 • FAX(217)834-3042 • immanuel-lcms@juno.com
**BROADVIEW—*BETHLEHEM*** (708)344-4987
David J Behling • NI • 2001 S 17th Ave Broadview IL 60153-2905
**BROOKFIELD—*ST PAUL*** (708)485-6987
Walter D Otten • H • NI • 9035 Grant Brookfield IL 60513 • FAX(708)485-7448
**BRUSSELS—*ST MATTHEW*** (618)883-2351
Lawrence E Meinzen • WS 10; SS 9; BC 9;* • H • SI • Hardin Rd HCR 82 Box 20A Brussels IL 62013 • schulzef@planet.com
**BUCKLEY—*ST JOHN*** (217)394-2444
Vacant • WS 9;* • H • EC/EL/HS • CI • 109 N Oak 60918 PO Box 6 Buckley IL 60918-0006 • FAX(217)394-2444 • stjohns@illicom.net
**BUFFALO GROVE—*LIVING CHRIST***
See Arlington Heights
**BUNKER HILL—*ZION*** (618)585-3606
Terry L Grebing • H • EC • SI • 609 E Warren St Bunker Hill IL 62014
**BURBANK—*HOLY TRINITY*** (708)598-8070
Robert J Nemoyer • WS 9;* • H • NI • 8659 S Sayre Burbank IL 60459-2259
**BURLINGTON—*ST JOHN*** (847)683-2338
Vacant • WS 9; BC 1030;* • H • NI • 13n535 French Rd 60109 PO Box 85 Burlington IL 60109-0085 • FAX(847)683-2521
**BURR RIDGE—*TRINITY*** (708)839-1200
Robert E Geaschel Michael W Sneath • WS 830 11; SS 945; BC UNKNOWN;* • H • EC/EL • NI • 11500 German Church Rd Burr Ridge IL 60521-6491 • FAX(708)839-8503
**CAHOKIA—*MOUNT CALVARY*** (618)337-9107
Jonathan C Winterfeldt • WS 1030; SS 915; BC 915;* • H • SI • 2300 Jerome Ln Cahokia IL 62206-2602 • FAX(618)337-9107 • mclclcms@aol.com
**CALUMET CITY—*ST JOHN*** (708)862-1920
Warren G Mandel • WS 1015; BC 9 • HS • NI • 520 Sibley Blvd Calumet City IL 60409-2614
**CALUMET PARK—*MOUNT CALVARY*** (708)389-1010
Vacant • WS 1045; SS 1210 • H • HS • NI • 1301 W Vermont Ave Calumet Park IL 60827-6427
**CAMPBELL HILL—*IMMANUEL*** (618)426-3154
Vacant • WS 8;* • H • SI • 1699 Westpoint Rd Campbell Hill IL 62916
***ST PETER*** (618)426-9091
Gregory J Schultz • WS 10; SS 9; BC 9 • H • HS • SI • 601 W Church St 62916 PO Box 69 Campbell Hill IL 62916-0069 • splccampbellhill@juno.com
**CANTON—*GRACE*** (309)647-5123
Kirk M Clayton • WS 1030; SS 915; BC 915;* • CI • 125 E Locust St Canton IL 61520-1924
**CARBONDALE—*OUR SAVIOR*** (618)549-1694
Robert W Gray Tich H Luu • WS 10 4; SS 9; BC 9 • H • SI • 700 S University Ave Carbondale IL 62901-2831 • lutheran@siu.edu
**CARLINVILLE—*ZION*** (217)854-8514
Harry C Sheets • H • EC • SI • 501 S Broad St Carlinville IL 62626
**CARLYLE—*BETHLEHEM***
See Ferrin
***MESSIAH*** (618)594-3912
Vacant • WS 10; SS 9; BC 9;* • H • SI • 1091 13th St Carlyle IL 62231-1157
**CARMI—*OUR SAVIOR*** (618)384-5291
Mark S Lohnes • H • SI • 1102 Jill St Carmi IL 62821-1561
**CAROL STREAM—*OUR SAVIOR*** (630)830-4833
Andrew M Koschmann John W Schultz(#) Jeffrey L Zoellick(#) • H • EC/EL/HS • NI • 1244 W Army Trail Rd Carol Stream IL 60188-9000 • FAX(630)483-3148 • www.oursavior.com
**CARPENTER—*ZION*** (618)656-4492
Vacant • H • SI • 62025- 6409 Quercus Grove Rd Edwardsville IL 62025-6165
**CARPENTERSVILLE—*FAITH*** (847)428-2079
Bruce W Meissner • WS 8; SS 915; BC 915;* • H • NI • Helm Rd At Navajo Dr 60110 PO Box 366 Carpentersville IL 60110-0366 • FAX(847)428-0358 • bdmeissnerfaith@cs.com
**CARROLLTON—*OUR REDEEMER*** (217)942-3168
Steven J Jacobsen • WS 8 1030; SS 915; BC 915 • H • SI • 208 7th St Carrollton IL 62016-1022 • RevJacobsen@excite.com
**CARY—*HOLY CROSS*** (847)639-1702
Robert M Hess E Timothy Frick • WS 8 1045; SS 930; BC 930;* • H • EC • NI • 2107 Three Oaks Rd Cary IL 60013-1628 • FAX(847)639-6702 • HCLChurch@ameritech.net
**CASEY—*TRINITY*** (217)932-2645
Vacant • H • CI • NE Second and Colorado Sts Casey IL 62420 • revdms@shawneelink.com
**CASEYVILLE—*SAINT PETER*** (618)398-2646
Keith E Brown Jr. • WS 1030; BC 930;* • SI • 8705 Bunkum Rd Caseyville IL 62232
**CENTRALIA—*TRINITY*** (618)532-2614
James K Gullen Perry W Schefelker • H • EC/EL • SI • 201 S Pleasant Ave Centralia IL 62801-3657 • FAX(618)532-4110
**CHAMPAIGN—*FRIENDSHIP/JOY*** (217)355-0454
Larry E Bell • * • H • CI • 3601 S Duncan Rd Champaign IL 61822-6707 • FAX(217)355-0467 • frndship@pdnt.com
***ST JOHN*** (217)359-1123
Mark R Elliott James F Wright • WS 8 1045; SS 930; BC 930;* • H • EC/EL • CI • 509 S Mattis Ave Champaign IL 61821-3630 • FAX(217)359-7972
***UNIVERSITY*** (217)344-1558
Rick R Milas • WS 1030;* • CI • 604 E Chalmers Champaign IL 61820
**CHANDLERVILLE—*SALEM*** (309)546-2434
Brian A Lesemann • CI • Mechanic St Chandlerville IL 62627
**CHANNAHON—*RIVER OF LIFE**** (815)467-0641
Vacant • H • NI • 24300 S Ford Rd Channahon 25313 W Eames Channahon IL 60410 • FAX(815)467-0642 • river@cbcast.com
**CHAPIN 3 NW—*ST PAUL*** (217)472-7891
Gene A Strattman • H • CI • 62628 RR 1 Box 186 Chapin IL 62628-9755
**CHARLESTON—*IMMANUEL*** (217)345-3008
Douglas H Fleischfresser • Gregory P Witto P Asst • WS 8; SS 920; BC 920 • H • EC • CI • 902 Cleveland Ave Charleston IL 61920-3441 • FAX(217)345-5059
**CHATHAM—*ST JOHN*** (217)483-2612
Glenn L Strohschein • WS 9; SS 1030; BC 1030;* • H • EC/HS • CI • N Main St 62629 PO Box 377 Chatham IL 62629-0377
**CHEBANSE—*ZION*** (815)697-2212
Vacant • WS 8; SS 915; BC 915 • H • EC/EL/HS • NI • 190 Concordia Dr Chebanse IL 60922-9761 • FAX(815)697-2212 • zionschool@dlogue.net
**CHENOA—*ST PAUL*** (815)945-5331
Jerome R Koch • * • H • CI • 800 S Division St Chenoa IL 61726-1371
**CHESTER—*ST JOHN*** (618)826-3545
Mark S Willig Martin R Springer • WS 745; SS 9; BC 9;* • H • EC/EL/HS • SI • 302 W Holmes St Chester IL 62233-1300
**CHESTNUT—*ZION*** (217)796-3386
Richard E Stamm • * • H • CI • 407 N Logan St 62518-6077 PO Box 107 Chestnut IL 62518-0107
**CHICAGO—*BEAUT SAVIOR*** (773)582-6470
La Mar Miller • WS 10; BC 9 • H • HS • NI • 5122 S Archer Ave Chicago IL 60632-4508 • FAX(773)582-6470
***BETHANY*** (773)561-9159
Lincoln C Winter • HS • EN • 1244 W Thorndale Ave Chicago IL 60660-3348
***BETHANY NORTH*** (773)637-3604
John H Lutz(EM) • WS 10; SS 11; BC 11 • H • HS • NI • 1701 N Narragansett Ave Chicago IL 60639-3825
***BETHEL*** (773)252-1104
John M Treude • WS 1030; SS 930; BC 930 • EC/EL/HS • NI • 1410 N Springfield Ave Chicago IL 60651-2042 • FAX(773)252-4852
***BETHESDA*** (773)743-6460
Paul E Bacon Shadrach Katari • WS 7; BC 9;* • EC/EL/HS • EN • 6803 N Campbell Ave Chicago IL 60645-4607 • FAX(773)743-4415
***BETHLEHEM*** (773)734-8223
Vacant • EL • NI • 10300 S Avenue H 60617-6050 10261 S Avenue H Chicago IL 60617-6008 • FAX(773)768-0390
***CHATHAM FIELDS*** (773)723-3661
Vacant • WS 1030; SS 9;* • H • HS • EN • 8050 S Saint Lawrence Ave Chicago IL 60619-3814
***CHRIST ENGLISH*** (773)637-4800
Vacant • H • EC/EL/HS • EN • 1511 N Long Ave Chicago IL 60651-1348 • FAX(773)622-4563 • rmgg59a@prodigy.com
***CHRIST KING*** (773)536-1984
John W Brazeal • WS 11; SS 930;* • H • EC/EL/HS • NI • 3701-3709 S Lake Park Ave 3701 S Lake Park Ave Chicago IL 60653-2012 • FAX(312)536-2387 • mrsgb@earthlink.net
***CONCORDIA*** (773)588-4040
A F F Windisch-Graetz • HS • NI • 2645 W Belmont Ave Chicago IL 60618-5912 • FAX(773)755-1867
***DR MARTIN LUTHER*** (773)776-8104
Steven M Massey • H • HS • S • 5344 S Francisco Ave Chicago IL 60632-2226 • smmassey@aol.com
***EBENEZER*** (773)762-0500
Vacant • WS 10; SS 12;* • NI • 1252 S Harding Ave 60623-1347 PO Box 6687 Chicago IL 60680-6687 • MMcComm@prodigy.net
***EPHPHATHA-DEAF*** (773)723-3232
Prentice D Marsh(DM) • H • EN • 7956 S M L King Dr Chicago IL 60619-3702
***FAITH*** (773)488-8286
Kevin E Dean Sr. • WS 11; SS 930;* • HS • EN • 8300 S Sangamon St Chicago IL 60620-3138 • FAX(773)488-0468
***FIRST BETHLEHEM*** (773)276-2338
James A Kellerman • WS 1045; SS 930;* • HS • NI • 1649 W Le Moyne St Chicago IL 60622-2240
***FIRST IMMANUEL*** (312)733-6886
John S Carrier Donald V Becker(EM) • H • HS • NI • 1124 S Ashland Ave Chicago IL 60607-4604 • FAX(312)733-2676
***FIRST ST PAUL*** (312)642-7172
Delayne H Pauling H D Brummer • H • HS • NI • 1301 N La Salle Dr Chicago IL 60610-1935 • FAX(312)642-1608
***GETHSEMANE*** (312)778-8821
Vacant • NI • 2735 W 79th St 60652-1739 2727 W 79th St Chicago IL 60652-1724
***GLORIA DEI*** (773)767-2771
Franklin H Giebel • WS 8;* • H • HS • NI • 5259 S Major Ave Chicago IL 60638-1503 • FAX(773)767-4670
***GOOD SHEPHERD*** (773)581-0096
Peter C Hoffmann • EC • EN • 4200 W 62nd St Chicago IL 60629-5042
***GRACE*** (773)762-1234
Vacant • HS • NI • 4106 W 28th St Chicago IL 60623-4358
***GRACE ENGLISH*** (773)637-1177
Sean M Esterline • WS 930 • EL/HS • EN • 2725 N Laramie Ave Chicago IL 60639-1615 • FAX(773)637-1188
***HOLY CROSS*** (773)523-3838
George J Mrochen • WS 1030; BC 930 • NI • 3116 S Racine Ave Chicago IL 60608-6405 • FAX(773)523-3838

***HOPE*** (773)776-7816
Robert F Burke • HS • EN • 6416 S Washtenaw Ave Chicago IL 60629-1734 • FAX(773)776-7832 • rfburke@worldnet.att.net
***IMMANUEL*** (773)221-6935
Vacant • WS 10; SS 9; BC 9 • HS • NI • 9037 41 S Houston Ave Chicago IL 60617-4312
***JEFFERSON PARK*** (773)545-5109
Charles R Aufdenkampe • * • HS • EN • 5009 N Northwest Hwy Chicago IL 60630-2237 • FAX(773)545-5109
***JEHOVAH-EL BUEN PAST*** (773)342-5854
Vacant • H • EC/EL/HS • NI • 3740 W Belden Ave Chicago IL 60647-2348 • FAX(773)342-6048
***LA SANTISIMA TRINIDA*** (773)521-2144
Vacant • NI • 2759 S Karlov Ave 60623-4438 4106 W 28th St Chicago IL 60623-4358
***LORD JESUS***
Vacant • NI • 3042 W 38th Pl Chicago IL 60632-2320
***MESSIAH*** (773)767-2727
Steven J Anderson • WS 9; SS 1030; BC 1030 • NI • 6159 S Monitor Ave Chicago IL 60638-4413
***MESSIAH*** (773)725-8903
Vacant • EC/EL/HS • NI • 6201 W Patterson Ave Chicago IL 60634-2529 • FAX(773)202-7671
***MOUNT GREENWOOD*** (773)445-6080
Louis R Vician • * • H • HS • NI • 10911 S Trumbull Ave Chicago IL 60655-3323 • revheinz@juno.com
***NAZARETH*** (773)737-7082
M C Groth • H • HS • NI • 3250 W 60th St Chicago IL 60629-3230
***OUR SAVIOR***
See Norwood Park
***OUR SAVIOR*** (773)631-1100
Stanley J Zyskowski Jr. • WS 9 • EC/EL/HS • EN • 6099 N Northcott Ave 60631-2447 6035 N Northcott Ave Chicago IL 60631-2413 • FAX(773)775-9265
***OUR SAVIOUR*** (773)736-1120
James P Stephens • EC/EL/HS • NI • 3457 N Neva Ave Chicago IL 60634-3610 • FAX(773)736-4851 • oslc00@juno.com
***PEACE*** (773)523-5790
Luther G Albrecht • HS • NI • 4300 S California Ave Chicago IL 60632-1233
***RESURRECTION*** (773)928-6311
Larry Frazier • H • EC/EL/HS • NI • 9349 S Wentworth Ave Chicago IL 60620-1428
***SAINT PAUL*** (773)721-1438
Richard E Robinson • WS 1030; SS 915;* • H • EC/EL/HS • NI • 7619 S Dorchester Ave Chicago IL 60619-3425 • FAX(773)721-1749 • stpaulev@juno.com
***SAINT PAUL*** (773)378-6644
Donald B Gourlay • Gretchen Krueger DEAC • EL/HS • NI • 857 N Menard Ave 60651-2660 846 N Menard Ave Chicago IL 60651-2663 • FAX(773)378-7442 • stpaul@ameritech.net
***ST JAMES*** (773)525-4990
Robert B Donovan • EC/EL/HS • NI • 2046 N Fremont St Chicago IL 60614-4312
***ST JOHN*** (773)736-1112
Robert P Degner Christopher L Farina • WS 8 11; SS 930; BC 930;* • H • EC/EL/HS • NI • 4939 W Montrose Ave Chicago IL 60641-1525 • FAX(773)736-3614
***ST JOHN DIVINE*** (773)238-2320
Vacant • H • EN • 10511 S Oakley Ave Chicago IL 60643-2525
***ST MARTINI*** (773)776-7610
Kevin L Wenker • NI • 1624 W 51st St Chicago IL 60609-4821
***ST MATTHEW*** (773)847-6458
Julio A Loza • H • NI • 2108 W 21st St Chicago IL 60608-2608 • FAX(773)847-6471 • jloza@juno.com
***ST MICHAEL*** (773)625-7165
Paul G Mumme • WS 1030;* • H • NI • 8200 W Addison St Chicago IL 60634-1950 • st.michael@aol.com
***ST PAUL***
See Norwood Park
***ST PETER*** (773)582-0470
William L Barthel • H • NI • 8550 S Kedvale Ave Chicago IL 60652-3608
***ST PHILIP*** (773)493-3865
Elstner C Lewis Jr. • WS 11; SS 930; BC 930;* • HS • NI • 6232 S Eberhart Ave Chicago IL 60637-3319 • FAX(773)493-8680
***ST PHILIP NORTH*** (773)561-9830
Christopher C Browne • WS 9 11;* • EC/EL/HS • NI • 2500 W Bryn Mawr Ave Chicago IL 60659-5104 • FAX(773)561-9831
***ST STEPHEN*** (773)783-0416
Vacant • HS • NI • 910 W 65th St Chicago IL 60621-1906
***TABOR*** (773)478-0196
Martin L Schlossman • WS 9; SS 1045; BC 1045 • NI • 3542 W Sunnyside Ave Chicago IL 60625-5931
***TIMOTHY*** (773)874-7333
James R Foley • EC/EL/HS • NI • 1700 W 83rd St Chicago IL 60620-4621 • FAX(773)874-7032
***TRINITY*** (773)646-3811
Vacant • HS • NI • 13200 S Burley Ave Chicago IL 60633-1438
***TRINITY*** (773)237-5045
Jeffrey Dire • WS 945;* • HS • NI • 2601 N Meade Ave Chicago IL 60639-1117 • FAX(773)237-2549 • trinitylutheran@aol.com
***UPTOWN*** (773)271-3760
Vacant • WS 11;* • H • EN • 4720 N Sheridan Rd Chicago IL 60640-5022 • FAX(773)271-8146
***ZION*** (773)233-1775
Vacant • HS • NI • 9901 S Winston Ave Chicago IL 60643-1325
***ZION*** (773)928-3530
Jimmy Mc Cants • EC/EL • NI • 356 E 109th St Chicago IL 60628-3662 • FAX(312)928-3465 • jrmccants@prodogy.net
**CHICAGO HEIGHTS—*ST PAUL*** (708)754-4493
David A Steuernagel William L Metzger • H • EC/EL • NI • 330 W Highland Dr Chicago Heights IL 60411-2043 • FAX(708)754-9807
**CICERO—*FAITH*** (708)652-6414
Michael E Michalk • WS 9 530;* • H • HS • NI • 3601 S 61st Ave Cicero IL 60804-4147 • pastorm@megsinet.net
***REDEEMER*** (708)652-9178
Robert A Sorensen Carlos Castillo(#) • WS 9 1130;* • HS • NI • 5247 W 23rd St Cicero IL 60804-2843 • robtsorens@aol.com
**CISSNA PARK—*IMMANUEL*** (815)457-2909
Vacant • WS 8;* • CI • 996 N State Route 49 Cissna Park IL 60924 • FAX(815)457-2615 • pastorh@localline2.com
***TRINITY*** (815)457-2739
Terry A Strom • WS 830;* • H • CI • 302 S Fourth St 60924 PO Box 207 Cissna Park IL 60924-0207 • stromt@localline2.com
**CLAYTON—*GOOD SHEPHERD*** (217)894-7717
Donald E Busboom • WS 9; SS 10; BC 10 • H • CI • 103 E Morgan 62324 PO Box 347 Clayton IL 62324-0347 • FRLC@Adams.net
**CLINTON—*CHRIST*** (217)935-5808
James Bloch • H • EC • CI • 701 S Mulberry St Clinton IL 61727-2480
**COAL VALLEY—*TRINITY*** (309)799-5650
Robert E Hagen • WS 845; SS 10; BC 10;* • H • CI • 2815 W 3rd St 61240-9661 PO Box 160 Coal Valley IL 61240-0160 • revhag@hotmail.com
**COLLINSVILLE—*GOOD SHEPHERD*** (618)344-3151
Michael P Walther Peter D Hoft • WS 1030; SS 915; BC 915;* • H • EC/EL/HS • SI • 1300 Belt Line Rd Collinsville IL 62234-4373 • FAX(618)344-3378
***HOLY CROSS*** (618)344-3145
William F Engfehr III Ronald A Jansen Fred H Kraemer • WS 8 1030; SS 915; BC 915;* • H • EC/EL/HS • SI • 304 South St Collinsville IL 62234-2619 • FAX(618)344-1222
***JERUSALEM*** (618)346-1925
Vacant • WS 10; SS 915; BC 915 • SI • 305 Collinsville Ave 100 Windridge Dr Collinsville IL 62234-4737
**COLONA—*BEAUT SAVIOR*** (309)949-2111
David C Anderson • H • CI • 5765 Poppy Garden Rd Colona IL 61241-8609
**COLUMBIA—*ST PAUL*** (618)281-4600
Steven C Theiss • WS 8 1030; SS 915; BC 915;* • H • EC • SI • 227 N Good Haven Dr Columbia IL 62236-1921 • FAX(618)281-3821 • stpauls@rdr.net
**CONANT—*TRINITY***
See Pinckneyville
**COTTAGE HILLS—*CONCORDIA*** (618)259-2911
Kevin M Jennings • WS 1015; SS 9; BC 9 • H • SI • 21 Circle Dr Cottage Hills IL 62018-1120 • revkev97@aol.com
**COUNTRY CLUB HILLS—*ST JOHN*** (708)798-4131
Dennis A Aubey • * • H • EC/EL • NI • 4247 183rd St Country Club Hills IL 60478-5337 • FAX(708)798-4193
**COUNTRYSIDE—*HOPE*** (708)354-6176
Randall Donahue • H • NI • 6455 Joliet Rd Countryside IL 60525-4643
**COVINGTON—*ST LUKE*** (618)478-5544
Timothy P Mueller • SI • UKNWN C/O St John Luth 15538 State Route 127 Nashville IL 62263-2374 • FAX(618)478-2042
**CRYSTAL LAKE—*IMMANUEL*** (815)459-1441
Edward B Bergen Thomas H Tews • Mary E Lightbody DCE • WS 8 11;* • H • EC/EL • NI • 178 Mc Henry Ave Crystal Lake IL 60014-6007 • FAX(815)459-1462 • ilc@mc.net
***PRINCE PEACE*** (815)455-3200
Paul R Schuth Larry D Rubeck • WS 8;* • H • EC • NI • 932 Mc Henry Ave Crystal Lake IL 60014-7449 • FAX(815)455-6323 • poplchurchmfwpreschool@juno.com
**DANVERS—*ZION*** (309)963-4825
Frank W Zimmerman • H • CI • 204 W North St 61732 PO Box 545 Danvers IL 61732-0545 • Fwz@frontiernet.net
**DANVILLE—*IMMANUEL*** (217)442-5675
Daniel H Fienen • WS 8 1030; SS 915;* • H • EC/EL • CI • 1930 N Bowman Avenue Rd Danville IL 61832-2298 • FAX(217)442-3827
***TRINITY*** (217)446-4300
Kent A Tibben • H • EC/EL • CI • 824 E Main St Danville IL 61832-5957
**DARIEN—*ST JOHN*** (630)969-7987
David M Bottorff Donald Kirst • WS 8 1045; SS 915; BC 930;* • H • EC • NI • 7214 S Cass Ave Darien IL 60561-3605 • FAX(630)969-8204 • stjohn7214@juno.com
**DARMSTADT—*TRINITY*** (618)475-3143
John P Lukomski • WS 9; SS 10 • H • HS • SI • 900 Belsha St New Athens IL 62264-1502
**DE KALB—*IMMANUEL*** (815)756-6669
E G Krause Michael R Thurau • WS 8 1030;* • H • EC • NI • 511 Russell Rd De Kalb IL 60115-2221 • FAX(815)756-9585 • office@godwithusilc.org
**DECATUR—*CONCORDIA*** (217)428-6421
Robert L Bruer • WS 9; SS 1015;* • H • EL • CI • 3303 E Maryland St Decatur IL 62521-4707 • rbruer@juno.com
***MOUNT CALVARY*** (217)428-0641
Michael Damery • H • EC/EL • CI • 2055 S Franklin Street Rd Decatur IL 62521-5269
***PILGRIM*** (217)877-2444
William K Abbott William B Abbott • WS 8 1045; SS 930;* • H • CI • 2155 N Oakland Ave Decatur IL 62526-3125 • FAX(217)877-2450 • plc@springnet1.com
***ST JOHN*** (217)875-3656
Russell J Weise Mark E Gruden • WS 8 930 11; SS 930; BC 930 • H • EC/EL • CI • 2727 N Union St Decatur IL 62526-3247 • FAX(217)875-7242
***ST PAUL*** (217)423-6955
Wray A Offermann Ronald D Pennekamp • Eric J Altenbernd DCE David F Ahles DCE • WS 8 930 1045; SS 1045 930; BC 1045 930;* • H • EC/EL • CI • 352 W Wood St Decatur IL 62522 • FAX(217)423-6959
***TRINITY*** (217)422-3630
Karl A Weber • H • EL • CI • 1960 E Johns Ave Decatur IL 62521-3105 • karlweber@juno.com
**DELAVAN—*CHRIST*** (309)244-7200
Marvin L Lorenz • WS 9; SS 10; BC 8 • CI • 306 N Locust St 61734 PO Box 477 Delavan IL 61734-0477
**DES PLAINES—*GOOD SHEPHERD*** (847)824-4923
Jeffery H Leichman • H • NI • 1177 Howard Ave Des Plaines IL 60018-2794 • FAX(847)824-7510 • gslambs@juno.com
***IMMANUEL*** (847)824-3652
Richard A Mau • WS 815;* • H • EC/EL • NI • 855 Lee St Des Plaines IL 60016-6407 • FAX(847)294-9640 • immanueldp@juno.com
**DIETERICH—*GRACE*** (217)925-5349
Vacant • * • H • CI • 206 Fayette St 62424-1015 PO Box 1 Dieterich IL 62424-0001
***ST JOHN*** (217)739-2252
Stephen P Gillet • WS 830; SS 930; BC 930 • H • CI • 22775 E 700th Ave 62424-2618 PO Box 18 Dieterich IL 62424-0018 • revspg@hotmail.com
**DIXON—*CHRIST OUR SAVIOR*** (815)284-4554
Vacant • WS 9; SS 1020 • H • NI • 2035 Il Route 26 Dixon IL 61021-9764
**DOLTON—*ST PAUL*** (708)849-6929
Michael D Udoekong • WS 9; SS 1030; BC 1030;* • H • EC/EL/HS • NI • 245 E 138th St Dolton IL 60419-1060 • FAX(708)849-2276
**DORSEY—*ST PETER***
See Prairietown
**DORSEY 2 NW—*EMMAUS*** (618)377-6221
George J Gude • WS 10; SS 9; BC 9;* • H • SI • 62021 5215 Loop Rd Dorsey IL 62021-1103
**DOWNERS GROVE—*IMMANUEL*** (630)968-3112
John R Prohl Steven M Hufford • WS 745 10 1115; SS 845; BC 9;* • H • EC • NI • 5211 Carpenter St Downers Grove IL 60515-4519 • FAX(630)968-3183 • ilchu@netzero.net
**DU QUOIN—*BETHEL*** (618)542-3418
Christopher S Esget • WS 10; SS 845; BC 845 • H • EC • SI • 699 W Main St Du Quoin IL 62832-9301
**DUNDEE—*BETHLEHEM*** (847)426-7311
Steven D Simon Frank E Hewitt(#) • * • H • EL/HS • NI • 401 W Main St Dundee IL 60118-2022 • FAX(847)426-4234
***IMMANUEL***
See East Dundee
***ST PETER*** (847)428-4054
Allan R Buss • WS 8;* • H • NI • 18N377 Galligan Rd Dundee IL 60118 • FAX(847)428-1640 • albussrev@aol.com
**DUNLAP—*EPIPHANY*** (309)243-5957
John A Frahm III • Colleen D Simpson DCE • H • CI • 12716 N Allen Rd 61525-9606 PO Box 182 Dunlap IL 61525-0182
**DWIGHT—*EMMANUEL*** (815)584-3433
Daniel F Ognoskie • * • H • NI • Rtes 47 And 17 325 E Mazon Ave Dwight IL 60420-1159 • FAX(815)584-1291 • emmandwi@core.
**DWIGHT 4 NE—*TRINITY*** (815)584-3407
Willis R Piepenbrink • WS 10 • H • NI • 515 E Stonewall Rd Dwight IL 60420 • FAX(815)584-3407
**EAST CARONDELET—*HOLY CROSS***
See Sugar Loaf Twp
**EAST DUNDEE—*IMMANUEL*** (847)428-4477
William P Yonker • WS 8 1045; SS 930; BC 930;* • EC/EL/HS • NI • Main And Van Buren 60118 407 Johnson St Dundee IL 60118-2305 • FAX(847)428-4580
**EAST MOLINE—*ST JOHN*** (309)792-0755
Kent A Umbarger Lester H Dumer(EM) • Elizabeth A Posey DEAC • WS 9; SS 1015; BC 1015;* • H • EC/HS • CI • 1450 30th Ave East Moline IL 61244-3831 • FAX(309)792-0776 • stjohns@qconline.com
**EAST MOLINE 5 NE—*ZION*** (309)496-2186
Gary A Wright • WS 9; SS 1015;* • H • EC/HS • CI • 61244 17628 Hubbard Rd East Moline IL 61244-9782 • FAX(309)469-9076 • zionlutheranchurch@juno.com
**EAST PEORIA—*ASCENSION*** (309)694-4047
Arthur H Baisch • WS 9; SS 1030; BC 1030 • H • CI • 1081 Upper Spring Bay Rd East Peoria IL 61611-9649
***ST PETER*** (309)699-5411
Vernon L Bettermann Thomas E Engel • H • CI • 200 Cole St 61611-2521 PO Box 2205 East Peoria IL 61611-0205 • FAX(309)699-9776
**EAST ST LOUIS—*UNITY*** (618)874-6600
Vacant • H • SI • 4200 Caseyville Ave East St Louis IL 62204-1807
**EDINBURG—*TRINITY*** (217)623-5549
Vacant • H • CI • 205 N Campbell 62531 PO Box 259 Edinburg IL 62531-0259
**EDWARDSVILLE—*TRINITY*** (618)656-2918
Terence R Groth Gary W Galen • WS 745 915 1045; SS 910;* • H • EC/EL/HS • SI • 600 Water St Edwardsville IL 62025-1764 • FAX(618)656-5941 • tlce@plantnet.com
***ZION***
See Carpenter
**EFFINGHAM—*ST JOHN*** (217)342-4334
Robert J Backhus • Larry L Brandt DCE • WS 8 1030; SS 915; BC 915 • H • EC • CI • 901 W Jefferson Ave Effingham IL 62401-2034 • FAX(217)342-6599 • jtolch@effingham.net

**EL PASO—*TRINITY*** (309)527-4333
Bruce Lakamp • WS 10; SS 9; BC 910 • H • CI • 595 W 3rd St El Paso IL 61738-1006

**ELGIN—*CALVARY*** (847)741-5433
Richard J Bellas • H • NI • 535 N Mc Lean Blvd Elgin IL 60123-3241

***GOOD SHEPHERD*** (847)741-7788
Roger J Pollock Martin W Balzer • Sheila K Rudat DCE • WS 8 930 1045; SS 930; BC 930;* • H • EL/HS • NI • 1111 Van St Elgin IL 60123-6016 • FAX(847)741-6904 • shepherd@foxvalley.net

***KING OF GLORY*** (847)931-1520
Mark C Schulz • WS 815 1045; BC 930;* • H • NI • 36W720 Hopps Rd Elgin IL 60123-8540

***ST JOHN*** (847)741-0814
Thomas A Niermann Clifford M Frederich • Jason W Huebner DCE • WS 8 1030; BC 915;* • EC/EL • NI • 101 N Spring St Elgin IL 60120-5519 • FAX(847)741-0859

**ELIZABETH—*ST PAUL*** (815)858-3334
Harvey E Nicholson • * • H • NI • 411 W Catlin St 61028 PO Box 506 Elizabeth IL 61028-0506

**ELK GROVE VILLAGE—*HOLY SPIRIT*** (847)437-5897
David T Stein • * • H • EC • EN • 150 Lions Dr Elk Grove Village IL 60007-4200 • FAX(847)437-5899 • dtsteinlb@aol.com

**ELMHURST—*IMMANUEL*** (630)832-1649
Mark P Bussert Stanley L Harding • WS 8;* • H • EC/EL/HS • NI • 142 E 3rd St Elmhurst IL 60126-2461 • FAX(630)832-5761 • immelm@mcs.net

***MESSIAH*** (630)279-4775
Bradford Maxon • * • EN • 130 W Butterfield Rd Elmhurst IL 60126-5073

***REDEEMER*** (630)834-1411
Richard D Drews Stephen A Knapp • WS 830;* • H • EN • 345 S Kenilworth Ave Elmhurst IL 60126-3409 • FAX(630)834-1462 • schafrhund@aol.com

**ELMWOOD PARK—*ZOAR*** (708)453-6486
Vacant • H • HS • NI • 2940 N 75th Ct Elmwood Park IL 60707-1123 • zelc@juno.com

**EUREKA—*OUR REDEEMER*** (309)467-5477
Joseph G Murphy • WS 9; SS 1015 • H • CI • 698 Reagan Dr 61530-9790 PO Box 273 Eureka IL 61530-0273

**EVANSTON—*BETHLEHEM*** (847)328-9454
Victor J Van Kanegan • H • NI • 1334 Wesley Ave Evanston IL 60201-4141 • FAX(847)328-9467 • bethleheml@aol.com

**EVANSVILLE—*ST PETER*** (618)853-2322
Vacant • SS 9;* • H • HS • SI • 900 Church St 62242-2050 PO Box 27 Evansville IL 62242-0027

**EVANSVILLE (RUMA)—*ST JOHN*** (618)282-6060
Vacant • * • H • HS • SI • 62242 8446 1st Rd Evansville IL 62242-1008

**FAIRFIELD—*CHRIST*** (618)847-3733
Vacant • SI • 912 W Delaware St Fairfield IL 62837-1411

**FAIRVIEW HEIGHT—*BETHANY***
See O Fallon

**FARMERSVILLE—*ZION*** (217)227-3504
Mark A Thompson • H • SI • 501 Nobbe St 62533 PO Box 19 Farmersville IL 62533-0019

**FERRIN—*BETHLEHEM*** (618)226-3550
Mitchel E Schuessler • SS 9; BC 9;* • H • EC • SI • 12903 Clara St Carlyle IL 62231-3837

**FISHER—*IMMANUEL***
See Osman

**FLORA—*FAITH*** (618)662-9500
Paul D Egger • WS 10; SS 9; BC 9 • H • CI • 62839-1013 600 West Twelfth St RR 1 Flora IL 62839-9802 • pdegger@wabash.net

**FOREST PARK—*ST JOHN*** (708)366-3226
Russell S Belisle • H • EC/EL/HS • NI • 305 Circle Ave Forest Park IL 60130-1609 • FAX(708)488-2194

**FORSYTH—*OUR REDEEMER*** (217)877-2967
Vacant • WS 9; SS 1015; BC 1015 • H • EL • CI • 155 W Forsyth Rd PO Box 259 Forsyth IL 62535-0259

**FRANKFORT—*GOOD SHEPHERD*** (815)469-1028
Kevin E Hahn Jay D Mather(#) • WS 9; BC 1015;* • H • NI • 295 W Sauk Trl Frankfort IL 60423-7779

**FRANKLIN PARK—*MOUNT CALVARY*** (847)678-5565
Paul G Mumme • WS 830;* • H • HS • NI • 3222 Rose St Franklin Park IL 60131-2145

***OUR SAVIOR DEAF***
See Wood Dale

**FREEBURG—*CHRIST OUR SAVIOR*** (618)539-5664
Bruce E Keseman • WS 9; SS 1020;* • H • HS • SI • 612 N State St Freeburg IL 62243-4000 • keseman@aol.com

**FREEPORT—*IMMANUEL*** (815)235-1993
Willis R Schwichtenberg • WS 8 1030; SS 915; BC 915;* • H • EC/EL • NI • 1964 W Pearl City Rd 61032-9332 1993 W Church St Freeport IL 61032-4600 • FAX(815)233-9158 • immanuelfrpt@mwci.net

***OUR REDEEMER*** (815)232-6934
Stephen F Precht • WS 9; SS 1030; BC 1030 • H • NI • 1320 S Blackhawk Ave Freeport IL 61032-6302 • FAX(815)233-2243 • ourredeemer@aeroinc.net

**GALESBURG—*MOUNT CALVARY*** (309)342-7083
Joseph R Cassady III • WS 10; SS 845; BC 845 • H • EC • CI • 1372 W Fremont St Galesburg IL 61401-2437 • mclc@galesburg.net

**GENESEO—*CONCORDIA*** (309)944-3993
Daniel A Olson • WS 8 1030; SS 915; BC 915;* • H • CI • 316 S Oakwood Ave Geneseo IL 61254-1445 • FAX(309)945-4400 • lcms@geneseo.net

**GENESEO 7 SW—*ST JOHN*** (309)949-2516
Robert A Woods • * • H • CI • 61254 8948 N 1900th Ave Geneseo IL 61254-8941 • revwoods@netexpress.net

**GENEVA—*FAITH*** (630)232-8420
Chris Nilges • WS 1045 8; SS 945; BC 945 • H • EC/EL/HS • NI • 60134 1745 Kaneville Rd Geneva IL 60134-1828 • FAX(630)232-7344

**GENOA—*TRINITY*** (815)784-2522
Harold W Schmidt Daniel C Berteau • WS 8 1030; BC 915;* • H • EC • NI • 33930 N State Rd 60135-8420 PO Box 7 Genoa IL 60135-0007 • FAX(815)784-5208 • trinity@tbcnet.com

**GILLESPIE—*REDEEMER*** (217)839-2717
Walter E Byerley(EM) Edward T Purdy(EM) • H • SI • 206 W Spruce St Gillespie IL 62033-1615

**GIRARD 2 N—*TRINITY*** (217)965-4816
Kit B Belk • WS 10; SS 9; BC 9;* • H • SI • 62640 32946 Route 4 Girard IL 62640-9516

**GLEN CARBON—*ST JAMES*** (618)288-6120
Edward K Wolfe • WS 1030; SS 9; BC 9;* • H • EC/HS • SI • 146 N Main St Glen Carbon IL 62034-1611

**GLENCOE—*TRINITY*** (847)835-3096
Vacant • WS 10 • NI • Hawthorn And Greenwood 60022 PO Box 157 Glencoe IL 60022-0157 • FAX(847)634-3986 • trinitygco@aol.com

**GLENDALE HEIGHTS—*FAMILY IN*** (630)653-5030
Stephen R Kass • Lisa A Kamis DCE • WS 8 1030; SS 915; BC 915 • H • NI • 1480 Bloomingdale Rd Glendale Heights IL 60139-2772 • fifcc@mcs.net

**GLENVIEW—*IMMANUEL*** (847)724-1034
David E Barber • * • H • EC/EL • NI • 1850 Chestnut Ave Glenview IL 60025-1688 • FAX(847)724-1038 • ilg3staff@familysafe.net

**GODFREY—*FAITH*** (618)466-3833
Curtis L Deterding • WS 9; SS 1030; BC 1030;* • H • EC/EL/HS • SI • 6809 Godfrey Rd Godfrey IL 62035-2222 • FAX(618)466-3839

**GOLCONDA—*OUR REDEEMER*** (618)683-8621
Gary K Harroun • H • SI • Franklin At Madison 62938 PO Box 580 Golconda IL 62938-0580

**GOLDEN—*HOLY CROSS*** (217)696-2642
Mark R Eddy • * • CI • 205 West Third St 62339 PO Box 116 Golden IL 62339-0116 • FAX(217)696-2642 • markeddy@adams.net

**GRANITE CITY—*CONCORDIA*** (618)451-9925
Brian Feicho • WS 1015; SS 9; BC 9 • H • HS • SI • 2305 Grand Ave Granite City IL 62040-4733 • info@concordialutheran.cc

***HOPE*** (618)876-7568
David Fielding • WS 930; SS 830; BC 830 • H • EC • SI • 3715 Wabash Ave Granite City IL 62040-3977

***ST JOHN*** (618)451-7788
Warren L Huffines • WS 1030; SS 9; BC 9;* • H • S • 2001 Saint Clair Ave Granite City IL 62040-6065 • FAX(618)451-5855 • StJohnGraniteCity@juno.com

**GRANT PARK 4 NW—*ZION*** (815)465-6011
Fred W Beck • * • H • NI • 60940 11456 N 11000E Rd Grant Park IL 60940-5067 • FAX(815)465-0042

**GRAYSLAKE—*LORD OF GLORY**** (847)548-5673
Glenn S Brauer • WS 8; SS 1030; BC 930 • H • EC • NI • 607 W Belvidere Rd Grayslake IL 60030 • FAX(847)548-6796

**GREEN VALLEY 6 N—*ST JOHN*** (309)348-3180
Thomas R Wenndt • WS 8 1045; SS 930; BC 930 • H • EC/EL • CI • 13443 Townline Rd Green Valley IL 61534-9216 • FAX(309)348-3678 • sandluth@dpc.net

**GREENVILLE—*OUR REDEEMER*** (618)664-0223
Jeffery D Nehrt • WS 1015; SS 9; BC 9 • H • SI • 813 E College Ave Greenville IL 62246-1530

**GURNEE—*BETHEL*** (847)244-9647
Lee S Clark • * • H • EC • NI • 5110 Grand Ave Gurnee IL 60031-1813 • leesclark@aol.com

**HAMPSHIRE—*ST PETER***
See Pinegree

***ST PETER***
See North Plato

***TRINITY*** (847)683-2238
Vacant • * • H • NI • 135 Terwilliger Ave Hampshire IL 60140-9603 • FAX(847)683-2238

**HARDIN—*ST PAUL*** (618)653-4649
Rueben J Ankney • WS 830;* • H • SI • S County Rd 62047 PO Box 429 Hardin IL 62047-0429

**HARVARD—*ST PAUL*** (815)943-5330
Michael D Pfingsten • * • H • NI • 1601 N Garfield Rd Harvard IL 60033-1749 • FAX(815)943-1522

**HARVEL—*TRINITY*** (217)229-3143
Clifford Adair • WS 10; SS 9 • H • SI • 402 N Monroe Box 207 Harvel IL 62538-0207

**HARVEY—*TRINITY*** (708)333-0580
Vacant • H • NI • 10 W 150th St Harvey IL 60426-2120 • c1tracy@harvey.liv.il.us

**HAVANA—*ST PAUL*** (309)543-4850
Martin W Liebmann Jr. • H • CI • 121 N Pearl St 62644-1409 PO Box 534 Havana IL 62644-0534 • FAX(309)543-1245 • stpaul@fgi.net

**HERRIN—*TRINITY*** (618)942-3401
Michael D Henson • H • EC • SI • 1000 N Park Ave Herrin IL 62948-2720

**HERSCHER—*TRINITY*** (815)426-2262
Gary L Ruckman • WS 8 1015; SS 9; BC 9;* • H • NI • 255 E 3rd St 60941-4414 PO Box 414 Herscher IL 60941-0414 • FAX(815)426-2390 • trinityher@juno.com

**HIGHLAND—*HOPE*** (618)654-7891
Leonard C Laetsch • WS 9;* • H • SI • 2745 Broadway Highland IL 62249-2431

**HIGHLAND PARK—*REDEEMER*** (847)831-2225
Jerald S Lindemann • WS 9;* • EC • NI • 1731 Deerfield Rd Highland Park IL 60035-3704 • FAX(847)831-2226 • rlchp@concentric.net

**HILLSBORO—*OUR SAVIOR*** (217)532-3463
Vacant • H • SI • 510 E Tremont St Hillsboro IL 62049-1802

**HILLSIDE—*HOPE*** (708)449-8688
Steven J Cornwell • SS 9 • NI • 5159 Madison Hillside IL 60162 • hopehillside@juno.com

***IMMANUEL*** (708)562-5590
Patrick Mc Kenzie • H • EL/HS • NI • 2317 S Wolf Rd Hillside IL 60162-2211 • FAX(708)562-6085

**HINCKLEY 5 NW—*IMMANUEL*** (815)286-3885
Donald E Balgeman • * • H • NI • 60520 12760 Lee Rd Hinckley IL 60520-6083 • FAX(815)286-3885 • ilc1@thestix.net

**HINSDALE—*ZION*** (630)323-0384
Vacant • * • H • HS • NI • 60521 204 S Grant St Hinsdale IL 60521-4052 • FAX(630)323-0694

**HODGKINS—*IMMANUEL*** (708)354-0692
Vacant • H • NI • 6605 Kane Ave Hodgkins IL 60525-7619 • FAX(708)448-0154 • dietrich@millnet.net

**HOFFMAN 1 N—*TRINITY*** (618)495-2545
Ronald E Oppen • WS 830;* • H • SI • 8700 Huey Rd UKNWN PO Box 200 Hoffman IL 62250-0200 • FAX(618)495-2692

**HOMEWOOD—*SALEM*** (708)798-1820
David W Speerbrecker • WS 830 11; SS 945; BC 945;* • H • EC • NI • 18324 Ashland Ave Homewood IL 60430-3403 • FAX(708)798-1590

**HOOPESTON—*GOOD SHEPHERD*** (217)283-7966
Wallace J Waite • WS 1030 • H • EC • CI • 302 N Market St Hoopeston IL 60942-1320 • goodshepherd@htb.net

**HOYLETON—*TRINITY*** (618)493-6226
Mark A Nebel • * • H • EC/EL • SI • 205 N Main St 62803-2005 PO Box 176 Hoyleton IL 62803-0176 • FAX(618)493-7754

**HUNTLEY—*TRINITY*** (847)669-5780
Charles W Kittel • H • EC • NI • 11008 N Church St 60142-6952 PO Box 186 Huntley IL 60142-0186 • FAX(847)669-5978 • trinityluth.huntley@juno.com

**INDIAN CREEK—*RISEN SAVIOR*** (847)367-9250
Andrew K Barkley • H • NI • 230 US Highway 45 Indian Creek IL 60061-4405 • FAX(847)367-9309 • rs-lc@juno.com

**ISLAND LAKE—*ST JOHN*** (847)526-7614
Bruce A Hoffmann • WS 9; SS 1015; BC 1015 • H • NI • 405 W State Rd # 176 60042-8450 PO Box 370 Island Lake IL 60042-0370 • FAX(847)526-7672 • gospel14all@yahoo.com

**ITASCA—*ST LUKE*** (630)773-0396
Danny W Tutwiler • Cynthia K Nelsen DCE • H • HS • NI • 410 S Rush St Itasca IL 60143-2130 • FAX(630)773-0786

**IUKA 4 SE—*TRINITY*** (618)323-6586
Gregory D Hyatt • WS 10; SS 930; BC 930 • H • SI • 62849 8250 Trinity Ln Iuka IL 62849-2420

**JACKSONVILLE—*CHRIST DEAF*** (217)793-1802
Vacant • H • CI • 104 Finley St 62650 C/O Rev Joel Cluver 1850 N Grand Ave W Springfield IL 62791

***JOY OF JESUS DEAF***
See Peoria

***OUR REDEEMER*** (217)243-3939
Gary R Schmidtke Alvin J Schmidt Oscar J Klinkerman(EM) • H • CI • 405 Massey Ln Jacksonville IL 62650-2615

***SALEM*** (217)243-3419
Peter R Brechbuhl Richard A Salcido • WS 8 1030; SS 915; BC 915;* • H • EC/EL • CI • 222 E Beecher Ave 62650-2513 PO Box 1057 Jacksonville IL 62651-1057 • FAX(217)245-0289 • salemlutheran@netscape.com

**JACOB—*CHRIST*** (618)763-4663
Vacant • WS 9; SS 1015; BC 1015 • EL • SI • 62950 184 W Jacob Rd Jacob IL 62950-2719

**JERSEYVILLE—*HOPE*** (618)498-3423
Vacant • H • SI • 1009 N State St Jerseyville IL 62052-1111

**JOLIET—*OUR SAVIOR*** (815)725-1606
Klaus M Mehrl William T Mitschke • WS 8 1045; SS 915; BC 915;* • EC • NI • 1910 Black Rd Joliet IL 60435-3423 • FAX(815)725-1689 • office.oslc.joliet.il@juno.com

***ST PETER*** (815)722-3567
Lee M Jany • * • H • EC/EL • NI • 310 N Broadway St Joliet IL 60435-7169 • FAX(815)722-6544

**KAMPSVILLE—*ST JOHN*** (618)653-4649
Rueben J Ankney • WS 1015; SS 915;* • H • SI • 316 Saint Louis Ave 62053 PO Box 305 Kampsville IL 62053-0305 • sjlc@jvil.com

**KANKAKEE—*ST PAUL*** (815)932-0312
Karl J Koeppen • WS 8 930 11; SS 930; BC 930;* • H • EC/EL • NI • 1580 Butterfield Trl Kankakee IL 60901-2933 • FAX(815)932-7588

**KEWANEE—*ST PAUL*** (309)852-2461
Burnell F Eckardt • WS 9; SS 1015; BC 1015;* • H • CI • 109 S Elm St Kewanee IL 61443-2340 • beckardt@inw.net

**LA GRANGE—*HOPE***
See Countryside

***ST JOHN*** (708)354-1690
James P Haberkost David L Smith • Brent D Stewart DCE • WS 815 1045; SS 930; BC 930 • H • NI • 505 S Park Rd La Grange IL 60525-6198 • FAX(708)354-4910

**LA ROSE—*TRINITY*** (309)248-7153
Kenneth J Mangold • CI • PO Box 115 La Rose IL 61541-0115

**LA SALLE—*SHEP OF VALLEY*** (815)224-4434
Vacant • H • NI • 1119 8th St La Salle IL 61301-1937

**LAFOX—*LORD OF LIFE*** (708)513-5325
Barry L Kolb • WS 8; SS 930; BC 11;* • H • EC/EL/HS • NI • 40 W 605 Rt 38 Elburn 60147 PO Box 70 Lafox IL 60147-0070 • FAX(708)513-7692 • docvmp@mailcity.com

**LAKE FOREST—*FAITH*** (847)234-1868
Mark R Schulz • WS 1030; SS 915;* • H • EC • NI • 680 W Deerpath Rd Lake Forest IL 60045-1611 • FAX(847)234-1929 • FaithLutheran.LakeForest@juno.com

**LAKE VILLA—*GOOD SHEPHERD*** (847)356-5158
John W Zellmer • WS 815 1045; BC 930;* • EC • NI • 25100 W Grand Ave Lake Villa IL 60046-9704

**LAKE ZURICH—*ST MATTHEW*** (847)438-7709
Harold O Krueger Carlton E Payne • WS 815 1045; SS 1030 930; BC 1030 930;* • H • EC/EL • NI • C/O Rev Harold O Krueger 24500 N Old Mc Henry Rd Lake Zurich IL 60047-8424 • FAX(847)438-0376 • stmatts@dls.net

**LANSING—*ST JOHN*** (708)895-9240
Paul W Krause • WS 8 1030; BC 915;* • H • EC/EL/HS • NI • 18100 Wentworth Ave Lansing IL 60438-3900 • FAX(708)895-9303

***TRINITY*** (708)474-7997
Robert D Koeppen • H • EC/EL/HS • NI • 2505 Indiana Ave Lansing IL 60438-2159 • FAX(708)474-0820

**LAWRENCEVILLE—*OUR SAVIOR*** (618)943-6680
J Kevin Wyckoff • H • CI • 15th And Collins 62439 PO Box 643 Lawrenceville IL 62439-0643 • jkevinw@midwest.net

**LEBANON—*MESSIAH*** (618)537-2300
Garry A Mc Cracken • H • EC • SI • 801 N Madison St 62254-1455 PO Box 21 Lebanon IL 62254-0021 • FAX(618)224-7240

**LEMONT—*ST MATTHEW*** (630)257-5000
Vacant • NI • 305 Lemont St Lemont IL 60439-3618 • FAX(630)257-5910 • stmatt@stmatt.com

**LENA—*ST JOHN*** (815)369-4035
Rick L Bader Donald H Hoffmann • WS 8 1030; SS 915; BC 915;* • H • NI • 625 Country Lane Dr 61048-9559 PO Box 216 Lena IL 61048-0216 • FAX(815)369-2535 • sjl@mwci.net

**LEXINGTON—*ST PAUL*** (309)365-5100
Edward F Doerner • H • EC • CI • 107 E Chatham St Lexington IL 61753-1018 • FAX(309)365-8251 • stpaul@davesworld.net

**LINCOLN—*FAITH*** (217)732-4901
Mark D Peters • H • CI • 2320 N Kickapoo Lincoln IL 62656-1334

***ZION*** (217)732-3946
Mark D Carnahan Kirk R Cunningham William W Adam(EM) • WS 8 1030; SS 920; BC 930;* • H • CI • 205 Pulaski St Lincoln IL 62656-2037 • FAX(217)732-5876 • mdc@abelink.com

**LINCOLNSHIRE—*TRINITY***
See Glencoe

**LINDENWOOD—*IMMANUEL*** (815)393-4500
J D Riddle • WS 9; BC 1030;* • H • NI • 16060 E Lindenwood Rd Lindenwood IL 61049-9724 • FAX(815)393-4500 • immanuel.lcms@tbcnet.com

**LISLE—*TRINITY*** (630)964-1272
Arthur H Beyer • H • EC • NI • 1101 Kimberly Way Lisle IL 60532-3175 • FAX(630)964-1468 • artbeyer@aol.com

**LITCHFIELD—*ZION*** (217)324-2033
Donald H Langhoff Jonathan C Bontke • WS 8 1030; SS 915;* • H • EC/EL • SI • 1301 N State St Litchfield IL 62056-1105 • FAX(217)324-3166

**LIVINGSTON—*HOLY CROSS*** (618)637-2146
Maurice H Alms • H • HS • SI • Church And Mullen Sts 62058 PO Box 397 Livingston IL 62058-0397

**LOCKPORT—*ST PAUL*** (815)838-1832
Mark H Hein • WS 9; SS 1045; BC 1045;* • H • EC • NI • 1500 S Briggs St Lockport IL 60441-4546 • FAX(815)838-1734 • St.PaulsLutheran@worldnet.att.net

**LODA—*IMMANUEL*** (217)386-2232
Edgar L Peters • WS 830;* • CI • 215 N Poplar St 60948 PO Box 338 Loda IL 60948-0338

**LOMBARD—*PEACE*** (630)627-1101
Duane S Feldmann Kenneth W Garazin • H • EC • NI • 21W500 Butterfield Rd Lombard IL 60148-5134 • FAX(630)627-1103 • peaceinfo@aol.com

***ST JOHN*** (630)629-2515
Thomas C Noll Patrick J Boomhower • H • EC/EL/HS • NI • 215 S Lincoln St Lombard IL 60148-2510 • FAX(630)629-2515

***TRINITY*** (630)629-8765
Randy R Emmons A A Das • H • EC/EL/HS • NI • 1165 Westmore Meyers Rd Lombard IL 60148-4174 • FAX(630)627-5676 • pastoremmons@mediaone.net

**LOUISVILLE—*ST JOHN*** (618)686-2971
Rollie Meyer • WS 10; SS 9; BC 9;* • H • CI • 62858 17684 E 1st Ave Louisville IL 62858-9469

**LYONS—*ZION*** (708)447-4499
David T Kluge • * • EC • NI • 7930 Ogden Ave Lyons IL 60534-1333

**MACHESNEY PARK—*CONCORDIA*** (815)633-4983
David A Uden(#) • WS 8 1045;* • H • EC/EL/HS • NI • 7424 N Second St Machesney Park IL 61115-2814 • FAX(815)633-1345

**MACOMB—*IMMANUEL*** (309)833-4286
Michael H Burdick • WS 830; SS 940; BC 940 • H • CI • 906 E Grant St Macomb IL 61455-3322 • FAX(309)833-2749 • milsc@wiu.edu

**MAHOMET—*CHRIST FAMILY**** (217)586-7022
David A Allen(DM) • WS 1015; SS 9; BC 9 • H • CI • 405 S Division St 61853-9227 PO Box 523 Mahomet IL 61853-0523 • Christfamily@pdnt.com

**MANITO—*TRINITY*** (309)968-6984
K M Simminger • H • CI • 110 S Park Ave Manito IL 61546-9284

**MANITO 6 SE—*ST PAUL*** (309)968-6614
Donald C Hinkel Jr. • WS 930; SS 830; BC 830 • H • CI • 61546 21819 County Rd N 3300 E Manito IL 61546-7983 • dhinkel@ntslink.net

**MANTENO—*RISEN SAVIOR*** (815)468-2011
Paul M Crolius • WS 8 1030; SS 915; BC 915 • NI • 499 Park St Manteno IL 60950-1026 • PCroliusjuno.com

**MARENGO—*ZION*** (815)568-6564
Glen W Borhart • Thomas L Heren DCE • WS 8 1030; SS 915; BC 930;* • H • EC/EL • NI • 412 Jackson St Marengo IL 60152 • FAX(815)568-0547

**MARION—*GOOD SHEPHERD*** (618)993-3649
William E Schmidt • WS 1015 745; SS 9; BC 9;* • H • SI • 1801 Westminster Dr Marion IL 62959-1441 • goodslc@hotmail.com

**MARKHAM—*MARKHAM*** (708)331-4885
Larry G Schneekloth • H • EC • EN • 160th and Clifton Park Ave Markham IL 60426

**MARSEILLES—*TRINITY*** (815)795-2031
David C Mumme • H • NI • 621 Union St Marseilles IL 61341-1623

**MARYVILLE—*ST JOHN*** (618)344-8989
Lee A Maxwell • WS 1015; SS 9; BC 9;* • H • EC/HS • SI • 7201 W Main St 62062-6707 PO Box 517 Maryville IL 62062-0517 • stjohnsluth@juno.com

**MASCOUTAH—*ZION*** (618)566-7345
Mark W Love • WS 10; SS 845 • H • EC • SI • 101 S Railway Mascoutah IL 62258 • FAX(618)566-9519 • zionlcms@accessus.net

**MASON CITY—*CHRIST*** (217)482-5168
Robert W Martinek • WS 9; SS 1015; BC 1015;* • H • EC • CI • 114 E Walnut St Mason City IL 62664-1164 • christlu@fgi.net

**MATTESON—*ST PAUL*** (708)720-0880
Matthew D Troester • WS 8 1045;* • H • NI • 6201 Vollmer Rd Matteson IL 60443-1058 • rtroester@aol.com

***ZION*** (708)747-1116
Dennis L Thompson Marvin Griffin • H • EC/EL/HS • NI • 3840 216th St Matteson IL 60443-2717 • FAX(708)747-1194

**MATTOON—*ST JOHN*** (217)234-4923
Bruce D Osborne Delton L Nack • WS 1015 8; SS 9; BC 9;* • H • EC/EL • CI • 200 Charleston Ave Mattoon IL 61938-4428 • FAX(217)234-4925 • osborne.stjohns@advant.net

**MATTOON 4N 2E—*ST PAUL*** (217)234-9880
Scott A Kozisek • WS 10; SS 845; BC 845 • H • CI • 61938 8975 E County Road 1200N Mattoon IL 61938-3458 • FAX(217)234-9880 • stpaulsluth@one-eleven.net

**MC HENRY—*FELLOWSHIP OF FAITH*** (815)759-0739
Rodney H Knoerr • Stephanie J Kosbab DCE • WS 1015; SS 9; BC 9 • H • NI • 1014 N River Rd Mc Henry IL 60050-5683 • FAX(815)759-0792 • fof@owc.net

***ZION*** (815)385-0859
Peter Diebenow • H • EC • NI • 4206 W Elm St Mc Henry IL 60050-4001 • FAX(815)385-0878

**MC LEANSBORO—*TRINITY*** (618)643-4229
Mark S Lohnes • SI • 404 S Marshall Mc Leansboro IL 62859

**MELROSE PARK—*APOSTLES*** (847)455-0903
John E Helmke • WS 815; SS 11; BC 930 • EC • NI • 10429 W Fullerton Ave Melrose Park IL 60164-1860 • FAX(847)455-0915

***ST PAUL*** (708)343-1000
Paul K Gossman Elias Martinez • H • EC/EL/HS • NI • 1025 Lake St Melrose Park IL 60160-4150 • FAX(708)343-8635 • spcrusad@flash.net

**MILAN—*ST MATTHEW*** (309)787-4295
Paul K Pett • Gregory G Mueller DCE • WS 8 1030; SS 915; BC 915;* • H • HS • CI • 115 12th Ave W Milan IL 61264-3037 • FAX(309)787-4291 • revpett@aol.com

**MILFORD—*OUR SAVIOR*** (815)889-4121
Don R Stuckwisch • WS 9; BC 1015;* • H • NI • 209 W Jones St 60953-1051 PO Box 188 Milford IL 60953-0188 • oursavior@excite.com

***ST PAUL***
See Woodworth

**MINIER—*GOOD SHEPHERD*** (309)392-2933
Frank W Zimmerman • H • CI • 101 E Garfield 61759 PO Box 858 Minier IL 61759-0858 • fwz@frontiernet.net

**MOKENA—*IMMANUEL*** (708)479-5600
David P Constien • WS 8;* • H • EC • NI • 10731 W La Porte Rd Mokena IL 60448-9284 • FAX(708)479-2248 • imm10731@netzero.net

**MOLINE—*HOLY CROSS*** (309)764-9720
John A Laux Eldor W Haake • WS 815; SS 930; BC 930 • H • CI • 4107 21st Ave Moline IL 61265-4580

**MOMENCE—*OUR SAVIOR*** (815)472-2829
Keith E Ge Rue • WS 10; BC 850;* • NI • 118 N Pine St Momence IL 60954-1512 • FAX(815)472-6321 • revgerue@techinter.com

**MONTGOMERY—*ST LUKE*** (630)892-9309
Peter Hoffman • WS 8; SS 930; BC 930;* • H • EC/EL • NI • 11 Pembrooke Rd Montgomery IL 60538-2016 • FAX(630)892-0166 • stlukes11@juno.com

***ST LUKE***
See Boulder Hill

**MORRISON—*ST PETER*** (815)772-3386
Michael L Winkelman • WS 930;* • H • EC/EL • NI • 601 N Jackson St Morrison IL 61270-3007 • FAX(815)772-7478 • stpeters@sanasys.com

**MORTON—*BETHEL*** (309)263-2417
Richard Benke Brian N Pape • WS 8 1045; SS 915; BC 930;* • H • EC/EL • CI • 425 N Missouri Ave Morton IL 61550-1708 • FAX(309)263-7902 • bethel@mtco.com

**MOUNT CARMEL—*HOPE*** (618)262-7373
Wayne N Woolery • WS 1030; SS 930; BC 930 • H • SI • 1512 N Cherry St Mount Carmel IL 62863-1855

**MOUNT OLIVE—*IMMANUEL*** (217)999-7442
Daniel Barbey • WS 10; SS 845; BC 845 • H • SI • 111 E Main St Mount Olive IL 62069-1703 • immanuel@ctnet.net or barbey@ctnet.net

**MOUNT PROSPECT—*ST JOHN*** (847)593-7670
Jeff G Gavin • * • H • EC/EL • NI • 1100 S Linneman Rd Mount Prospect IL 60056-4124 • FAX(847)593-2601 • jeffgavin@avenew.com

***ST PAUL*** (847)255-0332
William H Tucker Marc N Schwichtenberg David F Walker • Dari R Hartmann DCE • H • EC/EL • NI • 100 S School St Mount Prospect IL 60056-3317 • FAX(847)255-0948 • stpaulmp@aol.com

**MOUNT PULASKI—*ZION*** (217)792-5965
Paul E Droegemueller • H • EC/EL • CI • 203 S Vine St Mount Pulaski IL 62548-1256

**MOUNT STERLING—*FIRST*** (217)322-4237
Joseph V Eckman • H • CI • 111 W South St Mount Sterling IL 62353-1548

**MOUNT VERNON—*FAITH*** (618)242-4330
Josepha H Lecke • WS 8 1015; SS 915;* • H • SI • 1104 N 42nd St Mount Vernon IL 62864 • jlecke@hotmail.com

**MOUNT ZION—*MOUNT ZION*** (217)864-4958
Vacant • WS 1030; SS 930; BC 930 • H • CI • 1475 W Main St Mt Zion IL 62549-1371

**MURPHYSBORO—*IMMANUEL*** (618)684-3012
Vacant • WS 8 1030; SS 915; BC 915 • H • EC/EL • SI • 1915 Pine St Murphysboro IL 62966-1935 • FAX(618)684-5115

**NAPERVILLE—*BETHANY*** (630)355-2198
Timothy A Rossow Terry A Mc Reynolds Stephen Schumacher • Nick Malleos DCE • WS 8 930 11; SS 915; BC 930;* • H • NI • 1550 Modaff Rd Naperville IL 60565-6191 • FAX(630)355-2216

***WORD OF LIFE*** (630)355-9655
Donald W Moll • WS 9; SS 1020; BC 1020 • H • EC • NI • 879 Tudor Rd Naperville IL 60563-2100 • FAX(630)355-2220 • wol9655@juno.com

***ZION*** (630)904-1124
Vacant • WS 815; SS 930;* • H • EC • NI • 11007 Book Rd Naperville IL 60564-5306 • FAX(630)904-4149

**NASHVILLE—*ST JOHN***
See New Minden

***TRINITY*** (618)327-3311
Vacant • WS 8 1015; SS 915; BC 915;* • H • EC/EL • SI • 680 W Walnut St Nashville IL 62263-1158 • FAX(618)327-4540

**NEUNERT—*CHRIST***
See Jacpb 2 S

**NEW ATHENS—*ST PAUL*** (618)475-3143
John P Lukomski • WS 1030;* • H • SI • Church St 62264 900 Belsha St New Athens IL 62264-1502

***TRINITY***
See Darmstadt

**NEW BERLIN—*ST JOHN*** (217)488-3190
Robert L Barth • WS 10; SS 9; BC 9 • EL • CI • 300 E Gibson 62670 PO Box 197 New Berlin IL 62670-0197

**NEW HOLLAND—*ZION*** (217)445-2264
Michael A Kettner • H • CI • 105 Logan St 62671 PO Box 199 New Holland IL 62671-0199

**NEW LENOX—*TRINITY*** (815)485-6973
Douglas E Hoag • H • EC • EN • 508 N Cedar Rd New Lenox IL 60451-1408

**NEW MEMPHIS—*ST PETER*** (618)824-6366
David G Fletcher • SI • PO Box 261 New Memphis IL 62266-0261

**NEW MINDEN—*ST JOHN*** (618)478-5544
Timothy P Mueller • WS 10; SS 9; BC 9;* • H • EC/EL • SI • 62263 15538 State Route 127 Nashville IL 62263-2374 • FAX(618)478-2042

**NEWTON—*GOOD SHEPHERD*** (618)783-4105
Daniel M Smith • H • EC • CI • 110 Edwards St Newton IL 62448-1736 • revdms@shawneelink.com

**NILES—*ST JOHN*** (847)647-9867
Marvin F Mueller • * • HS • NI • 7429 N Milwaukee Ave Niles IL 60714-3707 • FAX(847)647-8132

**NOKOMIS—*TRINITY*** (217)563-2718
Bert H Eickhoff • WS 10; SS 845; BC 845;* • SI • 204 N Pine St Nokomis IL 62075-1230 • FAX(217)563-7371

**NOKOMIS 4 NW—*ST PAUL*** (217)563-2487
James E Norton • H • EL • SI • 62075 22009 E 19th Rd Nokomis IL 62075-3719 • FAX(217)563-2487 • norton5@nokomis.net

**NORMAL—*CHRIST*** (309)452-5609
Philip S Kaufmann • WS 8 1045; SS 925; BC 925;* • H • EC • CI • 311 N Hershey Rd Normal IL 61761-2295 • FAX(309)888-9085 • clcms@gte.net

***GOOD SHEPHERD***
See Bloomington

**NORRIDGE—*ZION*** (708)453-3514
Luther J Bajus • WS 930;* • H • HS • S • 8600 W Lawrence Ave Norridge IL 60706-2936 • FAX(708)456-8818

**NORTH PLATO—*ST PETER*** (847)464-5721
Edward A Davis • * • H • EC • NI • 43W301 Plank Rd Hampshire IL 60140-7901 • FAX(847)464-4204

**NORTHBROOK—*GRACE*** (847)498-3060
Vacant • * • H • EC • NI • 2245 Walters Ave Northbrook IL 60062-4596 • FAX(847)498-3061

***ST JOHN*** (847)296-5727
John W Walter • WS 9;* • H • NI • 3020 Milwaukee Ave Northbrook IL 60062-7120 • FAX(847)296-0036 • stjohn@icsp.net

**NORTHLAKE—*CHRIST*** (708)344-3185
David J Behling • H • NI • 111 S Harold Ave Northlake IL 60164-2510

**NORWOOD PARK—*ST PAUL*** (708)867-5044
Walter P Schoenfuhs • Rod M Krueger DCE • WS 815 1045; SS 930; BC 930;* • H • EC/EL • NI • UKNWN 5650 N Canfield Ave Chicago IL 60631-3318 • FAX(708)867-0083 • stpaul@chicago.avenew.com

**O FALLON—*BETHANY*** (618)632-6906
Douglas A Nicely • WS 8 1030; SS 915; BC 915;* • H • EC • SI • 62269 5600 Old Collinsville Rd Fairview Heights IL 62208-3741 • bethany@icss.net

***BLESSED SAVIOR*** (618)632-0126
Vernon K Lintvedt • WS 8 1045; SS 915; BC 915 • H • SI • 1205 N Lincoln Ave O Fallon IL 62269-1253 • bslchurch@intertek.net

**OAK LAWN—*FAITH*** (708)424-1059
Vacant • H • HS • NI • 9701 Melvina Ave Oak Lawn IL 60453-2717

***ST PAUL*** (708)423-1040
Daniel W Gensch John S Moeller • H • EC/EL/HS • NI • 4660 W 94th St Oak Lawn IL 60453-2513 • FAX(708)423-1588

***ZION*** (708)422-1433
John W Josupait • H • HS • NI • 9000 Menard Ave Oak Lawn IL 60453-1525 • FAX(708)422-1485

**OAK PARK—*CHRIST*** (708)386-3306
Martin R Noland • WS 10; BC 9 • H • EC/HS • NI • 607 Harvard St Oak Park IL 60304-2015 • christ³oakpark³lcms@juno.com

**OKAWVILLE—*IMMANUEL*** (618)243-6215
Vacant • WS 10; SS 9; BC 9 • H • EC/EL • SI • 206 E Schumacher St Okawville IL 62271-2212 • FAX(618)243-6142

**OKAWVILLE 4 E—*OLIVE BRANCH*** (618)243-5498
Vacant • H • SI • 62271 11265 State Route 177 Okawville IL 62271-1307 • GEMUEHLER@juno.com

**OLMSTED—*ST LUKE*** (618)742-8136
Carl H Miller • WS 10; SS 9; BC 9 • SI • PO Box 87 Olmsted IL 62970-0087

**ONARGA—*TRINITY*** (217)387-2381
Erich R Fickel • WS 1030;* • CI • 605 W Seminary Ave 60955-1053 PO Box 45 Onarga IL 60955-0045

**ONARGA 10 SE—*ST JOHN*** (815)457-2909
Vacant • * • H • HS • CI • 60955 1180 E 1000 N Rd Onarga IL 60955-7646 • FAX(815)457-2615 • pastorh@localline2.com

**ORLAND PARK—*CHRIST*** (708)349-0431
Walter A Ledogar Gregg W Bowen • H • EC • NI • 14700 S 94th Ave Orland Park IL 60462-2656 • FAX(708)349-0668

***LIVING WORD*** (708)403-9673
Steven A Lange • Jamie Harvan DCE • WS 8 1030; SS 920; BC 920 • H • EC • S • 16301 Wolf Rd Orland Park IL 60467-5331 • FAX(708)403-5869 • lwlc@aol.com

**OSMAN—*IMMANUEL*** (217)897-6170
Dean H Spooner • WS 10; SS 9; BC 9 • H • CI • 100 N Mc Lean County Rd UKNWN RR 1 Box 142 Fisher IL 61843-9501

**OTTAWA—*ZION*** (815)433-1408
Jeffrey J Corder • WS 9; SS 1030; BC 1030;* • H • EC • NI • 622 W Jefferson St Ottawa IL 61350-2737 • FAX(815)433-1408

**PALATINE—*IMMANUEL*** (847)359-1549
Robert H Clausen • Timothy J Hetzner DCE • WS 8 930 11;* • H • EC/EL • NI • 200 N Plum Grove Rd Palatine IL 60067-5298 • FAX(847)359-1583 • Immanuel@ilcp.org

***PRINCE PEACE*** (847)359-3451
Michael W Newman Scott E Christenson • WS 8 1045; SS 930; BC 930;* • H • NI • 1190 N Hicks Rd Palatine IL 60067-3745 • FAX(847)359-3471 • office@pop-lcms.org

**PANA—*ST PAUL*** (217)562-4731
Dean A Stolz • H • CI • 208 E 4th St Pana IL 62557-1652

**PARIS—*GRACE*** (217)466-1215
Jerry L Klug • WS 8 1030; SS 915; BC 915 • H • EC • CI • 711 S Main St 61944-2329 711 South Main PO Box 493 Paris IL 61944-0493 • FAX(217)466-1017 • cswernerf@tigerpaw.com

**PARK FOREST—*HOPE*** (708)748-1995
Michael J Heggen • * • H • EC/HS • NI • 424 Indianwood Blvd Park Forest IL 60466-2249 • FAX(708)748-1940 • hope@lincolnnet.net

**PARK RIDGE—*ST ANDREWS*** (847)823-6656
Gregory R Williamson • WS 830;* • H • EC/EL/HS • NI • 260 N Northwest Hwy Park Ridge IL 60068-3353 • FAX(847)823-1846

**PECATONICA—*ST JOHN*** (815)239-2400
Terry L Theiss • WS 9;* • NI • 1301 N Jackson St 61063-9518 PO Box 480 Pecatonica IL 61063-0480 • theiss@aeroinc.net

**PEKIN—*ST JOHN*** (309)347-2136
Mark A Miller Eric J Stefanski • Gordon A Buchholz DCE • H • EC/EL • CI • 711 Court St Pekin IL 61554-4735

***TRINITY*** (309)346-1391
Rodger P Abatie Kevin J Jenkins • WS 815 1045; SS 930; BC 930 • H • EC/EL • CI • 700 S 4th St Pekin IL 61554-4504

**PEORIA—*CHRIST*** (309)637-5309
Arthur I Schudde • WS 8; SS 930; BC 930 • H • CI • 2020 W Malone St Peoria IL 61605-3304 • FAX(309)637-6033 • info@christlutheranpeo.org

***HOLY CROSS*** (309)697-4832
Douglas O Handrich • WS 9; SS 1015; BC 1015 • H • EC • CI • 618 S Maxwell Rd Peoria IL 61607-1039

***IMMANUEL*** (309)691-3911
Craig S Stanford • WS 9; SS 1015;* • H • CI • 2110 W Northmoor Rd Peoria IL 61614-3337 • FAX(309)691-5277 • immanuelpeoria@aol.com

***JOY OF JESUS DEAF*** (217)243-2528
Vacant • H • CI • 135 NE Randolph Ave 61606-1920 104 Finley St Jacksonville IL 62650-1720

***MOUNT CALVARY*** (309)688-4321
Barry A Long • WS 8 1045; SS 930; BC 930 • H • EL • CI • 908 W Hanssler Pl Peoria IL 61604-2738 • FAX(309)688-3062 • mtcalevluth@juno.com

***REDEEMER*** (309)691-2333
Ronald C Miller Stephen E Hartman • Jeffry T Shoumaker DCE • WS 830 1045; SS 940; BC 945;* • H • EC/EL • CI • 6801 N Allen Rd Peoria IL 61614-2415 • FAX(309)691-4388

***TRINITY*** (309)676-4609
Ronald C Moritz Griffith F Pritchard • Scott M Rauch DCE • WS 8 1045; SS 930;* • H • EL • CI • 135 NE Randolph Ave Peoria IL 61606-1920 • FAX(309)676-4689

**PEOTONE—*GRACE**** (708)258-9136
Quentin M Genke(DM) • WS 10; SS 11; BC 11 • H • NI • 108 1/2 W Main St 60468 PO Box 895 Peotone IL 60468-0895 • FAX(708)258-0638 • grace³community@juno.com

**PETERSBURG—*BETHLEHEM*** (217)632-2453
Maurice R Low • CI • 120 W Monroe St 62675-1532 PO Box 197 Petersburg IL 62675-0197 • bethlehem9@juno.com

**PINCKNEYVILLE—*TRINITY*** (618)357-2818
Russell K Helbig • WS 830;* • H • SI • 2338 Mountain Lion Rd 62274-2819 C/O Zion Luth Church 508 Mill St Pinckneyville IL 62274-1654

***ZION*** (618)357-2818
Russell K Helbig • WS 10;* • H • SI • 508 Mill St Pinckneyville IL 62274-1654 • FAX(618)357-2818 • bismarck@midwest.net

**PINGREE GROVE—*ST PETER*** (847)464-5440
Vacant • H • NI • 14N205 Reinking Rd Hampshire IL 60140-8806

**PITTSFIELD—*ST PAUL*** (217)285-2566
Stephen Southward • H • CI • 1234 W Washington Pittsfield IL 62363

**PLAINFIELD—*PEACE*** (815)436-9847
Galen R Sollie • WS 9; SS 1015; BC 1015;* • H • NI • 415 W Main St Plainfield IL 60544-1869 • FAX(815)436-9887 • grsollie@peaceplainfield.org

**PLAINFIELD 6 NE—*ZION***
See Naperville

**PLANO—*LIVING HERITAGE*** (630)552-3926
Vacant • WS 8; SS 915;* • H • NI • 901 W Rt 34 Suite 105 Plano IL 60545 • FAX(630)552-3926 • livingheritage@prairienet.com

**PLEASANT PLAINS—*ZION*** (217)626-1282
Donald F Pritchard • H • HS • CI • 525 N Cartwright Pleasant Plains IL 62677

**PONTIAC—*TRINITY*** (815)842-1205
Clarence H Mankin • WS 10; SS 9; BC 9 • NI • 520 N Oak St Pontiac IL 61764-1738

**PRAIRIETOWN—*ST PETER*** (618)888-2250
James L Hennig • WS 10; SS 9; BC 9;* • H • EL • SI • UKNWN 7183 Renken Rd Dorsey IL 62021-1803 • FAX(618)888-2353 • splcasop@madisontelco.com

**PROSPECT HEIGHTS—*OUR*** (847)537-4430
Daniel J Teller • WS 830 10;* • H • EC/HS • NI • 304 W Palatine Rd Prospect Heights IL 60070-1199 • FAX(847)537-4480 • teller4ds@aol.com

**QUINCY—*OUR REDEEMER*** (217)223-1769
Larry D Troxel • WS 8 1015; SS 910; BC 910;* • CI • 2701 College Ave Quincy IL 62301-3558 • FAX(217)223-2392 • orlcqcy@rnet.com

***ST JAMES*** (217)222-8447
Marlin R Rempfer • WS 8 1030; SS 915; BC 915;* • H • EC/EL • CI • 17th And Jefferson 62301 900 S 17th St Quincy IL 62301-5542 • FAX(217)222-3415 • stjameschurch³quincy@yahoo.com

***ST JOHN*** (217)222-8579
Harold J Bender Jr. • WS 8 1030; SS 930;* • H • CI • 3340 State St Quincy IL 62301-5726 • lutheran@rnet.com

**RED BUD—*ST JOHN*** (618)282-3873
Donald A Schultz Rory G Seeger • WS 8 1030; SS 930; BC 930 • H • EC/EL/HS • SI • 508 Bloom St 62278-1702 104 E Sixth St Red Bud IL 62278-1746 • FAX(618)282-4087 • st.john62278@juno.com

**RED BUD 5 SE—*TRINITY*** (618)282-2883
Steven A Mac Dougall • * • H • EC/EL/HS • SI • 62278 10235 S Prairie Rd Red Bud IL 62278-4611 • FAX(618)282-4646 • stevem53@htc.net

**RENAULT—*HOLY CROSS*** (618)458-6680
Ralph E Laufer • * • H • HS • SI • 2033 Kaskaskia Rd 62279 PO Box 7 Renault IL 62279-0007 • holycros@htc.net

**RICHTON PARK—*IMMANUEL*** (708)748-0558
Vacant • WS 9;* • H • NI • 4800 Sauk Trl Richton Park IL 60471-1018 • FAX(708)748-6593

**RIVER FOREST—*RESURRECTION*** (708)209-3349
Vacant • H • HS • NI • C/O Concordia University 7400 Augusta St Box 44 G River Forest IL 60305-1402

**RIVER GROVE—*BETHLEHEM*** (708)453-1113
Roger B Gallup • WS 8 1030;* • H • EC/EL • NI • 2624 Oak St River Grove IL 60171-1696 • gallup57@juno.com

**RIVERTON—*IMMANUEL*** (217)629-8415
Michael A Koschmann • H • CI • 705 E Menard St 62561 PO Box 380 Riverton IL 62561-0380

**ROANOKE—*TRINITY*** (309)923-5251
Bruce W Scarbeary • WS 10; SS 845; BC 845 • H • CI • 202 W Lincoln 61561 PO Box 268 Roanoke IL 61561-0268

**ROBINSON—*OUR REDEEMER*** (618)546-5210
J Kevin Wyckoff • H • CI • 801 W Emmons St 62454-1639 PO Box 42 Robinson IL 62454-0042 • jkevinw@midwest.net

**ROCHELLE—*ST PAUL*** (815)562-2744
Mark A Nordman • WS 8 1030; SS 915; BC 915;* • H • EC/EL • NI • 1415 10th Ave Rochelle IL 61068-1233 • FAX(815)561-8074

**ROCHESTER—*GOOD SHEPHERD*** (217)498-7991
Arthur J Goldberger II • WS 10; SS 845; BC 845 • H • EC • CI • 1 Camelot Dr Rochester IL 62563-9203 • FAX(217)498-7991 • gslcrochil@juno.com

**ROCK FALLS—*GOOD SHEPHERD*** (815)625-3376
Daniel M Behmlander • WS 9; SS 1015; BC 1015 • H • EC/EL • NI • 435 Martin Rd Rock Falls IL 61071-1966

**ROCK ISLAND—*IMMANUEL*** (309)786-3391
Kevin J Cramm • WS 9; SS 1015; BC 1015;* • H • EC/EL • CI • 1925 5th Ave 61201-8105 3300 24th St Rock Island IL 61201-6296 • FAX(309)786-3392 • ILCMM@AOL.COM

**ROCKFORD—*CHRIST THE ROCK*** (815)332-7191
David L Meggers • WS 8 1030; SS 920; BC 920;* • H • EC/EL/HS • NI • 8330 Newburg Rd Rockford IL 61108-6935 • FAX(815)332-7703 • dmeggers@aol.com

***CONCORDIA***
See Machesney Park

***MOUNT OLIVE*** (815)399-3171
Kenneth E Krause • SS 11 930;* • H • EC/EL/HS • NI • 2001 N Alpine Rd Rockford IL 61107-1417 • FAX(815)399-3174 • kkatmto@juno.com

***REDEEMER*** (815)397-2227
Robert H Rub Jr. • WS 8 1030 6; SS 915; BC 915 • H • EC/EL/HS • NI • 827 16th St Rockford IL 61104-3322 • FAX(815)397-3191

***ROCKFORD DEAF*** (815)397-2227
Vacant • H • NI • 827 16th St Rockford IL 61104-3322

***ST PAUL*** (815)963-5435
Scott C Malme • H • EC/EL/HS • NI • 600 N Horsman St Rockford IL 61101-6612 • FAX(815)963-5435 • SMALME@JUNO.COM

**ROCKTON—*ST ANDREW*** (815)624-6051
Richard A Wagner • WS 8 1045;* • H • EL/HS • NI • 511 W Rockton Rd Rockton IL 61072-1640 • FAX(815)624-6051 • revrun@xta.com

**ROSCOE—*CHRIST OUR SAVIOR*** (815)623-2138
Kenneth R Scherer • WS 9;* • H • EL/HS • NI • 5506 Reimer Dr Roscoe IL 61073-7316

**ROSELLE—*ST JOHN***
See Schaumburg

***TRINITY*** (630)894-3263
Charles S Mueller Jr. James F Bach Stephen J Biegel Charles S Mueller Douglas R Warmann Thomas A Gibbons(#) • Steven W Moeller DCE Michael J Heinz DCE • WS 11; SS 8; BC 930;* • H • EL/HS • NI • 405 Rush St Roselle IL 60172-2228 • FAX(630)894-1430 • office@trinityroselle.com

**RUSHVILLE—*ST JOHN*** (217)322-4237
Joseph V Eckman • H • CI • 424 W Washington St Rushville IL 62681-1356

**SADORUS—*ST PAUL*** (217)598-2259
Warren E Miller • WS 10; BC 9;* • H • EC • CI • 101 E Church St 61872 PO Box 230 Sadorus IL 61872-0230 • FAX(217)598-2216 • stpaul96@juno.com

**SAINT CHARLES—*ST MARK*** (630)584-8638
Timothy P Silber • WS 815 1045; SS 930; BC 930 • H • EC/EL/HS • NI • 101 S 6th Ave Saint Charles IL 60174-2107 • FAX(630)584-8646 • stmarksstc@aol.com

**SAINT PETER—*ST PETER*** (618)349-8321
Stephen F Gallo • H • EL • CI • Hwy 185 62880 RR 1 Box 70B Saint Peter IL 62880-9721 • FAX(618)349-8321

**SALEM—*SALEM*** (618)548-3190
Douglas E Meyer • * • H • CI • 1401 Hawthorn Rd Salem IL 62881-1041 • FAX(618)548-3206

**SAN JOSE 6 W—*ST LUKE*** (217)482-5822
Marvin L Lorenz • WS 1030; SS 915;* • H • CI • 15757 N Cr 3600e 62682 PO Box 407 San Jose IL 62682-0407

**SAVOY—*FRIENDSHIP/JOY***
See Champaign

**SCHAUMBURG—*ST JOHN*** (847)524-9746
Mark J Brockhoff • H • EC • NI • 1800 S Rodenburg Rd Schaumburg IL 60193-3536 • FAX(847)524-6376

***ST PETER*** (847)885-3350
David P Hudak Fred C Ade • David A Cheatham DCE • H • EC/EL • NI • 208 E Schaumburg Rd Schaumburg IL 60194-3517 • FAX(847)885-1106

**SECOR—*ST JOHN*** (309)744-2255
Michael J Kolesar • WS 10; SS 9; BC 9;* • H • EC • CI • 212 N Second 61771 PO Box 229 Secor IL 61771-0229

**SHELBYVILLE—*HOLY CROSS*** (217)774-2952
Earl W Helmkamp • WS 1015; SS 9; BC 9;* • H • CI • 1201 N Chestnut St Shelbyville IL 62565-9362

**SHERMAN—*GOOD SHEPHERD*** (217)496-3149
James A Stuenkel • Cynthia M Good DCE • H • EC/HS • CI • 6086 Bus 55 62684 PO Box 237 Sherman IL 62684-0237 • FAX(217)496-2456 • goodshepherd@bullets.net

**SHOBONIER 4 E—*IMMANUEL*** (618)846-8383
Ronald C Simmons • WS 10; SS 9; BC 9 • H • CI • 900 N 1300 E 62885 RR 1 Box 179 Shobonier IL 62885-9739 • ilcaugsburg@juno.com

**SHOBONIER 8 SE—*ST PAUL*** (618)349-6392
Robert H Heimgartner(EM) • H • CI • Mm 800 N And Mm 1600 E 62885 RR 1 Box 131 Shobonier IL 62885-9724

**SHOREWOOD—*HOPE*** (815)741-2428
George A Klima • WS 8 1015;* • H • NI • C/O Rev George A Klima 305 E Black Rd Shorewood IL 60431-8665 • FAX(815)741-9958 • gklima@mediaone.net

**SHUMWAY—*FAITH*** (217)868-5484
Jason E Rensner • WS 10; SS 9; BC 9 • H • CI • 7707 E State Hwy 33 62461 PO Box 118 Shumway IL 62461-0118 • rensner@juno.com

**SIGEL—*ST PAUL*** (217)844-2019
Vacant • WS 930; SS 830; BC 830 • H • CI • PO Box 182 Sigel IL 62462-0182

**SKOKIE—*ST PAUL*** (847)673-5030
E L Jones III Michael A Croon • WS 8;* • H • EC/EL/HS • NI • 7870 Niles Center Rd 60077-2707 5201 Galitz St Skokie IL 60077-2737 • FAX(847)673-9828

***ST PAUL KOREAN*** (847)673-5030
Chang S Ko • H • NI • 5201 Galitz St Skokie IL 60077-2737

**SOUTH ELGIN—*KING OF GLORY***
See Elgin

**SOUTH HOLLAND—*GRACE*** (708)331-7706
Warren G Mandel • WS 845 • H • NI • 16500 Woodlawn East Ave South Holland IL 60473-2558

**SPARTA—*ST JOHN*** (618)443-3634
Bruce A Cameron • WS 9; SS 1015; BC 1015;* • H • EC/HS • SI • 1110 N Market St 62286-1018 PO Box 334 Sparta IL 62286-0334 • FAX(618)443-5695

**SPRING GROVE—*COMMUNITY FAITH*** (815)675-1074
John L Spangler • WS 9;* • NI • 3010 E Solon Rd PO Box 5 Spring Grove IL 60081 • FAX(815)675-9261

**SPRINGFIELD—*CONCORDIA*** (217)529-3307
Charles P Olander Carl E Cross Jr.(EM) • WS 815; SS 930; BC 930 • H • EC/EL/HS • CI • 2300 E Wilshire Rd Springfield IL 62703-4949 • FAX(217)529-3096 • concordia³spi@yahoo.com

**HOLY TRINITY** (217)528-9894
Vacant • CI • 119 N 15th St 117 N 15th St Springfield IL 62703-1021

**IMMANUEL** (217)528-5232
Theodore C Gall James F Ritter • WS 8 1030; SS 915; BC 930;* • H • EC/EL/HS • CI • 2750 E Sangamon Ave Springfield IL 62702-1419 • FAX(217)528-5232 • tedgall@eosinc.com

**OUR SAVIOR** (217)546-4531
Wayne P Hoffman Lawrence F Goetz • H • EC/EL/HS • CI • 2645 Old Jacksonville Rd Springfield IL 62704-3199 • FAX(217)546-0293 • osl@fgi.net

**TRINITY** (217)522-8151
Micheal M Strong Thomas G Radtke William C Schroeder • H • EC/EL/HS • CI • 220 S Second St Springfield IL 62701-1121 • FAX(217)522-7059 • trinity@eosinc.com

**STAUNTON—ZION** (618)635-2880
John D Reek Michael G Kloepping • WS 8 1030; SS 915; BC 915;* • H • EC/EL • SI • 311 S Elm St Staunton IL 62088-3100 • FAX(618)635-3994

**STEELEVILLE—ST MARK** (618)965-3192
Alan W Janneke Steven J Okpisz • H • EC/EL/HS • SI • 105 N Garfield St Steeleville IL 62288-1345 • stmark@egyptian.net

**STEELEVILLE 5 S—ST PAUL** (618)965-3831
Vacant • * • H • HS • SI • 62288 11854 Wine Hill Rd Steeleville IL 62288-3000

**STEGER—IMMANUEL** (708)754-2345
Vacant • WS 8 1030; SS 915; BC 915 • H • NI • 12 W 34th Pl Steger IL 60475-1640

**STERLING—MESSIAH** (815)625-2284
Duane Fluechtling • WS 9; SS 1030; BC 1030 • H • EC/EL • NI • 1601 Avenue F 61081-2240 614 W 16th St Sterling IL 61081-2230 • FAX(815)625-1804 • messiahlc@netscape.net

**STERLING 8 NW—OUR SAVIOR** (815)772-4345
Donald W Matthiessen • H • EC/EL • NI • 61081 21496 Hazel Rd Sterling IL 61081-9158

**STEWARDSON—TRINITY** (217)682-5722
Vacant • H • EC/EL • CI • 113 S Walnut St 62463-1323 PO Box 307 Stewardson IL 62463-0305 • FAX(217)682-5722

**STRASBURG—GRACE** (217)644-2452
Michael W Mohr • H • CI • N First And Locust 62465 PO Box 336 Strasburg IL 62465-0336 • pppadre@aol.com

**ST PAUL** (217)644-2661
Gary D Fortkamp • WS 10; SS 9; BC 9;* • H • CI • 511 S Walnut 62465 RR 1 Box 38 Strasburg IL 62465-9701 • StPaulLCMS@one-eleven.net

**STREAMWOOD—GRACE** (630)289-3996
James A Schroeder Mark A Frusti • WS 815 1045; BC 930;* • H • EC • NI • 780 S Bartlett Rd Streamwood IL 60107-1312 • FAX(630)289-7104

**STREATOR—HOLY TRINITY** (815)672-2393
John E Gutz • * • H • EC • S • 101 Trinity Dr Streator IL 61364-3119

**SUGAR LOAF TWP—HOLY CROSS** (618)538-5600
Allen L Braun • SI • UKNWN 7640 Triple Lakes Rd East Carondelet IL 62240-1716 • twilekn@htc.net

**SULLIVAN—FAITH** (217)728-7711
Paul G Mc Ghghy • WS 930; SS 815; BC 815;* • H • CI • Rr 32 South 61951 PO Box 109 Sullivan IL 61951-0109

**SUMMIT ARGO—ZION** (708)563-0777
Donald R Gerlach • * • H • NI • 5865 S Archer Rd Summit Argo IL 60501-1409

**SYCAMORE—ST JOHN** (815)895-4477
Donald R Phelps Marvin Metzger • H • NI • 327 S Main St Sycamore IL 60178-1825 • FAX(815)899-4477

**TAYLOR RIDGE 8 W—ZION** (309)795-1063
John E Hafermann • WS 815 1030; SS 920; BC 920 • H • CI • 61284 18121 134th Ave W Taylor Ridge IL 61284-9737 • zionlc@winco.net

**TAYLORVILLE—TRINITY** (217)824-8148
Rodney G Blomquist • H • EC • CI • 1010 N Webster St Taylorville IL 62568-1277

**THAWVILLE—ST PETER** (217)387-2381
Erich R Fickel • WS 830;* • H • HS • CI • 114 N Mc Neil St 60968 PO Box 157 Thawville IL 60968-0157

**THOMASBORO—PEACE** (217)643-3265
Vacant • * • H • CI • Arnold And Phillips 61878 PO Box 428 Thomasboro IL 61878-0428 • peace@pdnt.com

**THORNTON—ST PAUL** (708)877-6564
Vacant • WS 945; BC 830;* • H • HS • NI • 508 Chicago Rd Thornton IL 60476-1024 • St.Paul60476@Juno.com

**TINLEY PARK—TRINITY** (708)532-9395
Paul O J Strand Paul H Brunner Ronald D Rock • H • EC/EL • NI • 6850 159th St Tinley Park IL 60477-1629 • FAX(708)532-0750 • trinitypil@crf.cuis.edu

**TOPEKA 4 E—ST JOHN** (309)597-2442
Vacant • CI • 61567 RR 1 Box 218 Topeka IL 61567-9743

**TROY—ST PAUL** (618)667-6681
James G Zimmerman • WS 1015; SS 9; BC 9;* • H • EC/EL • SI • 106 N Border St Troy IL 62294-1137 • jzimmer555@aol.com

**TUSCOLA—IMMANUEL** (217)253-4341
Michael J Ruhlig • WS 9; SS 1015; BC 1015;* • H • CI • 600 E North Line Rd Tuscola IL 61953-1105 • FAX(217)253-4341 • immanuel.lutheran@netcare-il.com

**UNION—ST JOHN** (815)923-2733
Norman S Meyer • Lauren K Olsen DEAC • H • NI • 6821 Main St Union IL 60180-9673 • FAX(815)923-2734 • stjohnslutheranchurch@avenew.com

**URBANA—TRINITY** (217)367-8923
Jeffrey D Mc Pike • H • EC • CI • 701 E Florida Ave Urbana IL 61801-5950 • FAX(217)367-8928 • trinity@prairienet.org

**VANDALIA—HOLY CROSS** (618)283-1133
Lawrence W Saeger • WS 9; SS 1015; BC 1015;* • H • CI • 726 W Fillmore St Vandalia IL 62471-1209 • FAX(618)283-1890 • holycrss@swetland.net

**VARNA—ST PAUL** (815)853-4479
Peter M Glock • WS 830;* • H • CI • S Chestnut St 61375 PO Box 417 Wenona IL 61377-0417 • FAX(815)853-4479 • pmglock@maxiis.com

**VENEDY—ST SALVATOR** (618)824-6366
David G Fletcher • SI • 179 W Church St Venedy IL 62214-1253

**VILLA PARK—TRINITY** (630)834-3440
Thomas J Sanders Mark Post • H • EC • EN • 300 S Ardmore Ave Villa Park IL 60181-2699 • FAX(630)834-5232

**WALNUT—HOLY TRINITY** (815)379-2839
Roland Hischke • H • NI • Highway 92 E 61376 PO Box 550 Walnut IL 61376-0550

**WARSAW—CONCORDIA** (217)256-3215
Karl C Bollhagen • WS 930;* • H • CI • Eighth and Lafayette Warsaw IL 62379

**WASHBURN—ST JOHN** (309)248-7153
Kenneth J Mangold • H • CI • 400 N Jefferson Washburn IL 61570

**WASHINGTON—OUR SAVIOR** (309)444-4030
David A Likeness • H • EC • CI • 1209 Kingsbury Rd Washington IL 61571-1212 • FAX(309)444-8817

**WATERLOO—HOLY CROSS** (618)939-7094
Jon C Bischof • H • SI • 5765 Maeystown Rd Waterloo IL 62298-6539

**IMMANUEL** (618)939-6480
Antonin Troup Kyle J Sandersfeld • WS 745 1015; SS 9; BC 9;* • H • EC • SI • Church And Hoener St 62298 522 S Church St Waterloo IL 62298-1429 • FAX(618)939-7010

**WATSEKA—CALVARY** (815)432-4136
Dean L Bottjen • WS 9;* • H • EC • NI • 120 E Hickory St Watseka IL 60970-1339

**WAUKEGAN—PRINCE PEACE** (847)244-6522
John A Shumate • H • NI • 2720 N Mc Aree Rd Waukegan IL 60087-3555

**REDEEMER** 221
Wayne P Jahn • WS 9; SS UNKNOWN;* • EC • NI • 620 W Grove Ave Waukegan IL 60085-1847 • FAX(847)336-4891

**WAVERLY—CHRIST** (217)435-9685
Keith R Pereira • WS 10;* • CI • 185 E Tremont St Waverly IL 62692-1026 • katco@csj.net

**WENONA—ZION** (815)853-4479
Peter M Glock • WS 10;* • CI • 117 Walnut 61377 PO Box 417 Wenona IL 61377-0417 • FAX(815)853-4479 • pmglock@maxiis.com

**WEST CHICAGO—TRINITY** (630)231-1175
David P Balla • * • EC/EL • NI • 331 George St West Chicago IL 60185-3118 • FAX(630)231-6926 • trinitywc@netzero.net

**WEST FRANKFORT—ST PAUL** (618)932-3450
Joel Danner • WS 1030; SS 9; BC 9 • H • SI • Interstate 57 And Il Rt 149 62896 1 West Frankfort Plz West Frankfort IL 62896-4964

**WESTCHESTER—FAITH** (708)343-1030
Vacant • WS 9; SS 1015; BC 1015 • NI • 1124 Westchester Blvd 1118 Westchester Blvd Westchester IL 60154-2533

**WESTERN SPRINGS—GRACE** (708)246-0536
Mark A Lundgren • H • HS • NI • 4101 Wolf Rd Western Springs IL 60558-1451

**WESTMONT—BETHEL** (630)968-3232
Paul J Pfotenhauer • WS 9; BC 1030;* • H • NI • 36 N Grant St Westmont IL 60559-1606 • FAX(630)968-2030

**WHEATON—ST JOHN** (630)668-0701
Scott A Bruzek Eric F Allyn Dennis W Schlecht • Keith R Richard DCE • WS 745 9 1115; SS 1015; BC 1015;* • H • NI • 125 E Seminary Ave Wheaton IL 60187-5308 • FAX(630)871-9931 • sabruzek@cin.net

**WHEELER 6 NW—ST PAUL** (217)924-4498
Stephen P Gillet • WS 10; SS 9; BC 9 • H • CI • 13204 N 2300th St Wheeler IL 62479 • revspg@hotmail.com

**WILLOW SPRINGS—GRACE** (708)839-5255
David R Krampitz • WS 9 1030;* • H • HS • NI • 212 S Nolton Ave Willow Springs IL 60480-1443 • prdave63@aol.com

**WINCHESTER—CHRIST** (217)742-3919
Glenn R Niemann • WS 10; SS 9; BC 9 • H • CI • 125 W Jefferson St Winchester IL 62694-1049

**WINFIELD—CHRIST OUR SAVIOR** (630)665-5110
James J Plackner • H • NI • O S 501 Summit Dr Winfield IL 60190 • FAX(630)665-5262

**WOOD DALE—CALVARY** (630)766-2838
Carl W Bassett • WS 8; BC 915;* • H • EC/HS • NI • 107 N Wood Dale Rd 60191-2029 PO Box 175 Wood Dale IL 60191-0175 • FAX(630)766-8125 • lizakb@aol.com

**OUR SAVIOR DEAF** (708)766-2838
Vacant • H • NI • Wood Dale Rd And Montrose St 60191 C/O Calvary Lutheran Church PO Box 175 Wood Dale IL 60191-0175

**WOOD RIVER—ST PAUL** (618)259-0257
Martin A Schultz • SS 915; BC 915;* • H • EC/HS • SI • 1327 Vaughn Rd Wood River IL 62095-1851 • 2mschultz@home.com

**WOODSTOCK—ST JOHN** (815)338-5159
Larry J Trout • * • H • EC • NI • 401 Saint Johns Rd Woodstock IL 60098-2726 • FAX(815)338-9377 • stjohnws@stans.net

**WOODWORTH—ST PAUL** (815)889-4569
Vacant • WS 10; SS 9; BC 9 • H • EC/EL/HS • NI • UKNWN 113 W Woodworth Milford IL 60953-9632 • FAX(815)889-4364 • stpauls@colint.com

**WORDEN—ST PAUL** (618)633-2209
William C Weedon • WS 745 10; SS 9; BC 9;* • H • EL/HS • SI • 6969 W Frontage Rd 62097 PO Box 247 Hamel IL 62046-0247 • wmweedon@madisontelco.com

**TRINITY** (618)459-3991
Jeffrey A Gross • H • EC/EL/HS • SI • 512 Main St 62097-1214 PO Box 296 Worden IL 62097-0296 • marty144@midwest.net

**YORKVILLE—CROSS** (630)553-7335
Dan P Gilbert Brian M Truog • Brian L Jensen DCE • WS 8 1045; SS 930; BC 930;* • H • EC/EL • NI • 8609 Rt 47 60560 8609 State Route 47 Yorkville IL 60560-9751 • FAX(630)553-2580

## INDIANA

**ABOITE TOWNSHIP—ABOITE** (219)436-5673
Richard Pagan • H • HS • IN • UKNWN 10312 Aboite Center Rd Fort Wayne IN 46804-5436 • FAX(219)436-9990 • info@aboitelutheran.org

**ANDERSON—CHRIST** (765)642-2154
Mark D Whitsett • WS 1015; SS 9; BC 9 • H • IN • 716 Rainbow Blvd Anderson IN 46012-1467 • christluth1@juno.com

**ARCADIA—EMANUEL** (317)984-3651
Vacant • IN • 355 Shaffer St Arcadia IN 46030-9637

**AUBURN—TRINITY** (219)925-2440
Lloyd A Bickel • * • H • IN • 1801 N Main St Auburn IN 46706-1047 • trinity@locl.net

**AURORA—ST JOHN** (812)926-3337
Vacant • H • EC/EL • IN • 220 Mechanic St Aurora IN 47001-1322

**AUSTIN—BETHEL** (812)523-8234
Frederick A Mildenburger • * • IN • 101 N Church St 47102-1211 PO Box 98 Austin IN 47102-0098 • dtwnfam@voyager.net

**AVILLA—IMMANUEL** (219)897-2071
Dean R Bearman • WS 930; SS 830;* • H • IN • 113 W Albion St 46710-1002 PO Box 188 Avilla IN 46710-0188

**AVON—LIVING CHRIST** (317)718-0718
James A Myers • WS 1030; SS 915; BC 915 • H • IN • 5250 E US Highway 36 Ste 340 Avon IN 46123 • FAX(317)718-1309 • revjmyers@aol.com

**BEAN BLOSSOM 1/2 N—SHEPHERD** (812)988-8057
Ronnie D Maxwell • WS 1015; SS 9; BC 9 • H • IN • UKNWN 5802 N Old Settlers Rd Morgantown IN 46160-8833

**BEDFORD—CALVARY** (812)275-5488
Paul D Neuman • WS 1030; SS 930 • H • EC • IN • Hwy 37 At 39th St 47421 3705 Austin Dr Bedford IN 47421-9291 • FAX(812)275-5488

**BEECH GROVE—ASCENSION** (317)788-1118
Mark E Wagner • WS 1030; SS 915; BC 915 • H • HS • IN • 602 S 9th Ave Beech Grove IN 46107-2208 • bascension@aol.com

**BERNE—PEACE** (219)589-3848
Paul F Stohlmann Jr. • SS 915; BC 915;* • H • IN • 201 Fulton St Berne IN 46711-2139 • FAX(219)589-3848 • stohlmannberne@juno.com

**BLOOMINGTON—FAITH** (812)332-1668
Lawrence W Mitchell Patrick J Kuhlman • H • EC • IN • 2200 S High St Bloomington IN 47401-4313 • FAX(812)332-2206 • faithlu@bloomington.in.us

**UNIVERSITY** (812)336-5387
Richard L Woelmer • WS 1030;* • IN • 607 E 7th St Bloomington IN 47408-3835 • FAX(812)336-5387 • ulu@indiana.edu

**BREMEN—ST PAUL** (219)546-2332
Roger E Rohde Neil K Wonnacott • WS 8; SS 915; BC 915 • EC/EL • IN • 210 E South St Bremen IN 46506-1333

**BROWNSBURG—CHRIST** (317)852-3343
Gary A Dworak • H • EC • IN • 701 E Tilden Dr Brownsburg IN 46112-1718

**BROWNSTOWN—ST PETER** 235
Jack A Belk Jeffrey L Geisler • WS 8 1030; SS 915;* • H • EC/EL • IN • 403 W Bridge St Brownstown IN 47220-1303 • FAX(812)358-2524

**BROWNSTOWN 5 SE—ST PAUL** (812)358-2334
Kenneth G Keily • H • EL • IN • 47220 1165 E 400 S Brownstown IN 47220-9803

**CARMEL—CARMEL** (317)814-4252
Luther C Brunette Daniel D Schumm • Melissa C Seybert DCE Mark C Borcherding DCE • WS 1045; SS 815; BC 1035;* • H • EC/HS • IN • 4850 E 131st St Carmel IN 46033-9311 • FAX(317)814-4260 • cic³office@clearcall.net

**CEDAR LAKE—HOPE** (219)374-7913
Paul E Gramit • H • IN • 9010 W 141st Ave Cedar Lake IN 46303-8860

**CHESTERTON—ST PAUL** (219)926-1556
Robert E Duncan • WS 8 1030; SS 930 • H • IN • 106 E County Rd 1100 N Chesterton IN 46304 • FAX(219)926-2638 • red@niia.net

**CHURUBUSCO—FAITH** (219)693-6254
Lane A Burgland • WS 8 10; SS 9; BC 9;* • H • IN • 9251 E State Road 205 Churubusco IN 46723 • laburg@msn.com

**CLEAR LAKE—CLEAR LAKE**
See Fremont 5 E 1/2 N

**CLOVERDALE—GRACE** (765)795-3214
Howard J Gleason • WS 9; SS 1030;* • H • IN • 11234 South State Rd 42 Cloverdale IN 46120-0870 • FAX(765)795-6614 • grace@ccrtc.com

**COLUMBIA CITY—ZION** (219)244-5513
James A Haugen Sr. • WS 8 1015; SS 9; BC 9 • H • IN • 101 E North St Columbia City IN 46725-1401

**COLUMBIA CITY 6 SW—ST JOHN** (219)244-3712
David A Mommens • H • IN • 46725 2465 W Keiser Rd Columbia City IN 46725-8009 • FAX(219)244-5870 • dmommens@juno.com

**COLUMBUS—*GRACE*** (812)372-4859
John W Armstrong • WS 8; SS 915; BC 915 • H • EC • IN • 3201 Central Ave Columbus IN 47203-2253 • FAX(812)372-4862

***ST JOHN*** (812)342-3516
Karl H Rein • H • EL • IN • 16270 S 300 W Columbus IN 47201-9357

***ST PETER*** (812)372-1571
Wayne K Frost Mark R Teike Michael A Malinsky Dale H Trimberger • George Denholm DCE • WS 8 1030; SS 930; BC 930;* • H • IN • 719 5th St Columbus IN 47201-6306 • FAX(812)372-7556 • stpeters@hsonline.net

***ST PETER***
See Waymansville

**COLUMBUS 1 W—*FAITH*** (812)342-3587
Stewart G Schulz • H • EC • IN • 47201 6000 W State Road 46 Columbus IN 47201-4691 • FAX(812)342-7267 • faithlc@hsonline.net

**COLUMBUS 3 SE—*ST PAUL*** (812)376-6504
William Stache • H • EC • IN • 2555 S Rd 300 E Columbus IN 47201 • FAX(812)376-6504 • stpaullutheran@voyager.net

**CONNERSVILLE—*BETHANY*** (765)825-4061
Vacant • WS 1030; SS 915;* • H • IN • 2907 Virginia Ave Connersville IN 47331-3067

**CORUNNA 5 NW—*ZION*** (219)281-2286
Vacant • WS 10; SS 9;* • H • IN • 46730 0389 County Rd 12 Corunna IN 46730-9762

**CRAWFORDSVILLE—*HOLY CROSS*** (765)362-5599
Alfred J Hellert • H • IN • 1414 E Wabash Ave Crawfordsville IN 47933-2640

**CROSS PLAINS 3 E—*ST PAUL*** (812)667-5700
Donald A Sauls • WS 10; SS 9; BC 9 • H • IN • 47017 5588 E County Road 900 S Cross Plains IN 47017-8973

**CROWN POINT—*RESURRECTION***
See Merrillville

***TRINITY*** (219)663-1578
Hermann L Thoelke David P Kipp • Paul R Wendt DCE • WS 8 1045; SS 920; BC 920 • H • EC/EL • IN • 250 S Indiana Ave Crown Point IN 46307-4174 • FAX(219)663-9606 • trinluth@mail.icongrp.com

**CULVER—*TRINITY*** (219)842-3175
Robert O Bartz • * • H • IN • 330 Academy Rd Culver IN 46511 • trinitylutheran@culcom.net

**DANVILLE—*LIVING CHRIST***
See Avon

**DARMSTADT—*TRINITY*** (812)867-5279
Martin E Keller Mark A Moog(#) • WS 945; SS 830; BC 830;* • H • EC/EL • IN • UKNWN 1401 W Boonville New Harmony Evansville IN 47725-8663 • FAX(812)867-5333

**DECATUR—*ZION*** (219)724-7177
Donald W Biester John M Fuchs • H • IN • 10th and Monroe Sts Decatur IN 46733

**DECATUR 5N—*ST PETER*** (219)724-7533
Martin K Moehring • WS 9;* • EL • IN • 46733 1033 E 1100 N Decatur IN 46733-8407 • spl1845@adamswells.com

**DECATUR 6 NE—*IMMANUEL*** (219)724-7680
James G Bushur • WS 930; SS 830; BC 830;* • H • EL • IN • 46733 8538 N 500 E Decatur IN 46733-7120

**DECATUR 6 NW—*ST PAUL*** (219)547-4176
Daniel J Brege • WS 9;* • H • EC/EL • IN • 46733 4510 W 750 N Decatur IN 46733-7853

**DECATUR 7 NW—*ST JOHN*** (219)639-6178
Thomas L Olson • H • EC/EL • IN • 46733 11555 N US Highway 27 Decatur IN 46733-9799 • 74073.3430@compuserve.com

**DECATUR 8 NW—*ZION*** (219)547-4248
Daniel F Dahling • H • EC/EL • IN • 46733 10653 N 550 W Decatur IN 46733-7894 • zionfriedheim@decaturnet.com

**DEMOTTE—*FAITH*** (219)987-3730
Jared M Raebel • WS 8 1030; SS 915; BC 915 • H • EC • IN • 1700 S Halleck St 46310-9313 PO Box 396 Demotte IN 46310-0396 • lutheran@netnitco.net

**DENHAM—*ST PAUL*** (219)896-5090
Carl S Fitchett V • H • IN • Pulaski Cr 575w 46996 6692 N 575 W Winamac IN 46996-7973

**DILLSBORO—*ST JOHN***
See Farmers Retreat

***TRINITY*** (812)432-5406
Vacant • H • IN • 9901 Central Ave 47018 PO Box 578 Dillsboro IN 47018-0578

**DUDLEYTOWN—*EMANUEL*** (812)523-8234
Frederick A Mildenburger • H • IN • UKNWN 2174 S County Road 750 E Seymour IN 47274-9227 • dtwnelc@voyager.net

**DYER 2 S—*GRACE*** (219)865-1137
John C Kolb • WS 9;* • H • HS • IN • 46311 8303 Sheffield Ave Dyer IN 46311-2752 • FAX(219)865-1137 • gracedyer@tsrcom.com

**EAST CHICAGO—*ST PAUL*** (219)397-8933
R D Mues(EM) • EC • IN • 2001 Franklin St East Chicago IN 46312-3124

**EDWARDSVILLE—*SHEPHERD HILLS*** (812)945-2101
Mark L Darnstaedt • EC • IN • UKNWN 5231 State Road 62 Georgetown IN 47122-9227 • sothluth@juno.com

**ELKHART—*CROWN OF LIFE*** (219)262-9966
Vacant • WS 1030; BC 930 • H • EN • 53111 County Rd 15 N Elkhart IN 46514-8584

***TRINITY*** (219)522-1491
Robert G Schallhorn Jr. Spencer A Mielke Allen T Goebbert • H • EC/EL • IN • 400 S West Blvd 420 West Blvd S Elkhart IN 46514-2017 • FAX(219)522-0114 • trinity@trinityl.org

**EVANSTON 2 NE—*ST JOHN*** (812)547-2007
Jeffrey L Stuckwisch • WS 930; SS 830 • H • IN • 47531 RR 1 Box 149 Evanston IN 47531-9618

**EVANSVILLE—*CONCORDIA*** (812)422-0384
Philip T R Spomer • H • IN • 2451 Stringtown Rd Evansville IN 47711-3374 • duetspomer@aol.com

***IMMANUEL*** (812)867-5088
Kirk P Horstmeyer • WS 10 8; SS 845; BC 845;* • H • IN • 1925 Volkman Rd Evansville IN 47725-9476 • FAX(812)867-5088

***MESSIAH*** (812)985-2278
William R Randall • H • EC • IN • 7700 Middle Mount Vernon Rd Evansville IN 47712-3025

***OUR REDEEMER*** (812)476-9991
Thomas D Wenig Paul Rupprecht(#) • Richard W Soeken DCE • WS 8 1030; SS 915; BC 915 • H • EC/EL • IN • 1811 Lincoln Ave Evansville IN 47714-1505 • FAX(812)476-4561 • office@redeemerchurch.org

***OUR SAVIOUR*** (812)476-8707
Robert W Wurst Jr. • WS 915; SS 1030; BC 1030;* • H • IN • 6501 East Madison Ave Evansville IN 47715-5163 • oslc-evv@juno.com

***ST PAUL*** (812)422-5414
Walter W Ullman Robert L Hagan • WS 830 1030; SS 915; BC 915;* • H • EL • IN • 100 E Michigan St Evansville IN 47711-5428 • FAX(812)422-5363 • histwan@aol.com

***TRINITY***
See Darmstadt

***TRINITY*** (812)424-4785
Wade E Butler • WS 10; SS 845;* • H • EL • IN • 1000 W Illinois 47710 1026 W Illinois Evansville IN 47710-1114 • trinityevansville@msn.com

**FARMERS RETREAT—*ST JOHN*** (812)667-5281
Vacant • WS 10; SS 9; BC 9 • H • EC • IN • 7291 State Road 62 Dillsboro IN 47018-9139

**FISHERS—*FAMILY OF CHRIST*** (317)594-9157
Eugene F Wagner • H • EC/EL • IN • 11965 Allisonville Rd Fishers IN 46038-2315 • FAX(317)594-9155 • focl@oaktree.net

**FORT WAYNE—*ABOITE***
See Aboite Township

***ASCENSION*** (219)486-2226
John C Stube • WS 8 1030;* • H • EC/EL/HS • IN • 8811 Saint Joe Rd Fort Wayne IN 46835-1037 • church@fwi.com

***BETHANY*** (219)747-0713
Charles E Varsogea • WS 9; SS 1030 • H • EN • 2435 Engle Rd Fort Wayne IN 46809-1408 • FAX(219)747-8011 • bethanyfw@ourhouse.net

***BETHLEHEM*** (219)744-3228
Thomas E Eggold Gregory T Manning • WS 8 1045; SS 930; BC 930;* • H • EC/EL/HS • IN • 3705 S Anthony Blvd Fort Wayne IN 46806-4329 • FAX(219)744-3229 • bethlcms@gateway.net

***CONCORDIA*** (219)422-2429
Karl A Frincke Kenneth M Wise • WS 8 1030; SS 920; BC 920;* • H • EC/EL/HS • IN • 4245 Lake Ave Fort Wayne IN 46815-7219 • FAX(219)422-3415

***EMMANUEL*** (219)423-1369
Arnold E Piering • WS 8 1030; SS 915; BC 915;* • H • EC/EL • IN • 917 W Jefferson Blvd Fort Wayne IN 46802-4096 • FAX(219)426-6147 • pastor@emmanuellutheran.org

***EMMAUS*** (219)456-4573
Albert L Keller Jr. • * • H • EC/EL/HS • IN • 2320 Broadway Fort Wayne IN 46807-1198 • FAX(219)745-0104 • emmaus@elcs.org

***HOLY CROSS*** (219)483-3173
Richard M Koehneke John W Fair Edward H Fehskens • Kenneth M Schilf DCE • H • EL/HS • IN • 3425 Crescent Ave Fort Wayne IN 46805-1505 • FAX(219)471-6141

***MOUNT CALVARY*** (219)747-4121
Gerald C Hartke David C Adams • H • EC/EL/HS • IN • 1819 Reservation Dr Fort Wayne IN 46819-2000 • FAX(219)747-2564

***NEW LIFE*** (219)420-3024
Larry C Merino • H • HS • IN • 2424 S Coliseum Blvd Fort Wayne IN 46803-2940 • FAX(219)422-9180

***PEACE*** (219)744-3869
James R Teasdale • H • EC/EL/HS • IN • 4900 Fairfield Ave Fort Wayne IN 46807-3215 • FAX(219)456-7384

***PRAISE*** (219)490-7729
James R Cotter Fredrick C Hearn • WS 8 1030; SS 930;* • H • HS • EN • 1115 W Dupont Rd Fort Wayne IN 46825-1099 • PraiseLC@FWI.Com

***PROMISE*** (219)493-9953
Vacant • H • IN • 5303 Wheelock Rd 46835-9706 7323 Schwartz Rd Fort Wayne IN 46835 • FAX(219)749-8119 • office@promiseministries.org

***REDEEMER*** (219)744-2585
David H Petersen • WS 8 10; BC 9;* • H • HS • EN • 202 W Rudisill Blvd Fort Wayne IN 46807-2498

***SHEPHERD CITY*** (219)422-3790
Vacant • H • HS • IN • 1301 S Anthony Blvd Fort Wayne IN 46803-2107

***ST JOHN DEAF*** (219)483-3173
David S Bush • WS 930;* • H • IN • 3425 Crescent Ave Fort Wayne IN 46805-1505 • bushds@mail.ctsfw.edu

***ST MICHAEL*** (219)432-2033
Robert A Bruckner David R Moore • H • EC/EL/HS • EN • 2131 Getz Rd Fort Wayne IN 46804-1625

***ST PAUL*** (219)423-2496
Richard S Radtke John H Hamer • WS 845 11; SS 10; BC 10 • H • EL/HS • IN • 1126 S Barr St Fort Wayne IN 46802-3108 • FAX(219)423-2497 • splutheran@ctlnet.com

***ST PETER*** (219)749-5816
Steven M Ahlersmeyer Donald D Nord • WS 8 1030; BC 915;* • H • EL/HS • IN • 7710 E State Blvd Fort Wayne IN 46815-6505 • FAX(219)749-5816 • stpeterlc@aol.com

***TRINITY*** (219)422-7931
David A Easterday • * • H • EC/EL/HS • IN • 1636 Saint Marys Ave Fort Wayne IN 46808-3271 • FAX(219)969-4005 • pastoreasterday1@juno.com

***VERSAILLES****
Vacant • H • IN • C/O Indiana District Office 1145 Barr St Fort Wayne IN 46802-3135

***ZION*** (219)744-1389
Matthew C Harrison Paul M Kaiser • HS • IN • 2313 Hanna St Fort Wayne IN 46803-2477 • FAX(219)744-2421

**FORT WAYNE 3 SE—*EMMANUEL*** (219)447-3005
Albert R Bierlein James R Tews • BC 915;* • H • HS • IN • 46802 9909 Wayne Trce Fort Wayne IN 46816-9742 • FAX(219)447-3840

**FORT WAYNE 4 E—*GLORIA DEI*** (219)447-6819
Vacant • IN • 46802 C/O Mr Tom Gasper 6432 Parrott Rd Fort Wayne IN 46803-1960

**FORT WAYNE 4NW—*SUB BETHLEHEM*** (219)484-7873
Richard K Smith Matthew D Switzer • Sharon L Knippenberg DEAC • WS 8 1030; SS 930; BC 915;* • H • EC/EL/HS • IN • 46802 6318 W California Rd Fort Wayne IN 46818-9737 • FAX(219)483-9016 • sub3bethlehem@juno.com

**FORT WAYNE 5 S—*TRINITY*** (219)447-2411
Gregory S Cynova • WS 9; SS 1030 • H • EC/HS • IN • 7819 Decatur Rd Fort Wayne IN 46816-2604 • FAX(219)447-0962 • trinity1853@juno.com

**FRANKLIN—*GOOD SHEPHERD*** (317)736-7849
Roger R Hubbard • H • IN • Us 31 S 46131 PO Box 265 Franklin IN 46131-0265

**FREMONT—*PEACE*** (219)495-4306
Wayne C Berkesch • WS 8 10;* • H • EC • EN • 355 E State Road 120 Fremont IN 46737-9743 • FAX(219)495-5076 • peacefremontin@juno.com

**FREMONT 5 E 1/2 N—*CLEAR LAKE*** (219)495-9219
Kenneth P Redmann • WS 9; SS 10; BC 10;* • H • IN • 46737 270 Outer Drive Clear Lk Fremont IN 46737-9516 • FAX(219)495-9219 • cllutheran@dmci.net

**FREMONT 8 W 1 N—*LAKE GEORGE*** (219)833-6208
Vacant • H • IN • 46737 1540 W 800 N Fremont IN 46737-9655 • lkgeorge@luther95.org

**GARRETT—*ZION*** (219)357-4545
Herbert L Schumm • WS 10; SS 845; BC 845;* • H • EC • IN • 1349 S Randolph St Garrett IN 46738-1970 • zelcgarrett@juno.com

**GARY—*FAITH*** (219)844-0780
Peter A Bauernfeind • WS 9; SS 1030;* • H • IN • 2609 Colfax St Gary IN 46406-3033 • FAX(219)844-0780

***GOOD SHEPHERD*** (219)885-2109
Peter A Bauernfeind • WS 1045; SS 930; BC 930 • IN • 719 W 25th Ave Gary IN 46407-3534

***OUR SAVIOUR*** (219)887-5031
James A Wetzstein • WS 8; SS 1045 • H • IN • 1150 W 49th Ave Gary IN 46408-4100 • FAX(219)887-0435 • oslcgary@aol.com

***ST JOHN*** (219)944-0654
Charles P Schaum • WS 9; SS 1015; BC 1015 • IN • 2235 W 10th Ave Gary IN 46404-2263

***ST PHILIP*** (219)949-5150
Vacant • WS 11; SS 10;* • IN • 3545 W 20th Pl Gary IN 46404-2640

**GEORGETOWN—*SHEPHERD HILLS***
See Edwardsville

**GOODLAND—*TRINITY*** (219)297-3556
David R Mueller • H • IN • 217 W Jasper St 213 W Jasper St Goodland IN 47948-8006

**GOSHEN—*PRINCE PEACE*** (219)533-7705
Vacant • WS 8 1030; SS 915; BC 915 • H • IN • 18548 County Road 18 Goshen IN 46528-9562

**GRABILL—*PRINCE OF PEACE***
See Leo

**GREENCASTLE—*PEACE*** (765)653-6995
Alan J Barber • H • EC • IN • 218 S Bloomington St Greencastle IN 46135-1733 • FAX(765)653-6995

**GREENFIELD—*FAITH*** (317)462-4609
David A Koeneman • WS 915; SS 1030; BC 1030 • H • EC/HS • IN • 200 W Mc Kenzie Rd Greenfield IN 46140-1018 • FAX(317)467-1716

**GREENSBURG—*HOLY TRINITY*** (812)663-8192
Mark S Flory • H • IN • 1219 S Michigan Ave Greensburg IN 47240-7905

**GREENWOOD—*CONCORDIA*** (317)881-4477
Howard O Fabricius John A Flamme • WS 8 1030; SS 915; BC 915;* • H • EC/HS • IN • 305 N Howard Rd Greenwood IN 46142-3836 • FAX(317)881-4498 • concordia@concordia-lcms.org

***MOUNT OLIVE*** (317)422-9991
David R Mc Clean Bruce E Holstein • WS 9; SS 1030 • H • IN • 5171 W Smokey Row Rd Greenwood IN 46143-8664 • FAX(317)422-9976 • pastordave@lightdog.com

**HAMLET—*IMMANUEL***
See Tracy

***ST MATTHEW*** (219)867-2891
Timothy W Gravelyn • H • IN • 6 W Indiana Ave Hamlet IN 46532-9530

**HAMMOND—*CONCORDIA*** (219)844-5616
Paul E Speerbrecker • * • H • IN • 7441 Grand Ave Hammond IN 46323-2967 • concordialutheran@altavista.com

***TRINITY*** (219)932-4660
Karl C Davies • H • EC • IN • 7227 Hohman Ave Hammond IN 46324-1817

**HANNA—*FIRST*** (219)797-4855
Vacant • IN • 46340 PO Box 26 Hanna IN 46340-0026 • FAX(219)797-5004

**HARTFORD CITY—*PRINCE OF PEACE*** (765)348-3910
Chad D Trouten • WS 9; SS 1015 • H • IN • Mill And Van Cleve Sts 47348 PO Box 86 Hartford City IN 47348-0086 • weaserex@netusa1.net

**HEBRON—*ST MICHAEL*** (219)996-7681
Richard L Boshoven • * • H • IN • 805 S County Line Rd Hebron IN 46341-9037 • FAX(219)996-7681 • stm-lcms@netnitco.net

**HIGHLAND—*REDEEMER*** (219)838-4898
Arthur R Burkman • WS 8 1045; SS 915; BC 915;* • H • IN • 9009 Kennedy Ave Highland IN 46322-1950 • art.burkman@juno.com

**HOBART—*HOLY CROSS***
See Portage 2 S

***TRINITY*** (219)942-2589
Gary Nagy Marc L Freiberg • BC 930;* • H • EC/EL • IN • 900 Luther Dr Hobart IN 46342-5246 • FAX(219)942-7459 • nagyinhobart@cs.com

**HUDSON—*PRINCE PEACE*** (219)351-2144
Vacant • WS 9;* • H • EN • 10275 E 550 S Hudson IN 46747

**HUNTERTOWN—*OUR HOPE*** (219)637-3625
Philip J Schamehorn • WS 8 1045; SS 930; BC 930;* • H • EC • IN • 1826 Trinity Dr 46748 PO Box 36 Huntertown IN 46748-0036 • FAX(219)637-4673 • OHLC@aol.com

**HUNTINGTON—*ST PETER*** (219)356-6528
Vacant • WS 9; SS 1015; BC 1015 • H • EC/EL • IN • 648 N Lafontaine St 46750 605 Polk St Huntington IN 46750-1932 • FAX(219)356-5703

**INDIANAPOLIS—*CALVARY*** (317)783-2000
Arthur H Wehrmeister William T Yates • H • EC/EL/HS • IN • 6111 Shelby St Indianapolis IN 46227-4879 • FAX(317)783-7096 • admin@clcs.org

***CHRIST*** (317)357-8596
J S F Machina • WS 1025;* • H • HS • IN • 345 N Kitley Ave Indianapolis IN 46219-6216 • FAX(317)357-8658

***EMMANUEL*** (317)890-9338
Dale A Dumperth • WS 915; SS 1030 • H • HS • IN • 329 S Boehning St Indianapolis IN 46219-7909 • FAX(317)897-6375 • daled@mac.com

***EMMAUS*** (317)632-1486
W E Lauterbach • Linda A Smith DEAC • WS 10; SS 845; BC 845 • H • EC/EL/HS • IN • 1224 Laurel St Indianapolis IN 46203-1984 • FAX(317)632-2620 • emmaus@inct.net

***FIRST TIMOTHY*** (317)257-6383
Vacant • WS 930; SS 1045;* • IN • 2190 Lafayette Rd 46222-3142 PO Box 88465 Indianapolis IN 46208-0465 • cwsi@indynet.com

***HOLY CROSS*** (317)823-5801
John W Sattler Terry N Hursh • Heidi P Mielke DCE • WS 830 1045; SS 945; BC 945;* • H • EC/HS • IN • Ne Oaklandon And Fox Rd 8115 Oaklandon Rd Indianapolis IN 46236-8578 • FAX(317)826-0622 • hclc@hclc.in.lcms.org

***MESSIAH*** (317)858-3733
Richard E Kurth • Samuel K Leiter P Asst • WS 8 1045; SS 930;* • H • EC • IN • 6100 N Raceway Rd Indianapolis IN 46234-3037 • FAX(317)858-3735 • churchoffice@messiah-indy.org

***OUR SAVIOR*** (317)925-3737
Douglas G Kenny • WS 11; SS 930; BC 930 • H • EL/HS • IN • 261 W 25th St Indianapolis IN 46208-5688 • FAX(317)925-3744

***OUR SHEPHERD*** (317)271-9103
Ronald P May • Martin A Hasz DCE • H • EC/EL/HS • IN • 9101 W 10th St Indianapolis IN 46234-2006 • oshepherd@iquest.net

***PEACE DEAF*** (317)546-6094
Jerold D Munz • WS 1030; SS 915; BC 915 • H • IN • 6404 E 46th St Indianapolis IN 46226-3550 • peacedeaf@juno.com

***SAINT PAUL*** (317)787-4464
David A Shadday • WS 930 • H • EC/HS • IN • 3932 Mi Casa Ave Indianapolis IN 46237-3213 • FAX(317)787-4464 • stpaulsindy@juno.com

***ST JOHN*** (317)352-9196
Philip J Krupski • WS 8 1030; SS 930;* • H • EC/EL/HS • IN • 6630 Southeastern Ave Indianapolis IN 46203-5834 • FAX(317)352-9197 • stjohnindy@iquest.net

***ST PETER*** (317)638-7245
Douglas P Bock • WS 1015; SS 1015; BC 845 • HS • IN • 2525 E 11th St PO Box 11287 Indianapolis IN 46201-0287 • FAX(317)638-8528 • stpeterindy@lightdog.com

***TRINITY*** (317)897-0243
John A Herfurth • Gary M Truwe DCE • WS 830 11; SS 945;* • H • EC/EL/HS • IN • 8540 E 16th St Indianapolis IN 46219-2503 • FAX(317)897-5277 • Pastor@trinityindy.org

**IRELAND—*FAITH IN CHRIST*** (812)482-5285
Vacant • IN • Walnut At St James PO Box 97 Ireland IN 47545

**JASPER—*FAITH IN CHRIST***
See Ireland

**JONESVILLE—*ST PAUL*** (812)522-2180
Vacant • H • IN • 607-609 Mill St 47247 PO Box 122 Jonesville IN 47247-0122

**KENDALLVILLE—*ST JOHN*** (219)347-2158
Paul B Griebel Robert W Shriner • Joann E Grepke DEAC • WS 8; SS 915; BC 1045;* • H • EC/EL • IN • 301 S Oak St Kendallville IN 46755-1758 • FAX(219)347-1770

**KNOX—*OUR REDEEMER*** (219)772-4186
Timothy P Miller • Diane R Snyder DCE • H • EC • IN • 1600 S Heaton St Knox IN 46534-2318

**KOKOMO—*GOOD SHEPHERD*** (765)457-4968
Robert E Bohlmann • WS 1015; SS 9; BC 9 • H • IN • 121 Santa Fe Blvd Kokomo IN 46901-4060 • gslc-lcms@usa.net

***OUR REDEEMER*** (765)453-0969
William S Allison Scott G Sommerfeld Barry A Akers • H • EC/EL • IN • 705 E Southway Blvd Kokomo IN 46902-4384 • FAX(765)864-6470 • lcor@netusa1.net

***ZION*** (765)452-9168
Frederick E Davison • IN • 6843 W Rd 400 N Kokomo IN 46901

**KOUTS—*ST PAUL*** (219)766-2395
Kent G Wartick • WS 9 1115; SS 1015; BC 1015;* • IN • Rose And Elizabeth Sts PO Box 547 Kouts IN 46347-0547 • splckouts@in.freei.net

**LA CROSSE—*ST JOHN*** (219)754-2296
Joel S Zipay • H • IN • PO Box 359 La Crosse IN 46348-0359

**LA PORTE—*ST JOHN*** (219)362-3726
David A Schoop Richard J Ungrodt • WS 8 1045; SS 930; BC 930;* • H • EC/EL/HS • IN • 111 Kingsbury Ave La Porte IN 46350-5211 • FAX(219)362-2237 • stjohns@stjohns-lpin.org

***TRINITY*** (219)362-4932
Noel C Olse • WS 1015;* • EN • 907 Michigan Ave La Porte IN 46350-3504 • nco-trinity@juno.com

**LAFAYETTE—*ST JAMES*** (765)423-1616
Daniel P May David R French • WS 730 830 UNKNOWN 1; SS 945; BC 945;* • H • IN • 47901 800 Cincinnati St Lafayette IN 47901-1073 • FAX(765)742-4642 • pastormay@stjameslaf.org

**LAKE STATION—*REDEEMER*** (219)962-1609
Vacant • IN • 3930 Central Ave Lake Station IN 46405-2415

**LANESVILLE 2 S—*ST JOHN*** (812)952-3711
Richard A Heinz • WS 8 1030; SS 915; BC 915 • H • EC/EL • IN • 47136 1505 Saint Johns Church Rd NE Lanesville IN 47136-8568 • stjohns@otherside.com

**LAWRENCEBURG—*BETHLEHEM*** (812)537-0361
Vacant • EC • IN • 495 Ludlow St Lawrenceburg IN 47025-1532 • Bethluth@juno.com

**LEESVILLE—*EMMANUEL*** (812)966-2446
Larry G Mallett • WS 6 • IN • UKNWN PO Box 310 Medora IN 47260-0310

**LEO—*PRINCE OF PEACE*** (219)627-5621
David M Taylor • WS 9;* • H • IN • 46765 12640 St Joe Rd Grabill IN 46741-9412

**LIGONIER—*TRINITY*** (219)894-3667
Russell D Fuhrmann • IN • Fourth And Martin Sts 46767 PO Box 134 Ligonier IN 46767-0134

**LOGANSPORT—*ST JAMES*** (219)753-4227
Marvin R Hinkle • * • H • IN • Ninth And Spear 46947 430 9th St Logansport IN 46947-3533 • FAX(219)753-5432 • stjaslog@cqc.com

**LOWELL—*TRINITY*** (219)696-9338
Mark E Pflughoeft • H • IN • 631 W Commercial Ave 46356-2221 PO Box 236 Lowell IN 46356-0236 • FAX(219)696-0447

**MADISON—*FAITH*** (812)273-1371
Jeffery D Pflug • WS 1030; SS 915; BC 915 • H • IN • 3024 Michigan Rd Madison IN 47250-1801 • FAX(812)273-1371 • lcmsfaith@juno.com

**MARION—*ST JAMES*** (765)662-3092
Mark E Carlson • Philip J Rosel DCE • H • EC • IN • 1206 N Miller Ave Marion IN 46952-1535 • FAX(765)662-9197 • stjames@comteck.com

**MARTINSVILLE—*PRINCE PEACE*** (317)342-2004
Nathan L Janssen • WS 9; SS 1015 • H • EC/EL • IN • 3496 E Morgan St Martinsville IN 46151-8053 • njanssen@scican.net

**MEDARYVILLE—*ST MARK*** (219)843-3051
Vacant • WS 1130;* • H • IN • Us 421 PO Box 89 Medaryville IN 47957

**MEDORA—*EMMANUEL***
See Leesville

***GOOD SHEPHERD*** (812)966-2446
Larry G Mallett • WS 1030; SS 930; BC 945 • H • IN • 186 W Main St 47260 PO Box 310 Medora IN 47260-0310

**MERRILLVILLE—*RESURRECTION*** (219)942-6604
Robert C Breitbarth • WS 8; SS 915; BC 930;* • H • S • 46401 8061 E US Highway 30 Crown Point IN 46307-8824 • FAX(219)942-6604 • resurrectionlutheranchurch@usa.net

***TRINITY MEMORIAL*** (219)769-5376
G E Isenberg • WS 9;* • H • IN • 7950 Marshall St Merrillville IN 46410-5219 • FAX(219)769-1265 • trinity-pastor@ateze.com

**MICHIGAN CITY—*IMMANUEL*** (219)872-4048
David M Albertin • WS 8 1045; SS 930; BC 930;* • H • EC/HS • IN • 1237 E Coolspring Ave Michigan City IN 46360-6312 • FAX(219)872-4780 • david@cicinet.com

**MILFORD TOWNSHI—*PRINCE PEACE***
See Hudson

**MISHAWAKA—*ST PAUL***
See Woodland

***ST PETER*** (219)255-5585
Kenneth D Mangelsdorf • H • EC • IN • 437 E Dragoon Trl 46544-6633 PO Box 196 Mishawaka IN 46546-0196 • FAX(219)255-5585

**MONROEVILLE 6 SW—*ST JOHN*** (219)639-6404
Douglas M Christian • WS 815 1030;* • H • IN • 46773 12912 Franke Rd Monroeville IN 46773-9559 • FAX(219)639-7383

**MONTICELLO—*OUR SAVIOUR*** (219)583-5005
William A Parsons • WS 9; SS 1030; BC 1030 • H • IN • 122 Condo St Monticello IN 47960-1641 • FAX(219)583-3372

**MOORESVILLE—*HARVEST*** (317)834-9741
Vacant • WS 10; SS 9; BC 9;* • H • IN • 450 Saint Clair St Mooresville IN 46158 • FAX(317)834-9745 • harvest@surf-ici.com

**MORGANTOWN—*SHEPHERD HILLS***
See Bean Blossom 1/2 N

**MUNCIE—*GRACE*** (765)282-2537
Kevin A Karner Peter C Cage • H • IN • 610 N Reserve St Muncie IN 47303-3830 • FAX(765)284-2096 • gracelutheran2@juno.com

**MUNSTER—*ST PAUL*** (219)836-6270
Eric C Stumpf Scott D Bruick • Julie A Heck DEAC • H • EC/EL • IN • 8601 Harrison Ave Munster IN 46321-2398 • FAX(219)836-3724 • stpaul@mail.icongrp.com

**MURFREESBORO—*GRACE*** (615)893-0338
Carl R Wenck Jason A Dail • Becky L Bradfield DCE • WS 8 1045; SS 925; BC 925;* • H • MDS • 57130-2325 811 E Clark Blvd Murfreesboro TN 37130-2325 • FAX(615)893-1406 • graceoffice@aol.com

**NASHVILLE 1 1/2—*SHEPHERD HILLS***
See Bean Blossom 1/2 N on 135

**NEW ALBANY—*GRACE*** (812)944-1267
Bruce R Kischnick • WS 8 1030; SS 915 • H • EC • IN • 1787 Klerner Ln New Albany IN 47150-1986 • FAX(812)944-1889

**NEW HAVEN—*EMANUEL*** (219)749-2163
Paul E Shoemaker David O Stecker Scott A Zeckzer • WS 8 7;* • H • EL • IN • 800 Green St New Haven IN 46774-1610 • FAX(219)493-3425 • emanuelnh@juno.com

**NEW HAVEN 3 S—*MARTINI*** (219)749-0014
Herbert M Gerken • WS 9;* • H • EL • IN • 333 Moeller Rd New Haven IN 46774-1848

**NEW HAVEN 5 NE—*ST PAUL*** (219)749-5444
Ronald R Francis • H • EL • IN • 46774 1910 N Berthaud Rd New Haven IN 46774-9661 • garcreek@gateway.net

**NEW PALESTINE 3 NW—*ZION*** (317)861-5544
Ronald W Baumann • WS 8 1030; SS 915; BC 915 • H • EC/EL/HS • IN • 46163 6513 W 300 S New Palestine IN 46163-9748 • FAX(317)861-8153

**NEW SALISBURY—*EPIPHANY*** (812)347-3147
Vacant • H • EC • IN • 8600 Highway 135 NE New Salisbury IN 47161-8601

**NEWBURGH—*SHEP PARADISE*** (812)853-3972
Edwin J Carey • H • IN • 7811 Oak Grove Rd Newburgh IN 47630-2998

**NOBLESVILLE—*CHRIST*** (317)773-3669
Adrian L Piazza • H • EC • IN • 10055 E 186th St Noblesville IN 46060-1659

**NORTH JUDSON—*ST PETER*** (219)896-2025
Michael B Boyd • WS 9; BC 1015;* • H • IN • 810 W Talmer Ave North Judson IN 46366-1348 • FAX(219)896-2082

**NORTH VERNON—*LORD OF LIFE*** (812)346-6400
Gary Held • H • IN • 3330 N State Highway 3 47265-7290 PO Box 411 North Vernon IN 47265-0411 • rtremainl@hsonline.net

**OSSIAN—*NEW HOPE*** (219)622-7954
Paul M Doehrmann • * • H • EC • IN • 8824 N State Rd 1 46777 PO Box 341 Ossian IN 46777-0341

**OSSIAN 5 SE—*BETHLEHEM***
See Tocsin 2 NE

**OTIS—*ST PAUL***
Vacant • WS 9; SS 1015; BC 1015 • IN • 46391 PO Box 906 Westville IN 46391-0906

**PENDLETON—*ST MARK*** (765)778-3201
Howard Whitecotton III • H • IN • 6865 S 100 W Pendleton IN 46064-9387 • FAX(765)778-3201 • derstift@hotmail.com

**PERU—*ST JOHN*** (765)473-6659
Vacant • WS 815 11; SS 945;* • H • EC/EL • IN • 181 W Main St Peru IN 46970-2049 • FAX(765)473-6659

**PLYMOUTH—*CALVARY*** (219)936-2903
Steven J Resner • * • H • EC • IN • 1314 N Michigan St Plymouth IN 46563-1118 • FAX(219)936-5458 • calvary-lutheran@hotmail.com

**PORTAGE—*ST PETER*** (219)762-2673
Roy M Zerbe • WS 10; SS 845;* • H • IN • 6540 Central Ave Portage IN 46368-3102 • rhzerbe@excelonline.com

**PORTAGE 2 S—*HOLY CROSS*** (219)763-6343
Timothy A Engel • WS 9; SS 1015; BC 1015;* • IN • 46368 5402 US Highway 6 Hobart IN 46342-5420

**RENSSELAER—*ST LUKE*** (219)866-7681
Garry E Wickert • H • EC • IN • 704 E Grace St Rensselaer IN 47978-3299

**RENSSELAER 8 NW—*ST JOHN*** (219)866-8683
Vacant • IN • 47978 2787 N County Rd 700 W Rensselaer IN 47978-9093

**REYNOLDS—*ST JAMES*** (219)984-5421
Stephen E Koenig • H • EC • IN • 110 N Kenton St 47980-8162 PO Box 327 Reynolds IN 47980-0327

**ROANOKE—*FAITH*** (219)672-1140
Vacant • WS 830;* • H • IN • 3416 E 900 N 46783-9142 PO Box 219 Roanoke IN 46783-0219

**ROCHESTER—*ST JOHN*** (219)223-6898
James W Kreft • H • IN • Fourth And Jefferson Sts 46975 PO Box 712 Rochester IN 46975-0712

**SALEM—*FAITH*** (812)883-6127
William D O Connor • H • IN • PO Box 331 Salem IN 47167-0331

**SCHERERVILLE—*PEACE*** (219)322-5490
Daniel P Dierks • * • H • EC • IN • 144 W Parkway Dr Schererville IN 46375-2100

**SEYMOUR—*EMANUEL***
See Dudleytown

***IMMANUEL*** (812)522-3118
Ralph Blomenberg Philip E Bloch • WS 9 1115;* • H • EL • IN • S Walnut And Oak 47274 605 S Walnut St Seymour IN 47274-2921 • FAX(812)522-6675 • immanuel@hsonline.net

***REDEEMER*** (812)522-1837
Andrew J Currao Paul R Schlueter • H • IN • 504 N Walnut St Seymour IN 47274-1537 • FAX(812)524-9040 • redeemer@compuage.com

***ZION*** (812)522-1089
Mark G Press • WS 8 1030; SS 915; BC 915 • H • EC • IN • 1501 Gaiser Dr Seymour IN 47274-3627 • FAX(812)523-7526 • zionseymin@seidata.com

**SEYMOUR 9 SW—*ST JOHN*** (812)523-3559
Craig A Muhlbach • H • EL • IN • 47274 1108 S County Road 460 E Seymour IN 47274-9572

**SHELBYVILLE 1 N—*ST MARK*** (317)398-7990
Vacant • WS 1030;* • IN • 46176 1560 N Michigan Rd Shelbyville IN 46176-9386

**SOUTH BEND—*EMMAUS*** (219)287-4151
Don R Stuckwisch • H • EC • IN • 929 Milton St South Bend IN 46613-2825

***FAITH*** (219)288-3737
James C Link • H • EC • IN • 156 S Lombardy Dr South Bend IN 46619-1758 • FAX(219)289-0683 • faithlcmssb@netscape.net

***OUR REDEEMER*** (219)288-8288
Daniel A Streufert • H • EC • IN • 805 S 29th St South Bend IN 46615-2239

***ST PAUL*** (219)271-1050
Gregory K Fiechtner • * • H • EC • IN • 51490 Laurel Rd South Bend IN 46637-1018 • FAX(219)271-1051 • stpaulsb@juno.com

**SOUTHPORT—*CALVARY***
See Indianapolis

**SYRACUSE—*SHEP BY LAKES*** (219)528-6137
Raymond A Mueller • WS 930; SS 830; BC 830 • H • IN • 7449 E 1000 N Syracuse IN 46567 • FAX(219)834-3746

**TELL CITY—*EMMANUEL*** (812)547-4215
Robert K Hall • WS 10; SS 9; BC 9 • H • IN • 1105 Pestalozzi St 47586-1813 PO Box 116 Tell City IN 47586-0116 • emmanuel@psci.net

**TERRE HAUTE—*IMMANUEL*** (812)232-4972
Philip G Meyer • WS 1030; SS 9; BC 9 • EC • IN • 645 Poplar St Terre Haute IN 47807-4203 • FAX(812)234-3935 • Pastor@indynet.com

**TIPTON—*EMANUEL*** (765)675-4090
Kurt H Gremel • WS 815 1045; SS 930; BC 930 • H • EC • IN • 1385 S Main St 46072-8460 PO Box F Tipton IN 46072-0137 • FAX(765)675-4200

**TOCSIN 2 NE—*BETHLEHEM*** (219)597-7286
William R Brege • H • EL • IN • 46777 6514 E 750 N Ossian IN 46777-9631

**TRACY—*IMMANUEL*** (219)867-2891
Timothy W Gravelyn • H • IN • 46532 C/O St Matthew Luth Church 6 W Indiana Ave Hamlet IN 46532-9530

**VALLONIA 2 S—*TRINITY*** (812)358-3225
William D O Connor • WS 930;* • H • EL • IN • 47281 4381 S State Rd #135 Vallonia IN 47281-9801 • FAX(812)358-3225 • goirish@hsonline.net

**VALPARAISO—*FAITH MEMORIAL*** (219)462-7684
John M Albers • WS 8 1045; SS 930; BC 930 • H • HS • IN • 753 N Calumet Ave Valparaiso IN 46383-7903 • FAX(219)477-5304 • fmlc@nila.net

***HERITAGE*** (219)464-2810
Joseph A Ostafinski • WS 9; BC 1030;* • H • IN • 308 Washington St Valparaiso IN 46383-4734 • FAX(219)477-2677

***IMMANUEL*** (219)462-8207
Donald H Williams Stephen H Bongard Victor E Gebauer • Darlene E Mortimer DEAC • * • H • EC/EL/HS • IN • 1700 Monticello Park Dr Valparaiso IN 46383-3847 • FAX(219)531-2238

***PRINCE PEACE*** (219)464-4911
Joseph Molitoris • WS 9; SS 1030; BC 1030 • H • IN • 234 W Division Rd Valparaiso IN 46385

**VINCENNES—*ST JOHN*** (812)882-4662
John D Duke • WS 8 10; SS 9; BC 9;* • H • EL • IN • 707 N 8th St Vincennes IN 47591-3111 • FAX(812)882-5492

**VINCENNES 7 S—*ST PETER*** (812)882-8229
Nathan P Rastl • WS 10; SS 9; BC 9 • H • EL • IN • Old Decker Rd 47591 7000 S Decker Rd Vincennes IN 47591-9142 • nprastl@vincennes.net

**WABASH—*ZION*** (219)563-1886
Manfred W Fremder • WS 1030; SS 9; BC 915 • H • IN • 173 Hale Dr Wabash IN 46992

**WANATAH 4 SE—*ST JOHN*** (219)733-9475
Joel S Zipay • IN • 46390 15496 S 900 W Wanatah IN 46390-9614

**WARSAW—*REDEEMER*** (219)267-5656
Thomas W Vanselow • SS 915; BC 915;* • H • EC/EL • IN • 1720 E Center St Warsaw IN 46580-3602 • FAX(219)267-5242 • Redeemer³Warsaw@Juno.com

**WAWAKA—*RESTORATION***
Robert J Muller • IN • 9878 N 125 W Wawaka IN 46794

**WAYMANSVILLE—*ST PETER*** (812)342-4921
Wayne K Frost • IN • 11630 W 930 S Columbus IN 47201-8758

**WEST LAFAYETTE—*REDEEMER*** (765)463-5851
Joseph E Townsend • H • IN • Salisburg And Lindberg 47901 510 Lindberg Ave West Lafayette IN 47906-2033 • redeemer@indy.net

***UNIVERSITY*** (765)743-2472
James P Barton • WS 1230;* • IN • 100 S Chauncey Ave West Lafayette IN 47906-3695 • ululaf@aol.com

**WESTFIELD—*LORD OF LIFE*** (317)867-5673
Timothy P Krupski • WS 945; SS 830; BC 830 • IN • 800 E Main St 46074-9440 PO Box 1075 Westfield IN 46074-9998

**WESTVILLE—*ST PAUL***
See Otis

***TRINITY*** (219)785-2861
Thomas C Obersat • WS 9; BC 1015;* • H • IN • 402 Flynn Rd 46391 PO Box 315 Westville IN 46391-0315 • FAX(219)785-2861

**WHEATFIELD—*EMMANUEL*** (219)956-4513
Vacant • H • IN • Hwy 10 46392 PO Box 142 Wheatfield IN 46392-0142

**WHITING—*ST JOHN*** (219)659-3505
Vacant • WS 9 • IN • 1701 Cleveland Ave 1709 Cleveland Ave Whiting IN 46394-1616

***ST PAUL*** (219)659-0303
Kevin Bergmann • S • 1801 Atchison Ave Whiting IN 46394-1615

**WINAMAC—*ST LUKE*** (219)946-3501
Matthew B Woods • IN • 721 S Market St Winamac IN 46996-1550

***ST PAUL***
See Denham

**WOLCOTTVILLE 1 N—*MESSIAH*** (219)854-3129
Kevin R Loughran • WS 1030;* • H • IN • 46795 2955 E 700 S Wolcottville IN 46795-8957

**WOODBURN—*CHRIST*** (219)632-4821
Samuel D Schlie • * • H • EC/EL • IN • 4412 Park St 46797-9015 PO Box 127 Woodburn IN 46797-0127

**WOODBURN 3 NW—*ZION*** (219)632-4679
Vacant • WS 10 745 715; SS 9; BC 9;* • H • EC/EL • IN • 46797 7616 Bull Rapids Rd Woodburn IN 46797-9749

**WOODLAND—*ST PAUL*** (219)633-4888
Karl A Brenner • H • IN • UKNWN 15697 New Rd Mishawaka IN 46544-9753

**ZIONSVILLE—*ADVENT*** (317)873-6318
John W Fiene • H • EC • IN • 11250 N Michigan Rd Zionsville IN 46077-9207 • FAX(317)873-6369 • advent@iquest.net

## IOWA

**ADAIR—*IMMANUEL*** (515)742-3821
Peter J Haenftling • EC • IW • 709 Adair St Adair IA 50002-1121 • immluthch@juno.com

**ADAIR 4N 3W—*ST JOHN*** (515)742-3669
Peter J Haenftling • IW • 50002 3046 Union Ave Adair IA 50002-7500 • immluthch@juno.com

**ADEL—*FAITH*** (515)993-3848
Mark A Gerken • WS 8 1030; SS 915; BC 915;* • H • EC • IW • 602 S 14th St Adel IA 50003-1947 • faithadel@hotmail.com

**ALDEN—*ST PAUL*** (515)859-3901
Vacant • H • IE • 806 Mill St 50006 PO Box 27 Alden IA 50006-0027

***ZION***
Jay A Jaeger • SD • C/O St Paul Lutheran Church PO Box 27 Alden IA 50006-0027

**ALGONA—*TRINITY*** (515)295-3518
Steven D Turner Patrick E O Neal • WS 8 1030;* • H • EC • IW • 520 N Garfield St Algona IA 50511-1615 • FAX(515)295-3519 • trinity.algona@iowawest.org

**ALTA—*ST PAUL*** (712)284-1133
Kevin Huss • WS 930; SS 815; BC 815 • H • IW • Fourth and Division Alta IA 51002 • FAX(712)284-2482 • kvdahuss@ncn.net

**ALTA 8 SW—*ST JOHN*** (712)284-1450
Mark W Abraham • EC • IW • 51002 169 630th St Alta IA 51002-7447

**ALTOONA—*CHRIST KING*** (515)967-3349
Vacant • H • EC • IW • 600 1st Ave N Altoona IA 50009-1432 • FAX(515)967-3254 • ctkaltoona@aol.com

**AMES—*MEMORIAL*** (515)292-5005
Richard N Osslund Mark T Heilman • WS 830 11; BC 950;* • H • IW • 2228 W Lincoln Way Ames IA 50014-7185 • mlcames@aol.com

***ST PAUL*** (515)232-5838
Steven P Chellew • * • H • IW • 1435 Wilson Ave Ames IA 50010-5463 • general@stpaulames.org

**ANITA—*HOLY CROSS*** (712)762-3335
George A Krengel • * • EC • IW • 401 Maple St 50020-1134 704 Maple St Anita IA 50020

**ANKENY—*ST PAUL*** (515)964-1250
Edward R Grimm • H • EC • IW • 1100 SE Sharon Dr Ankeny IA 50021-3738 • pastorofst.paul@juno.com

**ANTHON—*TRINITY*** (712)373-5283
Michael D Harman • * • H • IW • 106 Arnold St Anthon IA 51004-8184

**ARCADIA—*ZION*** (712)689-2441
Carl L Noble • WS 10;* • EC • IW • 51430-1001 PO Box 59 118 W Tracy St Arcadia IA 51430-0059 • zionl@netins.net

**ARTESIAN—*ST PAUL***
See Waverly 10 NE

**ATKINS—*ST STEPHEN*** (319)446-7675
Vacant • WS 830;* • H • EC/EL • IE • 303 3rd Ave 52206-9758 PO Box 203 Atkins IA 52206-0203

**ATLANTIC—*ZION*** (712)243-2927
Allen D Hellwege • WS 8 1030; SS 915; BC 915 • H • EC • IW • 811 Oak St Atlantic IA 50022-1740 • zionluth@netins.net

**AUBURN—*ZION*** (712)688-2810
Vacant • WS 1030;* • IW • 3rd And Ash Sts 51433 PO Box 246 Auburn IA 51433-0246 • FAX(712)688-2810

**AUDUBON—*ST JOHN*** (712)563-3548
Bradley W Ketcham • * • EC • IW • 815 E Division St Audubon IA 50025-1318

***TRINITY*** (712)653-3611
Richard E Burrack(EM) • IW • 1405 Eagle Ave Audubon IA 50025-7494

**AURELLIA—*ST PAUL*** (712)434-2331
Larry G Lemke • WS 930; SS 1030; BC 1030 • H • IW • 501 Locust Aurelia IA 51005-0278 • spaurlia@netins.net

**AYRSHIRE—*ZION*** (712)425-3328
Neil E Hayen • WS 8; SS 9 • IW • 50515 C/O Trinity Lutheran Church PO Box 216 Mallard IA 50562-0216

**BATTLE CREEK—*ST JOHN*** (712)365-4477
Daniel T Torkelson • WS 9; BC 8;* • H • IW • 608 Fifth St 51006 PO Box 286 Battle Creek IA 51006-0286

**BATTLE CREEK 10 NW—*ST PAUL*** (712)365-4328
Thomas A Sabel • IW • 51006 2326 Story Ave Battle Creek IA 51006-8014

**BEDFORD—*ST TIMOTHY*** (712)523-2874
Vacant • H • IW • 1308 Madison St Bedford IA 50833-1039

**BELLE PLAINE—*FIRST*** (319)444-2849
Vacant • * • H • IE • 1523 Sunset Dr Belle Plaine IA 52208-1319 • flc@netins.net

**BENNETT—*ST PAUL*** (319)890-6619
Bruce H Miller • BC 9;* • H • IE • 260 E Fourth St PO Box J Bennett IA 52721-0348

**BETTENDORF—*OUR SAVIOR*** (319)332-5141
Keith A Piotter • WS 8 1045; SS 930 • H • EC/HS • IE • 3775 Middle Rd Bettendorf IA 52722-3315 • FAX(319)332-2117 • oursavior@qconline.com

**BLAIRSTOWN—*GRACE*** (319)454-6941
David P Rempfer • WS 10; SS 9; BC 9 • H • IE • 100 Locust NE 52209 PO Box 156 Blairstown IA 52209-0156 • gracetou@netins.net

**BOONE—*ST PAUL*** (515)432-4470
Vacant • WS 930;* • H • IW • 1/2 Mile W Of 17 On E 18 50036 281 Spruce Ln Boone IA 50036-7365 • FAX(515)432-4470

***TRINITY*** (515)432-5140
Lindsay W Watkins • WS 8 1030; SS 915; BC 915;* • H • EC/EL • IW • 712 12th St Boone IA 50036-2240 • FAX(515)432-1059

**BOUTON—*CHRIST***
Vacant • * • IW • 111 South St 50039 PO Box 100 Bouton IA 50039-0100

**BUCK GROVE—*ST JOHN*** (712)674-3323
Vacant • WS 815 • IW • PO Box 167 Dow City IA 51528-0167

**BUCKEYE—*ST PAUL*** (515)855-4240
Vacant • IE • Berlin And East Sts 50043 PO Box 2036 Buckeye IA 50043-2036

**BURLINGTON—*CONCORDIA*** (319)754-4246
Christopher A Roepke • WS 10; SS 845;* • H • EC • IE • 2901 Cliff Rd Burlington IA 52601-2410 • caroepke@aol.com

**BURT—*ST JOHN*** (515)924-3344
Vacant • WS 930; SS 830; BC 830;* • H • EC • IW • 109 Maple St 50522 PO Box 98 Burt IA 50522-0098

**CARLISLE—*HOLY CROSS*** (515)989-3841
John A Meyer • * • H • IW • 1100 Market St Carlisle IA 50047

**CARROLL—*ST PAUL*** (712)792-4354
Charles W Haake • WS 8 1030; BC 915;* • H • EC • IW • 19th And Highland Dr 1844 Highland Dr Carroll IA 51401-3573 • FAX(712)792-0514 • stpaulle@pionet.net

**CASEY—*ST JOHN*** (641)746-2734
Carl W Janssen • WS 9; SS 1015; BC 1015 • H • IW • 104 E 1st St 50048-1000 PO Box 73 Casey IA 50048-0073 • FAX(641)746-2734 • stjohn@netins.net

**CEDAR FALLS—*COLLEGE HILL*** (319)266-1274
Thomas G Ogilvie • * • IE • 2321 Walnut St Cedar Falls IA 50613-3860 • chlc.lcms@cfu.net

***OUR REDEEMER*** (319)266-2509
Michael R Knox • H • EC • IE • 904 Bluff St Cedar Falls IA 50613-3326

**CEDAR RAPIDS—*BETHANY*** (319)364-6026
Donald D Loesch(EM) • H • EC • IE • 2202 Forest Dr SE Cedar Rapids IA 52403-1654 • FAX(319)366-4891

***CONCORDIA*** (319)396-9035
Paul A Scheidt • Verlyn E Le Fevere DCE • WS 8;* • H • EC • IE • 4210 Johnson Ave NW Cedar Rapids IA 52405-4218

***KING OF KINGS*** (319)393-2438
Leon E Hauser • * • H • IE • 52403-1344 6621 C Ave NE Cedar Rapids IA 52402-1344 • FAX(319)393-5512 • kngkngwb@aol.com

***TRINITY*** (319)366-1569
Parker A Knoll • Carol M Goldfish DEAC • WS 8 1030; SS 915; BC 915;* • H • EC/EL • IE • 1363 1st Ave SW Cedar Rapids IA 52405-4891 • FAX(319)366-1569 • trinity@inav.net

***WORD OF GOD DF*** (319)362-5420
Roger K Altenberger • IE • 1515 29th St NE Cedar Rapids IA 52402-4007 • meka5@prodigy.net

**CENTER POINT—*ST JOHN*** (319)849-1251
David L Hansen • IE • 1115 Water St 52213-9314 PO Box 244 Center Point IA 52213-0244

**CHARITON—*TRINITY*** (515)774-8335
Vacant • WS 10; SS 845; BC 845 • H • IE • 825 N 7th St Chariton IA 50049-1331

**CHARLOTTE—*IMMANUEL*** (319)677-2756
Terrance K Ellis • WS 10; BC 9;* • H • IE • Hwy 136 235 First St 52731 PO Box 239 Charlotte IA 52731-0239

**CHARTER OAK—*ST JOHN*** (712)678-3630
Leonhardt Gebhardt • WS 10; SS 845; BC 9 • H • EC • IW • 104 Birch Ave 51439 PO Box 73 Charter Oak IA 51439-0073

***ST JOHN*** (712)678-3630
Leonhardt Gebhardt • WS 10; SS 845; BC 9 • H • EC • IW • First And Birch St 51439 PO Box 73 Charter Oak IA 51439-0073

**CHARTER OAK 5 N—*IMMANUEL*** (712)679-2701
Eugene W Ernst • * • IW • 51439 1512 130th St Charter Oak IA 51439-9801

**CHARTER OAK 7 NE—*ST PAUL*** (712)679-2701
Eugene W Ernst • * • IW • 51439 1743 G Ave Charter Oak IA 51439-9801

**CHEROKEE—*TRINITY*** (712)225-4332
Richard L Arndt • WS 9;* • H • IW • 230 N Roosevelt Ave Cherokee IA 51012-1971 • tlcchero@netins.net

**CLARINDA—*ST JOHN*** (712)542-3708
Gary D Jaeckle • WS 1030; SS 910; BC 910;* • H • EC • IW • 301 N 13th St Clarinda IA 51632-1755 • stjohnluth@clarinda.heartland.net

***ST PAUL*** (712)542-1505
Nathan S Dudley • WS 10; SS 11; BC 11 • H • EL • IW • 2463 State Hwy 2 51632 Box 128 E Yorktown IA 51656-9999 • ndudley@clarinda.heartland.net

**CLARINDA 7 NW—*IMMANUEL*** (712)542-3524
Kendall M Lampe • * • H • EL • IW • 1614 P Avenue Clarinda IA 51632

**CLEMONS—*ST JOHN*** (515)483-2578
Marvin L Flanscha • H • IE • 50247 1956 Durham Ave State Center IA 50247-9692

**CLINTON—*ST JOHN*** (319)242-5588
Wayne O Brinkmann • H • EC • IE • 416 Main Ave Clinton IA 52732-1938

***TRINITY*** (319)242-5328
Michael H Holm • WS 9; SS 1015; BC 1015 • H • IE • 656 5th Ave S Clinton IA 52732-4618 • FAX(319)242-5328

**CONROY—*TRINITY*** (319)662-4075
Gary L Sears • WS 930;* • H • EC/EL • IE • 626 8th Ave 52220 PO Box 66 Conroy IA 52220-0066 • glsears@avalon.net

**COON RAPIDS 6 NE—*TRINITY*** (712)684-5118
Vacant • WS 1030;* • IW • 50058 2174 B Ave Coon Rapids IA 50058-8514

**CORALVILLE—*PRINCE OF PEACE*** (319)338-1842
Mitchell E Otto • WS 1015; SS 9; BC 9 • H • IE • 1701 8th St Coralville IA 52241-1601 • popcoralville@juno.com

**CORNING—*REDEEMER*** (515)322-3498
Vacant • WS 1030; SS 915; BC 915 • H • IW • 800 17th St Corning IA 50841-1067

**CORRECTIONVILLE—*GRACE*** (712)372-4528
Michael D Harman • WS 1030 9;* • H • IW • 828 Driftwood Correctionville IA 51016

**COUNCIL BLUFFS—*FAITH*** (712)323-6445
Philip W Hanson • WS 8 1030; SS 915; BC 915 • H • EL • IW • 2100 S 11th St Council Bluffs IA 51501-7304 • FAX(712)323-0076 • faith@neonramp.com

***ST PAUL*** (712)322-4729
Gus A George • H • EL • IW • 239 Frank St Council Bluffs IA 51503-4545 • FAX(712)322-6226

***TIMOTHY*** (712)323-0693
Michael J Petri • WS 8 1030; SS 915; BC 915 • H • EC/EL • IW • 3112 W Broadway Council Bluffs IA 51501-3310 • FAX(712)323-7582 • timothylc@juno.com

**CRESTON—*TRINITY*** (515)782-5095
Vacant • WS 8; SS 945; BC 945 • H • EC • IW • 800 N Sumner Ave Creston IA 50801-1349

**CYLINDER—*ST LUKE*** (515)889-2769
David H Bergquist • WS 1015;* • H • IW • 5652 340th St Cylinder IA 50528-8078 • stluke.fairville@iowawest.org

**DAVENPORT—*HOLY CROSS*** (319)322-2654
Frederick H Schuster • H • EC/HS • IE • 1705 E Locust St Davenport IA 52803-3205

***IMMANUEL*** (319)324-6431
James R Shaw • H • EC/HS • IE • 3834 Rockingham Rd Davenport IA 52802-2598 • FAX(319)324-8899 • immanuel@lifeoftheworld.com

***RISEN CHRIST*** (319)386-2342
Kurt R Larson • H • EC/HS • IE • 6021 Northwest Blvd Davenport IA 52806-1848 • FAX(319)386-8969 • RisenChrist@mail.com

***TRINITY*** (319)323-8001
Michael E Vokt David A Grimm • Michael H Tanney DCE • WS 8 930 1050;* • H • HS • IE • 1122 W Central Park Ave Davenport IA 52804-1805 • FAX(319)324-9153 • trinity@lutheran.com

**DAYTON—*TRINITY*** (515)547-2431
Vacant • IW • 201 1st Ave NE Dayton IA 50530-7596

**DE WITT—*GRACE*** (319)659-9153
Galen F Drawbaugh Ronald H Goodsman • Michelle O Moorhead DCE • * • H • IE • 415 1oth St 52742 PO Box 156 De Witt IA 52742-0156 • FAX(319)659-3470 • glcms@netcis.net

**DEEP RIVER—*CALVARY*** (515)595-4265
Michael J Parris • IE • Church St And Hwy 85 52222 PO Box 71 Deep River IA 52222-0071

**DELAWARE—*ST PAUL*** (319)922-2364
Vacant • WS 9;* • IE • 200 S 4th St Delaware IA 52057 • FAX(319)922-2364

**DELOIT—*FAITH*** (712)675-4617
Hilmer J Hafner • WS 9; SS 8;* • H • IW • 51441 PO Box 216 Kiron IA 51448-0216 • revhjh@netins.net

**DENISON—*OUR SAVIOR*** (712)263-3282
David P Loeschen • WS 9; BC 10;* • H • EC • IW • 500 N 24th St Denison IA 51442-1704 • FAX(712)263-3744 • osluth@pionet.net

***ZION*** (712)263-2235
Kurt R Kaiser David M Sewing • WS 8 1030; SS 915; BC 915;* • H • IW • 1004 1st Ave S Denison IA 51442-2615 • FAX(712)263-6010 • zionls@frontiernet.net

**DENVER—*ST JOHN*** (319)984-5351
Donald C Illian • WS 10; SS 9; BC 9 • H • IE • 641 Lincoln St 50622-9789 PO Box 389 Denver IA 50622-0389 • pdillian@forbin.com

**DES MOINES—*CALVARY DEAF*** (515)262-3420
Vacant • WS 10; BC 1130 • H • IW • 3909 E 42nd St Des Moines IA 50317-8107 • FAX(515)262-3420 • marionjum@aol.com

***HOPE*** (515)265-2057
Timothy P Braun • WS 1045 815; BC 935 • H • EC • IW • 3857 E 42nd St Des Moines IA 50317-8105 • FAX(515)265-8775

***MOUNT OLIVE*** (515)277-8349
David P Mumm • WS 8 1030; SS 920; BC 920;* • H • IW • 5625 Franklin Ave Des Moines IA 50310-1099 • FAX(515)274-2723

***OUR SAVIOUR*** (515)244-9347
Thomas O Cole • WS 9;* • H • IW • 4003 2nd Ave Des Moines IA 50313-3507 • FAX(515)244-9347 • oslc2nd@juno.com

***PEACE*** (515)285-3769
Peter C Wegner • WS 8 1030; SS 915;* • H • IW • 5615 SW 14th St Des Moines IA 50315-4814 • peace5615@yahoo.com

***TRINITY*** (515)279-3609
Vacant • WS 9; SS 1015; BC 1015;* • H • IW • 3223 University Ave Des Moines IA 50311-3819 • FAX(515)274-6806 • trinitylc@aol.com

**DEXTER—*ZION*** (515)789-4295
Linden B Wendzel • H • IW • 309 Marshall St 50070 PO Box 127 Dexter IA 50070-0127

**DOW CITY—*BETHLEHEM*** (712)674-3323
Vacant • H • IW • 110 Logan St 51528 PO Box 167 Dow City IA 51528-0167

***ST JOHN***
See Buck Grove

**DUBUQUE—*OUR REDEEMER*** (319)588-1247
Kristian G Kincaid • H • EC • IE • 2145 John F Kennedy Rd Dubuque IA 52002-3817 • FAX(319)588-1247

***ST PAUL*** (319)556-7636
Robert W Weinhold • WS 9;* • H • IE • 2025 Jackson St Dubuque IA 52001-3520 • pastorweinhold@juno.com

**EAGLE GROVE—*MOUNT CALVARY*** (515)448-4668
Raymond J Salemink • * • IW • 400 W Broadway St 50533-1704 PO Box 194 Eagle Grove IA 50533-0194

**EARLY—*FAITH*** (712)273-5296
Vacant • H • IW • 202 E Sixth St 50535 PO Box 19 Early IA 50535-0019

**ELDORA—*ST PAUL*** (641)858-3225
David L Splett • WS 930; SS 830; BC 830 • H • EC • IE • 1105 Washington St Eldora IA 50627-1627 • FAX(641)858-2464 • godshous@netins.net

**ELDRIDGE—*PARK VIEW*** (319)285-9035
Robert H Bartel • H • EC • IE • 14 Grove Rd Eldridge IA 52748-9632

**ELMA—*ST PETER*** (515)393-2558
Vacant • H • IE • PO Box 346 Elma IA 50628-0346

**EMMETSBURG—*ST PAUL*** (712)852-2367
Dennis W Angland • * • H • EC • IW • 805 Harrison St Emmetsburg IA 50536-1522 • dwangland@ncn.net

**ESTHERVILLE—*IMMANUEL*** (712)362-3237
Glenn S Bohmer • WS 9; SS 1030; BC 1045;* • H • IW • 409 N 6th St 51334-1653 PO Box 43 Estherville IA 51334-0043

**EVANSDALE—*ST PAUL*** (319)232-7657
James E Moog • WS 10 • IE • 735 Central Ave Evansdale IA 50707-1613

**FAIRBANK—*ST JOHN*** (319)635-2181
Michael K Waples • WS 9; SS 1010 • H • EC • IE • 208 N 4th St 50629-8550 PO Box 465 Fairbank IA 50629-0465 • mkw@Fairbank.net

**FAIRFIELD—*IMMANUEL*** (515)472-5333
Thomas P Phillips • WS 8 1030;* • H • EC • IE • 1601 S Main St Fairfield IA 52556-2090

**FARNHAMVILLE—*HOLY TRINITY*** (515)544-3264
Steven K Benson • H • IW • 805 Garfield Ave 50538 PO Box 125 Farnhamville IA 50538-0125

**FAYETTE—*GRACE*** (319)425-3544
Carl J Richardson • WS 9; SS 10 • H • IE • 201 King St 52142-9729 PO Box 446 Fayette IA 52142-0446

**FENTON—*ST JOHN*** (515)889-2812
David P Schultz • H • EC • IW • 600 Ash 50539 PO Box 169 Fenton IA 50539-0169

**FONDA—*FIRST*** (712)468-2211
Kevin L Schnakenberg • H • IW • 50540 PO Box 280 Pomeroy IA 50575-0280

**FORT DODGE—*GOOD SHEPHERD*** (515)573-3174
Lyle D Hansen • * • H • IW • 1436 21st Ave N Fort Dodge IA 50501 • goodshep@frontiernet.net

***PRINCE PEACE*** (515)573-8618
Paul G Helmer • WS 9; BC 1015;* • H • EC • IW • 1023 S 27th St Fort Dodge IA 50501-6310 • FAX(515)573-8618 • princeofpeace.fortdodge@iowawest.com

***ST PAUL*** (515)955-7285
Allen W Henderson • WS 8 1030; SS 915; BC 915;* • H • EC/EL • IW • 419 S 12th St Fort Dodge IA 50501-4714 • FAX(515)955-2263 • stpaulfd@dodgenet.com

**FORT DODGE 7 NW—*TRINITY*** (515)546-6331
Donald D Mann • * • H • IW • 50501 1446 Johnson Ave Fort Dodge IA 50501-8589

**FORT MADISON—*OUR SAVIOR*** (319)372-7952
Steven C Rasmussen • WS 9; SS 1015; BC 1015 • H • IE • 2121 Avenue A Fort Madison IA 52627-2448

**FREDERICKSBURG—*ST PAUL*** (319)237-5759
Ronnie L Koch • SS 9;* • H • EC • IE • 222 S Washington Ave 50630-1010 PO Box 336 Fredericksburg IA 50630-0336 • paskoch@juno.com

**GALVA—*ST JOHN*** (712)282-4700
Vacant • WS 10; BC 9;* • H • IW • 406 Monona Galva IA 51020

**GARNER—*ST PAUL*** (515)923-2261
Clyde J Kieschnick Robert J Bronson • WS 8 1030; SS 915; BC 915;* • H • EC • IW • 810 State St 860 State St Garner IA 50438-1631 • FAX(515)923-0087 • stpaulia@ncn.net

**GARNER 5 NE—*ST JOHN*** (515)829-4493
Carl R Hedberg • * • IW • 50438 2406 260th St Garner IA 50438-8506

**GARRISON—*ST MARK*** (319)477-5141
Mark T Leckband • WS 8;* • H • IE • 101 N Walnut Ave Garrison IA 52229-9613

**GERMANTOWN—*ST JOHN*** (712)448-2637
Steven J Hayden • * • EC/EL • IW • 5092 480th St Paullina IA 51046-7532 • FAX(712)448-2637 • revhayden@hotmail.com

**GLADBROOK—*CHRIST*** (515)473-2527
Bruce L Zimmermann • IE • PO Box 43 Gladbrook IA 50635-0043

**GLENWOOD—*TRINITY*** (712)527-4667
Charles M Ramsey III • H • IW • 512 2nd St Glenwood IA 51534-1440

**GLIDDEN—*PEACE*** (712)659-3875
Alan J Miller • H • IW • PO Box 448 Glidden IA 51443-0448

**GRAND MOUND—*IMMANUEL*** (319)847-2631
Dennis A Arndt • * • H • IE • 706 Smith St 52751-9510 PO Box 166 Grand Mound IA 52751-0166

**GREENFIELD—*IMMANUEL*** (515)743-2116
Carl M Droegemueller • * • H • EC • IW • 505 NE Dodge St Greenfield IA 50849-1106 • immanuel.greenfield@iowawest.org

**GRINNELL—*IMMANUEL*** (515)236-6691
David T Brandt • H • IE • 229 11th Ave W Grinnell IA 50112-2606

**GUTHRIE CENTER—*IMMANUEL*** (515)747-3918
Dale F Glawatz • WS 9; SS 1015; BC 1015 • H • IW • 713 N 12th St Guthrie Center IA 50115-1514 • dglawatz@netins.net

**GUTTENBERG—*TRINITY*** (319)252-1476
Gregory J Eilers • H • IE • 106 S River Park Dr Guttenberg IA 52052-9298 • tlclcms@netins.net

**HAMPTON—*TRINITY*** (515)456-4816
Wayne P Dobratz • * • H • EC • IE • 16 12th Ave NE Hampton IA 50441-1113 • trinity@rconnect.com

**HARLAN—*PEACE*** (712)755-2970
Vacant • H • IW • 401 12th St 51537-1001 PO Box 467 Harlan IA 51537-0467

**HARRIS—*ST JOHN*** (712)832-3503
Virgil W Ewoldt • WS 845;* • IW • Henry And Proper Sts 51345 PO Box 103 Harris IA 51345-0103

**HARTLEY—*ST PAUL*** (712)728-2711
David E Ericksen • WS 9; SS 1015; BC 1015 • H • IW • 60 N Central Ave 51346-1140 PO Box 88 Hartley IA 51346-0088

**HASTINGS 5 NW—*ST JOHN*** (712)624-8891
Vacant • H • IW • 51540 56042 340th St Hastings IA 51540-4113

**HAWARDEN—*TRINITY*** (712)552-2743
Loren L Vogler • H • IW • 1103 Central Ave 51023-1814 PO Box 311 Hawarden IA 51023-0311 • trinity@acsnet.com

**HIAWATHA—*ZION*** (319)393-2013
Daniel L Krueger • WS 8 1030; SS 915; BC 915;* • H • IE • 201 1st Ave Hiawatha IA 52233-1601 • FAX(319)393-2012

**HINTON 5 E—*TRINITY*** (712)947-4435
David P Kottlowski • WS 930; BC 820;* • H • IW • 56024 29014 Lake Ave Hinton IA 51024-8578

**HOMESTEAD 4 SW—*ST JOHN*** (319)662-4124
Vacant • WS 8;* • H • EC/EL • IE • 56236 1930 V Ave Homestead IA 52236-8521

**HONEY CREEK 8 NE—*ST JOHN*** (712)545-3022
David R Kuhnle • IW • 51542 30907 Coldwater Ave Honey Creek IA 51542-4193 • drkuhnle@juno.com

**HORNICK—*ST JOHN*** (712)876-2686
Thomas A Sabel • IW • 157 Deer Run Trl 51026-8124 PO Box 68 Climbing Hill IA 51015-0068

**HUBBARD—*ST JOHN*** (515)864-2672
Matthew W Rueger • WS 10; SS 9; BC 9 • H • IE • 124 S Iowa St 50122 PO Box 267 Hubbard IA 50122-0267 • FAX(515)864-2672

**HUMBOLDT—*ZION*** (515)332-3279
Jerry K Raether Richard C Merrill • H • EC • IW • 1005 11th Ave N Humboldt IA 50548-1223

**IDA GROVE—*ST PAUL*** (712)364-2918
John E Schauer Michael W Saylor • H • IW • 100 7th St Ida Grove IA 51445-1644 • stpaulig@pionet.net

**INDEPENDENCE—*OUR REDEEMER*** (319)334-2745
Mark B Beesley • WS 1030; BC 930;* • H • IE • 112 3rd Ave NE 50644-1924 PO Box 275 Independence IA 50644-0275

**INDIANOLA—*MOUNT CALVARY*** (515)961-4321
Vacant • WS 8; SS 915; BC 915 • EC • IW • 805 N 1st St Indianola IA 50125-1301

**IOWA CITY—*OUR REDEEMER*** (319)338-5626
Timothy J Zimmermann Jonathan L Offt • WS 8 1030; SS 915; BC 915;* • H • EC • IE • 2301 E Court St Iowa City IA 52245-5217 • FAX(319)338-9171 • redeemer@ourredeemer.org

***ST PAUL CHAPEL & UNI*** (319)337-3652
Wilfred E Eckhardt • IE • 404 E Jefferson St Iowa City IA 52245-2410 • FAX(319)337-4102 • eckhardt@blue.weeg.uiowa.edu

**IOWA FALLS—*IMMANUEL*** (515)648-3805
Kenneth Krueger • H • IE • 313 Lee Ln Iowa Falls IA 50126-1542

**IRETON—*ST PAUL*** (712)278-2324
Warren L Prochnow • WS 9;* • H • IW • 602 Main St 51027-7423 PO Box 66 Ireton IA 51027-0066 • FAX(712)278-2324

**IRETON 4 SE—*ST JOHN*** (712)278-2543
Helmut H Schauland • H • IW • 51027 4755 Fir Ave Ireton IA 51027-7408

**JEFFERSON—*TRINITY*** (515)386-3517
David L Simonson • WS 930;* • H • IW • 801 W Lincolnway St Jefferson IA 50129-1618 • FAX(515)386-5262 • tlcjefia@netins.net

**JESUP—*GRACE*** (319)827-1257
James E Moog • WS 830 • IE • Sixth And Purdy 50648 PO Box 318 Jesup IA 50648-0318

**KEOKUK—*MESSIAH*** (319)524-6396
Vacant • IE • 22nd And Timea 52632 PO Box 63 Keokuk IA 52632-0063

**KEOSAUQUA—*OUR SAVIOUR*** (319)293-3405
Vacant • WS 9;* • H • IE • 1593 Highway 1 N 52565 PO Box 424 Keosauqua IA 52565-0424

**KEYSTONE—*ST JOHN*** (319)442-3514
Bruce J Kaltwasser • H • EC/EL • IE • 201 4th Ave 52249-9512 PO Box 176 Keystone IA 52249-0176

**KINGSLEY—*FIRST*** (712)378-2129
Michael V Gruhn • WS 9; SS 10; BC 1015 • IW • 406 S Main St 51028-5020 PO Box 306 Kingsley IA 51028-0306 • revgruhn@willinet.net

**KIRON—*ST JOHN*** (712)675-4881
Hilmer J Hafner • WS 1030; SS 915; BC 915;* • H • IW • Orchard And Main 51448 PO Box 216 108 Lime St Kiron IA 51448-0216 • FAX(712)675-4881 • revhjh@netins.net

**KNIERIM N1—*TRINITY*** (515)463-2244
John I Trewyn Sr. • WS 10;* • H • IW • 50552 3335 220th St Manson IA 50563-7593 • greenbay43@hotmail.com

**KNOXVILLE—*TRINITY*** (515)842-4724
Leon A Hodges • WS 1030 6;* • H • EC • IE • 814 W Pleasant St Knoxville IA 50138-2740

**LACONA 7 NE—*ST PAUL*** (515)947-4404
Randall D Cormeny • H • IE • 50451 2020 20th Pl Lacona IA 50139-8527

**LAKE CITY—*PILGRIM*** (712)464-3130
Erland Asmus • WS 9;* • H • IW • 720 E Main St Lake City IA 51449-1431 • idwcares@cal-net.net

**LAKE PARK—*CONCORDIA*** (712)832-3503
Virgil W Ewoldt • WS 1030 • IW • 306 E Fourth St 51347 PO Box 597 Lake Park IA 51347-0597

***TRINITY***
See Sioux Valley Twp MN

**LAKE VIEW—*EMMANUEL*** (712)657-3324
Herman W Kramer • H • IW • 115 2nd St 51450 PO Box 260 Lake View IA 51450-0260

**LARCHWOOD—*ENGLISH*** (712)477-2387
George Clausen • IW • 1690 130th St Larchwood IA 51241-7565

**LATIMER—*ST PAUL*** (515)579-6281
Randall D Bell • H • EC/EL • IE • 304 W Main St 50452 PO Box 697 Latimer IA 50452-0697

**LAWTON—*BETHEL*** (712)944-5580
Bruce W Jackson • * • H • IW • 322 Pine St 51030-1033 PO Box 218 Lawton IA 51030-0218 • bethel@netins.net

**LE MARS—*GRACE*** (712)546-5516
Larry C Fett • * • H • IW • 1430 7th Ave SE Le Mars IA 51031-2828 • FAX(712)546-5516

**LEON—*OUR SAVIOR*** (515)446-4138
Vacant • * • H • IW • 709 W 1st St Leon IA 50144-1167

**LIDDERDALE—*IMMANUEL*** (712)822-5512
Raymond H Reinbolt • H • IW • PO Box 100 Lidderdale IA 51452-0100

**LIVERMORE—*IMMANUEL*** (515)379-1287
Ronald E Krause • H • IW • 301 K Road 50558 PO Box 29 Livermore IA 50558-0029

**LOGAN—*IMMANUEL*** (712)644-2384
Jerald E Firby • WS 9; SS 1015; BC 1015 • H • IW • 311 E 6th St Logan IA 51546-1344 • immanuel@pionet.net

***ZION***
See Magnolia

**LONE ROCK—*IMMANUEL*** (515)925-3597
David H Bergquist • WS 9;* • H • IW • 2706 50th Ave Lone Rock IA 50559-8530 • immanual.lonerock@iowawest.org

**LOWDEN—*TRINITY*** (319)941-5853
John R Ranbarger • H • IE • 801 Washington Ave 52255-9539 PO Box 399 Lowden IA 52255-0399

**LU VERNE—*ZION*** (515)882-3555
Vacant • WS 10; SS 845; BC 10 • IW • 1002 Hayes St Lu Verne IA 50560-8701 • baboyce@trvnet.net

**LUZERNE—*ST PAUL*** (319)444-2378
William M Mons • WS 9; BC 10;* • EC/EL • IE • 107 Maple St Luzerne IA 52257-9601 • splcluzerne@juno.com

**MAGNOLIA—*ZION*** (712)644-3153
Werner F Wetzstein(EM) • IW • 51550 216 N 3rd Ave Logan IA 51546-1310

**MALLARD—*TRINITY*** (712)425-3328
Neil E Hayen • WS 10; SS 9;* • H • EC • IW • 810 Inman 50562 PO Box 216 Mallard IA 50562-0216 • nehayen@ncn.net

***ZION***
See Ayrshire

**MANCHESTER—*OUR SAVIOR*** (319)927-4860
David C Weber • * • H • IE • 116 Guetzko Ct Manchester IA 52057-1325 • FAX(319)927-4860 • oursaviorlutheran@juno.com

**MANILLA—*TRINITY*** (712)654-3031
Timothy P Geitz • WS 9; BC 1015;* • H • IW • 641 Third Ave 51454 PO Box 340 Manilla IA 51454-0340 • timgeitz@netins.net

**MANNING—*ZION*** (712)653-2352
Daniel J Vogel • WS 10; SS 845; BC 845;* • H • EC • IW • 1204 Center St Manning IA 51455-1531 • danvogel@pionet.net

**MANSON—*TRINITY***
See Knierim N1

**MAPLETON—*ST MATTHEW*** (712)882-1163
Scott T Fiege • WS 1045; BC 930;* • H • EC • IW • Fifth and Walnut Mapleton IA 51034

**MARCUS—*PEACE*** (712)376-4818
James L Gruber • * • H • IW • 300 E Spruce St 51035 PO Box 428 Marcus IA 51035-0428

**MARCUS 5 SW—*TRINITY*** (712)376-2666
Donald J Meyer • WS 10; SS 11; BC 11 • H • IW • 51035 5289 C Ave Marcus IA 51035-7034 • trinity@nwidt.com

**MARENGO—*ST JOHN*** (319)642-5452
Douglas V Morton • EC • IE • 780 Court Ave Marengo IA 52301-1433 • FAX(319)642-5452 • stjohns2@netins.net

**MARION—*ST PAUL*** (319)377-4687
Thomas E Hedtke • WS 8 1030; SS 915; BC 915 • H • IE • 915 27th St Marion IA 52302-3740 • office@stpaulsmarioniowa.org

**MARSHALLTOWN 9 SE—*TRINITY*** (515)479-2170
Fred L Berry • SS 9; BC 9;* • H • IE • 50158 2702 Dillon Rd Marshalltown IA 50158-9824

**MASON CITY—*BETHLEHEM*** (515)423-0438
Frederick J Wood • WS 8 1015; BC 915;* • H • EC • IE • 419 N Delaware Ave Mason City IA 50401-7009 • FAX(515)423-0459

***MESSIAH*** (515)423-2970
Vacant • H • IE • 2620 4th St SE 50401-4553 PO Box 478 Mason City IA 50401-0478 • FAX(515)829-3612 • korth@netins.net

**MAY CITY—*ST JOHN*** (712)735-4401
Paul E Johnson • WS 9; SS 10;* • IW • 6665 Frederick Ave 51354-7102 PO Box 128 May City IA 51349-0128

**MC GREGOR—*ST PAUL*** (319)873-3341
Gregory J Eilers • IE • 630 Main St 52157 PO Box 368 Mc Gregor IA 52157-0368 • tlclcms@netins.net

**MELCHER - DALLAS—*ST JOHN*** (515)947-6904
Randall D Cormeny • IE • 50062 PO Box 278 Melcher IA 50163-0278

**MILLERSBURG—*TRINITY*** (319)655-7822
Michael J Parris • IE • H Street 52308 PO Box 10 Millersburg IA 52308-0010

**MISSOURI VALLEY—*FIRST*** (712)642-2483
Daniel G Brammeier • WS 930;* • H • EC • IW • 724 N 8th St Missouri Valley IA 51555-1134 • Flutheran@aol.com

**MONTICELLO—*ST JOHN*** (319)465-4842
Vacant • H • EC • IE • 52310 18927 Highway 38 Monticello IA 52310-7764

**MOUNT AYR—*FIRST*** (515)464-2424
Vacant • H • IW • 1111 E Hwy 2 50854 PO Box 387 Mount Ayr IA 50854-0387

**MOUNT PLEASANT—*FAITH*** (319)385-8427
Keith A Haerer • H • EC • IE • 910 Maple Leaf Dr Mount Pleasant IA 52641-1405

**MOUNT VERNON—*ST PAUL*** (319)895-8772
Matthew W Vesey • WS 9;* • H • IE • 600 5th Ave S Mount Vernon IA 52314-1700

**MUSCATINE—*OUR SAVIOR*** (319)263-0347
Brian S Saunders • WS 8; SS 915; BC 915 • H • EC • IE • 2611 Lucas St Muscatine IA 52761-2109 • FAX(319)263-0347

**NEWELL—*ST PETER*** (712)272-3739
Donnie L Poole • WS 1030; SS 915; BC 915 • H • IW • 314 S Clark St 50568 PO Box 393 Newell IA 50568-0393

**NEWHALL—*ST JOHN*** (319)223-5593
Steven W Rempfer • * • H • EC/EL • IE • 310 Second St E 52315 PO Box 390 Newhall IA 52315-0390 • FAX(319)223-5201 • stjohnnewhall@freewwweb.com

**NEWTON—*OUR SAVIOR*** (515)792-1084
Jerry W Doellinger • WS 9;* • H • IE • 1900 N. 4 Ave. E 1900 N 4th Ave E Newton IA 50208-2563 • FAX(515)792-8410 • oursavr@pcpartner.net

**NORWALK—*CHRIST OUR SAVIOR*** (515)981-9145
Brady W Blasdel • WS 815 1045; SS 930;* • H • IW • 515 Sunset Dr PO Box 302 Norwalk IA 50211-0302 • FAX(520)438-6386 • christour@aol.com

**OAKLAND—*ST PAUL*** (712)482-3028
Vacant • WS 830;* • H • IW • 735 North Hwy St Oakland IA 51560-4532

**OCHEYEDAN—*ST PETER*** (712)758-3425
John S Rutowicz • WS 9; SS 10; BC 10 • IW • 1077 Pine St 51354-7526 PO Box 56 Ocheyedan IA 51354-0056 • stpeter-lcms@juno.com

**OCHEYEDAN 3 NW—*ZION*** (712)758-3185
Richard A Jordan • IW • 51354 1303 Tanager Ave Ocheyedan IA 51354-7008

**ODEBOLT—*TRINITY*** (712)668-4528
Albert H Buelow • SS 9; BC 9;* • H • IW • 612 S Dewey St 51458 PO Box 470 Odebolt IA 51458-0470 • ahgbuelow@juno.com

**OELWEIN—*PEACE*** (319)283-5778
Mark B Beesley • WS 8; SS 915;* • H • EC • IE • 1308 E Charles St Oelwein IA 50662-1962

**OGDEN—*ZION*** (515)275-2234
Stephen C Ude • WS 9; BC 1015;* • H • IW • 319 W Elm St 50212-2077 PO Box L Ogden IA 50212-0812 • Revsude@netins.net

**ORANGE CITY—*FAITH*** (712)737-2112
David H Daumer • * • H • IW • 710 8th St SE Orange City IA 51041-7451

**OSAGE—*TRINITY*** (515)732-4771
Christian F Gugel • WS 10; BC 9;* • H • IE • 402 State St Osage IA 50461-1939 • gugel@osage.net

**OSAGE 6 SW—*ST JOHN*** (515)732-4191
Vacant • * • IE • 1921 317th St 50461 PO Box 153 Osage IA 50461-0153 • gugel@osage.net

**OSCEOLA—*IMMANUEL*** (515)342-3121
Jay R Wheeler • H • EC • IW • 101 E View Pl Osceola IA 50213-1300 • ilcmsoi@pionet.net

**OSKALOOSA—*ST JOHN*** (515)673-6546
Stephen S Lane • WS 9; SS 1015; BC 1015 • H • IE • 2370 Merino Ave PO Box 1004 Oskaloosa IA 52577-1004

**OTTUMWA—*TRINITY*** (515)684-7279
Mathew A Andersen • H • EC • IE • 295 Shaul Ave Ottumwa IA 52501-4915

**PANORA 1 N—*ST THOMAS*** (515)755-2051
Dennis M Maaske • WS 1015; SS 9; BC 9 • H • IW • 2106 Hwy 4 50216 PO Box 509 Panora IA 50216-0509

**PAULLINA—*ST JOHN***
See Germantown

***ZION*** (712)448-3910
Karl F Eckhoff • WS 930;* • H • EC/EL • IW • 103 E Bertha 51046 PO Box 509 Paullina IA 51046-0509

**PERRY—*TRINITY*** (515)465-3272
Wayne J Ahrens • H • EC • IW • 2715 Iowa St Perry IA 50220-2414

**PERSIA—*TRINITY*** (712)488-2023
David R Kuhnle • H • IW • PO Box 86 Persia IA 51563-0086

**POLK CITY—*BEAUTIFUL SAVIOR*** (515)984-6146
Mark L Schwalenberg • H • EC • IW • 1701 W Jester Park Dr 50226 PO Box 24 Polk City IA 50226-0024 • bslcpolkc@aol.com

**POMEROY—*FIRST***
See Fonda

***IMMANUEL*** (712)468-2211
Kevin L Schnakenberg • IW • PO Box 280 Pomeroy IA 50575-0280

**QUIMBY—*PILGRIM*** (712)445-2549
Donald J Meyer • WS 8; SS 9; BC 9;* • H • IW • 301 N Main 51049 PO Box 146 Quimby IA 51049-0146 • pilgrim@nwidt.com

**READLYN—*IMMANUEL*** (319)279-3977
Harold H Block • * • EC/EL • IE • 2683 Quail Ave Readlyn IA 50668-9798

***ST PAUL*** (319)279-3961
Maurice D Ellwein • WS 9;* • H • EC/EL • IE • 50668 PO Box 57 120 W 4th St Readlyn IA 50668-0057 • FAX(319)279-3039 • readrev@netins.net

**RED OAK—*OUR SAVIOR*** (712)623-4600
Jerome Wagoner • H • IW • 2300 N 8th St 51566-1149 600 Hillcrest Dr Red Oak IA 51566

**REINBECK—*ST JOHN*** (319)345-2766
Bruce A Boyce • H • HS • IE • 207 Randall St Reinbeck IA 50669-1250 • FAX(319)345-2766

**REMSEN—*CHRIST*** (712)786-2225
Robert L Eggers • WS 9; SS 1015; BC 1030 • H • IW • 503 S Washington St 51050 PO Box 570 Remsen IA 51050-0570 • FAX(712)786-2227

**RICEVILLE—*ST PETER*** (515)985-2421
Vacant • H • IE • 105 W 6th St 50466-7536 PO Box 255 Riceville IA 50466-0255

**RICKETTS—*ST LUKE*** (712)679-2701
Eugene W Ernst • * • IW • PO Box 60 Ricketts IA 51460-0060

**ROCK RAPIDS—*PEACE*** (712)472-3226
George Clausen • H • IW • 902 S Carroll St Rock Rapids IA 51246-1945

**ROCKWELL CITY 5 E—*IMMANUEL*** (712)297-7708
John R Lohman • WS 9; BC 1015;* • IW • 50579 3010 270th St Rockwell City IA 50579-7513

**ROWAN 5E—*IMMANUEL*** (515)532-2729
Raymond J Salemink • BC 230;* • H • IW • Joint Highway 69 And 3 50470 PO Box 157 Rowan IA 50470-0157

**ROYAL—*TRINITY*** (712)933-2641
Theodore A Letzring(EM) • * • IW • 504 Church St 51357 PO Box 139 Royal IA 51357-0139 • catle@rconnect.com

**SAC CITY—*ST PAUL*** (712)662-7029
Mark D Selby • Kelly L Helm DCE • H • EC • IW • 1112 Baily St Sac City IA 50583-2003 • sacluth@pionet.net

**SAC CITY 9 SE—*ST PETER*** (712)662-7392
Vacant • IW • 50583 3541 300th St Sac City IA 50583-7536 • FAX(712)688-2810

**SANBORN—*ST JOHN*** (712)729-3800
Kenneth R Funke • WS 9; SS 1015; BC 1015 • H • IW • 305 Angie St 51248-1036 PO Box 250 Sanborn IA 51248-0250 • stjohns@mtcnet.net

**SCHALLER—*ST PAUL*** (712)275-4299
David E Hagen • * • H • IW • 402 E Third 51053 PO Box 368 Schaller IA 51053-0368

**SCHLESWIG—*IMMANUEL*** (712)676-2235
Merle F Mahnken Lee R Mentink(EM) • WS 8 1030; SS 915; BC 915 • H • EC • IW • 501 Glad St 51461 PO Box 27 Schleswig IA 51461-0027

**SERGEANT BLUFF—*SHEPHERD*** (712)943-4502
Michael C Wolfram • SS 915; BC 915;* • H • IW • 203 Port Neal Rd 51054 PO Box 36 Sergeant Bluff IA 51054-0036 • FAX(712)943-4506 • mcwolfram@aol.com

**SHELL ROCK—*PEACE*** (319)885-4440
Vacant • WS 915; SS 1015; BC 1015 • H • IE • 121 E Washington St Shell Rock IA 50670-0625 • dgahl@forbin.com

**SHELLSBURG—*ZION*** (319)436-2524
Mark T Leckband • IE • 209 Grand Ave Sw 52332 PO Box 268 Shellsburg IA 52332-0268

**SHENANDOAH—*TRINITY*** (712)246-1131
Steven W Teske • WS 1030;* • H • IW • 713 Church St Shenandoah IA 51601-1916

**SHERRILL—*ST MATTHEW***
Vacant • H • IE • 5350 Sherrill Rd Sherrill IA 52073-9610

**SIDNEY—*OUR SAVIOR*** (712)246-1131
Steven W Teske • WS 9;* • H • IW • 1000 Illinois 51652 PO Box 242 Sidney IA 51652-0242

**SIGOURNEY—*HOPE*** (515)622-3777
Vacant • H • IE • 315 Kelley St 52591-1159 PO Box 246 Sigourney IA 52591-0246

**SIOUX CITY—*BETHANY*** (712)255-4900
Arnold E Vehling(EM) • H • IW • 1201 Dubuque St Sioux City IA 51105-2658

***CALVARY*** (712)239-1575
Glen R Rachuy • Cindy L Storm DCE • H • IW • 4410 Central St Sioux City IA 51108

***CONCORDIA*** (712)252-2938
Donald O Schlesselman • WS 9; SS 1030; BC 1030 • H • IW • 2000 Military Rd Sioux City IA 51103-1702

***FAITH*** (712)258-4820
David W Fechner Paul C Mueller(EM) • WS 915;* • H • IW • 3101 Hamilton Blvd Sioux City IA 51104-2409 • FAX(712)279-0118

***REDEEMER*** (712)276-1125
Russell C Senstad • Lori R Potratz DCE • WS 745 915 1045; SS 915; BC 915;* • H • EC • IW • 3204 S Lakeport St Sioux City IA 51106-4599 • FAX(712)276-1146 • redeemer³church@yahoo.com

***ST PAUL*** (712)252-0338
Leo E Kostizen George P Zehnder • WS 815 1045; SS 930; BC 930;* • H • EC/EL • IW • 612 Jennings St Sioux City IA 51101-1918 • FAX(712)252-1141

**SIOUX RAPIDS—*FAITH*** (712)283-2212
Vacant • WS 8 • H • IW • 415 East Thomas 50585 PO Box 304 Sioux Rapids IA 50585-0304

**SOLON—*KING OF GLORY***
See Swisher 1 E

**SPENCER—*CHRIST KING*** (712)262-2244
David M Schoenknecht • WS 9; SS 1030; BC 1030;* • H • IW • 500 4th Ave SW Spencer IA 51301-6206 • schoenk@nwiowa.com

***FIRST ENGLISH*** (712)262-5598
Paul E Kaldahl • WS 8 1045; SS 930; BC 930 • H • EC • IW • 23 E 10th St Spencer IA 51301-4317 • FAX(712)262-8396 • felc@nwiowa.com

**SPIRIT LAKE—*IMMANUEL*** (712)336-1010
Phill E Andreasen Mark J Haller • * • H • IW • 2300 27th St 51360 PO Box 422 Spirit Lake IA 51360-0422 • FAX(712)336-5734 • imluthsl@rconnect.com

**SPRING FOUNTAIN—*ST JOHN***
See Sumner

**ST ANSGAR—*IMMANUEL*** (515)736-4782
Edward H Schmidt • WS 930;* • H • IE • 308 E 5th St 50472-9504 PO Box 429 St Ansgar IA 50472-0429 • ilsta@smig.net

**STANWOOD—*ST PAUL*** (319)942-3924
William R Riley • WS 10 • IE • Us 30 And Hwy 38 52337 PO Box 236 Stanwood IA 52337-0236

**STATE CENTER—*TRINITY*** (515)483-2682
Michael L Maddick • H • IE • 206 1st Ave N 50247-1010 PO Box 638 State Center IA 50247-0638

**STORM LAKE—*GRACE*** (712)732-5005
Steven M Schulz • WS 9; SS 1015; BC 1015 • H • EC • IW • 1407 W 5th St Storm Lake IA 50588-3007 • FAX(712)732-3791 • grace.stormlake@iowawest.org

***ST JOHN*** (712)732-2400
Douglas W Haynes • H • EC • IW • 402 Lake Ave Storm Lake IA 50588-2445 • FAX(712)732-2401 • stjohnsl@ncn.net

**STORM LAKE 12 NE—*ZION*** (712)732-5223
Thomas J Egger • WS 10; SS 845; BC 845 • H • IW • 50588 1725 555th St Storm Lake IA 50588-7763 • FAX(712)732-5323 • revkenschaeffer@juno.com

**SUMNER—*ST JOHN*** (319)578-3315
George A Volkert • WS 830; SS 930 • IE • 1490 Tahoe Ave 50674-9596 PO Box 163 Sumner IA 50674-0163

***ST PAUL*** (319)578-3315
George A Volkert • WS 10; SS 9; BC 9 • H • IE • 612 W 3rd St 50674-1324 PO Box 163 Sumner IA 50674-0163

**SUTHERLAND—*BETHEL*** (712)446-3630
Leroy E Riemer • * • H • IW • 502 Ash St 51058-7621 PO Box A Sutherland IA 51058-0901

**SWEA CITY—*OUR SAVIOR*** (515)272-4713
Donald H Winterrowd • H • EC • IW • 710 5th St N Swea City IA 50590-1025

**SWISHER 1 E—*KING OF GLORY*** (319)857-4241
Vacant • WS 830 • H • IE • 52338 2720 120th St NE Swisher IA 52338-9578 • FAX(319)857-4241

**TERRIL—*IMMANUEL*** (712)853-6162
Ralph C Shorey III • WS 9;* • IW • 206 Terril Ave 51364 PO Box 98 Terril IA 51364-0098 • revrcs3@ncn.net

**URBANDALE—*GLORIA DEI*** (515)276-1700
Daniel P Parsch Ronald D Burcham • WS 8 930 11; SS 930 • H • IW • 8301 Aurora Ave Urbandale IA 50322-2301 • FAX(515)276-5939

**UTE—*ST PAUL*** (712)885-2221
Edgar W Bode • WS 10;* • IW • 303 E 4th St 51060 PO Box 139 Ute IA 51060-0139

**VAN HORNE—*ST ANDREW*** (319)228-8325
Vacant • H • IE • 307 Third Ave 52346 PO Box 294 Van Horne IA 52346-0294

**VAN METER 4 S—*TRINITY*** (515)996-2093
Steven A Barker • WS 9; SS 1015; BC 1015 • IW • 50261 1193 Prairieview Ave Van Meter IA 50261-8575

**VENTURA—*REDEEMER*** (515)829-3615
Daird W Korth • WS 930; SS 1045; BC 1045 • H • EC • IE • 301 S Main St 50482 PO Box 138 Ventura IA 50482-0138 • FAX(515)829-3612 • korth@netins.net

**VICTOR—*ST JAMES*** (319)647-3375
Alan S Hafner • H • IE • 502 Washington St Victor IA 52347 • stjames@netins.net

**VICTOR 10 SE—*ST JOHN*** (319)685-4400
David E Mac Kain • IE • 52347 2654 Ave CC Victor IA 52347-8534

**VILLISCA—*MOUNT CALVARY*** (712)826-7202
Jerome Wagoner • IW • 107 S 5th Ave 50864-1130 PO Box 204 Villisca IA 50864-0204

**VINCENT 5 SW—*ST JOHN*** (515)356-4406
Carl W Van Nostrand • WS 830;* • IW • 50594 2980 170th St Vincent IA 50594-7533 • cwvn@netins.net

**VINTON—*TRINITY*** (319)472-5571
Clarke E Frederick • WS 9;* • H • EC • IE • 1002 E 13th St Vinton IA 52349-2385 • FAX(319)472-5571

**WALL LAKE—*PEACE*** (712)664-2961
Roger P Carlisle • H • IW • 406 Stuart St 51466-7016 PO Box 189 Wall Lake IA 51466-0189 • peacecar@netins.net

**WALNUT—*OUR SAVIOR*** (712)784-3644
Vacant • H • IW • 903 Antique City Dr 51577-3029 PO Box 344 Walnut IA 51577-0344

**WAPELLO—*ST PAUL*** (319)523-6951
Chris N Hinkle • WS 930;* • H • IE • 226 Washington St Wapello IA 52653-1527 • FAX(888)392-4832 • stpaulwapello@email.com

**WATERLOO—*CHRIST*** (319)233-1278
John C Drosendahl • H • HS • IE • 234 S Hackett Rd Waterloo IA 50701-1660

***CONCORDIA*** (319)233-4025
Robert W Olson • WS 915; SS 1030; BC 1030 • H • IE • 1005 W Parker St Waterloo IA 50703-2121

***FAITH*** (319)236-1771
Thomas C Wegener • H • IE • 1555 W Ridgeway Ave Waterloo IA 50701-4434 • FAX(319)236-1771

***GRACE*** (319)235-6705
Randolph W Mc Hone John M Moore • WS 8; SS 915; BC 915 • H • HS • IE • 1024 W 8th St Waterloo IA 50702-2208 • FAX(319)235-6735

***IMMANUEL*** (319)233-7052
Gerald C Kapanka • WS 8 1030; SS 915; BC 930;* • H • EC/EL/HS • IE • 207 Franklin St Waterloo IA 50703-3515 • FAX(319)232-6184 • immanulluth@home.com

**WAVERLY—*ST JOHN*** (319)352-2314
Larry R Sipe Jr. • WS 8 1030; SS 915 • H • HS • IE • 415 4th St SW Waverly IA 50677-3126 • FAX(319)352-2242 • pasarp@forbin.com

**WAVERLY 10 NE—*ST PAUL*** (319)352-5394
Keith Brustuen • WS 9; SS 1015;* • IE • 50677 2022 Larrabee Ave Waverly IA 50677-9517 • kskbrul8@hotmail.com

**WEBSTER CITY—*ST PAUL*** (515)832-3043
Travis J Schmidt • WS 10 3; SS 845; BC 845;* • H • EC • IW • 1005 Beach St Webster City IA 50595-1951 • FAX(515)832-3069 • stpaulwc@ncn.net

**WELLMAN—*GOOD SHEPHERD*** (319)646-2702
Vacant • IE • Fifth St And Fourth Ave 52356 PO Box 116 Wellman IA 52356-0116

**WELLSBURG—*ST JOHN*** (515)869-3838
Bruce L Zimmermann • IE • 806 S Washington 50680 PO Box Q Wellsburg IA 50680-0564

**WEST BEND—*PEACE*** (515)887-3261
Edward E Brandt • WS 10;* • H • IW • Hwy 15 S 50597 PO Box 100 West Bend IA 50597-0100 • FAX(515)887-2400 • brandt@ncn.net

**WEST DES MOINES—*SHEP/VALLEY***
Second Location See Clive

***SHEP/VALLEY*** (515)225-1623
John R Koczman Mark E Krause Arno H Melz(EM) • H • EC • IW • 3900 Ashworth Rd West Des Moines IA 50265-3048 • FAX(515)225-0871 • bgarrison@dwx.com

**WEST UNION—*GOOD SHEPHERD*** (319)422-3393
Victor P Young • WS 830; SS 945; BC 945 • H • EC • IE • 311 Hwy 150 S West Union IA 52175-1506 • vpyoung@trxinc.com

**WESTGATE—*ST PETER*** (319)578-8664
Vacant • EC • IE • Main And Church Sts 50681 PO Box 220 Westgate IA 50681-0220

**WHITTEMORE—*ST PAUL*** (515)884-2629
Michael D Botsford • H • IW • 513 Clay St 50598-5003 PO Box 248 Whittemore IA 50598-0248 • spwhitt@ncn.net

**WILLIAMSBURG—*ST PAUL*** (319)668-1266
Carl D Cloeter • WS 845; SS 10; BC 10;* • H • EC/EL • IE • 500 Clark St 52361-9602 PO Box 42 Williamsburg IA 52361-0042 • FAX(319)668-9436

**WILLIAMSBURG 6 NE—*IMMANUEL*** (319)668-2372
Richard A Meyer • H • EC/EL • IE • 52361 2920 225th St Williamsburg IA 52361-9536

**WILTON—*ZION*** (319)732-3651
Wayne P Fredericksen • WS 8 1030; SS 915; BC 915 • H • EC/EL • IE • 1000 Maurer St Wilton IA 52778-0404 • FAX(319)732-2106

**WIOTA 6 SE—*FIRST*** (712)774-5787
Theodore F Weishaupt • H • IW • 50274 70139 Memphis Wiota IA 50274-9722

**WOOLSTOCK—*ST PETER*** (515)839-5506
Carl W Van Nostrand • IW • Neville St 50599 PO Box 131 Woolstock IA 50599-0131 • cwcn@netins.net

## KANSAS

**ABILENE—*FAITH*** (785)263-1842
Timothy P Kersten • * • H • KS • 1600 N Buckeye Ave Abilene KS 67410-1540 • FAX(785)263-1842 • faithlut@ikansas.com

**ALICEVILLE—*ST JOHN*** (785)489-2534
Vacant • WS 9; SS 1015 • H • KS • UKNWN 114 2nd St Westphalia KS 66093-7108

**ALMA—*ST JOHN*** (785)765-3632
Vacant • WS 930 7; SS 830; BC 830 • H • EL • KS • 218 W Second St PO Box 365 Alma KS 66401-0365 • FAX(785)765-7777 • r.w.grimm@juno.com

**ALTA VISTA—*ST PAUL*** (785)499-6623
Larry D Brakenhoff • KS • 303 Main St 66834 PO Box 235 Alta Vista KS 66834-0235 • brakenhoff@cgtelco.net

**ANDOVER—*PEACE*** (316)733-2633
Vacant • H • KS • 410 Grace Ave 67002-9567 PO Box 492 Andover KS 67002-0492 • FAX(316)733-2633 • peaceevluth@juno.com

**ARGONIA—*ZION*** (316)435-6524
Daryl S Bahn • H • KS • Main And Cherry Sts 67004 PO Box 205 Argonia KS 67004-0205

**ARKANSAS CITY—*REDEEMER*** (316)442-5240
Mark D Boxman • WS 8 1030; SS 915 • H • KS • 320 W Central Ave Arkansas City KS 67005-2637 • rlcarkcity@kcisp.net

**ATCHISON—*TRINITY*** (913)367-2837
Robert M Ziegler • Esther M Barg DCE • WS 8 1030 630; SS 915; BC 915 • H • EC/EL • KS • 603 N 8th St Atchison KS 66002-1721 • FAX(913)367-4763 • trinitychurch@journey.com

**ATWOOD—*REDEEMER*** (785)626-3178
Vacant • WS 830;* • H • EC • KS • 808 S 1st St Atwood KS 67730-2108 • redluth@juno.com

**AUGUSTA—*CHRIST*** (316)775-7301
John A Einem Robert L Sweet • * • H • KS • 1500 Cron St Augusta KS 67010-1925 • FAX(316)775-7301 • christaugusta@networksplus.net

**BARNES 9 S—*ST PETER*** (785)763-4582
John P Drush • * • H • KS • 2647 3rd Rd Barnes KS 66933 • jpdrush@jbntelco.com

**BASEHOR—*ST MARTIN*** (913)724-2900
Arlin A Holtz • WS 10; SS 9;* • H • KS • 14308 Fairmount Rd Basehor KS 66007-5226

**BAZINE—*ST LUKE*** (785)398-2360
Vacant • * • H • KS • 102 W Washington St 67516-9622 PO Box 277 Bazine KS 67516-0277

**BONNER SPRINGS—*EMMAUS*** (913)441-3243
Gaylen A Burow • WS 9; SS 1015; BC 1015 • H • KS • 66012 12900 Kansas Ave Bonner Springs KS 66012-9203 • geeel@juno.com

**BREMEN 4 NE—*IMMANUEL*** (785)337-2472
Edward O Grimenstein • * • H • EC/EL • KS • 66412 570 3rd Rd Bremen KS 66412-8625 • grims@kansas.net

**BREMEN 8 NE—*BETHLEHEM*** (785)337-2472
Edward O Grimenstein • * • H • EC/EL • KS • 66412 564 3rd Rd Bremen KS 66412-9708 • grims@kansas.net

**BURLINGTON—*TRINITY*** (316)364-2283
Vacant • H • EC • KS • 902 Kennedy St Burlington KS 66839-1130

**CANEY—*TRINITY*** (316)879-5604
Vacant • H • KS • 108 N Bradley Ave Caney KS 67333-2441

**CANTON 7S 1W—*IMMANUEL*** (316)628-4801
Michael D Sharp • KS • 67428 703 26th Ave Canton KS 67428-8860

**CHANUTE—*ZION*** (316)431-1341
Scott A Lemmermann • * • H • EC • KS • 1202 W Main St Chanute KS 66720-1414 • zion@apexcorp.com

**CHENEY—*ST PAUL*** (316)542-0115
Kenneth M Kaufmann • WS 8 1030; SS 915; BC 915 • H • EC/EL • KS • 639 Lincoln St PO Box 397 Cheney KS 67025-0397 • stpauls@southwind.net

**CLAFLIN—*ZION*** (316)587-3698
Vacant • WS 1030; SS 915; BC 915 • H • KS • 121 Fifth St 67525 PO Box 415 Claflin KS 67525-0415

**CLAY CENTER—*ST PAUL*** (785)632-5301
Richard W Bruenger • Jeremy J Pera DCE • WS 815 1030; SS 930; BC 930 • H • KS • 816 9th St Clay Center KS 67432-2603 • spluther@kansas.net

**COFFEYVILLE—*ST PAUL*** (316)251-2927
Richard E Peckman • Carla J Brakhage DCE • WS 10; SS 845; BC 845 • H • EC • KS • 506 W 9th St 67337-5002 PO Box 263 Coffeyville KS 67337-0263 • FAX(316)251-3276 • stpaul@terraworld.net

**COLBY—*TRINITY*** (785)462-3497
Vacant • WS 1030; SS 915; BC 915;* • H • KS • 855 E 5th St Colby KS 67701-2623

**COUNCIL GROVE—*CALVARY*** (316)767-6772
Vacant • H • KS • 715 E Main St Council Grove KS 66846-1142 • bahnclone2@aol.com

**DEERFIELD—*IMMANUEL***
See Lakin

**DERBY—*FAITH*** (316)788-1715
Richard A Boyer • WS 815 1045; SS 930 • H • EC • KS • 214 S Derby Ave Derby KS 67037-1443 • faithderby@aol.com

**DIGHTON—*CHRIST KING*** (316)397-2179
Vacant • H • KS • 210 N Central Dighton KS 67839

**DODGE CITY—*HOLY CROSS*** (316)227-6204
Randall L Jahnke • H • KS • 2200 3rd Ave Dodge City KS 67801-2535 • hclc@midusa.net

**DOWNS—*ZION*** (913)454-3733
Timothy P Wangerin • WS 830; SS 930; BC 930 • H • KS • 1019 Blunt St Downs KS 67437-1511 • zlcdowns@nckcn.com

**DULUTH 5 NW OF ONAG—*ST PAUL*** (785)889-4486
Joseph W Davis Jr. • H • KS • 21185 Duluth Rd Duluth KS 66521

**EASTON 5 N—*ST JOHN*** (913)773-8591
Arnold G Twenhafel • H • KS • 66020 34771 243rd St Easton KS 66020-8039

**EL DORADO—*GRACE*** (316)321-2423
Vacant • WS 1030; SS 9; BC 9;* • H • KS • 1124 W Central Ave 67042-2122 PO Box 389 El Dorado KS 67042-0389

**ELKHART—*CHRIST*** (316)697-2284
James A Lucas • WS 11;* • H • KS • 813 S Baca 67950 PO Box 39 Elkhart KS 67950-0039 • FAX(316)697-2284 • jimlucas@elkhart.com

**ELLINWOOD—*ST JOHN*** (316)564-2044
James A Keltner • WS 8 1045 7; SS 9; BC 930 • H • EC • KS • 510 N Wilhelm Ellinwood KS 67526 • FAX(316)564-3024 • andykeltner@ellinwood.com

**ELLSWORTH—*IMMANUEL*** (913)472-4045
Vacant • WS 10; BC 9 • H • KS • 905 Stanberry St 67439-2231 PO Box 133 Ellsworth KS 67439-0133

**ELLSWORTH 7 NW—*ST PAUL*** (785)472-3712
Vacant • KS • 67439 449 13th Rd Ellsworth KS 67439-8638

**EMPORIA—*FAITH*** (316)342-3590
Clarence L Marquardt • WS 945; SS 830; BC 830;* • H • EC • KS • 1348 Trailridge Rd Emporia KS 66801-6142 • FAX(316)342-2414 • faithlu@valu-line.net

***MESSIAH*** (316)342-8181
Norbert D Tegtmeier • Elaine Whiteneck DCE Laura S Ulicky-Weerts DCE • WS 830 11; SS 945;* • H • KS • 1101 Neosho St Emporia KS 66801-2747

**ERIE—*GOOD SHEPHERD*** (316)244-5555
Vacant • H • KS • 603 N Mildfelt St Erie KS 66733-9570

**FAIRVIEW—*IMMANUEL***
Vacant • WS 8; SS 9; BC 9 • KS • 66425 C/O Rev L Boye 613 S 1st St Hiawatha KS 66434-2701

***ST PAUL*** (785)467-8810
Trenton D Christensen • WS 9; SS 10; BC 10 • EC • KS • 110 E Maple St 66425-9509 PO Box 158 Fairview KS 66425-0158

**FORT SCOTT—*TRINITY*** (316)223-3596
Larry H Block • WS 930; SS 1045; BC 1045 • H • EC • KS • 2824 S Horton Fort Scott KS 66701 • tlc@terraworld.net

**GARDEN CITY—*LA SANTA CRUZ*** (316)276-6212
Vacant • H • KS • 2009 N Main St Garden City KS 67846-3066

***TRINITY*** (316)276-3110
Lyle R Stuehrenberg • Cynthia J Lavrenz DCE Leland P Jackson DCE • WS 8 1030; SS 915; BC 915 • H • EC • KS • 1010 Fleming St Garden City KS 67846-6225 • FAX(316)276-3169 • tlcqck@odsgc.net

**GARDNER—*KING OF KINGS*** (913)856-2500
Craig R Boehlke • WS 8 1030; SS 915; BC 915 • H • EC • KS • 306 E Madison St PO Box 364 Gardner KS 66030-0364 • FAX(913)856-2500 • LutheranChurch@KingMail.net

**GARNETT—*TRINITY*** (785)448-6930
Vacant • H • KS • Third and Vine Sts Garnett KS 66032

**GIRARD—*TRINITY*** (316)724-8895
Mark E Wenzelburger • WS 1030; SS 915; BC 915 • H • KS • 109 W Saint John St Girard KS 66743-1226

**GREAT BEND—*OUR SAVIOUR*** (316)792-6901
Vacant • H • KS • 5860 Eisenhower Ave Great Bend KS 67530-3145

**GREENLEAF 3 SW—*BETHLEHEM*** (785)747-2407
David P Ersland • H • KS • 66943 2054 10th Rd Greenleaf KS 66943-9440

**GREENSBURG—*PEACE*** (316)723-2300
Lon E Landsmann • WS 11; SS 10;* • H • KS • Walnut And Iowa Sts 67054 321 S Walnut St Greensburg KS 67054-1746

**HANOVER 7 NE—*TRINITY*** (785)337-2665
Rodney D Fritz • * • H • KS • 66945 2942 27th Rd Hanover KS 66945-8885 • FAX(785)337-2675

**HAVEN 1 W—*ST PAUL*** (316)465-3427
Donald E Adolf • H • EC/EL • KS • 67543 8513 E Arlington Rd Haven KS 67543-8015

**HAYS—*MESSIAH*** (785)625-2057
Kenton G Rohrberg • KS • 20th And Main 67601 2000 Main St Hays KS 67601-2938 • mlc@dailynews.net

**HEPLER 6 SE—*IMMANUEL*** (316)395-2692
John J Stubenrouch Jr. • WS 1030; SS 9; BC 9;* • H • KS • 66746 673 W 680th Ave Hepler KS 66746-2119 • jstubenrouch@ckt.net

**HERINGTON—*OUR REDEEMER*** (785)258-3122
K C Dehning • WS 1030; SS 9; BC 9 • H • EC • KS • 802 E Trapp St Herington KS 67449-2850 • FAX(785)258-2528 • orlclcms@ikansas.com

***ZION***
See Latimer

**HERINGTON 4 NW—*ST JOHN*** (785)366-7386
Allen J Woelzlein • * • H • KS • 67449 2126 Highway 4 Herington KS 67449-8705

**HERINGTON 7 NW—*IMMANUEL*** (785)258-3003
Vacant • KS • 67449 2201 1000 Ave Herington KS 67449-8609

**HIAWATHA—*IMMANUEL***
See Fairview

***ZION*** (785)742-3995
Lawrence C Boye • WS 1030; SS 915; BC 915 • H • KS • 613 S 1st St Hiawatha KS 66434-2701

**HILL CITY—*GRACE*** (785)421-2481
Vacant • H • KS • 11th And Hill St 67642 PO Box 40 Hill City KS 67642-0040

**HILLSBORO—*ZION*** (316)947-3522
John A Ryding • WS 1030; SS 915; BC 915 • H • KS • 106 N Lincoln St Hillsboro KS 67063-1610 • zionluth@southwind.net

**HOISINGTON—*CONCORDIA*** (316)653-4644
Garry R Dassow • * • KS • 460 W 9th 67544 PO Box 86 Hoisington KS 67544-0086

**HOLTON—*TRINITY*** (785)364-2206
John J Deister • H • KS • 401 Cheyenne Holton KS 66436

**HOLYROOD—*ST PETER*** (913)252-3275
John W Sharp • H • KS • 209 N County Rd 67450-9603 PO Box 46 Holyrood KS 67450-0046

**HOXIE—*IMMANUEL*** (785)675-3608
Vacant • WS 830;* • H • KS • 1400 Locust 67740 PO Box 672 Hoxie KS 67740-0672

***IMMANUEL*** (785)675-3608
Vacant • WS 830;* • H • KS • 1400 Locust 67740 PO Box 672 Hoxie KS 67740-0672

**HUGOTON—*FAITH*** (316)544-2092
James A Lucas • WS 9;* • H • KS • 500 E 10th St Hugoton KS 67951-2816 • FAX(316)697-2284 • jimlucas@elkhart.com

**HUMBOLDT—*ST PETER*** (316)473-2343
David E Meier • WS 1030 815; SS 930; BC 930 • H • KS • 910 Amos St Humboldt KS 66748-1258 • FAX(316)473-3235 • dmeier@humboldtks.com

**HUNTER—*TRINITY*** (785)529-2715
Vacant • WS 845; SS 945 • H • KS • PO Box 128 Hunter KS 67452-0128

**HUTCHINSON—*CHRIST*** (316)665-8513
Michael C Brockman • WS 1015; SS 9; BC 9 • H • KS • 3600 N Monroe St Hutchinson KS 67502-2263

***OUR REDEEMER*** (316)662-5642
Thomas B Mendenhall • Henry A Blickhahn DCE • WS 830 11; SS 945; BC 945 • H • KS • 407 E 12th Ave Hutchinson KS 67501-5823 • FAX(316)662-4074

**INDEPENDENCE—*ZION*** (316)332-3300
Ronnie L Oldenettel • WS 1030; SS 915; BC 915;* • H • EC/EL • KS • 219 S 10th St 67301-3617 303 S 10th St Independence KS 67301 • FAX316)332-3302 • roldenettel@terraworld.net

**IOLA—*GRACE*** (316)365-6468
Bruce R Kristalyn • WS 1030; SS 9; BC 9 • H • EC • KS • 401 S Walnut St Iola KS 66749-3248 • gracelutheran@aceks.com

**JETMORE—*ST PAUL***
Vacant • * • KS • S Bowles St 67854 PO Box 97 Jetmore KS 67854-0097

**JUNCTION CITY—*IMMANUEL*** (913)238-6007
Vacant • WS 830; SS 945; BC 945 • H • KS • 630 S Eisenhower Dr Junction City KS 66441-3321

**JUNCTION CITY 6 SE—*ST PAUL*** (785)238-7619
Marvin L Barz • WS 10; BC 9 • H • KS • 66441 5805 Clarks Creek Rd Junction City KS 66441-8214

**KANSAS CITY—*BETHEL*** (913)299-6478
Raymond L Schiefelbein • WS 10; SS 9; BC 9;* • H • HS • KS • 2801 N 83rd St Kansas City KS 66109-1423 • FAX(913)299-1507 • bethel³lcms³kcks@yahoo.com

***FAITH*** (913)321-1326
Vacant • H • KS • 530 Quindaro Blvd Kansas City KS 66101-1458

***GRACE*** (913)281-1621
Vacant • * • H • EC/EL/HS • KS • 3333 Wood Ave Kansas City KS 66102-2137 • FAX(913)281-9243 • gracekck@aol.com

***IMMANUEL*** (913)831-4542
Vacant • H • EC • KS • 3232 Metropolitan Ave Kansas City KS 66106-2802

***OUR SAVIOUR*** (913)236-6228
Frank Eberhart • Heidi Werner DCE • H • EC/HS • KS • 4153 Rainbow Blvd Kansas City KS 66103-3110 • FAX(913)236-8522

***ST LUKE*** (913)281-3102
Michael N May • H • HS • KS • 722 Reynolds Ave Kansas City KS 66101-3421 • FAX(913)281-3558 • sllckc@msn.com

**KENSINGTON—*FIRST ST JOHN*** (785)476-2246
David L Hutson • WS 1030; SS 930; BC 930 • H • EC • KS • 332 N Adams Ave 66951-9751 PO Box 57 Kensington KS 66951-0057 • FAX(785)476-2283 • 1stjohn@ruraltel.net

**KINSLEY—*OUR REDEEMER*** (316)659-2262
David H Parks • WS 9; SS 10; BC 10 • KS • 201 Massachusetts Ave Kinsley KS 67547-1050

**LAKIN—*IMMANUEL*** (316)355-7161
Robert R Roberts • H • KS • 1304 Mattie 67860 PO Box 46 Lakin KS 67860-0046 • rroberts@pld.com

**LARNED—*GRACE*** (316)285-2013
Vacant • WS 1030; SS 930 • H • KS • 524 Carroll Ave Larned KS 67550-2923

**LATIMER—*ZION*** (785)466-2290
Vacant • KS • 106 Main St 67449-4036 2201 1000 Ave Herington KS 67449-8609

**LAWRENCE—*IMMANUEL-UNIV*** (785)843-0620
Donald L Miller Alan C Estby • WS 830 11; SS 945; BC 945 • H • EC • KS • 2104 W 15th St Lawrence KS 66049-2722 • FAX(785)843-1576 • immanluthch@juno.com

***REDEEMER*** (785)843-8181
Jay W Watson • H • KS • 2700 Lawrence Ave Lawrence KS 66047-3016 • rlc@lawrence.ixks.com

**LEAVENWORTH—*ST PAUL*** (913)682-0387
Van Edward Mease • WS 8 1030; SS 915; BC 915 • H • EC/EL • KS • 301 N 7th St 66048-1932 311 N 7th St Leavenworth KS 66048-1994 • FAX(913)682-1139 • stpaulchurch@grapevine.net

***TRINITY*** (913)682-7474
Kevin A Wilson David S Hall • WS 930 8 1045 11; SS 1030 930; BC 1030 930;* • H • EC • KS • 2101 10th Ave Leavenworth KS 66048-4210 • FAX(913)682-7767 • kcgilly@hotmail.com

**LEAWOOD—*LORD OF LIFE*** (913)681-5167
Thomas P Krause • David W Saving DCE • WS 8 1030; SS 930; BC 930 • H • EC • KS • 3105 W 135th St Leawood KS 66224-9540 • FAX(913)681-9143 • diane.s@leawoodlordoflife.com

**LIBERAL—*GRACE*** (316)624-5900
Andrew A Wehling • H • KS • 1200 W 11th St 67901-2309 PO Box 1253 Liberal KS 67905-1253 • FAX(316)624-5900 • glc@oz-online.net

**LINCOLN 10 SE—*ST PAUL*** (913)524-4046
Gary C Wolf • H • KS • 67455 RR 2 Box 40 Lincoln KS 67455-9521

**LINCOLN 3 S—*ST JOHN*** (785)524-4039
Gerald T Radtke • WS 1030; SS 930; BC 930 • H • KS • KS Hwy 14 67455 RR 2 Box 124 Lincoln KS 67455-9555 • FAX(785)524-4039 • stjlutheran@nckcn.com

**LINCOLNVILLE—*ST JOHN*** (316)924-5236
Alan R Stahlecker • * • H • KS • 220 Sixth St 66858 PO Box 157 Lincolnville KS 66858-0157

**LINN—*ZION*** (785)348-5332
David F Gruoner • WS 930; SS 1030; BC 1030 • H • EL • KS • 210 Church St 66953-9527 PO Box 343 Linn KS 66953-0343

**LINN 8 W—*IMMANUEL*** (785)348-5892
Vacant • H • EL • KS • 66953 712 Heritage Rd Linn KS 66953-9244

**LYONS—*GRACE*** (316)257-2204
Calvin L L Heureux • H • EC • KS • 1111 W Lincoln St Lyons KS 67554-3023

**MANHATTAN—*CHRIST*** (785)776-2227
Darrell Matthews • H • KS • 314K Tuttle Creek Blvd Manhattan KS 66502

***ST LUKE*** (785)539-2604
Joseph A Jones Eric R Wood • WS 830; SS 945;* • H • EC • KS • 330 Sunset Ave Manhattan KS 66502-3757 • stlukes@flinthills.com

**MARION—*OUR SAVIOR*** (316)382-2432
John A Ryding • WS 9; SS 10; BC 10 • H • KS • 320 S Cedar St Marion KS 66861-1330 • zionluth@southwind.net

**MARYSVILLE—*MOUNT CALVARY*** (785)562-2046
Donnie A Hofman • WS 10; SS 845; BC 845;* • H • EC/EL • KS • 1710 Jenkins St Marysville KS 66508-1348 • mtcalvary@oz-online.net

**MC FARLAND—*TRINITY*** (785)765-3755
Jeffrey D Geske • WS 10; SS 9; BC 9 • H • KS • 322 Main 66501 PO Box 67 Mc Farland KS 66501-0067

**MC PHERSON—*GRACE*** (316)241-1627
Vacant • H • KS • 800 E 1St St Mc Pherson KS 67460-3614 • FAX(316)241-8785 • cfiaime@mpks.net

**MEADE—*ST JOHN*** (316)873-2966
Lynn E Spencer • WS 1030; SS 930; BC 930 • H • KS • 208 E Grant St 67864 PO Box 587 Meade KS 67864-0587

**MEDICINE LODGE—*TRINITY*** (316)886-3397
Paul J Beyer • * • H • KS • 908 N Guffey St 67104-1062 PO Box 161 Medicine Lodge KS 67104-0161 • mltrinity@juno.com

**MISSION—*TRINITY*** (913)432-5441
LeRoy K Hovel Vernon E Oestmann • Deborah S Moore DCE • WS 815 945 11; SS 930; BC 945;* • H • EC • KS • 5601 W 62nd St Mission KS 66202-3532 • FAX(913)432-3530 • lee@tlcms.org

**MOUNDRIDGE—*ST JOHN*** (316)345-8729
Vacant • WS 930; SS 1030; BC 1045 • H • KS • 411 N Christian Ave 67107 PO Box 784 Moundridge KS 67107-0784

**NASHVILLE—*ST JOHN*** (316)246-5220
Paul J Beyer • SS 930;* • KS • 516 S Main St 67112-8003 PO Box 105 Nashville KS 67112-0105 • sjlcmsnash@juno.com

**NATOMA—*PEACE*** (785)885-4718
Donald R White • H • KS • 705 5th St 67651-9744 PO Box 292 Natoma KS 67651-0292

**NETAWAKA—*IMMANUEL*** (785)364-2206
John J Deister • KS • 302 Kansas St Netawaka KS 66516-9307

**NEWTON—*ZION*** (316)283-1441
Ronald F Gloe • WS 1030; SS 845;* • H • EC • KS • 225 S Poplar St 67114-3637 PO Box 885 Newton KS 67114-0885 • FAX(316)283-0950 • rfgloe@aol.com

**NORTON—*IMMANUEL*** (785)877-2430
David J Bretscher • KS • 814 N 2nd Ave Norton KS 67654-1320

**NORTONVILLE—*ST MATTHEW*** (913)886-6331
Rick J Twenhafel • WS 10; SS 9; BC 9 • H • KS • 312 Elm St 66060 PO Box 297 Nortonville KS 66060-0297 • twenhafel@hotmail.com

**OAKLEY—*IMMANUEL*** (785)672-3833
Theodore E Cook Sr. • WS 1030; SS 930; BC 930 • H • KS • 206 E 7th St Oakley KS 67748-1809 • immanueloakley@netscape.net

**OBERLIN—*ST JOHN*** (785)475-2333
Chad M Eckels • H • KS • 510 N Wilson Ave Oberlin KS 67749-1734

**OFFERLE 11 SW—*ZION*** (316)659-2078
David H Parks • WS 1045; SS 945; BC 945 • KS • 67563 13307 Jewell Rd Offerle KS 67563-9227

**OLATHE—*BEAUTIFUL SAV*** (913)780-6023
Earl J Zimmerman • Sarah B Hinkel DCE • H • KS • 13145 S Blackbob Rd Olathe KS 66062-1417 • FAX(913)780-0602 • bslcolathe@yahoo.com

***REDEEMER*** (913)764-2359
Ronald B Flentgen • Joel E Symmank DCE • WS 8 1045; SS 930; BC 930 • H • EC • KS • 920 S Alta Ln Olathe KS 66061-4105 • FAX(913)764-3038 • rlcolathe@planetkc.com

**OSWEGO—*ST PAUL*** (316)795-4887
Paul V Schnelle • KS • 522 5th St Oswego KS 67356-2104

**OTTAWA—*FAITH*** (785)242-1906
John M Duran • Peter A Lange DCE • WS 8 1030; SS 915 • H • EC • KS • 316 E 12th St Ottawa KS 66067-3605 • FAX(785)242-1906 • duran@ott.net

**OVERLAND PARK—*BETHANY*** (913)648-2228
Edward W Trost John F Niermann • Pamela R Nummela DCE Steven D Armbrust DCE • WS 8 930 11; SS 930; BC 11 930;* • H • EC/EL/HS • KS • 66204 9101 Lamar Ave Shawnee Mission KS 66207-2494 • FAX(913)648-2283 • khaden@bethanylutheran-op.org

***CHRIST*** (913)345-9700
Kenneth O Sype Jeffrey T Meyers • Arlyn Sprecher DCE • WS 815 935 11; SS 935;* • H • EC/HS • KS • 11720 Nieman Overland Park KS 66210 • FAX(913)345-9707 • clclenexa@aol.com

**PALMER—*ST JOHN*** (913)692-4228
Gene K Holtorf • * • H • EL • KS • 304 National Rd 312 National Rd Palmer KS 66962-8902 • gholtorf@midusa.net

**PAOLA—*FIRST*** (913)294-3476
Jerome K Peck • Mary E Ginkel DCE • WS 10; SS 845; BC 845;* • H • KS • 401 E Piankishaw St Paola KS 66071-1724 • FAX(913)294-0074 • flcsecjk@micoks.net

**PAOLA 9 SE—*TRINITY*** (913)849-3344
Kurt G Rutz • H • EL • KS • 66071 34868 Block Rd Paola KS 66071-6201

**PARSONS—*TRINITY*** (316)421-6479
Vacant • WS 1015; SS 9; BC 9 • H • KS • 2931 Crawford Ave 2911 Crawford Ave Parsons KS 67357-2443 • FAX(316)421-6479

**PHILLIPSBURG—*FIRST*** (785)543-5046
Joel S Hiesterman • WS 1030; BC 915;* • H • KS • 1035 First St Phillipsburg KS 67661 • jhiesterman@juno.com

**PITTSBURG—*ZION*** (316)231-4267
Steven L Anderson • H • KS • 102 W Jackson St Pittsburg KS 66762-5658 • FAX(316)231-4267 • zionpitt@grapevine.net

**PLAINVILLE—*FIRST*** (913)434-2874
Victor Samuel • WS 9;* • H • KS • 705 S Jefferson St Plainville KS 67663-3305

**POWHATTAN—*ZION*** (785)467-8810
Trenton D Christensen • WS 11; BC 1015 • KS • 202 W Main 66527 PO Box 121 Powhattan KS 66527-0121

**PRATT—*OUR SAVIOR*** (316)672-6203
Lon E Landsmann • WS 9; SS 8; BC 8 • H • EC • KS • Second And S Thompson 67124 PO Box 192 Pratt KS 67124-0192

**PRESTON—*ST PAUL*** (316)672-5354
Michael L Schotte • WS 10; SS 9; BC 9 • H • KS • 40291 NE 40th Ave 67583-8569 40307 NE 40th Ave Preston KS 67583-8572 • stpaulpreston@juno.com

**RAMONA—*TRINITY*** (785)366-7386
Allen J Woelzlein • * • H • KS • PO Box 8 Ramona KS 67475-0008

**SABETHA—*FIRST*** (785)284-3566
Mark J Janzen • H • EC • KS • 311 Cedar St 66534-2810 316 Spruce St Sabetha KS 66534-2823

**SALINA—*CHRIST KING*** (785)827-7492
Leroy H Pralle • WS 1030; BC 915;* • H • EC • KS • 111 W Magnolia Rd Salina KS 67401-7546

***TRINITY*** (785)823-7151
Robert C Schaedel Charles W Adams • Dana J Beck DCE • WS 830 11 7; SS 945; BC 945 • H • KS • 702 S 9th St Salina KS 67401-4807 • FAX(785)823-3898 • revrobcs@aol.com

**SCOTT CITY—*HOLY CROSS*** (316)872-2294
John W Riebhoff • WS 1015; SS 9; BC 9 • H • KS • 1102 Court St Scott City KS 67871-1815 • holy³cross³scks@yahoo.com

**STRONG CITY—*GRACE*** (316)273-8685
Vacant • H • KS • Chase And Central 66869 PO Box 366 Strong City KS 66869-0366

**SUMMERFIELD—*FIRST*** (913)244-6529
Vacant • H • NEB • Front St 66541 PO Box 70 Summerfield KS 66541-0070

**SYLVAN GROVE—*BETHLEHEM*** (913)526-7766
Robert H Wilson • H • KS • 308 N Indiana Ave 67481-8835 RR 2 Box 53 Sylvan Grove KS 67481-9408 • FAX(785)526-7416 • Taina@midusa.net

**TAMPA—*ST JOHN*** (785)965-2234
Clark M Davis • WS 930; SS 1030; BC 1030 • KS • 425 Main St 67483 PO Box 12 Tampa KS 67483-0012 • FAX(785)965-2604 • revclark@midusa.net

**TOPEKA—*CALVARY*** (785)286-1431
John R Hopkins • WS 8 1030; SS 915; BC 915 • H • KS • 4211 NW Topeka Blvd Topeka KS 66617-1765 • FAX(785)286-1516

***CHRIST*** (785)266-6263
David G Schemm • WS 1015; SS 9; BC 9 • H • EC/EL • KS • 3509 SW Burlingame Rd Topeka KS 66611-2049 • christlutheran3@juno.com

***FAITH*** (785)272-4214
Peter D Tremain Nathan E Schaus • James P Bradshaw DCE • H • EC/EL • KS • 1716 SW Gage Blvd Topeka KS 66604-3334

***HOPE*** (785)266-5206
John F Domsch • WS 930; SS 11; BC 11;* • H • EC • KS • 2636 SE Minnesota Ave Topeka KS 66605-1642 • hope@kspress.com

***PRINCE OF PEACE*** (785)271-0808
Arno H Meyer Waldemar J Friedrichs Neil F Buono • Kenneth D Lueders DCE • WS 830 11; SS 945; BC 945;* • H • EC • KS • 3625 SW Wanamaker Rd Topeka KS 66614-4566 • FAX(785)271-5324 • popeace@cjnetworks.com

***ST JOHN*** (785)354-7132
Peter K Lange Roger M Goetz Glenn R Bitter • Dennis L Hintz DCE Mark C Anderson DCE • H • EC/EL • KS • 901 SW Fillmore St Topeka KS 66606-1445 • FAX(785)354-7179

***ST PAUL*** (785)354-1908
Vacant • WS 930; SS 1045; BC 1045;* • EC/EL • KS • 2322 NE Laurent St Topeka KS 66616-1366

**UNKNOWN—*HOPE*** (913)631-6940
Paul T Hoppe Michael A Penikis • George W Nelson DCE • WS 8 930; SS 930; BC 930 • H • EC/EL • KS • 6308 Quivira Rd Shawnee KS 66216-2744 • FAX(913)268-9525 • hope@hopelutheran.org

**ULYSSES—*GRACE*** (316)356-3161
Patrick D Mason • WS 1030; BC 9;* • H • KS • 205 E Patterson Ulysses KS 67880 • grace@pld.com

**VASSAR—*ZION*** (785)828-4482
Thomas H Harries • WS 9; SS 1015; BC 1015 • H • KS • 23167 Topeka 66543 PO Box 88 Vassar KS 66543-0088

**WAMEGO—*MOUNT CALVARY*** (785)456-2444
James H Mayes • WS 9; SS 1015; BC 1015;* • H • KS • 17535 Say Rd Wamego KS 66547

**WATERVILLE 9 NW—*TRINITY*** (785)325-2506
Vacant • KS • 66548 PO Box 456 Waterville KS 66548-0456

**WATHENA—*CHRIST*** (785)989-3348
Mark P Eichler • WS 1015; SS 9; BC 9 • H • EC • KS • 2108 Hwy 36 Wathena KS 66090-0427

**WELLINGTON—*CALVARY*** (316)326-7715
Michael D Wolff • WS 1030; SS 915; BC 915 • H • KS • 1300 North C St Wellington KS 67152-4346

**WESTPHALIA—*ST JOHN***
See Aliceville

**WHEATON—*ST LUKE*** (785)396-4411
Kevin A Hahn • H • EC • KS • 129 Railroad St 131 Railroad St Wheaton KS 66551-9221 • FAX(785)396-4411 • dehningv@midusa.net

**WICHITA—*ASCENSION*** (316)722-4694
Keith E Kohlmeier Scott L Goltl • Derek J Broten DCE • WS 745 9 1115; SS 1010; BC 1010 • H • EC • KS • 842 N Tyler Rd Wichita KS 67212-3239 • FAX(316)729-7027 • ascenlut@swbell.net

***BETHANY*** (316)265-7415
Kenneth C Studtmann Devon W Woodyard • WS 8 1030; SS 915; BC 915;* • H • EC/EL • KS • 1000 W 26th St S Wichita KS 67217-2922 • FAX(316)265-0887 • becky.bethany@juno.com

***GRACE*** (316)685-6781
Richard L Zabel • R M Freed DCE • WS 8; SS 915; BC 915;* • H • KS • 3310 E Pawnee St Wichita KS 67218-5504 • jwgrace@juno.com

***HOLY CROSS*** (316)684-5201
Jeffrey Crane Michael E Reiners • Kent W Stephens DCO Rebecca L Brockman DCE • WS 815 11; SS 945; BC 945;* • H • KS • 600 N Greenwich Rd Wichita KS 67206-2633 • FAX(316)684-2847 • office@holycrosslutheran.net

***IMMANUEL*** (316)264-0639
Allen C Hoger • H • KS • 909 S Market St Wichita KS 67211-2214 • FAX(316)264-0593 • ilc.office@veracom.net

***RISEN SAVIOR*** (316)683-5538
Thomas E Harmon • WS 8 1030; SS 915; BC 915 • H • KS • K 96 And Woodlawn 67276 6770 E 34th St N Wichita KS 67226-2527 • FAX(316)683-5536 • risnsavior@aol.com

***ST ANDREW*** (316)838-0944
Clifford A Winter • WS 8 1045; SS 930; BC 930;* • H • KS • 2555 Hyacinth Ln Wichita KS 67204-5332 • FAX(316)838-0948 • standrews@feist.com

***TRINITY*** (316)685-1571
Luke D Russert • WS 1030; SS 9; BC 9 • H • KS • 611 S Erie St Wichita KS 67211-2904 • trinitywichita@juno.com

***UNIVERSITY CTR**** (316)684-5224
Vacant • H • KS • 3815 E 17th St N Wichita KS 67208-2039 • FAX(316)684-5224 • wsulc@juno.com

**WINFIELD—*TRINITY*** (316)221-9460
Roderick A Hathaway • H • EC/EL • KS • 910 Mound St Winfield KS 67156-3929 • FAX(316)221-3779 • trinity@hit.net

## KENTUCKY

**ASHLAND—*ST PAUL*** (606)324-3515
Mark A Kloha • H • OH • 1320 Bath Ave Ashland KY 41101-2628

**BOWLING GREEN—*HOLY TRINITY*** (270)843-9595
James A Bettermann • WS 8 1030; SS 910; BC 910 • H • EC/EL • MDS • 553 Ashmoor Ave Bowling Green KY 42101-3702 • FAX(270)843-7466 • htlc-bg@htlc-bg.org

**CRAB ORCHARD—*IMMANUEL***
See Stanford 10 S

**DANVILLE—*OUR SAVIOR*** (859)236-2970
David M Witten • WS 930; SS 1045; BC 1045 • H • IN • Hill N Dale And E Main 40422 839 Hilltop Rd Danville KY 40422-1140 • davidoslc@searnet.com

**DRY RIDGE—*IMMANUEL*** (859)428-1133
Vacant • WS 11; SS 945; BC 945 • OH • 3515 Dixie Hwy Dry Ridge KY 41035-8228

**ELIZABETHTOWN—*GLORIA DEI*** (270)766-1503
David S Tannahill • WS 1030;* • H • EC • IN • 1701 Ring Rd Elizabethtown KY 42701-9497 • FAX(270)769-5703 • glordei@ne.infi.net

**ERLANGER—*BETHANY*** (859)331-3501
Mark R Etter • WS 1030; SS 915; BC 915 • H • EC • OH • 3501 Turkeyfoot Rd Erlanger KY 41018-2670 • nkybethluth@netzero.net

**FLORENCE—*GOOD SHEPHERD*** (859)746-9066
Vacant • WS 9; SS 1015; BC 1015 • H • OH • 9066 Gunpowder Rd Florence KY 41042-8251 • FAX(859)746-9066 • gslc9066@aol.com

**FORT KNOX—*GLORIA DEI***
See Elizabethtown

**HENDERSON—*TRINITY*** (502)826-4337
Dennis E Ouellette • WS 8 1030; SS 915; BC 915;* • H • IN • 501 N Elm St Henderson KY 42420-2933 • trinity-ehr@juno.com

**HOPKINSVILLE—*FAITH*** (270)885-3969
James C Redmann • WS 1030; SS 915; BC 915;* • H • MDS • 405 Shelia Dr Hopkinsville KY 42240-1268 • FAX(270)885-3969 • faith-lutheran@prodigy.net

**LA GRANGE—*HOLY TRINITY*** (502)222-5827
Dale F Reusch • H • EC • IN • 2416 S Highway 53 La Grange KY 40031-9535

**LEITCHFIELD—*HOLY TRINITY*** (270)259-9241
Monty Gleitz(#) • H • IN • 889 Lilac Rd Leitchfield KY 42754-7612 • gleitzmd@juno.com

**LEXINGTON—*GOOD SHEPHERD*** (859)269-6517
Lohn M Johnson • WS 1030; SS 915;* • H • EC • IN • 425 Patchen Dr Lexington KY 40517-4312 • l.m.johns@juno.com

***OUR REDEEMER*** (606)299-9615
Patrick J Bayens • WS 1015; SS 9; BC 9 • H • IN • 2255 Eastland Pkwy Lexington KY 40505-2524 • FAX(606)299-9615 • orlcms@juno.com

***ST JOHN*** (606)277-6391
Vacant • WS 1030;* • H • EC • IN • 516 Pasadena Dr Lexington KY 40503-2217

**LOUISVILLE—*CONCORDIA*** (502)585-4459
Curtis H Peters • WS 10; SS 9; BC 9;* • H • IN • 40202-1711 1127 E Broadway Louisville KY 40204-1711 • FAX(502)585-1392 • mail@concordia.win.net

***FAITH*** (502)367-8513
Ronald L Richeson • H • IN • 7635 Old 3rd Street Rd Louisville KY 40214-5509 • FAX(502)368-2463 • faithksl@couriernet.infi.net

***OUR SAVIOR*** (502)426-1130
Timothy P Anderson Charles A Fausel • Todd M Clark DCE • WS 8 930 1045; SS 930; BC 930;* • H • IN • 8305 Nottingham Pkwy Louisville KY 40222-5539 • FAX(502)394-0648 • oslcoff@aol.com

***PEACE*** (502)239-0486
Donald C Dengler • WS 10;* • H • IN • 8913 Pennsylvania Run Rd Louisville KY 40228-2547 • FAX(520)395-3488 • revdcd@aol.com

***PILGRIM*** (502)458-4451
Donald R Garvue • H • IN • 4205 Gardiner View Ave Louisville KY 40213

***REDEEMER*** (502)776-5945
Vacant • WS 1030;* • H • IN • 3640 River Park Dr Louisville KY 40211-2919 • FAX(502)776-5945

**MAYSVILLE—*TRINITY*** (606)564-3566
Dean M Bauer • WS 930; SS 845; BC 845 • H • OH • 621 Parker Rd Maysville KY 41056-9620

**MURRAY—*IMMANUEL*** (502)753-6712
Vacant • H • MDS • 100 S 15th St Murray KY 42071-2368

**OWENSBORO—*PEACE*** (502)685-0249
Timothy J Henning • WS 10; SS 9; BC 9 • H • EC • IN • 2200 Carter Rd Owensboro KY 42301-4131

**PADUCAH—*ST PAUL*** (270)442-8343
Vacant • Denise E Sprengeler DCE • WS 8 930 1045; SS 930; BC 930 • H • MDS • 211 S 21st St Paducah KY 42003-3204 • st-paul@juno.com

**RADCLIFF—*GLORIA DEI***
See Elizabethtown

**SHELBYVILLE—*HOLY CROSS*** (502)647-3696
Henry H Loppnow • H • IN • 181 Old Seven Mile Pike Shelbyville KY 40065-8816

**SHEPHERDSVILLE—*DIVINE SAVIOR*** (502)543-2905
John C Lehenbauer • H • EC • IN • 1025 Hwy 61 N 40165 1025 N Buckman St Shepherdsville KY 40165-7926 • FAX(520)395-3810 • pastor@dslc.org

**STANFORD 10 S—*IMMANUEL*** (606)355-7590
Vacant • WS 1030 • H • IN • 40484 C/O H Brenda 1007 Kentucky Highway 39 N Crab Orchard KY 40419-9631

**WINCHESTER—*GRACE*** (859)745-2873
Benjamin G Lorenz • WS 915;* • H • EC • IN • 108 Hemlock Rd Winchester KY 40391-2342

## LOUISIANA

**ALEXANDRIA—*AUGUSTANA*** (318)445-0444
Vacant • SO • 2732 3rd St Alexandria LA 71302-6053

***REDEEMER*** (318)442-4325
Walter C Schmidt • WS 1030;* • H • SO • 4809 Masonic Dr Alexandria LA 71301-3327 • redeemlcms@juno.com

**BATON ROUGE—*CALVARY*** (225)355-3866
Vacant • H • SO • 5219 Greenwell St Baton Rouge LA 70805-1908

***CHAPEL CROSS*** (504)383-2962
Gary I Peterson • H • SO • 3235 Dalrymple Dr Baton Rouge LA 70802-6913

***GOOD SHEPHERD*** (225)766-4610
Paul N Anderson • SO • 5990 Perkins Rd Baton Rouge LA 70808-4113

***TRINITY*** (225)272-3110
Scott A Schmieding • H • EC/EL • SO • 10925 Florida Blvd Baton Rouge LA 70815-2009 • FAX(504)272-8504

**BOGALUSA—*ZION*** (504)732-4701
Vacant • WS 1030; SS 9;* • H • SO • 135 Rio Grande St 70427-2242 PO Box 1089 Bogalusa LA 70429-1089 • FAX(504)732-4702 • bobbelknap@aol.com

**BOSSIER CITY—*IMMANUEL*** (318)746-2215
Siegfried Kunz • WS 8 1030 8; SS 915; BC 915 • H • EC • SO • 2565 Airline Dr Bossier City LA 71111-5812 • FAX(318)746-2220 • immanu-el@juno.com

**CHALMETTE—*CHRIST*** (504)279-6795
Thomas R Johnson • H • SO • 3300 Jupiter Dr Chalmette LA 70043-6103 • FAX(504)271-9082 • lutheranchurch@aol.com

**CLINTON—*ZION*** (225)683-5592
Raymond C Huddle • WS 1030 8 • H • SO • 11007 Plank Rd 70722-3312 PO Box 281 Clinton LA 70722-0281

**COVINGTON—*HOLY TRINITY*** (504)892-6146
Mark R Muenchow Bradley S Aumann • Richard K Gutekunst DCE • WS 8 930 1045; SS 930; BC 930;* • H • EC • SO • 1 N Marigold Dr Covington LA 70433-9160 • FAX(504)892-3012 • htlc@neosoft.com

**CROWLEY—*FIRST*** (318)783-8713
Vacant • H • SO • 121 W 8th St 70526-3601 PO Box 1446 Crowley LA 70527-1446

**DE RIDDER—*REDEEMER*** (318)463-8427
Gary E Archbold • H • SO • 811 Shirley St De Ridder LA 70634-3821

**GONZALES—*ST JAMES*** (504)644-2432
Vacant • H • SO • 1415 E Highway 30 Gonzales LA 70737-4765

**GRETNA—*SALEM*** (504)367-5126
Keith R Brda Martin W Friedrich • H • EC/EL/HS • SO • 418 4th St Gretna LA 70053-5317 • FAX(504)367-5128

**HAMMOND—*ST PAUL*** (504)345-6008
Vacant • WS 10; SS 9; BC 9 • H • EC • SO • 707 W Dakota St Hammond LA 70401-2413 • FAX(504)345-6027 • stpaul@i-55.com

**HARAHAN—*FAITH*** (504)737-0448
David J Lofthus • H • EC/EL/HS • SO • 300 Colonial Club Dr Harahan LA 70123-4428 • FAX(504)739-9470

**HARVEY—*CHRIST OUR SAVIOR*** (504)348-1212
Jerald P Dulas • WS 9; SS 1015; BC 1015 • H • HS • SO • 3150 Destrehan Ave Harvey LA 70058-2049 • FAX(504)348-1212 • dulasjpd@juno.com

**HOUMA—*GRACE*** (504)879-1865
William M Childress • H • SO • 422 Valhi Blvd Houma LA 70360-6285

**IOTA—*ST JOHN*** (337)779-2760
Gary A Koopmann • SO • 222 And 228 Third St 70543 PO Box 125 Iota LA 70543-0125

**JENNINGS—*IMMANUEL*** (337)824-3546
Gary A Koopmann • H • SO • 114 N Cutting Ave 70546-6206 PO Box 530 Jennings LA 70546-0530

**LACOMBE—*THE VILLAGE*** (504)882-5727
Edgar W Homrighausen • WS 1015; SS 9; BC 9 • H • SO • 29180 Highway 190 70445-3172 PO Box 1219 Lacombe LA 70445-1219 • FAX(504)781-8388

**LAFAYETTE—*OUR REDEEMER*** (318)981-9731
Vacant • H • SO • 205 Touchet Rd Lafayette LA 70506-7809

***TRINITY*** (318)235-3607
Vacant • WS 1030; SS 915; BC 915 • H • SO • 1402 Johnston St Lafayette LA 70503-2026

**LAKE CHARLES—*ST JOHN*** (318)478-5666
Charles R Miller • WS 1030; SS 9;* • H • EC • SO • 600 University Dr Lake Charles LA 70605-5634 • FAX(318)478-8196 • lutheranrus@usunwired.net

***ST MATTHEW*** (318)436-9927
Vacant • H • SO • 810 N Shattuck St Lake Charles LA 70601-1750

**LEESVILLE—*TRINITY*** (337)239-2457
Gary E Archbold • WS 9; SS 1015; BC 1015 • H • SO • Hwy 8 E 71446 PO Box 65 Leesville LA 71496-0065

**MANSURA 3 N—*ST PAUL*** (318)253-9798
Vacant • H • SO • 577 Cocoville Rd Mansura LA 71350 • RGallersen@aol.com

**METAIRIE—*ATONEMENT*** (504)887-0225
Patrick K Carlson Mark D Kocsis • WS 8 1030; SS 915; BC 915;* • H • EL/HS • SO • 6205 Veterans Memorial Blvd Metairie LA 70003-3998 • FAX(504)887-7876 • churchoffice@alcs.org

***MONTE DE OLIVE*** (504)455-1541
Vacant • H • SO • 4105 David Dr Metairie LA 70003-3422

***MOUNT OLIVE*** (504)833-4963
Bradley A Drew • WS 8 1030; SS 915;* • H • EC/HS • SO • 315 Ridgelake Dr Metairie LA 70001-5315 • FAX(504)833-0154 • pastor@mtolive-lcms.org

**MONROE—*TRINITY*** (318)322-3507
Martin P Mc Comack • WS 1030; SS 915; BC 6;* • H • SO • 1301 Oliver Rd Monroe LA 71201-5017

**NATCHITOCHES—*CHRIST KING*** (318)352-8708
John E Karle • WS 1015; SS 9 • H • SO • 305 Royal St Natchitoches LA 71457-5708 • christus@worldnetla.net

**NEW ORLEANS—*BETHEL*** (504)943-5109
Vacant • H • SO • 3515 Louisa St New Orleans LA 70126-5806

***EPIPHANY***
Vacant • SO • 9004 Hickory St New Orleans LA 70118

***FIRST ENGLISH*** (504)779-9073
Vacant • H • HS • SO • 1228 Arts St 70117-7739 3864 17th St Ste 315 Metairie LA 70002 • FAX(504)779-9075

***GLORIA DEI*** (504)822-7229
Mark T Buetow • WS 1030; SS 915; BC 915 • H • HS • SO • 2021 S Dupre St New Orleans LA 70125-3610 • FAX(504)822-7229 • deibreak@juno.com

***HOLY CROSS*** (504)288-3437
Vacant • H • SO • 6154 Press Dr New Orleans LA 70126-2225

***MOUNT CALVARY*** (504)945-9981
Sidney J Ponseti • HS • SO • 2900 Grand Rte Saint John St New Orleans LA 70119-3025

***MOUNT ZION*** (504)522-9951
Stephen R Everette • H • HS • SO • 1401 Simon Bolivar Ave New Orleans LA 70113-2327

***OUR SAVIOR*** (504)242-0696
Vacant • WS 830 • H • SO • 3443 Esplanade Ave Second Floor Chapel 70119 4633 Knight Dr New Orleans LA 70127-3327

***PRINCE OF PEACE*** (504)242-2636
Edward A Scott Arthur L Porter • H • EC/EL/HS • SO • 9301 Chef Menteur Hwy New Orleans LA 70127-4137 • FAX(504)242-2659

***ST JOHN*** (504)482-2118
Jesus M Gonzales • H • EC/EL/HS • SO • 3937 Canal St New Orleans LA 70119-6002 • FAX(504)482-5869

***ST MATTHEW*** (504)945-6395
Sidney J Ponseti • H • HS • SO • 4127 Franklin Ave New Orleans LA 70122-6007

***ST PAUL*** (504)945-3741
Arthur D Yunker • WS 8 1030; SS 915; BC 915 • H • EC/EL/HS • SO • 2624 Burgundy St New Orleans LA 70117-7304 • FAX(504)945-3743

***ST PAUL*** (504)944-5401
James A Ertl • WS 7; SS 10;* • H • SO • 1625 Annette St New Orleans LA 70116-1322 • FAX(504)944-8214

***ST STEPHEN*** (504)394-4956
Mark C Hayman • WS 9; BC 1030;* • H • SO • 6336 Berkley Dr New Orleans LA 70131-4106 • FAX(504)394-4970 • st2nola@juno.com

***TRINITY*** (504)368-0411
Ronald M Loesel • WS 9; SS 10; BC 10 • H • HS • SO • 620 Eliza St New Orleans LA 70114-1123 • FAX(504)368-0425 • trntyluth@aol

***TRINITY*** (504)945-4447
Byron R Williams Sr. • H • EC/EL • SO • 5234 N Claiborne Ave New Orleans LA 70117-3604 • FAX(504)945-4485

***ZION*** (504)524-1025
Marvin D Otto • WS 1045 • HS • SO • 1924 Saint Charles Ave 70130-5317 1539 St Andrew St New Orleans LA 70130-5334

**PINEVILLE—*PRINCE PEACE*** (318)473-0812
Vacant • WS 1030; SS 9; BC 9 • H • SO • 2063 John H King Service Rd Pineville LA 71360-8219 • FAX(318)473-0812

**RUSTON—*ST PAUL*** (318)251-2389
Vacant • H • SO • 3000 N Trenton St 71270-6909 PO Box 752 Ruston LA 71273-0752

**SHREVEPORT—*FAITH*** (318)635-8084
Richard B Thompson • H • SO • 4727 Broadway Ave Shreveport LA 71109-6908 • dick@nwla.com

***OUR SAVIOR*** (318)686-2921
Rodney W Loose • WS 8; SS 915; BC 915 • H • SO • 2010 Bert Kouns Industr Loop Shreveport LA 71118-3315 • FAX(318)686-9783 • revloose@prodigy.net

***REDEEMER*** (318)868-5778
Vacant • H • SO • 1106 Shreveport Barksdale Hwy Shreveport LA 71105-2403

***ST PAUL*** (318)636-2310
Wesley M Toncre • WS 1030; SS 915; BC 915 • H • EC • SO • 4175 Lakeshore Dr Shreveport LA 71109-1936 • FAX(318)636-2384 • wtoncre@nwla.com

**SLIDELL—*BETHANY*** (504)643-3043
Rodney W Pasch Robert P Aumann Charles J Truax • WS 8; SS 1015 9;* • H • EC • SO • 627 Gause Blvd Slidell LA 70458 • FAX(504)643-1698 • bethanyl@neosoft.com

***LAMB OF GOD*** (504)847-9588
Vacant • SO • C/O Reverend Jan C Case 123 Honeywood Dr Slidell LA 70461

**SULPHUR—*TRINITY*** (337)625-3276
Ronald G Hampsten • WS 1015; SS 9; BC 9;* • H • SO • 1400 S Post Oak Rd Sulphur LA 70663-6014 • FAX(337)625-3276 • tlcron@ibm.net

**WEST MONROE—*CHRIST SERVANT*** (318)396-2198
Vacant • H • SO • 214 Oaklawn Dr West Monroe LA 71291

## MAINE

**CAPE ELIZABETH—*REDEEMER*** (207)799-5941
Edward J Balfour • H • NE • 126 Spurwink Ave Cape Elizabeth ME 04107-9610 • FAX(207)799-3111

**WATERVILLE—*RESURRECTION*** (207)872-5208
Paul Nielsen • SS 9;* • H • NE • 36 Cool St Waterville ME 04901-5220 • lcr@mint.net

## MARYLAND

**ACCIDENT—*ZION*** (301)746-8170
Wilfred L Karsten • WS 1030; SS 930; BC 930;* • H • EC • EA • 209 N Main St PO Box 171 Accident MD 21520-0171 • FAX(301)746-7375 • zion@gcnet.net

**ACCIDENT 4 NW—*ST JOHN*** (301)746-8466
Douglas R Kabell • WS 9 630; SS 1015; BC 1015 • EA • 21520 1065 Cove Rd Accident MD 21520-2015 • FAX(301)746-8466 • sjlcms@hotmail.com

**ANNAPOLIS—*ST PAUL*** (410)268-2400
Michael F Burt • WS 1030; SS 9; BC 9 • H • EC • SE • 31 Roscoe Rowe Blvd Annapolis MD 21401-1517 • FAX(410)268-2884 • splca@aol.com

**ARBUTUS—*HOLY NATIVITY*** (410)242-9441
James C Bredeson Roger W Fink • WS 815 940 11; SS 930; BC 1045 • H • EC/EL/HS • SE • 21227 1200 Linden Ave Baltimore MD 21227-2423 • FAX(410)242-0295

**BALTIMORE—*BEREA*** (410)675-5171
Vacant • SE • 2214-16 E Oliver St Baltimore MD 21213-3424

***BETHANY*** (410)644-7106
Vacant • WS 11; SS 945; BC 945;* • EL/HS • SE • 1022 Haverhill Rd Baltimore MD 21229-5114

***BETHLEHEM*** (410)488-4445
Martin S Gilliland • WS 8 1115; BC 945;* • H • EC/EL/HS • SE • 4815 Hamilton Ave Baltimore MD 21206-3899 • FAX(410)488-2599 • Bethelcb@aol.com

***CALVARY*** (410)426-4301
Daniel H Quiram Robert J Kretzschmar • EC/EL/HS • SE • 2625 E Northern Pkwy Baltimore MD 21214-1118 • FAX(410)426-7590

***CHRIST***
See Dundalk

***EMMANUEL***
See Catonsville

***FAITH***
See Middle River

***HOLY NATIVITY***
See Arbutus

***IMMANUEL*** (410)435-6861
Darrell P Nelson • EC/EL • SE • 5701 Loch Raven Blvd Baltimore MD 21239 • FAX(410)433-3646 • dpnelson@immanuellutheran.org

***MARTINI*** (410)752-7817
Elliott M Robertson • H • EL/HS • SE • 100 W Henrietta St Baltimore MD 21230-3610 • FAX(410)752-7817 • RobertsonE@erols.com

***MOUNT OLIVE*** (410)732-5160
Vacant • WS 10 • EL/HS • SE • 2999 Belair Rd 21213-1234 6202 Radecke Ave Baltimore MD 21206-2934

***NAZARETH*** (410)732-3125
Vacant • WS 10;* • H • EC/EL/HS • SE • 3401 Bank St Baltimore MD 21224-2302 • FAX(410)732-3125 • nazarethlutheran@altavista.com

***OUR SAVIOUR*** (410)235-9553
Gary L Fisher Terry E Greenwood • EC/EL/HS • SE • 3301 The Alameda Baltimore MD 21218-3008 • FAX(410)235-1913

***PILGRIM***
See Milford

***REDEEMER*** (410)644-6780
Vacant • EC/EL/HS • SE • 4211 Vermont Ave Baltimore MD 21229-3599 • FAX(410)644-6781 • redeemerlutheran@erols.com

***RESURRECTION***
See Brooklyn Park

***ST JAMES OF OVERLEA***
See Overlea

***ST MARK DEAF***
See Towson

***ST THOMAS*** (410)947-7258
Charles L Wildner • EL/HS • SE • 339 S Pulaski St Baltimore MD 21223-2924

**BEL AIR—*ADVENT***
See Forest Hill

***ST MATTHEW*** (410)879-6710
John F Kassouf Paul R Schmidt Jr. • WS 8 930 11; BC 11 930;* • H • EC • SE • 1200 E Churchville Rd Bel Air MD 21014-3412 • FAX(410)838-2974 • office@smlc.org

**BETHESDA—*PILGRIM*** (301)229-2800
Vacant • WS 830 11 • H • SE • 5500 Massachusetts Ave Bethesda MD 20816-1933 • FAX(301)320-7085 • pilluch@aol.com

**BOWIE—*FIRST*** (301)464-2599
Vacant • WS 9; SS 1015; BC 1015 • H • SE • 12710 Duckettttown Rd 20715 PO Box 120 West Station Bowie MD 20719-0120 • FAX(301)464-3005

***TRINITY*** (301)262-5475
Allen L Behnke William H Heffel • WS 830; SS 945; BC 945;* • H • SE • 6600 Laurel Bowie Rd Bowie MD 20715-1706 • FAX(301)352-9067 • abehnke@aol.com

**BROOKLYN PARK—*RESURRECTION*** (410)789-0415
Vincent S Hammel Sr.(#) • WS 9;* • H • SE • UKNWN 601 Hammonds Ln Baltimore MD 21225-3330

**BRYANS ROAD—*OUR SAVIOR*** (301)375-7507
Floyd P Duff • WS 1030; BC 915;* • H • SE • 7365 Indian Head Hwy 20616-3237 C/O 7963 Oakwood Ln Pomfret MD 20675 • FAX(301)375-7537 • oursavior@crosswinds.net

**CAMBRIDGE—*OUR SHEPHERD*** (410)228-7099
Adam G Kegel • * • H • SE • 1312 Race St 21613 PO Box 777 Cambridge MD 21613-0777

**CATONSVILLE—*EMMANUEL*** (410)744-0016
Robert L Mordhorst • WS 815 11;* • H • EC/EL • SE • 21228 929 Ingleside Ave Baltimore MD 21228-1316 • FAX(410)744-1199 • emmanuel@bellatlantic.net

***ST PAUL*** (410)747-1897
Stephen B Schafer • WS 815; SS 11 • H • EC/EL/HS • SE • 2001 Old Frederick Rd Catonsville MD 21228-4119 • FAX(410)747-7248 • stpaullc@aol.com

**CHARLOTTE HALL—*ST PAUL*** (301)884-5184
Vacant • WS 1030; SS 9; BC 9 • H • EC • SE • 20622 37707 New Market-Turner Rd Mechanicsville MD 20659-3075

**CHESTER—*GALILEE*** (410)643-6545
Charles A Braband • WS 9;* • H • SE • Kent Island 21619 1934 Harbor Dr Chester MD 21619-2102 • Brabands@friend.ly.net

**CHESTERTOWN—*TRINITY*** (410)778-2744
Michael C Hagebusch • WS 1015;* • H • SE • 101 Greenwood Ave Chestertown MD 21620-1405

**CUMBERLAND—*TRINITY*** (301)777-1800
Stephen C Sweyko • H • SE • 326 N Centre St Cumberland MD 21502-2228 • FAX(301)777-1800 • trinity@hereintown.net

**DUNDALK—*CHRIST*** (410)284-2850
Alvin L Newton • WS 1030;* • EL/HS • SE • 7041 Sollers Point Rd Dundalk MD 21222-3033 • christlutheran-d@juno.com

**EASTON—*IMMANUEL*** (410)822-5665
Kevin A Graudin • Ann M Thompson DCE • WS 9; SS 1015;* • H • EC • SE • 7215 Ocean Gtwy Easton MD 21601-4605 • FAX(410)763-7372 • imluch@shore.intercom

**ELDERSBURG—*FAITH*** (410)795-8082
James G Stoltenberg • * • H • SE • 1700 Saint Andrews Way Eldersburg MD 21784-6252 • FAX(410)795-8091 • faithlc@carr.org

**ELLICOTT CITY—*OUR SHEPHERD*** (410)730-8765
Vacant • WS 930; SS 1045;* • H • EL/HS • SE • Burleigh Manor Middle School 21042 8775 Cloudleap Ct - Suite 210 Columbia MD 21045-3045 • FAX(410)730-3455 • stjohn@erols.com

***TRINITY***
See West Friendship

**FREELAND—*REDEEMER***
See Parkton

**GAMBRILLS—*ST PAUL*** (410)721-2332
Thomas Krepps • * • H • SE • 1370 Defense Hwy 21054 PO Box 3386 Crofton MD 21114-0386

**GERMANTOWN—*MESSIAH*** (301)972-2130
R B Hill • WS 8 1030; SS 915; BC 915 • H • SE • 13901 Clopper Rd Germantown MD 20874-1406 • FAX(301)972-0256 • rburkhill@aol.com

**GLEN BURNIE—*ST PAUL*** (410)766-2283
Richard C Izzard John B Warther • * • H • EC/EL • SE • 308 Oak Manor Dr Glen Burnie MD 21061-5509 • FAX(410)766-2281 • preese@stpauls-lutheran.org

**GREENBELT—*HOLY CROSS*** (301)345-5111
Stephen H Mentz • WS 830 • H • SE • 6905 Greenbelt Rd Greenbelt MD 20770-3301 • FAX(301)220-0692 • myholycross@erols.com

**HAGERSTOWN—*CONCORDIA*** (301)797-5955
William R Burgett • WS 1015; SS 9; BC 9;* • H • SE • 17906 Garden Ln Hagerstown MD 21740-7908 • FAX(301)797-5955 • pastorb@peoplepc.com

**HANCOCK 5 W—*ST PAUL*** (301)678-7180
Timothy P Davis • WS 10; SS 845;* • H • SE • 3738 Resley Rd Hancock MD 21750 • stpaul@nfis.com

**HYATTSVILLE—*AFRICAN IMMIGRANT**** (301)277-2302
Vacant • H • SE • 3799 E West Hwy Hyattsville MD 20782-2007

***CHRISTOS SENOR DE VI**** (301)277-4729
Vacant • H • SE • 3799 E West Hwy Hyattsville MD 20782-2007

***REDEEMER*** (301)277-2302
Rudolf Kampia • WS 815 11; SS 945; BC 945 • H • EC/EL • SE • 3799 E West Hwy Hyattsville MD 20782-2007 • FAX(301)699-0071 • rkampia@erols.com

**KINGSVILLE—*ST PAUL*** (410)592-8100
Michael W Wollman Gary W Zieroth • WS 830 11; SS 945;* • H • EC/EL/HS • SE • 12022 Jerusalem Rd Kingsville MD 21087-1146 • FAX(410)592-3282 • rev.mike@juno.com

**LA PLATA—*GRACE*** (301)932-0963
Eric G Peterson Christopher L Otten • WS 8 930 11;* • H • EC/EL • SE • 1200 E Charles St 20646-3940 PO Box 446 La Plata MD 20646-0446 • FAX(301)934-1459 • gracelutheran@cccomp.com

**LANDOVER HILLS—*ASCENSION*** (301)577-0500
Frederick T Hedt • EC/EL • SE • 7415 Buchanan St Landover Hills MD 20784-2323 • FAX(301)577-9558 • ascenluth@aol.com

**LAUREL—*OUR SAVIOR*** (301)776-7670
Jon T Diefenthaler • WS 815 945 11; SS 930; BC 11;* • H • EC • SE • 20708 13611 Laurel Bowie Rd Laurel MD 20708-1563 • FAX(301)776-2872 • oslc@erols.com

**LEXINGTON PARK—*TRINITY*** (301)863-9512
Stephen W Updegrave • WS 815 11; SS 930; BC 930 • H • EC • SE • 46707 Shangri La Dr Lexington Park MD 20653-4135 • FAX(301)863-8185 • trinity@us.hsanet.net

**LONG GREEN—*ST JOHN BLENHEIM*** (410)592-8018
Paul W Richter • Karna R Hubbard DCE • WS 830;* • H • EC/EL/HS • SE • 13300 Manor Road Long Green MD 21092-9999 • FAX(410)592-5185 • pastor@stjohnslcms.org

**MARRIOTTSVILLE—*TRINITY*** (410)461-4313
William L F Gies • WS 915; SS 11; BC 11;* • H • SE • 1525 Marriotsville Rd 21104 10176 Baltimore Natl Pike #202 Ellicott City MD 21042-3652 • wlfg@@juno.com

**MIDDLE RIVER—*FAITH*** (410)687-7500
Vacant • EL/HS • SE • 21220 2200 Old Eastern Ave Baltimore MD 21220-4721

**MILFORD—*PILGRIM*** (410)484-6692
John H Betz • EL/HS • SE • UKNWN 7200 Liberty Rd Baltimore MD 21207-3801 • FAX(410)484-6692

**MOUNT RAINIER—*TRINITY*** (301)864-4340
Peter A Schiebel • * • EC/EL • SE • 4000 30th St Mount Rainier MD 20712-1803 • FAX(301)779-5629 • trinchurch@aol.com

**ODENTON—*FIRST*** (410)551-9189
Robert L Hinz • WS 8;* • H • EC • SE • 1306 Odenton Rd 21113-1512 PO Box 3 Odenton MD 21113-0003 • FAX(410)551-9189 *51 • flcodenton@toadnet.net

**OLNEY—*GOOD SHEPHERD*** (301)774-9125
Donald C Schaefer • Roberta S Hillhouse DEAC • WS 815 11; SS 930;* • H • EC • SE • 4200 Olney Laytonsville Rd 20832-1806 PO Box 280 Olney MD 20830-0280 • FAX(301)774-9649 • donalds807@aol.com

**OVERLEA—*ST JAMES OF OVERLEA*** (410)668-0158
J T Foelber • WS 915;* • EC/EL/HS • SE • UKNWN 8 W Overlea Ave Baltimore MD 21206-1026

**OWINGS MILLS—*CHRIST KING*** (410)356-3400
Harry M Krolus • H • SE • 515 Academy Ave Owings Mills MD 21117-1309 • FAX(410)356-3400 • ctklc@chesint.net

**OXON HILL—*OXON HILL*** (301)894-3773
Kenneth E Schnepp Jr. • WS 10; BC 845;* • H • SE • 20745 3415 Brinkley Rd Temple Hills MD 20748-7102 • FAX(301)894-2592 • ohluth@aol.com

**PARKTON—*REDEEMER*** (410)343-3112
James L Banach • SS 9; BC 9;* • H • SE • 20440 Downes Rd Parkton MD 21120-9165 • FAX(410)343-1665 • info@redeemerparkton.com

**PASADENA—*GALILEE*** (410)255-8236
Vacant • WS 8 1045; SS 915; BC 915;* • H • EC • SE • 4652 Mountain Rd Pasadena MD 21122-5463 • FAX(410)360-4303

**PRESTON—*IMMANUEL*** (410)673-7107
Neil E Andersen • WS 11; SS 945; BC 945 • H • EC • SE • 242 Main St 21655 PO Box 39 Preston MD 21655-0039 • FAX(410)673-1426

**ROCKVILLE—*CROSS*** (301)762-7565
Lester P Stano • * • H • EC • SE • 12801 Falls Rd Rockville MD 20854-6199 • FAX(301)762-0739 • lcc@radix.net

**SALISBURY—*BETHANY*** (410)742-1737
Kevin D Wackett • WS 815; SS 930; BC 945;* • H • SE • 817 Camden Ave Salisbury MD 21801-6231 • bethanylutheranc@aol.com

**SILVER SPRING—*CALVARY*** (301)589-4041
Larry W Schmidt • H • EL • SE • 9545 Georgia Ave Silver Spring MD 20910-1438 • FAX(301)589-0931

***CHRIST DEAF*** (301)937-1705
Vacant • SE • 9545 Georgia Ave Silver Spring MD 20910-1438 • FAX(301)589-0931

***ST ANDREW*** (301)942-6531
Mark A Hricko Edwin M Foster David L Pearcy • WS 815 930 11; SS 930; BC 930 • H • EC • SE • 12247 Georgia Ave Silver Spring MD 20902-5523 • FAX(301)942-0170 • lcsa@erols.com

**SUNDERLAND—*FIRST*** (410)257-3030
Vacant • WS 8 930 12;* • H • EC • SE • 6300 Southern Md Blvd 20689 PO Box 129 Sunderland MD 20689-0129 • FAX(605)590-5916 • firstlutheran@chesapeake.net

**TEMPLE HILLS—*OXON HILL***
See Oxon Hill

**TOWSON—*FIRST*** (410)825-8770
Gerald E Todd • WS 845 10; SS 845; BC 845;* • H • EL/HS • SE • 40 E Burke Ave Towson MD 21286-1124 • FAX(410)583-7416 • firsttowson@juno.com

***HOLY CROSS*** (410)825-7905
Guenter Schwab • * • H • EC/EL/HS • SE • 8516 Loch Raven Blvd Towson MD 21286-2303 • FAX(410)825-7905 • holycros@bcpl.net

***ST MARK DEAF*** (410)825-8772
Vacant • WS 815 • H • SE • 40 E Burke Ave Towson MD 21286-1124 • stmarkdeaf@juno.com

**UPPER MARLBORO—*CONCORDIA*** (301)372-6582
Vacant • H • EC • SE • 10201 Old Indian Head Rd Upper Marlboro MD 20772-7936

**WALKERSVILLE—*PEACE IN CHRIST*** (301)845-6300
David J Betzner • SS 950; BC 950 • H • SE • 8798 Adventure Ave Walkersville MD 21793-7804 • FAX(301)845-6800 • dbetzner@aol.com

## MASSACHUSETTS

**ACTON—*MOUNT CALVARY*** (978)263-5156
Vacant • James W Reed DCE • H • EC • NE • 472 Massachusetts Ave 01720-2937 PO Box 986 Acton MA 01720-0986 • FAX(978)264-0167 • mcalvary@ultranet.com

**BEDFORD—*OF THE SAVIOR*** (781)275-6013
Mark R Oien Mark R Clow • WS 830; SS 945;* • H • EC • NE • 426 Davis Rd Bedford MA 01730-1514 • FAX(781)275-9308 • lcsavior@tiac.net

**BOSTON—*FIRST*** (617)536-8851
Ingo R Dutzmann • WS 830; SS 945 • H • NE • 299 Berkeley St Boston MA 02116-2001 • FAX(617)247-9827 • flc@flc-boston.org

**BOSTON-ROSLINDALE—*TRINITY*** (617)327-8866
Vacant • NE • UKNWN 1195 Centre St # C Roslindale MA 02131-1010

**CANTON—*ST JAMES*** (781)828-0620
John W Hohe • WS 9 1030; SS 915;* • EC • NE • 214 York St Canton MA 02021-2466 • FAX(781)821-4752 • thehohes@mediaone.net

**CENTERVILLE—*OUR SAVIOR***
See Mashpee

**CLINTON—*TRINITY*** (978)365-6888
Richard P Bucher • NE • 117 Chace St Clinton MA 01510-3203

**DEDHAM—*ST LUKE*** (781)326-1346
Benjamin T Ball • EC • NE • 950 East St Dedham MA 02026-6335 • FAX(781)326-4094

**EASTHAMPTON—*TRINITY*** (413)527-3311
Vacant • WS 9; SS 9; BC 1015 • H • NE • 2 Clark St Easthampton MA 01027 • trinityem@yahoo.com

**FITCHBURG—*MESSIAH*** (978)343-7397
Phillip J Alexander • WS 930 815; SS 11; BC 11 • H • EC • NE • 750 Rindge Rd Fitchburg MA 01420-1312 • FAX(978)343-7397 • messiahlcms@aol.com

**HANOVER—*OF THE CROSS*** (781)826-5121
Robert H Pohl • WS 9;* • H • EC • NE • Route 139 02339 77 Rockland St # 54 Hanover MA 02339-2220

**HOLYOKE—*FIRST*** (413)534-7071
Timothy D Knapp • WS 9 1115; BC 1015;* • H • EC/EL • NE • 1810 Northampton St Holyoke MA 01040-1923 • FAX(413)534-7071 • flcsma@hotmail.com

**HYANNIS—*OUR SAVIOR***
See Mashpee

**LYNNFIELD—*MESSIAH*** (781)334-4111
David P Mahn • * • H • EC • NE • 708 Lowell St Lynnfield MA 01940-1643 • FAX(781)334-6557

**MASHPEE—*OUR SAVIOR*** (508)477-4966
Vacant • * • H • NE • 14 Cape Dr Mashpee MA 02649-3077

**QUINCY—*WOLLASTON*** (617)773-5482
Adolph H Wismar Jr. Richard M Law • NE • 550 Hancock St Quincy MA 02170-1922 • FAX(617)471-0235 • wollaston-lcms@worldspy.net

**RAYNHAM—*OF THE WAY*** (508)822-5900
Edwin T Harkey • WS 8 11; SS 930; BC 930;* • H • EC • NE • 110 Robinson St Raynham MA 02767-1921 • FAX(508)822-5900 • lcw@tmlp.com

**SCITUATE—*CHRIST*** (781)545-5271
Dean E Tegeler • H • NE • 460 Chief Justice Cushing Hwy Scituate MA 02066-3604

**SOUTHWICK—*CHRIST*** (413)569-5151
Jeffrey D King • WS 830 945 11; SS 945;* • H • EC • NE • 568 College Hwy PO Box 1107 Southwick MA 01077-1107 • FAX(413)569-5151

**SPRINGFIELD—*TRINITY*** (413)783-9112
James E Butler • * • H • NE • 400 Wilbraham Rd Springfield MA 01109-2723 • butlersix@att.net

**TAUNTON—*OF THE WAY***
See Raynham

**TOPSFIELD—*OUR SAVIOR*** (978)887-5701
Scott A Callaway • WS 8 1045; SS 915; BC 915 • H • NE • RR 1 01983-9801 478 Boston St Topsfield MA 01983-1225 • FAX(978)887-5701 • osaviorlc@aol.com

**WESTFIELD—*ST JOHN*** (413)568-1417
Michael R Gruel • * • H • NE • 60 Broad St Westfield MA 01085-2927 • FAX(413)568-1417

**WESTMINSTER—*OUR SAVIOR*** (978)874-2504
R M Hintze • WS 830 11; SS 945; BC 945 • H • NE • Rt 2a And 140 01473 PO Box 459 Westminster MA 01473-0459 • FAX(978)874-2479

## MICHIGAN

**ADA TWP—*ST MATTHEW*** (616)942-9091
William B Wagner • H • MI • 49301 5125 Cascade Rd SE Grand Rapids MI 49546-3726 • FAX(616)942-0252 • StMatthew@i2k.com

**ADDISON—*OF THE LAKES*** (517)547-4261
David R Gadbaw • Sheila M Thomack DCE Erik P Thomack DCE • WS 830 11 6; SS 945; BC 945 • H • MI • 8800 N Rollin Hwy Addison MI 49220-9727 • FAX(517)547-4262 • lcol@dmci.net

**ADRIAN—*HOPE*** (517)263-4317
Paul W Herter • WS 830 11; SS 945; BC 945 • H • MI • 5625 W US Highway 223 Adrian MI 49221-8431 • FAX(517)265-5432 • hopelcms@tc3net.com

***ST JOHN*** (517)265-6998
Joel H Sarrault • WS 830 11; SS 940; BC 945 • H • MI • 121 N Locust St 49221-2822 430 E Church St Adrian MI 49221-3002 • FAX(517)264-2512 • jsarrault@tc3net.com

**ALBION—*ST PAUL*** (517)629-8379
James A Waddell • H • EC • MI • 100 Luther Blvd Albion MI 49224-2056 • FAX(517)629-8802 • spelc@voyager.net

**ALGONAC—*FIRST*** (810)794-4642
Gerhard Mau • WS 1030; SS 1030;* • H • MI • 1623 Washington St Algonac MI 48001-1355

**ALLEN PARK—*ANGELICA*** (313)381-2080
Joel M Holls • WS 8 11; BC 930;* • H • EN • 8400 Park Ave Allen Park MI 48101-1544 • FAX(313)381-9903 • joholls@aol.com

***MOUNT HOPE*** (313)565-9445
Albert I Prouty • H • EC/EL/HS • MI • 5323 Southfield Rd Allen Park MI 48101-2855 • FAX(313)565-2426

**ALLENDALE—*ST JOHN*** (616)895-4826
James E Metcalf • * • H • MI • 49401 9628 48th Ave Jenison MI 49428-9528 • FAX(616)892-4826 • stjohnlu@iserv.net

**ALMA—*PEACE*** (517)463-5754
Terry W Kenitz Paul O Richert(EM) • WS 930;* • MI • 325 E Warwick Dr Alma MI 48801-1013

**ALPENA—*IMMANUEL*** (517)354-3443
David M Nickel James D Erickson • WS 8 1030; SS 915; BC 915;* • H • EC/EL • MI • 351 Wilson St Alpena MI 49707-1423 • FAX(517)354-0122

**AMASA—*SION*** (906)822-7810
Thomas R Mackey • WS 8;* • NW • 413 W Pine St Amasa MI 49903-9999

**AMELITH—*ST JOHN***
See Bay City 5 SW

**ANN ARBOR—*DIVINE SHEPHERD*** (734)761-7273
Vacant • H • EC • MI • 2600 Nixon Rd Ann Arbor MI 48105-1420 • FAX(734)761-7257 • divshep@aol.com

***PEACE*** (734)424-0899
Larry G Courson • WS 830; SS 945; BC 945;* • H • MI • 8260 Jackson Rd Ann Arbor MI 48103 • FAX(734)424-0481 • peacelutheran@provide.net

***ST LUKE*** (734)971-0550
David V Koch Mark E Schulz • Lloyd R Stuhr DCE Byron D Porisch DCE • WS 830 1045; SS 940; BC 940;* • H • HS • MI • 4205 Washtenaw Ave Ann Arbor MI 48108-1005 • FAX(734)971-6541 • StLukeAA@aol.com

***ST PAUL*** (734)665-9117
Parke G Frederick • Adolph E Zielke DCE Esther E Jurchen P Asst • WS 8 1045; SS 930; BC 930;* • H • HS • MI • 420 W Liberty St Ann Arbor MI 48103-4343 • FAX(734)665-9449 • information@stpaul.pvt.k12.mi.us

***UNIVERSITY CHAPEL**** (734)663-5560
Vacant • H • MI • 1511 Washtenaw Ave Ann Arbor MI 48104-3122 • FAX(734)663-4236 • lutheran@umich.edu

**ANN ARBOR 12 SW—*ST THOMAS*** (734)663-7511
John W Kayser • MI • 48104 10001 W Ellsworth Rd Ann Arbor MI 48103-9613

**ARCADIA—*TRINITY*** (231)889-3620
Vacant • * • H • MI • 17191 Third St 49613 PO Box 139 Arcadia MI 49613-0139 • trinityarcadia@net-port.com

**ARMADA—*OUR SAVIOUR*** (810)784-9088
Paul B Dancy • WS 8 1045;* • H • EL/HS • MI • 22511 West Main St Armada MI 48005-3207 • FAX(810)784-9771 • oslchurch@teleweb.net

**AU GRES—*ST JOHN*** (517)876-8910
Gary L Nehring • WS 9; BC 1015;* • H • MI • 206 N Court St 48703-9505 PO Box 763 Au Gres MI 48703-0763

**AUBURN—*GRACE*** (517)662-6161
David H Reed • WS 8 1030; BC 930;* • H • EL • MI • 303 Ruth St Auburn MI 48611-9463 • FAX(517)662-4791 • reedrev@voyager.net

**AUBURN 7 NW—*ZION*** (517)662-4264
Gregory A Schlicker Douglas J Stowe • * • H • EC/EL/HS • MI • 48611 1556 Seidler Rd Auburn MI 48611-9732 • FAX(517)662-7052 • zionluta@concentric.net

**BACH—*ST PETER*** (517)883-3524
Ernest C Wendt • * • MI • 9667 Bach Rd Sebewaing MI 48759-9566

**BAD AXE—*OUR SAVIOR*** (517)269-7642
Kenneth D Lueke • WS 815; BC 930;* • EC • MI • 123 W Irwin St Bad Axe MI 48413-1014

**BALDWIN—*GRACE*** (231)745-7521
David W Bogda • WS 11; SS 930; BC 930 • H • MI • 8636 S M 37 8636 S M37 Baldwin MI 49304-9781

**BATTLE CREEK—*REDEMPTION*** (616)964-2321
Dan L Seng • H • MI • 2450 Michigan Ave W Battle Creek MI 49017-1335

***ST MARK*** (616)964-0401
Carl W Schneider • WS 830 11; SS 945; BC 945;* • MI • 114 E Minges Rd Battle Creek MI 49015-4051 • FAX(616)965-4051 • StMart@net-link.net

***ST PAUL*** (616)968-3055
Gary L Siefert • * • H • MI • 349 Capital Ave NE Battle Creek MI 49017-4890 • FAX(616)968-2795 • stpaulbc@iserv.net

**BAY CITY—*FAITH*** (517)684-3430
Vacant • WS 8;* • H • EC/EL • MI • 3033 Wilder Rd Bay City MI 48706-2360 • FAX(517)684-3545

***IMMANUEL*** (517)893-4088
Leslie D Tyvela • WS 8 1030; SS 915; BC 915;* • H • EC/EL • MI • Lincoln And Tenth Sts 48708 300 N Sheridan St Bay City MI 48708-6600 • FAX(517)893-3719 • immanuel@concentric.net

***ST PAUL*** (517)686-7140
Paul D Theiss • David M Schultz DCE • WS 8 1030; BC 915;* • H • EC/EL/HS • MI • I75 And M84 48708 6100 WS Saginaw RD Bay City MI 48706 • FAX(517)684-0882 • pdtheiss@efortress.com

***ZION*** (517)894-2611
William H Allwardt Mark A Gerisch • * • H • EC/EL • MI • 510 W Ivy St Bay City MI 48706-5234 • FAX(517)893-0377 • zion/th@concentric.net

**BAY CITY 5 SW—*ST JOHN*** (517)686-0176
Stephen P Starke • WS 830 11; SS 950; BC 950 • H • EC/EL/HS • MI • 1664 Amelith Rd Bay City MI 48706-9378 • FAX(517)686-2169 • webmaster@st.john-amelith.org

**BAY CITY 8 W—*TRINITY*** (517)662-6093
David F Sherry • WS 830; SS 1030; BC 930 • EC/EL/HS • MI • 48708 5545 8 Mile Rd Bay City MI 48706-9711 • FAX(517)662-6173 • orca23@tir.com

**BELDING—*HOLY CROSS*** (616)794-1310
Gary W Jacobsen(#) • H • MI • 422 W High St Belding MI 48809-1130 • FAX(616)794-3285

**BELLAIRE—*HOPE*** (231)533-8129
Walter D Kreger • WS 9; BC 1030;* • H • MI • 2680 N Hwy M 88 49615 PO Box 160 Bellaire MI 49615-0160

**BENZONIA—*OUR SAVIOR*** (616)882-4326
Daniel L Henke • H • MI • 6790 Frankfort Hwy # M115 49616-9770 PO Box 227 Benzonia MI 49616-0227 • FAX(616)882-4002 • oursavior@coslink.net

**BERGLAND—*TRINITY*** (906)575-3512
Kevin K Ader • WS 915;* • H • NW • 404 Birch St 49910 PO Box 367 Bergland MI 49910-0367

**BERKLEY—*TRINITY*** (248)542-4654
David L Prout • WS 1030; BC 915;* • H • MI • 3238 Royal Ave Berkley MI 48072-1332 • FAX(248)542-0914

**BERRIEN SPRINGS—*TRINITY*** (616)473-1811
Lyle H Fritsch Gary C Williams • WS 8 1030; SS 915; BC 915;* • H • EC/EL • MI • 9123 George Ave Berrien Springs MI 49103-1622 • FAX(616)473-2322

**BEVERLY HILLS—*ASCEN O CHRIST*** (248)644-8890
Ronald R Farah • WS 8; BC 915;* • H • EN • 16935 W 14 Mile Rd Beverly Hills MI 48025-3223 • FAX(248)644-1181 • aocchurch@aol.com

***ASCEN O CHRIST***
See Birmingham

**BIG RAPIDS—*ST PETER*** (231)796-6684
Lee H Zabrocki • WS 8 1030; SS 915;* • H • EC/EL • MI • 408 W Bellevue St Big Rapids MI 49307-1310 • FAX(231)796-1186 • zabrocki@tucker-usa.com

**BILLINGS—*TRINITY*** (406)245-3984
David L Poovey James A Haugen Jr. • WS 8 1030; SS 915; BC 930;* • H • MT • 537 Grand Ave Billings MT 59101-5926 • FAX(406)245-3923 • trinity³billings@uswest.net

**BIRCH RUN—*CHRIST*** (517)624-9378
Kenneth O Schroeder • WS 9;* • H • MI • 8101 Poellet St 48415 PO Box 176 Birch Run MI 48415-0176 • FAX(517)624-2521

***ST MARTIN*** (517)624-9204
William P Eickhoff • WS 8 1045; SS 915; BC 915;* • H • MI • 10995 Canada Rd Birch Run MI 48415-9792 • FAX(517)624-0298

**BIRMINGHAM—*OUR SHEPHERD*** (248)646-6100
Ray E Scherbarth Ronald L Young • WS 8 930 11; SS 930; BC 930;* • H • EC/EL/HS • MI • 2225 E 14 Mile Rd Birmingham MI 48009-7258 • FAX(248)646-6176 • lcoslcb@ccaa.edu

***REDEEMER*** (248)644-4010
Randall J Schlak • WS 830;* • H • EC/HS • MI • 1800 W Maple Rd Birmingham MI 48009-1567 • FAX(248)644-1471 • rlutheran@aol.com

**BLOOMFIELD HILLS—*CROSS CHRIST*** (248)646-5886
Jon W Reusch Cory A Fanning • H • HS • MI • 1100 Lone Pine Rd Bloomfield Hills MI 48302-2817 • FAX(248)646-5968 • coclc@aol.com

**BOYNE CITY—*CHRIST*** (231)582-9301
Kenneth G Bernthal • Wayne A King DCE • H • MI • 1250 Boyne Ave Boyne City MI 49712-9655

**BRIDGEPORT—*FAITH*** (517)777-2600
William W Hessler • Linda Kirchner DCE/DCO • * • H • EC • MI • 4241 Williamson Rd 48722 PO Box 242 Bridgeport MI 48722-0242 • FAX(517)777-5069 • faithlc@concentric.net

**BRIDGMAN—*IMMANUEL*** (616)465-6031
James A Schouweiler • WS 8 1030 730; BC 915 • H • EC/EL • MI • 9650 Church St 49106-9525 PO Box 26 Bridgman MI 49106-0026 • FAX(616)465-6409 • immanuel.1896@juno.com

**BRIGHTON—*SHEP LAKES*** (810)227-5099
Paul G Werner K F Graves • Eric K Brei DCE • WS 815 945 1115; SS 945; BC 945;* • H • EC • MI • 2101 S Hacker Rd Brighton MI 48114-8764 • FAX(810)227-3566 • shepherd@ismi.net

**BRITTON 4 NE—*EMMANUEL*** (517)451-8148
James G Balzer • WS 10; SS 845; BC 845 • H • MI • 49229 9950 Ridge Hwy Britton MI 49229-9591 • FAX(517)451-8694 • elc@lni.net

**BROOKLYN 4 SE—*ST MARK*** (517)467-7565
Kelly D Smith Sr. • WS 9; SS 1015; BC 1015 • H • MI • Irish Hills (E Of M-50) 49230 11151 US Highway 12 Brooklyn MI 49230-9201 • FAX(425)732-7805 • lcstmark@ccaa.edu

**BUCHANAN—*ST PAUL*** (616)695-9061
Thomas M Nowak Daniel H Woodring • WS 10;* • MI • 212 W Front St 49107-1211 PO Box 129 Buchanan MI 49107-0129 • FAX(616)695-9061 • stpaulbuch@qtm.net.

***TRINITY***
See Glendora

**BULLOCK CREEK—*MESSIAH*** (517)835-7143
Gregory A Finke John E Langewisch • WS 8 930 11; SS 930; BC 930;* • H • EC • MI • 48640 1550 Poseyville Rd Midland MI 48640-9599 • FAX(517)835-5325 • messiah@messiahbc.org

**BURR OAK—*ST JOHN*** (616)489-5539
Kurt P Kuhlmann • WS 1030; SS 915; BC 930;* • H • MI • 226 W Main St 49030 PO Box 72 Burr Oak MI 49030-0072

**BURTON—*PILGRIM*** (810)744-1188
Daniel A Wonderly • * • H • EC • MI • 3222 S Genesee Rd Burton MI 48519-1424 • FAX(810)744-0452

**CADILLAC—*EMMANUEL*** (231)775-3261
Paul A Lauer • H • MI • 403 E North St PO Box 286 Cadillac MI 49601 • FAX(231)775-2754 • emmanuel@netonecom.net

**CALEDONIA 2 NW—*ST PAUL*** (616)891-8688
Robert A Gerke • WS 830; SS 945; BC 945 • H • MI • 49316 8436 Kraft Ave SE Caledonia MI 49316-9718 • FAX(616)891-0598 • stpaul@iserv.net

**CANTON—*CHRIST GOOD SHEPHERD*** (734)981-0286
Vacant • H • EC/HS • MI • 42690 Cherry Hill Rd Canton MI 48187-3402 • FAX(734)981-CHRI • ctgslc@juno.com

**CARLETON—*CHRIST OUR SHEPHERD***
See Newport

**CARO—*ST PAUL*** (517)673-4214
David E Hollender • Gregory S Arnett DCE • BC 945;* • H • MI • 503 S State St Caro MI 48723-1729 • FAX(517)673-5518 • stpaul@centuryinter.net

**CARROLLTON—*MESSIAH*** (517)753-7281
M S Sherouse • WS 930;* • H • EC/HS • MI • 48724 4640 N Michigan Ave Saginaw MI 48604-1013 • FAX(517)753-7905 • sherouse@prodigy.net

**CARSON CITY—*CALVARY*** (517)584-6068
Kenneth L Williamson • WS 1015;* • H • MI • 509 W Elm St 48811-9673 PO Box 703 Carson City MI 48811-0703 • klw@mvcc.com

**CASEVILLE—*GOOD SHEPHERD*** (517)856-4850
Vacant • WS 1030;* • H • MI • 7899 Crescent Beach Rd 48725 PO Box 640 Caseville MI 48725-0640

**CASS CITY—*GOOD SHEPHERD*** (517)872-2770
Gerald A Meyer • WS 930;* • H • MI • 6820 Main St 48726-9694 PO Box 164 Cass City MI 48726-0164

**CASSOPOLIS—*ST PAUL*** (616)445-3950
David E Weiss Daniel H Woodring • WS 9; SS 1015; BC 1030 • H • EC • MI • 305 W State St 49031-1009 PO Box 382 Cassopolis MI 49031-0382 • FAX(616)445-3350 • stpaul@beanstalk.net

**CEDAR—*BETHLEHEM***
See Glen Arbor

***ST PAUL***
See Good Harbor

**CENTREVILLE—*ST PAUL*** (616)467-4355
Mark E Gilson • WS 1045; SS 930; BC 930 • H • MI • 600 W Burr Oak St Centreville MI 49032-9781 • megilson@juno.com

**CENTREVILLE 6 SE—*SALEM*** (616)489-5539
Vacant • MI • 49032 23269 Banker Street Rd Sturgis MI 49091-9376

**CHARLEVOIX—*BETHANY*** (231)547-9446
Michael L Teuscher • WS 1030;* • H • MI • 1407 Bridge St 49720-1609 PO Box 602 Charlevoix MI 49720-0602

**CHARLOTTE—*FIRST*** (517)543-4360
Timothy W Olson • WS 830 11; SS 945;* • H • EC • MI • 550 E Shepherd St Charlotte MI 48813-2224 • FAX(517)543-9836 • flcrer@ia4u.net

**CHATHAM—*SION*** (906)439-5222
Kirk E Griebel • WS 1030; BC 915;* • H • NW • N5177 Hwy M-94 49816 PO Box 131 Chatham MI 49816-0131

**CHEBOYGAN—*ST JOHN*** (616)627-5149
Keith A Schneider • H • MI • 8757 N Straits Hwy Cheboygan MI 49721-9011

**CHELSEA—*OUR SAVIOR*** (734)475-1404
Dale A Grimm • George A Bruick II DCE • WS 815 1030; SS 930; BC 930 • H • EC • MI • 1515 S Main St Chelsea MI 48118-1433 • FAX(734)475-9197 • oslc2@juno.com

**CLARE—*PRINCE PEACE*** (517)386-2687
Robert L Barker • WS 1030;* • H • MI • 10333 S Clare Ave Clare MI 48617-9733 • popeace@glccomputers.com

**CLARKSTON—*ST TRINITY*** (248)625-4644
Vacant • Lance W Klotz DCO • H • EC • MI • 7925 Sashabaw Rd Clarkston MI 48348-2905 • FAX(248)625-2093 • newtrinity@aol.com

**CLINTON TOWNSHIP—*ST LUKE*** (810)791-1150
Mark E Sell Scot A Kinnaman Steven C Mahlburg • WS 745 10 1130;* • H • EC/EL/HS • MI • 21400 S Nunneley Rd Clinton Township MI 48035-1632 • FAX(810)791-1880 • stluke@flash.net

***TRINITY*** (810)463-2921
Harry C Henneman Mark H Gaertner • Kristin E Hardy DCE David E Brown DCE • WS 8; SS 930; BC 930;* • H • EC/EL/HS • MI • 38900 Harper Ave Clinton Township MI 48036-3222 • FAX(810)463-2389 • tlc@123.net

**CLIO—*MESSIAH*** (810)686-0740
Erwin Kostizen • WS 8 930 11; SS 11 930; BC 11 930;* • H • MI • 520 Butler St 48420-1268 PO Box 10 Clio MI 48420-0010 • FAX(810)686-4299 • ervkost@cs.com

**COLDWATER—*PRINCE PEACE***
See Quincy

***ST PAUL*** (517)278-8061
David L Gruenhagen • WS 9 1130; SS 1030 • H • EC • MI • 95 W State St Coldwater MI 49036-8825 • FAX(517)279-6232 • stpaullccw@cbpu.com

**COLOMA—*SALEM*** (616)468-6567
Mark A Steinke • WS 8 1030; BC 915;* • EC • MI • 275 Marvin 49038 PO Box 729 Coloma MI 49038-0729 • FAX(616)468-7729

**COLON—*ST PAUL*** (616)432-3807
Mark E Gilson • WS 9; SS 1015; BC 1015 • H • MI • 484 S Burr Oak Rd PO Box 264 Colon MI 49040-0264

**COMMERCE TWP—*OUR SAVIOR DF***
See Farmington Hills

**CONKLIN 3 NE—*TRINITY*** (616)899-2973
Mark A Oswald • WS 930; SS 1045; BC 1045;* • H • EL • MI • 49403 1351 Harding St Conklin MI 49403-9519 • FAX(616)899-2930 • drwacker@aalweb.net

**COOPERSVILLE—*GRACE*** (616)837-7831
Joel F Hoyer • WS 930; SS 1045; BC 1045 • H • MI • 300 Cleveland St E Coopersville MI 49404-9601 • joelffl@iserv.net

**COVINGTON—*TRINITY*** (906)355-2534
Mark C Reinsch • WS 9;* • NW • M-28 49919 PO Box 140 Covington MI 49919-0140

**DAVISON—*TRINITY*** (810)658-3000
Randall P Schultz Stephen C Stahlhut • WS 815 1045; SS 930; BC 930;* • H • MI • 706 W Flint St Davison MI 48423-1010 • FAX(810)653-4155 • trinitydavison@juno.com

**DE TOUR VILLAGE—*REDEEMER*** (906)297-5005
Dean R Muhle • H • MI • 210 Superior St 49725 PO Box 62 De Tour Village MI 49725-0062

**DE WITT—*HOPE*** (517)669-3930
Vacant • H • EC • MI • 48820 1180 W Herbison Rd Dewitt MI 48820-8308 • FAX(517)669-1580

**DEARBORN—*ATONEMENT*** (313)581-2525
Kenton R Gottschalk • WS 930; BC 830;* • EC/EL/HS • MI • 6961 Mead St Dearborn MI 48126-1787 • FAX(313)581-1156 • atone6961@aol.com

***EMMANUEL*** (313)565-4002
Rodney E Zwonitzer Joel R Baseley • WS 815; SS 940; BC 940;* • H • EC/EL/HS • MI • 800 S Military St Dearborn MI 48124-2120 • FAX(313)565-4330 • lcebaseb@ccaa.edu

***GUARDIAN*** (313)274-1414
David L Schrader David A Jung • WS 8 11; SS 930; BC 930;* • H • HS • MI • 24544 Cherry Hill St Dearborn MI 48124-1369 • FAX(313)274-2076 • lcschrd@ccaa.edu

***OUR REDEEMER*** (313)562-9246
Vacant • BC 915;* • H • EC • MI • 24931 Union St Dearborn MI 48124-4819 • FAX(313)562-9247

**DEARBORN HEIGHTS—*IMMANUEL*** (313)278-5755
Vacant • H • EC • MI • 27035 Ann Arbor Trl Dearborn Heights MI 48127-1061

**DETROIT—*BEREA*** (313)834-5901
Vacant • H • MI • 7047 Tireman St Detroit MI 48204-3438

***BETHANY*** (313)885-7721
Peter R Brueckner • WS 10; BC 9;* • EC/EL/HS • MI • 11475 E Outer Dr Detroit MI 48224-3226

***BETHLEHEM*** (313)554-3728
Theodore J Klein • MI • 1450 McKinstry St 48209-2456 2462 Riverwood Dr Port Huron MI 48060

***CHARITY*** (313)527-4337
Vacant • WS 1030;* • H • HS • MI • 17220 Kelly Rd Detroit MI 48224-1581

***EAST BETHLEHEM*** (313)892-2670
Robert H Sorenson • WS 9; SS 1030 • H • EL/HS • MI • 3510 E Outer Dr Detroit MI 48234-2658 • FAX(313)892-1754 • bobshirl@flash.net

***EPIPHANY*** (313)368-1260
Richard P Hillenbrand • * • MI • 933 W 7 Mile Rd Detroit MI 48203-1929 • FAX(313)368-4309 • elcofdet@aol.com

***EVERGREEN*** (313)584-0450
William F Danowski • WS 10; SS 10; BC 9 • H • MI • 8680 Evergreen Ave Detroit MI 48228-2922

***GOOD SHEPHERD*** (313)527-6353
Gene Evans • WS 1030 2;* • HS • EN • 14190 Edmore Dr 48205-1258 20247 Regent Dr Detroit MI 48205-1265

***GRACE***
See Redford Township

***GREENFLD PEACE*** (313)838-3366
Harold A Avers • WS 8 11; SS 930; BC 930 • EL • MI • 6980 W Outer Dr 48235-2858 7000 W Outer Dr Detroit MI 48235-3166 • FAX(313)838-8524

***HIST TRINITY*** (313)567-3100
David Eberhard • WS 830 930 11; SS 930; BC 930;* • H • HS • MI • 1345 Gratiot Ave Detroit MI 48207-2720 • FAX(313)567-3209 • Histtrin@aol.com

***HOLY CROSS*** (313)836-2272
James W Turner • WS 845 1115; SS 10; BC 10;* • MI • 14213 Whitcomb St Detroit MI 48227-2126

***MOUNT CALVARY*** (313)527-3366
Gerald E Grimm • WS 1030; SS 9; BC 9 • EC/EL/HS • MI • 17100 Chalmers Ave Detroit MI 48205-2862 • FAX(313)527-7535 • mtcal@voyager.net

***NAZARETH*** (313)897-8622
Vacant • MI • 4321 Vicksburg St Detroit MI 48204-2428

***NEW MT OLIVE*** (313)834-4396
Venice C Douglas • EC • EN • 8590 Esper St Detroit MI 48204-3183 • mtolive.com

***OUTER DR FAITH*** (313)341-4095
Roosevelt Gray • H • MI • 17500 James Couzens Fwy Detroit MI 48235-2642 • FAX(313)341-2926 • disciple@odflc.org

***PEACE*** (313)882-0254
Arnold H Brammeier • WS 10; SS 9; BC 9 • H • EC/EL/HS • MI • 15700 E Warren Ave Detroit MI 48224-3289 • FAX(313)882-5680

***REDEMPTION*** (313)526-5631
Arthur R Henne • WS 9; SS 1030; BC 1030 • H • HS • MI • 12411 E 7 Mile Rd Detroit MI 48205-2154 • arthenne@aol.com

***REDFORD*** (313)535-3733
Steven S Billings Richard A Zeile • WS 930; BC 11;* • H • HS • MI • 22159 Grand River Ave Detroit MI 48219-3228 • FAX(313)535-3734 • redfordluth@juno.com

***RESURRECTION*** (313)372-4902
Arthur M Casci • H • EC/HS • MI • 20531 Kelly Rd Detroit MI 48225-1209 • lcmresur@ccaa.edu

***ST JOHN*** (313)933-9360
Duane O Geary • WS 1030;* • H • EC/EL • MI • 4950 Oakman Blvd Detroit MI 48204-2684 • FAX(313)933-5842

***ST PHILIP*** (313)872-1010
David F Burgess • H • HS • MI • 2884 E Grand Blvd Detroit MI 48202-3130 • FAX(313)872-2010

***ST STEPHEN*** (313)841-7940
Vacant • WS 1030; BC 915;* • HS • MI • 8736 Chamberlain St 48209-1770 1235 Lawndale St Detroit MI 48209-1727 • FAX(313)841-7963

***ST TIMOTHY*** (313)535-1970
Paul A Wolff • H • EC/EL • MI • 19400 Evergreen Rd Detroit MI 48219-2025 • FAX(313)535-9732

***ZION*** (313)894-7450
John W Fenton • WS 9; SS 11;* • EN • 4315 Military St 4305 Military St Detroit MI 48210-2451 • FAX(313)894-7871 • zion@flash.net

**DEXTER—*PEACE***
See Ann Arbor

**DORR—*EPIPHANY*** (616)681-0791
Charles R Hogg Jr. • WS 915; BC 1045;* • H • EN • 4219 Park Ln 49323 PO Box 245 Dorr MI 49323-0245 • epiphany@accn.org

**DRAYTON PLAINS—*ST STEPHEN*** (248)673-6621
E D Evanson • WS 8 1045; SS 930; BC 930;* • H • EC/EL/HS • MI • 3795 Sashabaw 48330 PO Box 298020 Waterford MI 48329-8020 • FAX(248)673-6683

**DRUMMOND ISLAND—*DRUMMOND*** (906)493-5982
Vacant • WS 1030;* • H • MI • Channel Rd 49726 PO Box 269 Drummond Island MI 49726-0269 • FAX(906)493-5982

**DRYDEN 2 W—*HOLY REDEEMER*** (810)796-3951
Steven C Helms • WS 8;* • EC • MI • Dryden And Havens Rd 48428 4538 Dryden Rd Dryden MI 48428-9702 • FAX(810)796-2060 • holyred@tir.com

**EAST LANSING—*ASCENSION*** (517)337-9703
Patrick S Fodor • H • MI • 2780 Haslett Rd East Lansing MI 48823-2919 • FAX(517)337-4840 • ascension@acd.net

***MARTIN LUTHER CHAPEL*** (517)332-0778
David A Dressel • WS 7;* • H • EN • 444 Abbott Rd East Lansing MI 48823-3321 • FAX(517)332-4506 • dresseld@tcimet.net

**EASTPOINTE—*ST PETER*** (810)776-1663
Michael J Roth • H • EC/EL/HS • MI • 23000 Gratiot Ave Eastpointe MI 48021-1663 • FAX(810)771-2524

***ST THOMAS*** (810)772-3370
Mark W Hetzner Darryl L Andrzejewski • H • HS • MI • 23801 Kelly Rd Eastpointe MI 48021-3440

**ELK RAPIDS—*GRACE*** (231)264-5312
James E Weber • WS 930;* • H • MI • 10561 US 31 S Elk Rapids MI 49629 • dajweb@juno.com

**ENGADINE—*GRACE***
See Germfask

**ENGADINE 5 N—*BETHLEHEM*** (906)477-1011
John F Walker • H • MI • 49827 RR 1 Box 160 Engadine MI 49827-9726

**ESCANABA—*OUR SAVIOR*** (906)789-9350
Paul D Kelto • WS 8 1030;* • H • EC • NW • 2401 N Lincoln Rd 49829-9569 PO Box 1232 Escanaba MI 49829-6232

**ESSEXVILLE—*PILGRIM*** (517)893-7224
Carl F Trosien • H • EC • MI • 1705 Nebobish Ave Essexville MI 48732-1638

**FAIR HAVEN—*ST PETER*** (810)765-8161
Robert V Wagner • * • H • MI • 6745 Palms Rd 48023-2212 PO Box 230405 Fair Haven MI 48023-0405

**FAIRGROVE—*GRACE*** (517)693-6322
Stephen J Biegel • WS 930;* • H • MI • 1809 S Main St Fairgrove MI 48733-9554 • FAX(520)441-9516 • petersen@avci.net

**FARMINGTON HILLS—*OUR SAVIOR*** (248)684-7358
Vacant • H • MI • 28000 New Market Rd 48334-3335 3541 E Commerce Rd Commerce Twp MI 48382-1418

***PRINCE PEACE*** (248)553-3380
Thomas M Lange • H • HS • MI • 28000 New Market Rd Farmington Hills MI 48334-3335 • FAX(248)553-2809

***ST PAUL*** (248)474-0675
John W Meyer Carl E Mehl(EM) • WS 915; BC 1045;* • H • EC/EL/HS • MI • 20805 Middlebelt Rd Farmington Hills MI 48336-5545 • FAX(248)474-1945 • stpls@hotmail.com

**FENTON—*TRINITY*** (810)629-7861
Dean G Dumbrille • Lisa B Lindeman DCE • WS 845 11; BC 10;* • H • MI • 48430-2174 806 Main St PO Box 288 Fenton MI 48430 • FAX(810)629-9877

**FLAT ROCK—*COMMUNITY*** (734)782-0563
David P Gohn Michael S Heusel • WS 830 11; SS 10; BC 10;* • H • MI • 23984 Gibraltar Rd Flat Rock MI 48134-9411 • FAX(734)782-1541

**FLINT—*CALVARY*** (810)239-5651
Vacant • H • MI • 2210 N Franklin Ave Flint MI 48506-4434 • FAX(810)239-6534

***CHRIST KING*** (810)785-8371
Vacant • H • MI • 3499G W Carpenter Rd Flint MI 48504-1253

***NEW LIFE COMM*** (810)239-7127
Bradley J Yops • MI • Flint Institute Of Music 48502 1214 Maxine Flint MI 48503-2076 • FAX(810)239-7127

***OUR SAVIOR*** (810)789-1361
Bertrand J Cottam • MI • 6901 N Saginaw St Flint MI 48505-2276 • FAX(810)235-7120 • REVCOTT@TIR.COM

***PEACE*** (810)234-2423
James G Wilber • H • MI • 2051 W Maple Ave Flint MI 48507-3501 • FAX(810)234-5699

***REDEEMER*** (810)249-1380
Robert K Wahl • H • EC/EL • MI • 460 W Atherton Rd Flint MI 48507-2602 • FAX(810)249-1383

***ST MARK*** (810)736-6680
Gary L Beck • James M Mol P Asst • * • EC/EL • MI • 5073 Daly Blvd Flint MI 48506-1507 • FAX(810)736-6096

***ST PAUL*** (810)239-6200
Roger R Kilponen Steven R Maske • Kathleen A Schuck P Asst • WS 830 11; SS 945 • H • EC/EL • MI • 402 S Ballenger Hwy Flint MI 48532-3637 • FAX(810)239-5466

***UNITED/CHRIST*** (810)732-3730
Gilbert R Mabry • WS 1030;* • H • MI • G-6330 Corunna Rd Flint MI 48532

**FLUSHING—*HOLY CROSS*** (810)659-5926
Clifford F Bira • Sharlene A Kleinedler DCE • * • H • MI • 1209 Coutant St Flushing MI 48433-1708 • FAX(810)659-5964 • hclc@tir.com

**FORESTVILLE 2 W—*TRINITY*** (517)864-3745
Richard G Wilson • H • MI • 48434 5034 Bay City Forestville Rd Minden City MI 48456-9769 • trinity@hbch.com

**FOWLER—*ST PAUL*** (517)593-2066
Paul M Clark • * • H • MI • 329 N Sorrell St 48835-9297 PO Box 317 Fowler MI 48835-0317 • FAX(517)593-2066

**FRANKENLUST—*ST PAUL***
See Bay City

**FRANKENMUTH—*ST LORENZ*** (517)652-6141
Mark D Brandt Dale C Ahlschwede Gary L Bender Michael N Fitzgerald Joel C Kaiser • James C Anderson DCE • WS 8 1045; SS 925;* • H • EC/EL • MI • 1030 W Tuscola St 48734-9201 140 Churchgrove Rd Frankenmuth MI 48734-1038 • FAX(517)652-9071 • church@stlorenz.org

**FRASER—*ST JOHN*** (810)293-0333
John E Merrill Eric W Majeski • WS 8; SS 930; BC 930;* • H • EC/EL/HS • MI • 16339-14 Mile Rd Fraser MI 48026 • FAX(810)294-9565 • sjfraser@bignet.net

**FREMONT—*LIVING HOPE***
Vacant • MI • C/O PO Box 462 Fremont MI 49412-0462

***REDEEMER*** (231)924-2707
George W Brinley • H • MI • 49412 24 Southwoods Ave Fremont MI 49412-1750 • FAX(231)924-2707 • revgwbrinley@ncats.net

**GAYLORD—*TRINITY*** (517)732-4816
Vacant • H • EC • MI • 1354 S Otsego Ave 49735-7711 PO Box 542 Gaylord MI 49734-0542

**GERMFASK—*GRACE*** (906)586-6900
John F Walker • H • MI • RR 1 Box 50 Germfask MI 49836

**GLADWIN—*OUR SAVIOR*** (517)426-9689
Timothy M Verity • WS 10;* • H • MI • 331 Clendening Rd 48624-1054 PO Box 527 Gladwin MI 48624 • FAX(517)426-2324

**GLEN ARBOR—*BETHLEHEM*** (231)334-4180
Vacant • WS 930; BC 10;* • H • MI • 6012 S Lake St 49636-9724 PO Box 353 Glen Arbor MI 49636-0353

**GLENDORA—*TRINITY*** (616)422-2554
W J Lowmaster • WS 10; SS 845; BC 845;* • H • MI • 1733 Glendora Rd Buchanan MI 49107 • FAX(616)422-2554

**GLENNIE—*OUR SAVIOR*** (517)735-2710
Vacant • WS 9; BC 1030;* • H • MI • 3639 S M-65 Glennie MI 48737-0007

**GOOD HARBOR—*ST PAUL*** (231)228-6888
Thomas P Zimmerman • WS 930;* • H • MI • 49621 2943 S Manitou Trl Cedar MI 49621-9733 • tpzimm@prodigy.net

**GOODELLS—*HOPE*** (810)325-1169
Vacant • WS 11 • H • MI • 2792 Goodells Rd 48027-1409 PO Box 158 Goodells MI 48027-0158

**GOODRICH 6 E—*CHRIST*** (810)797-4602
John R Schreiber • * • H • MI • 5245 Hadley Rd Goodrich MI 48438-9699 • rev.schreiber@juno.com

**GRAND BLANC—*FAITH*** (810)694-9351
Wayne H Wentzel Gregory L Sawyer • WS 8 930 11; SS 930; BC 930;* • H • EC • MI • 12534 Holly Rd Grand Blanc MI 48439-1815 • FAX(810)694-3949

**GRAND HAVEN—*ST JOHN*** (616)842-4510
Dieter E Haupt Phillip A Baerwolf • WS 8 930 11;* • H • MI • 527 Taylor Ave Grand Haven MI 49417-2125

**GRAND RAPIDS—*HOPE*** (616)459-2941
Daniel J Gruenwald • * • H • EN • 100 Packard Ave SE Grand Rapids MI 49503-4439 • pastor@iserv.net

***IMMANUEL*** (616)454-3655
David A Davis Walter E Bunkowske • * • H • EC/EL • MI • 2 Michigan St NE Grand Rapids MI 49503 • FAX(616)454-3427 • ilc@iserv.net

***MESSIAH*** (616)363-2553
Terry E Hoese • Richard C Krueger P Asst • WS 830 11; SS 945; BC 945 • H • EC • MI • 2727 5 Mile Rd NE Grand Rapids MI 49525-1709 • FAX(616)363-7843 • messiahgr@juno.com

***MOUNT OLIVE*** (616)453-0803
Sean L Rippy • WS 930;* • H • MI • 3950 Leonard St NW Grand Rapids MI 49544-3628 • FAX(616)453-9450 • mt.olivegr@juno.com

***OUR SAVIOR*** (616)949-0710
David C Fleming • WS 815 11; SS 945; BC 945 • H • EC/EL • MI • 2900 Burton St SE Grand Rapids MI 49546-5153 • FAX(616)975-7840 • davidfleming1@juno.com

***REDEEMER*** (616)452-1529
Stephen A Wiggins Sr. • WS 11; SS 10;* • H • EC • MI • 1905 Madison Ave SE Grand Rapids MI 49507-2539 • FAX(616)452-1450 • redeemerlutheran@prodigy.net

***ST JAMES*** (616)363-7718
James H Blain • * • H • EC/EL • MI • 2040 Oakwood Ave NE Grand Rapids MI 49505-4170

***ST MATTHEW***
See Ada Twp

**GRANDVILLE—*BETHEL*** (616)534-3364
Glenn P Kopper • * • H • MI • 3655 Wilson Ave SW Grandville MI 49418-1869 • bethelutheran@juno.com

**GRAYLING—*MOUNT HOPE*** (517)348-5921
Vacant • H • MI • 905 N I 75 Business Loop 49738-6771 PO Box 483 Grayling MI 49738-0483 • FAX(517)348-0166 • mthope@freeway.net

**GREENVILLE—*MOUNT CALVARY*** (616)754-4886
Mark R Pflug • * • H • EC • MI • 908 W Oak St Greenville MI 48838-2149 • FAX(616)754-4886 • mclc@iserv.net

**GROSSE POINTE WOODS—*CHRIST*** (313)884-5090
Randy S Boelter Timothy A Holzerland • WS 815; BC 930;* • EC/HS • EN • 48236 20338 Mack Ave Grosse Pointe Woods MI 48236-1718 • FAX(313)884-5927

**HALE—*ST PAUL*** (517)728-4082
Vacant • H • MI • 407 S Washington St 48739-8501 PO Box 307 Hale MI 48739-0307

**HAMBURG—*ST PAUL*** (810)231-1033
Mark A Neumann • Michael F Hausch DCE • H • HS • MI • 7701 E M-36 48139 PO Box 490 Hamburg MI 48139-0490 • FAX(810)231-1016 • stpaul@cac.net

**HANCOCK—*SS PETER&PAUL*** (906)482-4750
David J Weber • H • NW • 323 Hancock St 49930-2005 307 Montezuma St Hancock MI 49930-2024 • FAX(906)482-7425 • >pastor@sspeterpaul-lcms.orgı

**HARBOR BEACH—*ZION*** (517)479-3615
Mark E Girardin • H • EC/EL • MI • 225 N 3rd St Harbor Beach MI 48441-1112 • FAX(517)479-6551

**HARBOR SPRINGS—** (231)526-6357
Vacant • WS 6;* • H • MI • Blackbird El Sch/421 E Lake St PO Box 712 Harbor Springs MI 49740

**HARRISON—*ST LUKE*** (517)539-6312
Warren W Graff • WS 1030; SS 915;* • H • MI • 616 S 4th St 48625-9149 PO Box 623 Harrison MI 48625-0623 • stluke@juno.com

**HARRISVILLE—*FAITH*** (517)724-7837
Vacant • WS 930; BC 1045;* • H • MI • 216 School Dr Harrisville MI 48740-9587 • dneigh@triton.net

**HARTLAND—*OUR SAVIOR*** (248)887-4300
Frank J Pies William E Thompson • Christopher I Thoma DCE • H • EC/EL/HS • EN • 13667 W Highland Rd Hartland MI 48353-3127 • FAX(248)887-3596

**HASLETT—*ST LUKE*** (517)339-9119
Raymond M Rohlfs • * • H • EC • MI • 5589 Van Atta Rd Haslett MI 48840-9726 • FAX(517)339-5430 • stlukehas@aol.com

**HAWKS—*FAITH*** (517)734-2891
Jack D Ferguson • MI • PO Box 131 Hawks MI 49743-0131

**HAZEL PARK—*HAZEL PARK*** (248)398-6363
Cameron K Steele • WS 10; BC 9;* • MI • 22910 Highland Ave Hazel Park MI 48030-1815 • FAX(248)398-3088 • hplc@juno.com

**HEMLOCK 3 NE—*ST PETER*** (517)642-8188
Martin J Hagenow Richard E Mundt • WS 8 1030;* • H • EC/EL/HS • MI • 48626 2461 N Raucholz Rd Hemlock MI 48626-9461 • FAX(517)642-9052 • spls@svol.org

**HEMLOCK 5 NW—*ZION*** (517)642-5909
Paul A Hauser • WS 930;* • H • EC/EL/HS • MI • 48626 17927 Dice Rd Hemlock MI 48626-9637 • FAX(517)642-4416

**HERRON—*ST PAUL*** (517)727-2496
Robert L Mikkelson • WS 930; BC 11;* • H • MI • 7716 Wolf Creek Rd Herron MI 49744-9752 • FAX(517)727-8086 • stpaulh@freeway.net

**HIGHLAND—*FAITH*** (248)887-5550
Terry A Claus • WS 830;* • H • MI • 3501 E Highland Rd Highland MI 48356-2824 • FAX(248)889-8115 • faithl@tir.com

**HILLMAN 6 N—*ST JOHN*** (517)742-4400
Vacant • H • MI • 49746 22000 County Rd 452 Hillman MI 49746-9547

**HILLSDALE—*ST PAUL*** (517)437-2762
Lee D Johnson • H • MI • 2551 W Bacon Rd Hillsdale MI 49242-9208 • pastordanjohnson@yahoo.com

**HOLLAND—*CHRIST OUR SAVIOR*** (616)738-0100
Rodney D Otto • * • H • MI • 3151 N 120th Ave Holland MI 49424 • FAX((616)738-2861 • pfordo7@iserv.net

***ZION*** (616)392-7151
John Westra • Erna I Schmid DEAC • * • H • EC • MI • 77 W 32nd St Holland MI 49423-5061 • FAX(616)392-7180

**HOLLY—*GETHSEMANE*** (248)634-9452
Roger D Gallert(#) • H • HS • MI • 961 E Maple St Holly MI 48442-1769

**HOLT—*MESSIAH*** (517)694-1280
John A Schinkel • Michael R Bridges DCE • WS 8 1030; SS 915; BC 915 • H • MI • 5740 Holt Rd Holt MI 48842-8645 • FAX(517)694-1492 • messiahholt@juno.com

**HOUGHTON LAKE—*ST JOHN*** (517)366-5164
William C Winter • WS 930; BC 11;* • H • MI • 2882 W Houghton Lake Dr Houghton Lake MI 48629-9297 • FAX(517)366-4420 • winterhaus@voyager.net

**HOWARD CITY 3 N—*BETHEL*** (231)937-4921
David W Heinert • WS 930; SS 1045;* • H • EC • MI • 49329 18669 W Howard City Edmore Rd Howard City MI 49329-9312 • FAX(231)937-4921 • bethelhc@pathwaynet.com

**HOWELL—*IMMANUEL*** (517)548-2066
Eric C Forss • H • EN • 1944 Oak Grove Rd 48843-8781 PO Box 656 Howell MI 48844-0656

**HUBBELL—*ST JOHN*** (906)296-1022
James K Fundum • WS 830;* • H • NW • 311 Guck St 49934 PO Box 486 Hubbell MI 49934-0486

**HUDSON—*OUR SAVIOUR*** (517)448-6271
Todd J Brunworth • H • MI • 751 N Maple Grove Ave Hudson MI 49247-1149

**HUDSONVILLE—*NEW HOPE*** (616)669-2790
Vacant • WS 930;* • H • MI • 3232 Port Sheldon St Hudsonville MI 49426-9317 • newhope17@juno.com

**HUNTINGTON WOODS—*HUNTINGTON*** (248)542-3007
Peter S Nickel • * • H • EC/HS • MI • 12935 W 11 Mile Rd Huntington Woods MI 48070-1023 • FAX(248)542-0709

**INKSTER—*OUR MASTER*** (313)565-5766
David G Huber • WS 10;* • MI • 821 Inkster Rd Inkster MI 48141-1214 • dghuber@aol.com

**IONIA—*ST JOHN*** (616)527-1250
Paul A Yanke • WS 930;* • H • EC/EL • MI • 617 N Jefferson St Ionia MI 48846-1230 • stjohns@ionia-mi.net

**IRON RIVER—*ST PAUL*** (906)265-4750
Thomas R Mackey • WS 1030; BC 915;* • H • EC • NW • 4221 W US Highway 2 49935-7981 PO Box 499 Iron River MI 49935-0499 • FAX(906)265-4750

**IRONWOOD—*TRINITY*** (906)932-3022
Todd I Frusti • * • H • EC • NW • E5104 E Margaret St Ironwood MI 49938-1536 • FAX(906)932-5583 • tlc@portup.com

**IRONWOOD 18 NW—*IMMANUEL*** (906)932-3022
Todd I Frusti • * • NW • Little Girls Point 49938 E1898 Brace Rd Ironwood MI 49938-9225

**ISHPEMING—*CHRIST KING*** (906)485-4432
Timothy M Ott • H • EC • NW • 440 Stoneville Rd Ishpeming MI 49849

**JACKSON—*REDEEMER*** (517)750-3100
R W Roper • WS 8 1045; SS 930; BC 930;* • H • MI • 3637 Spring Arbor Rd Jackson MI 49201-9301 • FAX(517)750-4590 • rlcofc@dmci.net

***TRINITY*** (517)784-3135
Galen E Grulke Douglas A Krengel • WS 1045 8; SS 930; BC 930;* • H • MI • 122 W Wesley Ave Jackson MI 49201-2227 • FAX(517)784-4344 • trinity.luth@dmci.net

**JENISON—*HOLY CROSS*** (616)457-2420
John A Bookshaw • H • EC • MI • 1481 Baldwin St Jenison MI 49428-8910 • FAX(616)457-4590

**JENISON 5 NW—*ST JOHN***
See Allendale

**KALAMAZOO—*IMMANUEL*** (616)345-8090
Vacant • BC 11;* • H • MI • 3000 W Main St Kalamazoo MI 49006-2956 • immanuel@voyager.net

***UNIVERSITY*** (616)349-1100
Vacant • * • H • MI • Kanley Chapel Wmu 49008 1720 W Michigan Ave Kalamazoo MI 49006-4431

***ZION*** (616)382-2360
Timothy W Seeber Larry E Brelje Louis W Grother(EM) • Christopher S Drager DCE • WS 8;* • H • EC • MI • 2122 Bronson Blvd Kalamazoo MI 49008-1905 • FAX(616)382-2367 • zionkazoo@net-link.net

**KALKASKA—*ST PAUL*** (231)258-9258
Ted N Turanski • WS 10;* • MI • Us 131 N 49646 PO Box 535 Kalkaska MI 49646-0535

**KENTWOOD—*ST MARK*** (616)455-5320
Donald E Schoenback Jr. • Thomas B Chester P Asst • H • EC/EL • MI • 1934 52nd St SE Kentwood MI 49508-4915 • FAX(616)455-8487

**KILMANAGH—*ST JOHN*** (517)883-2188
David P Lukefahr • WS 930; SS 1045; BC 1045 • MI • 9476 Kilmanagh Rd 48759 9456 Kilmanagh Rd Sebewaing MI 48759-9722

**KINCHLOE—*ST BARNABAS***
See Sault Ste Marie

**KINDE—*ST PETER*** (517)874-4181
Vacant • WS 8 • MI • 5098 Dwight St 48445 PO Box 177 Kinde MI 48445-0177

**KINGSFORD—*OUR REDEEMER*** (906)774-1844
Martin E Koeller • WS 10;* • H • NW • 420 W Breitung Ave Kingsford MI 49802-5508

**KINGSLEY—*ST JOHANNES*** (231)263-5800
Kelly D Todd • * • H • MI • 7861 Summit City Rd Kingsley MI 49649-9663 • FAX(231)263-4801 • toddkd@mail.ctsfw.edu

**KINGSTON—*CHRIST THE KING**** (810)648-2660
Vacant • H • MI • 5910 State St (M-46) 48741 PO Box 9 Kingston MI 48741-0009

**KINROSS—*ST PAUL*** (906)495-5849
Dean R Muhle • MI • 49752 16811 S Water Tower Dr Kincheloe MI 49788-1505

**LAKE ORION—*GOOD SHEPHERD*** (248)391-1170
James H Van Dellen Eric E Tritten • WS 830 11;* • H • EC • MI • 1950 S Baldwin Rd Lake Orion MI 48360-1016 • FAX(248)391-1680 • gslcorion@juno.com

**LAKEVIEW—*HOLY TRINITY*** (517)352-6374
Larry G Sheppard • WS 930; BC 1045;* • H • EN • 8890 Tamarack Rd Lakeview MI 48850-9120

**LAMBERTVILLE—*CHRIST KING*** (734)856-1461
Ronald P Scheer • WS 830 1030; BC 935;* • H • EC/HS • MI • 2843 Sterns Rd Lambertville MI 48144-9627

**LANSING—*CHRIST*** (517)482-2252
David L Thiele Richard A Mittwede(#) • H • EN • 122 S Pennsylvania Ave Lansing MI 48912-1802 • FAX(517)482-4719 • packerrev@voyager.net

***GOOD SHEPHERD*** (517)321-6100
Roger K Straub • WS 945;* • H • MI • 7000 W Saginaw Hwy Lansing MI 48917-1117 • shepherd@iserv.net

***OUR SAVIOR*** (517)882-8665
David P Maier Robert B Appold • WS 8 1045;* • H • MI • 1601 W Holmes Rd Lansing MI 48910-0354 • FAX(517)882-3477

***TRINITY*** (517)372-1631
Richard P Laeder • H • EC • MI • 501 W Saginaw St Lansing MI 48933-1043 • FAX(517)372-5026 • joannevw@juno.co

**LAPEER—*ST PAUL*** (810)664-6653
John C Kaiser Douglas A Krengel • Kimberly J Tedesco P Asst • WS 8;* • H • EC/EL • MI • 90 Millville Rd Lapeer MI 48446-1642 • FAX(810)245-4082

**LAURIUM—*ST PAUL*** (906)337-0231
James K Fundum • WS 1030;* • H • NW • 146 Tamarack St Laurium MI 49913-2046

**LELAND—*IMMANUEL*** (231)256-9464
Lawrence K Matro • WS 10; SS 830; BC 830;* • H • MI • 303 E Pearl St 49654 PO Box 436 Leland MI 49654-0436 • FAX(231)256-2052 • ilcleland@juno.com

**LESLIE—*GRACE*** (517)589-5239
James D Keat • H • EC • MI • 4279 Oak St 49251 PO Box 511 Leslie MI 49251-0511

**LEWISTON—*BETHLEHEM*** (517)786-3713
Vacant • WS 10;* • H • MI • 3805 W County Rd 612 49756 PO Box 827 Lewiston MI 49756-0827

**LEXINGTON—*ST MATTHEW*** (810)359-8411
Barry C Sheldon • WS 930;* • H • MI • 7155 Huron At Union 48450 PO Box 160 Lexington MI 48450-0160

**LINCOLN PARK—*CALVARY*** (313)381-6715
Calvin E Reinke • H • EC/EL/HS • MI • 3320 Electric Ave Lincoln Park MI 48146-3103 • FAX(313)381-3584

**LINDEN—*HOPE*** (810)735-4807
Lawrence M Eckart • H • MI • 7355 Silver Lake Rd 48451-8772 PO Box 524 Linden MI 48451-0524 • FAX(810)735-1942

**LINKVILLE—*ST PAUL*** (517)453-2271
Lee C Wenskay • H • MI • UKNWN 7292 Kilmanagh Rd Pigeon MI 48755-9544 • spaullvl@avci.net

**LIVONIA—*CHRIST OUR SAVIOR***
2nd Location

***CHRIST OUR SAVIOR*** (734)522-6830
Luther A Werth Robert F Bayer • Timothy A Bode DCO Dena M Black DCE • WS 830 11; SS 945; BC 945 • H • EC/HS • MI • 14175 Farmington Rd Livonia MI 48154-5422 • FAX(734)522-5949

**LOWELL 3E—*GOOD SHEPHERD*** (616)897-8307
Joseph Fremer • WS 10;* • H • MI • 49331 10305 Bluewater Hwy Lowell MI 49331-9281 • goodshep@iserv.net

**LUDINGTON—*PEACE*** (616)845-1985
Vacant • WS 915; SS 1015; BC 1015 • H • MI • 1650 N Jebavy Dr Ludington MI 49431-8618 • fosdic@t-one.net

***ST JOHN*** (231)843-9188
Vacant • H • MI • 209 N Rowe Street PO Box 209 Ludington MI 49431-1733

**MACOMB—*ST PETER*** (810)781-3434
Robert E Kasper Gregory M Lorenz • WS 8 930 11; SS 930; BC 930;* • H • EC/EL/HS • MI • 17051 24 Mile Rd Macomb MI 48042-2902 • FAX(810)781-9726

**MACOMB 5 NW—*IMMANUEL*** (810)286-4231
Michael J Lutz E Paul Burow Ronald H Jahnke(#) • WS 745 1015 1145;* • H • EC/EL/HS • MI • 47120 Romeo Plank-21 Mile Rd Macomb MI 48044-2809 • FAX(810)286-8645

**MANCELONA—*ST MATTHEW*** (616)587-5505
Daniel J Mc Vey • MI • 211 E Hinman 49659-9640 PO Box 469 Mancelona MI 49659-0469

**MANISTEE—*TRINITY*** (231)723-5149
Dennis D Rahn • H • EC/EL • MI • 420 Oak St Manistee MI 49660-1697 • FAX(231)723-9755 • trinityK8@voyager.net

**MANITOU BEACH—*OF THE LAKES***
See Addison

**MARENISCO—*MESSIAH*** (906)787-2491
Vacant • NW • PO Box 155 Marenisco MI 49947-0155

**MARLETTE—*OUR SAVIOR*** (517)635-7994
Eric S Kilmer • WS 9; SS 1030; BC 1030 8;* • H • EC • MI • 6770 W Marlette St Marlette MI 48453-9203 • FAX(517)635-8306 • OSL@centurytel.net

**MARQUETTE—*REDEEMER*** (906)228-9883
Paul A Weber Wesley Baumeister Edwin V Fitz(EM) • Betty J Knapp DEAC • H • EC • NW • 1700 W Fair Ave Marquette MI 49855-2569 • FAX(906)228-8912 • RlutheranC@aol.com

**MARSHALL—*CHRIST*** (616)781-5842
David E Boedecker • * • H • EC • MI • 440 West Dr N Marshall MI 49068-9619 • clcmarshall@juno.com

***ZION*** (616)781-8982
Vacant • H • MI • 135 W Green St Marshall MI 49068-1535 • FAX(616)781-3711

**MASON—*SAINT MARK*** (517)676-6685
Vacant • H • MI • 840 W Columbia St Mason MI 48854-1028

**MECOSTA—*CHAPEL LAKES*** (231)972-7891
Raymond Pollatz • WS 9; SS 1015; BC 1015;* • H • MI • 9407 90th Ave Mecosta MI 49332-9733 • FAX(231)972-7891

**MEMPHIS—*ST ANDREW*** (810)392-2392
Paul M Boerger • H • MI • 34830 Potter St 48041-4614 PO Box 282 Memphis MI 48041-0282 • FAX(810)392-7046 • standrew@klondyke.net

**MESICK—*FAITH*** (616)885-1072
Vacant • WS 1015; SS 9; BC 9 • H • EC • MI • 320 N Clark St 49668-9215 PO Box 603 Mesick MI 49668-0603

**MIDDLEVILLE—*GOOD SHEPHERD*** (616)795-2391
Edward A Sikora • WS 930; SS 11; BC 11 • H • MI • 908 W Main St Middleville MI 49333-9770 • revsikora@juno.com

**MIDLAND—*LORD OF NEW LIF*** (517)832-3667
Vacant • MI • 3489 N Eastman Rd Midland MI 48640

***MESSIAH***
See Bullock Creek

***OUR SAVIOR*** (517)832-3667
Thomas F Fischer • * • H • MI • 1501 N Saginaw Rd Midland MI 48640-2841 • FAX(517)832-3667 • tfischer@journey.com

***ST JOHN*** (517)835-5861
John C Pohanka Douglas K Janetzke • WS 8;* • H • EC/EL • MI • 505 E Carpenter St Midland MI 48640-5462 • FAX(517)835-2443 • stjohns505@aol.com

**MILAN—*ST PAUL*** (734)439-2806
Dale M Kleimola • WS 1015; SS 9; BC 9 • MI • 106 Dexter St Milan MI 48160-1310 • FAX(734)439-0601 • kleimola@msn.com

**MILFORD—*CHRIST*** (248)684-0895
Richard E Pape • * • H • EC • MI • 620 General Motors Rd Milford MI 48381-2218 • FAX(248)684-0895

**MILLINGTON—*ST PAUL*** (517)871-4581
James R Bruner Timothy J Bickel • WS 830 11;* • H • EC/EL • MI • 4941 Center St Millington MI 48746-9676 • FAX(517)871-5573

**MINDEN CITY—*TRINITY***
See Forestville 2 W

**MIO—*LIVING WATER***
Vacant • WS 930; SS 830;* • H • MI • 207 Fourth St 48647 PO Box 247 Mio MI 48647-0247

**MOLTKE—*IMMANUEL*** (517)734-3216
Paul G Ruediger • MI • UKNWN 7134 Church Hwy Rogers City MI 49779-9721

**MONROE—*GRACE*** (734)242-1401
Ronald C Schultz Daniel A Kempin • Larry H Rockensuess Sr. P Asst • WS 8 1030; SS 915; BC 915 • H • HS • MI • 630 N Monroe St Monroe MI 48162-2935 • FAX(734)243-2629 • gracelc@foxberry.net

***TRINITY*** (313)242-2308
Stanley R Au Buchon Jeffrey B Walsh • H • EC/EL/HS • MI • 323 Scott St Monroe MI 48161-2132 • FAX(313)241-6293 • www.foxberry.net/trinity

**MONROE 6 NW—*HOLY GHOST*** (734)241-0525
Larry K Loree Sr. • WS 815 1045;* • H • EC/EL/HS • MI • 2 Miles W Of Us Hwy 24 3589 Heiss Rd Monroe MI 48162-9458 • FAX(734) 242-2701 • holyghost@hglcms.org

**MONROE 9 SW—*IMMANUEL*** (734)269-2961
Bruce K Lucas • H • HS • MI • 48161 6272 W Albain Rd Monroe MI 48161-9501

**MONTAGUE—*ST JAMES*** (231)894-8471
John W Brooks • Cynthia L Inselmann DCE • WS 815;* • H • EC • MI • 8945 Stebbins St Montague MI 49437-1263 • FAX(231)893-0198 • stjamessue@aol.com

**MOUNT CLEMENS—*ST LUKE***
See Clinton Township

***ST PETER***
See Macomb

***TRINITY***
See Clinton Township

**MOUNT CLEMENS 5—*IMMANUEL***
See Macomb 5 NW

**MOUNT PLEASANT—*CHRIST/KING**** (517)773-5050
Samuel B Reith James M Krach • H • MI • Central Michigan University 48858 1401 S Washington St Mount Pleasant MI 48858-4280 • zion.mtpleasant@juno.com

***ZION*** (517)772-1516
Samuel B Reith James M Krach • WS 8; SS 915; BC 915 • EC • MI • 701 E Maple St Mount Pleasant MI 48858-2757 • FAX(517)772-7640 • zion.mtpleasant@juno.com

**MUNGER—*TRINITY-ST JAMES*** (517)659-2506
Theodore E Voll • WS 830 11; SS 945; BC 945;* • H • EC/EL • MI • 119 E Munger Rd 48747-9701 PO Box 156 Munger MI 48747-0156 • tsjl@voyager.net

**MUNISING—*GOOD SHEPHERD*** (906)387-3579
Vacant • WS 9;* • H • NW • Hwy M 28 East 49862 PO Box 275 Munising MI 49862-0275

**MUSKEGON—*OUR REDEEMER*** (231)773-2667
Robert J Conradt • WS 830 11; BC 945;* • H • EC/EL • MI • 1215 E Apple Ave Muskegon MI 49442-3745

***ST MARK*** (231)798-2197
Mark E Zimmerman • WS 815 1045; SS 930;* • H • EC • MI • 4475 Henry St Muskegon MI 49441-4927 • FAX(231)798-7448 • stmark2000@yahoo.com

***TRINITY*** (616)755-1292
Dennis L Lassanske • * • H • EC/EL • MI • 3225 Roosevelt Rd Muskegon MI 49441-3909 • FAX(616)755-6942

**NEW BALTIMORE—*CHRIST*** (810)725-1431
Barry L Mueller • H • MI • 50750 Walpole St New Baltimore MI 48047-4270

***GOOD SHEPHERD*** (810)949-9440
David M Ulm • WS 815;* • HS • MI • 31100 23 Mile Rd New Baltimore MI 48047-1863 • FAX(810)949-0720

**NEW BOSTON—*ST JOHN***
See Waltz

***ST PAUL*** (734)753-9048
D L Cullen Jr. • * • H • HS • MI • 19109 Craig St 48164 PO Box 274 New Boston MI 48164-0274 • FAX(734)753-9710

**NEW BUFFALO—*PRINCE PEACE*** (616)469-0380
David H Sidwell • H • MI • 1615 E Buffalo St New Buffalo MI 49117-1569 • FAX(616)469-0380 • poplcms@trek.alliance.net

**NEW HAVEN—*ST JOHN*** (810)749-5286
Edward J Steeh • H • EC/EL/HS • MI • 30844 27 Mile Rd New Haven MI 48048-1812 • sjluth@i-is.net

**NEWBERRY—*TRINITY*** (906)293-9340
Kenneth P Johnson • WS 11;* • MI • 711 Newberry Ave 49868-1504 111 E Ave B Newberry MI 49868 • tahqluth@sault.com

**NEWPORT—*CHRIST OUR SHEPHERD*** (734)586-6229
Stephen E Schilke • WS 930; SS 1045; BC 1045;* • H • HS • MI • 8212 N Telegraph Rd Newport MI 48166-8913 • FAX(734)586-3760 • cosluth@juno.com

**NILES—*ST PAUL*** (616)683-0771
Robert M Zagore Daniel H Woodring • WS 8 1045; SS 915; BC 930 • H • MI • 1340 Sycamore St 49120-2033 PO Box 766 Niles MI 49120-0766 • FAX(616)683-0782 • pastor@stpaullutheran.org

**NORTH BRANCH—*NW LIFE CHRIST*** (810)688-2747
Henry C Wesenberg • WS 1030;* • H • MI • 6007 Fish Lake Rd #L North Branch MI 48461-9715

**NORTHVILLE—*ST PAUL*** (248)349-3140
Thomas M Lubeck Christopher D Fairbairn • WS 830 11; BC 10;* • H • EC/EL/HS • MI • 201 Elm St Northville MI 48167-1260 • FAX(248)349-7493 • stpaulnorthville@ameritech.net

**NUNICA—*ST LUKE*** (616)837-6059
William C Lahrman • H • MI • 11261 South St 49448 PO Box 97 Nunica MI 49448-0097 • stluke@iserv.net

**ONAWAY—*HOLY CROSS*** (517)733-8412
Vacant • WS 1045 • H • MI • 3786 Glasier Rd 49765 PO Box 706 Onaway MI 49765-0706

**ONEKAMA—*NORWALK*** (231)889-3543
Paul A Pollatz • H • MI • 5471 Fairview 49675 PO Box 119 Onekama MI 49675-0119 • FAX(231)889-3543 • bluefoxone@aol.com

***TRINITY*** (231)889-3543
Paul A Pollatz • H • EC • MI • 5471 Fairview St 49675 PO Box 119 Onekama MI 49675-0119 • FAX(231)889-3543 • bluefoxdne@aol.com

**ONTONAGON—*ST PAUL*** (906)884-4008
Howard R Neider • WS 9;* • NW • 107 E River St 49953-1324 303 S 7th St Ontonagon MI 49953-1442 • sneider@goisd.k12.mi.us

**ORTONVILLE—*PRINCE OF PEACE*** (248)627-6222
Vacant • * • H • MI • 270 Grange Hall Rd 48462-8836 PO Box 156 Ortonville MI 48462-0156

**OSCODA—*TRINITY*** (517)739-9292
Thomas V Boehne • H • MI • 5625 N US Highway 23 Oscoda MI 48750-9792 • FAX(517)739-9295 • trinluth@voyager.net

**OSSINEKE—*GOOD SHEPHERD*** (517)471-5428
Vacant • WS 10; SS 9; BC 9;* • H • MI • 12365 US 23 S PO Box 175 Ossineke MI 49766-0175 • FAX(517)471-5428 • goodshep@freeway.net

**OTISVILLE—*ST TIMOTHY*** (810)631-4730
David H Hensler • WS 830 11; BC 945;* • H • MI • 450 Wilson Rd Otisville MI 48463-9737 • FAX(810)631-4730

**OWOSSO—*ST PHILIP*** (517)723-6238
Brian F Heidt • MI • 219 W Oliver St 48867-2317 PO Box 772 Owosso MI 48867-0772

**OXFORD—*HOLY CROSS*** (248)628-2011
Michael P Schulz • WS 10; BC 845;* • EC • MI • 136 S Washington St Oxford MI 48371-4975 • FAX(248)628-9966

**PALMS 1 NE—*ST JOHN*** (517)864-3663
Henry B Malone • EC • MI • 48465 6600 N Ruth Rd Palms MI 48465-9706 • FAX(517)864-3411 • peerhankl@aol.com

**PARADISE—*PARADISE*** (906)293-9340
Kenneth P Johnson • WS 9;* • MI • PO Box 251 Paradise MI 49768-0251 • tahqluth@sault.com

**PAW PAW—*TRINITY*** (616)657-4840
Carl W Weis Mark C Whittaker • Kevin D Otrhalik DCE • WS 815 930 11; SS 930 • H • EC/EL • MI • 721 Pine St Paw Paw MI 49079-1248 • FAX(616)657-3378 • churchoffice@trinitylutheran.com

**PETERSBURG—*ST PETER*** (313)279-1949
Ainslie B Wagner • * • H • EC • MI • 343 E Center St 49270-9702 PO Box 39 Petersburg MI 49270-0039

**PETOSKEY—*ZION*** (231)347-3438
Walter W Teske • WS 8 1030; SS 915;* • H • EC • MI • 500 W Mitchell St Petoskey MI 49770-2231

**PIGEON—*ST PAUL***
See Linkville

**PINCKNEY—*TRINITY*** (734)878-5977
Alan R Stadelman • WS 8 1045; SS 930; BC 930;* • H • MI • 5758 W M 36 Pinckney MI 48169-9716 • FAX(734)878-6261

**PINCONNING 2E OF 1—*ST JOHN*** (517)879-2377
Robert F Allmann • H • EC • MI • 48650 PO Box 56 Pinconning MI 48650-0056

**PLYMOUTH—*RISEN CHRIST*** (734)453-5252
David W Martin Hugh H Mc Martin(#) • Mary A Hibbard DEAC • * • H • HS • EN • 46250 Ann Arbor Rd W Plymouth MI 48170-3501 • FAX(734)453-0224

**PONTIAC—*ST PAUL*** (248)338-8618
Roger C Reckling • MI • 1133 Joslyn Ave Pontiac MI 48340-2868 • juno.comstpaul@juno.com

**PORT HOPE—*ST JOHN*** (517)428-4140
Vacant • H • EC/EL • MI • State And Second Sts 48468 PO Box 182 Port Hope MI 48468-0182 • FAX(517)428-4140

**PORT HURON—*FAITH*** (810)985-5733
Timothy M Eichberger • H • MI • 3455 Stone St Port Huron MI 48060-2158 • FAX(810)985-9388

***TRINITY*** (810)984-2993
Robert H Mann Terry Rosenau(#) • H • MI • 1517 10th St Port Huron MI 48060-5814 • FAX(810)982-3906 • joroman@advnet.net

**PORT SANILAC—*ST JOHN*** (810)622-9653
Donald P Veitengruber • H • MI • 246 N Ridge Rd 48469-9737 PO Box 625 Port Sanilac MI 48469-0625

**PORTAGE—*ST MICHAEL*** (616)327-7832
Paul R Naumann Steven E Thiel • WS 830;* • H • EC • MI • 7211 Oakland Dr Portage MI 49024-4151 • FAX(616)327-3148 • stmike@net-link.net

**PORTLAND—*ST ANDREW*** (517)647-4473
Edward W Filter • WS 830 11;* • H • EC • MI • I96 And Kent 48875 8867 Kent St Portland MI 48875-1986 • FAX(517)647-5153 • st.andrew@mvcc.com

**POSEN—*ST PAUL*** (517)734-3164
Vacant • MI • 12510 Alpena Rd Posen MI 49776

**PRESCOTT—*FAITH*** (517)873-4506
Virgil T Bening • WS 830;* • H • MI • 5815 Henderson Lake Rd 48756-9105 PO Box 4259 Prescott MI 48756-4259

**QUINCY—*PRINCE PEACE*** (517)639-8986
Vacant • WS 10; SS 9; BC 9 • H • MI • 295 N Ray Quincy Rd Quincy MI 49082-9744

**RAMSAY—*OUR REDEEMER*** (906)663-4318
Kevin K Ader • WS 10;* • H • NW • 49959 E8223 Sanders Rd Bessemer MI 49911-9706 • FAX(906)663-6330

**REDFORD—*HOSANNA-TABOR*** (313)937-2424
Lawrence E Witto Steven M Eggers G D Milz(#) • * • H • EC/EL/HS • MI • 9600 Leverne Redford MI 48239-2239 • FAX(313)937-2173 • htlcms@juno.com

**REDFORD TOWNSHIP—*GRACE*** (313)532-2266
Victor F Halboth Timothy P Halboth • H • HS • EN • 25630 Grand River Ave Redford Township MI 48240-1429 • FAX(313)532-0643 • glcms@prodigy.net

**REED CITY—*TRINITY*** (616)832-5392
Robert D Baerwolf • WS 8;* • H • EC/EL • MI • 139 W Church Ave Reed City MI 49677-1313 • FAX(616)832-5186

**REESE—*TRINITY*** (517)868-9901
Steven G Siegel • * • HS • MI • 9858 North St Reese MI 48757-9544 • FAX(517)868-3702 • lctlcs@ccaa.edu

**RICHMOND—*ST PETER*** (810)727-9693
Gerhardt A Doroh Randy D Lett • WS 8; BC 930;* • H • EC/EL/HS • MI • 67055 Gratiot Ave Richmond MI 48062-1929 • FAX(810)727-3370

**RICHVILLE—*ST MICHAEL*** (517)868-4791
David E Hakes Wes S Gillaspie • WS 745 1030; BC 9;* • H • EC/EL • MI • 3455 S Van Buren Rd 48768-0098 PO Box 98 Richville MI 48758-0098 • FAX(517)868-3391 • stm3455@aol.com

**RIVER ROUGE—*CHRIST*** (313)842-2036
Vacant • MI • 25 Louis St 48218-1254 PO Box 18103 River Rouge MI 48218-0103

**ROCHESTER—*LIVING WORD*** (248)651-5316
John E Kassen • Lisa M Glotzhober DCE • WS 9 1030;* • H • EC/HS • MI • 3838 N Rochester Rd Rochester MI 48306-1052 • FAX(248)608-9285 • livword@attglobal.net

***SHEPHERD HILLS***
See Rochester Hills

***ST JOHN*** (248)652-8830
Mark E Heuser Richard L Schlecht(EM) Donald A Ritter(#) • Richard E Webb DCE • H • HS • MI • 1011 W University Dr Rochester MI 48307-1862 • FAX(248)652-9916

**ROCHESTER HILLS—*CROWN OF LIFE*** (248)652-7720
Terry J Rebert • WS 830;* • H • MI • 2975 Dutton Rd Rochester Hills MI 48306-2347 • FAX(248)652-1387 • crownoflifelcms@ameritech.net

***GETHSEMANE*** (248)852-5510
Vacant • WS 8 1030; SS 915; BC 915;* • H • MI • 1892 E Auburn Rd Rochester Hills MI 48307-4801

***LIVING WORD***
See Rochester

***SHEPHERD HILLS*** (248)652-8420
Roland E Holder(#) • * • H • EN • 900 W Hamlin Rd Rochester Hills MI 48307-3432 • FAX(248)652-2076 • rholder@tir.com

**ROCKFORD—*ST PETER*** (616)866-1818
Thomas R Brazinsky • WS 815;* • H • EC • MI • 310 E Division St Rockford MI 49341-1358 • FAX(616)866-1258

**ROGERS CITY—*IMMANUEL***
See Moltke

***PEACE*** (517)734-7621
Kevin C Jones • WS 930;* • H • MI • 1401 M-68 Hwy Rogers City MI 49779-9792 • FAX(517)734-0441 • revkev@george.lhi.net

***ST JOHN*** (517)734-4522
Barton C Gray • WS 10;* • H • EC/EL • MI • 460 W Erie St Rogers City MI 49779-1633

**ROGERS CITY 6 S—*ST MICHAEL*** (517)734-3007
William Besler • EL • MI • 5918 M 451 Rd Rogers City MI 49779

**ROMEO—*GRACE FELLOWSH*** (810)752-9800
Lynn F Witt • * • H • MI • 7525 32 Mile Rd Romeo MI 48065-4272 • FAX(810)752-8996 • witt@ees.eesc.com

**ROSEVILLE—*BETHLEHEM*** (810)777-9128
Jeffrey M Fritz • WS 8 1030;* • H • EC/EL/HS • MI • 29675 Gratiot Ave Roseville MI 48066-4140 • FAX(810)777-9131

**ROYAL OAK—*OUR SAVIOR DF***
See Farminton Hills

***ST PAUL*** (248)541-0613
Daniel E Lochner • WS 815; SS 930; BC 930;* • H • EC/EL/HS • MI • 202 E 5th St Royal Oak MI 48067-2609 • FAX(248)541-6965

**SAGINAW—*BETHLEHEM*** (517)755-1144
Paul B Mc Cain Charles F Buckhahn • WS 8 1045;* • H • EC/EL/HS • MI • 808 Weiss St Saginaw MI 48602-5709 • FAX(517)755-3969 • pastor@bethlehemsaginaw.com

***GOOD SHEPHERD*** (517)793-8201
John W Rauh Paul R Hinz • WS 8; SS 915; BC 915;* • H • EC/HS • MI • 5335 Brockway Rd Saginaw MI 48603-4423 • FAX(517)793-9525 • goodshep@concentric.net

***HOLY CROSS*** (517)793-9723
Timothy J Loewe Eric A Lambart • H • EC/EL/HS • MI • 600 Court St Saginaw MI 48602-4249 • FAX(517)793-7441 • church@hclc.org

***MESSIAH***
See Carrollton

***PEACE***
Robert M Eggers • WS 8 930 11; SS 930; BC 11 930;* • H • HS • MI • 3427 Adams Ave Saginaw MI 48602-2902

***REDEEMER*** (517)753-2963
J R Herrod Cesar Sifuentes • WS 9 7; BC 1030;* • H • MI • 3829 Lamson St Saginaw MI 48601-4170 • FAX(517)753-5922

***ST MARK*** (517)781-3205
Daniel L Krause • WS 815 1045;* • H • EC/HS • MI • 2565 N Miller Rd Saginaw MI 48609-9532 • dnlkrs@excite.com

**SAGINAW 5 E—*IMMANUEL*** (517)754-0929
Donald O Neuendorf • WS 8 1015; BC 915;* • H • EC/EL/HS • MI • 8220 E Holland Rd Saginaw MI 48601-9479 • FAX(517)754-0454 • immanuel@frankentrost.org

**SAINT CHARLES—*NATIVITY*** (517)865-9964
Vacant • * • H • MI • 625 W Clinton St Saint Charles MI 48655

**SAINT CLAIR—*IMMANUEL*** (810)329-7174
Alan J Schwieger • WS 8 930 11;* • H • EC • MI • 415 N 9th St Saint Clair MI 48079-4847 • FAX(810)329-4104

**SAINT CLAIR SHORES—*REDEEMER*** (810)294-0640
Jack M Cascione • WS 8 1045; SS 915; BC 915;* • H • EC/HS • MI • 30003 Jefferson Ave Saint Clair Shores MI 48082-1737 • FAX(810)294-4063 • pastorcascione@juno.com

***ST PAUL*** (810)777-0215
David A Rutter • EN • 48080 22915 Greater Mack Ave St Clair Shrs MI 48080-2009 • FAX(810)777-0216 • st.pauls.scs@juno.com

**SAINT HELEN—*HOPE*** (517)389-7715
Randolph J Schnack • H • MI • 635 M 76 48656-7503 PO Box 297 Saint Helen MI 48656-0297

**SAINT JOHNS—*ST JOHN*** (517)224-6796
Vacant • WS 8; BC 915;* • H • MI • 511 E Sturgis St Saint Johns MI 48879-2045 • stjohnschurch@mintcity.com

**SAINT JOHNS 12 SW—*ST PETER*** (517)224-3178
Jeffrey E Heimsoth • WS 8 1030; SS 915; BC 915;* • H • EC/EL • MI • 48879 8990 Church Rd Saint Johns MI 48879-9230 • FAX(517)224-8962 • lcmstplc@abraham.ccaa.edu

**SAINT JOSEPH—*TRINITY*** (616)983-5000
Barry R Sommerfield Robert G Barber Jr. Thomas E Batsky Jon D Bendewald • WS 8 930 1030;* • H • EC/EL • MI • 715 Market St Saint Joseph MI 49085-1320 • FAX(616)983-8933 • trinity@parrett.net

**SALINE—*CHRIST KING*** (734)429-9200
Thomas L Schroeder • WS 815; SS 940; BC 940;* • H • HS • MI • 3255 Saline Waterworks Rd Saline MI 48176-9725 • FAX(734)944-5432 • mcneil@c-o-k-org.

**SAND LAKE—*RESURRECTION*** (616)636-5502
Vacant • WS 915; SS 1045;* • H • EC • MI • 180 Northland Dr 49343-9701 PO Box 172 Sand Lake MI 49343-0172 • saints@cmedic.net

**SANDUSKY—*HOLY REDEEMER*** (810)648-3190
Howard E Claycombe Jr. • SS 9 • H • EN • 85 E Miller Rd Sandusky MI 48471-9412

***PEACE*** (810)648-3241
Vacant • WS 830 1045; SS 945; BC 945 • EC • MI • 92 N Flynn St Sandusky MI 48471-1011 • FAX(810)648-3336 • peace@avci.net

**SANFORD—*ST PAUL*** (517)687-2209
Paul V Young • WS 930; BC 11;* • H • MI • 2045 Lynn St Sanford MI 48657-9213

**SAULT STE MARIE—*ST BARNABAS*** (906)632-7796
Charles B Burhop • H • MI • 113 E 14th Ave PO Box 308 Sault Ste Marie MI 49783 • cbburhop@up.net

**SAWYER—*TRINITY*** (616)426-3937
Kendall L Schaeffer • WS 830 11; SS 945; BC 945 • H • EC/EL • MI • 5791 Sawyer Rd 49125-9257 PO Box 247 Sawyer MI 49125-0247 • FAX(616)426-3151

**SCOTTVILLE—*OUR SAVIOR*** (231)757-2271
James E Schroeder • Karen M Trench DCE • * • H • EC • MI • 765 W US Highway 10 31 49454-9601 PO Box 66 Scottville MI 49454-0066 • FAX(231)757-4320 • oslcscot@t-one.net

**SEBEWAING—*IMMANUEL*** (517)883-3050
Albert W Bahr(EM) • WS 8 1030;* • H • EC/EL • MI • 800 E Bay St Sebewaing MI 48759-1642 • FAX(517)883-3556 • immanuel@avci.net

***ST JOHN***
See Kilmanagh

***ST PETER***
See Bach

**SHELBY 6 W—*ST STEPHEN*** (231)861-2952
Arthur J Bode • WS 830 1030; BC 930;* • H • MI • 49455 7410 W Johnson Rd Shelby MI 49455-9511

**SHELBY TOWNSHIP—*PEACE*** (810)731-4120
Murray W Brindle • WS 745 9 1115; SS 10; BC 10;* • H • EC/EL/HS • MI • 6580 24 Mile Rd Shelby Township MI 48316-3306 • FAX(810)731-8935

***SHEPHERDS GATE*** (810)731-4544
Jon A Bjorgaard • WS 9; SS 1030; BC 1030 • H • HS • MI • 12400 23 Mile Rd Shelby Township MI 48315-2620 • FAX(810)731-8658 • sgate@ameritech.net

**SOUTH LYON—*CROSS CHRIST*** (248)437-8810
Terry A Nelson • * • H • EC • MI • 24155 Griswold Rd South Lyon MI 48178-8932 • FAX(248)437-7708 • crosslut@bignet.net

**SOUTHGATE—*CHRIST KING*** (734)285-9695
Terry L Cashmer Jason D Cashmer Harry N Edenfield • WS 11; SS 830; BC 945;* • H • EC/EL/HS • MI • 15600 Trenton Rd Southgate MI 48195-2063 • FAX(734)285-4188 • staff@ctk-church.org

**SPRING L:AKE—*LAKESHORE*** (616)846-8556
Glenn Shelton • Christina L Simon DCE Steven A Scheer DCE • WS 9;* • H • MI • 16790 Van Wagoner Rd Spring Lake MI 49456-1351 • FAX(616)846-5540 • lakeshoreluth@novagate.com

**SPRING LAKE—*LAKESHORE***
See Ferrysburg

***ST MATTHEW*** (616)846-2490
George O Hamilton • WS 8 1030; SS 915; BC 915 • H • MI • 15395 Rannes Rd Spring Lake MI 49456-2238 • stmatthew@novagate.com

**STANDISH 3 W—*BETHLEHEM*** (517)846-4972
Daniel L Jansen • WS 9; BC 1030;* • H • MI • 48658 5606 Johnsfield Rd Standish MI 48658-9430 • dcjansen@sch-net.com

**STANTON 5 W—*HOPE*** (517)831-5594
Alsen K Wenzel • H • MI • 4741 Stanton Rd NW Stanton MI 48888

**STERLING HEIGHTS—*REDEMPTION*** (810)268-1080
John E Mackowiak • WS 830 11;* • H • HS • MI • 39051 Dodge Park Rd Sterling Heights MI 48313-5045 • FAX(810)268-1140 • lcrlc@abraham.ccaa.edu

***ST PAUL*** (810)247-4645
Walter A Keller • WS 8 1030;* • H • HS • MI • 42681 Hayes Rd Sterling Heights MI 48313-2914 • FAX(810)247-1476 • stpaullutheran7@netzero.com

**STEVENSVILLE—*CHRIST*** (616)429-7222
Philip Quardokus Kenneth M Ferrier • WS 8 1045; BC 930;* • H • EC/EL • MI • 4333 Cleveland Ave Stevensville MI 49127-9595 • FAX(616)429-3788 • clc@Christ-luth.org

**STURGIS—*SALEM***
See Centreville 6 SE

***TRINITY*** (616)651-6511
Michael A Klafehn Calvin J Kolzow Jr. • WS 1030 8; SS 915; BC 915;* • H • EC/EL • MI • 406 S Lakeview St Sturgis MI 49091-1953 • FAX(616)659-2909 • trinityl@trinity.pvt.k12.mi.us

**TAWAS CITY—*ZION*** (517)362-5712
Vacant • WS 8 1030;* • H • MI • 720 2nd St Tawas City MI 48763-9602 • zionlu@i-star.com
**TAYLOR—*OUR REDEEMER*** (313)291-4400
Samuel R Pranschke • WS 930;* • H • MI • 9601 Pardee Rd Taylor MI 48180-3546
***ST JOHN*** (734)287-2080
Stephen F Long • WS 8 1030; SS 915; BC 915;* • H • EC/EL/HS • MI • 13115 Telegraph Rd Taylor MI 48180-4645 • FAX(734)287-0532
**TRAVERSE CITY—*ST MICHAEL*** (616)947-5293
Timothy J Brand • H • EC • MI • 912 S Garfield Ave Traverse City MI 49686-3403 • stmichluth@aol.com
***TRINITY*** (231)946-2720
Donald V Engebretson Charles J Koehler • WS 830 11; BC 945;* • H • EC/EL • MI • 13th And Maple Sts 49684 1003 S Maple St Traverse City MI 49684-4025 • FAX(231)946-4796
**TRENTON—*ST PAUL*** (734)676-1565
Wayne A Pohl John L Bush • Kim D Schutt DCE Donald R Busse DCE • WS 11 830; SS 945; BC 945;* • H • EC/HS • MI • 2550 Edsel Dr Trenton MI 48183-2558 • FAX(734)676-1573 • info@stpaul.org
**TROY—*ALL NATIONS*** (248)689-4664
Vacant • MI • 37635 Dequindre Rd 48083-5709 C/O 35004 Michigan Ave Wayne MI 48184 • FAX(734)467-8669
***FAITH*** (248)689-4664
Warren B Arndt Paul W Arndt Timothy P Kade Frederick W Traugott • WS 915 11 915; SS 11; BC 915;* • H • EC/HS • MI • 37635 Dequindre Rd Troy MI 48083-5709 • FAX(248)689-1554 • jcasiglia@faithtroy.org
***ST AUGUSTINE*** (248)879-6400
John R Monson • WS 8; BC 1115;* • H • EC • MI • 5475 Livernois Rd Troy MI 48098-3251
**UNION CITY—*OUR SAVIOR*** (517)741-7643
David A Dodge • WS 930; BC 11;* • H • EC • MI • 405 Saint Joseph St Union City MI 49094-1244 • FAX(517)741-7643 • oslc.us@juno.com
**UNION LAKE—*PEACE***
See Waterford Twp
***ST MARK***
See West Bloomfield
**UNIONVILLE—*ST PAUL*** (517)674-8681
Michael S Allen • H • EC/EL • MI • 6356 Center St 48767-9784 PO Box 196 Unionville MI 48767-0196
**UTICA—*PEACE***
See Shelby Township
***SHEPHERDS GATE***
See Shelby Township
***TRINITY*** (810)731-4490
George E Black Mark J Hill Philip J Scharnitzke • WS 8 930 11; SS 930;* • H • EC/EL/HS • MI • 45160 Van Dyke Ave Utica MI 48317-5578 • FAX(810)731-1071 • trinitychurch@ameritech.net
**WALLED LAKE—*ST MATTHEW*** (248)624-7676
Paul M Moldenhauer Daniel C Meckes • Lavern R Kruse DCE Gary A Janetzke DCE • WS 8 815 1045 11; SS 930; BC 930;* • H • EC/EL/HS • MI • 2040 S Commerce Rd Walled Lake MI 48390-2412 • FAX(248)624-0685
**WALTZ—*ST JOHN*** (734)654-6366
William L Morris Dennis M Berkesch • WS 815 11; SS 930; BC 930;* • H • EC/EL/HS • MI • UKNWN 28320 Waltz Rd New Boston MI 48164-9607 • FAX(734)654-3675
**WARREN—*HOLY CROSS*** (810)751-2550
Richard H Rossow • H • MI • 30003 Ryan Rd Warren MI 48092-3324 • FAX(810)751-3926
***HOPE*** (810)979-9055
John M Duerr • WS 8 1045; SS 930; BC 930;* • H • HS • MI • 32400 Hoover Rd Warren MI 48093-1183 • FAX(810)979-5570 • hopelc@compserv.net
***PEACE*** (810)751-8010
E E Nevis • H • HS • MI • 11701 E 12 Mile Rd Warren MI 48093-3466 • FAX(810)751-8558
***TRINITY*** (810)755-6767
Paul C Monson • WS 830 11; BC 945;* • H • MI • 8150 Chapp Ave Warren MI 48089-1657 • FAX(810)755-6767
**WASHINGTON—*OUR REDEEMER*** (810)781-5567
Jeffrey G Draeger • WS 8 1030; SS 915; BC 915;* • H • EC • MI • 8600 27 Mile Rd Washington MI 48094-2303 • FAX(810)781-0672 • orlc@glis.net
**WATERFORD—*ST STEPHEN***
See Drayton Plains
**WATERFORD TWP—*PEACE*** (248)681-9360
William D Merrell • * • H • EC • MI • 48329 7390 Elizabeth Lake Rd Waterford MI 48327-3729
**WAYNE—*LIVING WORD*** (734)737-9566
Randall S Duncan • H • MI • 48184 39615 Randall Canton MI 48188 • FAX(734)737-9567 • livingword@mediaone.net
***ST MICHAEL*** (734)728-1950
Robert J Schultz Edwin Ott(#) • WS 8 930 11; SS 11 930; BC 11 930;* • H • HS • MI • 3003 Hannan Rd Wayne MI 48184-1009 • FAX(734)728-9569 • revschultz@juno.com
**WELLSTON—*BEAUTIFUL SAVIOR*** (231)723-2207
Vacant • MI • PO Box 47 Wellston MI 49686
**WEST BLOOMFIELD—*SHEPHERD*** (248)626-2121
Dennis G Fitzpatrick • H • EC • EN • 5300 W Maple Rd West Bloomfield MI 48322-3801 • FAX(248)626-0324
***ST MARK*** (248)363-0741
Allen D Lunneberg William C Grafe(EM) • Michael J Mathey DCE • WS 8 1030; BC 915 • H • MI • 7979 Commerce Rd West Bloomfield MI 48324-4716 • FAX(248)363-4755 • lunneberg.al@acd.net
**WEST BRANCH—*ST JOHN*** (517)345-0120
Carlo A Sgambelluri • H • MI • 155 Fairview West Branch MI 48661-9240 • pastorcas@aol.com
**WEST OLIVE—*UNITED*** (616)846-4790
Vacant • * • H • EC • MI • 15424 Lake Michigan Dr West Olive MI 49460-9520 • FAX(616)846-8707
**WESTLAND—*OUR SAVIOUR*** (313)728-3440
Vacant • H • MI • 29425 Annapolis Rd Westland MI 48186-5183
***SALEM NATIONAL*** (734)422-5550
Vacant • WS 10;* • H • HS • MI • 32430 Ann Arbor Trl Westland MI 48185-1474 • FAX(734)422-5550
***ST MATTHEW*** (734)425-0260
Gary D Headapohl Kurt E Lambart • WS 8; SS 930; BC 930;* • H • EC/EL/HS • MI • 5885 N Venoy Rd Westland MI 48185-2831 • FAX(734)425-7932 • 105256.2073@compuserve.com
**WHEELER 2 E—*IMMANUEL*** (517)842-3459
Larry A Warsinski • WS 930;* • H • MI • 48662 10020 E Monroe Rd Wheeler MI 48662-9743 • FAX(517)842-3089 • revlarry@rural-net.com
**WHITE CLOUD—*CHRIST*** (231)689-1704
Richard S Hoogerhyde • * • H • EC • MI • 701 S Evergreen Dr 49349-9568 PO Box 625 White Cloud MI 49349-1625
**WHITE LAKE—*CEDAR CREST*** (248)698-3820
Vacant • * • H • MI • 485 Farnsworth St White Lake MI 48386-3170
**WHITEHALL—*FAITH*** (231)893-7722
Micheal D Kroll • H • MI • 707 Alice St Whitehall MI 49461-1415 • FAX(231)894-6636
**WHITTEMORE—*GOOD NEWS MIN*** (517)756-2159
Vacant • WS 830 11; SS 945; BC 945 • H • MI • 3107 S M 65 48770-9792 PO Box 64 Whittemore MI 48770-0064
**WYANDOTTE—*TRINITY*** (734)282-5877
Neal S Groeling Ervin D Schachel(#) • WS 815 11; SS 940; BC 940;* • H • EC/EL/HS • MI • 505 Oak St 48192-5023 465 Oak St Wyandotte MI 48192-5819 • FAX(734)282-2707
**WYOMING—*GRACE*** (616)534-0805
Robert C Weidmayer • * • H • EC • EN • 150 50th St SW Wyoming MI 49548-5636 • FAX(616)534-2308 • gracelc@iserv.net
**YPSILANTI—*FAITH*** (313)482-9412
David K Gerke • H • MI • 1255 E Forest Ave Ypsilanti MI 48198-3911
***UNIVERSITY**** (313)483-8330
Vacant • H • MI • 812 Ann St Ypsilanti MI 48197-2486

## MINNESOTA

**ADA—*ZION*** (218)784-7103
Earl Schmidt • WS 9;* • H • MNN • W Third And Jamison Dr 300 5th St W Ada MN 56510 • zlca@rrv.net
**ADA 8 NE—*ST JOHNS*** (218)784-4644
David L Truenow • * • H • MNN • 56510 2948 240th Ave Ada MN 56510-9317 • truefour@means.net
**AFTON—*ST PETER*** (651)436-3357
Alan C Rehwaldt • Stacy A Winter DCE • * • H • EC • MNS • 880 Neal Ave S Afton MN 55001-9760 • stpeterafton@juno.com
**AITKIN—*ST JOHN*** (218)927-3170
David Becker • H • EC/EL • MNN • 324 3rd St NW Aitkin MN 56431-1229 • stjnlcms@mlecmn.net
**AITKIN 8 NW—*IMML IRON HUB*** (218)546-6910
Vacant • MNN • 26535 Iron Hub Rd Aitkin MN 56431
**AKELEY—*ST JOHN*** (218)652-3779
Vacant • H • MNN • PO Box 160 Akeley MN 56433-0160
**ALBANY—*IMMANUEL*** (612)845-2620
Frederick M Kutter • H • MNN • 23845 County Road 40 56307-9751 PO Box 340 Albany MN 56307
**ALBERT LEA—*ZION*** (507)373-8609
Paul J Aldrich • Timothy J Stroming DCE • WS 8;* • H • MNS • 924 Bridge Ave Albert Lea MN 56007-2351 • FAX(507)373-7114
**ALBERTVILLE—*LIFE IN CHRIST*** (612)497-3799
Michael A Trask • * • H • MNS • 5015 Main Ave NE Albertville MN 55301-9749
**ALEXANDRIA—*GOOD SHEPHERD*** (320)762-5152
Wade R Meyer • WS 9;* • H • MNN • 2702 State Highway 29 N Alexandria MN 56308-7928 • FAX(320)762-2897
***ST JAMES***
See Parkers Prairie 9 SW
***ZION*** (320)763-4842
Terry L Finnern • BC 930;* • H • EC/EL • MNN • 300 Lake St Alexandria MN 56308-1531 • FAX(320)763-3676 • zionluth@rea-alp.com
**ALEXANDRIA 12 NW—*EBENEZER*** (320)834-2546
Joel R Brutlag • * • MNN • 56308 5393 County Road 5 NW Alexandria MN 56308-9740
**ALPHA—*TRINITY*** (507)639-5645
Vacant • H • MNS • Main St 56111 RR 2 Box 61 Alpha MN 56111-9615
**ALPHA 9 N—*IMMANUEL*** (507)639-5645
Vacant • MNS • Jackson County Rd # 29 56111 RR 2 Box 61 Alpha MN 56111-9615
**AMBOY—*ST PAUL*** (507)674-3916
G Greg Hovland • MNS • 231 South St E 56010 C/O PO Box 415 Vernon Center MN 56090-0415 • FAX(507)549-3032 • pastorh@prairie.lakes.com
**ANDOVER—*FAMILY CHRIST*** (612)434-7337
Dennis S Perryman • Joy L Risher DCO Peter E Hiller DCE • * • H • MNS • 16045 Nightingale St NW Andover MN 55304-2522 • FAX(612)434-9232 • info@foclutheran.org
**ANNANDALE—*ZION*** (320)274-5226
Thomas J Queck • Grace V Rao DEAC • H • MNS • 360 Chestnut St E Annandale MN 55302-9594 • FAX(320)274-3800 • zionandl@1kdllink.net
**ANNANDALE 11 SE—*BETHLEHEM*** (320)963-3592
Leland D Bendix • WS 930; BC 1030;* • H • MNS • 55302 7809 County Rd 35W Annandale MN 55302-2615 • ldbend@lkdllink
**ANOKA—*MOUNT OLIVE*** (763)421-3223
Dennis L Heiden • Carl R Stroming DCE • WS 1030 8; SS 915; BC 915 • H • EC • MNS • 700 Western St Anoka MN 55303-2001 • FAX(763)576-9626 • mtolive@mtolive-anoka.org
**APPLE VALLEY—*MESSIAH***
See Lakeville
**APPLETON—*TRINITY*** (320)289-1342
George W Sagissor III • * • MNN • 27 E Thielke Ave Appleton MN 56208-1446 • FAX(320)289-1342
**APPLETON 8 N—*IMMANUEL*** (320)394-2358
Edwin L Parker • MNN • 56208 160 210th Ave SW Appleton MN 56208-9723
**ARDEN HILLS—*TRINITY*** (651)633-2402
Byron Northwick • Sheila A Schlechte DCE • WS 9; SS 1015; BC 1015 • H • HS • MNS • 3245 New Brighton Rd Arden Hills MN 55112-7914
**ARLINGTON—*PEACE*** (507)964-2959
W Kurt P Lehmkuhl • * • H • MNS • 514 Freedom Dr 55307-2006 PO Box 333 Arlington MN 55307-0333
***ST JOHN*** (507)964-2400
Luther A Koehler • * • MNS • 38595 State Highway 19 55307-9251 PO Box 363 Arlington MN 55307-0363
**ATWATER 3 N—*ST JOHN*** (320)974-8983
Russell J Grabau • WS 10; SS 9; BC 9;* • H • EL • MNS • 56209 19903 56th Ave NE Atwater MN 56209-9356 • FAX(320)974-8982
**AURORA—*REDEEMER*** (218)229-3208
Walter L Brill • WS 11 • MNN • Central Ave And Sixth St W 55705 500 Central Ave W Aurora MN 55705-1260
**AUSTIN—*HOLY CROSS*** (507)437-2107
Robert V Stohlmann • * • H • EC/EL • MNS • 300 16th St NE Austin MN 55912-4524
***ST JOHN*** (507)433-2642
William J Natzke • WS 9;* • H • MNS • 1200 13th Ave NW Austin MN 55912-1981 • stjohns@smig.net
**AVON—*IMMANUEL***
See Albany
**BABBITT—*GOOD SHEPHERD*** (218)827-2301
John Bonk • H • MNN • 10 Central Blvd Babbitt MN 55706-1133
**BACKUS—*EMMANUEL*** (218)947-4182
Vacant • H • EC/EL • MNN • Hwy 371 N 56435 PO Box 12 Backus MN 56435-0012
**BAGLEY—*REDEEMER*** (218)694-6258
Vacant • WS 930; BC 1045;* • H • MNN • 11 Red Lake Ave SW 56621-8732 PO Box E Bagley MN 56621-1004
**BARNESVILLE—*ST JOHN*** (218)354-7158
John H Knierim • WS 9; SS 1010; BC 1015;* • H • MNN • 1103 4th Ave SE 56514 PO Box 370 Barnesville MN 56514-0370 • knierim@rrt.net
**BARNUM—*EMMANUEL*** (218)389-6849
Vacant • H • MNN • 3756 Fair St 55707 PO Box 138 Barnum MN 55707-0138
**BATTLE LAKE—*LIFE**** (218)864-8253
Vacant • WS 1030; SS 930; BC 930 • H • MNN • 56515 PO Box 6 Battle Lake MN 56515-0006
**BAUDETTE—*BETHLEHEM*** (218)634-1532
Travis D Stolz • H • MNN • 310 W Main 56623 PO Box 694 Baudette MN 56623-0694
**BAXTER—*PRINCE OF PEACE*** (218)829-7092
Terry S Small • WS 9; SS 1015; BC 1030;* • H • EC/EL • MNN • 2100 Lynwood Dr N Baxter MN 56425-7922 • poplcms@brainerd.net
**BEARDSLEY—*BETHLEHEM*** (320)695-2401
Paul A Warnier • * • MNN • 56211 PO Box 318 Browns Valley MN 56219-0318
**BECKER—*GRACE*** (612)261-4244
David M Johnson(DM) • WS 9; SS 10 • MNN • Becker Community Ctr 11225 Julia Ln 55308-9364 PO Box 252 Becker MN 55308 • dmjohnson71@hotmail.com
**BELLINGHAM—*ST PETER*** (320)568-2651
Robert A Friedrich • WS 9; SS 10 • MNN • C/O Rev Robert A Friedrich RR 1 Box 133 Bellingham MN 56212-9749 • rafirene@info-link.net
**BELLINGHAM 5 SW—*TRINITY*** (320)568-2551
Robert A Friedrich • WS 1030; SS 9 • MNN • 56212 RR 1 Box 133 Bellingham MN 56212-9749 • rafirene@info-link.net
**BEMIDJI—*TRINITY*** (218)444-4441
Hyle R Anderson • WS 815 1045; SS 930; BC 930 • H • MNN • 123 29th St NE Bemidji MN 56601-4304 • FAX(218)444-4443 • trinity3@paulbunyan.net
**BENSON—*ST MARK*** (320)843-4131
Dennis J Mc Manus • WS 8;* • H • MNN • 1420 Nevada Ave Benson MN 56215-1136 • dmcmanus@fedtel.net
**BERTHA—*ST PAUL*** (218)924-4051
Vacant • H • MNN • 203 1st Ave Se 56437 PO Box 296 Bertha MN 56437-0296 • FAX(218)924-4050 • bhparish@wcta.net
**BETHEL 10 N W—*ZION***
See Crown 1 N
**BLACKDUCK—*HOLY TRINITY*** (218)835-4423
Allan D Wierschke • WS 930; SS 1045; BC 1045 • H • EC • MNN • 125 1st St Nw 56630 PO Box 219 Blackduck MN 56630-0219
**BLAINE—*KING OF GLORY*** (763)784-4229
Jeffrey A Lee • WS 8 1030;* • H • MNS • 10103 University Ave NE Blaine MN 55434-8014 • FAX(763)795-0134 • glorychurch@lynxus.com
**BLOOMINGTON—*HOLY EMMANUEL*** (952)888-2345
Dennis E Starr • Jill D Hartman DCE • WS 8 1030; BC 915;* • H • EC/HS • S • 201 E 104th St Bloomington MN 55420-5305 • FAX(952)888-2349
***MOUNT HOPE*** (612)888-5059
Vacant • * • H • EC/EL/HS • MNS • 3601 W Old Shakopee Rd Bloomington MN 55431-3544 • FAX(612)888-5059 • mthope@mail.com

***REDEMPTION*** (952)881-0035
Dennis M Drews • Janine A Zitzow DCE • WS 8;* • H • EC/EL/HS • MNS • 927 E Old Shakopee Rd Bloomington MN 55420-4551 • FAX(952)881-0035 • lcr927@aol.com

***ST MICHAEL*** (952)831-5276
Christopher R Dodge • James W Anderson DCE • WS 5 815 1045; SS 930; BC 930;* • H • EC • MNS • 9201 Normandale Blvd Bloomington MN 55437-1940 • FAX(952)831-5225 • stmike@pclink.com

**BLUE EARTH—*IMMANUEL*** (507)526-2072
Karl D Hollibaugh John W Otte • WS 8; SS 9 • MNS • 43103 120th St 56013-7628 PO Box 392 Blue Earth MN 56013-0392

***ST PAUL*** (507)526-7318
Karl D Hollibaugh John W Otte • WS 930; BC 1030;* • H • MNS • 305 E 5th St 56013-1929 PO Box 423 Blue Earth MN 56013-0423 • stpaul@bevcomm.net

**BOVEY—*MOUNT OLIVE*** (218)245-3983
Vacant • WS 1030;* • H • MNN • 301 3rd Ave 55709 PO Box 508 Bovey MN 55709-0508 • tschell@uslink.net

**BOYD—*REDEEMER*** (320)855-2554
Vacant • MNN • Boyd MN 56218

**BOYD 7 SW—*ZION*** (320)855-2554
Randy C Maland • MNN • 56218 RR 1 Box 24 Boyd MN 56218-9658

**BRAHAM—*ST STEPHEN*** (320)396-3103
Harvey G Johnson • * • H • MNN • 400 8th St SE Braham MN 55006-3071 • FAX(320)396-3103

**BRAINERD—*ZION*** (218)829-4317
Vacant • * • H • EC/EL • MNN • 220 N 8th St Brainerd MN 56401-3402 • FAX(218)829-6394

**BRECKENRIDGE—*GRACE*** (218)643-5286
Vacant • WS 9;* • H • MNN • 1100 Main St Breckenridge MN 56520-1036

**BREWSTER—*TRINITY*** (507)842-5982
David P Mc Donald • H • MNS • 1025 4th Ave 56119 PO Box 308 Brewster MN 56119-0308

**BROOK PARK—*EMMANUEL*** (612)384-6884
Michael E Breach • MNN • 55007 C/O St John Lutheran Church 3295 Velvet St Hinckley MN 55037-9631

**BROOKLYN CENTER—*TRIUNE GOD*** (763)561-6470
Peter E Preus • WS 8 1045; SS 930; BC 930;* • H • MNS • 5827 Humboldt Ave N Brooklyn Center MN 55430-2637 • FAX(612)585-0080

**BROOKLYN PARK—*ETERNAL HOPE*** (763)424-8245
Roger K Dramstad • * • H • MNS • 10508 Douglas Dr N Brooklyn Park MN 55443-1003 • eternalhopelutheran@juno.com

***GRACE*** (612)533-4411
Brendan S Prigge • WS 8 1045; SS 930; BC 930;* • H • MNS • 6810 Winnetka Ave N Brooklyn Park MN 55428-2156 • FAX(612)533-4434 • bprigge@gracelcms.org

**BROWNS VALLEY—*BETHLEHEM***
See Beardsley

***ZION*** (320)695-2401
Paul A Warnier • * • MNN • 106 1st St S 56219 PO Box 318 Browns Valley MN 56219-0318

**BROWNSDALE—*OUR SAVIOR*** (507)567-2329
Vacant • H • EC • MNS • 411 W Main St 55918-9714 PO Box 216 Brownsdale MN 55918-0216

**BROWNTON—*IMMANUEL*** (320)328-5522
Merle Kitzmann • Mavis J Smith DCE • * • H • EC • MNS • 700 Division St 55312 PO Box 147 Brownton MN 55312-0147

**BRUNO—*ST PAUL*** (320)233-6138
Matthew J Vrudny • * • H • MNN • 55712 C/O PO Box 60 Finlayson MN 55735-0060 • peaceluth@pinenet.com

**BUFFALO—*HOSANNA*** (763)682-3278
Bruce H Richardson • WS 9; BC 1115;* • H • EC • MNS • 1705 State Highway 25 N Buffalo MN 55313-1929

***ST JOHN*** (763)682-1883
James G Disney • WS 8;* • H • EC/HS • MNS • 302 2nd St NE 55313-1609 PO Box 238 Buffalo MN 55313-0238 • FAX(763)682-1936 • stjohns4@juno.com

**BURNSVILLE—*ASCENSION*** (952)890-3412
Donald W Mulfinger • Mark J Engelhardt DCE • * • H • MNS • 1801 E Cliff Rd Burnsville MN 55337-1394 • FAX(952)890-3417 • lcaburnsville@excite.com

***REDEEMER*** (612)432-7942
Kenneth P Kothe Richard L Buege Marcus O Drevlow • SS 9;* • H • MNS • 1301 County Road 42 E Burnsville MN 55306-4720

**BYRON—*MOUNT MORIAH*** (507)775-2460
Matthew L Lehman • WS 9;* • H • MNS • 923 2nd Ave NW Byron MN 55920-1333 • FAX(507)775-2460 • mountmoriah@bresnanlink.net

**CALLAWAY—*IMMANUEL*** (218)375-2786
James S Wasmuth • H • MNN • PO Box 98 Callaway MN 56521-0098

**CAMBRIDGE—*JOY*** (612)689-4355
David B Franzmeier • H • EC • MNN • 1155 Joy Cir Cambridge MN 55008-2637

**CAMPBELL—*ST PAUL*** (218)630-5377
Carl R Berner • H • MNN • 324 Connecticut Ave 56522 PO Box 38 Campbell MN 56522-0038 • buchs@runestone.net

**CANBY—*NICOLAI*** (507)223-5223
Randy C Maland • H • MNN • 103 Humphry Dr Canby MN 56220-9293

**CARVER—*TRINITY*** (612)448-3628
M K Perry • * • MNS • 417 Oak St N 55315 PO Box 124 Carver MN 55315-0124

**CASS LAKE—*ALL NATIONS*** (218)335-7767
Mark I Peske • WS 6; SS 630 • H • MNN • Pike Bay Town Hall Hwy 371 S 56633 PO Box 1230 Cass Lake MN 56633-1230

***IMMANUEL*** (218)335-6134
Darwin F Schauer(#) • WS 945;* • H • MNN • 3rd St E 56633 PO Box 506 Cass Lake MN 56633-0506

**CEYLON—*OUR SAVIOR*** (507)632-4596
David L Wetmore • MNS • 306 W Main St Ceylon MN 56121

**CEYLON 5 E—*ST PAUL*** (507)632-4674
Russel D Reimers • H • HS • MNS • 56121 RR 1 Box 47 Ceylon MN 56121-9719

**CHANHASSEN—*LIVING CHRIST*** (952)934-5110
Norman J Ruthenbeck Steven D Latzke • WS 8 1030; SS 915; BC 915;* • H • EC • MNS • 820 Lake Dr 55317-9324 PO Box 340 Chanhassen MN 55317-0340 • FAX(952)934-8155 • normanr@livingchrist.org

**CHASKA—*CHRIST VICTORIOUS*** (952)443-2993
Thomas P Braun • H • HS • MNS • 9860 Shady Oak Dr Chaska MN 55318-9338 • FAX(952)443-3624

***ST JOHN*** (612)448-2433
Kenneth R Klaus Gregory J Snow Martin R Cloeter(EM) • WS 8 930 1030;* • H • EC/EL/HS • MNS • 300 4th St E Chaska MN 55318 • FAX(612)448-9500

**CHATFIELD—*ST PAUL*** (507)867-4604
Clark A Jaeger • WS 9 • MNS • 116 Fillmore St SE Chatfield MN 55923-1219

**CHISAGO CITY—*LORD OF LAKES*** (612)462-3535
Craig C Bertram • * • H • MNN • Hwy 8 And Co Rd 23 55013 PO Box 334 Chisago City MN 55013-0334 • FAX(612)462-3535

**CHISHOLM—*GRACE*** (218)254-3466
Steven E Breitbarth • * • MNN • 508 9th St NW Chisholm MN 55719-1453 • breitfam@uslink.net

**CIRCLE PINES—*GOOD SHEPHERD*** (763)784-8417
Kenneth Harste • Matthew W Kuschel DCE • H • MNS • 1 Shepherd Ct Circle Pines MN 55014-1742 • FAX(763)783-0977 • sheepherder4@juno.com

**CLAREMONT—*PEACE*** (507)528-2345
Vacant • WS 9;* • H • MNS • Second And Oak 55924 PO Box 177 Claremont MN 55924-0177

**CLAREMONT 5 SW—*ST JOHN*** (507)528-2643
Giles Zimmer • * • H • MNS • 55924 4489 SE 84th Ave Claremont MN 55924-4532 • gzpz@clear.lakes.com

**CLARISSA—*ST MATTHEW*** (218)756-2395
Horst W Augustin • H • MNN • Howe And Leslie Sts 56440 PO Box 425 Clarissa MN 56440-0425

**CLEAR LAKE—*TRINITY*** (320)743-2919
Vacant • H • MNN • 209 Market St 55319 PO Box 152 Clear Lake MN 55319-0152

**CLOQUET—*HOPE*** (218)729-6380
Walter Lehenbauer • * • H • EL • MNN • 4093 Munger Shaw Rd Cloquet MN 55720-9255

***OUR REDEEMER*** (218)879-3380
Vacant • Sheila K Peterson DCO • WS 9;* • H • EC • MNN • 515 Skyline Blvd Cloquet MN 55720-1138

**COHASSET—*OUR REDEEMER*** (218)328-5165
William C Zeige • Joel R Zander DCE • WS 9; SS 1015; BC 1015;* • H • MNN • 35568 Foxtail Ln 55721 PO Box 8 Cohasset MN 55721-0008 • FAX(218)328-5165 • wzeige@grandnet.com

**COLOGNE 4 SW—*ZION*** (612)466-3379
Eric L Zacharias • * • H • EC/EL/HS • MNS • 55322 14745 County Road 153 Cologne MN 55322-9143

**COLUMBIA HEIGHTS—*ST MATTHEW*** (763)788-9427
Keith W Brutlag • Christine R Eid DCE • WS 8 930 11; SS 930; BC 930;* • H • MNS • 4101 Washington St NE Columbia Heights MN 55421-2818 • FAX(763)788-5772 • stmatt@pclink.com

**COON RAPIDS—*OLIVE BRANCH*** (612)755-2663
Richard L Lindeman • WS 830;* • H • EC • MNS • 2135 Northdale Blvd NW Coon Rapids MN 55433-3006 • FAX(612)755-2663

**CORRELL—*GRACE*** (320)596-2277
Edwin L Parker • MNN • PO Box 107 Correll MN 56227-0107

**COTTAGE GROVE—*ROSE OF*** (651)459-3551
Ronald F Hofmann • WS 9;* • H • EC • MNS • 7241 80th St S Cottage Grove MN 55016-3004 • FAX(651)459-3551 • roseofsharonluth@aol.com

**COURTLAND 3 SE—*IMMANUEL*** (507)359-2528
Wayne A Bernau • WS 930;* • H • EC/EL • MNS • County Rd 25 56021 RR 1 Box 41 Courtland MN 56021-9701

**CROOKSTON—*OUR SAVIOR*** (218)281-1239
Steven W Bohler • WS 745 1045; SS 9; BC 9;* • H • EC/EL • MNN • 217 S Broadway 56716-1953 PO Box 477 Crookston MN 56716-0477

**CROSBY—*ZION*** (218)546-6910
Vacant • H • EC/EL • MNN • 225 4th St NW Crosby MN 56441-1434 • FAX(218)546-6910

**CROSSLAKE—*MISSION CROSS*** (218)692-4228
David G Schoessow • WS 930; SS 830; BC 830 • H • EC/EL • MNN • Junction Hwy 3 And 103 13716 County Road 103 Crosslake MN 56442-2756 • motc@crosslake.net

**CROWN 1 N—*ZION*** (612)856-2099
Steven L Tischer • EC/EL • MNN • UKNWN 7515 269th Ave NW Saint Francis MN 55070-9345

**DAYTON—*BETHLEHEM*** (763)433-0646
Mervyn D Bauer • WS 9;* • H • MNS • 12000 S Diamond Lake Rd 55327-9735 PO Box 365 Champlin MN 55316-0365 • Revbauer@Minn.net

**DEER RIVER—*REDEEMER*** (218)246-8154
James W Anthony • MNN • PO Box 606 Deer River MN 56636-0606

**DENT—*IMMANUEL*** (218)758-2942
Larry O Schmidt • MNN • PO Box 127 Dent MN 56528-0127

**DENT 4 W—*ST JOHN*** (218)758-2942
Larry O Schmidt • H • MNN • 56528 PO Box 127 Dent MN 56528-0127

**DETROIT LAKES—*ZION*** (218)847-7630
Dan C Abrahams David G Hahn • WS 8 1030; BC 930;* • H • MNN • 1100 Lake Ave 56501-3408 PO Box 926 Detroit Lakes MN 56502-0926 • FAX(218)847-2952 • zionlcms@tekstar.com

**DODGE CENTER—*GRACE*** (507)374-2253
Robert A Lentz • WS 9;* • H • EC/EL • MNS • 404 Central Ave N Dodge Center MN 55927-9015 • FAX(507)374-2783

**DORSET—*FIRST ENGLISH*** (218)732-9466
Vacant • WS 9;* • H • MNN • UKNWN 20252 State 226 Park Rapids MN 56470-9803

**DULUTH—*CHRIST KING*** (218)624-3696
Timothy E Moe • H • EC • MNN • 4219 Grand Ave Duluth MN 55807-2748

***MISSION DEAF**** (715)845-4908
Vacant • H • MNN • 4219 Grand Ave 55807-2748 2628 W 2nd St #B Duluth MN 55806-1853

***MOUNT OLIVE*** (218)724-2500
David B Magruder Robert C Franck • * • H • MNN • 2012 E Superior St Duluth MN 55812-2137 • FAX(218)728-0801 • dulutheran@aol.com

***REDEEMER*** (218)626-1630
Vacant • * • H • MNN • 9503 Grand Ave Duluth MN 55808-1313 • FAX(815)371-4842 • redeemerlc@hotmail.com

**DUMONT—*ST JOHN*** (320)563-4004
Vacant • MNN • 202 Main St E 56236 PO Box 125 Dumont MN 56236-0125

**DUNNELL—*ST JOHN*** (507)695-2521
David L Wetmore • HS • MNS • PO Box 127 Dunnell MN 56127

**EAGAN—*CHRIST*** (651)454-4091
Donald R Schmiege • Nadine J Noble DCE • H • EC • MNS • 1930 Diffley Rd Eagan MN 55122-2203 • FAX(651)405-6881 • pastord@mr.net

***PRAISE*** (651)688-8794
Timothy J Rehwaldt • H • MNS • 670 Diffley Rd Eagan MN 55123-1603 • FAX(651)994-0155 • praiselutheran@uswest.net

***TRIN LONE OAK*** (651)454-7235
Vacant • WS 8 1030; SS 915; BC 915;* • H • EC/EL/HS • MNS • 2950 Highway 55 Eagan MN 55121-1521 • FAX(651)454-0109

**EAGLE BEND—*IMMANUEL*** (218)738-3431
Horst W Augustin • MNN • 308 South St W 56446-9579 PO Box 35 Eagle Bend MN 56446-0035

**EAST GRAND FORKS—*FIRST*** (218)773-0181
David E Laue • WS 9;* • H • EC • MNN • 203 5th St NW East Grand Forks MN 56721-1857 • lutheranfirst@hotmail.com

**EASTON—*ST PETER*** (507)787-2349
Vacant • WS 830;* • MNS • 48 Date St 56025-2005 PO Box 96 Easton MN 56025-0096

**EDEN PRAIRIE—*VICTORY*** (952)934-0956
Vacant • * • H • MNS • 16200 Berger Dr Eden Prairie MN 55347-2365 • FAX(952)934-7347 • lauriefromvictory@juno.com

**EDEN VALLEY—*ST PAUL*** (320)453-2472
Juan D Palm • WS 9; BC 1015;* • MNN • 852 Stearns Ave W 55329-9278 PO Box 59 Eden Valley MN 55329-0059 • stpauls@meltel.net

**EDINA—*CROSS VIEW*** (952)941-1094
Gerald P Coleman Christian D Bode Harold N Wendt • Lyle M Heggemeier DCE Audrey M Duensing DCE • WS 815 1045; SS 930; BC 930;* • H • EC/HS • MNS • 6645 Mc Cauley Trl Edina MN 55439-1074 • FAX(952)941-5513 • gerry@crossview.com

***ST PETER*** (952)927-8408
Mark W Shockey • BC 915;* • H • EC/EL/HS • MNS • 5421 France Ave S Edina MN 55410-2357 • FAX(952)926-6545 • caurich@stpeter.pvt.k12.mn.us

**ELBOW LAKE—*CHRIST*** (218)685-5213
Donald R Wagner • WS 830;* • H • MNN • 20 3rd Ave NE 56531-4424 PO Box 479 Elbow Lake MN 56531-0479

**ELDRED—*FIRST ENGLISH*** (218)281-1239
Steven W Bohler • WS 915 • MNN • 56523 C/O PO Box 477 Crookston MN 56716-0477

**ELGIN—*TRINITY*** (507)876-2671
Vacant • H • MNS • PO Box 247 Elgin MN 55932-0247 • aschroeder@juno.com

**ELGIN 6 NW—*IMMANUEL*** (507)876-2585
John G Fuchs • H • MNS • 55932 7134 Highway 247 NE Elgin MN 55932-9519 • potsdam@juno.com

**ELIZABETH—*ST JOHN*** (218)739-2538
Vacant • MNN • PO Box 799 Elizabeth MN 56533-0799

**ELK RIVER—*EMMANUEL*** (612)441-2555
Gary Rehborg • WS 8 1030;* • H • EC • MNN • 1506 Main St Elk River MN 55330-1827 • FAX(612)241-0731 • emmanuelluth@worldnet.att.net

**ELK RIVER 4 NE—*ST JOHN*** (763)441-3646
Wilfred L Pieper • Carl A Eliason DCE • WS 8;* • H • EC/EL • MNS • 55330 9231 Viking Blvd NW Elk River MN 55330-8019 • FAX(763)441-9858 • carlathome@juno.com

**ELK RIVER 4W—*LORD OF GLORY*** (763)263-3090
Mark W Halvorson • Scott D Brown DCE • WS 8 1030;* • H • MNN • 55330 19255 County Road 15 Elk River MN 55330-7920 • FAX(763)263-3090 • limitman@juno.com

**ELMORE—*TRINITY*** (507)943-3348
Vacant • H • MNS • 203 E North St PO Box 427 Elmore MN 56027-0427

**ELMORE 5 NE—*ST JOHN*** (507)943-3390
Vacant • WS 1045 • MNS • 3893 420th Ave Elmore MN 56027 • buchs@bevcomm.net

**ELY—*FIRST*** (218)365-3348
Vacant • WS 1030;* • H • MNN • 915 E Camp St Ely MN 55731-1607 • elyans@northernnet.com

**ELYSIAN—*BETHLEHEM*** (507)362-8381
Christopher P Meyer • H • MNS • PO Box 70 Elysian MN 56028-0070 • bell220@juno.com

**ESKO—*ST MATTHEW*** (218)879-3510
Vacant • H • MNN • 1 Elizabeth Ave Esko MN 55733-9630

**EUCLID—*ST PAUL*** (218)891-4581
Michael K Eminger • * • MNN • 56722 C/O Trinity Lutheran PO Box 247 Fisher MN 56723-0247
**EVANSVILLE 8 NE—*TRINITY*** (218)876-4021
Vacant • WS 9;* • H • MNN • C/O Dennis Meissner 17001 CO Rd 5 NW Evansville MN 56326
**EVERGREEN—*ST PAUL*** (218)334-8124
Anthony C Cloose • H • MNN • UKNWN 13084 Co Hwy 39 Frazee MN 56544
**EXCELSIOR—*OUR SAVIOR*** (952)474-5181
John C Zahrte • Jerry D Rosamond DCO • WS 8 930 11;* • H • EC/EL/HS • MNS • 23290 Highway 7 Excelsior MN 55331-3139 • FAX(952)470-1985 • oslcexcel@aol.com
**EYOTA—*OUR SAVIOR*** (507)545-2067
Lyle R Kath • * • H • MNS • 222 W Fourth St 55934 PO Box 417 Eyota MN 55934-0417 • lkath@people.com
**FAIR HAVEN—*CONCORDIA*** (320)236-7550
Norman A Hanan • H • MNN • UKNWN 13455 Bluffton Rd South Haven MN 55382-9098 • FAX(320)236-7552
**FAIRMONT—*IMMANUEL*** (507)238-1387
David P Anderson Wade A Daul • WS 8 1030;* • H • HS • MNS • 1200 N North Ave Fairmont MN 56031-1653 • FAX(507)238-2544 • immlcms@frontiernet.net
***ST PAUL*** (507)238-9491
Roger G Abernathy Thomas E Fast Vernon H Harley(EM) • H • HS • MNS • 211 Budd St Fairmont MN 56031-2904 • stpaulfmt@bevcomm.net
**FAIRMONT 10 NW—*ZION*** (507)235-5153
Robert C Trueblood • WS 10; SS 845; BC 845 • H • EC/EL/HS • MNS • 56031 1621 170th St Fairmont MN 56031-1305 • FAX(507)436-5547
**FARIBAULT—*PEACE*** (507)334-9610
Richard L Wilkie Paul A Philp • WS 8 1030;* • H • EC/EL • MNS • 213 6th Ave SW Faribault MN 55021-5836 • FAX(507)334-1726
***TRINITY*** (507)334-6579
Robert E Snyder Steven J Kuehne • Richard R Moen DCE • WS 8 1045 1; SS 930; BC 930;* • H • EC/EL • MNS • 530 4th St NW Faribault MN 55021-5033 • FAX(507)334-7982
**FARMINGTON—*TRINITY*** (651)463-7225
James A Markworth IV • * • H • MNS • 600 Walnut St Farmington MN 55024-1349 • FAX(651)463-7225
**FERGUS FALLS—*FAITH*** (218)736-5352
Craig M Palach • WS 9;* • H • MNN • 333 E Cedar Ave Fergus Falls MN 56537-1436
***TRINITY*** (218)736-4869
David F Knuth • WS 8; BC 915;* • H • EC/EL • MNN • 1150 W Cavour Fergus Falls MN 56537 • FAX(218)739-3667 • trichuFF@prairietech.net
**FERGUS FALLS 13 NE—*ST PAUL*** (218)739-9535
William J Stottlemyer • WS 9;* • MNN • 26141 300th St Fergus Falls MN 56537
**FERGUS FALLS 7 NE—*IMMANUEL*** (218)736-6228
William J Stottlemyer • WS 1030;* • MNN • 22083 Co Hwy 10 Fergus Falls MN 56537
**FINLAYSON—*PEACE*** (320)233-6138
Matthew J Vrudny • * • H • MNN • 2177 Hwy 18 55735 PO Box 60 Finlayson MN 55735-0060 • peaceluth@pinenet.com
***ST PAUL***
See Bruno
**FISHER—*ST PAUL***
See Euclid
***TRINITY*** (218)891-4581
Michael K Eminger • * • MNN • PO Box 247 Fisher MN 56723-0247
**FOLEY—*ST PAUL*** (612)968-6400
Michael K Dagel • MNN • 155 Dewey Street 56329 PO Box 338 Foley MN 56329-0338
**FOREST LAKE—*MESSIAH*** (612)464-6842
Theodore G Predoehl • WS 9;* • H • HS • EN • 807 Hwy 97 55025 PO Box 485 Forest Lake MN 55025-0485
**FOSSTON—*FIRST ENGLISH*** (218)435-6263
Vacant • WS 11 • MNN • 418 Granum Ave N Fosston MN 56542-1313
**FRAZEE—*BETHLEHEM*** (218)334-2866
William M Aufdenkamp • H • EC • MNN • 210 E Maple Ave 56544-4417 PO Box 335 Frazee MN 56544-0335 • bethlech@means.net
**FRAZEE 10 E—*ST PAUL***
See Evergreen
**FRAZEE 10 N—*ST JOHN***
See Height Of Land Twp
**FULDA—*ST PAUL*** (507)425-2258
Vacant • EC/EL • MNS • 400 N Maryland Ave 56131-1150 PO Box 384 Fulda MN 56131-0384
**GARFIELD—*ST JOHN*** (612)834-2248
William K Stockman(EM) • WS 9;* • H • MNN • 401 Park St 56332 PO Box 18 Garfield MN 56332-0018
***ST PAUL***
See Holmes City 3 NW
***TRINITY***
See Evansville 8 NE
**GARRISON 1 N—*SHEP OF LAKE*** (320)692-4581
Curtis L Foreman • H • EC/EL • MNN • Hwy 169 N 56450 PO Box 155 Garrison MN 56450-0155
**GAYLORD—*IMMANUEL*** (507)237-2380
David E Helmer • H • EC/EL • MNS • 312 Fifth St Gaylord MN 55334
**GAYLORD 5 NW—*ST JOHN*** (507)237-2782
Harold A Storm • WS 915 • H • MNS • 23677 491 Ave Gaylord MN 55334
**GEORGETOWN—*CHRIST*** (218)233-0692
Vacant • MNN • PO Box 177 Georgetown MN 56546-0177
**GIBBON 6 NW—*ST PETER*** (507)834-6484
Timothy R Gordish • * • EL/HS • MNS • 63924 240th St Gibbon MN 55335 • kb9lgj@leogate.kf9ug.ampr.org
**GLENCOE—*FIRST*** (320)864-5522
Harvey G Kath Vance G Becker • WS 8 1030; SS 915;* • H • EC/EL • MNS • 925 13th St E Glencoe MN 55336-1543 • FAX(320)864-6813 • firstev.lcms@juno.com
***GOOD SHEPHERD*** (320)864-6157
Philip W Penhallegon • Traci L Kohls DCE • WS 9; BC 10;* • H • MNS • 1407 Cedar Ave N Glencoe MN 55336-1137 • FAX(320)864-8519 • shepherd@xtratyme.com
**GOLDEN VALLEY—*GOLDEN VALLEY*** (763)544-2810
Philip P Wagner • Jennifer R Hall DCE • * • H • EC • MNS • 5501 Glenwood Ave Golden Valley MN 55422-5070 • FAX(763)542-7824 • gvlc@aol.com
**GOOD THUNDER—*ST JOHN*** (507)278-3635
Rudolph H Maurer Jr. • WS 9;* • H • EC/EL/HS • MNS • 311 Sherman St 56037-4021 PO Box 37 Good Thunder MN 56037-0037 • FAX(507)278-3966
**GOODHUE 10 E—*ST PETER*** (612)923-4622
Vacant • * • H • MNS • 55335 28961 365th St Goodhue MN 55027-8515
**GRAND RAPIDS—*FIRST*** (218)326-5453
Daniel M Domke Michael L Eckert • Diane M Meyer DCE • WS 8 1030; SS 915; BC 915 • H • EC • MNN • 735 NE 1st Ave Grand Rapids MN 55744-2613 • FAX(218)326-9729
**GRANITE FALLS—*ST PAUL*** (612)564-2221
Vacant • WS 11;* • H • MNN • 1050 10th Ave Granite Falls MN 56241-1229
**GREEN ISLE—*ST PAUL*** (507)326-3451
Herman R Hannemann • H • MNS • 240 Cleveland Ave 55027 PO Box 25 Green Isle MN 55338-0025
**GREEN ISLE 3 SW—*ZION*** (507)964-2911
Herman R Hannemann • MNS • 55338 PO Box 25 Green Isle MN 55338-0025
**GREY EAGLE—*MOUNT OLIVE***
See Upsala
***ST JOHN*** (320)285-2902
Ronald E Tibbetts • H • MNN • 203 Cedar St S 55338 PO Box 127 Grey Eagle MN 56336-0127
**GROVELAKE—*TRINITY*** (320)554-2161
Lawrence E Cain • MNN • Pope Co Hwy#39 56336 PO Box 36 Villard MN 56385-0036 • nrist@rea-alp.com
**HAM LAKE—*SPIRIT CHRIST*** (612)755-7234
Richard D Miller • * • H • MNS • 2749 Bunker Lake Blvd NE Ham Lake MN 55304-7133 • soclc3@hotmail.com
**HAMBURG 1 W—*EMANUEL*** (952)467-2788
Donald L Andrix • WS 915;* • EC/EL/HS • MNS • UKNWN 18175 County Road 50 Hamburg MN 55339-9406 • FAX(952)467-2473 • donchery@gv2.com
**HAMMOND—*ST JOHN*** (507)753-2388
John G Fuchs • H • MNS • 55339 RR 2 Box 449 Zumbro Falls MN 55991-9611 • potsdam@juno.com
**HARDWICK—*ZION*** (507)669-2855
Mark W Mumme • * • MNS • 305 2nd St 55991 PO Box 36 Hardwick MN 56134-0036
**HASTINGS—*SHEP VALLEY*** (612)437-7010
Bruce F King • WS 915; SS 1015; BC 1015 • H • EC • MNS • 1450 4th St W 55033-1599 PO Box 592 Hastings MN 55033-0592
**HAY CREEK TWP—*IMMANUEL*** (651)388-4577
Jonathan C Nack • H • EC/EL • MNS • 56134 24686 Old Church Rd Red Wing MN 55066-7613
**HEIGHT OF LAND TWP—*ST JOHN*** (218)847-5064
Vacant • WS 930 • H • MNN • 56544 37425 County Hwy 56 Frazee MN 56544-8836
**HENDERSON—*CENTENNIAL*** (507)248-3888
Jonathan H Vollrath • WS 9; SS 10; BC 1020 • H • MNS • 701 Locust St 56044-7704 PO Box 487 Henderson MN 56044-0487
**HENNING—*ST PAUL*** (218)583-2707
Ronald W Jobe • H • MNN • 700 Douglas Ave 56551-4110 PO Box 332 Henning MN 56551-0332
**HERMAN—*BETHLEHEM*** (320)677-2525
Carl R Berner • MNN • 206 Fourth St E UKNWN PO Box 192 Herman MN 56248-0192
**HERMANTOWN—*PEACE CHRIST*** (218)729-9473
Timothy J Ludwig • WS 9;* • H • MNN • 5007 Maple Grove Rd Hermantown MN 55811-1443 • pichrist@cpinternet.com
**HEWITT—*TRINITY*** (218)924-4051
Vacant • H • MNN • 524 Front St 56248 PO Box 116 Hewitt MN 56453-0116 • FAX(218)924-4050 • bhparish@wcta.net
**HIBBING—*GRACE*** (218)263-3955
Mark R Palmer • WS 8 1030; BC 915;* • MNN • 2104 6th Ave E Hibbing MN 55746-1821 • FAX(218)263-5683 • mbpalmer@the-bridge.net
**HILL CITY—*TRINITY*** (218)547-1825
Vacant • H • MNN • PO Box 299 Hill City MN 55748-0299 • FAX(218)697-2504
**HINCKLEY—*EMMANUEL***
See Brook Park
***ST PAUL*** (320)384-6267
Paul J Mundinger • H • EC • MNN • 405 2nd St NW 55037 PO Box 99 Hinckley MN 55037-0099 • FAX(320)384-6267
**HINCKLEY 12 NW—*ST JOHN*** (612)384-6884
Michael E Breach • H • MNN • 56453 3295 Velvet St Hinckley MN 55037-9631
**HOFFMAN—*ZION*** (320)986-2897
Donald R Wagner • WS 11;* • H • MNN • 106 6th St S 56339-8942 PO Box 367 Hoffman MN 56339-0367
**HOLLAND—*ST JAMES*** (507)347-3357
Evan G Schiller • WS 930;* • H • MNS • 300 Carter Ave PO Box 218 Holland MN 56139-0218 • eschiller@juno.com
**HOLLANDALE—*ST PAUL*** (507)889-4441
Vacant • WS 930; BC 1045;* • H • MNS • 202 Park Ave E 26045-0219 PO Box 219 Hollandale MN 56045-0219 • johnf@perling.com
**HOLLOWAY—*IMMANUEL*** (320)394-2452
Vacant • MNN • 510 Olivia St 56045 1750 30th St NW Holloway MN 56249
**HOLLOWAY 8 NW—*TRINITY*** (320)394-2306
Vacant • MNN • 1746 30th St Nw 1750 30th St NW Holloway MN 56249
**HOLMES CITY 3 NW—*ST PAUL*** (320)589-3857
Vacant • H • MNN • 56341 17651 Park Ln SW Kensington MN 56343-8130
**HOPKINS—*ZION*** (612)938-7661
Karl E Galik Howard A Krienke Roy R Karner(EM) Herman E Sieving(EM) • H • HS • MNS • 241 5th Ave N Hopkins MN 55343-7376 • FAX(612)938-7662 • z.church@worldnet.att.net
**HOWARD LAKE—*ST JAMES*** (320)543-2766
Michael J Nirva Martin T Schoenfeld • H • EL/HS • MNS • 1000 7th Ave 55349 PO Box 680 Howard Lake MN 55349-0680
**HUGO—*SHEPHERD FIELDS*** (612)429-1975
Vacant • H • EC • MNS • 6000 148th St N 55038-9309 PO Box 78 Hugo MN 55038-0078
**HUTCHINSON—*OUR SAVIOR*** (320)587-3318
Kevin W Oster • WS 8 1030; SS 915;* • H • EL • MNS • 800 Bluff St NE Hutchinson MN 55350-1313 • FAX(320)234-7861 • osl@hutchtel.net
***PEACE*** (320)587-3031
Gerhard H Bode Jonathan C Rathjen • Theodore G Stroming DCE Paul R Otte DCE Paul A Berg DCE • WS 8 920 1030;* • H • EC • MNS • 400 Franklin St SW Hutchinson MN 55350-2493 • FAX(320)587-1162 • peace@hutchtel.net
**HUTCHINSON 10 W—*ST JOHN*** (320)587-4853
Rodney W Dunker • * • H • EL • MNS • 55350 60929 110th St Hutchinson MN 55350-8204 • rdunk@juno.com
**INTERNATIONAL FALLS—*ST PAUL*** (218)283-8642
Vacant • WS 1115;* • H • MNN • 56649 1324 9th St Intl Falls MN 56649-2540 • FAX(218)283-8642
**INVER GROVE HEIGHTS—*OLD*** (651)457-3929
Daniel V Matasovsky • Robin R Kurth DCE • WS 8;* • H • HS • MNS • 2075 - E 70th St Inver Grove Heights MN 55077-2533 • FAX(651)457-4612 • emanueligh@uswest.net
**ISLE—*TRINITY*** (320)676-8774
Joel A Krueger • WS 830; SS 945; BC 10 • H • MNN • 880 Island Ave S 56342 PO Box 51 Isle MN 56342-0051
**JACKSON—*OUR REDEEMER*** (507)847-3693
Roger W Hett • H • MNS • 100 Kimball Ave Jackson MN 56143-1558 • hett@juno.com
**JANESVILLE—*TRINITY*** (507)231-5189
Larry J Griffin • WS 8 915 1030; BC 915;* • H • EC/EL • MNS • 412 N Main St Janesville MN 56048-9746 • FAX(507)231-6191 • trinity3@frontiernet.net
**JANESVILLE 9 S—*IMMANUEL*** (507)835-2621
Glenn L Korb • MNS • 56048 30266 35th St Janesville MN 56048-5505
**JASPER—*TRINITY*** (507)348-4186
Peter J Sestak • MNS • 409 Wall St E Jasper MN 56144-1123
**KILKENNY—*ST JOHN*** (507)685-2307
Michael S Wallace • WS 9;* • MNS • 56052 C/O Trinity Lutheran Church 10500 215th St W Morristown MN 55052-5083 • FAX(507)685-4346 • wallacmd@means.net
**KIMBALL—*ST JOHN*** (320)398-7151
David S Milz • WS 9;* • H • MNN • 14 Magnus Johnson St 55353 PO Box 307 Kimball MN 55353-0307 • stjohnslutheranch@msn.com
**LA CRESCENT—*MESSIAH*** (507)895-5673
Vacant • MNS • PO Box 156 La Crescent MN 55947-0156 • FAX(507)895-6594
**LAKE CITY—*BETHANY*** (651)345-2424
Vacant • * • H • EC • MNS • 525 S 6th St Lake City MN 55041-1705 • FAX(651)345-3939 • bethany.lc@juno.com
**LAKE CRYSTAL—*ST JOHN***
See Rapidan
***TRINITY*** (507)726-2739
James M Holthus • HS • MNS • 342 S Main St 56055-2118 PO Box 873 Lake Crystal MN 56055-0873
**LAKE GEORGE—*TRINITY*** (218)266-3330
Darwin F Schauer(#) • WS 8;* • H • MNN • 37115 US 71 56458 PO Box 1644 Lake George MN 56458-1644
**LAKE SHORE—*LIVING SAVIOR*** (218)963-9733
Vacant • WS 9;* • H • MNN • 8327 Interlachen Rd Lake Shore MN 56468
**LAKEFIELD—*IMMANUEL*** (507)662-5718
Gerald R Menk • WS 8 1030; SS 915; BC 915;* • H • HS • MNS • Fifth And Bush St 56150 PO Box 750 Lakefield MN 56150-0750 • FAX(507)662-5820 • immanuel@rconnect.com
**LAKEFIELD 6 N—*ST PETER*** (507)662-5862
Bart A Mueller • WS 845; SS 10; BC 10 • H • MNS • RR 2 Box 33 PO Box 1010 Lakefield MN 56150
**LAKEFIELD 6S 1E—*HOLY TRINITY*** (507)662-5938
Bart A Mueller • WS 1015; SS 9; BC 9 • MNS • RR 2 Box 33 PO Box 1010 Lakefield MN 56150
**LAKEFIELD 8 SW—*ST PAUL*** (507)853-4512
Ronald R Yungmann • WS 845; SS 10; BC 10 • H • MNS • 56150 RR 3 Box 113 Lakefield MN 56150-9332
**LAKEVILLE—*MESSIAH*** (612)431-5959
Timothy E Booth Scott M Randall(#) • WS 8 915;* • H • EC/HS • MNS • 16725 Highview Ave Lakeville MN 55044-9294 • FAX(612)431-5980
**LESTER PRAIRIE—*ST PAUL*** (320)395-2573
Grant T Bode • * • H • MNS • 124 Maple St N 55354 PO Box 38 Lester Prairie MN 55354-0038 • FAX(320)395-2037 • stpaullp@hutchtel.net
***ST PETER*** (612)395-2811
Gerald A Schwanke • * • MNS • 77 S Second Ave 55354 77 Second Ave S PO Box 217 Lester Prairie MN 55354-0217

**LEWISTON 2 N—*IMMANUEL*** (507)523-2228
William C Meilner • WS 815 1030; SS 930; BC 930 • H • EC/EL • MNS • 55952 RR 2 Box 63 Lewiston MN 55952-9615 • FAX(507)523-2228

**LEWISVILLE—*ZION*** (507)435-4181
Steve Bagnall • WS 10;* • HS • MNS • 102 Martin St E 56060 PO Box 235 Lewisville MN 56060-0235

**LEWISVILLE 4 NE—*TRINITY*** (507)435-2434
Steve Bagnall • WS 8;* • HS • MNS • 56060 C/O Zion Lutheran Church PO Box 235 Lewisville MN 56060-0235

**LITCHFIELD—*IMMANUEL*** (320)693-6155
Anthony T Bertram • WS 9;* • H • MNS • 175 W 11th St Litchfield MN 55355-1325

**LITTLE FALLS—*ZION*** (320)632-5792
Martin S Langemo • WS 815; BC 930;* • H • MNN • 411 3rd Ave NE Little Falls MN 56345-2745 • zionlf@littlefalls.net

**LONG PRAIRIE—*TRINITY*** (320)732-2238
William E Postel • WS 815 1030; SS 920; BC 920;* • H • EL • MNN • 610 2nd Ave SE Long Prairie MN 56347-1706 • FAX(320)732-3435

**LUVERNE—*ST JOHN*** (507)283-2316
Iver L Possehl • * • H • EC • MNS • 803 N Cedar St Luverne MN 56156-1320 • stjohn2@rconnect.com

**MADELIA—*SALEM*** (507)642-8414
Jack E Dahl • WS 845 11; BC 10;* • H • HS • MNS • 109 3rd St SE Madelia MN 56062-1821

**MADISON—*ST JOHN*** (320)598-7550
Terrill F Bramstedt • WS 9; BC 1015;* • H • MNN • 822 6th St Madison MN 56256-1109 • FAX(320)598-7550

**MAHNOMEN—*BETHLEHEM*** (218)935-2456
David L Truenow • EC • MNN • Munroe W And Fifth St 56557 PO Box 328 Mahnomen MN 56557-0207 • truefour@means.net

**MANKATO—*CAMPUS CHAPEL**** (507)387-6587
Monte L Meyer • H • MNS • 329 Ellis Ave Mankato MN 56001-4006 • lutheran@vax1.mankato.msus.edu

***HOSANNA*** (507)388-1766
Steven Kosberg • David M Zellar DCE DeAnn L Hopper DCE • WS 815;* • H • MNS • 105 Hosanna Dr Mankato MN 56001-5527 • FAX(507)388-2851 • skosberg@prairie.lakes.com

***OUR SAVIOR*** (507)345-5112
Charles E Ortloff • WS 8 1030;* • H • MNS • 1103 N Broad St Mankato MN 56001-3332 • FAX(507)345-5113 • oursav@mnic.net

***ST JOHN***
See Rapidan

**MAPLE GROVE—*SHEPHERD GROVE*** (763)425-5941
Mark G Stillman • * • H • EC/EL • MNS • 11875 W Eagle Lake Dr Maple Grove MN 55369-5529 • FAX(763)425-0622 • sotg@usinternet.com

***ST JOHN*** (763)420-2426
Steven C Briel Loel A Wessel • WS 8 1030;* • H • EC/EL • MNS • 9141 County Road 101 N Maple Grove MN 55311-1302 • FAX(763)420-7198

**MARBLE—*GRACE*** (218)247-7451
Timothy D Schellenbach • WS 9;* • H • MNN • 200 Ethel St 55764 PO Box 430 Marble MN 55764-0430 • FAX(218)247-7451 • tschell@uslink.net

**MARSHALL—*GOOD SHEPHERD*** (507)532-4857
Keith W Bicknase • WS 9;* • H • MNS • 1600 E College Dr Marshall MN 56256-2658

**MAYER—*ZION*** 245
Peter A Meier • WS 815 1030; BC 930;* • H • EC/EL/HS • MNS • 209 Bluejay Ave 55360 PO Box 88 Mayer MN 55360-0088 • FAX(612)657-2337 • zionmayer@mcg.net

**MC GRATH—*GRACE***
Joel A Krueger • MNN • HC 2 Box 43A Mc Grath MN 56350-9607

**MC GREGOR—*OUR SAVIOR*** (218)768-3198
Henry J Koopmann • WS 9;* • H • MNN • 2nd Ave 55760 135 S 1st St Mc Gregor MN 55760-9702 • FAX(218)768-3198

**MC INTOSH—*IMMANUEL*** (218)563-2235
Dean M Bell • MNN • 305 Jackson Ave Nw 56566 PO Box 128 Mc Intosh MN 56556-0128

**MEDFORD—*TRINITY*** (507)451-0447
Wayne A Krohe • * • MNS • 108 3rd St SW 55049-9573 PO Box 209 Medford MN 55049-0209

**MELROSE—*ST PAUL*** (612)256-3847
Reed J Stockman • * • H • MNN • 207 E 5th St N Melrose MN 56352-1176

**MENAHGA—*REDEEMER*** (218)564-4931
Bernhard W Lutz • H • MNN • Hwy 71 S 133 1st St Sw 56464 PO Box 306 Menahga MN 56464-0306

**MILACA—*ST PAUL*** (320)983-6703
Vernon H Dorn • WS 9;* • MNN • 260 3rd Ave SE Milaca MN 56353-1226

**MILTONA—*MOUNT CALVARY*** (218)943-5251
Vacant • MNN • 56354 19020 W Miltona Rd NE Parkers Prairie MN 56361-8143

**MINN LAKE 5 NE—*ST JOHN*** (507)462-3404
Michael W Mathews • * • MNS • Co Rd 161 And St Hwy 30 56068 62747 121st ST Minnesota Lake MN 56068-3159

**MINNEAPOLIS—*BEREA***
See Richfield

***FAITH*** (612)729-5463
Rodney E Ketcher • WS 9;* • H • HS • MNS • 3430 E 51st St Minneapolis MN 55417-1547 • FAX(612)729-1856

***GLORIA DEI*** (612)781-1989
Bruce A Brinkman • * • MNS • 3014 Mc Kinley St NE Minneapolis MN 55418-2318 • FAX(612)781-1982 • parsonb@isd.net

***GOLDEN VALLEY***
See Golden Valley

***HOLY CROSS*** (612)722-1083
Roger A Holland • * • H • MNS • 1720 E Minnehaha Pkwy Minneapolis MN 55407-3640

***IMMANUEL*** (612)522-5644
Yeddo A Gottel • WS 930;* • H • HS • MNS • 2201 Girard Ave N Minneapolis MN 55411-2548 • FAX(612)529-4152

***MESSIAH***
Mounds View

***MOUNT HOPE***
See Bloomington

***MOUNT ZION*** (612)824-1882
Dennis C Ahl • Terry D Schmeckpeper DCE • WS 830;* • H • EC • MNS • 5645 Chicago Ave Minneapolis MN 55417-2429 • FAX(612)824-4612

***PRINCE PEACE DF*** (612)331-2474
Daryl D Gehlbach • WS 1030;* • H • MNS • 1101 University Ave SE Minneapolis MN 55414-2212

***ST JAMES*** (612)824-8828
Gordon H Vogt • WS 10; SS 9; BC 9 • H • HS • MNS • 4854 Portland Ave Minneapolis MN 55417-1034 • FAX(612)824-8828

***ST MATTHEW***
See Columbia Heights

***ST PETER***
See Edinal

***TRINITY FIRST*** (612)870-9487
De Lloyd D Wippich • H • EC/EL/HS • MNS • 1115 E 19th St Minneapolis MN 55404-2035 • FAX(612)871-2353

***UNIV CHAPEL*** (612)331-2747
Vacant • WS 10; BC 845;* • H • MNS • 1101 University Ave SE Minneapolis MN 55414-2212 • FAX(612)331-4519 • lsf@tc.umn.edu

**MINNETONKA—*BETHLEHEM*** (952)934-9633
David P Buuck • WS 930;* • H • EC • MNS • 5701 Eden Prairie Rd Minnetonka MN 55345-5807 • FAX(952)934-9633 • dpbuuck@aol.com

***FAIRVIEW*** (952)935-2044
Vacant • WS 9; SS 1015; BC 1015 • H • EC • MNS • 4215 Fairview Ave Minnetonka MN 55343-8698

**MONTEVIDEO—*ST JOHN*** (612)269-6601
Richard Hamlow • MNN • 3090 40th Ave SW 56265-3042 4005 40th St Montevideo MN 56265

***ST PAUL*** (612)269-7145
Leo R Deitemeyer • WS 9;* • MNN • 321 N 5th St 56265-1505 PO Box 149 Montevideo MN 56265-0149

***TRINITY*** (612)367-2703
Richard Hamlow • MNN • 1055 20th St NE 56265-4069 4005 40th St SW Montevideo MN 56265-9331

**MOORHEAD—*OUR REDEEMER*** (218)233-7569
Bruce Noennig • H • EC • MNN • 1000 14th St S Moorhead MN 56560-3762 • redeemmhd@juno.com

**MOOSE LAKE—*ST PETER*** (218)485-4902
Vacant • WS 1030;* • H • MNN • 4600 West Rd Moose Lake MN 55767-9103

**MORA—*ZION*** (320)679-1094
Robert J Gehrke • David W Hinz DCE • H • EC • MNN • 401 Highway 65 S Mora MN 55051-1800 • FAX(320)679-1096 • zionlc@ncis.com

**MORRIS—*ZION*** (320)589-2744
Robert W Jarvis • * • H • MNN • 311 S Columbia Ave Morris MN 56267-1624 • Zion@inet-serv.com

**MORRISTOWN—*BETHLEHEM*** (507)685-4338
Eugene C Chase Jr. • WS 9; BC 1015;* • H • MNS • 406 W Franklin 55052 PO Box 346 Morristown MN 55052-0346

***ST JOHN***
See Kilkenny

**MORRISTOWN 4 NW—*TRINITY*** (507)685-2307
Michael S Wallace • WS 1030;* • EL • MNS • 55052 10500 215th St W Morristown MN 55052-5083 • FAX(507)685-4346 • wallacmd@means.net

**MOTLEY—*ST JOHN*** (218)352-6399
Vacant • WS 930; BC 830;* • H • EC/EL • MNN • Third And Eledredge 56466 PO Box 231 Motley MN 56466-0231

**MOUND—*MOUNT OLIVE*** (612)472-2756
Thomas L Evans • * • H • MNS • 5218 Bartlett Blvd Mound MN 55364-1748 • FAX(612)472-2783 • eagle³crest@msn.com

**MOUNDS VIEW—*MESSIAH*** (612)784-1786
Bruce G Fredericksen Daniel D Czech Eric E Klemme • H • EC • MNS • 2848 County Road H2 Mounds View MN 55112-3810 • FAX(612)784-1927 • messiah@citilink.com

**MOUNTAIN LAKE—*TRINITY*** (507)427-2451
Robert E Gardner • Kenneth W Bakalyar DCE • * • H • MNS • 1418 2nd Ave 56159-1422 PO Box 503 Mountain Lake MN 56159-0503 • FAX(507)427-2611 • tlcmountainlakemn@juno.com

**MUNGER—*HOPE***
See Cloquet

**NEW GERMANY—*ST MARK*** (612)353-2151
Vacant • H • EC/EL/HS • MNS • 510 E Broadway 55367 PO Box 69 New Germany MN 55367-0069

**NEW GERMANY 2 N—*ST JOHN*** (612)353-2109
Ronald L Mathison • EC/EL/HS • MNS • 55367 17725 53rd St New Germany MN 55367-9337

**NEW HOPE—*BEAUTIFUL SAVIOR***
See Plymouth

**NEW LONDON—*SHEPHERD OF THE*** (320)354-4594
David A Dauk • * • H • MNN • 21 Ash St NE PO Box 242 New London MN 56273-9567 • soth@kandi.net

**NEW ULM—*REDEEMER*** (507)233-3470
Robert D Hines • Deborah L Anderson DCE • WS 9 • H • MNS • 700 S Broadway St New Ulm MN 56073-3405 • FAX(507)359-7789 • redeemer@newulmtel.net

**NEW YORK MILLS—*TRINITY*** (218)385-2450
Vacant • Gary D Bach DCE • * • H • EC • MNN • 424 E Gilman Ave 56567-4514 PO Box J New York Mills MN 56567-0370 • FAX(218)385-4533 • trinity@wcta.net

**NIMROD—*NIMROD*** (218)472-3306
Raymond V Hendrickson • H • MNN • 56478 C/O Grace Lutheran Church 500 Wells Ave N Sebeka MN 56477

**NORTH BRANCH—*LIVING BRANCH**** (612)674-5576
Steven E Ferber(DM) • MNN • North Branch Middle Sch PO Box 922 North Branch MN 55056

**NORTH BRANCH 8 S W—*ST JOHN*** (612)444-5988
George A Krueger • WS 9;* • H • EC • MNN • 55056 28168 Jodrell St NE North Branch MN 55056-6310

**NORTH MANKATO—*GOOD SHEPHERD*** (507)388-4336
Greggory S Coop • WS 9; SS 1015; BC 1015 • H • MNS • 2101 Lor Ray Dr North Mankato MN 56003

**NORTHFIELD—*TRINITY*** (507)645-4438
Donald C Porter • H • MNS • 803 Winona St Northfield MN 55057-2515 • FAX(507)645-0658 • trinity@microassist.com

**NORTHROP—*ST JAMES*** (507)436-5289
Robert C Trueblood • WS 830;* • EC/EL/HS • MNS • 56031 PO Box 315 Northrop MN 56075-0315 • FAX(507)436-5547

**ODESSA—*TRINITY*** (320)273-2127
Edwin L Parker • MNN • PO Box 38 Odessa MN 56276-0038

**OGEMA—*TRINITY*** (218)375-2786
James S Wasmuth • MNN • PO Box 146 Ogema MN 56569-0146

**OGILVIE—*ST PAUL*** (320)272-4352
James W Hesse • * • H • MNN • 301 Church Ave Ogilvie MN 56358-9028

**OKABENA—*OUR REDEEMER*** (507)853-4648
Ronald R Yungmann • WS 1030; SS 9; BC 9 • H • MNS • 120 N Front St Okabena MN 56161

**ORMSBY—*GRACE*** (507)639-3051
Shawn P Ethridge • WS 845;* • MNS • 56162 C/O Immanuel Luth Church 2325 120th Ave Ormsby MN 56162-1209

**ORMSBY 5 SE—*IMMANUEL*** (507)639-3051
Shawn P Ethridge • WS 1030;* • H • HS • MNS • 56162 2325 120th Ave Ormsby MN 56162-1209

**ORTONVILLE—*TRINITY*** (320)839-3422
Richard A Boehnke • WS 830; SS 11; BC 945 • H • MNN • 341 Park St Ortonville MN 56278-1232

**OSAGE—*GETHSEMANE***
See Snellman

**OSAKIS—*REDEEMER*** (320)859-2769
Allan D Craig • H • MNN • PO Box 310 Osakis MN 56360-0310

**OSSEO—*ST PAUL*** (612)425-2238
Gregory C Tyler • H • MNS • 710 Broadway St E Osseo MN 55369-1636 • FAX(612)425-9026

**OSSEO 6W—*ST JOHN***
See Maple Grove

**OTTERTAIL—*ST PAUL***
See Richville

**OTTERTAIL 2 E—*ST JOHN*** (218)367-2470
Timothy B Vaughan • WS 930; BC 1045;* • H • MNN • 56571 RR 2 Box 674 Ottertail MN 56571-9606 • stjohnot@eot.com

**OWATONNA—*GOOD SHEPHERD*** (507)451-4125
John M Kallio • H • EC • MNS • 2500 7th Ave NE Owatonna MN 55060-1488 • goodshep@mnic.net

***REDEEMER*** (507)451-2720
David R Cloeter • H • MNS • 1054 Truman Ave Owatonna MN 55060-3540 • rlcowat@mnic.net

**PARK RAPIDS—*FIRST ENGLISH***
See Dorset

***ST JOHN*** (218)732-9783
Donald J Fondow James H Neubauer • WS 8 1030; BC 915;* • H • EC • MNN • Hwy 34 W 56470 803 W 1st St Park Rapids MN 56470-9532 • FAX(218)732-9783 • jimneu@unitelc.com

**PARKERS PRAIRIE—*IMMANUEL*** (218)338-2511
Kirk E Lee • WS 930;* • MNN • 709 S Douglas Ave 56361 PO Box 66 Parkers Prairie MN 56361-0066

***MOUNT CALVARY***
See Miltona

***MOUNT CALVARY***
See Miltona

**PARKERS PRAIRIE 6SW—*ST PAUL*** (218)943-4774
Vacant • H • MNN • 56361 19020 W Miltona Rd NE Parkers Prairie MN 56361-8143

**PARKERS PRAIRIE 7NW—*ZION*** (218)583-2482
Vacant • MNN • 56361 RR 2 Box 182 Parkers Prairie MN 56361-9638

**PARKERS PRAIRIE 9 SW—*ST JAMES*** (320)834-2547
Joel R Brutlag • * • H • MNN • 56361 C/O Ebenezer 5393 County Road 5 NW Alexandria MN 56308-9740

**PELICAN RAPIDS—*OUR REDEEMER*** (218)863-1897
Vacant • H • MNN • PO Box 711 Pelican Rapids MN 56572-0711

**PEQUOT LAKES—*GLORIA DEI*** (218)568-5668
Frank V Milo • WS 815 1030; SS 925; BC 925;* • H • EC/EL • MNN • 30609 State Hwy 371 56472 PO Box 126 Pequot Lakes MN 56472-0126 • FAX(218)568-5651 • gloriadi@uslink.net

**PERHAM—*ST PAUL*** (218)346-7725
Terry L Grzybowski • WS 8 1030; BC 915;* • H • EC/EL • MNN • 56573 500 6th Ave SW Perham MN 56573-1115 • stpauls1@eot.com

**PERHAM 11 NE—*ST JOHN*** (218)346-4301
Delbert H Meyer • WS 10; BC 11;* • MNN • 8 East On 8-3 North On 53 56573 RR 1 Box 360 Perham MN 56573-9770 • FAX(218)346-4301

**PINE CITY—*ZION*** (320)629-3683
Glen A Kleppe • WS 9;* • H • MNN • 400 6th St Pine City MN 55063-1646 • zionpinecity@juno.com

**PIPESTONE—*OUR SAVIOUR*** (507)825-4124
Thomas L Mickelson • * • H • MNS • 1102 7th Ave SW Pipestone MN 56164-1045 • tommicks@juno.com

***ST PAUL*** (507)825-5271
Vacant • WS 830;* • EC • MNS • 621 W Main St Pipestone MN 56164-1243 • FAX(507)825-2499 • stpaul@rconnect.com

**PLAINVIEW—*IMMANUEL*** (507)534-3700
David Frederickson Scott S Hirssig • H • EC/EL • MNS • 45 W Broadway Plainview MN 55964-1238
**PLATO—*ST JOHN*** (320)238-2338
Bruce H Laabs • WS 9;* • H • MNS • 216 Mc Leod Ave N Plato MN 55370-5427 • FAX(320)238-2550 • stjluth@hutchtel.net
**PLUMMER—*REDEEMER*** (218)253-4611
Vacant • WS 10; SS 11; BC 915 • H • MNN • 56748 RR 1 Box 323 Red Lake Falls MN 56750-9766
**PLYMOUTH—*BEAUTIFUL SAVIOR*** (612)550-1000
Thomas K Stoebig • Sheryl B Olson DCE William R Johnson DCE • WS 830 11; BC 945;* • H • EC • MNS • 5005 Northwest Blvd Plymouth MN 55442-3504 • FAX(612)383-0990 • info@beautifulsaviorlc.org
***GLORY OF CHRIST*** (612)478-6031
Klemet I Preus • H • MNS • 4040 Highway 101 N Plymouth MN 55446-2306
**PRINCETON 5 NE—*ZION*** (763)389--1286
Vacant • H • MNN • 55371 5972 70th Ave Princeton MN 55371-6403
**PRIOR LAKE—*HOLY CROSS*** (952)445-1779
Robert W Nowak • H • EC • MNS • 14085 Pike Lake Trl NE Prior Lake MN 55372-9024 • FAX(952)445-6997 • holycrosspl@juno.com
***ST PAUL*** (952)447-2117
John P Vaughn Timothy D Schiller • WS 9; BC 1015;* • H • EC/EL/HS • MNS • 5634 Luther Dr SE Prior Lake MN 55372-2030 • FAX(952)447-2119
**PRIOR LAKE 4 SW—*IMMANUEL*** (952)492-6010
Dan L Siedenburg • WS 9; SS 1015; BC 1015 • H • MNS • 55372 20200 Fairlawn Ave Prior Lake MN 55372-8846 • FAX(952)492-2810 • fishlakelutheran@christian.net
**RACINE 8 NW—*IMMANUEL*** (507)754-5783
Ronald B Prigge • SS 945;* • H • MNS • 55967 73278 310th St Racine MN 55967-9731
**RADIUM 1 S—*IMMANUEL*** (218)745-4766
Vacant • * • EC • MNN • 56762 PO Box 102 Warren MN 56762-0102
**RAMEY—*BETHANY*** (320)355-2604
John A Ramsbacher • H • MNN • UKNWN 34238 Nature Rd Foley MN 56329
**RANDALL—*ST PETER*** (320)749-2477
James M Lewis • H • MNN • 413 Parkview Dr 56475-2436 121 E Sixth St Randall MN 56475-9620
**RAPIDAN—*ST JOHN*** (507)278-3835
James M Holthus • H • MNS • UKNWN Rt 6 Box 590 Mankato MN 56001
**RED LAKE FALLS—*ST JOHN*** (218)253-2987
Vacant • WS 1030; SS 915; BC 915 • H • MNN • 702 Main Ave S 56750-4712 PO Box 387 Red Lake Falls MN 56750-0387
**RED WING—*CONCORDIA*** (651)388-5447
Ronald E Stehr • H • EC/EL • MNS • 1805 Bush St Red Wing MN 55066-3629
**RED WING 6 S—*IMMANUEL***
See Hay Creek Twp
**RICE—*SHEPHERD PINES*** (320)393-4295
Vacant • H • EL • MNN • 1950 125th St NW Rice MN 56367-9701 • FAX(320)393-4295
**RICHFIELD—*BEREA*** (612)861-7121
Randolph G Sherren Mark G Heine • * • H • MNS • 7538 Emerson Ave S Richfield MN 55423-3933 • FAX(612)869-5141 • berealutheran@worldnet.att.net
***MOUNT CALVARY*** (612)866-5405
Mark D Johnson Don A Stults • WS 8 1045; BC 930;* • H • EC/EL/HS • MNS • 6544 16th Ave S Richfield MN 55423-1750 • FAX(612)866-6005 • MC-
**RICHVILLE—*ST PAUL*** (218)367-2470
Timothy B Vaughan • MNN • 56576 C/O St John Luth RR 2 Box 674 Ottertail MN 56571-9606
**ROBBINSDALE—*PEACE*** (763)533-0570
Carleton E Zahn • * • EC • MNS • 4512 France Ave N Robbinsdale MN 55422-1306 • FAX(763)533-0026
***REDEEMER*** (763)533-2564
John M Dreyer • WS 9; BC 1030;* • H • EC • MNS • 4201 Regent Ave N Robbinsdale MN 55422-1257 • FAX(763)533-2564 • ologos@ibm.net
**ROCHESTER—*CHRIST*** (507)289-0271
Eric R Gawura • H • MNS • 2904 20th St SE Rochester MN 55904-6019
***GRACE*** (507)289-7833
Gregory N Heidorn • * • H • EC/EL • MNS • 800 E Silver Lake Dr Rochester MN 55906-4460 • FAX(507)289-2888 • gracerochester@aol.com
***HOLY CROSS*** (507)289-1354
Steven R Schauder • Ernest F Freudenburg DCO • WS 8;* • H • EC/EL • MNS • 2703 9th Ave NW Rochester MN 55901-2301 • FAX(507)289-4815 • holycros@infonet.isl.net
***REDEEMER*** (507)289-5147
James W Heining John C Schleicher • WS 8;* • H • MNS • 869 7th Ave SE Rochester MN 55904-7359 • FAX(507)289-7887 • redeemer.lutheran@worldnet.att.net
***TRINITY*** (507)289-1531
John A Rasmussen James L Kroonblawd • WS 8; SS 915; BC 930;* • H • EC/EL • MNS • 222 6th Ave SW Rochester MN 55902-2956 • FAX(507)287-9882 • office@trinitylutheranchurch.org
**ROSEAU—*OUR SAVIOR*** (218)463-3226
Vacant • WS 9; BC 1015;* • MNN • 204 4th Ave NE Roseau MN 56751-1140 • FAX(218)528-4555
**ROSEMOUNT 1 W—*OUR SAVIOR*** (651)423-2580
Neil G Ristow • WS 8 915 1030;* • H • EC • MNS • 55068 14980 Diamond Path W Rosemount MN 55068-4505 • FAX(651423-2581 • OSavior@email.msn.com
**ROSEMOUNT 4 E—*ST JOHN*** (651)423-2149
John Moe • H • MNS • 55068 14385 Blaine Ave E Rosemount MN 55068-5929 • sjrv@myhometown.net

**ROSEVILLE—*KING OF KINGS*** (651)484-5142
Alan J Braun • James F Bargmann DCE • WS 830 11; SS 945; BC 945;* • H • EC/EL/HS • MNS • 2330 Dale St N Roseville MN 55113-4510 • FAX(651)484-9206
**ROUND LAKE—*BETHEL*** (507)945-8102
Kevin L Werner • MNS • 501 Main St Round Lake MN 56167-9759 • KWerner@rconnect.com
**ROYALTON—*BETHANY***
See Ramey
***ST JOHN*** (320)584-8132
John A Ramsbacher • MNN • 56373 26733 63rd St Royalton MN 56373-3326
***ST PAUL*** (320)584-8367
John A Ramsbacher • WS 8; SS 910 • H • MNN • 13 S Driftwood St 56373 PO Box 216 Royalton MN 56373-0216
**RUSH CITY—*ST JOHN*** (320)358-3623
Vacant • WS 8; BC 915;* • H • MNN • 980 W 4th St 55069-9065 PO Box 368 Rush City MN 55069-0368
**RUSHFORD—*ST MARK*** (507)864-7111
William E Mueller • * • H • MNS • 104 E North St Rushford MN 55971-9131 • FAX(507)864-4017 • stmarks@means.net
**RUSHFORD 5N—*ST JOHN*** (507)864-2585
Frederick P Buth • * • MNS • 55971 RR 1 Box 71 Rushford MN 55971-9622
**RUSHMORE—*ST JOHN*** (507)478-4922
William W Stratman • H • MNS • 420 4th St 56168-9792 PO Box 128 Rushmore MN 56168-0128
**SABIN—*TRINITY*** (218)789-7259
Daniel E Wagner • WS 9;* • H • MNN • 100 2nd Ave W 56580 PO Box 198 Sabin MN 56580-0198 • FAX(218)789-7517
**SAINT CHARLES—*ST MATTHEW*** (507)932-4246
David K Hodel Michael B Hart • WS 8 1030; BC 920;* • H • MNS • 555 E 12th St Saint Charles MN 55972 • FAX(507)932-5345 • davidhodel@earthlink.net
**SAINT CLOUD—*FAITH*** (320)252-3315
Donald W Kirsch • * • H • EL • MNN • 3000 County Road 8 SE Saint Cloud MN 56304-8525 • FAX(320)252-3315 • ddjjjkir@aol.com
***HOLY CROSS*** (320)251-8416
David P Strohschein Paul W Dare • WS 8; BC 915;* • H • EL • MNN • 2555 Clearwater Rd Saint Cloud MN 56301-5954 • FAX(320)252-4006 • holycross@disciple.org
***LOVE OF CHRIST*** (320)253-7453
Kenneth E Ferber Steven L Hayden • H • EL • MNN • 5488 20th St N Saint Cloud MN 56303-0372 • FAX(320)251-5396 • pastorken@loveofchrist.org
***REDEEMER*** (320)252-8171
Peter R Holm • WS 8 1030; BC 915;* • H • EL • MNN • 2719 3rd St N Saint Cloud MN 56303-4224 • FAX(320)240-9353
**SAINT CLOUD TWP—*OUR SAVIOR*** (320)251-7821
Robert A Trinklein • SS 1030;* • H • MNN • 56301 2929 County Road 136 Saint Cloud MN 56301-9017 • FAX(320)251-7821 • oursaviors@juno.com
**SAINT JAMES—*ST JOHN***
See Truman 4 NE
**SAINT JAMES 10 SE—*ST JOHN*** (507)375-4228
Matthew L Rusert • EL/HS • MNS • South Branch 56081 RR 1 Box 90 Saint James MN 56081-9735
**SAINT LOUIS PARK—*ST LUKE*** (952)929-5507
William H Kirmsse • WS 9; SS 1030;* • H • MNS • 5524 W 41st St Saint Louis Park MN 55416-2847 • FAX(952)929-5508 • whkirmsse@uswest.net
**SAINT PAUL—*BETHEL*** (651)488-6681
Mark G Hayhurst • Brian R Scoles DCO • * • H • HS • MNS • 670 Wheelock Pkwy W Saint Paul MN 55117-4150 • FAX(651)488-3800 • winnie@bethel.bchub.com
***BETHLEHEM*** (651)776-4737
Robert H Krueger • * • EC/EL/HS • MNS • 655 Forest St Saint Paul MN 55106-4508 • bethstpaullcms@juno.com
***CRISTO EL REDENTOR**** (651)291-2757
Larry E Miller(DM) • WS 1045; SS 930;* • MNS • 784 Jackson St Saint Paul MN 55117-5539 • FAX(651)225-9052 • lmilleresq@aol.com
***EASTERN HGHTS*** (651)735-4202
Steven M Benson • H • EL/HS • MNS • 616 Ruth St N Saint Paul MN 55119-3936 • revsbenson@afo.net
***EMMAUS*** (651)489-9426
Roger A Rekstad • WS 830 11; BC 945;* • H • HS • MNS • 1074 Idaho Ave W Saint Paul MN 55117-3354 • FAX(651)489-9426 • emmaus@isd.net
***HMONG*** (612)644-7100
Vacant • H • MNS • 1566 Thomas Ave Saint Paul MN 55104-1823
***JEHOVAH*** (651)644-1421
Vacant • * • H • EC/EL/HS • MNS • 1566 Thomas Ave Saint Paul MN 55104-1823 • jehovahlutheranchurch@juno.com
***OUR SAVIOUR*** (651)774-2396
John F Perling • * • H • EL/HS • MNS • 674 Johnson Pkwy Saint Paul MN 55106-4731 • FAX(651)774-6759 • oslc@isd.net
***ST PETER*** (651)228-1482
John D Wende • * • H • HS • MNS • 530 Victoria St S Saint Paul MN 55102-3729 • FAX(651)312-0548 • stpeters@christianmail.net
***ST STEPHANUS*** (651)228-1486
James W Bender • Jack Carlos DCO • WS 1030; SS 915; BC 915 • H • EC/EL/HS • MNS • 739 Lafond Ave Saint Paul MN 55104-1604
***ZION*** (651)224-3331
Gregory S Musolf • HS • MNS • 784 Jackson St Saint Paul MN 55117-5539
**SAINT PAUL 3 N—*TRINITY***
See Arden Hills

**SANBORN—*TRINITY*** (507)342-5544
Jeffrey P Schulz • * • MNS • 20476 Laser Ave 56083-3012 665 Maple St Wabasso MN 56293-9690 • trinitysanborn@yahoo.com
**SARGEANT 2 SE—*ST JOHN*** (507)584-6358
Ronald B Prigge • * • H • MNS • 28959 630 Ave 55973 C/O Immanuel Lutheran Church 73278 310th St Racine MN 55967-9731
**SARTELL—*MESSIAH*** (320)252-5883
John E Beck • * • H • MNN • 320 4th Ave N Sartell MN 56377-1739 • FAX(320)252-2814 • messiahsartell@juno.com
**SAUK CENTRE—*ZION*** (320)352-3447
Rudolph E Bloemker • MNN • 316 Maple St Sauk Centre MN 56378-1223
**SAUK RAPIDS—*TRINITY*** (320)252-3670
Paul E Cloeter • Craig L Cooper DCO • WS 8 10; BC 915;* • H • EC/EL • MNN • 400 2nd Ave N Sauk Rapids MN 56379-1612 • FAX(320)202-1095 • trinity@cloudnet.com
**SAUK RAPIDS 9 NE—*ST JOHN*** (612)968-7047
Michael K Dagel • MNN • 56379 6855 Golden Spike Rd NE Sauk Rapids MN 56379-9715
**SEBEKA—*GRACE*** (218)837-5565
Raymond V Hendrickson • H • MNN • 500 Wells Ave N Sebeka MN 56477
***NIMROD***
See Nimrod
**SEBEKA 5 SE—*ZION***
Bernard R Gorentz(EM) • WS 1030; BC 945;* • MNN • C/O Mrs Pearl Kreklau 17911 260th St Sebeka MN 56477
**SHAKOPEE—*CHRIST*** (952)445-3545
Vacant • H • MNS • 1053 Jefferson St S Shakopee MN 55379-2048
**SHERBURN—*ST JOHN*** (507)764-5312
Steven D Wilson • Daryl D Hoewisch DCE • * • H • MNS • 317 S Main St 56171 PO Box 760 Sherburn MN 56171-0760 • matthew9@frontiernet.net
**SILVER BAY—*FAITH*** (218)226-3908
Dennis P Brostrom • WS 845;* • MNN • 105 Outer Dr Silver Bay MN 55614-1119
**SILVER CREEK—*IMMANUEL*** (612)878-2820
Vacant • MNS • 55380 11390 Elliot Ave NW Maple Lake MN 55358
**SIOUX VALLEY TWP—*TRINITY*** (507)839-3086
David L Steege • H • MNS • RR 2 Box 31 Lake Park IA 51347-9209
**SLAYTON—*TRINITY*** (507)836-8129
John T Stern • EC • MNS • 2105 King Ave Slayton MN 56172-1024
**SNELLMAN—*GETHSEMANE*** (218)573-3574
Arthur A Ohlwine • H • MNN • UKNWN 46913 St Hwy 34 Osage MN 56570-9733
**SOUTH HAVEN—*CONCORDIA***
See Fair Haven
**SOUTH ST PAUL—*CONCORDIA*** (651)451-0309
Neldo Schmidt • * • H • MNS • 255 W Douglas St South St Paul MN 55075-3414 • FAX(651)451-8730
**SPRING LAKE PARK—*PRINCE OF*** (763)786-1706
Dean W Gade Paul Strawn • WS 830 11;* • H • HS • MNS • 7700 Monroe St NE Spring Lake Park MN 55432-2741 • FAX(763)786-2473 • popeace@uswest.net
**SPRING VALLEY—*FIRST ENGLISH*** (507)346-2793
Robert J Burmeister • * • H • MNS • 217 W Grant St Spring Valley MN 55975-1139
**SPRINGFIELD—*ZION*** (507)723-6230
David H Preuss • WS 915; BC 1030;* • H • MNS • 122 W Central St # 163 Springfield MN 56087-1404 • davidpreuss@juno.com
**SQUAW LAKE—*CENTENNIAL*** (218)246-8154
James W Anthony • MNN • Hwy 46 56681 PO Box 395 Squaw Lake MN 56681-0395
**ST FRANCIS—*TRINITY*** (763)753-1234
Jack R Baumgarn David H Baumgarn • WS 8; SS 915; BC 915;* • H • EC/EL • MNS • 3812 229th Ave Nw 55070 PO Box 700 St Francis MN 55070-0700 • FAX(763)753-1234 • Trinitysf@juno.com
***ZION***
See Crown 1 N
**STAPLES—*TRINITY*** (218)894-2372
Robin A Collins • WS 9; BC 1030;* • H • EC/EL • MNN • 1000 4th St NE 56479-3101 HC 3 Box 12 Staples MN 56479-9502
**STEWARTVILLE—*ST JOHN*** (507)533-4420
Vacant • WS 10;* • H • EC • MNS • 111 2nd Ave NE Stewartville MN 55976-1203 • FAX(507)533-4502
**STILLWATER 5W—*RISEN CHRIST*** (651)770-3618
Vacant • WS 8;* • H • HS • MNS • 55082 9050 60th St N Stillwater MN 55082-8315
**STOCKTON—*GRACE*** (507)689-2777
Vacant • WS 830;* • H • MNS • 55987-3442 PO Box 197 Stockton MN 55988-0197
**SUPERIOR—*MISSION DEAF****
See Duluth
**SWANVILLE—*ST PETER*** (320)547-2928
John O Grein • H • MNN • 503 Berkey Ave 56382 PO Box 126 Swanville MN 56382-0126
**THIEF RIVER FALLS—*ST JOHN*** (218)681-4488
Donald G Kirchner • * • H • MNN • 101 Pine Ave S Thief River Falls MN 56701-3314 • stjohntrf@juno.com
**TRIMONT—*TRINITY*** (507)639-4111
Royce E Rinehart • WS 9; SS 1015; BC 1015 • H • HS • MNS • Hwy 4 And Main St 56176 PO Box 321 Trimont MN 56176-0321
**TROSKY—*ST JOHN*** (507)348-7661
Vacant • MNS • 210 Ridge St 56177 PO Box 57 Trosky MN 56177-0057

**TRUMAN—*ST PAUL*** (507)776-2801
Nathan J Rusert • WS 9; BC 1015 • H • HS • MNS • 110 E 4th St N Truman MN 56088-1132 • FAX(507)776-3060
**TRUMAN 4 NE—*ST JOHN*** (507)776-6487
Matthew L Rusert • EL/HS • MNS • 56088 RR 1 Box 90 Saint James MN 56081-9735
**TWIN VALLEY—*TRINITY*** (218)584-8440
Arvid M Salvhus • * • H • EC • MNN • Hwy 32 S 56684 PO Box 248 Twin Valley MN 56584-0248
**TWO HARBORS—*HOPE*** (218)834-5345
Dennis P Brostrom • WS 1045;* • H • MNN • 411 3rd Ave Two Harbors MN 55616-1628
**UPSALA—*MOUNT OLIVE*** (612)573-2630
Vacant • MNN • 201 Johnson St 56384 PO Box 322 Upsala MN 56384-0322
**VERGAS—*ST JOHN*** (218)342-2791
Michael D Wolters • WS 9; BC 8;* • H • MNN • 410 Scharf St 56587 RR 1 Box 39 Vergas MN 56587-9708
**VERGAS 2 SW—*ST PAUL*** (218)342-2379
Michael D Wolters • WS 1030; BC 915;* • H • MNN • Cnty Rd #4 Loon Lake 56587 RR 1 Box 39 Vergas MN 56587-9708
**VERNDALE—*REDEEMER*** (218)445-5313
William F Moeller • * • H • MNN • 22 Third St Nw 56481 306 NW Brown St Verndale MN 56481-9302
**VERNDALE 8 S—*IMMANUEL*** (218)924-2454
William F Moeller • * • H • MNN • Todd Co Rd 30 306 NW Brown St Verndale MN 56481
**VERNON CENTER—*ST PETER*** (507)549-3166
G Greg Hovland • H • MNS • 202 E Kendall St 56090 PO Box 415 Vernon Center MN 56090-0415 • FAX(507)549-3032 • pastorh@prairie.lakes.com
***TRINITY***
See Lewisville 4 NE
**VERNON CENTER 7 SW—*ST JOHN*** (507)549-3760
Craig A Cummins • EC/EL/HS • MNS • 56090 RR 1 Box 51 Vernon Center MN 56090-9721
**VICTORIA—*CHRIST VICTORIOUS***
See Chaska
**VILLARD—*ST JOHN*** (320)554-2161
Lawrence E Cain • H • MNN • 341 Commercial Ave 56385 PO Box 36 Villard MN 56385-0036
***TRINITY***
See Grovelake
**VIRGINIA—*TRINITY*** (218)741-1911
Walter L Brill • WS 9; BC 1030;* • H • MNN • 900 13th St S Virginia MN 55792-3250
**VIRGINIA 12 N—*GLORIA DEI*** (218)741-1977
Daniel F Clemons • H • MNN • UKNWN 6959 Highway 169 Virginia MN 55792-8040
**WABASSO—*BETHANY*** (507)342-5544
Jeffrey P Schulz • * • MNS • 665 Maple St Wabasso MN 56293- • bethanywabasso@yahoo.com
***TRINITY***
See Sanborn
**WACONIA—*TRINITY*** (952)442-4165
Dean E Mahlum Peter M Peitsch Craig T Mc Court(#) • WS 8; BC 915;* • H • EC/EL/HS • MNS • 601 E 2nd St Waconia MN 55387-1608 • FAX(952)442-4644 • office@trinitywaconia.org
**WADENA—*ST JOHN*** (218)631-3000
Vacant • * • H • EC • MNN • 710 Franklin Ave SW Wadena MN 56482-1755
**WALDORF—*FIRST*** (507)239-2431
Michael W Mathews • * • H • MNS • 120 3rd Ave 56091 PO Box 216 Waldorf MN 56091-0216
**WALKER—*IMMANUEL*** (218)547-3156
Vacant • WS 9;* • H • EC/EL • MNN • 4656 State 200 NW 56484-2619 PO Box 307 Walker MN 56484-0307
**WALTHAM 3 SW—*TRINITY*** (507)567-2272
Vacant • * • H • MNS • 29972 570th Ave 55982 57043 300th St Waltham MN 55982-7631 • jaluther@smig.net
**WARREN—*IMMANUEL***
See Radium 1 S
***ZION*** (218)745-4766
Vacant • * • H • EC • MNN • PO Box 102 Warren MN 56762-0102
**WARROAD—*BETHLEHEM*** (218)463-3226
Vacant • MNN • PO Box 595 Warroad MN 56763-0595
**WASECA—*ST PAUL*** (507)835-2647
Armand J Boehme • WS 8 1030; BC 915;* • H • MNS • 314 4th Ave NE Waseca MN 56093-2925 • FAX(507)835-8733 • stpaulwas@platec.net
**WASECA 5 SW—*TRINITY*** (507)835-2621
Glenn L Korb • MNS • 56093 31184 W Wilton River Rd Waseca MN 56093-5525
**WATERTOWN—*ST PAUL*** (952)955-1498
Paul D Krentz • WS 8; BC 915;* • H • EC/EL/HS • MNS • 505 Westminster Sw 55388 PO Box 697 Watertown MN 55388-0697 • FAX(952)955-3874
**WATERTOWN 3 E—*ST PETER*** (952)955-1679
Jay B Klein • * • H • EC/EL/HS • MNS • 2980 Navajo Ave Watertown MN 55388 • stpeterlc@juno.com
**WATERVILLE—*TRINITY*** (507)362-4454
Erwin W Meitz • * • H • MNS • 415 Lake St W Waterville MN 56096-1323
**WATERVILLE 8 NW—*ST PETER*** (507)362-8381
Christopher P Meyer • H • MNS • 56096 RR 2 Box 220 Waterville MN 56096-9542 • bell220@juno.com
**WAYZATA—*REDEEMER*** (612)473-1281
Robert L Nordlie • Larry L Finke DCE • WS 8;* • H • EC/EL • MNS • 115 Wayzata Blvd W Wayzata MN 55391-1541
**WEBSTER—*ST JOHN*** (612)652-2844
Jerry E Markel • MNS • 4376 41st St W Webster MN 55088-2105 • markelministry@juno.com
**WELLS—*CHRIST REDEEMER*** (507)553-3596
Vacant • H • MNS • Second Ave Nw 56097 PO Box 101 Wells MN 56097-0101

**WEST CONCORD—*ZION***
Robert A Lentz • H • MNS • 710 Third St 55985 14301 Grand Ave Burnsville MN 55306-5707
**WHEATON—*ST JOHN*** (320)563-4143
Vacant • H • MNN • 1603 Broadway Wheaton MN 56296-1052
**WHEATON 11 NE—*IMMANUEL*** (320)563-4891
Vacant • MNN • 56296 C/O St John Lutheran Church PO Box 125 Dumont MN 56236
**WHITE BEAR LAKE—*TRINITY*** (651)429-4293
John C Schildwachter • WS 8 930 11;* • H • EC/HS • MNS • 2480 S Shore Blvd White Bear Lake MN 55110-3898 • FAX(651)653-3634 • sstwbl@juno.com
**WILLMAR—*REDEEMER*** (320)235-4685
Steven M Bielenberg • WS 8 1045; BC 915;* • H • MNN • 1401 6th St SW Willmar MN 56201-4004 • FAX(320)235-1879 • redeemer@mail.tds.net
**WINDOM—*OUR SAVIOR*** (507)831-3522
Paul S Woebbeking • WS 8 1030; SS 905; BC 905 • H • EC • MNS • 1157 3rd Ave Windom MN 56101-1452 • FAX(507)831-5641 • lcoos@oursaviorslutheran.net
**WINNEBAGO—*OUR SAVIOR*** (507)893-3320
Vacant • WS 10;* • H • HS • MNS • 121 1st Ave SE 56098-1086 PO Box 455 Winnebago MN 56098-0455
**WINONA—*REDEEMER*** (507)452-3828
William E Flesch • * • H • EC • MNS • 1664 Kraemer Dr Winona MN 55987-2064 • FAX(507)452-3435 • redeluth@rconnect.com
***ST MARTIN*** (507)452-8879
Vacant • H • EC/EL • MNS • 328 E Broadway St Winona MN 55987-3700 • FAX(507)457-0884 • stmartin@hbci.com
**WINSTED—*ST JOHN*** (320)485-2522
Gerald L Boldt • MNS • 410 First St N 55395 PO Box 67 Winsted MN 55395-0067
**WOLF LAKE—*CHRIST*** (218)538-6694
Bernhard W Lutz • WS 1030;* • H • MNN • County Rd 45 56593 PO Box 305 Wolf Lake MN 56593-0305 • pjramsay@wcta.net
**WOLVERTON 13 SE—*CHRIST*** (218)557-8892
Vacant • * • MNN • RR Wolverton MN 56594
**WOOD LAKE 5 SE—*ST LUKE*** (507)485-3527
Randall C Moritz • MNN • 56297 5597 130th Ave Wood Lake MN 56297-1497
**WOODBURY—*ST JOHN*** (651)436-6621
Jonathan Marxhausen • * • H • HS • MNS • 1975 Saint Johns Dr Woodbury MN 55129-9462 • FAX(651)436-4131
***WOODBURY*** (651)739-5144
Dean W Nadasdy Paul J Pfotenhauer Orval E Goldsby Todd D Stocker • Chad J Starfeldt DCE • WS 8 1045; SS 930; BC 930;* • H • EC/EL • MNS • 7380 Afton Rd Woodbury MN 55125-1502 • FAX(651)739-3536 • office@woodburylutheran.org
**WORTHINGTON—*ST MATTHEW*** (507)376-6168
Robert A Schulze • WS 8 1030; SS 915; BC 915;* • H • MNS • 1505 Dover St Worthington MN 56187-1809 • FAX(507)376-6915
**WRENSHALL—*ST JOHN*** (218)384-4925
Kevin N Tiaden • WS 930; BC 815;* • H • MNN • 417 Alcohol Rd 55797-9043 PO Box 98 Wrenshall MN 55797-0098
**WRIGHT—*ST JOHN*** (218)357-2003
Henry J Koopmann • WS 1030;* • H • MNN • Pease Ave And 2nd St 1417 2nd St Wright MN 55798-0035 • FAX(218)768-3198
**WYKOFF—*ST JOHN*** (507)352-2296
Vacant • * • H • EC/EL • MNS • 241 Line St S 55990-9770 PO Box 128 Wykoff MN 55990-0128 • FAX(507)352-7671
**YOUNG AMERICA—*ST JOHN*** (612)467-2740
David W Winter Scott A Gustafson • H • EC/EL/HS • MNS • 101 2nd St SE Young America MN 55397-9778
**ZIMMERMAN—*FAITH COMMUNITY*** (763)856-3600
James S Walburg • WS 1030;* • H • MNN • Hwy 169 South 55398 PO Box 156 Zimmerman MN 55398-0156

## MISSISSIPPI

**BILOXI—*GOOD SHEPHERD*** (601)388-5767
Morris D Meseke • WS 1030; SS 915; BC 915 • H • EC • SO • 2004 Pass Rd Biloxi MS 39531-3126
**BRANDON—*GOOD SHEPHERD*** (601)992-4752
J R Sawyer • WS 8 1030; SS 915; BC 915;* • H • EC • SO • 6035 Hwy 25 39042 PO Box 5013 Brandon MS 39047-5013 • seelsorge@aol.com
**CLEVELAND—*GOOD SHEPHERD*** (601)846-0233
Weldon D Brinkley • WS 9;* • SO • 222 N 1st Ave 38732-2522 PO Box 386 Cleveland MS 38732-0386
**COLUMBUS—*OUR SAVIOR*** (601)328-1757
Leonard B Poppe • WS 1030 7; SS 915; BC 915 • SO • 1211 18th Ave N Columbus MS 39701-2305
**CORINTH—*PRINCE OF PEACE*** (662)287-1037
Vacant • H • SO • 4203 Shiloh Rd Corinth MS 38834-8619 • pop@avsia.com
**GREENVILLE—*FAITH*** (601)332-5093
Weldon D Brinkley • WS 11;* • H • SO • 38703 PO Box 5038 Greenville MS 38704-5038 • wbrinkle@deltaland.net
**GREENWOOD—*CHRIST KING*** (662)453-8323
Vacant • H • SO • 1509 Highway 82 W 38930-2717 PO Box 673 Greenwood MS 38935-0673
**GULFPORT—*HOLY TRINITY*** (601)896-5878
Gary W Weier Delbert W Gremmels(EM) • WS 1030; SS 9; BC 9;* • H • SO • 505 Cowan Rd Gulfport MS 39507-2024 • FAX(601)896-9363 • trinitygpt@juno.com
***ST MATTHEW*** (228)864-6264
Adam Cooper Jr. • WS 1045; SS 930;* • H • SO • 1301 31st Ave Gulfport MS 39501-1888 • m1919@bellsouth.net
**HATTIESBURG—*ST JOHN*** (601)583-4898
Vacant • WS 1030;* • H • SO • 2001 Hardy St Hattiesburg MS 39401-4919

**HOLLY SPRINGS—*ZION*** (601)252-4224
Vacant • WS 9; SS 10; BC 10 • H • SO • 945 Highway 311 38635-1343 310 S Cedar Hills Rd Holly Springs MS 38635-2720 • sliddy@centuryinter.net
**JACKSON—*CHRIST*** (601)366-2055
Allen J Kramp • WS 1030; SS 915; BC 915 • H • SO • 4423 I 55 N Jackson MS 39206-6102
***OUR REDEEMER*** (601)372-7256
Vacant • Cynthia A Namanny DCE • WS 1030 8; SS 915 • H • SO • 1735 Shady Lane Dr Jackson MS 39204-3526 • FAX(601)372-1887 • orlcms@bellsouth.net
***ST PAUL*** (601)982-1940
Vacant • SO • 2875 Medgar Evers Blvd Jackson MS 39213-7260
***ST PHILIP*** (601)353-0504
Mark A Griffin • WS 830; SS 935;* • SO • 1230 Isaiah Montgomery St Jackson MS 39203-3326 • hidolo@juno.com
**JACKSON (RESERVOIR)—*GOOD***
See Brandon
**MCCOMB—*TRINITY*** (601)684-5156
Vacant • WS 12; SS 1; BC 1 • H • SO • 1622 Virginia Ave 39648-4445 PO Box 732 Mc Comb MS 39649-0732
**MERIDIAN—*TRINITY*** (601)483-5457
Philip C Wottrich • WS 1030 8; SS 915; BC 915 • H • SO • 4805 Highway 39 N 39301 PO Box 3460 Meridian MS 39303-3460 • FAX(601)483-5457 • pastorwott@aol.com
**NATCHEZ—*FIRST*** (601)442-1397
William D Gassett • WS 9; SS 1015; BC 1015 • H • SO • 70 Sgt S Prentiss Dr Natchez MS 39120-4728 • lcms³natchez@hotmail.com
**OXFORD—*PEACE*** (662)234-6568
Bruce K Meier(#) • H • SO • 407 Jackson Ave W Oxford MS 38655-2637 • pbandmb@watervalley.net
**PASCAGOULA—*CHRIST*** (228)762-1754
Jon D Arbogast • WS 830 11; SS 945;* • H • SO • 3042 Pascagoula St 39567-4213 PO Box 877 Pascagoula MS 39568-0877 • clc1888@datasync.net
**PICAYUNE—*ST PAUL*** (601)798-4586
Tom P Willadsen • H • SO • 1309 Highway 11 S Picayune MS 39466-5508
**SOUTHAVEN—*PRINCE OF PEACE*** (601)393-3432
John M Doolittle • H • SO • 8089 US Highway 51 N Southaven MS 38671-4637
**STARKVILLE—*ST LUKE*** (662)323-3050
Marlo D Lemke • WS 1030; SS 930; BC 930 • H • SO • 1104 Hwy 25 S Starkville MS 39759-3906
**TUPELO—*HOLY TRINITY*** (662)842-0364
Richard C Kreitenstein • WS 9; SS 1045;* • H • SO • 1305 Lawhon St Tupelo MS 38804 • rckreit@ebicom.net
**VICKSBURG—*MESSIAH*** (601)636-1894
Gary D Osburn • H • SO • 301 Cain Ridge Rd Vicksburg MS 39180-6004
**WAVELAND—*OF THE PINES*** (601)467-6771
Vacant • H • SO • 309 Highway 90 Waveland MS 39576-2622

## MISSOURI

**AFFTON—*CHRIST MEMORIAL***
See Saint Louis
***REFORMATION*** (314)352-1355
David C Pelsue • WS 815 1045; SS 930; BC 930 • H • HS • MO • 63123 7910 Mackenzie Rd Saint Louis MO 63123-2721 • FAX(314)352-7652 • reformation@stl.com
***SALEM*** (314)352-4454
Michael P Scholz • John B Hagge DCE • WS 8 930 11; SS 930; BC 930;* • H • EC/EL/HS • MO • 8343 Gravois Rd Affton MO 63123-4735 • FAX(314)352-1030 • salemlc@aol.com
**ALMA—*TRINITY*** (660)674-2376
Frederick C Hertwig • * • H • MO • 310 N Waverly 64001 PO Box 276 Alma MO 64001-0276 • FAX(660)674-2747 • trinity@almanet.net
**ALTENBURG—*IMMANUEL*** (573)824-5636
Charles W Weber • H • MO • PO Box 26 Altenburg MO 63732-0026
***TRINITY*** (573)824-5287
Vacant • H • EL • MO • Church and Main Sts Altenburg MO 63732
**APPLETON CITY—*TRINITY*** (816)476-5438
Timothy C Brown • H • MO • 300 E 1st St Appleton City MO 64724-1006
**ARCADIA—*IMMANUEL***
See Pilot Knob
***ST PAUL***
See Ironton
**ARNOLD—*GOOD SHEPHERD*** (636)296-1292
Warren R Woerth • WS 9; SS 1030; BC 1030 • H • EC • MO • 2211 Tenbrook Rd Arnold MO 63010-1516 • goodshepamold@juno.com
***ST JOHN*** (314)464-0096
Steven J Benke • H • EC/EL/HS • MO • 3517 Jeffco Blvd Arnold MO 63010-3990 • FAX(314)464-8645
**AUGUSTA—*CHRIST*** (636)228-4642
Vacant • WS 10; SS 9; BC 9 • H • MO • 123 Church Rd Augusta MO 63332-1739
**AURORA—*GRACE*** (417)678-3603
Mark A Boettcher • H • MO • 1120 S Park Ave Aurora MO 65605-2459 • gracelc@mail.hdnet.k12.mo.us
**BABBTOWN—*ST JOHN***
See Meta 3 N
**BARNHART—*IMMANUEL*** (314)464-4114
Dennis W Schmidt • H • HS • MO • 6500 Metropolitan Blvd Barnhart MO 63012-1358
**BEAUFORT 2 N—*ST JOHN*** (573)484-3575
Vacant • WS 10; SS 9; BC 9 • H • MO • 2149 Lutheran Church Rd Beaufort MO 63013 • shirlin@usmo.com

**BELLE—*MOUNT CALVARY LUTHER*** (573)859-3934
Norman W Bahlow • WS 1030; SS 930; BC 930 • H • MO • 508 Taylor Ave PO Box 833 508 Taylor Ave Belle MO 65013-0833
**BELLEFONTAINE NEIGH—*GRACE*** (314)868-3232
David K Groth • Michael Kehe DCE • WS 8 1030; SS 915; BC 915;* • H • MO • UKNWN 10015 Lance Dr Saint Louis MO 63137-1564 • FAX(314)868-2485
**BELTON—*BETHLEHEM***
See Raymore
**BETHANY—*HOPE*** (660)425-3627
William L Gleason • H • MO • 1205 S 25th St Bethany MO 64424-2601
**BISMARCK—*ST JOHN*** (573)734-2156
Vacant • WS 845 • H • MO • 1146 Cedar St 63624-8902 PO Box 537 Bismarck MO 63624-0537
**BLACK JACK—*SALEM*** (314)741-6781
Mark Kluzek • Benjamin C Schumacher DCE • SS 915; BC 915;* • H • EC/EL • MO • UKNWN 5180 Parker Rd Florissant MO 63033-4653 • FAX(314)741-1797
**BLACKBURN—*BETHLEHEM***
See Mount Leonard
***ZION*** (785)538-4688
Timothy C Miille • MO • 313 W Third St 65321 PO Box 196 Blackburn MO 65321-0196
**BLUE SPRINGS—*TIMOTHY*** (816)228-5300
Francis M Lieb Theodore V Schubkegel • Steve A Jorgensen DCE • WS 8 915 1045; SS 915;* • H • EC/HS • MO • 425 NW R D Mize Rd Blue Springs MO 64014-2420 • FAX(816)228-5323 • timothylutheran@discoverynet.com
**BOLIVAR—*ZION*** (417)326-5506
Mark E Lavrenz • WS 11; SS 10; BC 10 • H • MO • 600 E Aldrich Rd PO Box 5 Bolivar MO 65613-0005 • zion7@microcore.net
**BONNE TERRE—*ST MATTHEW*** (573)358-3105
Thomas N Reeder Sr. • MO • 340 Summit St Bonne Terre MO 63628-1922
**BOONVILLE—*IMMANUEL*** (660)882-2208
Jerry A Riggert • WS 8; SS 915; BC 915 • H • EC • MO • Bingham Rd 65233 1001 Immanuel Dr Boonville MO 65233-1895 • FAX(660)882-9337 • immanluth@c-magic.com
**BOONVILLE 10 S—*TRINITY***
See Clarks Fork
**BOURBON—*CONCORDIA*** (573)732-4477
David N Zirpel • WS 8; SS 915; BC 915 • H • MO • 642 E Pine St 65441-8102 PO Box 359 Bourbon MO 65441-0359 • zirpel@fidnet.com
**BOWLING GREEN—*GOOD SHEPHERD*** (573)324-5405
Randy C Van Mehren • H • MO • 1806 W Main St 63334-1019 3405 Georgia St Louisiana MO 63353-2733
**BRANSON—*FAITH*** (888)777-3059
Michael D Wanner Timothy G Onnen(#) • WS 8 1030; SS 915; BC 915;* • H • EC • MO • 221 Malone Branson MO 65616-2011 • FAX(417)337-5201 • oslc@tri-lakes.net
**BRENTWOOD—*MOUNT CALVARY*** (314)968-2360
Darrell W Zimmerman • H • EC/EL • MO • 9321 Litzsinger Rd Brentwood MO 63144-2127 • FAX(314)968-4943 • mtcalvary@primary.net
**BRIDGETON—*BEAUT SAVIOR*** (314)291-2395
Thomas R Eckstein • WS 8 1030 10; SS 915; BC 915 • H • MO • 12397 Natural Bridge Rd Bridgeton MO 63044-2020 • FAX(314)291-2497 • beautsav@juno.com
***TRINITY*** (314)739-0022
Keith D Ellerbrock • WS 8 1045; SS 915; BC 915 • H • EL • MO • 3765 Mc Kelvey Rd Bridgeton MO 63044-2002 • KDBROCK777@aol.com
**BROOKFIELD—*ST PAUL*** (660)258-3673
Philip L Bach • WS 10; BC 9 • H • MO • 806 S Brunswick St 64628-2406 PO Box 125 Brookfield MO 64628-0125
**BRUNSWICK—*ST JOHN*** (660)548-3642
Glen A Drewitz • WS 10 • H • MO • 319 E Broadway St Brunswick MO 65236-1235 • stjohns@c-magic.com
**BUFFALO—*OUR SAVIOR*** (417)345-5856
Brian C Whittle • H • MO • 107 S Elder St Buffalo MO 65622-9753
**BUNCETON—*ZION***
See Lone Elm
**CABOOL—*HOLY CROSS***
See Houston
**CALIFORNIA—*ST PAUL*** (573)796-2735
Peter M Kurowski • WS 9; SS 1030; BC 1030 • H • MO • 207 N Owen St 65018-1125 PO Box 326 California MO 65018-0326
**CAMDENTON—*PEACE*** (573)873-6212
Robin D Fish Sr. • WS 9; SS 1030;* • H • MO • N Hwy 5 Greenview Mo 65020 HC 82 Box 6323 Camdenton MO 65020-8214 • peace@advertisnet.com
**CAMERON—*PRINCE PEACE*** (816)632-7904
Walter A Peckman • * • H • MO • 209 Little Brick St Cameron MO 64429-1262
**CAPE GIRARDEAU—*CHRIST*** (573)243-5639
Vacant • WS 10; SS 9 • H • MO • 248 Albert St 63703-5910 PO Box 72 Gordonville MO 63752-0072 • christch@marz.com
***GOOD SHEPHERD*** (573)335-3974
Barry L Pfanstiel • Gregory R Rommel DCE • WS 8 1030; SS 915 • H • MO • 1904 W Cape Rock Dr Cape Girardeau MO 63701-2625 • FAX(573)335-7610
***HANOVER*** (573)335-8583
Jeffrey E Sippy • WS 745 10; SS 9; BC 9 • H • MO • 2949 Perryville Rd Cape Girardeau MO 63701-1833 • FAX(573)335-4741 • hanover@clas.net
***ST ANDREW*** (573)334-3200
Paul J Short • H • MO • 804 N Cape Rock Dr Cape Girardeau MO 63701-3698 • FAX(573)335-8589 • pjshort@clas.net
***TRINITY*** (573)335-8224
Douglas C Breite David W Hintz • WS 8 1030; SS 915; BC 915;* • H • MO • 100 N Frederick St Cape Girardeau MO 63701-5610 • FAX(573)335-1146 • kim@t-lutheran.org
**CAPE GIRARDEAU 8 N—*TRINITY*** (314)334-4549
Mark D Martin • WS 10 745; BC 9;* • H • MO • Egypt Mills 63701 5665 County Rd 635 Cape Girardeau MO 63701-8748 • martin@showme.net
**CARROLLTON—*IMMANUEL*** (816)542-2064
Eric D Swyres • WS 10; SS 9; BC 9 • H • EC • MO • 402 S Folger St Carrollton MO 64633-1223
**CARTHAGE—*GOOD SHEPHERD*** (417)358-1325
James F Schnackenberg • WS 1045; SS 930; BC 930 • H • MO • 8975 County Ln 170 64836 PO Box 257 Carthage MO 64836-0257 • FAX(417)358-1381 • goodshep@janics.com
**CASCADE—*ZION***
See Gravelton
**CASSVILLE—*HOLY CROSS*** (417)847-2671
Vacant • H • MO • 305 W 7th St Cassville MO 65625-1437
**CEDAR HILL—*CEDAR HILL*** (314)274-4802
David A Bilgreen • H • MO • 8600 Silver Ln Cedar Hill MO 63016-1627
**CENTER—*TRINITY*** (573)565-2843
Vacant • H • MO • Routes Ee And J 63436 2227 Hwy EE Center MO 63436-9668
**CENTRALIA—*GOOD SHEPHERD*** (573)682-3941
Vacant • H • MO • 120 W Gano Chance Dr Centralia MO 65240-1695 • goodshepherd@bigfoot.com
**CHAFFEE—*ST PAUL*** (573)243-5395
Wayne W Schwiesow • WS 8; SS 9; BC 9 • H • MO • 201 Gray Ave Chaffee MO 63740-1403
**CHESTERFIELD—*KING OF KINGS*** (314)469-2224
Alan H Bachert Christopher J Watson • WS 8 1030; SS 915; BC 920 • H • EC • MO • 13765 Olive Blvd Chesterfield MO 63017-2601 • FAX(314)469-0601 • kokluth@kingofkingsluth.org
***LORD OF LIFE*** (636)532-0400
James C Rogers • WS 8 1030; SS 915; BC 915 • H • EC • MO • 15750 Baxter Rd Chesterfield MO 63017-4983 • FAX(636)536-2322 • jrogers@lordoflifelcms.org
**CHILLICOTHE—*ST JOHN*** (816)646-5944
Paul A Knittel • WS 845; SS 955; BC 955 • MO • 1001 Calhoun St 64601 PO Box 426 Chillicothe MO 64601-0426
**CLARKS FORK—*TRINITY*** (660)882-6253
Luther S Herman • WS 930 • H • MO • UKNWN 20209 Ellis Davis Rd Boonville MO 65233 • 1herman@c-magic.com
**CLINTON—*TRINITY*** (660)885-4728
Douglas D Punke • WS 10; SS 845; BC 845 • H • MO • 95 E Hwy 7 Clinton MO 64735-9557 • punke@lakeozark.net
**COLE CAMP—*MOUNT HULDA*** (660)668-3492
Mark F Laugavitz • WS 10; SS 915 • H • MO • RR 2 - Box 230 A Cole Camp MO 65325-9803
***TRINITY*** (816)668-2364
Randal G Ehrichs • WS 8 1030; SS 915; BC 915 • H • EL • MO • 108 E Butterfield Trl 65325-1119 PO Box H Cole Camp MO 65325-0168
**COLE CAMP 6 NW—*ST JOHN*** (816)668-3904
Erich L Kurz • WS 9; SS 815; BC 815 • H • EL • MO • 65325 PO Box 188 Cole Camp MO 65325-0188
**COLE CAMP 7 NE—*HOLY CROSS***
Erich L Kurz • WS 11; SS 1015; BC 1030 • H • EL • MO • 65325 PO Box 188 Cole Camp MO 65325-0188
**COLUMBIA—*ALIVE IN CHRIST*** (573)499-0443
Thomas K Brouwer • WS 9; SS 1030; BC 1030 • H • MO • 201 Southampton Dr Columbia MO 65203-3051 • FAX(573)499-0452 • office@aic.org
***CAMPUS*** (573)442-5942
David M Benson • Carolyn M Thompson DCE • H • MO • 304 S College Ave Columbia MO 65201-5024 • FAX(573)442-6930
***TRINITY*** (573)445-2112
Kenneth J Gerike Brian K Thieme • WS 8 1030; SS 915; BC 915;* • H • EC • MO • 2201 W Rollins Rd Columbia MO 65203-1433 • FAX(573)445-4078 • church@trinity-lcms.org
**CONCORDIA—*CHRIST***
See Sweet Springs 6 NE
***ST MATTHEW***
See Ernestville
***ST PAUL*** (660)463-2291
Gary R Clayton • WS 8 1030; SS 915; BC 915 • H • EC/EL • MO • 418 S Main St 64020 PO Box 60 Concordia MO 64020-0060 • FAX(660)463-7173 • splsrev@galaxyispc.com
**CONWAY 8 SE—*IMMANUEL*** (417)589-2402
Frederick Raedeke • MO • 8 Miles Se Hwy Zz To Rader 65632 3350 Wildwood Rd Niangua MO 65713-9712
**CORDER—*ZION*** (660)394-2322
Brett L Mueller • * • H • EC/EL • MO • 500 N Elizabeth PO Box 224 Corder MO 64021
**CORNING—*ST JOHN*** (660)683-5585
Donald W Craig John N Sellmeyer • MO • 112 Walters St Corning MO 64437
**CRAIG—*ST JOHN***
See Corning
**CRAIG 3 W—*ST PETER*** (660)683-5787
Donald W Craig John N Sellmeyer • H • MO • 64437 15371 Amber Dr Craig MO 64437-8174
**CREIGHTON—*TRINITY*** (816)499-2205
Timothy C Brown • MO • A Street 64739 PO Box 123 Creighton MO 64739-0123
**CRESTWOOD—*PRINCE OF PEACE*** (314)843-8448
Mark S H Smith • WS 815 1045; SS 930; BC 930 • H • EC/EL/HS • MO • 8646 New Sappington Rd Saint Louis MO 63126-1908 • FAX(314)843-5653
**CROSSTOWN—*ZION*** (573)547-8676
Robert W Schneider • MO • UKNWN 21202 Hwy C Perryville MO 63775 • FAX(573)824-5728
**CRYSTAL CITY—*IMMANUEL*** (314)937-5525
Virgil M Kelm • H • EC • MO • 205 Ward Ter 63019 PO Box 317 Crystal City MO 63019-0317
**CUBA—*ST PAUL*** (573)885-7234
Roger W Schnakenberg • H • MO • Maple Shade And Fleenor Rd 65453 730 Fleenor Rd Cuba MO 65453-9301
**DE SOTO—*GRACE*** (636)586-2487
Steven L Flo • WS 9; SS 1030; BC 1030 • H • MO • 121 W Kelley St De Soto MO 63020-2201 • FAX(636)586-5556 • sflo@usmo.com
**DES PERES—*ST PAUL*** (314)822-0447
David S Smith Jeremy J Schultz • WS 8 930 1045; SS 925; BC 925 • H • HS • MO • 63131 12345 Manchester Rd Saint Louis MO 63131-4316 • FAX(314)822-6574 • church@stpaulsdesperes.org
**DEXTER—*FAITH*** (573)624-4921
Daniel R Mc Quality • WS 930; SS 1045; BC 815 • H • MO • 1002 Saddle Spur Rd Dexter MO 63841-1846 • flc@bootheel.net
**DIGGINS—*ZION*** (417)767-4019
Dana M Wilkie • WS 1030; BC 930;* • H • MO • 65636 438 S Diggins Main St Seymour MO 65746 • nordana@juno.com
**DONIPHAN—*TRINITY*** (573)996-3061
Vacant • H • MO • RR 3 Box 2 Doniphan MO 63935-9401
**DRAKE 2 SE—*ST JOHN*** (573)437-2975
Norman H Dierking • WS 830; SS 930; BC 930 • H • MO • UKNWN 2840 Charlotte Church Rd Owensville MO 65066
**EL DORADO SPRINGS—*FAITH***
Johannes W Brann • WS 10; SS 9; BC 9 • H • MO • 64744 220 N Main St El Dorado Spgs MO 64744-1144
**ELDON—*BETHANY*** (573)392-4603
Steve G Riordan • WS 9; SS 1015; BC 1015 • H • MO • Grand At Jemphrey 1000 N Grand Eldon MO 65026
**ELK PRAIRIE—*PEACE*** (573)341-3482
Vacant • WS 10; BC 930 • H • MO • UKNWN PO Box 1573 Rolla MO 65402-1573
**ELLISVILLE—*ST JOHN*** (314)394-4100
Stephen D Hower Peter E Mueller David A Muench • WS 930 1115; BC 8;* • H • EC/EL/HS • MO • 15808 Manchester Rd Ellisville MO 63011-2208 • FAX(314)394-9853 • churchoffice@stjohnsellisville.org
**EMMA—*HOLY CROSS*** (660)463-7869
Walter P Snyder • WS 930; SS 830; BC 830 • H • EC/EL • MO • 504 N Elm 65327 PO Box 86 Emma MO 65327-0086 • augustana4@aol.com
**ERNESTVILLE—*ST MATTHEW*** (660)463-2719
Daniel S Rhodes • H • MO • UKNWN 2069 Hwy KK Concordia MO 64020-9504 • dsrhodes.almanet.net
**EUREKA—*ST MARK*** (636)938-4432
Darwin L Karsten John A Jameson Joseph D Sullivan • Michael A Patton DCE • WS 8 930 11; SS 930; BC 930 • H • EC/EL • MO • 500 Meramec Blvd Eureka MO 63025-1147 • FAX(314)215-0249 • stmarks@stmarkseureka.org
**EXCELSIOR SPRINGS—*MOUNT*** (816)637-5262
Vacant • WS 730; SS 845; BC 845 • H • MO • 1215 Baldwin Ln Excelsior Springs MO 64024-1189
**FARLEY—*ST JOHN*** (816)330-3314
Vacant • WS 1030; SS 930; BC 930 • H • MO • 98 Main St 64028 PO Box 117 Farley MO 64028-0117
**FARMINGTON—*ST PAUL*** (573)756-7872
Dino F Pacilli James T King • WS 8 1030; SS 915; BC 930;* • H • EC/EL • MO • 609 E Columbia St Farmington MO 63640-1309 • dbstpaul@yahoo.com
**FARRAR—*SALEM*** (573)824-5728
Robert W Schneider • H • MO • 299 PCR 328 Farrar MO 63746 • FAX(573)824-5728
**FAYETTE—*SHEPHERD OF THE HILL*** (660)248-3486
Vacant • H • MO • 402 Park Rd Fayette MO 65248-9187
**FENTON—*OUR SAVIOR*** (636)343-2192
Lawrence L Eatherton • WS 8 1030; SS 915; BC 915;* • H • EC/EL • MO • 1500 San Simeon Way Fenton MO 63026-3443 • FAX(636)343-9936 • ethrtn@aol.com
**FESTUS—*NEW HOPE*** (314)933-5015
George A Spicer • WS 8 1030; SS 930; BC 930 • H • MO • 1405 W Main St 63028-2057 PO Box 693 Festus MO 63028-0693 • FAX(314)933-5015 • gspicer@jcnl.com
**FLAT RIVER—*TRINITY***
See Park Hills
**FLORISSANT—*BLESSED SAVIOR*** (314)831-1300
Gary R Schack • WS 8 1030; SS 915; BC 915;* • H • MO • 2615 Shackelford Rd Florissant MO 63031-2005 • FAX(314)830-2364 • bslc@anet-stl.com
***SALEM***
See Black Jack
**FOREST GREEN 2 W—*SALEM*** (816)481-2249
Laurence H Carlson Jr. • MO • UKNWN RR 4 Box 4066 Salisbury MO 65281-9422
**FORSYTH—*SHEPHERD/LAKES*** (417)546-2246
Mickey D Wilkey • WS 1030; SS 9; BC 9 • H • MO • 13904 US Highway 160 65653-5157 PO Box 144 Forsyth MO 65653
**FREDERICKTOWN—*TRINITY*** (573)783-2740
Rick L Pettey • H • MO • E College And S Mine La Motte 63645 401 Armory St Fredericktown MO 63645-1343 • sthilary@mines.missouri.org
**FREEDOM—*PILGRIM*** (573)943-2261
Norman H Dierking • MO • Freedom Hwy 50 And N UKNWN PO Box 585 Linn MO 65051-0585

**FREISTATT—*TRINITY*** (417)235-7300
Steven A Becker • H • EC/EL • MO • 207 North Main Freistatt MO 65654-9999 • FAX(417)235-5931

**FRIEDHEIM—*TRINITY*** (636)788-2536
David M Burge • WS 930; SS 830; BC 830 • H • MO • 3700 County Road 415 Friedheim MO 63747-7454

**FROHNA—*CONCORDIA*** (573)824-5435
Wayne H Palmer • WS 9; SS 8; BC 8;* • H • EL • MO • 10172 Highway C Frohna MO 63748-9101

**FULTON—*ST PAUL*** (573)642-2856
David L Mueller • WS 1030; SS 915; BC 915;* • H • MO • 1703 Plaza Dr Fulton MO 65251-2461 • info@stpaulsluthfulton.org

**GLENCOE—*ST PAUL*** (314)273-6239
Douglas K Balzer • WS 9; SS 1030; BC 1030 • H • MO • 955 Hwy 109 63038-1401 PO Box 220 Grover MO 63040-0220

**GLENDALE—*GLENDALE*** (314)966-3220
Steven H Albers • Jolene R Siebarth DCE • WS 815 1045; SS 930; BC 930 • H • EC/EL/HS • MO • UKNWN 1365 N Sappington Rd Saint Louis MO 63122-1823 • FAX(314)966-3243 • glendale@postnet.com

**GORDONVILLE—*ST PAUL***
See Chaffee

**GORDONVILLE 2 SE—*ZION*** (573)204-1944
Wayne W Schwiesow • H • MO • 63752 176 County Road 226 Cape Girardeau MO 63701-9276

**GRANDVIEW—*HOLY TRINITY*** (816)763-3211
Dale D Sveom • H • EC/HS • MO • 5901 E 135th St Grandview MO 64030-3744 • holytrinity1@juno.com

**GRAVELTON—*ZION*** (573)783-2740
Rick L Pettey • MO • UKNWN Cascade MO 636322 • schilary@mines.missouri.org

**HANNIBAL—*ST JOHN*** (573)221-0615
Richard L Ingmire • H • EC/EL • EN • 1201 Lyon St Hannibal MO 63401-4115 • FAX(573)221-8384

**HANNIBAL 10 W 1 N—*IMMANUEL*** (573)221-7051
Kenneth G Schamber • WS 1030; SS 930; BC 930 • H • MO • 63401 6508 County Road 263 Hannibal MO 63401-6612 • FAX(573)248-8210 • immanluth@socket.net

**HARVESTER—*ZION*** (636)441-7425
Dennis L Schwab William G Rusnak Andrew C Steinke • H • EC/EL/HS • MO • UKNWN 3866 Harvester Rd Saint Charles MO 63304-2825 • FAX(636)441-7424

**HERMANN—*SHEPHERD HILLS*** (573)486-3335
Pete A Scheele • * • H • MO • 1952 W Hwy 100 Hermann MO 65041-4044 • ppascheele@yahoo.com

**HERMITAGE—*HOPE*** (417)745-2117
Brian C Whittle • H • MO • 510 W Highway 54 65668-9105 PO Box 346 Hermitage MO 65668-0346

**HIGGINSVILLE—*IMMANUEL*** (660)584-3541
Marcus R Jauss • WS 1015; SS 9; BC 9 • H • EC/EL • MO • 1501 Lipper Ave 64037 PO Box 267 Higginsville MO 64037-0267

**HIGH RIDGE 1 E—*HOPE*** (636)677-8788
Harold S Luckritz • WS 8 1030; SS 915; BC 915;* • H • EC/HS • MO • 63049 2308 Gravois Rd High Ridge MO 63049-2505 • FAX(636)677-3188 • hopelutheran3@juno.com

**HILLSBORO 5 NE—*ZION*** (314)789-2111
Robert L Mundahl • WS 8; SS 915; BC 915 • H • MO • 63050 9700 Zion Luth Church Rd Hillsboro MO 63050-3701 • FAX(636)797-5265 • revrlm@juno.com

**HOLTS SUMMIT—*GRACE*** (573)896-8824
Stephen N Krenz • WS 10; SS 9; BC 9 • H • MO • 618 Halifax Rd Holts Summit MO 65043-1752 • graceluth@juno.com

**HOUSTON—*HOLY CROSS*** (417)967-2204
David L Kettner • H • MO • 1419 S Sam Houston Blvd Houston MO 65483-2199

**IMPERIAL—*ST PAUL***
See Otto

**INDEPENDENCE—*MESSIAH*** (816)254-9405
Jeffrey E Lloyd Jon R Nicolaus • WS 8 1045; SS 930; BC 930 • H • EC/EL/HS • MO • 613 S Main St Independence MO 64050-4499 • FAX(816)254-9407 • messiah@oz.sunflower.org

***ST PAUL*** (816)373-5290
Gary D Stolle • Cory Smith DCE • WS 8 10 11; SS 9; BC 9 • H • EC/EL/HS • MO • 17200 E 39th St S Independence MO 64055-3832 • FAX(816)373-5863 • Gstplc@aol.com

**IRONTON—*ST PAUL*** (573)546-2171
Paul C Weisenborn • WS 845 7; SS 10; BC 10 • H • MO • 101 E Dent St Ironton MO 63650-1206 • stpaulslutheran@juno.com

**ISABELLA—*FAITH*** (417)273-4591
Vacant • H • MO • Hwy 160 North Side Of Hwy 65676 HC 1 Box 1380 Isabella MO 65676-9714

**JACKSON—*ST PAUL*** (573)243-2236
David P Johnson Robert M Henrichs • WS 8 1030; SS 915; BC 915;* • H • MO • 223 W Adams St Jackson MO 63755-2017 • FAX(573)243-6238 • stpaulch@showme.net

**JACKSON 7 SW—*IMMANUEL*** (573)243-0132
Vacant • WS 845; SS 10; BC 10 • H • MO • 63755 496 State Highway F Jackson MO 63755-7315

**JAMESTOWN—*IMMANUEL*** (660)882-6253
Luther S Herman • H • MO • 148 Cedar St Jamestown MO 65046 • 1herman@c-magic.com

**JEFFERSON CITY—*FAITH*** (573)636-4602
Anthony A Alter • WS 8; SS 1030 • H • MO • 2027 Industrial Dr Jefferson City MO 65109-0901 • FAX(917)477-7374 • faithjeffcity@juno.com

***TRINITY*** (573)636-6750
Jerome A Brownlee Sr. John A Hobratschk • WS 8 1030; SS 915;* • H • MO • 803 Swifts Hwy Jefferson City MO 65109-2547 • FAX(573)636-5613

**JEFFERSON CITY 12 S—*IMMANUEL*** (573)496-3451
Russell E Bowder Jr. • WS 930; SS 830; BC 830;* • H • EL • MO • 65101 8231 Tanner Bridge Rd Jefferson City MO 65101-9601 • FAX(573)496-3451

**JEFFERSON CITY 8 SE—*ST JOHN*** (573)395-4591
Gerald R Scheperle • H • MO • Us Hwy 50 In Schubert 65101 4409 Saint Johns Rd Jefferson City MO 65101-9564 • Rev.Mrs.Schep@juno.com

**JENNINGS—*ST JACOBI*** (314)388-0345
Paul H Schroeder • WS 9; BC 10 • H • EC • MO • 8646 Jennings Station Rd Jennings MO 63136-6306

**JONESBURG—*ST PAUL*** (636)488-5235
Steven L Dressler • H • MO • 204 Jones St 63351 PO Box 328 Jonesburg MO 63351-0328 • FAX(636)488-3367 • sdrev@jonesburg.net

**JOPLIN—*IMMANUEL*** (417)624-0333
Lowell D Rossow Donald E Stock • WS 8 1030; SS 920; BC 920 • H • EC/EL • MO • 2616 Connecticut Ave Joplin MO 64804-3027 • FAX(417)624-2774 • gracealone@clandjop.com

**KANSAS CITY—*ASCENSION***
See Raytown (Kan Cty)

***CALVARY*** (816)444-6908
Bryce A Bereuter • WS 8 1045; SS 930; BC 930 • H • EC/EL/HS • MO • 7500 Oak St Kansas City MO 64114-1945 • FAX(816)444-5696 • bbereuter@calvarykc.com

***CHAPEL/CROSS*** (816)942-4285
David M Spaeth • WS 930; SS 1030; BC 1030 • H • HS • MO • 10819 Wornall Rd Kansas City MO 64114-5069

***CHRIST***
See Platte Woods

***EL BUEN PASTOR**** (816)474-9049
David H Loza • WS 1030;* • H • MO • 1755 Jefferson St 64108-1103 PO Box 412594 Kansas City MO 64141-2594 • lmgskcmo@aol.com

***GOOD SHEPHERD*** (816)474-9049
David H Loza Ronald B Staples • Jane E Loza DEAC • WS 1030;* • H • MO • 1755 Jefferson St 64108-1104 PO Box 412594 Kansas City MO 64141-2594 • lmgskcmo@aol.com

***HOLY CROSS*** (816)452-9113
Mark S Nuckols Duane R Osterloth • WS 8 1045; SS 915; BC 915;* • H • EC/EL/HS • MO • 2003 NE Englewood Rd Kansas City MO 64118-5698

***IMMANUEL*** (816)561-0561
Albert G Engler • WS 1045; SS 930; BC 930 • H • HS • MO • 4203 Tracy Ave 4205 Tracy Ave Kansas City MO 64110-1243 • marilyn@mwis.net

***KING OF KINGS*** (816)436-7680
Paul E Schult • WS 8 1030; SS 915; BC 915 • H • EC/HS • MO • 1701 NE 96th St Kansas City MO 64155-2167 • FAX(816)436-2876

***OUR REDEEMER*** (816)241-2334
Vacant • WS 945 3; SS 11; BC 11 • H • HS • MO • 711 Benton Blvd Kansas City MO 64124-2529

***PEACE*** (816)353-3813
Keith B Ratcliffe • WS 8 930 11; SS 930; BC 930;* • H • EC/EL/HS • MO • 8240 Blue Ridge Blvd Kansas City MO 64138-1565 • FAX(816)353-3886 • peace@safe4kids.net

***ST JOHN*** (816)923-5646
Vacant • MO • 4545 Benton Blvd Kansas City MO 64130-2063

**KEARNEY—*TRINITY*** (816)628-6644
Drew A Newman • WS 9; SS 1030; BC 1030 • H • HS • MO • 1715 S Jefferson St 64060-8483 PO Box 440 Kearney MO 64060-0440 • gnuguy@prodigy.net

**KENNETT—*REDEEMER*** (314)888-4638
Vacant • MO • Harrison And Jones 63857 PO Box 823 Kennett MO 63857-0823

**KIMBERLING CITY—*SHEPHERD HILLS*** (417)739-2512
James F Troyke • WS 8 1030; SS 915; BC 915;* • H • MO • 103 Kimberling Blvd 65686 PO Box 484 Kimberling City MO 65686-0484

**KIRKSVILLE—*FAITH*** (660)665-6122
Mark L Appold • WS 1015; SS 9; BC 9 • EC/EL • MO • 1820 S Baltimore St Kirksville MO 63501-4504 • FAX(660)665-6122 • mappold@truman.edu

**KIRKWOOD—*CONCORDIA*** (314)822-7772
Vernon D Gundermann Charles B Kieschnick • James T Meyer DCE William C Leese DCE Benjamin F Freudenburg DCE David Christian DCE Jeremy M Becker DCE • H • EC/EL/HS • MO • 505 S Kirkwood Rd Kirkwood MO 63122-5925 • FAX(314)984-0086 • concrdia@il.net

**KNOB NOSTER—*FAITH*** (660)563-5973
Vacant • H • MO • 507 S Washington Ave 65336-1567 PO Box 42 Knob Noster MO 65336-0042 • faith@almanet.net

**LA GRANGE—*ST PETER*** (573)655-4416
Paul R Meseke • * • H • EC • MO • 300 N 7th St 63448-1100 RR 1 Box 152 La Grange MO 63448-9744

**LADUE—*VILLAGE*** (314)993-1834
John F Temple • Alan D Muck DCE • H • EC/HS • MO • 63155 9237 Clayton Rd Saint Louis MO 63124-1509 • FAX(314)993-8920

**LAKE OZARK—*CHRIST KING*** (573)365-5212
Ronald P Lehenbauer • H • MO • 1700 Bagnell Dam Blvd Lake Ozark MO 65049-9729 • FAX(573)365-5356 • revron@dam.net

**LAMAR—*GRACE*** (417)682-2257
Galen M Friedrichs • WS 1030; SS 915; BC 915 • H • MO • 64759-1125 Grace Lutheran Church 208 Poplar Lamar MO 64759 • glc@tiadon.com

**LEBANON—*TRINITY*** (417)532-2717
Vacant • WS 1030; SS 915; BC 915 • H • MO • 1300 Kent Dr Lebanon MO 65536-3583 • FAX(417)532-2717

**LEES SUMMIT—*BEAUT SAVIOR*** (816)524-7288
Nathaniel R Schwartz • WS 8 1030; SS 920; BC 920 • H • EN • 615 SE Todd George Rd Lees Summit MO 64063-4468 • FAX(816)524-6506

***ST MATTHEW*** (816)524-7068
John P Scharlemann • WS 8 1030; SS 915; BC 915 • H • EC/EL • MO • 700 NE Chipman Rd Lees Summit MO 64063-2571 • FAX(816)524-9012 • st.matt-lsmo@worldnet.att.net

**LEMAY—*GETHSEMANE*** (314)631-7331
Kenneth W Sievers Gary A Lampe • WS 8 1030; SS 915; BC 925;* • H • EL/HS • MO • 765 Lemay Ferry Rd Saint Louis MO 63125-1429 • FAX(314)631-0265

**LESLIE 8 NE—*EBENEZER*** (573)459-6432
William F Zastrow • WS 10; SS 9; BC 9;* • MO • 63056 9100 Highway Yy Leslie MO 63056-1101 • FAX(573)459-2203 • rungel@fidnet.com

**LEXINGTON—*GRACE*** (660)259-2932
Vacant • H • EC • MO • 806 13 Hwy 64067-1516 PO Box 69 Lexington MO 64067-0069

**LIBERTY—*ST STEPHEN*** (816)781-3377
Stephen C Streufert • WS 8 1030; SS 915; BC 915 • H • EC/HS • MO • 205 N Forest Ave Liberty MO 64068-1007 • FAX(816)792-0771 • sslc@oz.sunflower.org

**LINCOLN—*IMMANUEL*** (660)547-2496
Vacant • WS 830; SS 930 • H • MO • PO Box 278 Lincoln MO 65338-0278

***ZION*** (660)547-2259
Vacant • WS 830; SS 930 • H • MO • PO Box 278 Lincoln MO 65338-0278

**LINN—*PILGRIM***
See Freedom

**LOCKWOOD—*IMMANUEL*** (417)232-4642
Gary W Griffin • SS 915; BC 915;* • H • EL • MO • Fourth And Sycamore 65682 PO Box H Lockwood MO 65682-0363 • FAX(417)232-4476 • immanuelgodwithus@hotmail.com

**LOHMAN 2 S—*ST JOHN*** (573)782-3191
Warren P Brandt • H • MO • 65053 4420 Stringtown Rd Lohman MO 65053-9550

**LONE ELM—*ZION*** (816)838-6428
Vacant • H • EL • MO • UKNWN 9171 B Hwy Bunceton MO 65237-2123

**LONGTOWN—*ZION*** (314)547-2797
Paul R Winningham • H • MO • UKNWN 6483 S Hwy 61 Perryville MO 63775

**LOUISIANA—*TRINITY*** (573)754-6120
Randy C Van Mehren • WS 11; SS 10; BC 10 • H • MO • 3405 Georgia St Louisiana MO 63353-2750

**MACON—*ZION*** (660)385-4433
Eugene H Stueve • WS 10; SS 845; BC 845 • H • MO • 32405 Business Route 36 E Macon MO 63552-3846 • lstueve@mail.cyberusa.com

**MALDEN—*GRACE*** (573)276-3216
William J Mac Gregor(EM) • H • MO • W Burkhart At Stevenson 63863 PO Box 393 Malden MO 63863-0393

**MAPLEWOOD—*CONCORDIA*** (314)647-1215
Robert J Gebel • SS 915; BC 915;* • H • HS • MO • 7291 Sarah St Maplewood MO 63143-2404 • FAX(314)647-1215

**MARSHALL—*OUR REDEEMER*** (660)886-2270
Douglas A Dubisar • Christina M Meyer DCE • WS 8 1030; SS 915; BC 915;* • H • MO • 361 W Summit Ave Marshall MO 65340-2522 • FAX(660)886-9717 • our3redeemer@cdsinet.net

**MARSHFIELD—*ST PAUL*** (417)468-2577
John O Burger • WS 11; SS 930; BC 930 • H • EC/EL • MO • 609 N Locust St 65706-1212 PO Box 44 Marshfield MO 65706 • FAX(417)468-5005

**MARYLAND HEIGHTS—*ZION*** (314)739-6121
Robert A Sharp • WS 8 1030; SS 930; BC 930 • H • MO • 12075 Dorsett Rd Maryland Heights MO 63043-2403 • FAX(314)739-6121 • znmdhgts@juno.com

**MARYVILLE—*HOPE*** (660)582-3262
Theodore E Mayes • WS 10; SS 9; BC 9 • H • MO • 931 S Main St Maryville MO 64468-2645 • FAX(660)582-3262 • tjmayes@hotmail.com

**MEMPHIS—*ST PAUL*** (660)465-2669
Vacant • WS 1030;* • H • MO • PO Box 133 Memphis MO 63555-0133

**META 3 N—*ST JOHN*** (314)395-4591
Gerald R Scheperle • WS 8; SS 910; BC 910 • H • MO • 65058 HC 65 Box 79 Westphalia MO 65085-9711

**MEXICO—*ST JOHN*** (573)581-5655
James W Rhiver • WS 10; SS 845; BC 845 • H • MO • 1000 Dorcas St Mexico MO 65265-1129 • FAX(573)581-1173 • sklc@mexicomo.net

**MILAN—*PEACE*** (660)265-4104
Vacant • H • MO • Route E 63556 217 E 3rd St Milan MO 63556-1337 • FAX(660)265-4908

**MOBERLY—*ZION*** (660)263-3256
Gary R Hoffstetter • WS 10; SS 9; BC 9 • EC • MO • 1075 E Urbandale Dr Moberly MO 65270-1963

**MONETT—*ST JOHN*** (417)235-3416
W M Thompson • WS 10 730; SS 845; BC 9;* • H • EC • MO • 23237 Highway H Monett MO 65708 • FAX(417)235-8442 • stjohn@mo-net.com

**MONROE CITY—*OUR SAVIOR*** (573)735-3080
Kenneth G Schamber • WS 845; SS 945;* • H • MO • 110 5th St Monroe City MO 63456-1340 • FAX(573)248-8210 • immanluth@socket.net

**MOUND CITY—*CONCORDIA*** (816)442-3414
Donald W Craig John N Sellmeyer • H • MO • 1413 Nebraska St Mound City MO 64470-1527

**MOUNT LEONARD—*BETHLEHEM*** (785)538-4688
Timothy C Miille • MO • UKNWN PO Box 196 Blackburn MO 65321-0196

**NEOSHO—*FIRST*** (417)451-2464
William J Doubek III • WS 1030;* • H • MO • 431 Cemetery Rd Neosho MO 64850-8711 • FAX(417)451-2464

**NEVADA—*TRINITY*** (417)667-5676
Vacant • WS 745; SS 9;* • H • MO • 1630 N Ash St Nevada MO 64772-1106

**NEW HAVEN—*TRINITY*** (573)237-3026
Herman J Otten(X) • H • MO • 3277 Boeuf Lutheran Rd 63068-2213 PO Box 267 New Haven MO 63068-0267

**NEW HAVEN 6 SW—*BETHLEHEM*** (573)237-2602
Mark A Hawkinson • H • MO • 63068 3833 Boeuf Lutheran Rd New Haven MO 63068-2202 • FAX(573)237-4861 • hawkm@fidnet.com

**NEW MELLE—*ST PAUL*** (636)828-5616
Michael G Piper • WS 10; SS 845; BC 845;* • H • MO • 150 W Hwy D 63365 PO Box 70 New Melle MO 63365-0070 • FAX(636)828-4255 • stpaulnm@primary.net

**NEW WELLS—*IMMANUEL*** (573)833-6933
Walter F Patzwitz • WS 9; SS 815; BC 815 • H • EL • MO • 304 County Road 516 New Wells MO 63732-9111 • filioque@showme.net

**NIANGUA—*IMMANUEL***
See Conway 8 SE

**NORBORNE—*TRINITY*** (660)593-3721
Kim L Scharff • WS 10; SS 9; BC 9 • H • MO • 204 N Pine St Norborne MO 64668-1125 • kscharff@greenhills.net

**O FALLON—*HOLY CROSS*** (636)272-4505
Keith D Wachter • WS 745 1015; SS 9; BC 9 • H • HS • MO • 8945 Veterans Memorial Pkwy O Fallon MO 63366-3084

**OAK GROVE—*SHEP OF VALLEY*** (816)690-4020
Mark P Wenger • H • EC • MO • 600 SE 12th St Oak Grove MO 64075-9540

**OAKVILLE—*FAITH*** (314)846-8612
John S Brunette • David J Wacker DCE • WS 8 1045; SS 920; BC 920;* • H • EC/EL • MO • 6101 Telegraph Rd Saint Louis MO 63129-4655 • FAX(314)846-7157 • jbrunette@aol.com

**OLIVETTE—*IMMANUEL*** (314)993-2394
Ray G Mirly Paul W Rueckert Donald L Rousseau(#) • WS 8 1030; SS 915; BC 930;* • H • EC/EL/HS • MO • 63132 9733 Olive Blvd Saint Louis MO 63132-3003 • FAX(314)993-0311 • immanuel@stlnet.com

**OSAGE BEACH—*HOPE CHAPEL*** (573)348-2108
John C Dautenhahn Everett S Pepper • H • EC • MO • 1027 Industrial Dr Osage Beach MO 65065

**OTTO—*ST PAUL*** (636)942-4250
Russell E Koen • WS 745; SS 10 • H • MO • 63052 6550 State Rt 21 Imperial MO 63052-2940 • stpaullutheran@mailcity.com

**OVERLAND—*OUR REDEEMER*** (314)427-3444
Rodney A Wise • Todd C Stevens DCE • H • MO • 9135 Shelley Ave Overland MO 63114-4812 • FAX(314)427-8273

**OWENSVILLE—*ST JOHN***
See Drake 2 SE

***ZION*** (314)437-3581
Vacant • H • MO • Madison And Hickory 65066 PO Box 137 Owensville MO 65066-0137

**PAGEDALE—*GRACE*** (314)727-3030
Frank M Gallagher • H • MO • UKNWN 1425 Ferguson Ave Saint Louis MO 63133-1719

**PALMYRA—*ZION*** (573)769-2739
David Johnson • H • EC/EL • MO • 120 S Spring St Palmyra MO 63461-1484 • FAX(573)769-4022

**PARK HILLS—*TRINITY*** (573)431-3442
Ralph A Abernethy • WS 1030; SS 9; BC 915 • H • MO • 309 Taylor Ave 63601-2114 PO Box 471 Park Hills MO 63601-0471 • raasga@i1.net

**PARKVILLE—*CHRIST***
See Platte Woods

**PERRYVILLE—*IMMANUEL*** (573)547-8317
Craig D Otto Matthew T Marks • WS 730 10; BC 850;* • H • MO • 453 N West St Perryville MO 63775-1361 • FAX(573)547-7254 • lcmsperr@ldd.net

***ZION***
See Crosstown

***ZION***
See Longtown

**PEVELY—*ZION*** (314)475-4486
Vacant • WS 9; SS 1015; BC 1015;* • H • MO • 310 Central St 63070-2100 PO Box 29 Pevely MO 63070-0029

**PILOT KNOB—*IMMANUEL*** (573)546-3808
Vacant • H • MO • Ziegler St 63663 PO Box 26 Arcadia MO 63621-0026

**PINE LAWN—*BETHESDA*** (314)261-5381
David R Boisclair • WS 930; SS 1045; BC 1045 • H • MO • 6220 Bircher Ave Saint Louis MO 63121-3395

**PLATTE CITY—*OUR SAVIOR*** (816)858-5255
Robin D Fish Jr. • WS 9; SS 1030;* • H • MO • 14155 N Hwy Platte City MO 64079 • oslcpc@juno.com

**PLATTE WOODS—*CHRIST*** (816)741-0483
R R Krueger Tyler C Arnold • Kenneth W Erlandson DCE • WS 8 1045; SS 930; BC 930;* • H • EC • MO • 6700 NW 72nd St Platte Woods MO 64151-1600 • christlc@oz.sunflower.org

**PLEASANT HILL—*AMAZING GRACE*** (816)540-5150
Vacant • WS 930; SS 1045; BC 1045 • H • MO • 313 Cedar Pleasant Hill MO 64080

**POCAHONTAS—*TRINITY***
See Shawneetown

***ZION*** (573)833-6922
Howard W Mueller • H • MO • 264 Main St 63779 PO Box 60 Pocahontas MO 63779-0060

**POPLAR BLUFF—*ZION*** (573)785-3936
Larry L Feldt • WS 8 1030; SS 915; BC 915 • H • EC/EL • MO • 450 N Main St Poplar Bluff MO 63901-5150 • FAX(573)785-7273

**POTOSI—*REDEEMER***
Vacant • WS 1030 • H • MO • 312 E High St Potosi MO 63664

**PRAIRIE CITY—*ZION*** (660)598-6215
Philip B Wolf • WS 10; SS 9; BC 9 • H • EL • MO • UKNWN RR 1 Box 31 Rockville MO 64780-9022 • FAX(660)598-6215 • zionotlosage@juno.com

**PRAIRIE HOME—*IMMANUEL***
Luther S Herman • WS 11 • H • MO • 13002 Campbell Bridge Dr Prairie Home MO 65068-2025 • lherman@c-magic.com

**PRINCETON—*IMMANUEL*** (816)748-3022
Vacant • H • MO • 500 W Main St Princeton MO 64673-1138

**PURDY 3 NW—*ST JOHN*** (417)442-3836
Vacant • H • MO • 65734 RR 2 Purdy MO 65734-9802

**RAYMORE—*BETHLEHEM*** (816)322-3606
David M Reimnitz • H • EC • MO • Hwy 58 And Johnston Pkwy 64083 PO Box 1155 Raymore MO 64083-1155 • FAX(816)322-9673 • bethlehem@hhim.net

**RAYTOWN (KAN CTY)—*ASCENSION*** (816)358-1919
Vacant • WS 8 1045; SS 930; BC 930 • H • EC/EL/HS • MO • 64133 4900 Blue Ridge Blvd Kansas City MO 64133-2538 • FAX(816)358-0126 • bakers@crn.org

**REPUBLIC—*HOPE*** (417)732-7046
Vacant • WS 1030; SS 915; BC 9 • H • MO • 218 E State Route 174 Republic MO 65738 • FAX(417)732-7046 • hopelcrep@aol.com

**RICHMOND—*FAITH*** (816)776-5550
Charles D Hudson • WS 930; SS 1045;* • H • MO • 805 E Lexington St Richmond MO 64085-2907

**RIVERVIEW—*BEREA*** (314)868-9915
Vacant • WS 10; SS 830; BC 830;* • H • EN • 9915 Diamond Dr Saint Louis MO 63137-3637

**ROCKVILLE—*ZION***
See Prairie City

**ROLLA—*IMMANUEL*** (573)364-4525
Mark Mc Intyre Douglas A Ochner • * • H • EC/EL • MO • 801 W 11th St Rolla MO 65401-2103

***PEACE***
See Elk Prairie

***REDEEMER*** (573)364-7071
Gerald L Wittmaier • WS 9; SS 1030; BC 1030 • H • MO • 1701 Hwy 72 East Rolla MO 65401-3994 • FAX(573)364-6846 • redeemer@rollanet.org

**ROSEBUD—*IMMANUEL*** (573)764-2564
Frank J Coniglio • WS 10; SS 845; BC 845 • H • EL • MO • Highway 50 And First St 63091 229 Hwy 50 PO Box 290 Rosebud MO 63091-0290

**SAINT ANN—*HOPE*** (314)429-3808
Neil R Schmidt • WS 8 1045; SS 925; BC 925;* • H • EC/EL • MO • 10701 Saint Cosmas Ln Saint Ann MO 63074-2523 • FAX(314)429-3809 • fnp@hope--lutheran.org

**SAINT CHARLES—*HOLY CROSS*** (314)925-0670
Vacant • MO • 2809 Yale Blvd 63301-0456 PO Box 459 Saint Charles MO 63302-0459

***IMMANUEL*** (636)946-2656
Allen W Schade Roger B Henning Edward M Hummel Jeffrey D Kunze • WS 8 1045; SS 930; BC 930;* • H • EC/EL/HS • MO • 115 S 6th St Saint Charles MO 63301-2712 • FAX(636)946-0166

***OUR SAVIOR*** (636)947-8010
Thomas A Lampella Edward J Arle • H • EC/HS • MO • 2800 W Elm St Saint Charles MO 63301-4618 • FAX(636)947-1925

***ZION***
See Harvester

**SAINT CHARLES 6 N—*TRINITY*** (636)250-3350
Douglas A Gaunt • WS 8 1015; SS 915; BC 915 • H • EL/HS • MO • 5 Mi N Of Hwy 370 On Hwy 94 63301 4795 N Hwy 94 Saint Charles MO 63301-6406

**SAINT CLAIR—*HOLY TRINITY*** (636)629-3355
Craig B Fenske • H • EC • MO • 1500 S Outer Rd Saint Clair MO 63077-1000

**SAINT JAMES—*ST JOHN*** (573)265-3226
Paul E Goddard • WS 1030; SS 915; BC 915 • MO • 229 W James Blvd Saint James MO 65559-1214 • chalosi@rollanet.org

**SAINT JOSEPH—*ST PAUL*** (816)279-1110
Terry Weinhold Brandon J Luft • Bernard P Fortmeyer DCE • H • EC/EL • MO • 4715 Frederick Ave Saint Joseph MO 64506-3241 • FAX(816)279-1114

***ST PETER*** (816)279-8190
Kirk R Schmeisser • WS 9; SS 1015;* • H • MO • 3524 Saint Joseph Ave Saint Joseph MO 64505-1702

**SAINT LOUIS—*ABIDING SAVIOR***
See Saint Louis County

***ASCENSION*** (314)832-5600
Charles W Spomer • Arlo E Otto DCE • WS 8 930 11; BC 930;* • H • EC/EL/HS • MO • 5347 Donovan Ave Saint Louis MO 63109-2636 • FAX(314)832-5601

***BEREA***
See Riverview

***BETHANY*** (314)535-8736
Vacant • MO • 63155 4100 Natural Bridge Saint Louis MO 63115-3337

***BETHLEHEM*** (314)231-9615
John R Schmidtke • H • MO • 2153 Salisbury St Saint Louis MO 63107-3129

***CHAPEL CROSS***
See Saint Louis County

***CHRIST*** (314)776-0248
Vacant • Karen L Westbrooks DEAC • H • HS • MO • 3504 Caroline St Saint Louis MO 63104-1008

***CHRIST MEMORIAL*** (314)631-0304
Gregory K Smith William T Simmons Blake G Wolf • H • EC/EL • MO • 9712 Tesson Ferry Rd Saint Louis MO 63123-5322 • FAX(314)631-8583

***EBENEZER*** (314)388-2777
Allen E Schenk • WS 8; SS 915; BC 915 • H • EC/EL • MO • 1011 Theobald St Saint Louis MO 63147-1922 • FAX(314)388-4903 • ebenluth@stlnet.com

***EMMAUS*** (314)776-1274
Vacant • WS 9 • HS • MO • 2241 S Jefferson Ave 63104-2237 2617 Shenandoah Ave Saint Louis MO 63104-2311

***EPIPHANY*** (314)752-7065
Eldon K Winker • WS 8 1030; SS 915; BC 915 • H • HS • MO • 4045 Holly Hills Blvd Saint Louis MO 63116-2847 • FAX(314)752-7066 • epiphany@fastrans.net

***FAITH***
See Oakville

***FAITH***
See Velda City

***GETHSEMANE***
See Lemay

***GRACE CHAPEL***
See Bellefontaine Neigh

***HOLY CROSS*** (314)772-8633
James T Hoppes Robert W Lehr(#) • H • EL/HS • MO • 2650 Miami St Saint Louis MO 63118-3928 • FAX(314)772-0071 • hcstlou@inlink.com

***HOLY CROSS DF*** (314)533-6035
Richard A Moody • MO • 101 N Beaumont St Saint Louis MO 63103-2227 • FAX(314)533-6035 • revrmoody@aol.com

***HOLY SACRAMENT*** (314)371-4243
Frazier N Odom(DM) • MO • 4000 W Belle Pl Saint Louis MO 63108-3534

***HOPE*** (314)352-0014
Dennis F Lucero • WS 8 930 11 • H • EL/HS • MO • 5218 Neosho St Saint Louis MO 63109-2986 • FAX(314)352-1944

***IMMANUEL***
See Olivette

***IMMANUEL CHAPEL***
See Saint Louis County

***MESSIAH*** (314)772-4474
Jonathan C Lange • WS 8; SS 915; BC 915;* • H • EL/HS • MO • 2846 S Grand Blvd Saint Louis MO 63118-1033 • FAX(314)772-8554 • MessiahStL@aol.com

***MOUNT OLIVE*** (314)771-5714
Vacant • WS 1030; SS 9; BC 9 • H • MO • 4246 Shaw Blvd Saint Louis MO 63110-3527

***OUR REDEEMER*** (314)772-7169
Vacant • Luther A De Cuir DCE • H • MO • 2817 Utah St Saint Louis MO 63118-3007

***PEACE***
See Woodson Terrace

***PEACE***
See Saint Louis County

***PRINCE OF PEACE***
See Crestwood

***RESURRECTION***
See Sappington

***ST JOHN*** (314)773-0126
Gary D Dehnke • H • EL/HS • MO • 3738 Morganford Rd Saint Louis MO 63116-1615 • FAX(314)773-0126

***ST LUCAS*** (314)351-2628
Gerald L Kovac • WS 8 915 1030;* • EC/EL/HS • S • 7100 Morganford Rd Saint Louis MO 63116-2110 • FAX(314)351-1174 • stlucaslutheran@mail.com

***ST LUKE*** (314)353-9088
David L Dittmar • H • EC/EL/HS • MO • 3415 Taft Ave Saint Louis MO 63111-1431

***ST MATTHEW*** (314)261-7765
Vacant • EC/EL • MO • 5402 Wren Ave Saint Louis MO 63120-2442 • FAX(314)261-7707 • st.math@swbell.net

***ST PAUL*** (314)534-0372
Jay C Kilb • H • MO • 2137 E John Ave Saint Louis MO 63107-1313

***ST PAUL***
See Des Peres

***ST PETER***
See Spanish Lake

***ST PETER*** (314)535-3881
Vacant • WS 9 1115; SS 1115; BC 10 • HS • MO • 1126 S Kingshighway Blvd Saint Louis MO 63110-1528

***ST STEPHEN*** (314)531-1343
Frazier N Odom(DM) • WS 1015; BC 930 • MO • 515 Pendleton Ave Saint Louis MO 63108-3025

***ST TRINITY*** (314)353-3276
David A Liebnau • H • HS • MO • 7404 Vermont Ave 63111-3036 517 Koeln Ave Saint Louis MO 63111-3242

***TIMOTHY*** (314)781-8673
Ronald D Rall • H • EC/EL/HS • MO • 6704 Fyler Ave Saint Louis MO 63139-2239 • FAX(314)781-8704 • timothy@usmo.com

***TRANSFIGURATION*** (314)621-7845
Frazier N Odom(DM) • H • MO • 1807 Biddle St Saint Louis MO 63106-3540 • FAX(314)621-9390

***TRINITY*** (314)231-4092
David B Marth King K Schoenfeld • * • H • EL/HS • MO • 1805 S 8th St 63104-4007 812 Soulard St Saint Louis MO 63104-4036 • FAX(314)231-5430 • trinitysoulard@juno.com

***VILLAGE***
See Ladue

***ZION*** (314)231-0382
Vacant • WS 1030; SS 930; BC 930 • H • MO • 2500 N 21st St Saint Louis MO 63106-2409 • FAX(314)231-0453

**SAINT LOUIS COUNTY—*ABIDING*** (314)894-9703
James D Kirk Kevin M Wendt • WS 8 930 11;* • H • EC/EL • MO • UKNWN 4355 Butler Hill Rd Saint Louis MO 63128-3717 • FAX(314)894-0212 • aslc@worldinter.net

***CHAPEL CROSS*** (314)741-3737
Jonathan P Stein • Jeffery R Moeller DCE David M Funke DCE • H • EC • EN • Highway 367 And Interstate 27 UKNWN 11645 Benham Rd Saint Louis MO 63136-6112 • FAX(314)741-3746

***IMMANUEL CHAPEL*** (314)741-4700
Richard A Moore • WS 8 1045; SS 930; BC 930;* • H • EC • MO • UKNWN 11100 Old Halls Ferry Rd Saint Louis MO 63136-4632 • FAX(314)741-7236
***PEACE*** (314)892-5610
Dennis A Kastens • Allison J Sternberg DCE • WS 8 930 1030; SS 915; BC 915;* • H • EC/EL/HS • MO • UKNWN 737 Barracksview Rd Saint Louis MO 63125-5409 • FAX(314)892-7345 • peacelemay@aol.com
**SAINT PETERS—*CHAPEL CROSS*** (314)928-5885
Robert D Grams • H • HS • EN • 907 Jungermann Rd Saint Peters MO 63376-3094 • FAX(314)928-3688 • chapelofcross³sp@juno.com
***SPIRIT CHRIST*** (636)441-2552
Vacant • WS 9; SS 1030; BC 1030 • H • MO • 1615 Thoele Rd Saint Peters MO 63376-3053
**SAINT ROBERT—*FAITH***
See Waynesville 5E
**SAINTE GENEVIEVE—*HOLY CROSS*** (573)883-5361
Richard F Thur • WS 715 945; SS 830; BC 830 • H • MO • 200 Market St Sainte Genevieve MO 63670-1636
**SALEM—*SALEM*** (573)729-5512
David L Kettner • H • MO • 403 E State Route 32 Salem MO 65560-1862 • salemlch@rollanet.org
**SALISBURY—*IMMANUEL*** (660)388-5192
Willard J Kassulke • WS 1015; SS 9; BC 9;* • H • EC • MO • 124 W 3rd St Salisbury MO 65281-1445 • wkass@valley.net
***SALEM***
See Forest Green 2 W
**SARCOXIE—*TRINITY*** (417)548-2747
Vacant • MO • 300 S 9th St 64862-8094 PO Box 612 Sarcoxie MO 64862-0612
**SCOTT CITY—*EISLEBEN*** (573)264-2762
Robert B Azinger • WS 10; SS 845;* • H • MO • 432 Lutheran Ln Scott City MO 63780-2900 • FAX(573)264-2762
**SEDALIA—*OUR SAVIOR*** (660)827-0226
Ronald E Hoehne • T J Glaskey DCE • WS 8 1030; SS 915; BC 915 • H • MO • Us 50 Highway 65301 3700 W Broadway Blvd Sedalia MO 65301-2141 • FAX(660)829-1834 • revhols1@iland.net
***ST PAUL*** (660)826-1164
Kenneth L Tatkenhorst • WS 8 1030 12; SS 915; BC 915 • H • EC/EL • MO • Broadway And Massachusetts 65301 701 S Massachusetts Ave Sedalia MO 65301-4547 • FAX(660)826-1925 • pastor.tatkenhorst@sedaliastpauls.org
**SEYMOUR—*ZION***
See Diggins
**SHAWNEETOWN—*TRINITY*** (573)833-6976
Howard W Mueller • H • MO • UKNWN 175 Shawneetown Rd Jackson MO 63755-8227
**SHELBYVILLE—*MOUNT HOPE*** (573)221-7051
Vacant • WS 1030; SS 930; BC 930 • MO • 805 E Main St Shelbyville MO 63469-1426
**SHELL KNOB—*PEACE*** (417)858-3900
Elmer L Schnelle(EM) • H • MO • PO Box 407 Shell Knob MO 65747-0407
**SIKESTON—*CONCORDIA*** (573)471-5842
Alan J Wollenburg • WS 1030; SS 9;* • H • MO • Park And Wakefield Aves 63801 PO Box 146 Sikeston MO 63801-0146 • FAX(573)471-6794 • concluth@sbmu.net
**SLATER—*PEACE*** (660)529-2248
Vacant • MO • 408 N Porter Slater MO 65349
**SLATER 10 SE—*ST PAUL***
Vacant • H • MO • Rt 2 Slater MO 65349
**SPANISH LAKE—*ST PETER*** (314)741-2485
Gary T Schubert • MO • UKNWN 1120 Trampe Ave Saint Louis MO 63138-3014
**SPRINGFIELD—*FAITH*** (417)833-3749
Andrew J Spallek • Angeline R Reitmeier DEAC • WS 8 1030; SS 915; BC 915 • H • EC/EL • MO • 1517 E Valley Water Mill Rd Springfield MO 65803-3743 • FAX(417)833-3661 • aspall@atlascomm.net
***REDEEMER*** (417)881-5470
Wallace M Becker • WS 8 1045; SS 930; BC 930;* • H • EC/EL • MO • 2852 S Dayton Ave Springfield MO 65807-3644 • FAX(417)881-5470 • rlcoffice@pcis.net
***RIVER OF LIFE**** (417)881-2409
Vacant • H • EL • MO • 4560 S Campbell Springfield MO 65810 • FAX(417)881-2407 • jbuckman@usiw.net
***TRINITY*** (417)866-5878
William R Marler Martin E Conkling • WS 815 11; SS 945; BC 945 • H • EL • MO • 1415 S Holland Ave Springfield MO 65807-1813 • FAX(417)866-5629
**ST ROBERT—*FAITH*** (573)336-4464
Richard M Anderegg • WS 1030; SS 915; BC 915 • H • MO • 981 Highway Z Saint Robert MO 65584 • felc@rollanet.org
**STOCKTON—*ST ANDREW*** (417)276-3511
Mark E Lavrenz • H • MO • Highway 39 S 65785 PO Box 516 Stockton MO 65785-0516
**STOVER—*ST PAUL*** (573)377-2690
Cecil L Murdock • WS 10; SS 9; BC 9 • H • EC/EL • MO • 407 W Third 65078 PO Box 460 Stover MO 65078-0460 • FAX(573)377-2690 • rpete9@juno.com
**SULLIVAN—*ST MATTHEW*** (573)468-4245
Vacant • WS 1030; SS 915; BC 915 • H • EC • MO • 528 N Church St Sullivan MO 63080-1532 • stmattew@fidnet.com
**SUNRISE BEACH—*PEACE***
See Camdenton
**SUNSET HILLS—*RESURRECTION*** (314)843-6633
Michael A Bronner Dale R Kuhn • WS 8 930 11; SS 930; BC 930;* • H • EC/EL/HS • MO • 9907 Sappington Rd Saint Louis MO 63128-1644 • FAX(314)843-5154 • lcr@integritynetwork.net
**SWEET SPRINGS—*IMMANUEL*** (660)335-4141
David M Ritoch • H • MO • Main And Patrick 65351 PO Box 209 Sweet Springs MO 65351-0209 • dmritoch@mailandnews.com
**SWEET SPRINGS 6 NE—*CHRIST*** (660)335-4414
Walter O Umbach(EM) • H • MO • Liberty Township 65351 PO Box 993 Concordia MO 64020-0993
**TRENTON—*IMMANUEL*** (816)359-3076
Paul A Knittel • H • MO • 1711 Hillcrest Dr Trenton MO 64683-1116
**TROY—*TRINITY*** (636)528-4999
Thomas W Larson • WS 830 11; SS 945; BC 945;* • H • MO • 1307 W Boone St Troy MO 63379-2213 • FAX(636)528-2970
**UNION—*ST PAUL*** (636)583-2209
Robert L Kriete • WS 730 10; SS 845; BC 845 • H • EC • MO • 208 W Springfield Ave Union MO 63084-1757 • FAX(636)583-1155 • stpaul@fidnet.com
**UNIONTOWN—*GRACE*** (573)788-2342
Paul R Winningham • WS 10; SS 915; BC 915 • H • EC/EL • MO • 53 Grace Lane 63783 PO Box 105 Uniontown MO 63783-0105
**UNIVERSITY CITY—*ST JAMES*** (314)727-3253
Thomas A Baker • WS 10; SS 9; BC 9 • H • MO • 1401 N Hanley Rd University City MO 63130-1605 • FAX(314)727-3263 • tombaker@lawgospel.com
**VALLEY PARK—*ZION*** (636)225-7780
Steven J Hasenstein • WS 830 1130; BC 945;* • MO • 531 Meramec Station Rd Valley Park MO 63088-1130 • sjhazz8833@aol.com
**VAN BUREN—*IMMANUEL*** (573)323-4010
Vacant • H • MO • Us 60 W Of The Bridge 63965 PO Box 624 Van Buren MO 63965-0624
**VANDALIA—*ST JOHN*** (573)594-6640
Vacant • WS 1030; SS 915; BC 915 • H • MO • 414 S Main St Vandalia MO 63382-1831
**VELDA CITY—*FAITH*** (314)261-7070
David R Boisclair • WS 11; SS 10; BC 10 • HS • MO • 53121-5006 3000 Lucas And Hunt Rd Saint Louis MO 63121-5006
**VERSAILLES—*GRACE*** (573)378-5512
Vacant • WS 1015 • H • MO • 403 S Burke St Versailles MO 65084-1368
**WAPPAPELLO—*PEACE*** (314)243-7859
Walter E Fehrmann(EM) • MO • Civic Ctr Rd And Hwy D 63966 PO Box 215 Wappapello MO 63966-0215
**WARRENSBURG—*BETHLEHEM*** (660)747-6742
Roger Beese • WS 1030; SS 915; BC 915 • H • MO • 607 N Maguire St 64093-1419 PO Box 367 Warrensburg MO 64093-0367
**WARRENTON—*ST JOHN*** (636)456-2888
William R Dorow • WS 8; SS 915; BC 915;* • H • EC • MO • 950 S Highway 47 Warrenton MO 63383-2600 • FAX(636)456-0882 • warrlutheran@mocty.com
**WARSAW—*FAITH*** (660)438-6948
Lloyd J Helland • WS 8 1015; SS 915; BC 915 • H • MO • 1091 Walnut Dr 65355-3337 PO Box 876 Warsaw MO 65355-0876
**WASHINGTON—*FAITH*** (314)239-0554
Dennis R Schmelzer • H • MO • 4190 Bieker Rd Washington MO 63090-5368
***IMMANUEL*** (314)239-4705
Mark A Bangert Joel S Schultz • WS 8 1045; SS 930; BC 930;* • H • EC/EL • MO • 214 W 5th St Washington MO 63090-2304 • FAX(314)239-0589 • immanuel@midwestis.net
**WAVERLY—*IMMANUEL*** (816)493-2463
Brett L Mueller • MO • 116 W Kelling Ave 64096 PO Box 62 Waverly MO 64096-0062
**WEBSTER GROVES—*WEBSTER*** (314)961-5275
Joel T Christiansen Daniel J Teuscher • WS 8 930 1055; SS 930; BC 1055 930;* • H • EC/EL/HS • MO • 8749 Watson Rd Webster Groves MO 63119-5111 • FAX(314)961-5166 • info@webstergardenschurch.org
**WELDON SPRINGS 1E—*MESSIAH*** (314)926-9773
Dennis J Liebich Paul T Schult • H • EC/HS • MO • UKNWN 5911 Hwy 94 S St Charles MO 63304 • FAX(314)926-9924
**WELLSVILLE—*GRACE*** (573)684-2106
Derek J Cheek • WS 10 • H • MO • 528 W Hudson St Wellsville MO 63384-1210 • grace@yahoo.com
**WELLSVILLE 5 E—*TRINITY*** (573)684-2880
Vacant • WS 945; SS 845; BC 845 • H • MO • 63384 105 Trinity Church Rd Wellsville MO 63384-9560
**WENTZVILLE—*IMMANUEL*** (314)327-4416
Lloyd J Hackbarth Dwain E Sliger • H • EC/EL • MO • 317 W Pearce Blvd Wentzville MO 63385-1421 • FAX(314)327-5054
**WEST PLAINS—*IMMANUEL*** (417)256-3407
John W Gerlach • H • MO • 1051 Preacher Roe Blvd West Plains MO 65775-2926
**WESTPHALIA—*ST JOHN***
See Meta 3 N
**WOODSON TERRACE—*PEACE*** (314)427-5678
Wolfgang M Webern(EM) • WS 9; SS 1015; BC 1015;* • H • MO • 4055 Edmundson Rd Saint Louis MO 63134-3947 • peacewb@aol.com
**WRIGHT CITY—*GOOD SHEPHERD*** (636)745-2947
Vacant • WS 10; SS 1115; BC 1115 • H • EC • MO • 101 S Elm Ave 63390-1217 PO Box 44 Wright City MO 63390-0044

## MONTANA

**ANACONDA—*REDEEMER*** (406)846-1713
James D Wilson • H • MT • 1321 W 5th St Anaconda MT 59711-1812 • hayakawa@in-tch.com
**ANGLELA 1 N—*TRINITY***
See Rock Springs
**BELFRY—*ST JOHN*** (406)662-3776
Clark A Brown • MT • 103 Vaill 59008 C/O Dale Grebe HC 46 Box 14 Belfry MT 59008-9702 • FAX(406)662-3776
**BILLINGS—*CHRIST KING*** (406)252-9250
Timothy B Wilmot • H • MT • 759 Newman Ln Billings MT 59101
***HOPE*** (406)245-4605
Robert A Lane • WS 10; SS 830; BC 830 • H • MT • 1911 US Hwy 87 E Billings MT 59101-6651 • hopeluthbillings@juno.com
***MOUNT OLIVE*** (406)656-6687
Mark P Grunst Kenneth H Zoeller • H • EC • MT • 2336 Saint Johns Ave Billings MT 59102-4710 • FAX(406)656-1211 • mtolive@mcn.net
***OUR SAVIOR*** (406)252-5141
Vacant • WS 930;* • H • MT • 1603 Saint Andrews Dr Billings MT 59105-3863
**BOULDER—*FAITH*** (406)225-4442
Vacant • WS 11 • H • MT • 317 S Main St 59632 PO Box 586 Boulder MT 59632-0586 • geverson@juno.com
**BOZEMAN—*FIRST*** (406)586-5374
Bruce E Linderman Robert E Mitchell • WS 1115 10; SS 1015; BC 1015;* • H • EC • MT • 225 S Black Ave Bozeman MT 59715-4715 • FAX(406)586-1626 • 1sfmsu@mcn.net
**BRIDGER—*ST JOHN***
See Belfry
***ST PAUL*** (406)662-3776
Clark A Brown • WS 1030;* • MT • 302 Pryor St 59014 PO Box 310 Bridger MT 59014-0310 • FAX(406)662-3776
**BUTTE—*ST MARK*** (406)782-5935
Christopher E Wareham • WS 1030;* • MT • 223 S Montana St Butte MT 59701-1645
**CHINOOK—*ZION*** (406)357-2516
Alfred R Ebel • MT • 803 Illinois Ave 59523 PO Box 743 Chinook MT 59523-0743
**COLSTRIP—*MOUNT CALVARY*** (406)748-2516
Vacant • H • EC • MT • 430 Olive Dr 59323 PO Box 218 Colstrip MT 59323-0218
**COLUMBIA FALLS—*OUR REDEEMER*** (406)892-4074
Terry R Forke • WS 830 11; SS 945; BC 945 • H • MT • 640 7th St W 59912-3850 PO Box 2005 Columbia Falls MT 59912-2005
**CONDON 2 S—*FAITH*** (406)677-2281
Daniel A Wurster • WS 1115;* • H • MT • Condon Hwy 83 And Milepost 43 59826 PO Box 869 Seeley Lake MT 59868-0869
**CROW AGENCY—*CROW*** (406)638-2331
Daniel P Jacobs • H • MT • Crow Indian Reservation 59022 PO Box 335 Crow Agency MT 59002
**DEER LODGE—*ST JOHN*** (406)846-1755
James D Wilson • WS 11; BC 945;* • H • MT • 59722 410 Missouri Ave Deer Lodge MT 59722-1079 • hayakawa@in-tch.com
**DENTON—*OUR SAVIOR*** (406)566-2509
Robert L Weishoff • MT • 1102 Lehman 59430 PO Box 924 Denton MT 59430-0924
**ENNIS—*SHEPHERD HILLS*** (406)682-4910
Daniel L Freeman • H • MT • PO Box 785 Ennis MT 59729-0785
**EUREKA—*HOLY CROSS*** (406)296-2116
Christopher J Tabbert • H • MT • Hwy 93 N 59917 PO Box 332 Eureka MT 59917-0332 • chertab@kootenet.net
**FAIRFIELD—*ST JOHN*** (406)467-3325
Craig W Kellerman • WS 9; SS 1015;* • H • MT • PO Box 241 Fairfield MT 59436-0241
**FAIRVIEW—*ST JOHN*** (406)742-5332
Kent C Stenzel • WS 830;* • MT • 59221 C/O Trinity Lutheran 214 Lincoln Ave S Sidney MT 59270-3925 • tlc@lyrea.com
**FALLON—*GRACE*** (406)486-5545
James A Hageman Howard D Schreibeis • MT • PO Box 277 Fallon MT 59326-0277
**FORSYTH—*CONCORDIA*** (406)356-7614
John C Vallie • WS 10; BC 11;* • MT • 310 8th Ave N 59327 PO Box 1258 Forsyth MT 59327-1258
**FORT BENTON—*FIRST*** (406)622-3252
Vacant • WS 7; SS 6 • H • MT • PO Box 896 Fort Benton MT 59442-0896
**GLASGOW—*FAITH*** (406)228-8550
George L Draper • WS 830;* • H • MT • 909 8th Ave N Glasgow MT 59230-1635
**GLENDIVE—*OUR SAVIOR*** (406)377-3890
James A Hageman Howard D Schreibeis • H • MT • 322 N River Ave Glendive MT 59330-1749 • FAX(406)377-8825 • oslc@midrivers.com
**GREAT FALLS—*CHRIST DEAF*** (406)452-3884
Henry E Drummond • WS 930; SS 1030;* • H • MT • 1226 1st Ave N Great Falls MT 59401-3201 • FAX(406)761-7343 • Revdrummond@prodigy.net
***PEACE*** (406)761-7343
Henry E Drummond • * • H • MT • 3340 11th Ave S Great Falls MT 59405-5404 • FAX(406)761-7343 • revdrummond@prodigy.net
***TRINITY*** (406)452-2121
C F Grundmann • H • EC • MT • 1226 1st Ave N Great Falls MT 59401-3201 • FAX(406)761-5893 • http://www.trinity@mcn.net
**HAMILTON—*GRACE*** (406)363-1924
Glenn F Merritt • Rodney H Johnson DCE • * • H • EC • MT • 275 Hattie Ln Hamilton MT 59840-0927 • FAX(406)363-1925 • glc@cybernetl.com
**HARDIN—*REDEEMER*** (406)665-2239
James M Koss • H • MT • 323 N Crawford Ave 59034-1717 C/O 521 3rd St W Hardin MT 59034-1723
**HARLOWTON—*TRINITY*** (406)252-5141
Vacant • WS 2;* • MT • 2nd St Se And A Ave 59036 PO Box 665 Harlowton MT 59036-0665

**HAVRE—*ST PAUL*** (406)265-7637
Alfred R Ebel • WS 11;* • H • MT • 1100 11th Ave Havre MT 59501-4632 • ebel@hi-line.net

**HELENA—*FIRST*** (406)442-5367
Larry A Miller • WS 11 815; SS 945; BC 945;* • H • EC • MT • 2231 E Broadway St Helena MT 59601-4807 • FAX(406)442-5285

**HYSHAM—*TRINITY*** (406)356-7195
John C Vallie • MT • PO Box 466 Hysham MT 59038-0466 • revkev@mcn.net

**KALISPELL—*TRINITY*** (406)257-5683
Darold A Reiner Jerry D Schreck(#) • H • EC/EL • MT • 400 W California St Kalispell MT 59901-3935 • FAX(406)257-5684 • trinity@ptinet.net

**LAME DEER—*CIRCLE OF LIFE***
Vacant • MT • PO Box 458 Lame Deer MT 59043-0458

**LAUREL—*ST JOHN*** (406)628-4775
Arlo W Pullmann • WS 9;* • H • EC • MT • 417 W 9th St 59044-2040 PO Box 185 Laurel MT 59044-0185 • FAX(406)628-1591 • stjohnlaurelmt@juno.com

**LEWISTOWN—*ST PAUL*** (406)538-8563
Vacant • H • MT • 125 C St Lewistown MT 59457-2209

**LIBBY—*ST JOHN*** (406)293-4024
Eric M Christiansen • WS 1030; SS 915; BC 915 • H • EC • MT • 1017 Montana Ave Libby MT 59923-2015

**MILES CITY—*TRINITY*** (406)232-4983
James M Mavis • H • EC • MT • 221 S Center Ave Miles City MT 59301-4401

**MISSOULA—*FIRST*** (406)549-3311
David W Renfro • * • H • EC • MT • 2808 South Ave W Missoula MT 59804 • FAX(406)829-3528 • msla1lthrn@aol

***MESSIAH*** (406)549-9222
Raymond P Wiegert • * • H • EC • MT • 3718 Rattlesnake Dr Missoula MT 59802-3028 • FAX(406)543-4845 • mlc-lcms@in-tch.com

**PARK CITY—*ST PAUL*** (406)633-2356
Douglas S Thompson • H • EC • MT • 301 1st Ave SW 59063-9411 PO Box 188 Park City MT 59063-0188

**PLENTYWOOD—*TRINITY*** (406)765-1365
Vacant • H • MT • 212 N Maurice St Plentywood MT 59254-1531

**POLSON—*MOUNT CALVARY*** (406)883-4041
Eric M Nelson • WS 1030; SS 915; BC 915 • H • EC • MT • 1608 2nd St W Polson MT 59860-4005 • mtcalvry@centurytel.net

**POWER—*ZION*** (406)463-2541
Craig W Kellerman • WS 11; SS 950;* • H • MT • 302 Teton Ave 59468-9350 PO Box 265 Power MT 59468-0265 • FAX(406)463-2541

**ROCK SPRINGS—*TRINITY*** (406)232-4983
James M Mavis • MT • UKNWN PO Box 195 Angela MT 59312-0195

**RONAN—*ST PAUL*** (406)676-8280
Mark J Nicolaus • WS 1015; SS 9;* • H • EC • MT • 429 Terrace Lake Rd Ronan MT 59864-9812

**ROUNDUP—*ST PAUL*** (406)252-5141
Vacant • WS 6;* • H • MT • 1009 1st St W Roundup MT 59072-1830

**SAINT IGNATIUS—*ZION*** (406)745-4149
Vacant • WS 830; SS 945; BC 945 • H • MT • 300 N 2nd St 59865 PO Box 607 Saint Ignatius MT 59865-0607 • beefnkeep@blackfoot.net

**SAINT XAVIER—*ST JOHN**** (406)665-1618
Vacant • MT • 25 S Hardin St Xavier MT 59075

**SEELEY LAKE—*FAITH***
See Condon 2 S

***HOLY CROSS*** (406)677-2281
Daniel A Wurster • * • H • MT • Airport Rd 1.4 Mi E Of Hwy 83 59868 PO Box 869 Seeley Lake MT 59868-0869 • pastordan@blackfoot.net

**SIDNEY—*ST JOHN***
See Fairview

***TRINITY*** (406)482-2050
Kent C Stenzel • WS 1030;* • H • MT • 214 Lincoln Ave S Sidney MT 59270-3925 • tlc@lyrea.com

**STANFORD—*TRINITY*** (406)566-2723
Robert L Weishoff • MT • PO Box 57 Stanford MT 59479-0057

**STEVENSVILLE—*OUR SAVIOR*** (406)777-5625
Vacant • WS 1030 8; SS 915; BC 915 • H • EC • MT • 184 Pine Hollow Rd Stevensville MT 59870-6621 • FAX(406)777-5625 • oslc@cybernet1.com

**SUPERIOR—*TRINITY*** (406)822-4547
Myron E Wackler(EM) • H • MT • PO Box 790 Superior MT 59872-0790

**THREE FORKS—*GRACE*** (406)285-6865
Daniel L Freeman • H • EC • MT • 305 5th Ave 59752 PO Box 857 Three Forks MT 59752-0857

**WHITEFISH—*ST PETER*** (406)862-3008
Donald J Browne • * • H • MT • 201 Wisconsin Ave 59937-2306 PO Box 883 Whitefish MT 59937-0883

**WHITEHALL—*ZION*** (406)287-5446
Christopher E Wareham • WS 830;* • MT • 301 First W 59759 PO Box 84 Whitehall MT 59759-0084

**WOLF POINT—*TRINITY*** (406)653-2289
George L Draper • WS 11;* • MT • First And Benton 59201 PO Box 862 Wolf Point MT 59201-0862

**WORDEN—*OUR REDEEMER*** (406)252-5141
Vacant • WS 8;* • H • MT • PO Box 116 Worden MT 59088-0116

## NEBRASKA

**AINSWORTH—*ZION*** (402)387-1512
D G Williams • H • NEB • 318 E 4th St Ainsworth NE 69210-1621 • georgw01@nol.org

**ALBION—*ST PAUL*** (402)395-9972
Vernon R Knight(EM) • WS 9 • NEB • 4th And Columbia St 68620 330 W Columbia St Albion NE 68620-1447

**ALLIANCE—*IMMANUEL*** (308)762-4663
Martin T Schnare Richard C Mueller • WS 1030; SS 915; BC 915;* • H • WY • 1024 Box Butte Ave 69301-2520 PO Box 715 Alliance NE 69301-0715 • FAX(308)762-8218

**ALTONA—*FIRST TRINITY*** (402)375-2165
Keith K Kiihne • WS 1015;* • HS • NEB • UKNWN RR 1 Box 124 Wayne NE 68787-9766

**AMHERST—*ST PAUL***
See Venango

***TRINITY*** (308)826-3421
Jack L Gillam • WS 10; SS 9; BC 9 • H • NEB • Garfield And Cherry PO Box 157 Amherst NE 68812-0157 • FAX(308)826-4403 • jgillam@nebi.com

**ARAPAHOE—*TRINITY*** (308)962-7667
Carl R Lilienkamp • Mark Thuer DCE • WS 8 1030; SS 915; BC 915;* • H • NEB • 1005 9th St 68922 PO Box 385 Arapahoe NE 68922-0385 • FAX(308)962-7655

**ARLINGTON 4 N—*ST PAUL*** (402)478-4278
Michael L Rogers • * • H • EC/EL • NEB • 8951 County Rd 9 Arlington NE 68002 • FAX(402)478-5378 • stpaul@genesisnet.net

**ARNOLD—*ZION*** (308)848-2575
Benjamin P Eickhoff • H • NEB • 503 Court 69120 PO Box 46 Arnold NE 69120-0046

**ASHBY 9 S—*SWEDE VALLEY*** (308)458-2508
Vacant • WS 830; SS 930 • H • NEB • 69333 C/O Rev Greg Lucido PO Box 350 123 NE 69350-0350 • lucido@neb-sandhills.net

**ATKINSON—*IMMANUEL*** (402)925-2851
Donald E Erickson • H • NEB • Hwy 11 North 68713 HC 59 Box 39 Atkinson NE 68713-9407 • derick@inetnebr.com

**AUBURN—*TRINITY*** (402)274-4210
Vacant • WS 9; BC 1015 7;* • H • EC • NEB • 634 Alden Dr Auburn NE 68305-3013 • FAX(402)274-4204

**BANCROFT—*ST PAUL*** (402)648-7689
Terrence H Daberkow • WS 1030; SS 915; BC 915;* • H • NEB • 501 Park St 68004 PO Box 306 Bancroft NE 68004-0306 • splc@juno.com

**BANCROFT 6 SW—*ZION*** (402)648-7939
Vacant • EL • NEB • 20th And ‰Q‰ 68004 1710 20th Rd Bancroft NE 68004-4027 • gwrjar@gpdcom.net

**BARTLETT—*OUR SAVIOR*** (308)654-3349
Vacant • H • NEB • PO Box 95 Bartlett NE 68622-0095

**BATTLE CREEK—*ST JOHN*** (402)675-3155
Richard L Snow • WS 9;* • H • EC/EL/HS • NEB • 306 S Second 68715 PO Box 87 Battle Creek NE 68715-0087

**BAYARD—*MOUNT CALVARY*** (308)586-1300
Craig K Niemeier • * • WY • 1237 Ave A 69334 PO Box 488 Bayard NE 69334-0488 • mtcalv@actcom.net

**BEATRICE—*ST PAUL*** (402)228-1540
James E Fandrey Douglas D Irmer • WS 8 1030; SS 915; BC 915;* • H • EC/EL • NEB • 321 N 10th St Beatrice NE 68310-3014 • FAX(402)228-2576

**BEATRICE 8 NW—*FIRST TRINITY*** (402)228-0216
Mark D Rockenbach • WS 915; SS 1030; BC 1030 • EC • NEB • Hwy 4 68310 11668 West State Hwy 4 Beatrice NE 68310-7105

**BEEMER—*ST JOHN*** (402)528-7278
Vacant • WS 9; BC 10;* • NEB • 334 Lambrecht St 330 Lambrecht St Beemer NE 68716-4213 • beemer3@gpcom.net

***ZION-ST JOHN***
See Wisner 8 S

**BEEMER 4 S—*IMMANUEL*** (402)528-7253
Roger D Schepmann • * • H • NEB • 68716 1101 K Rd Beemer NE 68716-4014

**BELGRADE 6 SW—*PEACE*** (308)357-1046
Vacant • H • NEB • 68623 RR 1 Box 42 Belgrade NE 68623-9719

**BELLEVUE—*PILGRIM*** (402)291-2848
Daniel R Ritter • WS 8 930 1045; SS 930; BC 930 • H • EC • NEB • 2311 Fairview Rd Bellevue NE 68123-5318 • FAX(402)292-7836 • pilgrim@novia.net

**BERTRAND—*ST PAUL*** (308)472-5283
Vacant • H • NEB • 401 Marshfield 68927 PO Box 68 Bertrand NE 68927-0068

**BIG SPRINGS—*ZION*** (308)889-3632
Albert L Kasten Sr. • WS 1030;* • H • WY • W 4th And Pine 69122 PO Box 104 Big Springs NE 69122-0104

**BINGHAM—*BINGHAM*** (308)588-6222
Vacant • NEB • PO Box 518 Bingham NE 69335

**BLAIR—*TRINITY*** (402)426-2851
John W Emslie Jr. • WS 8 1030; SS 915; BC 915 • H • EC • NEB • 141 S 20th St Blair NE 68008-1884

**BLOOMFIELD—*FIRST TRINITY*** (402)373-4704
Phillip L Hannemann • WS 10;* • H • NEB • 402 E Main St 68718-2058 PO Box 540 Bloomfield NE 68718-0540 • trinone@bloomnet.com

**BLUE HILL—*CALVARY***
See Rosemont

***TRINITY*** (402)756-2102
James E Witt • WS 10; BC 9;* • H • NEB • 301 N Pine PO Box 355 Blue Hill NE 68930-0355 • jbwitt@gtmc.net

**BRIDGEPORT—*ST PAUL*** (308)262-0424
Craig K Niemeier • * • WY • 506 Main 69336 PO Box D Bridgeport NE 69336-0903

**BRULE—*ST JOHN*** (308)287-2394
Albert L Kasten Sr. • WS 815;* • H • WY • 6th And Oak 69127 PO Box 98 Brule NE 69127-0098

**BURTON—*GRACE*** (402)497-2507
Donald L Boettcher • H • NEB • 68777 HC 80 Box 29 Springview NE 68778-9804

**BURWELL—*ST JOHN*** (308)346-5060
Vacant • H • EC • NEB • 350 N 8th 68823 PO Box 595 Burwell NE 68823-0595 • juliemcbride@altavista.net

**BUTTE—*IMMANUEL*** (402)775-2194
Vacant • H • NEB • 241 Walnut St 68722 PO Box 260 Butte NE 68722-0260

**CAIRO—*CHRIST*** (308)485-4863
Glen D Keylon • WS 9; SS 1020 1120; BC 1030 1120 • H • HS • NEB • 503 W Medina St 68824 PO Box 9 Cairo NE 68824-0009 • christcairo@aol.com

**CAMBRIDGE—*ST PAUL*** (308)697-3725
Donald F Thompson • H • NEB • 719 Park Ave Cambridge NE 69022 • FAX(308)697-3625 • dontomp@csb.swnebr.net

**CAMPBELL—*TRINITY*** (402)756-8551
William F Caughey • * • H • NEB • 370 S Stewart 68932 PO Box 146 Campbell NE 68932-0146 • FAX(402)756-8551 • bcaughey@mail.gtmc.net

**CARROLL—*ST PAUL*** (402)585-4808
Vacant • WS 830; SS 930 • NEB • 411 Nebraska St (Carroll) 68723 C/O First Trinity Lutheran RR 1 box 124 Wayne NE 68787

**CEDAR BLUFFS—*ST MATTHEW*** (402)628-3015
Kenneth J Davidson • WS 9;* • H • NEB • 300 S 2nd St PO Box 8 Cedar Bluffs NE 68015-0008

**CEDAR RAPIDS—*ST JOHN*** (308)358-0370
Vacant • H • NEB • 111 S 3rd 68015 PO Box 361 Cedar Rapids NE 68627-0361

**CENTRAL CITY—*ST PAUL*** (308)946-2680
P B Rick • H • HS • NEB • 820 G Ave Central City NE 68826-1606

**CHADRON—*OUR SAVIOR*** (308)432-5698
Peter W Bertram • WS 10; SS 9; BC 9 • WY • 702 E 9th St Chadron NE 69337-2757

**CHAMBERS—*ST PAUL*** (402)482-5835
Allen C Bergstrazer • H • NEB • 106 W Wry 68725 PO Box 67 Chambers NE 68725-0067

**CHAPPELL—*ZION*** (308)874-2533
Vacant • WY • 650 5th St 69129 PO Box 307 Chappell NE 69129-0307

**CHESTER—*ST JOHN*** (402)324-8075
Vacant • WS 1030; SS 930; BC 930 • H • NEB • 805 Church St 68327 PO Box 211 Chester NE 68327-0211

**CLEARWATER—*CONCORDIA*** (402)485-2596
Daniel J Feusse • WS 9; SS 10; BC 10 • H • NEB • Second And Iowa 68726 PO Box 114 Clearwater NE 68726-0114

**COLUMBUS—*CHRIST*** (402)563-1314
John E Nelson Jr. • WS 10; SS 9; BC 9 • H • EC/EL • NEB • 8n 3e 32392 122nd Ave Columbus NE 68601 • FAX(402)564-6637 • jenelson@esu7.org

***IMMANUEL*** (402)564-0502
Richard P Bringewatt Roland A Jank(EM) • WS 8 1030; SS 915; BC 915;* • H • EC/EL • NEB • 2406 14th St 68601-5011 1470 24th Ave Columbus NE 68601-5017 • FAX(402)564-8851 • rbringe@gilligan.esuf.k12.ne.us

***PEACE*** (402)564-8311
Michael V Klatt Steven A Williams Ernest G Smith(EM) • WS 8; SS 915; BC 915;* • H • EC • NEB • 2720 28th St Columbus NE 68601-2418 • FAX(402)564-8643 • peacelc@megavision.com

**COLUMBUS 15 NW—*ST JOHN*** (402)285-0498
Brad E Birtell • WS 10; SS 9; BC 9 • H • EL • NEB • 68601 29452 Mason Rd Columbus NE 68601-9688 • FAX(402)285-0335 • sjlschl@megavision.com

**CONCORD 4 NE—*ST PAUL*** (402)375-3616
Brian W Handrich • H • NEB • 68728 58085 867th Rd Concord NE 68728-9800 • bhandri@midlands.net

**CORDOVA—*ST JOHN*** (402)576-3711
Arnold H Jurchen • NEB • 245 Nestor St 68330 PO Box 167 Cordova NE 68330-0167

**CRAWFORD—*BETHLEHEM*** (308)665-2058
James R Martin • WS 1030; SS 915;* • H • WY • 2nd And Reed Streets 69339 916 2nd St Crawford NE 69339-1226 • pwbmartin@panhandle.net

**CREIGHTON 3 N—*CHRIST*** (402)358-5298
Terell O Huber • WS 9; SS 10; BC 10 • H • NEB • 68729 101 Bazile Main St Creighton NE 68729-3838 • thubes@bloomnet.com

**CRETE—*BETHLEHEM*** (402)826-4359
Nathan P Ristvedt • WS 830 11; SS 945; BC 945 • H • EC • NEB • Eighth And Hawthorne Aves 68333 PO Box 249 Crete NE 68333-0249 • blutheran@alltelnet

**CRETE 4E 2S—*ST JOHN*** (402)826-3883
John M Heckmann • WS 8 1030; SS 915; BC 930 • H • NEB • 11400 W Panama Rd Crete NE 68333 • stjohn³kramer@alltel.net

**CROOKSTON—*ZION*** (402)425-3357
Rudolph H Schaff(#) • NEB • Oak And Main 69212 PO Box 47 Crookston NE 69212-0047

**CULBERTSON—*ST JOHN*** (308)278-2575
Bryan L Hopfensperger • WS 830; SS 930; BC 930;* • H • NEB • 712 Colorado 69024 PO Box 207 Culbertson NE 69024-0207

**CURTIS—*ST JOHN*** (308)367-4238
Paul M Warneke • H • NEB • Fifth And Wallace 69025 PO Box 64 Curtis NE 69025-0064

**DAVENPORT—*ST PETER*** (402)364-2182
H John Cotton • WS 9; SS 1015; BC 1015 • H • EC/EL • NEB • 208 W 10th St 68335 PO Box 160 Davenport NE 68335-0160

**DAVID CITY—*REDEEMER*** (402)367-3859
David W Palomaki • * • NEB • 695 N 9th St 68632-1417 PO Box 244 David City NE 68632-0244

**DAYKIN 5 E—*IMMANUEL*** (402)446-7357
Rick G Kanoy • WS 930; SS 1030; BC 1030 • H • NEB • 68338 72430 567th Ave Daykin NE 68338-3010

**DECATUR—*TRINITY*** (402)349-5541
Brion P Tolzman • * • H • NEB • 603 N 4th Ave 68020 PO Box 272 Decatur NE 68020-0272 • FAX(402)846-5935 • tolzie@huntel.net

**DESHLER—*ST PETER*** (402)365-4341
Duane L Fahr • WS 930;* • H • EL • NEB • 400 E Hebron 68340 PO Box 69 Deshler NE 68340-0069 • stpeter@gpcom.net

**DODGE—*IMMANUEL*** (402)693-2648
Vacant • NEB • PO Box 356 Dodge NE 68633-0356
**DONIPHAN—*ST PAUL*** (402)845-2340
Rodney A Armon • WS 8 1030; SS 915; BC 915 • H • EC • NEB • 207 N 4th St 68832 PO Box 185 Doniphan NE 68832-0185 • ch67bde@msn.com
**EAGLE—*IMMANUEL*** (402)781-2190
Scott T Porath • WS 9; SS 1015; BC 1015 • H • NEB • 1009 G St Eagle NE 68347-5048 • FAX(402)781-2190 • lcmseagle@juno.com
**ELGIN—*TRINITY*** (402)843-5874
Vacant • WS 8; SS 9;* • H • NEB • 200 N 5th St 68636 PO Box 378 Elgin NE 68636-0378
**ELK CREEK 5 SW—*ST PETER*** (402)335-2686
Robert H Schermbeck • NEB • 68348 RR 1 Box 159 Elk Creek NE 68348-9501
**ELKHORN—*LORD OF LIFE*** (402)289-3437
David H Linkugel • WS 8 1030; SS 915; BC 915 • H • NEB • 20844 Bonanza Blvd Elkhorn NE 68022-1800 • FAX(402)289-3437 • dlinkugel@aol.com
**ELWOOD—*OUR REDEEMER*** (308)785-2875
Richard D Boring • WS 10; SS 9; BC 9;* • H • NEB • 704 Smith Ave 68937-5214 PO Box 42 Elwood NE 68937-0042 • our³redeemer³elwood@yahoo.com
**FAIRBURY—*GRACE*** (402)729-5163
Charles O Schmidt • WS 830 11; SS 945; BC 945 • H • NEB • 1100 G St Fairbury NE 68352-1626 • gl92901@alltel.net
**FAIRFIELD—*SHEP OF PLAINS*** (402)726-2224
William F Larsen • H • NEB • 305 E 4th 68938 PO Box 42 Fairfield NE 68938-0042
**FALLS CITY—*CHRIST*** (402)245-3324
Dale W Bahls • H • NEB • 2310 Barada St 68355-1545 PO Box 421 Falls City NE 68355-0421 • FAX(402)245-4135
**FALLS CITY 6 N—*ST PAUL*** (402)245-4643
Merelyn R Snider • WS 1015; SS 9; BC 9;* • H • EC • NEB • 68355 RR 3 Box 102 Falls City NE 68355-9634 • FAX(402)245-4643 • pstrsnider@sentco.net
**FOSTER—*TRINITY*** (402)582-4587
Jerome P Leckband • WS 830; SS 930 • H • HS • NEB • RR 2 Box 544 Foster NE 68737
**FRANKLIN—*GRACE*** (308)425-3774
Bruce L Crabtree • H • EC • NEB • 1206 N St Franklin NE 68939-1343
**FREMONT—*GOOD SHEPHERD*** (402)721-8412
Timothy J Gierke • Pamela J Haltom DCE • H • NEB • 1544 E Military Ave 68025-4471 1440 E Military Ave Fremont NE 68025-5371 • FAX(402)753-0701 • goodshep@tvsonline.net
***TRINITY*** (402)721-5536
Phillip E Vance • WS 8 1030; SS 915;* • H • EC/EL • NEB • 1546 N Luther Rd Fremont NE 68025-3784 • FAX(402)721-5537
**FULLERTON—*MOUNT CALVARY*** (308)536-2635
Timothy W Wagner • WS 9; SS 1015; BC 1015 • NEB • 401 Irving St PO Box 7 Fullerton NE 68638-0007
**GARLAND—*IMMANUEL***
See Seward 7 E
***ZION*** (402)588-2229
Richard D Harre • H • NEB • 370 4th St 68360-9345 PO Box 106 Garland NE 68360
**GERING—*FAITH*** (308)436-4307
Richard H Neugebauer Ralph C Morris • H • WY • 2055 U St 69341-2034 PO Box 307 Gering NE 69341-0307 • FAX(308)436-3232
**GOEHNER—*HOLY CROSS*** (402)523-4705
Arnold H Jurchen • H • NEB • PO Box 92 Goehner NE 68364-0092
**GORDON—*GRACE*** (308)282-0584
Vacant • WS 10; SS 9; BC 9 • H • EC • WY • 801 N Elm St 69343-1138 PO Box 239 Gordon NE 69343-0239 • grace4u@bbc.net
**GRAND ISLAND—*CRISTO CORDERO*** (308)389-4611
Vacant • NEB • 512 E 2nd St & Vine Grand Island NE 68801
***GRACE*** (308)382-1190
Daniel G Bremer Herbert B Schutte(EM) • WS 8 1045; SS 930; BC 930 • H • EC/HS • NEB • 545 E Memorial Dr Grand Island NE 68801-7854 • gracluth@kdsi.net
***PEACE*** (308)384-5673
William R Voelker Roland W Going(EM) • WS 8 1035; SS 925; BC 925;* • H • EC/HS • NEB • 4018 Zola Ln Grand Island NE 68803-1520 • FAX(308)384-2001 • plchurch@computer-concepts.com
***TRINITY*** (308)382-0753
Martin P Schmidt Robert W Harms(EM) • Deborah K Drake DCO • WS 7 8 1030 1045; SS 1015; BC 1015 • H • HS • NEB • 212 W 12th St Grand Island NE 68801-3832 • FAX(308)384-6722 • triluthgi@cccusa.net
**GRANT—*ZION*** (308)352-4107
Vacant • WS 9; SS 1015 • H • NEB • 705 Central Ave 69140 PO Box 740 Grant NE 69140-0740 • dsewing@gpcom.net
**GRESHAM—*ST PETER*** (402)735-7333
Timothy A Prince • * • H • NEB • 2320 Hwy 69 Gresham NE 68367-7517 • FAX(402)735-7333 • revprince@hotmail.com
**GRETNA—*GOOD SHEPHERD*** (402)332-3345
Gary W Werling • WS 8 1030; SS 915; BC 915 • H • NEB • 20501 Hwy 370 68028 PO Box 39 20501 Hwy 370 Gretna NE 68028-0039 • FAX(402)332-3345
**GURLEY—*SALEM*** (308)884-2260
Vacant • WY • PO Box 117 Gurley NE 69141-0117
**HAMPTON—*ST PETER*** (402)725-3234
George E Damm • WS 10; SS 9; BC 9 • H • EC/EL • NEB • Third And H Sts 68843 PO Box 95 Hampton NE 68843-0095
**HAMPTON 2N 2E—*ZION*** (402)725-3320
Loren D Cooper • WS 10; SS 9; BC 9 • H • NEB • 68843 2306 E 16 Rd Hampton NE 68843-3702
**HARBINE 4 NE—*ZION*** (402)754-4522
Vacant • H • NEB • UKNWN 58115 718th Rd Jansen NE 68377-4014
**HARRISON—*REDEEMER***
James R Martin • H • WY • Third And Rose Sts 69346 PO Box 482 Harrison NE 69346-0482 • pwbmartin@panhandle.net
**HASTINGS—*FAITH*** (402)462-5044
Carl H Rehwaldt • Vicki L Fisher DCE • H • NEB • 837 Chestnut Ave Hastings NE 68901-4257 • faithlutheran@mailcity.com
***PEACE*** (402)462-9023
Donald E Boeschen • WS 8 1015; SS 9; BC 9 • H • NEB • 906 N California Ave Hastings NE 68901-4079 • FAX(402)463-3749 • peacelc@inebraska.com
***ZION*** (402)462-5015
Richard A Kothe • WS 8 1030; SS 915; BC 915;* • H • EC/EL/HS • NEB • 465 S Marian Rd Hastings NE 68901-7401 • FAX(402)462-5375 • goodrich@esu9.esu9.k12.ne.us
**HAY SPRINGS—*ZION*** (308)638-7575
Vacant • WS 11; BC 945;* • H • WY • S Main And S Third 69347 PO Box 177 Hay Springs NE 69347-0177
**HAZARD—*FAITH*** (308)452-3013
Dean A Hanson • NEB • PO Box 86 Hazard NE 68844-0086
**HEBRON—*FAITH*** (402)768-6837
Richard G Kelm • WS 9;* • H • NEB • 420 Charles Rd 68370-1023 PO Box 41 Hebron NE 68370
**HEBRON 7 W—*TRINITY*** (402)365-7636
Duane R Simonson • H • NEB • 68370 RR 2 Box 100A Hebron NE 68370-9536
**HOLDREGE—*MOUNT CALVARY*** (308)995-2208
Kenton J Birtell • David Wuggazer DCE • WS 830; SS 930; BC 945;* • H • NEB • 1419 East Ave Holdrege NE 68949-1325
**HOOPER—*ST JOHN*** (402)654-2338
Carl A Lehmann • * • H • NEB • 508 E Elk St 68031 PO Box A Hooper NE 68031-0599
**HOOPER 6 E—*IMMANUEL*** (402)654-3563
Rodney M Meske • WS 10; BC 9;* • H • EL • NEB • 68031 27052 Co Rd 12 Hooper NE 68031-5009 • FAX(402)654-2814 • rmeske@tusonline.net
**HOSKINS—*ZION*** (402)329-6720
Lynn A Riege • WS 1030; SS 915 • NEB • 55840 853rd Rd 68740-4002 RR 1 Box 250 Pierce NE 68767
**HOWELLS—*TRINITY*** (402)986-1254
Vacant • WS 830;* • H • NEB • 505 Ann St 68641-4078 PO Box 436 Howells NE 68641-0436
**HUBBELL—*ZION*** (402)324-8075
Vacant • WS 830;* • NEB • 203 Minnesota St 68375 PO Box 211 Chester NE 68327-0211
**HUMBOLDT—*FAITH*** (402)862-2437
Harold R Hintzman Jr. • WS 1030; SS 915; BC 915 • H • NEB • 940 Central Ave 68376-6112 RR 1 Box 57 Humboldt NE 68376-9711
**HUMPHREY—*ST PETER*** (402)246-2730
John P Hellwege Jr. • NEB • PO Box 325 Humphrey NE 68642
**HYANNIS—*SWEDE VALLEY***
Ashby 9 S
**HYANNIS 35 N—*FAITH**** (308)458-2508
Vacant • WS 7 • H • NEB • 69350 C/O Rev Greg Lucido PO Box 350 Hyannis NE 69350-0350 • lucido@neb-sandhills.net
**IMPERIAL—*ZION*** (308)882-5655
Robert A Frank • WS 945; SS 845; BC 845;* • H • NEB • 1305 N Broadway RR 2 Box 3H Imperial NE 69033 • zlcimpne@chase3000.com
**JAMISON—*IMMANUEL*** (402)832-5530
Donald L Boettcher • NEB • Main St UKNWN HC 74 Box 50 Newport NE 68759-9504
**JANSEN—*TRINITY*** (402)424-2335
Vacant • H • NEB • Broad St 68377 58115 718th Rd Jansen NE 68377-4014
***ZION***
See Harbine 4 NE
**JUNIATA 7 W 3 S—*ZION*** (402)756-5723
Harold L King Jr. • * • H • NEB • 4080 S Wanda Ave Juniata NE 68955 • FAX(402)756-5287 • revking@gtmc.net
**JUNIATA 8 NW—*CHRIST*** (402)744-4971
Gregory R Volzke • WS 10; SS 9; BC 9;* • H • EL • NEB • 68955 13175 W 70th St Juniata NE 68955-2138 • FAX(402)744-4971
**KEARNEY—*HOLY CROSS*** (308)237-2944
Russell L Sommerfeld Daniel E Heuer • H • EC • NEB • 3315 11th Ave Kearney NE 68845-8002 • FAX(308)237-2695 • holycross@kearney.net
***UNIVERSITY**** (308)236-8253
Vacant • H • NEB • 1814 W 24th St Kearney NE 68847-4904
***ZION*** (308)234-3410
North P Sherrill Jr. • H • NEB • 2421 Ave C 68847-4541 PO Box 778 Kearney NE 68847-0778 • FAX(308)236-8100
**KENESAW—*ST PAUL*** (402)752-3421
Paul S Duffy • * • H • NEB • 310 N 4th Ave 68956-1516 PO Box 36 Kenesaw NE 68956-0036
***ST PAUL***
See Lowell Twp
**KIMBALL—*ST JOHN*** (308)235-2582
Thomas C Jacobsen • H • WY • 601 Locust St Kimball NE 69145-1343
**LAUREL—*IMMANUEL*** (402)256-3314
William C Engebretsen • WS 10;* • H • NEB • Third And Alma Sts 68745 PO Box 597 Laurel NE 68745-0597
**LEIGH—*ZION*** (402)487-2502
Vacant • WS 10;* • H • EC • NEB • 405 Main St PO Box 215 Leigh NE 68643-0215
**LEXINGTON—*TRINITY*** (308)324-4341
Juan L Hormachea • Robert D Wiest DCE • WS 7;* • H • EC • NEB • 205 E 7th St 68850-2101 PO Box L Lexington NE 68850-0350 • FAX(308)324-6999 • trinitychurch@alltel.net
**LEXINGTON 15 N 4 W—*FIRST*** (308)324-6384
Vacant • * • NEB • 68850 42956 Buffalo Rd Lexington NE 68850-3450
**LINCOLN—*CALVARY*** (402)476-1567
Mark W Rosenau Roland A Hopmann(EM) • WS 8 1030; SS 915; BC 915 • H • EL/HS • NEB • 2788 Franklin St 2774 Franklin St Lincoln NE 68502-3231 • FAX(402)476-0881 • calvary@inetnebr.com
***CHRIST*** (402)483-7774
Luke R Schnake S T Williams Jr. Harold T Stelzer(EM) • Rhonda L Mc Clellan DCE Robert Ewell DCE • * • H • EC/EL/HS • NEB • 4325 Sumner St Lincoln NE 68506-1165 • FAX(402)483-7776 • clc@christlutheranchurch.org
***FAITH*** (402)466-6861
Mark T Hannemann Jerome A Troester • WS 1045; SS 745; BC 915;* • H • EC/EL/HS • NEB • 6345 Madison Ave Lincoln NE 68507-2598 • FAX(402)466-3857 • faith@inetnebr.com
***GOOD SHEPHERD*** (402)423-7639
Clint K Poppe • WS 8 1030; SS 915; BC 915 • H • EC/EL/HS • NEB • 40th St And Old Chenny Rd 68516 3825 Wildbriar Ln Lincoln NE 68516-4502 • FAX(402)423-0984 • goodshep1@net.zero.net
***HOLY SAVIOR*** (402)434-3325
Michael G Chaffee Burt L Garwood • WS 8 930 11; BC 930;* • H • EL/HS • NEB • 4710 N 10th St Lincoln NE 68521-4039 • FAX(402)434-3330 • hsoffice@aol.com
***IMMANUEL*** (402)474-6275
Donald E Cooper • WS 8 1045; SS 915; BC 930 • H • EC/EL/HS • NEB • 2001 S 11th St Lincoln NE 68502-2215 • FAX(402)474-6275 • immanuellutheran@juno.com
***MESSIAH*** (402)489-3024
Luther C Biggs Michael P Neidow John R Kunze • Warren A Viehl DCE • WS 8 6; SS 1030; BC 920 • H • EC/EL/HS • NEB • 1800 S 84th St Lincoln NE 68506-1870 • FAX(402)489-3093 • messiah@alltel.net
***REDEEMER*** (402)477-1710
Mark H Ebert John E Schmidt • WS 830 11; SS 945; BC 945 • H • EL/HS • EN • 510 S 33rd St Lincoln NE 68510-3304 • FAX(402)477-5240 • r174758@alltel.net
***TRINITY*** (402)474-0606
Duane R Voorman Jerome W Rossow Thomas H Pruitt(#) • WS 8 1030; SS 915;* • H • EC/EL/HS • NEB • 724 S 12th St Lincoln NE 68508-3217 • FAX(402)474-0666 • trinity-lincoln@juno.com
***UNIVERSITY CHAPEL**** (402)477-3997
William J Steinbauer • NEB • 1510 Q St Lincoln NE 68508-1647 • ulc@unlinfo.unl.edu
**LOUISVILLE—*ST PAUL***
See Weeping Water
**LOUISVILLE 3 SW—*IMMANUEL*** (402)234-5980
James H De Loach • WS 1030; SS 915;* • H • NEB • 68037 36712 Church Rd Louisville NE 68037-2918 • immanuel@alltel.net
**LOUP CITY—*IMMANUEL*** (308)745-0808
Shawn L Kitzing • H • NEB • First And N St 68853 PO Box 100 Loup City NE 68853-0100
**LOWELL TWP—*ST PAUL*** (308)647-6776
Timothy E Parker • H • NEB • UKNWN 2294 X Rd Kenesaw NE 68956-2517
**LYNCH—*CHRIST***
Duane C Miesner • WS 1045; SS 945 • NEB • 68746 C/O PO Box 308 Spencer NE 68777
**LYONS 4 SE—*ST JOHN*** (402)685-6260
Robert S Davis • NEB • 68038 1543 County Road 13 Lyons NE 68038-5020
**MADISON—*TRINITY*** (402)454-3532
Vacant • * • H • EC/EL/HS • NEB • 508 S Jackson St PO Box 367 Madison NE 68748-0367 • FAX(402)454-3408 • tlc@ncfcomm.com
**MADISON 8 SW—*ST JOHN*** (402)454-2823
James D Woelmer • * • EL • NEB • 68748 82660 547th Ave Madison NE 68748-6141 • jwoelmer@aol.com
**MALCOLM—*ST PAUL*** (402)796-2396
Todd A Schlechte • WS 10;* • H • NEB • 375 S Lincoln St 68402 PO Box 53 Malcolm NE 68402-0053
**MARTINSBURG—*TRINITY*** (402)945-2160
Gary H Klatt • WS 9; SS 1015; BC 1030 • H • NEB • 5106 Douglas St Ponca NE 68770-7019
**MC COOK—*PEACE*** (308)345-2595
Carl E Pullmann • WS 8 1030; SS 915; BC 915 • H • EC • NEB • 411 E 6th St 69001-3815 PO Box 240 Mc Cook NE 69001-0240
**MC COOK 9 SE—*ST JOHN*** (308)364-2706
Larry J Rodencal • H • NEB • 9 Se Mc Cook 69001 RR 3 Box 124 Mc Cook NE 69001-9539 • FAX(308)364-2706 • larroden@juno.com
**MEADOW GROVE—*ST MATTHEW*** (402)634-2933
Daniel J Welch • WS 1045;* • H • HS • NEB • 216 First St PO Box 48 Meadow Grove NE 68752-0048 • dwelch@ncfcomm.com
**MERNA—*IMMANUEL*** (308)643-2302
Vacant • WS 1030; SS 9 • NEB • 328 E Brotherton Ave 68856 PO Box 185 Merna NE 68856-0185
**MERRIMAN—*GRACE*** (308)684-3392
Vacant • WS 1115 • NEB • 2nd Ave And Main St 69218 PO Box 167 Merriman NE 69218-0167
**MILFORD—*GOOD SHEPHERD*** (402)761-3146
William C Ryden • WS 930; BC 1030;* • EC • NEB • 620 Second St 68405 PO Box 90 Milford NE 68405-0090 • FAX(402)761-3146

**MINDEN—*ST PAUL*** (308)832-1343
Donald H Becker • WS 1015; BC 9;* • H • NEB • 206 N Colorado Ave Minden NE 68959-1623 • stpaulminden@navix.net

**MORRILL—*TRINITY*** (308)247-2432
Vacant • WS 9; SS 1015; BC 1015;* • H • WY • 405 Jackson Ct 69358-2405 PO Box 185 Morrill NE 69358-0185 • FAX(308)247-2432 • foxtrot@prairieweb.com

**MURDOCK 2 N—*TRINITY*** (402)867-2916
Brent W Kuhlman • WS 1030; SS 930; BC 930 • H • NEB • 68407 31104 Church Rd Murdock NE 68407-2216

**NEBRASKA CITY—*CHRIST*** (402)873-6824
John H Schmidt • WS 9; SS 1010; BC 1010 • NEB • 2201 2nd Ave Nebraska City NE 68410-1809

**NELIGH—*GRACE*** (402)887-4791
David P Kuhfal • WS 1030; SS 915; BC 915;* • H • NEB • 508 K St Neligh NE 68756-1358 • dkuhfal@bloomnet.com

**NORFOLK—*CHRIST*** (402)371-1210
Frank R Maurer Steven R Heinsen Roger G Leavitt Jack H Thiesen V • WS 8 930 1045; SS 930; BC 930;* • H • EC/EL/HS • NEB • 605 S 5th St Norfolk NE 68701-5279 • FAX(402)371-1228 • clc@kdsi.net

***GRACE*** (402)371-1044
Ray S Wilke • H • HS • NEB • 416 Park Ave Norfolk NE 68701-5240

***MOUNT OLIVE*** (402)371-1238
Wilbur F Brink Glen E Gutz • WS 1030; BC 915;* • H • HS • NEB • 1212 S 2nd St Norfolk NE 68701-6324 • MtOlive@conpoint.com

***OUR SAVIOR*** (402)371-9005
Ronald E Holling Kenneth L Weander Jr. • WS 755 10; SS 850; BC 850;* • H • EC/HS • NEB • 2500 Norfolk Ave Norfolk NE 68701-4427 • FAX(402)371-1387 • oursav@conpoint.com

**NORTH BEND—*ST PETER*** (402)652-8215
Verdell D Schramm • WS 9; SS 1015; BC 1015;* • H • NEB • 920 Linden Dr 68649 PO Box 496 North Bend NE 68649-0496

**NORTH PLATTE—*BEAUT SAVIOR*** (308)534-7004
Robert C Kuefner Jr. • WS 915; SS 1030; BC 1030;* • H • EC • NEB • 402 S Baytree Ave North Platte NE 69101-4823 • FAX(308)534-3177 • pastkey@kdsi.net

***OUR REDEEMER*** (308)532-4753
Marion W Von Rentzell Fredrick A Simon • H • EC/EL • NEB • 1400 E D St North Platte NE 69101-5770 • orlc@kdsi.net

**O NEILL—*CHRIST*** (402)336-1884
Jerome H Meyer • Leah R Kortmeyer DCE • WS 9; SS 1010 • H • NEB • Seventh At E Clay 68763 PO Box 736 O Neill NE 68763-0736 • clc@inetnebr.com

**ODELL—*OUR SAVIOR*** (402)766-3688
Steven L Sommerer • NEB • 421 Maple St 68415 PO Box A Odell NE 68415-0130 • revsommerer@diller.net

**OGALLALA—*ST PAUL*** (308)284-2688
David F Dobbertien • SS 920; BC 920;* • EC/EL • NEB • 317 W 2nd St 69153-2501 312 W 3rd St Ogallala NE 69153-2522 • stpauls@megavision.com

***TRINITY*** (308)352-4079
Vacant • WS 10; SS 845; BC 845 • NEB • 69153 RFD 1 Box 289 A Ogallala NE 69153-9801

***ZION***
See Grant

**OGALLALA 10 SE—*ST JOHN*** (308)284-6015
Robert J Pierce • WS 1030; SS 930; BC 930 • H • NEB • 69153 466 Rd East G South Ogallala NE 69153-5332

**OMAHA—*ATONEMENT*** (402)571-3698
Gerald E Bossard • H • NEB • 4530 N 85th St Omaha NE 68134-3125

***BEAUT SAVIOR*** (402)331-7376
Daniel M Cloeter Keith H Grimm • James R Haack DCE • WS 8 930 1045; SS 930; BC 930;* • H • EC/EL • NEB • 9012 Q St Omaha NE 68127-3549 • FAX(402)331-1123

***BETHANY*** (402)558-6212
Patrick J Burt • WS 845; SS 10; BC 10 • H • EC • NEB • 5151 NW Radial Hwy Omaha NE 68104-4399 • FAX(402)561-6928

***BETHLEHEM DEAF*** (402)558-5672
Robert D Case • WS 10; SS 9;* • NEB • 5074 Lake St Omaha NE 68104-4314 • FAXA02-558-5672 • 73602.2062@compuserve.com

***CROSS*** (402)346-3203
Vacant • WS 1030; BC 915;* • H • EC/EL • NEB • 3101 S 20th St 68108-1903 2902 S 20th St Omaha NE 68108-1301 • FAX(402)342-6511

***DIVINE SHEPHER*** (402)895-1500
David L Block Douglas W Chinberg • David W Ricke DCE Timothy P Kightlinger DCE • WS 8 930 530; SS 930; BC 930 • H • EC/EL • NEB • 15005 Q St Omaha NE 68137-2525 • FAX(402)895-5377 • davelblock@aol.com

***HOPE*** (402)453-1583
Vacant • H • NEB • 2723 N 30th St Omaha NE 68111-3706

***KING OF KINGS*** (402)333-6464
Mark P Zehnder A L Gerner Daniel T Mc Dougall John M Sproul Roger P Theimer Jonathan B Trinklein • Robert A Broekemeier DCE • WS 8 930 11 6; SS 8; BC 930;* • H • EC/EL • NEB • 11615 I St Omaha NE 68137-1211 • FAX(402)333-0644 • seniorpastor@kingofkingsomaha.org

***LORD OF LIFE***
See Elkhorn

***MOUNT CALVARY*** (402)551-0244
Richard L Gudgel • * • EC/EL • NEB • 5529 Leavenworth St Omaha NE 68106-1349 • FAX(402)551-9299

***MOUNT OLIVE*** (402)455-8700
Roland A Jank Jr. • WS 9; SS 1020; BC 1020 • H • EC • NEB • 7301 N 28th Ave Omaha NE 68112-2816 • FAX(402)455-8701 • MountOlv@aol.com

***PACIFIC HILLS*** (402)391-9625
William G Moorhead • Larry R Biel DCE • WS 8 1030; SS 910; BC 910;* • H • EC/EL • NEB • 1110 S 90th St Omaha NE 68124-1202 • FAX(402)399-8929 • bmoorhead@westide66.org

***PEACE*** (402)553-8643
Vacant • WS 9;* • H • NEB • 3314 S 44th Ave Omaha NE 68105-3817

***ST JOHN*** (402)453-1335
Allen S Vomhof • WS 830 11; BC 945;* • NEB • 11120 Calhoun Rd Omaha NE 68152-1327 • FAX(402)455-5973 • stjohnlutheran@juno.com

***ST MARK*** (402)391-6148
Charles A Gierke James M Irwin John Northwall(EM) • WS 8 915 1045 1230; SS 915; BC 915;* • H • EC/EL • NEB • 1821 N 90th St Omaha NE 68114-1314 • FAX(402)399-1682 • stmark@st-marklcms.org

***ST PAUL*** (402)451-2865
Everett L Garwood • WS 8 1030; SS 915; BC 915;* • H • EC/EL • NEB • 5020 Grand Ave Omaha NE 68104-2367 • FAX(402)451-6816

***ZION*** (402)731-0743
Jose Flores Steven G Herfkens • H • EC/EL • NEB • 4001 Q St Omaha NE 68107-2462 • FAX(402)731-3121

***ZION WEST*** (402)493-1744
Thomas K Schmitt • WS 8 1030; SS 9; BC 930;* • H • EC/EL • NEB • 14205 Ida St Omaha NE 68142 • FAX(402)965-8706 • zionwest@aol.com

**ORCHARD—*ST PETER*** (402)893-2390
Philip M Heuser • WS 930; SS 1045; BC 1045 • H • NEB • 230 N Cherry St 68764 PO Box 117 Orchard NE 68764-0117 • pjheuser@juno.com

**ORCHARD 14 N—*ST PAUL*** (402)655-2246
Vacant • WS 8; SS 9; BC 9 • NEB • 68764 87127 512th Ave Orchard NE 68764-6403 • FAX(402)655-2254 • virginiavs@aol.com

**ORD—*ST JOHN*** (308)728-5111
Gerald W Roggow • WS 830 11; SS 950; BC 950 • H • EC • NEB • 725 S 14th St Ord NE 68862-1962

**OSMOND—*IMMANUEL*** (402)748-3301
Gary D Trowbridge • WS 930; SS 1030; BC 1030 • H • EC/HS • NEB • 808 Fulton 68765 PO Box 10 Osmond NE 68765-0010 • FAX(402)748-3301

**OXFORD—*ST JOHN*** (308)824-3269
George E Naylor • WS 1030; BC 915;* • H • NEB • 418 Globe St 68967 PO Box 68 Oxford NE 68967-0068 • gnaylor@swnebr.net

**PALISADE—*TRINITY*** (308)394-5522
Vacant • WS 830; SS 930 • NEB • 201 N Osborn 69040 PO Box 218 Palisade NE 69040-0218

***TRINITY*** (308)394-5522
Vacant • WS 830; SS 930 • NEB • 201 N Osborn 69040 PO Box 218 Palisade NE 69040-0218

**PALMER—*ST JOHN*** (308)894-3545
Robert G Schilling • H • NEB • 504 Utica Ave 68864 PO Box 157 Palmer NE 68864-0157 • stjohn@hamilton.net

**PAPILLION—*FIRST*** (402)339-3668
Martin R Greunke Philip G Houser • SS 915;* • H • EC • NEB • 332 N Washington St Papillion NE 68046-2360 • FAX(402)339-3693 • flcpapio@radiks.net

**PAWNEE CITY—*ZION*** (402)852-2671
Patrick J Riley • WS 9;* • H • NEB • 504 12th St NE Pawnee City NE 68420-3503 • FAX(402)852-2671 • zionlutheran2@juno.com

**PENDER 5S 2W—*ST JOHN*** (402)385-2447
Richard W Pingel • WS 9 730;* • H • NEB • 68047 2175 15th Rd Pender NE 68105-3817

**PIERCE—*ZION*** (402)329-4313
Gordon W Bruce John Hans K Trinklein • Laura J Ahlers DCE • H • EC/EL/HS • NEB • 520 E Main St Pierce NE 68767-1668

**PIERCE 3 NE—*ST JOHN*** (402)329-6720
Lynn A Riege • WS 845;* • H • NEB • 68767 RR 1 Box 250 Pierce NE 68767-9413

**PILGER—*ST JOHN*** (402)396-3478
Jeffrey L Bloom • WS 1015; SS 9; BC 9 • H • HS • NEB • 250 N Monroe 68768 PO Box 322 Pilger NE 68768-0322 • bloom5@juno.com

**PLAINVIEW—*ZION*** (402)582-3312
Daniel H Deardoff Sr. • * • H • EC/EL/HS • NEB • 102 N Sixth 68769 PO Box 159 Plainview NE 68769-0159 • zionplvw@plvwtelco.net

**PLATTE CENTER—*GRACE*** (402)246-2730
John P Hellwege Jr. • NEB • 216 First St 68653 PO Box 259 Platte Center NE 68653-0259

***ST PETER***
See Humphrey

**PLATTSMOUTH—*FIRST*** (402)296-2832
A N Friedmeyer • WS 9; SS 1015; BC 1015;* • H • NEB • 1025 Avenue D Plattsmouth NE 68048-1129 • FAX(402)296-2484 • firstluth@comweb.net

**PLEASANT DALE—*BETHLEHEM*** (402)795-3885
Louis E Griser • WS 9;* • H • NEB • 101 Maple 68423 PO Box 127 Pleasant Dale NE 68423-0127 • legriser@aol.com

**PLEASANTON—*GRACE*** (308)388-2755
Dean A Hanson • WS 10; SS 9; BC 9 • H • NEB • 29577 Highway 10 68866-3001 PO Box 218 Pleasanton NE 68866-0218 • gracelutheran@nebi.com

**POLK 4 SW—*IMMANUEL*** (402)765-7252
Kurt R Letcher • WS 930; SS 1045; BC 1045 • EL • NEB • 68654 2406 E 26th Rd Polk NE 68654-1702

**PONCA—*TRINITY***
See Martinsburg

**POTTER—*ST PAUL*** (308)879-4437
Vacant • WY • 4450 RD 89 Potter NE 69156-6637

**RAVENNA—*BETHLEHEM*** (308)452-3685
Steven R Schlund • WS 830; SS 930; BC 930;* • H • NEB • 324 Kufus Ave 68869-1218 PO Box 64 Ravenna NE 68869-0064 • sschlund@micrord.com

**RED CLOUD—*ZION*** (402)746-2859
Ronald K Kuehner • * • H • NEB • 802 N Franklin St Red Cloud NE 68970 • revron@gpcom.net

**RISING CITY 5 SE—*IMMANUEL*** (402)367-4685
David W Palomaki • WS 830;* • NEB • 910 31 Rd 910 31st Rd Rising City NE 68658

**ROCA—*FAITH/FATHERS*** (402)421-2222
Vacant • WS 9; SS 1030; BC 1030 • H • NEB • 15580 E 68430 PO Box 57 Roca NE 68430-0057

**ROSEMONT—*CALVARY*** (402)756-2568
William F Caughey • * • NEB • UKNWN RR 2 Box 100 Blue Hill NE 68930-9598 • FAX(402)756-8551 • bcaughey@mail.gtmc.net

**RUSHVILLE—*ST PAUL*** (308)327-2220
Vacant • WS 9; SS 1015; BC 1015 • WY • Fifth And S Main St PO Box 531 Rushville NE 69360-0531

**RUSKIN—*ST MARK*** (402)226-2391
Robert A Mrosko • WS 9; SS 1015; BC 1015 • H • NEB • 290 E Main St 68974 PO Box 97 Ruskin NE 68974-0097 • stmarkruskin@juno.com

**SAINT EDWARD—*FAITH*** (402)678-2878
Vernon R Knight(EM) • H • NEB • Sixth And Water 68660 PO Box 349 St Edward NE 68660-0349

**SAINT LIBORY 6 E—*ZION*** (308)687-6314
Karl P Ziegler • WS 1015; SS 9; BC 9 • H • EL/HS • NEB • 68872 1655 Worms Rd Saint Libory NE 68872-2906 • ziegworms@juno.com

**SAINT PAUL—*CHRIST*** (308)754-5135
John R Paulson • WS 9; SS 1030; BC 1030 • H • NEB • 1022 Elm St Saint Paul NE 68873-1906

**SARGENT—*PEACE*** (308)346-5060
Vacant • * • H • NEB • 1st And Della PO Box 246 Sargent NE 68874

**SCHUYLER—*IMMANUEL*** (402)352-2035
Norman E Porath • WS 1030; BC 915;* • H • NEB • 949 Road 7 68661-7195 632 Road 8 Schuyler NE 68661-7203 • immanuelschuyler@juno.com

***TRINITY*** (402)352-2307
Norman E Porath • WS 9; BC 10;* • NEB • 1617 Colfax St 68661-1439 PO Box 126 Schuyler NE 68661-0126 • FAX(402)352-8462 • np83710@alltel.net

**SCOTIA—*ZION*** (308)245-4151
Mark G Middendorf • WS 1030; BC 930;* • H • NEB • West Hwy 22 PO Box 334 Scotia NE 68875-0334 • FAX(308)245-4151 • mjmiddendorf@nctc.net

**SCOTTSBLUFF—*ST JAMES*** (308)632-8001
Barry G Warpness • H • WY • 1117 E 14th St Scottsbluff NE 69361-3311 • bgwarp@actcom.net

***ST JOHN*** (308)635-1722
Jeffery W Grams • WS 9; SS 1015; BC 1015;* • H • WY • 2220 Broadway Scottsbluff NE 69361-1970 • stjohns@actcom.net

**SCRIBNER—*ST PETER*** (402)664-3462
Donald E Brunner • H • NEB • Sixth And Baker Sts PO Box 409 Scribner NE 68057 • stpeter@tvsonline.net

**SEWARD—*ST JOHN*** (402)643-2983
Mark G Cutler Mark S Tewes • WS 730 9 1115; SS 1015; BC 1015;* • H • EC/EL • NEB • 919 N Columbia Ave Seward NE 68434-1557 • FAX(402)643-2985 • sjlc@navix.net

**SEWARD 7 E—*IMMANUEL*** (402)588-2602
Mark A Kophamer • H • NEB • 68434 1838 Alvo Rd Seward NE 68434-8082

**SHELTON—*ST PAUL*** (308)647-6733
Timothy E Parker • WS 1030;* • EC • NEB • 705 A St 68876-9669 PO Box 326 Shelton NE 68876-0326

***ZION*** (308)467-2343
Vacant • NEB • 53125 Grand Island Rd 68876-1781 24975 Sioux Rd Shelton NE 68876-1723

**SHICKLEY—*ZION*** (402)627-3795
Duane R Simonson • H • NEB • PO Box 135 Shickley NE 68436-0135

**SIDNEY—*ST PAUL*** (308)254-3144
Vacant • WS 8; BC 915;* • H • WY • 1424 Maple St 1432 15th Ave Sidney NE 69162

**SIDNEY 11 SE—*TRINITY*** (308)254-3062
Philip J Found • * • H • WY • 69162 11991 Road 6 Sidney NE 69162-4101

**SNYDER—*ST PETER*** (402)568-2571
Vacant • NEB • PO Box 67 Snyder NE 68664-0067

**SOUTH SIOUX CITY—*HOPE*** (402)494-1847
Charles E Horkey • WS 815 1045; SS 930; BC 930 • H • NEB • 218 W 18th St South Sioux City NE 68776-2713 • FAX(402)494-8304

**SPENCER—*IMMANUEL*** (402)589-1323
Duane C Miesner • WS 9; SS 10 • H • NEB • PO Box 308 Spencer NE 68777-0308 • FAX(402)589-1323 • dmiesner@inetnebr.com

**SPRINGFIELD—*OUR REDEEMER*** (402)253-2893
Thomas R Javor • WS 9;* • H • EC/EL • NEB • 305 N Third 68059 PO Box 529 Springfield NE 68059-0529

**SPRINGVIEW—*GRACE***
See Burton

**STANTON—*FAITH*** (402)439-2104
Timothy D Booth • H • HS • NEB • 506 16th 68779 PO Box 317 Stanton NE 68779-0317 • FAX(402)439-2461

**STAPLEHURST—*OUR REDEEMER*** (402)535-2625
Daniel W Myers • WS 9; SS 1015; BC 1015 • H • EC/EL • NEB • 3743 Marysville Rd Staplehurst NE 68439-8843 • revdmyers@alltel.net

**STERLING 2 W—*IMMANUEL*** (402)866-6661
Mark C Follett • H • NEB • Hwy 41 68443 RR 2 Box 69 Sterling NE 68443-9733

**SUMNER—*GRACE***
Vacant • * • H • NEB • PO Box 112 Sumner NE 68878-0112

**SUPERIOR—*CENTENNIAL*** (402)879-3137
Paul G Albrecht • WS 9; SS 10; BC 1015;* • H • NEB • 855 N Dakota St 68978-1203 PO Box 231 Superior NE 68978-0231 • FAX(402)879-3137 • pa32112@navix.net

**TECUMSEH—*ST JOHN*** (402)335-3816
Carlton K Hein • * • EC • NEB • 68450 PO Box 867 1260 Webster St Tecumseh NE 68450-0867
**THAYER—*ZION*** (402)362-3177
Lee D Seetin • NEB • UKNWN 1917 Road Q Waco NE 68460-9423
**THEDFORD—*TRINITY*** (308)645-2254
Vacant • WS 7; SS 6 • NEB • 408 Locust St 69166 PO Box 254 Thedford NE 69166-0254
**TILDEN—*IMMANUEL*** (402)368-5690
Michael A Awe • WS 1030; SS 915; BC 1130 915;* • H • EC/HS • NEB • 500 South Center St Tilden NE 68781-4728 • FAX(402)368-2158 • imnlluth@ncfcomm.com
**TILDEN 9 SE—*ST PAUL*** (402)634-2933
Daniel J Welch • WS 9; SS 1015;* • H • HS • NEB • 68781 C/O St Matthew Lutheran PO Box 48 Meadow Grove NE 68752-0048 • dwelch@ncfcomm.com
**TOBIAS 3 SE—*ZION*** (402)243-2353
Vacant • WS 9; SS 10; BC 10 • H • EC/EL • NEB • 2247 County Rd U Tobias NE 68453 • mr53603@navix.net
**UNKNOWN—*ST PAUL*** (402)756-5621
Harold L King Jr. • SS 915;* • H • NEB • 18260 West Sundown Rd PO Box 88 Holstein NE 68950-0088 • FAX(402)756-5287 • revking@gtmc.net
**UTICA—*ST PAUL*** (402)534-2200
Robert G Gadeken Harold E Malotky(EM) • WS 8 1030; SS 915; BC 915 • NEB • 975 D St 68456 PO Box 398 Utica NE 68456-0398 • FAX(402)534-2100
**VALENTINE—*OUR SAVIOR*** (402)376-2932
Vacant • * • NEB • 3rd And Hall 69201 PO Box 302 Valentine NE 69201-0302
**VENANGO—*ST PAUL*** (970)854-4310
Vacant • * • RM • PO Box 26 Venango NE 69168-0026
**VENUS—*ST PAUL***
See Orchard 14 N
**VERDIGRE—*BETHLEHEM*** (402)668-2846
Terell O Huber • WS 1030; SS 930 • H • NEB • 310 Quimby Ave 68783 PO Box 359 Verdigre NE 68783-0359 • thubes@bloomnet.com
**WACO—*PEACE*** (402)728-5227
Vacant • WS 9;* • NEB • PO Box 35 Waco NE 68460-0035
***ZION***
See Thayer
**WACO 2E 4.5S—*ST JOHN*** (402)728-5446
Paul T Kern • WS 9;* • H • EL • NEB • 68460 1011 A Rd U Waco NE 68460-9767 • FAX(402)728-5446
**WAHOO—*OUR REDEEMER*** (402)443-4450
Robert K Reimer • WS 9;* • H • NEB • 1245 N Locust St Wahoo NE 68066-1249
**WAKEFIELD—*ST JOHN*** (402)287-2385
Bruce L Schut • * • H • HS • NEB • 412 W Seventh St Wakefield NE 68784-5053
**WAKEFIELD 7 NW—*IMMANUEL*** (402)375-3616
Brian W Handrich • NEB • 57885 860 Rd Wakefield NE 68784 • bhandri@midlands.net
**WALTHILL—*TRINITY*** (402)846-5027
Brion P Tolzman • * • H • NEB • 207 N Broughton 68067 PO Box 252 Walthill NE 68067-0252 • FAX(402)846-5935 • tolzie@huntel.net
***TRINITY***
See Decatur
**WALTON 6 SE—*TRINITY*** (402)782-6515
Merlin D Holtzen • WS 10; SS 850; BC 850 • H • NEB • 162nd And Old Cheney Rd 68461 RR 1 Box 22 Walton NE 68461-9719 • retzlaff@unlserve.unl.edu
**WAUNETA—*REDEEMER*** (308)394-5522
Vacant • NEB • 233 S Arapahoe 69045 PO Box 278 Wauneta NE 69045-0278 • redwauneta@mailroom.com
**WAUNETA 13 SW—*ST PAUL*** (308)394-5562
Keith B Wellman • * • NEB • 8 W On Us 6 And 5 S On Hwy 61 69045 RR 2 Box 37 Wauneta NE 69045-9601 • byron@bwtelcom.net
**WAUSA 7 SW—*GOLGOTHA*** (402)586-2412
Daniel G Gifford • WS 1030; SS 930; BC 930 • NEB • 87242 543rd Ave 68786 501 S Hampton PO Box 240 Wausa NE 68786-0240 • dkgiff@bloomnet.com
**WAVERLY—*PEACE*** (402)786-2345
Kenneth D Hoover • WS 8 1030; SS 915; BC 915 • H • NEB • 9831 N 145th St Waverly NE 68462-1516 • peacewaverly@juno.com
**WAYNE—*FIRST TRINITY***
See Altona
***GRACE*** (402)375-1905
Jeffrey M Anderson • WS 1030 8; SS 915; BC 915;* • H • HS • NEB • 904 Logan St Wayne NE 68787-1449 • grace@bloomnet.com
***ST PAUL***
See Carroll
**WEEPING WATER—*ST PAUL*** (402)234-5980
James H De Loach • WS 830; SS 930 • H • NEB • 607 S Randolph St 68463-4403 C/O Immanuel 36712 Church Rd Louisville NE 68037-2918 • immanuel@alltel.net
**WEST POINT—*ST PAUL*** (402)372-2111
Robert C Hedtke • WS 830; BC 10;* • NEB • 434 N Lincoln St West Point NE 68788-1414 • FAX(402)372-5039 • stpaullutheran@alltel.net
**WILCOX—*ST JOHN*** (308)478-5466
Jeremy M Jacoby • WS 10; SS 1115; BC 1115 • H • NEB • 104 S Stocton 68982 PO Box 214 Wilcox NE 68982-0214
**WINSIDE—*ST PAUL*** (402)286-4929
Richard L Tino • WS 1030; SS 915; BC 915;* • H • HS • NEB • 218 Min 68790 PO Box 98 Winside NE 68790-0098
**WISNER—*ST PAUL*** (402)529-6583
James P Carretto • WS 1030; BC 915;* • H • HS • NEB • 509 13th St 68791-2232 PO Box 797 Wisner NE 68791-0797 • FAX(402)529-6005 • kelvin3@gpcom.net
**WISNER 8 S—*ZION-ST JOHN*** (402)529-6747
Roger D Schepmann • * • H • EC/EL • NEB • 68791 999 6th Rd Wisner NE 68791-3021
**WOOD RIVER—*GRACE*** (308)583-2820
Vacant • NEB • 11th And East St 68883 PO Box 327 Wood River NE 68883-0327 • sheinsen@kdsi.net
**WYMORE—*ST PETER*** (402)645-8215
Aaron M Witt • H • NEB • 10th And East St 68466 PO Box 3 Wymore NE 68466-0003
**YORK—*EMMANUEL*** (402)362-3655
Arthur Brinkmeyer Timothy J Marshall Douglas M Woltemath • WS 8 1030 630; SS 915; BC 915 • H • EC/EL • NEB • 806 Beaver York NE 68467 • FAX(402)362-5485
***FAITH*** (402)362-3000
Arthur P Schauer • WS 9; SS 1015; BC 1015;* • H • NEB • 1214 Ohio York NE 68467 • FAX(402)362-3821 • faithlcms@navix.net

## NEVADA

**BATAVIA—*ST PAUL*** (716)343-0488
Allen A Werk • WS 8 1045; SS 930; BC 930;* • H • EC/EL • EA • 31 Washington Ave Batavia NY 14020-2035 • FAX(716)344-0470 • werkasap@iinc.com
**BATTLE MOUNTAIN—*CHRISTS*** (702)635-5135
Mark A Kliewer • CNH • PO Box 953 Battle Mountain NV 89820-0953 • zion@the-onramp.net
**BOULDER CITY—*CHRIST*** (702)293-4332
Steven P Cluver • WS 9; BC 1020;* • H • EC/EL/HS • PSW • 1401 5th St Boulder City NV 89005-2301 • FAX(702)293-3221 • lutheran@anv.net
**CARSON CITY—*BETHLEHEM*** (702)882-5252
Paul E Deterding • WS 8 11; SS 930; BC 930 • H • EC/EL • CNH • 1837 N Mountain St Carson City NV 89703-2439 • FAX(702)882-9278
***SHEPHERD OF SIERRA***
Vacant • CNH • 3680 Highway 395 South Carson City NV 89705
**ELKO—*ST MARK*** (775)738-5436
Alan P Eisinger • * • H • EC • CNH • 277 Willow St Elko NV 89801-2851 • FAX(775)738-5456 • stmarkelko@ctnis.com
**ELY—*IMMANUEL*** (775)289-6353
Cary J Walter • WS 10; SS 9; BC 9 • CNH • 10th And Ave K 89301 PO Box 375 Ely NV 89301-0375 • immluth@the-onramp.net
**FALLON—*ST JOHN*** (702)423-4146
Robert L Porterfield Sr. • Edward W Morris DCE • H • EC • CNH • 1170 S Taylor St Fallon NV 89406-8837 • FAX(702)423-6596
**FERNLEY—*FERNLEY**** (702)575-4114
Vacant • H • CNH • 1320 Newlands Dr W 89408-9600 PO Box 1041 Fernley NV 89408-1041
**GARDNERVILLE—*TRINITY*** (775)782-8153
Vacant • WS 8 1030; SS 915; BC 915 • H • EC • CNH • 1480 Douglas Ave Gardnerville NV 89410-5103 • FAX(775)782-8154
**HAWTHORNE—*BETHANY*** (775)945-2332
Vacant • WS 11; SS 10;* • CNH • 204 C St 89415 PO Box 1207 Hawthorne NV 89415-1207 • harding3@oasisol.com
**HENDERSON—*OUR SAVIOR*** (702)565-9154
Edward V Bruning • H • EL/HS • PSW • 59 Lynn Ln 89015-7330 PO Box 91449 Henderson NV 89009-1449 • FAX(702)565-6246 • our3saviors@ccnmail.com
**JACKPOT—*HOPE**** (208)326-5450
Vacant • WS 2; BC 245;* • H • NOW • PO Box 801 Jackpot NV 89825-0801
**LAS VEGAS—*FAITH COMMUNITY*** (702)365-5070
Kenneth D Lieber • WS 9; SS 1015; BC 1015 • EL/HS • PSW • 7464 W Sahara Las Vegas NV 89117 • FAX(702)838-8866 • faithlasvegas@ad.com
***FRST GOOD SHEP*** (702)384-6106
Jason P Auringer • WS 815 11; BC 930;* • H • EL/HS • PSW • 301 S Maryland Pkwy Las Vegas NV 89101-5320 • FAX(702)384-2080 • fgslc@aol.com
***LAMB OF GOD*** (702)645-4998
Ronald G Folle • WS 8 1045; SS 930; BC 930;* • H • EC/EL/HS • PSW • 6220 N Jones Blvd Las Vegas NV 89130-1552 • FAX(702)645-7605 • loglc@lasvegas.net
***MOUNTAIN VIEW*** (702)360-8290
Terry L Brandenburg • WS 8; SS 930; BC 930;* • H • EC/EL/HS • PSW • 9550 W Cheyenne Las Vegas NV 89129 • FAX(702)360-2099 • pastor@mountainviewlc.org
***REDEEMER*** (702)642-7744
Vacant • WS 830 11; SS 945;* • H • EL/HS • PSW • 1730 N Pecos Rd Las Vegas NV 89115-0608 • FAX(702)642-7744
**LAUGHLIN—*LIVING CHRIST**** (520)763-3761
Robert O Wudy(EM) • WS 10 • H • PSW • Riverside Resort PO Box 2302 Laughlin NV 89029
**MESQUITE—*MESQUITE*** (702)346-5031
Vacant • SS 915; BC 915 • PSW • PO Box 1017 Mesquite NV 89024
**PAHRUMP—*SHEP/VALLEY*** (775)727-4098
Ronald P Mayer • H • PSW • 650 South Blagg Rd 89041 PO Box 2435 Pahrump NV 89041-2435
**RENO—*OUR SAVIOR***
See Sparks
***ST LUKE*** (775)825-0588
Michael R Benke • WS 830;* • H • CNH • 3835 Lakeside Dr Reno NV 89509-5239 • FAX(775)825-2979 • revofreno@aol.com
**ROUND MOUNTAIN—*GRACE**** (775)377-1445
Richard E Albers(#) • WS 9; SS 1015; BC 1015 • H • CNH • 93 Hadley Cir 89045 PO Box 1949 Round Mountain NV 89045-1949
**SPARKS—*OUR SAVIOR*** (702)358-0743
Ronald L Arnold • WS 9;* • H • CNH • 1900 1st St Sparks NV 89431-3270
**WINNEMUCCA—*ZION*** (775)623-3796
Mark A Kliewer • WS 8 1030; SS 915;* • H • EC • CNH • 3205 Highland Dr Winnemucca NV 89445-3573 • zion@the-onramp.net
**YERINGTON—*FAITH*** (702)463-5675
Vacant • H • CNH • 12 N West St 89447-2219 PO Box 861 Yerington NV 89447-0861 • harding3@oasisol.com

## NEW HAMPSHIRE

**EXETER—*FAITH*** (603)772-8803
Steven D Bartell • H • NE • 4 Elm St Exeter NH 03833-2703 • FAX(603)772-8898 • fthlthrn@nh.ultranet.com
**KEENE—*TRINITY*** (603)352-4446
James W Berry • Lisa Eberle DCE • * • H • EC/EL • NE • 28 Arch St Keene NH 03431-2236
**MANCHESTER—*IMMANUEL*** (603)622-1514
Robert H Piller • * • H • EC • NE • 673 Weston Rd Manchester NH 03103-3197 • FAX(603)622-5203 • secretary@immanuel-mnh.org
**NASHUA—*GRACE*** (603)888-7579
Michael H Meyer • * • H • NE • 130 Spit Brook Rd Nashua NH 03062-2642 • glcms@empire.net
**NEW IPSWICH—*OUR REDEEMER*** (603)878-1837
David A Batchelder • WS 10; BC 9;* • H • EC • NE • 200 Ashby Rd 03071-3707 PO Box 387 New Ipswich NH 03071-0387 • FAX(603)878-0891
**PETERBOROUGH—*GOOD SHEPHERD*** (603)924-4019
Vacant • WS 10 • H • NE • Rr 101 West 03458 PO Box 37 Peterborough NH 03458-0037
**TROY—*CHRIST*** (603)242-7283
Gerald Reiter • * • H • EC • NE • 4 Fitzwilliam Rd 03465-2309 PO Box 189 Troy NH 03465-0189

## NEW JERSEY

**ABSECON—*PEACE***
See Galloway Township
**BASKING RIDGE—*SOMERSET HILLS*** (908)766-2858
Robert A Kuppler • * • H • EC • NJ • 350 Lake Rd Basking Ridge NJ 07920-2121 • FAX(908)766-6546
**BLACKWOOD—*LUTHER MEMORIAL*** (856)227-2209
William R Klettke • WS 8 1030;* • H • NJ • 401 Erial Rd 08012 PO Box 186 Blackwood NJ 08012-0186
**BLAIRSTOWN—*GOOD SHEPHERD*** (908)362-9405
Robert C Klemm • * • H • EC • NJ • 168 State Route 94 Blairstown NJ 07825-2115 • FAX(908)362-9405
**BLOOMFIELD—*ST JOHN*** (973)429-8654
David B Hill • WS 10;* • H • NJ • 216 Liberty St Bloomfield NJ 07003-3432 • stjohnsrev1@prodigy.net
**BORDENTOWN TWP—*HOLY CROSS*** (609)298-2880
Timothy J Phillips • WS 1015; SS 9; BC 9 • H • EL • NJ • 08505 280 Crosswicks Rd Bordentown NJ 08505-2608 • FAX(609)298-1411 • hclcbrdn@bellatlantic.net
**BOUND BROOK—*ST JOHN*** (732)356-1038
Vacant • * • NJ • 319 Winsor St Bound Brook NJ 08805-1953
**BRIDGETON—*ST JOHN FIRST*** (856)451-0141
Dale R Johnston • WS 1015; BC 9;* • H • NJ • 61 Oak St 08302-2410 59 Oak St Bridgeton NJ 08302-1824 • FAX(856)358-6998 • johnstca@bellatlantic.net
**CARNEYS POINT—*TRINITY*** (609)299-4304
Vacant • H • NJ • 320 Georgetown Rd Carneys Point NJ 08069-2510 • FAX(609)299-4304
**CLARK—*ZION*** (732)382-7320
Andrew J Dzurovcik • H • EC • S • 559 Raritan Rd Clark NJ 07066-2233 • FAX(732)382-7512 • dzurovcik@aol.com
**CLIFFSIDE PARK—*TRINITY*** (201)943-0088
John H Schroter • H • NJ • 238 Columbia Ave Cliffside Park NJ 07010-2404
**CLIFTON—*ST JOHN*** (973)778-1412
Vacant • WS 9; BC 1015;* • H • NJ • 810 Broad St Clifton NJ 07013 • FAX(973)778-1412
***ST MATTHEW DF*** (973)614-9060
Eric R Ziegler • H • NJ • 63 Madison Ave Clifton NJ 07011-2716 • FAX(973)614-1737
**CLOSTER—*ST PAUL*** (201)768-6310
Robert W Holsten George E Lofmark(#) • H • NJ • 171 Closter Dock Rd Closter NJ 07624-1907 • FAX(201)768-6444 • weich52@ix.net.com.com
**DAYTON—*FAITH*** (908)329-8480
Ariel H Hidalgo • NJ • 410 Ridge Rd 08810-1324 PO Box 460 Dayton NJ 08810-0460
**EAST BRUNSWICK—*CHRIST*** (732)251-5454
Kenneth W Haupt • WS 830 10; SS 10 • H • EC • NJ • 114 Old Stage Rd East Brunswick NJ 08816-4818 • FAX(732)723-9026 • cmlc-ebnj@juno.com
**EAST RUTHERFORD—*IMMANUEL*** (201)939-2386
Barry L Casaday • NJ • 78 Washington Pl East Rutherford NJ 07073-1342
**ELIZABETH—*ST LUKE*** (908)352-5487
James F Pemberton • * • H • NJ • 7 Hillside Rd Elizabeth NJ 07208-1209 • jayfrank@juno.com
**ENGLISHTOWN—*ST THOMAS*** (908)431-3344
Kenneth Fosse • H • NJ • 07726 203 Taylors Mill Rd Manalapan NJ 07726-3201
**FAIR LAWN—*OUR SAVIOR*** (201)796-3007
Terry R Herzberg • * • H • EC • NJ • 22-15 Broadway Fair Lawn NJ 07410-3014 • FAX(201)796-7949 • oursavior3@juno.com
**FLEMINGTON—*ST PAUL*** (908)782-5120
Otto A Reinbacher • WS 815 945;* • H • EC/EL • NJ • 201 State Route 31 Flemington NJ 08822-5737 • FAX(908)782-1633
**FORDS—*OUR REDEEMER*** (732)738-7470
David L Yarrington Arthur R Kreyling(#) • WS 815; SS 930; BC 930 • H • EC/EL • NJ • 28 S 4th St Fords NJ 08863-1647 • FAX(732)738-6547

**GALLOWAY TOWNSHIP—*PEACE*** (609)748-1777
Joel C Elowsky(DM) • H • S • Great Creek And Pitney Rds 328 E Great Creek Rd Absecon NJ 08201-9621 • Joelowsky@Juno.com

**GARFIELD—*HOLY TRINITY*** (973)478-7434
Vacant • WS 10;* • H • EC • S • 340 Palisade Ave 07026-2808 85 Summit Ave Garfield NJ 07026-2815 • FAX(973)478-7434

**HACKETTSTOWN—*GETHSEMANE*** (908)852-2156
Ronald K Ewell • H • EC • NJ • 409 E Baldwin St Hackettstown NJ 07840-1422 • FAX(908)852-8556

**HAMBURG 2 SW—*PRINCE PEACE*** (973)827-5080
Stephen Vogt • H • EC • NJ • 3320 State Hwy 94 07419 PO Box 5 Hamburg NJ 07419-0005

**HAMPTON—*OUR SAVIOR***
See Perryville

**HARRISON—*ST JOHN*** (973)483-4938
Evan W Haener • * • NJ • 500 Davis Ave Harrison NJ 07029-1214

**HOPEWELL TWP—*ST PETER*** (609)466-0939
Stephen A Gewecke • WS 8;* • H • EC • NJ • Rt 518 And 579 Hopewell Twp 1608 Harbourton Rocktown Rd Lambertville NJ 08530-3004

**HOWELL—*PRINCE PEACE*** (732)363-0732
James R Pierce • WS 815 1015;* • H • NJ • 434 Aldrich Rd Howell NJ 07731-1862 • FAX(732)367-2544 • jrphwll@woldshare.net

**JACKSON—*PEACE IN CHRIST*** (732)928-2727
Phillip S Grovenstein • H • NJ • 256 Toms River Rd Jackson NJ 08527 • FAX(732)928-2727

**LAKEHURST—*REDEEMER*** (732)657-2828
Jeffrey E Skopak • Jennifer A Brown DCE • WS 830;* • H • EC • S • 2309 Highway 70 E Lakehurst NJ 08733-3641 • FAX(732)657-7462 • redeemer@adelphia.net

**LAMBERTVILLE—*ST PETER***
See Hopewell Twp

**LANOKA HARBOR—*VILLAGE*** (609)693-1333
Roy W Minnix • WS 1030 745;* • H • NJ • 701 Western Blvd Lanoka Harbor NJ 08734-1536 • FAX(609)693-6975 • anthrax573@aol.com

**LAWRENCEVILLE—*HOLY TRINITY*** (609)882-7891
Vacant • H • NJ • 2730 Princeton Pike Lawrenceville NJ 08648-3221 • FAX(609)882-7891 • holytrinitylutheranchurch@juno.com

**LIVINGSTON—*GRACE*** (973)992-0145
L R Vossler Jr. • H • NJ • 304 S Livingston Ave Livingston NJ 07039-3924 • FAX(917)677-7925 • glc07039@juno.com

**LYNDHURST—*ST MATTHEW*** (201)939-2134
Eric A Rieker • NJ • Valley Brook and Travers Lyndhurst NJ 07071-1812

**MAHWAH—*HOLY CROSS*** (201)529-2117
Dennis J Krueger • * • H • EC • NJ • 125 Glasgow Ter Mahwah NJ 07430-1635 • FAX(201)529-5538 • hcrevdk@aol.com

**MANCHESTER TWP—*REDEEMER***
See Lakehurst

**MAYWOOD—*ZION*** (201)843-5916
Vacant • WS 9; BC 1030;* • H • EC • NJ • 120 E Pleasant Ave Maywood NJ 07607-1319 • FAX(201)843-4109

**MEDFORD—*CALVARY*** (609)654-2489
Robert R Mueller • WS 10; BC 9;* • H • EC • NJ • Hwy 70 At 3 Eayrestown Rd 08055 3 Eayrestown Rd Medford NJ 08055-3940 • FAX(609)953-0432 • calvarynjd@aol.com

**MONTVILLE—*HOLY SPIRIT*** (973)263-1696
John M Rieker • H • NJ • 70 River Rd Montville NJ 07045-9449 • johnch1v29@aol.com

**MORRIS PLAINS—*TRINITY*** (973)538-7606
Daniel M Schmalz • H • NJ • 131 Mountain Way Morris Plains NJ 07950-2239 • FAX(973)538-6763

**MOUNT LAUREL—*CROWN OF LIFE*** (856)439-0104
Vacant • WS 10;* • H • EN • 65 Elbo Ln 08054 3 Bastian Dr Mount Laurel NJ 08054-3029

**MOUNTAIN LAKES—*KING OF KINGS*** (973)334-8333
Mark L Bartels • H • EC • NJ • Route 46 Mountain Lakes NJ 07046-9806 • FAX(973)334-8333

**NEW EGYPT—*ROSE OF SHARON*** (609)758-3680
Vacant • WS 9;* • EC • NJ • 18 Horverstown Rd Creamridge 08533 PO Box 72 New Egypt NJ 08533-0072

**NEW MILFORD—*ST MATTHEW*** (201)262-5092
Jack D Wangerin • NJ • 225 Center St 07646-1649 Center and St Matthews Way New Milford NJ 07646

**NEWARK—*CHRIST ASSEMBLY*** (973)268-7815
Vacant • NJ • 664 Broadway Newark NJ 07104

***REDEEMER*** (201)485-5557
Vacant • WS 9 • NJ • 664 Broadway Newark NJ 07104-3431

***ST MATTHEW DF***
See Clifton

**NEWTON—*REDEEMER*** (973)383-3945
Thomas E Diamond • BC 945;* • H • EC • NJ • 37 Newton Sparta Rd Newton NJ 07860-2745 • FAX(973)383-3954

**NORTH BERGEN—*OUR SAVIOUR*** (201)868-5948
Marcel Hart • NJ • 605 76th St North Bergen NJ 07047-4905

**OAK RIDGE—*HOLY FAITH*** (973)697-6060
Craig E Lutz • WS 9; BC 1030 930;* • H • EC • NJ • 104 Paradise Rd Oak Ridge NJ 07438-8936 • FAX(973)697-6060 • holyfaith@juno.com

**OLD BRIDGE—*GOOD SHEPHERD*** (732)679-8883
Norman L Johnson • * • H • EC • NJ • 3139 County Road 516 Old Bridge NJ 08857-2371 • FAX(732)679-8996 • pastorj@lc-goodshepherd.org

**PALISADES PARK—*GRACE*** (201)944-2107
Vacant • H • EN • 07650 129 Broad Ave Palisades Park NJ 07650-1456

***HOPE*** (201)944-2107
Michael Chung • EN • 9 E Homestead Ave Palisades Park NJ 07650

**PATERSON—*ST LUKE*** (201)279-8046
Vacant • H • NJ • 204 Madison Ave Paterson NJ 07524-1812

**PENNSAUKEN—*MARTIN LUTHER*** (856)665-0116
Larry M Vogel • WS 10; SS 845; BC 845;* • H • EC/EL • EN • 4100 Terrace Ave Pennsauken NJ 08109-1626 • FAX(856)665-0130

**PERRYVILLE—*OUR SAVIOR*** (908)735-2062
Ronald E Smith • * • H • NJ • UKNWN 142 Perryville Rd Hampton NJ 08827-4221

**PLAINFIELD—*MESSIAH*** (908)755-4525
Robert H Vogel • WS 11;* • H • EC • NJ • 630 E Front St Plainfield NJ 07060-1414

**POINT PLEASANT—*GOOD SHEPHERD*** (732)892-4492
Christian L Schonberg • WS 815 11; BC 930;* • H • NJ • 708 Ocean Rd Point Pleasant NJ 08742-4059 • FAX(732)899-3605

**POMPTON LAKES—*INCARNATION*** (973)835-5537
Vacant • H • NJ • 220 Hamburg Tpke Pompton Lakes NJ 07442-1802

***ST PAUL*** (973)278-6542
Robert J Palkewick • H • NJ • 220 Hamburg Tpke Pompton Lakes NJ 07442-1802

**PRINCETON—*MESSIAH*** (609)924-3642
John M Goerss • SS 9; BC 9;* • H • EN • 407 Nassau St Princeton NJ 08540-4603

**RANDOLPH—*GOOD SHEPHERD*** (973)366-4267
Vacant • H • NJ • 319 Quaker Church Rd Randolph NJ 07869-1314 • FAX(973)366-0883

**RARITAN—*ST PAUL*** (908)722-6111
Phillip T Miksad • H • S • 15 W Somerset St Raritan NJ 08869-2028 • ptmiksad@aol.com

**RIDGEWOOD—*BETHLEHEM*** (201)444-3600
Andrew D Nelson Louis C Meyer(EM) • * • H • NJ • 155 Linwood Ave Ridgewood NJ 07450-2623 • FAX(201)444-2549

**RINGWOOD—*CHRIST KING*** (973)962-6384
Thomas L Edge • H • EC • NJ • 50 Erskine Rd Ringwood NJ 07456-2150 • christtheking3@juno.com

**SMITHVILLE—*PEACE***
See Galloway Township

**SOMERSET—*HOLY TRINITY*** (732)873-2888
Donald M Hobratschk • WS 10;* • H • NJ • 1640 Amwell Rd Somerset NJ 08873-2862 • FAX(732)846-7379 • 70167.2523@compuserve.com

**STANHOPE—*OUR SAVIOR*** (973)347-1212
Arthur R Doring • EC • NJ • 143 Brooklyn Rd Stanhope NJ 07874-2869 • FAX(973)347-1818

**TINTON FALLS—*LUTHER MEMORIAL*** (732)542-2727
Paul R Huneke • * • H • NJ • 818 Tinton Ave Tinton Falls NJ 07724-2847 • phuneke@monmouth.com

**TRENTON—*BETHANY*** (609)883-2860
Philip R Matarazzo • SS 1030;* • H • EN • 1125 Parkside Ave Trenton NJ 08618-2625

***HOLY TRINITY***
See Lawrenceville

**UNION—*GRACE*** (908)686-3965
Donald L Brand • * • H • EC • NJ • 2222 Vauxhall Rd Union NJ 07083-5825 • FAX(908)686-5111

**VERONA—*CALVARY*** (973)239-0577
Gregg S Ramirez Erwin C Wackenhuth • * • H • NJ • 23 S Prospect St Verona NJ 07044-1507 • FAX(973)239-6703 • calvaryverona@earthlink.net

**WAYNE—*INCARNATION***
See Pompton Lakes

**WEST NEW YORK—*SAN PABLO*** (201)348-0004
Eric R Ziegler • EC • NJ • 5106 Palisade Ave West New York NJ 07093-1919 • FAX(201)348-0004

**WESTFIELD—*REDEEMER*** (908)232-1517
Paul E Kritsch Robert H Vogel • WS 830 11;* • H • EL • NJ • 229 Cowperthwaite Pl Westfield NJ 07090-4015 • FAX(908)317-9301

**WESTWOOD—*ZION*** (201)664-1325
Robert M Roegner • * • H • EC/EL • NJ • 155 2nd Ave Westwood NJ 07675-2133 • FAX(201)664-4393 • zionlutheranwwnj@yahoo.com

## NEW MEXICO

**ALAMOGORDO—*TRINITY*** (505)437-1482
David R Bergman • H • RM • 1505 College Ave Alamogordo NM 88310

**ALBUQUERQUE—*CHRIST*** (505)884-3876
Gregory G Werdin • WS 815 11; SS 945; BC 945 • H • EC/EL • RM • 7701 Candelaria Rd NE Albuquerque NM 87110-2752 • FAX(505)888-0655 • clc@lobo.net

***FAITH CHRIST*** (505)292-5673
Roger C Wohletz • H • RM • Chelwood At Indian School Rd 87101 1750 Faith Ct NE Albuquerque NM 87112-4630

***GRACE*** (505)823-9100
Randall L Golter • WS 9; SS 1030;* • H • RM • 7550 Eubank Blvd NE Albuquerque NM 87122-3200 • FAX(505)823-1681 • rlgolter@juno.com

***IMMANUEL*** (505)242-0616
Randy W Walquist • H • EL • RM • 300 Gold Ave SE Albuquerque NM 87102-3537 • FAX(505)242-0616 • prwalquist@aol.com

***OUR SAVIOR*** (505)836-7007
Michael D Erickson • WS 9; SS 1030; BC 930 • H • EC • RM • 4301 Atrisco Dr NW Albuquerque NM 87120-1662 • FAX(505)836-0082 • oslc@flash.net

***REDEEMER*** (505)256-9881
John Heffelfinger • H • RM • 210 Alvarado Dr SE Albuquerque NM 87108-2929 • FAX(505)268-6842 • rlchurch@flash.net

***SHEPHERD/HILLS***
See Rio Rancho

***TRINITY*** (505)344-9323
Vacant • H • RM • 4311 12th St NW Albuquerque NM 87107-3606 • rsenn@flash.net

**ANGEL FIRE—*CHRIST OUR SAV*** (505)377-2814
Charles L Keogh(DM) • H • RM • 13 Elliott Barker Ln 87710 PO Box 286 Angel Fire NM 87710-0286 • FAX(505)758-5944 • sdclc@laplaza.org

**ARTESIA—*IMMANUEL*** (505)748-1196
Paul E Neuberger • WS 830; BC 930;* • H • RM • 810 W Washington Ave 88210-2364 PO Box 1251 Artesia NM 88211-1251

**CARLSBAD—*IMMANUEL*** (505)885-5780
Paul E Neuberger • H • RM • 901 N Halagueno St Carlsbad NM 88220-5125 • neubs@caverns.com

**CEDAR CREST—*PRINCE OF PEACE*** (505)281-2430
John K Raess • WS 8 1030; SS 9; BC 9 • H • EC/EL • RM • 12121 Hwy N 14 87008 PO Box 1130 Cedar Crest NM 87008-1130 • FAX(505)281-2430 • jkraess@integrity.com

**CLOVIS—*IMMANUEL*** (505)763-4526
Scott R Blazek • H • EC • RM • 1021 N Prince St Clovis NM 88101-6152 • immanuel@pdrpip.com

**DEMING—*REDEEMER*** (505)546-3348
Gregory W Brown • WS 1030; BC 915;* • H • RM • 600 W Florida St 88030-4505 PO Box 261 Deming NM 88031-0261 • revgreg@zianet.com

**EDGEWOOD—*GOOD SHEPHERD*** (505)281-2013
Edward F Maas • H • RM • #5 Entrada Del Norte 87015 PO Box 1298 Edgewood NM 87015-1298 • FAX(505)281-2013 • gslcnm@juno.com

**FARMINGTON—*ZION*** (505)325-3420
Gary R Thur • H • RM • 1108 N Dustin Ave Farmington NM 87401-6166

**GALLUP—*TRINITY*** (505)863-3375
Gary A Bickner • * • H • RM • 1100 E Mesa Ave 87301-5449 PO Box 5150 Gallup NM 87305-5150

**GRANTS—*MOUNT CALVARY*** (505)287-2382
Armin F Stolp • * • H • RM • Chaco And Cordova 87020 PO Box 624 Grants NM 87020-0624

**HOBBS—*GRACE*** (505)393-4911
Michael K Erickson • WS 1030; SS 930; BC 930 • H • RM • 100 E Berry Dr Hobbs NM 88240-4418 • mkegrace@gte.net

**LAS CRUCES—*MISSION*** (505)522-0465
Ralph W E Patrick • WS 8; SS 915;* • H • EC • RM • 2752 N Roadrunner Pkwy Las Cruces NM 88011-8081 • FAX(505)532-5489 • mission@zianet.

**LAS VEGAS—*IMMANUEL*** (505)425-6833
Earnest J Hengst • H • RM • 2100 7th St Las Vegas NM 87701-4960

**LOS LUNAS—*CHRIST/KING*** (505)865-9226
Alan R Coleman • WS 9; SS 1030; BC 1030 • H • EL • RM • 700 Camelot Blvd SW Los Lunas NM 87031-8687

**LOVINGTON—*OUR SAVIOR*** (505)396-4549
Michael K Erickson • H • RM • 600 S 9th St Lovington NM 88260-4501

**PORTALES—*FAITH IN CHRIST*** (505)356-2510
Robby J Sandley • WS 9 • H • RM • 1024 W 14th Ln Portales NM 88130 • rsandley@yucca.net

**RANCHO DE TAOS—*CHRIST OUR SAV***
See Angel Fire

**RIO RANCHO—*CALVARY*** (505)892-9407
Donald H Neidigk • * • H • EC • RM • 305 Unser Blvd SE 87124-2473 PO Box 15595 Rio Rancho NM 87174-0595 • FAX(505)891-2080 • donald³neidigk@juno.com

***SHEPHERD/HILLS*** (505)891-7677
Robert J Pinta • WS 915; SS 11; BC 11;* • H • RM • 300 Frontage Rd NE Ste C 87124-1432 PO Box 15201 Rio Rancho NM 87174-0201 • FAX(505)891-7677 • rdscp@email.msn.com

**ROSWELL—*IMMANUEL*** (505)622-2853
Warren J Ruland • WS 9; SS 1020; BC 1020 • H • RM • 1405 N Sycamore Roswell NM 88201 • FAX(505)622-2853 • immanuelluthroswel@prodigy.net

**RUIDOSO—*SHEPHERD HILLS*** (505)258-4191
Kevin L Krohn • WS 1030; SS 930; BC 930;* • H • RM • 1120 Hull Rd Ruidoso NM 88345 • shlc@zianet.com

**SANTA FE—*IMMANUEL*** (505)983-7568
Douglas K Escue • * • H • EC • RM • 209 E Barcelona Rd Santa Fe NM 87501-4609 • FAX(505)983-2001 • dkescue@aol.com

**SILVER CITY—*MESSIAH*** (505)538-9446
Joseph E Pellegrino • WS 9; SS 1015;* • H • RM • 2501 N Swan St 88061-5806 PO Box 401 Silver City NM 88062-0401

**SOCORRO—*HOPE*** (505)835-9648
Douglas C May • WS 8; SS 920; BC 920 • H • RM • 908 Leroy Pl 87801-4744 PO Box 1907 Socorro NM 87801-1907 • dougmay@rt66.com

**SPRINGER—*IMMANUEL*** (505)483-2254
Earnest J Hengst • H • RM • 301 Summit Ave 87747 PO Box 213 Springer NM 87747-0213

**TAOS—*SANGRE DE CRISTO*** (505)758-5944
Charles L Keogh(DM) • H • RM • 116 Dona Ana Dr 87571 5712 NDCBU Taos NM 87571-6139 • FAX(505)758-5944 • sdclc@laplaza.org

**TRUTH CONSQ—*ST JOHN*** (505)894-3103
Theodore E Allwardt Sr. • WS 830;* • H • RM • 1220 Marshall St 87901-3685 1405 Tin St Truth/Consequences NM 87901-3659

## NEW YORK

**AKRON—*ST MICHAEL***
See Wolcottsville

**ALBANY—*CHRIST*** (518)456-1530
Paul G Behling • H • EC • AT • 1500 Western Ave Albany NY 12203-3525 • FAX(518)456-3526

***OUR SAVIOR***
See Colonie

***ST MATTHEW*** (518)436-8672
Vacant • WS 1030 • H • EC • AT • 75 Whitehall Rd Albany NY 12209-1436 • FAX(518)463-9417

***ST PAUL*** (518)463-0571
William G Hempel III • * • H • EC • AT • 475 State St Albany NY 12203-1004 • FAX(518)598-1447 • splc475@juno.com

**ALLEGANY—*ST JOHN*** (716)373-0025
Gerard F Le Feber • WS 10; SS 830; BC 830 • H • EA • 36 N 4th St Allegany NY 14706-1014

**AMHERST—*CALVARY*** (716)833-7300
Karl E Schmidt • H • EN • 4110 Bailey Ave Amherst NY 14226-2923

**AMITYVILLE—*ST PAUL*** (516)264-0763
David W Anglin • H • EL/HS • AT • 147 Park Ave Amityville NY 11701-3193 • FAX(516)264-0372

**ANGELICA—*ST PAUL***
See Town Of Allen

**ANGOLA—*ST JOHN*** (716)549-2144
Donald A Loos • H • EA • 962 Gold St Angola NY 14006-9607 • FAX(716)549-2144

**AQUEBOGUE—*OUR REDEEMER*** (631)722-4000
Charles R Byer • WS 8 1030; SS 915; BC 930 • H • EC/EL • AT • 265 Main Rd 11901 PO Box 960 Aquebogue NY 11931-0960

***OUR REDEEMER***
See Riverhead

**ASHFORD—*TRINITY*** (716)699-2265
William L Kay • H • EA • Dutch Hill Rd UKNWN PO Box 656 Ellicottville NY 14731-0656 • FAX(716)699-8402 • skitownchurch@juno.com

**AUBURN—*REDEEMER*** (315)252-7409
Vacant • H • EA • 10 Prospect St Auburn NY 13021-1610

**BAYSIDE—*GLORY KOREAN***
Vacant • AT • 210-10 Horace Harding Blvd Bayside NY 11364

***IMMANUEL CHINESE*** (718)229-4738
John C P Li Jukka A Kaariainen(DM) • H • AT • 21010 Horace Harding Expway Bayside NY 11364

***IMMANUEL KOREAN***
See Flushing

***REDEEMER*** (718)229-5770
Vacant • * • H • HS • AT • 3601 Bell Blvd Bayside NY 11361-2056 • FAX(718)229-5770

**BERGHOLTZ—*HOLY GHOST*** (716)731-5877
Philip N Sallach • WS 8; BC 9;* • H • EC/EL • EA • Niagara Rd UKNWN 6630 Luther St Niagara Falls NY 14304-2011 • FAX(716)731-3030 • lcmshg@aol.com

**BETHPAGE—*ST PAUL*** (516)931-8262
Vacant • * • H • EL/HS • AT • 449 Stewart Ave Bethpage NY 11714-2720 • FAX(516)827-0882

**BILLINGS—*ALL SAINTS***
See Lagrangeville

**BOSTON—*ST MARTIN*** (716)941-3335
Ronald R Sprehe • WS 1030;* • EA • 14025 8304 Cole Rd Colden NY 14033-9742 • FAX(716)941-9124

**BROCKPORT—*CONCORDIA*** (716)637-5930
Carl E Klug • H • EA • 6601 4th Section Rd Brockport NY 14420-2447 • FAX(716)637-5930

**BRONX—*GRACE*** (718)295-4766
Vacant • EL • AT • 2930 Valentine Ave Bronx NY 10458-2608 • FAX(718)365-2314

***OUR SAVIOUR*** (718)792-5665
Vacant • * • H • EC/EL • AT • 1734 Williamsbridge Rd Bronx NY 10461-6204 • FAX(718)409-3877 • ousalubn@aol.com

***REDEEMER*** (718)324-1288
Vacant • * • AT • 4360 Boyd Ave Bronx NY 10466-1804

***ST PAUL TREMONT*** (718)583-7978
Lynell H Carter • WS 11;* • AT • 1984 Crotona Ave Bronx NY 10457-5022

***TRINITY*** (718)828-1234
John R Hannah Dien A Taylor • WS 930 • EC/EL • AT • Watson And Olmstead 10431 2125 Watson Ave Bronx NY 10472-5401 • FAX(718)828-3474

**BRONXVILLE—*THE VILLAGE*** (914)337-0207
James C Zwernemann Robert E Hartwell • Meta J Johnson DCE • EC/EL • AT • 172 White Plains Rd Bronxville NY 10708-1954 • FAX(914)771-9711 • villagel@bestweb.net

**BROOKLYN—*GOOD SHEPHERD*** (718)338-5532
Frank G Ciampa • AT • 2142 New York Ave Brooklyn NY 11210-5424 • FAX(718)338-5532 • haroldhb@aol.com

***RISEN CHRIST*** (718)498-3848
Eugene A Koene • H • EC/EL • AT • 250 Blake Ave Brooklyn NY 11212-5502 • FAX(718)498-7786

***ST JOHN EVANGELIST*** (718)963-2100
Vacant • EL/HS • AT • 195 Maujer St Brooklyn NY 11206-1332

***ST MARK*** (718)453-4040
Paul Nordeen(X) • EC/EL/HS • AT • 626 Bushwick Ave Brooklyn NY 11206-6024 • FAX(718)455-5484

***ST MATTHEW*** (718)649-1879
Christoph M Schulze • AT • 1187 E 92nd St Brooklyn NY 11236-3926

***ST PAUL*** (718)443-2220
Christoph M Schulze • H • HS • AT • 592 Knickerbocker Ave Brooklyn NY 11221-4739

***ST PETER*** (718)647-1007
David H Benke • WS 10 1230; SS 10; BC 1130;* • EC/HS • AT • 105 Highland Pl Brooklyn NY 11208-1222 • FAX(718)647-9260

***TRINITY*** (718)745-0138
Michael A Bergbower • AT • 9020 3rd Ave Brooklyn NY 11209-5708

**BUFFALO—*BETHANY*** (716)832-3374
Vacant • EA • 2930 Bailey Ave Buffalo NY 14215-2835 • FAX(716)832-3374

***IMMANUEL*** (716)896-8035
Vacant • EA • 1084 E Lovejoy St Buffalo NY 14206-1127

***LA SANTA CRUZ*** (716)855-1090
Vacant • H • EA • 451 Niagara St 14201-1834 PO Box 209 Buffalo NY 14201-0209 • FAX(716)852-5407

***NAZARETH*** (716)876-1787
Paul R Koehn • WS 1030; SS 915; BC 915;* • H • EC/EL • EN • 265 Skillen St Buffalo NY 14207-1633 • FAX(716)876-7709

***OUR SAVIOR*** (716)885-1108
Vacant • H • EA • 26 Brunswick Blvd Buffalo NY 14208-1538 • FAX(716)883-5480

***SALEM*** (716)824-2787
Vacant • WS 1030;* • EA • 10 Mc Clellan Cir Buffalo NY 14220-1901 • FAX(716)824-3193

***ST PAUL*** (716)824-3326
Vacant • EA • 132 Scoville Ave 14206-2935 PO Box 3289 Buffalo NY 14240-3289 • FAX(716)824-3326

**CAIRO—*RESURRECTION*** (518)622-3286
Victor H Nelson • WS 815 1030; SS 915; BC 915;* • H • EC • AT • Rtes 23b And 32 12413 PO Box 563 Cairo NY 12413-0563 • resurrectionluch@cs.com

**CANANDAIGUA—*GOOD SHEPHERD*** (716)394-2760
Donald M Muller • WS 815 1030; SS 915; BC 915 • H • EC • EA • 320 S Pearl St 14424-1748 PO Box 690 Canandaigua NY 14424-0690 • FAX(716)394-2760 • rockyam@aol.com

**CENTEREACH—*OUR SAVIOR*** (516)588-2757
Ronald W Stelzer • H • EC/EL • AT • 140 Mark Tree Rd Centereach NY 11720-2220 • FAX(516)588-2617

**CENTRAL ISLIP—*GRACE*** (516)234-8524
Eddie Morales • H • EC • AT • 75 Calebs Path Central Islip NY 11722-1805

**CHEEKTOWAGA—*ST LUKE*** (716)633-6752
Chris C Wicher • WS 7;* • H • EC • EA • 900 Maryvale Dr Cheektowaga NY 14225-2702 • FAX(716)635-0718

**CHENANGO BRIDGE—*HOLY TRINITY*** (607)648-8104
David C Werly • WS 930; SS 1045; BC 1045 • H • EA • 216 Kattelville Rd 13745 PO Box 229 Chenango Bridge NY 13745-0229 • FAX(607)648-8104

**CLARENCE—*HOLY CROSS*** (716)634-2332
Keith E Enko • WS 1015;* • H • EA • 8900 Sheridan Dr Clarence NY 14031-1420 • FAX(716)634-2332

**CLYDE—*ST PAUL***
Vacant • EA • 48 Caroline St Clyde NY 14433-1315 • FAX(315)539-6225 • dstruss@flare.net

**COHOCTON—*ST PAUL*** (716)384-5667
Vacant • WS 9;* • H • EC • EA • 97 Maple Ave 14826-9712 PO Box 316 Cohocton NY 14826-0316 • FAX(716)384-5667 • stpaulcohocton@juno.com

**COLDEN—*REDEEMER*** (716)941-5419
James Murr • EA • Heath And Supervisor Ave 14033 8740 Supervisor Ave Colden NY 14033-9612 • FAX(716)941-6040

***ST MARTIN***
See Boston

**COLLEGE POINT—*ST JOHN*** (718)463-4790
Arthur L Gillespie • Daniel D Rath DCE • * • EL/HS • AT • 2201 123rd St 11356-2638 12307 22nd Ave College Point NY 11356-2644 • FAX(718)463-4795 • stjohnscpt@lutheran.com

**COLONIE—*OUR SAVIOR*** (518)459-2248
L K Cobb • WS 8 11; SS 945; BC 945 • H • EC/EL • AT • 12201 63 Mountain View Ave Albany NY 12205-2228 • FAX(518)459-1330 • info@oursaviorschurch.com

**CORNING—*FAITH*** (607)962-4970
Gerhard P Grabenhofer • WS 11; SS 930;* • EA • 71 W 1st St Corning NY 14830-2543

**CORONA—*EMANUEL*** (718)424-2211
Vacant • HS • AT • 3757 104th St Corona NY 11368-1947

**CORTLAND—*ST PAUL*** (607)753-7101
Thomas E Block • * • H • EC • EA • 122 Madison St 13045-1710 49 Hamlin St Cortland NY 13045-1706 • FAX(607)753-7101

**DELMAR—*BETHLEHEM*** (518)439-4328
Warren Winterhoff Mark A Mueller • * • H • AT • 85 Elm Ave Delmar NY 12054-3701 • blutheran@juno.com

**DEPEW—*ST JOHN*** (716)683-3947
Michael C Blackwell • * • H • EC • EA • 67 Litchfield Ave Depew NY 14043-3207 • FAX(716)683-3295

**DIX HILLS—*ST LUKE*** (516)499-8656
Charles W Froehlich Stanley G Macholz(EM) • * • H • EC/EL/HS • AT • 20 Candlewood Path Dix Hills NY 11746-5304 • FAX(516)462-6496 • cwkjf@aol.com

**DONAGAN HILLS—*ST MATTHEW***
See Staten Island

**EAST AURORA—*IMMANUEL*** (716)652-4240
Robert J Knepel • WS 8 1015; BC 9;* • H • EA • Pine St And Fillmore Ave 14052 43 Pine St East Aurora NY 14052-1821 • FAX(716)652-4240

**EAST AVON—*EPIPHANY*** (716)226-2200
Vacant • H • EA • 6050 Avon Rd East Avon NY 14414-2127 • FAX(716)226-2200

**EAST GREENBUSH—*LOVE*** (518)477-8685
Vacant • H • AT • Pheasant Ln And Middlesex Rd 12061 PO Box 118 East Greenbush NY 12061-0118

**EAST MEADOW—*CALVARY*** (516)735-1473
Vacant • WS 830 10; SS 10;* • H • EC/EL/HS • AT • Taylor Ave And Bush St 11554 36 Taylor Ave East Meadow NY 11554-2126 • FAX(516)735-1804

**EAST MORICHES—*CHRIST*** (631)878-2277
John G Fleischmann • * • AT • 100 Frowein Rd 11940 PO Box 580 East Moriches NY 11940-0580 • FAX(631)878-8672 • resqrev@gateway.net

**EDEN TWP—*ST PAUL*** (716)992-9112
Frederick C Jacobi • Steven W Durheim DCE • * • H • EA • 14057 3487 N Boston Rd Eden NY 14057-9507 • FAX(716)992-3113 • EAJ821@aol.com

**ELLICOTTVILLE—*ST PAUL*** (716)699-2265
William L Kay • H • EA • 6360 Route 242 E 14731-9504 PO Box 656 Ellicottville NY 14731-0656 • FAX(716)699-8402 • skitownchurch@juno.com

***TRINITY***
See Ashford

**ELMA—*FAITH*** (716)652-2221
Bruce B Morris • WS 9; SS 1030; BC 1030;* • H • EC • EA • Corner Of Bowen And Jamison Rd 14059 1230 Bowen Rd Elma NY 14059-8906 • FAX(716)652-2386

**ELMHURST—*ST MATTHEW DF*** (718)478-2108
Vacant • WS 11 • H • AT • 41-01 75th St Elmhurst NY 11373-1851 • FAX(718)478-7296 • stmattluth@juno.com

**FAIRPORT—*RISEN CHRIST***
See Rochester

**FARMINGTON TOWN OF—*ST JOHN*** (315)986-3045
Carl A Prostka • WS 830 11; SS 945 • H • EC • EA • 14425 153 Church Ave Farmington NY 14425-7025 • FAX(315)986-3045 • stjohns6@juno.com

**FILLMORE 10 SE—*ST PAUL***
See Town Of Allen

**FISHKILL—*OUR SAVIOR*** (845)897-4423
Jeffrey L Scheich • * • H • EC • AT • 1022 Route 52 12524-1619 1400 Route 52 Fishkill NY 12524 • FAX(419)715-4906 • oslcfish@aol.com

**FLUSHING—*ASCENSION***
See Jamaica

***CHAPEL REDEEMER*** (718)465-4236
Larry F Hendricks • BC 9;* • H • EC/EL/HS • AT • 220-16 Union Turnpike Flushing NY 11364-3543 • FAX(718)465-2808 • hendricksrev@msn.com

***RESURRECTION*** (718)463-4292
David A Elseroad • HS • AT • 4410 192nd St Flushing NY 11358-3434 • FAX(718)463-4677 • resurchurch@worldnet.att.net

***ST JOHN*** (718)463-2959
Ronald W Lehenbauer • WS 1030; SS 911; BC 911;* • HS • AT • 14746 Sanford Ave Flushing NY 11355-1254 • FAX(718)463-2959 • is40v31@aol.com

**FREDONIA—*ST PAUL*** (716)672-6731
George F Fyler III • H • EA • 334 Temple St Fredonia NY 14063-1018 • FAX(716)672-6731

**FULTON—*OUR SAVIOUR***
Vacant • H • EA • 13069 C/O Reverend David S Belasic 5111 Main St Williamsville NY 14221-5295

**GARDEN CITY—*RESURRECTION*** (516)746-4426
William J Meyer William A Harmon • * • H • EC/EL/HS • AT • 420 Stewart Ave Garden City NY 11530-4620 • FAX(516)746-6638 • choffice2@juno.com

**GLEN COVE—*TRINITY*** (516)676-1340
Jessie A Forrest • * • EC/EL/HS • AT • 74 Forest Ave Glen Cove NY 11542-2111

**GLENDALE—*REDEEMER*** (718)456-5292
Edward J Callahan • EC/EL/HS • AT • 6907 Cooper Ave Glendale NY 11385-7123 • FAX(718)821-3313

***ST JOHN*** (718)847-3188
William C Fischer • WS 845 1115;* • H • EC/EL/HS • AT • 8824 Myrtle Ave Glendale NY 11385-7821 • FAX(718)805-4735

**GLENS FALLS—*GOOD SHEPHERD*** (518)792-7971
William B Eberle • WS 8; SS 930; BC 930 • H • AT • 543 Glen St Glens Falls NY 12801-2207 • 9slc@netheaven.com

**GOWANDA—*IMMANUEL*** (716)532-4342
Travis S Grubbs • H • EC/EL • EA • 40 S Chapel St Gowanda NY 14070-1304 • FAX(716)532-9596

**HAMBURG—*GRACE*** (716)649-6581
Vacant • Robert J Brantsch DCE • WS 815 1045; SS 930; BC 930 • H • EA • S6220 Mc Kinley Pkwy Hamburg NY 14075-5330 • FAX(716)649-7733

**HAMLIN—*ST JOHN*** (716)964-2550
Thees C Hoft • WS 830 10;* • EC/EL • EA • 1107 Lake Rd West Fork Hamlin NY 14464-9601 • FAX(716)964-5859 • shepherd99@juno.com

**HAMPTON BAYS—*CHRIST OUR*** (631)728-3288
John A Kenreich • * • H • AT • 9 Terrace Dr Hampton Bays NY 11946-3518 • FAX(631)728-6716 • bkrouse@peconic.net

**HASTINGS-ON-HUDSON—*ST*** (914)478-1071
Andrew W Jagow Alan G Steinberg • H • AT • 10706 7 Farragut Ave Hastings On Hudson NY 10706-2304 • FAX(914)478-1071

**HAWTHORNE—*TRINITY*** (914)769-2546
Vacant • * • EC • AT • 292 Elwood Ave Hawthorne NY 10532-1861 • FAX(914)769-5326

**HENRIETTA—*PINNACLE*** (716)334-1392
Charles E Whited Jr. • WS 815 930 11; SS 930; BC 930;* • H • EC • EA • 14467 250 Pinnacle Rd Rochester NY 14623-1842 • FAX(716)334-6022 • revwhited@juno.com or revcew@flash.net

**HICKSVILLE—*TRINITY*** (516)931-2225
Wayne D Puls Michael W Cartwright • Marie A Dettling DCE • WS 815 945 1115;* • H • EC/EL/HS • AT • 40 W Nicholai St Hicksville NY 11801-3806 • FAX(516)931-6345

**HILTON—*ST PAUL*** (716)392-4000
Albert P Zoller • H • EC/EL • EA • 158 East Ave Hilton NY 14468-1318 • FAX(716)392-4001

**HOLBROOK—*ST JOHN*** (631)588-6050
William W Bloom • H • EC • AT • 1675 Coates Ave Holbrook NY 11741-2413 • FAX(631)588-8159

**HUDSON—*SAINT MARK***
Vacant • AT • 8 Storm Ave Hudson NY 12534

***ST MATTHEW*** (518)828-1172
Jeffrey N Webb • H • AT • 428 State St 12534-1914 PO Box 245 Hudson NY 12534-0245

**HYDE PARK—*ST TIMOTHY*** (845)229-2758
Vacant • WS 10;* • AT • 1348 Route 9G Hyde Park NY 12538-2139

**INTERLAKEN—*CHRIST*** (607)869-9734
Vacant • H • EA • 7966 Cr 153 On Cayuga Lake 8637 Route 89 Interlaken NY 14847 • FAX(607)869-5442

**ISLIP—*TRINITY*** (516)277-1555
David G Wackenhuth • SS 10;* • H • EC • AT • 111 Nassau Ave Islip NY 11751-3626 • FAX(516)277-3134

**ITHACA—*TRINITY*** (607)273-9017
Robert M Foote • SS 9; BC 9;* • H • EC • EA • 149 Honness Ln Ithaca NY 14850-6253 • FAX(607)273-9438 • trinity@baka.com

**JACKSON HEIGHTS—*HOLY*** (718)205-4711
Vacant • WS 11; SS 11; BC 2 • AT • 35-49 70 St 1Fl 35-49 70th St 2nd Fl Jackson Heights NY 11372-3939 • joshua$^3$k@hanmail.net

***HOLY MOUNTAIN KOREAN**** 
See Flushing

**JAMAICA—*ASCENSION*** (718)969-0484
Julius B Tusty(EM) • WS 11 • AT • 8010 Main St 11435-1217 C/O Rev J B Tusty 7589 Utopia Pkwy Flushing NY 11366-1526 • FAX(718)969-0484

***GRACE*** (718)526-6290
David R Udit • AT • 14412 89th Ave Jamaica NY 11435-3616

***REDEEMER***
See Saint Albans

***TRINITY*** (718)525-3689
Vacant • H • HS • AT • 17261 Baisley Blvd Jamaica NY 11434-2614 • FAX(718)525-3354

**JAMESTOWN—*CONCORDIA*** (716)664-4101
Vacant • H • EA • 80 City View Ave Jamestown NY 14701-7576

**KENMORE—*PILGRIM*** (716)875-5485
Ben Eder • H • EN • 44 Chapel Rd Kenmore NY 14217-2060 • FAX(716)875-5485 • beneder@aol.com

**KINGSTON—*GOOD SHEPHERD*** (914)338-5262
Vacant • WS 10;* • H • AT • 12401 470 Hurley Ave Hurley NY 12443-5121 • FAX(914)338-5262

**LAGRANGEVILLE—*ALL SAINTS*** (914)223-5288
Vacant • WS 930;* • H • AT • 133 Cross Rd Lagrangeville NY 12540-5201

**LATHAM—*RESURRECTION*** (518)785-8286
Gordon W Rakow • H • AT • 645 Watervliet Shaker Rd Latham NY 12110-3622 • FAX(518)785-8286

**LAURELTON—*GOOD SHEPHERD*** (718)528-5068
Steven M Roth • WS 11; SS 930;* • HS • AT • 13452 228 St Laurelton NY 11413-2441 • FAX(718)276-5444

**LEWISTON—*ESCARPMENT*** (716)297-2167
Vacant • WS 10;* • H • EA • 5287 Bronson Dr Lewiston NY 14092 • FAX(716)297-2167 • erengstorf@aol.com

**LOCKPORT—*IMMANUEL***
See Ridgewood

***MOUNT OLIVE*** (716)434-8500
William M Carney • H • EC • EA • 6965 Chestnut Ridge Rd Lockport NY 14094-3429

***TRINITY*** (716)434-3106
Otto G Struckmann • * • H • EA • 67 Saxton St Lockport NY 14094 • FAX(716)434-4440 • tlclockport@ny.freei.net

**LOCKPORT 11 NW—*ST PETER*** (716)433-9014
David J Musall • Beverly J Craig DEAC • H • EC/EL • EA • 14094 4169 Church Rd Lockport NY 14094-9724 • stpeternr@adelphia.net

**MACEDON 3 SW—*ST JOHN***
See Farmington Town Of

**MANHATTAN—*MOUNT ZION*** (212)862-8680
Vacant • AT • UKNWN 421 W 145th St New York NY 10031-5203

***ST MARK DEAF*** (718)478-2108
Vacant • AT • UKNWN C/O Mount Zion 421 W 145th St New York NY 10031-5203

***TRUE LIGHT*** (212)962-1482
Vacant • WS 1030 1230; SS 2;* • AT • UKNWN 195 Worth St New York NY 10013-4323 • FAX(212)962-0591 • truelightchurch@juno.com

**MASTIC BEACH—*GRACE*** (516)281-8196
Vacant • SS 11 915;* • H • AT • 240 Mastic Rd 11951-1624 PO Box 496 Mastic Beach NY 11951-0496 • FAX(516)281-7871 • grace1955@juno.com

**MEDINA—*TRINITY*** (716)798-0525
Peter A Lindemann • H • EA • 1212 West Ave 14103-1742 C/O 11530 Muzel Rd Medina NY 14103-9760 • FAX(716)798-0525 • palindemann@juno.com

**MENDON—*ST MARK*** (716)624-1766
David A Peterson • H • EA • 18 Victor Mendon Rd 14506-9727 PO Box 239 Mendon NY 14506-0239 • FAX(716)624-2217 • dpeter47@frontiernet.net

**MIDDLE ISLAND—*HOLY TRINITY*** (631)924-6991
Bruce A Nathan • WS 9 11;* • H • AT • Middle Island Yaphank Rd 11953 PO Box 36 Middle Island NY 11953-0036

**MIDDLEPORT—*HOLY CROSS*** (716)735-7209
David S Triplett • WS 815;* • H • EA • 133 Telegraph Rd 14105 PO Box 128 Middleport NY 14105-0128 • FAX(716)735-7209

**MIDDLETOWN—*FAMILY FAITH*** (914)692-7075
Edward J Grant • H • AT • Bahrenburg Rd 10940 24 Edinburgh Rd Middletown NY 10941-1744

**MONROE—*ST PAUL*** (845)782-5600
Dwayne H Mau • WS 8;* • H • EC/EL • AT • 21 Still Rd Monroe NY 10950-4107 • FAX(845)782-3703 • church@stpaulmonroeny.org

**MOUNT VERNON—*IMMANUEL*** (914)478-1071
Andrew W Jagow Alan G Steinberg • H • EC • AT • 17 E Grand St Mount Vernon NY 10552-2209

**NEW HYDE PARK—*TRINITY*** (516)354-8883
Victor J Rapp • * • H • EC/EL/HS • AT • 5 Durham Rd New Hyde Park NY 11040-2018 • FAX(516)488-2602

**NEW YORK—*ALL NATIONS**** (212)333-5583
Vacant • * • EC • AT • 417 W 57th St New York NY 10019 • FAX(212)333-5864 • cfanlcms@netzero.net

***MOUNT ZION***
See Manhattan

***ST MARK DEAF***
See Manhattan

***ST MATTHEW***
See New York

***ST MATTHEW*** (212)567-5948
Vacant • EC/EL • AT • 202 Sherman Ave 200 Sherman Ave New York NY 10034-3301 • FAX(212)569-2699

***TRUE LIGHT***
See Manhattan

**NEWARK—*REDEEMER*** (315)331-0662
William F Mugnolo • H • EA • 102 Hope Ave Newark NY 14513-1309 • FAX(315)331-0662

**NEWFANE—*FAITH*** (716)778-7981
Vacant • WS 10; SS 9 • H • EA • 2730 Transit Rd Newfane NY 14108-9703 • FAX(716)778-9725 • faithnewfane@juno.com

**NEWFANE 4 SW—*CONCORDIA*** (716)751-0310
Wayne F Jagow • WS 930;* • H • EA • 14108 3121 Beebe Rd Newfane NY 14108-9623 • FAX(716)751-0310

**NIAGARA FALLS—*GRACE*** (716)283-1843
Vacant • * • H • EA • 736 Cayuga Dr Niagara Falls NY 14304-3460 • FAX(716)283-1843

***HOLY GHOST***
See Bergholtz

***OUR SAVIOR*** (716)297-3880
Vacant • * • H • EA • 2759 Military Rd Niagara Falls NY 14304-1222 • FAX(716)297-6348

**NISKAYUNA—*IMMANUEL*** (518)346-1958
Steven C Ward • H • AT • 1850 Union St Niskayuna NY 12309-4502

**NORTH TONAWANDA—*REDEEMER*** (716)692-5734
David A Beutel • EC • EN • Falconer and Thompson Sts North Tonawanda NY 14120 • dabeutel@aol.com

***ST JOHN*** (716)693-9677
Ronald D Oravec • WS 1030;* • H • EC/EL • EA • 6950 Ward Rd North Tonawanda NY 14120-1413 • jn6950@wzrd.com

***ST MARK*** (716)693-3715
Paul D Doellinger • WS 8;* • H • EC/EL • EA • 1135 Oliver St North Tonawanda NY 14120-2637 • FAX(716)693-3932 • PaulDoellinger@cs.com

***ST MATTHEW*** (716)692-6862
Adolph W Moldenhauer • WS 8 1030; SS 915; BC 915 • H • EC/EL • EA • 875 Eggert Dr North Tonawanda NY 14120-3330 • FAX(716)692-0242

***ST PAUL*** (716)692-3255
Karl W Haeussler • WS 8 1045; SS 1030; BC 1030;* • EC/EL • EA • 453 Old Falls Blvd North Tonawanda NY 14120-3107 • FAX(716)692-3643 • khaeussler@aol.com

**OLD WESTBURY—*REDEEMER*** (516)333-3355
Kenneth N Hessel • WS 1015;* • H • EC/EL/HS • AT • 1 Old Westbury Rd Old Westbury NY 11568-1603 • FAX(516)333-7046 • redeemerli@yahoo.com

**OLEAN—*IMMANUEL*** (716)372-0650
Ronald S Semsel • WS 1030;* • H • EC • EA • 417 Laurens St Olean NY 14760-2515 • FAX(716)372-5824 • ilclcms@netsync.net

**ONEIDA—*REDEEMER***
Vacant • H • EA • PO Box 274 Oneida NY 13421-0274

**ORCHARD PARK—*ST JOHN*** (716)662-4747
Dennis T Conrad • Jennifer L Schneewind DCE • WS 8 1030; BC 915;* • H • EC • EA • 4536 S Buffalo St Orchard Park NY 14127-2915 • FAX(716)667-1290 • stjohns@buffnet.net

**OTTO—*IMMANUEL*** (716)257-9581
Vacant • H • EA • E Main St 14766 PO Box 18 Otto NY 14766-0018

**OWEGO—*ZION*** (607)687-1205
David D Heitner • WS 1030; SS 915; BC 930 • H • EC/EL • EA • 3917 Waverly Rd Owego NY 13827-2841 • FAX(607)687-6375 • zionlutheran@stny.rr.com

**PATCHOGUE—*EMANUEL*** (516)758-2240
Bruce E Rudolf • Joy Akeley • H • EC/EL • AT • 179 E Main St 11772-3103 PO Box 311 Patchogue NY 11772-0311 • FAX(516)758-2418

**PAWLING—*CHRIST KING*** (914)855-3169
David F Nuss • WS 930;* • H • AT • 14 Pine Dr Pawling NY 12564-1205 • dfnuss@aol.com

**PEEKSKILL—*OUR REDEEMER*** (914)737-0527
William P Terjesen • * • AT • 714 Hudson Ave Peekskill NY 10566-3318 • terjesen@bestweb.net

**PEKIN—*ST ANDREW*** (716)731-5863
Vacant • EA • UKNWN 3229 Upper Mountain Rd Sanborn NY 14132-9104 • FAX(716)731-5863 • gregbrehm@msn.com

**PENFIELD—*FAITH*** (716)381-3970
William H Flammann • * • H • EC • EA • 14526 2576 Browncroft Blvd Rochester NY 14625-1530 • FAX(716)381-6407

**PINE ISLAND—*ST PETER*** (845)258-4541
Elwood E Mather • SS 9;* • AT • 70 Little York Rd 10969 PO Box 147 Pine Island NY 10969-0147

**POTTERSVILLE—*SONRISE***
Vacant • AT • RR 9 PO Box Pottersville NY 12860

**PUTNAM VALLEY—*ST LUKE*** (914)528-8858
Vacant • EC/EL • AT • 67 Oscawana Lk Rd 10579-3004 PO Box 64 Putnam Valley NY 10579-0064

**QUEENS—*REDEEMER***
See Saint Albans

**QUEENS NYC—*EMMAUS***
See Ridgewood

**QUEENS VILLAGE—*GRACE*** (718)465-1010
Peter B Dorn • WS 815 1045;* • EL/HS • AT • 10203 Springfield Blvd 11429-1623 10005 Springfield Blvd Queens Village NY 11429-1619 • FAX(718)465-9069 • pbdorn@aol.com

**REGO PARK—*BETH EL MESSIANIC*** (718)520-0247
Vacant • * • AT • 9214 63rd Dr 11374-2927 PO Box 1060 Forest Hills NY 11375-8660 • FAX(718)520-0247 • aplohiseye@aol.com

***OUR SAVIOUR*** (718)897-4447
David J Born David G Demera • EC/EL/HS • AT • 9214 63rd Dr 11374-2927 6433 Woodhaven Blvd Rego Park NY 11374-5051 • FAX(718)830-9275 • djborn@aol.com

**RIDGEWOOD—*EMMAUS*** (718)821-5253
John A Stoudt • WS 9 1030;* • EC/HS • AT • 6010 67th Ave Ridgewood NY 11385-4536 • FAX(718)381-6719

***IMMANUEL*** (716)434-0521
David F C Wurster • H • EC • EA • 11385 7147 Ridge Rd Lockport NY 14094-9457 • FAX(716)434-0521

**ROCHESTER—*ALPHA DEAF*** (716)461-5320
Vacant • WS 11; BC 10;* • H • EA • 1969 S Clinton Ave Rochester NY 14618-5706 • FAX(716)461-5320

***FAITH***
See Penfield

***HOPE*** (716)723-4673
Arthur C Dueker Larry S Stojkovic • WS 830 945 1115; SS 945; BC 945 • H • EC • EA • 1301 Vintage Ln Rochester NY 14626-1760 • FAX(716)723-8549

***PINNACLE***
See Henrietta

***RISEN CHRIST*** (716)223-5757
Arnold W Deknatel • H • EC • EA • 14692 1000 Moseley Rd Fairport NY 14450-3852 • FAX(716)223-5757 • risenchrist@mlsonline.org

***ST MATTHEW*** (716)423-0410
Vacant • EA • 1015 Saint Paul St 14621-5253 PO Box 67304 Rochester NY 14617-7304 • FAX(716)423-2250 • stmatt@ggw.org

**ROME—*FAITH*** (315)336-7520
Vacant • EA • 8930 Turin Rd Rome NY 13440-7406

***ST JOHN*** (315)336-8090
Charles B Hanna • H • EC • EA • 502 W Chestnut St Rome NY 13440-2620 • FAX(315)336-8091 • st$^3$john$^3$lutheran@juno.com

**SAINT ALBANS—*REDEEMER*** (718)528-7084
Wayne E Lawrence • WS 1045; BC 930;* • EN • 11601 204th St Saint Albans NY 11412-3251

**SAINT JAMES—*ST JAMES*** (631)584-5212
Kenneth E Hansen • WS 830 11;* • H • EC • AT • Woodlawn And 2nd Ave 11780 PO Box 3 Saint James NY 11780-0003 • FAX(631)862-7809

**SANBORN—*ESCARPMENT***
See Lewiston

***ST ANDREW***
See Pekin

**SARATOGA SPRINGS—*ST PAUL*** (518)584-0904
James A Jaekel Adam C Wiegand • H • EC • AT • 149 Lake Ave Saratoga Springs NY 12866-2432 • FAX(518)584-2180 • stpaulss@juno.com

**SAYVILLE—*ST JOHN*** (631)589-3202
Harry T Schenkel III • WS 9 1045; BC 8;* • H • EC • AT • 48 Greene Ave Sayville NY 11782-2734 • FAX(631)589-1419

**SCARSDALE—*TRINITY*** (914)723-1998
Merlin D Rehm • * • H • EN • Crane Rd At Woodland Pl 10583 25 Crane Rd Scarsdale NY 10583-4251

**SCHENECTADY—*IMMANUEL***
See Niskayuna

***TRINITY*** (518)346-5646
Arthur R Downing • WS 1015;* • H • AT • 35 Furman St Schenectady NY 12304-1123

***ZION*** (518)374-1811
Paul F G Wildgrube Shawn L Dugan • WS 830;* • H • EC • AT • 153 Nott Ter Schenectady NY 12308-3130 • FAX(518)374-4438 • zion.lutheran@juno.com

**SENECA FALLS—*CALVARY*** (315)539-8053
Daniel P Strussenberg • H • EC • EA • 2414 Nys Rt 414 N Waterloo Ny 13148 2993 E Bayard Street Ext Seneca Falls NY 13148-9733 • FAX(315)539-6225 • dstruss@flare.net

**SETAUKET—*MESSIAH*** (631)751-1775
Charles Bell Alfred J Hofler • * • H • EC • AT • 465 Pond Path East Setauket NY 11733-0519 • FAX(631)751-1775 • messiah$^3$lutheran$^3$church1@juno.com

**SILVER CREEK—*TRINITY*** (716)934-2002
Theodore C Dallmann • EA • 15 Porter Ave Silver Creek NY 14136-1130 • FAX(716)934-9549 • revted@netsync.net

**SPENCERPORT—*TRINITY*** (716)352-3143
Charles E Alspaugh • H • EC • EA • 191 Nichols St Spencerport NY 14559-2160 • FAX(716)352-3143

**SPRINGVILLE—*SALEM*** (716)592-4893
Timothy A Bickel • WS 9; SS 1015;* • H • EC • EA • 91 W Main St Springville NY 14141-1057 • FAX(716)592-0800 • salem73@juno.com

**STAMFORD—*TRINITY*** (607)652-2711
Vacant • WS 930 • H • AT • Route 10 HC 1 Box 4-D Stamford NY 12167

**STATEN ISLAND—*CHRIST ASSEMBLY*** (718)556-2652
Vacant • * • AT • 27 Hudson St 10304 PO Box 204 Staten Island NY 10307 • FAX(718)420-9423 • aimlcms@aol.com

***ST JOHN*** (718)761-1600
Robert S Morris • WS 815 1045; SS 930; BC 930;* • EC/EL • AT • 216 Jewett Ave 10302-1837 663 Manor Rd Staten Island NY 10314-4523 • FAX(718)761-4962 • stjohnluthsiny@aol.com

***ST MATTHEW*** (718)351-0866
Allan H Fjordbotten • H • AT • 96 Alter Ave Staten Island NY 10304-3904

**STONY POINT—*ATONEMENT*** (914)942-0121
Vacant • H • AT • 71 Central Hwy 10980-2615 PO Box 622 Stony Point NY 10980-0622 • FAX(914)942-1787

**STUYVESANT—*ST JOHN*** (518)758-1891
Jeffrey N Webb • WS 11; SS 11;* • H • AT • 159 Rt 26a 159 Route 26A Stuyvesant NY 12173 • webb@berk.com
**SYLVAN BEACH—*GOOD SHEPHERD*** (315)762-4882
Vacant • H • EA • 15th Ave And Vienna Rd 13157 PO Box 786 Sylvan Beach NY 13157-0786
**SYRACUSE—*TRINITY*** (315)437-8203
Raymond V Kirk • H • EA • 140 Swansea Dr Syracuse NY 13206-1939 • FAX(315)463-6101
**TONAWANDA—*FIRST TRINITY*** (716)835-2220
Vacant • Susan M Steege DCE • WS 845 1115;* • H • EC/EL • EA • 1570 Niagara Falls Blvd Tonawanda NY 14150-8433 • FAX(716)833-6998 • ft1570@aol.com
***IMMANUEL*** (716)692-6200
Robert L Rickus • * • EA • 107 Scott St Tonawanda NY 14150-3428 • FAX(716)692-3435
**TOWN OF ALLEN—*ST PAUL***
Vacant • WS 10; SS 11 • H • EA • County Rd 15 PO Box 472 Angelica NY 14709-0472
**UTICA—*TRINITY*** (315)732-7869
Herbert H Grieves Jr. • * • H • EC • EA • 2620 Genesee St Utica NY 13502-6003 • FAX(315)732-7869 • trinl@juno.com
**VALLEY STREAM—*OUR SAVIOUR*** (516)825-5453
Alan F Steinke • EN • 888 Rockaway Ave 11581-2102 12 Dubois Ave Valley Stream NY 11581-2121 • FAX(516)825-5453
**VESTAL—*GRACE*** (607)748-0840
Donald H Mueller • * • H • EC • EA • 709 Main St Vestal NY 13850-3199 • FAX(607)748-0840 • gracelc@stny.rr.com
**WALDEN—*TRINITY*** (845)778-7119
Raymond D Cummings Robert E Griffin(EM) • WS 8; SS 940;* • H • EC • AT • 12586 2520 State Route 208 Walden NY 12586-2816 • FAX(845)778-1193 • rdc@frontiernet.net
**WARWICK—*GOOD SHEPHERD*** (914)986-3962
Kenneth J Susskraut • * • H • EC • AT • 95 Kings Hwy 10990-3112 PO Box 218 Warwick NY 10990-0218 • FAX(914)986-3050 • gslcwarwick@yahoo.com
**WELLSVILLE—*TRINITY*** (716)593-3311
Vacant • * • H • EC • EA • 470 N Main St Wellsville NY 14895-1043 • FAX(716)593-1194 • hkitzmann@juno.com
**WEST HENRIETTA—*ST MARK*** (716)334-4795
Gary W Bauch • * • H • EC • EA • 779 Erie Station Rd 14586 PO Box 287 West Henrietta NY 14586-0287 • FAX(716)334-4795
**WEST SENECA—*TRINITY*** (716)674-9188
Vacant • * • H • EC/EL • EA • 146 Reserve Rd West Seneca NY 14224-4016 • FAX(716)674-9188
**WHITESTONE—*IMMANUEL*** (718)747-1638
David C Mueller • * • EC/EL/HS • AT • 14940 11th Ave Whitestone NY 11357-1721 • FAX(718)747-1124
**WILLISTON PARK—*ST JOHN*** (516)742-5858
Martin J Schultheis • * • EL/HS • AT • 47 Winthrop St Williston Park NY 11596-0066 • FAX(516)746-0883 • st.johns.willistonpark@erols.com
**WOLCOTTSVILLE—*ST MICHAEL*** (716)542-9638
Vacant • * • H • EA • UKNWN 6379 Wolcottsville Rd Akron NY 14001-9002
**WOODSIDE—*CHRIST*** (718)639-3945
Vernon P Schultheis • WS 830 11;* • EL/HS • AT • 3357 58th St Woodside NY 11377-2216 • FAX(718)205-1426 • clcny@aol.com
**YONKERS—*BETHANY*** (914)965-2474
Andrew W Jagow Alan G Steinberg • * • AT • 26 Willow Pl 10701 PO Box 1429 Yonkers NY 10702-1429
***HOLY TRINITY*** (914)965-3884
James A Douthwaite • S • 60 Mulberry St Yonkers NY 10701-6004
***ST MARK*** (914)237-8199
Gary J Carstens • WS 10; SS 1015; BC 1115 • H • EC/EL • AT • 7 Saint Marks Pl Yonkers NY 10704-4011 • FAX(914)237-1346 • carstens@yni.net
**YOUNGSTOWN—*ST JOHN*** (716)745-3443
Kenneth F Curry • H • EA • 420 Lockport St 14174 PO Box 365 Youngstown NY 14174-0365

## NORTH CAROLINA

**ASHEVILLE—*EMMANUEL*** (828)252-1795
R M Nieting Robert O Liebmann • WS 8 915 11; SS 930; BC 930 • H • EC/EL • SE • 51 Wilburn Pl Asheville NC 28806-2752 • FAX(828)285-0064
**BURLINGTON—*REDEEMER*** (336)227-7092
Vacant • H • SE • 2306 Lacy St Burlington NC 27215-5343
**CARY—*RESURRECTION*** (919)851-7248
Paul D Kibler Richard L Browning • WS 8 1030 1045; SS 915;* • H • EC/EL • SE • 100 Lochmere Dr W Cary NC 27511-9129 • FAX(919)851-6411 • rlcoffice@rlcary.org
**CATAWBA—*REDEEMER*** (828)241-2371
Paul G Alms • H • SE • 200 S Main St 28609 PO Box 187 Catawba NC 28609-0187
**CHAPEL HILL—*ADVENT*** (919)968-7690
Robert A Bremer • WS 1030; SS 915; BC 915;* • H • EC • SE • 230 Erwin Rd Chapel Hill NC 27514-6855 • FAX(919)933-3233 • BobBremer@aol.com
**CHARLOTTE—*ALL SAINTS*** (704)523-4287
William D Beyer • WS 830 11;* • H • SE • 900 Seneca Pl Charlotte NC 28210-2926 • FAX(704)523-4420 • william.beyer@worldnet.att.net
***ASCENSION*** (704)372-7317
Richard H Runge • WS 830 11; SS 945; BC 945;* • H • EC/EL • SE • 1225 E Morehead St Charlotte NC 28204-2816 • FAX(704)372-7318 • Runge1225@aol.com
***CHAPEL DEAF*** (704)334-8319
Phillip M Mac Donald • H • SE • 1225 E Morehead St Charlotte NC 28204-2816 • FAX(704)372-7318 • mmacdon@juno.com
***MESSIAH*** (704)541-1624
Tim L Baldinger • Jodene A Baker DCE • WS 830 11; SS 945; BC 945 • H • EC • SE • 8300 Providence Rd Charlotte NC 28277-9752 • FAX(704)541-1292 • office@messiah-nc.org
***PRINCE OF PEACE*** (704)392-6098
Quentin G Poulson • WS 11; SS 945;* • H • SE • 3001 Beatties Ford Rd Charlotte NC 28216-3731 • FAX(704)392-6098 • popax@bellsouth.net
***RESURRECTION*** (704)377-6575
William Gittner • WS 9 11; SS 9;* • H • EC/EL • SE • 2825 Shenandoah Ave Charlotte NC 28205-6938 • FAX(704)377-6578 • res.luth.clt@juno.com
**CLAREMONT—*BETHEL*** (828)459-7378
Craig D Schultz • WS 1030; SS 915;* • H • SE • 5759 Bolick Rd Claremont NC 28610-8164 • FAX(828)459-7841
**CLYDE—*OUR SAVIOR*** (828)456-6493
John H Greene • WS 1030; SS 930;* • H • SE • 785 Paragon Pkwy Clyde NC 28721
**COLUMBUS—*TRINITY*** (828)859-0379
Matthew O Versemann • WS 10; SS 830; BC 830 • H • SE • 28722 3353 Hwy 176 Tryon NC 28782
**CONCORD—*GRACE*** (704)782-7620
Donald E Anthony • H • SE • 58 Chestnut Dr SW 28025-5244 PO Box 891 Concord NC 28026-0891 • FAX(704)795-5475 • lebuick@aol
***ST PETER*** (704)786-2507
Vacant • H • SE • 2400 Ward Ave Concord NC 28025
**CONOVER—*CONCORDIA*** (828)464-3324
Donald R Oldenburg • WS 815 1030; SS 930; BC 930 • H • EC/EL • SE • 216 5th Ave SE Conover NC 28613-1919 • FAX(828)464-3400 • donaldo@abts.net
***IMMANUEL*** (828)464-5813
Troy S Watford • H • SE • 2448 Emmanuel Church Rd 2440 Emmanuel Church Rd Conover NC 28613-9133
***ST JOHN*** (828)464-4071
Scott D Johnson • Melanie T Brunner DCE • WS 1030; SS 915;* • H • EC • SE • 2126 Saint Johns Church Rd 28613-8975 PO Box 575 Conover NC 28613-0575 • FAX(828)464-6590 • stjohnlc@twave.net
**CONOVER 8 N—*ST PETER*** (828)256-2970
Paul D Birner Paul D Sundbom • WS 815 1045; SS 930; BC 930 • H • EC • SE • 28613 6175 Saint Peters Church Rd Conover NC 28613-8752 • FAX(828)256-6633 • stplcms@twave.net
**DENVER—*LAKE NORMAN*** (704)483-2130
Ronald A Nichols • WS 9; SS 10; BC 1015 • H • SE • 1445 N Highway 16 Denver NC 28037-8638 • lakeshepherd@juno.com
**DURHAM—*GRACE*** (919)682-6030
James A Knuth Joseph M Dzugan Richard R Kuehn • H • SE • 824 N Buchanan Blvd Durham NC 27701-1542 • FAX(919)683-8309 • jaknuth@aol.com
**FAYETTEVILLE—*OUR REDEEMER*** (910)488-6010
Tod R Rappe • WS 1015; BC 9;* • H • SE • 1605 Van Buren Ave Fayetteville NC 28303-3751 • orluthrn@apcnet.com
**FRANKLIN—*RESURRECTION*** (828)524-5996
Gary M Brown • H • EC • SE • 38 Wayah St Franklin NC 28734-3329
**GOLDSBORO—*PEACE*** (919)778-2230
Michael P Thress • WS 11; SS 945;* • H • SE • 1002 Gardner Manor Dr Goldsboro NC 27534-7720
**GREENSBORO—*CROSS CHRIST*** (336)292-4770
Vacant • SE • 1505 New Garden Rd Greensboro NC 27410-2726 • crossofchrist@bellsouth.net
***EBENEZER*** (336)272-5321
Daniel G Koenig • WS 11 830; SS 945; BC 945 • H • SE • 310 S Tremont Dr Greensboro NC 27403-1739
***GRACE*** (336)272-1174
James A Mc Daniels • H • SE • 1315 E Washington St Greensboro NC 27401-3447 • FAX(336)272-1176
**HAVELOCK—*ST PAUL*** (252)447-3826
David M Meyer • WS 8 1030; SS 915; BC 915 • H • SE • 305 US Highway 70 W Havelock NC 28532-9433 • stpaul@connect.net
**HENDERSONVILLE—*MOUNT PISGAH*** (828)692-7027
Lawrence C Rabon Jr. • WS 1030 8; SS 9;* • H • SE • 2606 Chimney Rock Rd Hendersonville NC 28792 • FAX(828)692-7667 • mtpisgahlcms@juno.com
**HICKORY—*AUGUSTANA*** (828)328-6706
Williard E Mueller • WS 1030; SS 930; BC 930;* • H • SE • 1523 16th St SE Hickory NC 28602-9608 • augustana@sandtech.net
***CHRIST*** (828)328-1483
Richard L Schwandt David Ludwig • WS 1030; SS 9;* • H • SE • 324 2nd Ave SE Hickory NC 28602-3043 • FAX(828)328-9841 • clchickory@twave.net
***ST STEPHEN*** (828)256-9865
David J Guelzow Paul J Fitzpatrick • WS 8; SS 930; BC 11 • H • EC/EL • SE • 2304 Springs Rd NE Hickory NC 28601-3066 • FAX(828)256-7994 • sslcms@twave.net
**HICKORY NE—*OUR SAVIOR*** (828)256-5469
William D Seaman • WS 830 11; SS 945; BC 945;* • H • SE • 28603 2160 35th Avenue Dr NE Hickory NC 28601-9264 • FAX(828)256-2160 • osluth@twave.net
**HIGH POINT—*GRACE*** (336)886-4947
Vacant • H • SE • 808 N Centennial St High Point NC 27262-4218
***ST LUKE*** (252)885-6412
Vacant • SE • 820 Leonard Ave 27260-5228 PO Box 238 High Point NC 27261-0238
**JACKSONVILLE—*CALVARY*** (910)353-4016
Joel W Kettner • WS 830 11; SS 10; BC 10 • H • EC • SE • 206 Pine Valley Rd Jacksonville NC 28546-8237 • calvluth@onslowonline.net
**KANNAPOLIS—*MOUNT CALVARY*** (704)932-2864
Vacant • WS 11; SS 945;* • H • SE • 204 N Little Texas Rd 28083-6352 PO Box 250 Kannapolis NC 28082-0250 • FAX(704)932-7092
**KERNERSVILLE—*FOUNTAIN LIFE*** (336)993-4447
Jeffrey G Wuertz • WS 830 11; SS 945; BC 945 • H • EC • SE • 323 Hopkins Rd Kernersville NC 27284-9374 • FAX(336)993-0941 • foljw@aol.com
**KINSTON—*FAITH*** (252)523-6033
Ronald A Fletcher • H • SE • 709 W Vernon Ave Kinston NC 28501-3743 • faith@icomnet.com
**MARION—*ST MATTHEW*** (704)652-7699
Bruce C Alkire • SE • 307 W Court St Marion NC 28752-3911
**NAGS HEAD—*GRACE BY SEA*** (252)441-1530
Vacant • WS 930; SS 11;* • H • EC • SE • 4212 S Croatan Hwy PO Box 1356 Nags Head NC 27959-1356 • gracelu@juno.com
***GRACE BY SEA*** (252)441-1530
Vacant • WS 930; SS 11;* • H • EC • SE • 4212 S Croatan Hwy PO Box 1356 Nags Head NC 27959-1356 • gracelu@juno.com
**NEWTON—*HOLY CROSS*** (828)464-3791
C D Moser • H • SE • 612 S College Ave Newton NC 28658-3416 • cdavid@twave.net
**NEWTON 2 E—*MOUNT OLIVE*** (828)464-2407
Vacant • H • SE • 2103 Mount Olive Church Rd Newton NC 28658
**NORLINA—*ST PAUL***
See Ridgeway 1 E
**RALEIGH—*HOPE***
See Wake Forest
***OUR SAVIOR*** (919)832-8822
Kevin W Martin • Kathryn R Gosswein DEAC • WS 830 11; SS 945;* • H • EL • SE • 1500 Glenwood Ave Raleigh NC 27608-2338 • FAX(919)832-8852 • ktgoss@aol.com
**RIDGEWAY 1 E—*ST PAUL*** (252)456-2747
Vacant • WS 11 • H • SE • 27570 RR1 Box 570 Norlina NC 27563
**SALISBURY—*CROWN IN GLORY*** (704)633-0067
Vacant • H • SE • PO Box 1384 Salisbury NC 28145-1384 • FAX(704)633-0067
**SOUTHERN PINES—*ST JAMES*** (910)692-2515
Vacant • H • SE • 983 W New Hampshire Ave Southern Pines NC 28387-3921
**STATESVILLE—*HOLY TRINITY*** (704)873-3591
Peter W Varvaris • WS 10; SS 845; BC 845 • H • SE • 465 Hartness Rd Statesville NC 28677-3314 • FAX(704)873-8146 • pvarvaris@conninc.com
**TAYLORSVILLE—*ST PAUL*** (828)632-2695
Donald R Hunter • WS 11; SS 945;* • H • SE • 323 1st Ave SW 28681-2401 PO Box 535 Taylorsville NC 28681-0535 • InChrist2@twave.net
**TAYLORSVILLE 5 N—*SALEM*** (828)632-4863
Ray R Ohlendorf • WS 10; SS 9; BC 9 • H • SE • 4005 NC Hwy 16 N 28681 4046 NC Hwy 16 North Taylorsville NC 28681-9015 • rohlendorf@juno.com
**TRYON—*TRINITY***
See Columbus
**WAKE FOREST—*HOPE*** (919)554-8109
Preston E Wagner • H • EC/EL • SE • 701 S Main St Wake Forest NC 27587-2826 • FAX(919)554-0412 • pwag@aol.com
**WAYNESVILLE—*OUR SAVIOR***
See Clyde
**WILMINGTON—*MESSIAH*** (910)791-7040
Mark H Spelzhausen • WS 830 11; SS 945;* • H • SE • 3302 S College Rd Wilmington NC 28412-0906 • FAX(910)791-7620 • messiahlcms@juno.com
**WILSON—*OUR REDEEMER*** (252)243-6706
Vacant • WS 11; SS 945 • SE • 612 NE Vance St C/O Tim Collingwood 2212 Woodcroft Dr Wilson NC 27893
**WINSTON-SALEM—*ST JOHN*** (336)725-1651
Philip C Mc Lain Kevin L Armbrust • H • EC/EL • SE • 27102 2415 Silas Creek Pkwy Winston Salem NC 27103-4820 • FAX(336)725-1603 • church@stjohnsws.org
***ST MARK*** (336)724-0035
William T Parson • SE • 27102 1151 E 14th St Winston Salem NC 27105-6610

## NORTH DAKOTA

**ADRIAN—*TRINITY*** (701)778-5181
Vacant • H • ND • 8895 56th St SE Adrian ND 58472-0121
**ANAMOOSE—*ST MARTIN*** (701)465-3704
Vacant • H • ND • PO Box 179 Anamoose ND 58710-0179
**BARNEY—*PEACE*** (701)439-2429
Vacant • H • ND • 300 Main St 58008-4005 PO Box 142 Barney ND 58008-0142
**BEACH—*ST PAUL*** (701)872-4700
Alan R Kornacki Jr. • WS 1015;* • H • ND • 387 S Central Ave 58621-4002 PO Box 549 Beach ND 58621-0549
***ST PETER***
See Belfield
**BELFIELD—*ST PETER*** (701)872-4700
Alan R Kornacki Jr. • ND • 3710 128th Ave SW Belfield ND 58622-9235
**BEULAH—*CONCORDIA*** (701)873-4388
Toby H Heller • WS 9; BC 1015;* • H • ND • 801 Beacon Ln 58523 PO Box 189 Beulah ND 58523-0189
**BINFORD 8 SW—*ZION***
Charles E Johnson • ND • 58416 PO Box 55 Sutton ND 58484-0055
***ZION***
Charles E Johnson • ND • 7 Mi S 1 1/2 Mi W Of Binford 58416 PO Box 55 Sutton ND 58484-0055
**BISMARCK—*BETHEL*** (701)255-1433
Timothy A Jenks • WS 930; SS 1045; BC 11 • H • EC/EL • ND • 615 E Turnpike Ave Bismarck ND 58501-1733 • bethelbismarck@hotmail.com

***SHEP VALLEY*** (701)258-4231
Lester J Wolfgram • * • H • EC/EL • ND • 801 E Denver Ave 58504-6575 PO Box 2564 Bismarck ND 58502-2564 • FAX(701)258-1095 • sotv@nd.freei.net

***ZION*** (701)223-8286
Thomas R Marcis Bradley R Stoltenow • WS 745 9 11; SS 10; BC 10 9 • H • EC/EL • ND • 413 E Avenue D Bismarck ND 58501-3949 • FAX(701)258-2146 • zionlcms@btigate.com

**BOTTINEAU—*OUR SAVIOR*** (701)228-3021
Dean F Rothchild • WS 11; SS 945; BC 10;* • H • ND • 715 10th St E Bottineau ND 58318-1823

***ZION***
See Gardena

**CARRINGTON—*GRACE*** (701)652-2204
Vacant • * • H • ND • 95 1st St N PO Box 436 Carrington ND 58421-0436 • gracesp@daktel.com

**CAVALIER—*OUR SAVIOR*** (701)265-4408
Adam L Scheblein • * • H • ND • 508 Division Ave N 58220-4902 PO Box 88 Cavalier ND 58220-0088 • scheblei@polarcomm.com

**COOPERSTOWN—*GRACE*** (701)797-3444
Charles E Johnson • WS 11;* • H • ND • 1010 Burrel Ave SE PO Box 674 Cooperstown ND 58425-0674

**CRYSTAL 3 NE—*ST JOHN*** (701)657-2253
Vacant • ND • 58222 8294 Highway 18 Crystal ND 58222-9662

**DEVILS LAKE—*ST PETER*** (701)662-2245
Roger J Leonhardt • WS 1030;* • H • ND • Seventh Ave And 7th St 58301 PO Box 834 Devils Lake ND 58301-3050

***ST PETER*** (701)662-2245
Roger J Leonhardt • WS 1030;* • H • ND • 7th St 58301 PO Box 834 Devils Lake ND 58301-3050

**DICKINSON—*REDEEMER*** (701)483-4463
Todd W Smelser • WS 9; BC 1015;* • H • EC • ND • 711 10th Ave W Dickinson ND 58601-3716 • rlc4him@pop.ctctel.com

**DRAYTON—*TRINITY*** (701)454-3988
Bernhard M Seter • ND • 307 N Main St 58225-4613 PO Box 25 Drayton ND 58225-0025

**EDGELEY—*ZION*** (701)493-2537
Alan Eppen • WS 10; SS 11; BC 11 • H • ND • 110 2nd Ave W 58433-7104 PO Box 96 Edgeley ND 58433-0096

**ELLENDALE—*ZION*** (701)349-4147
Dennis B O Neill • WS 930; BC 1045 • H • ND • 121 2nd St S 58436 PO Box 793 Ellendale ND 58436-0793

**FAIRMOUNT—*FIRST ENGLISH*** (701)474-5854
Ronald R Carnicom • ND • 201 3rd St S 58030-4101 PO Box 295 Fairmount ND 58030-0295

**FARGO—*BEAUT SAVIOR*** (701)293-1047
David S Wagner • H • ND • 2601 23rd Ave S Fargo ND 58103-5018 • FAX(701)293-3857 • bslc@i29.net

***GRACE*** (701)232-1516
Arthur P Weidner • Ruth K Drum DEAC • H • ND • 821 5th Ave S Fargo ND 58103-1841 • art.weidner@juno.com

***IMMANUEL*** (701)293-7979
Roger M Sedlmayr Bernard M Worral • WS 815 11; SS 940; BC 940 • H • ND • 1258 Broadway Fargo ND 58102-2637 • rsed1613@aol.com

**FLAXTON—*ST PAUL*** (701)386-2246
Scott E Simpson • ND • 7353 109th St NW Flaxton ND 58737-9724 • simpson1@ndak.net

**FORBES—*BETHLEHEM*** (701)357-7521
Lyle E Klemz • ND • PO Box 95 Forbes ND 58439-0095

**GARDENA—*ZION*** (701)359-4461
Joel L Brandvold • * • H • ND • UKNWN C/O Mr A Hasenwinkel 816 Thompson St Bottineau ND 58318-1726

**GARRISON—*PEACE*** (701)463-2073
Paul R Nelson • WS 930; BC 1030;* • H • ND • 505 2nd St NW Garrison ND 58540-7330

**GLEN ULLIN—*ZION*** (701)348-3172
Loren W Strum • WS 11; SS 10; BC 10 • H • ND • 111 S 2nd St 58631-7301 PO Box 129 Glen Ullin ND 58631-0129

**GLENBURN 9 SW—*LYNCH IMMANUEL*** (701)727-4994
Vacant • WS 10;* • H • EC • ND • Hwy 83 North Of Minot Afb 58740 18301 Hwy 83 N Glenburn ND 58740-9557 • lynch@ndak.net

**GOLDEN VALLEY—*ST JAMES*** (701)938-4575
Vacant • WS 9; SS 845;* • ND • 220 Mercer Co Road 5 Golden Valley ND 58541

**GRAFTON—*ZION ENGLISH*** (701)352-2869
Bernhard M Seter • H • ND • 1100 Hill Ave Grafton ND 58237-2228 • bernie@polarcomm.com

**GRAND FORKS—*IMMANUEL*** (701)775-7125
Bradley D Viken • * • H • EC • ND • 1710 Cherry St Grand Forks ND 58201-7344 • FAX(701)775-4356 • ilc@gfherald.infi.net

***REDEEMER*** (701)772-0706
David E Laue • H • ND • 815 N 20th St 58203-0764 2230 7th Ave N Grand Forks ND 58203-2907

***WITTENBERG CHPL**** (701)772-3992
Mark J Buchhop • WS 1030; BC 930;* • H • ND • 3120 5th Ave N Grand Forks ND 58203-2824 • FAX(701)772-5991 • mbuchhop@sage.und.nodak.edu

**GRANDIN—*GRACE*** (701)484-5549
Vacant • WS 9; SS 10 • ND • PO Box 139 Grandin ND 58038-0139

**GRASSY BUTTE—*REDEEMER*** (701)863-6845
Vacant • WS 7; BC 6 • H • ND • PO Box 161 Grassy Butte ND 58634-0161

**GREAT BEND—*TRINITY*** (701)545-7422
Ronald R Carnicom • ND • 206 School St 58039-4024 PO Box 145 Great Bend ND 58039-0145

**GWINNER—*ZION*** (701)678-2401
Kirk Douglas • ND • 107 S Main St 58040-4103 PO Box 118 Gwinner ND 58040-0118

**HALLIDAY—*ST PAUL*** (701)938-4575
Vacant • ND • 106 First St N C/O Albert Weidner PO Box 5 Halliday ND 58636

**HANKINSON—*IMMANUEL*** (701)242-7834
Vacant • WS 8 1030; SS 915 • ND • 305 2nd Ave NE 58041-4017 PO Box 440 Hankinson ND 58041-0440 • hjjordin@hankinson.means.net

**HANKINSON 6 NW—*ST JOHN*** (701)242-7741
Vacant • WS 915; SS 1015 • ND • County Rd 1 58448 PO Box 440 Hankinson ND 58041-0440 • hjjordin@rrt.net

**HANNOVER—*ST PETER*** (701)794-8705
Gregory A Zillinger • * • H • ND • 2095 Highway 31 Hannover ND 58563

**HAZEN—*ST MATTHEW*** (701)748-5561
David K Suelzle • WS 830 • H • ND • 302 3rd St NW 58545-4111 PO Box 523 Hazen ND 58545-0523 • stmatthazennd@westriv.com

**HAZEN 20 NE—*TRINITY*** (701)442-3409
Thomas L Puffe • ND • Hwy 200 58545 PO Box 757 Underwood ND 58576-0757

**HILLSBORO—*ST JOHN*** (701)436-4692
Vacant • H • ND • 58045 PO Box 99 Hillsboro ND 58045-0099

**HOPE—*TRINITY*** (701)945-2575
Charles E Johnson • WS 9;* • H • ND • C/O Mr Clark Lemley RR 1 Box 50 Hope ND 58046-9753

**JAMESTOWN—*CONCORDIA*** (701)252-2819
Robert A Leiste • * • H • ND • 502 1st Ave N Jamestown ND 58401-3303 • FAX(701)252-1165 • concord@buffalocity.net

**KENSAL—*ST PAUL*** (701)435-2873
Vacant • H • ND • 510 2nd Ave 58455-4033 C/O St Paul Lutheran PO Box 195 Wimbledon ND 58492-0195

**KONGSBERG—*ST JOHN*** (701)463-2004
Vacant • WS 130 • ND • 3037 10th Ave N Voltaire ND 58792

**KRAMER—*ZION*** (701)359-4461
Joel L Brandvold • WS 9;* • H • ND • 560 Rudolph St 58748 PO Box 86 Kramer ND 58748-0086

**KULM—*ST PAUL*** (701)647-2257
Alan Eppen • WS 830 • ND • 213 1st Ave SW 58456-7108 PO Box M Kulm ND 58456-0228

**LA MOURE—*TRINITY*** (701)883-5029
Vacant • WS 9; SS 1015 • H • ND • 215 SE 2nd St 58458 PO Box 569 Lamoure ND 58458-0569

**LAKOTA—*GRACE*** (701)247-2625
Roger J Leonhardt • H • ND • 415 West ‰C‰ 58344 PO Box 645 Lakota ND 58344-0645

**LANGDON—*REDEEMER*** (701)256-2314
Charles Sheffler • ND • 1210 11th Ave Langdon ND 58249-1916

**LEHR—*GRACE*** (701)378-2565
Lyle E Klemz • H • ND • 221 East St S 58460-4012 PO Box 128 Lehr ND 58460-0128

**LIDGERWOOD—*HOLY CROSS*** (701)538-4688
Joseph E Crosswhite III • ND • PO Box I Lidgerwood ND 58053-1109

***ZION***
See Claire City 6 NE SD

**LIDGERWOOD 6 SE—*IMMANUEL*** (701)538-4849
Douglas C Wanderer • * • ND • 58053 9690 Hwy I8 Lidgerwood ND 58053-9774

**LISBON—*REDEEMER*** (701)683-4349
Donald R Polege • WS 845;* • H • ND • 801 Forest St 58054-4238 PO Box 582 Lisbon ND 58054-0582 • FAX(701)683-4463 • redeemer@corpcomm.net

**MANDAN—*MESSIAH*** (701)663-8545
James A Baneck • WS 9; SS 1030; BC 1030;* • H • EC/EL • ND • 1020 Boundary Rd NW Mandan ND 58554-1615 • jabmessiahmandan@aol.com

**MAX—*ST MATTHEW*** (701)679-2755
Paul R Nelson • WS 11; SS 10; BC 10 • H • ND • Main St Max ND 58759

**MC CLUSKY—*ST JOHN*** (701)363-2636
Arie D Bertsch • WS 10; SS 11; BC 11 • H • ND • 103 Ave F W PO Box 635 Mc Clusky ND 58463-0635

**MICHIGAN—*ZION*** (701)259-2296
Vacant • WS 6 • ND • PO Box 336 Michigan ND 58259-0336 • pastbutch@polar.polarcomm.com

**MINOT—*OUR SAVIOR*** (701)852-6404
Paul A Krueger • WS 830 11; BC 945;* • H • ND • 3705 11th St SW Minot ND 58701-8303 • FAX(701)838-2060 • oslc@minot.ndak.net

***ST MARK*** (701)839-4663
Carlyle L Roth • * • H • ND • 2209 4th Ave NW Minot ND 58703-2916

***ST PAUL*** (701)852-2821
Vacant • Rita C Footh DEAC • H • ND • 200 Burdick Expy E Minot ND 58701-4436 • saint@minot.com

**MINOT AFB—*LYNCH IMMANUEL***
See Glenburn 9 SW

**MONANGO—*ST PAUL*** (701)349-5313
Lyle E Klemz • H • ND • 302 2nd Ave Monango ND 58436-4007

**MUNICH—*ZION*** (701)682-5126
Charles Sheffler • H • ND • PO Box 130 Munich ND 58352-0130

**NAPOLEON—*ST MATTHEW***
Vacant • ND • 404 Broadway 58561-7012 RR 1 Box 176A Napoleon ND 58561-9801

**NEW ROCKFORD—*EMMANUEL*** (701)947-2303
Vacant • ND • 529 2nd Ave S New Rockford ND 58356-1617

**NEW SALEM—*ZION***
See Glen Ullin

***ZION*** (701)843-7202
Loren W Strum • WS 9;* • ND • 407 N 5th St 58563-4050 PO Box 37 New Salem ND 58563-0376 • FAX(701)783-7202 • zionlutheran@usa.net

**NIAGARA—*ST ANDREW*** (701)397-5713
Vacant • H • ND • PO Box 70 Niagara ND 58266-0070

**OAKES—*ST JOHN*** (701)742-2595
Patrick E O Brien • WS 1015; BC 910;* • H • ND • 120 S 9th St 58474-1729 PO Box 188 Oakes ND 58474-0188 • FAX(701)742-3008

**PETTIBONE—*OUR SAVIOR*** (701)273-4862
Vacant • H • ND • 104 N Main St 58475 PO Box 155 Pettibone ND 58475-0155

**PILLSBURY—*TRINITY***
See Hope

**ROCK LAKE—*ALL NATIONS*** (701)266-5361
Don L Kirklen • WS 9;* • H • ND • 22 S Sibley St PO Box 216 Rocklake ND 58365-0216 • FAX(701)266-5280 • anlcrl@utma.com

**ROLLA—*IMMANUEL*** (701)477-5122
Don L Kirklen • H • ND • 10 1st Ave SE 58367-7035 PO Box 37 Rolla ND 58367-0037

**RUGBY—*ST PAUL*** (701)776-6739
Dean R Poellet • H • ND • 320 SW Eighth Rugby ND 58368-1623 • lcmsstpaul@stellarnet.com

**SAINT THOMAS 8 NW—*ST PAUL*** (701)257-6747
Vacant • * • ND • 58276 8750 144th Ave NE Saint Thomas ND 58276-9730

**SAWYER—*ST PETER*** (701)624-5688
Larry D Marschner • * • H • ND • Main St 58781 PO Box 285 Sawyer ND 58781-0285

**STIRUM—*IMMANUEL*** (701)753-7651
Kirk Douglas • H • ND • 11897 Highway 13 58069-9537 PO Box 118 Gwinner ND 58040-0118

**SYKESTON—*ST PAUL*** (701)984-2293
Vacant • ND • 37 Hughes Ave NW 58486 PO Box 445 Sykeston ND 58486-0445 • gracesp@daktel.com

**TOLLEY—*TRINITY*** (701)386-2246
Scott E Simpson • ND • 202 Bertleson 58787 PO Box 127 Tolley ND 58787-0127 • simpson1@ndak.net

**TOWNER—*FAITH*** (701)537-5815
Daryl G Rothchild • WS 8; SS 915 • H • ND • 405 1st St SW 58788 PO Box 180 Towner ND 58788-0180

**UNDERWOOD—*ST JOHN*** (701)442-5467
Thomas L Puffe • ND • 137 Summit 58576 PO Box 757 Underwood ND 58576-0757

***TRINITY***
See Hazen 20 NE

**UPHAM 11 NW—*ST JOHN*** (701)272-6287
Daryl G Rothchild • ND • 58789 PO Box 5 Upham ND 58789-0005

**UPHAM 9 W—*BETHLEHEM*** (701)272-6276
Daryl G Rothchild • ND • 58789 PO Box 5 Upham ND 58789-0005

**VOLTAIRE—*ST JOHN***
See Kongsberg

**WAHPETON—*IMMANUEL*** (701)642-6910
Alan R Werth • * • H • ND • 420 3rd Ave N Wahpeton ND 58075-4421

**WATFORD CITY—*OUR REDEEMER*** (701)842-4632
Vacant • ND • C/O Judy Fitzgerald RR 1 Box 2C Watford City ND 58854-9702

**WEST FARGO—*ST ANDREW*** (701)282-4195
Clark H Jahnke Kevin C Zellers • Kenneth W Koehler DCE • H • ND • 1005 1st St E West Fargo ND 58078-3005 • FAX(701)282-4204 • chjahnke@aol.com

**WILLISTON—*CONCORDIA*** (701)572-9021
Lester J Reinke • H • ND • 1805 Main St Williston ND 58801-3543

**WILLOW CITY—*ST PAUL*** (701)366-4604
Dean R Poellet • ND • 199 Main St Willow City ND 58384-4105 • lcmsstpaul@stellarnet.com

**WILLOW CITY 7 W—*IMMANUEL***
Dean F Rothchild • ND • 58384 649 81st St NE Willow City ND 58384-9128

**WIMBLEDON—*ST PAUL***
See Kensal

***ST PAUL*** (701)435-2848
Vacant • H • ND • 305 Gibson St 58492-4050 PO Box 195 Wimbledon ND 58492-0195

**WOODWORTH—*REDEEMER*** (701)752-4110
Vacant • H • ND • 223 2nd Ave NE 58496-7129 PO Box 86 Woodworth ND 58496-0086

## OHIO

**AKRON—*CONCORDIA*** (330)535-1330
Richard O Bartholomew • H • EC • EN • 724 Sumner St Akron OH 44311-1660 • FAX(330)535-1433 • Pastor@CELC.org

***FAIRLAWN*** (330)836-7286
Charles D Lentner Robert W Graul • Peter J Le Borious DCE • H • EC • EN • 3415 W Market St Akron OH 44333-3307

***GOOD SHEPHERD*** (330)784-4564
Vacant • EN • 2254 Triplett Blvd Akron OH 44312-2357

***GRACE*** (330)864-4244
Vacant • H • EN • 989 N Portage Path Akron OH 44313-5859

***HOPE*** (330)644-3522
Jack A Kozak • WS 1030; BC 915;* • H • EC • OH • 999 Portage Lakes Dr Akron OH 44319-1538 • jakozak@bright.net

***ST JOHN*** (216)773-4128
Michael Maciupa • H • OH • 550 E Wilbeth Rd Akron OH 44301-2365 • mmaciupa@aol.com

***ZION*** (330)253-3136
John G Eiwen Dennis D Schwalenberg • WS 8; SS 9; BC 9;* • EL • OH • 139 S High St Akron OH 44308-1410 • FAX(330)253-3615

**AMHERST—*ST PAUL*** (440)988-4157
Gary D Bernath • Kendis D Bender DCE • WS 830 11; SS 945;* • H • EC • OH • 115 Central Dr Amherst OH 44001-1601 • FAX(440)988-5436 • stpaul@apk.net

**AMLIN—*ST JOHN***
See Dublin
**ANTWERP—*MOUNT CALVARY*** (419)258-6505
William C Emrick • H • OH • 3497 US 24 45813-9416 PO Box D Antwerp OH 45813
**ARCHBOLD 3 N—*ST JAMES*** (419)445-4750
James C Strawn • WS 930; SS 825;* • H • OH • 43502 22881 Monroe St Archbold OH 43502-9486
**ASHTABULA—*ZION*** (440)964-9483
Timothy J Landskroener • WS 1030; SS 9; BC 9 • H • OH • 2310 W 9th St Ashtabula OH 44004-2526
**AURORA—*HOPE*** (330)562-9660
Dennis C Mann(DM) • * • H • EC • OH • 456 S Chillicothe Rd Aurora OH 44202-8824 • FAX(330)562-9092 • hopelc@nccw.net
**AVON—*FAITH*** (216)934-4710
Roger W Daene • H • EC/HS • OH • Garden and Lakeland Drs Avon OH 44011-1170
**BEAVERCREEK—*LORD OF LIFE*** (937)431-0643
Timothy P Bohlmann • WS 1030; SS 9; BC 9 • H • OH • 3625 Dayton Xenia Rd 45432-2828 PO Box 340515 Beavercreek OH 45434-0515 • pastortimbo@worldnett.att.net
**BOWLING GREEN—*COMMUNITY OF*** (419)352-5101
Ronald R Rosenkaimer II • Christopher J Patterson DCO • H • OH • 1124 E Wooster St Bowling Green OH 43402-3224 • FAX(419)352-4901 • comchrist@wcnet.org
**BRECKSVILLE—*COMMUNITY HOPE*** (440)546-9360
Vacant • WS 9 1045; SS 1045 9 • H • OH • 4470 Oakes Rd Brecksville OH 44141-2562 • FAX(440)546-0365 • communityofhope@juno.com
**BRUNSWICK—*ST MARK*** (330)225-3110
John H Diener • WS 815 11; SS 945; BC 945;* • H • EC/EL/HS • OH • 1330 N Carpenter Rd Brunswick OH 44212-3113 • FAX(330)225-4380 • dienerjmmm@aol.com
**CELINA—*LORD OF LIFE**** (419)584-0071
Vacant • OH • Lake Area 7706 State Rt 703 Celina OH 45822
**CHAGRIN FALLS—*VALLEY*** (440)247-0390
Daniel D Esala Mark E Berg • Duane M Dukles DCE • WS 830 1045; SS 945; BC 945 • H • EC • OH • 87 E Orange St Chagrin Falls OH 44022-2732 • FAX(440)247-0125 • valleyluth@aol.com
**CHARDON—*PEACE*** (216)286-3310
Donald W Heino • H • EC • OH • 12686 Bass Lake Rd Chardon OH 44024-8316
**CHESTERLAND—*ST MARK*** (216)729-1668
Gary P Lissy • WS 815 1030; BC 930;* • H • EC • OH • 11900 Chillicothe Rd Chesterland OH 44026-1934 • FAX(216)729-1669 • stmarklutheran@juno.com
**CHILLICOTHE—*OUR SAVIOR*** (614)775-2470
Allen D Wolka • H • EC • OH • 151 University Dr Chillicothe OH 45601-2117
***OUR SAVIOR****
See Portsmouth
**CHUCKERY—*ST PAUL*** (937)349-2405
Gerald D Matzke • * • H • EL • OH • 7960 State Route 38 Milford Center OH 43045-9722 • FAX(937)349-5939
**CINCINNATI—*CHRIST*** (513)385-8342
Andrew Norris Scott A Ashmon • WS 1015; SS 9; BC 9 • H • EC • OH • 3301 Compton Rd Cincinnati OH 45251-2507 • FAX(513)385-8342 • anorris@christ-lcms.org
***CONCORDIA*** (513)861-9552
Michael R Korte • WS 8 1030; SS 915; BC 915 • H • EC/EL • OH • 1133 Clifton Hills Ave Cincinnati OH 45220-1405 • FAX(513)861-9552 • concormrk@aol.com
***GRACE*** (513)661-5166
Philip H Dumke • WS 8 1030; SS 915; BC 915 • H • OH • 3628 Boudinot Ave Cincinnati OH 45211-4922 • FAX(513)661-3728
***IMMANUEL*** (513)961-3407
Milton T Berner • OH • 544 Rockdale Ave Cincinnati OH 45229
***MESSIAH***
See Greenhills
***OUR REDEEMER***
See Silverton
***PEACE***
See Green Twp
***PRINCE PEACE*** (513)621-7265
Chris E Johnson • OH • 1524 Race St Cincinnati OH 45210-1712 • FAX(513)621-7265
***ST PAUL*** (513)271-4147
David P Lampman Peter D Kelm • H • EC/EL • OH • 5433 Madison Rd Cincinnati OH 45227-1507 • FAX(513)271-8558 • cincyrev@fuse.net
***TRINITY*** (513)385-7024
David D Reedy • WS 1030; SS 930; BC 915 • H • OH • 5921 Springdale Rd Cincinnati OH 45247-3433 • pastrdav@goodnews.net
***ZION*** (513)231-2253
Harold H G Oliver • Christopher T Graves DCE • WS 8 930 1045; SS 930; BC 930 • H • OH • 1175 Birney Ln Cincinnati OH 45230-3720 • FAX(513)231-2076
**CLEVELAN D—*HOLY CROSS*** (216)252-2348
Myron K Prok James A Herbolsheimer • WS 8 1015 11; SS 915; BC 915 • H • EL/HS • EN • 4260 Rocky River Dr Cleveland OH 44135-1948
**CLEVELAND—*CHRIST*** (216)961-6060
Lloyd E Gross Dean C Kavouras • WS 1030; BC 9;* • H • EL/HS • OH • 3271 W 43rd St Cleveland OH 44109-1063
***CHRIST DEAF*** (216)781-8571
Gary Lawson • H • HS • OH • 2203 Superior Ave Cleveland OH 44114
***COMMUNITY OF PRAISE****
Vacant • OH • C/O Saint Paul Lutheran Church PO Box 603756 Cleveland OH 44103-0756
***EL BUEN PASTOR*** (216)631-4634
Wilfredo C Rivera • H • EL/HS • OH • 2059 W 28th St Cleveland OH 44113-4066
***IGLESIA CRISTIANA HI*** (216)651-0236
Luis A Torres Sr. • HS • EN • 2970 W 30th St Cleveland OH 44113-5003
***IGLESIA LUTERANA EL***
Vacant • OH • 2059 W 28th Street Cleveland OH 44138-1303
***IMMANUEL*** (216)781-9511
Horst Hoyer S J Lemanski • H • HS • OH • 2928 Scranton Rd Cleveland OH 44113-5322 • FAX(216)781-4171 • pfarrerhh@aol.com
***MOUNT CALVARY*** (216)671-2099
Walter J Kovac • * • EC/EL/HS • OH • 12826 Lorain Ave Cleveland OH 44111-2611
***OUR SAVIOR***
See Mayfield Heights
***ST JAMES*** (216)351-6499
Paul W Hoffman • WS 8 1030; SS 915; BC 915;* • H • EC/HS • OH • 4771 Broadview Rd Cleveland OH 44109-4669 • FAX(216)351-7815 • stjamescleve@juno.com
***ST JOHN*** (216)531-1156
Walther P Marcis • H • EL/HS • OH • 17403 Nottingham Rd Cleveland OH 44119-2901
***ST LUKE*** (216)631-4120
Robert G Schoenheider • WS 10 • OH • 8601 Sauer Ave Cleveland OH 44102-3824 • FAX(216)651-0601
***ST MARK*** (216)749-3545
Gary L Miller • WS 930; SS 830; BC 830;* • H • EL/HS • OH • 4464 Pearl Rd Cleveland OH 44109-4224 • FAX(216)749-4270 • glmiller@corplink.net
***ST PAUL*** (216)361-0400
Vacant • HS • OH • 1486 E 55th St 44103-1307 PO Box 603756 Cleveland OH 44103-0756 • FAX(216)361-6912
***ST PHILIP*** (216)991-0655
Bertram B Lewis • * • HS • OH • 11315 Regalia Ave Cleveland OH 44104-5727 • FAX(216)991-5900
***TRINITY*** (216)281-1700
Jeffrey D Johnson • WS 930 11 10;* • EC/EL/HS • OH • 2045 W 30th St 2031 W 30th St Cleveland OH 44113-4009
***UNITY*** (216)741-2085
John Vavroch • WS 930; SS 11; BC 11 • H • HS • OH • 4542 Pearl Rd Cleveland OH 44109-4876
***ZION*** (216)861-2179
John W Milligan • HS • OH • 2062 E 30th St Cleveland OH 44115-2625 • FAX(216)861-2179
**CLEVELAND HEIGHTS—*MOUNT OLIVE*** (216)381-2873
Vacant • * • H • HS • EN • 2392 Noble Rd Cleveland Heights OH 44121-1473
**COLUMBIA STATION—*HOSANNA*** (440)236-8900
Donald L Bojens • WS 1030; BC 915;* • HS • OH • 13485 W River Rd Columbia Station OH 44028-9523 • FAX(440)236-8977 • hosannalc@n2net.net
**COLUMBUS—*ATONEMENT*** (614)451-1880
Daniel C Bell • H • EC • OH • 1621 Francisco Rd Columbus OH 43220-2536 • churchlady@atonementchurch.com
***BETHANY*** (614)866-7755
George T Zoebl • WS 830 11;* • H • EC • OH • 1000 Noe Bixby Rd Columbus OH 43213-3526 • FAX(614)367-1398 • bethany@computelnet.com
***CONCORDIA*** (614)878-7800
Vacant • WS 1030; SS 915; BC 915 • H • OH • 225 Schoolhouse Ln Columbus OH 43228-1216 • FAX(614)853-1795
***HOLY CROSS DEAF*** (614)885-3362
Edwin L Bergstresser II • WS 1030;* • H • OH • 360 Morse Rd Columbus OH 43214-1722 • FAX(614)885-0632 • columbusdeaflutheranchurch@juno.com
***ST JAMES*** (614)878-5158
Jay R Decker John A Hood • WS 8 930 11; SS 930; BC 930 • H • OH • 5660 Trabue Rd Columbus OH 43228-9500 • FAX(614)878-5443 • revjdecker@aol.com
***UNIV CHAPEL*** (614)291-9317
Vacant • * • H • OH • 45 E 13th Ave Columbus OH 43201-1807
***ZION*** (614)444-3456
Peter R Reetz Christopher L Atwell • WS 8 1030; SS 915; BC 915 • H • OH • 766 S High St Columbus OH 43206-1909 • FAX(614)443-4818 • preetz@asacomp.com
**CONDIT—*HOPE*** (614)965-1685
Robert V Riggs • H • OH • 15370 Meredion State Rd UKNWN PO Box 255 Sunbury OH 43074-0255
**CONVOY 1 S—*REDEEMER*** (419)749-2167
Lee H Genter • WS 930; SS 1030;* • H • OH • 6727 St Rt 49 45317 PO Box 10 Convoy OH 45832-0010 • redeemer@wcoil.com
**CUYAHOGA FALLS—*REDEEMER*** (330)923-1445
Keith J Johnson Larry L Leuthaeuser • Janet Juliano DCE • H • EC/EL • OH • 2141 5th St Cuyahoga Falls OH 44221-3213 • FAX(330)923-4517
**DAYTON—*CONCORDIA*** (937)299-1912
Vacant • WS 8 1030; SS 915; BC 915 • H • EC • OH • 250 Peach Orchard Ave Dayton OH 45419-2642 • FAX(937)299-6618 • concordialuther@aol.com
***EMMANUEL***
See Kettering
***MOUNT CALVARY*** (937)836-2238
Vacant • WS 1030; SS 9;* • H • OH • 9100 N Main St Dayton OH 45415-1123 • FAX(937)836-1518 • mtcalvary1@earthlink.net
***ST MATTHEW***
See Huber Heights
**DEFIANCE—*CHRIST OUR SAVIOR*** (419)782-6688
Terry L Cripe • H • OH • 301 Carter Rd Defiance OH 43512-3509
***ST JOHN*** (419)782-5766
Donald L Luhring • WS 8 930 11; SS 930; BC 930;* • H • EC/EL • OH • 655 Wayne Ave Defiance OH 43512-2659 • FAX(419)782-0954 • sjl@defnet.com
***ST STEPHEN*** (419)395-1507
Roger E Disbro • * • OH • 30304 New Bavaria Rd 30316 New Bavaria Rd Defiance OH 43512-8942
**DELHI HILLS—*PEACE***
See Green Twp
**DUBLIN—*ST JOHN*** (614)889-2284
David K Reimann Gerald P Heimlich • H • EC • OH • 6135 Rings Rd Dublin OH 43016-6718 • FAX(614)760-0412
**EDGERTON 2E 1.5S—*ZION*** (419)298-2594
Mark D Kleckner • H • OH • 43517 01018 Cicero Rd Edgerton OH 43517-9514 • FAX(419)298-2594 • mdkleck@bright.net
**ELMORE—*TRINITY*** (419)862-3461
Stephen Lutz • WS 8 1045; SS 930 • H • EC • OH • 412 Fremont St 43416 PO Box 22 Elmore OH 43416-0022
**ELYRIA—*GRACE*** (440)322-5497
Henry E Baum • H • EC • EN • 9685 E River Rd Elyria OH 44035-8147 • FAX(440)322-5497
***ST JOHN*** (216)324-4070
Dennis L Schmidt • SS 845;* • H • EC • OH • 1140 W River Rd N Elyria OH 44035-2897 • FAX(216)324-4070 • sjlc@ohio.net
**EUCLID—*BETHLEHEM*** (216)531-5990
Craig H Bode • WS 1015; SS 9; BC 9 • H • OH • 24490 Euclid Ave Euclid OH 44117-1711 • FAX(216)692-1421 • bethlehemluth@juno.com
***SHORE HAVEN*** (216)731-4100
Dennis R Juengel • WS 10; SS 845; BC 9;* • H • EC/HS • OH • 280 E 222nd St Euclid OH 44123-1719 • FAX(216)731-6821
**FAIRBORN—*BETHLEHEM*** (937)878-0651
Manfred K Rembold • WS 8 1045; SS 930; BC 930 • H • OH • 1240 S Maple Ave Fairborn OH 45324-3648 • FAX(937)878-8794 • bethlehem7@aol.com
**FAIRPORT HARBOR—*IMMANUEL*** (440)357-7446
Donald L Tompkins • WS 1030; SS 930; BC 930 • EL • OH • 325 Sixth St Fairport Harbor OH 44077-5650 • dltompkins@ncweb.com
**FINDLAY—*CONCORDIA*** (419)422-4209
Gerry W Mohr • WS 1015; SS 9; BC 9 • OH • 1431 E 6th St Findlay OH 45840-6450 • concordialutheranchurch@altavista.com
**FLORIDA—*ST PETER*** (419)762-5075
Douglas R Corniels • WS 10; SS 9; BC 9 • H • EC • OH • Cty Rd 17d 107 E School St Napoleon OH 43545-9802
**GARFIELD HEIGHTS—*ST JOHN*** (216)587-4222
Vern L Bok • WS 830 11; BC 945;* • H • EC/EL/HS • OH • 11333 Granger Rd Garfield Heights OH 44125-2851 • FAX(216)518-0941 • stjohnluthgh@juno.com
**GENEVA—*ST JOHN*** (440)466-2473
Charles E Althoff • WS 845 11; BC 10;* • H • EC/EL • OH • 811 S Broadway 44041-9146 811 South Broadway PO Box 500 Geneva OH 44041-0500 • FAX(440)415-0659
**GRAFTON—*TRINITY*** (440)748-2154
Mark L Viets • * • H • EC • OH • 38307 Royalton Rd Grafton OH 44044-9184
**GRANVILLE—*PILGRIM*** (614)587-0345
Daniel J Ruff • H • OH • 309 Broadway W Granville OH 43023-1121 • pilgrim309@juno.com
**GREEN TWP—*PEACE*** (513)941-5177
Joel D Kotila • WS 1030; SS 915; BC 915 • H • OH • 44232 1451 Ebenezer Rd Cincinnati OH 45233-4954 • joelkotila@aol.com
**GREENHILLS—*MESSIAH*** (513)825-4768
Michael F Volk • Steven M Hackmann DCE • WS 830 1045; SS 930; BC 930;* • H • OH • UKNWN 10416 Bossi Ln Cincinnati OH 45218-1508 • FAX(513)825-4778 • messiahgnh@aol.com
**HAMILTON—*IMMANUEL*** (513)893-6792
Kenneth M Kueker • WS 8 1030; SS 915; BC 915 • H • EC/EL • OH • 1285 Main St Hamilton OH 45013-1621 • FAX(513)863-2502 • imlutheran@aol.com
**HAMLER 3 N—*IMMANUEL*** (419)274-4811
Douglas A De Witt • WS 10; SS 9; BC 9 • H • OH • 43524 G-983 SR 109 Hamler OH 43524-9773 • imlutheran@skybiz.com
**HARRISON—*AMAZING GRACE*** (513)367-5094
Clayton G Vail • WS 1030; SS 915 • H • OH • 45030-8714 9961 New Haven Rd Harrison OH 45030
**HIGHLAND HEIGHTS—*BEAUTIFUL*** (440)684-1109
Vacant • * • H • OH • 5775 Highland Rd 44143 PO Box 21205 South Euclid OH 44121
**HOLGATE—*ST JOHN*** (419)264-4641
Theodore L Rellstab • EC • OH • 501 S Wilhelm St 43527-9760 PO Box 97 Holgate OH 43527-0097
**HUBER HEIGHTS—*SAINT TIMOTHY*** (937)233-2443
Dennis L Dobbins • WS 1030; SS 9 • H • EC • OH • 5040 Rye Dr Huber Heights OH 45424-4397 • FAX(937)233-0028 • sttim@juno.com
***ST MATTHEW*** (937)233-4632
David P Nehring Theodore L Scheidt • WS 930; SS 1045;* • H • OH • 5566 Chambersburg Rd Huber Heights OH 45424-3850 • FAX(937)233-4632 • st³matthew³ev@msn.com
**HUDSON—*GLORIA DEI*** (330)650-6550
Ronald E Duer John W Welge • H • EC • OH • 2113 Ravenna St Hudson OH 44236-3451 • FAX(330)650-6685
**INDEPENDENCE—*CONCORDIA*** (216)524-2188
Mark C Wilkens • H • HS • OH • 6705 Brecksville Rd Independence OH 44131-4833
**KENT—*FAITH*** (330)673-6633
Thomas P Mroch Kent D Pierce • Wade Johnson DCE • * • OH • 931 E Main St Kent OH 44240-2548 • FAX(330)673-1240 • faithlcms@nls.net

**KETTERING—*EMMANUEL*** (937)434-1798
Philip J Esala Paul W Stanko(EM) • WS 815 11; SS 930; BC 930 • H • EC/EL • OH • 4865 Wilmington Pike Kettering OH 45440-2092 • FAX(937)434-2234 • discoverus@emmanuellc.org

**LAKEWOOD—*GETHSEMANE*** (216)521-0434
Vacant • WS 730 9 1115; SS 1015; BC 1015 • EC/EL/HS • OH • 14560 Madison Ave Lakewood OH 44107-4324 • FAX(216)521-2173 • gelc@en.com

***PENTECOST*** (216)221-6265
Donald M Hayas • H • EC/HS • S • 13303 Madison Ave Lakewood OH 44107-4812

***PILGRIM*** (216)521-8842
Vacant • WS 1045;* • H • HS • OH • 14224 Detroit Ave Lakewood OH 44107-4472

***SS PETER&PAUL*** (216)221-7286
Robert E Matej • HS • S • 13030 Madison Ave Lakewood OH 44107-4931

***ST PAUL*** (216)521-5610
Norbert Folwaczny • WS 730 845 1115; SS 10; BC 10;* • EC/EL/HS • OH • 15501 Detroit Ave Lakewood OH 44107-3851 • FAX(216)226-4082 • stpaullkwd@aol.com

**LANCASTER—*EMANUEL*** (740)653-1847
Mark R Raddatz • WS 745; SS 9; BC 9 • H • OH • 231 E Mulberry St 43130-3164 PO Box 2270 Lancaster OH 43130-5270 • FAX(740)653-1880 • emauel@greenapple.com

***REDEEMER*** (740)653-4083
John C Davidson • WS 1015; SS 9; BC 9 • H • EC • OH • 1400 Concordia Dr Lancaster OH 43130-2003 • FAX(740)653-0801 • redeemer@ameritech.net

**LANDEN—*KING OF KINGS*** (513)398-6089
Anthony A Cook • WS 815 930 11; SS 930; BC 930 • H • EC • OH • UKNWN 3621 Socialville Foster Rd Mason OH 45040-9335 • FAX(513)459-9896 • pastor@kingofkings-lcms.org

**LIBERTY CENTER—*ST PAUL*** (419)533-3041
Randolph L Gragg • WS 10; SS 830;* • EC • OH • 8074 County Road T Liberty Center OH 43532-9735 • FAX(810)461-1855 • spelc@henry-net.com

**LIBERTY TOWNSHIP—*ROYAL*** (513)779-4740
Joel C Morgan • WS 1030; SS 915; BC 915 • H • OH • 7127 Dutchland Pkwy Liberty Township OH 45044-9096 • FAX(513)779-4740 • royalredmr@aol.com

**LIMA—*IMMANUEL*** (419)222-2541
Gary J Childs Michael A Phillips • WS 8 1030; SS 915;* • H • EL • OH • 2120 Lakewood Ave Lima OH 45805-3171 • FAX(419)229-2416 • immanuel@wcoil.com

**LODI—*CHRIST KING*** (330)948-3000
Christopher T Cahill • H • S • 8080 Lafayette Rd 44254-9611 PO Box 183 Lodi OH 44254-0183 • FAX(330)948-2515

**LOGAN—*TRINITY*** (740)385-3220
Danny R Koch • WS 1045; SS 915; BC 915 • H • OH • 430 N Mulberry St 43138-1336 PO Box 586 Logan OH 43138-0586 • dannyvalkoch@juno.com

**LORAIN—*PRINCIPE DE PAZ*** (440)277-0777
Juan A Gonzalez • H • OH • 1607 E 31st St Lorain OH 44055-1709 • FAX(440)282-2381 • egm777@centuryinter.net

***SS PETER&PAUL*** (216)233-5166
Edgar O Anthony • * • H • S • 1500 Lincoln Blvd Lorain OH 44055-3137

***ZION*** (440)282-8418
Kevin K Saylor • H • EC • OH • 5100 Ashland Ave Lorain OH 44053-3418 • FAX(440)282-8418

**MADISON—*HOLY CROSS*** (440)428-3759
Howard A Davis • H • EL • OH • 3050 Mc Mackin Rd Madison OH 44057-2768

**MAINVILLE—*OUR REDEEMER***
See Silverton

**MANSFIELD—*FAITH*** (419)756-4665
Denis J Wittenberger • WS 1030; SS 915;* • H • OH • 1685 Lexington Ave Mansfield OH 44907-2906 • FAX(419)756-4665 • faithlcms@aol.com

**MANTUA—*CHRIST*** (330)274-2849
Douglas E Riley • WS 10;* • OH • 10827 N Main St 44255 PO Box 737 Mantua OH 44255-0737

**MAPLE HEIGHTS—*ZION*** (216)475-2267
John T Vitello • H • HS • OH • 5754 Dunham Rd Maple Heights OH 44137-3663

**MARION—*GETHSEMANE**** (740)375-0599
Vacant • WS 1030; SS 915;* • H • OH • 240 W Church St 43302-4126 PO Box 111 Marion OH 43301-0111 • FAX(740)382-1609 • brett³cornelius@hotmail.com

**MARYSVILLE 4 SE—*ST JOHN*** (937)644-5540
Thomas S Hackett Jack D Heino • WS 8 1030; SS 915; BC 915 • H • EC/EL • OH • 43040 12809 State Route 736 Marysville OH 43040-9056 • FAX(937)644-1086 • stjohnsl@postbox.esu.k12.oh.us

**MASON—*KING OF KINGS***
See Landen

**MASSILLON—*ST JOHN*** (330)837-4645
John L Telloni • WS 8 1030; SS 915; BC 915 • H • EC/EL • S • 1900 Wales Rd NE Massillon OH 44646-4172 • FAX(330)837-2918 • stjohnmass@aol.com

**MAYFIELD HEIGHTS—*OUR SAVIOR*** (440)442-4455
Robert C Reinhardt • WS 9 1030;* • H • HS • OH • 2154 SOM Center Rd Cleveland OH 44124-4232 • FAX(440)442-4995

**MEDINA TOWNSHIP—*PRINCE PEACE*** (330)723-8293
Daniel R Haberkost • H • EN • 44256 3355 Medina Rd Medina OH 44256-9631

**MENTOR—*FAITH*** (440)255-2229
Ronald P Le Pere • Tina M Ziemnick DCE • * • H • EL • OH • 8125 Mentor Ave Mentor OH 44060-5744 • FAX(440)255-4186 • flc@stratos.net

***GOOD SHEPHERD*** (216)257-7822
Vacant • WS 815 1045;* • H • EL • OH • 7643 Lakeshore Blvd Mentor OH 44060-3364 • FAX(216)257-0970

**MIDDLETOWN—*MESSIAH*** (513)422-2441
Thomas W Chopp • WS 1030; SS 9; BC 9 • H • EC • OH • 4715 Holly Ave Middletown OH 45044-5314 • tomshopp@infinet.com

**MILFORD—*ST MARK*** (513)575-0292
William A Dierks Michael K Heidle • H • EC • OH • 5849 Buckwheat Rd Milford OH 45150-2459

**MILFORD CENTER—*ST PAUL***
See Chuckery

**MOUNT HOPE—*ST JOHN*** (330)674-5191
Wayne H Giesler • WS 915; SS 1015; BC 1015 • OH • 8084 State Rte 241 44660 PO Box 11 Mount Hope OH 44660-0011 • wgiesler@aol.com

**NAPOLEON—*ST PAUL*** (419)592-3535
Norman A Koy Peter C Marcis • Kurt F Mews DCE Harold A Frerich DCE • WS 8 920 1045;* • H • EC/EL • OH • 1075 Glenwood Ave Napoleon OH 43545-1250 • FAX(419)592-0652 • stpaulnap@yahoo.com

***ST PETER***
See Florida

**NAPOLEON 5 S—*ST PAUL*** (419)264-5511
Douglas R Corniels • WS 830; SS 945 • OH • Sr 108 43545 107 E School St Napoleon OH 43545-9217

**NAPOLEON 6 NW—*ST JOHN*** (419)598-8961
Stephen J Niermann • WS 9; BC 10;* • H • EL • OH • 43545 16035 County Road U Napoleon OH 43545-9753 • FAX(419)598-8518

**NEWARK—*OUR SAVIOR*** (614)366-6459
Vacant • H • OH • 1137 Sharon Valley Rd Newark OH 43055-1761 • pastorchris@alltel.net

**NORTH CANTON—*HOLY CROSS*** (330)499-3307
James W Menke William D Hugo • Michael S Creutz DCE • WS 815; SS 930; BC 11 • H • EC • OH • 44711 7707 Market Ave N Canton OH 44721-1642 • FAX(330)499-2319 • holycrossluth@juno.com

**NORTH JACKSON—*GETHSEMANE*** (330)538-2630
James A Oester • WS 9; SS 1015; BC 1015 • H • OH • 1110 N Salem Warren Rd North Jackson OH 44451-9602 • FAX(330)538-0569 • passher@netzero.net

**NORTH OLMSTED—*ASCENSION*** (440)777-6365
Roger R Stuenkel Daniel G Wenger(X) • WS 11 830;* • H • EC/HS • EN • 28081 Lorain Rd North Olmsted OH 44070-4026 • FAX(440)777-1609 • ascendno@juno.com

**NORTH RIDGEVILLE—*SHEPHERD*** (440)327-7321
Paul R Oberhaus • WS 1015; SS 9; BC 9;* • EC • OH • 34555 Center Ridge Rd North Ridgeville OH 44039-3155

**NORTH ROYALTON—*ROYAL*** (440)237-7958
James P Martin David S Luecke • WS 945 1115; BC 815;* • H • EC/EL/HS • OH • 11680 Royalton Rd North Royalton OH 44133-4461 • FAX(440)237-6992 • royalredeemer@compuserve.com

**NORTHFIELD—*EPIPHANY*** (330)467-7710
Christian F Just • WS 8 930;* • H • EN • 10503 Valley View Rd Northfield OH 44067-1430 • FAX(330)467-7710

**NORTON—*ST MATTHEW*** (216)825-4100
John D Mashek • H • S • 5451 Cleve Mass Rd Norton OH 44203-7823 • johnma@raex.com

**OBERLIN—*GRACE*** (440)775-3271
Richard J Docekal • H • EN • 310 W Lorain St Oberlin OH 44074-1028

**OHIO CITY 9 NW—*ST THOMAS*** (419)495-2408
Eric L Ebb • WS 9; SS 1015; BC 1015;* • H • OH • 45874 6299 German Church Rd Ohio City OH 45874-9527

**OREGON—*PRINCE PEACE*** (419)691-9407
Donald E Weiss • WS 10; SS 9; BC 9 • H • EC • OH • 4155 Pickle Rd Oregon OH 43616-4135 • FAX(419)691-8406 • dewpophome@aol.com

**PAINESVILLE—*ZION*** (440)357-5174
Kenton G Wendorf James R Zinkowich Ottomar E Bickel(EM) • WS 815 11; SS 945; BC 945;* • H • EL • OH • 508 Mentor Ave Painesville OH 44077-2628 • FAX(440)357-7158 • pkent508@aol.com

**PAINESVILLE 2 E—*ST PAUL*** (440)354-3000
Eric R Linthicum • Peggy A Backs DEAC • WS 815 1030; SS 915; BC 915;* • H • EC/EL • OH • 44077 250 Bowhall Rd Painesville OH 44077-5219 • FAX(440)354-7085 • stpauls@oh.verio.com

**PARMA—*BETHANY*** (440)884-1230
Daniel J Wegrzyn Joseph D Love • H • EC/EL/HS • OH • 6041 Ridge Rd Parma OH 44129-4498 • FAX(440)884-9813

***BETHLEHEM*** (440)845-2230
Robert L Green • WS 815; SS 930; BC 930 • H • EC/HS • OH • 7500 State Rd Parma OH 44134-6102 • bethlehem7500@aol.com

***CALVARY*** (440)845-0070
Todd A Biermann • WS 830 11; SS 945; BC 945 • H • S • 6906 W Pleasant Valley Rd Parma OH 44129-6745 • FAX(440)845-7499 • calvary.parma@lutheran.com

***HOLY TRINITY*** (216)741-2602
John R Schonkaes • H • S • 6220 Broadview Rd Parma OH 44134-3113 • FAX(216)741-2602 • JSchonkaes112@msn.com

**PERRYSBURG 2 S—*SHEP OF VALLEY*** (419)874-6939
John M Rutz • WS 1015; SS 9; BC 9 • H • OH • 43551 13101 5 Point Rd Perrysburg OH 43551-1341 • mewinter@juno.com

**PICKERINGTON—*DIVINE SHEPHERD****
Vacant • H • OH • 12800 Wheaton Ave NW Pickerington OH 43147 • divine³shepherd³lcms@yahoo.com

**PLEASANT CITY—*HOLY TRINITY*** (614)685-5991
Vacant • WS 930 4 • H • S • PO Box 309 Pleasant City OH 43772-0309

**PORTSMOUTH—*OUR SAVIOR**** (740)775-2470
Vacant • H • OH • 9th And Gallia 45662 151 University Dr Chillicothe OH 45601-2117

**RIDGEVILLE CORNERS—*ST JOHN*** (419)267-5180
Dale B Kern • WS 1015 8; SS 9; BC 9;* • H • OH • 43555 23120 US Highway 6 Stryker OH 43557-9452 • FAX(419)267-5266 • dkern@bright.net

***ZION*** (419)267-3429
Alvia M Martis • * • H • OH • 20-141 County Rd X 43555 PO Box 37 Ridgeville Corners OH 43555-0037 • FAX(419)267-3470 • zionreva@bright.net

**ROCKY RIVER—*ST THOMAS*** (440)331-2680
Eric L Van Scyoc • WS 815; SS 930 • H • EC/EL/HS • OH • 21211 Detroit Rd Rocky River OH 44116-2213 • FAX(440)331-2681 • stthomasrr@netzero.net

**SHAKER HEIGHTS—*ST PETER*** (216)561-2511
Jeffrey B Stephens • WS 815 1045; SS 930; BC 930 • HS • OH • 18000 Van Aken Blvd Shaker Heights OH 44122-4807 • FAX(216)561-4003 • stpeters@stratos.net

**SHEFFIELD VILLAGE—*HOPE*** (440)949-2620
Gary D Georgi • WS 830 11 • H • EC • OH • 4792 Oster Rd Sheffield Village OH 44054-1446 • FAX(440)949-5749 • hope2000@bright.net

**SHERWOOD 3 NW—*ST JOHN*** (419)899-2850
Robert D Eble • H • OH • 43556 9088 Openlander Rd Sherwood OH 43556-9751 • stjohnsh@bright.net

**SIDNEY—*REDEEMER*** (937)492-2461
Kenneth R Castor • WS 9; SS 1015;* • H • OH • 300 W Mason Rd Sidney OH 45365 • rlc1@bright.net

**SILVERTON—*OUR REDEEMER*** (513)697-7335
Timothy Patten John W Mitchell Jr. • H • OH • UKNWN 6734 S State Route 48 Maineville OH 45039-9775 • FAX(513)697-6397 • ouredeemer@aol.com

**SOLON—*OUR REDEEMER*** (440)248-4066
V P Woods Mark G Matzke • Christopher E Rennison DCE • WS 8 915 1030; SS 1030 915; BC 1030 915 • H • EC • OH • 7196 Som Center Rd Solon OH 44139-4230 • FAX(440)248-9413 • ourredeemerlutheran@earthlink.net

**SOUTH EUCLID—*ST JOHN*** (216)381-1513
Allen R Trapp • WS 830 11; SS 945; BC 10 • EC/EL/HS • OH • 4386 Mayfield Rd South Euclid OH 44121-3608 • FAX(216)381-1564

**SPRINGFIELD—*RISEN CHRIST*** (937)323-3688
Gordon P Bohlmann • WS 8 1030; SS 915; BC 915 • H • EC • OH • 41 E Possum Rd Springfield OH 45502-9477 • FAX(937)323-3746

**ST MARYS—*LORD OF LIFE****
See Celina

**STEUBENVILLE—*ST MARK*** (740)264-2561
Kenneth A Greenwald • H • S • 133 Lovers Ln Steubenville OH 43953

**STRONGSVILLE—*ST JOHN*** (440)234-5806
Thomas M Sharpe • H • HS • OH • 8888 Prospect Rd Strongsville OH 44136-1209 • FAX(440)234-5821 • tsharpe@stratos.net

**STRYKER—*ST JOHN***
See Ridgeville Corners 3W

**SUGAR GROVE 3 E—*TRINITY*** (740)746-8316
Danny R Koch • WS 815; SS 930; BC 930 • H • OH • 43155 7120 Sponagle Rd Sugar Grove OH 43155-9780 • dannyvalkoch@juno.com

**SUNBURY—*HOPE***
See Condit

**SYLVANIA—*KING OF GLORY*** (419)882-6488
Vacant • WS 830 1030; SS 915;* • H • EN • 6517 Brint Rd Sylvania OH 43560-3114 • FAX(419)882-6488 • kingof.glory@sylvania.sev.org

**TALLMADGE—*TALLMADGE*** (330)633-4775
David R Zachrich • Amber L Styskal DCE • WS 8 1030; SS 915; BC 915 • H • EC • OH • 44278 759 East Ave Tallmadge OH 44278-2566 • FAX(330)633-4846 • tallmadgeluthchurch@juno.com

**THOMPSON—*GRACE*** (216)298-3822
Ross W Fees • H • EL • OH • 8091 Plank Rd Thompson OH 44086-9537

**TIFFIN—*REDEEMER*** (419)447-7794
Jan S Kucera • H • OH • 1065 S Washington St Tiffin OH 44883-3492

**TOLEDO—*CONCORDIA*** (419)382-0410
Douglas H Meilander • H • EC • OH • 3636 S Detroit Ave Toledo OH 43614-4412 • FAX(419)382-6383

***GLORIA DEI*** (419)536-2020
Frederick A Anson • WS 1015;* • H • OH • 5845 Elmer Dr Toledo OH 43615-2705 • gloriadeiluthch@juno.com

***GOOD SHEP DEAF*** (419)536-3370
Shirrel Petzoldt • WS 1030; BC 930;* • OH • 5859 Elmer Dr Toledo OH 43615-2705

***GOOD SHEPHERD*** (419)474-0529
Bradford E Scott • WS 1030; SS 9; BC 9 • H • EL • EN • 3934 W Laskey Rd Toledo OH 43623-3705 • FAX(419)474-0520

***HOLY CROSS*** (419)476-6256
Peter M Burfeind • EN • 700 Eleanor Ave Toledo OH 43612-2308

***IMMANUEL*** (419)726-3991
Timothy A Daene • WS 930;* • EC • OH • 710 Buckeye St Toledo OH 43611-3805

***ST PHILIP*** (419)475-2835
Paul G Baumann Richard W Sansbury(#) • WS 1030; SS 9; BC 9 • H • EC • OH • 3002 Upton Ave Toledo OH 43606-3964 • FAX(419)472-9032

***TRINITY*** (419)385-2651
Charles E Brandt Edward B Andrada James Tsang(DM) • H • EC/EL • OH • 4560 Glendale Ave Toledo OH 43614-1907 • FAX(419)385-2636 • cbrandt@trinity.pvt.k12.oh.us

**VALLEY CITY—*ST PAUL*** (330)483-4119
Dennis D Murawski • * • H • OH • 1377 Lester Rd 44280-9443 PO Box 455 Valley City OH 44280-0455 • ddm@mail.ohio.net

**VAN WERT—*EMMANUEL*** (419)238-4992
William E Barlow • WS 9; SS 1015; BC 1015 • H • OH • 705 S Washington St Van Wert OH 45891-2354

**VERMILION—*ST MATTHEW*** (440)967-9886
James J Peter • WS 1030;* • H • OH • 15617 Mason Rd 44089-9206 PO Box 323 Vermilion OH 44089-0323 • FAX(440)967-0724

**WAPAKONETA—*LORD OF LIFE****
See Celina

**WAPAKONETA 3 SE—*ST JOHN*** (419)738-6746
Michael A Nicol • WS 10; SS 850; BC 850 • H • OH • 45895 15321 Pusheta Rd Wapakoneta OH 45895-8413 • FAX(419)738-6746 • stjohnlc@bright.net

**WARREN—*TRINITY*** (330)372-1897
Norman H Schinkel • H • OH • 2742 North Rd NE Warren OH 44483-3049

**WAUSEON—*EMMAUS*** (419)335-7446
Thomas S Lutz • WS 745 1015; SS 9; BC 9 • H • EC • OH • 841 N Shoop Ave Wauseon OH 43567-1800 • FAX(419)335-7446

**WAUSEON 3 S—*ST LUKE*** (419)335-9170
Richard W Behnke • WS 10; SS 9; BC 9 • H • OH • 1588 Sr 108 43567 1640 State Route 108 Wauseon OH 43567-9446 • FAX(419)335-9170 • rbehnke@bright.net

**WELLINGTON—*BETHANY*** (440)647-5300
Dale B Huelsman • WS 1015; SS 9; BC 9 • H • OH • 231 E Hamilton St Wellington OH 44090-1115

**WEST CHESTER—*ROYAL REDEEMER***
See Liberty Township

**WESTLAKE—*ST PAUL*** (440)835-3050
Larry F Wesolik David D Buegler • WS 9 1030; SS 1030 9; BC 1030 9;* • H • EL/HS • OH • 27993 Detroit Rd Westlake OH 44145-2149 • FAX(440)835-8216 • stpaul$^3$luth@ameritech.net

**WILLOUGHBY—*TRINITY*** (440)942-7766
Robert Schuler • H • OH • 37728 Euclid Ave Willoughby OH 44094-5926 • FAX(440)942-2021

**WILLOWICK—*BETHEL*** (440)943-5000
Keith A Knupp • * • H • OH • 32410 Willowick Dr Willowick OH 44095-3809 • FAX(440)943-0008 • bethellc.lcms@juno.com

**WILLSHIRE 3 E—*ZION*** (419)495-2398
Tim B Zechiel • H • OH • 45898 17434 Schumm Rd Willshire OH 45898-9837 • FAX(419)495-2350 • zionschumm@juno.com

**WOOSTER—*CONCORDIA*** (330)262-2456
Wayne H Giesler • WS 11;* • H • OH • 2343 Star Dr Wooster OH 44691-9019 • wgiesler@aol.com

**YOUNGSTOWN—*CONCORDIA*** (330)792-1805
Joel R Kurz • WS 1030; SS 930; BC 930 • S • 125 N Brockway Ave Youngstown OH 44509-2317

***IMMANUEL*** (330)747-1628
Kenneth D Kelly • * • H • OH • 485 Redondo Rd Youngstown OH 44504-1461 • Immanluth@aol.com

***REDEEMER*** (216)799-7823
Vacant • WS 1030; SS 9; BC 9 • H • OH • 44501 2305 S Canfield Niles Rd Austintown OH 44515-5007

***ST MARK*** (330)788-8995
Robert F Shonholz • * • H • EC • OH • 280 Mill Creek Dr Youngstown OH 44512-1405 • FAX(330)788-8995 • shonconn@aol.com

***VICTORY*** (330)747-2491
Hosea J Ekong • WS 11; SS 10;* • H • OH • 2110 Glenwood Ave Youngstown OH 44511-1531 • hoseaekong@juno.com

**ZANESVILLE—*TRINITY*** (740)453-0744
Larry R Kudart Keith A Lingsch • H • OH • 128 S 7th St Zanesville OH 43701-4304

## OKLAHOMA

**ADA—*FIRST*** (580)332-3433
Gary R Brandt • H • OK • 1319 E 18th St Ada OK 74820-4308 • FAX(580)332-3433 • gbrandt@juno.com

**ADAIR—*BETHLEHEM*** (918)785-2994
John C Polk Sr. • SS 1015 • H • OK • RR 1 Box 2750 Adair OK 74330-9727

**ALTUS—*FAITH*** (580)482-2222
William S Geis • H • OK • 2401 N Park Ln Altus OK 73521-2221 • FAX(580)846-5672 • wsgeis@lutheranok.com

**ALVA—*ZION*** (405)327-0510
Joel T Picard • WS 1030; SS 930;* • H • EC • OK • 218 Maple St Alva OK 73717-2836 • zlcalva@pldi.net

**APACHE—*ST PETER*** (580)588-2480
Vacant • H • OK • 321 E Franklin 73006 PO Box 762 Apache OK 73006-0762

**ARDMORE—*TRINITY*** (580)223-3048
Robert M Hinckley • H • OK • 1624 Harris St NW Ardmore OK 73401-1412 • lutheran@brightok.net

**BARTLESVILLE—*REDEEMER*** (918)333-6022
Vacant • Jonathan D Schultz DCE • WS 815 1045; SS 930; BC 930 • H • EC • OK • 3700 SE Woodland Rd Bartlesville OK 74006-4531 • FAX(918)333-2691 • redeembul@aol.com

**BEAVER—*PEACE*** (316)873-2966
Lynn E Spencer • OK • PO Box 323 Beaver OK 73932-0323

**BETHANY—*OUR SAVIOR*** (405)495-1605
Willard H Stark(EM) • Christopher W Schwenneker DCE • H • OK • 6501 NW 23rd St Bethany OK 73008-4701 • FAX(405)495-8386

**BLACKWELL—*TRINITY*** (580)363-4026
Robert D Alexander • WS 1030; SS 915 • H • EC • OK • 125 Vinnedge Ave 74631-4836 PO Box 545 Blackwell OK 74631-0545 • FAX(580)363-2464 • tlc@kskc.net

**BLACKWELL 6 NE—*ST JOHN*** (405)363-4603
Ernest Quillen(#) • H • OK • 74631 1998 North S St Ponca City OK 74601

**BOISE CITY—*HOPE*** (405)544-2420
John A Miller • H • OK • 408 W Main St Boise City OK 73933

**BRECKINRIDGE—*IMMANUEL*** (580)446-5521
Arthur M Mc Cormick • WS 1030; SS 930; BC 930 • H • OK • 418 Cty Rd UKNWN RR 6 Box 529B Enid OK 73701-9523 • Immanuel.breckinridge@juno.com

**BROKEN ARROW—*IMMANUEL*** (918)258-5506
Arthur J Spomer Dennis R Hilken • H • EC/EL • OK • 216 Luther Dr Broken Arrow OK 74012-1405 • FAX(918)251-8365 • general@immanuelba.org

***TRINITY*** (918)455-5750
Vacant • Cynthia L Twillman DCE • WS 8 1045; SS 930; BC 930 • H • OK • 5750 S Elm Pl Broken Arrow OK 74011-4823 • FAX(918)455-7726 • tlcba@aol.com

**BUFFALO—*ZION*** (580)735-2733
Joseph P Andrajack Jr. • WS 1030; SS 930;* • H • OK • S Hwy 64 73834 PO Box 632 Buffalo OK 73834-0632

**CHELSEA—*ZION*** (918)789-2110
Vacant • H • OK • 211 W 10th St 74016-1835 PO Box 271 Chelsea OK 74016-0271

**CHICKASHA—*FIRST*** (405)224-1552
David B Thompson • H • OK • 828 Minnesota Ave Chickasha OK 73018

**CLAREMORE—*REDEEMER*** (918)341-1429
Mark E Carter • WS 1030; SS 9; BC 9 • H • EC • OK • 220 N Seminole Ave Claremore OK 74017-8425

**COVINGTON—*ST JOHN*** (405)864-7965
Jerry D Brown • WS 1045; SS 930; BC 930 • H • OK • PO Box 92 Covington OK 73730-0092

**CUSHING—*OUR REDEEMER*** (918)225-4646
Vacant • H • OK • 730 E Cherry St Cushing OK 74023-4046

**DAVIS—*HOPE****
See Sulphur

**DUNCAN—*GOOD SHEPHERD*** (580)255-3267
David A Reese • WS 8 1030; SS 915; BC 915 • H • OK • 2401 N Country Club Rd 73533-3315 1008 W Plato Rd Duncan OK 73533-3216 • FAX(580)255-3001 • gslc@texhoma.net

**EDMOND—*HOLY TRINITY*** (405)348-3292
Barrie E Henke • WS 815 1045; SS 930;* • H • EC • OK • 308 NW 164th St Edmond OK 73013-2006 • FAX(405)348-8458 • htlcok@flash.net

***ST MARK*** (405)340-0192
Peter T Heckmann • WS 1015; SS 9; BC 9 • H • EC • OK • 1501 N Bryant Ave Edmond OK 73034-3250 • FAX(405)340-0142 • stmarkluth@ionet.net

**EL RENO—*TRINITY*** (405)262-7116
Bruce C Morant • WS 1030; SS 915;* • H • OK • 500 S Country Club Rd El Reno OK 73036-4302

**ELK CITY—*CHRIST*** (580)225-2266
William S Geis • H • OK • 1023 W 2nd St Elk City OK 73644-4612 • FAX(580)225-5672 • wsgeis@lutheranok.com

**ENID—*IMMANUEL***
See Breckinridge

***REDEEMER*** (405)234-6622
Dwayne J Schroeder • WS 8 1030; SS 915 • H • OK • 215 S Cleveland St Enid OK 73703-5304 • redeemer-enid@juno.com

***ST PAUL*** (580)234-6646
Kenneth E Wade • Stephen E Wiederkehr DCE • H • EC/EL • OK • 1626 E Broadway Ave Enid OK 73701-4539 • FAX(580)234-6692 • stpaulsenid@juno.com

**ENID 8 WNW—*TRINITY*** (580)855-2554
Gary L Hendrickson • WS 1030; BC 930;* • H • OK • RR 2 Box 357 Enid OK 73703-9734 • FAX(580)855-2554 • g$^3$hendrickson@juno.com

**EUFAULA—*GOOD SHEPHERD*** (918)689-2169
Roland C Hartmann • WS 9 • OK • Eunice Burns Rd 74432 PO Box 687 Eufaula OK 74432-0687

**FAIRLAND—*ST PAUL*** (918)676-3059
Leo G Schroeder(#) • H • EC • OK • Washington And Pine 74343 PO Box 219 Fairland OK 74343-0219 • stpaulluthch@rectec.net

**FAIRMONT—*ZION*** (580)358-2291
Timothy D Dorsch • H • EC • OK • RR 1 Box 16 Fairmont OK 73736-9701 • dorschtd@juno.com

**GARBER—*IMMANUEL*** (405)863-2722
Joseph L Myers • H • OK • Ponca And Arapaho 73738 PO Box 59 Garber OK 73738-0059 • imlutheran@juno.com

**GRANITE—*ST JOHN*** (580)535-4662
Vacant • H • OK • Ada And Parker 73547 PO Box 56 Granite OK 73547-0056 • FAX(580)846-5672 • wsgeis@lutheranok.com

**GUTHRIE—*OUR SAVIOR***
Vacant • OK • PO Box 1552 Guthrie OK 73044

***ZION*** (405)282-3914
Merlyn C Lohrke • WS 1045; SS 930; BC 930 • H • OK • 424 E Warner Ave 73044-3348 PO Box 996 Guthrie OK 73044-0996

**GUYMON—*TRINITY*** (580)338-3820
Mark A Wescoatt • WS 1030; SS 915;* • H • EC • OK • 1212 N Crumley St Guymon OK 73942-3643 • wescott@ptsi.net

**HINTON—*ST JOHN*** (405)542-6472
Earl D Philipp • OK • Enid And Spencer 73047 PO Box 8 Hinton OK 73047-0008

**HOOKER—*ST JOHN*** (580)652-2683
Christopher M Boehnke • WS 1030; SS 930 • H • OK • Hickory And Jackson 73945 PO Box 65 Hooker OK 73945-0065

**KINGFISHER—*EMMANUEL*** (405)375-3431
David L Krepel • H • OK • Main St And Douglas Ave 73750 124 W Douglas Ave Kingfisher OK 73750-4123 • dlklcms@aol.com

**KREBS—*TRINITY*** (918)426-4544
Robert A Dibell • WS 1030; SS 915; BC 915 • H • OK • 74554 RR 6 Box 777 Mc Alester OK 74501-9251

**LAHOMA—*ZION*** (580)796-2243
Velmer H Goebel • WS 1045; SS 930; BC 930 • H • EC • OK • Oklahoma And 5th St 73754 PO Box 128 Lahoma OK 73754-0128

**LAWTON—*HOLY CROSS*** (580)357-7684
Donald R Howard • WS 8 1030; SS 915;* • H • EC • OK • 2105 NW 38th St Lawton OK 73505-1809 • FAX(580)357-7684 • holycros@sirinet.net

***ST JOHN*** (580)353-0556
Richard Mayer Keith W Schweitzer Herman R Mayer • WS 9 11; SS 9; BC 11;* • H • EC • OK • 102 SW 7th St Lawton OK 73501-3922 • FAX(580)353-0646 • keithlcms@aol.com

**LONE WOLF—*ST JOHN*** (580)846-5459
William S Geis Ronald E Boelte(#) • H • OK • Second At Evans 73655 PO Box 326 Lone Wolf OK 73655-9998 • FAX(580)846-5672 • wsgeis@lutheranok.com

**MIAMI—*MOUNT OLIVE*** (918)542-4681
Donald G Kirchhoff • WS 1030; SS 915; BC 915;* • H • EC/EL • OK • 2337 N Main St Miami OK 74354-1621 • FAX(918)542-4681 • mtolive@rectec.net

**MIDWEST CITY—*GOOD SHEPHERD*** (405)732-2585
John A Ellington Michael J Reckling Kevin L Yoakum • H • EC/EL • OK • 700 N Air Depot Blvd Midwest City OK 73110-3763 • FAX(405)732-3977 • pastore2@juno.com

**MOORE—*ST JOHN*** (405)794-5462
Paul A Hartman • WS 8 1030; SS 915; BC 915 • H • EC • OK • 1032 NW 12th St Moore OK 73160-1604 • FAX(405)794-5690 • sjlcmoore@aol.com

**MUSKOGEE—*FIRST*** (918)683-4673
Wayne M Schuett • WS 1030; SS 915;* • H • OK • 428 E Broadway St Muskogee OK 74403-5111 • FAX(918)682-9533 • flcmusk@intellex.com

**MUSTANG—*CHRIST*** (405)376-3116
Terrance S Adamson • WS 1030 8; SS 915;* • H • EC/EL • OK • 501 N Clear Springs Rd 73064-1518 PO Box 98 Mustang OK 73064-0098 • FAX(405)376-3118 • christlc@swbell.net

**NEWKIRK—*ST JOHN*** (405)362-3750
Ernest Quillen(#) • H • OK • 7th And Magnolia 74647 209 S Plum Newkirk OK 74647-4019

**NORMAN—*TRINITY*** (405)321-3443
David R Nehrenz • Carole A Prime DCE • H • EC/EL • OK • 603 Classen Blvd Norman OK 73071-5007 • nehrenznet@aol.com

**OKARCHE—*ST JOHN*** (405)263-7311
John D Walther • WS 1015; SS 9; BC 9;* • H • EC/EL • OK • 408 W Colorado 73762-9121 PO Box 66 Okarche OK 73762-0066 • FAX(405)263-7656 • johnwalther@hotmail.com

**OKLAHOMA CITY—*FAITH*** (405)632-5744
W R Rains(#) • WS 1015; SS 9; BC 9 • H • OK • 2512 S Shartel Ave Oklahoma City OK 73109-1725 • faithokc@aol.com

***IMMANUEL*** (405)525-5793
Clinton R Mc Mullin • WS 815 1030; SS 915; BC 915 • H • OK • 1800 NW 36th St Oklahoma City OK 73118-3229 • FAX(405)528-8967 • immluth@juno.com

***MESSIAH*** (405)946-0681
Steven M Larsen Marvin A Henschel • Myron D Harms DCE • H • EC/EL • OK • 3600 NW Expressway Oklahoma City OK 73112-4410 • FAX(405)946-0682 • pastor@messiahokc.org

***ZION*** (405)722-7472
Ronald E Christie • H • OK • 7701 W Britton Rd Oklahoma City OK 73132-1514

**OKMULGEE—*TRINITY*** (918)756-6046
Myles R Schultz • WS 1045; SS 930 • H • OK • 1314 E 6th St Okmulgee OK 74447-4712 • tlcok74447@aol.com

**OWASSO—*FAITH*** (918)272-9858
William R Diekelman Harold J Klawitter(EM) • WS 8 1030; SS 915;* • H • EC/EL • OK • 9222 N Garnett Rd Owasso OK 74055-4424 • FAX(918)272-4629 • okpres@aol.com

**PONCA CITY—*FIRST*** (580)762-1111
Thomas G Ramsey • Heidi K Gillum DCE • WS 830 11 630; SS 945; BC 945 • H • EC/EL • OK • 1101 N 4th St Ponca City OK 74601-2724 • FAX(580)762-1111 • sowramsey@yahoo.com

***ST JOHN***
See Blackwell 6 NE

**POND CREEK—*FIRST*** (580)532-6531
Vacant • H • OK • 5th And W Birch 73766 PO Box 218 Pond Creek OK 73766-0218 • firstluth@juno.com

**PRYOR—*ST JOHN*** (918)825-1926
Mark R Erler • WS 9; SS 1030; BC 1030 • H • OK • 607 SE 9th St Pryor OK 74361-7028

**SALLISAW—*TRINITY*** (918)775-6753
Vacant • H • OK • HC 61 Box 50 Sallisaw OK 74955-9420

**SHATTUCK—*CHRIST*** (580)938-5208
Gary W Mc Clellan • H • OK • Third And Charles 73858 PO Box 456 Shattuck OK 73858-0456

**SHAWNEE—*REDEEMER*** (405)273-6286
Lenny Szeto • H • OK • 39307 Mac Arthur St Shawnee OK 74804-2485

**STILLWATER—*ZION*** (405)372-3703
Carlton L Riemer • WS 1030 8; SS 915;* • H • OK • 504 S Knoblock St Stillwater OK 74074-3026 • FAX(405)372-0372 • zionluth@provalue.net

**SULPHUR—*HOPE**** (580)369-5527
Vacant • WS 745; SS 845;* • H • OK • Third And Claremore 73086 C/O Melbourne Jones 1204 E Ellis Davis OK 73030 • gbrandt@juno.com

**TAHLEQUAH—*FIRST*** (918)456-5070
Bruce A Alberts • WS 1045; SS 930;* • H • EC • OK • 2111 Mahaney Ave Tahlequah OK 74464-5761 • FAX(518)456-5070 • first$^3$luth@intellex.com

**TEXHOMA—*ST PAUL*** (405)423-7224
Vacant • H • OK • 416 N Second 73949 PO Box 465 Texhoma OK 73949-0465

**TULSA—*CHRIST THE REDEEMER*** (918)492-6451
John F Raddatz • WS 815 1045; SS 930; BC 930 • H • EC • OK • 2550 E 71st St Tulsa OK 74136-5531 • FAX(918)492-3524 • ctrluth@ionet.net

***GOOD SHEPHERD*** (918)622-2905
Leonard E Busch • WS 1030 830; SS 930;* • H • EC/EL • OK • 8730 E Skelly Dr Tulsa OK 74129-3422 • FAX(918)622-3805 • gslcoffc@gslctulsa.org

***GRACE*** (918)592-2999
James R Haner • Charles E Eaton DCE • WS 10; SS 9; BC 9 • H • EC/EL • OK • 2331 E 5th Pl Tulsa OK 74104-2632 • FAX(918)592-3017 • jhaner@swbell.net

***OUR SAVIOR*** (918)836-3752
Timothy P Dreier • WS 8 1045; SS 930; BC 930 • H • EC/EL • OK • 146 S Sheridan Rd Tulsa OK 74112-1719 • FAX(918)836-4538 • knotbrad@oursaviorlutheran.com

**TUTTLE—*LAMB OF GOD*** (405)381-2695
Vacant • H • OK • 3 Nw 1st 73089 PO Box 506 Tuttle OK 73089-0506

**VINITA—*MESSIAH*** (918)256-3223
Clemens H Hartfield(EM) • WS 10; SS 9; BC 9 • H • OK • 460 N Wilson St 74301-2433 PO Box 392 Vinita OK 74301-0392

**WATONGA—*MOUNT CALVARY*** (580)623-5099
Matthew J Larson • WS 1045; SS 930; BC 930 • H • OK • 621 N Leach Ave Watonga OK 73772-2823 • mtcalvary@pldi.net

**WELLSTON—*ST PAUL*** (405)356-4203
Chad L Bird • WS 1030; SS 915; BC 915 • H • OK • 706 Birch 74881 PO Box 333 Wellston OK 74881-0333 • torahman@juno.com

**WOODWARD—*TRINITY*** (580)256-2524
Guillaume J S Williams • WS 930; SS 1030;* • H • OK • 1518 14th St Woodward OK 73801-4418

## ONTARIO

**PORT CREDIT—*ST MARK***
See Mississauga

## OREGON

**ALBANY—*HOLY CROSS*** (541)928-0214
Bruce G Ley • WS 1030; SS 915; BC 915 • H • NOW • 2515 Queen Ave SE Albany OR 97321-6861 • FAX(541)928-0200

***IMMANUEL*** (541)926-3495
Robert M Bjornstad • WS 1030 • H • NOW • 154 Madison St SE Albany OR 97321-3009

**ALOHA—*BETHLEHEM*** (503)649-3380
Jonathan M Dinger • Robert B Fossum DCE • WS 8 11 5; SS 930; BC 930 • H • EC/EL • NOW • 97005 18865 SW Johnson St Aloha OR 97006-3164 • FAX(503)649-1530 • bethlehem@usinternet.com

**ASHLAND—*GRACE*** (541)482-1661
Anthony J Schultz • WS 10; SS 845; BC 845 • H • EC/EL • NOW • 660 Frances Ln Ashland OR 97520-3410 • FAX(541)482-2860 • grace75552@aol.com

**BEAVERTON—*PILGRIM*** (503)644-4656
Michael P Bailey • Andrea Gehrke DCE • H • EC/EL • NOW • 5650 SW Hall Blvd Beaverton OR 97005-3918 • FAX(503)644-8182

**BEND—*TRINITY*** (541)382-1832
Robert F Luinstra David A Carnahan • WS 8 11; SS 945; BC 945;* • H • EC/EL • NOW • 97701 1034 NE 11th St Bend OR 97701-4402 • FAX(541)389-9171 • saints@bendcable.com

**BURNS—*FIRST EVANGELICAL*** (503)573-6391
Vacant • H • NOW • 349 S Egan Ave Burns OR 97720-2281

**CENTRAL POINT—*GLORIA DEI*** (541)664-3724
David D Keil • WS 930; SS 11; BC 11 • H • NOW • 745 N 10th St Central Point OR 97502-2167 • FAX(541)664-3724 • gdlchurch@juno.com

**CLACKAMAS—*CHRIST THE VINE*** (503)658-5650
Kalvin L Waetzig • WS 8 11; SS 945; BC 945 • H • EC/EL/HS • NOW • 18677 SE Highway 212 Clackamas OR 97015-6703 • FAX(503)658-3081 • kwaet@aol.com

**COOS BAY—*CHRIST*** (541)267-3851
Vacant • WS 1030; SS 915; BC 915 • H • EC/EL • NOW • 1835 N 15th St Coos Bay OR 97420-2159

**CORNELIUS 3 S—*ST PETER*** (503)357-3863
George B Putnam • WS 1015; SS 9; BC 9;* • H • EC/EL • NOW • 97113 4265 SW Golf Course Rd Cornelius OR 97113-6017 • FAX(503)357-6418 • stpeters@teleport.com

**CORVALLIS—*SHEP VALLEY*** (541)753-2816
Patrick W Chuinard • WS 845;* • H • NOW • 2650 NW Highland Dr Corvallis OR 97330-3631 • FAX(541)752-8065 • svlc@proaxis.com

***ZION*** (541)757-0946
Raymond W Waetjen • * • H • EC/EL • NOW • 2745 NW Harrison Blvd Corvallis OR 97330-5207 • FAX(541)754-8254 • zion@proaxis.com

**COTTAGE GROVE—*TRINITY*** (541)942-2373
Gerald L Rabe • * • H • EC • NOW • 675 S 7th St Cottage Grove OR 97424-2502 • FAX(541)942-5321 • tlclcms@efn.org

**EAGLE POINT—*ST JOHN*** (541)826-4334
Ronald T Norris • WS 1030; SS 9;* • H • EC • NOW • 42 Alta Vista Rd 97524-9622 PO 1049 Eagle Point OR 97524

**ESTACADA—*PEACE*** (503)630-4049
Kirk A Hille Oscar A Marquardt(EM) • WS 11;* • H • EC/EL/HS • NOW • 29455 SE Eagle Creek Rd 97023-9720 PO Box 930 Estacada OR 97023-0930

**EUGENE—*GRACE*** (541)342-4844
Philip H Schoenherr • * • H • EC/EL • NOW • 710 E 17th Ave Eugene OR 97401-4438 • FAX(541)342-2241 • glc@efn.org

***MESSIAH***
See Santa Clara

**FOREST GROVE—*MOUNT OLIVE*** (503)357-2511
Daniel C Bohlken • WS 845 11; SS 10; BC 10 • EC/EL • NOW • 97116 2327 17th Ave Forest Grove OR 97116-2405

**GRANTS PASS—*ST PAUL*** (541)476-2565
Steven D Stork • WS 10 • EC • NOW • 865 NW Fifth St Grants Pass OR 97526-1530

**GRESHAM—*REDEEMER*** (503)665-5414
Eric T Lange • WS 1015; SS 9; BC 9;* • H • EC/EL/HS • NOW • 795 E Powell Blvd Gresham OR 97030-7615 • FAX(503)665-1297 • rdmr-lcms@juno.com

**HERMISTON—*BETHLEHEM*** (541)567-6811
Mark E Adams • * • H • EC • NOW • 515 SW 7th St Hermiston OR 97838-2203

**HILLSBORO—*TRINITY*** (503)640-1693
Timothy L Huber Bruce A Rumsch • David A Crisi DCE • WS 8;* • H • EC/EL • NOW • 152 NE 5th Ave 97124-3102 527 E Main St Hillsboro OR 97123-4136 • FAX(503)640-1342 • trinityor@aol.com

***ZION*** (503)640-8914
Erwin Wichner • H • EC/EL • NOW • 30900 NW Evergreen Rd Hillsboro OR 97124-1806 • FAX(503)681-8944

**HOOD RIVER—*IMMANUEL*** (541)386-3046
Vacant • H • NOW • 904 State St Hood River OR 97031-1878 • hdrvluth@aol.com

**JUNCTION CITY—*SHEP OF VALLEY*** (541)998-6659
Roger O Sylwester • WS 11; SS 11;* • H • NOW • 29357 Lingo Ln Junction City OR 97448-9648

**KENO—*SAVING GRACE*** (503)882-4629
Frank W Burget(EM) • WS 11; BC 945 • H • NOW • 15681 Highway 66 Keno OR 97627-9705

**KLAMATH FALLS—*ZION*** (541)884-6793
Paul C Frerichs • WS 8; SS 915; BC 915;* • H • EC • NOW • 1025 High St Klamath Falls OR 97601-2831 • FAX(541)884-6793 • zionlutchl@juno.com

**LA GRANDE—*FAITH*** (541)963-2831
Wilfred Nitz • WS 10; SS 9; BC 9 • H • NOW • 104 S 12th St La Grande OR 97850-3300 • FAX(541)963-0541

**LA PINE 2 N—*FAITH***
Vacant • WS 1030; SS 915; BC 915 • H • NOW • 53215 S Huntington Rd 97739 PO Box 1280 La Pine OR 97739-1280

**LAKE OSWEGO—*TRIUMP KING*** (503)636-3436
Daniel Faragalli • WS 1015; SS 915 • EC • NOW • 4700 Lamont Way Lake Oswego OR 97035-5426 • Faragalli2@aol.com

**LAKEVIEW—*FIRST*** (541)947-3944
Vacant • WS 1030 130; SS 330; BC 1230 • NOW • Highway 395 North 97630 PO Box 69 Lakeview OR 97630-0003

**LEBANON—*BETHLEHEM*** (541)258-6393
Edwin A Rumerfield • WS 1030; SS 9 • NOW • 434 E Grant St 97355-4428 900 Cleveland St Lebanon OR 97355-4422

**LINCOLN CITY—*ST PETER*** (541)994-8793
Lawrence F Rohlfing • WS 1030; SS 9; BC 9 • H • NOW • 1226 SW 13th St 97367-2527 PO Box 169 Lincoln City OR 97367-0169

**MC MINNVILLE—*ST JOHN*** (503)472-6677
Vacant • H • EC/EL • NOW • 2142 NE Mc Donald Ln Mc Minnville OR 97128-3231 • stjohn@viclink.com

**MEDFORD—*ST PETER*** (541)772-4395
William H Lehmann III • WS 8 1045; SS 930; BC 930 • H • EC • NOW • 1020 E Main St Medford OR 97504-7449

**MILWAUKIE—*BEAUTIFUL SAVIOR***
See Portland

**MOLALLA—*GRACE*** (503)829-2250
Leroy C Rittenbach • * • H • NOW • 510 May Street 97038 PO Box 329 Molalla OR 97038-0329

**MONMOUTH—*FAITH*** (503)838-3459
Vacant • * • H • EC/EL • NOW • 200 Monmouth Independence Hwy 97361-1726 PO Box 327 Monmouth OR 97361-0327 • faithlc@open.org

**MOUNT ANGEL 3 E—*TRINITY*** (503)634-2437
Ronald Hues • H • EL • NOW • 97362 15534 E Marquam Rd NE Mount Angel OR 97362-9715 • rdhues@mollalla.net

**MYRTLE POINT—*ST JAMES*** (541)572-5665
Daniel G Martin • H • NOW • Railroad And Cedar 97458 PO Box 157 Myrtle Point OR 97458-0157

**NEWPORT—*ALL NATIONS*** (541)265-2503
Tim J Renstrom • WS 11; BC 945;* • NOW • 358 NE 12th St Newport OR 97365-2217

**OAKRIDGE—*ST LUKE*** (541)782-2030
Ronald L Leder • WS 10;* • H • NOW • 47477 Teller Rd 97463-9718 PO Box 674 Oakridge OR 97463-0674

**ONTARIO—*PILGRIM*** (541)889-5458
Fred P Schuett • H • NOW • Second St And First Ave 97914 PO Box 96 Ontario OR 97914-0096

**OREGON CITY—*TRINITY*** (503)656-4504
Michael D Kasting Paul L Heinlein Lornell L Ruthenbeck(EM) • * • EC/EL/HS • NOW • 1201 JQ Adams St Oregon City OR 97045-1457 • FAX(503)656-2438 • trinityoregoncty@cs.com

**PHILOMATH—*PEACE*** (541)929-5504
Jack B Flachsbart • * • H • NOW • 2540 Applegate St Philomath OR 97370-9366

**PLEASANT HILL—*PLEASANT HILL*** (541)747-8913
Vacant • H • EC/EL • NOW • 84421 Gaupp Ln Pleasant Hill OR 97455-9610 • FAX(541)747-8164 • phlclcm@cmc.net

**PORTLAND—*ASCENSION*** (503)665-8821
Vacant • Lance R Eads DCE • WS 830 11; SS 945; BC 945;* • H • EC/EL/HS • NOW • 1440 SE 182nd Ave Portland OR 97233-5009

***BEAUTIFUL SAVIOR*** (503)788-7000
Charles J Roluffs Mark C Bertermann • H • EC • NOW • 9800 SE 92nd Ave Portland OR 97266-7088 • FAX(503)788-8468 • bslc@worldaccessnet.com

***CALVARY*** (503)774-8335
Donald L Frerichs • WS 9; SS 1015; BC 1015 • H • EC/EL/HS • NOW • 8040 SE Woodstock Blvd 8026 SE Woodstock Blvd Portland OR 97206-5876 • FAX(503)788-5011

***GOOD SHEPHERD*** (503)244-4558
Glenn R Zander • David C Hoover DCE • H • EC/EL/HS • NOW • 3405 SW Alice St Portland OR 97219-5334 • FAX(503)244-1396 • forgivn@agora.rdrop.com

***HOLY CROSS*** (503)254-8705
Vacant • * • H • EC/EL/HS • NOW • 8705 E Burnside St Portland OR 97216-1552 • FAX(503)254-0955

***HOPE DEAF*** (503)252-0706
David L Carstens • H • NOW • 11100 NE Skidmore St Portland OR 97220-2466 • HopeLcDeaf@juno.com

***IMMANUEL*** (503)236-7823
Sidney V Johnson • WS 1030; SS 9;* • H • EC/EL/HS • NOW • 7810 SE 15th Ave Portland OR 97202-6014 • FAX(503)236-1410 • immport@teleport.com

***MARTIN LUTHER MEMORI*** (503)281-7036
Herman Hawkins • H • NOW • 4219 NE Mlk Jr Blvd 97211-3441 PO Box 11231 Portland OR 97211-0231

***OUR SAVIOR*** (503)257-9409
Vacant • H • EC/EL/HS • NOW • 11100 NE Skidmore St Portland OR 97220-2466 • FAX(503)251-8416

***PRINCE OF PEACE*** (503)645-1211
Dan T Wehrspann • WS 8 1030; SS 915; BC 915 • H • EC/EL • NOW • 14175 NW Cornell Rd Portland OR 97229-5406 • FAX(503)531-2534 • PofPLC@aol.com

***ST JOHN*** (503)289-9557
Tyrus H Miles • * • H • NOW • 4227 N Lombard St Portland OR 97203-4737 • FAX(503)289-6247 • lutheran@st-john-lutheran.com

***ST MICHAEL*** (503)282-0000
Orlando E Trier • WS 830;* • H • EC/EL/HS • NOW • 6700 NE 29th Ave Portland OR 97211-6654 • FAX(503)282-1336

***TRINITY*** (503)288-6403
Mark E Hoelter • Jonathan D Cleveland DCE • WS 8 1030; BC 915;* • H • EC/EL/HS • NOW • 5520 NE Killingsworth St Portland OR 97218-2416 • FAX(503)288-1095 • office@trinityportland.org

***ZION*** (503)221-1343
Stephen C Krueger • WS 11; BC 945;* • H • NOW • 1015 SW 18th Ave Portland OR 97205-1708 • FAX(503)228-6484 • zion@teleport.com

**REDMOND—*EMMAUS*** (541)548-1473
Willis C Jenson • H • NOW • 2260 SW Salmon Ave 97756-9556 PO Box 825 Redmond OR 97756-0173

**REEDSPORT—*BEAUTIFUL SAVIOR*** (541)271-2633
Wilbur L Gehrke • H • EC • NOW • 2160 Elm Ave Reedsport OR 97467-1135

**ROGUE RIVER—*FAITH*** (541)582-0457
Norman G Nibblett • WS 8; SS 915; BC 915 • H • NOW • 8582 Rogue River Hwy 97537 PO Box 428 Rogue River OR 97537-0428 • FAX(541)582-6284 • lcmsrr@so-oregon.net

**ROSEBURG—*ST PAUL*** (541)673-7212
Phillip L Brandt • WS 10; SS 845;* • H • EC/EL • NOW • 750 W Keady Ct Roseburg OR 97470-2749 • FAX(541)677-9561 • stpaul@rosenet.net

**SAINT HELENS—*CALVARY*** (503)397-1739
Edwin H Rosenthal Jr. • H • EC • NOW • 58251 S Division Rd Saint Helens OR 97051-3240 • Calvary.lutheran.church.LCMS@juno.com

**SALEM—*MESSIAH*** (503)362-4960
Vacant • WS 10 • H • EL • NOW • 4965 Indiana Ave NE Salem OR 97305-2983

***PEACE*** (503)362-8500
Vacant • WS 915;* • H • EL • NOW • 1525 Glen Creek Rd NW Salem OR 97304-2726

***REDEEMER*** (503)393-7121
Vacant • WS 8 1030; SS 915 • H • EC/EL • NOW • 4663 Lancaster Dr NE 97305 PO Box 17128 Salem OR 97305-7128 • FAX(503)393-8705 • redeemer@open.org

***ST JOHN*** (503)588-0171
John B Luttmann • H • EC/EL • NOW • 1350 Court St NE Salem OR 97301-4127 • FAX(503)585-2801

**SANDY—*IMMANUEL*** (503)668-6232
Matthew P Hempeck • WS 930; SS 1045; BC 1045 • H • EC/EL/HS • NOW • 39901 Pleasant St 97055 PO Box 686 Sandy OR 97055-0686 • immanulc@juno.com

**SANTA CLARA—*MESSIAH*** (541)688-0735
Kelly C Bedard • WS 9; SS 1015; BC 1015;* • H • EC/EL • NOW • UKNWN 3280 River Rd Eugene OR 97404-1766 • kjbedard@prodigy.net

**SCAPPOOSE—*GRACE*** (503)543-6555
Thomas R Schoenborn • WS 9;* • H • EC • NOW • 51737 Columbia River Hwy Scappoose OR 97056-4409 • gracelutheran@columbia-center.org

**SEASIDE—*FAITH*** (503)738-7223
Vacant • H • EC • NOW • 1115 Broadway St Seaside OR 97138-7817

**SENECA—*REDEEMER*** (541)575-2348
Robert J Ravell • WS 10 • H • NOW • 97873 627 SE Hillcrest Rd John Day OR 97845-1228

**SHERIDAN—*TRINITY*** (503)843-4747
Fred A Storteboom • H • NOW • 311 SE Schley St 97378-1949 PO Box 128 Sheridan OR 97378-0128

**SHERWOOD 1 NW—*ST PAUL*** (503)625-6648
Vernon G Sandersfeld William T Hering • * • H • EC/EL • NOW • 97140 17190 SW Scholls Sherwood Rd Sherwood OR 97140-8725 • FAX(503)625-8976 • vsandds@aol.com

**SPRINGFIELD—*BETHANY*** (541)726-7365
Andrew W Eckert • H • EC/EL • NOW • 3360 Game Farm Rd Springfield OR 97477-7521

***HOPE*** (541)746-1255
John W Luther • H • EC/EL • NOW • 1369 B St Springfield OR 97477-4817 • FAX(541)741-3999 • hopel@ix.netcom.com

**STAYTON—*CALVARY*** (503)769-6144
Joel T Nickel • WS 8 1030;* • H • EC/EL • NOW • 198 Fern Ridge Rd SE Stayton OR 97383-1257 • FAX(503)767-6144 • calvarylutheran@earthlink.net
**SUTHERLIN—*ST JOHN*** (541)459-3701
Vacant • WS 1015 • H • NOW • 1100 W 6th Ave 97479-9698 PO Box 620 Sutherlin OR 97479-0620
**SWEET HOME—*BETHEL*** (541)367-2881
Vacant • H • NOW • 3000 Long St Sweet Home OR 97386-2910 • wcarjs@peak.org
**THE DALLES—*FAITH*** (503)296-3586
Jerry D Powers • H • NOW • 2810 W 10th St The Dalles OR 97058-4237
**TIGARD—*OUR REDEEMER*** (503)524-6646
Paul A Linnemann • WS 8 1045; SS 930; BC 930;* • H • EC/EL • NOW • 12256 SW 135th Ave Tigard OR 97223-1550 • FAX(503)213-5937 • office@orlc.net
**TILLAMOOK—*REDEEMER*** (503)842-4823
Vacant • H • NOW • 302 Grove Ave Tillamook OR 97141-2130 • FAX(503)815-1771
**TOLEDO—*ST MARK*** (541)336-5233
Tim J Renstrom • WS 9; BC 815;* • NOW • 247 SE 4th St Toledo OR 97391-1616
**TROUTDALE—*RIVER OF LIFE***
Kirk A Hille • NOW • 2477 SW Cherry Park Rd Troutdale OR 97060
**TUALATIN—*LIVING SAVIOR*** (503)692-3490
Joel J Brauer Shawn F Hazel • Heidi B Frank DCE • WS 8 930;* • H • EC • NOW • 8740 SW Sagert St Tualatin OR 97062-9116 • FAX(503)691-6508 • lslc@transport.com
**VENETA—*CHRIST*** (541)935-1335
Roger O Sylwester • WS 9; SS 1015 • H • NOW • 25157 Luther Ln 97487 PO Box 338 Veneta OR 97487-0338 • FAX(541)935-1335
**WALDPORT—*OUR SAVIOR*** (541)563-7729
David W Chamberlain • WS 930; SS 1015;* • H • NOW • 38 N Bayview Rd-Hwy #101 97394 PO Box 2458 Waldport OR 97394-2458
**WOODBURN—*HOPE*** (503)981-0400
Bruce R Zagel • Ralph L Petersen DCE • WS 1030; SS 915; BC 915 • H • EC/EL • NOW • 211 Parr Rd 97071-5557 PO Box 355 Woodburn OR 97071-0355 • FAX(503)981-0400

## PENNSYLVANIA

**ALBION—*HOLY TRINITY*** (814)756-3426
Manfred O Poeppel • WS 1030; SS 930; BC 930 • H • EC • EA • 80 3rd Ave Albion PA 16401-1366 • FAX(814)756-3426 • pfredp@juno.com
**ALLENTOWN—*CONCORDIA***
See Macungie
**AMBLER—*GLORIA DEI***
See Blue Bell
**ARNOLD—*JOHN HUSS*** (412)335-1735
Jerome E Panzigrau • S • 1539 Kenneth Ave Arnold PA 15068-4216
**AVELLA—*PENTECOST***
Vacant • WS 130; BC 1230 • H • EA • 81 Browntown Rd Avella PA 15312
**BEAVER FALLS—*MOUNT OLIVE*** (724)843-0952
John L Pingel • WS 815; SS 915; BC 915 • H • EC • EA • 2679 Darlington Rd Beaver Falls PA 15010-1239 • FAX(724)843-1921 • mtolive@lollatlantic.net
**BETHLEHEM—*CONCORDIA*** (610)691-7625
Raymond A Malec Frank F Gruber Sr.(#) • WS 1045;* • H • EC • S • 1240 E 4th St Bethlehem PA 18015-2010 • FAX(610)861-0846 • concordiabeth@enter.net
**BLOOMSBURG—*FAMILY OF CHRIST**** (570)784-2900
Vacant • WS 11; SS 945; BC 945 • H • EA • 164B W Ninth St 17815 PO Box 202 Bloomsburg PA 17815-0202 • FAX(570)784-2900 • amurphy@planetx.bloomu.edu
**BLUE BELL—*GLORIA DEI*** (215)646-0848
Donald R Ortner • WS 930 • H • EN • 6024 Butler Pike Blue Bell PA 19422-2603
**BRACKENRIDGE—*ST JOHN*** (412)226-2244
Vacant • S • Mile Lock Ln and Parkside Dr Brackenridge PA 15014
**BRADDOCK—*IMMANUEL*** (412)271-1995
Vacant • WS 1015; SS 9; BC 9 • H • EC • EA • 420 5th St Braddock PA 15104-1530 • FAX(412)271-1984
***ST PAUL*** (412)271-9300
Vacant • H • S • 215 11th St Braddock PA 15104
**BRADFORD—*GRACE*** (814)362-3244
Eddie R Scheler • Scott L Jung DCE • WS 815 1045; SS 930; BC 930;* • H • EA • 79 Mechanic St Bradford PA 16701-1241 • FAX(814)362-6085 • gracecare@penn.com
**BRENTWOOD—*CONCORDIA*** (412)881-3005
Scott E Stiegemeyer • BC 9;* • H • EA • 3109 Brownsville Rd Pittsburgh PA 15227-2429 • stiegemeyer@att.net
**BRIDGEVILLE—*ZION*** (412)221-4776
Martin J Homan • WS 8; SS 915; BC 915;* • H • EC/EL • EA • 3197 Washington Pike Bridgeville PA 15017-1423 • FAX(412)220-9741
**BRUSHTON—*UNITY COMMUNITY*** (412)731-2811
Reholma Mc Cants • EC • EA • 7825 1/2 Hamilton PO Box 56913 Pittsburgh PA 15208-0913 • FAX(412)731-7686
**BUTLER—*FAITH*** (724)285-5893
Allan E Opper • WS 1030; SS 915; BC 915;* • H • EN • 241 Freeport Rd Butler PA 16002-3630 • FAX(724)285-5893
**CABOT 2 NW—*ST LUKE*** (724)352-2777
Barry J Keurulainen James A Beversdorf • WS 815 1045 11; SS 930; BC 930;* • H • EC/EL • EA • 16023 330 Hannahstown Rd Cabot PA 16023-2204 • FAX(724)352-2355 • stluke2@juno.com
**CAMP HILL—*CALVARY***
See Mechanicsburg
**CARLISLE—*CALVARY***
See Mechanicsburg
**CENTRAL CITY—*SS PETER&PAUL*** (814)539-0123
Daniel A Hahn Jr. • S • 879 Main St Central City PA 15926-1221
**COLUMBIA—*ST PAUL*** (717)684-9520
H G Reichel • WS 9; BC 1015 • H • SE • 555 Locust St 17512-1225 PO Box 501 Columbia PA 17512-0501
**CROYDON—*ST LUKE*** (215)788-8951
James A Eckert • H • EC • EA • 1305 State Rd Croydon PA 19021-6126 • FAX(215)788-3838
**DICKSON CITY—*ST STEPHEN*** (570)489-2462
Vacant • WS 930; SS 11; BC 11 • S • 701 W Lackawanna Ave 25 Hillcrest Dr Olyphant PA 18447-1338
**DOWNINGTOWN—** (610)383-0889
George A Mather • H • EN • 213 E Reeceville Rd 19335-1124 PO Box 182 Downingtown PA 19335 • FAX(610)383-0889 • faith@icdc.com
**EASTON 2 N—*FAITH*** (610)253-1625
Gregory S Tafel • WS 8; SS 915;* • H • EC • EA • 18045 2012 Sullivan Trl Easton PA 18040-8338 • FAX(610)253-6158 • faithlcms@fast.net
**ELKINS PARK—*PILGRIM*** (215)379-3072
Karl E Stumpf • H • EA • 20 E Church Rd Elkins Park PA 19027-2241 • karlstu@aol.com
**ERIE—*TRINITY*** (814)452-4888
Mark L Sallach Donald E Sallach • WS 9 6;* • H • EN • 14 E 38th St 16504-1558 PO Box 3248 Erie PA 16508-0248 • FAX(814)456-1703
**FAIRHOPE—*TRINITY***
See Glen Savage
**FOREST HILLS—*CHRIST*** (412)271-7173
Ernest J Knoche Jr. • WS 815 11 7; SS 945; BC 945 • H • EC/EL • EA • UKNWN 400 Barclay Ave Pittsburgh PA 15221-4036 • FAX(412)271-4921 • revejk@hotmail.com
**GIRARD—*FAITH*** (814)774-2040
Vacant • H • EC • EA • 824 Main St E 16417-1722 PO Box 56 Girard PA 16417-0056 • FAX(814)774-2040
**GLEN SAVAGE—*TRINITY*** (814)733-4553
John F Jenista • WS 1030; SS 930; BC 930 • EA • UKNWN 630 Church Rd Fairhope PA 15538-1811
**GLENSHAW—*BETHEL*** (412)486-5777
Arthur E Litke • WS 1015; SS 9; BC 9 • H • EC • EA • 301 Scott Ave Glenshaw PA 15116-1697 • FAX(412)487-8328 • bethel@pgh.net
**HARRISBURG—*CALVARY***
See Mechanicsburg
**HAVERTOWN—*CALVARY*** (610)789-9518
Vacant • WS 9;* • EC • EA • Chatham Drive And Myrtle Ave 19083 PO Box 1032 Havertown PA 19083-0032 • Calvary@lutheran.com
**HAZLETON—*ST JOHN*** (570)459-6423
Scott D Kruse • H • EC • S • 223 W 6th St Hazleton PA 18201-4250 • stjohns@ccomm.com
**HERNDON—*FAITH***
See Mandata
**HERSHEY—*CALVARY***
See Mechanicsburg
**HOP BOTTOM—*GRACE*** (570)289-4468
Kim E Bode • EC • EA • S Greenwood St 26 S Greenwood St Hop Bottom PA 18824 • FAX(570)289-4468 • hbgrace@epix.net
**JOHNSTOWN—*HOLY CROSS*** (814)539-0123
Daniel A Hahn Jr. • S • 711 Chestnut St Johnstown PA 15906-2535
**LANCASTER—*MOUNT CALVARY***
See Lititz
**LEVITTOWN—*HOPE*** (215)946-3467
Andrew C Lissy • H • EC/EL • EA • 2600 Haines Rd Levittown PA 19055-1808 • FAX(215)946-5926 • hopelevtnpa@juno.com
**LITITZ—*MOUNT CALVARY*** (717)560-6751
Thomas K Spahn • WS 8 1045; SS 915; BC 915 • H • EC • EN • 308 Petersburg Rd Lititz PA 17543-9367 • FAX(717)560-2193 • mcelc@juno.com
**MACUNGIE—*CONCORDIA*** (610)965-3265
Raymond A Malec • WS 9;* • H • S • 2623 Brookside Rd Macungie PA 18062-9045 • FAX(610)861-0846
**MALVERN—*CHRIST MEMORIAL*** (610)644-4508
Vacant • H • EC • EA • 89 Line Rd Malvern PA 19355-2879 • FAX(610)644-4677 • cmlcs@chesco.com
**MANDATA—*FAITH*** (717)758-4970
Roy A Wicke(#) • WS 1030; SS 915;* • H • EC • EA • UKNWN RR 1 Box 818 Herndon PA 17830-9766 • FAX(717)758-4970
**MC KEES ROCKS—*ST MARK*** (412)331-5513
John Sound • EA • 107 Broadway St 15136-3401 PO Box 314 Mc Kees Rocks PA 15136-0314 • revsound@aol.com
**MC KEESPORT—*CONCORDIA*** (412)672-6711
Vacant • H • EA • 908 Evans Ave Mc Keesport PA 15132-2009 • FAX(412)672-6711 • revdlw@aol.com
**MECHANICSBURG—*CALVARY*** (717)697-9771
Thomas D Kraus • WS 1030; SS 9; BC 9 • H • EC • EN • 208 Woods Dr 17055-2634 PO Box 374 Mechanicsburg PA 17055-0374 • FAX(717)697-139 • calvary³lutheran@juno.com
**MILLVALE—*ST JOHN*** (412)821-6266
Eric R Andrae • WS 9; BC 1030;* • EC • EA • 15290 501 North Ave Pittsburgh PA 15209-2305 • FAX(412)821-0179
**MONROEVILLE—*TRINITY*** (412)372-9046
Richard D Carner • H • EC • EA • 2555 Haymaker Rd Monroeville PA 15146-3507 • FAX(412)372-9046
**MORRISDALE—*ST JOHN***
See Munson 1 E
**MOUNT LEBANON—*OUR SAVIOR*** (412)561-7299
Vacant • EN • 15290 698 Country Club Dr Pittsburgh PA 15228-2644
**MOUNT POCONO—*OUR SAVIOR*** (570)839-9868
Vacant • WS 830 11; BC 945;* • H • EC • EA • 675 Belmont Ave Mount Pocono PA 18344-1014 • FAX(570)839-9868
**MUNSON 1 E—*ST JOHN*** (814)345-5741
Larry W Gerdes • Nancy L Lingenfelter DEAC • WS 1030;* • H • EC • EA • Munson-Winburne Rd Forrest 16860 RR 2 Box 322 Morrisdale PA 16858-9103 • FAX(814)345-5741 • lardeb@csrlink.net
**MURRYSVILLE—*CALVARY*** (724)327-2898
Charles C Minetree III • WS 8 1030; SS 915; BC 915 • H • EC • EA • 4725 Old William Penn Hwy Murrysville PA 15668-2012 • FAX(724)327-2878 • calvarylut@aol.com
**NEW CASTLE—*CHRIST*** (724)658-8009
David W Ernst • H • EA • 1302 E Washington St New Castle PA 16101-4416
**NEW KENSINGTON—*ST PAUL*** (724)339-2829
Vacant • WS 1045; BC 930;* • H • EC • EA • 1001 Knollwood Rd New Kensington PA 15068-5315 • FAX(724)339-8905
**NEW SEWICKLEY TOWNS—*PRINCE*** (724)728-3881
Roger D Nuerge • WS 1015; SS 9; BC 9;* • H • EC • EA • UKNWN 60 Rochester Rd Freedom PA 15042-9364 • FAX(724)728-6708 • popluth@bellatlantic.net
**NORTH EAST—*ST PAUL*** (814)725-4395
David R Kuchta • H • EA • 30 Clinton St North East PA 16428-1254 • FAX(814)725-4395
**OAKMONT—*REDEEMER*** (412)828-9323
Mark C Sheafer • WS 1045; SS 930; BC 930 • H • EC/EL • EN • Pennsylvania Ave And 13th St 15139 1261 Pennsylvania Ave Oakmont PA 15139-1140 • FAX(412)828-1860 • churchoffice@redeemer-oakmont.org
**OIL CITY—*CHRIST*** (814)677-4484
William A Schreiber • * • H • EC • EA • 1029 Grandview Rd Oil City PA 16301-1226 • FAX(814)677-4484 • wschreiber@mail.cosmosbbs.com
**PENN HILLS—*EPIPHANY*** (412)241-1313
John H Weldon • WS 1030 915; BC 915;* • H • EA • 11200 Frankstown Rd Penn Hills PA 15235-3005 • FAX(412)241-6513
***GRACE*** (412)793-1394
Berton L Greenway • WS 1015; SS 9;* • EA • 2931 Universal Rd Penn Hills PA 15235-2655 • FAX(412)793-0529 • revgreenway@juno.com
**PHILADELPHIA—*CHRIST ASSEMBLY*** (215)726-9649
David L Goodine(DM) • EA • 6139 Harley Ave 19142-3411 PO Box 19207 Philadelphia PA 19143-0207 • FAX(215)726-1442
***GLORIA DEI***
See Blue Bell
***HOLY CROSS*** (215)242-0530
Elder Mc Cants • EA • 500 E Mount Pleasant Ave Philadelphia PA 19119-1232
***NAZARETH*** (215)744-7843
Walter E Koller • WS 9 11; SS 930 • EC • EA • 1357 E Luzerne St Philadelphia PA 19124-5358
***ST LUKE*** (215)745-8922
Roger A Newton • WS 1030;* • EC • EN • 7200 Castor Ave Philadelphia PA 19149-1106
***ST PHILIP*** (215)878-2911
Howard M Alexander • * • H • EA • 5210 Wyalusing Ave 19131-5040 53rd and Wyalusing Ave Philadelphia PA 19131 • FAX(215)877-9626
**PITTSBURGH—*ASCENSION*** (412)364-4463
Paul L Rist • WS 830;* • H • EA • 8225 Peebles Rd Pittsburgh PA 15237-5713 • FAX(412)369-0599 • ascenson@fyi.net
***CHRIST***
See Forest Hills
***CONCORDIA***
See Brentwood
***FAITH*** (412)621-4713
Stephen M Niermann • EA • 3171 Ewart Dr Pittsburgh PA 15219-5740 • FAX(412)621-4713
***FIRST***
See Sharpsburg
***FIRST TRINITY*** (412)683-4121
Douglas H Spittel • EA • 531 N Neville St Pittsburgh PA 15213-2812 • FAX(412)683-3725 • trinity@fyi.net
***GOOD SHEPHERD OF SOU*** (412)884-3232
Vacant • * • H • EC • EA • 418 Maxwell Dr Pittsburgh PA 15236-2040 • FAX(412)884-3233
***HOPE***
See Upper St Clair
***MOUNT CALVARY***
See West View
***OUR SAVIOR***
See Mount Lebanon
***ST JOHN***
See Millvale
***ST MATTHEW*** (412)321-7720
Bryan G Borger • Scott P Nagy DCE • WS 1015; SS 9; BC 9 • EC/EL • EA • 600 E North Ave Pittsburgh PA 15212-4845 • FAX(412)321-3515 • revborger@aol.com
***ST THOMAS*** (412)766-7810
Vacant • EA • 3164 Sorento St Pittsburgh PA 15212-2460
***TRINITY DEAF*** (412)731-2550
Vacant • EA • 409 Swissvale Ave Pittsburgh PA 15221-3542 • FAX(412)731-2550 • ruppertm@bellatlantic.net
***UNITY COMMUNITY***
See Brushton
***ZION*** (412)621-2720
Scott A Kuntz • EA • 37th And Bandera St 15290 237 37th St Pittsburgh PA 15201-1815 • FAX(412)621-2720 • revsak@juno.com

**PITTSTON—*ST JOHN*** (570)655-2505
Russell R Kerns • WS 9; SS 10; BC 10 • EA • 9 Wood St 18640-2028 PO Box 541 Pittston PA 18640-0541 • FAX(570)655-5295 • spalaima@netscape.net
**PUNXSUTAWNEY—*MARTIN LUTHER*** (814)938-9792
Howard F Grether II • WS 1115; SS 10;* • EA • 230 N Penn St Punxsutawney PA 15767
***SALEM***
See Troutville 2 E
**RIDLEY PARK—*ST MARK*** (610)534-0746
G T Downs • H • EC • EA • 628 E Chester Pike 19078-1701 PO Box 285 Ridley Park PA 19078-0285
**SCRANTON—*IMMANUEL*** (570)342-3374
Robert H Marshall Jr. • WS 10; SS 11; BC 1115 • H • EA • 238 Reese St Scranton PA 18508-1449 • ilc.scranton@juno.com
***PEACE*** (717)343-9828
Vacant • H • EA • 2506 N Main Ave Scranton PA 18508-1606
**SHARON—*SS PETER&PAUL*** (724)347-3620
Paul M Sajban • EC • S • 699 Stambaugh Ave Sharon PA 16146
**SHARPSBURG—*FIRST*** (412)782-2272
George R Hansell Jr. • WS 10; BC 9;* • H • EC/EL • EA • 15290 600 Clay St Pittsburgh PA 15215-2204 • FAX(412)782-3093 • grh61655@aol.com
**SLIPPERY ROCK—*ALL SAINTS*** (724)794-4334
Vacant • H • EN • 351 S Main St 16057-1250 PO Box 104 Slippery Rock PA 16057-0104 • aslc4u@aol.com
**SPRINGFIELD—*ST JOHN*** (610)543-3100
Robert W Tauscher • EN • 25 Scenic Rd Springfield PA 19064-1951
**STATE COLLEGE—*GOOD SHEPHERD*** (814)234-8177
A D Sailer • SS 915 • H • EC • EA • 851 N Science Park Rd State College PA 16803-2225 • FAX(814)234-0877 • nittanylutheran1@netzero.net
**TROUTVILLE 2 E—*SALEM*** (814)938-9792
Vacant • H • EA • 15886 PO Box 77 Luthersberg PA 15848
**TUNKHANNOCK—*ST PAUL*** (570)836-2301
Keith D Blom • WS 9;* • H • EA • 654 SR 6 W Tunkhannock PA 18657-6620 • FAX(570)836-2301 • stpaul99@epix.net
**UNIVERSAL—*GRACE***
See Penn Hills
**UPPER ST CLAIR—*HOPE*** (724)941-9441
Neville Mirtschin • WS 9; SS 1020; BC 1030;* • EC • EN • 2799 Old Washington Rd Pittsburgh PA 15241-1999 • hope4u8@juno.com
**WARMINSTER—*GRACE*** (215)672-8181
Terry J Jobst • WS 1015; BC 10;* • H • EC • EN • 1169 W Street Rd PO Box 196 Warminster PA 18974-0520 • FAX(215)672-8180 • terryjobst@aol.com
**WELLSBORO—*TRINITY*** (717)724-2316
Peter A De Vantier • H • EC/EL • EA • West Ave and Luther Ln Wellsboro PA 16901 • FAX(717)723-1053
**WEST VIEW—*MOUNT CALVARY*** (412)931-4500
John Sound • EA • 15290 285 Highland Ave Pittsburgh PA 15229-1707 • revsound@aol.com
**WILKES BARRE—*ST MATTHEW*** (570)822-8233
Vacant • WS 730;* • H • S • 667 N Main St 663 N Main St Wilkes Barre PA 18705-1732 • stmattlut@aol.com
**WILKES-BARRE—*ST PETER*** (570)823-7332
Vacant • H • EA • 18701 1000 S Main St Wilkes Barre PA 18702-4028 • jag715@msn.com
**YORK—*FIRST ST JOHN*** (717)843-8597
Larry A Schaefer • WS 1030; SS 915; BC 915;* • H • SE • 140 W King St York PA 17401-1307 • FAX(717)843-8597 • larry1942@aol.com
***GOOD SHEPHERD*** (717)854-1325
H G Reichel • WS 11; SS 930; BC 930 • H • SE • Salem Ave And S Hartley 17404 PO Box 1083 York PA 17405-1083
***ST JOHN*** (717)840-0382
Dennis C Quackenboss Patrick J Cox • * • H • EC/EL • SE • 2580 Mount Rose Ave York PA 17402-7854 • FAX(717)840-1845 • stjohn-yorkpa@blazenet.net

## RHODE ISLAND

**ASHAWAY—*TRINITY*** (401)377-4340
Vacant • H • EC • NE • Rr 216 And Wellstown Rd 02804 110 High St Ashaway RI 02804-1504
**GREENVILLE—*OUR REDEEMER***
See Smithfield
**PROVIDENCE—*ST PAUL*** (401)941-5100
Leon W Schultz Alfred R Saeger Jr.(EM) • WS 10;* • H • NE • 445 Elmwood Ave Providence RI 02907-1735
**SMITHFIELD—*OUR REDEEMER*** (401)232-7575
Larry A Nichols • * • H • NE • 54 Cedar Swamp Rd Smithfield RI 02917 • FAX(401)233-2414 • lnick52623@aol.com

## SOUTH CAROLINA

**ANDERSON—*ABIDING SAVIOR*** (864)225-6438
Howard F Jones • * • H • SE • 1905 E Greenville St Anderson SC 29621-2036 • FAX(864)225-3550
***GREENWOOD****
See Greenwood
**CHARLESTON—*CALVARY*** (843)766-3113
Robert W Duddleston • WS 10; SS 845;* • H • SE • Hwy 7 29423 1400 Manor Blvd Charleston SC 29407-3910 • FAX(419)793-5088 • calvaryl@juno.com
**COLUMBIA—*HOLY SPIRIT*** (803)786-6389
Vacant • WS 11; BC 945;* • H • EC/EL • SE • 2015 Lorick Ave Columbia SC 29203-7247
***HOLY TRINITY*** (803)799-7224
Carl A Voges • WS 1030; BC 930;* • H • SE • 2200 Lee St 29205-1710 PO Box 5692 Columbia SC 29250-5692 • holtri@mindspring.com
***MOUNT OLIVE*** (803)781-5845
Paul C Sizemore • WS 8 1030; SS 915; BC 915 • H • SE • 1541 Lake Murray Blvd 29212 PO Box 7 Irmo SC 29063-0007 • FAX(803)781-3821 • pastorpcs@aol.com
**FLORENCE—*INCARNATE WORD*** (843)662-9639
Clifford W Gade • WS 1030; BC 930;* • H • SE • 1900 2nd Loop Rd 29501-6123 PO Box 1176 Florence SC 29503-1176 • FAX(843)673-0881 • cwghg@aol.com
**GREENWOOD—*GREENWOOD**** (864)227-0088
John M Nickerson(DM) • WS 11; SS 10; BC 10 • H • SE • 228 Northcreek Rd 29649 303 Beechwood Cir 303 Beachwood Cir Greenwood SC 29646 • pastorn@innova.net
**HILTON HEAD ISLAND—*ISLAND*** (843)689-5200
Vacant • WS 9; SS 1015; BC 1015 • H • EC • SE • 4400 Main St 29928 PO Box 22297 Hilton Head SC 29925-2297 • islutheran@hargray.com
**MYRTLE BEACH—*HOLY LAMB*** (803)236-1344
Leroy M Hansen • WS 10; SS 10; BC 9 • H • EC • SE • 2541 Forestbrook Rd Myrtle Beach SC 29579-7936 • holylamb@juno.com
***RISEN CHRIST*** (843)272-5845
Carl M Gnewuch • WS 830 1030; SS 930;* • H • EC/EL • SE • Briarcliffe 29577 10595 Hwy 17 N Myrtle Beach SC 29572-5712 • FAX(843)272-4039 • risenchrist@prodigy.net
**SENECA—*ETERNAL SHEPHERD*** (864)882-3209
George M Coffman • WS 8 1030; SS 915 • H • SE • 220 Carson Rd Seneca SC 29678-0804 • FAX(864)882-5512
**SIMPSONVILLE—*IMMANUEL*** (864)297-5815
Jeffrey M Van Osdol • H • EC • SE • 2820 Woodruff Rd Simpsonville SC 29681-4806 • FAX(864)297-1771
**SPARTANBURG 2 NE—*LAMB OF GOD*** (864)579-2062
John R Rickert • WS 1030; SS 9; BC 9 • H • SE • 1645 Fernwood Glendale Rd Spartanburg SC 29307-3137
**SUMMERVILLE—*GRACE*** (843)871-5444
Vacant • H • SE • 1600 Old Trolley Rd Summerville SC 29485-8275
**UNKNOWN—*GOOD SHEPHERD*** (864)244-5825
Steven M Saxe • WS 10; BC 9;* • H • SE • 1601 N Pleasantburg Dr Greenville SC 29609-4019

## SOUTH DAKOTA

**ABERDEEN—*OUR SAVIOR*** (605)225-7106
Terry W Naasz • WS 8 1030;* • H • SD • 624 N Jay St Aberdeen SD 57401-2911
***ST PAUL*** (605)225-1847
Ronald H Laue Monty A Dell(#) • WS 8;* • H • SD • 214 7th Ave SW 57401-5950 PO Box 787 Aberdeen SD 57402-0787
**ABERDEEN 13 SW—*ST JOHN*** (605)225-1847
Ronald H Laue Monty A Dell(#) • WS 915;* • SD • 57401 37900 140th St Aberdeen SD 57401-8730
**AGAR—*ST JOHN***
Richard W Milbrandt • WS 9;* • H • SD • 17865 SD Hwy 1804 Agar SD 57520-5900 • revrwm@sullybuttes.net
**ALCESTER—*PEACE*** (605)934-2365
Richard L Luttmann • * • H • SD • 106 Church St Alcester SD 57001-9305
**ALEXANDRIA—*ST MARTIN*** (605)239-4421
Thomas D Christopher • SD • Fifth And Poplar 57311 PO Box 126 Alexandria SD 57311-0126
**ANDOVER—*ZION*** (605)298-5610
Lloyd W Redhage • H • SD • PO Box 16 Andover SD 57422-0016
**ARMOUR—*REDEEMER*** (605)724-2489
Nabil S Nour • WS 930;* • SD • 403 3rd St 57313 PO Box 158 Armour SD 57313-0158 • FAX(605)724-2489 • nabilsnour@juno.com
**AURORA—*FIRST ENGLISH*** (605)693-3491
Terry L Martin • * • H • SD • 214 Hull St PO Box 344 Aurora SD 57002-0344
**AVON—*ZION*** (605)286-3402
Vacant • H • SD • 314 Pine St 57315 PO Box 243 Avon SD 57315-0243
**BLACK HAWK—*DIVINE SHEPHERD*** (605)787-6438
David E Schwan • WS 915; SS 1015; BC 1015 • H • SD • 7308 Wedgewood Dr Black Hawk SD 57718-9693 • schwan@rapidmet.com
**BLUNT—*TRINITY*** (605)962-6489
Vacant • H • SD • 108 W Fair St 57522 PO Box 98 Blunt SD 57522-0098
**BRANDON—*BLESSED REDEEMER*** (605)582-2396
Michael L Kumm • WS 8 1030; BC 915;* • H • EC • SD • 705 S Sioux Blvd 57005-1731 PO Box 289 Brandon SD 57005-0289 • FAX(605)582-6870 • brlc@splitrocktel.net
**BRITTON—*ST JOHN*** (605)448-5235
Russell A Reed • H • SD • 401 N Main 57430 PO Box J Britton SD 57430-0622
**BROOKINGS—*MOUNT CALVARY*** (605)692-2678
Richard A Townes • SD • 629 9th Ave Brookings SD 57006-1523 • FAX(605)692-8353 • lsfjacks@brookings.net
***PEACE*** (605)692-5272
Timothy J Rynearson • WS 1015; SS 845 • H • EC • SD • 1910 12th St S Brookings SD 57006-1428 • peaceluth@choicetech.net
**CANISTOTA—*ZION*** (605)296-3166
Albert F Althoff Jr. • WS 930; SS 1045; BC 1045;* • H • EC • SD • 350 W Elm 57012 640 N Fourth Canistota SD 57012-9701
**CENTERVILLE—*FIRST ENGLISH*** (605)563-2904
Jay A Jaeger • SD • PO Box 129 Centerville SD 57014-0129
**CHAMBERLAIN—*ZION*** (605)734-6874
Larry I Geyer • SD • 314 S Main St Chamberlain SD 57325-1521 • zionlcms@sd.cybernex.net
**CHESTER—*REDEEMER*** (515)753-9565
Daniel S Johnson • WS 8 1030 12; BC 915;* • H • IE • 204 3rd St 57016-0096 1600 S Center St Marshalltown IA 50158-5919 • daniel1johnson@mcleoadusa.net
***ST JOHN*** (605)489-2370
Dwaine D Doremus • * • SD • 204 3rd St PO Box 96 Chester SD 57016-0096
**CLAIRE CITY 6 NE—*ZION*** (701)538-4849
Douglas C Wanderer • * • ND • 57224 C/O Immanuel 9690 Highway 18 Lidgerwood ND 58053-9774
**CLEARFIELD—*REDEEMER*** (605)842-1352
Donavon W Heithold • * • H • SD • 57580 C/O Christ Lutheran 730 E 6th St Winner SD 57580-2027
**COLUMBIA—*ST JOHN*** (605)396-2349
Vacant • H • SD • 23 N James St Columbia SD 57433
**CORONA—*TRINITY*** (605)432-6137
Glenn A Schultz • WS 1030; SS 915 • SD • PO Box 93 Corona SD 57227-0093
**CREIGHTON 1 N—*EMMANUEL*** (605)457-3171
Ray A Greenseth • WS 11;* • SD • 20 Miles North Of Wall 57729 PO Box 327 Wall SD 57790-0327
**CRESBARD—*CONCORDIA*** (605)324-3318
Gregory S Hinners • * • H • SD • 307 Swift Ave 57435 PO Box 106 Cresbard SD 57435-0106
***IMMANUEL***
See Wecota 2 NE
**CUSTER—*OUR REDEEMER*** (605)673-4361
Robert L Anderson • WS 9;* • SD • 744 Harney St PO Box 907 Custer SD 57730-0907
***OUR SAVIOR***
See Hill City
**DAKOTA DUNES—*HOLY CROSS*** (605)232-9117
Glen D Wurdeman • H • EC • SD • 149 Bison Trl 57049 PO Box 1902 North Sioux City SD 57049-1902 • FAX(605)235-1688
**DEADWOOD—*GRACE*** (605)578-2219
Gordon L Goldammer • H • SD • 827 Main St Deadwood SD 57732-1012
**DELMONT—*ZION*** (605)779-5181
Richard D Weeman • WS 10 • SD • PO Box 204 Delmont SD 57330-0204
**DELMONT 7 S—*ST PAUL*** (605)779-5181
Richard D Weeman • SD • 57330 40265 293rd St Delmont SD 57330-6908
**DIMOCK 8 W—*IMMANUEL***
Vacant • H • SD • 57331 40201 270th St Dimock SD 57331-5202
**DOLAND—*REDEEMER*** (605)472-0730
Peter M Utecht • WS 11 • SD • 57436 225 E 1st St Redfield SD 57469-1211
**DRAPER—*ST PAUL*** (605)669-2406
David G Otten • WS 11 • SD • 57531 C/O Messiah Lutheran PO Box 469 Murdo SD 57559-0469
**EMERY—*ST JOHN*** (605)449-9289
John T P Werner • * • H • SD • 201 N 5th St 57332 42654 272nd Street Emery SD 57332-5306 • johnwerner@basec.net
**EMERY 13 SW—*ST PETER*** (605)825-4222
John T P Werner • * • SD • 57332 42654 272nd St Emery SD 57332-5306 • johnwerner@basec.net
**FAIRFAX—*TRINITY*** (605)654-2371
Clark H Gies • H • SD • 57335 C/O Rev Clark H Gies PO Box 506 Wagner SD 57380-0506
**FERNEY—*ST PAUL*** (605)395-6420
Lloyd W Redhage • * • H • SD • 301 S 2nd Ave 57439-0831 PO Box 835 Ferney SD 57439-0835 • FAX(605)395-6949
**FLANDREAU—*REDEEMER*** (605)997-3848
Vacant • H • SD • 508 W 1st Ave Flandreau SD 57028-1004
**FREEMAN—*ST PAUL*** (605)925-7219
John W Farden • WS 930;* • H • SD • 7th And Relanto 57029 PO Box 96 Freeman SD 57029-0096 • stpaul@gwtc.net
**GETTYSBURG—*EMMANUEL*** (605)765-9201
Kevin D Moore • SD • 601 E Logan Ave Gettysburg SD 57442-1615
**GREGORY—*ST JOHN*** (605)835-9214
Wade M Harr • WS 10; SS 11; BC 9 • H • SD • 211 Church Ave Gregory SD 57533-1516
**GROTON—*ST JOHN*** (605)397-2386
Craig N Grams • * • H • SD • 308 N Second 57445 PO Box 348 Groton SD 57445-0348
**HAMILL—*ZION*** (605)842-1352
Donavon W Heithold • * • H • SD • 57534 C/O Christ Lutheran 730 E 6th St Winner SD 57580-2027
**HARROLD—*IMMANUEL*** (605)875-3480
Vacant • * • SD • 201 E 2 St 57536 31848 207th St Harrold SD 57536-6105
**HARTFORD 4 SE—*TRINITY*** (605)526-3572
Vacant • H • SD • 57033 46448 263rd St Hartford SD 57033-6909
**HECLA 8 W—*PEACE***
Vacant • SD • RFD Hecla SD 57446
**HILL CITY—*OUR SAVIOR*** (605)673-4361
Robert L Anderson • WS 1045;* • H • SD • PO Box 356 Hill City SD 57745-0356
**HOT SPRINGS—*BETHESDA*** (605)745-4834
Dana A Brooks • WS 9; BC 1015 8;* • H • EL • SD • 1537 Baltimore Ave Hot Springs SD 57747-2205 • FAX(605)745-5374 • bethesda@gwtc.net
**HOWARD—*ST JOHN*** (605)772-5252
Robert E Behling • WS 930;* • H • SD • 502 S Main St 57349-8773 PO Box 607 Howard SD 57349-0607
**HURON—*MOUNT CALVARY*** (605)352-7121
Dale L Sattgast Lew A Koch • WS 8 1030; SS 915; BC 915;* • H • EC • SD • 688 Dakota Ave S Huron SD 57350-2857 • mtcalvhuronsd@santel.net

**IPSWICH—*GOOD SHEPHERD***
Raymond L Pomplun • WS 845;* • SD • Hwy 12 57451 PO Box 415 Ipswich SD 57451-0415
**LEBANON—*CHRIST*** (605)765-9201
Kevin D Moore • SD • 57455 C/O 601 E Logan Gettysburg SD 57442
**LEOLA—*ST PAUL*** (605)439-3531
Raymond L Pomplun • WS 1030;* • SD • Sherman St 57456 PO Box 317 Leola SD 57456-0317
**MADISON—*OUR SAVIOR*** (605)256-4483
Warren W Uecker • H • SD • 1010 N Washington Ave 57042-1101 RR 1 Madison SD 57042-9801
**MANSFIELD 5 SW—*TRINITY*** (605)887-3632
Vacant • * • SD • 14908 377th Ave Mansfield SD 57460 • djhasel@adco2.net
**MARION—*BETHESDA*** (605)648-3968
Wesley H Hafner • WS 9; SS 1015 • H • SD • PO Box 358 Marion SD 57043-0358
**MENNO—*IMMANUEL*** (605)387-5188
Vacant • SD • 255 W Juniper 57045 PO Box 467 Menno SD 57045-0467
**MIDLAND 10 SE—*ST PETER*** (605)843-2274
Glenn R Denke • WS 11;* • H • SD • 57552 HC 62 Box 140 Midland SD 57552-9707
**MILBANK—*EMANUEL*** (605)432-9555
Mark A Erickson Dennis L Schultz • H • EC • SD • 701 S 1st St Milbank SD 57252-2803
**MILBANK 8 SE—*BETHLEHEM*** (605)623-4281
Vacant • SD • 57252 PO Box 38 Revillo SD 57259-0038
**MILESVILLE—*FIRST*** (605)859-2721
Vacant • SD • 57553 C/O Our Redeemer PO Box 964 Philip SD 57567-0964
**MITCHELL—*ZION*** (605)996-7530
Patrick R Sparling Victor E Dorn • * • H • SD • 620 E 3rd Ave 57301-2754 PO Box 236 Mitchell SD 57301-0236 • FAX(605)996-7470 • zionluth@sunrisenet.com
**MONTROSE—*ST JOHN*** (605)363-5023
Albert F Althoff Jr. • WS 8;* • H • SD • 201 E Clark St 57048-2040 PO Box 295 Montrose SD 57048-0295
**MURDO—*MESSIAH*** (605)669-2406
David G Otten • WS 9;* • H • SD • PO Box 469 Murdo SD 57559-0469
***ST PAUL***
See Draper
**NORRIS 6 SE—*ST JOHN*** (605)462-6169
Glenn R Denke • WS 8; SS 9;* • SD • 57560 HC 75 Box 22 Norris SD 57560-9405
**NORTH SIOUX CITY—*HOLY CROSS***
See Dakota Dunes
**ONIDA—*HOLY CROSS*** (605)258-2207
Richard W Milbrandt • WS 1030;* • H • SD • 408 S Main St 57564 PO Box 49 Onida SD 57564-0049 • revrwm@sullybuttes.net
**PARKER—*FIRST ENGLISH*** (605)297-4452
Wesley H Hafner • WS 9; SS 10 • SD • PO Box 117 Parker SD 57053-0117
**PARKSTON—*FAITH*** (605)928-3876
Vacant • H • SD • 201 W Cherry 57366 PO Box 609 Parkston SD 57366-0609
**PHILIP—*OUR REDEEMER*** (605)859-2721
Vacant • H • EC • SD • 200 S West Ave 57567 PO Box 964 Philip SD 57567-0964
**PIERRE—*FAITH*** (605)224-2216
Jon B Urbach • H • EC • SD • 714 N Grand Ave Pierre SD 57501-1723 • FAX(605)224-2226 • Faith@DTGNET.com
**PLANKINTON—*ST PAUL*** (605)942-7364
Vacant • * • H • SD • 109 W State St 57368 PO Box 127 Plankinton SD 57368-0127
**PRESHO—*ZION*** (605)895-2334
David L Putz • H • SD • 141 Main Ave 57568 PO Box 266 Presho SD 57568-0266
**RAPID CITY—*BETHLEHEM*** (605)343-2011
William A Paepke • WS 815 1045; SS 930; BC 930;* • H • SD • 1630 Rushmore St Rapid City SD 57702-3370 • bethlehm@rapidcity.net
***OUR REDEEMER*** (605)388-0032
Raymond H Adams • WS 8; SS 9; BC 9 • H • SD • 610 St Francis St 57701 PO Box 3308 Rapid City SD 57709
***PEACE*** (605)342-8943
Robert G Bailey • WS 815 1045; BC 930;* • H • EC • SD • 219 E Saint Anne St Rapid City SD 57701-5665 • peacelutheranrc@juno.com
***ZION*** (605)342-5749
Duane M Duley • WS 8 1045; SS 930; BC 930;* • H • EC/EL • SD • 4550 S Highway 16 Rapid City SD 57701-8913 • FAX(605)342-4469 • zion@rapidnet.com
**REDFIELD—*MESSIAH*** (605)472-0730
Peter M Utecht • WS 845;* • SD • 225 E 1st St Redfield SD 57469-1211
***REDEEMER***
See Doland
**RELIANCE—*TRINITY*** (605)895-2334
David L Putz • SD • PO Box 943 Reliance SD 57569-0943
**REVILLO—*BETHLEHEM***
See Milbank 8 SE
***ST JOHN*** (605)623-4281
Vacant • * • SD • 100 S Dillman Ave 57259-2107 PO Box 38 Revillo SD 57259-0038
**SCOTLAND—*ST PAUL*** (605)583-2506
Vacant • WS 1030 • SD • 940 S First 57059 PO Box 484 Scotland SD 57059-0484
**SENECA—*ST PAUL*** (605)436-6236
Vacant • * • SD • 310 Elm St C/O Mr Rick Hoefert PO Box 25 Seneca SD 57473-0025
**SIOUX FALLS—*CHRIST*** (605)338-3769
Michael W Henrichs • WS 9; SS 1015 • H • EC/EL • SD • 4801 E 6th St Sioux Falls SD 57110-1261
***FAITH*** (605)332-3401
Scott C Sailer • WS 8 1045; SS 915; BC 915;* • H • EC/EL • SD • 601 N Cliff Ave Sioux Falls SD 57103-0849 • FAX(605)332-3334
***LORD OF LIFE*** (605)371-3501
John K Dawson Joel E Sund • WS 6 815 1045; SS 930; BC 940;* • H • EC/EL • SD • 2600 S Sycamore Ave Sioux Falls SD 57110-5968 • FAX(605)371-3592 • pastor@lordoflife.org
***MEMORIAL*** (605)334-7133
Aaron J Asmus • WS 8 1030; SS 915; BC 915 • H • SD • 5000 S Western Ave Sioux Falls SD 57108 • FAX(605)334-7177 • dinmlc@yahoo.com
***OUR REDEEMER*** (605)338-6957
Gene A Ott Dean H Duncan • H • EC/EL • SD • 2200 S Western Ave Sioux Falls SD 57105-3426 • FAX(605)338-9889 • orlc@sd.cybernex.net
***RESURRECTION*** (605)361-6631
Leonard S Spiehs • WS 930; BC 1050;* • H • EC/EL • SD • 5500 W 26th St Sioux Falls SD 57106-0606 • FAX(605)361-6575 • res5500@gateway.net
***TRINITY DEAF*** (605)330-0724
Matthew W Nix(DM) • WS 9;* • H • SD • 4801 E 6th St Sioux Falls SD 57110-1261 • mw³nix@yahoo.com
***ZION*** (605)338-5226
Timothy J Heupel Alexander Whitfield • WS 8 945 11; SS 9; BC 9;* • H • EC • SD • 1400 S Duluth Ave Sioux Falls SD 57105-1711 • FAX(605)338-8936 • hipe@ideasign.com
**SISSETON—*EMANUEL*** (605)698-7116
Larry G Johnson • WS 9;* • SD • 321 7th Ave E 57262-2146 PO Box 247 Sisseton SD 57262-0247
**SPEARFISH—*ST PAUL*** (605)642-2929
Gene D Bauman • * • H • SD • 846 N 7th St Spearfish SD 57783-2102 • stpspear@mato.com
**SPENCER—*TRINITY*** (605)246-2760
Thomas D Christopher • WS 830;* • H • SD • 416 Fuller 57374 PO Box 350 Spencer SD 57374-0350
**SPRINGFIELD—*OUR SAVIOR*** (605)369-2386
Joseph Howlett • SD • Twelfth And Elm 57062 PO Box 426 Springfield SD 57062-0426
**STRATFORD—*ST PAUL*** (605)887-3632
Vacant • WS 745;* • H • SD • PO Box 448 Stratford SD 57474-0448
**TRIPP—*EMMAUS*** (605)935-6725
Vacant • H • EC • SD • 400 S Dobson 57376 PO Box M Tripp SD 57376-0463 • jtroeste@santel.net
**TYNDALL—*ST JOHN*** (605)589-3195
Joseph Howlett • H • SD • 108 W 23rd 57066 PO Box 13 Tyndall SD 57066-0013
**UTICA 7 NE—*MARTINUS*** (605)665-5171
Vacant • SD • 57067 43804 300th St Utica SD 57067-5520
**VERMILLION—*CONCORDIA*** (605)624-3459
Michael C Boykin • * • H • SD • 7 S University St Vermillion SD 57069-3211 • concordia@dtgnet.com
**WAGNER—*ST JOHN*** (605)384-3500
Clark H Gies • H • SD • 110 High Ave NW 57380-9366 PO Box 506 Wagner SD 57380-0506
***TRINITY***
See Fairfax
**WALL—*FIRST*** (605)279-2453
Ray A Greenseth • WS 9;* • H • SD • 504 Norris St 57790 PO Box 327 Wall SD 57790-0327
**WATERTOWN—*MOUNT OLIVE*** (605)886-5671
Robert C Westad • WS 9;* • H • SD • 715 2nd St NE Watertown SD 57201-1611 • mtolive@dailypost.com
**WAUBAY—*ZION*** (605)947-4538
Larry G Johnson • WS 11;* • SD • 735 Fifth Ave 57273 PO Box 46 Waubay SD 57273-0046
**WECOTA 2 NE—*IMMANUEL*** (605)324-3318
Gregory S Hinners • * • H • SD • 57438 C/O Concordia Lutheran PO Box 106 Cresbard SD 57435-0106
**WENTWORTH—*ST PETER*** (605)483-3129
Dwaine D Doremus • * • SD • 321 S Main Ave PO Box 125 Wentworth SD 57075-0125
**WESSINGTON—*CONCORDIA*** (605)458-2290
Vacant • WS 1130; SS 1030;* • EC • SD • 57381 380 Wessington St S Wessington SD 57381-0030
**WESSINGTON SPRINGS—*ZION*** (605)539-1297
Daryl G Tompkins • WS 930 • H • SD • 312 Barrett Ave 57382 PO Box 308 Wessingtn Spg SD 57382-0308 • FAX(605)539-9142 • pastordaryl@sullybuttes.net
**WHITE—*ZION*** (605)629-4201
Terry L Martin • SD • 5th And Sherwood Ave 57276 PO Box 601 White SD 57276-0601 • martinru@itcel.com
**WHITE LAKE—*TRINITY*** (605)249-2333
Vacant • SD • 304 S Johnston St 57383-2251 PO Box 6 White Lake SD 57383-0006
**WILMOT—*OUR SAVIOR*** (605)938-4398
Glenn A Schultz • WS 9; SS 10 • SD • PO Box 7 Wilmot SD 57279-0007
**WINNER—*CHRIST*** (605)842-0780
Donavon W Heithold • WS 10 • H • SD • 798 E 5th St 57580-2021 730 E 6th St Winner SD 57580-2027
***REDEEMER***
See Clearfield
***ZION***
See Hamill
**WOLSEY—*ST JOHN*** (605)883-4972
Nathan P Henschen • WS 1045; BC 930;* • H • EC • SD • 241 Commercial Ave NE 57384-2107 PO Box 445 Wolsey SD 57384-0445
**WOONSOCKET—*MOUNT OLIVE*** (605)539-1297
Daryl G Tompkins • WS 8 • H • SD • 57385 PO Box 308 Wessingtn Spg SD 57382-0308 • FAX(605)539-9142 • pastordaryl@sullybuttes.net
**YALE—*TRINITY*** (605)599-2961
Nathan P Henschen • WS 845 • H • SD • PO Box 37 Yale SD 57386-0037
**YANKTON—*ST JOHN*** (605)665-7337
David E Gunderson Paul G Wenz • Elizabeth A Peters DCE • WS 8 1030; SS 915; BC 915 • H • EC • SD • 1009 Jackson St Yankton SD 57078-3336 • FAX(605)665-7293 • stjohns@willinet.net

## TENNESSEE

**ATHENS—*ATHENS*** (423)745-9419
Jan T Munch • WS 8; SS 915;* • H • EC • MDS • 710 Forrest Ave 37303-2721 PO Box 841 Athens TN 37371-0841 • jmunch@usit.net
**BRISTOL—*TRINITY*** (423)764-6872
Arthur M Kaufmann • WS 830 1045; SS 940; BC 940 • H • MDS • 1545 Bluff City Hwy Bristol TN 37620-6018 • pastog-k@yahoo.com
**BURNS—*ST JOHN*** (615)446-2332
John P Gierke • WS 9; SS 1030; BC 1030;* • H • MDS • 2300 Highway 96 Burns TN 37029-6273 • FAX(615)446-0023 • stjohnlc@bellsouth.net
**CHATTANOOGA—*CROSS OF CHRIST*** (423)877-7447
Barry C Hildebrandt • H • MDS • 3204 Hixson Pike Chattanooga TN 37415-5424 • FAX(423)870-2990
***FIRST*** (423)629-5990
Vacant • H • MDS • 2800 Mc Callie Ave Chattanooga TN 37404-3902 • FAX(423)629-1508 • pastor@lutheran-first.org
***GOOD SHEPHERD*** (423)629-4661
Clifford L Herd • WS 8 1030; SS 915; BC 915 • H • MDS • 822 Belvoir Ave Chattanooga TN 37412-2508 • FAX(423)629-1431 • clifford@gslc-chatt.org
***ST PHILIP*** (423)267-1475
Meredith B Jackson • WS 11; SS 10;* • H • MDS • 51 W 25th St Chattanooga TN 37408-2902 • FAX(423)629-8963
**CLARKSVILLE—*GRACE*** (931)647-6750
Larry A Peters • Jo Ann A Thomack DCE • WS 815; SS 930; BC 945 • H • MDS • 2041 Madison St Clarksville TN 37043-5058 • FAX(931)645-3374 • gracelutheranch@juno.com
**CLEVELAND—*FIRST*** (423)472-6811
Robert G Seaton • WS 815 1045; SS 930; BC 930 • H • MDS • 195 Mc Intire Ave NE Cleveland TN 37312-5450 • firstluthcl@wingnet.net
**COLLIERVILLE—*FAITH*** (901)853-4673
Douglas B Barnett • Alta M Hook DCE • WS 830; SS 945; BC 945 • H • EC • MDS • 507 N Byhalia Rd Collierville TN 38017-1301 • FAX(901)853-5015
**COLUMBIA—*TRINITY*** (931)388-0790
Harlan J Heiserman • Michael A Fulbright DCE • WS 8 1030; SS 915 • H • EC • MDS • 5001 Trotwood Ave Columbia TN 38401-5048 • FAX(931)388-0557 • trinity@galis.com
**COOKEVILLE—*HEAVENLY HOST*** (931)526-3423
Vacant • WS 10 8; SS 9; BC 9 • H • EC/EL • MDS • 777 S Willow Ave Cookeville TN 38501-3806 • FAX(931)526-3423 • hhlc@cookeville.com
**CORDOVA—*GRACE CELEBRATION*** (901)737-6010
Mark D Brunette • WS 1030; SS 915; BC 915;* • H • MDS • Ecs 7600 Macon Rd Cordora 8601 Trinity Rd Cordova TN 38018 • FAX(901)737-6084 • gracecele1@aol.com
**CORDOVA/BARTLETT—*IMMANUEL***
See Memphis
**CROSSVILLE—*SHEPHERD HILLS*** (931)484-3461
David W Wollenburg • Richard L Weyhrich DCE • WS 8 1030; SS 915; BC 915 • H • MDS • 1461 Sparta Hwy Crossville TN 38555-5751 • FAX(931)707-0042 • shepherdofhills@tnaccess.com
**DAYTON 7N—*PRINCE PEACE*** (423)775-3525
Ocie N Behringer(EM) • H • MDS • 7 Miles N On Us 27 37321 PO Box 195 Dayton TN 37321-0195
**DICKSON—*ST JOHN***
See Burns
**DYERSBURG—*TRINITY*** (901)285-9691
Robert E Cheney(EM) • H • MDS • 1500 US Highway 51 Byp N Dyersburg TN 38024-2867
**ELIZABETHTON—*REDEEMER*** (423)543-1132
Robert J Mader • WS 10; SS 9; BC 9 • H • MDS • 234 W F St Elizabethton TN 37643-3110 • FAX(423)915-0030 • mader603@aol.com
**FRANKLIN—*FAITH*** (615)791-1880
Douglas L Kallesen • H • EC • MDS • 415 Franklin Rd Franklin TN 37069-8207 • FAX(615)790-8746 • faith³franklin@juno.com
**GALLATIN—*TRINITY*** (615)452-3352
David Maki • H • EC • MDS • 720 Lock 4 Rd Gallatin TN 37066-3435 • FAX(615)452-3358 • trinitygallatin@juno.com
**GATLINBURG—*SAINT PAUL***
See Sevierville
**GERMANTOWN—*AMAZING GRACE**** (901)737-3933
Vacant • H • MDS • 7771 Poplar Pike 38138 823 Exocet Suite 102 Cordova TN 38018
**HARROGATE—*CHRIST*** (423)869-4359
Arthur F Avery(EM) • WS 1030; SS 930; BC 930 • H • MDS • 190 Forge Ridge Rd 37752-7806 PO Box 4069 Harrogate TN 37752-4069 • FAX(240)332-2419 • joybirdi@juno.com
**HERMITAGE—*EMMANUEL*** (615)883-7533
Jeffrey P Shanks • WS 830 1045; SS 930; BC 930;* • H • MDS • 1003 Hickory Hill Ln Hermitage TN 37076-1906 • pastor@emmanuel-hermitage.org
**JACKSON—*CONCORDIA*** (901)668-0757
Luther N Hasz • WS 8 1030; SS 915; BC 915 • H • EC • MDS • 637 Wallace Rd Jackson TN 38305-4229 • FAX(901)668-7820 • concluth@usit.net
**JOHNSON CITY—*BETHLEHEM*** (423)926-5261
Steven L Harmon • WS 1045; SS 915; BC 915;* • H • MDS • 201 E Watauga Ave Johnson City TN 37601-4629 • FAX(423)926-0102 • spharmon@juno.com

**KINGSPORT—*CONCORDIA*** (423)247-3582
Paul F Becker • H • MDS • 725 Truxton Dr Kingsport TN 37660-5603 • FAX(423)247-1563 • bygrace@preferred.com

**KINGSTON—*REDEEMER*** (865)376-7647
Michael M Miller • H • MDS • 37763 1658 Roane State Hwy Harriman TN 37748-8303

**KNOXVILLE—*CHRISTUS VICTOR*** (865)687-6622
Donald P Glass • WS 815 1030; SS 930;* • H • MDS • 4110 Central Avenue Pike 37912-4305 PO Box 12132 Knoxville TN 37912-0132 • FAX(865)687-9206 • cvlcms@korrnet.org

***FIRST*** (423)524-0366
Paul J Bushur • H • MDS • 1207 N Broadway St Knoxville TN 37917-6530 • flcsknox@aol.com

***GRACE*** (865)691-2823
Richard M Elseroad Lane B Reuter • Christopher L Henze DCE • WS 815 11; SS 945; BC 945;* • H • MDS • 9076 Middlebrook Pike Knoxville TN 37923-1557 • FAX(865)691-4895 • glc@esper.com

**LOUDON—*CHRIST OUR SAVIOR*** (865)458-9407
Vacant • WS 930; BC 1045;* • H • MDS • 336 Lakeside Plz Loudon TN 37774-5534 • lallison@prodigy.net

**MADISON—*ASCENSION*** (615)868-2346
Mark A Koch • WS 8 1030; SS 915;* • H • EL • MDS • 610 W Old Hickory Blvd Madison TN 37115-3514 • FAX(615)868-7674 • revmkoch@juno.com

**MARYVILLE—*PRAISE**** (865)982-0102
Vacant • H • MDS • 536 E Broadway Maryville TN 37804

**MC MINNVILLE—*SHEPHERD HILLS*** (931)473-2757
Vacant • WS 8 • H • MDS • 105 Edgewood Ave Mc Minnville TN 37110-1565

**MEMPHIS—*BEAUT SAVIOR*** (901)362-6080
Dan D Elkins • WS 1015; SS 9;* • H • EC • MDS • 5740 Winchester Rd Memphis TN 38115-4711 • FAX(901)362-6040 • bslc@vantek.net

***CHRIST KING*** (901)682-8404
Charles J Neugebauer Mark D Goble • WS 830; SS 945 • H • EC/EL • MDS • 5296 Park Ave Memphis TN 38119-3506 • FAX(901)682-7687 • betteh@juno.com

***CROSS/CALVARY*** (901)396-5566
Vacant • WS 10; SS 9; BC 9 • H • EC/EL • MDS • 4327 Elvis Presley Blvd Memphis TN 38116-6405 • FAX(901)395-0171 • crosscali@juno.com

***ETERL MERCY DF*** (901)332-5723
Paul D Tessaro • WS 11; SS 930;* • H • MDS • 4327 Elvis Presley Blvd Memphis TN 38116-6405 • FAX(901)332-3013 • revpt@juno.com

***IMMANUEL*** (901)373-4486
Michael R Bingenheimer Lonnie R Jacobsen Ronald F Halamka(EM) • WS 8 930 11; SS 11 930; BC 11 930 • H • MDS • 6325 Raleigh La Grange Rd Memphis TN 38134-6907 • FAX(901)373-4487 • immanuel@ilcmemphis.org

***INSPIRATIONAL FAITH**** (901)357-1468
Vacant • MDS • 3595 N Thomas St Memphis TN 38127 • FAX(901)357-1648

***MESSIAH*** (901)386-3401
Don L Schmidt • H • MDS • 3743 Austin Peay Hwy Memphis TN 38128-3721

***REDEEMER*** (901)327-3234
Vacant • WS 1015; SS 9; BC 9 • EC • MDS • 294 S Highland St Memphis TN 38111-4558 • FAX(901)327-3234

***TRINITY*** (901)525-1056
Ronald J Wiese Philip Schmidt • H • MDS • 210 Washington Ave Memphis TN 38103-1910 • FAX(901)525-0697 • tlc1memphi@aol.com

**MORRISTOWN—*OUR SAVIOR*** (423)586-8818
Jack T Robinson(EM) • WS 1030; SS 915; BC 915 • H • MDS • 2717 Buffalo Trl Morristown TN 37814-5907 • oslc@usit.net

**MURFREESBORO—*FREEDOM*** (615)217-2520
Vacant • H • MDS • 811 East Clark Blvd Murfreesboro TN 37130

**NASHVILLE—*ASCENSION***
See Madison

***CONCORDIA*** (615)292-0982
Vacant • WS 1030; SS 915 • MDS • 3501 Central Ave Nashville TN 37205-2341

***CROSS OF LIFE*** (615)641-6091
D Thomas King Jr. • WS 8 1030; SS 9; BC 9 • H • MDS • 37229 2304 Hobson Pike Antioch TN 37013-1109 • FAX(615)641-6092

***EMMANUEL***
See Hermitage

***OUR SAVIOR*** (615)833-1500
Daniel D Otto James H Rockey • WS 8; SS 930; BC 930 • H • EC • MDS • 5110 Franklin Rd Nashville TN 37220-1814 • danotto@juno.com

***REDEEMER*** (615)646-3150
Chris Powell • WS 1030; SS 915; BC 930 • H • MDS • 800 Bellevue Rd Nashville TN 37221-2702 • RLCNash@aol.com

**OAK RIDGE—*FAITH*** (865)483-5431
James P Evers • WS 1030; SS 915;* • H • MDS • 1300 Oak Ridge Turnpike Oak Ridge TN 37830-6445 • FAX(865)483-1202 • faithlc@icx.net

**PARIS—*CHRIST*** (901)642-6620
Vacant • WS 1030; SS 915; BC 915 • H • MDS • 412 W Wood St Paris TN 38242-3949 • strukken@aeneas.net

**PIGEON FORGE—*SAINT PAUL***
See Sevierville

**RALEIGH—*MESSIAH***
See Memphis

**SEVIERVILLE—*SAINT PAUL*** (865)429-6023
Linsey H Dettmer • WS 1030; BC 930;* • H • MDS • 1610 Pullen Rd 37862-6122 PO Box 4578 Sevierville TN 37864-4578 • dettmer@esper.com

**SEYMOUR—*HOLY TRINITY*** (865)573-8731
John E Johnson • WS 10 • H • MDS • 11212 Chapman Hwy Seymour TN 37865-4804

**TULLAHOMA—*FAITH*** (931)455-3510
Martin S Nutter • WS 8 1030; SS 915; BC 915 • H • EC • MDS • 101 Bragg Cir Tullahoma TN 37388-2975 • FAX(931)455-1862 • faithlcms@cafes.net

**UNION CITY—*FAITH*** (901)885-9562
Stewart A Marshall • WS 8 10; SS 915 • H • MDS • 2012 E Reelfoot Ave Union City TN 38261-6010 • faithlcuctn@earthlink.net

**WARTBURG—*ST PAUL*** (423)346-3554
Robert D Pfaff • WS 845 11; SS 10; BC 10 • H • EC • MDS • 222 Church St 37887 PO Box 67 Wartburg TN 37887-0067

**WHITE HOUSE—*PRINCE OF PEACE**** (615)672-3300
Gregory S Rachuy(DM) • WS 1030; SS 915; BC 915 • H • MDS • 2826B Highway 31W 37188 PO Box 1528 PO Box 1528 White House TN 37188-1528 • pstr1999@aol.com

## TEXAS

**ABILENE—*OUR SAVIOR*** (915)692-6163
Laverne A Janssen • H • TX • 4933 S 7th St Abilene TX 79605-2643 • FAX(915)692-6521 • oslc@camalott.com

***ZION*** (915)677-7801
Norman E Steinke • WS 1030; SS 915; BC 915 • H • TX • 79603 1011 Briarwood St Abilene TX 79603-4709 • FAX(915)677-0946 • zionlcms@camalott.com

**ALAMO—*ZION*** (956)787-1584
Dwayne A Johnson • * • H • TX • 226 S Alamo Rd 78516 PO Box 805 Alamo TX 78516-0805 • FAX(956)787-1584 • howanitz@juno.com

**ALBANY—*TRINITY*** (915)762-2557
Donald P Loeschen • WS 1030; SS 930; BC 930 • H • TX • 733 Hwy 180 E 76430 PO Box 567 Albany TX 76430-0567

**ALICE—*TRINITY*** (512)664-6231
Del O King • WS 1030; SS 915; BC 915 • H • TX • Fifth And Woodlawn 78332 PO Box 1258 Alice TX 78333-1258 • delking1@juno.com

**ALLEN—*IMMANUEL*** (972)390-0156
Paul D Neumann • TX • PO Box 183 Allen TX 75013-0183

**ALPINE—*REDEEMER*** (915)837-5428
Richard W Schroeder • WS 11; SS 930; BC 930 • H • TX • 1003 W Holland 79830 PO Box 1287 Alpine TX 79831-1287

**AMARILLO—*CHRIST*** (806)351-0458
Scott E Herbert • WS 8 1045; SS 930; BC 930 • H • TX • 2400 N Coulter 79124 PO Box 10225 Amarillo TX 79116-0225 • FAX(806)351-0458 • christlutheran@arn.net

***PRINCE PEACE*** (806)359-7700
John H Elser • H • TX • 6900 Hillside Rd Amarillo TX 79109-7182 • FAX(806)359-7719 • pop@amaonline.com

***TRINITY*** (806)352-5629
Mark A Cattau • WS 8 1030; SS 920; BC 920 • H • EC/EL • TX • 5005 I-40 W Amarillo TX 79106-4756 • FAX(806)353-7785 • tls@arn.net

**ANDERSON—*ZION*** (409)873-2175
Daniel R Schoessow • WS 10; SS 9 • H • TX • 455 FM 149 W 77830 PO Box 409 Anderson TX 77830-0409 • FAX(409)873-2175 • dans409@aol.com

**ANDREWS—*FAITH*** (915)523-4015
Vacant • H • TX • 1005 NW 2nd St Andrews TX 79714-3513 • FAX(915)523-6705

**ANGLETON—*GOOD SHEPHERD*** (409)849-2223
Vacant • H • TX • 1601 W Henderson Rd Angleton TX 77515-2910

**ARANSAS PASS—*FAITH*** (361)758-3145
William K Schuster(EM) • TX • 938 W Lott Ave Aransas Pass TX 78336-4120

**ARLINGTON—*BEAUT SAVIOR*** (817)465-3164
David J Hintze • WS 915; SS 1045; BC 8 • H • HS • TX • 5851 New York Ave Arlington TX 76018 • FAX(817)465-1761 • bslc2@airmail.net

***GRACE*** (817)274-1626
Bradley P Beckman Rudy Herbrich • Sheryl M Hansen DCE • WS 802 925 1050; SS 925; BC 925 • H • EC/EL/HS • TX • 210 W Park Row Dr Arlington TX 76010-4318 • FAX(817)861-0193 • gracearl@yahoo.com

***HOLY CROSS*** (817)451-7561
David L Bahn Clinton L Pluenneke • WS 810; SS 1050 930; BC 1050 930 • H • EC • TX • 4400 W Arkansas Ln Arlington TX 76016-6337 • FAX(817)429-6944 • holycross@hclc.net

**ATHENS—*ST JOHN*** (903)675-9598
Scott W Kirchoff • WS 1030; SS 9;* • TX • 1401 W Corsicana St 75751-2225 PO Box 1778 Athens TX 75751-1778 • FAX(903)677-8369 • lcmsathens@aol.com

**ATLANTA—*REDEEMER*** (903)796-9030
Vacant • WS 10; BC 9 • H • TX • Laws Chapel Rd FR 2328 75551 PO Box 882 Atlanta TX 75551-0882

**AUSTIN—*BEAUT SAVIOR*** (512)443-4947
Milferd J Meyer • WS 1045; SS 930; BC 930 • H • TX • 6830 S Pleasant Valley Rd Austin TX 78744-5314

***BETHANY*** (512)442-4870
Walter W Harms William B Knippa • WS 8 930 9 1050; SS 1030 930; BC 1030 930 • H • EC • TX • 6215 Manchaca Rd Austin TX 78745-4927 • FAX(512)462-9784

***CHRIST*** (512)442-5844
John C Stennfeld • Jill A Moyer DCE • WS 815 1045; SS 930; BC 930 • H • TX • 300 E Monroe St Austin TX 78704-2427 • FAX(512)707-8082 • christ.lutheran@juno.com

***HOPE*** (512)926-8574
David A Leeland • H • EC/EL • TX • 6414 N Hampton Dr Austin TX 78723-2043 • FAX(512)926-0708

***JESUS DEAF*** (512)442-1715
Mark W Seeger • H • TX • 1307 Newton St Austin TX 78704-3028 • markjlcd@aol.com

***MOUNT OLIVE*** (512)288-2370
Paul E Meyer • H • EC • TX • 7416 W Highway 71 Austin TX 78735-8202 • FAX(512)288-2375 • info@mountolivelutheran.org

***OUR SAVIOR*** (512)836-9600
Keith P Gravesmill • WS 8; SS 930; BC 930 • H • EC/EL • TX • 1513 E Yager Ln Austin TX 78753-7117 • FAX(512)836-4660 • oslc@io.com

***REDEEMER*** (512)459-1500
David N Schroder Kevin T Westergren • Randall J Kerkman DCE Travis M Hartjen DCE • WS 8 930 1045; SS 930; BC 930;* • H • EC/EL • TX • 1500 W Anderson Ln Austin TX 78757-1453 • FAX(512)459-6779 • pastor@redeemer.net

***ST PAUL*** (512)472-8301
Fred C Gersch • Mark R Rhoads DCE • H • EC/EL • TX • 3501 Red River St Austin TX 78705-1831 • FAX(512)469-0785 • fgersch@prismnet.com

***TRINITY*** (512)453-3835
Paul R Harris • WS 1030; SS 915; BC 915 • H • TX • 1207 W 45th St Austin TX 78756-3325

***UNIVERSITY**** (512)472-5461
Norbert A Firnhaber • * • H • TX • 2100 San Antonio Austin TX 78705-5522 • FAX(512)472-1199 • ulc@uts.cc.utexas.edu

**AZLE—*GOOD SHEPHERD*** (817)237-4822
Stanley W Geisler • WS 930; SS 11; BC 11 • H • TX • 1313 SE Parkway St Azle TX 76020-4024 • gslr@juno.com

**BALLINGER—*BETHEL*** (915)942-9275
Vacant • WS 9 • TX • 1701 N Broadway St Ballinger TX 76821-2415 • tbaden@aol.com

**BASTROP—*PRINCE OF PEACE*** (512)303-5267
Henry H Biar • WS 10; SS 845; BC 845 • TX • 927 Main St Bastrop TX 78602 • FAX(512)321-1703 • hbiar@netscape.net

**BAY CITY—*OUR SAVIOR*** (409)244-2055
Vacant • H • TX • 1900 Hammon Rd 77414-8538 PO Box 1020 Bay City TX 77404-1020

**BAYTOWN—*REDEEMER*** (281)422-2207
Richard T Turner Jr. • WS 1015; SS 9; BC 9 • H • EC • TX • 1200 E Lobit St Baytown TX 77520-5348 • FAX(281)427-3517

**BEAUMONT—*REDEEMER*** (409)892-3286
Harvey F Kelm Jr. • WS 8; SS 920; BC 920 • H • EC • TX • 4330 Crow Rd Beaumont TX 77706-6998 • FAX(409)924-8300 • fkelm@gtis.net

***ST JOHN*** (409)840-9915
Douglas D Rathgeber • WS 1030; SS 9; BC 9 • H • TX • 2955 S Major Dr Beaumont TX 77707-5121 • FAX(409)840-9915 • bmtstjohn@sat.net

**BEDFORD—*CONCORDIA*** (817)283-3560
Roger H Grummer • WS 1030; SS 915; BC 915 • H • TX • 3705 Harwood Rd Bedford TX 76021-4013 • Shepherd@concordialutheran.org

**BELLMEAD—*ST PAUL*** (254)799-3211
Walter F Albers Joel T Boesche • Tracy L Pressel DCE • WS 8; SS 915 • H • TX • 76702 1301 Hogan Ln Waco TX 76705-2571 • FAX(254)412-0529 • stpaulms@iamerica.net

**BELTON—*PRINCE PEACE*** (254)939-0824
Robert Budewig • WS 1015; SS 9; BC 9 • H • TX • 1215 S Wall St 76513-2157 PO Box 306 Belton TX 76513-0306 • FAX(254)933-2704 • popeace@stonemedia.com

**BIG SPRING—*ST PAUL*** (915)267-7163
Steve C Stutz • WS 8 1045; SS 930;* • H • TX • 810 Scurry St Big Spring TX 79720-2725 • FAX(915)267-8876 • stpaul@crcom.net

**BISHOP—*ST PAUL*** (361)584-2778
Gilbert A Franke • WS 10; SS 9; BC 9 • H • EC/EL • TX • 801 E Main St Bishop TX 78343-2720 • FAX(361)584-2691 • bishopaul@juno.com

**BOERNE—*MESSIAH*** (830)755-4300
Mark J Dankis • WS 1030; SS 915 • H • TX • 9401 Dietz Elkhorn Rd Boerne TX 78015-4933 • FAX(830)981-8035

**BONHAM—*ZION*** (903)583-5155
Loren A Du Bois • WS 10 • H • TX • 1205 Albert Broadfoot St Bonham TX 75418-2951

**BORGER—*GOOD SHEPHERD*** (806)274-2455
Vacant • WS 630; SS 515 • TX • PO Box 656 Borger TX 79008-0656 • gdshep@amaonline.com

***TRINITY*** (806)273-7546
Vacant • WS 1030; SS 915; BC 915 • H • TX • 212 W Jefferson St 79007-4748 PO Box 545 Borger TX 79008-0545 • FAX(806)273-7546 • tlc279@juno.com

**BOWIE—*ST PETER*** (940)872-1886
Belvin R Brummett • WS 1045; SS 945;* • H • TX • 806 Lindsey 76230 PO Box 133 Bowie TX 76230-0133 • luthrvivit@juno.com

**BRADY—*MOUNT CALVARY*** (915)597-2498
Archie Harlow(#) • H • TX • Highway 87 W 76825 HC 70 Box 77 Brady TX 76825-9730

**BRENHAM—*GRACE*** (979)836-3475
Matthew P Jacobs William H Holzer • WS 8 1015; SS 915; BC 915 • H • EC/EL • TX • 1212 W Jefferson St Brenham TX 77833-2943 • FAX(979)836-0510 • grace@pointecom.net

**BRENHAM/WM PENN—*BETHLEHEM*** (409)836-7303
Vacant • WS 10; SS 9; BC 9 • H • TX • 77833 10202 FM 1935 Brenham TX 77833-0100

**BRIDGEPORT—*TRINITY*** (817)683-5604
Gerald W Peterman Sr. • H • TX • 1307 10th St 76426-2311 PO Box 247 Bridgeport TX 76426-0247

**BROWNSVILLE—*EL CALVARIO*** (956)546-2350
Steven Morfitt • Lori L Bachmann DCE • TX • 1157 E Monroe St Brownsville TX 78520-5842

***TRINITY*** (956)542-7024
David R Byler • WS 1030; SS 915;* • H • EC • TX • 901 Boca Chica Blvd Brownsville TX 78520-8304 • FAX(956)546-3237

**BROWNWOOD—*GRACE*** (915)646-2045
Philip J Graf Sr. • WS 1015; SS 9; BC 9 • H • TX • 1401 1st St Brownwood TX 76801-4201 • pgraf@web-access.net

**BRYAN—*BETHEL*** (979)822-2742
Neil M Bockelmann • Randall R Moerbe DCE • H • TX • 410 Bethel Ln Bryan TX 77802-1005 • FAX(979)691-1257 • office@bethel-lutheran-church.org

**BUCHANAN DAM—*GENESIS*** (512)793-6800
Kenneth W Baisden(EM) • H • TX • 15946 E State Highway 29 78609-4421 PO Box 994 Buchanan Dam TX 78609

**BURKBURNETT—*GRACE*** (940)569-2277
Vacant • WS 8; SS 915; BC 915 • H • TX • 410 E 3rd St 76354-3439 306 N Avenue D Burkburnett TX 76354-3413

**BURLESON—*CHARITY*** (817)295-8621
Kent A Heimbigner • WS 10; SS 830; BC 830 • H • EC • TX • 1101 SW Wilshire Blvd Burleson TX 76028-5718 • FAX(817)295-1985 • ICXCNIKA@flashnet.com

**CANYON—*ST PAUL*** (806)655-4086
Vacant • WS 830; SS 10; BC 10 • TX • 2600 4th Ave Canyon TX 79015-4148 • FAX(806)655-3870 • stpaul@amaonline.com

**CARROLLTON—*PRINCE PEACE*** (972)447-9887
Stephen A Wagner C Wayne Hamit F Paul Liersemann Jr. • WS 8 930 11; SS 930; BC 930 • H • EC/EL • TX • 4000 Midway Rd Carrollton TX 75007-1903 • FAX(972)447-9881 • mailbox@popcarrollton.org

**CEDAR PARK—*GOOD SHEPHERD*** (512)258-6227
Richard R Goodwill Jonathan A Goeke • WS 8 930 11; SS 930; BC 11;* • H • EC • TX • 700 W Whitestone Blvd Cedar Park TX 78613-2119 • FAX(512)258-2335 • Goodslc@aol.com

**CENTERVILLE—*OUR SAVIOR*** (903)536-2019
Russell A Etzel • WS 1030; SS 930; BC 930 • H • TX • 171 Hwy 75 N 75833 PO Box 505 Centerville TX 75833-0505

**CHANNELVIEW—*GRACE*** (713)452-7982
Vacant • TX • Sheldon And Ridlon 77530 PO Box 88 Channelview TX 77530-0088

**CHILDRESS—*TRINITY*** (806)256-2355
James Sturgis Jr. • WS 8; SS 915; BC 915 • TX • 402 3rd St NW 79201-3741 C/O William Haseloff Jr 2007 Country Club Dr Childress TX 79201-2211

**CISCO—*REDEEMER*** (254)442-2090
Martin J Kaufmann • WS 1030; SS 930; BC 930 • H • EC • TX • 1711 Conrad Hilton Ave Cisco TX 76437-4856 • redeemer@mac.com

**CLARKSVILLE—*ST JOHN***
Vacant • H • TX • Highway 82 W 75426 RR 1 Box 340 Clarksville TX 75426-9719

**CLEBURNE—*ASCENSION*** (817)645-9452
Joseph M Ardy • WS 8 1015; SS 915; BC 915 • H • TX • 205 S Ridgeway Dr Cleburne TX 76031-4699 • FAX(817)645-5300 • ascensionlc@hotmail.com

**CLEVELAND—*GOOD SHEPHERD*** (281)592-6803
Vacant • WS 9; SS 1015; BC 1015 • H • TX • 900 Plum Grove Rd 77327-9805 RR 5 Box 1 Cleveland TX 77327-9000

**CLIFTON—*IMMANUEL*** (254)675-3281
Gregory D Knippa • WS 1030; SS 915; BC 915 • H • TX • 911 W 3rd St Clifton TX 76634-1401 • FAX(254)675-3281 • immanuel@htcomp.net

**COLLEGE STATION—*HOLY CROSS*** (409)764-3992
Michael A Hafer • WS 8; SS 915; BC 915 • H • TX • 1200 Foxfire Dr College Station TX 77845-5614 • FAX(979)693-2950 • hclutheran@aol.com

***UNIV CHAPEL**** (979)846-6687
Larry G Krueger • WS 1030; BC 930 • H • TX • At Texas A And M 77840 315 College Main College Station TX 77840-1225 • FAX(979)846-6687 • ulctamu@txcyber.com

**COLLEYVILLE—*CROWN OF LIFE*** (817)421-5683
David R Jung Gregory Beutel • WS 830 11; SS 945; BC 945;* • H • EL • TX • 6605 Pleasant Run Rd Colleyville TX 76034-6609 • FAX(817)421-9263 • church@crownoflife.org

**COMMERCE—*TRINITY*** (214)886-6810
Charles F Rogers • TX • 1502 Monroe St Commerce TX 75428-2568

**CONROE—*ST MARK*** (409)756-6335
David C Quail George F Borghardt III • H • EC/HS • TX • 2100 Tickner St Conroe TX 77301-1341 • FAX(409)756-3796

**COPPELL—*CHRIST OUR SAVIOR*** (972)462-0225
Richard A Mohr • Mary E Hildebrandt DCE • WS 805 11; SS 11 • H • EC/EL • TX • 140 Heartz Rd Coppell TX 75019 • FAX(972)468-0881

**COPPERAS COVE—*TRINITY*** (254)547-2225
Vacant • H • TX • 518 E Highway 190 Copperas Cove TX 76522-2959

**COPPERAS COVE 4 NW—*IMMANUEL*** (254)547-3498
Robert W Wagner • WS 1030; SS 930; BC 930;* • H • TX • 76522 922 Lutheran Church Rd Copperas Cove TX 76522-7443 • rwagner@seacove.net

**CORPUS CHRISTI—*LORD OF LIFE*** (361)937-8158
Alfred W Schubert • WS 8 1045; SS 930; BC 930 • H • EC • TX • 1318 Flour Bluff Dr Corpus Christi TX 78418-5104 • FAX(361)937-1796

***MESSIAH*** (361)387-7748
Kevin D Lentz • WS 10; SS 845; BC 845 • H • TX • 4102 Trinity River Dr Corpus Christi TX 78410-5674 • FAX(361)387-7748 • RevKlentz@juno.com

***MOUNT OLIVE*** (361)991-3416
Ronald A Bogs • WS 1030 8; SS 915; BC 915 • H • EC • TX • 5101 Saratoga Blvd Corpus Christi TX 78413-2812 • FAX(361)991-8851 • mountolive@lutheran.com

***NUESTRO SALVADOR*** (512)857-5673
William A Sielk • WS 815 1045; SS 930;* • H • TX • 6102 Greenwood Dr Corpus Christi TX 78417-3301 • FAX(512)853-2484 • OurSaviorLutheranChurch@juno.com

***TRINITY*** (361)884-4041
Alston s Kirk • WS 9 11; SS 10; BC 10;* • H • TX • 808 Louisiana Ave Corpus Christi TX 78404-2807 • FAX(361)884-7733 • cptkirk6@flash.net

**CORSICANA—*FAITH*** (903)874-8795
Peter C Kolb • WS 1030; SS 915; BC 915 • H • TX • 3824 W Highway 22 Corsicana TX 75110-2464 • FAX(903)874-8795 • faithch@airmail.net

**CROCKETT—*GRACE*** (409)544-3508
Jonathan F Meyer • H • TX • W Loop 304 And Halls Bluff Rd 75835 RR 3 Box 569-G Crockett TX 75835-9803

**CROSBY 5 N—*OUR SHEPHERD*** (281)324-2422
Victor L Frank • WS 8 1045; SS 915; BC 915 • H • EL • TX • 77532 19704 FM 2100 Rd Crosby TX 77532-3701 • FAX(281)324-4478

**CYPRESS—*ST JOHN*** (281)373-0503
Gregg A Stanton Duane R Bamsch • WS 8 930 11; SS 930; BC 930 • H • EC/HS • TX • 15235 Spring Cypress Rd 77429-6379 PO Box 159 Cypress TX 77410-0159 • FAX(281)373-5102 • sharingthegift@evl.net

**DALHART—*GRACE*** (806)244-2606
John A Miller • WS 11; SS 10;* • H • TX • 1311 E 16th St 79022-5105 PO Box 1025 Dalhart TX 79022-1025

**DALLAS—*BETHEL*** (214)348-0420
Donald A Berg Randall Haedge • Melody L Boersma DCE • WS 8 1045; SS 1045 930; BC 1045 930 • H • EC/EL/HS • TX • 11211 E Northwest Hwy Dallas TX 75238-3826 • FAX(214)348-7756 • bethel@airmail.net

***HOLY CROSS*** (214)358-4396
Donald G Little • Angela M Nitz DCE Jonathan M Fischer DCE • WS 8; SS 930; BC 930 • H • EC/EL/HS • TX • 11425 Marsh Ln Dallas TX 75229-2637 • FAX(214)358-4393

***HOPE*** (214)321-6584
Thomas W House • H • TX • 2835 Peavy Rd Dallas TX 75228-4772

***JOHN BEVERLEY DEAF**** (972)271-1408
Vacant • H • TX • 7611 Park Ln Dallas TX 75225-2028

***LORD OF LIFE***
See Plano

***OUR REDEEMER*** (214)368-1371
Vacant • WS 8 1030; SS 915; BC 915;* • H • EC/EL/HS • TX • 7611 Park Ln Dallas TX 75225-2028 • FAX(214)368-1473

***OUR SAVIOR*** (214)331-6105
Vacant • H • TX • 3621 W Clarendon Dr Dallas TX 75211-6055

***ST PAUL*** (214)371-9429
John A Nunes • WS 11 8; SS 930;* • H • TX • 5725 S Marsalis Ave Dallas TX 75241-1906 • jnunes@cphnet.org

***TRINITY*** (214)327-2729
Harold V Meissner • WS 1015 1230; SS 9; BC 9;* • H • TX • 7112 Gaston Ave Dallas TX 75214-4111 • FAX(214)327-3919 • a0006256@airmail.net

***ZION*** (214)363-1639
Robert C Preece Keith A Speaks Garland E Gotoski(EM) • WS 8 1030 6; SS 910 • H • EC/EL/HS • TX • 6121 E Lovers Ln Dallas TX 75214-2029 • FAX(214)361-2049 • zionlcms@ziondallas.org

**DEER PARK—*CHRIST REDEEM*** (713)479-2201
Walter A Dube • WS 1030; SS 915; BC 915 • H • TX • 77536 8909 Spencer Hwy La Porte TX 77571-3600

**DEL RIO—*CRISTO EL SALVADOR**** (830)775-9904
Gary E Martin(DM) • H • TX • 204 Wernett St Del Rio TX 78840 • gmart74@webnology.com

***GRACE*** (830)775-5797
John O Feierabend • WS 1030;* • H • TX • 201 Western Dr Del Rio TX 78840-3037 • gracelcms@hotmail.com

**DENISON—*GRACE*** (903)465-1016
Michael J Mattil • WS 1015; SS 9; BC 9 • H • TX • 2411 Woodlake Rd Denison TX 75021 • FAX(903)465-5255 • glcdenison@texoma.net

**DENTON—*ST PAUL*** (940)387-1575
Russell W Tieken • H • EC • TX • 703 N Elm St Denton TX 76201-6903 • FAX(940)566-0005 • st.paul.lcms@juno.com

**DESOTO—*CROSS CHRIST*** (972)223-9340
Craig R Schinnerer John E De Young • John D Mull DCE • WS 8 1030 6; SS 915; BC 915 • H • EC/EL/HS • TX • 512 N Cockrell Hill Rd 75115-3602 PO Box 306 De Soto TX 75123-0306 • FAX(972)223-8432 • coc96@airmail.net

**DEVINE—*DIVINE SAVIOR*** (210)663-3735
Dale L Brynestad • WS 10; SS 845; BC 845 • H • TX • Mount Vernon And Ingram Rd 78016 PO Box 143 Devine TX 78016-0143

**DIME BOX 3 W—*TRINITY*** (979)884-1471
Vacant • WS 9; SS 1015; BC 1015 • H • TX • H 21 At Old Dime Box 77853 Rt 1 Box 172-A Dime Box TX 77853-9801 • FAX(979)884-0441

**DUMAS—*ST JOHN*** (806)935-2974
Vacant • H • TX • 207 S Meredith Ave Dumas TX 79029-3836 • luthrvivit@juno.com

**EDEN—*TRINITY*** (915)869-4031
Robert E Boyce • H • TX • 14 Mason St 76837 PO Box 245 Eden TX 76837-0245

**EDNA—*ST PAUL*** (361)782-3037
Robert E Le Blanc • WS 1030; SS 915; BC 915 • H • TX • 108 E Gayle St Edna TX 77957-3754

**EL PASO—*ASCENSION*** (915)833-1009
James A Dunn • Robert A Lambeth DCE • WS 8 1030; SS 915; BC 915 • H • EC • RM • 6520 Loma De Cristo Dr El Paso TX 79912-7301 • FAX(915)581-3216 • eplighthaus@aol.com

***GRACE*** (915)755-1322
Alvey A Yates • H • RM • 9301 Diana Dr El Paso TX 79924-6412 • bj634@rgfn.epcc.edu

***OUR SAVIOR*** (915)591-9311
Glenn A Weber • WS 830 11; SS 945; BC 945 • H • EC • RM • 10200 Album Ave El Paso TX 79925-5439 • FAX(915)590-0851 • sweber370@aol.com

***SAN PABLO*** (915)858-2588
Karl P Heimer-Cotera Jose O Ruiz • H • RM • 301 S Schutz Dr El Paso TX 79907-6514 • FAX(915)858-2708 • heimerkarl@aol.com

***ST MATTHEW*** (915)857-7492
Daniel J Sattelmeier • WS 8; SS 930 • H • EC • RM • 11995 Montwood Dr El Paso TX 79936-0708 • FAX(915)857-2679 • stmattelpaso@juno.com

***ZION*** (915)566-4667
Charles O Canada • WS 10; SS 845; BC 845 • H • EC • RM • 2800 Pershing Dr El Paso TX 79903-2411 • FAX(915)566-6677 • zion@whc.net

**ELGIN—*GRACE*** (512)281-3367
Bryan C Sullivan • H • TX • 801 W 11th St Elgin TX 78621-2006 • FAX(512)285-9409

**EOLA—*MOUNT CALVARY*** (915)942-9275
Vacant • TX • PO Box 636 Eola TX 76937-0636 • tbaden@aol.com

**EULESS—*CONCORDIA***
See Bedford

**FAIRFIELD—*TRINITY*** (903)389-4005
Jerry D Bagwell • WS 10; SS 9 • H • TX • 1100 E Commerce St Fairfield TX 75840-2010

**FARWELL 8 S E—*ST JOHN***
See Lariat

**FEDOR—*TRINITY***
See Lexington 10 S

**FLOWER MOUND—*EMMANUEL**** (972)777-7975
Vacant • TX • PO Box 270085 Flower Mound TX 75027-0085

***LAMB OF GOD*** (972)539-5200
Vacant • Jill S Beck DCE • WS 8 1030; SS 915; BC 915 • H • EC • TX • 1401 Cross Timbers Rd Flower Mound TX 75028-1276 • FAX(972)539-8194

**FORT STOCKTON—*FAITH*** (915)336-3925
Richard W Schroeder • WS 830; SS 930; BC 830 • TX • 705 N Rio St 79735-4821 PO Box 1481 Fort Stockton TX 79735-1481

**FORT WORTH—*CHRIST*** (817)370-6242
Randall C Bard • WS 9; SS 1020; BC 1020 • H • TX • 4409 Sycamore School Rd Fort Worth TX 76133 • FAX(817)370-8600 • christlutheran³fortworth@hotmail.com

***REDEEMER*** (817)560-0030
David A Grassley • H • EC/EL • TX • 4513 Williams Rd Fort Worth TX 76116-8809 • FAX(817)560-0031 • redeemer@flash.net

***RESURRECTION*** (817)560-1870
Vacant • H • TX • 9200 Chapin Rd 76116-6611 PO Box 121483 Fort Worth TX 76121 • skypilot22@juno.com

***ST PAUL*** (817)332-2281
John A Messmann Edmund D Auger • Douglas D Widger DCE Sue A Davis DCE • WS 8 1050 11; SS 930; BC 930 • H • EC/EL • TX • 1800 West Fwy Fort Worth TX 76102-5930 • FAX(817)332-2640 • stpaul@flash.net

**FREDERICKSBURG—*RESURRECTION*** (830)997-9408
Lee R Kunkel • H • EL • TX • 2215 N Llano St Fredericksburg TX 78624-2955 • preach@ktc.com

**FRIENDSWOOD—*HOPE*** (281)482-7943
Ralph W Hobratschk Mark F Lasch • WS 8 11; SS 945; BC 945;* • H • EC/EL/HS • TX • 1804 S Friendswood Dr 77546-5412 PO Box 1076 Friendswood TX 77549-1076 • FAX(281)482-4371 • rhobratschk@cs.com

**GAINESVILLE—*FAITH*** (940)668-7147
Scott A Sundbye • WS 10; SS 9;* • H • TX • 1823 Luther Ln 76240-2481 PO Box 1199 Gainesville TX 76241-1199 • FAX(940)668-7147 • sundbye@texoma.net

**GALENA PARK—*PEACE*** (713)674-3111
Carlos M Segovia • WS 930; SS 11; BC 11 • TX • 1810 11th St Galena Park TX 77547-2908 • FAX(713)674-3111

**GALVESTON—*ST JOHN*** (409)762-2702
M A Taylor • H • TX • 1121 39th St Galveston TX 77550-3901 • patmostx@juno.com

**GARLAND—*CONCORDIA*** (972)495-4714
Kenneth M Krippner • WS 8 1030; SS 915 • H • EC/EL/HS • TX • 5702 N Jupiter Rd Garland TX 75044-3601 • FAX(972)496-1133 • cncordia@aol.com

***PEACE*** (972)278-5868
Vacant • WS 10; SS 845; BC 845 • H • TX • 2929 S 1st St Garland TX 75041-3440 • FAX(972)271-5778 • peacel@airmail.net

***TREE OF LIFE*** (972)226-6086
Thomas J Thierfelder • WS 8 1030; SS 915 • H • EL/HS • TX • 6318 Lyons Rd Garland TX 75043-6318 • FAX(972)226-1545 • Church@TreeOfLifeLCMS.org

**GATESVILLE—*FIRST*** (817)865-6903
Vacant • TX • 1608 W Main St Gatesville TX 76528-1002

***ST PAUL***
See The Grove

**GEORGETOWN—*FAITH*** (512)863-7332
John F Selle George W Lowrey • WS 1030 8; SS 915; BC 915;* • H • EC • TX • 4010 Williams Dr Georgetown TX 78628-1342 • FAX(512)819-0430 • jfselle@gtwn.net

***ZION***
See Walburg

**GIDDINGS—*IMMANUEL*** (409)542-2918
Wilbern C Michalk John F Davis • H • EC/EL • TX • 299 N Leon St Giddings TX 78942-2635 • FAX(409)542-0348

***ST JOHN***
See Lincoln 2 SW

***ST PAUL***
See Serbin

**GRAHAM—*FAITH*** (817)549-5155
Gerald W Peterman Sr. • WS 1045; SS 930;* • H • TX • 1618 Hwy 380 E Graham TX 76450-2406 • janpete@wf.net

**GRANBURY—*OUR SAVIOR*** (817)573-5011
John R Austin • WS 8 1030; SS 915; BC 915 • H • TX • 1101 Old Cleburne Rd Granbury TX 76048-2500 • FAX(817)573-1922 • oslc@itexas.net

**GRAND PRAIRIE—*FAITH*** (972)264-2511
Jonathan C Schroeder • H • HS • TX • 2200 SW 3rd St Grand Prairie TX 75051-4801 • FAX(972)264-2512

**GROVES—*ST PAUL*** (409)962-1133
Stephen S Linck • WS 10; SS 845; BC 845 • H • EC • TX • 5801 W Jefferson St Groves TX 77619-3724 • FAX(409)962-2007 • stpaul@pernet.net

**GUN BARREL CITY—*ST PETER*** (903)887-0436
Scott A Schaller • WS 1030; SS 915; BC 915 • H • TX • 130 Luther Ln Gun Barrel City TX 75147-9358 • FAX(903)887-7436 • splcgbc@stoutinternet.com

**HAMILTON—*ST JOHN*** (254)386-3158
Timothy J Carr Mark C Hass • WS 1030 8; SS 915; BC 915 • H • EC • TX • Hwy 22 E At Cheyenne Mesa Rd 76531 122 Cheyenne Mesa Rd Hamilton TX 76531-9801 • FAX(254)386-3159 • cteamcarr@htcomp.net

**HAMILTON 8 SE—*ST PAUL*** (817)386-5976
Vacant • H • TX • 76531 RR 1 Box 131 Hamilton TX 76531-9702

**HARLINGEN—*OUR REDEEMER*** (210)423-8142
Donald Neumann • WS 11;* • H • TX • 1210 W Grant Ave Harlingen TX 78550-6328

***ST PAUL*** (956)423-3924
C D Von Stroh Timothy J Droegemueller • WS 8 1045; SS 930; BC 930;* • H • EC/EL • TX • 602 Morgan Blvd Harlingen TX 78550-5143 • FAX(956)423-3942 • stpaulhar@aol.com

**HARROLD—*IMMANUEL*** (940)886-2342
Robert W Holaday • TX • 19113 County Road 132 E Harrold TX 76364-3730

**HASLET—*HOLY SHEPHERD*** (817)439-2100
Dennis M Kitzmann • WS 1030; SS 9;* • H • TX • 1500 Hwy 156 S PO Box 406 Haslet TX 76052 • FAX(817)439-2100

**HEREFORD—*IMMANUEL*** (806)364-1668
Erik W Stadler • H • TX • 100 Avenue B Hereford TX 79045-4315

**HILLSBORO—*CHRIST*** (254)582-5782
Russell A Nebhut • H • TX • 915 Corsicana Hwy Hillsboro TX 76645-2927 • FAX(254)582-8447 • texrev@hillsboro.net

**HONEY GROVE—*SAINT LUKE*** (903)378-3081
Vacant • H • TX • PO Box 25 Honey Grove TX 75446-0025 • FAX(903)378-2994 • tobybyrd@lstarnet.com

**HONEY GROVE 7 NW—*ST JAMES*** (903)378-2779
Walter W Snyder • WS 1030; SS 930; BC 930 • H • TX • Fm 1396 At Allens Chapel RR 1 Box 53A Windom TX 75492-9702

**HOUSTON—*BEAUT SAVIOR*** (281)445-2203
C M Snow • WS 8; SS 930;* • H • EC • TX • 161 West Rd Houston TX 77037-1144 • FAX(281)445-2966 • bslc@worldnet.att.net

***BETHANY*** (713)695-2933
Donn P Williams • WS 9; SS 1030; BC 1030 • H • EC/EL/HS • TX • 522 Lindale St Houston TX 77022-5557 • FAX(713)695-2726 • bethluthsch@juno.com

***BETHLEHEM*** (713)864-9716
Vacant • H • EL/HS • TX • 737 E 12th 1/2 St Houston TX 77008-7119

***CALVARY*** (713)633-7276
Willie C Lucas • H • EC/EL/HS • TX • 10635 Homestead Rd Houston TX 77016-2703

***CHRIST*** (281)458-3231
Todd A Dittloff • WS 8 1045; SS 930; BC 930 • H • EC/EL/HS • TX • 6603 Uvalde Rd Houston TX 77049-4501 • FAX(281)458-4625

***CHRIST MEMORIAL*** (281)497-0250
J M Kuehnert • Mark J Sperry DCE • H • EC • TX • 14200 Memorial Dr Houston TX 77079-6702 • FAX(281)497-1424 • cmlc@juno.com

***CONCORDIA*** (713)462-4040
Roy L Southard • WS 9; SS 1015; BC 1015 • H • TX • 4115 Blalock Rd Houston TX 77080-1499 • FAX(713)462-3012 • concordialutheran@juno.com

***CROSSPOINT***
See Katy

***EPIPHANY*** (713)896-1773
Michael F Welmer • WS 8 1045; SS 930; BC 930;* • H • EC/EL/HS • TX • 8101 Senate St Houston TX 77040-1277 • FAX(713)896-7568 • epiphanylu@aol.com

***FAMILY/FAITH*** (281)855-2950
John M Ramey • WS 830 11; SS 945; BC 945 • H • TX • 16710 FM 529 Rd Houston TX 77095-1312 • FAX(281)855-8301 • familyfath@aol.com

***GETHSEMANE*** (713)688-5227
John W Cain • WS 8 1030; SS 915 • H • EC • TX • 4040 Watonga Blvd Houston TX 77092-5321 • FAX(713)688-5235 • cain@texas.net

***GLORIA DEI*** (281)333-4535
John H Kieschnick Brad D Heintz Jonathan R Thomas Bruce G Collet(#) • Nicole D Stewart DCE Jonathan D Jordening DCE • WS 805 930 11 6; SS 805; BC 805 • H • EC/EL/HS • TX • 18220 Upper Bay Rd Houston TX 77058-4198 • FAX(281)335-0574 • gloriadei@gdlc.org

***HOLY CROSS*** (713)524-0192
James E Martin • H • TX • 2702 Rosalie St Houston TX 77004-1632

***HOLY THREE IN ONE*** (713)468-1815
Lawrence A Lieder • H • TX • 8311 Waterbury St 77201 1515 Hillendahl Blvd Houston TX 77055-3411 • FAX(713)468-6735 • c3in1@worldnet.att.net

***IMMANUEL*** (713)864-2651
Timothy J Steckling • WS 815 1045; SS 1030;* • H • EC/EL/HS • TX • 306 E 15th St Houston TX 77008-4239 • FAX(713)861-8787 ext 21 • ils@swbell.net

***MEMORIAL*** (713)782-6079
Scott R Murray John B Day • H • EC/EL • TX • 5800 Westheimer Rd Houston TX 77057-5617 • FAX(713)975-1684 • smurray@mlchouston.org

***MESSIAH*** (713)861-3072
Richard L Schuller • WS 9; SS 1015; BC 1015 • H • EC/EL/HS • TX • 816 Roy St Houston TX 77007-5248 • FAX(713)861-7952 • messiahlutheran@earthlink.net

***MOUNT CALVARY*** (713)680-1419
Samuel Cosby • WS 1015; SS 9; BC 9 • H • EC • TX • 1055 W Tidwell Rd Houston TX 77091-4349 • FAX(713)680-1449 • theskypilot@worldnet.att.net

***MOUNT OLIVE*** (281)922-5673
Randy W Ledbetter • H • EC/EL/HS • TX • 10310 Scarsdale Blvd Houston TX 77089-5665 • FAX(281)922-5914 • pastor.molc@urvip.net

***OUR REDEEMER*** (713)694-7433
Lawrence E Kelm • H • EC/EL • TX • 215 Rittenhouse St Houston TX 77076-1709 • FAX(713)699-1032

***OUR SAVIOR*** (713)290-9087
Laurence L White Thomas H Glammeyer • Jeffery S Armstrong DCE • WS 930; SS 1045;* • H • EC/EL/HS • TX • 5000 W Tidwell Rd 77091-4633 PO Box 925188 Houston TX 77292-5188 • FAX(713)290-0224 • church@osl.cc

***PILGRIM*** (713)666-3693
Allen J Bauer Harold A Heckmann(EM) • WS 815 1045; SS 930; BC 930;* • H • EC/EL • TX • 8601 Chimney Rock Rd Houston TX 77096-1304 • FAX(713)666-4385

***SAN PEDRO*** (713)228-2579
Vacant • EC/EL/HS • TX • 1501 Houston Ave Houston TX 77007-4135

***ST ANDREW*** (713)468-9565
Harold L Fleischhauer • WS 8 1030; SS 915; BC 915 • H • EC • TX • 1353 Witte Rd Houston TX 77055-4003 • FAX(713)468-9566 • office@standrew-lcms.org

***ST JOHN*** (713)923-5757
Claudio Perez Sr. • BC 1030;* • H • EL/HS • TX • 6601 Sherman St Houston TX 77011-3523 • FAX(713)923-7017

***ST LUKE*** (281)442-2180
Vacant • WS 9; SS 1015; BC 1015;* • H • TX • 11025 Aldine Westfield Rd Houston TX 77093-3215

***ST MARK*** (713)468-2623
William E Dasch Kenneth M Burkhard Steven J Misch David V Schultz • WS 8 930 1045; SS 930; BC 930;* • H • EC/EL/HS • TX • 1515 Hillendahl Blvd Houston TX 77055-3411 • FAX(713)468-6735 • info@stmarkhouston.org

***ST MATTHEW*** (713)526-5731
John F Stelling • H • TX • 5315 Main St Houston TX 77004-6810 • FAX(713)524-1709

***ST MATTHEW WESTFIELD***
See Spring

***ST PHILIP*** (713)771-8907
Ninh H Nguyen • WS 815 11; SS 940; BC 940 • H • EC • TX • 9745 Bissonnet St Houston TX 77036-8007 • FAX(713)771-8922

***ST TIMOTHY*** (281)469-2457
Steven H Henze • Jaylene M Miller DCE Richard A Leslie DCE • H • EC/HS • TX • 14225 Hargrave Rd Houston TX 77070-3843 • FAX(281)469-2921 • sttimlcs@flash.net

***TRINITY*** (713)224-0684
Brian R Bestian Donald G Black • H • EL/HS • TX • 800 Houston Ave Houston TX 77007-7710 • FAX(713)224-0685 • bomeme@aol.com

***VIETNAMESE*** (713)771-3207
Ninh H Nguyen • TX • 9745 Bissonnet Houston TX 77036

**HUMBLE—*LAMB OF GOD*** (281)446-8427
Mark C Behring Noel S Parker • Timothy P Kaufmann DCE Joy C Kaufmann DCE • WS 8 1030; SS 915; BC 915;* • H • EC • TX • 1400 Bypass 1960 E Humble TX 77338 • FAX(281)446-0289

**HUNTSVILLE—*FAITH*** (409)295-5298
Reinhard H Wuensche David J Thies • H • EC/EL • TX • 111 Sumac Rd Huntsville TX 77340-8943 • FAX(409)295-8266 • faithlc@lcc.net

**HURST—*PEACE*** (817)284-1677
Walter E Waiser Michael B Sheldon • John A Welte DCE • WS 8; SS 11 930; BC 11 930 • H • EC • TX • 941 Bedford-Euless Rd Hurst TX 76053-3808 • FAX(817)284-3731 • peace@peacechurch.org

**IOWA PARK—*GOOD SHEPHERD*** (817)592-5605
Vacant • WS 10; SS 9; BC 9 • H • TX • 801 N 1st St 76367-1543 PO Box 386 Iowa Park TX 76367-0386

**IOWA PARK 10 N—*TRINITY*** (940)569-3097
Robert W Holaday • TX • 76367 11867 FM 1813 Iowa Park TX 76367-5427

**IRVING—*OUR REDEEMER*** (972)255-0595
Michael Mc Farland • WS 8 1030; SS 9; BC 9;* • H • TX • 2505 W Northgate Dr Irving TX 75062-3264 • FAX(972)258-6757 • staff@orlc.org

**JASPER—*ST PAUL*** (409)384-8317
Vacant • H • TX • Hwy 190 W 75951 PO Box 1080 Jasper TX 75951-1080

**KATY—*CROSSPOINT*** (281)398-6464
Bill R Woolsey • Daniel L Hauser DCE • WS 1015; SS 1015 • H • EC • TX • Nottingham Country Elem Sch 77449 700 S Westgreen Blvd Katy TX 77450-2799 • FAX(281)398-6464 • crosspt@crosspt.org

***MEMORIAL*** (281)391-0171
I M Newman Jr. • Jason A Christ DCE • WS 8 1030; SS 915;* • H • EC • TX • 5810 3rd St Katy TX 77493-2425 • FAX(281)391-7579 • memorial@mlckaty.com

**KELLER—*MESSIAH*** (817)431-2345
Glenn E Huebel Christopher J Bramich • WS 8 1045; SS 930; BC 930 • H • EC • TX • 1308 Whitley Rd Keller TX 76248-3016 • FAX(817)431-6640 • glhuebel@gte.net

**KERMIT—*ZION*** (915)586-5236
Michael H Fickenscher Melvin G Herring(EM) • WS 9;* • H • TX • 400 Ne Ave 79745 PO Box 516 Kermit TX 79745-0516

**KERRVILLE—*HOLY CROSS*** (830)257-4433
Rolf E Larsen • WS 10; SS 845; BC 845 • H • EC/EL • TX • 204 Spence St Kerrville TX 78028-5131 • FAX(830)895-1772 • rellcl@ktc.com

***HOSANNA*** (830)257-6767
Joseph M Watson • WS 1030; SS 915; BC 915 • H • TX • 134 Camp Meeting Rd Kerrville TX 78028 • FAX(830)257-4283

**KILGORE—*PILGRIM*** (903)984-4333
Joseph C Lowery(EM) • WS 1045; SS 930; BC 930 • H • TX • 713 Florey St Kilgore TX 75662-3503 • FAX(903)984-4333

**KILLEEN—*GRACE*** (254)634-5858
Michael E Ramming Robert N Harbin • WS 830 945 1115; SS 830 945; BC 830 945;* • H • EC/EL • TX • 1007 Bacon Ranch Rd Killeen TX 76542-2744 • FAX(254)634-5475 • gracelcmskilleentx@juno.com

**KINGSBURY—*EVANGELISTS*** (830)639-4906
William F Shupe • WS 1030; SS 915; BC 915 • H • TX • 7745 Kingsbury Rd 78638-2043 PO Box 176 Kingsbury TX 78638-0176 • wmfred@ix.netcom.com

**KINGSVILLE—*ST PAUL*** (361)592-6531
Allan C Eckert • WS 9; SS 1015; BC 1015 • H • TX • 521 E Doddridge At Tenth 78363 PO Box 1581 Kingsville TX 78364-1581 • FAX(361)592-4134 • aceckert@juno.com

**KINGWOOD—*CHRIST KING*** (281)360-7936
Allen F Doering Doyle J Theimer • John H Williams DCE • SS 940;* • H • EC • TX • 3803 W Lake Houston Pkwy Kingwood TX 77339-5209 • FAX(281)360-2965 • info@christ-the-king.com

**LA GRANGE—*MOUNT CALVARY*** (979)968-3938
Dennis J Bragdon • WS 9; SS 1015;* • H • EC • TX • 800 N Franklin St La Grange TX 78945-1620 • dbragdon@cvtv.net

**LAGO VISTA—*CHRIST OUR SAVIOR*** (512)267-7121
John P Ellwanger • WS 1030; SS 915; BC 915;* • H • TX • 21900 Fm 1431 78645 PO Box 4973 Lago Vista TX 78645-0009 • FAX(512)267-7702

**LAKE JACKSON—*ST MARK*** (409)297-2667
Vacant • H • EC • TX • 501 Willow Dr 77566-4700 PO Box 858 Lake Jackson TX 77566-0858 • FAX(409)299-3291 • stmarksec@computron.net

**LAMESA—*GRACE*** (806)872-2858
Vacant • WS 9; SS 1015 • H • TX • 1002 N 11th St Lamesa TX 79331-3638

**LAMPASAS—*FAITH*** (512)556-3514
Phillip L Phifer • * • H • TX • Old Austin Rd And Sunflower 76550 PO Box 884 Lampasas TX 76550-0884

**LAREDO—*FAITH*** (956)722-2601
Vacant • WS 11; BC 930;* • H • TX • 2419 N Seymour Ave Laredo TX 78040-3430 • FAX(210)791-6830

**LARIAT—*ST JOHN*** (806)825-2409
David V Symm • WS 930; SS 1045; BC 1045 • H • EC • TX • 8 Miles E On Us Hwy 84 UKNWN RR 1 Box 146 Farwell TX 79325-9753

**LEXINGTON—*ST JAMES*** (979)773-2634
Wayne E Schumpe • WS 1030; SS 930; BC 10 • H • TX • 320 N Rockdale St 78947-9645 PO Box 247 Lexington TX 78947-0247

**LEXINGTON 10 S—*TRINITY*** (979)773-2634
Wayne E Schumpe • WS 830; SS 8; BC 8 • H • TX • Fm 1624 At Fedor 78947 PO Box 247 Lexington TX 78947-0247

**LINCOLN—*CHRIST***
See Loebau

**LINCOLN 2 SW—*ST JOHN*** (512)253-6350
Dale E Bohm • H • EC/EL • TX • Fm 1624 78948 RR 1 Box 280 Giddings TX 78942-9723

**LITTLEFIELD—*EMMANUEL*** (806)385-3260
Vacant • H • TX • 409 W 3rd St Littlefield TX 79339-3311

**LIVINGSTON—*TRINITY*** (936)327-3239
Victor L Winkelman • WS 1030; SS 9; BC 9 • H • EC • TX • 221 Pan American Way 77351 PO Box 1163 Livingston TX 77351-1163 • revwink@livingston.net

**LOEBAU—*CHRIST*** (409)884-0333
Herbert A Keistman • WS 1030; SS 930; BC 10 • H • TX • UKNWN RR 1 Box 190 4654 CR 114 Lincoln TX 78948-9726

**LONGVIEW—*OUR REDEEMER*** (903)758-2019
Adrian L Bacarisse • WS 8; SS 930; BC 930;* • H • TX • 1300 Judson Rd Longview TX 75601-3913 • FAX(903)757-0554 • redeemeronhilllongview@worldnet.att.net

**LUBBOCK—*CHRIST*** (806)799-0162
Mark A Paul • WS 830 11; SS 945; BC 945 • H • TX • 7800 Indiana Ave 79423-1802 PO Box 6304 Lubbock TX 79493-6304 • FAX(806)799-2273

***HOPE*** (806)798-2747
Jack A Schneider • Clinton C Colwell DCE • H • EC • TX • 5700 98th St Lubbock TX 79424-4458 • FAX(806)798-3019 • hope@llano.net

***REDEEMER*** (806)744-6178
Jay B Beyer • H • EC • TX • 2221 Avenue W Lubbock TX 79411-1023 • FAX(806)744-3889 • redeemer@rlcms.org

***UNIVERSITY**** (806)763-3644
Vacant • H • TX • C/O Karla Konrad 2615 19th St Lubbock TX 79410-1502 • lubbocklsf@juno.com

**LUFKIN—*FIRST*** (936)634-7468
Frank D Starr • WS 1015; SS 9; BC 9 • H • TX • 1001 Atkinson Dr Lufkin TX 75901-3133 • FAX(936)634-7468 • flc42@juno.com

**LYONS—*IMMANUEL*** (409)272-8968
Vacant • WS 9 • H • TX • Silver Maple And Church St 77863 PO Box 293 Lyons TX 77863-0293

**MAGNOLIA—*ST PAUL*** (281)259-7818
W C Campbell • WS 1015; SS 9; BC 9 • H • TX • 18230 FM 1488 Rd 77354-8557 PO Box 553 Magnolia TX 77353-0553 • FAX(281)259-2079

**MALONE 3 N—*SALEM*** (254)533-2330
James D Heiser • WS 1030; SS 930; BC 930;* • H • TX • 718 HCR 3424 E Malone TX 76660 • FAX(254)533-2357 • salemtx@aol.com

**MANHEIM—*EBENEZER*** (512)253-6636
Herbert A Keistman • WS 8; SS 9; BC 9 • H • TX • 4146 W Highway 21 Paige TX 78659-4222

**MANSFIELD—*ST JOHN*** (817)473-4889
Terry D Beltz • Jerry D Hays DCE • WS 8 1030; SS 915; BC 915 • H • EC • TX • 1218 E Debbie Ln Mansfield TX 76063-3378 • FAX(817)473-3661 • stjohnluthman@startelegram.com

**MARLIN—*GRACE*** (254)803-2475
Gerald N Epperson • WS 10; SS 9; BC 9 • H • EC • TX • 432 Houghton Ave Marlin TX 76661-2342 • marlinrev@hot1.net

**MART—*GRACE*** (254)876-2314
David G Jeske • H • TX • 814 E Texas Ave Mart TX 76664-1520 • FAX(254)876-2314 • dgjeske@aol.com

**MC ALLEN—*EL BUEN PASTOR*** (956)686-6673
Roberto Simental • WS 8 1030; SS 915;* • H • TX • 1929 Pecan Blvd Mc Allen TX 78501-6730

***ST PAUL*** (956)682-2345
Duane E Kirchner Erich F Brauer(EM) • Melanie L Dehning DCE • WS 8 1045; SS 930; BC 930;* • H • TX • 300 W Pecan Blvd Mc Allen TX 78501-2397 • FAX(956)682-7148 • stpaulmca@juno.com

**MC KINNEY—*OUR SAVIOR*** (972)542-6802
Craig A Du Bois Timothy E Morris • WS 830 1045; SS 930; BC 930 • H • EC • TX • 2708 W Virginia Pkwy Mc Kinney TX 75070-4916 • FAX(972)548-9673 • duboisca@prodigy.net

**MENARD—*GRACE*** (915)396-4947
Vacant • WS 9; SS 10;* • H • TX • PO Box 715 Menard TX 76859-0715 • boyce@wcc.net

**MERCEDES—*IMMANUEL*** (956)565-1518
Dale C Lehfeldt Robert O Waters(#) • WS 1030; SS 915; BC 9;* • H • EC • TX • 705 W 3rd St 703 W 3rd St Mercedes TX 78570-3005 • imluthschool@excelonlc.com

***MISION EMANUEL**** (512)565-4678
Edmund J Weber(DM) • H • TX • C/O Rev Ed Weber 257 S Washington Ave Mercedes TX 78570-3036

**MEXIA—*FAITH*** (254)562-7756
Curtis W Schneider • H • TX • 401 S Highway 14 76667-3540 PO Box 1456 Mexia TX 76667-1456 • faith@glade.net

**MIDLAND—*GRACE*** (915)697-3221
Robert J Pase • H • EC • TX • 3000 W Golf Course Rd Midland TX 79701-2998 • FAX(915)697-3536 • glc@marshill.com

***HOLY CROSS*** (915)570-8149
Philip M Konz • WS 1030; SS 915; BC 915 • H • TX • 5400 N Big Spring St Ste A Midland TX 79705-3026 • FAX(915)570-7123 • holycross@lx.net

**MIDLOTHIAN—*MESSIAH*** (972)723-1069
Patrick T Erickson • WS 1045; SS 930 • H • EC • TX • 111 Roundabout Dr Midlothian TX 76065-3620 • FAX(972)775-4007 • mlcmid@flash.net

**MINERAL WELLS—*ST MARK*** (817)325-4282
George P Ascher • WS 1030; SS 915; BC 915 • H • TX • 76067 1201 SE 25th Ave Mineral Wells TX 76067-6731 • stmark@txol.net

**MONAHANS—*ST PAUL*** (915)943-5888
Michael H Fickenscher Melvin G Herring(EM) • H • TX • 1500 S Main St Monahans TX 79756-6008

**MOUNT PLEASANT—*GOOD*** (903)572-4470
Vacant • H • TX • 2820 W Ferguson Rd Mount Pleasant TX 75455-6518

**NACOGDOCHES—*REDEEMER*** (409)564-6729
James E Otte • H • TX • 2306 Appleby Sand Rd Nacogdoches TX 75961-3630 • FAX(409)564-6729 • rlcnac@yahoo.com

**NASSAU BAY—*GLORIA DEI***
See Houston

**NAVASOTA—*TRINITY*** (936)825-6851
Donald M Kasper • WS 8 1030; SS 920; BC 920 • H • EC • TX • 1530 E Washington Ave Navasota TX 77868-3243 • FAX(936)825-6851 • kasper@tca.net

**NAVASOTA 11 SE—*SALEM*** (409)825-2239
Vacant • H • TX • Fr 2988 Near Fr 362 77868 RR 1 Box 482 Navasota TX 77868-9709

**NEDERLAND—*HOLY CROSS*** (409)722-1609
Francis Schroeder • Kristy L Witek DCE • WS 1030; SS 9; BC 9 • H • EC • TX • 2711 Helena Ave Nederland TX 77627-6901 • FAX(409)722-1194 • francis.schroeder@gte.net

**NEW BRAUNFELS—*CROSS*** (830)625-3666
Donald D Fraker • WS 8 1030; SS 915 • H • EC/EL • TX • 169 S Hickory Ave New Braunfels TX 78130-5821 • FAX(830)625-5019 • lutheran@sat.net

**NEW CANEY—*GRACE*** (281)689-0206
B B Blakelock • H • TX • PO Box 505 New Caney TX 77357-0505

**NOACK—*CHRIST***
See Taylor 8 SE

**NORTH RICHLANDH—*ZION***
See Watauga

**NORTH ZULCH 3 S—*BETHLEHEM*** (936)399-5563
Vacant • WS 945; SS 830; BC 830 • H • TX • 77872 5084 Church Ln North Zulch TX 77872-9714 • wd5iqr@txcyber.com

**ODEM—*TRINITY***
See West Sinton

**ODESSA—*EMMANUEL*** (915)366-9311
Vacant • WS 11; SS 10; BC 10 • H • TX • 6450 E Highway 191 Odessa TX 79762-5241 • FAX(915)366-6731

***HOLY CROSS***
See Midland

***REDEEMER*** (915)337-5451
A D Kelm • WS 830 11; SS 945; BC 945 • H • TX • 824 E 18th St Odessa TX 79761-1306 • FAX(915)580-5452 • adkelm@apex2000.net

**OLNEY—*ST LUKE*** (940)564-5466
Vacant • WS 1030; SS 930; BC 930;* • H • TX • 1302 W Oak St 76374-1314 PO Box 626 Olney TX 76374-0626 • FAX(940)564-5466 • stluke@brazosnet.com

**ORANGE—*GRACE*** (409)883-5145
Vacant • H • TX • 2300 Eddleman Rd Orange TX 77632-4405 • FAX(409)882-0034 • glc@ih2000.net

**OWASSO—*SAN PABLO**** (713)673-7862
Vacant • WS 1030; SS 12; BC 12;* • H • EC/EL • TX • 77020-5355 PO Box 15281 Houston TX 77220-5281 • FAX(713)673-4439 • mjunkans@wtez.net

**OZONA—*FAITH*** (915)392-3148
Charles E Huffman • H • TX • 801 First St 76943 PO Box 818 Ozona TX 76943-0818

**PAIGE 7 NE—*EBENEZER***
See Manheim

**PALACIOS—*OUR REDEEMER*** (512)972-3852
Vacant • H • TX • PO Box 943 Palacios TX 77465-0943

**PALESTINE—*BETHLEHEM*** (903)729-6362
Vacant • H • TX • 1515 S Loop 256 Palestine TX 75801-5857 • FAX(903)729-6362 • blc75801@juno.com

**PAMPA—*ZION*** (806)669-2774
Leif R Hasskarl • WS 1030; SS 910 • H • TX • 1200 Duncan St Pampa TX 79065-4736

**PARIS—*GRACE*** (903)784-3753
Jerry L Conley • WS 930; SS 1030; BC 1030 • H • TX • 739 19th St SE Paris TX 75460-7512

**PASADENA—*GOOD SHEPHERD*** (281)479-1091
John L Thompson • WS 8; SS 930; BC 930 • H • TX • 4116 Pasadena Blvd Pasadena TX 77503-3535 • FAX(281)479-1134 • GSLCpastx@aol.com

***ZION*** (281)478-5849
David L Sawhill Richard C Pfaff • WS 8 1045; SS 930; BC 930 • H • EC/EL/HS • TX • 4116 Pasadena Blvd 77503-3535 PO Box 5665 Pasadena TX 77508-5665 • FAX(281)478-5843 • dsawhill@ghgcorp.com

**PATTISON—*CHRIST*** (281)934-8218
William L Schwertlich • WS 1030; SS 9; BC 9 • TX • 35906 Royal Rd 77466 PO Box 507 Pattison TX 77466-0507 • swordly@aol.com

**PEARLAND—*EPIPHANY*** (281)485-7833
Jon D Salminen Ryan R Rupe • WS 8 930 11; SS 930; BC 930 • H • EC • TX • 5515 W Broadway St Pearland TX 77581-3739 • FAX(281)485-5040 • pastor³jon@epiphanypearland.org

**PEARSALL—*ST PETER*** (830)334-2336
Robert E Gentet • WS 1030; SS 930; BC 930 • H • TX • 819 E Brazos St Pearsall TX 78061-3705 • FAX(210)967-4861

**PERRYTON—*BETHLEHEM*** (806)435-3522
Vernon L Appel(#) • H • TX • 611 S Grinnell Perryton TX 79070-2817

**PLAINVIEW—*ST PAUL*** (806)293-1697
Gerald L Boerger • H • TX • 901 Oakland St Plainview TX 79072-7055 • FAX(806)293-8420 • stpaulsplv@door.net

**PLANO—*FAITH*** (972)423-7447
Robert W Hill Michael A Frick • WS 8 1045; SS 930; BC 930;* • H • TX • 1701 E Park Blvd Plano TX 75074-5123 • FAX(972)423-9618 • church@faith.plano.tx.us

***LORD OF LIFE*** (972)867-5588
John T Lindner • Ryan W Meyer DCE • WS 8 1045; SS 930 • H • TX • 3601 W 15th St Plano TX 75075-7741 • FAX(972)985-5588 • office@lol-plano.org

***ST PAUL*** (972)618-4266
Vacant • WS 8 1030; SS 915 • H • EC • TX • 6565 Independence Pkwy Plano TX 75023-3402 • FAX(972)208-1801 • stpaul1@airmail.net

**PORT ARTHUR—*ST MARK*** (409)982-8032
Vacant • H • TX • 201 4th St Port Arthur TX 77640-6447

***TRINITY*** (409)983-1130
Timothy J Dinger Dung V Do • WS 9 1145; SS 1030; BC 1030 • H • TX • 448 San Augustine Ave 2400 5th St Port Arthur TX 77640-6779 • FAX(409)983-1295 • trinitylupa@yahoo.com

**PORT ISABEL—*FISHERS OF MEN*** (956)943-2005
Vacant • WS 830 • H • TX • 603 S Tarnava St Box 8918 Port Isabel TX 78578 • fishersofmen12@juno.com

**RANKIN—*IMMANUEL*** (915)337-5451
Vacant • WS 530; SS 430; BC 430 • H • TX • 705 N Elizabeth 79778 PO Box 527 Rankin TX 79778-0527

**RAYMONDVILLE—*MOUNT CALVARY*** (956)689-2224
Walter A Pohland • WS 815 1030; SS 915; BC 915 • H • TX • E Wood Avenue & Eighth St Raymondville TX 78580 • mclc@vsta.com

**REFUGIO—*TRINITY*** (512)526-4555
Vacant • H • TX • PO Box 183 Refugio TX 78377-0183

**RICHARDSON—*CONCORDIA***
See Garland

***MESSIAH*** (972)234-6972
Victor J Kollmann • David E Rahberg DCE • WS 830 11; SS 945; BC 945 • H • EC/EL/HS • TX • 1245 W Belt Line Rd Richardson TX 75080-5851 • FAX(972)234-6975 • messiah@messiahlutheran.com

**RIESEL 3 E—*TRINITY*** (254)896-6043
Alfred E Gallmeier • H • EC • TX • 76682 PO Box 447 Riesel TX 76682-0447 • FAX(254)896-7105

**ROANOKE—*HOLY SHEPHERD***
See Haslet

**ROCKDALE—*GRACE*** (512)446-2978
Vacant • H • TX • Wilcox And Bell 76567 PO Box 1416 Rockdale TX 76567-1416

**ROCKPORT—*PEACE*** (512)729-7264
Vacant • WS 1030; SS 915; BC 915 • H • TX • 1302 W Market St Rockport TX 78382-6212 • FAX(512)729-5852

**ROCKWALL—*OUR SAVIOR*** (972)771-8118
Richard G Mayerhoff • WS 8 1045; SS 915; BC 915 • H • TX • 3003 Horizon Rd Rockwall TX 75032-5818 • rmayerhoff@rockwall.net

**ROSEBUD—*FIRST*** (254)583-7505
Walter Chelmo • WS 10; SS 9; BC 9 • H • TX • 103 West Avenue E 76570 PO Box 503 Rosebud TX 76570-0503 • wchelmo@prodigy.net

**ROSENBERG—*TRINITY*** (281)341-1451
Wayne A Schueler • WS 8 1015; SS 9 • H • TX • 1512 Louise St Rosenberg TX 77471-4523 • FAX(281)232-3803 • waysch@swbell.net

**ROUND ROCK—*KING OF KINGS*** (512)255-0829
Vacant • Robert L Grady DCE • WS 8 1045; SS 930 • H • EC • TX • 17000 Smyers Ln Round Rock TX 78681 • FAX(512)255-4582 • robgrady@aol.com

**ROWLETT—*CROWN OF LIFE*** (972)475-1348
Tom C Hadley • WS 8 1030; SS 915; BC 915 • H • EC • TX • 4301 Miller Rd Rowlett TX 75088-5811 • FAX(972)412-6686 • pastor@crownoflife-lcms.org

**SAN ANGELO—*TRINITY*** (915)944-8660
Chester L Mc Cown • H • EC/EL • TX • 3536 Ymca Dr San Angelo TX 76904-7154 • FAX(915)223-9770

**SAN ANTONIO—*COMMUNITY*** (210)648-0081
Vacant • TX • 5063 Rigsby Ave San Antonio TX 78222-1304

***CONCORDIA*** (210)479-1477
William G Thompson • Robert J D Ambrosio DCE • H • EC/EL/HS • TX • 16801 Huebner Rd San Antonio TX 78258-4456 • FAX(210)479-9348 • concordia@satx.com

***CROWN OF LIFE*** (210)490-6886
Mark D Barz • Cathy M Meyer DEAC • WS 8 1045; SS 920; BC 930 • H • EC/HS • TX • 19291 Stone Oak Pkwy San Antonio TX 78258-3216 • FAX(210)490-1552 • crownoflifesa@juno.com

***HOLY CROSS*** (210)532-1300
Roger A Hotopp John H Kaster(#) • WS 1015; SS 9; BC 9 • H • HS • TX • 3118 S New Braunfels Ave San Antonio TX 78210-5254

***IGLESIA*** (210)732-7223
Vacant • H • TX • 1826 Basse Rd San Antonio TX 78213 • FAX(210)732-9288

***IMMANUEL*** (210)923-2233
Theodore H Vogel(EM) • H • TX • 130 Saipan Pl San Antonio TX 78221-2927

***KING OF KINGS*** (210)656-6508
Henry H Biar Sr. John M Young • WS 8 1045; SS 930; BC 930 • H • EC • TX • 13888 Dreamwood Dr San Antonio TX 78233-4913 • FAX(210)656-7012 • KingOfKings@Lutheran.com

***MOUNT CALVARY*** (210)824-8748
Kim T De Vries Millard Watson(#) • WS 830 11; SS 945; BC 945 • H • HS • TX • 308 Mount Calvary Dr San Antonio TX 78209-4846 • FAX(210)804-0052 • mt.calvary@vshops.net

***MOUNT OLIVE*** (210)674-1973
James E Sturgis Sr. • H • EC • TX • 8138 Westshire Dr San Antonio TX 78227-2548 • FAX(210)674-3105

***REDEEMER*** (210)732-4112
James C Martin • WS 10; SS 845;* • H • EC/EL/HS • TX • 2507 Fredericksburg Rd San Antonio TX 78201-3711 • FAX(210)735-2868 • PastorMartin@juno.com

***SAN ESTEBAN**** (210)921-1474
Vacant • SS 930; BC 930 • H • TX • 203 Burgess St San Antonio TX 78211-1361

***SHEPHERD HILLS*** (210)614-3742
Daniel G Mueller Michael J Meissner Douglas W Koehler • WS 8 1045 7; SS 930; BC 930;* • H • EC/EL/HS • TX • 78240 6914 Wurzbach Rd San Antonio TX 78240-3832 • FAX(210)692-7554 • church@shlutheran.org

***ST PAUL*** (210)532-7341
Charles P Boerger • WS 9 1030; SS 1030; BC 1030 • H • EC • TX • 2302 S Presa St San Antonio TX 78210-2840 • FAX(210)534-2998 • stpaullu@swbell.net

**SAN BENITO—*ST JOHN*** (956)399-3422
Marcus R Mueller • WS 1030; SS 930; BC 930;* • H • TX • 1000 N Crockett St San Benito TX 78586-5208 • FAX(956)399-3735 • stjohnsanbtx@acnet.net

**SAN MARCOS—*GRACE*** (512)392-4241
Bruce A Peffer • H • TX • 1250 Belvin St San Marcos TX 78666-4181 • FAX(512)392-4250 • grace@itouch.net

**SCHULENBURG—*ZION*** (979)743-3842
Bernard J Schey • WS 10; SS 9; BC 9 • H • TX • 103 Keuper Ave Schulenburg TX 78956-1128 • FAX(979)743-3842 • zionburg@yahoo.com

**SEALY—*TRINITY*** (979)885-2211
Dale D Leland Mark B Anderson • WS 8 1015; SS 9; BC 9 • H • EC • TX • 402 Atchison St Sealy TX 77474-2702 • FAX(979)885-7003 • tlcsealy@clearsail.net

**SEGUIN—*GRACE*** (830)379-1690
Edward P Giese • WS 10; SS 845; BC 845 • H • EC • TX • 935 E Mountain St Seguin TX 78155-5010

**SERBIN—*ST PAUL*** (979)366-9650
Michael G Buchhorn • WS 830; SS 930; BC 930 • H • EC/EL • TX • 1572 CR 211 RR 2 Box 152 Giddings TX 78942-9769 • FAX(979)366-2200

**SEYMOUR—*TRINITY*** (817)888-3330
Vacant • H • TX • 500 S Main St 76380-3008 PO Box 53 Seymour TX 76380-0053

**SHAMROCK—*TRINITY*** (806)256-2355
James Sturgis Jr. • H • TX • 900 S Main St Shamrock TX 79079-2818

**SMITHVILLE—*GRACE*** (512)237-2108
James M Richardson Sr. • WS 10; SS 845; BC 845 • H • EC • TX • 308 Byrne St Smithville TX 78957-1617 • FAX(512)237-3051 • gracelutheran@smithsys.net

**SONORA—*HOPE*** (915)387-5366
Vacant • H • TX • 419 E 2nd St Sonora TX 76950

**SPRING—*RESURRECTION*** (281)353-4413
Stephen J Sohns James M Jobst • Thomas W Keithley DCE • WS 815 11; SS 945; BC 945 • H • EC/HS • TX • 1612 Meadow Edge Ln Spring TX 77388-6227 • FAX(281)353-1642 • usbad.com

***ST MATTHEW WESTFIELD*** (281)443-2304
David L Adler • H • TX • 77373 21434 E Hardy Rd Houston TX 77073-2200 • FAX(281)443-8463

**SPRING 5 W—*TRINITY*** (281)376-5773
Richard C Noack Roy A Kieschnick Jeffrey D Patterson • Michael S Hinckfoot DCE • WS 8 1050 11; SS 930; BC 930;* • H • EC/EL/HS • TX • 77373 18926 Klein Church Rd Klein TX 77379-4951 • FAX(281)251-7021 • trinity805@aol.com

***TRINITY***
See Spring 5 W

**STEPHENVILLE—*FAITH*** (254)968-2710
Thomas R Konz • WS 815 1045; SS 930;* • H • TX • 3000 Northwest Loop Stephenville TX 76401-1642 • FAX(254)968-2344 • flc@our-town.com

**SUGAR LAND—*FAITH*** (281)242-7729
Kenneth E Sinclair • WS 8 1030; SS 915;* • H • TX • 800 Brooks St Sugar Land TX 77478-3816 • FAX(281)242-8749 • information@flcsl.org

***FISHERS OF MEN*** (281)242-7711
Thomas N Van Duzer Lonnie Gonzales • WS 1045 830; SS 930; BC 830;* • H • EC • TX • 2011 Austin Pkwy Sugar Land TX 77479-1254 • FAX(281)242-2164 • office@fishersofmen.org

**SULPHUR SPRINGS—*OUR SAVIOR*** (903)885-5787
George W Shaffer • H • TX • 1000 Texas St Sulphur Springs TX 75482-4254 • FAX(903)885-3107 • gwshaffer@bluebonnet.net

**SWEENY—*ST LUKE*** (409)548-3535
Edward L Boineau • H • TX • 1402 North Main 77480 PO Box 97 Sweeny TX 77480-0097

**SWEETWATER—*FAITH*** (915)235-2773
Dale O Snyder • WS 1045; SS 930; BC 930 • H • TX • 1607 Josephine St Sweetwater TX 79556-3521 • faith@camalott.com

**TAYLOR—*TRINITY*** (512)352-6958
Martin Doering • WS 10; SS 9; BC 9 • H • EC • TX • 3505 N Main 76574 PO Box 72 Taylor TX 76574-0072

**TAYLOR 8 SE—*CHRIST*** (512)898-2471
Vernon M Appel(EM) • H • TX • 6730 Fm 112 Taylor 76574 PO Box 146 Thorndale TX 76577-0146 • appel@totalaccess.net

**TEMPLE—*IMMANUEL*** (254)773-3898
Alan D Struckmeyer Brian L Bibler • WS 8 930 1045;* • H • EC/EL • TX • 2109 W Avenue H Temple TX 76504-5216 • FAX(254)773-2844

**TEXARKANA—*FIRST*** (903)792-5253
Richard S Cody • WS 8 1030; SS 915; BC 915;* • H • TX • 4600 Texas Blvd Texarkana TX 75503-3029 • FAX(903)794-0999 • revcody@txk.net

**TEXAS CITY—*PEACE*** (409)938-1277
David H Tessmann • WS 1030; SS 915; BC 915 • H • TX • 9111 Emmett F Lowry Expy Texas City TX 77591-2101 • FAX(409)938-7764 • revdht@aol.com

**THE GROVE—*ST PAUL*** (254)986-2607
Christopher E Offen • H • TX • UKNWN 220 The Grove Rd Gatesville TX 76528-4205 • FAX(254)986-1478

**THE WOODLANDS—*LIVING WORD*** (281)363-4860
Alvin H Franzmeier • John R Wengel DCE • H • EC/HS • TX • 9500 N Panther Creek Dr The Woodlands TX 77381 • FAX(281)363-3447 • Franzie3@juno.com

**THORNDALE—*ST PAUL*** (512)898-2711
James K Mann • WS 8 10; SS 9; BC 9 • H • EC/EL • TX • 101 North Third St 76577 PO Box 369 Thorndale TX 76577-0369 • FAX(512)898-5298 • splcthorndale@hotmail.com

**THREE RIVERS—*ST PAUL***
Vacant • TX • Leroy And Caves PO Box 548 Three Rivers TX 78071

**TOMBALL—*ZION*** (281)351-5757
R J Teichmiller Ronald C Paseur • WS 8 1030; SS 915; BC 915 • H • EC/EL/HS • TX • 907 Hicks St Tomball TX 77375-4125 • FAX(281)255-8696 • revtike@juno.com

**TOMBALL 3 W—*SALEM*** (281)351-8223
Wayne E Graumann Douglas Dommer H M Neumann Craig E Whitson • WS 930; SS 1050; BC 1050 720;* • H • EC/EL/HS • TX • 77375 22601 Lutheran Church Rd Tomball TX 77375-3716 • FAX(281)351-6711 • slconline@salem4u.com

**TYLER—*TRINITY*** (903)593-1526
Art L Hill • WS 8 1030; SS 920; BC 920 • H • EC • TX • 2001 Hunter St Tyler TX 75701-4828 • FAX(903)593-7664 • tlc@tyler.net

**UVALDE—*TRINITY*** (830)278-9474
Vacant • H • EC • TX • 762 N Getty St Uvalde TX 78801-4302 • tlcchurch@peppersnet.com

**VERNON—*ST PAUL*** (940)552-2495
Rossetter T Leavitt • WS 1030; SS 930; BC 930 • H • EC • TX • 4405 Hospital Dr Vernon TX 76384-4022 • FAX(940)552-6616

**VERNON 12 SW—*ZION*** (940)552-7164
Kenneth J Bersche • H • TX • 76384 14570 FM 2074 Vernon TX 76384-8655 • zionvtx@cst.net

**VICTORIA—*GRACE*** (361)573-2232
Jay E Simonsen • Bruce Milbrath DCE • WS 8 1030; SS 915; BC 915 • H • TX • 605 E Locust Ave Victoria TX 77901-3933 • FAX(361)573-0867 • grace@tisd.net

**WACO—*PEACE*** (254)420-4729
Stephen P Rynearson • WS 9; SS 1015; BC 1015;* • H • TX • 9301 Panther Way 76712-8674 PO Box 307 Hewitt TX 76643-0307 • FAX(254)420-4729 • peacelc@calpha.com

***ST MARK*** (254)754-0644
James M Price • H • TX • 2000 Clay Ave Waco TX 76706-2722

***ST PAUL***
See Bellmead

***TRINITY*** (817)772-4225
Donald L Olson Jr. • WS 9; SS 1030; BC 1030 • H • TX • 6125 Bosque Blvd Waco TX 76710-4170 • FAX(254)772-2576 • dlolson@texasinternet.com

**WALBURG—*ZION*** (512)863-3065
John M Davenport Keith D Aschenbeck • WS 8 1030; SS 915; BC 915 • H • EC/EL • TX • 78673 6001 FM 1105 Georgetown TX 78626 • FAX(512)869-5659 • zion@texas.net

**WALLIS—*ST PAUL*** (979)478-6741
Raymond D Spitzenberger • WS 9; SS 1030; BC 1030 • TX • 506 Cedar 77485 PO Box 427 Wallis TX 77485-0427

**WARDA—*HOLY CROSS*** (409)242-3333
Thomas W Hoyt • WS 8 1030; SS 915; BC 915 • H • TX • FM 1482 78960 PO Box 69 Warda TX 78960-0069 • FAX(409)242-3416 • hclwarda@cvtv.net

**WATAUGA—*ZION*** (817)427-2909
David G Loeffler • WS 1030; SS 9; BC 9 • H • TX • 6416 Watauga Rd 76148-3325 PO Box 48399 Watauga TX 76148-0399 • zionlutherantexas@hotmail.com

**WAXAHACHIE—*CHRIST KING*** (972)938-1633
Norman R Finke • WS 8; SS 915; BC 915 • H • HS • TX • 301 W US Highway 287 Byp Waxahachie TX 75165-5073 • FAX(972)938-1633 • pastor@christtheking.net

**WEATHERFORD—*TRINITY*** (817)613-1939
Kenneth R Watson • WS 1015; SS 9; BC 9 • H • TX • 1500 W Ball St Weatherford TX 76086-2816 • tlcwford@aol.com

**WEST SINTON—*TRINITY*** (361)364-2367
Brian K Cummins • H • TX • 7912 Fm 796 UKNWN RR 1 Box 98 Odem TX 78370

**WESTFIELD—*ST MATTHEW***
See Spring

**WHARTON—*ST JOHN*** (979)532-2336
William B Sharp • WS 10; SS 9; BC 9 • H • TX • 614 Pecan St Wharton TX 77488-4012 • pastor@wcnet.net

**WHITNEY—*OUR SAVIOR*** (254)694-3234
Francis W Mennenga • WS 10; SS 9; BC 9 • H • TX • 117 HCR 2129 East 76692 PO Box 917 Whitney TX 76692-0917 • FAX(254)694-9654 • oursavior@whitneytx.net

**WICHITA FALLS—*OUR REDEEMER*** (940)692-3690
Charles Paulson • H • EC • TX • 4605 Cypress Ave Wichita Falls TX 76310-2540 • FAX(940)692-0382 • orlc@wf.net

***ST PAUL*** (940)322-6112
Thomas V Handrick • WS 1015; SS 9; BC 9 • TX • 1419 11th St 76301-4406 PO Box 126 Wichita Falls TX 76307-0126 • FAX(940)322-6135 • splcwftx@wf.quik.com

**WILLS POINT—*HOLY CROSS*** (903)873-6700
Vacant • SS 8; BC 8;* • TX • 235 N 4th St 75169-2042 PO Box 861 Wills Point TX 75169-0861

**WILSON—*ST PAUL*** (806)628-6471
David W Rohde • WS 1015; SS 915; BC 915 • TX • 16th And Houston Sts 79381 PO Box 136 Wilson TX 79381-0136 • FAX(806)628-6471 • wilsonSP@juno.com

**WINCHESTER—*ST MICHAEL*** (979)242-3444
Henry C Wied Sr. • WS 9; SS 1015; BC 1015 • H • TX • 700 Frio St Winchester TX 78945-5235 • FAX(979)242-3444

**WINDOM—*ST JAMES***
See Honey Grove 7 NW

**WINNIE—*HOPE*** (409)296-2377
Donald O Kroll • WS 930; SS 1030; BC 1030 • H • TX • 1322 9th St 77665 PO Box 701 Winnie TX 77665-0701 • FAX(409)296-3326 • hope@datarecall.net

**WOODVILLE—*FAITH*** (409)283-7171
Vacant • WS 9; SS 8; BC 8 • H • TX • 704 W Holly St Woodville TX 75979-5130

**ZAPATA—*ABIDING SAVIOR*** (956)765-6113
Vacant • WS 1030; SS 915; BC 915 • H • TX • 14th And Mier PO Box 5746 Zapata TX 78076

## UTAH

**BOUNTIFUL—*CROSS CHRIST*** (801)295-7677
Donal C Widger • WS 1030; SS 915; BC 915 • H • EC/HS • RM • 1840 S 75 E Bountiful UT 84010-5544 • crossofchrist-utah@juno.com

**CEDAR CITY—*TRINITY*** (435)586-7103
Vacant • H • RM • 410 E 1935 N 84720-9735 PO Box 1527 Cedar City UT 84721-1527

**KANAB—*MOUNT ZION*** (435)644-3541
Vacant • H • RM • 1518 S Hwy 89A Kanab UT 84741

**LAYTON—*TRINITY*** (801)544-5770
Kurt M Hering(#) • WS 9; SS 1030 • H • EC • RM • 385 W Golden Ave Layton UT 84041-2312 • tlcms@freewwweb.com

**LOGAN—*HOLY TRINITY*** (435)752-1453
Vacant • RM • 581 N 7th E Logan UT 84321-4256

**MOAB—*GRACE*** (435)259-5017
Richard A Evans(#) • H • RM • 360 W 400 N Moab UT 84532-2354 • gracelc@timp.net

**MURRAY—*CHRIST*** (801)262-4354
Merlyn D Wagner Kristian J Erickson • H • EC/EL/HS • RM • 240 E 5600 S Murray UT 84107-6113 • FAX(801)266-8799

**OGDEN—*ST PAUL*** (801)392-6368
Gary G Trickey • James D Ritter DCE • BC 945;* • H • EC/EL • RM • 3329 Harrison Blvd Ogden UT 84403-1228 • FAX(801)392-7562 • gtrickey@stpaullcms.org

**PROVO—*ST MARK*** (801)225-5777
Ronald E Saatkamp • WS 10 • H • RM • 464 W 3700 N Provo UT 84604-4955 • FAX(801)434-9624 • r.saatkamp@worldnet.att.net

**RICHFIELD—*GOOD SHEPHERD*** (435)896-8050
Donald R Schulz(DM) • WS 1045; SS 10;* • H • RM • 1270 W 1700 S 1270 W 1700 Richfield UT 84701 • FAX(435)896-8050 • prdon@gbasin.net

**ROOSEVELT—*FAITH***
Vacant • RM • 65 E Lagoon St # 120-8 Roosevelt UT 84066-2809

**SAINT GEORGE—*OUR SAVIOR*** (435)652-3040
Vacant • H • EN • 245 N 200 W 84770-2711 PO Box 599 St George UT 84771-0599

***TRINITY*** (435)628-1850
John Manweiler • WS 10; SS 9; BC 9 • H • EL • RM • 2260 Red Cliff Dr St George UT 84790-8153 • trinityl@infowest.com

**SALT LAKE CITY—*REDEEMER*** (801)467-4352
David A Fischer • WS 8 1030;* • H • EL/HS • RM • 1955 E Stratford Ave Salt Lake City UT 84106-4151 • FAX(801)463-7904

***ST JOHN*** (801)364-2873
Bryan N Lindemood • WS 10; BC 845;* • EC/HS • RM • 1030 S 500 E 84105-1120 475 Herbert Ave Salt Lake City UT 84111-4737 • st.johns.lutheran.slc@juno.com

**SANDY—*GRACE*** (801)572-6375
Mark G Below D T Brandt • WS 815 11 7; SS 945; BC 945 • H • EC/EL/HS • RM • 1815 E 9800 S Sandy UT 84092-3856 • FAX(801)553-2403 • church@glcs-lcms.org

**TOOELE—*FIRST*** (435)882-1172
Glenn D Kalthoff • WS 1030; SS 915; BC 915 • H • HS • RM • 349 N 7th St 84074-1978 PO Box 738 Tooele UT 84074-0738

**VERNAL—*OUR SAVIOUR*** (435)789-1421
Roger D Sterle • WS 11;* • H • RM • 357 S 500 W 84078-3046 PO Box 342 Vernal UT 84078-0342 • dsterle@iwworks.com

## VERMONT

**RUTLAND—*MESSIAH*** (802)775-0231
George M Gustke • H • NE • 42 Woodstock Ave Rutland VT 05701-3517

**SOUTH BURLINGTON—*COMMUNITY*** (802)864-5537
Jefrey S Jensen • WS 830 11; BC 945;* • H • EC • NE • 1560 Williston Rd South Burlington VT 05403-6477 • FAX(802)864-5537 • clc1560@juno.com

**WILLIAMSTOWN—*WILLIAMSTOWN*** (802)479-1164
Calvin W Kemp • WS 10; SS 1115;* • H • NE • 2846 Graniteville Rd Graniteville VT 05654 • kempcw@aol.com

## VIRGINIA

**ALEXANDRIA—*BETHANY*** (703)765-8255
Karl K Schmidt • H • EC • SE • 2501 Beacon Hill Rd Alexandria VA 22306-1609 • FAX(703)765-0307 • office@bethany-lcms.org

***IMMANUEL*** (703)549-0155
Vacant • WS 10; SS 9; BC 9 • H • EL • SE • 1801 Russell Rd Alexandria VA 22301-1934

***ST JOHN*** (703)971-2210
John S Meehan Bernard F Nass • WS 8 1030;* • H • EC • SE • 5952 Franconia Rd Alexandria VA 22310-4404 • FAX(703)971-9258 • stjohnslc@sjlc.com

**AMELIA—*ST PAUL***
Robert H Wind(EM) • H • SE • Eggleston St 23002 4721 West Creek Rd Amelia Ct Hse VA 23002-2109

**ARLINGTON—*OUR SAVIOR*** (703)892-4846
Wayne J Lehrer • WS 815 930 11; SS 940; BC 940 • H • EL • SE • 825 S Taylor St Arlington VA 22204-1461 • FAX(703)892-4847 • wlehrer@aol.com

**ASHBURN—*OUR SAVIORS WAY*** (703)858-9254
William B Mann V • WS 830 11; SS 945; BC 945 • H • EC • SE • 43115 Waxpool Rd Ashburn VA 20148 • FAX(703)729-9149 • oswlc@aol.com

**ASHLAND—*HOLY CROSS*** (804)798-6830
Terrance A Naumann • WS 1030; SS 9; BC 9 • H • SE • 11515 Ashcake Rd Ashland VA 23005-3062 • FAX(804)798-6330 • hclcashva@aol.com

**CALLAO—*GOOD SHEPHERD*** (804)529-5948
Richard J Finck • H • SE • 1717 Hampton Hall Rd 22435-2609 PO Box 576 Callao VA 22435-0576 • FAX(804)529-6012

**CHARLOTTESVILLE—*IMMANUEL*** (804)295-4038
Vacant • WS 830 11; SS 945;* • H • SE • 2416 Jefferson Park Ave Charlottesville VA 22903-3622 • FAX(804)295-4038 • iimanu@juno.com

**CHESAPEAKE—*FAITH*** (757)436-5832
Christian G Morales • WS 1030; SS 915; BC 915 • H • EN • PO Box 1443 Chesapeake VA 23327-1443

**CHESTER—*GRACE*** (804)748-6058
Vacant • WS 815 1045; SS 930 • H • SE • 13028 Harrowgate Rd 23831-4521 PO Box 1436 Chester VA 23831-8436 • glcoffice@aol.com

**DANVILLE—*CHRIST KING*** (804)836-6888
James O Kleinfelter • WS 11; SS 945; BC 945 • H • EC • SE • 1172 Franklin Tpke Danville VA 24540-1328 • ctklc@gamewood.net

**EMPORIA—*ST JOHN BAPTIST*** (804)634-4515
Vacant • H • EC • S • Highway 58 W 23847 1351 W Atlantic St Emporia VA 23847-2863 • FAX(804)634-4515

**FAIRFAX STATION—*LIVING SAVIOR*** (703)352-1421
Frederick G Klein • WS 830 11; SS 945; BC 945 • H • EC • SE • 5500 Ox Rd Fairfax Station VA 22039-1020 • FAX(703)352-1421 • secretary@livsavluthch.org

**FALLS CHURCH—*ST PAUL*** (703)573-0295
Mark A Shaltanis • * • H • EC • SE • 7426 Idylwood Rd Falls Church VA 22043-2915 • FAX(703)573-3273 • stpaulsoff@aol.com

**FARMVILLE—*ST JOHN*** (804)392-6767
Donald R Ortner • H • SE • 1375 S Main St 23901-2351 1421 Gilliam Dr Farmville VA 23901-2353 • FAX(804)223-6347

**FREDERICKSBURG—*REDEEMER*** (540)898-4748
Robert A Koehler • WS 8; SS 915; BC 915;* • H • EC • SE • 5120 Harrison Rd Fredericksburg VA 22408-1803 • FAX(540)891-9106 • rlclcms@erols.com

**HALLWOOD—*ST PAUL SHORE*** (757)824-0325
Vacant • WS 11; SS 10; BC 10;* • H • EC • SE • 28281 Main St Hallwood VA 23359-2624 • stpauls@intercom.net

**HAMPTON—*EMMANUEL*** (757)865-7800
Paul F Napier • WS 1030; SS 9; BC 9 • H • EC/EL • SE • 23 Semple Farm Rd Hampton VA 23666-1456 • pnap2000@aol.com

**HOPEWELL—*NAZARETH*** (804)458-7994
Michael O Kane • WS 11; SS 945; BC 945;* • H • SE • 1711 Grant St Hopewell VA 23860-3655

**KING GEORGE—*PEACE*** (540)775-9131
Richard J Finck • H • EC • SE • 10365 Luther Ln 22485-3860 PO Box 317 King George VA 22485-0317 • FAX(540)775-9131

**LYNCHBURG—*OUR SAVIOR*** (804)384-6651
James S Bloker • WS 11; SS 945 • H • SE • 2940 Link Rd Lynchburg VA 24503-3253

**MANASSAS—*HOPE*** (703)361-8732
Allan E Hudspith • H • SE • 10391 Sudley Manor Dr Manassas VA 20109-2962 • hopelc-ms@erols.com

**MEHERRIN 1 E—*ST MATTHEW*** (804)736-8219
Vacant • H • SE • 23954 PO Box 91 Meherrin VA 23954-0091

**MEHERRIN 2 NE—*ST PAUL***
Frank G Koehler(EM) • H • SE • Free State Road 23954 PO Box 69 Meherrin VA 23954-0069

**MIDLOTHIAN—*MT ZION KOREAN**** (804)763-1941
Vacant • WS 1130 4; SS 1130; BC 7;* • SE • 2306 Garrison Place Ct 23112 C/O Redeemer Luth Church 9400 Redbridge Rd Richmond VA 23236-3566 • FAX(804)763-1941 • pauljchung@hotmail.com

***NEW HOPE**** (804)330-9549
Vacant • WS 930;* • SE • 23113 2013 Esquire Rd Richmond VA 23235 • FAX(804)330-9549 • seelong@worldnet.att.net

***REDEEMER*** (804)272-7973
James R Byork Matthew D Bean Robert G Heckmann(EM) • WS 830 11; SS 945; BC 945 • H • EC • SE • 23232 9400 Redbridge Rd Richmond VA 23236-3566 • FAX(804)272-6310

**NEWPORT NEWS—*RESURRECTION*** (757)596-5808
William H Hollar Jr. • WS 830 11; SS 945; BC 945 • H • SE • 765 J Clyde Morris Blvd Newport News VA 23601-1513 • FAX(757)596-5010 • rlc@erols.com

**NORFOLK—*CHRIST*** (757)853-5655
Lawrence J Zimmermann • WS 10; SS 845; BC 845 • H • SE • 6510 N Military Hwy Norfolk VA 23518-5238 • FAX(757)858-5094 • ‹christnorfolk@juno.com

***TRINITY*** (757)489-2551
James P O Connor • WS 11 830; SS 940;* • H • EC/EL • SE • 6001 Granby St Norfolk VA 23505-4816 • FAX(757)489-8413 • lhtrinity@aol.com

***UNITY*** (804)627-3498
Vacant • H • SE • 2801 E Princess Anne Rd Norfolk VA 23504-3110

**PORTSMOUTH—*REDEEMER*** (757)397-8362
Thomas E Becker • WS 11; SS 930;* • H • SE • 1901 Airline Blvd Portsmouth VA 23701-2901

**POWHATAN—*KING OF KINGS*** (804)598-2641
Michael Brondos(EM) • WS 830; SS 930 • H • SE • 3840 Old Buckingham Rd 23139-7922 PO Box 719 Powhatan VA 23139-0719 • rmitchel@amel.tds.net

**RESTON—*GOOD SHEPHERD*** (703)437-5020
Monte E Frohm Peter T Luedemann Gerald E Kuhn(EM) • WS 8 1045;* • H • EC • SE • 1516 Moorings Dr Reston VA 20190-4242 • FAX(703)689-0032 • pastor@goodshepherd-lutheran.org

**RICHMOND—*BETHLEHEM*** (804)353-4413
Gary C Olson Otto L Wood • EC/EL • SE • 1100 W Grace St Richmond VA 23220-3613 • FAX(804)353-4632

***NEW HOPE****
See Midlothian

***RESURRECTION*** (804)321-7291
Vacant • H • SE • 2500 Seminary Ave Richmond VA 23220-1532

***ST PAUL***
See Sandston

***TRINITY*** (804)270-4626
W Philip Bruening Douglas C Romig • BC 945;* • H • EC • SE • 2315 Parham Rd Richmond VA 23229 • FAX(804)747-5113 • pbrue@erols.com

**RICHMOND 3 S W—*REDEEMER***
See Bon Air

**ROANOKE—*GOOD SHEPHERD*** (540)774-8746
Vacant • WS 1015; SS 915 • H • EC • SE • 1887 Electric Rd Roanoke VA 24018-1618

**SANDSTON—*ST PAUL*** (804)222-5416
Rodney E Bitely • H • SE • 23150 4700 Oakleys Ln Richmond VA 23231-2916

**SPRINGFIELD—*LIGHT/WORLD**** (703)916-7881
Suk H Lee(DM) • WS 130; SS 130; BC 330;* • SE • 8304 Old Keene Mill Rd 22152-1640 7822 Sutter Ln #3 Annandale VA 22003

***PRINCE OF PEACE*** (703)451-5855
John R Denninger Richard T Hinz Ralph E Wiechmann Helmut H Wiechmann(EM) • WS 815 11; SS 945;* • H • EC • SE • 8304 Old Keene Mill Rd Springfield VA 22152-1640 • FAX(703)569-0978

**STAFFORD—*LIVING HOPE**** (540)657-4105
Vacant • WS 10; SS 9; BC 9;* • SE • 100 Wood Dr 22554 PO Box 219 Garrisonville VA 22463 • FAX(413)487-0576 • hisjoy4u@msn.com

**TRIANGLE—*CONCORDIA*** (703)221-3703
James R Knill • WS 1030; SS 9; BC 9 • H • SE • 3637 Graham Park Rd PO Box 336 Triangle VA 22172-0336 • FAX(703)221-7366 • conlutri@doubled.com

**VIRGINIA BEACH—*HOPE*** (757)424-4848
Thomas R Clocker • WS 8 11;* • H • EC • SE • 5350 Providence Rd Virginia Beach VA 23464-4100 • FAX(757)424-7626 • hopelutheran1@juno.com

***PRINCE OF PEACE*** (757)340-8420
Edwin J Nicklas • H • EC • SE • 424 Kings Grant Rd Virginia Beach VA 23452-6921 • FAX(757)340-8421 • poplcvb@erols.com

**WARSAW—*GOOD SHEPHERD***
See Callao

**WAYNESBORO—*BETHANY-TRINITY*** (540)942-4361
Philip W Ressler • SS 945 • H • EC • SE • 712 W Main St 22980-4349 100 Maple Ave Waynesboro VA 22980-4607 • FAX(540)942-5574

**WILLIAMSBURG—*KING OF GLORY*** (757)258-9701
Thomas R Zehnder • WS 8; SS 915; BC 915 • H • EC • SE • 4897 Longhill Rd Williamsburg VA 23188-1572 • FAX(757)564-9810 • klutheran@aol.com

**WINCHESTER—*OUR SAVIOR*** (540)667-1459
Albert F Quoss • WS 10; SS 9;* • SE • 672 Virginia Ave 22601-5612 PO Box 2253 Winchester VA 22604-1453

**WOODBRIDGE—*GRACE*** (703)494-4600
Keith W Loesch • WS 815 11; SS 945; BC 945;* • H • SE • 2466 Longview Dr Woodbridge VA 22191-2139 • FAX(703)494-4600 • gracelc@doubled.com

## WASHINGTON

**ABERDEEN—*CALVARY*** (360)532-3980
Richard J Peterson Thomas A Graves • H • EC • NOW • 2515 Sumner Ave 98520-4316 PO Box 1957 Aberdeen WA 98520-0324 • FAX(360)532-2596 • calvary@techline.com

**ALGONA—*NEW HOPE***
See Pacific

**AUBURN—*NEW HOPE***
See Pacific

***ZION*** (253)833-5940
Terence M Dill • WS 1030;* • H • EC/HS • NOW • 98002 1305 17th St SE Auburn WA 98002-6934 • zionlcms@juno.com

**BASIN CITY—*MESSIAH***
See Mesa 6W

**BATTLE GROUND—*PRINCE OF PEACE*** (360)687-7455
Paul L Tuchardt • H • EC • NOW • 14208 NE 249th St Battle Ground WA 98604-9772

**BELLEVUE—*ALL SAINTS*** (425)881-2925
Roger H Dallman • WS 630;* • H • NOW • 5501 148th Ave NE Bellevue WA 98007-3024 • FAX(425)702-2131 • allsaints-lcms.com

***CHRIST THE KING*** (425)746-1711
Keith H Eilers • H • HS • NOW • 3730 148th Ave SE Bellevue WA 98006-1698 • FAX(425)401-8552 • ic-ctk@uswest.net

***PILGRIM*** (425)454-1162
James V Rehder • WS 830; SS 945; BC 945 • H • EC/HS • NOW • 10420 SE 11th St Bellevue WA 98004-6852 • FAX(425)637-7016 • staff@pilgrimlutheran.org

**BELLINGHAM—*REDEEMER*** (360)384-5923
Richard H Husman • WS 8 1030; SS 915; BC 915 • H • EC • NOW • 858 W Smith Rd Bellingham WA 98226-9613 • FAX(360)380-3378 • avisma@gte.net

***TRINITY*** (206)734-2770
Douglas Iben • Sara B Bormuth DEAC • WS 8 9 1030 • H • EC • NOW • 119 Texas St Bellingham WA 98225-3725 • FAX(206)734-2795 • church@trinitybellingham.org

**BENTON CITY—*ST JOHN*** (509)588-4081
Vacant • H • NOW • 1000 Irma Ave 99320 PO Box 515 Benton City WA 99320-0515

**BINGEN—*OUR SAVIOR*** (509)493-2499
Paul R Bundschuh • WS 9;* • H • NOW • PO Box 237 Bingen WA 98605-0237 • bundschuh@juno.com

**BONNEY LAKE—*OUR REDEEMER*** (253)862-0715
Rodney D Riveness • WS 9 1030 • H • EC/HS • NOW • 12407 214th Ave E 98390-7266 PO Box 7127 Bonney Lake WA 98390-0903 • FAX(253)862-0715

**BOTHELL—*EPIPHANY***
See Kenmore

***ST JAMES*** (425)745-9859
James B Jenson • H • NOW • 19510 Bothell Everett Hwy 98012-7117 PO Box 12806 Mill Creek WA 98082-0806

**BREMERTON—*MEMORIAL*** (360)377-0161
Richard W Andrus • WS 9; BC 1030;* • H • EC • NOW • 916 Veneta Ave Bremerton WA 98337-1341

***PEACE*** (360)377-6253
Jeffrey H Pulse • WS 8 1045; SS 930; BC 930;* • H • EC/EL • NOW • 1234 NE Riddell Rd Bremerton WA 98310-3637 • FAX(360)377-0686

**BREWSTER—*HOPE*** (509)689-3106
Vacant • WS 11; SS 10;* • NOW • 5th And W Indian Ave 98812 PO Box 1084 Brewster WA 98812-1084

**CHEHALIS—*PEACE*** (360)748-4108
Herman J Williams Larry W Bergman • H • EC • NOW • 2071 Bishop Rd Chehalis WA 98532-8712

**COULEE CITY—*BETHEL***
William D Goodin • WS 9; SS 10;* • NOW • Second At Main 99115 PO Box 446 Coulee City WA 99115-0446

***SALEM***
See Marlin

**DAYTON—*MISSION****
See Pomeroy

***REDEEMER*** (509)382-4662
Gregory Bye • * • H • NOW • 601 S 3rd St Dayton WA 99328-1513

**DEER PARK—*FAITH*** (509)276-5268
Steven J Brehmer • H • EC • NOW • 214 S Weber Rd 99006-9056 PO Box 1428 Deer Park WA 99006-1428 • dpfaith@juno.com

**DES MOINES—*RESURRECTION***
See Seattle

***RESURRECTION*** (206)824-2978
Richard W Gerken David M Dorpat • WS 8 1030; SS 915; BC 915 • H • NOW • 134 S 206th St Des Moines WA 98198-2815 • FAX(206)824-2979

**EAST WENATCHEE—*FAITH*** (509)884-7623
Bernhard J Huesmann • Mark L Schoepp DCE • WS 930; BC 11;* • H • NOW • 171 Eastmont Ave East Wenatchee WA 98802-5303 • FAX(509)884-7623 • faithlc@nwi.net

**EDMONDS—*ST TIMOTHY*** (425)743-2323
Jerrold Collins • WS 815 1030; BC 915;* • H • EC • NOW • 5124 164th St SW Edmonds WA 98026-4833 • FAX(425)745-4744 • jc12045@aol.com

**EPHRATA—*OUR SAVIOR*** (509)754-3468
Grant Francis • WS 11; SS 945; BC 945;* • H • EC • NOW • 98823 471 Southeast Blvd Ephrata WA 98823-2286

**EVERETT—*GRACE*** (425)353-1852
Robert C Hendrix • H • NOW • 8401 Holly Dr Everett WA 98208-1805

***IMMANUEL*** (425)252-7038
Kyle D Heck Kyle D Castens • WS 9; SS 1030 • H • NOW • 2521 Lombard Ave Everett WA 98201-3025 • FAX(425)258-2729 • revheck@gte.net

**FEDERAL WAY—*FED WAY KOREAN*** (253)839-6034
Ben C Song • NOW • 405 S 312th St Federal Way WA 98003-4032

***LIGHT OF CHRIST*** (253)874-2517
Theodore Werfelmann • WS 8;* • H • EC • NOW • 2400 SW 344th St Federal Way WA 98023-3032 • FAX(253)874-2517 • loc@thelight.org

***ST LUKE*** (253)941-3000
Victor V Hippe Christopher M Davis • Mark A Weinmeister DCE • WS 8 11 930;* • H • EC/HS • NOW • 515 S 312th St Federal Way WA 98003-4033 • FAX(253)941-8994 • church@stlukesfedway.org

**GIG HARBOR—*KING OF GLORY***
See Purdy

**GRAHAM—*ST PAUL*** (253)847-3084
Vacant • WS 830 11; SS 945;* • H • HS • NOW • 22419 108th Ave E 98338 PO Box 1186 Graham WA 98338-1186

**GRAND COULEE—*ZION*** (509)633-2566
William D Goodin • WS 11;* • H • NOW • 348 Mead St 99133 PO Box 4 Grand Coulee WA 99133-0004

**GRANITE FALLS—*CHAPEL ON HILL*** (360)691-2467
Vacant • WS 10; SS 9; BC 9 • H • NOW • 205 W Galena PO Box 344 Granite Falls WA 98252-0344

**GREENACRES—*HOPE*** (509)924-1630
Craig M Wulf • * • H • NOW • 17909 E Broadway Ave Greenacres WA 99016-9513

**KENMORE—*EPIPHANY*** (425)488-9606
Mark A Lieske David E Reinke • Heather C Ulrich DCE • WS 815 11; SS 940; BC 940 • H • EC/EL • NOW • 16450 Juanita Dr NE Kenmore WA 98028-4208 • FAX(425)488-3212 • epiphany@epiphanyonline.org

**KENNEWICK—*BETHLEHEM*** (509)586-1062
Arthur C Rasch • WS 8 1045; SS 915; BC 915 • H • EC/EL • NOW • 221 S Benton St Kennewick WA 99336-3902 • FAX(509)586-3388 • revrasch@aol.com

**KENT—*PEACE*** (253)631-3454
William A Beversdorf • Gerod R Bass DCE • WS 8;* • H • EC • NOW • 18615 SE 272nd St Kent WA 98042-5484 • FAX(253)639-4686

**KINGSTON—*FAITH*** (360)297-2736
Vacant • NOW • PO Box 1603 Kingston WA 98346-1603

**KIRKLAND—*ST PAUL***
See Woodinville

**KLICKITAT—*GRACE*** (509)369-4972
Paul R Bundschuh • WS 11; SS 1215; BC 1215 • NOW • PO Box 66 Klickitat WA 98628-0066 • bundschuh@juno.com

**LACEY—*FAITH*** (360)491-3552
Vacant • WS 830 11; SS 945;* • H • EC/EL/HS • NOW • 7075 Pacific Ave SE Lacey WA 98503-1473 • FAX(360)459-3784

**LAKE STEVENS—*LAMB OF GOD*** (425)334-5064
Vacant • WS 930; SS 1045; BC 1045 • H • NOW • 3923 103rd Ave SE Everett WA 98205

**LONGVIEW—*GRACE*** (360)423-3720
Barry J Stueve • WS 1030; SS 1030; BC 915 • H • NOW • 2725 Dover St Longview WA 98632-2006 • FAX360)423-2114

**MARLIN—*SALEM***
Donald G Smith • WS 8 • H • NOW • 98832 C/O Gordon Peterson PO Box 831 Coulee City WA 99115-0831

**MARYSVILLE—*MESSIAH*** (360)659-4112
Kurt D Onken • WS 8 1030; SS 915; BC 915 • H • EC • NOW • 9209 State Ave Marysville WA 98270-2214 • FAX(360)659-4113 • messiah-lcms@juno.com

**MERCER ISLAND—*REDEEMER*** (206)232-1711
William K Clements • H • NOW • 6001 Island Crest Way Mercer Island WA 98040-4518 • FAX(206)275-1424 • redeemer@jps.net

**MESA 6W—*MESSIAH*** (509)269-4618
Arthur H Werfelmann • WS 9;* • H • NOW • 99343 291 Loen Dr Basin City WA 99343-9559

**MILL CREEK—*ST JAMES***
See Bothell

**MILTON—*BEAUT SAVIOR*** (253)922-6977
Douglas A Good • WS 8 1030; SS 915; BC 915 • H • EC/EL • NOW • 2306 Milton Way 98354-9311 PO Box 1326 Milton WA 98354-1326

**MONROE—*PEACE*** (206)794-7230
Mark E Griesse • * • H • EC • NOW • 202 Dickinson Rd Monroe WA 98272-2127 • peacelc@worldshare.net

**MOSES LAKE—*GRACE*** (509)765-3131
Danny J Kunkel • H • NOW • 303 E Nelson Rd 98837-2363 217 E Nelson Rd Moses Lake WA 98837-2365 • FAX(509)764-2343 • graceluth³moseslake@atnet.net

**MOUNT VERNON—*TRINITY*** (360)428-0290
Robert E Bendick • * • H • NOW • 301 S 18th St Mount Vernon WA 98274-4660 • FAX(360)428-0467

**MOUNTLAKE TERRACE—*MOUNT ZION*** (425)778-3577
Franklin W Paine Jr. Richard F Green • WS 930;* • H • EC/EL • NOW • 21428 44th Ave W Mountlake Terrace WA 98043-3509 • mtzionlutheran@hotmail.com

**NEAH BAY—*MAKAH*** (206)645-2523
Vacant • H • NOW • PO Box 600 Neah Bay WA 98357-0600

**OAK HARBOR—*CONCORDIA*** (360)675-2548
Raymond L Hagan • * • H • EC • NOW • 590 N Oak Harbor St Oak Harbor WA 98277-4497

**ODESSA—*ZION-EMMANUEL*** (509)982-2402
Donald G Smith • * • H • NOW • 4279 State Route 21 N Odessa WA 99159 • zeodessa@odessaoffice.com

**OKANOGAN—*OUR SAVIOR*** (509)422-2652
John R Ramsey • WS 10; BC 9;* • H • NOW • 2262 Burton Ave RR 2 Okanogan WA 98840-9802 • vjrams@televar.com

**OLYMPIA—*FAITH***
See Lacey

***TRINITY*** (360)357-6574
Vacant • WS 830 11; SS 10; BC 10 • H • NOW • 2020 Franklin St SE Olympia WA 98501-2953

**OROVILLE—*FAITH*** (509)476-2426
Vacant • WS 9;* • H • NOW • 1011 Ironwood St 98844-9696 PO Box 338 Oroville WA 98844-0338

**OTHELLO—*PARADISE*** (509)488-3881
Vacant • H • NOW • 1212 E Pine St Othello WA 99344-1237

**PACIFIC—*NEW HOPE*** (253)351-0450
Mark Gause • H • HS • NOW • 603 3rd Ave SE Pacific WA 98047-1431

**PASCO—*TRINITY*** (509)547-3466
Arthur H Werfelmann • WS 11; SS 930; BC 930 • H • NOW • 1015 N 28th Ave Pasco WA 99301-3996 • revartw@aol.com

**POMEROY—*MISSION**** (509)382-4662
Gregory Bye • WS 8;* • H • NOW • 710 High St 99347 C/O Redeemer Lutheran 601 S 3rd St Dayton WA 99328-1513

**PORT ANGELES—*ST MATTHEW*** (360)457-4122
Philip K Ritter • WS 8 1030; SS 915; BC 915 • H • EC • NOW • 132 E 13th St Port Angeles WA 98362-7818 • FAX(360)457-2836 • stmatt@olypen.com

**PROSSER—*MESSIAH*** (509)786-2011
Stephen E Larson • WS 930 630; SS 1045; BC 1045;* • H • EC • NOW • 801 Luther Ln Prosser WA 99350-1549 • messiah@bentonrea.com

**PULLMAN—*CONCORDIA*** (509)332-2830
Dudley E Nolting • H • NOW • 1015 NE Orchard Dr Pullman WA 99163-4618 • dnolting@turbonet.com

**PURDY—*KING OF GLORY*** (253)857-4574
David J Meyer • WS 10; SS 9; BC 9;* • H • EC • NOW • UKNWN 6411 154th St NW Gig Harbor WA 98332-9016 • FAX(253)857-4574 • kingog1@juno.com

**PUYALLUP—*IMMANUEL*** (253)848-4548
John C Biermann • Amy L Vande Voort-Schweim DCE • WS 8 1030; SS 915; BC 915 • H • EC/EL/HS • NOW • 720 W Main Ave Puyallup WA 98371-5320 • FAX(253)848-3147 • pjbiermann@aol.com

**QUINCY—*CHRIST SAVIOR*** (509)785-4350
Jeffry D Berndt • H • EC • NOW • 214 Deacon Ave 98848-8836 PO Box 5325 George WA 98824-0325

**RENTON—*BETHLEHEM*** (425)255-9772
Gene W Baade • WS 10;* • H • EC/HS • NOW • 1024 Monroe Ave NE Renton WA 98056-3424 • FAX(425)255-9903 • blc@eskimo.com

**RENTON 3 S—*KING OF KINGS*** (425)226-1480
Kenneth M Wyneken • WS 6;* • H • EC • NOW • 98058 18207 108th Ave SE Renton WA 98055-6440 • FAX(425)226-4119 • pastorken@king-of-kings.org

**REPUBLIC—*TRINITY*** (509)775-2617
Vacant • WS 11 • H • NOW • 118 E Delaware Ave 99166-8757 PO Box 615 Republic WA 99166-0615

**RICHLAND—*REDEEMER*** (509)943-4967
Laurence L Meyer • WS 815 11; SS 930; BC 930 • H • NOW • 520 Thayer Dr Richland WA 99352-4126 • FAX(509)943-4967 • lmeyer1016@aol.com

**SEABECK—*EVERGREEN*** (360)830-4180
Hal G Ross • * • H • EC • NOW • 3200 Seabeck Holly Rd NW 98380-9257 PO Box 740 Seabeck WA 98380-0740

**SEATTLE—*AGAPE*** (206)634-3370
Theodore L Wuerffel • NOW • 4130 University Way NE Seattle WA 98105-6214 • agape@u.washington.edu

***AMAZING GRACE*** (206)723-5526
David-Paul Zimmerman • H • EL • NOW • 10056 Renton Ave S Seattle WA 98178-2255 • FAX(425)226-4089 • davpauzim@msn.com

***ATONEMENT*** (206)244-3020
Andrew E Northrop • WS 9; SS 1030; BC 1030 • H • NOW • 740 S 128th St Seattle WA 98168-2728

***BEACON*** (206)322-0251
Vacant • WS 1030 9; SS 915;* • H • HS • NOW • 1720 S Forest St Seattle WA 98144-5819 • FAX(206)322-3353

***BEAUT SAVIOR*** (206)246-9533
George J Burza • WS 8 1015; BC 9;* • H • EC • NOW • 16919 33rd Ave S Seattle WA 98188-3134 • FAX(206)246-9534 • bslcms@aol.com

***CALVARY*** (206)937-6590
Paul E Winterstein • H • HS • NOW • 3420 SW Cloverdale St Seattle WA 98126-3761 • calvarylutheran@juno.com

***GOOD SHEPHERD*** (206)325-2733
John M Barich • WS 11; SS UNKNOWN; BC 10 • H • EC/EL/HS • NOW • 2116 E Union St 98122-2954 PO Box 22639 Seattle WA 98122-0639 • lcgs22@juno.com

***HOPE*** (206)937-9330
Vacant • Jeffrey D Kranich DCE • H • EC/EL/HS • NOW • 4456 42nd Ave SW Seattle WA 98116-4223 • FAX(206)937-9332 • hopedesk@aol.com

***MESSIAH*** (206)524-0024
Ernie V Lassman Robert A Rogers • WS 8; SS 915; BC 915 • H • EC/EL • NOW • 7050 35th Ave NE Seattle WA 98115-5917 • FAX(206)524-4119

***MOUNT OLIVE*** (206)783-8699
Vacant • WS 845 11; SS 950; BC 950 • H • EC/EL • NOW • 7750 21st Ave NW Seattle WA 98117-4310 • mtolive@tcmnet.com

***OUR SAVIOR*** (206)363-0110
David W Blair • H • EC/EL • NOW • 12509 27th Ave NE Seattle WA 98125-4309 • FAX(206)440-1619 • oslcsea@tcmnet.com

***TRINITY*** (206)324-1066
Donald D Schatz • WS 10; BC 830;* • H • EC/EL/HS • NOW • E Highland Dr And 10th Ave E 1200 10th Ave E Seattle WA 98102-4324 • FAX(206)324-0805 • trinluth@aalweb.net

***W WASH DEAF*** (206)935-2920
Vacant • WS 11; BC 10 • NOW • 766 John St Seattle WA 98109-5112

***ZION*** (206)782-6734
Lloyd H Willweber • WS 10; SS 845; BC 845;* • H • EC/EL/HS • NOW • 7109 Aurora Ave N Seattle WA 98103-5343 • zionlu@aol.com

**SEAVIEW—*ST JOHN*** (360)642-4930
Harold J Bauder • WS 9; SS 930;* • H • NOW • 5000 N Place 98644 PO Box 271 Seaview WA 98644-0271 • hermy@pacifier.com

**SELAH—*PEACE*** (509)697-4353
Allan R Johnston • WS 8 1045;* • H • NOW • 98942 91 Wernex Loop Rd Selah WA 98942-9463

**SEQUIM—*FAITH*** (360)683-4803
Steven A Eaton • WS 830; SS 945; BC 945 • H • EC • NOW • 4th And Cedar Sts 98382 PO Box 925 Sequim WA 98382-0925 • FAX(360)683-1206

**SHELTON—*MOUNT OLIVE*** (360)426-6353
James L Markus • WS 1030; SS 915;* • H • EC • NOW • 206 Wyandotte Ave Shelton WA 98584-3638 • jimarkus@aol.com

**SNOHOMISH—*SHEPHERD HILLS*** (360)668-7881
Kerry D Reese • Steven K Endicott DCE • WS 8 1045; SS 930; BC 930 • H • EC • NOW • 9225 212th St SE Snohomish WA 98296-7164 • FAX(425)485-8171 • shephill@wwdb.org

***SHEPHERD HILLS***
See Maltby

***ZION*** (360)568-2700
Richard E Flath • WS 8 1030; SS 915; BC 915 • H • EC/EL • NOW • 329 Avenue A 98290-2836 331 Union Ave Snohomish WA 98290-2825 • FAX(360)568-2878 • zelc@firetrail.com

**SPOKANE—*BEAUTIFUL SAVIOR*** (509)747-6806
Timothy C Cartwright • Marlys K Cartwright DCE • H • EC/EL • NOW • 4320 S Conklin St Spokane WA 99203-6237

***FAITH DEAF*** (509)326-9052
Martin A Hewitt • WS 1045; BC 930 • NOW • 2733 W Northwest Blvd Spokane WA 99205-2381 • hewitt81ma@aol.com

***GLORIA DEI*** (509)327-1914
Vacant • WS 930; SS 10; BC 11 • H • NOW • 3307 W Rowan Ave Spokane WA 99205-5974

***HOLY CROSS*** (509)483-4218
Mark W Benning • Sarah J Syverson DCE • WS 8 11; SS 930; BC 930 • H • EC/EL • NOW • 7307 N Nevada St Spokane WA 99208-5516 • FAX(509)483-4293

***HOPE***
See Greenacres

***PILGRIM*** (509)325-5738
Kendall E Goodfellow • Timothy R Eitreim DCE • WS 8 1045; SS 930; BC 930;* • H • EC/EL • NOW • 2733 W Northwest Blvd Spokane WA 99205-2300 • FAX(509)326-4701 • pilgrim@nextdim.com

***REDEEMER*** (509)926-6363
Philip E Streufert David C Stuenkel • David C Noll DCE Ellsworth Anderson DCE • WS 8 930;* • H • EC • NOW • 3606 S Schafer Rd Spokane WA 99206-9518 • FAX(509)926-4573

***ST JOHN*** (509)747-0984
Vacant • H • EC/EL • NOW • 2 W 3rd Ave Spokane WA 99204-0108 • FAX(509)747-6471

**SUMNER—*OUR REDEEMER***
See Bonney Lake

**SUNNYSIDE—*CALVARY*** (509)837-5662
Mark Hein • H • EC • NOW • 804 S 11th St 98944-2402 PO Box 507 Sunnyside WA 98944-0507

**TACOMA—*FIRST KOREAN*** (253)474-1430
David M Stephen • NOW • 5401 S Lawrence St Tacoma WA 98409-5431

***GOOD SHEPHERD*** (253)473-4848
Daniel J Gerken • Richard D Johnson DCE • WS 8 1030; SS 915; BC 915 • H • EC/EL • NOW • 140 E 56th St Tacoma WA 98404-1299 • FAX(253)473-4849 • gslct@juno.com

***GRACE*** (253)472-7105
Richard H Tietjen • WS 10; SS 845; BC 845;* • H • NOW • 6202 S Tyler St Tacoma WA 98409-2521 • gracetacom@aol.com

***OUR SAVIOR*** (253)531-2112
Daryl C Wildermuth • Arthur R Langdon DCE • WS 8 930 11; SS 930; BC 930;* • H • EC/EL • NOW • 4519 112th St E Tacoma WA 98446-5229 • FAX(253)531-2997 • oslc@oslc.com

***PRINCE OF PEACE*** (253)584-2565
John D Schmidt • * • H • HS • NOW • 10333 Bridgeport Way SW Tacoma WA 98499-2300 • FAX(253)983-8975 • poplkwd@tcmnet.com

***ZION*** (253)752-1264
David H Schmidt • WS 8 1030; SS 915; BC 915 • H • EC/EL • NOW • 3410 6th Ave Tacoma WA 98406-5402 • FAX(253)759-1776 • ziontacwa@juno.com

**TONASKET—*HOPE*** (509)486-2254
Vacant • WS 11;* • H • NOW • 623 S Whitcomb 98855-8801 PO Box 607 Tonasket WA 98855-0607

***IMMANUEL*** (509)485-3342
Vacant • H • NOW • 1608 Tonasket Havillah Rd Tonasket WA 98855-9411 • FAX(509)485-3342

**TOPPENISH—*CRISTO DEL VALLE*** (509)865-3935
Jorge Garcia • H • NOW • 603 Washington Ave 98948-1145 PO Box 919 Toppenish WA 98948

**VANCOUVER—*GOOD SHEPHERD*** (360)254-5158
Theodore C Moeller • WS 10; BC 915 • H • NOW • 16001 NE 34th ST Vancouver WA 98682-8473 • FAX(360)254-1679 • flock@pacifier.com

***GRACE*** (360)892-7850
Vacant • WS 830; BC 945;* • H • EC/EL/HS • NOW • 9900 E Mill Plain Blvd Vancouver WA 98664-3966 • gracelc@pacifier.com

***MEMORIAL*** (360)695-7501
Daniel J Adams Theodore W Will Jr. • Katrina L Barnes DCE • WS 8 930 11; SS 930; BC 930 • H • EC/EL/HS • NOW • 2700 E 28 St 98661 2602 E 28th St Vancouver WA 98661-4528 • FAX(360)993-2797 • office@mlc.org

***ST JOHN*** (360)573-1461
William H Stuenkel Gary M Hagen • Craig C Neumiller DCE • H • EC/EL/HS • NOW • 11005 NE Highway 99 Vancouver WA 98686-5620 • FAX(360)574-8726

**WALLA WALLA—*TRINITY*** (509)525-2493
Stephen P Juergensen • H • EC • NOW • 109 S Roosevelt St Walla Walla WA 99362-2432

**WASHOUGAL—*ST MATTHEW*** (360)835-5533
Lawrence R Locke • WS 830 11; SS 945; BC 945 • H • NOW • 716 17th St Washougal WA 98671-1506 • FAX(360)835-7755 • stmatthewchurchoffice@juno.com

**WENATCHEE—*ST PAUL*** (509)662-8790
Timothy J Scharr • WS 1015; SS 9; BC 9;* • H • EC/EL • NOW • 312 Palouse St Wenatchee WA 98801-2641 • FAX(509)662-5274 • stpaulswenatchee@aol.com

**WOODINVILLE—*FRIENDS*** (425)481-5818
Vacant • H • NOW • 13109 Avondale Rd Ne 98072 PO Box 1912 Woodinville WA 98072-1912

***ST PAUL*** (425)481-5068
Vacant • H • NOW • 15326 158th Ave NE Woodinville WA 98072-8974

**YAKIMA—*BETHLEHEM*** (509)457-5822
Arden D Walz • * • H • NOW • 801 Tieton Dr Yakima WA 98902-3531 • FAX(509)457-5824

***MOUNT OLIVE*** (509)966-2190
Ralph T Joeckel • WS 8 1030; SS 915; BC 915;* • H • EC • NOW • 7809 Tieton Dr Yakima WA 98908-1543 • FAX(509)972-4932 • pastortoby@mtolivechurch.org

## WEST VIRGINIA

**HUNTINGTON—*OUR REDEEMER*** (304)529-7365
Jeffrey F Henry • WS 10; SS 1130;* • H • EC • OH • 3043 Washington Blvd Huntington WV 25705-1632 • innocentsmith@hotmail.com

**PARKERSBURG—*ST PAUL*** (304)428-5826
Vacant • WS 8 1045; SS 915; BC 915 • H • EC • OH • 3500 Broad St Parkersburg WV 26104-2118 • stpaullcms@juno.com

**SOUTH CHARLESTON—*REDEEMER*** (304)744-6251
Kirk D Dueker • H • OH • 270 Staunton Ave SW South Charleston WV 25303-2523 • FAX(304)744-2499 • redeemerluth@juno.com

## WISCONSIN

**ABBOTSFORD—*CHRIST*** (715)223-4315
Paul C Hunsicker Sr. • WS 9;* • H • EC • NW • 308 W Linden St 54405-9583 PO Box 489 Abbotsford WI 54405-0489 • FAX(715)223-8183 • clcabby@pcpros.net

**ADAMS—*IMMANUEL*** (608)339-6102
John R Krebs • WS 8 1030;* • H • SW • 243 N Linden St 53910-9574 PO Box 219 Adams WI 53910-0219 • FAX(608)339-6102

***ST JOHN***
See Quincy

***UNITED/CHRIST***
See Dellwood

**ADELL—*EMMANUEL*** (920)994-9005
Bryan R Osladil • H • HS • SW • 326 Center Ave 53001 PO Box 107 Adell WI 53001-0107

***ST STEPHEN***
See Batavia

**ALGOMA 3 W—*ST JOHN*** (920)487-2335
John C Neugebauer • WS 930;* • H • NW • Highway 54 Rankin 54201 E5221 Church Rd Algoma WI 54201-9683

**ALMA CENTER—*GRACE*** (715)964-2203
Ricky D Bertels • * • H • NW • 136 W Main 54611 PO Box 156 Alma Center WI 54611-0156 • pastorgl@discover-net.net

**ALMENA—*ST MATTHEW*** (715)357-3267
Norman F Peterson • H • NW • 305 Clinton St S 54805-7134 PO Box 128 Almena WI 54805-0128 • pztzrszn@win.bright.net

**ALMENA 9 S—*SILVER CREEK*** (715)357-3267
Norman F Peterson • H • NW • Hwy D East Of Clayton 54805 PO Box 128 Almena WI 54805-0128 • pztzrszn@win.bright.net

**ALMOND—*ST JOHN*** (715)366-2480
Daniel C Iwinski • * • H • NW • 1165 County Road D 54909-9778 PO Box 126 Almond WI 54909-0126 • stjohnsalmond@hotmail.com

**ALTOONA—*BETHLEHEM*** (715)832-9953
David B Karolus • * • H • EC • NW • 2245 Hayden Ave Altoona WI 54720-1548 • FAX(715)832-6761 • bethch@execpc.com

**AMERY—*REDEEMER*** (715)268-7283
Paul H Wiegert • * • H • NW • 600 Keller Ave S Amery WI 54001-1252 • rlcpo@spacestar.net

**AMHERST—*ST PAUL*** (715)824-3314
Dale R Critchley • * • H • EC • NW • 203 Grant St Amherst WI 54406-0028 • stpauls@wi-net.com

**ANIWA—*ZION***
See Wausau 12 NE

**ANTIGO—*PEACE*** (715)623-2200
Joseph A Marsh Randall A Neal William P Volm • David C Reineke DCE • WS 8 1030; SS 920; BC 920;* • H • EC/EL • NW • 300 Lincoln St Antigo WI 54409-1346 • FAX(715)627-4117

**ANTIGO 7 E—*ST PETER*** (715)623-6921
Vacant • WS 9; SS 10; BC 10 • H • NW • N2891 County Rd S Antigo WI 54409

**APPLETON—*CELEBRATION*** (920)734-7779
Rex A Rinne • * • H • EC/EL • NW • 3100 E Evergreen Dr Appleton WI 54913-9206 • FAX(920)734-7890 • celebration.lutheran@juno.com

***FAITH*** (920)739-9191
Paul R Brinkman Mark H Abram Daniel P Thews • Kathleen R Lane DCE • WS 8;* • H • NW • 601 E Glendale Ave Appleton WI 54911-2944 • FAX(920)739-6030 • faithwi@aol.com

***GOOD SHEPHERD*** (920)734-9643
Thomas A Part Timothy K Spilker • Byron J Schroeder DCE Leann J Johnson DCE • H • EC • NW • 2220 E College Ave Appleton WI 54915-3146 • FAX(920)734-3544 • goodshep.athenet.net

**ARLINGTON—*ST PETER*** (608)635-4825
Marion L Hendrickson • WS 8 1030;* • H • EC • SW • 303 Park St 53911 PO Box 45 Arlington WI 53911-0045 • FAX(608)635-2753 • lars62@juno.com

**ASHLAND—*ZION*** (715)682-6075
Martin C Kaarre • WS 1030;* • H • EL • NW • 1111 11th Ave W 54806-2846 PO Box 31 Ashland WI 54806-0031

**ATHENS—*ST JOHN*** (715)536-1810
John P Nelson • WS 10;* • H • EC • NW • 486 County Rd F Athens WI 54411 • stjohn@dwave.net

***TRINITY*** (715)257-7526
Donn H Radde • SS 1015; BC 1015;* • H • EC/EL • NW • Elm And Caroline 54411 PO Box 100 Athens WI 54411-0100

**AUBURNDALE—*ST JOHN*** (715)652-2213
David J Dahlke • NW • 10571 George Ave Auburndale WI 54412

**AUGUSTA—*GRACE*** (715)286-2116
Carlton W Kangas • H • EC • NW • 814 Hudson St Augusta WI 54722-9015 • FAX(715)286-5039 • grace5039@aol.com

**AUGUSTA 6 NW—*ST PETER*** (715)286-2116
Carlton W Kangas • NW • Hwy Jj And V 54722 814 Hudson St Augusta WI 54722-9015 • FAX(715)286-5039 • grace5039@aol.com

**AURORAVILLE 1 N—*IMMANUEL*** (920)361-1812
Brian M Beardsley • H • SW • N2506 State Road 49 Berlin WI 54923-8360

**BARABOO—*OUR SAVIOR*** (608)356-9792
Timothy A Anderson • WS 9; SS 1015; BC 1015 • H • EC • SW • 1120 Draper St Baraboo WI 53913-1229 • oslcb@chorus.net

**BARRON—*SALEM*** (715)537-3011
Ronald W Mueller • H • EC • NW • 1360 E La Salle Ave Barron WI 54812-1636

**BATAVIA—*ST STEPHEN*** (414)994-9060
William L Robinson • SW • UKNWN RR 1-N1510 Hwy 28 Adell WI 53001-9801

**BEAR CREEK—*GRACE*** (715)752-4855
Steven N Pockat • WS 845;* • NW • 409 W Willow St 54922-9773 PO Box 187 Bear Creek WI 54922-0187

**BEAR CREEK 5 W—*TRINITY*** (715)752-3601
Steven N Pockat • H • NW • 54922 E8010 State Road 22 Bear Creek WI 54922-9665

**BEAVER DAM—*PEACE*** (414)887-1272
John G Breitwisch • H • SW • 400 Hillcrest Dr Beaver Dam WI 53916-2422

**BELGIUM—*ST MARK*** (414)285-3820
Elmer R Lisch • H • SW • 200 Park St 53004-9659 PO Box 175 Belgium WI 53004-0175

**BELOIT—*MESSIAH*** (608)365-4724
Dennis L Pingel • H • SW • 1531 Townline Ave Beloit WI 53511-3245 • FAX(608)365-5767

***ST JOHN*** (608)362-8595
William W Wagner • Harry N Schilf DCE • H • SW • 1000 Bluff St Beloit WI 53511-5167

***TRINITY*** (608)362-3607
Edward H May • WS 815 11; SS 940; BC 940;* • H • EL/HS • SW • 1850 Cranston Rd Beloit WI 53511-2544 • trinity@ticon.net

**BERLIN—*IMMANUEL***
See Auroraville 1 N

***ST JOHN*** (920)361-9935
Kenneth N Hinrichs • WS 8;* • H • EC/EL • SW • 168 Mound St Berlin WI 54923-1729 • FAX(920)361-3095

***TRINITY***
See Borth 1 S

**BIG FALLS—*ST LUKE*** (920)596-3241
Jeffrey A Smiles • WS 830;* • NW • 54926 N7534 Church St Manawa WI 54949-9691

**BIRNAMWOOD—*ST PAUL*** (715)449-2101
Allen E Geil • H • EC • NW • N9035 US Highway 45 54414-9000 PO Box 208 Birnamwood WI 54414-0208

**BLACK RIVER FALLS—*ST JOHN*** (715)284-7003
Vacant • WS 9;* • H • NW • 351 W Jefferson St Blk River Fls WI 54615-1063

**BOAZ—*ST PAUL*** (608)647-6905
Vacant • SW • UKNWN 1060 N Central Ave PO Box 230 Richland Center WI 53581-0230 • FAX(608)647-4499 • seaver@mwt.net

**BONDUEL—*ST PAUL*** (715)758-8559
Timothy J Shoup Leonard P Wildauer • H • EC/EL • NW • 400 E Green Bay St 54107-9268 PO Box 395 Bonduel WI 54107-0395 • FAX(715)758-6352

**BONDUEL 4 NW—*ST PAUL*** (715)745-2299
David P Miller • WS 9;* • H • NW • 54107 W4496 County Rd E Bonduel WI 54107-8740 • rvmiller@frontiernet.net

**BORTH 1 S—*TRINITY*** (920)361-1812
Brian M Beardsley • H • SW • W 561 County Rd Xx UKNWN N2506 State Road 49 Berlin WI 54923-8360

**BOSCOBEL—*HICKORY GROVE*** (608)375-5441
William A Stark • H • SW • 15934 County Road T 53805-9537 C/O Rev William A Stark 1108 Yahn Ave Boscobel WI 53805-1700

**BOULDER JUNCTION—*TRINITY*** (715)385-2267
Donald J Dominkowski • H • NW • 10289 Old K Rd 54512 PO Box 24 Boulder Junction WI 54512-0024 • FAX(715)385-9286 • trinityluthch@centuryinter.net

**BOWLER—*ST PAUL*** (715)793-4608
David M Dukovan • WS 9;* • H • NW • 201 Wall St 54416 PO Box 18 Bowler WI 54416-0018

**BOYCEVILLE—*GRACE***
See Connorsville

***HOLY TRINITY*** (715)643-3182
Louis C Kerestes • H • S • C/O Rev Louis Kerestes N11568 County Road O Boyceville WI 54725-9472

***ST JOHN*** (715)643-2785
Kevin L Leidich • * • H • NW • Hwy 170 54725 804 Saint John St Boyceville WI 54725-9581

**BOYD—*ST PETER*** (715)289-4521
Raymond J Bell • WS 1030;* • NW • 206 E Murray St 54726-9004 PO Box 9 Cadott WI 54727-0009 • FAX(715)289-4521

**BREED—*EMMANUEL*** (920)842-4600
Paul A Scheunemann • WS 1030;* • H • NW • UKNWN 13346 County Road Aa Suring WI 54174-9750

**BRILLION—*ST BARTHOLOMEW*** (920)756-3031
Mark L Krueger • * • H • SW • 105 Horn St Brillion WI 54110-1505 • stbart@pitnet.net

**BROOKFIELD—*BROOKFIELD*** (262)783-4270
Roger V Heintz Alan E Klatt • Kenneth L Jacques DCO • WS 745 915 1045; BC 915;* • H • HS • SW • 18500 W Burleigh Rd Brookfield WI 53045-2525 • FAX(262)783-4616 • blc@netstream.net

***IMMANUEL*** (262)781-7140
Daniel S Schneider • WS 8;* • H • EC/EL/HS • SW • 13445 Hampton Rd Brookfield WI 53005-7513 • FAX(262)781-5460 • immanuel@execpc.com

**BROWN DEER—*ST PAUL*** (414)355-5030
Vacant • SS 9; BC 1015;* • H • SW • 8080 N 47th St Brown Deer WI 53223-3727 • FAX(414)354-7230

**BURLINGTON—*OUR SAVIOR*** (262)763-3281
Robert W Bolling Stephen M King • WS 8 1045; SS 930; BC 930 • H • EC • SW • 417 S Kane St Burlington WI 53105-2111 • FAX(262)763-5716 • pwt50@yahoo.com

**BURNETT—*ZION*** (920)689-2280
James N Daugherty • * • H • SW • N8523 Front St 53922-9636 PO Box 185 Burnett WI 53922-0185

**BURNETT 2 N—*IMMANUEL*** (920)689-2361
Floyd E Gogolin • * • H • SW • 53922 N9520 State Road 26 Burnett WI 53922-9785 • FAX(920)689-2361

**BUTTERNUT—*ST PAUL*** (715)769-3731
John A Deitz • WS 9; BC 1015;* • H • NW • 301 N Second St 54514 PO Box 158 Butternut WI 54514-0158

**CABLE—*TRINITY*** (715)798-3417
Vacant • WS 9;* • H • NW • Spruce And Townhall 54821 PO Box 145 Cable WI 54821-0145

**CADOTT—*ST JOHN*** (715)289-4521
Raymond J Bell • WS 9;* • H • NW • 215 E Seminary St 54727 PO Box 9 Cadott WI 54727-0009 • FAX(715)289-4521

***ST PETER***
See Cadott

**CAMERON—*ST JOHN*** (715)458-2602
James A Vanek • H • NW • 1115 W Main St Cameron WI 54822-9797

**CAMPBELLSPORT—*SAINT JOHN***
See New Fane

**CAROLINE 2 E—*IMMANUEL*** (715)787-3653
Carl L Krueger(#) • HS • NW • 54928 W10947 Upper Red Lake Rd Gresham WI 54128-8994

**CAROLINE 2 W—*ST JOHN*** (715)787-3653
Carl L Krueger(#) • H • NW • 54928 W10947 Upper Red Lake Rd Gresham WI 54128-8994

**CASCADE—*ST PAUL*** (920)528-8094
Richard M Bidinger • * • H • EC • SW • 509 Milwaukee Ave 53011 PO Box 167 Cascade WI 53011-0167 • rbidinge@excel.net

**CECIL—*HOPE*** (715)745-2494
David P Miller • WS 1030;* • NW • 108 James St 54111 W4496 County Highway E Bonduel WI 54107 • rvmiller@frontiernet.net

**CECIL 3 E—*IMMANUEL*** (715)745-2364
Steven D Hyvonen • WS 1030;* • H • HS • NW • W3110 White Clay Lake W3110 White Clay Lake Dr Cecil WI 54111

**CEDARBURG—*FIRST IMMANUEL*** (262)377-6610
Randolph H Raasch Wilmer H Reichmann Chris A Schwanz • WS 730 9 1030 1010; SS 9; BC 9;* • H • EC/EL • SW • W67N622 Evergreen Blvd Cedarburg WI 53012-1848 • FAX(262)377-9606

**CENTER—*ZION*** (608)876-6667
Wilfred J Grieser • WS 9; BC 1015;* • SW • 2129 N Church Rd Evansville WI 53536-9549

**CHELSEA—*TRINITY*** (715)748-4181
Randal R Jeppesen • WS 11;* • NW • W5127 Elm St Chelsea 54451 W5334 Dassow Ave Medford WI 54451-8785

**CHILI—*CHRIST*** (715)238-7422
Vacant • NW • N5740 Maple St 54420-9256 W2880 Granton Rd Granton WI 54436-8876 • FAX(715)238-7422

**CHILTON—*ST LUKE*** (414)849-9803
Vacant • SW • W3102 Killsnake Rd Chilton WI 53014-9736

***ST MARTIN*** (920)849-4421
Wayne K Huebner • WS 8;* • H • SW • 717 Memorial Dr Chilton WI 53014-1576 • FAX(920)849-4421 • stmartinlc@mail.tds.net

**CHIPPEWA FALLS—*FAITH*** (715)723-7754
William C Plautz • WS 745 1015;* • H • EC • NW • 733 Woodward Ave Chippewa Falls WI 54729-3283

***ZION*** (715)723-6380
Gary G Paul • WS 9 • H • EC • NW • 110 E Grand Ave Chippewa Falls WI 54729-2525

**CLAYTON—*IMMANUEL*** (715)986-4927
John A Wilman • * • NW • 124 Church St 54004-3352 C/O Zion Luth Church PO Box 32 Turtle Lake WI 54889-0032

**CLEGHORN—*ZION*** (715)878-4512
Roger D Eden • WS 8 10;* • H • EC • NW • Hwy 93 At Hh UKNWN PO Box 3033 Eau Claire WI 54702-3033 • FAX(715)878-4161

**CLINTON—*CHRIST*** (608)676-4994
William J Uffenbeck • * • H • SW • 300 High St PO Box 308 Clinton WI 53525-0308

**CLINTONVILLE—*ST JOHN***
See Shawano 6 S

***ST MARTIN*** (715)823-6538
Vilas E Mazemke Thomas W Vanderbilt • WS 8 1030; SS 915; BC 915;* • H • EC/EL • NW • 100 S Clinton Ave Clintonville WI 54929-1610 • FAX(715)823-1464 • stml@frontiernet.net

**CLYMAN—*ZION*** (414)696-3495
Vacant • WS 830; BC 730;* • H • SW • 700 Main St 53016 PO Box 220 Clyman WI 53016-0220 • pickhardt@netwurx.net

**COLBY—*ZION*** (715)223-2166
M G Neumann • WS 8 1030;* • H • EC • NW • 301 N 2nd St 54421-9653 PO Box 438 Colby WI 54421

**COLBY 7 NW—*ST PAUL*** (715)223-3525
DuWayne Schneider • WS 930; BC 1045;* • NW • 54421 N13510 County Rd E Colby WI 54421-9268

**COMSTOCK—*CHRIST***
See Pipe Lake

**CONNORSVILLE—*GRACE*** (715)643-3182
Louis C Kerestes • H • NW • Highway 64 UKNWN C/O Rev Kerestes N11568 County Road O Boyceville WI 54725-9472

**CRANDON—*GOOD SHEPHERD*** (715)478-3555
Sheldon L Kerstner • WS 1015;* • H • EC • NW • Hwy 32 And 55 54520 PO Box 146 Crandon WI 54520-0146

**CUDAHY—*ST JOHN*** (414)481-0520
Carl H Krueger Jr. Richard V Schauer • WS 8 1045; SS 915; BC 915;* • H • EC • S • 4850 S Lake Dr Cudahy WI 53110-1743 • FAX(414)481-0736 • selcdist@selc.lcms.org

**CUMBERLAND—*ST PAUL*** (715)822-8690
Stephen C Miller • H • NW • Hwy 48 1 Mile E Of Cumberland 54829 743 22 1/2 Ave Cumberland WI 54829-9792 • FAX(715)822-5018 • tekonsha@marcus³online.net

**DANBURY—*TRINITY*** (715)866-7191
Richard J Schreiber • WS 830;* • H • NW • 54830 C/O Our Redeemer Luth PO Box 85 Webster WI 54893-0085

**DANCY—*ST JOHN*** (715)457-2405
Stephen M Mueller • * • NW • UKNWN 2291 Church Rd Mosinee WI 54455-9356

**DE PERE—*HOPE*** (920)336-9582
Allen R Stoll • WS 7;* • HS • NW • 705 S Michigan St 54115-3268 715 S Superior St De Pere WI 54115-3277 • arsnal@yahoo.com

**DEER PARK—*ST PAUL*** (715)269-5126
Timothy J Coppersmith • WS 1045; BC 7;* • H • NW • 214 North St W 54007-9701 PO Box 100 Deer Park WI 54007-0100 • stpaul@win.bright.net

**DEER PARK 10 S—*ST JOHN***
See Forest 1 E

**DEERBROOK—*ST MATTHEW*** (715)627-7989
Jerome W Hahn • NW • N 5674 CTH E Deerbrook WI 54424

**DELAVAN—*HOLY CROSS DEAF*** (414)728-5980
Vacant • SW • 404 W Walworth Ave 53115-1032 C/O 6502 Mound Rd Delavan WI 53115

***OUR REDEEMER*** (262)728-4266
Robert P Rickman • WS 8 1030;* • H • EC/EL • SW • 416 W Geneva St Delavan WI 53115-1631 • FAX(262)728-5581

**DELLWOOD—*UNITED/CHRIST*** (608)339-7187
T C Nelson • H • SW • 1857 Hwy Z 53927 PO Box 152 Dellwood WI 53927-0152 • FAX(608)564-7966 • tchristian@maqs.net

**DORCHESTER—*ST PETER*** (715)654-5055
Jerome A Freimuth • WS 9; BC 1015;* • H • NW • 265 S 3rd St Dorchester WI 54425-9562 • stpeter@pcpros.net

**DURAND—*ST JOHN*** (715)672-8787
Daniel M Pfaffe • H • NW • 315 E Montgomery St Durand WI 54736-1436

**EAGLE RIVER—*OUR SAVIOR*** (715)479-6226
William J Trosien • Catherine A Wurster DEAC • WS 10;* • H • NW • 223 Silver Lake Rd 54521 PO Box 365 Eagle River WI 54521-0365 • savior@newnorth.net

**EAST TROY—*GOOD SHEPHERD*** (262)642-3310
Philip M Vangen • WS 8 1030; BC 915;* • H • EC/EL • SW • State Hwy 20 And Emery St 53120 1936 Emery St East Troy WI 53120-1131 • FAX(262)642-3310 • gsl@netwurx.net

**EAU CLAIRE—*EPIPHANY*** (715)835-9155
Brent L Parrish • H • NW • 3031 Epiphany Ln Eau Claire WI 54703-6924 • FAX(715)835-9166 • bparr45955@aol.com

***OUR REDEEMER*** (715)835-5239
Joel A Hoelter • Connie L Johnson DEAC • WS 8 915 1030;* • H • EC • NW • 601 Fall St Eau Claire WI 54703-3157 • FAX(715)835-0585 • redeemer@discover-net.net

***PEACE*** (715)834-2486
Mark W Schulz Chad M Ott • David L Forke DCE • H • NW • 501 E Fillmore Ave Eau Claire WI 54701-6536 • FAX(715)834-5604 • info@peace-lutheran.org

***ST MATTHEW*** (715)834-4028
Steven D Rutter • H • NW • 1915 Hogeboom Ave Eau Claire WI 54701-4356

***ZION***
See Cleghorn

**EDGAR 5 W—*ST JOHN*** (715)352-2888
Roger R Moldenhauer • WS 10;* • NW • 54426 W1145 Huckleberry St Edgar WI 54426-9739

**EDGERTON—*ST JOHN*** (608)884-3515
David K Jacob • WS 8 1030 • H • SW • 207 E High St Edgerton WI 53534-2111

**ELAND—*ZION*** (715)253-3939
David M Dukovan • WS 1045;* • H • NW • N7630 Pine St Eland WI 54427-9581

**ELCHO—*ST LUKE*** (715)275-3152
Jerome W Hahn • WS 1045;* • H • NW • PO Box 25 Elcho WI 54428-0025

**ELEVA—*ZION***
See Cleghorn

**ELKHART LAKE—*GRACE*** (414)876-2341
Matthew J Graminske • H • SW • 210 N Lincoln Hwy 67 53020 PO Box 262 Elkhart Lake WI 53020-0262

**ELM GROVE—*ELM GROVE*** (262)797-2970
Harold L Senkbeil Carl J Egloff Larry W Myers • Todd A Miller DCE • WS 8;* • H • HS • SW • 945 Terrace Dr 945 N Terrace Dr Elm Grove WI 53122-2035 • FAX(262)797-2977 • hsenkbeil@egl.org

**EMBARRASS—*ZION*** (715)823-3889
Todd R Jerabek • H • NW • 118 Church St 54933 PO Box 197 Embarrass WI 54933-0197

**EMBARRASS 3 NW—*ST PETER*** (715)823-4966
Todd R Jerabek • WS 10;* • NW • N2730 Pella Opening Rd 54933 C/O Zion Lutheran Church PO Box 197 Embarrass WI 54933-0197

**EVANSVILLE—*ZION***
See Center

**FAIRCHILD—*ST PAUL*** (715)334-4763
Ricky D Bertels • WS 8; SS 9;* • H • NW • 324 Oak St 54741-8259 C/O Lyle Abrahamson PO Box 42 Fairchild WI 54741-0042

**FAIRCHILD 5 W—*ZION*** (715)334-5582
Vacant • NW • 54741 320 Oak St Fairchild WI 54741-8259

**FALL CREEK—*ST PAUL*** (715)877-2117
Larry G Borgelt • * • H • EC • NW • 721 S State St Fall Creek WI 54742-9794 • FAX(715)877-3256 • lbcross@execpc.com

**FALL CREEK 12 NE—*BETHLEHEM*** (715)877-3249
Mark R Mischnick • WS 1030;* • H • NW • Hwy D And Sr 27 54742 E19675 State Road 27 Fall Creek WI 54742-5217 • FAX(715)877-3249

**FALL CREEK 3 S—*ST JOHN*** (715)877-3150
Vacant • WS 9; SS 1015; BC 1015 • H • NW • 54742 S7870 County Road JJ Fall Creek WI 54742-4215 • FAX(715)831-0188 • w0aih@ecol.net

**FALL CREEK 7 NE—*ZION*** (715)877-3128
Mark R Mischnick • WS 9;* • H • NW • Hwy Q At 150th 54742 E19675 State Road 27 Fall Creek WI 54742-5217 • FAX(715)877-3128

**FOND DU LAC—*HOPE*** (920)922-5130
David J Lieske David C Jensen • Tammy L Brehmer • * • H • EC • SW • 260 Vincent St Fond Du Lac WI 54935-5331 • FAX(920)922-9832 • hope@vbe.com

**FOREST 1 E—*ST JOHN*** (715)269-5126
Timothy J Coppersmith • WS 9; BC 7;* • H • NW • 54123 PO Box 100 Deer Park WI 54007-0100 • stpaul@win.bright.net

**FORESTVILLE—*ST PETER*** (920)856-6420
David J Luhrs • * • NW • 316 W Main St 54213-9644 PO Box 85 Forestville WI 54213-0085

**FORT ATKINSON—*PEACE*** (920)563-8050
Donald G Fehlauer(DM) • WS 9; SS 1015; BC 1015 • H • SW • 1661 Janesville Ave Fort Atkinson WI 53538-2727

**FRANKLIN—*RISEN SAVIOR*** (414)529-5647
Douglas R Groenewold • WS 815 1045; BC 930;* • H • EC/HS • SW • 9501 W Drexel Ave Franklin WI 53132-9627 • FAX(414)529-5673

**FREDERIC—*IMMANUEL*** (715)327-8608
Robin O Fink(EM) • WS 10; SS 845 • H • NW • 201 1st Ave S Frederic WI 54837-8919

**FREDONIA—*ST JOHN*** (414)692-2734
Robert C Zick • H • EC • SW • 824 Fredonia Ave Fredonia WI 53021-9412 • FAX(414)692-3297 • rczick@yahoo.com

**FREMONT—*ST PAUL*** (414)446-3251
John E Schmidt • H • EC • NW • 107 Tustin Rd Fremont WI 54940-9412

**FREMONT 6 SE—*ZION*** (920)667-4301
John E Schmidt • WS 915;* • H • NW • 2 Miles S Of Readfield 54940 E9016 Marsh Rd Fremont WI 54940-8828 • zionfre@juno.com

**GERMANTOWN—*FAITH*** (414)251-8250
Thomas C Kaul • WS 9;* • H • EC • SW • W172N11187 Division Rd Germantown WI 53022-4066 • FAX(262)502-9157

**GILLETT 3 N W—*IMMANUEL*** (920)855-2899
Vacant • WS 10;* • NW • 11639 County Rd H Gillett WI 54124 • immchrist@ez-net.com

**GILLETT 4 SE—*ST JOHN RIVERSIDE*** (414)855-2625
John V Laatsch • H • HS • NW • 5686 Hwy 32 54124 W2253 State Highway 22 Pulcifer WI 54124-9407

**GILLETT 8 NW—*CHRIST*** (920)855-2899
Vacant • WS 830;* • H • NW • 6905 Red Bank Rd 11639 County Rd H Gillett WI 54124 • immchrist@ez-net.com

**GILMAN—*ZION*** (715)447-8262
Steven J Haag • NW • 205 N Fifth Ave Gilman WI 54433-0036 • Hendzel@yahoo.com

**GILMANTON—*TRINITY*** (715)946-3291
Vacant • H • NW • PO Box 14 Gilmanton WI 54743-0014

**GLEASON—*LUTHER MEMORIAL*** (715)873-4592
Steven L Anderson • H • NW • N5302 Town Hall Rd 54435-9209 PO Box 39 Gleason WI 54435-0039

***OUR SAVIOR***
See Jeffris/Bundy

**GLENBEULAH—*ZION*** (920)893-8888
Matthew J Graminske • SW • 220 W Main St 53023-1153 226 E Main St Glenbeulah WI 53023 • zion@bytehead.com

**GLENDALE—*ST JOHN*** (414)352-4150
Glenn D Meyer • H • EC/EL/HS • SW • 7877 N Port Washington Rd Glendale WI 53217-3132 • FAX(414)352-4221 • sj1@execpc.com

**GLIDDEN—*TRINITY*** (715)264-3961
Michael A Paholke • WS 9;* • H • NW • 529 Lenz Rd 54527 PO Box 161 Glidden WI 54527-0161 • trinity@wageswebworks.com

**GRAFTON—*ST PAUL*** (262)377-4659
Larry Prahl Marvin J Moss John G Suelflow • WS 8 925 1045;* • H • EC/EL • SW • 701 Washington St Grafton WI 53024-1842 • FAX(262)377-7808 • splgrafton@aol.com

**GRANTON—*ZION*** (715)238-7422
Vacant • H • NW • W2880 Granton Rd Granton WI 54436-8876 • FAX(715)238-7422 • sangran@usa.net

**GRANTSBURG—*CHRIST***
See Pipe Lake

**GREEN BAY—*CHRIST OF BAY*** (920)468-4246
David N Boettcher • WS 1015;* • H • HS • NW • 450 Laverne Dr Green Bay WI 54311-5706

***FAITH*** (920)435-5524
Keith R Jones Peter A Speckhard • WS 8;* • H • EC • NW • 2335 S Webster Ave Green Bay WI 54301-2123 • FAX(920)435-6050

***OUR SAVIOUR*** (920)468-4065
Arthur A Callesen David H Hatch • WS 745 915 1030; SS 915;* • H • EC/HS • NW • 120 S Henry St Green Bay WI 54302-3405 • FAX(920)468-5757 • oslc@oslc-gb.org

***PILGRIM*** (920)494-1979
Gregory E Hoffmann • Cherie A Theis DCE • H • EC/EL/HS • NW • 1731 Saint Agnes Dr Green Bay WI 54304-3059 • FAX(920)494-2079 • john@pilgrimluth.com

***REDEEMER*** (920)499-1033
John C Poppe • * • H • EC/EL/HS • NW • 210 S Oneida St 54303-1923 205 Hudson St Green Bay WI 54303-1947 • FAX(920)496-0795 • revpoppe205@cs.com

**GREEN VALLEY 2 NW—*ST JOHN*** (715)745-2314
Bruce L Blocker • WS 1030; SS 915 • H • NW • 54127 W1294 Nauman Rd Cecil WI 54111-9338

**GREENDALE—*OUR SHEPHERD*** (414)421-2060
Douglas W Schroeder Paul R Schroeder • H • HS • SW • 76th And Parkview 53129 PO Box 77 Greendale WI 53129-0077 • FAX(414)421-7927

**GREENFIELD—*MOUNT ZION*** (414)282-4900
Aaron A Koch • H • EC • SW • 3820 W Layton Ave Greenfield WI 53221-2038

***OUR FATHER*** (414)282-8220
Roger A Janke Karl F Fabrizius • WS 8; BC 930;* • H • EC/EL/HS • SW • 6025 S 27th St Greenfield WI 53221-4804 • FAX(414)282-9737

**GREENLEAF—*ZION***
See Wayside

**GREENVILLE—*SHEPHERD HILLS*** (920)757-5722
Paul L Shackel Eric R Wenger • WS 8;* • H • EC • NW • N1615 Meadowview Ln Greenville WI 54942-9625 • FAX(920)757-0461 • office@shepherdhills.org

**GRESHAM—*ZION*** (715)787-4387
Richard R Buhrke • H • HS • NW • 740 Main St 54128 PO Box 325 Gresham WI 54128-0325

**GRESHAM 3 NE—*IMMANUEL***
Steven D Hyvonen • * • NW • 54128 N7915 Big Lake Rd Gresham WI 54128-8922

**GRESHAM 4 NW—*OUR SAVIOR*** (715)526-5280
Roy W Rinehard • H • NW • 54128 PO Box 57 Gresham WI 54128-0057

**HALES CORNERS—*HALES CORNERS*** (414)529-6700
Michael S Ernst Keith L Johnson Wayne R Rasmussen James E Thelen • H • EC/EL/HS • EN • 12300 W Janesville Rd Hales Corners WI 53130-1247 • FAX(414)529-6710

**HANCOCK 6 SE—*GRACE*** (715)249-3043
Arthur C Senn(EM) • WS 10; SS 9 • H • SW • W10805 Cty Rd B-C Hancock WI 54943

**HANOVER—*IMMANUEL*** (608)879-2059
David H Zimdars • SW • 8212 High St 53542 PO Box 497 Hanover WI 53542-0497

***ZION***
See Center

**HARSHAW—*FAITH*** (715)282-5550
Hans-Juergen W Heisinger • WS 830; SS 930;* • NW • 9160 Church Rd 54529-9735 PO Box 94 Harshaw WI 54529-0094

**HARTFORD—*DIVINE SAVIOR*** (262)673-5140
Thomas E Feiertag • H • SW • 3200 Highway K South Hartford WI 53027-9206 • FAX(262)673-0877 • divineslc@nconnect.net

**HARTLAND—*DIVINE REDEEMER*** (414)367-8400
Allan A Jahneke • H • HS • SW • 31385 W Hill Rd Hartland WI 53029 • FAX(414)367-9410

**HAVEN—*GRACE*** (414)565-2186
Ronald D Pederson • BC 630;* • H • HS • SW • W1264 County Road FF Haven WI 53083-5138

**HAYWARD—*TRINITY*** (715)634-2260
Albert S Oren • WS 930;* • H • NW • 10576 Gresylon Dr Hayward WI 54843

**HEWITT—*IMMANUEL*** (715)384-5153
Dean T Pingel • H • NW • 7735 Yellowstone Dr Hewitt WI 54441-9026

**HIGHLAND—*CHRIST*** (608)739-4017
Mark R Meier • SW • 303 Main St 53543-9768 PO Box 555 Muscoda WI 53573-0555

**HILBERT—*ST PETER*** (414)853-3217
Gary Rokenbrodt • H • EC/EL • SW • 43 N Third St 54129 PO Box 381 Hilbert WI 54129-0381

***TRINITY***
See Potter 1 S

**HILLPOINT—*ST PAUL*** (608)727-3841
Robert W Butler • * • H • SW • E 4171 Village Rd Hillpoint WI 53937

**HORICON—*ST STEPHEN*** (920)485-6687
Daniel J Seehafer • WS 8;* • H • EC/EL • SW • 103 S Cedar St 53032-1407 505 N Palmatory St Horicon WI 53032-1008 • FAX(920)485-2545 • ststephen@ststephen-lcms.org

**HORICON 4 E—*ST JOHN*** (920)387-3775
Vacant • H • SW • 53032 N7074 Highway D Horicon WI 53032-9750 • stjohns@nconnect.net

**HOULTON—*FAMILY OF CHRIST**** (715)549-6140
Jon T Haakana(DM) • H • MNS • 277 County Rd E Houlton WI 54082

**HOWARDS GROVE—*TRINITY*** (920)565-3349
Darrel R Bergelin • H • EC • SW • W 2776 STH 32 Howards Grove WI 53083-9801 • FAX(920)565-4592 • darrelbergelin@juno.com

**HUDSON—*TRINITY*** (715)386-9313
Daniel C Bruch Raymond E Wiebold • WS 8 930 11; BC 930;* • H • EC/EL • MNS • 1205 6th St Hudson WI 54016-1341 • FAX(715)386-9707 • trinity@tlchudson.org

**IRMA—*FAITH***
See Harshaw

***ST PAUL*** (715)536-5069
Hans-Juergen W Heisinger • NW • N6537 Old Highway 51 54442-9776 PO Box 7 Irma WI 54442-0007

**JACKSON—*LIVING WORD*** (414)677-1685
Timothy R Niekerk • WS 9; BC 1030;* • H • SW • 4466 Hwy P-Suite 205 53037-9634 PO Box 307 Jackson WI 53037 • FAX(414)677-8357 • livingword@hnet.net

**JANESVILLE—*MOUNT CALVARY*** (608)754-4145
R T Colgrove • Janice Thurner DEAC • WS 915;* • H • EC • SW • 2940 Mineral Point Ave Janesville WI 53545-3297 • FAX(608)754-0781

***OUR SAVIOR*** (608)754-8448
David H Zimdars • WS 1015 • H • SW • 2015 Kellogg Ave Janesville WI 53546-3905

***ST MARK*** (608)754-8115
Randall B Senn • WS 9 1030; SS 9 • H • EN • 2921 Mount Zion Ave Janesville WI 53545-1338 • FAX(608)755-1646 • stmark@ticon.net

***ST PAUL*** (608)754-4471
Paul H Garchow David P Ramel • WS 8 1030;* • H • EC/EL • SW • 210 S Ringold St Janesville WI 53545-4167 • FAX(608)754-4050

**JEFFRIS/BUNDY—*OUR SAVIOR*** (715)362-2323
Allen O Montgomery(#) • WS 9;* • H • NW • UKNWN W516 County Road D Gleason WI 54435-9649 • albea@newnorth.net

**JUNCTION CITY—*ST PAUL*** (715)457-2405
Stephen M Mueller • WS 1030;* • H • NW • 1225 Main St Junction City WI 54443-9729 • smueller@hotmail.com

**KAUKAUNA—*BETHANY*** (414)766-1452
Walter A Steinbach • Nicole L Kunda DCE/DCO • H • NW • 124 W 10th St Kaukauna WI 54130-2720 • bethany34@juno.com

**KENNAN—*ZION*** (715)474-6664
Gary D Lodholz • WS 1030;* • NW • W 10363 Main St Kennan WI 54537-8930

**KENOSHA—*GOOD SHEPHERD***
See Pleasant Prairie

***LAMB OF GOD*** (414)652-4695
John M Berg • H • SW • PO Box 487 Kenosha WI 53141-0487 • revberg@execpc.com

***MESSIAH*** (262)551-8182
Todd A Peperkorn • WS 9; SS 1015; BC 1015 • H • EC/HS • SW • 2026 22nd Ave Kenosha WI 53140-4601 • FAX(262)597-5168 • tpeperkorn@worldnet.att.net

**KEWASKUM—*SAINT JOHN***
See New Fane

**KOHLER—*BETHANY*** (920)457-4681
Kenneth L Loehrke Sr. • * • H • HS • SW • 222 Church St Kohler WI 53044-1503 • bethany@bytehead.com

**LA CROSSE—*FAITH*** (608)782-3696
James T Cumming • * • H • SW • 1407 Main St La Crosse WI 54601-4262

**LA VALLE—*ZION*** (608)985-7477
Tyge C Zucker • H • SW • 200 Union St 53941 PO Box 140 La Valle WI 53941-0140

**LA VALLE 5 NE—*ST PAUL*** (608)985-7276
Tyge C Zucker • H • SW • 53941 PO Box 140 La Valle WI 53941-0140

**LADYSMITH—*ST JOHN*** (715)532-5780
Brent G Berkesch • H • EC • NW • 515 College Ave W Ladysmith WI 54848-2107

**LAKE GENEVA—*GLORIA DEI*** (414)248-8058
Vacant • WS 9; BC 1030 • SW • 428 Walworth St 53147-1516 PO Box 156 Lake Geneva WI 53147-0156

**LAKE MILLS—*CHRIST*** (920)648-2190
Vacant • WS 9;* • EN • 403 Mulberry St 53551-1350 PO Box 566 Lake Mills WI 53551

**LAMPSON—*CHRIST*** (715)466-4516
Gerald A Creighton • WS 9;* • H • NW • Cty Hwy F 1/2 Mile E Of Us 53 W5523 County Highway F Trego WI 54888-9239 • FAX(715)466-5204

**LAND O LAKES—*HOPE*** (906)544-2259
Vacant • H • NW • 1756 Hwy 45 54540 PO Box 477 Land O Lakes WI 54540-0477

**LAONA—*ST JOHN*** (715)674-3836
Sheldon L Kerstner • WS 830;* • H • NW • Hwy 8 North 54541 4833 W 5th Laona WI 54541-9643

**LEBANON—*ST PETER*** (920)925-3547
Vacant • WS 8;* • H • EL • SW • W4661 County MM 53047 PO Box 115 Lebanon WI 53047-0115

**LOGANVILLE—*ST JOHN*** (608)727-2000
Robert W Butler • * • H • SW • 380 E Walnut St 53943 PO Box 94 Loganville WI 53943-0094

**LUXEMBURG—*ST JOHN*** (920)845-5250
Vacant • NW • 413 Saint John St 54217 PO Box 219 Luxemburg WI 54217-0219

**LUXEMBURG 5 S—*ST PAUL*** (920)845-5248
A E Batiansila • H • EC/EL/HS • NW • N4108 County Road AB Luxemburg WI 54217 • FAX(920)845-9075

**LYNDON STATION—*ST LUKE*** (608)666-4091
Vacant • H • SW • 377 Rogers St 53944 PO Box 337 Lyndon Station WI 53944-0337 • hirev@palacenet.net

**MADISON—*CALVARY CHAPEL*** (608)255-7214
Vacant • * • H • SW • Lake And State 701 State St Madison WI 53703-1017 • FAX(608)255-1857 • calvary@chorus.net

***CHRIST MEMORL*** (608)271-2811
Jeffrey S Meyer • H • EC • SW • 2833 Raritan Rd Madison WI 53711-5232 • FAX(608)271-2849 • cmlc@chorus.net

***IMMANUEL*** (608)257-5401
David J Susan • * • H • SW • 1021 Spaight St Madison WI 53703-3589 • FAX(608)257-8875 • immanluth@juno.com

***LIVING CHRIST*** (608)829-2136
Daniel C Kowert • WS 9; BC 1030;* • H • EC • SW • 110 N Gammon Rd Madison WI 53717-1301 • FAX(608)829-3513 • kowert@living-christ.org

***MOUNT OLIVE*** (608)238-5656
Larry D Thies Robert A Boehler • WS 8 1030; BC 915;* • H • EC • SW • 4018 Mineral Point Rd Madison WI 53705-5126 • FAX(608)238-5714 • molc@execpc.com

***SILENT DEAF***
Vacant • SW • 1909 Huxley St Madison WI 53704-3430 • wpalmer182@aol.com

***ST PAUL*** (608)244-8077
Mark C Kufahl • H • SW • 2126 N Sherman Ave Madison WI 53704-3999 • FAX(608)244-8086 • stpauluth@juno.com

**MANAWA—*ST LUKE***
See Big Falls

***ST PAUL*** (920)596-2837
Horst W Jordan Kevin M Arndt • WS 815 1030; BC 730 930;* • H • EC/EL • NW • 742 Depot St Manawa WI 54949-9564

**MANAWA 4N—*ST MARK*** (920)596-3241
Jeffrey A Smiles • WS 1015;* • H • NW • 54949 N7534 Church St Manawa WI 54949-9691 • stmarksymco@juno.com

**MANITOWOC—*REDEEMER*** (920)684-3989
Richard C Miller Benjamin C Squires • WS 1;* • H • EC • SW • 1712 Menasha Ave Manitowoc WI 54220-1839 • FAX(920)684-3277 • redeemer@manty.com

**MAPLE—*FAITH*** (715)363-2516
Vacant • H • MNN • County Hwy F 54854 PO Box 187 Maple WI 54854-0187

**MARENGO 3 SW—*ST PAUL*** (715)278-3271
Vacant • WS 8;* • H • NW • 54855 RR 1 Box 28A Marengo WI 54855-9801

**MARINETTE—*FAITH*** (715)735-6506
Martin J Frusti • WS 9; BC 1030;* • H • EC • NW • 4009 Irving St Marinette WI 54143-1001 • revmarty@cybrzn.com

**MARSHFIELD—*CHRIST*** (715)384-3535
Mark A Krueger Daryn A Bahn • Tammy J Schwartz DCE • WS 8;* • H • EC • NW • 1208 W 14th St Marshfield WI 54449-3369 • FAX(715)384-6945 • christlu@tznet.com

***IMMANUEL*** (715)384-5121
Robert A Brandt • WS 8 1030;* • H • EC/EL • NW • 604 S Chestnut Ave Marshfield WI 54449-3606 • FAX(715)389-2963 • immanuel@tznet.com

**MATTOON—*ST JOHN*** (715)489-3471
Jeffrey Krueger • H • NW • 304 Flint Ave 54450 PO Box 260 Mattoon WI 54450-0260

**MAYVILLE—*ST JOHN*** (920)387-3568
Edward A Blonski • * • H • EC/EL • SW • 7 N Walnut St 53050-1507 450 Bridge St Mayville WI 53050-1550 • FAX(920)387-2852 • Eblonski@stjohns-lcms.org

**MAYVILLE 3 E—*IMMANUEL*** (920)387-5363
Eldor J Harmann • WS 8; SS 915; BC 915 • H • EC/EL • SW • N 8092 County Hwy AY Mayville WI 53050 • imluth@internetwis.com

**MEDFORD 5 NE—*TRINITY*** (715)748-4181
Randal R Jeppesen • WS 9;* • H • NW • W5334 Dassow Ave Medford WI 54451-8785

**MELLEN—*IMMANUEL*** (715)274-2751
Martin R Eden • NW • 101 Thomas Ave 54546 PO Box 18 Mellen WI 54546-0018 • reveden@mellen.baysat.net

**MENASHA—*TRINITY*** (920)722-2662
Timothy L Kinne • * • SW • 300 Broad St 54952-3045 PO Box 445 Menasha WI 54952-0445 • FAX(920)722-7692

**MENOMONEE FALLS—*GRACE*** (262)251-0670
Warren A Granke Roy R Peterson • WS 8 930 11;* • H • EC/EL/HS • SW • N87W16171 Kenwood Blvd Menomonee Falls WI 53051-2914 • FAX(262)251-8263

***PRINCE PEACE*** (262)251-3360
Norman A Timmermann • * • H • EC • EN • W156N7149 Pilgrim Rd Menomonee Falls WI 53051-5029 • FAX(262)251-3168 • natimmer@execpc.com

***ZION*** (262)781-8133
David B Paape Matthew Roeglin • WS 8 1045; SS 930; BC 930;* • H • EC/EL/HS • SW • W188N4868 Emerald Hills Dr Menomonee Falls WI 53051-6416 • FAX(262)781-4656

**MENOMONIE—*FAITH*** (715)235-1653
Curtis W Brooks • H • NW • 2220 21st St S Menomonie WI 54751

**MEQUON—*BEAUT SAVIOR*** (262)242-6650
Philip J Hillenbrand • WS 9; BC 1015;* • H • SW • 11313 N Riverland Rd # 35W Mequon WI 53092-2713 • FAX(262)242-6650 • bslcmequon @yahoo.com

***TRINITY*** (262)242-2045
Robert H Lindau Robert E Johnson • WS 8;* • H • EC/EL/HS • SW • UKNWN 10729 W Freistadt Rd Mequon WI 53097-2503 • FAX(262)242-4407 • trinluth@execpc.com

***TRINITY***
See Mequon

**MERCER—*FAITH*** (715)476-2626
James A Radichel • WS 9 730;* • H • NW • 2701 W Kichaks Landing Rd 54547 PO Box 145 Mercer WI 54547-0145 • FAX(715)476-0150

**MERRILL—*ST JOHN*** (715)536-4722
Alden J Beversdorf Kelly J Leary • WS 8 7;* • H • EC/EL • NW • 1104 E 3rd St Merrill WI 54452-2530 • FAX(715)539-3381 • abever@stjohn.merrill.wi.us

***ST JOHN***
See Athens

***TRINITY*** (715)536-5482
Kenneth L Albers Bryan G Lundquist • WS 8 1030; SS 915; BC 915;* • H • EL • NW • 107 N State St Merrill WI 54452-2244 • FAX(715)539-2911 • trinluth@dwave.net

**MERRILL - PINE RIVE—*ST PAUL*** (715)536-8459
David M Kaarre • H • NW • 54452 W2608 County Road P Merrill WI 54452-9564

**MERRILL 5 S—*FAITH*** (715)536-5443
Kevin J Hoogland • WS 10; BC 9;* • H • NW • 54452 15425 County Road K S Merrill WI 54452-9110

**MERRILL 9 W—*IMMANUEL*** (715)536-7242
Vacant • WS 930;* • H • NW • 54452 N1660 Leafy Grove Rd Merrill WI 54452-9323

**MILAN—*BETHLEHEM*** (715)352-2888
Roger R Moldenhauer • WS 830;* • H • NW • 54453 2290 Eldred Ave Athens WI 54411

**MILLADORE—*ST LUKE***
See Sherry

**MILWAUKEE—*BEAUTIFUL SAVIOR*** (414)871-6744
Larry A Jost • * • H • EC/EL/HS • SW • 3205 N 85th St Milwaukee WI 53222-3793 • FAX(414)871-6864

***BENEDICTION*** (414)463-9158
Donald T Hougard • * • H • HS • SW • 8475 W Fond du Lac Ave Milwaukee WI 53225-2803 • FAX(414)463-8338 • pastor@benediction-lcms.org

***BEREA*** (414)466-9220
Larry A Hauser • H • EC/EL/HS • SW • 4873 N 107th St Milwaukee WI 53225-3904 • FAX(414)466-2863 • berea@execpc.com

***BETHANY*** (414)444-3131
Eberhard G Klatt • H • HS • SW • 2031 N 38th St Milwaukee WI 53208-1862

***BETHLEHEM*** (414)342-3585
Jon F Leider • HS • SW • 2466 W Mc Kinley Ave Milwaukee WI 53205-2437 • FAX(414)342-0086

***CHAPEL CROSS*** (414)481-1880
David A Wood • * • H • HS • SW • 3353 S Whitnall Ave Milwaukee WI 53207-2797 • FAX(414)481-1821 • dawood@execpc.com

***CHRIST MEMORIAL*** (414)461-3253
James G Kroemer • EC/EL/HS • SW • 3105 W Thurston Ave Milwaukee WI 53209-4137

***COVENANT*** (414)464-2410
John G Koch Steven J Voigt • Dennis E Wallinger DCE • H • EC/EL/HS • SW • 8121 W Hope Ave Milwaukee WI 53222-1930 • FAX(414)464-1942

***DIVINE SHEPHERD*** (414)321-0730
Vacant • WS 9;* • H • HS • SW • 9741 W Beloit Rd Milwaukee WI 53227-4220 • FAX(414)321-5733

***EBENEZER*** (414)383-0710
Robert L Alsleben • HS • EN • 1127 S 35th St Milwaukee WI 53215-1409 • balsleben@aol.com

***EMMAUS*** (414)444-6090
Clifford L Bischoff • EC/EL/HS • SW • 2818 N 23rd St Milwaukee WI 53206-1645 • FAX(414)444-3336

***GOSPEL*** (414)562-1890
Byrene K Haney • WS 10; SS 845; BC 845;* • HS • SW • 1535 W Capitol Dr Milwaukee WI 53206-2935 • FAX(414)562-6760

***GRACE*** (414)384-3520
George J Richter Jr. • H • HS • SW • 3030 W Oklahoma Ave Milwaukee WI 53215-4351 • www.gracelch@execpc.com

***HOLY GHOST*** (414)264-0372
Wilbert L Sallach • HS • SW • 547 W Concordia Ave 541 W Concordia Ave Milwaukee WI 53212-1946

***HOPE*** (414)342-0471
Jon F Leider • H • HS • SW • 1115 N 35th St Milwaukee WI 53208-2802

***LAYTON PARK*** (414)383-1066
Timothy J Benninghoff • HS • EN • 2820 W Grant St Milwaukee WI 53215-2444

***LUTHER MEMORIAL***
See Shorewood

***MISS OF CHRIST*** (414)264-4050
Vacant • H • HS • SW • 912 W Center St 53206-3203 PO Box 6499 Milwaukee WI 53206 • FAX(414)264-4237

***MOUNT CALVARY*** (414)873-3931
Thomas J Eggebrecht • WS 8 1030; BC 915;* • H • EC/EL/HS • SW • 2862 N 53rd St Milwaukee WI 53210-1613 • FAX(414)873-0567 • eggebrecht@aol.com

***MOUNT OLIVE*** (414)771-3580
John W M Struve Nathan R Jansen Mark E Wangerin • WS 745 9 11; BC 1010;* • H • HS • SW • 5327 W Washington Blvd Milwaukee WI 53208-1798 • FAX(414)771-3855 • mtolive@execpc.com

***NAZARETH*** (414)354-2650
Thomas C Piel Michael C Golberg(#) • H • EC/EL/HS • SW • 8242 N Granville Rd Milwaukee WI 53224-2754

***OKLAHOMA AVE*** (414)543-3580
Donald E Meyer • WS 8;* • HS • SW • 5335 W Oklahoma Ave Milwaukee WI 53219-4416 • FAX(414)543-3610 • oalcs@execpc.com

***OUR SAVIOR***
See Whitefish Bay

***SHEPHERD OF THE RIDG*** (414)357-8490
Daniel C Voth • WS 9; SS 1030; BC 1030 • H • HS • SW • 9455 N 76th St Milwaukee WI 53223-1043 • FAX(414)357-8499 • sotr@execpc.com

***SHERMAN PARK*** (414)445-5185
Vacant • WS 915;* • H • EC • EN • 2703 N Sherman Blvd Milwaukee WI 53210-2426 • FAX(414)445-6556 • shermpkl@aol.com

***ST MARK*** (414)258-7118
Allen L Pingel • H • SW • 550 N 95th St Milwaukee WI 53226-4435

***ST MARTINI*** (414)645-4094
Jerome A Stecker • WS 10; BC 845;* • H • EL/HS • SW • S 16th St 1520 S Cesar E Chavez Dr Milwaukee WI 53204-2715 • FAX(414)645-4094

***ST PETER-IMMANUEL*** (414)353-6800
Donald P Weiss • WS 8 1030;* • H • EC/EL/HS • SW • 7801 W Acacia St Milwaukee WI 53223-5621 • FAX(414)353-5510

***ST STEPHEN*** (414)384-8620
Timothy D May • WS 9 1130; SS 1015; BC 1015 • H • HS • SW • 1136 S 5th St 53204-2449 420 W Scott St Milwaukee WI 53204-2455 • FAX(414)384-8872 • ststephn@execpc.com

***TRINITY*** (414)271-2219
Hunter Hofmann • HS • SW • 1046 N 9th St 1026 N 9th St Milwaukee WI 53233-1412 • FAX(414)271-1530

***WALTHER MEMORIAL*** (414)444-4133
William G Fenker • * • H • HS • SW • 4040 W Fond Du Lac Ave Milwaukee WI 53216-3645

**MINOCQUA—*ROCK OF AGES*** (715)356-3848
Walter L Geist • H • NW • 10441 Hwy 70w 54548 PO Box 1131 Minocqua WI 54548-1131 • FAX(715)356-4726 • revgeist@yahoo.com

**MODENA—*ST PAUL*** (715)946-3749
Vacant • H • NW • 54755 W1320 County Road D Mondovi WI 54755-7900

**MONDOVI—*ZION*** (715)926-3664
Vacant • * • H • NW • 264 E Main St Mondovi WI 54755-1633 • FAX(715)926-4471 • zionluth@win.bright.net

**MONDOVI 9 SW—*ST PAUL*** (716)926-5973
Vacant • H • NW • Steinke Vly Rd • Town Of Canton W1143 Cty Rd A Mondovi WI 54755

**MONONA—*MONONA*** (608)222-7071
William J Pekari • H • SW • 4411 Monona Dr Monona WI 53716-1048

**MONTELLO 7 E—*TRINITY*** (920)293-4477
Vacant • SW • 20th Ct And Fern Dr Mecan Twp 53949 C/O St John Luth N7691 15th Dr Neshkoro WI 54960-8125

**MOSINEE—*ST JOHN***
See Dancy

**MOUNT MORRIS 3 NE—*IMMANUEL*** (920)987-5804
Vacant • SS 9;* • SW • UKNWN PO Box 346 Poy Sippi WI 54967-0346 • FAX(920)987-5804 • getagrip@vbc.com

**MOUNTAIN—*ST MATTHEW***
See White Lake

***TABOR*** (715)276-7707
Paul A Scheunemann • WS 830;* • H • NW • 14153 Church Rd 54149-9555 PO Box 67 Mountain WI 54149-0067 • tabor@ez-net.com

**MUSCODA—*ST PETER*** (608)739-4017
Vacant • H • SW • 210 W Beech St 53573 PO Box 555 Muscoda WI 53573-0555

**NECEDAH—*ST JAMES*** (608)565-7252
John A Siedschlag Sr. • WS 1030; BC 930;* • H • SW • 1106 S Main St 54646-8207 PO Box 350 Necedah WI 54646-0352 • stjames.luth@tds.net

***ST PAUL***
See New Miner 3 Ne

**NEENAH—*NEW HOPE*** (920)725-4354
Jeffery S Prewitt • WS 8 1030; BC 915;* • H • SW • 1368 Cold Spring Rd Neenah WI 54956-1108 • FAX(920)725-4058 • newhope@vbe.com
***PEACE*** (920)725-0510
Terry L Ahlemeyer • WS 9;* • H • SW • 1228 S Park Ave Neenah WI 54956-4252 • FAX(920)725-0625 • peace@athenet.net
**NEKOOSA—*BETHLEHEM*** (715)886-4081
Carl M Kummer Delbert R Rossin • H • NW • 316 Buehler Ave Nekoosa WI 54457-1370 • FAX(715)886-4094
**NESHKORO—*ST PAUL***
See Westfield 8 Ne
***TRINITY***
See Montello 7 E
***ZION*** (920)293-4312
Gerald A Dament • WS 9;* • H • SW • 227 N State St 54960-9501 PO Box 18 Neshkoro WI 54960-0018
**NESHKORO 7 SW—*ST JOHN*** (920)293-4477
Vacant • WS 830 1030 • SW • Hwy 22 And County E 54960 N7691 15th Dr Neshkoro WI 54960-8125
**NEW BERLIN—*BLESSED SAVIOR*** (262)786-6465
Timm L Griffin Gary A Plopper(#) • WS 8; SS 915; BC 915;* • H • EC/HS • SW • 15250 W Cleveland Ave New Berlin WI 53151-3728 • FAX(262)786-6799 • bslc@execps.com
***PEACE*** (262)679-1441
A Mark Schudde • * • H • EC/HS • EN • 17651 W Small Rd New Berlin WI 53146-5530 • FAX(262)679-0292 • pschudde@peacelutheran.org
**NEW FANE—*SAINT JOHN*** (414)626-2309
Mark W Eckert • SW • N665 Hwy S Kewaskum WI 53040-1112 • FAX(414)626-2309 • stjohn@hnet.net
**NEW HOLSTEIN—*ZION*** (920)898-5250
Michael C Cook • H • SW • 1702 Van Buren St New Holstein WI 53061-1334 • zionhwi@dotnet.com
**NEW MINER 3 NE—*ST PAUL*** (608)565-7252
John A Siedschlag Sr. • WS 8;* • H • SW • N15296 19th Ave UKNWN PO Box 350 Necedah WI 54646
**NEW RICHMOND—*ST LUKE*** (715)246-4861
John W Schenck • * • H • EC • NW • 365 W River Dr New Richmond WI 54017-1435 • FAX(715)246-2109 • stlukenr@frontiernet.net
**NORTH FOND DU LAC—*DIVINE*** (920)923-1532
Allen H Bramstadt • WS 9;* • H • EC • SW • Hwy 175 And Polk St 1081 Van Dyne Rd North Fond Du Lac WI 54937-9777
**NORTH PRAIRIE—*ST JOHN*** (414)392-2170
Mark A Gefaller • WS 8 1030; SS 915; BC 915;* • H • EC • SW • 312 N Main St North Prairie WI 53153-9728 • FAX(414)392-3270 • stjohnchurch@prodigy.net
**OAK CREEK—*GRACE*** (414)762-8990
Dean A Dummer • WS 8 1030; BC 915;* • H • EC/EL/HS • SW • 3381 E Puetz Rd 53154-3552 8537 S Pennsylvania Ave Oak Creek WI 53154-3333 • FAX(414)762-3702 • dadummer@excepc.com
**OCONOMOWOC—*ST PAUL*** (414)567-5001
Paul L Borgman Ronald P Krug • WS 8 1030; BC 915;* • H • EC/EL/HS • SW • 210 E Pleasant St Oconomowoc WI 53066-3050 • FAX(414)567-1207
**OCONOMOWOC 9 N—*ST JOHN*** (414)474-4749
Gary W Tillmann • * • H • SW • 53066 N1245 Hwy 67 Oconomowoc WI 53066-9539
**OCONTO—*ZION*** (920)834-5037
Bruce L Blocker • WS 9;* • H • NW • 1700 Superior Ave 54153-2010 PO Box 259 Oconto WI 54153-0259
**OMRO—*GRACE*** (920)685-2621
John C Brogaard • WS 8 1030; SS 915; BC 915 • H • EC • SW • 720 Jackson Ave Omro WI 54963-1718 • FAX(920)685-6786 • glc@northnet.net
**ONALASKA—*SHEPHERD HILLS*** (608)783-0330
Lionel O Skamser David E Wiist • * • H • EC • SW • 1215 Redwood St 54650-2368 PO Box 416 Onalaska WI 54650-0416 • FAX(608)783-1876
**ONEIDA—*ZION*** (414)869-2777
Vernon F Heim • * • H • HS • NW • 453 Rose Hill Dr 54155-9025 749 Silver Creek Dr Oneida WI 54155-9051 • FAX(414)869-2777 • zionev@netnet.net
**OSCEOLA—*SHEP OF VALLEY***
See Saint Croix Falls
**OSHKOSH—*GOOD SHEPHERD*** (920)231-0530
Thomas W Bye • WS 745 1030; BC 9;* • H • SW • 2450 W 9th Ave Oshkosh WI 54904-8050 • FAX(920)231-0530 • gsluth@execpc.com
***HMONG*** (414)235-7440
Yia Z Vang(DM) • H • SW • 370 Bowen St Oshkosh WI 54901-5157 • FAX(414)426-8725 • yzvang@aol.com
***TRINITY*** (920)235-7440
Marvin J Ahlborn • WS 8;* • H • EC/EL • SW • 370 Bowen St Oshkosh WI 54901-5157 • FAX(920)235-6940
**OSSEO—*ST PAUL***
See Whitehall 5 N
**OSSEO 8 NW—*ST PETER*** (715)597-2431
Dennis L Voss • * • H • NW • Township Of Clear Creek Wi 54758 E11770 County Road Hh Osseo WI 54758-8850
**OXFORD—*ST JOHN*** (608)586-5877
David W Totsky • WS 103;* • H • SW • 330 E Vallette St PO Box 127 Oxford WI 53952-0127 • FAX(608)586-4848
**PACKWAUKEE—*TRINITY*** (608)589-5138
David W Totsky • H • SW • W5940 Chestnut 53953 PO Box 628 Packwaukee WI 53953-0628
**PARK FALLS—*PEACE*** (715)762-4541
Vacant • * • H • EC • NW • 600 2nd Ave N Park Falls WI 54552-1327 • FAX(715)762-4533
**PEWAUKEE—*LAMB OF GOD*** (414)691-3828
Bruce Harrmann • WS 9 6;* • H • HS • SW • N 19 W 25050 Bluemound Rd Pewaukee WI 53072-5806 • FAX(262)691-4119 • lambofgod7@juno.com
***SHEPHERD HILLS*** (414)691-0700
Thomas R Wink • WS 8 1030; BC 915;* • H • SW • N36W24130 Pewaukee Rd 53072-2655 PO Box 238 Pewaukee WI 53072-0238 • FAX(414)691-1627
**PHILLIPS—*TRINITY*** (715)339-3495
Gary D Lodholz • WS 830;* • H • NW • 103 Trinity Dr Phillips WI 54555-1524 • trinzion@win.bright.net
**PICKEREL—*ST JOHN*** (715)484-8145
Charles F Kramer • WS 9;* • H • NW • N8934 Hwy 55 And Co Hwy A 54465 W5338 Clark Ln Pickerel WI 54465-9716 • W5338@newnorth.net
**PIPE LAKE—*CHRIST*** (715)822-3096
James A Vanek • H • NW • Polk County Rds Gandt UKNWN 12110 Pickerel Pt Grantsburg WI 54840-8410
**PITTSVILLE—*ST JOHN*** (715)884-2211
Vacant • WS 9;* • H • NW • 8313 2nd St Pittsville WI 54466-9544 • FAX(715)884-2211
**PITTSVILLE 12 W—*ST PAUL*** (715)884-2211
Vacant • WS 1030;* • H • NW • Hwy 73 54466 C/O St John Lutheran Church 8313 2nd St Pittsville WI 54466-9544
**PLATTEVILLE—*APOSTLES FISHE*** (608)348-9901
Frank X Kinast Jr. • WS 930;* • H • SW • 6732 Hwy 81 N Platteville 53818 PO Box 755 Platteville WI 53818-0755 • FAX(608)348-4900 • apostles@pcii.net
**PLEASANT PRAIRIE—*GOOD*** (262)694-4405
Donald L Hackbarth • * • H • EC • SW • 4311 104th St Pleasant Prairie WI 53158-3723 • FAX(262)694-0964
**PLOVER—*BEAUTIFUL SAVIOR*** (715)341-2898
Steven A Hulke • WS 930;* • H • NW • 3210 Maple Dr 54467-3657 PO Box 336 Plover WI 54467-0336 • FAX(715)342-5642
**PLUM CITY—*IMMANUEL*** (715)647-2555
Daniel M Pfaffe • WS 1030;* • NW • First Ave E Plum City WI 54761
**PLYMOUTH—*ST JOHN*** (920)893-3071
Ricky P Schroeder Thomas R Burton • H • EC/EL • SW • 222 N Stafford St Plymouth WI 53073-1839 • FAX(920)892-2845 • sjlc@danet.net
**PORT EDWARDS—*TRINITY*** (715)887-3021
Daniel L Bohn • WS 9; SS 1015;* • H • EC • NW • 990 3rd St Port Edwards WI 54469-1250
**PORT WASHINGTON—*ST JOHN*** (414)284-2131
John E Klieve Derek M Wolter • EC/EL • SW • 403 W Foster St Port Washington WI 53074-2111 • FAX(414)284-3935
**PORTAGE—*ST JOHN*** (608)742-2387
Alan G Boeck Todd C Riordan • * • H • EC/EL • SW • 850 Armstrong St Portage WI 53901-1601 • FAX(608)742-7154 • lutheran@centurytel.net
**POTTER 1 S—*TRINITY*** (920)853-3656
Kurt S Taylor • H • EC/EL • SW • 54160 N6078 W River Rd Hilbert WI 54129-9428 • koort@tds.net
**POY SIPPI—*EMMAUS*** (920)987-5229
Frederick L Mueller • * • H • SW • N 4494 Hwy 49 54967 PO Box 346 Poy Sippi WI 54967-0346 • FAX(920)987-5229
***IMMANUEL***
See Mount Morris 3 Ne
**PRENTICE—*TRINITY*** (715)428-2851
Duane A Jalas • WS 10; SS 845; BC 845 • H • NW • W4594 US Highway 8 Prentice WI 54556-9610
**PRINCETON—*CALVARY*** (920)295-4747
William R Lewis • WS 8;* • H • SW • 202 S Farmer St 54968-9051 PO Box 11 Princeton WI 54968-0011 • FAX(920)295-3421 • calvary@vbe.com
**PULASKI—*ST JOHN*** (920)822-3511
Steven G Kline G J Dobratz • WS 8; SS 915; BC 915;* • H • HS • NW • 910 S St Augustine 54162 PO Box 620 Pulaski WI 54162-0620 • FAX(920)822-1582 • revkline@aol.com
**PULCIFER—*ST JOHN*** (715)745-6464
John V Laatsch • H • NW • W2240 Hwy 22 54124 W2253 State Highway 22 Pulcifer WI 54124-9407
**QUINCY—*ST JOHN*** (608)339-7869
Richard R Sunderlage • * • H • EL • SW • 5 Miles N Of Hwy 82/Cty Rd Z 2823 County Road Z Adams WI 53910-9768
**RACINE—*CHAPEL CROSS*** (414)886-4000
Daniel R Feldscher • * • H • SW • 1426 Fancher Rd Racine WI 53406-2406
***CHRIST KING*** (414)639-5849
Mark S Kastner • WS 8; SS 9 • H • HS • SW • 53402 3357 La Salle St Racine WI 53402-3857
***GRACE*** (262)633-4831
Randal A Poppe Thomas E Chryst • * • H • EC/EL/HS • SW • 3700 Washington Ave Racine WI 53405-2944 • FAX(262)633-3832 • glracine@execpc.com
***HOLY CROSS*** (262)554-7010
David H Behling • WS 9; SS 1015; BC 1015 • H • EC/EL/HS • SW • 5230 Biscayne Ave 53406 3350 Lathrop Ave Racine WI 53405-4711
***PEACE*** (262)884-7633
Randall L Glander • WS 1015; SS 9; BC 9;* • H • EC/EL/HS • EN • 1619 N Newman Rd Racine WI 53406 • FAX(262)884-7636 • peacelcrac@mixcom.com
***PENTECOST*** (414)633-9674
Vacant • H • EC/EL/HS • S • 2213 Coolidge Ave Racine WI 53403-3119
***PRIMERA IGLESIA*** (414)633-4622
Vacant • H • SW • C/O Latinoamericana 2408 Durand Ave Racine WI 53403-3065
***PRINCE PEACE*** (262)639-1277
Daniel L Hinrichs • WS 8 1030; SS 915; BC 915;* • H • EC/HS • SW • 4340 6 Mile Rd Racine WI 53402-9621 • FAX(262)639-8144
***REDEEMER*** (414)639-3200
Mark S Kastner • H • HS • SW • 4649 Lora St Racine WI 53402-2775
***ST JOHN*** (262)637-7011
Daniel B Quinn • * • H • EC/EL/HS • SW • 1501 Erie St 53402-4830 510 Kewaunee St Racine WI 53402-5002
***TRINITY*** (414)632-2900
Daniel G Heinert Stephen E Jennings • WS 8; SS 915; BC 915;* • H • EC/EL/HS • SW • 2035 Geneva St Racine WI 53402-4627 • FAX(414)632-3838 • sjenn@execpc.com
**RANDOM LAKE—*IMMANUEL*** (414)994-9060
William L Robinson • H • SW • W8497 Brazelton Dr Random Lake WI 53075-1106
**RANDOM LAKE 2 N—*ST JOHN*** (920)994-2228
Bryan R Osladil Gregory R Laska(#) • EL/HS • SW • W5406 CTH SS Random Lake WI 53075 • FAX(920)994-9721
**REEDSBURG—*ST PETER*** (608)524-4512
Kevin J Kohnke • WS 1030 8;* • H • SW • 345 N Pine St Reedsburg WI 53959-1667
**REESEVILLE—*IMMANUEL*** (920)927-5734
Donald E Steinberg • WS 9;* • H • SW • 210 Lincoln Ave 53579 PO Box 272 Reeseville WI 53579-0272
**REESEVILLE 3 SW—*TRINITY*** (920)927-5762
Vacant • H • SW • 53579 N2296 County Road I Reeseville WI 53579-9615
**RHINELANDER—*OUR SAVIOR***
See Jeffris/Bundy
***ST MARK*** (715)362-2470
Jeff G Shearier • * • H • EC • NW • 17 S Baird Ave Rhinelander WI 54501-3502 • FAX(715)362-2037 • stmark@newnorth.net
**RIB MOUNTAIN—*RIB MOUNTAIN*** (715)845-2313
Thomas F Hoelter • WS 10 730;* • H • EC • NW • 54470 3010 Eagle Ave Wausau WI 54401-7345
**RICE LAKE—*FIRST*** (715)234-7505
Gerald L Bernecker • WS 8 1030; SS 915; BC 915 • H • EC • NW • 15 E Sawyer St Rice Lake WI 54868-2560 • first@discover-net.net
***IMMANUEL*** (715)236-7743
Vacant • WS 10;* • H • NW • 2476 27th St Rice Lake WI 54868
**RICHLAND CENTER—*ST LUKE*** (608)647-6905
Wade M Seaver • WS 9;* • H • SW • 1096 N Main St 53581-1426 1060 N Central Ave PO Box 230 Richland Center WI 53581-0230 • FAX(608)647-4499 • seaver@mwt.net
***ST PAUL***
See Boaz
**RIPON—*MESSIAH*** (414)748-3882
Bryan Fritsch • H • SW • 500 Mayparty Dr Ripon WI 54971-1030
**RIVER FALLS—*LUTHER MEMORIAL*** (715)425-2675
Vacant • * • H • NW • Fourth St And Cascade Ave 54022 420 S 4th St River Falls WI 54022-2413 • lmpastor@pressenter.com
**SAINT CROIX FALLS—*SHEP OF*** (715)483-1186
Mark K Schoen • WS 9;* • H • NW • 140 S Madison St Saint Croix Falls WI 54024
**SAUKVILLE—*PEACE*** (414)284-3608
Vacant • H • SW • 598 W Hillcrest Rd Saukville WI 53080-2548
**SCHOFIELD—*MOUNT OLIVE*** (715)359-5546
Raymond R Connor David K Zandt • Michelle D Potts DCE Randall D Fischer DCE • WS 8 1030; SS 915;* • H • EC • NW • 54476 6205 Alderson St Weston WI 54476-3905 • FAX(715)359-9245 • rconnor@mtolivewest.org
**SHARON—*TRIUNE*** (414)882-4000
Gary V Gehlbach • H • EC • SW • N1584 County Road K Sharon WI 53585-9723 • gehlbach@hughestech.net
**SHAWANO—*ST JAMES*** (715)524-4815
William H Otte Michael J Schram Fred T Zimmermann William A Uttech • WS 730 9 1030;* • H • EC/EL • NW • 324 S Andrews St Shawano WI 54166-2406 • FAX(715)524-4876 • elcsj@frontiernet.net
**SHAWANO 4 NW—*ST JAKOBI*** (715)524-4347
Timothy H Lamkin Sr. • * • HS • NW • 54166 W8089 County Road A Shawano WI 54166-5944
**SHAWANO 6 S—*ST JOHN***
Roland M Golz • NW • 54166 RR 2 Clintonville WI 54929-9802
**SHAWANO 6 W—*ST PAUL*** (715)524-2350
Richard R Buhrke • HS • NW • 54166 W9304 Oak Ave Shawano WI 54166-6239
**SHAWANO 9 W—*ST JOHN*** (715)524-4382
Roland M Golz • NW • 54166 N897 County Road U Shawano WI 54166-8931
**SHEBOYGAN—*BETHLEHEM*** (920)452-4331
James L Hartman Alan D Kubow • WS 8 1030; SS 915; BC 915;* • H • EC/EL/HS • SW • 1121 Georgia Ave Sheboygan WI 53081-5311 • FAX(920)452-0209
***CHRIST*** (920)457-9205
Vacant • WS 10;* • H • HS • SW • 3816 S 12th St Sheboygan WI 53081-7298 • christlutheranchurch1@juno.com
***GOOD SHEPHERD*** (920)452-8759
Martinho Q Sander • Janine M Bergeron DCE • WS 8 1030;* • H • HS • SW • 1614 S 23rd St Sheboygan WI 53081-5018 • FAX(920)452-6268 • gsluther@execpc.com
***IMMANUEL*** (920)452-7266
Vacant • * • H • EC/EL/HS • SW • 1634 Illinois Ave Sheboygan WI 53081-4826 • FAX(920)452-0102 • imanuelc@bytehead.com
***LUTHER MEMORIAL*** (414)458-1322
Bradley A Smith • WS 9;* • H • SW • 1127 Eisner Ave Sheboygan WI 53083-3056 • luthermemorial@juno.com
***OUR REDEEMER*** (920)452-0717
David C Cecil • * • H • HS • SW • 3027 Wilgus Ave Sheboygan WI 53081-3692

***OUR SAVIOR*** (920)452-4005
Marcus H Powers Robert W Steele • WS 8;* • H • HS • SW • 917 Mead Ave Sheboygan WI 53081-6361 • FAX(920)452-1492 • oslcshb@bytehead.com

***ST MARK*** (920)458-4343
Dean D Pittelko • * • H • EC • EN • 1019 N 7th St Sheboygan WI 53081-4019 • FAX(920)458-3484 • StMark@excel.net

***ST PAUL*** (414)452-6829
Alan R Kretschmar Bert A Thompson • H • EC/EL/HS • SW • 1810 N 13th St Sheboygan WI 53081-2525 • FAX(414)452-2382

***TRINITY*** (920)458-8246
Timothy J Mech • WS 8 1045;* • H • EC/EL/HS • SW • 824 Wisconsin Ave Sheboygan WI 53081-4030 • FAX(920)458-8267 • tls@tcbi.com

**SHEBOYGAN 3 S—*TRINITY*** (920)458-8881
Frederick K Jabs • WS 830;* • H • HS • SW • 53081 6522 S Business Dr Sheboygan WI 53081-8917 • FAX(920)803-5157 • tlctw@intella.net

**SHEBOYGAN FALLS—*ST PAUL*** (920)467-6449
Donald E Hasse Thomas P Gudmundson • WS 8;* • H • EC/HS • SW • 730 County Road Ppp 53085-1864 PO Box 185 Sheboygan Falls WI 53085-0185 • FAX(920)467-4239 • stpaulsf@bytehead.com

**SHELDON—*TRINITY*** (715)452-5359
Steven J Haag • NW • W5568 Main St 54766-9794 PO Box 144 Sheldon WI 54766-0144

**SHERRY—*ST LUKE*** (715)652-2213
David J Dahlke • NW • UKNWN 8478 Hetze Rd Milladore WI 54454-9710

**SHOREWOOD—*LUTHER MEMORIAL*** (414)332-5732
Kenneth W Wieting • WS 9; BC 1015;* • H • SW • 3833 N Maryland Ave Milwaukee WI 53211-2431 • FAX(414)332-3696 • lutherm@execpc.com

**SPENCER—*TRINITY*** (715)659-4006
Karl A Rose • WS 10;* • H • NW • Clark At Pearl 54479 PO Box 109 Spencer WI 54479-0109

**SPOONER—*FAITH*** (715)635-8167
Timothy W Roser • WS 8 1030; BC 915;* • H • EC • NW • W7148 Luther Rd Spooner WI 54801-8676

**STANLEY—*EPIPHANY*** (715)644-5899
Robert S Wilcken • WS 1030;* • H • NW • 114 W Oak St 54768-1042 PO Box 96 Stanley WI 54768-0096

**STEVENS POINT—*BEAUTIFUL SAVIOR***
See Plover

***ST PAUL*** (715)344-5664
Bob A Barnes Mark D Friedrich Jonathan A Wessel • WS 8 930 11;* • H • EC/EL • NW • 1919 Wyatt Ave Stevens Point WI 54481-3650 • FAX(715)344-5240 • stpaul@coredcs.com.

**STOUGHTON—*GOOD SHEP BY LK*** (608)873-5924
Thomas E Petersen • H • SW • 1860 Hwy 51 53589 PO Box 338 Stoughton WI 53589-0338 • Lutheran@TDS.net

**STURGEON BAY—*PRINCE PEACE*** (920)743-7750
Mark A Wenzel • WS 10; BC 9;* • H • NW • 1756 Michigan St Sturgeon Bay WI 54235-1412 • princeofpeace@msq.dcwis.com

**STURTEVANT—*FAITH*** (262)886-2522
Jeffrey E Mortenson • * • H • EC/EL/HS • SW • 8500 Durand Ave Sturtevant WI 53177-2003

**SULLIVAN 2 E—*ST JOHN*** (414)593-8630
John A Schmidt • H • SW • 53178 W407 Highway 18 Sullivan WI 53178-9708

**SUN PRAIRIE—*BETHLEHEM*** (608)837-7446
James A Pingel • David P Sauer DCE • WS 8 1030; BC 915;* • H • SW • 1700 Broadway Dr Sun Prairie WI 53590-1748 • FAX(608)825-2268 • bethlehem@bethlehemlc.org

**SUPERIOR—*CHRIST*** (715)398-3680
Vacant • * • H • MNN • 320 N 28th St E Superior WI 54880

***TRI-LAKES**** (715)374-2013
Vacant • MNN • 7872 S County Rd 4 54880 6930 S County Rd S Lake Nebagamon WI 54849-9102

**SURING—*EMMANUEL***
See Breed

***MOUNT OLIVE*** (920)842-2488
Vacant • H • NW • 206 N Burk 54174 PO Box 247 Suring WI 54174-0247

**SURING 3 SE—*TRINITY*** (414)842-2005
Russell J Kampfer • WS 830 • NW • 54174 8905 Saint Johns Rd Suring WI 54174-9706 • FAX(414)842-4443

**SURING 3 W—*ST JOHN*** (920)842-4443
Russell J Kampfer • WS 10; BC 9;* • EC/EL • NW • 54174 8945 Saint Johns Rd Suring WI 54174-9706 • FAX(920)842-4443

**SUSSEX—*PEACE*** (262)246-3200
Peter C Bender Matthew W Gatchell(#) • WS 745 1030; SS 915; BC 915;* • H • EC/EL • SW • 53089-3622 PO Box 123 W240 N6145 Maple Ave Sussex WI 53089-0123 • FAX(262)246-8455 • church@peacesussex.org

**SYMCO—*ST MARK***
See Manawa 4n

**THORP—*ST PAUL*** (715)669-5608
Robert S Wilcken • WS 9;* • H • NW • 203 E Rusch St 54771-9220 PO Box 327 Thorp WI 54771-0327 • pastorob@!discover-net.net

**THREE LAKES—*GRACE*** (715)546-2262
James A Radichel • WS 1130;* • NW • 6948 E School 54562 PO Box 216 Three Lakes WI 54562-0216

**TIGERTON—*ST JOHN*** (715)535-2281
Clifford Kessen • WS 930;* • H • NW • 502 Cedar St 54486-9502 PO Box 68 Tigerton WI 54486-0068

**TOMAH—*GOOD SHEPHERD*** (608)374-2444
John C Wille • WS 815 1045; SS 930; BC 930;* • H • SW • 1221 La Grange Ave Tomah WI 54660-2908 • FAX(608)374-2444 • goodshep@mwt.net

**TOMAHAWK—*ST PAUL*** (715)453-5391
Mark A Schoenherr • WS 8;* • H • NW • 12 E Wisconsin Ave Tomahawk WI 54487-1331 • FAX(715)453-5313

**TOWNSEND—*ST JOHN*** (715)276-7214
Gary C Bratz • Scott P Wycherley DCE • H • NW • 17963 State Rd 32 54175 PO Box 78 Townsend WI 54175-0078 • FAX(715)276-7214

**TREGO—*CHRIST***
See Lampson

**TURTLE LAKE—*IMMANUEL***
See Clayton

***ZION*** (715)986-4927
John A Wilman • BC 915;* • H • NW • 300 Martin Ave W 54889 Box 32 Turtle Lake WI 54889-0032

**TWO RIVERS—*GOOD SHEPHERD*** (920)793-1716
William R Kilps • * • H • EC • SW • 3234 Mishicot Rd Two Rivers WI 54241-1556 • goodshepherd@lsol.net

**UNION GROVE—*ST PAUL*** (414)878-2600
James F Keuch • WS 8 1030; SS 915;* • H • EC/HS • SW • 1610 Main St Union Grove WI 53182-1703 • FAX(414)878-2600 • stpaullcms@aol.com

**VESPER—*TRINITY*** (715)569-4114
Douglas A Schalow • * • H • NW • 6412 Michigan St S 54489 PO Box 57 Vesper WI 54489-0057

**VESPER 3 S—*ST PAUL*** (715)469-4307
Donald O Wesener(EM) • H • NW • Cor Cnty Tr D And Hwy 13n 54489 5065 Spruce Rd Vesper WI 54489-9724

**WALDO 3 NE—*ST THOMAS*** (920)458-8881
Frederick K Jabs • WS 1015;* • HS • SW • N4079 County Trunk Hwy M 53093 PO Box 117 Waldo WI 53093-0117

**WALES—*BETHLEHEM*** (262)968-2194
Erik K Cloeter • Jeffrey M Soeldner DCE Sandra J Rades • WS 8;* • H • EC • SW • 470 N Oak Crest Dr Wales WI 53183-9711 • FAX(262)968-5356 • blc@execpc.com

**WATERFORD—*ST PETER*** (262)534-3639
Frederick A Bischoff • H • EC • SW • 145 S 6th St Waterford WI 53185-4441 • FAX(262)534-2571 • www.stpeters@setnet.net

**WATERTOWN—*FAITH*** (920)261-8060
Vacant • H • EC/EL • EN • 626 Milford St Watertown WI 53094-6020 • FAX(920)261-8060

***GOOD SHEPHERD*** (920)261-2570
Richard L Thompson • WS 8 1030; BC 915;* • H • EL • SW • 1611 E Main St Watertown WI 53094-4109 • FAX(920)261-2769 • gslc@execpc.com

**WATERTOWN 10 SE—*ST STEPHEN*** (920)699-3433
Vacant • H • SW • N6848 Islandview Rd Watertown WI 53094

**WAUKESHA—*BEAUTIFUL SAVIOR*** (414)542-2496
Timothy J Bruss Peter A Schmidt • WS 8;* • H • EC/EL • SW • 1205 S East Ave Waukesha WI 53186-6666 • FAX(414)542-8574 • bslc@ticon.net

***CHRIST THE LIFE*** (262)547-1817
John T Kelling • WS 10;* • H • EC/EL/HS • SW • 3031 Summit Ave Waukesha WI 53188-2660 • FAX(262)547-7394 • christthelife@hotmail.com

***LAMB OF GOD***
See Pewaukee

**WAUNAKEE—*CONCORDIA*** (608)849-6130
Vacant • SW • 110 W 2nd St Waunakee WI 53597-1336 • tjrhwldt@itis.com

**WAUPACA—*CALVARY*** (715)258-3530
Vacant • WS 8 1030;* • H • NW • E1887 King Rd Waupaca WI 54981-8302

**WAUPACA 9 SE—*EMMAUS*** (715)258-3193
Vacant • NW • 54981 N180 County Road A Waupaca WI 54981-9061

**WAUPUN—*PELLA*** (920)324-3321
Kenneth M Spence • Jeffrey M Pool DCE • H • EC • SW • 315 S Madison St Waupun WI 53963-2002 • FAX(920)324-9734 • pastorjim@internetwis.com

**WAUSAU—*CHRIST*** (715)848-2040
Stephen K Wipperman • WS 830;* • H • NW • 1300 Town Line Rd Wausau WI 54403-6584 • FAX(715)849-3233 • stevew@ministers.net

***RIB MOUNTAIN***
See Rib Mountain

***ST MARK*** (715)848-5511
Bruce B Lamont • H • EC • NW • 600 Stevens Dr Wausau WI 54401-2977

***TRINITY*** (715)842-0769
Gary G Schultz Keith R Haldeman Dennis W Pegorsch Herbert O Praeuner(EM) • WS 730 9 1030; SS 9; BC 9;* • H • NW • 501 Stewart Ave Wausau WI 54401-4562 • FAX(715)843-7278

**WAUSAU 12 NE—*ZION*** (715)845-2014
Nathan M Meador • H • EC • NW • Wausau 12 Ne 54403 E7195 Star Rd Aniwa WI 54408-9622 • Nmeador@Dwave.net

**WAUSAU 6 NE—*ST PETER*** (715)675-9901
Gregory S Michel • WS 830; BC 930;* • H • NW • 54403 7505 N 33rd St Wausau WI 54403-9402 • sptr@dwave.net

***TRINITY*** (715)675-9901
Gregory S Michel • WS 10 • NW • 54403 4103 N 69th St Wausau WI 54403-9612 • sptr@dwave.net

**WAUSAU 8 E—*ST JOHN*** (715)842-5212
Mark J Lewis • WS 745 1015; SS 9; BC 9;* • EC/EL • NW • 8 Miles East Of Wausau 54403 E10723 County Road Z Wausau WI 54403-8915 • revdad@aol.com

**WAUTOMA—*TRINITY*** (920)787-2891
Frank G Frye • H • SW • S Scott And W Elm 54982 PO Box 915 Wautoma WI 54982-0915

**WAUTOMA 7 NW—*GRACE***
See Hancock 6 Se

**WAUWATOSA—*OUR REDEEMER*** (414)258-4555
Mark A Mueller Gene G Henke • WS 8 930 11; BC 930;* • H • EC/EL/HS • SW • 10025 W North Ave Wauwatosa WI 53226-2501 • FAX(414)258-5775 • church@orlctosa.org

***PILGRIM*** (414)476-0735
Paul H Peckman Thomas N Reeder Jr. • H • EC/EL/HS • SW • 6817 W Center St 53210-1255 2664 N 68th St Wauwatosa WI 53213-1310 • FAX(414)476-2820 • apostlesatpilgrim@juno.com

**WAYSIDE—*ZION*** (920)864-2463
Dennis Sundell • * • H • EC/EL/HS • NW • UKNWN 8378 County Rd W Greenleaf WI 54126-9468 • FAX(920)864-2684 • wayzion@netnet.net

**WEBSTER—*OUR REDEEMER*** (715)866-7191
Richard J Schreiber • WS 1030;* • H • NW • 26681 Lakeland Ave N 54893-8112 PO Box 85 Webster WI 54893-0085

***TRINITY***
See Danbury

**WEST ALLIS—*EMMANUEL DEAF*** (414)321-8430
William Palmer(DM) • H • SW • 2306 S 98th St West Allis WI 53227-2224 • FAX(414)321-5379 • wpalmer182@aol.com

***GREENFIELD PK*** (414)774-3019
Paul R Koester • H • EN • 1236 S 115th St West Allis WI 53214-2238

***ST PAUL*** (414)541-6250
Thomas R Acton John K Lescow • Leon C Jameson DCE • WS 8 1030; SS 915; BC 915;* • H • EC/EL/HS • SW • 7821 W Lincoln Ave West Allis WI 53219-1767 • FAX(414)541-2205 • acton@splcwa.org

***TRINITY*** (414)321-3640
Thomas I Krueger • H • EC • SW • 2500 S 68th St West Allis WI 53219-2613 • FAX(414)321-6470

**WEST BEND—*PILGRIM*** (414)334-0375
Joseph M Fisher • BC 915;* • H • SW • 462 Meadowbrook Dr West Bend WI 53090 • FAX(414)334-2424 • revjfish@nconnect.net

***SAINT ANDREW*** (262)335-4200
Bryan T O Connor • * • H • EC • SW • 7750 Highway 144 N West Bend WI 53090 • FAX(262)335-4175 • standrew@alexssa.net

***ST JOHN*** (262)334-4901
Daniel W Kelm J B Clark Jr. Calvin F Seban • WS 8 1030; SS 915; BC 915;* • H • EC/EL • SW • 809 S 6th Ave West Bend WI 53095-4613 • FAX(262)334-3094 • stjohns@hnet.net

**WEST BLOOMFIELD—*CHRIST*** (920)987-5283
Randolf D Blech • WS 930;* • H • EC/EL • SW • UKNWN N6412 State Rd 49 Weyauwega WI 54983-9804

**WEST SALEM—*PRINCE OF PEACE*** (608)786-3938
Michael J Hylton • WS 930; SS 1045; BC 1045 • H • SW • 475 S Mark St 54669 1045 Robin Ct West Salem WI 54669-1919 • popws@prodigy.net

**WESTFIELD—*IMMANUEL*** (608)296-2088
Dennis L Boettcher • WS 10;* • H • SW • 210 S Charles St 53964-9144 PO Box 397 Westfield WI 53964-0397 • FAX(608)296-2088

**WESTFIELD 8 NE—*ST PAUL*** (920)293-4477
Vacant • SW • 10th Rd And 11th Rd 53964 C/O St John Luth N7691 15th Dr Neshkoro WI 54960-8125

**WESTON—*MOUNT OLIVE***
See Schofield

***MOUNT OLIVE***
See Schofield

**WEYAUWEGA—*CHRIST***
See West Bloomfield

**WHITE LAKE—*ST MATTHEW*** (715)882-3111
Steven C Vaudt • WS 10;* • H • NW • 138 Bissell St 54491 PO Box 238 White Lake WI 54491-0238

**WHITEFISH BAY—*OUR SAVIOR*** (414)332-4458
Garland R Wittmayer • HS • SW • 6021 N Santa Monica Blvd Whitefish Bay WI 53217-4660

**WHITEHALL 5 N—*ST PAUL*** (715)597-2431
Dennis L Voss • * • H • NW • Hale Wi 54773 E11770 County Road Hh Osseo WI 54758-8850

**WHITEWATER—*CALVARY/UNIV**** (414)473-5274
Donald M Stein(DM) • H • EC • SW • 234 N Prince St Whitewater WI 53190-1311 • FAX(414)473-5689 • cmpspstr@idcnet.com

**WILD ROSE—*ST PAUL*** (920)622-3280
Vacant • WS 830;* • H • SW • 420 Park Ave 54984-6813 PO Box 240 Wild Rose WI 54984-0240

**WISCONSIN DELLS—*TRINITY*** (608)253-3241
Dennis R Schueler • * • H • EC/EL • SW • 728 Church St Wisconsin Dells WI 53965-1517 • FAX(608)254-7585

**WISCONSIN RAPIDS—*IMMANUEL*** (715)423-3260
Gary D Baumann Mark J Drengler • WS 730 9 1030;* • H • EC/EL • NW • 160 8th St N 54494-4543 111 11th St N Wisconsin Rapids WI 54494-4598 • FAX(715)423-2853 • imluthsc@wctc.net424-4638

***ST LUKE*** (715)423-5990
Timothy E Wenger David P Albers • Martha A Parris DCE • WS 1030 745; SS 915;* • H • EC • NW • 2011 10th St S Wisconsin Rapids WI 54494-6302 • FAX(715)423-5936 • stlukes1@tznet.com

**WISCONSIN RPDS 6 SE—*ST JOHN*** (715)423-7788
Paul G Mueller • WS 830;* • H • NW • 54494 8020 Southpark Rd Wisconsin Rapids WI 54494-9639 • stjohns@wctc.net

**WISCONSIN RPDS 6NW—*ST JOHN*** (715)421-3566
Douglas A Schalow • NW • 54494 3805 Saint Johns Rd Wisconsin Rapids WI 54495-9250

**WITHEE—*ST JOHN*** (715)229-4211
Thomas E Myhre • WS 8;* • H • NW • 204 Division St 54498-9787 PO Box 354 Withee WI 54498-0354

**WITTENBERG—*ST PAUL*** (715)253-2790
John D Pavel • H • NW • 701 S Home St 54499 PO Box 267 Wittenberg WI 54499-0267

**ZACHOW—*ZION*** (715)758-8978
Steven D Hyvonen • NW • N 4431 County F 54182 PO Box 33 Zachow WI 54182-0033

## WYOMING

**BIG PINEY—*PEACE***
See Marbleton

**BUFFALO—*PRINCE PEACE*** (307)684-5470
Kirk L Peters • H • WY • 1200 Fort St Buffalo WY 82834-2407

**BURNS—*IMMANUEL*** (307)245-3390
Bradley D Heinecke • WS 11;* • WY • 203 S Washington 82053 C/O Grace English Lutheran Ch PO Box 670 Pine Bluffs WY 82082

**CASPER—*MOUNT HOPE*** (307)234-8428
John E Hill • H • EC/EL • WY • 2300 S Hickory St Casper WY 82604-3430 • mthope@trib.com

***TRINITY*** (307)234-0568
David A Boehnke • WS 9; SS 1015; BC 1015 • H • WY • 1240 S Missouri Ave Casper WY 82609-2924

**CHEYENNE—*KING OF GLORY*** (307)632-1247
Mark J Maas • WS 845; SS 10;* • H • WY • 8806 Yellowstone Rd Cheyenne WY 82009-1132 • FAX(307)632-0609 • mmaas@wyoming.com

***OUR SAVIOR*** (307)632-2580
Richard O Boche Joel P Fritsche • WS 8 1030; SS 915; BC 915;* • H • EC • WY • 5101 Dell Range Blvd Cheyenne WY 82009-5653 • oslc.@sisna.com

***TRINITY*** (307)635-2802
David A Caspersen Michael W Barnes • WS 8 1045; SS 930; BC 930;* • H • EC/EL • WY • 1111 E 22nd St Cheyenne WY 82001-3932 • FAX(307)778-0799

**CODY—*CHRIST KING*** (307)587-5680
Timothy D Klug • WS 9; SS 1015; BC 1015 • H • EC • WY • 1207 Stampede Ave 82414-4223 PO Box 355 Cody WY 82414-0355

**CROWHEART—*CROWHEART**** (307)332-4537
Vernon C Boehlke(DM) • WY • 82512 PO Box 416 Fort Washakie WY 82514-0416 • vboehlke@wyoming.com

**DOUGLAS—*ZION*** (307)358-2810
Vacant • H • EC • WY • 601 S 9th St Douglas WY 82633-2704

**DUBOIS—*MOUNT CALVARY*** (307)455-2733
Sam J Christensen • H • WY • 516 W Ramshorn 82513 PO Box 707 Dubois WY 82513-0707 • revsjc@juno.com

**EMBLEM—*ZION*** (307)765-2878
Lowell N Kayser • WS 11;* • H • WY • PO Box 70 Emblem WY 82422

**EVANSTON—*OUR SAVIOUR*** (307)789-0042
Jonathan G Lange • WS 9; SS 1030; BC 1030 • H • WY • 49 Straight And Narrow Dr Evanston WY 82930-4880 • jglange@allwest.net

**FORT BRIDGER—*SHEP OF VALLEY*** (307)782-6802
Daniel L Mulholland • H • WY • 306 Uinta County Rd 224 82933 PO Box 280 Fort Bridger WY 82933-0280

**FORT WASHAKIE—*CROWHEART****
See Crowheart

***WIND RIVER**** (307)332-4537
Vacant • WY • 14695 Us 287 N 82514 PO Box 416 Fort Washakie WY 82514-0416 • vboehlke@wyoming.com

**GILLETTE—*FAITH*** (307)682-7227
Randy K Asburry • WS 8;* • H • WY • 7103 Robin Dr Gillette WY 82718 • faith@vcn.com

***TRINITY*** (307)682-4886
Nathan M Brandt Scott G Firminhac • WS 8 930 11;* • H • EC • WY • 1001 E 9th St 82716-4502 PO Box 485 Gillette WY 82717-0485 • FAX(307)686-0365 • trinity@vcn.com

**GLENROCK—*OUR REDEEMER*** (307)436-8691
Vacant • H • WY • 939 W Birch 82637 PO Box 884 Glenrock WY 82637-0884

**GREEN RIVER—*EMMANUEL*** (307)875-2598
Paul J Cain Jr. • WS 930;* • H • WY • 901 Trona Dr Green River WY 82935-4046

**GREYBULL—*GRACE*** (307)765-2866
Lowell N Kayser • WS 9; BC 8;* • H • WY • 501 6th Ave N 82426-1833 PO Box 309 Greybull WY 82426-0309

**HANNA—*GRACE*** (307)325-6747
Lee A Wisroth • * • H • WY • Second And Main 82327 PO Box 53 Hanna WY 82327-0053 • wizzy@union-tel.com

**JACKSON—*REDEEMER*** (307)733-3409
Matthew M Richardt • * • H • WY • 275 N Willow 83002 PO Box 1016 Jackson WY 83001-1016 • FAX(307)733-3409 • redeemer@wyoming.com

**KEMMERER—*ST PAUL*** (307)877-4210
Jonathan M Vanderhyde • WS 9; SS 10 • H • WY • Sage And Opal Sts 83101 PO Box 472 Kemmerer WY 83101-0472 • FAX(307)877-4210 • jvhyde@allwest.net

**LANDER—*BETHEL*** (307)332-4320
Donald L Johnson • WS 930; BC 830;* • H • WY • 626 Shoshone St Lander WY 82520-3626 • bethellutheran@wyoming.com

**LARAMIE—*ST ANDREW*** (307)745-5892
Marcus T Zill • WS 10; BC 845;* • H • WY • 1309 E Grand Ave Laramie WY 82070-4137 • pastor@standrewslcms.org

***ZION*** (307)745-9262
Shawn L Kumm • Karen L Gabriel DCE • * • H • WY • 406 S 19th St Laramie WY 82070-4308 • FAX(307)745-9262 • lcmszion@usa.net

**LOVELL—*ST JOHN*** (307)548-7127
Christopher Brandt • * • H • WY • 70 E 5th St Lovell WY 82431-1902 • FAX(307)548-7127

**LUSK—*ST PAUL*** (307)334-2336
Vacant • H • WY • Fifth And S Linn 82225 PO Box 1245 Lusk WY 82225-1245 • bschroed@wyoming.com

**MARBLETON—*PEACE*** (307)276-3843
Donald E Storrud • * • H • WY • 1st And Winkelman 83113 PO Box 674 Big Piney WY 83113-0674 • dostorr@wyoming.com

**MOORCROFT—*BETHLEHEM*** (307)756-9452
Vacant • WY • 204 W Goshen St 82721 PO Box 190 Moorcroft WY 82721-0190 • FAX(307)686-0365 • nbrandt@wyoming.com

**PINE BLUFFS—*GRACE ENGLISH*** (307)245-3390
Bradley D Heinecke • WS 930;* • WY • 417 W Eighth 82082 PO Box 670 Pine Bluffs WY 82082-0670

**PINEDALE—*OUR SAV!OR*** (307)367-2612
Donald E Storrud • H • WY • 512 N Tyler 82941 PO Box 148 Pinedale WY 82941-0148 • dostorr@wyoming.com

**POWELL—*IMMANUEL*** (307)754-3168
Larry A Veland • WS 9; SS 1015; BC 1015 • H • EC • WY • 223 E 5th St Powell WY 82435-1906 • immanuel@wavecom.net

**RAWLINS—*CHRIST*** (307)324-4168
Terry W Wiley • * • H • WY • Colorado And Kendrick 82301 Box 397 Rawlins WY 82301-0397 • clc@trib.com

**RIVERTON—*TRINITY*** (307)856-9340
Daniel C Praeuner Bret Schroeder • H • EC/EL • WY • 419 E Park Ave Riverton WY 82501-3650 • FAX(307)856-9454 • tls@trib.com

**ROCK SPRINGS—*TRINITY*** (307)362-5088
Daniel G Holthus • WS 8; SS 915; BC 915 • EC • WY • 1001 9th St Rock Springs WY 82901-5414 • trinitylcrs@allwest.net

**SARATOGA—*PLATTE VALLEY*** (307)326-5449
Lee A Wisroth • WS 9; SS 1010; BC 1010;* • H • WY • 513 S 1st 82331 PO Box 385 Saratoga WY 82331-0385 • wizzy@union-tel.com

**SHERIDAN—*IMMANUEL*** (307)674-6434
William C Heine • * • H • WY • 1300 W 5th St Sheridan WY 82801-2704 • FAX(307)674-6435 • sgodwin@wyoming.com

**SUNDANCE—*MOUNT CALVARY*** (307)283-1170
Vacant • WY • 706 S Fourth St 82729 PO Box 6 Sundance WY 82729-0006

**THERMOPOLIS—*ST PAUL*** (307)864-2205
John M Christensen • WS 9; SS 1030; BC 1030;* • H • WY • 288 Hwy 20 S Thermopolis WY 82443-2726 • jchriste@wyoming.com

**TORRINGTON—*OUR SAVIOR*** (307)532-5801
Marvin L Temme • WS 9; SS 1015; BC 1015 • H • EC • WY • 2973 E B St Torrington WY 82240-2039

**WHEATLAND—*TRINITY*** (307)322-3291
David L Anderson • WS 9;* • H • WY • 1004 Willow St 82201-2114 PO Box 216 Wheatland WY 82201-0216 • FAX(307)322-3896 • daanders@wyoming.com

**WORLAND—*ST LUKE*** (307)347-2293
Lee E Rupert • H • WY • 525 S 6th St Worland WY 82401-3910 • sllc@trib.com

**WRIGHT—*HOPE*** (307)464-0373
Randy K Asburry • WS 1030;* • H • WY • 357 Willow Creek Dr 82732 PO Box 147 Wright WY 82732-0147

## BAHAMAS

**NASSAU—*NASSAU*** (242)323-4107
Samuel M Boodle • WS 11;* • H • FG • 119 John F Kennedy Dr PO Box N-4794 Nassau • FAX(242)323-4107

## ONTARIO CANADA

**AURORA—*CHRIST*** (905)727-3311
Milford C Murray • EN • 7 Lacey Ct Aurora ON L4G 5H2

**BRADFORD—*HOLY TRINITY*** (705)775-3412
Paul G Jamnicky • S • 53 Miller Park Ave Bradford ON L3Z 1M7 • FAX(705)436-7518

**CHATHAM—*OUR SAVIOUR*** (519)352-1860
Mark S Story • H • S • 445 Mc Naughton Ave W Chatham ON N7L 4K3 • FAX(519)352-2175

**KINGSVILLE—*NATIVITY*** (313)838-0854
Vacant • S • 21 Spruce St Kingsville ON N9Y 1G2

**KITCHENER—*HOPE*** (519)893-5290
Richard A Thrift • * • EN • 30 Shaftsbury Dr Kitchener ON N2A 1N6 • FAX(519)579-4595 • hopelc@myrealbox.com

**MISSISSAUGA—*ST MARK*** (905)278-2122
Vacant • H • EC • EN • 130 Mineola Rd E Mississauga ON L5G 2E5 • FAX(905)278-6751

**MITCHELL—*GRACE*** (519)348-9082
Joshua T Ball • * • EN • 108 St David St PO Box 607 Mitchell ON N0K 1N0 • FAX(519)348-4676

**NORTH YORK—*ST LUKE*** (416)221-8900
J Derek Mathers Dusan Toth • * • H • EN • 3200 Bayview North York ON M2M 3R7 • FAX(416)221-8685 • stluke@idirect.ca

**PEMBROKE—*ST JOHN*** (613)735-6332
Edward F Radke • * • H • EN • 357 Miller St Pembroke ON K8A 5Y8 • FAX(613)735-6741 • stjohnspembroke@on.aibn.com

**SARNIA—*REDEEMER*** (519)337-6615
Roger C Ellis • H • EN • 429 Indian Rd N Sarnia ON N7T 7G3 • FAX(519)337-1750

**SCARBOROUGH—*ST MATTHEW*** (416)431-9252
Vacant • * • H • EN • 3159 Lawrence Ave E Scarborough ON M1H 1A1 • FAX(416)431-4729 • st.matthews@on.aibn.com

**TORONTO—*ST JOHN*** (416)536-3108
Michael P Drews • EN • 274 Concord Ave Toronto ON M6H 2P5 • FAX(416)536-3108

***ST PAUL*** (416)656-5259
Ladislav P Kozak • S • 1442 Davenport Rd Toronto ON M6H 2H8 • 1pkozak@sympatico.ca

**WINDSOR—*GETHSEMANE*** (519)969-7561
Robert E Voelker • * • H • EN • 1921 Cabana Rd W Windsor ON N9G 1C7 • FAX(519)969-0747 • rev@mnsi.net

***PEACE*** (519)945-1344
Arthur W Schiemann • * • H • EN • 1985 Rossini Blvd 1971 Rossini Blvd Windsor ON N8W 4P6 • FAX(519)945-5811 • partsch41@hotmail.com

## QUEBEC CANADA

**MONTREAL—*ASCENSION*** (514)272-8570
Mark N Koehler • WS 9; SS 1115; BC 8;* • S • 865 Jarry St W Montreal PQ H3N 1G8 • FAX(514)948-6006 • mkoehler@ascensionchurch.ca

## HONG KONG

**REPULSE BAY—*OF ALL NATIONS*** 011-852-2812-0375
Dale A Koehneke • WS 1015;* • H • NOW • 8 South Bay Close Repulse Bay • FAX011-852-2812-9508 • can@hkis.edu.hk

# MINISTERS OF RELIGION—ORDAINED

Corrected to October 18, 2000

Individuals on this listing were on the official ordained member roster of the Synod as of the above date, i.e., held membership in the Synod in conformity with Articles V and VI of the Constitution of The Lutheran Church–Missouri Synod.

Any congregation or other calling entity must contact the appropriate district president to find out whether an individual whose name is listed in this section is currently eligible for a call or service in the church.

Ordained Minster records are formatted in the following order:

Name, mailing address, phone number, e-mail, district, position held, where serving, an asterisk (*) indicates that he is serving in more positions, or status EM or CAND (See NOTE)), office phone number

In parenthesis: (Rostering Entity, Year of graduation or colloquy, and graduate degrees).

NOTE: If a minister is on Candidate status, the month and year such status was granted will appear in place of position held. Those individuals whose CAND status was extended one additional year by the Council of Presidents (Handbook, Bylaw 2.19) will be listed with two dates, the initial month and year candidate status was granted and the month and year on which the one-year extension was given.

## KEY TO ABBREVIATIONS

Candidate (CAND) =a minister who is not currently performing the duties of any of the offices of ministry specified in Bylaw 2.15, and is eligible to do so.

Emeritus (EM)= retired

### Rostering Entity

BY=Bethany, Mankato, MN (ELC)
CL=Columbus, OH (ALC)
CS=Christ Seminary (AELC)
ED=Edmonton (LCC)
EU=European schools
FW=Fort Wayne, IN (LCMS)
GE=Gettysburg, PA (LCA)
GB=Greensboro, NC (LCMS)
HK=Hong Kong (LCMS)
KO=Korea (LCMS)
LS=Luther Theo. Sem., St. Paul, MN (ALC/ELCA)
LT=Lutheran Theo. Sem., Phil., PA (LCA)
M=Bethany, Mankato, MN (ELS)
ME=Mequon, WI (WELS)
(before 1962 Thiensville)
MX=Monterrey, Mex. (LSM)
NG=Papua New Guinea
PA=Porto Alegre, Brazil (ELCB)
PC=Berkeley, CA (LCA)
SC=St. Catharines, ON (LCC)
SK=Saskatoon, SK (LCA/ELCC)
SL=St. Louis, MO (LCMS)
SPR=Springfield, IL (LCMS)
TH=Thiensville, WI (WELS)
TR=Trinity, Columbus, OH (ALC/ELCA)
TW=Taiwan (LCMS)
VB=Villa Ballester, Argentina (LCMS)
WB=Wartburg, Dubuque, IA (ALC)
WH=Westfield House Cambridge, Eng. (ELCE)
AR=Alternate Route
CQ=Colloquized
CSCQ=Christ Seminary, Approved by Colloquy Committee

### Position Titles

Assoc=Associate Pastor
Asst=Assistant Pastor
Aux=Auxiliary Ministry
CC P=Campus Congregation Pastor
CCRA=Cooperative Church Related Agency
Cmp P=Campus Pastor
D Adm=District Administrator
D Ex/S=District Executive or Staff
Df Min=Deaf Missionary
D Miss=District Missionary
END=Endorsed by Synod
IndC P=Independent Congregation Pastor
Inst C=Institutional Chaplain
LHS=Lutheran High School Faculty or Staff
M Chap=Military Chaplain/Dir of Rel Ed
O-Miss=Other Missionary
O-Sp Min=Other Special Ministry
P Df=Pastor to Deaf
RSO=Recognized Service Organization
S Adm=Synodical Administrator
S Ex/S=Synodical Executive or Staff
S HS/C=Synodical High School/College/Univ/Seminary
S Miss=Synodical Missionary
Sn/Adm=Senior or Administrative Pastor
SP=Sole Pastor
Sp S=Special School or Spec Lutheran Classes

### Missouri Synod Districts

AT=Atlantic
CNH=Calif.-Nev.-Hawaii
CI=Central Illinois
EA=Eastern
EN=English
FG=Florida-Georgia
IN=Indiana
IE=Iowa East
IW=Iowa West
KS=Kansas
MI=Michigan
MDS=Mid-South
MNN=Minnesota North
MNS=Minnesota South
MO=Missouri
MT=Montana
NE=New England
NEB=Nebraska
ND=North Dakota
NJ=New Jersey
NW=North Wisconsin
NI=Northern Illinois
NOW=Northwest
OH=Ohio
OK=Oklahoma
PSW=Pacific Southwest
RM=Rocky Mountain
S=SELC District
SD=South Dakota
SE=Southeastern
SI=Southern Illinois
SO=Southern
SW=South Wisconsin
TX=Texas
WY=Wyoming

## A

**ABATIE RODGER P REV** (913)648-4260
10001 Roe Ave Overland Park KS 57105-7109 • revabatie@ntslink.net • CI • Sn/Adm • Trinity Pekin IL • (309)346-1391 • (FW 1977 MA MDIV)

**ABBOTT NORMAN V REV** (210)696-5275
3430 Quakertown Dr San Antonio TX 78230-3338 • nabbott3430@juno.com • TX • EM • (SL 1941)

**ABBOTT WILLIAM BROCK REV** (217)877-5413
2155 N Oakland Ave Decatur IL 62526 • CI • Assoc • Pilgrim Decatur IL • (217)877-2444 • (FW 1992 MDIV)

**ABBOTT WILLIAM K REV** (217)875-1115
2 Dakota Dr Decatur IL 62526-2331 • CI • Sn/Adm • Pilgrim Decatur IL • (217)877-2444 • (SPR 1976 MDIV)

**ABEL ARNOLD J REV** (541)753-2939
32483 Oakville Rd SW Spc 17 Albany OR 97321-9439 • NOW • EM • (SL 1939)

**ABEL LOUIS H REV** (954)493-8204
730 NE 47th Ct Oakland Park FL 33334-3230 • louisabel@aol.com • FG • SP • Trinity Fort Lauderdale FL • (954)463-2450 • (CQ 1983 MAR)

**ABERNATHY ROGER GLEN REV** (507)238-9335
112 Linden Dr Fairmont MN 56031-2179 • pastora@bevcomm.net • MNS • Sn/Adm • St Paul Fairmont MN • (507)238-9491 • (FW 1992 MDIV)

**ABERNETHY RALPH ADOLPHUS REV** (573)431-4552
700 S School St Desloge MO 63601-3636 • raasga@i1.net • MO • SP • Trinity Park Hills MO • (573)431-3442 • (FW 1996 MDIV)

**ABRAHAM MARK W REV** (712)284-1443
165 630th St Alta IA 51002-7447 • IW • SP • St John Alta IA • (712)284-1450 • (FW 1999 MDIV)

**ABRAHAM STANLEY R REV** (408)685-3052
3005 Mar Vista Dr Aptos CA 95003-3652 • sabraham@cruzio.com • CNH • SP • Mount Calvary Soquel CA • (831)475-6962 • (SL 1972 MA MDIV)

**ABRAHAMS DAN C REV** (218)847-1083
1348 Pelican Ln Detroit Lakes MN 56501-8901 • abefam@lakesnet.net • MNN • Assoc • Zion Detroit Lakes MN • (218)847-7630 • (SL 1971 MDIV)

**ABRAM HENRY C REV** (561)286-5594
7905 SE Federal Hwy Hobe Sound FL 33455-7012 • bethelluthchurch@aol.com • FG • SP • Bethel Hobe Sound FL • (561)546-5399 • (SL 1950 MDIV)

**ABRAM MARK H REV** (920)991-0411
3405 N Mariah Ln Appleton WI 54911 • NW • Assoc • Faith Appleton WI • (920)739-9191 • (SL 1982 MDIV)

**ABRAM MICHAEL R REV** (408)267-7345
3096 Brunetti Pl San Jose CA 95125-6300 • michael@holycrosslosgatos.org • CNH • Asst • Holy Cross Los Gatos CA • (408)356-3525 • (SL 1998 MDIV MS)

**ACKERMAN JAMES L REV** (810)749-9738
28706 27 Mile Rd New Haven MI 48048-1769 • jjackerman@cov.com • MI • EM • (SL 1957)

**ACTON THOMAS R REV** (414)427-7151
8781 West Lake Pointe Dr Franklin WI 53132 • acton@splcwa.org • SW • Sn/Adm • St Paul West Allis WI • (414)541-6250 • (FW 1979 MED MDIV)

**ADAIR CLIFFORD REV** (217)229-4434
C/O Trinity Luth Church PO Box 207 Harvel IL 62538-0207 • cadair@cillnet.com • SI • SP • Trinity Harvel IL • (217)229-3143 • (SL 1987 MDIV)

**ADAM WILLIAM W REV** (217)732-9127
315 Williamette Ave Lincoln IL 62656-3026 • CI • EM • (SPR 1959)

**ADAMS CHARLES W REV** (785)822-0642
2601 E Key Ave Salina KS 67401-7649 • revcwa@aol.com • KS • Assoc • Trinity Salina KS • (785)823-7151 • (SL 1986 MDIV)

**ADAMS DANIEL J REV** (360)263-5266
C/O Memorial Luth Church 2700 E 28th St Vancouver WA 98661-4528 • dan@mlc.org • NOW • Assoc • Memorial Vancouver WA • (360)695-7501 • (SK 1984 MDIV)

**ADAMS DAVID C REV**
10429 Bitterroot Ct Fort Wayne IN 46804 • IN • Assoc • Mount Calvary Fort Wayne IN • (219)747-4121 • (SL 1991 MDIV)

**ADAMS DAVID L DR** (314)505-7144
C/O Concordia Seminary 801 De Mun Ave St Louis MO 63105 • adamsd@csl.edu • MO • SHS/C • Missouri Saint Louis MO • (314)317-4550 • (SL 1981 MDIV MST PHD)

**ADAMS MARK E REV** (541)567-8874
1205 S First St Hermiston OR 97838 • NOW • SP • Bethlehem Hermiston OR • (541)567-6811 • (FW 1989 MDIV)

**ADAMS RAYMOND H REV** (605)399-9575
2404 Maple Ave Rapid City SD 57701-7156 • SD • SP • Our Redeemer Rapid City SD • (605)388-0032 • (FW 1984 MDIV)

**ADAMS RICKY L REV** (510)538-4829
1838 B St Hayward CA 94541 • revlipps@aol.com • CNH • SP • Grace Hayward CA • (510)581-6620 • (SL 1985 MDIV)

**ADAMSON TERRANCE SEAN REV**
PO Box 98 Mustang OK 73064 • tadamson@cleanweb.net • OK • SP • Christ Mustang OK • (405)376-3116 • (SL 1992 MDIV STM)

**ADE FRED C REV** (312)884-6926
216 E Schaumburg Rd Schaumburg IL 60194-3517 • NI • Assoc • St Peter Schaumburg IL • (847)885-3350 • (SPR 1969 BCHE)

**ADER KEVIN K REV** (906)663-4995
E8193 Sanders Rd Bessemer MI 49911-9706 • preachermankev@netscape.net • NW • SP • Our Redeemer Bessemer MI* • (906)663-4318 • (FW 1991 MDIV)

**ADLER DAVID L REV** (281)443-2304
21434 E Hardy Rd Houston TX 77073-2200 • adlerdavidl@aol.com • TX • SP • St Matthew Westfield Houston TX • (281)443-2304 • (SL 1979 MDIV)

**ADOLF DONALD E REV** (316)465-3423
8609 E Arlington Rd Haven KS 67543-8187 • KS • SP • St Paul Haven KS • (316)465-3427 • (FW 1989 MDIV)

**AHART NEAL K REV** (417)847-2885
407 Merideth St Cassville MO 65625-4106 • MO • EM • (CQ 1978 MDIV)

**AHL DENNIS C REV** (612)824-7992
5701 10th Ave S Minneapolis MN 55417-2405 • MNS • Sn/Adm • Mount Zion Minneapolis MN • (612)824-1882 • (SL 1968)

**AHL KENNETH L REV** (414)786-0533
21825 Locksley Ln Brookfield WI 53045-4719 • SE • EM • (SL 1932 MDIV DD)

**AHLBORN MARVIN J REV** (920)232-1634
2660 Templeton Pl Oshkosh WI 54904-8314 • SW • SP • Trinity Oshkosh WI • (920)235-7440 • (CQ 1983 MDIV)

**AHLEMEYER ERIC M REV** (970)544-6785
1235 Mountain View Dr Aspen CO 81611 • RM • SP • Messiah Aspen CO • (970)925-7725 • (FW 2000 MDIV)

**AHLEMEYER TERRY L REV** (920)725-3868
1223 Lynrose Ln Neenah WI 54956-4277 • tahlemeyer@excite.com • SW • SP • Peace Neenah WI • (920)725-0510 • (CQ 1979 MA)

**AHLERSMEYER STEVEN M REV** (219)492-5580
5234 W Arlington Park Blvd Fort Wayne IN 46835 • stevena@one.net • IN • Sn/Adm • St Peter Fort Wayne IN • (219)749-5816 • (FW 1989 MDIV)

**AHLERSMEYER THOMAS R REV** (216)227-2190
14805 Detroit Ave Ste 250 Lakewood OH 44107-3921 • jlatra@aol.com • OH • Tchr • LHS West Rocky River OH • (440)333-1660 • (FW 1979 MDIV PHD)

**AHLMAN DAVID J REV** (303)940-7199
14292 W 70th Pl Arvada CO 80004-5905 • RM • Sn/Adm • Peace Arvada CO • (303)424-4454 • (FW 1983 MDIV)

**AHLSCHWEDE DALE C REV** (517)652-6852
1020 W Tuscola St Frankenmuth MI 48734-9101 • dahlschwede@stlorenz.org • MI • Assoc • St Lorenz Frankenmuth MI • (517)652-6141 • (SPR 1972 MDIV)

**AHO ORVILLE E REV** (218)825-8474
1271 Chrestnut Dr S Baxter MN 56425 • MNN • EM • (SPR 1947)

**AHRENS DANIEL L REV** (715)332-5157
W1018 Old Lodge Ln Winter WI 54896 • mdahrens@win.bright.net • NW • EM • (SPR 1960 MDIV)

**AHRENS WAYNE J REV** (515)465-3272
C/O Trinity Lutheran Church 2715 Iowa St Perry IA 50220-2414 • trinity@iowalink.com • IW • SP • Trinity Perry IA • (515)465-3272 • (FW 1990 MDIV)

**AKERS BARRY ALLEN REV** (765)457-5539
3608 E 100 S Kokomo IN 46902 • pastorakers@redeemerkokomo.org • IN • Asst • Our Redeemer Kokomo IN • (765)453-0969 • (SL 1991 MDIV)

**ALB LARRY A REV** (213)226-4945
Psychiatric Hospital-USC 1937 Hospital Pl Los Angeles CA 90033 • PSW • 06/1991 06/2000 • (FW 1982 MDIV MD DMIN)

**ALBACH WILLIAM H REV** (509)928-5333
722 N Burns Rd Spokane WA 99216-4005 • billa@on-ramp.ior.com • NOW • EM • (SL 1938 MA)

**ALBERS DAVID P REV** (715)423-1759
C/O St Luke Luth Church 2011 10th St S Wisconsin Rapids WI 54494-6302 • djalbers@tznet.com • NW • Assoc • St Luke Wisconsin Rapids WI • (715)423-5990 • (SL 1984 MDIV)

**ALBERS DUANE K REV** (941)723-3180
6401 64th Ln E Palmetto FL 34221 • FG • SP • Faith Parrish FL • (941)776-1395 • (SPR 1970)

**ALBERS JAMES W REV** (219)462-4640
303 Highland Dr Valparaiso IN 46383-1925 • jim.albers@valpo.edu • IN • END • Indiana Fort Wayne IN • (SL 1963 MDIV STM THD)

**ALBERS JOHN M REV** (219)462-4029
1206 Napoleon St Valparaiso IN 46383-3432 • fmlc@niia.net • IN • SP • Faith Memorial Valparaiso IN • (219)462-7684 • (SL 1989 MDIV)

**ALBERS KENNETH L REV** (715)536-9797
2705 Crescent Dr Merrill WI 54452-3235 • pka34@aol.com • NW • Sn/Adm • Trinity Merrill WI • (715)536-5482 • (SL 1980 MDIV)

**ALBERS PAUL J REV** (501)915-0293
16 Macotera Pl Hot Springs Village AR 71909 • paulruth@mail.com • MDS • EM • (SL 1962 MDIV DMIN)

**ALBERS RONALD W P REV** (262)786-5272
620 Hi View Ct Elm Grove WI 53122 • albersrw@aol.com • SW • EM • (SPR 1960 MDIV)

**ALBERS STEVEN H REV** (314)965-6578
2250 Ferncliff Ln Kirkwood MO 63122-5117 • alberssteven@hotmail.com • MO • SP • Glendale Saint Louis MO • (314)966-3220 • (SL 1970 MDIV MA)

**ALBERS VICTOR G REV** (516)354-8471
222 Carlton Ter Garden City NY 11530-5027 • AT • EM • (SL 1939 MDIV MA)

**ALBERS WALTER F REV** (254)799-4661
1309 Crestline St Waco TX 76705-2505 • stpaul@iamerica.net • TX • Sn/Adm • St Paul Waco TX • (254)799-3211 • (SPR 1971)

**ALBERT GARY M REV** (715)384-2855
1125 Ridge Rd Marshfield WI 54449-1214 • NW • Tchr • Immanuel Marshfield WI • (715)384-5121 • (CQ 1982 MAR)

**ALBERTIN DAVID M DR** (216)874-5740
106 Pontiac Dr Michigan City IN 46360-2737 • david@cicinet.com • IN • SP • Immanuel Michigan City IN • (219)872-4048 • (SL 1965 MDIV PHD)

**ALBERTS BRUCE A REV** (918)453-9411
903 Cecelia Ave Tahlequah OK 74464 • OK • SP • First Tahlequah OK • (918)456-5070 • (SL 1999 MDIV)

**ALBRECHT ARDON D REV** (310)829-4113
C/O Pilgrim Luth Church 1730 Wilshire Blvd Santa Monica CA 90403-5510 • amenmail@aol.com • PSW • SP • Pilgrim Santa Monica CA • (310)829-4113 • (SL 1962 MDIV MS LITTD)

**ALBRECHT LUTHER G REV** (815)293-0934
632 Driftwood Ave Romeoville IL 60446 • albrechtlg@aol.com • NI • SP • Peace Chicago IL • (773)523-5790 • (SL 1967 MDIV)

**ALBRECHT PAUL G REV** (402)879-3631
837 N Dakota St Superior NE 68978-1203 • pa32112@alltel.net • NEB • SP • Centennial Superior NE • (402)879-3137 • (CQ 1993 MDIV)

**ALBRECHT THOMAS D REV** (515)573-5999
1311 25th Ave N Fort Dodge IA 50501-7228 • IW • EM • (FW 1979)

**ALBRECHT VERN H REV** (402)397-5350
1815 N 93rd Ct Omaha NE 68114-1203 • NEB • EM • (SL 1951)

**ALDRICH BRADLEY C** (972)731-8264
12103 Rosedown Ln Frisco TX 75035-7753 • TX • D Miss • Texas Austin TX • (SL 2000 MDIV)

**ALDRICH PAUL J REV** (507)373-8547
1918 Bayview Dr Albert Lea MN 56007-2131 • paldrich@smig.net • MNS • SP • Zion Albert Lea MN • (507)373-8609 • (SL 1985 MDIV)

**ALEMAN RAUL REV** (414)632-4592
PO Box 514 Sturtevant WI 53177-0514 • SW • EM • (CQ 1980 MDIV MST)

**ALEXANDER HOWARD M REV** (215)635-9240
16 Dewey Rd Cheltenham PA 19012 • revlite97@aol.com • EA • SP • St Philip Philadelphia PA • (215)878-2911 • (CQ 1997 MED)

**ALEXANDER PETER C REV** (619)226-0939
4329 Loma Riviera Ct San Diego CA 92110-5504 • pa676@compuserve.com • PSW • 08/1999 • (SL 1973 MDIV)

**ALEXANDER PHILLIP J REV** (978)342-6562
706 Rindge Rd Fitchburg MA 01420 • messiahlcms@aol.com • NE • SP • Messiah Fitchburg MA • (978)343-7397 • (FW 1999 MDIV)

**ALEXANDER ROBERT D REV** (580)363-4026
256 Russell St Blackwell OK 74631 • pastor³bob³o³link@yahoo.com • OK • SP • Trinity Blackwell OK • (580)363-4026 • (SL 1985 MDIV)

**ALKIRE BRUCE C REV** (704)652-4277
15 Viewpoint Dr Marion NC 28752-3766 • SE • SP • St Matthew Marion NC • (704)652-7699 • (CQ 1989)

**ALLAN KENNETH H REV** (931)707-7304
122 Cromwell Ln Crossville TN 38558-7144 • marken@usit.net • MDS • EM • (SL 1957 MA)

**ALLEN DAVID A REV** (217)586-7223
212 Evergreen Ct Mahomet IL 61853 • therev@juno.com • CI • D Miss • Christ Family Mahomet IL • (217)586-7022 • (SPR 1973 MDIV)

**ALLEN FRED H REV**
305 Mohnton Lawn Ct Mohnton PA 19540-1342 • IN • 09/1999 • (SL 1968 MDIV)

**ALLEN MICHAEL S REV** (517)674-8656
6374 Marvin Unionville MI 48767-9701 • pastora@avci.net • MI • SP • St Paul Unionville MI • (517)674-8681 • (FW 1984 MDIV)

**ALLEN RICHARD B REV**
PO Box 1827 Palmer AK 99645-1827 • NOW • EM • (SL 1959)

**ALLISON WILLIAM S REV** (765)457-0346
1201 Arundel Dr Kokomo IN 46901-3920 • lcor@netusal.net • IN • Sn/Adm • Our Redeemer Kokomo IN • (765)453-0969 • (SL 1981 MDIV)

**ALLMANN JOHN A REV** (970)330-7465
3324 W 26th St Greeley CO 80634 • jamlka@aol.com • RM • EM • (SL 1959 MDIV)

**ALLMANN ROBERT F REV** (517)879-5204
4513 N Mackinaw Rd Pinconning MI 48650 • MI • SP • St John Pinconning MI • (517)879-2377 • (SPR 1972 MDIV)

**ALLSHOUSE WILLIAM N REV** (303)457-9023
13158 Bellaire Ct Thornton CO 80241-2299 • ltcch@uswest.net • RM • SP • Summit Peace Brighton CO • (303)452-0448 • (FW 1978 MDIV)

**ALLSING RICHARD C REV** (619)462-2561
6100 Samuel St La Mesa CA 91942-2556 • rcalls@home.com • PSW • SP • St Paul San Diego CA • (619)272-6363 • (SL 1966 MDIV)

**ALLWARDT THEODORE E SR. REV** (505)894-3103
C/O St John Luth Church 1405 Tin St Truth Consq NM 87901-3659 • RM • SP • St John Truth/Consequences NM • (505)894-3103 • (SL 1958)

**ALLWARDT WILLIAM H REV** (517)686-4273
3903 Sequin Dr Bay City MI 48706-2045 • zionlth@concentric.net • MI • Sn/Adm • Zion Bay City MI • (517)894-2611 • (SPR 1973 MDIV)

**ALLYN ERIC F REV** (630)752-0847
1613 Burning Trl Wheaton IL 60187 • efallyn@cin.net • NI • Assoc • St John Wheaton IL • (630)668-0701 • (FW 1978 MDIV)

**ALMS MAURICE H REV**
PO Box 448 Livingston IL 62058-0448 • SI • SP • Holy Cross Livingston IL • (618)637-2146 • (SL 1972 STM)

**ALMS PAUL GREGORY REV** (828)241-2373
C/O Redeemer Lutheran Church PO Box 187 Catawba NC 28609-0187 • SE • SP • Redeemer Catawba NC • (828)241-2371 • (FW 1992 MDIV)

**ALMS RICHARD L REV** (410)465-1621
2198 Mount Hebron Ct Ellicott City MD 21042-1848 • SE • Southeastern Alexandria VA • (SL 1960 MDIV MED PHD)

**ALMSTEDT QUENTIN P REV** (636)922-9322
1616 Burnside Ln St Charles MO 63303-8437 • MO • EM • (SPR 1969 MA MDIV)

**ALPERS ARLIN E REV** (816)322-5287
209 W Laredo Trl Raymore MO 64083-8517 • MO • EM • (SL 1953)

**ALSLEBEN ROBERT L REV** (414)604-1545
12016 W Verona Ct West Allis WI 53227-3868 • balsleben@aol.com • EN • SP • Ebenezer Milwaukee WI • (414)383-0710 • (SL 1968 MDIV)

**ALSOP DANIEL T REV** (661)822-7333
349 Holly Dr Tehachapi CA 93561 • alsop@bnis.com • PSW • SP • Good Shepherd Tehachapi CA • (661)822-6817 • (FW 1987 MDIV MMFC)

**ALSPAUGH CHARLES E REV** (716)352-1443
PO Box 92 Spencerport NY 14559-0092 • EA • SP • Trinity Spencerport NY • (716)352-3143 • (SPR 1968 MDIV)

**ALTENBERGER ROGER K REV** (319)377-0999
339 Windsor Dr NE Cedar Rapids IA 52402-1570 • meka5@prodigy.net • IE • P Df • Word Of God Df Cedar Rapids IA • (319)362-5420 • (FW 1995 MDIV)

**ALTER ANTHONY A REV** (573)761-5710
2015 Autumn Ln Jefferson City MO 65109-1801 • aaalter@juno.com • MO • SP • Faith Jefferson City MO • (573)636-4602 • (SL 1991 MDIV)

**ALTHOFF ALBERT F JR. REV** (605)296-3230
C/O Zion Luth Church RR 1 Box 4 Canistota SD 57012-9701 • SD • SP • Zion Canistota SD* • (605)296-3166 • (CQ 1989 MAR)

**ALTHOFF CHARLES E REV** (440)466-4026
811 S Broadway Geneva OH 44041-9146 • turnip@ncweb.com • OH • SP • St John Geneva OH • (440)466-2473 • (FW 1979 MDIV)

**ALVARADO LUIS A REV**
2525 Alemany Blvd San Francisco CA 94112 • CNH • D Miss • Calif/Nevada/Hawaii San Francisco CA • (415)468-2336 • (CQ 2000)

**AMAN NORMAN REV** (517)836-2674
6325 Deepwood Dr Alger MI 48610-9376 • MI • EM • (SPR 1961 MDIV)

**AMEISS WILLIAM H REV** (630)668-7866
1119 Santa Rosa Ave Wheaton IL 60187-3830 • ni³ameisswh@ni.lcms.org • NI • DP • Northern Illinois Hillside IL* • (SPR 1963 MED)

**AMES RICHARD W REV** (414)637-9948
5521 Alburg Ave Racine WI 53406-1115 • camper@wi.net • EN • EM • * • (SPR 1956 MS)

**ANACKER ARTHUR W REV** (608)981-2503
N9603 Anacker Rd Portage WI 53901-8806 • SW • EM • * • (SPR 1962)

**ANCIRA MARIO E REV** (510)235-1775
5737 Ravine Way Richmond CA 94805 • mancira@earthlink.net • CNH • SP • Mount Zion Richmond CA • (510)233-2299 • (FW 1997 MDIV)

**ANDEREGG RICHARD MARK REV** (573)336-4339
991 Highway Z Saint Robert MO 65584 • anderegg@rollanet.org • MO • SP • Faith Saint Robert MO • (573)336-4464 • (SL 1996 MS MDIV)

**ANDERSEN MATHEW A REV**
295 Shaul Ave Ottumwa IA 52501-4915 • IE • SP • Trinity Ottumwa IA • (515)684-7279 • (FW 1988 MDIV)

**ANDERSEN NEIL E REV** (410)673-7107
PO Box 39 Preston MD 21655-0039 • andersenne@aol.com • SE • SP • Immanuel Preston MD • (410)673-7107 • (SL 1981 MDIV)

**ANDERSON ALLEN D REV** (970)945-2744
60 Cardinal Ln Glenwood Springs CO 81601-2702 • RM • SP • Holy Cross Glenwood Springs CO • (970)945-6871 • (FW 1981 MDIV)

**ANDERSON DARRYL A REV** (314)963-0482
122 Oak Tree Dr Saint Louis MO 63119-4760 • mrchappie@webtv.net • MO • Missouri Saint Louis MO • (314)317-4550 • (SPR 1972 MDIV)

**ANDERSON DAVID C REV** (309)787-3190
406 Bruce Ave Milan IL 61264-3355 • acxiv@geneseo.net • CI • SP • Beaut Savior Colona IL • (309)949-2111 • (FW 1993 MDIV)

**ANDERSON DAVID L REV**
1413 9th Ave North Fort Dodge IA 50501 • IE • EM • (SPR 1962)

**ANDERSON DAVID LYNN REV** (307)322-4969
1304 10th St Wheatland WY 82201-2312 • daanders@wyoming.com • WY • SP • Trinity Wheatland WY • (307)322-3291 • (FW 1990 MDIV)

**ANDERSON DAVID P REV** (507)238-4597
1210 N North Ave Fairmont MN 56031 • pastoranderson@yahoo.com • MNS • Sn/Adm • Immanuel Fairmont MN • (507)238-1387 • (LS 1981 MDIV)

**ANDERSON GARY M REV** (904)968-2773
426 Pinebrook Cir Cantonment FL 32533-7679 • SO • EM • (CQ 1985 MAR)

**ANDERSON HYLE R REV** (218)759-9273
2800 Arrowhead Cir NW Bemidji MN 56601-8276 • hyleand@paulbunyan.net • MNN • SP • Trinity Bemidji MN • (218)444-4441 • (FW 1979 MDIV)

**ANDERSON JEFFREY M REV** (402)375-4528
901 Logan St Wayne NE 68787-1448 • grace@bloomnel.com • NEB • Sn/Adm • Grace Wayne NE • (402)375-1905 • (SL 1988 MDIV)

**ANDERSON JEFFREY O REV** (330)922-4283
1834 Cromwell Dr Akron OH 44313 • janderson@sbstone.com • EN • 01/1992 01/2000 • (SL 1972 MDIV)

**ANDERSON JON K REV** (219)486-4212
4211 Meridith Dr Fort Wayne IN 46815-5136 • IN • Tchr • Concordia LHS Fort Wayne IN • (219)483-1102 • (FW 1990 MS MDIV)

**ANDERSON MARK A REV** (815)626-3990
2900 W Science Ridge Rd Sterling IL 61081-9315 • NI • Df Min • Northern Illinois Hillside IL • (SL 1986 MDIV)

**ANDERSON MARK BISHOP REV** (409)885-2780
920 Fowlkes St Sealy TX 77474-3421 • texasred@c-com.net • TX • Assoc • Trinity Sealy TX • (979)885-2211 • (SL 1996 MDIV)

**ANDERSON MARVIN C REV** (661)822-3123
20875 Oak St Tehachapi CA 93561-8814 • warbucks@cybersurfers.net • PSW • EM • (SPR 1962)

**ANDERSON MARVIN G REV** (313)529-2095
131 Kimberly Ln Dundee MI 48131-1333 • MI • EM • (SPR 1969 MDIV)

**ANDERSON PAUL NORMAN DR** (225)201-9043
645 N Parkview Pl Baton Rouge LA 70815-4442 • SO • SP • Good Shepherd Baton Rouge LA • (225)766-4610 • (SL 1991 MA MDIV PHD)

**ANDERSON PAUL W E REV** (215)242-0530
C/O Holy Cross Lutheran Church 500 E Mount Pleasant Ave Philadelphia PA 19119-1232 • panderson9.@aol.com • EN • Good Shepherd Baton Rouge LA • (225)766-4610 • (CQ 1982 MA)

**ANDERSON ROBERT L REV** (605)673-2981
504 Buckhorn Dr Custer SD 57730-1629 • SD • SP • Our Redeemer Custer SD* • (605)673-4361 • (SPR 1974 MDIV)

**ANDERSON STEVEN J REV** (773)581-5238
6147 South Mason Chicago IL 60638 • sjanders@juno.com • NI • SP • Messiah Chicago IL • (773)767-2727 • (SL 1999 MDIV)

**ANDERSON STEVEN L REV** (715)873-4565
C/O Luther Memorial Luth Ch PO Box 39 Gleason WI 54435-0039 • NW • SP • Luther Memorial Gleason WI • (715)873-4592 • (SPR 1974 MDIV)

**ANDERSON STEVEN LYLE REV** (316)231-2053
109 Westfield Rd Pittsburg KS 66762-8624 • zionpitt@grapevine.net • KS • SP • Zion Pittsburg KS • (316)231-4267 • (FW 1985 MDIV)

**ANDERSON TIMOTHY A REV** (608)356-5744
1210 Winnebago Cir Baraboo WI 53913-1283 • andrfam1@chorus.net • SW • SP • Our Savior Baraboo WI • (608)356-9792 • (FW 1993 MDIV MBA)

**ANDERSON TIMOTHY P REV** (502)327-9835
9801 Stonehenge Way Louisville KY 40222 • tpandrsn@aol.com • IN • Sn/Adm • Our Savior Louisville KY • (502)426-1130 • (CQ 1980 MDIV)

**ANDERSON WAYNE A REV** (760)253-2335
PO Box 412 Hinkley CA 92347-0412 • PSW • SP • Concordia Barstow CA • (760)256-2036 • (SPR 1975 MDIV)

**ANDERSON WAYNE B REV** (661)724-2386
PO Box 250 Lake Hughes CA 93532-0250 • PSW • SP • First Palmdale CA • (661)947-6230 • (FW 1981 MDIV)

**ANDRADA EDWARD B REV** (419)389-1879
C/O Trinity Lutheran Church 4560 Glendale Ave Toledo OH 43614-1907 • cnp³trnluth@mavca2.mavca.ohio.gov • OH • Assoc • Trinity Toledo OH • (419)385-2651 • (SL 1993 MDIV)

**ANDRAE ERIC R REV** (412)441-2487
5700 Bunkerhill St #702 Pittsburgh PA 15206-1166 • ericandrae@hotmail.com • EA • SP • St John Pittsburgh PA • (412)821-6266 • (SL 1997 MDIV)

**ANDRAJACK JOSEPH P JR. REV** (580)735-2381
407 Lucia Buffalo OK 73834 • OK • SP • Zion Buffalo OK • (580)735-2733 • (SL 1999 MDIV)

**ANDREASEN PHILL E REV** (712)336-6520
711 19th St Spirit Lake IA 51360-1507 • imluthsl@rconnect.com • IW • Sn/Adm • Immanuel Spirit Lake IA • (712)336-1010 • (SPR 1975 MDIV)

**ANDRESEN RONALD MERLE REV** (719)495-6572
15975 Herring Rd Black Forest CO 80908 • NW • 11/1999 • (CQ 1992 MDIV MDIV)

**ANDRIX DONALD L REV** (952)467-3788
18169 County Road 50 Hamburg MN 55339-9406 • donchery@gv2.com • MNS • SP • Emanuel Hamburg MN • (952)467-2788 • (SL 1973 MDIV)

**ANDRUS DAVID S REV** (314)822-1990
10235 Richview Dr Saint Louis MO 63127-1430 • dave.andrus@lcms.org • MO • S Ex/S • Missouri Saint Louis MO • (314)317-4550 • (SL 1985 MDIV)

**ANDRUS RICHARD W REV** (360)275-7314
5997 Broussard Ln W Bremerton WA 98312-9741 • NOW • SP • Memorial Bremerton WA • (360)377-0161 • (SL 1997 MDIV)

**ANDRZEJEWSKI DARRYL L REV** (810)778-4978
18494 Michael Ave Eastpointe MI 48021-1333 • skiwing@aol.com • MI • Assoc • St Thomas Eastpointe MI • (810)772-3370 • (FW 1993 MDIV)

**ANGLAND DENNIS W REV** (712)852-4235
1805 18th St Emmetsburg IA 50536-2153 • dwangland@ncn.net • IW • SP • St Paul Emmetsburg IA • (712)852-2367 • (SPR 1974 MDIV)

**ANGLE JOHN S REV** (248)476-5399
35967 Hardenburg Rd Farmington Hills MI 48331-3826 • MI • EM • (SL 1947 MA)

**ANGLIN DAVID W REV**
130 Union Ave Amityville NY 11701-3026 • AT • SP • St Paul Amityville NY • (516)264-0763 • (SL 1983 MDIV)

**ANKNEY RUEBEN J REV** (618)653-4649
PO Box 305 Kampsville IL 62053-0305 • sjlc@jvil.com • SI • SP • St John Kampsville IL* • (618)653-4649 • (FW 1989 MDIV)

**ANSON FREDERICK A REV** (419)531-2786
2540 N Holland Sylvania Rd Toledo OH 43615-2708 • gloriadeiluthch@juno.com • OH • SP • Gloria Dei Toledo OH • (419)536-2020 • (CQ 1981 MDIV)

**ANSORGE BERNARD H REV** (256)533-1218
2000 Joseph Cir NE Huntsville AL 35811-2418 • ansorgebh@aol.com • SO • SP • Ascension Huntsville AL • (256)536-9987 • (SL 1963 MDIV)

**ANTHONY DONALD EUGENE REV** (704)795-5475
C/O Grace Lutheran Church PO Box 891 Concord NC 28026-0891 • lebuick@aol.com • SE • SP • Grace Concord NC • (704)782-7620 • (SL 1988 MDIV)

**ANTHONY EDGAR O REV** (440)458-8605
18 Waterfall Dr Grafton OH 44044-1520 • S • SP • SS Peter&Paul Lorain OH • (216)233-5166 • (CQ 1995 MNS)

**ANTHONY JAMES W REV** (218)246-8154
C/O Redeemer Luth Church PO Box 606 Deer River MN 56636-0606 • MNN • SP • Redeemer Deer River MN* • (218)246-8154 • (FW 1987 MDIV)

**ANTON CARL J REV** (860)561-3825
1655 Boulevard W Hartford CT 06107 • AntonCJ@aol.com • NE • Sn/Adm • Bethany West Hartford CT • (860)521-5076 • (SPR 1976 MED MDIV)

**APPEL VERNON M REV** (512)898-2471
PO Box 146 Thorndale TX 76577-0146 • TX • EM • (SL 1950)

**APPOLD MARK L REV** (660)665-7344
27 Overbrook Dr Kirksville MO 63501-2771 • mappold@truman.edu • MO • SP • Faith Kirksville MO • (660)665-6122 • (SL 1961 THD)

**APPOLD ROBERT BEN REV** (517)694-1421
4701 Sycamore St Holt MI 48842-1574 • rbappold@oursaviorchurch.org • MI • Assoc • Our Savior Lansing MI • (517)882-8665 • (SL 1983 MDIV)

**ARAND CHARLES P REV** (314)391-2810
597 Woodlyn Xing Ballwin MO 63021-7466 • MO • SHS/C • Missouri Saint Louis MO • (314)317-4550 • (SL 1984 STM MDIV THD)

**ARBOGAST JON D REV** (228)497-3854
2507 Bayou Bend Rd Gantier MS 39553 • ceejaya@sprintmail.com • SO • SP • Christ Pascagoula MS • (228)762-1754 • (SL 1998 MDIV)

**ARCHBOLD GARY E REV** (337)462-6204
1910 Donna Dr Deridder LA 70634-4552 • SO • SP • Redeemer De Ridder LA* • (318)463-8427 • (SPR 1975 MDIV)

**ARDY JOSEPH M REV** (817)641-0327
1403 Surry Place Dr Cleburne TX 76031-6503 • pastorjoe205@hotmail.com • TX • SP • Ascension Cleburne TX • (817)645-9452 • (SL 1991 MDIV)

**ARFT JORDAN E REV** (512)668-3450
PO Box 1430 Alice TX 78333-1430 • TX • EM • (SPR 1949)

**ARLE EDWARD J DR** (636)947-3763
2705 El Camino Dr Saint Charles MO 63301-1387 • ejarle@juno.com • MO • Assoc • Our Savior Saint Charles MO • (636)947-8010 • (SL 1970 MDIV DMIN)

**ARMBRUST KEVIN L REV** (336)631-8039
1460 Kenwood St Winston-Salem NC 27103 • SE • Assoc • St John Winston Salem NC • (336)725-1651 • (SL 1999 MDIV)

**ARMON RODNEY A REV** (402)845-2339
C/O St Paul Luth Church PO Box 185 Doniphan NE 68832-0185 • ch67bde@msn.com • NEB • SP • St Paul Doniphan NE • (402)845-2340 • (SL 1984 MDIV)

**ARMOUR THOMAS P REV** (941)949-2103
9332 Lake Abby Ln Bonita Springs FL 34135 • tpa.laa.ret@worldnet.att.net • NJ • EM • (SL 1956 DMIN)

**ARMSTRONG JOHN W REV**
Grace Lutheran Church 3201 Central Ave Columbus IN 47203-2253 • armstrng@hsonline.net • IN • Sn/Adm • Grace Columbus IN • (812)372-4859 • (SL 1986 MDIV STM)

**ARMSTRONG R RICHARD REV** (727)526-8025
1340 48th Ave NE Saint Petersburg FL 33703-4116 • rrarms@aol.com • FG • SP • Grace Saint Petersburg FL • (727)527-1168 • (SL 1979 MDIV)

**ARNDT DENNIS A REV** (319)847-3245
C/O Immanuel PO Box 166 Grand Mound IA 52751-0166 • revdaa@netins.net • IE • SP • Immanuel Grand Mound IA • (319)847-2631 • (SPR 1969 MDIV)

**ARNDT GERALD REV** (715)294-4092
282 State Road 35 Osceola WI 54020-4108 • MNS • EM • (SL 1955)

**ARNDT KEVIN M REV** (920)596-1698
410 Grove St Manawa WI 54949 • NW • Assoc • St Paul Manawa WI • (920)596-2837 • (SL 1992 MDIV)

**ARNDT PAUL W REV** (810)689-4664
C/O Faith Lutheran Church 37635 Dequindre Rd Troy MI 48083-5709 • MI • Assoc • Faith Troy MI • (248)689-4664 • (FW 1992 MDIV)

**ARNDT RICHARD LARRY REV** (561)968-7837
3727 Woods Walk Blvd Lake Worth FL 33467-2361 • FG • SP • St Peter Belle Glade FL • (407)996-2205 • (SL 1965 MDIV)

**ARNDT RICHARD LOUIS REV** (712)225-2880
1477 Harrison Dr Cherokee IA 51012-7237 • IW • SP • Trinity Cherokee IA • (712)225-4332 • (SPR 1976 MDIV)

**ARNDT WARREN B REV** (248)524-9559
2775 Saratoga Dr Troy MI 48083-2647 • MI • Sn/Adm • Faith Troy MI • (248)689-4664 • (SPR 1967 MDIV)

**ARNHOLT BRADLEY PAUL REV**
5141 Yosemite Dr Columbus GA 31907-1728 • IN • 04/1999 • (FW 1996 MDIV)

**ARNOLD RONALD L REV** (702)359-0198
2730 Springland Dr Sparks NV 89434-2642 • CNH • SP • Our Savior Sparks NV • (702)358-0743 • (SL 1972 MDIV)

**ARNOLD TODD WAYNE REV** (520)474-7449
509 W Wade Ln Payson AZ 85541-4761 • todd509@futureone.com • EN • SP • Shepherd Pines Payson AZ • (520)474-5440 • (SL 1996 MDIV)

**ARNOLD TYLER C REV** (816)746-2407
7304 NW Maple Ln Platte Woods MO 64151 • taarnold24@juno.com • MO • Asst • Christ Platte Woods MO • (816)741-0483 • (SL 1999 MDIV)

**ARP GARY M REV** (319)352-2198
2603 Easton Ave Waverly IA 50677-9233 • pasarp@forbin.com • IE • DP • Iowa East Marion IA • (SPR 1966)

**ARP WALLY M REV** (407)699-5268
1209 Winter Springs Blvd Winter Springs FL 32708 • wmarp@stlukes-oviedo.org • S • Sn/Adm • St Luke Oviedo FL • (407)365-3408 • (FW 1988 MDIV)

**ARTELT THOMAS A REV** (706)310-1523
1090 Woodridge Ln Watkinsville GA 30677 • tartelt@aol.com • FG • 08/1999 • (CQ 1988 MSW MDIV)

**ARTIGAS CRISTIANO REV** (602)582-8801
232 W Oraibi Dr Phoenix AZ 85027-4774 • PSW • D Miss • Santo Tomas Phoenix AZ • (602)276-5078 • (CQ 1980)

**ASBURRY RANDY K REV** (307)682-8071
1990 Wolff Rd Gillette WY 82718 • rasburry@vcn.com • WY • SP • Hope Wright WY* • (307)464-0373 • (SL 1990 MA MDIV MST)

**ASCHBRENNER ARNOLD R REV** (316)682-0979
1920 Farmstead St Wichita KS 67208-1746 • KS • EM • * • (SPR 1945)

**ASCHENBECK KEITH D REV**
1204 Brazos St Belton TX 76513-3794 • TX • Asst • Zion Georgetown TX • (512)863-3065 • (SL 1999 MDIV)

**ASCHER GEORGE P REV** (817)573-0643
2409 Forest Hill Ln Granbury TX 76048 • aerie@itexas.net • TX • SP • St Mark Mineral Wells TX • (817)325-4282 • (SPR 1971 MDIV MA DMIN)

**ASHER JOSEPH G REV** (219)459-9256
1902 Ardmore Ave Apt 8 Fort Wayne IN 46802-4815 • jga44@hotmail.com • IN • 12/1994 12/1999 • (FW 1984 MMIN MDIV)

**ASHMON SCOTT A REV** (513)923-9386
3311 Compton Rd Cincinnati OH 45251-2507 • sashmon@christ-lcms.org • OH • Asst • Christ Cincinnati OH • (513)385-8342 • (SL 1996 MDIV MST)

**ASMUS AARON J REV** (605)988-0062
6509 S Mogen Ave Sioux Falls SD 57108-5709 • asmuspa@juno.com • SD • SP • Memorial Sioux Falls SD • (605)334-7133 • (SL 1986 MDIV)

**ASMUS ERLAND REV** (712)464-3458
103 Circle Dr Lake City IA 51449-1430 • IW • SP • Zion Auburn IA • (712)688-2810 • (CQ 1981)

**ASMUS GERHARDT C REV** (701)273-4108
PO Box 155 Pettibone ND 58475-0155 • glasmus@juno.com • ND • EM • (SL 1956 MDIV)

**ASTALOS RONALD F REV** (810)385-7214
3557 Krafft Rd Fort Gratiot MI 48059 • ronarudo@aol.com • EN • EM • (SPR 1962 MDIV)

**ATROPS DAVID A REV** (805)388-3308
2909 E Dwight Ave Camarillo CA 93010-3603 • pastor@peacelcms.org • PSW • 08/2000 • (SL 1968 MDIV)

**ATSINGER VICTOR A REV** (352)243-1173
14725 Indian Ridge Trl Clermont FL 34711-8197 • TX • EM • (SPR 1964 MDIV)

**ATWELL CHRISTOPHER LEE REV**
C/O Zion Lutheran Church 766 S High St Columbus OH 43206 • atwell7@prodigy.net • OH • Asst • Zion Columbus OH • (614)444-3456 • (FW 1993 MDIV)

**AU BUCHON STANLEY R REV** (734)241-5526
C/O Trinity Luth Church 323 Scott St Monroe MI 48161-2132 • MI • Assoc • Trinity Monroe MI • (313)242-2308 • (SL 1972 MDIV)

**AUBEY DENNIS A DR** (708)957-4491
4251 183rd St Country Club Hills IL 60478-5337 • docaubey@juno.com • NI • SP • St John Country Club Hills IL • (708)798-4131 • (SL 1974 DMIN)

**AUERNHAMER MARK E REV** (716)778-5149
6135 Judy St Newfane NY 14108-1107 • meauern@juno.com • EA • 06/1999 • (SL 1995 MDIV)

**AUFDENKAMP WILLIAM M REV** (218)334-2866
213 Maple Ave E Frazee MN 56544 • bethlech@means.net • MNN • SP • Bethlehem Frazee MN • (218)334-2866 • (SL 1987 MDIV)

**AUFDENKAMPE CHARLES R REV** (773)763-3549
5516 N Parkside Ave Chicago IL 60630-1210 • EN • SP • Jefferson Park Chicago IL • (773)545-5109 • (SPR 1971 MA)

**AUFDERHEIDE HOWARD FRED DR** (619)223-5052
4728 Cape May Ave San Diego CA 92107-2226 • PSW • EM • (CQ 1992 MDIV MDIV MA DMIN)

**AUFDERHEIDE STAN M REV**
Concordia University Foundatio 2811 NE Holman St Portland OR 97211-6099 • PSW • M Chap • Pacific Southwest Irvine CA • (949)854-3232 • (CQ 1983 MTH)

**AUGER EDMUND D REV** (817)569-6369
6112 Ridgeway St Fort Worth TX 76116 • augerfam@aol.com • TX • Assoc • St Paul Fort Worth TX • (817)332-2281 • (FW 1985 MDIV)

**AUGUSTIN HORST W REV** (218)738-3912
306 South St W Eagle Bend MN 56446-9579 • MNN • SP • Immanuel Eagle Bend MN* • (218)738-3431 • (SL 1969 MDIV)

**AUMANN BRADLEY S REV** (504)639-0023
164 W Pinewood Dr Slidell LA 70458-1363 • SO • Assoc • Holy Trinity Covington LA • (504)892-6146 • (SL 1997 MDIV)

**AUMANN ROBERT P REV** (504)639-0023
419 Country Club Blvd Slidell LA 70458 • SO • Asst • Bethany Slidell LA • (504)643-3043 • (SPR 1969 MDIV)

**AUMANN ROGER F REV** (734)397-2095
44243 Cherbourg St Canton MI 48188-1712 • MI • EM • (CQ 1980 MS)

**AURICH LEONARD H REV** (816)478-0068
14809 Covington Rd Independence MO 64055-4924 • dlaurich@aol.com • MO • EM • (SPR 1957)

**AURINGER JASON P REV** (702)869-1979
301 S Maryland Pkwy Las Vegas NV 89101-5320 • Revorange@aol.com • PSW • SP • Frst Good Shep Las Vegas NV • (702)384-6106 • (SL 1995 MDIV)

**AUSTERMANN HAROLD W REV**
135 Commercial St Lone Rock WI 53556 • SW • 02/1999 • (SL 1970)

**AUSTIN JOHN R REV** (817)573-9125
702 Old Cleburne Rd Granbury TX 76048-2537 • oslc@itexas.net • TX • SP • Our Savior Granbury TX • (817)573-5011 • (FW 1986 MDIV)

**AVE-LALLEMANT M PETER REV** (404)907-3969
5860 W Fayetteville Rd College Park GA 30349-6170 • peteave@aol.com • FG • SP • Christ East Point GA • (404)767-2892 • (SL 1972 MDIV)

**AVERS HAROLD A REV** (313)534-0493
17555 Warwick St Detroit MI 48219-3514 • hafriend@aol.com • MI • SP • Greenfld Peace Detroit MI • (313)838-3366 • (SL 1968 MDIV)

**AVERY ARTHUR F C REV** (423)869-5934
PO Box 4069 180 Scott St Harrogate TN 37752-7300 • joybirdie@juno.com • MDS • EM • (SPR 1960 MDIV)

**AWE MICHAEL A REV** (402)368-9929
Immanuel Lutheran Church 500 S Center Tilden NE 68781-4726 • the1rev@juno.com • NEB • SP • Immanuel Tilden NE • (402)368-5690 • (SL 1989 MDIV)

**AZINGER ROBERT B REV**
418 Lutheran Ln Scott City MO 63780 • MO • SP • Eisleben Scott City MO • (573)264-2762 • (FW 1991 MDIV)

**AZZAM EDWARD B REV** (256)233-2536
27885 Azalea Trl Athens AL 35613-5612 • shazzam@hiwaay.net • SO • EM • (SPR 1952 MA)

**AZZAM TIMOTHY P REV** (616)273-9098
61146 Shorewood Dr Three Rivers MI 49093-9308 • paradox@net-link.net • MI • SP • St Peter Three Rivers MI • (616)278-8415 • (SL 1982 MDIV)

## B

**BAADE GENE W REV** (425)271-6481
824 Lynnwood Ave NE Renton WA 98056-3805 • gjbaade@eskimo.com • NOW • SP • Bethlehem Renton WA • (425)255-9772 • (SPR 1970 MDIV MA)

**BABEL MILAN J REV** (414)633-9674
6406 Larchmont Dr Racine WI 53406-5124 • S • EM • (SL 1959)

**BABIN KENNETH L REV** (352)376-2062
C/O First Lutheran Church 1801 NW 5th Ave Gainsville FL 32603-1624 • kbabin1966@aol.com • FG • Assoc • First Gainesville FL • (352)376-2062 • (SL 1997 MDIV)

**BACARISSE ADRIAN L REV** (903)758-6978
2 Clayton Pl Longview TX 75605-4142 • abacarisse@worldnet.att.net • TX • SP • Our Redeemer Longview TX • (903)758-2019 • (SPR 1966 MDIV)

**BACH J EINAR REV** (816)425-7279
Bethany Care Center Room 212 Bethany MO 64424-2628 • MO • EM • (SPR 1941)

**BACH JAMES F DR** (630)894-3263
405 S Rush St Roselle IL 60172-2294 • jbach@trinityroselle.com • NI • Asst • Trinity Roselle IL • (630)894-3263 • (SL 1968 MA MDIV PHD)

**BACH PHILIP L REV** (660)258-2450
St Paul Lutheran Church PO Box 125 Brookfield MO 64628-0125 • aethelfrith@hotmail.com • MO • SP • St Paul Brookfield MO • (660)258-3673 • (FW 1989 MDIV)

**BACHERT ALAN H REV** (314)391-0985
1133 Quails Nest Rd Ballwin MO 63021-6007 • kokluth@inlink.com • MO • Sn/Adm • King Of Kings Chesterfield MO • (314)469-2224 • (SPR 1969 MDIV DMIN)

**BACHMAN JAMES V REV** (949)854-8002
1530 Concordia West Irvine CA 92612-3299 • james.bachman@cui.edu • PSW • SHS/C • Pacific Southwest Irvine CA • (949)854-3232 • (SL 1972 MDIV MA PHD)

**BACHMAN KARL D REV** (808)550-2632
PO Box 22434 Honolulu HI 96823-2434 • bachman@lava.net • CNH • 08/1997 08/2000 • (SL 1974 MDIV)

**BACKHUS ROBERT J REV** (217)347-7275
1003 N Martin St Effingham IL 62401-1783 • jtolch@effingham.net • CI • Asst • St John Effingham IL • (217)342-4334 • (SPR 1969 MDIV)

**BACON PAUL E REV**
C/O Bethesda Lutheran Church 6803 N Campbell Chicago IL 60645 • EN • SP • Bethesda Chicago IL • (773)743-6460 • (SL 1967 MDIV STM DMIN)

**BADER RICK L REV** (815)369-2213
203 E Aspen Ct PO Box 216 Lena IL 61048-0216 • sjl@mwci.net • NI • Sn/Adm • St John Lena IL • (815)369-4035 • (SL 1980 MDIV)

**BAEPLER RICHARD P REV** (219)462-9629
555 Woodlawn Valparaiso IN 46383-3346 • IN • END • Indiana Fort Wayne IN • (SL 1954 MDIV PHD)

**BAEPLER WALTER J REV** (631)581-0290
45 Wavecrest Dr Islip NY 11751-4015 • AT • EM • (SL 1947)

**BAERWALD REUBEN C REV** (630)584-7561
39 White Oak Cir Saint Charles IL 60174-4164 • reuben.baerwald@worldnet.att.net • NI • EM • (SL 1949 MDIV)

**BAERWOLF PHILLIP ANDREW REV** (616)844-0145
18220 Swiss Dr Apt 1 Spring Lake MI 49456-9408 • pbaerwolf@sjls.com • MI • Assoc • St John Grand Haven MI • (616)842-4510 • (SL 1995 MDIV)

**BAERWOLF ROBERT D REV** (616)832-4613
123 W Church Ave Reed City MI 49677-1313 • MI • SP • Trinity Reed City MI • (616)832-5392 • (SL 1965 MDIV)

**BAESE DAVID P REV** (719)635-3873
C/O Redeemer Lutheran Church 2215 N Wahsatch Colorado Springs CO 80907-6939 • RM • Redeemer Colorado Springs CO • (719)633-7661 • (SL 1970 MST)

**BAESE WALTER J REV** (719)942-3505
11388 US Highway 50 Howard CO 81233-9677 • eljim@bwn.net • RM • EM • (SL 1955)

**BAGNALL STEVE REV** (507)435-2201
118 Martin St East Lewisville MN 56060 • jbagnall@frontiernet.net • MNS • SP • Zion Lewisville MN • (507)435-4181 • (FW 1998 MDIV)

**BAGWELL JERRY DON REV** (903)389-2652
580 Sherwood Fairfield TX 75840 • TX • SP • Trinity Fairfield TX • (903)389-4005 • (FW 1981 MDIV)

**BAHLOW NORMAN W REV** (573)859-6800
506 Taylor Ave PO Box 833 Belle MO 65013-0833 • MO • SP • Mount Calvary Luther Belle MO • (573)859-3934 • (SL 1965 MDIV)

**BAHLS DALE W REV** (402)245-4618
2318 Mc Lean St Falls City NE 68355-1706 • NEB • SP • Christ Falls City NE • (402)245-3324 • (FW 1987 MDIV)

**BAHN DARYL S REV** (316)435-6585
PO Box 235 Argonia KS 67004-0205 • KS • SP • Zion Argonia KS • (316)435-6524 • (SL 1993 MDIV)

**BAHN DARYN ANDREW REV** (715)384-7968
300 North Adams Ave Marshfield WI 54449-1708 • dbahn@commplusis.net • NW • Assoc • Christ Marshfield WI • (715)384-3535 • (SL 1992 MDIV)

**BAHN DAVID L REV** (817)457-0380
3411 Viscount Dr Arlington TX 76016-2339 • pastordavid@hclc.net • TX • Sn/Adm • Holy Cross Arlington TX • (817)451-7561 • (FW 1979 MDIV DMIN)

**BAHN STANLEY G REV** (715)762-4533
W7855 Simon Rd Fifield WI 54524 • bahnsg@win.bright.net • NW • EM • (SL 1965 MDIV)

**BAHR ALBERT W REV** (517)674-2401
3221 Bay St PO Box 177 Unionville MI 48767-9700 • MI • EM • (SL 1949 MDIV)

**BAHR DONALD G REV** (254)622-2533
RR 1 Box 171 Clifton TX 76634-9712 • bahrdgr@juno.com • TX • EM • (CQ 1982 MED MAR)

**BAHR FERDINAND O REV** (414)481-9502
4444 S Burrell St Milwaukee WI 53207-5024 • ferdobahr@aol.com • SW • EM • (SPR 1959 MDIV DMIN)

**BAILES DAVID RAY REV**
2796 West Battle Creek Cove Memphis TN 38134 • MDS • D Miss • Mid-South Cordova TN • (FW 1996 MDIV)

**BAILEY CLARK R REV** (661)823-0191
19621 Rose Ave Tehachapi CA 93561-8966 • PSW • EM • (SL 1953 MDIV)

**BAILEY MICHAEL P REV** (503)848-2466
C/O Pilgrim Lutheran Church 5650 SW Hall Blvd Beaverton OR 97005-3918 • mpbailey@cyberhighway.net • NOW • SP • Pilgrim Beaverton OR • (503)644-4656 • (FW 1986 MDIV)

**BAILEY ROBERT G REV** (605)343-2051
916 Clark St Rapid City SD 57701 • bailey.dr-rg@juno.com • SD • Sn/Adm • Peace Rapid City SD • (605)342-8943 • (SPR 1969 MDIV)

**BAIRD RANDY M REV** (918)250-1176
6230 S 86th East Ave Apt N Tulsa OK 74133-1360 • rbaird@pccompsoft.net • OK • 11/1997 11/1999 • (FW 1988 MDIV)

**BAISCH ARTHUR H REV** (309)822-8812
77 S Riverview Dr East Peoria IL 61611-9644 • CI • SP • Ascension East Peoria IL • (309)694-4047 • (CQ 1991 MDIV MA)

**BAISDEN KENNETH W REV** (915)388-0984
PO Box 89 Kingsland TX 78639-0089 • kilobrav@moment.net • TX • EM • (SPR 1975 MDIV)

**BAJUS LUTHER J REV** (708)453-3514
4825 N Ridgewood Ave Norridge IL 60656-2940 • ljbselc@aol.com • S • SP • Zion Norridge IL • (708)453-3514 • (SL 1953)

**BAKALYAR DONOVAN A REV** (906)265-9825
178 Stanley Lake Dr Iron River MI 49935-9359 • NW • EM • (SPR 1942 MDIV)

**BAKER CLAUDE H REV** (818)352-6821
C/O Faith Luth Church PO Box 577 Tujunga CA 91043-0577 • PSW • SP • Faith Tujunga CA • (818)352-4444 • (SL 1966 MDIV)

**BAKER DAVID W REV** (970)332-4718
4975 E 117th Ave Denver CO 80233-1886 • RM • 10/1997 10/1999 • (FW 1986 MDIV)

**BAKER GARTH L REV** (314)364-1445
1873 Osage Dr Rolla MO 65401 • carolyn@umr.edu • MO • EM • (SPR 1963)

**BAKER HERBERT A REV** (920)458-0997
3319 Superior Ave Sheboygan WI 53081 • SW • EM • (SL 1939 MDIV)

**BAKER OTTO E REV** (570)992-0679
HC 1 Box 261 Brodheadsville PA 18322 • rbob@ptd.net • NJ • EM • (SPR 1963 MDIV)

**BAKER ROBERT C REV** (561)978-9830
660 17th Ave Vero Beach FL 32962 • robcbaker@juno.com • FG • SP • Of The Redeemer Vero Beach FL • (561)567-8193 • (SL 1998 MDIV)

**BAKER RONALD M REV** (719)471-4485
1210 Chambers Dr Colorado Springs CO 80904-1216 • RM • SP • Rock Of Ages Colorado Springs CO • (719)632-9394 • (FW 1987 MDIV)

**BAKER THOMAS A REV**
1405 Anna Ave University City MO 63130-1611 • lawgospel@lawgospel.com • MO • SP • St James University City MO • (314)727-3253 • (SL 1971 MDIV STM MA DMIN)

**BALDINGER TIM L REV** (704)845-4521
900 Sunnyview Cir Matthews NC 28105-2801 • pastor@messiah-nc.org • SE • SP • Messiah Charlotte NC • (704)541-1624 • (SPR 1975 MDIV)

**BALDWIN CHARLES S DR** (336)882-5672
2104 Setliff Dr High Point NC 27265-9594 • charlesb@northstate.net • SE • EM • (SL 1963 MS MDIV DMIN)

**BALDWIN HAROLD RICHARD REV** (719)269-1236
2511 Pear St Canon City CO 81212-2667 • revhrbaldy@aol.com • RM • SP • St John Canon City CO • (719)275-0111 • (CQ 1995)

**BALDWIN MARK J REV** (515)987-5585
150 Windfield Pkwy Waukee IA 50263 • chapmjb@aol.com • IW • Inst C • Iowa West Fort Dodge IA • (FW 1984 MDIV)

**BALFOUR EDWARD J REV** (207)799-3111
150 Mitchell Rd Cape Elizabeth ME 04107-1212 • mbalfou1@maine.rr.com • NE • SP • Redeemer Cape Elizabeth ME • (207)799-5941 • (FW 1988 MDIV)

**BALGEMAN DONALD E REV** (815)286-7223
12530 Lee Rd Hinckley IL 60520-6082 • balgeman@thestix.net • NI • SP • Immanuel Hinckley IL • (815)286-3885 • (SPR 1975 MDIV)

**BALKE JAMES W REV**
4825 S Katelyn Cir #204 Milwaukee WI 53220-5399 • pastorjim@luther95.org • EN • 05/2000 • (SL 1971 MDIV DMIN)

**BALL BENJAMIN T REV** (781)828-0119
32 Fuller St Canton MA 02021-1925 • pastorball@stlukeslcms.org • NE • SP • St Luke Dedham MA • (781)326-1346 • (SL 1999 MDIV)

**BALL JOSHUA T**
PO Box 607 Mitchell ON N0K 1N0 CANADA • EN • SP • Grace Mitchell ON CANADA • (519)348-9082 • (SL 2000 MDIV)

**BALLA DAVID PAUL REV** (630)820-2824
2755 Prairieview Ln S Aurora IL 60504-2321 • revdballa@aol.com • NI • SP • Trinity West Chicago IL • (630)231-1175 • (SL 1992 MDIV)

**BALLAS KENNETH M REV** (203)531-4455
290 Delavan Ave Greenwich CT 06830-5946 • S • SP • St Paul Greenwich CT • (203)531-8466 • (SL 1961 STM)

**BALZER DOUGLAS K REV** (314)273-6239
C/O St Paul Lutheran Church 1018 Highway 109 Glencoe MO 63038-1401 • MO • SP • St Paul Grover MO • (314)273-6239 • (SPR 1973 MDIV STM)

**BALZER JAMES G REV** (517)451-5315
10925 Welch Rd Britton MI 49229-9566 • elc@lni.net • MI • SP • Emmanuel Britton MI • (517)451-8148 • (CQ 1997 MED)

**BALZER MARTIN W REV** (847)741-1130
1121 Van St Elgin IL 60123-6016 • martywb@aol.com • NI • Assoc • Good Shepherd Elgin IL • (847)741-7788 • (SL 1974 MDIV)

**BAMSCH DUANE R REV**
C/O St John Lutheran Church PO Box 159 Cypress TX 77410-0159 • TX • Assoc • St John Cypress TX • (281)373-0503 • (FW 1999 MDIV)

**BANACH JAMES L REV** (717)235-5714
11 Harrison Rd New Freedom PA 17349-9488 • pjbanach@aol.com • SE • SP • Redeemer Parkton MD • (410)343-3112 • (FW 1979 MDIV)

**BANECK JAMES A REV** (701)663-2738
504 15th St NE Mandan ND 58554-2162 • jabmessiahmandan@aol.com • ND • SP • Messiah Mandan ND • (701)663-8545 • (FW 1987 MDIV)

**BANGERT MARK ALAN DR** (636)390-3920
114 E 2nd St Washington MO 63090-2504 • mbangert@midwestis.net • MO • Sn/Adm • Immanuel Washington MO • (314)239-4705 • (SL 1985 MDIV DMIN)

**BANGERT MARTIN W REV** (414)529-9011
W135S6752 Fleetwood Rd Muskego WI 53150-3317 • mwbang@execpc.com • EN • EM • (SL 1957 MDIV STM)

**BANKEN ROBERT E REV** (253)845-0350
305 19th St NW Puyallup WA 98371 • gbanken@iname.com • NOW • EM • (SPR 1962)

**BARBER ALAN JOHN REV** (317)653-8020
1900 Wildwood Dr Greencastle IN 46135-9255 • IN • SP • Peace Greencastle IN • (765)653-6995 • (FW 1983 MDIV JD)

**BARBER DAVID E REV**
1625 Longmeadow Glenview IL 60025 • NI • Sn/Adm • Immanuel Glenview IL • (847)724-1034 • (SL 1991 MDIV)

**BARBER DONALD ANTHONY REV** (719)547-9480
703 S Aguilar Dr Pueblo West CO 81007-1701 • RM • SP • Our Savior Pueblo West CO • (719)547-2300 • (FW 1996 MDIV)

**BARBER ROBERT G JR. REV** (616)429-4220
5962 De Morrow Rd Stevensville MI 49127 • pbbugman@parrett.net • MI • Assoc • Trinity Saint Joseph MI • (616)983-5000 • (SL 1988 MDIV)

**BARBEY DANIEL REV** (217)999-5202
601 E 3rd St S Mount Olive IL 62069-1823 • barbey@ctnet.net • SI • SP • Immanuel Mount Olive IL • (217)999-7442 • (SL 1986 MDIV MA)

**BARCKHOLTZ STEVEN ARTHUR REV** (760)934-4223
PO Box 841 Mammoth Lakes CA 93546-0841 • mllutheran@qnet.com • PSW • SP • Mammoth Lakes Mammoth Lakes CA • (760)934-4051 • (SL 1992 MDIV)

**BARD RANDALL CLINTON REV** (817)346-8611
4409 Sycamore School Rd Fort Worth TX 76133 • fastpastor@hotmail.com • TX • SP • Christ Fort Worth TX • (817)370-6242 • (SL 1997 MDIV)

**BARG EDGAR E REV** (715)532-4841
205 Douglas Dr Ladysmith WI 54848-1163 • bessie@ladysmith.net • NW • EM • (SL 1953)

**BARICH JOHN M REV** (206)320-9480
1415 22nd Ave Seattle WA 98122-2909 • tbarich@sprynet.com • NOW • SP • Good Shepherd Seattle WA • (206)325-2733 • (SL 1997 MDIV)

**BARKER ROBERT L REV** (517)386-5374
417 John R St Clare MI 48617-1266 • rbarker@bigfoot.com • MI • SP • Prince Peace Clare MI • (517)386-2687 • (FW 1980 MDIV)

**BARKER STEVEN A REV** (515)996-2736
1193 Prairieview Ave Van Meter IA 50261-8575 • amsdorf@aol.com • IW • SP • Trinity Van Meter IA • (515)996-2093 • (FW 1998 MDIV)

**BARKLEY ANDREW K REV** (847)367-9250
C/O Risen Savior Luth Church 230 US Highway 45 Indian Creek IL 60061-4405 • sermon8r@juno.com • NI • SP • Risen Savior Indian Creek IL • (847)367-9250 • (FW 1985 MDIV)

**BARKOW ROLAND R REV** (616)273-7117
17160 Gentzler Dr Three Rivers MI 49093-9681 • r-c-barkow@juno.com • MI • EM • (SL 1959 MDIV MA)

**BARLOW WILLIAM E D REV** (419)232-3852
106 Boyd Ave Van Wert OH 45891 • wedbar@aol.com • OH • SP • Emmanuel Van Wert OH • (419)238-4992 • (CQ 1982)

**BARNER PERRY V REV** (920)713-3660
1133 Moraine Way Apt 7 Green Bay WI 54303-4471 • NW • 07/1994 07/1999 • (SL 1986 MDIV)

**BARNES BOB A REV** (715)341-6090
5292 Forest Cir S Stevens Point WI 54481-5606 • holyman@coredcs.com • NW • Sn/Adm • St Paul Stevens Point WI • (715)344-5664 • (SPR 1965 MDIV)

**BARNES MICHAEL W REV** (307)778-6186
4911 Griffith Ave Cheyenne WY 82009-5518 • WY • Asst • Trinity Cheyenne WY • (307)635-2802 • (FW 1984 MDIV)

**BARNETT DOUGLAS B REV**
1053 Courtfield Cove Collierville TN 38017 • MDS • SP • Faith Collierville TN • (901)853-4673 • (SL 1979 MDIV)

**BARNETT WILBUR E REV** (213)225-8442
4205 Sea View Ln Los Angeles CA 90065-3349 • PSW • EM • (SL 1957 STM)

**BARNETTE NORMAN B JR. REV** (714)893-4551
12081 Stonegate Ln Garden Grove CA 92845 • abarn39860@cs.com • PSW • EM • (FW 1986 MDIV)

**BARNHART JERRY W REV** (559)622-9112
2627 W Midvalley Ave #89 Visalia CA 93277-9384 • pasjerry-jan@msn.com • CNH • EM • (CQ 1985 MAR MBA)

**BARON DONALD W REV** (808)396-8173
430E Haleloa Pl Honolulu HI 96821-2254 • donbaron56@juno.com • CNH • SP • Good Shepherd Honolulu HI • (808)523-2927 • (LS 1959 MDIV MA)

**BARRY ALVIN L REV** (314)965-9000
1333 S Kirkwood Rd Saint Louis MO 63122-7226 • MO • S Adm • Missouri Saint Louis MO • (314)317-4550 • (TH 1956 MTH DD)

**BARTEL ROBERT H REV** (319)285-9252
14 Grove Rd Eldridge IA 52748-9632 • khakhea@@juno.com • IE • SP • Park View Eldridge IA • (319)285-9035 • (SL 1976 MDIV)

**BARTELL STEVEN D REV** (603)778-7172
3 Clara St Exeter NH 03833-4002 • bartells@nh.ultranet.com • NE • SP • Faith Exeter NH • (603)772-8803 • (FW 1983 MDIV)

**BARTELS DENNIS L REV** (305)620-3525
5761 NW 201 Ln Miami FL 33015 • dennisb@holycrossministries.com • FG • Sn/Adm • Holy Cross North Miami FL • (305)893-0371 • (SL 1982 MDIV)

**BARTELS ERNEST DR** (701)642-6222
1208 3rd Ave N Wahpeton ND 58075-4106 • ND • EM • (SPR 1950 MDIV MTH DRS DMIN PHD)

**BARTELS MARK L REV** (973)586-1823
474 W Main St Rockaway NJ 07866-3730 • mlbartels@aol.com • NJ • SP • King Of Kings Mountain Lakes NJ • (973)334-8333 • (CQ 1980 MDIV)

**BARTELS RALPH REV** (717)764-5847
1520 Church Rd York PA 17404-1502 • NE • EM • (CQ 1982 MA MAR)

**BARTELS WILLIAM H REV** (315)331-0818
928 Peirson Ave Newark NY 14513-9164 • EA • EM • (SL 1957 STM MDIV)

**BARTELT ANDREW H REV** (314)752-3779
7569 Terri Lynn Dr Saint Louis MO 63123-1675 • bartelta@csl.edu • MO • SHS/C • Missouri Saint Louis MO • (314)317-4550 • (SL 1976 MDIV MA PHD)

**BARTELT STEPHEN R REV** (262)784-0814
4295 S Longview Dr New Berlin WI 53151-9217 • sbartelt@execpc.com • SW • Tchr • Martin LHS Greendale WI • (414)421-4000 • (SL 1971 MDIV MPAD MMU)

**BARTELT VICTOR A REV** (414)259-7970
Camillus Terrace 530 N 103rd St Apt 34 Wauwatosa WI 53226 • SW • EM • (SL 1942 MDIV DD)

**BARTH GREGORY J P REV** (805)522-0014
3274 Hereford Ct Simi Valley CA 93063-1325 • church@our-redeemer.org • PSW • SP • Our Redeemer Winnetka CA • (818)341-3460 • (SL 1978 MDIV)

**BARTH HOWARD CHARLES REV** (310)534-8008
2212 W 232nd St # A Torrance CA 90501-5720 • PSW • SP • St Matthew Harbor City CA • (310)326-1958 • (CQ 1995)

**BARTH HOWARD G REV** (816)524-3945
1812 NW Rose Ct Lees Summit MO 64081-1177 • MO • EM • (SL 1939)

**BARTH KARL L REV** (262)789-5184
13330 W Bluemound Rd Apt 3 Elm Grove WI 53122-2536 • SW • S Ex/S • South Wisconsin Milwaukee WI • (414)464-8100 • (SL 1947 MDIV DD)

**BARTH ROBERT L REV** (217)488-6072
C/O St John Luth Church PO Box 197 New Berlin IL 62670-0197 • barthfamily@juno.com • CI • SP • St John New Berlin IL • (217)488-3190 • (SPR 1973 MDIV)

**BARTH WALTHER L REV** (219)486-5313
5815 Bayside Dr Fort Wayne IN 46815-8552 • IN • EM • (SL 1935)

**BARTHEL WILLIAM L REV** (847)228-1731
630 Cordial Dr Des Plaines IL 60018-5508 • a954995@aol.com • NI • SP • St Peter Chicago IL • (773)582-0470 • (SL 1971 MDIV)

**BARTHOLOMEW RICHARD O REV** (330)699-5012
12857 Hoover Ave NW Uniontown OH 44685-8421 • pastor@celc.org • EN • SP • Concordia Akron OH • (330)535-1330 • (CQ 1993)

**BARTLING FREDERICK DR** (651)698-7331
1401 Hartford Ave Saint Paul MN 55116-1668 • fbart@worldnet.att.net • MNS • EM • (SL 1953 MDIV MA DART)

**BARTLING WALTER J REV** (404)636-7050
2986 Briarlake Rd Decatur GA 30033-1014 • FG • EM • (SL 1948 PHD)

**BARTON JAMES P REV** (765)463-2437
755 Cumberland Ave W Lafayette IN 47906-1523 • ululaf@aol.com • IN • Cmp P • University West Lafayette IN • (765)743-2472 • (SPR 1973 MDIV)

**BARTZ HERBERT H REV** (408)736-7142
713 Santa Rosa St Sunnyvale CA 94086-3469 • helenbgood@aol.com • CNH • EM • (SL 1943)

**BARTZ PAUL A REV** (612)854-8317
8080 12th Ave S Apt 208 Bloomington MN 55425 • pabartz@aol.com • MNS • 10/1998 • (FW 1977 MDIV)

**BARTZ ROBERT O REV** (219)294-3191
56661 Wedgewood Ct N Elkhart IN 46516-5810 • IN • O Sp Min • Trinity Culver IN • (219)842-3175 • (SL 1981 MDIV)

**BARZ MARK D REV** (210)497-3938
1311 Summit Crk San Antonio TX 78258-1912 • mbarzcol@juno.com • TX • SP • Crown Of Life San Antonio TX • (210)490-6886 • (SL 1982 MDIV)

**BARZ MARVIN L REV** (785)238-7619
5805 Clarks Creek Rd Junction City KS 66441-8214 • papabarz@tfsksu.net • KS • SP • St Paul Junction City KS • (785)238-7619 • (SPR 1957)

**BASELEY JOEL R REV** (313)730-9094
2000 N York St Dearborn MI 48128-1249 • markv01@flash.net • MI • Assoc • Emmanuel Dearborn MI • (313)565-4002 • (SL 1988 MDIV MS)

**BASS DAVID R REV** (559)642-3139
28530 Creek Rd Coarsegold CA 93614-9100 • familybass@juno.com • CNH • EM • (SL 1974 STM)

**BASSETT CARL W REV** (630)860-1570
190 Oakwood Dr Wood Dale IL 60191-1952 • lizakb@aol.com • NI • SP • Calvary Wood Dale IL • (630)766-2838 • (FW 1987 MDIV)

**BATCHELDER DAVID A REV** (603)878-2661
51 Hakala Dr New Ipswich NH 03071 • lynndave@netzero.net • NE • SP • Our Redeemer New Ipswich NH • (603)878-1837 • (FW 1990 MDIV)

**BATIANSILA A E REV** (920)845-5248
N4118 County Rd AB Luxemburg WI 54217-7925 • NW • SP • St Paul Luxemburg WI • (920)845-5248 • (SPR 1965 MDIV)

**BATSKY THOMAS E REV** (616)428-7243
3790 Blenheim Rd St Joseph MI 49085-9415 • trinity@parrett.net • MI • Assoc • Trinity Saint Joseph MI • (616)983-5000 • (FW 1981 MDIV)

**BAUCH GARY W REV** (716)359-4179
98 Mickens Bnd West Henrietta NY 14586-9561 • gbauch56@rochester.rr.com • EA • SP • St Mark West Henrietta NY • (716)334-4795 • (FW 1987 MDIV)

**BAUDER HAROLD J REV** (360)642-8347
PO Box 271 Seaview WA 98644-0271 • hermy@pacifier.com • NOW • SP • St John Seaview WA • (360)642-4930 • (SPR 1963 MDIV)

**BAUE FREDERIC W REV** (314)835-9145
908 Brownell Ave Saint Louis MO 63122-3202 • fbaue@cs.com • EN • END • English Farmington MI • (SL 1981 MDIV PHD)

**BAUER ALLEN J REV** (713)666-3693
2227 Cypress Run Dr Sugarland TX 77478-5289 • TX • Sn/Adm • Pilgrim Houston TX • (713)666-3693 • (CQ 1980)

**BAUER BENJAMIN T REV** (520)885-2040
3774 N Sandrock Pl Tucson AZ 85750-2229 • pegbauer@aol.com • EN • EM • (SL 1949)

**BAUER DEAN M REV** (606)564-6157
79 Bryant Cir Maysville KY 41056 • ctsrev@maysvilleky.net • OH • SP • Trinity Maysville KY • (606)564-3566 • (FW 1999 MDIV)

**BAUER DENNIS D REV** (406)477-6791
PO Box 458 Lame Deer MT 59043-0458 • MT • D Miss • Montana Billings MT • (SL 1982 MDIV)

**BAUER ERHART L REV** (503)254-6032
215 SE 76th Ave Portland OR 97215-1465 • aeb503@aol.com • NOW • EM • (SL 1959 MDIV MED LLD)

**BAUER FRANK J REV** (617)773-1280
245 Sea St Apt 32 Quincy MA 02169-2575 • NE • EM • (SL 1943 MDIV)

**BAUER JACK A REV**
1582 Osowaw Blvd Spring Hills FL 34607 • FG • EM • (SL 1961 MA MA)

**BAUER JAMES D REV** (303)716)1078
6969 W Yale #64 Denver CO 80227 • pastorbauer@uswest.net • RM • Sn/Adm • Trinity Denver CO • (303)934-2103 • (SPR 1976 MDIV)

**BAUER JOHN A REV** (719)526-5279
1259 Suncrest Way Colorado Springs CO 80906-5051 • bauerja@carson.army.mil • RM • M Chap • Rocky Mountain Aurora CO • (SL 1970 MA MDIV DMIN)

**BAUER KENNETH B DR** (707)765-0946
1736 E Madison St Petaluma CA 94954-2323 • CNH • EM • (SPR 1965 MDIV MS DMIN)

**BAUER MERVYN D REV** (763)433-0646
177 Yoho Dr Anoka MN 55303-1904 • revbauer@minn.net • MNS • SP • Bethlehem Champlin MN • (763)433-0646 • (SPR 1969)

**BAUER STEVEN MARTIN REV** (303)393-0247
1410 Dexter St Denver CO 80220-2459 • RM • Tchr • Denver Lutheran High Denver CO • (303)934-2345 • (SL 1981 MDIV)

**BAUER WALTER R REV** (765)966-8837
501 Henley Rd S Richmond IN 47374-6765 • IN • EM • (SL 1953 MDIV)

**BAUERNFEIND PETER ARNOLD REV** (219)989-9125
C/O Faith Luth Church 2609 Colfax St Gary IN 46406-3033 • IN • SP • Good Shepherd Gary IN* • (219)885-2109 • (SL 1995 MDIV)

**BAUM HENRY E REV** (440)365-7290
341 Pemberton Ave Elyria OH 44035 • hbaum@alltel.net • EN • SP • Grace Elyria OH • (440)322-5497 • (FW 1980 MDIV STM DMIN)

**BAUMAN GENE D REV** (605)644-9412
2 Swan Ln Spearfish SD 57783 • stpspear@mato.com • SD • SP • St Paul Spearfish SD • (605)642-2929 • (SL 1979 MDIV)

**BAUMANN GARY D REV** (715)423-4506
1911 Pleasant View Dr Wisconsin Rapids WI 54494-2046 • NW • Assoc • Immanuel Wisconsin Rapids WI • (715)423-3260 • (CQ 1985 MAR)

**BAUMANN HERMAN E REV** (334)986-8277
26653 US Highway 98 Elberta AL 36530-2713 • SO • EM • (SPR 1952 MDIV)

**BAUMANN PAUL G REV** (419)539-7091
2721 Goddard Rd Toledo OH 43606-3056 • OH • SP • St Philip Toledo OH • (419)475-2835 • (SPR 1972 MDIV)

**BAUMANN RONALD W REV** (317)861-6855
5601 S 450 W New Palestine IN 46163-9533 • IN • SP • Zion New Palestine IN • (317)861-5544 • (SL 1964 MDIV)

**BAUMEISTER WESLEY REV** (906)475-7124
596 M 35 Negaunee MI 49866 • BoHusker1@aol.com • NW • Assoc • Redeemer Marquette MI • (906)228-9883 • (SL 1998 MDIV)

**BAUMGARN DAVID HANS REV** (763)753-9479
22918 Ambassador Blvd NW Saint Francis MN 55070-9312 • TrinitySF@juno.com • MNS • Assoc • Trinity St Francis MN • (763)753-1234 • (FW 1996 MDIV)

**BAUMGARN JACK R REV** (612)753-2451
23926 Nightingale St NW Saint Francis MN 55070-9648 • MNS • Sn/Adm • Trinity St Francis MN • (763)753-1234 • (SPR 1967 MDIV)

**BAUMGARTEL ALLAN P REV** (323)755-2541
C/O Faith Luth Church PO Box 73658 Los Angeles CA 90003-4012 • PSW • D Miss • Faith Los Angeles CA • (323)755-2541 • (SL 1970 MDIV)

**BAUMGARTNER ERWIN J REV** (505)522-0951
1654 Thunderbird St Las Cruces NM 88011-4966 • RM • EM • (SL 1958)

**BAUMGARTNER GEORGE A REV** (505)541-1909
1082 Nena Ct Las Cruces NM 88005 • RM • EM • (SL 1953)

**BAUMGARTNER JOHN D REV** (559)781-8145
649 Mc Comb Ave Porterville CA 93257-1513 • jbaumj@ocsnet.net • CNH • SP • Mount Olive Lindsay CA • (209)562-4879 • (FW 1991 MDIV)

**BAYENS PATRICK J REV** (606)223-8756
3817 Gillespies Gln Lexington KY 40514-1133 • invocavit@aol.com • IN • SP • Our Redeemer Lexington KY • (606)299-9615 • (FW 1977 MDIV PHD)

**BAYER ROBERT F REV** (734)542-9520
36969 Lancaster Livonia MI 48154-1815 • MI • Asst • Christ Our Savior Livonia MI • (734)522-6830 • (FW 1977 MDIV)

**BEALE LESLIE C REV** (910)528-5713
PMB 137 102 Rainbow Dr Livingston TX 77399-1002 • faithdefender@earthlink.net • SE • EM • (SL 1959)

**BEAN MATTHEW D REV**
305 Smoketree Ter Richmond VA 23236 • SE • Asst • Redeemer Richmond VA • (804)272-7973 • (SL 2000 MDIV)

**BEARDSLEY BRIAN M REV** (920)361-9470
C/O Immanuel Lutheran Church N2406 State Rd 29 Berlin WI 54923 • brianmbeards@yahoo.com • SW • SP • Immanuel Berlin WI* • (920)361-1812 • (SL 1991 MDIV)

**BEARMAN DEAN R REV** (219)351-4602
9660 E 520 S Wolcottville IN 46795 • IN • SP • Immanuel Avilla IN • (219)897-2071 • (SL 1967 MDIV)

**BEARSS MAC L REV** (972)712-3693
3417 Tulip Ln Rowlett TX 75088-7021 • TX • 11/1998 • (FW 1985 MDIV EDS)

**BEASLEY DERRICK K REV** (352)861-8211
8820 SW 40 Ave Ocala FL 34476 • thebeasleys@juno.com • SE • Immanuel Avilla IN • (219)897-2071 • (SL 1998 MDIV)

**BEATTIE DANIEL ROYCE REV** (515)246-9955
1241 12th St Des Moines IA 50314 • pmebeattie@aol.com • IW • O Miss • Iowa West Fort Dodge IA • (FW 1996 MDIV)

**BECERRA ROBERTO A REV** (616)847-7124
11622 152nd Ave West Olive MI 49460-9619 • robbecerra@hotmail.com • MI • EM • (FW 1987 MDIV)

**BECK ALFRED H REV** (503)665-7524
955 Birdsdale Gresham OR 07030 • NOW • EM • (SL 1949)

**BECK EARLE T REV** (248)334-3746
3134 Beacham Dr Waterford MI 48329-4504 • MI • EM • (CQ 1963 MED)

**BECK FRED W REV** (815)465-2186
11456 N 11000E Rd Grant Park IL 60940-5067 • NI • SP • Zion Grant Park IL • (815)465-6011 • (FW 1992 MDIV)

**BECK GARY L DR** (810)736-2981
5415 N Belsay Rd Flint MI 48506-1251 • MI • SP • St Mark Flint MI • (810)736-6680 • (FW 1983 MDIV DMIN)

**BECK GORDON A REV** (314)863-7713
7541 Teasdale Ave University Ctiy MO 63146 • gbeck3334@cs.com • MO • 02/1995 02/2000 • (SL 1966 MA MA STM)

**BECK HUBERT F REV** (512)292-3595
3628 Aspen Creek Pkwy Austin TX 78749-6972 • hujubeck@airmail.net • TX • EM • (SL 1956 MDIV)

**BECK JOHN E REV** (320)251-3433
312 4th Ave N Sartell MN 56377-1739 • Je6beck@juno.com • MNN • SP • Messiah Sartell MN • (320)252-5883 • (FW 1979 MDIV)

**BECK JOHN L REV** (203)346-4615
9 Glynn Ave Middletown CT 06457-3711 • NE • EM • (SL 1959 MDIV)

**BECK PAUL R REV** (517)792-2494
5350 Brockway Rd Saginaw MI 48603-4422 • pngbeck@concentric.net • MI • EM • (SL 1952 MDIV)

**BECKER BERNARD H REV** (651)777-5937
2582 Bittersweet Ln Saint Paul MN 55109-2104 • MNS • EM • (SL 1948)

**BECKER DAVID REV** (218)927-3922
404 4th St NW Aitkin MN 56431-1216 • stjnlcms@mlecmn.net • MNN • SP • St John Aitkin MN • (218)927-3170 • (SL 1982 MDIV)

**BECKER DONALD H REV** (308)832-2142
228 N Colorado Ave Minden NE 68959-1623 • sp04122@navix.net • NEB • SP • St Paul Minden NE • (308)832-1343 • (SL 1969 MDIV)

**BECKER DONALD V REV** (708)848-1549
606 S Scoville Ave Oak Park IL 60304-1406 • becker32@worldnet.att.net • NI • EM • (SL 1954)

**BECKER GILBERT C REV** (918)333-6618
1400 Harris Dr Bartlesville OK 74006-5417 • OK • EM • (SPR 1945)

**BECKER MATTHEW L REV** (503)288-9371
6454 NE 38th Ave Portland OR 97211 • mbecker@cu-portland.edu • NOW • SHS/C • Northwest Portland OR • (SL 1988 MA MDIV)

**BECKER NORBERT V REV** (314)849-3045
8746 Villa Crest Dr Saint Louis MO 63126-1954 • beckgb@juno.com • MO • EM • (SL 1946 STM DD)

**BECKER PAUL FREDERICK REV** (423)392-0626
2020 Malvern Dr Kingsport TN 37660-5093 • beckerpm657@pol.net • MDS • SP • Concordia Kingsport TN • (423)247-3582 • (SL 1985 MDIV MST)

**BECKER RICHARD ALAN REV** (217)636-7043
RR 3 Box 73A Petersburg IL 62675-9528 • CI • SP • Immanuel Athens IL • (217)636-8469 • (SL 1975 MDIV)

**BECKER ROBERT REV** (812)346-1449
RFD # 5 Box 454 North Vernon IN 47265 • IN • 04/2000 • (FW 1984)

**BECKER STEVEN A REV** (417)235-3019
215 N Main Friestatt MO 65654 • MO • SP • Trinity Freistatt MO • (417)235-7300 • (SL 1978 MDIV)

**BECKER THOMAS E REV** (757)686-0380
2920 Sir Walter Cres Chesapeake VA 23321-5730 • onesabre@aol.com • SE • SP • Redeemer Portsmouth VA • (757)397-8362 • (CQ 1979 MDIV)

**BECKER VANCE G REV** (612)864-3573
310 Wacker Dr Glencoe MN 55336-3011 • lvbecker@hutchtel.net • MNS • Assoc • First Glencoe MN • (320)864-5522 • (SL 1982 MDIV)

**BECKER WALLACE M REV** (417)890-9189
3612 W Birchwood Pl Springfield MO 65807-0981 • wbecker@pcis.net • MO • Assoc • Redeemer Springfield MO • (417)881-5470 • (SL 1988 MDIV)

**BECKMAN BRADLEY P REV**
210 W Park Row Dr Arlington TX 76010-4318 • Bpbeckman@aol.com • TX • Sn/Adm • Grace Arlington TX • (817)274-1626 • (SL 1992 MDIV)

**BECKMANN WILLIAM C REV** (708)584-0593
1531 Jewel Ave Saint Charles IL 60174-4534 • wbeckmann2@juno.com • EN • EM • (SL 1958 MDIV MA)

**BECKSTROM ROBERT REV** (818)967-0068
542 E Covina Blvd Covina CA 91722-2953 • PSW • EM • (CQ 1978)

**BEDARD KELLY C REV** (541)688-8434
4876 Briars St Eugene OR 97404-1115 • kjbedard@prodigy.net • NOW • SP • Messiah Eugene OR • (541)688-0735 • (SL 1988 MDIV)

**BEESE ROGER REV** (660)747-5047
12 SE 215th Rd Warrensburg MO 64093-7500 • rogerbz@aol.com • MO • SP • Bethlehem Warrensburg MO • (660)747-6742 • (SL 1967 MDIV STM)

**BEESLEY MARK B REV** (319)283-2442
1323 Elm St Oelwein IA 50662 • bishop1@sbtek.net • IE • SP • Peace Oelwein IA* • (319)283-5778 • (SL 1990 MDIV)

**BEGIN ROBERT M REV** (949)586-9748
20702 El Toro Rd Apt 489 Lake Forest CA 92630 • PSW • EM • * • (SL 1990 MDIV)

**BEHLING DAVID H REV** (262)554-1407
5111 Biscayne Ave Racine WI 53406 • SW • SP • Holy Cross Racine WI • (262)554-7010 • (SPR 1969)

**BEHLING DAVID J REV**
PO Box 317 Elmhurst IL 60126-0317 • NI • SP • Bethlehem Broadview IL* • (708)344-4987 • (SL 1966 MDIV)

**BEHLING EDWARD F REV** (218)736-1027
24620 N Wall Lake Dr Fergus Falls MN 56537-9746 • MNN • EM • * • (SPR 1955)

**BEHLING GERALD JOHN REV** (715)276-6546
16609 Peaceful Ln Townsend WI 54175-9590 • gbehling@ez-net.com • NW • EM • * • (SL 1980 MDIV MS)

**BEHLING HENRY W REV** (501)922-2268
16 N Badalona Dr Hot Springs AR 71909-2614 • hbbehling@webtv.net • MDS • EM • * • (SPR 1958 MDIV)

**BEHLING PAUL G REV** (518)456-1538
9 Victoria Dr Guilderland NY 12084-9759 • behlipg@nycap.rr.com • AT • SP • Christ Albany NY • (518)456-1530 • (SL 1958 MDIV)

**BEHLING ROBERT E REV** (605)772-5684
PO Box 302 Howard SD 57349 • rbehling@splitrocktel.net • SD • SP • St John Howard SD • (605)772-5252 • (FW 1985 MDIV)

**BEHM GARY H REV** (314)535-9495
4382 Westminster Pl Saint Louis MO 63108-2624 • MO • 08/1996 08/2000 • (SL 1972 MDIV STM)

**BEHMLANDER DANIEL M REV** (815)625-9435
C/O Good Sheph Luth Church 435 Martin Rd Rock Falls IL 61071-1966 • NI • SP • Good Shepherd Rock Falls IL • (815)625-3376 • (FW 1984 MDIV)

**BEHNKE ALLEN L REV** (301)262-6320
12410 Madeley Ln Bowie MD 20715-2903 • abehnke@aol.com • SE • Sn/Adm • Trinity Bowie MD • (301)262-5475 • (SL 1973 MDIV)

**BEHNKE GORDON E REV** (909)925-2319
601 N Kirby St Spce 577 Hemet CA 92545-5959 • PSW • EM • (SPR 1941)

**BEHNKE JAMES E REV** (520)803-6810
4964 Laguna Sierra Vista AZ 85650 • jimbehnke@juno.com • PSW • EM • (SL 1981 MDIV)

**BEHNKE RICHARD W REV** (419)335-9170
C/O St Luke Luth Church 1640 State Route 108 Wauseon OH 43567-9446 • rbehnke@bright • net • OH • SP • St Luke Wauseon OH • (419)335-9170

**BEHNKE ROBERT R REV** (503)281-3273
4265 NE Halsey St #212 Portland OR 97213 • SE • EM • (SPR 1958)

**BEHNKEN DUANE P REV** (760)433-2770
1900 S Nevada St Oceanside CA 92054-6418 • dbehnken@aol.com • PSW • SP • Immanuel Oceanside CA • (760)433-2770 • (SL 1972 MDIV)

**BEHNKEN JOHN W REV** (505)293-4693
10508 Arvilla Ave NE Albuquerque NM 87111-5004 • RM • EM • (SL 1940)

**BEHNKEN KEN REV** (702)746-5323
3242 Pleasant Hills Dr Reno NV 89523 • kenandeun@juno.com • CNH • EM • (SL 1953)

**BEHNKEN KENNETH W REV** (949)951-3476
27161 Puerta Del Oro Mission Viejo CA 92691-4421 • behnkenk@aol.com • PSW • D Ex/S • Pacific Southwest Irvine CA* • (949)854-3232 • (SL 1964 MDIV DMIN)

**BEHRHORST WALLACE D REV** (316)229-8521
910 E 9th Ave Winfield KS 67156-3032 • KS • EM • * • (SL 1950 MDIV MA)

**BEHRING MARK C REV** (281)812-2912
18802 Preakness Palm Cir Humble TX 77346-8179 • drbehring@aol.com • TX • Sn/Adm • Lamb Of God Humble TX • (281)446-8427 • (SL 1972 MDIV DMIN)

**BEHRINGER OCIE N REV** (423)775-3525
205 Troy Dr Dayton TN 37321-4204 • MDS • EM • (SL 1946 MDIV)

**BEHRMANN FRED W REV** (650)872-1676
860 Glenview Dr San Bruno CA 94066-2722 • FredBehr@aol.com • CNH • EM • (SL 1949)

**BEIDERWIEDEN JOHN H REV** (309)543-6880
316 E Adams St Havana IL 62644-1415 • CI • EM • (SL 1940 MDIV)

**BEINKE ROBERT D REV** (203)847-1252
C/O St Peter Luth Church 208 Newtown Ave Norwalk CT 06851-2316 • pastor@stpeterlc.norwalk.ct.us • NE • SP • St Peter Norwalk CT • (203)847-1252 • (FW 1986 MDIV)

**BEINS PAUL A REV** (314)869-5080
9711 Perch Dr Saint Louis MO 63136-1930 • sbeins@epconline.com • MO • EM • (SL 1961)

**BEK EDWIN C REV** (920)458-0836
2720 N 31st St Sheboygan WI 53083-3619 • SW • EM • (SPR 1954)

**BEKEMEIER LUTHER W REV** (253)582-6979
10701 Hill Terrace Dr SW Lakewood WA 98498-4338 • lbekemeier@cs.com • NOW • EM • (SL 1952 MDIV)

**BELASIC DAVID S REV** (716)675-0331
92 W Cavalier Dr Cheektowaga NY 14227-3526 • dbelasiced@aol.com • EA • EM • (SPR 1963 MAR MDIV DMIN)

**BELISLE RUSSELL S REV** (708)493-0839
5646 Murray Dr Berkeley IL 60163-1454 • NI • Assoc • St John Forest Park IL • (708)366-3226 • (FW 1988 MDIV)

**BELK JACK A REV** (812)358-4120
402 W Bridge St Brownstown IN 47220-1304 • IN • Sn/Adm • St Peter Brownstown IN • 235 • (SPR 1975 MDIV)

**BELK KIT B REV** (217)965-3736
C/O Trinity Lutheran Church 32946 Route 4 Girard IL 62640-9516 • SI • SP • Trinity Girard IL • (217)965-4816 • (SPR 1973 MDIV)

**BELL CHARLES REV**
RR #1 Box 89M Mattituck NY 11952 • AT • Sn/Adm • Messiah East Setauket NY • (631)751-1775 • (SL 1975 MDIV)

**BELL DANIEL C REV** (614)457-9030
4236 Waddington Rd Columbus OH 43220-4447 • pastorbell@atonementchurch.com • OH • SP • Atonement Columbus OH • (614)451-1880 • (SPR 1965 MDIV)

**BELL DEAN M REV** (218)784-4827
1943 220th St Hendrum MN 56550-9544 • revbell@means.net • MNN • SP • Immanuel Mc Intosh MN • (218)563-2235 • (CQ 1996)

**BELL GARY A REV** (707)751-0406
321 Raymond Dr Benicia CA 94510 • CNH • SP • Benicia Benicia CA • (707)746-0201 • (FW 1988 MDIV)

**BELL LARRY E REV** (217)586-4900
706 Colony Grv Mahomet IL 61853-9566 • frndship@pdnt.com • CI • SP • Friendship/Joy Champaign IL • (217)355-0454 • (SL 1993 MDIV)

**BELL RANDALL D REV** (515)579-6281
PO Box 697 Latimer IA 50452-0697 • IE • SP • St Paul Latimer IA • (515)579-6281 • (FW 1986 MDIV)

**BELL RAYMOND J REV** (715)289-4968
221 E Seminary St PO Box 242 Cadott WI 54727 • NW • SP • St John Cadott WI* • (715)289-4521 • (CQ 1993 MDIV)

**BELLAS RICHARD J REV** (847)608-8804
534 N Weston Ave Elgin IL 60123-3339 • NI • Sn/Adm • Calvary Elgin IL • (847)741-5433 • (SL 1998 MDIV)

**BELOW MARK G REV** (801)562-5716
9301 S Burgundy Sandy UT 84070 • tiggerbuster@earthlink.net • RM • Sn/Adm • Grace Sandy UT • (801)572-6375 • (FW 1990 MDIV)

**BELTON VICTOR J REV** (404)244-8200
C/O Peace Lutheran Church 1679 Columbia Dr Decatur GA 30032-4615 • pastorbo@aol.com • FG • SP • Peace Decatur GA • (404)289-1474 • (SL 1986 MDIV)

**BELTZ DEWYTH D REV** (719)531-7224
7625 Julynn Rd Colorado Springs CO 80919-4228 • TX • EM • (SL 1952)

**BELTZ HENRY F REV** (763)789-9387
953-42 1/2 Avenue NE Columbia Heights MN 55421 • MNS • EM • (SL 1940)

**BELTZ TERRY D REV** (817)473-8635
1012 Hickory Ct Mansfield TX 76063-2907 • tbeltz@luther95.net • TX • SP • St John Mansfield TX • (817)473-4889 • (SL 1981 MDIV)

**BELTZ WALTER W REV** (320)230-8950
1414 11th Ave N Saint Cloud MN 56303-1911 • MNN • EM • (SL 1936)

**BELZ KENNETH C REV** (515)993-5301
60 River Vista Dr Adel IA 50003 • IW • EM • (SPR 1964)

**BENDER GARY L REV** (517)652-7769
1637 S Beyer Rd Saginaw MI 48601 • gbender@stlorenz.org • MI • Assoc • St Lorenz Frankenmuth MI • (517)652-6141 • (SPR 1976 MDIV MS)

**BENDER HAROLD J JR. REV** (217)222-0141
3340 State St Quincy IL 62301-5726 • lutheran@rnet.com • CI • SP • St John Quincy IL • (217)222-8579 • (SL 1993 MDIV)

**BENDER JAMES W REV** (651)487-0331
989 Lafond Ave Saint Paul MN 55104-2111 • bendegg@peoplepc.com • MNS • SP • St Stephanus Saint Paul MN • (651)228-1486 • (SL 1991 MDIV)

**BENDER PETER C REV** (414)628-4976
4200 Elmwood Rd Colgate WI 53017-9702 • prbender@peacesussex.org • SW • SP • Peace Sussex WI • (262)246-3200 • (FW 1987 MDIV)

**BENDEWALD DONALD E REV** (410)866-3055
1525 Customs Rd Baltimore MD 21237-1603 • pdbendy@aol.com • SE • EM • (SL 1961 MDIV)

**BENDEWALD JON D REV** (616)429-4139
4741 Beechnut Dr St Joseph MI 49085 • bendewaldjl@juno.com • MI • Asst • Trinity Saint Joseph MI • (616)983-5000 • (CQ 1997 MDIV)

**BENDICK ROBERT E REV** (360)848-0232
17873 Valley Ridge Ln Mount Vernon WA 98274-4660 • NOW • SP • Trinity Mount Vernon WA • (360)428-0290 • (SL 1965 MDIV MED)

**BENDIX LELAND D REV** (320)963-3592
7809 County Rd 35W Annandale MN 55302 • ldbend@lkdllink.net • MNS • SP • Bethlehem Annandale MN • (320)963-3592 • (FW 1977 MDIV)

**BENEDIX GARY SCOTT REV** (208)326-3182
PO Box 33 Filer ID 83328-0033 • peace@filertel.com • NOW • SP • Peace Filer ID • (208)326-5450 • (SL 1968 MDIV)

**BENEDUM THOMAS JOHN REV** (314)996-1728
408 Stryker Ct Ballwin MO 63021-4402 • thomas.benedum@lcms.org • MO • S Ex/S • Missouri Saint Louis MO • (314)317-4550 • (SL 1969 MDIV)

**BENING VIRGIL T REV** (517)836-2899
2471 N Melita Rd Sterling MI 48659-9771 • MI • SP • Faith Prescott MI • (517)873-4506 • (SPR 1970 MDIV)

**BENJAMIN SCOTT E REV**
6315 Johnson St Mc Farland WI 53558-9228 • lrms@peterlink.ru • SW • 09/1998 • (FW 1989 MDIV)

**BENKE DAVID H REV** (718)229-1262
61-26 211th St Oakland Gardens NY 11364-2119 • dhbad@aol.com • AT • SP • St Peter Brooklyn NY* • (718)647-1007 • (SL 1972 MDIV DMIN LLD)

**BENKE MICHAEL R REV** (775)857-7723
2355 Parkway Dr Reno NV 89502-9590 • revofreno@aol.com • CNH • SP • St Luke Reno NV • (775)825-0588 • (SL 1973 MDIV)

**BENKE RICHARD REV** (309)266-8511
633 E Polk St Morton IL 61550-1712 • CI • Sn/Adm • Bethel Morton IL • (309)263-2417 • (SL 1962 MDIV)

**BENKE ROBERT J REV**
1233 Carroll St Paul MN 55104 • eqpk62a@prodigy.com • MNS • Cmp P • Minnesota South Burnsville MN • (SL 1985 MDIV)

**BENKE STEVEN J REV** (314)464-2592
1570 Donnybrook Ln Imperial MO 63052-3083 • sjbenke@msn.com • MO • Assoc • St John Arnold MO • (314)464-0096 • (SL 1990 MDIV)

**BENKEN F RICHARD REV** (203)245-2703
13 Stonewall Ln Madison CT 06443-2236 • rbenken@snet.net • NE • EM • (SPR 1955)

**BENNER ROGER L REV**
PMB 7010 170 Rainbow Dr Livingston TX 77399-1070 • CNH • EM • (FW 1977 MDIV)

**BENNETT DENNIS H REV** (828)324-0192
7360 RH Rd Hickory NC 28602 • denjanben@earthlink.net • SE • 08/1990 08/2000 • (FW 1984 MDIV)

**BENNING MARK W REV** (509)483-4218
7307 N Nevada Spokane WA 99208 • NOW • SP • Holy Cross Spokane WA • (509)483-4218 • (FW 1982 MDIV)

**BENNINGHOFF TIMOTHY J REV** (414)383-9646
2169 S 28th St Milwaukee WI 53215-2423 • lxthus821@aol.com • EN • SP • Layton Park Milwaukee WI • (414)383-1066 • (SPR 1975 MDIV)

**BENSCOTER RANDALL K REV** (907)357-8022
PO Box 871069 Wasilla AK 99687-1069 • randyben@mtaonline.net • NOW • SP • Lamb Of God Wasilla AK • (907)357-8077 • (FW 1979 MDIV)

**BENSON CHRISTOPHER** (707)837-8712
1012 Ventana Dr Windsor CA 95492 • CNH • Assoc • Vineyard of Faith Windsor CA • (707)837-8712 • (SL 2000 MDIV)

**BENSON DAVID M REV** (573)446-0240
3005 W Rollins Rd Columbia MO 65203 • pastordaveb@juno.com • MO • SP • Campus Columbia MO • (573)442-5942 • (SL 1979 MDIV)

**BENSON KENNETH H REV** (815)586-4572
507 E Plumb Ransom IL 60470 • benson³kenneth@html.com • NI • EM • (SL 1949)

**BENSON STEVEN K REV** (515)544-3229
3670 350th St Farnhamville IA 50538 • IW • SP • Holy Trinity Farnhamville IA • (515)544-3264 • (FW 1987 MDIV)

**BENSON STEVEN M REV** (651)731-0956
2127 Margaret St Saint Paul MN 55119-3923 • revsbenson@afo.net • MNS • SP • Eastern Hghts Saint Paul MN • (651)735-4202 • (SL 1985 MDIV)

**BENTRUP ROLLAND L REV** (606)297-1604
397 Ky Route 1559 Nippa KY 41240-9223 • bentrupr@foothills.net • OH • EM • (SL 1953 MTH)

**BENTZ ROBERT W REV** (623)214-9551
13450 W Prospect Dr Sun City West AZ 85375-4843 • PSW • EM • (SPR 1952 MDIV)

**BEREUTER BRYCE A REV** (816)361-0329
9909 Wayne Ave. Kansas City MO 64131-3402 • bbereuter@calvarykc.com • MO • SP • Calvary Kansas City MO • (816)444-6908 • (SL 1988 MDIV)

**BERG DONALD A REV** (214)271-1714
2409 Country Club Pkwy Garland TX 75041-2117 • garlandrev@aol.com • TX • Sn/Adm • Bethel Dallas TX • (214)348-0420 • (SPR 1968 MDIV)

**BERG HENRY F REV** (217)643-7702
205 Lincoln Thomasboro IL 62878 • CI • EM • (SL 1966 MDIV)

**BERG JOHN M REV** (414)654-1116
6233 64th St Kenosha WI 53142-2913 • revberg@execpc.com • SW • SP • Lamb Of God Kenosha WI • (414)652-4695 • (FW 1993 MDIV)

**BERG MARK E REV**
87 E Orange St Chagrin Falls OH 44022-2732 • OH • Assoc • Valley Chagrin Falls OH • (440)247-0390 • (FW 1990 MDIV)

**BERG RICHARD W REV** (815)877-2897
4865 Burningtree Dr Rockford IL 61114-5311 • reuberg@gateway.net • NI • EM • (CQ 1983 MAR MED)

**BERGBOWER MICHAEL A REV**
29 89th St Brooklyn NY 11209 • AT • SP • Trinity Brooklyn NY • (718)745-0138 • (SL 1973 MDIV)

**BERGELIN DARREL L REV** (920)565-3349
W2780 Highway 32 Howards Grove WI 53083-5236 • darrelbergelin@juno.com • SW • SP • Trinity Howards Grove WI • (920)565-3349 • (SPR 1976 MDIV)

**BERGEN CARL A REV** (444)354-5841
5700 Emerald Ct Mentor OH 44060-1870 • NJ • EM • (SL 1927 DD)

**BERGEN EDWARD B REV** (815)459-1956
141 Maple St Crystal Lake IL 60014-5918 • revcorvette1@yahoo.com • NI • Sn/Adm • Immanuel Crystal Lake IL • (815)459-1441 • (SL 1969 MA)

**BERGEN RONALD L REV** (330)922-9923
C/O Ohio District Office PO Box 38277 Olmsted Falls OH 44138-0277 • odprez@aol.com • OH • DP • Ohio Olmsted Falls OH • (SL 1961 MDIV STM)

**BERGER RICHARD A REV** (480)671-3657
2208 W Baseline Ave Lot 75 Apache Junction AZ 85220-9511 • rbergerwindfall@aol.com • PSW • EM • (CQ 1982 MAR MAR)

**BERGMAN DAVID R REV** (505)434-5459
1205 Mc Kinley Ave Alamogordo NM 88310-4250 • dandsberg@zianet.com • RM • SP • Trinity Alamogordo NM • (505)437-1482 • (SL 1979 MDIV)

**BERGMAN LARRY W REV** (360)978-6389
470 Dluhosh Rd Onalaska WA 98570-9606 • NOW • Asst • Peace Chehalis WA • (360)748-4108 • (SPR 1972 DMIN)

**BERGMAN MARVIN M REV** (402)643-3724
1610 N Columbia Ave Seward NE 68434-1111 • NEB • EM • (SL 1959 MDIV MED EDD PHD)

**BERGMANN DAVID P REV** (915)599-1398
10009 Trinidad Dr El Paso TX 79925-6075 • RM • EM • (SL 1948 MDIV)

**BERGMANN KEVIN REV** (219)659-3505
1809 Atchison Ave Whiting IN 46394-1615 • S • SP • St Paul Whiting IN • (219)659-0303 • (FW 1988 MDIV)

**BERGMANN MARK W REV** (321)359-8194
1353 Haven Dr Oviedo FL 32765-5205 • FG • EM • (SL 1950 MDIV DMIN DD)

**BERGQUIST DAVID H REV** (515)925-3582
2708 50th Ave Lone Rock IA 50559-8530 • david.bergquist@iowawest.org • IW • SP • Immanuel Lone Rock IA* • (515)925-3597 • (FW 1985 MDIV)

**BERGSTRAZER ALLEN C REV** (402)482-5789
Box 156 Chambers NE 68725 • NEB • SP • St Paul Chambers NE • (402)482-5835 • (SL 1999 MDIV)

**BERGSTRESSER EDWIN L II REV** (614)885-3362
C/O Holy Cross Deaf Luth Chur 360 Morse Rd Columbus OH 43214-1722 • edwinlot@ameritech.net • OH • SP • Holy Cross Deaf Columbus OH • (614)885-3362 • (SL 1984 MDIV)

**BERGSTROM MARTIN E REV** (707)422-2787
C/O Trinity Luth Church 2075 Dover Ave Fairfield CA 94533-2346 • CNH • SP • Trinity Fairfield CA • (707)425-2944 • (SL 1986 MDIV)

**BERGT ROBERT R REV** (314)727-1296
6425 San Bonita Ave Saint Louis MO 63105-3117 • rbergt@aol.com • IN • EM • (SL 1955 MST MDIV)

**BERKELAND MARVIN A REV** (651)345-2629
1101 N Garden St Lake City MN 55041-1901 • MNS • EM • (LS 1952)

**BERKESCH BRENT G REV** (715)532-3034
515 College Ave W Ladysmith WI 54848-2107 • NW • SP • St John Ladysmith WI • (715)532-5780 • (SL 1985 MDIV)

**BERKESCH DENNIS M DR** (313)654-0170
27104 Bryan New Boston MI 48164 • summit@cdlcorp.com • MI • Assoc • St John New Boston MI • (734)654-6366 • (SPR 1975 MDIV MA DMIN)

**BERKESCH WAYNE C REV** (219)495-4040
215 Deborah Dr Fremont IN 46737 • inberk@gte.net • EN • SP • Peace Fremont IN • (219)495-4306 • (CQ 1987 MDIV MA)

**BERLIN VON ERIC REV** (937)492-2024
80 E Mason Rd Sidney OH 45365 • OH • 09/2000 • (FW 1990 MDIV)

**BERNARD DAVID E REV** (716)384-5575
St Paul Lutheran Church 93 Maple Ave PO Box 316 Cohocton NY 14826-0316 • revdber@frontiernet.net • EA • SP • St Paul Cohocton NY • (716)384-5667 • (CQ 2000)

**BERNATH GARY D REV** (440)985-2016
133 Central Dr Amherst OH 44001-1601 • OH • SP • St Paul Amherst OH • (440)988-4157 • (SL 1968 MDIV)

**BERNAU WAYNE A REV** (507)359-2528
C/O Immanuel Luth Church RR 1 Box 41 Courtland MN 56021-9701 • MNS • SP • Immanuel Courtland MN • (507)359-2528 • (SL 1981)

**BERNDT BRUCE E REV** (507)776-3434
309 N 2nd Ave E Truman MN 56088-1129 • MNS • Tchr • Martin Luther Northrop MN • (507)436-5249 • (FW 1982 MDIV)

**BERNDT JEFFRY D REV** (509)785-8010
PO Box 5393 George WA 98824-0393 • NOW • SP • Christ Savior George WA • (509)785-4350 • (SL 1990 MDIV)

**BERNDT JUAN REV** (708)366-8377
837 Hannah Ave Forest Park IL 60130-2005 • NI • EM • (VB 1950 MDIV DD)

**BERNDT LEANDER P REV** (502)479-3343
3025 Meadowview Cir Louisville KY 40220 • pancho38@earthlink.net • IN • EM • (SL 1965 MS MDIV)

**BERNDT MANFRED HELMUTH REV** (208)237-5945
1396 Lavine Dr Pocatello ID 83201-2941 • mnjberndt@aol.com • NOW • Sn/Adm • Grace Pocatello ID • (208)237-0467 • (SL 1962 MDIV STM THD)

**BERNECKER GERALD L REV** (715)234-4979
1326 Kern Ave Rice Lake WI 54868 • first@discover-net.net • NW • SP • First Rice Lake WI • (715)234-7505 • (SL 1983 MDIV)

**BERNER CARL R REV** (320)677-8896
Box 195 Herman MN 56248-0195 • MNN • SP • Bethlehem Herman MN* • (320)677-2525 • (SL 1993 MDIV)

**BERNER CARL W REV** (530)873-0284
6365 Glendale Dr Magalia CA 95954-9514 • CNH • EM • * • (SL 1958)

**BERNER MILTON T REV** (513)231-0267
7682 Clough Pike Cincinnati OH 45244-2936 • OH • SP • Immanuel Cincinnati OH • (513)961-3407 • (SL 1965 MDIV JD)

**BERNER TIMOTHY ARTHUR REV** (651)484-8429
Concordia Academy 2400 N Dale St Roseville MN 55113 • MNS • Tchr • Concordia Academy Roseville MN • (612)484-8429 • (SL 1994 MDIV)

**BERNET ERNEST WALTER REV**
2108 Mims St Fort Worth TX 76112 • ebernetics@aol.com • TX • 06/2000 • (SL 1992 MDIV STM)

**BERNHARDT ROBERT H REV** (262)242-2631
11924 N Granville Rd Mequon WI 53097-2806 • SW • EM • (SL 1956)

**BERNINGHAUS GILBERT B REV** (406)463-2245
C/O Zion Luth Church PO Box 214 Power MT 59468-0214 • MT • EM • (CQ 1994)

**BERNSTEIN JOHN I REV** (719)531-9848
8320 Sutterfield Dr Colorado Springs CO 80920-6206 • jibernie@aol.com • RM • Asst • Holy Cross Colorado Springs CO • (719)596-0661 • (SL 1971 MDIV PHD)

**BERNTHAL AUGUST REV** (941)293-5354
665 W Lake Otis Dr SE Winter Haven FL 33880-3559 • FG • EM • (SL 1950 MDIV DD)

**BERNTHAL DAVID H DR**
505 Hamilton Shore Court N Winter Haven FL 33881 • dpbernthal@prodigy.net • FG • SP • Trinity Athens GA • (706)546-1280 • (CQ 1971 DMIN MAT)

**BERNTHAL ERWIN J REV** (402)489-6517
7005 Shamrock Rd Unit 101 Lincoln NE 68506-2980 • NEB • EM • (SL 1935)

**BERNTHAL HUBERT L REV** (501)925-3329
9221 Grimes Dr Rogers AR 72756-8182 • MDS • EM • (SL 1956)

**BERNTHAL KENNETH G REV** (231)582-7346
1103 BC - EJ Rd Boyne City MI 49712 • MI • SP • Christ Boyne City MI • (231)582-9301 • (SL 1970 MDIV)

**BERNTHAL RICHARD H REV** (810)655-4898
6341 Lady Jeanette Dr Swartz Creek MI 48473-8819 • MI • EM • (SL 1953 MA)

**BERRY FRED L REV**
C/O Trinity Luth Church 2702 Dillon Rd Marshalltown IA 50158-9824 • IE • SP • Trinity Dillon Marshalltown IA • (515)479-2170 • (SL 1990 MDIV)

**BERRY JAMES W REV** (603)352-446
22 Andover St Keene NH 03431-2832 • NE • SP • Trinity Keene NH • (603)352-4446 • (FW 1990 MDIV)

**BERSCHE KENNETH JAY REV** (940)552-2954
14567 FM 2074 Vernon TX 76384-8659 • TX • SP • Zion Vernon TX • (940)552-7164 • (SL 1994 MDIV)

**BERTEAU DANIEL CHRISTIAN REV** (815)784-4086
16126 Hemlock Rd Genoa IL 60135-8513 • dberteau@tbcnet.com • NI • Assoc • Trinity Genoa IL • (815)784-2522 • (SL 1996 MDIV)

**BERTELS GARY LEONARD SR. REV** (708)338-2289
1651 Charleston Ct Melrose Park IL 60160-2416 • crfbertelgl@curf.edu • NI • SHS/C • Northern Illinois Hillside IL • (CQ 1976 MA MA PHD)

**BERTELS RICKY D REV** (715)964-2203
C/O Grace Lutheran Church PO Box 156 Alma Center WI 54611-0156 • pastorgl@discover-net.net • NW • SP • Grace Alma Center WI* • (715)964-2203 • (SL 1986 MDIV)

**BERTERMANN MARK C REV** (503)659-0908
11616 SE 35th Ave Milwaukie OR 97222-6766 • pm@bslc.com • NOW • Assoc • Beautiful Savior Portland OR • (503)788-7000 • (SPR 1972 MDIV)

**BERTRAM ANTHONY T REV** (320)693-7715
1015 N Miller Ave Litchfield MN 55355-1206 • MNS • SP • Immanuel Litchfield MN • (320)693-6155 • (FW 1989 MDIV)

**BERTRAM CRAIG C REV** (651)408-9611
PO Box 334 Chisago City MN 55013-0334 • cnmbert@msn.com • MNN • SP • Lord Of Lakes Chisago City MN • (612)462-3535 • (SL 1993 MDIV)

**BERTRAM EDWARD G REV** (314)376-5113
4972 Country Club Dr High Ridge MO 63049 • edwardb845@aol.com • MO • S Ex/S • Missouri Saint Louis MO • (314)317-4550 • (SL 1960)

**BERTRAM PETER W REV** (308)432-3526
808 E 9th St Chadron NE 69337-2759 • pbertram@panhandle.net • WY • SP • Our Savior Chadron NE • (308)432-5698 • (FW 1981 MDIV)

**BERTSCH ARIE D REV** (701)363-2636
815 2nd St East PO Box 635 Mc Clusky ND 58463-0635 • ND • SP • St John Mc Clusky ND • (701)363-2636 • (FW 1998 MDIV)

**BESALSKI ROBERT C REV** (352)376-1392
4520 NW 16th Pl Gainesville FL 32605-3488 • ebesalski@aol.com • FG • EM • (SL 1958 MDIV MED)

**BESEL GORDON W REV** (501)621-6488
706 Valley West Dr Rogers AR 72756-1769 • gbesel@arkansas.net • MDS • SP • Holy Trinity Rogers AR • (501)636-1135 • (SL 1979 MDIV MED)

**BESEL KEITH LEROY REV** (303)464-0310
3220 S Princess Cir Broomfield CO 80020-5413 • kbesel@ctrlc.org • RM • SP • Christ The Rock Broomfield CO • (303)438-5569 • (SL 1996 MDIV)

**BESLER WILLIAM REV** (517)734-3007
C/O St Michael Luth Church 5918 M 451 Rd Rogers City MI 49779 • MI • SP • St Michael Rogers City MI • (517)734-3007 • (CQ 1981 MED)

**BESTIAN BRIAN R REV** (713)224-0684
C/O Trinity Lutheran Church 800 Houston Ave Houston TX 77007-7792 • b.bestian@tmls.org • TX • Sn/Adm • Trinity Houston TX • (713)224-0684 • (SL 1987 MDIV)

**BESTUL DENNIS E REV** (408)255-1764
1191 Cordelia Ave San Jose CA 95129-4211 • bestul@earthlink.net • CNH • Sn/Adm • Our Savior Cupertino CA • (408)252-0345 • (SPR 1974 MDIV)

**BETKE NORMAN E REV** (517)426-3516
4552 Oberlin Rd Gladwin MI 48624-8955 • nbetke@mich.com • IE • EM • (SPR 1959)

**BETKER BRUCE R REV** (808)235-3467
46-369 Haiku Rd # 1 Kaneohe HI 96744-4257 • btbetker@worldnet.att.net • CNH • SP • St Mark Kaneohe HI • (808)247-4565 • (SL 1973 MDIV)

**BETOW BURTON C REV** (218)825-0532
1215 11th St SE Brainerd MN 56401-4103 • MNN • EM • (SPR 1952)

**BETTERMANN JAMES A REV** (270)796-8320
C/O Holy Trinity Luth Church 553 Ashmoor Ave Bowling Green KY 42101-3702 • rbetter1@aol.com • MDS • SP • Holy Trinity Bowling Green KY • (270)843-9595 • (FW 1983 MDIV)

**BETTERMANN VERNON L REV** (309)699-5411
C/O St Peter Luth Church PO Box 2205 East Peoria IL 61611-0205 • headpadre@aol.com • CI • Sn/Adm • St Peter East Peoria IL • (309)699-5411 • (SL 1967 MDIV)

**BETZ JOHN HANDLEY REV**
14 Thomas Craddock Ct Pikesville MD 21208-7305 • SE • SP • Pilgrim Baltimore MD • (410)484-6692 • (FW 1997)

**BETZNER DAVID J REV** (301)694-8761
6958 Sundays Ln Frederick MD 21702-2116 • SE • SP • Peace In Christ Walkersville MD • (301)845-6300 • (SL 1969 MDIV)

**BEUSCHLEIN CARL W REV** (541)312-2346
60061 Cheyenne Rd Bend OR 97702 • NOW • EM • (SL 1959 MDIV)

**BEUTEL DAVID A REV** (716)731-8136
6138 Baer Rd Sanborn NY 14132-9264 • EN • SP • Redeemer North Tonawanda NY • (716)692-5734 • (SPR 1975 MDIV)

**BEUTEL GREGORY REV** (817)306-0698
7937 Firefly Dr Fort Worth TX 76137-1223 • horkma@worldnet.att.net • TX • Assoc • Crown of Life Colleyville TX • (817)421-5683 • (SL 1998 MDIV)

**BEVERSDORF ALDEN J REV** (715)536-1512
1001 E 6th St Merrill WI 54452-1412 • abever@stjohn.merrill.wi.us • NW • Sn/Adm • St John Merrill WI • (715)536-4722 • (SL 1968 MDIV MURP)

**BEVERSDORF JAMES A REV** (724)352-0108
329 Hannahstown Rd Cabot PA 16023-2203 • jim42bon@pgh.net • EA • Assoc • St Luke Cabot PA • (724)352-2777 • (SL 1969 MDIV)

**BEVERSDORF WILLIAM A REV** (253)630-4475
25221 161st Pl SE Covington WA 98042 • NOW • SP • Peace Kent WA • (253)631-3454 • (SL 1982 MDIV)

**BEYER ARTHUR H REV** (864)944-8542
202 Safe Harbor Cir Salem SC 29676 • artbeyer@aol.com • NI • Sn/Adm • Trinity Lisle IL • (630)964-1272 • (SL 1964 DMIN)

**BEYER CHARLES E REV** (517)684-0545
3314 Boy Scout Rd Bay City MI 48706-1249 • neb1@efortress.com • MI • EM • (SL 1963 MA)

**BEYER ELMER E REV**
2441 Blueberry Dr Oxnard CA 93030-1536 • EN • EM • (SL 1941)

**BEYER EUGENE A REV** (480)502-5116
10432 E Pinnacle Peak Rd Scottsdale AZ 85255-9400 • PSW • EM • (SL 1954)

**BEYER JAMES D REV** (707)538-3390
556 Saint Mary Dr Santa Rosa CA 95409-3260 • jim@stmarklc.org • CNH • Sn/Adm • St Mark Santa Rosa CA • (707)545-1230 • (FW 1977 MDIV)

**BEYER JAY B REV** (806)796-1290
2313 52nd St Lubbock TX 79412-2507 • beyer3family@juno.com • TX • SP • Redeemer Lubbock TX • (806)744-6178 • (SL 1993 MDIV)

**BEYER JONATHAN M REV** (501)262-5917
208 Brentwood St Hot Springs AR 71901-8102 • jkbeyer@netzero.net • MDS • SP • First Hot Springs AR • (501)525-0322 • (SL 1985 MDIV)

**BEYER MARK E REV** (805)983-0094
1820 Holly Ave Oxnard CA 93030-6233 • mbeyer1@gte.com • PSW • Sn/Adm • St John Oxnard CA • (805)983-0330 • (SPR 1976 MDIV)

**BEYER MICHAEL R REV**
2031 La Salle Ct Chula Vista CA 91913-3118 • PSW • SP • Of Joy Chula Vista CA • (619)482-1214 • (SL 1991 MDIV)

**BEYER PAUL J REV** (316)246-5220
PO Box 195 Nashville KS 67112-0105 • pjbeyer@juno.com • KS • SP • Trinity Medicine Lodge KS* • (316)886-3397 • (FW 1993 MDIV)

**BEYER PHILIP J REV**
1 Paulownia Rcho Sta Marg CA 92688-1328 • PSW • D Miss • Mount Hope Rancho St Margarita CA • (949)459-1463 • (FW 1983 MDIV)

**BEYER TIMOTHY P REV** (310)694-6437
9422 Mikinda Ave La Habra CA 90631-2467 • PSW • SP • Hope Whittier CA • (562)943-3888 • (FW 1983)

**BEYER WILLIAM DAVIS REV** (704)523-5965
840 Seneca Pl Charlotte NC 28210-2924 • william.beyer@worldnet.att.net • SE • SP • All Saints Charlotte NC • (704)523-4287 • (SL 1996 MDIV)

**BEYERS BURNELL REV** (402)727-9324
2237 Teakwood Dr Fremont NE 68025-6801 • NEB • EM • (TH 1953)

**BIAR HENRY H REV**
504 Elm Bastrop TX 78602-2518 • TX • SP • Prince Of Peace Bastrop TX • (512)303-5267 • (SL 1992 MDIV)

**BIAR HENRY H SR. DR** (210)656-5425
5138 Campe Verde Dr San Antonio TX 78233-5402 • kingluthch@aol.com • TX • Sn/Adm • King Of Kings San Antonio TX • (210)656-6508 • (SL 1960 MDIV MSED DMIN)

**BIBERDORF RICHARD W REV** (314)428-5503
2335 Kratky Rd Apt C Saint Louis MO 63114-1782 • biberdorf4@juno.com • CNH • 10/1999 • (SL 1983 MDIV)

**BIBLER BRIAN L REV** (254)780-9908
10 Triton Dr Belton TX 76513-6460 • blbibler@bigfoot.com • TX • Assoc • Immanuel Temple TX • (254)773-3898 • (FW 1986 MDIV)

**BICKEL ADOLF M REV** (419)598-8711
UO 94 Rd 16 Napoleon OH 43545 • OH • EM • (SL 1945)

**BICKEL CRAIG L REV** (850)479-9449
4419 Eastpointe Dr Pensacola FL 32514-6610 • fl-bics@juno.com • SO • Sn/Adm • Grace Pensacola FL • (850)476-5667 • (FW 1992 MDIV)

**BICKEL ELDOR F REV** (517)646-8668
10223 Lafayette Ln Dimondale MI 48821-9548 • eldotbickel@juno.com • MI • EM • (SL 1949)

**BICKEL EMIL L REV** (573)547-8456
121 Independence Dr Perryville MO 63775-1496 • MO • EM • (SL 1930)

**BICKEL KURT A REV** (419)749-2831
5398 Mentzer Rd Convoy OH 45832-8804 • kabickel@bright.net • OH • EM • (SL 1953 MDIV)

**BICKEL LLOYD A REV** (219)925-1995
C/O Trinity Lutheran Church 1801 N Main St Auburn IN 46706-1047 • IN • SP • Trinity Auburn IN • (219)925-2440 • (SL 1971 MDIV)

**BICKEL OTTOMAR E REV** (440)392-6413
5700 Emerald Ct #257 Mentor OH 44060-1870 • OH • EM • (SL 1942 MDIV)

**BICKEL PAUL V REV** (410)661-1028
1805 Cromwood Rd Baltimore MD 21234-2701 • SE • Tchr • Baltimore LHS Baltimore MD • (410)825-2323 • (CQ 1982 MAR)

**BICKEL PHILIP M REV** (651)487-1260
1167 Ryan Ave W Roseville MN 55113 • pmbickel@aol.com • MNS • 08/1996 08/2000 • (SPR 1975 MDIV DMISS)

**BICKEL TIMOTHY A REV** (716)592-3857
9141 Cattaraugus St Springville NY 14141 • tpbickel@juno.com • EA • SP • Salem Springville NY • (716)592-4893 • (SL 1998 MDIV)

**BICKEL TIMOTHY J REV** (517)871-5015
8581 Fulmer Rd Millington MI 48746-9702 • timothyjbickel@hotmail.com • MI • Assoc • St Paul Millington MI • (517)871-4581 • (SL 1971 MDIV)

**BICKNASE KEITH W REV** (507)532-3982
604 Roosevelt St Marshall MN 56258-1952 • MNS • SP • Good Shepherd Marshall MN • (507)532-4857 • (SL 1998 MDIV)

**BICKNER GARY A REV** (505)722-3283
711 S Navajo Dr Gallup NM 87301-5548 • gmbick@cia-g.com • RM • SP • Trinity Gallup NM • (505)863-3375 • (SL 1983 MDIV)

**BIDINGER RICHARD M REV** (920)528-8094
C/O St Paul Luth Church PO Box 167 Cascade WI 53011-0167 • rbidinge@excel.net • SW • SP • St Paul Cascade WI • (920)528-8094 • (SL 1986 MDIV)

**BIEGEL STEPHEN J REV**
C/O Trinity Lutheran Church 405 Rush St Roselle IL 60172-2228 • NI • Asst • Trinity Roselle IL • (630)894-3263 • (SPR 1976 MDIV)

**BIEGNER PAUL R REV** (218)828-1313
207 Hawkins Dr Brainerd MN 56401-3916 • riverev@brainerd.net • MNN • EM • (SL 1957 MST)

**BIEL RONALD D REV** (941)394-3317
204 Shadowridge Ct Marco Island FL 34145-3622 • rbiel4golf@aol.com • FG • SP • Marco Marco Island FL • (941)394-0332 • (SL 1969 STM MDIV)

**BIELEFELD EARL A REV** (602)454-2908
2609 W Southern Ave - #10 1337 W 11th St Tempe AZ 85282 • bielefeld@access1.net • PSW • SP • Beautiful Savior Tempe AZ • (480)967-2660 • (SPR 1967 MDIV)

**BIELEFELDT WALTER F REV** (281)351-0894
1000 Hicks St Apt 313 Tomball TX 77375-4154 • TX • EM • (SL 1938)

**BIELENBERG ALBERT E REV** (321)639-6617
104 Riverside Dr #C-305 Cocoa FL 32922-7859 • apbiel@aol.com • FG • EM • (SL 1954)

**BIELENBERG STEVEN M REV** (612)214-9117
806 5th St SW Willmar MN 56201-3417 • sbielen@mail.tds.net • MNN • SP • Redeemer Willmar MN • (320)235-4685 • (SL 1988 MDIV)

**BIER LOUIS H REV** (781)326-5774
169 Nahatan St Westwood MA 02090-3607 • NE • M Chap • New England Springfield MA • (SPR 1959 MDIV MED)

**BIERLEIN ALBERT R REV** (219)447-6615
7902 Newlin Dr Fort Wayne IN 46816-2781 • albierlein@hotmail.com • IN • Sn/Adm • Emmanuel Fort Wayne IN • (219)447-3005 • (SL 1971 MDIV)

**BIERMAN EDWARD A REV** (650)568-0368
4000 Farm Hill Blvd Apt 112 Redwood City CA 94061-1006 • ed@biermans.com • CNH • 10/1996 10/1999 • (SL 1991 MDIV)

**BIERMANN HERBERT L REV** (616)393-9679
838 York St Holland MI 49423 • MI • EM • (SPR 1962)

**BIERMANN JOEL D REV** (314)353-0149
7116 Rhodes Ave Saint Louis MO 63123 • lam323@juno.com • MI • 08/1998 08/2000 • (SL 1987 MDIV)

**BIERMANN JOHN C REV** (253)770-8656
2517 14th Street Pl SE Puyallup WA 98374-6106 • jcbiermann@aol.com • NOW • SP • Immanuel Puyallup WA • (253)848-4548 • (SPR 1973 MDIV)

**BIERMANN TODD A REV** (440)884-0186
3327 Park Dr Parma OH 44134-4644 • tabiermann@juno.com • S • SP • Calvary Parma OH • (440)845-0070 • (SL 1990 MDIV)

**BIESENTHAL BRUCE W REV**
1690 22nd St Apt M Wheaton IL 60187-7775 • NI • 11/1994 11/1999 • (SL 1976)

**BIESENTHAL W LEROY REV** (314)965-4747
2137 Mason Green Dr Ballwin MO 63011-4419 • MO • EM • (SL 1948 MDIV DLITT)

**BIESTER DONALD W REV** (219)728-2970
1143 W 500 N Decatur IN 46733-9519 • IN • Sn/Adm • Zion Decatur IN • (219)724-7177 • (SL 1960 MDIV)

**BIGGS DONALD L REV** (717)848-6978
2276 N Point Dr York PA 17402-1954 • rev.biggs@juno.com • SE • EM • (SL 1956)

**BIGGS LUTHER C REV** (402)483-5540
7641 Myrtle St Lincoln NE 65806-3148 • lbiggs1558@aol.com • NEB • Sn/Adm • Messiah Lincoln NE • (402)489-3024 • (SL 1984 MDIV)

**BIJJIGA JAYA P REV** (314)963-0029
2465 Cecelia Ave Saint Louis MO 63144-2512 • bijaimna@aol.com • NI • O Miss • Northern Illinois Hillside IL • (CQ 1995 MA)

**BILGREEN DAVID A DR** (636)285-8808
10991 Blackhawk Ln Dittmer MO 63023-2662 • db.12@aol.com • MO • SP • Cedar Hill Cedar Hill MO • (314)274-4802 • (FW 1983 MDIV DMIN)

**BILLINGS STEVEN S REV**
8477 Honey Ln Canton MI 48187 • ssbillings@earthlink.net • MI • Sn/Adm • Redford Detroit MI • (313)535-3733 • (FW 1991 MDIV)

**BILLOW WILLIAM D REV** (662)324-1536
103 Edgewood Dr Starkville MS 39759-2317 • SO • EM • (CQ 1982 MA)

**BINGENHEIMER MICHAEL R REV** (901)385-1997
3133 Hill Lake Dr Bartlett TN 38135-2585 • gobing@hotmail.com • MDS • SP • Immanuel Memphis TN • (901)373-4486 • (SL 1986 MDIV)

**BINGENHEIMER ROY W REV** (417)847-4091
1009 Hickory Wildwood Estates Cassville MO 65625-2001 • bingmail@mo-net.com • MDS • EM • (SL 1959)

**BINZ CURTIS A REV** (707)894-1850
PO Box 455 Cloverdale CA 95425-0455 • CNH • SP • Grace Cloverdale CA • (707)894-2330 • (SL 1999 MDIV)

**BIRA CLIFFORD F REV** (810)659-4145
1250 Bonnie Sue Dr Flushing MI 48433-1475 • cfbcib@aol.com • MI • SP • Holy Cross Flushing MI • (810)659-5926 • (FW 1981 MDIV)

**BIRD CHAD L REV** (405)356-2170
PO Box 628 Wellston OK 74881-0628 • torahman@juno.com • OK • SP • St Paul Wellston OK • (405)356-4203 • (FW 1996 MDIV MST)

**BIRD GEARY F REV** (706)376-2316
514 Eagle Heights Rd Canon GA 30520-4176 • SE • EM • (SPR 1971 THD)

**BIRD RALPH E REV** (501)455-4414
20 Butterfly Cove Little Rock AR 72209 • MDS • EM • (SL 1947)

**BIRNER CHARLES R REV** (714)768-9059
23841 Via El Rocio Mission Viejo CA 92691-3519 • cbirner@home.com • PSW • EM • (SL 1947 MDIV)

**BIRNER DAVID C REV**
955 Millpond Rd Valparaiso IN 46385-6121 • 103601.2023@compuserve.com • MO • S Ex/S • Missouri Saint Louis MO • (314)317-4550 • (CQ 1986 MDIV)

**BIRNER EDWARD H REV** (301)474-9200
13N Ridge Rd Greenbelt MD 20770-0706 • ehbirner@cs.com • SE • EM • (SL 1953)

**BIRNER PAUL D REV** (828)256-4967
1582 Haupt Strasse Conover NC 28613-0396 • stplcms@twave.net • SE • Sn/Adm • St Peter Conover NC • (828)256-2970 • (SL 1985 MDIV)

**BIRTELL BRAD EVAN REV** (402)285-0498
C/O St John Lutheran Church 39452 Mason Rd Columbus NE 68601-9749 • NEB • SP • St John Columbus NE • (402)285-0498 • (SL 1992 MDIV)

**BIRTELL KENTON JAY REV** (308)995-2208
1402 East Ave Dr Holdrege NE 68601 • NEB • SP • Mount Calvary Holdrege NE • (308)995-2208 • (SL 1995 MDIV)

**BISCHOF JON CHARLES REV** (618)939-7094
5765 Maeystown Rd Waterloo IL 62298-6539 • SI • SP • Holy Cross Waterloo IL • (618)939-7094 • (SL 1991 MDIV STM)

**BISCHOFF CLIFFORD L REV** (414)442-2062
2811 N 23 St Milwaukee WI 53206-1645 • bishlark@classic.msn.com • SW • SP • Emmaus Milwaukee WI • (414)444-6090 • (SL 1971 MDIV)

**BISCHOFF FREDERICK A REV** (414)534-3493
602 Aber Dr Waterford WI 53185-4404 • SW • SP • St Peter Waterford WI • (262)534-3639 • (FW 1981 MDIV)

**BISCHOFF LESTER L REV** (618)483-5317
6252 E 600th Ave Altamont IL 62411 • CI • EM • (SPR 1952)

**BISCHOFF WILLIAM H REV** (314)739-5354
12026 Avery Ln Bridgeton MO 63044-3529 • whbischoff@aol.com • MO • EM • (SL 1957 MDIV)

**BISHOP DANIEL JOHN REV** (217)997-5973
PO Box 49 Arenzville IL 62611-0047 • CI • SP • Trinity Arenzville IL • (217)997-5534 • (FW 1992 MDIV)

**BITELY RODNEY E REV** (804)559-3185
8060 Kiwi Lane Mechanicsville VA 23111 • SE • SP • St Paul Richmond VA • (804)222-5416 • (SL 1999 MDIV)

**BITTER GLENN RAY REV** (785)232-0962
2414 SE Alexander Dr Topeka KS 66605-1856 • glennbitter@bigfoot.com • KS • Asst • St John Topeka KS • (785)354-7132 • (SPR 1967 MDIV)

**BITTNER PAUL E REV** (715)832-8510
1616 South St Eau Claire WI 54701-6634 • w0aih@ecol.net • NW • EM • (SPR 1958 MDIV)

**BJORGAARD JON A REV** (810)948-2480
12400 23 Mile Rd Shelby Township MI 48315-2620 • jonbjorgaard@shepherdsgate.com • MI • SP • Shepherds Gate Shelby Township MI • (810)731-4544 • (SL 1986 MDIV)

**BJORNSTAD KRISTIAN G REV**
C/O Peace Lutheran Church 2506 N Main Ave Scranton PA 18508-1606 • EA • Shepherds Gate Shelby Township MI • (810)731-4544 • (ED 1994 MDIV)

**BJORNSTAD ROBERT M REV** (541)924-0367
2517 NW Gibson Hill Rd Albany OR 97321-1131 • yasurebjorn@cs.com • NOW • SP • Immanuel Albany OR • (541)926-3495 • (CQ 1981 MDIV)

**BLACK DONALD G REV** (713)782-6307
7719 Meadowvale Dr Houston TX 77063-6211 • TX • Assoc • Trinity Houston TX • (713)224-0684 • (SL 1958)

**BLACK GEORGE E REV** (810)677-1167
3293 Barnaby Dr Shelby Twp MI 48316-4807 • revmrblack@hotmail.com • MI • Sn/Adm • Trinity Utica MI • (810)731-4490 • (FW 1977 MDIV DMIN)

**BLACKWELL MICHAEL C REV** (716)681-5499
54 Paula Dr Cheektowaga NY 14225-4432 • mjblackwell@webtv.net • EA • SP • St John Depew NY • (716)683-3947 • (SL 1971 MDIV)

**BLAIN JAMES H REV** (616)361-0808
400 Sligh Blvd NE Grand Rapids MI 49505-3511 • MI • SP • St James Grand Rapids MI • (616)363-7718 • (SL 1977 MDIV)

**BLAIR DAVID W REV** (425)778-3041
2925 227th St SW Brier WA 98036-8147 • oslcsea@tcmnet.com • NOW • SP • Our Savior Seattle WA • (206)363-0110 • (SL 1981 MDIV)

**BLAKELOCK B BRUCE REV** (281)359-5359
2018 Lakeville Dr Kingwood TX 77339 • TX • SP • Grace New Caney TX • (281)689-0206 • (SPR 1966)

**BLANCO CHARLES W REV** (303)857-4903
889 S Hoover Ave Fort Lupton CO 80621-1254 • cwblanco@worldnet.att.net • RM • SP • Mount Calvary Fort Lupton CO • (303)857-6827 • (SL 1983 MDIV STM)

**BLANK RUDOLPH H REV**
C/O Jet Cargo Intnl M 182 PO Box 20010 Miami FL 33102-0010 • NI • S Miss • Northern Illinois Hillside IL • (SL 1959 MDIV DD)

**BLANKE JONATHAN A REV** (314)505-7673
One Founders Way - Apt B St Louis MO 63105 • j.blanke@worldnet.att.net • SE • S Miss • Southeastern Alexandria VA • (SL 1992 MDIV)

**BLANKE NEAL R REV** (760)373-4068
PO Box 2337 California City CA 93504-0337 • PSW • D Miss • Trinity California City CA • (760)373-4068 • (FW 1988 MDIV)

**BLANKE NORWOOD M REV** (909)988-3438
1347 S Vine Pl Ontario CA 91762-5751 • PSW • Sn/Adm • Redeemer Ontario CA • (909)986-2615 • (SPR 1964 MDIV)

**BLANKENBUEHLER LORENZ REV** (412)352-4308
112 Marwood Rd Apt 351 Cabot PA 16023-2229 • EA • EM • (SL 1943 MDIV)

**BLASDEL BRADY W REV** (515)256-0692
4830 Candlewick Dr Norwalk IA 50211 • IW • SP • Christ Our Savior Norwalk IA • (515)981-9145 • (SL 1998 MDIV)

**BLASKE MARVIN O REV** (320)369-4101
9366 85th Ave Milaca MN 56353-4524 • MNN • EM • (SPR 1955)

**BLATNICKY EDWIN J REV** (815)730-1291
321 S Park Dr Joliet IL 60436-2044 • NI • EM • (SPR 1959 MDIV)

**BLAU RONALD E REV** (623)933-7175
14210 N Bolivar Dr Sun City AZ 85351-2939 • ronblau@juno.com • PSW • EM • (SL 1959 MDIV)

**BLAU TIMOTHY A REV** (949)737-6613
1530 Concordia Irvine CA 92612-3203 • ttblau@yahoo.com • PSW • Assoc • Salem Orange CA • (714)633-2366 • (SL 1992 MDIV)

**BLAZEK SCOTT R REV** (505)769-0693
5 Pineway Blvd Clovis NM 88101-8464 • immanuel@pdrpip.com • RM • SP • Immanuel Clovis NM • (505)763-4526 • (SL 1975 MDIV)

**BLECH RANDOLF D REV** (920)987-5283
N6404 State Road 49 Weyauwega WI 54983-5618 • randdb@pitnet.net • SW • SP • Christ Weyauwega WI • (920)987-5283 • (FW 1981 MDIV)

**BLEICK ROY H REV** (815)398-1867
7190 Weathered Oak Ln Rockford IL 61107 • MO • EM • (SPR 1954 MDIV)

**BLEKE EARL H REV** (414)567-4152
W358N5971 Misty Ct Oconomowoc WI 53066-2436 • ebleke@blhs.org • SW • D Ex/S • South Wisconsin Milwaukee WI* • (414)464-8100 • (SL 1976 MDIV MSW)

**BLEMASTER RICHARD E REV** (716)542-2410
191 Golden Pond Ests Akron NY 14001-9223 • EA • EM • * • (SL 1958 MDIV)

**BLESI ROGER D REV** (253)639-9921
14419 SE 251st Pl Kent WA 98042 • blesi@hotmail.com • NOW • Df Min • Northwest Portland OR • (FW 1998 MDIV)

**BLIESE KARL REV**
4880 N 900 E Whitestown IN 46075-9315 • IN • O Sp Min • Indiana Fort Wayne IN • (CQ 1984)

**BLIESE WILLIAM M REV** (937)299-3805
3072 Gracemore Ave Dayton OH 45420-1258 • bliwil@webtv.net • OH • EM • (SL 1955 MDIV DMIN)

**BLOCH JAMES REV** (217)935-3246
600 W Leander St Clinton IL 61727-2101 • CI • SP • Christ Clinton IL • (217)935-5808 • (SPR 1970)

**BLOCH PHILIP E REV** (812)523-8415
1237 Hickory Hill Rd Seymour IN 47274-2619 • pmbloch@hotmail.com • IN • Assoc • Immanuel Seymour IN • (812)522-3118 • (SL 1990 MDIV)

**BLOCK DAVID L REV** (402)894-0389
17474 Riviera Dr Omaha NE 68136-1991 • davelblock@aol.com • NEB • Sn/Adm • Divine Shepher Omaha NE • (402)895-1500 • (SL 1969 MS MDIV DMIN)

**BLOCK HAROLD H REV** (319)279-3667
2689 Quail Ave Readlyn IA 50668-9798 • hnblock@netins.net • IE • SP • Immanuel Readlyn IA • (319)279-3977 • (CQ 1991 MAR MSIMT MSPS)

**BLOCK KENNETH B REV** (402)643-3324
1261 N 1st St Seward NE 68434-1224 • kblock@seward.cune.edu • NEB • SHS/C • Nebraska Seward NE • (SL 1963 MDIV MST MLAT MCLGR)

**BLOCK LARRY H REV** (316)223-0844
419 W 8th St Fort Scott KS 66701-2570 • tlc@terraworld.net • KS • SP • Trinity Fort Scott KS • (316)223-3596 • (SL 1996 MDIV)

**BLOCK THOMAS E REV** (607)756-7614
24 William St Cortland NY 13045 • EA • SP • St Paul Cortland NY • (607)753-7101 • (SL 1977 MDIV)

**BLOCKER BRUCE L REV**
Zion Lutheran Church PO Box 259 Oconto WI 54153-0259 • NW • SP • Zion Oconto WI* • (920)834-5037 • (FW 1990 MDIV)

**BLOEDEL DAVID L REV** (805)566-1806
1480 Manzanita St Carpinteria CA 93013 • faithlc@juno.com • PSW • SP • Faith Carpinteria CA • (805)684-4707 • (SL 1967 MDIV)

**BLOEMKER RUDOLPH E REV** (320)352-5240
300 Maple St Sauk Centre MN 56378-1223 • MNN • SP • Zion Sauk Centre MN • (320)352-3447 • (CQ 1981 MAR MA)

**BLOKER JAMES S REV** (804)525-5876
202 Sheffey Dr Forest VA 24551-2314 • jbloker@centralva.net • SE • SP • Our Savior Lynchburg VA • (804)384-6651 • (FW 1983 MDIV)

**BLOM KEITH D REV** (570)836-7420
8 Jeanne Dr Tunkhannock PA 18657-9523 • stpaul99@epix.net • EA • SP • St Paul Tunkhannock PA • (570)836-2301 • (FW 1982 MDIV)

**BLOMENBERG RALPH REV** (812)523-3460
580 Nottingham Dr Seymour IN 47274-1940 • immanuel@hsonline.net • IN • Sn/Adm • Immanuel Seymour IN • (812)522-3118 • (SL 1981 MDIV)

**BLOMQUIST RODNEY G REV** (217)824-4705
717 Glacier Dr Taylorville IL 62568-9105 • CI • SP • Trinity Taylorville IL • (217)824-8148 • (FW 1980 MDIV)

**BLONSKI EDWARD A REV** (920)387-0257
650 Green Bay Dr Mayville WI 53050-1708 • reved@internetwis.com • SW • Assoc • St John Mayville WI • (920)387-3568 • (SL 1995 MDIV)

**BLOOM JEFFREY L REV** (402)396-9705
C/O St John Lutheran Church 210 N Monroe St PO Box 322 Pilger NE 68768-0322 • bloom5@juno.com • NEB • SP • St John Pilger NE • (402)396-3478 • (SL 1998 MDIV)

**BLOOM NEIL D REV** (208)687-1809
PO Box 1031 Rathdrum ID 83858-1031 • nbloom@dmi.net • NOW • SP • Shepherd Hills Rathdrum ID • (208)687-1809 • (CQ 1993 MDIV)

**BLOOM WILLIAM W REV** (516)981-7113
67 Avenue A Holbrook NY 11741-1431 • AT • Sn/Adm • St John Holbrook NY • (631)588-6050 • (SL 1965 DMIN)

**BLUHM G DAVID REV** (704)871-1514
6203 St. Peter's Church Rd Conover NC 28613 • SE • EM • (SL 1985 MDIV JD)

**BLUM RUDOLPH P REV**
PO Box 3163 Teaneck NJ 07666-9103 • NJ • EM • (SL 1934)

**BLUMENKAMP EDWIN W REV** (217)434-8650
13 Hooken Quarter Fowler IL 62338-9731 • CI • EM • (SPR 1955)

**BLUNCK PAUL H REV** (619)286-7272
6820 1/2 Mission Gorge Rd San Diego CA 92120-2437 • MT • EM • (SPR 1957 MED)

**BOARTS MATTHEW A REV** (405)733-2577
PO Box 45963 Tinker AFB OK 73145 • mabbts@prodigy.net • TX • M Chap • Texas Austin TX • (FW 1995 MDIV)

**BOCHE RICHARD O REV** (307)634-1524
7520 Drummond Ave Cheyenne WY 82009-2206 • rboche@wyoming.com • WY • Sn/Adm • Our Savior Cheyenne WY • (307)632-2580 • (SL 1973 MA MDIV)

**BOCK DOUGLAS P REV** (317)889-4337
4506 Tarragon Dr Indianapolis IN 46237-3672 • revdbock@aol.com • IN • SP • St Peter Indianapolis IN • (317)638-7245 • (CQ 1994 MBA)

**BOCK GORDON EUGENE REV** (320)563-4522
607 11th St N Wheaton MN 56296-1100 • MNN • EM • (SPR 1973 STM MA)

**BOCKELMANN NEIL M REV** (409)822-2742
C/O Bethel Luth Church 410 East Ln Bryan TX 77802-1005 • TX • SP • Bethel Bryan TX • (979)822-2742 • (SL 1972 MDIV)

**BODA SAMUEL REV** (618)288-5683
216 Westglen Dr Glen Carbon IL 62034-1006 • S • EM • (SL 1948 STM THD)

**BODE ARTHUR J REV** (616)861-2952
C/O St Stephen Lutheran Church 7410 W Johnson Rd Shelby MI 49455-9511 • MI • Sn/Adm • St Stephen Shelby MI • (231)861-2952 • (FW 1988 MDIV)

**BODE CHRISTIAN DANIEL REV** (612)593-5319
1321 Independence Ave S St Louis Park MN 55426-1867 • chris@crossview.com • MNS • Asst • Cross View Edina MN • (952)941-1094 • (SL 1996 MDIV)

**BODE CRAIG H REV** (216)692-0256
1622 Beverly Hills Dr Euclid OH 44117-1950 • bethlehemluth@juno.com • OH • SP • Bethlehem Euclid OH • (216)531-5990 • (FW 1980 MDIV)

**BODE DAVID A REV** (218)346-6409
PO Box 604 Brainerd MN 56401-0604 • MNN • DP • Minnesota North Brainerd MN • (SL 1963 MRE)

**BODE EDGAR W REV** (712)885-2667
PO Box 139 Ute IA 51060-0139 • charis811@juno.com • IW • SP • St Paul Ute IA • (712)885-2221 • (SL 1968 MDIV)

**BODE GERHARD F REV** (918)687-6902
2024 Sallie Ave Muskogee OK 74403-5848 • gerbode@oknetl.net • OK • EM • (CQ 1965 DD)

**BODE GERHARD H REV** (320)587-3031
22543 Unit Ave Hutchinson MN 55350-4111 • MNS • Sn/Adm • Peace Hutchinson MN • (320)587-3031 • (SPR 1966 MDIV)

**BODE GRANT T REV**
118 Maple St N PO Box 490 Lester Prairie MN 55354-0490 • stpaullp@hutchtel.net • MNS • SP • St Paul Lester Prairie MN • (320)395-2573 • (FW 1994 MDIV)

**BODE HAROLD H REV** (440)944-1861
2250 Par Ln #117 Willoughby Hills OH 44094 • haroldhb@earthlink.net • OH • EM • (SPR 1963)

**BODE KIM E REV** (570)289-4081
28 S Greeenwood Hop Bottom PA 18824 • hbgrace@epix.net • EA • SP • Grace Hop Bottom PA • (570)289-4468 • (SPR 1976 MDIV)

**BODE RICHARD P REV** (095)455-7110
C/O Russis Luth Hour Minis 37 666 5th Ave Suite 572 New York NY 10103 • KS • Grace Hop Bottom PA • (570)289-4468 • (SL 1959 MA STM THD)

**BODLEY ARTHUR L REV** (850)944-3357
401 Thorn Ct Pensacola FL 32526-1166 • NI • EM • (GB 1961)

**BODLEY CHRISTOPHER RAYNARD** (407)292-7491
C/O Our Savior Luth Church 1750 Bruton Blvd Orlando FL 32805-5132 • FG • SP • Our Savior Orlando FL • (407)295-0261 • (FW 1992 MDIV)

**BODLEY SIMON REV** (314)367-3404
5624 Bartmer Ave Saint Louis MO 63112-2822 • MO • Missouri Saint Louis MO • (314)317-4550 • (GB 1957 MA LLD)

**BODLING KURT A REV** (914)793-1973
214 Midland Ave Tuckahoe NY 10707-4308 • kab@concordia-ny.edu • AT • SHS/C • Atlantic Bronxville NY • (914)337-5700 • (SL 1980 MDIV STM MS)

**BOECHE HAROLD A REV** (714)877-4426
C/O First Luth Church 9315 Citrus Ave Fontana CA 92335-5563 • PSW • O Sp Min • First Fontana CA • (909)823-3457 • (SL 1958)

**BOECK ALAN G REV** (608)742-8441
214 Highland Ave Portage WI 53901-1550 • SW • Sn/Adm • St John Portage WI • (608)742-2387 • (FW 1981 MDIV)

**BOECK RICHARD J JR. REV** (414)871-1209
3218 N 48th St Milwaukee WI 53216-3344 • rboeck@execpc.com • SW • 11/1991 05/2000 • (FW 1978 STM MDIV)

**BOECLER PAUL A O REV** (616)957-2033
3144 E Gatehouse Dr SE Grand Rapids MI 49546-7010 • AT • EM • (SL 1956 MDIV MA STM)

**BOEDECKER DAVID E REV** (616)781-9054
701 E Mansion St Marshall MI 49068-1239 • dboedecker@prodigy.net • MI • SP • Christ Marshall MI • (616)781-5842 • (SL 1979 MDIV)

**BOEDECKER ROBERT C REV** (414)632-9375
1921 Menomonee Ave Racine WI 53406-2331 • kkqm69e@juno.com • SW • EM • (SL 1945 MDIV)

**BOEDER CHARLES F REV** (507)825-4342
904 5th Ave SE Pipestone MN 56164-1715 • SD • EM • (ME 1958)

**BOEDER ROYAL E REV** (618)458-6608
PO Box 117 Maeystown IL 62256-0117 • SI • 04/1997 04/2000 • (SL 1989 MDIV)

**BOEGL SIGMUND W REV** (360)275-0877
12561 E State Highway 106 Belfair WA 98528-8543 • sboegl@earthlink.net • NOW • EM • (SL 1958)

**BOEHLER ROBERT A REV** (608)233-3759
2237 Hollister Ave Madison WI 53705-5313 • jboehler@mailbag.com • SW • Assoc • Mount Olive Madison WI • (608)238-5656 • (FW 1984 MDIV)

**BOEHLKE ALVIN A REV** (330)928-8364
322 Orrville Ave Cuyahoga Falls OH 44221-1535 • OH • Inst C • Ohio Olmsted Falls OH • (SL 1962)

**BOEHLKE CRAIG R REV** (913)856-7425
219 E Colleen Dr Gardner KS 66030-1279 • pyradome@handtech.com • KS • SP • King Of Kings Gardner KS • (913)856-2500 • (SL 1990 MDIV)

**BOEHLKE MELVIN R REV** (254)939-9248
2218 S Herrington St Belton TX 76513-4563 • TX • EM • (SPR 1946)

**BOEHLKE VERNON C REV** (307)856-7123
420 Gabes Rd Pavillion WY 82523 • vboehlke@wyoming.com • WY • D Miss • Crowheart Fort Washakie WY • (307)332-4537 • (CQ 1993)

**BOEHME ARMAND J REV** (507)835-1943
705 17th Ave NE Waseca MN 56093-2746 • stpaulwa@platec.net • MNS • SP • St Paul Waseca MN • (507)835-2647 • (SPR 1974 STM STM)

**BOEHNE THOMAS V REV** (517)739-4449
4751 Nelson Ln Oscoda MI 48750-9720 • trinluth@voyager.net • MI • SP • Trinity Oscoda MI • (517)739-9292 • (FW 1989 MA)

**BOEHNKE ARNOLD F REV** (719)599-9739
5820 Flintridge Dr Apt 231 Colorado Springs CO 80918-1878 • RM • EM • (SL 1937)

**BOEHNKE CHRISTOPHER M REV**
C/O St Johns Lutheran Church PO Box 65 Hooker OK 73945 • OK • SP • St John Hooker OK • (580)652-2683 • (SL 2000 MDIV)

**BOEHNKE DAVID A REV** (307)234-4461
3941 Washakie St Casper WY 82609-2395 • WY • SP • Trinity Casper WY • (307)234-0568 • (SL 1968 MDIV)

**BOEHNKE RICHARD A REV** (320)839-2184
541 Stephens Ave Ortonville MN 56278-1353 • MNN • SP • Trinity Ortonville MN • (320)839-3422 • (SL 1965 MDIV)

**BOEHNKE ROLAND W REV** (913)262-3712
6348 Dearborn Dr Mission KS 66202-4240 • revb@kcnet.com • KS • EM • (SL 1954)

**BOELTER FRED J REV** (219)447-5860
6723 S Anthony Blvd Apt E 304 Fort Wayne IN 46816-2045 • IN • EM • (SL 1933)

**BOELTER RANDY SCOTT REV**
806 Cadieux Rd Grosse Pointe MI 48230-1232 • EN • Sn/Adm • Christ King Grosse Pointe Woods MI • (313)884-5090 • (SL 1983 MDIV)

**BOERGER CHARLES F REV** (810)229-2494
981 Alpine Dr Brighton MI 48116-1765 • MI • EM • (SL 1947)

**BOERGER CHARLES PAUL REV** (512)532-7799
2627 Sally Gay Dr San Antonio TX 78223-2239 • carlos-b@swbell.net • TX • Sn/Adm • St Paul San Antonio TX • (210)532-7341 • (FWSR 1977 MDIV)

**BOERGER GERALD L REV** (806)293-2855
913 Oakland Plainview TX 79072 • gboerger@door.net • TX • SP • Zion Plainview NE* • (402)582-3312 • (FW 1977 MDIV)

**BOERGER JOHN A REV**
180 Lane 101 Lake Minifenokee Fremont IN 46737-9173 • fayjohn@aol.com • MI • EM • * • (SL 1956)

**BOERGER PAUL M REV** (810)392-2392
775 Kinney Rd PO Box 282 Memphis MI 48041-0282 • standrew@mail.klondyke.net • MI • SP • St Andrew Memphis MI • (810)392-2392 • (SL 1979 MDIV)

**BOERNKE DEAN H REV** (303)659-2689
C/O Zion Luth Church 1400 Skeel St Brighton CO 80601-2336 • dboernke@hotmail.com • RM • SP • Zion Brighton CO • (303)659-2339 • (SPR 1973 MDIV)

**BOESCHE JOEL T DR** (254)857-9728
104 Truffles Ct Waco TX 76712 • drjtb@netzero.net • TX • Assoc • St Paul Waco TX • (254)799-3211 • (FW 1987 MDIV THD)

**BOESCHEN DONALD E REV** (402)463-4850
306 Forest Blvd Hastings NE 68901-4029 • dboeschen@aol.com • NEB • SP • Peace Hastings NE • (402)462-9023 • (SL 1968 MDIV)

**BOETCHER KENNETH F REV** (253)847-5925
8917 222nd Street Ct E Graham WA 98338-8000 • kboetc2144@aol.com • NOW • EM • (SL 1955 MDIV)

**BOETTCHER DAROLD F REV** (303)366-1827
12034 E Maple Ave Aurora CO 80012 • bvdpadre@aol.com • RM • EM • (SL 1961 MDIV)

**BOETTCHER DAVID N REV** (920)465-6232
3109 Saint Gregory Dr Green Bay WI 54311-5952 • boettrn@aol.com • NW • SP • Christ Of Bay Green Bay WI • (920)468-4246 • (SL 1967 MDIV MA)

**BOETTCHER DENNIS LEE REV** (920)457-9205
1530 Falcon Way Sheboygan Falls WI 53085-3332 • boettden@yahoo.com • SW • SP • Immanuel Westfield WI • (608)296-2088 • (FW 1993 MDIV)

**BOETTCHER DONALD L REV** (402)589-1097
RR 2 Box 110 Spencer NE 68777-9744 • NEB • SP • Grace Springview NE* • (402)497-2507 • (CQ 1994)

**BOETTCHER FREDERICK N DR** (262)783-6712
N50W16326 Pin Oak Ct Menomonee Falls WI 53051-6650 • fritzee@execpc.com • SW • EM • * • (SL 1952 MDIV STM DMIN)

**BOETTCHER LOREN A REV** (573)339-0365
1419 N Clark St Cape Girardeau MO 63701-3717 • MO • EM • * • (SL 1958 MDIV)

**BOETTCHER LOWELL F REV** (605)341-6886
1809 Copperdale Dr Rapid City SD 57703-4745 • SD • EM • * • (SL 1963 MDIV)

**BOETTCHER MARK A REV** (417)678-5358
823 Rosemary Ave Aurora MO 65605-1871 • MO • SP • Grace Aurora MO • (417)678-3603 • (SL 1985 MDIV)

**BOGARDUS LARRY D REV** (805)650-2741
146 Brentwood Ave Ventura CA 93001 • PSW • SP • First Ventura CA • (805)643-5586 • (CQ 1999)

**BOGDA DAVID W REV** (231)745-3036
8636 S M37 Baldwin MI 49304-9781 • MI • SP • Grace Baldwin MI • (231)745-7521 • (FW 1999 MA MDIV)

**BOGS RONALD ALLEN REV** (361)853-1643
3133 Crest Colony Ln Corpus Christi TX 78415-2437 • bogshome@juno.com • TX • SP • Mount Olive Corpus Christi TX • (361)991-3416 • (SL 1992 MDIV)

**BOHEIM KEITH D REV** (636)447-7836
42 S Weston Ct Saint Charles MO 63303-1934 • kdboh@aol.com • MO • 07/1995 07/2000 • (SL 1979 MDIV)

**BOHLER STEVEN W REV** (218)281-1744
800 S Washington Crookston MN 56716 • sbohler@rrv.net • MNN • SP • Our Savior Crookston MN* • (218)281-1239 • (FW 1993 MDIV)

**BOHLKEN DANIEL C REV** (503)359-3585
C/O Mt Olive Luth Church 2327 17th Ave Forest Grove OR 97116-2405 • danandsan@wwdb.cc • NOW • SP • Mount Olive Forest Grove OR • (503)357-2511 • (SPR 1976 MDIV)

**BOHLKEN PHILIP J REV**
1824 Dainesway Valparaiso IN 46383-3868 • pbohlken@rmci.net • NOW • SP • Grace Caldwell ID • (208)459-4191 • (SL 1972 MDIV)

**BOHLMANN GORDON P REV** (937)325-5120
3120 E Leffel Ln Springfield OH 45505-4528 • agape@glasscity.net • OH • SP • Risen Christ Springfield OH • (937)323-3688 • (SL 1964 MTH MED)

**BOHLMANN RALPH A REV** (314)821-7781
12836 Stump Rd Des Peres MO 63131-2145 • ralphbohlmann@msn.com • MO • EM • (SL 1956 MDIV STM PHD DD)

**BOHLMANN ROBERT E REV** (765)457-6330
1308 Doud Dr Kokomo IN 46902-5848 • rebmlb65@usa.net • IN • SP • Good Shepherd Kokomo IN • (765)457-4968 • (SL 1967 MDIV)

**BOHLMANN TIMOTHY PAUL REV** (937)431-1264
3440 Crab Orchard Dr Beavercreek OH 45430-1407 • pastortimbo@worldnet.att.net • OH • SP • Lord Of Life Beavercreek OH • (937)431-0643 • (SL 1992 MDIV)

**BOHLMANN VICTOR A REV** (903)769-5297
4507 Peaceful Woods Trl Rt 1 Box 920 Big Sandy TX 75755-9625 • vicbecky@risecom.net • TX • EM • (SL 1961 MDIV MA)

**BOHM DALE E REV**
RR 1 Box 280 Giddings TX 78942-9723 • TX • SP • St John Giddings TX • (512)253-6350 • (SL 1989)

**BOHMER GLENN S REV** (712)362-4897
623 17th Ave N Estherville IA 51334-1022 • IW • SP • Immanuel Estherville IA • (712)362-3237 • (FW 1986 MDIV)

**BOHN BRIAN G REV** (402)375-2282 909 Main St Wayne NE 68787 • bgbohn@bloomnet.com • NEB • 08/2000 • (SL 1997 MDIV)

**BOHN DANIEL LEE REV** (715)887-3538 221 Verbunker Ave Port Edwards WI 54469 • NW • SP • Trinity Port Edwards WI • (715)887-3021 • (FW 1987 MDIV)

**BOHREN DENNIS M REV** 3405 N Cortez Ct Chandler AZ 85224 • PSW • S Ex/S • Pacific Southwest Irvine CA • (949)854-3232 • (FW 1984 MDIV MS)

**BOINEAU EDWARD L REV** (409)345-6313 305 Freeman Blvd W Columbia TX 77486 • eboineau@orbitworld.com • TX • SP • St Luke Sweeny TX • (409)548-3535 • (SL 1997 MDIV)

**BOISCLAIR DAVID R REV** (314)664-9450 3733 Bamberger #1Fl Saint Louis MO 63116-4621 • MO • SP • Faith Saint Louis MO* • (314)261-7070 • (SL 1982 MDIV STM)

**BOJARZIN HENRY W REV** 51 Old Orchard St Williamsville NY 14221-2105 • EN • EM • * • (SPR 1962 MMU)

**BOJENS DONALD L REV** (440)236-8977 13455 W River Rd Columbia Station OH 44028-9523 • hosannalc@n2net.net • OH • SP • Hosanna Columbia Station OH • (440)236-8900 • (CQ 1991)

**BOK VERN L REV** (216)328-0746 3223 Forest Overlook Dr Seven Hills OH 44131-3744 • bokul@juno.com • OH • SP • St John Garfield Heights OH • (216)587-4222 • (SL 1971 MDIV)

**BOK WILBERT E REV** (419)899-4515 404 S Harrison St PO Box 336 Sherwood OH 43556-0336 • webok@bright.net • OH • EM • (SL 1950 MDIV)

**BOLDT GERALD L REV** (320)485-2202 PO Box 276 Winsted MN 55395-0276 • MNS • SP • St John Winsted MN • (320)485-2522 • (CQ 1996 MA)

**BOLIN RICHARD L REV** (618)669-2563 PO Box 397 Pocahontas IL 62275-0397 • SI • EM • (SL 1953)

**BOLLAND RICHARD A REV** (970)731-9891 2132 Lake Forest Cir Pagosa Springs CO 81147-8835 • RM • SP • Our Savior Pagosa Springs CO • (970)731-4668 • (FW 1986 MDIV MSED)

**BOLLHAGEN JAMES G REV** (219)483-2339 8 Tyndale Pl Fort Wayne IN 46825-4936 • bollhagenjg@mail.ctsfw.edu • IN • SHS/C • Indiana Fort Wayne IN • (SL 1971 STM MDIV THD)

**BOLLHAGEN KARL C REV** (217)256-3289 810 Main St Warsaw IL 62379 • CI • SP • Concordia Warsaw IL • (217)256-3215 • (FW 1998 MDIV)

**BOLLING RICHARD E REV** (402)201-5978 2603 Morrie Dr Bellevue NE 68123 • MNN • EM • (SPR 1968 MDIV)

**BOLLING ROBERT W REV** (262)763-6039 2424 Fairfield Ln Burlington WI 53105-9118 • pwt50@yahoo.com • SW • SP • Our Savior Burlington WI • (262)763-3281 • (FW 1981 MDIV)

**BOLLMANN JOHN F REV** (708)974-1397 8225 Willow Dr Palos Hills IL 60465-2562 • NI • EM • (SPR 1952)

**BOLSTAD ARTHUR C REV** (314)298-0414 4195 Gallatin Ln Bridgeton MO 63044-1927 • holycross@email.com • MO • 04/1998 04/2000 • (FW 1981 MA MDIV MRE MST MS MA)

**BOLT RANDY G REV** (719)647-0546 991 W Stallion Dr Pueblo West CO 81007-1931 • boltlutz@juno.com • RM • SP • Trinity Pueblo CO • (719)544-3016 • (SL 1983 MDIV)

**BOLTE DAVID J REV** (623)935-2339 C/O Trinity Lutheran Church 830 E Plaza Cir Litchfield Park AZ 85340-4915 • drbolte@aol.com • PSW • SP • Trinity Litchfield Park AZ • (623)935-4665 • (FW 1990 MDIV)

**BOMBA JAMES M REV** (713)463-3226 15010 Britterige St Houston TX 77084-2016 • TX • EM • (SPR 1954)

**BOMBERGER GARY D REV** 305 W/HC 587 Utah Ave Bldg 18200 Vandenberg AFB CA 93437-6309 • gary.bomberger@vandenberg.af.mil • FG • M Chap • Florida-Georgia Orlando FL • (SPR 1975 MDIV)

**BOND DALE A SR. REV** (417)725-0007 504 Hightower St Nixa MO 65714-9463 • MO • SP • Family Christ Nixa MO • (863)385-7848 • (SL 1976 MDIV)

**BONGARD RONALD A REV** (651)688-9439 4170 Hilltop Ln Eagan MN 55123-1495 • rbongard@webtv.net • MNS • EM • (SPR 1962 MDIV)

**BONGARD STEPHEN H REV** (219)462-8690 4203 Onyx Ct Valparaiso IN 46385 • shb@immanuel.pvt.k12.in.us • IN • Assoc • Immanuel Valparaiso IN • (219)462-8207 • (SL 1989 MDIV)

**BONGO EBENGO REV** 81 NW 163rd St Miami FL 33169 • FG • 06/1997 06/2000 • (CQ 1995 MDIV)

**BONK JOHN REV** (218)984-3529 4910 Waisanen Rd Embarrass MN 55732-8347 • MNN • SP • Good Shepherd Babbitt MN • (218)827-2301 • (SL 1987)

**BONTKE JONATHAN C REV** (217)324-6617 1314 N State St Litchfield IL 62056 • revbontke@msn.com • SI • Asst • Zion Litchfield IL • (217)324-2033 • (SL 1997 MST MDIV)

**BOODLE SAMUEL M REV** 119 John F Kennedy Dr Box N 4794 Nassau BAHAMAS • sboodle@cob.edu.bs • FG • SP • Nassau Nassau BAHAMAS • (242)323-4107 • (FW 2000 MDIV)

**BOOKSHAW JOHN A REV** 4121 Honeyvale St SW Grandville MI 49418-3103 • MI • Sn/Adm • Holy Cross Jenison MI • (616)457-2420 • (SL 1982 MDIV)

**BOOMHOWER PATRICK J REV** 150 W Saint Charles Rd #526 Lombard IL 60148-2280 • NI • Assoc • St John Lombard IL • (630)629-2515 • (FW 1993 MDIV)

**BOONE ARTHUR E REV** (086)692-270 C/O Jet Cargo Intnl M 182 PO Box 20010 Miami FL 33102-0010 • MI • S Miss • Michigan Ann Arbor MI • (SL 1984)

**BOOS WERNER K REV** (303)973-0411 7364 W Walden Dr Littleton CO 80123-5469 • buddykb@mindspring.com • RM • Assoc • Our Father Littleton CO • (303)779-1332 • (SL 1971 MDIV STM DPSY)

**BOOTH TIMOTHY D REV** (402)439-2461 PO Box 206 Stanton NE 68779-0206 • ltbooth@stanton.net • NEB • SP • Faith Stanton NE • (402)439-2104 • (FW 1991 MDIV)

**BOOTH TIMOTHY E REV** 17011 Kings Court Lakeville MN 55044 • tbooth@isd.net • MNS • Sn/Adm • Messiah Lakeville MN • (612)431-5959 • (FW 1977 MDIV)

**BORCHARD TERRANCE H REV** C/O S I L PO Box 232 Ukarumpa Via Lae Papua NEW GUINEA • SD • S Miss • South Dakota Sioux Falls SD • (SL 1969 MDIV)

**BORCHELT HERBERT E REV** (330)528-0334 2039 Fairway Blvd Hudson OH 44236-1345 • OH • EM • (SL 1958 MDIV)

**BORCHELT RAY L REV** (678)937-9756 3662 South Marlborough Dr Tucker GA 30084 • praybor@juno.com • FG • SP • St Mark Tucker GA • (404)938-4541 • (CQ 1995 MED)

**BORCHERDING ALAN W REV** 481 Dana Meadows Ln Ballwin MO 63021 • ic³borcheaw@lcms.org • MO • S Ex/S • Missouri Saint Louis MO • (314)317-4550 • (SL 1982 MDIV PHD)

**BORCHERDING CHARLES D REV** (402)421-2034 1802 Normandy Ln Lincoln NE 68512-1425 • EN • EM • (SPR 1965)

**BORCHERS DENNIS R REV** (219)749-0171 6727 Lake Valley Ct Fort Wayne IN 46815-7920 • drwho@juno.com • IN • Tchr • Concordia LHS Fort Wayne IN • (219)483-1102 • (SPR 1973 MDIV)

**BORCHERS RICHARD W REV** (414)256-6899 8220 Harwood Ave Apt 401 Wauwatosa WI 53213-2532 • richborchers@yahoo.com • SW • EM • (SL 1955)

**BORGELT LARRY G REV** (715)877-2701 741 S Liberty St Fall Creek WI 54742 • NW • SP • St Paul Fall Creek WI • (715)877-2117 • (FW 1980 MDIV)

**BORGER BRYAN G REV** (412)321-6286 3332 Perrysville Ave Pittsburgh PA 15214-2209 • revborger@aol.com • EA • SP • St Matthew Pittsburgh PA • (412)321-7720 • (SL 1990 MDIV)

**BORGES GARY F REV** (503)370-8958 1860 Summit Ave NW Salem OR 97304-2716 • NOW • EM • (SPR 1960 MDIV)

**BORGHARDT GEORGE F III** C/O St Mark Lutheran Church 2100 Tickner St Conroe TX 77301-1341 • TX • Asst • St Mark Conroe TX • (409)756-6335 • (SL 2000 MDIV)

**BORGMAN PAUL L REV** (414)567-7131 N53W35748 Hillview Ct Oconomowoc WI 53066-3238 • billy@cedar.net • SW • Sn/Adm • St Paul Oconomowoc WI • (414)567-5001 • (SL 1972 MDIV STM DMIN)

**BORGSTEDE MICHAEL R REV** C/O Mount Olive Lutheran 11500 E Iliff Ave Aurora CO 80014-1177 • mrborgs@juno.com • RM • St Paul Oconomowoc WI • (414)567-5001 • (SL 1997 MDIV)

**BORHART GLEN W DR** (815)568-6738 710 Stanford Dr Marengo IL 60152-3065 • borharts@yahoo.com • NI • Sn/Adm • Zion Marengo IL • (815)568-6564 • (FW 1979 MDIV DMIN)

**BORING RICHARD D REV** (308)785-2797 C/O Our Redeemer Luth Church PO Box 42 Elwood NE 68937-0042 • rb63846@alltel.net • NEB • SP • Our Redeemer Elwood NE • (308)785-2875 • (SL 1993 MDIV)

**BORMANN CURT A REV** (734)429-9305 223 Nichols Dr Saline MI 48176-1018 • MI • EM • (SL 1935 MDIV)

**BORN CHARLES H REV** (512)388-4020 1612 Woods Blvd Round Rock TX 78681-2150 • TX • EM • (SL 1949 LLD)

**BORN CLARENCE H REV** (206)723-7557 9624 56th Ave S Seattle WA 98118-5713 • chborn@seanet.com • NOW • EM • (SPR 1952 MDIV)

**BORN DAVID J REV** (718)896-7850 63-13 Dieterle Cres Rego Park NY 11374-4822 • djborn@aol.com • AT • Sn/Adm • Our Saviour Rego Park NY • (718)897-4447 • (SL 1973 MDIV)

**BORST STEVEN BRUNO REV** (714)998-9523 3040 E Meadow Grove Rd Orange CA 92867 • borst@cui.edu • PSW • Cmp P • Pacific Southwest Irvine CA • (949)854-3232 • (SL 1992 MDIV)

**BOSHOVEN RICHARD L** (219)996-7671 805 South County Line Rd Hebron IN 46341-9037 • IN • SP • St Michael Hebron IN • (219)996-7681 • (SL MDIV)

**BOSSARD GERALD E DR** (402)697-3915 15712 Shamrock Rd Omaha NE 68118 • gebossard@aol.com • NEB • SP • Atonement Omaha NE • (402)571-3698 • (FW 1999)

**BOTHWELL JAMES R REV** (707)431-8065 553 Fieldcrest Dr Healdsburg CA 95448-3364 • goodshepherd@metro.net • CNH • SP • Good Shepherd Healdsburg CA • (707)433-3835 • (FW 1983 MDIV)

**BOTSFORD MICHAEL D REV** (515)884-2629 502 Clay Whittemore IA 50518 • IW • SP • St Paul Whittemore IA • (515)884-2629 • (CQ 1998 MDIV)

**BOTTJEN DEAN L REV** (815)432-5381 419 N 4th St Watseka IL 60970-1317 • mtnest@capstonebank.com • NI • SP • Calvary Watseka IL • (815)432-4136 • (SL 1975 MDIV)

**BOTTOMS DENNIS W REV** (562)867-2058 13609 Ardis Ave Bellflower CA 90706-2305 • revdenn@csn.com • PSW • SP • Good Shepherd Downey CA • (562)803-4459 • (SPR 1972 MDIV)

**BOTTORFF CHRIS A REV** (219)661-9228 136 Tenbrook Dr Crown Point IN 46307 • NI • 07/1999 • (SL 1983 MDIV)

**BOTTORFF DAVID M REV** (630)969-6726 7222 Cass Ave Darien IL 60561-3605 • stjohn7214@juno.com • NI • Sn/Adm • St John Darien IL • (630)969-7987 • (SL 1979 MDIV)

**BOUMAN JAMES D REV** (847)296-8512 1326 Margret St Des Plaines IL 60018-1523 • NI • EM • (SL 1957 MDIV)

**BOWDER RUSSELL E JR. REV** (573)636-3346 1018 Carol St Jefferson City MO 65101-3604 • rfbowder@midamerica.net • MO • SP • Immanuel Jefferson City MO • (573)496-3451 • (SL 2000 MDIV MED)

**BOWDITCH MARK A REV** (808)234-0225 45-537 Alokahi Pl Kaneohe HI 96744 • mbowditch@aol.com • CNH • Tchr • St Mark Kaneohe HI • (808)247-5589 • (FW 1990 MDIV)

**BOWEN GREGG W REV** (708)349-4826 9124 170th St Orland Hills IL 60477-7264 • NI • Asst • Christ Orland Park IL • (708)349-0431 • (SL 1989 MDIV)

**BOWLDS JOHN BRADLEY REV** (606)224-0458 3314 Snaffle Rd Lexington KY 40513 • IN • 08/1999 • (SL 1997 MDIV)

**BOWLES RAY E REV** (409)345-4567 RR 1 Box 42 CC Damon TX 77430 • TX • EM • (SL 1947 MDIV)

**BOXDORFER ELMER C REV** (909)780-0602 6708 Rycroft Dr Riverside CA 92506-5315 • PSW • EM • (SL 1932)

**BOXMAN MARK D REV** (316)441-0961 312 W Central Ave Arkansas City KS 67005-2637 • KS • SP • Redeemer Arkansas City KS • (316)442-5240 • (FW 1987 MDIV)

**BOYCE BRUCE A REV** 103 Upper Ridge Reinbeck IA 50669-1250 • baboyce@trvnet.net • IW • SP • St John Reinbeck IA • (319)345-2766 • (FW 1988 MDIV)

**BOYCE ROBERT E REV** (915)869-5369 PO Box 245 Eden TX 76837-0245 • boyce@wcc.net • TX • SP • Trinity Eden TX • (915)869-4031 • (FW 1982 MDIV)

**BOYD DAVID A REV** 17910 Prairie Ave Torrance CA 90504-3713 • PSW • SP • Ascension Torrance CA • (310)793-0071 • (SL 1991 MDIV)

**BOYD MICHAEL B REV** (219)896-2025 307 E Weninger North Judson IN 46366 • IN • SP • St Peter North Judson IN • (219)896-2025 • (FW 1997 MDIV)

**BOYE GARY P REV** (303)745-4458 1429 S Laredo St Aurora CO 80017-4005 • Hhtbear@aol.com • RM • SP • St Andrew Denver CO • (303)371-7014 • (SL 1976 MDIV)

**BOYE LAWRENCE C REV** (785)742-3445 615 S 1st St Hiawatha KS 66434-2701 • KS • SP • Zion Hiawatha KS • (785)742-3995 • (SL 1972 MDIV)

**BOYER CURT W REV** PO Box 357 Crescent City IL 60928 • NI • 05/1998 05/2000 • (FW 1989 MDIV)

**BOYER RICHARD A REV** (316)788-0554 13 Madapalla Ct Derby KS 67037-9515 • faithderby@aol.com • KS • SP • Faith Derby KS • (316)788-1715 • (SL 1961 MDIV)

**BOYKIN MICHAEL C REV** 11 S University St Vermillion SD 57069-3211 • mboykin@msn.com • SD • SP • Concordia Vermillion SD • (605)624-3459 • (FW 1983 MDIV MS DMIN)

**BOYSEN ALBERT M REV** (901)754-1476 7622 Dexter Hills Dr Cordova TN 38018-8712 • alboyboysen@hotmail.com • MDS • EM • (SL 1958 MDIV)

**BRABAND CHARLES A REV** (410)643-3066 2710 Cecil Dr Chester MD 21619-2134 • brabands@friend.ly.net • SE • SP • Galilee Chester MD • (410)643-6545 • (SL 1971 MDIV)

**BRACK DELMER W REV** (316)733-8204 630 N Broadview Ln Andover KS 67002-9753 • TX • EM • (SL 1952 MA)

**BRACK LA VERN L REV** (702)228-1411 340 Dockside Ct Las Vegas NV 89145-4794 • PSW • EM • (SL 1952)

**BRACK ORLETT D REV** (605)336-6559 3305 E 31st St Sioux Falls SD 57103-4407 • SD • EM • (SL 1946)

**BRADLEY RICHARD E DR** (727)596-4186 19725 Gulf Blvd #8 Indian Shores FL 33785-2329 • rickshare@aol.com • FG • SP • Rogate Clearwater FL • (727)531-2761 • (FW 1981 MDIV DMIN)

**BRADSHAW DENNIS NEIL REV** (805)983-1619 1200 Maria Way Oxnard CA 93030-5045 • PSW • D Miss • Centro Cristiano Oxnard CA • (805)240-0074 • (SL 1983 MDIV)

**BRADTKE TRAUGOTT P REV** (715)384-4246 700 W 4th St Marshfield WI 54449-2603 • NW • EM • (TH 1943)

**BRADY CHARLES N REV** (323)564-1634 8145 San Miguel Ave South Gate CA 90280-2522 • cnbrady007@aol.com • PSW • SP • Redeemer South Gate CA • (323)588-0934 • (FW 1978 MDIV)

**BRAEM RICHARD G REV** (503)649-6775 18975 SW Johnson St Aloha OR 97006-3162 • NOW • EM • (SL 1953)

**BRAEUNIG LOTHAR REV** (503)587-0591
585 Winter St NE #410 Salem OR 97301 • PSW • EM • (SL 1931 MA)

**BRAGDON DENNIS J REV** (979)968-6337
840 N Franklin St La Grange TX 78945-1620 • dbragdon@cvtv.net • TX • SP • Mount Calvary La Grange TX • (979)968-3938 • (SL 1982 MDIV)

**BRAKENHOFF LARRY D REV** (785)499-5333
PO Box 235 Alta Vista KS 66834-0235 • brakenhoff@cgtelco.net • KS • SP • St Paul Alta Vista KS • (785)499-6623 • (SL 1974 MDIV)

**BRAMICH CHRISTOPHER J REV**
C/O Messiah Lutheran Church 1308 Whitley Rd Keller TX 76248 • TX • Asst • Messiah Keller TX • (817)431-2345 • (SL 2000 MDIV)

**BRAMMEIER ARNOLD H REV** (313)885-7923
4141 Audubon Rd Detroit MI 48224-2750 • MI • Sn/Adm • Peace Detroit MI • (313)882-0254 • (SL 1965 MDIV)

**BRAMMEIER DANIEL G REV** (712)642-2871
723 N 9th St Missouri Valley IA 51555-1134 • flutheranc@aol.com • IW • SP • First Missouri Valley IA • (712)642-2483 • (FW 1994 MDIV)

**BRAMMEIER JAMES E REV** (847)519-0258
2070 Carling Rd Hoffman Estates IL 60195-2601 • NI • 09/2000 • (SL 1968 MDIV)

**BRAMMER DAVID H REV** (716)693-0023
173 Dexter Ter Tonawanda NY 14150-4720 • EA • EM • (SL 1955 MDIV MSW)

**BRAMSTADT ALLEN H REV** (920)921-8630
1085 Van Dyne Rd North Fond du Lac WI 54937-9777 • SW • SP • Divine Savior North Fond Du Lac WI • (920)923-1532 • (SL 1997 MDIV)

**BRAMSTEDT PAUL W REV** (618)234-3954
2405 E B Street Rd Belleville IL 62221-4202 • bramstet@apci.net • SI • EM • (SL 1955 STM DMIN)

**BRAMSTEDT TERRILL F REV** (320)598-3965
521 9th Ave Madison MN 56256-1134 • MNN • SP • St John Madison MN • (320)598-7550 • (SL 1973 MDIV)

**BRAND DONALD L REV** (908)686-4269
C/O Grace Luth Church 2222 Vauxhall Rd Union NJ 07083-5825 • shepherd4u@usa.net • NJ • SP • Grace Union NJ • (908)686-3965 • (FW 1977 MDIV)

**BRAND TIMOTHY JOHN REV** (616)933-7112
C/O St Michael Lutheran Church 1030 Centre St Traverse City MI 49686-3403 • tsbrand@aol.com • MI • SP • St Michael Traverse City MI • (616)947-5293 • (FW 1996 MDIV)

**BRANDEL HAROLD R REV** (904)789-8058
1109 Cambridge St Deltona FL 32725-3655 • FG • EM • (CQ 1975)

**BRANDENBURG TERRY L REV** (702)658-0813
3204 Paragon Pointe St Las Vegas NV 89129-6702 • pastor@mountainviewlc.org • PSW • SP • Mountain View Las Vegas NV • (702)360-8290 • (SPR 1976 MDIV)

**BRANDMIRE WAYNE H REV** (509)452-4542
1212 S 33rd Ave Yakima WA 98902-4921 • NOW • EM • (SL 1957)

**BRANDON RICHARD D REV** (503)375-7379
1601 Almond Ln NW Salem OR 97304-1101 • tupela@juno.com • NOW • EM • (SPR 1971 MTH MDIV)

**BRANDT CHARLES E REV** (419)382-8855
4559 Shadowood Ln Toledo OH 43614 • brandtcl@aol.com • OH • Sn/Adm • Trinity Toledo OH • (419)385-2651 • (FW 1980 MTH)

**BRANDT CHRISTOPHER REV** (307)548-7127
C/O St John Lutheran Church 70 E 5th St Lovell WY 82431-1902 • mtbrandt@juno.com • WY • SP • St John Lovell WY • (307)548-7127 • (SL 1981 MDIV)

**BRANDT D TIMOTHY REV** (801)523-1793
10446 Leilani Dr Sandy UT 84070-0959 • timbrandt@juno.com • RM • Asst • Grace Sandy UT • (801)572-6375 • (SL 1991 MDIV)

**BRANDT DAVID T REV** (515)236-3688
1919 Spencer St Grinnell IA 50112-1035 • IE • SP • Immanuel Grinnell IA • (515)236-6691 • (SL 1982 MDIV)

**BRANDT DENNIS A REV** (618)465-3423
3605 Gary Ave Alton IL 62002 • SI • 09/1994 09/1999 • (SL 1985 MDIV JD)

**BRANDT EDWARD EARL REV** (515)887-6991
PO Box 235 West Bend IA 50597-0235 • brandt@ncn.net • IW • SP • Peace West Bend IA • (515)887-3261 • (SL 1994 MDIV)

**BRANDT ELDON L REV** (812)372-9597
3325 Woodland Pkwy Columbus IN 47203-1615 • IN • EM • (SL 1949)

**BRANDT GARY RAY REV** (580)436-3829
RR 1 Box 124 Ada OK 74820-9710 • gbrandt@juno.com • OK • SP • First Ada OK • (580)332-3433 • (SL 1995 MDIV MBA)

**BRANDT MARK D REV** (517)652-6141
C/O St Lorenz Lutheran Church 140 Churchgrove Rd Frankenmuth MI 48734-1097 • mbrandt@stlorenz.org • MI • Sn/Adm • St Lorenz Frankenmuth MI • (517)652-6141 • (SL 1980 MDIV)

**BRANDT MAYNARD H REV** (660)285-3383
36399 Highway E Green Ridge MO 65332-3407 • mhbrandt@ihand.net • MO • EM • (SPR 1954)

**BRANDT NATHAN M REV** (307)682-9173
117 Overland Trl Gillette WY 82716-4626 • nbrandt@wyoming.com • WY • Sn/Adm • Trinity Gillette WY* • (307)682-4886 • (SL 1980 MDIV)

**BRANDT PHILLIP L REV** (541)957-9132
932 Oakview Roseburg OR 97470 • psbrandt@wmni.net • NOW • SP • St Paul Roseburg OR • (541)673-7212 • (SL 1991 MDIV MA)

**BRANDT ROBERT A REV** (715)389-8048
411 Evergreen Ave S Marshfield WI 54449-3214 • NW • Sn/Adm • Immanuel Marshfield WI • (715)384-5121 • (SPR 1970 MDIV)

**BRANDT RUDOLPH C REV** (270)783-8179
308 St Albans Dr Bowling Green KY 42103-4737 • MDS • EM • (SL 1947)

**BRANDT WARREN P REV** (573)782-3216
4422 Stringtown Rd Lohman MO 65053-9550 • MO • SP • St John Lohman MO • (573)782-3191 • (FW 1985)

**BRANDVOLD JOEL L REV** (701)263-4062
10451 Co Rd 49 Bottineau ND 58318-7024 • shr@ndak.net • ND • SP • Zion Kramer ND* • (701)359-4461 • (FW 1988 MDIV)

**BRANN JOHANNES W REV** (417)876-9807
220 N Main St El Dorado Springs MO 64744-1144 • MO • SP • Faith El Dorado Spgs MO • (CQ 1994 MDIV)

**BRASSIE STUART W REV** (636)458-9078
2313 Winegarden Ct Wildwood MO 63011-1808 • S.Brassiestl.com • MO • D Ex/S • Missouri Saint Louis MO • (314)317-4550 • (FW 1977 MDIV DMIN)

**BRATZ GARY C REV** (715)276-3802
C/O St John Luth Church PO Box 78 Townsend WI 54175-0078 • gsbratz@ez-net.com • NW • SP • St John Townsend WI • (715)276-7214 • (SL 1966)

**BRAUER ERICH F REV** (956)782-9460
1001 W Ridge Rd Apt 102 Pharr TX 78577-5706 • TX • EM • (SL 1935 MDIV MA DD)

**BRAUER GLENN S REV** (847)548-1867
1148 Williamsburg Cir Grayslake IL 60030-7904 • brauer@lnd.com • NI • SP • Lord Of Glory Grayslake IL • (847)548-5673 • (SL 1980 MDIV)

**BRAUER JAMES L REV** (636)394-5519
516 Sulphur Springs Rd Ballwin MO 63021-5152 • brauerj@csl.edu • MO • SHS/C • Missouri Saint Louis MO • (314)317-4550 • (SL 1964 STM MDIV MSMU PHD)

**BRAUER JOEL J REV** (503)684-9342
8550 SW Avon St Tigard OR 97224 • jbrauer@transport.com • NOW • Sn/Adm • Living Savior Tualatin OR • (503)692-3490 • (SL 1973 MDIV MA)

**BRAUER MARTIN JAMES REV** (661)252-0622
24616 Town Center Dr #4304 Valencia CA 91355 • mbrauer@thevine.net • PSW • SP • Bethlehem Santa Clarita CA • (661)252-0622 • (SL 1994 MDIV)

**BRAUER MARTIN W REV** (314)918-8069
715 Imse Dr Apt 201 Webster Groves MO 63119-4977 • mbrauer@worldnet.att.net • MO • EM • (SL 1947 STM)

**BRAUER NORMAN E REV** (503)692-9106
17929 SW 105th Ct Tualatin OR 97062-9404 • NOW • EM • (SL 1943 MDIV)

**BRAUN ALAN J REV** (651)483-3157
2975 Highpointe Curv Roseville MN 55113-2169 • MNS • SP • King Of Kings Roseville MN • (651)484-5142 • (SL 1968 MDIV)

**BRAUN ALLEN L** (618)286-3254
1246 Muskopf Pl Dupo IL 62239-1410 • SI • SP • Holy Cross East Carondelet IL • (618)538-5600 • (SL 2000 MDIV)

**BRAUN HAROLD C REV** (651)770-0939
3150 Glen Oaks Ave Apt 310 White Bear Lake MN 55110-5675 • MNS • EM • (SL 1938)

**BRAUN RODDY L REV** (703)743-5050
13665 Paddock Ct Gainesville VA 20155 • rbchron@juno.com • SE • EM • (SL 1960 STM THD)

**BRAUN THOMAS P REV** (952)442-3922
1622 Coney Ln Waconia MN 55387 • MNS • SP • Christ Victorious Chaska MN • (952)443-2993 • (FW 1982 MDIV)

**BRAUN TIMOTHY P REV** (515)967-2846
601 22nd Ave SW Altoona IA 50009 • t.braun@worldnet.att.net • IW • SP • Hope Des Moines IA • (515)265-2057 • (FW 1982 MDIV)

**BRAUN WAYNE M REV** (414)692-6124
835 Fredonia Ave Fredonia WI 53021-9412 • wayne³braun@cuw.edu • SW • SHS/C • South Wisconsin Milwaukee WI • (414)464-8100 • (SL 1984 MDIV DMIN)

**BRAUNER DOUGLAS P REV**
4125 Constitution Ave Colorado Springs CO 80909-1662 • pdoug@aol.com • RM • Assoc • Holy Cross Colorado Springs CO • (719)596-0661 • (SL 1982 MDIV)

**BRAUNERSREUTHER JON M REV** (806)358-2294
6704 Garwood Rd Amarillo TX 79109 • braunersreuther@txdistlcms.org • TX • D Ex/S • Texas Austin TX • (SL 1989 MDIV)

**BRAY DAVID D REV** (715)887-2844
840 Fawn Ln Port Edwards WI 54469-1163 • NW • 08/1998 • (FW 1982 MA)

**BRAZEAL JOHN W REV** (773)536-1984
C/O Christ The King Luth Ch 3701 S Lake Park Ave Chicago IL 60653-2012 • mrsgb@earthlink.net • NI • SP • Christ King Chicago IL • (773)536-1984 • (CQ 1994 MA)

**BRAZINSKY THOMAS R REV** (616)866-4632
210 E Main St Rockford MI 49341-1069 • MI • SP • St Peter Rockford MI • (616)866-1818 • (CQ 1985 MA)

**BRDA KEITH R REV** (504)391-1079
5161 Carlisle Court New Orleans LA 70131 • KandEBrda@aol.com • SO • Sn/Adm • Salem Gretna LA • (504)367-5126 • (SL 1983 MDIV)

**BREACH MICHAEL EUGENE REV** (320)384-6273
C/O St John Lutheran Church 3295 Velvet St Hinckley MN 55037-9631 • MNN • SP • St John Hinckley MN* • (612)384-6884 • (FW 1992 MDIV)

**BRECH DENNIS E REV** (303)499-1104
4320 Grinnell Ave Boulder CO 80303-6611 • RM • SP • Mount Hope Boulder CO • (303)499-9800 • (SPR 1973 MDIV)

**BRECHBUHL PETER R REV** (217)245-7116
12 Manassas Ave Jacksonville IL 62650-1065 • CI • Sn/Adm • Salem Jacksonville IL • (217)243-3419 • (SL 1984 MDIV STM)

**BREDEMEIER HERBERT G REV** (219)486-2925
5807 Lassiter Mill Fort Wayne IN 46835-8813 • IN • EM • (SL 1935 MA MS LLD LLD)

**BREDEMEYER WILLIAM H REV** (713)452-7947
16227 Palm St Channelview TX 77530-2804 • TX • EM • (SPR 1964)

**BREDESON JAMES C REV** (410)536-9065
1236 Poplar Ave Baltimore MD 21227-2612 • revjimhnlc@aol.com • SE • Sn/Adm • Holy Nativity Baltimore MD • (410)242-9441 • (SL 1982 MDIV)

**BREGE CLIFFORD P REV** (517)734-7300
4895 M-68 Hwy Rogers City MI 49779 • MI • EM • (SPR 1954)

**BREGE DANIEL J REV** (219)547-4256
4520 W 750 N Decatur IN 46733-7853 • IN • SP • St Paul Decatur IN • (219)547-4176 • (FW 1982 MDIV)

**BREGE WILLIAM R REV** (219)597-7265
6541 E 750 N Ossian IN 46777-9631 • IN • SP • Bethlehem Ossian IN • (219)597-7286 • (FW 1985 MDIV)

**BREHMER CHARLES A REV** (661)588-8585
7720 Feather River Dr Bakersfield CA 93308-6446 • cab13@lightspeed.net • CNH • EM • (SL 1962 MDIV MA)

**BREHMER STEVEN J REV** (509)276-9575
PO Box 2203 Deer Park WA 99006 • sjakbreh@juno.com • NOW • SP • Faith Deer Park WA • (509)276-5268 • (SL 1999 MDIV)

**BREIGHT RONALD M REV** (608)524-3399
203 S Albert Ave Reedsburg WI 53959-1842 • rbreight@jvlnet.com • SW • 02/1993 02/1999 • (SL 1990 MDIV)

**BREIMEIER KENNETH H REV** (616)889-5539
PO Box 197 Arcadia MI 49613-0197 • MO • EM • (SL 1949 MDIV MA PHD)

**BREITBARTH ROBERT C REV**
C/O Resurrection Lutheran 8061 E Lincoln Hwy Crown Point IN 46307-8824 • S • SP • Resurrection Crown Point IN • (219)942-6604 • (FW 1980 MDIV)

**BREITBARTH STEVEN E REV** (218)254-2702
313 4th St NW Chisholm MN 55719-1508 • breitfam@uslink.net • MNN • SP • Grace Chisholm MN • (218)254-3466 • (FW 1980 MDIV)

**BREITE DOUGLAS C REV** (573)651-3038
2811 Thomas Dr Cape Girardeau MO 63701 • dcbreite@juno.com • MO • Sn/Adm • Trinity Cape Girardeau MO • (573)335-8224 • (SL 1988 MDIV)

**BREITWISCH JOHN G REV** (414)885-5698
420 S Roosevelt Dr Beaver Dam WI 53916-2445 • SW • SP • Peace Beaver Dam WI • (414)887-1272 • (SL 1970 MDIV)

**BRELJE LARRY E REV** (616)375-8223
6387 Saybrook Dr Kalamazoo MI 49009-9176 • MI • Assoc • Zion Kalamazoo MI • (616)382-2360 • (SL 1960)

**BRELJE MILFORD C REV** (815)399-7147
1312 Coolidge Pl Rockford IL 61107-2213 • NI • EM • (SL 1950 MDIV STM MS)

**BREMER DANIEL G REV** (308)389-4837
537 Memorial Dr Grand Island NE 68801-7854 • gracluth@kdsi.net • NEB • SP • Grace Grand Island NE • (308)382-1190 • (SL 1984 MDIV)

**BREMER NOLAN R REV** (503)281-2026
6315 NE 27th Ave Portland OR 97211-6069 • nbremer@cu-portland.edu • NOW • SHS/C • Northwest Portland OR • (SL 1964 MDIV MLS)

**BREMER RICHARD A REV** (217)323-3865
10856 IL Route 125 Beardstown IL 62618-7780 • rbrem@cityscape.net • CI • SP • Saint John Beardstown IL • (217)323-1288 • (FW 1983 MDIV)

**BREMER ROBERT A REV** (919)929-0705
20056 Long Chapel Hill NC 27514 • bobbremer@aol.com • SE • SP • Advent Chapel Hill NC • (919)968-7690 • (SL 1965 MDIV)

**BREN DONALD J REV** (406)538-3654
1104 W Main St Lewistown MT 59457-2302 • MT • EM • (SPR 1965)

**BRENNAN JOSEPH M REV** (303)438-9325
115 Agate Way Broomfield CO 80020-2309 • revjoe@mho.net • RM • Assoc • Beaut Savior Broomfield CO • (303)469-1785 • (FW 1991 MDIV)

**BRENNER DONALD J REV** (619)596-0750
2363 Grafton St El Cajon CA 92020-1317 • djbrenner@aol.com • PSW • SP • Faith San Diego CA • (619)582-1068 • (SL 1966 MDIV DMIN)

**BRENNER KARL A REV** (219)291-3639
17432 Battles Rd South Bend IN 46614-9104 • IN • SP • St Paul Mishawaka IN • (219)633-4888 • (SL 1969)

**BRESE ERWIN A REV** (716)297-5764
8366 Ziblut Ct Niagara Falls NY 14304-1855 • EA • EM • (SL 1961 MDIV STM STM DMIN)

**BRETSCHER DAVID J REV** (785)877-5413
1110 Nixon Dr Norton KS 67654-1130 • KS • SP • Immanuel Norton KS • (785)877-2430 • (SL 1992 MDIV)

**BRETSCHER PAUL G REV** (219)462-4907
807 Linwood Ave Valparaiso IN 46383-6533 • pbretscher@juno.com • IN • EM • (SL 1945 STM MA MA THD)

**BREUDIGAM BRUCE C REV** (330)345-5673
3783 Friendsville Rd #4 Wooster OH 44691 • OH • 08/1998 08/2000 • (FW 1994 MDIV)

**BREWER MICHAEL K REV** (909)989-7453
6265 Terracina Ave Rancho Cucamonga CA 91737-6919 • mkbrewer@linkline.com • PSW • Sn/Adm • Shepherd Hills Alta Loma CA • (909)989-6500 • (FW 1976 MDIV)

**BREWER RICHARD P REV** (925)933-0876
263 Croyden Dr Pleasant Hill CA 94523-3516 • revrpb@aol.com • CNH • EM • (SL 1958)

**BREZNEN JACK REV**
148 Farm Rd New Canaan CT 06840-6326 • S • SP • Trinity Stamford CT • (203)966-3070 • (SPR 1976)

**BRIDGES H LANE REV** (860)582-3415
25 Sherwood Rd Bristol CT 06010-2678 • pastor.b@snet.net • NE • Sn/Adm • Immanuel Bristol CT • (860)583-5649 • (FW 1980 MDIV)

**BRIEL STEVEN C REV** (612)420-2257
17425 83rd Ave N Maple Grove MN 55311-1755 • scbriel@aol.com • MNS • Sn/Adm • St John Maple Grove MN • (763)420-2426 • (SPR 1975 STM)

**BRIGGS RONALD JUNIOR REV** (803)506-3144
3420 Green View Parkway Sumter SC 29150 • EN • EM • (CQ 1995)

**BRIGHTON DAVID C REV** (912)218-2812
106 Holly Pointe Warner Robins GA 31088-6761 • pastor³brighton@yahoo.com • FG • SP • Mount Calvary Warner Robins GA • (912)922-1418 • (SL 1982 MDIV)

**BRIGHTON LOUIS A REV** (314)677-5947
2541 Belmont Dr High Ridge MO 63049-2421 • bellebright@worldnet.att.net • MO • EM • (SL 1952 MDIV STM PHD)

**BRIGHTON MARK A REV** (714)854-8002
1530 Concordia Irvine CA 92612-3203 • brightma@cui.edu • PSW • SHS/C • Pacific Southwest Irvine CA • (949)854-3232 • (SL 1986 MDIV MA)

**BRILL PAUL H REV**
4444 Reservoir Blvd Rm 31 Columbia Heights MN 55421-3255 • MNN • EM • (SL 1930)

**BRILL WALTER L REV** (218)741-2103
910 13th St S Virginia MN 55792-3250 • wlbrill@the-bridge.net • MNN • SP • Trinity Virginia MN* • (218)741-1911 • (SL 1967 MDIV)

**BRILLINGER OTTO A REV** (812)667-6939
7280 St Rd 62 Dillsboro IN 47018-9139 • obrillinger@juno.com • IN • EM • * • (SPR 1964)

**BRINDLE MURRAY W REV** (810)226-0048
19663 Lloyd Clinton Township MI 48038 • murraybrindle@worldnet.att.net • MI • SP • Peace Shelby Township MI • (810)731-4120 • (CQ 1991)

**BRINGEWATT RICHARD P REV** (402)563-4185
215 S Calle Colombo Columbus NE 68601 • richb@megavision.com • NEB • Sn/Adm • Immanuel Columbus NE • (402)564-0502 • (SL 1986 MDIV)

**BRINK KURT W REV**
7250 Arthur Blvd Apt 269 Merrillville IN 46410-3772 • RM • EM • (SPR 1941)

**BRINK PAUL W DR**
1617 W 5th St Storm Lake IA 50588 • IW • O Miss • Iowa West Fort Dodge IA • (FW 1978 MDIV DMISS)

**BRINK WILBUR FRANK REV** (402)379-2203
2207 Sunset Ave Norfolk NE 68701-4545 • NEB • Sn/Adm • Mount Olive Norfolk NE • (402)371-1238 • (CQ 1994 MS)

**BRINKLEY DAVID R REV** (626)286-8520
1124 E Lastunas D Sangabriel CA 91776 • PSW • SP • First Temple City CA • (626)287-0968 • (CQ 1999)

**BRINKLEY THOMAS J REV**
6825 Triple Lakes Rd Saginaw MN 55779 • MNN • S Miss • Minnesota North Brainerd MN • (FW 1996)

**BRINKLEY WELDON DELMADGE REV** (601)843-0035
636 N Bayou Ave Cleveland MS 38732-2054 • wbrinkle@deltaland.net • SO • SP • Good Shepherd Cleveland MS* • (601)846-0233 • (CQ 1994)

**BRINKMAN BRUCE A REV** (612)781-9698
3022 Mc Kinley St NE Minneapolis MN 55418-2318 • parsonb@isd.net • MNS • SP • Gloria Dei Minneapolis MN • (612)781-1989 • (SL 1966 MDIV)

**BRINKMAN F PETER REV** (608)243-8912
40 Golf Course Rd Madison WI 53704-1423 • fpb@peacecouncil.org • SW • EM • (SL 1960 STM)

**BRINKMAN PAUL R REV** (920)731-2729
4809 N Gardenwood Ln Appleton WI 54913-7645 • prbfaith@aol.com • NW • Sn/Adm • Faith Appleton WI • (920)739-9191 • (SL 1967 MDIV)

**BRINKMANN NORMAN G REV** (201)664-6807
21 Lotus St Westwood NJ 07675-2309 • NJ • EM • (SPR 1960 STM)

**BRINKMANN WAYNE O REV** (319)242-4513
422 Main Ave Clinton IA 52732-1938 • IE • SP • St John Clinton IA • (319)242-5588 • (SL 1973 MDIV)

**BRINKMEYER ARTHUR REV** (402)362-2777
908 S Hutchins Ave York NE 68467-4024 • NEB • Sn/Adm • Emmanuel York NE • (402)362-3655 • (CQ 1978 MAD)

**BRINLEY GEORGE W REV** (616)924-1986
24 Southwoods Ave Fremont MI 49412-1750 • revgwbrinley@ncats.net • MI • SP • Redeemer Fremont MI • (231)924-2707 • (SPR 1973 MDIV)

**BRISBOIS TIMOTHY R REV** (641)393-2381
417 Main St Elma IA 50628 • brisbois@n-connect.net • IE • 06/2000 • (FW 1990 MDIV)

**BRISTOL E MICHAEL REV** (317)889-0216
4339 Tarragon Dr Indianapolis IN 46237-3667 • IN • Inst C • Indiana Fort Wayne IN • (SPR 1970 MDIV)

**BRITTON WILLIAM J REV** (937)644-1693
PO Box 617 Marysville OH 43040-0617 • OH • EM • (SPR 1952)

**BROCKHOFF DANIEL A REV** (727)581-4602
3820 Mc Kay Creek Dr Largo FL 33770-4566 • dbrockhoff@worldnet.att.net • FG • EM • (SL 1954 MDIV)

**BROCKHOFF DAVID D REV** (914)667-1807
15 Locust Ln Mount Vernon NY 10552-1327 • brockhoff@netzero.net • AT • D Miss • Atlantic Bronxville NY • (914)337-5700 • (SL 1985 MDIV DMIN)

**BROCKHOFF HAROLD E REV** (918)369-3303
11205 So 94 East Ave Bixby OK 74008-1776 • hebrock@juno.com • OK • EM • (SL 1950)

**BROCKHOFF MARK J REV** (847)895-0088
C/O St John Lutheran Church 1800 S Rodenburg Rd Schaumburg IL 60193-3536 • NI • SP • St John Schaumburg IL • (847)524-9746 • (SL 1982 MDIV)

**BROCKHOFF ROBERT A REV** (502)241-4435
7311 Lark Rd Crestwood KY 40014-9451 • IN • Indiana Fort Wayne IN • (SL 1965 MDIV)

**BROCKMAN MICHAEL C REV** (316)665-8513
1502 N Hendricks Hutchinson KS 67501 • KS • SP • Christ Hutchinson KS • (316)665-8513 • (FW 1984 MDIV)

**BROCKMAN WAYNE R REV** (510)237-9432
5838 N Arlington Blvd San Pablo CA 94806-4250 • wrbrockman@earthlink.net • CNH • SP • Trinity Richmond CA • (510)223-8822 • (SL 1973 MDIV)

**BROCKMANN JAMES E REV** (602)684-8678
5558 E Player Pl Mesa AZ 85215 • pjb3436@gateway.net • PSW • EM • (SL 1959 MDIV)

**BROCKOPP DANIEL C REV** (608)742-8551
900 West Pleasant St Portage WI 53901 • EN • EM • (SPR 1961 STM)

**BROCKOPP DAVID W REV** (218)253-4611
RR 1 Box 323 Red Lake Falls MN 56750-9766 • MNN • EM • (SPR 1960)

**BROCKOPP ELROY D REV** (314)843-0576
9216 Medallion Ct Saint Louis MO 63126-2527 • MO • EM • (SPR 1954)

**BROECKER MARK F REV**
C/O St John Lutheran Church PO Box 436 Yuma CO 80759-0436 • RM • Trinity Richmond CA • (510)223-8822 • (SL 1972 MDIV)

**BROESKE DONALD E REV** (562)799-4233
13270 N Fairfield Ln # 174H Seal Beach CA 90740 • PSW • EM • (SPR 1947 MAT)

**BROGAARD JOHN C REV** (920)685-5830
683 Grant Ave Omro WI 54963-1358 • brogaard@northnet.net • SW • SP • Grace Omro WI • (920)685-2621 • (SL 1970 MDIV)

**BRONDOS ANDREW D REV** (901)757-2432
1413 Hawkcrest Cv N Cordova TN 38018-5770 • andrewbrondos@cs.com • MDS • EM • (SL 1955 MDIV)

**BRONDOS JOEL A REV** (219)744-2541
229 W Maplegrove Ave Fort Wayne IN 46807-2835 • stimme@aol.com • IN • Prin • Zion Fort Wayne IN • (219)744-1389 • (SL 1984 MDIV STM)

**BRONDOS MICHAEL REV** (804)320-1232
9370 Donachy Dr Richmond VA 23235-4902 • SE • EM • (SPR 1946 MED)

**BRONES DANA ALLEN REV**
C/O Bethlehem Lutheran Church 1423 8th Ave N Jacksonville FL 32250-3555 • FG • Assoc • Bethlehem Jacksonville Beach FL • (904)249-5418 • (SL 1983 MDIV)

**BRONNER MICHAEL A REV**
1035 Winter Park Dr Fenton MO 63026-5690 • MO • Sn/Adm • Resurrection Saint Louis MO • (314)843-6633 • (CQ 1996 MA)

**BRONSON ROBERT J REV** (515)923-2589
740 State St Garner IA 50438-1543 • IW • Assoc • St Paul Garner IA • (515)923-2261 • (FW 1991 MDIV)

**BROOKS CURTIS WAYNE REV** (715)233-0195
2020 2nd St E Menomonie WI 54751 • cwbrooks@juno.com • NW • SP • Faith Menomonie WI • (715)235-1653 • (FW 1995 MDIV)

**BROOKS DANA A REV** (605)745-6637
C/O Bethesda Luth Church 1537 Baltimore Ave Hot Springs SD 57747-2205 • brooksfam5@juno.com • SD • SP • Bethesda Hot Springs SD • (605)745-4834 • (SL 1988 MDIV)

**BROOKS ERNEST H REV** (630)543-6909
141 W Army Trl Blvd Addison IL 60101 • ehb23@aol.com • NI • Sn/Adm • St Paul Addison IL • (630)543-6909 • (FW 1998 MDIV)

**BROOKS GARY D REV** (804)764-7801
Hq ACC/HCR 216 Sweeney Blvd Suite 114 Langley AFB VA 23665-2793 • gdbrooks@aol.com • SI • M Chap • Southern Illinois Belleville IL • (SPR 1975 MDIV)

**BROOKS JOHN W REV** (616)861-0747
9020 W William St Shelby MI 49455-9371 • MI • SP • St James Montague MI • (231)894-8471 • (FW 1985 MDIV)

**BROOKS L JAMES REV** (770)339-4413
1425 Sever Rd Lawrenceville GA 30043-5235 • FG • EM • (LS 1953 MED)

**BROOKS M THOMAS REV** (417)546-3908
PO Box 281 Forsyth MO 65653 • t-mbrooks@inter-linc.net • KS • EM • (SL 1963 MDIV)

**BROSTROM DENNIS P REV** (218)226-4773
107 Outer Dr Silver Bay MN 55614 • MNN • SP • Faith Silver Bay MN* • (218)226-3908 • (CQ 1999 MDIV)

**BROUWER THOMAS KENT REV** (573)817-3311
201 Southampton Dr Columbia MO 65203-3051 • pastortom@aic.org • MO • Assoc • Alive in Christ Columbia MO • (573)499-0443 • (SL 1995 MDIV)

**BROWN CARL A REV** (901)357-1481
2970 Everest St Memphis TN 38127-7814 • cblbbrown@aol.com • MDS • D Miss • Mid-South Cordova TN • (FW 1997 MDIV)

**BROWN CLARK A REV** (406)662-3776
PO Box 316 Bridger MT 59014 • cbrown0696@aol.com • MT • SP • St Paul Bridger MT* • (406)662-3776 • (FW 1999 MDIV)

**BROWN GARY M REV** (828)369-3993
79 Wayah St #C Franklin NC 28734-3328 • parsonguy@aol.com • SE • SP • Resurrection Franklin NC • (828)524-5996 • (SL 1994 MDIV)

**BROWN GREGORY WILLIAM REV** (505)546-4091
1608 S Bryant DR Deming NM 88030-6104 • revgreg@zianet.com • RM • SP • Redeemer Deming NM • (505)546-3348 • (FW 1991 MDIV)

**BROWN JAMES P REV** (805)476-9106
8595 Untreiner Ave Pensacola FL 32534-1831 • SO • SP • St Matthew Pensacola FL • (850)477-0567 • (SPR 1973 MDIV)

**BROWN JERRY D REV** (580)864-7803
PO Box 92 Covington OK 73730 • jdbrown8@pldi.net • OK • SP • St John Covington OK • (405)864-7965 • (CQ 1983)

**BROWN JOHN M REV** (205)682-9749
C/O Holy Cross Luth Church 4 Brown St Camden AL 36726-2006 • SO • SP • Holy Cross Camden AL • (334)682-9552 • (GB 1955)

**BROWN KEITH E JR.** (618)624-0920
301 Frey Ln Fairview Heights IL 62208 • brown@lcms.org • TX • SP • Saint Peter Caseyville IL • (618)398-2646 • (SL 2000 MDIV)

**BROWN ROBERT E REV** (231)861-2995
2737 Hillcrest Dr New Era MI 49446 • rbbrown3618@yahoo.com • MI • EM • (CQ 1987 MA MA)

**BROWN ROBERT J REV** (305)296-4904
6800 Maloney Ave Lot 41 Key West FL 33040-8112 • SI • EM • (SPR 1971 MDIV)

**BROWN TIMOTHY C REV** (816)476-5672
308 E 1st St Appleton City MO 64724-1006 • tcbrown@iland.net • MO • SP • Trinity Appleton City MO* • (816)476-5438 • (SL 1989 MDIV)

**BROWN WARREN R REV** (317)894-3282
7508 W US Highway 40 Cumberland IN 46229-4221 • IN • EM • * • (SL 1960)

**BROWNE CHRISTOPHER C REV** (773)561-9468
2454 W Bryn Mawr Ave Chicago IL 60659 • NI • SP • St Philip North Chicago IL • (773)561-9830 • (SL 2000 MDIV)

**BROWNE DONALD J REV** (406)862-3008
200 Colorado Ave Whitefish MT 59937-0883 • MT • SP • St Peter Whitefish MT • (406)862-3008 • (CQ 1987 MDIV)

**BROWNING RICHARD L REV** (919)567-2526
221 Springside Dr Holly Springs NC 27511 • PastorRichard@RLCary.org • SE • Assoc • Resurrection Cary NC • (919)851-7248 • (SL 1998 MDIV)

**BROWNLEE JEROME A SR. DR** (573)635-5969
809 Swifts Hwy Jefferson City MO 65109-2547 • jlbrownlee@aol.com • MO • Sn/Adm • Trinity Jefferson City MO • (573)636-6750 • (FW 1978 MDIV DMIN)

**BRUBAKER JAMES A REV** (907)789-4117
2500 Sunset Dr Juneau AK 99801-9371 • faithjno@alaska.net • NOW • SP • Faith Juneau AK • (907)789-7568 • (SL 1976 MA)

**BRUCE GORDON W REV** (402)329-4524
704 E Florence St Pierce NE 68767-1613 • NEB • Sn/Adm • Zion Pierce NE • (402)329-4313 • (FW 1987 MDIV)

**BRUCH DANIEL CHARLES REV** (715)386-6483
621 Hickory Rd Hudson WI 54016-1838 • drdbruch@pressenter.com • MNS • SP • Trinity Hudson WI • (715)386-9313 • (FW 1978 MDIV MSO DMIN PHD DSC)

**BRUCKNER ROBERT A REV** (219)432-4697
10704 Jenn Ridge Dr Fort Wayne IN 46804-4988 • pilopack@cs.com • EN • Sn/Adm • St Michael Fort Wayne IN • (219)432-2033 • (SPR 1972 MDIV)

**BRUECKNER ALLEN F REV** (920)866-3524
4484 Nicolet Dr Green Bay WI 54311 • rpolak@flash.net • SW • EM • (SPR 1952)

**BRUECKNER PETER R REV** (810)773-5344
20840 Maple St St Clair Shrs MI 48081-2112 • brueckner@mich.com • MI • SP • Bethany Detroit MI • (313)885-7721 • (CQ 1993 MDIV)

**BRUEGGEMANN EUGENE V REV** (970)221-0899
123 Harvard St Fort Collins CO 80525 • brueggie@aol • RM • EM • (SL 1950 MDIV)

**BRUENGER ALVIN J REV** (913)672-4561
505 S Center Oakley KS 67748 • albrueng@ruraltel.net • KS • EM • (SL 1959 MST)

**BRUENGER RICHARD W REV** (913)632-3465
2220 8th St Clay Center KS 67432 • bruenger@kansas.net • KS • SP • St Paul Clay Center KS • (785)632-5301 • (SPR 1972 MDIV)

**BRUENING GEORGE J REV** (785)273-5769
2719 SW James St Topeka KS 66614-2230 • KS • EM • (SL 1941 MA DD)

**BRUENING W PHILIP REV** (804)741-1364
10307 Windbluff Dr Richmond VA 23233-3617 • pbrue@erols.com • SE • Sn/Adm • Trinity Richmond VA • (804)270-4626 • (SL 1968 MDIV DMIN)

**BRUENJES IRVIN H REV** (701)222-1035
1028 Mouton Ave Bismarck ND 58501-5531 • irvinb@aol.com • ND • EM • (SL 1960 MDIV)

**BRUER ROBERT L REV** (217)362-6210
1928 S 32nd Pl Decatur IL 62521 • rbruer@juno.com • CI • SP • Concordia Decatur IL • (217)428-6421 • (FW 1982 MDIV)

**BRUESKE ROBERT E REV** (320)834-2805
8100 County Rd 8 NW Alexandria MN 56308 • merabrue@juno.com • MNN • 04/1987 04/2000 • (SL 1963 MDIV STM)

**BRUICK SCOTT DENNIS REV** (219)923-1228
8440 White Oak Ave Munster IN 46321-2398 • sbruick@mail.icongrp.com • IN • Assoc • St Paul Munster IN • (219)836-6270 • (SL 1995 MDIV)

**BRUMME CARL A REV** (423)764-3418
1012 Holston Ave Bristol TN 37620-3517 • MDS • EM • (SPR 1952)

**BRUMMER H DAVID REV** (630)782-0727
798 Emroy Ave Elmhurst IL 60126-1712 • davidbrummer@hotmail.com • NI • Assoc • First St Paul Chicago IL • (312)642-7172 • (SPR 1965 MDIV)

**BRUMMETT BELVIN R REV** (940)872-8821
1207 Anetta St Bowie TX 76230-3301 • luthrvivit@juno.com • TX • SP • St Peter Bowie TX • (940)872-1886 • (SL 1988 MDIV)

**BRUNDIGE FRANK N REV** (323)773-3056
C/O San Pedro Y San Pablo 6430 Colmar Ave Bell Gardens CA 90201-1798 • PSW • D Miss • SS Pedro/Pablo Bell Gardens CA • (323)773-3056 • (FW 1987 MDIV)

**BRUNER JAMES RICHARD REV** (517)871-2407
8843 Fulmer Rd Millington MI 48746-8708 • MI • Sn/Adm • St Paul Millington MI • (517)871-4581 • (SL 1991 MDIV)

**BRUNETTE DUANE A REV**
2711 Bayview Dr Eustis FL 32726-6960 • brunette@cde.com • FG • EM • (SL 1959 STM DMIN)

**BRUNETTE JOHN S REV** (314)846-2975
7020 Briar Bluff Dr Saint Louis MO 63129-5534 • jbrunette@aol.com • MO • SP • Faith Saint Louis MO • (314)846-8612 • (SL 1987 MDIV)

**BRUNETTE LUTHER C REV** (317)814-4252
C/O Carmel Luth Church 4850 E 131st St Carmel IN 46033-9311 • lbrunette@clearcall.net • IN • Sn/Adm • Carmel Carmel IN • (317)814-4252 • (SL 1980 STM)

**BRUNETTE MARK D REV** (901)737-6010
2060 Bohemia Cv Cordova TN 38018-3577 • pmb1017@aol.com • MDS • SP • Grace Celebration Cordova TN • (901)737-6010 • (SL 1983 MDIV)

**BRUNING ALTON J REV** (216)524-4401
7562 Brecksville Rd Cleveland OH 44131-6535 • abruning@cyberdrive.net • OH • EM • (SPR 1965)

**BRUNING EDWARD VICTOR REV** (702)264-0917
C/O Our Savior Luth Church PO Box 91449 Henderson NV 89009-1449 • ed-bruning@ccnmail.com • PSW • SP • Our Savior Henderson NV • (702)565-9154 • (SL 1985 MDIV MBA)

**BRUNNER DONALD E REV** (402)664-3432
PO Box 409 Scribner NE 68057-0409 • NEB • SP • St Peter Scribner NE • (402)664-3462 • (SPR 1974 MDIV)

**BRUNNER JOHN G REV** (610)873-8530
199 Plaza Dr Downingtown PA 19335-3364 • cmlcs@chesco.com • EA • DP • Eastern Williamsville NY • (716)634-5111 • (SL 1972 DMIN)

**BRUNNER PAUL H REV** (708)532-9395
C/O Trinity Luth Church 6850 159th St Tinley Park IL 60477-1629 • NI • Asst • Trinity Tinley Park IL • (708)532-9395 • (SL 1960)

**BRUNOLD WILLIAM LUCAS REV** (818)840-8629
2007 N Parish Pl Burbank CA 91504 • wlbrunold@aol.com • PSW • SP • First Burbank CA • (818)848-7432 • (FW 1978 MDIV)

**BRUNOW EUGENE W REV** (219)749-7517
6612 Durango Dr Fort Wayne IN 46815-7851 • IN • D Ex/S • Indiana Fort Wayne IN* • (CQ 1982 MED)

**BRUNS PAUL C REV** (815)399-8174
1117 Eastview Rd Rockford IL 61108-4127 • drpbruns@execpc.com • NI • S Miss • Northern Illinois Hillside IL • (SL 1964 MDIV DD)

**BRUNWORTH TODD J REV** (517)448-8827
C/O Our Savior Luth Church 751 N Maple Grove Ave Hudson MI 49247-1149 • MI • SP • Our Saviour Hudson MI • (517)448-6271 • (SL 1976 MDIV)

**BRUSCO STEPHEN R JR. REV** (603)357-7453
11 Emerson Brook Dr Gilsum NH 03448-7500 • NE • EM • (SL 1956 MDIV)

**BRUSIUS RONALD W REV** (941)731-1247
1204 Buena Vista Dr Fort Myers FL 33903-1544 • rbrusius@aol.com • FG • EM • (SPR 1968 MDIV)

**BRUSS ELDOR A REV** (636)464-7127
1643 Shadwell Dr Barnhart MO 63012-2627 • bruss-2@msn.com • MO • EM • (SL 1956 MDIV)

**BRUSS TIMOTHY J REV** (262)547-3596
1411 E Roberta Ave Waukesha WI 53186-6817 • tjbruss@ticon.net • SW • Sn/Adm • Beautiful Savior Waukesha WI • (414)542-2496 • (SL 1971 MDIV)

**BRUSTUEN KEITH REV** (319)352-0998
2028 Larrabee Ave Waverly IA 50677-9043 • kskbru18@hotmail.com • IE • SP • St Paul Waverly IA • (319)352-5394 • (SL 1988 MDIV)

**BRUTLAG JOEL ROBERT REV** (612)834-2547
C/O Ebenezer Luth Church 5393 County Road 5 NW Alexandria MN 56308-9740 • jandcbrutlag@juno.com • MNN • SP • Ebenezer Alexandria MN* • (320)834-2546 • (FW 1992 MDIV)

**BRUTLAG KEITH W REV**
1328 Hillcrest Dr NE Fridley MN 55432-5825 • keithbrutlag@juno.com • MNS • SP • St Matthew Columbia Heights MN • (763)788-9427 • (SPR 1975 MDIV)

**BRUZEK SCOTT A REV** (630)668-9926
2S065 Burning Trl Wheaton IL 60187-7842 • bruzek@stjohnwheaton.org • NI • Sn/Adm • St John Wheaton IL • (630)668-0701 • (SL 1985 MDIV PHD)

**BRYNESTAD DALE L REV** (830)663-2659
507 Wedgewood Devine TX 78016 • TX • SP • Divine Savior Devine TX • (210)663-3735 • (SL 2000 MDIV)

**BUCHER RICHARD P REV** (978)365-9571
125 Chace St Clinton MA 01510-3203 • revbucher@aol.com • NE • SP • Trinity Clinton MA • (978)365-6888 • (FW 1985 MDIV)

**BUCHHEIMER JOHN R REV** (904)249-4905
209 Tallwood Rd Jaxville Bch FL 32250-2985 • FG • Sn/Adm • Bethlehem Jacksonville Beach FL • (904)249-5418 • (SL 1955 MED)

**BUCHHOLZ HENRY V REV** (218)346-6725
840 1st St W Richville MN 56576-9702 • hmbhive@eot.com • MNN • EM • (SPR 1963)

**BUCHHOP MARK J REV** (701)775-6151
2344 W Springbrook Ct Grand Forks ND 58201-5251 • mbuchhop@sage.und.nodak.edu • ND • Cmp P • Wittenberg Chpl Grand Forks ND • (701)772-3992 • (FW 1979 MDIV)

**BUCHHORN MICHAEL G REV** (979)366-2219
RR 2 Box 152 Giddings TX 78942 • buchhorn@totalaccess.net • TX • SP • St Paul Giddings TX • (979)366-9650 • (FW 1989 MDIV)

**BUCHHORN RALPH H REV**
300 Santa Fe Dr Encinitas CA 92024-5131 • clothcop@aol.com • PSW • SP • St Mark Encinitas CA • (760)753-4776 • (FW 1982 MDIV)

**BUCHMANN ROLF A REV** (860)644-3221
20 Aroda Dr South Windsor CT 06074-1358 • our.savior.lutheran@snet.net • NE • Sn/Adm • Our Savior South Windsor CT • (860)644-3350 • (SPR 1968 MDIV)

**BUCK BENJAMIN A REV** (507)345-6637
235 Heather Lane Mankato MN 56001-5682 • ben.buck@juno.com • MNS • EM • (CQ 1950 MA PHD)

**BUCK GEORGE REV** (440)845-5128
1800 Winchester Dr Parma OH 44134-4837 • OH • EM • (SL 1960)

**BUCK RAYMOND REV** (303)659-1640
240 S 22nd Ave Brighton CO 80601-2586 • RM • EM • (SL 1940)

**BUCKA JOHN D REV** (909)737-3564
C/O Grace Lutheran Church 1000 West Wilson St Banning CA 92220 • PSW • SP • Grace Banning CA • (909)849-3232 • (SPR 1964 MDIV)

**BUCKERT MARK P REV** (716)385-1274
396 East St Pittsford NY 14534-3645 • FG • 03/1999 • (SL 1977 MDIV MSED)

**BUCKHAHN CHARLES F REV** (517)249-0494
1109 Elmdale Dr Saginaw MI 48602-2961 • cfbuckhahn@aol.com • MI • Assoc • Bethlehem Saginaw MI • (517)755-1144 • (SL 1978 MDIV)

**BUCKMAN ALLAN R REV** (314)487-4240
4875 Towne South Rd Saint Louis MO 63128-2841 • MO • S Ex/S • Missouri Saint Louis MO • (314)317-4550 • (SL 1965 MDIV MA DMISS)

**BUCKMAN JAMES D REV** (417)823-3743
5149 S Chatsworth Springfield MO 65810 • jbuckman@usiw.net • MO • D Miss • Missouri Saint Louis MO* • (314)317-4550 • (SL 1996 MDIV)

**BUCKMAN JAMES R REV** (715)886-3852
360 Wood Ave Nekoosa WI 54457-1366 • injc2@yahoo.com • NW • EM • * • (SL 1956)

**BUCKMAN ROBERT A REV** (715)423-3490
641 18th St S Wisconsin Rapids WI 54494-5118 • NW • EM • * • (SL 1960)

**BUDEWIG ROBERT REV** (254)771-1002
3502 Buffalo Trl Temple TX 76504 • rbudewig@stonemedia.com • TX • SP • Prince Peace Belton TX • (254)939-0824 • (CQ 1975 MDIV DMIN)

**BUDKE CLARENCE E REV** (828)456-7992
157 Jarvis St Waynesville NC 28786-4424 • cebudke@aol.com • SE • EM • (SPR 1960)

**BUECHELER RANDALL A REV** (909)336-3156
C/O Mt Calvary Lutheran Church PO Box 250 Lake Arrowhead CA 92352-0250 • PSW • SP • Mount Calvary Lake Arrowhead CA • (909)337-1412 • (FW 1987 MDIV)

**BUEGE RICHARD L REV** (507)388-5454
327 Floral Ave Mankato MN 56001-4010 • MNS • Asst • Redeemer Burnsville MN • (612)432-7942 • (SPR 1955)

**BUEGE WILLIAM A REV** (623)972-5917
10101 W Palmeras Dr Apt 105 Sun City AZ 85373-2084 • PSW • EM • (SL 1936 DD)

**BUEGEL JOHN E REV** (651)683-0191
2250 Field Stone Dr Mendota Heights MN 55120-1918 • buegel@csp.edu • MNS • SHS/C • Minnesota South Burnsville MN • (SL 1960 MDIV MA)

**BUEGLER DAVID D DR** (440)937-5598
4321 Jaycox Rd Avon OH 44011 • dbuegler@ameritech.net • OH • Assoc • St Paul Westlake OH • (440)835-3050 • (SPR 1972 MDIV LLD)

**BUEHNER THEO W REV** (812)944-3634
3417 Deerwood Dr New Albany IN 47150-2116 • IN • EM • (SL 1955)

**BUELOW ALBERT H REV** (712)668-4528
C/O Trinity Luth Church PO Box 470 Odebolt IA 51458-0470 • ahgbuelow@juno.com • IW • SP • Trinity Odebolt IA • (712)668-4528 • (SL 1960 MLS MST)

**BUELTMANN DAVID J REV** (217)364-4513
8687 Hilltop Ct Dawson IL 62520 • cidlcms@eosinc.com • CI • DP • Central Illinois Springfield IL • (SPR 1968 MDIV MA)

**BUETOW MARK T REV** (504)827-5600
C/O Gloria Dei Lutheran Church 2021 S Dupre New Orleans LA 70125 • SO • SP • Gloria Dei New Orleans LA • (504)822-7229 • (SL 2000 MDIV)

**BUETTNER HARVEY J REV** (360)312-9060
5209 La Bounty Rd Ferndale WA 98248-8918 • NOW • EM • (CQ 1993)

**BUGTONG LEONARDO R REV** (808)678-1664
94-1036 Leihaku St Waipahu HI 96797-5256 • lrbugtong@juno.com • CNH • EM • (CQ 1973 STM)

**BUHRKE RICHARD R REV** (715)526-2349
W9318 Oak Ave Shawano WI 54166-6239 • rrbuhrke@frontiernet.net • NW • SP • St Paul Shawano WI* • (715)524-2350 • (SL 1978 MDIV)

**BUMBY NORMAN A REV** (207)892-5526
220 Fort Hill Rd Gorham ME 04038-2254 • EN • Inst C • English Farmington MI • (SPR 1964)

**BUNDSCHUH PAUL ROBERT REV** (509)369-4972
PO Box 66 Klickitat WA 98628-0066 • bundschuh@juno.com • NOW • SP • Grace Klickitat WA* • (509)369-4972 • (SPR 1971 MDIV)

**BUNKOWSKE EUGENE W REV** (219)482-1783
5724 Lancashire Ct Fort Wayne IN 46825-5910 • ewbunkowske@msn.com • IN • SHS/C • Indiana Fort Wayne IN • (SL 1960 MDIV DLITT PHD DLITT DD)

**BUNKOWSKE PAUL A REV** (701)241-4610
3525 11th St S Apt 308 Fargo ND 58104 • ND • EM • (SPR 1964)

**BUNKOWSKE WALTER E REV**
C/O Immanuel Lutheran Church 2 Michigan St NE Grand Rapids MI 49503 • ilc@iserv.net • MI • Asst • Immanuel Grand Rapids MI • (616)454-3655 • (FW 1997 MDIV)

**BUNNETT ROBERT W REV** (562)420-7366
4843 Adenmoor Ave Lakewood CA 90713-2303 • PSW • EM • (SL 1959 MAR)

**BUNNETT THOMAS T REV** (619)299-2890
5389 Wilshire Dr San Diego CA 92116 • tbunnettpacbell.net • PSW • EM • (SL 1962 MDIV MA)

**BUNTING DAVID L REV** (530)458-4943
C/O Bethlehem Luth Church 1600 Wescott Rd Colusa CA 95932-3228 • CNH • SP • Bethlehem Colusa CA • (530)458-4943 • (FW 1989 MDIV)

**BUNZEL FREDERICK J REV** (860)355-2630
40 Twin Oaks New Milford CT 06776-5400 • NE • SP • Trinity New Milford CT • (860)354-3450 • (SL 1977 MDIV)

**BUONO NEIL F REV** (785)228-1729
2510 SW Staffordshire Topeka KS 66614 • KS • Asst • Prince Of Peace Topeka KS • (785)271-0808 • (SL 1999 MDIV)

**BURCE WILLARD L REV** (715)874-6447
8103 W Folsom St Eau Claire WI 54703-9657 • wburce@discover-net.net • NW • EM • (SL 1947 STM THD DD)

**BURCH DON EDWARD REV** (317)329-0070
8856 Doral E Dr Apt G Indianapolis IN 46250-4126 • EN • EM • (SL 1964 MDIV)

**BURCH HERBERT W REV** (502)254-1196
Unit-3301 APO AA 34024-3301 • herburch@pronet.net.gt • NEB • S Miss • Nebraska Seward NE • (FW 1998 MDIV)

**BURCHAM RONALD D REV** (515)270-9463
5421 NW 93rd St Johnston IA 50131 • burcham.ron@gd-lc.org • IW • D Ex/S • Iowa West Fort Dodge IA* • (SL 1988 MDIV)

**BURDICK MICHAEL H REV** (309)836-1095
1191 Stacy Ln Macomb IL 61455-2646 • milsc@wiu.edu • CI • SP • Immanuel Macomb IL • (309)833-4286 • (SL 1988 MDIV)

**BURFEIND PETER MARK REV**
2450 Westbrook Dr Toledo OH 43613 • EN • SP • Holy Cross Toledo OH • (419)476-6256 • (SL 1996 MDIV)

**BURG CHRISTIAN G REV** (305)821-2839
7969 W 16th Ave Hialeah FL 33014-3345 • FG • SP • St Andrew Hialeah FL • (305)821-3622 • (SL 1998 MDIV)

**BURGDORF DONALD A REV** (352)684-3854
7388 Philatelic Dr Springhill FL 34606 • FG • EM • (SL 1960)

**BURGDORF LAWRENCE A REV** (314)429-3714
2615 Poe Ave Saint Louis MO 63114-1412 • schwanfnd@aol.com • MO • EM • (SL 1956)

**BURGE DAVID M REV** (573)788-2677
3642 County Rd 415 Friedheim MO 63747-7453 • MO • SP • Trinity Friedheim MO • (636)788-2536 • (FW 1978 MDIV)

**BURGER JOHN O REV** (417)468-2577
C/O St Paul Luth Church 609 N Locust St # 44 Marshfield MO 65706-1212 • MO • SP • St Paul Marshfield MO • (417)468-2577 • (SL 1990 MDIV)

**BURGER MARK M REV** (501)996-2154
PO Box 425 Greenwood AR 72936-0425 • mmbrgr@juno.com • MDS • SP • Grace Greenwood AR • (501)996-7747 • (CQ 1993 MA MED)

**BURGESS DAVID F REV** (810)739-2804
C/O St Philip Luth Church 2884 E Grand Blvd Detroit MI 48202-3130 • kawika2@home.com • MI • SP • St Philip Detroit MI • (313)872-1010 • (FW 1981 MDIV)

**BURGET FRANK W REV** (503)882-8202
1235 Hilton Dr Klamath Falls OR 97603-5254 • NOW • EM • (SPR 1963 MDIV)

**BURGETT WILLIAM R REV** (301)393-5651
457 Links View Dr Hagerstown MD 21740-2901 • pastorb@peoplepc.com • SE • SP • Concordia Hagerstown MD • (301)797-5955 • (SL 1989 MDIV DMIN)

**BURGLAND LANE A DR** (219)693-7969
323 Windsor Dr Churubusco IN 46723-1207 • laburg@msn.com • IN • SP • Faith Churubusco IN • (219)693-6254 • (SL 1979 MDIV STM THD)

**BURHOP CHARLES B REV** (906)495-2273
73 Wood Lake Rd Kincheloe MI 49788-1301 • cbburhop@up.net • MI • SP • St Barnabas Sault Ste Marie MI • (906)632-7796 • (FW 1980 MDIV)

**BURK KEITH H REV** (402)243-2395
Zion Lutheran Church 2247 County Rd 400 Tobias NE 68453 • khburk@alltel.net • NEB • SP • Nebraska Seward NE • (SC 1998 MDIV)

**BURK STEWART A REV** (301)592-7922
3727 Dance Mill Rd Phoenix MD 21131-2117 • SE • EM • (SL 1939)

**BURKE ROBERT F REV** (773)239-1587
9627 S Hamilton Ave Chicago IL 60643-1630 • rfburke@worldnet.att.net • EN • SP • Hope Chicago IL • (773)776-7816 • (SL 1965 MDIV)

**BURKEY RICHARD D DR** (619)462-5211
C/O Christ Lutheran Church 7929 La Mesa Blvd La Mesa CA 91941-5029 • richburkey@aol.com • PSW • Sn/Adm • Christ La Mesa CA • (619)462-5211 • (SL 1985 MDIV DMIN)

**BURKHARD KENNETH M REV** (713)935-0650
8308 Winningham Ln Houston TX 77055-7530 • kburkhard@p.d.q.net • TX • Assoc • St Mark Houston TX • (713)468-2623 • (FW 1982 MDIV)

**BURKMAN ARTHUR R REV** (219)922-4546
9329 Erie St Highland IN 46322-2741 • art.burkman@juno.com • IN • SP • Redeemer Highland IN • (219)838-4898 • (SPR 1971 MDIV)

**BURMEISTER CLYDE J REV** (612)577-0607
11015 57th Ave N Plymouth MN 55442-1623 • MNS • EM • (SPR 1962 MDIV)

**BURMEISTER ROBERT J REV** (507)346-2315
305 Pearl St Spring Valley MN 55975 • pearl@deskmedia.com • MNS • SP • First English Spring Valley MN • (507)346-2793 • (SL 1973 MDIV)

**BURNS JAMES D REV** (501)982-4922
19 Blackwell St Jacksonville AR 72076-3012 • jburns@aristotle.net • MDS • SP • Hope Jacksonville AR • (501)982-1333 • (SL 1990 MDIV)

**BURNS JUSTIN J REV** (636)528-5038
1201 White Oak Ct Troy MO 63379-2282 • MO • EM • (SPR 1970)

**BUROW E PAUL REV**
C/O Immanuel Lutheran Church 47120 Romeo Plank Rd Macomb MI 48044 • MI • Assoc • Immanuel Macomb MI • (810)286-4231 • (SPR 1966 MDIV)

**BUROW GAYLEN A REV** (913)441-0884
C/O Emmaus Luth Church 12900 Kansas Ave Bonner Springs KS 66012-9203 • geeel@juno.com • KS • SP • Emmaus Bonner Springs KS • (913)441-3243 • (SL 1973 MDIV)

**BURRACK RICHARD E REV** (712)653-3611
C/O Trinity Luth Church 1405 Eagle Ave Audubon IA 50025-7494 • IW • EM • (WBS 1951)

**BURRESON KENT JORGEN REV**
17 Seminary Terrace Saint Louis MO 63105 • kent.j.burreson.1@nd.edu • MO • SHS/C • Missouri Saint Louis MO • (314)317-4550 • (SL 1992 MDIV STM MA)

**BURROUGHS ALBERT C REV** (913)235-3805
1915 SW Oakley Ave Topeka KS 66604-3254 • KS • EM • (SL 1938 MDIV)

**BURT MICHAEL F REV** (410)518-9886
1213 Finneans Run Arnold MD 21012-1877 • murtmb@annapolis.net • SE • SP • St Paul Annapolis MD • (410)268-2400 • (SL 1969 MDIV)

**BURT PATRICK J REV** (402)551-7934
5823 Lake St Omaha NE 68104-4153 • NEB • SP • Bethany Omaha NE • (402)558-6212 • (SL 1991 MDIV)

**BURTON KENNETH WILLIAM III REV** (501)337-5226
620 Overman St Malvern AR 72104 • kwburton3@juno.com • MDS • SP • St Luke Malvern AR* • (501)337-9616 • (SL 1999 MDIV)

**BURTON THOMAS R REV** (920)893-8271
420 Wilson St Plymouth WI 53073-1052 • SW • Assoc • St John Plymouth WI • (920)893-3071 • (SL 1969 STM)

**BURTZLAFF PAUL STEVEN REV** (352)732-3494
2575 SE 28th St Ocala FL 34471-6273 • burtz7@aol.com • FG • Assoc • St John Ocala FL • (352)629-1794 • (SL 1993 MDIV MA)

**BURZA GEORGE J REV** (206)242-7319
16615 10th Ave SW Burien WA 98166-2935 • gburza@aol.com • NOW • SP • Beaut Savior Seattle WA • (206)246-9533 • (SL 1985 MDIV)

**BUSBOOM DONALD E REV** (217)894-6360
C/O Good Shepherd Luth Church PO Box 347 Clayton IL 62324-0347 • frlc@adams.net • CI • SP • Good Shepherd Clayton IL • (217)894-7717 • (SPR 1970 MDIV)

**BUSBY WALTER L REV** (904)797-2093
230 Cornell Rd Saint Augustine FL 32086 • wbusby@bellsouth.net • FG • EM • (SPR 1962)

**BUSCH LEONARD E REV** (918)252-1565
9310 E 96th St Tulsa OK 74133-6120 • OK • SP • Good Shepherd Tulsa OK • (918)622-2905 • (SL 1985 MDIV)

**BUSCH LEWIS M REV** (760)353-2935
750 W Holt Ave El Centro CA 92243-3228 • busl@juno.com • PSW • SP • Grace El Centro CA • (760)352-5715 • (SL 1992 MDIV)

**BUSH DAVID S REV** (219)485-0541
C/O St John Deaf Luth Church 3425 Crescent Ave Fort Wayne IN 46805-1505 • bushds@mail.ctsfw.edu • IN • P Df • St John Deaf Fort Wayne IN • (219)483-3173 • (FW 1978 MDIV)

**BUSH GENE H REV** (661)871-8928
3200 Sunview Dr Bakersfield CA 93306-2354 • CNH • EM • (SL 1960 MDIV)

**BUSH JOHN L REV** (734)783-8991
25177 Alicia Brownstown MI 48134 • MI • Assoc • St Paul Trenton MI • (734)676-1565 • (SL 2000)

**BUSH JULIUS B REV** (314)822-3630
411 Gill Ave Kirkwood MO 63122-4433 • MO • EM • (SL 1955)

**BUSH LELAND E REV** (870)238-0860
4525 N Washington St Forrest City AR 72335 • MDS • SP • Faith Forrest City AR • (870)633-8312 • (CQ 1998)

**BUSHUR JAMES GEORGE REV** (219)724-8891
8535N 500 E Decatur IN 46733-7120 • jblb23@adamswells.com • IN • SP • Immanuel Decatur IN • (219)724-7680 • (FW 1993 MDIV STM)

**BUSHUR PAUL J REV**
1146 Whitesburg Knoxville TN 37918 • MDS • SP • First Knoxville TN • (423)524-0366 • (FW 1989 MDIV)

**BUSS ALLAN R REV** (847)428-8722
255 Tollview Ter Gilberts IL 60136-9749 • albussrev@aol.com • NI • SP • St Peter Dundee IL • (847)428-4054 • (FW 1990 MDIV)

**BUSS GARY L REV** (970)241-2255
647 Karen Lee Dr Grand Junction CO 81504-5233 • gbusstar@aol.com • RM • Sn/Adm • Messiah Grand Junction CO • (970)245-2838 • (SL 1983 MDIV)

**BUSS WALTER E REV** (402)371-6448
2507 Westside Ave Norfolk NE 68701-4451 • NEB • EM • (SL 1941)

**BUSSERT MARK P REV** (630)941-7611
C/O Immanuel Luth Church 142 E 3rd St Elmhurst IL 60126-2461 • immelm@mcs.net • NI • Sn/Adm • Immanuel Elmhurst IL • (630)832-1649 • (SL 1981 MDIV)

**BUSSERT PAUL E REV** (712)262-8895
701 4th Ave SE Spencer IA 51301-5432 • bussertp@mymailstation.com • IW • EM • (SL 1940)

**BUSSERT WALTER E REV** (785)840-0392
1510 Saint Andrews Dr Apt G 7 Lawrence KS 66047-1626 • KS • EM • (SL 1934)

**BUTH FREDERICK P REV** (507)864-2585
Rt 1 Box 71 Rushford MN 55971-9622 • frbuth@juno.com • MNS • SP • St John Rushford MN • (507)864-2585 • (SL 1970 MDIV)

**BUTLER JAMES E REV** (413)782-6032
148 Hartford Ter Springfield MA 01118-1538 • butlersix@worldnet.att.net • NE • SP • Trinity Springfield MA • (413)783-9112 • (SL 1985 MDIV DMIN)

**BUTLER ROBERT W REV** (608)727-3841
PO Box 9 Hillpoint WI 53937-0009 • SW • SP • St Paul Hillpoint WI* • (608)727-3841 • (SPR 1974 MA)

**BUTLER WADE ERIC REV** (812)464-1104
1020 W Illinois Evansville IN 47110 • webmaster@trinityevansville.org • IN • SP • Trinity Evansville IN • (812)424-4785 • (CQ 1991 MDIV)

**BUTT JAMES C REV** (808)537-5243
1717 Mott-Smith Dr Apt 2712 Honolulu HI 96822-2850 • jbutt@co.honolulu.hi.us • CNH • Asst • Our Redeemer Honolulu HI • (808)946-4223 • (CQ 1992 MDIV JD)

**BUTTKE KERRY D REV** (815)439-8004
12739 S Elizabeth Dr Plainfield IL 60544-7414 • EN • 09/1993 09/1999 • (FW 1985 MDIV)

**BUTZ LEE A REV** (317)873-9769
45 Clay Ct Zionsville IN 46077-1821 • lbutz84865@aol.com • IN • EM • (SL 1950)

**BUUCK DAVID P REV** (952)939-9173
4100 Tonkawood Ln Minnetonka MN 55345-1840 • dpbuuck@aol.com • MNS • SP • Bethlehem Minnetonka MN • (952)934-9633 • (SL 1971 MDIV)

**BUUCK LEROY E REV** (931)484-7204
119 Friar Ln Crossville TN 38558-8501 • lebdjb@tnaccess.com • MDS • EM • (SL 1945)

**BUUCK R JOHN DR** (414)466-2774
4242 N 99th St Milwaukee WI 53222-1402 • wiu@wiu-usa.edu • SW • EM • (CQ 1990 MA PHD)

**BYARS ANDREW K REV** (520)717-0572
1202 Green Ln Prescott AZ 86305-5231 • acmbyars@computerlink.com • PSW • SP • Shepherd Hills Prescott AZ • (520)778-9122 • (SL 1990 MDIV)

**BYE GREGORY REV** (509)382-4662
C/O Redeemer Luth Church 601 S 3rd St Dayton WA 99328-1513 • bye@bmi.net • NOW • SP • Redeemer Dayton WA* • (509)382-4662 • (SL 1975 MDIV)

**BYE THOMAS W REV** (920)235-8440
1610 Deerfield Dr Oshkosh WI 54904-8276 • tbye@execpc.com • SW • SP • Good Shepherd Oshkosh WI • (920)231-0530 • (FW 1981 MDIV)

**BYER CHARLES RAY REV** (631)727-2510
102 Timber Dr Calverton NY 11933 • pastorbyer@juno.com • AT • SP • Our Redeemer Aquebogue NY • (631)722-4000 • (SL 1983 MDIV)

**BYERLEY WALTER E REV** (217)839-4394
20178 Washer Rd Mount Olive IL 62069 • SI • EM • (CQ 1982)

**BYERS GARY W REV** (618)235-0612
805 Penhurst Pl Belleville IL 62221-7942 • zion96@aol.com • SI • Sn/Adm • Zion Belleville IL • (618)233-2299 • (SPR 1974 MDIV)

**BYLER DAVID R REV** (956)541-3907
901 Boca Chica Blvd Brownsville TX 78520-8304 • strukken@aol.com • TX • SP • Trinity Brownsville TX • (956)542-7024 • (SL 1997 MDIV)

**BYLER GARY L REV** (623)546-6590
19832 W Pinnacle Peak Rd Surprise AZ 85387 • KS • EM • (FW 1977 MDIV)

**BYNUM GORDON W DR** (763)441-3718
420 Rush Ave Elk River MN 55330-1851 • bynum001@tc.umn.edu • EN • 08/1988 08/2000 • (SL 1986 MCMU MDIV PHD)

**BYORK JAMES R REV** (804)897-5307
C/O Redeemer Lutheran Church 9400 Redbridge Rd Richmond VA 23236-3566 • jrbyork@juno.com • SE • Sn/Adm • Redeemer Richmond VA • (804)272-7973 • (SL 1970 MDIV)

## C

**CAGE PETER C REV** (765)284-2097
720 W Ashland Ave Muncie IN 47303 • pccage@juno.com • IN • Asst • Grace Muncie IN • (765)282-2537 • (FW 1991 MDIV)

**CAHILL CHRISTOPHER T REV** (330)948-2458
656 Wooster St Lodi OH 44254-1326 • revcahill@aol.com • S • D Ex/S • SELC Cudahy WI* • (SL 1980 MDIV)

**CAIN JOHN WILLIAM REV** (281)807-3668
C/O Gethsemane Lutheran Church 4040 Watonga Houston TX 77092-5321 • cain@texas.net • TX • Sn/Adm • Gethsemane Houston TX • (713)688-5227 • (SL 1996 MDIV)

**CAIN LAWRENCE E REV**
PO Box 36 Villard MN 56385-0036 • MNN • SP • St John Villard MN* • (320)554-2161 • (CQ 1989)

**CAIN PAUL J JR. REV** (307)875-2598
351 Sunset Green River WY 82935 • WY • SP • Emmanuel Green River WY • (307)875-2598 • (SL 2000 MDIV)

**CALLAHAN EDWARD JOSEPH REV** (718)417-5831
62-18 80th Ave Glendale NY 11385-6839 • stsabbas@earthlink.net • AT • SP • Redeemer Glendale NY • (718)456-5292 • (SL 1991 MDIV)

**CALLAWAY SCOTT A REV** (978)887-5253
C/O Our Savior Luth Church 478 Boston St Topsfield MA 01983-1225 • psacallaway@mediaone.net • NE • SP • Our Savior Topsfield MA • (978)887-5701 • (SL 1988 MDIV)

**CALLESEN ARTHUR A DR** (920)468-4819
1862 Melon Ave Green Bay WI 54302-3449 • callesen@netnet.net • NW • Assoc • Our Saviour Green Bay WI • (920)468-4065 • (SPR 1965 DMIN)

**CALLIES DAVID W REV** (901)753-5144
8135 Aspen Pine Cv Germantown TN 38138-4110 • dcallies@aol.com • MDS • DP • Mid-South Cordova TN • (SL 1965 MDIV)

**CALLIES ELMER W REV** (901)753-5144
8135 Aspen Pine Cv Germantown TN 38138-4110 • MDS • EM • (SL 1936)

**CAMANN FRANCIS E REV** (715)823-5438
27 E 14th St Clintonville WI 54929-1314 • NW • EM • (SPR 1972 MDIV)

**CAMERON BRUCE A REV** (618)443-2067
PO Box 334 Sparta IL 62286-0334 • bcameron@midwest.net • SI • SP • St John Sparta IL • (618)443-3634 • (SL 1979 STM MDIV)

**CAMERON IVORY C REV** (205)681-4479
PO Box 94051 Birmingham AL 35220-4051 • SO • EM • (CQ 1964 MDIV)

**CAMERON PHILIP J REV** (303)469-3097
3236 W 11th Avenue Ct Broomfield CO 80020-6753 • pastorphil@rslc.org • RM • SP • Risen Savior Broomfield CO • (303)469-3521 • (SL 1983 MDIV)

**CAMIN BALDWIN A REV** (208)324-7923
39 W 600 S Jerome ID 83338-6010 • pastorc@magiclink.com • NOW • SP • St Paul Jerome ID • (208)324-2842 • (SPR 1967 MDIV)

**CAMPBELL CHARLES FRED REV** (618)826-3605
110 Allan St Chester IL 62233-2226 • frednjun@midwest.net. • SI • EM • (SPR 1975 MDIV)

**CAMPBELL DAVID E REV** (541)482-2999
6470 Highway 99 S Ashland OR 97520-9754 • NOW • EM • (SPR 1963 DMIN)

**CAMPBELL PHILLIP A REV** (314)965-9000
1206 Meramec Heights Dr Ballwin MO 63021-7711 • phillip.campbell@lcms.org • MO • S Ex/S • Missouri Saint Louis MO • (314)317-4550 • (SL 1971 MDIV DMIN)

**CAMPBELL SCOTT C REV** (303)466-6846
5613 W 118th Pl Broomfield CO 80020-5928 • RM • EM • (SPR 1972 MDIV)

**CAMPBELL W CLAYTON REV**
31119 Alice Ln Tomball TX 77375-4060 • TX • SP • St Paul Magnolia TX • (281)259-7818 • (FW 1994 MDIV)

**CANADA CHARLES O REV** (915)821-4893
4308 Loma De Oro Dr El Paso TX 79934-3709 • zion@whc.net • RM • SP • Zion El Paso TX • (915)566-4667 • (SL 1971 MDIV MS)

**CANION DANIEL A REV** (512)448-1843
8104 B Dowling Cv Austin TX 78745 • trinity240@aol.com • TX • EM • (SPR 1966)

**CANJURA HECTOR ARNOLDO REV** (708)652-6136
3716 S 60th Ct Cicero IL 60804-4114 • NI • D Miss • Northern Illinois Hillside IL • (MX 1978 MDIV)

**CARDARO ROBERT G REV** (713)485-9628
4319 Morris Ct Pearland TX 77584-4901 • TX • Inst C • Texas Austin TX • (SPR 1957)

**CAREY EDWIN J REV** (812)853-5346
8300 Stonegate Dr Newburgh IN 47630-2731 • IN • SP • Shep Paradise Newburgh IN • (812)853-3972 • (SPR 1964)

**CAREY RALPH W REV** (616)667-1522
259 Covington Ct SW Grandville MI 49418-3297 • MI • EM • (SL 1957)

**CARIO DONALD A REV** (716)352-8416
4436 Canal Rd Spencerport NY 14559-9516 • dacario@aol.com • EA • EM • (SPR 1968 MDIV)

**CARLISLE ROGER P REV** (712)664-2323
405 Center PO Box 189 Wall Lake IA 51466-0189 • peacecar@netins.net • IW • SP • Peace Wall Lake IA • (712)664-2961 • (FW 1983 MDIV)

**CARLSON ANDREW J REV**
C/O Gadbury PO Box 55680 North Pole AK 99705 • buchs@runestone.net • NOW • M Chap • Northwest Portland OR • (SL 1997 MDIV)

**CARLSON KENNETH G REV** (301)279-2868
11501 Brandy Hall Ln Gaithersburg MD 20878-2425 • kencarlson@aol.com • SE • D Ex/S • Southeastern Alexandria VA • (SL 1967 MDIV)

**CARLSON LAURENCE H JR. REV**
RR 4 Box 4066 Salisbury MO 65281 • MO • SP • Salem Salisbury MO • (816)481-2249 • (SPR 1970 MDIV)

**CARLSON MARK E REV** (765)662-0981
4897 N Brooke Dr Marion IN 46952-9725 • IN • SP • St James Marion IN • (765)662-3092 • (SL 1983 MDIV)

**CARLSON PATRICK K REV** (504)887-7988
2904 Lexington Dr Metairie LA 70002-7028 • patcarlson@earthlink.net • SO • Sn/Adm • Atonement Metairie LA • (504)887-0225 • (SPR 1975 MDIV DMIN)

**CARLSON STEVEN C REV** (310)798-2724
825 11th St Manhattan Beach CA 90266 • marysteve@earthlink.net • PSW • SP • First Manhattan Beach CA • (310)545-5653 • (FW 1982 MDIV)

**CARLSON THOMAS H REV** (202)588-1820
1700 17th St NW Apt 609 Washington DC 20009-2419 • SE • EM • (SPR 1965)

**CARLTON RICK C REV** (941)992-3400
22632 Fountain Lakes Blvd Estero FL 33928-2328 • rccarlton@aol.com • FG • SP • Hope Bonita Springs FL • (941)992-6952 • (FW 1980 MDIV DMIN)

**CARNAHAN DAVID A REV** (541)617-9649
1034 NE 11th St Bend OR 97701-4402 • celtic@transport.com • NOW • Assoc • Trinity Bend OR • (541)382-1832 • (SL 1985 MDIV)

**CARNAHAN MARK D REV** (217)732-6116
1301 Rutledge Dr Lincoln IL 62656-1259 • 9ofus@abelink.com • CI • SP • Zion Lincoln IL • (217)732-3946 • (FW 1985 MDIV)

**CARNER RICHARD D REV**
C/O Trinity Lutheran Church 2555 Haymaker Rd Monroeville PA 15146-3507 • EA • SP • Trinity Monroeville PA • (412)372-9046 • (SL 1990 MDIV)

**CARNEY WILLIAM M REV** (716)434-0174
7064 Northview Dr Lockport NY 14094-5335 • pcdpmm@wzrd.com • EA • SP • Mount Olive Lockport NY • (716)434-8500 • (SC 1986 MDIV)

**CARNICOM RONALD R REV** (701)545-7413
PO Box 145 Great Bend ND 58039-0145 • rrcarnic@rrt.net • ND • SP • Trinity Great Bend ND* • (701)545-7422 • (FW 1989 MDIV)

**CAROW ALBERT H REV** (503)357-4201
3138 Watercrest Rd Forest Grove OR 97116-1038 • NOW • EM • * • (SPR 1952)

**CARR TIMOTHY J REV** (254)386-3158
122 Cheyenne Mesa Rd Hamilton TX 76531-9801 • cteamcarr@htcomp.net • TX • Sn/Adm • St John Hamilton TX • (254)386-3158 • (FW 1988 MDIV)

**CARR WILLIAM W REV** (314)505-7664
6701 San Bonita Ave Apt 2AW Saint Louis MO 63105-3061 • revbillcarr@juno.com • SE • 07/1994 07/2000 • (SL 1983 MDIV STM)

**CARRETTO JAMES P REV** (402)529-3512
C/O St Paul Lutheran Church PO Box 797 Wisner NE 68791-0797 • kelvin3@prontomail.com • NEB • SP • St Paul Wisner NE • (402)529-6583 • (FW 1981 MDIV)

**CARRIER JOHN S REV** (708)788-6554
3421 Wenonah Ave Berwyn IL 60402-3349 • pjsc@prodigy.net • NI • SP • First Immanuel Chicago IL • (312)733-6886 • (SL 1983 MDIV)

**CARSTENS DAVID LEROY REV** (503)667-6703
19805 NE Holladay St Portland OR 97230-7941 • hopelcdeaf@juno.com • NOW • P Df • Hope Deaf Portland OR • (503)252-0706 • (SPR 1970 MDIV MS)

**CARSTENS GARY J REV** (914)237-8199
C/O St Mark Lutheran Church 7 Saint Marks Pl Yonkers NY 10704-4011 • carstens@yni.net • AT • SP • St Mark Yonkers NY • (914)237-8199 • (CQ 1982 MAR DMIN PHD)

**CARTER LYNELL H REV**
C/O St Pauls Church of Tremont 1984 Crotona Ave Bronx NY 10457-5022 • AT • SP • St Paul Tremont Bronx NY • (718)583-7978 • (CQ 1987 MTH MTH)

**CARTER MARK E REV**
16660 Hummingbird Ln Clarekmore OK 74017-0486 • OK • SP • Redeemer Claremore OK • (918)341-1429 • (CQ 1999 MDIV)

**CARTER MICHAEL D REV** (314)268-1168
4405 W Pine Blvd Apt 501 Saint Louis MO 63108-2355 • mca8562077@aol.com • MO • Missouri Saint Louis MO • (314)317-4550 • (FW 1991 MDIV)

**CARTER RICHARD E REV** (651)645-7800
1175 Englewood Ave Saint Paul MN 55104-1412 • carter@luther.csp.edu • MNS • SHS/C • Minnesota South Burnsville MN • (SL 1980 MED MDIV STM THD)

**CARTER STEPHEN J REV** (314)846-7473
6240 Kings Ferry Pl Saint Louis MO 63129-5044 • MO • S Ex/S • Missouri Saint Louis MO • (314)317-4550 • (SL 1966 MDIV STM DMIN)

**CARTWRIGHT MICHAEL W** (516)931-1647
99 W Nicholai St Hicksville NY 11801-3806 • AT • Asst • Trinity Hicksville NY • (516)931-2225 • (SL 2000 MDIV)

**CARTWRIGHT TIMOTHY C REV**
4106 E 42nd Ave Spokane WA 99223 • NOW • SP • Beautiful Savior Spokane WA • (509)747-6806 • (SL 1985 MDIV)

**CARUANA PETER A REV** (719)520-9870
832 E Pikes Peak Ave Colorado Springs CO 80903-3636 • RM • EM • (SPR 1970)

**CARY BRYAN S REV** (719)852-5420
PO Box 605 Monte Vista CO 81144-0605 • bscary@aol.com • RM • SP • St Peter Monte Vista CO • (719)852-3424 • (FW 1988 MDIV MS MBA)

**CASACHAHUA OSCAR D REV** (201)614-1746
5106 Palisade Ave West New York NJ 07093-1919 • NJ • 09/1992 09/1999 • (FW 1981)

**CASADAY BARRY L REV** (609)758-8076
75 Hill Rd Allentown NJ 08501-1411 • NJ • SP • Immanuel East Rutherford NJ • (201)939-2386 • (CQ 1986)

**CASCI ARTHUR M REV** (810)773-7615
16494 Collinson Ave Eastpointe MI 48021-3024 • lcmresur@ccaa.edu • MI • SP • Resurrection Detroit MI • (313)372-4902 • (SL 1984 MDIV)

**CASCIONE JACK M REV** (810)294-1988
31011 Greater Mack Ave St Clair Shrs MI 48082-1446 • PastorCascione@Juno.com • MI • Sn/Adm • Redeemer Saint Clair Shores MI • (810)294-0640 • (CQ 1981 MFA MDIV MFA)

**CASE JAN C REV** (504)282-2632
PO Box 8396 New Orleans LA 70182-8396 • SO • D Ex/S • Southern New Orleans LA • (SL 1984 MDIV PHD)

**CASE ROBERT DICK REV**
5074 Lake St Omaha NE 68104 • 73602.2062compuserve • NEB • SP • Bethlehem Deaf Omaha NE • (402)558-5672 • (CQ 1978 MA MA)

**CASH ERIC REV** (870)670-4120
PO Box 298 Horseshoe Bend AR 72512-0298 • MDS • EM • (SL 1947)

**CASHMER JASON D REV**
12450 Devoe Southgate MI 48195 • MI • Assoc • Christ King Southgate MI • (734)285-9695 • (SL 1993 MDIV)

**CASHMER TERRY L REV** (734)281-3773
13690 Argyle St Southgate MI 48195-1929 • staff@ctk-church.org • MI • Sn/Adm • Christ King Southgate MI • (734)285-9695 • (SPR 1971)

**CASPERSEN DAVID A REV** (307)637-4947
5131 Bowie Dr Cheyenne WY 82009-4936 • WY • Sn/Adm • Trinity Cheyenne WY • (307)635-2802 • (SPR 1969 MDIV)

**CASSADY JOSEPH R III REV** (309)341-3752
507 Isle Royale Rd Galesburg IL 61401 • mtcav@gallafinriver.net • CI • SP • Mount Calvary Galesburg IL • (309)342-7083 • (SL 1999 MDIV)

**CASSIDY JOHN S JR. REV** (415)587-2525
2525 Alemany Blvd San Francisco CA 94112 • CNH • SP • Bethel San Francisco CA • (415)587-2525 • (SL 1971 MDIV)

**CASTELLANI JOHN A REV** (440)338-3447
13993 E Willard Dr Novelty OH 44072-9734 • jcaste9901@aol.com • EN • 03/2000 • (SPR 1969 MA)

**CASTENS KYLE D REV** (360)691-3173
13613 Tastad Rd Arlington WA 98223 • NOW • Assoc • Immanuel Everett WA • (425)252-7038 • (SL 2000 MDIV)

**CASTENS LOUIS C REV** (770)975-0358
3798 Pine Brook Dr Acworth GA 30102-1539 • FG • EM • (SL 1939 MDIV)

**CASTOR KENNETH R REV** (937)492-7345
3051 N Kuther Rd Sidney OH 45365 • OH • SP • Redeemer Sidney OH • (937)492-2461 • (FW 1998 MDIV)

**CATTAU MARK A REV** (806)351-2278
5000 Albert Ave Amarillo TX 79106-4739 • mcattau@juno.com • TX • SP • Trinity Amarillo TX • (806)352-5629 • (SL 1986 MDIV)

**CAUGHEY WILLIAM F REV** (402)756-8551
C/O Trinity Lutheran Church PO Box 146 Campbell NE 68932-0146 • bcaughey@mail.gtmc.net • NEB • SP • Trinity Campbell NE* • (402)756-8551 • (FW 1997 MDIV)

**CAVENER JAMES H REV** (402)551-1266
641 N 47th St Omaha NE 68132-2511 • jcavener@unomaha.edu • NEB • Cmp P • Trinity Campbell NE • (FW 1988 MDIV MA)

**CECIL DAVID CHARLES REV** (414)459-9119
3007 Wilgus Ave Sheboygan WI 53081-3692 • dccecil@thesurf.com • SW • SP • Our Redeemer Sheboygan WI • (920)452-0717 • (FW 1996 MDIV)

**CHA KYUNG JIN REV** (310)834-5337
48 Camelback Ave N Carson CA 90745-5613 • PSW • D Miss • Ark Noah Korean Carson CA • (310)834-5337 • (CQ 1995)

**CHADWICK ROBERT L REV** (810)695-0659
448 Sandehurst Dr Grand Blanc MI 48439-1556 • revrlclc@aol.com • MI • EM • (CQ 1983 MAR)

**CHAFFEE MICHAEL G REV** (402)477-1937
1836 Old Glory Rd Lincoln NE 68521-1550 • hsoffice@aol.com • NEB • Sn/Adm • Holy Savior Lincoln NE • (402)434-3325 • (SL 1983 MDIV)

**CHAMBERLAIN DAVID WAYNE REV** (541)563-4624
PO Box 754 Waldport OR 97394 • eph289@casco.net • NOW • SP • Our Savior Waldport OR • (541)563-7729 • (SPR 1969 MDIV)

**CHAN DAVID TZE-MING REV** (650)756-5989
87 Montebello Dr Daly City CA 94015-4723 • dtchanl@juno.com • CNH • SP • Holy Spirit San Francisco CA • (415)771-6658 • (SL 1996 MDIV)

**CHAN TERRENCE C REV** (415)871-0307
103 Aldenglen Dr S San Fran CA 94080-3284 • ptcnewlife@aol.com • EN • D Miss • New Life Chinese San Francisco CA • (415)681-5433 • (CQ 1986 MAR)

**CHASE EUGENE C JR. REV** (507)685-4390
C/O Bethlehem Luth Church PO Box 346 Morristown MN 55052-0346 • eccjrdr@juno.com • MNS • SP • Bethlehem Morristown MN • (507)685-4338 • (FW 1981 MDIV DMIN)

**CHEEK DEREK J REV** (573)684-2106
516 W Hudson St Wellsville MO 63384 • MO • SP • Grace Wellsville MO • (573)684-2106 • (FW 1999 MDIV MA)

**CHELLEW STEVEN P REV** (515)232-5449
1411 Wilson Ave Ames IA 50010 • pastor@stpaulames.org • IW • SP • St Paul Ames IA • (515)232-5838 • (FW 1990 MDIV)

**CHELLEW WILLIAM A REV** (414)567-1327
922 State St Apt 6 Oconomowoc WI 53066-3884 • NW • EM • (SL 1957)

**CHELMO WALTER REV** (254)772-4478
1533 Northcrest Dr Waco TX 76710-1041 • wchelmo@prodigy.net • TX • SP • First Rosebud TX • (254)583-7505 • (SPR 1955)

**CHEN WEN-FU REV** (626)442-7191
5403 N Robinhood Ave Temple City CA 91780 • PSW • D Miss • First Temple City CA • (626)287-0968 • (CQ 1998)

**CHENEY ROBERT E REV** (901)644-7007
4520 County Home Rd Paris TN 38242 • cheney@aeneas.net • MDS • EM • (CQ 1980 MA)

**CHILDRESS WILLIAM M REV** (504)868-7077
509 Galveston Dr Houma LA 70360-6270 • auggie@internet8.net • SO • SP • Grace Houma LA • (504)879-1865 • (SPR 1975 MDIV DMIN)

**CHILDS GARY J REV** (419)991-0327
C/O Immanuel Luth Church 2120 Lakewood Ave Lima OH 45805-3171 • gchilds@wcoil.com • OH • Sn/Adm • Immanuel Lima OH • (419)222-2541 • (FW 1981 MDIV)

**CHINBERG DOUGLAS W REV** (402)894-1937
14724 Madison Cir Omaha NE 68137-3945 • dwchinberg@aol.com • NEB • Assoc • Divine Shepher Omaha NE • (402)895-1500 • (SL 1989 MDIV MSED)

**CHITTICK BARR T REV**
4020 Palm Dr Punta Gorda FL 33950-7330 • FG • SP • Faith Punta Gorda FL • (941)639-6309 • (FW 1987 MDIV)

**CHO EUN-KYOO REV** (708)933-1023
4841 Kirk St Apt 2E Skokie IL 60077-3048 • NI • 12/1997 12/1999 • (KO 1978 MTH)

**CHOPP THOMAS W REV** (513)422-1934
1509 Rayview Dr Middletown OH 45044-6733 • tomchopp@infinet.com • OH • SP • Messiah Middletown OH • (513)422-2441 • (SPR 1976 MDIV)

**CHORMANN WILLIAM T REV** (407)858-9144
2512 Miscindy Pl Orlando FL 32806-7315 • wchormann@netscape.net • FG • EM • (FW 1990 MDIV)

**CHRIST MARK E REV** (208)326-4650
3557 N 1825 E Buhl ID 83316-6358 • mechrist@filertel.com • NOW • SP • Clover Trinity Buhl ID • (208)326-4950 • (SL 1989 MDIV)

**CHRISTENSEN JOHN M REV** (307)864-9354
116 S 11th St Thermopolis WY 82443-2525 • jchriste@wyoming.com • WY • SP • St Paul Thermopolis WY • (307)864-2205 • (FW 1987 MDIV)

**CHRISTENSEN KENNETH DEAN REV** (626)292-2435
280 S Charlotte Ave San Gabriel CA 91776-1658 • PSW • SP • First El Monte CA • (626)448-0767 • (FW 1994 MDIV)

**CHRISTENSEN LYNN WILSON REV** (307)358-2557
1059 Durango Dr Douglas WY 82633 • revlwc@juno.com • WY • M Chap • Wyoming Sheridian WY • (FW 1994 MDIV)

**CHRISTENSEN SAM J REV** (307)455-3888
Mt Calvary Luth Ch PO Box 707 Dubois WY 82513 • revsjc@juno.com • WY • SP • Mount Calvary Dubois WY • (307)455-2733 • (SPR 1976 MDIV)

**CHRISTENSEN TRENTON DAVID REV** (913)467-8810
112 E Maple St Fairview KS 66425-9509 • tjahchri@jbntelco.com • KS • SP • St Paul Fairview KS* • (785)467-8810 • (FW 1995 MDIV)

**CHRISTENSON SCOTT ERIC REV** (847)359-6658
239 W Kenilworth Ave Palatine IL 60067 • pastorc@pop-lcms.org • NI • Assoc • Prince Peace Palatine IL • (847)359-3451 • (FW 1996 MDIV)

**CHRISTIAN DOUGLAS M REV** (219)639-3293
C/O St John Luth Church 12912 Franke Rd Monroeville IN 46773-9559 • IN • SP • St John Monroeville IN • (219)639-6404 • (FW 1983 MDIV)

**CHRISTIANSEN DONALD A REV** (636)272-8433
743 Montbrook Dr O Fallon MO 63366-2417 • dchristi@mail.win.org • MO • EM • (SL 1950 MDIV)

**CHRISTIANSEN ERIC M REV** (406)293-4024
C/O St John Lutheran Church 1017 Montana Ave Libby MT 59923-2015 • patch@libby.org • MT • SP • St John Libby MT • (406)293-4024 • (FW 1991 MDIV)

**CHRISTIANSEN HERMAN REV** (847)888-4156
1007 Lincolnshire Ct Apt B Elgin IL 60120-7144 • hc1007@gateway.net • NI • EM • (SPR 1960)

**CHRISTIANSEN JOEL T REV**
9129 Rusticwood Trl Saint Louis MO 63126-2213 • joel@webstergardenschurch.org • MO • Sn/Adm • Webster Gardens Webster Groves MO • (314)961-5275 • (SL 1982 MDIV)

**CHRISTIANSEN KEITH P REV** (660)463-4012
213 S Main St Concordia MO 64020-9669 • kchristiansen@almanet.net • MO • Tchr • St Paul Concordia MO • (660)463-2238 • (FW 1983 MDIV)

**CHRISTIE RONALD E REV**
C/O Zion Lutheran Church 7701 W Britton Rd Oklahoma City OK 73132-1514 • OK • SP • Zion Oklahoma City OK • (405)722-7472 • (FW 1987 MDIV)

**CHRISTOPHER THOMAS D REV** (605)239-4754
PO Box 126 Alexandria SD 57311 • thomas@sd.cybernex.net • SD • SP • Trinity Spencer SD* • (605)246-2760 • (FW 1990 MDIV)

**CHRYST THOMAS E REV** (262)752-0785
2914 Green St Racine WI 53402 • glracine@execpc.com • SW • Assoc • Grace Racine WI • (262)633-4831 • (SL 1999 MDIV)

**CHU BILL S REV** (510)758-5169
3100 Pinole Valley Rd Pinole CA 94564-1823 • revbchu@aol.com • CNH • SP • Our Savior Pinole CA • (510)758-1961 • (SL 1996 MDIV)

**CHUINARD PATRICK W REV** (503)754-8112
1545 NW 27th St Corvallis OR 97330-2448 • svlcpat@proaxis.com • NOW • SP • Shep Valley Corvallis OR • (541)753-2816 • (FW 1986 MDIV)

**CHUN YE YN REV**
3042 12th Los Angeles CA 90006 • PSW • D Miss • Pacific Southwest Irvine CA • (949)854-3232 • (CQ 1995)

**CHUNG MICHAEL REV** (201)585-8380
Hope Lutheran Church 9 E Homestead Ave Palisades Park NJ 07650 • EN • SP • Hope Palisades Park NJ • (201)944-2107 • (CQ 1995)

**CHUNG PAUL J REV** (804)763-1941
C/O Redeemer Lutheran Church 9400 Redbridge Rd Richmond VA 23236 • pauljchung@hotmail.com • SE • 01/2000 • (CQ 1997 MDIV)

**CIAMPA FRANK GENE REV** (718)338-5532
2142 New York Ave Brooklyn NY 11210 • AT • SP • Good Shepherd Brooklyn NY • (718)338-5532 • (FW 2000 MDIV)

**CIZMAR THOMAS JOHN REV** (818)362-7847
15910 Joseph Ct Sylmar CA 91342-1123 • thepromise@earthlink.net • PSW • SP • Celebration Sylmar CA • (818)367-4699 • (CQ 1998 MDIV)

**CLAASEN DONALD K REV** (707)822-0083
610 Park Ave Arcata CA 95521-6518 • dclaasen@northcoast.com • CNH • EM • (SL 1948 MA)

**CLAIBORNE ROBERT D REV** (818)342-2578
6961 Nestle Ave Reseda CA 91335-4545 • rclaiborne@socal.rr.com • PSW • SP • Trinity Reseda CA • (818)342-1633 • (FW 1983 MDIV)

**CLANCY BRYANT E REV** (314)394-6713
643 Highland Glen Dr Ballwin MO 63021-7318 • ic³clancybe@stl • MO • S Ex/S • Missouri Saint Louis MO • (314)317-4550 • (GB 1961 DMIN LLD)

**CLANCY ROBERT A REV** (973)423-0756
136 Grand Ave Hawthorne NJ 07506-1915 • taela@msn.com • S • 06/1999 • (SL 1988 STM MDIV MPHIL)

**CLARK J BLAIR JR. REV** (262)335-4213
3227 Windsor Pl West Bend WI 53090 • blair.23@gateway.net • SW • Assoc • St John West Bend WI • (262)334-4901 • (SL 1987 MDIV)

**CLARK LEE S REV** (847)244-8683
1098 Fuller Rd Gurnee IL 60031-1802 • leesclark@aol.com • NI • SP • Bethel Gurnee IL • (847)244-9647 • (SL 1969 MDIV)

**CLARK MOSES J REV** (334)446-3664
C/O Ebenezer Luth Church PO Box 369 Atmore AL 36504-0369 • SO • EM • (GB 1955)

**CLARK PAUL M REV** (517)593-2354
PO Box 317 Fowler MI 48835-0317 • revpmclark@voyager.net • MI • SP • St Paul Fowler MI • (517)593-2066 • (FW 1988 MDIV)

**CLAUS ARNOLD F REV** (407)269-9371
3464 Dove Ct Titusville FL 32796-3751 • ma@qnc.net • FG • EM • (SPR 1949)

**CLAUS TERRY A REV** (248)887-5369
4096 Ashford St White Lake MI 48383-1702 • MI • SP • Faith Highland MI • (248)887-5550 • (SL 1971 MDIV)
**CLAUSEN GEORGE REV** (712)472-3114
910 S Carrol St Rock Rapids IA 51246-1945 • gclausen@heartlandtel.com • IW • SP • Peace Rock Rapids IA* • (712)472-3226 • (FW 1983 MDIV)
**CLAUSEN JULIUS B REV** (909)944-4861
10801 Lemon Ave #1515 Alta Loma CA 91737 • PSW • Tchr • Pacific Southwest Irvine CA • (949)854-3232 • (SL 1975 MDIV MA)
**CLAUSEN MARVIN W REV** (870)431-5340
374 Lake Dr Lakeview AZ 72642-7108 • NI • 04/1997 04/2000 • (SL 1960 MDIV)
**CLAUSEN ROBERT H REV** (847)359-3632
468 W Auburn Woods Ct Palatine IL 60067-2400 • robertclausen@juno.com • NI • Assoc • Immanuel Palatine IL • (847)359-1549 • (SL 1952 MFA)
**CLAUSING DEAN F REV** (870)879-0580
6207 Timber Lake Dr Pine Bluff AR 71603 • dfclausing@mailcity.com • MDS • SP • Trinity Pine Bluff AR • (870)534-4316 • (CQ 1979)
**CLAWSON RONALD A REV** (916)684-5728
8927 Generations Ct Elk Grove CA 95758 • CNH • EM • (SL 1961 MDIV)
**CLAYCOMBE HOWARD E JR. REV** (810)648-3749
491 S Sandusky Rd Sandusky MI 48471 • m2stars@greatlakes.net • EN • SP • Holy Redeemer Sandusky MI • (810)648-3190 • (SL 1954 MDIV MTH)
**CLAYTON GARY R REV** (660)463-2175
C/O St Paul Luth Church PO Box 60 Concordia MO 64020-0060 • splsrev@galaxyispc.com • MO • SP • St Paul Concordia MO • (660)463-2291 • (SPR 1971 MDIV MA)
**CLAYTON KIRK M** (309)647-5431
138 Pecan St Canton IL 61520 • SI • SP • Grace Canton IL • (309)647-5123 • (SL 2000 MDIV)
**CLEMENS EDWARD EMIL REV** (320)654-8938
301 17th Ave N Sartell MN 56377-1675 • MNN • 06/1994 06/2000 • (SL 1991 MDIV)
**CLEMENTS WILLIAM K REV** (206)236-6271
7749 85th Pl SE Mercer Island WA 98040-5730 • karl7749@aol.com • NOW • SP • Redeemer Mercer Island WA • (206)232-1711 • (SL 1976 DMIN)
**CLEMONS DANIEL F REV** (218)749-5421
6959 Highway 169 Virginia MN 55792-8040 • MNN • SP • Gloria Dei Virginia MN • (218)741-1977 • (FW 1990 MDIV)
**CLOCKER THOMAS R REV**
5137 Stratford Chase Dr Virginia Beach VA 23464-5531 • clocker@erols.com • SE • SP • Hope Virginia Beach VA • (757)424-4848 • (FW 1991 MDIV)
**CLOETER CARL D REV** (319)668-2352
204 Westwood Rd Williamsburg IA 52361 • IE • SP • St Paul Williamsburg IA • (319)668-1266 • (SL 1979 MDIV)
**CLOETER DANIEL M REV** (402)339-3112
6517 S 107th St Omaha NE 68127 • bslc@radiks.net • NEB • Sn/Adm • Beaut Savior Omaha NE • (402)331-7376 • (FW 1978 MDIV)
**CLOETER DAVID C REV** (218)367-3083
RR 2 Box 243 Ottertail MN 56571 • dccloete@djam.com • MNN • EM • (SPR 1963 MS)
**CLOETER DAVID R REV** (507)451-7996
1716 Greenwood Pl Owatonna MN 55060-1373 • MNS • SP • Redeemer Owatonna MN • (507)451-2720 • (FW 1980 MDIV)
**CLOETER ERIK K REV**
C/O Bethlehem Luth Church 470 Oak Crest Dr Wales WI 53138-9711 • SW • SP • Bethlehem Wales WI • (262)968-2194 • (SL 2000 MDIV)
**CLOETER MARTIN R REV** (952)448-2520
1391 Broadview Ave Chaska MN 55318-1703 • mrcloeter@aol.com • MNS • EM • (CQ 1967)
**CLOETER O H REV** (507)334-8466
12 Saint James Bay Faribault MN 55021-6755 • MNS • EM • (SL 1945 LITTD)
**CLOETER PAUL E REV** (320)654-6319
2045 E Highview Dr Sauk Rapids MN 56379-2629 • pecloeter@cloudnet.com • MNN • Sn/Adm • Trinity Sauk Rapids MN • (320)252-3670 • (FW 1982 MDIV)
**CLOOSE ANTHONY C REV** (218)334-8125
13084 County Hwy 39 Frazee MN 56544-9028 • MNN • SP • St Paul Frazee MN • (218)334-8124 • (FW 1995 MDIV)
**CLOW MARK R REV** (978)589-9488
20 Old Lowell Rd Westford MA 01886 • NE • Assoc • Of The Savior Bedford MA • (781)275-6013 • (SL 1998 MDIV)
**CLUVER JOEL A REV** (217)674-3405
PO Box 48 Latham IL 62543-0048 • CI • D Ex/S • Central Illinois Springfield IL* • (SPR 1975 MDIV)
**CLUVER STEVEN PAUL REV** (702)294-1582
1446 Bronco Rd Boulder City NV 89005-3104 • lutheran@anv.net • PSW • SP • Christ Boulder City NV • (702)293-4332 • (SPR 1969 MDIV)
**COBB L KENN REV** (518)459-4850
59 Mountain View Ave Colonie NY 12205-2803 • kenncobb@aol.com • AT • SP • Our Savior Albany NY • (518)459-2248 • (SL 1981 MDIV)
**COCHRANE ROBERT S REV** (314)677-2667
2113 Wildwind Ln High Ridge MO 63049-1729 • MO • 05/1984 05/2000 • (SL 1979 MDIV)
**CODAY TERRY J REV** (870)780-6375
1001 Illinois St Blytheville AR 72315-1428 • MDS • SP • First Blytheville AR • (870)763-6339 • (SL 1996 MDIV)
**CODY RICHARD SCOTT REV** (903)792-8042
4220 Olive St Texarkana TX 75503-3023 • revcody@txk.net • TX • SP • First Texarkana TX • (903)792-5253 • (SL 1996 MDIV)
**COFFEY JIMMY B JR. REV** (203)862-4090
38 Field Point Rd Greenwich CT 06830-5338 • revjimc@optonline.net • NE • SP • First Greenwich CT • (203)869-0032 • (FW 1998 MDIV)
**COFFMAN GEORGE M REV** (864)882-3306
1602 Cherokee Dr Seneca SC 29672-8076 • hobbit@carol.net • SE • SP • Eternal Shepherd Seneca SC • (864)882-3209 • (SL 1988 MDIV MA)
**COLE THOMAS ORA REV** (515)288-1250
4010 1st St Des Moines IA 50313-3548 • IW • SP • Our Saviour Des Moines IA • (515)244-9347 • (FW 1985 MDIV)
**COLEMAN ALAN RICHARD REV** (505)866-5867
33 Bunton Rd Belen NM 87002-8293 • revalanc@aol.com • RM • SP • Christ/King Los Lunas NM • (505)865-9226 • (FW 1993 MDIV)
**COLEMAN GERALD P REV** (952)941-1094
678 Johnson Pkwy Saint Paul MN 55106-4731 • gerry@crossview.com • MNS • Sn/Adm • Cross View Edina MN • (952)941-1094 • (SL 1988 MDIV MMU)
**COLES DAVID REV**
Concordia Institute Caixa Postal 60754 05786-990SaoPaulo SP BRAZIL • NE • S Miss • New England Springfield MA • (FW 1986 MDIV MPHIL PHD)
**COLGROVE R THOMAS REV** (608)754-6903
2928 Harvard Dr Janesville WI 53545-6702 • rtomcole@juno.com • SW • SP • Mount Calvary Janesville WI • (608)754-4145 • (FW 1981 MS MDIV)
**COLLIER C PHILIP REV** (626)357-6966
1210 S Mayflower Ave #C Monrovia CA 91016-4081 • PSW • SP • Peace South Gate CA • (323)569-8185 • (CQ 1987 MDIV MAT)
**COLLIER JOHN S REV** (716)244-2701
37 Lansdale St Rochester NY 14620-1517 • EA • EM • (SL 1958)
**COLLIN RICHARD W REV** (208)528-0110
6118 S Foxrun Dr Idaho Falls ID 83402-5875 • rwcollin@aalweb.net • NOW • SP • St John Idaho Falls ID • (208)522-5650 • (SPR 1971 MDIV)
**COLLINS JERROLD REV** (425)742-8628
6116 Norma Beach Rd Edmonds WA 98026 • jc12045@aol.com • NOW • SP • St Timothy Edmonds WA • (425)743-2323 • (FW 1978 MDIV)
**COLLINS ROBERT H REV** (708)339-5705
17000 Greenwood Ave South Holland IL 60473-3538 • NI • EM • (SPR 1963 MDIV STM)
**COLLINS ROBIN A REV** (218)894-3681
1021 5th St NE Staples MN 56479-9502 • MNN • SP • Trinity Staples MN • (218)894-2372 • (FW 1994 MDIV)
**COMPTON DANE WERLEY REV** (320)834-2184
6517 County Rd 22 NW Garfield MN 56332-8137 • MNN • EM • (SPR 1968)
**CONIGLIO FRANK J REV** (573)764-3587
PO Box 257 Rosebud MO 63091-0257 • MO • SP • Immanuel Rosebud MO • (573)764-2564 • (SL 1986 MDIV MAT)
**CONKLING MARTIN E REV** (417)882-5120
5202 S Elisabeth Ave Springfield MO 65810 • martconk@earthlink.net • MO • Asst • Trinity Springfield MO • (417)866-5878 • (SL 2000 MDIV)
**CONLEY JERRY LEE REV**
C/O Grace Lutheran Church 739 19th St SE Paris TX 75460-7512 • mrjcrev@usa.net • TX • SP • Grace Paris TX • (903)784-3753 • (FW 1986 MDIV)
**CONNER CHARLES REV** (636)586-2007
112 W Lakeview De Soto MO 63020 • mom@brick.net • MO • EM • (SL 1959 MDIV)
**CONNOR RAYMOND R REV** (715)355-7016
9406 Woodland Weston WI 54476 • rctmconnor@aol.com • NW • Sn/Adm • Mount Olive Weston WI • (715)359-5546 • (FW 1981 MDIV)
**CONRAD DANIEL E REV**
Apdo 3468 El Trigal Zona 2002 Valencia Edo Carabob VENEZUELA • MI • S Miss • Michigan Ann Arbor MI • (FW 1984 MDIV)
**CONRAD DENNIS T REV** (716)662-4747
17 Timberlake Dr Orchard Park NY 14127-3569 • EA • SP • St John Orchard Park NY • (716)662-4747 • (SL 1972 MDIV)
**CONRADO ALFONSO REV** (818)981-1038
9214 Wakefield Ave Panorama City CA 91402-1424 • PSW • D Miss • St John Orchard Park NY* • (CQ 1999)
**CONRADT ROBERT J REV** (231)773-0408
1085 Roberts St Muskegon MI 49442-4163 • rjameson@aol.com • MI • SP • Our Redeemer Muskegon MI • (231)773-2667 • (FW 1979 MDIV)
**CONROE JON WALLACE REV**
668 NE Alexis Ct Hillsboro OR 97124 • NOW • M Chap • Northwest Portland OR • (SL 1993 MDIV)
**CONSTABLE CLAUDE H REV** (307)245-3063
705 Maple Box 454 Pine Bluffs WY 82082 • KS • EM • (CQ 1994 MDIV)
**CONSTIEN ARTHUR J REV** (708)345-9254
207 Augusta St Maywood IL 60153-1028 • NI • EM • (SL 1959 MDIV)
**CONSTIEN DAVID P REV** (815)722-4890
3005 Carlyle Ct New Lenox IL 60451-8619 • cdcdpc@netzero.net • NI • SP • Immanuel Mokena IL • (708)479-5600 • (SL 1989 MDIV)
**CONSTIEN STEPHEN J REV** (941)646-7912
5130 Cimarron Dr Lakeland FL 33813 • sjconstien@juno.com • FG • Assoc • St Paul Lakeland FL • (863)644-7710 • (SL 1989 MDIV)
**CONSTIEN VICTOR A DR** (314)843-5285
8519 General Grant Ln Saint Louis MO 63123-1202 • vaconstien@aol.com • MO • EM • (SL 1952 STM MDIV LLD)
**COOK ANTHONY ALLAN REV** (513)754-0055
424 Kings Mills Rd Mason OH 45040-9335 • culinarius@discipleshop.net • OH • Assoc • King Of Kings Mason OH • (513)398-6089 • (SL 1994 MDIV)
**COOK EDWIN H REV** (308)324-6384
1006 N Jefferson St Lexington NE 68850-2028 • NEB • EM • (CQ 1977 MED)
**COOK MICHAEL CHRISTOPHER REV** (920)898-5369
1702 Van Buren St New Holstein WI 53061 • SW • SP • Zion New Holstein WI • (920)898-5250 • (FW 1994 MDIV)
**COOK RICHARD P REV** 00-267-399-348
Private Bag II T Thamaga BOTSWANA • richardcook@info.bw • MO • S Miss • Missouri Saint Louis MO • (314)317-4550 • (FW 1987 MDIV MS)
**COOK STEVEN T REV** (253)472-1010
4530 S J St Tacoma WA 98418 • cooksve@aa.net • NOW • 01/1997 01/2000 • (FW 1980 MDIV)
**COOK THEODORE E SR. REV** (913)672-4339
214 E 7th St Oakley KS 67748-1809 • tedcook@ruraltel.net • KS • SP • Immanuel Oakley KS • (785)672-3833 • (SL 1987 MDIV)
**COOLEY JAMES P REV** (316)224-2313
726 S Margrave St Fort Scott KS 66701-2853 • jcooley@cpol.net • KS • EM • (FW 1977 MDIV)
**COOP GREGGORY S REV** (507)388-4127
149 Mary Circle North Mankato MN 56003 • MNS • SP • Good Shepherd North Mankato MN • (507)388-4336 • (SL 1989 MDIV)
**COOPER ADAM JR. REV** (228)896-9243
C/O St Matthew Luth Ch 1301 31st Ave Gulfport MS 39501-1888 • st-matthew@juno.com • SO • SP • St Matthew Gulfport MS • (228)864-6264 • (SL 1966 MDIV STM)
**COOPER DONALD E REV** (402)435-3522
1408 SW 15th St Lincoln NE 68522-1503 • NEB • SP • Immanuel Lincoln NE • (402)474-6275 • (FW 1980 MED MDIV)
**COOPER LOREN D REV** (402)725-3320
2306 E 16 Rd Hampton NE 68843-3702 • NEB • SP • Zion Hampton NE • (402)725-3320 • (FW 1990 MDIV)
**COOPER PAUL E REV** (714)257-9537
712 Lantana Ave Sun City AZ 92821 • revpec@aol.com • PSW • EM • (SPR 1969 MDIV MA)
**COPPERSMITH MICHAEL JOHN DR** (760)321-9343
24 Lincoln Pl Rancho Mirage CA 92270 • mike@oursaviors.org • PSW • SP • Our Savior Palm Springs CA • (760)327-5611 • (SL 1980 MDIV DMIN)
**COPPERSMITH TIMOTHY J** (715)269-5600
121 Park St Deer Park WI 54007 • NW • SP • St Paul Deer Park WI* • (715)269-5126 • (SL 2000 MDIV)
**CORCORAN HENRY A REV** (303)759-3902
2811 E Colorado Ave Denver CO 80210-3557 • hcorky@juno.com • RM • SP • Christ Triumphant Denver CO • (303)758-3375 • (FW 1981 MED MDIV)
**CORDER JEFFREY J REV**
C/O Zion Lutheran Church 622 W Jefferson St Ottawa IL 61350-2737 • NI • SP • Zion Ottawa IL • (815)433-1408 • (SL 1986 MDIV)
**CORDES DAROWIN E REV** (616)723-4887
601 Harvard Ln Manistee MI 49660-1633 • MI • EM • (SL 1970 MA)
**CORDES MELVIN J REV** (713)462-4075
10108 Kempwood Dr Apt 1148 Houston TX 77080-3709 • TX • EM • (SL 1939)
**CORDES ROBERT C REV** (616)676-2001
2301 Honey Creek Ave NE Ada MI 49301-9514 • revinbob@aol.com • MI • EM • (SL 1960 MDIV)
**CORMENY RANDALL D REV** (515)947-6904
C/O St John Luth Church PO Box 278 Melcher-Dallas IA 50163-0278 • IE • SP • St John Melcher IA* • (515)947-6904 • (SL 1994 MDIV)
**CORNIELS DOUGLAS R REV** (419)762-5585
107 E School St Napoleon OH 43545-9217 • OH • SP • St Peter Napoleon OH* • (419)762-5075 • (SPR 1972 MDIV)
**CORNWELL STEVEN J REV** (708)547-8662
1458 Morris Ave Berkeley IL 60163-1320 • sjcornwell@cs.com • NI • SP • Hope Hillside IL • (708)449-8688 • (FW 1986 MDIV)
**COSBY SAMUEL REV** (281)807-7651
11126 Lark Brook Lane Houston TX 77065-3314 • theskypilot@worldnet.att.net • TX • SP • Mount Calvary Houston TX • (713)680-1419 • (SL 1971 MDIV)
**COSTELLO JOHN M REV** (919)870-8021
1204 Hillwood Ct Raleigh NC 27615-3424 • costeljm@bellsouth.net • SE • EM • (SPR 1957)
**COTTAM BERTRAND J REV** (810)659-1865
7176 Randee St Flushing MI 48433-8817 • revcott@tir.com • MI • SP • Our Savior Flint MI • (810)789-1361 • (FW 1987 MDIV)
**COTTER JAMES R REV** (219)493-6263
2610 Knollridge Dr Fort Wayne IN 46815-7749 • pastorc@praiselc.org • EN • SP • Praise Fort Wayne IN • (219)490-7729 • (FW 1980 MDIV)
**COTTON H JOHN REV** (402)364-2211
PO Box 187 Davenport NE 68335 • NEB • SP • St Peter Davenport NE • (402)364-2182 • (SL 1998 MDIV)
**COTTRELL BRUCE C REV** (918)665-0138
8235 E 32 Pl Tulsa OK 74145 • OK • EM • (SL 1971 MDIV)
**COUCH MARK T REV** (727)302-9093
5887 27th Ave N Saint Petersburg FL 33710 • mmcouch@cft.net • FG • SP • Our Savior Saint Petersburg FL • (727)344-2684 • (SL 1995 MDIV)
**COUCH WILLIAM L JR. REV** (865)584-7678
5117 Yosemite Trl Knoxville TN 37909-1842 • bcouch@korrnet.org • MDS • Cmp P • Mid-South Cordova TN • (SPR 1963)
**COUNTS R PAUL REV** (256)828-9110
384 Thompson Ln Hazel Green AL 35750-7766 • pscounts@bellsouth.net • SO • EM • (CQ 1990 MDIV)

**COURSON LARRY G REV** (734)426-1169
4701 Birch Ln Dexter MI 48130-8554 • peacelutheran@provide.net • MI • SP • Peace Ann Arbor MI • (734)424-0899 • (CQ 1979 MDIV MDIV)

**COX J ARTHUR REV** (814)362-9924
465 Interstate Pkwy Bradford PA 16701-2733 • EA • EM • (SPR 1975 DMIN)

**COX JOSEPH L REV** (636)447-7511
4 Newberry Ct St Peters MO 63376 • MO • Tchr • LHS St Charles Saint Peters MO • (636)928-5100 • (SL 2000 MDIV)

**COX PATRICK J REV** (717)246-8097
780 Blossom Hill Ln Dallastown PA 17313 • SE • Assoc • St John York PA • (717)840-0382 • (SL 1999 MDIV)

**COX RONALD L REV**
14721 Whitecap Blvd Apt 226 Corpus Christi TX 78418 • SD • M Chap • South Dakota Sioux Falls SD • (SL 1988 MDIV)

**COYNE JONATHAN J REV** (650)854-7057
1051 Cloud Ave Menlo Park CA 94025-6203 • revjon@ispchannel.com • CNH • SP • Bethany Menlo Park CA • (650)854-5897 • (FW 1991 MDIV)

**COYNER CONRAD H REV** (707)538-7257
26 Tiffany Pl Santa Rosa CA 95409 • CNH • EM • (SL 1943)

**COYNER EDWIN L REV** (336)996-4088
216 Baxter Kernersville NC 27284 • SO • EM • (SL 1939)

**CRABBE KELLY JAMES REV** (303)716-0538
12931 W Florida Dr Lakewood CO 80228 • coloradocrabs@juno.com • RM • SP • Concordia Lakewood CO • (303)989-5260 • (FW 1984 MDIV)

**CRABTREE BRUCE LEE REV** (308)425-3387
411 12th Ave Franklin NE 68939 • crabhaus@gtmc.net • NEB • SP • Grace Franklin NE • (308)425-3774 • (SL 1997 MDIV)

**CRAIG ALLAN DUANE REV**
328 Sinclair Lewis Ave Sauk Centre MN 56378-1343 • familycraig@juno.com • MNN • SP • Redeemer Osakis MN • (320)859-2769 • (FW 1994 MDIV)

**CRAIG DONALD W REV** (660)442-5664
1413 Nebraska Mound City MO 64470-1527 • dwcraig4315@hotmail.com • MO • Assoc • St Peter Craig MO* • (660)683-5787 • (FW 1990)

**CRAMM KEVIN JAY REV**
2300 18th Ave Rock Island IL 61201 • CI • SP • Immanuel Rock Island IL • (309)786-3391 • (FW 1983)

**CRANDALL TED L REV** (843)522-1815
24 Mystic Cir Beaufort SC 29902-6624 • bfh1tlc@bfh10.med.navy.mil • NE • M Chap • New England Springfield MA • (FW 1990 MDIV)

**CRANE JEFFREY REV** (316)684-3593
6601 Abbotsford Dr Wichita KS 67206-1123 • jscranel@aol.com • KS • Sn/Adm • Holy Cross Wichita KS • (316)684-5201 • (SPR 1968 MDIV DMIN)

**CRAVER JAMES F REV** (512)218-8026
2005 Rosemary Ln Round Rock TX 78664-7113 • jcraver@aol.com • TX • 09/1999 • (SL 1987 MDIV)

**CREIGHTON GERALD A REV** (715)466-4634
W5518 Cty Hwy F Trego WI 54888-9239 • NW • SP • Christ Trego WI • (715)466-4516 • (SL 1971 MDIV)

**CRIPE TERRY L REV** (419)784-3478
1969 Redwood Dr Defiance OH 43512-3475 • tcripe@defnet.com • OH • SP • Christ Our Savior Defiance OH • (419)782-6688 • (SPR 1974 MDIV MTH)

**CRIPPEN JACK P REV** (918)342-4006
13225 S Walnut Rd Claremore OK 74017 • OK • EM • (SPR 1967)

**CRITCHETT DANIEL REV**
15145 SE Brackenbush Rd Clackamas OR 97015-5356 • NOW • 09/1996 09/1999 • (SL 1981 MDIV)

**CRITCHLEY DALE R REV** (715)824-3314
223 Grant St Amherst WI 54406-0028 • dale@stpaulsamherst.org • NW • SP • St Paul Amherst WI • (715)824-3314 • (SL 1998 MDIV)

**CROCKETT DELL J REV** (314)645-2611
6948 Winona Ave St Louis MO 63109-1174 • dnacrockett@excelonline.com • MO • EM • (SL 1957)

**CROLIUS PAUL MARK REV** (815)468-7360
228 E 3rd St Manteno IL 60950-1310 • pcrolius@juno.com • NI • SP • Risen Savior Manteno IL • (815)468-2011 • (SL 1993 MDIV)

**CROLL EDGAR A REV** (417)882-9334
1034 S Gelven Ave Springfield MO 65804-0612 • MO • EM • (SL 1953)

**CROLL GILBERT M REV** (410)665-7716
2612 Matthews Dr Baltimore MD 21234-2636 • SE • EM • (SPR 1956)

**CROOK NORRIS C REV**
55 Tangerine Ct Lehigh Acres FL 33936-7231 • FG • EM • (SPR 1947 MA PHD)

**CROON MICHAEL ALAN REV**
7860 Niles Center Rd Skokie IL 60077-2707 • NI • Assoc • St Paul Skokie IL • (847)673-5030 • (FW 1996 MDIV)

**CROSMER ARTHUR J REV** (208)733-5642
667 Navajo Loop Twin Falls ID 83301-6873 • NOW • EM • (SL 1949 MAR)

**CROSS CARL E JR. REV** (217)529-1538
60 Glen Aire Dr Springfield IL 62703 • ccross@warpnet.net • CI • EM • (CQ 1986)

**CROSSAN ROBERT D REV** (909)927-3285
1126 E Johnston Ave Hemet CA 92543-8101 • PSW • M Chap • Pacific Southwest Irvine CA • (949)854-3232 • (CQ 1982 MDIV)

**CROSSWHITE JOSEPH E III REV**
Holy Cross Lutheran Church PO Box 1 Lidgerwood ND 58053-1109 • ND • SP • Holy Cross Lidgerwood ND • (701)538-4688 • (SL 2000 MDIV)

**CROWN STEWART D REV** (650)327-4729
1230 Fulton St Palo Alto CA 94301 • pastorcrown@juno.com • CNH • SP • Trinity Palo Alto CA • (650)853-1295 • (SL 1989 MDIV STM)

**CROWTHER J NEVIN REV** (651)426-1655
282 Chelsea St Mahtomedi MN 55115-2080 • MNS • EM • (SPR 1971)

**CRUIKSHANK THOMAS G REV** (573)581-7684
1211 Dorcas Mexico MO 65265-1015 • MO • EM • (SPR 1962)

**CULLEN D LEE JR. REV** (734)753-9374
37002 Ellis St PO Box 274 New Boston MI 48164-0274 • MI • SP • St Paul New Boston MI • (734)753-9048 • (FW 1992 MDIV)

**CUMMING JAMES T REV** (608)788-0915
2147 Hoeschler Dr La Crosse WI 54601-6870 • revcummg@execpc.com • SW • SP • Faith La Crosse WI • (608)782-3696 • (SPR 1964 MDIV)

**CUMMINGS RAYMOND D REV** (845)778-7077
25 Highland Ave Walden NY 12586-1429 • rdc@frontiernet.net • AT • SP • Trinity Walden NY • (845)778-7119 • (SPR 1965)

**CUMMINS BRIAN K REV** (361)364-4922
RR 1 Box 98 Odem TX 78370 • acts20@juno.com • TX • SP • Trinity Odem TX • (361)364-2367 • (FW 1998 MDIV)

**CUMMINS CRAIG A REV** (507)549-3860
C/O St John Luth Church RR 1 Box 51 Vernon Center MN 56090-9721 • cacwcreek@juno.com • MNS • SP • St John Vernon Center MN • (507)549-3760 • (FW 1997 MDIV)

**CUNNINGHAM J ROBERT REV** (217)523-0227
3036 Buena Vista Dr Springfield IL 62707-6900 • CI • EM • (SL 1964 MDIV)

**CUNNINGHAM JOSEPH R REV** (219)476-0054
2655 Calavevas Valparasio IN 46385-5380 • Joseph.Cunningham@valpo.edu • IN • END • Indiana Fort Wayne IN • (FW 1984 MDIV)

**CUNNINGHAM KIRK ROBERT REV** (217)732-8212
211 S Logan Lincoln IL 62656 • CI • Asst • Zion Lincoln IL • (217)732-3946 • (SL 1994 MDIV)

**CURLEY PATRICK W REV** (626)974-9798
1181 N Fairvale Ave Covina CA 91722 • PSW • SP • St John Covina CA • (626)332-3142 • (FW 1989 MDIV)

**CURRAO ANDREW J REV** (812)524-9294
1432 Robinhood Dr Seymour IN 47274-1537 • IN • Sn/Adm • Redeemer Seymour IN • (812)522-1837 • (SL 1991 MDIV)

**CURRY KENNETH F REV** (716)745-7120
510 3rd St Youngstown NY 14174-1238 • EA • SP • St John Youngstown NY • (716)745-3443 • (SPR 1971 MDIV)

**CUSSON BRADLEY G REV** (303)426-1282
2104 Miller St Lakewood CO 80215-1320 • RM • SP • Mount Zion Denver CO • (303)429-0165 • (FW 1987)

**CUTLER MARK G REV** (402)646-2001
603 S Evergreen Dr Seward NE 68434-2249 • mjlbrj@juno.com • NEB • Sn/Adm • St John Seward NE • (402)643-2983 • (SL 1988 MDIV)

**CUTLER ROBERT E REV** (208)898-0352
2352 N Glennfield Way Meridian ID 83642 • recutler@earthlink.net • NOW • SP • Christ Meridian ID • (208)888-1622 • (SL 1997 MDIV MA)

**CWIRLA WILLIAM M REV** (626)336-3249
1843 Pontenova Ave Hacienda Heights CA 91745-3524 • wcwirla@earthlink.net • PSW • SP • Holy Trinity Hacienda Heights CA • (626)333-9017 • (SL 1990 MDIV STM)

**CYNOVA GREGORY S REV** (219)447-0962
7821 Decatur Rd Fort Wayne IN 46816-2604 • gscynova@juno.com • IN • SP • Trinity Fort Wayne IN • (219)447-2411 • (CQ 1980 MAR)

**CZAPLEWSKI DANIEL P DR**
1621 NE 56th St Fort Lauderdale FL 33334 • czapled@concentric.net • FG • SP • Peace Fort Lauderdale FL • (954)772-8010 • (SL 1990 MDIV MA EDD)

**CZECH DANIEL D REV** (612)784-2354
7665 Bacon Dr NE Fridley MN 55432-3623 • MNS • Assoc • Messiah Mounds View MN • (612)784-1786 • (SL 1989 MDIV)

## D

**DABERKOW TERRENCE H REV** (402)648-7400
PO Box 306 Bancroft NE 68004-0306 • NEB • SP • St Paul Bancroft NE • (402)648-7689 • (CQ 1995)

**DAEKE DUANE O REV** (414)527-4868
4929 N 53rd St Milwaukee WI 53218-4313 • SW • 11/1984 11/1999 • (SL 1976 MDIV)

**DAENE ROGER WILLIAM REV** (440)934-1831
C/O Faith Lutheran Church Garden & Lakeland Drives Avon OH 44011-4710 • OH • SP • Faith Avon OH • (216)934-4710 • (SC 1995 MDIV)

**DAENE TIMOTHY ALLEN REV** (419)727-1588
1967 N Michigan St Toledo OH 43611-3720 • tdaene@yahoo.com • OH • SP • Immanuel Toledo OH • (419)726-3991 • (FW 1994 MDIV)

**DAGEL MICHAEL K REV** (320)968-7047
7440 Ronneby Rd NE Foley MN 56329-9270 • MNN • SP • St Paul Foley MN* • (612)968-6400 • (FW 1980 MA)

**DAHL DAVID C REV** (303)565-7433
C/O Trinity Luth Church PO Box 989 Cortez CO 81321-0989 • RM • SP • Trinity Cortez CO • (303)565-9346 • (SL 1967 MDIV)

**DAHL JACK E REV** (507)642-3709
141 3rd St SE Madelia MN 56062-1821 • MNS • SP • Salem Madelia MN • (507)642-8414 • (CQ 1985 MA MA)

**DAHLING DANIEL F REV** (219)547-4534
C/O Zion Lutheran Church 10653 N 550 W Decatur IN 46733-7894 • zionfriedheim@decaturnet.com • IN • SP • Zion Decatur IN • (219)547-4248 • (FW 1983 MDIV)

**DAHLKE DAVID JAMES REV** (715)652-6324
10541 North Rd #202 Auburndale WI 54412-9050 • djdahlke@tznet.com • NW • SP • St John Auburndale WI* • (715)652-2213 • (SL 1992 MDIV)

**DAHLKE JAMES E REV** (660)463-7044
313 College Dr PO Box 203 Concordia MO 64020 • revjed@yahoo.com • MO • SHS/C • St Paul Concordia MO • (660)463-2238 • (FW 1981 MDIV)

**DAHMANN ROY L REV** (510)276-3860
633 Hacienda Ave San Lorenzo CA 94580-2944 • CNH • P Df • Memorial-Deaf Fremont CA • (510)656-0694 • (SPR 1975 MDIV)

**DAIL JASON A REV** (615)217-2520
1726 Cason Trl Murfreesboro TN 37128 • MDS • Asst • Grace Murfreesboro TN • (615)893-0338 • (SL 2000 MDIV)

**DAKE MELVIN L REV** (715)344-5283
3100 Center St Stevens Point WI 54481-4214 • NW • EM • (SPR 1944)

**DALLMAN ROGER H REV** (425)337-1661
5423 151st Pl SE Everett WA 98208 • rdallman@allsaints-lcms.com • NOW • SP • All Saints Bellevue WA • (425)881-2925 • (SPR 1976 MDIV DMIN)

**DALLMANN THEODORE C REV** (716)934-2002
C/O Trinity Luth Church 15 Porter Ave Silver Creek NY 14136-1130 • revted@netsync.net • EA • SP • Trinity Silver Creek NY • (716)934-2002 • (SL 1966 MDIV)

**DALY THOMAS RICHARD REV**
52614 W Esch Trl Maricopa AZ 85239-4547 • CI • EM • (SPR 1972)

**DALY THOMAS ROBERT REV** (309)662-0269
7 Bandecon Way Bloomington IL 61704 • CI • SP • Our Redeemer Bloomington IL • (309)662-3935 • (FW 1984)

**DAMENT GERALD A J REV** (920)293-4312
C/O Zion Luth Church 219 N State St # 18 Neshkoro WI 54960-9501 • lerev@wirural.net • SW • SP • Zion Neshkoro WI • (920)293-4312 • (FW 1984 MDIV)

**DAMERY MICHAEL REV**
Mount Calvary Luth Church 2055 S Franklin Decatur IL 62521-5269 • CI • SP • Mount Calvary Decatur IL • (217)428-0641 • (SL 1998 MS MA)

**DAMM GEORGE E REV** (402)725-3224
PO Box 94 Hampton NE 68843-0094 • NEB • SP • St Peter Hampton NE • (402)725-3234 • (SL 1985 MDIV)

**DANCY PAUL B DR** (810)677-9665
54817 Pimenta Dr Macomb MI 48042-2219 • pdancy@lhsa.net • MI • SP • Our Saviour Armada MI • (810)784-9088 • (FW 1980 MDIV DMIN)

**DANIEL DAVID PAUL REV** (4217)6383-5309
Tematinska 4 851 05 Bratislava SLOVAKIA • dpdaniel@internet.sk • S • S Miss • SELC Cudahy WI • (SPR 1966 MDIV MA PHD)

**DANIEL ROBERT J REV** (636)207-0887
2 Somme Ct Manchester MO 63021-5630 • MO • EM • (SL 1949)

**DANIEL THEODORE A REV** (313)838-0854
15100 Glastonbury Ave Detroit MI 48223-3601 • MI • EM • (SL 1944)

**DANIEL THOMAS A REV** (330)724-7830
622 S Firestone Blvd Akron OH 44301-3125 • S • EM • (SL 1946 MDIV)

**DANIELSEN GARY L DR** (770)447-0070
C/O Luth Ministries of Georgia 756 W Peachtree St NW Atlanta GA 30308-1138 • garyldan@mindspring.com • FG • O Sp Min • Florida-Georgia Orlando FL • (SL 1973 MDIV DMIN)

**DANIELSEN RALPH N REV** (715)832-0012
904 E Lexington Blvd Eau Claire WI 54701-6426 • NW • EM • (SL 1944)

**DANKIS MARK J DR** (830)981-8929
202 Kendall Pkwy Boerne TX 78015-8345 • gdankis@texas.net • TX • SP • Messiah Boerne TX • (830)755-4300 • (SL 1983 MDIV DMIN)

**DANNENBERG DONALD G REV** (909)823-5623
9732 Tamarind Ave Bloomington CA 92316-1645 • dgd@earthlink.net • PSW • SP • First Fontana CA • (909)823-3457 • (SPR 1962 MA PHD)

**DANNENBRING RICHARD A REV** (714)992-6075
1431 Cheltenham Ln La Habra CA 90631-7418 • rdann-enbring@clcs-brea.com • PSW • SP • Christ Brea CA • (714)529-2984 • (SL 1973 MDIV)

**DANNENFELDT PAUL T REV** (410)647-2921
93 Roads End Ln Severna Park MD 21146-4633 • Bishop173@juno.com • SE • EM • (SL 1949)

**DANNER BERNARD L REV** (847)368-3034
C/O Lutheran Home 800 W Oakton St Room 208 H Arlington Heights IL 60004 • NI • EM • (SL 1941)

**DANNER JOEL REV** (618)932-2022
1 West Frankfort Plz West Frankfort IL 62896-4964 • SI • SP • St Paul West Frankfort IL • (618)932-3450 • (SL 1988 MDIV)

**DANOWSKI WILLIAM F REV** (313)945-1517
C/O Evergreen Luth Church 8680 Evergreen Ave Detroit MI 48228-2922 • MI • SP • Evergreen Detroit MI • (313)584-0450 • (SL 1991 MDIV)

**DARE PAUL W REV**
918 Ranae Ln #210 Saint Cloud MN 56301 • MNN • Assoc • Holy Cross Saint Cloud MN • (320)251-8416 • (SL 2000 MDIV)

**DARGATZ ROBERT A REV** (714)633-5746
2534 Burly Ave Orange CA 92869-3611 • rmdargatz@earthlink.net • PSW • SP • Immanuel Orange CA • (714)538-2373 • (SPR 1976 MDIV STM)

**DARKOW FRED C REV** (316)221-4765
2027 Holloway Ln Winfield KS 67156-8988 • KS • EM • (SPR 1960 MDIV)

**DARNSTAEDT MARK L REV** (812)951-0005
1230 Oakes Rd Georgetown IN 47122 • IN • SP • Shepherd Hills Georgetown IN • (812)945-2101 • (SL 1981 MDIV)

**DAS A ANDREW** (630)617-3541
190 Prospect Ave Elmhurst IL 60126 • NI • Assoc • Trinity Lombard IL • (630)629-8765 • (FW 2000 MDIV)

**DASCH WILLIAM E REV** (713)468-2623
C/O St Mark Luth Church 1515 Hillendahl Blvd Houston TX 77055-3411 • bdasch@stmarkhouston.org • TX • Sn/Adm • St Mark Houston TX • (713)468-2623 • (SPR 1973 MDIV MS EDD)

**DASSOW GARRY R REV** (316)653-7739
367 W 10th St Hoisington KS 67544-1715 • KS • SP • Concordia Hoisington KS • (316)653-4644 • (SL 1965 MDIV)

**DAUB JAMES M REV** (407)260-1259
110 Southcot Dr Casselberry FL 32707 • revdaub@hotmail.com • FG • Asst • Ascension Casselberry FL • (407)831-7788 • (SL 1999 MDIV)

**DAUGHERTY ERVIN A JR. REV** (913)782-2935
1113 S Stagecoach Pl Olathe KS 66062-2217 • edaugh6966@aol.com • KS • Inst C • Kansas Topeka KS • (FW 1984 MDIV MED)

**DAUGHERTY JAMES N REV** (920)689-2280
PO Box 185 Burnett WI 53922-0185 • SW • SP • Zion Burnett WI • (920)689-2280 • (FW 1980 MDIV)

**DAUK DAVID ANTHONY REV** (320)354-4103
216 1st Ave NW New London MN 56273-9560 • dvdauk@mail.tds.net • MNN • SP • Shepherd of the Hill New London MN • (320)354-4594 • (SL 1994 MDIV)

**DAUL WADE A REV** (507)235-8188
1320 N Park St Fairmont MN 56031-2625 • wdaul@frontiernet.net • MNS • Assoc • Immanuel Fairmont MN • (507)238-1387 • (SL 1993 MDIV)

**DAUM HAROLD R REV** (605)384-5857
PO Box 665 Wagner SD 57380 • SD • EM • (SL 1956)

**DAUMER DAVID H REV** (712)737-8727
606 Kansas Ave SW Orange City IA 51041-1539 • daumer@rconnect.com • IW • SP • Faith Orange City IA • (712)737-2112 • (FW 1983 MDIV)

**DAUTENHAHN JOHN C REV** (573)348-3619
RR 1 Box 739 Osage Beach MO 65065-9742 • MO • Sn/Adm • Hope Chapel Osage Beach MO • (573)348-2108 • (SPR 1963)

**DAVENPORT JOHN M REV** (512)819-9102
RR 2 Box 75B Georgetown TX 78626-9792 • TX • Sn/Adm • Zion Georgetown TX • (512)863-3065 • (SL 1983 MDIV)

**DAVIDENAS EUGENE D REV** (808)969-3033
595 Kapiolani St Hilo HI 96720-3936 • christhilo@juno.com • CNH • SP • Christ Hilo HI • (808)935-8612 • (SPR 1975 MDIV)

**DAVIDSON JOHN C DR** (740)653-6005
420 Sells Rd Lancaster OH 43130-8733 • davgang@greenapple.com • OH • SP • Redeemer Lancaster OH • (740)653-4083 • (FW 1982 MDIV STM DMIN)

**DAVIDSON KENNETH J REV** (402)628-3333
207 S 2nd St PO Box 8 Cedar Bluffs NE 68015-0008 • kjdavidson@huskerfan.com • NEB • SP • St Matthew Cedar Bluffs NE • (402)628-3015 • (SL 1987 MDIV)

**DAVIES KARL CLEVEN REV** (219)932-4940
7255 Hohman Ave Hammond IN 46324-1817 • krcleven@aol.com • IN • SP • Trinity Hammond IN • (219)932-4660 • (SPR 1971 MDIV)

**DAVIS CHRISTOPHER M** (253)839-7614
31256 8th Ave S Federal Way WA 98003 • NOW • Assoc • St Luke Federal Way WA • (253)941-3000 • (SL 2000 MDIV)

**DAVIS CLARK M REV** (913)965-2234
C/O St John Luth Church PO Box 12 Tampa KS 67483-0012 • revclark@midusa.net • KS • SP • St John Tampa KS • (785)965-2234 • (FW 1980 MDIV)

**DAVIS DAVID A REV** (616)285-9818
4671 Braeburn SE Grand Rapids MI 49546 • MI • Sn/Adm • Immanuel Grand Rapids MI • (616)454-3655 • (SL 1983 MDIV)

**DAVIS EDWARD A REV** (847)683-0525
PO Box 276 Burlington IL 60109-0276 • NI • SP • St Peter Hampshire IL • (847)464-5721 • (SL 1980 MDIV)

**DAVIS HOWARD A REV** (440)354-0376
8159 Auburn Rd Painesville OH 44077-9179 • revhd@hotmail.com • OH • SP • Holy Cross Madison OH • (440)428-3759 • (SPR 1962)

**DAVIS JOHN F REV** (281)347-2728
1876 County Rd 213 Giddings TX 78942 • TX • Assoc • Immanuel Giddings TX • (409)542-2918 • (SL 1993 MDIV)

**DAVIS JOHN H REV**
PO Box 221 Catherine AL 36728-0221 • SO • EM • (CQ 1985)

**DAVIS JOSEPH WALTER JR. REV** (913)889-4486
21780 Rolling Prairie Rd Duluth KS 66521-9449 • KS • SP • St Paul Duluth KS • (785)889-4486 • (SL 1996 MDIV)

**DAVIS LARRY F REV** (352)371-4419
8114 SW 53rd Place Gainesville FL 32608 • LDavis2645@aol.com • FG • SP • Good Shepherd Chiefland FL • (352)493-4597 • (SPR 1968 MA)

**DAVIS RICHARD J REV** (253)887-8140
751 Oakhurst Dr Pacific WA 98047 • skypilot31@hotmail.com • NOW • SP • Of The Cross Kent WA • (253)854-3240 • (FW 1980 MDIV)

**DAVIS ROBERT S REV** (402)685-6260
C/O St John Lutheran Church 1543 County Rd 13 Lyons NE 68038-5020 • NEB • SP • St John Lyons NE • (402)685-6260 • (SL 1998 MDIV)

**DAVIS TIMOTHY P REV** (301)678-7180
3740 Resley Rd Hancock MD 21750 • stpaul@nfis.com • SE • SP • St Paul Hancock MD • (301)678-7180 • (SL 1998 MDIV)

**DAVIS WARREN H REV** (850)476-5725
7041 Kelvin Ter Pensacola FL 32503-7356 • wdavis0919.aol.com • SO • SP • Jehovah Pensacola FL • (850)433-2091 • (SPR 1973 MDIV)

**DAVISON FREDERICK ELWOOD** (765)452-9168
6823 W 400 N Kokomo IN 46901 • IN • SP • Zion Kokomo IN • (765)452-9168 • (FW 2000 MDIV)

**DAVISON TONY REV** (847)299-4593
1477 Thacker St #203 Des Plaines IL 60016-8614 • NI • D Ex/S • Northern Illinois Hillside IL • (SPR 1964 MSED MDIV MBA DED PHD)

**DAWSON JOHN K REV** (605)371-4015
4904 E Blueridge Dr Sioux Falls SD 57110-5534 • pastor@lordoflifelutheran.org • SD • Sn/Adm • Lord Of Life Sioux Falls SD • (605)371-3501 • (FW 1988 MDIV)

**DAY JOHN BART REV** (713)974-0595
9622 Fairdale Ln Houston TX 77063 • revday@aol.com • TX • Assoc • Memorial Houston TX • (713)782-6079 • (SL 1997 MDIV)

**DE LOACH JAMES HOWARD REV** (402)234-5985
C/O Immanuel Lutheran Church 36712 Church Rd Louisville NE 68037-2918 • jdeloach@alltel.net • NEB • SP • Immanuel Louisville NE* • (402)234-5980 • (SL 1991 MDIV)

**DE LOYE GERALD J DR** (715)552-3797
4010 House Rd #4 Eau Claire WI 54701-8170 • gjd3213@execpc.com • SW • South Wisconsin Milwaukee WI • (414)464-8100 • (SPR 1967 MDIV MS MA PHD DMIN)

**DE RAMUS DAVID T REV** (334)872-9999
PO Box 2005 Selma AL 36702-2005 • dtd4real@earthlink.net • SO • SHS/C • Southern New Orleans LA • (SPR 1965)

**DE ROSA RUDY A REV** (570)839-1428
PO Box 212 Mount Pocono PA 18344 • EA • Southern New Orleans LA • (FW 1993 MDIV)

**DE SOTO KENNETH J REV** (770)887-6383
3950 Starr Creek Rd Cumming GA 30040 • revkendesoto@juno.com • FG • D Miss • Florida-Georgia Orlando FL • (FW 1989 MDIV)

**DE VANTIER PETER A REV** (570)724-4892
C/O Trinity Luth Church West Ave & Luther Ln Wellsboro PA 16901 • EA • SP • Trinity Wellsboro PA • (717)724-2316 • (SC 1989 MTH)

**DE VRIES KIM T REV** (210)653-0602
5522 Crosswind Dr San Antonio TX 78239-1903 • ktdevries@vshops.net • TX • SP • Mount Calvary San Antonio TX • (210)824-8748 • (SL 1976 MDIV)

**DE WERFF ROBERT E DR** (651)482-1840
1087 Westcliff Curve Saint Paul MN 55126-1403 • dewerff@genesis.csp.edu • MNS • SHS/C • Minnesota South Burnsville MN • (SL 1973 MDIV DED)

**DE WITT DOUGLAS A REV** (419)274-1084
983 State Rt 109 #G Hamler OH 43524-9773 • imlutheran@skybiz.com • OH • SP • Immanuel Hamler OH • (419)274-4811 • (FW 1998 MDIV)

**DE WITT EDWARD JAMES REV** (941)927-8770
4010 Westfield D Ct Sarasota FL 34237 • FG • SP • Concordia Sarasota FL • (941)365-0844 • (SL 1995 MDIV)

**DE YOUNG JOHN E REV** (972)223-7725
512 N Cockrell De Soto TX 75123 • revjohnplum@juno.com • TX • Assoc • Cross Christ De Soto TX • (972)223-9340 • (SL 1989 MDIV)

**DEMOSS WALTER L REV** (630)264-1022
513 S Calumet Ave Aurora IL 60506-5301 • walt@lbt.org • NI • Northern Illinois Hillside IL • (SPR 1968 MDIV)

**DEAN KEVIN E SR. DR** (312)873-4996
8308 S Sangamon St Chicago IL 60620-3138 • EN • SP • Faith Chicago IL • (773)488-8286 • (CQ 1983 DMIN)

**DEARDOFF DANIEL H SR. REV** (402)582-3222
PO Box 159 Plainview NE 68769-0159 • deardoffgang@plvwtelco.net • NEB • SP • Zion Plainview NE • (402)582-3312 • (SL 1984 MDIV)

**DEARDOFF ROBERT E REV** (907)283-3244
505 Pine Ave Kenai AK 99611-7556 • sonlc@ptialaska.net • NOW • SP • Star Of North Kenai AK • (907)283-4153 • (SL 1982 MDIV)

**DECKER DANIEL J REV**
1725 White Oak Dr Chaska MN 55318-1444 • MNS • D Ex/S • Minnesota South Burnsville MN • (FW 1983 MDIV)

**DECKER JAY R REV** (614)527-9257
1817 Hobbes Dr Hilliard OH 43026-8216 • revjdecker@aol.com • OH • Sn/Adm • St James Columbus OH • (614)878-5158 • (SL 1966 MDIV)

**DECKER THOMAS R REV** (253)968-1125
2393 Stryker Ave Ft Lewis WA 98433 • tom.decker@nw.amedd.army.mil • PSW • M Chap • Pacific Southwest Irvine CA • (949)854-3232 • (SL 1969 MDIV)

**DECKER WAYNE D REV** (440)937-5765
34509 Heatherwood Ave Avon OH 44011-2489 • OH • 06/1997 06/2000 • (SL 1981 MDIV)

**DEDE JOHN REV** (352)365-0831
36320 W Spring Lake Blvd Fruitland Park FL 34731-5309 • FG • EM • (SL 1956 MDIV)

**DEGNER KURT E REV** (530)273-7043
PO Box 924 Grass Valley CA 95945-0924 • revdeg@prodigy.net • CNH • SP • Grace Grass Valley CA • (530)273-7043 • (CQ 1982 MDIV)

**DEGNER MARK R REV** (303)980-9994
5735 W Atlantic Pl #302 Lakewood CO 80227-2529 • mrdegner@mindspring.com • RM • 06/1996 06/2000 • (SL 1977 MDIV)

**DEGNER ROBERT P REV** (773)736-3053
4933 W Montrose Chicago IL 60641 • degner2000@aol.com • NI • Sn/Adm • St John Chicago IL • (773)736-1112 • (SPR 1965)

**DEHNING K C REV** (785)258-3521
300 South H St Herington KS 67449-2850 • orlcrev@ikansas.com • KS • SP • Our Redeemer Herington KS • (785)258-3122 • (FW 1991 MDIV)

**DEHNKE GARY D REV** (314)481-6271
4060 Toenges Ave Saint Louis MO 63116-2840 • gdehnke@aol.com • MO • SP • St John Saint Louis MO • (314)773-0126 • (FW 1984 MDIV)

**DEINERT ALLEN R REV** (760)356-5302
821 Oak Ave Holtville CA 92250-1632 • deinert@aol.com • PSW • SP • St Paul Holtville CA • (760)356-4315 • (FW 1977 MDIV MST)

**DEISTER JOHN JEROME REV** (785)364-3436
804 New York Ave Holton KS 66436 • cdeister@mail.holton.k12.ks.us • KS • SP • Trinity Holton KS* • (785)364-2206 • (SL 1997 MDIV)

**DEITEMEYER LEO R REV** (320)269-8612
1211 N 4th St Montevideo MN 56265 • MNN • SP • St Paul Montevideo MN • (612)269-7145 • (SPR 1971 MDIV)

**DEITZ JOHN A REV** (715)769-3127
PO Box 158 Butternut WI 54514-0158 • NW • SP • St Paul Butternut WI • (715)769-3731 • (FW 1994 MDIV)

**DEKNATEL ARNOLD W REV** (716)425-9736
67 Princeton Ln Fairport NY 14450-9021 • risenchrist@mlsonline.com • EA • SP • Risen Christ Fairport NY • (716)223-5757 • (FW 1979 MDIV DMIN)

**DELGEHAUSEN L E REV** (225)756-5274
5414 Highland Ridge Dr Baton Rouge LA 70817-2837 • SO • EM • (SPR 1960 MS)

**DEMCHUK ROBERT W REV** 815-929-9303
1633 Waterberry Dr Bourbonnais IL 60914 • rwdsrrev@worldnet.att.net • NI • SP • Good Shepherd Bourbonnais IL • (815)935-2663 • (SL 1991 MDIV)

**DEMEL MARK W REV** (760)728-5001
1544 Linda St Fallbrook CA 92028-2427 • mwd4nu@aol.com • PSW • SP • Zion Fallbrook CA • (760)728-8288 • (FW 1982 MDIV)

**DEMERA DAVID G REV** (718)746-0541
17-35 147th St Whitestone NY 11357-3052 • AT • Assoc • Our Saviour Rego Park NY • (718)897-4447 • (SL 1980 MDIV)

**DEMERITT CARL F JR. REV** (513)245-1856
5345 Orchard Valley Cincinnati OH 45239 • demericf@healthall.com • OH • Inst C • Ohio Olmsted Falls OH • (FW 1983 MDIV MA MA)

**DEN OUDEN ROBERT P REV**
5648 Jefferson Ave Chino CA 91710-3602 • anchovie@gte.net • PSW • SP • Immanuel Chino CA • (909)628-2823 • (SL 1985 MDIV)

**DENGLER DONALD C REV** (502)425-6778
3803 Burning Bush Rd Louisville KY 40241-1612 • revdcd@aol.com • IN • SP • Peace Louisville KY • (502)239-0486 • (CQ 1985)

**DENKE GLENN R REV** (605)462-6169
C/O St John Lutheran Church HCR 75 Box 22 Norris SD 57560-9405 • SD • SP • St John Norris SD* • (605)462-6169 • (FW 1982 MDIV)

**DENNINGER JOHN R REV** (703)455-3552
7209 Trappers Pl Springfield VA 22153-1333 • giraffeman@aol.com • SE • Sn/Adm • Prince Of Peace Springfield VA • (703)451-5855 • (SL 1980 MDIV)

**DENNIS MARSHALL H REV** (219)939-2452
8981 E 5th Ave Apt 202 Gary IN 46403-3309 • IN • 09/1996 09/1999 • (CQ 1985 JD)

**DEQUIN HENRY C REV** (815)758-7265
808 Normal Rd Dekalb IL 60115-1612 • hdequin@niu.edu • NI • EM • (SL 1949 MDIV STM MLS PHD)

**DESENS MERWIN C REV** (913)432-0759
6210 Robinson St Apt 2 Overland Park KS 66202 • MO • EM • (SL 1959)

**DETERDING CURTIS L REV** (618)467-0425
4625 Storeyland Dr Alton IL 62002 • curtisdeterding@hotmail.com • SI • SP • Faith Godfrey IL • (618)466-3833 • (SL 1987 MDIV)

**DETERDING DAROLD W REV** (618)467-2077
5006 Bedford Dr Alton IL 62002-6947 • SI • EM • (SPR 1966)

**DETERDING JOHN G REV** (517)652-8829
7345 W Ronrick Pl Frankenmuth MI 48734-9107 • MI • EM • (SL 1947 DD)

**DETERDING PAUL E REV** (775)885-7674
1840 Ivy St Carson City NV 89703 • CNH • Sn/Adm • Bethlehem Carson City NV • (702)882-5252 • (SL 1978 MDIV STM THD)

**DETTMER LINSEY H REV** (423)453-2274
632 Zion Hill Rd Sevierville TN 37876-1434 • dettmer@esper.com • MDS • SP • Saint Paul Sevierville TN • (865)429-6023 • (SPR 1970 MDIV)

**DETVILER TIMOTHY JAMES REV** (714)744-1678
1423 E Lael Dr Orange CA 92866 • PSW • Cmp P • Lutheran HS/Orange C Orange CA • (714)998-5151 • (SL 1996 MDIV)

**DEVAN EDWARD J REV** (717)757-6964
4264 Webster Dr York PA 17402-3331 • SE • EM • (SPR 1957)

**DEVANTIER PAUL W REV**
C/O Bethesda Lutheran Homes 700 Hoffman Dr Watertown WI 53094 • devantier@primary.net • SW • Lutheran HS/Orange C Orange CA • (714)998-5151 • (SL 1972 MS MDIV LLD)

**DEY ARTHUR REV** (702)252-4588
5795 W Flamingo Rd Apt 107 Las Vegas NV 89103-2362 • CNH • EM • (SL 1945)

**DEYE ARMIN U REV** (507)452-5465
90 Knopp Valley Trail Dr Winona MN 55987 • MNS • EM • (SL 1939)

**DI GREGORIO PHILIP J REV** (208)634-5905
C/O Our Savior Luth Church PO Box 912 Mc Call ID 83638-0912 • NOW • SP • Our Savior Mc Call ID • (208)634-5905 • (FW 1977 MDIV MA)

**DIAMOND THOMAS E REV** (973)383-9303
21 Elm St Newton NJ 07860-2015 • NJ • SP • Redeemer Newton NJ • (973)383-3945 • (SL 1976 MDIV MA)

**DIAZ JOHN ARROYO REV** (956)712-0704
1113 Topaz Trl Laredo TX 78045 • TX • 06/2000 • (FW 1995 MDIV)

**DIBELL ROBERT A REV** (918)426-6704
1802 Mockingbird Ln Mc Alester OK 74501 • dibell5@hotmail.com • OK • SP • Trinity Mc Alester OK • (918)426-4544 • (CQ 1984 MA)

**DICKINSON CHARLES W REV** (573)546-3990
PO Box 323 Arcadia MO 63621 • MO • EM • (CQ 1982)

**DICKINSON RICHARD C REV** (314)531-0998
4325 Delmar Blvd Saint Louis MO 63108-2625 • MO • EM • (GB 1952 PHD)

**DIEBENOW PETER REV** (815)759-9539
1941 N Orleans St #1D Mc Henry IL 60050 • peted@wans.net • NI • SP • Zion Mc Henry IL • (815)385-0859 • (SL 1969 MDIV)

**DIEFENTHALER JON T REV** (410)309-1253
7311 Shady Glen Dr Columbia MD 21046 • jtdiefen@aol.com • SE • Sn/Adm • Our Savior Laurel MD • (301)776-7670 • (SL 1969 MDIV MA PHD)

**DIEKELMAN WILLIAM R REV** (918)272-3639
807 N Elm Pl Owasso OK 74055-5564 • okpres@aol.com • OK • Sn/Adm • Faith Owasso OK* • (918)272-9858 • (SL 1973 MDIV)

**DIEKROGER WALTER E REV** (614)772-1873
231 Chestnut St Chillicothe OH 45601-2402 • OH • Inst C • Ohio Olmsted Falls OH • (SL 1973 MDIV)

**DIENER JOHN HENRY REV** (330)220-5950
1554 Devonshire Dr Brunswick OH 44212-4401 • dienerjmmm@aol.com • OH • SP • St Mark Brunswick OH • (330)225-3110 • (FW 1994 MDIV)

**DIENST MARTIN P REV** (802)878-2579
100 Ridge Rd Williston VT 05495-9781 • NE • EM • (SL 1944)

**DIERKER ELDRED W REV** (310)677-7653
1145 Walnut St Inglewood CA 90301-3835 • PSW • EM • (SL 1941 PHD)

**DIERKING NORMAN H REV** (573)943-2234
C/O Pilgrim Lutheran Church PO Box 585 Linn MO 65051-0585 • MO • SP • Pilgrim Linn MO* • (573)943-2261 • (SL 1973 MDIV MSW)

**DIERKS DANIEL P REV** (219)322-8944
430 York Rd Schererville IN 46375-2328 • IN • SP • Peace Schererville IN • (219)322-5490 • (FW 1983 MDIV)

**DIERKS REINHOLD F REV** (319)766-2085
PO Box 164 Oakville IA 52646-0164 • IE • EM • (SL 1956 STM)

**DIERKS WILLIAM A REV** (513)575-0426
5710 Larkspur Dr Milford OH 45150-2429 • OH • Sn/Adm • St Mark Milford OH • (513)575-0292 • (SL 1960 MDIV)

**DIETRICH ADAM A REV** (708)448-0110
12505 S Harold Ave Palos Heights IL 60463-1321 • dietrich@millnet.net • NI • EM • (SPR 1962 MDIV MA)

**DIETRICH HERMAN K REV** (614)847-9607
249 Meadowlark Ln Columbus OH 43214-1244 • OH • EM • (SL 1955)

**DIETZ PAUL T REV** (414)252-4777
W158N6301 Cherry Hill Dr Menomonee Falls WI 53051-5731 • ptcbdietz/@bigplanet.com • SW • EM • (SL 1949 MLS MDIV MA LITTD)

**DIETZ WILLIAM F A REV** (520)684-2358
680 W Smoketree St Wickenburg AZ 85390-1134 • SD • EM • (FW 1978 MDIV)

**DIGGS HOMER L REV**
272 Foster Rd Henderson NC 27536-7582 • SW • EM • (CQ 1984)

**DILL BRIAN R REV** (520)745-9170
6162 E 20th St Tucson AZ 85711-5218 • pastrdill@aol.com • EN • Assoc • Faith Tucson AZ • (520)326-2262 • (SL 1966 MDIV)

**DILL TERENCE M REV** (253)333-0487
1307 17th St SE Auburn WA 98002 • NOW • SP • Zion Auburn WA • (253)833-5940 • (FW 1977)

**DIMIT ANDREW W REV** (970)522-4902
725 Fairhurst St Sterling CO 80751-4525 • RM • SP • First English Sterling CO • (970)522-5142 • (FW 1986 MDIV)

**DINDA RICHARD J REV** (512)836-8456
1103 E Applegate Dr Austin TX 78753-4005 • TX • EM • (SL 1951 MLS MA MLAS DLITT)

**DINEEN RUSSELL H REV**
2145 S Coronado Dr Sierra Vista AZ 85635-5540 • PSW • SP • Immanuel Sierra Vista AZ • (520)458-3883 • (SL 1995 MDIV)

**DINGEL ARTHUR C REV** (920)458-5870
2731 Henry St Sheboygan WI 53081-6719 • SW • EM • (SL 1958)

**DINGER JONATHAN MARK REV** (503)642-0295
20556 SW Rosa Dr Aloha OR 97007-1032 • bethlehem@usinternet.com • NOW • SP • Bethlehem Aloha OR • (503)649-3380 • (SL 1995 MDIV)

**DINGER TIMOTHY J REV** (409)962-5546
3819 Purdue Ave Port Arthur TX 77642-2353 • TX • SP • Trinity Port Arthur TX • (409)983-1130 • (CQ 1982)

**DINGLER WILLIAM B REV** (636)225-3105
1340 Crossings Ct # A Ballwin MO 63021-7688 • MO • EM • (SPR 1959)

**DINKEL EMIL L REV** (602)378-3665
7146 S Pintek Ln Hereford AZ 85615-9528 • PSW • SP • Hope Bisbee AZ • (530)432-5504 • (SL 1956)

**DIRE JEFFREY REV** (630)810-0893
7100 Powell St Downers Grove IL 60516-3776 • NI • SP • Trinity Chicago IL • (773)237-5045 • (CQ 1985 MA PHD)

**DISBRO ROGER E REV** (419)395-2278
St Stephen Luth Church 30316 New Bavaria Rd Defiance OH 43512-8942 • revred@defnet.com • OH • SP • St Stephen Defiance OH • (419)395-1507 • (SL 1982 MDIV)

**DISCHER GERALD R REV** (409)825-3762
620 Grimes St Navasota TX 77868-3913 • jerry@rvctexas.com • TX • EM • (SPR 1961 MDIV)

**DISCHER NORMAN E REV** (612)469-1601
9606 Upper 205th St W Lakeville MN 55044-8853 • MNS • EM • (SL 1957)

**DISHOP JAMES L REV** (941)435-7212
800 Banyan Blvd Naples FL 34102-5112 • FG • EM • (SL 1956 STM MDIV)

**DISNEY JAMES G REV**
PO Box 238 Buffalo MN 55313-0238 • MNS • Sn/Adm • St John Buffalo MN • (763)682-1883 • (SL 1985 MDIV)

**DISSEN DAVID V REV** (573)334-5736
211 Hillview St Cape Girardeau MO 63703-6327 • dd@clas.net • MO • EM • (SL 1959)

**DITTLOFF TODD A REV** (713)450-1125
62 Moonridge Dr Houston TX 77015-1706 • todd@hal-pc.org • TX • SP • Christ Houston TX • (281)458-3231 • (SPR 1976 MDIV)

**DITTLOFF WAYNE A REV** (713)649-8768
8503 Dover St Houston TX 77061-2105 • TX • EM • (SPR 1954 MDIV)

**DITTMANN ROBERT LOUIS REV** (334)433-6432
507 Church St Mobile AL 36602-2004 • rdittmob@juno.com • SO • EM • (SL 1952)

**DITTMAR DAVID L REV** (314)352-3036
7316 Coronado Ave Saint Louis MO 63116-3053 • MO • SP • St Luke Saint Louis MO • (314)353-9088 • (CQ 1995)

**DITTMER TERRY K REV** (314)781-7580
1723 Mc Cready Ave Richmond Heights MO 63117-2105 • MO • S Ex/S • Missouri Saint Louis MO • (314)317-4550 • (SPR 1974 MDIV)

**DO DUNG VAN REV** (409)983-3273
5229 5th St Port Arthur TX 77642-1112 • TX • Assoc • Trinity Port Arthur TX • (409)983-1130 • (CQ 1997)

**DOAN DANIEL H REV** (920)361-1192
214 S Brooklyn St Berlin WI 54923-1933 • patchs@rbe.com • SW • EM • (CQ 1985 MDIV)

**DOBBERFUHL GERHARD P REV** (281)292-2981
123 Sandpebble Dr The Woodlands TX 77381-3247 • gdobberfuhl@yahoo.com • TX • EM • (SL 1945)

**DOBBERSTEIN PAUL M REV** (630)832-7534
179 Evergreen Ave Elmhurst IL 60126-2612 • pastorpaullcms@flashcom.net • NI • 03/1994 03/2000 • (SL 1981 MDIV MLS)

**DOBBERTIEN DAVID F REV** (308)284-0947
409 E 9th St Ogallala NE 69153-1507 • revddobb@hotmail.com • NEB • SP • St Paul Ogallala NE • (308)284-2688 • (CQ 1996)

**DOBBINS DENNIS L REV** (937)669-0083
6670 Deer Meadows Dr Huber Heights OH 45424 • dldobb1953@aol.com • OH • SP • Saint Timothy Huber Heights OH • (937)233-2443 • (FW 1999)

**DOBRATZ G JEFFREY REV** (414)822-1535
8198 S Chase Rd Pulaski WI 54162-9640 • gdobratz@aol.com • NW • Assoc • St John Pulaski WI • (920)822-3511 • (FW 1995 MDIV)

**DOBRATZ WAYNE P REV** (515)456-2184
1510 3rd St NE Hampton IA 50441-1206 • trinity@rconnect.com • IE • SP • Trinity Hampton IA • (515)456-4816 • (CQ 1985 MDIV)

**DOCEKAL RICHARD JOHN REV** (440)775-3271
C/O Grace Lutheran Church 310 W Lorain St Oberlin OH 44074 • richdocekal@hotmail.com • EN • SP • Grace Oberlin OH • (440)775-3271 • (FW 1994 MDIV)

**DOCTOR LUTHER M REV** (208)765-5313
1820 Golf Course Rd Apt 214 Coeur D Alene ID 83815-1630 • NOW • EM • (SL 1937 MDIV)

**DODGE CHRISTOPHER R REV** (612)946-1801
8329 Kingslee Rd Bloomington MN 55438-1267 • stmike@pclink.com • MNS • Sn/Adm • St Michael Bloomington MN • (952)831-5276 • (SL 1979 MDIV)

**DODGE DAVID A REV** (517)741-8211
207 South St Union City MI 49094-9351 • drdodge@juno.com • MI • SP • Our Savior Union City MI • (517)741-7643 • (FW 1999 MAMS MDIV)

**DOEHRMANN PAUL M REV**
5429 Gustin Rd Woodburn IN 46797 • IN • SP • New Hope Ossian IN • (219)622-7954 • (FW 2000)

**DOELLINGER JERRY W REV** (515)792-7669
801 E 16th St N Newton IA 50208-2423 • oursavr@pcpartner.net • IE • SP • Our Savior Newton IA • (515)792-1084 • (SL 1972 MDIV)

**DOELLINGER PAUL D REV** (716)693-0411
57 Washington St North Tonawanda NY 14120-6543 • pauldoellinger@cs.com • EA • SP • St Mark North Tonawanda NY • (716)693-3715 • (SL 1969 MDIV)

**DOERING ALLEN F REV** (281)360-4672
3314 Golden Willow Dr Humble TX 77339-1291 • ald@christ-the-king.com • TX • Sn/Adm • Christ King Kingwood TX • (281)360-7936 • (SL 1983 MDIV)

**DOERING MARTIN REV** (512)365-8021
1301 Sagewood Dr Taylor TX 76574-7010 • boi749@aol.com • TX • SP • Trinity Taylor TX • (512)352-6958 • (CQ 1976 MDIV)

**DOERNER EDWARD F REV** (309)365-2401
117 Hilton Dr Lexington IL 61753-1003 • stpaul@davesworld.net • CI • SP • St Paul Lexington IL • (309)365-5100 • (FW 1991 MDIV)

**DOERR DALE D REV** (316)365-3732
1602 Redbud Ln Iola KS 66749-1949 • KS • EM • (SPR 1969 MDIV)

**DOHRMAN THOMAS E REV** (850)383-1760
1527 Belleau Wood Dr Tallahassee FL 32312 • FG • SP • University Tallahassee FL • (850)224-6059 • (SL 1968 MA)

**DOHRMANN REINHOLD G REV** (712)243-2462
24 Fair Ridge Cir Atlantic IA 50022-2848 • IW • EM • (SL 1938)

**DOKA KENNETH J DR** (845)462-5837
85 Alda Dr Poughkeepsie NY 12603-5421 • AT • 08/1996 08/2000 • (SL 1973 MDIV PHD)

**DOLAK GEORGE REV** (412)224-8892
105 Mc Williams Dr Natrona Heights PA 15065-2316 • S • EM • (SL 1957)

**DOMINGUEZ RUBEN REV** (847)288-0310
2816 Landen Dr Melrose Park IL 60164-1544 • rubentee@worldnet.att.net • NI • SHS/C • Northern Illinois Hillside IL • (MX 1978 MA MTH)

**DOMINKOWSKI DONALD J REV** (715)385-2267
C/O Trinity Luth Church PO Box 24 Boulder Junction WI 54512-0024 • trinityluthch@centuryinter.net • NW • SP • Trinity Boulder Junction WI • (715)385-2267 • (SPR 1963)

**DOMKE DANIEL M REV** (218)326-3848
715 NE 1st Ave Grand Rapids MN 55744 • revdomke@uslink.net • MNN • Sn/Adm • First Grand Rapids MN • (218)326-5453 • (SL 1983 MDIV)

**DOMMER DOUGLAS REV** (281)351-6166
31118 Alice Ln Tomball TX 77375-4059 • ddommer@salem4u.com • TX • Assoc • Salem Tomball TX • (281)351-8223 • (SL 1981 MDIV)

**DOMMER RONALD G REV** (608)779-1398
120 Heritage Ln Onalaska WI 54650 • MNS • EM • (SL 1958)

**DOMSCH JOHN F REV** (785)266-8435
3735 SW Plaza Dr Apt 105 Topeka KS 66609 • jdomsch@inlandnet.net • KS • SP • Hope Topeka KS • (785)266-5206 • (SL 1968 MDIV)

**DONAHUE RANDALL REV** (630)968-4393
639 Maple Ave Lisle IL 60532 • CNH • SP • Hope Countryside IL • (708)354-6176 • (SL 1998 MDIV)

**DONLEY BRUCE CHARLES REV** (334)962-4338
12855 Perdido St Lillian AL 36549 • revbdonley@aol.com • SO • SP • Shep Of Bay Lillian AL • (334)962-7682 • (FW 1988 MDIV)

**DONNAN JOHN M REV** (208)934-5355
1480 Mt View Dr PO Box 525 Gooding ID 83330 • NOW • SP • Calvary Gooding ID • (208)934-5355 • (FW 1993 MDIV)

**DONNER PAUL H REV** (270)442-5218
4137 Rustic Ave Paducah KY 42001-5329 • MDS • EM • (SL 1957 MDIV)

**DONOFRIO CRAIG J REV** (860)446-0779
378 Meridian St Ext Apt 24 Groton CT 06340 • reverendme@aol.com • NE • SP • Our Redeemer New London CT • (860)444-6529 • (SL 1998 MDIV)

**DONOVAN ROBERT BICKFORD REV** (773)281-4231
2046 N Fremont St Chicago IL 60614-4312 • revdonovan@aol.com • NI • SP • St James Chicago IL • (773)525-4990 • (SL 1996 MDIV)

**DONSBACH ALTON C REV** (940)387-1592
1426 Kendolph Dr Denton TX 76205-6936 • TX • EM • (SL 1950 MA)

**DOOLITTLE JOHN M REV**
8106 Elmbrook Southaven MS 38671 • SO • SP • Prince Of Peace Southaven MS* • (601)393-3432 • (FW 1998 MDIV)

**DOREMUS DWAINE D REV** (605)483-3230
209 Centennial PO Box 125 Wentworth SD 57075-0125 • SD • SP • St Peter Wentworth SD* • (605)483-3129 • (FW 1986 MDIV)

**DORING ARTHUR R REV** (973)347-3293
28 Musconetcong Ave Stanhope NJ 07874-2936 • NJ • SP • Our Savior Stanhope NJ • (973)347-1212 • (SL 1958)

**DORN HILBERT H REV** (804)748-4236
4608 Riderwood Way Chester VA 23831-4326 • glcoffice@aol.com • SE • EM • (SL 1963 MDIV)

**DORN LOUIS O DR** (201)385-6165
32 Larch Ave Dumont NJ 07628-1223 • louisdorn@cs.com • NJ • O Sp Min • New Jersey Mountainside NJ • (SL 1953 STM MA THD)

**DORN OSCAR H REV** (701)255-6805
1030 N 5th St Bismarck ND 58501-3911 • ND • EM • (SL 1932)

**DORN PAUL C REV** (203)763-0067
PO Box 887 Enfield CT 06083-0887 • lcor@portone.com • NE • EM • (SL 1959 MDIV STM)

**DORN PETER B REV** (718)465-4142
219-21 102nd Ave Queens Village NY 11429-1611 • pbdorn@aol.com • AT • SP • Grace Queens Village NY • (718)465-1010 • (SL 1982 MDIV)

**DORN VERNON H REV** (320)983-3481
425 2nd St SE Milaca MN 56353-1226 • MNN • SP • St Paul Milaca MN • (320)983-6703 • (SPR 1969 MDIV)

**DORN VICTOR E REV** (605)996-4530
820 W Birch Ave Mitchell SD 57301-3228 • SD • Asst • Zion Mitchell SD • (605)996-7530 • (SPR 1969 MDIV)

**DORNER MICHAEL H REV** (612)728-0443
5715 14th Ave S Minneapolis MN 55417 • dorner@csp.edu • MNS • SHS/C • Minnesota South Burnsville MN • (SL 1995 MBA MDIV STM)

**DOROH DAVID A REV** (256)766-9601
624 N Poplar St Florence AL 35630-4634 • dadoroh@juno.com • SO • SP • Our Redeemer Florence AL • (256)764-3902 • (CQ 1976 MDIV)

**DOROH GERHARDT A REV** (810)727-2888
8903 Bartel Rd Columbus MI 48063-4305 • MI • Sn/Adm • St Peter Richmond MI • (810)727-9693 • (SL 1971 MDIV)

**DOROW MAYNARD W REV** (651)628-4934
4385 Arden View Ct Arden Hills MN 55112 • dorow@genesis.csp.edu • MNS • EM • (SL 1956 MDIV STM DD)

**DOROW WILLIAM R REV**
15 Squaw Ct Warrenton MO 63383-7039 • MO • SP • St John Warrenton MO • (636)456-2888 • (FW 1989 MDIV)

**DORPAT DAVID M REV** (206)878-8305
20435 1st Pl S Des Moines WA 98198-2802 • NOW • Assoc • Resurrection Des Moines WA • (206)824-2978 • (SL 1957)

**DORR PAUL H REV** (217)243-2528
C/O Christ Deaf Luth Ch 104 Finley St Jacksonville IL 62650-1720 • CI • EM • (SPR 1965 MDIV MS)

**DORRE RALPH O REV** (760)320-4130
697 S Beverly Dr Palm Springs CA 92264-8240 • proralph458@cs.com • AT • EM • (SL 1956 MA)

**DORSCH TIMOTHY D REV** (580)358-2535
RR 1 Box 16 Fairmont OK 73736-9701 • dorschtd@juno.com • OK • SP • Zion Fairmont OK • (580)358-2291 • (SL 1973 MDIV)

**DORTH JEFFREY D REV**
C/O St Paul Lutheran Church 1635 Chester Dr Tracy CA 95376-2927 • CNH • SP • St Paul Tracy CA • (209)835-7438 • (FW 1988 MDIV)

**DOST TIMOTHY P REV**
1103 Gilmore Ave Wilona MN 55987 • tpdost@msn.com • NOW • 07/1999 • (SL 1985 MDIV MA PHD)

**DOSTERT WILLIAM A REV**
2161 White Birch Dr Mears MI 49436-0106 • MI • EM • (CQ 1979 MA)

**DOUBEK WILLIAM J P III REV** (417)451-0371
1001 N Summit St Neosho MO 64850-1095 • namvetrev@janics.com • MO • SP • First Neosho MO • (417)451-2464 • (SL 1985 MDIV DMIN)

**DOUCHES ANTHONY J REV** (863)533-6264
830 Trish Place Bartow FL 33830 • tonycaro@gateway.net • FG • SP • Redeemer Bartow FL • (863)533-6054 • (SL 1967 MDIV)

**DOUGLAS KIRK REV** (701)678-2084
PO Box 118 Gwinner ND 58040 • ND • SP • Zion Gwinner ND* • (701)678-2401 • (FW 1998 MDIV)

**DOUGLAS VENICE C REV** (313)834-6197
13030 Mac Kenzie St Detroit MI 48228-4011 • EN • Sn/Adm • New Mt Olive Detroit MI • (313)834-4396 • (FW 1979)

**DOUTHWAITE JAMES ARTHUR REV** (914)375-0418
56 Mulberry St Yonkers NY 10701-6004 • revjdoc@aol.com • S • SP • Holy Trinity Yonkers NY • (914)965-3884 • (FW 1994 MDIV)

**DOUTHWAITE WILLIAM III REV** (904)446-4308
48 Barkley Ln Palm Coast FL 32137-8836 • wdouth@pcfl.net • EN • SP • Shepherd Coast Palm Coast FL • (904)446-2481 • (FW 1986 MDIV)

**DOWDY KENNETH L REV** (920)682-0063
1207 E Cedar Ave Manitowoc WI 54220-1329 • SW • EM • (SPR 1976 MDIV)

**DOWNING ARTHUR R REV** (518)346-8107
1129 Mc Clellan Schenectady NY 12309-5627 • artdattlc@aol.com • AT • SP • Trinity Schenectady NY • (518)346-5646 • (SL 1968 MDIV)

**DOWNS G TRAVIS REV** (610)534-0746
415 Swarthmore Ave Folsom PA 19033-1715 • EA • SP • St Mark Ridley Park PA • (610)534-0746 • (SL 1982 MDIV)

**DRAEGER HAROLD S DR** (650)365-7208
881 Chesterton Ave Redwood City CA 94061-1203 • hdraeger@mindspring.com • CNH • SP • Redeemer Redwood City CA • (650)366-5892 • (SPR 1971 MDIV MS DMIN)

**DRAEGER JEFFREY G REV** (810)781-5567
341 Salem Dr S Romeo MI 48065 • MI • SP • Our Redeemer Washington MI • (810)781-5567 • (SL 1988 MDIV)

**DRAKE PAUL REV** (248)546-9311
454 Leroy Ave Ferndale MI 48220 • cvojinov@aol.com • EN • 05/1996 05/2000 • (FW 1989 MDIV)

**DRAMSTAD ROGER K REV** (763)493-5450
617 2nd Ave NE Osseo MN 55369-1107 • rdramsta@isd.net • MNS • SP • Eternal Hope Brooklyn Park MN • (763)424-8245 • (SL 1976 MDIV)

**DRANKWALTER RICHARD H REV** (352)799-8036
518 Underwood Ave Brooksville FL 34601-1209 • drank@gate.net • FG • SP • Christ Brooksville FL • (352)796-8331 • (SPR 1970 MDIV)

**DRAPER GEORGE L REV** (406)653-3099
731 Knapp St Wolf Point MT 59201 • frgeorge@midrivers.com • MT • SP • Trinity Wolf Point MT* • (406)653-2289 • (FW 1999 MDIV)

**DRAWBAUGH GALEN F REV** (319)659-8880
1414 Royal Oak Ct De Witt IA 52742 • jgd@internetwis.com • IE • Sn/Adm • Iowa East Marion IA* • (SL 1966 MDIV)

**DREES D BRUCE REV** (512)793-4000
402 Long Mountain Dr Burnet TX 78611 • TX • EM • * • (FW 1988 MS MDIV)

**DREHER STEVEN L REV** (719)530-9153
1204 E St Salida CO 81201 • Stevendreher@bemail.com • RM • SP • First Salida CO • (719)539-4311 • (FW 1981 MDIV DMIN)

**DREIER TIMOTHY P REV** (918)663-8529
2604 S 96th East Ave Tulsa OK 74129-7022 • OK • SP • Our Savior Tulsa OK • (918)836-3752 • (SL 1986 MDIV)

**DRENGLER MARK J REV** (715)421-0186
140 10th St N Wisconsin Rapids WI 54494-4546 • medreng@tznet.com • NW • Assoc • Immanuel Wisconsin Rapids WI • (715)423-3260 • (SL 1991 MDIV)

**DRESSEL DAVID A REV** (517)332-4681
922 Whitman Dr East Lansing MI 48823-2473 • dresseld@pilot.msu.edu • EN • Cmp P • Martin Luther Chapel East Lansing MI • (517)332-0778 • (SL 1968 MDIV MA MTH)

**DRESSLER STEVEN L REV** (636)488-5808
C/O St Paul Luth Church PO Box 328 Jonesburg MO 63351-0328 • sdrev@jonesburg.net • MO • SP • St Paul Jonesburg MO • (636)488-5235 • (SL 1989 MDIV)

**DRESSLER WALDIMAR W REV** (317)889-4321
4005 W Smith Valley Rd Greenwood IN 46142-9004 • IN • EM • (SL 1951)

**DRETKE JAMES P REV** (219)486-1093
6600 N Clinton St Fort Wayne IN 46825-4996 • jpdretke@aol.com • PSW • D Miss • Pacific Southwest Irvine CA • (949)854-3232 • (SL 1956 MDIV MA DMISS)

**DREVLOW FERDINAND A REV** (904)767-3785
1919 Papaya Dr South Daytona FL 32119-1821 • FG • EM • (SPR 1951)

**DREVLOW MARCUS O REV**
23039 S Lakeshore Dr Richton Park IL 60471 • MNS • Asst • Redeemer Burnsville MN • (612)432-7942 • (SL 1982 MA MDIV)

**DREW BRADLEY A REV**
315 Ridgelake Dr Metairie LA 70001-5315 • bradleydrew@mtolive-lcms.org • SO • SP • Mount Olive Metairie LA • (504)833-4963 • (FW 1989 MDIV)

**DREWITZ GLEN A REV** (660)548-3621
701 Harrison St Brunswick MO 65236-1388 • stjohns@c-magic.com • MO • SP • St John Brunswick MO • (660)548-3642 • (FW 1979 MDIV)

**DREWS DENNIS M REV** (612)529-3596
5255 Triton Dr Golden Valley MN 55422-2709 • lcr927@aol.com • MNS • SP • Redemption Bloomington MN • (952)881-0035 • (SL 1971 MDIV)

**DREWS MICHAEL P REV** (416)588-1671
848 Shaw St Toronto ON M6G 3M2 CANADA • drewsfamily@attcanada.net • EN • Sn/Adm • St John Toronto ON CANADA • (416)536-3108 • (SL 1967 MDIV)

**DREWS RICHARD D REV** (630)833-4433
318 Arlington Ave Elmhurst IL 60126-3506 • schafrhund@aol.com • EN • Sn/Adm • Redeemer Elmhurst IL • (630)834-1411 • (SL 1961 STM DMIN)

**DREWS RICHARD T REV** (847)816-7454
912 Cambridge Dr Libertyville IL 60048-3434 • lbrtd@worldnet.att.net • NI • 07/1986 07/2000 • (SL 1972 MDIV)

**DREYER JOHN MICHAEL REV** (612)533-2564
C/O Redeemer Lutheran Church 4201 Regent Ave N Robbinsdale MN 55422-1257 • MNS • SP • Redeemer Robbinsdale MN • (763)533-2564 • (FW 1992 MDIV)

**DROEGE THOMAS A REV** (770)393-0273
3928 Locklear Ct Doraville GA 30360-1304 • tdroege@emory.edu • FG • EM • (SL 1956 MA MA PHD)

**DROEGEMUELLER BERYL D DR** (760)724-1080
2836 Hutchison St Vista CA 92084-1714 • bdrags@aol.com • PSW • Sn/Adm • Faith Vista CA • (760)724-7700 • (SPR 1967 MDIV LLD)

**DROEGEMUELLER CARL M REV** (515)743-2262
608 NE 5th St Greenfield IA 50849-1119 • pastord@iowawest.org • IW • SP • Immanuel Greenfield IA • (515)743-2116 • (SL 1967 MDIV)

**DROEGEMUELLER PAUL E REV** (217)792-3359
219 E Cooke St Mount Pulaski IL 62548-1209 • drgmller43@juno.com • CI • SP • Zion Mount Pulaski IL • (217)792-5965 • (SL 1969 MDIV)

**DROEGEMUELLER TIMOTHY J REV** (956)565-6325
630 Moonlake Dr N Weslaco TX 78596 • TX • Assoc • St Paul Harlingen TX • (956)423-3924 • (SL 1999 MDIV)

**DROSENDAHL JOHN CHARLES REV** (319)226-3032
256 S Hackett Rd Waterloo IA 50701 • IE • SP • Christ Waterloo IA • (319)233-1278 • (SL 1992 MDIV)

**DROUTZ PAUL N REV** (770)277-3041
476 Huff St Apt 10 Lawrenceville GA 30045-6947 • FG • 11/1981 11/1999 • (SL 1979 MDIV)

**DRUM GERARD W REV** (716)384-5455
3 S Dansville St Cohocton NY 14826-9750 • gwdrum@wycol.com • EA • EM • (SL 1959)

**DRUMMOND HENRY E REV** (406)771-8116
2922 1st Ave N Great Falls MT 59401-3404 • revdrummond@prodigy.net • MT • SP • Christ Deaf Great Falls MT* • (406)452-3884 • (FW 1995 MDIV)

**DRUSH JOHN P REV** (785)763-4582
2649 3rd Rd Barnes KS 66933-9718 • jpdrush@jbnteloo.com • KS • SP • St Peter Barnes KS • (785)763-4582 • (SPR 1968 MDIV)

**DU BOIS CRAIG A REV** (214)540-5411
2907 Post Oak Ln Mc Kinney TX 75070-3640 • TX • Sn/Adm • Our Savior Mc Kinney TX • (972)542-6802 • (SL 1981 MDIV)

**DU BOIS KEITH REV** (254)542-7141
Rt 1 Box 282 Kempner TX 76539 • TX • EM • (SPR 1968)

**DU BOIS LOREN A REV** (903)378-3777
RR #1 Box 61 A Windom TX 75492 • rev.bev.dubois@fonninelectric.com • TX • SP • Zion Bonham TX • (903)583-5155 • (FW 1986 MDIV)

**DUBBELDE DAVID V REV** (219)749-6319
7427 Bent Willow Dr Fort Wayne IN 46815-8717 • dave.dd@in.lcms.org • IN • D Ex/S • Indiana Fort Wayne IN* • (SPR 1969 MDIV)

**DUBBERKE EDWIN H REV** (314)481-6377
5825 Holly Hills Ave Saint Louis MO 63109-3410 • MO • EM • * • (SPR 1956)

**DUBE WALTER A REV** (409)938-7094
2703 Meadow Ln La Marque TX 77568-5045 • wadube@swbell.net • TX • SP • Christ Redeem La Porte TX • (713)479-2201 • (SPR 1963 MDIV)

**DUBISAR DOUGLAS A REV** (816)886-9699
833 Watermill Rd Marshall MO 65340-2817 • dadubisar@cdsinet.net • MO • SP • Our Redeemer Marshall MO • (660)886-2270 • (FW 1988)

**DUBKE DALLAS D REV** (530)529-1773
PO Box 726 Red Bluff CA 96080-0726 • CNH • SP • St Paul Red Bluff CA* • (530)527-3414 • (FW 1979 MDIV)

**DUCHOW GILBERT J DR** (859)586-4875
4875 Elkwood Dr Burlington KY 41005-9774 • duke4875@aol.com • OH • SP • Good Shepherd Florence KY • (859)746-9066 • (SL 1968 MDIV DMIN)

**DUCHOW MARCUS T REV**
C/O Lincoln Comm Nursing Home RR 1 Box 302 Lincoln MO 65338-9770 • MO • EM • (SL 1932)

**DUCHOW ROBERT M REV** (518)797-3624
PO Box 215 Westerlo NY 12193-0215 • AT • EM • (SL 1960)

**DUDDLESTON ROBERT W REV** (803)766-8518
2315 Vanderbilt Dr Charleston SC 29414-7027 • geduddleston@juno.com • SE • SP • Calvary Charleston SC • (843)766-3113 • (SL 1967 MDIV)

**DUDER CLYBURN REV** (512)929-9037
1906 Ridgemont Dr Austin TX 78723-2639 • duderc@concordia.edu • TX • SHS/C • Texas Austin TX • (SPR 1966 MDIV MA PHD)

**DUDLEY NATHAN S REV** (712)542-1065
PO Box 205 Yorktown IA 51656-0205 • ndudley@clarinda.heartland.net • IW • SP • St Paul Yorktown IA • (712)542-1505 • (FW 1997 MDIV)

**DUEKER ARTHUR C DR** (716)723-4673
C/O Hope Lutheran Church 1301 Vintage Ln Rochester NY 14626-1760 • EA • Sn/Adm • Hope Rochester NY • (716)723-4673 • (SL 1958 MDIV DD)

**DUEKER KIRK D REV** (304)744-2805
608 Highland Ave South Charleston WV 25303-2033 • OH • Sn/Adm • Redeemer South Charleston WV • (304)744-6251 • (SL 1993 MDIV)

**DUER RONALD E REV** (330)653-2778
C/O Gloria Dei Lutheran Church 2113 Ravenna Rd Hudson OH 44236-3451 • OH • Sn/Adm • Gloria Dei Hudson OH • (330)650-6550 • (SL 1964 MDIV MA STM DMIN)

**DUERR GEORGE F REV** (760)387-2732
348 Arboles Dr Bishop CA 93514-7652 • geojoyduerr@yahoo.com • PSW • EM • (SL 1953)

**DUERR JOHN M REV** (810)264-8810
31415 Saratoga Ave Warren MI 48093-1660 • hopelc@compuserv.net • MI • Sn/Adm • Hope Warren MI • (810)979-9055 • (SL 1982 MDIV)

**DUERR KERWIN L REV** (714)635-8757
1636 W Cris Ave Anaheim CA 92802-2418 • pastorduerr@yahoo.com • PSW • SP • Prince Peace Anaheim CA • (714)774-0993 • (FW 1977 MDIV)

**DUERR WILLIAM L REV** (714)846-3270
6291 Farinella Dr Huntington Beach CA 92647-4200 • durbilt@aol.com • PSW • Sn/Adm • Redeemer Huntington Beach CA • (714)846-6330 • (SPR 1967 MDIV)

**DUESCHER STEVEN J REV** (858)566-3516
8605 Lynx San Diego CA 92126-1828 • livingwatersd@juno.com • EN • SP • Living Water San Diego CA • (858)792-7691 • (SL 1985 MDIV)

**DUEY WILLIAM E REV** (630)553-2937
206B Hillcrest Ave Yorkville IL 60560-1187 • NI • D Ex/S • Northern Illinois Hillside IL • (SL 1961 MED MDIV)

**DUFF FLOYD P REV** (301)934-2627
7963 Oakwood Ln Pomfret MD 20675 • fpduff@iwon.com • SE • SP • Our Savior Pomfret MD • (301)375-7507 • (SL 1955)

**DUFFY PAUL S REV** (402)752-3536
C/O St Paul Lutheran Church PO Box 36 Kenesaw NE 68956 • NEB • SP • St Paul Kenesaw NE • (402)752-3421 • (FW 1998 MDIV)

**DUGAN SHAWN L REV**
4 Stoney Creek Dr Clifton Park NY 12065-6638 • shawndugan@juno.com • AT • Assoc • Zion Schenectady NY • (518)374-1811 • (SL 1997 MDIV)

**DUITSMAN JOHN EARL REV**
21812 Mohican Ave Apple Valley CA 92307 • PSW • S Miss • Pacific Southwest Irvine CA • (949)854-3232 • (CQ 1995)

**DUKE JOHN D REV** (812)895-0289
C/O St John Lutheran Church 707 N 8th St Vincennes IN 47591-3111 • lutheran@bestonline.net • IN • SP • St John Vincennes IN • (812)882-4662 • (SPR 1974 MDIV)

**DUKOVAN DAVID M REV** (715)793-4608
101 First St Bowler WI 54416 • NW • SP • St Paul Bowler WI* • (715)793-4608 • (SL 1999 MDIV)

**DULAS JERALD P REV** (504)491-7849
6325 Mandeville St New Orleans LA 70122 • dulasjpd@juno.com • SO • SP • Christ Our Savior Harvey LA • (504)348-1212 • (FW 1998 MDIV)

**DULEY DUANE M REV** (605)341-1896
614 Crestview Dr Rapid City SD 57702-2039 • circuitrider@prodigy.net • SD • Sn/Adm • Zion Rapid City SD • (605)342-5749 • (FW 1980 MDIV)

**DUMBRILLE DEAN GLEN REV** (810)750-1415
14393 Appletree Ln Fenton MI 48430-1430 • MI • SP • Trinity Fenton MI • (810)629-7861 • (FW 1991 MDIV)

**DUMER LESTER H REV** (309)792-9478
1222 Forty Seventh Ave Ct East Moline IL 61244 • CI • EM • (SPR 1964 MDIV)

**DUMKE PHILIP H REV** (513)941-0963
2831 Hocking Dr Cincinnati OH 45233-4226 • phil5du@fuse.net • OH • Sn/Adm • Grace Cincinnati OH • (513)661-5166 • (SL 1966 MDIV)

**DUMMER DEAN A REV** (414)423-5850
8201 S 35th St Franklin WI 53132-9389 • dadummer@execpc.com • SW • SP • Grace Oak Creek WI • (414)762-8990 • (SL 1981 MDIV)

**DUMPERTH DALE ALLEN REV** (317)897-6124
Emmanuel Lutheran Church 329 S Boehning St Indianapolis IN 46219-7909 • IN • SP • Emmanuel Indianapolis IN • (317)890-9338 • (FW 1992 MDIV)

**DUNCAN DEAN H REV** (605)332-8310
2221 S Willow Ave Sioux Falls SD 57105 • bishop2@sd.cybernex.net • SD • Assoc • Our Redeemer Sioux Falls SD • (605)338-6957 • (FW 1991 MDIV)

**DUNCAN RANDALL S REV** (734)397-3040
39615 Randall St Canton MI 48188-1550 • liveword@aol.com • MI • SP • Living Word Canton MI • (734)737-9566 • (FW 1993 MDIV)

**DUNCAN ROBERT E REV** (219)926-6506
787 Dodge Trl Westville IN 46391-9410 • IN • SP • St Paul Chesterton IN • (219)926-1556 • (FW 1980 MDIV MS)

**DUNKER KARL J REV** (706)863-8949
402 Aumond Rd Augusta GA 30909 • kjdunker@aol.com • FG • Sn/Adm • Our Redeemer Augusta GA • (706)733-6076 • (SPR 1966 MDIV)

**DUNKER RODNEY WADE REV** (320)587-4853
60883 110th St Hutchinson MN 55350 • rdunk@juno.com • MNS • SP • St John Hutchinson MN • (320)587-4853 • (FW 1996 MDIV)

**DUNN CHARLES R REV**
6137 N Talman Ave Chicago IL 60659 • PSW • 04/1996 04/2000 • (FW 1982 MDIV)

**DUNN JAMES A REV**
1400 Plaza Verde El Paso TX 79912 • jldunn5@earthlink.net • RM • SP • Ascension El Paso TX • (915)833-1009 • (SL 1984 MDIV)

**DUNN M CRAIG REV** (313)384-7133
PO Box 1422 Monroe MI 48161-6422 • cdunn1@juno.com • MI • 12/1998 • (SL 1997 MDIV)

**DUNSETH THOMAS W REV**
1223 Valley Cir Rochester Hills MI 48309-1781 • MI • S Miss • Michigan Ann Arbor MI • (FW 1993 MDIV)

**DURAN JOHN M REV** (913)242-6102
1116 S College St Ottawa KS 66067-3618 • duran@ott.net • KS • SP • Faith Ottawa KS • (785)242-1906 • (SPR 1970 MDIV)

**DURHAM DENNIS J REV** (707)539-6471
532 Lombard Ave Santa Rosa CA 95409 • CNH • Assoc • St Mark Santa Rosa CA* • (707)545-1230 • (CQ 1999)

**DURKOVIC JOHN G REV** (714)542-0784
C/O Trinity Luth Ch 902 S Broadway Santa Ana CA 92701-5647 • jpapucho@pacbell.net • PSW • SP • Trinity Santa Ana CA • (714)542-0784 • (SPR 1969 MDIV)

**DUTZMANN INGO ROLF REV** (617)536-8851
24 Laneway St Taunton MA 02780 • flc@flc-boston.org • NE • SP • First Boston MA • (617)536-8851 • (SL 1980 STM MDIV MA)

**DWORAK GARY A REV** (317)271-4034
8815 Ellington Dr Indianapolis IN 46234-2219 • christluthchurch@juno.com • IN • SP • Christ Brownsburg IN • (317)852-3343 • (SPR 1967 MA MDIV STM)

**DWYER CURTIS E REV**
C/O St John Lutheran Church PO Box 235 Lafe AR 72436-0235 • cdwyer@pionet.net • MDS • Christ Brownsburg IN • (317)852-3343 • (SL 1996 MDIV)

**DWYER GREGORY REV**
228 Cutler St Watertown CT 06795-2217 • chemnitz@unidial.com • NE • SP • Shepherd/Hills Bantam CT • (860)567-1433 • (SL 1992 MDIV)

**DYE LAWRENCE J REV** (719)347-0385
965 Boulder St Calhan CO 80808-8665 • dyelj@aol.com • RM • Asst • Immanuel Colorado Springs CO • (719)636-5011 • (FW 1991 MA MDIV)

**DZUGAN JOSEPH MARK REV** (919)528-8169
2056 Ferbow St Creedmoor NC 27522 • jmdzugan@aol.com • SE • Assoc • Grace Durham NC • (919)682-6030 • (SL 1995 MDIV)

**DZUROVCIK ANDREW J REV** (732)388-4551
566 Oak Ridge Rd Clark NJ 07066-2124 • dzurovcik@aol.com • S • SP • Zion Clark NJ • (732)382-7320 • (SL 1973 MDIV)

## E

**EARHART GEORGE R REV** (305)763-6286
70 NW 33rd St Oakland Park FL 33309-6020 • FG • SP • Grace Fort Lauderdale FL • (954)763-6286 • (SL 1983 MDIV)

**EASTERDAY DAVID A REV** (219)478-1468
3718 Nokomis Rd Fort Wayne IN 46809-1430 • pastoreasterday1@juno.com • IN • Sn/Adm • Trinity Fort Wayne IN • (219)422-7931 • (FW 1994 MDIV)

**EATHERTON LAWRENCE L REV** (636)861-3591
1600 Valley Park Rd Fenton MO 63026-2147 • MO • SP • Our Savior Fenton MO • (636)343-2192 • (CQ 1983 MAR)

**EATON STEVEN A REV** (360)683-4803
PO Box 925 Sequim WA 98382-0925 • NOW • SP • Faith Sequim WA • (360)683-4803 • (SL 1986 MDIV)

**EBB ERIC L REV** (419)749-9404
5693 Monmouth Rd Convoy OH 45832-8943 • OH • SP • St Thomas Ohio City OH • (419)495-2408 • (FW 1999 MDIV)

**EBEL ALFRED R REV** (406)265-2115
1000 11th Ave Havre MT 59501 • ebel@hi-line.net • MT • SP • St Paul Havre MT* • (406)265-7637 • (CQ 1988 MA MAD)

**EBELING HENRY C REV** (414)774-5057
7700 W Portland Ave Wauwatosa WI 53213-3190 • SW • EM • * • (SL 1946)

**EBERHARD DAVID DR** (313)567-3100
C/O Historic Trinity Luth Ch 1345 Gratiot Ave Detroit MI 48207-2720 • Histtrin@aol.com • MI • Sn/Adm • Hist Trinity Detroit MI • (313)567-3100 • (SL 1959 MTH LITTD)

**EBERHART FRANK REV** (913)236-6257
3515 W 47th Pl Roeland Park KS 66205-1510 • holyword@sky.net • KS • SP • Our Saviour Kansas City KS • (913)236-6228 • (SL 1967 MDIV)

**EBERLE RODEL J REV** (507)352-2291
PO Box 245 Wykoff MN 55990-0245 • MNS • EM • (SL 1948)

**EBERLE WILLIAM B REV** (518)761-7168
85 Mc Cormack Dr Lake George NY 12845-3423 • chbill@aol.com • AT • SP • Good Shepherd Glens Falls NY • (518)792-7971 • (SL 1960 MED)

**EBERT DAVID F REV** (830)990-0512
221 Timberidge Fredericksburg TX 78624 • TX • EM • (SL 1957)

**EBERT MARK H REV** (402)423-0632
4315 Bingham Cir Lincoln NE 68516-2948 • revmhe@alltel.net • EN • Sn/Adm • Redeemer Lincoln NE • (402)477-1710 • (SL 1983 MDIV)

**EBERT PHILIP S REV** (503)370-9338
2455 Commercial St NE Salem OR 97303-6618 • NOW • 02/1997 02/2000 • (FW 1991 MDIV)

**EBKE RICHARD C REV** (712)366-9339
21824 Green Valley Ave Council Bluffs IA 51503-4110 • IW • EM • (SL 1956)

**EBLE ROBERT D REV** (419)899-2358
11984 Lockwood Rd Sherwood OH 43556 • OH • SP • St John Sherwood OH • (419)899-2850 • (FW 1986 MDIV MA)

**EBS DAVID W REV** (210)341-9787
11623 Intrigue Dr San Antonio TX 78216-3071 • davidebs@yahoo.com • TX • EM • (SL 1957 STM)

**ECKARDT BURNELL F REV** (309)852-2460
440 S Vine St Kewanee IL 61443-2966 • beckardt@inw.net • CI • SP • St Paul Kewanee IL • (309)852-2461 • (FW 1981 MDIV STM PHD)

**ECKART LAWRENCE M REV** (248)442-9956
C/O Hope Lutheran Church PO Box 524 Linden MI 48451-0524 • MI • SP • Hope Linden MI • (810)735-4807 • (SL 1984 MDIV)

**ECKELKAMP MICHAEL A L DR** (760)741-5717
C/O Gloria Dei Lutheran Church 1087 W Country Club Ln Escondido CA 92026-1101 • pastor@gloriadeilc.com • PSW • SP • Gloria Dei Escondido CA • (760)743-2478 • (SL 1991 STM MDIV)

**ECKELMAN ROBERT D REV** (303)654-1021
210 Aspen Dr Brighton CO 80601-2905 • reveck@aol.com • RM • EM • (SL 1958 MDIV)

**ECKELS CHAD M REV** (785)475-2944
504 N Wilson Oberlin KS 67749-1734 • KS • SP • St John Oberlin KS • (785)475-2333 • (SL 1998 MDIV)

**ECKERT ALLAN C REV** (361)592-4095
815 S 10th St Kingsville TX 78363 • aceckert@juno.com • TX • SP • St Paul Kingsville TX • (361)592-6531 • (FW 1999 MDIV)

**ECKERT ANDREW WILLIAM REV** (541)744-3849
3360 Game Farm Rd Springfield OR 97477-7521 • NOW • SP • Bethany Springfield OR • (541)726-7365 • (SL 1996 MDIV)

**ECKERT JAMES ARTHUR REV** (215)945-4801
1970 New Rodgers Rd A6 Levittown PA 19056 • jaestm96@aol.com • EA • SP • St Luke Croydon PA • (215)788-8951 • (SL 1983 MDIV STM)

**ECKERT LEROY J REV** (618)785-2344
C/O St John Luth Church PO Box 162 Baldwin IL 62217-0162 • leenlois@egyptian.net • SI • SP • St John Baldwin IL • (618)785-2344 • (SL 1965 MDIV)

**ECKERT MARK W REV** (414)626-8398
C/O St John Luth Church N665 Highway S Kewaskum WI 53040-1112 • meckert@hnet.net • SW • SP • Saint John Kewaskum WI • (414)626-2309 • (FW 1986 MDIV)

**ECKERT MICHAEL L REV** (218)326-1666
328 NW 10th St Grand Rapids MN 55744-2557 • mleckert@uslink.net • MNN • Assoc • First Grand Rapids MN • (218)326-5453 • (FW 1983 MDIV)

**ECKERT STEPHEN A REV**
C/O Our Savior Lutheran Church 4725 S Bradley Rd Santa Maria CA 93455-5051 • CNH • SP • Our Savior Santa Maria CA • (805)937-1116 • (SL 1986 MA MA)

**ECKERT TIMOTHY CHARLES REV** (319)359-7105
2550 E 32nd St Davenport IA 52807-2366 • qcdeaf@mciworld.com • IE • P Df • Iowa East Marion IA • (SL 1996 MDIV)

**ECKHARDT EUGENE L REV** (785)379-9659
5443 SE 44th Ct Tecumseh KS 66542-9752 • KS • EM • (SL 1950)

**ECKHARDT WILFRED E REV** (319)338-3386
514 N Linn St Iowa City IA 52245-2157 • eckhardt@blue.weeg.uiowa.edu • IE • Cmp P • St Paul Chapel & Uni Iowa City IA • (319)337-3652 • (SL 1963 MDIV)

**ECKHOFF KARL F REV** (712)448-2026
517 S Cannon Paullina IA 51046 • kfejle@pionet.net • IW • SP • Zion Paullina IA • (712)448-3910 • (SL 1990 MDIV)

**ECKHOFF RAYNOLD H REV** (253)756-7913
3214 N Vassault St Tacoma WA 98407-1528 • rayeckhoff@yahoo.com • NOW • EM • (SL 1954 MDIV)

**ECKMAN JOSEPH V REV**
114 N Jackson St Rushville IL 62681-1314 • CI • SP • St John Rushville IL* • (217)322-4237 • (FW 1991 MDIV)

**ECKSTEIN THOMAS ROBERT REV** (314)514-7821
1726 Parkway Acres Ct Maryland Heights MO 63043 • eckstein@fastlynx.com • MO • SP • Beaut Savior Bridgeton MO • (314)291-2395 • (SL 1991 MDIV)

**ECKSTROM CORY J REV** (402)333-0420
12016 William Plaza Apt 213 Omaha NE 68144 • coryecks@aol.com • NEB • Df Min • Bethlehem Deaf Omaha NE • (402)558-5672 • (SL 1996 MDIV)

**EDDLEMAN JAMES L REV**
1630 Dolan Dr Memphis TN 38116-5202 • MDS • EM • (GB 1955)

**EDDY MARK ROLAND REV** (217)696-2642
C/O Holy Cross Luth Ch PO Box 116 Golden IL 62339-0116 • markeddy@adams.net • CI • SP • Holy Cross Golden IL • (217)696-2642 • (FW 1983 MDIV STM)

**EDEN MARTIN R REV** (715)274-2751
C/O Immanuel Luth Church PO Box 18 Mellen WI 54546 • reveden@mellen.baysat.net • NW • SP • Immanuel Mellen WI • (715)274-2751 • (FW 1995 MDIV)

**EDEN ROGER D REV** (715)836-9502
3345 E Meadows Pl Eau Claire WI 54701 • NW • SP • Zion Eau Claire WI • (715)878-4512 • (SL 1965 MDIV)

**EDENFIELD HARRY N REV** (734)479-6337
19545 Wherle Dr Brownstown MI 48192-8533 • medenfield@juno.com • MI • Assoc • Christ King Southgate MI • (734)285-9695 • (CQ 1983 MAR MAT)

**EDER BEN REV** (716)833-9698
239 Fayette Ave Buffalo NY 14223-2709 • beneder@aol.com • EN • SP • Pilgrim Kenmore NY • (716)875-5485 • (FW 1985 MDIV)

**EDGE JAMES M REV** (256)837-3058
109 McDermotts Way Madison AL 35758 • jmedge@prodigy.net • SO • SP • Faith Madison AL • (256)830-5600 • (CQ 1998 MS MA)

**EDGE THOMAS L REV** (973)962-7142
222 Skylands Rd Ringwood NJ 07456-2905 • NJ • SP • Christ King Ringwood NJ • (973)962-6384 • (SL 1960 MDIV)

**EFRAIMSON CARL R REV**
6855 Cory Pl Colorado Springs CO 80915-4253 • RM • EM • (SPR 1958)

**EGGEBRECHT THOMAS J REV** (414)875-7263
3347 N 58th St Milwaukee WI 53216 • eggebrecht@aol.com • SW • SP • Mount Calvary Milwaukee WI • (414)873-3931 • (SL 1991 MDIV)

**EGGER PAUL D REV** (618)662-4673
433 E 2nd St Flora IL 62839-2517 • CI • SP • Faith Flora IL • (618)662-9500 • (FW 1990 MDIV)

**EGGER THOMAS J REV** (712)732-5323
1727 555th St Storm Lake IA 50588 • IW • SP • Zion Storm Lake IA • (712)732-5223 • (SL 2000 MDIV)

**EGGERS ROBERT L REV** (712)786-2436
C/O Christ Lutheran Church PO Box 570 Remsen IA 51050-0570 • reggers@usd.edu • IW • SP • Christ Remsen IA • (712)786-2225 • (SL 1985 MDIV)

**EGGERS ROBERT M REV** (517)790-7598
6418 Belmar Dr Saginaw MI 48603-3474 • berte@cris.com • MI • Assoc • Peace Saginaw MI • (SPR 1970 STM)

**EGGERS STEVEN M REV** (248)347-7602
22554 Terrace Ct Apt 204 Novi MI 48375-4679 • drsteve@ameritech.net • MI • Assoc • Hosanna-Tabor Redford MI • (313)937-2424 • (SL 1981 STM)

**EGGERT EDWARD F REV** (262)782-0987
2330 S Ronke Ln New Berlin WI 53151-2962 • SW • EM • (SL 1950)

**EGGERT JOHN C REV** (503)331-1884
5020 NE 32nd Ave Apt #3 Portland OR 97211 • jeggert@cu-portland.edu • NW • S Miss • North Wisconsin Wausau WI • (SL 1985 MDIV)

**EGGOLD PAUL H REV** (414)421-8988
7409 Devonshire Ave Greendale WI 53129-2241 • pseggold@wauknet.com • EN • Inst C • English Farmington MI • (SL 1961 MDIV)

**EGGOLD THOMAS E REV** (219)744-3228
C/O Bethlehem Luth Church 3705 S Anthony Blvd Fort Wayne IN 46806-4329 • blcrw@juno.com • IN • Sn/Adm • Bethlehem Fort Wayne IN • (219)744-3228 • (CQ 1985 MA)

**EGLOFF CARL J REV** (262)782-8151
21345 Ann Rita Dr Brookfield WI 53045-1638 • SW • Assoc • Elm Grove Elm Grove WI • (262)797-2970 • (SPR 1959 MA)

**EGOLF RALPH C DR** (573)348-2140
6404 Alpine Ln Osage Beach MO 65065-9663 • MO • EM • (SPR 1942 MA PHD)

**EHLERS DONALD D REV** (217)356-3525
2204 Glenoak Dr Champaign IL 61821-6222 • ddehlers@aol.com • CI • EM • (SPR 1960 MDIV STM)

**EHLERS HARVEY I REV** (320)255-0443
1020 7th Ave N Sauk Rapids MN 56379-2345 • MNN • EM • (SPR 1959)

**EHLERS JAMES M REV** (608)274-1696
15 Kessel Ct Apt 34 Madison WI 53711 • SW • EM • (SL 1948)

**EHLERS JEFFERY J REV** 0116625035840
205/20 Chaiyakiat 1 Ngam Wong Wan Rd Bangkok 10210 THAILAND • ehlers@mozart.inet.co.th • FG • S Miss • Florida-Georgia Orlando FL • (SL 1985 MDIV DMIN)

**EHLKE JOHN W REV** (619)670-3322
10804 Buggywhip Dr Spring Valley CA 91978-1906 • jgehlke@aol.com • PSW • SP • Atonement Spring Valley CA • (619)670-7174 • (SL 1973 MDIV)

**EHRFURTH CARL P REV** (414)592-0249
1456 Servais St Green Bay WI 54304-3138 • NW • EM • (SPR 1953)

**EHRICHS RANDAL GENE REV** (660)668-2364
PO Box H Cole Camp MO 65325-0168 • revmopar@iland-net • MO • SP • Trinity Cole Camp MO • (816)668-2364 • (SL 1992 MDIV)

**EHRKE DONALD W** (970)668-2181
PO Box 3720 Dillon CO 80435 • RM • SP • Christ Breckenridge CO* • (970)453-8019 • (FW 2000 MDIV)

**EICHBERGER TIMOTHY M REV** (810)982-4305
2001 Jack Pine Ln Port Huron MI 48060-1561 • MI • SP • Faith Port Huron MI • (810)985-5733 • (SL 1972 MDIV)

**EICHELBERGER ALBERT REV** (865)693-9293
2114 Scenic Ridge Cv Knoxville TN 37923-1229 • tennlke@aol.com • PSW • EM • (SPR 1960)

**EICHLER MARK P REV** (785)985-2252
515 W Chestnut St Troy KS 66087 • KS • SP • Christ Wathena KS • (785)989-3348 • (SL 1985 MDIV)

**EICKHOFF BENJAMIN P REV** (308)645-2530
HC 58 Box 4E Thedford NE 69166 • beickho@neb-sandhills.net • NEB • SP • Zion Arnold NE • (308)848-2575 • (CQ 1994)

**EICKHOFF BERT H REV** (217)563-2728
201 N Pine St Nokomis IL 62075-1230 • SI • SP • Trinity Nokomis IL • (217)563-2718 • (SL 1988 MDIV)

**EICKHOFF WILLIAM P REV** (517)624-4656
10905 Canada Rd Birch Run MI 48415-9792 • greick@aol.com • MI • SP • St Martin Birch Run MI • (517)624-9204 • (SL 1987 MDIV STM)

**EICKMANN JERROLD A REV** (636)391-5452
1344 Haute Loire Dr Ballwin MO 63011-2959 • MO • SHS/C • Missouri Saint Louis MO • (314)317-4550 • (SL 1964 MDIV)

**EICKMANN ROBERT E JR. REV** (517)238-5411
426 Lake Dr Coldwater MI 49036-9533 • reeickmann@yahoo.com • IN • 10/1994 11/1999 • (SL 1981 MDIV)

**EIFERT CLARENCE C REV** (630)668-9419
203 E Seminary Ave Wheaton IL 60187-5309 • ceifert@stjohnwheaton.org • NI • EM • (SPR 1954 MDIV)

**EIFERT EDGAR H REV** (507)334-7463
510 1st St SW Faribault MN 55021-5804 • MNS • EM • (SL 1934)

**EIFERT EDWIN W REV** (952)893-0654
5631 W 98 1/2 St Bloomington MN 55437-2208 • eeifert@prodigy.net • MNS • EM • (SL 1950)

**EIFERT HERBERT N REV** (713)944-5301
2514 Huckleberry Ln Pasadena TX 77502-5453 • TX • EM • (SL 1960 MDIV)

**EILERS GREGORY J REV** (319)252-2498
102 S River Pk Dr Guttenberg IA 52052 • tlclcms@netins.net • IE • SP • Trinity Guttenberg IA* • (319)252-1476 • (FW 1996 MDIV)

**EILERS KEITH H REV**
18803 SE 60th St Issaquah WA 98027-8638 • pastorkeilers@uswest.net • NOW • SP • Christ The King Bellevue WA • (425)746-1711 • (SL 1970 MDIV)

**EINEM EDWARD H REV** (734)464-9312
37625 Bristol Ct Livonia MI 48154-1260 • eeinem@mindspring.com • MI • EM • (SPR 1962)

**EINEM HAROLD E REV** (414)329-9994
11964 W Coldspring Rd Greenfield WI 53228 • EN • EM • (SPR 1963)

**EINEM JOHN A REV** (316)775-1976
1501 Cron Augusta KS 67010 • KS • Sn/Adm • Christ Augusta KS • (316)775-7301 • (SC 1989 MDIV)

**EISBERG CLARENCE H REV** (209)725-9082
3856 N Gardner Ave Merced CA 95340-9344 • reveis@cyberlynk.com • CNH • SP • St Paul Merced CA • (209)383-3301 • (SL 1973 MDIV)

**EISINGER ALAN P REV** (775)753-8700
279 Willow St Elko NV 89801-2851 • nevadaal@hotmail.com • CNH • SP • St Mark Elko NV • (775)738-5436 • (FW 1983 MDIV)

**EISSFELDT RICHARD A REV** (727)347-7276
5950 Bayview Cir S Gulfport FL 33707-3930 • eissfer@worldnet.att.net • FG • EM • (SL 1962 MDIV MSW)

**EIWEN JOHN G REV** (330)784-5912
316 Ellen Ave Akron OH 44305-3979 • jgeiwen@aol.com • OH • Sn/Adm • Zion Akron OH • (330)253-3136 • (SL 1968 MDIV STM)

**EKONG HOSEA J REV** (330)782-9304
3311 Glenwood Ave Youngstown OH 44511 • hoseaekong@juno.com • OH • SP • Victory Youngstown OH • (330)747-2491 • (SL 1999 MDIV)

**ELAM CAREY PAUL REV** (334)244-8600
6107 Margo Pl Montgomery AL 36117 • cpelam@aol.com • SO • SP • St Paul Montgomery AL • (334)272-6214 • (SL 1984 MDIV)

**ELBERT THOMAS J JR. REV** (402)561-6645
508 S 68th St Omaha NE 68106 • tjelbert@juno.com • OK • M Chap • Oklahoma Tulsa OK • (SL 1988 MDIV)

**ELGERT LOUIS G REV** (352)854-8592
10450 SW 99th Ct Ocala FL 34481-9076 • momlillie@aol.com • FG • EM • (SPR 1952)

**ELIASON GILBERT MARLAN REV** (907)356-3611
914 Erwin Ct Fort Wainwright AK 99703 • eliason@mosquitonet.com • S • M Chap • SELC Cudahy WI • (SL 1992 MDIV MA)

**ELKINS DAN DOUGLAS REV** (662)895-6577
12089 Thompson Dr Olive Branch MS 38654-8398 • rev.elkins@vantek.net • MDS • SP • Beaut Savior Memphis TN • (901)362-6080 • (FW 1978)

**ELLERBROCK KEITH D REV** (636)940-9233
2913 N Kristopher Bnd Saint Charles MO 63303-3167 • kdbrock777@aol.com • MO • SP • Trinity Bridgeton MO • (314)739-0022 • (SL 1985 MDIV)

**ELLERMANN JOHN E REV** (504)641-0684
1566 Wildwood Ln Slidell LA 70458-3146 • jellermann@nternet.com • SO • EM • (SL 1953)

**ELLING NORMAN B REV** (317)826-9620
7226 N Orchard Dr Indianapolis IN 46236-3126 • IN • EM • (SPR 1955)

**ELLINGTON JOHN A REV** (405)737-4847
3405 Ridgehaven Dr Midwest City OK 73110-3731 • pastore@juno.com • OK • Sn/Adm • Good Shepherd Midwest City OK • (405)732-2585 • (SL 1987 MDIV)

**ELLIOTT MARK R REV** (217)239-3830
308 S Fair St Champaign IL 61821-3123 • CI • Sn/Adm • St John Champaign IL • (217)359-1123 • (FW 1984 MDIV)

**ELLIS ROGER C REV** (519)542-6219
948 Dagan Sarnia ON N7S 1Y5 CANADA • rcellis@rivernet.net • EN • SP • Redeemer Sarnia ON CANADA • (519)337-6615 • (SL 1972 MDIV DMIN)

**ELLIS TERRANCE K REV** (319)677-2759
C/O Immanuel Luth Church PO Box 239 Charlotte IA 52731-0239 • IE • SP • Immanuel Charlotte IA • (319)677-2756 • (FW 1985 MDIV)

**ELLIS VERN W REV** (618)483-3554
202 S Edwards St Altamont IL 62411-1208 • CI • EM • (SPR 1968)

**ELLIS WILLIAM F JR. REV** (916)332-4001
4812 Porto Dr Antelope CA 95843 • belllis@earthlink.net • CNH • SP • Zion North Highlands CA • (916)332-4001 • (SL 1984 MDIV)

**ELLWANGER JOHN P REV** (512)452-4281
7406 Barcelona Dr Austin TX 78752-2005 • johnellwanger.yahoo.com • TX • SP • Christ Our Savior Lago Vista TX • (512)267-7121 • (SL 1956 MDIV)

**ELLWEIN MAURICE D REV** (319)279-3531
211 Lobeck Ave PO Box 57 Readlyn IA 50668 • readrev@netins.net • IE • SP • St Paul Readlyn IA • (319)279-3961 • (SL 1972 MDIV)

**ELMSHAUSER JAMES M REV** (719)765-4483
PO Box 187 Flagler CO 80815-0187 • RM • SP • Zion Flagler CO* • (719)765-4460 • (SL 1972 MDIV)

**ELOWSKY EARL W REV** (517)742-2070
17574 Avalon Dr Hillman MI 49746-8243 • ewelowsk@freeway.net • MI • EM • * • (SPR 1960 MDIV)

**ELOWSKY JOEL C REV** (609)748-8008
109 S Concord Absecon NJ 08201 • joelowsky@juno.com • S • D Miss • Peace Absecon NJ • (609)748-1777 • (SL 1990 STM MDIV)

**ELROD J MURRAY REV** (530)673-9135
C/O First Lutheran Church 850 Cooper Ave Yuba City CA 95991-3849 • CNH • SP • First Yuba City CA • (530)673-8894 • (SL 1968 MDIV)

**ELSER JOHN HANS REV** (806)354-2366
1606 Armstrong St Amarillo TX 79106-2332 • TX • SP • Prince Peace Amarillo TX • (806)359-7700 • (SL 1992 MDIV)

**ELSEROAD DAVID A REV** (718)463-0190
189-28 45th Rd Flushing NY 11358-3415 • resurchurch@worldnet.att.net • AT • SP • Resurrection Flushing NY • (718)463-4292 • (SL 1976 MDIV)

**ELSEROAD KEVIN P REV** (770)740-8021
6470 Maid Marion Close Alpharetta GA 30202-6402 • KElseroad@mindspring.com • EN • SP • Christ Shepherd Alpharetta GA • (770)475-0640 • (SL 1981 MDIV)

**ELSEROAD RICHARD M REV** (423)671-3939
1128 Terra Rosa Dr Knoxville TN 37932-2558 • relseroad@usa.net • MDS • Sn/Adm • Grace Knoxville TN • (865)691-2823 • (SL 1979 MDIV)

**ELSNER ROBERT C REV** (813)855-6713
C/O St Matthew Luth Church 5601 Hanley Rd Tampa FL 33634-4905 • FG • SP • St Matthew Tampa FL • (813)884-3097 • (SPR 1962 MDIV)

**EMINGER MICHAEL KEVIN REV** (218)891-4775
PO Box 247 Fisher MN 56723-0247 • meminger@rrv.net • MNN • SP • Trinity Fisher MN* • (218)891-4581 • (FW 1991 MDIV)

**EMMEL PAUL W REV** (920)336-2216
418 Ridgeview Ter Green Bay WI 54301-1515 • NW • EM • * • (SL 1965 MST MPSY)

**EMMONS RANDY R REV** (630)792-9103
21 W 205 Ahlstrand Lombard IL 60148 • NI • SP • Trinity Lombard IL • (630)629-8765 • (FW 1997 MDIV)

**EMMRICH DAVID N REV** (320)259-1577
201 4th St S Saint Cloud MN 56301 • emmrich@stcloudstate.edu • MNN • Cmp P • Minnesota North Brainerd MN • (SL 1989 MA MDIV STM)

**EMRICK WILLIAM C REV** (419)258-9585
C/O Mt Calvary Lutheran Church PO Box 1024 Antwerp OH 45813 • wcemrick@bright.net • OH • SP • Mount Calvary Antwerp OH • (419)258-6505 • (FW 1986 MDIV)

**EMSLIE JOHN W JR. REV** (402)426-1800
2026 Lincoln St Blair NE 68008-1836 • revcycle@huntel.net • NEB • SP • Trinity Blair NE • (402)426-2851 • (CQ 1986 MA)

**ENDRIHS JAMES EDWARD REV** (334)393-4240
C/O Christ The King Luth Churc 208 E Watts St Enterprise AL 36330-1813 • jendrihs@aol.com • SO • SP • Christ King Enterprise AL • (205)347-6716 • (SL 1996 MDIV)

**ENGEBRETSEN WILLIAM C REV** (402)256-3314
C/O Immanuel Luth Church PO Box 597 Laurel NE 68745-0597 • engebretsen@mail.laurel.esu1.k12.ne.us • NEB • SP • Immanuel Laurel NE • (402)256-3314 • (FW 1994 MDIV)

**ENGEBRETSON DONALD V REV** (231)946-6043
1021 S Maple St Traverse City MI 49684-4025 • frzeke@aol.com • MI • Sn/Adm • Trinity Traverse City MI • (231)946-2720 • (FW 1987 MDIV)

**ENGEL RICHARD S REV** (904)998-9287
11048 Raley Creek Dr S Jacksonville FL 32225-2325 • legne@juno.com • FG • SP • Grace Jacksonville FL • (904)928-9136 • (SL 1977 MDIV)

**ENGEL RONALD P REV** (561)468-6837
5509 Buchanan Dr Fort Pierce FL 34982-7419 • tllbia25@aol.com • FG • SP • Trinity Fort Pierce FL • (561)461-7272 • (SL 1970 MDIV)

**ENGEL THOMAS EDWARD REV** (309)698-0512
120 Turnron Pl East Peoria IL 61611 • CI • Assoc • St Peter East Peoria IL • (309)699-5411 • (SL 1994 MDIV)

**ENGEL TIMOTHY A REV** (219)764-4246
5849 Carnation Portage IN 46368 • tengel@netnitco.net • IN • SP • Holy Cross Hobart IN • (219)763-6343 • (SL 1989 MDIV)

**ENGELBRECHT EDWARD A REV**
1519 E 3rd Pkwy Washington MO 63090 • MO • S Ex/S • Missouri Saint Louis MO • (314)317-4550 • (SL 1993 MDIV STM)

**ENGELBRECHT LUTHER T REV** (206)706-1348
610 NW 73rd St Seattle WA 98117-4951 • ltengelbrecht@webtv.net • NOW • EM • (SL 1953 MDIV STM)

**ENGFEHR WILLIAM F III REV** (618)345-5360
19 Ramsgate Collinsville IL 62234-4872 • engfehr@sprintmail.com • SI • Sn/Adm • Holy Cross Collinsville IL • (618)344-3145 • (SL 1978 MDIV)

**ENGLER ALBERT G REV** (816)333-5880
7220 Baltimore Ave Kansas City MO 64114-5716 • pastage@cysource.com • MO • SP • Immanuel Kansas City MO • (816)561-0561 • (SL 1960 MDIV)

**ENGLER THOMAS E REV**
C/O Luth Church in Korea CPO Box 1239 Seoul 100-612 100-612 KOREA • tengler@chollian.net • MO • S Miss • Missouri Saint Louis MO • (314)317-4550 • (SL 1990 MDIV STM)

**ENKO KEITH E REV**
10760 Stage Rd Clarence NY 14031-2317 • EA • SP • Holy Cross Clarence NY • (716)634-2332 • (SL 1982 MDIV)

**EPPEN ALAN REV** (701)493-2531
PO Box 95 Edgeley ND 58433-0095 • ND • SP • Zion Edgeley ND* • (701)493-2537 • (FW 1983 MDIV)

**EPPERSON GERALD N REV** (254)803-2497
619 E Royal Oaks Dr Marlin TX 76661-2226 • marlinrev@hot1.net • TX • SP • Grace Marlin TX • (254)803-2475 • (FW 1993 MDIV)

**ERBE RONALD A REV** (203)661-8062
1 Putnam Hill Apt 4H Greenwich CT 06830-5703 • NE • EM • (SL 1960 MSW MDIV)

**ERBER DAVID M REV**
PO Box 448 Ikom Cross River St NIGERIA • MI • S Miss • Michigan Ann Arbor MI • (FW 1986 MDIV)

**ERDMAN ALAN REV** (314)534-1515
4201 Lindell Blvd Saint Louis MO 63108-2915 • alane@lfcs.org • MO • Missouri Saint Louis MO • (314)317-4550 • (CQ 1979 MDIV STM)

**ERDMAN LEONARD E REV** (715)355-4295
7010 Ross Ave Schofield WI 54476-1650 • NW • EM • (SPR 1956)

**ERICKSEN DAVID E REV** (712)728-2890
50 N Central Ave Hartley IA 51346 • IW • SP • St Paul Hartley IA • (712)728-2711 • (SPR 1976 MDIV)

**ERICKSON DONALD E REV** (402)925-5652
C/O Immanuel Luth Church HC 59 Box 39 Atkinson NE 68713-9407 • derick@inetnebr.com • NEB • SP • Immanuel Atkinson NE • (402)925-2851 • (SL 1986 MDIV)

**ERICKSON ERICK E REV** (612)536-7862
4819 Azelia Ave N Apt 7 Brooklyn Center MN 55429-3804 • MNS • EM • (SPR 1947)

**ERICKSON JAMES D REV** (517)356-4018
2738 S 3rd Ave Alpena MI 49707-3315 • erickson@freeway.net • MI • Assoc • Immanuel Alpena MI • (517)354-3443 • (SL 1982 MDIV)

**ERICKSON JOHN B REV** (623)412-5902
4001 W Beardsley Rd Glendale AZ 85308-4713 • circleride@aol.com • PSW • SP • Atonement Glendale AZ • (623)582-8785 • (SPR 1976 MDIV)

**ERICKSON KRISTIAN J REV** (801)288-9443
222 E 5600 S Salt Lake City UT 84107-6113 • RM • Asst • Christ Murray UT • (801)262-4354 • (SL 1986)

**ERICKSON MARK A REV** (605)432-6095
706 S 1st St Milbank SD 57252 • SD • Assoc • Emanuel Milbank SD • (605)432-9555 • (FW 1986 MDIV)

**ERICKSON MICHAEL D REV** (505)836-7007
C/O Our Savior Luth Ch 4301 Atrisco Dr NW Albuquerque NM 87120-1662 • RM • SP • Our Savior Albuquerque NM • (505)836-7007 • (FW 1979 MDIV)

**ERICKSON MICHAEL K REV** (505)393-2822
103 E Berry Dr Hobbs NM 88240-4417 • mkegrace@gte.net • RM • SP • Grace Hobbs NM* • (505)393-4911 • (SL 1993 MDIV)

**ERICKSON PATRICK THERON REV** (972)775-8734
404 Westview Ter Midlothian TX 76065-2034 • mlcinmid@flash.net • TX • SP • Messiah Midlothian TX • (972)723-1069 • (SL 1986 MDIV)

**ERICKSON ROBERT L REV** (708)747-4849
236 Indiana St Park Forest IL 60466-1166 • NI • EM • (SL 1962 MDIV)

**ERKKINEN ERIC J REV** (703)492-6149
3171 Ironhorse Dr Lake Ridge VA 22192 • erkk51@aol.com • NE • M Chap • New England Springfield MA • (SL 1977 MDIV)

**ERLER MARK ROBERT REV** (918)825-6235
1316 SE 17th St Pryor OK 74361-8211 • merler@viagrafix.net • OK • SP • St John Pryor OK • (918)825-1926 • (SL 1991 MDIV)

**ERMELING VERNON F REV** (602)277-4665
6718 N 20th St Phoenix AZ 85016-1102 • vermeling@juno.com • EN • Assoc • Christ Phoenix AZ • (602)955-4830 • (CQ 1982 MED)

**ERNST DAVID W REV**
169 Kittery Ridge New Castle PA 16101 • EA • SP • Christ New Castle PA • (724)658-8009 • (CQ 1997)

**ERNST EUGENE W REV** (712)676-2293
3319 Keystone Ave Ida Grove IA 51445-8138 • geneviv@pionet.net • IW • SP • Immanuel Charter Oak IA* • (712)679-2701 • (SL 1972 MDIV)

**ERNST MICHAEL S REV** (414)422-9319
S79W15273 Foxboro Pl Muskego WI 53150-7722 • mikeerns@execpc.com • EN • Sn/Adm • Hales Corners Hales Corners WI • (414)529-6700 • (SL 1973 MDIV)

**ERNST ROBERT G REV** (631)325-8266
PO Box 146 388 A Montauk Hwy Eastport NY 11941-0146 • AT • EM • (SL 1959 MA MA)

**ERNSTMEYER MILTON SIEBERT REV** (843)272-3910
147 Cabana Rd Myrtle Beach SC 29572-5604 • mernstmeyer@aol.com • SE • EM • (SL 1943 MDIV MA MST DD)

**ERSLAND DAVID PAUL REV** (785)747-2407
2054 10th Rd Greenleaf KS 66943-9440 • KS • SP • Bethlehem Greenleaf KS • (785)747-2407 • (CQ 1995 MDIV)

**ERTL JAMES A REV** (504)944-5401
C/O St Paul Lutheran Church 1625 Annette St New Orleans LA 70116-1322 • SO • SP • St Paul New Orleans LA • (504)944-5401 • (SL 1971 MDIV DMIN)

**ESALA DANIEL D REV** (440)543-4506
17886 Lost Trail Chagrin Falls OH 44023 • danesala@aol.com • OH • Sn/Adm • Valley Chagrin Falls OH • (440)247-0390 • (SL 1982 MDIV)

**ESALA H PAUL REV** (520)744-5064
7871 W Morning Light Way Tucson AZ 85743-5475 • EN • EM • (SPR 1944 MDIV)

**ESALA LUTHER P REV** (520)579-7140
3356 W Quarter Moon Pl Tucson AZ 85741-1247 • esala@rtd.com • EN • SP • Messiah Tucson AZ • (520)744-6984 • (SL 1973 MDIV STM)

**ESALA PHILIP J REV** (937)438-3990
333 Blackstone Dr Centerville OH 45459-4307 • philesala@emmanuellc.org • OH • SP • Emmanuel Kettering OH • (937)434-1798 • (SL 1984 MDIV JD)

**ESALA TOIVO A REV** (218)385-4042
RR 1 Box 51A New York Mills MN 56567-9999 • MNN • EM • (SPR 1945 MA)

**ESCHELBACH MICHAEL A DR** (708)771-8300
1135 Bonnie Brae River Forest IL 60305 • NI • SHS/C • Northern Illinois Hillside IL • (FW 1985 MDIV PHD)

**ESCUE DOUGLAS K REV** (505)983-8050
207 E Barcelona Rd Santa Fe NM 87501-4609 • dkescue@aol.com • RM • SP • Immanuel Santa Fe NM • (505)983-7568 • (SL 1986 MDIV)

**ESGET CHRISTOPHER S REV** (618)542-3418
699 W Main Du Quoin IL 62832 • csesget@onecliq.net • SI • SP • Bethel Du Quoin IL • (618)542-3418 • (FW 1997 MDIV)

**ESPINOSA ALFONSO O REV** (949)699-3309
C/O St Paul Lutheran Church 1190 Morningside Dr Laguna Beach CA 92651-3038 • chirhoae@aol.com • PSW • SP • St Paul Laguna Beach CA • (949)494-7998 • (FW 1991 MDIV)

**ESSIG ERHARDT H REV** (219)484-5916
1905 Colony Dr Fort Wayne IN 46825-5009 • IN • EM • (SL 1936 MA PHD)

**ESSIG ERNST H REV** (313)884-9134
20655 Country Club Dr Harper Woods MI 48225-1651 • MI • EM • (SL 1935)

**ESTBY ALAN C REV** (785)832-9575
2700 Inverness Ct Lawrence KS 66047-1891 • raestby@ukans.edu • KS • Assoc • Immanuel-Univ Lawrence KS • (785)843-0620 • (CQ 1998)

**ESTERLINE SEAN M REV** (773)745-9410
5139 W Parker Ave Chicago IL 60639 • EN • SP • Grace English Chicago IL • (773)637-1177 • (FW 2000 MDIV)

**ESTOK DANIEL M REV** (407)366-4168
1321 Haven Dr Oviedo FL 32765-5204 • S • EM • (SL 1947 MDIV)

**ETHRIDGE SHAWN P REV** (507)639-3051
2323 120th Ave Ormsby MN 56162 • MNS • SP • Immanuel Ormsby MN* • (507)639-3051 • (SL 1998 MDIV)

**ETTER MARK R REV**
345 Jerlou Ln Edgewood KY 41017-2614 • etter@prodigy.net • OH • SP • Bethany Erlanger KY • (859)331-3501 • (SL 1983 MDIV)

**ETTNER DANN J REV** (602)943-6909
1027 E Palmaire Ave Phoenix AZ 85020-5320 • revdann@azlutheran.org • PSW • Sn/Adm • Mount Calvary Phoenix AZ • (602)263-0402 • (SL 1983 MDIV)

**ETZEL LENHART E REV** (810)732-8833
3056 Red Barn Rd Flint MI 48507-1252 • MI • EM • (SPR 1952 MDIV)

**ETZEL RUSSELL ALVIN REV** (903)536-4037
PO Box 794 Centerville TX 75833-0794 • oslc@risecom.net • TX • SP • Our Savior Centerville TX • (903)536-2019 • (SL 1992 MDIV)

**ETZLER ANDREW ROBERT REV** (573)682-3702
612 Tarr St Centralia MO 65240-1734 • revetzler@aol.com • MO • 06/2000 • (FW 1995 MDIV)

**ETZOLD HERMAN A REV** (402)643-2526
445 N Columbia Ave Seward NE 68434-1601 • he91422@alltel.net • NEB • EM • (SL 1942 MST MDIV MSED DMIN)

**EVANS GENE REV** (313)521-7323
14642 Bringard Dr Detroit MI 48205-1246 • EN • SP • Good Shepherd Detroit MI • (313)527-6353 • (SPR 1971)

**EVANS JACK W REV** (570)275-5052
30 Fairland Dr Danville PA 17821-9385 • patmos@aol.danville • EA • EM • (SPR 1966 MDIV)

**EVANS THOMAS L REV** (952)472-2151
5200 Bartlett Blvd Mound MN 55364-1748 • eagle$^3$crest@msn.com • MNS • SP • Mount Olive Mound MN • (612)472-2756 • (SL 1989 MDIV)

**EVANSON CHARLES J REV**
3026 Long Iron Dr Evansville IN 47725-8009 • cjevanson36@worldnet.att.net • EN • SHS/C • English Farmington MI • (CQ 1964)

**EVANSON E DALE REV** (248)673-8149
4496 Meigs St Waterford MI 48329-1815 • be1owat@moa.net • MI • Sn/Adm • St Stephen Waterford MI • (248)673-6621 • (SL 1960 MDIV)

**EVERETTE STEPHEN R REV** (504)368-7925
1001 Greenspoint Dr New Orleans LA 70114-4936 • revev@compuserve.com • SO • SP • Mount Zion New Orleans LA • (504)522-9951 • (FW 1994 MDIV)

**EVERS JAMES P REV** (865)483-6444
106 Beechwood Ct Oak Ridge TN 37830-7867 • lmrvrs@icx.net • MDS • SP • Faith Oak Ridge TN • (865)483-5431 • (SL 1967 MDIV)

**EVERS TIMOTHY C REV** (303)259-0567
C/O St Paul Luth Church PO Box 2282 Durango CO 81302-2282 • RM • SP • St Paul Durango CO • (970)247-0357 • (SL 1967 MDIV)

**EVERSON GALE R REV** (406)227-8326
3835 Chokecherry St East Helena MT 59635-3404 • geverson@juno.com • MT • Inst C • Montana Billings MT • (FW 1978 MDIV)

**EVERTSEN THEODORE A REV** (207)873-7319
4 Ursula St Waterville ME 04901-4630 • NE • 06/1985 06/2000 • (CQ 1979)

**EWELL RONALD KARL REV**
801 East Baldwin St Hackettstown NJ 07840-1422 • NJ • SP • Gethsemane Hackettstown NJ • (908)852-2156 • (CQ 1997 MDIV DMIN)

**EWOLDT VIRGIL W REV** (712)337-3812
1819 190th St Milford IA 51351-7297 • IW • SP • Concordia Lake Park IA* • (712)832-3503 • (FW 1986)

**EYER RICHARD C REV** (414)332-0649
4933 N Newhall St Milwaukee WI 53217-6049 • richard.eyer@cuw.edu • SW • SHS/C • South Wisconsin Milwaukee WI • (414)464-8100 • (SL 1965 MDIV DMIN)

## F

**FABRICIUS HOWARD O REV** (317)881-3899
7809 Broadview Dr Indianapolis IN 46227-8040 • hbfab@surf-ici.com • IN • Assoc • Concordia Greenwood IN • (317)881-4477 • (SPR 1965)

**FABRIZIUS KARL F REV** (414)529-3999
7390 Hill Valley Ct Greendale WI 53129-2725 • fabriz@execpc.com • SW • Assoc • Our Father Greenfield WI • (414)282-8220 • (FW 1984 MDIV PHD)

**FABRY JOSEPH P REV** (419)429-1161
1437 Autumn Dr Findlay OH 45840 • EN • EM • (SL 1954)

**FACKLER WILLIAM J REV** (818)351-9269
3665 Landfair Rd Pasadena CA 91107-2120 • wfackler@aol.com • PSW • EM • (SL 1947)

**FAERBER RICHARD B REV** (760)722-7373
702 Eucalyptus St Oceanside CA 92054-5108 • PSW • EM • (SL 1943)

**FAGA ROBERT O REV**
10808 Foothill Blvd Ste 160 PMB #110 Rancho Cucamonga CA 91730-3889 • PSW • EM • (SPR 1961)

**FAHR DUANE L REV** (402)365-4245
PO Box 69 Deshler NE 68340-0069 • stpeter@gpcom.net • NEB • SP • St Peter Deshler NE • (402)365-4341 • (SL 1991 MDIV)

**FAIR JOHN W REV** (219)471-7539
5706 Inland Trl Fort Wayne IN 46825-5909 • fairjohn@juno.com • IN • Assoc • Holy Cross Fort Wayne IN • (219)483-3173 • (FW 1982 MDIV)

**FAIRBAIRN CHRISTOPHER DAVID REV**
201 Elm St Northville MI 48167-1260 • chrislisa@foxberry.net • MI • Assoc • St Paul Northville MI • (248)349-3140 • (FW 1995 MDIV)

**FAIRCHILD JOE C REV**
835 Kennedy Ave Virginia Beach VA 23451 • SE • EM • (FW 1977 MDIV)

**FAIROW GREGORY L REV** (414)616-2888
4074 N 89th St Milwaukee WI 53222-1723 • gfairow@ameritech.net • SW • D Miss • St Paul Northville MI • (SL 1996 MDIV)

**FAITH GARY J REV** (256)413-0437
807 Woodmar Dr Gadsden AL 35906-5849 • gfaith@mindspring.com • SO • SP • Trinity Gadsden AL • (256)546-1712 • (SL 1986 MDIV)

**FAJEN JOHN H REV** (314)966-5944
1406 Windward Ridge Dr Saint Louis MO 63127-1137 • MO • EM • (SL 1955 MDIV LITTD)

**FALE JOHN A REV** (402)379-0784
1710 Imperial Rd Norfolk NE 68701-2641 • jfale@frhs.org • NEB • Inst C • Nebraska Seward NE • (FW 1985 MDIV)

**FAMULINER LOREN E REV** (501)885-2323
RR 1 Box 96 Knoxville AR 72845-9003 • MDS • EM • (FW 1985)

**FANDREY JAMES E REV** (402)223-3544
1807 Washington St Beatrice NE 68310-2529 • NEB • Sn/Adm • St Paul Beatrice NE • (402)228-1540 • (FW 1980 MDIV MTH)

**FANGMEIER TIMOTHY J REV** (704)641-5811
PO Box 1877 Davidson NC 28036 • fang835@aol.com • SE • D Ex/S • Southeastern Alexandria VA • (SPR 1971 MDIV)

**FANNING ALLEN REV**
1004 N Chestnut Shelbyville IL 62565 • CI • EM • (SPR 1970)

**FANNING CORY A REV** (248)865-0809
4115 Meadow Way Bloomfield Hills MI 48301 • MI • Asst • Cross Christ Bloomfield Hills MI • (248)646-5886 • (FW 1997 MDIV)

**FARAGALLI DANIEL REV** (503)639-7422
19295 Marlin Ct Lake Oswego OR 97035-8049 • faragall2@aol.com • NOW • SP • Triump King Lake Oswego OR • (503)636-3436 • (CQ 1996 MDIV MAR)

**FARAH RONALD R REV** (248)645-0179
672 Westbourne Dr Bloomfield Hills MI 48301-3453 • rontalitha@aol.com • EN • SP • Ascen O Christ Beverly Hills MI • (248)644-8890 • (SL 1963 MA MDIV)

**FARDEN JOHN W REV** (605)925-7333
618 E 8th St Freeman SD 57029-2039 • mmfarden@gwtc.net • SD • SP • St Paul Freeman SD • (605)925-7219 • (SPR 1969 MDIV)

**FARINA CHRISTOPHER L REV** (773)427-5228
4861 W Berenice Ave Chicago IL 60641-3502 • NI • Assoc • St John Chicago IL • (773)736-1112 • (FW 1999 MDIV)

**FARMER STEVEN PAUL REV** (210)732-0831
3253 Hillcrest Dr Apt 37B San Antonio TX 78201 • hayreow@msn.com • TX • 06/1999 • (SL 1994 MDIV)

**FARNSWORTH KENNETH WALTER** (813)662-0937
2913 S John Moore Rd Brandon FL 33511-7139 • imlc@ij.net • FG • SP • Immanuel Brandon FL • (813)689-1787 • (FW 1992 MDIV)

**FAST THOMAS E REV**
C/O Saint Paul Lutheran Church 211 Budd St Fairmont MN 56031 • MNS • Assoc • St Paul Fairmont MN • (507)238-9491 • (SL 1988 MDIV)

**FASZHOLZ JOHN E REV** (573)859-6945
18338 Maries Rd - 308 Belle MO 65013-9606 • MO • EM • (SL 1958 MDIV MED)

**FASZHOLZ THOMAS O REV** (630)530-3717
200 Michigan Apt 227 Elmhurst IL 60126 • NI • SHS/C • Northern Illinois Hillside IL • (SL 1964 MDIV MA)

**FAULKNER DAVID ALAN REV** (314)752-5872
503 E Washington St Millstadt IL 62260-1231 • revfaulkner2000@yahoo.com • SI • SP • Trinity Millstadt IL • (618)476-3101 • (SL 1996 MDIV MA)

**FAUSEL CHARLES ALLEN REV** (502)228-2189
12109 Valley Dr Goshen KY 40026 • oslcfausel@aol.com • IN • Assoc • Our Savior Louisville KY • (502)426-1130 • (FW 1993 MDIV)

**FAUST WILLIAM J REV** (775)746-1875
1865 Quail Run Rd Reno NV 89523-1827 • CNH • EM • (SPR 1960)

**FECHNER DAVID W REV** (712)255-0746
3110 Norman Dr Sioux City IA 51104-2837 • dfech@aol.com • IW • D Ex/S • Iowa West Fort Dodge IA* • (SL 1971 MDIV)

**FECHNER RAYMOND W REV** (515)277-4302
3900 Lower Beaver Rd Des Moines IA 50310-4725 • IW • EM • * • (SL 1939)

**FEDDERSEN EARL P REV** (636)629-3690
1722 Day Dr Saint Clair MO 63077-2507 • IC$^3$FEDDEREP@LCMS.ORG • MO • S Ex/S • Missouri Saint Louis MO • (314)317-4550 • (SL 1968 MDIV)

**FEDDERSEN ELMER A REV** (673)712-7056
13733 Quay St NW Apt 107 Andover MN 55304-3647 • SI • EM • (SPR 1935)

**FEDERWITZ DALE G REV** (630)897-0660
PO Box 2050 Aurora IL 60507-2050 • DAFederwitz@compuserve.com • PSW • Asst • Emmaus Alhambra CA • (626)289-3664 • (FW 1995 MDIV)

**FEDERWITZ ROCKY L REV** (920)563-0040
344 Jones Ave Fort Atkinson WI 53538 • rckwtz@idcnet.com • NI • 12/1998 • (FW 1989 MDIV)

**FEEDER DAVID W REV** (970)667-9377
1213 Heather Dr Loveland CO 80537-8050 • davidfeeder@prodigy.net • RM • SP • Mount Olive Loveland CO • (970)669-7350 • (SPR 1969 MDIV)

**FEES ROSS W REV**
C/O Grace Lutheran Church 8091 Plank Rd Thomspon OH 44086 • rfees@compuserve.com • OH • SP • Grace Thompson OH • (216)298-3822 • (SL 1967 MDIV)

**FEHLAUER DONALD G REV** (920)563-4038
1503 Montclair Pl Fort Atkinson WI 53538-3102 • fehlauer@ticon.net • SW • D Miss • Peace Fort Atkinson WI • (920)563-8050 • (SL 1989 MDIV)

**FEHNER JAMES R REV** (702)254-6205
8237 Ocean Terrace Way Las Vegas NV 89128-7456 • PSW • EM • (SL 1949 MDIV)

**FEHNER WALTER M REV** (562)422-8196
1081 E 66th Way Long Beach CA 90805-1551 • PSW • EM • (SL 1937)

**FEHRMANN JOHN R REV** (612)427-8749
3601 Sunset Rd N Brooklyn Park MN 55443-1214 • MNS • Minnesota South Burnsville MN • (SPR 1976 MDIV)

**FEHRMANN WALTER E REV** (573)243-7859
1021 Cathy Dr Jackson MO 63755-1958 • fehrmann@showme.net • MO • EM • (SL 1945)

**FEHSKENS EDWARD H REV** (219)484-2713
1126 Northlawn Dr Fort Wayne IN 46805-2116 • powhite@juno.com • IN • Assoc • Holy Cross Fort Wayne IN • (219)483-3173 • (FW 1981 MDIV)

**FEICHO BRIAN REV**
3407 Maryville Rd Granite City IL 62040 • SI • SP • Concordia Granite City IL • (618)451-9925 • (FW 1984 MDIV)

**FEICKERT ROLAND K REV** (618)483-5571
5534 E 600th Ave Altamont IL 62411-9721 • CI • SP • Zion Altamont IL • (618)483-5571 • (SL 2000 MDIV)

**FEIERABEND JOHN O REV** (830)774-0162
112 Tenderfoot Trl Del Rio TX 78840-2327 • jfkfbfjf@hotmail.com • TX • SP • Grace Del Rio TX • (830)775-5797 • (SPR 1961)

**FEIERTAG THOMAS E REV** (414)673-2985
C/O Divine Savior Luth Church 3200 Highway K Hartford WI 53027-9206 • feiertag@nconnect.net • SW • SP • Divine Savior Hartford WI • (262)673-5140 • (FW 1978 MDIV)

**FELDMANN DUANE S REV** (630)428-4336
2508 Woodcliff Ct Lisle IL 60532 • dsfeldmann@aol.com • NI • Sn/Adm • Peace Lombard IL • (630)627-1101 • (CQ 1980 MDIV)

**FELDSCHER DANIEL R REV** (414)886-3825
8812 Mary Dr Racine WI 53406-3124 • danruthf@wi.net • SW • SP • Chapel Cross Racine WI • (414)886-4000 • (SL 1969 MDIV)

**FELDT LARRY L REV** (573)785-2952
529 W Relief St Poplar Bluff MO 63901-5203 • MO • SP • Zion Poplar Bluff MO • (573)785-3936 • (FW 1998 MDIV)

**FELLER ROBERT F REV** (520)531-0928
10191 N Hatteras Place Tucson AZ 85737-6934 • PSW • EM • (SL 1958 MSW)

**FELTEN VICTOR C REV** (219)477-5891
3303 Pines Village Cir # 129 Valparaiso IN 46383-2691 • EN • EM • (SL 1935 MDIV)

**FELTON CHARLES W REV** (219)749-7437
8816 Middleboro Pl New Haven IN 46774-1062 • cwfelton@juno.com • IN • EM • (SL 1949)

**FENKER WILLIAM G REV** (414)871-6602
6601 W Chambers St Milwaukee WI 53210-1330 • SW • SP • Walther Memorial Milwaukee WI • (414)444-4133 • (FW 1982 MDIV)

**FENSKE CRAIG B REV** (314)629-1533
221 Katherine Ln Saint Clair MO 63077-3412 • MO • SP • Holy Trinity Saint Clair MO • (636)629-3355 • (FW 1986 MDIV)

**FENTON EUGENE L REV** (909)887-2548
5536 Dahlia St San Bernardino CA 92407-2425 • nfen2000@juno.com • PSW • SP • Trinity San Bernardino CA • (909)882-2989 • (CQ 1978)

**FENTON JOHN W REV** (313)361-3433
4305 Military St Detroit MI 48210-2451 • zion@flash.net • EN • SP • Zion Detroit MI • (313)894-7450 • (FW 1989 MDIV STM)

**FERBER KENNETH E REV** (612)259-5393
2803 Island View Ct Saint Cloud MN 56301-5922 • pastorken@loveofchrist.org • MNN • SP • Love Of Christ Saint Cloud MN • (320)253-7453 • (SL 1981 MDIV)

**FERBER STEVEN E REV** (320)358-3418
PO Box 428 Rush City MN 55069 • MNN • D Miss • Living Branch North Branch MN • (612)674-5576 • (SL 1989)

**FERGUSON JACK D REV** (517)734-7855
PO Box 92 Hawks MI 49743-0092 • revferg@lhi.net • MI • SP • Holy Cross Onaway MI • (517)733-8412 • (SL 1972 MDIV MA)

**FERGUSON RANDALL L REV** (262)377-4152
N42W5493 Spring St Cedarburg WI 53012-2516 • randall.ferguson@cuw.edu • SW • SHS/C • South Wisconsin Milwaukee WI • (414)464-8100 • (SL 1987 MDIV MA PHD)

**FERGUSON WILLIAM A REV**
26410 Columbia St Hemet CA 92544-6299 • wb6cgs@aol.com • PSW • SP • St John Hemet CA • (909)925-7756 • (FW 1982 MDIV)

**FERRIER KENNETH M REV** (616)429-8995
1646 Roberts Dr Saint Joseph MI 49085-9512 • MI • Assoc • Christ Stevensville MI • (616)429-7222 • (SL 1983 MDIV)

**FERRY PATRICK T DR** (414)463-7397
10408 W Hillside Ave Wauwatosa WI 53222-2323 • patrick.ferry@cuw.edu • SW • SHS/C • South Wisconsin Milwaukee WI • (414)464-8100 • (FW 1987 MDIV PHD)

**FETT LARRY C REV** (712)546-4943
1531 3rd Ave SE Le Mars IA 51031-2764 • IW • SP • Grace Le Mars IA • (712)546-5516 • (FW 1983 MDIV)

**FEUERHAHN RONALD R REV** (314)863-4725
13 S Seminary Ter Clayton MO 63105-3013 • MO • SHS/C • Missouri Saint Louis MO • (314)317-4550 • (SL 1963 MDIV MPHIL PHD)

**FEUSSE DANIEL J REV** (402)485-2619
PO Box 114 Clearwater NE 68726-0114 • seelsorg@aol.com • NEB • SP • Concordia Clearwater NE • (402)485-2596 • (SL 1998 MDIV)

**FEY JOHN W C REV** (314)664-2054
2710 S Grand Blvd Apt 800 Saint Louis MO 63118-1009 • EN • EM • (SPR 1929)

**FIBELKORN JOHN E REV** (909)625-1324
380 W Baseline Rd Claremont CA 91711-1751 • fibelkorn@msn.com • PSW • SP • St Luke Claremont CA • (909)624-8898 • (SL 1962)

**FICHTELMAN DONALD R REV** (865)577-7993
807 Carter St Seymour TN 37865-5156 • MDS • EM • (SPR 1958)

**FICK BURNEAL REV** (630)851-0418
326 Jackson St Aurora IL 60505-4368 • revb-j-fick@worldnet.att.net • NI • SP • Emmanuel Aurora IL • (630)851-2200 • (SPR 1973 MDIV)

**FICKEL ERICH R REV** (217)387-2381
PO Box 67 Thawville IL 60968-0067 • CI • SP • St Peter Thawville IL* • (217)387-2381 • (FW 1999 MDIV)

**FICKEN JOCK E REV** (630)844-3378
C/O St Paul Luth Church 555 E Benton St Aurora IL 60505-4440 • jficken@saintpauls.net • NI • Sn/Adm • St Paul Aurora IL • (630)820-3450 • (SL 1982 MDIV DMIN)

**FICKENSCHER CARL C II DR** (219)452-3473
2 Martin Luther Dr Fort Wayne IN 46825-4996 • fickenschercc@mail.ctsfw.edu • IN • SHS/C • Indiana Fort Wayne IN • (FW 1984 MBA MDIV PHD)

**FICKENSCHER MICHAEL H REV** (915)943-7745
1305 S Kenneth Monahans TX 79756 • TX • SP • Zion Kermit TX* • (915)586-5236 • (SL 1998 MDIV)

**FICKENSCHER ROBERT F REV** (209)478-8651
4 W Banbury Dr Stockton CA 95207-5704 • pastorrff@aol.com • CNH • EM • * • (SL 1963 MDIV)

**FIECHTNER GREGORY K REV** (219)277-7501
51610 Trowbridge Ln South Bend IN 46637-1361 • IN • SP • St Paul South Bend IN • (219)271-1050 • (FW 1977 MDIV)

**FIEGE CALVIN R REV** (949)493-7307
3413 Via Loro San Clemente CA 92672-3534 • pswfiege@psw.lcms.org • PSW • EM • (SL 1948 MDIV)

**FIEGE SCOTT T DR** (712)882-1876
506 Walnut St Mapleton IA 51034 • fiege@pionet.net • IW • SP • St Matthew Mapleton IA • (712)882-1163 • (SL 1982 MDIV DMIN)

**FIEHLER DANIEL G REV** (804)589-6444
124 Jefferson Dr W Palmyra VA 22963-2110 • SE • EM • (SL 1942)

**FIELDING DAVID DR** (618)876-1625
3243 Westchester Dr Granite City IL 62040-5117 • SI • SP • Hope Granite City IL • (618)876-7568 • (SL 1970 STM MDIV MA THD)

**FIELDS THOMAS M REV** (303)756-2932
5680 E Bates Ave Denver CO 80222-7019 • tnjf@aol.com • RM • SP • Univ Hills Denver CO • (303)759-0161 • (SL 1972 MDIV)

**FIENE JOHN W REV** (317)873-9587
670 W Pine St Zionsville IN 46077-1727 • advent@iquest.net • IN • SP • Advent Zionsville IN • (317)873-6318 • (FW 1980 MDIV STM)

**FIENE LEONARD R REV** (812)988-8889
7544 Ogle Rd Freetown IN 47235 • lrfiene@earthlink.net • IN • EM • (SL 1955 STM MDIV)

**FIENEN DANIEL H REV** (217)446-4607
C/O Immanuel Lutheran Church 1930 N Bowman Ave Rd Danville IL 61834-7492 • dhfienen@hotmail.com • CI • SP • Immanuel Danville IL • (217)442-5675 • (FW 1978 MA MDIV)

**FIGULY JEROME C REV** (904)725-7017
702 D Orleans Ct Jacksonville FL 32211-7157 • FG • EM • (SPR 1957 MA)

**FIGUR NILO LUTERO REV** (512)323-0820
1705 Raven Dr Austin TX 78752 • TX • SHS/C • Texas Austin TX • (PA 1974 MA MDIV)

**FILBERT BERNHARD W REV** (231)938-0996
4448 Audubon Ln Traverse City MI 49686-3886 • MI • EM • (SL 1961 MDIV STM)

**FILTER EDWARD W REV** (517)647-6189
6824 Maynard Rd Portland MI 48875-9605 • MI • SP • St Andrew Portland MI • (517)647-4473 • (CQ 1989 MAR)

**FINCH ROBERT L REV** (507)645-2801
300 N Plum St Northfield MN 55057 • robertfinch@webtv.net • MNS • EM • (CQ 1993)

**FINCK RICHARD J REV** (703)775-9344
13179 Bradley Ln King George VA 22485-4309 • SE • SP • Peace King George VA* • (540)775-9131 • (SL 1975 MDIV)

**FINGERLIN HENRY F REV** (303)794-0401
2909 E Weaver Pl Littleton CO 80121-2961 • revhff@aol.com • RM • EM • * • (SL 1954)

**FINK ROBIN O REV** (715)924-4004
PO Box 173 Chetek WI 54728-0173 • NW • EM • * • (SPR 1961)

**FINK ROGER W REV** (410)561-2326
2615 Pot Spring Rd Lutherville MD 21093-2733 • SE • Asst • Holy Nativity Baltimore MD • (410)242-9441 • (SL 1960 MA MDIV PHD)

**FINK RONALD FRANK REV** (828)733-7161
3254 Land Harbor Newland NC 28657 • FG • EM • (SPR 1964 LLD)

**FINKE GREGORY A REV** (517)839-2818
985 E Gordonville Rd Midland MI 48640-8382 • MI • Sn/Adm • Messiah Midland MI • (517)835-7143 • (SL 1989 MDIV)

**FINKE NORMAN R REV** (972)937-5924
109 Noel St Waxahachie TX 75165-1333 • pastor@christtheking.net • TX • SP • Christ King Waxahachie TX • (972)938-1633 • (CQ 1992 MDIV)

**FINKE ROLAND G REV** (501)922-2451
31 La Granja Cir Hot Springs AR 71909-2652 • MDS • EM • (SPR 1934)

**FINNERN TERRY L REV** (320)763-4842
9311 Park Lane Dr NE Alexandria MN 56308 • zionluth@rea-alp.com • MNN • SP • Zion Alexandria MN • (320)763-4842 • (SPR 1974 MDIV)

**FINSTERLE GEORGE F REV** (804)493-0569
49 Grove Dr Montross VA 22520-8506 • SE • EM • (SPR 1965)

**FIRBY JERALD E REV** (712)642-2842
914 Longview Dr Missouri Valley IA 51555-1154 • jfirby@uswest.net • IW • SP • Immanuel Logan IA • (712)644-2384 • (FW 1986)

**FIRMINHAC SCOTT GARY REV** (307)686-1973
C/O Trinity Lutheran Church PO Box 485 Gillette WY 82717-0485 • cfirminhac@vcn.com • WY • Asst • Trinity Gillette WY • (307)682-4886 • (SL 1996 MDIV)

**FIRNHABER NORBERT A REV** (512)258-8577
11503 Dosshills Dr Austin TX 78750-2560 • ulc@uts.cc.utexas.edu • TX • Cmp P • University Austin TX • (512)472-5461 • (SL 1970 MDIV MA DMIN)

**FIRNHABER STUART F REV** (909)696-6913
40265 Via Francisco Murrieta CA 92562 • reverend40@aol.com • PSW • EM • (SPR 1969 MA MDIV)

**FISCHER ARNOLD E REV** (406)452-1682
1601 9th St NW Apt 102 Great Falls MT 59404-1843 • MT • EM • (SL 1957)

**FISCHER CARL O REV** (360)398-1650
1300 E Axton Rd Bellingham WA 98226-9755 • fischtime@aol.com • NOW • EM • (SL 1949)

**FISCHER DAVID A REV** (801)272-1420
5138 Gurene Dr Salt Lake City UT 84117-6904 • dfischer@redeemer-slc.org • RM • SP • Redeemer Salt Lake City UT • (801)467-4352 • (SPR 1974 MDIV)

**FISCHER DONALD G REV** (219)358-1907
38 Quayle Run Huntington IN 46750-9083 • donald@fwi.com • IN • EM • (CQ 1982)

**FISCHER GLENN EDWARD REV** (205)446-6432
660 Duncan Ln Leighton AL 35646-9611 • SO • SP • Christ King Muscle Shoals AL • (205)381-3560 • (FW 1991 MDIV)

**FISCHER JOHN G REV** (352)344-5942
3203 S Skyline Dr Inverness FL 34450-7427 • jjfisch@citrus.infi.net • FG • SP • First Inverness FL • (352)726-1637 • (SL 1968 MDIV)

**FISCHER KENNETH E REV** (636)207-6920
155 Romine Cir Ballwin MO 63011-3017 • MO • EM • (SL 1959)

**FISCHER RANDY JAMES REV** (618)251-2549
15 Magnolia East Alton IL 62024 • fishpond@juno.com • SI • SP • Messiah Alton IL • (618)465-5343 • (SL 1992 MDIV)

**FISCHER ROBERT F REV** (219)668-3635
200 W South St Angola IN 46703-1906 • bobvary@locl.net • IN • 12/1999 • (FW 1988 MDIV)

**FISCHER THOMAS A REV** (319)386-6594
1411 W 43rd St Davenport IA 52806-4521 • IE • EM • (SL 1965 MDIV)

**FISCHER THOMAS F REV** (517)689-5489
2730 E Bombay Rd Midland MI 48642-7380 • tfischer@journey.com • MI • SP • Our Savior Midland MI • (517)832-3667 • (SL 1983 MDIV MS)

**FISCHER WILLIAM C REV**
78-31 76th St Glendale NY 11385-7442 • AT • SP • St John Glendale NY • (718)847-3188 • (SL 1978)

**FISCHER WILLIAM E REV** (414)896-0144
1703 Sycamore Dr Waukesha WI 53189-7244 • SW • EM • (SL 1950 MA)

**FISH ROBIN D SR. REV** (573)374-2276
202 Laurie Hts Dr Laurie MO 65037-6101 • cuda@lakepc.com • MO • SP • Peace Camdenton MO • (573)873-6212 • (FW 1980 MDIV)

**FISH ROBIN D JR. REV** (816)858-3120
1147 Hampton Ln PO Box 2172 Platte City MO 64079 • MO • SP • Our Savior Platte City MO • (816)858-5255 • (FW 2000 MDIV)

**FISHER GARY L REV** (410)243-0933
4028 Deepwood Rd Baltimore MD 21218-1403 • SE • Sn/Adm • Our Saviour Baltimore MD • (410)235-9553 • (SL 1968 MDIV)

**FISHER JOSEPH M REV** (262)335-6736
616 Meadowbrook Dr West Bend WI 53090 • revjfish@nconnect.net • SW • SP • Pilgrim West Bend WI • (414)334-0375 • (FW 1994 MDIV)

**FISHER WALTER F REV** (254)675-2865
1507 W 9th St Apt C Clifton TX 76634-1834 • TX • EM • (SL 1947 STM)

**FITCH LA VERNE J REV** (979)743-4812
1104 Summit St Schulenburg TX 78956-1346 • fitchphd@cvtv.net • TX • EM • (SPR 1960 MAR MED PHD)

**FITCHETT CARL S V REV** (219)896-2344
4013 W 700 N Winamac IN 46996 • IN • SP • St Paul Winamac IN • (219)896-5090 • (CQ 1980)

**FITZ EDWIN V REV** (906)343-6760
332 Shot Point Dr Marquette MI 49855-9554 • NW • EM • (SL 1947 MA MED)

**FITZGERALD MICHAEL NEAL REV** (517)652-4858
9135 Bender Rd Frankenmuth MI 48734 • MI • Assoc • St Lorenz Frankenmuth MI • (517)652-6141 • (FW 1994 MDIV)

**FITZPATRICK DENNIS G REV**
7300 S Tratham Ct West Bloomfield MI 48322-4109 • celtic7@netzero.net • EN • SP • Shepherd King West Bloomfield MI • (248)626-2121 • (CQ 1984)

**FITZPATRICK PAUL J REV** (828)256-1530
2378 - 24th Street Ln NE Hickory NC 28601 • padrefitz@tware.net • SE • Assoc • St Stephen Hickory NC • (828)256-9865 • (CQ 1980 MDIV MS)

**FITZPATRICK ROBERT L REV** (734)953-3761
8951 Norman Ave Livonia MI 48150 • jansbob@juno.com • EN • D Ex/S • English Farmington MI • (SL 1970 MDIV)

**FJORDBOTTEN ALLAN H REV** (718)351-0866
C/O St Matthew Luth Church 96 Alter Ave Staten Island NY 10304-3904 • AT • SP • St Matthew Staten Island NY • (718)351-0866 • (SL 1979 MDIV)

**FLACHSBART JACK B REV** (541)929-7970
PO Box 36 Philomath OR 97370-0036 • jjrevtek@cs.com • NOW • SP • Peace Philomath OR • (541)929-5504 • (SL 1974 MDIV)

**FLAMMANN WILLIAM H REV** (716)388-9658
19 Edenfield Rd Penfield NY 14526-1975 • pstrwhf@rochester.rr.com • EA • SP • Faith Rochester NY • (716)381-3970 • (CQ 1983 MDIV)

**FLAMME JOHN A REV**
305 N Howard Rd Greenwood IN 46142-3836 • IN • Assoc • Concordia Greenwood IN • (317)881-4477 • (FW 1992 MDIV)

**FLANNERY MICHAEL L REV** (719)495-9054
12745 N Holmes Colorado Springs CO 80908 • RM • Sn/Adm • Holy Cross Colorado Springs CO • (719)596-0661 • (SL 1976 MDIV)

**FLANSCHA MARVIN L REV** (515)483-2753
1948 Durham Ave State Center IA 50247-9692 • IE • SP • St John State Center IA • (515)483-2578 • (SPR 1966)

**FLATH RICHARD E REV** (360)568-6580
1425 Lakeview Drive Snohomish WA 98290-1845 • NOW • SP • Zion Snohomish WA • (360)568-2700 • (SL 1976 MDIV)

**FLEISCHFRESSER DOUGLAS H REV** (217)234-4582
C/O Immanuel Lutheran Church 902 Cleveland Ave Charleston IL 61920-3441 • packiskewl@aol.com • CI • SP • Immanuel Charleston IL • (217)345-3008 • (SL 1987 MDIV)

**FLEISCHHAUER HAROLD L REV** (832)467-0320
15722 Honolulu Houston TX 77040 • hlf@hal-pc.org • TX • Sn/Adm • St Andrew Houston TX • (713)468-9565 • (SL 1964 MDIV)

**FLEISCHMANN JOHN GEORGE REV** (516)874-3725
119 Ocean Ave Center Moriches NY 11935 • 75413.424@compuserve.com • AT • SP • Christ East Moriches NY • (631)878-2277 • (SL 1986 MDIV)

**FLEISCHMANN THOMAS GERALD REV** (920)892-2211
N5451 State Rd 57 Plymouth WI 53073-4235 • SW • Inst C • South Wisconsin Milwaukee WI • (414)464-8100 • (FW 1993 MDIV)

**FLEMING DAVID C REV** (616)554-0426
4545 Meadowlawn Dr SE Kentwood MI 49512-5413 • davidflemingl@juno.com • MI • SP • Our Savior Grand Rapids MI • (616)949-0710 • (FW 1986 MDIV)

**FLENTGEN RONALD B REV** (913)782-6279
1102 W Wabash Ter Olathe KS 66061-3928 • rlcpastor@planetkc.com • KS • SP • Redeemer Olathe KS • (913)764-2359 • (SPR 1964 MDIV)

**FLESCH WILLIAM E REV** (507)452-2560
720 49th Ave Winona MN 55987-1229 • redeluth@rconnect.com • MNS • SP • Redeemer Winona MN • (507)452-3828 • (SPR 1972 MA MDIV)

**FLETCHER DAVID G L REV** (618)622-0259
179 W Church St Venedy IL 62214-0586 • SI • SP • St Salvator Venedy IL* • (618)824-6366 • (CQ 1984 MDIV)

**FLETCHER RONALD A REV** (252)522-1392
1204 Meadowood Dr Kinston NC 28501-2140 • fletch7@icomnet.com • SE • SP • Faith Kinston NC • (252)523-6033 • (SL 1964 MA)

**FLO STEVEN L REV** (636)586-7775
5555 Paw Paw Ln De Soto MO 63020-4754 • sflo@usmo.com • MO • SP • Grace De Soto MO • (636)586-2487 • (FW 1990 MDIV)

**FLOHRS ROBERT J REV** (480)854-8645
2957 E Nance Mesa AZ 85213 • beachrev@aol.com • PSW • SP • St Luke Mesa AZ • (480)969-4414 • (FW 1985 MDIV)

**FLOR EUGENIO W REV** (954)747-1641
9969 Nob Hill Ct Sunrise FL 33351-4614 • FG • 10/1990 10/1999 • (PA 1973)

**FLORES GILBERTO BRIONES REV** (915)447-6759
1212 S Park St Pecos TX 79772-5717 • TX • D Miss • Texas Austin TX • (CQ 1996)

**FLORES JOSE REV** (402)926-2748
Zion Ev Lutheran Church So 4001 Q St Omaha NE 68107-2462 • pastorjose@compuserve.com • NEB • Sn/Adm • Zion Omaha NE • (402)731-0743 • (CQ 1996)

**FLORSCHUETZ DUANE W REV** (512)868-2621
194 Whispering Wind Dr Georgetown TX 78628-4506 • duanewf@email.msn.com • TX • EM • (SPR 1971 MDIV)

**FLORY MARK S REV** (812)663-9293
1036 E Israel St Greensburg IN 47240-2404 • IN • SP • Holy Trinity Greensburg IN • (812)663-8192 • (FW 1983 MDIV)

**FLOYD DAVID A REV** (805)995-2432
25 13th St Cayucos CA 93430 • surfingpastor@hotmail.com • CNH • 09/2000 • (FW 1997 MDIV)

**FLUECHTLING DUANE REV** (815)622-3076
614 W 16th St Sterling IL 61081-2230 • flick@cin.net • NI • SP • Messiah Sterling IL • (815)625-2284 • (CQ 1981 MDIV)

**FLUEGGE GLENN KEVIN** (760)749-0858
29317 Twain Way Valley Center CA 92082 • PSW • D Miss • Pacific Southwest Irvine CA • (949)854-3232 • (CQ 2000)

**FLUEGGE WILTON H REV** (810)781-9398
16665 Shale Ct Macomb Twp MI 48042 • MI • EM • (SPR 1946)

**FOARD HOWARD A REV**
5448 Garden Ave Pennsauken NJ 08109-4708 • NI • EM • (GB 1949 MED DD)

**FODOR PATRICK S REV** (517)339-9367
5802 Montebello Ave Haslett MI 48840-8208 • jndamascus333@cs.com • MI • SP • Ascension East Lansing MI • (517)337-9703 • (SC 1993 MDIV)

**FOELBER J THOMAS REV**
9701 Harding Ave Parkville MD 21234-2662 • jtfs@erols.com • SE • SP • St James of Overlea Baltimore MD • (410)668-0158 • (FW 1990 MAR)

**FOELBER PAUL F REV** (407)366-9884
1376 Haven Dr Oviedo FL 32765-5202 • paulfoelber@msn.com • FG • EM • (SL 1950 PHD)

**FOELBER ROBERT E REV** (562)596-5409
1740 Sunningdale Rd 16 H Seal Beach CA 90740 • PSW • EM • (SL 1947 MA)

**FOERSTER BARRY C REV** (626)852-6735
1181 E Hollyvale #1 Azusa CA 91702 • PSW • SP • Faith Pasadena CA • (626)351-5413 • (SPR 1967)

**FOGLE WILLIAM F REV**
720 7th Ave NE #A16 Hickroy NC 28601-3959 • SE • EM • (SPR 1960)

**FOLEY JAMES R REV** (773)221-6151
9031 S Houston Ave Chicago IL 60617-4312 • NI • SP • Timothy Chicago IL • (773)874-7333 • (SL 1969 MDIV)

**FOLLE RONALD G REV** (702)656-9639
5028 Drifting Creek Ave Las Vegas NV 89130-1552 • PSW • SP • Lamb Of God Las Vegas NV • (702)645-4998 • (SPR 1968 MDIV)

**FOLLETT MARK CLIFTON REV** (402)866-6601
C/O Immanuel Lutheran Church RR 2 Box 69 Sterling NE 68443-9733 • NEB • SP • Immanuel Sterling NE • (402)866-6661 • (SL 1997 MDIV)

**FOLWACZNY NORBERT REV** (216)521-5600
1433 Arthur Ave Lakewood OH 44107-3801 • stpaullkwd@aol.com • OH • SP • St Paul Lakewood OH • (216)521-5610 • (FW 1977 MDIV)

**FONDOW DONALD J REV** (218)732-9236
18626 Estate Dr Park Rapids MN 56470-9803 • MNN • Sn/Adm • St John Park Rapids MN • (218)732-9783 • (SL 1979 MDIV)

**FONTAINE RAYMOND A REV** (219)981-4235
5322 W 300 North La Porte IN 46350 • rfontain@iunhaw1.iun.indiana.edu • NI • EM • (SL 1969 MDIV MA DMIN)

**FOOTE ROBERT M REV** (607)273-5169
129 Whitetail Dr Ithaca NY 14850-9482 • trinity@baka.com • EA • SP • Trinity Ithaca NY • (607)273-9017 • (FW 1985 MDIV)

**FOREMAN CURTIS L REV**
PO Box 155 Garrison MN 56450-0155 • cforeman@wcta.net • MNN • SP • Shep Of Lake Garrison MN • (320)692-4581 • (SPR 1966 MDIV)

**FORKE TERRY R REV** (406)892-4074
C/O Our Redeemer Luth Church PO Box 2005 Columbia Falls MT 59912-2005 • MT • SP • Our Redeemer Columbia Falls MT • (406)892-4074 • (SL 1982 STM)

**FORREST JESSIE ALLEN REV**
C/O Trinity Lutheran Church 74 Forest Ave Glen Cove NY 11542-2111 • AT • SP • Trinity Glen Cove NY • (516)676-1340 • (SL 1995 MDIV)

**FORSS DON N REV** (920)528-8478
N3379 Scenic Dr Cascade WI 53011 • forss@excel.net • SW • EM • (CQ 1986 MST)

**FORSS ERIC CHARLES REV** (517)545-0245
515 W Highland Rd Apt E7 Howell MI 48843-1173 • EN • SP • Immanuel Howell MI • (517)548-2066 • (CQ 1995 MDIV MA)

**FORTKAMP GARY D REV** (217)644-2226
512 S Walnut RR 1 Box 38 Strasburg IL 62465 • stpaullcms@one-eleven.net • CI • SP • St Paul Strasburg IL • (217)644-2661 • (SPR 1966)

**FOSS DAVID K REV** (219)485-6874
7104 Tanbark Ln Fort Wayne IN 46835-1847 • IN • 03/1993 03/2000 • (FW 1991 MDIV)

**FOSS RICHARD A REV** (310)510-2323
326 Sunny Ln PO Box 1505 Avalon CA 90704-1505 • rfoss@ispchannel.com • PSW • Asst • Our Savior Arcadia CA • (626)447-7690 • (SL 1984 MDIV)

**FOSSE KENNETH REV** (732)792-1638
C/O St Thomas Lutheran Church 203 Taylors Mill Rd Manalapan NJ 07726-3201 • frskull@aol.com • NJ • SP • St Thomas Manalapan NJ • (908)431-3344 • (CQ 1980 MDIV)

**FOSTER EDWIN M REV** (301)549-3211
15105 Cedar Tree Dr Burtonsville MD 20866-1152 • emfoster2@yahoo.com • SE • Assoc • St Andrew Silver Spring MD • (301)942-6531 • (SL 1981 MDIV)

**FOUND PHILIP JONATHAN REV** (308)254-3062
11991 Road 6 Sidney NE 69162-4101 • WY • SP • Trinity Sidney NE • (308)254-3062 • (CQ 1996)

**FOUNTAIN DOUGLAS E DR** (407)969-0896
261 Ohio Rd Lake Worth FL 33467-4821 • drdougfountain@netscape.net • FG • SP • Epiphany Lake Worth FL • (407)968-3627 • (FW 1983 MDIV PHD)

**FOUST PAUL J DR** (407)977-1297
1303 Haven Dr Oviedo FL 32765-5203 • revgoodnews@aol.com • FG • EM • (SPR 1945 DD)

**FOUST PAUL MARTIN REV** (407)889-5958
6430 Lakeville Rd Orlando FL 32818-8817 • FG • SP • Zion Orlando FL • (407)293-5616 • (SPR 1973 MTH)

**FOX CHARLES A REV** (909)902-9067
2334 Parkview Ln Chino Hills CA 91709-1767 • pastorchip@aol.com • PSW • D Miss • Loving Savior Chines Chino Hills CA* • (909)597-5771 • (SL 1981 MDIV STM)

**FRAHM JOHN A III REV**
12716 N Allen Rd PO Box 182 Dunlap IL 61525-0182 • CI • SP • Epiphany Dunlap IL • (309)243-5957 • (SC 1998 MDIV)

**FRAHM JOHN H REV** (512)255-8378
3904 Woodchester Ln Austin TX 78727-2936 • jhfrahm@texas.net • TX • SHS/C • Texas Austin TX • (SPR 1976 MS MDIV PHD)

**FRAHM RUSSELL G REV** (321)454-3477
280 E Merritt Island Merritt Island FL 32953 • faithmi@faithcaring.org • FG • SP • Faith Merritt Island FL • (321)452-4080 • (SL 1982 MAR PHD)

**FRAKER DONALD D REV** (830)620-4723
1107 River Rock New Braunfels TX 78130-2410 • revdfraker@nbtx.com • TX • SP • Cross New Braunfels TX • (830)625-3666 • (SL 1983 MDIV)

**FRANCIS GRANT REV** (509)754-0154
500 D St SE Ephrata WA 98823-2242 • francis6@2fast.net • NOW • SP • Our Savior Ephrata WA • (509)754-3468 • (SL 1983 MDIV)

**FRANCIS RONALD R REV**
9615 Hidden Village Pl Fort Wayne IN 46835-9348 • R.L.Francis@fwi.com • IN • SP • St Paul New Haven IN • (219)749-5444 • (SL 1984 MDIV MS PHD)

**FRANCK ROBERT C REV** (218)724-1969
515 W Saint Marie St Duluth MN 55811-2417 • revfranck@aol.com • MNN • Assoc • Mount Olive Duluth MN • (218)724-2500 • (FW 1991 MDIV)

**FRANCKOWIAK MICHAEL S REV** (559)594-4270
400 Sequoia Dr Exeter CA 93221-1232 • mbsfranck@juno.com • CNH • SP • Trinity Exeter CA • (559)592-4070 • (SL 1999 MDIV)

**FRANK ARNOLD W REV** (480)941-1149
7013 E Willetta St Scottsdale AZ 85257-3319 • awalfran@juno.com • EN • Assoc • Christ Phoenix AZ • (602)955-4830 • (SL 1968 MDIV)

**FRANK DONALD E REV** (219)833-6138
1100 Lane 301 Lake George Fremont IN 46737-8921 • IN • EM • (SL 1955)

**FRANK PAUL L REV** (503)252-8174
3601 NE 141st Ave Portland OR 97230-3625 • NOW • EM • (SL 1949)

**FRANK ROBERT A REV** (308)882-5170
RR 2 Box 3G Imperial NE 69033-9701 • revraf@chase3000.com • NEB • Sn/Adm • Zion Imperial NE • (308)882-5655 • (FW 1986 MDIV)

**FRANK VICTOR L REV** (281)355-8128
2410 Sweetgum Hill Ct Spring TX 77388-5446 • TX • SP • Our Shepherd Crosby TX • (281)324-2422 • (SPR 1975 MDIV)

**FRANKE GILBERT A REV** (512)584-2142
1003 Juniper Ave Bishop TX 78343-1835 • bishopaul@juno.com • TX • SP • St Paul Bishop TX • (361)584-2778 • (SL 1972 MDIV)

**FRANKE MATTHEW P REV** (702)652-2950
99 ABW/HC 4302 N Washington Blvd Nellis AFB NV 89191-7031 • matthew.franke@nellis.af.mil • MNS • M Chap • Minnesota South Burnsville MN • (SL 1996 MDIV)

**FRANZEN NORMAN N REV** (714)996-6934
601 W Santa Fe Ave #H60 Placentia CA 92870-5850 • nfranzen@stpaulsorg.org • PSW • Assoc • St Paul Orange CA • (714)637-2640 • (WBS 1962 MDIV)

**FRANZEN ROGER L REV**
3441 Dupont Ave S Apt #303 Minneapolis MN 55408-4072 • MNS • Tchr • Luth HS Of Greater M Bloomington MN • (612)854-0224 • (SPR 1976 MDIV)

**FRANZMEIER ALVIN H REV** (281)353-7459
1922 Long Shadow Ln Spring TX 77388-6225 • franzie3@swbell.net • TX • SP • Living Word The Woodlands TX • (281)363-4860 • (SL 1957 MDIV MTH DREL)

**FRANZMEIER DAVID B REV**
2965 Juniper St S Cambridge MN 55008 • MNN • SP • Joy Cambridge MN • (612)689-4355 • (SL 1968 MDIV)

**FRANZMEIER WILBUR C REV**
6 E Marie Ave D W St PAUL MN 55118 • dgfwcf@juno.com • MNS • EM • (SL 1950 MDIV)

**FRAZELL JAY W REV** (630)766-9218
C/O Zion Luth Church 865 S Church Rd Bensenville IL 60106-2904 • NI • 08/2000 • (SL 1969 MDIV)

**FRAZEN SIDNEY J REV** (708)246-5832
111 Acacia Dr Apt 401 Indianhead Park IL 60525-9061 • NI • EM • (CQ 1983)

**FRAZIER LARRY REV** (708)849-8490
14832 State St Dolton IL 60419-1519 • NI • SP • Resurrection Chicago IL • (773)928-6311 • (CQ 1994)

**FREDERICH CLIFFORD M REV** (847)310-0107
2255 Briar Ct Hoffman Estates IL 60195-2166 • cfrederich@aol.com • NI • Assoc • St John Elgin IL • (847)741-0814 • (SL 1981 MDIV MST)

**FREDERICK CLARKE E REV** (319)472-2898
1503 H Ave Vinton IA 52349-1555 • czfred@severewx.com • IE • SP • Trinity Vinton IA • (319)472-5571 • (SPR 1973 MDIV)

**FREDERICK PARKE G REV** (734)665-7912
2871 Aurora St Ann Arbor MI 48105-1414 • pfrederick@stpaul.pvt.k12.mi.us • MI • Sn/Adm • St Paul Ann Arbor MI • (734)665-9117 • (SPR 1959 MDIV)

**FREDERICKSEN WAYNE P REV** (319)732-2177
1010 Maurer St Wilton IA 52778-9563 • iafreds@netins.net • IE • SP • Zion Wilton IA • (319)732-3651 • (SL 1991 MDIV)

**FREDERICKSON BRUCE G REV** (763)786-2723
7571 Brigadoon Pl NE Minneapolis MN 55432-3625 • brucef6300@aol.com • MNS • Sn/Adm • Messiah Mounds View MN • (612)784-1786 • (SPR 1972 MDIV)

**FREDERICKSON DAVID REV** (507)534-4160
45 W Broadway Plainview MN 55964-1238 • MNS • Sn/Adm • Immanuel Plainview MN • (507)534-3700 • (SL 1987)

**FREDERKING MARTIN A REV**
4517 S Cooper Pl Tampa FL 33611-2107 • FG • EM • (SL 1952)

**FREED JOHN H REV** (713)462-7597
9730 Railton St Houston TX 77080-1237 • jr9730@msn.com • TX • EM • (SL 1959)

**FREED JOHN W REV** (410)442-2921
870 Windriver Dr Sykesville MD 21784-5502 • annfreed@smart.net • SE • Southeastern Alexandria VA • (SL 1951 MA MDIV)

**FREEMAN DANIEL L REV** (406)285-4649
PO Box 850 Three Forks MT 59752-0850 • MT • SP • Grace Three Forks MT* • (406)285-6865 • (SL 1999 MDIV)

**FREIBERG MARC L REV** (219)962-8056
29 Cleveland Ave Hobart IN 46342-1006 • IN • Asst • Trinity Hobart IN • (219)942-2589 • (FW 2000 MDIV)

**FREIMUTH JEROME A REV** (715)654-5738
266 S 3rd St Dorchester WI 54425-9562 • jayfreimuth@hotmail.com • NW • SP • St Peter Dorchester WI • (715)654-5055 • (SL 1979 MDIV)

**FREITAG ALFRED J DR** (818)241-0252
329 E Mountain St Glendale CA 91207-1339 • ajfreitag@aol.com • PSW • EM • (CQ 1969 MA EDD)

**FREITAG JOHN PAUL REV** (865)769-2581
9705 Cortez Dr Knoxville TN 37923 • jpfreitag@mindspring.com • MDS • 11/1997 06/2000 • (SL 1970 MDIV)

**FREMDER ALFRED L REV** (480)473-0401
22036 N 44th Pl Phoenix AZ 85050-6847 • MO • EM • (SL 1945 MA PHD)

**FREMDER MANFRED W REV** (219)563-3408
541 Bond St Wabash IN 46992-2107 • IN • SP • Zion Wabash IN • (219)563-1886 • (FW 1990 MDIV)

**FREMER JOSEPH REV** (616)897-5790
424 N Hudson Lowell MI 49331 • goodshep@iserv.net • MI • SP • Good Shepherd Lowell MI • (616)897-8307 • (SL 1982 MDIV)

**FRENCH DAVID RAY REV** (765)474-2525
2301 Manitoba Dr Lafayette IN 47909 • IN • Asst • St James Lafayette IN • (765)423-1616 • (FW 1992 MDIV)

**FRENK ERDMANN A REV** (407)332-6196
104 Marla Ln Longwood FL 32750-2729 • egfrenk@c.s.com • FG • EM • (SL 1949 STM MDIV)

**FRERICHS DONALD L REV** (503)760-4583
2912 SE 141st Ave Portland OR 97236-2604 • calvary@integrityonline.com • NOW • SP • Calvary Portland OR • (503)774-8335 • (SPR 1968)

**FRERICHS PAUL CHRISTIAN REV** (541)850-6651
5507 Bel Aire Dr Klamath Falls OR 97603 • zionpastor@juno.com • NOW • SP • Zion Klamath Falls OR • (541)884-6793 • (SL 1994 MDIV)

**FRERKING HORACE R REV** (816)254-3769
C/O Mrs John Kuddes 12009 Oak Ridge Rd Independence MO 64052-2827 • MO • EM • (SL 1928)

**FRERKING JOHN L REV** (561)848-4737
Faith Lutheran Church 555 US Highway 1 North Palm Beach FL 33408-4901 • efrerking@sprintmail.com • FG • Sn/Adm • Faith North Palm Beach FL • (561)848-4737 • (SL 1967 MDIV MDIV)

**FRERKING KENNETH L REV** (573)446-1306
1703 Apple Valley Ct Columbia MO 65202-3873 • MO • EM • (SL 1957 MDIV MA PHD)

**FRERKING ROBERT D REV** (813)779-8776
3416 Pyrite Dr Zephyrhills FL 33540 • SE • EM • (SL 1961 MDIV MA)

**FRESE FRANK A REV** (209)951-3524
PO Box 99128 Stockton CA 95209-0128 • CNH • EM • (SL 1936)

**FRESE KENNETH WALTER REV** (310)398-3741
3778 Ashwood Ave Los Angeles CA 90066-3516 • frstluthrn@aol.com • PSW • SP • First Venice CA • (310)821-2740 • (SL 1969 MDIV)

**FREUDENBURG ALLEN P REV** (501)884-3824
148 Pine Hill Rd Fairfield Bay AR 72088 • alfreud@juno.com • MDS • EM • (CQ 1988 MAR LITTD)

**FREUDENBURG GERALD V REV** (309)691-5022
5118 N Merrimac Ave Peoria IL 61614-4658 • tgltyty2@aol.com • CI • EM • (SL 1959 MST)

**FREY DAVID F REV** (217)682-5457
RR 1 Box 23E Stewardson IL 62463-9713 • CI • EM • (CQ 1987)

**FRIAS BARTOLOME RAFAEL REV** (305)238-1408
21015 SW 125th PL Miami FL 33177 • FG • EM • (CQ 1993)

**FRICK E TIMOTHY REV** (847)639-6397
C/O Holy Cross Luth Church 2107 Three Oaks Rd Cary IL 60013-1626 • etfrick@mc.net • NI • Assoc • Holy Cross Cary IL • (847)639-1702 • (SPR 1974 MDIV)

**FRICK MICHAEL A REV** (972)398-9837
3108 Oswego Dr Plano TX 75074 • mafrick@faith.plano.tx.us • TX • Asst • Faith Plano TX • (972)423-7447 • (CQ 1989 MDIV)

**FRICKE GARY H REV** (303)838-2528
PO Box 635 Bailey CO 80421-0635 • pasnurse@bwn.net • RM • SP • Shep Rockies Bailey CO • (303)838-2161 • (FW 1980 MDIV BCHE)

**FRICKE MILTON E REV** (808)877-5412
783 Makalii St Kahului HI 96732-2618 • CNH • SP • Emmanuel Kahului HI* • (808)877-3037 • (SL 1968 MDIV)

**FRIEDMEYER A NORMAN REV** (402)296-2570
1111 Earls Ct Plattsmouth NE 68048-1329 • nandjfried@comweb.net • NEB • SP • First Plattsmouth NE • (402)296-2832 • (FW 1981 MDIV)

**FRIEDRICH BRIAN L REV** (402)643-4380
503 Bader Ave Seward NE 68434-1127 • bfriedrich@seward.cune.edu • NEB • SHS/C • Nebraska Seward NE • (SL 1986 MDIV)

**FRIEDRICH CARL H REV** (612)442-4785
433 W 5th St Waconia MN 55387-1744 • MNN • EM • (SL 1937 MDIV)

**FRIEDRICH HENRY W REV** (515)295-2387
121 S Finn Dr Algona IA 50511 • ehfried@ncn.net • ND • EM • (SL 1953)

**FRIEDRICH MARK D REV** (715)341-7298
180 Black Forest Dr Plover WI 54467 • mdf@coredcs.com • NW • Assoc • St Paul Stevens Point WI • (715)344-5664 • (SL 1986 MDIV)

**FRIEDRICH MARTIN W REV** (504)340-1254
3804 N Deerwood Dr Harvey LA 70058-2123 • SO • Asst • Salem Gretna LA • (504)367-5126 • (SL 1949 MDIV)

**FRIEDRICH ORVAL REV** (515)393-2427
217 Grove St Elma IA 50628-8021 • MO • EM • (WBS 1968)

**FRIEDRICH PAUL L REV** (218)583-2788
710 Holden Ave Henning MN 56551-9601 • MNN • EM • (SL 1940)

**FRIEDRICH ROBERT A REV** (320)568-2551
C/O Trinity Luth Church RR 1 Box 133 Bellingham MN 56212-9749 • rafirene@info-link.net • MNN • SP • Trinity Bellingham MN* • (320)568-2551 • (SL 1962)

**FRIEDRICH RONALD E REV** (972)271-1408
234 Trailridge Dr Garland TX 75043-2334 • r.friedrich@juno.com • TX • 04/1998 04/2000 • * • (SL 1976 MDIV)

**FRIEDRICH WILLIAM E REV** (618)684-2699
917 Roberta Dr Murphysboro IL 62966-2914 • SI • EM • * • (SL 1955 MDIV)

**FRIEDRICHS DAVID W REV** (313)885-3134
528 Cadieux Rd Grosse Pointe MI 48230-1509 • 105006.430@compuserve.com • MI • EM • * • (SPR 1952 PHD)

**FRIEDRICHS GALEN M REV**
210 Poplar St Lamar MO 64759 • MO • SP • Grace Lamar MO • (417)682-2257 • (FW 1993 MDIV)

**FRIEDRICHS ROLAND G REV** (281)320-0386
17314 Granberry Gate Dr Tomball TX 77375 • TX • EM • (SPR 1954)

**FRIEDRICHS WALDEMAR J REV** (913)271-6266
3036 SW Lincolnshire Rd Topeka KS 66614-4408 • KS • Assoc • Prince Of Peace Topeka KS • (785)271-0808 • (CQ 1999)

**FRIEDRICHSMEYER EUGENE O REV** (314)918-8181
619 Deerhurst Saint Louis MO 63119 • SI • EM • (CQ 1994 MED)

**FRIESE FOREST F REV** (310)772-2675
22325 Yale St St Clair Shrs MI 48081-2039 • MI • EM • (SPR 1941)

**FRINCKE HERMAN R REV** (716)385-8569
72 Greenwood Pk Pittsford NY 14534 • 73072.151@compuserve.com • EA • EM • (SL 1936 DD)

**FRINCKE KARL A REV** (219)486-7486
3231 Solitude Pl Fort Wayne IN 46815-6225 • KFrincke.aol.com • IN • Sn/Adm • Concordia Fort Wayne IN • (219)422-2429 • (SL 1975 MDIV)

**FRITH MARK T REV**
C/O Beautiful Savior Lutheran 13145 S Blackbob Rd Olathe KS 66062-1417 • mtfrith@yahoo.com • KS • Concordia Fort Wayne IN • (219)422-2429 • (SL 1990 MDIV)

**FRITSCH BRYAN REV** (920)748-2242
526 Mayparty Dr Ripon WI 54971-1030 • SW • SP • Messiah Ripon WI • (414)748-3882 • (SL 1985 MDIV)

**FRITSCH LYLE H REV** (616)471-4874
9030 N Main St Berrien Springs MI 49103-1414 • MI • Sn/Adm • Trinity Berrien Springs MI • (616)473-1811 • (FW 1982 MDIV)

**FRITSCHE JOEL P REV** (307)632-2580
335 Storey Blvd #2 Cheyenne WY 82009 • WY • Assoc • Our Savior Cheyenne WY • (307)632-2580 • (SL 2000 MDIV)

**FRITZ JEFFREY M REV** (810)296-7285
32500 Kelly Rd Roseville MI 48066-1060 • MI • SP • Bethlehem Roseville MI • (810)777-9128 • (SL 1968 MDIV)

**FRITZ JOHN A REV** (708)898-7782
1541 Reckinger Rd Aurora IL 60505-1625 • NI • SP • Hope Aurora IL • (630)898-6754 • (SL 1984 MDIV)

**FRITZ JOHN D REV** (281)493-5552
11306 Pecan Creek Dr Houston TX 77043-4614 • erfjdf@aol.com • TX • EM • (SL 1950 STM MDIV)

**FRITZ MARVIN R REV** (815)654-2631
3269 City View Dr Rockford IL 61101-9523 • NI • EM • (SL 1948)

**FRITZ RODNEY D REV** (785)337-2665
C/O Trinity Lutheran Church 2942 27th Rd Hanover KS 66945-8885 • KS • SP • Trinity Hanover KS • (785)337-2665 • (SL 1980 MDIV)

**FRITZE ANDREW J REV** (316)221-0102
1320 Wheat Rd Winfield KS 67156-4704 • KS • EM • (SL 1952)

**FRIZELLE THOMAS A REV** (907)688-2157
C/O Our Redeemer Luth Ch PO Box 670150 Chugiak AK 99567 • frizelle@alaska.net • NOW • SP • Our Redeemer Chugiak AK • (907)688-2157 • (FW 1995 MDIV)

**FROBE ROGER P REV** (428)265-2271
209 Stratford Way Signal Mountain TN 37377-2522 • charissima@mindspring.com • MDS • EM • (SL 1963 STM MDIV)

**FROEHLICH CHARLES D REV** (708)366-5542
7229 Division St River Forest IL 60305-1221 • NI • EM • (SL 1955 STM)

**FROEHLICH CHARLES W REV** (516)462-5998
18 Candlewood Path Dix Hills NY 11746-5304 • cwkjf@aol.com • AT • SP • St Luke Dix Hills NY • (516)499-8656 • (SL 1974 MDIV)

**FROEHLICH RONALD G REV** (414)462-5510
9502 W Ruby Ave Wauwatosa WI 53225-4813 • rgfjaf@gateway.net • NE • EM • (SL 1956)

**FROELICH KEVIN M REV** (320)839-3446
315 Jackson Ave Ortonville MN 56278 • froelichkm@hotmail.com • MNN • 06/1999 • (SL 1982 MDIV)

**FROH CHARLES E REV** (650)349-8265
808 W Hillsdale Ave San Mateo CA 94403 • CNH • SP • Grace San Mateo CA • (650)345-9068 • (SL 1977 MDIV)

**FROHM MONTE E REV** (703)787-9619
11612 Chapel Cross Way Reston VA 20194-1242 • pastor@goodshepherd-lutheran.org • SE • Sn/Adm • Good Shepherd Reston VA • (703)437-5020 • (SL 1968 MDIV)

**FROST WAYNE K REV**
11750 W 930 S Columbus IN 47201 • IN • SP • St Peter Columbus IN* • (812)372-1571 • (SL 2000 MDIV)

**FRUSTI JONATHAN M REV**
Chaplain USS Coronado AGF 11 FPO AP 96662-3330 Newport RI 96662-3330 • frusti.jonathan@chaplain.navy.mil • MNS • M Chap • Minnesota South Burnsville MN • (FW 1980 MDIV THM)

**FRUSTI MARK A REV** (630)837-4342
26 Ridge Cir Streamwood IL 60107-1751 • NI • Asst • Grace Streamwood IL • (630)289-3996 • (FW 1983 MDIV)

**FRUSTI MARTIN J REV** (906)864-3031
1504 7th St Menominee MI 49858-2814 • Revmarty@cybrzn.com • NW • SP • Faith Marinette WI • (715)735-6506 • (FW 1992 MDIV)

**FRUSTI TODD I REV** (906)932-3771
E5120 E Margaret St Ironwood MI 49938-1536 • tfrusti@portup.com • NW • SP • Trinity Ironwood MI* • (906)932-3022 • (FW 1993 MDIV)

**FRY HENRY J REV** (320)274-3586
11698 Knowles Ave NW Annandale MN 55302 • MNS • EM • * • (SL 1958)

**FRY VICTOR G REV** (612)496-2662
1270 Sapphire Ln Shakopee MN 55379-3702 • MNS • EM • * • (SPR 1962 MDIV)

**FRYE FRANK G REV** (920)787-3471
120 W Division St Wautoma WI 54982-8468 • fgfrye@vbe.com • SW • SP • Trinity Wautoma WI • (920)787-2891 • (FW 1983 MDIV)

**FUCHS JOHN G REV** (507)876-2585
C/O Immanuel Lutheran Church 7134 Highway 247 NE Elgin MN 55923-9519 • MNS • SP • Immanuel Elgin MN* • (507)876-2585 • (SL 1965 MDIV STM)

**FUCHS JOHN M REV** (219)724-2324
918 Nuttman Ave Decatur IN 46733-1543 • IN • Assoc • Zion Decatur IN • (219)724-7177 • (SL 1993 MDIV)

**FUEHLER KENNETH MARTIN REV** (864)286-9073
6 Doverdale Rd Greenville SC 29615 • revkmf@aol.com • FG • 03/1997 03/2000 • (SL 1970 MDIV MS)

**FUERBRINGER KENNETH P REV** (805)492-2444
C/O Thousand Oaks Healthcare 93 W Avenida De Los Arboles Thousand Oaks CA 91360-2939 • PSW • EM • (SL 1959 MST)

**FUHLBRIGGE KARL A REV** (734)242-0593
94 Linswood Dr Monroe MI 48162-3170 • kmfuhlbrigge@earthlink.net • OH • EM • (CQ 1983 MDIV)

**FUHRMANN RUSSELL D REV** (219)894-7549
301 W Union St Ligonier IN 46767 • rfuhrman@ligtel.com • IN • Sn/Adm • Trinity Ligonier IN • (219)894-3667 • (FW 1982 MDIV)

**FUNCK STEPHEN H REV** (410)661-1763
3201 Hiss Ave Baltimore MD 21234 • signdovesf@aol.com • SE • O Sp Min • Southeastern Alexandria VA • (SL 1968 MDIV)

**FUNDUM JAMES KENT REV** (906)337-2871
201 Tamarack St Laurium MI 49913 • NW • SP • St Paul Laurium MI* • (906)337-0231 • (FW 1990 MDIV)

**FUNKE KENNETH R REV** (712)729-3336
306 Emily St Box 250 Sanborn IA 51248-0250 • kenfunke@mtc1.mtcnet.net • IW • SP • St John Sanborn IA • (712)729-3800 • (FW 1980 MDIV)

**FUQUA THOMAS KENT REV** (770)914-1538
300 Monroe Rd Mc Donough GA 30252-3663 • kf6634@mindspring.com • FG • SP • Lord Of Life Stockbridge GA • (770)474-3668 • (CQ 1975 MDIV)

**FYLER GEORGE F III REV** (716)679-0260
20 Birchwood Dr Fredonia NY 14063 • revgff@netsync.net • EA • SP • St Paul Fredonia NY • (716)672-6731 • (SL 1970 MST)

## G

**GAAL ALBERT H REV**
5111 Main St Buffalo NY 14221-5203 • EA • EM • (SL 1958 MDIV)

**GABBERT LAMBERT G REV** (813)657-8132
1105 Callista Ave Valrico FL 33594-7061 • l-cgabbert@juno.com • FG • EM • (SL 1956)

**GABRAM GORDON O REV** (757)229-4199
102 Arena St Williamsburg VA 23185-8315 • SE • EM • (SPR 1951 MDIV MA)

**GADBAW DAVID R REV** (517)688-9727
11780 N Lake Side Dr Jerome MI 49249-9749 • MI • SP • Of The Lakes Addison MI • (517)547-4261 • (FW 1991 MDIV)

**GADDINI DAVID CHRISTIAN**
929 W Locust Apt 303 Belvidere IL 61008 • NI • Inst C • Northwest Portland OR • (SL 2000 MDIV)

**GADE CLIFFORD W REV** (843)673-0788
601 Mc Keithan Rd Florence SC 29501 • cwghg@aol.com • SE • SP • Incarnate Word Florence SC • (843)662-9639 • (SPR 1962)

**GADE DEAN R REV**
2700 Eastside Rd Ukiah CA 95482-9642 • CNH • 09/1998 • (SPR 1963 MDIV)

**GADE DEAN W REV** (612)869-5150
6615 Stevens Ave S Richfield MN 55423-2469 • dgade60@hotmail.com • MNS • SP • Prince Of Peace Spring Lake Park MN • (763)786-1706 • (SL 1995 MDIV)

**GADE DWAIN M REV** (616)228-7875
3752 S Bay Bluffs Dr Cedar MI 49621-9434 • MI • EM • (SL 1947 MA EDS)

**GADEKEN ROBERT G REV** (402)534-3594
PO Box 505 Utica NE 68456 • NEB • SP • St Paul Utica NE • (402)534-2200 • (SL 1985 MA MDIV)

**GAERTNER MARK H REV** (810)783-3050
127 Lois Ln Mount Clemens MI 48043-2248 • gaertner@123.net • MI • Asst • Trinity Clinton Township MI • (810)463-2921 • (SL 1971 MDIV)

**GAGE RAYMOND W REV** (910)739-0132
2707 Alamac Rd Lumberton NC 28358-8218 • SE • 08/1995 08/2000 • (FW 1977 MDIV)

**GAHL RICHARD W REV** (440)835-3386
6451 Columbia Rd Olmsted Falls OH 44138-1303 • rgahl@aol.com • OH • D Ex/S • Ohio Olmsted Falls OH* • (SL 1965 MDIV)

**GAINES LLOYD DOUGLAS SR. REV** (301)856-1378
8309 Deerstill Way Clinton MD 20735-3365 • LGaines@se.lcms.org • SE • D Ex/S • Southeastern Alexandria VA • (SL 1984 MDIV)

**GALCHUTT GARY C REV** (763)784-9316
1351 78th Cir Spring Lake Park MN 55432-2849 • MNS • EM • (SL 1958 MDIV STM)

**GALEN ALBERT W REV** (407)365-5991
2004 Outer Circle Dr Oviedo FL 32765-6536 • FG • EM • (SL 1930)

**GALEN GARY W DR** (618)667-6307
# 3 Parklane Dr Troy IL 62294 • garygalen4@yahoo.com • SI • Assoc • Trinity Edwardsville IL • (618)656-2918 • (SL 1971 MDIV DMIN)

**GALIK KARL E REV**
C/O Zion Lutheran Church 241 5th Ave N Hopkins MN 55343 • 73143.1165@compuserve.com • MNS • Sn/Adm • Zion Hopkins MN • (612)938-7661 • (SL 1982 MDIV MS)

**GALL JOHN D REV** (717)938-6143
20 Highland Cir Etters PA 17319-9713 • NE • EM • (SL 1947 MA STM)

**GALL THEODORE C REV** (217)753-4316
2229 Dunwich St Springfield IL 62702-3141 • tedgall@eosinc.com • CI • Sn/Adm • Immanuel Springfield IL • (217)528-5232 • (SL 1979 MDIV)

**GALLAGHER FRANK MICHAEL REV** (573)763-5768
Star Rt Box 46-C Chamois MO 65024 • MO • SP • Grace Saint Louis MO • (314)727-3030 • (SL 1986 MDIV MFA MA)

**GALLMEIER ALFRED E REV** (254)896-6043
264 CR 143 Riesel TX 76682-9412 • TX • SP • Trinity Riesel TX • (254)896-6043 • (CQ 1982 MED)

**GALLO STEPHEN F REV**
C/O St Peter Lutheran Church RR 1 Box 70B St Peter IL 62880-9721 • CI • SP • St Peter Saint Peter IL • (618)349-8321 • (SL 1983 MDIV)

**GALLUP ROGER B REV** (708)456-9028
C/O Bethlehem Luth Church 2624 N Oak St River Grove IL 60171-1696 • gallup57@juno.com • NI • SP • Bethlehem River Grove IL • (708)453-1113 • (FW 1986 MDIV MA)

**GALSTER LENARD REV** (541)957-8888
1081 Black Oak Dr Roseburg OR 97470-9204 • NOW • EM • (SPR 1960)

**GANO DENNIS R REV**
1826 N Harvard Blvd Apt 4 Los Angeles CA 90027-3628 • PSW • SP • Bethany Los Angeles CA • (323)662-4176 • (SL 1978 MMU)

**GARAZIN KENNETH W REV** (630)653-6281
27W144 Wallace Ave Wheaton IL 60187-7833 • kgarazin@aol.com • NI • Asst • Peace Lombard IL • (630)627-1101 • (SL 1972 MDIV)

**GARBER DANIEL LEE REV** (402)654-2968
1862 Co Rd E Hooper NE 68031-2142 • NEB • 06/1994 03/2000 • (FW 1990 MDIV)

**GARBER REUBEN L REV** (931)565-3030
529 Pollock Hollow Rd Minor Hill TN 38473-5460 • revb@igiles.net • SO • EM • (SL 1958 MDIV)

**GARCHOW PAUL H REV** (608)756-0814
615 Sussex Dr Janesville WI 53546-1915 • garchow@aol.com • SW • Sn/Adm • St Paul Janesville WI • (608)754-4471 • (FW 1978 MDIV)

**GARCIA ALBERT L DR** (262)243-4236
12800 N Lake Shore Dr Mequon WI 53097-2418 • albert.garcia@cuw.edu • SW • SHS/C • South Wisconsin Milwaukee WI • (414)464-8100 • (SPR 1974 MTH MDIV PHD)

**GARCIA ERNESTO L REV** (956)682-4697
2100 Harvey St Mc Allen TX 78501-6105 • TX • Inst C • Texas Austin TX • (SPR 1966)

**GARCIA JORGE REV**
C/O Cristo Del Valle Lutheran PO Box 919 Toppenish WA 98948 • NOW • SP • Cristo Del Valle Toppenish WA • (509)865-3935 • (CQ 1989)

**GARD DANIEL L REV** (219)486-0957
6317 Kiwanis Dr Fort Wayne IN 46835-2185 • garddl@aol.com • IN • SHS/C • Indiana Fort Wayne IN • (FW 1984 MDIV MA PHD)

**GARDNER ROBERT E REV** (507)427-3735
1016 10th St N PO Box 503 Mountain Lake MN 56159-1006 • bgardner@rconnect.com • MNS • SP • Trinity Mountain Lake MN • (507)427-2451 • (SPR 1976 MDIV)

**GARRELS DENNIS E REV** (314)351-6652
4506 Tennessee Ave Saint Louis MO 63111-1050 • MO • 02/1985 02/2000 • (FW 1978 MDIV)

**GARRETT GERALD G REV** (909)681-9125
10493 Latour Ln Mira Loma CA 91752-2840 • garrettg@ix.netcom.com • PSW • EM • (SPR 1975 MDIV)

**GARRISON BRADLEY G REV** (734)433-9734
13460 E Old US 12 Chelsea MI 48118 • revbgarr@aol.com • IW • 10/1999 • (FW 1984 MDIV)

**GARTNER ALLEN A REV** (616)957-5172
2425 Okemos Dr SE Grand Rapids MI 49506-5302 • EN • EM • (SL 1957 MTH MDIV MA)

**GARTON HORACE W REV** (501)776-0879
2005 N Fox Trl Benton AR 72015-2075 • gart@juno.com • MDS • Assoc • Zion Alexander AR • (501)316-1100 • (SPR 1968)

**GARVUE DONALD R REV** (502)459-9212
1929 Meadowcreek Dr Louisville KY 40218-2401 • Dfgarvue@aol.com • IN • SP • Pilgrim Louisville KY • (502)458-4451 • (SPR 1964 MDIV)

**GARWOOD BURT L REV** (402)438-6711
1550 Hartland Rd Lincoln NE 68521 • bgarwood1@juno.com • NEB • Assoc • Holy Savior Lincoln NE • (402)434-3325 • (SL 1999 MDIV)

**GARWOOD EVERETT L REV** (402)457-4246
5320 Hartman Ave Omaha NE 68104-1748 • e.garwoodl@juno.com • NEB • SP • St Paul Omaha NE • (402)451-2865 • (FW 1978 MDIV)

**GARWOOD RONALD M REV** (307)234-2078
2040 W 39th St Casper WY 82604-5058 • wypres@aol.com • WY • DP • Wyoming Sheridian WY • (FW 1983 MDIV DD)

**GASSETT WILLIAM D REV** (601)442-4074
20 Newman Rd Natchez MS 39120-9203 • pharos@altavista.net • SO • SP • First Natchez MS • (601)442-1397 • (SL 1982 MDIV)

**GAST JAMES R REV** (920)458-0868
4431 S 15th St Sheboygan WI 53081-7707 • SW • EM • (SL 1966 MDIV)

**GATZ DALE G REV** (914)876-5572
404 Sepasco Center St Rhinebeck NY 12572-2239 • dgatz@thewartburg.org • AT • Atlantic Bronxville NY • (914)337-5700 • (SL 1968 MDIV DMIN)

**GATZ WILLIAM A REV** (517)784-8338
1631 Duguid Rd Jackson MI 49203-5457 • wtgatz@dmci.net • MI • EM • (SPR 1961)

**GAU JAMES A REV** (614)833-6248
11130 Saylor Rd Pickerington OH 43147-9413 • OH • 03/1996 03/2000 • (SL 1989 MDIV)

**GAUGER REUEL C REV** (940)564-3416
1015 W Hamilton St PO Box 777 Olney TX 76374-0777 • gauger@brazosnet.com • TX • EM • (SPR 1963)

**GAULKE EARL H REV** (314)822-3991
2447 Camberwell Ct Saint Louis MO 63131-2118 • MO • EM • (SL 1956 MA MDIV PHD DD)

**GAULKE STEPHEN E REV** (770)385-8219
205 Doubles Dr Covington GA 30016-1740 • sgaulke@bellsouth.net • FG • D Miss • Florida-Georgia Orlando FL • (SL 1984 MDIV STM)

**GAUNT DOUGLAS A REV** (636)250-3050
4795 N Highway 94 Saint Charles MO 63301-6406 • MO • SP • Trinity Saint Charles MO • (636)250-3350 • (FW 1986 MDIV)

**GAUSE MARK REV** (253)939-5759
747 37th St SE # A1 Auburn WA 98002-8010 • NOW • SP • New Hope Pacific WA • (253)351-0450 • (SL 1984 MDIV)

**GAUSMAN CARL R REV** (509)326-7184
3107 W Cleveland Ave Spokane WA 99205-3912 • carlgaus@aol.com • NOW • EM • (CQ 1982)

**GAVIN JEFF G REV** (847)439-2232
1111 S Linneman Rd Mt Prospect IL 60056-4167 • NI • SP • St John Mount Prospect IL • (847)593-7670 • (FW 1982 MDIV)

**GAWURA ERIC R REV**
2904 - 20th St SE Rochester MN 55904-6019 • MNS • SP • Christ Rochester MN • (507)289-0271 • (SL 2000 MDIV)

**GE RUE KEITH EDWARD REV** (815)472-6321
12202 E Gregg Blvd Momence IL 60954-3425 • revgerue@techinter.com • NI • SP • Our Savior Momence IL • (815)472-2829 • (FW 1994 MDIV)

**GEACH JOHN T DR** (209)586-5613
23828 Oxbow Ln S Sonora CA 95370-9516 • CNH • 01/1993 01/2000 • (SPR 1963 DMIN)

**GEARY DUANE O REV** (248)967-4427
21727 Stratford Ct Oak Park MI 48237 • MI • SP • St John Detroit MI • (313)933-9360 • (SPR 1966)

**GEASCHEL ROBERT EARL REV** (708)839-4170
11480 German Church Rd Burr Ridge IL 60521-6459 • armydad2@aol.com • NI • Sn/Adm • Trinity Burr Ridge IL • (708)839-1200 • (SL 1996 MDIV)

**GEBAUER ETHAN C REV**
105 Ash St Susanville CA 96130-4539 • CNH • SP • St Paul Susanville CA • (530)257-2223 • (SPR 1969 MDIV)

**GEBAUER RONALD F REV**
SITAG PO Box 986 Honiara SOLOMON ISLANDS • gebauer@sitag.org.sb • OH • 06/1989 06/2000 • (FW 1985 MDIV MBA)

**GEBAUER VICTOR E REV** (612)879-9555
122 W Franklin Ave Ste 522 Minneapolis MN 55404-2454 • vgebauer@lutheranmusicprogram.org • IN • Assoc • Immanuel Valparaiso IN • (219)462-8207 • (SL 1964 MDIV PHD)

**GEBEL ROBERT JOHN REV** (314)352-7557
7834 Navajoe St St Louis MO 63123 • gebelrsml@juno.com • MO • SP • Concordia Maplewood MO • (314)647-1215 • (SL 1996 MDIV)

**GEBHARDT LEONHARDT REV** (712)678-3618
C/O St John Luth Church PO Box 73 Charter Oak IA 51439-0073 • gsgeb@frontiernet.net • IW • SP • St John Charter Oak IA • (712)678-3630 • (SPR 1970 MDIV)

**GEERDES BERNARD C REV** (813)345-1992
6060 Shore Blvd S Apt 710 Saint Petersburg FL 33707-5846 • bgeer3@juno.com • FG • EM • (SL 1947)

**GEFALLER MARK A REV** (262)392-2170
312 N Main St North Prairie WI 53153-9728 • navybluegold@prodigy.net • SW • SP • St John North Prairie WI • (414)392-2170 • (FW 1985 MDIV)

**GEFFERT MELVIN R REV** (715)457-6701
2158 Du Bay Dr Mosinee WI 54455-9367 • NW • EM • (SPR 1946 MDIV)

**GEHLBACH DARYL D REV** (763)561-0767
7207 Girard Ave N Brooklyn Center MN 55430-1148 • dgehlbach@aol.com • MNS • P Df • Prince Peace Df Minneapolis MN • (612)331-2474 • (SL 1983 MDIV)

**GEHLBACH GARY V REV** (414)296-1804
N1584 A Cty K Sharon WI 53585 • gehlbach@hughestech.net • SW • SP • Triune Sharon WI • (414)882-4000 • (SL 1987 MDIV)

**GEHRKE FREDERICK H REV** (414)328-0884
2754 S 69th St Milwaukee WI 53219-2905 • SW • EM • (SL 1943)

**GEHRKE ROBERT J REV** (320)679-1093
313 Clark St Mora MN 55051-1501 • gehrkerl@ncis.com • MNN • SP • Zion Mora MN • (320)679-1094 • (SL 1982 MDIV)

**GEHRKE WILBUR L REV** (541)271-2895
2150 Elm Ave Reedsport OR 97467-1135 • gehrke@presys.com • NOW • SP • Beautiful Savior Reedsport OR • (541)271-2633 • (SL 1971 MDIV)

**GEHRS GERHARD A REV**
6262 Soledad Dr Riverside CA 92504-1523 • PSW • P Df • Mt Calvary Df Riverside CA • (714)689-8380 • (SL 1960 MA)

**GEIDEL ARTHUR W REV** (845)254-5317
PO Box 341 Bonnieview Dr Pine Hill NY 12465-0341 • ageidel@catskill.net • AT • EM • (SPR 1954)

**GEIGER OREN H REV** (209)668-2270
2225 Temple Ave Turlock CA 95382-1843 • CNH • EM • (SPR 1945)

**GEIL ALLEN E REV** (715)449-3289
C/O St Paul Ev Luth Ch PO Box 208 Birnamwood WI 54414-0208 • NW • SP • St Paul Birnamwood WI • (715)449-2101 • (CQ 1994 MS)

**GEIS WILLIAM S REV** (580)846-9928
PO Box 326 Lone Wolf OK 73655-0326 • wsgeis@lutheranok.com • OK • SP • Christ Elk City OK* • (580)225-2266 • (SL 1990 MDIV)

**GEISLER HERBERT G REV** (734)973-9859
2905 Carlton St Ann Arbor MI 48108-1211 • revgeis@aol.com • MI • EM • * • (SPR 1973 MA MDIV MA)

**GEISLER JEFFREY L REV** (812)358-5269
301 W Spring St Brownstown IN 47220-1315 • IN • Assoc • St Peter Brownstown IN • 235 • (FW 1997 MDIV)

**GEISLER JOHN H REV** (714)921-4535
6555 E Via Fresco Anaheim CA 92807-4914 • PSW • EM • (SL 1946 MDIV)

**GEISLER STANLEY W REV** (817)270-1447
432 Schooner Dr Azle TX 76020-4918 • gslr@juno.com • TX • SP • Good Shepherd Azle TX • (817)237-4822 • (SL 1965 MDIV)

**GEIST WALTER L REV** (715)356-6749
162 Woodland Ln Woodruff WI 54568-9411 • revgeist@yahoo.com • NW • SP • Rock Of Ages Minocqua WI • (715)356-3848 • (SL 1972 MDIV)

**GEISTLINGER JACK A REV** (707)252-4978
2492 Cabernet Ct Napa CA 94558-2504 • CNH • Rock Of Ages Minocqua WI • (715)356-3848 • (SL 1965 DMIN)

**GEITZ DARREL W REV** (502)543-3325
215 Gibnaltar Dr Shepherdsville KY 40165-6242 • dwgeitz@alltel.net • IN • EM • (SL 1956 MDIV)

**GEITZ TIMOTHY P REV** (712)654-6444
PO Box 455 Manilla IA 51454-0455 • timgeitz@netins.net • IW • SP • Trinity Manilla IA • (712)654-3031 • (SL 1987 MDIV)

**GENKE QUENTIN M REV** (708)258-0093
PO Box 83 Peotone IL 60468-0083 • gracepeotone@juno.com • NI • D Miss • Grace Peotone IL • (708)258-9136 • (SL 1998 MDIV)

**GENSCH DANIEL W REV** (708)430-0633
9105 S 87th Ave Hickory Hills IL 60457-1710 • joyjan@aol.com • NI • Sn/Adm • St Paul Oak Lawn IL • (708)423-1040 • (SL 1974 MDIV)

**GENTER LEE H REV** (419)749-4268
6699 State Route 49 Convoy OH 45832-9107 • redeemer@wcoil.com • OH • SP • Redeemer Convoy OH • (419)749-2167 • (FW 1987 MDIV)

**GENTET ROBERT E REV** (210)967-4736
305 Cloudmont Dr San Antonio TX 78239 • regentet@ratedg.com • TX • SP • St Peter Pearsall TX • (830)334-2336 • (SL 1993 MDIV MS)

**GENTZKE ROBERT W REV** (417)725-0952
1150 W Vineyard Dr Nixa MO 65714-8213 • MO • EM • (SPR 1957 MDIV)

**GENZEN GARY C REV** (352)314-0514
PO Box 491901 Leesburg FL 34749-1901 • ggenzen@aol.com • FG • SP • Bethany Leesburg FL • (352)787-7275 • (SPR 1970 MDIV DMIN)

**GEORG DANIEL E REV**
1409 Normandy Ln Allen TX 75002 • TX • 04/2000 • (FW 1981 MDIV STM)

**GEORGE GUS A REV** (712)322-7243
170 Nicholas Council Bluffs IA 51503 • IW • SP • St Paul Council Bluffs IA • (712)322-4729 • (CQ 1977 MDIV)

**GEORGI GARY D REV** (440)934-3424
36451 N Reserve Cir Avon OH 44011-2821 • hope2000@bright.net • OH • SP • Hope Sheffield Village OH • (440)949-2620 • (SL 1971 MDIV)

**GERDES EVERETT E REV** (505)556-0122
2853 Cloud Croft Cir Las Cruces NM 88011 • Everettgerdes@aol.com • TX • EM • (SL 1955 MDIV)

**GERDES LARRY W REV** (814)345-6390
C/O St John Luth Church RR 2 Box 322 Morrisdale PA 16858-9103 • lardeb@csrlink.net • EA • SP • St John Morrisdale PA • (814)345-5741 • (CQ 1982 MED)

**GERDES TIMOTHY A REV** (810)279-0905
340 S Third St Apt C San Jose CA 95112 • CNH • Asst • First Immanuel San Jose CA • (408)292-5404 • (SL 1999 MDIV)

**GERHARDT ARTHUR H REV** (518)456-5309
6 Witte Rd Albany NY 12203-4963 • gerhardtardith@aol.com • AT • EM • (SL 1941 MST)

**GERHOLD CHARLES ROLAND REV** (570)253-5326
RR 3 Box 2475 Honesdale PA 18431-9563 • NJ • EM • (SL 1942 LLD)

**GERIKE ERNEST L REV** (309)454-6504
711 S Cottage Ave Apt 106 Normal IL 61761-4337 • CI • EM • (SL 1944 MDIV)

**GERIKE GERHARDT J C REV** (863)683-4037
Bobs Landing Mobile Home Park # 24 Babson Park FL 33827-9681 • MO • EM • (SL 1935 MDIV)

**GERIKE HENRY V REV** (314)505-7463
801 De Mun Ave Saint Louis MO 63105-3168 • hvghalfsch@aol.com • EN • D Miss • English Farmington MI • (SL 1991 MDIV MCMU)

**GERIKE KENNETH J REV** (573)445-1200
12 Dundee Dr Columbia MO 65203-1213 • revkgerike@email.com • MO • Sn/Adm • Trinity Columbia MO • (573)445-2112 • (SL 1975 MDIV)

**GERISCH MARK A REV** (517)894-2611
C/O Zion Lutheran Church 510 W Ivy St Bay City MI 48706-5234 • MI • Assoc • Zion Bay City MI • (517)894-2611 • (FW 1987 MDIV)

**GERKE DAVID K REV** (313)483-9784
1275 E Forest Ave Ypsilanti MI 48198-3911 • MI • SP • Faith Ypsilanti MI • (313)482-9412 • (FW 1982 DMIN)

**GERKE ROBERT A REV** (616)891-9175
8392 Kraft Ave SE Caledonia MI 49316-9403 • rgerke@aol.com • MI • Sn/Adm • St Paul Caledonia MI • (616)891-8688 • (FW 1986 MA)

**GERKEN DANIEL J REV** (253)770-9115
6016 85th St E Puyallup WA 98371-6461 • gslct@juno.com • NOW • SP • Good Shepherd Tacoma WA • (253)473-4848 • (CQ 1979 MDIV)

**GERKEN ERWIN A REV** (253)845-1025
902 18th St SW Puyallup WA 98371-6642 • eagerken@tcmnet.com • NOW • EM • (SL 1945 DMIN)

**GERKEN HERBERT M REV** (219)447-5658
2716 Palisade Dr Fort Wayne IN 46806-5321 • hmgerken@email.com • IN • SP • Martini New Haven IN • (219)749-0014 • (SL 1966 MDIV)

**GERKEN MARK A REV** (515)993-3527
1311 Pleasant St Adel IA 50003-2006 • mrdsj@juno.com • IW • Sn/Adm • Faith Adel IA • (515)993-3848 • (SL 1982 MDIV)

**GERKEN OSCAR A REV** (352)357-2308
1602 Alan Dr Eustis FL 32726-5002 • oscartracy@aol.com • FG • EM • (SL 1948 DMIN)

**GERKEN PHILIP J REV** (301)762-3904
2315 Ring St Rockville MD 20851-1523 • SE • EM • (SL 1951)

**GERKEN RICHARD W REV** (206)242-3516
17837 7th Pl SW Seattle WA 98166-3655 • NOW • Sn/Adm • Resurrection Des Moines WA • (206)824-2978 • (SL 1965 MDIV)

**GERLACH DONALD R REV** (708)563-0777
5859 S Archer Rd Summit Argo IL 60501-1409 • NI • SP • Zion Summit Argo IL • (708)563-0777 • (SPR 1961 MDIV)

**GERLACH JOHN W REV** (417)257-7669
2614 Paula Dr West Plains MO 65775-1553 • MO • SP • Immanuel West Plains MO • (417)256-3407 • (FW 1988 MDIV)

**GERNER A LEROY REV** (402)891-8676
15813 Gertrude St Omaha NE 68136-1046 • leroy@kingofkingsomaha.org • NEB • Assoc • King Of Kings Omaha NE • (402)333-6464 • (SL 1983 MDIV)

**GERSCH FRED C REV** (512)891-0234
3924 Sendero Dr Austin TX 78735 • fgersch@prismnet.com • TX • SP • St Paul Austin TX • (512)472-8301 • (SPR 1967 MDIV)

**GESCH ROY G REV** (949)448-0234
72 La Mirage Cir Aliso Viejo CA 92656-4226 • royndot@aol.com • PSW • EM • (SL 1944)

**GESCHKE EDWARD M REV** (815)436-7425
23556 W Fern St Plainfield IL 60544 • NI • EM • (SPR 1971)

**GESKE FREDERICK E REV** (612)824-1263
5728 10th Ave S Minneapolis MN 55417-2406 • MNS • EM • (SL 1938)

**GESKE JEFFREY D REV** (785)765-3620
315 Main St PO Box 83 Mc Farland KS 66501-0083 • jdgeske@aol.com • KS • SP • Trinity Mc Farland KS • (785)765-3755 • (SL 1999 MDIV)

**GESKE STEVEN ROGER REV** (912)477-5728
1165 Chisholm Trl Macon GA 31220-3709 • rev.geske@mylink.net • FG • SP • Holy Trinity Macon GA • (912)474-8393 • (SL 1996 MDIV)

**GESTERLING DONALD LE ROY REV** (320)695-2385
PO Box 3l2 Browns Valley MN 56219-0312 • MNN • EM • (SPR 1955 MDIV)

**GEWECKE STEPHEN A REV** (609)466-3490
1606 Harbourton Rocktown Rd Lambertville NJ 08530-3004 • NJ • SP • St Peter Lambertville NJ • (609)466-0939 • (SL 1985 MDIV)

**GEYER LARRY I REV** (605)734-5305
100 W Kellam Ave Chamberlain SD 57325-1514 • SD • SP • Zion Chamberlain SD • (605)734-6874 • (FW 1981 MDIV)

**GIBBS JEFFREY A REV** (314)721-2714
10 N Seminary Ter Saint Louis MO 63105-3011 • gibbsj@csl.edu • MO • SHS/C • Missouri Saint Louis MO • (314)317-4550 • (FW 1979 STM MDIV PHD)

**GIBSON GEORGE JR. REV** (409)690-7504
1508 Front Royal Dr College Station TX 77845-4001 • gibaccess@aol.com • TX • EM • (SL 1964 MDIV)

**GIBSON MICHAEL E REV** (408)262-0506
C/O Mt Olive Luth Church 1989 E Calaveras Blvd Milpitas CA 95035-6041 • mike@mt-olive.org • CNH • SP • Mount Olive Milpitas CA • (408)262-0506 • (SL 1984 MDIV DMIN)

**GIEBEL FRANKLIN H REV** (312)284-0926
5243 S Major Ave Chicago IL 60638-1503 • revfhg@juno.com • NI • SP • Gloria Dei Chicago IL • (773)767-2771 • (SPR 1976 MDIV)

**GIECK WILLIAM R REV** (206)839-8036
29822 11th Ave SW Federal Way WA 98023-8210 • saint³bill@mns.com • NOW • EM • (SPR 1956 MA)

**GIERKE CHARLES A REV** (402)697-8215
15726 Westchester Cir Omaha NE 68118-2037 • prgierke@st-marklcms.org • NEB • Sn/Adm • St Mark Omaha NE • (402)391-6148 • (SPR 1967 MDIV)

**GIERKE EUGENE V REV** (402)643-6524
1126 Eastridge Dr Seward NE 68434-1330 • nebpres@aol.com • NEB • DP • Nebraska Seward NE • (SPR 1971 MDIV)

**GIERKE JOHN PETER REV** (615)740-0386
108 Eastdale Ln Dickson TN 37055-2959 • jpgierke@bellsouth.net • MDS • SP • St John Burns TN • (615)446-2332 • (SL 1996 MDIV)

**GIERKE TIMOTHY J REV** (402)727-6207
2012 Phelps Ave Fremont NE 68025-4522 • goodshep@tvsonline.net • NEB • Sn/Adm • Good Shepherd Fremont NE • (402)721-8412 • (SL 1976 MDIV)

**GIES CLARK H REV** (605)384-5680
PO Box 506 Wagner SD 57380-0506 • giescj@charles-mix.com • SD • SP • St John Wagner SD* • (605)384-3500 • (SPR 1966 MDIV)

**GIES WILLIAM L F REV** (410)465-7583
8636 Spruce Run Ct Ellicott City MD 21043-6945 • wlfg@juno.com • SE • SP • Trinity Ellicott City MD • (410)461-4313 • (SL 1989 MDIV)

**GIESCHEN CHARLES A REV** (219)484-0144
8610 Oakcliff Ct Fort Wayne IN 46825-7137 • gieschenca@mail.ctsfw.edu • IN • SHS/C • Indiana Fort Wayne IN • (FW 1984 MTH MDIV PHD)

**GIESCHEN THEODORE C REV** (541)388-2867
2400 Mountain Willow Dr Bend OR 97701-8287 • NOW • EM • (SPR 1950)

**GIESE BURTON F REV** (480)981-2949
4275 E Harwell Cir Higley AZ 85236-8005 • PSW • SP • Eternal Life Mesa AZ • (602)985-0224 • (SL 1959)

**GIESE CURTIS P REV**
411 Pine Brae St Ann Arbor MI 48105-2743 • giesec@ccaa.edu • MI • SHS/C • Michigan Ann Arbor MI • (SL 1989 MDIV STM MPHIL PHD)

**GIESE EDWARD P REV** (830)303-4331
154 Twin Oak Rd Seguin TX 78155 • eandrgiese@juno.com • TX • SP • Grace Seguin TX • (830)379-1690 • (FW 1998 MDIV)

**GIESE GORDON W REV** (715)355-2638
510 Lawrence Ave Rothschild WI 54474-1236 • NW • EM • (SL 1961)

**GIESEKE HAROLD J REV** (541)338-4267
3355 N Delta Hwy Unit 193 Eugene OR 97408-5916 • NOW • EM • (SL 1934)

**GIESLER WAYNE H REV** (330)262-5737
C/O Concordia Lutheran Church 2343 Star Dr Wooster OH 44691-9019 • wgiesler@aol.com • OH • SP • Concordia Wooster OH* • (330)262-2456 • (SPR 1962 MDIV)

**GIFF LARRY A REV** (507)825-5539
318 4th St SW Pipestone MN 56164-1504 • MNS • 11/1995 11/1999 • * • (SL 1973 MDIV)

**GIFFORD DANIEL GEORGE REV** (402)586-2411
501 S Hampton PO Box 240 Wausa NE 68786 • dkgiff@bloomnet.com • NEB • SP • Golgotha Wausa NE • (402)586-2412 • (SL 1996 MDIV)

**GILBERT DAN PAUL REV** (630)553-6781
700 Morgan St Yorkville IL 60560-1644 • crossyorkg@juno.com • NI • Assoc • Cross Yorkville IL • (630)553-7335 • (SL 1977 MDIV)

**GILLAM JACK L REV** (308)826-4403
107 North Cherry PO Box 157 Amherst NE 68812 • jgillam@nebi.com • NEB • SP • Trinity Amherst NE • (308)826-3421 • (SL 1999 MDIV)

**GILLASPIE WES S REV** (517)868-4217
PO Box 152 Richville MI 48758-0152 • wessgill@aol.com • MI • Assoc • St Michael Richville MI • (517)868-4791 • (FW 1986 MDIV)

**GILLESPIE ARTHUR L REV** (718)961-3037
2207 123rd St College Point NY 11356-2638 • AT • SP • St John College Point NY • (718)463-4790 • (SL 1970 MDIV)

**GILLET STEPHEN PAUL REV** (217)924-4688
13234 N 2300th St Wheeler IL 62479 • rev5pg@hotmail.com • CI • SP • St Paul Wheeler IL* • (217)924-4498 • (FW 1995 MDIV)

**GILLILAND MARTIN S REV** (410)686-3130
8912 Philadelphia Rd Baltimore MD 21237 • Bethelcb@aol.com • SE • SP • Bethlehem Baltimore MD • (410)488-4445 • (SL 1998 MDIV)

**GILMORE ROZELL REV** (503)284-0848
3909 N Overlook Ter Portland OR 97227 • NOW • EM • (CQ 1982 MAR)

**GILSON MARK E REV** (616)467-6222
C/O St Paul Lutheran Church 600 W Burr Oak St Centreville MI 49032-9781 • megilson@juno.com • MI • SP • St Paul Colon MI* • (616)432-3807 • (FW 1997 MDIV)

**GIMBEL JAMES R REV** (618)345-8048
9 Fairlane Dr Collinsville IL 62234-5406 • jim.gimbel@cph.org • MO • S Ex/S • Missouri Saint Louis MO • (314)317-4550 • (SL 1985 MDIV)

**GINTER RONALD A REV** (716)542-1210
159 Golden Pond Estates Akron NY 14001 • EA • EM • (SPR 1962)

**GIOVENCO JOSEPH V REV** (217)243-2111
1042 E Morton Ave #65 Jacksonville IL 62650-3302 • giovenco@fgi.net • NW • EM • (FW 1982 MDIV)

**GIRARDIN MARK E REV**
216 North Third Harbor Beach MI 48441 • MI • SP • Zion Harbor Beach MI • (517)479-3615 • (FW 1977 MDIV)

**GITTNER WILLIAM REV** (704)365-1418
736 Wingrave Dr Charlotte NC 28270-5934 • wgittner@juno.com • SE • Sn/Adm • Resurrection Charlotte NC • (704)377-6575 • (SPR 1966 MDIV)

**GLADE EUGENE C REV** (507)387-4928
133 E Glencrest Dr Mankato MN 56001-4508 • MNS • EM • (SL 1958 MDIV)

**GLADE WILFRED W REV** (562)947-1160
11936 Hartdale Ave La Mirada CA 90638-1512 • arrie44@aol.com • PSW • SP • Peace Pico Rivera CA • (562)949-5203 • (SL 1971 MDIV)

**GLAMANN JOHN V DR** (941)678-0144
1170 Yarnell Ave Lake Wales FL 33853-3921 • FG • SP • Lake Wales Lake Wales FL • (863)676-4715 • (SL 1974 MDIV DMIN)

**GLAMMEYER THOMAS H REV** (281)587-8072
6610 Greenvale Ln Houston TX 77066-3825 • TX • Asst • Our Savior Houston TX • (713)290-9087 • (SPR 1955 MDIV)

**GLANDER DENNIS E REV** (810)359-2055
5239 Independence Ln Lexington MI 48450-9293 • MI • EM • (SPR 1965)

**GLANDER RANDALL L REV** (262)637-5240
2131 Carlisle Ave Racine WI 53404-2111 • rlgatpeace@mixcom.com • EN • SP • Peace Racine WI • (262)884-7633 • (FW 1990 MDIV)

**GLASPIE JAMES J REV**
PSC 821 Box 1 FPO AE 09421-0001 • e.glaspie@virgin.net • CNH • M Chap • Calif/Nevada/Hawaii San Francisco CA • (415)468-2336 • (SL 1986 MDIV)

**GLASS DONALD P REV** (865)281-0013
5907 Wade Ln Knoxville TN 37912-3302 • dpg5907@juno.com • MDS • SP • Christus Victor Knoxville TN • (865)687-6622 • (SPR 1964)

**GLAWATZ DALE F REV** (641)747-2055
709 N 12th St Guthrie Center IA 50115-1514 • dglawatz@netins.net • IW • SP • Immanuel Guthrie Center IA • (515)747-3918 • (FW 1988 MTH)

**GLEASON HOWARD JESS REV** (765)795-6590
302 Hurst Ave Cloverdale IN 46120-9148 • grace@ccrtc.com • IN • SP • Grace Cloverdale IN • (765)795-3214 • (SL 1995 MDIV)

**GLEASON WILLIAM L REV** (660)425-2334
2104 Central St Bethany MO 64424-1247 • wgleason@netins.net • MO • SP • Hope Bethany MO • (660)425-3627 • (SL 1985 MDIV)

**GLICK DENNIS W DR** (561)393-6225
79 SW 15th Ave Boca Raton FL 33486-4457 • dglick@cyberfalcom.com • FG • Sn/Adm • St Paul Boca Raton FL • (561)395-0433 • (SPR 1972 MDIV DMIN)

**GLIENKE HERMAN J REV** (305)888-4486
1701 Apache St Miami Springs FL 33166-3217 • hermdel@earthlink.net • FG • EM • (SL 1952 MDIV)

**GLOCK DELMAR J REV** (904)252-4667
444 S Beach St Daytona Beach FL 32114-5004 • FG • EM • (SL 1950)

**GLOCK PETER M REV** (815)853-4479
C/O Zion Luth Church PO Box 417 Wenona IL 61377-0417 • pmglock@maxiis.com • CI • SP • Zion Wenona IL* • (815)853-4479 • (SL 1991 MDIV)

**GLOCK RICHARD C REV** (520)472-7062
717 E Skyway Ct Payson AZ 85541-3336 • rglock@altavista.com • EN • EM • * • (SL 1954)

**GLOE RONALD F REV** (316)283-1441
C/O Zion Luth Church 225 S Poplar St # 885 Newton KS 67114-3637 • rfgloe@aol.com • KS • SP • Zion Newton KS • (316)283-1441 • (FW 1980 MDIV)

**GLOVER JOHN E REV** (209)951-8892
9818 Northridge Way Stockton CA 95209-5031 • CNH • Assoc • St Andrew Stockton CA • (209)957-8750 • (SL 1991 MDIV)

**GNEWUCH CARL M REV** (843)361-0568
810 Arbor Ln North Myrtle Beach SC 29582 • cgnewuch@aol.com • SE • SP • Risen Christ Myrtle Beach SC • (843)272-5845 • (SL 1991 MDIV)

**GNEWUCH DONALD E DR** (312)366-0638
7712 Monroe St Forest Park IL 60130-1725 • crfgnewucd@cuis.crf.edu • NI • SHS/C • Northern Illinois Hillside IL • (SL 1961 MDIV PHD)

**GOBLE MARK DAVID REV** (901)751-1630
1068 Fox Trace Cv Cordova TN 38018 • markgoble@aol.com • MDS • Assoc • Christ King Memphis TN • (901)682-8404 • (SL 1997 MDIV)

**GOCKEN RONALD E REV**
12620 232nd Ave E Buckley WA 98321-9582 • rgocken@msn.com • NOW • EM • (SL 1963 MDIV)

**GODDARD PAUL E REV** (573)265-3167
221 W James Blvd Saint James MO 65559-1214 • chalosi@rollanet.org • MO • SP • St John Saint James MO • (573)265-3226 • (FW 1986 MDIV)

**GOEBBERT ALLEN T REV**
53619 Sweetspire Trl Elkhart IN 46514-9032 • amgoebbert@coolsky.com • IN • Asst • Trinity Elkhart IN • (219)522-1491 • (SL 1979 MDIV)

**GOEBEL RICHARD F REV** (651)488-5378
71 Geranium Ave W Saint Paul MN 55117-4906 • dfgoebel@secondharvest.org • MNS • EM • (SL 1961 MDIV LITTD)

**GOEBEL VELMER H REV** (405)796-2283
C/O Zion Luth Church PO Box 128 Lahoma OK 73754-0128 • VGoebel@juno.com • OK • SP • Zion Lahoma OK • (580)796-2243 • (CQ 1982 MS)

**GOEHNER EDWARD C REV** (615)889-5476
805 Withers Pl Hermitage TN 37076 • ednelliemae@juno.com • MDS • EM • (SL 1951)

**GOEHRING IRWIN D REV** (909)652-5880
1363 Cherry Dr Hemet CA 92545-7755 • PSW • EM • (SL 1960)

**GOEKE JONATHAN ANDREW REV**
3745 Newland Dr Round Rock TX 78681 • pjlousjc@aol.com • TX • Assoc • Good Shepherd Cedar Park TX • (512)258-6227 • (SL 1996 MDIV)

**GOERSS JOHN M DR** (609)921-3608
86 Snowden Ln Princeton NJ 08540-3939 • EN • SP • Messiah Princeton NJ • (609)924-3642 • (SL 1970 MDIV MS DMIN)

**GOETZ GEROLD W REV** (320)732-3788
604 3rd St S Long Prairie MN 56347-1631 • redeemd@rea-alp.com • MNN • IndC P • Minnesota North Brainerd MN • (SPR 1966 MDIV)

**GOETZ LAWRENCE FRANKLIN REV** (217)726-8515
2206A Lexington Dr Springfield IL 62704 • CI • Assoc • Our Savior Springfield IL • (217)546-4531 • (SL 1994 MDIV)

**GOETZ LLOYD H REV** (407)365-2681
2038 Inner Circle Dr Oviedo FL 32765-8707 • FG • EM • (SL 1936 DD)

**GOETZ ROGER M REV** (785)273-0613
1918 SW Arrowhead Rd Topeka KS 66604-3725 • rmgoetz@stjohnlcmstopeka.org • KS • Assoc • St John Topeka KS • (785)354-7132 • (SPR 1967 MDIV STM)

**GOFF DENNISON J REV** (863)648-9858
1714 Tierra Alta Ddr Lakeland FL 33813-1433 • FG • Sn/Adm • St Paul Lakeland FL • (863)644-7710 • (SL 1986 MDIV MA)

**GOGL G LEON REV** (503)257-4168
1749 NE 157th Ave Portland OR 97230-5328 • NOW • EM • (SL 1960 MS)

**GOGOLIN FLOYD E REV** (920)689-2361
N9520 Hwy 26 Burnett WI 53922 • SW • SP • Immanuel Burnett WI • (920)689-2361 • (SL 1963)

**GOHDES MELVIN J REV** (715)257-9249
7251 Nehrbass Rd Athens WI 54411-9751 • NW • EM • (SPR 1953 MA)

**GOHN DAVID P REV** (313)782-0147
C/O Community Lutheran Church 23984 Gibraltar Rd Flat Rock MI 48134-9411 • dgohn@wdl.net • MI • Sn/Adm • Community Flat Rock MI • (734)782-0563 • (CQ 1980)

**GOING ROLAND W REV** (308)384-2142
3417 Graham Ave Grand Island NE 68803-6526 • NEB • EM • (SPR 1948)

**GOING THOMAS A REV** (812)376-6788
5047 Countess Dr Columbus IN 47203-2817 • IN • EM • (SPR 1958 MDIV)

**GOLDAMMER GORDON L REV** (605)578-2449
C/O Grace Luth Church 827 Main St Deadwood SD 57732-1012 • SD • SP • Grace Deadwood SD • (605)578-2219 • (FW 1978 MDIV)

**GOLDBERGER ARTHUR J II REV** (217)498-8345
8 Camelot Dr Rochester IL 62563-9203 • goldberger@eosinc.com • CI • SP • Good Shepherd Rochester IL • (217)498-7991 • (CQ 1984)

**GOLDBERGER ARTHUR J SR. REV** (217)732-3950
10 Riggs Dr Lincoln IL 62656-1014 • ajg-lrg@juno.com • CI • EM • (SPR 1951)

**GOLDHAMMER MAURICE W REV** (303)986-6904
10230 W Exposition Dr Lakewood CO 80226-3918 • RM • SP • Redeemer Denver CO • (303)934-5447 • (SL 1965 MDIV)

**GOLDSBY ORVAL E REV** (651)731-4723
6568 Falstaff Ter Woodbury MN 55125-2429 • wlc@isd.net • MNS • Assoc • Woodbury Woodbury MN • (651)739-5144 • (SL 1981 MDIV)

**GOLISCH JOHN E REV** (847)398-3181
912 S Maple St Mount Prospect IL 60056-4338 • golischje@juno.com • NI • EM • (SL 1957 MDIV STM PHD)

**GOLKE FRED W REV** (763)784-5513
5114 Long Lake Rd Mounds View MN 55112-4823 • golke@juno.com • MNS • EM • (SL 1955 MDIV)

**GOLTER RANDALL L REV** (505)299-0376
2825 Tennessee St NE Albuquerque NM 87110-3707 • pastor@gracelutheran-nm.org • RM • SP • Grace Albuquerque NM • (505)823-9100 • (SL 1984 MDIV)

**GOLTERMANN ELMER M REV**
W275 N2345 Oak Ct Pewaukee WI 53072 • SW • EM • (SL 1937)

**GOLTERMANN SAMUEL I REV** (314)842-7394
5160 Deerfield Circle Dr Apt 3 Saint Louis MO 63128-2981 • MO • EM • (SL 1948 DD)

**GOLTL SCOTT L REV** (316)722-3691
12714 Taft St Wichita KS 67235-8434 • scottgoltl@netzero.com • KS • Assoc • Ascension Wichita KS • (316)722-4694 • (SL 1993 MDIV)

**GOLTZ GORDON K REV** (616)957-4863
3767 Bradford St NE Grand Rapids MI 49525-3324 • pastorpete@netscape.net • MI • EM • (SL 1962 MDIV)

**GOLZ ROLAND M REV** (715)787-3674
PO Box 181 Gresham WI 54128-0181 • rollie@ezwebtech.com • NW • SP • St John Shawano WI* • (715)524-4382 • (CQ 1973 MA)

**GONZALES JESUS M REV**
Ideal Trailer Ct 720 Lee St Lot 9 Kenner LA 70062 • SO • Assoc • St John New Orleans LA • (504)482-2118 • (CQ 1984)

**GONZALES LONNIE REV** (281)313-3646
2910 Grants Lake Blvd # 1407 Sugar Land TX 77479 • TX • Assoc • Fishers Of Men Sugar Land TX • (281)242-7711 • (SL 2000 MDIV)

**GONZALEZ JUAN A REV** (440)282-2381
5802 Colony Ct Lorain OH 44053-4102 • egm777@centuryinter.net • OH • SP • Principe De Paz Lorain OH • (440)277-0777 • (SC 1988 MDIV)

**GONZALEZ ROBERT F REV** (636)343-9045
1026 Winter Park Dr Fenton MO 63026 • robert.gonzalez@lcms.org • MO • S Ex/S • Missouri Saint Louis MO • (314)317-4550 • (CQ 1982 DD)

**GONZALEZ VICENTE R REV** (216)631-4634
2059 W 28th St Cleveland OH 44113-4066 • OH • EM • (CQ 1988)

**GOOD DOUGLAS A REV** (253)922-6977
C/O Beautiful Savior Lutheran 2306 Milton Way - PO Box 1326 Milton WA 98354-1326 • chev327@juno.com • NOW • Sn/Adm • Beaut Savior Milton WA • (253)922-6977 • (FW 1984 MDIV)

**GOODFELLOW KENDALL EDWARD** (509)467-2099
8527 N Pamela St Spokane WA 99208-9656 • keg@nextdim.com • NOW • SP • Pilgrim Spokane WA • (509)325-5738 • (SPR 1969 MDIV)

**GOODIN WILLIAM D DR** (509)633-2767
517 Roosevelt Dr Grand Coulee WA 99133-9742 • NOW • SP • Zion Grand Coulee WA* • (509)633-2566 • (SPR 1970 MDIV MTH DMIN THD)

**GOODINE DAVID LEE REV** (610)924-0320
3600 Red Lion Rd Apt 64A Philadelphia PA 19114 • plm1111@abl.com • EA • D Miss • Christ Assembly Philadelphia PA • (215)726-9649 • (FW 1989 MDIV)

**GOODSMAN RONALD H REV** (319)323-3245
1354 8th Ave S Clinton IA 52732 • pastorgoodsman@aol.com • IE • SP • Grace De Witt IA • (319)659-9153 • (SL 1971 MDIV)

**GOODWILL RICHARD R REV** (512)248-9294
2029 Inverness Dr Round Rock TX 78681 • prgoodwill@aol.com • TX • Sn/Adm • Good Shepherd Cedar Park TX • (512)258-6227 • (FW 1987 MDIV)

**GORDISH TIMOTHY R REV** (507)834-6484
63888 240 St Gibbon MN 55335 • MNS • SP • St Peter Gibbon MN • (507)834-6484 • (FW 1998 MDIV)

**GORENTZ BERNARD R REV** (218)732-9670
11214 Fisher Ln Park Rapids MN 56470-9450 • MNN • EM • (SL 1944)

**GORKLO JOHN P REV** (303)814-2906
4087 Ashcroft Ave Castle Rock CO 60104-8763 • RM • 10/1996 10/1999 • (CQ 1983 MDIV)

**GORRELL LARRY N REV** (909)925-3274
1563 Chateau Ct San Jacinto CA 92583-5731 • PSW • EM • (SPR 1971 MDIV MED)

**GOSSMAN PAUL K REV** (708)343-1000
1025 W Lake St Melrose Park IL 60160 • paul@gossman.org • NI • Sn/Adm • St Paul Melrose Park IL • (708)343-1000 • (SL 1985 MDIV PHD)

**GOTFREDSON LARRY L REV** (707)762-7425
1988 Rainier Cir Petaluma CA 94954 • lgtfrdsn@pacbell.net • CNH • SP • St John Petaluma CA • (707)762-4466 • (SL 1986 MDIV)

**GOTOSKI GARLAND E REV** (972)240-6031
3925 Larkin Ln Garland TX 75043-2502 • ggotoski@gte.net • TX • EM • (CQ 1989 MDIV)

**GOTSCH RICHARD J DR** (847)272-4116
2344 Maple Ave Northbrook IL 60062-5210 • eliznrich@aol.com • NI • EM • (SL 1957 MDIV STM STD)

**GOTTBERG ARMIN C REV** (214)750-0578
10320 Stone Canyon #204S Dallas TX 75230 • gottberg@juno.com • TX • EM • (SL 1938)

**GOTTBERG GERALD W REV** (402)263-5870
2268 E Lake Dr Union NE 68455-2602 • NEB • EM • (SPR 1963)

**GOTTEL YEDDO A REV** (612)544-1770
7700 Winsdale St N Golden Valley MN 55427-4055 • MNS • SP • Immanuel Minneapolis MN • (612)522-5644 • (CQ 1995)

**GOTTSCHALK KENTON R REV** (313)582-0623
26827 Sheahan Dearborn Heights MI 48127 • pastorkeng@juno.com • MI • SP • Atonement Dearborn MI • (313)581-2525 • (SL 1978 MDIV)

**GOURLAY DONALD B REV** (708)386-2229
413 Division St Oak Park IL 60302-1438 • dgourlay.aol.com • NI • SP • Saint Paul Chicago IL • (773)378-6644 • (SL 1964 MA MDIV DMIN)

**GOWEN MITCHELL W REV** (808)488-0664
98-325 Koauka St Aiea HI 96701-4433 • oslc@aloha.net • CNH • SP • Our Savior Aiea HI • (808)488-3654 • (FW 1988 MDIV)

**GRABAU RUSSELL JOSEPH REV** (320)974-8983
19921 56th Ave NE Atwater MN 56209 • MNS • SP • St John Atwater MN • (320)974-8983 • (SL 1992 MDIV)

**GRABENHOFER GERHARD P REV** (607)962-9743
352 W Third St Corning NY 14830 • EA • SP • Faith Corning NY • (607)962-4970 • (FW 1993 MDIV)

**GRAEBNER STEVEN M REV** (941)641-3980
PO Box 2892 Clewiston FL 33440-2892 • graebner@gate.net • FG • 05/1997 05/2000 • (SL 1986 MDIV)

**GRAEF DAVID A REV** (219)477-4294
340 Arlington Ct Valparaiso IN 46383-9531 • IN • EM • (CQ 1975 MAR)

**GRAF ARTHUR E REV** (806)795-9583
4302 64th St Lubbock TX 79413-5112 • aegraf • TX • EM • (SL 1937 MTH DD)

**GRAF HERBERT C REV** (936)441-2812
8 Village Hill Dr Conroe TX 77304-3526 • TX • EM • (SPR 1956)

**GRAF PHILIP J SR. REV** (915)646-2045
C/O Grace Luth Church 1401 1st St Brownwood TX 76801-4201 • pgraf@web-access.net • TX • SP • Grace Brownwood TX • (915)646-2045 • (FW 1995 MDIV)

**GRAFE WILLIAM C REV** (248)363-4252
3533 Elder Rd S Orchard Lake MI 48324-2529 • lwceg@aol.com • MI • EM • (SL 1953 PHD)

**GRAFF PAUL L REV** (661)252-2146
19310 San Leandro Dr Santa Clarita CA 91321 • 102415.1716@compuserve.com • PSW • SP • Good Shepherd Inglewood CA • (310)671-7644 • (SL 1966 MDIV)

**GRAFF WARREN W REV** (517)539-6637
C/O St Luke Luth Church 616 S 4th St # 623 Harrison MI 48625-9149 • wwgraff@juno.com • MI • SP • St Luke Harrison MI • (517)539-6312 • (SL 1991 STM MDIV)

**GRAGG RANDOLPH LEWIS REV** (419)533-3295
8054 Cty Rd T Liberty Center OH 43532-9735 • duckeye@defnet.com • OH • SP • St Paul Liberty Center OH • (419)533-3041 • (FW 1992 MDIV)

**GRAHAM MICHAEL D REV** (630)906-1343
509 Mountain St Aurora IL 60505-2206 • NI • 09/1995 09/1999 • (FW 1979 MDIV)

**GRAMINSKE MATTHEW J REV** (920)893-8888
226 E Main St Glenbeulah WI 53023 • mjgrami@megavision.com • SW • SP • Zion Glenbeulah WI* • (920)893-8888 • (FW 1991 MDIV)

**GRAMIT PAUL E REV** (219)374-4959
9010 W 141st Ave Cedar Lake IN 46303 • IN • SP • Hope Cedar Lake IN • (219)374-7913 • (FW 1998 MDIV)

**GRAMMES RICHARD A REV** (412)486-8527
205 Wadsworth Dr Glenshaw PA 15116-2721 • diclov@bellatlantic.net • EA • EM • (CQ 1983 MAR)

**GRAMS CRAIG N REV** (605)397-2386
C/O St John Luth Church PO Box 348 Groton SD 57445-0348 • SD • SP • St John Groton SD • (605)397-2386 • (FW 1978 MDIV)

**GRAMS JEFFERY WALLACE REV** (308)635-1723
2218 Broadway Scottsbluff NE 69361 • jgrams@bigfoot.com • WY • SP • St John Scottsbluff NE • (308)635-1722 • (SL 1995 MDIV)

**GRAMS ROBERT D REV** (314)922-0733
473 Chelsea Ct Saint Charles MO 63304-5568 • bobgrams@inlink.com • EN • SP • Chapel Cross Saint Peters MO • (314)928-5885 • (SL 1994 MDIV)

**GRANKE WARREN A REV** (262)251-7621
N90W16555 Roosevelt Dr Menomonee Falls WI 53051-2135 • SW • Sn/Adm • Grace Menomonee Falls WI • (262)251-0670 • (CQ 1989)

**GRANT EDWARD J REV** (914)692-7075
24 Edinburgh Rd Middletown NY 10941-1744 • revgrant@warwick.net • AT • SP • Family Faith Middletown NY • (914)692-7075 • (CQ 1987 MDIV)

**GRASER ALFRED P REV** (518)792-2420
537 Glen St Glens Falls NY 12801-2207 • algraser@aol.com • AT • EM • (SL 1957)

**GRASSINGER TIMOTHY L REV** (719)262-9441
5450 Saddle Rock Rd Colorado Springs CO 80918-5227 • tim.grassinger@juno.com • RM • Sn/Adm • Immanuel Colorado Springs CO • (719)636-5011 • (SPR 1965 MDIV)

**GRASSLEY DAVID A REV** (817)249-1539
321 Sexton Ln Fort Worth TX 76126-3116 • grassley@flash.net • TX • SP • Redeemer Fort Worth TX • (817)560-0030 • (FW 1985 MDIV)

**GRATZ WILLIAM H REV**
507 David Dr Bremerton WA 98310-2935 • NOW • 11/1992 11/1999 • (FW 1984 MDIV)

**GRAUDIN ARTHUR F REV** (314)727-4477
6417 San Bonita Ave Clayton MO 63105-3117 • MO • EM • (SL 1950 MDIV DREL)

**GRAUDIN JOHN E REV** (843)689-3794
2 Sunflower Ct Hilton Head SC 29926-1713 • johnedg@juno.com • SE • EM • (SL 1954 MDIV)

**GRAUDIN KEVIN A REV** (410)820-5612
5505 Marlan Dr Trappe MD 21673-1908 • kgraudin@shore.intercom.net • SE • SP • Immanuel Easton MD • (410)822-5665 • (SL 1983 MDIV)

**GRAUL ROBERT W REV** (330)873-9502
308 Caladonia Ave Akron OH 44333-3712 • pasgraul@juno.com • EN • Assoc • Fairlawn Akron OH • (330)836-7286 • (CQ 1980 MDIV)

**GRAUMANN WAYNE E REV** (281)351-5281
16020 Lutheran School Rd Tomball TX 77375 • wayne@salem4u.com • TX • Sn/Adm • Salem Tomball TX • (281)351-8223 • (SPR 1974 MDIV)

**GRAUMANN WILLIAM S REV** (559)222-5034
5515 N Fresno #104 Fresno CA 93710 • wgrmnn@earthlink.net • PSW • EM • (SL 1937 MDIV DD)

**GRAUPNER HERBERT H REV** (231)780-2969
2042 Seminole Rd Muskegon MI 49441-4226 • MI • EM • (SL 1956)

**GRAVELYN TIMOTHY W REV**
6 W Indiana Ave Hamlet IN 46532-9530 • IN • SP • St Matthew Hamlet IN* • (219)867-2891 • (FW 1991 MDIV)

**GRAVES K FRANK REV** (810)229-2068
7193 Summit Ridge Brighton MI 48116-8277 • gravesb@ismi.net • MI • Assoc • Shep Lakes Brighton MI • (810)227-5099 • (SL 1972 MDIV DMIN)

**GRAVES RICHARD P REV** (573)774-3157
19535 Salem Rd Waynesville MO 65583 • gravesr@wood.army.mil • MDS • M Chap • Mid-South Cordova TN • (SL 1989 MDIV)

**GRAVES THOMAS A REV** (360)533-3718
1208 Friedlander Dr Aberdeen WA 98520 • NOW • Assoc • Calvary Aberdeen WA • (360)532-3980 • (FW 1999 MS MDIV)

**GRAVESMILL KEITH P REV** (512)733-0259
1172 Southern Pl Round Rock TX 78664 • caleb@flash.net • TX • SP • Our Savior Austin TX • (512)836-9600 • (SL 1988 MDIV)

**GRAY BARTON C REV** (517)734-0046
336 W Erie St Rogers City MI 49779-1631 • MI • SP • St John Rogers City MI • (517)734-4522 • (SPR 1970 MDIV)

**GRAY ROBERT W REV** (618)549-4327
835 Thunderstorm Rd Carbondale IL 62901-7341 • lutheran@siu.edu • SI • Sn/Adm • Our Savior Carbondale IL • (618)549-1694 • (SL 1973 MDIV)

**GRAY ROOSEVELT REV**
17500 James Couzens Hwy Detroit MI 48235-2642 • MI • SP • Outer Dr Faith Detroit MI • (313)341-4095 • (FW 1988 MDIV)

**GREBING TERRY L REV** (618)585-4774
621 E Warren St Bunker Hill IL 62014 • SI • SP • Zion Bunker Hill IL • (618)585-3606 • (SL 1982 MDIV)

**GREDVIG RODGER J REV** (619)571-7118
6548 Alcala Knolls Dr San Diego CA 92111-6947 • pgredvig@access1.net • PSW • SP • Peace San Diego CA • (858)268-4688 • (SPR 1972 MDIV)

**GREEAR JAMES NOAH REV** (414)774-0017
2217 N 103 St Wauwatosa WI 53216 • SW • Inst C • South Wisconsin Milwaukee WI • (414)464-8100 • (SL 1991 MDIV)

**GREEN ANDREW REV**
167 Park Ave Naugatuck CT 06770 • NE • SP • St Paul Naugatuck CT • (203)729-8610 • (SL 2000 MDIV)

**GREEN KENNETH D II REV** (561)734-7101
6313 Bengal Cir Boynton Beach FL 33437-3209 • blessed1@gate.net • FG • Assoc • Trinity Delray Beach FL • (561)278-1737 • (SL 1994 MDIV)

**GREEN LOWELL C REV** (716)684-0132
62 Leni Ln Buffalo NY 14225-4420 • lgreen@acsu.buffalo.edu • EA • EM • (WBS 1949 DTH)

**GREEN RICHARD F REV** (206)789-0546
8317 Earl Ave NW Seattle WA 98117-4531 • NOW • Assoc • Mount Zion Mountlake Terrace WA • (425)778-3577 • (SPR 1974)

**GREEN ROBERT L REV** (440)842-0694
4925 Ocala Dr Parma OH 44134-6339 • revrgreen@aol.com • OH • SP • Bethlehem Parma OH • (440)845-2230 • (FW 1996 MDIV)

**GREEN THOMAS REV** ~~(718)828-2696~~
1801 Seminole Ave Bronx NY 10461-1830 • AT • EM • (SL 1955 MDIV MA PHD)

**GREEN TIMOTHY REV** (215)877-9218
5327 W Columbia Ave Philadelphia PA 19131 • EN • 07/1997 07/2000 • (FW 1984 MDIV)

**GREENE JOHN H REV** (828)627-6634
1030 Redfield Dr Clyde NC 28721 • johnlisa@primeline.com • SE • SP • Our Savior Clyde NC • (828)456-6493 • (SL 1994 MDIV)

**GREENE ROBERT C REV** (512)863-2181
31013 La Quinta Dr Georgetown TX 78628-1174 • bobg2@igg-tx.net • TX • EM • (SPR 1963)

**GREENE STEVEN R REV** (505)777-2325
C/O Shep Of Vly Luth Ministry PO Box 204 Navajo NM 87328-0204 • RM • D Miss • Rocky Mountain Aurora CO • (FW 1980)

**GREENSETH RAY A REV** (605)279-2458
C/O First Luth Church 19615 Geigle Rd Creighton SD 57729 • SD • SP • First Wall SD* • (605)279-2453 • (SL 1982 MDIV)

**GREENTHANER EDWARD R REV** (520)885-9125
10162 E Lucille Dr Tucson AZ 85730-6135 • PSW • EM • * • (CQ 1987)

**GREENWALD KENNETH A REV** (740)264-6004
129 Lovers Ln Steubenville OH 43953-3465 • kengree@clover.net • S • SP • St Mark Steubenville OH • (740)264-2561 • (SL 1984 MDIV)

**GREENWAY BERTON L REV** (412)793-1394
2939 Universal Rd Penn Hills PA 15235 • revgreenway@juno.com • EA • SP • Grace Penn Hills PA • (412)793-1394 • (FW 1988 MDIV)

**GREENWOOD TERRY E REV** (808)573-6209
1071 Mac Ohu St Makawao HI 96768-9346 • terryg@maritgateway.com • SE • Asst • Our Saviour Baltimore MD • (410)235-9553 • (SPR 1973 MDIV)

**GREIN JOHN O REV** (320)547-2403
C/O St Peter Luth Church PO Box 126 Swanville MN 56382-0126 • jkgrein@fallsnet.com • MNN • SP • St Peter Swanville MN • (320)547-2928 • (FW 1983 MDIV)

**GREINKE KENNETH W REV** (314)394-1163
423 Sorrento Dr Ballwin MO 63021-6424 • IC3greinkkw@lcms.org • MO • S Ex/S • Missouri Saint Louis MO • (314)317-4550 • (SL 1965 MDIV)

**GRELL DAVID E REV** (518)475-1125
104 Elm Ave Delmar NY 12054 • NJ • 11/1999 • (SL 1982 MDIV)

**GREMEL KURT H REV** (317)675-4901
2816 S 200 W Tipton IN 46072 • IN • SP • Emanuel Tipton IN • (765)675-4090 • (CQ 1980 MED)

**GREMMELS DELBERT W REV** (228)388-3272
2588 Audubon Pl Biloxi MS 39531-3707 • delbertwg@aol.com • SO • EM • (SL 1955 MDIV MA)

**GRENINGER FREDERICK C REV** (607)962-4970
54 Corning Blvd Corning NY 14830-2024 • EA • EM • (CQ 1962 MDIV)

**GRESE EVERETT G REV** (901)758-2701
8060 Arbor Bend Ln Apt 108 Cordova TN 38018-6767 • MDS • EM • (SL 1942)

**GRESS C SCOTT REV** (561)369-2967
1446 B SW 25th Ave Boynton Beach FL 33426-7425 • sgress@earthlink.net • FG • Sn/Adm • Trinity Delray Beach FL • (561)278-1737 • (SL 1988 MDIV)

**GRETHER HOWARD F II REV** (814)938-9792
230 N Penn St Punxsutawney PA 15767 • revgrether@juno.com • EA • SP • Martin Luther Punxsutawney PA • (814)938-9792 • (FW 1999 MDIV)

**GREUNKE DEAN REV** (815)436-1327
2215 N Kelly Ave Apt 1 Plainfield IL 60544-8924 • NI • EM • (SL 1958 MDIV MAR)

**GREUNKE MARTIN R REV** (402)593-7320
906 Chisholm Trl Papillion NE 68046-3756 • mgreunke@aol.com • NEB • Sn/Adm • First Papillion NE • (402)339-3668 • (SPR 1969 MDIV)

**GREXA PAUL REV** (330)448-6131
239 Joshua Dr Brookfield OH 44403-9619 • S • EM • (SPR 1953)

**GRIEBEL KIRK E REV** (906)439-5547
C/O Sion Lutheran Church PO Box 131 Chatham MI 49816-0131 • elksgriebel@mail.tds.net • NW • SP • Sion Chatham MI • (906)439-5222 • (SL 1985 MDIV)

**GRIEBEL PAUL B REV** (219)347-4329
312 S Oak St Kendallville IN 46755-1759 • IN • Sn/Adm • St John Kendallville IN • (219)347-2158 • (SL 1973 MDIV)

**GRIESER WILFRED J REV** (608)423-4184
1771 Hillside Rd Cambridge WI 53523 • wgrieser@bminet.com • SW • SP • Zion Evansville WI • (608)876-6667 • (SPR 1962 MS)

**GRIESSE ELMER E REV** (360)786-8258
1111 Archwood Dr SW #399 Olympia WA 98502 • griessefe@aol.com • NOW • EM • (SL 1943 STM MDIV MA)

**GRIESSE MARK E REV** (360)794-7230
695 Park Ln Monroe WA 98272 • griesseme@aol.com • NOW • SP • Peace Monroe WA • (206)794-7230 • (SL 1992 MDIV)

**GRIESSE WILBERT E REV** (501)646-8234
3009 S 34th St Fort Smith AR 72903-4471 • MDS • EM • (SL 1940 MDIV DD)

**GRIEVES HERBERT H JR. REV** (315)797-3800
506 Tamarack St Utica NY 13502-1322 • hgrievesjr@cs.com • EA • SP • Trinity Utica NY • (315)732-7869 • (SPR 1968 MDIV)

**GRIFFIN DALE E DR** (314)821-3765
254 Elm Ave Saint Louis MO 63122-4718 • dgrif10500@aol.com • MO • EM • (SPR 1944 STM MDIV MED LITTD)

**GRIFFIN GARY W REV** (417)232-4509
PO Box 462 Lockwood MO 65682-0462 • immanuelgodwithus@hotmail.com • MO • SP • Immanuel Lockwood MO • (417)232-4642 • (CQ 1991 MSED)

**GRIFFIN LARRY J DR** (507)234-6942
410 N Main St Janesville MN 56048-9746 • trinity3@frontiernet.net • MNS • Sn/Adm • Trinity Janesville MN • (507)231-5189 • (FW 1980 MDIV DMIN)

**GRIFFIN MARK A REV** (601)362-8440
4580 Old Canton Rd Jackson MS 39211-5934 • SO • SP • St Philip Jackson MS • (601)353-0504 • (FW 1995 MDIV)

**GRIFFIN MARVIN REV**
17730 Pheasant Ln Country Club Hills IL 60478-4984 • NI • Assoc • Zion Matteson IL • (708)747-1116 • (CQ 1981)

**GRIFFIN ROBERT E REV** (845)778-1407
54 Wileman Ave Walden NY 12586-1038 • AT • EM • (SL 1958 MDIV)

**GRIFFIN TIMM L REV** (414)782-6802
15300 W Glendale Dr New Berlin WI 53151-2916 • timmgrif@execpc.com • SW • SP • Blessed Savior New Berlin WI • (262)786-6465 • (SL 1982 MDIV DMIN)

**GRIFFIN WILLIAM H REV** (616)469-0654
16050 Lakeshore Rd Union Pier MI 49129-9333 • NI • EM • (GB 1951)

**GRIME PAUL J REV** (636)256-8328
322 Woodlawn Terrace Ct Ballwin MO 63021-8336 • paul.grime@lcms.org • MO • S Ex/S • Missouri Saint Louis MO • (314)317-4550 • (FW 1986 MDIV STM MMU PHD)

**GRIMENSTEIN EDWARD O REV** (785)337-2472
564 3rd Rd Bremen KS 66412 • grims@kansas.net • KS • SP • Immanuel Bremen KS* • (785)337-2472 • (FW 1999 MDIV)

**GRIMM DALE A REV** (734)433-5419
4791 Cottonwood Ln Chelsea MI 48118-9546 • imgrimm@ibm.net • MI • SP • Our Savior Chelsea MI • (734)475-1404 • (FW 1980 MDIV)

**GRIMM DAVID AARON REV** (319)445-0355
4712 N Main St Davenport IA 52806-4122 • pdgtlc@juno.com • IE • Assoc • Trinity Davenport IA • (319)323-8001 • (SL 1992 MDIV)

**GRIMM EDWARD R REV**
602 SE 2nd St Ankeny IA 50021-3788 • lutheranpastor@uswest.net • IW • SP • St Paul Ankeny IA • (515)964-1250 • (FW 1996 MDIV)

**GRIMM GERALD E REV** (810)977-9595
11591 Arden Warren MI 48093-1105 • MI • SP • Mount Calvary Detroit MI • (313)527-3366 • (SL 1969 MA MDIV)

**GRIMM GERALD J REV** (570)823-6737
9 Glendale Dr Mountaintop PA 18707 • jag715@msn.com • EA • EM • (SPR 1964 MDIV)

**GRIMM KEITH H REV** (402)758-0465
13424 Valley St Omaha NE 68144 • NEB • Assoc • Beaut Savior Omaha NE • (402)331-7376 • (SL 1991 MDIV)

**GRIMM ROBERT W REV** (913)765-3607
706 Iowa St Alma KS 66401-9504 • r.w.grimm@juno.com • KS • SP • St John Alma KS • (785)765-3632 • (FW 1985 MDIV)

**GRISER LOUIS EARL REV** (402)795-3770
417 Pine St PO Box 93 Pleasant Dale NE 68423-0193 • legriser@aol.com • NEB • SP • Bethlehem Pleasant Dale NE • (402)795-3885 • (CQ 1974 MED)

**GROELING NEAL S REV** (734)282-5877
441 Chestnut St Wyandotte MI 48192 • groeling@concentric.net • MI • Sn/Adm • Trinity Wyandotte MI • (734)282-5877 • (SL 1987 MDIV)

**GROENEWOLD DOUGLAS R REV** (262)679-7335
577 W19786 Sanctuary Dr Muskego WI 53150 • cpnb13a@prodigy.com • SW • SP • Risen Savior Franklin WI • (414)529-5647 • (SL 1967 MDIV)

**GROENKE LLOYD E REV** (636)583-2657
61 Edwards Cir Union MO 63084-2044 • MO • EM • (SL 1955)

**GROERICH JAMES G REV** (303)935-9285
2796 S Wolff St Denver CO 80236-2009 • RM • EM • (SL 1951 MDIV)

**GROH CARL W REV** (501)329-3854
Peace Lutheran Church 800 S Donaghey Ave Conway AR 72032-6735 • MDS • SP • Peace Conway AR • (501)329-3854 • (SL 1989 MDIV)

**GROHN DENNIS R REV** (712)274-7557
2606 S Mulberry St Sioux City IA 51106-3403 • mside4@aol.com • IW • O Sp Min • Iowa West Fort Dodge IA • (SPR 1974 MDIV)

**GROLL DOUGLAS R DR** (773)622-1879
1724 N Rutherford Ave Chicago IL 60707-3941 • drgroll@worldnet.att.net • NI • SHS/C • Northern Illinois Hillside IL • (SL 1966 MDIV DD)

**GRONBACH ARTHUR F REV** (757)824-9829
PO Box 632 Atlantic VA 23303-0632 • SE • EM • (SL 1957 MDIV)

**GROSS GORDON A REV** (719)530-0789
940 Maple Salida CO 81201 • big144@bemail.com • RM • EM • (SL 1957)

**GROSS JEFFREY A REV** (618)459-3979
505 South Main St Worden IL 62097-1219 • SI • SP • Trinity Worden IL • (618)459-3991 • (FW 1989 MDIV)

**GROSS JOHN P REV**
699 Washington Blvd Roseville CA 95678-1567 • revgross@aol.com • CNH • SP • St Matthew Roseville CA • (916)773-5771 • (FW 1988)

**GROSS LLOYD E REV** (216)459-0767
5901 Graydon Dr Seven Hills OH 44131-1907 • revleg@aol.com • OH • Sn/Adm • Christ Cleveland OH • (216)961-6060 • (SL 1968 MST)

**GROSS RICHARD E REV** (503)644-5489
13345 SW 22nd St Beaverton OR 97008-5026 • NOW • EM • (SL 1947)

**GROTELUSCHEN NORMAN L REV** (901)854-4192
360 Fairwoods Dr Collierville TN 38017-3541 • MDS • EM • (SL 1949 MDIV)

**GROTH CHARLES A REV** (859)266-7464
3376 Monavesta Rd Lexington KY 40502 • kycgroth@aol.com • IN • S Miss • Indiana Fort Wayne IN • (SPR 1975 MDIV)

**GROTH DAVID KARL REV** (314)868-3055
1446 Blackhurst Dr Saint Louis MO 63137-1531 • MO • SP • Grace Chapel Saint Louis MO • (314)868-3232 • (SL 1992 MDIV STM)

**GROTH HARVEY W REV** (314)631-1702
9847 Coventry Ln Saint Louis MO 63123-4313 • grothrevharvmarge@yahoo.com • MO • EM • (SPR 1969 MDIV)

**GROTH JEROME H REV** (920)743-0206
4158 Snake Island Rd Sturgeon Bay WI 54235-8427 • EN • EM • (SL 1960)

**GROTH M CHARLES REV** (312)737-7082
C/O Nazareth Luth Church 3250 W 60th St Chicago IL 60629-3230 • NI • SP • Nazareth Chicago IL • (773)737-7082 • (SL 1961)

**GROTH TERENCE R REV** (618)692-0314
1925 Vassar Dr Edwardsville IL 62025-2664 • trgroth@yahoo.com • SI • Sn/Adm • Trinity Edwardsville IL • (618)656-2918 • (SL 1979 MDIV MST)

**GROTHE FREDERICK REV** (616)536-2481
1601 Walpole Dr # B Chesterfield MO 63017-4626 • MO • EM • (SL 1937 MA)

**GROTHE ROBERT LEE REV** (253)946-0957
31416 11th Pl S Federal Way WA 98003-5310 • rgrothe@tcmnet.com • NOW • 01/1995 01/2000 • (FW 1981 MA)

**GROTHEER KURT V REV** (847)259-9075
21 S Maple St Mt Prospect IL 60056-3227 • NI • EM • (SL 1937 MDIV)

**GROTHER LOUIS W REV** (616)344-2417
4309 Sunnybrook Dr Kalamazoo MI 49008-3344 • MI • EM • (SL 1937 MA MDIV)

**GROTHMAN FLOYD W REV** (715)424-4480
1400 River Run Dr Apt 209 Wisconsin Rapids WI 54494-5429 • NW • EM • (SPR 1950)

**GROVENSTEIN PHILLIP S REV** (732)833-2329
256 Toms River Rd Jackson NJ 08527 • chemnitznj@aol.com • NJ • SP • Peace In Christ Jackson NJ • (732)928-2727 • (FW 1985 MDIV)

**GRUBBS TRAVIS S REV** (716)532-1953
32 Orchard Pl Gowanda NY 14070 • revtgrubbs@cs.com • EA • SP • Immanuel Gowanda NY • (716)532-4342 • (FW 1981 MDIV)

**GRUBER JAMES L REV**
PO Box 428 Marcus IA 51035-0428 • jigruber@nwidt.com • IW • SP • Peace Marcus IA • (712)376-4818 • (FW 1978 MDIV)

**GRUDEN MARK E REV** (217)428-9976
66 Nolen Dr Decatur IL 62521 • CI • Assoc • St John Decatur IL • (217)875-3656 • (SL 2000 MDIV)

**GRUEL MICHAEL R REV** (413)562-2805
125 Glenwood Dr Westfield MA 01085-4920 • NE • SP • St John Westfield MA • (413)568-1417 • (SL 1967 MDIV)

**GRUELL EUGENE F REV** (530)938-4088
17716 Mount Blanch Dr Weed CA 96094-9307 • gruell@snowcrest.net • TX • EM • (SL 1946 DD)

**GRUEN DARALD A REV** (847)265-2450
2312 E Sand Lake Rd Lindenhurst IL 60046-7862 • 9gruens@concentric.net • NI • IndC P • Northern Illinois Hillside IL • (CQ 1996)

**GRUENBAUM PHILIP L REV** (630)896-2430
901 Prairie St Aurora IL 60506-5419 • NI • Inst C • Northern Illinois Hillside IL • (CQ 1989)

**GRUENHAGEN DAVID L REV** (517)278-8851
30 Douglas Ave Coldwater MI 49036 • gruenhagen@cbpv.com • MI • SP • St Paul Coldwater MI • (517)278-8061 • (CQ 1988 MED)

**GRUENWALD DANIEL J REV** (616)363-4005
2438 College Ave NE Grand Rapids MI 49505-3639 • pastor@iserv.net • EN • SP • Hope Grand Rapids MI • (616)459-2941 • (FW 1983 MDIV)

**GRUETZNER JAMES M REV** (810)652-6718
777 Oakbrook Rdg Rochester Hills MI 48307-1043 • MI • EM • (SL 1956)

**GRUHN MICHAEL V REV** (712)378-3417
C/O First Luth Church PO Box 306 Kingsley IA 51028-0306 • revgruhn@willinet.net • IW • SP • First Kingsley IA • (712)378-2129 • (CQ 1981 MED)

**GRULKE GALEN E REV** (517)768-9175
C/O Trinity Lutheran Church 122 W Wesley St Jackson MI 49201-2227 • ggrulke@dmci.net • MI • Sn/Adm • Trinity Jackson MI • (517)784-3135 • (CQ 1991 MDIV)

**GRUMM M H REV**
4608 Lawrenceville Hwy Tucker GA 30084-2903 • FG • EM • (SL 1931 LLD)

**GRUMMER ROGER H REV** (817)283-1735
1400 Fair Oaks Blvd Euless TX 76039-2727 • rgrummer@flash.net • TX • SP • Concordia Bedford TX • (817)283-3560 • (SPR 1961 MA DMIN)

**GRUND TERRY L REV** (205)655-4560
2029 Gadsden Hwy Birmingham AL 35235-3230 • SO • O Sp Min • Redeemer Birmingham AL • (205)853-5739 • (SL 1990 MDIV)

**GRUNDMANN C FRED REV** (406)771-7716
1200 32nd St S #87 Great Falls MT 59405-5343 • MT • SP • Trinity Great Falls MT • (406)452-2121 • (CQ 1979 MDIV)

**GRUNDMEIER RUSSELL M REV** (605)338-2454
1705 S Melanie Ln Sioux Falls SD 57103-3641 • SD • EM • (SPR 1950)

**GRUNOW ROBERT ADELBERT REV** (352)683-2196
Timber Pines 2286 Augusta Dr Spring Hill FL 34606 • digrag@aol.com • FG • EM • (SL 1949 MAR MA MA MA STM DMIN)

**GRUNOW WM PAUL REV** (510)351-4628
1334 Devonshire Ave San Leandro CA 94579-1348 • EN • SP • Christ San Leandro CA • (510)351-4628 • (SL 1940 MA MA)

**GRUNST MARK P REV** (406)669-3125
4035 Buffalo Trail Rd Molt MT 59057-2131 • MT • Sn/Adm • Mount Olive Billings MT • (406)656-6687 • (FW 1981 MDIV)

**GRUONER DAVID F REV** (785)348-5316
202 Church St Box 343 Linn KS 66953-9527 • kdbjgruoner@juno.com • KS • SP • Zion Linn KS • (785)348-5332 • (SL 1979 MDIV)

**GRZYBOWSKI TERRY L REV** (218)346-6090
555 6th Ave SW Perham MN 56573-1668 • gbo@djam.com • MNN • SP • St Paul Perham MN • (218)346-7725 • (SL 1982 MDIV)

**GUDE GEORGE J DR** (618)377-6246
5221 Loop Rd Dorsey IL 62021-1103 • SI • SP • Emmaus Dorsey IL • (618)377-6221 • (SL 1967 MDIV MST THD)

**GUDEL JOSEPH P REV** (219)485-7256
5714 Evard Rd Fort Wayne IN 46835-1771 • IN • Tchr • Concordia LHS Fort Wayne IN • (219)483-1102 • (CQ 1991 MA)

**GUDGEL RICHARD L REV** (402)393-5585
8620 Pacific St Omaha NE 68114-5230 • randbgudgel@juno.com • NEB • SP • Mount Calvary Omaha NE • (402)551-0244 • (CQ 1990 MED MAR)
**GUDMUNDSON THOMAS P REV** (920)803-9201
2319 N 40th St Sheboygan WI 53083-3504 • stpaulsf@bytehead.com • SW • Assoc • St Paul Sheboygan Falls WI • (920)467-6449 • (SL 1981 MDIV)
**GUEBERT PAUL N REV** (562)944-3575
14864 Fairvilla Dr La Mirada CA 90638-3008 • guebertpm@juno.com • PSW • EM • (SL 1947)
**GUELZOW DAVID J REV** (828)326-9294
960 36th Avenue Cir NE Hickory NC 28601-9663 • davidguelzow@twave.net • SE • Sn/Adm • St Stephen Hickory NC • (828)256-9865 • (SL 1990 MS MDIV)
**GUELZOW JAMES R REV** (813)963-3419
5513 Raven Ct Tampa FL 33625-1919 • FG • SP • Messiah Tampa FL • (813)961-2182 • (SL 1974 MDIV)
**GUELZOW NATHAN J REV**
C/O Holy Cross Lutheran Church 760 N Sun Dr Lake Mary FL 32746 • S • Asst • Holy Cross Lake Mary FL • (407)333-0797 • (SL 2000 MDIV)
**GUETERSLOH RALPH A REV**
2015 S 127th Cir Omaha NE 68144 • rgueter@aol.com • NEB • 06/2000 • (SL 1967 MRE MDIV)
**GUETTLER RONALD H REV** (248)585-9485
235 Orchard View Dr Royal Oak MI 48073-3321 • MI • EM • (SL 1957)
**GUGEL CHRISTIAN F REV** (515)732-1241
415 State St Osage IA 50461-1939 • gugel@osage.net • IE • SP • Trinity Osage IA • (515)732-4771 • (FW 1987 MDIV)
**GULLEN JAMES K REV** (618)533-5208
38 Edgewood Ln N Centralia IL 62801-3707 • SI • Sn/Adm • Trinity Centralia IL • (618)532-2614 • (FW 1982 MDIV)
**GUMZ BERNARD C REV** (920)923-4311
37 University Dr Fond Du Lac WI 54935-2935 • SW • EM • (SL 1940)
**GUNDERLACH DAVID P REV** (757)440-0275
1244 Mindoro St Norfolk VA 23511-1212 • davjoy@norfolk.infi.net • EA • M Chap • Eastern Williamsville NY • (716)634-5111 • (SL 1974 MDIV MA)
**GUNDERMANN MILTON W REV** (808)247-1402
46-146 Nahiku St Kaneohe HI 96744-3630 • CNH • EM • (SPR 1951)
**GUNDERMANN VERNON D REV** (314)984-9472
34 Cedarbrook Ln Kirkwood MO 63122-5211 • gundermn@i1.net • MO • Sn/Adm • Concordia Kirkwood MO • (314)822-7772 • (SL 1963 MDIV)
**GUNDERSON DAVID E REV** (605)665-6869
2010 Ross St Yankton SD 57078-1851 • gunersn@willinet.net • SD • Sn/Adm • St John Yankton SD • (605)665-7337 • (SL 1981 MDIV)
**GUNDLACH THEODORE E REV** (414)637-1968
1135 Blaine Ave Racine WI 53405-2904 • SW • EM • (CQ 1965)
**GUNTER GEORGE REV**
1686 Whitestone Rd Spring Valley CA 91977-5421 • PSW • D Miss • Shield Faith San Diego CA • (619)286-6440 • (CQ 1986 MDIV)
**GUNTHER EUGENE C REV** (314)388-2488
1630 Orchid Ave Saint Louis MO 63147-1415 • heypastor/aol.com • MO • EM • (SPR 1938)
**GURNEY HUGO V REV** (303)669-7221
1904 W 24th St Loveland CO 80538-3034 • NOW • EM • (SPR 1933 PHD)
**GUSEWELLE MONTE W REV** (510)632-1592
6018 Brann St Oakland CA 94605-1544 • guse13@aol.com • CNH • SP • Our Redeemer Oakland CA • (510)632-4841 • (SL 1973 MDIV)
**GUSSICK ROBERT F REV** (623)972-3455
11001 N 99th Ave Peoria AZ 85345-2405 • EN • EM • (SL 1941 MDIV DMIN)
**GUSTAFSON CHARLES REV** (203)699-8942
312 Sharon Dr Cheshire CT 06410-4250 • coachrev@juno.com • NE • SP • Cheshire Cheshire CT • (203)272-5106 • (SL 1979 MDIV)
**GUSTAFSON SCOTT ARTHUR REV** (612)467-2962
115 Muirfield Cir Young America MN 55397 • MNS • Assoc • St John Young America MN • (612)467-2740 • (SL 1996 MDIV)
**GUSTKE GEORGE M REV** (802)775-1384
C/O Messiah Lutheran Church 42 Woodstock Ave Rutland VT 05701-3517 • NE • SP • Messiah Rutland VT • (802)775-0231 • (SPR 1960)
**GUTZ GLEN E REV** (402)565-4885
RR 1 Box 97 Hoskins NE 68740-9747 • g4tero@yahoo.com • NEB • Assoc • Mount Olive Norfolk NE • (402)371-1238 • (SL 1998 MDIV)
**GUTZ JOHN E REV** (815)673-1635
102 Trinity Dr Streator IL 61364-3120 • S • SP • Holy Trinity Streator IL • (815)672-2393 • (SL 1988 MDIV)
**GUTZ LUTHER R REV** (208)765-2560
4301 N Ramsey Rd Trlr D20 Coeur D Alene ID 83815-8450 • lutherg@nicon.org • NOW • Inst C • Northwest Portland OR • (SPR 1968 MDIV MCOUN PHDREL)

### H

**HAACK LON R REV** (415)567-0175
2200 Pacific Ave 7B San Francisco CA 94115-1433 • lrhaack@aol.com • CNH • SP • Resurrection San Rafael CA • (415)479-1334 • (SPR 1973 STM MA)
**HAACK MILTON G REV** (612)729-2507
3457 11th Ave S Minneapolis MN 55407-2130 • MNS • EM • (SPR 1952)
**HAAG STEVEN JOHN REV**
C/O Trinity Lutheran Church PO Box 144 Sheldon WI 54766-0144 • shaag@centurytel.net • NW • SP • Trinity Sheldon WI* • (715)452-5359 • (SL 1994 MDIV)
**HAAK HERMAN D REV** (320)272-4132
1393 220th Ave Ogilvie MN 56358-3909 • MNN • EM • * • (SPR 1945)
**HAAK LOEL G DR** (623)931-6645
4034 W Hatcher Phoenix AZ 85051-3245 • lghaak@juno.com • PSW • Sn/Adm • Christ Redeemer Phoenix AZ • (623)934-3286 • (SL 1964 MDIV MST DMIN)
**HAAKANA JON T REV** (715)386-9183
905 Colonial Dr Hudson WI 54016-1935 • MNS • D Miss • Family Of Christ Houlton WI • (715)549-6140 • (SL 1983 MDIV)
**HAAKE CHARLES W REV** (712)792-9990
C/O St Paul Luth Church 19th & Highland Dr Carroll IA 51401 • stpaulle@pionet.net • IW • SP • St Paul Carroll IA • (712)792-4354 • (SL 1968 MDIV)
**HAAKE ELDOR W REV** (309)764-6811
4108 21st Ave Moline IL 61265-4506 • CI • Assoc • Holy Cross Moline IL • (309)764-9720 • (SPR 1948 DD)
**HAARA DAVID M REV** (813)994-1953
8740 Ashworth Tampa FL 33647 • haara@aol.com • S • D Miss • Family Of Christ Tampa FL • (813)558-9343 • (SL 1989 MA MDIV)
**HAAS MARK W REV** (916)927-9725
10 Rock Hill Ct Sacramento CA 95833-1012 • mhaasrev@aol.com • CNH • SP • Peace Sacramento CA • (916)927-5934 • (CQ 1986 MAR MED)
**HAAS ROLAND R REV** (562)598-5063
11372 Davenport Rd Los Alamitos CA 90720-3017 • PSW • EM • (SL 1952 MS MA)
**HAASE DONALD R REV** (520)722-2580
3905 N Placita Hondonada Tucson AZ 85750-2355 • bunnywaltz@aol.com • EN • Sn/Adm • Faith Tucson AZ • (520)326-2262 • (SL 1972 MS MDIV)
**HABERKOST DANIEL R REV** (330)725-6025
2831 Stiegler Rd Medina OH 44256-9431 • EN • SP • Prince Peace Medina OH • (330)723-8293 • (FW 1986 MDIV MA)
**HABERKOST JAMES P REV** (708)354-9515
544 Sunset Ave La Grange IL 60525-6117 • NI • Sn/Adm • St John La Grange IL • (708)354-1690 • (SL 1959 MA)
**HABERMAS DAVID J REV** (920)233-2225
1145 Devonshire Dr Oshkosh WI 54901-6233 • habermas@northnet.net • SW • EM • (SL 1965 MDIV MSED STM)
**HABERSTOCK PAUL J H REV** (708)957-5719
1139 Leavitt Ave #208 Flossmoor IL 60422-1540 • chaplainph@aol.com • NI • Inst C • Northern Illinois Hillside IL • (CQ 1972 MED)
**HACKBARDT D MICHAEL REV** (216)398-1127
5418 Northcliff Ave Cleveland OH 44144-4021 • bible@godsword.org • EN • O Sp Min • English Farmington MI • (FW 1986 MDIV)
**HACKBARTH DONALD L REV** (262)694-3273
C/O Good Sheph Luth Church 4311 104th St Pleasant Prairie WI 53158-3723 • dhackbar@aol.com • SW • SP • Good Shepherd Pleasant Prairie WI • (262)694-4405 • (FW 1978 MDIV DMIN)
**HACKBARTH LLOYD J REV** (636)327-6697
509 Spring Meadow Dr Wentzville MO 63385 • MO • Sn/Adm • Immanuel Wentzville MO • (314)327-4416 • (SL 1961 MDIV)
**HACKETT THOMAS S REV** (937)642-8805
16561 Kendall Rd Marysville OH 43040-8900 • stjohnsl@postbox.esu.k12.oh.us • OH • Sn/Adm • St John Marysville OH • (937)644-5540 • (SPR 1976 MDIV)
**HACKLER ROBERT G REV** (217)345-2006
7058 N County Rd 1380E Charleston IL 61920 • CI • EM • (SL 1950 MED)
**HACKMANN E EDWARD DR** (505)891-4966
826 Thunder Rd SE Rio Rancho NM 87124-3197 • deogloria@juno.com • RM • EM • (SL 1947 MDIV MA PHD)
**HACKNEY DANIEL M REV**
C/O Our Savior Lutheran Church 1001 S Patrick Dr Satellite Beach FL 32937 • FG • SP • Our Savior Satellite Beach FL • (321)777-0232 • (SL 1998 MDIV)
**HADLEY TOM C REV** (972)412-4564
3408 Lilac Ln Rowlett TX 75089-3445 • pastor@crownoflife-lcms.org • TX • SP • Crown Of Life Rowlett TX • (972)475-1348 • (SL 1977 MDIV)
**HAEDGE RANDALL REV** (972)270-6674
822 Arrowhead Dr Garland TX 75043-5001 • phragmos@yahoo.com • TX • Assoc • Bethel Dallas TX • (214)348-0420 • (SL 1982 MDIV)
**HAEGER MARTIN A REV** (815)937-9027
1055 S Myrtle Ave Kankakee IL 60901-5457 • nidsouth@aol.com • NI • D Ex/S • Northern Illinois Hillside IL • (FW 1981 MA MDIV)
**HAENER EVAN W REV** (201)483-4938
504 Davis Ave Harrison NJ 07029-1214 • NJ • SP • St John Harrison NJ • (973)483-4938 • (FW 1991 MDIV STM)
**HAENFTLING JAMES F REV** (231)585-7095
PO Box 805 Gaylord MI 49735-0805 • jimjean@avci.net • MI • EM • (SL 1964 MDIV)
**HAENFTLING PETER JAMES REV** (515)742-3464
713 Adair St Adair IA 50002-1121 • immluthch@juno.com • IW • SP • Immanuel Adair IA* • (515)742-3821 • (FW 1996 MDIV)
**HAERER KEITH A REV** (319)385-2390
C/O Faith Lutheran Church 910 E Mapleleaf Dr Mount Pleasant IA 52641-1405 • IE • SP • Faith Mount Pleasant IA • (319)385-8427 • (FW 1994 MDIV)
**HAERTEL ROBERT N REV** (502)458-7180
2807 Montrose Ave Louisville KY 40205 • IN • EM • (SL 1949)
**HAERTLING DANIEL C REV** (760)738-1561
1901 Bear Valley Oaks Escondido CA 92025-6300 • PSW • 09/1992 09/1997 • (SL 1958)
**HAEUSSLER KARL W REV** (716)298-9249
202 Beckwith Ave Niagara Falls NY 14304-1103 • khaeussler@aol.com • EA • SP • St Paul North Tonawanda NY • (716)692-3255 • (FW 1988 MDIV)
**HAFEMAN GREG S REV** (970)310-7774
1440 Grand Ave Windsor CO 80550-5815 • RM • 08/1999 • (FW 1985 MDIV)
**HAFEMANN DONALD V REV** (915)682-1919
2004 Hughes St Midland TX 79705-8332 • TX • EM • (SL 1941)
**HAFER MICHAEL ALBERT REV** (409)694-3161
1304 Austin Ave College Station TX 77845 • HCLutheran@aol.com • TX • SP • Holy Cross College Station TX • (409)764-3992 • (SL 1992 MDIV)
**HAFERMANN JOHN E REV** (309)795-1063
C/O Zion Luth Church 18121 134th Ave W Taylor Ridge IL 61284-9737 • zionlc@winco.net • CI • SP • Zion Taylor Ridge IL • (309)795-1063 • (FW 1992 MDIV)
**HAFNER ALAN S REV** (319)647-3364
508 Washington St Victor IA 52347 • stjames@netins.net • IE • SP • St James Victor IA • (319)647-3375 • (FW 1989 MDIV)
**HAFNER CARL W REV** (805)238-3269
8337 Shirdon Pl Paso Robles CA 93446 • CNH • 08/1996 08/2000 • (CQ 1979 MDIV)
**HAFNER HILMER J REV** (712)675-4617
C/O St John Luth Church 108 Lime St # 216 Kiron IA 51448-7600 • IW • SP • St John Kiron IA* • (712)675-4881 • (CQ 1986 MED MAR EDS)
**HAFNER WESLEY H REV**
C/O Trinity Luth Church 14912 377th Ave Mansfield SD 57460 • SD • SP • Bethesda Marion SD* • (605)648-3968 • (FW 1994 MDIV)
**HAGAN RAYMOND L REV** (209)679-3808
925 Misty Trl Oak Harbor WA 98277-8243 • rayhagan@msn.com • NOW • SP • Concordia Oak Harbor WA • (360)675-2548 • (FW 1978 MDIV)
**HAGAN ROBERT LEE REV** (812)471-3669
2232 E Chandler Ave Evansville IN 47714 • haganlee@aol.com • IN • Assoc • St Paul Evansville IN • (812)422-5414 • (SL 1996 MDIV)
**HAGEBUSCH MICHAEL C REV** (410)778-2744
206 Pine St Chestertown MD 21620-1412 • SE • SP • Trinity Chestertown MD • (410)778-2744 • (SL 1971 MDIV MA)
**HAGEMAN JAMES A REV**
702 Windham Sq Glendive MT 59330-2644 • MT • Sn/Adm • Our Savior Glendive MT* • (406)377-3890 • (FW 1985 MDIV)
**HAGEMEIER FRED W REV** (501)646-7654
3606 Southview Dr Fort Smith AR 72903-6453 • MDS • O Sp Min • Mid-South Cordova TN • (SL 1962 MED DED DED)
**HAGEN DAVID E REV**
C/O St Paul Lutheran Church PO Box 368 Schaller IA 51053 • IW • SP • St Paul Schaller IA • (712)275-4299 • (SL 2000 MDIV)
**HAGEN GARY M REV** (360)574-4772
10620 NW 26th Ave Vancouver WA 98685 • NOW • Asst • St John Vancouver WA • (360)573-1461 • (SL 1987 MDIV)
**HAGEN LEVINE K REV** (505)892-2591
579 Archibeque Ave SE Rio Rancho NM 87124-3248 • RM • EM • (BY 1948)
**HAGEN ROBERT E REV** (309)799-7464
712 E 3rd St Coal Valley IL 61240-9413 • CI • SP • Trinity Coal Valley IL • (309)799-5650 • (SPR 1976 MDIV)
**HAGENOW MARTIN J REV** (517)642-3772
484 Ault St Hemlock MI 48626-9320 • hagenows@svol.org • MI • Sn/Adm • St Peter Hemlock MI • (517)642-8188 • (CQ 1980)
**HAGER HARRY A REV** (573)324-3285
1008 Southway Ct Bowling Green MO 63334-2438 • MO • EM • (SPR 1961)
**HAGLER BRIAN D REV** (217)253-9227
807 E Wilson St Tuscola IL 61953-1541 • olorin@net66.com • CI • 01/1999 • (FW 1986 MDIV)
**HAHN DANIEL ANTHONY JR. REV** (814)539-0123
C/O Holy Cross Luth Church 711 Chestnut St Johnstown PA 15906-2535 • 7hahns@msn.com • S • SP • Holy Cross Johnstown PA* • (814)539-0123 • (SL 1995 MDIV)
**HAHN DAVID GORDON REV**
1424 Corbett Rd Detroit Lakes MN 56501-4523 • MNN • Assoc • Zion Detroit Lakes MN • (218)847-7630 • (SL 1995 MDIV)
**HAHN ERNEST N REV** (905)279-1020
3081 Grenville Dr Mississauga ON L5A 2P6 CANADA • EN • EM • (SL 1952 STM MA MDIV DD)
**HAHN FREDERICK F REV** (303)789-3991
3945 S Galapago St Englewood CO 80110-4522 • RM • EM • (SL 1938)
**HAHN JAMES H REV** (818)368-7412
16991 Timber Ridge Dr Granada Hills CA 91344-1137 • PSW • SP • Our Savior First Granada Hills CA • (818)363-9505 • (FW 1979 MDIV)
**HAHN JEROME W REV** (715)627-7989
C/O St Matthew Luth Church N5674 CTH E Deerbrook WI 54424 • NW • SP • St Matthew Deerbrook WI* • (715)627-7989 • (SPR 1975 MDIV)
**HAHN KENNETH S REV** (805)485-5268
1035 W Roderick Ave Oxnard CA 93030-4126 • kenkathyh@aol.com • PSW • Assoc • St John Oxnard CA • (805)983-0330 • (SL 1972 MDIV)
**HAHN KEVIN A REV** (785)396-4411
131 Railroad St Wheaton KS 66551 • KS • SP • St Luke Wheaton KS • (785)396-4411 • (SL 2000 MDIV)

**HAHN KEVIN ELDOR REV**
7458 W Wishing Well Dr Frankfort IL 60423-8736 • NI • SP • Good Shepherd Frankfort IL • (815)469-1028 • (SL 1995 MDIV)

**HAHN THOMAS J REV**
C/O St John Lutheran Church 8313 - 2nd St Pittsville WI 54466-9544 • NW • Good Shepherd Frankfort IL • (815)469-1028 • (CQ 1985 MDIV)

**HAIGHT ELMER REV** (509)662-1956
1114 Foothills Ln Wenatchee WA 98801-1498 • DotHaight@aol.com • NOW • EM • (SPR 1968)

**HAKE ROGERS K DR** (219)234-7714
203 Swanson Cir NE South Bend IN 46615-2549 • rhake@michiana.org • IN • EM • (SL 1959 MDIV PHD)

**HAKES DAVID E REV** (517)868-9625
1667 Kern Rd Reese MI 48757-9454 • davidhakes@aol.com • MI • Sn/Adm • St Michael Richville MI • (517)868-4791 • (SPR 1963 MDIV)

**HALAMKA RONALD F REV** (901)682-3282
1073 Estate Dr Memphis TN 38119-4908 • MDS • EM • (SL 1959 MDIV MST DST)

**HALBOTH TIMOTHY P REV** (248)426-7719
34915 Drake Heights Dr Farmington MI 48335-3301 • glcms@prodigy.net • EN • Assoc • Grace Redford Township MI • (313)532-2266 • (SL 1989 MDIV)

**HALBOTH VICTOR F REV** (313)537-7576
25156 Pembroke Ave Redford MI 48240-1049 • EN • Sn/Adm • Grace Redford Township MI • (313)532-2266 • (SL 1957 MDIV)

**HALDEMAN KEITH R REV** (715)842-9165
712 Ross Ave Wausau WI 54403-6973 • haldemank@trinitynet.org • NW • Assoc • Trinity Wausau WI • (715)842-0769 • (SL 1994 MDIV)

**HALL CHRISTOPHER D REV** (205)759-9150
800 Energy Center Blvd #4502 Northport AL 35473 • SO • SP • University Tuscaloosa AL • (205)752-8784 • (SL 2000 MDIV)

**HALL DAVID S REV** (913)680-1121
1624 Shawnee Leavenworth KS 66048 • dshall@birch.net • KS • Assoc • Trinity Leavenworth KS • (913)682-7474 • (SL 1998 MDIV)

**HALL LESTER H REV** (405)842-6519
2329 NW 49th St Oklahoma City OK 73112-8365 • OK • EM • (SPR 1953)

**HALL ROBERT K REV** (812)547-9967
1105 Pestalozzi St Tell City IN 47586-1813 • IN • SP • Emmanuel Tell City IN • (812)547-4215 • (SPR 1970 MDIV)

**HALL RODNEY N REV** (408)266-0198
1835 Nelson Way San Jose CA 95129 • CNH • SP • St Mark Sunnyvale CA • (408)736-6605 • (CQ 1990 MA)

**HALLER MARK J REV** (712)336-8896
407 21st St Spirit Lake IA 51360-0422 • busybee@rconnect.com • IW • Assoc • Immanuel Spirit Lake IA • (712)336-1010 • (FW 1998 MDIV)

**HALLERBERG JAMES W REV** (619)437-1255
C/O Resurrection Luth Church 1111 5th St Coronado CA 92118-1807 • jwhaller@san.rr.com • PSW • SP • Resurrection Coronado CA • (619)435-1000 • (SL 1966 MDIV STM)

**HALLMAN GERHARDT F REV** (219)223-4690
5820E CR 350S Rochester IN 46975 • IN • EM • (CQ 1981 MAR)

**HALLMAN RICHARD C REV** (360)416-6772
1120 S 25th St Trlr 13 Mount Vernon WA 98274-4760 • NOW • EM • (CQ 1980)

**HALLMANN JAMES A REV** (990)925-6121
C/O Prince Of Peace Luth Ch 701 N Sanderson Ave Hemet CA 92545-1523 • peej@lasercom.net • PSW • Sn/Adm • Prince Peace Hemet CA • (909)925-6121 • (FW 1977 MDIV)

**HALM D RAY REV** (541)388-4559
20486 Timberline Ct Bend OR 97702-9303 • PSW • SHS/C • Pacific Southwest Irvine CA • (949)854-3232 • (CQ 1978 MDIV MA DED DD)

**HALVORSON LYLE W REV** (812)323-7411
1006 E Commons Dr Bloomington IN 47401 • OH • EM • (SL 1943)

**HALVORSON MARK W REV** (952)368-4774
1790 Park Ridge Dr Chaska MN 55318 • markannh@aol.com • MNN • SP • Lord Of Glory Elk River MN • (763)263-3090 • (SL 1985)

**HAMER BRIAN JOHN REV** (813)643-4692
1815 Princeton Lakes Dr #704 Brandon FL 33511-2233 • revhamer@prodigy.net • FG • SP • Christ King Riverview FL • (813)677-1332 • (FW 1995 MDIV)

**HAMER JOHN H REV** (219)485-9768
7006 Putt Ln Fort Wayne IN 46835-4049 • IN • Assoc • St Paul Fort Wayne IN • (219)423-2496 • (FW 1982 MA MDIV)

**HAMILTON GEORGE O REV** (616)844-5361
16229 Pine Hollow Ave Spring Lake MI 49456-2254 • mahamilton@novagate.com • MI • SP • St Matthew Spring Lake MI • (616)846-2490 • (SL 1986 MDIV JD)

**HAMILTON WENDELL R REV** (402)727-7528
1350 E 11th St Fremont NE 68025-4450 • NEB • EM • (SPR 1950)

**HAMIT C WAYNE REV** (972)355-3773
3520 Spring Meadow Ln Flower Mound TX 75028 • TX • Assoc • Prince Peace Carrollton TX • (972)447-9887 • (FW 1988 MDIV)

**HAMLOW RICHARD REV** (612)269-5486
C/O St John Luth Church 4005 40th Ave SW Montevideo MN 56265-3617 • MNN • SP • St John Montevideo MN* • (612)269-6601 • (SL 1966 MDIV)

**HAMPSTEN RONALD G REV** (337)626-1636
1916 Linda Ave Sulphur LA 70663-7118 • SO • SP • Trinity Sulphur LA • (337)625-3276 • (FW 1979 MDIV)

**HANAN NORMAN A REV** (320)236-7729
C/O Concordia Luth Church 13455 Bluffton Rd South Haven MN 55382-9098 • mhanan@lkdllink.net • MNN • SP • Concordia South Haven MN • (320)236-7550 • (CQ 1982 MED MA)

**HANDRICH BRIAN W REV** (402)375-3616
C/O Immanuel Lutheran Church 57885 860 Rd Wakefield NE 68784 • bhandri@midlands.net • NEB • SP • Immanuel Wakefield NE* • (402)375-3616 • (SL 1997 MDIV)

**HANDRICH DOUGLAS O REV** (309)697-1840
5927 W Fairview Rd Peoria IL 61607-1012 • CI • SP • Holy Cross Peoria IL • (309)697-4832 • (FW 1991 MDIV)

**HANDRICK THOMAS V REV** (940)767-1986
1526 South Winds Dr Wichita Falls TX 76302-2930 • handrick@wf.quik.com • TX • SP • St Paul Wichita Falls TX • (940)322-6112 • (FW 1978 MDIV)

**HANEBUTT ROBERT L REV** (530)676-1224
2435 Sandpiper Way Cameron Park CA 95682-9227 • CNH • EM • (SPR 1951)

**HANER JAMES R DR** (918)744-0013
PO Box 50527 Tulsa OK 74150-0527 • jhaner@swbell.net • OK • Sn/Adm • Grace Tulsa OK • (918)592-2999 • (SL 1966 MDIV DMIN)

**HANEY BYRENE KEITH REV** (414)871-6275
2550 N 48th St Milwaukee WI 53210-2845 • kmhaney@execpc.com • SW • SP • Gospel Milwaukee WI • (414)562-1890 • (SL 1993 MDIV)

**HANFT ADRIAN E REV**
C/O Our Father Lutheran Church 6335 S Holly St Littleton CO 80121-3555 • ahanft2@juno.com • RM • Assoc • Our Father Littleton CO • (303)779-1332 • (SL 1997 MS MA MDIV)

**HANKE KARL W REV** (816)350-8699
4301 S Cottage Ave Independence MO 64055-4506 • MO • 03/1996 03/2000 • (SPR 1964)

**HANNA CHARLES B REV** (315)337-2299
5329 Rome New London Rd Rome NY 13440-8329 • EA • Sn/Adm • St John Rome NY • (315)336-8090 • (SPR 1976 MDIV)

**HANNAH JOHN R REV** (718)892-7268
2130 Watson Ave Bronx NY 10472-5402 • hannahj39@aol.com • AT • Sn/Adm • Trinity Bronx NY • (718)828-1234 • (SL 1965 MTH DMIN)

**HANNEMAN HARVEY D REV** (316)686-9696
2176 South Terrace Dr Wichita KS 67218 • harveyhanneman@webtv.net • KS • EM • (SL 1964 MDIV)

**HANNEMANN HERMAN R REV** (507)326-7081
PO Box 25 Green Isle MN 55338-0025 • MNS • SP • St Paul Green Isle MN* • (507)326-3451 • (SL 1960 MDIV MAR)

**HANNEMANN MARK T REV** (402)489-2785
327 Taylor Park Dr Lincoln NE 68510-2346 • mthannemann@cs.com • NEB • Sn/Adm • Faith Lincoln NE • (402)466-6861 • (SL 1984 MDIV DMIN)

**HANNEMANN NORMAN A REV** (402)371-4568
605 Adare Rd Norfolk NE 68701-5410 • NEB • EM • (SL 1948)

**HANNEMANN PHILLIP L REV** (402)373-2225
PO Box 536 Bloomfield NE 68718-0536 • hannephil@yahoo.com • NEB • SP • First Trinity Bloomfield NE • (402)373-4704 • (SPR 1975 MDIV)

**HANNENBERG DARRYL S REV** (970)240-1803
1025 York St Montrose CO 81401-5155 • hannberg@rmi.net • RM • SP • Hope Montrose CO • (970)249-8811 • (FW 1989 MDIV)

**HANNUSCH HUGO A REV** (210)344-3337
1202 Morey Peak Dr San Antonio TX 78213-1725 • TX • EM • (SL 1943)

**HANS RICHARD J REV** (218)963-1217
6578 Cadwell Ave NW Brainerd MN 56401-8713 • rrjh23@brainerd.net • MNN • D Ex/S • Minnesota North Brainerd MN • (FW 1986 MTH)

**HANSEL WILFERD A REV** (828)252-6158
700 Biltmore Ave Apt 307 Ashville NC 28803 • EN • EM • (SL 1956)

**HANSELL GEORGE R JR. REV** (412)486-0644
403 Laurel Hill Rd Allison Park PA 15101-3830 • grh61655@aol.com • EA • SP • First Pittsburgh PA • (412)782-2272 • (FW 1981 MDIV)

**HANSEN DAVID D REV** (678)377-9559
C/O Holy Cross Lutheran Church 377 Valley Hill Rd Riverdale GA 30274-2757 • dthansen@stsi.net • FG • SP • Holy Cross Riverdale GA • (770)478-9324 • (SL 1985 MDIV)

**HANSEN DAVID L REV** (319)849-1845
1115 Water St #244 Center Point IA 52213-9314 • dchansen@cedar-rapids.net • IE • SP • St John Center Point IA • (319)849-1251 • (SL 1981 MDIV)

**HANSEN DONALD G REV** (949)858-1880
26 Regato Rnch Snta Marg CA 92688-3000 • PSW • EM • (SPR 1960 MS)

**HANSEN KENNETH E REV** (631)584-6257
193 Woodlawn Ave Saint James NY 11780-2528 • fafherkc@aol • AT • SP • St James Saint James NY • (631)584-5212 • (SL 1964 STM MDIV)

**HANSEN LEROY M REV** (843)236-7393
2557 Hunters Trl Myrtle Beach SC 29579-8404 • SE • SP • Holy Lamb Myrtle Beach SC • (803)236-1344 • (CQ 1998)

**HANSEN LYLE D REV** (515)576-1676
1464 21St Ave N Fort Dodge IA 50501 • rvhansen@frontier.net • IW • SP • Good Shepherd Fort Dodge IA • (515)573-3174 • (FW 1981 MA MDIV)

**HANSON BRUCE C REV** (334)602-5300
10654 Deakle Ct Grand Bay AL 36541 • bp.hanson@prodigy.net • SO • SP • Our Savior Mobile AL • (334)661-4524 • (SL 1971 MDIV)

**HANSON CARL MARTIN REV**
Chung Te Rd Sec 2 Ln 346 Alley 25 #20 11 F Taichung 406 TAIWAN • crlhan@ms17.hinet.net • IW • S Miss • Iowa West Fort Dodge IA • (SL 1996 MDIV STM)

**HANSON DEAN A REV**
PO Box 211 Pleasanton NE 68866-0211 • NEB • SP • Grace Pleasanton NE* • (308)388-2755 • (SL 1992 MDIV)

**HANSON PHILIP W REV** (712)527-5193
56742 230th St Glenwood IA 51534-6068 • phanson@neonramp.com • IW • SP • Faith Council Bluffs IA • (712)323-6445 • (SL 1966 MDIV)

**HANUS THEODORE R REV** (863)993-3435
722 W Whidden St Arcadia FL 34266-3547 • tedjonhanus@hotmail.com • FG • SP • Grace Arcadia FL • (863)494-7008 • (SL 1964 MDIV)

**HAPPEL E H REV** (847)516-1532
243 S Wulff St Cary IL 60013-2529 • NI • EM • (SL 1944 DD)

**HARBIN ROBERT N REV** (254)634-5858
C/O Grace Lutheran Church 1007 Bacon Ranch Rd Killeen TX 76542 • gracelcmskilleentx@juno.com • TX • Assoc • Grace Killeen TX • (254)634-5858 • (SL 1998 MDIV)

**HARDING MICHAEL S REV** (602)548-8468
1419 W Libby St Phoenix AZ 85023-2590 • pmsh@aol.com • PSW • SP • The Master Phoenix AZ • (602)997-7439 • (SL 1985 MDIV)

**HARDING STANLEY L REV** (630)832-5442
330 Ridgeland Ave Elmhurst IL 60126-2228 • immelm@mcs.net • NI • Assoc • Immanuel Elmhurst IL • (630)832-1649 • (SL 1986 MDIV MA)

**HARGER BURTON M REV** (715)236-7017
904 Colan Blvd Rice Lake WI 54868-8545 • revbmh@win.bright.net • NW • EM • (SPR 1960)

**HARKEY EDWIN T REV** (508)923-6388
22 Forest Park Dr Lakeville MA 02347-1626 • harkeyrama@tmlp.com • NE • SP • Of The Way Raynham MA • (508)822-5900 • (SL 1987 MDIV)

**HARLEY VERNON H REV** (507)235-9348
511 Tilden St Fairmont MN 56031-4116 • MNS • EM • (SPR 1940)

**HARM FREDERICK R DR** (732)849-4690
19 Amesbury Rd Whiting NJ 08759-3243 • mcfrh@aol.com • NJ • EM • (CQ 1962 MS DMIN PHD DD)

**HARM RUDOLPH H REV** (636)629-4445
1300 Highacres Dr Saint Clair MO 63077-2104 • rharm@mail.usmo.com • MO • EM • (CQ 1952 MDIV STM PHD)

**HARMAN MICHAEL D REV** (712)373-5283
504 S 1st Ave Anthon IA 51004-8173 • IW • SP • Trinity Anthon IA* • (712)373-5283 • (FW 1987 MDIV)

**HARMAN VINCENT RONALD REV** (520)317-0560
2242 E San Marcos Dr Yuma AZ 85365-3219 • christyuma@aol.com • PSW • SP • Christ Yuma AZ • (520)726-0773 • (SL 1995 MDIV)

**HARMANN ELDOR J REV** (920)387-5363
N 8092 Cty Hwy AY Mayville WI 53050 • SW • SP • Immanuel Mayville WI • (920)387-5363 • (SL 1961 MDIV)

**HARMELINK DANIEL NATHAN REV** (714)841-7620
16531 Kellog Cir # A Huntington Beach CA 92647-4419 • missio@earthlink.net • PSW • Assoc • Redeemer Huntington Beach CA • (714)846-6330 • (SL 1993 MDIV)

**HARMON CRAIG R REV** (219)483-9242
9613 W Cook Rd Fort Wayne IN 46818-9452 • NI • 06/1998 06/2000 • (FW 1981)

**HARMON STEVEN L REV** (423)926-2521
119 E Watauga Ave Johnson City TN 37601 • spharmon@juno.com • MDS • SP • Bethlehem Johnson City TN • (423)926-5261 • (SL 1987 MDIV)

**HARMON THOMAS E REV** (316)744-2978
4217 Country Ln Wichita KS 67220-1747 • risnsavior@aol.com • KS • SP • Risen Savior Wichita KS • (316)683-5538 • (FW 1983 MDIV)

**HARMON WILLIAM A REV** (516)292-5433
42 Marlborough Rd West Hempstead NY 11552 • harmons2@juno.com • AT • Assoc • Resurrection Garden City NY • (516)746-4426 • (SL 1998 MDIV)

**HARMS DAVID G REV** (503)645-1735
15568 NW Oakhills Dr Beaverton OR 97006-5507 • revdharms@aol.com • NOW • EM • (SPR 1963)

**HARMS ELVIN R REV** (618)656-9105
1335 Mary Dr Edwardsville IL 62025-4210 • elalharmsedus@juno.com • SI • Southern Illinois Belleville IL • (SL 1977 MED MDIV)

**HARMS ERHARD H REV** (217)463-1484
132 Concordia Dr Paris IL 61944-2379 • erhar22@tigerpaw.com • CI • EM • (SL 1941)

**HARMS GERALD E REV** (352)237-0031
6238 SW 100th Loop Ocala FL 34476 • jnjatocala@aol.com • FG • EM • (SPR 1969)

**HARMS GERHARD W F REV** (760)747-4784
1145 Barham Dr SPC 68 San Marcos CA 92078-4538 • PSW • EM • (CQ 1965)

**HARMS ROBERT W F REV** (308)381-4674
PO Box 401 Grand Island NE 68802-0401 • NEB • EM • (SL 1947)

**HARMS WALTER W REV** (512)282-2626
11303 Menodora Dr Austin TX 78748-1842 • TX • Sn/Adm • Bethany Austin TX • (512)442-4870 • (SL 1958 STM)

**HARNAPP HARLAN L REV** (303)466-0880
960 Coral St Broomfield CO 80020-3529 • RM • EM • (SL 1957 MDIV DD)

**HARPER WALTER J REV**
47 Quaker Ridge Rd Bethel CT 06801 • NE • Assoc • Immanuel Danbury CT • (203)748-3320 • (SL 2000 MDIV)

**HARR WADE M REV** (605)835-9214
211 Church Ave Gregory SD 57533-1516 • SD • SP • St John Gregory SD • (605)835-9214 • (SL 1993 MDIV)

**HARRE ALAN F REV** (219)462-3758
3900 Hemlock St Valparaiso IN 46383-1814 • alan.harre@valpo.edu • IN • END • Indiana Fort Wayne IN • (SL 1966 MDIV MA PHD)
**HARRE RICHARD D REV**
PO Box 241 Seward NE 68434-0241 • NEB • SP • Zion Garland NE • (402)588-2229 • (SL 1993 MDIV MBA)
**HARRE RICHARD R REV** (217)438-6826
1211 W Jackson Auburn IL 62615 • trinitylcms@auburnctnet.com • CI • SP • Trinity Auburn IL • (217)438-6820 • (SL 1968 MDIV)
**HARRIES THOMAS H REV** (785)828-4846
C/O Zion Luth Church PO Box 88 Vassar KS 66543-0088 • KS • SP • Zion Vassar KS • (785)828-4482 • (CQ 1992 MA)
**HARRIS JAMES N REV** (520)632-8962
20030 E Prickly Pear Dr Mayer AZ 86333-2140 • PSW • D Miss • Mountain Of Faith Mayer AZ • (602)632-8785 • (SL 1985 MDIV)
**HARRIS LAWRENCE H REV** (419)353-1401
18978 Mercer Rd Bowling Green OH 43402-9244 • OH • EM • (SL 1964 MDIV MA)
**HARRIS MARLIN L REV** (618)744-9719
2239 A Bridlewood Pl Scott AFB IL 62225 • marlin.harris@scott.af.mil • MNN • M Chap • Minnesota North Brainerd MN • (FW 1981 MDIV)
**HARRIS PAUL ROBERT REV** (512)453-3835
1207 W Forty Fifth St Austin TX 78756 • TX • SP • Trinity Austin TX • (512)453-3835 • (FW 1983 MDIV)
**HARRISON MATTHEW CARL REV** (219)744-5937
C/O Zion Lutheran Church 2313 Hanna St Fort Wayne IN 46803-2477 • veloescher@aol.com • IN • Sn/Adm • Zion Fort Wayne IN • (219)744-1389 • (FW 1991 MDIV STM)
**HARRMANN BRUCE REV**
3501 N 98th St Milwaukee WI 53222-2409 • SW • SP • Lamb Of God Pewaukee WI • (414)691-3828 • (SPR 1975 MDIV)
**HARROUN GARY K REV** (618)683-3407
PO Box 637 Golconda IL 62938-0637 • gharroun@shawneelink.com • SI • SP • Our Redeemer Golconda IL • (618)683-8621 • (FW 1987)
**HARSTE KENNETH REV** (763)786-2969
3839 97th Ave NE Circle Pines MN 55014-2516 • sheepherder4@juno.com • MNS • SP • Good Shepherd Circle Pines MN • (763)784-8417 • (FW 1983 MDIV)
**HART LEIGH G REV** (402)561-1630
4923 Cass #2 Omaha NE 68132 • NEB • O Miss • Nebraska Seward NE • (SL 1999 MDIV)
**HART MARCEL REV** (201)869-2447
C/O Our Savior Luth Church 605 76th St North Bergen NJ 07047-4905 • NJ • SP • Our Saviour North Bergen NJ • (201)868-5948 • (FW 1985)
**HART MICHAEL B REV** (507)932-0084
670 E 4th St St Charles MN 55972 • MNS • Assoc • St Matthew Saint Charles MN • (507)932-4246 • (SL 1989 MDIV)
**HARTENBERGER MARTIN J REV** (505)237-0373
1217 Blue Quail NE Albuquerque NM 87112 • RM • EM • (SL 1941)
**HARTER JEFFREY M REV**
460 Park St New Germany MN 55367-9718 • MNS • Inst C • Minnesota South Burnsville MN • (FW 1983 MDIV)
**HARTFIELD ALAN R REV** (616)473-2246
9124 George St Apt #2 Berrien Springs MI 49103-1654 • SE • EM • (SL 1968 MDIV)
**HARTFIELD CLEMENS H REV** (918)785-4615
RR 2 Box 840 Adair OK 74330-9416 • chartcove@rectec.net • OK • EM • (SL 1956)
**HARTFIELD PAUL W REV** (979)366-2220
RR 2 Box 165 Giddings TX 78942 • TX • EM • (SPR 1963)
**HARTFIELD ROBERT L REV** 011-493084109783
Kamillenstr 50 12203 Berlin GERMANY • rlhlcms@aol.com • CI • S Miss • Central Illinois Springfield IL • (SPR 1967 MDIV)
**HARTKE GERALD C REV** (219)478-4998
8620 Hempford Dr Fort Wayne IN 46819-2264 • hartke@mtcalvarylutheran.com • IN • Sn/Adm • Mount Calvary Fort Wayne IN • (219)747-4121 • (SL 1976 MDIV)
**HARTMAN JACK L REV** (716)632-4921
110 Dolphin Dr Butler PA 16002-3502 • EA • Inst C • Eastern Williamsville NY • (716)634-5111 • (SL 1976 MDIV)
**HARTMAN JAMES L REV** (920)452-9597
2215 N 34th St Sheboygan WI 53083-4306 • SW • Sn/Adm • Bethlehem Sheboygan WI • (920)452-4331 • (FW 1982 MDIV)
**HARTMAN PAUL A REV** (405)799-3962
613 SW 155th Pl Oklahoma City OK 73170 • kardiaish@aol.com • OK • SP • St John Moore OK • (405)794-5462 • (SPR 1965)
**HARTMAN STEPHEN E REV** (309)243-9121
759 W Wonderview Dr Dunlap IL 61525-9433 • revshartman@aol.com • CI • Assoc • Redeemer Peoria IL • (309)691-2333 • (FW 1986 MDIV)
**HARTMAN THEODORE E REV** (925)449-5628
1189 Riesling Cir Livermore CA 94550-5704 • oslc@pacbell.net • CNH • SP • Our Savior Livermore CA • (925)447-1246 • (SPR 1975 MDIV)
**HARTMANN ROLAND C REV** (918)689-4457
120 Broadway Ave Eufaula OK 74432-2647 • OK • SP • Good Shepherd Eufaula OK • (918)689-2169 • (SL 1987 MDIV)
**HARTNER HARLAN J REV** (913)722-4070
6416 Reeds Dr Mission KS 66202-4220 • KS • EM • (SL 1938)
**HARTNER TIMOTHY J REV** (954)252-9252
6215 Hawkes Bluff Ave Davie FL 33331-3423 • timothy@stpaulweston.org • FG • SP • St Paul Weston FL • (954)384-9096 • (CQ 1986 MDIV)
**HARTRICK PAUL W REV** (920)446-3252
PO Box 414 Fremont WI 54940-0414 • NW • EM • (SPR 1965 MDIV MA)
**HARTUNG BRUCE M DR** (314)996-1396
1333 S Kirkwood Saint Louis MO 63122-7295 • bruce.hartung@lcms.org • MO • S Ex/S • Missouri Saint Louis MO • (314)317-4550 • (SL 1967 MDIV STM PHD)
**HARTWELL ROBERT E REV** (914)725-6818
49 Homestead Ave Scarsdale NY 10583-5842 • Revhartwel@aol.com • AT • Assoc • The Village Bronxville NY • (914)337-0207 • (FW 1993 MDIV)
**HARTWIG JOHN D REV** (540)389-5291
123 Niblick Dr Salem VA 24153-6817 • SE • 05/1999 • (SL 1968)
**HARTWIG RAYMOND L DR** (314)664-6962
1333 SKirkwood Rd Saint Louis MO 63122-7226 • raymond.hartwig@lcms.org • MO • S Ex/S • Missouri Saint Louis MO • (314)317-4550 • (SL 1971 MDIV DD)
**HARVALA LARRY S REV** (701)652-2008
1714 Gold Dr S #203 Fargo ND 58103 • ND • DP • North Dakota Fargo ND • (FW 1980 MDIV)
**HASBARGEN ROY M REV** (320)363-1107
32314 Terry Rd Avon MN 56310-9694 • MNN • EM • (SPR 1959)
**HASE RICHARD A REV**
203 Prize Taker Ct Pasadena MD 21122-3875 • rickhase@aol.com • SE • 03/1996 03/2000 • (SPR 1975 MDIV)
**HASELHUHN DON MARTIN REV**
C/O Trinity Lutheran Church 902 Kennedy St Burlington KS 66839-1130 • KS • North Dakota Fargo ND • (SL 1994 MDIV)
**HASENSTEIN STEVEN J REV** (314)394-9520
502 Wyncrest Dr Manchester MO 63011-4410 • MO • SP • Zion Valley Park MO • (636)225-7780 • (SL 1973 MDIV)
**HASKELL KENNETH F REV** (316)221-6539
19219 111th Rd Winfield KS 67156-7880 • thehaskells@terraworld.net • KS • EM • (SL 1961)
**HASS LEROY DR** (414)771-8198
8325 W Wisconsin Ave Wauwatosa WI 53213-3351 • SW • EM • (SPR 1946 MDIV PHD)
**HASS MARK CHRISTIAN REV**
RR 3 Box 306 815 N Rice Hamilton TX 76531 • 2wyrms@htcomp.net • TX • Assoc • St John Hamilton TX • (254)386-3158 • (FW 1996 MDIV)
**HASS ROBERT C REV** (203)239-6635
125 Scrub Oak Rd North Haven CT 06473-1111 • NE • SP • Zion Wallingford CT • (203)269-6847 • (FW 1980 MDIV)
**HASSE DONALD E REV** (920)467-3042
628 Giddings Ave Sheboygan Falls WI 53085-1710 • dphasse@bytehead.com • SW • Sn/Adm • St Paul Sheboygan Falls WI • (920)467-6449 • (SL 1965 MDIV)
**HASSELBRING PAUL L REV**
C/O New Life Lutheran Church PO Box 82311 Pembroke Pines FL 33082 • FG • SP • New Life Pembroke Pines FL • (954)473-4353 • (FW 1999 MDIV MS)
**HASSKARL LEIF R REV** (806)669-7845
C/O Zion Lutheran Church 1200 Duncan Pampa TX 79065-4736 • leifh@juno.com • TX • SP • Zion Pampa TX • (806)669-2774 • (FW 1997 MDIV)
**HASSOLD WILLIAM J REV** (407)366-6285
1505 Chipmunk Ln Oviedo FL 32765-8709 • sarwilha@atlantic.net • FG • EM • (SL 1948 STM THD)
**HASZ LUTHER N REV** (901)423-5383
380 Henderson Rd Jackson TN 38305-9558 • lushorse@aol.com • MDS • SP • Concordia Jackson TN • (901)668-0757 • (SL 1966 MDIV)
**HATCH DAVID H REV** (414)465-8118
887 Saint Charles Dr Green Bay WI 54311-5829 • oslc@netnet.net • NW • Assoc • Our Saviour Green Bay WI • (920)468-4065 • (FW 1982 MDIV)
**HATHAWAY RODERICK A REV** (316)221-0646
810 E 9th Ave Winfield KS 67156-2942 • KS • SP • Trinity Winfield KS • (316)221-9460 • (FW 1985 MDIV)
**HATTSTAEDT OTTO H REV** (303)527-6798
53 Pan American Ave Paonia CO 81428-2010 • RM • SP • Immanuel Paonia CO • (970)527-3232 • (CQ 1984 MDIV)
**HAUBEIN WENDELL L REV** (417)777-4480
1560 S Sunset Ave Bolivar MO 65613-2293 • rwendell@ipa.net • MO • EM • (CQ 1981 MAR)
**HAUG DON D REV**
PO Box 273 Shrewsbury PA 17361 • lori-don@juno.com • SE • EM • (SL 1964 MDIV)
**HAUGEN JAMES A JR. REV**
1628 Clark Ave Billings MT 59102 • jhaugen445@aol.com • MT • Assoc • Trinity Billings MT • (406)245-3984 • (FW 1998 MDIV)
**HAUGEN JAMES A SR. REV** (219)244-4778
1444 W Business 30 Columbia City IN 46725-8717 • IN • SP • Zion Columbia City IN • (219)244-5513 • (SL 1972 MDIV)
**HAUGEN PAUL J REV** (712)328-3763
203 Wildwood Rd Council Bluffs IA 51503-5362 • IW • O Sp Min • Iowa West Fort Dodge IA • (SL 1990 MDIV)
**HAUGHT DAVID P REV**
PO Box 476 Mullan ID 83846-0476 • NOW • SP • Emmanuel Mullan ID* • (208)744-1324 • (FW 1987)
**HAUPT DIETER E REV** (616)846-7875
521 Marion Ave Grand Haven MI 49417-2104 • MI • Sn/Adm • St John Grand Haven MI • (616)842-4510 • (SL 1975 MDIV)
**HAUPT JAMES F REV** (210)344-8454
507 Downshire San Antonio TX 78216 • TX • EM • (SPR 1962)
**HAUPT KENNETH W REV** (732)257-6557
295 Summerhill Rd East Brunswick NJ 08816-4201 • NJ • SP • Christ Memorial East Brunswick NJ • (732)251-5454 • (SL 1970 STM)
**HAUPTMAN AUGUST L REV** (909)860-1960
23026 Paseo De Terrado Apt 4 Diamond Bar CA 91765-4480 • PSW • EM • (SPR 1948)
**HAUSCH THOMAS JAMES DR** (208)938-0752
398 N Sierra View Way Eagle ID 83616-4600 • NOW • SP • Friendship Meridian ID • (208)288-2404 • (SPR 1973 MDIV DMIN)
**HAUSCHILD DANIEL C REV** (858)268-4075
2750 Wheatstone St Space 177 San Diego CA 2 • PSW • SP • Holy Cross San Diego CA • (858)273-2886 • (SPR 1973 MDIV)
**HAUSER DALE A JR. REV** (815)577-8110
6450 Adamic Ln Plainfield IL 60955-9774 • pastorh@localline2.com • NI • Holy Cross San Diego CA • (858)273-2886 • (FW 1981 MDIV)
**HAUSER J GEORGE REV** (414)464-2306
4157 N 96th St Milwaukee WI 53222-1528 • SW • EM • (SL 1955)
**HAUSER LARRY A REV** (414)463-8277
4870 N 108th St Milwaukee WI 53225-3802 • berea@execpc.com • SW • SP • Berea Milwaukee WI • (414)466-9220 • (SL 1971 MDIV)
**HAUSER LEON E REV** (319)294-0271
7811 Burr Ridge Ct NE Cedar Rapids IA 52402-6729 • kngkngwb@aol.com • IE • SP • King Of Kings Cedar Rapids IA • (319)393-2438 • (SPR 1969 MDIV)
**HAUSER LUTHER H REV** (209)732-5729
711 S Edwards Ct Visalia CA 93277-2217 • CNH • EM • (SPR 1945 MA)
**HAUSER PAUL ALAN REV**
3940 Iva Rd Hemlock MI 48626 • MI • SP • Zion Hemlock MI • (517)642-5909 • (SL 1983 MDIV)
**HAUSMANN WILLIAM J REV** (610)681-5596
PO Box 471 Gilbert PA 18331-0471 • NJ • EM • (SL 1955 MDIV STM MA PHD)
**HAWKINS DANIEL D REV** (630)906-0046
343 Wildwood Dr N Aurora IL 60542 • NI • D Miss • Northern Illinois Hillside IL • (SL 1994 MDIV)
**HAWKINS HERMAN REV**
12997 SW Timara Ln Tigard OR 97224 • revherm@aol.com • NOW • SP • Martin Luther Memori Portland OR • (503)281-7036 • (SL 1985 MDIV)
**HAWKINSON MARK A REV** (573)237-2940
3833 Boeuf Lutheran Rd New Haven MO 63068-2202 • hawkam@fidnet.com • MO • SP • Bethlehem New Haven MO • (573)237-2602 • (SPR 1975 MDIV)
**HAWLEY JAMES F REV** (307)684-5369
955 N Burritt Ave Buffalo WY 82834-1403 • WY • EM • (SPR 1956)
**HAWLICHECK ARTHUR REV**
75 Great Pond Rd #237 Simsbury CT 06070-1905 • AT • EM • (SL 1937 MDIV)
**HAYAS DONALD M REV** (440)356-2964
20968 Woodstock Rd Fairview Park OH 44126 • S • SP • Pentecost Lakewood OH • (216)221-6265 • (SPR 1970 MDIV)
**HAYDEN STEVEN J REV** (712)448-2630
5086 480th St Paullina IA 51046-7532 • revhayden@hotmail.com • IW • SP • St John Paullina IA • (712)448-2637 • (SL 1986 MDIV)
**HAYDEN STEVEN L REV**
C/O Love of Christ Lutheran 5488 20th St N Saint Cloud MN 56303-0372 • MNN • Assoc • Love Of Christ Saint Cloud MN • (320)253-7453 • (SL 2000 MDIV)
**HAYDON KENNETH C REV** (501)253-7835
8 Thomas Dr Eureka Spgs AR 72632-9724 • kchaydon@ipa.net • MDS • SP • Grace Holiday Island AR* • (501)253-9040 • (SL 1968 MDIV)
**HAYEN NEIL E REV** (712)425-3328
PO Box 216 Mallard IA 50562-0216 • nehayen@ncn.net • IW • SP • Trinity Mallard IA* • (712)425-3328 • (CQ 1994)
**HAYHURST MARK G REV**
878 W Arlington Ave St Paul MN 55117 • hay³mark@juno.com • MNS • SP • Bethel Saint Paul MN • (651)488-6681 • (FW 1989 MDIV)
**HAYMAN MARK C REV**
C/O St Stephen Lutheran Church 6336 Berkley Dr New Orleans LA 70131 • st2nola@juno.com • SO • SP • St Stephen New Orleans LA • (504)394-4956 • (CS 1975 MDIV)
**HAYNES DOUGLAS W REV** (712)732-6598
C/O St John Lutheran Church 402 Lake Ave Storm Lake IA 50588-2445 • fairway@ncn.net • IW • SP • St John Storm Lake IA • (712)732-2400 • (SL 1972 MDIV)
**HAYNES JASON M REV** (909)948-7401
11531 Mt Hood Ct Rancho Cucamonga CA 91737 • soth@linkline.com • PSW • Asst • Shepherd Hills Alta Loma CA • (909)989-6500 • (SL 1999 MDIV)
**HAZEL FREDERICK G III REV** (520)836-6338
1748 E Catalina St Casa Grande AZ 85222 • PSW • SP • Trinity Casa Grande AZ • (520)836-2451 • (SL 1982 MDIV)
**HAZEL SHAWN FREDERICK REV** (503)692-3490
8153 SW Seminole Trl Tualatin OR 97062-8127 • hazels@transport.com • NOW • Assoc • Living Savior Tualatin OR • (503)692-3490 • (SL 1997 MDIV)
**HEADAPOHL GARY D REV** (313)522-4576
31478 Rosslyn Ave Garden City MI 48135-1344 • MI • Sn/Adm • St Matthew Westland MI • (734)425-0260 • (FW 1984 MDIV)
**HEARN FREDRICK C REV**
5140-9 Stonehedge Blvd Fort Wayne IN 46825 • EN • Assoc • Praise Fort Wayne IN • (219)490-7729 • (FW 1993 MDIV)
**HECK JACK D REV** (308)468-5525
14 El Charman Lk Gibbon NE 68840-9504 • jcheck@nctc.net • NEB • EM • (SPR 1963)
**HECK JOEL D REV** (512)339-7002
12062 Lincolnshire Dr Austin TX 78758 • heckyes@aol.com • TX • SHS/C • Texas Austin TX • (SPR 1974 MDIV MTH THD)

**HECK KYLE DAVID REV**
7224 49th Pl NE Marysville WA 98270-8825 • revheck@gte.net • NOW • Sn/Adm • Immanuel Everett WA • (425)252-7038 • (SL 1992 MDIV)

**HECKERT JAKOB K REV** (734)665-2697
419 Pine Brae Dr Ann Arbor MI 48105-2743 • heckej@ccaa.edu • MI • EM • (SL 1960 MED STM MA THD)

**HECKMANN EUGENE E REV** (281)955-9034
11314 Hillside Glen Trl Houston TX 77065-5026 • eeheckmann@juno.com • TX • EM • (SL 1958 MDIV)

**HECKMANN GARY W REV** (931)526-3046
1340 Sherwood Ln Cookeville TN 38501-1148 • gwheckmann@netscape.net • MDS • 09/1990 09/1999 • (SL 1972 MDIV)

**HECKMANN HAROLD A REV** (713)721-2331
5611 Burlinghall Dr Houston TX 77035-2623 • hheckmann@juno.com • TX • EM • (SL 1945 MDIV)

**HECKMANN JOHN M REV** (402)826-5281
11440 W Panama Rd RR 1 Box 66 Crete NE 68333-9608 • NEB • SP • St John Crete NE • (402)826-3883 • (SL 1985 MDIV)

**HECKMANN PETER TIM REV** (405)359-8380
1205 Alexanders Trl Edmond OK 73003-4373 • pheckmann@juno.com • OK • SP • St Mark Edmond OK • (405)340-0192 • (SL 1992 MDIV)

**HECKMANN ROBERT E DR** (605)743-5612
27078 Saddlerock Pl Harrisburg SD 57032 • ezzodad@pol.net • SD • 07/1991 07/2000 • (SL 1984 MDIV MA MD)

**HECKMANN ROBERT G REV** (804)740-3437
10402 Brookmont Dr Richmond VA 23233-2521 • rghmch@aol.com • SE • EM • (SL 1951 STM DMIN)

**HECKSEL STANTON R REV** (952)891-2158
14317 Glenda Dr Apple Valley MN 55124-5507 • shecksel@webtv.net • MNS • EM • (SL 1958 MDIV)

**HEDBERG CARL R REV** (515)829-4493
2406 260th St Garner IA 50438-8506 • IW • SP • St John Garner IA • (515)829-4493 • (SL 1981 MDIV)

**HEDSTROM ROGER F REV** (480)982-8266
2122 S Goldfield Rd Apache Junctian AZ 85217-0868 • revrog@netzero.net • PSW • SP • Mountain View Apache Junction AZ • (480)982-8266 • (SL 1969 MDIV)

**HEDT FREDERICK T REV** (301)577-0500
4100 Elsie Ct Landover Hills MD 20784-2397 • hedt@aol.com • SE • SP • Ascension Landover Hills MD • (301)577-0500 • (SL 1974 MDIV)

**HEDTKE ROBERT C REV** (402)372-5321
431 N Colfax West Point NE 68788 • hedtkerc@aol.com • NEB • Sn/Adm • St Paul West Point NE • (402)372-2111 • (SPR 1973 MDIV)

**HEDTKE THOMAS E REV** (319)377-1552
995 S 26th St Marion IA 52302-5062 • tmjhedtke@aol.com • IE • SP • St Paul Marion IA • (319)377-4687 • (SPR 1972 MDIV)

**HEERBOTH PAUL M REV** (314)894-8613
5253 Brass Lantern Pl Saint Louis MO 63128-3501 • pheerboth@aol.com • MO • EM • (SL 1948 DD)

**HEFFEL WILLIAM H REV** (301)352-4124
16321 Lea Dr Bowie MD 20715 • SE • Assoc • Trinity Bowie MD • (301)262-5475 • (SL 1988 MDIV)

**HEFFELFINGER JOHN REV** (505)898-5356
PO Box 81832 Albuquerque NM 87198 • jkheffel@flash.net • RM • SP • Redeemer Albuquerque NM • (505)256-9881 • (FW 1979 MDIV)

**HEFTA DONALD R REV** (813)936-2017
C/O St John S Luth Church 10401 N Florida Ave Tampa FL 33612-6708 • stjohn1@usinternet.com • FG • SP • St John Tampa FL • (813)935-5648 • (FW 1984 MDIV)

**HEGGEN MICHAEL J REV** (708)754-0563
3319 Hopkins Ave Steger IL 60475 • heggens@juno.com • NI • SP • Hope Park Forest IL • (708)748-1995 • (SL 1973 MDIV)

**HEIDE VOLKER SIEGMUND REV**
90 Fawn Brook Cir Madison CT 06443-2442 • NE • SP • Madison Madison CT • (203)245-4145 • (SL 1990 MDIV)

**HEIDEN DENNIS LEE REV**
5970 142nd Ave NW Ramsey MN 55303 • pastor@mtolive-anoka.org • MNS • Sn/Adm • Mount Olive Anoka MN • (763)421-3223 • (SL 1983 MDIV)

**HEIDER GEORGE C REV** (708)771-9023
946 Clinton Pl River Forest IL 60305-1504 • heider@curf.edu • NI • SHS/C • Northern Illinois Hillside IL • (SL 1979 MDIV PHD)

**HEIDLE MICHAEL K REV** (513)576-0286
1280 Eagle Ridge Dr Milford OH 45150-9613 • spikerev@aol.com • OH • Asst • St Mark Milford OH • (513)575-0292 • (FW 1990 MDIV)

**HEIDORN GREGORY N REV** (507)252-9661
2311 Viking Dr NW Rochester MN 55901 • ggnheidorn@aol.com • MNS • SP • Grace Rochester MN • (507)289-7833 • (SK 1981 MDIV)

**HEIDORN NORMAN W REV** (651)631-0993
1381 Skillman Ave W Saint Paul MN 55113-5813 • nheidorn@mediaone.net • MNS • EM • (SPR 1952)

**HEIDT BRIAN F REV**
789 Johnson St Owosso MI 48867-3820 • MI • SP • St Philip Owosso MI • (517)723-6238 • (FW 1993 MDIV MA)

**HEIKKILA GUNARD W REV** (218)462-2464
C/O Trinity Lutheran Church PO Box 237 Deer Creek MN 56527-0237 • MNN • SP • Trinity Deer Creek MN • (218)462-2465 • (SPR 1965)

**HEILMAN MARK L REV** (610)644-5165
4 Valleybrook Rd Paoli PA 19301-1914 • EA • EM • (SL 1946)

**HEILMAN MARK T REV** (515)232-4595
2010 Stevenson Dr Ames IA 50010-4322 • mkheilman@aol.com • IW • Assoc • Memorial Ames IA • (515)292-5005 • (SL 1984 MDIV)

**HEIM VERNON F REV** (920)869-2777
749 Silver Creek Dr Oneida WI 54155-9051 • zionev@netnet.net • NW • SP • Zion Oneida WI • (414)869-2777 • (SL 1971 MDIV)

**HEIMBIGNER KENT A REV** (817)426-0783
820 Lisa St Burleson TX 76028 • icxcnika@flash.net • TX • Sn/Adm • Charity Burleson TX • (817)295-8621 • (SL 1989 STM MDIV)

**HEIMER-COTERA KARL P REV** (915)858-4625
C/O San Pablo Luth Church 301 S Schutz Dr El Paso TX 79907-6514 • heimerkarl@aol.com • RM • SP • San Pablo El Paso TX • (915)858-2588 • (SPR 1971 MDIV)

**HEIMGARTNER ROBERT H REV** (618)349-6392
C/O St Paul Luth Church RR 1 Box 131 Shobonier IL 62885-9724 • CI • EM • (SPR 1948)

**HEIMLICH GERALD P REV** (614)275-0780
1684 Hale Ct Columbus OH 43228-7024 • gphrev@aol.com • OH • Assoc • St John Dublin OH • (614)889-2284 • (CQ 1972)

**HEIMSOTH ELTON N REV** (630)627-4871
1155 S Church Ave Lombard IL 60148-4123 • NI • EM • (SPR 1963)

**HEIMSOTH JEFFREY E REV** (517)224-3212
8964 Church Rd Saint Johns MI 48879-9230 • lcmstplc@abraham.ccaa.edu • MI • SP • St Peter Saint Johns MI • (517)224-3178 • (SL 1987 MDIV)

**HEIN BRUCE REV**
C/O Rocky Mountain District 14334 E Evans Aurora CO 80014 • RM • S Miss • Rocky Mountain Aurora CO • (FW 2000 MDIV)

**HEIN CARLTON K REV** (402)335-4125
217 S 13th St Tecumseh NE 68450-2231 • st62912@navix.net • NEB • SP • St John Tecumseh NE • (402)335-3816 • (SL 1993 MDIV)

**HEIN HAROLD A REV** (847)742-6254
473 Lowell Dr South Elgin IL 60177-2927 • NI • EM • (SPR 1952)

**HEIN HUGO REV** (541)764-3005
455 Seagrove Loop Lincoln City OR 97367-5307 • NOW • EM • (SL 1953)

**HEIN MARK H REV** (815)834-1156
1512 S Briggs St Lockport IL 60441-4546 • m.h.hein@worldnet.att.net • NI • SP • St Paul Lockport IL • (815)838-1832 • (FW 1992 MDIV MA)

**HEIN MARK REV** (509)837-5622
C/O Calvary Luth Church PO Box 507 Sunnyside WA 98944-0507 • NOW • SP • Calvary Sunnyside WA • (509)837-5662 • (SL 1986 MDIV)

**HEIN STEVEN A REV** (719)598-7446
Shepherd Of The Springs HS 9550 Otero Ave Colorado Springs CO 80920 • heinsa@ix.netcom.com • RM • Prin • Shep of the Springs Colorado Springs CO • (719)598-7446 • (SPR 1971 MTH MDIV PHD)

**HEINE HERMAN H REV** (219)497-0169
4709 Blade Ct Fort Wayne IN 46818-9039 • IN • EM • (SL 1943 MA)

**HEINE MARK G REV** (952)892-7084
14620 Fieldcrest Ln Burnsville MN 55306-6915 • mgh715@yahoo.com • MNS • Assoc • Berea Richfield MN • (612)861-7121 • (SL 1988 MDIV)

**HEINE V PAUL REV** (314)723-5301
629 Norma Dr Saint Charles MO 63301-8804 • MO • EM • (SL 1944 MDIV)

**HEINE WILLIAM C REV** (307)674-9196
910 Idaho Ave Sheridan WY 82801 • billheine@wyoming.com • WY • SP • Immanuel Sheridan WY • (307)674-6434 • (SL 1986 MDIV)

**HEINECKE BRADLEY D REV** (307)245-3242
C/O Grace English Luth Church PO Box 670 Pine Bluffs WY 82082-0674 • bhein@juno.com • WY • SP • Grace English Pine Bluffs WY* • (307)245-3390 • (FW 1982 MDIV)

**HEINERT DANIEL G REV** (262)633-7232
2029 Geneva St Racine WI 53402-4627 • SW • Sn/Adm • Trinity Racine WI • (414)632-2900 • (SL 1967 MDIV)

**HEINERT DAVID W REV** (231)937-9133
18669 W M-46 Howard City MI 49329-9312 • bethelhc@pathwaynet.com • MI • SP • Bethel Howard City MI • (231)937-4921 • (SL 1967 MST)

**HEINEY TIMOTHY M REV**
Lutheran Mission BP 438 Conakry Guinea WEST AFRICA • luthmiss@mirinet.net.gn • MI • S Miss • Michigan Ann Arbor MI • (FW 1983 MDIV)

**HEINICKE MARTIN W REV** (208)336-0111
3201 Scenic Dr Boise ID 83703-4718 • NOW • EM • (SL 1950 MDIV)

**HEINING JAMES W DR** (507)282-6955
1020 Rocky Creek Dr NE Rochester MN 55906-8344 • jamesheining@hotmail.com • MNS • Sn/Adm • Redeemer Rochester MN • (507)289-5147 • (SL 1976 MDIV DMIN)

**HEINITZ KENNETH L REV** (708)386-3337
1040 Erie St Apt 408 Oak Park IL 60302-1920 • NI • EM • (SL 1952 STM MDIV PHD)

**HEINLEIN DALE V REV** (303)625-2369
C/O Emmanuel Luth Church 652 E 5th St Rifle CO 81650-2908 • RM • SP • Emmanuel Rifle CO • (970)625-2369 • (FW 1984 MDIV)

**HEINLEIN HAROLD E REV** (941)369-3635
3204 3rd St E Lehigh Acres FL 33972-5582 • harold1022@aol.com • FG • EM • (SL 1947 MDIV)

**HEINLEIN PAUL L REV**
C/O Trinity Lutheran Church 1201 JQ Adams Oregon City OR 97045-1457 • heinlein@teleport.com • NOW • Asst • Trinity Oregon City OR • (503)656-4504 • (SL 1990 MDIV MA)

**HEINO DONALD W REV** (440)286-7300
11917 Bean Rd Chardon OH 44024-9097 • OH • SP • Peace Chardon OH • (216)286-3310 • (SPR 1961)

**HEINO JACK D REV** (513)644-5540
C/O St John Lutheran Church 12809 State Route 736 Marysville OH 43040-9056 • stjohnsl@postbox.esu.k12.oh.us • OH • Assoc • St John Marysville OH • (937)644-5540 • (SL 1988 MDIV)

**HEINS JOHN L REV** (734)944-3200
5985 Bellwether Dr Saline MI 48176 • MI • EM • (SL 1958 DD)

**HEINS PAUL C REV** (410)455-5447
29 Dunvegan Rd Catonsville MD 21228 • pcheins@bigfoot.com • SE • 08/1995 08/2000 • (SL 1968 MDIV)

**HEINSEN STEVEN ROBERT REV** (402)371-5706
1807 N Eastwood Norfolk NE 68701 • clcsteve@kdsi.net • NEB • Assoc • Christ Norfolk NE • (402)371-1210 • (SL 1996 MDIV)

**HEINTZ BRAD D REV**
305 Lazy Hollow Dr League City TX 77573-1725 • pastrbrad@epiphany-lcms.org • TX • Assoc • Gloria Dei Houston TX • (281)333-4535 • (SL 1992 MDIV)

**HEINTZ NORMAN H REV** (616)861-2009
8967 W Chippewa Trl Shelby MI 49455-9533 • ncheintz@voyager.net • MI • EM • (SPR 1957)

**HEINTZ ROGER V REV** (262)781-5519
4720 Parkhurst Dr Brookfield WI 53045-1127 • rheintz@goblc.org • SW • Sn/Adm • Brookfield Brookfield WI • (262)783-4270 • (SPR 1970 MDIV)

**HEINTZEN ERICH H III DR** (813)384-1908
2080 Dolphin Blvd S Saint Petersburg FL 33707-3812 • beheintzen@msn.com • FG • EM • (SPR 1961 MDIV MA DED)

**HEINZ RICHARD ANDREW REV** (812)952-1903
1440 Saint Johns Church Rd NE Lanesville IN 47136-8536 • RevFrHeinz@aol.com • IN • SP • St John Lanesville IN • (812)952-3711 • (SL 1995 MDIV)

**HEISER JAMES D REV** (254)533-2330
RR 1 Box 285 Malone TX 76660-9720 • TX • SP • Salem Malone TX • (254)533-2330 • (SL 1998 MDIV)

**HEISERMAN HARLAN J REV** (931)381-1942
4271 Trousdale Ln Columbia TN 38401 • heiserm@galis.com • MDS • SP • Trinity Columbia TN • (931)388-0790 • (FW 1983 MDIV)

**HEISINGER HANS-JUERGEN W REV** (715)536-4626
C/O St Paul Lutheran Church PO Box 7 Irma WI 54442-0007 • heisinge@exepc.com • NW • SP • St Paul Irma WI* • (715)536-5069 • (SL 1979 MDIV)

**HEITHOLD DONAVON W REV** (605)842-1352
730 E 6th Winner SD 57580 • heithold@gwtc.net • SD • SP • Christ Winner SD* • (605)842-0780 • (SL 1997 MDIV MS)

**HEITNER DAVID D REV**
C/O Zion Lutheran Church 3917 Waverly Rd Owego NY 13827-2841 • EA • SP • Zion Owego NY • (607)687-1205 • (FW 1986 MDIV)

**HEITSHUSEN SCOTT ERIC REV** (407)422-5704
C/O Trinity Lutheran Church 123 E Livingston St Orlando FL 32801-1598 • revscott@trinitydowntown.org • FG • SP • Trinity Orlando FL • (407)422-5704 • (SL 1996 MDIV)

**HELBERG ROBERT W REV** (419)599-4995
PO Box 362 Napoleon OH 43545-0362 • OH • EM • (SL 1945)

**HELBIG RUSSELL K REV** (618)357-2818
315 West Chester Pinckneyville IL 62274 • bismarck@midwest.net • SI • SP • Zion Pinckneyville IL* • (618)357-2818 • (SL 1994 MDIV)

**HELD GARY REV**
PO Box 411 North Vernon IN 47265 • IN • SP • Lord Of Life North Vernon IN • (812)346-6400 • (SL 2000 MDIV)

**HELD HAROLD F REV** (724)658-0053
909 Ryan Ave New Castle PA 16101-4409 • EA • EM • (SL 1937)

**HELLAND LLOYD J REV** (660)438-9487
PO Box 876 Warsaw MO 65355-0876 • helland@iland.net • MO • SP • Faith Warsaw MO • (660)438-6948 • (SL 1990 MDIV)

**HELLER DAVID R REV** (808)689-4334
91-1006 Kailoa St Ewa Beach HI 96706 • MI • M Chap • Michigan Ann Arbor MI • (FW 1979 MDIV)

**HELLER RICHARD A REV** (847)823-4767
1832 W Crescent Ave Park Ridge IL 60068-3878 • grbart@aol • NI • Northern Illinois Hillside IL • (FW 1985 MDIV MA)

**HELLER TOBY H REV** (701)873-4223
PO Box 189 Beulah ND 58523-0189 • thheller@westriv.com • ND • SP • Concordia Beulah ND • (701)873-4388 • (FW 1990 MDIV)

**HELLERT ALFRED J REV** (317)291-1464
6113 Meadowood Dr Indianapolis IN 46224-3218 • IN • SP • Holy Cross Crawfordsville IN • (765)362-5599 • (SL 1961 MDIV)

**HELLING MELBOURNE F REV** (605)338-7134
905 S Ruby Pl Sioux Falls SD 57106-3447 • SD • EM • (SPR 1962)

**HELLMAN VICTOR T REV** (920)324-9212
500 S Grove St Waupun WI 53963-2227 • SW • EM • (SL 1957)

**HELLMERS CLIFFORD N JR. REV** (205)988-3138
238 Crest Lake Dr Hoover AL 35244 • dee.and.cliff.hellmers@worldnet.att.net • SO • SP • Vestavia Hills Birmingham AL • (205)823-1883 • (SL 1972 MDIV)

**HELLMERS DWIGHT D REV** (303)986-7155
1079 S Johnson Way Lakewood CO 80226-4045 • dchellmers@aalweb.net • RM • SP • St Luke Golden CO • (303)233-5658 • (SPR 1974 MDIV STM)

**HELLWEGE ALLEN D REV** (712)243-2474
401 E 8th St Atlantic IA 50022-1716 • zionluth@netins.net • IW • SP • Zion Atlantic IA • (712)243-2927 • (SL 1967 MDIV)

**HELLWEGE JOHN P JR. REV** (402)246-2118
PO Box 259 Platte Center NE 68653 • NEB • SP • Grace Platte Center NE* • (402)246-2730 • (SL 1999 STM MDIV)

**HELMER DAVID E REV** (507)237-5331
C/O Immanuel Luth Church PO Box 448 Gaylord MN 55334-0448 • MNS • SP • Immanuel Gaylord MN • (507)237-2380 • (CQ 1979 MED)

**HELMER PAUL G REV** (515)573-5558
2620 15th Ave N Fort Dodge IA 50501-2124 • paul.helmer@iowawest.org • IW • Sn/Adm • Prince Peace Fort Dodge IA • (515)573-8618 • (SL 1967 MDIV MA)

**HELMICH CLARENCE W REV** (615)826-1239
3494 New Hope Rd Hendersonville TN 37035 • MDS • EM • (SL 1960 MDIV)

**HELMKAMP EARL WADE REV** (217)774-3353
1201 N Chestnut Shelbyville IL 62565 • CI • SP • Holy Cross Shelbyville IL • (217)774-2952 • (SL 1987 MDIV)

**HELMKE JOHN E REV** (708)488-0880
1345 Elgin Ave Forest Park IL 60130 • jehaaldr@aol.com • NI • SP • Apostles Melrose Park IL • (847)455-0903 • (SL 1963 MDIV STM)

**HELMS STEVEN C REV** (810)796-2871
4538 Dryden Rd Dryden MI 48428-9702 • shelms@tir.com • MI • SP • Holy Redeemer Dryden MI • (810)796-3951 • (SL 1984 MDIV)

**HEMENWAY WILLIAM B REV** (714)631-1611
C/O Christ Luth Church 760 Victoria St Costa Mesa CA 92627-2968 • PSW • Sn/Adm • Christ Costa Mesa CA • (949)631-1611 • (SL 1969 MDIV)

**HEMPECK MATTHEW PAUL REV**
C/O Immanuel Lutheran Church PO Box 686 Sandy OR 97055 • NOW • SP • Immanuel Sandy OR • (503)668-6232 • (SL 1992 MDIV)

**HEMPEL JOEL R REV** (314)968-7263
1409 Eddystone Pl Webster Groves MO 63119-4825 • joelhempel@aol.com • MO • Missouri Saint Louis MO • (314)317-4550 • (SPR 1971 MDIV MA MCOUN)

**HEMPEL WILLIAM G III DR** (518)456-3238
4 Joseph Ter Albany NY 12203-4236 • whempel@ix.netcom.com • AT • SP • St Paul Albany NY • (518)463-0571 • (SL 1968 MDIV MSED DMIN)

**HEMPELMANN L DEAN REV** (636)458-2964
2825 Westridge Oaks Ct Wildwood MO 63040 • l.hempelmann@lcms.org • MO • S Ex/S • Missouri Saint Louis MO • (314)317-4550 • (SL 1965 MDIV STM PHD)

**HEMSATH ROBERT WILLIAM REV** (208)237-4216
C/O Faith Lutheran Church 856 W Eldredge Rd Pocatello ID 83201-5525 • rmhemway@nicoh.com • NOW • SP • Faith Pocatello ID* • (208)237-2391 • (SL 1996 MDIV)

**HENDERSON ALLEN W REV** (515)955-7285
1004 N 31st PL Fort Dodge IA 50501-2920 • pastoral@dodge.net • IW • Sn/Adm • St Paul Fort Dodge IA • (515)955-7285 • (SL 1989 MDIV)

**HENDERSON SAMUEL C REV**
26360 Berg Rd-Apt 218 Southfield MI 48034 • MI • EM • (CQ 1986 MA)

**HENDRICKS LARRY FRED REV** (718)464-1803
217-30 Peck Ave #30 Queens Village NY 11427-1118 • hendricksrev@msn.com • AT • SP • Chapel Redeemer Flushing NY • (718)465-4236 • (SC 1992 MDIV)

**HENDRICKS REINHOLD MERTON REV** (360)373-0664
PO Box 2211 Bremerton WA 98310-0261 • mahm2211@home.com • NOW • EM • (CQ 1981 MDIV MBA MDIV)

**HENDRICKSON GARY L REV** (580)855-2554
C/O Trinity Luth Church Rt 2 Box 357 Enid OK 73703-9734 • g³hendrickson@juno.com • OK • SP • Trinity Enid OK • (580)855-2554 • (SL 1990 MDIV)

**HENDRICKSON JOHN H REV** (651)489-9435
1020 West Roselawn Roseville MN 55113 • lmpastor@pressenter.com • MNS • 10/1999 • (SL 1968 MDIV MED)

**HENDRICKSON MARION LARS REV** (608)635-4441
211 Curtis St PO Box 147 Arlington WI 53911-0147 • lars62@juno.com • SW • SP • St Peter Arlington WI • (608)635-4825 • (SL 1986 MDIV MS STM)

**HENDRICKSON RAYMOND V REV**
57884 175th St Menahga MN 56464 • revray@wcta.net • MNN • SP • Grace Sebeka MN* • (218)837-5565 • (SL 1981 MDIV)

**HENDRIKSON JAMES L REV** (608)868-4853
872 E Highway #59 Milton WI 53563 • SW • EM • * • (SPR 1966)

**HENDRIX ROBERT C REV** (425)347-5301
8614 7th Ave SE Everett WA 98208-2042 • NOW • SP • Grace Everett WA • (425)353-1852 • (SL 1984 MDIV)

**HENDRY THOMAS E REV** (760)365-4472
7962 Elk Trl Yucca Valley CA 92284-3320 • thendry@telis.org • PSW • SP • Good Shepherd Yucca Valley CA • (760)365-2548 • (SPR 1972 MDIV DMIN)

**HENGST EARNEST J REV** (505)425-5006
C/O Immanuel Luth Church 2100 7th St Las Vegas NM 87701-4960 • RM • SP • Immanuel Las Vegas NM* • (505)425-6833 • (SL 1981 MDIV)

**HENKE BARRIE EMIL REV** (405)359-0009
16317 Del Mar Dr Edmond OK 73013-2008 • bhenke@flash.net • OK • SP • Holy Trinity Edmond OK • (405)348-3292 • (SPR 1973 MDIV)

**HENKE DANIEL L REV** (616)882-4326
C/O Our Savior Luth Church PO Box 227 Benzonia MI 49616-0227 • oursavior@coslink.net • MI • SP • Our Savior Benzonia MI • (616)882-4326 • (FW 1984 MDIV)

**HENKE GENE G REV** (414)790-9410
3405 N Brookfield Rd Brookfield WI 53045-2520 • padre2000@peoplepc.com • SW • Assoc • Our Redeemer Wauwatosa WI • (414)258-4555 • (FW 1978 MDIV)

**HENKELL JAMES D REV** (805)499-3657
1115 Amberton Ln Newbury Park CA 91320 • RevJH@aol.com • PSW • Sn/Adm • St Paul Agoura Hills CA • (818)889-1620 • (SL 1998 MDIV)

**HENNE ARTHUR R REV** (313)526-4316
11630 Rossiter St Detroit MI 48224-1681 • arthenne@aol.com • MI • SP • Redemption Detroit MI • (313)526-5631 • (CQ 1991 MMU)

**HENNEMAN HARRY C REV** (810)468-5003
38944 Farmcrest St Clinton Twp MI 48036-3218 • henneman@123.net • MI • Sn/Adm • Trinity Clinton Township MI • (810)463-2921 • (SL 1966 MDIV)

**HENNIG HENRY L REV** (912)256-3271
Harmony Ct - #3271 173 Bennette Ave Council Bluffs IA 51503-5166 • PSW • EM • (SL 1930)

**HENNIG JAMES L REV** (618)888-2356
7187 Renken Rd Dorsey IL 62021-9710 • pjdjajm@juno.com • SI • SP • St Peter Dorsey IL • (618)888-2250 • (SL 1993 MDIV)

**HENNING J C REV** (281)367-3959
28902 Pinehill Dr Spring TX 77381-1116 • TX • EM • (SL 1958 MS)

**HENNING JAMES E REV** (616)949-7696
351 Eastmoor Ave SE Grand Rapids MI 49546-2274 • MI • 10/1995 10/1999 • (SL 1970 DMIN)

**HENNING ROGER B REV** (636)477-8493
605 River Bend Estates Dr St Charles MO 63303-6061 • rhenning@immanuelluth.org • MO • Assoc • Immanuel Saint Charles MO • (636)946-2656 • (CQ 1986 MA)

**HENNING TIMOTHY J REV** (270)688-0378
2604 Bittel Rd Owensboro KY 42301 • IN • SP • Peace Owensboro KY • (502)685-0249 • (FW 1999 MDIV)

**HENNINGFIELD CRAIG W REV** (303)798-0711
9662 S Timber Hawk Cir Apt 21 Highlands Ranch CO 80126-7146 • chenning1@aol.com • RM • Sn/Adm • Shepherd Hills Littleton CO • (303)798-0711 • (SL 1986 MDIV)

**HENNINGS KENNETH M REV** (512)251-4639
1009 Twin Creek Dr Pflugerville TX 78660-2849 • hennings@txdistlcms.org • TX • D Ex/S • Texas Austin TX* • (SL 1973 MDIV)

**HENRICHS MICHAEL WILLIAM REV** (605)988-0956
4201 S Ash Grove Ave Sioux Falls SD 57103-4909 • SD • SP • Christ Sioux Falls SD • (605)338-3769 • (SL 1995 MDIV STM)

**HENRICHS ROBERT M REV** (314)243-7090
221 S Union Ave Apt 1 Jackson MO 63755-1967 • rmhenrichs@prodigy.net • MO • Assoc • St Paul Jackson MO • (573)243-2236 • (SL 1976 MDIV)

**HENRICKSON CHARLES M REV** (314)351-2098
7606 Terri Lynn Dr Affton MO 63123 • henrick@swbell.net • MO • 08/1999 • (SL 1990 MDIV STM)

**HENRY JEFFREY F REV** (304)522-3751
3043 Washington Blvd Huntington WV 25705-1632 • innocentsmith@hotmail.com • OH • SP • Our Redeemer Huntington WV • (304)529-7365 • (FW 1999 MA MDIV)

**HENRY PATRICK D REV** (520)574-3611
7760 S Caesar Dr Tucson AZ 85747-5119 • debpat@azstarnet.com • EN • SP • Mount Olive Tucson AZ • (520)298-0996 • (FW 1985 MDIV)

**HENSCHEL MARVIN A REV** (405)722-5285
7320 NW 114th St Oklahoma City OK 73162-2703 • OK • Asst • Messiah Oklahoma City OK • (405)946-0681 • (SL 1960 MED MDIV)

**HENSCHEN NATHAN P REV** (605)883-4200
241 Commercial Ave NW Wolsey SD 57384 • velvet106@home.com • SD • SP • St John Wolsey SD* • (605)883-4972 • (SL 1996 MDIV)

**HENSLER DAVID H REV** (810)686-7431
2115 E Dodge Rd Clio MI 48420-9746 • sharryk@ameritech.net • MI • SP • St Timothy Otisville MI • (810)631-4730 • (FW 1991 MDIV)

**HENSLIN DAVID D REV** (507)282-9342
1704 Lakeview Dr SW Rochester MN 55902-4228 • davehenslin@juno.com • MNS • 02/1999 • (FW 1983 MDIV)

**HENSON MICHAEL DAVID REV**
605 Indian Hill Dr Herrin IL 62948-4324 • mdhauz@midwest.net • SI • SP • Trinity Herrin IL • (618)942-3401 • (SL 1991 MDIV)

**HENTZ ROBERT D REV** (562)691-2829
1440 Pamela Ln La Habra CA 90631-3254 • PSW • EM • (SL 1959)

**HENZE STEVEN H REV**
14225 Hargrave Rd Houston TX 77070-3843 • TX • SP • St Timothy Houston TX • (281)469-2457 • (SL 1981 MDIV)

**HERBERT SCOTT EDWARD REV** (806)622-9590
2100 S Fork Ave Amarillo TX 79118-5200 • christlutheran@am.net • TX • SP • Christ Amarillo TX • (806)351-0458 • (SL 1995 MDIV)

**HERBOLSHEIMER JAMES A REV** (216)676-0336
4260 Rocky River Dr Cleveland OH 44135 • cj-herb@prodigy.net • EN • Assoc • Holy Cross Cleveland OH • (216)252-2348 • (SL 1977 MDIV)

**HERBRICH RUDY REV** (817)861-5224
2500 High Oak Dr Arlington TX 76012-3542 • herbrich1@juno.com • TX • Assoc • Grace Arlington TX • (817)274-1626 • (CQ 1981 MAR)

**HERD CLIFFORD LEROY REV**
832 Belvoir Crest Dr Chattanooga TN 37412-2010 • goodshepherds@cs.com • MDS • SP • Good Shepherd Chattanooga TN • (423)629-4661 • (SL 1969 MDIV MED)

**HERFKENS STEVEN G REV** (402)455-4442
2912 N 50th St Omaha NE 68104-3776 • NEB • Asst • Zion Omaha NE • (402)731-0743 • (FW 1980 MDIV)

**HERFURTH JOHN A REV** (317)352-9926
2565 S Ritter Ave Indianapolis IN 46203-5653 • pastor@trinityindy.org • IN • SP • Trinity Indianapolis IN • (317)897-0243 • (SL 1982 MDIV)

**HERFURTH LAWRENCE E REV** (716)731-4015
2650 Kenneth Ct Niagara Falls NY 14304-4605 • EA • EM • (SPR 1945)

**HERING EARL R REV** (541)929-5702
2545 Applegate St Philomath OR 97370-9366 • NOW • EM • (SL 1962 MDIV)

**HERING JEFFREY P REV** (716)359-4248
93 Elaine Dr Rochester NY 14623-5341 • jphcpm@rit.edu • EA • Cmp P • Eastern Williamsville NY • (716)634-5111 • (CQ 1979)

**HERING WILLIAM T REV** (503)625-6648
St Paul Lutheran Church 17190 SW Scholls Sherwood Rd Sherwood OR 97140-8725 • NOW • Assoc • St Paul Sherwood OR • (503)625-6648 • (FW 1991 MDIV)

**HERMAN DARVIN A REV** (864)879-6534
332 Cornelson Dr Greer SC 29651-1268 • rev.nyou@juno.com • SE • EM • (SL 1956)

**HERMAN DON O REV** (530)676-5533
PO Box 1992 Cameron Park CA 95682-1992 • CNH • EM • (SPR 1955)

**HERMAN GERALD L REV** (520)399-1323
3949 S Via de Cristal Green Valley AZ 85614-5861 • Glhrmn@aol.com • NW • EM • (SL 1962 MDIV)

**HERMAN LUTHER S REV** (660)882-6253
20209 Ellis Davis Rd Boonville MO 65233-4022 • lherman@c-magic.com • MO • SP • Trinity Boonville MO* • (660)882-6253 • (SL 1967 MDIV)

**HERMANN RORY M REV** (904)827-1588
88 Keith St St Augustine FL 32084 • rory@net-magic.net • OH • M Chap • Ohio Olmsted Falls OH • (FW 1979 MDIV MA)

**HERMETZ HAROLD G REV** (256)739-0976
923 Morgan Ave SW Cullman AL 35055-4616 • hermetz@hiwaay.net • SO • Assoc • St Paul Cullman AL • (256)734-3575 • (SL 1958 MDIV)

**HERNANDEZ CARLOS REV** (314)843-5165
PO Box 50117 Clayton MO 63105-5117 • prcarlos@aol.com • MO • S Ex/S • Missouri Saint Louis MO • (314)317-4550 • (SL 1969 STM)

**HERNDON JAMES N REV** (419)832-6047
14223 Harrison Rd Grand Rapids OH 43522-9669 • jnhlcms@hotmail.com • OH • EM • (SL 1973 MDIV)

**HERPOLSHEIMER ARTHUR H REV** (402)643-4272
2652 E Seward Rd Unit 20 Seward NE 68434-8032 • SI • EM • (SL 1935)

**HERRING MELVIN G REV** (281)495-6340
15323 Rio Plaza Houston TX 77083 • melinda4@flash.net • TX • EM • (SL 1957)

**HERRING ROBERT G REV** (501)452-9892
9712 E Pointe Dr Fort Smith AR 72903-7135 • bherring@alltel.net • MDS • SP • Bethel Fort Smith AR • (501)452-1521 • (SL 1978 MDIV)

**HERRMANN JOHN V REV** (209)533-2087
20660 Gopher Dr Sonora CA 95370-9097 • johnh@sonnet.com • CNH • SP • St Matthew Sonora CA • (209)532-4639 • (SPR 1975 MDIV)

**HERRMANN OTTO DAVID REV** (909)672-4627
28333 Valley Blvd #A L 2102 Sun City CA 92586 • EN • EM • (SL 1925 MDIV)

**HERROD J ROBERT REV** (517)754-2280
C/O Redeemer Lutheran Church 3829 Lamson St Saginaw MI 48601-4170 • pastorherrod@juno.com • MI • Sn/Adm • Redeemer Saginaw MI • (517)753-2963 • (FW 1992 MDIV)

**HERTER PAUL W REV** (517)264-4171
5653 Forrister Rd Adrian MI 49221-9422 • hopelcms@tc3net.com • MI • SP • Hope Adrian MI • (517)263-4317 • (FW 1981 MDIV)

**HERTWIG FREDERICK A REV** (660)668-3940
RR 2 Box 343 Lincoln MO 65338-9581 • MO • EM • (SL 1945)

**HERTWIG FREDERICK C REV** (816)674-2413
C/O Trinity Lutheran Church PO Box 276 Alma MO 64001-0276 • MO • SP • Trinity Alma MO • (660)674-2376 • (SL 1976 MDIV)

**HERZBERG TERRY R REV** (201)797-6372
31-06 Morlot Ave Fair Lawn NJ 07410 • therzberg@worldnet.att.net • NJ • SP • Our Savior Fair Lawn NJ • (201)796-3007 • (CQ 1980 MDIV)

**HERZOG JAMES M REV** (817)542-1206
RR 3 Box 166A Killeen TX 76542-9310 • TX • EM • (SPR 1962)

**HERZOG JOHN A DR** (810)777-2652
15764 S Park Ave Eastpointe MI 48021-1635 • jherzog@lhsa.com • MI • Tchr • Michigan Ann Arbor MI • (SPR 1974 MDIV MA PHD)

**HESS ROBERT M REV** (847)639-7702
PO Box 218 Cary IL 60013-0218 • NI • Sn/Adm • Holy Cross Cary IL • (847)639-1702 • (SL 1953 STM MDIV MAR)

**HESS RUSSELL IRWIN REV** (916)983-5743
C/O Mount Olive Lutheran Ch 320 Montrose Dr Folsom CA 95630-2720 • rhess@ttns.net • CNH • SP • Mount Olive Folsom CA • (916)985-2984 • (SL 1983 MDIV)

**HESS STEVEN J REV** (941)768-2193
6441 Emerald Pines Cir Fort Myers FL 33912 • pastorhess@earthlink.net • FG • Assoc • Zion Fort Myers FL • (941)481-4040 • (SL 1980 MDIV)

**HESSE DONLEY D REV** (501)243-9077
300 9th St Mena AR 71953-3030 • MDS • EM • (SL 1957)

**HESSE JAMES W REV** (320)272-4416
604 E Rutherford St Ogilvie MN 56358 • revjim2000@hotmail.com • MNN • SP • St Paul Ogilvie MN • (320)272-4352 • (FW 1993 MDIV)

**HESSEL KENNETH N REV** (516)333-1082
1 Old Westbury Rd Old Westbury NY 11568-1603 • khessel@earthlink.net • AT • SP • Redeemer Old Westbury NY • (516)333-3355 • (SL 1987 MDIV)

**HESSEL THEODORE E REV** (414)332-2813
8949 N 97th St Apt A120 Milwaukee WI 53224-5711 • SW • EM • (SPR 1953)

**HESSLER WILLIAM W REV** (517)777-2648
4235 Williamson Rd PO Box 242 Bridgeport MI 48722 • wwh0211@gateway.net • MI • SP • Faith Bridgeport MI • (517)777-2600 • (SL 1977 MDIV)

**HETT ROGER W REV** (507)847-2974
400 Morrison Ave Jackson MN 56143-1262 • MNS • SP • Our Redeemer Jackson MN • (507)847-3693 • (SL 1966 MDIV)

**HETZEL BRIAN J REV** (816)224-1156
1108 SW Granite Creek Dr Blue Springs MO 64015-6723 • bjhetz@juno.com • MO • D Miss • Missouri Saint Louis MO • (314)317-4550 • (SL 1992 MDIV)

**HETZNER MARK W REV** (810)777-3576
23142 Hayes Ave Eastpointe MI 48021-1542 • MI • Sn/Adm • St Thomas Eastpointe MI • (810)772-3370 • (CQ 1983 MA)

**HEUER DANIEL E REV** (308)234-4139
3908 Ave F Kearney NE 68847-2649 • dheuer@kearney.net • NEB • Assoc • Holy Cross Kearney NE • (308)237-2944 • (SL 1993 MDIV)

**HEUMANN ALVIN E REV** (407)366-5694
2122 Sunbird Ct Oviedo FL 32765-5208 • FG • EM • (SL 1945)

**HEUPEL TIMOTHY J REV** (605)335-8071
3809 E 23rd St Sioux Falls SD 57103-3528 • SD • Sn/Adm • Zion Sioux Falls SD • (605)338-5226 • (FW 1978 MDIV)

**HEUSEL MICHAEL S DR** (734)994-4107
2691 Bedford Rd Ann Arbor MI 48104-4009 • mheusel@mediaone.net • MI • Asst • Community Flat Rock MI • (734)782-0563 • (SL 1982 MDIV DMIN)

**HEUSER MARK E REV** (248)299-5506
936 Golfview Ct Rochester Hills MI 48307-1007 • mheuser@stjohnrochester.org • MI • Assoc • St John Rochester MI • (248)652-8830 • (SL 1999 MA)

**HEUSER PHILIP M REV** (402)893-5221
C/O St Peter Lutheran Church PO Box 117 Orchard NE 68764 • pjheuser@juno.com • NEB • SP • St Peter Orchard NE • (402)893-2390 • (SL 1998 MDIV MA)

**HEUSMANN JOHN HENRY REV**
8561 Old Blairsville Rd #21 Wadesville IN 47638-9753 • IN • 03/2000 • (FW 1980 MDIV)

**HEWITT MARTIN A REV** (509)466-8844
11916 N Stevens Ct Spokane WA 99218-2839 • hewitt81ma@aol.com • NOW • P Df • Faith Deaf Spokane WA • (509)326-9052 • (SL 1963 MDIV)

**HEYNE WALTER M REV** (407)365-8182
2076 Woodpecker Ln Oviedo FL 32765 • FG • EM • (SL 1926 STM MED)

**HICKS EUGENE W REV** (785)258-2892
614 N Broadway Herington KS 67449-1707 • KS • EM • (SPR 1963 MDIV)

**HIDALGO ARIEL HERNAN REV** (732)274-0252
34 Dawn Ct Monmouth Junction NJ 08852 • yeye@home.com • NJ • SP • Faith Dayton NJ • (908)329-8480 • (CQ 1996)

**HIESTERMAN JOEL S REV** (785)543-2865
602 7th St Phillipsburg KS 67661-2124 • jhiesterman@juno.com • KS • SP • First Phillipsburg KS • (785)543-5046 • (FW 1979 MDIV)

**HILDEBRANDT BARRY C REV** (423)877-7954
C/O Cross Christ Luth Church 3204 Hixson Pike Chattanooga TN 37415-5424 • crossofchristlcms@juno.com • MDS • SP • Cross Of Christ Chattanooga TN • (423)877-7447 • (SL 1973 MDIV)

**HILDEBRANDT RUSSELL C REV** (501)851-0749
106 Cannes Ct Maumelle AR 72113-6595 • rhildebrandt@aristotle.net • MDS • Sn/Adm • Christ Little Rock AR • (501)663-5232 • (FW 1985 MDIV DMIN)

**HILGENDORF HILBERT P REV** (920)923-5159
429 Austin Ln Fond Du Lac WI 54935-5331 • SW • EM • (SPR 1956)

**HILGENDORF M D REV** (262)377-1792
1910 Cedar Dr Grafton WI 53024-2704 • SW • EM • (SPR 1955 MDIV MA PHD DMIN)

**HILGENDORF PAUL A REV** (503)669-0257
PO Box 1073 Gresham OR 97030 • pah@hevanet.com • NOW • EM • (SPR 1949 MDIV)

**HILGERT DAVID W REV** (636)397-4270
125 Heron Ct Saint Peters MO 63376-5038 • dwhilgert@aol.com • MO • 04/1993 04/2000 • (SL 1984 MDIV)

**HILKEN DENNIS R REV** (918)459-2610
216 Luther Dr Broken Arrow OK 74012-9051 • dhilken@immanuelba.org • OK • Assoc • Immanuel Broken Arrow OK • (918)258-5506 • (FW 1993 MDIV)

**HILL ART L REV** (903)534-1974
505 Bentley Ct Tyler TX 75703 • artkimhill@juno.com • TX • Assoc • Trinity Tyler TX • (903)593-1526 • (SL 1982 MDIV)

**HILL DAVID BRUCE REV** (973)338-4919
98 Sadler Rd Bloomfield NJ 07003-5319 • stjohnsrev1@prodigy.net • NJ • SP • St John Bloomfield NJ • (973)429-8654 • (SL 1983 MDIV)

**HILL GARY E REV** (850)769-1731
5214 Teri Ln Panama City FL 32404-6735 • pastorghill@aol.com • SO • SP • Good Shepherd Panama City FL • (850)871-6311 • (SL 1977 MDIV)

**HILL JOHN E REV** (307)237-2829
3630 Navarre Casper WY 82604 • mthope@trib.com • WY • SP • Mount Hope Casper WY • (307)234-8428 • (FW 1990 MDIV)

**HILL MARK J REV** (248)601-1456
207 Arlington Rochester Hills MI 48307 • hill³mrk@hotmail.com • MI • Assoc • Trinity Utica MI • (810)731-4490 • (SL 1980 MDIV DMIN)

**HILL R BURK REV** (301)947-3232
22000 Goshen School Rd Gaithersburg MD 20882-1402 • rburkhill@aol.com • SE • SP • Messiah Germantown MD • (301)972-2130 • (SPR 1971 MDIV)

**HILL RICHARD L REV** (757)397-2859
246 Mount Vernon Ave Portsmouth VA 23707-1623 • SE • 06/1995 06/2000 • (SL 1970 MDIV)

**HILL ROBERT W REV** (972)423-5204
2825 E Parker Rd Plano TX 75074-7503 • rhill@faith.plano.tx.us • TX • Sn/Adm • Faith Plano TX • (972)423-7447 • (SPR 1961)

**HILL WILLIAM A REV** (517)321-7182
1106 Dillon Cir Lansing MI 48917-4059 • MI • EM • (CQ 1981 MAR)

**HILLE KIRK A REV** (503)465-8654
1606 SE Larch Way Gresham OR 97080 • river@roll.org • NOW • SP • Peace Estacada OR* • (503)630-4049 • (SL 1999 MDIV)

**HILLE WILTON E REV** (509)534-5862
624 E 7th Ave Spokane WA 99202-2422 • hillews@msn.com • NOW • EM • * • (CQ 1973 MA)

**HILLENBRAND PHILIP J REV** (414)512-1067
4805 W Willow Rd Mequon WI 53092 • philiph@ameritech.net • SW • SP • Beaut Savior Mequon WI • (262)242-6650 • (SL 1985 MDIV)

**HILLENBRAND RICHARD P REV** (313)868-9171
114 W Grixdale Detroit MI 48203-4556 • rphofmi@aol.com • MI • SP • Epiphany Detroit MI • (313)368-1260 • (SL 1982 MDIV)

**HILLER MICHAEL J REV** (303)693-8416
3075 S Quintero Way Aurora CO 80013-2250 • mikehiller@pwcic.org • RM • SP • Peace W Christ Aurora CO • (303)693-5618 • (FW 1978 MDIV DMIN)

**HILLMER GERHARDT R REV** (608)238-9846
213 Marinette Trl Madison WI 53705-4718 • gbhillmer@aol.com • SW • EM • (TH 1942 MA)

**HILLMER J CARL REV** (608)221-1886
3045 Waunona Way Madison WI 53713-2273 • hillmerjc@cs.com • SW • EM • (TH 1959 MA)

**HILLMER SIGMUND W REV** (319)232-7927
707 1/2 W 7th St Waterloo IA 50702-1513 • IE • EM • (TH 1945)

**HILMER RONALD P REV** (314)227-2819
404 Crestbury Dr Manchester MO 63011-4308 • roncarerev@msn.com • MO • Missouri Saint Louis MO • (314)317-4550 • (CQ 1970 MAR)

**HILPERT RODNEY A REV** (530)642-8500
C/O First Lutheran Church 1200 Pinecrest Ct Placerville CA 95667 • flcp@jps.net • CNH • Assoc • First Placerville CA • (530)622-3022 • (SL 1972 MDIV)

**HILSABECK HOWARD R REV** (314)332-9947
608B Linda Ln Wentzville MO 63385-1029 • MO • EM • (SL 1957 STM)

**HINCHEY DONALD F REV** (303)773-9857
10906 E Berry Ave Englewood CO 80111-3904 • dfhinchey@aol.com • RM • Sn/Adm • Our Father Littleton CO • (303)779-1332 • (SL 1969 STM DMIN)

**HINCK DAVID E REV** (702)384-6106
7400 W Flamingo Rd Apt 2002 Las Vegas NV 89117-4367 • PSW • EM • (SL 1967 MDIV)

**HINCKLEY ROBERT M REV** (580)226-4386
725 Wallace NW Ardmore OK 73401-1412 • lutheran@brightok.net • OK • SP • Trinity Ardmore OK • (580)223-3048 • (SL 1996 MDIV)

**HINES ROBERT D REV** (507)354-6745
717 S State St New Ulm MN 56073-3577 • MNS • SP • Redeemer New Ulm MN • (507)233-3470 • (FW 1989 MDIV)

**HINKEL DONALD C JR. REV** (309)968-6614
21830 N County Rd 3300E Manito IL 61546-9529 • dhinkel@ntslink.net • CI • SP • St Paul Manito IL • (309)968-6614 • (CQ 1976)

**HINKLE CHRIS N REV**
300 Roy El Ct Wapello IA 52653-1346 • Chris³N³Hinkle@xcite.com • IE • SP • St Paul Wapello IA • (319)523-6951 • (SL 1981 MDIV)

**HINKLE MARVIN R REV** (219)753-4209
422 9th St Logansport IN 46947-3533 • IN • SP • St James Logansport IN • (219)753-4227 • (CQ 1979 MS)

**HINMAN DAVID GERALD REV** (941)792-1876
C/O Hope Lutheran Church 4635 26th St Bradenton FL 34207 • cocoabomb@juno.com • FG • SP • Hope Bradenton FL • (941)755-3256 • (FW 1994 MDIV)

**HINNERS GREGORY S REV**
C/O Concordia Lutheran Church PO Box 106 Cresbard SD 57435-0106 • henricus@nvc.net • SD • SP • Concordia Cresbard SD* • (605)324-3318 • (FW 1998 MDIV)

**HINRICHS DANIEL L REV** (262)681-0382
5527 N Meadows Dr Racine WI 53402-1751 • SW • SP • Prince Peace Racine WI • (262)639-1277 • (SPR 1972 MDIV)

**HINRICHS KENNETH N REV** (920)361-2986
358 N Wisconsin St Berlin WI 54923-1102 • revkenhi@yahoo.com • SW • Sn/Adm • St John Berlin WI • (920)361-9935 • (FW 1992 MED MDIV)

**HINRICHS MARVIN F REV** (501)751-5885
1710 Westwood Ave Springdale AR 72762-4012 • MDS • EM • (SL 1948 MDIV)

**HINTZ DAVID W REV** (573)335-8916
20 N Benton St Cape Girardeau MO 63701-5421 • dwh@t-lutheran.org • MO • Assoc • Trinity Cape Girardeau MO • (573)335-8224 • (FW 1994 MDIV)

**HINTZ LARRY L REV** (626)358-6073
425 Greenbank Duarte CA 91010 • falahintz@aol.com • PSW • SP • First Monrovia CA • (626)357-3543 • (SL 1980 MDIV)

**HINTZE DAVID J REV** (817)468-4854
2401 Heathercrest Dr Arlington TX 76018-2521 • djhintze@aol.com • TX • SP • Beaut Savior Arlington TX • (817)465-3164 • (FW 1977 MDIV)

**HINTZE OTTO C REV** (314)843-9913
9239 Laurel Hill Dr Saint Louis MO 63126-2819 • ochintze@juno.com • MO • EM • (SL 1948 MDIV STM DTH LITTD)

**HINTZE R MICHAEL REV** (978)874-2504
C/O Our Savior Luth Church PO Box 459 Westminster MA 01473-0459 • NE • SP • Our Savior Westminster MA • (978)874-2504 • (FW 1977 MDIV)

**HINTZMAN HAROLD R JR. REV** (402)862-2436
RR 1 Box 57 Humboldt NE 68376-9711 • NEB • SP • Faith Humboldt NE • (402)862-2437 • (SL 1975 MDIV)

**HINZ ALFRED J REV** (402)584-2481
PO Box 123 Dixon NE 68732-0123 • CNH • EM • (SL 1944)

**HINZ CLARENCE R REV** (810)463-3770
20855 S Miles St Clinton Township MI 48036-1951 • MI • EM • (SPR 1976 MED)

**HINZ DAVID W REV** (907)790-4234
9367 Rivercourt Way Juneau AK 99801-9629 • dwjlhinz@gci.net • NOW • EM • (SL 1956 MDIV MA)

**HINZ FREDERICK C REV** (540)710-0891
13 Olde Plantation Dr Fredericksburg VA 22407-2404 • fchinz@aol.com • AT • EM • (SL 1950 MDIV MA LLD)

**HINZ PAUL R REV**
2561 Hemmeter Rd Saginaw MI 48603-3019 • MI • Asst • Good Shepherd Saginaw MI • (517)793-8201 • (SL 1991 MDIV)

**HINZ RICHARD T DR** (540)373-5378
15 Osprey Ln Fredericksburg VA 22405-3481 • SE • Assoc • Prince Of Peace Springfield VA • (703)451-5855 • (SL 1959 MDIV LLD DD)

**HINZ ROBERT L REV** (410)672-0632
1307 Beverly Ave Odenton MD 21113-1532 • microtuspenn@erols.com • SE • SP • First Odenton MD • (410)551-9189 • (SL 1977 MDIV)

**HINZ THOMAS P REV** (414)327-2368
2324 S 81st St Milwaukee WI 53219-1728 • TomHinz@juno.com • SW • EM • (SPR 1951 MDIV)

**HINZ TIMOTHY M REV** (352)372-3009
930 NW 37th Ter Gainesville FL 32605-4942 • timminz@aol.com • FG • Sn/Adm • First Gainesville FL • (352)376-2062 • (SL 1991 MDIV)

**HINZ VERN D REV** (517)423-5502
1418 Sauk Trl Tecumseh MI 49286-1634 • vernhinz@umich.edu • MI • EM • (SPR 1961 MA DMIN)

**HINZE DENNIS A REV** (810)463-2012
297 Riverside Dr Clinton Twp MI 48036-3261 • MI • 10/1989 10/1999 • (FW 1979 MDIV)

**HIPENBECKER DENNIS REV** (414)475-9012
12220 W Ripley Ave Wauwatosa WI 53226-3828 • SW • EM • (SPR 1965)

**HIPPE VICTOR V DR** (253)838-7500
33750 29th Ct SW Federal Way WA 98023-7718 • vichip@stlukesfedway.org • NOW • Sn/Adm • St Luke Federal Way WA • (253)941-3000 • (SL 1971 MDIV DMIN)

**HIRSCH JOHN M REV** (512)238-7484
2033 Inverness Dr Round Rock TX 78681-2600 • jhirsch@txdistlcms.org • TX • D Ex/S • Texas Austin TX • (SPR 1972 MDIV MA DMIN)

**HIRSCH THOMAS W REV** (909)548-0735
6133 Walnut Ave Chino CA 91710-2773 • drtdub@hotmail.com • PSW • 04/1994 04/2000 • (SL 1975 MDIV DMIN)

**HIRSSIG SCOTT S REV**
C/O Immanuel Lutheran Church 45 W Broadway Plainview MN 55964-1238 • MNS • Assoc • Immanuel Plainview MN • (507)534-3700 • (SL 1999 MDIV)

**HIRST JOHN C REV** (863)357-1734
1750 NE 131st Ln Okeechobee FL 34972-8539 • FG • SP • Peace Okeechobee FL • (863)763-5042 • (SL 1981 MDIV)

**HISCHKE ROLAND REV** (815)379-9458
105 Fairview Ct PO Box 550 Walnut IL 61376-0550 • NI • SP • Holy Trinity Walnut IL • (815)379-2839 • (SPR 1963 MDIV)

**HISCHKE W F REV** (618)346-6962
962 N Bluff Rd Collinsville IL 62234 • SI • EM • (SL 1957 MDIV MA DMIN)

**HOAG DOUGLAS E REV** (815)723-7642
2707 Dougall Rd Joliet IL 60433 • 102670.1341@compuserve.com • EN • SP • Trinity New Lenox IL • (815)485-6973 • (FW 1993 MDIV)

**HOARD SAMUEL L REV** (407)423-5291
3323 Gulfstream Rd Orlando FL 32805-5828 • FG • EM • (SL 1957 MSW MDIV)

**HOBRATSCHK DONALD M REV** (732)846-8978
PO Box 5533 Somerset NJ 08875-5533 • 70167.2523@compuserve.com • NJ • SP • Holy Trinity Somerset NJ • (732)873-2888 • (SL 1966 MDIV DMIN)

**HOBRATSCHK JOHN A REV** (573)636-6685
1216 Jefferson St Jefferson City MO 65109-2410 • jhobratsch@socket.net • MO • Assoc • Trinity Jefferson City MO • (573)636-6750 • (SL 1970 MDIV)

**HOBRATSCHK RALPH WAYNE REV** (281)482-4160
Hope Lutheran Church PO Box 1076 Friendswood TX 77549-1076 • rhobratschk@cs.com • TX • Sn/Adm • Hope Friendswood TX • (281)482-7943 • (SL 1976 MDIV)

**HOBUS ROBERT A DR** (417)886-6684
1705 W Primrose St Springfield MO 65807-4482 • rohbus@juno.com • EN • EM • (SL 1949 STM MDIV DMIN)

**HODDE JOHN F REV** (818)249-9088
5012 Verwood Ave Glendale CA 91214-1054 • jfhodde@cs.com • PSW • SP • Zion Glendale CA • (818)243-3119 • (SL 1963 MDIV)

**HODEL DAVID KURT REV** (507)932-4570
567 East 12th St Saint Charles MN 55972-1601 • davidhodel@earthlink.net • MNS • Sn/Adm • St Matthew Saint Charles MN • (507)932-4246 • (FW 1992 MDIV)

**HODEL RONALD K REV** (949)493-5333
32792 David Cir Dana Point CA 92629-1058 • PSW • SP • Faith Capistrano Beach CA • (949)496-1901 • (FW 1981 MDIV)

**HODGES LEON A REV** (515)842-3322
1006 W Robinson St Knoxville IA 50138-2823 • IE • SP • Trinity Knoxville IA • (515)842-4724 • (SPR 1962)

**HODSON JOHN L REV**
6992 Cora Lee Dr Belvidere IL 61008 • IW • 03/1999 • (SL 1998 MDIV)

**HOECKER PAUL M REV** (580)765-0099
1208 Memory Ln Ponca City OK 74601-1082 • NI • 04/1999 • (SL 1986 MDIV)

**HOEFER HERBERT E REV** (503)251-0070
2412 NE 163rd Ave Portland OR 97230 • hhoefer@cu-portland.edu • NOW • SHS/C • Northwest Portland OR • (SL 1974 STM MDIV DED)

**HOEFERKAMP DONALD E REV** (314)843-1138
10718 Meath Dr Saint Louis MO 63123-4954 • MO • EM • (SL 1958 MDIV)

**HOEFERKAMP HAROLD REV** (334)968-5698
1701 Regency Rd Apt 113 Gulf Shores AL 36542-3404 • SO • EM • (CQ 1980 MAR)

**HOEHNE RONALD E REV** (660)826-5185
403 W 20th St Sedalia MO 65301-7221 • revholsl@iland.net • MO • SP • Our Savior Sedalia MO • (660)827-0226 • (CQ 1978 MDIV)

**HOEHNER ROBERT P REV** (414)306-8757
1300 Vogt Dr West Bend WI 53095-4991 • hoehner@swd.lcms.org • SW • D Ex/S • South Wisconsin Milwaukee WI • (414)464-8100 • (SL 1972 MDIV)

**HOELTER JOEL A REV** (715)831-8562
609 Fall St Eau Claire WI 54703-3157 • jhoelter@werewolf.net • NW • SP • Our Redeemer Eau Claire WI • (715)835-5239 • (SL 1979 MDIV)

**HOELTER MARK E REV** (503)253-0942
16452 NE Fargo St Portland OR 97230-5528 • hoelterm@teleport.com • NOW • SP • Trinity Portland OR • (503)288-6403 • (SL 1972 MDIV MSED)

**HOELTER THOMAS F REV** (715)355-4876
5401 Rose Ave Wausau WI 54401-7574 • thoel@home.dwave.net • NW • SP • Rib Mountain Wausau WI • (715)845-2313 • (SL 1973 MDIV)

**HOEMANN GERALD L REV** (760)922-4958
581 Seville Ln Blythe CA 92225-1045 • zionblythe@juno.com • PSW • SP • Zion Blythe CA • (760)922-7321 • (SL 1963 MDIV)

**HOEMANN J PAUL REV** (708)865-9230
1015 N 2nd Ave Maywood IL 60153-1010 • NI • D Miss • Northern Illinois Hillside IL • (SL 1999 MDIV)

**HOEMANN RICHARD L J REV** (315)637-5453
125 Shady Lane Fayetteville NY 13066-1530 • rljhoemann@gateway.net • EA • EM • (SL 1958 MDIV)

**HOENER KENNETH E REV** (724)327-2830
3481 N Hills Rd Murrysville PA 15668-1323 • EA • EM • (SPR 1956)

**HOERLE DARREL D REV** (417)682-5043
1204 E 10th St Lamar MO 64759-2114 • MO • EM • (SL 1958 MDIV)

**HOESE TERRY E REV** (616)361-1384
1435 Mayfield Ct NE Grand Rapids MI 49525-2300 • tehoese@iserv.net • MI • SP • Messiah Grand Rapids MI • (616)363-2553 • (CQ 1979 MED)

**HOESMAN C WILLIAM REV** (734)998-2907
3773 Geddes Rd Ann Arbor MI 48105 • mc$^3$pres@mc.lcms.org • MI • DP • Michigan Ann Arbor MI • (SPR 1970 MSED MDIV)

**HOFENER ROBERT H REV** (216)845-2207
4410 Stary Dr Parma OH 44134-5831 • OH • EM • (SPR 1960)

**HOFFERBER MARK JAMES REV** (618)659-2315
1130 Nassau Dr Edwardsville IL 62025 • zionhoff@ezl.com • SI • Asst • Zion Bethalto IL • (618)377-8314 • (SL 1995 MDIV)

**HOFFMAN PAUL W REV** (440)885-4857
7900 Hollenbeck Cir Parma OH 44129-6214 • OH • SP • St James Cleveland OH • (216)351-6499 • (SL 1975 MDIV DMIN)

**HOFFMAN PETER REV** (630)554-7689
112 Fox Chase Dr S Oswego IL 60543-7106 • petrospetros@juno.com • NI • SP • St Luke Montgomery IL • (630)892-9309 • (CQ 1992 MDIV)

**HOFFMAN ROBERT A REV** (760)375-7444
731 N Sanders St Ridgecrest CA 93555-3527 • PSW • SP • Our Savior Ridgecrest CA • (760)375-7921 • (SL 1966 MA MDIV)

**HOFFMAN WAYNE P REV** (217)698-8125
1809 Strawberry Ln Springfield IL 62707-8077 • CI • Sn/Adm • Our Savior Springfield IL • (217)546-4531 • (SPR 1975 DMIN)

**HOFFMANN BRUCE A REV** (847)526-7614
C/O St John Luth Church PO Box 370 Island Lake IL 60042-0370 • maruce@juno.com • NI • SP • St John Island Lake IL • (847)526-7614 • (SPR 1972 MDIV)

**HOFFMANN DONALD H REV** (815)369-4501
518 Quail Dr Lena IL 61048-9232 • NI • Assoc • St John Lena IL • (815)369-4035 • (SPR 1953)

**HOFFMANN FRANKLIN L REV** (715)276-3064
11690 Martha Ln Crivitz WI 54114 • NW • EM • (SL 1957)

**HOFFMANN GEORGE W REV** (541)265-3174
172 NW 58th St Newport OR 97365-1141 • gwdh@newportnet.com • NOW • EM • (SL 1951)

**HOFFMANN GREGORY E REV** (414)592-8509
1722 Carroll Ave Green Bay WI 54304-3803 • greg@pilgrimluth.com • NW • Assoc • Pilgrim Green Bay WI • (920)494-1979 • (FW 1982 MDIV)

**HOFFMANN OSWALD C J REV** (314)918-1130
705 S Laclede Station Rd #465 Saint Louis MO 63119-4969 • MO • EM • (SL 1936 MA LLD DD LHD)

**HOFFMANN PAUL G REV** (408)723-3004
5386 Southbridge Ct San Jose CA 95118-3052 • paul@holycrosslosgatos.org • CNH • Sn/Adm • Holy Cross Los Gatos CA • (408)356-3525 • (SL 1971 MDIV MA)

**HOFFMANN PETER C REV** (708)849-2583
209 E 138th St Dolton IL 60419-1060 • EN • SP • Good Shepherd Chicago IL • (773)581-0096 • (SL 1968 MDIV)

**HOFFMASTER PAUL D REV** (330)666-1312
3496 Yellow Creek Rd Akron OH 44333 • EN • EM • (CQ 1954)

**HOFFSCHNEIDER DALE W REV** (805)271-0356
5321 Barrymore Dr Oxnard CA 93033-8535 • PSW • EM • (SPR 1962 MLS)

**HOFFSTETTER GARY R REV** (660)263-3176
526 Meadowbrook Dr Moberly MO 65270-2451 • MO • SP • Zion Moberly MO • (660)263-3256 • (SL 1976 MDIV)

**HOFLER ALFRED J REV** (516)473-6924
123 South St Port Jefferson NY 11777-1814 • AT • Asst • Messiah East Setauket NY • (631)751-1775 • (SL 1961 MDIV MSW)

**HOFMAN DONNIE A REV** (913)562-2046
C/O Mt Calvary Luth Church 1710 Jenkins St Marysville KS 66508-1348 • KS • SP • Mount Calvary Marysville KS • (785)562-2046 • (CQ 1989)

**HOFMAN MARION C REV** (970)874-4956
1156 Grand Ave Delta CO 81416-2037 • RM • SP • Redeemer Delta CO • (970)874-3052 • (SL 1961)

**HOFMANN HUNTER REV** (262)375-3819
W56 N491 Highland Dr Cedarburg WI 53012-2556 • SW • SP • Trinity Milwaukee WI • (414)271-2219 • (FW 1994 MDIV)

**HOFMANN RONALD F REV** (651)458-0359
7573 Jeffery Ave S Cottage Grove MN 55016-2232 • chof1943@aol.com • MNS • SP • Rose Of Sharon Cottage Grove MN • (651)459-3551 • (SPR 1964 STM)

**HOFT PETER D** (618)343-1815
816 Westwood Village Maryville IL 62062-5745 • SI • Assoc • Good Shepherd Collinsville IL • (618)344-3151 • (SL 2000 MDIV)

**HOFT THEES C REV** 964-8103
C/O St John Lutheran Church 1107 Lake Rd West Fork Hamlin NY 14464-9601 • shepherd99@juno.com • EA • SP • St John Hamlin NY • (716)964-2550 • (SL 1974 MDIV)

**HOGER ALLEN C REV** (316)744-6699
4649 N Farmstead Wichita KS 67220 • KS • SP • Immanuel Wichita KS • (316)264-0639 • (CQ 1979 MDIV)

**HOGER DONALD R REV** (845)229-7404
20 Roosevelt Rd Hyde Park NY 12538-2319 • hoger@msn.com • AT • EM • (SL 1954 MDIV)

**HOGG CHARLES ROBERT JR. DR** (616)681-0791
8246 Harlow Ave PO Box 173 Byron Twp MI 49315 • pastor$^3$hogg@hotmail.com • EN • SP • Epiphany Dorr MI • (616)681-0791 • (FW 1983 MDIV PHD)

**HOHE JOHN W REV** (781)821-1598
3 Standish Way Canton MA 02021-1217 • thehohes@mediaone.net • NE • SP • St James Canton MA • (781)828-0620 • (SL 1982 MDIV)

**HOHENSTEIN KENNETH F REV** (509)764-5263
1223 S Balsam St Apt 56 Moses Lake WA 98837 • kfhohnst@nwi.net • NOW • EM • (SPR 1976 MDIV)

**HOHLE ELMER M REV** (512)515-6071
506 Oak Ln Liberty Hill TX 78642-4530 • TX • EM • (SL 1957)

**HOKANA STEVEN C REV**
PO Box 61167 Fairbanks AK 99706-1167 • hokanamo@northnet.org • SE • M Chap • Southeastern Alexandria VA • (SL 1987 MDIV)

**HOKE JAMES L REV**
Univ of Maryland Unit 21293 APO AE 09102 • jhoke@aol.com • NEB • S Miss • Nebraska Seward NE • (FW 1980 MDIV PHD)

**HOLADAY ROBERT W REV** (940)569-3097
C/O Trinity L C of Clara 11867 FM 1813 Iowa Park TX 76367 • trinclara@aol.com • TX • SP • Immanuel Harrold TX* • (940)886-2342 • (CQ 2000 MDIV)

**HOLBIRD DOYLE REV** (618)565-2626
PO Box 102 Gorham IL 62940-0102 • SO • Immanuel Harrold TX • (940)886-2342 • (FW 1985 MDIV)

**HOLDORF KENNETH P REV**
9815 Asheboro Frisco TX 75035 • kholdorf@gte.net • TX • EM • (SL 1964 MED MDIV)

**HOLLAND RICHARD A REV** (407)359-6982
2133 Fox Sparrow Ct Oviedo FL 32765-5211 • FG • EM • (SPR 1962 MDIV MA)

**HOLLAND ROGER A REV** (612)722-1000
1708 E Minnehaha Pkwy Minneapolis MN 55407-3640 • MNS • SP • Holy Cross Minneapolis MN • (612)722-1083 • (SL 1969 MDIV STM)

**HOLLAR WILLIAM H JR. REV** (757)989-0739
1276 Springwell Pl Newport News VA 23608-7713 • rlc@erols.com • SE • SP • Resurrection Newport News VA • (757)596-5808 • (FW 1979 MDIV)

**HOLLENDER DAVID E REV** (517)673-8804
1664 Cedar Knoll Ln Caro MI 48723-9524 • stpaul@centuryinter.net • MI • Sn/Adm • St Paul Caro MI • (517)673-4214 • (SPR 1966)

**HOLLIBAUGH KARL D REV** (507)526-7318
305 E 5th St Blue Earth MN 56013 • stpaul@bevcomm.net • MNS • Sn/Adm • St Paul Blue Earth MN* • (507)526-7318 • (SL 1993 MDIV MTH)

**HOLLING RONALD E REV** (402)371-8895
2507 Madison Ave Norfolk NE 68701-4445 • pastorholling@oursav.org • NEB • Sn/Adm • Our Savior Norfolk NE • (402)371-9005 • (SL 1970 MDIV)

**HOLLS JOEL M REV** (313)388-5008
14555 Cleveland Ave Allen Park MI 48101-2107 • joholls@aol.com • EN • SP • Angelica Allen Park MI • (313)381-2080 • (SPR 1976 MDIV)

**HOLM MICHAEL H REV** (319)242-8158
919 7th Ave N Clinton IA 52732-3520 • IE • SP • Trinity Clinton IA • (319)242-5328 • (FW 1984 MDIV)

**HOLM PETER R REV** (320)203-1637
428 N 28th Ave Saint Cloud MN 56303-3748 • holmpm@astound.net • MNN • Assoc • Redeemer Saint Cloud MN • (320)252-8171 • (SPR 1976 MDIV)

**HOLM WALTER E REV** (847)299-2678
1165 Southwest Pl Des Plaines IL 60016-6229 • NI • EM • (SPR 1950)

**HOLMES EDGAR W REV** (215)854-0148
6803 Emlen St #308 Philadelphia PA 19119-2635 • EA • EM • (CQ 1979 MTH MTH PHD)

**HOLST ROBERT A REV** (651)641-8211
275 Syndicate St N Saint Paul MN 55104-5436 • holst@csp.edu • MNS • SHS/C • Minnesota South Burnsville MN • (SL 1961 MDIV STM PHD)

**HOLSTEIN BRUCE E REV**
Mount Olive Lutheran Church 5171 W Smokey Row Rd Greenwood IN 46143-8664 • bruce@reliable-net.net • IN • Assoc • Mount Olive Greenwood IN • (317)422-9991 • (SPR 1974)

**HOLSTEIN GILBERT J REV** (316)683-0489
2608 Clover Ln Wichita KS 67216-2265 • KS • EM • (SL 1961 MDIV STM)

**HOLSTEIN LOWELL J REV** (813)962-0658
4722 Southbreeze Dr Tampa FL 33624-1634 • FG • 01/1989 01/2000 • (SL 1961)

**HOLSTEIN ROBERT W REV** (623)974-6861
10113 W Sombrero Cir Sun City AZ 85373-1147 • holstein32@aol.com • PSW • EM • (SL 1958 MDIV)

**HOLSTEIN SYLVESTER W REV** (712)263-3359
114th S 20th Denison IA 51442-2253 • IW • EM • (SL 1932)

**HOLSTEN ROBERT W REV** (201)767-4542
417 High St Closter NJ 07624-2005 • NJ • SP • St Paul Closter NJ • (201)768-6310 • (SL 1984 MDIV)

**HOLT PAUL V REV** (415)532-8817
3311 Madera Ave Oakland CA 94619-3415 • CNH • SP • Pilgrim Oakland CA • (510)531-3715 • (SPR 1975)

**HOLT WILBERT V REV** (415)752-2444
614 6th Ave San Francisco CA 94118-3805 • CNH • EM • (SPR 1945)

**HOLTHUS DANIEL G REV** (307)362-6605
225 Sunflower Ln Rock Springs WY 82901-4375 • WY • SP • Trinity Rock Springs WY • (307)362-5088 • (FW 1999 MDIV)

**HOLTHUS JAMES M REV** (507)726-6587
341 Murphy PO Box 873 Lake Crystal MN 56055-0873 • MNS • SP • Trinity Lake Crystal MN* • (507)726-2739 • (SL 1992 MDIV)

**HOLTORF GENE KENT REV** (913)692-4228
C/O St John Luth Church 312 National Rd Palmer KS 66962-9606 • KS • SP • St John Palmer KS • (913)692-4228 • (FW 1993 MDIV MS MS)

**HOLTORF PAUL C REV** (402)643-6605
1437 N 1st St Seward NE 68434-1013 • NEB • SHS/C • Nebraska Seward NE • (SL 1991 MDIV MED PHD)

**HOLTZ ALAN E REV** (618)349-8747
305 Holman PO Box 155 Saint Peter IL 62880-0155 • CI • EM • (SPR 1963)

**HOLTZ ARLIN A REV** (913)432-2333
4300 W 55th St Roeland Park KS 66205-2431 • KS • SP • St Martin Basehor KS • (913)724-2900 • (SL 1948 MDIV)

**HOLTZ LOWELL D REV**
W11204 2nd St Medford WI 54451 • NW • EM • (CQ 1986)

**HOLTZEN MERLIN D REV** (402)782-6505
C/O Trinity Luth Church 5315 S 162nd St Walton NE 68461-9719 • tah21@aol.com • NEB • SP • Trinity Walton NE • (402)782-6515 • (CQ 1994 MED)

**HOLZ HERBERT F REV** (603)487-2910
PO Box 552 New Boston NH 03070-0552 • NE • EM • (SPR 1957)

**HOLZ RICHARD W REV** (303)730-7636
1064 E Fremont Cir N Littleton CO 80122-1479 • rholz@du.edu • RM • Assoc • Shepherd Hills Littleton CO • (303)798-0711 • (SL 1982 MDIV)

**HOLZER WILLIAM H REV**
3112 Wood Creek Rd Brenham TX 77833-0613 • wwwholzer@phoenix.net • TX • Assoc • Grace Brenham TX • (979)836-3475 • (SL 1989 MDIV)

**HOLZERLAND TIMOTHY A REV**
4363 Kensington Ave Detroit MI 48224-2736 • EN • Assoc • Christ King Grosse Pointe Woods MI • (313)884-5090 • (SL 1991 MDIV)

**HOMAN MARTIN J REV** (412)221-0363
3199 Washington Pike Bridgeville PA 15017-1423 • mjhoman@earthlink.net • EA • SP • Zion Bridgeville PA • (412)221-4776 • (SL 1980 MDIV STM MTH)

**HOMP GERALD A REV** (715)675-6521
4310 Ashland Ave Wausau WI 54403-2210 • NW • EM • (SPR 1957)

**HOMRIGHAUSEN EDGAR W REV** (504)781-8388
147 Kelly Dr Slidell LA 70458-5403 • ed-marge@bellsouth.net • SO • SP • The Village Lacombe LA • (504)882-5727 • (SPR 1950 DD)

**HONG KUN WON REV**
987 S Gramercy Pl Los Angeles CA 90019 • PSW • D Miss • First Van Nuys CA • (818)989-5844 • (CQ 1997)

**HONG YOUNG-HWAN REV** (213)384-2295
C/O Trinity Central Luth Ch 987 S Gramercy Pl Los Angeles CA 90019-2155 • PSW • SP • Trinity Central Los Angeles CA • (323)732-4444 • (KO 1970 MTH MDIV PHD)

**HONIG JAMES K REV** (941)649-8378
780 Banyan Blvd Naples FL 34102-5110 • jashonig@mindspring.com • FG • SP • Grace Naples FL • (941)261-7421 • (SL 1987 MDIV STM)

**HONIG WALTER A REV** (309)691-2910
7019 N Galena Rd Peoria IL 61614-2205 • CI • EM • (SL 1927)

**HOOD JOHN A REV** (614)876-7367
5200 Citrus Dr Hilliard OH 43026-9215 • revjhood@hotmail.com • OH • Assoc • St James Columbus OH • (614)878-5158 • (SL 1994 MDIV)

**HOOGERHYDE RICHARD S REV** (616)689-6292
1407 E Swain St White Cloud MI 49349-9206 • MI • SP • Christ White Cloud MI • (231)689-1704 • (FW 1988 MDIV)

**HOOGLAND KEVIN J REV** (715)536-1192
W5640 County Road Ff Merrill WI 54452-7834 • NW • SP • Faith Merrill WI • (715)536-5443 • (SL 1984 MDIV)

**HOOPER BRIAN W REV**
10236 Wateridge Suite 193 San Diego CA 92121-2732 • PSW • Cmp P • University La Jolla CA • (858)453-0561 • (SL 1984 MDIV)

**HOOVER DAVID W REV** (503)674-7637
1430 SW Spence Ct Troutdale OR 97060 • dhooverdam@aol.com • NOW • D Ex/S • Northwest Portland OR • (SL 1971 MDIV)

**HOOVER FREDERICK M REV** (559)595-1332
894 Suzanne Ct Dinuba CA 93618 • CNH • SP • First Dinuba CA • (559)591-0375 • (SL 1999 MDIV)

**HOOVER KENNETH D REV** (402)786-3414
14320 Carlson Ct Waverly NE 68462-1522 • peacewaverly@juno.com • NEB • SP • Peace Waverly NE • (402)786-2345 • (SL 1983 MDIV)

**HOPFENSPERGER BRYAN LEE REV**
PO Box 207 Culbertson NE 69024 • NEB • SP • St John Culbertson NE • (308)278-2575 • (SL 2000 MDIV)

**HOPKINS JOHN RICHARD REV** (785)286-3782
4115 NW Fielding Rd Topeka KS 66618-2626 • indianlancer@peoplepc.com • KS • Sn/Adm • Calvary Topeka KS • (785)286-1431 • (SL 1995 MDIV)

**HOPMANN ROLAND A REV** (402)488-7216
2751 Scott Ave Lincoln NE 68506-3259 • rahopmann@aol.com • NEB • EM • (SL 1947)

**HOPPE HECTOR E REV** (636)386-0940
717 Rockridge Dr Ballwin MO 63021 • hector@cphnet.org • MO • S Ex/S • Missouri Saint Louis MO • (314)317-4550 • (VB 1977 STM MDIV)

**HOPPE PAUL T REV** (913)631-9494
12201 W 72nd St Shawnee KS 66216-3623 • pthoppe@aol.com • KS • Sn/Adm • Hope Shawnee KS • (913)631-6940 • (SL 1972 MDIV)

**HOPPES JAMES T REV** (314)776-7534
2626 Miami St Saint Louis MO 63118-3928 • hcstlou@inlink.com • MO • SP • Holy Cross Saint Louis MO • (314)772-8633 • (SPR 1965 MDIV)

**HORKEY CHARLES E REV** (402)494-7680
513 E 39th St South Sioux City NE 68776-3447 • NEB • Sn/Adm • Hope South Sioux City NE • (402)494-1847 • (SL 1984 MDIV)

**HORMACHEA JUAN L REV** (308)324-7399
1708 N Cleveland St Lexington NE 68850-2721 • jhormachea@alltel.net • NEB • Assoc • Trinity Lexington NE • (308)324-4341 • (CQ 1987 MDIV MDIV)

**HORN DAVID K REV**
127 15th St E Glencoe MN 55336 • davehorn@email.com • MNN • 07/1999 • (SL 1986 MDIV)

**HORN JEFFREY PAUL REV** (626)794-2294
C/O Mt Olive Lutheran CH 1118 N Allen Ave Pasadena CA 91104-3206 • refjeffhorn@juno.com • PSW • SP • Mount Olive Pasadena CA • (626)794-2294 • (FW 1996 MDIV)

**HORN ORVILLE H REV** (940)569-4085
401 Mistletoe St Burkburnett TX 76354-2629 • ohorn@earthlink.net • TX • EM • (FW 1977)

**HORN OSCAR H REV** (281)392-1353
1550 Katy Flewellen Rd #1511 Katy TX 77494-6324 • TX • EM • (SL 1939)

**HORN RUSSELL L REV**
14479 Lake Wildwood Dr Penn Valley CA 95946-9570 • revrhorn@horn-net.com • CNH • 10/1998 • (SL 1993 MDIV)

**HORNBOSTEL ALVIN C REV** (913)236-4034
1843 S 31st St Apt D Kansas City KS 66106-2875 • KS • EM • (SL 1938)

**HORNIG EDWARD R REV** (205)887-3901
C/O Trinity Luth Church 446 S Gay St Auburn AL 36830-5937 • SO • SP • Trinity Auburn AL • (334)887-3901 • (SL 1970 MDIV)

**HORNIG JURAINE J REV** (605)399-3687
602 Alta Vista Dr Rapid City SD 57701 • SD • EM • (SL 1957 MDIV)

**HORNISH ARTHUR H REV** (205)351-9049
1601 12th St SE Decatur AL 35601-5139 • SO • EM • (CQ 1991 MDIV)

**HORSTMEYER KIRK P REV** (812)867-6812
C/O Immanuel Luth Church 1925 Volkman Rd Evansville IN 47725-9476 • IN • SP • Immanuel Evansville IN • (812)867-5088 • (FW 1984 MTH)

**HOTOPP ROGER A REV**
Holy Cross Lutheran Church 3118 S New Braunfels Ave San Antonio TX 78210-5254 • Rev3Rah@yahoo.com • TX • SP • Holy Cross San Antonio TX • (210)532-1300 • (FW 1979 MDIV)

**HOUGARD DONALD T REV** (414)760-7261
9615 W Kaul Ave Milwaukee WI 53225-1620 • dhougard@execpc.com • SW • SP • Benediction Milwaukee WI • (414)463-9158 • (FW 1988 MDIV)

**HOUGE CLAUDE G REV**
PO Box 43 Gambaga NR GHANA • houge@africanline.com.gh • NEB • S Miss • Nebraska Seward NE • (CQ 1996)

**HOUPPERT ERNEST R REV**
PO Box 6936 Charlottsville VA 22906-6936 • SE • 05/1994 05/2000 • (SL 1985 MDIV)

**HOUSE THOMAS WENDELL REV**
C/O Hope Lutheran Church 2835 Peavy Rd Dallas TX 75228-4772 • t.house@juno.com • TX • SP • Hope Dallas TX • (214)321-6584 • (FW 1996 MDIV)

**HOUSER GLENN D REV** (509)935-8929
2175 Dry Creek Rd # C Chewelah WA 99109-9712 • NOW • 11/1992 11/1999 • (FW 1986 MDIV MD)

**HOUSER PHILIP GIDEON REV** (402)339-3668
903 Overland Trl Papillion NE 68046 • philip.houser@prodigy.net • NEB • Assoc • First Papillion NE • (402)339-3668 • (CQ 1996 MDIV)

**HOUSER WILLIAM G REV** (360)678-4305
1300 Leahy Dr Coupeville WA 98239-9799 • NOW • EM • (SPR 1951 MDIV MA MA PHD)

**HOUSKA CHARLES L REV**
C/O All Saints Lutheran Church PO Box 2626 Blairsville GA 30514-2626 • revc@aol.com • FG • SP • All Saints Blairsville GA • (706)745-7777 • (SL 1967 MDIV)

**HOVEL LEROY K REV** (913)341-6812
8108 Dearborn Dr Prairie Village KS 66208-4825 • hov3@kcnet.com • KS • Sn/Adm • Trinity Mission KS • (913)432-5441 • (SL 1972 MDIV)

**HOVLAND G GREG REV** (507)549-3386
PO Box 296 Vernon Center MN 56090-0296 • pastorh@prairie.lakes.com • MNS • SP • St Peter Vernon Center MN* • (507)549-3166 • (SL 1997 MDIV)

**HOWANITZ DARRELL K REV** (219)749-9925
1822 N Tyland Blvd New Haven IN 46774 • howanitz@juno.com • IN • Indiana Fort Wayne IN • (FW 1993 MDIV)

**HOWARD DONALD R REV** (580)536-0894
210 NW 74th St Lawton OK 73505 • OK • SP • Holy Cross Lawton OK • (580)357-7684 • (FW 1999)

**HOWARD RICHARD A REV**
818 N 11th Ave Melrose Park IL 60160-4116 • NI • 08/1998 08/2000 • (CQ 1987 MED MAR)

**HOWE PAUL F REV** (502)942-2295
1125-A 13th Cav Rd Fort Knox KY 40121 • howep@ftknox-emh19.army.mil • MNN • M Chap • Minnesota North Brainerd MN • (SPR 1972 MDIV)

**HOWEN RUSSELL H REV** (530)541-8509
2453 Del Norte S Lake Tahoe CA 96150 • CNH • EM • (SL 1957)

**HOWER STEPHEN D REV** (636)451-5471
230 Killarney Ln Pacific MO 63069-2469 • josh1v7@aol.com • MO • Sn/Adm • St John Ellisville MO • (314)394-4100 • (FW 1978 MDIV)

**HOWLETT JOSEPH REV**
C/O Our Savior Luth Church PO Box 426 Springfield SD 57062-0426 • SD • SP • Our Savior Springfield SD* • (605)369-2386 • (FW 1985 MDIV)

**HOYER DWAYNE C REV** (822)794-6274
Inst Chaplains Office 34th ASG PSC 303 Box 75 APO AP 96204-3075 • ilcseool@att.co.kr • FG • S Miss • Florida-Georgia Orlando FL • (SL 1964 MDIV DMIN)

**HOYER HORST REV** (216)398-5552
1723 Tampa Ave Cleveland OH 44109-4427 • pfarrerhh@aol.com • OH • Sn/Adm • Immanuel Cleveland OH • (216)781-9511 • (SL 1955 MDIV)

**HOYER JOEL F REV** (616)837-1442
250 Cleveland St E Coopersville MI 49404-9601 • joelffl@iserv.net • MI • SP • Grace Coopersville MI • (616)837-7831 • (SL 1985 MDIV)

**HOYER MARTIN O REV** (573)392-8449
19083 Hobbs Rd Barnett MO 65011 • marthoy@socket.net • MO • EM • (SL 1959 MDIV MS)

**HOYER MARVIN E REV** (630)221-0148
545 E Thornhill Dr - Apt 104 Carol Stream IL 60188-2719 • mehoyer@msn.com • NI • EM • (SL 1965 MDIV)

**HOYER PAUL M REV** (407)322-2552
301 Washington Ave Lake Mary FL 32746-3507 • S • Sn/Adm • Holy Cross Lake Mary FL • (407)333-0797 • (SL 1980 MDIV)

**HOYER VICTOR O REV** (515)986-3339
508 N Harvey St Grimes IA 50111-2018 • iowahoyers@aol.com • IW • EM • (SL 1945 MA)

**HOYT THOMAS W REV** (979)242-5505
PO Box 69 Warda TX 78960-0069 • hoyt@cvtv.net • TX • SP • Holy Cross Warda TX • (409)242-3333 • (FW 1982)

**HRACHOVINA DAVID A REV** (208)344-4577
5191 Cassia St Boise ID 83705-1952 • dodarock@aol.com • NOW • SP • Good Shepherd Boise ID • (208)343-7212 • (FW 1978 MDIV)

**HRICKO MARK A REV** (301)490-7083
9413 Tall Window Way Columbia MD 21046-2058 • markhricko@yahoo.com • SE • Sn/Adm • St Andrew Silver Spring MD • (301)942-6531 • (FW 1985 MDIV)

**HSU WILL C REV** (714)761-3517
5445 Riva Ct Cypress CA 90630 • PSW • D Miss • Concordia Cerritos CA • (562)926-7416 • (CQ 1998)

**HU JOSEPH S REV** (307)637-8169
5118 Jane Ln Cheyenne WY 82009-5312 • WY • EM • (CQ 1961)

**HUBBARD L ALAN REV** (707)786-9353
C/O St Mark Luth Church PO Box 1016 Ferndale CA 95536-1016 • CNH • SP • St Mark Ferndale CA • (707)786-9353 • (SL 1992 MDIV)

**HUBBARD ROGER R REV** (317)736-1911
2074 Galaxy Dr Franklin IN 46131-7974 • IN • SP • Good Shepherd Franklin IN • (317)736-7849 • (FW 1984 MDIV)

**HUBER CURTIS E REV**
6489 S Sheridan Ave Tacoma WA 98408-4713 • EN • EM • (SL 1953 MDIV PHD)

**HUBER DAVID G REV** (313)565-5766
C/O Our Master Luth Church 821 Inkster Rd Inkster MI 48141-1214 • dghuber@aol.com • MI • SP • Our Master Inkster MI • (313)565-5766 • (SL 1967 MDIV)

**HUBER JOHN G DR** (858)459-8855
809 Colima St La Jolla CA 92037-8037 • john.huber@ecunet.org • PSW • EM • (SL 1958 MDIV MTH DMIN)

**HUBER ROLAND W REV** (206)426-5017
128 W Birch St Shelton WA 98584-1729 • NOW • EM • (SL 1946)

**HUBER TERELL O REV** (402)358-3623
101 Bazile Main St Creighton NE 68729-3838 • thubes@bloomnet.com • NEB • SP • Christ Creighton NE* • (402)358-5298 • (FW 1982 MDIV)

**HUBER TIMOTHY L REV** (503)693-7875
681 NE Goldie Dr Hillsboro OR 97124-2120 • TrinityTim@aol.com • NOW • Sn/Adm • Trinity Hillsboro OR • (503)640-1693 • (SPR 1974 MDIV)

**HUBER WALTER H REV** (214)378-6050
7027 Chipperton Dr Dallas TX 75225-1706 • TX • EM • (SL 1945 MTH MED)

**HUDAK DAVID P REV** (847)885-2398
C/O St Peter Luth Church 208 E Schaumburg Rd Schaumburg IL 60194-3517 • dphstp@aol.com • NI • Sn/Adm • St Peter Schaumburg IL • (847)885-3350 • (SPR 1976 MDIV)

**HUDDLE RAYMOND CLIFFORD REV** (225)683-4121
12526 Cedar St PO Box 615 Clinton LA 70722 • SO • SP • Zion Clinton LA • (225)683-5592 • (CQ 1969 MAR)

**HUDSON CHARLES DAVID REV** (816)470-2442
308 Morningside Ter Richmond MO 64085-1940 • phoebadius@aol.com • MO • SP • Faith Richmond MO • (816)776-5550 • (FW 1995 MDIV)

**HUDSPITH ALLAN E REV** (703)257-7581
9317 Amaryllis Ave Manassas VA 20110-6653 • hopelc-ms@erols.com • SE • SP • Hope Manassas VA • (703)361-8732 • (SL 1994 MDIV)

**HUEBEL GLENN E REV** (817)656-1987
6812 Mesa Dr N Richlnd Hls TX 76180-4444 • glhuebel@gte.net • TX • Sn/Adm • Messiah Keller TX • (817)431-2345 • (FW 1980 MDIV)

**HUEBNER ROBERT G REV** (719)548-8725
3725 Deep Haven Dr Colorado Springs CO 80920-4510 • rhueb11226@aol.com • RM • EM • (SL 1952 MA MDIV LLD)

**HUEBNER WAYNE KENNETH REV** (920)849-7867
304 Oak St Chilton WI 53014-1570 • stmartinlc@mail.tds.net • SW • SP • St Martin Chilton WI • (920)849-4421 • (SL 1992 MDIV)

**HUELSE ROBERT L REV** (816)373-6324
3905 Christopher Cir Independence MO 64055-4169 • bbhuelse@kctera.com • MO • EM • (SL 1957)

**HUELSMAN DALE B REV** (440)647-3736
126 Grand Ave Wellington OH 44090-1328 • OH • SP • Bethany Wellington OH • (440)647-5300 • (FW 1983 MDIV)

**HUENER WILLIAM C REV** (630)968-3113
210 56th St Downers Grove IL 60516-1533 • NI • EM • (SL 1952)

**HUERTA HERIBERTO REV** (512)675-2734
2107 W Vale San Antonio TX 78227-2822 • TX • EM • (CQ 1970)

**HUES RONALD REV** (503)634-2751
15534 E Marquam Rd NE Mount Angel OR 97362-9715 • NOW • SP • Trinity Mount Angel OR • (503)634-2437 • (FW 1976 MDIV)

**HUESMANN BERNHARD J REV** (509)884-8519
173 Eastmont Ave East Wenatchee WA 98802-5303 • bghuesmann@hotmail.com • NOW • SP • Faith East Wenatchee WA • (509)884-7623 • (FW 1991 MDIV)

**HUFFINES WARREN L REV**
2017 St Clair Ave Granite City IL 62040-6065 • S • SP • St John Granite City IL • (618)451-7788 • (SL 1999 MDIV)

**HUFFMAN CHARLES ELVIN REV** (915)392-2017
PO Box 518 Ozona TX 76943-0518 • TX • SP • Faith Ozona TX • (915)392-3148 • (CQ 1995)

**HUFFORD STEVEN MARTIN REV** (630)681-8028
ON631 Knollwood Dr Wheaton IL 60187-3015 • NI • Asst • Immanuel Downers Grove IL • (630)968-3112 • (SL 1995 MDIV)

**HUGGINS MARVIN A REV** (314)487-9884
5732 White Pine Dr Saint Louis MO 63129-2936 • marvinh@pobox.com • MO • S Ex/S • Missouri Saint Louis MO • (314)317-4550 • (SL 1970 MDIV)

**HUGHES JAMES N II REV** (630)584-8832
304 S 6th Ave Saint Charles IL 60174-2904 • NI • 06/1993 06/2000 • (CQ 1978 MDIV)

**HUGHES WILLIAM J III REV** (847)253-0031
1123 N Ridge Ave Arlington Hts IL 60004-4603 • whughes@luhome.org • NI • Inst C • Northern Illinois Hillside IL • (SPR 1959 MA MDIV)

**HUGHEY BARRY STEPHENSON REV** (636)225-1497
1287 Lombez Dr Manchester MO 63021-5606 • ventexmo@msn.com • MO • S Ex/S • Missouri Saint Louis MO • (314)317-4550 • (SL 1968 MDIV)

**HUGO WILLIAM DEMPSEY REV** (330)497-7094
1456 Jonathan Ave North Canton OH 44721 • wdh@nls.net • OH • Assoc • Holy Cross Canton OH • (330)499-3307 • (SL 1996 MDIV)

**HULKE STEVEN A REV** (715)341-9909
2002 Frontenac Ave Stevens Point WI 54481-4124 • NW • SP • Beautiful Savior Plover WI • (715)341-2898 • (SL 1987 MDIV)

**HULLINGER ROBERT N REV** (513)641-1024
1739 Bella Vista St Cincinnati OH 45237-5705 • ohionews12@aol.com • OH • EM • (SL 1958 MTH MDIV)

**HUMMEL EDWARD M REV** (636)916-5222
3009 Blanchette Dr Saint Charles MO 63301-0705 • ehummel@immanuelluth.org • MO • Assoc • Immanuel Saint Charles MO • (636)946-2656 • (SL 1968 MDIV)

**HUMMEL HORACE D REV** (760)746-5945
2166 Shadetree Ln Escondido CA 92029-5305 • hdhummel@home.com • PSW • EM • (SL 1951 STM MDIV PHD)

**HUNEKE PAUL R REV** (732)542-9047
57 Parmly Rd Tinton Falls NJ 07724-2845 • phuneke@monmouth.com • NJ • SP • Luther Memorial Tinton Falls NJ • (732)542-2727 • (CQ 1976 MAR)

**HUNSICKER PAUL C SR. REV** (715)223-3669
307 W Pine St Abbotsford WI 54405 • ontarget@pcpros.net • NW • SP • Christ Abbotsford WI • (715)223-4315 • (SL 1984 MDIV DMIN)

**HUNT CLIFFORD D REV**
813 M and O Station Rd Millstadt IL 62260-1367 • SI • EM • (SPR 1963)

**HUNTER DONALD R REV** (828)632-3724
C/O St Paul Lutheran Church PO Box 535 Taylorsville NC 28681-0535 • inchrist2@twave.net • SE • SP • St Paul Taylorsville NC • (828)632-2695 • (FW 1990 MDIV)

**HUNTER KENT R REV** (219)281-2688
347 County Road 20 Corunna IN 46730-9766 • kenthunter@churchdoctor.org • IN • 01/1987 01/2000 • (SL 1973 MDIV PHD DMIN)

**HUNTINGTON DENNIS E REV** (317)787-7571
2053 E Legrande Ave Indianapolis IN 46203-4161 • IN • 01/1995 01/2000 • (SPR 1975 MDIV)

**HURSH TERRY N REV** (317)578-3656
8839 Green Branch Ln Indianapolis IN 46256-9739 • IN • Asst • Holy Cross Indianapolis IN • (317)823-5801 • (CQ 1993 MDIV JD)

**HUSCHER FREDERICK J REV** (909)928-9313
27650 Benigni Ave Romoland CA 92585-9616 • PSW • EM • (SPR 1964)

**HUSFELD MONROE R REV** (979)826-4488
1825 Tenth St Hempstead TX 77445-6039 • TX • 04/1998 04/2000 • (SPR 1951)

**HUSMAN RICHARD H REV** (206)384-0976
3712 Sinclair Dr Ferndale WA 98248 • rhusman@gte.net • NOW • SP • Redeemer Bellingham WA • (360)384-5923 • (FW 1979 MDIV)

**HUSS KEVIN REV** (712)284-2482
301 W 4th St Alta IA 51002-1319 • kvdahuss@ncn.net • IW • SP • St Paul Alta IA • (712)284-1133 • (SL 1988 MDIV)

**HUSSMANN REX REV** (706)291-6930
310 Clark Dr Rome GA 30161-6036 • FG • 01/1977 01/2000 • (SL 1967 MTH MDIV)

**HUTSON DAVID LEE REV** (913)476-2640
329 N Adams PO Box 24 Kensington KS 66951-0024 • 1stjohn@ruraltel.net • KS • SP • First St John Kensington KS • (785)476-2246 • (SL 1981 MDIV)

**HUWE RALPH A REV** (520)445-0195
1962 Ventnor Cir Prescott AZ 86301-5594 • rbhuwe@futureone.com • PSW • EM • (SPR 1966 MDIV)

**HUXHOLD PAUL F REV** (630)739-4176
412 Justine Ave Bolingbrook IL 60440-2221 • NI • EM • (SL 1939)

**HYATT GREGORY D REV** (618)323-6586
8250 Trinity Ln Iuka IL 62849-2420 • ghyatt@midwest.net • SI • SP • Trinity Iuka IL • (618)323-6586 • (FW 1994 MDIV)

**HYLTON MICHAEL JON REV** (608)786-3939
1045 Robin Ct West Salem WI 54669-1919 • popws@prodigy.net • SW • SP • Prince Of Peace West Salem WI • (608)786-3938 • (FW 1992 MDIV)

**HYVONEN STEVEN DALE REV** (715)745-6908
W3122 White Clay Dr Lake Dr Cecil WI 54111-9545 • hyvo1@frontiernet.net • NW • SP • Immanuel Cecil WI* • (715)745-2364 • (FW 1994 MDIV)

## I

**IBEN DOUGLAS DR** (360)714-1912
1919 Rhododendron Way Bellingham WA 98226-4561 • NOW • SP • Trinity Bellingham WA • (206)734-2770 • (CQ 1981 DMIN)

**IBEN HAROLD A REV** (503)255-2682
2222 NE 132nd Ave Portland OR 97230-3002 • NOW • EM • (SL 1941)

**IHLENFELD PAUL C REV** (262)966-0860
W326 N6591 Sylvian Dr Hartland WI 53029 • EN • 09/2000 • ( STM)

**ILLIAN DONALD C REV** (319)984-5912
C/O St John Luth Church PO Box 389 Denver IA 50622-0389 • pdillian@forbin.com • IE • SP • St John Denver IA • (319)984-5351 • (SPR 1964)

**ILLICK FREDERICK S REV** (301)932-6578
7382 Glen Albin Rd La Plata MD 20646-5906 • fmillick@juno.com • SE • EM • (SL 1960 MDIV)

**ILTEN JAMES B REV** (630)932-8286
47 N Elizabeth St Lombard IL 60148-2201 • ilich29@aol.com • NI • D Ex/S • Northern Illinois Hillside IL • (SL 1962 STM)

**ILTEN PHILIP H REV** (805)498-7583
561 Walter Ave Newbury Park CA 91320-5069 • filten@aol.com • PSW • EM • (SL 1961 MDIV)

**IMME JON REV** (213)899-3950
11660 Fenton Lake View Ter CA 91342 • PSW • D Miss • Peace Lake View Ter CA • (213)899-3950 • (SL 1977)

**INGMIRE RICHARD L REV** (573)221-1522
1 Locust Ln Hannibal MO 63401-3073 • EN • SP • St John Hannibal MO • (573)221-0615 • (SPR 1966)

**IRELAN CHRISTOPHER JOHN REV** (847)797-5779
2406 Martin Ln Rolling Meadows IL 60008-2752 • chrisirelan@juno.com • NI • 09/1998 • (FW 1993 MDIV)

**IRMER DOUGLAS D REV** (402)223-4925
315 N 10th St Beatrice NE 68310-3014 • irmer@yahoo.com • NEB • Assoc • St Paul Beatrice NE • (402)228-1540 • (FW 1985 MDIV)

**IRWIN JAMES M REV**
5017 Terrace Dr Omaha NE 68134 • prirwin@st-marklcms.org • NEB • Assoc • St Mark Omaha NE • (402)391-6148 • (SL 1997 MDIV)

**ISENBERG G E REV** (219)942-8049
9420 Sullivan Ln Crown Point IN 46307-8625 • trinity-pastor@ateze.com • IN • SP • Trinity Memorial Merrillville IN • (219)769-5376 • (SL 1958 MDIV)

**ISENBERG WESLEY W REV** (508)394-3349
129 Driftwood Ln South Yarmouth MA 02664-1013 • NI • SHS/C • Northern Illinois Hillside IL • (SL 1956 MDIV PHD)

**ISLER ALBERT C REV** 001-49-622-788-1410
HQ VCA Unit #29060 APO AE 09081 • vcachaplin@vca.vcorps.army.mil • TX • M Chap • Texas Austin TX • (SL 1967 MDIV MTH)

**ISRAEL JOHN W REV** (970)203-1652
4515 Filbert Dr Loveland CO 80538-1734 • RM • EM • (SL 1956)

**ISTA MYRON W REV** (415)492-3405
113 Holmes Ave San Rafael CA 94903-2813 • mtista@juno.com • CNH • SP • Trinity San Rafael CA • (415)454-4135 • (SL 1973 MA)

**IVERSON EDWIN REV**
285 Camp St Platteville WI 53805 • SD • 02/2000 • (SP 1975)

**IVERSON THEODORE A REV** (925)376-3631
134 Oxford Dr Moraga CA 94556-1722 • cnhcef@pacbell.net • CNH • D Ex/S • Calif/Nevada/Hawaii San Francisco CA • (415)468-2336 • (SL 1958 MDIV)

**IWINSKI DANIEL C REV** (715)366-4644
1169 County Rd D Almond WI 54909 • iwinski@uniontel.net • NW • SP • St John Almond WI • (715)366-2480 • (FW 2000 MDIV)

**IZZARD RICHARD C REV** (410)384-9501
329 Gordon Ave Severna Park MD 21146 • rizzard@stpauls-lutheran.org • SE • Sn/Adm • St Paul Glen Burnie MD • (410)766-2283 • (SPR 1969 MDIV)

## J

**JABS FREDERICK K REV** (920)458-8512
6502 S Business Dr Sheboygan WI 53081 • pfkjabs@hotmail.com • SW • SP • Trinity Sheboygan WI* • (920)458-8881 • (FW 1980 MDIV)

**JACK EDWARD E REV** (910)989-4580
101 Erskine Ct Jacksonville NC 28540-3819 • ejack73@earthlink.net • MI • M Chap • Michigan Ann Arbor MI • (FW 1982 MDIV)

**JACKSON BRUCE W REV** (712)944-5544
PO Box 177 Lawton IA 51030-0177 • IW • SP • Bethel Lawton IA • (712)944-5580 • (FW 1989 MDIV)

**JACKSON JOHN P REV** (334)928-5713
16 Echo Ln Fairhope AL 36532-1455 • jajuson@aol.com • SO • SP • Redeemer Fairhope AL • (334)928-8397 • (FW 1979 MDIV)

**JACKSON MEREDITH B REV** (423)624-9375
110 Belvoir Ave Chattanooga TN 37411 • jaypbsig@sprintmail.com • MDS • SP • St Philip Chattanooga TN • (423)267-1475 • (FW 1999 MBA MDIV)

**JACKSON PAUL H REV**
C/O St Pauls Lutheran Church PO Box 465 Texhoma OK 73949-0465 • paul.jackson@cph.org • MO • 07/2000 • (SL 1979 MLS MDIV STM)

**JACKSON ROBERT L REV** (501)248-7145
738 Elm Springs Rd Springdale AR 72762-2745 • MDS • EM • (SPR 1962)

**JACOB DAVID KARL REV** (254)539-5380
52348-1 Cayuga Ct Fort Hood TX 76544 • david.jacob@hood.army.mil • SW • SP • St John Edgerton WI • (608)884-3515 • (SL 1994 MDIV)

**JACOB RICKY A REV** (402)878-2450
PO Box 413 Winnebago NE 68071-0413 • rezrevrj@huntel.net • NEB • D Miss • Nebraska Seward NE • (SL 1987 MDIV)

**JACOB ROY A REV** (501)767-5468
108 Woodcliff Ter Hot Springs AR 71913-8994 • rjacob@hsnp.com • MDS • EM • (SL 1955)

**JACOBI FREDERICK C REV** (716)992-3113
7650 Sisson Hwy Eden NY 14057-9508 • eaj821@aol.com • EA • SP • St Paul Eden NY • (716)992-9112 • (SL 1964 MDIV)

**JACOBS DANIEL P REV** (406)638-2331
PO Box 335 Crow Agency MT 59022-0335 • MT • SP • Crow Crow Agency MT • (406)638-2331 • (FW 1986 MDIV)

**JACOBS MATTHEW P REV** (979)277-0505
140 New Wehdem Rd Brenham TX 77833-8106 • jacobs@bluebon.net • TX • Sn/Adm • Grace Brenham TX • (979)836-3475 • (FW 1989 MDIV)

**JACOBS ROBERT C REV** (941)775-4543
8505 Naples Heritage Dr #18 Naples FL 34112 • messiahlutheran@worldnet.att.net • FG • SP • Messiah Naples FL • (941)455-2520 • (SPR 1964)

**JACOBSEN FRANK A REV** (415)751-6184
786 30th Ave San Francisco CA 94121-3520 • CNH • EM • (SL 1937)

**JACOBSEN JACK E REV** (727)372-7949
4705 Cavendish Dr New Port Richey FL 34655-1482 • MNS • EM • (CQ 1981 MTH PHD)

**JACOBSEN LONNIE R** (901)372-3821
6717 Elmore Woods Ln Memhis TN 38134 • MDS • Assoc • Immanuel Memphis TN • (901)373-4486 • (SL 2000 MDIV)

**JACOBSEN STEVEN J REV** (217)942-6826
321 Locust St Carrollton IL 62016 • revjacobsen@excite.com • SI • SP • Our Redeemer Carrollton IL • (217)942-3168 • (SL 1995 MDIV)

**JACOBSEN THOMAS C REV** (308)235-4273
615 Locust St Kimball NE 69145-1343 • WY • SP • St John Kimball NE • (308)235-2582 • (SL 1961 MDIV)

**JACOBSMEYER HAROLD W REV** (214)942-4822
1217 Arizona Ave Dallas TX 75216-1021 • TX • EM • (SL 1949)

**JACOBY JEREMY MICHAEL REV** (308)478-5274
C/O St John Lutheran Church PO Box 214 Wilcox NE 68982-0214 • NEB • SP • St John Wilcox NE • (308)478-5466 • (SL 1997 MDIV)

**JAECH EMIL G REV** (503)254-0703
13440 NE Shaver St Portland OR 97230-2628 • emjaech@pacifier.com • NOW • EM • (SPR 1938 DD)

**JAECKLE GARY D REV** (712)542-3601
700 N 14th St Clarinda IA 51632-1117 • gjaeckle@hotmail.com • IW • Sn/Adm • St John Clarinda IA • (712)542-3708 • (SL 1973 MDIV)

**JAEGER CLARK A REV** (507)867-4126
C/O St Paul Luth Church 116 Fillmore St SE Chatfield MN 55923-1219 • MNS • SP • St Paul Chatfield MN • (507)867-4604 • (SPR 1961)

**JAEGER JAY ARTHUR REV**
C/O First English Luth Ch PO Box 129 Centerville SD 57014 • SD • SP • First English Centerville SD* • (605)563-2904 • (SL 1997 MDIV)

**JAEGER RALPH REV**
2814 Leslie Ct Laramie WY 82072-2992 • WY • EM • * • (CQ 1991)

**JAEGER ROBERT F REV** (210)699-3744
3735 Newrock Dr San Antonio TX 78230-3205 • TX • EM • * • (SL 1946 MDIV)

**JAEKEL JAMES A REV** (518)584-5501
25 Stonehedge Dr Gansevoort NY 12831-2705 • stpaulss@juno.com • AT • Sn/Adm • St Paul Saratoga Springs NY • (518)584-0904 • (SL 1968 MDIV)

**JAGOW ANDREW W REV**
15 Farragut Hastings On Hudson NY 10706 • AT • SP • St Matthew Hastings On Hudson NY* • (914)478-1071 • (SL 1998 MDIV)

**JAGOW FREDERICK WM REV** (707)838-1666
152 Cornell St Windsor CA 95492-8742 • CNH • EM • * • (SPR 1956 MDIV)

**JAGOW WAYNE F REV** (716)434-2022
6310 Ridge Rd Lockport NY 14094-1017 • wayne.jagow@niagaracounty.com • EA • SP • Concordia Newfane NY • (716)751-0310 • (SL 1969 MDIV)

**JAHN WAYNE P REV** (847)623-7784
618 Grove Ave Waukegan IL 60085-1847 • NI • SP • Redeemer Waukegan IL • 221 • (SL 1999 MDIV)

**JAHNEKE ALLAN A REV** (262)367-8572
3719 Campbell Trce Hartland WI 53029-8826 • SW • Sn/Adm • Divine Redeemer Hartland WI • (414)367-8400 • (SL 1976 MDIV)

**JAHNKE CLARK H REV** (701)281-9367
325 Cherry Ct West Fargo ND 58078-2923 • chjahnke@aol.com • ND • Sn/Adm • St Andrew West Fargo ND • (701)282-4195 • (SL 1989 MDIV)

**JAHNKE RANDALL L REV** (316)227-6179
2217 Post Ave Dodge City KS 67801-2555 • pastorrj@midusa.net • KS • SP • Holy Cross Dodge City KS • (316)227-6204 • (SL 1984 MDIV)

**JALAS DUANE A REV** (715)428-2835
W4594 US Hwy 8 Prentice WI 54556-9610 • dajalas@win.bright.net • NW • SP • Trinity Prentice WI • (715)428-2851 • (CQ 1998 MBA)

**JAMES HAROLD REV** (334)452-0427
2351 Crestwood Cir Mobile AL 36617-2710 • SO • EM • (CQ 1980 MDIV)

**JAMES ROGER B REV**
22838 Springfield Center Rd Grabill IN 46741 • IN • 05/1999 • (SL 1991 MDIV)

**JAMESON JOHN A REV** (636)938-3274
221 Walden Ct Eureka MO 63025-1130 • pastorjohn@stmarkseureka.org • MO • Assoc • St Mark Eureka MO • (636)938-4432 • (SL 1990 MDIV)

**JAMNICKY PAUL G REV** (705)436-7518
2155 Raynor Court Box 3680 Stroud ON L0L 2M0 CANADA • S • SP • Holy Trinity Bradford ON CANADA • (705)775-3412 • (SPR 1960)

**JANETZKE DOUGLAS K REV** (517)837-8361
4205 Bluebird Dr Midland MI 48640-2129 • prjanetzke@aol.com • MI • Assoc • St John Midland MI • (517)835-5861 • (SPR 1974 MDIV DMIN)

**JANK ORVILLE J REV** (715)675-2187
3826 Henry St Wausau WI 54403-2225 • NW • EM • (SL 1956)

**JANK ROLAND A JR. REV** (402)455-9711
6928 Florence Blvd Omaha NE 68112-3414 • rajankjr@juno.com • NEB • SP • Mount Olive Omaha NE • (402)455-8700 • (SL 1974 MDIV)

**JANK ROLAND A REV** (402)564-9271
3384 33rd Ave Columbus NE 68601-1414 • NEB • EM • (SL 1945 MDIV)

**JANKE ORTWIN R REV** (916)447-9030
2701 Capitol Ave # 211 Sacramento CA 95816 • CNH • EM • (SL 1931)

**JANKE PAUL B REV** (916)363-6983
9688 Rudway Ct Sacramento CA 95827-1129 • apjanke@aol.com • CNH • Calif/Nevada/Hawaii San Francisco CA • (415)468-2336 • (SL 1961 DMIN)

**JANKE ROGER A REV** (414)571-5029
425 W Aspen Dr Unit 4 Oak Creek WI 53154-4442 • rmjanke@nconnect.net • SW • Sn/Adm • Our Father Greenfield WI • (414)282-8220 • (SL 1964 MDIV STM)

**JANNEKE ALAN WENDEL DR** (618)965-9276
603 W Illinois St Steeleville IL 62288-1323 • ajanneke@egyptian.net • SI • Sn/Adm • St Mark Steeleville IL • (618)965-3192 • (SL 1981 MDIV DMIN)

**JANS GREGORY D REV** (801)777-2106
75 ABW HC 5711 E Ave Hill AFB UT 84056-5302 • gnljans@juno.com • SI • SP • Southern Illinois Belleville IL • (SL 1988 MDIV)

**JANSEN DANIEL LAURIN REV** (517)846-4972
C/O Bethlehem Lutheran Church 5606 Johnsfield Rd Standish MI 48658-9430 • dcjansen@sch-net.com • MI • SP • Bethlehem Standish MI • (517)846-4972 • (SL 1992 MDIV)

**JANSEN NATHAN R REV** (414)871-6332
6132 W Richmond Ave Milwaukee WI 53210-2142 • najansen@hotmail.com • SW • Assoc • Mount Olive Milwaukee WI • (414)771-3580 • (SL 1994 MDIV)

**JANSEN RONALD A REV** (618)346-9170
6935 Clay School Rd Collinsville IL 62234-7523 • rknaas@aol.com • SI • Assoc • Holy Cross Collinsville IL • (618)344-3145 • (SL 1967 MDIV)

**JANSSEN ARLO T REV** (520)364-9287
7068 N Bond Rd Mc Neal AZ 85617 • tedj@primenet.com • EN • SP • Peace Valley Benson AZ • (520)586-3171 • (SPR 1955 MA)

**JANSSEN CARL WARNER REV** (641)746-2724
802 Russell St Casey IA 50048-1025 • stjohn@netins.net • IW • SP • St John Casey IA • (641)746-2734 • (FW 1986 MDIV)

**JANSSEN IHNO A REV** (510)945-8910
1023 Rudgear Rd Walnut Creek CA 94596-6425 • shirleytill@juno.com • EN • EM • (SL 1945 MA PHD DD)

**JANSSEN LAVERNE A REV** (915)698-4499
2301 Darrell Dr Abilene TX 79606-3601 • TX • SP • Our Savior Abilene TX • (915)692-6163 • (SL 1977 MAR STM)

**JANSSEN NATHAN L REV** (317)342-5288
2985 Little Hurricane Rd Martinsville IN 46151-8581 • njanssen@scican.net • IN • SP • Prince Peace Martinsville IN • (317)342-2004 • (FW 1989 MDIV)

**JANSSEN RONALD H DR** (770)486-8901
St Paul Luth Church 700 Ardenlee Prkwy Peachtree City GA 30269 • rjanssen@mindspring.com • FG • SP • St Paul Peachtree City GA • (770)487-0339 • (SPR 1972 MDIV DD)

**JANY LEE M REV** (815)725-3132
616 Apollo Dr Joliet IL 60435-5120 • shirlleej@dell.net • NI • SP • St Peter Joliet IL • (815)722-3567 • (CQ 1991 MAR MAR MSED)

**JANZ MARVIN P REV** (905)775-4567
2881 14th Line RR 1 Gilford ON L0L 1R0 CANADA • wkapralik@sprint.ca • EN • EM • (SL 1959)

**JANZEN MARK JOEL REV** (785)284-2368
203 Ohio St Sabetha KS 66534-2423 • >wecare@jbntelco.comı • KS • SP • First Sabetha KS • (785)284-3566 • (SL 1995 MDIV)

**JANZOW F SAMUEL REV** (708)445-8127
339 Home Ave Apt 3F Oak Park IL 60302-3438 • NI • EM • (SL 1936 MA PHD)

**JANZOW JOEL MARK REV**
29 Wanda Ct Troy NY 12180-8523 • AT • Inst C • Atlantic Bronxville NY • (914)337-5700 • (SPR 1976 MDIV)

**JANZOW W THEOPHIL REV** (402)489-8817
7515 Sherman St Lincoln NE 68506-4656 • tedjanzow@webtv.net • NEB • EM • (SL 1944 MDIV MA PHD DD)

**JARVIS ROBERT W REV** (320)589-4665
311 S Columbia Ave Morris MN 56267-1624 • zion@inet-serv.com • MNN • SP • Zion Morris MN • (320)589-2744 • (SL 1990 MDIV)

**JASPER JAMES W REV** (216)381-5757
1443 Dorsh Rd Cleveland OH 44121 • EN • Inst C • English Farmington MI • (CQ 1993 MAR)

**JASPER LOUIS R REV** (315)331-0963
1259 Summit Dr Newark NY 14513-8903 • ljasper@usadatane.net • AT • S Miss • Atlantic Bronxville NY • (914)337-5700 • (SL 1959 MA MED EDD DD)

**JASTER JOHN E REV** (520)757-3525
C/O Good Sheph Luth Church 3958 N Bank St Kingman AZ 86401-2727 • PSW • SP • Good Shepherd Kingman AZ • (520)757-3525 • (SL 1962 MDIV)

**JASTRAM DANIEL N REV** (651)699-7986
1320 Hartford Ave Saint Paul MN 55116-1623 • jastram@csp.edu • MNS • SHS/C • Minnesota South Burnsville MN • (FW 1983 MA MDIV PHD)

**JASTRAM NATHAN R REV** (262)512-0244
3317 W Colette Ct Mequon WI 53092-2306 • nathanjastram@mail.com • NI • SHS/C • South Wisconsin Milwaukee WI • (414)464-8100 • (FW 1984 MDIV PHD)

**JASTRAM ROBERT J REV** (218)826-6305
31180 Mc Arthur Rd Underwood MN 56586-9720 • robertjastram@juno.com • MNN • EM • (SPR 1952)

**JAUSS MARCUS R REV** (660)584-6677
109 E 12th St Higginsville MO 64037-1116 • lsjauss@ctcis.net • MO • SP • Immanuel Higginsville MO • (660)584-3541 • (SL 1984 MDIV)

**JAVOR THOMAS R REV** (402)253-2716
C/O Our Redeemer Luth Church PO Box 529 Springfield NE 68059-0529 • sjavor@radiks.net • NEB • SP • Our Redeemer Springfield NE • (402)253-2893 • (FW 1987 MDIV)

**JEAN EDOUANE REV** (561)499-4954
3449 Place Valencay Delray Beach FL 33444 • FG • O Sp Min • Emmanuel Haitian Delray Beach FL • (651)276-0205 • (CQ 1991 MDIV)

**JENISTA JOHN FRANCIS REV** (814)733-4553
161 Fochtman Rd Berlin PA 15530-9314 • EA • SP • Trinity Fairhope PA • (814)733-4553 • (CQ 1994)

**JENKINS DONALD F REV**
16498 Highway 48 Rea MO 64480-1715 • MO • EM • (SPR 1963)

**JENKINS KEVIN J REV** (309)671-5677
525 Martin Luther King Jr Dr Apt 1D Peoria IL 61605-2368 • CI • Assoc • Trinity Pekin IL • (309)346-1391 • (SL 1989 MDIV)

**JENKINS RONALD L REV** (806)795-5600
3413 68th Dr Lubbock TX 79413-6121 • TX • EM • (SPR 1962 MDIV)

**JENKS KENNETH C REV**
3542 Texas Ave Simi Valley CA 93063-1423 • PSW • SP • Canoga Park Canoga Park CA • (818)348-5714 • (SL 1963 MDIV)

**JENKS TIMOTHY A REV**
517 E Turnpike Ave Bismarck ND 58501-1731 • ND • SP • Bethel Bismarck ND • (701)255-1433 • (FW 1990 MDIV)

**JENKS TODD ALLEN DR** (321)269-5860
4230 Pondapple Dr Titusville FL 32796 • jenkst@warner.edu • FG • SP • Good Shepherd Titusville FL • (321)267-4323 • (FW 1991 MDIV PHD)

**JENNINGS KEVIN M REV** (618)258-1826
C/O Concordia Lutheran Church 21 Circle Dr Cottage Hills IL 62018 • revkev97@aol.com • SI • SP • Concordia Cottage Hills IL • (618)259-2911 • (SL 1997 MDIV)

**JENNINGS LANCE R REV** (907)338-0183
3656 Bisquier Dr Anchorage AK 99508-4870 • NOW • 09/1998 • (CQ 1979 MDIV)

**JENNINGS STEPHEN E REV** (414)633-9636
1112 Goold St Racine WI 53402-4558 • stevejjj@aalweb.net • SW • Assoc • Trinity Racine WI • (414)632-2900 • (FW 1986 MDIV)

**JENNRICH WALTER A REV** (414)445-5004
5002 W Keefe Ave Milwaukee WI 53216-2942 • EN • EM • (SL 1946 MA MDIV PHD)

**JENSEN DAVID C REV** (920)923-4316
191 Prairie Ct Fond Du Lac WI 54935-4584 • hope@vbe.com • SW • Asst • Hope Fond Du Lac WI • (920)922-5130 • (SL 1976 MDIV)

**JENSEN JEFREY STEVEN REV** (802)862-7017
28 Barber Ter South Burlington VT 05403 • PastorJefrey1@juno.com • NE • SP • Community South Burlington VT • (802)864-5537 • (SL 1995 MDIV)

**JENSEN ROBERT A REV** (217)523-1855
1820 N 20th St Springfield IL 62702-3006 • CI • 09/1984 11/2000 • (SPR 1974 MDIV)

**JENSON JAMES B REV** (206)337-0567
2914 116th St SE Everett WA 98208-6105 • NOW • SP • St James Mill Creek WA • (425)745-9859 • (CQ 1981 MST)

**JENSON WILLIS C REV**
C/O Emmaus Lutheran Church PO Box 825 Redmond OR 97756-0173 • NOW • SP • Emmaus Redmond OR • (541)548-1473 • (FW 1989 MDIV)

**JEON KWANG HEE REV** (213)739-8844
3970 W Ingraham St #302 Los Angeles CA 90005 • PSW • D Miss • Emmaus Redmond OR • (CQ 1997)

**JEPPESEN RANDAL R REV** (715)748-0826
W5334 Dassow Ave Medford WI 54451-8785 • mapleleaf@tds.net • NW • SP • Trinity Medford WI* • (715)748-4181 • (FW 1988 MDIV)

**JERABEK TODD R REV** (715)823-4966
C/O Zion Lutheran Church PO Box 197 Embarrass WI 54933-0197 • tjerabek@frontiernet.net • NW • SP • Zion Embarrass WI* • (715)823-3889 • (FW 1993 MDIV)

**JESKE ALVIN REV** (320)594-3034
RR 1 Box 211A Browerville MN 56438-9518 • alkjineden@juno.com • MNN • EM • * • (SPR 1972 MDIV)

**JESKE BRUCE E REV** (619)424-6166
866 Imperial Beach Blvd Imperial Beach CA 91932-2703 • stjameslutheranchurch@home.com • PSW • SP • St James Imperial Beach CA • (619)424-6166 • (SL 1968 MA)

**JESKE DAVID G REV** (254)876-3175
104 S Carpenter St Mart TX 76664-1536 • dgjeske@aol.com • TX • SP • Grace Mart TX • (254)876-2314 • (SL 1964 MST)

**JESSE RICHARD F REV** (937)497-0812
179 Tranquility Ct Sidney OH 45365-1555 • OH • EM • (SL 1941 MA)

**JI WON YONG REV** (314)727-6336
950 Morehouse Ln Saint Louis MO 63130-2156 • MO • EM • (SL 1952 DTH)

**JILG PAUL H REV** (501)227-6380
315 Brookside Dr Little Rock AR 72205-2329 • jilgsr@aol.com • MDS • EM • (SPR 1956)

**JIROVEC DYMANN L REV** (309)452-9207
1320 Hanson Dr Normal IL 61761-1923 • dljirov@ilstu.edu • CI • Cmp P • Central Illinois Springfield IL • (FW 1980 MDIV)

**JOBE RONALD W REV** (218)583-2707
C/O St Paul Luth Church 700 Douglas Ave # 332 Henning MN 56551-4110 • MNN • SP • St Paul Henning MN • (218)583-2707 • (SL 1974 MDIV)

**JOBST JAMES MARVIN REV** (281)355-9656
4002 Postwood Dr Spring TX 77388-4952 • TX • Asst • Resurrection Spring TX • (281)353-4413 • (SL 1995 MDIV)

**JOBST TERRY J REV** (215)491-3396
C/O Grace Lutheran Church PO Box 196 Warminster PA 18974-0520 • terryjobst@aol.com • EN • SP • Grace Warminster PA • (215)672-8181 • (SL 1981 MDIV)

**JOECKEL DAVID B DR** (817)265-6146
1719 S Pecan St Arlington TX 76010-4360 • djoeckel@aol.com • TX • EM • (SL 1958 MDIV DMIN)

**JOECKEL MARK TOBIAS REV**
1860 Larkspur Dr Arlington TX 76013-3480 • TX • D Miss • Texas Austin TX • (SL 1992 MDIV)

**JOECKEL RALPH TOBIAS REV** (509)965-7096
7805 Tieton Dr Yakima WA 98908 • pastortoby@mtolivechurch.org • NOW • SP • Mount Olive Yakima WA • (509)966-2190 • (FW 1981 MDIV)

**JOERSZ JERALD C REV** (314)837-6910
16702 Edisto Ct Florissant MO 63034-1021 • ic³joerszjc@lcms.org • MO • S Ex/S • Missouri Saint Louis MO • (314)317-4550 • (SL 1968 STM MDIV LLD)

**JOESTEN LEROY B REV** (847)698-3045
12 N Merrill St Park Ridge IL 60068-3522 • NI • Inst C • Northern Illinois Hillside IL • (SL 1967 MDIV)

**JOHANN SIMON SUNG-CHIL REV** (718)886-1128
3381 164th St Flushing NY 11358-1441 • EN • SP • Immanuel Korean Flushing NY • (718)460-5736 • (CQ 1980 DMIN DREL)

**JOHANNES WALTER C REV** (815)932-5739
20 Norman St Kankakee IL 60901-6030 • MO • EM • (SPR 1946)

**JOHANSEN JOHN REV** (307)382-4909
224 H St Rock Springs WY 82901-6433 • jjohanse@wyoming.com • WY • EM • (SPR 1967 MDIV)

**JOHNS DAVID REV** (417)782-5886
727 Plaza Dr Joplin MO 64804-3961 • KS • EM • (CQ 1975 MMU DMU)

**JOHNSON BARKLIE A REV** (407)860-0037
659 Sagamore Dr Deltona FL 32738-8722 • FG • EM • (SPR 1969)

**JOHNSON CHARLES E REV** (701)797-2334
PO Box 674 1008 Barrel Ave SE Cooperstown ND 58425-0674 • johnsonrevckr@mlgc.com • ND • SP • Grace Cooperstown ND* • (701)797-3444 • (SL 1974 MDIV)

**JOHNSON CHRIS E REV** (513)621-7265
C/O Prince Of Peace Luth Ch 1524 Race St Cincinnati OH 45210-1712 • cejtsjasj@msn.com • OH • SP • Prince Peace Cincinnati OH • (513)621-7265 • (SL 1981 MDIV)

**JOHNSON DANIEL Q REV** (319)373-2680
6829 Brentwood Dr NE Cedar Rapids IA 52402-1543 • dqj@home.com • IE • EM • (SPR 1955)

**JOHNSON DANIEL S REV** (515)753-9565
C/O Redeemer Luth Church 1600 S Center St Marshalltown IA 50158-5919 • prdan@ibm.net • IE • Sn/Adm • Redeemer Marshalltown IA • (515)753-9565 • (SL 1990 MDIV)

**JOHNSON DAVID A REV** (314)845-8761
115 Shetland Dr Saint Louis MO 63125-3631 • MO • S Ex/S • Missouri Saint Louis MO • (314)317-4550 • (SL 1989 MDIV)

**JOHNSON DAVID CLIFFORD REV** (817)489-1677
5905 Oak Hill Rd Wautaga TX 76148 • TX • 10/1996 10/1999 • (FW 1986 MDIV)

**JOHNSON DAVID M REV** (612)261-0389
11225 Julia Ln Becker MN 55308-9364 • MNN • D Miss • Grace Becker MN • (612)261-4244 • (FW 1987 MDIV)

**JOHNSON DAVID P REV** (573)243-6046
1015 Leigh Ann Ct Jackson MO 63755-2596 • stpaulch@showme.net • MO • Sn/Adm • St Paul Jackson MO • (573)243-2236 • (FW 1979 MDIV)

**JOHNSON DAVID REV**
C/O Zion Lutheran Church 210 S Spring St Palmyra MO 63461-1484 • pastorj@nemonet.com • MO • SP • Zion Palmyra MO • (573)769-2739 • (FW 1988 MDIV)

**JOHNSON DONALD L REV** (307)332-5964
1030 Riverview Dr Lander WY 82520-2069 • WY • SP • Bethel Lander WY • (307)332-4320 • (SPR 1966)

**JOHNSON DONALD LEE REV** (414)457-7406
1615 S 17th St Sheboygan WI 53081-5127 • johnson@lutheranhigh.com • SW • Tchr • Lutheran HS Sheboygan WI • (920)452-3323 • (FW 1978 MDIV)

**JOHNSON DONALD W REV**
978 Brooks Ct Maplewood MN 55109-1951 • NOW • O Miss • Northwest Portland OR • (SPR 1973)

**JOHNSON DWAYNE A REV**
PO Box 3559 Alamo TX 78516 • TX • SP • Zion Alamo TX • (956)787-1584 • (SL 1988 MDIV)

**JOHNSON G EDWARD REV**
108 190th Ave SE #25 Puyallup WA 98372 • NOW • Inst C • Northwest Portland OR • (CQ 1999)

**JOHNSON HAROLD G REV** (831)427-2695
346 Moore St Santa Cruz CA 95060-2516 • CNH • EM • (SL 1947)

**JOHNSON HARRY N REV** (908)221-0747
19 Post Ter Basking Ridge NJ 07920-2430 • hardorj@aol.com • NJ • EM • (LT 1955 MDIV)

**JOHNSON HARVEY G REV**
41212 Ural St NE Braham MN 55006-3048 • MNN • SP • St Stephen Braham MN • (320)396-3103 • (SPR 1967 PHD)

**JOHNSON JAMES P REV** (805)687-9627
1123 Crestline Dr Santa Barbara CA 93105-4603 • PSW • SP • Good Shepherd Goleta CA • (805)967-1416 • (SL 1965 MDIV)

**JOHNSON JAMES ROBERT SR. REV** (410)257-1487
3719 30th St Chesapeake Beach MD 20732 • revJRJSR@aol.com • SE • 12/1999 • (FW 1992 MDIV MS)

**JOHNSON JEFFREY D REV** (216)252-9278
3542 Lloyd Rd Cleveland OH 44111-4678 • OH • SP • Trinity Cleveland OH • (216)281-1700 • (FW 1992 MDIV)

**JOHNSON JOHN D REV** (561)738-5433
C/O Son Life Luth Church 9301 Jog Rd Boynton Beach FL 33437-3653 • pastorjohnd@juno.com • FG • SP • Son Life Boynton Beach FL • (561)738-5433 • (SL 1987 MDIV)

**JOHNSON JOHN E REV** (865)573-1078
PO Box 1059 Seymour TN 37865-1059 • jakota@esper.com • MDS • SP • Holy Trinity Seymour TN • (865)573-8731 • (SPR 1970 MDIV)

**JOHNSON JOHN F REV** (314)721-5409
One Seminary Terr N St Louis MO 63105 • johnsonj@csl.edu • MO • SHS/C • Missouri Saint Louis MO • (314)317-4550 • (CQ 1975 MA MDIV PHD DTH)

**JOHNSON JOHN F REV** (727)381-1037
5950 Pelican Bay Plz S#110 3 Saint Petersburg FL 33707-3961 • FG • EM • (SPR 1946 MST)

**JOHNSON JOHN FOSTER REV**
1306 Vermont Ave NW Washington DC 28083-6352 • jfjohnson@prodigy.net • SE • SP • Mount Olivet Washington DC • (202)667-5357 • (SL 1988 MDIV)

**JOHNSON KEITH J REV**
2762 Cedar Hill Rd Cuyahoga Falls OH 44223-1226 • OH • Sn/Adm • Redeemer Cuyahoga Falls OH • (330)923-1445 • (CQ 1978)

**JOHNSON KEITH L REV** (414)529-4758
5222 S Menard Dr New Berlin WI 53151-8187 • www.hcl.org • EN • Assoc • Hales Corners Hales Corners WI • (414)529-6700 • (SL 1966 MDIV DMIN)

**JOHNSON KENNETH P REV** (906)293-5707
111 East Ave B Newberry MI 49868 • tahqluth@sault.com • MI • SP • Trinity Newberry MI* • (906)293-9340 • (SL 1993 MDIV)

**JOHNSON LARRY G REV** (605)947-4538
C/O Zion Luth Church PO Box 46 Waubay SD 57273-0046 • rjohn57273@aol.com • SD • SP • Emanuel Sisseton SD* • (605)698-7116 • (FW 1979 MDIV)

**JOHNSON LEE D REV** (517)439-0179
2651 W Bacon Rd Hillsdale MI 49242-9208 • pastordanjohnson@yahoo.com • MI • SP • St Paul Hillsdale MI • (517)437-2762 • (SL 1981 MDIV)

**JOHNSON LOHN M REV** (859)273-4850
653 Southpoint Dr Lexington KY 40515 • l.m.johns@juno.com • IN • SP • Good Shepherd Lexington KY • (859)269-6517 • (SL 1984 MDIV STM)

**JOHNSON MARK D REV** (612)866-5715
6501 16th Ave S Richfield MN 55423-1751 • MNS • Sn/Adm • Mount Calvary Richfield MN • (612)866-5405 • (FW 1977 MDIV)

**JOHNSON MICHAEL A SR. REV** (205)836-6657
629 Sundale Dr Birmingham AL 35232 • johnsonjohnmic@aol.com • SE • SP • Pilgrim Birmingham AL* • (205)251-3451 • (FW 1999 MDIV)

**JOHNSON NORMAN L REV** (201)679-3942
46 Bushnell Rd Old Bridge NJ 08857-2322 • NJ • SP • Good Shepherd Old Bridge NJ • (732)679-8883 • (SL 1966 MDIV DMIN)

**JOHNSON PAUL E REV**
PO Box 128 May City IA 51349 • IW • SP • St John May City IA • (712)735-4401 • (SL 1980 MDIV MA)

**JOHNSON RICHARD E REV** (845)297-6155
16 Fox Hill Rd Wappingers Falls NY 12590-3808 • AT • EM • (SPR 1957)

**JOHNSON ROBERT E REV** (414)250-1987
N111W16328 Catskill Ln Germantown WI 53022-4019 • johnsore@execpc.com • SW • Assoc • Trinity Mequon WI • (262)242-2045 • (SPR 1972 MDIV)

**JOHNSON RUSSEL P JR. REV**
C/O Loving Shepherd Luth Ch PO Box 1402 Hiram GA 30141 • padre669@aol.com • EN • SP • Loving Shepherd Hiram GA • (770)439-0800 • (SL 1966 MDIV)

**JOHNSON SCOTT D REV** (828)465-5972
10 Maple Ct Newton NC 28658 • stjohnlc@twave.net • SE • SP • St John Conover NC • (828)464-4071 • (FW 1987 MDIV)

**JOHNSON SIDNEY V REV** (503)656-3141
2435 Saddle Ct West Linn OR 97068-2517 • immport@teleport.com • NOW • SP • Immanuel Portland OR • (503)236-7823 • (SL 1964 MA)

**JOHNSON STEVEN P REV** (509)891-0839
C/O Messiah Lutheran Church 608 N Spokane St Post Falls ID 83854 • NOW • SP • Messiah Post Falls ID • (208)777-2887 • (FW 1979 MDIV)

**JOHNSON THOMAS R REV**
3616 Pecan Dr Chalmette LA 70043-1548 • SO • SP • Christ Chalmette LA • (504)279-6795 • (SL 1988 MDIV)

**JOHNSON WILLIAM A REV** (830)885-7355
483 Rebecca Springs Rd Spring Branch TX 78070-3513 • bjej@gvtc.com • TX • EM • (SPR 1956)

**JOHNSTON ALLAN R REV** (509)697-7353
60 Lyle Ln Selah WA 98942-9450 • NOW • SP • Peace Selah WA • (509)697-4353 • (SPR 1976 MDIV DMIN)

**JOHNSTON DALE R REV** (856)358-0542
2 Tiverstock Dr Pittsgrove NJ 08318-3037 • johnstca@bellatlantic.net • NJ • SP • St John First Bridgeton NJ • (856)451-0141 • (SPR 1971 MDIV MA)

**JOHNSTON GORDON E REV** (518)374-3053
857 Harris Dr Niskayuna NY 12309-3009 • fjohnston@empire.net • AT • EM • (SL 1956)

**JOHNSTON PAUL I REV** (405)329-2770
511 Shawnee St Norman OK 73071-4630 • paratus1@aol.com • OK • 08/1999 • (SL 1985 MDIV MA PHD)

**JOHNSTON THOMAS D REV** (402)371-6410
1102 S 10th St Norfolk NE 68701-5707 • NEB • EM • (SPR 1961)

**JOHNSTONE DOUGLAS V REV** (714)636-7284
9341 Tudor Ln Garden Grove CA 92841-3426 • pastrdug@aol.com • PSW • D Ex/S • Pacific Southwest Irvine CA • (949)854-3232 • (SL 1970 MDIV)

**JOLLIFF BRUCE H REV** (615)689-0684
4411 Plummer Dr Knoxville TN 37918-1324 • MDS • EM • (CQ 1983)

**JONAS ARNOLD T REV** (209)223-4508
312 Hoffman St Jackson CA 95642 • PSW • EM • (SL 1935)

**JONAS HERMAN W REV** (602)922-4463
16827 N 62nd Pl Scottsdale AZ 85254-7316 • PSW • SP • St Mark Phoenix AZ • (602)992-1980 • (CQ 1978 MDIV)

**JONES BRANDON SCOTT REV** (562)596-1089
C/O St Paul Lutheran Church 2283 Palo Verde Ave Long Beach CA 90815 • Brandon34@aol.com • PSW • SP • St Paul Long Beach CA • (562)596-4409 • (FW 1998 MDIV)

**JONES CHARLES E REV** (847)202-1804
3540 Wilshire Dr Palatine IL 60067-4764 • NI • SHS/C • Northern Illinois Hillside IL • (SL 1967 MDIV)

**JONES DANIEL G REV** (501)279-7619
111 Woodland Dr Searcy AR 72143-9662 • jonesd@cswnet.com • MDS • SP • Our Shepherd Searcy AR • (501)268-1613 • (SL 1982 MDIV)

**JONES DOUGLAS D REV** (310)692-6100
10304 Cliota St Whittier CA 90601-1710 • PSW • SP • St John Montebello CA • (323)728-8410 • (FW 1989 MDIV)

**JONES E LEE III REV** (847)674-9836
5201 George St Skokie IL 60077-2743 • elj3@avenew.com • NI • Sn/Adm • St Paul Skokie IL • (847)673-5030 • (FW 1983 MDIV MED)

**JONES HOWARD FRANCIS REV** (864)964-0347
C/O Abiding Savior Luth Church 1905 E Greenville St Anderson SC 29621-2036 • SE • SP • Abiding Savior Anderson SC • (864)225-6438 • (FW 1992 MDIV)

**JONES JOSEPH A DR** (785)776-5145
C/O St Luke Lutheran Church 330 Sunset Ave Manhattan KS 66502-3757 • stlukes@flinthills.com • KS • SP • St Luke Manhattan KS • (785)539-2604 • (SPR 1975 MDIV DMIN)

**JONES KEITH R REV** (920)435-5524
C/O Faith Luth Church 2335 S Webster Ave Green Bay WI 54301-2123 • kkjones@netnet.net • NW • Sn/Adm • Faith Green Bay WI • (920)435-5524 • (SL 1988 MDIV)

**JONES KEVIN C REV** (517)734-4795
470 W Ontario St Rogers City MI 49779-2038 • revkev@george.lhi.net • MI • SP • Peace Rogers City MI • (517)734-7621 • (SL 1988 MDIV)

**JONES RICHARD J REV**
C/O Grace Lutheran Church PO Box 496 Mastic Beach NY 11951-0496 • AT • Peace Rogers City MI • (517)734-7621 • (SL 1991 MDIV)

**JONES RONALD W REV** (914)779-1227
3 Concordia Pl Bronxville NY 10708 • AT • 02/2000 • (SL 1970 STM MDIV MA EDD)

**JONES STANLEY E REV** (501)855-7295
5 Boyce Ln Bella Vista AR 72714-5552 • stanjones@mc2k.com • MDS • EM • (SL 1956)

**JONES TODD A REV** (501)855-6228
5 Hope Dr Bella Vista AR 72715-1687 • pastorj@faithbentonville.com • MDS • SP • Faith Bentonville AR • (501)273-9419 • (SL 1989 MDIV)

**JORDAN DONALD A REV** (510)724-0611
2078 Blackwood Dr San Pablo CA 94806-1005 • jordan2078@earthlink.net • CNH • SP • Rollingwood San Pablo CA • (510)223-1932 • (SL 1983 MDIV)

**JORDAN HORST W REV**
335 High St Manawa WI 54949-9215 • NW • Sn/Adm • St Paul Manawa WI • (920)596-2837 • (SPR 1966 MDIV)

**JORDAN RICHARD A REV** (712)758-3185
1307 Tanager Ave Ocheyedan IA 51354-7008 • rjordan@earthlink.net • IW • SP • Zion Ocheyedan IA • (712)758-3185 • (SL 1981)

**JORDENING VICTOR REV** (308)324-7188
1811 Ridgeway Dr Apt 104 Lexington NE 68850-1192 • NEB • EM • (SL 1936)

**JORDING HOWARD J DR** (701)242-7576
PO Box 247 Hankinson ND 58041-0247 • hjjordin@rrt.net • ND • EM • (SL 1958 MDIV DMIN THD)

**JOSE RODERICK DESMOND REV** (715)824-5254
PO Box 146 Nelsonville WI 54458-0146 • NW • EM • (BY 1955)

**JOST LARRY A DR** (414)871-6820
3225 N 85th St Milwaukee WI 53222-3706 • SW • SP • Beautiful Savior Milwaukee WI • (414)871-6744 • (FW 1981 MS MDIV DMIN)

**JOSUPAIT JOHN W REV** (708)349-7313
10439 Songbird Cir Orland Park IL 60467-8470 • jwjosupait@msn.com • NI • SP • Zion Oak Lawn IL • (708)422-1433 • (SPR 1961 MDIV MA)

**JOW PATRICK REV**
1339 S Concord Ln Glendora CA 91740-5150 • PSW • Assoc • Emmaus Alhambra CA • (626)289-3664 • (SL 1986 MDIV)

**JUDGE JOSEPH B REV**
1713 Braemore Ct Kernersville NC 27284-8617 • judgnot@aol.com • SE • 07/1999 • (SL 1984 MDIV)

**JUDISCH DOUGLAS REV**
C/O Concordia Seminary 6600 N Clinton St Fort Wayne IN 46825-4916 • IN • SHS/C • Indiana Fort Wayne IN • (SL 1971 MDIV PHD)

**JUEDES JOHN P REV** (909)864-7400
7400 Yellow Jasmine Dr Highland CA 92346-3862 • messiah7@empirenet.com • PSW • SP • Messiah Highland CA • (909)862-2923 • (SL 1981 MDIV DMIN)

**JUENGEL DENNIS R REV** (216)486-4479
24271 Yosemite Dr Euclid OH 44117-1864 • OH • SP • Shore Haven Euclid OH • (216)731-4100 • (FW 1987 MDIV)

**JUENGEL RALPH F REV** (562)690-6136
2461 Gregory Lane La Habra CA 90631 • RevJuenem@juno.com • PSW • EM • (SL 1956 MDIV)

**JUERGENSEN EUGENE W REV** (406)248-2629
1156 Ponderosa Dr Billings MT 59102-2455 • dejuer@juno.com • MT • EM • (SL 1953 MDIV)

**JUERGENSEN STEPHEN P REV** (509)525-6678
1214 Francis Ave Walla Walla WA 99362-2418 • NOW • SP • Trinity Walla Walla WA • (509)525-2493 • (SL 1985 MDIV DMIN)

**JUNG DAVID A REV** (313)278-3964
213 N Denwood St Dearborn MI 48128-1509 • lcjungd@ccaa.edu • MI • Assoc • Guardian Dearborn MI • (313)274-1414 • (FW 1982 MDIV)

**JUNG DAVID R REV** (817)788-0659
6865 Dogwood Ct Fort Worth TX 76180-2050 • djung@fastlane.net • TX • Sn/Adm • Crown of Life Colleyville TX • (817)421-5683 • (FW 1984 MDIV)

**JUNGE ROLF A REV** (503)361-0011
3434 El Dorado Ct S Salem OR 97302 • NOW • 04/1996 04/2000 • (FW 1977 MDIV MBA)

**JUNGKUNTZ FREDERICK H O REV**
W 2091 Church Dr Watertown WI 53094 • SW • EM • (CQ 1985)

**JUNKANS ERVIN A REV** (573)893-4535
1723 Centennial Rd Jefferson City MO 65101 • eajunkans@juno.com • MO • EM • (SPR 1963 MDIV MED)

**JUNKIN ROBERT L REV** (209)862-0649
1531 Canyon Creek Dr Newman CA 95360-1441 • junkin@jps.net • CNH • SP • St James Newman CA • (209)862-3438 • (FW 1977 MDIV)

**JURCHEN ARNOLD H REV** (402)576-3711
245 Nestor Cordova NE 68330 • NEB • SP • St John Cordova NE* • (402)576-3711 • (SPR 1973 MDIV)

**JURKOWSKI MARK A REV** (909)697-1943
20717 Hillsdale Rd Riverside CA 92508 • revskeeilc@yahoo.com • PSW • Assoc • Immanuel Riverside CA • (909)682-7613 • (SL 1993 MDIV)

**JUST ARTHUR A REV** (219)471-2258
7 Tyndale Pl Fort Wayne IN 46825-4936 • aajustjr@aol.com • IN • SHS/C • Indiana Fort Wayne IN • (FW 1980 MDIV PHD)

**JUST CHRISTIAN F REV** (330)467-7147
1567 Meadowlawn Dr Macedonia OH 44056-1439 • revcfj@apk.net • EN • SP • Epiphany Northfield OH • (330)467-7710 • (SL 1973 MDIV)

## K

**KAARIAINEN JUKKA A REV** (718)372-6728
109E Bay 40th St Brooklyn NY 11214 • AT • D Miss • Immanuel Chinese Bayside NY* • (718)229-4738 • (SL 2000 MDIV)

**KAARRE DAVID M REV** (715)536-8459
C/O St Paul Luth Church W 2608 County Rd P Merrill WI 54452 • NW • SP • St Paul Merrill WI • (715)536-8459 • (FW 1986 MDIV)

**KAARRE MARTIN C REV** (715)682-4420
619 9th Ave W Ashland WI 54806 • kaarre@ncis.net • NW • SP • Zion Ashland WI • (715)682-6075 • (FW 1980 MDIV)

**KABEL JAMES A REV** (707)825-0529
1096 Diamond Drive Arcata CA 95521 • jkabel3@aol.com • CNH • SP • Arcata Arcata CA • (707)822-5117 • (SL 1967 MDIV)

**KABELL DOUGLAS R REV** (301)746-8466
1019 Cove Rd Accident MD 21520 • sjlcms@hotmail.com • EA • SP • St John Accident MD • (301)746-8466 • (FW 1982 MDIV)

**KACER DANIEL J REV** (812)926-3137
401 Maple St Aurora IN 47001-1589 • djkacer@seidata.com • IN • EM • (FW 1977 MDIV)

**KACHMAREK KASIMIR REV** (503)640-4903
1360 SW 345th Ave Hillsboro OR 97123 • kazikak@aol.com • NOW • Inst C • Northwest Portland OR • (SL 1966 MDIV)

**KACZOR RICHARD J REV** (785)625-8821
109 W 18th St Hays KS 67601-3325 • kaczor@hotmail.com • KS • D Ex/S • Kansas Topeka KS • (SL 1964 MDIV MSW)

**KADE TIMOTHY P REV** (248)689-4664
C/O Faith Lutheran Church 37635 Dequindre Rd Troy MI 48083-5709 • tkade@faithtroy.org • MI • Assoc • Faith Troy MI • (248)689-4664 • (FW 1996 MDIV)

**KADEN KENNETH P REV** (651)484-6396
3090 Avon St N Saint Paul MN 55113-1901 • MNS • EM • (SL 1954 MDIV MA LITTD)

**KAEDING HUGO C DR** (828)687-7821
102 Silverrod Ln Asheville NC 28803-8674 • lpn3444@home.com • SE • EM • (SPR 1968 MSEE MDIV DMIN)

**KAELBERER ERIC V REV** (909)756-2789
539 N Acacia Rialto CA 92376 • ekbj@earthlink.net • PSW • SP • Grace Rialto CA • (909)875-3163 • (FW 1985 MDIV)

**KAELBERER JOHN H REV** (360)437-7768
140 Dogleg Ln Port Ludlow WA 98365-9581 • NOW • EM • (CQ 1985 MDIV MA)

**KAESTNER HAROLD REV** (303)522-3040
14042 Greenway Dr Sterling CO 80751-9052 • RM • EM • (SL 1949)

**KAH JOHN P III REV**
C/O St Peter Lutheran Church 111 W Olive St Arlington Heights IL 60004-4797 • jdkah@flash.net • NI • Assoc • St Peter Arlington Heights IL • (847)259-4114 • (FW 1980 MDIV)

**KAHLE RAYMOND F REV** (972)641-1124
2005 Huntington Dr Grand Prairie TX 75051-3734 • kahle@flash.net • TX • EM • (SPR 1961 MDIV MA)

**KAISER JOEL C REV** (517)652-4091
576 Franconian Dr E Frankenmuth MI 48734 • jkaiser@stlorenz.com • MI • Assoc • St Lorenz Frankenmuth MI • (517)652-6141 • (FW 1993 MDIV)

**KAISER JOHN C REV** (810)667-0082
C/O St Paul Luth Church 90 Millville Rd Lapeer MI 48446-1642 • MI • Sn/Adm • St Paul Lapeer MI • (810)664-6653 • (FW 1980 MDIV)

**KAISER KURT R REV** (712)263-6896
1989 N Ave Denison IA 51442-7451 • IW • Sn/Adm • Zion Denison IA • (712)263-2235 • (CQ 1984)

**KAISER PAUL MATTHEW REV** (219)426-5718
1707 N Anthony Blvd Fort Wayne IN 46805-5105 • propterchr@aol.com • IN • Assoc • Zion Fort Wayne IN • (219)744-1389 • (FW 1992 MDIV)

**KALBHEN WALTER C REV**
6101 N Sheridan Rd Unit 6B Chicago IL 60660-2874 • EN • EM • (SL 1959 MDIV)

**KALDAHL PAUL E REV** (712)262-3596
815 6th St SW Spencer IA 51301-6255 • kaldahlrev@hotmail.com • IW • SP • First English Spencer IA • (712)262-5598 • (FW 1988 MDIV)

**KALLESEN DOUGLAS L REV** (615)794-1033
110 Churchill Pl Franklin TN 37067-4435 • MDS • SP • Faith Franklin TN • (615)791-1880 • (SL 1983 MDIV)

**KALLIO HAROLD N REV** (520)680-7784
3630 Blue Colt Dr Lake Havasu City AZ 86406-4274 • PSW • EM • (SPR 1957 MDIV MED)

**KALLIO JOHN M REV** (507)451-3788
1310 Cherry St Owatonna MN 55060-1961 • MNS • SP • Good Shepherd Owatonna MN • (507)451-4125 • (SPR 1964)

**KALSOW LARRY D REV** (843)228-7775
148 Laurel Bay Boulevard Beaufort SC 29906-3613 • kalsowld@islc.net • KS • M Chap • Kansas Topeka KS • (SPR 1976 STM)

**KALTHOFF GLENN D REV** (435)833-0769
C/O First Lutheran Church PO Box 738 Tooele UT 84074-0738 • joglenn@uswest.net • RM • SP • First Tooele UT • (435)882-1172 • (SL 1964)

**KALTHOFF JAMES W REV** (314)230-9866
14960 Manor Lake Dr Chesterfield MO 63017-7816 • MO • DP • Missouri Saint Louis MO • (314)317-4550 • (SPR 1963 DD)

**KALTWASSER AURELIUS O REV** (219)747-2472
PO Box 9506 Fort Wayne IN 46899-9506 • aokhck@fortwayne.infi.net • IN • EM • (SPR 1933)

**KALTWASSER BRUCE J REV** (319)442-3639
PO Box 144 Keystone IA 52249-0144 • stjnluth@netins.net • IE • SP • St John Keystone IA • (319)442-3514 • (FW 1983 MDIV)

**KAMMAN HAROLD W REV** (405)692-2212
10113 S Carter Ct Oklahoma City OK 73159-7029 • hwkamman@juno.com • OK • EM • (SL 1950 MDIV)

**KAMMRATH MARVIN F REV** (217)644-3022
PO Box 386 Strasburg IL 62465-0386 • CI • EM • (SL 1940)

**KAMPFER RUSSELL J REV** (414)842-2005
C/O St John Luth Church 8905 Saint Johns Rd Suring WI 54174-9706 • NW • SP • St John Suring WI* • (920)842-4443 • (SL 1991)

**KAMPIA RUDOLF REV** (301)614-0918
8800 58th Ave Berwyn Heights MD 20740-4308 • rkampia@erols.com • SE • SP • Redeemer Hyattsville MD • (301)277-2302 • (SL 1973 MDIV)

**KAMPRATH STEPHEN P REV** (850)505-9975
9680 Coachman Ct Pensacola FL 32514 • sk812@gateway.net • SO • SP • Immanuel Pensacola FL • (850)438-8138 • (CQ 1981)

**KAMRATH ROBERT F REV** (970)264-6279
PO Box 3697 Pagosa Springs CO 81147-3697 • k-nine3@juno.com • TX • EM • (SL 1954)

**KANE MICHAEL O REV** (804)458-8937
1710 W City Point Rd Hopewell VA 23860 • carpenter-shop@juno.com • SE • SP • Nazareth Hopewell VA • (804)458-7994 • (FW 1991 MDIV)

**KANG MAN SUK REV** (714)827-9120
3114 W Paso Robles Dr Anaheim CA 92804-1724 • PSW • D Miss • True Love Korean Fullerton CA • (714)992-5008 • (FW 1990 MDIV)

**KANGAS CARLTON W REV** (715)286-2562
E 21110 Cty Hwy SD Augusta WI 54722 • Kangas5472@aol.com • NW • SP • Grace Augusta WI* • (715)286-2116 • (FW 1980 MDIV)

**KANOY RICK G REV** (402)446-7357
C/O Immanuel Lutheran Ch 72430 567th Ave Daykin NE 68338 • NEB • SP • Immanuel Daykin NE • (402)446-7357 • (SL 1997 MDIV)

**KAPANKA GERALD C REV** (319)226-3926
C/O Immanuel Lutheran Church 207 Franklin St Waterloo IA 50703-3515 • IE • SP • Immanuel Waterloo IA • (319)233-7052 • (FW 1989 MDIV)

**KAPFER RICHARD G REV** (515)573-8299
2981 15th Ave NE Fort Dodge IA 50501-2127 • IW • EM • (SPR 1963 LITTD)

**KAPPEL MARC A REV** (904)291-9623
3261 Avalon Dr Middleburg FL 32068 • FG • SP • St Peter Orange Park FL • (904)282-8876 • (SL 2000 MDIV)

**KAPPELER EUGENE D REV** (318)387-0762
1402 Roselawn Ave Monroe LA 71201 • ckappeler@aol.com • SO • EM • (SL 1959)

**KAPPLER STEVE A REV** (623)975-7123
14226 W White Rock Dr Sun City West AZ 85375-5643 • col2@futureone.com • PSW • SP • Crown Of Life Sun City West AZ • (623)546-6228 • (SL 1967 MDIV)

**KARCH JOHN D REV** (706)232-5723
1 Villamar Dr NW Rome GA 30165-8899 • FG • SP • Holy Trinity Rome GA • (706)232-7257 • (FW 1980 MDIV)

**KARLE JOHN ERIC REV** (318)352-4810
407 St Clair Ave Natchitoches LA 71457-5843 • christus@worldnetla.net • SO • SP • Christ King Natchitoches LA • (318)352-8708 • (SL 1994 MDIV)

**KARNER KEVIN A REV** (765)759-5120
3100 N Countryview Dr Muncie IN 47304 • kkarner@juno.com • IN • Sn/Adm • Grace Muncie IN • (765)282-2537 • (FW 1989 MDIV)

**KARNER ROY R REV** (763)323-8604
2609 Rivers Bluff Ln Anoka MN 55303-6282 • MNS • EM • (SL 1954)

**KAROLUS DAVID B REV** (715)832-7350
2241 Hayden Ave Altoona WI 54720 • dkarolus@execpc.com • NW • SP • Bethlehem Altoona WI • (715)832-9953 • (SL 1989 MDIV)

**KARSTEN DARWIN L REV** (636)938-5637
313 Wallach Dr Eureka MO 63025-2111 • pastordar@stmarkseureka.org • MO • Sn/Adm • St Mark Eureka MO • (636)938-4432 • (SL 1969 MDIV)

**KARSTEN WILFRED L REV** (301)746-8215
PO Box 157 Accident MD 21520-0157 • zion@gcnet.net • EA • SP • Zion Accident MD • (301)746-8170 • (SL 1983 STM DMIN)

**KASISCHKE DEAN B REV** (561)967-8152
8420 Blue Cypress Dr Lake Worth FL 33467-6243 • FG • EM • (SL 1945)

**KASISCHKE DONALD D REV** (561)439-4308
C/O Our Savior Luth Church 1615 Lake Ave Lake Worth FL 33460-3670 • FG • Asst • Our Savior Lake Worth FL • (561)582-4430 • (SL 1973 MDIV PHD)

**KASPAR DONALD L REV** (409)295-6092
2119 Avenue R Huntsville TX 77340-4920 • TX • Inst C • Texas Austin TX • (SPR 1965 MDIV MA)

**KASPER DONALD M REV** (936)825-8056
130 Thane St Navasota TX 77868-3730 • kasper@tca.net • TX • SP • Trinity Navasota TX • (936)825-6851 • (SL 1982 MDIV)

**KASPER ROBERT E REV** (810)786-0255
13011 27 Mile Rd Washington MI 48094 • robkasper@juno.com • MI • Sn/Adm • St Peter Macomb MI • (810)781-3434 • (SL 1983 MDIV DMIN)

**KASS ROBERT E REV** (847)568-0690
8933 Forestview Rd Evanston IL 60203-1910 • NI • EM • (SPR 1953)

**KASS STEPHEN ROBERT REV** (630)260-3679
507 Heather Ln Carol Stream IL 60188 • srkass@mcs.net • NI • SP • Family In Faith Glendale Heights IL • (630)653-5030 • (FW 1994 MDIV)

**KASSEN JOHN E REV** (248)969-0242
1450 Athlone St Oxford MI 48371-6002 • livword@attglobal.net • MI • SP • Living Word Rochester MI • (248)651-5316 • (FW 1979 MDIV)

**KASSOUF JOHN F REV** (410)879-6710
1200 Churchville Rd Bel Air MD 21014 • office@smlc.org • SE • Sn/Adm • St Matthew Bel Air MD • (410)879-6710 • (CQ 1992 STM MA)

**KASSULKE WILLARD J REV** (660)388-5935
201 E 4th St Salisbury MO 65281-1340 • wkass@cvalley.net • MO • SP • Immanuel Salisbury MO • (660)388-5192 • (SL 1965 MDIV)

**KAST EDWARD L REV** (517)791-4172
4449 Windemere Dr Saginaw MI 48603-1272 • MI • EM • (SL 1962 MDIV)

**KASTEN ALBERT LEROY SR. REV**
PO Box 111 Big Springs NE 69122-0111 • 100523.3262@compuserve.com • WY • SP • Zion Big Springs NE* • (308)889-3632 • (FW 1995 MDIV)

**KASTEN DOUGLAS L REV**
8439 Huey Rd Centralia 62801 COTE D'IVOIRE • doug³kasten@sil.org • NEB • 05/1991 05/2000 • * • (SL 1988 MA MDIV)

**KASTENS DENNIS A DR** (314)892-0888
5101 Kings Park Dr Saint Louis MO 63129-3353 • dakastens@aol.com • MO • SP • Peace Saint Louis MO • (314)892-5610 • (SL 1965 MDIV LITTD)

**KASTER DALE W REV** (904)928-9901
4562 Bannons Walk Ct Jacksonville FL 32258-2189 • jaxdale@aol.com • EN • SP • Celebration Jacksonville FL • (904)928-9901 • (SL 1989 MDIV)

**KASTING MICHAEL D REV** (503)722-7518
Trinity Lutheran Church 1201 JQ Adams St Oregon City OR 97045-1457 • NOW • Sn/Adm • Trinity Oregon City OR • (503)656-4504 • (SL 1972 MDIV)

**KASTNER MARK S REV** (262)639-4801
3357 La Salle St Racine WI 53402-3856 • kastner5@execpc.com • SW • SP • Christ King Racine WI* • (414)639-5849 • (FW 1982 MDIV)

**KATARI SHADRACH REV** (773)509-0241
PO Box 59812 Chicago IL 60659-0812 • katari@megsinet.net • EN • Asst • Bethesda Chicago IL • (773)743-6460 • (CQ 1997 THM MA)

**KATH HARVEY G REV** (320)864-6007
1406 10th St E Glencoe MN 55336-2405 • hkath@juno.com • MNS • Sn/Adm • First Glencoe MN • (320)864-5522 • (SL 1964 MDIV)

**KATH LYLE REUBEN REV** (507)545-2461
PO Box 417 Eyota MN 55934-0417 • lkath@people.com • MNS • SP • Our Savior Eyota MN • (507)545-2067 • (FW 1992 MDIV)

**KAUFMANN ARTHUR MORROW REV** (423)652-0550
6038 Old Jonesboro Rd Bristol TN 37620-3057 • MDS • SP • Trinity Bristol TN • (423)764-6872 • (SPR 1968 MDIV MBA)

**KAUFMANN CLIFFORD C REV** (503)620-0476
14785 SW 109th Ave Apt 3 Tigard OR 97224-3225 • NOW • 10/1993 10/1999 • (SL 1965 MDIV)

**KAUFMANN KENNETH M REV** (316)542-0170
C/O St Paul Luth Church PO Box 397 Cheney KS 67025-0397 • stpauls@southwind.net • KS • SP • St Paul Cheney KS • (316)542-0115 • (SL 1975 MDIV)

**KAUFMANN LOUIS A REV** (419)445-6809
500 Haven Dr Room 235 Archbold OH 43502 • OH • EM • (SPR 1938)

**KAUFMANN MARTIN JOHN REV** (254)442-2451
1610 Conrad Hilton Ave Cisco TX 76437-4856 • heisrisn@flash.net • TX • SP • Redeemer Cisco TX • (254)442-2090 • (FW 1997 MDIV)

**KAUFMANN PHILIP S REV** (309)662-1770
2802 Kolby Ct Bloomington IL 61704-1513 • kaufs4@aol.com • CI • SP • Christ Normal IL • (309)452-5609 • (SPR 1972 MDIV)

**KAUL THOMAS C REV** (414)771-2141
2234 N 61st St Milwaukee WI 53213-1502 • SW • SP • Faith Germantown WI • (414)251-8250 • (SL 1985 MDIV)

**KAUSCH GEORGE K REV** (503)672-2508
235 W Center St Roseburg OR 97470-2313 • NOW • Inst C • Northwest Portland OR • (SL 1957)

**KAUTH ROLAND C REV** (904)463-6745
C/O Joel Kauth 4869 Huntsmen Pl Fontana CA 92336 • lerokauth@netscape.net • NOW • EM • (SL 1959)

**KAUTSCH CLEO O REV** (712)364-3497
802 Valley View Dr Apt 2C Ida Grove IA 51445-1734 • IW • EM • (SL 1938)

**KAVASCH PAUL M REV** (714)447-4340
2101 Nutwood Ave Fullerton CA 92831-3529 • PSW • EM • (SL 1940)

**KAVASCH ROBERT W REV** (702)616-9612
481 Eagle Vista Dr Henderson NV 89012-4513 • kavasch@aol.com • EN • EM • (SL 1955)

**KAVOURAS DEAN C REV** (216)459-1499
5948 W 24th St Parma OH 44134-3003 • action@multiverse.com • OH • Asst • Christ Cleveland OH • (216)961-6060 • (SL 1978 MDIV)

**KAY WILLIAM L REV** (716)699-4106
8151 Irish Hill Rd West Valley NY 14171-9603 • wlkay@juno.com • EA • SP • St Paul Ellicottville NY* • (716)699-2265 • (CQ 1980 MDIV)

**KAYSER JOHN WALTER REV** (734)913-8691
10069 W Ellsworth Rd Ann Arbor MI 48103-9613 • dannydog@provide.net • MI • SP • St Thomas Ann Arbor MI • (734)663-7511 • (SL 1995 MDIV)

**KAYSER LOWELL N REV** (307)765-2878
409 5th Ave N Greybull WY 82426-1817 • WY • SP • Grace Greybull WY* • (307)765-2866 • (SPR 1972 MDIV)

**KEARNEY CHANNING REV**
PSC 479 Box 105 FPO AP 96269-0105 • chapclk@javanet.com • NOW • M Chap • Northwest Portland OR • (FW 1991 MDIV)

**KEAT JAMES D REV**
5230 State Rd Leslie MI 49251-9733 • jameskeat@juno.com • MI • SP • Grace Leslie MI • (517)589-5239 • (CQ 1990 MGC)

**KEBSCHULL ALLEN C REV** (914)395-1962
20 Fairview Ave Tuckahoe NY 10707-4143 • akebschull@aol.com • AT • EM • (SPR 1967 MSED MDIV)

**KECK MARTIN W REV** (310)762-2924
1001 West Cressey #109 Compton CA 90222-3837 • rev2mwk@webtv.net • PSW • EM • (SL 1949)

**KEEKLEY HAROLD F REV** (715)325-3990
283 Lincoln Ct Nekoosa WI 54457-8153 • EN • EM • (SL 1950)

**KEENAN JACK W REV** (480)786-3132
1720 W Winchester Way Chandler AZ 85248-0973 • jandmkeenan@home.com • PSW • EM • (SPR 1965 MA MDIV PHD)

**KEGEL ADAM G REV** (410)943-0365
5704 French Farm Rd East New Market MD 21631-1671 • agkegel@juno.com • SE • SP • Our Shepherd Cambridge MD • (410)228-7099 • (CQ 1993 MS MBA MTH)

**KEHRBERG WILLARD E REV** (612)276-0663
4300 W River Pkwy #178 Minneapolis MN 55406-3677 • MNS • EM • (ME 1943 PHD)

**KEHRET DAVID H REV** (219)464-5096
C/O Valparaiso University Valparaiso IN 46383 • dkehret@exodus.valpo.edu • IN • Cmp P • Indiana Fort Wayne IN • (SL 1967 MA MDIV)

**KEIL DAVID D REV** (541)664-4607
1020 Arroyo Dr Central Point OR 97502-2102 • dart64@juno.com • NOW • SP • Gloria Dei Central Point OR • (541)664-3724 • (SPR 1975 MDIV)

**KEILY KENNETH G REV** (812)358-2334
C/O St Paul Lutheran Church 1165 E 400 S Brownstown IN 47220-9803 • IN • SP • St Paul Brownstown IN • (812)358-2334 • (FW 1988 MDIV)

**KEINATH EDGAR M REV** (812)522-4448
450 Manor Dr Seymour IN 47274-2216 • IN • Indiana Fort Wayne IN • (FW 1977 MDIV)

**KEIPER EDWIN E REV** (512)291-9997
2915 Windcliff Way Austin TX 78748 • TX • EM • (SPR 1948)

**KEISKER WALTER J REV** (314)335-0158
2825 Bloomfield Rd Cape Girardeau MO 63703-6303 • MO • EM • (SL 1923 DD)

**KEISTMAN HERBERT ARNOLD REV** (979)542-2378
4146 W Hwy 21 RR 1 Box 23 Lincoln TX 78948 • keistman@juno.com • TX • SP • Ebenezer Paige TX* • (512)253-6636 • (FW 1996 MDIV)

**KELLER ALBERT L JR. REV** (219)486-4487
6230 Shell Dr Fort Wayne IN 46835-2162 • emmaus@elcs.org • IN • SP • Emmaus Fort Wayne IN • (219)456-4573 • (FW 1983 MDIV MA)

**KELLER ELFRED T REV** (608)781-4132
1301 Wilson St Onalaska WI 54650-3105 • SW • EM • (SL 1951)

**KELLER MARTIN E REV** (812)963-8336
5267 Chastain Dr Evansville IN 47720 • mkeller@evansville.net • IN • SP • Trinity Evansville IN • (812)867-5279 • (CQ 1990 MTH)

**KELLER WALTER A REV** (810)566-1439
15022 Annapolis Dr Sterling Hts MI 48313-3624 • MI • SP • St Paul Sterling Heights MI • (810)247-4645 • (SL 1981 STM MDIV)

**KELLER WALTER E REV** (219)462-2850
1705 Chicago St Valparaiso IN 46383-5122 • walter.keller@valpo.edu • IN • EM • (SL 1955 STM PHD)

**KELLER WILLIAM H REV** (970)330-7098
1980 44th Ave Greeley CO 80634-3318 • revkeller@ctos.com • RM • Sn/Adm • Trinity Greeley CO • (970)330-1203 • (SL 1969 MDIV)

**KELLER WILLIAM LAMONT REV** (573)329-4325
7 Pick Pl Fort Leonard Wood MO 65473 • wlklak@juno.com • MNS • M Chap • Minnesota South Burnsville MN • (SL 1996 MDIV)

**KELLERMAN CRAIG W REV** (406)463-2519
PO Box 203 Power MT 59468 • cwkellerman@juno.com • MT • SP • Zion Power MT* • (406)463-2541 • (CQ 1998)

**KELLERMAN JAMES A REV** (773)725-4249
3040 N Kilbourn Ave Chicago IL 60641-5362 • jkellrmn@hotmail.com • NI • SP • First Bethlehem Chicago IL • (773)276-2338 • (FW 1988 MA MDIV PHD)

**KELLERMAN LEROY W REV** (360)786-0449
1204 Bay St SW Tumwater WA 98512-1107 • NOW • EM • (SL 1961)
**KELLERMAN MERVIN A REV** (208)466-5808
312 17th Ave S Nampa ID 83651-4356 • makellerman@juno.com • NOW • EM • (SL 1953)
**KELLERMAN ROBERT REV** (314)422-7545
128 Rainbow Dr PMB 2818 Livingston TX 77351-9330 • jkelle4410@aol.com • MDS • EM • (CQ 1984 MA)
**KELLEY PHILLIP B REV** (520)876-5334
126 E Ocotilla St Casa Grande AZ 85222-2525 • PSW • 01/1995 01/2000 • (SPR 1974 MDIV)
**KELLING JOHN T REV** (414)549-2150
1908 Avalon Dr Waukesha WI 53186-2802 • jtkelling@peoplepc.com • SW • SP • Christ The Life Waukesha WI • (262)547-1817 • (SL 1995 MSED)
**KELLOGG CHRISTOPHER E REV** (719)546-0414
1726 Sheridan Rd Pueblo CO 81001-1615 • papak@bemail.com • RM • SP • Bethany Pueblo CO • (719)544-5269 • (SL 1982 MDIV)
**KELLY ADRIAN R REV** (813)884-4894
7204 Beasley Rd Tampa FL 33615-2102 • chapkelly@juno.com • FG • EM • (SPR 1966 MDIV MED)
**KELLY KENNETH D REV** (216)395-1356
C/O Immanuel Luth Church 485 Redondo Rd Youngstown OH 44504-1461 • immanluth@aol.com • OH • SP • Immanuel Youngstown OH • (330)747-1628 • (FW 1982 MED MDIV)
**KELM A DEAN REV** (915)362-1179
3120 Deering Dr Odessa TX 79762-5012 • adkelm@apex2000.net • TX • Sn/Adm • Redeemer Odessa TX • (915)337-5451 • (SPR 1965 MDIV)
**KELM DANIEL W REV** (414)335-9877
600 Bender Rd West Bend WI 53095-2212 • dankelm@hnet.net • SW • Sn/Adm • St John West Bend WI • (262)334-4901 • (CQ 1995 MDIV)
**KELM HARVEY F JR. REV** (409)751-4678
6330 Austin Cir Lumberton TX 77657-7529 • fkelm@clearsail.net • TX • SP • Redeemer Beaumont TX • (409)892-3286 • (SL 1985 MDIV)
**KELM LAWRENCE E REV** (713)445-3313
215 Rittenhouse Rd Houston TX 77076 • TX • SP • Our Redeemer Houston TX • (713)694-7433 • (SL 1965 MDIV)
**KELM PETER D REV** (513)891-1614
3837 St Johns Terrace Deer Park OH 45236 • OH • Asst • St Paul Cincinnati OH • (513)271-4147 • (SL 2000 MDIV)
**KELM RICHARD G REV** (402)768-6080
260 Belmont Dr Hebron NE 68370 • NEB • SP • Faith Hebron NE • (402)768-6837 • (FW 1999 MDIV)
**KELM VIRGIL M REV** (636)937-4264
103 Crystal Meadow Dr Crystal City MO 63019-1346 • kelm7@postnet.com • MO • SP • Immanuel Crystal City MO • (314)937-5525 • (FW 1982 MDIV)
**KELTNER JAMES A REV** (316)564-2018
412 W 5th St Ellinwood KS 67526-1307 • andykeltner@ellinwood.com • KS • SP • St John Ellinwood KS • (316)564-2044 • (SL 1984 MDIV)
**KELTO PAUL D REV** (906)428-1322
5986 Rivers 22nd Rd Gladstone MI 49837-8921 • NW • SP • Our Savior Escanaba MI • (906)789-9350 • (FW 1987 MDIV)
**KEMP CALVIN W REV** (802)479-1164
2846 Graniteville Rd Graniteville VT 05654-9608 • kempcw@aol.com • NE • SP • Williamstown Graniteville VT • (802)479-1164 • (FW 1996 MDIV MS)
**KEMPFERT FREDERICK REV** (712)284-2730
409 W 9th St Alta IA 51002-1510 • IW • EM • (TH 1950)
**KEMPFERT MERRILL R REV** (702)396-6805
5475 Campbell Rd Las Vegas NV 89129-3433 • kempferts@aol.com • RM • 01/1999 • (SL 1968 MDIV MA)
**KEMPFF GERHARD F REV** (509)922-3831
18016 E Riverway Ave Greenacres WA 99016-8522 • gerbet@juno.com • NOW • EM • (SL 1951)
**KEMPIN DANIEL ALLAN REV** (734)241-4126
321 Smith St Monroe MI 48161-2364 • kempin@michigannet.com • MI • Assoc • Grace Monroe MI • (734)242-1401 • (SL 1995 MDIV STM)
**KENITZ TERRY W REV** (517)772-2672
15038 E Gaylord St Mount Pleasant MI 48858-3631 • antiquer@sensible-net.com • MI • SP • Peace Alma MI • (517)463-5754 • (FW 1990 MDIV)
**KENNY DOUGLAS G REV** (317)873-1636
80 N 3rd St Zionsville IN 46077-1554 • revkenesq@aol.com • IN • SP • Our Savior Indianapolis IN • (317)925-3737 • (FW 1993 MDIV JD)
**KENREICH JOHN A REV** (516)653-4530
55 Old Country Rd East Quogue NY 11942-3801 • AT • SP • Christ Our Saviour Hampton Bays NY • (631)728-3288 • (SL 1965)
**KENT THOMAS G REV** (303)403-4480
9508 W 65th Ave Arvada CO 80004-5257 • RM • 01/1989 01/2000 • (CQ 1980 MA)
**KENYON CLIFFORD REV** (949)583-7868
26562 Avenida Veronica Mission Viejo CA 92691-3331 • PSW • 05/1991 05/2000 • (CQ 1981 MDIV)
**KEOGH CHARLES L REV** (505)751-7073
5796 NDCBU Taos NM 87571 • sdclc@laplaza.org • RM • D Miss • Sangre De Cristo Taos NM* • (505)758-5944 • (SL 1979 MDIV STM)
**KEREKES ROBERT S REV** (423)681-2315
2339 Sir Edward Ln Maryville TN 37803 • Belkerk@aol.com • MDS • EM • * • (SL 1951 DMIN)
**KERESTES LOUIS C REV** (715)643-3182
N 111568 Cty Rd O Boyceville WI 54725 • S • SP • Holy Trinity Boyceville WI* • (715)643-3182 • (SPR 1960 MDIV)
**KERN DALE B REV** (419)267-5180
23120 US Highway 6 Stryker OH 43557-9452 • dkern@bright.net • OH • SP • St John Stryker OH • (419)267-5180 • (SL 1971 MDIV)
**KERN HERBERT M REV** (516)731-8833
2301 5th St East Meadow NY 11554-1911 • AT • EM • (SL 1941)
**KERN PAUL T REV** (402)728-5416
1011 Road U Waco NE 68460-9159 • pk90413@navix.net • NEB • SP • St John Waco NE • (402)728-5446 • (SPR 1972 MDIV)
**KERNER JAMES L REV** (860)647-0136
PO Box 155 Suffield CT 06078-0155 • prkerner@erols.com • NE • SP • Good Shepherd Suffield CT • (860)668-2790 • (SL 1983 MDIV)
**KERNS RUSSELL R REV** (717)655-2505
C/O St John Luth Church 9 Wood St Pittston PA 18640-2028 • EA • SP • St John Pittston PA • (570)655-2505 • (CQ 1981)
**KERSTEN TIMOTHY PAUL REV** (785)263-0520
400 NE 95th St Abilene KS 67410-1540 • tkersten1@juno.com • KS • SP • Faith Abilene KS • (785)263-1842 • (SL 1995 MDIV)
**KERSTNER SHELDON L REV** (715)674-3836
C/O St John Lutheran Church 4833 5th St Laona WI 54541-9643 • NW • SP • St John Laona WI* • (715)674-3836 • (FW 1986 MDIV)
**KESEMAN BRUCE EDWARD REV** (618)539-5630
313 Saint Clair Ct Freeburg IL 62243-1207 • keseman@aol.com • SI • SP • Christ Our Savior Freeburg IL • (618)539-5664 • (SL 1990 MDIV STM)
**KESSELMAYER DARWOOD J REV** (309)346-4320
1116 S 4th St Pekin IL 61554-4512 • CI • EM • (SL 1955)
**KESSEN CLIFFORD REV** (715)535-2281
C/O St John Luth Church PO Box 68 Tigerton WI 54486-0068 • NW • SP • St John Tigerton WI • (715)535-2281 • (SPR 1966)
**KESSLER RICHARD W REV** (817)629-2009
RR 2 Box 60A Cisco TX 76437-9625 • TX • EM • (SPR 1971)
**KETCHAM BRADLEY W REV** (712)563-2759
906 E Division St Audubon IA 50025 • IW • SP • St John Audubon IA • (712)563-3548 • (FW 1989 MDIV)
**KETCHER RODNEY E REV** (612)729-8542
5101 36th Ave S Minneapolis MN 55417-1518 • MNS • SP • Faith Minneapolis MN • (612)729-5463 • (SL 1986 MDIV)
**KETTLER EARL C REV** (937)432-9363
6515 Sorrento Ct Dayton OH 45459 • ekettler@erinet.com • SE • EM • (SL 1947 MDIV)
**KETTNER DAVID L REV** (573)729-6271
1106 Bay Ct Salem MO 65560-2808 • salemlch@rollanet.org • MO • SP • Salem Salem MO* • (573)729-5512 • (FW 1989 MDIV)
**KETTNER JOEL W REV** (910)346-9383
120 Epworth Dr Jacksonville NC 28546-5808 • jkettner@onslowonline.net • SE • SP • Calvary Jacksonville NC • (910)353-4016 • (SL 1965 MDIV)
**KETTNER MICHAEL ALLEN REV** (217)445-2431
PO Box 199 New Holland IL 62671-0199 • CI • SP • Zion New Holland IL • (217)445-2264 • (FW 1992 MDIV)
**KETTNER PAUL L REV** (757)479-4884
1600 Dylan Dr Virginia Beach VA 23464-6705 • pilnek@juno.com • SE • EM • (SL 1959 MDIV)
**KETTNER VERNON R DR** (530)258-2347
PO Box 784 Chester CA 96020-0784 • church@psln.com • CNH • SP • Our Savior Chester CA* • (530)258-2347 • (SPR 1968 DMIN)
**KETURAKAT CHARLES W REV** (760)489-0273
286 Boleroridge Pl Escondido CA 92026-1246 • PSW • EM • * • (TH 1947 MA DMIN)
**KEUCH JAMES F REV** (414)878-2054
1618 Main St Union Grove WI 53182-1721 • stpaullcms@aol.com • SW • SP • St Paul Union Grove WI • (414)878-2600 • (FW 1986 MDIV DMIN)
**KEUCK RICHARD L REV** (307)746-3377
45 Crestline Dr Newcastle WY 82701-9742 • WY • 12/1998 • (FW 1990 MDIV)
**KEURULAINEN BARRY J REV** (724)352-3841
125 Cobham Ln Cabot PA 16023-9725 • barryk4@juno.com • EA • Sn/Adm • St Luke Cabot PA • (724)352-2777 • (FW 1978 MDIV)
**KEURULAINEN JAMES E REV** (781)329-5263
15 Calvin Rd Dedham MA 02026-6405 • NE • DP • New England Springfield MA • (SPR 1974 MDIV)
**KEYL RUDOLF J S REV** (540)662-2151
110 Walls Cir Winchester VA 22602-6939 • SE • EM • (SPR 1955)
**KEYLON GLEN D REV** (308)485-4716
C/O Christ Lutheran Church 503 West Medina Cairo NE 68824 • revfarm@aol.com • NEB • SP • Christ Cairo NE • (308)485-4863 • (SL 1993 MDIV)
**KIBLER PAUL D REV** (919)362-8362
1208 Maple Ave Apex NC 27502-1550 • pastorpaul@rlcary.org • SE • Sn/Adm • Resurrection Cary NC • (919)851-7248 • (CQ 1979 MDIV)
**KIBLER RAY F REV** (909)596-5086
4249 La Junta Dr Claremont CA 91711-2351 • PSW • Sn/Adm • Emmaus Alhambra CA • (626)289-3664 • (CQ 1999)
**KIECK HAROLD W REV**
5465 W Box R St Tucson AZ 85713 • RM • EM • (SL 1945)
**KIEFER JOHN M REV** (815)426-2650
C/O Zion Lutheran Church 11478 W State Route 17 Bonfield IL 60913-7290 • NI • SP • Zion Bonfield IL • (815)426-2650 • (FW 1983 MTH)
**KIEHL ERICH H REV** (314)965-0719
364 Mark Dr Saint Louis MO 63122-1423 • MO • EM • (SL 1945 STM THD)
**KIEHL PAUL G REV** (314)741-3035
11035 Perham Dr Saint Louis MO 63136-4604 • MO • EM • (SL 1945 MDIV)
**KIESCHNICK CHARLES B REV** (314)849-6354
9938 Heatherton Dr Saint Louis MO 63123-4923 • clkies@aol.com • MO • Asst • Concordia Kirkwood MO • (314)822-7772 • (SL 1991 MDIV)
**KIESCHNICK CLYDE J REV** (515)923-3217
810 State St Garner IA 50438 • ckiesch@yahoo.com • IW • Sn/Adm • St Paul Garner IA • (515)923-2261 • (SL 1990 MDIV)
**KIESCHNICK GERALD B DR** (512)218-1970
1917 Plantation Cv Round Rock TX 78681-2167 • txpres@txdistlcms.org • TX • DP • Texas Austin TX • (SPR 1970 MDIV JD)
**KIESCHNICK JOHN H REV** (281)333-3539
C/O Gloria Dei Luth Church 18220 Upper Bay Rd Houston TX 77058-4108 • jkieschnick@gdlc.org • TX • Sn/Adm • Gloria Dei Houston TX • (281)333-4535 • (SPR 1970 MDIV)
**KIESCHNICK ROY A REV** (281)350-5117
18214 Mantana Dr Spring TX 77388-5049 • TX • Assoc • Trinity Klein TX • (281)376-5773 • (SL 1969)
**KIESEL MARTIN E REV** (203)264-8762
172 Grandview Rd Southbury CT 06488-1968 • NE • SP • St John Waterbury CT • (203)754-7618 • (SL 1979 MDIV)
**KIESSLING RICHARD E REV** (503)492-4036
2350 SW 257th Ave Apt B204 Troutdale OR 97060-3700 • rkiessling@cu-portland.edu • NOW • O Sp Min • Northwest Portland OR • (SL 1967 MDIV)
**KIETZMAN HARVEY H REV** (218)652-3341
RR 2 Box 27A Akeley MN 56433-9612 • MNN • EM • (SPR 1972)
**KIIHNE KEITH K REV** (402)375-1291
RR 1 Box 124 Wayne NE 68787 • kkiihne@bloomnet.com • NEB • SP • First Trinity Wayne NE • (402)375-2165 • (SL 1962 MDIV)
**KILB JAY C REV** (314)534-0372
C/O St Paul Lutheran Church 2137 E John Ave Saint Louis MO 63107-1313 • MO • SP • St Paul Saint Louis MO • (314)534-0372 • (SL 1972 MDIV)
**KILIAN M VICTOR REV** (254)933-3205
2610 Riverside Trl Temple TX 76502-5900 • vkilian@vmm.com • TX • EM • (SPR 1960 MDIV)
**KILLION RUSSELL D REV** (334)281-3346
3818 Malabar Rd Montgomery AL 36116-4606 • SO • EM • (SPR 1953)
**KILLION TIMOTHY W REV** (205)330-1162
C/O Holy Cross Lutheran Church 4222 Harper Circle Northport AL 35473 • SO • SP • Holy Cross Tuscaloosa AL • (205)553-8004 • (FW 1998 MDIV)
**KILMER ERIC S REV** (517)635-2969
6764 W Marlette Rd Marlette MI 48453-9203 • MI • SP • Our Savior Marlette MI • (517)635-7994 • (CQ 1989 MAR)
**KILPONEN ROGER R REV** (810)603-2863
834 Layman Creek Cir Grand Blanc MI 48439 • MI • Sn/Adm • St Paul Flint MI • (810)239-6200 • (FW 1978 MDIV MA)
**KILPS WILLIAM R REV** (920)793-3368
3504 Pierce Ct Two Rivers WI 54241-1858 • wrkilps@lsol.net • SW • SP • Good Shepherd Two Rivers WI • (920)793-1716 • (FW 1982 MDIV)
**KIM CHANG SOO REV** (858)513-0191
12612 Oak Knoll Rd Apt J15 Poway CA 92064-5544 • PSW • D Miss • Christ Cnrstne San Diego CA • (619)566-1860 • (CQ 1997 MDIV)
**KIM DONG JOON REV**
1644 4th Ave Los Angeles CA 90019-6129 • PSW • D Miss • Brazilian Los Angeles CA • (213)732-4444 • (CQ 1997)
**KIM HYO JONG REV**
506 Judith Ann Pl Fairview Heights IL 62208-2451 • SI • Asst • Zion Belleville IL • (618)233-2299 • (SL 1995 STM MDIV)
**KIM IN CHUL REV**
153 N Rampart Blvd Los Angeles CA 90026-4721 • PSW • D Miss • Pacific Southwest Irvine CA • (949)854-3232 • (CQ 1995)
**KIM JOSHUA Y REV** (718)205-4711
35-49 70th St Jackson Heights NY 11372 • AT • D Miss • Atlantic Bronxville NY • (914)337-5700 • (KO 1975)
**KIM PHILIP SUNGMIN REV**
249-21 64th Ave # 2 Upper Little Neck NY 11362 • AT • D Miss • Atlantic Bronxville NY • (914)337-5700 • (CQ 1993)
**KIMARI WALLACE JAMES REV**
9225 Carlton Hills Blvd Ste 30 Santee CA 92071-2980 • EN • SP • Christ King Santee CA • (619)448-5515 • (FW 1991 MDIV)
**KIMBALL ALBERT L REV** (812)882-7772
2333 E Navaho Dr Vincennes IN 47591-1920 • IN • EM • (FW 1977 MDIV)
**KIMBALL LES L REV**
116 S Grant Hinsdale IL 60521-4051 • lkimball@juno.com • NI • S Miss • Northern Illinois Hillside IL • (SPR 1968 MDIV)
**KIMBERLEY WYATT A REV** (706)549-7201
518 Cherokee Rdg Athens GA 30606-1826 • FG • EM • (SPR 1944)
**KINAST FRANK X JR. REV** (608)348-5442
1165 Lancaster St Platteville WI 53818 • apostles@pcii.net • SW • SP • Apostles Fishe Platteville WI • (608)348-9901 • (SL 1995 MDIV)
**KINCAID KRISTIAN G REV** (319)582-2157
1695 Lawndale St Dubuque IA 52001-4239 • IE • SP • Our Redeemer Dubuque IA • (319)588-1247 • (FW 1987 MDIV)

**KIND DAVID ARTHUR REV** (219)483-0385
5 Tyndale Pl Fort Wayne IN 46825 • kindfamily@email.msn.com • IN • SHS/C • Indiana Fort Wayne IN • (FW 1996 MDIV)

**KINDSCHY CLARENCE A REV** (623)566-2425
9295 W Sierra Pinta Dr Peoria AZ 85382-0985 • akind@altavista.com • PSW • EM • (SPR 1967 MDIV)

**KINDSCHY LOWELL B REV** (805)686-9315
3240 Sandy Ln Santa Ynez CA 93460-9767 • locorush@cwo.com • PSW • SP • Shep Of Valley Santa Ynez CA • (805)688-8938 • (FW 1978 MDIV)

**KING BRUCE F REV** (612)437-7010
C/O Shepherd of the Valley PO Box 592 Hastings MN 55033-0592 • MNS • SP • Shep Valley Hastings MN • (612)437-7010 • (FW 1989 MDIV MA)

**KING D THOMAS JR. REV** (615)366-7156
2957 Nautilus Dr Nashville TN 37217-4306 • revking@bellsouth.net • MDS • SP • Cross Of Life Antioch TN • (615)641-6091 • (CQ 1980 MDIV)

**KING DEL O REV** (361)547-1011
HCR 1 Box 1060 Sandia TX 78383-9504 • TX • SP • Trinity Alice TX • (512)664-6231 • (SL 1999)

**KING HAROLD L JR. REV** (402)756-5285
4080 S Wanda Ave Juniata NE 68955 • revking@gtmc.net • NEB • SP • St Paul Holstein NE* • (402)756-5621 • (FW 1982 MDIV)

**KING JAMES T REV**
916 Michigan Farmington MO 63640 • river@cbcast.com • MO • Assoc • St Paul Farmington MO • (573)756-7872 • (SL 1997 MDIV)

**KING JEFFREY D REV** (413)569-5151
C/O Christ Luth Church PO Box 1107 Southwick MA 01077-1107 • jking@clcsouthwick.org • NE • SP • Christ Southwick MA • (413)569-5151 • (SL 1984 MDIV)

**KING ROBERT H REV** (573)635-6538
901 Roland Ct Jefferson City MO 65101-3576 • MO • EM • (GB 1949 MED MA PHD)

**KING STEPHEN MATTHEW REV** (262)763-3883
970 Dorothy Ct Unit 7D Burlington WI 53105 • SW • Assoc • Our Savior Burlington WI • (262)763-3281 • (SL 2000 MDIV)

**KINNAMAN SCOT A REV** (810)791-9119
18798 Florence Roseville MI 48066 • kinnaman@ispn.net • MI • Assoc • St Luke Clinton Township MI • (810)791-1150 • (FW 1995 MDIV)

**KINNE LAWRENCE A REV** (248)347-3310
24347 Hampton Hill St Novi MI 48375-2613 • MI • EM • (SPR 1952)

**KINNE TIMOTHY L REV** (920)720-5925
949 Bridgewood Dr Neenah WI 54956-3711 • allthekinnes@worldnet.att.net • SW • SP • Trinity Menasha WI • (920)722-2662 • (FW 1989 MMED MDIV)

**KINNEE L EARL REV**
1512 E Gardner Ln Apt #5 Peoria Heights IL 61614-3660 • bugbug5@juno.com • IE • 02/1995 02/2000 • (SL 1988 MDIV)

**KINSER J RUSSELL REV** (512)267-9306
117 Comanche Dr Lago Vista TX 78645-8623 • TX • EM • (SPR 1968)

**KIPP DAVID PAUL REV** (219)662-4108
920 W South St Crown Point IN 46307 • trinluth@mail.icongrp.com • IN • Assoc • Trinity Crown Point IN • (219)663-1578 • (CQ 1992 MDIV)

**KIRBY PETER NATHAN REV** (876)925-9745
45 Oleander Ave Oaklands Kingston 8 JAMAICA • kirbypn@cwjamaica.com • SI • S Miss • Southern Illinois Belleville IL • (SL 1994 MDIV)

**KIRCHHOFF DONALD G REV** (918)542-9611
325 I St NW Miami OK 74354-5435 • mtolive@rectec.net • OK • SP • Mount Olive Miami OK • (918)542-4681 • (SL 1968 MDIV)

**KIRCHNER DONALD E REV** (217)935-4616
24 Kirkwood Dr Clinton IL 61727-2440 • CI • EM • (SPR 1954)

**KIRCHNER DONALD G REV** (218)683-3404
118 Belleville Ct Thief River Falls MN 56701 • dgkirch@bigfoot.com • MNN • SP • St John Thief River Falls MN • (218)681-4488 • (SL 1999 MDIV)

**KIRCHNER DUANE E REV** (956)687-1974
108 E Lark Ave Mc Allen TX 78504-2013 • kirchner@quik.com • TX • Sn/Adm • St Paul Mc Allen TX • (956)682-2345 • (SL 1972 MDIV)

**KIRCHOFF SCOTT W REV**
C/O St John Lutheran Church PO Box 1778 Athens TX 75751-1778 • TX • SP • St John Athens TX • (903)675-9598 • (FW 1995 MDIV)

**KIRK ALSTON SHEPHERD REV** (361)993-2526
737 Brock Dr Corpus Christi TX 78412-3010 • captkirk6@juno.com • TX • SP • Trinity Corpus Christi TX • (361)884-4041 • (SL 1964 MTH)

**KIRK JAMES D REV** (314)845-9033
4769 Titan Ct Saint Louis MO 63128-3012 • aslc@worldinter.net • MO • Sn/Adm • Abiding Savior Saint Louis MO • (314)894-9703 • (SL 1985 MDIV)

**KIRK JOHN E REV**
1165 Bon Accord Ln Fallon NV 89406-5846 • CI • M Chap • Central Illinois Springfield IL • (SPR 1975 MDIV)

**KIRK RAYMOND V REV**
5783 Mountain Laurel Dr 140 Swansea Dr East Syracuse NY 13057 • EA • SP • Trinity Syracuse NY • (315)437-8203 • (SL 1972 MDIV)

**KIRKEIDE DUWAYNE D REV** (303)591-9133
5472 Kay Cir Colorado Springs CO 80917-3811 • kirkeideduwayne@hotmail.com • RM • SP • Redeemer Colorado Springs CO • (719)633-7661 • (SL 1971 MDIV)

**KIRKLEN DON LEE REV** (701)477-6767
PO Box 668 Rolla ND 58367-0668 • kirklen@utma.com • ND • SP • Immanuel Rolla ND* • (701)477-5122 • (CQ 1984 MED)

**KIRMSSE WILLIAM H REV** (612)938-0437
8800 W 35th St Saint Louis Park MN 55426-3859 • whkirmsse@uswest.net • MNS • SP • St Luke Saint Louis Park MN • (952)929-5507 • (SL 1970 MDIV)

**KIRSCH DONALD W REV** (320)251-1951
2688 14 1/2 Ave SE Saint Cloud MN 56304-9539 • ddjjjkir@aol.com • MNN • SP • Faith Saint Cloud MN • (320)252-3315 • (SPR 1970 MDIV)

**KIRST DONALD REV** (630)972-1396
235 Capitol Dr Bolingbrook IL 60440-2513 • donkirst@yahoo.com • NI • Assoc • St John Darien IL • (630)969-7987 • (SL 1959)

**KISCHNICK BRUCE R REV** (812)949-9014
2463 Birch Dr Clarksville IN 47129-1286 • IN • Sn/Adm • Grace New Albany IN • (812)944-1267 • (CQ 1991 MED)

**KISTLER DANIEL LEROY REV**
847 Dell Rd Pacifica CA 94044 • CNH • SP • Our Savior Pacifica CA • (650)359-1550 • (SL 1997 MA MDIV)

**KITTEL CHARLES W REV** (847)669-5735
PO Box 865 Huntley IL 60142-0865 • NI • SP • Trinity Huntley IL • (847)669-5780 • (SL 1970 MDIV)

**KITZING SHAWN L** (308)745-1585
PO Box 461 Loup City NE 68853 • NEB • SP • Immanuel Loup City NE • (308)745-0808 • (SL 2000 MDIV)

**KITZMANN DENNIS M REV** (817)847-7383
405 Lottie Ln Saginaw TX 76179 • TX • SP • Holy Shepherd Haslet TX • (817)439-2100 • (CQ 1995)

**KITZMANN HAROLD L REV** (716)593-9544
300 N Main St Wellsville NY 14895-1037 • hkitzmann@juno.com • EA • EM • (SL 1964 STM MTH MDIV THD)

**KITZMANN MERLE REV** (320)328-4094
C/O Immanuel Luth Church PO Box 147 Brownton MN 55312-0147 • MNS • SP • Immanuel Brownton MN • (320)328-5522 • (SL 1964 STM)

**KJERGAARD CARLTON F REV** (913)780-5468
13920 S Raintree Dr Olathe KS 66062-1917 • KS • EM • (SL 1954)

**KLAFEHN MICHAEL A REV** (616)659-1655
406 S Lakeview Ave Sturgis MI 49091 • klafehn@aol.com • MI • Sn/Adm • Trinity Sturgis MI • (616)651-6511 • (SPR 1975 MDIV)

**KLAGES CECIL A REV** (616)842-3016
1204 Hillcrest St Grand Haven MI 49417-2154 • cklages@webtv.net • MI • EM • (SL 1945 MA)

**KLAMMER ENNO E REV** (503)588-3917
1553 Chukar Ct NW Salem OR 97304-2001 • ennok@open.org • NOW • EM • (SL 1953 MDIV MA)

**KLANN H RICHARD REV** (904)357-3560
34245 Parkview Ave Eustis FL 32736-7230 • mklann@aol.com • MO • EM • (SL 1938 MA PHD DD)

**KLATT ALAN E REV** (414)545-3678
2164 S 77th St West Allis WI 53219-1130 • alklatt@aol.com • SW • Assoc • Brookfield Brookfield WI • (262)783-4270 • (SL 1988 MDIV)

**KLATT EBERHARD G REV** (414)444-0100
2503 N 47th St Milwaukee WI 53210-2928 • ebklatt@juno.com • SW • Sn/Adm • Bethany Milwaukee WI • (414)444-3131 • (SL 1960 MDIV)

**KLATT GARY H REV** (402)945-2625
C/O Trinity Lutheran Chuch 5106 Douglas St Ponca NE 68770-7019 • ghksk@nntc.net • NEB • SP • Trinity Ponca NE • (402)945-2160 • (FW 1985 MDIV)

**KLATT MICHAEL V REV** (402)564-2859
3377 Mimick Ln Columbus NE 68601-1473 • NEB • Sn/Adm • Peace Columbus NE • (402)564-8311 • (SL 1982 MDIV)

**KLATTENHOFF WILBUR H REV** (505)298-0939
3101 Vermont St NE Albuquerque NM 87110-2450 • RM • EM • (SL 1944)

**KLAUCK ROLAND M DR** (203)746-6604
5 Old Bridge Rd E New Fairfield CT 06812-3211 • jk931 • NE • SP • Good Shepherd New Fairfield CT • (203)746-9022 • (SL 1964 MDIV DMIN)

**KLAUS KENNETH R REV** (612)448-7855
1427 Valley View Rd Chaska MN 55318-1735 • krklau19@mail.idt.net • MNS • Sn/Adm • St John Chaska MN • (612)448-2433 • (SPR 1974 MTH DTH)

**KLAUSMEIER ARNO M REV** (414)342-1754
1171 N 44 St Milwaukee WI 53208-2726 • SW • EM • (SL 1957 STM MLS MMU)

**KLAUSMEIER ARTHUR P REV** (219)471-1179
3215 River Forest Dr Fort Wayne IN 46805-2237 • arsuti@aol.com • IN • O Sp Min • Indiana Fort Wayne IN • (CQ 1982 MAR)

**KLAWITTER HAROLD J REV** (918)627-2158
7818 E 22nd Pl Tulsa OK 74129-2416 • OK • EM • (SL 1950)

**KLECKNER MARK D REV** (419)298-2594
C/O Zion Luth Church 1018 Cicero Rd Edgerton OH 43517-9514 • mdkleck@bright.net • OH • SP • Zion Edgerton OH • (419)298-2594 • (SL 1992 MDIV MST JD)

**KLEIDON NORBERT REV** (303)457-3298
2002 E 129th Dr Thornton CO 80241-1908 • n.kleidon@worldnet.att.net • RM • EM • (SPR 1967 MDIV DMIN)

**KLEIMOLA DALE M REV** (734)439-7455
12544 Carpenter Rd Milan MI 48160 • kleimola@msn.com • MI • SP • St Paul Milan MI • (734)439-2806 • (SL 1979 MDIV DMIN)

**KLEIN ADOLPH A REV**
6337 Jackson St Pittsburgh PA 15206-2231 • MI • EM • (SPR 1932)

**KLEIN BERT A REV** (512)272-8901
6617 Bramber Ln Austin TX 78754-5714 • bklein6617@aol.com • TX • Inst C • Texas Austin TX • (SL 1970 MDIV DMIN)

**KLEIN BRENT A REV**
Credo Okinawa Unit 35028 FPO AP 96373-5028 • chapklein@aol.com • NW • M Chap • North Wisconsin Wausau WI • (SL 1987 MDIV)

**KLEIN FREDERICK G REV** (703)250-4658
5914 Burnside Landing Dr Burke VA 22015-2519 • secretary@livsavluthch.org • SE • SP • Living Savior Fairfax Station VA • (703)352-1421 • (SL 1968 MDIV MCED)

**KLEIN JAY B REV** (952)955-2006
3030 Navajo Ave Watertown MN 55388 • stpeterlc@juno.com • MNS • SP • St Peter Watertown MN • (952)955-1679 • (SL 1999 MDIV)

**KLEIN KURT A REV** (352)873-3735
8862-D SW 92nd St Ocala FL 34481-9249 • FG • EM • (WBS 1954)

**KLEIN THEODORE J REV** (810)985-7622
2462 Riverwood Dr Port Huron MI 48060-2656 • MI • SP • Bethlehem Port Huron MI • (313)554-3728 • (SL 1953)

**KLEINFELTER JAMES O REV** (804)836-2132
1172C Franklin Tpke Danville VA 24540-1328 • ctklc@gamewood.net • SE • SP • Christ King Danville VA • (804)836-6888 • (SL 1983 MDIV)

**KLEINHANS THEODORE J REV** (920)734-4783
1710 S Bluemound Dr Appleton WI 54914-4141 • NW • EM • (SL 1950 MDIV MA MA)

**KLEINSCHMIDT DONALD W REV** (219)485-0057
9526 Mount Creek Cv Fort Wayne IN 46835-9490 • IN • EM • (SL 1964 MDIV)

**KLEMM ROBERT C REV** (908)362-7381
62 Stony Brook Rd Blairstown NJ 07825-9319 • 73611.156.compuserve.com • NJ • SP • Good Shepherd Blairstown NJ • (908)362-9405 • (SL 1961)

**KLEMME ERIC ERNEST REV** (612)784-1786
2848 County Rd H2 Mounds View MN 55112 • lastrev@hotmail.com • MNS • Assoc • Messiah Mounds View MN • (612)784-1786 • (SL 1994 MDIV)

**KLEMP JOHN A REV** (920)361-4513
248 E Marquette St Berlin WI 54923 • SW • EM • (SL 1958)

**KLEMP PAUL A REV** (952)442-5926
309 E 1st St Waconia MN 55387-1531 • MNS • EM • (SL 1965 MDIV)

**KLEMSZ SCOTT C REV** (219)471-8110
8 Wycliffe Place Fort Wayne IN 46825 • klemsz@ctsfw.edu • IN • SHS/C • Indiana Fort Wayne IN • (FW 1997 MDIV)

**KLEMZ LYLE E REV** (701)378-2534
C/O Grace Lutheran Church PO Box 128 Lehr ND 58460-0128 • ND • SP • Grace Lehr ND* • (701)378-2565 • (SPR 1964)

**KLEMZ ROGER E REV** (763)682-4787
PO Box 363 Buffalo MN 55313 • MNS • EM • * • (SPR 1958)

**KLENK ELMER E REV** (281)255-2562
800 Alma St Tomball TX 77375-4513 • TX • EM • * • (SL 1938 MDIV)

**KLENZ HOWARD R REV** (414)789-9727
16355 Gebhardt Rd Brookfield WI 53005-5169 • SW • EM • * • (SL 1959 MDIV)

**KLEPATZ HERBERT R REV** (615)287-9140
603 Kendrick Ct La Vergne TN 37086 • MDS • EM • * • (SL 1957)

**KLEPPE GLEN A REV** (320)629-2242
930 8th Ave W Pine City MN 55063-1820 • MNN • SP • Zion Pine City MN • (320)629-3683 • (FW 1994 MDIV)

**KLEPPER HARRY W REV** (956)787-4025
814 Fannin Box 4006 Alamo TX 78516-4006 • klepperhg@juno.com • TX • EM • (CQ 1979 MS)

**KLETTKE WILLIAM R REV** (856)227-0296
45 Silver Birch Rd Turnersville NJ 08012-1929 • klett9@aol.com • NJ • SP • Luther Memorial Blackwood NJ • (856)227-2209 • (SL 1973 MDIV)

**KLETZIEN EDWARD F REV** (715)258-0415
E2262 Circle Dr Waupaca WI 54981-8362 • NW • Inst C • North Wisconsin Wausau WI • (CQ 1982 MDIV)

**KLEWIN THOMAS W REV** (902)658-2405
RR 1 Box 58 Crapaud PE C0A 1J0 CANADA • NE • EM • (SL 1945 MA MA STM)

**KLIETZ SHELDON H REV** (406)251-6399
2520 Sunridge Ct Missoula MT 59803-2646 • MT • EM • (SL 1960)

**KLIEVE JOHN E REV** (414)284-4439
430 W Jefferson St Port Washington WI 53074-2111 • revklieve@excite.com • SW • Sn/Adm • St John Port Washington WI • (414)284-2131 • (FW 1983 MDIV)

**KLIEWER MARK A REV** (775)623-0212
3225 N Highland Dr Winnemucca NV 89445-3905 • zion@the-onramp.net • CNH • SP • Zion Winnemucca NV* • (775)623-3796 • (FW 1987 MDIV)

**KLIMA GEORGE A REV** (815)725-8552
1304 Edgerton Dr Joliet IL 60435-3743 • gklima@mediaone.net • NI • SP • Hope Shorewood IL • (815)741-2428 • (SPR 1969 MDIV)

**KLINE DUWAYNE L REV** (360)658-5878
14727 43rd Ave NE Unit 94 Marysville WA 98271-8936 • NOW • EM • (SPR 1962 MA MTH DD)

**KLINE STEVEN G REV** (920)822-3511
8248 S Chase Rd Pulaski WI 54162 • revkline@aol.com • NW • Sn/Adm • St John Pulaski WI • (920)822-3511 • (SL 1992 MDIV)

**KLINGEBIEL ROBERT W REV** (716)778-8120
6261 Charlotteville Rd Newfane NY 14108-9709 • aallcms50@aol.com • EA • EM • (SL 1950 MDIV)

**KLINKENBERG TIMOTHY M REV** (714)639-4320
1423 E Dana Pl Orange CA 92866-1736 • prtim@aol.com • PSW • Sn/Adm • St John Orange CA • (714)288-4400 • (SL 1991 MDIV)

**KLINKERMAN OSCAR J REV** (217)245-9814
617 W Greenwood Ave Jacksonville IL 62650-3104 • CI • EM • (SL 1931)

**KLIPP WALTER J REV** (970)378-1590
2004 21st Ave Greeley CO 80631 • RM • EM • (SL 1945)

**KLOEHN GORDON A REV** (509)448-7216
5411 S Martin St Spokane WA 99223-8243 • gakloehn@aol.com • NOW • EM • (SL 1963 MDIV)

**KLOEPPING MICHAEL GENE REV** (618)635-4882
307 S Elm Staunton IL 62088-1964 • SI • Assoc • Zion Staunton IL • (618)635-2880 • (SL 1997 MDIV)

**KLOHA JEFFREY J REV**
#20 Seminary Terrace Saint Louis MO 63105 • klohaj@csl.edu • MO • SHS/C • Missouri Saint Louis MO • (314)317-4550 • (SL 1992 STM MDIV)

**KLOHA MARK A REV** (606)325-1919
1403 29th St Ashland KY 41101-4064 • nrkloh0@pop.uky.edu • OH • SP • St Paul Ashland KY • (606)324-3515 • (SL 1979 MDIV)

**KLOPFER FRED EARL REV** (614)837-5605
232 Gender Rd Canal Winchester OH 43110-9735 • OH • EM • (CQ 1993)

**KLOPKE PAUL J REV** (847)577-7133
C/O Living Christ Luth Church 625 E Dundee Rd Arlington Hts IL 60004-1541 • NI • SP • Living Christ Arlington Heights IL • (847)577-7133 • (SL 1991 MDIV)

**KLOTZ GREGORY D REV**
C/O Jet Cargo Intnl M 182 PO Box 20010 Miami FL 33102-0010 • NI • S Miss • Northern Illinois Hillside IL • (SL 1984 MDIV MTH)

**KLUCK HERBERT L REV** (830)990-0104
601 Tanya St Fredericksburg TX 78624-2682 • TX • EM • (SL 1953 MDIV)

**KLUG ALVIN T REV** (520)284-5926
205 Appaloosa Dr Sedona AZ 86351-9334 • EN • EM • (SL 1938)

**KLUG CARL E REV** (716)637-5613
6605 4th Section Rd Brockport NY 14420-2447 • ceklug@frontiernet.net • EA • SP • Concordia Brockport NY • (716)637-5930 • (SL 1973 MDIV)

**KLUG EUGENE F REV** (219)492-2988
2846 Northgate Blvd Apt 3 Fort Wayne IN 46835-2926 • IN • EM • (SL 1942 MDIV MA DTH DTH)

**KLUG JERRY L REV** (217)466-0820
11407 Blackhawk Dr Paris IL 61944 • jlk@tigerpaw.com • CI • SP • Grace Paris IL • (217)466-1215 • (SL 1968 MDIV)

**KLUG TIMOTHY D REV** (307)587-1377
1702 Cedar View Dr Cody WY 82414-4231 • WY • SP • Christ King Cody WY • (307)587-5680 • (FW 1989 MDIV STM)

**KLUGE DAVID T REV** (708)447-9350
4033 Prescott Ave Lyons IL 60534-1330 • NI • SP • Zion Lyons IL • (708)447-4499 • (SL 1965 MDIV)

**KLUHSMAN MERRILL M REV** (913)294-5617
723 Redbud Dr Paola KS 66071-1178 • kluhsman@grapevine.net • KS • EM • (SL 1958)

**KLUTH DAVID L REV** (512)218-1732
2508 Plantation Dr Round Rock TX 78681-2609 • kluthd@concordia.edu • TX • SHS/C • Texas Austin TX • (SL 1977 MDIV MA)

**KLUZEK MARK REV** (314)839-1806
9 Les Cherbourg Ct Florissant MO 63034-2256 • kluzekmark@juno.com • MO • Assoc • Salem Florissant MO • (314)741-6781 • (SL 1996 MDIV)

**KNAACK WILLIAM LYLE REV** (715)845-4908
1201 Prospect Ave Wausau WI 54403-6662 • billknaack@aol.com • NW • Df Min • North Wisconsin Wausau WI • (FW 1994 MDIV)

**KNAPP JAMES D REV** (303)986-8063
13126 W Green Mountain Dr Lakewood CO 80228-3513 • RM • SP • Wheat Ridge Wheat Ridge CO • (303)424-3161 • (FW 1982 MDIV MS)

**KNAPP STEPHEN A REV** (773)643-2980
1100 E 55th St Chicago IL 60615-5112 • sknapp@mcs.net • EN • Asst • Redeemer Elmhurst IL • (630)834-1411 • (SPR 1976 MDIV THM)

**KNAPP TIMOTHY D REV** (413)527-8806
39 Cook Rd Southampton MA 01073-9495 • Revtknapp@aol.com • NE • SP • First Holyoke MA • (413)534-7071 • (FW 1983 MDIV)

**KNAUFT JESS M REV**
21421 Howard Ave Torrance CA 90503 • jknauft@concentric.net • PSW • SP • Immanuel Redondo Beach CA • (310)540-4435 • (FW 1986 MDIV)

**KNAUS RHEINOLD F REV** (714)637-0337
316 W Brentwood Ave Orange CA 92865-2235 • PSW • EM • (SL 1938)

**KNEER DENNIS C REV** (920)261-3431
205 N Monroe St Watertown WI 53094-7644 • dkneer@blhs.org • SW • South Wisconsin Milwaukee WI • (414)464-8100 • (FW 1986 MDIV)

**KNEPEL ROBERT J REV** (716)655-5616
2420 W Blood Rd East Aurora NY 14052-1126 • rknepel@buffnet.net • EA • SP • Immanuel East Aurora NY • (716)652-4240 • (SL 1973 MDIV)

**KNEPPER GRANT A REV** (520)572-6616
9523 N Mission Valley Pl Tucson AZ 85743 • gknep@worldnet.att.net • EN • Asst • Faith Tucson AZ • (520)326-2262 • (FW 1998 MDIV)

**KNEPPER THEODORE C REV** (870)422-7668
522 E Pine St Lead Hill AR 72644-9513 • rev.knepper@juno.com • MDS • EM • (SPR 1958 MDIV)

**KNESER BRIAN N REV** (407)469-4552
C/O Woodlands Lutheran Church 15749 County Road 455 Montverde FL 34756-3775 • kneser5@digital.net • FG • SP • Woodlands Montverde FL • (407)469-2525 • (FW 1981 MDIV DMIN)

**KNICK DONALD E REV** (507)282-4457
2247 30th Ave NW Rochester MN 55901-7626 • dknick2857@aol.com • MNS • EM • (SPR 1950)

**KNIEF LOUIS C REV** (309)637-3037
724 S Pleasant St Peoria IL 61604-5951 • shepherd@davesworld.net • CI • EM • (SL 1960)

**KNIERIM JOHN HECHT REV** (218)354-2360
PO Box 725 Barnesville MN 56514-0725 • knierim@rrt.net • MNN • SP • St John Barnesville MN • (218)354-7158 • (CQ 1997 MDIV)

**KNIGHT VERNON R REV**
302 N 7th St Edward NE 68660 • NEB • EM • (SL 1959)

**KNILL JAMES R DR** (703)221-3220
4160 Eby Dr Dumfries VA 22026-2401 • conlutri@doubled.com • SE • SP • Concordia Triangle VA • (703)221-3703 • (SL 1964 MDIV DMIN)

**KNIPPA CLARENCE W REV** (918)742-1563
2813 E 56th Pl Tulsa OK 74105-7401 • OK • EM • (SL 1973 DD)

**KNIPPA GREGORY DUANE REV** (254)675-2459
302 N Ave R Clifton TX 76634-1250 • immanuel@htcomp.net • TX • SP • Immanuel Clifton TX • (254)675-3281 • (SL 1998 MDIV)

**KNIPPA M ERIC REV** (618)943-2073
2111 Maple St Lawrenceville IL 62439-2073 • CI • EM • (SL 1951 MA)

**KNIPPA WILLIAM B REV** (512)282-0234
12505 Red Mesa Holw Austin TX 78739-7535 • TX • Assoc • Bethany Austin TX • (512)442-4870 • (SL 1973 MA PHD)

**KNIPPEL CHARLES T REV** (618)259-1477
263 Oakley Pl East Alton IL 62024-1655 • charlestk@stlnet.com • EN • EM • (SL 1952 STM MDIV PHD)

**KNIPPENBERG KEITH J REV** (219)482-1996
4625 Golfview Dr Fort Wayne IN 46818-9344 • sknip@prodigy.net • IN • 08/1985 08/2000 • (SPR 1962)

**KNITTEL PAUL A REV**
RR 1 Box 333 Chillicothe MO 64601-9615 • MO • SP • St John Chillicothe MO* • (816)646-5944 • (SL 1976)

**KNOCHE ERNEST J JR. REV** (412)271-1308
400 Barclay Ave Pittsburgh PA 15221-4036 • revejk@hotmail.com • EA • SP • Christ Pittsburgh PA • (412)271-7173 • (FW 1978 MS MDIV)

**KNOERR RODNEY HOWARD REV** (815)653-1747
1014 N River Rd Mc Henry IL 60050-5863 • fofpastor@owc.net • NI • SP • Fellowship Of Faith Mc Henry IL • (815)759-0739 • (FW 1995 MDIV DDS)

**KNOKE HENRY A REV** (480)924-3546
5647 E University Dr Mesa AZ 85205 • RM • EM • (SL 1939 MDIV)

**KNOLHOFF WAYNE J REV** (319)377-4609
7007 Chelsea Dr NE Cedar Rapids IA 52402-1447 • revwjknolhoff@compuserve.com • IE • D Ex/S • Iowa East Marion IA* • (SL 1983 MDIV MED)

**KNOLL PARKER A REV** (319)396-7491
119 Norwick Rd SW Cedar Rapids IA 52404-1143 • trinity@inau.net • IE • Assoc • Trinity Cedar Rapids IA • (319)366-1569 • (SL 1977 MDIV)

**KNOPPEL GENE K REV** (714)892-0643
15502 Cabot Cir Huntington Beach CA 92647-2802 • PSW • EM • (SPR 1956 MDIV)

**KNOTEK JAMES H REV** (909)674-6047
33830 Breckenridge Trl Wildomar CA 92595-8484 • PSW • EM • (SPR 1969 MDIV MA)

**KNOX MICHAEL R REV** (319)266-0933
922 Bluff St Cedar Falls IA 50613 • knoxcf@cfu.net • IE • SP • Our Redeemer Cedar Falls IA • (319)266-2509 • (FW 1987 MDIV)

**KNUDSON GARRETT L REV**
C/O Woodlands Luth Church 15333 CR 455 Montverde FL 34756-3702 • FG • D Miss • Woodlands Montverde FL • (407)469-2525 • (SL 2000 MDIV)

**KNUPP KEITH A REV** (440)943-3475
30540 Willowick Dr Willowick OH 44095 • ksknupp@juno.com • OH • SP • Bethel Willowick OH • (440)943-5000 • (FW 1998 MDIV)

**KNUTESON DALE H REV** (317)996-3936
5580 State Road 39 N Martinsville IN 46151-9178 • IN • EM • (SPR 1965 MDIV MS)

**KNUTH DAVID FRANCIS REV**
617 W Beech Fergus Falls MN 56537 • MNN • Assoc • Trinity Fergus Falls MN • (218)736-4869 • (FW 1996 MDIV)

**KNUTH EDWARD REV**
PO Box 98 Wautoma WI 54982-1198 • SD • 08/1998 08/2000 • (SL 1985 MDIV)

**KNUTH JAMES A REV** (919)682-6030
C/O Grace Lutheran Church 824 N Buchanan Blvd Durham NC 27701-1542 • jaknuth@aol.com • SE • Sn/Adm • Grace Durham NC • (919)682-6030 • (SL 1967 MDIV)

**KO CHANG SU REV**
C/O St Paul Korean Church 5201 Galitz St Skokie IL 60077-2737 • NI • SP • St Paul Korean Skokie IL • (847)673-5030 • (CQ 1981)

**KOBERG SERGEI S REV** (925)828-0575
7592 Interlachen Ave San Ramon CA 94583-4019 • CNH • Sn/Adm • St Philip Dublin CA • (925)828-2117 • (SL 1963 MDIV)

**KOBS DARRELL C REV** (501)967-1788
1016 Lancelot Dr Russellville AR 72801-5750 • kobs@cei.net • MDS • SP • St John Russellville AR • (501)968-1309 • (SL 1975 MDIV)

**KOCH AARON A REV** (414)281-5643
3840 W Layton Ave Greenfield WI 53221-2038 • akoch@execpc.com • SW • SP • Mount Zion Greenfield WI • (414)282-4900 • (SL 1990 MDIV)

**KOCH ALAN ROGER REV** (818)808-0630
15117 Greenleaf St Sherman Oaks CA 91403 • jkochcali@aol.com • EN • SP • Sherman Oaks Sherman Oaks CA • (818)789-0215 • (CQ 1994 MED)

**KOCH ALTON R REV**
Koch & Colonial Manor PO Box 266 Columbus Junction IA 52738-0266 • OH • EM • (SL 1936)

**KOCH DANNY R REV** (740)746-8316
7120 Sponagle Rd Sugar Grove OH 43155-9780 • dannyvalkoch@juno.com • OH • SP • Trinity Sugar Grove OH* • (740)746-8316 • (SL 1981 MDIV)

**KOCH DAVID V REV** (734)668-6358
2705 Ember Way Ann Arbor MI 48104-6463 • stlukeaa@aol.com • MI • Sn/Adm • St Luke Ann Arbor MI • (734)971-0550 • (SL 1966 MDIV)

**KOCH GLENN A REV** (623)878-9212
7407 W Dahlia Dr Peoria AZ 85381-5382 • gmkoch@juno.com • PSW • EM • (SPR 1962 MDIV MA)

**KOCH J ROBERT REV** (920)391-9999
2590 Hillside Heights Dr Green Bay WI 54311 • koch9999@webtv.net • NW • EM • (SPR 1962 MA PHD)

**KOCH JEROME R REV** (815)945-4941
404 Davis St Chenoa IL 61726-1303 • CI • SP • St Paul Chenoa IL • (815)945-5331 • (FW 1988 MDIV)

**KOCH JOHN G REV** (414)438-1838
10307 W Park Ridge Ave Wauwatosa WI 53222-2340 • cjkoch@earthlink.com • SW • Sn/Adm • Covenant Milwaukee WI • (414)464-2410 • (SL 1966 MDIV)

**KOCH KARL W REV** (614)890-1679
5445 Aqua St Columbus OH 43229-3915 • mentorkarl@hotmail.com • OH • EM • (SL 1959 MA STM MDIV)

**KOCH LEW ALAN REV** (605)353-6044
642 Dakota Ave S Huron SD 57350-2857 • SD • Asst • Mount Calvary Huron SD • (605)352-7121 • (SL 1996 MDIV)

**KOCH MARK A REV** (615)868-7141
720 Jessica Taylor Dr Madison TN 37115-5580 • revmkoch@juno.com • MDS • SP • Ascension Madison TN • (615)868-2346 • (FW 1992 MDIV)

**KOCH MARVIN O REV** (903)465-7728
1014 Woodlawn Blvd Denison TX 75020-5250 • TX • EM • (SPR 1951 MDIV)

**KOCH ROBERT A REV** (303)453-1912
10701 N Pecos - #1002 Northglenn CO 80234 • RM • 09/1992 09/1999 • (SPR 1975)

**KOCH ROBERT J REV** (925)679-1026
38 Oak Villa Ct Oakley CA 94561-4222 • robge@juno.com • CNH • EM • (TH 1943)

**KOCH ROBERT W REV** (219)267-5754
611 N Johnson St Warsaw IN 46580-3135 • rwkoch@angelfire.com • IN • EM • (SPR 1958 MDIV)

**KOCH ROLAND A REV** (253)475-4525
6836 E Grandview Ave Tacoma WA 98404-5038 • NOW • EM • (SL 1938)

**KOCH ROLAND O REV** (612)927-6099
4820 Aspasia Ln Edina MN 55435-4070 • MNS • EM • (SL 1945)

**KOCH RONALD E REV** (408)842-7444
C/O Good Shepherd Luth Church 1735 Hecker Pass Rd Gilroy CA 95020-8837 • goodshep@hotcity.com • CNH • SP • Good Shepherd Gilroy CA • (408)842-2713 • (SL 1972 MDIV MA)

**KOCH RONNIE L REV** (319)237-6118
PO Box 336 Fredericksburg IA 50630-0336 • paskoch@juno.com • IE • SP • St Paul Fredericksburg IA • (319)237-5759 • (FW 1996 MDIV MA)

**KOCH WILLARD E REV** (507)662-6269
209 W Menage Ave Lakefield MN 56150-9361 • wwekoch@hotmail.com • MNS • EM • (SL 1944)

**KOCSIS MARK D REV** (504)464-4699
4208 Arizona Ave Kenner LA 70065-1310 • SO • Assoc • Atonement Metairie LA • (504)887-0225 • (SL 1987 MDIV)

**KOCZMAN JOHN R REV** (515)327-8995
1259 65th St West Des Moines IA 50266-5751 • jrkoczman@aol.com • IW • Sn/Adm • Shep/Valley West Des Moines IA • (515)225-1623 • (FW 1983 MDIV)

**KOEHLER ARTHUR P REV**
4550 N Flowing Wells Rd # 1 2 Tucson AZ 85705-2359 • PSW • EM • (SPR 1939)

**KOEHLER CHARLES J REV** (616)941-2054
2971 Silver Farms Ln Traverse City MI 49684 • MI • Asst • Trinity Traverse City MI • (231)946-2720 • (SL 1997 MDIV)

**KOEHLER DOUGLAS W REV** (210)614-3742
6914 Wurzbach San Antonio TX 78240 • TX • Asst • Shepherd Hills San Antonio TX • (210)614-3742 • (SL 1995 MDIV)

**KOEHLER EDWARD J REV** (218)746-3419
9131 29th Ave SW Pequot Lakes MN 56472-2011 • (218)746-3419 • MNN • EM • (SL 1960 MST)

**KOEHLER FRANK G REV** (804)458-7333
3303 Warsaw Ave Hopewell VA 23860-1752 • SE • EM • (SL 1938)

**KOEHLER FREDERICK F REV** (941)543-2009
2130 Valparaiso Blvd North Fort Myers FL 33917-6788 • davidjets@cs.com • FG • EM • (SL 1957 STM)

**KOEHLER JAMES A REV** (360)769-0730
9468 SE Southworth Dr Port Orchard WA 98366-8854 • NOW • EM • (SL 1957 MA)

**KOEHLER LUTHER A REV** (507)964-2400
PO Box 363 Arlington MN 55307 • MNS • SP • St John Arlington MN • (507)964-2400 • (SL 1954)

**KOEHLER MARK NATHAN REV** (514)272-8570
C/O Ascension Lutheran Church 855 Jarry St W Montreal PQ H3N 1G8 CANADA • mkoehler@ascensionchurch.ca • S • SP • Ascension Montreal PQ CANADA • (514)272-8570 • (SL 1983 MDIV)

**KOEHLER ROBERT A REV** (540)786-4594
5045 Tara Dr Fredericksbrg VA 22407-6547 • SE • SP • Redeemer Fredericksburg VA • (540)898-4748 • (SPR 1972 MDIV)

**KOEHLER ROBERT T REV** (320)632-6548
603 E Broadway Little Falls MN 56345-3245 • MNN • EM • (SL 1948 MDIV)

**KOEHLINGER VERNON D REV** (314)968-4484
825 Greeley Ave Saint Louis MO 63119 • vdkoeh.pas@juno.com • MO • 05/1998 05/2000 • (SL 1986 MDIV)

**KOEHN PAUL R REV** (716)876-1787
269 Skillen St Buffalo NY 14207-1633 • EN • SP • Nazareth Buffalo NY • (716)876-1787 • (SL 1985 MDIV)

**KOEHNEKE DALE A REV** 011-852-2873-3585
14 Shouson Hill Rd W Apt 2B Hong Kong HONG KONG • koehneke@mysite.com.hk • NOW • SP • Of All Nations Repulse Bay HONG KONG • 011-852-2812-0375 • (CQ 1978 MDIV)

**KOEHNEKE RICHARD M REV** (219)484-0923
2529 Springfield Ave Fort Wayne IN 46805-1547 • richmart1@juno.com • IN • Sn/Adm • Holy Cross Fort Wayne IN • (219)483-3173 • (SL 1971 MDIV)

**KOELLER MARTIN E REV** (906)774-5368
W8855 W Lakeview Dr Iron Mountain MI 49801-9305 • lkoeller@hotmail.com • NW • SP • Our Redeemer Kingsford MI • (906)774-1844 • (SL 1979 MDIV DMIN)

**KOEN RUSSELL E REV** (314)942-3760
4090 State Rd M Imperial MO 63052-2940 • koeni@prodigy.net • MO • SP • St Paul Imperial MO • (636)942-4250 • (SL 1983 MDIV)

**KOENE EUGENE A REV** (718)346-9308
815 Linden Blvd Brooklyn NY 11203-3517 • AT • SP • Risen Christ Brooklyn NY • (718)498-3848 • (SL 1971 MDIV)

**KOENEMAN DAVID A REV** (317)326-4473
2415 Osman Ln Greenfield IN 46140-8423 • dkoeneman@prodigy.net • IN • SP • Faith Greenfield IN • (317)462-4609 • (FW 1991 MDIV)

**KOENIG CLIFFORD W REV** (816)358-5647
12011 E 55th Ter Kansas City MO 64133-3028 • ckoenigkc@aol.com • MO • EM • (CQ 1972 MSED MA)

**KOENIG DANIEL G REV** (336)668-4132
3649 Cherry Hill Dr Greensboro NC 27410-9141 • SE • SP • Ebenezer Greensboro NC • (336)272-5321 • (SL 1970 MDIV MA DMIN)

**KOENIG DAVID R REV** (419)782-5556
1040 Wayne Ave Defiance OH 43512-2831 • OH • EM • (SL 1952 STM)

**KOENIG DONALD F REV** (425)385-2646
11413 36th Dr SE Everett WA 98208 • dfkrrh@aol.com • NOW • EM • (SL 1950 MDIV)

**KOENIG KEVIN A REV** (941)371-1611
6416 Samoa Dr Sarasota FL 34241-5635 • goodshep@gte.net • FG • SP • Good Shepherd Sarasota FL • (941)921-3673 • (SL 1978 MDIV)

**KOENIG STEPHEN E REV** (219)984-5626
104 N Kenton St PO Box 315 Reynolds IN 47980-0315 • plkoenig@home.ffni.com • IN • SP • St James Reynolds IN • (219)984-5421 • (SL 1971 MDIV)

**KOENIG WAYNE W REV**
5151 Boardwalk Dr Dr - H 1 Fort Collins CO 80525 • rmkwwk@cs.com • RM • EM • (SL 1961 MDIV)

**KOENKER ERNEST B REV**
5851 Brannen Dr Huntington Beach CA 92649-4607 • PSW • EM • (SL 1946 PHD)

**KOEPCHEN HENRY L REV** (516)941-9319
PO Box 2326 Setauket NY 11733-0735 • AT • EM • (SL 1957 MDIV LLD)

**KOEPCHEN PAUL K REV** (941)768-1656
6560 Saint Ives Ct Fort Myers FL 33912-1539 • pkkoepchen@aol.com • FG • EM • (SL 1952 MDIV)

**KOEPKE FRANK F REV** (503)661-5669
558 SW Eastman Pkwy Gresham OR 97080-6802 • joandk@hevanet.com • NOW • EM • (SPR 1955 MDIV)

**KOEPKE LE ROY R REV** (608)254-7411
4130 W 8th Ave Wisconsin Dells WI 53965-8502 • SW • EM • (SL 1944 MDIV)

**KOEPP REINHARD W REV** (320)328-5374
PO Box 363 Brownton MN 55312-9308 • MNS • EM • (SL 1942)

**KOEPPEN KARL JAMES REV** (815)932-1545
1474 W Budd Blvd Kankakee IL 60901-4506 • KKoeppen@juno.com • NI • Assoc • St Paul Kankakee IL • (815)932-0312 • (SL 1996 MDIV)

**KOEPPEN ROBERT D REV** (708)895-4034
18521 Wildwood Apt 2B Lansing IL 60438 • NI • SP • Trinity Lansing IL • (708)474-7997 • (SPR 1968 MDIV)

**KOERBER CARL A REV** (757)430-1270
3801 Donnington Dr Virginia Beach VA 23456 • carolste@exis.net • SE • EM • (SL 1937)

**KOESSEL EUGENE H REV** (810)445-6290
15265 Grovedale St Roseville MI 48066 • gggeno@juno.com • MI • EM • (CQ 1982)

**KOESSEL FRANCIS O REV** (352)796-7727
7015 Windmere Rd Brooksville FL 34602 • fkoessel@cnnet.com • FG • EM • (SPR 1961)

**KOESTER PAUL R REV** (414)257-1447
1214 S 115th St West Allis WI 53214-2238 • gplc@execpc.com • EN • SP • Greenfield Pk West Allis WI • (414)774-3019 • (SL 1972 MDIV MS)

**KOHL BRIAN DALE REV** (316)322-7555
338 Hunton Rd El Dorado KS 67042-3012 • solac@powwwer.net • KS • 08/2000 • (SL 1996 MDIV)

**KOHL CARROLL C REV** (915)263-2764
615 Colgate Ave Big Spring TX 79720-3405 • stpaul@xroadstx.com • TX • EM • (SPR 1961 MDIV MTH)

**KOHLMEIER KEITH E REV** (316)722-4694
422 S Prescott Ct Wichita KS 67209-3502 • kekohl@southwind.net • KS • Sn/Adm • Ascension Wichita KS • (316)722-4694 • (FW 1978 MDIV)

**KOHLMEIER THEODORE W REV** (505)521-8153
251 N Roadrunner Pkwy Apt 1305 Las Cruces NM 88011-7017 • lrkprtwk@aol.com • RM • EM • (CQ 1980)

**KOHLMEIER WILLIAM G REV** (303)794-0529
291 W Davies Ave N Littleton CO 80120-4288 • wkohlmeier@aol.com • RM • SP • Christ Denver CO • (303)722-1424 • (CQ 1973 MA)

**KOHLMEYER PHILLIP REV** (925)676-1426
1306 Gragg Ln Concord CA 94518-3919 • pkohlmeyer@aol.com • CNH • 12/1972 07/2000 • (SL 1966 MDIV)

**KOHNKE KEVIN J REV** (608)524-7857
E8057 E Lake Virginia Rd Reedsburg WI 53959 • kjkohnke@yahoo.com • SW • Assoc • St Peter Reedsburg WI • (608)524-4512 • (FW 1991 MDIV)

**KOHRT DARRIN LYNN REV** (970)506-1542
4326 W 22nd St Greeley CO 80634 • RM • Sn/Adm • Gloria Christi Greeley CO • (970)353-2554 • (FW 1996 MDIV)

**KOIS DARREL K REV** (515)967-5005
1105 3rd Ave SE Altoona IA 50009-2005 • pastorkois@aol.com • IW • EM • (SL 1986 MDIV)

**KOKE LOUIS I REV** (989)835-3153
301 Sandy Ridge Ct Midland MI 48640-3412 • louiskoke@hotmail.com • MI • EM • (SPR 1960 STM)

**KOLANDER KEVIN L REV** (909)246-2337
30177 Rim Rock Pl Canyon Lake CA 92587-7967 • firstluth@le.klever.net • PSW • SP • First Lake Elsinore CA • (909)674-2757 • (FW 1989 MDIV)

**KOLASCH BRUCE W REV** (208)652-7571
C/O Zion Lutheran Church PO Box 387 Ashton ID 83420-0387 • bluekoal@aol.com • NOW • SP • Zion Ashton ID • (208)652-7438 • (FW 1986 MDIV)

**KOLB BARRY L DR** (630)365-0017
817 N 1st St Elburn IL 60119-8971 • docvmp@mailcity.com • NI • SP • Lord Of Life Lafox IL • (708)513-5325 • (CQ 1986 MED MAR MBA DMIN)

**KOLB ERWIN J REV** (314)842-0019
12429 Matthews Ln Saint Louis MO 63127-1345 • ervkolb@netzero.net • MO • EM • (SL 1949 MST MSED THD)

**KOLB JOHN C REV** (219)864-3977
8307 Sheffield Ave Dyer IN 46311 • jckolb@gateway.net • IN • SP • Grace Dyer IN • (219)865-1137 • (SL 1968 STM MDIV)

**KOLB PETER CARL REV** (903)872-6033
331 S 42nd St Corsicana TX 75110 • TX • SP • Faith Corsicana TX • (903)874-8795 • (SL 2000 MDIV)

**KOLB PETER L REV** (407)957-4473
3126 Harvest Ln Kissimmee FL 34744-9219 • pmkolb@netzero.net • FG • SP • Grace Saint Cloud FL • (407)892-4653 • (SL 1985 MDIV)

**KOLB ROBERT A REV** (314)647-5865
7110 Clayton Rd Saint Louis MO 63117-1505 • MO • SHS/C • Missouri Saint Louis MO • (314)317-4550 • (SL 1967 MDIV STM MA PHD)

**KOLBERG OLIVER E REV** (520)378-1439
3100 Oakmont Dr Sierra Vista AZ 85650-5154 • oak52@theriver.com • NW • EM • (SPR 1951)

**KOLESA SCOTT T REV** (504)443-7210
10 Jasmine Lane St Rose LA 70087 • stk0l@gnofn.org • SO • 10/1996 • (SPR 1975 MDIV)

**KOLESAR MICHAEL J REV** (309)744-2256
208 N Second St Secor IL 61771 • CI • SP • St John Secor IL • (309)744-2255 • (FW 2000 MDIV)

**KOLK CHARLES G REV** (763)421-8377
286 Yoho Dr Anoka MN 55303-1901 • MNS • 03/1997 03/2000 • (SL 1972 MDIV)

**KOLKMAN ALLEN DR** (760)433-9250
C/O Shepherd Of Valley Luth Ch 4510 N River Rd Oceanside CA 92057-5116 • lcmspastor@aol.com • PSW • SP • Shep Of Valley Oceanside CA • (760)433-9250 • (FW 1977 MDIV DMIN)

**KOLLER WALTER E REV** (215)379-3575
600 Croyden Rd Cheltenham PA 19012-1616 • EA • SP • Nazareth Philadelphia PA • (215)744-7843 • (SL 1953)

**KOLLMANN ALVIN V REV** (618)344-5197
100 Windridge Dr Collinsville IL 62234-4737 • SI • EM • (SL 1954 MST LITTD)

**KOLLMANN VICTOR J REV** (972)618-4369
3524 Santana Ln Plano TX 75023-3705 • victor@messiahlutheran.com • TX • Sn/Adm • Messiah Richardson TX • (972)234-6972 • (SL 1981 MDIV DMIN)

**KOLLMEYER ARTHUR T REV** (727)576-0212
8701 40th Ln Pinellas Park FL 33782-5813 • artk@ij.net • FG • EM • (SL 1947)

**KOLLMEYER DAVID L REV** (618)826-5787
811 State St Chester IL 62233 • kollmyr@midwest.net • SI • Inst C • Southern Illinois Belleville IL • (SL 1982 MDIV)

**KOLLMEYER GLEN C REV**
4355 S National #402 Springfield MO 65810 • OK • EM • (SL 1947)

**KOLZOW CALVIN J JR. REV** (616)651-2169
69503 Franklin Cir Sturgis MI 49091-9523 • MI • Assoc • Trinity Sturgis MI • (616)651-6511 • (FW 1987 MDIV)

**KONRAD ALLEN E REV** ¢27-31-705-9718
PO Box 2544 New Germany 3620 SOUTH AFRICA • onamission@eastcoast.co.za • NW • S Miss • North Wisconsin Wausau WI • (SPR 1966 MDIV)

**KONZ J LOUIS REV** (281)449-1307
5022 Debeney Dr Houston TX 77039-4813 • heloukom@juno.com • TX • EM • (SL 1944 MDIV)

**KONZ PHILIP M REV** (915)520-5759
4213 Greenbriar Dr Midland TX 79707-5460 • TX • SP • Holy Cross Midland TX • (915)570-8149 • (SL 1983 MDIV)

**KONZ THOMAS R REV** (254)968-6164
207 Maple Ln Stephenville TX 76401-2229 • tcpkonz@erathinet • TX • SP • Faith Stephenville TX • (254)968-2710 • (SL 1986 MDIV)

**KOOPMANN GARY A REV** (337)824-4206
408 1st St Jennings LA 70546-5432 • koopmann@cfweb.net • SO • SP • Immanuel Jennings LA* • (337)824-3546 • (SL 1984 MDIV)

**KOOPMANN HENRY J REV** (218)768-3602
120 3rd St S Mc Gregor MN 55760-9702 • MNN • SP • Our Savior Mc Gregor MN* • (218)768-3198 • (FW 1989 MDIV)

**KOPATZ PERRY A REV** (480)759-6464
16446 S 29th St Phoenix AZ 85048-8559 • EN • SP • Family Of Christ Phoenix AZ • (480)759-4047 • (FW 1980 MDIV)

**KOPHAMER MARK A REV** (402)588-2602
1838 Alvo Rd Seward NE 68434 • NEB • SP • Immanuel Seward NE • (402)588-2602 • (FW 1989 MDIV)

**KOPITSKE HARLEY L REV** (715)758-8284
W4962 State Highway 156 Bonduel WI 54107-8601 • bingsu@ezwebtech.com • NW • EM • (SPR 1960 MDIV)

**KOPPER GLENN P REV** (616)538-4523
3765 Thunderbird Ave SW Grandville MI 49418-2246 • thekop@juno.com • MI • SP • Bethel Grandville MI • (616)534-3364 • (SL 1974 MDIV)

**KORB GLENN L REV** (507)835-2621
C/O Trinity Lutheran Church 31184 W Wilton River Rd Waseca MN 56093-5525 • MNS • SP • Trinity Waseca MN* • (507)835-2621 • (FW 1978 MTH)

**KORBY KENNETH F REV** (360)417-2924
928 W 15th St Port Angeles WA 98363-7230 • EN • EM • * • (SL 1948 STM MDIV THD)

**KORINEK ALAN W REV** (806)767-9516
2213 37th St Lubbock TX 79412-1110 • SO • 08/1996 08/2000 • * • (SL 1981 MDIV MA)

**KORNACKI ALAN R JR. REV**
C/O Saint Paul Lutheran Church PO Box 549 Beach ND 58621-0549 • ND • SP • St Paul Beach ND* • (701)872-4700 • (SC 2000 MDIV)

**KORTE CARL E REV** (309)662-6741
19 Crystal Ct Bloomington IL 61704 • CI • EM • * • (SL 1950 MDIV)

**KORTE MICHAEL R REV** (513)481-4425
2896 Morningridge Dr Cincinnati OH 45211 • concormrk@aol.com • OH • SP • Concordia Cincinnati OH • (513)861-9552 • (FW 1986 MDIV)

**KORTH DAIRD W REV** (641)829-3624
C/O Redeemer Lutheran Church PO Box 138 Ventura IA 50482-0138 • korth@netins.net • IE • SP • Redeemer Ventura IA • (515)829-3615 • (FW 1981 MDIV)

**KORYTKOWSKI ROBERT A REV** (208)983-2316
402 NE 3rd St Grangeville ID 83530-2272 • NOW • SP • Trinity Grangeville ID • (208)983-0562 • (CQ 1980 MDIV)

**KOSBERG CHARLES T REV** (850)893-3270
2924 Edenderry Dr Tallahassee FL 32308-2634 • ckosberg756@cs.com • FG • SP • Epiphany Tallahassee FL • (904)385-7373 • (SPR 1971 MDIV)

**KOSBERG JERRY M REV** (480)460-7629
778 E Mountain Sage Dr Phoenix AZ 85048-4425 • pswkosbergj@psw.lcms.org • PSW • D Ex/S • Pacific Southwest Irvine CA • (949)854-3232 • (SL 1972 MDIV MA)

**KOSBERG KEVIN C REV** (719)687-0404
1450 Blackfoot Trl Woodland Park CO 80863-8316 • RM • SP • Faith Woodland Park CO • (719)687-2303 • (SL 1989)

**KOSBERG STEVEN REV** (507)386-1399
109 Thro Ave Mankato MN 56001-5540 • skosberg@prairie.lakes.com • MNS • SP • Hosanna Mankato MN • (507)388-1766 • (CQ 1985 MDIV)

**KOSCHMANN ANDREW M REV** (630)289-8210
1892 Pastoral Ln Hanover Park IL 60103-6743 • akosch57@aol.com • NI • SP • Our Savior Carol Stream IL • (630)830-4833 • (SL 1983 MDIV)

**KOSCHMANN MICHAEL A REV** (217)629-8415
C/O Immanuel Lutheran Church Box 380 Riverton IL 62561 • CI • SP • Immanuel Riverton IL • (217)629-8415 • (SL 1981 MDIV)

**KOSCHMANN PAUL H REV** (217)245-6254
611 Westwinds Dr Jacksonville IL 62650-3613 • CI • EM • (CQ 1982 MED)

**KOSS JAMES MICHAEL REV** (406)665-2945
PO Box 384 Hardin MT 59034-0384 • MT • SP • Redeemer Hardin MT • (406)665-2239 • (FW 1996 MDIV)

**KOSTER RAYMOND W REV** (718)836-0180
150 95th St Apt 5E Brooklyn NY 11209-7226 • AT • EM • (SL 1952 MTH MA)

**KOSTIZEN ERWIN REV** (810)686-5534
C/O Messiah Luth Ch PO Box 10 Clio MI 48420-0010 • ervkost@cs.com • MI • SP • Messiah Clio MI • (810)686-0740 • (SL 1965 MDIV)

**KOSTIZEN LEO E REV** (712)252-7737
3320 Pawnee Pl Sioux City IA 51104-1864 • lekostizen@aol.com • IW • Sn/Adm • St Paul Sioux City IA • (712)252-0338 • (SL 1972 MDIV)

**KOTHE KENNETH P REV** (952)890-3560
604 Pheasant Run Burnsville MN 55337-3606 • kennkatie@juno.com • MNS • Sn/Adm • Redeemer Burnsville MN • (612)432-7942 • (SPR 1976 MDIV)

**KOTHE RICHARD A REV** (402)462-6378
421 S Saint Joseph Ave Hastings NE 68901-6145 • NEB • SP • Zion Hastings NE • (402)462-5015 • (SPR 1976 MDIV)

**KOTHE RICHARD W REV** (612)452-5816
4373 Lodgepole Dr Saint Paul MN 55122-1849 • rwk@net-info.com • MNS • 08/1997 08/2000 • (FW 1982 MDIV)

**KOTILA JOEL DAVID REV** (513)598-1938
3651 Summerdale Ln Cincinnati OH 45248-3129 • OH • SP • Peace Cincinnati OH • (513)941-5177 • (FW 1995 MDIV)

**KOTTLOWSKI DAVID PETER REV** (712)947-4896
29016 Lake Ave Hinton IA 51024-8578 • IW • SP • Trinity Hinton IA • (712)947-4435 • (FW 1996 MDIV)

**KOVAC GERALD L REV** (314)416-7580
4301 Rockspur Ct Saint Louis MO 63128-4705 • S • D Ex/S • SELC Cudahy WI* • (SL 1965 MDIV)

**KOVAC JOHN D REV** (402)643-6490
946 N 5th St Seward NE 68434-1524 • NEB • EM • * • (SL 1947)

**KOVAC WALTER J REV**
32649 Bridgestone Dr North Ridgeville OH 44039-4395 • OH • SP • Mount Calvary Cleveland OH • (216)671-2099 • (SL 1961)

**KOWERT DANIEL C REV** (608)836-3136
8905 Timber Wolf Trl Madison WI 53717-2726 • kowert@living-christ.org • SW • SP • Living Christ Madison WI • (608)829-2136 • (SL 1984 MDIV)

**KOY NORMAN A REV** (419)599-0933
80 Capri Dr Napoleon OH 43545-2249 • koyco@henry-net.com • OH • Sn/Adm • St Paul Napoleon OH • (419)592-3535 • (CQ 1987 MAR)

**KOZAK JACK A REV** (330)644-4366
C/O Hope Lutheran Church 999 Portage Lakes Dr Akron OH 44319-1538 • jakozak@bright.net • OH • SP • Hope Akron OH • (330)644-3522 • (FW 1990 MDIV)

**KOZAK LADISLAV PETER REV** (416)656-5259
1442 Davenport Rd Toronto ON M6H 2H8 CANADA • S • SP • St Paul Toronto ON CANADA • (416)656-5259 • (CQ 1992 STM)

**KOZISEK SCOTT A REV** (217)234-9380
8955 E County Road 1200N Mattoon IL 61938-3458 • skozisek@hotmail.com • CI • SP • St Paul Mattoon IL • (217)234-9880 • (FW 1994 MDIV)

**KRACH HAROLD F REV** (941)639-3833
273 Coldeway Dr #D10 Punta Gorda FL 33950 • MI • EM • (SL 1945)

**KRACH JAMES M**
701 E Maple St Mount Pleasant MI 48858-2757 • MI • Asst • Zion Mount Pleasant MI* • (517)772-1516 • (SL 2000 MDIV)

**KRAEMER FRED H REV** (618)345-1326
1002 Lester Collinsville IL 62234 • SI • Asst • Holy Cross Collinsville IL • (618)344-3145 • (SL 1986 MDIV)

**KRAFT DONALD A REV** (901)664-4956
439 Wallace Rd Jackson TN 38305-2836 • halo2gcs@aol.com • AT • EM • (SL 1952 MPAD)

**KRAFT PHILIP H REV** (215)672-2037
676 Cheryl Dr Warminster PA 18974-2159 • pkhr@home.com • EN • EM • (SL 1957 MDIV)

**KRAFT RONALD A REV** (909)684-3549
2855 David St Riverside CA 92506-4131 • rkos1@msn.com • PSW • Asst • Shep Of Valley Moreno Valley CA • (909)924-4688 • (SL 1961)

**KRAHN ROBERT A REV** (918)458-1079
1829 Notty Acres Dr Tahlequah OK 74464 • OK • EM • (CQ 1984)

**KRAMER CHARLES F REV** (715)484-8145
C/O St John Lutheran Church W5338 Clark Ln Pickerel WI 54465-9716 • w5338@newnorth.net • NW • SP • St John Pickerel WI • (715)484-8145 • (SL 1971 MDIV)

**KRAMER HERMAN W REV** (712)657-2219
102 Madison St PO Box 260 Lake View IA 51450-0260 • IW • SP • Emmanuel Lake View IA • (712)657-3324 • (SL 1961)

**KRAMER HOWARD W REV** (505)532-0731
4532 Paseo Azul Las Cruces NM 88011 • hvkramer@cybermesa.com • RM • EM • (SL 1948 MDIV MA STM PHD)

**KRAMER JAMES F REV** (408)279-8231
1329 Arbor Park Ct San Jose CA 95126-4246 • james³the³preacher@juno.com • CNH • SP • Trinity San Jose CA • (408)377-4411 • (SPR 1975 MDIV)

**KRAMER KENNETH J REV** (520)625-5730
2028 S Santa Carla Dr Green Valley AZ 85614 • EN • 05/1999 • (SL 1982 MDIV)

**KRAMER LOREN T REV** (949)240-9751
25582 Goldenspring Dr Dana Point CA 92629-1535 • pswltk@aol.com • PSW • EM • (SL 1959 MDIV DD)

**KRAMER ROBERT L REV** (618)529-4449
3350 N Reed Station Rd De Soto IL 62924-3407 • SI • EM • (SPR 1972 MDIV MS JD)

**KRAMIN HOWARD F REV**
Lutheran Brotherhood 401 Commercial Ct Ste F Venice FL 34292-1652 • kramin.fl@worldnet.att.net • FG • EM • (SPR 1964 MED MDIV)

**KRAMP ALLEN J REV**
C/O Christ Lutheran Church 4423 I-55 N Jackson MS 39206 • revkramp@hotmail.com • SO • SP • Christ Jackson MS • (601)366-2055 • (FW 1994 MDIV)

**KRAMPITZ DAVID R REV** (708)482-3572
535 Blackstone Ave La Grange IL 60525-6103 • prdave63@aol.com • NI • SP • Grace Willow Springs IL • (708)839-5255 • (SL 1959 MDIV)

**KRANS GLEN A REV** (910)353-5050
213 Baytree Dr Jacksonville NC 28546 • grafec@gibralter.net • SE • M Chap • Southeastern Alexandria VA • (SL 1973 MDIV DMIN)

**KRAUS THOMAS D REV** (717)737-9551
6112 Wallingford Way Mechanicsburg PA 17050-7324 • EN • SP • Calvary Mechanicsburg PA • (717)697-9771 • (SL 1960 MA DD)

**KRAUSE ARTHUR C REV** (352)242-1886
12528 Lake Ridge Cir Clermont FL 34711-8584 • ackcrk@aol.com • FG • EM • (CQ 1963 MA)

**KRAUSE DANIEL LOUIS REV** (517)642-2526
7779 Rockcress Dr Freeland MI 48623-8419 • MI • SP • St Mark Saginaw MI • (517)781-3205 • (SL 1992 MDIV)

**KRAUSE DAVID WILLIAM DR**
107 Castle Ct Fairfield Bay AR 72088 • vistrak@win.bright.net • MDS • EM • (CQ 1994 MMU PHD)

**KRAUSE E GEORGE REV** (815)756-7607
312 W Hillcrest Dr Dekalb IL 60115-2344 • pk@godwithusilc.org • NI • Sn/Adm • Immanuel De Kalb IL • (815)756-6669 • (SL 1952 STM)

**KRAUSE FRED C REV** (616)984-5329
10639 W Briggs Rd Trufant MI 49347-9726 • MI • EM • (SPR 1968 MA)

**KRAUSE KENNETH E REV** (815)226-4752
1903 Spring Brook Ave Rockford IL 61107-1543 • kkatmto@juno.com • NI • SP • Mount Olive Rockford IL • (815)399-3171 • (SL 1986 MDIV)

**KRAUSE MARK E REV**
14432 Briarwood Ln Urbandale IA 50323 • mekrause40@aol.com • IW • Assoc • Shep/Valley West Des Moines IA • (515)225-1623 • (SL 1987 MDIV STM)

**KRAUSE MARTIN H REV** (507)528-2598
PO Box 177 Claremont MN 55924-0177 • orgnlme@lakes.com • MNS • EM • (SPR 1954)

**KRAUSE PAUL E REV** (316)221-4123
1121 Mound St Winfield KS 67156-3932 • KS • EM • (SL 1943)

**KRAUSE PAUL W REV** (708)747-3224
258 Marquette St Park Forest IL 60466-1951 • paulwk@juno.com • NI • SP • St John Lansing IL • (708)895-9240 • (SL 1968 MDIV)

**KRAUSE ROGER L REV** (303)840-8942
8094 E Inspiration Dr Parker CO 80138-8625 • rmdpres@aol.com • RM • DP • Rocky Mountain Aurora CO • (SPR 1974 MDIV DVM)

**KRAUSE RONALD EMIL REV** (515)379-2416
PO Box 29 Livermore IA 50558-0029 • rkrause@jumpgate.net • IW • SP • Immanuel Livermore IA • (515)379-1287 • (SL 1988 MDIV)

**KRAUSE THEODORE C REV** (404)516-2645
1001 Longwood Dr Woodstock GA 30189-1532 • chated@aol.com • CI • EM • (SL 1949)

**KRAUSE THOMAS P REV** (913)649-8135
10319 Walmer St Overland Park KS 66212-1742 • tom.k@lgawoodlordoflife.com • KS • SP • Lord Of Life Leawood KS • (913)681-5167 • (SL 1972 MDIV)

**KRAUSS EDWARD L REV** (727)527-8157
1982 75th Ave N St Petersburg FL 33702 • dredlk@juno.com • MI • EM • (SL 1962 MDIV DMIN)

**KREBS JOHN R REV** (608)339-6136
PO Box 219 Adams WI 53910-0219 • jnks87@hotmail.com • SW • SP • Immanuel Adams WI • (608)339-6102 • (FW 1987 MDIV MED)

**KREBS ROGER L REV**
10485 6th St NE Blaine MN 55434-1562 • MNN • 06/2000 • (FW 1995 MDIV)

**KREFT JAMES W REV** (219)223-4344
1217 Lakeshore Dr Rochester IN 46975-2412 • IN • SP • St John Rochester IN • (219)223-6898 • (SL 1981 MDIV)

**KREGER WALTER D REV** (231)533-6227
7730 Briar Ln Bellaire MI 49615-0160 • MI • SP • Hope Bellaire MI • (231)533-8129 • (SL 1968)

**KREITENSTEIN RICHARD C REV** (662)840-7456
907 Nixon Cir Tupelo MS 38801-6485 • rckreit@ebicom.net • SO • SP • Holy Trinity Tupelo MS • (662)842-0364 • (FW 1988 MDIV)

**KREKELER CARL H REV** (520)722-8948
8060 E Broadway Blvd Apt 111 Tucson AZ 85710-3907 • EN • EM • (SL 1945 PHD)

**KRENGEL DOUGLAS A REV**
C/O Saint Paul Lutheran Church 90 Millville Rd Lapeer MI 48446-1642 • MI • Assoc • St Paul Lapeer MI • (810)664-6653 • (SL 1991 MDIV MA)

**KRENGEL GEORGE A REV** (712)762-4301
704 Maple St Anita IA 50020-1136 • IW • SP • Holy Cross Anita IA • (712)762-3335 • (SPR 1948)

**KRENNING WILLIAM REV** (253)924-1164
2500 S 370th St Unit 58 Federal Way WA 98003-7624 • wkrenning@aol.com • NOW • EM • (SL 1956)

**KRENTZ ARNO EMIL REV** (314)968-1114
798 Eckrich Pl Webster Groves MO 63119 • arnokrentz@aol.com • MO • EM • (SL 1947 MDIV MA)

**KRENTZ EUGENE L REV** (847)587-4442
36395 N Tara Ct Ingleside IL 60041-8576 • NI • EM • (SPR 1958 MDIV MA PHD)

**KRENTZ HAROLD H REV** (630)543-1044
137 Army Trail Rd Addison IL 60101 • NI • EM • (CQ 1979 MA)

**KRENTZ PAUL D REV** (952)955-5097
844 Southview St SE Watertown MN 55388 • MNS • SP • St Paul Watertown MN • (952)955-1498 • (SL 1989 MDIV)

**KRENZ STEPHEN N REV** (573)896-9271
209 Franklin St Holts Summit MO 65043-2503 • graceluth@juno.com • MO • SP • Grace Holts Summit MO • (573)896-8824 • (SL 1994 MDIV)

**KRENZKE RICHARD L REV** (217)774-2763
608 W 12th St N Shelbyville IL 62565-1075 • dickrenzke@one-eleven.net • CI • EM • (SPR 1968 MDIV MA)

**KREPEL DAVID L REV** (405)375-3543
C/O Emmanuel Lutheran Church 124 W Douglas Ave Kingfisher OK 73750-4123 • dlklcms@aol.com • OK • SP • Emmanuel Kingfisher OK • (405)375-3431 • (SL 1984 MDIV)

**KREPPS THOMAS REV**
St Paul Lutheran Church PO Box 3386 Crofton MD 21114-0386 • SE • SP • St Paul Crofton MD • (410)721-2332 • (SL 1987 MDIV)

**KRESKEN ALBERT S REV** (803)272-5844
151 Cabana Rd Myrtle Beach SC 29572-5604 • SE • EM • (SPR 1962 PHD)

**KRETSCHMAR ALAN R REV** (920)457-2947
2217 N 23rd St Sheboygan WI 53083-4444 • akretsch@execpc.com • SW • Sn/Adm • St Paul Sheboygan WI • (414)452-6829 • (SL 1984 MDIV)

**KRETZMANN GERHARD R REV** (219)347-5463
123 S Morton St Kendallville IN 46755-1634 • IN • EM • (SL 1941)

**KRETZMANN OTTO H REV** (830)896-0244
426 Meadow View Ln Kerrville TX 78028-5609 • TX • EM • (SL 1955 MDIV)

**KRETZSCHMAR DONALD C REV** (630)668-3878
1206 Dawes Ave Wheaton IL 60187-6724 • kretzmar@aol.com • NI • Inst C • Northern Illinois Hillside IL • (SL 1969 MDIV)

**KRETZSCHMAR FELIX H REV**
1820 S 75th St Apt 213 West Allis WI 53214-5716 • SW • EM • (SL 1931)

**KRETZSCHMAR MARTIN H REV** (612)482-1235
183 Little Canada Rd E Apt 202 Saint Paul MN 55117-1337 • NW • EM • (SL 1941)

**KRETZSCHMAR ROBERT J REV** (410)661-8339
9701 Red Clover Ct Baltimore MD 21234-1804 • bobkretzs@aol.com • SE • Assoc • Calvary Baltimore MD • (410)426-4301 • (SL 1969 MS MDIV)

**KREUTZ EUGENE W REV** (916)939-4268
1484 Sutter Creek Dr El Dorado Hills CA 95762-4060 • EN • EM • (SL 1952)

**KREYLING PAUL C REV** (410)838-1499
1004 Chantery Dr Bel Air MD 21015-6322 • iggyk@juno.com • SE • EM • (SL 1945 MDIV)

**KRIEFALL DANIEL REV** (636)271-8346
1230 Little Calvey Crk Robertsville MO 63072 • MO • 04/1999 • (CQ 1983 MDIV DMIN)

**KRIEFALL LUTHER H REV** (212)666-4723
29 Claremont Ave # 11N New York NY 10027-6802 • AT • Cmp P • Atlantic Bronxville NY • (914)337-5700 • (SL 1957 MA PHD)

**KRIEFALL THEODORE A REV** (360)866-0661
2020 Franklin Olympia WA 98501 • NOW • EM • (SL 1960 MDIV)

**KRIEGER EUGENE L REV** (616)949-5165
1755 Ridgewood Ave SE Grand Rapids MI 49506-5051 • MI • EM • (SL 1955 MDIV)

**KRIEGER HERBERT J REV**
3196 Washington Pike Bridgeville PA 15017-1414 • EA • EM • (SPR 1953 MDIV)

**KRIEGER TIMOTHY O REV** (714)962-5571
C/O Faith Lutheran Church 8200 Ellis Ave Huntington Beach CA 92646-1839 • tkrieger@faithhb.org • PSW • SP • Faith Huntington Beach CA • (714)962-5571 • (SL 1980 MDIV)

**KRIENKE HOWARD A REV** (952)934-4205
15302 Boulder Creek Dr Minnetonka MN 55345-6510 • z.shepherd@worldnet.att.net • MNS • Assoc • Zion Hopkins MN • (612)938-7661 • (SL 1972 MDIV)

**KRIETE ROBERT L REV** (636)583-9705
8 Katerina Ct Union MO 63084-2461 • rkricte@fidmail.com • MO • SP • St Paul Union MO • (636)583-2209 • (FW 1984 MTH)

**KRIGER ROBERT A REV** (510)222-5341
4505 Fran Way Richmond CA 94803-2425 • CNH • EM • (SL 1968 MDIV)

**KRINGEL ARTHUR D REV** (302)736-0744
770 Oak Dr Dover DE 19904-4342 • artk770@aol.com • SE • SP • St John Dover DE • (302)734-7078 • (SL 1969 MDIV)

**KRINGEL RAY R REV** (805)925-9679
416 E Fesler St Santa Maria CA 93454-4510 • CNH • SP • Grace Santa Maria CA • (805)925-3818 • (SL 1968 MDIV)

**KRIPPNER KENNETH M REV** (972)495-2545
3237 Creek Bend Garland TX 75044 • kmkrippner@aol.com • TX • SP • Concordia Garland TX • (972)495-4714 • (SL 1988 MDIV)

**KRISTALYN BRUCE R REV** (316)365-2496
1407 N Kentucky St Iola KS 66749-1935 • kristalyn@aceks.com • KS • SP • Grace Iola KS • (316)365-6468 • (FW 1989 MDIV)

**KRISTO ARNE REV** (757)424-9560
6025 Clear Springs Rd Virginia Beach VA 23464-4637 • arnekristo@aol.com • SE • EM • (SL 1945 MDIV)

**KRITSCH PAUL E REV** (908)232-3073
107 Glenside Ave Scotch Plains NJ 07076 • paulkritsch@hotmail.com • NJ • Sn/Adm • Redeemer Westfield NJ • (908)232-1517 • (SL 1973 MDIV)

**KRITZER KEVIN LEE REV**
C/O Fountain Of Life Luth Ch 710 S Kolb Rd Tucson AZ 85710-4941 • PSW • Sn/Adm • Fountain Life Tucson AZ • (520)747-1213 • (SL 1992 MDIV)

**KROEMER JAMES G DR** (414)354-5096
9440 N Bethanne Dr Milwaukee WI 53223-1210 • SW • SP • Christ Memorial Milwaukee WI • (414)461-3253 • (SL 1980 MA MDIV PHD)

**KROENING ELMER H REV** (913)685-1426
2024 W 139th St Leawood KS 66224-4537 • KS • EM • (SL 1944)

**KROGEN RICHARD A REV** (612)757-2770
231 104th Lane NW Coon Rapids MN 55448-5042 • revrak@mailcity.com • MNS • 03/2000 • (SPR 1964)

**KROHE WAYNE ALBERT REV** (507)451-0447
108 3rd St SW Medford MN 55049-9573 • MNS • SP • Trinity Medford MN • (507)451-0447 • (FW 1986)

**KROHN KEVIN L REV** (505)257-5296
212 Barcus Rd Ruidoso NM 88345-6839 • shlc@zianet.com • RM • SP • Shepherd Hills Ruidoso NM • (505)258-4191 • (SL 1987 MDIV)

**KROHN ORVILLE E REV** (505)622-1055
708 A La Fonda Dr Roswell NM 88201-7733 • orvkrohn@hotmail.com • RM • EM • (SL 1953)

**KROHN PAUL E REV** (651)463-2993
19268 Enchanted Way Farmington MN 55024-8083 • MNS • EM • (SL 1949)

**KROLL C DOUGLAS DR** (909)624-0405
524 Foxpark Dr Claremont CA 91711-3630 • drdkroll@aol.com • PSW • 02/1999 • (LS 1980 MDIV MA DPH)

**KROLL DONALD O REV** (409)296-2081
PO Box 1684 Winnie TX 77665-1684 • kroll@datarecall.net • TX • SP • Hope Winnie TX • (409)296-2377 • (SPR 1966)

**KROLL MICHEAL D REV** (616)893-7722
C/O Faith Lutheran Church 707 Alice St Whitehall MI 49461-1415 • MI • SP • Faith Whitehall MI • (231)893-7722 • (FW 1990 MDIV)

**KROLL ROLAND REV** (208)585-2694
23155 Lansing Ln Middleton ID 83644-5631 • krollr@msn.com • NOW • EM • (SPR 1966 MDIV)

**KROLUS HARRY M REV** (410)871-0712
668 Geneva Dr Westminster MD 21157-4607 • krol07@aol.com • SE • SP • Christ King Owings Mills MD • (410)356-3400 • (SL 1984 MDIV)

**KROMPART DONALD H REV** (410)208-6057
1044 Ocean Pkwy Ocean Pines MD 21811-1662 • dkrompart@msn.com • SE • SP • Peace Smyrna DE • (302)653-4312 • (SPR 1964)

**KROMPHARDT ARNOLD E REV** (727)372-6455
9543 Conservation Dr New Port Richey FL 34655 • kromp@worldnet.att.net • EA • EM • (SPR 1955 LLD)

**KROONBLAWD JAMES L REV** (507)287-3281
826 26th St NW Rochester MN 55901 • MNS • Assoc • Trinity Rochester MN • (507)289-1531 • (SL 1986 MDIV)

**KROUT LOREN R REV** (815)895-2723
1411 E Stonehenge Dr Sycamore IL 60178-2661 • NI • EM • (SL 1957 MDIV)

**KRUECKEBERG DAVID E REV** (708)530-5204
353 Emroy Ave Elmhurst IL 60126-2427 • EN • D Miss • English Farmington MI • (SPR 1969 MDIV)

**KRUEGER CARL ARTHUR REV** (508)758-6425
16 Knollwood Dr Mattapoisett MA 02739-1551 • cana@vcn.com • NE • EM • (SL 1973 MDIV)

**KRUEGER CARL HENRY JR. REV** (414)481-1000
4035 E Munkwitz Ave Cudahy WI 53110-1715 • selcpres@selc.lcms.org • S • DP • SELC Cudahy WI* • (SPR 1974 MDIV)

**KRUEGER DALE B REV** (616)375-0114
3706 Barrington Dr Kalamazoo MI 49006-5477 • pastorkrueger@aalweb.net • MI • EM • * • (SL 1957 MDIV)

**KRUEGER DANIEL L REV**
321 Carnaby Dr NE Cedar Rapids IA 52402 • IE • SP • Zion Hiawatha IA • (319)393-2013 • (SL 1981 MDIV)

**KRUEGER DELMAR O REV** (217)443-0631
22218 N 1750 E Rd Danville IL 61834 • CI • EM • (SL 1954 MDIV)

**KRUEGER DENNIS J REV** (201)529-2117
C/O Holy Cross 129 Glasgow Terrace Mahwah NJ 07430-1635 • hcrevdk@aol.com • NJ • SP • Holy Cross Mahwah NJ • (201)529-2117 • (SC 1986 MDIV)

**KRUEGER EDWIN A REV** (209)835-2486
1130 Freedom Ct Tracy CA 95376-4729 • revrev@inreach.com • CNH • D Ex/S • Calif/Nevada/Hawaii San Francisco CA • (415)468-2336 • (SL 1971 MDIV)

**KRUEGER FREDERICK H REV** (715)723-7778
751 S Main St Chippewa Falls WI 54729-3219 • chap@werewolf.net • NW • EM • (SL 1943)

**KRUEGER GEORGE A REV** (612)444-7122
28200 Jodrell St NE North Branch MN 55056 • kruegerev@juno.com • MNN • SP • St John North Branch MN • (612)444-5988 • (SPR 1967 MDIV)

**KRUEGER HAROLD O REV** (262)877-4005
11631 344th Ave Twin Lakes WI 53181-9387 • NI • Sn/Adm • St Matthew Lake Zurich IL • (847)438-7709 • (SL 1950 MDIV)

**KRUEGER JEFFREY REV**
304 Flint Ave Matton WI 54450 • NW • SP • St John Mattoon WI • (715)489-3471 • (CQ 1984)

**KRUEGER JOEL A REV** (320)676-3435
PO Box 51 Isle MN 56342-0051 • kruegjl@ecenet.com • MNN • SP • Trinity Isle MN* • (320)676-8774 • (SL 1997 MDIV)

**KRUEGER JOHN W DR** (480)753-1212
6562 W Ivanhoe Ct Chandler AZ 85226 • glc@primenet.com • PSW • SP • Gethsemane Tempe AZ • (480)839-0906 • (SL 1972 MDIV DMIN)

**KRUEGER KARL REV** (954)434-0253
5851 Bristol Ln Davie FL 33331-3242 • FG • EM • (SL 1949 MDIV)

**KRUEGER KENNETH REV** (515)648-2792
323 Lee Ln Iowa Falls IA 50126-1542 • kenk@cnsinternet.com • IE • SP • Immanuel Iowa Falls IA • (515)648-3805 • (SPR 1971 MDIV)

**KRUEGER LARRY G REV** (979)822-7381
2105 Sleepy Hollow Ln Bryan TX 77807 • ulctamu@txcyber.com • TX • Cmp P • Univ Chapel College Station TX • (979)846-6687 • (SL 1986 MDIV)

**KRUEGER MARK A REV** (715)387-2207
309 Meadow Ln Marshfield WI 54449-3115 • mass@tznet.com • NW • Sn/Adm • Christ Marshfield WI • (715)384-3535 • (CQ 1976 MDIV)

**KRUEGER MARK L REV** (920)756-3912
566 S Main St Brillion WI 54110-1433 • SW • SP • St Bartholomew Brillion WI • (920)756-3031 • (SL 1984 MDIV)

**KRUEGER PAUL A REV** (701)852-6404
C/O Our Savior Lutheran Church 3705 11th St SW Minot ND 58701-8303 • paulk@minot.ndak.net • ND • SP • Our Savior Minot ND • (701)852-6404 • (FW 1987 MDIV)

**KRUEGER R ROBERT REV**
6609 N Camden Ave Kansas City MO 64151-1998 • MO • Sn/Adm • Christ Platte Woods MO • (816)741-0483 • (SPR 1961)

**KRUEGER RALPH E REV** (412)795-1015
6024 Bolte Dr Verona PA 15147-3204 • EA • EM • (SL 1940)

**KRUEGER RAYMOND A REV** (507)289-4705
804 Nine One-half St NE Rochester MN 55906 • MNS • EM • (SL 1939)

**KRUEGER ROBERT H REV** (651)738-2549
11 Battle Creek Ct Saint Paul MN 55119-4903 • rhklmkll@juno.com • MNS • SP • Bethlehem Saint Paul MN • (651)776-4737 • (SPR 1971 MDIV)

**KRUEGER ROY R REV** (828)464-8162
1006 2nd St SE Conover NC 28613-1808 • SE • EM • (SPR 1956)

**KRUEGER STEPHEN C REV** (503)221-1343
8293 SW Canyon Ln Portland OR 97225-3923 • zion@teleport.com • NOW • SP • Zion Portland OR • (503)221-1343 • (CQ 1993 MDIV)

**KRUEGER THEODORE E REV** (608)742-6221
708 Cass St Portage WI 53901-1618 • Krueger@palacenet.net • SW • EM • (SPR 1956 MDIV)

**KRUEGER THOMAS I REV** (414)327-7610
2520 S 68th St Milwaukee WI 53219-2613 • SW • SP • Trinity West Allis WI • (414)321-3640 • (SL 1983 MDIV)

**KRUEGER WILLARD L REV** (623)566-8776
9634 W Wescott Dr Peoria AZ 85382-2627 • PSW • EM • (SPR 1969)

**KRUELLE CARL H REV** (302)453-0287
48 Sanford Dr Newark DE 19713-4029 • SE • SP • Our Redeemer Newark DE • (302)737-6176 • (SPR 1963)

**KRUG EUGENE O REV** (828)466-9958
205 Geitner Ave Newton NC 28658 • FG • EM • (SPR 1947)

**KRUG RONALD P REV** (414)367-0271
620 Pleasant Dr Hartland WI 53029-1242 • krugrb@execpc.com • SW • Assoc • St Paul Oconomowoc WI • (414)567-5001 • (SL 1973 MDIV)

**KRUGER DAVID F REV** (206)623-8193
Consultation To Clergy 911 Stewart St Seattle WA 98101 • dkrugerctc@aol.com • NOW • O Sp Min • Northwest Portland OR • (SL 1972 MDIV DMIN)

**KRUGER ROGER A DR** (402)572-5165
8042 Newport Ave Omaha NE 68122 • rkruger@radiks.net • NEB • Nebraska Seward NE • (SL 1968 MDIV DMIN)

**KRUGLER RICHARD A REV** (360)574-2057
900 NW 95th St Vancouver WA 98665-6427 • rkrugler@pacifier.com • NOW • EM • (SL 1949)

**KRUPP EARL F REV** (509)327-4146
6711 N Cedar Rd Apt 116 Spokane WA 99208-7124 • NOW • EM • (SL 1945)

**KRUPSKI OTTO F REV** (219)485-7920
9502 Mound Creek Cove Fort Wayne IN 46835 • ogkrupski@aol.com • IN • EM • (SPR 1952)

**KRUPSKI PHILIP J REV** (317)357-0519
7830 Softwood Ct Indianapolis IN 46239 • pkrupski@netusal.net • IN • Sn/Adm • St John Indianapolis IN • (317)352-9196 • (FW 1989 MDIV)

**KRUPSKI TIMOTHY P REV** (317)776-3782
227 Wintergreen Dr Noblesville IN 46060-6742 • tpkrupski@aol.com • IN • SP • Lord Of Life Westfield IN • (317)867-5673 • (FW 1982 MDIV)

**KRUSE DAVID A REV** (770)740-1349
140 Clipper Bay Dr Alpharetta GA 30005-4218 • dkruse3542@aol.com • EN • EM • (SL 1957 MDIV)

**KRUSE EUGENE REV** (660)784-3303
PO Box 235 Gilliam MO 65330 • ekruse@mid-mo.net • RM • EM • (SPR 1971 MDIV)

**KRUSE LOREN D REV** (320)875-4300
410 130 Ave SE Murdock MN 56271-9676 • MNN • EM • (SPR 1969 MDIV)

**KRUSE SCOTT D REV**
C/O St John Lutheran Church 621 Vine Hazleton PA 18201 • S • SP • St John Hazleton PA • (570)459-6423 • (SL 2000 MDIV)

**KUBE BERNHARD O REV** (541)459-5653
722 NW Tanglewood St Sutherlin OR 97479-9015 • bkube@wizzards.net • NOW • EM • (SPR 1964 MDIV)

**KUBOW ALAN D REV** (414)452-7129
1929 S 16th St Sheboygan WI 53081-5743 • alkubow@juno.com • SW • Assoc • Bethlehem Sheboygan WI • (920)452-4331 • (FW 1981 MDIV)

**KUCENSKI WILLIAM A REV** (815)562-8561
921 N Main St Rochelle IL 61068-1629 • kucenski@rochelle.net • NI • EM • (SL 1957 MDIV)

**KUCERA EDWARD A REV** (724)342-6130
2442 Romar Dr Hermitage PA 16148-2837 • S • EM • (SL 1959 MDIV)

**KUCERA JAN S REV** (419)448-9477
25 Orchard Park Tiffin OH 44883-3430 • OH • SP • Redeemer Tiffin OH • (419)447-7794 • (SPR 1974 MDIV MA)

**KUCERA JOHN S REV** (330)837-4540
3485 Briardale Dr NW Massillon OH 44646-2811 • S • EM • (SL 1946)

**KUCHARIK JOHN J REV**
2037 Inner Circle Dr Oviedo FL 32765-8708 • S • EM • (SL 1941)

**KUCHTA DAVID R REV** (814)725-9918
31 S Washington St North East PA 16428-1516 • fivek@velocity.net • EA • SP • St Paul North East PA • (814)725-4395 • (SL 1988 MDIV)

**KUDART LARRY R REV** (740)452-8832
507 Imlay Dr Zanesville OH 43701-2323 • kudart8@prodigy.net • OH • Sn/Adm • Trinity Zanesville OH • (740)453-0744 • (SL 1964 MDIV)

**KUDDES JEFFREY MARK REV** (870)548-2228
C/O St Pauls Ev Lutheran Chur PO Box 419 Gillett AR 72055-0419 • MDS • SP • St Paul Gillett AR* • (870)548-2554 • (SL 1992 MDIV)

**KUDICK RONALD J REV** (623)582-9882
18828 N 20th Dr Phoenix AZ 85027-5255 • PSW • EM • * • (SL 1960 MDIV)

**KUEBLER KARL E REV** (716)249-0043
500 Hahnemann Trl #115 Pittsford NY 14534-2356 • EA • EM • * • (SL 1936)

**KUEFNER ROBERT CHARLES JR. REV** (308)534-0218
615 S Elm St North Platte NE 69101-5230 • pastkey@kdsi.net • NEB • Sn/Adm • Beaut Savior North Platte NE • (308)534-7004 • (SL 1995 MDIV)

**KUEGELE FREDERICK R REV** (817)626-0132
1005 Springer Ave Fort Worth TX 76114-2730 • TX • EM • (SL 1941)

**KUEHN CLARENCE T REV** (215)283-7020
1701 Foulkeways Gwynedd PA 19436-1034 • ted.kuehn@gateway.net • NE • EM • (SL 1950 STM MED)

**KUEHN GILBERT A REV** (813)996-6041
23920 Nene Cir Land O Lakes FL 34639-3811 • kuehn@ebuffalo.net • FG • SP • Holy Trinity Lutz FL • (813)949-7173 • (SL 1969 MA)

**KUEHN RICHARD R REV** (919)682-6960
918 Englewood Ave Durham NC 27701-1152 • SE • Asst • Grace Durham NC • (919)682-6030 • (SL 1969 MDIV MED)

**KUEHN ROGER R REV** (925)757-5182
1201 Saint Francis Dr Antioch CA 94509-4626 • CNH • SP • Saint Andrew Antioch CA • (925)757-1672 • (SL 1969 MDIV)

**KUEHNE STEVEN J REV** (507)332-2512
22085 Dalton Ave Faribault MN 55021-7558 • MNS • Asst • Trinity Faribault MN • (507)334-6579 • (FW 1977 MDIV)

**KUEHNER RONALD K REV** (402)746-7303
840 N Franklin Red Cloud NE 68970 • revron@gpcom.net • NEB • SP • Zion Red Cloud NE • (402)746-2859 • (SL 1986 MS MDIV)

**KUEHNERT ARTHUR T REV** (505)722-0016
3715 Ciniza Dr Gallup NM 87301-4543 • RM • EM • (SL 1939 MDIV DD)

**KUEHNERT ELDOR P REV** (828)465-7144
403 10th Street Cir NW Conover NC 28613-2415 • eldorpkuehnert@aol.com • SE • EM • (SL 1945)

**KUEHNERT J MARK REV** (281)579-2729
1118 Barkston Dr Katy TX 77450-4220 • kuehnertho@aol.com • TX • SP • Christ Memorial Houston TX • (281)497-0250 • (SL 1963 MDIV DMIN)

**KUEHNERT PHILIP R REV** (907)456-7660
1170 Pickering Dr Fairbanks AK 99709-5762 • 75557.1653@compuserve.com • NOW • SP • Zion Fairbanks AK • (907)456-7660 • (SL 1969 MDIV MA THD)

**KUEHNERT RICHARD E REV** (504)464-6433
3144 Iowa Ave Kenner LA 70065 • rkuehnert@juno.com • MDS • EM • (SL 1957 MDIV DMIN)

**KUEKER KENNETH M REV** (513)868-3264
4102 Mill Crest Dr Hamilton OH 45011 • broken777@aol.com • OH • SP • Immanuel Hamilton OH • (513)893-6792 • (FW 1980 MDIV MSW)

**KUERSCHNER VICTOR H REV** (920)923-6316
431 Austin Ln Fond du Lac WI 54935 • kuersch@internetwis.com • SW • EM • (SL 1961)

**KUFAHL MARK CHARLES REV** (608)245-9732
1214 Melby Dr Madison WI 53704-1738 • stpaulluth@juno.com • SW • SP • St Paul Madison WI • (608)244-8077 • (SL 1989 MDIV STM)

**KUHFAL DAVID PAUL REV** (303)887-4855
109 F St Neligh NE 68756-1643 • dkuhfal@bloomnet.com • NEB • SP • Grace Neligh NE • (402)887-4791 • (SL 1992 MDIV)

**KUHL CHARLES W REV** (517)883-3471
486 9th St Sebewaing MI 48759-1209 • MI • EM • (SPR 1965)

**KUHLMAN BRENT W REV** (402)867-2916
31112 Church Rd Murdock NE 68407-2216 • bb55841@alltel.net • NEB • SP • Trinity Murdock NE • (402)867-2916 • (SL 1990 MDIV STM)

**KUHLMAN MARVIN W REV** (612)722-9611
1616 E 51st St Minneapolis MN 55417-1230 • MNS • EM • (SPR 1959 MS MS)

**KUHLMAN NATHAN A** (573)339-7313
417 Marrosean Dr #11 Cape Girardeau MO 63701 • MO • Assoc • St Andrew Cape Girardeau MO • (573)334-3200 • (SL 2000 MDIV)

**KUHLMAN PATRICK J REV**
3400 S Sare Rd Apt 1421 Bloomington IN 47401-8013 • IN • Asst • Faith Bloomington IN • (812)332-1668 • (SL 2000 MDIV)

**KUHLMANN KURT PAUL REV** (616)489-5124
PO Box 72 Burr Oak MI 49030-0072 • MI • SP • St John Burr Oak MI • (616)489-5539 • (SL 1995 MDIV)

**KUHLMANN MARVIN E REV** (816)331-1220
204 Johnston Pkwy Raymore MO 64083-9250 • MO • EM • (SL 1963 MDIV)

**KUHLMANN ROBERT T REV** (806)383-7700
325 Fairlane St Amarillo TX 79108-4215 • rek68@aol.com • TX • EM • (SL 1957 MST MDIV)

**KUHN DALE R REV** (314)962-6312
119 Waverly Pl Saint Louis MO 63119-3726 • dkuhn@careandcounseling.org • MO • Asst • Resurrection Saint Louis MO • (314)843-6633 • (SL 1973 MDIV MA STM)

**KUHN DONALD A REV** (734)847-3511
1168 Birchwood Dr Temperance MI 48182-9550 • MI • EM • (SPR 1956)

**KUHN GERALD E REV** (703)573-8367
2301 Barbour Rd Falls Church VA 22043-2941 • SE • EM • (SL 1949 MA MDIV DD)

**KUHN HENRY P REV** (712)284-2282
310 Lake St Alta IA 51002-1451 • shkuhn@pionet.net • IW • EM • (SL 1960 MDIV)

**KUHN ROBERT T REV** (636)394-4015
522 Oak Ridge Trails Ct Ballwin MO 63021-4414 • elderones@aol.com • MO • S Adm • Missouri Saint Louis MO • (314)317-4550 • (SL 1963 MDIV DD)

**KUHN WESLEY J REV** (601)388-5915
2293 Windsor Ct Biloxi MS 39532-3101 • weskay@aol.com • SO • EM • (SL 1945 MDIV)

**KUHNLE DAVID R REV** (712)545-9307
C/O St John Lutheran Church 30907 Coldwater Ave Honey Creek IA 51542-9739 • IW • SP • St John Honey Creek IA* • (712)545-3022 • (SL 1987 MDIV)

**KUKER LESTER H REV** (219)464-9865
2308 Linden Dr Valparaiso IN 46383-2333 • IN • EM • * • (SPR 1940)

**KUMM MICHAEL L** (605)582-7642
216 S Cardinal Dr Brandon SD 57005 • SD • SP • Blessed Redeemer Brandon SD • (605)582-2396 • (SL 2000 MDIV)

**KUMM SHAWN L REV** (307)742-8534
420 S 19th St Laramie WY 82070-4308 • lcmszion@usa.net • WY • SP • Zion Laramie WY • (307)745-9262 • (SL 1990 MDIV)

**KUMMER CARL M REV** (715)886-4123
1026 W 5th St Nekoosa WI 54457-1054 • NW • Sn/Adm • Bethlehem Nekoosa WI • (715)886-4081 • (SL 1961)

**KUMMER DAVID J REV**
C/O Grace Lutheran Church 1111 S Conyer St Visalia CA 93277 • CNH • Assoc • Grace Visalia CA • (559)734-7694 • (SL 2000 MDIV)

**KUMMER PAUL W REV** (904)654-5946
821 N Lakeside Dr Destin FL 32541-2039 • gracelutheran@destin • SO • SP • Grace Destin FL • (904)654-1679 • (SL 1989 MDIV)

**KUNKEL DANNY JOE REV** (509)765-3131
303 E Nelson Rd Moses Lake WA 98837-2365 • graceluth³moseslake@atnet.net • NOW • SP • Grace Destin FL* • (SL 1973 MDIV)

**KUNKEL LEE R REV** (830)997-8920
111 W Travis St Fredericksburg TX 78624-3850 • preach@ktc.com • TX • SP • Resurrection Fredericksburg TX • (830)997-9408 • (SL 1985 MDIV)

**KUNTZ ARNOLD G REV** (714)894-4282
5751 Richmond Ave Garden Grove CA 92845-2020 • PSW • EM • (SL 1950 MDIV LLD DD)

**KUNTZ JOHN P REV** (949)859-8838
22972 Springwater Lake Forest CA 92630-5417 • jimkuntz@aol.com • PSW • EM • (SL 1957 MDIV MA)

**KUNTZ SCOTT ALLAN REV** (412)822-7659
1105 Geyer Rd Pittsburgh PA 15209 • revsak@juno.com • EA • SP • Zion Pittsburgh PA • (412)621-2720 • (FW 1995 MDIV)

**KUNZ ROBERT E REV** (360)694-5686
1417 NE 63rd St Vancouver WA 98665-0208 • bob³kunz@juno.com • NOW • Inst C • Northwest Portland OR • (SPR 1952)

**KUNZ ROBERT T REV** (719)384-7400
1609 Raton Ave La Junta CO 81050-3420 • RM • SP • Trinity La Junta CO • (719)384-6555 • (SL 1954 MDIV)

**KUNZ SIEGFRIED REV** (318)746-2036
2410 Melrose Bossier City LA 71111 • SJKunz@aol.com • SO • SP • Immanuel Bossier City LA • (318)746-2215 • (SPR 1963 MA MDIV MA)

**KUNZE JEFFREY DAVID REV** (636)447-7972
10 Crescent Woods Dr St Peters MO 63376-3070 • jkunze@immanuelluth.org • MO • Assoc • Immanuel Saint Charles MO • (636)946-2656 • (SL 1991 MDIV)

**KUNZE JOHN RAYMOND REV**
6100 Vine St M69 Lincoln NE 68505 • jrkunze@juno.com • NEB • Asst • Messiah Lincoln NE • (402)489-3024 • (SL 1996 MDIV)

**KUPPLER ROBERT A REV** (908)604-2425
77 Keats Rd Basking Ridge NJ 07920-2618 • prbobkup@aol.com • NJ • SP • Somerset Hills Basking Ridge NJ • (908)766-2858 • (CSCQ 1977 MDIV)

**KUROWSKI PETER M DR** (573)796-2383
602 Crystal Ln California MO 65018 • MO • SP • St Paul California MO • (573)796-2735 • (SL 1978 MDIV DMIN)

**KURTH HOMER H REV** (660)674-2256
113 W Lincoln Alma MO 64001 • MO • EM • (SL 1939)

**KURTH RICHARD E REV** (317)329-1440
5632 Rains Ln Indianapolis IN 46254-5089 • richardkurth@messiah-indy.org • IN • SP • Messiah Indianapolis IN • (317)858-3733 • (SL 1970 MDIV)

**KURZ ERICH L REV** (816)668-2193
Rt 2 Box 104 Cole Camp MO 65325 • bekurz@juno.com • MO • SP • Holy Cross Cole Camp MO* • (FW 1988 MDIV)

**KURZ GEORGE E REV** (206)878-5619
1116 S 244th Pl Des Moines WA 98198-3891 • NOW • EM • * • (SL 1939 MST)

**KURZ JOEL R REV** (330)270-5823
4200 Pembrook Apt 9 Youngstown OH 44515 • S • SP • Concordia Youngstown OH • (330)792-1805 • (FW 1997 MDIV)

**KURZWEG BERNHARD F REV** (850)893-3732
3639 Barbary Dr Tallahassee FL 32308-3001 • FG • EM • (SL 1951 STM)

**KUSEL RONALD J REV** (562)425-2186
3520 Ladoga Ave Long Beach CA 90808-2952 • www.firstlutheran@juno.com • PSW • Sn/Adm • First Long Beach CA • (562)437-8532 • (SL 1964 MDIV DMIN)

**KUSTER THEODORE F REV** (612)825-1256
3446 1st Ave S Minneapolis MN 55408-4505 • theokuster@aol.com • MNS • S Miss • Minnesota South Burnsville MN • (CQ 1982 MA)

**KUTSCHER LEONARD R REV** (314)842-5731
5118 Kennerly Pines Ct Saint Louis MO 63128-2771 • MO • EM • (SL 1956 MDIV MA)

**KUTTER FREDERICK M REV** (320)597-2132
26245 County Rd 9 Richmond MN 56368-8026 • MNN • SP • Immanuel Albany MN • (612)845-2620 • (FW 1986 MDIV)

**KUZNIK ROLLIN F REV** (847)515-1801
12951 Applewood Dr Huntley IL 60142 • saintj-alg@worldnet.att.net • NI • Sn/Adm • St John Algonquin IL • (847)658-9300 • (SL 1968 MDIV)

**KWON YOUNG MAN REV**
3756 Cardiff Ave - Apt 321 Los Angeles CA 90034-8811 • PSW • D Miss • Pacific Southwest Irvine CA • (949)854-3232 • (CQ 1995)

## L

**L HEUREUX CALVIN LEROY REV**
C/O Grace Lutheran Church 1111 W Lincoln St Lyons KS 67554-3023 • blessdec@midusa.net • KS • SP • Grace Lyons KS • (316)257-2204 • (FW 1991 MDIV)

**LA DASSOR LARRY D REV** (218)694-6258
129 6th St NE Bagley MN 56621-1004 • MNN • 05/2000 • (SL 1967 MDIV)

**LA FONTAINE RALPH E REV** (701)250-1350
3405 Montreal St #3 Bismarck ND 58501-0458 • ND • EM • (CQ 1958 MDIV)

**LABORE RICHARD D REV** (314)961-7283
1421 Woodhue Dr Saint Louis MO 63126-1334 • rlabore@ci.crestwood.mo.us • MO • Tchr • LHS South Saint Louis MO • (314)631-1400 • (SL 1958 MDIV STM PHD)

**LAABS BRUCE H REV** (320)238-2338
216 Mc Leod Ave N Plato MN 55370-5427 • MNS • SP • St John Plato MN • (320)238-2338 • (SL 1985 MDIV)

**LAABS ERNST A REV** (734)525-4186
28910 Plymouth Rd Livonia MI 48150-2337 • OH • EM • (SPR 1940)

**LAATSCH JAMES F REV** (608)635-2866
PO Box 47 Arlington WI 53911-0047 • SW • EM • (SL 1967 MDIV)

**LAATSCH JOHN V REV** (715)745-4710
W2253 State Highway 22 Pulcifer WI 54124-9407 • NW • SP • St John Pulcifer WI* • (715)745-6464 • (FW 1986 MDIV)

**LABRENZ PAUL E REV** (510)523-7314
812 Lincoln Ave Alameda CA 94501-3422 • CNH • EM • * • (SPR 1964 DMIN)

**LACH NOBLE P REV**
147 Creekshire Cres Newport News VA 23603-1352 • EN • EM • * • (SL 1963 MDIV)

**LAEDER RICHARD P REV**
2133 Wayland Dr Lansing MI 48917-1370 • dicklaeder@aalweb.net • MI • SP • Trinity Lansing MI • (517)372-1631 • (FW 1986 MDIV)

**LAESCH NORMAN T REV** (949)951-8148
24721 Daphne E Mission Viejo CA 92691-4723 • padreviejo@msn.com • PSW • Tchr • Lutheran HS/Orange C Orange CA • (714)998-5151 • (SL 1955 MDIV)

**LAESCH THEODORE L SR. DR** (931)456-6616
112 Britton Ln Fairfield Glade TN 38558-8639 • NI • EM • (SL 1960 STM MDIV DD LLD)

**LAESCH THEODORE L JR. REV** (408)347-8273
1413 Danby Ave San Jose CA 95132 • tmlaesch@juno.com • CNH • SP • Christ The Life San Jose CA • (408)259-1670 • (SL 1998 STM MDIV)

**LAETSCH LEONARD C REV** (618)654-7891
1022 8th St Highland IL 62249-1602 • SI • SP • Hope Highland IL • (618)654-7891 • (SL 1967 MDIV)

**LAHRMAN WILLIAM C REV** (616)837-6020
PO Box 203 Nunica MI 49448-0203 • blahrman@juno.com • MI • SP • St Luke Nunica MI • (616)837-6059 • (FW 1983 MDIV)

**LAI HENRY H S REV** (510)471-1856
2621 Nevada St Union City CA 94587 • CNH • SP • First Trinity Oakland CA • (510)534-1630 • (CQ 1987)

**LAKAMP BRUCE REV** (309)527-4334
C/O Trinity Lutheran Church 595 W 3rd St El Paso IL 61738-1006 • CI • SP • Trinity El Paso IL • (309)527-4333 • (SPR 1968 MDIV)

**LAKSO THOMAS E REV** (870)241-3778
PO Box 184 Ulm AR 72170-0184 • tllakso@futura.net • MDS • SP • Zion Ulm AR • (870)241-3778 • (FW 1983 MED MDIV)

**LAMB JAMES I REV** (515)382-2077
1229 S G Ave Bldg B Nevada IA 50201 • jlamb@lutheransforlife.org • IW • 09/1998 • (SL 1982 MDIV DMIN)

**LAMB RICHARD EUGEN REV**
2521 52nd St Lubbock TX 79413-4401 • ricalamb@juno.com • TX • Inst C • Texas Austin TX • (SL 1996 MDIV)

**LAMBART ERIC A REV** (517)797-3802
202 S Charles St Saginaw MI 48602-2505 • 75640.3340@compuserve.com • MI • Asst • Holy Cross Saginaw MI • (517)793-9723 • (SL 1978 MDIV)

**LAMBART KURT E REV** (734)513-9703
28484 Balmoral Garden City MI 48135 • sklambart@aol.com • MI • Assoc • St Matthew Westland MI • (734)425-0260 • (SL 1996 MDIV)

**LAMKIN TIMOTHY HAROLD SR. REV** (715)526-9036
W8089 County Road A Shawano WI 54166-5944 • lamkin5@frontiernet.net • NW • SP • St Jakobi Shawano WI • (715)524-4347 • (FW 1995 MDIV)

**LAMMERT RICHARD A REV** (219)484-2889
3 Coverdale Pl Fort Wayne IN 46825-4928 • thelammerts@mail.fwi.com • IN • SHS/C • Indiana Fort Wayne IN • (FW 1998 MDIV)

**LAMONT BRUCE B REV**
C/O Saint Mark Lutheran Church 600 Stevens Dr Wausau WI 54401-2977 • NW • SP • St Mark Wausau WI • (715)848-5511 • (SL 1987)

**LAMPE GARY A REV**
12670 Bay Shore Dr Florissant MO 63033-5103 • MO • Asst • Gethsemane Saint Louis MO • (314)631-7331 • (SL 1978 MDIV)

**LAMPE KENDALL M REV**
1612 P Ave Clarinda IA 51632-9719 • IW • SP • Immanuel Clarinda IA • (712)542-3524 • (CQ 1988 MED)

**LAMPE KENNETH E REV** (870)425-3550
231 Cody Creek Dr Mountain Home AR 72653-5580 • kel@mtnhome.com • MDS • Sn/Adm • Redeemer Mountain Home AR • (870)425-6071 • (SL 1973 MDIV)

**LAMPELLA THOMAS A REV** (636)949-8534
3345 W Adams St Saint Charles MO 63301-0506 • tlampella@aol.com • MO • Sn/Adm • Our Savior Saint Charles MO • (636)947-8010 • (SL 1984 MDIV)

**LAMPITT CARL R REV** (256)352-5216
1629 Edmondson Rd NE Hanceville AL 35077-5552 • SO • EM • (SPR 1962 MDIV)

**LAMPMAN DAVID PAUL REV** (513)232-5269
2437 Coveyrun South Cincinnati OH 45230-1477 • cincyrev@fuse.net • OH • SP • St Paul Cincinnati OH • (513)271-4147 • (SC 1995 MDIV)

**LANDGRAF PAUL D REV** (319)323-6812
805 Tremont Ave Davenport IA 52803-5636 • landgraf@ia.freei.net • IE • D Miss • Iowa East Marion IA • (SL 1990 MDIV STM)

**LANDSKROENER JOHN C REV** (419)385-6771
3122 Winston Blvd Toledo OH 43614-3846 • OH • EM • (SL 1952)

**LANDSKROENER TIMOTHY J REV** (440)964-6164
1015 Allen Ave Ashtabula OH 44004-2543 • OH • SP • Zion Ashtabula OH • (440)964-9483 • (SL 1994 MDIV)

**LANDSMANN LON EMERSON REV**
114 S Thompson St Pratt KS 67124-2917 • revlands@juno.com • KS • SP • Our Savior Pratt KS* • (316)672-6203 • (FW 1994 MDIV)

**LANE ROBERT A REV** (406)256-0570
22 Nightingale Dr Billings MT 59101 • RLane20614@aol.com • MT • SP • Hope Billings MT • (406)245-4605 • (SL 1998 MDIV)

**LANE STEPHEN S REV** (641)673-3321
2368 Merino Ave Oskaloosa IA 52577 • slane@kdsi.net • IE • SP • St John Oskaloosa IA • (515)673-6546 • (FW 1983 MDIV STM)

**LANG EDWARD M REV** (314)849-3393
9120 Fort Donelson Dr Saint Louis MO 63123-1921 • EdLangShowMe@juno.com • MO • D Ex/S • Missouri Saint Louis MO* • (314)317-4550 • (SL 1959 MDIV)

**LANG MARCUS T REV** (707)987-3930
20352 Powder Horn Rd Middletown CA 95461-8724 • CNH • EM • * • (SL 1945 MDIV MA)

**LANG WALTER J H REV** (206)241-8988
1239 SW132nd Ln Apt 821 Seattle WA 98146-3119 • whjlang@juno.com • NOW • EM • * • (SL 1937)

**LANGE ALVIN H REV** (573)893-3643
623 Sue Dr Jefferson City MO 65109-0556 • ahlange@juno.com • MO • EM • * • (SL 1962 STM MDIV)

**LANGE EDWIN F REV** (512)629-4859
665 Floral B 3 New Braunfels TX 78130 • TX • EM • * • (SL 1937)

**LANGE ERIC T REV** (503)492-4004
4181 NE El Camino Dr Gresham OR 97030-1750 • rdmr-lcms@juno.com • NOW • SP • Redeemer Gresham OR • (503)665-5414 • (FW 1988 MDIV STM)

**LANGE GEORGE H REV** (219)497-7042
1221 Big Horn Pl Fort Wayne IN 46825-3419 • ghlange@fwi.com • IN • EM • (SPR 1960)

**LANGE HARVEY D REV** (262)783-5746
17540 Windemere Rd Brookfield WI 53045-2646 • hlange0412@aol.com • SW • EM • (SL 1955 MDIV STM THD)

**LANGE JAMES A REV** (314)845-3794
3772 Southern Manor Dr Saint Louis MO 63125 • jglange@dellnet.com • MO • EM • (CQ 1982)

**LANGE JONATHAN C REV** (314)776-4993
38 Lindorf Belleville IL 62223 • MO • Asst • Messiah Saint Louis MO • (314)772-4474 • (SL 1997)

**LANGE JONATHAN GEORGE REV** (307)789-1687
148 Springbrook Dr Evanston WY 82930-4768 • jglange@allwest.net • WY • SP • Our Saviour Evanston WY • (307)789-0042 • (FW 1990 MDIV)

**LANGE MICHAEL R REV** (925)516-4196
971 Oak St Brentwood CA 94513-1242 • 72642.3450@compuserve.com • CNH • SP • Resurrection Brentwood CA • (925)634-5180 • (SL 1988 MDIV)

**LANGE PETER K REV** (785)379-5268
734 SE Tecumseh Rd Tecumseh KS 66542-9313 • pklange@cjnetworks.com • KS • Sn/Adm • St John Topeka KS • (785)354-7132 • (FW 1988 MDIV STM)

**LANGE ROBERT E REV** (636)349-8024
1605 Littleton Ct Fenton MO 63026-3014 • robertelan@aol.com • MO • EM • (SL 1959 MDIV)

**LANGE ROGER A REV** (218)589-8810
RR 1 Box 233 11695 Bankers Dr Dalton MN 56324-9748 • revnms@prtel.com • MNS • EM • (SL 1961)

**LANGE STEVEN A REV** (708)460-5264
15661 Peachtree Dr Orland Park IL 60462-7717 • revslange@aol.com • S • SP • Living Word Orland Park IL • (708)403-9673 • (SL 1982 MDIV)

**LANGE THOMAS MARK REV** (248)476-7475
20916 Birchwood St Farmington MI 48336 • btlange@wcic.cioe.com • MI • SP • Prince Peace Farmington Hills MI • (248)553-3380 • (SL 1995 MDIV)

**LANGE WILLIAM H REV** (309)688-3635
2611 W Westport Rd Peoria IL 61615-4111 • wlange@ntslink.net • CI • EM • (SL 1954 MDIV)

**LANGEMO MARTIN S REV** (320)632-3234
400 4th St NE Little Falls MN 56345-2725 • MNN • SP • Zion Little Falls MN • (320)632-5792 • (SPR 1964)

**LANGEWISCH DAVID JOHN REV** (303)989-1475
11230 W Ford Dr Lakewood CO 80226-3766 • RM • Sn/Adm • Bethlehem Lakewood CO • (303)238-7676 • (SL 1991 MDIV)

**LANGEWISCH JOHN E REV** (517)832-2629
1683 E Miller Rd Midland MI 48640-8942 • messiahbc@aol.com • MI • Assoc • Messiah Midland MI • (517)835-7143 • (SL 1974 MDIV)

**LANGHANS C F REV** (812)659-3263
PO Box 386 Lyons IN 47443-0386 • IN • EM • (SL 1942)

**LANGHOFF DONALD H REV** (217)324-5926
810 N Monroe St Litchfield IL 62056-1539 • shepherd@npwt.net • SI • Sn/Adm • Zion Litchfield IL • (217)324-2033 • (SPR 1971 MDIV)

**LAPACKA THOMAS J REV** (661)298-5706
26832 Madigan Dr Santa Clarita CA 91351 • PSW • SP • Prince Of Peace Castaic CA • (661)298-5706 • (FW 1998 MA)

**LAPP ORLEN W REV** (613)735-6790
PO Box 854 Randburg 2125 SOUTH AFRICA • EN • EM • (SL 1958 MA)

**LAREVA JAMES P REV** (714)997-7397
363 N Fern St Orange CA 92867-7806 • PSW • EM • (SPR 1961 MDIV)

**LARRABEE EUGENE EDWIN REV** (507)867-0012
Rt 1 Box 90 Wykoff MN 55990 • MNN • EM • (SPR 1949)

**LARSEN JAMES F REV** (661)398-2176
5618 Halifax St Bakersfield CA 93309-4532 • CNH • SP • Grace Bakersfield CA • (661)324-4315 • (FW 1986 MDIV)

**LARSEN LARRY J REV**
4825 E Bay Dr Clearwater FL 34624-6800 • FG • P Df • Rogate Deaf Clearwater FL • (813)536-3862 • (SPR 1976 MDIV)

**LARSEN PETER E REV** (734)996-3413
2394 Delaware Ct Ann Arbor MI 48103 • lcmlarsp@ccaa.edu • MI • D Ex/S • Michigan Ann Arbor MI • (SL 1965 MDIV DMIN)

**LARSEN ROLF E REV** (830)895-1772
700 Mockingbird Ln Kerrville TX 78028-2927 • rellcl@ktc.com • TX • SP • Holy Cross Kerrville TX • (830)257-4433 • (FW 1982 MDIV)

**LARSEN STEVEN M REV**
C/O Messiah Lutheran Church 3600 Northwest Expwy Oklahoma City OK 73112-4410 • OK • Sn/Adm • Messiah Oklahoma City OK • (405)946-0681 • (FW 1983 MDIV)

**LARSEN WILLIAM F REV** (402)726-2546
PO Box 7 Fairfield NE 68938-0007 • NEB • SP • Shep Of Plains Fairfield NE • (402)726-2224 • (FW 1991 MDIV)

**LARSON CLIFFORD G REV** (361)992-5588
6202 Durant Cir Corpus Christi TX 78414-3016 • cprest@aol.com • TX • EM • (SL 1951)

**LARSON DARYL N REV** (813)376-4477
3218 Player Dr New Port Richey FL 34655-2120 • FG • Inst C • Florida-Georgia Orlando FL • (FW 1988 MA)

**LARSON ELMER C REV** (920)898-4784
2117 Randolph Ave New Holstein WI 53061-1033 • SW • EM • (SPR 1953)

**LARSON JAMES E REV** (316)431-6512
RR 2 Box 285 Chanute KS 66720-9441 • KS • EM • (SL 1957 MDIV)

**LARSON JOHN R REV** (303)420-8918
9348 W 67th Ave Arvada CO 80004-3016 • apastor@peacelutheran.net • RM • Assoc • Peace Arvada CO • (303)424-4454 • (SL 1983 MDIV)

**LARSON KENNETH E REV** (561)967-4140
232 Henthorne Dr Palm Springs FL 33461-2010 • ken³larson42@hotmail.com • FG • SP • Redeemer West Palm Beach FL • (561)832-8705 • (FW 1977 MDIV DD)

**LARSON KURT RUSSELL REV**
2407 N Myrtle St Davenport IA 52804-1817 • kmdal@msn.com • IE • SP • Risen Christ Davenport IA • (319)386-2342 • (FW 1992 MDIV)

**LARSON MARK C REV** (303)695-8001
Rocky Mountain District Office PO Box 441395 Aurora CO 80044-1395 • RM • Risen Christ Davenport IA • (319)386-2342 • (SL 1988 MDIV)

**LARSON MATTHEW JAMES REV** (580)623-4884
501 Skyview Dr Watonga OK 73772-2823 • mjlarson1@juno.com • OK • SP • Mount Calvary Watonga OK • (580)623-5099 • (SL 1997 MDIV)

**LARSON RAYMOND EVERET SR. REV**
100th ASG CMR 415 Box 3656 APO AE 09114 • raymond.larson@cmtymail.100asg.army.mil • NW • M Chap • North Wisconsin Wausau WI • (SPR 1975)

**LARSON STEPHEN E REV** (509)786-3523
815 Luther Ln Prosser WA 99350-1549 • messiah@bentonrea.com • NOW • SP • Messiah Prosser WA • (509)786-2011 • (FW 1981 MDIV)

**LARSON THOMAS W REV** (636)462-6321
222 John St Troy MO 63379-1342 • eccleneedle@juno.com • MO • SP • Trinity Troy MO • (636)528-4999 • (SL 1982 MDIV)

**LARSON VINCENT S REV** (719)632-3994
2025 Alpine Dr Colorado Springs CO 80909 • RM • SP • Resurrection Colorado Springs CO • (719)392-7045 • (SPR 1973 MSFLM MDIV)

**LARSON WALLACE A REV** (218)233-2327
1022 Belsly Blvd Apt 102 Moorhead MN 56560-5018 • MNN • EM • (LS 1953 MDIV)

**LASCH MARK FREDERICK REV**
9222 N Garnett Rd Owasso OK 74055-4424 • TX • Assoc • Hope Friendswood TX • (281)482-7943 • (SL 2000 MDIV)

**LASHLEY DALE L REV** (909)927-0921
42112 Bancroft Way Hemet CA 92544-8403 • laledashly@juno.com • PSW • Assoc • Prince Peace Hemet CA • (909)925-6121 • (SL 1993 MDIV)

**LASKY DALE G REV** (219)462-3591
2259 Hayes Leonard Rd Valparaiso IN 46385 • IN • EM • (SL 1954 STM MDIV PHD)

**LASSANSKE DENNIS L REV** (616)755-6226
3042 Chapel Ct Muskegon MI 49441-3751 • dlassans@remc4.k12.mi.us • MI • SP • Trinity Muskegon MI • (616)755-1292 • (SL 1972 MDIV)

**LASSANSKE RAYMOND O REV** (904)432-8194
6414 Fairview Dr Pensacola FL 32505-2059 • rlassanske@aol.com • SO • EM • (SL 1945)

**LASSMAN ERNIE V REV** (206)526-8820
7056 35th Ave NE Seattle WA 98115-5917 • NOW • Assoc • Messiah Seattle WA • (206)524-0024 • (FW 1978 MDIV STM)

**LAST DAVID A REV** (256)736-6018
405 13th St SE Cullman AL 35055 • fenixdal@yahoo.com • SO • Sn/Adm • St Paul Cullman AL • (256)734-3575 • (SL 1978 MDIV)

**LATHAM MARK E REV**
St John Lutheran Church 1128 Poplar St Buhl ID 83316-1636 • revswim@aol.com • NOW • SP • St John Buhl ID • (208)543-4282 • (FW 1985 MDIV)

**LATTERNER RICHARD RAY REV**
13075 Florida Ct Apple Valley MN 55124-7943 • MNS • Minnesota South Burnsville MN • (FW 1994 MDIV)

**LATZKE STEVEN DONALD REV** (952)368-9571
855 Walnut Pl Chaska MN 55318 • slatzke@excite.com • MNS • Assoc • Living Christ Chanhassen MN • (952)934-5110 • (SL 2000 MA)

**LAU DONALD W REV** (612)866-1941
6326 Vincent Ave S Richfield MN 55423-1024 • MNS • EM • (TH 1945)

**LAU SHIU MING REV**
12134 Beckford Est Maryland Heights MO 63043 • MO • O Miss • Missouri Saint Louis MO • (314)317-4550 • (CQ 1999)

**LAUE DAVID E REV** (218)773-8775
16 James Cir SE East Grand Forks MN 56721-2272 • MNN • SP • First East Grand Forks MN* • (218)773-0181 • (SL 1991 MDIV)

**LAUE RONALD H REV** (605)225-0844
PO Box 787 Aberdeen SD 57402-0787 • SD • Sn/Adm • St Paul Aberdeen SD* • (605)225-1847 • (SL 1963 MDIV)

**LAUER JAMES P REV** (757)850-8649
214 Woodburn Dr Hampton VA 23664-1961 • lauerjpb@aol.com • SE • EM • * • (SL 1960 MDIV)

**LAUER PAUL A REV** (231)775-2949
1822 Chestnut Street Cadillac MI 49601 • pnalauer@netonecom.net • MI • SP • Emmanuel Cadillac MI • (231)775-3261 • (SL 1991 MDIV)

**LAUFER RALPH E REV** (618)458-7177
C/O Holy Cross Lutheran Church PO Box 7 Renault IL 62279-0007 • rlaufer@htc.net • SI • SP • Holy Cross Renault IL • (618)458-6680 • (SL 1986 MDIV)

**LAUGAVITZ MARK F REV** (660)668-3492
RR 2 Box 230A Cole Camp MO 65325-9273 • MO • SP • Mount Hulda Cole Camp MO • (660)668-3492 • (SL 1980 MDIV)

**LAUNHARDT LOUIS H REV** (573)243-7338
1025 Bella Vista Dr Jackson MO 63755-7846 • launhrdt@showme.net • MO • EM • (SL 1958 MDIV)

**LAURENT GULFREY N REV** (310)635-7610
19316 Northwood Ave Carson CA 90746-2737 • pstr2gwen@aol.com • PSW • EM • (GB 1941 MED)

**LAUTENSCHLAGER ADAM D REV** (805)526-9505
1524 Glacier St Simi Valley CA 93063-3131 • PSW • EM • (SL 1940 MA)

**LAUTERBACH W EUGENE REV** (317)784-4339
130 Canna Rd Indianapolis IN 46217-3831 • genlau@aol.com • IN • SP • Emmaus Indianapolis IN • (317)632-1486 • (SL 1955)

**LAUX JOHN A REV** (309)764-0287
Holy Cross Lutheran Church 4107 21st Ave Moline IL 612654580 • CI • Sn/Adm • Holy Cross Moline IL • (309)764-9720 • (FW 1987 MDIV)

**LAVCEK EMIL REV** (724)335-2483
212 Sunset Dr Lower Burrell PA 15068-3221 • S • EM • (SL 1945)

**LAVRENZ MARK E REV** (417)326-3907
PO Box 5 704 E Lindon St Bolivar MO 65613-0005 • rnss4@microcure.net • MO • SP • Zion Bolivar MO* • (417)326-5506 • (FW 1991 MDIV)

**LAW RICHARD M REV** (617)472-9643
10 Mount Vernon St Quincy MA 02169-1631 • richlaw@ix.netcom.com • NE • Assoc • Wollaston Quincy MA • (617)773-5482 • (HK 1969 MSW)

**LAWRENCE WAYNE E REV** (718)528-7084
116-12 204th St Saint Albans NY 11412-3252 • EN • SP • Redeemer Saint Albans NY • (718)528-7084 • (SL 1998 MDIV)

**LAWRENZ RONALD H REV** (713)460-5431
2830 Stetson Houston TX 77043 • TX • EM • (SPR 1950 MDIV)

**LAWSON GARY REV** (216)381-5778
4797 Lindsey Ln Richmond Heights OH 44143-2926 • OH • P Df • Christ Deaf Cleveland OH • (216)781-8571 • (FW 1984 MDIV)

**LAWSON SCOTT WILLIAM REV** (909)679-6007
29984 Oakbridge Dr Sun City CA 92586-4449 • sjlawsonfaml.@yahoo.com • PSW • SP • Good Shepherd Menifee CA • (909)672-6675 • (FW 1991 MDIV)

**LE BLANC ROBERT EARL REV** (512)782-3015
508 S Wells St Edna TX 77957-3741 • TX • SP • St Paul Edna TX • (361)782-3037 • (FW 1996 MDIV)

**LE FEBER GERARD FRANK REV** (716)372-9220
1545 Four Mile Rd Allegany NY 14706-9798 • lefeeb@localnet.com • EA • SP • St John Allegany NY • (716)373-0025 • (SL 1972 MDIV MA)

**LE PERE RONALD P REV** (440)953-8350
8032 Brentwood Rd Mentor OH 44060-5508 • lepere@juno.com • OH • SP • Faith Mentor OH • (440)255-2229 • (SL 1971 MDIV)

**LEACH RONALD D REV** (303)426-0309
8433 Chase St Arvada CO 80003-1433 • RM • EM • (SPR 1958)

**LEARY KELLY J REV** (715)536-3859
1002 E 8th St Merrill WI 54452-1111 • veritas9@juno.com • NW • Assoc • St John Merrill WI • (715)536-4722 • (SL 1995 MDIV)

**LEAVITT ROGER GLEN REV** (402)371-5043
1007 N 10th St Norfolk NE 68701 • NEB • Assoc • Christ Norfolk NE • (402)371-1210 • (FW 1996 MDIV)

**LEAVITT ROSSETTER T REV** (940)553-3816
2709 Oaklawn Dr Vernon TX 76384-6416 • TX • SP • St Paul Vernon TX • (940)552-2495 • (SL 1981 MDIV)

**LEBAHN MERLE E REV** (952)431-6776
7770 Glenda Ct Apple Valley MN 55124-6330 • MNS • EM • (CQ 1984 MAR)

**LEBER DONALD E REV** (909)987-5484
6950 Center Ave Alta Loma CA 91701-5265 • revleber@aol.com • PSW • O Sp Min • Pacific Southwest Irvine CA • (949)854-3232 • (SPR 1963)

**LECKBAND JEROME P** (402)329-4262
RR #2 Box 544 Foster NE 68737 • NEB • SP • Trinity Foster NE • (402)582-4587 • (FW 2000 MDIV)

**LECKBAND MARK THOMAS REV** (319)477-3785
102 N Spruce Ave Garrison IA 52229-9616 • leckbnd@netins.net • IE • SP • St Mark Garrison IA* • (319)477-5141 • (SL 1996 MDIV)

**LECKBAND ROYCE C REV** (507)662-5003
401 S Griffin St Lakefield MN 56150-9455 • MNS • EM • * • (SPR 1964)

**LECKE JOSEPHA H REV** (618)244-7521
706 N 18th St Mount Vernon IL 62864-2867 • jlecke@isbe.accessus.net • SI • SP • Faith Mount Vernon IL • (618)242-4330 • (FW 1978 MDIV)

**LEDBETTER RANDY W REV** (281)485-7955
PO Box 788 Pearland TX 77588-0788 • ranled19@idt.net • TX • SP • Mount Olive Houston TX • (281)922-5673 • (FW 1986 MDIV)

**LEDEBUHR ARTHUR A REV** (423)843-9853
1911 Crystal Lake Ln Hixson TN 37343-3513 • MDS • EM • (SL 1949)

**LEDER RONALD L REV** (541)782-3756
76428 Ks Dr Oakridge OR 97463-9508 • NOW • SP • St Luke Oakridge OR • (541)782-2030 • (SL 1958 MDIV)

**LEDIC PETER REV**
C/O Messiah Lutheran Church 2305 Camino Tassajara Danville CA 94526-4402 • pjl603@adamswells.com • EN • SP • Messiah Danville CA • (925)736-2270 • (FW 1982 MDIV)

**LEDOGAR WALTER A REV** (708)349-8085
C/O Christ Lutheran Church 14700 S 94th Ave Orland Park IL 60462-2656 • ledo@mc.net • NI • Sn/Adm • Christ Orland Park IL • (708)349-0431 • (SL 1964 MDIV)

**LEE DANIEL W REV** 011-852-2140-6368
Flat F Block 5 Cotton Tree Ct New Town Plz Shatin Ctr Street Shatin NT ARGENTINA • dwclee@yahoo.com.hk • NOW • S Miss • Northwest Portland OR • (HK 1978 MED MED)

**LEE DONG KIE REV** (949)559-4376
2 Willow Tree Ln Irvine CA 92612 • donklee@juno.com • PSW • D Miss • Northwest Portland OR • (CQ 1997 MA)

**LEE DU PYO REV** (909)924-8419
11650 Perris Blvd Moreno Valley CA 92557-6536 • PSW • D Miss • Grace Korean Moreno Valley CA • (909)924-4688 • (FW 1989 MDIV DMIN)

**LEE JEFFREY A REV** (763)786-5344
7820 Eastwood Rd Mounds View MN 55112-4311 • glorychurch@lynxus.com • MNS • SP • King Of Glory Blaine MN • (763)784-4229 • (FW 1987 MDIV)

**LEE KIRK E REV** (218)338-5351
PO Box 66 Parkers Prairie MN 56361-0066 • MNN • SP • Immanuel Parkers Prairie MN • (218)338-2511 • (SL 1989 MDIV)

**LEE KWANG MAN REV** (213)387-3499
C/O Young Kwang Luth Church 1233 S Vermont Ave Los Angeles CA 90006-2714 • PSW • D Miss • Young Kwang Los Angeles CA • (213)387-3499 • (CQ 1995)

**LEE R KEITH REV** (828)726-8355
1701 Greenbrooke Rd Hudson NC 28638-9581 • klee@conninc.com • SE • EM • (SPR 1956 MDIV)

**LEE SIMMON MYUNG REV** (510)635-1710
955 Karol Way #15 San Leandro CA 94577 • CNH • D Miss • Calif/Nevada/Hawaii San Francisco CA • (415)468-2336 • (CQ 1998 MTH)

**LEE SOO MIN REV** (818)762-9506
1211 S Mariposa Ave #4 Los Angeles CA 90006-3234 • PSW • D Miss • Young Kwang Los Angeles CA • (213)387-3499 • (CQ 1990)

**LEE STEPHEN CLIFFGARD REV** (877)487-1717
C/O Peace Officer Ministries PO Box 63177 Colorado Springs CO 80962-3177 • stevelee.pom@juno.com • RM • O Sp Min • Shepherd Hills Littleton CO • (303)798-0711 • (FW 1992 MDIV)

**LEE SUK HAE REV**
7822 Sutter Ln #3 Annandale VA 22003 • kleeh@concentric.net • SE • D Miss • Light/World Annandale VA • (703)916-7881 • (CQ 1998)

**LEE YONG MO REV** (619)497-0524
3944 Georgia St San Diego CA 92103-3505 • PSW • D Miss • Pacific Southwest Irvine CA • (949)854-3232 • (CQ 1995 MTH PHD)

**LEELAND DAVID A REV** (512)252-0788
810 Indian Run Dr Pflugerville TX 78660-3971 • lutheran@swbell.net • TX • SP • Hope Austin TX • (512)926-8574 • (SL 1981 MDIV)

**LEEMAN KARL K REV** (573)334-7078
187 Estate Dr #159 Cape Girardeau MO 63701-9494 • MO • EM • (SPR 1963 MDIV)

**LEENERTS ROGER W REV** (314)894-0551
5072 Peyton Place Ct Saint Louis MO 63128-2901 • NI • EM • (SPR 1963)

**LEHENBAUER ALBERT W REV** (847)394-3862
1313 Village Dr Arlington Hts IL 60004-8105 • vml1313@juno.com • NI • EM • (BTSEM 1943 DED)

**LEHENBAUER JOEL D REV** (636)583-5672
1776 Oak Parc Union MO 63084-3607 • ic³lehenbjd@lcms.org • MO • S Ex/S • Missouri Saint Louis MO • (314)317-4550 • (SL 1984 MDIV STM)

**LEHENBAUER JOHN C REV** (502)921-2443
471 Peaceful Way Shepherdsville KY 40165 • jlky@juno.com • IN • SP • Divine Savior Shepherdsville KY • (502)543-2905 • (FW 1986 MDIV)

**LEHENBAUER OSMAR O DR** (219)490-1386
1306 Big Horn Pl Fort Wayne IN 46825-3420 • ozkay1@home.com • IN • EM • (SPR 1954 LLD)

**LEHENBAUER RONALD P REV** (573)365-4913
501 Cherokee Rd Lake Ozark MO 65049-9335 • revron@dam.net • MO • SP • Christ King Lake Ozark MO • (573)365-5212 • (SL 1991 MDIV)

**LEHENBAUER RONALD W REV** (718)359-7022
150-12 28th Ave Flushing NY 11354-1550 • is40v31@aol.com • AT • SP • St John Flushing NY • (718)463-2959 • (SL 1967 STM DMIN)

**LEHENBAUER VICTOR H REV** (702)648-9029
1341 Nye St Las Vegas NV 89106-1986 • vmlbauer@earthlink.net • PSW • EM • (SL 1954 MDIV)

**LEHENBAUER WALTER REV** (218)729-5468
6310 Maple Grove Rd Cloquet MN 55720-9250 • wlehenba@cpinternet.com • MNN • SP • Hope Cloquet MN • (218)729-6380 • (FW 1981 MDIV)

**LEHFELDT DALE C REV** (956)565-3444
701 W 3rd St Mercedes TX 78570-3005 • TX • SP • Immanuel Mercedes TX • (956)565-1518 • (SPR 1963 MDIV)

**LEHMAN MATTHEW L REV** (507)775-6325
200 7th St NW Byron MN 55920 • pastormatt@bresnanlink.net • MNS • SP • Mount Moriah Byron MN • (507)775-2460 • (SL 1997 MDIV)

**LEHMANN CARL ALAN REV** (402)654-2338
PO Box A Hooper NE 68031-0599 • NEB • SP • St John Hooper NE • (402)654-2338 • (FW 1995 MDIV)

**LEHMANN RICHARD P REV**
C/O Heavenly Host LC 777 S Willow Cookeville TN 38501-3806 • MDS • EM • (SL 1935 MS)

**LEHMANN SIEGFRIED J REV** (573)556-6279
3916 Buckingham Pk Jefferson City MO 65109-6478 • lehmann@computerland.net • MO • EM • (SL 1955)

**LEHMANN WILLIAM H JR. DR** (509)548-6838
9481 E Leavenworth Rd Leavenworth WA 98826-9358 • EN • EM • (SL 1951 MDIV MA PHD)

**LEHMANN WILLIAM HENRY III REV**
1020 E Main St Medford OR 97504-7449 • NOW • SP • St Peter Medford OR • (541)772-4395 • (SL 1986 MDIV)

**LEHMKUHL W KURT P REV** (507)964-2883
510 Circle Ln Arlington MN 55307-0965 • mooncool@frontiernet.com • MNS • SP • Peace Arlington MN • (507)964-2959 • (SL 1971 STM)

**LEHR MILTON O REV** (352)683-8938
8051 Wooden Dr Spring Hill FL 34606-6802 • FG • SP • Forest Oaks Spring Hill FL • (352)683-9731 • (SL 1958 MDIV)

**LEHRER WAYNE J REV** (703)892-4846
C/O Our Savior Lutheran Church 825 S Taylor St Arlington VA 22204 • wlehrer@aol.com • SE • SP • Our Savior Arlington VA • (703)892-4846 • (SL 1969 MA MDIV)

**LEICHMAN JEFFERY H REV** (847)635-7916
1905 Maple Ave Des Plaines IL 60018 • seraph@innocent.com • NI • SP • Good Shepherd Des Plaines IL • (847)824-4923 • (SL 1998 MA MDIV)

**LEIDER JON F REV** (414)475-6866
4472 N 110th St Milwaukee WI 53225-4408 • SW • SP • Hope Milwaukee WI* • (414)342-0471 • (FW 1981)

**LEIDHOLDT JAMES H REV** (217)999-7483
410 N Oak St Mount Olive IL 62069-1300 • SI • EM • * • (SL 1958 MDIV)

**LEIDICH KEVIN LEE REV** (715)643-7701
360 Railroad Ave Boyceville WI 54725-9504 • NW • SP • St John Boyceville WI • (715)643-2785 • (SL 1994 MDIV)

**LEIGEBER PAUL A REV** (870)579-2438
C/O Zion Lutheran Church PO Box 40 Waldenburg AR 72475-0040 • leigeber@mailexcite.com • MDS • SP • Zion Waldenburg AR • (870)579-2276 • (SL 1987 MDIV)

**LEIGHTY FRED LE ROY REV**
929 E Van Buren Columbia City IN 46725 • revfleighty@yourcon.net • IN • 09/2000 • (FW 1996 MDIV)

**LEIMER WELDON H REV** (714)827-3145
1267 S Berkley St Anaheim CA 92804-4607 • PSW • Sn/Adm • Holy Cross Cypress CA • (714)527-7225 • (FW 1983 MDIV MA)

**LEINHOS STEVEN J REV** (909)676-1492
C/O New Community Lutheran Ch 30470 Pauba Rd Temecula CA 92592-6214 • nclc@temecula.com • PSW • SP • New Community Temecula CA • (909)676-1492 • (SL 1985 MDIV)

**LEISING EMIL P REV** (775)267-3993
PO Box 2974 Carson City NV 89702-2974 • CNH • EM • (SL 1940)

**LEISTE ROBERT A REV** (701)252-5039
1109 8th St SW Jamestown ND 58401-4506 • ND • SP • Concordia Jamestown ND • (701)252-2819 • (FW 1984 MDIV)

**LEIV LEO REV** (503)695-5429
39400 E Knieriem Rd Corbett OR 97019-9795 • NOW • IndC P • Northwest Portland OR • (SK 1957)

**LEJA ALFRED E REV** (320)251-7796
1615 15th Ave SE Apt 223 Saint Cloud MN 56304-3309 • MNN • EM • (SL 1938 MA PHD)

**LELAND DALE D REV** (979)885-3379
803 5th St Sealy TX 77474-2613 • revdale98@aol.com • TX • Sn/Adm • Trinity Sealy TX • (979)885-2211 • (SL 1980 MDIV)

**LEMANSKI S JAY REV** (216)781-9512
2928 Scranton Rd Cleveland OH 44113-5322 • jlemanski@juno.com • OH • Assoc • Immanuel Cleveland OH • (216)781-9511 • (SL 1995 MDIV MA)

**LEMKE ERVIN R DR** (262)783-4080
N50W16414 Maple Crest Ln Menomonee Falls WI 53051-6664 • relemke@utechworld.com • SW • EM • (SL 1944 MTH LITTD)

**LEMKE LARRY G REV** (712)434-5867
PO Box 278 Aurelia IA 51005-0278 • IW • SP • St Paul Aurelia IA • (712)434-2331 • (CQ 1990)

**LEMKE LAYTON L REV** (952)467-4496
17200 104th St Young America MN 55397-9430 • MNS • EM • (SPR 1962)

**LEMKE MARLO D REV** (662)320-4894
107 Oakridge Starkville MS 39759-4150 • SO • SP • St Luke Starkville MS • (662)323-3050 • (SL 1963 MDIV)

**LEMMERMANN SCOTT A REV** (316)431-2318
920 S Ashby Chanute KS 66720 • last5@juno.com • KS • SP • Zion Chanute KS • (316)431-1341 • (SL 1993 MDIV MS)

**LEMMERMANN WALTER C REV** (636)933-5072
616 Santschi Dr Herculaneum MO 63048 • walt-pat@juno.com • MO • EM • (SPR 1955)

**LENK GENE A REV** (412)931-9057
11 Pearl Ave Pittsburgh PA 15229-2126 • EA • EM • (CL 1960)

**LENSER RUDI P REV**
2322 E Cedarwood Ct Spokane WA 99223-7609 • CNH • EM • (SPR 1952)

**LENTNER CHARLES D REV** (330)659-3709
3006 Burnbrick Rd Richfield OH 44286-9717 • EN • Sn/Adm • Fairlawn Akron OH • (330)836-7286 • (SL 1967 STM)

**LENTZ KEVIN D REV** (361)241-4160
3917 Dunstain St Corpus Christi TX 78410 • revklentz@juno.com • TX • SP • Messiah Corpus Christi TX • (361)387-7748 • (SL 1990 MDIV)

**LENTZ ROBERT A REV** (507)374-2906
306 Central Ave N Dodge Center MN 55927 • MNS • SP • Zion Burnsville MN* • (FW 1977 MDIV)

**LENZ LLOYD L REV** (308)458-2785
PO Box 166 Hyannis NE 69350-0166 • NEB • EM • * • (CQ 1994 MDIV)

**LEONHARDT ROGER J REV** (701)662-3267
308 E 14th St Devils Lake ND 58301 • ND • SP • St Peter Devils Lake ND* • (701)662-2245 • (SL 1965 MDIV)

**LEOSCHKE FLOYD L REV** (815)398-5715
1907 S Trainer Rd Rockford IL 61108-6826 • fdlusky@compuserve.com • NI • EM • * • (CQ 1982 MA)

**LEPPER GEORGE A REV** (805)489-9617
PO Box 450 Grover Beach CA 93483-0450 • prgl7@aol.com • CNH • SP • Peace Arroyo Grande CA • (805)489-2708 • (FW 1984 MDIV)

**LESCOW JOHN K REV** (414)464-8569
2040 Elm Tree Rd Elm Grove WI 53122-1116 • SW • Assoc • St Paul West Allis WI • (414)541-6250 • (SL 1966 MSW MTH)

**LESEMANN BRIAN ALBERT REV** (309)546-2434
C/O St John Lutheran Church 13961 CR 1100 N Bath IL 62617 • banblesemann@juno.com • CI • SP • St John Bath IL* • (309)546-2434 • (SL 1993 MDIV)

**LESEMANN BRUCE H REV**
PO Box 154 General Santos City 9500 PHILIPPINES • lesemann@dv.weblinq.com • SI • S Miss • Southern Illinois Belleville IL • (SL 1997 MDIV)

**LESS KEITH G REV** (727)443-0772
1680 Nursery Rd Clearwater FL 33756-2437 • firebird@ij.net • FG • Assoc • First Clearwater FL • (727)447-4504 • (SL 1984 MDIV)

**LESSING ROBERT R REV** (314)505-7148
#18 Seminary Terrace Saint Louis MO 63105 • lessingr@csl.edu • MO • SHS/C • Missouri Saint Louis MO • (314)317-4550 • (SL 1985 STM MDIV)

**LESSMANN RICHARD P REV** (256)574-2326
2606 Clemons Rd Scottsboro AL 35769-3307 • rpjless@aol.com • SO • Sn/Adm • Grace Huntsville AL • (256)881-0552 • (SL 1961 MDIV MA DMIN)

**LETCHER KURT RUSSEL REV** (402)765-7255
2402 E 26th Rd Polk NE 68654 • il55727@alltel.net • NEB • SP • Immanuel Polk NE • (402)765-7252 • (FW 1997 MDIV)

**LETT RANDY DONALD REV** (810)392-2046
81325 Cole St Memphis MI 48041-4455 • MI • Assoc • St Peter Richmond MI • (810)727-9693 • (FW 1983 MDIV)

**LETZRING THEODORE A REV** (712)284-1090
218 570th St Alta IA 51002-7550 • catle@rconnect.com • IW • EM • (SPR 1956 MDIV)

**LEUTHAEUSER LARRY LEE REV** (330)670-9038
2035 Glengary Rd Fairlawn OH 44333 • larryleut@hotmail.com • OH • Assoc • Redeemer Cuyahoga Falls OH • (330)923-1445 • (SL 1966 MDIV)

**LEVENHAGEN DONALD E REV** (402)721-7055
2026 N Howard St Fremont NE 68025-2853 • e11hagen@teknetwork.com • NEB • EM • (SL 1959 MAR)

**LEVERENZ EDWIN W REV** (941)377-5143
4532 Citation Ln Sarasota FL 34233-5036 • libned1909@aol.com • FG • EM • (SL 1932 MDIV MA PHD)

**LEWER RICHARD F REV** (870)597-4601
5560 Highway 34 E Marmaduke AR 72443-9734 • MDS • EM • (CQ 1974 MA)

**LEWIS BERTRAM B REV** (216)531-9337
372 Royal Oak Blvd Richmond Heights OH 44143 • fairchild.bclew@juno.com • OH • SP • St Philip Cleveland OH • (216)991-0655 • (CQ 1990 MA)

**LEWIS DAVID A REV** (256)350-2998
2005 Franklin Ave SW Decatur AL 35603-1016 • stpaulsdal@aol.com • SO • Sn/Adm • St Paul Decatur AL • (256)353-8759 • (SL 1988 MDIV)

**LEWIS DAVID I REV** (707)464-9394
PO Box 2073 Crescent City CA 95531 • bobcatlew@aol.com • CNH • SP • Grace Crescent City CA • (707)464-4712 • (SL 1994 MDIV STM)

**LEWIS ELSTNER C JR. REV** (773)476-0446
7501 S Saint Louis Ave Chicago IL 60652-1417 • NI • SP • St Philip Chicago IL • (773)493-3865 • (CQ 1998)

**LEWIS JAMES M REV** (320)749-2755
C/O Saint Peter Luth Church 121 E Sixth St Randall MN 56475 • MNN • SP • St Peter Randall MN • (320)749-2477 • (FW 1996 MDIV)

**LEWIS LAWRENCE A REV** (760)247-5693
13026 Iroquois Rd Apple Valley CA 92308 • clergy68@hotmail.com • PSW • 04/1993 04/2000 • (SPR 1968)

**LEWIS MARK J REV** (715)843-5604
E10723 County Road Z Wausau WI 54403-8915 • revdad@aol.com • NW • SP • St John Wausau WI • (715)842-5212 • (FW 1985 MDIV)

**LEWIS WILLIAM R REV** (920)295-6682
W5288 Oxbow Trl Princeton WI 54968-8301 • wmjoy@vbe.com • SW • SP • Calvary Princeton WI • (920)295-4747 • (SL 1963 MAR)

**LEY BRUCE G REV** (541)812-0684
1800 47th Ave SE Albany OR 97321-7103 • pastorley@proaxis.com • NOW • SP • Holy Cross Albany OR • (541)928-0214 • (FW 1994 MDIV)

**LI JOHN C P REV** (718)454-7608
86-60 188 St Jamaica Estates New York NY 11423-1110 • AT • SP • Immanuel Chinese Bayside NY • (718)229-4738 • (TW 1964)

**LIBBY FREDERICK J DR** (219)497-9194
4546 Craftsbury Cir Apt C Fort Wayne IN 46818-2054 • EN • EM • (CQ 1986 MA MAR PHD)

**LICHTSINN EDMUND W REV** (712)732-6781
905 Pierce Dr Storm Lake IA 50588-2740 • edluwit@ncn.net • IW • EM • (SL 1943)

**LICHTSINN WALTER E REV** (623)584-5369
12923 W Copperstone Dr Sun City West AZ 85375-4849 • whlixin@juno.com • PSW • EM • (SL 1940)

**LIDBOM ROY A REV** (727)848-1471
5551 Tennessee Ave New Port Richey FL 34652-2929 • FG • Sn/Adm • Faith New Port Richey FL • (727)849-4418 • (SPR 1969 MDIV)

**LIEB FRANCIS M REV** (816)229-1904
725 NW 6th Ter Blue Springs MO 64014-2407 • flieb@juno.com • MO • Sn/Adm • Timothy Blue Springs MO • (816)228-5300 • (SL 1971 MDIV)

**LIEBER KENNETH D REV** (702)248-4536
7560 Parnell Ave Las Vegas NV 89147-4850 • faithlasvegas@aol.com • PSW • SP • Faith Community Las Vegas NV • (702)365-5070 • (SL 1998 MDIV)

**LIEBICH DENNIS J REV** (314)928-1093
13 Mill Spring Ct Saint Peters MO 63376-7022 • liebich@postnet.com • MO • Sn/Adm • Messiah St Charles MO • (314)926-9773 • (SL 1986 MDIV)

**LIEBMANN MARTIN W JR. REV** (309)543-2086
227 E Market Havana IL 62644 • stpaul@fgi.net • CI • SP • St Paul Havana IL • (309)543-4850 • (FW 1983 MDIV)

**LIEBMANN ROBERT O REV** (828)232-4703
10 Crestview Ct Asheville NC 28806 • pastor-bob7@juno.com • SE • Asst • Emmanuel Asheville NC • (828)252-1795 • (SL 1999 MDIV)

**LIEBNAU DAVID A REV** (314)961-4151
934 Briarton Dr Saint Louis MO 63126-1102 • MO • SP • St Trinity Saint Louis MO • (314)353-3276 • (SL 1973 MDIV)

**LIEDER LAWRENCE A REV** (281)351-9646
11114 Olde Mint House Tomball TX 77375-7029 • larrytx@worldnet.att.net • TX • SP • Holy Three In One Houston TX • (713)468-1815 • (FW 1987 MDIV)

**LIEDER WALTER F REV** (507)454-6334
121 N Baker St Winona MN 55987-2235 • MNS • EM • (SL 1931)

**LIEFELD DAVID R REV** (636)397-9614
3 Outpost Ct Saint Peters MO 63376-5007 • dliefeld@concentric.net • EN • EM • (LS 1975 MDIV MTH MA)

**LIERSEMANN F PAUL JR. REV** (972)394-1973
1600 E Peters Colony Rd Carrollton TX 75007-3901 • paull@popcarrollton.org • TX • Assoc • Prince Peace Carrollton TX • (972)447-9887 • (SL 1973 MDIV)

**LIESE MICHAEL DAVID REV** (309)446-3436
PO Box 297 Brimfield IL 61517-0297 • CI • SP • St Paul Brimfield IL • (309)446-3233 • (SL 1995 MDIV)

**LIESKE BRUCE J REV** (407)359-0449
1826 Seneca Blvd Winter Springs FL 32708-5530 • blieske7@cs.com • FG • D Miss • Florida-Georgia Orlando FL • (SPR 1969 MDIV MTH MS)

**LIESKE DAVID J REV** (414)924-5210
1027 S Park Ave Fond Du Lac WI 54935-8033 • hope@vbe.com • SW • Sn/Adm • Hope Fond Du Lac WI • (920)922-5130 • (SL 1972 MDIV DMIN)

**LIESKE H WILLIAM REV** (828)687-9281
264 Rocky Mountain Way Arden NC 28704-8445 • beksel@juno.com • SE • EM • (SL 1941 MDIV)

**LIESKE MARK A REV** (425)488-7926
15704 63rd Ave NE Kenmore WA 98028-4319 • mlieske@tcmnet.com • NOW • Sn/Adm • Epiphany Kenmore WA • (425)488-9606 • (SL 1970 MDIV)

**LIESKE MARTIN W REV** (952)926-7489
4605 W 44th St Edina MN 55424-1003 • MNS • EM • (SL 1935 MDIV LITTD)

**LIESKE RICHARD P REV** (517)694-6418
2450 Featherstone Dr Lansing MI 48911-6494 • lieskeri@pilot.msu.edu • MI • SHS/C • Michigan Ann Arbor MI • (SL 1985 MDIV MA)

**LIKENESS DAVID A REV** (309)444-3465
1207 Kingsbury Rd Washington IL 61571-1212 • CI • SP • Our Savior Washington IL • (309)444-4030 • (SL 1968 MDIV)

**LIKENS JAMES D REV** (314)481-7603
5250A Neosho Saint Louis MO 63109-2963 • grandpajim@grandpajim.com • MO • 01/1998 02/2000 • (FW 1982 MDIV)

**LILIENKAMP CARL R REV** (308)962-7934
PO Box 623 Arapahoe NE 68922-0623 • clilienkamp@chooselife.com • NEB • Sn/Adm • Trinity Arapahoe NE • (308)962-7667 • (SL 1977 MDIV DMIN)

**LILLICH VICTOR O REV** (509)972-4295
4701 Clinton Way Yakima WA 98908 • vjlillich@juno.com • NOW • EM • (SL 1959)

**LIM EDMUND T H REV** (219)486-9827
6807 Hunterdon Cove Ft Wayne IN 46835 • IN • D Miss • Indiana Fort Wayne IN • (CQ 1996 STM)

**LIM MICHAEL E REV** (719)597-0604
2728 Casden Cir Colorado Springs CO 80909-6108 • RM • SP • Korean First Colorado Springs CO • (719)393-1940 • (CQ 1997)

**LIMMER HARLAN L REV** (650)347-2862
1320 Lincoln Ave Burlingame CA 94010-3414 • revjol@aol.com • CNH • SP • Trinity Burlingame CA • (650)347-6661 • (FW 1985 MDIV MED)

**LINCK STEPHEN S REV** (409)963-3578
4125 Coke Rd Port Arthur TX 77642 • stpaul@pernet.net • TX • SP • St Paul Groves TX • (409)962-1133 • (FW 1989 MDIV)

**LINCKS HOWARD J REV** (518)392-4395
130 Hudson Ave Chatham NY 12037-1429 • AT • EM • (SPR 1940)

**LIND MAURICE WM REV** (515)393-2558
PO Box 346 Elma IA 50628-0346 • IE • 08/1995 08/2000 • (FW 1979 MDIV)

**LIND STEVEN D REV**
8875 N 600 E Ossian IN 46777-9634 • NW • 11/1999 • (FW 1994 MDIV)

**LINDAU ROBERT H REV** (262)512-0465
11911 N Granville Rd Mequon WI 53097-2807 • revlin45@execpc.com • SW • Sn/Adm • Trinity Mequon WI • (262)242-2045 • (CQ 1980 MAR MMU)

**LINDEMAN RICHARD L REV** (612)754-7750
1733 122nd Ave NW Coon Rapids MN 55448-1947 • richardlindeman@xc.org • MNS • SP • Olive Branch Coon Rapids MN • (612)755-2663 • (SPR 1976 MDIV STM)

**LINDEMANN ALBERT H REV** (817)569-0307
1022 Jan Lee Dr Burkburnett TX 76354-2916 • TX • EM • (SL 1936 MA)

**LINDEMANN JERALD S REV** (708)831-3130
1717 Deerfield Rd Highland Park IL 60035-3704 • rlchp@concentric.net • NI • SP • Redeemer Highland Park IL • (847)831-2225 • (SPR 1964 MDIV)

**LINDEMANN PETER A REV** (716)798-5740
11530 Munzel Rd Medina NY 14103-9760 • palindemann@juno.com • EA • SP • Trinity Medina NY • (716)798-0525 • (SL 1972 MDIV)

**LINDEMOOD BRYAN N REV** (801)532-3963
1024 S 500 E Salt Lake City UT 84111 • RM • SP • St John Salt Lake City UT • (801)364-2873 • (SL 2000 MDIV)

**LINDENMEYER WILLIAM D REV** (714)894-4886
6281 Santa Barbara Ave Garden Grove CA 92845-1246 • revlindy@aol.com • PSW • Assoc • Holy Cross Cypress CA • (714)527-7225 • (FW 1981 MDIV)

**LINDERMAN BRUCE E REV** (406)586-5041
3150 Prairie Smoke Rd Bozeman MT 59715-8701 • lutheranbobcats@yahoo.com • MT • Assoc • First Bozeman MT • (406)586-5374 • (SL 1976 MDIV)

**LINDERMAN JAMES R REV** (512)280-5024
4701 Indian Wells Dr Austin TX 78747-1407 • texvpres@aol.com • TX • EM • (SL 1960 MA)

**LINDNER ERNEST G REV** (281)379-5857
9531 Magnolia Ridge Dr Houston TX 77070-1936 • ernie10453@aol.com • TX • Inst C • Texas Austin TX • (SPR 1962)

**LINDNER JOHN T REV** (972)867-5588
3601 W 15th St Plano TX 75075-7741 • jlindner@lol-plano.org • TX • SP • Lord of Life Plano TX • (972)867-5588 • (FW 1981 MDIV)

**LINDSAY KENNETH M REV** (920)894-7434
925 Adams St Kiel WI 53042-1217 • EN • EM • (SL 1946)

**LINEBERGER LAWRENCE R REV** (919)562-8835
1137 Chilmark Ave Wake Forest NC 27587-5334 • lrline@mindspring.com • SE • EM • (SL 1961 MDIV)

**LINEBERGER RICHARD W REV** (904)629-1794
C/O St John Lutheran Church 1915 SE Lake Weir Rd Ocala FL 34471-5424 • FG • Sn/Adm • St John Ocala FL • (352)629-1794 • (SL 1985 MDIV)

**LINEN ELMER E REV** (218)631-1536
821 Harmony Ln Wadena MN 56482-1949 • MNN • EM • (SPR 1952 MDIV MRE)

**LING TIMOTHY K REV** (510)638-6908
5825 Bollinger RD Cupertino CA 95014-3536 • revrevling@aol.com • CNH • SP • Faith Chinese Cupertino CA • (408)252-0552 • (HK 1977)

**LINGSCH KEITH A REV** (740)453-0481
1175 Pfeifer Dr Zanesville OH 43701-1351 • bowmankal@globalco.net • OH • Asst • Trinity Zanesville OH • (740)453-0744 • (FW 1996 MDIV)

**LINK JAMES C REV** (219)289-0683
26222 Whippoorwill Dr South Bend IN 46619-4590 • jimlink@sprintmail.com • IN • SP • Faith South Bend IN • (219)288-3737 • (FW 1997 MDIV)

**LINKUGEL DAVID H REV** (402)289-3631
21479 Brentwood Rd Elkhorn NE 68022-2050 • dlinkugel@aol.com • NEB • SP • Lord Of Life Elkhorn NE • (402)289-3437 • (FW 1985 MDIV)

**LINN HAROLD A REV** (502)451-5745
2117 Boulevard Napoleon Louisville KY 40205-1833 • IN • EM • (SPR 1961 MDIV)

**LINNEMANN PAUL ARTHUR REV** (503)591-8977
17575 SW Oak St Aloha OR 97007-3912 • office@orlc.net • NOW • SP • Our Redeemer Tigard OR • (503)524-6646 • (CQ 1995 MA MA)

**LINSE EUGENE W REV** (636)285-4835
7325 Scenic Ct Cedar Hill MO 63016-3432 • MO • EM • (SL 1944 MA MA PHD PHD)

**LINTHICUM ERIC RODGER REV** (440)354-9328
260 Bowhall Rd Painesville OH 44077-5219 • ericlinthicum@oh.verio.com • OH • SP • St Paul Painesville OH • (440)354-3000 • (FW 1996 MDIV)

**LINTVEDT VERNON K REV** (618)624-9346
120 White Pine Ave O Fallon IL 62269-2508 • bslchurch@intertek.net • SI • SP • Blessed Savior O Fallon IL • (618)632-0126 • (SL 1990 MDIV)

**LISCH ELMER R REV** (920)894-4525
1232 1st St Kiel WI 53042 • ealisch@juno.com • SW • SP • St Mark Belgium WI • (414)285-3820 • (CQ 1983)

**LISSY ANDREW C REV** (215)945-2778
55 Turf Rd Levittown PA 19056-1519 • alissyhope@juno.com • EA • SP • Hope Levittown PA • (215)946-3467 • (SL 1985 MDIV MA)

**LISSY GARY PAUL REV** (440)461-2296
1613 Crestwood Rd Mayfield Heights OH 44124-3332 • revgarylissy@earthlink.net • OH • SP • St Mark Chesterland OH • (216)729-1668 • (SC 1995 MDIV)

**LIST PETER ANDREW REV** (314)725-2518
6447 Clayton Rd 1W Saint Louis MO 63117-1867 • machts.gut@usa.net • MO • 02/1997 • (SL 1995 MDIV)

**LITKE ARTHUR E REV** (412)486-5962
108 Arden Dr Glenshaw PA 15116-1602 • lit5@aol.com • EA • SP • Bethel Glenshaw PA • (412)486-5777 • (FW 1981 MDIV)

**LITTERER CHARLES E REV** (423)543-8501
PO Box 1043 Elizabethton TN 37644-1043 • littererˢcharles@juno.com • MDS • EM • (SL 1959 MDIV)

**LITTLE DONALD G REV** (972)716-9985
4532 Myerwood Ln Dallas TX 75244-7515 • TX • SP • Holy Cross Dallas TX • (214)358-4396 • (SPR 1973 MDIV)

**LITTMANN PAUL G REV**
67 Preston Dr Cranston RI 02910 • NE • EM • (SL 1947 STM MTH)

**LLERENA EDUARDO A REV**
6771 SW 13th Ter Miami FL 33144-5524 • FG • EM • (CQ 1966 MDIV)

**LLOYD JEFFREY E REV** (816)833-0091
9512 E 30th St Independence MO 64052 • lloydpastor@hotmail.com • MO • Assoc • Messiah Independence MO • (816)254-9405 • (SPR 1972 MDIV)

**LOBER JOHN A REV** (803)798-2614
1622 Saint Michaels Rd Columbia SC 29210-6010 • SE • EM • (SPR 1969 MDIV MA)

**LOBIEN GEORGE F REV** (757)258-5699
108 Westchester Way Williamsburg VA 23188-7525 • globien@aol.com • SE • EM • (SL 1960 STM THD)

**LOCHHAAS PHILIP H REV** (636)227-1396
922 Dutch Mill Dr Ballwin MO 63011-3548 • phloch@aol.com • MO • EM • (SL 1948 LITTD)

**LOCHNER DANIEL E REV** (248)483-5339
28510 Lathrup Blvd Lathrup Village MI 48076-2806 • delochner@earthlink.net • MI • SP • St Paul Royal Oak MI • (248)541-0613 • (SPR 1975 MDIV)

**LOCKE LAWRENCE R REV** (360)335-0311
C/O St Matthew Luth Ch 715 17th St Washougal WA 98671-1506 • locke@worldaccessnet.com • NOW • SP • St Matthew Washougal WA • (360)835-5533 • (FW 1984 MDIV)

**LODHOLZ GARY DALE REV** (715)762-4438
W7814 Simon Rd Fifield WI 54524-9465 • llodh@win.bright.net • NW • SP • Trinity Phillips WI* • (715)339-3495 • (SL 1973 MDIV)

**LOEBER HENRY A REV** (201)791-0519
19-06 Berdan Ave Fair Lawn NJ 07410-2117 • NJ • EM • * • (SL 1955 MA)

**LOEFFLER DAVID G REV**
5665 Rockport Ln Haltom City TX 76137-2117 • pastorˢloeffler@hotmail.com • TX • SP • Zion Watauga TX • (817)427-2909 • (SL 1984 MDIV MS)

**LOEHRKE KENNETH L SR. REV** (920)452-9563
143 Grafton Ct Kohler WI 53044-1507 • SW • SP • Bethany Kohler WI • (920)457-4681 • (SPR 1971 MDIV)

**LOESCH DONALD D REV**
240 15th Ave Court Hiawatha IA 52233 • IE • EM • (SL 1960 MDIV DMIN)

**LOESCH JEREMY D REV** (614)853-3827
1190 Wimbeldon Blvd Columbus OH 43228 • OH • SP • Concordia Columbus OH • (614)878-7800 • (SL 2000 MDIV)

**LOESCH KEITH W REV** (703)494-0602
3397 Flint Hill Pl Woodbridge VA 22192-7100 • j14loesch@aol.com • SE • Sn/Adm • Grace Woodbridge VA • (703)494-4600 • (SL 1967 MDIV)

**LOESCH NATHAN O REV** (949)215-7413
24511 Aguirre Mission Viejo CA 92692 • PSW • EM • (SL 1955)

**LOESCHEN DAVID P REV** (712)263-6430
1026 Oak Park Blvd Denison IA 51442 • IW • SP • Our Savior Denison IA • (712)263-3282 • (FW 1984 MDI)

**LOESCHEN DONALD P REV** (915)762-3227
PO Box 103 Albany TX 76430-0103 • dloeschen@aol.com • TX • SP • Trinity Albany TX • (915)762-2557 • (SL 1976 MDIV)

**LOESCHKE DAVID R REV**
Immanuel Luth Church PO Box 116 Haxtum CO 80731-0116 • RM • SP • Immanuel Haxtun CO* • (970)774-6236 • (FW 1985)

**LOESCHMAN ALBERT J REV** (396)399-4001
5413 Church Ln North Zulch TX 77872-9714 • wd5iqr@txcyber.com • TX • EM • * • (SL 1965 MDIV)

**LOESEL ANDREW E REV** (360)318-8139
8384 Double Ditch Rd Lynden WA 98264 • a.loesel@att.worldnet.net • MI • 05/1999 • * • (SPR 1969 MDIV)

**LOESEL BERTHOLD J REV**
1021 Cathy Dr Jackson MO 63755-1958 • MO • EM • * • (SL 1932)

**LOESEL RONALD MARK REV** (504)398-0700
3521 Mimosa Ct New Orleans LA 70131-8304 • rmloesel@aol.com • SO • SP • Trinity New Orleans LA • (504)368-0411 • (SL 1994 MDIV)

**LOEST ADEN E REV** (847)244-1989
625 S Dilger Ave Apt 103 Waukegan IL 60085-7083 • NI • EM • (SL 1959)

**LOEST MARK A REV** (618)327-3391
747 W Vernor St Nashville IL 62263-1120 • mloest@chi.lcms.org • MO • S Ex/S • Trinity Nashville IL* • (618)327-3311 • (FW 1988 MDIV STM)

**LOEWE TIMOTHY J REV** (517)497-0301
5725 Constance Dr Saginaw MI 48603 • pastor@hclc.org • MI • Sn/Adm • Holy Cross Saginaw MI • (517)793-9723 • (FW 1993 MDIV)

**LOFGREN RICHARD S REV** (219)447-6333
9627 Marion Center Rd Fort Wayne IN 46816-9750 • lofrs@aol.com • TX • 07/1998 07/2000 • (SL 1986 MDIV MA)

**LOFTHUS DAVID J REV** (504)456-7382
1605 Mason Smith Ave Metairie LA 70003-5013 • SO • SP • Faith Harahan LA • (504)737-0448 • (FW 1989 MDIV)

**LOFTIS JOSEPH N REV** (219)493-8377
1407 Melbourne Dr New Haven IN 46774-2649 • IN • 05/1995 05/2000 • (FW 1993 MDIV THD)

**LOGID MARK J REV** 39-081-568-5255
Credo Europe PSC 817 Box 14 FPO AE 09622-1014 • logidm@naples.navy.mil • FG • M Chap • Florida-Georgia Orlando FL • (SL 1982 MDIV MA)

**LOHMAN JOHN R REV** (712)297-5097
C/O Immanuel Lutheran Church 3010 270th St Rockwell City IA 50579-7513 • IW • SP • Immanuel Rockwell City IA • (712)297-7708 • (CQ 1982)

**LOHMEYER RICHARD G REV** (850)934-3834
1370 Calcutta Dr Gulf Breeze FL 32561-3439 • revˢjudy@sprynet.com • SO • SP • Good Shepherd Gulf Breeze FL • (850)932-3263 • (SL 1988 MDIV)

**LOHNES MARK S REV**
138 11th St Carmi IL 62821-1314 • SI • SP • Our Savior Carmi IL* • (618)384-5291 • (SL 1984)

**LOHNES PAUL D REV** (217)283-6967
507 Judson Ave Hoopeston IL 60942-1220 • lefty1@htb.net • CI • EM • * • (CQ 1988)

**LOHRKE MERLYN C REV** (405)282-5260
1313 E Prairie Grove Rd Guthrie OK 73044-6801 • OK • SP • Zion Guthrie OK • (405)282-3914 • (SL 1964 MDIV)

**LOHRMANN KURT T REV** (703)866-7853
5815 Rexford Dr Apt B Springfield VA 22152-4000 • MI • EM • (SL 1935)

**LONDENBERG DAVID L REV** (830)663-3423
C/O LCMS Bd for Mission Serv 1333 S Kirkwood Rd Saint Louis MO 63122 • TX • S Miss • Texas Austin TX • (SPR 1969 MDIV STM)

**LONG BARRY ALBERT REV** (309)693-7653
C/O Mount Calvary Ev Lutheran 908 W Hanssler Place Peoria IL 61604-2738 • PRBLong@aol.com • CI • SP • Mount Calvary Peoria IL • (309)688-4321 • (CQ 1997 MDIV)

**LONG CHARLES MILTON REV** (804)330-9549
2013 Esquire Rd Richmond VA 23235-3523 • seelong@worldnet.att.net • SE • D Miss • Southeastern Alexandria VA • (SL 1992 MDIV MS)

**LONG STEPHEN F REV** (313)287-2080
25005 Northline Rd Taylor MI 48180 • MI • Sn/Adm • St John Taylor MI • (734)287-2080 • (FW 1993 MDIV)

**LONGSHORE HAL REX REV** (503)350-1356
14507 SW Grayling Ln Beaverton OR 97007-3668 • NOW • EM • (SL 1966 MDIV)

**LONSBERRY KEITH B REV** (623)583-7919
10525 Kingswood Cir Sun City AZ 85351 • lons@futureone.com • PSW • SP • Fountain of Life Sun City AZ • (623)933-8246 • (FW 1978 MDIV)
**LOOCK LAMBERT E REV** (626)303-4995
1223 S Magnolia Ave Monrovia CA 91016-4019 • PSW • 03/1988 03/2000 • (SL 1959 MDIV)
**LOOS DONALD A REV** (716)549-1062
70 High St Angola NY 14006-1318 • EA • SP • St John Angola NY • (716)549-2144 • (SL 1976 MDIV)
**LOOSE GEORGE A REV** (407)366-9698
1323 Haven Dr Oviedo FL 32765-5204 • geoloose@aol.com • FG • EM • (SL 1945 STM DD)
**LOOSE RODNEY W REV** (318)687-8347
9714 Amblewood Ln Shreveport LA 71118-5052 • RevLoose@prodigy.net • SO • SP • Our Savior Shreveport LA • (318)686-2921 • (SL 1966 MDIV)
**LOPEZ JOHNNY J REV**
2514 Park Dr Santa Ana CA 92707-3317 • PSW • D Miss • Igl Cristo Rey Orange CA • (714)633-8891 • (CQ 1987)
**LOPEZ PEDRO L REV** (414)633-5442
3014 Gilson St Racine WI 53403-2820 • SW • D Miss • South Wisconsin Milwaukee WI • (414)464-8100 • (CQ 1995)
**LOPPNOW HENRY H REV** (502)647-0278
201 Glenway Dr Shelbyville KY 40065-8830 • IN • SP • Holy Cross Shelbyville KY • (502)647-3696 • (CQ 1993 MSED)
**LOREE LARRY K SR. REV** (734)240-0279
3589 Heiss Rd Monroe MI 48162 • peacemaker45@earthlink.net • MI • Sn/Adm • Holy Ghost Monroe MI • (734)241-0525 • (SC 1990 MDIV)
**LORENZ BENJAMIN G REV** (859)737-1581
1 Woodland Dr Winchester KY 40391 • lorenzbg@meginc.com • IN • SP • Grace Winchester KY • (859)745-2873 • (SL 1977 MDIV)
**LORENZ DENNIS L REV** (208)667-3599
C/O Christ The King Luth Ch 1700 E Pennsylvania Ave Coeur D Alene ID 83814-5563 • NOW • Assoc • Christ King Coeur D Alene ID • (208)664-9231 • (SPR 1963 MDIV)
**LORENZ GREGORY M REV** (810)677-3474
52910 Romeo Plank Rd Macomb MI 48042-3509 • gregoyo@worldnet.att.net • MI • Assoc • St Peter Macomb MI • (810)781-3434 • (SL 1989 MDIV)
**LORENZ MARVIN L REV** (309)244-7209
PO Box 477 Delavan IL 61734-0477 • CI • SP • Christ Delavan IL* • (309)244-7200 • (FW 1977 MDIV)
**LOTTES WILBUR P REV**
615 N Pike Rd Cabot PA 16023-2215 • EA • EM • * • (SL 1939)
**LOUDENBACK G DONALD REV** (409)830-8073
902 Carlee Dr Brenham TX 77833-5006 • gdloudenback@mail.esc4.com • TX • EM • * • (FW 1977 MDIV)
**LOUDERBACK MARK Q L REV** (912)489-8297
505 Pleasant Point Rd Statesboro GA 30458-4160 • mqll@bulloch.com • FG • SP • St Paul Statesboro GA • (912)681-2481 • (SL 1997 MDIV)
**LOUGHRAN KEVIN R REV**
2925 E 700 S Wolcottville IN 46795-8957 • IN • SP • Messiah Wolcottville IN • (219)854-3129 • (FW 1993 MDIV)
**LOUISSAINT ELIE REV** (407)641-8980
2935 Donald Rd Lake Worth FL 33461-1709 • elie1020@yahoo.com • FG • O Sp Min • Salem Haitian Lake Worth FL • (407)586-5691 • (CQ 1991)
**LOUM JOHN S REV** (219)447-5771
1649 Hobson Rd Fort Wayne IN 46805 • IN • D Miss • Indiana Fort Wayne IN • (CQ 1999)
**LOVE DONALD G REV**
4173 Van Gassler Rd Cloquet MN 55720-9149 • MNN • 08/1999 • (FW 1989 MDIV)
**LOVE JOSEPH DAVID REV** (440)845-1552
3107 Priscilla Ave Cleveland OH 44134-4232 • OH • Assoc • Bethany Parma OH • (440)884-1230 • (SL 1996 MDIV)
**LOVE MARK W REV** (618)566-2709
102 S Railway St Mascoutah IL 62258-1934 • mdl1195@accessus.net • SI • SP • Zion Mascoutah IL • (618)566-7345 • (FW 1992 MDIV)
**LOW MAURICE ROBERT REV** (217)632-2922
PO Box 315 Petersburg IL 62675-0315 • rlow@fgi.net • CI • SP • Bethlehem Petersburg IL • (217)632-2453 • (FW 1977 MDIV)
**LOWERY JOSEPH C REV** (214)297-6085
2013 S Lake Harris Rd Lot 34 White Oak TX 75693-2355 • TX • EM • (SPR 1970)
**LOWMASTER W JAMES REV** (616)422-2685
1371 W Glendora Rd Buchanan MI 49107 • revjimlow@earthlink.net • MI • SP • Trinity Buchanan MI • (616)422-2554 • (FW 1986 MDIV)
**LOWREY GEORGE W REV** (512)868-9709
3202 Lonesome Trl Georgetown TX 78628 • lowrey@totalaccess.net • TX • Assoc • Faith Georgetown TX • (512)863-7332 • (SL 1994 MDIV)
**LOZA DAVID H REV** (913)262-7239
10210 W 56th St Merriam KS 66203-2358 • MO • Asst • El Buen Pastor Kansas City MO* • (816)474-9049 • (SL 1984 MDIV)
**LOZA JULIO A REV** (773)283-4360
3424 N Oak Park Ave Chicago IL 60634-3719 • jloza@juno.com • NI • SP • St Matthew Chicago IL • (773)847-6458 • (LS 1969 MDIV)
**LUBBEN DARRELL M REV** (517)799-5639
3736 Manistee St Saginaw MI 48603-3143 • MI • EM • (SL 1953)
**LUBBEN HENRY C REV**
74 Kennedy Rd Manchester CT 06450 • 102151.3403 • NE • SP • Zion Manchester CT • (860)649-4243 • (SPR 1964)
**LUBBEN LOWELL L REV** (651)454-9182
4060 Blackhawk Rd Eagan MN 55122 • lubbendor@aol.com • MNS • EM • (SL 1959 MDIV)
**LUBECK THOMAS M REV** (248)349-0588
38124 S Vista Dr Livovia MI 48157 • tlubeck@ameritech.net • MI • Sn/Adm • St Paul Northville MI • (248)349-3140 • (FW 1982 MDIV)
**LUBKEMAN AUGUST H REV** (360)692-3693
393 NW San Juan Dr Bremerton WA 98311 • augjunelubkeman@earthlink.net • NOW • EM • (SL 1957)
**LUCAS BRUCE KENNETH REV** (734)269-6049
6272 W Albain Rd Monroe MI 48161-9503 • vergferm@bignet.net • MI • SP • Immanuel Monroe MI • (734)269-2961 • (FW 1995 MMU MDIV)
**LUCAS GLENN A REV** (323)735-1083
2535 9th Ave Los Angeles CA 90018-1708 • pastorg@pacificnet.net • PSW • SP • St Paul Los Angeles CA • (323)731-8384 • (SL 1987 MDIV)
**LUCAS JAMES A REV** (316)697-2284
PO Box 37 Elkhart KS 67950-0037 • jimlucas@elkhart.com • KS • SP • Christ Elkhart KS* • (316)697-2284 • (FW 1980 MDIV)
**LUCAS WILLIE C REV**
C/O Calvary Luthran Church 10635 Homestead Rd Houston TX 77016 • socrates14@aol.com • TX • SP • Calvary Houston TX • (713)633-7276 • (FW 1979 MDIV)
**LUCERO DENNIS F DR** (314)771-8461
3892 Fairview Ave Saint Louis MO 63116-4705 • dflucero@aol.com • MO • SP • Hope Saint Louis MO • (314)352-0014 • (SL 1985 MDIV DMIN)
**LUCHTERHAND KARL J REV**
2339 Jerome Blvd Racine WI 53403-2451 • SW • Tchr • Lutheran High School Racine WI • (414)637-6538 • (FW 1984 MDIV)
**LUCIDO GREGORY J REV** (308)458-2508
PO Box 350 Hyannis NE 69350 • NEB • D Miss • Nebraska Seward NE • (SL 2000 MDIV)
**LUCKRITZ HAROLD S REV** (314)677-4132
C/O Hope Lutheran Church 2308 Gravois Rd High Ridge MO 63049-2505 • MO • SP • Hope High Ridge MO • (636)677-8788 • (SPR 1975 MDIV)
**LUDWIG ALAN GRANT REV** (219)452-2100
6600 N Clinton St Fort Wayne IN 46825-4996 • professor@mail.nsk.ru • IN • SHS/C • Indiana Fort Wayne IN • (SL 1989 MDIV STM)
**LUDWIG ARNOLD W REV** (715)479-6229
1527 Sandstone Cir Eagle River WI 54521-9391 • NW • EM • (SL 1954)
**LUDWIG DAVID G SR. REV** (407)306-0492
5999 Lakepointe Dr Unit 602 Orlando FL 32822-3786 • FG • EM • (SL 1959)
**LUDWIG DAVID REV** (828)324-7879
1974 12th Street Pl NE Hickory NC 28601-1649 • ludwig@lrc.edu • SE • Asst • Christ Hickory NC • (828)328-1483 • (SL 1965 MDIV PHD)
**LUDWIG EUGENE M REV** (503)434-9456
3023 NE Maloney Dr Mc Minnville OR 97128-2250 • willgene@onlinemac.com • NOW • EM • (SL 1959)
**LUDWIG PAUL W DR** (803)781-7900
236 White Falls Dr Columbia SC 29212-1232 • luap236@juno.com • SE • EM • (SL 1951 MTH MDIV DMIN)
**LUDWIG RICHARD C REV** (352)753-7573
2106 Santo Domingo Dr Lady Lake FL 32159-9557 • dickludwig@atlantic.net • FG • EM • (SL 1961 MED MDIV)
**LUDWIG TIMOTHY J REV** (218)729-5722
5101 Country Rd Hermantown MN 55810-9701 • pichrist@cpinternet.com • MNN • SP • Peace Christ Hermantown MN • (218)729-9473 • (SL 1985 MDIV)
**LUDWIG WILLIAM A REV** (206)524-2283
6547 46th Ave NE Seattle WA 98115-7629 • NOW • EM • (SPR 1959 MDIV)
**LUECK CHAD DOUGLAS REV** (309)821-0512
2707 Essington St Bloomington IL 61704-6533 • revbci@yahoo.com • CI • SP • Good Shepherd Bloomington IL • (309)662-8905 • (FW 1991 MDIV)
**LUECK DWAYNE M REV** (715)355-4554
2607 Marigold Rd Wausau WI 54401-9343 • dmlu@aol.com • NW • D Ex/S • North Wisconsin Wausau WI* • (SL 1979 MDIV)
**LUECKE DAVID L REV** (703)943-4431
700 Lovers Ln Waynesboro VA 22980-3528 • dmluecke@cfw.com • SE • EM • * • (SL 1956 DREL)
**LUECKE DAVID S REV** (440)838-1985
9419 Misty Oakes Dr Broadview Hts OH 44147-3125 • dsluecke@aol.com • OH • Assoc • Royal Redeemer North Royalton OH • (440)237-7958 • (SL 1967 MDIV MBA PHD)
**LUECKE GEORGE L REV** (817)274-9592
8025 John T White Rd Fort Worth TX 76120-3611 • TX • EM • (SL 1951 MDIV)
**LUECKE JAMES R REV** (940)779-3403
937 Longscamp Rd Graford TX 76449 • patjim21@wf.net • TX • EM • (SL 1955 MDIV)
**LUECKE MARK G REV** (330)492-0527
4023 Vernon Ave NW Canton OH 44709-1774 • OH • O Sp Min • Ohio Olmsted Falls OH • (SL 1986 MDIV)
**LUECKE MARTIN J REV** (828)692-4498
153 Wendy Lane Hendersonville NC 28792 • humbird65@juno.com • SE • EM • (SL 1959)
**LUEDEMANN PETER T REV** (703)444-3908
21067 Ethan Ct Sterling VA 20164 • SE • Asst • Good Shepherd Reston VA • (703)437-5020 • (SL 1998 MDIV)
**LUEDEMANN RONALD S REV** (760)247-3972
12410 Havasupi Rd Apple Valley CA 92308 • lronanne@aol.com • PSW • SP • Faith Hesperia CA • (760)244-5943 • (SL 1999 MDIV JD)
**LUEDERS CARL E REV** (515)752-0864
109 Meadow Ln Marshalltown IA 50158 • lueder4@ibm.net • IE • EM • (SPR 1952)
**LUEDTKE CARL F REV** (920)231-4123
2990 County Road GG Oshkosh WI 54904-9758 • NW • EM • (SL 1941)
**LUEHMANN ALFRED J REV** (218)828-0880
Box 152 Gaylord MN 55334 • MNN • EM • (SL 1960 MDIV)
**LUEKE KENNETH D REV** (517)269-6357
134 W Butler St Bad Axe MI 48413-1001 • axeman@hdtinfo.com • MI • SP • Our Savior Bad Axe MI • (517)269-7642 • (SL 1981 MDIV)
**LUEKER CARL M H REV** (870)492-6236
46 Sunshine Cir Mountain Home AR 72653-6802 • MDS • EM • (SPR 1946)
**LUEKER ERWIN L REV** (661)725-2225
1017 Princeton St Delano CA 93215-2447 • CNH • SP • Our Saviour Delano CA* • (661)725-2225 • (SL 1970 MDIV MA PHD)
**LUFT BRANDON J REV** (816)233-9206
2301 Briarcliff St Joseph MO 64503 • MO • Asst • St Paul Saint Joseph MO • (816)279-1110 • (SL 2000 MDIV)
**LUHRING DONALD L REV** (419)782-5766
655 Wayne Ave Defiance OH 43512-2659 • sjl@defnet.com • OH • SP • St John Defiance OH • (419)782-5766 • (SL 1969 MA)
**LUHRS DAVID J REV** (920)856-6420
C/O St Peter Lutheran Church PO Box 85 Forestville WI 54213-0085 • jluhrs@itol.com • NW • SP • St Peter Forestville WI • (920)856-6420 • (SPR 1970 MDIV)
**LUINSTRA ROBERT F REV** (541)382-1832
1034 NE 11th St Bend OR 97701 • NOW • Sn/Adm • Trinity Bend OR • (541)382-1832 • (SPR 1971 MDIV)
**LUKE HAROLD H REV** (816)356-8754
5013 Osage Ave Kansas City MO 64133 • MO • EM • (SL 1948 MDIV)
**LUKEFAHR DAVID P REV** (517)883-2188
9456 Kilmanagh Rd Sebewaing MI 48759-9722 • luke@avci.com • MI • SP • St John Sebewaing MI • (517)883-2188 • (SL 1998 MDIV)
**LUKOMSKI JOHN P REV** (618)475-3143
C/O St Paul Luth Ch 900 Belsha St New Athens IL 62264-1502 • lukomski@apci.net • SI • SP • St Paul New Athens IL* • (618)475-3143 • (FW 1978 MDIV STM)
**LUMPP DAVID A REV**
2838 Lakeview Ave Saint Paul MN 55113-2033 • lumpp@luther.csp.edu • MNS • SHS/C • Minnesota South Burnsville MN • (SL 1979 MDIV STM THD)
**LUNDGREN MARK ANDREW REV**
4121 Wolf Rd Western Springs IL 60558-1451 • NI • SP • Grace Western Springs IL • (708)246-0536 • (SL 1992 MDIV)
**LUNDI MARTIN E REV** (714)514-4049
318 Country Club Dr Naples FL 34110-1144 • melundi@aol.com • EN • EM • (SPR 1964 MDIV)
**LUNDQUIST BRYAN G REV** (715)536-6653
C/O Trinity Lutheran Church 107 N State St Merrill WI 54452-2244 • NW • Assoc • Trinity Merrill WI • (715)536-5482 • (FW 1996 MDIV)
**LUNICK DONALD W REV** (912)238-0371
112 Hunter Lane Savannah GA 31405 • bardonlu.com • FG • EM • (SPR 1962 MA)
**LUNNEBERG ALLEN D REV** (248)623-2590
5534 S Rainbow Ln Waterford MI 48329-1559 • lunneberg.al@acd.net • MI • SP • St Mark West Bloomfield MI • (248)363-0741 • (FW 1979 MDIV)
**LUTHER JOHN W REV** (541)988-1616
942 S 32nd Pl Springfield OR 97478 • hopel@ix.netcom.com • NOW • SP • Hope Springfield OR • (541)746-1255 • (SL 1988 MDIV)
**LUTTMANN JOHN B REV** (503)362-6927
4525 Sunland St SE Salem OR 97302 • NOW • SP • St John Salem OR • (503)588-0171 • (SPR 1971 MDIV)
**LUTTMANN RICHARD L REV** (605)934-1832
C/O Peace Lutheran Church 106 Church St Alcester SD 57001-9305 • revrll@eastplains.net • SD • SP • Peace Alcester SD • (605)934-2365 • (SPR 1969)
**LUTZ ARLEIGH L REV** (715)845-5169
1250 Sunset Dr Wausau WI 54401-4255 • alljnwd@aol.com • NW • DP • North Wisconsin Wausau WI • (SPR 1963 DD)
**LUTZ BERNHARD W DR** (218)993-2911
PO Box 302 Crane Lake MN 55725 • brlutz@wcta.net • MNN • EM • (SPR 1967 MDIV DMIN)
**LUTZ CARL E REV**
PO Box 302 Crane Lake MN 55725-0302 • celutz@earthlink.net • PSW • EM • (SL 1959 MS MDIV STM)
**LUTZ CLINTON J REV** (707)576-1148
1829 Cody Ct Santa Rosa CA 95403 • pastorc@stluke-lcms.org • CNH • Assoc • St Luke Santa Rosa CA • (707)545-6772 • (SL 1997 MDIV)
**LUTZ CRAIG EDWARD REV** (973)697-2872
13 Sandlor Ter Oak Ridge NJ 07438-8922 • clutz@nac.net • NJ • SP • Holy Faith Oak Ridge NJ • (973)697-6060 • (SL 1989 MDIV)
**LUTZ DONALD A REV** (319)668-9887
406 W Walnut Williamsburg IA 52361 • IE • EM • (SL 1955)
**LUTZ DONALD H REV** (812)280-8159
1710 Na Charlestown Rd # 9 Jeffersonville IN 47130-9729 • IN • EM • (SL 1954)
**LUTZ EDWARD F REV** (651)489-5924
1068 Iowa Ave W Saint Paul MN 55117-3361 • MNS • EM • (SL 1950 MDIV)
**LUTZ JOHN H REV** (312)725-6132
4567 N Narragansett Ave Chicago IL 60630-3029 • NI • EM • (SL 1945)

**LUTZ MICHAEL J REV** (810)739-3568
8665 Elizabeth Ann St Utica MI 48317-4329 • seniorpa@rust.net • MI • Sn/Adm • Immanuel Macomb MI • (810)286-4231 • (SL 1972 MDIV)

**LUTZ STEPHEN REV** (419)862-0015
C/O Trinity Lutheran Church 412 Fremont St Elmore OH 43416-0022 • sthesaas@accesstoledo.com • OH • SP • Trinity Elmore OH • (419)862-3461 • (FW 1991 MDIV)

**LUTZ THOMAS S REV** (419)335-2556
801 N Shoop Wauseon OH 43567-1800 • emmaus@freewwweb.com • OH • SP • Emmaus Wauseon OH • (419)335-7446 • (FW 1993 MDIV)

**LUTZE JOHN ERNST REV** (920)452-1472
928 Wisconsin Ave Apt 313 Sheboygan WI 53081-3950 • SW • EM • (SL 1939 MDIV)

**LUTZE KARL E REV** (219)462-8043
4 Old Orchard Ln Valparaiso IN 46383-6565 • karlelutze@home.com • IN • EM • (SL 1945)

**LUU TICH HOA REV** (618)549-5893
305 Robinson Cir Apt B-H Carbondale IL 62901 • SI • Asst • Our Savior Carbondale IL • (618)549-1694 • (SL 1995 MDIV)

**LYDICK ROBERT R REV** (888)298-9048
303 Alanna Cir Panama City Beach FL 32408 • fortbob@juno.com • SO • SP • Christ Our Sav Panama City Beach FL • 888-298-9048 • (FW 1997 MDIV)

**LYONS HOWARD D SR. REV** (701)838-3674
1700 7th St NW Minot ND 58703 • turtle@minot.com • ND • EM • (FW 1986 MDIV)

**LYTLE JEFFREY SCOTT REV** (910)355-9430
210 Princeton Dr Jacksonville NC 28546-8424 • chapusn@worldnet.att.net • SW • M Chap • South Wisconsin Milwaukee WI • (414)464-8100 • (FW 1994 MDIV)

## M

**MAACK DAVID R REV**
PSC 9 Box 3238 APO AE 09123 • maackd@chaplain.usaf.org • SE • M Chap • Southeastern Alexandria VA • (SL 1983 MSED MDIV)

**MAACK ROY A REV** (410)426-4911
6619 Birchwood Ave Baltimore MD 21214-1108 • roymsed@aol.com • SE • EM • (SL 1956 MDIV JD)

**MAAS DUANE N REV** (250)301-8936
2262 Westmead Dr SW Decatur AL 35603 • stpaulsdm@aol.com • SO • Assoc • St Paul Decatur AL • (256)353-8759 • (FW 1978 MDIV)

**MAAS EDWARD F REV** (505)281-9342
PO Box 297 Edgewood NM 87015-0297 • gslcnm@juno.com • RM • SP • Good Shepherd Edgewood NM • (505)281-2013 • (CQ 1991 MA)

**MAAS MARK J REV** (307)778-6698
C/O King Of Glory Luth Church 8806 Yellowstone Rd Cheyenne WY 82009-1132 • mmaas@wyoming.com • WY • SP • King of Glory Cheyenne WY • (307)632-1247 • (FW 1987 MDIV)

**MAASKE DENNIS M REV** (402)558-3446
670 N 58th St Omaha NE 68132 • IW • SP • St Thomas Panora IA • (515)755-2051 • (SL 1968 MDIV)

**MAASS ROBERT W REV** (619)466-7071
8726 Tommy Dr San Diego CA 92119-2014 • EN • EM • (SL 1968 MDIV)

**MAASSEL RICHARD G REV** (219)489-0453
10118 Fawns Frd Fort Wayne IN 46825-2079 • IN • EM • (SL 1957 MST)

**MABRY GILBERT R REV** (810)233-4683
2952 Clement St Flint MI 48504-3042 • MI • SP • United/Christ Flint MI • (810)732-3730 • (SPR 1972 MDIV)

**MAC DONALD PHILLIP MICHAEL REV** (704)532-1452
6215 Farm Pond Ln Charlotte NC 28212-1756 • mmacfamly@aol.com • SE • P Df • Chapel Deaf Charlotte NC • (704)334-8319 • (FW 1986 MDIV)

**MAC DOUGALL STEVEN ALAN REV** (618)282-2882
10241 S Prairie Rd Red Bud IL 62278-4611 • stevem53@htc.net • SI • SP • Trinity Red Bud IL • (618)282-2883 • (FW 1992 MDIV)

**MAC GREGOR WILLIAM J REV** (573)683-4067
2827 W 404th Rd Bertrand MO 63823-9179 • MO • EM • (SL 1957)

**MAC KAIN DAVID ELLIOTT REV** (319)685-4050
C/O St John Lutheran Church 2654 CC Ave Victor IA 52347-8534 • IE • SP • St John Victor IA • (319)685-4400 • (FW 1995 MDIV)

**MAC LACHLAN NEAL F REV** (303)444-9022
C/O Mt Zion Lutheran Church 1680 Balsam Ave Boulder CO 80304-3539 • RM • SP • Mount Zion Boulder CO • (303)443-4151 • (SPR 1964 MDIV MA)

**MACKENZIE CAMERON A REV** (219)484-7039
6 Tyndale Pl Fort Wayne IN 46825-4936 • IN • SHS/C • Indiana Fort Wayne IN • (CQ 1981 STM MA MA PHD)

**MACHINA J S FRANK REV** (317)353-1248
6720 E Pleasant Run Pkwy North Dr Indianapolis IN 46219-3432 • IN • Sn/Adm • Christ Indianapolis IN • (317)357-8596 • (SL 1962)

**MACHOLZ STANLEY G REV** (631)277-1497
105 S Ocean Ave 20 Candlewood Path Dix Hills NY 11746-5398 • gmacholz@compuserve.com • AT • EM • (SPR 1952)

**MACHULA LYNN A REV** (320)252-5795
5150 15th St NE Sauk Rapids MN 56379-9615 • MNN • 07/1991 07/2000 • (SPR 1976 MDIV MA)

**MACIUPA MICHAEL REV** (216)773-4128
C/O St John Lutheran Church 550 E Wilbeth Rd Akron OH 44301-2365 • mmaciupa@aol.com • OH • SP • St John Akron OH • (216)773-4128 • (FW 1981 MA MCHME)

**MACK ALVIN C REV** (949)854-9125
5 Lago Norte Irvine CA 92612-2605 • PSW • EM • (SL 1938 MDIV)

**MACK DANIEL C REV** (949)360-6142
6 Carey Ct Aliso Viejo CA 92656-4297 • dmackattak@aol.com • PSW • SP • St Mark Anaheim CA • (714)535-9742 • (SL 1986 MDIV)

**MACK JAMES W REV** (706)235-3254
113 Echota Cir Rome GA 30165-3558 • FG • EM • (SL 1950 MDIV)

**MACKENSEN GORDON R REV**
4873 Sunrise Valley Dr El Cajon CA 92020-8260 • EN • EM • (SPR 1944 MA MCOUN DD)

**MACKEY THOMAS R REV** (906)265-5493
193 Section 16 Rd Iron River MI 49935 • NW • SP • St Paul Iron River MI* • (906)265-4750 • (CQ 1998)

**MACKIE ROGER L REV** (507)389-9780
1726 Orchid Dr N North Mankato MN 56003-1429 • rlmackie@mctcnet.net • MNS • 08/1996 08/2000 • * • (SL 1982 MDIV)

**MACKOWIAK JOHN E REV** (810)412-5705
45517 Spagnuolo Rd Macomb MI 48044-4551 • MI • SP • Redemption Sterling Heights MI • (810)268-1080 • (FW 1977 MDIV)

**MADDICK MICHAEL L REV** (515)477-8389
1244 190th St # A State Center IA 50247-9609 • IE • SP • Trinity State Center IA • (515)483-2682 • (FW 1985 MDIV)

**MADDOX RICHARD REV** (219)462-8694
1658 Stoney Creek Ct Valparaiso IN 46383-6143 • IN • END • Indiana Fort Wayne IN • (SL 1981 JD)

**MADER MYRON G REV** (352)854-8502
3737 SW 57th Ct Ocala FL 34474-9439 • FG • EM • (SL 1957 MDIV)

**MADER ROBERT J REV** (423)915-0030
603 Marboro Dr Johnson City TN 37601-2431 • mader603@aol.com • MDS • SP • Redeemer Elizabethton TN • (423)543-1132 • (SPR 1969 MDIV)

**MAGARINO AURELIO REV** (301)754-0676
10225 Douglas Ave Silver Spring MD 20902-5001 • SE • O Miss • Christos Senor de Vi Hyattsville MD • (301)277-4729 • (CQ 1996)

**MAGER JOHN G REV** (814)226-9213
19 Fairview Ave Clarion PA 16214-8815 • CNH • EM • (SL 1943 MDIV STM MA MLS)

**MAGRUDER DAVID B REV** (218)723-1194
811 S Lake Ave Duluth MN 55802-2403 • dulutheran@aol.com • MNN • Sn/Adm • Mount Olive Duluth MN • (218)724-2500 • (SL 1990 MDIV)

**MAHLBURG STEVEN CHRISTOPHER** (810)792-2139
21430 S Nunneley Rd Clinton Twp MI 48035-1632 • zauber@juno.com • MI • Assoc • St Luke Clinton Township MI • (810)791-1150 • (SL 1995 MDIV)

**MAHLUM DEAN E REV** (612)442-4882
632 E 2nd St Waconia MN 55387-1607 • MNS • Sn/Adm • Trinity Waconia MN • (952)442-4165 • (FW 1987 MDIV)

**MAHN DAVID P REV** (781)828-6598
5 Cynthia Rd Canton MA 02021-1308 • davidmahn@hotmail.com • NE • SP • Messiah Lynnfield MA • (781)334-4111 • (SL 1967 MDIV MBA)

**MAHNKE EDWARD J REV** (713)723-2486
5238 Wigton Dr Houston TX 77096-5113 • edmahnke@aol.com • TX • EM • (SL 1943 MDIV DD LITTD)

**MAHNKE RONALD W REV** (701)852-6606
516 28th Ave SW Minot ND 58701-7065 • ND • Inst C • North Dakota Fargo ND • (SL 1968 MCOUN MDIV)

**MAHNKEN MERLE F REV** (712)676-2242
PO Box 6 Schleswig IA 51461-0006 • mfmahnken@juno.com • IW • SP • Immanuel Schleswig IA • (712)676-2235 • (SL 1991 MDIV)

**MAHSMAN DAVID L REV** (314)965-1110
142 Edwin Ave Saint Louis MO 63122-4835 • david.mahsman@lcms.org • MO • S Ex/S • Missouri Saint Louis MO • (314)317-4550 • (FW 1983 MDIV STM)

**MAIER DAVID P E REV** (517)887-1121
2573 Ayrshire Dr Lansing MI 48911-6489 • dpemaier@oursaviorchurch.org • MI • Sn/Adm • Our Savior Lansing MI • (517)882-8665 • (FW 1982 MA MDIV)

**MAIER PAUL L REV** (616)375-3967
8383 West Main St Kalamazoo MI 49009 • paul.maier@wmich.edu • MI • EM • (SL 1955 MA PHD LLD LITTD)

**MAIER SIMON REV** (425)644-7599
13849 SE 10th St Bellevue WA 98005-3717 • NOW • EM • (SL 1948)

**MAIER WALTER A DR** (219)637-5170
12017 Westwind Dr Fort Wayne IN 46845-1341 • IN • SHS/C • Indiana Fort Wayne IN • (SL 1948 STM MA THD LHD)

**MAIER WALTER A III REV** (219)483-7275
5017 Lonesome Oak Trl Fort Wayne IN 46845-9103 • maierwa3@mail.ctsfw.edu • IN • SHS/C • Indiana Fort Wayne IN • (FW 1978 MDIV PHD)

**MAIN RAYMOND H REV** (317)786-7583
1002 E Bradbury Ave Indianapolis IN 46203-4205 • IN • Inst C • Indiana Fort Wayne IN • (SL 1966 MDIV)

**MAIRE JULIAN F REV**
11673 Dorothy Ln Warren MI 48093-8915 • EN • 01/1987 01/2000 • (SL 1983 MDIV)

**MAJER WILLIAM JOSEPH REV** (847)259-5043
310 N Stratford Rd Arlington Hts IL 60004-6405 • bmajer@aol.com • EN • Assoc • Faith Arlington Hts IL • (847)253-4839 • (SPR 1973 MDIV)

**MAJESKI ERIC W REV**
30788 Roselawn Dr Warren MI 48093-5946 • MI • Assoc • St John Fraser MI • (810)293-0333 • (FW 1993 MDIV)

**MAKI DAVID REV** (615)230-9816
120 Canterbury Close Gallatin TN 37066 • maki3family@yahoo.com • MDS • SP • Trinity Gallatin TN • (615)452-3352 • (FW 1982 MDIV)

**MALACH WARREN R REV** (206)528-0269
5036 22nd Ave NE Apt 101 Seattle WA 98105-5731 • NOW • 08/1991 11/1999 • (FW 1982 MDIV)

**MALAND RANDY C REV** (507)223-5223
302 N Pine Canby MN 56220 • MNN • SP • Zion Boyd MN* • (320)855-2554 • (FW 1995 MDIV)

**MALEC RAYMOND A REV** (610)866-5981
1240 E Fourth St Bethlehem PA 18015 • malecr@aol.com • S • Sn/Adm • Concordia Macungie PA* • (610)965-3265 • (SL 1983 MDIV)

**MALINSKY MICHAEL A REV** (812)375-9575
3810 Waycross Dr Columbus IN 47203 • assistem@mindspring.com • IN • Assoc • St Peter Columbus IN • (812)372-1571 • (SL 1977 MDIV)

**MALLETT LARRY G REV** (812)966-2446
C/O Good Shepherd Luth Church PO Box 310 Medora IN 47260-0310 • IN • SP • Good Shepherd Medora IN* • (812)966-2446 • (FW 1985 MDIV)

**MALME SCOTT C REV** (815)398-6458
2022 Birchwood Dr Rockford IL 61107-1809 • NI • Assoc • St Paul Rockford IL • (815)963-5435 • (SL 1992 MDIV STM)

**MALMSTROM RICHARD ERIC REV** (805)525-6825
906 E Virginia Terrace Santa Paula CA 93060 • PSW • SP • Our Redeemer Ojai CA* • (805)646-2064 • (FW 2000 MDIV)

**MALONE C ROBERT REV** (773)737-1416
C/O Luther Hs South 3130 W 87th St Chicago IL 60652-3454 • NI • Tchr • Luther HS South Chicago IL • (773)737-1416 • (SL 1980 MDIV)

**MALONE HENRY B REV** (517)864-3663
C/O St John Lutheran Church 6600 Ruth Rd Palms MI 48465-9706 • peerhank1@aol.com • MI • SP • St John Palms MI • (517)864-3663 • (SL 1994 MDIV)

**MALOTKY ARDEN H REV** (952)442-5397
8975 Island View Rd Waconia MN 55387-9605 • MNS • EM • (SL 1953)

**MALOTKY HAROLD E REV** (402)534-2050
PO Box 446 Utica NE 68456-0446 • hm50841@navix.net • NEB • EM • (SL 1942)

**MALOTKY RAYMOND P REV** (863)324-1631
212 Shore Loop Winter Haven FL 33884-2575 • FG • EM • (SL 1956)

**MALTZ MYRON C REV** (580)336-2668
1316 N 7th St Perry OK 73077-2235 • mcmaltz@hotmail.com • OK • SP • Christ Perry OK • (580)336-2347 • (SPR 1967 MDIV STM)

**MALTZAHN ROBERT F DR** (850)926-9074
15 Kelley Ct Crawfordville FL 32327-3020 • malt2@aol.com • FG • EM • (SL 1957 DMIN)

**MANDEL WARREN G REV** (708)862-2111
514 Sibley Blvd Calumet City IL 60409 • wgmonsibley@netscape.net • NI • SP • Grace South Holland IL* • (708)331-7706 • (SL 1968 MDIV)

**MANDLEY JASON LOUIS REV** (517)742-3474
22000 County Rd 452 Hillman MI 49746 • MI • SP • Minnesota North Brainerd MN • (FW 1996 MDIV)

**MANGELSDORF KENNETH D REV** (219)255-6096
2402 Lincoln Way E Mishawaka IN 46544-3313 • kdmangelsdorf@aol.com • IN • Sn/Adm • St Peter Mishawaka IN • (219)255-5585 • (SL 1964 MDIV STM)

**MANGOLD KENNETH J REV**
109 E Church St Box 437 Washburn IL 61570 • CI • SP • St John Washburn IL* • (309)248-7153 • (SL 1998 MDIV)

**MANGONE CHARLES R REV** (817)547-5554
RR 1 Box 2208 Kempner TX 76539-9504 • TX • EM • * • (FW 1981 MDIV)

**MANILA JOHN K REV**
COMFLEACT PSC 473 BOX 10 FPO AP 96349-1102 • NOW • M Chap • Northwest Portland OR • (FW 1989 MDIV)

**MANKIN CLARENCE H REV** (217)648-2637
PO Box 778 Atlanta IL 61723-0778 • NI • SP • Trinity Pontiac IL • (815)842-1205 • (FW 1985 MDIV)

**MANN DENNIS C REV** (330)562-2784
335 Chatham Dr Aurora OH 44202-7811 • hopelc@nccw.net • OH • D Miss • Hope Aurora OH • (330)562-9660 • (CQ 1992 MAR)

**MANN DONALD DALE REV** (515)546-4790
1444 Johnson Ave Fort Dodge IA 50501-8589 • IW • SP • Trinity Fort Dodge IA • (515)546-6331 • (SPR 1968 MDIV)

**MANN H ALBERT REV** (513)877-2231
8309 Morrow Rossburg Rd Morrow OH 45152-8375 • hagm@msn.com • OH • EM • (SL 1954 MDIV)

**MANN JAMES K REV** (512)898-5278
105 Regina Ct PO Box 642 Thorndale TX 76577-0642 • prjimmann@hotmail.com • TX • SP • St Paul Thorndale TX • (512)898-2711 • (CQ 1980 MDIV)

**MANN ROBERT H REV** (810)982-3319
3034 E Village Ln Port Huron MI 48060-1827 • joroman@advnet.net • MI • SP • Trinity Port Huron MI • (810)984-2993 • (SL 1968 MDIV)

**MANN WILLIAM B V REV** (703)729-2286
20269 Rosedale Ct Ashburn VA 20147-3317 • oswlc@aol.com • SE • SP • Our Saviors Way Ashburn VA • (703)858-9254 • (SL 1985 MDIV)

**MANNING GREGORY T** (219)426-0904
1716 Cody St Fort Wayne IN 46805 • IN • Assoc • Bethlehem Fort Wayne IN • (219)744-3228 • (FW 2000 MDIV)

**MANNING MARK L REV** (714)685-9046
2710 N Gaff St Orange CA 92865-2920 • PSW • Assoc • St Paul Orange CA • (714)637-2640 • (SL 1998 MDIV)

**MANNS RICHARD W REV** (508)362-1591
24 Surrey Ln Barnstable MA 02630-1501 • NE • EM • (SL 1947 MDIV)

**MANSKE CHARLES L DR** (949)551-4484
14782 Elm Ave Irvine CA 92606-2658 • uscluther@aol.com • PSW • EM • (SL 1957 MDIV MA PHD)

**MANTEUFEL THOMAS REV** (314)727-5016
1067 Wilson Ave Saint Louis MO 63130-2236 • manteufelt@csl.edu • MO • SHS/C • Missouri Saint Louis MO • (314)317-4550 • (SL 1968 MDIV STM PHD)

**MANUS RICHARD M REV** (636)305-0822
306 Jefferson Circle Dr Fenton MO 63026 • richard.manus@lcms.org • MO • S Ex/S • Missouri Saint Louis MO • (314)317-4550 • (SL 1970 MDIV MA DMIN)

**MANWEILER JOHN REV**
2260 Red Cliffs Dr St George UT 84790-8153 • RM • SP • Trinity St George UT • (435)628-1850 • (FW 1988 MDIV)

**MAPPES MARTIN L REV** (812)944-6835
5369 State Road 62 Georgetown IN 47122-9227 • IN • EM • (SL 1954 MDIV)

**MARCIS ALBERT M REV** (440)842-1589
6800 W Pleasant Valley Rd Parma OH 44129-6743 • S • EM • (SL 1954 DD)

**MARCIS PETER C REV** (419)599-5609
610 Cripple Creek Ct Napoleon OH 43545-2223 • marcis@henry-net.com • OH • Assoc • St Paul Napoleon OH • (419)592-3535 • (SL 1987 MDIV)

**MARCIS T RICHARD SR. REV** (330)220-9056
4506 Patricia Dr Brunswick OH 44212-2090 • trichmarcissr@aol.com • MI • EM • (SL 1956)

**MARCIS THOMAS R REV** (701)258-4075
1982 N 20th St Bismarck ND 58501-2368 • tmarcisjr@aol.com • ND • Sn/Adm • Zion Bismarck ND • (701)223-8286 • (SL 1986 MDIV)

**MARCIS WALTHER P REV** (216)481-1578
17619 Nottingham Rd Cleveland OH 44119-2905 • OH • SP • St John Cleveland OH • (216)531-1156 • (SL 1961 MDIV MA DMIN)

**MARG GEORGE C REV** (573)346-3898
RR 3 Box 3460 Camdenton MO 65020-9719 • MO • EM • (SL 1949 MDIV MA)

**MARHENKE LARRY E REV** (972)572-7832
8906 Bluestem Circle Dallas TX 75249-1106 • larry-sonya³marhenke@juno.com • TX • 12/1997 • (SPR 1965)

**MARINCIC SCOTT M REV** (419)425-3025
719 Carnahan Ave Findlay OH 45840-5639 • marincic@friendlynet.com • OH • 08/1998 08/2000 • (FW 1987 MDIV)

**MARKEL JERRY E REV** (612)652-2844
4386 41st St W PO Box 69 Webster MN 55088 • MNS • SP • St John Webster MN • (612)652-2844 • (SPR 1969)

**MARKS MARTIN L REV**
1921 Calgary Trl Little Rock AR 722121-540 • MDS • SP • Lord Of Life Little Rock AR • (501)223-2292 • (SL 1997 MDIV)

**MARKS MATTHEW T REV**
532 Brinkman Dr Perryville MO 63775 • MO • Assoc • Immanuel Perryville MO • (573)547-8317 • (SL 2000 MDIV)

**MARKUS JAMES L REV** (360)426-3290
40 E North Haven Ct Shelton WA 98584-8500 • jimarkus@aol.com • NOW • SP • Mount Olive Shelton WA • (360)426-6353 • (SL 1986 MDIV)

**MARKWORTH JAMES A IV REV** (612)463-2501
18236 Embers Ave Farmington MN 55024-9258 • MNS • SP • Trinity Farmington MN • (651)463-7225 • (SL 1974 MDIV)

**MARKWORTH RICHARD C REV** (352)753-2371
409 Aldama Ave Lady Lake FL 32159-9283 • rmmarkwo@atlantic.net • FG • SP • Trinity Summerfield FL • (352)307-4500 • (SPR 1967 MDIV)

**MARLER WILLIAM R REV** (417)883-7188
3111 W Tracy Ct Springfield MO 65807-8173 • wrmarler@pcls.net • MO • Sn/Adm • Trinity Springfield MO • (417)866-5878 • (SL 1983 MDIV)

**MAROZIK JOHN R REV** (707)938-1191
925 Arguello Ct Sonoma CA 95476-5455 • grammaann@vom.com • CNH • EM • (SL 1960)

**MARQUARDT CLARENCE L REV** (316)342-8144
2520 Loma Vista Dr Emporia KS 66801-5856 • KS • SP • Faith Emporia KS • (316)342-3590 • (SL 1970 MDIV)

**MARQUARDT ELVIN H REV** (623)972-0258
14202 N Crown Point Ct Sun City AZ 85351-2339 • PSW • EM • (SL 1947)

**MARQUARDT JEFFREY DAVID REV**
C/O Trinity Lutheran Church 1330 Fiske Blvd S Rockledge FL 32955-2318 • tlcspastor@iol15.com • FG • SP • Trinity Rockledge FL • (407)636-5431 • (SL 1994 MDIV)

**MARQUARDT MARTIN J REV** (319)396-7854
3731 Knight Dr SW Cedar Rapids IA 52404 • IE • EM • (SL 1959 MAT)

**MARQUARDT OSCAR A REV** (503)669-6624
2150 SW 18th Ct Gresham OR 97080-9716 • NOW • EM • (SPR 1952)

**MARQUARDT RUDOLPH H REV** (507)433-1238
1200 20th St NE Austin MN 55912-4155 • MNS • EM • (SL 1936)

**MARQUART KURT REV** (219)485-8901
7113 Tanbark Ln Fort Wayne IN 46835-1846 • EN • SHS/C • English Farmington MI • (SL 1959 MDIV MA)

**MARSCHKE PAUL REV** (734)662-9586
3017 Bolgos Cir Ann Arbor MI 48105-1512 • marscp@ccaa.edu • MI • SHS/C • Michigan Ann Arbor MI • (SL 1963 MDIV MA PHD)

**MARSCHNER LARRY D REV** (701)624-5341
203 1st Ave E PO Box 285 Sawyer ND 58781-0285 • ND • SP • St Peter Sawyer ND • (701)624-5688 • (SPR 1972 MDIV)

**MARSH JOSEPH A REV** (715)623-3481
W10084 Dennis Ln Antigo WI 54409-9005 • jmarsh@newnorth.net • NW • Assoc • Peace Antigo WI • (715)623-2200 • (SPR 1976 MDIV)

**MARSH PRENTICE D REV** (773)994-8685
8448 S Indiana Ave Chicago IL 60619-5607 • pdmarsh@flash.net • EN • D Miss • Ephphatha-Deaf Chicago IL • (773)723-3232 • (CQ 1981 MA)

**MARSH WILLIAM H REV** (205)385-2144
2140 Hwy 162 Pine Hill AL 36769 • SO • SP • Epiphany Arlington AL* • (334)385-2435 • (CQ 1982)

**MARSHALL FRANK T REV** (904)765-1133
1503 Carbondale Dr N Jacksonville FL 32208-1514 • FG • SP • St Paul Jacksonville FL • (904)765-4219 • (SPR 1973 MDIV)

**MARSHALL JAMES B REV** (334)476-1468
306 E Lourdes Cir Mobile AL 36617-2407 • jmarshall@bellsouth.net • SO • SP • Faith Mobile AL • (205)471-1629 • (GB 1961 MA JD)

**MARSHALL ROBERT H JR. REV** (570)342-3374
C/O Immanuel Lutheran Ch 238 Reese St Scranton PA 18508-1449 • rhmjr-ilc@juno.com • EA • SP • Immanuel Scranton PA • (570)342-3374 • (FW 1987 MDIV)

**MARSHALL STEWART A REV** (901)885-6591
1200 Highland Ave Union City TN 38261-4409 • sangrant@usa.net • MDS • SP • Faith Union City TN • (901)885-9562 • (SL 1982 MDIV)

**MARSHALL TIMOTHY J REV**
650 E 12th St - Apt D202 York NE 68467 • timnsun@ix.netcom.com • PSW • Asst • Abiding Savior Lake Forest CA* • (949)830-1460 • (SL 1997 MDIV)

**MARSHALL ULMER REV** (334)343-7273
6405 Saint Thomas Ct Mobile AL 36618-3242 • gmarsh-6247@amol.com • SO • SP • Trinity Mobile AL* • (334)456-7929 • (SPR 1973 MDIV)

**MARSTON WILLIAM M REV** (309)692-7475
6001 N Hamilton Rd Peoria IL 61614-3352 • CI • EM • * • (SPR 1966)

**MARTEN JAMES R REV** (573)996-5151
510 Lafayette Doniphan MO 63935 • MO • 03/1992 03/2000 • * • (CQ 1988 MA)

**MARTEN WILLIAM G REV** (303)745-6242
2560 S Sable Way Aurora CO 80014-2438 • billmarten@juno.com • RM • EM • * • (SL 1961 MDIV)

**MARTENS ELDEN H REV** (406)862-5927
216 Bear Trl Whitefish MT 59937-8427 • MT • EM • * • (SPR 1942)

**MARTENS RAY F REV** (512)219-9131
6003 Sierra Grande Dr Austin TX 78759-5181 • rfmartens@juno.com • TX • EM • * • (SL 1956 MDIV STM DST)

**MARTENS ROBERT J REV** (815)624-4271
136 E Russell St Rockton IL 61072-2942 • rmar23501@aol.com • SW • EM • * • (SPR 1950)

**MARTH DAVID B REV** (314)772-6795
2422 S 18th St Saint Louis MO 63104-4303 • dbmarth@aol.com • MO • Sn/Adm • Trinity Saint Louis MO • (314)231-4092 • (SL 1973 MDIV)

**MARTH WALTER D REV** (320)587-8563
860 Oak St NE Hutchinson MN 55350-1275 • MNS • EM • (SL 1959)

**MARTIN CLARENCE L REV** (901)372-2969
6605 Stephan Ridge Cove Bartlett TN 38135 • mncmartin@msn.com • MDS • Trinity Saint Louis MO • (314)231-4092 • (CQ 1997)

**MARTIN DANIEL G REV** (541)572-2924
257 Miller Ln Myrtle Point OR 97458 • martind82840@peoplepc.com • NOW • SP • St James Myrtle Point OR • (541)572-5665 • (SPR 1971 MDIV)

**MARTIN DAVID W REV** (734)453-5252
45720 Larchmont Canton MI 48187 • EN • SP • Risen Christ Plymouth MI • (734)453-5252 • (FW 1987 MDIV)

**MARTIN FRANK H REV** (770)386-8545
28 Engineer Ln SW Cartersville GA 30120-6181 • marbunch9@cs.com • FG • SP • Savior Of All Cartersville GA • (770)387-0379 • (FW 1989 MDIV)

**MARTIN GARY E REV** (830)775-7375
126 Alta Vista Dr Del Rio TX 78840-2658 • gary2martin@freewwweb.com • TX • D Miss • Cristo El Salvador Del Rio TX • (830)775-9904 • (SPR 1974 MDIV)

**MARTIN GEROLD R REV** (636)797-4432
60 Shepherds Way Hillsboro MO 63050-2605 • SW • EM • (TH 1932)

**MARTIN JAMES C REV** (512)523-6763
9434 Arden Bnd San Antonio TX 78250-2712 • pastor³martin@juno.com • TX • Sn/Adm • Redeemer San Antonio TX • (210)732-4112 • (FW 1989 MDIV)

**MARTIN JAMES E REV**
3431 Arbor St Houston TX 77004-6302 • TX • SP • Holy Cross Houston TX • (713)524-0192 • (SPR 1969)

**MARTIN JAMES P REV** (440)237-1940
12339 Drake Rd North Royalton OH 44133-5427 • rrchurch@aol.com • OH • Sn/Adm • Royal Redeemer North Royalton OH • (440)237-7958 • (SPR 1973 MDIV)

**MARTIN JAMES R REV** (308)665-1394
916 2nd St Crawford NE 69339 • pwbmartin@panhandle.net • WY • SP • Bethlehem Crawford NE* • (308)665-2058 • (FW 1999 MDIV)

**MARTIN JUAN M REV**
3000 NW 75th Ave Hollywood FL 33024-2712 • FG • SP • Prince Peace Hollywood FL* • (305)983-8599 • (CQ 1976 STM)

**MARTIN KENNETH A REV** (217)465-2709
21 Concordia Dr Paris IL 61944 • CI • EM • * • (SPR 1954)

**MARTIN KEVIN WAYNE REV** (919)787-0497
5105 Talton Cir Raleigh NC 27612 • SE • SP • Our Savior Raleigh NC • (919)832-8822 • (CQ 1992 MDIV MA)

**MARTIN MARK D REV** (314)334-2656
392 County Rd 627 Cape Girardeau MO 63701-8748 • martin@showme.net • MO • SP • Trinity Cape Girardeau MO • (314)334-4549 • (SL 1991 MDIV)

**MARTIN MICHAEL R REV**
2744 Brentwood Ave East Lansing MI 48823-4717 • michael.martin@grafix-net.com • MI • Inst C • Michigan Ann Arbor MI • (FW 1979 MDIV EDS)

**MARTIN MURRAY W REV** (914)747-4097
31 Milford St Hawthorne NY 10532-1801 • AT • EM • (SL 1959)

**MARTIN RONALD L REV** (714)998-5013
1895 N Shattuck Pl Orange CA 92865-4640 • rmartin@stpaulsorg.org • PSW • Sn/Adm • St Paul Orange CA • (714)637-2640 • (SPR 1973 MDIV)

**MARTIN TERRY L REV**
PO Box 601 White SD 57276-0601 • SD • SP • Zion White SD* • (605)629-4201 • (SL 1973 MDIV DMIN)

**MARTIN THEODORE A REV** (978)422-8104
31 Gates Rd Sterling MA 01564-1407 • NE • EM • * • (SL 1939 MDIV MST)

**MARTIN WAYNE S REV** (217)726-0975
5212 Wildcat Run Springfield IL 62707-7802 • bmartin839@aol.com • CI • EM • * • (CQ 1992 MRE)

**MARTINEK ROBERT W REV**
114 E Walnut St Mason City IL 62664-1164 • CI • SP • Christ Mason City IL • (217)482-5168 • (FW 1988 MDIV)

**MARTINEZ ELIAS REV**
1640 Clinton Ct Melrose Park IL 60160-2421 • NI • Assoc • St Paul Melrose Park IL • (708)343-1000 • (CQ 1995)

**MARTIS ALVIA MCEWEN REV** (419)267-3349
20-129 Cty Rd X PO Box 282 Ridgeville Corners OH 43555 • zionreva@bright.net • OH • SP • Zion Ridgeville Corners OH • (419)267-3429 • (FW 1996 MDIV)

**MARXHAUSEN JONATHAN REV** (612)702-0467
2432 Lamplight Dr Woodbury MN 55125 • marxy@juno.com • MNS • SP • St John Woodbury MN • (651)436-6621 • (SL 1991 MDIV)

**MASAKI NAOMICHI REV** (314)505-7720
12 D Founders Way Clayton MO 63105 • nmasaki@sprynet.com • NJ • 11/1997 11/1999 • (FW 1991 MA MDIV STM)

**MASAKI SHIGERU REV** (812)378-3880
3201 Thomas Trce Columbus IN 47203-2846 • smasaki@christianliving.net • IN • D Miss • Indiana Fort Wayne IN • (CQ 1994 MDIV MDIV)

**MASCHKE ROBERT O REV** (414)452-8593
656 School St Kohler WI 53044-1430 • SW • EM • (SPR 1945 MDIV)

**MASCHKE TIMOTHY H DR** (262)375-3592
1624 N Pine St Grafton WI 53024-2041 • timothy.maschke@cuw.edu • SW • SHS/C • South Wisconsin Milwaukee WI • (414)464-8100 • (SL 1974 MDIV STM PHD DMIN)

**MASHEK JOHN D REV** (330)825-2220
1281 Gardner Blvd Norton OH 44203-6668 • johnma@raex.com • S • SP • St Matthew Norton OH • (216)825-4100 • (FW 1980 MDIV)

**MASKE STEVEN R REV** 810)659-6124
728 Hickorywood Flushing MI 48433 • MI • Asst • St Paul Flint MI • (810)239-6200 • (SL 2000 MDIV)

**MASON JOHN S REV** (800)248-1930
C/O Gloria Dei Lutheran Church 7601 SW 39th St Davie FL 33328-2716 • FG • Florida-Georgia Orlando FL • (SL 1997 MDIV)

**MASON JOSEPH E REV**
18160 Cottonwood Rd # 437 Sunriver OR 97707-9317 • NOW • 10/1993 10/1999 • (FW 1983 MDIV)

**MASON PATRICK DENNIS REV** (316)356-4651
945 N Missouri St Ulysses KS 67880 • grace@pld.com • KS • SP • Grace Ulysses KS • (316)356-3161 • (FW 1983 MDIV)

**MASSEY STEVEN M REV**
5344 S Francisco Ave Chicago IL 60632-2226 • S • SP • Dr Martin Luther Chicago IL • (773)776-8104 • (SL 1988)

**MAST MICHAEL WM REV** (540)288-0945
2 Silverthorn Ct Stafford VA 22554 • hisjoy4u@msn.com • SE • D Miss • Southeastern Alexandria VA • (SL 1978 MDIV)

**MATARAZZO PHILIP R REV** (609)883-3872
1105 Parkside Ave Ewing NJ 08618 • pastor@bethanylutherannj.org • EN • SP • Bethany Trenton NJ • (609)883-2860 • (SL 2000 MDIV)

**MATASOVSKY DANIEL V REV** (612)457-3586
7060 Babcock Trl Inver Grove MN 55077-2510 • MNS • Sn/Adm • Old Emanuel Inver Grove Heights MN • (651)457-3929 • (SPR 1965)

**MATEJ ROBERT E REV** (216)521-7948
13028 Madison Ave Lakewood OH 44107-4931 • S • SP • SS Peter&Paul Lakewood OH • (216)221-7286 • (SPR 1962)

**MATEJKA RAYMOND A REV** (708)343-4809
734 Portsmouth Westchester IL 60154 • NI • EM • (SPR 1965)

**MATELSKI HARRY A REV** (310)531-4076
5228 Verdura Ave Lakewood CA 90712-2228 • EN • M Chap • English Farmington MI • (FW 1979 MDIV)

**MATHER ELWOOD E REV** (845355-3220
25 Castle High Rd Middletown NY 10940-6788 • martinusl@aol.com • AT • SP • St Peter Pine Island NY • (845)258-4541 • (SL 1979 MDIV MA PHD)

**MATHER GEORGE A REV** (610)380-3391
255 Baker Rd Coatesville PA 19320-1403 • faith@icdc.com • EN • SP • Faith/Brandywine Downingtown PA • (610)383-0889 • (FW 1989 MDIV)

**MATHERS J DEREK REV** (416)221-5711
3202 Bayview Ave North York ON M2M 3R7 CANADA • stluke@idirect.ca • EN • Sn/Adm • St Luke North York ON CANADA • (416)221-8900 • (SC 1984 MDIV)

**MATHEWS MICHAEL WILLIAM REV** (507)239-2446
PO Box 116 Waldorf MN 56091-0116 • mickmwm@aol.com • MNS • SP • First Waldorf MN* • (507)239-2431 • (SL 1993 MDIV)

**MATHISON RONALD L REV**
17725 53rd St New Germany MN 55367-9337 • MNS • SP • St John New Germany MN • (612)353-2109 • (CQ 1988)

**MATRANGA GEORGE J REV** (916)427-0800
6372 Driftwood St Sacramento CA 95831-1044 • revmat@lanset.com • CNH • SP • Our Savior Sacramento CA • (916)451-2855 • (SL 1964 MDIV MA)

**MATRO LAWRENCE K REV** (231)271-3637
8876 E Bahle Rd Suttons Bay MI 49682-9142 • ilcleland@juno.com • MI • SP • Immanuel Leland MI • (231)256-9464 • (FW 1984 MDIV)

**MATSON RONALD P REV** (708)453-5357
2932 N 75th Ct Elmwood Park IL 60707-1123 • revmatson@juno.com • NI • EM • (SPR 1966 MED MDIV)

**MATTHEWS DARRELL REV** (913)592-9982
22404 S Cedar Niles Rd Spring Hill KS 66083-9003 • revmatt2@juno.com • KS • SP • Christ Manhattan KS • (785)776-2227 • (CQ 1985 MEAD MED)

**MATTHEWS MARK A REV** (708)749-8899
3138 Home Ave Berwyn IL 60402-2910 • theoldrev@hotmail.com • EN • SP • Concordia Berwyn IL • (708)484-9784 • (FW 1985 MAR)

**MATTHIAS ELMER W REV** (714)572-9737
17370 Golden Maple Ln Yorba Linda CA 92886-5194 • PSW • EM • (SL 1945 MDIV DMIN)

**MATTHIES RICHARD J REV** (303)755-8573
10062 E Wyoming Pl Apt 2218 Denver CO 80231 • RM • EM • (SPR 1963)

**MATTHIESSEN DONALD W REV** (815)772-4345
C/O Our Savior Luth Church 21496 Hazel Rd Sterling IL 61081-9158 • NI • SP • Our Savior Sterling IL • (815)772-4345 • (SPR 1975)

**MATTIL MICHAEL J REV** (903)868-2680
1200 Cimmaron Trl Sherman TX 75092-4702 • revmattil@texoma.net • TX • SP • Grace Denison TX • (903)465-1016 • (SL 1984 MDIV)

**MATTSON DANIEL LLOYD REV** (314)892-2653
4808 Laketon Ct Saint Louis MO 63128-3915 • dan.mattson@lcms.org • MO • S Ex/S • Missouri Saint Louis MO • (314)317-4550 • (SL 1968 MA MDIV PHD)

**MATTSON JOHN M REV** (216)259-5789
4145 S Ridge Rd Perry OH 44081-9612 • OH • EM • (SPR 1958)

**MATTSON LEONARD D REV** (813)494-9147
1905 SE Maple Dr Arcadia FL 34266-7465 • FG • 10/1991 10/1999 • (SL 1970 MDIV)

**MATZAT DONALD G REV** (724)743-4251
1006 Woodridge Dr Canonsburg PA 15317 • MO • EM • (SL 1965)

**MATZAT WILLIAM A DR** (573)335-6540
1908 W Cape Rock Dr Cape Girardeau MO 63701-2625 • matzatb@hotmail.com • MO • Inst C • Missouri Saint Louis MO • (314)317-4550 • (SL 1967 MDIV DMIN)

**MATZKE BRUCE R REV**
3912 W 97th Pl Westminster CO 80031-2630 • RM • Assoc • Gethsemane Northglenn CO • (303)451-6895 • (FW 1990 MDIV)

**MATZKE GERALD D REV** (937)349-6001
7978 State Route 38 Milford Center OH 43045-9722 • revgmatzke1@juno.com • OH • SP • St Paul Milford Center OH • (937)349-2405 • (CQ 1981)

**MATZKE MARK G REV** (330)995-2658
475 Sycamore Ln Apt 207 Aurora OH 44202 • ourredeemerlutheran@earthlink.net • OH • Asst • Our Redeemer Solon OH • (440)248-4066 • (FW 1998 MDIV)

**MATZKE MARVIN L REV** (309)527-6806
475 E Clay St El Paso IL 61738-1506 • CI • EM • (SPR 1949 MDIV)

**MAU DWAYNE H REV** (914)497-7202
12 Cranbury Rd Washingtonville NY 10992-9998 • stpauldm@ny.frontiercomm.net • AT • SP • St Paul Monroe NY • (845)782-5600 • (SL 1968 MDIV MED LLD)

**MAU GERHARD REV** (810)794-4642
1625 Washington St Algonac MI 48001-1355 • MI • SP • First Algonac MI • (810)794-4642 • (FW 1983 MDIV)

**MAU JON C REV** (719)276-2280
489 Glenmoor Rd Canon City CO 81212-2719 • j.mau@juno.com • RM • Inst C • Rocky Mountain Aurora CO • (SL 1994 MDIV)

**MAU RICHARD A REV** (847)391-9284
1780 E Algonquin Des Plaines IL 60016 • ilc60016@juno.com • NI • SP • Immanuel Des Plaines IL • (847)824-3652 • (FW 1999 MSED)

**MAULELLA ROBERT J REV** (305)252-0691
8791 SW 124th St Kendall FL 33176 • rob-lindamaulella@juno.com • FG • SP • Concordia Miami FL • (305)235-6123 • (SL 1997 MDIV)

**MAURER FRANK R REV** (402)371-9149
1213 Greenlawn Dr Norfolk NE 68701-2638 • fmaurer@ncfcomm.com • NEB • Sn/Adm • Christ Norfolk NE • (402)371-1210 • (FW 1980 MDIV DMIN)

**MAURER RUDOLPH H JR. REV** (507)278-3169
PO Box 36 Good Thunder MN 56037-0037 • rudymaurer@ao1.com • MNS • SP • St John Good Thunder MN • (507)278-3635 • (FW 1983 MDIV)

**MAVIS JAMES MICHAEL REV** (406)232-4983
205 S Center Miles City MT 59301-4401 • mavl@midrivers.com • MT • SP • Trinity Miles City MT* • (406)232-4983 • (FW 1993 MDIV)

**MAXFIELD JOHN A REV** (609)919-0796
208 Loetscher Pl 3A Princeton NJ 08540 • jjmaxfield@juno.com • NJ • 09/1999 • * • (FW 1989 MDIV MA)

**MAXON BRADFORD REV** (630)530-0537
150 W Harrison St Elmhurst IL 60126-5021 • maxonhere@aol.com • EN • SP • Messiah Elmhurst IL • (630)279-4775 • (CQ 1984 MDIV)

**MAXWELL LEE A REV**
PO Box 517 Maryville IL 62062-0517 • lmaxwell@inlink.com • SI • SP • St John Maryville IL • (618)344-8989 • (SL 1983 MA THD THD)

**MAXWELL RONNIE D REV** (317)878-9149
136 Clear Spring Ln Trafalgar IN 46181 • IN • SP • Shepherd Hills Morgantown IN • (812)988-8057 • (FW 1997 MDIV)

**MAY DANIEL P REV** (765)474-6897
1905 Beck Ln Lafayette IN 47909-3109 • pastormay@stjameslaf.org • IN • Sn/Adm • St James Lafayette IN • (765)423-1616 • (SPR 1970 MDIV)

**MAY DOUGLAS C REV** (505)835-9648
915 Bursum Pl Socorro NM 87801-4710 • dougmay@rt66.com • RM • SP • Hope Socorro NM • (505)835-9648 • (SPR 1965 MDIV)

**MAY EDWARD H REV** (608)362-2851
1830 Cranston Rd Beloit WI 53511-2544 • ehmay@hotmail.com • SW • SP • Trinity Beloit WI • (608)362-3607 • (SPR 1975 MDIV)

**MAY MICHAEL N REV** (913)281-1886
712 Reynolds Ave Kansas City KS 66101-3421 • sllckc@msn.com • KS • SP • St Luke Kansas City KS • (913)281-3102 • (SL 1971 MDIV)

**MAY RONALD P REV** (317)481-8454
6813 Thousand Oaks Ln Indianapolis IN 46214 • rpmay3@iquest.net • IN • SP • Our Shepherd Indianapolis IN • (317)271-9103 • (FW 1989 MDIV)

**MAY TIMOTHY DOUGLAS REV** (414)604-8817
3642 S 83rd St Milwaukee WI 53220 • maytk@execpc.com • SW • SP • St Stephen Milwaukee WI • (414)384-8620 • (SL 1991 MDIV)

**MAY WILBUR T REV** (785)475-3124
104 S Griffith Oberlin KS 67749-2308 • KS • EM • (SL 1948 STM)

**MAYER HERMAN R REV** (501)795-2733
8243 Barron Rd Bentonville AR 72712-9153 • OK • Asst • St John Lawton OK • (580)353-0556 • (SL 1945 MMIN)

**MAYER MARTIN E REV** (619)722-6926
78989 Quiet Springs Dr Palm Desert CA 92211-1583 • PSW • EM • (SL 1936)

**MAYER RICHARD REV** (405)353-5804
5547 NW Eisenhower Dr Lawton OK 73505-5826 • OK • Sn/Adm • St John Lawton OK • (580)353-0556 • (SL 1982 MTH)

**MAYER ROBERT F REV** (517)675-7584
8908 W Scenic Lake Dr Laingsburg MI 48848-9748 • bobfmayer@aol.com • EN • EM • (SL 1954 MDIV STM)

**MAYER RONALD P REV** (775)727-4690
PO Box 2016 Pahrump NV 89041-2016 • PSW • SP • Shep/Valley Pahrump NV • (775)727-4098 • (SL 1973 MDIV)

**MAYERHOFF PAUL D REV** (501)851-8760
PO Box 13365 Maumelle AR 72113-0365 • pmayerhoff@yahoo.com • MDS • SP • Shepherd Peace Maumelle AR • (501)851-4546 • (SPR 1970 MDIV)

**MAYERHOFF RICHARD G REV** (972)771-9894
15 Hillside Dr Rockwall TX 75087-6826 • rmayerhoff@rockwall.net • TX • SP • Our Savior Rockwall TX • (972)771-8118 • (SL 1969 MDIV)

**MAYES JAMES H REV** (785)456-7291
4504 Horizon Trl Wamego KS 66547 • KS • SP • Mount Calvary Wamego KS • (785)456-2444 • (SL 1976 MTH)

**MAYES THEODORE E REV** (816)582-4372
710 Highland Ave Maryville MO 64468-2712 • tjmayes@hotmail.com • MO • SP • Hope Maryville MO • (660)582-3262 • (SL 1976 MDIV STM)

**MAYNARD ARTHUR FRANK REV** (619)390-5307
15543 Meadow Oaks Ln El Cajon CA 92021-2566 • maynards@incom.net • EN • SP • Inter Mountain Pine Valley CA* • (619)473-8604 • (CQ 1994)

**MAZAK RICHARD A DR** (828)441-7925
2374 24th Street Ln NE Hickory NC 28601-9101 • mazak@lrc.edu • SE • 06/1991 06/2000 • * • (SL 1958 MA MA PHD)

**MAZEMKE VILAS E REV** (715)823-2596
E8848 Velte Rd Clintonville WI 54929-9022 • mazemke@mail.cli.earthreach.com • NW • Sn/Adm • St Martin Clintonville WI • (715)823-6538 • (SPR 1969 STM)

**MC BRIDE LORENZO REV**
4108 Bonnie Ln Mobile AL 36609-6054 • SO • SP • Mount Calvary Mobile AL • (205)471-4200 • (CQ 1994)

**MC BRIDE THOMAS J REV** (813)662-0338
518 Rooks Rd Seffner FL 33584-3940 • rev3mcbride@hotmail.com • FG • EM • (SPR 1969)

**MC CABE H HERBERT REV** (920)262-9521
445 S Concord Ave Watertown WI 53094-7307 • sanherb@globaldialog.com • SW • EM • (CQ 1973 MA)

**MC CAIN PAUL B REV** (517)792-7309
5177 Narcissus Dr Saginaw MI 48603-1147 • revpbm@aol.com • MI • Sn/Adm • Bethlehem Saginaw MI • (517)755-1144 • (FW 1989 MDIV)

**MC CAIN PAUL T REV** (314)965-9000
1333 S Kirkwood Rd Saint Louis MO 63122-7226 • paul.mccain@lcms.org • MO • S Ex/S • Missouri Saint Louis MO • (314)317-4550 • (FW 1988 MDIV)

**MC CANTS ELDER REV** (210)661-2596
6302 Mission Hills Dr San Antonio TX 78244-1568 • eldenclm@aol.com • EA • Asst • Holy Cross Philadelphia PA • (215)242-0530 • (FW 1977 MDIV)

**MC CANTS JIMMY REV** (312)928-3530
10855 S Calumet Ave Chicago IL 60628-3610 • jrmccants@prodogy.net • NI • SP • Zion Chicago IL • (773)928-3530 • (FW 1982 MDIV)

**MC CANTS REHOLMA REV**
50 A Sandune Ct Pittsburgh PA 15239 • EA • SP • Unity Community Pittsburgh PA • (412)731-2811 • (FW 1979)

**MC CLEAN CHARLES L REV** (617)742-6126
34 Lime St Boston MA 02108 • EN • 09/1999 • (SL 1967 MST)

**MC CLEAN DAVID R REV** (317)780-7413
830 Woodhill Dr Indianapolis IN 46227-2125 • pastordave@lightdog.com • IN • Sn/Adm • Mount Olive Greenwood IN • (317)422-9991 • (SL 1986 MDIV)

**MC CLELLAN GARY WAYNE REV** (580)938-5208
PO Box 456 Shattuck OK 73858-0456 • OK • SP • Christ Shattuck OK • (580)938-5208 • (SL 1992 MDIV)

**MC CLURE GARRY D REV** (520)881-2252
2012 E Monte Vista Dr Tucson AZ 85719-2874 • EN • D Miss • English Farmington MI • (SL 1969 MDIV)

**MC COMACK MARTIN PAUL REV**
113 Oak Circle Monroe LA 71203 • SO • SP • Trinity Monroe LA • (318)322-3507 • (FW 1989 MDIV)

**MC CORMICK ARTHUR M REV** (580)446-5540
RR 6 Box 517 Enid OK 73701 • OK • SP • Immanuel Enid OK • (580)446-5521 • (SL 1999 MDIV)

**MC COWN CHESTER L REV** (915)468-5201
C/O Trinity Lutheran Church 3536 Ymca Dr San Angelo TX 76904-7154 • cnomcown@wcc.net • TX • Assoc • Trinity San Angelo TX • (915)944-8660 • (SL 1969 MDIV)

**MC COY JAMES R REV** (810)629-9626
813 North Rd Fenton MI 48430 • MI • EM • (CQ 1977 MA)

**MC COY MICHAEL L REV** (208)365-5214
403 S Hayes Ave Emmett ID 83617-2971 • NOW • SP • Our Redeemer Emmett ID • (208)365-5231 • (FW 1984 STM MDIV)

**MC CRACKEN GARRY A REV**
801 N Madison St Lebanon IL 62254-1455 • SI • SP • Messiah Lebanon IL • (618)537-2300 • (SL 1998 MDIV MA)

**MC CRILLIS WALTER C II REV** (850)892-9269
566 Paradise Island Dr De Funiak Springs FL 32433 • wnmccrillis@dfsi.net • SO • EM • (FW 1983 MA MDIV)

**MC CUNE SAMUEL W REV** (716)836-4061
124 Morris Ave Buffalo NY 14214-1610 • EA • EM • (SPR 1962 MDIV)

**MC DANIELS JAMES A REV** (336)272-1174
2008 Chelsea Ln Greensboro NC 27406-3211 • jmcdani631@aol.com • SE • SP • Grace Greensboro NC • (336)272-1174 • (CQ 1977 MDIV)

**MC DERMOTT LAWRENCE JOSEPH** (785)434-2846
406 S Cochran St Plainville KS 67663 • KS • EM • (CQ 1993 MDIV)

**MC DONALD DAVID P REV** (507)842-5667
PO Box 362 Brewster MN 56119-0362 • MNS • SP • Trinity Brewster MN • (507)842-5982 • (SL 1999 MDIV)

**MC DONALD GILBERT K REV** (248)674-1564
4770 Pine Knob Ln Clarkston MI 48346-4055 • MI • Tchr • LHS Northwest Rochester Hills MI • (810)852-6677 • (SPR 1973 MDIV)

**MC DONALD ROBERT A REV** (760)753-2246
7974 Los Pinos Cir Carlsbad CA 92009-9135 • mcdonaldfamily@excite.com • PSW • D Miss • Redeemer By The Sea Carlsbad CA • (760)431-8990 • (FW 1978 MDIV)

**MC DOUGALL DANIEL T REV** (402)333-6464
16822 Holmes Cir Omaha NE 68135-1455 • NEB • Assoc • King Of Kings Omaha NE • (402)333-6464 • (SL 1981 MDIV)

**MC FARLAND MICHAEL REV**
1421 Cooper Dr Irving TX 75061-5527 • TX • SP • Our Redeemer Irving TX • (972)255-0595 • (SL 1983 MDIV DMIN)

**MC GHGHY HUGH R REV** (660)438-3416
850 Circle Dr Warsaw MO 65355-3221 • MO • EM • (CQ 1978 MED)

**MC GHGHY PAUL G REV** (217)728-4759
12 Eastlawn Dr Sullivan IL 61951-1614 • 4mcghghy@cu-online.com • CI • SP • Faith Sullivan IL • (217)728-7711 • (SL 1978 MDIV)

**MC HONE RANDOLPH W REV** (319)235-6705
C/O Grace Lutheran Church 1024 W 8th St Waterloo IA 50702-2208 • IE • Sn/Adm • Grace Waterloo IA • (319)235-6705 • (SPR 1974 MDIV)

**MC INTYRE DAVID R REV**
207 La Ruisseau Louisville KY 40223-3107 • pasmc@gte.net • IN • 06/2000 • (SL 1979 MDIV)

**MC INTYRE MARK REV** (573)364-0397
55 Rolla Gardens Dr Rolla MO 65401-3908 • mmac@fidnet.com • MO • Sn/Adm • Immanuel Rolla MO • (573)364-4525 • (SL 1991 MDIV)

**MC KELVEY DONALD B REV** (618)537-4329
620 Hillcrest Dr Lebanon IL 62254 • naej@peaknet.net • SI • EM • (CQ 1987)

**MC KENZIE MARK L REV** (909)886-6755
1426 Wrightwood Dr San Bernardino CA 92407-5010 • PSW • SP • La Santisma Tri San Bernardino CA • (909)882-5952 • (FW 1985 MDIV)

**MC KENZIE PATRICK REV** (708)531-0477
2300 Mayfair Ave Westchester IL 60154-5044 • NI • SP • Immanuel Hillside IL • (708)562-5590 • (SL 1984 MDIV)

**MC KILLOP DON C REV** (011)886-9350
PO Box 854 Randburg Gauteng2125 SOUTH AFRICA • elfjhb@hixnet.co.za • SD • 09/1997 09/1999 • (FW 1982 MDIV)

**MC KINESS JOHN C REV** (319)351-0760
708 18th Ave Coralville IA 52241-1606 • IE • EM • (SPR 1966 MDIV)

**MC KNIGHT DAVID M REV** (515)782-3006
C/O Trinity Lutheran Church 800 N Sumner Ave Creston IA 50801-1349 • dmckn16@creston.heartland.net • SE • 12/1999 • (SL 1979 MDIV)

**MC LAIN PHILIP C REV** (919)765-9546
2940 Burlwood Dr Winston Salem NC 27103-6208 • SE • Sn/Adm • St John Winston Salem NC • (336)725-1651 • (FW 1984 MDIV)

**MC MANUS DENNIS J REV** (320)843-4439
C/O St Mark Lutheran Church 1420 Nevada Ave Benson MN 56215-1136 • dmcmanus@fedtel.net • MNN • SP • St Mark Benson MN • (320)843-4131 • (SL 1987 MDIV)

**MC MILLAN WHITFIELD M REV** (210)496-7350
2710 Stone Edge St San Antonio TX 78232-4218 • whitmac@stic.net • TX • EM • (SL 1953 MA MA)

**MC MILLER DANIEL FREDERICK REV**
124 N 87th St Milwaukee WI 53226-4610 • SW • S Miss • South Wisconsin Milwaukee WI • (414)464-8100 • (CQ 1996 MDIV)

**MC MILLER ROBERT J REV** (623)876-4033
9711 W Edward Dr Sun City AZ 85351-3632 • rdadmac@acninc.net • PSW • 12/1994 • (SL 1955 MDIV)

**MC MILLIAN RIC L REV** (501)329-7895
2900 Saddletop Conway AR 72032-5533 • mcmillian@conwaycorp.net • MDS • SP • Saint Matthew Conway AR • (501)329-2227 • (FW 1985 MDIV)

**MC MULLIN CLINTON R REV** (405)917-1744
4109 NW 61st St Oklahoma City OK 73112 • mcmokc@aol.com • OK • SP • Immanuel Oklahoma City OK • (405)525-5793 • (SL 1990 MDIV)

**MC NAMARA JERRY F REV** (770)499-1587
2277 Northbrook Rdg NW Kennesaw GA 30152-7301 • jerry.mcnamara@pastors.com • FG • SP • Living Hope Kennesaw GA • (770)425-6726 • (SL 1991 MDIV)

**MC PEEK SAMUEL E REV**
C/O Our Redeemer Lutheran 205 Touchet Rd Lafayette LA 70506-7809 • sampastorl@aol • SO • Living Hope Kennesaw GA • (770)425-6726 • (SL 1982 MDIV)

**MC PHERSON DANIEL P REV** (561)840-0037
433 Driftwood Rd North Palm Beach FL 33408-4811 • faithnpbd@aol.com • FG • Asst • Faith North Palm Beach FL • (561)848-4737 • (SL 1998 MDIV)

**MC PIKE JEFFREY D REV** (217)337-7842
708 E Sunnycrest Dr Urbana IL 61801-5965 • n9cqs@iname.com • CI • SP • Trinity Urbana IL • (217)367-8923 • (FW 1988 MDIV)

**MC QUALITY DANIEL R REV** (573)624-6581
308 Williams Dr Dexter MO 63841 • flc@bootheel.net • MO • SP • Faith Dexter MO • (573)624-4921 • (FW 1999 MDIV)

**MC QUILLAN KIRK ALBERT REV** (256)891-0608
9341 US Highway 431 Albertville AL 35950-5504 • kirk@airnet.net • SO • SP • Christ Albertville AL • (256)891-0608 • (SL 1991 MDIV)

**MC REYNOLDS TERRY A REV** (630)416-8137
2271 Norwich Ct Naperville IL 60565-3102 • mcreynolds@ntsource.com • NI • Assoc • Bethany Naperville IL • (630)355-2198 • (SL 1985 MDIV)

**MC VEY DANIEL J REV** (616)587-5505
PO Box 469 Mancelona MI 49659 • MI • SP • St Matthew Mancelona MI • (616)587-5505 • (CQ 1982)

**MC VEY TODD J REV** (608)276-9167
2914 Salem Dr Madison WI 53713-2167 • tmcvey@chorus.net • SW • 12/1990 • (SL 1984 MDIV)

**MC WHIRTER JOHN A REV**
505 White Oak Ln Kingsport TN 37663-2551 • jlmcwhirter@juno.com • MDS • EM • (CQ 1980 MED)

**MEADOR NATHAN MICHAEL REV** (715)845-2719
E7263 Star Rd Aniwa WI 54408 • nmeador@dwave.net • NW • SP • Zion Aniwa WI • (715)845-2014 • (SL 1996 MDIV)

**MEALWITZ PETER E DR** (440)322-8246
125 Oakley Green Dr Elyria OH 44035-8850 • EN • EM • (SL 1960 MDIV DMIN)

**MEASE ROCKY W REV** (316)788-9627
467 S Westview Dr Derby KS 67037-1337 • chaprm@aol.com • KS • Inst C • Kansas Topeka KS • (SL 1981 MDIV MA)

**MEASE VAN EDWARD REV** (913)758-0703
804 N 18th St Leavenworth KS 66048-1100 • stpaulchurch@grapevine.net • KS • Sn/Adm • St Paul Leavenworth KS • (913)682-0387 • (FW 1984 MDIV)

**MECH GREGORY ALAN REV** (402)643-2444
407 N 1st St Seward NE 68434-1803 • NEB • SHS/C • Nebraska Seward NE • (SL 1986 MDIV)

**MECH TIMOTHY J REV** (920)467-1724
4589 Hunters Glen Dr Sheboygan WI 53083 • tdmech@excel.net • SW • Sn/Adm • Trinity Sheboygan WI • (920)458-8246 • (SL 1989 MDIV)

**MECKES DANIEL C REV** (248)624-7676
2040 South Commerce Rd Walled Lake MI 48390 • n-jamm@juno.com • MI • Assoc • St Matthew Walled Lake MI • (248)624-7676 • (FW 1989 MDIV)

**MEDLEY J ELMER JR. REV** (954)578-9511
5161 NW 81st Ave Lauderhill FL 33351 • twomedleys@juno.com • SE • EM • (SPR 1961)

**MEEHAN JOHN S REV** (703)922-1833
5606 Cornish Way Alexandria VA 22315 • jsmeehan@erols.com • SE • Sn/Adm • St John Alexandria VA • (703)971-2210 • (SL 1988 MDIV MCED)

**MEGGERS DAVID L REV** (815)226-7098
7140 Mill Rd Rockford IL 61108-2632 • dmeggers@aol.com • NI • SP • Christ The Rock Rockford IL • (815)332-7191 • (SL 1988 MDIV)

**MEHL CARL E REV** (248)553-4677
28382 Kendallwood Dr Farmington Hills MI 48334-2629 • cemehl@aol.com • MI • EM • (SL 1940 MDIV)

**MEHL CLEMENS H REV** (417)232-5002
RR 3 Box 37A Lockwood MO 65682-9556 • MO • EM • (SL 1941)

**MEHL DUANE P REV** (302)998-4856
1123 Flint Hill Rd Wilmington DE 19808-1911 • SE • EM • (SL 1957 MDIV MA PHD)

**MEHL JOHN L REV** (636)349-8024
1605 Littleton Ct Fenton MO 63026-3014 • mehl@glasnet.ru • KS • S Miss • Kansas Topeka KS • (SL 1985 MDIV)

**MEHL LAMBERT J REV** (660)463-2637
PO Box 849 Concordia MO 64020-0849 • MO • EM • (SL 1930 MED MA DED)

**MEHL PAUL M REV** (501)793-2592
650 Lonoke Ln Batesville AR 72501-8093 • 72614.2513compuserve • MDS • SP • Hope Batesville AR • (870)793-3078 • (SL 1986 MDIV)

**MEHRL KLAUS M REV** (815)741-1932
720 Westshore Dr Shorewood IL 60431-9478 • kmmehr@aol.com • NI • Sn/Adm • Our Savior Joliet IL • (815)725-1606 • (SL 1983 MDIV)

**MEICHSNER JAMES H REV** (320)202-8003
520 6th Ave N Sauk Rapids MN 56379-2022 • jhmeichsner@juno.com • MNN • EM • (SPR 1958 MDIV)

**MEIER DAVID E REV** (316)473-2675
901 N 10th St Humboldt KS 66748-1021 • dmeier@humboldtks.com • KS • SP • St Peter Humboldt KS • (316)473-2343 • (FW 1978 MDIV)

**MEIER HARLAN D REV** (308)785-3100
606 Calvert PO Box 82 Elwood NE 68937-0082 • NEB • EM • (SL 1952)

**MEIER MARK RAYMOND REV**
Christ Lutheran Church PO Box 555 Muscoda WI 53573-0555 • mark³meier2@mail.ccs.kl2.ia.us • SW • SP • St Peter Muscoda WI • (608)739-4017 • (FW 1994 MDIV)

**MEIER PETER A REV** (612)657-2182
PO Box 88 Mayer MN 55360-0088 • pkmeier@prodigy.net • MNS • SP • Zion Mayer MN • 245 • (FW 1982 MDIV)

**MEIER RONALD W REV** (920)589-4213
4977 Stevens Ln Oshkosh WI 54904-6853 • revron@milwpc.com • SW • EM • (SPR 1965 MDIV)

**MEIER WILLIAM E REV** (920)787-4707
W6264 Retreat Cir Wautoma WI 54982 • EN • EM • (SL 1962 MDIV)

**MEILAENDER GILBERT C REV** (616)789-0185
715 W Mansion St Marshall MI 49068-1409 • MI • EM • (SL 1937)

**MEILAENDER GILBERT REV** (219)462-6984
1901 Rockcastle Park Dr Valparaiso IN 46383-3832 • EN • English Farmington MI • (SL 1972 MDIV PHD)

**MEILANDER DOUGLAS H REV** (419)893-9080
1261 Hugo St Maumee OH 43537-3113 • OH • SP • Concordia Toledo OH • (419)382-0410 • (SL 1972 MDIV)

**MEILNER WILLIAM C REV** (507)523-2228
RR 2 Box 63 Lewiston MN 55952-9615 • MNS • SP • Immanuel Lewiston MN • (507)523-2228 • (FW 1983 MDIV)

**MEINHART WALTER F REV** (503)691-9323
11475 SW Elmer Ct Tualatin OR 97062-7082 • NOW • 03/1986 03/2000 • (SL 1971 MDIV)

**MEINZEN LAWRENCE E REV** (618)656-1616
1378 Biscay Dr Edwardsville IL 62025-5103 • SI • SP • St Matthew Brussels IL • (618)883-2351 • (CQ 1968 MAR)

**MEINZEN LUTHER W REV** (636)225-1429
1469 Ganso Ct Fenton MO 63026-3615 • Lumeinzen@juno.com • MO • EM • (SL 1946 MDIV STM THD THD)

**MEISSNER ALVIN G REV** (817)939-3206
509 E 27th Ave Belton TX 76513-1619 • TX • EM • (SL 1958)

**MEISSNER BRUCE W REV** (847)428-2082
2501 Helm Rd Carpentersville IL 60110-1305 • NI • SP • Faith Carpentersville IL • (847)428-2079 • (SL 1963 MDIV)

**MEISSNER HAROLD V DR** (214)328-1346
8332 Moorcroft Dr Dallas TX 75228-5940 • a0006256@airmail.net • TX • SP • Trinity Dallas TX • (214)327-2729 • (SPR 1962 MDIV DMIN)

**MEISSNER MICHAEL JAMES REV** (210)561-0851
13935 S Village Dr San Antonio TX 78249-2512 • TX • Assoc • Shepherd Hills San Antonio TX • (210)614-3742 • (SL 1996 MDIV)

**MEISSNER REUBEN F REV** (651)453-9228
7272 Brendon Ave Inver Grove Heights MN 55076 • MNS • EM • (SL 1953 MDIV)

**MEITZ ERWIN W REV** (507)362-8133
C/O Trinity Lutheran Church 415 Lake St W Waterville MN 56096-1323 • MNS • SP • Trinity Waterville MN • (507)362-4454 • (FW 1982 MDIV)

**MELCHIOR EDWARD F REV** (314)631-0301
8431 Weber Trail Dr Saint Louis MO 63123-4649 • MO • EM • (SPR 1958 MDIV)

**MELINAT THEODORE C REV** (517)879-3195
2770 N Garfield Rd Pinconning MI 48650-8965 • tedm@lcfsmi.org • MI • EM • (SL 1958 MSW MDIV)

**MELZ ARNO H REV**
4125 75th St Urbandale IA 50322 • IW • EM • (SPR 1962)

**MENAGH JASON C REV** (406)222-9551
86 Loch Leven Rd Livingston MT 59047-9128 • dachsie@mcn.net • MT • EM • (FW 1987 MDIV)

**MENDELMAN G HOLMES REV**
12B Queen Anne Way Chester MD 21619 • 73551.1742@compuserve.com • SE • EM • (SL 1956 MDIV)

**MENDENHALL THOMAS B REV** (316)665-4025
2601 Arizona St Hutchinson KS 67502-5123 • padre@mindspring.com • KS • SP • Our Redeemer Hutchinson KS • (316)662-5642 • (SL 1973 MDIV)

**MENGSTEAB YOHANNES A REV** (301)595-5373
11813 Macon St Beltsville MD 20705 • ymengsert@aol.com • SE • O Miss • African Immigrant Hyattsville MD • (301)277-2302 • (SL 1991 MDIV MTH)

**MENK GERALD R REV** (507)662-5868
511 Chicago St # 1001 Lakefield MN 56150-1168 • immanuel@rconnect.com • MNS • SP • Immanuel Lakefield MN • (507)662-5718 • (CQ 1981)

**MENKE JAMES W REV** (330)966-7404
2603 Cottington Cir NW North Canton OH 44720-5703 • jmenke@juno.com • OH • Sn/Adm • Holy Cross Canton OH • (330)499-3307 • (SL 1983 MDIV)

**MENNENGA FRANCIS W REV** (254)622-2985
HC 99 Box 127A8 Clifton TX 76634-9409 • oursavior@whitneytx.net • TX • SP • Our Savior Whitney TX • (254)694-3234 • (SPR 1960 MDIV)

**MENNICKE AUGUST T REV** (763)413-9490
15504 Larch St NW Andover MN 55304-2745 • MNS • EM • (SL 1955 MDIV DD LITTD)

**MENNICKE DAVID G REV** (321)783-8386
109 Boca Ciega Rd Cocoa Beach FL 32931-2601 • clccc@earthlink.net • FG • SP • Christ Cape Canaveral FL • (321)783-3303 • (SL 1965 MDIV MST)

**MENNICKE VICTOR O REV** (941)922-6259
6122 Approach Ln Sarasota FL 34238-5743 • luthy3@aol.com • FG • EM • (CQ 1982 MA)

**MENSING RICKY CARL REV** (602)575-4064
8540 N Rancho Catalina Ave Tucson AZ 85704-7344 • rccm@azstarnet.com • EN • Sn/Adm • Ascension Tucson AZ • (520)297-3095 • (SL 1983 MDIV)

**MENTINK LEE R REV** (712)282-4241
200 Crawford St PO Box 221 Galva IA 51020-0221 • lmentink@netins.net • IW • EM • (LS 1964 MDIV)

**MENTZ MARLIN A REV** (770)947-8586
2992 Concord Way Douglasville GA 30135 • FG • EM • (SL 1947 STM STD)

**MENTZ STEPHEN H REV** (301)805-8397
8401 Triple Crown Rd Bowie MD 20715-4568 • shmvlm@aol.com • SE • SP • Holy Cross Greenbelt MD • (301)345-5111 • (SL 1979 MDIV STM)

**MENZEL WALTER E REV** (413)593-0015
109 Partridge Ln Chicopee MA 01022-1138 • NE • EM • (SPR 1944)

**MERDINYAN WALLACE REV** (860)443-7382
611 Ocean Ave G4 New London CT 06320-4449 • NE • EM • (SL 1950)

**MERINO LARRY CHARLES REV** (219)471-5603
2226 Lawndale Dr Fort Wayne IN 46805-3727 • IN • SP • New Life Fort Wayne IN • (219)420-3024 • (FW 1992 MDIV)

**MERITT KELLY-RAY REV** (718)822-4495
2090 E Tremont Ave Apt 10H Bronx NY 10462-5752 • kelly-ray.meritt@med.va.gov • AT • M Chap • Atlantic Bronxville NY • (914)337-5700 • (SL 1980 MDIV)

**MERKENS GUIDO DR** (210)828-1447
330 Jeanette Dr San Antonio TX 78216-7415 • TX • EM • (SL 1951 MDIV DD)

**MERLO ALEX L REV**
648 S 4th St Aurora IL 60505-5175 • NI • Assoc • Emmanuel Aurora IL* • (630)851-2200 • (CQ 1996)

**MERRELL GENE E REV** (510)614-8584
14242 Outrigger Dr San Leandro CA 94577-6419 • blgem@earthlink.net • CNH • EM • * • (SL 1957)

**MERRELL WILLIAM D REV** (248)623-0717
3915 Percy King Rd Waterford MI 48329-1369 • MI • SP • Peace Waterford MI • (248)681-9360 • (SL 1971 MDIV)

**MERRILL JOHN E REV** (810)773-5798
19610 Rock St Roseville MI 48066-2629 • MI • Sn/Adm • St John Fraser MI • (810)293-0333 • (CQ 1987)

**MERRILL RICHARD CHARLES REV** (515)332-3121
311 11th St N Humboldt IA 50548-1631 • rmerrill@trvnet.net • IW • Asst • Zion Humboldt IA • (515)332-3279 • (FW 1991 MDIV)

**MERRILL THEODORE H REV** (701)852-4260
5801 19th Ave NW Minot ND 58703 • merrill@minot.com • ND • North Dakota Fargo ND • (FW 1981 MDIV)

**MERRITT GLENN F REV** (406)363-1924
405 South 4th St Hamilton MT 59840-0927 • revrun99@aol.com • MT • SP • Grace Hamilton MT • (406)363-1924 • (FW 1985 MDIV)

**MERZ ROBERT J REV** (360)373-9979
1139 Perry Ave Bremertown WA 98310 • NOW • EM • (SPR 1965)

**MESCHKE MARK WILLIAM REV** (618)345-1512
231 S Wilson Heights Rd Collinsville IL 62234-5117 • dotmarkm@plantnet.com • MO • Tchr • Lutheran North Saint Louis MO • (314)389-3100 • (SL 1995 MDIV MED)

**MESEKE ERVIN G REV** (618)283-0553
113 W Randolph St Vandalia IL 62471-2334 • SI • EM • (SPR 1939)

**MESEKE GILBERT F REV** (219)897-3369
10733 E 450 S Laotto IN 46763-9710 • IN • EM • (SPR 1953)

**MESEKE MORRIS D REV** (228)594-9521
2243 Club Moss Cir Biloxi MS 39532 • SO • SP • Good Shepherd Biloxi MS • (601)388-5767 • (SL 1992 MDIV)

**MESEKE PAUL R REV** (573)655-4416
Rt 1 Box 152 La Grange MO 63448-1100 • MO • SP • St Peter La Grange MO • (573)655-4416 • (FW 1999 MDIV)

**MESKE RODNEY M REV** (402)654-3564
27068 County Rd 12 Hooper NE 68031-5009 • rmeske@tvsonline.net • NEB • SP • Immanuel Hooper NE • (402)654-3563 • (SPR 1974 MDIV)

**MESSMANN JOHN A REV** (817)346-3367
4351 Dove Meadow Ct Fort Worth TX 76133-7040 • messmann@flash.net • TX • Sn/Adm • St Paul Fort Worth TX • (817)332-2281 • (SL 1982 DMIN)

**MESSMANN WARREN E REV** (219)484-6538
2721 Vance Ave Fort Wayne IN 46805-2409 • wemessmann@aol.com • IN • 07/1991 07/2000 • (FW 1977)

**METCALF JAMES E REV** (616)895-7648
9654 48th Ave Jenison MI 49428-9528 • stjohnlu@iserv.net • MI • SP • St John Jenison MI • (616)895-4826 • (SL 1978 MDIV)

**METCALF MAX P REV** (360)693-6744
6810 Dogwood Dr Vancouver WA 98663 • metcalfmax@dellnet.com • NOW • EM • (SL 1960 STM STM)

**METZ ERWIN A REV** (281)376-2732
15818 Whipple Tree Dr Houston TX 77070-1637 • TX • EM • (SL 1950 MED)

**METZGER DANIEL J REV** (316)684-3415
3934 E Elm St Wichita KS 67208-3405 • danielmetzger@juno.com • IE • 01/1995 01/2000 • (FW 1990 MDIV)

**METZGER MARVIN REV** (815)562-2193
4083 S Center Rd Rochelle IL 61068-9777 • NI • Assoc • St John Sycamore IL • (815)895-4477 • (FW 1990 MDIV)

**METZGER WILLIAM L REV** (708)283-9765
330 W Highland Dr Chicago Heights IL 60411-2043 • wlmetzger@juno.com • NI • Assoc • St Paul Chicago Heights IL • (708)754-4493 • (SL 1983 MDIV)

**METZLER NORMAN P J DR** (360)254-1874
1909 NE 107th Ave Vancouver WA 98664 • nmetzler@cu-portland.edu • NOW • SHS/C • Northwest Portland OR • (SL 1967 MDIV STM DTH)

**MEYER ALBERT E REV** (262)786-1513
18415 Countryside Court Brookfield WI 53045 • pmjung@netzero.net • AT • EM • (SL 1930 MDIV MA LLD LHD)

**MEYER ARNO H REV** (785)271-1923
3742 SW Arvonia Pl Topeka KS 66610-1356 • revarno@cjnetworks.com • KS • Sn/Adm • Prince Of Peace Topeka KS • (785)271-0808 • (SL 1964 MDIV DMIN)

**MEYER ARTHUR W REV** (757)523-8963
5733 Hamlet Rd Virginia Beach VA 23464-2211 • artztoy@earthlink.net • SE • EM • (SL 1945)

**MEYER C RODGER REV** (770) 642-5469
9165 Martin Rd Roswell GA 30076 • FG • 04/2000 • (SL 1959 THD)

**MEYER CHARLES A REV** (909)787-6223
1056 Leconte Dr Riverside CA 92507-5932 • meyer46@earthlink.net • PSW • 05/1990 05/2000 • (SL 1973 MDIV)

**MEYER CHRISTOPHER P REV** (507)362-8038
Rt 2 Box 220 Waterville MN 56096 • MNS • SP • St Peter Waterville MN* • (507)362-8381 • (FW 1999 MDIV)

**MEYER DALE A REV**
624 Tillotson St Collinsville IL 62234-3640 • SI • St Peter Waterville MN • (507)362-8381 • (SL 1973 MDIV PHD DD)

**MEYER DAVID J** (253)857-4574
6411 154th St NW Gig Harbor WA 98332 • NOW • SP • King Of Glory Gig Harbor WA • (253)857-4574 • (SL 2000 MDIV)

**MEYER DAVID M REV** (480)357-1504
723 S 7th St Mesa AZ 85208 • SE • SP • St Paul Havelock NC • (252)447-3826 • (SL 1964)

**MEYER DAVID P REV** (402)643-4704
111 N Columbia Ave Seward NE 68434-2229 • dm35945@navix.net • NEB • SHS/C • Nebraska Seward NE • (SL 1963 STM PHD)

**MEYER DAVID R REV** (262)334-5071
440 Meadowbrook Dr West Bend WI 53090-2416 • SW • EM • (SL 1961 MDIV)

**MEYER DELBERT H REV** (218)346-4301
C/O St John Luth Church RR 1 Box 360 Perham MN 56573-9770 • delmeyer@juno.com • MNN • SP • St John Perham MN • (218)346-4301 • (SL 1971 MDIV)

**MEYER DONALD E REV** (414)327-2391
3130 S 53rd St Milwaukee WI 53219-4520 • dales@execpc.com • SW • SP • Oklahoma Ave Milwaukee WI • (414)543-3580 • (SPR 1966 MDIV MED)

**MEYER DONALD G REV** (302)875-1005
740 Millsboro Rd Laurel DE 19956-1214 • SE • SP • Christ Seaford DE • (302)629-9755 • (SPR 1965)

**MEYER DONALD J REV** (712)376-2666
Trinity Lutheran Church 5290 C Ave Marcus IA 51035-7034 • trinity@nwidt.com • IW • SP • Trinity Marcus IA* • (712)376-2666 • (FW 1997 MDIV)

**MEYER DOUGLAS E REV** (618)548-2115
101 Hawthorn Estates Rd Salem IL 62881-1034 • demeyer@midwest.net • CI • SP • Salem Salem IL • (618)548-3190 • (FW 1981 MDIV)

**MEYER EDWARD A REV** (859)543-0636
325 Forest Hill Dr Lexington KY 40509-1972 • eamlrm@juno.com • IN • EM • (SPR 1952 DD)

**MEYER EDWARD ANDREW REV** (850)271-9587
4018 Torino Way Panama City FL 32405 • SO • Assoc • Trinity Panama City FL • (850)763-2412 • (FW 1997 MDIV)

**MEYER EDWARD F REV** (828)459-1131
2653 Birdie Ln Conover NC 28613-9454 • SE • EM • (SL 1957 MDIV)

**MEYER EDWARD H REV** (636)447-3993
261 Cedar Grove Dr Saint Charles MO 63304-7379 • MO • EM • (SL 1946)

**MEYER ELDOR W REV** (316)724-6375
PO Box 315 Girard KS 66743-0315 • meyere@ckt.net • KS • EM • (SPR 1964 MDIV MS DD)

**MEYER ERWIN M REV** (785)348-5892
712 Heritage Rd Linn KS 66953-9244 • KS • EM • (CQ 1962 MMU)

**MEYER GERALD ALAN REV** (517)872-1847
4283 Maple St Cass City MI 48726-1622 • MI • SP • Good Shepherd Cass City MI • (517)872-2770 • (CQ 1985)

**MEYER GLENN D REV** (414)238-9383
11639 N Saint James Ln Mequon WI 53092-2853 • gd-meyer@execpc.com • SW • Sn/Adm • St John Glendale WI • (414)352-4150 • (FW 1981 MDIV)

**MEYER HENRY E REV**
1801 E Upriver Dr Apt 371 Spokane WA 99207-5155 • MT • EM • (SL 1942) .

**MEYER JEFFREY SCOTT REV** (608)848-5830
104 Melody Cir Verona WI 53593-1454 • SW • SP • Christ Memorl Madison WI • (608)271-2811 • (SL 1992 MDIV)

**MEYER JEROME H REV** (402)336-2340
PO Box 736 O Neill NE 68763-0736 • clc@inetnebr.com • NEB • SP • Christ O Neill NE • (402)336-1884 • (SL 1968 MDIV)

**MEYER JOHN A REV** (515)989-0511
1040 Market St Carlisle IA 50047-9701 • IW • SP • Holy Cross Carlisle IA • (515)989-3841 • (SL 1989 MDIV)

**MEYER JOHN E REV** (314)821-0565
1541 Breezeridge Dr Des Peres MO 63131-4212 • MO • EM • (SL 1944 MA STM)

**MEYER JOHN W REV** (313)534-2785
26371 Barbara Redford MI 48239-2902 • jajmeyer@aol.com • MI • SP • St Paul Farmington Hills MI • (248)474-0675 • (CQ 1978 MED)

**MEYER JOHN-PAUL REV** (916)624-4973
5445 5th St Rocklin CA 95677-2526 • jpmeyer@pacbell.net • CNH • SP • Holy Cross Rocklin CA • (916)624-8185 • (SPR 1974 MDIV MA)

**MEYER JONATHAN F REV** (936)546-7102
207 Pecan Dr Crockett TX 75835 • TX • SP • Grace Crockett TX • (409)544-3508 • (SL 2000 MDIV)

**MEYER JOSEPH MARSH REV** (480)357-7665
C/O Hosanna Lutheran Church 9601 E Brown Rd Mesa AZ 85207-4400 • joeluthrn@aol.com • PSW • SP • Hosanna Mesa AZ • (480)984-1414 • (SL 1995 MDIV)

**MEYER LAURENCE L REV** (509)946-1016
518 Thayer Dr Richland WA 99352-4126 • lmeyer1016@aol.com • NOW • SP • Redeemer Richland WA • (509)943-4967 • (SL 1966 MDIV)

**MEYER LEALAND L REV** (480)894-2610
C/O Alleluia Lutheran Church 1034 S Mill Ave Tempe AZ 85281-5606 • alleluia@asu.edu • PSW • Cmp P • Alleluia Tempe AZ • (480)894-2610 • (SL 1973 MDIV)

**MEYER LOUIS C REV** (201)445-2151
239 N Walnut St Ridgewood NJ 07450-2628 • NJ • EM • (SL 1940 MDIV STM)

**MEYER MERLIN C REV** (203)267-6796
72A Heritage Southbury CT 06488 • EN • EM • (SPR 1948)

**MEYER MICHAEL H REV** (603)883-1126
67 Robin Hood Rd Nashua NH 03062-2189 • NE • SP • Grace Nashua NH • (603)888-7579 • (FW 1984 MDIV)

**MEYER MILFERD J REV** (512)303-4046
RR 1 Box 280C Cedar Creek TX 78612-9735 • revmick@freewwaeb.com • TX • SP • Beaut Savior Austin TX • (512)443-4947 • (CQ 1979)

**MEYER MONTE L REV**
Rt 9 Box 271 Mankato MN 56001 • MNS • Cmp P • Campus Chapel Mankato MN • (507)387-6587 • (FW 1987 MDIV)

**MEYER NORMAN C REV** (314)389-2730
7242 Canterbury Dr Saint Louis MO 63121-2607 • nandemeyer@aol.com • MO • EM • (SL 1949 MDIV)

**MEYER NORMAN S REV** (815)568-5531
17106 Garden Valley Rd Woodstock IL 60098-9155 • janeemeyer@auenew.com • NI • SP • St John Union IL • (815)923-2733 • (SL 1970 MDIV)

**MEYER PAUL E REV** (512)892-5263
5103 Trail West Dr Austin TX 78735-6331 • pastor@mountolivelutheran.org • TX • SP • Mount Olive Austin TX • (512)288-2370 • (SL 1981 MDIV)

**MEYER PAUL W REV** (714)538-5001
C/O Salem Luth Church 6500 E Santiago Canyon Rd Orange CA 92869-1533 • salemlcms@aol.com • PSW • Sn/Adm • Salem Orange CA • (714)633-2366 • (CQ 1978 MA MA DED)

**MEYER PAUL DR** (925)933-9657
32 Los Banos Ct Walnut Creek CA 94598-3101 • pcmeyer@juno.com • CNH • EM • (SL 1955 DMIN)

**MEYER PHILIP G REV** (812)232-8341
2140 Poplar St Terre Haute IN 47803-2169 • pastor@indynet.net • IN • SP • Immanuel Terre Haute IN • (812)232-4972 • (SL 1971 MDIV)

**MEYER RICHARD A REV** (319)668-2372
2980 225th St Williamsburg IA 52361 • IE • SP • Immanuel Williamsburg IA • (319)668-2372 • (FW 1986)

**MEYER RICHARD G REV** (214)902-9262
10436 Cromwell Dr Dallas TX 75229-5948 • TX • Inst C • Texas Austin TX • (SL 1992 MDIV DMIN)

**MEYER RICHARD H REV** (504)944-8051
2701 Dauphine St New Orleans LA 70117-7321 • rhm02@gnofn.org • SO • EM • (SL 1947 MDIV MA DD)

**MEYER RICHARD Z REV** (310)454-3471
16790 Edgar St Pacific Plsds CA 90272-3225 • richzmeyer@aol.com • PSW • EM • (SL 1952 MST)

**MEYER ROBERT F REV** (925)924-1317
5740 Belleza Dr Pleasanton CA 94588 • bakmeyer@aol.com • CNH • SP • Trinity Walnut Creek CA • (925)935-3360 • (SL 1964 MDIV MLS STM)

**MEYER ROBERT L REV** (219)749-7433
6807 Forestwood Dr Fort Wayne IN 46815-7717 • IN • EM • (SL 1955)

**MEYER ROLLIE REV** (618)686-2455
C/O St John Luth Church RR 4 Box 223 Louisville IL 62858-9469 • CI • SP • St John Louisville IL • (618)686-2971 • (FW 1985)

**MEYER RONALD E REV** (262)784-5232
14248 Waters Edge Trl New Berlin WI 53151-9508 • meyer@swd.lcms.org • SW • DP • South Wisconsin Milwaukee WI • (414)464-8100 • (SL 1969 MDIV DD)

**MEYER THOMAS F REV** (714)533-6787
105 S Normandy Ct Anaheim CA 92806-3625 • pstrtmeyer@aol.com • PSW • Sn/Adm • Zion Anaheim CA • (714)535-1169 • (SPR 1972 MDIV)

**MEYER VERNON JAMES REV**
2908 1st St SE Minot ND 58701-7166 • ND • 06/1994 06/2000 • (SL 1988 MDIV)

**MEYER VIRGIL F REV** (972)624-0391
3824 Acacia Trail The Colony TX 78056 • TX • EM • (SL 1951 MDIV)

**MEYER WADE R REV**
1415 Lake Crest Dr Alexandria MN 56308 • MNN • SP • Good Shepherd Alexandria MN • (320)762-5152 • (SL 1990 MDIV)

**MEYER WALTER H REV**
10176 Beekman Place Dr Houston TX 77043-4314 • KS • EM • (SL 1948)

**MEYER WILLARD V REV** (618)377-9815
4 Ridgewood Ct Bethalto IL 62010-1190 • willyrev@aol.com • SI • Sn/Adm • Zion Bethalto IL • (618)377-8314 • (SL 1969 STM STM)

**MEYER WILLIAM F REV** (636)405-1192
524 Eagles Nest Ct Wildwood MO 63011-1774 • william.meyer@lcms.org • MO • S Ex/S • Missouri Saint Louis MO • (314)317-4550 • (SL 1966 MDIV MA PHD)

**MEYER WILLIAM J REV** (516)248-2540
7 Devereaux Pl Garden City NY 11530-4605 • WandMMeyer@aol.com • AT • Sn/Adm • Resurrection Garden City NY • (516)746-4426 • (SL 1963 MDIV)

**MEYER WILLIAM JOSEPH REV** (334)342-8755
C/O Holy Cross Lutheran Church 3900 Airport Blvd Mobile AL 36608-1622 • SO • SP • Holy Cross Mobile AL • (334)342-8755 • (SL 1974 MDIV)

**MEYERS JEFFREY T REV** (913)438-4797
11807 W 99th Pl Overland Park KS 66214-2432 • KS • Assoc • Christ Overland Park KS • (913)345-9700 • (SL 1989 MA SPA)

**MEYLE ROLAND O REV** (414)268-0789
1619 Parkway Dr Port Washington WI 53074-1139 • SW • S Miss • South Wisconsin Milwaukee WI • (414)464-8100 • (SPR 1963 MDIV)

**MEYR RONALD K REV** (407)636-5504
756 Harrier Ct Rockledge FL 32955-6329 • rmeyr04@aol.com • S • SP • Faith Rockledge FL • (321)636-5504 • (SL 1980 MDIV)

**MEYR VICTOR HERBERT REV** (651)458-8801
8286 Jewel Ave S Cottage Grove MN 55016-4985 • MNS • EM • (SPR 1974 MDIV)

**MICHAEL GERHARD C JR. REV** (407)856-2485
1800 Wind Harbor Rd Orlando FL 32809-6847 • gmjrflga@aol.com • FG • DP • Florida-Georgia Orlando FL • (SL 1965 MDIV MTH)

**MICHAEL GERHARD C REV** (320)543-3940
PO Box 397 Howard Lake MN 55349-0397 • MNS • EM • (SL 1930 LITTD)

**MICHAELSON CRAIG ALAN REV** (520)298-5163
9202 E Chirco Pl Tucson AZ 85710 • cmamjm@uswest.net • PSW • Assoc • Fountain Life Tucson AZ • (520)747-1213 • (SL 1994 MDIV)

**MICHALK MICHAEL E REV** (708)780-1834
3237 S Austin Blvd Cicero IL 60804 • pasform@megsinet.net • NI • SP • Faith Cicero IL • (708)652-6414 • (SL 1990 MDIV)

**MICHALK THEODORE A REV** (979)542-0075
313 Edgewood Ave Giddings TX 78942-3607 • trkmichalk@juno.com • TX • EM • (SL 1945 MDIV)

**MICHALK WILBERN C REV** (979)542-0139
RR 1 Box 151 Giddings TX 78942-9712 • wmichalk@bluebon.net • TX • Sn/Adm • Immanuel Giddings TX • (409)542-2918 • (SPR 1963)

**MICHEL GREGORY S REV** (715)675-7143
1608 Woodland Ridge Rd Wausau WI 54403 • gsmichel@att.net • NW • SP • Trinity Wausau WI* • (715)675-9901 • (SL 1996 MDIV)

**MICKAN ELDOR L REV** (915)388-4685
214 Mesquite Dr Kingsland TX 78639-9579 • TX • EM • * • (SPR 1945)

**MICKELSON THOMAS L REV** (507)825-3028
1112 7th Ave SW Pipestone MN 56164-1045 • MNS • SP • Our Saviour Pipestone MN • (507)825-4124 • (CQ 1978 MDIV)

**MICKOW VERNON H REV** (414)542-7622
2225 Woodfield Cir Waukesha WI 53188-4715 • SW • EM • (SPR 1953 MDIV)

**MIDDENDORF MARK G REV** (308)245-3151
Zion Lutheran Church PO Box 334 Scotia NE 68875-0334 • mjmiddendorf@nctc.net • NEB • SP • Zion Scotia NE • (308)245-4151 • (SL 1998 MDIV)

**MIDDENDORF MARVIN L REV** (520)722-5891
8110 E Speedway Blvd Apt 7376 Tucson AZ 85710-1781 • MNS • EM • (SL 1953 STM MA THD)

**MIDDENDORF MICHAEL P DR** (512)832-0703
4504 Abelia Dr Austin TX 78727-5865 • middendm@concordia.edu • TX • SHS/C • Texas Austin TX • (SL 1987 MDIV STM THD)

**MIELKE SPENCER A REV** (219)293-1481
1901 Aspin Dr Elkhart IN 46514-1401 • pastormielke@trinityl.org • IN • Assoc • Trinity Elkhart IN • (219)522-1491 • (SL 1998 MDIV)

**MIESNER DONALD R DR** (914)793-5141
6 Concordia Pl Bronxville NY 10708-1802 • drm@concordia-ny.edu • AT • SHS/C • Atlantic Bronxville NY • (914)337-5700 • (SL 1959 STM MA MDIV THD)

**MIESNER DUANE C REV** (402)589-1160
C/O Immanuel Lutheran Church Po Box 308 Spencer NE 68777-0308 • dmiesner@inetnebr.com • NEB • SP • Immanuel Spencer NE* • (402)589-1323 • (FW 1998 MDIV)

**MIESNER WILLIS E REV** (573)547-8720
254 N Walnut St Perryville MO 63775-1937 • MO • EM • * • (SPR 1968)

**MIETZNER LEONARD G REV** (208)436-6610
1105 8th St Rupert ID 83350-1526 • NOW • SP • Trinity Rupert ID • (208)436-3413 • (SL 1957)
**MIGUET STEPHEN EDWARD REV**
100 Mohigan Cir Boca Raton FL 33487-1520 • FG • Asst • St Paul Boca Raton FL • (561)395-0433 • (CQ 1999)
**MIILLE TIMOTHY CHARLES REV**
313 W 3rd Blackburn MO 65321 • MO • SP • Zion Blackburn MO* • (785)538-4688 • (FW 1996 MDIV)
**MIKKELSON ROBERT L REV** (517)727-3273
7706 Wolf Creek Rd Herron MI 49744 • blsmik@freeway.net • MI • SP • St Paul Herron MI • (517)727-2496 • (CQ 1996)
**MIKSAD PHILLIP T REV** (908)725-1651
705 Rhine Blvd Raritan NJ 08869-1213 • ptmiksad@aol.com • S • SP • St Paul Raritan NJ • (908)722-6111 • (CQ 1979 MDIV)
**MIKULASTIK ROBERT J REV** (203)521-4539
108 Meadowbrook Rd W Hartford CT 06107-2532 • rjmikl@aol • NE • Assoc • Bethany West Hartford CT • (860)521-5076 • (SPR 1976 STM)
**MILAS RICK R REV** (217)359-5630
1109 Foothill Dr Champaign IL 61821 • CI • SP • University Champaign IL • (217)344-1558 • (FW 1979 MDIV)
**MILBRANDT RICHARD W REV** (605)258-2667
PO Box 49 Onida SD 57564-0049 • revrwm@sullybuttes.net • SD • SP • Holy Cross Onida SD* • (605)258-2207 • (FW 1989 MDIV)
**MILBRATH GERALD L REV** (515)573-3525
PO Box 1501 Fort Dodge IA 50501-1501 • IW • EM • * • (SPR 1958)
**MILDENBURGER FREDERICK A REV** (812)523-8234
2202 S County Road 750 E Seymour IN 47274-9227 • dtwnfam@voyager.net • IN • SP • Emanuel Seymour IN* • (812)523-8234 • (SL 1965 MDIV)
**MILES DONALD G REV** (303)743-0777
9167 E Floyd Pl Denver CO 80231-4671 • secondmile@aol.com • RM • EM • * • (CQ 1982 MA DED)
**MILES TYRUS H REV** (503)289-5357
7313 N Washburne Ave Portland OR 97217-5859 • snoopy1@teleport.com • NOW • SP • St John Portland OR • (503)289-9557 • (SL 1964 MDIV)
**MILLER ALAN JAY REV** (712)659-3875
C/O Peace Luth Church 208 Arizona St # 448 Glidden IA 51443-1019 • IW • SP • Peace Glidden IA • (712)659-3875 • (FW 1991 MDIV)
**MILLER ALBERT H REV** (512)261-0990
406 Eagle Lakeway TX 78734-5005 • TX • EM • (SL 1950 MDIV MA MED EDD DD)
**MILLER BRUCE H REV** (319(890-6619
256 E Fourth St PO Box J Bennett IA 52721 • bhmklm@gateway.net • IE • SP • St Paul Bennett IA • (319)890-6619 • (SL 1999 MDIV)
**MILLER CARL H REV** (618)742-8136
PO Box 87 Olmsted IL 62970-0087 • SI • SP • St Luke Olmsted IL • (618)742-8136 • (SPR 1974 MSED MDIV)
**MILLER CHAD M REV** (281)238-0850
1502 Pecan Crossing Richmond TX 77469 • life4u@wt.net • TX • 04/1999 • (SL 1983 MDIV)
**MILLER CHANNING E REV** (816)228-3681
201 SW 26th St Blue Springs MO 64015-3339 • MO • EM • (SPR 1944 MDIV)
**MILLER CHARLES R REV** (318)477-9928
111 Orchard Dr Lake Charles LA 70605-4441 • milsack1@juno.com • SO • SP • St John Lake Charles LA • (318)478-5666 • (SL 1987 MDIV)
**MILLER DAVID P REV** (715)745-2299
C/O St Paul Luth Church W4496 County Rd E Bonduel WI 54107-8740 • rvmiller@frontiernet.net • NW • SP • St Paul Bonduel WI* • (715)745-2299 • (CQ 1991 MAR MA)
**MILLER DONALD L REV** (785)842-6181
3128 Lance Ct Lawrence KS 66049-1903 • dlm59@earthlink.net • KS • Sn/Adm • Immanuel-Univ Lawrence KS • (785)843-0620 • (SL 1967 MDIV)
**MILLER FRED M REV** (612)333-3195
1510 11th Ave S Apt 605 Minneapolis MN 55404-1736 • MNS • EM • (SL 1934)
**MILLER GARY L REV** (216)741-5072
1708 Cypress Ave Cleveland OH 44109-4410 • glmiller@corplink.net • OH • SP • St Mark Cleveland OH • (216)749-3545 • (FW 1990 MDIV)
**MILLER HARRY F REV** (818)343-1833
19137 Bassett St Reseda CA 91335-3801 • PSW • EM • (SL 1944)
**MILLER JAMES PATRICK REV** (760)743-2975
933 Homestead Pl Escondido CA 92026 • PSW • Asst • Grace Escondido CA • (760)745-0831 • (SL 2000 MDIV)
**MILLER JEFFREY J REV** (636)207-8996
721 Windy Ridge Dr Ballwin MO 63021-7707 • jeff1812@aol.com • MO • S Ex/S • Missouri Saint Louis MO • (314)317-4550 • (SPR 1971 MDIV)
**MILLER JOHN A REV**
C/O Grace Lutheran Church PO Box 1025 Dalhart TX 79022-1025 • TX • SP • Grace Dalhart TX* • (806)244-2606 • (SPR 1973 MDIV)
**MILLER KIRK D REV** (334)774-8828
105 Alcuri Dr Ozark AL 36360 • SO • SP • Prince Peace Ozark AL • (334)774-6758 • (SL 1993 MDIV)
**MILLER LA MAR REV** (773)838-1926
4959 S Tripp Ave Chicago IL 60632 • NI • SP • Beaut Savior Chicago IL • (773)582-6470 • (SL 1951 MED DMIN)
**MILLER LARRY A REV** (775)782-2369
1575 Wildrose Dr Minden NV 89423-4049 • tlctherev@aol.com • CNH • EM • (SPR 1963)
**MILLER LARRY ALLEN REV** (406)227-5207
3827 Chokecherry St East Helena MT 59635-3404 • revvery@aol.com • MT • SP • First Helena MT • (406)442-5367 • (FW 1983 MDIV)
**MILLER LARRY E REV** (612)291-2757
1395 Beech St Saint Paul MN 55106-4836 • MNS • D Miss • Cristo El Redentor Saint Paul MN • (651)291-2757 • (FW 1979 MDIV)
**MILLER LOUIS JULIUS REV** (501)565-0786
10509 Diamond Dr Little Rock AR 72209-8311 • MDS • 12/1995 12/1999 • (CQ 1994)
**MILLER MARK A REV** (309)346-1381
1024 S 4th St Pekin IL 61554-4510 • markmiller2@juno.com • CI • Sn/Adm • St John Pekin IL • (309)347-2136 • (FW 1983 MDIV)
**MILLER MICHAEL M REV** (865)882-1967
324 Sunset Ln Harriman TN 37748-5431 • mixer@gateway.net • MDS • SP • Redeemer Harriman TN • (865)376-7647 • (SL 1987 MDIV STM)
**MILLER PAUL E REV** (760)329-0186
65661 Avenida Dorado Dsrt Hot Spgs CA 92240-1535 • ichthus@theprovider.com • PSW • SP • Christ Dsrt Hot Spgs CA • (760)329-9292 • (FW 1980 MDIV)
**MILLER RICHARD A REV** (302)737-6744
33 Windy Ct Newark DE 19713-2820 • faithc2@juno.com • SE • EM • (SPR 1974 MDIV)
**MILLER RICHARD CHARLES REV** (920)682-4183
1856 Michigan Ave Manitowoc WI 54220-3140 • rmiller@lsol.net • SW • Sn/Adm • Redeemer Manitowoc WI • (920)684-3989 • (SL 1971 MDIV)
**MILLER RICHARD D REV** (763)755-7234
C/O Spirit Christ Luth Church 2749 Bunker Lake Blvd NE Ham Lake MN 55304-7133 • soclc3@hotmail.com • MNS • SP • Spirit Christ Ham Lake MN • (612)755-7234 • (SPR 1974 MDIV)
**MILLER RICHARD P REV** (941)481-8690
3577 Knollwood Rd Fort Myers FL 33919-6414 • rpmrey@aol.com • FG • Sn/Adm • Zion Fort Myers FL • (941)481-4040 • (SL 1964 MDIV)
**MILLER RICK L REV** (719)254-6064
952 Washington Ave Rocky Ford CO 81067-2433 • RM • 08/1991 08/2000 • (FW 1987 MDIV)
**MILLER ROBERT S REV** (407)977-0689
1512 Fountain Dr Oviedo FL 32765-8688 • rami327210@aol.com • FG • EM • (SL 1945 MDIV)
**MILLER RONALD C REV** (309)693-0336
905 Baybrook Ct Peoria IL 61615-1066 • revmiller@hotmail.com • CI • Sn/Adm • Redeemer Peoria IL • (309)691-2333 • (SPR 1970 MDIV)
**MILLER STEPHEN C REV** (715)822-8168
1075 11th Ave Cumberland WI 54829-9110 • tekonsha@excite.com • NW • SP • St Paul Cumberland WI • (715)822-8690 • (FW 1977 MDIV)
**MILLER TIMOTHY P REV** (219)772-3572
C/O Our Redeemer Luth Church 1600 S Heaton St Knox IN 46534-2318 • TimMill@skye.net • IN • SP • Our Redeemer Knox IN • (219)772-4186 • (SL 1981 MDIV)
**MILLER WARREN E (JACK) DR** (217)598-2216
C/O St Paul Luth Church PO Box 230 Sadorus IL 61872-0230 • jactun@juno.com • CI • SP • St Paul Sadorus IL • (217)598-2259 • (SL 1985 MDIV DMIN)
**MILLHORN HENRY ORVILLE REV** (614)664-6697
PO Box 91 New Marshfield OH 45766 • hootowl@eurekanet.com • EN • Cmp P • English Farmington MI • (SL 1970)
**MILLIGAN JOHN W REV** (216)341-1591
3715 Washington Park Blvd Newburgh Heights OH 44105 • OH • SP • Zion Cleveland OH • (216)861-2179 • (SL 1980 MDIV MED)
**MILLS PETER E REV** (219)471-1787
PO Box 15922 Fort Wayne IN 46885-5922 • millspe@earthlink.net • IN • 01/1999 • (FW 1996 MDIV JD)
**MILNER GEORGE E JR. REV** (323)255-4622
5212 Dahlia Dr Los Angeles CA 90041-1407 • gnedmilner@cs.com • EN • Sn/Adm • Eagle Rock Los Angeles CA • (323)255-4622 • (SPR 1966)
**MILO FRANK V REV** (218)568-5663
PO Box 658 Pequot Lakes MN 56472-0658 • gloriadi@uslink.net • MNN • SP • Gloria Dei Pequot Lakes MN • (218)568-5668 • (SL 1979 MDIV)
**MILZ DAVID S REV** (320)398-6108
PO Box 437 Kimball MN 55353-0437 • dsmilz@prodigy.net • MNN • SP • St John Kimball MN • (320)398-7151 • (SL 1994 MDIV)
**MINETREE CHARLES C III REV** (724)468-3488
578 Monticello Dr Delmont PA 15626-1374 • cminetree@aol.com • EA • SP • Calvary Murrysville PA • (724)327-2898 • (SL 1987 MDIV)
**MINNIX ROY W REV** (609)971-7020
C/O Village Luth Church 701 Western Blvd Lanoka Harbor NJ 08734-1536 • anthrax573@aol.com • NJ • SP • Village Lanoka Harbor NJ • (609)693-1333 • (SL 1973 MS MDIV)
**MIRELES BONIFACIO R REV** (916)682-1706
7632 Clement Cir Sacramento CA 95828-4310 • CNH • EM • (CQ 1980)
**MIRLY HERBERT H REV** (704)377-3024
2900 Belvedere Ave Charlotte NC 28205-3708 • hmirly@juno.com • SE • EM • (SL 1945)
**MIRLY RAY G REV** (314)569-0725
1618 Fahrpark Ct Saint Louis MO 63146-4765 • rmirly@worldnet.att.net • MO • Sn/Adm • Immanuel Saint Louis MO • (314)993-2394 • (CQ 1977 MAR)
**MIRTSCHIN NEVILLE REV** (724)941-3673
2799 Old Washington Rd Uppr St Clair PA 15241-1999 • EN • SP • Hope Pittsburgh PA • (724)941-9441 • (CQ 1972)
**MISCH C BEN REV** (520)836-1889
1232 E Avenida Fresca Casa Grande AZ 85222-1002 • bentek@c2i2.com • PSW • EM • (SPR 1954)
**MISCH STEVEN JON REV** (713)468-2623
C/O St Mark Luth Church 1515 Hillendahl Blvd Houston TX 77055-3411 • smisch@flash.net • TX • Assoc • St Mark Houston TX • (713)468-2623 • (SL 1982 MDIV)
**MISCHNICK MARK R REV** (715)877-2046
E19775 State Rd # 27 Fall Creek WI 54742-5200 • northrev@execpc.com • NW • SP • Bethlehem Fall Creek WI* • (715)877-3249 • (CQ 1998)
**MISKIMEN ROBERT I REV** (307)638-3880
2228 E Pershing Blvd Cheyenne WY 82001-4111 • purlyrim@earthlink.net • WY • EM • * • (SPR 1952)
**MISTEREK WALLACE F REV** (503)661-3926
550 NW Eleven Mile Ct Gresham OR 97030-5253 • waldem@juno.com • NOW • EM • * • (SL 1953 MA)
**MITCHELL CHRISTOPHER W REV** (314)843-2529
8921 Westhaven Ct Saint Louis MO 63126-2328 • chris.mitchell@cph.org • MO • S Ex/S • Missouri Saint Louis MO • (314)317-4550 • (SL 1987 MA MDIV PHD)
**MITCHELL HAROLD R REV** (408)723-1091
3560 Steval Pl San Jose CA 95136-1439 • CNH • EM • (SPR 1955)
**MITCHELL HERBERT D REV** (727)441-1754
51 Island Way Condo 608 Clearwater FL 33767 • script@ij.net • FG • SP • Faith Dunedin FL • (727)733-2657 • (SL 1966 DMIN)
**MITCHELL JEROME K REV** (219)486-8085
3919 Hedwig Dr Fort Wayne IN 46815-5120 • IN • 09/1999 • (FW 1990 MDIV)
**MITCHELL JOHN W JR. REV** (513)754-1101
6712 Pondfield Ln Mason OH 45040-8525 • johnmitc@excite.com • OH • Asst • Our Redeemer Maineville OH • (513)697-7335 • (SL 1987 MDIV)
**MITCHELL LAWRENCE W REV** (812)339-9275
720 E Eddington Ct Bloomington IN 47401-8739 • IN • Sn/Adm • Faith Bloomington IN • (812)332-1668 • (SPR 1974 MDIV)
**MITCHELL ROBERT E REV** (406)587-5307
1145 Cherry Dr Bozeman MT 59715-5918 • lsfmsu@mcn.net • MT • Assoc • First Bozeman MT • (406)586-5374 • (CQ 1995 MED)
**MITKOS LESLIE J JR. REV** (618)635-3143
116 W Henry St Staunton IL 62088-1967 • ljmjr55@hotmail.com • SI • 10/1999 • (FW 1976 MDIV DMIN)
**MITSCHKE HERMAN W REV** (760)944-6253
955 Sealane Dr Encinitas CA 92024-5036 • PSW • Assoc • Our Redeemer San Diego CA • (619)262-0757 • (SL 1950)
**MITSCHKE KENNETH R REV** 210-566-1650
1531 Jasmine Dr Schertz TX 78154-3738 • kenmits@wireweb.net • TX • D Miss • Texas Austin TX • (SL 1987 MDIV)
**MITSCHKE WILLIAM T REV** (815)725-1341
2500 Hacker Dr Joliet IL 60435 • NI • Sn/Adm • Our Savior Joliet IL • (815)725-1606 • (SL 1958 MDIV)
**MITTELSTAEDT NEIL A REV** (905)271-9466
1606 Crestview Ave Mississauga ON L5G 3P8 CANADA • mittel@ljci.com • EN • D Miss • English Farmington MI • (SC 1989 MDIV)
**MITTELSTAEDT ROBERT O REV** (760)329-9720
11018 Rhodesia Ave Sunland CA 91040 • PSW • EM • (SPR 1945 MA)
**MOCK GEORGE W REV** (480)945-7918
4814 N Granite Reef Rd Scottsdale AZ 85251-1725 • PSW • EM • (SL 1955 MDIV)
**MOE JOHN REV** (612)423-2149
C/O St John Luth Church 14385 Blaine Ave E Rosemount MN 55068-5929 • moexx016@tc.umn.edu • MNS • SP • St John Rosemount MN • (651)423-2149 • (SL 1982 MDIV)
**MOE TIMOTHY E REV** (218)624-9310
314 N 43rd Ave W Duluth MN 55807-1553 • MNN • SP • Christ King Duluth MN • (218)624-3696 • (SL 1990 MDIV)
**MOEHRING JAMES E REV** (231)889-4015
PO Box 170 Arcadia MI 49613-0170 • MI • EM • (SPR 1952 MDIV)
**MOEHRING MARTIN K REV** (219)724-7552
1034 E 1100 N Decatur IN 46733-8407 • mkmgbp@adamswells.com • IN • SP • St Peter Decatur IN • (219)724-7533 • (FW 1982 MDIV)
**MOELLER ERIC J REV** (708)209-1615
1123 Bonnie Brae #2 River Forest IL 60305 • NI • SHS/C • Northern Illinois Hillside IL • (SL 1989 MDIV MA PHD)
**MOELLER JOHN S REV** (708)423-3414
9901 S Kolmar Oak Lawn IL 60453 • jomamo@juno.com • NI • Asst • St Paul Oak Lawn IL • (708)423-1040 • (SL 1999 MDIV)
**MOELLER THEODORE C REV** (360)882-0273
14621 NE 49th Cir Vancouver WA 98682 • flock@pacifier.com • NOW • SP • Good Shepherd Vancouver WA • (360)254-5158 • (SK 1982 MDIV)
**MOELLER WILLIAM F REV** (218)445-5751
306 N W Brown St Verndale MN 56481-9303 • MNN • SP • Immanuel Verndale MN* • (218)924-2454 • (SL 1993 MDIV)
**MOELLER WILLIAM F REV** (320)834-2467
13342 Krohnfeldt Beach Rd NW Alexandria MN 56308-9735 • moeller@gctel.com • MNN • EM • * • (SL 1960 MDIV)
**MOELLERING RALPH L REV**
632 Kearney St #1 El Cerrito CA 94530 • EN • EM • * • (SL 1946 MDIV MST MA PHD)
**MOHN MARTIN G REV**
PO Box 673 Black River Falls WI 54615-0673 • NW • 05/1999 • * • (FW 1992 MDIV)
**MOHN TRUMAN P REV** (612)822-6660
4832 Dupont Ave S Minneapolis MN 55409-2326 • MNS • EM • * • (LS 1944 MDIV MED)

**MOHR GARY W REV** (510)538-0941
23400 Mona Marie Ct Hayward CA 94541-3572 • thegoodrev@juno.com • CNH • SP • Good Shepherd Hayward CA • (510)782-0872 • (CQ 1991 MDIV)

**MOHR GERRY W REV** (419)422-3910
1425 6th St Findlay OH 45840-6450 • OH • SP • Concordia Findlay OH • (419)422-4209 • (FW 1977 MDIV MSED)

**MOHR MICHAEL W REV** (217)644-2452
PO Box 336 Strasburg IL 62465-0336 • CI • SP • Grace Strasburg IL • (217)644-2452 • (SL 1998 MDIV)

**MOHR RICHARD A REV** (972)471-0861
200 River Rd Coppell TX 75019-6232 • rich@coslcs.org • TX • SP • Christ Our Savior Coppell TX • (972)462-0225 • (SPR 1974 MDIV)

**MOLDENHAUER ADOLPH W REV** (716)693-4012
394 Rosebrock St N Tonawanda NY 14120-4156 • EA • SP • St Matthew North Tonawanda NY • (716)692-6862 • (SL 1953 MDIV DD)

**MOLDENHAUER PAUL M REV** (248)624-8290
2020 S Commerce Rd Walled Lake MI 48390-2412 • pastorpaul@st-matthew.org • MI • Sn/Adm • St Matthew Walled Lake MI • (248)624-7676 • (FW 1981 MDIV)

**MOLDENHAUER ROGER R REV** (715)352-2888
W1143 Huckleberry St Edgar WI 54426-9739 • RogerM27@aol.com • NW • SP • St John Edgar WI* • (715)352-2888 • (SL 1965 MDIV)

**MOLITORIS CRAIG L REV**
Flat B #12 Wiltshire Rd Kowloon Tong HONG KONG • lcmsclm@ctimail.com • MO • S Miss • Missouri Saint Louis MO • (314)317-4550 • (SL 1985 MDIV STM MA)

**MOLITORIS JOHN REV** (412)795-3238
136 Cypress Hill Dr Pittsburgh PA 15235-2610 • EA • EM • (SL 1952)

**MOLITORIS JOSEPH REV** (219)464-4437
1506 Wood St Valparaiso IN 46383-5146 • IN • SP • Prince Peace Valparaiso IN • (219)464-4911 • (SPR 1962)

**MOLL DONALD W REV** (630)879-8342
272 S Forest Ave Batavia IL 60510 • woldmoll@juno.com • NI • SP • Word Of Life Naperville IL • (630)355-9655 • (CQ 1970 MED MAR)

**MOLL JAMES P REV** (402)365-4181
PO Box 9 Deshler NE 68340-0009 • jemoll@gpcom.net • NEB • EM • (CQ 1977 MED)

**MOLL ROBERT L REV** (847)382-3292
312 Tower Rd Barrington IL 60010-4257 • NI • Sn/Adm • St Matthew Barrington IL • (847)382-7002 • (CQ 1982 MAR MED)

**MOLNAR S CHRISTOPHER REV** (805)543-8327
C/O Zion Luth Church 1010 Foothill Blvd San Luis Obispo CA 93405-1816 • chaplain@fix.net • CNH • SP • Zion San Luis Obispo CA • (805)543-8327 • (SL 1979 MDIV MST)

**MOLZAN HAROLD G REV** (517)734-3164
812 Linden St Rogers City MI 49779-1123 • MI • EM • (SPR 1947)

**MOMMENS AUGUST W REV** (308)687-6443
1649 Worms Rd Saint Libory NE 68872 • NEB • EM • (SPR 1952)

**MOMMENS DAVID A REV** (219)248-8065
C/O St John Luth Church 2465 W Keiser Rd Columbia City IN 46725-8009 • dmommens@juno.com • IN • SP • St John Columbia City IN • (219)244-3712 • (FW 1984 MDIV)

**MONS WILLIAM MAXIMILLIAN REV** (319)444-2793
103 Maple St Luzerne IA 52257-9601 • splcluzerne@juno.com • IE • SP • St Paul Luzerne IA • (319)444-2378 • (SL 1996 MDIV)

**MONSON JOHN R REV** (248)879-0464
135 Mc Kinley Rd Troy MI 48098-2966 • MI • SP • St Augustine Troy MI • (248)879-6400 • (SL 1961 MAR MA)

**MONSON PAUL C REV**
C/O Trinity Lutheran Church 8150 Chapp Warren MI 48089-1657 • MI • SP • Trinity Warren MI • (810)755-6767 • (SL 1997 MDIV)

**MONTGOMERY JOHN WARWICK DR** 01144-207-5831210
No 9 Four Crane Ct Fleet St London EC4A 2EJ ENGLAND • 106612.1066@compuserve.com • NOW • EM • (CQ 1965 MPHIL MA PHD THD)

**MOODY RICHARD A REV** (636)343-9389
90 W Lakewood Dr Fenton MO 63026 • revrmoody@aol.com • MO • P Df • Holy Cross Df Saint Louis MO • (314)533-6035 • (SL 1979 MDIV)

**MOOG JAMES E REV** (319)291-6930
741 Central Ave Evansdale IA 50707-1613 • wdgb87@aol.com • IE • SP • St Paul Evansdale IA* • (319)232-7657 • (SL 1976 MDIV)

**MOON HARRY H B REV** (714)995-3251
9034 Stacie Ln Anaheim CA 92804-6380 • PSW • D Miss • Pacific Southwest Irvine CA • (949)854-3232 • (CQ 1990 MDIV)

**MOON MARVIN D REV** (805)928-1452
135 S E St Lompoc CA 93436-6810 • CNH • SP • Bethany Lompoc CA • (805)736-8615 • (CQ 1988 PHD)

**MOON SHANG IK REV** (949)559-1881
13842 Typee Way Irvine CA 92620-3274 • moonsi@cui.edu • PSW • SHS/C • Pacific Southwest Irvine CA • (949)854-3232 • (SL 1963 MA MDIV PHD)

**MOORE DAVID R REV** (219)432-7397
8420 Creekside Pl Fort Wayne IN 46804-2701 • drmoore@aol.com • EN • Assoc • St Michael Fort Wayne IN • (219)432-2033 • (FW 1986 MDIV STM)

**MOORE DONALD A REV** (407)464-5967
2266 Lake Marion Dr Apopka FL 32712 • stpaullcms@netzero.net • FG • SP • St Paul Apopka FL • (407)889-2634 • (SL 1999 MDIV)

**MOORE JEFFERY C REV** (314)727-9592
16 N Seminary Ter Saint Louis MO 63105-3011 • revjcmoore@aol.com • MO • SHS/C • Missouri Saint Louis MO • (314)317-4550 • (SL 1980 MDIV STM)

**MOORE JOHN MICHAEL REV** (319)235-5589
4958 William Dr Waterloo IA 50701 • IE • Assoc • Grace Waterloo IA • (319)235-6705 • (SL 1986 MDIV)

**MOORE KEVIN D REV**
601 E Logan Ave Gettysburg SD 57442-1615 • SD • SP • Emmanuel Gettysburg SD* • (605)765-9201 • (SL 1990 MDIV)

**MOORE RICHARD A REV** (314)741-5207
1516 Surfside Dr Saint Louis MO 63138-2341 • MO • SP • Immanuel Chapel Saint Louis MO • (314)741-4700 • (SL 1985 MDIV)

**MOORE THOMAS L REV** (407)977-0973
2069 Bluejay Ln Oviedo FL 32765-8610 • FG • EM • (SPR 1970)

**MOORHEAD WILLIAM G REV** (402)339-2676
5648 Bay Meadows Rd Omaha NE 68127-3518 • bmoorhead@westside66.org • NEB • Sn/Adm • Pacific Hills Omaha NE • (402)391-9625 • (SL 1973 MDIV DMIN)

**MORALES CHRISTIAN G REV** (757)548-6484
472 Albemarle Dr PO Box 1443 Chesapeake VA 23322 • EN • SP • Faith Chesapeake VA • (757)436-5832 • (CQ 1978)

**MORALES EDDIE REV**
105 Applegate Dr Central Islip NY 11722 • AT • SP • Grace Central Islip NY • (516)234-8524 • (FW 1999 MDIV)

**MORANT BRUCE C REV** (405)262-1552
400 S Country Club Rd El Reno OK 73036 • bcmorant@aol.com • OK • SP • Trinity El Reno OK • (405)262-7116 • (SL 1998 MDIV MA)

**MORDHORST ROBERT L REV** (410)947-7656
4639 Briarclift Rd Baltimore MD 21229-1412 • rmord@bellatlantic.net • SE • Sn/Adm • Emmanuel Baltimore MD • (410)744-0016 • (SL 1965 MDIV DMIN)

**MOREHOUSE MICHAEL A REV** (520)349-8440
15879 N Twin Lakes Dr Tucson AZ 85739-8895 • pastormorehouse@juno.com • EN • SP • Catalina Tucson AZ • (520)825-9255 • (FW 1998 MDIV)

**MORENO MICHAEL P REV**
USS Cleveland FPO AP 96662-1710 • mmoreno@ncfcomm.com • NEB • M Chap • Nebraska Seward NE • (FW 1990 MDIV)

**MORFITT STEVEN REV** (512)548-0579
C/O El Calvario Luth Church 1157 E Monroe St Brownsville TX 78520-5842 • TX • SP • El Calvario Brownsville TX • (956)546-2350 • (SL 1982)

**MORGAN JOEL C REV** (513)759-2946
5757 Mc Carthy Ct West Chester OH 45044-9096 • jolmorg@aol.com • OH • SP • Royal Redeemer Liberty Township OH • (513)779-4740 • (FW 1988 MDIV MS)

**MORIARITY DANIEL T REV** (602)569-0946
3608 E Renee Dr Phoenix AZ 85050-6358 • dtmort@aol.com • PSW • Assoc • St Mark Phoenix AZ • (602)992-1980 • (SL 1974 MDIV)

**MORITZ RANDALL CLARE REV** (507)485-3351
C/O St Luke Lutheran Church 5595 130th Ave Wood Lake MN 56297-1497 • rmoritz@rconnect.com • MNN • SP • St Luke Wood Lake MN • (507)485-3527 • (SL 1997 MDIV)

**MORITZ RONALD C REV** (309)683-1163
1111 W Brookforest Peoria IL 61615 • CI • Sn/Adm • Trinity Peoria IL • (309)676-4609 • (SPR 1972 MDIV MS)

**MORITZ VICTOR E REV** (504)282-9983
4423 Dreux Ave New Orleans LA 70126-3505 • SO • EM • (SPR 1952 MDIV)

**MORNER DENNIS D REV** (520)775-4061
4881 N Hobo Cir Prescott Valley AZ 86314-5157 • dmorner@northlink.com • PSW • SP • Trinity Prescott Valley AZ • (520)772-8845 • (FW 1981 MDIV)

**MORRIS BRUCE B REV** (716)652-0256
640 Jamison Rd Elma NY 14059-9526 • EA • SP • Faith Elma NY • (716)652-2221 • (FW 1981 MDIV)

**MORRIS RALPH C REV** (308)436-2662
1755 Flaten Ave Gering NE 69341-1844 • rm82311@navix.net • WY • Asst • Faith Gering NE • (308)436-4307 • (FW 1978 MDIV)

**MORRIS ROBERT S REV** (718)761-7250
37 Gansevoort Blvd Staten Island NY 10314-4023 • morris7553@aol.com • AT • Sn/Adm • St John Staten Island NY • (718)761-1600 • (SL 1979 MDIV)

**MORRIS TIMOTHY E REV** (972)547-0200
4510 Wedgewood Dr Mc Kinney TX 75070-7756 • TX • Assoc • Our Savior Mc Kinney TX • (972)542-6802 • (SL 1998 MDIV)

**MORRIS WILLIAM L DR** (734)654-2890
28428 Nieman Rd New Boston MI 48164-9640 • wmmorris@cdlcorp.com • MI • Sn/Adm • St John New Boston MI • (734)654-6366 • (FW 1986 MDIV DMIN)

**MORROW EDWIN L REV** (765)474-9855
204 Buckingham Cir Lafayette IN 47905-6921 • IN • SP • Grace Lafayette IN • (765)474-1887 • (FW 1991 MDIV)

**MORTENSON JEFFREY E REV** (262)886-2370
3112 91st St Sturtevant WI 53177-2726 • SW • SP • Faith Sturtevant WI • (262)886-2522 • (SL 1983 MDIV)

**MORTHOLE DONALD G REV** (540)432-9759
3450 Dawn Dr Harrisonburg VA 22801-2689 • d.g.morthole@juno.com • SE • EM • (SL 1956 MED)

**MORTON DOUGLAS V REV** (319)642-7216
1295 Howard Ave Marengo IA 52301-1117 • dmluther@netins.net • IE • SP • St John Marengo IA • (319)642-5452 • (SL 1979 MDIV)

**MORTON R WAYNE REV**
HC 62 Box 46166 Pinetop AZ 85935-9666 • EN • SP • Shep Mountains Pinetop AZ • (520)367-1183 • (FW 1994 MDIV)

**MOSEMANN BRIAN M REV**
C/O Concordia River Forest 7400 Augusta St River Forest IL 60305-1499 • NI • SHS/C • Northern Illinois Hillside IL • (SL 1991 MDIV MST)

**MOSER C DAVID REV** (704)464-6110
608 S College Ave Newton NC 28658-3416 • cdavid@twave.net • SE • SP • Holy Cross Newton NC • (828)464-3791 • (TR 1979 MDIV)

**MOSLEY LELAND K REV** (510)792-4399
4436 Glidden Way Fremont CA 94536-7325 • fkmosley@ix.netcom.com • CNH • EM • (SPR 1961)

**MOSS MARK E REV**
CMR 411 Box 1911 APO AE 09112 • mossm@cmtymail.100asg.army.mil • MNS • M Chap • Minnesota South Burnsville MN • (FW 1986 MDIV)

**MOSS MARVIN J REV** (414)376-4240
817A Washington St Grafton WI 53024-1844 • pastormoss@aol.com • SW • Assoc • St Paul Grafton WI • (262)377-4659 • (SL 1991 MDIV)

**MOSSMAN DONALD J REV** (734)971-3375
2805 Towner Blvd Ann Arbor MI 48104-6547 • mossmd@ccaa.edu • MI • SHS/C • Michigan Ann Arbor MI • (SPR 1964 MA MDIV PHD)

**MOWRY TIMOTHY E REV** (616)943-9623
5816 Joanne Ct Traverse City MI 49684-8650 • pastortim@aliens.com • MI • SP • Redeemer Interlochen Interlochen MI • (616)276-6372 • (SL 1972 MDIV)

**MOYER JOHN V REV** (517)264-2001
2364 Kenwood Dr Adrian MI 49221-3629 • jmoyer@tc3net.com • EN • EM • (SPR 1961 STM)

**MOYER THOMAS E REV** (217)726-7714
3032 S Lincoln Ave Springfield IL 62704-4952 • temoyer@juno.com • CI • Central Illinois Springfield IL • (FW 1985 MDIV)

**MOZOLAK SAMUEL P REV** (440)333-3153
4267 W 215th St Fairview Park OH 44126-1854 • samoze@juno.com • S • EM • (SPR 1940 MA)

**MROCH PAUL G REV** (812)476-1433
2100 Adams Ave Evansville IN 47714-3013 • IN • EM • (SL 1932)

**MROCH THOMAS P REV** (330)676-1306
2511 Mallory Ln Stow OH 44224-1989 • tcmroch@aol.com • OH • Sn/Adm • Faith Kent OH • (330)673-6633 • (SL 1971 MDIV)

**MROCHEN GEORGE J REV** (312)523-3838
C/O Holy Cross Luth Church 3116 S Racine Ave Chicago IL 60608-6405 • gmrochen@aol.com • NI • SP • Holy Cross Chicago IL • (773)523-3838 • (SPR 1976 MDIV)

**MROSKO ROBERT ANDREW REV** (402)226-2311
PO Box 95 Ruskin NE 68974-0097 • rm10956@alltel.net • NEB • SP • St Mark Ruskin NE • (402)226-2391 • (SL 1997 MDIV)

**MUCHOW DONALD K REV** (512)301-0431
5725 Galsworthy Ct Austin TX 78739 • mondon1@juno.com • SE • EM • (SL 1962 MDIV DD LHD)

**MUDGE RONALD R REV** (507)372-4053
804 W Shore Dr Worthington MN 56187-3013 • mela@africaonline.co.ci • MNS • S Miss • Minnesota South Burnsville MN • (SL 1996 MDIV)

**MUEHLER CRAIG GARY REV**
PO Box 874 Concordia MO 64020-0874 • CKMuehler@aol.com • SD • M Chap • North Dakota Fargo ND • (SL 1988 MDIV)

**MUEHLER GARY A REV**
RR 3 Box 104 Cole Camp MO 65325-9141 • MO • EM • (SPR 1966 MDIV)

**MUELLER ADAM REV** (314)334-9982
3418 Julie Dr Cape Girardeau MO 63701-4937 • MO • EM • (CQ 1970 MDIV)

**MUELLER ALVIN W REV** (309)692-5938
7019 N Galena Rd Peoria IL 61614 • CI • EM • (SL 1930 DD)

**MUELLER ARMAND J REV** (618)282-4474
319 Indiana St Red Bud IL 62278-1814 • SI • EM • (SL 1957 MDIV)

**MUELLER ARNOLD G REV** (936)321-8258
14168 Old Conroe Rd Conroe TX 77384-3207 • TX • EM • (SL 1945)

**MUELLER BARRY L REV** (810)727-2640
70521 Karen St Richmond MI 48062-1024 • MI • SP • Christ New Baltimore MI • (810)725-1431 • (FW 1988 MDIV)

**MUELLER BART ALLEN REV** (507)662-5032
RR 2 Box 33 Lakefield MN 56150-9717 • MNS • SP • St Peter Lakefield MN* • (507)662-5862 • (SL 1986 MDIV)

**MUELLER BRETT L REV** (660)394-8770
PO Box 146 Corder MO 64021-0146 • revblm@juno.com • MO • SP • Zion Corder MO* • (660)394-2322 • (SL 1993 MDIV)

**MUELLER CHARLES R REV** (508)877-5934
198 Maravista Ave East Falmouth MA 02536-7331 • NE • EM • * • (SL 1949 MA MSW)

**MUELLER CHARLES S JR. REV** (630)894-1541
305 Catalpa Roselle IL 60172-2403 • pjr@trinityroselle.com • NI • Sn/Adm • Trinity Roselle IL • (630)894-3263 • (SL 1982 MDIV)

**MUELLER CHARLES S REV** (630)540-5263
308 Patricia Ln Bartlett IL 60103 • chassenior@aol.com • NI • Asst • Trinity Roselle IL • (630)894-3263 • (SL 1953 LLD)

**MUELLER DANIEL G REV** (512)684-7826
7711 Susan Elaine St San Antonio TX 78240-3626 • dmueller@swbell.net • TX • Sn/Adm • Shepherd Hills San Antonio TX • (210)614-3742 • (SL 1975 MDIV DMIN)

**MUELLER DAVID A REV** (305)743-6873
11231 5th Ave - Gulf Marathon FL 33050 • cdmue@aol.com • FG • EM • (SL 1964 MSED MDIV)

**MUELLER DAVID C REV** (718)767-4361
11-10 150th St Whitestone NY 11357-1746 • dmrev@aol.com • AT • SP • Immanuel Whitestone NY • (718)747-1638 • (SL 1965 MDIV MA)

**MUELLER DAVID E REV** (302)762-5471
1204 Bruce Rd Wilmington DE 19803-4202 • davidmueller@dol.net • SE • SP • Concordia Wilmington DE • (302)478-3004 • (SPR 1971 MDIV MTH)

**MUELLER DAVID L REV** (573)642-3820
1701 Plaza Dr Fulton MO 65251-2461 • dmueller@ktis.net • MO • SP • St Paul Fulton MO • (573)642-2856 • (SL 1981 MDIV)

**MUELLER DAVID R** (219)
213 W Jasper Goodland IN 47948-8006 • IN • SP • Trinity Goodland IN • (219)297-3556 • (FW 2000 MDIV)

**MUELLER DONALD H REV** (607)748-0840
C/O Grace Lutheran Church 709 Main St Vestal NY 13850-3157 • rdvmm@aol.com • EA • SP • Grace Vestal NY • (607)748-0840 • (SL 1968 MDIV MPH DVM)

**MUELLER ELDOR H REV** (815)622-5091
1421 W 21st St Sterling IL 61081-4501 • NI • EM • (SL 1938)

**MUELLER FREDERICK L REV** (920)987-5804
C/O Emmaus Luth Church PO Box 346 N 4490 Poy Sippi WI 54967-0346 • getagrip@vbe.com • SW • SP • Emmaus Poy Sippi WI • (920)987-5229 • (SL 1982 MDIV)

**MUELLER GILBERT E REV** (319)355-3694
2515 E Pleasant St Davenport IA 52803 • gibretired@aol.com • IE • EM • (SL 1958 STM MDIV)

**MUELLER HENRY C REV** (320)259-6810
901 12th Ave S Saint Cloud MN 56301-5249 • MNN • EM • (SL 1963 MDIV EDS)

**MUELLER HERBERT C JR. REV** (618)939-7130
102 Front St Waterloo IL 62298-1727 • sidpreshcm@aol.com • SI • DP • Southern Illinois Belleville IL • (SL 1979 MDIV)

**MUELLER HERMAN W REV** (760)723-3390
861 Shade Tree Ln Fallbrook CA 92028-3566 • PSW • EM • (SL 1946 MDIV)

**MUELLER HOWARD E REV** (314)631-2400
4515 Canoe Dr Saint Louis MO 63123-5725 • muellhe@aol.com • MO • EM • (SL 1940 MDIV LITTD)

**MUELLER HOWARD W REV** (573)833-6922
PO Box 56 Pocahontas MO 63779-0056 • muellerh@showme.net • MO • SP • Zion Pocahontas MO* • (573)833-6922 • (SL 1961)

**MUELLER JAMES L REV**
3818 S Western Ave # PMB413 Sioux Falls SD 57105-6511 • jim-mona@juno.com • MO • EM • * • (SL 1959)

**MUELLER JAMES W REV** (925)686-5161
4627 Lincoln Dr Concord CA 94521-1334 • circassiancat@msn.com • CNH • SP • First Concord CA • (925)671-9942 • (SL 1969 MDIV)

**MUELLER JEFFREY E REV** (707)837-9452
9763 Dawn Way Windsor CA 95492-8879 • vof@vof.org • CNH • Sn/Adm • Vineyard of Faith Windsor CA • (707)837-8712 • (SL 1993 MDIV)

**MUELLER JOHN F REV** (517)249-4115
4351 Bradford Dr Saginaw MI 48603 • muelljf@svol.org • MI • Tchr • Valley Saginaw MI • (517)790-1676 • (SL 1982 MDIV)

**MUELLER JOHN H REV** (209)522-8890
3612 Chiburis Ct Modesto CA 95356 • CNH • SP • Grace Modesto CA • (209)522-8890 • (SL 1982 MDIV)

**MUELLER JOHN W REV** (314)845-2975
3523 Chaplou Dr Saint Louis MO 63129-2317 • ic³muellejw@lcms.org • MO • S Ex/S • Missouri Saint Louis MO • (314)317-4550 • (SL 1978 MDIV)

**MUELLER KENNARD O REV**
C/O Peace Lutheran Church PO Box 320060 Dunnellon FL 34432-0060 • FG • SP • Peace Dunnellon FL • (352)489-5881 • (SPR 1965 MDIV)

**MUELLER LE ROY F REV** (320)839-2447
312 Jackson Ave Ortonville MN 56278-1451 • MNN • EM • (SL 1952)

**MUELLER MARCUS R REV** (956)399-8242
1095 N Dowling St San Benito TX 78586-5221 • muellersbtx@acnet.net • TX • SP • St John San Benito TX • (956)399-3422 • (CQ 1985)

**MUELLER MARK A REV** (414)679-5850
S75W17717 Harbor Cir Muskego WI 53150-9187 • http://www/ods.net/.orlc • SW • Sn/Adm • Our Redeemer Wauwatosa WI • (414)258-4555 • (SL 1976 MDIV)

**MUELLER MARK ALAN REV** (518)767-2131
180 Maple Ave Selkirk NY 12158 • stlmueller@aol.com • AT • Asst • Bethlehem Delmar NY • (518)439-4328 • (SL 1999 MDIV)

**MUELLER MARTIN E REV** (507)281-2656
1410 Cascade St NW Rochester MN 55901-7751 • MNS • EM • (SL 1957 MDIV)

**MUELLER MARTIN E A REV**
18449 Greenmadow Dr Clinton Township MI 48038-5231 • SW • EM • (SL 1931 MTH)

**MUELLER MARVIN F REV** (847)470-1205
7800 N Harlem Ave Niles IL 60714-3202 • Marvmuel@aol.com • NI • SP • St John Niles IL • (847)647-9867 • (SL 1961 MST)

**MUELLER NORBERT H DR** (972)470-0267
13035 Chandler Dr Dallas TX 75243-2448 • TX • EM • (SL 1954 STM MDIV DMIN)

**MUELLER ORVAL D REV** (504)242-5769
7801 Newcastle St New Orleans LA 70126-1629 • orvmueller@aol.com • SO • DP • Southern New Orleans LA • (SL 1964 MDIV)

**MUELLER PAUL C REV** (712)276-5385
5223 Wellington Ct Sioux City IA 51106-4245 • paulynmueller@aol.com • IW • EM • (SL 1946)

**MUELLER PAUL G REV** (715)423-8649
1710 Plum St Wisconsin Rapids WI 54494-5173 • stjohns@wctc.net • NW • SP • St John Wisconsin Rapids WI • (715)423-7788 • (SL 1964)

**MUELLER PAUL WALTER DR** (651)487-5514
1820 Onacrest Ct Maplewood MN 55117-2329 • mueller@csp.edu • MNS • SHS/C • Minnesota South Burnsville MN • (SL 1983 MDIV MTH DMISS)

**MUELLER PETER E REV** (636)273-4463
219 Strecker Farms Ct Wildwood MO 63011-2089 • pmueller@stjohnsellisville.org • MO • Assoc • St John Ellisville MO • (314)394-4100 • (CQ 1998 MTH MTH)

**MUELLER PETER L REV** (913)239-9607
HHC 3rd BDE 1st AD Fort Riley KS 66442 • petros555@juno.com • MI • M Chap • Michigan Ann Arbor MI • (SL 1984 MDIV)

**MUELLER RANDALL F REV** (949)951-2155
23666 Via Navarra Mission Viejo CA 92691-3636 • rmueller@gslh.org • PSW • O Sp Min • Pacific Southwest Irvine CA • (949)854-3232 • (SL 1973 MDIV DMIN)

**MUELLER RANDOLPH E REV** (319)472-4174
205 Lutheran Home Ct Vinton IA 52349-1169 • IE • EM • (SL 1941)

**MUELLER RAYMOND A REV** (219)834-3706
403 N Hickory W North Webster IN 46555 • IN • SP • Shep by Lakes Syracuse IN • (219)528-6137 • (SL 1954 MDIV MST)

**MUELLER RICHARD C REV** (308)762-9208
1042 Duncan Ave Alliance NE 69301-2630 • rmueller@premaonline.com • WY • Asst • Immanuel Alliance NE • (308)762-4663 • (SL 1990 MDIV)

**MUELLER ROBERT G REV** (727)535-3910
3881 El Camino Ct Largo FL 33771-2776 • FG • EM • (SL 1954 MDIV)

**MUELLER ROBERT R ANDREW REV** (609)654-5386
1 Eayrestown Rd Medford NJ 08055 • enxristo@aol.com • NJ • SP • Calvary Medford NJ • (609)654-2489 • (FW 1988 MA MDIV)

**MUELLER RONALD A REV** (937)848-2733
2427 Portage Path Bellbrook OH 45305-1738 • OH • EM • (SL 1958 MDIV)

**MUELLER RONALD R REV** (352)237-2233
C/O Our Redeemer Lutheran Ch 5200 SW State Rd 200 Ocala FL 34474-5737 • ourredeemer@netzero.net • FG • SP • Our Redeemer Ocala FL • (352)237-2233 • (SL 1965 MDIV)

**MUELLER RONALD W REV** (715)537-3080
1347 E La Salle Ave Barron WI 54812-1637 • NW • SP • Salem Barron WI • (715)537-3011 • (SPR 1973 MDIV STM)

**MUELLER STEPHEN M REV** (715)457-2405
C/O St Paul Lutheran Church 1225 Main St Junction City WI 54443-9729 • smueller@hotmail.com • NW • SP • St Paul Junction City WI* • (715)457-2405 • (SL 1982 MDIV)

**MUELLER STEVEN PAUL REV** (949)588-0774
22132 Broken Bow Dr Lake Forest CA 92630-5708 • steve-mueller@cui.edu • PSW • SHS/C • Pacific Southwest Irvine CA • (949)854-3232 • (FW 1990 MDIV STM PHD)

**MUELLER THEODORE C REV** (707)575-3994
421 Denton Way Santa Rosa CA 95401-4810 • pastorT@stluke-lcms.org • CNH • Sn/Adm • St Luke Santa Rosa CA • (707)545-6772 • (SPR 1965)

**MUELLER THEODORE H REV** (630)810-9123
5146 Belden Ave Apt D1 Downers Grove IL 60515-4765 • tmueller01@sprynet.com • NI • EM • (CQ 1979 PHD)

**MUELLER THOMAS H REV** (805)610-1684
1211 Echo Ct Paso Robles CA 93446 • thmpls@aol.com • CNH • SP • Of The Redeemer Atascadero CA • (805)466-9350 • (SPR 1975 MDIV)

**MUELLER TIMOTHY P REV** (618)478-5544
15516 State Route 127 Nashville IL 62263-2374 • SI • SP • St John Nashville IL* • (618)478-5544 • (SL 1987 MDIV)

**MUELLER WILLIAM E REV** (507)864-7821
202 N Mill St Rushford MN 55971-9133 • pbjmller@means.net • MNS • SP • St Mark Rushford MN • (507)864-7111 • (SL 1994 MDIV)

**MUELLER WILLIARD E REV** (828)324-5495
1910 19th Street Pl NE Hickory NC 28601-0539 • wemuell@twave.net • SE • SP • Augustana Hickory NC • (828)328-6706 • (SL 1955 STM)

**MUENCH DAVID A REV** (636)405-2757
497 Thunderhead Canyon Dr Wildwood MO 63011 • MO • Assoc • St John Ellisville MO • (314)394-4100 • (SL 1986 MDIV MS)

**MUENCH HERBERT E REV** (636)949-8183
64 N Trumbull Circle St Charles MO 63301 • MO • EM • (CQ 1977 MAR)

**MUENCH PAUL E REV** (512)462-0914
6904 Meadow Run 3500 N I 35 Austin TX 78745 • pmu6909440@aol.com • TX • SHS/C • Texas Austin TX • (SL 1972 MDIV MTH PHD)

**MUENCHOW FRED A REV** (618)483-6475
2 S Edwards St Altamont IL 62411-1204 • CI • SP • Immanuel Altamont IL • (618)483-6395 • (SL 1961 MA)

**MUENCHOW MARK R REV** (504)727-3160
1337 Sycamore Pl Mandeville LA 70448 • muenchow@compsurf.com • SO • Sn/Adm • Holy Trinity Covington LA • (504)892-6146 • (SL 1990 MDIV)

**MUES R DEAN REV** (219)465-6800
210 Kraus Dr Valparaiso IN 46373 • IN • EM • (SPR 1962)

**MUGNOLO WILLIAM F REV** (315)331-0662
C/O Redeemer Lutheran Church 102 Hope Ave Newark NY 14513-1309 • rlc102@juno.comm • EA • SP • Redeemer Newark NY • (315)331-0662 • (SC 1990)

**MUHLBACH CRAIG ALAN REV**
1015 S Cty Rd 460 E Seymour IN 47274 • IN • SP • St John Seymour IN • (812)523-3559 • (SL 1992 MDIV)

**MUHLE DEAN RAY REV** (906)495-7165
61 Parkside Kincheloe MI 49788 • MI • SP • St Paul Kincheloe MI* • (906)495-5849 • (SL 1992 MDIV)

**MUHLENBRUCH JACK K DR** (314)487-6939
775 Gradient Dr Saint Louis MO 63125-5215 • MO • EM • * • (SL 1944 PHD)

**MULDER DAVID P DR** (314)965-5610
688 Trailcrest Ct Saint Louis MO 63122-2240 • david.mulder@lcms.org • MO • S Ex/S • Missouri Saint Louis MO • (314)317-4550 • (FW 1978 MDIV DMIN)

**MULFINGER DONALD W REV** (952)435-6058
213 Stevens Ct Burnsville MN 55306-5075 • mdmulfing@aol.com • MNS • SP • Ascension Burnsville MN • (952)890-3412 • (CQ 1980 MDIV)

**MULHOLLAND DANIEL L REV** (307)782-6802
PO Box 280 Fort Bridger WY 82933 • smulholl@union-tel.com • WY • SP • Shep Of Valley Fort Bridger WY • (307)782-6802 • (FW 1997 MDIV)

**MULLER DONALD M REV** (716)394-7648
245 Prospect St Canandaigua NY 14424-1609 • rockyam@aol.com • EA • SP • Good Shepherd Canandaigua NY • (716)394-2760 • (SL 1973 MDIV)

**MULLER LYLE D REV** (501)760-1021
2061 Marion Anderson Rd Hot Springs Nat Pk AR 71913-7522 • mmlm97@aol.com • MDS • EM • (SL 1961 MDIV DD)

**MULLER RICHARD E REV** (219)483-0899
3 Tyndale Pl Fort Wayne IN 46825-4936 • kayrich@gateway.net • IN • SHS/C • Indiana Fort Wayne IN • (CQ 1979 MA MA MDIV)

**MULLER ROBERT JOHN REV**
9878 N 125 W Wawaka IN 46794 • IN • SP • Restoration Wawaka IN • (SL 1971 MDIV)

**MULLER TIMOTHY B REV** (714)738-1381
C/O Our Savior Lutheran Church 1521 W Orangethorpe Ave Fullerton CA 92833-4533 • PSW • SP • Messiah Buena Park CA* • (714)521-7705 • (FW 1984 MDIV)

**MUMM DAVID P REV** (515)331-1770
3615 49th St Des Moines IA 50310 • davidmumm@aol.com • IW • Sn/Adm • Mount Olive Des Moines IA • (515)277-8349 • (SL 1981 MDIV)

**MUMM GEORGE A REV** (262)338-8251
818 S 6th Ave West Bend WI 53095-4614 • SW • EM • (SPR 1955 MDIV)

**MUMME DAVID C REV** (815)795-2020
422 Liberty St Marseilles IL 61341 • dgmumme@uti.com • NI • SP • Trinity Marseilles IL • (815)795-2031 • (FW 1997 MDIV)

**MUMME MARK W REV** (507)669-2480
C/O Zion Luth Church 305 Second St Hardwick MN 56134 • MNS • SP • Zion Hardwick MN • (507)669-2855 • (FW 2000 MDIV)

**MUMME PAUL G REV** (847)678-8483
3224 Rose St Franklin Park IL 60131-2145 • revmumme@worldnet.att.net • NI • SP • Mount Calvary Franklin Park IL* • (847)678-5565 • (FW 1998 MDIV)

**MUNCH JAN T REV** (423)745-0440
1812 Cherokee St Athens TN 37303-2364 • jmunch@usit.net • MDS • SP • Athens Athens TN • (423)745-9419 • (FW 1976 MDIV)

**MUNDAHL ROBERT L REV** (636)797-5265
9700 Zion Lutheran Church Rd Hillsboro MO 63050-3701 • revrlm@juno.com • MO • SP • Zion Hillsboro MO • (314)789-2111 • (FW 1982 MDIV)

**MUNDINGER GEORGE W REV** (913)722-4280
2200 W 51st St Mission Woods KS 66205-2048 • KS • EM • (SL 1951 MA)

**MUNDINGER PAUL J REV**
St Paul Lutheran Church PO Box 99 Hinckley MN 55037-0099 • MNN • SP • St Paul Hinckley MN • (320)384-6267 • (FW 1998 MDIV)

**MUNDT RICHARD EARL REV** (517)642-8346
C/O St Peter Lutheran Church 2461 N Raucholz Rd Hemlock MI 48626-8467 • MI • Assoc • St Peter Hemlock MI • (517)642-8188 • (SPR 1973 MDIV)

**MUNNICHA KHAMPHEUY TIMOTHY** (770)478-9494
377 Valley Hill Rd Riverdale GA 30274 • FG • D Miss • Florida-Georgia Orlando FL • (CQ 1991)

**MUNZ JEROLD D REV** (317)576-9828
7569 Farm View Cir East Dr Indianapolis IN 46256 • JDMunz@aol.com • IN • P Df • Peace Deaf Indianapolis IN* • (317)546-6094 • (SL 1972 MDIV)

**MURAWSKI DENNIS D REV** (330)483-4119
2256 Lester Rd PO Box 455 Valley City OH 44280-0455 • ddm@mail.ohio.net • OH • SP • St Paul Valley City OH • (330)483-4119 • (SL 1974 MDIV)

**MURDAUGH GEORGE E REV** (770)978-4072
2897 Jenny Way Lawrenceville GA 30244-5716 • gmurdaugh@hotmail.com • FG • SP • Oak Road Lilburn GA • (770)979-6391 • (SL 1984 MDIV MTH)

**MURDOCK CECIL L REV** (573)377-2824
PO Box 460 Stover MO 65078-0460 • MO • SP • St Paul Stover MO • (573)377-2690 • (FW 1999)

**MURPHY HADYN Z REV** (859)879-8803
309 Ridgewood Dr Versailles KY 40383-1434 • profrn@hotmail.com • IN • 06/1999 • (FW 1993 MDIV MA)

**MURPHY JOSEPH GABRIEL REV** (309)467-2505
520 W Sunset Dr Eureka IL 61530-1039 • jmurphy@mtco.com • CI • SP • Our Redeemer Eureka IL • (309)467-5477 • (FW 1994 MDIV)

**MURR JAMES REV** (716)941-5419
C/O Redeemer Luth Church 8740 Supervisor Ave Colden NY 14033-9612 • EA • SP • Redeemer Colden NY • (716)941-5419 • (SL 1992 MDIV)

**MURRAY JAMES E REV** (702)346-5031
786 Peartree Ln Mesquite NV 89027 • PSW • EM • (SPR 1962 MTH MDIV DMIN)

**MURRAY MILFORD C REV** (905)713-2730
7 Chadburne Cres Aurora ON L4G 4T4 CANADA • melmurray@aol.com • EN • SP • Christ Aurora ON CANADA • (905)727-3311 • (SL 1962 MDIV)

**MURRAY SCOTT R REV** (713)782-6079
C/O Memorial Lutheran Church 5800 Westheimer Rd Houston TX 77057-5617 • smurray531@aol.com • TX • SP • Memorial Houston TX • (713)782-6079 • (FW 1983 MDIV MA PHD)

**MUSALL DAVID J REV** (716)433-9014
4169 Church Rd Lockport NY 14094-9724 • EA • SP • St Peter Lockport NY • (716)433-9014 • (SL 1961)

**MUSGROVE ALVIN W REV** (281)469-8261
10814 Perigrine Dr Houston TX 77065-3168 • TX • EM • (SL 1958 MDIV)

**MUSKE CLARENCE REV** (612)693-7508
619 E 5th St Litchfield MN 55355-1806 • chorma@hutchtel.net • MNS • EM • (SL 1940)

**MUSOLF GREGORY SCOTT REV** (612)755-6709
633 108th Ave NW Coon Rapids MN 55448 • MNS • SP • Zion Saint Paul MN • (651)224-3331 • (FW 1991 MDIV)

**MYERS DANIEL W REV** (402)535-2712
C/O Our Redeemer Luth Church 3743 Marysville Rd Staplehurst NE 68439-8843 • revdmyers@alltel.net • NEB • SP • Our Redeemer Staplehurst NE • (402)535-2625 • (SL 1990 MDIV)

**MYERS JAMES A REV** (317)272-4239
273 Overlook Court Avon IN 46123 • revjmyers@aol.com • IN • SP • Living Christ Avon IN • (317)718-0718 • (FW 1999 MDIV)

**MYERS JOHN W REV** (417)532-2717
PO Box 735 Lebanon MO 65536-0735 • MO • 02/1989 • (SPR 1971)

**MYERS JOSEPH L REV** (405)863-2722
C/O Immanuel Luth Church PO Box 59 Garber OK 73738-0059 • immanuel@pldi.net • OK • SP • Immanuel Garber OK • (405)863-2722 • (FW 1995 MDIV)

**MYERS L WAYNE REV** (321)452-0990
1760 Porpoise St Merritt Island FL 32952-5640 • lwm326@aol.com • FG • EM • (SPR 1952)

**MYERS LARRY W REV** (414)774-9725
2163 N 73rd St Wauwatosa WI 53213-1812 • meyerslw@mixcom.com • SW • Assoc • Elm Grove Elm Grove WI • (262)797-2970 • (SL 1972 MDIV MA PHD)

**MYERS ROBERT F DR** (330)722-1777
4447 Grand Teton Dr Medina OH 44256 • thdir1@juno.com • OH • D Ex/S • Ohio Olmsted Falls OH • (SL 1968 MDIV DMIN)

**MYHRE THOMAS E REV** (715)229-2212
PO Box 10 Withee WI 54498-9705 • ptom101@tds.net • NW • SP • St John Withee WI • (715)229-4211 • (FW 1982 MDIV)

## N

**NA THALANG PORNPROM REV** 0116625741749
67/505 Chuan Chuen-Bangkaen Changwaltana Rd/Don Muang Bangkok 10210 THAILAND • cgmlcms@external.oit.ac.th • ND • 05/1997 • (SL 1991 MDIV)

**NAASZ TERRY W REV** (605)229-2514
1505 Cedar Dr Aberdeen SD 57401-1120 • naaszta@nvc.net • SD • SP • Our Savior Aberdeen SD • (605)225-7106 • (FW 1981 MDIV)

**NACK DELTON L REV** (217)234-4748
417 Hickory Ln Mattoon IL 61938-2027 • delka9tdt@aol.com • CI • Assoc • St John Mattoon IL • (217)234-4923 • (CQ 1982 MS)

**NACK JONATHAN COREY REV** (651)388-4577
24686 Old Church Rd Red Wing MN 55066-7613 • jnack@win.bright.net • MNS • SP • Immanuel Red Wing MN • (651)388-4577 • (SL 1994 MDIV)

**NACK RICHARD REV** (573)445-4673
1700 Forum Blvd Apt 1502 Columbia MO 65203-5480 • MO • EM • (SPR 1954)

**NADASDY DEAN W REV**
9255 Pinehurst Rd Woodbury MN 55125 • dnadasdy.aol.com • MNS • Sn/Adm • Woodbury Woodbury MN • (651)739-5144 • (SL 1973 MDIV MA DLIT)

**NAEGELE WARREN L REV** (760)433-3259
3513 Ponderosa Dr Oceanside CA 92054-1612 • wnnn@nctimes.net • PSW • EM • (SL 1958 MA DMIN)

**NAFZGER SAMUEL H REV** (314)390-0284
4315 Green Briar Ct Washington MO 63090-5747 • ic³nafzgesh@lcms.org • MO • S Ex/S • Missouri Saint Louis MO • (314)317-4550 • (SL 1965 MDIV THD)

**NAGEL HERBERT H REV** (630)963-0742
4906 Montgomery Ave Downers Grove IL 60515-3418 • NI • EM • (SL 1934)

**NAGEL NORMAN E REV** (314)963-1219
790 Eckrich Pl St Louis MO 63119-4971 • nageln@csl.edu • MO • SHS/C • Missouri Saint Louis MO • (314)317-4550 • (SL 1953 MDIV PHD DD)

**NAGLER STEPHEN L REV** (315)642-1335
32059 US Rte 11 Philadelphia NY 13673 • ssnagler72@aol.com • CNH • M Chap • Calif/Nevada/Hawaii San Francisco CA • (415)468-2336 • (SPR 1973 MDIV)

**NAGY GARY REV** (219)947-1360
903 State St Hobart IN 46342-5267 • nagyinhobart@cs.com • IN • Sn/Adm • Trinity Hobart IN • (219)942-2589 • (FW 1978 MDIV)

**NAPIER CARL H JR. REV** (301)434-4718
8608 20th Ave Adelphi MD 20783-2111 • SE • EM • (SL 1947 MDIV MED)

**NAPIER PAUL F REV** (757)851-3278
302 Gaines Mill Ln Hampton VA 23669-1427 • pnap2000@aol.com • SE • SP • Emmanuel Hampton VA • (757)865-7800 • (SL 1980 MDIV)

**NARR EDWIN J REV** (612)353-2237
5950 Upland Ave New Germany MN 55367-9514 • enarr18788@aol.com • MNS • EM • (SPR 1957 MDIV)

**NARRING DANA A REV**
22707 Waters Edge Blvd #52 Land O Lakes FL 34639 • dnarring@juno.com • FG • Asst • Concordia Sarasota FL • (941)365-0844 • (SL 1996)

**NASS BERNARD F DR** (703)317-0523
4210 Wilton Woods Ln Alexandria VA 22310-2944 • bnass@sjlc.com • SE • Assoc • St John Alexandria VA • (703)971-2210 • (SL 1960 MDIV MS MA DMIN)

**NATHAN BRUCE A REV** (631)758-0964
2200 Race Ave Medford NY 11763-1818 • banathan@aol.com • AT • SP • Holy Trinity Middle Island NY • (631)924-6991 • (FW 1980 MDIV)

**NATONICK GEORGE REV** (301)306-7269
7202 Buchanan St Landover Hills MD 20784-2236 • gwnatonick@gallua.gallaudet.edu • SE • 09/1999 • (SL 1968 MDIV MSPED)

**NATZKE NORMAN F REV** (303)249-7126
65791 Lincoln Rd Montrose CO 81401-8337 • RM • EM • (SL 1948)

**NATZKE ROYAL W REV** (262)377-2028
N78 W7064 Oak St Cedarburg WI 53012-1124 • rnatzke@execpc.com • EN • EM • (SL 1960 MA MDIV DMIN)

**NATZKE WILLIAM J REV** (507)433-2974
1401 10th St NW Austin MN 55912-1875 • wjnatzke@smig.com • MNS • SP • St John Austin MN • (507)433-2642 • (SL 1968 MDIV)

**NAU JOHN F REV** (601)268-6106
3106 Jamestown Rd Hattiesburg MS 39402-2331 • SO • EM • (SL 1936 MA MA PHD)

**NAU LOUIS Y REV** (314)352-2694
6940 Hampton Ave St Louis MO 63109 • lynau@attglobal.net • MO • St John Austin MN • (507)433-2642 • (SPR 1954 MA PHD)

**NAUMANN FREDERICK A REV** (402)645-3949
412 W Broad St Blue Springs NE 68318 • ltmbigfred@juno.com • NEB • EM • (SL 1957 STM)

**NAUMANN GEORGE R REV** (717)757-2255
3321 Minton Dr York PA 17402-9104 • SE • EM • (SPR 1940)

**NAUMANN PAUL R DR** (616)383-1749
1749 Greenbriar Dr Portage MI 49024-5771 • naumann@net-link.net • MI • Sn/Adm • St Michael Portage MI • (616)327-7832 • (SL 1984 STM MDIV DMIN)

**NAUMANN TERRANCE A REV** (804)550-3809
10434 Rapidan Way Ashland VA 23005-3313 • terrynaum@aol.com • SE • SP • Holy Cross Ashland VA • (804)798-6830 • (SPR 1976 MDIV)

**NAUSS ALLEN H DR** (714)997-7867
261 N Malena Dr Orange CA 92869-3214 • shaker38@aol.com • PSW • EM • (SL 1948 MED MDIV PHD)

**NAUSS MILTON J REV** (843)671-7317
13 Wisteria Ln Hilton Head SC 29928-4210 • SE • EM • (SL 1946 DD)

**NAYLOR GEORGE E REV** (308)824-3437
PO Box 68 Oxford NE 68967-0068 • NEB • SP • St John Oxford NE • (308)824-3269 • (SL 1998 MDIV)

**NEAGLEY RICHARD L REV** (860)582-4062
12 Maple St Terryville CT 06786 • rcrd4n@juno.com • NE • SP • Holy Trinity Terryville CT • (860)582-0723 • (SL 1976 MDIV)

**NEAL RANDALL A REV** (715)623-3977
1440 9th Ave Antigo WI 54409-1325 • neal1440@newnorth.net • NW • Assoc • Peace Antigo WI • (715)623-2200 • (SPR 1976 MDIV)

**NEBEL MARK A REV** (618)493-6134
C/O Trinity Lutheran Church PO Box 176 Hoyleton IL 62803-0176 • SI • SP • Trinity Hoyleton IL • (618)493-6226 • (SL 1989 MA MDIV STM)

**NEBHUT RUSSELL A REV** (254)582-0715
101A Old Brandon Rd Hillsboro TX 76645-2328 • texrev@hillsboro.net • TX • SP • Christ Hillsboro TX • (254)582-5782 • (SL 1992 MDIV)

**NEEB ROBERT V REV** (937)643-1605
3762 Waterbury Dr Kettering OH 45439-2470 • OH • EM • (CQ 1961 MDIV)

**NEEB ROGER J REV** (817)284-8581
1137 Zelda Dr Hurst TX 76053-4137 • TX • EM • (SL 1956)

**NEELS DENNIS J REV** (907)235-1090
318 Lee Dr Homer AK 99603-7518 • dneels@xyz.net • NOW • SP • Christ Hillsboro TX* • (SPR 1973 MDIV)

**NEFF BRUCE REV** (559)322-5230
640 Decatur Ave Clovis CA 93611 • caparson@aol.com • CNH • SP • Emmanuel Fresno CA • (559)485-5780 • (FW 1983 MDIV)

**NEFF KARL M REV** (517)345-6943
2828 Lake George Rd West Branch MI 48661-9316 • MI • EM • (CQ 1988 MDIV)

**NEHRENZ DAVID R REV** (405)360-9396
902 Carey Dr Norman OK 73069-4545 • nehrenznet@aol.com • OK • SP • Trinity Norman OK • (405)321-3443 • (FW 1982 MDIV)

**NEHRING DAVID P REV** (937)429-3432
3686 Westwind Dr Dayton OH 45440-3530 • dnehring@earthlink.net • OH • Assoc • St Matthew Huber Heights OH • (937)233-4632 • (SL 1966 MPAD MDIV STM)

**NEHRING GARY LEE REV** (517)876-4506
PO Box 763 Au Gres MI 48703-0763 • MI • SP • St John Au Gres MI • (517)876-8910 • (SL 1997 MDIV)

**NEHRT JEFFERY D REV** (618)664-4056
812 E Oak St Greenville IL 62246-1547 • SI • SP • Our Redeemer Greenville IL • (618)664-0223 • (SL 1993 MDIV)

**NEIDER HOWARD R REV** (906)884-4788
303 S 7th St Ontonagon MI 49953-1442 • sneider@goisd.k12.mi.us • NW • SP • St Paul Ontonagon MI • (906)884-4008 • (SL 1989 MDIV)

**NEIDIGK DONALD H REV** (505)890-8528
PO Box 45151 Rio Rancho NM 87174-5151 • donald³neidigk@juno.com • RM • SP • Calvary Rio Rancho NM • (505)892-9407 • (CQ 1985 MDIV)

**NEIDOW MICHAEL P REV** (402)484-8218
7937 Broadview Dr Lincoln NE 68505-2720 • mike.neidow@alltel.net • NEB • Assoc • Messiah Lincoln NE • (402)489-3024 • (SL 1984 MDIV)

**NEISCH WALDEMAR O REV** (810)630-0069
7414 Cross Creek Dr Swartz Creek MI 48473-1497 • MI • EM • (SL 1956 MDIV)

**NEISWENDER DONALD R REV**
C/O Saint Matthew Lutheran Ch 99 Franklin Sq New Britain CT 06051-2606 • NE • EM • (SPR 1965 MDIV MA STM)

**NELESEN JAMES H REV** (805)532-1049
C/O Faith Luth Church PO Box 377 Moorpark CA 93020-0377 • PSW • SP • Faith Moorpark CA • (805)532-1049 • (SL 1963 MA MDIV)

**NELSEN LOUIS E JR. REV** (504)893-9541
94 Gardenia Dr Covington LA 70433-9168 • SO • EM • (SPR 1954)

**NELSEN RAYMOND E REV** (503)492-2037
1108 SE 210th Ave Gresham OR 97030-2329 • NOW • EM • (SL 1977 MDIV)

**NELSON ANDREW D REV** (201)445-4704
165 Linwood Ave Ridgewood NJ 07450 • NJ • SP • Bethlehem Ridgewood NJ • (201)444-3600 • (SL 1984 MDIV MS)

**NELSON CARL E REV** (562)694-4945
1061 Concord Way La Habra CA 90631 • nelsce@netscape.net • PSW • EM • (SL 1960 MDIV)

**NELSON DARRELL PAUL REV** (410)435-5631
203 Churchwardens Rd Baltimore MD 21212-2937 • dpnelson@immanuellutheran.org • SE • SP • Immanuel Baltimore MD • (410)435-6861 • (SPR 1966 MDIV)

**NELSON DEWAYNE RAY JR. REV** (913)451-3344
4707 College Blvd Ste 202 Leawood KS 66211-1611 • nelsondr@worldnet.att.net • TX • 02/1999 • (SL 1973 MDIV MS)

**NELSON ERIC MATTHEW REV** (406)883-5906
24 A Ave Polson MT 59860-4071 • MT • SP • Mount Calvary Polson MT • (406)883-4041 • (SL 1995 MST MDIV)

**NELSON JOHN EDWARD JR. REV** (402)563-3884
Christ Lutheran Church 32392 122nd Ave Columbus NE 68601-9774 • jenelson@es47.org • NEB • SP • Christ Columbus NE • (402)563-1314 • (SL 1992 MDIV)

**NELSON JOHN EDWARD SR. REV** (206)542-4969
1550 NW 195th St #112 Seattle WA 98177 • johnn@kcmsmail.com • NOW • Inst C • Northwest Portland OR • (SPR 1973 MDIV)

**NELSON JOHN P REV** (715)443-2279
16460 NOUGART dR Athens WI 54411 • NW • SP • St John Athens WI • (715)536-1810 • (FW 1999 MDIV)

**NELSON PAUL R REV** (701)463-2004
C/O Peace Luth Church 505 2nd St NW Garrison ND 58540-7330 • ND • SP • Peace Garrison ND* • (701)463-2073 • (FW 1981 MTH)

**NELSON RICHARD A REV** (817)599-7196
301 Oakridge Dr Weatherford TX 76086-2931 • TX • EM • * • (SPR 1954)

**NELSON RICHARD E REV**
C/O Mr Lee Yohn 422 Fairway Dr Mechanicsburg PA 17055-5713 • sandrich@gol.com • IW • S Miss • Iowa West Fort Dodge IA • (FW 1983 MA MDIV MIR)

**NELSON RONALD E REV** (314)638-7131
9826 Affton View Ct Saint Louis MO 63123-6273 • ic³nelsonre@lcms.org • MO • S Ex/S • Missouri Saint Louis MO • (314)317-4550 • (CQ 1991 MED)

**NELSON T CHRISTIAN REV**
1660 County Road Z Arkdale WI 54613-9515 • SW • SP • United/Christ Dellwood WI • (608)339-7187 • (SPR 1976 MDIV)

**NELSON TERRY A REV** (248)486-4335
24085 Griswold Rd South Lyon MI 48178-8932 • MI • SP • Cross Christ South Lyon MI • (248)437-8810 • (FW 1980 MDIV)

**NELSON VICTOR H REV** (518)622-0438
299 Bailey Rd Purling NY 12470-9709 • AT • SP • Resurrection Cairo NY • (518)622-3286 • (FW 1984 MDIV MS)

**NEMEC MICHAEL C REV**
PO Box 025207 Miami FL 33102 • MI • S Miss • Michigan Ann Arbor MI • (FW 2000 MDIV)

**NEMOYER ROBERT J REV** (708)458-4052
8205 S 76th Ave Bridgeview IL 60455-1601 • nemoyer@juno.com. • NI • SP • Holy Trinity Burbank IL • (708)598-8070 • (SL 1983 MDIV MA)

**NENOW CHARLES D REV** (425)828-0265
7924 125th Ln NE Kirkland WA 98033-8247 • NOW • EM • (SL 1960)

**NERGER EDWIN A REV** (219)483-4466
2610 Santa Rosa Dr Fort Wayne IN 46805-3933 • IN • EM • (SL 1939 MDIV LLD)

**NESTLER ROBERT B REV** (785)286-2871
617 NW 43rd St Topeka KS 66617-1302 • KS • EM • (CQ 1978 MAR)

**NETLAND LANCE A REV** (404)377-9730
203 Jefferson Pl Decatur GA 30030-3654 • lancenet@aol.com • FG • O Sp Min • Florida-Georgia Orlando FL • (SL 1971 MTH MDIV)

**NETTLING KENNETH J REV** (913)321-1326
530 Quindaro Blvd Kansas City KS 66101 • KS • O Miss • Faith Kansas City KS* • (913)321-1326 • (CQ 1997 MS)

**NEUBAUER JAMES HOWARD REV** (218)732-5621
210 Court St Park Rapids MN 56470-1412 • MNN • Assoc • St John Park Rapids MN • (218)732-9783 • (SL 1994 MDIV)

**NEUBERGER PAUL E REV** (505)887-3372
905 N Halagueno St Carlsbad NM 88220-5125 • neubs@caverns.com • RM • SP • Immanuel Carlsbad NM* • (505)885-5780 • (SL 1987 MDIV MA)

**NEUENDORF DONALD O REV** (517)752-6413
1220 S Mueller Rd Saginaw MI 48601-9457 • don@neuendorfs.com • MI • SP • Immanuel Saginaw MI • (517)754-0929 • (FW 1985 MDIV)

**NEUGEBAUER CHARLES J REV**
2082 Donnington Cv Memphis TN 38138-4612 • MDS • Sn/Adm • Christ King Memphis TN • (901)682-8404 • (FW 1983)

**NEUGEBAUER JOHN C REV** (920)487-2335
E5217 Church Rd Algoma WI 54201-9683 • NW • SP • St John Algoma WI • (920)487-2335 • (SL 1973 MDIV)

**NEUGEBAUER RICHARD H REV** (308)436-4306
C/O Faith Lutheran Church 1815 R St Gering NE 69341-2665 • WY • Sn/Adm • Faith Gering NE • (308)436-4307 • (SL 1987 MDIV)

**NEUMAN PAUL DANIEL REV** (812)278-9473
Rt 1 Box 353A Williams IN 47470 • neumanp@freewwweb.com • IN • SP • Calvary Bedford IN • (812)275-5488 • (FW 1984 MDIV)

**NEUMANN DONALD REV**
1210 W Grant Ave Harlingen TX 78550 • texrevdonald@msn.com • TX • SP • Our Redeemer Harlingen TX • (210)423-8142 • (FW 1992 MDIV)

**NEUMANN FRED W REV** (512)891-9087
6501 Brush Country Rd Apt 109 Austin TX 78749-1406 • TX • EM • (SPR 1965 MDIV)

**NEUMANN H MARK REV** (281)255-2255
17710 Jeanie Dr Tomball TX 77375-5773 • mneumann@salem4u.com • TX • Assoc • Salem Tomball TX • (281)351-8223 • (FW 1991 MS MDIV)

**NEUMANN LEONARD C REV** (812)895-1476
226 S 6th St Vincennes IN 47591 • neumann@charter.net • IN • 08/1987 08/2000 • (SL 1965 MDIV)

**NEUMANN M G REV** (715)223-3094
PO Box 438 Colby WI 54421-0438 • lofgren@tznet.com • NW • SP • Zion Colby WI • (715)223-2166 • (FW 1980 MDIV)

**NEUMANN MARK ALAN REV** (810)231-1033
PO Box 490 Hamburg MI 48139-0490 • neumann@cac.net • MI • SP • St Paul Hamburg MI • (810)231-1033 • (SL 1984 MDIV)

**NEUMANN PAUL D REV**
1107 Mill Run Dr Allen TX 75002-1913 • TX • SP • Immanuel Allen TX • (972)390-0156 • (SL 1982 MDIV)

**NEUMANN TIMOTHY L REV** (517)354-7510
132 W Clark Alpena MI 49707 • tneumann@mailroom.com • NEB • 12/1999 • (SL 1997 MDIV)

**NEUMANN WILBUR F REV**
17922 Dayspring Dr Park Rapids MN 56470 • MNN • EM • (SL 1959 MDIV)

**NEVIS E ENWOOD REV** (810)759-2402
3808 Pearl Ave Warren MI 48091 • revnevis@cs.com • MI • Sn/Adm • Peace Warren MI • (810)751-8010 • (SL 1999 MDIV)

**NEWMAN DREW A REV** (816)630-8119
2006 Lynn Rd Excelsior Springs MO 64024-9702 • gnuguy@prodigy.net • MO • SP • Trinity Kearney MO • (816)628-6644 • (FW 1985 MDIV)

**NEWMAN I MELVIN JR. REV** (281)391-2253
1014 Avenue C Katy TX 77493-2406 • pmel@mlckaty.com • TX • Sn/Adm • Memorial Katy TX • (281)391-0171 • (SPR 1972 MDIV)

**NEWMAN LEONARD W REV** (517)687-2244
3373 N Stark Rd Midland MI 48642-7943 • MI • EM • (SPR 1953)

**NEWMAN MICHAEL W REV** (847)705-1989
354 N Lytle Dr Palatine IL 60067-5548 • mnewman@pop-lcms.org • NI • SP • Prince Peace Palatine IL • (847)359-3451 • (SL 1987 MDIV)

**NEWTON ALVIN L REV** (410)866-4763
1815 Greencastle Dr Rosedale MD 21237 • alvinnewton@sprintmail.com • SE • SP • Christ Dundalk MD • (410)284-2850 • (SL 1969 MDIV)

**NEWTON ROBERT D REV** (408)629-3080
4448 Windsor Park Dr San Jose CA 95136 • firstimmanuel@cs.com • CNH • Sn/Adm • First Immanuel San Jose CA • (408)292-5404 • (FW 1977 MDIV PHD)

**NEWTON ROGER ALLEN REV** (215)342-2208
C/O St Lukes Lutheran Church 7200 Castor Ave Philadelphia PA 19149-1106 • EN • SP • St Luke Philadelphia PA • (215)745-8922 • (CQ 1997)

**NGUYEN NINH HUU REV** (281)568-2896
11803 Moonmist Dr Houston TX 77072-1841 • vietlcms@aol.com • TX • Asst • Vietnamese Houston TX* • (713)771-3207 • (CQ 1992)

**NGUYEN WYNN T REV** (714)636-5185
11880 Dorada Ave Garden Grove CA 92840-5501 • PSW • S Miss • Pacific Southwest Irvine CA • (949)854-3232 • (CQ 1984 MAR)

**NIBBLETT NORMAN G REV** (503)582-0087
435 Nugget Dr Rogue River OR 97537-9518 • lcmsrr@so-oregon.net • NOW • SP • Faith Rogue River OR • (541)582-0457 • (FW 1988 MDIV)

**NICELY DOUGLAS A REV** (618)566-8505
514 W South St Mascoutah IL 62258-1921 • bethany@icss.net • SI • SP • Bethany Fairview Heights IL • (618)632-6906 • (SL 1977 MDIV)

**NICHOLS GERALD L REV** (972)644-7984
2005 Portsmouth Dr Richardson TX 75082-4837 • pastorjunglejev@aol.com • TX • EM • (SL 1960 MA)

**NICHOLS JERROLD L REV** (219)436-0754
5210 Homestead Rd Fort Wayne IN 46814 • IN • EM • (SL 1961 MDIV)

**NICHOLS LARRY A REV** (401)231-6564
27 Riverview Ave Smithfield RI 02917-1723 • lnich52623@aol.com • NE • SP • Our Redeemer Smithfield RI • (401)232-7575 • (CQ 1988 MDIV)

**NICHOLS RONALD A REV** (704)483-5654
7146 Forney Hill Rd Denver NC 28037 • lakeshepherd@juno.com • SE • SP • Lake Norman Denver NC • (704)483-2130 • (SPR 1972 MDIV)

**NICHOLSON HARVEY E REV** (815)858-2493
PO Box 485 Elizabeth IL 61028-0485 • NI • SP • St Paul Elizabeth IL • (815)858-3334 • (SPR 1974 MDIV)

**NICHOLSON PAUL E REV** (210)690-9442
2023 Indian Meadows Dr San Antonio TX 78230-0910 • pnicholson@juno.com • IE • EM • (SPR 1963 STM)

**NICHOLUS ROBERT H REV** (650)854-8300
2181 Camino A Los Cerros Menlo Park CA 94025-6533 • CNH • 12/1990 12/1999 • (SL 1969 MDIV)

**NICKEL DAVID M REV** (517)356-1500
2161 Ralph Ave Alpena MI 49707-1415 • MI • Sn/Adm • Immanuel Alpena MI • (517)354-3443 • (SL 1960 MDIV)

**NICKEL JOEL T REV** (503)769-6144
C/O Calvary Luth Church 198 Fern Ridge Rd SE Stayton OR 97383-1257 • NOW • SP • Calvary Stayton OR • (503)769-6144 • (SL 1965 MDIV)

**NICKEL PETER S REV** (248)542-8887
12762 Lasalle Huntington Woods MI 48070 • revnrn@aol.com • MI • SP • Huntington Wds Huntington Woods MI • (248)542-3007 • (CQ 1982)

**NICKEL RONALD P REV** (303)223-6643
3001 Rustic Ct Fort Collins CO 80526-2673 • RM • SP • St John Fort Collins CO • (970)482-5316 • (CQ 1978 PHD)

**NICKEL TIMOTHY M REV** (716)964-8305
C/O Mason 1874 N Hamlin Rd Hamlin NY 14464-9725 • tmnickel@aol.com • EA • S Miss • Eastern Williamsville NY • (716)634-5111 • (SL 1970 MDIV)

**NICKERSON JOHN M DR** (864)227-0088
303 Beechwood Cir Greenwood SC 29646 • pastorn@innova.net • SE • D Miss • Greenwood Greenwood SC • (864)227-0088 • (SPR 1958 MDIV MA EDD DMIN)

**NICKLAS EDWIN J REV** (757)486-4213
384 Golden Maple Dr Virginia Beach VA 23452-6783 • poplcvb@erols.com • SE • SP • Prince Of Peace Virginia Beach VA • (757)340-8420 • (CQ 1979 MDIV)

**NICKODEMUS STEPHEN REV** (208)263-7516
C/O Christ Our Rdmr Luth Chur 1900 W Pine St Sandpoint ID 83864-9328 • corlc@micron.net • NOW • SP • Christ Our Rede Sandpoint ID • (208)263-7516 • (SL 1982 MDIV)

**NICOL LLOYD E REV** (513)349-2675
29 Commercial St PO Box 223 Milford Center OH 43045-0223 • lmnicol@sjl.org • OH • EM • (CQ 1983)

**NICOL MICHAEL A REV** (419)738-6746
15321 Pusheta Rd Wapakoneta OH 45895-8413 • stjohnlc@bright.net • OH • SP • St John Wapakoneta OH • (419)738-6746 • (FW 1986 MDIV MA)

**NICOLAUS JON R REV** (816)795-8517
2429 Viking Dr Independence MO 64057-1392 • jonicolaus@aol.com • MO • Assoc • Messiah Independence MO • (816)254-9405 • (SL 1984 MDIV)

**NICOLAUS MARK J REV** (406)676-8223
113 4th Ave SE Ronan MT 59864-2824 • MT • SP • St Paul Ronan MT • (406)676-8280 • (SPR 1970 MDIV)

**NICOLAUS MARVIN F REV** (414)994-9689
W5566 County SS Random Lake WI 53075-1236 • SW • EM • (SL 1934)

**NIEDERBRACH WILLARD E REV** (909)658-1200
5001 W Florida #452 Hemet CA 92545 • willflo@gte.net • PSW • EM • (SPR 1962)

**NIEDNER FREDERICK A REV** (503)524-3182
10500 SW Tarpan Dr Beaverton OR 97008-8102 • fredesniedner@webtv.net • NOW • EM • (SL 1944 DD)

**NIEDNER FREDERICK A JR. REV** (219)462-5161
1402 Crosscreek Rd Valparaiso IN 46383-2074 • fred.niedner@valpo.edu • IN • END • Indiana Fort Wayne IN • (SL 1971 STM MDIV THD)

**NIEKERK TIMOTHY ROGER REV** (414)677-8987
W209 N16531 Cairn Ct Jackson WI 53037 • SW • SP • Living Word Jackson WI • (414)677-1685 • (SL 1997 MDIV)

**NIELSEN GLENN A DR** (314)725-5960
6 N Seminary Ter Saint Louis MO 63105-3011 • profnielsen@juno.com • MO • SHS/C • Missouri Saint Louis MO • (314)317-4550 • (SL 1981 STM MA MDIV PHD)

**NIELSEN PAUL REV** (207)872-5094
4 Martin Ave Waterville ME 04901-4626 • NE • SP • Resurrection Waterville ME • (207)872-5208 • (FW 1993 MDIV)

**NIELSEN RICHARD J REV** (219)749-1096
3315 Blackfoot Ct Fort Wayne IN 46815-6409 • rcnhoosier@cs.com • IN • EM • (CQ 1984 MAR)

**NIEMAN HENRY F REV** (520)342-0447
13538 E 50th St Yuma AZ 85367-8508 • PSW • EM • (SL 1956 MDIV)

**NIEMANN GLENN ROY REV** (217)742-9281
335 E Jefferson St Winchester IL 62694-1136 • CI • SP • Christ Winchester IL* • (217)742-3919 • (SL 1996 MDIV)

**NIEMEIER CRAIG K REV** (308)262-0339
PO Box 625 Bridgeport NE 69336-0903 • WY • SP • St Paul Bridgeport NE* • (308)262-0424 • (SL 1998 MDIV)

**NIEMOELLER MARK A REV** (219)747-1180
1021 Olympia Dr Fort Wayne IN 46819-1417 • IN • 11/1996 11/1999 • * • (FW 1979 MDIV)

**NIERMANN HENRY W REV** (316)672-5331
523 Welton St Pratt KS 67124-1358 • KS • EM • * • (SL 1956)

**NIERMANN JOHN F REV** (816)361-8916
1247 W 72nd Ter Kansas City MO 64114-1241 • KS • Assoc • Bethany Shawnee Mission KS • (913)648-2228 • (SL 1959 MDIV MA)

**NIERMANN STEPHEN J REV** (419)598-8181
T-721 Co Rd 16 Napoleon OH 43545 • snierman@sjl.org • OH • SP • St John Napoleon OH • (419)598-8961 • (FW 1985 MDIV)

**NIERMANN STEPHEN M REV** (412)244-1145
2341 Mc Nary Blvd Pittsburgh PA 15235-2779 • EA • SP • Faith Pittsburgh PA • (412)621-4713 • (SL 1991 MDIV)

**NIERMANN THOMAS A REV** (847)695-2136
715 Wright Ave Elgin IL 60120-8517 • nierman@attglobal.net • NI • Sn/Adm • St John Elgin IL • (847)741-0814 • (SL 1969 MDIV)

**NIERMANN WALTER E REV** (714)751-5529
3410 S Main St Apt H1 Santa Ana CA 92707-4359 • PSW • EM • (SL 1935)

**NIERMANN WALTER H REV** (319)396-0843
207 Cynthia St SW Cedar Rapids IA 52404-6076 • whnnmrs@aol.com • IE • EM • (SL 1952 MDIV)

**NIETFELD DANNY L REV** (402)682-0858
706 Vannorman Dr Bellevue NE 68005-2555 • NEB • 07/1996 07/2000 • (SL 1972 MDIV)

**NIETING EDMUND P REV** (219)464-8608
2207 Linden Dr Valparaiso IN 46383-2330 • IN • EM • (SL 1948 MDIV)

**NIETING R MARK REV** (828)255-8383
21 Wilburn Rd Asheville NC 28806-2748 • nieting@aol.com • SE • Sn/Adm • Emmanuel Asheville NC • (828)252-1795 • (CQ 1986)

**NILGES CHRIS REV** (630)262-8220
2301 Pepper Valley Dr Geneva IL 60134-1752 • NI • SP • Faith Geneva IL • (630)232-8420 • (SL 1985 MDIV)

**NIRVA MICHAEL JOHN REV** (320)543-3832
PO Box 680 Howard Lake MN 55349-0680 • MNS • Sn/Adm • St James Howard Lake MN • (320)543-2766 • (FW 1991 MDIV MA)

**NISSEN NORMAN E REV** (218)736-0562
13854 200 St Fergus Falls MN 56537-7236 • MNN • EM • (SL 1958 MDIV)

**NITZ WILFRED REV** (541)963-2052
408 L Ave La Grande OR 97850-1322 • wilnitz@eoni.com • NOW • SP • Faith La Grande OR • (541)963-2831 • (CQ 1980)

**NIX MATTHEW WILLIAM REV** (605)335-7078
6205 N Purple Martin Ave Sioux Falls SD 57107-1120 • SD • D Miss • Trinity Deaf Sioux Falls SD • (605)330-0724 • (SL 1993 MDIV)

**NOACK RICHARD C DR** (281)379-3314
6310 Elmgrove Rd Spring TX 77389-3618 • noacks@usa.net • TX • Sn/Adm • Trinity Klein TX • (281)376-5773 • (SL 1974 MDIV DMIN)

**NOBLE CARL L REV** (712)689-2541
200 W Tracy St PO Box 59 Arcadia IA 51430 • zionl@netins.net • IW • SP • Zion Arcadia IA • (712)689-2441 • (SL 1983 MDIV)

**NOENNIG BRUCE REV** (218)287-4851
1210 25th Ave South Moorhead MN 56560 • noennighome@juno.com • MNN • Sn/Adm • Our Redeemer Moorhead MN • (218)233-7569 • (CQ 1981)

**NOLAND MARTIN R DR** (708)386-5609
C/O Christ Luth Church 607 Harvard St Oak Park IL 60304-2015 • 75113.2703@compuserve.com • NI • SP • Christ Oak Park IL • (708)386-3306 • (FW 1983 MDIV STM MPHIL PHD)

**NOLL THOMAS C REV** (630)495-7050
9 S Edgewood Ave Lombard IL 60148-2804 • NI • Sn/Adm • St John Lombard IL • (630)629-2515 • (CQ 1983 MED MAR MLS)

**NOLTING DUDLEY E REV** (509)332-7137
1750 NE Lower Dr Pullman WA 99163-4600 • dnolting@turbonet.com • NOW • SP • Concordia Pullman WA • (509)332-2830 • (SPR 1973 MDIV)

**NOON THOMAS R REV** (205)923-7186
1409 67th St W Birmingham AL 35228-1528 • SO • SP • St Paul Birmingham AL • (205)324-2063 • (SPR 1971 MDIV MHST)

**NORD DONALD D REV** (219)493-8557
1604 Randford Pl Fort Wayne IN 46815-7635 • dondnord@aol.com • IN • Assoc • St Peter Fort Wayne IN • (219)749-5816 • (FW 1990 MDIV)

**NORD RANDOLPH D REV** (319)393-1000
236 Johnson Ave NW Cedar Rapids IA 52405 • dronfive@prodigy.net • IE • O Sp Min • Iowa East Marion IA • (FW 1982 MDIV)

**NORDEN AL J REV** (402)489-5010
245 Piazza Ter Lincoln NE 68510-2049 • NEB • EM • (SL 1943)

**NORDEN ERWIN H REV** (626)791-3324
2254 Galbreth Rd Pasadena CA 91104-3314 • PSW • EM • (SL 1936)

**NORDLIE ROBERT L DR** (763)553-9290
17020 39th Ave N Plymouth MN 55446 • drrln@aol.com • MNS • Sn/Adm • Redeemer Wayzata MN • (612)473-1281 • (SPR 1975 MDIV DMIN)

**NORDLING JOHN G REV**
5305 Lake Charles St Waco TX 76710 • TX • 08/1999 • (SL 1985 MDIV MA PHD)

**NORDMAN MARK A REV** (815)562-6155
1333 Sunset Terrace Rochelle IL 61068 • nordman@rochelle.net • NI • Sn/Adm • St Paul Rochelle IL • (815)562-2744 • (SL 1987 MDIV)

**NORDQUIST WALLACE DEAN REV** (651)674-0896
4542 Egret Ln North Branch MN 55056 • nordquistfamily@hotmail.com • MNN • EM • (SL 1964 MDIV)

**NORRIS ANDREW REV** (513)858-2174
5895 Windermere Ln Fairfield OH 45014-3751 • anorris@christ-lcms.org • OH • Sn/Adm • Christ Cincinnati OH • (513)385-8342 • (WES 1989)

**NORRIS RICHARD A REV** (863)699-0768
114 Mc Kinley Ave NE Lake Placid FL 33852-5874 • trinity@htn.com • FG • SP • Trinity Lake Placid FL • (863)465-5253 • (FW 1983 MDIV)

**NORRIS RONALD T REV** (541)826-3367
PO Box 173 Eagle Point OR 97524-0173 • rnorris@wave.net • NOW • SP • St John Eagle Point OR • (541)826-4334 • (FW 1991 MDIV)

**NORRIS THOMAS G REV**
50 Woodsworth Ln Pleasant Hill CA 94523-3314 • revnorris@aol.com • CNH • SP • Faith Pleasant Hill CA • (925)685-7353 • (SL 1990 MDIV)

**NORTHROP ANDREW E REV** (206)439-8034
21021 4th Pl S Des Moines WA 98198-3618 • northrop@transport.com • NOW • SP • Atonement Seattle WA • (206)244-3020 • (FW 1981 MDIV DMIN)

**NORTHWALL JOHN DR** (402)330-2720
913 Palamino Rd Omaha NE 68154-3440 • jnorthwall@uswest.net • NEB • EM • (CQ 1994 MA STM PHD)

**NORTHWICK BYRON REV** (612)636-6018
3247 New Brighton Rd Saint Paul MN 55112-7914 • bnorthwick@juno.com • MNS • SP • Trinity Arden Hills MN • (651)633-2402 • (FW 1981 MDIV PHD)

**NORTON JAMES E REV** (217)563-2487
C/O St Paul Luth Church 22009 E 19th Rd Nokomis IL 62075-3719 • norton5@nokomis.net • SI • SP • St Paul Nokomis IL • (217)563-2487 • (SL 1979 MDIV)

**NORTON WILLIAM D REV** (907)479-5514
4392 Bishop Cir Fairbanks AK 99709 • iamamc@mosquitonet.com • NOW • O Sp Min • Northwest Portland OR • (CQ 1977)

**NOSKE FERDINAND H REV** (410)893-1923
902 Buckland Pl Bel Air MD 21014-6844 • revferdn@aol.com • SE • EM • (SL 1956)

**NOTHWEHR ROLLAND R REV** (816)827-0399
2502 Anderson Ave Sedalia MO 65301-6708 • MO • EM • (SPR 1964)

**NOUR NABIL SUBHI REV** (605)724-2722
PO Box 158 Armour SD 57313-0158 • SD • SP • Redeemer Armour SD • (605)724-2489 • (SL 1994 MDIV)

**NOVOTNEY ROBERT L REV** (920)849-2778
417 Manhattan St Chilton WI 53014-1565 • SW • EM • (SL 1956 MDIV)

**NOWAK ROBERT W REV** (952)440-8095
15153 Oak Ridge Cir SE Prior Lake MN 55372-1915 • revrwn@juno.com • MNS • SP • Holy Cross Prior Lake MN • (952)445-1779 • (FW 1979 MDIV)

**NOWAK THOMAS M REV** (616)695-9061
PO Box 129 Buchanan MI 49107 • stpaulbuch@qtm.net • MI • Sn/Adm • St Paul Buchanan MI • (616)695-9061 • (SL 1989 MDIV)

**NUCKOLS MARK S REV** (816)452-8692
2003 NE Englewood Rd Kansas City MO 64118-5627 • MO • Sn/Adm • Holy Cross Kansas City MO • (816)452-9113 • (FW 1989 MDIV)

**NUECHTERLEIN LOUIS G REV** (203)272-6294
6 Ives Hill Ct Cheshire CT 06410-3914 • NE • EM • (SL 1953 MDIV)

**NUERGE ROGER D REV** (724)869-1936
675 Moonridge Dr Freedom PA 15042-2633 • EA • SP • Prince Peace Freedom PA • (724)728-3881 • (CQ 1983 MDIV)

**NUFFER RICHARD THOMAS REV** (219)483-1241
2530 Foxchase Run Fort Wayne IN 46825-3971 • nufferrt@mail.ctsfw.edu • IN • SHS/C • Indiana Fort Wayne IN • (FW 1993 MDIV JD)

**NUNES JOHN A REV** (214)375-7722
940 Wood River Rd Dallas TX 75232 • TX • SP • St Paul Dallas TX • (214)371-9429 • (SC 1991 MDIV)

**NUNEZ HIRAM REV** (314)352-8184
4232 South 37th St St Louis MO 63116 • MO • O Miss • Missouri Saint Louis MO • (314)317-4550 • (CQ 1999)

**NUSS DAVID F REV** (845)855-0915
44 Pine Dr Pawling NY 12564-1208 • dfnuss@aol.com • AT • SP • Christ King Pawling NY • (914)855-3169 • (FW 1981 MDIV)

**NUTTER MARTIN S REV** (931)455-6756
202 Meadowbrook Dr Tullahoma TN 37388-4103 • MDS • SP • Faith Tullahoma TN • (931)455-3510 • (SL 1979 MDIV)

**NUTZMANN LA VERN W REV** (517)428-4509
7921 Market St Port Hope MI 48468-9636 • MI • EM • (SPR 1946)

**NYE FERRY L REV** (334)265-3492
2003 Cahaba Dr Montgomery AL 36108 • SO • SP • Trinity Montgomery AL • (334)262-4326 • (FW 1999 MDIV)

**NYGAARD SPENCER M REV** (941)492-6311
977 Lakeside Ct Venice FL 34293-1927 • EN • EM • (SL 1960 MDIV MTH)

## O

**O BRIEN PAT F A REV** (727)530-9270
2429 Harn Blvd Clearwater FL 33764-2908 • pfa0@aol.com • FG • Sn/Adm • First Clearwater FL • (727)447-4504 • (SPR 1970 MDIV)

**O BRIEN PATRICK E REV** (701)742-2305
PO Box 188 Oakes ND 58474-0188 • ND • SP • St John Oakes ND • (701)742-2595 • (SPR 1975 MA)

**O CONNOR BRYAN T REV** (414)334-7854
3137 Kristine Ln West Bend WI 53090 • SW • SP • Saint Andrew West Bend WI • (262)335-4200 • (CQ 1991 MED MAR)

**O CONNOR JAMES P REV** (757)440-9444
1060 Algonquin Rd Norfolk VA 23505 • jocon76517@aol.com • SE • SP • Trinity Norfolk VA • (757)489-2551 • (SL 1965 MDIV)

**O CONNOR WILLIAM DANIEL REV** (812)358-2708
4381 S State Rd 135 Vallonia IN 47281-9716 • goirish@hsonline.net • IN • SP • Trinity Vallonia IN* • (812)358-3225 • (FW 1994 MDIV)

**O NEAL PATRICK E REV** (515)295-8668
405 N Phillips St Algona IA 50511 • patrick.oneal@iowawest.org • IW • Asst • Trinity Algona IA • (515)295-3518 • (SL 1999 MDIV)

**O NEILL DENNIS B REV** (701)349-4465
C/O Zion Lutheran Church PO Box 793 Ellendale ND 58436-0793 • ND • SP • Zion Ellendale ND • (701)349-4147 • (FW 1980 MDIV)

**O SHONEY GLENN R REV** (314)256-3367
1730 Warmington Ct Ballwin MO 63021-5873 • MO • S Ex/S • Missouri Saint Louis MO • (314)317-4550 • (SPR 1962 MDIV LLD LLD)

**O SULLIVAN ROBERT H REV**
4684 Reinhardt Dr Oakland CA 94619-2948 • CNH • SP • Bethlehem Berkeley CA • (510)848-8821 • (CQ 1993 MDIV)

**O'CONNOR JOHN ALBERT REV** (315)339-0094
4268 Wood Creek Rd Rome NY 13440 • jaoconn@aol.com • EA • EM • (SL 1962)

**OBERDECK JOHN W DR** (314)726-5615
9 N Seminary Ter Saint Louis MO 63105-3010 • oberdeckj@csl.edu • MO • SHS/C • Missouri Saint Louis MO • (314)317-4550 • (SL 1979 MDIV MSED PHD)

**OBERDIECK DAVID LEE REV** (501)794-3916
7310 Davidwood Dr Benton AR 72015-9588 • dcjkk@juno.com • MDS • SP • First Benton AR • (501)315-4311 • (SL 1993 MDIV)

**OBERHAUS PAUL R REV** (440)327-9462
34555 Center Ridge Rd North Ridgeville OH 44039-3155 • PrPaulOber@aol.com • OH • SP • Shepherd Ridge North Ridgeville OH • (440)327-7321 • (CQ 1995)

**OBERHEU ROBERT C REV**
600 1725 Rd Delta CO 81416-2832 • WY • EM • (SPR 1958 MDIV)

**OBERMUELLER NOLAN W REV** (307)674-8571
PO Box 331 Big Horn WY 82833-0331 • WY • EM • (SL 1945)

**OBERSAT THOMAS FRANK REV** (219)785-2861
C/O Trinity Luth Church PO Box 315 Westville IN 46391-0315 • IN • SP • Trinity Westville IN • (219)785-2861 • (FW 1991 MED MDIV)

**OCHNER DOUGLAS A REV** (573)364-2239
517 E 2nd St Rolla MO 65401-3931 • dochner@hotmail.com • MO • Assoc • Immanuel Rolla MO • (573)364-4525 • (SL 1998 MDIV)

**ODOM FRAZIER N REV** (314)388-5036
1640 Grape Ave Saint Louis MO 63147-1406 • frazierodom@aol.com • MO • D Miss • Holy Sacrament Saint Louis MO* • (314)371-4243 • (GB 1960 MAR DMIN)

**OELTJEN ROBERT STEGER REV** (303)637-7101
2427 Cherry Cir Brighton CO 80601-3453 • rsopro@juno.com • RM • Tchr • North Lutheran Broomfield CO • (720)887-9031 • (SL 1991 MDIV)

**OERMANN ERVIN R REV** (904)777-1501
5326 Ortega Forest Dr Jacksonville FL 32210-8218 • FG • EM • (SL 1953)

**OESCH EUGENE A DR** (903)856-1958
RR 2 Box 154A Pittsburg TX 75686-9420 • gpoesch@internetwork.net • TX • EM • (SL 1955)

**OESCH NORBERT C DR** (714)639-6400
936 E Wilson Ave Orange CA 92867-5030 • plincoesch@aol.com • PSW • O Sp Min • Pacific Southwest Irvine CA • (949)854-3232 • (SL 1966 MA DMIN)

**OESTER JAMES ALLEN REV** (330)399-8283
4424 Tod Ave SW Warren OH 44481 • OH • SP • Gethsemane North Jackson OH • (330)538-2630 • (FW 1995 MDIV)

**OESTMANN VERNON E REV** (913)381-8750
4508 W 91st St Shawnee Mission KS 66207-2610 • vern@tlcms.org • KS • Assoc • Trinity Mission KS • (913)432-5441 • (CQ 1979 MDIV)

**OETTING J LOUIS REV** (830)510-6366
258 Backhaus Rd Pipe Creek TX 78063-5614 • TX • EM • (SL 1958 MDIV)

**OFFEN CHRISTOPHER E REV** (254)986-2905
250 The Grove Rd Gatesville TX 76528 • TX • SP • St Paul Gatesville TX • (254)986-2607 • (SL 1997 MDIV)

**OFFERMANN WRAY A REV** (217)422-7474
289 S Linden Ave Decatur IL 62522-2566 • offermann@prodigy.net • CI • Sn/Adm • St Paul Decatur IL • (217)423-6955 • (SL 1971 MDIV)

**OFFT JONATHAN L REV** (319)355-8889
Davenport Lutheran Home 1130 W 53rd St Davenport IA 52806 • IE • Asst • Our Redeemer Iowa City IA • (319)338-5626 • (SL 1996 MDIV)

**OGILVIE THOMAS GUY REV** (319)277-7206
2906 W 4th St Cedar Falls IA 50613-6605 • rev.togilvie@cfu.net • IE • SP • College Hill Cedar Falls IA • (319)266-1274 • (SL 1995 MDIV)

**OGNOSKIE DANIEL F REV** (815)584-1023
315 E Mazon Ave Dwight IL 60420-1103 • emmandwi@core.com • NI • SP • Emmanuel Dwight IL • (815)584-3433 • (SPR 1975 MDIV)

**OHLDE CARROLL REV** (785)267-5479
3517 SE 35th St Topeka KS 66605-3137 • KS • D Ex/S • Kansas Topeka KS • (SL 1968 MA PHD)

**OHLENDORF RAY R REV** (828)632-4863
4046 NC Hwy 16 N Taylorsville NC 28681 • rohlendorf@juno.com • SE • SP • Salem Taylorsville NC • (828)632-4863 • (FW 1979 MDIV)

**OHLWINE ARTHUR A** (218)573-3574
46913 St Hwy 34 Osage MN 56570 • MNS • SP • Gethsemane Osage MN • (218)573-3574 • (SL 2000 MDIV)

**OIE THOMAS REV** (734)844-3495
45085 Horseshoe Cir Canton MI 48187 • MI • Inst C • Michigan Ann Arbor MI • (CQ 1981 MTH STM DMIN)

**OIEN MARK R REV** (617)275-1164
424 Davis Rd Bedford MA 01730-1514 • NE • SP • Of The Savior Bedford MA • (781)275-6013 • (SPR 1976 MDIV MA)

**OKAMOTO JOEL PHILIP REV** (314)918-8617
870 Atalanta Ave Saint Louis MO 63119-2077 • okamotoj@csl.edu • MO • SHS/C • Missouri Saint Louis MO • (314)317-4550 • (SL 1996 STM MDIV DTH)

**OKAMOTO TOSHIO REV** (517)669-9323
11517 River Dr De Witt MI 48820 • MI • EM • (SL 1956)

**OKPISZ STEVEN J REV**
507 E Broadway Steeleville IL 62288 • sokpisz@egyptian.net • SI • Assoc • St Mark Steeleville IL • (618)965-3192 • (SL 1994 MDIV)

**OKUBO MASON K REV** (714)543-5244
1606 E Avalon Santa Ana CA 92705 • PSW • SHS/C • Pacific Southwest Irvine CA • (949)854-3232 • (SL 1999)

**OLANDER CHARLES P REV** (217)529-8842
8 Red Oak Ln Springfield IL 62707-8742 • CI • SP • Concordia Springfield IL • (217)529-3307 • (FW 1978 MDIV)

**OLDENBURG DONALD R REV** (828)466-3049
612 4th Ave NE Conover NC 28613-1617 • donaldo@abts.net • SE • SP • Concordia Conover NC • (828)464-3324 • (FW 1977 MDIV)

**OLDENETTEL RONNIE L REV** (316)332-3300
C/O Zion Luth Church 303 S 10th St Independence KS 67301-3617 • roldenettel@terraworld.net • KS • SP • Zion Independence KS • (316)332-3300 • (FW 1981 MDIV)

**OLDSEN GILBERT REV** (716)343-1712
427 E Main St Apt 210 Batavia NY 14020-2527 • EA • EM • (SL 1933)

**OLIMB CURTIS A REV** (701)772-7561
2092 Prairie Rose Ct Grand Forks ND 58201-5802 • olimb2092@aol.com • ND • EM • (CQ 1980 MAR)

**OLIVER HAROLD H G REV** (513)231-0715
6967 Moorfield Dr Cincinnati OH 45230-2223 • holiver@zionlc.org • OH • SP • Zion Cincinnati OH • (513)231-2253 • (SL 1969 MDIV MED)

**OLIVER STEPHEN P REV** 011-886-3-571-0023
China Lutheran Seminary #11 Lane 51 Tahsueh Rd Hsinchu 300 TAIWAN • steve.oliver@bigfoot.com • IW • M Chap • Iowa West Fort Dodge IA • (SL 1986 MDIV STM)

**OLLEK KENNETH L REV** (503)393-0507
4714 18th Ave NE Salem OR 97303-2202 • NOW • EM • (SL 1961)

**OLSE NOEL C REV** (219)324-5365
1405 Illinois Ave LaPorte IN 46350-2913 • nco-trinity@juno.com • EN • SP • Trinity La Porte IN • (219)362-4932 • (FW 1998 MDIV)

**OLSEN CLIFFORD T REV** (936)295-9242
341 Elkins Lk Huntsville TX 77340-7308 • TX • EM • (SPR 1964)

**OLSEN JEFFREY A REV** (219)749-0887
3810 Sugarhill Ct New Haven IN 46774-2730 • IN • 04/1988 04/2000 • (SL 1972 MDIV)

**OLSEN STEVEN W REV** (515)225-7984
5317 Meadow Pl West Des Moines IA 50266-6325 • AT • 08/2000 • (CQ 1980 MDIV)

**OLSON DANIEL ALAN REV**
318 S Oakwood Ave Geneseo IL 61254-1445 • potsdam@juno.com • CI • SP • Concordia Geneseo IL • (309)944-3993 • (FW 1995 MDIV)

**OLSON DONALD L JR. REV** (254)751-1026
1417 White River Dr Waco TX 76712-3259 • dlolson@texasinternet.com • TX • SP • Trinity Waco TX • (817)772-4225 • (SL 1973 MDIV)

**OLSON EDWARD G REV** (715)678-2363
PO Box 10 Stetsonville WI 54480-0010 • NW • 10/1976 10/1999 • (SPR 1967 MDIV)

**OLSON GARY C REV** (804)320-3779
C/O Bethlehem Luth Church 1100 W Grace St Richmond VA 23220-3613 • SE • SP • Bethlehem Richmond VA • (804)353-4413 • (FW 1984 MDIV)

**OLSON JEREMIAH REV** (651)450-1564
1035 15th Ave N South St Paul MN 55075 • MNN • Bethlehem Richmond VA • (804)353-4413 • (CQ 1997 MDIV PHD)

**OLSON MARLOW J REV** (518)356-2646
3570 Carman Rd Schenectady NY 12303-5313 • AT • 08/1982 10/1999 • (SL 1972 MDIV)

**OLSON N VERNER REV** (510)558-9442
760 Richmond St El Cerrito CA 94530-3207 • revnvern@aol.com • CNH • SP • Grace El Cerrito CA • (510)525-9004 • (SL 1979 MDIV)

**OLSON ROBERT W REV** (715)659-4762
300 W Main St Spencer WI 54479-9793 • NW • EM • (SPR 1950)

**OLSON ROBERT W REV** (319)233-0812
1027 W Parker St Waterloo IA 50703 • IE • SP • Concordia Waterloo IA • (319)233-4025 • (SL 1957 MDIV)

**OLSON ROGER WILLIAM REV** (219)485-8417
2511 Kingston Pt Fort Wayne IN 46815-8526 • olsonrw@aol.com • IN • Inst C • Indiana Fort Wayne IN • (FW 1984 MDIV)

**OLSON THOMAS L REV** (219)639-7177
C/O St John Luth Church 11555 N US Highway 27 Decatur IN 46733-9799 • 74073@compuserve.com • IN • SP • St John Decatur IN • (219)639-6178 • (FW 1982 MDIV MA STM)

**OLSON TIMOTHY W REV**
2871 Old Hickory Ln Charlotte MI 48813 • flcrev@ia4u.net • MI • SP • First Charlotte MI • (517)543-4360 • (FW 1994 MDIV)

**OLSON WAYNE F REV** (317)784-7449
860 Yosemite Dr Indianapolis IN 46217 • shantiwoso@aol.com • IN • Inst C • Indiana Fort Wayne IN • (SL 1961 MDIV)

**OLSON WILLIAM REV** (704)365-3601
7000 Pleasant Dr Charlotte NC 28211-4740 • SE • EM • (SPR 1961 MTH)

**ONDOV DANIEL J REV** (406)656-6348
2039 Forest Park Dr Billings MT 59102-2819 • ondov@mcn.net • MT • EM • (SL 1948 DMIN)

**ONGSTAD CHRIS DUANE REV** (708)388-1113
11812 S Kolin Ave Alsip IL 60803-2178 • S • SP • Holy Cross Alsip IL • (708)597-5209 • (SL 1981 MDIV)

**ONKEN KURT DEAN REV** (360)659-6038
4309-2 88th St NE Marysville WA 98270 • athanasius65@juno.com • NOW • SP • Messiah Marysville WA • (360)659-4112 • (FW 1996 MDIV)

**OPPEN RONALD E REV** (618)495-2904
8702 Huey Rd Centralia IL 62801-7538 • SI • SP • Trinity Hoffman IL • (618)495-2545 • (SL 1984 MDIV)

**OPPER ALLAN E REV** (724)352-3375
PO Box 272 Saxonburg PA 16056-0272 • EN • SP • Faith Butler PA • (724)285-5893 • (FW 1983 MDIV)

**OPSAHL BRUCE H REV** (610)381-3610
RR 3 Box 3495 Saylorsburg PA 18353-9749 • NJ • EM • (SPR 1952 MAR)

**ORAVEC RONALD DAVID REV** (716)692-6809
2897 Lemke Dr North Tonawanda NY 14120-1111 • hitzonok@prodigy.net • EA • SP • St John North Tonawanda NY • (716)693-9677 • (SL 1971 MDIV)

**OREA HIRAM CORIA REV** (214)369-2515
5729 Caruth Haven Ln Apt 216 Dallas TX 75206-1947 • TX • D Miss • Texas Austin TX • (CQ 1993 MDIV)

**OREN ALBERT S REV** (715)634-3972
15664 Parkland Dr Hayward WI 54843 • NW • SP • Trinity Hayward WI • (715)634-2260 • (FW 1999)

**ORMAN RICHARD L REV** (760)741-0676
1109 Hoover St Escondido CA 92027-1412 • richmel@quixnet.net • PSW • 12/1975 12/1999 • (SL 1964 MDIV)

**OROZCO JULIO A REV**
9735 Sumac Rd #406 Desplaines IL 60016 • NI • 08/1994 08/2000 • (SPR 1973 MDIV)

**ORTIZ LUIS E REV** (310)477-3748
2477 Sawtelle Blvd Apt E Los Angelos CA 90064 • CNH • 12/1997 12/1999 • (CQ 1987 MA)

**ORTLOFF CHARLES E REV** (507)625-9461
963 Belvista Dr North Mankato MN 56003-3607 • MNS • Sn/Adm • Our Savior Mankato MN • (507)345-5112 • (FW 1977 MDIV)

**ORTNER DONALD R DR** (804)392-6767
1421 Gilliam Dr Farmville VA 23901-2353 • EN • Asst • Gloria Dei Blue Bell PA* • (215)646-0848 • (ME 1947 MS MA PHD)

**OSBORNE BRUCE D REV**
407 N 35 St Mattoon IL 61938 • CI • Sn/Adm • St John Mattoon IL • (217)234-4923 • (FW 1989 MDIV)

**OSBURN GARY DAVID REV** (601)638-6830
4273 Highway 80 Vicksburg MS 39180-7746 • grado@magnolia.net • SO • SP • Messiah Vicksburg MS • (601)636-1894 • (SL 1992 MDIV)

**OSCHWALD JEFFREY A REV**
Ta Hsueh Rd # 82 19-4 Hsinchu 300 TAIWAN • oschwald@gcn.net.tw • IN • S Miss • Indiana Fort Wayne IN • (FW 1983 MA MDIV PHD)

**OSLADIL BRYAN R REV** (920)994-8200
402 Center Ave Adell WI 53001-1116 • bosladil@execpc.com • SW • SP • Emmanuel Adell WI* • (920)994-9005 • (FW 1988 MDIV)

**OSSLUND RICHARD N REV** (515)292-7542
110 Lynn Ave Ames IA 50014-7107 • rnosslund@aol.com • IW • Sn/Adm • Memorial Ames IA • (515)292-5005 • (SL 1970 STM THD)

**OSTAFINSKI JOSEPH A REV** (219)464-2810
C/O Heritage Luth Church 308 Washington St Valparaiso IN 46383-4734 • IN • SP • Heritage Valparaiso IN • (219)464-2810 • (FW 1988 MDIV MSW)

**OSTER KEVIN WADE REV** (320)587-8910
545 Lincoln Ave SW Hutchinson MN 55350-2352 • revkev1@hutchtel.net • MNS • SP • Our Savior Hutchinson MN • (320)587-3318 • (FW 1994 MDIV)

**OSTERLOTH DUANE R REV** (816)454-9271
2000 NE 55th Ter Kansas City MO 64118 • MO • Asst • Holy Cross Kansas City MO • (816)452-9113 • (FW 1997 MDIV)

**OSTGREN STANLEY M REV** (316)435-6442
PO Box 156 Argonia KS 67004-0156 • KS • EM • (CQ 1993 MDIV)

**OSTRUSKE NEAL J REV** (510)886-7362
401 Harder Rd Hayward CA 94544-2932 • CNH • EM • (SL 1940)

**OSWALD ARTHUR A REV** (920)451-4625
2315 Silver Leaf Ln Sheboygan WI 53083-2736 • SW • EM • (SL 1947)

**OSWALD MARK ARTHUR REV** (616)899-2426
1351 Harding St Conklin MI 49403 • MI • SP • Trinity Conklin MI • (616)899-2973 • (FW 1991 MDIV)

**OSWALD ORVAL M REV** (530)677-2887
2825 Waverly Dr Cameron Park CA 95682-9256 • CNH • EM • (SL 1950 MDIV DD)

**OSWALD WALLACE C REV** (715)479-8707
5649 Silver Shore Ln Eagle River WI 54521-9620 • SW • EM • (SL 1957)

**OTT CHAD M REV** (715)838-0672
3513 E Meadows Pl Eau Claire WI 54701 • NW • Assoc • Peace Eau Claire WI • (715)834-2486 • (SL 2000 MDIV)

**OTT GENE A REV** (605)338-7988
2212 S Western Ave Sioux Falls SD 57105-3426 • gott713508@aol.com • SD • Sn/Adm • Our Redeemer Sioux Falls SD • (605)338-6957 • (FW 1985 MDIV)

**OTT HAROLD A REV** (317)887-9760
5414 Chesterton Pl Indianapolis IN 46237-9303 • IN • EM • (SL 1932)

**OTT NORMAN W REV** (602)641-9344
5639 E Encanto St Mesa AZ 85205-5520 • njott98@aol.com • PSW • EM • (SL 1954 MDIV)

**OTT TIMOTHY MICHAEL REV** (906)485-4012
1765 S Rose St Ishpeming MI 49849-2740 • cohotim@aol.com • NW • SP • Christ King Ishpeming MI • (906)485-4432 • (SL 1973 MDIV)

**OTTE GREGORY REV** (714)997-7878
553 S Shasta Way Orange CA 92869-5242 • PSW • 09/1988 09/1997 • (SPR 1967 MDIV MTH)

**OTTE HAROLD W REV** (763)780-8079
2970 Highway 10 NE Mounds View MN 55112-4077 • MNS • EM • (CQ 1972 DED)

**OTTE JAMES E REV** (409)569-0103
930 Millard Dr Nacogdoches TX 75961-2627 • TX • SP • Redeemer Nacogdoches TX • (409)564-6729 • (SL 1980 MDIV MED)

**OTTE JOHN W REV** (507)526-4446
310 E 4th St Blue Earth MN 56013 • MNS • Assoc • St Paul Blue Earth MN* • (507)526-7318 • (SL 2000 MDIV)

**OTTE WILLIAM HAROLD REV** (715)524-5956
111 Lange Ct Shawano WI 54166-3605 • whotte@frontiernet.net • NW • Sn/Adm • St James Shawano WI • (715)524-4815 • (SL 1972 MDIV STM)

**OTTEN CHRISTOPHER LEE REV** (301)638-9832
4020 Windsor Heights Pl White Plains MD 20695 • christopher@otten.com • SE • Assoc • Grace La Plata MD • (301)932-0963 • (SL 1995 MDIV)

**OTTEN DAVID GENE REV** (605)669-2832
PO Box 469 Murdo SD 57559-0469 • davidotten@hotmail.com • SD • SP • Messiah Murdo SD* • (605)669-2406 • (FW 1996 MDIV)

**OTTEN DAVID L REV** (910)938-7380
2nd BN 8th MAR PSC Box 20103 Camp Lejeune NC 28542-0103 • otter59@hotmail.com • NEB • M Chap • Nebraska Seward NE • (SL 1984 MDIV)

**OTTEN WALTER D REV** (708)485-7074
9044 Sheridan Ave Brookfield IL 60513-1628 • NI • SP • St Paul Brookfield IL • (708)485-6987 • (SL 1959 MDIV)

**OTTEN WILLIAM H REV**
885 Augusta Dr Rochester Hills MI 48309-1533 • MI • EM • (SPR 1965 MDIV)

**OTTO CRAIG DOUGLAS REV** (314)547-6002
706 Lincoln Ct Perryville MO 63775-1469 • MO • Sn/Adm • Immanuel Perryville MO • (573)547-8317 • (SL 1995 MDIV)

**OTTO DANIEL D REV** (615)834-3135
404 Fieldcrest Dr Nashville TN 37211-4320 • danotto@juno.com • MDS • Sn/Adm • Our Savior Nashville TN • (615)833-1500 • (SL 1961 MDIV)

**OTTO EDGAR J REV** (414)228-7457
500 W Bradley Rd # C234 Milwaukee WI 53217-2638 • SW • EM • (SPR 1951 MAR)

**OTTO MARVIN D REV** (504)466-0581
15 Traminer Dr Kenner LA 70065-1133 • SO • SP • Zion New Orleans LA • (504)524-1025 • (SPR 1964)

**OTTO MITCHELL E REV** (319)887-9479
1025 20th Ave Coralville IA 52241 • pastor-otto@juno.com • IE • SP • Prince Of Peace Coralville IA • (319)338-1842 • (FW 1996 MDIV)

**OTTO RODNEY D DR** (616)249-8249
5432 Sand Dune Ct SW Grandville MI 49418-9226 • pfordo7@iserv.net • MI • SP • Christ Our Savior Holland MI • (616)738-0100 • (SL 1969 MDIV DMIN)

**OTTO WILLIAM H REV** (262)242-2461
2311 W Ranch Rd # 116N Mequon WI 53092-3132 • wotto2536@aol.com • SW • EM • (SL 1961 MDIV)

**OUELLETTE DENNIS E REV** (502)831-2148
1024 Homestead Trail Henderson KY 42420 • deouellette@hcc-uky.campus.mci.net • IN • SP • Trinity Henderson KY • (502)826-4337 • (CQ 1997 MA)

## P

**PAAPE DAVID B REV** (262)781-6654
N51W17197 Maple Crest Ln Menomonee Falls WI 53051-7522 • repaa@aol.com • SW • SP • Zion Menomonee Falls WI • (262)781-8133 • (FW 1977 MDIV)

**PAAVOLA DANIEL E REV** (920)668-8710
504 Van Altena Ave Cedar Grove WI 53013 • SW • SHS/C • South Wisconsin Milwaukee WI • (414)464-8100 • (FW 1983 MTH MDIV)

**PABOR LOUIS L REV** (512)345-1488
3800 Crowncrest Cv Austin TX 78759-8601 • pastor-pabor@aol.com • TX • EM • (SL 1940 MDIV)

**PACHECO HECTOR H REV** (773)975-8992
1523 W Cullom Ave Apt 2E Chicago IL 60613-1205 • NI • Inst C • Northern Illinois Hillside IL • (CQ 1960 MTH MDIV)

**PACILLI DINO F REV** (573)756-8410
511 W College St Farmington MO 63640-2433 • dpacilli@fxnet.missouri.org • MO • Sn/Adm • St Paul Farmington MO • (573)756-7872 • (SL 1994 MDIV)

**PADILLA BENSESLADO CRUZ REV** (916)846-2585
1763 Grace Rd Gridley CA 95948-9485 • gracelutheran@man2net.com • CNH • SP • Grace Gridley CA • (530)846-4736 • (CQ 1991)

**PAEPKE WILLIAM A REV** (605)787-5672
2042 Mountain Shadow Rd PO Box 285 Piedmont SD 57769 • abpep42@rapidcity.net • SD • SP • Bethlehem Rapid City SD • (605)343-2011 • (SL 1968 MDIV)

**PAGAN RICHARD REV**
6433 Spy Glass Run Fort Wayne IN 46804-4239 • IN • Sn/Adm • Aboite Fort Wayne IN • (219)436-5673 • (FW 1979 MDIV)

**PAGE FRED LOYD REV** (626)919-1530
C/O Immanuel First Lutheran Ch 512 S Valinda Ave West Covina CA 91790-3007 • chinofour@aol.com • PSW • SP • Immanuel First West Covina CA • (818)919-1530 • (FW 1994 MDIV)

**PAGE JAMES WILLIAM REV** (909)898-1330
1019 Meadow View Ct Corona CA 92880 • revpage@aol.com • PSW • SP • Grace Corona CA • (909)737-3217 • (CQ 1995 MA)

**PAGEL PETER REV**
C/O Faith Lutheran Church PO Box 1280 La Pine OR 97739-1280 • NOW • SP • Faith La Pine OR • (ED 1989 MDIV)

**PAHOLKE MICHAEL ALLEN REV** (715)264-3721
C/O Trinity Luth Church PO Box 161 Glidden WI 54527-0161 • NW • SP • Trinity Glidden WI • (715)264-3961 • (FW 1994 MDIV)

**PAINE FRANKLIN W JR. REV** (425)778-2782
2940 217th Pl SW Brier WA 98036-8045 • fwpainejr@cs.com • NOW • Sn/Adm • Mount Zion Mountlake Terrace WA • (425)778-3577 • (CQ 1982 MS MDIV)

**PALACH CRAIG MICHAEL REV** (218)736-7717
RR 4 Box 123 Fergus Falls MN 56537-9356 • revcmp@prtel.com • MNN • SP • Faith Fergus Falls MN • (218)736-5352 • (FW 1995 MDIV)

**PALKA JOHN M REV** 228-70-84-51
B P 53 Dapaong Togo WEST AFRICA • lcmstogo2@togotel.net.tg • NI • S Miss • Northern Illinois Hillside IL • (FW 1991 MDIV)

**PALKEWICK ROBERT J REV** (973)423-3535
32 Richard St North Haledon NJ 07508-2430 • NJ • SP • St Paul Pompton Lakes NJ • (973)278-6542 • (FW 1977 MDIV)

**PALM JUAN D REV** (320)453-3096
PO Box 583 862 Stearns Ave W Eden Valley MN 55329-0583 • MNN • SP • St Paul Eden Valley MN • (320)453-2472 • (FW 1999 MDIV)

**PALMER MARK R REV** (218)262-6240
3841 E 2nd Ave Hibbing MN 55746-2910 • mbpalmer@the-bridge.net • MNN • SP • Grace Hibbing MN • (218)263-3955 • (SL 1987 MDIV)

**PALMER WAYNE H REV**
10200 Highway C Frohna MO 63748-9103 • MO • SP • Concordia Frohna MO • (573)824-5435 • (FW 1992 MDIV)

**PALMER WILLIAM REV** (414)384-2160
2228 S 33rd St Lowr Milwaukee WI 53215-2414 • wpalme182@aol.com • SW • D Miss • Emmanuel Deaf West Allis WI • (414)321-8430 • (FW 1984 MDIV)

**PALOMAKI DAVID W REV** (402)367-6136
880 M St David City NE 68632-1146 • NEB • SP • Redeemer David City NE* • (402)367-3859 • (SL 1987 MDIV)

**PALOMAKI THOMAS E REV** (218)547-2146
PO Box 1384 5938 Honeysuckle Ln NW Walker MN 56484 • MNN • EM • * • (SPR 1958)

**PANKOW BERNARD J REV** (408)946-1370
2067 Morrill Ave San Jose CA 95132-1128 • panbj@worldnet.att.net • CNH • EM • * • (SL 1942 MA)

**PANKOW EDWARD R REV** (517)642-8333
2750 N Raucholz Rd Hemlock MI 48626-9680 • MI • EM • * • (SL 1952 MDIV)

**PANKRATZ A W REV** (517)821-5606
504 Beacon Ln Roscommon MI 48653-8778 • pankratz@triton.net • MI • EM • * • (SL 1954)

**PANNIER CLARENCE W REV** (319)359-1919
1814 E 38th St #6A Davenport IA 52807-1377 • IE • EM • * • (SPR 1962)

**PANNING JOHN F REV** (616)399-5083
2726 132nd Ave Holland MI 49424-9205 • 110425.574@compuserve.com • MI • EM • * • (SL 1953 MA MDIV)

**PANZIGRAU JEROME E REV** (724)337-8450
149 Glenview Dr New Kensington PA 15068 • S • SP • John Huss Arnold PA • (412)335-1735 • (SL 2000 MDIV)

**PAPE BRIAN N REV**
681 Fillmore Dr Morton IL 61550 • CI • Assoc • Bethel Morton IL • (309)263-2417 • (SL 1999 MDIV)

**PAPE JAMES C REV** (501)876-0800
18 Thirsk Ln Bella Vista AR 72714 • pape@specent.com • MDS • EM • (SL 1957)

**PAPE NEIL F REV** (850)477-1792
1698 Spalding Cir Pensacola FL 32514-8300 • neilpape@quixnet.net • SO • EM • (SL 1960 DMIN)

**PAPE RICHARD E REV** (248)684-4027
990 Squire Ln Milford MI 48381 • MI • SP • Christ Milford MI • (248)684-0895 • (SL 1975 MDIV)

**PARDIECK DAVID C REV** (480)839-0510
6830 S Butte Ave Tempe AZ 85283-4150 • PSW • EM • (SL 1961 MDIV)

**PARK PAUL Y REV** (818)244-9315
5700 Etiwanda Ave Unit 281 Tarzana CA 91356 • PSW • D Miss • Zion Korean Glendale CA • (818)244-9315 • (FW 1990 MTH MDIV DD)

**PARK THOMAS C REV** (219)622-6711
806 N Melching Dr Apt B Ossian IN 46777-8900 • IN • EM • (SPR 1963)

**PARKER EDWIN LEE REV** (320)273-2127
C/O Trinity Luth Church PO Box 38 Odessa MN 56276-0038 • MNN • SP • Trinity Odessa MN* • (320)273-2127 • (FW 1994 MDIV)

**PARKER MARION K REV** (936)441-7503
1901 N Thompson Conroe TX 77301-1241 • mk³parker@bigfoot.com • TX • 05/1986 05/2000 • * • (SPR 1970 MDIV)

**PARKER NOEL SEAN REV**
1400 Bypass 1960 E Humble TX 77338 • TX • Assoc • Lamb Of God Humble TX • (281)446-8427 • (SL 1996 MDIV)

**PARKER TIMOTHY EDWIN REV** (308)647-6776
C/O St Paul Luth Church PO Box 326 Shelton NE 68876-0326 • takepar@juno.com • NEB • SP • St Paul Shelton NE* • (308)647-6733 • (FW 1994 MDIV)

**PARKS ALLEN E REV** (219)416-0511
632 Chesteron Tr Fort Wayne IN 46825-1110 • aparks1569@aol.com • IN • EM • * • (SL 1963)

**PARKS DAVID H REV** (316)659-2078
C/O Zion Lutheran Church 13307 Jewell Rd Offerle KS 67563-9227 • KS • SP • Zion Offerle KS* • (316)659-2078 • (SPR 1968 MDIV)

**PARODI HECTOR L REV**
1357 E Luzerne St Philadelphia PA 19124 • EA • D Miss • Eastern Williamsville NY • (716)634-5111 • (OTHER 1999)

**PARRIS MICHAEL J REV** (319)655-7823
PO Box 10 Millersburg IA 52308-0010 • IE • SP • Trinity Millersburg IA* • (319)655-7822 • (FW 1987 MDIV)

**PARRISH BRENT L REV** (715)834-7294
1814 Vine St Eau Claire WI 54703-4930 • bparr45955@aol.com • NW • Sn/Adm • Epiphany Eau Claire WI • (715)835-9155 • (SL 1989 MDIV)

**PARSCH DANIEL PAUL REV** (515)276-4452
C/O Gloria Dei Lutheran Church 8301 Aurora Ave Urbandale IA 50322-2301 • parsch.dan@gd-lc.org • IW • Sn/Adm • Gloria Dei Urbandale IA • (515)276-1700 • (SL 1971 MDIV)

**PARSCH DAVID H REV** (407)277-8872
212 Thyme Ct Orlando FL 32825-3648 • FG • SP • Resurrection Orlando FL • (407)855-1393 • (SL 1968 MDIV)

**PARSCH TIMOTHY J REV** (727)535-5323
2187 Egret Dr Clearwater FL 33764 • toaster@tampabay.rr.com • FG • SP • Bethel Clearwater FL • (727)799-3010 • (SL 1974 MDIV)

**PARSHALL DANIEL W REV** (503)674-8172
21962 NE Lachenview Ln Fairview OR 97024-8775 • NOW • EM • (SPR 1964)

**PARSON WILLIAM T REV** (336)767-7813
3420 Cumberland Rd Winston Salem NC 27105-3307 • wtp@aol.com • SE • SP • St Mark Winston Salem NC • (336)724-0035 • (SPR 1975 MDIV)

**PARSONS DANIEL C DR** (714)523-0717
14642 Gandesa Rd La Mirada CA 90638-4416 • parsons4u@aol.com • PSW • 01/1996 01/2000 • (FW 1983 MDIV DMIN MAT)

**PARSONS WILLIAM A REV** (219)583-3372
128 Condo St Monticello IN 47960 • IN • SP • Our Saviour Monticello IN • (219)583-5005 • (FW 1998 MDIV)

**PART THOMAS A REV**
150 S Lee St Appleton WI 54915-2732 • NW • Assoc • Good Shepherd Appleton WI • (920)734-9643 • (SL 1974)

**PARVIZ KEVIN D REV** (314)647-8214
6603 Wise Ave St Louis MO 63139 • brthrlove1@aol.com • MO • D Miss • Missouri Saint Louis MO • (314)317-4550 • (SL 1998 MDIV)

**PASCH RODNEY W REV** (504)645-9455
1418 Washington Ct Slidell LA 70458-2144 • rod³pasch@yahoo.com • SO • Sn/Adm • Bethany Slidell LA • (504)643-3043 • (SL 1981 MDIV)

**PASE ROBERT J REV**
3000 W Golf Course Rd Midland TX 79701-2998 • TX • SP • Grace Midland TX • (915)697-3221 • (SL 1989 MDIV)

**PASEUR RONALD C REV** (281)357-5793
25115 Kingsdown Dr Spring TX 77389 • rpaseur@selec.net • TX • Assoc • Zion Tomball TX • (281)351-5757 • (SL 1990 MDIV)

**PATRICK RALPH W E REV** (505)522-0082
3107 Enchanted Dr Las Cruces NM 88011-4906 • mission@zianet.com • RM • SP • Mission Las Cruces NM • (505)522-0465 • (FW 1988 MDIV)

**PATSCHECK ARTHUR F REV** (760)363-7511
49159 Tamarisk Dr Morongo Valley CA 92256-9732 • PSW • 03/1994 03/2000 • (SPR 1974 MDIV)

**PATT RICHARD W REV** (414)771-7460
9999 W North Ave Unit 107 Wauwatosa WI 53226 • EN • EM • (SL 1960 MDIV)

**PATTEN HOWARD J REV** (785)478-1648
4217 SW Aylesbury Rd Topeka KS 66610-1584 • patten@kslcms.org • KS • DP • Kansas Topeka KS • (SL 1961 MDIV)

**PATTEN TIMOTHY REV** (513)774-0115
6734 Midnight Sun Dr Maineville OH 45039-8840 • chesheads@aol.com • OH • Sn/Adm • Our Redeemer Maineville OH • (513)697-7335 • (SL 1995 MDIV)

**PATTERSON CRAIG A REV** (303)346-8403
9392 S Burlington Ln Highlands Ranch CO 80126 • pastorcap@hotmail.com • RM • SP • Immanuel Englewood CO • (303)781-5887 • (FW 1978 MDIV)

**PATTERSON JEFFREY D REV** (281)528-0021
17323 Bent Cypress Dr Spring TX 77388-5767 • pattersons@vonl.com • TX • Assoc • Trinity Klein TX • (281)376-5773 • (FW 1986 MDIV)

**PATZWITZ WALTER F REV** (573)833-6933
320 County Road 516 New Wells MO 63732-9111 • filioque@showme.net • MO • SP • Immanuel New Wells MO • (573)833-6933 • (SL 1983 MDIV)

**PAUL GARY G REV** (715)720-9963
13964 95th Ave Chippewa Falls WI 54729-5107 • minifarm1@juno.com • NW • SP • Zion Chippewa Falls WI • (715)723-6380 • (FW 1980 MDIV DMIN)

**PAUL MARK ARTHUR REV** (806)794-8731
6604 Brentwood Ave Lubbock TX 79424-1509 • TX • SP • Christ Lubbock TX • (806)799-0162 • (SL 1975 MDIV)

**PAUL MICHAEL JOHN REV** 011-853-522-397
Estrada da Vitoria 24 Edificio Long Chu Terrace B 8 Macau MACAU • paulm@macau.ctm.net • SI • S Miss • Southern Illinois Belleville IL • (SL 1996 MDIV)

**PAUL RICHARD D DR** (714)999-1690
1801 E Santa Ana St Anaheim CA 92805-4309 • revpaul@surfside.net • PSW • 04/1992 04/2000 • (SPR 1970 MDIV MA DMIN)

**PAUL ROBERT W REV** (906)482-2647
RR 1 Box 628A Houghton MI 49931-9736 • rwpaul@portup.com • NW • EM • (SL 1958 MDIV MAR)

**PAULING CLARENCE H REV** (612)689-1124
909 S Dellwood St Apt 119 Cambridge MN 55008-2139 • MNN • EM • (SL 1934)

**PAULING DELAYNE H REV** (312)944-1452
1615 N Cleveland Ave Apt 1N Chicago IL 60614-5647 • NI • Sn/Adm • First St Paul Chicago IL • (312)642-7172 • (SL 1960)

**PAULING RUCLARE D REV** (707)425-2887
3535 Astoria Cir Fairfield CA 94533-3310 • ruclare@aol.com • CNH • 03/1983 10/1998 • (SL 1961 MDIV)

**PAULISON MICHAEL E REV** (970)522-9395
800 Clark St Sterling CO 80751-2824 • trinity@trinitysterling.org • RM • SP • Trinity Sterling CO • (970)522-5942 • (SL 1990 MDIV)

**PAULS TIMOTHY J REV** (208)898-9692
1885 E Oakcrest Meridian ID 83642 • tntpauls@rmci.net • NOW • Assoc • Good Shepherd Boise ID • (208)343-7212 • (SL 1993 MDIV)

**PAULSON CHARLES REV** (940)691-2493
4826 Dickens St Wichita Falls TX 76308-5249 • cpaulson42@aol.com • TX • SP • Our Redeemer Wichita Falls TX • (940)692-3690 • (SL 1982 MDIV MA)

**PAULSON JOHN R REV** (308)754-4588
505 Grant St Saint Paul NE 68873-1926 • NEB • SP • Christ Saint Paul NE • (308)754-5135 • (SL 1986 MDIV)

**PAULSON WARREN L REV** (517)796-9360
2013 Cascade Ridge Dr Jackson MI 49203 • MI • EM • (SPR 1958 MDIV)

**PAULUS EUGENE R REV** (909)793-1150
805 E Colton Ave Redlands CA 92374-3634 • PSW • EM • (SPR 1964 MDIV)

**PAULUS LARRY C REV** (219)639-6564
PO Box 73759 Kowloon Central HONG KONG • IE • 09/1994 09/1999 • (CQ 1989 MDIV)

**PAVEL JAN REV** (612)727-1015
3816 E 55th St Minneapolis MN 55417-2248 • MNS • EM • (SL 1949 MDIV MA)

**PAVEL JOHN D REV** (715)253-2701
500 W College Ave Wittenberg WI 54499-9196 • NW • SP • St Paul Wittenberg WI • (715)253-2790 • (SL 1981 MDIV)

**PAYNE CARLTON E REV** (847)726-7808
24530 N Old Mc Henry Rd Lake Zurich IL 60047-8424 • paspayne@aol.com • NI • Asst • St Matthew Lake Zurich IL • (847)438-7709 • (FW 1989 MDIV)

**PAYNE MATTHEW A REV** (626)914-8068
1012 S Danehurst Ave Glendora CA 91740 • revdog@yahoo.com • PSW • SP • Trinity Covina CA • (626)337-2971 • (FW 1989 MDIV)

**PEARCY DAVID L REV** (301)527-1743
15512 Norman Dr Darnestown MD 20878-3574 • SE • Asst • St Andrew Silver Spring MD • (301)942-6531 • (SL 1971 STM MDIV)

**PEARSON CHARLES W JR. REV** (818)951-8188
Gethsemane Lutheran Church 2723 Orange Ave La Crescenta CA 91214-2124 • cpear1@aol.com • PSW • SP • Gethsemane La Crescenta CA • (818)248-3738 • (SPR 1972)

**PECK JEROME K REV** (913)557-5009
709 Rosewood Ct Paola KS 66071 • flynrev1@micoks.net • KS • SP • First Paola KS • (913)294-3476 • (SL 1973 MDIV)

**PECKMAN PAUL H REV** (262)781-9664
N65W14452 Redwood Dr Menomonee Falls WI 53051-5170 • peckmfwi@execpc.com • SW • Sn/Adm • Pilgrim Wauwatosa WI • (414)476-0735 • (SL 1975 MDIV DMIN)

**PECKMAN RICHARD E REV** (316)251-3611
510 W 9th St Coffeyville KS 67337-5002 • peckman@terraworld.net • KS • SP • St Paul Coffeyville KS • (316)251-2927 • (SL 1975 MDIV)

**PECKMAN WALTER A REV** (816)632-2493
1106 Sam G Hiner Dr Cameron MO 64429 • MO • SP • Prince Peace Cameron MO • (816)632-7904 • (SL 1972 MDIV)

**PEDERSON JOE ED REV**
HHB 4/27 Field Artillery Unit 23735 Box 37 APO AE 09034-3735 • 427fachap@427fahg.1ad.army.mil • WY • M Chap • Wyoming Sheridian WY • (SL 1987 DMIN)

**PEDERSON RONALD DOUGLAS REV** (920)565-2062
W1268 Cty Rd FF Haven WI 53083 • rpeders@bythead.com • SW • SP • Grace Haven WI • (414)565-2186 • (FW 1995 MDIV)

**PEFFER BRUCE A REV**
3 Wildflower Way Wimberley TX 78676-3100 • TX • SP • Grace San Marcos TX • (512)392-4241 • (SL 1986 MDIV)

**PEGORSCH DENNIS W REV** (715)675-4074
4210 Hilltop Rd Wausau WI 54403-2235 • NW • Assoc • Trinity Wausau WI • (715)842-0769 • (SL 1967 MSW DMIN)

**PEITSCH PETER M REV** (612)442-5612
1432 Wood Duck Rd Waconia MN 55387-1140 • p3c2mp@juno.com • MNS • Assoc • Trinity Waconia MN • (952)442-4165 • (FW 1985 MDIV)

**PEKARI RANDALL L REV** (860)643-4390
29 Diane Dr Vernon CT 06066 • NE • Assoc • Our Savior South Windsor CT • (860)644-3350 • (SL 1999 MDIV)

**PEKARI WILLIAM J REV** (608)224-1446
1914 Dolores Dr Madison WI 53716-2318 • wpekari@execpc.com • SW • SP • Monona Monona WI • (608)222-7071 • (SL 1972 MDIV)

**PELLEGRINO JOSEPH EDWARD REV**
405 E 25th St Silver City NM 88061-5707 • RM • SP • Messiah Silver City NM • (505)538-9446 • (SL 1995 MDIV)

**PELSUE DAVID C REV** (314)352-1355
6325 De Mara Dr Affton MO 63123-3301 • reformation@stlnet.com • MO • SP • Reformation Saint Louis MO • (314)352-1355 • (SL 1981 MDIV)

**PEMBERTON JAMES F REV** (908)289-0983
7 Hillside Rd Elizabeth NJ 07208 • jayfrank@juno.com • NJ • SP • St Luke Elizabeth NJ • (908)352-5487 • (SL 1999 MDIV)

**PENHALLEGON PHILIP W REV** (320)864-5263
1805 9th St E Glencoe MN 55336 • MNS • SP • Good Shepherd Glencoe MN • (320)864-6157 • (SL 2000 MDIV)

**PENIKIS MICHAEL ARTHUR REV** (810)694-9351
C/O Faith Lutheran Church 12534 Holly Rd Grand Blanc MI 48439-1815 • KS • Assoc • Hope Shawnee KS • (913)631-6940 • (FW 2000 MDIV)

**PENNEKAMP EUGENE F REV** (316)231-0105
1704 Colonial Dr Pittsburg KS 66762-3510 • KS • EM • (SL 1949)

**PENNEKAMP RONALD DAVID REV** (217)424-9997
2812 S Forrest Ln Decatur IL 62521-5415 • rpenne5253@aol.com • CI • Assoc • St Paul Decatur IL • (217)423-6955 • (CQ 1994)

**PEPERKORN TODD A REV** (262)551-9081
2044 24th Ave Kenosha WI 53140-4604 • TPeperkorn@worldnet.att.net • SW • SP • Messiah Kenosha WI • (262)551-8182 • (FW 1996 MDIV STM)

**PEPOON JOHN MARK REV** (972)317-2111
1333 Brazos Blvd Lewisville TX 75077-7612 • TX • EM • (SPR 1961 MDIV)

**PEPPER EVERETT S REV** (573)873-9658
27 Kathryn Ct Camdenton MO 65020 • MO • Assoc • Hope Chapel Osage Beach MO • (573)348-2108 • (SL 2000 MDIV)

**PERA CLEMENS W REV** (206)932-2566
4720 47th Ave SW Seattle WA 98116-4306 • perawest@foxinternet.net • NOW • EM • (SL 1957 MDIV)

**PERA GERHARD A REV** (716)624-1635
80 Monroe St Honeoye Falls NY 14472-1029 • EA • EM • (SL 1954)

**PERA VICTOR H REV** (414)562-5167
4191 N 15th St Milwaukee WI 53209-6908 • pera@execpc.com • SW • EM • (SL 1957 MDIV)

**PEREIRA KEITH R REV** (217)435-9685
181 E Tremont St Waverly IL 62692-1026 • katco@csj.net • CI • SP • Christ Waverly IL • (217)435-9685 • (SL 1985 MDIV)

**PEREZ ANGEL REV** (787)833-7782
PO Box 3085 Mayaguez PR 00681-3085 • luterano@caribe.net • OK • O Miss • Oklahoma Tulsa OK • (CQ 1986)

**PEREZ CLAUDIO SR. REV** (713)926-4621
7439 Azalea St Houston TX 77023-2706 • TX • SP • St John Houston TX • (713)923-5757 • (CQ 1995 MDIV)

**PEREZ-ARCHE ERWIN REV** (305)553-7530
C/O Bay Shore Luth Church 5051 Biscayne Blvd Miami FL 33137-3217 • epereza@aol.com • FG • SP • Bay Shore Miami FL • (305)758-1344 • (SL 1992 MDIV)

**PEREZ-LOPEZ BENITO REV** (305)227-4733
10301 SW 45th St Miami FL 33165-5611 • bperez6950@aol.com • FG • D Miss • Hospital de Alma Homestead FL • (305)247-0459 • (CQ 1995)

**PERLING JOHN FRIEDRICH REV**
C/O Our Savior Lutheran 674 Johnson Parkway St Paul MN 55106 • johnf@perling.com • MNS • SP • Our Saviour Saint Paul MN • (651)774-2396 • (SL 1997 MDIV)

**PERLING R JOHN REV** (310)277-2144
C/O Mt Calvary Lutheran Church 436 S Beverly Dr Beverly Hills CA 90212-4402 • rjohn@perling.com • PSW • SP • Mount Calvary Beverly Hills CA* • (310)277-1164 • (SL 1965 MDIV)

**PERRY M KEITH REV** (612)368-7550
PO Box 42 Carver MN 55315-0042 • pstrperry@aol.com • MNS • SP • Trinity Carver MN • (612)448-3628 • (CQ 1996 MA)

**PERRYMAN DENNIS S REV** (612)767-4441
16045 Nightingale St NW Andover MN 55304-2522 • PastorDsp@aol.com • MNS • Sn/Adm • Family Christ Andover MN • (612)434-7337 • (SPR 1975 MDIV)

**PESKE GERALD W REV** (763)271-4713
1305 E7th St Apt 359 Monticello MN 55362-8174 • MNS • EM • (SPR 1950 MDIV)

**PESKE MARK I REV** (218)755-9132
1015 Bemidji Ave N Bemidji MN 56601-2830 • MNN • Assoc • All Nations Cass Lake MN • (218)335-7767 • (FW 1997 MDIV)

**PETER DAVID J REV** (314)721-8324
21 Seminary Terrace St Louis MO 63105 • PeterD@csl.edu • MO • SHS/C • Missouri Saint Louis MO • (314)317-4550 • (SL 1987 MDIV DMIN)

**PETER JAMES J REV** (440)967-6397
4483 Mapleview Dr Vermilion OH 44089-3407 • daylily325@aol.com • OH • SP • St Matthew Vermilion OH • (440)967-9886 • (SPR 1969)

**PETERMAN GERALD W SR. REV** (940)549-8337
RR 1 Box 348 Graham TX 76450-9719 • janpete@digitalpassage.com • TX • SP • Faith Graham TX* • (817)549-5155 • (CQ 1984)

**PETERS CURTIS H REV** (812)948-8711
1605 Hedden Ct New Albany IN 47150-2571 • curtandpam@earthlink.net • IN • SP • Concordia Louisville KY • (502)585-4459 • (SL 1969 MDIV PHD)

**PETERS EDGAR L REV** (217)379-3778
962 E Summer St Paxton IL 60957-1800 • CI • SP • Immanuel Loda IL • (217)386-2232 • (CQ 1994 MDIV)

**PETERS EDMUND A REV** (219)232-7436
1910 Peachtree Ln South Bend IN 46617-1835 • pastorpeters@trinityl.org • IN • EM • (SL 1950)

**PETERS EDWARD F REV** (610)251-2586
93 N Bacton Hill Rd Lot B-3 Frazer PA 19355-1001 • NW • S Miss • North Wisconsin Wausau WI • (SL 1957 STM THD)

**PETERS GREG REV**
12095 W Bowles Pl Littleton CO 80127-2317 • RM • Sn/Adm • Hosanna Littleton CO • (303)973-1706 • (CQ 1981)

**PETERS KIRK L REV**
Prince Of Peace Luth Church 1200 Fort St Buffalo WY 82834 • WY • SP • Prince Peace Buffalo WY • (307)684-5470 • (FW 1998 MDIV)

**PETERS LARRY A REV** (931)645-5890
203 Rachel Ct Clarksville TN 37043-1763 • lapatglc@juno.com • MDS • SP • Grace Clarksville TN • (931)647-6750 • (FW 1980 MDIV)

**PETERS MARK D REV** (217)732-8095
1 Meadow Lane Lincoln IL 62656 • mpeters@colint.com • CI • SP • Faith Lincoln IL • (217)732-4901 • (FW 1980 MDIV)

**PETERSEN DAVID H REV**
4024 S Harrison Fort Wayne IN 46807 • petersen@avci.net • EN • SP • Redeemer Fort Wayne IN • (219)744-2585 • (FW 1996 MDIV)

**PETERSEN JOHN M REV** (719)687-8763
2990 Sunnywood Ave Woodland Park CO 80863-9423 • RM • EM • (SPR 1973 MDIV)

**PETERSEN LORMAN M REV** (920)830-6866
No A204 2600 S Heritage Woods Dr Appleton WI 54915-1408 • NW • EM • (SL 1940 MST THD)

**PETERSEN REYNOLD B REV** (320)859-3857
PO Box 411 Osakis MN 56360-0411 • MNN • EM • (SPR 1973 MDIV)

**PETERSEN ROBERT L REV** (320)763-6763
13144 Maple Cir Dr SE Glenwood MN 56334 • revpetersen@juno.com • MNN • EM • (SL 1965 MDIV)

**PETERSEN THOMAS E REV** (512)452-1038
6709 Shoal Creek Blvd Austin TX 78757-4380 • TX • EM • (SL 1956 MDIV)

**PETERSEN THOMAS EDGAR REV** (608)873-5718
817 Johnson St Stoughton WI 53589-1317 • Lutheran@tds.net • SW • SP • Good Shep By Lk Stoughton WI • (608)873-5924 • (CQ 1988 MDIV)

**PETERSON CARL L REV** (706)565-0066
5141 Yosemite Dr Columbus GA 31907-1728 • FG • SP • Redeemer Columbus GA • (706)322-5026 • (FW 1989 MDIV)

**PETERSON CLIFFORD H REV** (914)779-5392
1 Concordia Pl Bronxville NY 10708-1802 • chp@concordia-ny.edu • AT • SHS/C • Atlantic Bronxville NY • (914)337-5700 • (SL 1953 STM DED)

**PETERSON DAVID A REV** (716)226-8735
23 Pine View Hts Avon NY 14414-1340 • dpeter47@frontiernet.net • EA • SP • St Mark Mendon NY • (716)624-1766 • (FW 1987 STM)

**PETERSON ERIC G REV** (301)277-5366
6501 Adelphi Rd Hyattsville MD 20782-2009 • epeter7574@aol.com • SE • Sn/Adm • Grace La Plata MD • (301)932-0963 • (SL 1970 MED MDIV DMIN)

**PETERSON GARY I REV** (504)769-7148
550 Lee Dr Apt 105 Baton Rouge LA 70808-4908 • SO • Cmp P • Chapel Cross Baton Rouge LA • (504)383-2962 • (SL 1993 MDIV)

**PETERSON GERALD REV** (612)571-8655
776 63rd Ave NE Fridley MN 55432-5043 • MNS • EM • (CQ 1980 MTH)

**PETERSON H LEROY REV** (932)906-1978
100 W Michigan Ave Ironwood MI 49938 • NW • EM • (SPR 1968)

**PETERSON HOWARD M REV** (509)624-9411
3003 S Bernard St Spokane WA 99203-1737 • NOW • EM • (SL 1957)

**PETERSON IVAN E REV** (314)293-0708
6575 Towne Woods Dr Saint Louis MO 63129-4521 • ipjp72@aol.com • MO • 06/1998 06/2000 • (SL 1971 MDIV)

**PETERSON KEVIN M REV** (303)288-6170
6790 Monaco St Commerce City CO 80022-2875 • RM • SP • Our Saviour Commerce City CO • (303)288-9577 • (FW 1999 MDIV)

**PETERSON NORMAN F REV** (715)357-6135
C/O St Matthew Luth Church PO Box 128 Almena WI 54805-0128 • pztzrszn@win.bright.net • NW • SP • St Matthew Almena WI* • (715)357-3267 • (SPR 1972 MDIV)

**PETERSON RICHARD J REV** (360)532-4943
621 3rd Ave Aberdeen WA 98520-1914 • revpete@techline.com • NOW • Sn/Adm • Calvary Aberdeen WA • (360)532-3980 • (SL 1964 MDIV)

**PETERSON ROY R REV** (414)644-6872
4620 Lakeview Circle Slinger WI 53086-9520 • revpete@execpc.com • SW • Assoc • Grace Menomonee Falls WI • (262)251-0670 • (CQ 1998 MA)

**PETERSON RUSSELL J REV** (920)682-0146
1231 S 32nd St Manitowoc WI 54220-5407 • SW • EM • (SPR 1966)

**PETERSON STANLEY R REV** (707)254-9510
3075 Beecham St Napa CA 94558-3005 • CNH • SP • Faith Napa CA • (707)224-4214 • (SL 1963 MDIV)

**PETERSON WENDELL P REV** (715)675-5822
2524 N 76th Ave Wausau WI 54401-9779 • petersonw@G2A.net • NW • O Sp Min • North Wisconsin Wausau WI • (SL 1966 STM MDIV)

**PETRI MICHAEL J REV**
245 Canterbury Cir Council Bluffs IA 51503 • revpetri@dct.com • IW • SP • Timothy Council Bluffs IA • (712)323-0693 • (SL 1983 MDIV)

**PETRICH DAVID J DR**
1402 S 4th St Apt 2 Marshall MN 56258-2264 • MNN • 01/2000 • (FW 1985 MDIV)

**PETROWSKY ARTHUR E REV** (719)596-5654
6689 Showhorse Ct Colorado Springs CO 80922 • RM • EM • (SL 1957)

**PETT PAUL K REV** (309)787-2531
509 Bruce Ave Milan IL 61264-3358 • revpett@aol.com • CI • Sn/Adm • St Matthew Milan IL • (309)787-4295 • (FW 1990 MDIV)

**PETTEY RICK L REV** (573)783-2740
401 Armory St Fredericktown MO 63645-1343 • MO • SP • Trinity Fredericktown MO* • (573)783-2740 • (FW 1991 MDIV)

**PETZKE KARL G REV** (208)773-9160
238 Sunset Dr Post Falls ID 83854-9525 • kmpetzke@juno.com • NOW • EM • * • (SPR 1972 MA MDIV)

**PETZOLDT SHIRREL REV** (419)531-3457
4908 San Joaquin Dr Toledo OH 43615-6106 • OH • P Df • Good Shep Deaf Toledo OH • (419)536-3370 • (CQ 1976 MDIV)

**PEYMANN DONALD R DR** (713)729-5574
5647 Wigton Houston TX 77096 • peymann@pdq.net • TX • D Miss • Texas Austin TX • (SPR 1969 MDIV)

**PFAFF RICHARD C REV** (281)464-2447
10803 Kirkwell Drive Houston TX 77089-3004 • txpfaff@flash.net • TX • Assoc • Zion Pasadena TX • (281)478-5849 • (SL 1983 MDIV)

**PFAFF ROBERT D REV** (423)346-7704
PO Box 766 Wartburg TN 37887-0766 • MDS • SP • St Paul Wartburg TN • (423)346-3554 • (SL 1983 MDIV)

**PFAFFE DANIEL M REV** (715)672-5616
608 3rd Ave E Durand WI 54736-1417 • NW • SP • St John Durand WI* • (715)672-8787 • (FW 1990 MDIV)

**PFANSTIEL BARRY L REV** (573)334-2870
1063 Stewart Dr Cape Girardeau MO 63701-3537 • barryp@ldd.net • MO • SP • Good Shepherd Cape Girardeau MO • (573)335-3974 • (SL 1974 MDIV)

**PFEFFER DEAN R REV** (813)752-1164
4327 Kipling Ave Plant City FL 33567-7225 • pastorpfeffer@juno.com • FG • SP • Hope Plant City FL • (813)752-4622 • (SL 1994 MDIV MPAD)

**PFEIFFER GILBERT H REV** (727)733-8298
860 Virginia St Apt 211 Dunedin FL 34698-6733 • AT • EM • (SL 1935)

**PFEIL ROBERT A REV**
C/O Bridget Bell W7644 West Lane Fond du Lac WI 54937 • bobpfeil@elcat.kg • NW • S Miss • North Wisconsin Wausau WI • (FW 1984 MDIV)

**PFINGSTEN MICHAEL D REV** (815)943-0820
C/O St Paul Lutheran Church 1601 N Garfield Rd Harvard IL 600339-174 • pfngs104@mc.net • NI • SP • St Paul Harvard IL • (815)943-5330 • (FW 1988 MDIV)

**PFLIEGER RICHARD C SR. DR** (515)957-9945
922 Robin Cir Altoona IA 50009-2711 • rmpflieger@aol.com • IE • EM • (SL 1961 MDIV DMIN)

**PFLUEGER IRVIN E REV** (561)369-0499
1180 SW 24th Ave Boynton Beach FL 33426-7450 • NJ • EM • (SPR 1955)

**PFLUEGER JAMES K REV**
13633 183rd St Cerritos CA 90703-8940 • PSW • SP • Concordia Cerritos CA • (562)926-7416 • (SL 1970 MDIV)

**PFLUG JEFFERY D REV** (812)273-5716
323 Hillcrest Dr Madison IN 47250-2921 • jdpflug@juno.com • IN • SP • Faith Madison IN • (812)273-1371 • (SL 1993 MDIV)

**PFLUG MARK R REV** (616)754-4886
C/O Mt Calvary Luth Church 908 W Oak St Greenville MI 48838-2149 • mclc@iserv.net • MI • SP • Mount Calvary Greenville MI • (616)754-4886 • (SL 1966 MDIV)

**PFLUGER RONALD M REV** (501)855-0272
C/O Bella Vista Lutheran Churc 1990 Forest Hills Blvd Bella Vista AR 72714-2389 • Rspfluger@aol.com • MDS • SP • Bella Vista Bella Vista AR • (501)855-0272 • (SPR 1973 MDIV)

**PFLUGHOEFT DARREN M REV** (808)676-9446
94-1125 Ka Uka Blvd Apt D-303 Waipahu HI 96797-4426 • dcpflug@gateway.net • CNH • SP • Trinity Wahiawa HI • (808)621-6033 • (FW 1999 MDIV)

**PFLUGHOEFT MARK E REV** (219)696-0447
621 W Commercial Ave Lowell IN 46356-2221 • pflugs@comnetcom.net • IN • SP • Trinity Lowell IN • (219)696-9338 • (FW 1980 MDIV)

**PFOTENHAUER PAUL E REV** (831)475-2916
2600 Monterey Ave Soquel CA 95073-2804 • pfoty@sasquatch.com • CNH • EM • (SL 1952 MA MDIV)

**PFOTENHAUER PAUL J REV** (651)739-1522
7217 Coachwood Rd Woodbury MN 55125-1541 • pfotenhauer@juno.com • MNS • Sn/Adm • Woodbury Woodbury MN • (651)739-5144 • (SPR 1958 MAR MAR)

**PFOTENHAUER PAUL JAY REV** (630)964-3987
4930 Douglas Rd Downers Grove IL 60515-3818 • raechel4pj@earthlink.net • NI • SP • Bethel Westmont IL • (630)968-3232 • (SL 1992 MDIV)

**PHELPS DONALD REYNOLDS REV** (815)895-8478
330 S Main St Sycamore IL 60178 • drp1216@aol.com • NI • Sn/Adm • St John Sycamore IL • (815)895-4477 • (SL 1996 MDIV)

**PHIFER PHILLIP L REV** (512)556-0422
PO Box 884 Lampasas TX 76550-0884 • pjphifer@ltex.net • TX • SP • Faith Lampasas TX • (512)556-3514 • (SL 1998 MDIV)

**PHILIPP EARL D REV** (405)354-6008
1005 Oakwood Dr Yukon OK 73099-4842 • OK • SP • St John Hinton OK • (405)542-6472 • (SL 1965 MDIV)

**PHILIPP JOHN C REV** (847)336-8346
825 Hickory St Waukegan IL 60085-3835 • NI • Inst C • Northern Illinois Hillside IL • (SPR 1972 MDIV MS)

**PHILLIPS MICHAEL A REV** (419)229-2345
2120 Lakewood Ave Lima OH 45805 • maphil@wcoil.com • OH • Assoc • Immanuel Lima OH • (419)222-2541 • (SL 1992 MDIV)

**PHILLIPS THOMAS PETER REV** (515)472-6441
710 W Tyler Ave Fairfield IA 52556-4049 • tomrevph@kdsi.net • IE • SP • Immanuel Fairfield IA • (515)472-5333 • (SL 1991 MDIV)

**PHILLIPS TIMOTHY J REV** (609)324-7964
11 Holloway Ln Bordentown NJ 08505 • hclcbrdn@bellatlantic.net • NJ • SP • Holy Cross Bordentown NJ • (609)298-2880 • (SL 1989 MDIV)

**PHILP PAUL A REV** (507)333-5436
2 S W Aspen CT Faribault MN 55021 • psphilp@means.net • MNS • Assoc • Peace Faribault MN • (507)334-9610 • (SL 1999 MDIV)

**PHIPPS RALPH A DR** (561)732-4964
2504 SW 23rd Cranbrook Dr Boynton Beach FL 33436-5708 • ralphaphi@juno.com • FG • EM • (SL 1954 LITTD)

**PIAZZA ADRIAN L REV** (317)773-3669
1294 Clinton St Noblesville IN 46060-1659 • revpiazza@earthlink.com • IN • Sn/Adm • Christ Noblesville IN • (317)773-3669 • (SL 1989 MDIV)

**PIAZZA CHARLES T REV** (765)289-3905
4205 N Redding Rd Muncie IN 47304-1340 • IN • EM • (SPR 1964)

**PICARD JOEL T REV** (580)327-0877
826 3rd St Alva OK 73717 • OK • SP • Zion Alva OK • (405)327-0510 • (SL 1997 MDIV)

**PICK WAYNE T REV** (870)863-9398
104 Alderman Dr El Dorado AR 71730-2936 • wdjsp@ipa.net • MDS • SP • Our Savior El Dorado AR • (870)862-1443 • (SL 1979 MDIV)

**PICKETT ARTHUR REV** (440)247-4585
3841 Wiltshire Rd Chagrin Falls OH 44022-1151 • OH • EM • (SPR 1962)

**PICKHARDT MICHAEL A REV** (262)569-9352
W202 Valley Rd Oconomowoc WI 53066 • pickhardt@netwurx.net • SW • Asst • St Paul Oconomowoc WI • (414)567-5001 • (SL 1987 MDIV)

**PIEL THOMAS C REV** (414)357-6257
8156 N Granville Rd Milwaukee WI 53224-2947 • SW • SP • Nazareth Milwaukee WI • (414)354-2650 • (SL 1976 MDIV)

**PIEPENBRINK KENNETH G REV** (623)561-8892
21523 N 57th Ave Glendale AZ 85308-6228 • PSW • SP • King Of Kings Phoenix AZ • (602)973-0500 • (SPR 1962)

**PIEPENBRINK WILLIS R REV** (815)584-3407
515 E Stonewall Rd Dwight IL 60420-9656 • NI • SP • Trinity Dwight IL • (815)584-3407 • (CQ 1983 MA)

**PIEPER WALTER A REV**
500 Waterman Ave #202 Mount Dora FL 32757-9567 • FG • EM • (SPR 1930)

**PIEPER WILFRED L REV** (612)441-6236
18174 Hudson St NW Elk River MN 55330-1840 • MNS • SP • St John Elk River MN • (763)441-3646 • (SL 1990 MA)

**PIEPKORN GARY A REV**
625-C Perimeter Rd Mountainview CA 94043 • gary.piepkorn@onizuka.af.mil • TX • M Chap • Texas Austin TX • (FW 1981 MDIV)

**PIEPLOW CHARLES F REV** (205)591-7386
931 42nd St S Birmingham AL 35222-4235 • chuck.pieplow@bhs.ala • SO • Inst C • Southern New Orleans LA • (SL 1967 MDIV)

**PIEPLOW RICHARD E REV** (912)244-0143
C/O Messiah Luth Church 500 Baytree Rd Valdosta GA 31602-2810 • messiah@planttel.net • FG • SP • Messiah Valdosta GA • (912)244-0143 • (CQ 1980 MDIV)

**PIERCE EARL J REV** (515)240-6835
633 39th St Des Moines IA 50312-3309 • ejpierce@aol.com • IW • D Ex/S • Iowa West Fort Dodge IA • (SL 1987 MDIV)

**PIERCE JAMES R REV** (732)363-0621
650 Aldrich Rd Howell NJ 07731-1913 • jrphwll@worldshare.net • NJ • SP • Prince Peace Howell NJ • (732)363-0732 • (SL 1970 STM MDIV)

**PIERCE KENT D REV** (330)678-8204
1090 Munroe Falls Kent Rd Kent OH 44240 • kpierce@kent.edu • OH • Cmp P • Faith Kent OH • (330)673-6633 • (SL 1999 MDIV)

**PIERCE ROBERT J REV** (308)284-6015
470 Rd East G S Ogallala NE 69153-5332 • NEB • SP • St John Ogallala NE • (308)284-6015 • (SL 1966)

**PIERING ARNOLD EDWARD REV** (219)483-7441
3430 Woodrow Ave Fort Wayne IN 46805-2218 • pastor@emmanuellutheran.org • IN • Sn/Adm • Emmanuel Fort Wayne IN • (219)423-1369 • (CQ 1996 MA)

**PIERSON MARION F REV** (440)327-6036
32472 Sourbrook Ln North Ridgeville OH 44039-2376 • OH • EM • (SPR 1959)

**PIERSON RICHARD A REV** (970)332-4718
514 Dexter St Wray CO 80758 • rapierson@plains.net • RM • SP • Calvary Wray CO • (970)332-4630 • (SL 1972 MDIV)

**PIES FRANK J REV** (248)887-9695
13895 Hibner Rd Hartland MI 48353-2414 • EN • Sn/Adm • Our Savior Hartland MI • (248)887-4300 • (SPR 1972 MDIV STM DMIN)

**PIESCER MICHAEL A REV** (03)3261-5266
Tokyo Lutheran Center 1-2-32 Fujimi Chiyoda ku Tokyo 102-0071 JAPAN • mpiescer@tke.att.ne.jp • CNH • Inst C • Calif/Nevada/Hawaii San Francisco CA • (415)468-2336 • (SL 1998 MDIV)

**PIKALEK THOMAS J REV** (701)239-4813
1116 7th St N Fargo ND 58102-2602 • ND • 06/1996 06/2000 • (SL 1973)

**PILLACK ROLAND E REV** (515)276-6492
4048 42nd St Des Moines IA 50310-2816 • IW • EM • (SPR 1970 MDIV MED)

**PILLER ROBERT H REV** (603)644-1857
627 Weston Rd Manchester NH 03103-3197 • rhpiller@mediaone.net • NE • SP • Immanuel Manchester NH • (603)622-1514 • (SC 1986 MDIV)

**PINGEL ALLEN L REV** (414)258-7118
570 N 95th St Milwaukee WI 53226-4435 • SW • SP • St Mark Milwaukee WI • (414)258-7118 • (SL 1985 MDIV)

**PINGEL DEAN T REV** (715)384-7673
906 W 6th St Marshfield WI 54449-3503 • NW • SP • Immanuel Hewitt WI • (715)384-5153 • (SL 1985 MDIV)

**PINGEL DENNIS L REV** (608)362-1614
2740 N Wood Dr Beloit WI 53511-2225 • SW • SP • Messiah Beloit WI • (608)365-4724 • (SL 1969 MDIV)

**PINGEL GILBERT H REV** (803)738-8166
3703 Custer Loop Columbia SC 29206-5332 • gpingel322@aol.com • NI • M Chap • Northern Illinois Hillside IL • (SL 1965 MDIV)

**PINGEL JAMES A DR** (608)837-8345
1183 Abbott Ln Sun Prairie WI 53590-8901 • apingel@chorus.net • SW • SP • Bethlehem Sun Prairie WI • (608)837-7446 • (SL 1965 MDIV DMIN)

**PINGEL JOHN L REV** (412)847-8727
230 Stuber Rd New Brighton PA 15066-3328 • EA • SP • Mount Olive Beaver Falls PA • (724)843-0952 • (SL 1983 MDIV MA)

**PINGEL RICHARD W REV** (402)385-2605
C/O St John Lutheran Church 2175 15th Rd Pender NE 68047-4407 • rwpingel@midlands.net • NEB • SP • St John Pender NE • (402)385-2447 • (SL 1971 MDIV)

**PINNT WALTER M REV** (402)371-8196
411 Blaine St Norfolk NE 68701-5380 • wmpinnt@conpoint.com • NEB • EM • (SL 1950)

**PINTA ROBERT JOHN REV** (505)891-3809
761 Comanche Rd SE Rio Rancho NM 87124-3068 • rdjcp@email.msn.com • RM • SP • Shepherd/Hills Rio Rancho NM • (505)891-7677 • (CQ 1995 MTH)

**PIOTTER ALAN G DR** (707)996-8481
474 Linda Dr Sonoma CA 95476-5659 • revbigal@vom.com • CNH • SP • Faith Sonoma CA • (707)996-7365 • (SL 1969 MDIV DMIN)

**PIOTTER KEITH ALAN REV** (319)332-7046
3106 Dundee Ln Bettendorf IA 52722-3329 • IE • SP • Our Savior Bettendorf IA • (319)332-5141 • (SL 1991 MDIV)

**PIPER MICHAEL G REV** (636)828-5060
154 W Hwy D PO Box 334 New Melle MO 63365-0334 • stpaulnm@primary.net • MO • SP • St Paul New Melle MO • (636)828-5616 • (FW 1988 MDIV)

**PITCHER JOHN C REV** (360)658-5885
8010 55th Ave NE Marysville WA 98270-3166 • NOW • EM • (FW 1990 MDIV)

**PITTELKO DEAN D REV** (920)451-1549
1643 Settlement Trl Sheboygan WI 53081 • pastordp@excel.net • EN • SP • St Mark Sheboygan WI • (920)458-4343 • (SL 1988 MDIV)

**PITTELKO ROGER D DR** (847)437-3008
85 Brantwood Ave Elk Grove Village IL 60007 • emep@juno.com • EN • SHS/C • English Farmington MI • (SL 1957 MDIV MST DMIN DD)

**PLACKNER JAMES J REV** (630)462-8584
OS 455 Summit Winfield IL 60190 • plackner@megsinet.net • NI • SP • Christ Our Savior Winfield IL • (630)665-5110 • (SL 1967 MDIV)

**PLATH WILLIAM H REV** (916)393-0833
637 Riverlake Way Sacramento CA 95831-1122 • glc-lcms@msn.com • CNH • SP • Greenhaven Sacramento CA • (916)428-8449 • (CQ 1985 MDIV)

**PLATZER MARTIN M DR** (770)476-9374
2711 Whippoorwill Cir Duluth GA 30097 • FG • Inst C • Florida-Georgia Orlando FL • (SL 1972 MDIV MTH DMIN)

**PLAUTZ WILLIAM C REV** (715)723-6273
735 Woodward Ave Chippewa Falls WI 54729-3283 • NW • Sn/Adm • Faith Chippewa Falls WI • (715)723-7754 • (FW 1981 MDIV)

**PLEDGER PHILLIP M REV** (909)790-1863
C/O Good Shepherd Luth Ch 34215 Avenue E Yucaipa CA 92399-2577 • ppledger@cybertime.net • PSW • SP • Good Shepherd Yucaipa CA • (909)790-1863 • (FW 1984 MDIV)

**PLESS JOHN T REV** (219)492-2159
5007-7 Truemper Way Fort Wayne IN 46835 • plessjt@mail.ctsfw.edu • IN • SHS/C • Indiana Fort Wayne IN • (CQ 1983 MDIV)

**PLITT CARVEL V REV** (707)984-8805
47275 Redwood Hwy 101N PO Box 34 Laytonville CA 95454-0034 • CNH • EM • (SPR 1952 MA)

**PLUENNEKE CLINTON L REV**
5951 Wisdom Creek Rd Dallas TX 75249-2823 • cpluenneke@aol.com • TX • Assoc • Holy Cross Arlington TX • (817)451-7561 • (SL 1998 MDIV)

**PLUMP JOHN T REV** (909)532-9781
PO Box 331 La Verne CA 91750-0331 • PSW • 12/1994 • (FW 1980 MDIV)

**PLVAN GEORGE D REV** (804)634-0722
309 Weaver Ave Emporia VA 23847-1231 • gdplvn@3rddoor.com • S • EM • (SL 1956 MDIV)

**POCKAT STEVEN N** (715)752-4854
E 7759 State Hwy 22 Bear Creek WI 54922 • NW • SP • Trinity Bear Creek WI* • (715)752-3601 • (FW 2000 MDIV)

**PODOLL LYNN A REV** (217)834-3121
2401 County Rd 400 N Broadlands IL 61816 • podoll@newman.net • CI • SP • Immanuel Broadlands IL • (217)834-3289 • (SL 1967 MDIV)

**POEDEL DAVID G DR** (520)762-1139
3180 E Cardenas Dr Vail AZ 85641-9641 • padredave@juno.com • EN • SP • Holy Trinity Tucson AZ • (520)294-8851 • (CQ 2000 MED DMIN)

**POELLET DEAN R REV** (701)776-5385
711 4th Ave SW Rugby ND 58368 • ND • SP • St Paul Rugby ND* • (701)776-6739 • (FW 1999 MDIV)

**POELLOT LUTHER REV** (314)487-1598
753 Buckley Rd Saint Louis MO 63125-5347 • MO • EM • * • (SL 1937 LITTD)

**POEPPEL MANFRED O REV** (814)756-0806
102 Norton Rd Albion PA 16401-1014 • pfredp@juno.com • EA • SP • Holy Trinity Albion PA • (814)756-3426 • (SL 1995 MDIV)

**POERSCHKE JAMES P REV** (310)375-9349
4653 Rockbluff Dr Rllng Hls Est CA 90274-1513 • PSW • SP • Mount Olive Rancho Palos Verdes CA • (310)377-8541 • (SL 1960 MDIV)

**POGANSKI DAVID F REV** (530)887-1934
249 Nation Dr Auburn CA 95603-3629 • dfpogostpaul@neworld.net • CNH • SP • St Paul Auburn CA • (530)885-5378 • (FW 1980 MDIV DMIN)

**POGANSKI DONALD J REV** (805)524-4166
250 E Telegraph Rd Spc 165 Fillmore CA 93015-2157 • CNH • EM • (SPR 1955)

**POGGEMEIER WILLIS F REV** (417)235-3623
7739 Lawrence 2190 Monett MO 65708-9117 • MO • EM • (SL 1958)

**POHANKA JOHN C REV** (517)631-6388
1104 Airfield Ln Midland MI 48642-4766 • jpohanka@aol.com • MI • Sn/Adm • St John Midland MI • (517)835-5861 • (SL 1973 STM)

**POHL GARY L REV** (210)481-1464
22307 Navasota Cir San Antonio TX 78259-2602 • garyp@lfot.org • TX • 05/1999 • (SPR 1971 MTH)

**POHL MERLIN S REV** (334)427-0444
1723 E By Pass Apt B3 Andalusia AL 36420-2419 • SO • SP • New Hope Andalusia AL • (334)427-1584 • (CQ 1963 MED MED)

**POHL ROBERT H REV** (781)826-3263
541 Broadway Hanover MA 02339-2743 • NE • SP • Of The Cross Hanover MA • (781)826-5121 • (SL 1972 MDIV)

**POHL WAYNE A REV**
30227 Willow Springs Rd Flat Rock MI 48134-2747 • MI • Sn/Adm • St Paul Trenton MI • (734)676-1565 • (SPR 1966 MDIV)

**POHLAND WALTER A REV** (956)689-6169
180 E Wood Ave Raymondville TX 78580-3044 • pohland@vsta.com • TX • SP • Mount Calvary Raymondville TX • (956)689-2224 • (SL 1988 MDIV)

**POHLERS DONALD L REV**
2613 Marengo Dr Perry IA 50220-2419 • CI • EM • (SL 1964 STM MDIV)

**POHLIG JAMES N REV** (704)843-5295
6219 Dogwood Ln Waxhaw NC 28173 • jim-annie3pohlig@sil.org • SE • 06/1988 06/2000 • (SL 1977 MDIV MA)

**POHLOD GEORGE M REV** (216)221-0209
3554 Palmer Drive Rocky River OH 44116 • OH • EM • (SL 1959 MDIV)

**POLACK WILLIAM GUSTAVE IV REV** (303)424-1375
8417 W 79th Pl Arvada CO 80005-4326 • RM • EM • (SL 1939 MED MDIV)

**POLANSKY ROGER W REV**
1058 Double Eagle Ave SE Rochester MN 55904-8020 • MNS • EM • (SL 1957)

**POLEGE DONALD R REV** (701)683-5347
PO Box 582 Lisbon ND 58054-0582 • dpolege@corpcomm.net • ND • SP • Redeemer Lisbon ND • (701)683-4349 • (SL 1988 MDIV)

**POLK JOHN C SR. REV** (918)743-1119
1643 E 55th Pl Tulsa OK 74105-6924 • OK • SP • Bethlehem Adair OK • (918)785-2994 • (SPR 1959)

**POLLATZ PAUL A REV** (618)889-3543
C/O Norwalk Luth Church PO Box 119 Onekama MI 49675-0119 • MI • SP • Trinity Onekama MI* • (231)889-3543 • (SPR 1969 MDIV)

**POLLATZ RAYMOND REV** (616)972-7812
8125 Highland Trl Stanwood MI 49346-9756 • rpollatz@juno.com • MI • SP • Chapel Lakes Mecosta MI • (231)972-7891 • (SPR 1965 MDIV)

**POLLEX PAUL A REV** (519)631-1924
15 St Joseph St St Thomas ON N5R 1S8 CANADA • EN • SP • Chapel Lakes Mecosta MI • (SPR 1965 MDIV)

**POLLOCK ROGER J REV** (847)464-1702
40W119 Sturbridge Way Elgin IL 60123-8637 • rogerpo@aol.com • NI • Sn/Adm • Good Shepherd Elgin IL • (847)741-7788 • (SPR 1975 MDIV)

**POLZIN JOSEPH M REV** (770)516-1688
1768 Blackwillow Dr Marietta GA 30066-1952 • jo10nis@aol.com • FG • SP • Timothy Woodstock GA • (770)928-2812 • (SL 1985 MDIV)

**POMPLUN RAYMOND L REV** (605)225-7099
821 16th Ave NE Aberdeen SD 57401-1444 • SD • SP • St Paul Leola SD* • (605)439-3531 • (SL 1961 MDIV)

**PONSETI SIDNEY J REV** (504)888-5481
4008 Taft Park Metairie LA 70002-4454 • SO • SP • Mount Calvary New Orleans LA* • (504)945-9981 • (SPR 1962 MDIV)

**POOCK DONALD F REV**
303 N Lake St Aurora IL 60506 • NI • S Miss • Northern Illinois Hillside IL • (SPR 1972 STM)

**POOL CHARLES H REV** (616)228-6783
7201 S Cedarview Ln Cedar MI 49621-8509 • gpool@remci.k12.mi.us • MI • EM • (SL 1945 MA)

**POOL JOHN M REV** (316)722-3811
9100 W 9th St N Wichita KS 67212-4108 • KS • EM • (SPR 1962)

**POOLE DONNIE L REV** (712)272-3739
C/O St Peter Lutheran Church PO Box 393 Newell IA 50568-0393 • IW • SP • St Peter Newell IA • (712)272-3739 • (FW 1990 MDIV)

**POOLE JOHN D REV** (704)784-4560
359 Cozart Ct SW Concord NC 28025-5495 • SE • EM • (GB 1952)

**POOVEY DAVID L REV** (406)896-0681
5715 Kaitlin Rd Billings MT 59101-9378 • dlpoovey@uswest.net • MT • Sn/Adm • Trinity Billings MT • (406)245-3984 • (CQ 1979 MDIV)

**POPE JOHN F REV** (602)978-1254
4542 W Wagoner Rd Glendale AZ 85308-1525 • jfpope@aol.com • PSW • EM • (SL 1969 MDIV)

**POPP KEVIN REV** (314)428-2624
2620 White Manor Ct Saint Louis MO 63114 • kevpopp@aol.com • MO • 03/2000 • (SL 1981 MDIV STM)

**POPP MILTON N REV** (520)567-5954
4760 N Valancius Way Rimrock AZ 86335-5725 • PSW • EM • (SPR 1950 MDIV)

**POPPE CLINT K REV** (402)420-6367
705 Glenarbor Cir Lincoln NE 68512-1744 • huskerfan76@netzero.net • NEB • SP • Good Shepherd Lincoln NE • (402)423-7639 • (SL 1998 MDIV)

**POPPE JOHN C REV** (920)499-7574
1658 Orchid Ln Green Bay WI 54313-6077 • revpoppe205@cs.com • NW • Sn/Adm • Redeemer Green Bay WI • (920)499-1033 • (SPR 1970 MDIV)

**POPPE LEONARD B REV** (601)328-5987
C/O Our Savior Luth Church 1211 18th Ave N Columbus MS 39701-2305 • pastor-poppe@hotmail.com • SO • SP • Our Savior Columbus MS • (601)328-1757 • (FW 1987 MDIV)

**POPPE RANDAL A REV** (262)633-9592
1123 Monroe Ave Racine WI 53405-2849 • rcpoppe@juno.com • SW • Sn/Adm • Grace Racine WI • (262)633-4831 • (FW 1983 MDIV)

**POPPE RAYMOND A REV** (319)885-6678
26012 Silver Ln Shell Rock IA 50670-9333 • IE • EM • (LS 1958)

**PORATH NORMAN E REV** (402)352-8462
310 W 19th St Schuyler NE 68661-1172 • np83710@alltel.net • NEB • SP • Trinity Schuyler NE* • (402)352-2307 • (SPR 1965 MTH)

**PORATH SCOTT T REV** (402)781-2776
100 South 4th Eagle NE 68347 • revporath@alltel.net • NEB • SP • Immanuel Eagle NE • (402)781-2190 • (FW 1991 MDIV)

**PORTER ARTHUR L REV** (504)243-1277
10501 Curran Blvd - Apt 18G New Orleans LA 70127-5156 • SO • Assoc • Prince Of Peace New Orleans LA • (504)242-2636 • (FW 2000 MDIV)

**PORTER DONALD C REV** (507)645-4438
803 Winona St Northfield MN 55057-2515 • porter@rconnect.com • MNS • SP • Trinity Northfield MN • (507)645-4438 • (FW 1980 MDIV)

**PORTER MICHAEL H REV** (219)462-5157
3602 Candlewood Dr Valparaiso IN 46385-8986 • IN • O Sp Min • Indiana Fort Wayne IN • (SL 1984 MDIV)

**PORTERFIELD ROBERT L SR. REV** (775)867-5900
5112 Rivers Edge Dr Fallon NV 89406-5209 • CNH • SP • St John Fallon NV • (702)423-4146 • (SL 1982 MDIV)

**POSSEHL IVER L REV** (507)283-8396
1406 Victory Cir Luverne MN 56156-2116 • ipossehl@rconnect.com • MNS • Assoc • St John Luverne MN • (507)283-2316 • (FW 1982 MDIV)

**POST MARK REV**
C/O Trinity Lutheran Church 300 S Ardmore Ave Villa Park IL 60181 • EN • Assoc • Trinity Villa Park IL • (630)834-3440 • (SL 2000 MDIV)

**POSTEL WILLIAM E REV** (320)732-2779
410 4th St S Long Prairie MN 56347-1615 • wmpostel@rea-alp.com • MNN • SP • Trinity Long Prairie MN • (320)732-2238 • (CQ 1981 MAR)

**POTRATZ KENNETH J REV** (262)781-8435
N53 W14432 Aberdeen Dr Menomonee Falls WI 53051-6866 • kenpotra@gte.net • SW • EM • (CQ 1967 MDIV)

**POTTER JEFFREY R REV** (208)825-5022
1092 S Eden Rd Eden ID 83325-5216 • NOW • SP • Trinity Eden ID • (208)825-5277 • (FW 1987 MDIV)

**POTTHOFF WILLIAM F REV** (253)864-8121
PO Box 731222 Puyallup WA 98373-0050 • NOW • EM • (SL 1960 MA)

**POULOS GEORGE EVANGELOS JR.** (305)251-1959
21721 SW 97 Court Miami FL 33190 • FG • SP • Trinity Miami FL • (305)216-0030 • (CQ 1997 MDIV)

**POULSON QUENTIN G REV** (704)392-7503
4306 Lothar Ridge Ln Charlotte NC 28216-3269 • popax@bellsouth.net • SE • SP • Prince Of Peace Charlotte NC • (704)392-6098 • (SC 1993 MDIV)

**POURCHOT DANIEL REV** (514)735-9389
5955 Wilderton #3J Montreal PQ H3S 2V1 CANADA • EN • EM • (SL 1951 MA THD)

**POWELL CHRIS REV** (615)646-9398
1006 General George Patton Rd Nashville TN 37221-2587 • MDS • SP • Redeemer Nashville TN • (615)646-3150 • (SPR 1974 MDIV)

**POWERS GREGORY JOHN REV**
5260 Stonehedge Blvd Apt 2 Fort Wayne IN 46835-3008 • IN • SHS/C • Indiana Fort Wayne IN • (FW 1992 MDIV)

**POWERS JERRY D REV** (541)296-4584
C/O Faith Lutheran Church 2810 W 10th St The Dalles OR 97058-4237 • revjerr@skyride.net • NOW • SP • Faith The Dalles OR • (503)296-3586 • (FW 1992 MDIV)

**POWERS LLOYD D REV** (480)471-7727
25232 N Abajo Dr Rio Verde AZ 85263 • pastorldp@aol.com • PSW • EM • (SL 1960 MDIV)

**POWERS MARCUS H REV** (920)458-1930
918 Custer Ave Sheboygan WI 53081-6368 • mhpowers@hotmail.com • SW • Sn/Adm • Our Savior Sheboygan WI • (920)452-4005 • (SL 1993 MDIV)

**PRAEUNER DANIEL C REV**
610 E Park Ave Riverton WY 82501-3655 • WY • Assoc • Trinity Riverton WY • (307)856-9340 • (FW 1993 MDIV)

**PRAEUNER HERBERT O REV** (715)845-3268
5712 Lombardy Dr Wausau WI 54401-8059 • praeuner@dwave.net • NW • EM • (SL 1956 MDIV)

**PRAGMAN JAMES H REV** (507)625-1777
200 Opal Ln Mankato MN 56001-5896 • jpragman@prairie.lakes.com • MNS • D Ex/S • Minnesota South Burnsville MN • (SL 1964 MDIV MST THD)

**PRAHL LARRY REV** (262)375-2049
535 Greenfield Dr Grafton WI 53024-1118 • njp1730@aol.com • SW • Sn/Adm • St Paul Grafton WI • (262)377-4659 • (CQ 1983 MED MAR)

**PRALLE LEROY H REV** (785)825-6210
2657 Quail Hollow Dr Salina KS 67401 • KS • SP • Christ King Salina KS • (785)827-7492 • (CQ 1982 MA)

**PRANGE ANTON A REV** (831)394-2163
1073 Paloma Rd Monterey CA 93940-5634 • aprange@juno.com • CNH • SP • Faith Seaside CA • (831)394-1312 • (SL 1967 MDIV)

**PRANGE ERWIN E REV** (612)452-6634
259 Hidden Vly Minnesota City MN 55959-1232 • SE • EM • (SL 1954 MST STM)

**PRANGE PAUL T REV** (314)739-7301
11452 Nora Ct Bridgeton MO 63044-3173 • paulandcarol@prodigy.net • MO • EM • (SL 1963 MDIV)

**PRANGE R DONALD REV** (540)869-6517
5141 Middle Rd Winchester VA 22602-2787 • coramej@visuallink.com • SE • EM • (SL 1957)

**PRANSCHKE SAMUEL R REV** (313)299-0732
24904 Hayes St Taylor MI 48180 • MI • SP • Our Redeemer Taylor MI • (313)291-4400 • (FW 2000)

**PRAULINS JANIS REV** (416)685-3190
C/O Latvian Luth Church 301 Queenston St St Catharines ON L2P 2X5 CANADA • EN • EM • (EU 1940 MTH)

**PRECHT FRED L REV** (618)235-2472
21 Cobblestone Ln Swansea IL 62226-2485 • SI • EM • (SL 1940 MMU STM THD DD)

**PRECHT STEPHEN F REV** (815)233-6234
1040 Appaloosa Dr Freeport IL 61032-7216 • revprecht@aol.com • NI • SP • Our Redeemer Freeport IL • (815)232-6934 • (SL 1980 MDIV)

**PRECUP J L REV** (858)270-7874
5112 New Haven Rd San Diego CA 92117-1934 • TX • M Chap • Texas Austin TX • (SL 1972 MDIV THM)

**PREDOEHL THEODORE G REV** (651)481-0291
208 Nature Way Little Canada MN 55117-1762 • tpredoehl@aol.com • EN • SP • Messiah Forest Lake MN • (612)464-6842 • (SL 1964 MDIV MSED)

**PREECE ROBERT C DR** (972)907-9057
10334 Cimmaron Trl Dallas TX 75243-2520 • rpreece@ziondallas.org • TX • SP • Zion Dallas TX • (214)363-1639 • (SL 1973 MDIV DMIN)

**PREISINGER DON C REV** (760)746-7958
11446 Kaywood Cir Escondido CA 92026-8407 • donpreisinger@home.com • PSW • EM • (SL 1948 MDIV MA MDIV)

**PRELLOP ALFRED C REV** (504)275-0757
1258 Lakemont Dr Baton Rouge LA 70816-1220 • jarprel@ix.netcom.com • SO • EM • (SL 1964 MDIV)

**PRENZLOW ELMER J C SR. REV** (715)568-5683
15794 225th Ave Bloomer WI 54724 • NW • EM • (TH 1953 MS MA DPSY)

**PRESS GOTTFRIED G REV** (334)673-8759
22 Lonie Young Cir Dothan AL 36303-2939 • SO • EM • (SL 1946)

**PRESS MARK G C REV** (812)522-4741
428 Persimmon Dr Seymour IN 47274-8674 • zionseymin@seidata.com • IN • SP • Zion Seymour IN • (812)522-1089 • (FW 1977 MDIV)

**PRESUHN GERALD E REV** (715)375-3510
8725 S Lyman Lake Rd South Range WI 54874 • MNN • EM • (SL 1964 MDIV)

**PREUS DANIEL REV** (314)849-6125
9228 Lavant Dr Saint Louis MO 63126-2714 • dpreus@chi.lcms.org • MO • S Ex/S • Missouri Saint Louis MO • (314)317-4550 • (SPR 1975 MDIV STM)

**PREUS JACOB A O REV** (949)725-3199
1 Charity Irvine CA 92612 • preus@cui.edu • PSW • SHS/C • Pacific Southwest Irvine CA • (949)854-3232 • (SL 1980 STM MDIV THD)

**PREUS KLEMET I REV**
C/O Glory of Christ LC 4040 Hwy 101 N Plymouth MN 55446-2306 • klemjan@worldnet.att.net • MNS • SP • Glory Of Christ Plymouth MN • (612)478-6031 • (SPR 1976 MST)

**PREUS PETER E REV**
7755 Polaris Ln Maple Grove MN 55311 • MNS • SP • Triune God Brooklyn Center MN • (763)561-6470 • (FW 1982 MDIV)

**PREUSS DAVID H DR** (507)723-6230
209 W Central St Springfield MN 56087-1404 • davidpreuss@juno.com • MNS • SP • Zion Springfield MN • (507)723-6230 • (SL 1965 MDIV DMIN)

**PREUSS GERALD F REV** (760)344-6165
1017 Calle Luna Brawley CA 92227 • GFP051338@aol.com • PSW • EM • (CQ 1993 MMFC)

**PREWITT JEFFERY S REV** (414)725-1445
1285 Cooke Rd Neenah WI 54956-1967 • newhope@vbe.com • SW • SP • New Hope Neenah WI • (920)725-4354 • (FW 1983 MDIV)

**PRICE GEORGE W REV** (512)542-7024
15 Winter Haven Ln Brownsville TX 78521 • TX • EM • (SPR 1963)

**PRICE JAMES MICHAEL REV** (254)754-0644
1901 La Porte Dr Waco TX 76710-2545 • TX • SP • St Mark Waco TX • (254)754-0644 • (SL 1997 MDIV)

**PRIESS EDGAR M REV** (816)781-2390
1317 Craig Dr Liberty MO 64068-1307 • MO • EM • (SL 1949)

**PRIESZ PAUL A REV**
18125 American Beauty Dr #175 Santa Clanta CA 91351 • PSW • EM • (SPR 1949)

**PRIFOGLE MITCHELL J REV** (702)643-0718
3289 Queen St Las Vegas NV 89115-0400 • PSW • EM • (SL 1938 MDIV)

**PRIGGE BRENDAN S REV** (763)533-4411
C/O Grace Lutheran Church 6810 Winnetka Ave N Brooklyn Park MN 55428-2156 • bprigge@gracelcms.org • MNS • SP • Grace Brooklyn Park MN • (612)533-4411 • (SL 1991 MDIV)

**PRIGGE RONALD B REV** (507)754-5782
73278 310th St Racine MN 55967 • MNS • SP • Immanuel Racine MN* • (507)754-5783 • (SL 2000 MDIV)

**PRINCE TIMOTHY ANDREW REV** (402)735-7236
2320 Hwy 69 Gresham NE 68367 • revprince@hotmail.com • NEB • SP • St Peter Gresham NE • (402)735-7333 • (SL 1996 MDIV)

**PRINZ DAVID C REV** (707)644-6260
C/O First Redeemer Lutheran Ch 912 Florida St Vallejo CA 94590-5512 • CNH • SP • First Vallejo CA • (707)644-6260 • (CQ 1982)

**PRITCHARD DONALD F REV** (217)626-1444
531 N Cartwright Pleasant Plains IL 62677 • revdfp@aol.com • CI • SP • Zion Pleasant Plains IL • (217)626-1282 • (FW 1988 MDIV MSED)

**PRITCHARD GRIFFITH F REV** (309)685-1247
4819 Grandview Dr Peoria Heights IL 61614 • CI • Assoc • Trinity Peoria IL • (309)676-4609 • (FW MDIV)

**PROCHNOW WARREN L REV** (712)278-2207
602 Main PO Box 66 Ireton IA 51027 • prochnow@bigfoot.com • IW • SP • St Paul Ireton IA • (712)278-2324 • (SL 2000 MDIV)

**PROHL JOHN R REV** (630)960-2970
4101 Main St Downers Grove IL 60515-2141 • NI • Sn/Adm • Immanuel Downers Grove IL • (630)968-3112 • (CQ 1977 MDIV)

**PROK MYRON K REV** (216)228-0776
2085 Wascana Ave Cleveland OH 44107-6129 • EN • SP • Holy Cross Cleveland OH • (216)252-2348 • (SPR 1967 MDIV)

**PROSTKA CARL A REV** (315)986-3968
975 Wayneport Rd Macedon NY 14502-9733 • stjohns6@juno.com • EA • SP • St John Farmington NY • (315)986-3045 • (SL 1971 MDIV)

**PROUT DAVID L DR** (248)542-4654
3238 Royal Blvd Berkley MI 48072-1332 • MI • SP • Trinity Berkley MI • (248)542-4654 • (SL 1983 MDIV MA MA PHD)

**PROUTY ALBERT I REV** (313)562-7137
5325 Southfield Rd Allen Park MI 48101-2855 • MI • Sn/Adm • Mount Hope Allen Park MI • (313)565-9445 • (SPR 1964 MDIV)

**PROWATZKE ARMIN P REV** (414)548-6392
2224 Gatekeeper Ct Waukesha WI 53188-1533 • SW • EM • (SL 1959)

**PUERTO JOSE G REV** (305)225-0851
11715 SW 18th St Apt 401 Miami FL 33175-1693 • FG • EM • (SPR 1965)

**PUESCHEL ALEC EDMUND REV** (904)998-9711
7645 Sentry Oak Cir Jacksonville FL 32256 • holycrosslc@cxp.com • FG • SP • Holy Cross Jacksonville FL • (904)724-3210 • (FW 1997 MDIV)

**PUFFE PAUL J REV** (512)244-7750
13207 Rampart St Austin TX 78727-3255 • ppuffe@compuserve.com • TX • SHS/C • Texas Austin TX • (SL 1979 MDIV MA)

**PUFFE THOMAS L REV** (701)442-3409
C/O St John Lutheran Church PO Box 757 Underwood ND 58576-0757 • ND • SP • St John Underwood ND* • (701)442-5467 • (FW 1993 MDIV)

**PUIG CARLOS H REV** (281)240-6579
2418 Burkdale Dr Sugar Land TX 77478-6061 • chpuig@ev1.net • TX • EM • * • (CQ 1978)

**PULLMANN ARLO W REV** (406)628-4466
908 5th Ave Laurel MT 59044-1908 • anpullmann@juno.com • MT • SP • St John Laurel MT • (406)628-4775 • (SL 1987 MDIV)

**PULLMANN CARL E REV** (308)534-5925
401 S Baytree Ave North Platte NE 69101-4824 • NEB • SP • Peace Mc Cook NE • (308)345-2595 • (SL 1956)

**PULLMANN DONALD J REV** (303)745-9292
3300 S Tamarac Dr Apt 1-110 Denver CO 80231-4325 • RM • 02/1993 02/2000 • (SPR 1975 MDIV)

**PULS ARTHUR H REV** (619)659-3275
2666 Columbine Rd Alpine CA 91901-1333 • pulsa@juno.com • PSW • EM • (SPR 1962)

**PULS KENTON A REV** (760)873-3640
C/O Grace Lutheran Church 711 N Fowler St Bishop CA 93514-2617 • PSW • SP • Grace Bishop CA • (760)872-9791 • (FW 1987 MDIV)

**PULS TIMOTHY R REV** (219)484-4726
4 Tyndale Pl Fort Wayne IN 46825-4936 • pulstr@mail.ctsfw.edu • IN • SHS/C • Indiana Fort Wayne IN • (FW 1989 STM MDIV)

**PULS WAYNE D REV** (516)496-9656
48 Meadowbrook Rd Syosset NY 11791-2116 • PulsNY@aol.com • AT • Sn/Adm • Trinity Hicksville NY • (516)931-2225 • (FW 1984 MDIV)

**PULSE JEFFREY H REV** (360)692-8771
6765 Chico Way NW Bremerton WA 98312-1025 • jeffp@nobodeez.com • NOW • Sn/Adm • Peace Bremerton WA • (360)377-6253 • (FW 1984 MDIV STM)

**PUMMILL BRIAN L REV** (870)257-4169
55 Wahoo Dr Cherokee Village AR 72529 • bkpummill@hotmail.com • MDS • SP • Peace Cherokee Village AR • (870)257-3957 • (SL 1989 MDIV)

**PUNKE DOUGLAS D REV** (660)885-5363
609 E Bodine Ave Clinton MO 64735 • punke@lakeozark.net • MO • SP • Trinity Clinton MO • (660)885-4728 • (FW 1998 MDIV)

**PURDY EDWARD T REV** (217)839-2906
415 W Chestnut St Gillespie IL 62033-1510 • SI • EM • (SPR 1964)

**PUTNAM GEORGE B REV** (503)359-2300
4373 SW Golf Course Rd Cornelius OR 97113-6018 • stpeters@teleport.com • NOW • SP • St Peter Cornelius OR • (503)357-3863 • (FW 1982 MDIV MS)

**PUTTLER JAMES D REV** (808)456-0247
98-1850 Kaahumanu St Apt S Pearl City HI 96782-3814 • darryl@poi.net • NOW • M Chap • Northwest Portland OR • (SPR 1976 MDIV MA)

**PUTZ DAVID L REV** (605)895-2334
143 Main Ave Box 266 Presho SD 57568 • david@wcenet.com • SD • SP • Zion Presho SD* • (605)895-2334 • (FW 1999 MDIV)

## Q

**QUACKENBOSS DENNIS C REV** (717)755-9471
3320 Cranmere Ln York PA 17402-4205 • denniscq@blazenet.net • SE • Sn/Adm • St John York PA • (717)840-0382 • (SL 1970 MDIV)

**QUAIL DAVID C REV** (409)756-7109
916 Manchester Dr Conroe TX 77304-2713 • TX • Sn/Adm • St Mark Conroe TX • (409)756-6335 • (SPR 1976 MDIV)

**QUALMAN WILLIAM A REV** (863)299-5977
327 Ave C SE Winter Haven FL 33880-3245 • waqgrace@gte.net • FG • SP • Grace Winter Haven FL • (863)293-8447 • (SL 1979 MDIV)

**QUANDT WALTER H REV** (760)956-2654
12456 Kokomo Ct Victorville CA 92392-6781 • PSW • EM • (SL 1965 MDIV)

**QUARDOKUS PHILIP REV** (616)429-9309
1448 Castle Ct Saint Joseph MI 49085-9727 • quardok@andrews.edu • MI • Sn/Adm • Christ Stevensville MI • (616)429-7222 • (SL 1977 MDIV)

**QUEBE STANLEY A REV** (559)325-8486
8396 N Dearing Ave Fresno CA 93720-0439 • saquebe@aol.com • CNH • EM • (SL 1954)

**QUECK THOMAS J REV** (320)274-2230
350 Chestnut St E Annandale MN 55302-9594 • zionandl@lkdllink.net • MNS • SP • Zion Annandale MN • (320)274-5226 • (FW 1983 MDIV)

**QUILL GRANT C J REV** (608)524-4975
1111 12th St Reedsburg WI 53959-1003 • SW • EM • (SPR 1947)

**QUILL TIMOTHY C J REV** (219)471-7577
4918 Oak Knob Run Fort Wayne IN 46845-8940 • quilltim@aol.com • IN • SHS/C • Indiana Fort Wayne IN • (SL 1980 MDIV STM MPHIL)

**QUINN DANIEL B REV** (414)681-8410
2920 Cherry Tree Racine WI 53402-1318 • revdbquinns@aol.com • SW • Sn/Adm • St John Racine WI • (262)637-7011 • (SL 1990 MDIV STM)

**QUIRAM A GERALD REV** (405)732-2585
700 N Air Depot Blvd Midwest City OK 73110-3763 • OK • EM • (SPR 1960)

**QUIRAM DANIEL H REV** (410)339-7979
908 Crestwick Rd Baltimore MD 21286 • quiramd@aol.com • SE • Sn/Adm • Calvary Baltimore MD • (410)426-4301 • (SL 1968 MDIV)

**QUITMEYER H HUGO REV** (330)865-4616
2951 Greenspire Ln Fairlawn OH 44333-9103 • OH • EM • (SL 1935)

**QUOSS ALBERT F REV** (703)323-1120
5105 Claytonia Ct Annandale VA 22003 • SE • SP • Our Savior Winchester VA • (540)667-1459 • (SPR 1974 MDIV)

## R

**RAABE BERNARD O REV** (480)396-9288
5648 E Holmes Ave Mesa AZ 85206 • MO • EM • (SPR 1947 MDIV DD)

**RAABE PAUL R REV** (314)505-7128
5 N Seminary Ter Clayton MO 63105-3010 • raabep@csl.edu • MO • SHS/C • Missouri Saint Louis MO • (314)317-4550 • (SL 1979 MDIV MA PHD)

**RAAP GEORGE P REV** (608)362-2263
2405 Dewey Ave Beloit WI 53511-2426 • SW • EM • (SPR 1954)

**RAASCH RANDOLPH H REV** (262)377-7655
W71N706 Harrison Ave Cedarburg WI 53012-1007 • rraasch@fils.org • SW • Sn/Adm • First Immanuel Cedarburg WI • (262)377-6610 • (SL 1982 MDIV)

**RABE GERALD L REV** (541)942-4355
600 Lincoln Ave Cottage Grove OR 97424-2850 • tlclcms@efn.org • NOW • SP • Trinity Cottage Grove OR • (541)942-2373 • (CQ 1988)

**RABE W GAIL REV** (847)634-3659
207 Rivershire Ln Apt 202 Lincolnshire IL 60069-3808 • trinitygco@aol.com • NI • EM • (SL 1958 MDIV)

**RABON LAWRENCE C JR. REV** (828)697-5494
3106 Hickory Hill Rd Hendersonville NC 28792 • larryrabon@aol.com • SE • SP • Mount Pisgah Hendersonville NC • (828)692-7027 • (FW 1984 MDIV)

**RACHUY GLEN RAYMOND REV** (712)274-0485
1600 S Palmetto St Sioux City IA 51106-1936 • IW • Asst • Calvary Sioux City IA • (712)239-1575 • (CQ 1986 MDIV)

**RACHUY GREGORY S REV** (615)672-4724
604 Highland Dr White House TN 37188 • pstr1999@aol.com • MDS • D Miss • Prince Of Peace White House TN • (615)672-3300 • (CQ 1999)

**RADDATZ JOHN F REV** (918)491-9441
7835 S 66th East Ave Tulsa OK 74133-3406 • OK • Sn/Adm • Christ The Redeemer Tulsa OK • (918)492-6451 • (FW 1982 MDIV)

**RADDATZ MARK R REV** (614)654-5275
420 N Maple St Lancaster OH 43130 • mrraddatz@juno.com • OH • SP • Emanuel Lancaster OH • (740)653-1847 • (SL 1983 MDIV STM)

**RADDE DONN H REV** (715)257-9919
616 Elm St Athens WI 54411-9700 • NW • SP • Trinity Athens WI • (715)257-7526 • (SL 1970 MDIV)

**RADICHEL JAMES A REV** (715)476-2430
PO Box 201 Mercer WI 54547-0201 • NW • SP • Faith Mercer WI* • (715)476-2626 • (CQ 2000)

**RADKE EDWARD F REV** (613)732-2893
755 Cecelia St Pembroke ON K8A 8H5 CANADA • EN • SP • St John Pembroke ON CANADA • (613)735-6332 • (SL 1969 MDIV)

**RADLOFF ROY T REV** (605)371-0418
5004 E Fernwood Dr Sioux Falls SD 57110-5500 • SD • EM • (SPR 1957)

**RADTKE GERALD T REV** (785)524-4039
C/O St John Luth Church RR 2 Box 124 Lincoln KS 67455-9555 • stjlutheran@nckcn.com • KS • SP • St John Lincoln KS • (785)524-4039 • (SL 1970 MDIV)

**RADTKE RICHARD S REV** (219)483-0650
5014 Honey Oak Run Fort Wayne IN 46845-9485 • rcradtke@fwi.com • IN • Sn/Adm • St Paul Fort Wayne IN • (219)423-2496 • (SPR 1968 MDIV)

**RADTKE THOMAS G REV** (217)525-6279
515 S Macarthur Blvd Springfield IL 62704-1744 • revtom4@aol.com • CI • Assoc • Trinity Springfield IL • (217)522-8151 • (FW 1978 MDIV)

**RAEBEL JARED M REV** (219)987-2190
C/O Faith Luth Church PO Box 396 Demotte IN 46310-0396 • lutheran@netnitco.net • IN • SP • Faith Demotte IN • (219)987-3730 • (SL 1987 MDIV)

**RAEBEL ROGER E REV** (218)359-1097
227 Hazelwood Ave New Ulm MN 56073-2023 • MNS • EM • (SL 1954)

**RAEDEKE FREDERICK REV** (314)894-1428
C/O Immanuel Lutheran Church 3350 Wildwood Rd Niangua MO 65713-9712 • fritz@good-news.net • MO • SP • Immanuel Niangua MO • (417)589-2402 • (SL 1982 MDIV)

**RAEDEKE NORMAN L REV** (303)452-6401
12935 Dexter St Thornton CO 80241-2203 • beatitudesr2@juno.com • RM • Sn/Adm • Gethsemane Northglenn CO • (303)451-6895 • (SL 1961)

**RAESS JOHN K REV** (505)296-2377
14312 Arcadia Rd NE Albuquerque NM 87123-2401 • jkraess@integrityonline1.com • RM • SP • Prince Of Peace Cedar Crest NM • (505)281-2430 • (SL 1964 MDIV)

**RAETHER JERRY K REV** (515)332-1303
802 8th St S Humboldt IA 50548-2241 • IW • Sn/Adm • Zion Humboldt IA • (515)332-3279 • (FW 1977 MDIV)

**RAETZ DAVID W REV**
3254 Coastal Hwy Crawfordville FL 32327-4200 • revraetz@aol.com • FG • 09/1999 • (SPR 1967)

**RAFFERTY CHARLES RONALD REV** (970)641-1860
PO Box 662 Gunnison CO 81230-0662 • mtcalvary@westelk.com • RM • SP • Mount Calvary Gunnison CO • (970)641-1860 • (FW 1991 MDIV)

**RAHE GARY A REV** (303)854-2614
C/O Zion Lutheran Church 240 S High School Ave Holyoke CO 80734-1727 • RM • SP • Zion Holyoke CO • (970)854-2615 • (SPR 1975 MDIV)

**RAHN DENNIS DARYL REV**
1520 Red Apple Rd Manistee MI 49660 • MI • SP • Trinity Manistee MI • (231)723-5149 • (FW 1996 MDIV)

**RAHN JAMES ELWOOD REV** (714)832-9477
1282 Veeh Dr Tustin CA 92780-5140 • rahnje@cui.edu • PSW • SHS/C • Pacific Southwest Irvine CA • (949)854-3232 • (CQ 1995 MA MS EDD)

**RAHN ROBERT L REV** (810)264-7317
34354 Burstyn Dr Sterling Heights MI 48312 • rrahn@lhfmissions.org • MI • Michigan Ann Arbor MI • (SL 1961 MDIV)

**RAKOW GORDON W REV** (518)785-8286
C/O Luth Ch Of Resurrection 645 Watervliet Shaker Rd Latham NY 12110-3622 • grrake@aol.com • AT • SP • Resurrection Latham NY • (518)785-8286 • (SPR 1973 MDIV)

**RALL EUGENE E REV** (319)243-8791
2715 N 4th St Clinton IA 52732-1833 • IE • EM • (SL 1956)

**RALL RONALD DEAN REV** (314)781-2177
6949 Pernod Ave Saint Louis MO 63139-2117 • Rallpela@aol.com • MO • SP • Timothy Saint Louis MO • (314)781-8673 • (SL 1973 MDIV STM)

**RALLISON JOHN C REV**
220 Pleasant Hill Dr Clermont FL 34711 • sslc@flash.net • FG • Assoc • Prince Of Peace Orlando FL • (407)277-3945 • (SL 1995 MDIV)

**RALPH EDWARD M REV** (706)543-2760
565 Belmont Rd Athens GA 30605-4907 • FG • EM • (SPR 1964 MDIV)

**RAMEL DAVID P REV** (608)741-1785
375 Greendale Dr Janesville WI 53546 • pdram5@spsflames.k12.wi.us • SW • Assoc • St Paul Janesville WI • (608)754-4471 • (SL 1989 MDIV)

**RAMEY JOHN M REV** (713)855-8060
16313 Wellers Way Houston TX 77095-3900 • miker3900@aol.com • TX • Sn/Adm • Family/Faith Houston TX • (281)855-2950 • (SL 1984 THD)

**RAMIREZ GREGG S REV** (973)239-0490
C/O Calvary Luth Church 23 S Prospect St Verona NJ 07044-1507 • calvaryverona@earthlink.net • NJ • Sn/Adm • Calvary Verona NJ • (973)239-0577 • (SL 1985 MDIV)

**RAMMING MICHAEL E REV** (254)634-5697
Lonely Oaks Rd RT 1 Box 11 Killeen TX 76542-9801 • meramming@juno.com • TX • Sn/Adm • Grace Killeen TX • (254)634-5858 • (SL 1969 MDIV)

**RAMSBACHER JOHN ALLEN REV** (320)584-8132
26733 63rd St Royalton MN 56373 • MNN • SP • St John Royalton MN* • (320)584-8132 • (SL 1996 MDIV)

**RAMSEY CHARLES M III REV** (712)527-9046
1012 N Walnut St Glenwood IA 51534-1440 • chckrmsy@aol.com • IW • SP • Trinity Glenwood IA • (712)527-4667 • (SL 1988 MCRT MDIV)

**RAMSEY DANIEL JOHN REV** 011-22522412370
C/O Mission Lutherienne Africa BP 129 Toulepleu WEST AFRICA • d-sramsey@onebox.com • NOW • S Miss • Northwest Portland OR • (SL 1994 MDIV)

**RAMSEY JOHN R REV** (509)826-0961
610 N Main St Omak WA 98841 • vjrams@televar.com • NOW • SP • Our Savior Okanogan WA • (509)422-2652 • (SPR 1963)

**RAMSEY THOMAS G REV** (580)765-4568
1001 W Grand Ponca City OK 74601 • sowramsey@yahoo.com • OK • SP • First Ponca City OK • (580)762-1111 • (SL 1988 MDIV)

**RAMTHUN MARVIN W REV** (810)664-7830
1614 Indian Rd Lapeer MI 48446-8054 • MI • EM • (SPR 1969)

**RANBARGER JOHN R REV**
553 Remingtron Pt Apt 104 Greenwood IN 46143-8049 • tlclowdn.netins.net • IE • SP • Trinity Lowden IA • (319)941-5853 • (FW 1982 MDIV)

**RANDALL WILLIAM R REV** (812)985-5441
700 Crestmont Dr Evansville IN 47712-9681 • brgm3@aol.com • IN • SP • Messiah Evansville IN • (812)985-2278 • (FW 1982 MDIV)

**RANTA HILLARD K REV** (707)822-2165
1786 Zehndner Ave Arcata CA 95521-5464 • CNH • EM • (SPR 1952 MA)

**RANTA W ARNOLD REV** (618)826-4965
30 Skyline Dr Chester IL 62233-1831 • wardir@webtv.net • SI • EM • (SPR 1951 MA)

**RAPP VICTOR JOHN REV** (516)354-1478
9 Durham Rd New Hyde Park NY 11040-2018 • AT • SP • Trinity New Hyde Park NY • (516)354-8883 • (SPR 1973 STM)

**RAPPE TOD ROGER REV** (910)488-6010
1605 Van Buren Ave Fayetteville NC 28303-3751 • orluthrn@amil.apcnet.com • SE • SP • Our Redeemer Fayetteville NC • (910)488-6010 • (FW 1991 MDIV)

**RASCH ARTHUR C REV** (509)586-8551
4506 S Kent St Kennewick WA 99337-4510 • revrasch@aol.com • NOW • SP • Bethlehem Kennewick WA • (509)586-1062 • (SL 1966 MDIV)

**RASCH LYLE H REV** (513)245-0547
3791 Sagebrush Ln Cincinnati OH 45251-1405 • lhrasch@aol.com • OH • EM • (BY 1952 MDIV)

**RASMUSSEN ERVIN B REV** (480)949-5325
8552 E Pinchot Ave Scottsdale AZ 85251-7312 • levapfi@futureone.com • EN • EM • (SPR 1957 MDIV)

**RASMUSSEN JOHN A REV** (507)292-9767
525 SW 3rd St Rochester MN 55902 • MNS • Sn/Adm • Trinity Rochester MN • (507)289-1531 • (SPR 1968 MA MDIV)

**RASMUSSEN STEVEN C REV** (319)372-4650
302 12th St Fort Madison IA 52627 • stevetta@interl.net • IE • SP • Our Savior Fort Madison IA • (319)372-7952 • (FW 1990 MDIV)

**RASMUSSEN WAYNE R REV** (414)464-4492
8903 W Hope Ave Milwaukee WI 53222-1743 • EN • Assoc • Hales Corners Hales Corners WI • (414)529-6700 • (CQ 1990 MA)

**RASSBACH JAMES W REV** (314)843-3714
5000 Fernhill Dr Saint Louis MO 63128-2929 • jim.rassbach@lcms.org • MO • S Ex/S • Missouri Saint Louis MO • (314)317-4550 • (SPR 1966 MA MDIV)

**RAST LAWRENCE ROBERT REV** (219)471-1013
6600 N Clinton St Fort Wayne IN 46825-4916 • Rastlr@mail.ctsfw.edu • IN • SHS/C • Indiana Fort Wayne IN • (FW 1990 MDIV STM MA)

**RASTL MARVIN L REV** (219)482-9874
2624 Santa Rosa Dr Fort Wayne IN 46805-3933 • IN • EM • (SPR 1947)

**RASTL NATHAN P REV** (812)886-9965
6926 S Decker Rd Vincennes IN 47591-9145 • nprastl@vincennes.net • IN • SP • St Peter Vincennes IN • (812)882-8229 • (FW 1988 MDIV)

**RATCLIFFE KEITH B REV** (816)356-7035
8816 Elm Ave Kansas City MO 64138-4737 • peace@safe4kids.net • MO • SP • Peace Kansas City MO • (816)353-3813 • (SL 1979 MDIV)

**RATCLIFFE KERMIT H REV** (414)365-1288
9119 N 70th St Milwaukee WI 53223-2115 • kermit.ratcliffe@con.edu • SW • SHS/C • South Wisconsin Milwaukee WI • (414)464-8100 • (SPR 1966 MDIV STM DMIN)

**RATH JOHN H REV** (785)272-1821
2136 SW Meadow Ln Topeka KS 66614-1442 • KS • EM • (SL 1956 MDIV)

**RATHGEBER BENJAMIN G REV** (817)517-5358
1209 Wedgewood St Cleburne TX 76031-4623 • loisr@hpnc.com • TX • EM • (SL 1958)

**RATHGEBER DOUGLAS D REV** (409)832-3006
5390 Cambridge Dr Beaumont TX 77707-2048 • bmtstjohn@sat.net • TX • SP • St John Beaumont TX • (409)840-9915 • (SL 1970 MDIV)

**RATHJEN H DOUGLAS REV** (540)381-4867
695 Tarrytown Christiansburg VA 24073-7633 • drathjen@usit.net • SE • 03/1999 • (SL 1964 MDIV)

**RATHJEN HAROLD JOHN REV** (870)741-9330
PO Box 662 Harrison AR 72602-0662 • hjr@alltel.net • RM • 05/1999 • (SL 1992 MDIV)

**RATHJEN JONATHAN CHRISTOPHER** (320)587-1018
556 2nd Ave SW Hutchinson MN 55350-2302 • MNS • Assoc • Peace Hutchinson MN • (320)587-3031 • (SL 1995 MDIV)

**RATTELMULLER GEORGE H REV** (573)445-1667
4701 W Georgetown Dr Columbia MO 65203-0411 • MO • EM • (SL 1956 MDIV MST)

**RAU CARL R REV** (910)396-4373
XVIII Airborne Corps Chaplains Office Fort Bragg NC 28307-5000 • IN • M Chap • Indiana Fort Wayne IN • (FW 1984 MDIV)

**RAU HAROLD M REV** (636)458-6914
18123 Sunny Top Ct Wildwood MO 63038-1461 • hmrau@earthlink.net • MO • 01/1997 01/2000 • (FW 1982 MDIV)

**RAUBER ROLAND J REV** (505)867-9195
2163 Cimmarron Ct NE Rio Rancho NM 87124-6400 • RM • EM • (SL 1944)

**RAUH JOHN WM REV** (517)781-0558
581 Timberwood Ln Saginaw MI 48609-8507 • goodshep@concentric.net • MI • SP • Good Shepherd Saginaw MI • (517)793-8201 • (SL 1964 MDIV)

**RAUHUT DONALD E REV** (517)238-2119
13271 Iyopawa Island Rd Coldwater MI 49036-8748 • IN • EM • (SL 1960 MDIV)

**RAUSCHEK CHARLES A REV** (909)606-5353
6290 Narcissus Ln Chino Hills CA 91709 • lsothlc@aviastar.net • PSW • SP • Loving Savior Chino Hills CA • (909)597-4668 • (SPR 1964 MA)

**RAUSCHER PAUL N REV**
C/O Luth Church of Providence 1696 Providence Blvd Deltona FL 32725 • FG • SP • Providence Deltona FL • (904)789-3300 • (FW 1980 MDIV)

**RAUTENSHILDS ARNOLDS G REV** (630)832-4910
135 Green Leaf Dr Oak Brook IL 60523 • rautensild@aol.com • NI • EM • (CQ 1951)

**RAVELL ROBERT J REV** (503)517-2348
C/O Redeemer Luth Church 627 SE Hillcrest Rd John Day OR 97845-1228 • NOW • SP • Redeemer John Day OR • (541)575-2348 • (FW 1982 MDIV)

**REAGAN WILLIAM M REV** (210)499-4333
15019 Digger Dr San Antonio TX 78247-3046 • billreagan@aol.com • TX • D Ex/S • Texas Austin TX • (SL 1983 MDIV)

**REBENSAL ROBERT F REV** (909)481-8515
9022 San Bernardino Rd Rancho Cucamonga CA 91730 • robber7@aol.com • PSW • SP • Redeemer Perris CA • (909)657-3662 • (FW 1997 MDIV)

**REBENTISCH KRIS S REV** (402)643-3978
1204 N 2nd St Seward NE 68434-1233 • rebentisch@juno.com • CNH • 11/1999 • (SL 1988 MDIV MA)

**REBERT TERRY J REV** (248)393-7360
3676 Bald Mountain Rd Lake Orion MI 48360 • MI • SP • Crown Of Life Rochester Hills MI • (248)652-7720 • (SL 1980 MSW)

**RECKLING MICHAEL JOHN REV**
PSC 599 Box 5146 FPO AP 96377-5146 • OK • Asst • Good Shepherd Midwest City OK • (405)732-2585 • (SL 1996 MDIV)

**RECKLING ROGER C REV** (810)247-7171
13739 Bowling Green Dr Sterling Hts MI 48313-3509 • pastor@missourisynod.com • MI • SP • St Paul Pontiac MI • (248)338-8618 • (SPR 1970)

**RECKS JOHN F REV** (217)222-7371
1301 Jackson St Quincy IL 62301-6736 • CI • EM • (SL 1960 MDIV STM)

**REDDEL EUGENE L REV** (412)443-6719
3149 Haberlein Rd Gibsonia PA 15044-8258 • EA • Inst C • Eastern Williamsville NY • (716)634-5111 • (SL 1965 MDIV)

**REDEKER MICHAEL JAMES REV** (314)727-4938
6501 San Bonita Ave #1 Clayton MO 63105 • john112526@aol.com • MO • SHS/C • Missouri Saint Louis MO • (314)317-4550 • (SL 1995 MDIV)

**REDEKER WILLIAM N REV** (920)458-5856
1435 Camelot Blvd Sheboygan WI 53081-7511 • SW • EM • (SL 1958 MDIV)

**REDER F DONALD REV** (573)335-1954
904 N Fountain St Cape Girardeau MO 63701-6911 • MO • EM • (CQ 1978)

**REDHAGE LLOYD W REV** (605)298-5695
C/O Zion Lutheran Church PO Box 16 Andover SD 57422-0016 • sheepcircles@hotmail.com • SD • SP • Zion Andover SD* • (605)298-5610 • (FW 1983 MDIV)

**REDIEHS ROBERT E DR** (217)446-9005
1425 Woodridge Dr Danville IL 61832-1669 • rediehs@prairienet.org • CI • O Sp Min • Central Illinois Springfield IL • (SL 1958 STM MDIV PHD)

**REDIGER FRED A REV** (317)984-5243
PO Box 396 Arcadia IN 46030-0396 • IN • EM • (SL 1938)

**REDMANN JAMES C REV** (502)886-1497
1208 Pin Oak Dr Hopkinsville KY 42240-5116 • faith-lutheran@prodigy.net • MDS • SP • Faith Hopkinsville KY • (270)885-3969 • (SPR 1975 MDIV)

**REDMANN KENNETH PAUL REV** (219)833-4538
2380 N Saint Andrews Ct Angola IN 46703-8518 • cllutheran@dmci.net • IN • SP • Clear Lake Fremont IN • (219)495-9219 • (FW 1996 MDIV)

**REDMANN LOUIS J REV** (210)680-8469
8818 Queen Hts San Antonio TX 78250-2314 • ljredmann@aol.com • TX • EM • (CQ 1985)

**REED DAVID H REV** (517)662-7900
307 Ruth St Auburn MI 48611-9463 • reedrev@voyager.net • MI • SP • Grace Auburn MI • (517)662-6161 • (FW 1983 MDIV)

**REED MARTY EDWARD REV** (209)535-3707
10328 Rd 256 Terra Bella CA 93270-9722 • mreed@cwia.com • CNH • SP • Zion Terra Bella CA • (559)535-4952 • (SL 1993 MDIV)

**REED PHILLIP D REV**
655 North Park Blvd #139 Grapevine TX 76051-6958 • pdreed@earthlink.net • TX • 05/1998 • (FW 1986 MDIV)

**REED RUSSELL ALLAN REV** (605)448-5103
C/O St John Luth Church PO Box J Britton SD 57430-0622 • revreed@brittonsd.com • SD • SP • St John Britton SD • (605)448-5235 • (SL 1995 MDIV)

**REEDER THOMAS N JR. REV** (262)255-2070
W158 N8365 Steven Mack Cr #C5 Menomonee Falls WI 53051 • yunmei@juno.com • SW • Asst • Pilgrim Wauwatosa WI • (414)476-0735 • (SL 1999 MDIV)

**REEDER THOMAS N SR. REV** (573)358-2417
310 Summit St Bonne Terre MO 63628 • MO • SP • St Matthew Bonne Terre MO • (573)358-3105 • (SPR 1968)

**REEDY DAVID D REV**
C/O Trinity Lutheran Church 5921 Springdale Rdd Cincinnati OH 45247-3433 • pastrdav@goodnews.net • OH • SP • Trinity Cincinnati OH • (513)385-7024 • (SL 1996 MDIV)

**REEHL CHARLES W REV**
N9680 Van Dyne Rd Van Dyne WI 54979-9344 • SW • 11/1989 11/1998 • (CQ 1979)

**REEHL JOHN D REV** (308)384-3792
1623 W Anna St Grand Island NE 68801-6303 • NEB • EM • (SL 1960 MDIV MA)

**REEK JOHN DIRK REV**
C/O Zion Lutheran Church 311 S Elm St Staunton IL 62088-3100 • revdreek@aol.com • SI • Sn/Adm • Zion Staunton IL • (618)635-2880 • (SPR 1974 STM MDIV)

**REES JAMES R REV** (812)284-5697
2450 Mallard Run Jeffersonville IN 47130-8032 • rjrrees@netscape.net • IN • 07/2000 • (FW 1982 MDIV)

**REESE DAVID ALLEN REV** (580)255-0941
1008 W Plato Rd Duncan OK 73533 • gslc@texhoma.net • OK • D Ex/S • Oklahoma Tulsa OK* • (SL 1991 MDIV MED)

**REESE KERRY D REV** (425)338-2886
12618 47th Dr SE Everett WA 98208-9624 • revreese@integrityol.com • NOW • SP • Shepherd Hills Snohomish WA • (360)668-7881 • (SL 1980 MDIV STM)

**REESE WALTER T REV** (360)568-7806
PO Box 578 Snohomish WA 98291 • NOW • EM • (CQ 1982)

**REETZ PETER R REV** (614)868-5148
6950 Tanya Ter Reynoldsburg OH 43068-1777 • preetz@asacomp.com • OH • Sn/Adm • Zion Columbus OH • (614)444-3456 • (SPR 1972 MDIV)

**REHBORG GARY REV** (763)241-4870
20936 Ogden St NW Elk River MN 55330 • emmanuel³luth@worldnet.att.net • MNN • SP • Emmanuel Elk River MN • (612)441-2555 • (FW 1985 MDIV)

**REHDER JAMES V REV** (425)454-1162
1026 104th Ave SE Belkvue WA 98004-6848 • NOW • SP • Pilgrim Bellevue WA • (425)454-1162 • (SL 1976 MDIV)

**REHLEY JAMES W REV** (541)757-0784
645 NW 35th St Corvallis OR 97330-4914 • jwrehley@juno.com • NOW • EM • (SPR 1963 MDIV)

**REHM MERLIN D REV** (914)723-1998
38 Orchard St Eastchester NY 10709 • EN • SP • Trinity Scarsdale NY • (914)723-1998 • (TH 1959 THD)

**REHMER NORMAN J REV** (319)447-0506
2365 Winchester Marion IA 52302-6136 • iderehmer@aol.com • IE • D Ex/S • Iowa East Marion IA • (CQ 1986 MA MAR)

**REHMER RUDOLPH F REV** (317)463-1455
157 Linda Ln W Lafayette IN 47906-1611 • IN • EM • (SL 1944 MDIV MA DD)

**REHRER RONALD LEROY REV**
7127 Louise Ave Van Nuys CA 91406-3551 • ronr007@earthlink.net • PSW • D Ex/S • Pacific Southwest Irvine CA • (949)854-3232 • (SL 1973 MDIV MA)

**REHWALDT ALAN C REV** (651)730-9251
1550 Parkwood Dr Apt 311 Woodbury MN 55125-3108 • a.c.rehwaldt@juno.com • MNS • SP • St Peter Afton MN • (651)436-3357 • (SL 1987 MDIV MS)

**REHWALDT CARL H REV** (402)462-9460
846 Chestnut Ave Hastings NE 68901-4258 • crehwaldt@inebraska.com • NEB • Sn/Adm • Faith Hastings NE • (402)462-5044 • (SL 1969 MDIV DMIN)

**REHWALDT EDGAR F REV** (218)568-8759
PO Box 624 Nisswa MN 56468-0624 • MNN • EM • (SL 1945)

**REHWALDT TIMOTHY J REV**
C/O Praise Lutheran Church 670 Diffley Rd Eagan MN 55123-1603 • pastorrehwaldt@uswest.net • MNS • SP • Praise Eagan MN • (651)688-8794 • (FW 1984 MDIV)

**REHWINKEL EUGENE A REV** (941)923-4484
1935 Mid Ocean Cir Sarasota FL 34239-3412 • FG • EM • (SL 1959 MDIV)

**REICH CHARLES TRAVIS REV** (352)331-3064
1610 NW 89th Ter Gainesville FL 32606-6788 • creich@juno.com • FG • SP • Abiding Savior Gainesville FL • (352)331-4409 • (SL 1996 MDIV)

**REICH RAYMOND D REV**
744 Getty St Uvalde TX 78801 • TX • EM • (SPR 1958)

**REICHEL CHARLES E REV** (706)234-0678
1097 Mt Alto Rd Rome GA 30165-4325 • excelassist@cs.com • SO • O Sp Min • St Peter Gadsden AL • (205)492-6941 • (SL 1969 MA MDIV PHD)

**REICHEL H GENE REV** (717)755-7364
110 Southview Dr York PA 17402 • hgreichel@prodigy.net • SE • SP • Good Shepherd York PA* • (717)854-1325 • (SL 1964 MDIV)

**REICHMANN WILMER H REV** (414)376-1942
N41 W5913 Hamilton Rd Cedarburg WI 53012-2433 • wilreichmann@fils.org • SW • Assoc • First Immanuel Cedarburg WI • (262)377-6610 • (SL 1969 MDIV)

**REIDENBACH KENNETH H REV** (828)267-1261
1330 5th St NE #131 Hickory NC 28601-2704 • SE • EM • (SL 1958)

**REIMANN DAVID K REV** (614)876-8780
5526 Cara Ct Dublin OH 43016-8700 • pdreim@aol.com • OH • Sn/Adm • St John Dublin OH • (614)889-2284 • (SL 1983 MDIV MMU)

**REIMER ROBERT K REV** (308)357-1303
RR 1 Box 66 Belgrade NE 68623-9731 • NEB • SP • Our Redeemer Wahoo NE • (402)443-4450 • (CQ 1982 MTH MDIV)

**REIMERS RUSSEL D REV** (507)632-4674
C/O St Paul Luth Church RR 1 Box 47 Ceylon MN 56121-9719 • MNS • SP • St Paul Ceylon MN • (507)632-4674 • (FW 1993 MDIV)

**REIMNITZ ALWIN M REV** (701)223-9065
1105 Prairie Dr Bismarck ND 58501-2431 • ND • EM • (SL 1950 DD)

**REIMNITZ CHARLES A DR** (402)330-8836
14925 Dorcas Cir Omaha NE 68144-2033 • careimnitz@aol.com • NEB • EM • (SL 1954 MA PHD)

**REIMNITZ DAVID M REV** (816)331-7012
215 Hillcrest Rd Belton MO 64012-1818 • dreimnitz@juno.com • MO • SP • Bethlehem Raymore MO • (816)322-3606 • (SL 1986 MDIV)

**REIMNITZ ELMER REV** (805)581-7058
2508 Lowell Ct Simi Valley CA 93065-5800 • PSW • EM • (PA 1942 STM DD)

**REIMNITZ ELROI REV** (805)498-5933
3883 San Marcos Ct Newbury Park CA 91320-3725 • PSW • SP • Redeemer Thousand Oaks CA • (805)498-4813 • (SL 1971 MDIV THD)

**REIMNITZ STEWART N REV** (619)271-7088
7971 Calico St San Diego CA 92126-3001 • PSW • SP • Christ Cnrstne San Diego CA • (619)566-1860 • (SL 1964)

**REIMNITZ WESLEY E REV** (217)546-0614
19 Guilford Dr Springfield IL 62707-8013 • wgreimnitz@eosinc.com • CI • D Ex/S • Central Illinois Springfield IL* • (FW 1980 MDIV MS)

**REIMOLD JOHN I REV** (870)670-4248
404 Mohawk Dr Horseshoe Bend AR 72512-1930 • MDS • EM • * • (CQ 1979 MED)

**REIN KARL HELMUT REV** (812)342-4854
16150 S 300 W Columbus IN 47201-9357 • IN • SP • St John Columbus IN • (812)342-3516 • (FW 1995 MDIV)

**REINBACHER OTTO A REV** (215)794-2043
515 Clydesdale Dr New Hope PA 18938 • NJ • Sn/Adm • St Paul Flemington NJ • (908)782-5120 • (SL 1961 MDIV MBA MS)

**REINBOLT DONALD D REV** (317)894-8810
10933 Mount Vernon Trl N Indianapolis IN 46229-3512 • IN • EM • (SL 1949)

**REINBOLT RAYMOND H REV** (712)822-5513
C/O Immanuel Luth Church PO Box 100 Lidderdale IA 51452-0100 • IW • SP • Immanuel Lidderdale IA • (712)822-5512 • (SL 1971 STM)

**REINDERS DOUGLAS ROBERT REV**
2402 Hansen Ave Racine WI 53405-2519 • SW • S Miss • South Wisconsin Milwaukee WI • (414)464-8100 • (FW 1995 MDIV)

**REINEMANN LEWIS R REV** (218)722-3752
1801 Stanford Ave Duluth MN 55811-2021 • MNN • EM • (SPR 1956 MDIV)

**REINER DAROLD A REV** (406)756-6124
2457 Mission Trail Rd Kalispell MT 59901-2248 • reiner@centurytel.net • MT • SP • Trinity Kalispell MT • (406)257-5683 • (CQ 1972 MAR MED)

**REINERS MICHAEL E REV** (316)218-0763
C/O Holy Cross Lutheran Church 600 N Greenwich Rd Wichita KS 67206-2633 • pastorreiners@holycrosslutheran.net • KS • Asst • Holy Cross Wichita KS • (316)684-5201 • (FW 1988 MDIV)

**REINHARDT HAROLD L REV** (253)584-2558
10819 Glenwood Dr SW Lakewood WA 98498-4330 • chhlrein@aol.com • NOW • EM • (SL 1949 MA)

**REINHARDT LARRY L REV** (636)861-0289
1301 Point Mariner Dr Fenton MO 63026-6917 • ic³reinhall@lcms.org • MO • S Ex/S • Missouri Saint Louis MO • (314)317-4550 • (CQ 1973)

**REINHARDT ROBERT C REV** (440)543-2187
8120 Stoneybrook Dr Chagrin Falls OH 44023-4847 • bobjoarein@aol.com • OH • SP • Our Savior Cleveland OH • (440)442-4455 • (SL 1960 MDIV)

**REINHARDT RONALD A REV** (256)353-3481
1311 Noble Ave SW Decatur AL 35601-3643 • ronhardt@hiwaay.net • SO • EM • (SL 1958 MDIV)

**REINHARDT WILLIAM B REV** (407)365-2338
C/O Lutheran Haven 1344 Haven Dr Oviedo FL 32765-5213 • reinclergy@aol.com • FG • EM • (SL 1956 MDIV)

**REINHEIMER DANIEL D REV** (252)426-3503
3 Green Ct E Hartford NC 27944 • NJ • EM • (SL 1958 MST MDIV)

**REINISCH RICHARD O REV** (503)284-1558
5705 NE 25th Ave Portland OR 97211-6107 • dreinisch@cu-portland.edu • NOW • EM • (SL 1948 MDIV MA MA PHD)

**REINKE CALVIN E REV** (313)381-4474
3320 Electric Ave Lincoln Park MI 48146 • creinke@globelbiz.net • MI • Sn/Adm • Calvary Lincoln Park MI • (313)381-6715 • (FW 1979 MDIV)

**REINKE CHRIS J REV** (907)243-2250
9300 Emerald St Anchorage AK 99515-1058 • chrisjrein@aol.com • NOW • SP • Beaut Savior Anchorage AK • (907)522-3899 • (SPR 1969 MDIV DMIN LLD)

**REINKE CLARENCE F JR. REV** (561)586-7599
1709 22nd Ave N Lake Worth FL 33460-6049 • joshreinke@prodigy.net • FG • Sn/Adm • Our Savior Lake Worth FL • (561)582-4430 • (SL 1995 MDIV MS)

**REINKE DAVID E REV** (425)771-1781
9117 185th Pl SW Edmonds WA 98026-5731 • NOW • Asst • Epiphany Kenmore WA • (425)488-9606 • (SL 1971 MDIV)

**REINKE GERALD R REV** (208)238-7048
2785 Kootemi Pocatello ID 83201 • gkreinke@aol.com • NOW • D Miss • Northwest Portland OR • (SL 1992 MDIV)

**REINKE JOHN P REV** (608)752-0229
610 Lyndhurst Dr Janesville WI 53546 • revreinke@aol.com • SW • Northwest Portland OR • (SL 1989 MDIV)

**REINKE LANGDON J REV** (770)942-4128
6656 N Seminole Dr Douglasville GA 30135-3250 • langdonreinke@juno.com • FG • SP • Prince Peace Douglasville GA • (770)942-4681 • (SL 1993 MDIV)

**REINKE LESTER JAY REV** (701)572-7084
2122 1st Ave E Williston ND 58801-3507 • ljreinke@dia.net • ND • SP • Concordia Williston ND • (701)572-9021 • (SL 1987 MDIV)

**REINSCH MARK C REV** (906)355-2555
C/O Trinity Lutheran Church PO Box 140 Covington MI 49919-0140 • NW • SP • Trinity Covington MI • (906)355-2534 • (FW 1997 MDIV)

**REISER GREGG ALAN REV** (303)345-6540
762 Date Ave Akron CO 80720-1328 • RM • SP • Trinity Akron CO • (303)345-2303 • (FW 1991 MDIV)

**REISS HAROLD H REV** (303)494-7311
420 S 40th St Boulder CO 80303-5420 • revreiss@aol.com • RM • EM • (SPR 1954)

**REISTER WILLIAM P REV** (904)768-1618
3845 Dexter Dr N Jacksonville FL 32218 • wmreister@aol.com • FG • SP • Our Redeemer Jacksonville FL • (904)766-4728 • (SL 1981 MDIV)

**REITER CARL C REV** (602)856-5138
15409 W Indianola Ave Goodyear AZ 85338-8584 • ccr@phnx.uswest.net • PSW • EM • (SL 1956 MDIV)

**REITER GERALD REV** (603)242-3834
94 S Main St Troy NH 03465-2315 • grreiter@webtv.net • NE • SP • Christ Troy NH • (603)242-7283 • (CQ 1983 MAR MA)

**REITH FERDINAND H REV** (402)643-6144
1738 Meadow Ln Seward NE 68434-1039 • NEB • EM • (SL 1933 MDIV)

**REITH MERLIN L REV** (623)934-1438
Saint Paul Lutheran Church 6301 W Indian School Rd Phoenix AZ 85033-3326 • PSW • SP • St Paul Phoenix AZ • (623)846-2228 • (SL 1964 MST)

**REITH SAMUEL B REV** (517)775-6228
1105 E Bellows St Mount Pleasant MI 48858-3604 • sbreith@juno.com • MI • Sn/Adm • Zion Mount Pleasant MI* • (517)772-1516 • (SL 1983 MDIV)

**REKSTAD ROGER A REV** (651)604-9373
1241 Rose Place Roseville MN 55113 • internet.rrekstad@isd.net • MNS • SP • Emmaus Saint Paul MN • (651)489-9426 • (SL 1971 MDIV)

**RELLSTAB THEODORE L REV** (419)264-2962
PO Box 97 Holgate OH 43527-0097 • rellstab@henry-net.com • OH • SP • St John Holgate OH • (419)264-4641 • (FW 1980 MDIV)

**REMBOLD MANFRED K REV** (937)767-2548
53 Yellow Spr/Fairfield Rd Yellow Springs OH 45387-9718 • marnatha@aol.com • OH • SP • Bethlehem Fairborn OH • (937)878-0651 • (SPR 1976 MDIV)

**REMPFER DAVID P REV** (319)454-6951
PO Box 156 Blairstown IA 52209-0156 • rempfam@netins.net • IE • SP • Grace Blairstown IA • (319)454-6941 • (SL 1982 MDIV)

**REMPFER MARLIN R REV** (217)223-5682
2721 Ken Ray Quincy IL 62301 • revremp@juno.com • CI • SP • St James Quincy IL • (217)222-8447 • (SL 1979 MDIV)

**REMPFER STEVEN W REV** (319)223-5594
C/O St John Luth Church 310 Second St E Newhall IA 52315 • srempfer@cedar-rapids.net • IE • SP • St John Newhall IA • (319)223-5593 • (SL 1986 MDIV MA)

**RENFRO DAVID W REV** (406)721-5280
1825 Mullan Trl Missoula MT 59808 • pastordrenfro@aol.com • MT • SP • First Missoula MT • (406)549-3311 • (FW 1986 MDIV)

**RENGSTORF DWIGHT E REV**
PO Box 1292 Crown Point IN 46308-1292 • lucypug@mail.icongrp.com • IN • Indiana Fort Wayne IN • (SPR 1971 MDIV)

**RENGSTORF ELTON J REV** (716)754-7541
4969 Creek Road Ext Lewiston NY 14092-1838 • erengstorf@aol.com • EA • EM • (SL 1956)

**RENKEN GERALD L REV** (501)751-4796
1701 Glen St Springdale AR 72762-1605 • MDS • SP • Salem Springdale AR • (501)751-9359 • (SPR 1963 MDIV)

**RENKEN GLENN E REV** (217)347-3357
2709 Pine Hurst St Effingham IL 62401-4907 • CI • EM • (SPR 1964)

**RENNER MARTIN REV** (941)574-1165
1044 SE 21st Ave Cape Coral FL 33990-1932 • FG • SP • Good Shepherd Fort Myers FL • (941)995-7711 • (SL 1958)

**RENNER MARVIN J REV** (920)568-3617
427 Commonwealth Dr Fort Atkinson WI 53538-1582 • marvrenner@aol.com • EN • EM • (SL 1949)

**RENNING WAYNE A REV**
C/O St John Lutheran Church RR 1 Box 340 Clarksville TX 75426-9719 • TX • Good Shepherd Fort Myers FL • (941)995-7711 • (SPR 1966 DMIN)

**RENSNER JASON EDWARD REV** (217)342-6047
700 E Goidon Effingham IL 62401 • rensner@juno.com • CI • SP • Faith Shumway IL • (217)868-5484 • (SL 1991 MDIV)

**RENSTROM TIM JEROME REV** (541)265-4046
C/O All Nations Luth Ch 358 NE 12th Newport OR 97365 • NOW • SP • All Nations Newport OR* • (541)265-2503 • (SL 1997 MDIV)

**REPP ARTHUR C REV** (314)741-7449
5080 Craigmont Dr Florissant MO 63033-7316 • EN • EM • * • (SL 1961 MDIV)

**RESCH RICHARD C REV** (219)484-2125
3218 Eastbrook Dr Fort Wayne IN 46805-1710 • IN • SHS/C • Indiana Fort Wayne IN • (FW 1988 MDIV MMU)

**RESCHKE MARK C REV** (714)726-3438
31878 Del Obisop St San Juan Capistrano CA 92675-3223 • PSW • M Chap • Pacific Southwest Irvine CA • (949)854-3232 • (SL 1989 MDIV)

**RESNER STEVEN J REV** (219)936-2903
C/O Calvary Lutheran Church 1314 N Michigan St Plymouth IN 46563-1118 • prresner@hotmail.com • IN • SP • Calvary Plymouth IN • (219)936-2903 • (FW 1991 MDIV)

**RESNER WALTER A REV** (316)221-2629
2111 John Mark Dr Winfield KS 67156-1611 • KS • EM • (SPR 1952)

**RESSLER PHILIP W REV** (540)942-7889
213 Skyland Ave Waynesboro VA 22980 • SE • SP • Bethany-Trinity Waynesboro VA • (540)942-4361 • (SL 2000 MDIV)

**REUNING DANIEL G REV** (219)485-2143
6218 Stony Brook Dr Fort Wayne IN 46835-2384 • deandanbarb@juno.com • EN • EM • (SL 1960 MSMU)

**REUNING WALTER H REV** (617)332-0042
19 Salisbury Rd Newton MA 02458-1947 • NE • EM • (SL 1956)

**REUSCH DALE F REV**
2001 Deer Park Cir Crestwood KY 40014-9149 • IN • SP • Holy Trinity La Grange KY • (502)222-5827 • (SL 1979)

**REUSCH JON W REV** (248)932-5374
4435 Westover Dr West Bloomfield MI 48323-2875 • jonreusch@aol.com • MI • Sn/Adm • Cross Christ Bloomfield Hills MI • (248)646-5886 • (CQ 1981)

**REUSCHER ELMER A REV** (407)323-0810
2444 S Palmetto Ave Sanford FL 32771-4400 • reuschere@worldnet.att.net • FG • SP • Redeemer Sanford FL • (407)322-3552 • (SL 1963 MDIV)

**REUTER LANE BROOKS REV** (865)560-0078
C/O Grace Lutheran Church 9076 Middlebrook Pike Knoxville TN 37923 • lbreuter@usa.net • MDS • Assoc • Grace Knoxville TN • (865)691-2823 • (SL 1996 MDIV)

**REUTZ FREDERICK W REV** (713)383-2360
7311 Bois D Arc Ln Baytown TX 77521-5033 • TX • EM • (CQ 1959)

**REYNOLDS JOHN D REV** (770)413-0802
2546 Rockbridge Rd Stone Mountain GA 30087-3613 • jreyno1920@aol.com • EN • SP • First Stone Mountain GA • (770)413-2375 • (FW 1998 MDIV)

**REYNOLDS TERRENCE P REV** (703)834-1217
12025 Meadowville Ct Herndon VA 20170-2608 • reynoldt@gunet.georgetown.edu • SE • 09/1991 09/1999 • (SPR 1972 MTH MDIV PHD)

**RHIVER JAMES W REV** (573)581-3080
1908 Beacon St Mexico MO 65265-1110 • MO • SP • St John Mexico MO • (573)581-5655 • (CQ 1981 MED)

**RHODE PAUL G REV** (303)776-9817
2828 Mountain View Ave Longmont CO 80503-2313 • RM • SP • Eternal Savior Lafayette CO • (303)665-6105 • (FW 1981 MDIV)

**RHODES DANIEL SCOTT REV** (660)463-7192
2095 Hwy KK Concordia MO 64020 • MO • SP • St Matthew Concordia MO • (660)463-2719 • (SL 1994 MDIV)

**RICE RICHARD R REV** (415)387-7401
495 Ninth Ave San Francisco CA 94118-2915 • revrrice@aol.com • CNH • Assoc • Zion San Francisco CA • (415)221-7500 • (SL 1985 MDIV)

**RICE STEVEN DANIEL REV** (614)876-6123
5456 Ramblehurst Ct Columbus OH 43221-5910 • srice5456@aol.com • OH • Ohio Olmsted Falls OH • (SL 1972 MDIV)

**RICHARDSON BRUCE HARLAN REV** (763)682-0921
204 17th St S Buffalo MN 55313 • b.richardson@toast.net • MNS • SP • Hosanna Buffalo MN • (763)682-3278 • (SL 1996 MDIV)

**RICHARDSON CARL JOHN REV** (319)425-4237
200 Vine St Fayette IA 52142-9733 • IE • SP • Grace Fayette IA • (319)425-3544 • (CQ 1984 MDIV)

**RICHARDSON GLENN W REV** (716)542-9607
7881 Moore Rd Akron NY 14001-9726 • glenn7881@aol.com • EA • 02/1989 02/2000 • (SPR 1976 MDIV)

**RICHARDSON JAMES M SR.** (512)237-2902
707 Bishop St Smithville TX 78957 • TX • SP • Grace Smithville TX • (512)237-2108 • (SL 2000 MDIV)

**RICHARDT MATTHEW MARK REV** (307)733-6629
C/O Redeemer Lutheran Church PO Box 1016 Jackson WY 83001 • redeemer@wyoming.com • WY • SP • Redeemer Jackson WY • (307)733-3409 • (FW 1995 MDIV)

**RICHERT PAUL O REV** (313)665-1729
6655 Jackson Rd Trl 633 Ann Arbor MI 48103 • MI • EM • (SL 1951)

**RICHESON RONALD LEE REV** (502)995-0499
8804 Gladstonberry Place Louisville KY 40258 • faithpas@couriernet.infi.net • IN • SP • Faith Louisville KY • (502)367-8513 • (SL 1991 MDIV)

**RICHMEYER EDWARD J REV** (505)622-4395
1610 S Michagan Roswell NM 88201-3747 • RM • EM • (SPR 1966 MA)

**RICHTER ELDOR W REV** (847)255-8847
714 E Hackberry Dr Arlington Hts IL 60004 • rick520juno.com • NI • EM • (SL 1957 MDIV)

**RICHTER GEORGE J JR. REV** (262)938-9614
1365 N Calhoun Rd Brookfield WI 53005-5565 • gracelch@execpc.com • SW • SP • Grace Milwaukee WI • (414)384-3520 • (SPR 1968 MDIV)

**RICHTER JAMES F REV**
Living Savior Luth Church 2159 Azalea Dr Lawrenceville GA 30043-2635 • urforgiven@altavista.com • FG • SP • Living Savior Lawrenceville GA • (770)237-3232 • (SL 1995 MDIV)

**RICHTER LEO M REV** (410)833-1666
1818 Emory Rd Reisterstown MD 21136-4015 • SE • EM • (SL 1957 MA)

**RICHTER PAUL W REV** (410)666-5833
1022 Bosley Rd Cockeysville MD 21030-3114 • pastor@stjohnslcms.org • SE • SP • St John Blenheim Long Green MD • (410)592-8018 • (SL 1976 MDIV)

**RICHTER ROBERT L DR** (850)444-9918
3151 Leesburg Square Pensacola FL 32504 • bobsue65@dellnet.com • SO • Asst • Grace Pensacola FL • (850)476-5667 • (SL 1960 MDIV MS DMIN)

**RICHTER THEODORE M REV** (334)671-1263
716 Evert Dr Dothan AL 36301 • trich716@ala.net • SO • SP • Trinity Dothan AL • (334)792-9745 • (CQ 1985 MDIV)

**RICHY JOHN M REV** (708)354-7951
729 N Spring Ave La Grange Park IL 60526-1474 • NI • 07/1995 07/2000 • (CQ 1985 MTH MDIV DMIN)

**RICK P BRADLEY REV** (308)946-2713
804 G Ave Central City NE 68826-1606 • NEB • SP • St Paul Central City NE • (308)946-2680 • (FW 1987 MDIV)

**RICKER JOHN S REV**
157 Marilyn Dr Swansea IL 62226-4250 • SI • EM • (SL 1946)

**RICKERT JOHN ROBERT REV** (864)582-4059
769 Kenmore Dr Spartanburg SC 29303 • jrickert@quik.com • SE • SP • Lamb Of God Spartanburg SC • (864)579-2062 • (FW 1987 MDIV)

**RICKMAN ROBERT P REV** (414)728-2247
205 Spring Dr Delavan WI 53115-1636 • SW • P Df • Our Redeemer Delavan WI • (262)728-4266 • (SL 1978 MDIV)

**RICKUS RICHARD H REV** (501)228-0075
6 Coral Ct Little Rock AR 72212-2207 • erickus@aristotle.net • MDS • SP • First Little Rock AR • (501)372-1023 • (SL 1987 MS MDIV)

**RICKUS ROBERT L REV** (716)695-2959
250 Rogers Ave Tonawanda NY 14150-5273 • rick4219@aol.com • EA • SP • Immanuel Tonawanda NY • (716)692-6200 • (SL 1965 STM)

**RIDDERING WAYNE W REV** (719)783-0392
308 S 3rd St Westcliffe CO 81252-9502 • dedeptl@ris.net • RM • SP • Hope Westcliffe CO • (719)783-9773 • (FW 1978 MDIV)

**RIDDLE J DEREK REV** (815)393-4784
16062 E Lindenwood Rd Lindenwood IL 61049-9724 • riddle@tbcnet.com • NI • SP • Immanuel Lindenwood IL • (815)393-4500 • (SL 1998 MDIV)

**RIEBHOFF JOHN W REV** (316)872-5771
1303 Elizabeth St Scott City KS 67871-1938 • lovegod@ruraltel.net • KS • SP • Holy Cross Scott City KS • (316)872-2294 • (FW 1981 MDIV DVM)

**RIECK JOHN W REV** (818)248-3337
4732 Rosemont Ave La Crescenta CA 91214-3145 • PSW • EM • (SL 1957 MDIV)

**RIEDEL E PAUL REV** (208)467-1705
2106 Carey Pl Nampa ID 83651-7563 • NOW • EM • (SL 1943)

**RIEDEL HUBERT W REV** (715)479-4927
2049 E Anvil Lake Rd Eagle River WI 54521 • OH • EM • (SL 1950)

**RIEGE LYNN A REV** (402)329-6720
RR 1 Box 250 Pierce NE 68767-9413 • NEB • SP • St John Pierce NE* • (402)329-6720 • (CQ 1999)

**RIEHL KARL W REV** (519)685-9767
35 Piers Cres London ON N6E 1Z1 CANADA • EN • EM • * • (SL 1945)

**RIEKER ERIC A REV** (201)933-5867
295 Travers Pl Lyndhurst NJ 07071-1821 • ourcrew@aol.com • NJ • SP • St Matthew Lyndhurst NJ • (201)939-2134 • (FW 1981 MDIV)

**RIEKER ERIC H REV** (518)758-1204
32 Sunset Ave Kinderhook NY 12106-2317 • erieker@aol.com • AT • EM • (SPR 1951)

**RIEKER JOHN M REV** (973)334-5611
98 Pine Brook Rd Towaco NJ 07082-1523 • john213a@aol.com • NJ • SP • Holy Spirit Montville NJ • (973)263-1696 • (FW 1979 MDIV)

**RIEMAN DONALD A REV** (307)587-5712
198 Carter View Dr Cody WY 82414-8849 • WY • EM • (FW 1978)

**RIEMER CARLTON L REV** (405)624-8875
410 N Manning St Stillwater OK 74075-7915 • cariemer@provalue.net • OK • SP • Zion Stillwater OK • (405)372-3703 • (SL 1967 MDIV MA)

**RIEMER FREDERICK M REV** (903)860-3662
3102 Hwy 115 Scroggins TX 75480 • revriem@juno.com • TX • EM • (SPR 1956)

**RIEMER HILBERT W REV**
C/O Lutheran Church in Korea CPO Box 1239 Seoul 100-612 KOREA • riemer@chollian.net • SW • S Miss • South Wisconsin Milwaukee WI • (414)464-8100 • (SL 1961 MDIV LITTD)

**RIEMER LEROY E REV** (712)446-3428
107 W Washington St PO Box A Sutherland IA 51058-0901 • IW • SP • Bethel Sutherland IA • (712)446-3630 • (SL 1970 MDIV)

**RIEMER MILTON H REV** (512)453-3465
1602 Northridge Dr Austin TX 78723-2524 • TX • EM • (SL 1958 MDIV MA PHD JD)

**RIES THOMAS K REV** (612)435-1924
14905 1st Ave S Burnsville MN 55306-6452 • ries@csp.edu • MNS • SHS/C • Minnesota South Burnsville MN • (SL 1980 MDIV MBA)

**RIESS WALTER C REV** (517)652-4150
PO Box 232 Frankenmuth MI 48734-0232 • MO • EM • (SL 1950)

**RIETHMEIER HUBERT G REV** (423)510-0912
1112 Steeplechase Dr Chattanooga TN 37421-4433 • riethmei@chatt.mindspring.com • MDS • 06/1999 • (SL 1972 MDIV)

**RIFFEL ELMER L REV** (813)949-3865
17124 Orangewood Dr Lutz FL 33549-4504 • eriffel@gte.net • FG • EM • (SPR 1970 MDIV)

**RIGGERT JERRY A REV** (660)882-7209
1026 Wingate Boonville MO 65233 • immanluth@c-magic.com • MO • SP • Immanuel Boonville MO • (660)882-2208 • (FW 1978 MDIV)

**RIGGERT RICHARD L REV** (916)621-2398
1169 School St Placerville CA 95667-4733 • rich.riggert@poboxes.com • CNH • Assoc • First Placerville CA • (530)622-3022 • (CQ 1997)

**RIGGERT ROBERT D REV** (712)653-2104
810 Nishnabotna Dr Manning IA 51455 • bob.riggert@iowawest.org • IW • D Ex/S • Iowa West Fort Dodge IA • (CQ 1982 MED MAR)

**RIGGS ROBERT V REV** (740)965-9622
PO Box 186 203 Hawthorne Rd Sunbury OH 43074-9493 • dkmriggs@aol.com • OH • SP • Hope Sunbury OH • (614)965-1685 • (SL 1983 MDIV)

**RILEY DOUGLAS E REV** (330)274-8608
PO Box 125 Mantua OH 44255-0125 • djriley@nls.com • OH • SP • Christ Mantua OH • (330)274-2849 • (SL 1964 MDIV)

**RILEY DWIGHT D REV** (870)673-4422
602 Circle Lane Stuttgart AR 72160-5825 • davvic@mursuky.campus.cwix.net • MDS • Assoc • St John Stuttgart AR • (870)673-2858 • (FW 1993 MDIV)

**RILEY NATHAN R REV** (714)637-6158
1414 E Concord Ave Orange CA 92867-3853 • pasrileynr@aol.com • PSW • SP • Hephatha Anaheim CA • (714)637-0887 • (SPR 1975 MDIV)

**RILEY PATRICK J REV** (402)852-2669
1430 E St Pawnee City NE 68420 • NEB • SP • Zion Pawnee City NE • (402)852-2671 • (SL 1983 MDIV)

**RILEY WILLIAM R REV** (319)366-8046
1033 26th St SE Cedar Rapids IA 52403-3415 • wrbaylorkid@cs.com • IE • SP • St Paul Stanwood IA • (319)942-3924 • (CQ 1978 MRE)

**RIMBACH JAMES A REV**
C/O Concordia Theol Seminary 68 Begonia Rd Yau Yat Chuen Kowloo HONG KONG • NOW • S Miss • Northwest Portland OR • (SL 1965 MDIV STM PHD)

**RINEHARD ROY W REV** (715)526-5280
N6927 River Dr Shawano WI 54166-4222 • NW • SP • Our Savior Gresham WI • (715)526-5280 • (SL 1964 MA MDIV STM DED)

**RINEHART ROYCE E REV** (507)639-4111
PO Box 321 Trimont MN 56176 • revroyce³2000@yahoo.com • IE • SP • Trinity Trimont MN • (507)639-4111 • (SPR 1973 MDIV MDIV)

**RING GEORGE C REV** (515)284-1209
3215 Cedar Ct Des Moines IA 50320-1945 • ganddring@msn.com • IW • EM • (SPR 1946)

**RINGERS KEITH JOHN REV** (334)986-5782
12521 Chicago St Elberta AL 36530-2543 • kringers@gulftel.com • SO • SP • St Mark Elberta AL • (334)986-8133 • (SL 1984 MDIV)

**RINGHARDT WESLEY H REV** (501)293-4483
PO Box 220 London AR 72847-0220 • MDS • EM • (SL 1955)

**RINKER CRAIG W REV** (504)828-3802
C/O Concordia Univ-New Orleans 3229 36th St - Suite 210 Metairie LA 70001 • rinkercw@aol.com • SO • SHS/C • Southern New Orleans LA • (SL 1971 MDIV STM PHD)

**RINNE REX A REV** (920)734-7779
C/O Celebration Luth Church 3100 E Evergreen Dr Appleton WI 54913-9206 • cellcrex@juno.com • NW • SP • Celebration Appleton WI • (920)734-7779 • (SPR 1975 MDIV)

**RIORDAN STEVE G REV** (573)392-4603
C/O Bethany Lutheran Church 1000 N Grand Eldon MO 65026 • MO • SP • Bethany Eldon MO • (573)392-4603 • (SL 1999 MDIV)

**RIORDAN TODD C REV** (608)742-0479
124 E Marion St Portage WI 53901 • riordans@jvlnet.com • SW • Assoc • St John Portage WI • (608)742-2387 • (SL 1996 MDIV)

**RIPPE BRUCE W REV** (303)650-6815
11419 County Road 36 Platteville CO 80651-8620 • RM • Inst C • Rocky Mountain Aurora CO • (SL 1976 MDIV)

**RIPPY SEAN L REV**
628 Bayberry Pointe Dr NW #K Grand Rapids MI 49544-4612 • washmount@aol.com • MI • SP • Mount Olive Grand Rapids MI • (616)453-0803 • (SL 1998 MDIV)

**RISCHE HENRY R REV** (970)586-5591
1160 Lakeshore Dr Estes Park CO 80517-7113 • RM • SP • Mount Calvary Estes Park CO • (970)586-4646 • (SL 1961 MDIV)

**RISCHE JOHN R REV** (520)578-0047
5730 W Triangle Dr Tucson AZ 85713 • EN • EM • (SPR 1968)

**RISCHE SCOTT F REV** (619)593-7832
421 Vista Del Escuela El Cajon CA 92019-1211 • s.rische@worldnet.att.net • EN • SP • First El Cajon CA • (619)444-7444 • (SL 1988 MDIV)

**RIST PAUL L REV** (412)487-9638
4691 Hidden Pond Dr Allison Park PA 15101 • ascension@fyi.net • EA • Sn/Adm • Ascension Pittsburgh PA • (412)364-4463 • (SL 1979 MDIV)

**RIST RICHARD W REV** (907)694-3498
18901 Mountain Point Dr Eagle River AK 99577-8586 • zionpastor@gci.net • NOW • SP • Zion Anchorage AK • (907)338-3838 • (SL 1976 MDIV)

**RISTOW LEONARD E REV** (915)235-4158
806 E 14th St Sweetwater TX 79556-2506 • lristow@earthlink.net • TX • EM • (SPR 1954)

**RISTOW NEIL G REV** (612)405-1309
635 Waterview Cv Eagan MN 55123-2180 • ristow7@aol.com • MNS • SP • Our Savior Rosemount MN • (651)423-2580 • (SL 1986 MDIV)

**RISTVEDT JAMES W REV** (903)928-2304
26 Back Gate Rd Palestine TX 75801-9645 • TX • Inst C • Texas Austin TX • (SPR 1965 MDIV)

**RISTVEDT NATHAN PAUL REV** (402)826-3645
639 Michelle Crete NE 68333 • natennellbob@juno.com • NEB • SP • Bethlehem Crete NE • (402)826-4359 • (SL 1992 MDIV)

**RITOCH DAVID MICHAEL REV** (660)335-6528
108 Medallion Dr Sweet Springs MO 65351-1419 • dmritoch@mailandnews.com • MO • SP • Immanuel Sweet Springs MO • (660)335-4141 • (SL 1996 MDIV)

**RITT DAVID H DR** (734)432-0075
16431 Levan Livonia MI 48154-2035 • EDPresl@aol.com • EN • DP • English Farmington MI • (SPR 1969 MDIV DD)

**RITTENBACH LEROY C REV** (503)266-9632
830 S Pine St Canby OR 97013-8773 • NOW • SP • Grace Molalla OR • (503)829-2250 • (SPR 1969 MDIV STM)

**RITTER DANIEL R REV** (402)293-8948
13304 S 28th St Omaha NE 68123 • NEB • Sn/Adm • Pilgrim Bellevue NE • (402)291-2848 • (SL 1985 MDIV)

**RITTER JAMES F REV** (217)726-9904
136 Lost Tree Springfield IL 62704 • CI • Asst • Immanuel Springfield IL • (217)528-5232 • (SL 1984 MDIV)

**RITTER PHILIP K REV** (360)452-9239
233 E Panorama Ln Port Angeles WA 98362-1915 • paritter@ocypen.com • NOW • SP • St Matthew Port Angeles WA • (360)457-4122 • (SL 1975 MDIV)

**RITTER RONALD A REV** (760)723-7738
2037 E Mission Rd Fallbrook CA 92028-1806 • anr@tfb.com • PSW • 10/1995 10/1999 • (SPR 1970)

**RITTMANN CLARENCE REV** (605)882-3478
109 19th St NE Apt 11 Watertown SD 57201-2891 • clarence@dailypost.com • SD • EM • (SL 1928 DD)

**RIVENESS RODNEY D REV** (253)862-6622
11415 221st Ave E Sumner WA 98390-7857 • rdriveness@uswest.net • NOW • SP • Our Redeemer Bonney Lake WA • (253)862-0715 • (CQ 1983 MDIV)

**RIVERA WILFREDO C REV**
2059 W 28th St Cleveland OH 44113-4066 • OH • SP • El Buen Pastor Cleveland OH • (216)631-4634 • (CQ 1988)

**RIVETT EDWARD JAMES REV** (618)964-1413
1268 St Vincent Lane Marion IL 62959 • ejrivett@midwest.net • EN • Inst C • English Farmington MI • (CQ 1977 MSW MDIV)

**ROBAK WARD A REV**
11813 East 37th St Spokane WA 99206 • immanuellc@aol.com • EA • Inst C • Northwest Portland OR • (SC 1993 MDIV)

**ROBARGE DARYL B REV** (602)486-0464
7718 W Brown St Peoria AZ 85345-6798 • revdbr@pop.phnx.uswest.net • PSW • SP • Apostles Peoria AZ • (623)979-3497 • (SL 1974 MDIV)

**ROBATZEN DAVID A REV** (850)484-4546
5760 Leesway Blvd Pensacola FL 32504-7728 • pstrdavid@aol.com • SO • SP • Resurrection Pensacola FL • (850)456-5340 • (SL 1988 MDIV)

**ROBBERT GEORGE S REV** (314)862-7234
709 S Skinker Blvd Apt 701 Saint Louis MO 63105-3225 • MO • EM • (SL 1948 STM MA MDIV PHD)

**ROBBINS DOUGLAS A REV** (979)884-1471
C/O Trinity Lutheran Church Rt 1 Box 172 A Dime Box TX 77853 • TX • EM • (SPR 1960)

**ROBERSON JAMES R REV** (423)689-1142
3903 Harris Rd Knoxville TN 37918-6416 • doulosxp@aol.com • MDS • EM • (SPR 1963 MDIV)

**ROBERTS BRADLEY D REV** (559)252-8423
250 S Clovis Ave Apt 113 Fresno CA 93727-4219 • CNH • EM • (SL 1985 MDIV)

**ROBERTS BRIAN D REV**
St Luke Lutheran Church 2021 State Road 426 Oviedo FL 32765 • brian³maui@msn.com • S • Asst • St Luke Oviedo FL • (407)365-3408 • (FW 1988 MDIV)

**ROBERTS DONALD S REV** (305)743-5742
C/O Martin Luther Chapel 325 122nd Street Gulf Marathon FL 33050-3503 • FG • SP • Martin Luther Marathon FL • (305)289-0700 • (SL 1986 MDIV MRC)

**ROBERTS KENNETH H REV**
11459 Scripps Creek Dr San Diego CA 92131 • pastorkenr@juno.com • PSW • SP • Mount Olive Poway CA • (858)748-3871 • (SL 1981 MDIV)

**ROBERTS ROBERT RICHARD REV** (316)355-6117
PO Box 461 Lakin KS 67860-0461 • rroberts@pld.com • KS • SP • Immanuel Lakin KS • (316)355-7161 • (SPR 1973 STM MDIV MS)

**ROBERTS ROBERT ROLAND REV** (530)877-8226
1723 Lazy Oaks Cir Paradise CA 95969-3619 • rrrcar@aol.com • CNH • EM • (CQ 1982)

**ROBERTS TODD W REV** (525)596-1856
C/O Good Shepherd Luth Church Paseo de las Palmas 1910 Lomas de Chapultepec 11000 DF MEXICO • skypilot@acnet.net • NI • S Miss • Northern Illinois Hillside IL • (SPR 1975 MDIV)

**ROBERTS WALTER W REV** (616)895-6058
5962 Bauer Rd Hudsonville MI 49426-9598 • MI • EM • (SPR 1964 MDIV)

**ROBERTSON ELLIOTT M REV**
1338 S Hanover St Baltimore MD 21230-4221 • robertsone@aol.com • SE • SP • Martini Baltimore MD • (410)752-7817 • (FW 1985 MDIV)

**ROBINSON GEOFFREY L REV** (618)483-6646
6267 N 200th St Altamont IL 62411-9512 • geoff@altamont.net • CI • SP • Bethlehem Altamont IL • (618)483-6756 • (SL 1982 MDIV)

**ROBINSON JACK T REV** (706)858-0468
416 Evans Rd Rossville GA 30741-2412 • MDS • EM • (CQ 1984 MA PHD)

**ROBINSON JAMES W REV** 011-49-631-3608825
HHC 21st TSC Unit #23203 Box 472 APO AE 09263 • RobinsonJ@hq.21tsc.army.mil • RM • M Chap • Rocky Mountain Aurora CO • (SL 1972 MDIV)

**ROBINSON PAUL W REV** (314)725-3770
7 N Seminary Ter Saint Louis MO 63105-3010 • MO • SHS/C • Missouri Saint Louis MO • (314)317-4550 • (SL 1989 MDIV STM)

**ROBINSON RICHARD ERIC REV** (708)757-1972
1745 215th Pl Sauk Village IL 60411-4403 • rob2son@juno.com • NI • SP • Saint Paul Chicago IL • (773)721-1438 • (CQ 1994)

**ROBINSON WILLIAM L REV** (414)994-9060
W8497 Brazelton Dr Random Lake WI 53075-1106 • SW • SP • Immanuel Random Lake WI* • (414)994-9060 • (SL 1963)

**ROCK ROBERT L REV** (417)533-7794
325 Brook Lebanon MO 65536 • stoney@leblink.com • MO • EM • * • (SL 1945)

**ROCK RONALD D REV** (708)633-8824
7645 163rd St Tinley Park IL 60477-1430 • rdrock@juno.com • NI • Asst • Trinity Tinley Park IL • (708)532-9395 • (FW 1993 MDIV)

**ROCKEMANN LARRY W REV** (314)863-5753
8 N Seminary Terrace St Louis MO 63105-3010 • rockemannl@csl.edu • MO • SHS/C • Missouri Saint Louis MO • (314)317-4550 • (SL 1978 MDIV)

**ROCKENBACH MARK D REV** (402)228-2342
11666 W State Hwy 4 Beatrice NE 68310 • revrock@alltel.net • NEB • SP • First Trinity Beatrice NE • (402)228-0216 • (SL 1998 MDIV)

**ROCKEY JAMES H REV** (615)837-7854
1628 Celebration Way Nashville TN 37211 • JRockey@juno.com • MDS • Asst • Our Savior Nashville TN • (615)833-1500 • (SL 1998 MDIV)

**ROCKEY JONATHAN REV** (907)746-5131
HC 3 Box 9552 Palmer AK 99645-9804 • jonrock@pobox.alaska.net • NOW • SP • St John Palmer AK • (907)745-3338 • (SL 1979 MDIV)

**ROCKROHR CARL E REV** (314)727-5197
C/O Concordia Seminary 801 De Mun Ave St Louis MO 63105-3168 • rev-c-rockrohr@bigfoot.com • MO • 06/1998 06/2000 • (SL 1989 MDIV STM)

**ROCKROHR DAVID K REV** (414)445-0230
2338 N 55th St Milwaukee WI 53210-2741 • SW • EM • (SPR 1963 MDIV)

**RODECK ALVIN W REV** (540)562-0508
2834 Emissary Dr Roanoke VA 24019-3330 • arodeck@roanoke.infi.net • SE • EM • (SPR 1970)

**RODECK RONALD R REV** (806)794-1861
3806 95th St Lubbock TX 79423-3918 • TX • EM • (SL 1961 MDIV MS)

**RODENCAL LARRY J REV** (308)364-2706
C/O St John Luth Church RR 3 Box 124 Mc Cook NE 69001-9539 • larroden@juno.com • NEB • SP • St John Mc Cook NE • (308)364-2706 • (SL 1981 MDIV)

**RODEWALD ALFRED REV** (660)463-7909
PO Box 531 Concordia MO 64020-0531 • awrodewald@almanet.net • MO • EM • (SPR 1953)

**ROEDER EUGENE P SR. REV** (530)269-0133
5885 Lone Star Oaks Ct Auburn CA 95602-9280 • bgroeder@foothill.com • CNH • EM • (SL 1950)

**ROEGLIN MATTHEW**
3030 N Fairwood Ct Wauwatosa WI 53222-4020 • SW • Assoc • Zion Menomonee Falls WI • (262)781-8133 • (SL 2000 MDIV)

**ROEGNER ROBERT M REV** (201)263-1865
149 Second Ave Westwood NJ 07675-2132 • NJ • Sn/Adm • Zion Westwood NJ • (201)664-1325 • (FW 1981 MDIV)

**ROEHRS ROLAND H REV** (941)426-1563
3085 Pan American Blvd North Port FL 34287-1762 • jean@home.com • FG • EM • (SPR 1954)

**ROEHRS STEPHEN P REV**
642 Greenwich Dr Aiken SC 29803 • FG • Asst • Our Redeemer Augusta GA • (706)733-6076 • (SL 1971 MDIV)

**ROELLIG HAROLD F REV** (503)623-3506
14520 Ferns Corner Rd Monmouth OR 97361-9652 • harold.roellig@mciworld.com • NOW • EM • (SL 1957 PHD)

**ROEMER CARL E REV** (607)773-4404
47 Andrea Dr Apt D Vestal NY 13850-2281 • croemer@binghamton.edu • EA • Inst C • Eastern Williamsville NY • (716)634-5111 • (SPR 1964 MDIV THD)

**ROEPKE CHRISTOPHER A REV** (319)752-8146
1306 Madison Ave Burlington IA 52601-6336 • caroepke@aol.com • IE • SP • Concordia Burlington IA • (319)754-4246 • (SL 1989 MDIV)

**ROETHEMEYER ROBERT V REV** (219)637-5888
223 Eagle Point Ct Fort Wayne IN 46845-1182 • roethemeyerrv@mail.ctsfw.edu • IN • SHS/C • Indiana Fort Wayne IN • (SL 1986 MLS MDIV)

**ROEVER KENNETH H REV**
N1507 2nd St Rd Watertown WI 53098-3939 • SW • EM • (TH 1953)

**ROGERS CHARLES F DR** (214)886-4406
6224 C Z 4400 Commerce TX 75428-9717 • cfrogers@koyote.com • TX • SP • Trinity Commerce TX • (214)886-6810 • (SL 1973 MDIV MS DED)

**ROGERS EDWARD B REV** (334)774-3400
100 Heather Dr Ozark AL 36360-9220 • EBR@prodigy.net • SO • EM • (SPR 1963 MDIV)

**ROGERS JAMES C REV** (636)391-6828
818 Whispering Village Cir Ballwin MO 63021-4483 • JRogers@LordOfLifeLCMS.org • MO • SP • Lord Of Life Chesterfield MO • (636)532-0400 • (SL 1973 MDIV)

**ROGERS MICHAEL L REV** (402)478-4537
Rt 5 Box 298F Bemidji MN 56601 • NEB • SP • St Paul Arlington NE • (402)478-4278 • (SPR 1972 MDIV DMIN)

**ROGERS RAY M REV**
215 Choptank Ave Cambridge MD 21613-1626 • SE • Southeastern Alexandria VA • (SL 1982 MDIV)

**ROGERS RICHARD S REV**
CMR 415 Box 4684 APO AE 09114 • SRRogers@t-online.de • SE • M Chap • Southeastern Alexandria VA • (SL 1981 MDIV STM)

**ROGERS ROBERT A REV** (206)297-2959
346 N 101ST ST Seattle WA 98133 • robrogl@aol.com • NOW • Assoc • Messiah Seattle WA • (206)524-0024 • (SL 1990 MDIV)

**ROGERS THOMAS J DR** (949)472-6109
24411 Corta Cresta Dr Lake Forest CA 92630-3914 • aslcpastor@aol.com • PSW • Sn/Adm • Abiding Savior Lake Forest CA • (949)830-1460 • (CQ 1980 MDIV DMIN)

**ROGGOW GERALD W REV**
St John Lutheran Church 725 S 14th St Ord NE 68862-1962 • gwrjar@cornhusker.net • NEB • SP • St John Ord NE • (308)728-5111 • (CQ 1992 MDIV MED)

**ROHDE DAVID W REV** (806)628-6584
C/O St Paul Luth Church PO Box 136 Wilson TX 79381-0136 • rohdedw@aol.com • TX • SP • St Paul Wilson TX • (806)628-6471 • (FW 1984 MDIV)

**ROHDE ROGER E REV** (219)546-2236
609 S Morningside Dr Bremen IN 46506-1415 • rogerrohde@juno.com • IN • Sn/Adm • St Paul Bremen IN • (219)546-2332 • (FW 1977 MDIV)

**ROHE HERBERT W REV** (417)667-5036
RR 3 Box 156 Nevada MO 64772-9427 • MO • EM • (SL 1945)

**ROHLFING LAWRENCE F REV** (541)994-8531
2517 NW Neptune Ave Lincoln City OR 97367-4105 • NOW • SP • St Peter Fisherman Lincoln City OR • (541)994-8793 • (SL 1957 MDIV)

**ROHLFS RAYMOND M REV** (517)655-3835
1156 E Sherwood Rd Williamston MI 48895-9441 • rohlfsrj@aol.com • MI • SP • St Luke Haslett MI • (517)339-9119 • (SL 1983 MDIV)

**ROHLWING DANIEL E REV** (970)949-1296
C/O Gracious Savior Luth Ch PO Box 250 Edwards CO 81632-0250 • drohlwing@vchs.org • RM • Sn/Adm • Gracious Savior Edwards CO • (970)926-3550 • (FW 1983 MDIV)

**ROHRBERG KENTON G REV**
C/O Messiah Lutheran Church 2000 Main St Hays KS 67601-2938 • mlcl@ruraltel.net • KS • SP • Messiah Hays KS • (785)625-2057 • (CQ 1980 MDIV)

**ROHWER GARY E REV** (818)789-0215
9008 Gothic Ave North Hills CA 91343-4127 • poblola@ibelieve.com • PSW • D Miss • Pacific Southwest Irvine CA • (949)854-3232 • (FW 1986 MDIV)

**ROJAS ROBERTO E REV** (407)207-0559
214 N Dean Rd Orlando FL 32825-3706 • amigorojas@aol.com • FG • O Miss • Florida-Georgia Orlando FL • (CQ 1981 MA)

**ROKENBRODT GARY REV**
43 N 3 St PO Box 504 Hilbert WI 54129-0504 • SW • SP • St Peter Hilbert WI • (414)853-3217 • (SL 1981)

**ROKKE RALPH M REV** (612)869-9261
5837 Pleasant Ave Minneapolis MN 55419-2306 • rrokke@pclink.com • MNS • Assoc • Minnesota South Burnsville MN • (CQ 1997 MST DMIN)

**ROLF JOHN D REV** (303)422-5362
8152 Kline St Arvada CO 80005-5202 • jdrolf@aol.com • RM • EM • (SPR 1955)

**ROLF RICHARD R REV** (716)592-4713
412 E Main St Springville NY 14141-1425 • richrudi7@yahoo.com • EA • EM • (SL 1958 MDIV)

**ROLF ROBERT F REV** (440)845-9281
22701 Lake Rd - Apt 410 Rocky River OH 44116 • OH • EM • (SL 1941 MA)

**ROLLEFSON STACY DEAN REV** (530)246-8979
Trinity Lutheran Church 2440 Hilltop Dr Redding CA 96002-0506 • stacerollefson@juno.com • CNH • SP • Trinity Redding CA • (530)221-6686 • (FW 1992 MDIV)

**ROLLINGS DERAL E REV** (334)968-8154
PO Box 791 Gulf Shores AL 36547-0791 • SO • SP • St Jude By Sea Gulf Shores AL • (334)968-JUDE • (SL 1981 MDIV)

**ROLUFFS CHARLES J REV** (503)788-9808
9675 SE Otty Pl Portland OR 97266-7029 • NOW • Sn/Adm • Beautiful Savior Portland OR • (503)788-7000 • (SPR 1960 MDIV)

**ROMA RON T REV** (314)849-8488
5137 Suson Way Ct Saint Louis MO 63128-4531 • MO • Tchr • LHS South Saint Louis MO • (314)631-1400 • (SL 1980 MDIV MED)

**ROMBERG DAVID F REV** (931)456-8007
101 Hilton Ln Fairfield Glade TN 38558-8689 • dromberg@citlink.net • EN • EM • (SL 1960)

**ROMIG DOUGLAS C REV**
8511 Lansdowne Rd Richmond VA 23229-3224 • Revromig@ctos.com • SE • Assoc • Trinity Richmond VA • (804)270-4626 • (SL 1995 MDIV)

**ROMULUS JOSEPH REV**
Delmar #9 • Rue du Cosquer #10 Port-au-Prince HAITI • FG • D Miss • Florida-Georgia Orlando FL

**ROPER R WILLIAM REV** (517)750-9360
1963 Elmhurst Ln Jackson MI 49201-9301 • rwroper@dmci.net • MI • SP • Redeemer Jackson MI • (517)750-3100 • (CQ 1977 MDIV)

**ROSCHE KENNETH L REV** (414)892-7501
124 Broadway St Apt 7 Sheboygan Falls WI 53085-1353 • EN • 01/1984 • (SPR 1964 MED)

**ROSCHKE EDGAR M REV** (513)821-1452
7605 View Place Dr Cincinnati OH 45224-1437 • OH • EM • (SL 1937 MA MA)

**ROSCHKE FRANCIS E REV** (719)599-7005
6627 Foxdale Cir Colorado Springs CO 80919-1770 • faroschke@aol.com • RM • EM • (SL 1947 DMIN)

**ROSCHKE HAROLD A REV** (319)352-2835
708 3rd Ave SW Waverly IA 50677-2912 • IE • EM • (SL 1936)

**ROSCHKE NORBERT F REV** (409)722-5076
2811 Memphis Ave Nederland TX 77627-6731 • TX • EM • (SL 1941)

**ROSE DAVID R REV** (707)263-4742
852 Central Park Ave Lakeport CA 95453-4230 • drrose@jps.net • CNH • SP • First Lucerne CA* • (707)274-5572 • (SL 1974 MDIV)

**ROSE KARL A REV** (715)659-5598
PO Box 109 Spencer WI 54479 • kpjrose@commplusis.net • NW • SP • Trinity Spencer WI • (715)659-4006 • (SPR 1974 MDIV)

**ROSE MARTIN W REV** (715)234-3282
2372 20 1/4 St Rice Lake WI 54868-9783 • NW • EM • (SL 1943)

**ROSE ROBERT H REV** (845)446-5998
20 Cedar Ln Highland Falls NY 10928-1523 • AT • EM • (SL 1957)

**ROSEMAN JAMES N REV** (843)237-7789
1718 Hawthorn Dr Pawleys Island SC 29585-8160 • James.Roseman@eudoramail.com • SE • EM • (SPR 1961 DMIN)

**ROSEMAN RICHARD Y REV** (305)852-5961
108 Ocean Dr Tavernier FL 33070-2340 • dfcpr@ndak.net • FG • SP • Immanuel Tavernier FL • (305)852-8711 • (SPR 1964 MDIV)

**ROSEN EDGAR R REV** (540)932-8920
100 Waverley Dr - Apt C2 Waynesboro VA 22980 • enbrosen@intelos.net • SE • EM • (SPR 1963)

**ROSENAU GRAEME M REV** (562)941-4658
14717 Fairvilla Dr La Mirada CA 90638-3006 • graemem@aol.com • PSW • EM • (SL 1959 MDIV DMIN)

**ROSENAU MARK W REV** (402)476-6819
4333 N 15th St Lincoln NE 68521-1904 • calvary@inetnebr.com • NEB • SP • Calvary Lincoln NE • (402)476-1567 • (CQ 1997)

**ROSENAU STANLEY W REV** (507)835-3233
208 14th Ave NE Waseca MN 56093-2780 • MNS • EM • (SPR 1953)

**ROSENBLADT W ROD REV** (714)734-6827
1971 Blueberry Way Tustin CA 92780-3908 • PSW • SHS/C • Pacific Southwest Irvine CA • (949)854-3232 • (CQ 1987)

**ROSENKAIMER RONALD R II REV**
118 Williams St Bowling Green OH 43402-3256 • OH • SP • Community Of Christ Bowling Green OH • (419)352-5101 • (FW 1992 MDIV)

**ROSENTHAL EDWIN H JR. REV** (503)397-6765
58241 S Division Rd Saint Helens OR 97051-3240 • Calvary.lutheran.lcms@juno.com • NOW • SP • Calvary Saint Helens OR • (503)397-1739 • (CQ 1992 MDIV)

**ROSENTHAL TIMOTHY S REV** (580)480-0312
471 Jasmine Altus AFB Altus OK 73521 • dr.t.rose@juno.com • MO • M Chap • Missouri Saint Louis MO • (314)317-4550 • (SL 1988 STM MDIV MMU DMIN)

**ROSENTRETER DONALD G REV** (702)564-8222
3524 Humble Ave Midland TX 79707-6609 • >drose@marshill.comı • PSW • 07/1993 07/2000 • (SL 1977 MDIV)

**ROSENVINGE DOUGLAS A REV** (352)688-9694
2132 Orchard Park Dr Spring Hill FL 34608-4970 • acolyte@juno.com • FG • SP • Hope Hudson FL • (727)863-6446 • (FW 1981 MDIV)

**ROSER TIMOTHY W REV** (715)635-2008
W7190 Luther Rd Spooner WI 54801-8676 • NW • SP • Faith Spooner WI • (715)635-8167 • (SL 1989 MDIV STM)

**ROSER WILLIAM K REV** (920)261-3191
1416 Oak St Watertown WI 53098-1135 • wkroser@execpc.com • SW • EM • (SPR 1958)

**ROSIN ROBERT L REV** (314)505-7134
19 N Seminary Ter Saint Louis MO 63105-3011 • MO • SHS/C • Missouri Saint Louis MO • (314)317-4550 • (SL 1976 MDIV PHD)

**ROSIN WALTER L REV** (715)524-2655
1623 S Spruce Ct Shawano WI 54166 • we³be@ezwebtech.com • NW • EM • (SL 1953 MDIV THD LHD)

**ROSIN WILBERT H REV** (314)894-6082
4787 Chapel Hill Dr Saint Louis MO 63128-2405 • MO • EM • (SL 1947 MDIV PHD)

**ROSNAU ALAN PAUL REV** (602)788-6013
5959 E Phelps Rd Scottsdale AZ 85254-9224 • PSW • Asst • Shepherd Desert Scottsdale AZ • (480)860-1188 • (SL 1985 MDIV)

**ROSNAU PAUL O REV** (626)336-8248
15316 Cristalino St Hacienda Heights CA 91745-5923 • PSW • EM • (SL 1956 MDIV)

**ROSS HAL G REV** (360)377-6253
7737 Vineyards Ln NE #B201 Bremerton WA 98311-8707 • hal.lonnie@rossemail.com • NOW • SP • Evergreen Seabeck WA • (360)830-4180 • (FW 1996 MDIV)

**ROSS HAROLD E REV** (815)337-3518
12212 Mc Cannon Rd Woodstock IL 60098 • rosshe@megsinet.net • NI • Evergreen Seabeck WA • (360)830-4180 • (SL 1961)

**ROSS WILLIAM A REV** (513)722-8233
1283 Cross Creek Dr Loveland OH 45140 • OH • EM • (SPR 1952)

**ROSSIN DELBERT R REV** (715)325-6026
1065 Kings Way Nekoosa WI 54457 • drossrim@wctc.net • NW • Assoc • Bethlehem Nekoosa WI • (715)886-4081 • (SL 1963 MDIV)

**ROSSINGTON MARK W REV** (714)685-9956
6235 E Twin Peak Cir Anaheim CA 92807-4850 • mrossington@zionanaheim.org • PSW • Assoc • Zion Anaheim CA • (714)535-1169 • (FW 1993 MDIV MA)

**ROSSOW EDWIN J REV** (407)365-5567
2036 W State Road 426 Oviedo FL 32765-8825 • S • EM • (SL 1956)

**ROSSOW FRANCIS C REV** (314)727-5159
6501 San Bonita Ave Apt 2 Saint Louis MO 63105-3198 • MO • EM • (SL 1948 MDIV MA)

**ROSSOW JEROME W REV** (402)327-8020
4135 Teri Lane Lincoln NE 68502 • jr44538@navix.net • NEB • Assoc • Trinity Lincoln NE • (402)474-0606 • (SPR 1968 MDIV)

**ROSSOW LOWELL D REV** (417)624-3756
2605 Vermont Ave Joplin MO 64804-2958 • fisherofmen44@hotmail.com • MO • Sn/Adm • Immanuel Joplin MO • (417)624-0333 • (SL 1970 MDIV)

**ROSSOW RICHARD H REV** (810)751-2058
3607 Common Rd Warren MI 48092-6004 • lcmrossr@ccaa.edu • MI • SP • Holy Cross Warren MI • (810)751-2550 • (CQ 1990 MAR)

**ROSSOW ROBERT REV** (714)974-5519
305 W Brentwood Ave Orange CA 92865 • rossowr@cui.edu • PSW • SHS/C • Pacific Southwest Irvine CA • (949)854-3232 • (SL 1986 MDIV)

**ROSSOW TIMOTHY A REV** (630)778-0601
306 Westbury Ct Naperville IL 60565-2230 • trossow@bethanylcs.org • NI • Sn/Adm • Bethany Naperville IL • (630)355-2198 • (SL 1985 MDIV MA)

**ROTH CARLYLE L REV** (701)838-4663
1511 Glacial Dr Minot ND 58703-1222 • ND • Sn/Adm • St Mark Minot ND • (701)839-4663 • (SPR 1975)

**ROTH CLARENCE L REV** (610)381-2219
RR 3 Box 3494 Saylorsburg PA 18353-9749 • clroth@webtv.com • AT • EM • (SPR 1944)

**ROTH DELBERT R REV** (828)256-5070
3120 44th Avenue Dr NE Hickory NC 28601-9743 • delroth@twave.net • SE • EM • (SPR 1958)

**ROTH JOHN D REV** (559)741-0646
3108 S Jacob St Visalia CA 93277-7424 • revjroth@lightspeed.net • CNH • Sn/Adm • Grace Visalia CA • (559)734-7694 • (SL 1987 MDIV)

**ROTH MICHAEL J REV** (810)498-9137
22900 Gratiot Ave Eastpointe MI 48021-1654 • michaeljroth@hotmail.com • MI • Sn/Adm • St Peter Eastpointe MI • (810)776-1663 • (FW 1986 MDIV)

**ROTH STEVEN MARK REV**
36-29 Bell Blvd Bayside NY 11361-2056 • AT • SP • Good Shepherd Laurelton NY • (718)528-5068 • (CQ 1996)

**ROTH VICTOR M REV** (507)362-8529
115 Lake St W Waterville MN 56096-1466 • MNS • EM • (SPR 1953 MDIV)

**ROTHCHILD DARYL G REV** (701)839-8320
525 17th St SW Minot ND 58701-3523 • darylpeg@minot.ndak.net • ND • SP • Bethlehem Upham ND* • (701)272-6276 • (FW 1984 MDIV)

**ROTHCHILD DEAN F REV** (701)228-2935
715 7th St E Bottineau ND 58318-1419 • dfcpr@ndak.net • ND • SP • Our Savior Bottineau ND* • (701)228-3021 • (FW 1982 MDIV)

**ROTNEM ROBERT L M REV** (209)358-3471
C/O Holy Cross Lutheran Church 1495 Underwood Ave Atwater CA 95301-2745 • protokos@elite.net • CNH • SP • Holy Cross Atwater CA • (209)358-3471 • (FW 1989 MDIV)

**ROTTMANN ELLIS T REV** (636)225-6734
1211 Eagleshire Dr Manchester MO 63021-6851 • etrottmann@worldnet.att.net • MO • EM • (SL 1956 MDIV DMIN)

**ROTTMANN ERIK J REV** (217)754-3517
1585 Trinity Rd Bluffs IL 62621-9603 • rottmann@bluffsnet.com • CI • SP • Trinity Bluffs IL • (217)754-3517 • (FW 1996 MDIV)

**ROWAN ROBERT H REV** (701)250-9115
34 Santee Rd Lincoln ND 58504-9180 • ND • EM • (CQ 1985)

**ROWE DANIEL REV** (805)226-8878
2102 Summit Dr Paso Robles CA 93446 • danrowe@juno.com • CNH • SP • Trinity Paso Robles CA • (805)238-3702 • (SL 1985 MDIV)

**ROWLAND ROBERT C REV** (916)391-3463
6425 Greenhaven Dr Sacramento CA 95831-1613 • CNH • P Df • Valley Deaf Sacramento CA • (916)391-3463 • (SPR 1974 MDIV)

**ROWOLD HENRY L REV** (314)727-1608
4 Seminary Ter Saint Louis MO 63105-3011 • rowoldh@csl.edu • MO • SHS/C • Missouri Saint Louis MO • (314)317-4550 • (SL 1964 MDIV STM THD)

**ROWOLDT PAUL L REV** (402)564-5744
3731 Lakeview Ln Columbus NE 68601-7321 • NEB • EM • (CQ 1992 MDIV DMIN)

**ROWOLDT WALTER E REV** (402)483-2855
2405 S 60th St Lincoln NE 68506-3500 • EN • EM • (CQ 1996)

**ROYER WILLIAM M REV** (623)587-8154
1949 E Rosemonte Dr Phoenix AZ 85024-3053 • billroyer@hotmail.com • PSW • EM • (SPR 1956 MDIV)

**RUB ROBERT H JR. REV** (815)398-4759
4863 Alpine Park Dr Rockford IL 61108-2212 • rhrubjr@cs.com • NI • Sn/Adm • Redeemer Rockford IL • (815)397-2227 • (SPR 1966 MDIV)

**RUBECK LARRY D REV** (815)455-7323
907 Hawthorne Dr Crystal Lake IL 60014-8358 • NI • Assoc • Prince Peace Crystal Lake IL • (815)455-3200 • (SL 1994 MDIV)

**RUBEL WARREN G REV** (219)462-6450
913 Jefferson St Valparaiso IN 46383-5005 • wrubel@valpo.edu • IN • EM • (SL 1952 MDIV MA PHD)

**RUBKE DAVID A REV**
C/O Trinity Lutheran Church 800 N Sumner Ave Creston IA 50801-1349 • davidr@hiwaay.net • IW • Prince Peace Crystal Lake IL • (815)455-3200 • (FW 1984 MDIV)

**RUBKE WALTER C REV** (707)571-7673
816 Benton St Santa Rosa CA 95404-3708 • wlrubke@pon.net • CNH • EM • (SL 1948 MDIV MA PHD)

**RUCKMAN GARY L REV** (815)426-2176
PO Box 426 Herscher IL 60941-0426 • trinityher1@juno.com • NI • SP • Trinity Herscher IL • (815)426-2262 • (FW 1986 MDIV)

**RUDNICK MILTON LEROY DR**
5518 Lachman Ave NE Albertville MN 55301 • MNS • EM • (SL 1952 STM)

**RUDOLF BRUCE E REV** (516)654-3426
26 Rose Ave Patchogue NY 11772-2826 • AT • SP • Emanuel Patchogue NY • (516)758-2240 • (SL 1966 MDIV)

**RUDOLPH LAWRENCE P REV** (619)286-2819
4522 Collwood Ln San Diego CA 92115-2018 • lerudolph@netzero.net • PSW • EM • (SL 1941 MA)

**RUDOW ALLEN A REV**
PMB14173 241 Rainbow Dr Livingston TX 77399-2041 • allenr@access1.com • PSW • EM • (SL 1960 MDIV MA)

**RUDOW EUGENE C REV** (810)254-7941
49107 Cranberry Ct Shelby Twp MI 48315 • brudow725@aol.com • MI • EM • (CQ 1988 MAR MMTH)

**RUECKERT PAUL W REV** (314)434-2942
12723 Markaire Dr Saint Louis MO 63146-4416 • prueckert@stlnet.com • MO • Assoc • Immanuel Saint Louis MO • (314)993-2394 • (SL 1996 MDIV MS)

**RUEDIGER PAUL G REV** (517)734-3216
C/O Immanuel Luth Church (Moltke) 7134 Church Hwy Rogers City MI 49779 • ruedigerp@juno.com • MI • SP • Immanuel Rogers City MI • (517)734-3216 • (CQ 1982 MAR MA)

**RUEGER MATTHEW W REV** (515)864-2766
PO Box 267 Hubbard IA 50122-0267 • mrueger@netins.net • IE • SP • St John Hubbard IA • (515)864-2672 • (FW 1990 MDIV)

**RUEHRDANZ WALTER E REV** (847)818-8565
203 S Edward St Mt Prospect IL 60056-3415 • NI • EM • (SL 1949)

**RUETER GARY D REV** (785)478-4265
3975 SW King Arthurs Rd Topeka KS 66610-1540 • garyr@kslcms.org • KS • D Ex/S • Kansas Topeka KS • (SPR 1972 MDIV)

**RUFF DANIEL JOHN REV** (740)587-3453
10 Samson Pl Granville OH 43023-1166 • djruff@juno.com • OH • SP • Pilgrim Granville OH • (614)587-0345 • (FW 1984 MDIV)

**RUFF PAUL A REV** (941)753-7303
4654 La Jolla Dr Bradenton FL 34210-3931 • parruff@aol.com • FG • EM • (SL 1960 MDIV)

**RUFF ROGER O REV** (410)836-9168
1303 Cheshire Ln Bel Air MD 21014-2553 • rrooo8@juno.com • SE • SP • Advent Forest Hill MD • (410)838-5967 • (SL 1965 MDIV MED)

**RUHBUSCH WILLIAM H REV** (715)359-9757
6209 Alta Verde St Schofield WI 54476-3917 • NW • EM • (SPR 1963)

**RUHL LORNE C REV** (810)227-2367
195 Breezeway Dr Brighton MI 48116-8704 • MI • EM • (SL 1944)

**RUHL MICHAEL R REV** (734)426-2314
5918 Dexter Pinckney Rd Dexter MI 48130-8539 • evangelman@aol.com • MI • D Ex/S • Michigan Ann Arbor MI* • (SL 1971 MDIV)

**RUHLIG EDWARD M REV**
2173 Clover St NE Palm Bay FL 32905 • MI • EM • * • (SL 1937)

**RUHLIG ERWIN A REV** (217)636-7710
RR 2 Box 104F Athens IL 62613-9224 • eruhlig@juno.com • CI • EM • * • (SPR 1961)

**RUHLIG MICHAEL JOHN REV** (217)253-4539
706 E Northline Rd Tuscola IL 61953 • CI • SP • Immanuel Tuscola IL • (217)253-4341 • (FW 1995 MDIV)

**RUHNKE CHARLES D REV** (305)720-9663
7801 S Colony Cir Bldg 10103 Tamarac FL 33321-3996 • FG • 08/1988 08/2000 • (SL 1962 MED)

**RUIZ JOSE OVALLE REV** (915)593-4892
806 Los Surcos Rd El Paso TX 79907-2713 • RM • Asst • San Pablo El Paso TX • (915)858-2588 • (CQ 1996)

**RUIZ SAMUEL ISAIAS REV** (219)464-8760
152 College St Valparaiso IN 46383 • insruiz@aol.com • IN • D Miss • San Pablo El Paso TX • (SC 1996 MDIV)

**RULAND WARREN J REV** (505)625-8797
2705 Resolana Dr Roswell NM 88201-1340 • RM • SP • Immanuel Roswell NM • (505)622-2853 • (CQ 1988 MRE)

**RUMERFIELD EDWIN A REV** (541)258-2710
910 Cleveland St Lebanon OR 97355-4422 • rumerfield@dswebnet.com • NOW • SP • Bethlehem Lebanon OR • (541)258-6393 • (SPR 1969)

**RUMPEL WILLIAM A REV**
214 W 5th St Valley Center KS 67147-2613 • TX • EM • (SPR 1957)

**RUMSCH BRUCE A REV** (503)648-3362 3146 SE Brian St Hillsboro OR 97123-7014 • trinityor@aol.com • NOW • Assoc • Trinity Hillsboro OR • (503)640-1693 • (FW 1978 MDIV)

**RUMSCH WILBUR A REV** (503)981-4465 1954 Umpqua Rd Woodburn OR 97071-2725 • warums@web-ster.com • NOW • EM • (SPR 1953 MAR MDIV DMIN)

**RUMSEY JOHN C REV** (619)429-6506 1237 East Ln Imperial Beach CA 91932-3229 • PSW • EM • (SPR 1957)

**RUNGE BRIAN E REV** (904)609-0130 33 Berwick Cir Shalimar FL 32579-2019 • brunge358@aol.com • SO • SP • Good Shepherd Shalimar FL • (850)651-1022 • (SL 1985 MDIV)

**RUNGE EDGAR G REV** (407)359-1431 1354 Haven Dr Oviedo FL 32765-5213 • irmarunge@aol.com • SE • EM • (SL 1936)

**RUNGE EDWARD W REV** (314)867-1437 247 Coburg Dr Saint Louis MO 63137-3946 • EN • EM • (SPR 1963)

**RUNGE RICHARD H REV** (704)372-7317 2802 Watch Hill Ct Charlotte NC 28210-7971 • runge1225@aol.com • SE • SP • Ascension Charlotte NC • (704)372-7317 • (SPR 1969 DMIN)

**RUNTSCH TIMOTHY D REV** (970)686-2833 781 Pioneer Pl Windsor CO 80550-5954 • runtsch@redeemer-lutheran.org • RM • SP • Redeemer Fort Collins CO • (970)225-9020 • (SL 1990 MDIV)

**RUPE RYAN R REV** (281)489-0332 4002 Spring Meadow Dr Pearland TX 77584-9364 • ryanrupe@yahoo.com. • TX • Assoc • Epiphany Pearland TX • (281)485-7833 • (SL 1998 MDIV)

**RUPERT LEE ELIOT REV** (307)347-6235 1912 Gregg Ave Worland WY 82401 • WY • SP • St Luke Worland WY • (307)347-2293 • (SL 1991 MDIV)

**RUPP ROBERT G REV** (850)456-6428 312 E Winthrop Ave Pensacola FL 32507-3670 • bobruppmel3@juno.com • SO • Sn/Adm • Redeemer Pensacola FL • (850)455-0330 • (SPR 1969 MDIV)

**RUPPERT MARK A REV** (412)243-7220 C/O Trinity Deaf Luth Church 409 Swissvale Ave Pittsburgh PA 15221-3542 • ruppertm@bellatlantic.net • EA • Df Min • Trinity Deaf Pittsburgh PA • (412)731-2550 • (FW 1997 MDIV)

**RUSCHKE PALMER G H REV** (651)784-8922 1208 Ravenswood Ct Shoreview MN 55126-8607 • joyb2u@juno.com • MNS • EM • (SL 1956 STM DMIN)

**RUSERT LYLE D DR** (507)239-2217 PO Box 96 Waldorf MN 56091-0096 • MNS • EM • (SPR 1953 MDIV DTH)

**RUSERT MATTHEW L REV** (507)375-4228 C/O St John Luth Church RR 1 Box 90 Saint James MN 56081-9735 • sbranch@ureach.com • MNS • SP • St John Saint James MN* • (507)375-4228 • (FW 1985 MDIV)

**RUSERT NATHAN J REV** (507)776-2725 413 N 1st Ave West Truman MN 56088-1132 • njrusert@juno.com • MNS • SP • St Paul Truman MN • (507)776-2801 • (FW 1987 MDIV)

**RUSH JAMES MCCALL REV** (559)338-2972 37994 Ruth Hill Rd Squaw Valley CA 93675-9643 • CNH • EM • (SPR 1973 MDIV)

**RUSNAK WILLIAM GARY REV** (636)397-6687 1225 Golden Harvest Dr Saint Peters MO 63376-5209 • brusnak@stlnet.com • MO • Assoc • Zion Saint Charles MO • (636)441-7425 • (SL 1996 MA MDIV)

**RUSSELL BRUCE E REV** (303)443-7836 7005 Lake View Pt Longmont CO 80503-8738 • RM • SP • Divine Savior Longmont CO • (303)652-2419 • (FW 1982)

**RUSSELL RANDALL H REV** (540)548-0251 4000 Doran Rd Fredericksburg VA 22407 • k.russell@mindspring.com • EA • M Chap • Eastern Williamsville NY • (716)634-5111 • (FW 1991 MDIV)

**RUSSERT ARLYN A REV** (541)967-7145 875 NW Lawnridge St Albany OR 97321-1319 • NOW • EM • (SL 1954 MDIV)

**RUSSERT LUKE D REV** (316)689-8987 637 S Erie St Wichita KS 67211-2904 • lrussert@kscable.com • KS • SP • Trinity Wichita KS • (316)685-1571 • (FW 1984 MDIV)

**RUSSERT LUTHER E REV** (815)468-2077 357 W 7th St Manteno IL 60950-1181 • NI • EM • (SL 1952)

**RUSSERT MARTIN L REV** (402)371-5502 1106 Eldorado Rd Unit D Norfolk NE 68701-3079 • NEB • EM • (SL 1948 MDIV)

**RUSSOW HOWARD E REV** 23333 S Torrence Ave Crete IL 60417 • IN • EM • (TH 1939)

**RUSSOW JAMES R REV** (209)478-4228 1962 Pontelli Ct Stockton CA 95207-8811 • jnbrussow@aol.com • CNH • SP • Trinity Stockton CA • (209)464-1936 • (SPR 1973 MDIV DMIN)

**RUTHENBECK LORNELL L REV** (503)656-8997 1530 Windsor Dr Gladstone OR 97027-2649 • NOW • EM • (SPR 1948)

**RUTHENBECK NORMAN J REV** (952)934-6880 7497 Saratoga Dr Chanhassen MN 55317-9771 • normanr@livingchrist.org • MNS • Sn/Adm • Living Christ Chanhassen MN • (952)934-5110 • (SPR 1965 MDIV)

**RUTKOWSKY WALTER F REV** (517)652-8384 732 W Genesee St Frankenmuth MI 48734-1317 • MI • EM • (SL 1935)

**RUTOWICZ JOHN S REV** (712)758-3425 1079 Pine St Ocheyedan IA 51354 • IW • SP • St Peter Ocheyedan IA • (712)758-3425 • (FW 2000 MDIV)

**RUTT DOUGLAS L DR** (219)471-0836 2 Coverdale Dr Fort Wayne IN 46825 • ruttdl@mail.ctsfw.edu • IN • SHS/C • Indiana Fort Wayne IN • (FW 1986 MDIV DMISS)

**RUTTER DAVID ALLAN REV** (810)778-7422 22134 Colony St St Clair Shores MI 48080-2025 • EN • SP • St Paul St Clair Shrs MI • (810)777-0215 • (FW 1993 MDIV)

**RUTTER EDWARD J REV** (701)642-8523 820 8th Ave N Wahpeton ND 58075-3813 • ND • EM • (SPR 1954)

**RUTTER STEVEN D REV** (715)834-1132 1808 Sherwin Ave Eau Claire WI 54701 • rutter@ecol.net • NW • SP • St Matthew Eau Claire WI • (715)834-4028 • (FW 1984 MDIV)

**RUTZ JOHN M REV** C/O Shepherd Of The Valley LC 13101 Five Point Rd Perrysburg OH 43551 • OH • SP • Shep Of Valley Perrysburg OH • (419)874-6939 • (SL 1987 MDIV)

**RUTZ KARL W REV** (612)645-4245 1269 Shryer Ave W Saint Paul MN 55113-5935 • MNS • EM • (SL 1956 MDIV MA THD)

**RUTZ KURT G REV** (913)849-3711 C/O Trinity Lutheran Church 34868 Block Rd Paola KS 66071-6201 • KS • SP • Trinity Paola KS • (913)849-3344 • (FW 1984 MDIV)

**RUTZ WAYNE E REV** (219)493-7506 1825 Berwick Ln New Haven IN 46774-2019 • EN • EM • (SL 1967 MDIV)

**RUX JAROLD D REV** (314)843-8273 11542 Concord Village Ave Saint Louis MO 63128 • ic³ruxjd@lcms.org • MO • S Ex/S • Missouri Saint Louis MO • (314)317-4550 • (SPR 1976 MDIV)

**RYDEN WILLIAM C REV** (402)761-3151 630 Park Ave Milford NE 68405 • gs63413@ltec.net • NEB • SP • Good Shepherd Milford NE • (402)761-3146 • (SL 1998 MDIV)

**RYDING EUGENE C REV** (312)824-3411 8811 Old So State Rd 37 Bloomington IN 47403 • IN • EM • (SL 1946 MDIV JD)

**RYDING JOHN A REV** (316)947-3070 114 N Lincoln St Hillsboro KS 67063-1610 • zionluth@southwind.net • KS • SP • Zion Hillsboro KS* • (316)947-3522 • (SL 1977 MDIV MS)

**RYNEARSON RODNEY R REV** (314)487-9015 4101 Behnke Ct Saint Louis MO 63129-2712 • rodryn@aol.com • MO • S Ex/S • Missouri Saint Louis MO • (314)317-4550 • (SL 1959 MDIV MED DED)

**RYNEARSON STEPHEN P REV** (254)666-7506 809 Cheyenne Trl Hewitt TX 76643-3240 • slrynearson@mciworld.com • TX • SP • Peace Hewitt TX • (254)420-4729 • (SL 1987 MDIV)

**RYNEARSON TIMOTHY J REV** (605)692-1894 1018 4th St Brookings SD 57006 • peaceluth@choicetech.net • SD • SP • Peace Brookings SD • (605)692-5272 • (SL 1985 MDIV STM)

## S

**SAATKAMP RONALD E REV** (801)224-1106 909 E 640 N Orem UT 84097-4227 • r.saatkamp@worldnet.att.net • RM • SP • St Mark Provo UT • (801)225-5777 • (FW 1987 MDIV MBA)

**SABEL THOMAS A REV** (712)365-4328 2338 Story Ave Battle Creek IA 51006-8014 • tjsabel@pionet.net • IW • SP • St John Climbing Hill IA* • (712)876-2686 • (SL 1993 MDIV)

**SABO ANDREW REV** (913)648-1949 9200 Somerset Dr Overland Park KS 66207-2451 • KS • EM • * • (SL 1945)

**SACHS JONATHAN BAUER REV** (519)253-1805 1400 Ouellette Ave #1203 Windsor ON N8X 4T4 CANADA • sachs@xmail.com • S • 07/1997 07/2000 • * • (SL 1994 MDIV MA)

**SACKSCHEWSKY RALPH A REV** (860)456-2210 786 Storrs Rd Storrs Mansfield CT 06268-2627 • ralphs@connix.com • NE • D Ex/S • New England Springfield MA* • (CQ 1981)

**SAEGER ALFRED R JR. REV** (904)756-5091 1574 Town Park Dr Port Orange FL 32119-1270 • NE • EM • * • (SL 1949 STM MA)

**SAEGER LAWRENCE W REV** (618)283-8766 PO Box 101 Vandalia IL 62471-0101 • lsaeger@hotmail.com • CI • SP • Holy Cross Vandalia IL • (618)283-1133 • (SPR 1970 MDIV MA)

**SAEGER MAYNARD H REV** (909)986-3247 1527 N Boulder Ave Ontario CA 91762-1211 • PSW • EM • (SPR 1972 MA)

**SAEZ ALFRED R REV** (805)492-2514 2539 Young Ave Thousand Oaks CA 91360-1845 • PSW • EM • (SL 1943 MA PHD)

**SAGER WILLIAM A REV** (931)431-0079 1158-B Dent Ct Fort Campbell KY 42223-3404 • sagerw@emh2.campbell.army.mil • TX • M Chap • Texas Austin TX • (FW 1985 MDIV)

**SAGISSOR GEORGE W III REV** (320)289-1341 160 N Bordson St Appleton MN 56208-1404 • MNN • SP • Trinity Appleton MN • (320)289-1342 • (SPR 1975 MDIV)

**SAILER A DAVID REV** (814)235-0904 113 Rhaubert Cir State College PA 16801-7249 • adnasail@penn.com • EA • SP • Good Shepherd State College PA • (814)234-8177 • (SL 1968 MDIV)

**SAILER SCOTT C REV** (605)330-0849 2105 S Lincoln Ave Sioux Falls SD 57103-2333 • scottsailer@aol.com • SD • SP • Faith Sioux Falls SD • (605)332-3401 • (SL 1985 MDIV)

**SAINT PIERRE RUPERT A REV** (334)990-4801 210 Royal Lane Fairhope AL 36532 • SO • EM • (SPR 1960 DMIN)

**SAJBAN PAUL MARTIN REV** (412)347-7209 SS Peter/Paul Luth Church 699 Stambaugh Ave Sharon PA 16146 • S • SP • SS Peter&Paul Sharon PA • (724)347-3620 • (FW 1994 MDIV)

**SALAY JOHN-PAUL REV** (219)492-9468 4720 Druid Hills Dr Apt 112 Fort Wayne IN 46835 • EN • 06/1999 • (FW 1996 MDIV)

**SALCIDO RICHARD A REV** (217)243-7915 3 Greenbriar Dr Jacksonville IL 62650-1709 • salcido1@ispchannel.com • CI • Assoc • Salem Jacksonville IL • (217)243-3419 • (CQ 1991)

**SALEMINK RAYMOND J** (515)448-3255 208 Court Ave Eagle Grove IA 50533 • IW • SP • Mount Calvary Eagle Grove IA* • (515)448-4668 • (FW 2000 MDIV)

**SALESKA JOHN W REV** (219)483-2041 10720 Bayou Blvd Fort Wayne IN 46845-9400 • IN • SHS/C • Indiana Fort Wayne IN • (SL 1954 MED)

**SALESKA TIMOTHY E DR** (314)862-0498 12 Seminary Terrace St Louis MO 63105 • saleskat@csl.edu • MO • SHS/C • Missouri Saint Louis MO • (314)317-4550 • (SL 1982 MDIV MPHIL PHD)

**SALLACH DONALD E REV** (814)866-7662 5465 Patton St Erie PA 16509-2668 • EN • Assoc • Trinity Erie PA • (814)452-4888 • (SL 1955 MDIV)

**SALLACH MARK L REV** (814)824-5155 8833 Old Wattsburg Rd Erie PA 16510-5060 • EN • Sn/Adm • Trinity Erie PA • (814)452-4888 • (SL 1981 MDIV)

**SALLACH PHILIP N REV** (716)731-2720 C/O Holy Ghost Luth Church 6637 Luther St Niagara Falls NY 14304-2010 • EA • SP • Holy Ghost Niagara Falls NY • (716)731-5877 • (SPR 1975)

**SALLACH WILBERT L REV** (414)445-8955 3334 N 46th St Milwaukee WI 53216-3331 • SW • SP • Holy Ghost Milwaukee WI • (414)264-0372 • (SPR 1947)

**SALMINEN BRYAN R REV** (314)726-2183 #21 N Seminary Ter Clayton MO 63105-3010 • casey1386.aol.com • MO • SHS/C • Michigan Ann Arbor MI • (SL 1986 MDIV MED PHD)

**SALMINEN JON D REV** (713)997-2327 2322 Colleen Dr Pearland TX 77581-5413 • TX • Sn/Adm • Epiphany Pearland TX • (281)485-7833 • (SL 1989 MDIV)

**SALOMON ESAUL REV** (619)656-1108 583 Via La Paloma Chula Vista CA 91910-7947 • PSW • O Sp Min • Pacific Southwest Irvine CA • (949)854-3232 • (CQ 1982 MAIS MAR DMIN)

**SALVHUS ARVID M REV** (218)584-8440 C/O Trinity Luth Church PO Box 248 Twin Valley MN 56584-0248 • asalvhus@tvutel.com • MNN • SP • Trinity Twin Valley MN • (218)584-8440 • (FW 1986 MA)

**SAMMETINGER CARL A REV** (828)891-3539 200 Timberlake Ct Apt G-2 Etowah NC 28729-8713 • SE • EM • (SL 1951)

**SAMPSON MARLIN J REV** (530)677-6655 5616 Meesha Ln Placerville CA 95667-7740 • mjsampson@directcon.net • CNH • EM • (SPR 1951)

**SAMUEL VICTOR REV** 401 S Wyoming St Plainville KS 67663-2520 • KS • SP • First Plainville KS • (913)434-2874 • (CQ 1997)

**SANDATE ISIDRO REV** C/O First Immanuel 374 S 3rd St San Jose CA 95112-3648 • CNH • Asst • First Immanuel San Jose CA • (408)292-5404 • (FW 1996)

**SANDBERG DARRILL D REV** (916)632-9507 5505 Darby Rd Rocklin CA 95765 • www.dsandberg@starstream.net • CNH • EM • (SPR 1962 MDIV)

**SANDER MARTINHO Q REV** (920)208-9333 1642 S 23rd St Sheboygan WI 53081-5018 • revsander@aol. • SW • SP • Good Shepherd Sheboygan WI • (920)452-8759 • (CQ 1984)

**SANDERS THOMAS J REV** (708)456-5479 2334 N 77th Ave Elmwood Park IL 60707-3041 • trinluthup@aol.com • EN • Sn/Adm • Trinity Villa Park IL • (630)834-3440 • (FW 1978 MDIV)

**SANDERSFELD KYLE JOHN REV** 216 Norma Ave Waterloo IL 62298-1528 • SI • Assoc • Immanuel Waterloo IL • (618)939-6480 • (FW 1997 MDIV)

**SANDERSFELD VERNON G REV** (503)625-9792 17116 SW Scholls Sherwood Rd Sherwood OR 97140-8725 • vsandds@aol.com • NOW • Sn/Adm • St Paul Sherwood OR • (503)625-6648 • (SL 1983 MDIV)

**SANDERSON STEPHEN C REV** (520)343-2958 3012 W 14th St Yuma AZ 85364-4276 • steve1945@sprynet.com • PSW • SP • St Paul Sherwood OR* • (FW 1981 MDIV)

**SANDLEY ROBBY JOE REV** (505)356-0799 1010 E Amazon St Portales NM 88130-5528 • rsandley@yucca.net • RM • SP • Faith In Christ Portales NM • (505)356-2510 • (SL 1996 MDIV)

**SANDMANN DONALD W REV** 319 Northwest Passage Trl Fort Wayne IN 46825 • donsand@aol.com • NJ • DP • New Jersey Mountainside NJ • (SL 1963 MDIV STM DMIN LLD)

**SANDMANN RUDOLPH D REV** (330)929-7480 2180 Bailey Rd Cuyahoga Falls OH 44221-3418 • OH • EM • (SPR 1943)

**SANTAMARIA JORGE REV** (308)385-4739 216 W 21st Grand Island NE 68801 • santamaria@computer-concepts.com • NEB • O Miss • Cristo Cordero De Di Grand Island NE • (308)389-4611 • (SC 1993 MDIV)

**SANTANA LUIS M REV** (305)642-2860 621 Beacom Blvd Miami FL 33135 • FG • SP • St Matthew Miami FL • (305)642-2860 • (FW 1988 MDIV)

**SARESKY EDWARD L REV** 26724 Raquet Cir Leesburg FL 34748 • edls@prodigy.net • EA • EM • (SL 1953)

**SARRAULT JOEL H REV** (517)266-8540
2674 Oakwood Adrian MI 49221 • jsarrault@tc3net.com • MI • SP • St John Adrian MI • (517)265-6998 • (SL 1988 MDIV)

**SARRIA RICARDO H REV** (562)776-5262
9619 Samoline Ave Downey CA 90240-3246 • PSW • D Miss • Pacific Southwest Irvine CA • (949)854-3232 • (CQ 1982)

**SATTELMEIER DANIEL J REV** (915)849-3062
C/O St Matthews Lutheran Ch 11995 Montwood Dr El Paso TX 79936-0708 • stmattlelpaso@juno.com • RM • SP • St Matthew El Paso TX • (915)857-7492 • (SL 1975 MDIV)

**SATTELMEIER GLENN REV** (517)786-2016
PO Box 813 Lewiston MI 49756-0813 • MI • EM • (SPR 1962 MDIV)

**SATTGAST DALE L REV** (605)352-7824
20723 396th Ave Huron SD 57350-5040 • dsatt@santel.net • SD • Sn/Adm • Mount Calvary Huron SD • (605)352-7121 • (SL 1980 MDIV)

**SATTLER JOHN W REV** (317)823-8118
7470 Geist Valley Blvd Indianapolis IN 46236-9794 • jws@hclc.in.lcms.org • IN • Sn/Adm • Holy Cross Indianapolis IN • (317)823-5801 • (SL 1979 MDIV)

**SAUDER FREDERICK C REV** (715)832-6271
2217 Vienna Ter Eau Claire WI 54703-6074 • alfreds@execpc.com • NW • EM • (SPR 1963 MDIV)

**SAUER DAVID MICHAEL REV** (510)632-2112
1033 Begier Ave San Leandro CA 94577-3023 • splcdave@juno.com • CNH • SP • St Peter San Leandro CA • (510)638-7017 • (SL 1973 MDIV)

**SAUER JOHN A REV** (818)982-7758
6906 Bluebell Ave North Hollywood CA 91605-5129 • sauerpowr3@aol.com • PSW • SP • First Van Nuys CA • (818)989-5844 • (SL 1966 MDIV JD)

**SAUER ROBERT C REV** (314)925-0862
2716 Norwich Dr Saint Charles MO 63301-1344 • MO • EM • (SPR 1948 MDIV DD)

**SAULS DONALD A REV** (812)667-5700
5588 E Cty Rd 900 S Cross Plains IN 47017 • IN • SP • St Paul Cross Plains IN • (812)667-5700 • (FW 1984 MDIV)

**SAULS OTTIS L REV** (812)522-5983
717 S Walnut St Seymour IN 47274-2923 • osauls@compuage.com • IN • EM • (SL 1950)

**SAUNDERS BRIAN S REV** (319)263-0639
1103 Westwood Ln Muscatine IA 52761-2244 • revsaunders@eiccd.cc.ia.us • IE • SP • Our Savior Muscatine IA • (319)263-0347 • (FW 1990 MDIV)

**SAVAGE LEON E REV**
PSC 80 Box 10004 APO AP 96367-0004 • treker509@aol.com • CNH • M Chap • Calif/Nevada/Hawaii San Francisco CA • (415)468-2336 • (SL 1981 MDIV)

**SAWHILL DAVID L REV** (713)475-1547
2224 Walnut Ln Pasadena TX 77502-4045 • dsawhill@ghgcorp.com • TX • Sn/Adm • Zion Pasadena TX • (281)478-5849 • (SL 1981 MDIV)

**SAWHILL LAWRENCE W REV** (402)466-0595
6100 Vine St Apt W150 Lincoln NE 68505-2872 • lwsawhill@wwdb.org • NEB • EM • (SPR 1951)

**SAWYER GREGORY L REV** (810)953-9260
1105 Townline Ct Grand Blanc MI 48439 • faithgbm@tir.com • MI • Assoc • Faith Grand Blanc MI • (810)694-9351 • (SL 1991 MDIV PHD)

**SAWYER J RICHARD REV** (601)992-9741
117 Christy Ln Brandon MS 39047 • seelsorge@aol.com • SO • SP • Good Shepherd Brandon MS • (601)992-4752 • (SL 1987 MDIV)

**SAXE STEVEN M REV**
40 Wood Pointe Dr #64 Scottswood Greenville SC 29615 • sjsaxe@juno.com • SE • SP • Good Shepherd Greenville SC • (864)244-5825 • (SL 1987 MDIV)

**SAYLOR KEVIN K REV** (440)960-2594
5102 Ashland Ave Lorain OH 44053 • OH • SP • Zion Lorain OH • (440)282-8418 • (FW 1981 MDIV)

**SAYLOR MICHAEL W REV** (712)364-3266
1101 Park Lane Ida Grove IA 51445 • saylor@pionet.net • IW • Assoc • St Paul Ida Grove IA • (712)364-2918 • (FW 1999 MDIV)

**SAYRE ROGER B REV** (614)836-8000
3813 Big Walnut Dr Groveport OH 43125-9281 • rbrookssayre@cs.com • OH • 09/1990 09/1999 • (FW 1988 MDIV)

**SAYRE THOMAS M REV** (630)897-0660
C/O Lutheran Bible Translators PO Box 2050 Aurora IL 60507-2050 • revsay@aol.com • NI • O Sp Min • Northern Illinois Hillside IL • (FW 1986 MDIV)

**SCAER DAVID P REV** (219)637-6201
1912 Brandywine Trl Fort Wayne IN 46845-1578 • dpscaer@juno.com • IN • SHS/C • Indiana Fort Wayne IN • (SL 1960 MDIV THD)

**SCAER PAUL J REV** (215)438-8495
4000 Gypsy Lane #611 Philadelphia PA 19144 • scaerp@pond.com • EN • 11/1998 • (SL 1972 MSLS)

**SCAER PETER JAMES REV** (219)480-0169
1914 Wendmere Ln Fort Wayne IN 46825 • pjscaer@yahoo.com • IN • SHS/C • Indiana Fort Wayne IN • (FW 1992 MDIV MA)

**SCANSEN JERRY P REV** (503)393-2138
4252 Prairie Star Ct NE Salem OR 97305-2390 • revjer@home.net • NOW • EM • (SL 1993 MDIV)

**SCAR WILLIAM A REV** (203)264-9591
711B Heritage Vlg Southbury CT 06488-1606 • NE • EM • (SL 1945 MDIV MA)

**SCAR WILLIAM C DR** (310)548-4448
1536 W 25th St San Pedro CA 90732-4402 • EN • Inst C • English Farmington MI • (SL 1971 MDIV DMIN)

**SCARBEARY BRUCE W REV** (309)923-7646
704 N Jefferson St PO Box 687 Roanoke IL 61561-0687 • CI • SP • Trinity Roanoke IL • (309)923-5251 • (FW 1989 MDIV)

**SCHAADT JOHN P REV** (847)368-3081
800 W Oakton St #318H Arlington Hts IL 60004-4602 • EN • EM • (TH 1948)

**SCHAAR CHRISTOPHER G REV** (626)335-4465
920 Starcrest Dr Glendora CA 91740-4743 • firstpasa@aol.com • PSW • SP • First Pasadena CA • (626)793-1139 • (SL 1994 MDIV)

**SCHAARSCHMIDT MARK F REV** (860)628-8108
84 Bridlepath Dr Southington CT 06489-4046 • revmark@javanet.com • NE • 05/1984 05/2000 • (FW 1979 MDIV)

**SCHABACKER MARTIN C REV** (707)426-3345
773 Meadowlark Dr Fairfield CA 94533-2313 • CNH • EM • (SL 1940)

**SCHABACKER THEODORE T REV** (602)985-7403
5545 E Decatur St Mesa AZ 85205-6521 • PSW • EM • (SL 1935 MA)

**SCHACK C EARL REV** (209)847-0607
C/O St Luke Lutheran Church 120 West Ave Oakdale CA 95361-3840 • CNH • SP • St Luke Oakdale CA* • (209)847-0607 • (SPR 1950)

**SCHACK GARY ROBERT REV** (314)830-2364
3214 Carefree Ln Florissant MO 63033 • gschack@anet-stl.com • MO • SP • Blessed Savior Florissant MO • (314)831-1300 • (CQ 1996 EDD)

**SCHACKEL JAMES H REV** (503)581-0363
3491 Lake Vanessa Cir NW Salem OR 97304-9553 • salemjim@aol.com • NOW • EM • (SL 1960 MDIV)

**SCHADE ALLEN W REV** (636)946-3546
821 Laurel Ln Saint Charles MO 63301-0716 • aschade@immanuelluth.org • MO • Sn/Adm • Immanuel Saint Charles MO • (636)946-2656 • (SPR 1973 MDIV)

**SCHAEDEL ROBERT C REV** (785)826-9257
101 W Neal Ave Salina KS 67401-7842 • revrobcs@aol.com • KS • Sn/Adm • Trinity Salina KS • (785)823-7151 • (SL 1972 MDIV)

**SCHAEFER DONALD C REV** (301)774-0618
3421 Damascus Rd Brookeville MD 20833-1210 • donalds807@aol.com • SE • SP • Good Shepherd Olney MD • (301)774-9125 • (CQ 1975 MDIV)

**SCHAEFER HENRY L REV**
7104 N Deschutes Dr Spokane WA 99208 • NOW • EM • (SL 1955)

**SCHAEFER HENRY MATTHEW REV** (501)847-7242
3118 Forest Dr Bryant AR 72022 • revschaefer@juno.com • MDS • Asst • Zion Alexander AR • (501)316-1100 • (SL 1996 MDIV)

**SCHAEFER LARRY ALLAN REV** (717)741-5454
2790 Chestnut Run Rd York PA 17402-8858 • larry1942@aol.com • SE • SP • First St John York PA • (717)843-8597 • (CQ 1996 MRE MED)

**SCHAEFER MARK ALLAN REV** (818)735-9945
5304 Mark Ct Agoura Hills CA 91301 • PSW • Asst • St Paul Agoura Hills CA • (818)889-1620 • (SL 2000 MDIV)

**SCHAEFER MAX L REV** (503)968-8024
15920 SW Oak Meadow Ln Tigard OR 97224-5640 • amysch@juno.com • NOW • EM • (SL 1956 MDIV)

**SCHAEFER THEODORE P REV** (714)761-4522
8901 Holder St Buena Park CA 90620 • PSW • SP • Bethel Buena Park CA • (714)527-4776 • (SL 1991 MDIV)

**SCHAEFFER KENDALL L REV** (616)426-8931
PO Box 142 Sawyer MI 49125 • revkenschaeffer@aol.com • MI • SP • Trinity Sawyer MI • (616)426-3937 • (FW 1989 MDIV)

**SCHAEFFER ROBERT B REV** (815)544-2816
1102 Luther Ave Belvidere IL 61008-4593 • revschaef@juno.com • NI • 11/1998 • (SPR 1972 MDIV)

**SCHAETZLE GEORGE D REV**
5580 Bridgetown Rd Apt #2 Cincinnati OH 45248 • geoschaetzlerev@hotmail.com • EN • 06/1997 06/2000 • (CQ 1981 MDIV)

**SCHAFER EDMUND E REV** (850)482-4691
C/O Ascension Lutheran Church 3975 Highway 90 Marianna FL 32446-8922 • SO • SP • Ascension Marianna FL • (850)482-4691 • (CQ 1988 MA MA)

**SCHAFER STEPHEN B REV**
2001 Old Frederick Rd Catonsville MD 21228-4119 • SE • SP • St Paul Catonsville MD • (410)747-1897 • (SL 1985 MDIV)

**SCHAFFER HARVEY L REV** (360)459-4443
4603 Yorkshire Dr SE Olympia WA 98513-4863 • hls65@worldnet.att.net • PSW • EM • (SPR 1961 MS)

**SCHAIBLE H JOHN REV** (714)679-8560
27283 Terrytown Rd Sun City CA 92586-3210 • PSW • EM • (TH 1952 STM)

**SCHAIBLEY ROBERT W REV** (719)282-9367
8174 Ferncliff Dr Colorado Springs CO 80920-1514 • lutheran@ix.netcom.com • RM • SP • Shep Springs Colorado Springs CO • (719)598-7446 • (SPR 1972 MDIV)

**SCHALK GERALD REV** (847)516-3390
217 Lexington Ave Fox River Grv IL 60021-1856 • stmatthewbarrington@ameritech.net • NI • Assoc • St Matthew Barrington IL • (847)382-7002 • (CQ 1980 MED MAR STD)

**SCHALLER GILBERT REV** (612)724-1888
6532 16th Ave S #208 Minneapolis MN 55423-1776 • MNS • EM • (TH 1935)

**SCHALLER ROBERT W REV** (602)944-3487
1112 W Lawrence Ln Phoenix AZ 85021-4435 • PSW • EM • (SL 1936)

**SCHALLER SCOTT A**
261 Harbor Dr Gun Barrel City TX 75147 • TX • SP • St Peter Gun Barrel City TX • (903)887-0436 • (SL 2000 MDIV)

**SCHALLHORN ROBERT G JR. REV** (219)293-4027
433 Aspin Dr Elkhart IN 46514-1428 • pastor@trinityl.org • IN • Sn/Adm • Trinity Elkhart IN • (219)522-1491 • (SL 1977 MDIV MA)

**SCHALM ROGER B REV** (520)726-5144
2281 E 26th Way Yuma AZ 85365-3261 • rbschalm@aol.com • PSW • EM • (SPR 1964 MDIV MSED MA)

**SCHALOW DOUGLAS A REV** (715)569-4878
6550 Cameron Ave E Vesper WI 54489 • NW • SP • Trinity Vesper WI* • (715)569-4114 • (CQ 1993 MDIV MDIV)

**SCHAMBER KENNETH G REV** (573)221-7051
C/O Immanuel Luth Church 6508 County Road 263 Hannibal MO 63401-6612 • immanluth@socket.net • MO • SP • Immanuel Hannibal MO* • (573)221-7051 • (SL 1974 MDIV)

**SCHAMEHORN PHILIP J REV** (219)489-7179
1310 Windsor Woods Blvd S Fort Wayne IN 46845-1078 • ohlcms@aol.com • IN • SP • Our Hope Huntertown IN • (219)637-3625 • (FW 1985 MDIV)

**SCHAMENS KENNETH W REV** (352)335-8780
8723 SW 45th Blvd Gainesville FL 32608-4138 • kenschamen@aol.com • FG • EM • (CQ 1982 MAR MA MA)

**SCHAPER GARY G REV** (636)458-4381
2438 Indian Tree Run Wildwood MO 63038-1516 • schaperg@csl.edu • MO • S Ex/S • Missouri Saint Louis MO • (314)317-4550 • (SL 1966 DMIN)

**SCHARDT WAYNE M REV** (281)292-0306
21 Buttonbush Ct The Woodlands TX 77380-0924 • TX • EM • (SL 1948)

**SCHARFF KIM L REV** (660)593-3354
202 N Pine St Norborne MO 64668-1125 • kscharff@greenhills.net • MO • SP • Trinity Norborne MO • (660)593-3721 • (FW 1981 MDIV MMU)

**SCHARLEMANN HERBERT K REV** (618)495-2270
110 W 5th St Hoffman IL 62250-1000 • SI • EM • (TH 1953 DMIN)

**SCHARLEMANN JOHN P REV** (816)524-7068
700 NE Chipman Lees Summit MO 64063 • st.matt-lsmo@worldnet.net • MO • SP • St Matthew Lees Summit MO • (816)524-7068 • (SL 1982 MDIV)

**SCHARNITZKE PHILIP J REV** (810)254-1426
7412 Flickinger Dr Shelby Twp MI 48317 • Scharnitzke@worldnet.att.net • MI • Assoc • Trinity Utica MI • (810)731-4490 • (SL 1993 MDIV)

**SCHARR TIMOTHY J REV** (509)664-8994
1231 Columbine St Wenatchee WA 98801-3149 • timothoess@aol.com • NOW • SP • St Paul Wenatchee WA • (509)662-8790 • (FW 1984 MDIV)

**SCHASER RUDOLF C REV** (314)965-9270
428 Julian Pl Kirkwood MO 63122-2917 • 111schaserc@1hm.org • MO • St Paul Wenatchee WA • (509)662-8790 • (SL 1965 MDIV MA)

**SCHATZ DONALD D REV** (425)673-0831
18403 74th Pl W Edmonds WA 98026-5552 • dl5smap@aol.com • NOW • SP • Trinity Seattle WA • (206)324-1066 • (FW 1980 MDIV DMIN)

**SCHAUDER STEVEN R REV** (507)280-8278
3360 Geselle Ln NW Rochester MN 55901-6952 • gbpastor@holycross-church.org • MNS • SP • Holy Cross Rochester MN • (507)289-1354 • (SL 1981 MDIV)

**SCHAUER ARTHUR P REV** (402)362-3159
1604 E 13th St York NE 68467-2116 • artscha@navix.net • NEB • SP • Faith York NE • (402)362-3000 • (SL 1970 MDIV)

**SCHAUER JOHN E REV** (712)364-3617
400 Main St Ida Grove IA 51445-1322 • jeslks@pionet.net • IW • Sn/Adm • St Paul Ida Grove IA • (712)364-2918 • (SL 1969 MDIV)

**SCHAUER KENNETH E REV** (907)688-5395
PO Box 671792 Chugiak AK 99567-1792 • kenschau@aol.com • NOW • D Miss • Denali Chugiak AK • (907)688-5395 • (SL 1968 MDIV)

**SCHAUER RICHARD V REV** (414)764-6923
6240 S Elaine Ave Cudahy WI 53110-2919 • rschauer@selc.lcms.org • S • Asst • St John Cudahy WI • (414)481-0520 • (SL 1991 MDIV)

**SCHAULAND HELMUT H REV** (712)546-5219
215 Central Ave SW Le Mars IA 51031-2035 • IW • SP • St John Ireton IA • (712)278-2543 • (SL 1945)

**SCHAULAND THEODORE E REV** (970)669-2160
706 S Dotsero Dr Loveland CO 80537-6727 • RM • EM • (SL 1938)

**SCHAUM CHARLES P** (219)938-0448
7516 Oak Ave Gary IN 46403 • IN • SP • St John Gary IN • (219)944-0654 • (SL 1998 MDIV)

**SCHAUS NATHAN EUGENE REV** (785)271-0172
3206 SW Arrowhead Rd Topeka KS 66614 • KS • Assoc • Faith Topeka KS • (785)272-4214 • (SL 2000 MDIV)

**SCHEBLEIN ADAM L REV** (701)265-4408
C/O Our Savior Luth Ch 508 Division Ave N # 88 Cavalier ND 58220-4902 • scheblei@polarcomm.com • ND • SP • Our Savior Cavalier ND • (701)265-4408 • (SL 1992 MDIV)

**SCHECK ELMER E REV** (262)569-8198
N55W35949 Lisbon Rd Oconomowoc WI 53066-2431 • SW • EM • (SL 1955)

**SCHECK JOHN F REV** (503)378-7209
2215 Hayden St NE Salem OR 97301-4466 • johnnans@open.org • NOW • EM • (SL 1955 MA PHD)

**SCHEDLER HERMAN C REV** (414)242-6619
614 Sunny Ln Thiensville WI 53092-1449 • SW • EM • (SL 1923)

**SCHEDLER MARVIN J REV** (919)469-9659
900 Vickie Dr Cary NC 27511-5832 • mschedle@bellsouth.net • SE • EM • (SPR 1961)

**SCHEDLER WALTER F REV** (715)372-8466
6360 Lake Ahmeek RD Iron River WI 54847-9622 • MNN • EM • (SL 1935)

**SCHEDLER WALTER J REV** (408)247-0804
2091 Holly Branch Ct Santa Clara CA 95050-3487 • wjschedler@aol.com • CNH • Asst • Our Savior Cupertino CA • (408)252-0345 • (FW 1992 MDIV)

**SCHEELE PETE ALAN REV** (573)486-3021
101 W 14th St Hermann MO 65041 • ppascheele@yahoo.com • MO • SP • Shepherd Hills Hermann MO • (573)486-3335 • (FW 1996 MDIV)

**SCHEER HAROLD A REV** (319)337-4855
C/O Univ Hospitals C 124 200 Hawkins Dr Iowa City IA 52242-1046 • harold-scheer@uiowa.edu • IE • Inst C • Iowa East Marion IA • (SPR 1970 MDIV)

**SCHEER R WILLIAM REV** (616)924-4072
24 W Pine St Fremont MI 49412-1528 • MI • EM • (CQ 1962 MCOUN)

**SCHEER RAYMOND P REV** (504)892-1239
72 Iris St Covington LA 70433-9156 • SO • EM • (SL 1963 MDIV)

**SCHEER RODNEY R REV** (619)566-1679
8871 Keremeos Way San Diego CA 92126-1419 • PSW • O Sp Min • Christ Chrstne San Diego CA • (619)566-1860 • (SL 1959 MDIV MA PHD)

**SCHEER RONALD P REV** (734)847-1346
1129 Cumberland Dr Temperance MI 48182 • scheerclr@voyager.net • MI • SP • Christ King Lambertville MI • (734)856-1461 • (CQ 1979 MED)

**SCHEFELKER PERRY W REV** (618)533-0447
519 Tracy Ter Centralia IL 62801 • SI • Assoc • Trinity Centralia IL • (618)532-2614 • (SL 1973 MDIV)

**SCHEICH JEFFREY L REV** (402)483-7774
5141 Larkwood Rd Lincoln NE 68516 • AT • SP • Our Savior Fishkill NY • (845)897-4423 • (SL 1985 MDIV)

**SCHEIDT PAUL A REV** (319)396-6139
214 Stoney Creek Rd NW Cedar Rapids IA 52405-5317 • edie5138@aol.com • IE • SP • Concordia Cedar Rapids IA • (319)396-9035 • (SL 1961 STM)

**SCHEIDT THEODORE L REV** (937)275-4960
1735 Benson Dr Dayton OH 45406-4030 • scheidtl@earthlink.net • OH • Assoc • St Matthew Huber Heights OH • (937)233-4632 • (SL 1964 MDIV STM MS)

**SCHEIMANN RICHARD W REV** (219)462-3158
905 Vale Park Rd Apt D3 Valparaiso IN 46383-2626 • scheiman@niia.net • IN • EM • (SL 1950 PHD)

**SCHEIPS ALFRED T REV** (407)359-8729
2112 Toucan Ct Oviedo FL 32765-5210 • FG • EM • (SL 1937 MA LITTD LITTD)

**SCHELER EDDIE RAY REV**
32 Bates St Bradford PA 16701 • EA • SP • Grace Bradford PA • (814)362-3244 • (FW 1991 MDIV)

**SCHELLENBACH TIMOTHY D REV** (218)247-7407
PO Box 430 Marble MN 55764-0430 • tschell@uslink.net • MNN • SP • Grace Marble MN • (218)247-7451 • (FW 1996 MDIV)

**SCHELLING JAMES B REV** (630)893-2598
139 W Devon Ave Roselle IL 60172-1109 • NI • EM • (SL 1959)

**SCHELTER HERMAN J REV** (281)955-7753
12518 Mile Dr Houston TX 77065-1302 • TX • EM • (SPR 1944 MDIV)

**SCHEMM DAVID G REV** (316)729-5599
3509 Burlingame Rd Topeka KS 66611 • jsign@aol.com • KS • SP • Christ Topeka KS • (785)266-6263 • (SPR 1974 MDIV)

**SCHEMM MILTON R REV** (248)813-9747
6833 Granger Dr Troy MI 48098 • MI • EM • (SL 1956)

**SCHEMPF MICHAEL D REV** (920)261-3050
C/O Bethesda Lutheran Home 700 Hoffman Dr Watertown WI 53094-6204 • mschempf@blhs.org • SW • South Wisconsin Milwaukee WI • (414)464-8100 • (FW 1982 MDIV)

**SCHENCK JOHN W REV** (715)246-9768
530 Chestnut Dr New Richmond WI 54017-6564 • NW • SP • St Luke New Richmond WI • (715)246-4861 • (SL 1973 MDIV)

**SCHENK ALLEN E REV** (314)869-2408
2316 Ada Wortley Ave Saint Louis MO 63136-5071 • MO • SP • Ebenezer Saint Louis MO • (314)388-2777 • (SL 1973 MDIV STM)

**SCHENKEL HARRY THEODORE III REV** (631)567-4572
19 Loop Dr Sayville NY 11782-1512 • revhts3@banet.net • AT • SP • St John Sayville NY • (631)589-3202 • (FW 1995 MDIV)

**SCHEPERLE GERALD R REV** (573)395-4591
4409 Saint Johns Rd Jefferson City MO 65101-9564 • MO • SP • St John Jefferson City MO* • (573)395-4591 • (FW 1980 MDIV)

**SCHEPMAN TIMOTHY W REV** (310)414-0050
901 Mc Carthy Ct El Segundo CA 90245-2447 • scheptim@aol.com • PSW • SP • St John El Segundo CA • (310)615-1072 • (FW 1983 MDIV)

**SCHEPMANN DANIEL WAYNE REV** (501)954-8238
2702 Millbrook Rd Little Rock AR 72227 • revschep@clutheran.org • MDS • Assoc • Christ Little Rock AR • (501)663-5232 • (SL 1996 MDIV)

**SCHEPMANN ROGER D REV** (402)528-7253
C/O Immanuel Luth 1101 K Rd Beemer NE 68716-4014 • NEB • SP • Immanuel Beemer NE* • (402)528-7253 • (CQ 1982 MA)

**SCHERBARTH RAY E REV** (248)288-4244
541 N Manitou Ave Clawson MI 48017-1476 • pod-ray@juno.com • MI • Sn/Adm • Our Shepherd Birmingham MI • (248)646-6100 • (FW 1984 MDIV)

**SCHERER ARTHUR W DR** (410)744-0481
11 Colgate Ct Baltimore MD 21228-5336 • arthurs20@aol.com • SE • DP • Southeastern Alexandria VA • (SL 1964 MDIV DMIN)

**SCHERER HENRY A REV** (530)662-1122
387 Quail Dr Woodland CA 95695-5873 • CNH • SP • St Paul Woodland CA • (530)662-1935 • (CQ 1979)

**SCHERER KENNETH R REV** (815)624-6118
12954 Portsmough Ln Roscoe IL 61073-8644 • NI • SP • Christ Our Savior Roscoe IL • (815)623-2138 • (SPR 1965)

**SCHERMBECK ROBERT H REV**
C/O St Peter Lutheran Church RR 1 Box 159 Elk Creek NE 68348-9501 • NEB • SP • St Peter Elk Creek NE • (402)335-2686 • (SL 1982 MDIV MSFLM)

**SCHETTENHELM JOHN G REV** (203)795-3916
C/O Zion Luth Church 780 Grassy Hill Rd Orange CT 06477-1653 • NE • SP • Zion Orange CT • (203)795-3916 • (SL 1982 MDIV)

**SCHEUNEMANN PAUL A REV** (715)276-6439
14162 Church Rd PO Box 74 Mountain WI 54149-0074 • sch-mann@juno.com • NW • SP • Emmanuel Suring WI* • (920)842-4600 • (SL 1980 MDIV)

**SCHEURICH GEORGE R REV** (410)486-8676
7415 Eldon Ct Baltimore MD 21208-5823 • SE • 10/1994 10/1999 • * • (CQ 1982 MDIV)

**SCHEVE MARK REV** (440)352-3232
135 Overlook Rd Painesville OH 44077-5383 • OH • 10/1981 10/1999 • * • (SL 1976 MDIV MA)

**SCHEY BERNARD J REV** (409)743-3323
102 Emma St Schulenburg TX 78956-1011 • TX • SP • Zion Schulenburg TX • (979)743-3842 • (FW 1985 MDIV)

**SCHEYDER PAUL L REV** (281)251-7713
5215 Cobble Ln Spring TX 77379 • TX • Tchr • Concordia LHS Tomball TX • (281)351-2547 • (FW 1990 MDIV)

**SCHICK RICHARD W REV** (510)724-5456
128 Banion Ct San Pablo CA 94806-1629 • CNH • EM • (SPR 1948)

**SCHIEBEL PETER A REV** (202)829-8432
1671 Madison St NW Washington DC 20011 • pascts97@aol.com • SE • SP • Trinity Mount Rainier MD • (301)864-4340 • (FW 1997 MDIV)

**SCHIEBINGER DARRELL D REV**
509 Crabtree Ct Fort Mill SC 29708-8305 • ddschieb@worldnet.att.net • SE • EM • (SL 1955 PHD DSOC)

**SCHIEFELBEIN HERBERT A REV** (406)677-2143
PO Box 716 Seeley Lake MT 59868-0716 • MT • EM • (SL 1952)

**SCHIEFELBEIN RAYMOND L REV** (816)795-8722
18200 E 27th Ter S Independence MO 64057-1520 • schrayron@earthlink.net • KS • SP • Bethel Kansas City KS • (913)299-6478 • (SPR 1971 MDIV MSED DMIN)

**SCHIEFER ELMER B REV** (660)838-6428
9195 B Hwy Bunceton MO 65237 • MO • EM • (SL 1950)

**SCHIELKE FREDERICK W REV** (314)845-9358
132 W Marseille Dr Saint Louis MO 63129-3462 • fschielke@cs.com • MO • 06/2000 • (SPR 1970 MDIV)

**SCHIEMANN ARTHUR W REV** (519)945-1344
C/O Peace Luth Church 1971 Rossini Blvd Windsor ON N8W 4P6 CANADA • partsch41@hotmail.com • EN • SP • Peace Windsor ON CANADA • (519)945-1344 • (SL 1968 MDIV)

**SCHILDWACHTER JOHN C REV** (651)429-7779
2193 Park Ave White Bear Lake MN 55110-2320 • sstwbl@juno.com • MNS • Sn/Adm • Trinity White Bear Lake MN • (651)429-4293 • (SPR 1972 MDIV)

**SCHILKE STEPHEN E REV** (734)243-3603
426 Country Dr Monroe MI 48162 • schilkes@juno.com • MI • SP • Christ Our Shepherd Newport MI • (734)586-6229 • (CQ 1998 MA)

**SCHILLER EVAN G REV** (507)347-3260
301 Carter Holland MN 56139 • eschiller@juno.com • MNS • SP • St James Holland MN • (507)347-3357 • (CQ 1982 MAR)

**SCHILLER TIMOTHY DEAN REV**
5530 Woodside Rd Prior Lake MN 55372 • T.D.Schiller@juno.com • MNS • Assoc • St Paul Prior Lake MN • (952)447-2117 • (SL 1995 MDIV)

**SCHILLING DAVID D REV** (808)257-2686
H & S CO 1/3 Box 63006 MCBH Kaneohe Bay HI 96863-3006 • schillingdd@mcbh.usmc.mil • SO • M Chap • Southern New Orleans LA • (SL 1988 MDIV)

**SCHILLING DAVID E REV** (909)924-4688
C/O Shep Of Valley Luth Church 11650 Perris Blvd Moreno Valley CA 92557-6536 • schiltonyt@aol.com • PSW • Sn/Adm • Shep Of Valley Moreno Valley CA • (909)924-4688 • (SL 1965 MDIV)

**SCHILLING ROBERT G REV** (308)894-3545
PO Box 213 Palmer NE 68864-0157 • stjohn@hamilton.net • NEB • SP • St John Palmer NE • (308)894-3545 • (SL 1983 MDIV)

**SCHILLINGER DAVID R REV**
C/O Holy Cross Luth Church 724 Big Tree Rd South Daytona FL 32119-2754 • FG • SP • Holy Cross South Daytona FL • (904)767-6542 • (CQ 1980)

**SCHILLINGER GILBERT H REV**
8716 Sweet Blossom Ct Fort Wayne IN 46835 • IN • EM • (CQ 1982 MED MAR)

**SCHILLO ERIC L REV** (515)576-2318
234 9th Ave N Fort Dodge IA 50501-2411 • IW • Iowa West Fort Dodge IA • (SPR 1975 MS MS MDIV)

**SCHINDLER VERNON L REV** (605)357-8220
119 N Marquette Ave Sioux Falls SD 57110-1290 • sdpres@aol.com • SD • DP • South Dakota Sioux Falls SD • (SL 1967 MDIV)

**SCHINKEL JOHN A REV** (517)694-2766
4683 Sycamore St Holt MI 48842-1573 • messiahholt@juno.com • MI • SP • Messiah Holt MI • (517)694-1280 • (SL 1979 MDIV)

**SCHINKEL NORMAN H REV** (330)856-6280
7826 Castle Rock Dr NE Warren OH 44484-1409 • OH • SP • Trinity Warren OH • (330)372-1897 • (SL 1960 MDIV)

**SCHINNERER CARL F REV** (810)286-5372
42221 Todd Mark Ln Apt 111 Clinton Township MI 48038-6809 • MI • EM • (SL 1948)

**SCHINNERER CRAIG R REV** (972)299-6051
808 Lemons Dr Cedar Hill TX 75104-7270 • crschinn@aol.com • TX • Sn/Adm • Cross Christ De Soto TX • (972)223-9340 • (SL 1983 MDIV)

**SCHINNERER RICHARD A REV** (909)626-4308
833 Manchester Ct Claremont CA 91711-2919 • rschinn@aol.com • PSW • EM • (SL 1954 MDIV)

**SCHIPUL ROBERT F REV** (203)355-0800
14 White Swan Dr New Milford CT 06776-2347 • NE • Inst C • New England Springfield MA • (SPR 1975 MDIV)

**SCHIRMER BERTRAM I REV** (618)826-3447
PO Box 346 2281 Old Plank Rd Chester IL 62233-1163 • bertnbetty@aol.com • SI • EM • (SPR 1971)

**SCHKADE LANDON L JR. REV** (780)417-2970
21 Wilson Crescent Sherwood Park AB T8A 3L1 CANADA • NOW • 09/2000 • (FW 1984 MDIV)

**SCHKADE RAY C REV** (512)926-8695
7101 Creighton Ln Austin TX 78723-1539 • rschkade@aol.com • TX • EM • (SPR 1954 MA)

**SCHLAK RANDALL J REV** (248)680-9028
2381 Paris Dr Troy MI 48083 • MI • Sn/Adm • Redeemer Birmingham MI • (248)644-4010 • (FW 1990 MDIV)

**SCHLAK RICHARD K REV**
C/O Jet Cargo Internl M-182 PO Box 20010 Miami FL 33102-0010 • NI • S Miss • Northern Illinois Hillside IL • (SL 1986 MDIV)

**SCHLECHT DENNIS W REV** (630)879-0967
810 Aster Ct North Aurora IL 60542-8909 • opanoma@juno.com • NI • Assoc • St John Wheaton IL • (630)668-0701 • (SL 1961 MDIV STM)

**SCHLECHT GLEN A REV** (970)663-7929
3306 Franklin Ave Loveland CO 80538-7612 • gschlecht@juno.com • RM • Sn/Adm • Immanuel Loveland CO • (970)667-4506 • (SL 1989 MDIV)

**SCHLECHT RICHARD L REV** (248)651-6965
622 Lockport Rd Rochester Hills MI 48307-3764 • MI • EM • (SL 1945 DD)

**SCHLECHTE ROGER E REV** (303)233-7870
2664 Taft Ct Lakewood CO 80215-7042 • reschl@aol.com • RM • SP • Emmaus Denver CO • (303)433-3303 • (FW 1977 MDIV)

**SCHLECHTE TODD ALAN REV** (402)796-2147
141 N Exeter PO Box 201 Malcolm NE 68402 • toddschlechte@prodigy.net • NEB • SP • St Paul Malcolm NE • (402)796-2396 • (FW 1994 MDIV)

**SCHLEEF DIETRICH N REV** (323)751-0862
3442 W 83rd St Inglewood CA 90305-1607 • revschleef@luther95.net • PSW • SP • Faith Inglewood CA • (323)750-3552 • (CQ 1975)

**SCHLEEF EVERETT W REV** (330)297-6770
5242 Lakewood Rd Ravenna OH 44266-9564 • OH • Inst C • Ohio Olmsted Falls OH • (SL 1968 MDIV)

**SCHLEGEL ALBERT P REV** (219)447-6303
6701 S Anthony Blvd # 401 Fort Wayne IN 46816-2012 • IN • EM • (SPR 1928)

**SCHLEGEL RONALD J REV** (843)280-9489
1001 Coral Reef Dr North Myrtle Beach SC 29582-2896 • ronjonronjon@yahoo.com • SE • EM • (SL 1959 MDIV)

**SCHLEGELMILCH OTTO REV** (651)454-4033
2020 Zircon Ln Eagan MN 55122-2804 • MNS • EM • (SPR 1934 MST)

**SCHLEICHER JOHN C REV** (507)289-6626
553 21st St NE Rochester MN 55906-4253 • johnschleicher@hotmail.com • MNS • Assoc • Redeemer Rochester MN • (507)289-5147 • (SPR 1975 MDIV)

**SCHLENSKER DANIEL A REV** (530)758-4546
980 Anderson Cir Woodland CA 95776 • danasker@juno.com • CNH • SP • Our Faith Davis CA • (530)758-4546 • (SL 1999 MDIV MAT)

**SCHLESSELMAN DONALD O REV** (712)252-9092
2203 Helmer St Sioux City IA 51103-1741 • IW • SP • Concordia Sioux City IA • (712)252-2938 • (SL 1995 MDIV)

**SCHLESSMANN PHILLIP C REV** (407)636-5526
832 Mallard Rd Cocoa FL 32926-2318 • pschle3284@aol.com • FG • EM • (SPR 1953)

**SCHLICKER GREGORY ALAN REV** (517)662-7463
2064 Carter Rd Midland MI 48642-9228 • schlicks@tir.com • MI • Sn/Adm • Zion Auburn MI • (517)662-4264 • (SL 1988 MDIV)

**SCHLIE DAVID REV** (219)478-1444
6959 Hiltonia Dr Fort Wayne IN 46819-1325 • IN • EM • (CQ 1966 MAR)

**SCHLIE SAMUEL DAVID REV** (219)632-1348
24503 Slusher Rd Woodburn IN 46797 • IN • SP • Christ Woodburn IN • (219)632-4821 • (CQ 1996 MSED)

**SCHLIEBE MARTIN J REV** (505)892-1984
920 Riverview Dr SE Apt 146 Rio Rancho NM 87124-0909 • RM • EM • (SL 1931)

**SCHLIEPSIEK RICHARD S REV**
808 Seven Lakes N West End NC 27376 • rickschliep@ac.net • SE • D Miss • Southeastern Alexandria VA • (SL 1968 MHST)

**SCHLOSSMAN MARTIN L REV** (773)866-1722
4512 N Drake Ave Chicago IL 60625-5904 • cmifamily@aol.com • NI • SP • Tabor Chicago IL • (773)478-0196 • (CQ 1982)

**SCHLOTE LOY GENE REV**
15 Wheeler Ave Joliet IL 60436-1529 • lschlote@accessus.net • NI • Tabor Chicago IL • (773)478-0196 • (SL 1983 MDIV)

**SCHLUETER PAUL R REV** (812)524-1153
304 Manor Heights Dr Seymour IN 47274 • pjschluerer@bigfoot.com • IN • Assoc • Redeemer Seymour IN • (812)522-1837 • (SL 1999 MDIV)

**SCHLUND STEVEN R REV** (308)452-3605
323 Buell Ave Ravenna NE 68869-1203 • sschlund@micrord.com • NEB • SP • Bethlehem Ravenna NE • (308)452-3685 • (SL 1983 MDIV)

**SCHMALZ DANIEL M REV** (973)697-9955
17 Pine Hollow Ct Oak Ridge NJ 07438-9179 • latte97@aol.com • NJ • SP • Trinity Morris Plains NJ • (973)538-7606 • (SL 1968 MDIV)

**SCHMEISSER KIRK R REV** (816)232-8339
1024 Magnolia St St Joseph MO 64505-1604 • MO • SP • St Peter Saint Joseph MO • (816)279-8190 • (FW 1984 MDIV)

**SCHMELDER WILLIAM J REV** (636)928-4301
266 Cedar Grove Dr Saint Charles MO 63304-7347 • MO • EM • (SL 1960 STM MDIV)

**SCHMELZER DENNIS RYAN REV** (314)390-2333
1202 Fawn Ln Washington MO 63090-5372 • MO • SP • Faith Washington MO • (314)239-0554 • (CQ 1995)

**SCHMICK VICTOR L REV** (804)737-6896
313 Treva Rd Sandston VA 23150-2126 • SE • EM • (SPR 1962 MDIV DMIN)

**SCHMID JOHN B REV** (816)353-8161
8144 James A Reed Rd Kansas City MO 64138-1464 • MO • EM • (SL 1957 MDIV)

**SCHMID MICHAEL A REV**
3521 Linda Vista Ave Napa CA 94558 • pstrmike@fcs.net • CNH • Assoc • St John Napa CA • (707)255-0119 • (FW 1990 MDIV)

**SCHMIDT ALVIN J REV** (217)243-4637
7 Audubon Dr Jacksonville IL 62650-2773 • schmidt@hilltop.ic.edu • CI • Asst • Our Redeemer Jacksonville IL • (217)243-3939 • (SPR 1963 MDIV MA PHD)

**SCHMIDT CHARLES O REV** (402)729-5118
1616 G St Fairbury NE 68352-1340 • cs91923@alltel.net • NEB • Sn/Adm • Grace Fairbury NE • (402)729-5163 • (CQ 1982 MAR MSFLM)

**SCHMIDT DARYL M REV** (719)632-3797
1219 N 31st St Colorado Springs CO 80904-1240 • RM • EM • (SL 1943)

**SCHMIDT DAVID H REV** (253)756-9590
5728 N 12th St Tacoma WA 98406-2713 • NOW • SP • Zion Tacoma WA • (253)752-1264 • (SL 1966 MDIV)

**SCHMIDT DAVID P REV** (636)225-0356
1215 Summerhawk Ln Fenton MO 63026-6941 • david.schmidt@lfnd.org • MO • S Ex/S • Missouri Saint Louis MO • (314)317-4550 • (SL 1963 MDIV)

**SCHMIDT DENNIS L REV** (440)365-3551
660 Augdon Dr Elyria OH 44035-3032 • dschmidt@ohio.net • OH • SP • St John Elyria OH • (216)324-4070 • (SL 1973 MDIV)

**SCHMIDT DENNIS W REV** (314)892-0653
4616 Longspur Dr Saint Louis MO 63128-2316 • MO • SP • Immanuel Barnhart MO • (314)464-4114 • (SL 1986 MA MAR)

**SCHMIDT DON L REV**
3743 Austin Peay Hwy Memphis TN 38128-3721 • hhlc@midtenn.net • MDS • SP • Messiah Memphis TN • (901)386-3401 • (FW 1977 MDIV)

**SCHMIDT DONALD W REV**
PSC 3 Box 477 APO AP 96266 • donseoul@hotmail.com • MDS • EM • (SPR 1963)

**SCHMIDT EARL REV** (218)784-7101
300 5th St W Ada MN 56510-1014 • zlca@rrv.net • MNN • SP • Zion Ada MN • (218)784-7103 • (SL 1966 MA)

**SCHMIDT EDWARD A REV** (314)837-8687
4023 Browning Dr Florissant MO 63033-4009 • EN • EM • (SL 1948 MDIV)

**SCHMIDT EDWARD H REV** (515)736-4753
C/O Immanuel Lutheran Church PO Box 429 St Ansgar IA 50472-0429 • IE • SP • Immanuel St Ansgar IA • (515)736-4782 • (FW 1989 MDIV)

**SCHMIDT EUGENE E REV** (785)478-3078
3617 SW Kings Forest Rd Topeka KS 66610-1553 • eueschmidt@aol.com • KS • EM • (SL 1955 MDIV LLD)

**SCHMIDT G DANIEL REV** (303)651-6581
2834 15th Ave Longmont CO 80503-1746 • RM • EM • (SPR 1954 MDIV MA)

**SCHMIDT GALE D REV** (602)863-9219
218 E Waltann Lane Phoenix AZ 85022-3038 • gschmidt@azlink.com • PSW • EM • (SL 1962 MDIV)

**SCHMIDT GERHARDT K REV** (314)569-0556
1660 Schulte Rd Saint Louis MO 63146-4863 • jerrymarilyn@juno.com • MO • EM • (SL 1943)

**SCHMIDT HAROLD V REV** (206)485-9582
3333 228th St SE Unit 15 Bothell WA 98021-8952 • NOW • EM • (SL 1934)

**SCHMIDT HAROLD W REV** (815)784-2292
233 N Washington St PO Box 7 Genoa IL 60135-0007 • hschmidt@tbcnet.com • NI • Sn/Adm • Trinity Genoa IL • (815)784-2522 • (SL 1958)

**SCHMIDT JAMES A REV** (805)967-0889
944 N Patterson Ave Santa Barbara CA 93111-1110 • PSW • Assoc • Good Shepherd Goleta CA • (805)967-1416 • (SL 1962 MDIV)

**SCHMIDT JOHN ARTHUR REV** (414)593-2346
C/O St John Lutheran Church W407 Highway 18 Sullivan WI 53178-9708 • SW • SP • St John Sullivan WI • (414)593-8630 • (FW 1979 MDIV)

**SCHMIDT JOHN D REV** (206)582-4043
PO Box 99967 Tacoma WA 98499-0967 • 71174.23@compuserve.com • NOW • SP • Prince Of Peace Tacoma WA • (253)584-2565 • (SL 1969)

**SCHMIDT JOHN E REV** (920)982-1112
E9016 Marsh Rd Fremont WI 54940 • jjjschmidt@pitnet.net • NW • Sn/Adm • St Paul Fremont WI* • (414)446-3251 • (SL 1962)

**SCHMIDT JOHN ERICH REV**
4110 Paxton Lincoln NE 68521 • EN • Assoc • Redeemer Lincoln NE • (402)477-1710 • (SL 1992 MDIV)

**SCHMIDT JOHN H REV** (402)873-7277
2221 2nd Ave Nebraska City NE 68410 • NEB • SP • Christ Nebraska City NE • (402)873-6824 • (FW 1986 MDIV)

**SCHMIDT JOHN L REV**
C/O Christ The King Luth Ch 1700 Pennsylvania Ave Coeur d Alene ID 83814 • revjls@aol.com • NOW • Sn/Adm • Christ King Coeur D Alene ID • (208)664-9231 • (FW 1977 MDIV)

**SCHMIDT KARL ERIC REV** (716)835-7567
184 Grandview Ave Tn Of Tona NY 14223-3043 • EN • SP • Calvary Amherst NY • (716)833-7300 • (FW 1985 MA)

**SCHMIDT KARL K REV** (703)360-4112
4316 Southwood Dr Alexandria VA 22309-2825 • SE • SP • Bethany Alexandria VA • (703)765-8255 • (SL 1961 STM LLD)

**SCHMIDT KARL W REV** (847)255-1452
1212 W Nichols Rd Arlington Hts IL 60004-1334 • Kschmidt@kiwi.dep.anl.gov • NI • Sn/Adm • St Peter Arlington Heights IL • (847)259-4114 • (SL 1978 MDIV)

**SCHMIDT LARRY O REV** (218)758-2942
C/O Immanuel Luth Church PO Box 127 Dent MN 56528-0127 • MNN • SP • Immanuel Dent MN* • (218)758-2942 • (FW 1990 MDIV)

**SCHMIDT LARRY W REV** (301)946-2614
10801 Drumm Ave Kensington MD 20895-2305 • SE • Sn/Adm • Calvary Silver Spring MD • (301)589-4041 • (SL 1962 MDIV)

**SCHMIDT LAWRENCE A REV** (319)393-5658
2540 Amber Dr NE Cedar Rapids IA 52402-3318 • schmidtduo@juno.com • IE • EM • (CQ 1977 MED)

**SCHMIDT LELAND P REV** (712)274-1599
2721 S Cornelia St Sioux City IA 51106-3341 • chaplee@aol.com • IW • Inst C • Iowa West Fort Dodge IA • (SL 1971 MDIV)

**SCHMIDT MARTIN J REV** (407)880-2163
2121 East Lake Dr Zellwood FL 32798-9732 • gladmartz@webtv.net • FG • EM • (SPR 1953 MA DED)

**SCHMIDT MARTIN P REV** (308)395-8551
3019 Sothman Dr Grand Island NE 68801 • mschmidt@ginetworks.com • NEB • Sn/Adm • Trinity Grand Island NE • (308)382-0753 • (SL 1982 MDIV)

**SCHMIDT MICHAEL JOHN REV** (480)585-8007
29305 N Scottsdale Rd Scottsdale AZ 85262 • mjschmidt@lanset.com • PSW • SP • Desert Foothills Scottsdale AZ • (480)585-8007 • (SL 1995 MDIV STM)

**SCHMIDT NEIL R REV** (314)427-1053
10745 Saint Cosmas Ln Saint Ann MO 63074-2523 • MO • SP • Hope Saint Ann MO • (314)429-3808 • (SL 1959)

**SCHMIDT NELDO REV** (612)552-7277
225 W Douglas St S Saint Paul MN 55075 • MNS • SP • Concordia South St Paul MN • (651)451-0309 • (PA 1983)

**SCHMIDT PAUL M REV** (503)653-0640
11383 SE 64th Ave Milwaukie OR 97222-2329 • penqueen2@aol.com • NOW • EM • (SL 1955 STM)

**SCHMIDT PAUL R REV** (402)486-1362
4210 Clifford Dr Lincoln NE 68506-4967 • NEB • EM • (SPR 1950)

**SCHMIDT PAUL R JR. REV** (410)879-6710
C/O St Matthew Luth Church 1200 E Churchville Rd Bel Air MD 21014-3412 • SE • Asst • St Matthew Bel Air MD • (410)879-6710 • (SL 1988 MDIV)

**SCHMIDT PAUL RONALD SR. REV** (217)235-5596
421 Briar Ln Mattoon IL 61938-2037 • CI • EM • (SL 1956)

**SCHMIDT PETER A REV** (262)513-0775
650 S Greenfield Ave Waukesha WI 53186-6739 • pastorpschmidt@juno.com • SW • Assoc • Beautiful Savior Waukesha WI • (414)542-2496 • (SL 1989 MDIV STM)

**SCHMIDT PHILIP REV** (901)274-1340
2088 Hallwood Dr Memphis TN 38107-4706 • MDS • Assoc • Trinity Memphis TN • (901)525-1056 • (SPR 1968 MDIV)

**SCHMIDT RALPH G REV** (402)643-4776
1051 Eastridge Dr Seward NE 68434-1327 • NEB • SHS/C • Nebraska Seward NE • (SL 1973 MDIV)

**SCHMIDT RAYMOND D REV** (973)786-7455
28 Hemlock Ave Newton NJ 07860-9713 • NJ • EM • (SPR 1952 MRE)

**SCHMIDT REUBEN J DR** (608)527-5975
707 Haslen Ave New Glarus WI 53574-9417 • reuben@utelco.tds.net • EN • EM • (SL 1944 MDIV DD)

**SCHMIDT RICHARD W REV** (619)421-2812
744 Cholla Rd Chula Vista CA 91910-6614 • pastorrschmidt@juno.com • PSW • SP • Concordia Chula Vista CA • (619)422-6606 • (SL 1993 MDIV)

**SCHMIDT ROBERT A REV** (608)221-4618
4602 Camden Rd Madison WI 53716-1749 • SW • EM • (SL 1948)

**SCHMIDT ROBERT F REV** (503)288-9371
C/O Concordia College 2811 NE Holman St Portland OR 97211-6067 • NOW • SHS/C • Northwest Portland OR • (SL 1960 STM MA MDIV PHD)

**SCHMIDT STEPHEN C REV** (605)336-1880
100 W 37th St Sioux Falls SD 57105-5702 • SD • 01/1994 01/2000 • (CQ 1983)

**SCHMIDT TRAVIS J REV** (515)832-4610
1005 Beach St Webster City IA 50595-1951 • pastorts@ncn.net • IW • SP • St Paul Webster City IA • (515)832-3043 • (FW 1989 MDIV)

**SCHMIDT WALTER C REV** (318)442-5388
1716 Simmons St Alexandria LA 71301-3733 • redeemlcms@juno.com • SO • SP • Redeemer Alexandria LA • (318)442-4325 • (SL 1965 MDIV)

**SCHMIDT WARREN W REV** (870)698-0075
606 Eagle Mountain Blvd Batesville AR 72501-4210 • MDS • EM • (SL 1961 STM)

**SCHMIDT WILLIAM E REV** (618)997-6868
1109 Laura Ln Marion IL 62959-1528 • pastorwschmidt@midamer.net • SI • SP • Good Shepherd Marion IL • (618)993-3649 • (SL 1965 MDIV)

**SCHMIDT WILLIAM P REV** (352)483-2716
1989 Meadowside Dr Eustis FL 32726-2329 • schmidt774@aol.com • FG • Sn/Adm • Faith Eustis FL • (352)589-5433 • (SL 1984 MDIV)

**SCHMIDTKE GARY R REV** (217)245-0438
214 Brookside Dr Jacksonville IL 62650-1029 • CI • Sn/Adm • Our Redeemer Jacksonville IL • (217)243-3939 • (SL 1972 MDIV)

**SCHMIDTKE JOHN R REV** (314)869-7830
9941 Norbridge Ln Saint Louis MO 63137-1402 • MO • SP • Bethlehem Saint Louis MO • (314)231-9615 • (SL 1987 MDIV)

**SCHMIDTKE RICHARD L REV** (503)257-3640
3363 NE 133rd Ave Portland OR 97230-2810 • NOW • 08/1987 08/2000 • (SL 1971 MDIV)

**SCHMIEDING SCOTT ALAN REV** (225)272-9854
1802 South Flannery Baton Rouge LA 70816 • revschmieding@bitworx.com • SO • Sn/Adm • Trinity Baton Rouge LA • (225)272-3110 • (SL 1991 MDIV STM)

**SCHMIEGE DONALD R REV** (612)890-1813
11906 River Hills Cir Burnsville MN 55337-3314 • pastord@mr.net • MNS • Sn/Adm • Christ Eagan MN • (651)454-4091 • (SPR 1975 MDIV)

**SCHMIEGE ERICK H REV** (218)741-2329
801 9th St N Apt 307 Virginia MN 55792 • ehschm@lcp2.net • MNN • EM • (SPR 1944)

**SCHMIEL DAVID G DR** (941)947-5839
27670 Bay Point Ln Apt 3 Bonita Springs FL 34134-3918 • FG • EM • (TH 1957 THD)

**SCHMIESING EARL W REV** (410)329-6891
19716 Middletown Rd Freeland MD 21053-9405 • SE • EM • (SL 1946 MDIV)

**SCHMITT DAVID R REV** (314)647-3537
1107 Ralph Ter Richmond Heights MO 63117-1528 • schmittd@csl.edu • EN • SHS/C • English Farmington MI • (SL 1988 MDIV MA)

**SCHMITT THOMAS KEVIN REV** (402)496-8849
14205 Ida St Omaha NE 68142-1667 • Ppcreature@aol.com • NEB • SP • Zion West Omaha NE • (402)493-1744 • (SL 1991 MDIV)

**SCHMOOCK ENNO A REV** (909)654-1815
1345 Trenton Cir San Jacinto CA 92583-5161 • EN • EM • (SL 1942 MDIV)

**SCHMOOCK NORMAN W REV** (760)245-6712
13228 Kirkwood Dr Victorville CA 92392 • schmoock@oak-tree.net • PSW • SP • Zion Victorville CA • (760)245-9725 • (CSCQ 1974 MDIV)

**SCHNACK RANDOLPH J REV** (517)389-3305
PO Box 297 Saint Helen MI 48656-0297 • rjs45@theglobe.com • MI • SP • Hope Saint Helen MI • (517)389-7715 • (FW 1981 MDIV)

**SCHNACKENBERG JAMES F REV** (417)451-3819
1346 E Mc Kinney St Neosho MO 64850-8530 • goodshep@janics.com • MO • SP • Good Shepherd Carthage MO • (417)358-1325 • (SL 1971 MDIV)

**SCHNAKE LUKE R REV** (402)420-7301
7301 S 41st St Lincoln NE 68516 • clc@christlutheranchurch.org • NEB • Sn/Adm • Christ Lincoln NE • (402)483-7774 • (FW 1978 MDIV DMIN)

**SCHNAKENBERG KEVIN LOUIS REV**
C/O Immanuel Lutheran Church PO Box 280 Pomeroy IA 50575-0280 • IW • SP • Immanuel Pomeroy IA* • (712)468-2211 • (SL 1996 MDIV)

**SCHNAKENBERG ROGER W REV** (573)885-4453
760 Fleenor Rd Cuba MO 65453-9718 • MO • SP • St Paul Cuba MO • (573)885-7234 • (CQ 1984 MSED)

**SCHNARE MARTIN T REV** (308)762-7745
1015 Box Butte Ave Alliance NE 69301-2519 • altarboy@btigate.com • WY • Sn/Adm • Immanuel Alliance NE • (308)762-4663 • (SL 1984 MDIV)

**SCHNEEKLOTH LARRY G REV** (708)596-5398
3332 W 160th St Markham IL 60426-4504 • larschneek@excite.com • EN • SP • Markham Markham IL • (708)331-4885 • (SPR 1967 MA PHD)

**SCHNEGELBERGER KENT E REV** (303)776-0640
1351 Francis St Longmont CO 80501-2511 • kschnege@concentric.net • RM • SP • Messiah Longmont CO • (303)776-2573 • (SL 1975 MDIV MA)

**SCHNEIDER ARNOLD W REV** (651)499-0289
408 Bluebird Ln Delray Beach FL 33445-1738 • FG • EM • (SPR 1937)

**SCHNEIDER CARL W REV** (616)965-1078
113 Wahwahtaysee Way Battle Creek MI 49015-4058 • carlsbcmi@cs.com • MI • SP • St Mark Battle Creek MI • (616)964-0401 • (SL 1981 MDIV)

**SCHNEIDER CURTIS W REV** (254)562-0632
900 La Villeta Mexia TX 76667 • faith@glade.net • TX • SP • Faith Mexia TX • (254)562-7756 • (CQ 1977 MDIV)

**SCHNEIDER DANIEL S REV** (262)502-3519
N77W15511 Crossway Dr Menomonee Falls WI 53051-4297 • schneid6@execpc.com • SW • Sn/Adm • Immanuel Brookfield WI • (262)781-7140 • (FW 1980 MDIV)

**SCHNEIDER DAVID J REV** (314)505-7675
Concordia Apartments Founders Way 1-D St Louis MO 63105 • EN • S Miss • English Farmington MI • (SL 1960 STM MDIV)

**SCHNEIDER DONALD D REV**
1075 El Monte Ave Mountain View CA 94040 • pstrdon@jps.net • CNH • SP • St Paul Mountain View CA • (650)967-0666 • (SL 1994 MDIV)

**SCHNEIDER DUWAYNE REV** (906)544-2259
C/O Hope Lutheran Church PO Box 477 Land O Lakes WI 54540-0477 • NW • SP • St Paul Colby WI • (715)223-3525 • (SPR 1965)

**SCHNEIDER E WILLIAM REV** (254)698-4095
803 Wolf Trail Harker Heights TX 76548 • EA • M Chap • Eastern Williamsville NY • (716)634-5111 • (SL 1982 MDIV)

**SCHNEIDER EDWARD L REV** (210)490-5095
1147 Custer Pass San Antonio TX 78232-3420 • TX • EM • (SL 1949 MDIV MST)

**SCHNEIDER JACK A REV** (806)799-1615
4505 80th St Lubbock TX 79424-3207 • Hope@llano.net • TX • SP • Hope Lubbock TX • (806)798-2747 • (SL 1974 MDIV)

**SCHNEIDER KEITH A REV** (616)627-6994
8213 Lakewood Cheboygan MI 49721 • MI • SP • St John Cheboygan MI • (616)627-5149 • (SPR 1973 MDIV)

**SCHNEIDER NORMAN A REV** (314)831-8485
4379 Varano Dr Florissant MO 63033-6922 • MO • EM • (SL 1962 MDIV MED)

**SCHNEIDER PAUL HENRY REV**
4740 N Hwy 83 Franktown CO 80116-9664 • RM • SP • Trinity Franktown CO • (303)841-8620 • (SL 1995 MDIV)

**SCHNEIDER ROBERT W REV** (314)824-5108
315 PCR 328 Farrar MO 63746-9999 • schneiderrobert@hotmail.com • MO • SP • Salem Farrar MO* • (573)824-5728 • (FW 1990 MDIV)

**SCHNEIDER TERRELL J REV**
1701 N Chestnut Ave Apt 111 Marshfield WI 54449-1427 • NW • 07/1996 07/1999 • * • (SPR 1966 MTH)

**SCHNELLE ELMER L REV** (417)739-2720
154 Fishers Cove Rd Kimberling Cy MO 65686 • MO • EM • * • (SPR 1949)

**SCHNELLE PAUL V REV** (417)358-9252
409 E Highland Ave Carthage MO 64836-3312 • KS • SP • St Paul Oswego KS • (316)795-4887 • (SL 1957)

**SCHNEPP KENNETH E JR. REV** (301)574-2774
9404 Grandhaven Ave Upper Marlboro MD 20772-5248 • pkrailshep@aol.com • SE • SP • Oxon Hill Temple Hills MD • (301)894-3773 • (SL 1973 STM MDIV)

**SCHNUTE WM C REV** (760)758-8601
1506 Oak Dr Spc 90 Vista CA 92084-3512 • PSW • EM • (SL 1937 MST)

**SCHOECH THOMAS K REV**
1614 E Swan Cir Brentwood MO 63144 • thomas.schoech@gte.net • MI • 08/2000 • (SL 1979 MDIV)

**SCHOECH WALTER F REV** (561)833-0104
1133 Oak St West Palm Beach FL 33405-2011 • FG • EM • (SL 1939)

**SCHOEDEL WALTER M REV** (314)822-8379
734 Eckrich Pl St Louis MO 63119-4971 • wschoedel@aol.com • MO • EM • (SL 1949 MS MDIV STM)

**SCHOEN MARK K REV** (715)483-1184
118 Blanding Woods Rd St Croix Falls WI 54024 • revschoen@yahoo.com • NW • SP • Shep Of Valley Saint Croix Falls WI • (715)483-1186 • (FW 1985 MDIV)

**SCHOENBACK DONALD E JR. REV** (616)827-9198
2122 Gettysburg Dr SE Kentwood MI 49508-6513 • MI • Assoc • St Mark Kentwood MI • (616)455-5320 • (SL 1982 MDIV)

**SCHOENBORN ERNEST F REV** (210)521-6811
Stonefield Estates 9630 Elmstone Drive San Antonio TX 78254-6724 • TX • EM • (SL 1955 MED MED)

**SCHOENBORN THOMAS R REV** (503)543-3229
51636 SW Snyder Ct Scappoose OR 97056-4467 • angel@columbia-center.org • NOW • SP • Grace Scappoose OR • (503)543-6555 • (SL 1968 MDIV)

**SCHOENFELD KING K REV** (314)863-0152
6124 Westminster Pl Saint Louis MO 63112-1210 • king@creativecomm.com • MO • Asst • Trinity Saint Louis MO • (314)231-4092 • (SL 1967 MDIV)

**SCHOENFELD MARTIN THOMAS REV** (320)543-3148
PO Box 680 Howard Lake MN 55349-0680 • MNS • Assoc • St James Howard Lake MN • (320)543-2766 • (SL 1995 MDIV)

**SCHOENFELDT HOWARD J REV** (703)433-2652
22355 Providence Village Dr Apt 318 Sterling VA 20164 • SE • EM • (SL 1938 STM)

**SCHOENFUHS WALTER P REV** (708)867-8216
7901 W Seminole St Chicago IL 60631-2935 • schoenfuhsland@chicago.avenew.com • NI • SP • St Paul Chicago IL • (708)867-5044 • (FW 1979 MDIV)

**SCHOENFUHS WALTER P SR. REV** (410)931-3516
3905 Darleigh Rd Apt 3A Baltimore MD 21236-5809 • speciosuspes@aol.com • SE • EM • (SL 1954 MDIV STM MA)

**SCHOENHEIDER ROBERT G REV** (440)427-9232
27024 Oakwood Dr #111E Olmsted Township OH 44138 • OH • EM • (SL 1954)

**SCHOENHERR MARK A REV** (715)453-1217
1217 E King Rd Tomahawk WI 54487-2004 • schoenherr@juno.com • NW • Sn/Adm • St Paul Tomahawk WI • (715)453-5391 • (SPR 1975 MDIV)

**SCHOENHERR PHILIP H REV** (541)484-6362
2365 Chambers St Eugene OR 97405-1860 • glc@efn.org • NOW • Sn/Adm • Grace Eugene OR • (541)342-4844 • (SL 1973 MDIV)

**SCHOENKNECHT DAVID M REV** (712)262-7232
1603 1st Ave E Spencer IA 51301-4339 • schoenk@nwiowa.com • IW • SP • Christ King Spencer IA • (712)262-2244 • (SL 1984 MDIV)

**SCHOENROCK HARLAN R REV** (407)951-1613
496 High Point Ct Melbourne FL 32901-8634 • FG • SP • Redeemer Melbourne FL • (321)723-4152 • (SL 1970 MDIV)

**SCHOESSOW DANIEL RAY REV** (409)873-2175
C/O Zion Luth Church PO Box 409 Anderson TX 77830-0409 • dans409@aol.com • TX • SP • Zion Anderson TX • (409)873-2175 • (FW 1992 MDIV)

**SCHOESSOW DAVID G REV** (218)692-2049
38453 Ox Lake Landing Crosslake MN 56442-9310 • schoesso@crosslake.net • MNN • SP • Mission Cross Crosslake MN • (218)692-4228 • (SL 1981 MDIV)

**SCHOEWE DONALD REV** (218)442-6881
28413 675 Ave Roosevelt MN 56673 • nschowe@wiktel.com • MNN • EM • (SL 1963)

**SCHOEWE THEODORE M REV** (507)452-2788
415 W 8th St Winona MN 55987-2935 • tmschoewe@hbcl.com • MNS • EM • (SPR 1945)

**SCHOLL LOUIS N REV** (519)969-7052
3500 Askin Blvd Windsor ON N9E 3J9 CANADA • EN • EM • (SL 1959 MDIV)

**SCHOLLE RAYMOND W JR. REV** (440)572-0904
20364 Arlington Dr Strongsville OH 44136 • OH • 09/2000 • (SL 1994 MDIV)

**SCHOLZ ALFRED REV**
1434 Pirates Cv Houston TX 77058-4039 • aloisscholz@compuserve.com • TX • EM • (SL 1952 MDIV)

**SCHOLZ HARRY G REV** (503)682-8655
11266 SW Churchill Wilsonville OR 97070-9571 • NOW • EM • (SPR 1956 MA)

**SCHOLZ JOHN G REV** (541)773-6090
3095 Crystal Mountain Ave Medford OR 97504-1902 • scholzje@aol.com • NOW • EM • (SL 1952 MDIV)

**SCHOLZ MICHAEL P REV** (314)843-7229
9821 Hedgebrook Ln Saint Louis MO 63126-3212 • MO • Assoc • Salem Affton MO • (314)352-4454 • (SL 1984 MDIV)

**SCHOLZ RICHARD J REV** (503)654-7702
10963 SE 92nd Ave Portland OR 97266-7456 • NOW • EM • (SPR 1951)

**SCHOMBURG DELL B REV** (503)390-6313
4824 Schaefer Ct NE Salem OR 97305-3649 • schoms@open.org • NOW • Inst C • Northwest Portland OR • (CQ 1980)

**SCHONBERG CHRISTIAN L REV** (732)714-0715
803 Catherine St Point Pleasant NJ 08742-4080 • NJ • SP • Good Shepherd Point Pleasant NJ • (732)892-4492 • (SL 1984 MDIV)

**SCHONKAES JOHN REGINALD REV**
3019 Liggett Dr Cleveland OH 44134-2609 • jschonkaes@aol.com • S • SP • Holy Trinity Parma OH • (216)741-2602 • (SL 1997 MDIV)

**SCHOOF ARMOND D REV** (734)241-6082
765 Ruff Dr Monroe MI 48162-3581 • MI • EM • (CQ 1979 MED)

**SCHOOLCRAFT ROGER P REV** (501)521-3496
2533 E Lancer St Fayetteville AR 72703-4336 • rps3942@aol.com • MDS • SP • St John Fayetteville AR • (501)443-3609 • (SL 1969 MDIV)

**SCHOOLER EUGENE E REV** (231)723-8574
115 Piney Rd Manistee MI 49660-9221 • NOW • 08/1991 08/2000 • (SPR 1961)

**SCHOOP DAVID A REV** (219)393-5038
388 E 650 S La Porte IN 46350-9363 • IN • Sn/Adm • St John La Porte IN • (219)362-3726 • (CQ 1980 MAR)

**SCHOPPA ROY M REV** (909)359-6147
4535 Albion Dr Riverside CA 92503-2623 • royschoppa@aol.com • PSW • EM • (SPR 1959 PHD)

**SCHORNHORST RONALD L REV** (706)484-9855
PO Box 1060 Greensboro GA 30642 • lolc@negia.net • FG • SP • Florida-Georgia Orlando FL* • (SL 1972 MDIV)

**SCHOTTE MICHAEL L REV** (316)672-6015
40307 NE 40th Ave Preston KS 67583-8572 • stpaulnatrona@juno.com • KS • SP • St Paul Preston KS • (316)672-5354 • (FW 1991 MDIV)

**SCHOUWEILER JAMES A REV** (616)465-5970
9732 Karen Ct Bridgman MI 49106-9780 • pneumaj@aol.com • MI • Sn/Adm • Immanuel Bridgman MI • (616)465-6031 • (SL 1984 MDIV)

**SCHRADER DARWIN P REV** (618)397-8454
88 Circle Dr Fairview Heights IL 62208-3303 • SI • 10/1986 10/1999 • (SL 1973 MDIV MA PHD)

**SCHRADER DAVID L REV** (313)561-7575
205 N Denwood St Dearborn MI 48128-1509 • lcschrd@ccaa.edu • MI • Sn/Adm • Guardian Dearborn MI • (313)274-1414 • (SPR 1969 MDIV)

**SCHRADER DENVER L REV** (314)965-4672
10 Pitman Pl Kirkwood MO 63122-6121 • MO • EM • (SPR 1968 MDIV)

**SCHRAGE DONALD K REV** (602)837-9195
16867 E Malta Dr Fountain Hills AZ 85268-5008 • tlcfhaz@msn.com • PSW • SP • Trinity Fountain Hills AZ • (602)837-0130 • (SPR 1974 MDIV)

**SCHRAM MICHAEL J REV** (715)524-8725
313 S Washington St Shawano WI 54166 • eleos4u@frontiernet.net • NW • Assoc • St James Shawano WI • (715)524-4815 • (SL 1999 MDIV)

**SCHRAMM FREDERICK J REV**
PO Box 70450 Fairbanks AK 99707-0450 • NOW • Assoc • Zion Fairbanks AK • (907)456-7660 • (SL 1970 MDIV DMIN)

**SCHRAMM MARTIN G REV** (949)586-6499
20 Tierra Vista Laguna Hills CA 92653 • schramm@cui.edu • PSW • SHS/C • Pacific Southwest Irvine CA • (949)854-3232 • (CQ 1983 MDIV MA MA PHD)

**SCHRAMM NORMAN W REV**
450 W Sunwest Dr # 10C Casa Grande MN 85222 • MNS • EM • (SL 1949)

**SCHRAMM VERDELL DENNIS REV** (402)652-8550
C/O St Peter Lutheran Church PO Box 496 North Bend NE 68649-0496 • veschram@gpcom.net • NEB • SP • St Peter North Bend NE • (402)652-8215 • (CQ 1997)

**SCHRANK JEFFERY T DR** (602)787-0881
4302 E Blanche Dr Phoenix AZ 85032 • jschrank@juno.com • EN • Sn/Adm • Christ Phoenix AZ • (602)955-4830 • (FW 1988 MDIV DMIN)

**SCHRANK ROBERT J REV** (801)268-4277
1109 Chevy Chase Dr Salt Lake City UT 84117-7207 • rjschrank@juno.com • RM • EM • (SL 1954)

**SCHREIBEIS HOWARD D REV** (406)377-6861
511 N Taylor Ave Glendive MT 59330-2639 • schreib@midrivers.com • MT • Assoc • Our Savior Glendive MT* • (406)377-3890 • (FW 1985 MDIV)

**SCHREIBER JOHN R REV** (810)797-4792
5245 Hadley Rd Goodrich MI 48438-9640 • rev.schreiber@juno.com • MI • SP • Christ Goodrich MI • (810)797-4602 • (SPR 1976 MDIV)

**SCHREIBER MARK J REV**
5355 Walker Horse Dr Jacksonville FL 32257 • FG • M Chap • Florida-Georgia Orlando FL • (FW 1977 MDIV DMIN)

**SCHREIBER OTTO T REV** (920)387-5671
520 Seitz Ave Mayville WI 53050 • SW • EM • (SL 1937)

**SCHREIBER RICHARD J REV**
7420 Maple St W PO Box 85 Webster WI 54893-0085 • rjslcms@win.bright.net • NW • SP • Our Redeemer Webster WI* • (715)866-7191 • (SL 1983 MDIV)

**SCHREIBER WILLIAM A REV**
32 Paul Revere Rd Oil City PA 16301-1199 • EA • SP • Christ Oil City PA • (814)677-4484 • (CQ 1980 MDIV)

**SCHREIBER WILLIAM REV** (702)247-9303
4201 S Decatur Blvd Apt 3194 Las Vegas NV 89103-5893 • CNH • EM • (CL 1967)

**SCHRIEBER PAUL L DR** (314)389-2389
2800 Clearview Dr Saint Louis MO 63121-4506 • schrieberp@csl.edu • MO • SHS/C • Missouri Saint Louis MO • (314)317-4550 • (SPR 1975 MDIV THD)

**SCHRODER DAVID N REV** (512)255-8114
4008 Palomar Ln Austin TX 78727-2948 • dschroder@redeemer.net • TX • Sn/Adm • Redeemer Austin TX • (512)459-1500 • (SL 1972 MDIV)

**SCHROEDER ALBERT H REV** (970)587-2366
PO Box 128 Johnstown CO 80534-0128 • alfloco@cs.com • RM • Asst • Immanuel Loveland CO • (970)667-4506 • (SL 1958 MDIV MA)

**SCHROEDER ARTHUR F REV** (303)341-1321
650 S Clinton St Apt 7-D Denver CO 80231-1546 • chaplart@aol.com • RM • EM • (SL 1944 MST)

**SCHROEDER BRET REV** (307)856-3650
C/O Trinity Lutheran Church 502 E Lincoln Riverton WY 82501 • bschroed@wyoming.com • WY • Assoc • Trinity Riverton WY • (307)856-9340 • (SL 1991 MDIV)

**SCHROEDER DONALD K REV** (678)560-0906
3621 Clubwood Trl Marietta GA 30068-4028 • donschro31@aol.com • FG • EM • (SL 1957 STM)

**SCHROEDER DOUGLAS W REV** (414)421-6016
6016 Clover Ln Greendale WI 53129-2418 • SW • Sn/Adm • Our Shepherd Greendale WI • (414)421-2060 • (SL 1988 MDIV)

**SCHROEDER DWAYNE J REV** (580)234-6655
210 S Arthur St Enid OK 73703-5317 • djschroeder@juno.com • OK • SP • Redeemer Enid OK • (405)234-6622 • (SL 1991 MDIV)

**SCHROEDER FRANCIS REV**
Holy Cross Lutheran Church 2711 Helena Ave Nederland TX 77627-6901 • francis.schroeder@gte.net • TX • SP • Holy Cross Nederland TX • (409)722-1609 • (SL 1984 MDIV)

**SCHROEDER HENRY C REV** (904)854-9502
8665 SW 92nd Ln Apt F Ocala FL 34481-9232 • FG • EM • (SL 1945)

**SCHROEDER JAMES A REV** (847)695-8313
2025 Valley Creek Dr Elgin IL 60123-2687 • friarjim1@aol.com • NI • Sn/Adm • Grace Streamwood IL • (630)289-3996 • (SL 1965 MDIV)

**SCHROEDER JAMES E REV** (616)757-9311
4353 N US Highway 31 Scottville MI 49454-9660 • MI • SP • Our Savior Scottville MI • (231)757-2271 • (SPR 1976 STM)

**SCHROEDER JOHN E REV** (314)352-3058
4991 Miami St Saint Louis MO 63139-1215 • MO • EM • (SL 1949)

**SCHROEDER JONATHAN COLIN REV** (972)264-2511
2200 SW 3rd St Grand Prairie TX 75051-4801 • TX • SP • Faith Grand Prairie TX • (972)264-2511 • (SL 1999 MDIV)

**SCHROEDER KENNETH O REV** (517)624-7243
PO Box 121 Birch Run MI 48415-0121 • MI • SP • Christ Birch Run MI • (517)624-9378 • (SL 1969 MDIV)

**SCHROEDER LAMBERT H REV** (208)467-6653
108 N Brent Ave Nampa ID 83687-8610 • hschro@yahoo.com • NOW • EM • (SPR 1963 MED)

**SCHROEDER MARK A REV** (636)938-3837
172 Rockwood Place Ct Eureka MO 63025-1161 • mark.schroeder@lcms.org • MO • S Ex/S • Missouri Saint Louis MO • (314)317-4550 • (SL 1984 MDIV)

**SCHROEDER MARTIN L REV** (909)778-2570
5231 Wenatchee Way Riverside CA 92509 • martin.schroeder@painewebber.com • PSW • SP • Trinity Montclair CA • (909)626-6552 • (FW 1997 MDIV)

**SCHROEDER PAUL H REV** (314)385-2342
7219 Jenwood Ave Jennings MO 63136-1215 • phschr@aol.com • MO • SP • St Jacobi Jennings MO • (314)388-0345 • (SPR 1975 MDIV)

**SCHROEDER PAUL R REV** (414)421-4221
C/O Our Shepherd Luth Ch PO Box 77 Greendale WI 53129-0077 • SW • Asst • Our Shepherd Greendale WI • (414)421-2060 • (SL 1958)

**SCHROEDER RANDALL A REV** (219)637-2084
232 Red Eagle Pass Fort Wayne IN 46845-1175 • schroede@gateway.net • IN • SHS/C • Indiana Fort Wayne IN • (FW 1986 MDIV MED PHD)

**SCHROEDER RICHARD W REV** (915)336-6263
306 S Mesquite St Fort Stockton TX 79735-6104 • TX • SP • Faith Fort Stockton TX* • (915)336-3925 • (SL 1967 MDIV)

**SCHROEDER RICKY P REV** (414)358-0491
10232 W Green Tree Rd Milwaukee WI 53224-4436 • rps10232@netzero.net • SW • Sn/Adm • St John Plymouth WI • (920)893-3071 • (FW 1986 MDIV)

**SCHROEDER ROBERT H REV** (517)886-0992
7211 Creekside Dr Lansing MI 48917-9691 • MI • EM • (SL 1955)
**SCHROEDER ROBERT J REV** (562)947-6462
10323 Larrylyn Dr Whittier CA 90603-2613 • revbob@gte.net • PSW • Sn/Adm • Trinity Whittier CA • (562)699-7431 • (SL 1975 MDIV)
**SCHROEDER ROY P DR** (517)332-0495
5190 Park Lake Rd East Lansing MI 48823-3885 • royschroeder@juno.com • MI • EM • (SL 1954 STM THD)
**SCHROEDER STEPHEN E REV** (912)925-4369
C/O Trinity Luth Church 12391 Mercy Blvd Savannah GA 31419-3436 • tlcpastor@juno.com • FG • SP • Trinity Savannah GA • (912)925-4839 • (SL 1970 MDIV)
**SCHROEDER THOMAS L REV** (734)439-7050
13099 Petersburg Rd Milan MI 48160 • MI • SP • Christ King Saline MI • (734)429-9200 • (CQ 1984 MAR)
**SCHROEDER WAYNE CARL REV**
Congregational Services 8100 West Capitol Dr Milwaukee WI 53222-1981 • trinity@inav.net • SW • Christ King Saline MI • (734)429-9200 • (SL 1969 MDIV)
**SCHROEDER WILLIAM C REV** (217)787-3749
1721 W Iles Ave Springfield IL 62704-4832 • wildbill141@juno.com • CI • Assoc • Trinity Springfield IL • (217)522-8151 • (SL 1976 MDIV)
**SCHROEDER WINFRED A REV** (360)882-3955
2911 SE Village Loop #169 Vancouver WA 98683 • NOW • EM • (SL 1937)
**SCHROETER HAROLD W REV** (210)655-7619
6515 Gulf Strm San Antonio TX 78239-2813 • TX • EM • (SPR 1954)
**SCHROTER JOHN H REV**
C/O Trinity Luth Church 238 Columbia Ave Cliffside Park NJ 07010-2404 • NJ • SP • Trinity Cliffside Park NJ • (201)943-0088 • (SL 1992 MDIV)
**SCHRUHL JOE E REV** (510)655-8289
58 Fairview Ave Piedmont CA 94610-1016 • CNH • Sn/Adm • Zion Piedmont CA • (510)530-4213 • (SPR 1969)
**SCHUBERT ALFRED W REV**
1318 Flour Bluff Dr Corpus Christi TX 78418-5104 • adase@worldnet.att.net • TX • SP • Lord Of Life Corpus Christi TX • (361)937-8158 • (SL 1989 MDIV)
**SCHUBERT ALFRED W JR. REV** (601)264-9042
105 Bellmont Dr Hattiesburg MS 39402-1916 • aschuber@netdoor.com • SO • EM • (SL 1962 MDIV)
**SCHUBERT GARY T REV**
C/O St Peter Lutheran Church 1120 Trampe Ave Saint Louis MO 63138-3014 • MO • SP • St Peter Saint Louis MO • (314)741-2485 • (SL 1963 MDIV)
**SCHUBERT JEFFERY S REV** (636)227-3753
16136 Pine Terrace Dr Ballwin MO 63021-6082 • jeffery.schubert@lcms.org • MO • S Ex/S • Missouri Saint Louis MO • (314)317-4550 • (SL 1981 MDIV)
**SCHUBERT JOHN R REV** (480)963-6105
Epiphany Lutheran Church 800 W Ray Rd Chandler AZ 85225-3120 • pastorz@telesouth1.com • PSW • Missouri Saint Louis MO • (314)317-4550 • (SL 1999 MDIV)
**SCHUBKEGEL THEODORE V REV** (816)228-8037
207 SW Lake Vill Blvd Blue Springs MO 64014 • schubatbs@aol.com • MO • Assoc • Timothy Blue Springs MO • (816)228-5300 • (SPR 1976 MDIV)
**SCHUCHARD BRUCE G DR** (314)725-5232
11 N Seminary Ter St Louis MO 63105-3011 • schuchardb@csl.edu • MO • SHS/C • Missouri Saint Louis MO • (314)317-4550 • (FW 1984 STM MDIV PHD)
**SCHUDDE A MARK REV** (262)650-9160
2109 Springbrook South Waukesha WI 53186 • kmschu-d@execpc.com • EN • SP • Peace New Berlin WI • (262)679-1441 • (SL 1985 MDIV)
**SCHUDDE ALBERT L REV** (360)424-6709
1904 N 33rd Pl Mount Vernon WA 98273-8945 • NOW • EM • (SL 1958)
**SCHUDDE ARTHUR I REV** (309)697-1444
1910 S Akorn Ct Peoria IL 61607-1301 • CI • Sn/Adm • Christ Peoria IL • (309)637-5309 • (SL 1965 MDIV)
**SCHUDLICH GERALD E REV** (616)723-2207
3209 River Rd Manistee MI 49660-9713 • revges@webtv.net • MI • EM • (SL 1959 MDIV)
**SCHUELEIN VIRGIL L REV**
2270 Castlegate Dr N Apt 817 Castle Rock CO 80104-8341 • RM • EM • (SL 1958 MED)
**SCHUELER DENNIS R REV** (608)253-2651
528 Bauer St Wisconsin Dells WI 53965-1701 • SW • SP • Trinity Wisconsin Dells WI • (608)253-3241 • (SL 1976 MDIV)
**SCHUELER WAYNE A REV** (281)344-8546
4518 Meadowbend Dr Richmond TX 77469-9072 • was25@juno.com • TX • SP • Trinity Rosenberg TX • (281)341-1451 • (FW 1982 MDIV)
**SCHUESSLER DEANE L REV** (651)731-4451
6626 Falstaff Rd Woodbury MN 55125-3804 • deanejul@pclink.com • MNS • EM • (SL 1958 MDIV DMIN)
**SCHUESSLER MICHAEL JOSEPH REV** (712)252-0776
3500 Nebraska Sioux City IA 51104 • lcmos@aol.com • IW • O Miss • Iowa West Fort Dodge IA • (SL 1994 MDIV)
**SCHUESSLER MITCHEL E REV** (618)226-3547
C/O Bethlehem Luth Church (Ferrin) 12903 Clara St Carlyle IL 62231 • revmitchel@yahoo.com • SI • SP • Bethlehem Carlyle IL • (618)226-3550 • (SL 1987 MDIV)
**SCHUESSLER RALPH F REV**
PO Box 1185 Newton NC 28658-1185 • SE • EM • (SL 1932 MA)
**SCHUETT FRED P REV** (541)889-5674
4404 Bellows Dr Ontario OR 97914-8492 • NOW • SP • Pilgrim Ontario OR • (541)889-5458 • (SL 1965 MTH)
**SCHUETT SCOTT R REV** (860)642-6191
269 Babcock Hill Rd Lebanon CT 06249-1303 • fm106@earthlink.net • NE • SP • Redeemer Lebanon CT • (860)423-4320 • (FW 1980 MDIV)
**SCHUETT WAYNE M REV** (918)687-0150
428 E Broadway St Muskogee OK 77403-5111 • flcmusk@intellex.com • OK • SP • First Muskogee OK • (918)683-4673 • (FW 1985 MDIV)
**SCHUETTE RONALD H REV** (305)271-3903
11060 SW 59th Ter Miami FL 33173-1110 • rhschuette@hotmail.com • FG • SP • St Paul Miami FL • (305)271-3171 • (SL 1963 MDIV)
**SCHUETZ ALFRED L REV** (303)368-5899
13992 E Marina Dr Apt 211 Aurora CO 80014-3750 • RM • EM • (SL 1941)
**SCHUFREIDER JEFFREY L REV** (415)967-0666
C/O First Lutheran Church 350 Dolores Way S San Francisco CA 94080 • st-paul.org.pastor@st-paul.org • CNH • SP • First S San Francisco CA • (415)583-5131 • (FW 1979 MDIV)
**SCHULDHEISS ALLEN REV** (406)755-5922
122 Sherry Ln Kalispell MT 59901-2548 • MT • EM • (SL 1935)
**SCHULENBURG HERBERT J REV** (760)240-2887
11111 Sandy Ln Apple Valley CA 92308-9339 • PSW • EM • (SL 1933)
**SCHULER MARK T DR** (651)641-0264
1288 Marshall Ave Saint Paul MN 55104-6448 • schuler@csp.edu • MNS • SHS/C • Minnesota South Burnsville MN • (SL 1981 STM MDIV THD)
**SCHULER ROBERT REV** (216)255-1822
7996 Buckthorn Dr Mentor OH 44060-7445 • OH • SP • Trinity Willoughby OH • (440)942-7766 • (SL 1969 MED)
**SCHULINGKAMP WARREN JOHN REV** (225)647-0496
1613 E John Alan St Gonzales LA 70737-4998 • SO • 10/1999 • (FW 1992 MDIV MS)
**SCHULLER DAVID S DR** (937)276-2542
1743 Philadelphia Dr Dayton OH 45406-4012 • OH • EM • (SL 1950 STM MDIV PHD DD)
**SCHULLER RICHARD L REV** (713)692-0597
412 Kelley Houston TX 77007-4135 • TX • SP • Messiah Houston TX • (713)861-3072 • (FW 1982)
**SCHULT PAUL E REV** (816)734-4559
1726 NE Chowning Dr Kansas City MO 64155-3782 • pschult@swbell.net • MO • SP • King Of Kings Kansas City MO • (816)436-7680 • (FW 1983 MDIV)
**SCHULT PAUL TIMOTHY REV** (314)928-1651
1258 Stephenridge Saint Charles MO 63304 • schult@postnet.com • MO • Assoc • Messiah St Charles MO • (314)926-9773 • (SL 1995 MDIV)
**SCHULTE EDWARD N REV** (313)622-8653
1073 N Lakeshore Rd PO Box 621 Port Sanilac MI 48469-0621 • EN • EM • (SPR 1941)
**SCHULTHEIS MARTIN J REV**
39 Winthrop St Williston Park NY 11596 • AT • SP • St John Williston Park NY • (516)742-5858 • (SL 1998 MDIV)
**SCHULTHEIS VERNON P REV** (718)429-6413
3338 75th St Jackson Heights NY 11372-1143 • vernsny@aol.com • AT • SP • Christ Woodside NY • (718)639-3945 • (SL 1969 MDIV)
**SCHULTZ ANTHONY J REV** (541)482-5004
C/O Grace Lutheran Church 660 Frances Ln Ashland OR 97520-3410 • minton143@aol.com • NOW • SP • Grace Ashland OR • (541)482-1661 • (SL 1979 MDIV)
**SCHULTZ ARTHUR L REV** (937)438-9879
8365 Saint Francis Ct Centerville OH 45458-2761 • OH • EM • (SPR 1946 MDIV)
**SCHULTZ CLARENCE L REV**
100 Stardust Dr #104 Sherman IL 62684-9763 • OK • EM • (SPR 1930)
**SCHULTZ CRAIG D REV** (828)459-7378
5759 Bolick Rd Claremont NC 28610 • pastorpac@aol.com • SE • SP • Bethel Claremont NC • (828)459-7378 • (SL 1975 MDIV)
**SCHULTZ DALE E REV** (801)635-9631
831 N 20 W # 2411 Hurricane UT 84737-1704 • RM • EM • (SPR 1954)
**SCHULTZ DAVID P REV** (515)889-2881
203 2nd St Fenton IA 50539 • IW • SP • St John Fenton IA • (515)889-2812 • (FW 1999 MDIV)
**SCHULTZ DAVID V REV** (281)448-5449
6211 Woodland Forest Dr Houston TX 77088-4031 • dschultz@stmarkhouston.org • TX • Assoc • St Mark Houston TX • (713)468-2623 • (CQ 1988 MDIV)
**SCHULTZ DENNIS L REV** (605)432-9492
803 S 5th St Milbank SD 57252-3012 • dpschult@tnics.com • SD • Assoc • Emanuel Milbank SD • (605)432-9555 • (SL 1968 MDIV)
**SCHULTZ DONALD A REV** (618)282-3022
803 S Main St Red Bud IL 62278-1216 • rev³don@juno.com • SI • Sn/Adm • St John Red Bud IL • (618)282-3873 • (SL 1961 MDIV)
**SCHULTZ FREDERICK W REV** (904)677-3146
1207 Parkside Dr Ormond Beach FL 32174-3942 • ricdelsch@aol.com • FG • SP • Trinity Holly Hill FL • (904)255-7580 • (FW 1984 MDIV MED)
**SCHULTZ GARY G REV** (715)848-6092
330 N 12th Ave Wausau WI 54401-4260 • garygs@pcpros.net • NW • Sn/Adm • Trinity Wausau WI • (715)842-0769 • (SL 1987 MDIV)
**SCHULTZ GERALD N REV** (407)876-3151
9204 Sabal Palm Cir Windermere FL 34786-8815 • FG • SP • Christ King Orlando FL • (407)876-2771 • (SL 1963 MDIV DMIN)
**SCHULTZ GLENN A REV** (605)432-6031
PO Box 82 Corona SD 57227 • SD • SP • Trinity Corona SD* • (605)432-6137 • (SL 1970 MDIV)
**SCHULTZ GREGORY J REV** (618)426-3741
PO Box 246 Campbell Hill IL 62916-0246 • gmbmesch@egyptian.net • SI • SP • St Peter Campbell Hill IL • (618)426-9091 • (SL 1989 MDIV)
**SCHULTZ JEREMY J REV** (636)225-9128
243 Valley View Ridge Dr Valley Park MO 63088 • MO • Asst • St Paul Saint Louis MO • (314)822-0447 • (SL 1998 MDIV)
**SCHULTZ JOEL S A REV** (636)390-0439
4508 Scarecrow Ln Washington MO 63090 • JASchultz@juno.com • MO • Assoc • Immanuel Washington MO • (314)239-4705 • (SL 2000 MDIV)
**SCHULTZ JOSEPH A REV** (715)833-2424
3415 Markgraff Rd Fall Creek WI 54742-9399 • NW • EM • (SPR 1954 STM)
**SCHULTZ KURTIS D REV** (205)956-1340
764 Abigail Ln Birmingham AL 35210-2902 • flcbal@msn.com • SO • SP • First Birmingham AL • (205)933-0380 • (FW 1979 MDIV)
**SCHULTZ LEON W REV** (401)737-4651
26 Grand Ave Warwick RI 02889-5807 • letz874810@aol.com • NE • SP • St Paul Providence RI • (401)941-5100 • (SL 1983 MDIV)
**SCHULTZ MARK A REV**
205/20 Soi Chaiyakiat 1 Ngam Wong Wan Road Bangkok 10210 THAILAND • schultzs@cscoms.com • MT • S Miss • Montana Billings MT • (FW 1983 MDIV)
**SCHULTZ MARTIN A REV** (618)259-4332
1301 Vaughn Rd Wood River IL 62095-1851 • zmschultz@home.com • SI • SP • St Paul Wood River IL • (618)259-0257 • (SL 1988 MDIV MA)
**SCHULTZ MYLES R REV** (918)758-0669
1310 E 6th St Okmulgee OK 74447-4712 • mylesschultz@aol.com • OK • SP • Trinity Okmulgee OK • (918)756-6046 • (FW 1990 MDIV)
**SCHULTZ OLIVER M REV** (715)874-6521
7621 Blue Valley Dr S Eau Claire WI 54703-9175 • NW • EM • (SPR 1952 MDIV)
**SCHULTZ RANDALL P REV** (810)653-5365
624 Oda St Davison MI 48423-1022 • schultz5@internet4all.net • MI • Sn/Adm • Trinity Davison MI • (810)658-3000 • (SL 1979 MDIV)
**SCHULTZ RICHARD J REV** (314)355-6281
11720 Hidden Lake Dr #2G-242 Saint Louis MO 63138-1749 • MO • EM • (SL 1945 MED MDIV DD)
**SCHULTZ ROBERT J DR** (734)697-4088
47286 Hull Rd Belleville MI 48111 • schult98@pilot.msu.edu • MI • Sn/Adm • St Michael Wayne MI • (734)728-1950 • (SL 1971 MDIV MS DMIN)
**SCHULTZ RONALD C REV** (313)241-1607
618 N Monroe St Monroe MI 48162-2935 • ronschultz@foxberry.net • MI • Sn/Adm • Grace Monroe MI • (734)242-1401 • (FW 1983 MDIV)
**SCHULTZ RONALD L REV** (414)361-0686
236 E Park Ave Berlin WI 54923-1639 • SW • EM • (TH 1958)
**SCHULTZ WALTER G REV** (507)533-8080
110 Fourth St NE Apt 204 Stewartville MN 55976 • MNS • EM • (SPR 1934)
**SCHULTZ WILLIAM F REV** (706)745-4739
2315 Crawford Rd Blairsville GA 30512-6709 • FG • EM • (SPR 1965 MA)
**SCHULTZ WILLIAM K REV** (408)629-2460
6881 Ivegill Ct San Jose CA 95119-1836 • revwkschultz@juno.com • CNH • SP • Resurrection Santa Clara CA • (408)241-2728 • (FW 1985 MDIV)
**SCHULTZ WILLIAM M REV** (320)252-5221
7109 41st Ave Clear Lake MN 55319-9637 • MNN • EM • (SPR 1947)
**SCHULTZE EDWIN L REV** (503)363-8276
7241 Hilda St SE Salem OR 97301-9255 • schu6342@aol.com • NOW • EM • (SPR 1965 MDIV MCOUN)
**SCHULZ DONALD C REV** (715)536-7823
1011 Jefferson St Merrill WI 54452-3023 • NW • EM • (SPR 1950)
**SCHULZ DONALD RICHARD REV** (801)896-8460
1070 S 800 W Richfield UT 84701-3049 • prdon@gbasin.net • RM • D Miss • Good Shepherd Richfield UT • (435)896-8050 • (FW 1991 MDIV)
**SCHULZ JEFFREY P REV** (507)342-2350
665 Maple St Wabasso MN 56293-9690 • jpschulz@rconnect.com • MNS • SP • Bethany Wabasso MN* • (507)342-5544 • (SL 1997 MDIV)
**SCHULZ JOHN P REV** (865)690-6464
1605 Blackwood Dr Knoxville TN 37923-1104 • MDS • EM • * • (SL 1957 MDIV)
**SCHULZ M L REV** (707)462-2523
560 Park Blvd Ukiah CA 95482-3701 • mlschulz@pacific.net • CNH • SP • Faith Ukiah CA • (707)462-2618 • (SL 1991 MDIV)
**SCHULZ MARK CARL REV** (847)429-9395
1298 Evergreen Ln Elgin IL 60123 • schulzmc@mc.net • NI • SP • King Of Glory Elgin IL • (847)931-1520 • (CQ 1995 MA)
**SCHULZ MARK E REV** (734)434-8022
6587 Crane Rd Ypsilanti MI 48197-8851 • mschulz@stlukeaa.org • MI • Assoc • St Luke Ann Arbor MI • (734)971-0550 • (SC 1984 MDIV)
**SCHULZ MARK R REV** (847)234-8906
688 W Deerpath Rd Lake Forest IL 60045-1611 • mschulz37@aol.com • NI • SP • Faith Lake Forest IL • (847)234-1868 • (SL 1986 MDIV DMIN)
**SCHULZ MARK W DR** (715)833-0920
820 Pamela Pl Eau Claire WI 54701-7301 • mark@peace-lutheran.org • NW • Sn/Adm • Peace Eau Claire WI • (715)834-2486 • (SL 1982 MDIV DMIN)
**SCHULZ MICHAEL PAUL REV** (248)969-0531
136 South Washington Oxford MI 48371-4975 • MI • SP • Holy Cross Oxford MI • (248)628-2011 • (SL 1973 MDIV)

**SCHULZ NORMAN L REV** (205)595-7578
1127 Cresthill Dr Birmingham AL 35213-1418 • SO • SP • Hope Birmingham AL • (205)956-1930 • (SL 1964 MDIV)
**SCHULZ REINHARDT E REV** (626)286-1317
5212 Golden West Ave Temple City CA 91780-3246 • PSW • EM • (SL 1936)
**SCHULZ ROBERT C REV** (219)996-5953
68 Mediterranean Ave Hebron IN 46341-9113 • IN • EM • (SL 1935)
**SCHULZ STEVEN MICHAEL REV** (712)732-9307
504 Gran Drive Storm Lake IA 50588 • smschulz@ncn.net • IW • SP • Grace Storm Lake IA • (712)732-5005 • (SL 1991 MDIV)
**SCHULZ STEWART G REV** (812)375-0877
3906 Sycamore Dr Columbus IN 47203-1163 • schulz@hsonline.net • IN • Sn/Adm • Faith Columbus IN • (812)342-3587 • (SL 1977 MDIV MA MTH)
**SCHULZ VICTOR P REV** (850)438-3869
1212 E Lakeview Ave Pensacola FL 32503-5326 • SO • EM • (SPR 1949)
**SCHULZ WALLACE R REV** (636)271-4444
4751 Chateau Ln Pacific MO 63069-2942 • wschulz@mvp.net • MO • Faith Columbus IN • (812)342-3587 • (SPR 1973 MDIV)
**SCHULZE CHRISTOPH M** (718)649-1707
1182 E 93rd St Brooklyn NY 11236-3929 • AT • SP • St Paul Brooklyn NY* • (718)443-2220 • (FW 2000)
**SCHULZE PAUL E REV** (352)694-5674
1909 SE 37th Circle Ct Ocala FL 34471-5651 • AT • EM • * • (SL 1953)
**SCHULZE ROBERT A REV** (507)372-2821
621 - 9th St Worthington MN 56187 • rbschulze@aol.com • MNS • SP • St Matthew Worthington MN • (507)376-6168 • (SPR 1975 MDIV)
**SCHUMACHER FRED JR. REV** (405)942-5497
3720 NW 62nd St Oklahoma City OK 73112-1420 • OK • EM • (SL 1948 MDIV MT)
**SCHUMACHER MICHAEL D REV** (208)463-9897
3718 Brenan Dr Nampa ID 83686-5041 • NOW • SP • Zion Nampa ID • (208)466-6746 • (SL 1987 MDIV)
**SCHUMACHER STEPHEN REV** (630)428-9174
1122 Catalpa Ln Naperville IL 60540 • sschumacher@bethanylcs.org • NI • Assoc • Bethany Naperville IL • (630)355-2198 • (SL 1985 MDIV)
**SCHUMACHER STEVEN R REV**
136 Fleetwood Rd Bristol CT 06010 • NE • Assoc • Immanuel Bristol CT • (860)583-5649 • (FW 1987 MDIV)
**SCHUMACHER WARREN W REV** (503)648-4318
2254 NE 13th Ave Hillsboro OR 97124-1363 • wshoebox@aol.com • NOW • DP • Northwest Portland OR • (SPR 1965 LLD)
**SCHUMACHER WILLIAM W REV** (314)968-8973
2929 Collier Ave Saint Louis MO 63144-2613 • schumacherw@csl.edu • MO • SHS/C • Missouri Saint Louis MO • (314)317-4550 • (SL 1985 MDIV STM)
**SCHUMM DANIEL DAVID REV** (317)818-9232
5743 Cantigny Way N Carmel IN 46033-8650 • rev@email.com • IN • Asst • Carmel Carmel IN • (317)814-4252 • (SL 1983 MDIV)
**SCHUMM DONALD REV**
PO Box 504 Holgate OH 43527-0504 • MI • EM • (SPR 1945)
**SCHUMM HERBERT L REV** (219)357-3537
1351 S Randolph St Garrett IN 46738-1970 • revhschumm@juno.com • IN • SP • Zion Garrett IN • (219)357-4545 • (FW 1979 MDIV)
**SCHUMM MARK E REV** (520)297-3290
8000 N El Tovar Pl Tucson AZ 85704-3325 • meschumm@aol.com • EN • Assoc • Ascension Tucson AZ • (520)297-3095 • (SL 1998 MDIV)
**SCHUMM RICHARD G REV** (949)495-3599
24201 Via Aquara Laguna Niguel CA 92677-2133 • rgschumm@quik.com • PSW • EM • (SPR 1959 MDIV)
**SCHUMM WILLIAM E REV** (360)679-9459
2047 W Pinewood Way Oak Harbor WA 98277-8519 • NOW • EM • (SL 1959 MDIV)
**SCHUMPE WAYNE E REV** (979)773-2634
C/O St James Lutheran Church PO Box 247 Lexington TX 78947-0247 • TX • SP • St James Lexington TX* • (979)773-2634 • (CQ 1971 MAR)
**SCHURB KEN R REV** (636)391-8352
408 Iron Warrior Ln Manchester MO 63011-4334 • kenschurb@aol.com • MO • S Ex/S • Missouri Saint Louis MO • (314)317-4550 • (FW 1982 MDIV STM MA)
**SCHURLE DARRELL WAYNE REV** (303)659-4072
380 S 20th Ave Brighton CO 80601-2522 • dwschurle@ctos.com • RM • 02/1998 02/2000 • (CQ 1992 MDIV MA)
**SCHURTER DENNIS D REV** (940)383-4066
1320 Greenbriar St Denton TX 76201-1788 • dennis.schurter@mhmr.state.tx.us • TX • Inst C • Texas Austin TX • (SL 1968 MDIV DMIN)
**SCHUSCHKE GARY STEVEN REV**
C/O St Luke Lutheran Church 2021 W State Rd Oviedo FL 32765 • S • Asst • St Luke Oviedo FL • (407)365-3408 • (SL 2000 MDIV)
**SCHUSTER FREDERICK H REV** (319)332-4348
3997 Keeneland Ct Bettendorf IA 52722-2106 • IE • Sn/Adm • Holy Cross Davenport IA • (319)322-2654 • (SL 1960 MDIV DMIN)
**SCHUSTER WILLIAM K REV** (361)855-9442
4513 Essex Dr Corpus Christi TX 78413-3109 • wkschuster@juno.com • TX • EM • (SL 1944 MDIV)
**SCHUT BRUCE L REV** (402)287-2289
702 Maple St Wakefield NE 68784-5054 • NEB • SP • St John Wakefield NE • (402)287-2385 • (FW 1984 MDIV)
**SCHUTH LOUIS W REV** (217)463-3603
122 Concordia Dr Paris IL 61944-2379 • CI • EM • (SL 1938)
**SCHUTH PAUL R REV** (815)455-4322
952 Mc Henry Ave Crystal Lake IL 60014 • NI • SP • Prince Peace Crystal Lake IL • (815)455-3200 • (SPR 1973 MDIV)
**SCHUTT CHARLES K REV** (810)463-2036
23500 Denton Rd Apt #198 Clinton Twp MI 48036-3422 • MI • EM • (SPR 1964)
**SCHUTTE DENNIS C REV** (509)485-1915
C/O Immanuel Luth Church 1608 Tonasket Havillah Rd Tonasket WA 98855-9411 • MNN • Prince Peace Crystal Lake IL • (815)455-3200 • (SL 1993 MDIV)
**SCHUTTE HERBERT B REV** (308)381-7148
2404 N Howard Ave Grand Island NE 68803-1955 • NEB • EM • (SPR 1962)
**SCHUTZ ROLAND D DR** (608)839-1757
430 Ollie St Cottage Grove WI 53527-9623 • schutz75@chorus.net • SW • D Miss • South Wisconsin Milwaukee WI • (414)464-8100 • (FW 1977 MDIV DMIN)
**SCHWAB DENNIS L REV** (314)928-7994
125 Fort Sumter Way Saint Charles MO 63303-6147 • MO • Sn/Adm • Zion Saint Charles MO • (636)441-7425 • (CQ 1978 MED)
**SCHWAB GUENTER REV** (410)828-0473
6754 Glenkirk Rd Baltimore MD 21239-1410 • guenterschwab @netscape.net • SE • SP • Holy Cross Towson MD • (410)825-7905 • (SL 1965 MDIV MCED)
**SCHWALENBERG DENNIS D REV** (330)644-9914
470 Bobwhite Trl Akron OH 44319 • voxuantron@prodigy.net • OH • Assoc • Zion Akron OH • (330)253-3136 • (SL 1980 MDIV)
**SCHWALENBERG MARK LYNN REV** (515)984-6075
1000 W Broadway St Polk City IA 50226-1008 • markpolkc@aol.com • IW • SP • Beautiful Savior Polk City IA • (515)984-6146 • (SL 1991 MDIV)
**SCHWAN DAVID E REV** (605)787-4388
7201 Timberline Rd Black Hawk SD 57718-9686 • schwan@rapidnet.com • SD • SP • Divine Shepherd Black Hawk SD • (605)787-6438 • (FW 1977 MDIV MA)
**SCHWAN PAUL W REV** (317)862-3807
5832 S Franklin Rd Indianapolis IN 46239-9560 • IN • EM • (SL 1947 MA MDIV)
**SCHWANDT HERBERT A REV** (301)736-9442
9532 Noble Dr Upper Marlboro MD 20772-9424 • SE • EM • (SPR 1960 MA)
**SCHWANDT JAMES L REV** (253)891-0607
15613 67th St Ct E Sumner WA 98390 • NOW • EM • (SL 1957 MDIV)
**SCHWANDT RICHARD L REV** (828)322-5078
C/O Christ Lutheran Church 324 2nd Ave SE Hickory NC 28602-3043 • clchickory@twave.net • SE • Sn/Adm • Christ Hickory NC • (828)328-1483 • (SL 1982 MDIV)
**SCHWANE WALTER H REV** (217)854-9242
411 Sumner St Carlinville IL 62626-1465 • SI • EM • (SL 1938)
**SCHWANKE GERALD A REV** (612)395-2029
PO Box 217 Lester Prairie MN 55354-0217 • MNS • SP • St Peter Lester Prairie MN • (612)395-2811 • (FW 1989 MDIV)
**SCHWANKE WAYNE L REV** (304)728-6433
RR 3 Box 120 N3 Kearneysville WV 25430-9413 • SE • 03/1991 03/2000 • (FW 1987 MDIV)
**SCHWANZ CHRIS A REV** (262)377-6610
9025 Oakridge Ln Cedarburg WI 53012-9388 • cschwanz@fils.org • SW • Assoc • First Immanuel Cedarburg WI • (262)377-6610 • (FW 1989 MDIV)
**SCHWARTZ NATHANIEL R REV** (816)246-6797
601 NE Adams Dr Lees Summit MO 64086-6260 • pastor@beautifulsavior-lsmo.org • EN • SP • Beaut Savior Lees Summit MO • (816)524-7288 • (SL 1989 MDIV STM)
**SCHWARTZ ROGER A REV** (706)297-7314
9354 Sherwood St Toccoa GA 30577 • FG • SP • Trinity Toccoa GA • (706)886-6723 • (SL 2000 MDIV)
**SCHWARTZ VERNON H REV** (231)924-0032
111 W Pine St Fremont MI 49412-1529 • MI • EM • (SPR 1950)
**SCHWARTZKOPF ELMER J REV** (618)965-9118
4570 Ballpark Rd Steeleville IL 62288-2814 • elmerj@midwest.net • SI • EM • (SL 1945 MDIV)
**SCHWARTZKOPF LUTHER E REV** (760)872-1030
2206 Galloway Ave Bishop CA 93514-2018 • PSW • EM • (SL 1945)
**SCHWEIM F ARTHUR REV** (253)848-7105
118 18th St NW Puyallup WA 98371-5220 • NOW • 06/1977 10/1997 • (SPR 1962 MSED)
**SCHWEITZER KEITH W REV**
St John Lutheran Church 102 SW 7th St Lawton OK 73501-3922 • keithlcms@aol.com • OK • Assoc • St John Lawton OK • (580)353-0556 • (SL 1989 MDIV)
**SCHWENGEL KENNETH E REV** (301)262-3159
4005 Woodrow Ln Bowie MD 20715-1244 • schwenge@erols.com • SE • EM • (SL 1952 MDIV)
**SCHWERTFEGER HAROLD A REV** (414)241-4663
945 W Heritage Ct Apt 112 Mequon WI 53092-6056 • SW • EM • (SL 1940)
**SCHWERTLICH WILLIAM L REV** (281)375-6547
C/O Christ Lutheran Church PO Box 507 Pattison TX 77466-0507 • swordly@aol.com • TX • SP • Christ Pattison TX • (281)934-8218 • (SL 1982 MDIV)
**SCHWICHTENBERG MARC N REV** (847)392-9060
413 N Pine St Mount Prospect IL 60056 • schwich@aol.com • NI • Assoc • St Paul Mount Prospect IL • (847)255-0332 • (FW 1997 MDIV)
**SCHWICHTENBERG WILLIS R REV** (815)235-8689
321 N Holly Ave Freeport IL 61032-3508 • pastorswitz@mwci.net • NI • SP • Immanuel Freeport IL • (815)235-1993 • (SPR 1972 MDIV DMIN)
**SCHWIEGER ALAN J REV** (313)329-4502
961 Vine St Saint Clair MI 48079-5453 • ajspastor@adunet.net • MI • SP • Immanuel Saint Clair MI • (810)329-7174 • (FW 1979 MDIV)
**SCHWIEGER FLOYD J REV** (307)548-7030
472 W 7th St Apt B8 Lovell WY 82431-1538 • WY • EM • (SL 1945)
**SCHWIESOW WAYNE WILLIAM REV** (573)243-5395
138 Cty Rd 226 Cape Girardeau MO 63701 • MO • SP • Zion Cape Girardeau MO* • (573)204-1944 • (FW 1992 MDIV MS)
**SCHWOLERT NORMAN W REV** (972)539-0887
2204 Ellis Dr Flower Mound TX 75028-7552 • TX • EM • * • (SPR 1958 MTH)
**SCOTT ALAN D REV** (520)669-6349
1500 S Ocotillo Ave Parker AZ 85344-6234 • pastoral@ispchannel.com • EN • SP • Messiah Parker AZ • (520)669-8964 • (FW 1983 MDIV)
**SCOTT BRADFORD E REV** (419)824-9868
6807 Gettysburg Dr Sylvania OH 43560-3246 • scottbe@juno.com • EN • SP • Good Shepherd Toledo OH • (419)474-0529 • (SL 1982 MDIV)
**SCOTT CHARLES R REV**
PO Box 791 Moundridge KS 67107-0791 • KS • 09/2000 • (FW 1992 MDIV)
**SCOTT EDWARD A REV** (504)726-0315
247 Cross Gates Blvd Slidell LA 70461 • mail4scott@aol.com • SO • Sn/Adm • Prince Of Peace New Orleans LA • (504)242-2636 • (CQ 1980 MDIV)
**SCUDDER MICHAEL R REV** (219)471-7401
6 Wycliffe Pl Fort Wayne IN 46825 • prscoot@juno.com • IN • SHS/C • Indiana Fort Wayne IN • (FW 1994 MDIV)
**SCUDIERI ROBERT J REV** (314)436-9729
1826 S 8th St Saint Louis MO 63104-4061 • namissions@aol.com • EN • D Ex/S • English Farmington MI* • (SL 1971 STM STM DMIN)
**SEABAUGH TIMOTHY M** (850)455-2897
304 E Winthrop Pensacola FL 32507 • SO • Asst • Redeemer Pensacola FL • (850)455-0330 • (SL 2000 MDIV)
**SEALS TIMOTHY L REV**
9001 La Verne Dr Rancho Cucamonga CA 91701-4887 • PSW • Cmp P • Univ Chapel Los Angeles CA • (310)208-4579 • (FW 1984)
**SEAMAN GERALD W REV** (407)322-2827
736 Silverwood Dr Lake Mary FL 32746-4917 • seamanj@ix.netcom.com • FG • D Ex/S • Florida-Georgia Orlando FL* • (SL 1964 MDIV)
**SEAMAN WILLIAM D REV** (828)256-5569
C/O Our Savior Luth Church 2160 35th Avenue Dr NE Hickory NC 28601-9264 • osluth@twave.net • SE • SP • Our Savior Hickory NC • (828)256-5469 • (SL 1971 MDIV MA DMIN)
**SEARS GARY L REV** (319)662-4108
C/O Trinity Lutheran Church PO Box 66 Conroy IA 52220-0066 • glsears@avalon.net • IE • SP • Trinity Conroy IA • (319)662-4075 • (FW 1987 MDIV)
**SEATON ROBERT G REV** (423)473-9250
2825 Julian Dr NE Cleveland TN 37312 • MDS • SP • First Cleveland TN • (423)472-6811 • (SL 1982 MDIV)
**SEAVER WADE M REV** (608)647-6905
1060 N Central Ave PO Box 230 Richland Center WI 53581 • seaver@mwt.net • SW • SP • St Luke Richland Center WI • (608)647-6905 • (FW 1999 MDIV)
**SEBAN CALVIN F REV** (414)255-7656
N86 W15852 Riverside Bluff Menomonee Falls WI 53051 • SW • Assoc • St John West Bend WI • (262)334-4901 • (SL 1968 MDIV MS)
**SECKER PHILIP J REV** (203)429-6739
76 Willowbrook Rd Storrs Mansfield CT 06268-2205 • psecker@snet.net • NE • Cmp P • Hope Storrs Mansfield CT • (860)429-5409 • (SL 1963 MDIV MST THD)
**SEDLMAYR ROGER M REV** (701)297-0838
90 Cedar Ave Fargo ND 58102-1638 • rsedl613@aol.com • ND • Sn/Adm • Immanuel Fargo ND • (701)293-7979 • (SL 1986 MDIV)
**SEDORY ELMER J REV** (616)424-5934
50256 E Lake Shore Dr Dowagiac MI 49047-8400 • MI • EM • (SL 1948)
**SEEBER TIMOTHY W REV** (616)327-0974
6148 Rothbury St Portage MI 49024-2389 • seebfam@ix.netcom.com • MI • Sn/Adm • Zion Kalamazoo MI • (616)382-2360 • (CQ 1984 MDIV)
**SEEGER MARK W REV** (512)251-3125
2000 Magic Hill Dr Pflugerville TX 78660-8175 • markjlcd@aol.com • TX • P Df • Jesus Deaf Austin TX • (512)442-1715 • (FW 1979 MDIV)
**SEEGER RORY G** (618)282-8222
317 Middle St Red Bud IL 62278 • SI • Assoc • St John Red Bud IL • (618)282-3873 • (SL 2000 MDIV)
**SEEGERS CONRAD J REV** (920)261-8012
1141 Hus Dr Apt 100 Watertown WI 53098-3236 • SW • EM • (SL 1940)
**SEEHAFER DANIEL J REV** (920)485-0517
N 7479 Old Hwy 28 Horicon WI 53032-9736 • seehafer@ststephen-lcms.org • SW • Asst • St Stephen Horicon WI • (920)485-6687 • (FW 1997 MDIV)
**SEETIN LEE D REV** (402)362-1558
435 Cedar Thayer Comm Waco NE 68460 • NEB • SP • Zion Waco NE • (402)362-3177 • (SL 1985 MDIV)
**SEEVERS CHARLES J DR** (952)249-1383
1144 Hollybrook Dr Wayzata MN 55391 • seevers@uswest.net • MNS • EM • (SL 1949 MS PHD)
**SEGOVIA CARLOS M REV** (713)472-2534
3500 Red Bluff Rd Apt 268 Pasadena TX 77503-3325 • TX • Asst • Peace Galena Park TX • (713)674-3111 • (CQ 1983)
**SEIBLE ROBERT D REV**
2370 Harbor View Dr Martinez CA 94553-3313 • CNH • SP • Christ Martinez CA • (925)228-5120 • (SL 1983 MDIV)

**SEIDLER SCOTT KENNETH REV**
C/O Immanuel Lutheran Church 407 Johnson St East Dundee IL 60118-2305 • NI • Christ Martinez CA • (925)228-5120 • (SL 1996 MDIV)

**SEIFERTH LARRY G REV** (501)753-6824
C/O Trinity Lutheran Church 3802 Olive Little Rock AR 72116-8748 • pastrmoe@aol.com • MDS • SP • Trinity N Little Rock AR • (501)753-6824 • (SL 1982 MDIV)

**SEITZ LANE R DR** (612)440-9777
8109 139th St Savage MN 55378 • mnspres@aol.com • MNS • DP • Minnesota South Burnsville MN • (SPR 1974 MDIV DMIN LITTD)

**SELBY MARK D REV** (712)662-4875
410 S 11th St Sac City IA 50583 • sacluth@pionet.net • IW • SP • St Paul Sac City IA • (712)662-7029 • (FW 1996 MDIV)

**SELF LES H REV** (916)393-1976
7537 Rio Mondego Dr Sacramento CA 95831-4640 • revles@jps.net • CNH • SP • Trinity Sacramento CA • (916)456-8701 • (FW 1986 MDIV)

**SELL MARK E REV**
162 Riverside Dr Mount Clemens MI 48043 • MI • Sn/Adm • St Luke Clinton Township MI • (810)791-1150 • (FW 1988 STM MDIV)

**SELLE CARL F REV** (414)987-5454
PO Box 305 Poy Sippi WI 54967-0305 • SW • EM • (SL 1937)

**SELLE CARL RICHARD REV** (715)677-4877
3177 State Hwy 66 Rosholt WI 54473-9529 • selleism@ccaa.edu • NW • Cmp P • North Wisconsin Wausau WI • (SL 1969 MDIV)

**SELLE JOHN F REV** (512)863-3634
405 W Esparada Dr Georgetown TX 78628-1359 • jfselle@gtwn.net • TX • Sn/Adm • Faith Georgetown TX • (512)863-7332 • (SL 1971 MDIV)

**SELLE ROBERT F REV** (920)987-5454
PO Box 305 Poy Sippi WI 54967-0305 • selle@wirural.net • NW • O Miss • North Wisconsin Wausau WI • (SL 1970 MDIV)

**SELLE ROBERT V REV** (941)267-9576
19168 Dogwood Rd Fort Myers FL 33912-3615 • bobselle@aol.com • FG • O Sp Min • Florida-Georgia Orlando FL • (SL 1983 MDIV)

**SELLMEYER JOHN N REV** (660)683-5716
15356 Amber Dr Craig MO 64437-8174 • MO • Assoc • St Peter Craig MO* • (660)683-5787 • (SPR 1974 MDIV)

**SELTZ GREGORY P REV**
1530 Concordia West Irvine CA 92612-3299 • gpseltz@aol.com • PSW • SHS/C • Pacific Southwest Irvine CA • (949)854-3232 • (SL 1986 MDIV STM)

**SEMSEL RONALD STEPHEN REV** (716)372-6968
3791 Karl Rd Allegany NY 14706-9632 • cwsoldier@juno.com • EA • SP • Immanuel Olean NY • (716)372-0650 • (SL 1969 MDIV)

**SENG DAN L REV** (616)965-5210
134 Robin Ave N Battle Creek MI 49017-1037 • danseng@ameritech.net • MI • SP • Redemption Battle Creek MI • (616)964-2321 • (SPR 1968 MDIV)

**SENKBEIL HAROLD L REV** (262)782-8845
2680 El Rancho Dr Brookfield WI 53005-4543 • hsenkbeil@egl.org • SW • Sn/Adm • Elm Grove Elm Grove WI • (262)797-2970 • (SPR 1971 MDIV STM)

**SENN ARTHUR C REV** (262)268-9026
807 W Lincoln Port Washington WA 53074 • SW • EM • (SL 1952)

**SENN RANDALL BRYAN REV** (608)757-8396
607 Margate Dr Janesville WI 53546-2034 • herr³pastor1@yahoo.com • EN • SP • St Mark Janesville WI • (608)754-8115 • (SL 1996 MDIV MED)

**SENNE EDGAR P REV** (219)462-8508
1207 Ohio St Valparaiso IN 46383-3705 • esenne@exodus.valpo.edu • IN • EM • (SL 1957 MDIV MED MA)

**SENSTAD RUSSELL C REV** (712)276-1125
4211 Eldorado Ct Sioux City IA 51106-3620 • IW • Assoc • Redeemer Sioux City IA • (712)276-1125 • (SL 1992 MDIV)

**SENTER JOHN D REV** (636)390-4918
6261 Yellow Brick Rd Washington MO 63090-4346 • jnlsntr@usmo.com • MO • EM • (SL 1956)

**SEPMEYER MERLIN REV** (931)484-7668
125 Shoreline Dr Crossville TN 38555-8983 • MDS • EM • (CQ 1981 MDIV)

**SESTAK PETER J REV** (507)348-3481
409 Wall St E Jasper MN 56144-1123 • MNS • SP • Trinity Jasper MN • (507)348-4186 • (SL 1977 MDIV)

**SETER BERNHARD M REV** (701)352-1791
1100 Hill Ave Grafton ND 58237-2228 • bernie@polar.polarcomm.com • ND • SP • Zion English Grafton ND* • (701)352-2869 • (SL 1978 MDIV)

**SETO LESTER T REV** (707)446-2274
C/O Bethany Lutheran Church 621 S Orchard Ave Vacaville CA 95688-4335 • lesterseto@aol.com • CNH • SP • Bethany Vacaville CA • (707)451-6675 • (SL 1985 MDIV)

**SETTGAST LELAND REV** (714)630-3478
2875 E Virginia Ave Anaheim CA 92806-4443 • drlee1000@aol.com • IW • O Miss • Iowa West Fort Dodge IA • (SPR 1964 MA PHD DD)

**SEWING DAVID MARK REV** (712)263-8469
514 N 20th Denison IA 51442 • dsewing@frontiernet.net • IW • Assoc • Zion Denison IA • (712)263-2235 • (SL 1997 MDIV)

**SEYING LAOKOUXANG REV** (651)776-7703
499 Iowa Ave E Saint Paul MN 55101-3024 • seying@luther.csp.edu • MNS • O Sp Min • Minnesota South Burnsville MN • (FW 1991 MDIV)

**SGAMBELLURI CARLO A REV** (517)345-0122
129 N Fairview St West Branch MI 48661-9240 • csgambelluri@voyager.net • MI • SP • St John West Branch MI • (517)345-0120 • (FW 1989 MDIV)

**SHACKEL PAUL L REV** (920)722-6686
1140 Pomer Way Menasha WI 54952-1730 • pshackel@shepherdhills.org • NW • Sn/Adm • Shepherd Hills Greenville WI • (920)757-5722 • (SL 1973 MDIV)

**SHACKELL MAURICE G REV** (616)781-4479
383 Boyer Ct Marshall MI 49068-1184 • maurycarol@aol.com • MI • EM • (SL 1955)

**SHADDAY DAVID A REV** (317)784-9872
5432 Antoneli Ln Indianapolis IN 46237-2352 • pdshad@juno.com • IN • SP • Saint Paul Indianapolis IN • (317)787-4464 • (FW 1984 MDIV)

**SHAFFER GEORGE WILLIAM REV** (903)438-9613
216 Lou Ave Sulphur Springs TX 75482 • gwshaffer@bluebonnet.net • TX • SP • Our Savior Sulphur Springs TX • (903)885-5787 • (FW 2000 MDIV)

**SHALTANIS JOEL A REV** (909)947-8729
2800 E Riverside Dr #57 Ontario CA 91761 • PSW • SP • St Paul Pomona CA • (909)623-6368 • (SL 2000 MDIV)

**SHALTANIS MARK ALAN REV** (703)573-6008
7426 Idylwood Rd Falls Church VA 22043-2915 • prmarkspfc@aol.com • SE • SP • St Paul Falls Church VA • (703)573-0295 • (SL 1993 MDIV)

**SHANE HOWARD O REV**
401 E Lotta St Sioux Falls SD 57105-7109 • sdexec@midco.net • SD • D Ex/S • South Dakota Sioux Falls SD • (CQ 1978 MAR)

**SHANKS JEFFREY P REV** (615)885-4137
840 Chandler Grove Dr Hermitage TN 37076-1210 • jashanks@home.com • MDS • SP • Emmanuel Hermitage TN • (615)883-7533 • (FW 1989 MDIV)

**SHARP JOHN W REV** (785)252-3214
PO Box 46 Holyrood KS 67450-0046 • jcsharp@midusa.net • KS • SP • St Peter Holyrood KS • (913)252-3275 • (SL 1998 MDIV)

**SHARP MICHAEL D REV** (316)628-4801
RR 1 Box 104 Canton KS 67428-9509 • KS • SP • Immanuel Canton KS • (316)628-4801 • (FW 1982 MDIV)

**SHARP ROBERT ALLAN REV** (314)579-6060
12322 Montsouris Dr Creve Coeur MO 63141-7420 • znmdhgts@juno.com • MO • SP • Zion Maryland Heights MO • (314)739-6121 • (SL 1996 MDIV)

**SHARP WILLIAM BARRY REV** (979)532-0925
613 Pecan St Wharton TX 77488-4011 • pastor@wcnet.net • TX • SP • St John Wharton TX • (979)532-2336 • (FW 1992 MBA MDIV)

**SHARPE THOMAS MICHAEL REV** (440)891-9076
8714 Fair Rd Strongsville OH 44149-1229 • tsharpe@stratos.net • OH • SP • St John Strongsville OH • (440)234-5806 • (SL 1992 MDIV)

**SHAW JAMES E REV** (512)267-3824
3404 American Dr The Island-Villa 1307 Lago Vista TX 78645 • TX • EM • (SPR 1959 DD)

**SHAW JAMES R REV** (319)445-1068
3605 N Birchwood Ave Davenport IA 52806-5127 • jrshaw@wans.net • IE • SP • Immanuel Davenport IA • (319)324-6431 • (FW 1999 MDIV)

**SHAW JONATHAN E REV** (915)568-2644
7757 Luz de Camino Way El Paso TX 79912 • shawje@occh-nt.army.mil • MO • M Chap • Southeastern Alexandria VA • (FW 1984 MDIV MA)

**SHEAFER MARK C REV** (412)795-7144
1617 Galeton Dr Verona PA 15147-2826 • EN • SP • Redeemer Oakmont PA • (412)828-9323 • (FW 1988 MDIV)

**SHEARIER JEFF G REV** (715)369-5784
616 N Stevens St Rhinelander WI 54501 • revnjeff@yahoo.com • NW • SP • St Mark Rhinelander WI • (715)362-2470 • (SL 1997)

**SHEARIER JEFFREY E REV** (303)755-2403
2523 S Eagle St Aurora CO 80014-2426 • pjshearier@idcomm.com • RM • Sn/Adm • Mount Olive Aurora CO • (303)755-9123 • (SL 1984 MDIV MA)

**SHEETS HARRY C REV** (217)854-3946
509 S Broad St Carlinville IL 62626-2113 • SI • SP • Zion Carlinville IL • (217)854-8514 • (SL 1987 MDIV)

**SHEFFLER CHARLES REV** (701)256-2336
C/O Redeemer Luthern Church 1210 11th Ave Langdon ND 58249-1916 • therev@utma.com • ND • SP • Redeemer Langdon ND* • (701)256-2314 • (SL 1991 MDIV)

**SHELDON BARRY C REV** (313)359-7184
PO Box 160 Lexington MI 48450-0160 • MI • SP • St Matthew Lexington MI • (810)359-8411 • (FW 1983)

**SHELDON MICHAEL B REV** (817)788-1480
Peace Lutheran Church 941 Bedford Euless Rd Hurst TX 76053 • TX • Assoc • Peace Hurst TX • (817)284-1677 • (SL 1997 MDIV)

**SHELTON GLENN REV**
16228 Heritage Trl Spring Lake MI 49456 • glennms@novagate.com • MI • SP • Lakeshore Fellowship Spring Lake MI • (616)846-8556 • (FW 1986 MDIV)

**SHEPPARD LARRY G REV** (517)352-6374
8890 W Tamarack Rd Lakeview MI 48850 • EN • SP • Holy Trinity Lakeview MI • (517)352-6374 • (FW 1999 MDIV)

**SHEROUSE M SAMUEL REV** (517)753-1575
4205 Lorraine Ave Saginaw MI 48604-1638 • sherouse@earthlink.net • MI • SP • Messiah Saginaw MI • (517)753-7281 • (SL 1977 MDIV)

**SHEROUSE PAUL L REV**
PSC 41 Box 5668 APO AE 09464 • paul.sherouse@lakenheath.af.mil • MO • M Chap • Missouri Saint Louis MO • (314)317-4550 • (SL 1983 MDIV)

**SHERREN RANDOLPH G REV** (952)835-6445
9851 Edgewood Rd S Minneapolis MN 55438-1754 • MNS • Sn/Adm • Berea Richfield MN • (612)861-7121 • (SPR 1973 MDIV MA)

**SHERRILL NORTH P JR. REV** (308)237-2740
2521 30th Ave Kearney NE 68845-4017 • npsherrill@nebi.com • NEB • Sn/Adm • Zion Kearney NE • (308)234-3410 • (FW 1979 MDIV)

**SHERRY DAVID F REV** (517)662-7640
5545 8 Mile Rd Bay City MI 48706-9711 • orca23@tir.com • MI • SP • Trinity Bay City MI • (517)662-6093 • (FW 1982 MDIV)

**SHEWMAKER RUSSELL L REV** (870)933-8869
511 W Thomas Jonesboro AR 72401 • pilgrim@bscn.com • MDS • SP • Pilgrim Jonesboro AR • (870)935-2001 • (SL 1987 MDIV)

**SHIBATA GEORGE T REV** 03-3716-7095
5-12-5 Shimo-Meguro Meguro-ku Tokyo 153 JAPAN • CNH • EM • (SL 1945 MDIV DD)

**SHIELDS RANDALL W REV** (734)996-4399
403 Pine Brae St Ann Arbor MI 48105-2743 • MI • Cmp P • Michigan Ann Arbor MI • (SPR 1972 MDIV MST THD)

**SHIFFLETT WALLACE H REV**
4304 Mc Corkle Rd Memphis TN 38116-7002 • SE • Michigan Ann Arbor MI • (FW 1994 MDIV)

**SHIMKUS WILLIAM E REV** (208)522-7267
801 Buckboard Ln Idaho Falls ID 83402-2441 • pastor1@srv.net • NOW • SP • Hope Idaho Falls ID • (208)529-8080 • (CQ 1978 MDIV)

**SHIPPERT PAUL REV** (716)652-0103
148 Blake Hill Rd East Aurora NY 14052-2602 • EA • EM • (SL 1950 MSED)

**SHOCKEY MARK W REV** (952)944-5606
10510 Buckingham Dr Eden Prairie MN 55347-2942 • markshockey@mn.rr.com • MNS • SP • St Peter Edina MN • (952)927-8408 • (SL 1989 MDIV)

**SHOEMAKER DAVID T REV** (209)532-4406
15830 Ridgefield Ct Sonora CA 95370-8755 • svalleylut.aol.com • CNH • EM • (SPR 1965 MDIV)

**SHOEMAKER PAUL E REV** (219)749-6007
9820 Winding Shores Dr New Haven IN 46774-2806 • Shoe9820@aol.com • IN • Sn/Adm • Emanuel New Haven IN • (219)749-2163 • (FW 1978 MDIV)

**SHONHOLZ ROBERT F REV** (330)629-2335
144 Brainard Dr Boardman OH 44512-2801 • shonconn@aol.com • OH • SP • St Mark Youngstown OH • (330)788-8995 • (FW 1996 MDIV)

**SHOREY RALPH CHESTER III REV** (712)853-6162
310 N State St PO Box 98 Terril IA 51364-0098 • revrcs3@ncn.net • IW • SP • Immanuel Terril IA • (712)853-6162 • (SL 1995 MST MDIV)

**SHORT PAUL J REV** (573)335-1188
3054 N Church St Cape Girardeau MO 63701-2680 • pjshort@clas.net • MO • Sn/Adm • St Andrew Cape Girardeau MO • (573)334-3200 • (SPR 1974 MDIV)

**SHOUP TIMOTHY J REV** (715)758-7303
PO Box 543 Bonduel WI 54107-0543 • tjshoup@ezwebtech.com • NW • Sn/Adm • St Paul Bonduel WI • (715)758-8559 • (SL 1987 MDIV)

**SHRINER ROBERT W DR** (219)343-0071
6233 E Beck Lake Rd N Kendallville IN 46755-9359 • rshriner@noble.cioe.com • IN • Assoc • St John Kendallville IN • (219)347-2158 • (FW 1987 MDIV DMIN)

**SHUMATE JOHN A REV** (847)244-3234
10182 W Bairstow Ave Waukegan IL 60087-2451 • NI • SP • Prince Peace Waukegan IL • (847)244-6522 • (SPR 1976 MDIV)

**SHUPE WILLIAM F REV** (830)303-1570
12565 FM 3353 Kingsbury TX 78638-1727 • wmfred@ix.netcom.com • TX • SP • Evangelists Kingsbury TX • (830)639-4906 • (FW 1984 MDIV)

**SHUTA RICHARD J REV** (734)663-6052
C/O Concordia College 4090 Geddes Rd Ann Arbor MI 48105-2750 • MI • SHS/C • Michigan Ann Arbor MI • (SPR 1964 MPHIL PHD)

**SIDWELL DAVID H REV** (616)426-3170
6519 Ravenswood Sawyer MI 49125-9133 • revdsid@aol.com • MI • SP • Prince Peace New Buffalo MI • (616)469-0380 • (SL 1997 MDIV)

**SIEBRASS LOWELL L REV** (909)359-6017
8479 Garfield St Riverside CA 92504-2961 • PSW • Sn/Adm • Immanuel Riverside CA • (909)682-7613 • (SL 1964 MDIV)

**SIEDENBURG DAN L REV** (952)492-2485
20200 Fairlawn Ave Prior Lake MN 55372-8846 • dpsied@frontiernet.net • MNS • SP • Immanuel Prior Lake MN • (952)492-6010 • (FW 1980 MDIV)

**SIEDSCHLAG JOHN A SR. REV** (608)565-7641
PO Box 388 Necedah WI 54646-0388 • jvsiedschlag@tds.net • SW • SP • St James Necedah WI* • (608)565-7252 • (CQ 1982)

**SIEFERT GARY L REV** (616)968-6163
15 Crest Dr Battle Creek MI 49017-3317 • glsiefert@prodigy.net • MI • Sn/Adm • St Paul Battle Creek MI • (616)968-3055 • (FW 1996 MDIV)

**SIEFKES WILLIAM F REV** (714)772-9661
904 S Echo Pl Anaheim CA 92804-4510 • PSW • EM • (SL 1946)

**SIEGEL STEVEN G REV** (517)868-9529
9814 North St Reese MI 48757-9544 • stevkar@internet4all.net • MI • Sn/Adm • Trinity Reese MI • (517)868-9901 • (SL 1998 MDIV)

**SIEGFRIED ARTHUR W REV** (509)662-2464
3685 School St Wenatchee WA 98801-9006 • NOW • EM • (SL 1958)

**SIELK WILLIAM ALAN REV** (361)887-6141
C/O Our Savior Luth Ch 6102 Greenwood Dr Corpus Christi TX 78417-3301 • TX • SP • Nuestro Salvador Corpus Christi TX • (512)857-5673 • (FW 1985 MDIV)

**SIEMS PAUL A REV** (316)264-5964
1937 S Fern St Wichita KS 67213-3543 • alltree@southwind.net • SD • 02/1999 • (SL 1989 MDIV)

**SIERRA LAZARO JAVIER REV** (660)829-2484
30665 Randy Dr Sedalia MO 65301 • javier@iland.net • MO • O Miss • Missouri Saint Louis MO • (314)317-4550 • (CQ 1999)

**SIESS KENNETH J REV** (651)690-4538
1460 Lincoln Ave Saint Paul MN 55105-2235 • kesiess@usfamily.net • MNS • EM • (SL 1956 MDIV DMIN)

**SIEVEKING PAUL G REV** (712)276-4484
1122 Summit Ave Fort Dodge IA 50501 • IW • DP • Iowa West Fort Dodge IA • (SL 1976 MDIV)

**SIEVERS KENNETH W REV** (314)892-5246
155 Bridgeview Ln Saint Louis MO 63129-3401 • MO • Sn/Adm • Gethsemane Saint Louis MO • (314)631-7331 • (SL 1972 MDIV)

**SIEVERS PHILIP W REV** (208)382-4942
PO Box 940 Cascade ID 83611-0940 • siemtmin@cyberhighway.net • NOW • SP • Shep Mountains Cascade ID • (208)382-4422 • (SL 1971 MDIV MA)

**SIEVING HERMAN E REV** (612)938-7504
231 5th Ave N Hopkins MN 55343-7376 • MNS • EM • (SPR 1929)

**SIFUENTES CESAR REV** (517)799-7342
C/O Redeemer Luth Ch 3829 Lamson St Saginaw MI 48601-4170 • MI • Assoc • Redeemer Saginaw MI • (517)753-2963 • (CQ 1982 MSS)

**SIGMON STEPHEN D REV** (919)768-4883
5025 Timbrook Ln Winston Salem NC 27103-6015 • SE • 07/1997 07/2000 • (SPR 1970 MDIV)

**SIKORA EDWARD A REV** (616)795-3920
1014 Greenwood Middleville MI 49333 • MI • SP • Good Shepherd Middleville MI • (616)795-2391 • (SL 1999 MDIV)

**SILBER TIMOTHY P REV** (630)443-4680
1706 Larson Ave St Charles IL 60174 • NI • SP • St Mark Saint Charles IL • (630)584-8638 • (SL 1984 MDIV)

**SIMCAK ANDREW JR. REV** (281)477-6194
14215 Ravenhurst Ln Houston TX 77070 • simcak@flash.net • TX • EM • (SL 1955)

**SIMENTAL ROBERTO REV** (956)668-9359
C/O El Buen Pastor L C 1929 Pecan Blvd Mc Allen TX 78501-6730 • TX • SP • El Buen Pastor Mc Allen TX • (956)686-6673 • (CQ 1999)

**SIMMINGER K MICHAEL REV** (309)968-7867
101 S Park Ave Manito IL 61546-9285 • revkms@ntslink.net • CI • SP • Trinity Manito IL • (309)968-6984 • (SPR 1970 MDIV)

**SIMMONS ARTHUR G REV** (314)353-8867
5756 Tholozan Ave Saint Louis MO 63109-1560 • 111simmonag@lhm.org • MO • Trinity Manito IL • (309)968-6984 • (SL 1970 MDIV)

**SIMMONS CHARLES F REV**
2900 145th St W Apt 600 Rosemount MN 55068-4957 • MNN • EM • (SPR 1971)

**SIMMONS RAYMOND L REV** (724)443-5520
10720 Babcock Blvd Gibsonia PA 15044-8976 • SE • EM • (CQ 1986 MDIV)

**SIMMONS RONALD C REV** (618)846-8282
RR 1 Box 178 Shobonier IL 62885-9739 • datasimmons@juno.com • CI • SP • Immanuel Shobonier IL • (618)846-8383 • (FW 1985)

**SIMMONS WILLIAM T REV** (314)544-4508
8333 Weber Trail Dr Saint Louis MO 63123-4645 • wtsimmons@primary.net • MO • Assoc • Christ Memorial Saint Louis MO • (314)631-0304 • (FW 1979 MBA MDIV)

**SIMON ARTHUR R REV** (301)927-5519
3907 Newton St Brentwood MD 20722-2132 • art.simon@zzapp.org • SE • EM • (SL 1956 STM)

**SIMON DONALD E REV**
19225 N Cave Creek Rd #41 Phoenix AZ 85024 • d.simon@juno.com • SI • EM • (SL 1950 MDIV)

**SIMON FREDRICK A REV** (308)534-6942
1404 Burlington Blvd North Platte NE 69101-5731 • psimon@kdsi.net • NEB • Assoc • Our Redeemer North Platte NE • (308)532-4753 • (SL 1984 MDIV)

**SIMON HENRY A REV** (618)397-1206
132 N 82nd St Belleville IL 62223-2121 • hsimon@the-word.net • SI • Sn/Adm • Signal Hill Belleville IL • (618)397-1407 • (SL 1972 MDIV)

**SIMON HENRY E REV** (920)832-9322
345 W Highland Park Ave #526 Appleton WI 54911 • NW • EM • (SL 1944 LITTD)

**SIMON JOHN M REV** (562)903-7877
C/O Bethany Luth Church 4644 Clark Ave Long Beach CA 90808-1203 • clergytax@aol.com • PSW • Asst • Bethany Long Beach CA • (562)421-4711 • (SPR 1967 MDIV)

**SIMON STEVEN D REV** (847)426-8508
111 N 4th St West Dundee IL 60118-2007 • mrnkp@foxvalley.net • NI • Sn/Adm • Bethlehem Dundee IL • (847)426-7311 • (FW 1983 MDIV)

**SIMONSEN JAY ERIC REV** (361)574-9884
204 Alamogordo Dr Victoria TX 77904-3717 • simonsen@tisd.net • TX • SP • Grace Victoria TX • (361)573-2232 • (FW 1978 MDIV MED)

**SIMONSON CHARLES K REV** (805)834-1412
10615 Rising Sun Dr Bakersfield CA 93312-2922 • ckscfuw@aol.com • CNH • 10/1999 • (SPR 1976 MDIV)

**SIMONSON DAVID L REV** (515)386-8215
306 S Locust St Jefferson IA 50129-2230 • tlcjefia@netins.net • IW • SP • Trinity Jefferson IA • (515)386-3517 • (SL 1985 MDIV)

**SIMONSON DUANE R REV** (402)365-7636
C/O Trinity Lutheran Ch RR 2 Box 100A Hebron NE 68370-9536 • dsimonsonlll@yahoo.com • NEB • SP • Trinity Hebron NE* • (402)365-7636 • (CQ 1976 MED)

**SIMPSON SCOTT E REV** (701)386-2419
PO Box 127 Tolley ND 58787-0127 • simpson1@ndak.net • ND • SP • Trinity Tolley ND* • (701)386-2246 • (SL 1999 MDIV)

**SIMS HERBERT A REV** (708)209-1120
7622 Madison St #501 Forest Park IL 60190-1466 • NI • EM • * • (CQ 1965 MA PHD)

**SIMS TIMOTHY E REV** (219)493-1153
925 Koehlinger Dr New Haven IN 46774-1711 • intsims@aol.com • IN • DP • Indiana Fort Wayne IN • (SL 1964 MDIV)

**SINCEBAUGH NORMAN C REV**
1877 26th Ave Southwest Backus MN 56435 • ND • 08/2000 • (SPR 1962 LITTD)

**SINCLAIR KENNETH E REV** (409)387-2200
8130 Blase Rd Rosenberg TX 77471-8590 • pastorken@flcsl.org • TX • SP • Faith Sugar Land TX • (281)242-7729 • (SL 1971 MDIV)

**SIPE LARRY RAY JR. REV**
2603 Easton Ave Waverly IA 50677-9233 • pastorsipe@juno.com • IE • Assoc • St John Waverly IA • (319)352-2314 • (FW 1996 MDIV)

**SIPES PHILLIP L REV** (714)282-8003
306 E Riverdale Ave Orange CA 92865-1204 • PSW • Assoc • St John Orange CA • (714)288-4400 • (FW 1979 MDIV)

**SIPES TIMOTHY A REV**
619 Cedar Ave Apt 12 Long Beach CA 90802-1226 • PSW • EM • (SL 1984 MA)

**SIPPY JEFFREY E REV** (573)651-4002
1561 Briarcliff Dr Cape Girardeau MO 63701-2652 • caj3@ldd.net • MO • SP • Hanover Cape Girardeau MO • (573)335-8583 • (SL 1988 MDIV)

**SIREK STEVEN B REV** (402)488-4390
5625 La Salle Lincoln NE 68516 • sbsirek1@hotmail.com • NEB • Tchr • Lincoln Luth Jr/Sr H Lincoln NE • (402)467-5404 • (CQ 1997 MA MA)

**SITTMANN GUSTAV E REV** (828)294-6596
5217 Olde School Dr Hickory NC 28602-8283 • SE • EM • (SL 1949)

**SIZEMORE PAUL C REV** (803)407-9811
1704 Quail Valley East Columbia SC 29212 • pastorpcs@aol.com • SE • SP • Mount Olive Irmo SC • (803)781-5845 • (SL 1981 MDIV)

**SKAMSER LIONEL O REV**
914 Starlite Dr Holment WI 54636-7318 • SW • Sn/Adm • Shepherd Hills Onalaska WI • (608)783-0330 • (SPR 1960)

**SKEESICK DALE A REV**
1315 Lexington Dr Collinsville IL 62234-4348 • SI • Shepherd Hills Onalaska WI • (608)783-0330 • (SL 1992 MDIV)

**SKELTON BRUCE A REV**
840 N 11th St Grand Junction CO 81501-3218 • RM • Assoc • Messiah Grand Junction CO • (970)245-2838 • (FW 1992 MED MDIV)

**SKIBBE CECIL H REV** (812)336-8128
908 S Sowders Sq Bloomington IN 47401-8757 • IN • EM • (SPR 1947)

**SKOPAK JEFFREY ERIC REV** (732)341-5326
371 Grande River Blvd Toms River NJ 08755-1192 • revskopak@aol.com • S • Sn/Adm • Redeemer Lakehurst NJ • (732)657-2828 • (SL 1992 MDIV)

**SKOV CLARE B REV** (970)587-9067
PO Box 905 Johnstown CO 80534 • c.t.skov@juno.com • RM • SP • Holy Cross Windsor CO* • (970)686-5599 • (CQ 1982 MS MDIV PHD)

**SKOV FREDERICK A REV** (303)755-4307
18730 E Oregon Dr Aurora CO 80017-5406 • fasnjs@worldnet.att.net • RM • EM • * • (SL 1955 MDIV)

**SKOV RICHARD H REV** (860)434-8057
176 Four Mile River Rd Old Lyme CT 06371-1325 • sskov@uconect.net • NE • EM • * • (SL 1957 MDIV)

**SKOV STEPHEN EDWARD REV** (805)569-1132
1043 Portesuello Ave Santa Barbara CA 93105-4616 • stall5@aol.com • PSW • SP • Emanuel Santa Barbara CA • (805)687-3734 • (SPR 1968 MDIV)

**SKOVGAARD ERIC C REV**
395 Bald Eagle Dr Vacaville CA 95688 • CNH • D Miss • Calif/Nevada/Hawaii San Francisco CA • (415)468-2336 • (SL 2000 MDIV)

**SLATER THOMAS K REV** (707)442-9472
3526 Nevada St Eureka CA 95503-4932 • CNH • SP • Trinity Eureka CA • (707)442-4939 • (FW 1987 MDIV)

**SLIGER DWAIN EDWIN REV** (314)240-2715
49 Royal Oaks Dr O Fallon MO 63366-1025 • MO • Assoc • Immanuel Wentzville MO • (314)327-4416 • (SL 1994 MDIV)

**SLUBERSKI THOMAS R REV** (914)793-7219
26 Dusenberry Rd Bronxville NY 10708-2421 • sluberski@aol.com • AT • SHS/C • Atlantic Bronxville NY • (914)337-5700 • (SL 1966 MDIV MA THD)

**SMALL TERRY SCOTT REV** (218)828-4835
2010 Graydon Ave Brainerd MN 56401 • tsmall@brainerd.net • MNN • SP • Prince Of Peace Baxter MN • (218)829-7092 • (SL 1995 MDIV)

**SMELSER TODD W REV** (701)225-5878
1068 7th St W Dickinson ND 58601-4739 • ND • SP • Redeemer Dickinson ND • (701)483-4463 • (SL 1984 MDIV)

**SMIDT DONALD D REV** (602)548-8536
Connecting Generations Inc 1535 E Meadow Ln Phoenix AZ 85022 • gnerations@aol.com • PSW • 03/2000 • (SPR 1968 MDIV)

**SMILES JEFFREY A REV** (920)596-1929
N7530 Church St Manawa WI 54949-9691 • stmarksymco@juno.com • NW • SP • St Mark Manawa WI* • (920)596-3241 • (SL 1994 MDIV)

**SMITH ANDREW DANIEL REV**
100 Lisbon Ct Apt 101 Virginia Beach VA 23462-3188 • andrew³smith19@excite.com • MI • M Chap • Michigan Ann Arbor MI • (SL 1997 MDIV)

**SMITH BRADLEY A REV** (414)452-4333
1117 Eisner Ave Sheboygan WI 53083-3056 • SW • SP • Luther Memorial Sheboygan WI • (414)458-1322 • (FW 1988 MDIV)

**SMITH BRIAN KEITH REV**
3125 Crooked Creek Dr Diamond Bar CA 91765 • PSW • P Df • Pilgrim Deaf Los Angeles CA • (213)389-9940 • (SL 1995 MDIV)

**SMITH CHARLES A REV** (513)943-9689
C/O Dept Veterans Aff Med Ctr 3200 Vine St Cincinnati OH 45220-2251 • SE • Pilgrim Deaf Los Angeles CA • (213)389-9940 • (FW 1977 MDIV)

**SMITH CHARLES O REV** (314)996-1680
PO Box 229008 Saint Louis MO 63122 • chuck.smith@lfnd.org • MO • S Ex/S • Missouri Saint Louis MO • (314)317-4550 • (SPR 1963 MA MDIV)

**SMITH DANIEL MIKE REV** (618)783-2102
110 Edwards St Newton IL 62448-1736 • revdms@shawneelink.com • CI • SP • Good Shepherd Newton IL • (618)783-4105 • (SL 1992 MDIV)

**SMITH DAVID L REV** (708)354-1690
1429 Williams Westmont IL 60559 • marnie-rev@juno.com • NI • Assoc • St John La Grange IL • (708)354-1690 • (FW 1998 MA)

**SMITH DAVID S REV** (314)256-0325
601 Huntley Heights Ballwin MO 63021 • MO • Sn/Adm • St Paul Saint Louis MO • (314)822-0447 • (SL 1978 MDIV DMIN)

**SMITH DONALD G REV**
Rt 1 Box M Odessa WA 99159 • zeodessa@odessaoffice.com • NOW • SP • Zion-Emmanuel Odessa WA* • (509)982-2402 • (FW 1993 MDIV)

**SMITH ERNEST G REV** (402)564-5314
2514 30th St Columbus NE 68601-1844 • kaspar@plattevalley.net • NEB • EM • * • (SL 1954)

**SMITH FREDERICK V REV** (423)892-8470
1403 Fore Winds Hl Ooltewah TN 37363-9425 • KS • 05/1992 05/1999 • * • (SL 1979 MA MA MDIV)

**SMITH GREGORY KENT REV** (314)843-6002
8619 Grantwood Trails Ct Saint Louis MO 63123-1146 • MO • Sn/Adm • Christ Memorial Saint Louis MO • (314)631-0304 • (SL 1975 MDIV)

**SMITH GUY BRAGDON REV** (501)571-4591
2344 N Juneway Ter Fayetteville AR 72703-2915 • MO • EM • (SL 1952 MED)

**SMITH HARRY D REV** (423)892-8470
1403 Fore Winds Hl Ooltewah TN 37363-9425 • MDS • EM • (SL 1948 MST)

**SMITH JONATHAN M REV** (757)436-4587
740 Willow Brook Rd Chesapeake VA 23320-3557 • Chaplain@home.com • IW • M Chap • Iowa West Fort Dodge IA • (SL 1985 MDIV)

**SMITH KELLY DALTON SR. REV** (517)592-4272
7790 Jefferson Brooklyn MI 49230-9796 • havoc@frontiernet.net • MI • SP • St Mark Brooklyn MI • (517)467-7565 • (FW 1991 MDIV)

**SMITH LAWRENCE J REV** (319)372-6860
3527 Southland St SW Cedar Rapids IA 52404-4620 • IE • 07/1996 07/2000 • (FW 1977)

**SMITH MARK S H REV** (314)849-5811
9029 Laurel Crest Dr Saint Louis MO 63126-2412 • MO • SP • Prince Of Peace Saint Louis MO • (314)843-8448 • (SL 1979 STM MDIV DMIN)

**SMITH RICHARD K REV** (219)484-2932
3020 Peppertree Trl Fort Wayne IN 46808-3834 • IN • Sn/Adm • Sub Bethlehem Fort Wayne IN • (219)484-7873 • (SL 1981 MDIV)

**SMITH ROBERT E REV** (760)347-8389
43629 Hollyhock St Indio CA 92201-1998 • revs455@aol.com • PSW • SP • Trinity Indio CA • (760)347-3971 • (FW 1985 MDIV)

**SMITH ROBERT ERNEST REV** (219)471-5019
5 Wycliffe Pl Fort Wayne IN 46825-4937 • smithre@mail.ctsfw.edu • IN • SHS/C • Indiana Fort Wayne IN • (SL 1985 MDIV MLS)

**SMITH ROBERT W REV** 011-822-330-3114
C/O Seoul Foreign School 55 Yonhi Dong Seoul 120-113 KOREA • rwsmith@crusader.sfs-h.ac.kr • MI • S Miss • Michigan Ann Arbor MI • (FW 1986 MDIV MED)

**SMITH RONALD E REV** (908)713-9601
123 Black Brook Rd Hampton NJ 08827-2519 • NJ • SP • Our Savior Hampton NJ • (908)735-2062 • (SL 1961)

**SMITH STEVEN N REV** (708)343-8384
C/O Concordia University 7400 Augusta St River Forest IL 60305-1402 • crfsmithsn@curf.edu • NI • Cmp P • Northern Illinois Hillside IL • (SL 1989 STM MDIV)

**SMITH WILEY JAMES REV** (909)794-0402
1566 Campus Ave Redlands CA 92374-3908 • PSW • SP • Christ King Redlands CA • (909)793-5703 • (FW 1995 MDIV)

**SNEATH MICHAEL W REV** (815)588-2509
17459 Sauk Dr Lockport IL 60441-7688 • NI • Assoc • Trinity Burr Ridge IL • (708)839-1200 • (SL 1998 MDIV)

**SNIDER MERELYN R REV** (402)245-2162
St Paul Lutheran Church RR 3 Box 102 Falls City NE 68355-9634 • pstrsnider@sentco.net • NEB • SP • St Paul Falls City NE • (402)245-4643 • (CQ 1998)

**SNOW C MICHAEL DR** (713)353-9387
3615 Cypresswood Dr Spring TX 77388-5725 • ccsnow@pdq.net • TX • SP • Beaut Savior Houston TX • (281)445-2203 • (SL 1980 MDIV DMIN)

**SNOW EDWARD E REV** (904)646-0455
2352 Brentfield Rd W Jacksonville FL 32225-1541 • FG • EM • (SL 1958 MED)

**SNOW GREGORY J** (952)361-0186
2619 Rachel Ct Chaska MN 55318 • MNS • Asst • St John Chaska MN • (612)448-2433 • (SL 2000 MDIV)

**SNOW RICHARD L REV** (402)675-1444
303 S 2nd St PO Box 119 Battle Creek NE 68715 • rs62247@navix.net • NEB • Sn/Adm • St John Battle Creek NE • (402)675-3155 • (SL 1987 MDIV)

**SNOW SCOTT A REV** (815)962-8267
4555 Trail Ridge Rd Rockford IL 61101-6041 • snow61957@aol.com • NI • D Ex/S • Northern Illinois Hillside IL • (SL 1983 MDIV)

**SNYDER DALE O REV** (915)235-2097
1608 Silas St Sweetwater TX 79556 • faith@camalott.com • TX • SP • Faith Sweetwater TX • (915)235-2773 • (SL 1998 MDIV)

**SNYDER RICHARD H REV** (310)635-8632
C/O St Philip Luth Church 1110 N Dwight Ave Compton CA 90222-3833 • PSW • SP • St Philip Compton CA • (310)635-8632 • (SL 1981 MDIV)

**SNYDER ROBERT E REV** (507)332-2671
1108 Candy Ln Faribault MN 55021-3201 • revbobs@juno.com • MNS • Sn/Adm • Trinity Faribault MN • (507)334-6579 • (SL 1966 MDIV)

**SNYDER WALTER PHILLIP REV** (660)463-7553
PO Box 12 Emma MO 65327-0012 • xrysostom@aol.com • MO • SP • Holy Cross Emma MO • (660)463-7869 • (SL 1992 MDIV)

**SNYDER WALTER W DR** (903)378-2088
RR 1 Box 53A Windom TX 75492-9702 • TX • SP • St James Windom TX • (903)378-2779 • (SPR 1958 STM STM THD)

**SODTKE PAUL F REV** (519)690-0132
210 Millbank Dr London ON N6C 4W1 CANADA • psodtke@sympatico.ca • EN • 06/1990 09/1999 • (SK 1977 STM MDIV)

**SOELDNER O ARNOLD REV** (314)843-1225
8900 Fox Park Dr Saint Louis MO 63126-2312 • MO • EM • (SL 1945)

**SOHN EDWIN C REV** (510)635-8637
1094 Oakes Blvd San Leandro CA 94577-3042 • ejsohn@saber.net • CNH • EM • (SL 1946 MDIV)

**SOHN PAUL H REV** (515)964-2064
403 SE Delaware Ave Unit 202 Ankeny IA 50021-6410 • lpsohn@cs.com • IW • EM • (SL 1943 MDIV)

**SOHN WALTER G REV** (651)483-3843
252 County Road F W Saint Paul MN 55126-2358 • waltergsohn@yahoo.com • MNS • EM • (SL 1945 MDIV STM)

**SOHNS STEPHEN J REV** (281)350-4687
18207 Navajo Trail Dr Spring TX 77388-9008 • usbad@aol.com • TX • Sn/Adm • Resurrection Spring TX • (281)353-4413 • (FW 1984 MDIV)

**SOHNS WILBERT J REV** (254)986-1131
13610 S State 36 Hwy Gatesville TX 76528-4264 • TX • EM • (SL 1959 DD)

**SOLLIE GALEN R REV** (815)254-6723
25110 W Pauline Dr Plainfield IL 60544-8206 • grsollie@peaceplainfield.org • NI • SP • Peace Plainfield IL • (815)436-9847 • (FW 1978 MDIV)

**SOLON ROLANDO L REV**
La Santa Cruz Luth Mission 2747 Whittier Blvd Los Angeles CA 90023-1469 • PSW • 03/1996 03/2000 • (CQ 1994 MDIV)

**SOLTIS THOMAS REV** (440)582-6140
491 Tollis Pkwy Apt 176E Cleveland OH 44147-1824 • S • EM • (SL 1956)

**SOMMER ALAN J REV** (530)672-2040
3600 Santos Cir Cameron Park CA 95682 • absommer@jps.net • CNH • SP • Light Of Hills Cameron Park CA • (530)677-9536 • (SL 1990 MDIV)

**SOMMERER STEVEN LANCE REV**
C/O Our Savior Lutheran Church PO Box A Odell NE 68415-0130 • NEB • SP • Our Savior Odell NE • (402)766-3688 • (SL 1997 MDIV)

**SOMMERFELD RUSSELL L REV** (308)234-3370
3304 11th Ave Kearney NE 68845-8022 • rsommerfeld@kearney.net • NEB • Sn/Adm • Holy Cross Kearney NE • (308)237-2944 • (SL 1980 MDIV)

**SOMMERFELD SCOTT G REV** (765)864-0957
3602 Robin Dr Kokomo IN 46902-4432 • lcor@netusa1.net • IN • Assoc • Our Redeemer Kokomo IN • (765)453-0969 • (SL 1987 MDIV)

**SOMMERFIELD BARRY R REV** (616)465-6065
2760 Southfork Dr Stevensville MI 49127-9220 • MI • Sn/Adm • Trinity Saint Joseph MI • (616)983-5000 • (FW 1985 MA MTH)

**SOMMERFIELD BRUCE R REV** (863)385-7848
500 Summit Dr Sebring FL 33870-2340 • fls@strayo.net • FG • SP • Faith Sebring FL • (941)385-7848 • (SL 1961 MTH)

**SON SUNGKWON REV** (512)218-4455
515 E Palm Valley Blvd Apt 1428 Round Rock TX 78664 • TX • D Miss • Texas Austin TX • (FW 1999 MDIV)

**SONG BEN C DR** (253)838-4599
33502 11th Pl SW Federal Way WA 98023-5310 • cbensong@hotmail.com • NOW • SP • Fed Way Korean Federal Way WA • (253)839-6034 • (CQ 1980 MTH)

**SONG JOSEPH C REV** (779)664-2227
3750 Patterstone Dr Alpharetta GA 30022 • FG • D Miss • Florida-Georgia Orlando FL • (CQ 1999)

**SONNENBERG ROGER R REV** (626)445-8613
531 Monte Vista Rd Arcadia CA 91007-6062 • PSW • Sn/Adm • Our Savior Arcadia CA • (626)447-7690 • (SL 1971 MDIV MA)

**SONNTAG DONALDO REV** (501)770-4570
623 Kinkade Pl Lowell AR 72745 • dson230757@hotmail.com • MDS • D Miss • Living Savior Lowell AR • (501)770-2124 • (PA 1984 MTH MA)

**SORENSEN DAVID E REV** (414)425-6502
8073 S Chapel Hill Dr Franklin WI 53132-2429 • d.sorensen@juno.com • SW • Inst C • South Wisconsin Milwaukee WI • (414)464-8100 • (FW 1977 MDIV)

**SORENSEN JOHN K REV** (760)751-8881
10375 Cerveza Baja Dr Escondido CA 92026-6929 • friarabbey@aol.com • EN • EM • (SL 1956 MA MDIV)

**SORENSEN ROBERT A REV** (708)795-1844
1844 Grove Ave Berwyn IL 60402-1736 • robtsorens@aol.com • NI • SP • Good Shepherd Berwyn IL* • (708)788-9054 • (SL 1989 MDIV MFA)

**SORENSEN THOMAS A REV** (214)357-8534
3627 Whitehall Dr Dallas TX 75229-2655 • TX • EM • * • (SPR 1958 MA)

**SORENSON JAMES H REV** (831)449-3404
328 Rhine Court Salinas CA 93906 • revjhs@redshift.com • CNH • SP • Our Savior Salinas CA • (831)422-6352 • (SL 1968 MDIV)

**SORENSON ROBERT H REV** (810)978-2160
35275 Brighton Dr Sterling Hts MI 48310-7410 • bobshirl@flash.net • MI • SP • East Bethlehem Detroit MI • (313)892-2670 • (SPR 1965)

**SOUND JOHN REV** (412)369-0423
117 Manor Rd Pittsburgh PA 15237-5209 • revsound@aol.com • EA • SP • Mount Calvary Pittsburgh PA* • (412)931-4500 • (FW 1991 MDIV MA MS MPAD)

**SOUTHARD ROY L DR** (713)690-4541
C/O Concordia Lutheran Church 4115 Blalock Rd Houston TX 77080-1413 • concordialutheran@juno.com • TX • SP • Concordia Houston TX • (713)462-4040 • (FW 1983 MDIV MED DED)

**SOUTHWARD STEPHEN REV**
301 S Walnut St Pittsfield IL 62363 • CI • SP • St Paul Pittsfield IL • (217)285-2566 • (SL 1983)

**SOWERS TIMOTHY E REV**
HHC 1-4IN BN Unit 28211 PO Box 284 APO AE 09173 • sowerst@hotmail.com • SO • M Chap • Southern New Orleans LA • (SL 1985 MDIV)

**SPAETH DAVID MICHAEL REV** (816)765-1892
10929 Bales Ave Kansas City MO 64137-2101 • dspaeth@mwis.net • MO • SP • Chapel/Cross Kansas City MO • (816)942-4285 • (CQ 1986 MAR MAR)

**SPAETH MARC D REV**
C/O Shepherd of the Desert LCh PO Box 343 Page AZ 86040-0343 • RM • SP • Shepherd Deser Page AZ • (520)645-9398 • (SL 1984 MDIV)

**SPAHN THOMAS K REV** (717)581-5836
243 Kingsbridge Lititz PA 17543 • EN • SP • Mount Calvary Lititz PA • (717)560-6751 • (SL 1965 MDIV)

**SPALLEK ANDREW J REV** (417)833-2330
3968 N Bannister Ave Springfield MO 65803-4803 • aspall@atlascomm.net • MO • SP • Faith Springfield MO • (417)833-3749 • (SL 1987 MDIV MBA STM)

**SPALTEHOLZ HANS REV** (503)281-8560
6200 NE 29th Ave Portland OR 97211-6036 • hspalteholz@cu-portland.edu • NOW • EM • (SL 1955 MA MA STM)

**SPANGLER JOHN L REV** (920)498-4085
1802 Chateau Dr Green Bay WI 54304-3113 • john@pilgrimluth.com • NI • SP • Community Faith Spring Grove IL • (815)675-1074 • (FW 1978 MDIV DST)

**SPANNAUS RUBEN E REV** (206)935-2359
5402 49th Ave SW Seattle WA 98136-1016 • NOW • EM • (SL 1938)

**SPARLING PATRICK R REV** (605)996-3065
709 E 13th Ave Mitchell SD 57301 • revpat@sunrisenet.com • SD • Cmp P • Community Faith Spring Grove IL* • (SL 1993 MDIV)

**SPARLING PAUL W REV** (973)538-2704
11 Holly Dr Morris Plains NJ 07950-2708 • NJ • EM • * • (SL 1954 MTH)

**SPATZEK CARLTON C REV** (813)633-1131
2325 Del Webb Blvd E Sun City Center FL 33573-6953 • FG • EM • * • (SL 1955 MDIV)

**SPEAKS KEITH A REV** (214)221-4124
6121 E Lovers Lane Dallas TX 75214 • speaks@flash.net • TX • Assoc • Zion Dallas TX • (214)363-1639 • (SL 1990 MDIV)

**SPECKHARD PETER A REV** (920)430-4944
1245 Grignon St Green Bay WI 54301 • NW • Assoc • Faith Green Bay WI • (920)435-5524 • (SL 1997 MDIV)

**SPEERBRECKER DAVID W REV** (708)206-1854
18320 Ashland Ave Homewood IL 60430-3403 • dwspeer@juno.com • NI • SP • Salem Homewood IL • (708)798-1820 • (SL 1980 MDIV DMIN)

**SPEERBRECKER PAUL E REV** (219)844-3934
7327 Colorado Ave Hammond IN 46323 • pespeer1@juno.com • IN • SP • Concordia Hammond IN • (219)844-5616 • (SL 1979 MDIV)

**SPEERS DAVID R REV** (618)483-6993
C/O St Paul Lutheran Church RR 2 Box 231 Altamont IL 62411-9652 • CI • SP • St Paul Altamont IL • (618)483-6993 • (FW 1989 MDIV)

**SPELZHAUSEN MARK H REV** (910)392-9379
4517 Dean Dr Wilmington NC 28405-2429 • messiahlcms@juno.com • SE • SP • Messiah Wilmington NC • (910)791-7040 • (SL 1972 MDIV)

**SPENCE KENNETH M** (920)324-3210
400 S Madison Waupun WI 53963 • SW • Assoc • Pella Waupun WI • (920)324-3321 • (FW 2000 MDIV)

**SPENCER LYNN E REV** (316)873-2966
C/O St John Lutheran Church PO Box 587 Meade KS 67864-0587 • KS • SP • St John Meade KS* • (316)873-2966 • (FW 1981 MDIV)

**SPENN MELVIN F REV** (254)876-2384
1515 E Kensington St Mart TX 76664-1818 • TX • EM • * • (CQ 1961)

**SPICER GEORGE A REV** (314)931-3912
1429 Alexander Dr Festus MO 63028-1045 • MO • SP • New Hope Festus MO • (314)933-5015 • (SL 1997 MDIV)

**SPIEHS LEONARD SCOTT REV** (605)362-8749
5509 W 23rd St Sioux Falls SD 57106-0405 • revlspiehs@aol.com • SD • SP • Resurrection Sioux Falls SD • (605)361-6631 • (FW 1991 MDIV)

**SPIEKERMAN VICTOR J REV** (517)939-8176
8288 Crapo Lake Rd Johannesburg MI 49751-9511 • MI • EM • (SL 1948)

**SPILKER TIMOTHY K REV** (920)954-0902
1224 Montclaire Ct Appleton WI 54915-2804 • timspilker@aol.com • NW • Assoc • Good Shepherd Appleton WI • (920)734-9643 • (SPR 1971 MDIV)

**SPILMAN ROBERT C REV** (716)631-9212
C/O Lutheran Service Society PO Box 1963 Williamsville NY 14231-1963 • EA • Eastern Williamsville NY • (716)634-5111 • (SL 1972 MDIV MDIV)

**SPITTEL DOUGLAS H REV**
535 N Neville St Pittsburgh PA 15213-2812 • spittel1913@duq3.cc.duq.edu • EA • SP • First Trinity Pittsburgh PA • (412)683-4121 • (FW 1990 MDIV)

**SPITZ MARK D REV** (314)835-1413
836 Culloden Kirkwood MO 63122 • mds1701@ix.netcom.com • MO • First Trinity Pittsburgh PA • (412)683-4121 • (SL 1985 MDIV)

**SPITZACK MAYNARD A REV** (507)664-0962
106 E Mill St Dundas MN 55019 • MNS • EM • (SPR 1975 MDIV)

**SPITZENBERGER RAYMOND D DR** (979)335-6170
PO Box 575 515 Todd St East Bernard TX 77435 • spitz575@wcnet.net • TX • SP • St Paul Wallis TX • (979)478-6741 • (CQ 2000 MA DART DART)

**SPLETT DAVID L REV** (641)858-3719
1109 Washington St Eldora IA 50627-1627 • godshous@netins.net • IE • SP • St Paul Eldora IA • (641)858-3225 • (SL 1977 MDIV)

**SPLITGERBER WILLIAM F REV** (352)243-5754
4114 Hammersmith Dr Clermont FL 34711-6979 • wsplitgerber@earthlink.net • FG • EM • (SL 1960 MDIV)

**SPOMER ARTHUR J DR** (918)215-1902
3708 N Battle Creek Dr Broken Arrow OK 74012-0742 • aspomer@immanuelba.org • OK • Sn/Adm • Immanuel Broken Arrow OK • (918)258-5506 • (SL 1964 MA MDIV DMIN)

**SPOMER CHARLES W REV** (314)351-7142
6360 Devonshire Ave Saint Louis MO 63109-2215 • spo.mer@juno.com • MO • SP • Ascension Saint Louis MO • (314)832-5600 • (SL 1973 MDIV)

**SPOMER NORMAN F REV** (651)454-2373
1953 Timber Wolf Trl N Eagan MN 55122-2229 • MNS • EM • (SL 1947)

**SPOMER PHILIP T R REV** (812)471-4227
3043 Elmridge Dr Evansville IN 47711-2856 • duetspomer@aol.com • IN • SP • Concordia Evansville IN • (812)422-0384 • (FW 1987 MDIV)

**SPOONER DEAN HOWARTH REV** (217)863-2014
202 S Walnut St Bondville IL 61815-0118 • englishmix@yahoo.com • CI • SP • Immanuel Fisher IL • (217)897-6170 • (FW 1995 MDIV)

**SPREE FLOYD H REV** (314)842-9850
9712 Grantview Forest Dr Saint Louis MO 63123-3953 • MO • EM • (SL 1958)

**SPREHE RONALD R REV** (716)941-3335
8292 Cole Rd Colden NY 14033-9742 • nyhillrev@aol.com • EA • SP • St Martin Colden NY • (716)941-3335 • (CQ 1980 MDIV)

**SPREIER JOHN E REV** (904)241-1600
2950 Sanctuary Blvd Jaxville Bch FL 32250-2566 • FG • EM • (SPR 1961 MS)

**SPRENGELER ERWIN C REV** (425)369-9524
3935 226th Pl SE #313 Issaquah WA 98029-5251 • esprengeler@wcn.net • NOW • EM • (SL 1963 MDIV)

**SPRENGLER DONALD H REV** (715)623-0924
W6231 Hattes Ln Bryant WI 54418 • NW • EM • (SPR 1962 MDIV)

**SPRICK DONOVAN J REV** (636)391-5561
578 Spragues Mill Ct Ballwin MO 63011-3327 • MO • EM • (SL 1962 MDIV)

**SPRICK LLOYD E REV** (913)252-3317
PO Box 147 Holyrood KS 67450-0147 • KS • EM • (SL 1962 MDIV)

**SPRINGER MARTIN R REV** (618)826-3830
303 Ben St Chester IL 62233 • revspringer@aol.com • SI • Assoc • St John Chester IL • (618)826-3545 • (SL 2000 MDIV)

**SPRINGER NORMAN R REV** (813)788-1760
5621 Beech St Zephyrhills FL 33540-4505 • FG • SP • Our Savior Zephyrhills FL • (813)782-1369 • (SPR 1965 MDIV)

**SPROUL JOHN M REV** (402)894-2437
17411 Y St Omaha NE 68135 • John@KingofKingsomaha.org • NEB • Assoc • King Of Kings Omaha NE • (402)333-6464 • (SC 1988 MDIV)

**SPURGAT OTTO R REV** (302)645-2046
214 Holly Ln Lewes DE 19958-9637 • SE • EM • (CQ 1962 MA)

**SQUARE ARTHUR E REV**
506B Ramey St Edwardsville IL 62025-1519 • MO • EM • (CQ 1971)

**SQUIRES BENJAMIN CHARLES REV** (920)682-7401
619 Pine St Manitowoc WI 54220 • SW • Assoc • Redeemer Manitowoc WI • (920)684-3989 • (SL 2000 MDIV)

**ST JEAN THOMAS REV** (562)941-0245
14312 Hawos Whittier CA 90604 • tstjean@aol.com • PSW • SP • Faith Whittier CA • (562)941-0245 • (CQ 1983 MDIV)

**STACHE WILLIAM REV** (812)372-2459
2725 Wedgewood Dr Columbus IN 47203-3341 • IN • SP • St Paul Columbus IN • (812)376-6504 • (SL 1960 MDIV)

**STADELMAN ALAN R REV** (734)878-0815
721 Putnam St Pinckney MI 48169-8010 • hge@livingonline.com • MI • SP • Trinity Pinckney MI • (734)878-5977 • (FW 1990 MDIV)

**STADLER ERIK W REV**
253 E 28th St Apt B Littlefield TX 79339-5640 • TX • SP • Immanuel Hereford TX • (806)364-1668 • (FW 1998 MDIV)

**STAHL MARTIN R REV** (619)556-2860
3200 Santo Rd San Diego CA 92124 • IN • M Chap • Indiana Fort Wayne IN • (SPR 1976 MDIV)

**STAHLECKER ALAN ROY REV** (316)924-5440
C/O St John Luth Church PO Box 157 Lincolnville KS 66858-0157 • revalanstahlecker@hotmail.com • KS • SP • St John Lincolnville KS • (316)924-5236 • (FW 1993 MDIV)

**STAHLHUT STEPHEN C REV** (810)735-4707
410 Riverside Dr Linden MI 48451-9090 • MI • Asst • Trinity Davison MI • (810)658-3000 • (SL 1974 MDIV)

**STAHLKE LEONARD E REV** (512)926-5839
7300 Fred Morse Dr Austin TX 78723-1613 • TX • SHS/C • Texas Austin TX • (SL 1958 MDIV STM)

**STAHNKE AUGUST C REV** (805)937-5781
295 N Broadway # 114 Santa Maria CA 93455 • pastorgus@aol.com • CNH • EM • (SPR 1937)

**STALLINGS S SCOTT REV**
PO Box 597 Richmond TX 77406-0597 • TX • 03/1996 03/2000 • (SPR 1970 MDIV)

**STALLWORTH BENJAMIN F REV** (334)928-1069
19707 Greeno Rd Fairhope AL 36532 • SO • 12/1991 12/1999 • (FW 1988 MDIV)

**STAM BRUCE L REV** (507)775-2867
942 1st Ave NW Byron MN 55920-1410 • MNS • 05/1996 05/2000 • (SL 1973 MDIV MED MAT)

**STAMM RICHARD E REV** (217)796-3386
PO Box 107 Chestnut IL 62518-0107 • CI • SP • Zion Chestnut IL • (217)796-3386 • (CQ 1994 MA)

**STAMM SHAWN OWEN REV** (661)917-1280
C/O Resurrection Luth Church 42217 55th St West Quartz Hill CA 93536-3669 • PSW • SP • Resurrection Quartz Hill CA • (661)943-8433 • (FW 1996 MDIV)

**STANDLEY JOHN M REV** (916)638-4245
3500 Data Dr - #275 Rancho Cordova CA 95670 • CNH • SP • Cordova Rancho Cordova CA • (916)363-5687 • (SL 2000 MDIV)

**STANFORD CRAIG S REV**
233 Jay St East Peoria IL 61611-1804 • CI • SP • Immanuel Peoria IL • (309)691-3911 • (FW 1991 MDIV)

**STANGOHR CLARENCE W REV** (414)458-0504
1427 Saint Clair Ave Sheboygan WI 53081-3235 • SW • EM • (CQ 1971)

**STANKO PAUL W REV** (937)434-0474
2127 Springmill Rd Dayton OH 45440-2815 • paul@discoverus@emmanuel.org • OH • EM • (SL 1945 MDIV)

**STANLEY VINCENT C REV**
7445 Wise Ave St Louis MO 63117-1621 • MO • Missouri Saint Louis MO • (314)317-4550 • (SL 2000 MDIV)

**STANO LESTER P REV** (301)527-0106
436 Winter Walk Dr Gaitheresburg MD 20878-5785 • lessp@aol.com • SE • SP • Cross Rockville MD • (301)762-7565 • (SPR 1973 MBA MDIV)

**STANTON GREGG A REV** (281)251-9984
14306 Cypress Valley Dr Cypress TX 77429-6310 • TX • Sn/Adm • St John Cypress TX • (281)373-0503 • (FW 1989 MDIV)

**STANTON SANFORD D REV**
3315 Pursell Ln Pensacola FL 32526-9516 • SO • SP • Trinity Cantonment FL • (904)968-0078 • (SL 1992 MDIV)

**STAPLES RONALD B REV** (816)836-4264
12025 Mar Bec Trl Independence MO 64052-3850 • MO • Assoc • Good Shepherd Kansas City MO • (816)474-9049 • (SL 2000 MDIV)

**STARK PAUL MATTHEW REV**
891 W Blaine St Riverside CA 92507-3927 • PSW • SP • Gethsemane Riverside CA • (909)684-6446 • (SL 1995 MDIV)

**STARK WILLARD H REV** (405)789-1897
2909 N Holloway Ave Bethany OK 73008-4636 • OK • EM • (SL 1948 MDIV)

**STARK WILLIAM A REV** (608)375-5441
1108 Yahn Ave Boscobel WI 53805-1700 • SW • SP • Hickory Grove Boscobel WI • (608)375-5441 • (SL 1964 MDIV)

**STARKE STEPHEN P REV** (517)686-4184
1704 Amelith Rd Bay City MI 48706-9337 • spstarke@concentric.net • MI • SP • St John Bay City MI • (517)686-0176 • (FW 1983 MDIV)

**STARR DENNIS E REV** (612)806-0114
4119 Pebblebrook Cir Bloomington MN 55437-2106 • S • SP • Holy Emmanuel Bloomington MN • (952)888-2345 • (FW 1983 MDIV)

**STARR FRANK D REV** (936)634-2465
906 Copeland St Lufkin TX 75904-4901 • flc42@juno.com • TX • SP • First Lufkin TX • (936)634-7468 • (SL 1967 MDIV MA)

**STAUDACHER THEODORE L REV** (913)286-1391
3928 NW Morley Rd Topeka KS 66618-3515 • tstaud@inlandnet.net • KS • EM • (SL 1962 MDIV)

**STAUFFER W ROGER REV** (517)687-5404
991 W Walter Rd Sanford MI 48657-9335 • stauffers@tm.net • MI • Inst C • Michigan Ann Arbor MI • (SL 1982 MDIV)

**STAWICKI GARY THOMAS REV**
827 Top Of The Thumb Ln Ellison Bay WI 54210 • NW • 12/1999 • (CQ 1992 MDIV)

**STECHHOLZ DAVID P REV** (650)615-0255
335 Valverde Dr S San Fran CA 94080-5624 • stecholz@infinex.com • EN • SP • West Portal San Francisco CA • (415)661-0242 • (FW 1978 MDIV)

**STECHHOLZ ERWIN H REV** (716)624-2650
PO Box 238 Mendon NY 14506 • EA • EM • (SPR 1940)

**STECKER DAVID O REV** (219)493-1899
9910 N Country Knls New Haven IN 46774-1906 • IN • Assoc • Emanuel New Haven IN • (219)749-2163 • (FW 1998 MDIV)

**STECKER JEROME A REV** (414)358-2593
2841 S 44th St Milwaukee WI 53219-3405 • SW • SP • St Martini Milwaukee WI • (414)645-4094 • (SL 1976 MDIV)

**STECKLING LARRY L REV**
RORC/ELCENTER 78 Kazybek Bl Almaty 480091 KAZAKHSTAN • steckling@itte.kz • NW • S Miss • North Wisconsin Wausau WI • (SL 1982 MDIV)

**STECKLING TIMOTHY J REV** (713)895-8459
1431 Arlington St Houston TX 77008-4566 • TX • SP • Immanuel Houston TX • (713)864-2651 • (SL 1998 MDIV)

**STEEGE DAVID L REV** (507)839-3086
RR 2 Box 31 Lake Park IA 51347 • MNS • SP • Trinity Lake Park IA • (507)839-3086 • (SL 1998 MDIV)

**STEEGE MARK W REV** (210)696-0016
11906 Flaming Star San Antonio TX 78249-2446 • marksteege@aol.com • TX • EM • (SL 1957 MDIV MSW)

**STEEH EDWARD J REV** (810)749-8636
30880 Clark St New Haven MI 48048-1812 • MI • SP • St John New Haven MI • (810)749-5286 • (FW 1995 MDIV)

**STEELE CAMERON K REV** (248)548-1345
623 E Evelyn Ave Hazel Park MI 48030-3104 • cksteele@flash.net • MI • SP • Hazel Park Hazel Park MI • (248)398-6363 • (FW 1993 MDIV)

**STEELE ROBERT W REV** (920)208-7895
3808 S 17th St Sheboygan WI 53081-7142 • rjrsnsteele@dellnet.com • SW • Assoc • Our Savior Sheboygan WI • (920)452-4005 • (FW 1997 MDIV)

**STEELE WALTER ROBERT REV** 81-611-722-8699
USS Monterey CG61 FPO AE 09578-1181 • walter³steele@hotmail.com • SE • M Chap • Southeastern Alexandria VA • (FW 1994 MDIV)

**STEENBOCK ELMER G REV** (541)267-4451
1125 Oakway Dr Coos Bay OR 97420-1932 • NOW • EM • (SPR 1962 MDIV)

**STEFANSKI ERIC J REV** (309)346-2536
500 S 8th St Pekin IL 61554-4710 • revski@cat41.org • CI • Assoc • St John Pekin IL • (309)347-2136 • (FW 1989 MDIV)

**STEFFEN LEE W REV** (828)369-7812
565 Waterfall Dr Franklin NC 28734-3958 • lsteffen@macon.main.nc.us • SE • EM • (SL 1945)

**STEFFEN NORMAN L REV** (785)865-0872
1915 Marvonne Rd Lawrence KS 66047-2323 • KS • EM • (SL 1954 MDIV STM)

**STEFFENS EARL L REV** (912)386-8463
1007 Davis Ave Tifton GA 31794-4049 • FG • SP • Peace Tifton GA • (912)382-7344 • (SL 1974 MDIV)

**STEHR JOHN W REV** (612)442-2759
351 W 4th St Waconia MN 55387-1709 • MNS • EM • (SL 1935 MDIV)

**STEHR RONALD E REV** (651)388-4822
33300 Kolshorn Ln Red Wing MN 55066-7602 • MNS • SP • Concordia Red Wing MN • (651)388-5447 • (SL 1972 MDIV)

**STEIN DAVID T REV** (708)771-5588
550 Clinton Pl River Forest IL 60305-1910 • dtsteinlb@aol.com • EN • SP • Holy Spirit Elk Grove Village IL • (847)437-5897 • (SL 1961 STM MA PHD)

**STEIN DONALD M REV** (920)568-1105
1116 W Cramer St Fort Atkinson WI 53538-1033 • cmpspstr@idcnet.com • SW • D Miss • Calvary/Univ Whitewater WI • (414)473-5274 • (FW 1978 MDIV)

**STEIN JONATHAN P REV** (314)355-5341
6655 Mignon Dr Florissant MO 63033-5031 • EN • SP • Chapel Cross Saint Louis MO • (314)741-3737 • (SL 1960 MDIV MA)

**STEINBACH ALAN H REV** (804)527-1762
4001 Harcourt Ln Richmond VA 23233-1777 • ahsteinba@aol.com • SE • EM • (CQ 1988 MSCT MA PHD)

**STEINBACH WALTER A REV** (920)766-5882
310 W Henry St Kaukauna WI 54130-3466 • wsteinb727@aol.com • NW • SP • Bethany Kaukauna WI • (414)766-1452 • (SL 1971 MDIV)

**STEINBAUER WILLIAM JOSEPH REV** (402)421-9434
3535 Canyon Rd Lincoln NE 68516-5731 • bsteinbauer@hotmail.com • NEB • Cmp P • University Chapel Lincoln NE • (402)477-3997 • (SL 1992 MDIV)

**STEINBECK ALLEN L REV** (309)452-3142
7 Brookwood Dr Normal IL 61761-4011 • CI • Assoc • Trinity Bloomington IL • (309)828-6265 • (SL 1988 MDIV)

**STEINBECK ARNOLD G REV** (831)372-5085
399 Grant Ave Monterey CA 93940-3854 • steinarn@aol.com • CNH • SP • Bethlehem Monterey CA • (831)373-1523 • (SPR 1960)

**STEINBERG ALAN G REV** (914)923-0166
27 Camp Woods Grounds Camp Woods Rd Ossining NY 10562 • AT • Asst • St Matthew Hastings On Hudson NY* • (914)478-1071 • (FW 1999 MA MDIV PHD)

**STEINBERG DONALD E REV** (920)927-5726
PO Box 451 Reeseville WI 53579-0451 • SW • SP • Immanuel Reeseville WI • (920)927-5734 • (FW 1986 MDIV)

**STEINBRONN ANTHONY J REV**
PO Box 3427 Rustenburg 0300 SOUTH AFRICA • steinbro@intekom.co.za • IN • S Miss • Indiana Fort Wayne IN • (SL 1982 MDIV STM DMISS)

**STEINBRONN REUBEN A REV** (505)275-0896
1308 Stutz Dr NE Albuquerque NM 87112-6235 • RM • EM • (SPR 1974 MDIV)

**STEINER MARK G REV**
6811 Chestnut Ave Falls Church VA 22042 • MO • M Chap • Northern Illinois Hillside IL • (SL 1982 MA MA STM MDIV)

**STEINKAMP GEORGE P REV** (218)864-5999
308 Bowman St E Battle Lake MN 56515-4104 • stein@prtel.com • MNN • EM • (SL 1959 MDIV)

**STEINKE ALAN F REV** (516)825-5921
C/O Our Saviour Luth Church 12 Dubois Ave Valley Stream NY 11581-2121 • EN • SP • Our Saviour Valley Stream NY • (516)825-5453 • (SL 1971 MDIV MSW)

**STEINKE ANDREW C REV** (636)272-7566
5 Chambers Ct O Fallon MO 63366 • aksteink@gte.net • MO • Assoc • Zion Saint Charles MO • (636)441-7425 • (SL 1998 MDIV)

**STEINKE MARK A REV** (616)468-5935
492 Park St Coloma MI 49038-9485 • salempastor@hotmail.com • MI • SP • Salem Coloma MI • (616)468-6567 • (FW 1985 MDIV)

**STEINKE NORMAN E REV**
11 Hoylake Dr Abilene TX 79606-5127 • TX • SP • Zion Abilene TX • (915)677-7801 • (SPR 1963)

**STEINKE PAUL D REV** (718)852-1625
379 Sackett St # 1 Brooklyn NY 11231-4703 • paul.steinke@med.nyu.edu • AT • Inst C • Atlantic Bronxville NY • (914)337-5700 • (SL 1961 MALS MDIV)

**STEINKE PETER L REV** (512)342-8684
11713 Astoria Dr Austin TX 78733 • TX • 08/1996 08/2000 • (SL 1964 STM MED DREL)

**STEINKE RICHARD G REV** (515)278-9460
3416 Patricia Dr Urbandale IA 50322 • richterrysteinke@netscape.net • IW • Inst C • Iowa West Fort Dodge IA • (SL 1973 MDIV)

**STEINKE ROBERT C REV**
8665 Cypress Lakes Blvd New Port Richey FL 34653 • revstein@aol.com • FG • Assoc • Faith New Port Richey FL • (727)849-4418 • (SL 1969 MDIV)

**STEINMANN ANDREW E REV**
C/O Concordia University 7400 Augusta St River Forest IL 60305 • crf.steinmae@crf.cuis.edu • NI • SHS/C • Northern Illinois Hillside IL • (FW 1981 MDIV PHD)

**STELLING JOHN F REV** (713)526-5731
5315 Main St Houston TX 77004-6878 • jkstell@flash.net • TX • SP • St Matthew Houston TX • (713)526-5731 • (SL 1965 MDIV)

**STELMACHOWICZ MICHAEL J REV** (512)339-8630
12408 Blossomwood Dr Austin TX 78727-5302 • ulbramjs@family.net • TX • EM • (SL 1957 MED MDIV PHD)

**STELTER HERBERT W REV** (920)452-3570
928 Wisconsin Ave Apt 316 Sheboygan WI 53081-3951 • SW • EM • (TH 1945)

**STELZER HAROLD T REV** (402)423-6023
3150 Jasper Ct Lincoln NE 68516-1635 • NEB • EM • (CQ 1966 MED)

**STELZER RONALD W REV** (631)736-6718
28 Belair Rd Selden NY 11784-1755 • rwstelzer@aol.com • AT • Sn/Adm • Our Savior Centereach NY • (516)588-2757 • (SL 1980 MDIV MST)

**STELZER WILBERT W REV** (512)863-5356
109 Woodland Rd Georgetown TX 78628-3036 • TX • EM • (SL 1944 MA)

**STENBECK MARK C REV** (530)877-7571
6428 Pentz Rd Paradise CA 95969-3626 • mstenbeck@aol.com • CNH • SP • Our Savior Paradise CA • (530)877-7321 • (SPR 1976 MDIV)

**STENNETT ARTHUR R REV** (216)633-2255
89 West Ave Tallmadge OH 44278-2249 • EN • EM • (SPR 1961 MED PHD)

**STENNFELD FRED H REV** (415)584-2664
5505 Diamond Heights Blvd San Francisco CA 94131-2642 • soth@hooked • net • CNH • SP • Shepherd Hills San Francisco CA • (415)586-3424

**STENNFELD JOHN C REV** (512)899-9223
4607 Yellow Rose Trl Austin TX 78749-1655 • jcs442@yahoo.com • TX • SP • Christ Austin TX • (512)442-5844 • (SL 1989 MDIV)

**STENZEL KENT CHARLES REV** (406)482-2050
214 S Lincoln Ave Sidney MT 59270-3925 • tlc@lyrea.com • MT • SP • Trinity Sidney MT* • (406)482-2050 • (SL 1973 MDIV)

**STEPHAN LUKE F REV** (734)741-9278
3203 Dunwoodie Ln Ann Arbor MI 48105 • Luke³Stephan@earthlink.net • MI • Michigan Ann Arbor MI • (SL 1967 MSW MDIV)

**STEPHEN DAVID MARTIN REV** (253)952-6823
35921 23rd Pl S Federal Way WA 98003-9174 • NOW • SP • First Korean Tacoma WA • (253)474-1430 • (CQ 1979)

**STEPHENS JAMES P REV** (773)589-1976
3450 N Panama Ave Chicago IL 60634-2923 • NI • SP • Our Saviour Chicago IL • (773)736-1120 • (SL 1967 MDIV)

**STEPHENS JEFFREY B REV** (216)561-2511
C/O St Peter Luth Church 18000 Van Aken Blvd Shaker Heights OH 44122-4807 • stpeters@stratos.net • OH • SP • St Peter Shaker Heights OH • (216)561-2511 • (FW 1983 MDIV DMIN)

**STERLE ROGER D REV** (801)789-1421
PO Box 342 Vernal UT 84078-0342 • dsterle@iwworks.com • RM • SP • Our Saviour Vernal UT* • (435)789-1421 • (SPR 1976 MDIV)

**STERN JOHN T REV** (507)836-6643
2010 Broadway Ave Slayton MN 56172-1135 • MNS • SP • Trinity Slayton MN • (507)836-8129 • (SL 1970 MDIV)

**STERNBERG JOHN R REV** (503)624-4827
13209 SW 61st Ave Portland OR 97219-8062 • jrst@cyberhighway.net • NOW • EM • (SL 1945 MDIV)

**STEUERNAGEL DAVID A REV** (708)672-3391
148 Denell Dr Crete IL 60417-1013 • NI • Sn/Adm • St Paul Chicago Heights IL • (708)754-4493 • (SL 1963 MED MDIV)

**STEVENS LELAND R REV** (505)434-4224
403 Sunglow Ave Alamogordo NM 88310-4126 • RM • EM • (SL 1953 MDIV MA PHD)

**STEVENS ROBERT JAMES REV**
28330 Lilac Rd Valley Center CA 92082-5415 • PSW • SP • Light Valley Valley Center CA • (760)749-9733 • (FW 1994 MDIV)

**STEWART SCOTT ALAN REV**
PO Box 104 Raymond IL 62560-0104 • SO • 08/1998 08/2000 • (SL 1991 MDIV)

**STEYER EDWARD A REV** (501)239-5151
4902 Wise St Paragould AR 72450-3743 • MDS • EM • (SPR 1961)

**STEYER MARTIN W REV** (805)739-0901
1837 Duke Dr Santa Maria CA 93454 • CNH • EM • (SL 1952 MDIV)

**STIEGEMEYER SCOTT EDMUND REV** (412)881-1131
3112 Clermont Ave Pittsburgh PA 15227 • stiegemeyer@worldnet.att.net • EA • SP • Concordia Pittsburgh PA • (412)881-3005 • (FW 1995 MDIV)

**STIEMKE FREDERICK A REV** (828)299-1534
3703 Trinity Ct Asheville NC 28805-0401 • fjstiemke@ioa.com • SE • EM • (SL 1955 DD)

**STIER DONALD L REV** (612)440-6055
15055 Aquilla Ave S Prior Lake MN 55372-9248 • donstier@juno.com • MNS • 11/1995 11/1999 • (FW 1987 MDIV)

**STIER LARRY E REV** (318)742-0608
2239 Windsor Ct Bossier City LA 71111-5443 • larrystier@aol.com. • SO • Inst C • Southern New Orleans LA • (SL 1964 MDIV)

**STIEVE JOHN W REV**
4954 N Claremont Ave #Garden Chicago IL 60625-1912 • pex63@msn.com • EN • SP • Risen Savior Green Valley AZ • (520)625-2612 • (SL 1970 MDIV)

**STILL WAYMAN L REV** (941)351-5227
3909 Oak Grove Dr Sarasota FL 34243-2808 • wayman-nita@msn.com • FG • SP • Beaut Savior Sarasota FL • (941)355-2798 • (SPR 1972)

**STILLMAN MARK G REV** (612)424-5393
9660 99th Ave N Maple Grove MN 55369-3819 • pmstills@aol.com • MNS • SP • Shepherd Grove Maple Grove MN • (763)425-5941 • (SL 1986 MDIV)

**STILWELL S JAMES REV**
2625 Midway Branch Dr #101 Odenton MD 21113-2319 • stilwellrj@aol.com • SE • EM • (SPR 1964 MDIV)

**STIRDIVANT DAVID M REV** (909)797-4067
35525 Wildwood Canyon Rd Yucaipa CA 92399-5128 • PSW • EM • (SL 1948 DD)

**STISSER LEE H REV** (813)805-2499
3705 Kensington Ave Tampa FL 33629 • FG • SP • Holy Trinity Tampa FL • (813)839-6847 • (SC 1991 MDIV)

**STOCK DONALD EDWARD REV** (417)781-4798
3801 Norman Dr Joplin MO 64804-4052 • MO • Asst • Immanuel Joplin MO • (417)624-0333 • (SL 1992 MDIV)

**STOCKER TODD DAVID REV** (651)578-3091
6700 Buckingham Rd Woodbury MN 55125 • tkstocker@usfamily.net • MNS • Assoc • Woodbury Woodbury MN • (651)739-5144 • (SL 1998 MDIV)

**STOCKMAN REED JOEL REV** (320)256-3840
C/O St Paul Lutheran Church 519 N 4th Ave E Melrose MN 56352-1176 • stockman@melrose.means.net • MNN • SP • St Paul Melrose MN • (612)256-3847 • (SL 1986 MDIV)

**STOCKMAN ROBERT E REV** (602)983-2224
619 S Copper Dr Apache Junction AZ 85220-5034 • PSW • EM • (SL 1960 MDIV THD)

**STOCKMAN WILLIAM K REV** (218)943-2337
18508 E Lake Vermont Rd NE Parkers Prairie MN 56361-8140 • MNN • EM • (SL 1955)

**STOEBIG THOMAS K REV** (612)550-0317
11900 44th Pl N Plymouth MN 55442-2745 • tstoebig@beautifulsaviorlc.org • MNS • SP • Beautiful Savior Plymouth MN • (612)550-1000 • (SL 1982 MDIV)

**STOEHR WALDEMAR C REV**
114 S Cedar St Horicon WI 53032 • SW • EM • (SL 1945)

**STOEPPELWERTH HENRY P REV** (540)825-6387
15528 Bradford Rd Culpeper VA 22701-4228 • SE • EM • (SL 1957 MA)

**STOHLMANN DAVID H DR** (707)528-4122
2289 Valley West Court Santa Rosa CA 95401-5735 • davjoy@juno.com • CNH • SP • Mount Olive Sebastopol CA • (707)823-6316 • (SL 1970 MDIV MA MTH DMIN)

**STOHLMANN JOHN S REV** (718)461-8246
21-12 123rd St #3R College Point NY 11356 • stohljss@juno.com • AT • Tchr • Martin Luther Maspeth NY • (718)894-4000 • (SL 1999 MDIV)

**STOHLMANN PAUL F JR. REV** (219)589-3609
725 Forest Park Dr Berne IN 46711-1706 • stohlmannberne@juno.com • IN • SP • Peace Berne IN • (219)589-3848 • (SPR 1970 MDIV MA)

**STOHLMANN ROBERT V REV** (507)433-4405
703 2nd St NW Austin MN 55912-3016 • MNS • SP • Holy Cross Austin MN • (507)437-2107 • (SL 1963)

**STOHLMANN STEPHEN C REV** (651)770-4027
2850 Helen St N North Saint Paul MN 55109-1610 • stohlmann@csp.edu • MNS • SHS/C • Minnesota South Burnsville MN • (SL 1968 MDIV MA PHD)

**STOHS EUGENE E REV** (913)268-4948
4712 Stearns Ln Shawnee Msn KS 66203-1173 • KS • 05/1998 • (SL 1967 MDIV MPHIL)

**STOHS MILTON E REV** (314)868-3644
1227 Blodgett Dr Saint Louis MO 63137-1342 • MO • EM • (SL 1953 MDIV)

**STOJKOVIC LARRY S REV** (716)723-4673
130 Mount Ridge Cir Rochester NY 14616-4830 • EA • Assoc • Hope Rochester NY • (716)723-4673 • (SC 1987 MDIV)

**STOLL ALLEN R REV** (920)336-9582
715 S Superior St De Pere WI 54115-3277 • arsnal@yahoo.com • NW • SP • Hope De Pere WI • (920)336-9582 • (CQ 1994)

**STOLL HENRY L REV** (870)239-3977
1904 Glendale St Paragould AR 72450-4834 • MDS • EM • (SPR 1963)

**STOLLE GARY D REV** (816)373-5290
17200 E 39th St S Independence MO 64055-3832 • Gstplc@aol.com • MO • Sn/Adm • St Paul Independence MO • (816)373-5290 • (SL 1977 MDIV)

**STOLP ARMIN F REV** (505)287-2772
725 Gunnison Ave Grants NM 87020-2939 • RM • SP • Mount Calvary Grants NM • (505)287-2382 • (SL 1956)

**STOLTENBERG JAMES G REV** (410)795-4571
5613 Old Washington Rd Sykesville MD 21784-8617 • jamess267@aol.com • SE • SP • Faith Eldersburg MD • (410)795-8082 • (SPR 1974 MDIV)

**STOLTENOW BRADLEY R REV** (701)223-4993
2501 East Blvd Bismarck ND 58501 • brszionbis@aol.com • ND • Assoc • Zion Bismarck ND • (701)223-8286 • (FW 1988 MDIV DMIN)

**STOLZ DEAN A REV** (217)562-2816
302 E 4th St Pana IL 62557-1654 • CI • SP • St Paul Pana IL • (217)562-4731 • (FW 1980 MDIV)

**STOLZ TRAVIS D REV** (218)634-2808
112 3rd Ave NW PO Box 694 Baudette MN 56623-0694 • khs@wiktel.com • MNN • SP • Bethlehem Baudette MN • (218)634-1532 • (FW 1999 MDIV)

**STOPPENHAGEN NORMAN W REV** (562)869-7899
7821 Kingbee St Downey CA 90242-3419 • normstop@aol.com • PSW • SP • Messiah Downey CA • (562)923-1215 • (SL 1967 MDIV)

**STORK STEVEN D REV**
1840 Foothill Blvd Grants Pass OR 97526-3852 • NOW • SP • St Paul Grants Pass OR • (541)476-2565 • (FW 1982 MDIV)

**STORM HAROLD A REV** (507)237-2782
23633 491st Ave Gaylord MN 55334 • MNS • SP • St John Gaylord MN • (507)237-2782 • (FW 1983 MDIV)

**STORM HAROLD W REV** (407)877-0932
410 Orlando Ave Apt 20A Ocoee FL 34761-2957 • FG • EM • (SL 1948)

**STORRUD DONALD E REV** (307)367-2612
C/O Our Savior Luth Church PO Box 148 Pinedale WY 82941-0148 • dostorr@wyoming.com • WY • SP • Our Savior Pinedale WY* • (307)367-2612 • (FW 1983 MDIV)

**STORTEBOOM FRED A REV** (503)843-2180
PO Box 313 Sheridan OR 97378-0313 • NOW • SP • Trinity Sheridan OR • (503)843-4747 • (CQ 1982)

**STORY MARK S REV** (519)380-9586
274 Lark St Chatham ON N7L 1G8 CANADA • S • SP • Our Saviour Chatham ON CANADA • (519)352-1860 • (CQ 1999 MDIV MTH)

**STOTERAU LARRY ALLEN REV** (480)838-1014
631 W Straford Dr Chandler AZ 85225-1415 • stoterau@psw.lcms.org • PSW • Sn/Adm • Epiphany Chandler AZ • (480)963-6105 • (SL 1973 MDIV)

**STOTTLEMYER WILLIAM J REV** (218)736-5005
22001 County Hwy 10 Fergus Falls MN 56537-7903 • revstott@prairietech.net • MNN • SP • Immanuel Fergus Falls MN* • (218)736-6228 • (FW 1990 MDIV)

**STOUDT JOHN ANWYL REV** (718)366-9231
77-02 82nd St Glendale NY 11385-7635 • AT • SP • Emmaus Ridgewood NY • (718)821-5253 • (SC 1992 MDIV MA)

**STOWE DOUGLAS JOHN REV** (517)662-4579
1392 Seidler Rd Auburn MI 48611 • MI • Assoc • Zion Auburn MI • (517)662-4264 • (SL 1996 STM)

**STRADE BRUCE REV** (503)579-6605
15780 Nurrelet Dr Beaverton OR 97007 • toplfs@aol.com • NOW • Northwest Portland OR • (SL 1966 STM)

**STRADTMAN CLARENCE W REV** (262)728-3022
N4901 Dam Rd Delavan WI 53115 • SW • EM • (SL 1935 MDIV)

**STRAND AHLERT J C JR. REV** (830)895-5453
333 Water St Apt D 2 Kerrville TX 78028 • TX • EM • (FW 1978 MDIV)

**STRAND AHLERT J C REV** (972)283-4322
5120 Cliff Haven Dr Dallas TX 75236-2237 • MDS • EM • (SPR 1957 MAR)

**STRAND GREGORY A REV**
C/O Portland Lutheran School 740 SE 182nd Portland OR 97233-4960 • NOW • Northwest Portland OR • (SL 2000 MDIV)

**STRAND PAUL O J REV** (708)532-2633
6850 159th St Tinley Park IL 60477-1629 • NI • Sn/Adm • Trinity Tinley Park IL • (708)532-9395 • (FW 1979)

**STRASEN LUTHER G REV** (219)747-9317
1003 Crestway Dr Fort Wayne IN 46819-1436 • lgsfw@aol.com • IN • EM • (SL 1958 MDIV)

**STRATMAN WILLIAM WARNER REV** (507)478-4335
PO Box 128 - 502 4th St Rushmore MN 56168 • MNS • SP • St John Rushmore MN • (507)478-4922 • (FW 2000 MDIV)

**STRATTMAN GENE ARTHUR REV** (217)472-7651
1930 Saint Pauls Church Rd Chapin IL 62628-4011 • CI • SP • St Paul Chapin IL • (217)472-7891 • (CQ 1994)

**STRAUB ROGER K REV** (517)626-7000
9960 W Herbison Rd Eagle MI 48822-9718 • MI • SP • Good Shepherd Lansing MI • (517)321-6100 • (SL 1977 MDIV)

**STRAWN JAMES C REV** (419)446-2217
C/O St James Lutheran Church 22881 Monroe St Archbold OH 43502-9486 • OH • SP • St James Archbold OH • (419)445-4750 • (FW 1988 MDIV)

**STRAWN PAUL REV** (320)963-3697
4292 114th St NW Maple Lake MN 55358-6038 • strawn@lkdllink.net • MNS • SP • Prince Of Peace Spring Lake Park MN • (763)786-1706 • (FW 1992 MDIV)

**STREIT JOHN C REV** (313)532-8971
16035 Negaunee Redford MI 48239-3946 • EN • EM • (SL 1939 MED)

**STRELOW LLOYD REV** (909)925-4559
767 Genesee Dr Hemet CA 92544-1888 • ljstrelow@earthlink.net • PSW • SP • Shep Of Valley Anza CA • (909)763-4226 • (SPR 1965 MDIV DMIN)

**STRELOW THEODORE N REV** (336)449-9208
813 Alamance St Gibsonville NC 27249-2710 • SE • EM • (SL 1963 MDIV)

**STREUFERT CARL A REV** (716)634-5625
4555 Hedgewood Dr Williamsville NY 14221-6122 • castas@buffnet.net • EA • EM • (SL 1951 STM)

**STREUFERT DANIEL A REV** (219)291-8297
3121 Chelsea Ct South Bend IN 46614-2207 • IN • SP • Our Redeemer South Bend IN • (219)288-8288 • (SL 1966 MDIV)

**STREUFERT NORBERT A REV** (651)429-4095
4150 Thornhill Ln Vadnais Heights MN 55127-3610 • MNS • EM • (SL 1953 STM)

**STREUFERT PHILIP E REV** (509)922-1385
4910 S Gillis Way Ct Spokane WA 99206-9440 • NOW • Sn/Adm • Redeemer Spokane WA • (509)926-6363 • (CQ 1976 STM)

**STREUFERT STEPHEN C REV** (816)407-9744
1013 Lindenwood Ln Liberty MO 64068 • MO • SP • St Stephen Liberty MO • (816)781-3377 • (SL 1972 MDIV)

**STREUFERT VICTOR B REV** (913)227-3418
105 W Green St Lindsborg KS 67456-1709 • vstreufert@ks-usa.net • KS • EM • (SL 1955 PHD)

**STREUFERT WALDEMAR B REV** (217)342-6417
2909 S Park St Effingham IL 62401-2924 • CI • EM • (SL 1941 STM THD)

**STRICKERT PAUL G REV** (972)907-2351
1613 Mayflower Dr Richardson TX 75081-4602 • TX • EM • (SL 1942 MDIV)

**STRICKERT ROBERT H REV** (770)396-6816
1664 Bethesda Ct Atlanta GA 30338-6102 • estrickert@mindspring.com • FG • 01/1999 • (SL 1956 MST)

**STRICKERT WALTER F REV** (636)532-3954
15124 Isleview Dr Chesterfield MO 63017-7741 • MO • EM • (SL 1941)

**STRINGER GREGORY S REV** (510)668-1987
4618 Stratford Ave Fremont CA 94538 • stringergta1@juno.com • CNH • SP • Our Savior Fremont CA • (510)657-3191 • (SL 1982 MDIV)

**STROHSCHEIN ARNOLD REV** (941)637-0643
2816 Caribbean Dr Punta Gorda FL 33950 • FG • EM • (SL 1946)

**STROHSCHEIN DAVID P REV** (320)252-1470
2913 Golf View Ct Saint Cloud MN 56301-5988 • revdps@aol.com • MNN • Sn/Adm • Holy Cross Saint Cloud MN • (320)251-8416 • (SL 1977 MDIV)

**STROHSCHEIN GLENN L REV** (217)483-4617
524 Teal Dr Chatham IL 62629-9791 • CI • SP • St John Chatham IL • (217)483-2612 • (SPR 1972)

**STROHSCHEIN JONATHAN REV** (320)274-8467
190 Lake Dr E Annadale MN 55302 • MNN • 09/1998 • (SL 1982 MDIV)

**STROHSCHEIN MARCUS T REV** (320)274-5588
645 Cedar Cir Annandale MN 55302-9417 • MNS • EM • (SPR 1947)

**STROM TERRY ALAN REV** (815)457-2041
PO Box 290 Cissna Park IL 60924-0290 • stromt@localline2.com • CI • SP • Trinity Cissna Park IL • (815)457-2739 • (SL 1995 MDIV)

**STROMING KARL B REV** (218)732-1143
20095 County 24 Park Rapids MN 56470-9336 • MNN • EM • (SL 1950)

**STRONG MICHEAL M DR** (217)522-3821
1508 S Whittier Ave Springfield IL 62704-3747 • strong@eosinc.com • CI • Sn/Adm • Trinity Springfield IL • (217)522-8151 • (SPR 1971 MDIV DMIN)

**STROUD KENYON L REV** (979)731-1163
9732 Elmo Weedon Loop Bryan TX 77808 • lstroud@bop.gov • TX • Inst C • Texas Austin TX • (SL 1987 MDIV DMIN)

**STRUBBE JOSEPH H REV** (714)557-5891
3473 Venetian Dr Costa Mesa CA 92626-1625 • PSW • Assoc • Christ Costa Mesa CA • (949)631-1611 • (CQ 1994 MA MMU)

**STRUCKMANN OTTO G REV** (716)434-5675
7589 Fairview Dr Lockport NY 14094-1609 • ottostruckmann@free1.net • EA • SP • Trinity Lockport NY • (716)434-3106 • (SL 1959)

**STRUCKMEYER ALAN D REV** (254)774-8829
3902 Antelope Trl Temple TX 76504-3608 • allinstr@hotmail.com • TX • Sn/Adm • Immanuel Temple TX • (254)773-3898 • (SL 1986 MDIV)

**STRUM LOREN W REV** (701)843-7718
316 N 5th St New Salem ND 58563-0037 • lstrum@btigate.com • ND • SP • Zion New Salem ND* • (701)843-7202 • (SL 1988 MDIV)

**STRUSSENBERG DANIEL P REV** (315)568-8395
2993 E Bayard St Ext Seneca Falls NY 13148-9707 • dstruss@flare.net • EA • SP • Calvary Seneca Falls NY • (315)539-8053 • (CQ 1983 MAR)

**STRUVE JOHN W M REV** (414)771-8909
3030 N Fairwood Ct Wauwatosa WI 53222-4020 • jstruve@execpc.com • SW • Sn/Adm • Mount Olive Milwaukee WI • (414)771-3580 • (SL 1974 MDIV)

**STUBE JOHN C REV** (219)486-2226
C/O Ascension Luth Church 8811 Saint Joe Rd Fort Wayne IN 46835-1037 • church@fwi.com • IN • SP • Ascension Fort Wayne IN • (219)486-2226 • (FW 1981 MS MDIV)

**STUBENROUCH JOHN J JR. REV** (316)395-2010
673 W 680th Ave Helper KS 66746-2119 • jstubenrouch@ckt.net • KS • SP • Immanuel Hepler KS • (316)395-2692 • (SL 1998 MSED MDIV)

**STUCKMEYER C DAVID REV** (847)253-4402
424 S Pine Ave Arlington Hts IL 60005-2056 • EN • Sn/Adm • Faith Arlington Hts IL • (847)253-4839 • (SL 1961 MDIV)

**STUCKWISCH ALLEN D REV** (501)452-5596
2802 S Dallas Fort Smith AR 72901 • MDS • SP • First Fort Smith AR • (501)785-2886 • (SL 1987)

**STUCKWISCH DON R REV**
C/O Our Savior Lutheran Church PO Box 188 Milford IL 60953-0188 • revdonsan@excite.com • NI • SP • Our Savior Milford IL • (815)889-4121 • (CQ 1980 MAR)

**STUCKWISCH DON RICHARD REV** (219)299-9115
225 E Woodside St South Bend IN 46614-1115 • IN • SP • Emmaus South Bend IN • (219)287-4151 • (FW 1993 MDIV)

**STUCKWISCH JEFFREY L REV** (812)547-2007
RR 1 Box 149 Evanston IN 47531-9618 • jstuckwi@psci.net • IN • SP • St John Evanston IN • (812)547-2007 • (SL 1991 MDIV)

**STUDT DONALD O REV** (219)699-7458
12440 S County Rd 700 E Galveston IN 46932-8719 • IN • EM • (SPR 1965 MDIV)

**STUDTMANN KENNETH C DR** (316)945-9483
3107 S Mount Carmel St Wichita KS 67217-1243 • KS • Sn/Adm • Bethany Wichita KS • (316)265-7415 • (SL 1960 MDIV DMIN)

**STUEBE MARTIN C REV**
1895 SE Currin Dr Hillsboro OR 97123-5118 • NOW • EM • (SL 1939)

**STUEHRENBERG DARRELL REV** (954)473-1115
7601 SW 39th St Davie FL 33328-2716 • gloriadei@juno.com • FG • SP • Gloria Dei Davie FL • (954)475-0683 • (CQ 1980)

**STUEHRENBERG LYLE R REV** (316)275-5042
2601 Belmont Pl Garden City KS 67846 • lrst@gcnet.com • KS • SP • Trinity Garden City KS • (316)276-3110 • (SL 1970 MDIV)

**STUEMPFIG EWALD L REV** (319)472-5499
203 Lutheran Home Ct Vinton IA 52349-1169 • IE • EM • (SL 1933)

**STUENKEL DAVID C REV** (509)927-0250
12902 E 25th Ave Spokane WA 99216-0333 • stuenkel@iea.com • NOW • Assoc • Redeemer Spokane WA • (509)926-6363 • (SL 1972 MDIV)

**STUENKEL JAMES A REV** (217)496-2771
2659 Windfall Dr Sherman IL 62684-9542 • goodshepherd@bullets.net • CI • SP • Good Shepherd Sherman IL • (217)496-3149 • (CQ 1983 MAR)

**STUENKEL ROBERT E REV** (303)494-1438
2775 Emerson Ave Boulder CO 80303-6342 • stuenkel@stripe.colorado.edu • RM • Cmp P • University Boulder CO • (303)443-8720 • (SL 1964 STM STM)

**STUENKEL ROGER R REV**
32905 Mills Rd North Ridgeville OH 44039-2351 • rstuenkel@aol.com • EN • SP • Ascension North Olmsted OH • (440)777-6365 • (SL 1970 MDIV)

**STUENKEL WALTER W REV** (602)625-8139
1460 N Rio Sonora Green Valley AZ 85614-4007 • EN • EM • (SL 1936 PHD DD)

**STUENKEL WILLIAM H REV** (360)573-5791
12204 NE 96th Ave Vancouver WA 98662-1152 • gails@teleport.com • NOW • Sn/Adm • St John Vancouver WA • (360)573-1461 • (CQ 1986 MA)

**STUEVE BARRY J REV** (360)578-2074
PO Box 2626 Longview WA 98632-8663 • blnmstueve@juno.com • NOW • SP • Grace Longview WA • (360)423-3720 • (SL 1988 MDIV)

**STUEVE DENNIS W REV** (909)629-4700
77 Rolling Ridge Dr Phillips Ranch CA 91766-4730 • mtcal@juno.com • PSW • SP • Mount Calvary Diamond Bar CA • (909)861-2740 • (SL 1980 MDIV)

**STUEVE EUGENE H REV** (660)385-2211
1112 Rustic Dr Macon MO 63552 • lstueve@mail.cyberusa.com • MO • SP • Zion Macon MO • (660)385-4433 • (CQ 1976 MDIV)

**STULTS DON ALAN REV** (612)866-8445
6920 Clinton Ave Richfield MN 55423-2448 • god.rules@usfamily.net • MNS • Assoc • Mount Calvary Richfield MN • (612)866-5405 • (SL 1996 MDIV)

**STUMPF ERIC CLINTON DR** (219)934-9067
10348 Manlou Dr Munster IN 46321 • estumpf@mail.1congrp.com • IN • Sn/Adm • St Paul Munster IN • (219)836-6270 • (SL 1973 MDIV DMIN)

**STUMPF KARL E REV** (215)245-0258
1915 Ironwood Ln Bensalem PA 19020-4425 • karlstu@aol.com • EA • SP • Pilgrim Elkins Park PA • (215)379-3072 • (SPR 1972 MDIV)

**STURGIS JAMES EDWARD SR. REV** (210)688-9150
15306 Geronimo Loop San Antonio TX 78254-1717 • TX • Sn/Adm • Mount Olive San Antonio TX • (210)674-1973 • (CQ 1994)

**STURGIS JAMES JR. REV** (806)256-5056
819 South Houston Shamrock TX 79079 • TX • SP • Trinity Shamrock TX* • (806)256-2355 • (FW 1999 MDIV)

**STURTZ ARLYN L REV** (334)660-2038
5022 Perin Rd Mobile AL 36693-3143 • asturtz@aol.com • SO • SP • Grace Mobile AL • (334)433-2749 • (SL 1973 MA PHD)

**STUTZ STEVE C REV** (915)268-1370
2702 Central Dr Big Spring TX 79720 • scstutz@hotmail.com • TX • SP • St Paul Big Spring TX • (915)267-7163 • (SL 1998 MDIV)

**SUEHS A VICTOR REV** (314)285-2993
21 Deborah Rd Hillsboro MO 63050-1937 • MO • EM • (SPR 1955)

**SUELFLOW EDWIN S REV** (262)238-8642
12024 N Wasaukee Rd Mequon WI 53097-2527 • edenmsuel@juno.com • SW • EM • (SL 1948 DD)

**SUELFLOW JOHN G REV** (262)377-3785
1406 Fox Ln Grafton WI 53024-9702 • jjsilflo@execpc.com • SW • Assoc • St Paul Grafton WI • (262)377-4659 • (SL 1962 MDIV)

**SUELZLE DAVID K REV** (701)748-2292
PO BOX 523 Hazen ND 58545-0523 • dsuelzle@westriv.com • ND • SP • St Matthew Hazen ND • (701)748-5561 • (SL 1982 MDIV)

**SUHR MARVIN E REV** (719)260-6194
6235 Ashton Park Pl Colorado Springs CO 80919-4813 • mdsuhr@altavista.com • RM • EM • (SL 1952 MDIV)

**SULLIVAN BRYAN C REV** (512)281-2705
801 W 11th St Elgin TX 78621-2006 • TX • SP • Grace Elgin TX • (512)281-3367 • (FW 1978 MDIV)

**SULLIVAN JOSEPH DEAN REV** (636)938-7307
604 Williams Dr Eureka MO 63025 • pastorjoe@stmarkseureka.org • MO • Assoc • St Mark Eureka MO • (636)938-4432 • (SL 1999 MDIV)

**SUND JOEL ERIC REV**
C/O Lord Of Life Lutheran Ch 2600 S Sycamore Ave Sioux Falls SD 57110-5968 • Jmiller@cs.com • SD • Assoc • Lord Of Life Sioux Falls SD • (605)371-3501 • (SL 1993 MDIV)

**SUNDBOM PAUL D**
C/O St Peters Luth Church 6175 St Peters Church Rd Conover NC 28613 • SE • Asst • St Peter Conover NC • (828)256-2970 • (FW 2000 MDIV)

**SUNDBYE SCOTT ALAN REV** (940)612-5552
764 Cty Rd 147 Gainesville TX 76240-7132 • sundbye@texoma.net • TX • SP • Faith Gainesville TX • (940)668-7147 • (FW 1995 MDIV)

**SUNDELL DENNIS REV** (920)864-2463
C/O Zion Lutheran Church 8378 County Rd W Greenleaf WI 54126-9468 • NW • Sn/Adm • Zion Greenleaf WI • (920)864-2463 • (FW 1985 MDIV)

**SUNDERLAGE RICHARD R REV** (608)339-0337
N2515 11th Ave Adams WI 53910 • SW • SP • St John Adams WI • (608)339-7869 • (FW 1982 MDIV)

**SUNDERMAN BRYON L REV** (979)265-3348
309 Van Winkle St Lake Jackson TX 77566-3132 • TX • 01/1999 • (FW 1984 MDIV)

**SURBURG RAYMOND F REV** (219)486-3442
800 Bell Trace Cir Apt 360 Bloomington IN 47408-4414 • IN • EM • (SL 1933 MA MRE THD PHD DD)

**SUSAN DAVID J REV** (608)246-4216
2210 Lakeland Ave Madison WI 53704-5637 • djsusan@juno.com • SW • Sn/Adm • Immanuel Madison WI • (608)257-5401 • (SL 1971 MDIV)

**SUSSKRAUT KENNETH J REV** (914)986-3962
55 Southern Ln Warwick NY 10990-1919 • RevK@Warwick.net • AT • SP • Good Shepherd Warwick NY • (914)986-3962 • (CQ 1978 MDIV)

**SUTTERER PAUL R REV** (703)878-6920
15746 Widewater Dr Dumfries VA 22026-1212 • FG • EM • (SPR 1966)

**SUTTERER STEVEN E REV** (800)991-7715
C/O St Joseph Hospital 611 Saint Joseph Ave Marshfield WI 54449-1832 • sutteres@mfldclin.edu • NW • Inst C • North Wisconsin Wausau WI • (SL 1984 MDIV)

**SVEOM DALE D REV** (816)322-8327
810 Minnie Ave Belton MO 64012-4732 • MO • SP • Holy Trinity Grandview MO • (816)763-3211 • (SL 1981 MDIV)

**SWAN MELVIN F REV** (660)463-2755
27484 Becker Rd Concordia MO 64020-7138 • MO • EM • (SPR 1963)

**SWANSON RICHARD M REV** (805)659-3459
981 Phoenix Ave Ventura CA 93004-2253 • PSW • 04/1998 04/2000 • (SL 1971 MDIV)

**SWEARER ROBERT J REV**
737 Queens Grant Palmetto Dunes Hilton Head SC 29938 • RM • Sn/Adm • Immanuel Colorado Springs CO • (719)636-5011 • (SL 1983 MDIV)

**SWEET ROBERT L REV**
2124 Willow Dell Dr Seabrook TX 7586-3309 • revbsweet@juno.com • KS • Asst • Christ Augusta KS • (316)775-7301 • (SL 1992 MDIV)

**SWEYKO STEPHEN C REV** (301)264-4064
12904 New Row Rd NW Mount Savage MD 21545-1026 • SE • SP • Trinity Cumberland MD • (301)777-1800 • (SL 1998 MDIV)

**SWINFORD JAMES S REV** (623)544-9635
16416 N Naegel Surprise AZ 85374 • PSW • SP • Mount Zion Peoria AZ • (623)825-9221 • (FW 1989 MDIV)

**SWITZER MATTHEW D REV** (219)490-5080
6021 Blackstone Dr Fort Wayne IN 46818 • somedayson@juno.com • IN • Assoc • Sub Bethlehem Fort Wayne IN • (219)484-7873 • (FW 2000 MDIV)

**SWYRES ERIC DAVID REV** (816)542-1989
1218 Hillcrest Dr Carrollton MO 64633-1526 • MO • SP • Immanuel Carrollton MO • (816)542-2064 • (SL 1996 MDIV)

**SYLVESTER HELMUTH A REV** (702)263-7221
PO Box 91046 Henderson NV 89009-1046 • CNH • EM • (SL 1938 MBA)

**SYLWESTER ROGER O REV** (541)607-1271
4139 Hampshire Ln Eugene OR 97404 • NOW • SP • Shep Of Valley Junction City OR* • (541)998-6659 • (SL 1965 MDIV)

**SYMM DAVID V REV** (806)825-3074
RR 1 Box 146 Farwell TX 79325-9753 • dvsymm@wtrt.net • TX • SP • St John Farwell TX • (806)825-2409 • (FW 1983 MDIV)

**SYMMANK C LEO REV** (504)488-9491
6844 Louis Xiv St New Orleans LA 70124-3332 • SO • EM • (SL 1953 MA)

**SYMMANK CHARLES R REV** (541)779-6256
181 Shaniko Ct Medford OR 97504 • symmcj@aol.com • NOW • EM • (SL 1956 MA DMIN)

**SYMMANK H MELVIN REV** (972)271-4089
1718 Merrimac Trl Garland TX 75043-1229 • symmank1@airmail.net • TX • 07/1997 07/2000 • (SL 1965 MDIV)

**SYPE KENNETH O REV** (913)492-5493
10343 Westgate St Overland Park KS 66215-2252 • mstrpastor@aol.com • KS • Sn/Adm • Christ Overland Park KS • (913)345-9700 • (SL 1970 MDIV)

**SZCZESNY JONATHAN DAVID REV** (515)993-5014
9051 Somerset Rd SE Thornville OH 43076 • IW • M Chap • Iowa West Fort Dodge IA • (FW 1997 MDIV)

**SZEDLAK ERNO L REV** (715)831-6418
2831 Clark Pl Eau Claire WI 54701 • NW • EM • (SPR 1964)

**SZETO LENNY REV** (405)273-6286
39307 Mac Arthur St Shawnee OK 74804-2485 • OK • SP • Redeemer Shawnee OK • (405)273-6286 • (SL 1999 MDIV)

## T

**TABBERT CHRISTOPHER J REV** (406)296-0117
PO Box 332 Eureka MT 59917-0332 • MT • SP • Holy Cross Eureka MT • (406)296-2116 • (FW 1998 MDIV)

**TAFEL GREGORY S REV** (610)515-1753
2012 Sullivan Trl Easton PA 18040 • rvgtafel@cs.com • EA • SP • Faith Easton PA • (610)253-1625 • (SC 1997 MDIV)

**TAGLAUER JAMES R REV** (504)486-9588
149 26th St New Orleans LA 70124-1314 • SO • EM • (CQ 1974 MA MED)

**TAGLAUER KENNETH C REV** (870)424-4382
229 Chaperal Mountain Home AR 72653-5449 • MDS • Assoc • Redeemer Mountain Home AR • (870)425-6071 • (SPR 1970 MDIV)

**TALLEY PHILLIP REV** (512)643-7133
847 Cliff Dr Portland TX 78374 • TX • D Miss • Texas Austin TX • (SL 1998 MDIV)

**TALSMA DALE A REV**
5224 N Stony Run Ln Fort Wayne IN 46825 • lcn³jos@sil.org • MI • S Miss • Michigan Ann Arbor MI • (SL 1985 MDIV)

**TANNAHILL DAVID S REV** (270)234-0082
1215 Kelly Dr Elizabethtown KY 42701 • drtanna@kvnet.org • IN • SP • Gloria Dei Elizabethtown KY • (270)766-1503 • (SC 1986 MDIV)

**TAPE JOHN W REV** (314)416-0909
5225 Hettinger Ct Saint Louis MO 63128-3525 • ljtape@aol.com • MO • 05/1986 05/2000 • (FW 1980 MDIV MTH THD)

**TASLER ROBERT L REV** (303)798-6859
8187 S Pennsylvania Ct Littleton CO 80122-2855 • pbt45@ecentral.com • RM • SP • Epiphany Littleton CO • (303)798-6859 • (SL 1971 MDIV)

**TASSLER MELVIN J REV** (402)477-2114
3429 N St Lincoln NE 68510-1528 • EN • EM • (SL 1941 DD)

**TATKENHORST KENNETH L REV** (660)827-6320
2701 Southwest Blvd Sedalia MO 65301 • pastor.tatkenhorst@sedaliastpauls.org • MO • SP • St Paul Sedalia MO • (660)826-1164 • (CQ 1992 MDIV)

**TAUSCHER ROBERT W SR. REV** (850)871-6370
6510 Lake Dr Panama City FL 32404-8319 • SO • EM • (SPR 1952)

**TAUSCHER ROBERT W REV** (610)328-3991
126 Old State Rd Springfield PA 19064-1728 • btauscher@aol.com • EN • SP • St John Springfield PA • (610)543-3100 • (FW 1980 MDIV)

**TAUSZ RALPH GERHARD REV** (847)288-9545
2235 N Ruby St Melrose Park IL 60164 • NI • SP • Apostles Melrose Park IL • (312)455-0903 • (FW 2000 MDIV)

**TAYKOWSKI THEODORE R REV** (219)493-1436
1916 Montgomery Ct Fort Wayne IN 46815-7447 • IN • EM • (SL 1958)

**TAYLOR DAVID M REV** (219)623-2363
12919 Fackler Rd Monroeville IN 46773-9539 • IN • SP • Prince Of Peace Grabill IN • (219)627-5621 • (FW 1989 MDIV)

**TAYLOR DERIC ARMON REV** (914)337-9300
171 White Plains Rd Bronxville NY 10708-3101 • dat@concordia-ny.edu • AT • Cmp P • Atlantic Bronxville NY • (914)337-5700 • (SL 1992 MDIV)

**TAYLOR DIEN A REV**
2158 Watson Ave Bronx NY 10472 • AT • Asst • Trinity Bronx NY • (718)828-1234 • (SL 2000 MDIV)

**TAYLOR DONALD L REV** (612)445-6955
1064 Merritt St Shakopee MN 55379-2922 • revdont@aol.com • MNS • EM • (SL 1964 MDIV)

**TAYLOR KURT SCOTT REV** (920)853-3656
C/O Trinity Luth Church (Potter) N6078 W River Rd Hilbert WI 54129 • koort@tds.net • SW • SP • Trinity Hilbert WI • (920)853-3656 • (SL 1992 STM MDIV)

**TAYLOR M ALAN REV** (409)770-9891
115 Tarpon Galveston TX 77550 • patmostx@juno.com • TX • SP • St John Galveston TX • (409)762-2702 • (FW 1993 MDIV)

**TAYLOR MICHAEL S REV** (334)970-1813
146 Pennbrooke Loop Foley AL 36535-1600 • mikesuet@gulftel.com • SO • SP • St Paul Foley AL • (334)943-6931 • (FW 1984 MDIV)

**TEACHENOR MONROE S REV** (510)654-4471
5905 Claremont Ave Oakland CA 94618-1220 • CNH • EM • (SPR 1952 MA)

**TEASDALE JAMES R REV** (219)456-7103
245 E Pettit Ave Fort Wayne IN 46806-3004 • pjrthome@aol.com • IN • Sn/Adm • Peace Fort Wayne IN • (219)744-3869 • (FW 1983 MDIV)

**TEGELER DEAN E REV** (617)337-1295
540 Commercial St Weymouth MA 02188-3705 • NE • SP • Christ Scituate MA • (781)545-5271 • (SL 1954 MST)

**TEGTMEIER DENNIS H REV** (310)714-6777
2424 Ocean Park #4 Santa Monica CA 90405 • DrDTeg@aol.com • PSW • 08/1997 08/2000 • (SPR 1966 MA MA MDIV)

**TEGTMEIER NORBERT D REV** (316)343-1819
1907 Casa Loma Dr Emporia KS 66801-5829 • KS • SP • Messiah Emporia KS • (316)342-8181 • (FW 1979 MDIV)

**TEGTMEIER VICTOR D REV** (920)262-9188
N9227 Ash Rd Watertown WI 53094-9565 • SW • EM • (SL 1962)

**TEICHMILLER R JEROME REV** (281)351-1077
606 N Magnolia St Tomball TX 77375-4448 • revtike@juno.com • TX • Sn/Adm • Zion Tomball TX • (281)351-5757 • (SPR 1973 MDIV)

**TEIGEN MARTIN A REV** (507)344-8087
208 Wilson Way Mankato MN 56001 • margen@mctcnet.net • MNS • D Miss • Minnesota South Burnsville MN • (CQ 1997 STM MDIV)

**TEIKE MARK R REV** (812)376-9364
1012 Tanager Dr Columbus IN 47203-1928 • mteike@stpeters-columbus.org • IN • Sn/Adm • St Peter Columbus IN • (812)372-1571 • (SL 1983 MDIV)

**TEKLEGIORGIS TUQUABO H REV** (215)879-0053
1219 N 57th St Philadelphia PA 19131-4104 • EA • 06/1993 06/2000 • (FW 1989)

**TELLER DANIEL J REV** (847)419-9373
416 Sussex Ct Buffalo Grove IL 60089-4457 • teller4ds@aol.com • NI • SP • Our Redeemer Prospect Heights IL • (847)537-4430 • (FW 1990 MDIV)

**TELLONI JOHN L REV** (330)830-2179
3642 Wales Ave NW Apt B Massillon OH 44646-1847 • jlt3750@aol.com • S • SP • St John Massillon OH • (330)837-4645 • (FW 1977 MDIV)

**TEMME ELTON H REV** (402)462-6909
1803 W 8th St Hastings NE 68901-4216 • NEB • EM • (SL 1958)

**TEMME HUBERT REV** (727)372-3645
6618 Garden Palm Ct New Port Richey FL 34655-5117 • htemme2@gte.net • FG • EM • (CQ 1968)

**TEMME MARVIN L REV** (307)532-7650
221 Lupine Dr Torrington WY 82240-3504 • mltemme@prairieweb.com • WY • SP • Our Savior Torrington WY • (307)532-5801 • (SL 1973 MDIV)

**TEMME NORMAN L REV** (828)696-8539
306 High Point Ln Hendersonville NC 28791-1202 • ntemme@ioa.com • SE • EM • (SL 1945 MDIV DD)

**TEMPLE EVAN J REV** (916)723-6001
8176 Woodlake Hills Dr Orangevale CA 95662-3728 • etemple@juno.com • CNH • EM • (SPR 1958)

**TEMPLE JOHN FRANKLIN REV** (314)989-0939
9241 Clayton Rd St Louis MO 63124 • MO • SP • Village Saint Louis MO • (314)993-1834 • (SPR 1973 MA MDIV)

**TENSMEYER WILFRIED H REV** (208)765-6111
4301 N Ramsey Rd Trlr C-19 Coeur D Alene ID 83814-8440 • NOW • EM • (SPR 1942)

**TERHUNE PAUL C REV** (818)852-9485
1419 E Dalton Ave Glendora CA 91741-3139 • PSW • SP • Hope Glendora CA • (626)335-5315 • (CQ 1977 MA)

**TERJESEN WILLIAM P REV** (914)737-0527
The Luth Church Of Our Redeeme 714 Hudson Ave Peekskill NY 10566-3318 • terjesen@bestweb.net • AT • SP • Our Redeemer Peekskill NY • (914)737-0527 • (CQ 1991 MDIV)

**TESCH PHILIP C REV** (651)695-1692
132 Wheeler St S Saint Paul MN 55105-1925 • tesch@csp.edu • MNS • SHS/C • Minnesota South Burnsville MN • (SPR 1975 MDIV JD)

**TESKE HERBERT J REV**
174 Linden Ln Chicago Heights IL 60411-2119 • NI • EM • (SPR 1955 MDIV)

**TESKE MARTIN E REV** (281)343-0585
1714 Bumelia Ct Sugar Land TX 77479 • TX • O Miss • Texas Austin TX • (SL 1966 MDIV MTH)

**TESKE PAUL N E REV** (203)254-7471
11 Rustic Ln Westport CT 06880-6340 • S • SP • St Paul Westport CT • (203)227-7441 • (SPR 1976)

**TESKE STEVEN W REV** (712)246-2488
408 W Summit Ave Shenandoah IA 51601-2336 • srteske@shenessex.heartland.net • IW • SP • Trinity Shenandoah IA* • (712)246-1131 • (FW 1988 MDIV)

**TESKE THOMAS W REV** (303)460-8193
3827 W 98th Pl Westminster CO 80030-2619 • tteske@earthlink.net • RM • SP • King Of Kings Arvada CO • (303)425-7096 • (SL 1970 MDIV DMIN)

**TESKE WALTER W REV** (616)348-3787
809 W Sheridan St Petoskey MI 49770-2859 • MI • SP • Zion Petoskey MI • (231)347-3438 • (SL 1972)

**TESSARO CHARLES REV**
Luth Church Of Nigeria Onne PO Box 109 Nchia Eleme LGA Rivers State NIGERIA • lcn³jos@sil.org • MI • S Miss • Michigan Ann Arbor MI • (FW 1984 MDIV)

**TESSARO PAUL DEAN DAVIS REV** (901)363-9791
6496 Trysting Oak Dr Memphis TN 38141-0470 • revpt@juno.com • MDS • P Df • Eterl Mercy Df Memphis TN • (901)332-5723 • (SL 1992 MDIV)

**TESSIN SCOTT MATTHEW REV** (314)379-1305
2610 Babble Creek Lane O Fallon MO 63366 • pastors@faithalive.org • MO • D Miss • Missouri Saint Louis MO • (314)317-4550 • (SL 1994 MDIV)

**TESSMANN DAVID H REV** (409)938-3612
7926 Larkspur Dr Texas City TX 77591 • revdht@aol.com • TX • SP • Peace Texas City TX • (409)938-1277 • (SPR 1969 MDIV MTH)

**TETZLOFF RICHARD D REV** (314)225-3839
819 Kentridge Ct Ballwin MO 63021-7568 • MO • Missouri Saint Louis MO • (314)317-4550 • (SPR 1963 MDIV)

**TEUSCHER DANIEL J REV** (314)849-1086
9832 Emil Ave Saint Louis MO 63126-3207 • danjudy@aol.com • MO • Assoc • Webster Gardens Webster Groves MO • (314)961-5275 • (SPR 1963)

**TEUSCHER HAROLD J REV** (480)895-5745
9625 E Eddystone Ct Sun Lakes AZ 85248-7162 • ssluth@ipxnet.com • PSW • SP • Risen Savior Sun Lakes AZ • (480)895-6782 • (SL 1961 MAS STM MDIV)

**TEUSCHER MICHAEL L REV** (231)547-9919
221 W Carpenter Ave Charlevoix MI 49720-1613 • MI • SP • Bethany Charlevoix MI • (231)547-9446 • (SL 1982 MDIV)

**TEWES MARK S REV** (402)646-2264
3162 Mc Kelvie Rd Seward NE 68434-7515 • NEB • Assoc • St John Seward NE • (402)643-2983 • (SL 1989 MDIV)

**TEWS DAVID E REV** (870)670-4814
1405 Oklahoma St Horseshoe Bend AR 72512-4055 • cen77616@mail.centurytel.net • MDS • SP • Shepherd Hills Horseshoe Bend AR • (870)670-5482 • (SL 1968 MDIV)

**TEWS JAMES R REV** (219)447-4368
9921 Wayne Trce Fort Wayne IN 46816-9742 • IN • Asst • Emmanuel Fort Wayne IN • (219)447-3005 • (CQ 1998)

**TEWS JOHN M REV** (515)465-5403
2323 Willis Ave #8 Perry IA 50220-2148 • IW • EM • (SL 1938 MDIV)

**TEWS MARK WILLIAM REV**
PSC 558 Box 3782 FPO AP 96375-3782 • TX • M Chap • Texas Austin TX • (SL 1992 MDIV)

**TEWS THOMAS A REV** (334)621-1151
9638 Sherwood Ct Daphne AL 36526-8054 • rev80@aol.com • SO • SP • Ascension Daphne AL • (334)626-7500 • (SL 1980 MDIV)

**TEWS THOMAS H REV** (815)459-1447
163 Pomeroy Ave Crystal Lake IL 60014-5947 • NI • Asst • Immanuel Crystal Lake IL • (815)459-1441 • (SL 1971 MDIV DMIN)

**THEIL STEPHEN L REV** (480)585-5954
25919 N 115th Way Scottsdale AZ 85255-5778 • slt@aol.com • PSW • Sn/Adm • Shepherd Desert Scottsdale AZ • (480)860-1188 • (SPR 1970 MDIV MA)

**THEILE KENNETH W REV** (513)782-6409
642 Maple Trce Cincinnati OH 45246-4166 • OH • EM • (CQ 1982 STM THD)

**THEIMER DOYLE J REV** (281)360-9310
4531 Echo Falls Dr Kingwood TX 77345 • djtheimer@juno.com • TX • Assoc • Christ King Kingwood TX • (281)360-7936 • (SL 1990 MDIV)

**THEIMER ROGER P REV** (402)894-2584
7217 Audrey St Omaha NE 68138-5933 • NEB • Assoc • King Of Kings Omaha NE • (402)333-6464 • (SL 1984 MDIV)

**THEISS HARRY R REV** (701)348-3904
PO Box 475 Glen Ullin ND 58631-0475 • ND • EM • (SL 1953 MDIV)

**THEISS LOUIS C REV** (573)547-3717
529 E St Maries St Perryville MO 63775-2036 • MO • EM • (SPR 1953 MDIV)

**THEISS PAUL D REV** (517)684-9927
2704 Ziegler Rd Bay City MI 48706-9355 • pdtheiss@juno.com • MI • Sn/Adm • St Paul Bay City MI • (517)686-7140 • (SL 1977 MDIV)

**THEISS STEVEN C REV** (618)281-5518
229 N Good Haven Dr Columbia IL 62236-1921 • SI • SP • St Paul Columbia IL • (618)281-4600 • (SL 1981 MDIV MED)

**THEISS TERRY L REV** (815)239-2554
PO Box 480 Pecatonica IL 61063-0480 • theiss@aeroinc.net • NI • SP • St John Pecatonica IL • (815)239-2400 • (SL 1981 MDIV)

**THELEN JAMES E REV** (414)321-4126
12300 W Janesville Rd Hales Corners WI 53130-2350 • EN • Assoc • Hales Corners Hales Corners WI • (414)529-6700 • (SL 1989 MDIV)

**THERWANGER-TATONE HAROLD L** (708)209-3502
1136 N Harlem Ave River Forest IL 60305 • crftherwah@curf.edu • NI • Hales Corners Hales Corners WI • (414)529-6700 • (SL 1987 MDIV)

**THEWS DANIEL P REV** (920)739-9191
C/O Faith Lutheran Church 601 E Glendale Ave Appleton WI 54911-2944 • dthews3427@aol.com • NW • Assoc • Faith Appleton WI • (920)739-9191 • (SL 1989 MDIV)

**THIEL STEVEN E REV** (616)321-0122
3345 Davcliff Portage MI 49024-3130 • thiel@net-link.net • MI • Assoc • St Michael Portage MI • (616)327-7832 • (FW 1992 MDIV)

**THIELE DAVID L REV** (517)321-5183
3323 Aragon Dr Lansing MI 48906-3504 • packerrev@voyager.net • EN • SP • Christ Lansing MI • (517)482-2252 • (SL 1981 MDIV)

**THIELE GERALD L REV** (940)552-2038
10955 Center Dr Vernon TX 76384 • gthiele@cst.net • TX • EM • (SL 1959 MDIV)

**THIELE KARL REV** (863)859-0516
PO Box 91274 Lakeland FL 33804-1274 • karlnatalie@cs.com • FG • EM • (SL 1955 MA MA)

**THIELE WALDEMAR A REV** (916)421-5600
1 Miranda Ct Sacramento CA 95822-3207 • wathlf@excite.com • CNH • EM • (SL 1942)

**THIEM ALFRED E REV** (701)293-6127
2618 18th St S Fargo ND 58103-6604 • ND • Inst C • North Dakota Fargo ND • (SL 1949 MDIV)

**THIEMANN EUGENE A REV** (970)282-7763
5643 Hummel Ln Ft Collins CO 80525 • gthiemann@home.com • NJ • EM • (SPR 1962 MDIV PHD)

**THIEME BRIAN K REV** (573)886-9433
520 N Crater Lake Dr Columbia MO 65201-6871 • MO • Assoc • Trinity Columbia MO • (573)445-2112 • (SL 1993 MDIV)

**THIEME JOHN A REV** (303)776-1789
640 Alpine St Longmont CO 80501 • coslongmont@juno.com • RM • SP • Christ Our Savior Longmont CO • (303)776-1789 • (SL 1988 MDIV)

**THIEME OTTO G REV** (847)368-3044
C/O Lutheran Home 800 W Oakton St # 218 H Arlington Heights IL 60004-4602 • NI • EM • (SL 1935)

**THIERFELDER DAVID F REV** (480)816-0850
PO Box 698 Waldport OR 97394-0698 • NOW • EM • (SPR 1962 MA)

**THIERFELDER THOMAS J REV** (972)226-6086
6318 Lyons Rd Garland TX 75043-6624 • pastor@treeoflifelcms.org • TX • SP • Tree Of Life Garland TX • (972)226-6086 • (FW 1993 MDIV)

**THIES DANIEL E REV** (850)626-5626
5733 Lorng Dr Milton FL 32570 • SO • SP • Eternal Trin Milton FL • (850)623-5780 • (FW 2000 MDIV)

**THIES DAVID J** (936)295-5298
107 Leighanne St Huntsville TX 77340 • TX • Assoc • Faith Huntsville TX • (409)295-5298 • (FW 2000 MDIV)

**THIES GERARD L REV** (417)886-2844
3060 W Village Ter Springfield MO 65810-1245 • MO • EM • (SL 1948)

**THIES JOHN A REV** (334)986-5857
26575 US Highway 98 Elberta AL 36530-2711 • SO • EM • (SPR 1960)

**THIES LARRY D REV** (608)271-5935
5817 Crabapple Ln Madison WI 53711-3436 • molc@execpc.com • SW • Sn/Adm • Mount Olive Madison WI • (608)238-5656 • (SL 1973 MDIV)

**THIESEN JACK H V REV** (402)371-8732
1807 Sunset Ave Norfolk NE 68701-7337 • NEB • Asst • Christ Norfolk NE • (402)371-1210 • (SL 1962 MDIV)

**THOELKE HERMANN LOTHAR REV** (219)663-6456
763 Trenton St Crown Point IN 46307-5213 • thoelke@juno.com • IN • Sn/Adm • Trinity Crown Point IN • (219)663-1578 • (SL 1965 MDIV)

**THOELKE ROBERT L REV** (509)545-8480
315 S 27th Ave Pasco WA 99301-4765 • lcmsbob@3-cities.com • NOW • EM • (SPR 1957)

**THOMACK ALWIN W REV** (217)324-4801
500 E Jones St Litchfield IL 62056-2498 • SI • EM • (WBS 1952 MDIV)

**THOMAS CRAIG B REV** (303)412-9277
9230 Knox Ct Westminster CO 80030 • RM • Assoc • Beaut Savior Broomfield CO • (303)469-1785 • (FW 1992 MDIV)

**THOMAS GLEN D REV** (314)727-5004
52 Arundel Pl Saint Louis MO 63105-2278 • revgdt@aol.com • MO • SHS/C • Missouri Saint Louis MO • (314)317-4550 • (SL 1982 STM)

**THOMAS JONATHAN ROBERT REV** (281)282-0924
14244 Oak Chase Dr Houston TX 77062-2037 • jthomas@gdlc.org • TX • Assoc • Gloria Dei Houston TX • (281)333-4535 • (SL 1994 MDIV)

**THOMAS RAYMOND K REV** (970)586-3017
1020 Lakeshore Dr Estes Park CO 80517-7158 • estesrkt@aol.com • RM • EM • (SL 1959)

**THOMAS STEVEN C REV** (208)278-5650
104 W Blvd New Plymouth ID 83655 • thomas.s.c@worldnet.alt.net • NOW • SP • Concordia Weiser ID* • (208)549-2563 • (SL 1999 MDIV)

**THOMAS STEVEN E REV** (920)324-2359
N2543 Banner Rd Waupun WI 53963-8901 • stthomas@powerweb.net • SW • Inst C • South Wisconsin Milwaukee WI • (414)464-8100 • (FW 1978 MDIV)

**THOMASON WARREN J REV** (941)475-1905
7021 Denmark St Englewood FL 34224-9501 • FG • SP • Redeemer Englewood FL • (941)475-2410 • (SC 1990 MDIV)

**THOMPSON BERT ANTHONY REV** (920)208-1695
924 Lincoln Ave Sheboygan WI 53081-2645 • SW • Assoc • St Paul Sheboygan WI • (414)452-6829 • (FW 1996 MDIV)

**THOMPSON CALVIN J REV** (256)881-1629
14003 Wyandotte Dr SW Huntsville AL 35803-2536 • calndee@aol.com • MNN • EM • (FW 1977 MDIV)

**THOMPSON DAVID BROOKS REV** (405)224-3918
1428 W Minnesota Ave Chickasha OK 73018-2954 • ecobill@swbell.net • OK • SP • First Chickasha OK • (405)224-1552 • (FW 1996 MDIV)

**THOMPSON DENNIS L REV** (708)748-9205
C/O Zion Lutheran Church 3840 216th St Matteson IL 60443-2717 • dennis95@aol.com • NI • SP • Zion Matteson IL • (708)747-1116 • (SL 1977 MDIV)

**THOMPSON DONALD F REV** (308)697-3625
RR 3 Box 40 Cambridge NE 69022-9203 • dontomp@csb.swnebr.net • NEB • SP • St Paul Cambridge NE • (308)697-3725 • (FW 1990 MDIV)

**THOMPSON DOUGLAS K REV** (734)728-4554
33024 Shawnee St Westland MI 48185-2710 • tkmtkd90@hotmail.com • MI • EM • (FW 1977 MDIV)

**THOMPSON DOUGLAS SCOTT REV** (406)633-2356
PO Box 7 Park City MT 59063 • bump@mcn.net • MT • SP • St Paul Park City MT • (406)633-2356 • (SL 1997 MDIV)

**THOMPSON GREGORY NOEL REV** (303)438-1333
10086 Zenobia Ct Westminster CO 80030-2536 • RM • Sn/Adm • Beaut Savior Broomfield CO • (303)469-1785 • (FW 1992 MDIV)

**THOMPSON JOHN L REV**
3530 Cape Forest Dr Kiingwood TX 77345-1654 • TX • Asst • Good Shepherd Pasadena TX • (281)479-1091 • (FW 1986 MDIV)

**THOMPSON MARK A REV** (217)227-3504
C/O Zion Lutheran Church PO Box 19 Farmersville IL 62533-0019 • SI • SP • Zion Farmersville IL • (217)227-3504 • (SL 1998 MDIV)

**THOMPSON RICHARD B REV** (318)525-1966
3312 Sandra Dr Shreveport LA 7119 • dick@nwla.comet • SO • SP • Faith Shreveport LA • (318)635-8084 • (SPR 1964 MA)

**THOMPSON RICHARD L REV** (920)262-1802
404 Bradley St Watertown WI 53094-5313 • rlt@execpc.com • SW • Sn/Adm • Good Shepherd Watertown WI • (920)261-2570 • (SPR 1973 MDIV DD)

**THOMPSON W MART REV** (417)235-3977
1111 14th St Monett MO 65708-1309 • cmt@mo-net.com • MO • SP • St John Monett MO • (417)235-3416 • (SL 1988 MDIV)

**THOMPSON WILLIAM E REV**
13667 W Highland Rd Hartland MI 48353-3127 • loehe@tir.com • EN • Assoc • Our Savior Hartland MI • (248)887-4300 • (FW 1988 MDIV)

**THOMPSON WILLIAM G REV** (210)493-9070
C/O Concordia Luth Church 16801 Huebner Rd San Antonio TX 78258-4456 • williamt@concordia-satx.com • TX • Sn/Adm • Concordia San Antonio TX • (210)479-1477 • (SPR 1973 MDIV DMIN)

**THOMSON JOHN M REV** (218)924-4050
PO Box 296 Bertha MN 56437 • MNN • 12/1999 • (FW 1993 MDIV)

**THORMODSON JEFFREY LUTHER REV**
C/O Board For Mission Ser Lcms 1333 S Kirkwood Rd Saint Louis MO 63122-7226 • jthormodson@excite.com • FG • S Miss • Florida-Georgia Orlando FL • (SL 1995 MDIV)

**THRESS EDWIN WILLIAM REV** (302)628-5379
715 W Ivy Dr Seaford DE 19973 • edellenthress@juno.com • SE • EM • (SL 1960 MDIV)

**THRESS MICHAEL PAUL REV** (919)751-2834
309 Jeannine Dr Goldsboro NC 27534-8892 • shellymike@juno.com • SE • SP • Peace Goldsboro NC • (919)778-2230 • (SL 1997 MDIV)

**THRIFT RICHARD A REV** (519)579-5786
96 Crosby Dr Kitchener ON N2B 2L2 CANADA • aw-ratz@softhome.net • EN • SP • Hope Kitchener ON CANADA • (519)893-5290 • (SC 1984 MDIV)

**THUR GARY R REV** (505)325-3420
1108 N Dustin Farmington NM 87401 • RM • SP • Zion Farmington NM • (505)325-3420 • (SL 1971 MDIV)

**THUR MELVIN E REV** (920)356-0078
204 Mc Kinley Beaver Dam WI 53916-1938 • thur@internetwes.com • SW • EM • (SL 1963 MDIV)

**THUR RICHARD F REV** (573)883-2260
735 Gettinger St Sainte Genevieve MO 63670-1901 • MO • SP • Holy Cross Sainte Genevieve MO • (573)883-5361 • (SL 1967 MDIV)

**THURAU MICHAEL R REV** (815)748-4713
3 Lee Ct Dekalb IL 60115-2630 • mrt@tbcnet.com • NI • Assoc • Immanuel De Kalb IL • (815)756-6669 • (SL 1987 MDIV MS)

**THYR ELMER D REV** (702)782-0255
877 Longleaf Pl Minden NV 89423 • CNH • EM • (SL 1952)

**TIADEN KEVIN NORMAN REV** (218)878-0763
110 14th St Cloquet MN 55720 • memmingen@aol.com • MNN • SP • St John Wrenshall MN • (218)384-4925 • (SL 1998 MDIV)

**TIBBEN KENT A REV** (217)446-2321
1429 Woodridge Dr Danville IL 61832-1669 • danetibb@aol.com • CI • Sn/Adm • Trinity Danville IL • (217)446-4300 • (FW 1992 MDIV)

**TIBBETTS RONALD EUGENE REV** (320)285-2297
PO Box 127 Grey Eagle MN 56336-0127 • MNN • SP • St John Grey Eagle MN • (320)285-2902 • (SL 1992 MDIV)

**TIEKEN RUSSELL W REV** (940)565-6369
2400 Natchez Trace Denton TX 76205-2932 • TX • SP • St Paul Denton TX • (940)387-1575 • (SL 1981 MDIV)

**TIEMAN LARRY W REV** (770)777-1269
2505 Clairview St Alpharetta GA 30004 • lstieman@att.net • FG • SP • Rivercliff Atlanta GA • (770)993-4316 • (SL 1991 MDIV)

**TIEMAN TERRY D REV** (901)753-7063
1736 Edgeburge Ln Cordova TN 38018-3550 • ttieman@aol.com • MDS • D Ex/S • Mid-South Cordova TN • (SL 1983 MDIV DMIN)

**TIEMANN DELBERT C DR** (716)334-3366
79 Barnfield Rd Pittsford NY 14534-2543 • EA • EM • (SPR 1956 DD)

**TIETJEN RICHARD H REV** (253)564-2028
4416 61st Ave W Tacoma WA 98466-6327 • rstietjen@aol.com • NOW • SP • Grace Tacoma WA • (253)472-7105 • (SL 1965 MDIV)

**TIETJEN WALTER C REV** (510)489-4611
35014 Clover St Union City CA 94587-5317 • cnhpres@aol.com • CNH • DP • Calif/Nevada/Hawaii San Francisco CA • (415)468-2336 • (SL 1961 DD)

**TILLMANN GARY W REV** (920)474-4749
St John Lutheran Church N 1245 St Johns Way Oconomowoc WI 53066-9539 • SW • SP • St John Oconomowoc WI • (414)474-4749 • (SL 2000 MDIV)

**TIMBO IBRAHIM S REV** (301)420-4075
2031 Brooks Dr Forestville MD 20747 • SE • O Miss • Southeastern Alexandria VA • (FW 1999 MDIV)

**TIMLER FERDINAND R REV** (920)849-9436
42 W Grand St Chilton WI 53014-1131 • SW • EM • (SPR 1961 MDIV)

**TIMM TERRY A REV**
C/O Angie Timm 1316 Galeth Apt A Norfolk NE 68701 • lcmsspb@neva.spb.ru • NEB • S Miss • Nebraska Seward NE • (SPR 1976 MDIV)

**TIMMER WILLIAM R SR. REV** (920)261-2027
N7976 High Rd Watertown WI 53094-9407 • SW • EM • (SPR 1968 MDIV)

**TIMMERMANN NORMAN ALVIN REV** (262)253-0417
W148N7346 Woodland Dr Menomonee Falls WI 53051-4518 • natimmer@exec.pc • EN • SP • Prince Peace Menomonee Falls WI • (262)251-3360 • (CQ 1980 MDIV)

**TIN DAVID S G REV** (415)664-5826
7 Lake Forest Ct San Francisco CA 94131-1024 • CNH • EM • (CQ 1986 MDIV)

**TINO JAMES C REV**
C/O Jet Cargo Intnl M 182 PO Box 20010 Miami FL 33102-0010 • MI • S Miss • Michigan Ann Arbor MI • (FW 1988 MDIV)

**TINO RICHARD L REV** (402)286-4157
C/O St Paul Luth Church PO Box 98 Winside NE 68790-0098 • antinomian@juno.com • NEB • SP • St Paul Winside NE • (402)286-4929 • (FW 1991 MDIV)

**TIPPIN EDWARD G REV** (228)255-4209
7814 Maui Ct Diamondhead MS 39525-3634 • SO • EM • (SPR 1952)

**TIRMENSTEIN LOUIS C REV** (513)867-8683
5 Patriot Crescent Hamilton OH 45013 • lctirmenstein@juno.com • OH • EM • (SL 1937 MDIV)

**TISCHER STEVEN LAVERNE REV** (763)444-8697
6525 261st Ave NW Saint Francis MN 55070-9345 • MNN • SP • Zion Saint Francis MN • (612)856-2099 • (FW 1993 MDIV)

**TODD GERALD E REV**
502 Fairway Ct Towson MD 21286-1124 • SE • SP • First Towson MD • (410)825-8770 • (SL 1977 MDIV)

**TODD GREGORY N REV** (718)815-4338
450 USS Florida CT#6 Straten Island NY 10305 • gntodd@hotmail.com • SI • M Chap • Southern Illinois Belleville IL • (SL 1988 MDIV)

**TODD KELLY D** (231)263-4800
6873 Carrollwood Ln Kingsley MI 49649 • MI • SP • St Johannes Kingsley MI • (231)263-5800 • (FW 2000)

**TOELKE CARL H JR. DR** (314)822-2668
1426 Dublin Dr Saint Louis MO 63126-1626 • chtoelke@aol.com • MO • S Ex/S • Missouri Saint Louis MO • (314)317-4550 • (SL 1965 MDIV MSW DMIN PHD)

**TOENJES ALAN M REV** (847)888-1102
335 Pleasant Dr South Elgin IL 60177-2141 • hjtoenjes@hotmail.com • NI • Northern Illinois Hillside IL • (SL 1991 MDIV STM)

**TOENSING MAYNARD L REV** (708)946-9020
28054 S Yates Ave Beecher IL 60401 • NI • SP • St John Beecher IL • (708)946-2561 • (SL 1992 MDIV)

**TOEPPER WESLEY A REV** (301)567-7070
5803 Black Hawk Dr Forest Heights MD 20745-1210 • toepper@erols.com • SE • EM • (SL 1962 MDIV)

**TOLLEFSON RICHARD C REV** (253)549-2791
1078 Paiute Trl Fox Island WA 98333-9627 • NOW • EM • (SPR 1962)

**TOLZMAN BRION P REV** (402)846-5935
206 N Broughton PO Box 252 Walthill NE 68067-0252 • tolzie@huntel.net • NEB • SP • Trinity Walthill NE* • (402)846-5027 • (SL 1986 MDIV)

**TOMASOVIC PAUL REV** (210)673-8688
4917 Ravenswood Dr #43B HCC San Antonio TX 78227-4300 • TX • EM • * • (SL 1936 MA)

**TOMESCH HARALD REV** (414)540-6402
380 E Mac Arthur Rd Fox Point WI 53217 • htomesch@bach.cuw.edu • SW • SHS/C • South Wisconsin Milwaukee WI • (414)464-8100 • (SC 1981 MTH MDIV THD)

**TOMHAVE GREGORY J REV** (320)252-8171
Redeemer Luth Church 2719 N Third St Saint Cloud MN 56303 • MNN • 05/1999 • (FW 1987 MDIV)

**TOMPKINS DARYL G REV** (605)539-1297
C/O Zion Lutheran Church PO Box 308 Wessington Springs SD 57382-0308 • pastordaryl@sullybuttes.net • SD • SP • Zion Wessingtn Spg SD* • (605)539-1297 • (SL 1997 MDIV)

**TOMPKINS DONALD L REV** (440)354-3432
537 Greenside Dr Painesville OH 44077-4879 • dltompkins@ncweb.com • OH • SP • Immanuel Fairport Harbor OH • (440)357-7446 • (SPR 1967 MDIV)

**TONACK DONALD P REV** (503)926-2820
2154 Meadow Pl SE Albany OR 97321-5560 • NOW • EM • (SL 1980 MDIV)

**TONCRE WESLEY M REV** (318)631-7580
5734 Lakefront Dr Shreveport LA 71119-3915 • wtoncre@nwla.com • SO • SP • St Paul Shreveport LA • (318)636-2310 • (SL 1962 MDIV DMIN)

**TONN RANDELL E REV** (956)765-6197
1005 Blossum Blvd PO Box 1007 Za Pata TX 78076 • randytonn@juno.com • EN • EM • (SL 1959 STM)

**TOOPES ANDREW W REV** (501)847-6511
208 Morningside Dr Bryant AR 72022-3274 • revatoopes@juno.com • MDS • Sn/Adm • Zion Alexander AR • (501)316-1100 • (FW 1983 MDIV)

**TORGLER ROBERT H REV** (865)458-8732
109 Kawatuska Way Loudon TN 37774-2636 • SE • EM • (SL 1951 MDIV)

**TORKELSON DANIEL T REV** (712)365-2590
600 Fifth St Battle Creek IA 51006 • lthpastr@pionet.net • IW • SP • St John Battle Creek IA • (712)365-4477 • (SL 1997 MST MDIV)

**TORMOEHLEN ALGER J REV**
3122 Country Bluff Dr Saint Charles MO 63301-3741 • MO • EM • (CQ 1977 MED)

**TORNOW HANS R REV** (630)543-2959
202 N Country Club Dr Addison IL 60101-2109 • NI • EM • (SPR 1946)

**TORNOW LOTHAR V REV** (714)549-3233
2414 S Manitoba Dr Santa Ana CA 92704-5012 • PSW • EM • (SL 1948)

**TORRES LUIS A SR. REV** (216)281-8250
3286 W 44th St Cleveland OH 44109-1074 • EN • SP • Iglesia Cristiana Hi Cleveland OH • (216)651-0236 • (CQ 1986)

**TOTH DUSAN REV** (416)221-0418
55 Allview Cres Willowdale ON M2J 2R4 CANADA • dusan@pathcom.com • EN • Asst • St Luke North York ON CANADA • (416)221-8900 • (EU 1961 MA)

**TOTSKY DAVID W REV** (608)586-4848
142 E Vallete St PO Box 141 Oxford WI 53952-0141 • dtots@maqs.net • SW • SP • St John Oxford WI* • (608)586-5877 • (FW 1989 MDIV STM)

**TOTTEN MICHAEL R REV** (510)481-7018
16079 Via Harriet San Lorenzo CA 94580-1919 • CNH • SP • Hope San Leandro CA • (510)351-7410 • (FW 1979 MDIV PHD)

**TOWNES RICHARD ARTHUR REV** (605)692-6983
621 9th Ave Brookings SD 57006-1523 • revrat@brookings.net • SD • SP • Mount Calvary Brookings SD • (605)692-2678 • (FW 1994 MDIV)

**TOWNSEND JOSEPH E REV** (765)463-6702
81 Peregrine Ct W Lafayette IN 47906 • redeemer@integrityonline32.com • IN • SP • Redeemer West Lafayette IN • (765)463-5851 • (FW 1980 MDIV)

**TRAHMS VERNON T REV** (623)546-8270
21925 N Montego Dr Sun City West AZ 85375-2941 • e.v.trahms@prodigy.net • PSW • EM • (SL 1953 MDIV)

**TRAPP ALLEN R REV** (440)845-9821
5221 Sequoia Dr Parma OH 44134-6133 • OH • SP • St John South Euclid OH • (216)381-1513 • (SL 1972 MDIV)

**TRAPP THOMAS H REV** (651)645-2223
1698 Hubbard Ave Saint Paul MN 55104-1130 • ttrapp@csp.edu • MNS • SHS/C • Minnesota South Burnsville MN • (SL 1971 MDIV DTH)

**TRASK MICHAEL A REV** (612)497-1386
5270 Lannon Ave NE Albertville MN 55301 • 72056.3406@compserve.com • MNS • SP • Life In Christ Albertville MN • (612)497-3799 • (SL 1986 MDIV)

**TRAUGOTT FREDERICK W REV** (248)528-9340
4221 Marywood Dr Troy MI 48098-3652 • MI • Assoc • Faith Troy MI • (248)689-4664 • (SPR 1969 MDIV MA)

**TRAUTMANN KARL H REV** (810)795-3743
2133 E 14 Mile Rd # 110 Sterling Hts MI 48310-5904 • MI • EM • (SL 1941)

**TRAVIS MARTIN L REV** (217)942-3205
327 Church St Carrollton IL 62016-1124 • SI • EM • (SPR 1955 MDIV STM)

**TREGLOWN DONALD E REV**
PO Box 81039 8000 Davao City PHILIPPINES • tregfam@interasia.com.ph • EN • S Miss • English Farmington MI • (FW 1987 MDIV)

**TREICHEL HERBERT W REV** (612)645-3044
1272 Dayton Ave Saint Paul MN 55104-6438 • MNS • EM • (CQ 1970 MA MS)

**TREMAIN PETER D REV** (913)228-0804
6448 SW Castle Ln Topeka KS 66614-4391 • KS • Sn/Adm • Faith Topeka KS • (785)272-4214 • (SL 1969 MDIV DMIN)

**TREMAIN RICHARD D REV** (812)342-3902
4085 W 200 S Columbus IN 47201-9636 • rtremain@hsonline.net • IN • EM • (SL 1955 MS)

**TREUDE JOHN M REV** (773)252-1104
1410 N Springfield Ave Chicago IL 60651-2042 • NI • SP • Bethel Chicago IL • (773)252-1104 • (SL 1985 MDIV)

**TREWYN JOHN I SR. REV** (515)463-2341
3337 220th St Manson IA 50563 • greenbay43@hotmail.com • IW • SP • Trinity Manson IA • (515)463-2244 • (SL 1998 MDIV)

**TRICKEY GARY G REV** (801)479-3541
4875 Kiwana Dr Ogden UT 84403-4213 • gtrickey@stpaullcms.org • RM • SP • St Paul Ogden UT • (801)392-6368 • (CQ 1983 MED)

**TRIEGLAFF EUGENE E DR** (414)245-1677
821 Legend Dr Lake Geneva WI 53147-5015 • NI • EM • (SL 1961 MA)

**TRIER ORLANDO E REV** (503)288-6528
6439 NE 35th Pl Portland OR 97211-7271 • otrier@cu-portland.edu • NOW • SP • St Michael Portland OR • (503)282-0000 • (SL 1971 MDIV)

**TRIMBERGER DALE H REV** (812)378-3362
3960 Waycross Dr Columbus IN 47203-3526 • IN • Assoc • St Peter Columbus IN • (812)372-1571 • (SPR 1966 MDIV)

**TRINKLEIN EDGAR A REV** (863)644-6140
1882 Stella Ct S Lakeland FL 33813-2477 • etrink@juno.com • FG • EM • (SL 1957 MDIV)

**TRINKLEIN JOHN HANS KARL REV** (402)329-4527
516 E Nebraska St Pierce NE 68767-1632 • zionhans@ptcnet.net • NEB • Assoc • Zion Pierce NE • (402)329-4313 • (SL 1995 MDIV MA)

**TRINKLEIN JONATHAN B REV** (402)891-2680
7019 Joyce St Omaha NE 68138 • jbtsmt@aol.com • NEB • Assoc • King Of Kings Omaha NE • (402)333-6464 • (SL 1981 MDIV)

**TRINKLEIN ROBERT A REV** (320)363-1323
PO Box 88 Saint Joseph MN 56374-0088 • anewme777@juno.com • MNN • SP • Our Savior Saint Cloud MN • (320)251-7821 • (FW 1978 MA)

**TRIPLETT DAVID S REV** (716)735-7970
4250 Freeman Rd Middleport NY 14105-9640 • brodave3@juno.com • EA • SP • Holy Cross Middleport NY • (716)735-7209 • (FW 1980 MDIV)

**TRITTEN ERIC E REV**
791 Laird Rd Lake Orion MI 48362 • tribefans@juno.com • MI • Assoc • Good Shepherd Lake Orion MI • (248)391-1170 • (SL 1998 MDIV)

**TROESTER JEROME A REV** (402)465-4642
8124 Leighton Ave Lincoln NE 68507 • jtroeste@santel.net • NEB • Assoc • Faith Lincoln NE • (402)466-6861 • (SL 1983 MDIV)

**TROESTER MATTHEW D REV** (708)479-6986
19555 Willowfield Ct Mokena IL 60448-1788 • mdtroester@sprintmail.com • NI • SP • St Paul Matteson IL • (708)720-0880 • (SL 1984 MDIV)

**TROSIEN CARL F REV** (517)893-5266
1611 Nebobish Ave Essexville MI 48732-1611 • trosien5@concentric.net • MI • SP • Pilgrim Essexville MI • (517)893-7224 • (SL 1978 MDIV)

**TROSIEN WILLIAM J REV** (715)479-6757
1379 Bluebird Ln Eagle River WI 54521-9775 • NW • SP • Our Savior Eagle River WI • (715)479-6226 • (SL 1980 MDIV)

**TROST EDWARD WM REV** (913)894-2389
11216 W 106th St Overland Park KS 66214-2668 • et@tfs.net • KS • Sn/Adm • Bethany Shawnee Mission KS • (913)648-2228 • (SL 1967 MDIV)

**TROUP ANTONIN REV** (618)939-8379
520 S Church St Waterloo IL 62298-1429 • SI • Sn/Adm • Immanuel Waterloo IL • (618)939-6480 • (SL 1984 MDIV)

**TROUT LARRY JAMES REV** (815)338-7831
523 St Johns Rd Woodstock IL 60098 • lutheran.church@mindspring.com • NI • Assoc • St John Woodstock IL • (815)338-5159 • (SL 1995 MDIV)

**TROUTEN CHAD DAVID REV** (765)348-3910
403 W Main St Hartford City IN 47348-2014 • weaserex@netusa1.net • IN • SP • Prince of Peace Hartford City IN • (765)348-3910 • (FW 1995 MDIV)

**TROVALL CARL CURTIS REV** (512)251-0728
17223 Village Glen Rd Pflugerville TX 78660-1859 • trovallc@concordia.edu • TX • SHS/C • Texas Austin TX • (SL 1987 MDIV)

**TROWBRIDGE GARY D REV** (402)748-3649
PO Box 38 Osmond NE 68765-0038 • olddogs@huntel.net • NEB • SP • Immanuel Osmond NE • (402)748-3301 • (FW 1977 MDIV)

**TROXEL LARRY D REV** (217)224-9000
2823 Payson Hts Dr Quincy IL 62301-6431 • troxel@rnet.com • CI • Sn/Adm • Our Redeemer Quincy IL • (217)223-1769 • (SPR 1970 MDIV)

**TROYKE JAMES F REV** (417)739-5757
116 Shiloh Ln Kimberling City MO 65686-9763 • troyke@tri-lakes.net • MO • SP • Shepherd Hills Kimberling City MO • (417)739-2512 • (SL 1972 MDIV)

**TRUAX CHARLES J REV** (504)643-9760
1331 Patriot Dr Slidell LA 70458-2131 • candcin@accesscom.net • SO • Asst • Bethany Slidell LA • (504)643-3043 • (SL 1972 MDIV)

**TRUEBLOOD ROBERT CAIRL REV** (507)235-2644
1623 170th St Fairmont MN 56031-1305 • didache@bigfoot.com • MNS • SP • Zion Fairmont MN* • (507)235-5153 • (FW 1988 MDIV)

**TRUEMPER DAVID G REV** (219)464-1351
1557 Sherwood Dr Valparaiso IN 46385-2806 • david.truemper@valpo.edu • IN • END • Indiana Fort Wayne IN • (SL 1965 MDIV STM PHD)

**TRUENOW DAVID LUTHER REV** (218)784-4712
C/O Saint John Luth Ch 2948 240th Ave Ada MN 56510-9521 • truefour@means.net • MNN • SP • St Johns Ada MN* • (218)784-4644 • (SL 1996 MDIV)

**TRUOG BRIAN M REV** (630)553-5809
8545 State Route 47 Yorkville IL 60560-9751 • btruog@juno.com • NI • Assoc • Cross Yorkville IL • (630)553-7335 • (SL 1982 MDIV STM)

**TRUOG OTTO N REV** (316)283-8718
1509 Westborough Dr Newton KS 67114-1479 • KS • EM • (SPR 1944)

**TSANG JAMES REV** (419)866-1772
C/O Trinity Lutheran Church 4560 Glendale Ave Toledo OH 43614 • OH • D Miss • Trinity Toledo OH • (419)385-2651 • (CQ 1980 MDIV MTH)

**TUCHARDT PAUL L REV** (360)687-4170
C/O Prince Of Peace Luth Ch 14208 NE 249th St Battle Ground WA 98604-9772 • NOW • SP • Prince Of Peace Battle Ground WA • (360)687-7455 • (SPR 1962)

**TUCKER WILLIAM H REV** (847)255-9191
7 N Maple St Mt Prospect IL 60056 • friartuc@aol.com • NI • Sn/Adm • St Paul Mount Prospect IL • (847)255-0332 • (FW 1987 MDIV)

**TUMBUAN DINO F REV** (562)422-4843
6025 Cerritos Ave Long Beach CA 90805-3051 • PSW • SP • St John Long Beach CA • (323)423-3547 • (CQ 1989 MDIV MS)

**TURANSKI TED N REV** (231)258-8189
PO Box 524 Kalkaska MI 49646 • MI • SP • St Paul Kalkaska MI • (231)258-9258 • (SL 1972 MDIV)

**TURNER JAMES W REV** (248)356-1351
22986 Park Place Dr Southfield MI 48034-2661 • MI • SP • Holy Cross Detroit MI • (313)836-2272 • (CQ 1997 MA)

**TURNER RICHARD T JR. REV** (281)422-2960
1405 Coyote Ln Baytown TX 77521-3511 • Pastor$^3$Turner@juno.com • TX • SP • Redeemer Baytown TX • (281)422-2207 • (FW 1988 MDIV)

**TURNER STEVEN D REV** (515)295-3680
605 N Church St Algona IA 50511-1708 • steve.turner@iowawest.org • IW • Sn/Adm • Trinity Algona IA • (515)295-3518 • (FW 1985 MDIV)

**TURNER WALLACE B REV** (619)292-4863
10858 Rueda Ct San Diego CA 92124-2125 • wtu8584760@ol.com • PSW • EM • (SL 1962 MDIV DMIN)

**TURSIC RICHARD ERNEST REV**
China Ministry Team 12 Wiltshire Rd Kowloon Tong HONG KONG • OH • S Miss • Ohio Olmsted Falls OH • (FW 1996 MDIV)

**TUSCHLING CHARLES FREDERICK** (616)977-5920
3604 E Fulton St GAE # 130 Grand Rapids MI 49546-1384 • tuschling@yahoo.com • MI • EM • (SL 1950 MSW)

**TUSTY JULIUS B REV** (718)969-0484
75-89 Utopia Pkwy Flushing NY 11366-1526 • AT • EM • (SL 1939 MDIV MA)

**TUTWILER DANNY W REV** (708)773-2324
404 N Rush St Itasca IL 60143-1846 • dtutlyn@aol.com • NI • Sn/Adm • St Luke Itasca IL • (630)773-0396 • (SL 1982 MDIV DMIN)

**TWENHAFEL ARNOLD G REV** (913)773-8591
34748 243rd St Easton KS 66020-8039 • KS • SP • St John Easton KS • (913)773-8591 • (SL 1947 MED)

**TWENHAFEL RICK JOHN REV** (913)886-6430
C/O St Matthew Lutheran Church PO Box 297 Nortonville KS 66060-0297 • twenhafel@hotmail.com • KS • SP • St Matthew Nortonville KS • (913)886-6331 • (SL 1994 MDIV)

**TYLER GREGORY C REV** (763)494-9464
9463 Teakwood Ln N Maple Grove MN 55369-7121 • MNS • SP • St Paul Osseo MN • (612)425-2238 • (FW 1987 MDIV)

**TYLER JAMES W REV** (661)871-0927
3104 Vassar St Bakersfield CA 93306-2540 • CNH • SP • Bethany Bakersfield CA • (661)399-3532 • (CQ 1968)

**TYVELA LESLIE D REV** (517)892-8245
1600 10th St Bay City MI 48708-6743 • MI • SP • Immanuel Bay City MI • (517)893-4088 • (SPR 1968 MDIV MA)

## U

**UDE DONALD E REV** (254)939-7920
3766 Smoke Signal Rd Belton TX 76513-5615 • TX • EM • (SL 1958 MDIV)

**UDE STEPHEN C REV**
PO Box L Ogden IA 50212-0812 • IW • SP • Zion Ogden IA • (515)275-2234 • (SPR 1971 MDIV)

**UDE WILLIS P REV** (828)696-8144
110 Thrashing Rock Dr Hendersonville NC 28739-9388 • texaspreacher@juno.com • TX • EM • (SL 1951 MA)

**UDIT DAVID RAMARACK REV** (718)526-6290
89-24 145th St Jamaica NY 11435-3620 • AT • SP • Grace Jamaica NY • (718)526-6290 • (CQ 1995 MA DMIN)

**UDOEKONG MICHAEL D REV** (708)849-6979
C/O St Paul Lutheran Church 245 E 138th St Dolton IL 60419-1060 • NI • SP • St Paul Dolton IL • (708)849-6929 • (SL 1996 MDIV)

**UECKER WARREN W REV** (605)256-4372
904 NE 5th St Madison SD 57042-2418 • SD • SP • Our Savior Madison SD • (605)256-4483 • (SL 1981)

**UECKERT WARREN C REV** (602)526-9578
C/O Peace Luth Church 3430 N 4th St Flagstaff AZ 86004-1764 • PSW • SP • Peace Flagstaff AZ • (520)526-9578 • (SPR 1975 MST)

**UFFENBECK WILLIAM J REV** (608)676-4994
208 High St PO Box 308 Clinton WI 53525-9476 • SW • Sn/Adm • Christ Clinton WI • (608)676-4994 • (SL 1971 MDIV)

**UHLES PAUL F REV** (254)622-8156
Cedar Shores Estates Rt 1 Box 611 Morgan TX 76671-9716 • uhlespl@hillsboro.net • TX • EM • (SPR 1953 MDIV MA)

**UHLIG JOHN P REV** (760)435-2405
Carlsbad By The Sea 2855 Carlsbad Blvd Apt N113 Carlsbad CA 92008 • revjpu@juno.com • CNH • EM • (SL 1937 PHD)

**UHLIG WALTER D REV** (913)268-8194
7405 Larsen Ln Shawnee KS 66203-4533 • wuhlig@compuserve.com • KS • EM • (SL 1938 MDIV STM MA)

**ULLMAN WALTER W REV** (812)477-8244
2600 E Powell Ave Evansville IN 47714-2548 • walter.ullman@gte.net • IN • Sn/Adm • St Paul Evansville IN • (812)422-5414 • (SL 1973 MDIV MA)

**ULM DAVID M REV** (810)949-5082
28448 Raleigh Cres Chesterfield MI 48051-2309 • MI • SP • Good Shepherd New Baltimore MI • (810)949-9440 • (FW 1980 MDIV)

**ULMER MARVIN W REV** (660)547-3885
400 Crescent Dr PO Box 274 Lincoln MO 65338-0274 • mjulmer@iland.net • MO • EM • (SPR 1965 MA MDIV)

**ULRICH EDWARD C REV** (503)648-6164
2590 NE Anna Hillsboro OR 97124-3204 • NOW • EM • (SPR 1953)

**ULRICH LESLIE E REV** (206)361-7914
19236 25th NE Seattle WA 98155 • NOW • EM • (SL 1958 MDIV)

**UMBACH ARTHUR M REV** (804)897-0160
2711 Valley Springs Rd Powhatan VA 23139-5237 • arthuru@aol.com • SE • D Ex/S • Southeastern Alexandria VA • (SL 1969 MDIV)

**UMBACH WALTER O REV** (660)463-1169
509 Sandia Dr PO Box 993 Concordia MO 64020-0993 • MO • EM • (CQ 1983 MA)

**UMBARGER KENT A REV** (309)757-7613
1316 29th Ave Moline IL 61265 • k$^3$alan$^3$u@yahoo.com • CI • SP • St John East Moline IL • (309)792-0755 • (FW 1987 MDIV)

**UNGER RALPH E REV** (810)751-3778
11299 Irene Ave Warren MI 48093-6543 • oxunger@aol.com • MI • EM • (SL 1956 MDIV)

**UNGRODT RICHARD JAMES REV** (219)393-5287
3645 S Wayne Dr La Porte IN 46350-9262 • ungrodt@adsnet.net • IN • Asst • St John La Porte IN • (219)362-3726 • (FW 1981 MDIV)

**UPDEGRAVE STEPHEN W REV** (301)475-7814
40965 Knight Rd Leonardtown MD 20650-2211 • prsteveup@aol.com • SE • SP • Trinity Lexington Park MD • (301)863-9512 • (FW 1989 MDIV)

**URBACH DONALD E DR** (320)864-4427
1406 Armstrong Ave Glencoe MN 55336-1227 • MNS • EM • (CQ 1989 PHD)

**URBACH JON BRADFORD REV** (605)224-2838
803 N Grand Ave Pierre SD 57501-1605 • jburbach@dtgnet.com • SD • Sn/Adm • Faith Pierre SD • (605)224-2216 • (SL 1971 MDIV)

**URBAN OTTO H REV**
PMB 15663 256 Rainbow Dr Livingston TX 77399-2056 • TX • EM • (SL 1957 MA)

**UTECH WILLIAM G REV** (636)230-8696
937 Forest Lake Ct Ballwin MO 63021-6064 • utechw@csl.edu • S • SHS/C • Missouri Saint Louis MO • (314)317-4550 • (SL 1985 MDIV STM)

**UTECHT ANDREW EMIL REV** (605)747-2448
PO Box 558 Rosebud SD 57570 • SD • D Miss • South Dakota Sioux Falls SD • (FW 1997 MDIV)

**UTECHT PETER MATTHEW REV**
221 East 1st St Redfield SD 57469 • church1@fia.net • SD • SP • Messiah Redfield SD* • (605)472-0730 • (FW 1994 MDIV)

**UTECHT ROBERT E REV** (605)584-2729
HC 37 Box 2432 Lead SD 57754-9721 • momdadu@juno.com • SD • O Miss • South Dakota Sioux Falls SD • (SPR 1953)

**UTTECH GARY REUBEN DR** (715)453-5865
104 S 2nd St Tomahawk WI 54487-1205 • revbo@newnorth.net • NW • Inst C • North Wisconsin Wausau WI • (CQ 1994 MDIV DMIN)

**UTTECH WILLIAM A REV** (715)526-2537
466 S Lincoln St Apt 4 Shawano WI 54166-2466 • NW • Asst • St James Shawano WI • (715)524-4815 • (SL 1933)

## V

**VAHLE MICHAEL T REV** (520)634-7256
PO Box 793 Clarkdale AZ 86324-0793 • PSW • SP • Faith Cottonwood AZ • (520)634-7876 • (FW 1981 MDIV)

**VAIL CLAYTON G REV** (513)202-9203
109 Circle Dr Harrison OH 45030-2803 • OH • SP • Amazing Grace Harrison OH • (513)367-5094 • (FW 1978 MDIV)

**VAJDA JAROSLAV J REV** (314)892-9473
3534 Brookstone South Dr Saint Louis MO 63129-2900 • S • EM • (SL 1944 MDIV)

**VALERIANO MERNILO CLEMENTE** (510)441-8798
3240 San Andreas Dr Union City CA 94587-2719 • CNH • 12/1994 12/1999 • (CQ 1992 MDIV)

**VALLEJO GABRIEL ENRIQUE REV** (408)729-8832
611 Detroit Ct San Jose CA 95133-2054 • CNH • Assoc • First Immanuel San Jose CA • (408)292-5404 • (CQ 1996)

**VALLIE JOHN C REV**
C/O Concordia Luth Church PO Box 1258 Forsyth MT 59327 • MT • SP • Concordia Forsyth MT* • (406)356-7614 • (SL 2000 MDIV)

**VAN DELLEN JAMES H REV** (248)391-4625
2407 Browning Dr Lake Orion MI 48360-1809 • pastorvan@juno.com • MI • Sn/Adm • Good Shepherd Lake Orion MI • (248)391-1170 • (SPR 1970 MDIV)

**VAN DER BLOEMEN THOMAS G REV** (970)635-9842
1964 E 16th St Loveland CO 80538-4361 • tmvan@prodigy.net • RM • EM • (TH 1956 MDIV DMIN)

**VAN DUZER THOMAS N REV** (281)980-3132
3039 Pasture Ln Sugar Land TX 77479-1800 • vanduzet@flash.net • TX • Sn/Adm • Fishers Of Men Sugar Land TX • (281)242-7711 • (SL 1979 MDIV)

**VAN FOSSAN KURT A REV** (303)657-3558
6244 Quitman St Arvada CO 80003 • kurt.vanfossan@intellink.net • RM • SP • Faith Denver CO • (303)455-5878 • (SL 1987 MDIV)

**VAN KANEGAN VICTOR J REV** (847)864-0561
1406 Wilder St Evanston IL 60202-1181 • NI • SP • Bethlehem Evanston IL • (847)328-9454 • (FW 1982 MA)

**VAN MEHREN RANDY C REV**
115 Marys Dr Louisiana MO 63353 • MO • SP • Trinity Louisiana MO* • (573)754-6120 • (FW 1997 MDIV)

**VAN NOSTRAND CARL W REV** (515)356-4406
C/O St John Lutheran Church 2980 170th St Vincent IA 50594-7533 • cwvn@netins.net • IW • SP • St John Vincent IA* • (515)356-4406 • (SL 1992 MDIV)

**VAN OSDOL JEFFREY M REV** (864)297-5815
2820 Woodruff Rd Simpsonville SC 29681 • revjvan@bellsouth.net • SE • SP • Immanuel Simpsonville SC • (864)297-5815 • (FW 1992 MDIV)

**VAN PATTEN PAUL LYLE JR. DR** (580)233-3449
1913 W Oklahoma Enid OK 73703 • OK • 06/1998 06/2000 • (FW 1996 MDIV PHD)

**VAN SCYOC ERIC L REV** (440)331-2680
C/O St Thomas Luth Church 21211 Detroit Rd Rocky River OH 44116-2213 • vanscyoce@aol.com • OH • Sn/Adm • St Thomas Rocky River OH • (440)331-2680 • (SL 1987 MDIV)

**VANCE PHILLIP E REV** (402)727-7901
1022 Edearl Ln Fremont NE 68025 • im4stlcards@yahoo.com • NEB • Sn/Adm • Trinity Fremont NE • (402)721-5536 • (FW 1993 MDIV)

**VANDER WERF MARC REV** (303)471-1931
9331 S Desert Willow Rd Highlands Ranch CO 80129 • RM • SP • Holy Cross Highlands Ranch CO • (303)683-1300 • (CQ 1981 MAR)

**VANDERBILT THOMAS W REV** (715)823-2588
157 N Clinton Ave Clintonville WI 54929-1248 • tsvandy@frontiernet.net • NW • Asst • St Martin Clintonville WI • (715)823-6538 • (SL 1997 MDIV)

**VANDERHYDE CHARLES ARTHUR** (303)739-0378
881 Ursula St Aurora CO 80011-6655 • cvanderhyde@juno.com • RM • EM • (SL 1961 MDIV)

**VANDERHYDE JONATHAN M REV** (307)877-3696
805 Antelope Kemmerer WY 83101 • jvhyde@hotmail.com • WY • SP • St Paul Kemmerer WY • (307)877-4210 • (FW 1989 MDIV)

**VANEK JAMES A REV** (715)327-8931
12110 Pickerel Pt Grantsburg WI 54840-8410 • NW • SP • Christ Grantsburg WI* • (715)822-3096 • (SL 1965 MDIV)

**VANG YIA ZONG REV** (414)426-8725
415 Boyd St Oshkosh WI 54901-5135 • yzvang@aol.com • SW • D Miss • Hmong Oshkosh WI • (414)235-7440 • (SL 1993 MDIV)

**VANGEN PHILIP MARK REV** (262)642-9337
3242 Superior Ave East Troy WI 53120-1100 • pvangen@netwurx.net • SW • SP • Good Shepherd East Troy WI • (262)642-3310 • (CQ 1988 MDIV STM)

**VANSELOW THOMAS W REV** (219)268-1721
618 N Harrison St Warsaw IN 46580 • tvanselow@juno.com • IN • SP • Redeemer Warsaw IN • (219)267-5656 • (FW 1989 MDIV)

**VARGA ERNEST L REV** (518)877-5370
5 Garrison Ln Ballston Lake NY 12019-1219 • AT • Inst C • Atlantic Bronxville NY • (914)337-5700 • (FW 1979 MDIV)

**VARSOGEA CHARLES EVERETT REV** (219)747-0714
2435 Engle Rd Fort Wayne IN 46809-1408 • cvarsogea@home.com • EN • SP • Bethany Fort Wayne IN • (219)747-0713 • (FW 1995 MDIV)

**VARVARIS PETER WILLIAM REV** (704)873-7326
518 Stinson Ct Statesville NC 28677-3314 • pvarvaris@conninc.com • SE • SP • Holy Trinity Statesville NC • (704)873-3591 • (SL 1997 MDIV)

**VASCONCELLOS A PAUL REV** (402)643-4095
1480 Karol Kay Blvd Seward NE 68434-1197 • NEB • SHS/C • Nebraska Seward NE • (SL 1964 MDIV MED MS PHD)

**VAUDT ERWIN REV** (507)943-3173
PO Box 26 Elmore MN 56027-0026 • MNS • EM • (SL 1945)

**VAUDT STEVEN C REV** (715)882-2919
PO Box 238 White Lake WI 54491-0238 • NW • SP • St Matthew White Lake WI • (715)882-3111 • (CQ 1982 MDIV)

**VAUGHAN TIMOTHY BRYAN REV** (218)367-2473
C/O St John Luth Church RR 2 Box 674 Ottertail MN 56571-9606 • revtv@digitaljam.com • MNN • SP • St John Ottertail MN* • (218)367-2470 • (FW 1992 MDIV)

**VAUGHN JOHN P REV** (612)440-2720
17120 Pheasant Meadow Ln SW Prior Lake MN 55372-2760 • pastorjpv@aol.com • MNS • Sn/Adm • St Paul Prior Lake MN • (952)447-2117 • (FW 1978 MDIV)

**VAVROCH JOHN REV** (440)871-2714
26707 Normandy Rd Bay Village OH 44140-2321 • OH • SP • Unity Cleveland OH • (216)741-2085 • (SPR 1963 MA)

**VEDDER LAWRENCE M REV** (208)733-5196
1339 Evergreen Dr Twin Falls ID 83301-3422 • immanuel@ltlink.com • NOW • SP • Immanuel Twin Falls ID • (208)733-7820 • (CQ 1988)

**VEHLING ARNOLD E REV**
C/O Bethany Luth Church 1201 Dubuque St Sioux City IA 51105-2658 • IW • EM • (SL 1936)

**VEHLING JAMES J REV** (954)966-2727
3916 Jefferson St Hollywood FL 33021-7314 • vehlingj@msn.com • FG • SP • St Mark Hollywood FL • (954)922-7568 • (SL 1966 MDIV MA)

**VEIT BENJAMIN F REV** (405)353-3113
1728 NW 31st St Lawton OK 73505-3845 • revben@aol.com • OK • EM • (SL 1957 MA)

**VEITENGRUBER DONALD P REV** (810)622-9653
PO Box 625 Port Sanilac MI 48469-0625 • veitengd@iserv.net • MI • SP • St John Port Sanilac MI • (810)622-9653 • (SL 1964 STM)

**VELAND LARRY A REV** (307)754-8287
454 Hamilton Way Powell WY 82435-3112 • heb13-20@warecom.net • WY • SP • Immanuel Powell WY • (307)754-3168 • (CQ 1984 MS)

**VENZKE RODGER R REV** (314)531-5972
4422 Westminster Pl Saint Louis MO 63108-1813 • rodger.venzke@lcms.org • SE • S Ex/S • Southeastern Alexandria VA • (SL 1961 MS MTH STM)

**VERITY TIMOTHY M REV** (517)426-2815
1590 N Shaw Rd Gladwin MI 48624-8751 • MI • SP • Our Savior Gladwin MI • (517)426-9689 • (FW 1982 MDIV)

**VERNAVA MICHAEL N REV** (559)582-8057
195 E Sherwood Dr Hanford CA 93230-1261 • CNH • SP • First Hanford CA • (559)582-2463 • (FW 1989 MDIV)

**VERSEMANN MATTHEW OLIVER REV** (828)894-5518
PO Box 1356 Columbus NC 28722 • SE • SP • Trinity Tryon NC • (828)859-0379 • (SL 1991 MDIV)

**VESEY MATTHEW W REV**
C/O Saint Paul Lutheran Church 600 5th Ave S Mount Vernon IA 52314-1757 • IE • SP • St Paul Mount Vernon IA • (319)895-8772 • (FW 1993 MDIV)

**VETTER EUGENE H REV** (623)584-9416
18211 N Alyssum Dr Sun City West AZ 85375-5022 • ehjlvetter@aol.com • PSW • EM • (SL 1950 MDIV MS)

**VICIAN LOUIS R** (708)532-5918
7421 W 161st St Tinley Park IL 60477 • NI • SP • Mount Greenwood Chicago IL • (773)445-6080 • (FW 2000)

**VICK CALVIN T REV** (864)268-0406
10 Guyton St Greenville SC 29615-1932 • SE • EM • (SL 1964 MDIV MA)

**VIEKER JON D REV** (636)225-6052
1025 Villaview Dr Manchester MO 63021 • jon.vieker@lcms.org • MO • S Ex/S • Missouri Saint Louis MO • (314)317-4550 • (SL 1987 MDIV MST)

**VIERGUTZ WILLIAM H REV**
C/O Trinity Lutheran Church 338 7th St Burlington CO 80807-1971 • RM • SP • Trinity Burlington CO • (719)346-7401 • (SL 1987 MDIV)

**VIESELMEYER DEAN M REV** (714)838-3573
14652 Danborough Rd Tustin CA 92780-6756 • vieseldm@cui.edu • PSW • SHS/C • Pacific Southwest Irvine CA • (949)854-3232 • (SPR 1974 MS MDIV PHD)

**VIETS MARK L REV** (440)748-3673
38363 Royalton Rd Grafton OH 44044-9184 • mkbrbviets@mciworld.com • OH • SP • Trinity Grafton OH • (440)748-2154 • (SL 1970 MDIV)

**VIGIL LEOPOLDO REV** (956)423-1335
1610 E Jackson Ave Harlingen TX 78550-7318 • TX • EM • (MX 1959)

**VIKEN BRADLEY DONALD REV** (701)775-4554
729 S 25th St Grand Forks ND 58201-4153 • blviken@hotmail.com • ND • SP • Immanuel Grand Forks ND • (701)775-7125 • (SL 1992 MDIV)

**VINCENT ARTHUR M DR** (704)846-9299
11616 Sir Francis Drake Dr Charlotte NC 28277-5800 • arm³inc@compuserve.com • SE • EM • (SL 1946 MDIV MST DMIN)

**VINCENT ERIK J REV** (216)354-4146
405 New Fourth St Fairport Hbr OH 44077 • anja.erik@gateway.net • OH • EM • (SPR 1955 MDIV)

**VINOVSKIS WALDEMAR R REV** (510)733-6413
5201 Park Blvd Piedmont CA 94611-3328 • wrvinovskis@cs.com • CNH • Assoc • Zion Piedmont CA • (510)530-4213 • (SL 1992 MDIV)

**VISOKY PAUL REV** (717)824-2202
12 Pine Rd Plains PA 18705-2221 • visoky@intergrafix.net • S • EM • (SPR 1957)

**VISSCHER EDWARD F REV** (407)889-9856
1071 Encourte Grn Apopka FL 32712-2101 • edvisscher@aol.com • FG • EM • (SL 1959)

**VISSER ROBERT M REV** (916)726-7219
7066 Lynnetree Way Citrus Heights CA 95610-3932 • CNH • EM • (SL 1946)

**VITELLO JOHN T REV** (216)662-5366
C/O Zion Lutheran Church 5754 Dunham Rd Maple Heights OH 44137-3663 • OH • SP • Zion Maple Heights OH • (216)475-2267 • (FW 1983 MDIV)

**VO MINH CHAU NGOC REV** (314)835-0063
17 Ponca Trail Kirkwood MO 63122 • MO • O Miss • Missouri Saint Louis MO • (314)317-4550 • (SL 1992 MDIV)

**VOELKER ROBERT E REV** (519)250-9398
3835 Aristotle Cres Windsor ON N9G 2P1 CANADA • rev@mnsi.net • EN • SP • Gethsemane Windsor ON CANADA • (519)969-7561 • (FW 1984 MDIV)

**VOELKER WILLIAM R REV** (308)384-9213
4215 Arizona Ave Grand Island NE 68801-1006 • plchurch@computer-concepts.com • NEB • Sn/Adm • Peace Grand Island NE • (308)384-5673 • (SL 1970 MDIV)

**VOELZ JAMES W REV** (314)863-8704
14 S Seminary Ter Saint Louis MO 63105-3013 • voelzjames@stlnet.com • MO • SHS/C • Missouri Saint Louis MO • (314)317-4550 • (SL 1971 MDIV PHD)

**VOELZKE PAULUS E REV** (310)315-1887
1625 Franklin St Apt A Santa Monica CA 90404-4222 • PSW • EM • (SL 1956 MTH)

**VOGEL DANIEL J REV** (712)653-2351
C/O Zion Lutheran Church 519 12th St Manning IA 51455 • danvogel@pionet.net • IW • Sn/Adm • Zion Manning IA • (712)653-2352 • (FW 1982 MDIV)

**VOGEL GUY A REV** (651)776-4187
1463 Winthrop St N Saint Paul MN 55119-3065 • birdguy@netzero.net • MNS • EM • (SL 1963 MDIV)

**VOGEL LARRY M REV** (856)858-1344
635 Bettlewood Ave Collingswood NJ 08108-3004 • revogelnj@juno.com • EN • SP • Martin Luther Pennsauken NJ • (856)665-0116 • (SL 1981 MDIV)

**VOGEL LEROY E REV** (507)346-2614
PO Box 111 Spring Valley MN 55975-0111 • MNS • EM • (SL 1961 STM)

**VOGEL LUTHER E REV** (816)524-2058
436 SW Sunset Dr Lees Summit MO 64081-2313 • EN • EM • (SPR 1953)

**VOGEL ROBERT H REV** (908)687-9169
C/O Redeemer Lutheran Church 229 Cowperthwaite Pl Westfield NJ 07090 • meengel@aol.com • NJ • Assoc • Redeemer Westfield NJ* • (908)232-1517 • (FW 1999 MED)

**VOGEL THEODORE H REV** (830)334-4843
PO Box 617 Pearsall TX 78061-0617 • TX • EM • * • (SPR 1947)

**VOGELSANG WILLIAM R REV** (760)745-7771
2335 Amber Ln Escondido CA 92026-1230 • wrvogcmvog@home.com • PSW • SP • Community Escondido CA • (760)739-1650 • (FW 1978 MDIV)

**VOGES CARL A REV** (803)788-6656
129 Pond Ridge Rd Columbia SC 29223-7007 • holtri@mindspring.com • SE • SP • Holy Trinity Columbia SC • (803)799-7224 • (SPR 1966 MTH)

**VOGES ETHAN C REV** (253)639-3719
22317 126th Pl SE Kent WA 98031-9696 • alethan@aol.com • NOW • O Sp Min • Northwest Portland OR • (SL 1965 MDIV)

**VOGLER LOREN L REV** (712)552-1151
PO Box 311 Hawarden IA 51023-0311 • IW • SP • Trinity Hawarden IA • (712)552-2743 • (SL 1966)

**VOGT GORDON H REV** (612)824-8828
4842 Portland Ave Minneapolis MN 55417-1034 • MNS • SP • St James Minneapolis MN • (612)824-8828 • (SL 1959 MDIV)

**VOGT STEPHEN REV** (973)827-7437
251 Wheatsworth Rd Hamburg NJ 07419 • popchurch@juno.com • NJ • SP • Prince Peace Hamburg NJ • (973)827-5080 • (SL 1982 MDIV)

**VOGTS KEVIN D REV** (414)512-0372
9914 W Huntington Mequon WI 53097-3827 • Kevin³Vogts@cuw.edu • SW • SHS/C • South Wisconsin Milwaukee WI • (414)464-8100 • (SL 1986 MDIV)

**VOIGT ARNOLD J REV** (303)798-7887
1701 W Caley Ave Littleton CO 80120-3109 • arnievoigt@aol.com • RM • SP • Ascension Littleton CO • (303)794-4636 • (SL 1965 MDIV)

**VOIGT STEVEN J REV** (414)461-5820
4251 N 86th St Milwaukee WI 53222-1703 • voigt5@execpc.com • SW • Assoc • Covenant Milwaukee WI • (414)464-2410 • (SL 1991 MDIV)

**VOIGTMANN JAMES LEE REV** (217)793-5234
44 Arabian Spur Springfield IL 62702-1565 • CI • 02/1997 02/2000 • (CQ 1994)

**VOITKO PAUL A REV** (732)892-2109
610 Atlantic Ave Pt Pleasant NJ 08742-3005 • NJ • EM • (SL 1951)

**VOKT MICHAEL E REV** (319)355-9909
2202 E 33rd St Davenport IA 52807 • mvokt@netscape.net • IE • Sn/Adm • Trinity Davenport IA • (319)323-8001 • (SL 1986 MDIV)

**VOLK MICHAEL F REV** (513)931-0306
873 Southmeadow Cir Cincinnati OH 45231 • mvolk5@aol.com • OH • SP • Messiah Cincinnati OH • (513)825-4768 • (SL 1971 MDIV)

**VOLKER THOMAS G REV** (618)394-0702
1A Pearson Dr Apt #15 Fairview Heights IL 62208 • tomshlc@the-word.net • SI • Asst • Signal Hill Belleville IL • (618)397-1407 • (SL 1997 MDIV)

**VOLKERT GEORGE A REV** (319)578-8841
315 N Guilford St Sumner IA 50674-1029 • IE • SP • St Paul Sumner IA* • (319)578-3315 • (SL 1980 MDIV)

**VOLKERT ROBERT W REV** (218)845-2872
49400 405th Pl Palisade MN 56469-2226 • MNN • EM • * • (SPR 1970 MDIV)

**VOLL THEODORE E REV** (517)659-3422
PO Box 156 Munger MI 48747-0156 • MI • SP • Trinity-St James Munger MI • (517)659-2506 • (SL 1975 MDIV)

**VOLLRATH JONATHAN H REV** (507)248-3888
PO Box 487 Henderson MN 56044-0487 • MNS • SP • Centennial Henderson MN • (507)248-3888 • (SL 1998 MDIV)

**VOLM WILLIAM PAUL REV** (715)623-2786
W9834 County Road D Antigo WI 54409-8860 • wpvolm@newnorth.net • NW • Asst • Peace Antigo WI • (715)623-2200 • (SPR 1973 MDIV)

**VOLMER ALFRED F REV** (408)356-1595
103 Cherrystone Ct Los Gatos CA 95032-3554 • CNH • EM • (SPR 1946 MDIV)

**VOLZ PAUL M REV**
1929 Metlock Ln Oklahoma City OK 73160-5639 • IE • Peace Antigo WI • (715)623-2200 • (SL 1956 MDIV)

**VOLZ WALTER D REV** (954)581-8954
7521 NW 8th Ct Plantation FL 33317-1017 • oslc@gate.net • FG • SP • Our Savior Plantation FL • (954)473-6888 • (SL 1961 STM)

**VOLZKE GREGORY R REV** (402)744-4961
13115 W 70th Juniata NE 68955-2138 • NEB • SP • Christ Juniata NE • (402)744-4971 • (CQ 1993)

**VOMHOF ALLEN S REV** (402)455-9363
4519 Kelby Rd Omaha NE 68152-1303 • alvomhof@juno.com • NEB • SP • St John Omaha NE • (402)453-1335 • (FW 1986 MDIV)

**VON DIELINGEN PAUL REV** (314)352-6244
6438 Mardel Ave Saint Louis MO 63109-1356 • vondie@vtechworld.com • MO • EM • (SL 1941)

**VON RENTZELL MARION W REV** (308)532-6551
1821 Burlington Blvd North Platte NE 69101-6602 • NEB • Sn/Adm • Our Redeemer North Platte NE • (308)532-4753 • (SL 1964 MDIV)

**VON SEGGERN ARLEIGH FRED REV** (502)943-0518
5655 Corley Apt A Fort Knox KY 40121 • IN • M Chap • Indiana Fort Wayne IN • (FW 1992 MDIV)

**VON STROH C DEAN REV** (956)412-6915
2702 Jeff St Harlingen TX 78550-3354 • TX • Sn/Adm • St Paul Harlingen TX • (956)423-3924 • (SPR 1968 MDIV MA)

**VOORHEES DAVID L REV** (517)482-3444
2201 Lyman Dr Lansing MI 48912-3415 • MI • EM • (SL 1949 MA)

**VOORMAN DUANE R REV** (402)484-8598
5016 Randolph St Lincoln NE 68510-3852 • NEB • Sn/Adm • Trinity Lincoln NE • (402)474-0606 • (FW 1983 MDIV)

**VOSS DENNIS L REV** (715)597-3293
E11775 Cty Hwy HH Osseo WI 54758-8851 • dlvoss@win.bright.net • NW • SP • St Peter Osseo WI* • (715)597-2431 • (FW 1999 MDIV)

**VOSS HANS A REV** (919)556-3635
241 Evesham Ct Wake Forest NC 27587-6400 • havoss2000@yahoo.com • NE • EM • * • (SL 1945)

**VOSS THEOPHIL H REV** (330)785-0703
386 N Firestone Blvd Akron OH 44301 • OH • EM • * • (SL 1946 MED)

**VOSSLER L RICHARD JR. DR** (973)992-2843
3 Berkeley Ter Livingston NJ 07039 • richard³vossler@juno.com • NJ • SP • Grace Livingston NJ • (973)992-0145 • (SL 1985 MDIV DMIN)

**VOTH DANIEL C REV** (414)355-7812
10000 W Fountain Ave #1905 Milwaukee WI 53224-3227 • SW • SP • Shepherd Of The Ridg Milwaukee WI • (414)357-8490 • (FW 1999 MDIV)

**VRUDNY MATTHEW J REV** (320)233-6133
C/O Peace Lutheran Church PO Box 60 Finlayson MN 55735-0060 • peaceluth@pinenet.com • MNN • SP • Peace Finlayson MN* • (320)233-6138 • (SL 1990 MDIV)

**VRUDNY WALTER J REV** (408)484-1162
22276 Davenrich St Salinas CA 93908-1011 • CNH • EM • * • (SL 1946)

**VU KINH (KENNETH) TON REV** (714)534-3413
11894 Dorada Ave Garden Grove CA 92840-5501 • vukinh@yahoo.com • PSW • SP • Vietnamese Garden Grove CA • (714)537-4245 • (FW 1995 MDIV)

W

**WACHHOLZ DEAN C REV** (219)471-9477
1 Martin Luther Dr Fort Wayne IN 46825-4935 • wachholtzdc@mail.ctsfw.edu • IN • SHS/C • Indiana Fort Wayne IN • (SPR 1972 MDIV)

**WACHHOLZ EDWARD R REV** (409)836-9032
C/O Immanuel Luth Ch-Lyons 1801 Old Mill Creek Rd Brenham TX 77833-9152 • TX • EM • (CQ 1994 MSW MDIV)

**WACHHOLZ WILLIAM H REV** (402)643-2352
657 Bader Ave Seward NE 68434-1149 • NEB • SHS/C • Nebraska Seward NE • (SL 1972 MDIV MA MA DMIN)

**WACHTER KEITH D REV** (314)980-4268
809 Whispering Windsong O Fallon MO 63366 • MO • SP • Holy Cross O Fallon MO • (636)272-4505 • (SL 1980 MDIV)

**WACKENHUTH DAVID G REV** (516)277-0082
186 Country Village Ln East Islip NY 11730-3708 • thear2@aol.com • AT • Sn/Adm • Trinity Islip NY • (516)277-1555 • (CQ 1986 MA)

**WACKENHUTH ERWIN C REV** (973)276-3058
Crane's Mill 459 Passaic Ave Apt 307 West Caldwell NJ 017006-746 • NJ • Asst • Calvary Verona NJ • (973)239-0577 • (CQ 1993)

**WACKER DAVID L REV**
114 Van Dr Kathleen GA 31047-2202 • MDS • EM • (SL 1955)

**WACKETT KEVIN DAVID REV** (410)742-1737
C/O Bethany Luth Church 817 Camden Ave Salisbury MD 21801-6231 • bethanylutheranc@juno.com • SE • SP • Bethany Salisbury MD • (410)742-1737 • (FW 1986 MDIV)

**WACKLER JOHN V REV** (580)223-0326
1916 10th Ave NW Ardmore OK 73401-2206 • OK • EM • (SPR 1954)

**WACKLER MYRON E REV** (406)251-5958
2320 43rd St Missoula MT 59803-1117 • MT • EM • (SPR 1947)

**WADDELL JAMES ALAN REV** (517)629-8929
C/O St Paul Lutheran Church 100 Luther Blvd Albion MI 49224-2056 • spelc@voyager.net • MI • SP • St Paul Albion MI • (517)629-8379 • (SL 1991 MDIV MA STM)

**WADE KENNETH EARL REV** (405)234-6666
1210 S Hayes St Enid OK 73703-6726 • kewade@peakonline.com • OK • SP • St Paul Enid OK • (580)234-6646 • (SL 1968 MDIV)

**WADEWITZ WERNER K REV** (219)483-1930
5559 N Clinton St Fort Wayne IN 46825 • IN • EM • (SL 1937 STM MA)

**WAECH OSWALD A REV** (909)989-1774
10210 Baseline Rd Spc 69 Alta Loma CA 91701-6037 • PSW • EM • (SL 1936 DD)

**WAECHTER LEANDER M REV** (803)781-2481
5912 Ellisor St Columbia SC 29212-2112 • SE • EM • (SL 1945 MDIV MST)

**WAETJEN RAYMOND W DR** (541)994-2337
1611 NE 11th St Lincoln City OR 97367-3410 • zion@proaxis.com • NOW • SP • Zion Corvallis OR • (541)757-0946 • (SL 1967 MDIV DMIN)

**WAETZIG KALVIN L REV** (503)669-3672
653 SE 18th Ln Gresham OR 97080-9332 • kwaet@aol.com • NOW • SP • Christ The Vine Clackamas OR • (503)658-5650 • (SL 1986 MDIV)

**WAGEMAN HAROLD F REV** (903)895-0025
2340 County Rd 4156 N Overton TX 75684 • TX • EM • (SL 1952)

**WAGENER KENNETH C REV** (314)464-5780
1031 Thames Dr Imperial MO 63052-2377 • kenw@cphnet.org • MO • S Ex/S • Missouri Saint Louis MO • (314)317-4550 • (SL 1986 MDIV MA)

**WAGNER AINSLIE B REV** (734)279-1108
C/O St Peter Lutheran Church PO Box 39 Petersburg MI 49270-0039 • lam@cass.net • MI • SP • St Peter Petersburg MI • (313)279-1949 • (FW 1983 MDIV MS)

**WAGNER ARNOLD O REV** (618)327-4453
556 W Hill St Nashville IL 62263-1513 • SI • EM • (SL 1945)

**WAGNER CHARLES E REV** (205)923-2609
1700 St Charles Ave SW Birmingham AL 35211 • SO • 11/1999 • (SL 1965 MDIV)

**WAGNER DANIEL E REV** (218)789-7406
8501 80th Ave S Sabin MN 56580-9516 • lcmsdwagner2@mbusa.net • MNN • SP • Trinity Sabin MN • (218)789-7259 • (SL 1984 MDIV)

**WAGNER DAVID S REV** (701)232-1215
3720 15th St S Fargo ND 58104-6353 • ND • SP • Beaut Savior Fargo ND • (701)293-1047 • (SL 1987 MDIV)

**WAGNER DONALD R REV** (218)685-5205
PO Box 446 Elbow Lake MN 56531 • wags@paulbbunyan.net • MNN • SP • Christ Elbow Lake MN* • (218)685-5213 • (SL 1990 MDIV)

**WAGNER EUGENE F REV** (317)773-9627
54 S 10th St Noblesville IN 46060-2809 • focl@oaktree.net • IN • SP • Family Of Christ Fishers IN • (317)594-9157 • (FW 1986 MDIV)

**WAGNER MARK ERIK REV** (317)788-9023
602 S 9th Ave Beech Grove IN 46107-2208 • markewagnr@aol.com • IN • SP • Ascension Beech Grove IN • (317)788-1118 • (FW 1996 MS MDIV)

**WAGNER MERLYN D REV** (801)255-4739
625 E Pioneer Ave Sandy UT 84070-1168 • binksu@juno.com • RM • Sn/Adm • Christ Murray UT • (801)262-4354 • (SPR 1962 MDIV)

**WAGNER OSWALD F REV** (503)287-7264
3575 NE Ainsworth St Portland OR 97211-7364 • NOW • EM • (SL 1944)

**WAGNER PAUL L REV** (631)261-3909
47 West St Northport NY 11768-1249 • AT • EM • (SL 1957 STM)

**WAGNER PAUL ROBERT REV** (860)446-9593
237 Gales Ferry Rd Groton CT 06340-2737 • flcqroton@aol.com • NE • SP • Faith Groton CT • (860)445-0483 • (SL 1992 MDIV)

**WAGNER PHILIP P REV** (612)550-9635
14830 41st Ave N Plymouth MN 55446-2753 • MNS • SP • Golden Valley Golden Valley MN • (763)544-2810 • (SL 1982 MDIV)

**WAGNER PRESTON E REV** (919)556-4658
2304 Welsh Tavern Way Wake Forest NC 27587-6689 • pwag@aol.com • SE • SP • Hope Wake Forest NC • (919)554-8109 • (SPR 1972 MDIV)

**WAGNER RICHARD ALAN REV** (815)624-7792
515 W Rockton Rd Rockton IL 61072-1640 • NI • SP • St Andrew Rockton IL • (815)624-6051 • (SL 1973 MDIV)

**WAGNER RICHARD F REV** (512)462-2725
1704 Nelms Dr #811 Austin TX 78744-4234 • TX • EM • (SL 1953 STM)

**WAGNER ROBERT V REV** (810)765-4161
7255 Meisner Rd China MI 48054-3009 • rwagner@ees.eesc.com • MI • SP • St Peter Fair Haven MI • (810)765-8161 • (FW 1980 MDIV)

**WAGNER ROBERT W REV** (254)547-7257
920 Lutheran Church Rd Copperas Cove TX 76522-7443 • rwagner@seacove.net • TX • SP • Immanuel Copperas Cove TX • (254)547-3498 • (SL 1984 MDIV)

**WAGNER RONALD A REV** (618)236-2125
12 Justice Dr Belleville IL 62226-5179 • SI • 12/1995 12/1999 • (SL 1983 MDIV)

**WAGNER STEPHEN A REV** (972)492-2315
1923 Westminster Dr Carrollton TX 75007-2411 • sawagner@airmail.net • TX • Sn/Adm • Prince Peace Carrollton TX • (972)447-9887 • (SL 1973 MDIV)

**WAGNER TIMOTHY WAYNE REV** (308)536-2728
PO Box 263 Fullerton NE 68638-0263 • NEB • SP • Mount Calvary Fullerton NE • (308)536-2635 • (FW 1995 MDIV)

**WAGNER WILLIAM B REV**
C/O St Matthew Luth Church 5125 Cascade Rd SE Grand Rapids MI 49546-3726 • MI • SP • St Matthew Grand Rapids MI • (616)942-9091 • (SL 1988 MDIV)

**WAGNER WILLIAM W REV** (608)362-8755
2491 Dewey Ave Beloit WI 53511-2462 • w3inbeloit@aol.com • SW • Sn/Adm • St John Beloit WI • (608)362-8595 • (SPR 1975 MDIV)

**WAGONER JEROME REV** (712)542-4241
1860 N Ave Clarinda IA 51632-4562 • IW • SP • Our Savior Red Oak IA* • (712)623-4600 • (SPR 1971 MDIV)

**WAHL HAROLD IRVIN REV** (630)837-5671
1112 E Devon Ave Bartlett IL 60103-4760 • hiwahl@aol.com • NI • SP • Immanuel Bartlett IL • (630)837-1166 • (FW 1977 MDIV)

**WAHL JOHN F REV** (831)475-9369
2435 Felt St Spc 44 Santa Cruz CA 95062-4237 • CNH • EM • (SL 1939 MLS)

**WAHL RANDOLPH C REV** (308)352-2279
PO Box 20051 Wickenburg AZ 85358 • PSW • SP • Redeemer Wickenburg AZ • (520)684-2729 • (FW 1997 MDIV)

**WAHL ROBERT K REV** (810)579-7729
5473 Copley Sq Grand Blanc MI 48439 • MI • SP • Redeemer Flint MI • (810)249-1380 • (SL 1981 MDIV)

**WAHLERS ARTHUR G REV** (503)282-4286
6405 NE 26th Ave Portland OR 97211-6050 • awahlers@mail2.cu-portland.edu • NOW • EM • (SL 1946 MA DED)

**WAHLERS LORENZ F REV** (314)638-2139
4449 Fatima Dr Saint Louis MO 63123-6749 • EN • EM • (SL 1937 MDIV)

**WAIDELICH CARL W REV**
2203 London Ave Lincoln Park MI 48146-3467 • cwwaidelich@aol.com • MI • EM • (SPR 1968)

**WAISER WALTER E REV** (817)284-1677
C/O Peace Luth Church 941 W Bedford Euless Rd Hurst TX 76053-3808 • fisher@peacechurch.org • TX • Sn/Adm • Peace Hurst TX • (817)284-1677 • (CQ 1975 MTH)

**WAITE WALLACE J REV** (217)283-5403
802 S 3rd St Hoopeston IL 60942-1808 • CI • SP • Good Shepherd Hoopeston IL • (217)283-7966 • (SL 1980)

**WAKELAND MICHAEL S REV**
APDO Postal 5714 Guadalajara 5 Jalisco MEXICO • wakelandms@aol.com • SI • S Miss • Southern Illinois Belleville IL • (FW 1987 MDIV)

**WALBURG JAMES S REV** (763)389-3387
C/O Faith Community Luth Ch PO Box 156 Zimmerman MN 55398-0156 • MNN • SP • Faith Community Zimmerman MN • (763)856-3600 • (SPR 1975 MDIV)

**WALK KERMIT H REV** (708)331-3023
2 W - 150th St Harvey IL 60426-2120 • NI • 07/1999 • (SPR 1966 MDIV)

**WALKER DAVID F REV** (847)398-5237
14 N Owen St Mt Prospect IL 60056-2532 • NI • Assoc • St Paul Mount Prospect IL • (847)255-0332 • (SL 1958 MDIV)

**WALKER JOHN F REV**
RR 1 Box 160 Engadine MI 49827-9726 • MI • SP • Bethlehem Engadine MI* • (906)477-1011 • (FW 1995 MDIV)

**WALLACE MICHAEL SCOTT REV** (507)685-2307
C/O Trinity Luth Church 10500 215th St W Morristown MN 55052-5083 • wallacmd@means.net • MNS • SP • Trinity Morristown MN* • (507)685-2307 • (FW 1994 MDIV)

**WALLIS MATTHEW REV**
C/O Orlando Luth Academy 550 Econlockhatchee Trl Orlando FL 32825 • FG • Cmp P • Orlando Lutheran Aca Orlando FL • (407)275-7750 • (SL 2000 MDIV)

**WALQUIST RANDY W REV** (505)821-4498
6608 Mia St NE Albuquerque NM 87109-3632 • prwalquist@aol.com • RM • SP • Immanuel Albuquerque NM • (505)242-0616 • (SL 1978 MDIV)

**WALSH JEFFREY B REV**
5038 Robinwood Dr Monroe MI 48161 • jwalsh@tlsmonroe.org • MI • Assoc • Trinity Monroe MI • (313)242-2308 • (FW 1984 MDIV)

**WALTA ARNOLD H REV** (253)815-0818
37601 37th Ave S Auburn WA 98001-8739 • ahw6@juno.com • NOW • EM • (SL 1958)

**WALTER CARY J REV** (775)289-6353
PO Box 375 Ely NV 89301-0375 • CNH • SP • Immanuel Ely NV • (775)289-6353 • (FW 1999 MDIV)

**WALTER JAMES CARL REV** (501)225-8843
7807 Evergreen Dr Little Rock AR 72227-5909 • MDS • SP • Grace Little Rock AR • (501)663-3631 • (SL 1991 MDIV)

**WALTER JODY ROGER REV** (715)536-6514
N1882 County Rd M Merrill WI 54452-9312 • voneis@worldnet.att.net • NW • 08/2000 • (FW 1992 MDIV)

**WALTER JOHN WILLIAM REV**
2978 Milwaukee Ave Northbrook IL 60062-7118 • NI • SP • St John Northbrook IL • (847)296-5727 • (SPR 1973 MDIV)

**WALTER NORMAN E REV** (623)977-6450
8505 W Charleston Ave Peoria AZ 85382-8071 • PSW • EM • (SL 1956 MDIV)

**WALTERS RALPH M REV** (512)281-5219
PO Box 266 1113 Robin Rd Elgin TX 78621-0266 • TX • EM • (CQ 1990)

**WALTHER GALAN D REV** (734)528-1434
4115 Rolling Meadow Ln Ypsilanti MI 48197 • walthergd@mc.lcms.org • MI • D Ex/S • Michigan Ann Arbor MI • (SL 1980 MA MDIV)

**WALTHER HERBERT G REV** (919)477-6421
5114 Long Leaf Dr Durham NC 27712-2218 • holyjoe121@juno.com • SE • EM • (TH 1947 MDIV)

**WALTHER JEFFREY H REV** (218)878-1246
9 Elizabeth Ave Esko MN 55733 • walthernet@aol.com • MNN • SHS/C • Minnesota North Brainerd MN • (FW 1989 MDIV)

**WALTHER JOHN D REV** (405)263-7656
410 Colorado Ave Okarche OK 73762 • johnwalther@hotmail.com • OK • SP • St John Okarche OK • (405)263-7311 • (FW 1990 MDIV)

**WALTHER MICHAEL P REV** (618)346-1786
432 Chapel Dr Collinsville IL 62234-4369 • michaelpwalther@netscape.net • SI • Sn/Adm • Good Shepherd Collinsville IL • (618)344-3151 • (SL 1984 MDIV STM)

**WALTON GREGORY S REV** (770)579-6537
3713 Oak Springs Trace Marietta GA 30066 • gsw1@mindspring.com • FG • SP • Faith Marietta GA • (770)973-8877 • (SL 1987 MDIV)

**WALZ ARDEN D REV** (509)573-9205
803 Tieton Dr Yakima WA 98902 • ajwalz1@juno.com • NOW • SP • Bethlehem Yakima WA • (509)457-5822 • (SL 1968 MDIV)

**WALZ EDGAR REV** (219)483-8316
1915 Colony Dr Fort Wayne IN 46825-5009 • IN • EM • (SL 1937 MDIV MA DED)

**WALZ ORVILLE C REV** (402)643-4884
711 E Pinewood Ave Seward NE 68434-1131 • owalz@seward.cune.edu • NEB • SHS/C • Nebraska Seward NE • (CQ 1982 DED)

**WANDERER DOUGLAS CRAIG REV** (701)538-4849
C/O Immanuel Luth Church 9690 Highway 18 Lidgerwood ND 58053-9774 • ND • SP • Immanuel Lidgerwood ND* • (701)538-4849 • (FW 1995 MDIV)

**WANG CHIENPING PAUL REV** (909)598-9580
3004 Crooked Creek Dr Diamond Bar CA 91765 • PSW • 01/1997 01/2000 • * • (SL 1987 MDIV)

**WANGERIN JACK D REV** (201)262-0466
234 Grand St New Milford NJ 07646-1635 • NJ • SP • St Matthew New Milford NJ • (201)262-5092 • (SL 1955)

**WANGERIN MARK E REV** (414)259-9837
2532 N 124th St Apt 253 Wauwatosa WI 53226-1030 • wangerme@execpc.com • SW • Assoc • Mount Olive Milwaukee WI • (414)771-3580 • (SL 1978 STM)

**WANGERIN NORMAN P DR** (414)351-6254
1821 W Daisy Ln Milwaukee WI 53209-2117 • SW • EM • (SL 1948 MDIV MA MST DD)

**WANGERIN TIMOTHY P REV**
C/O Zion Lutheran Church 1019 Blunt St Downs KS 67437-1511 • timw@par1.net • KS • SP • Zion Downs KS • (913)454-3733 • (ED 1990 MDIV)

**WANGERIN WALTER M SR. DR** (719)328-0392
2731 Quail Ridge Pt Colorado Springs CO 80906 • RM • EM • (SL 1942 MSED PHD)

**WANNER MICHAEL D REV** (417)336-5628
221 Malone Branson MO 65616-2457 • oslc@tri-lakes.net • MO • SP • Faith Branson MO • (888)777-3059 • (FW 1985 MDIV)

**WAPLES MICHAEL KEITH REV** (319)635-2247
PO Box 465 206 N Fourth St Fairbank IA 50629-0465 • mkw@fairbank.net • IE • SP • St John Fairbank IA • (319)635-2181 • (FW 1996 MDIV)

**WARD DOUGLAS C REV** (802)863-8014
57 Maple St Apt 421 Burlington VT 05401-4770 • NE • EM • (SPR 1974 MDIV)

**WARD STEVEN C REV** (518)346-7198
2339 Shirl Ln Niskayuna NY 12309-5919 • revward@minister.com • AT • SP • Immanuel Niskayuna NY • (518)346-1958 • (SL 1997 MDIV)

**WAREHAM CHRISTOPHER E REV**
3029 Irene St Butte MT 59701-6325 • MT • SP • St Mark Butte MT* • (406)782-5935 • (SL 1980 MDIV)

**WARGO PAUL E REV** (810)773-7534
15722 Semrau Ave Eastpointe MI 48021-1622 • paulwargo@juno.com • MI • Tchr • LHS North Macomb MI • (810)781-9151 • (CQ 1980 MED)

**WARMANN DOUGLAS RALPH REV** (630)351-3489
323 Orchard Ter Roselle IL 60172-3005 • doug@trinityroselle.com • NI • Asst • Trinity Roselle IL • (630)894-3263 • (CQ 1995 MDIV)

**WARMBIER MICHAEL G REV** (208)756-2141
RR 1 Box 104 AB Salmon ID 83467-9701 • warmbier@dmi.net • MT • SP • Shep Of Valley Salmon ID • (208)756-4429 • (SL 1985 MDIV)

**WARNECK RICHARD H REV** (314)862-3410
15 S Seminary Ter Saint Louis MO 63105-3013 • MO • SHS/C • Missouri Saint Louis MO • (314)317-4550 • (SL 1960 MDIV MST PHD)

**WARNECK WALTER J JR. DR** (912)598-8129
2 Cranes Nest Ct Savannah GA 31411-2127 • FG • O Sp Min • Florida-Georgia Orlando FL • (SL 1971 MDIV MTH DMIN)

**WARNEKE ANTON C REV** (320)762-9039
2010 Lake Park Ave # D Alexandria MN 56308-8599 • MNN • EM • (SPR 1941)

**WARNEKE LLOYD C REV** (303)420-8542
5430 Field Ct Arvada CO 80002-3040 • RM • EM • (SL 1953)

**WARNEKE PAUL M REV** (308)367-4588
602 E 6th St PO Box 64 Curtis NE 69025 • warneke@curtis-nc.com • NEB • SP • St John Curtis NE • (308)367-4238 • (FW 1996 MDIV)

**WARNER JEFFERY PHILIP REV**
409 N Little St Wathill NE 68067-5003 • jw61028@navix.net • NEB • O Sp Min • Nebraska Seward NE • (SL 1995 MDIV)

**WARNIER PAUL A REV** (320)695-2401
C/O Zion Lutheran Church PO Box 318 Browns Valley MN 56219-0318 • revpaw@prtel.com • MNN • SP • Zion Browns Valley MN* • (320)695-2401 • (SL 1981 MDIV)

**WARNKE MATTHEW L REV** (619)237-1325
701 Kettner Blvd #27 San Diego CA 92101 • mlwarnke@aol.com • IW • M Chap • Iowa West Fort Dodge IA • (FW 1983 MDIV MTH)

**WARPNESS BARRY G REV** (308)783-1150
C/O St James Lutheran Church 1117 E 14th St Scottsbluff NE 69361-3311 • bgwarp@actcom.net • WY • SP • St James Scottsbluff NE • (308)632-8001 • (FW 1986 MDIV)

**WARREN WILLIAM REV** (907)522-6321
2563 Brookstone Loop Anchorage AK 99515-2714 • w3finnrev@aol.com • NOW • SP • Anchorage Anchorage AK • (907)272-5323 • (CQ 1983)

**WARSINSKI LARRY A REV** (517)842-5964
10010 E Monroe Wheeler MI 48662 • revlarry@rural-net.com • MI • SP • Immanuel Wheeler MI • (517)842-3459 • (FW 1978 MDIV)

**WARTHER JOHN B DR** (410)969-4116
308 Oak Manor Dr Glen Burnie MD 21061-5509 • jbwarther@prodigy.net • SE • Assoc • St Paul Glen Burnie MD • (410)766-2283 • (SL 1988 MDIV DMIN)

**WARTICK KENT G REV** (219)766-2395
C/O St Paul Luth Church PO Box 547 Kouts IN 46347-0547 • splckouts@in.freei.net • IN • SP • St Paul Kouts IN • (219)766-2395 • (SL 1985 MDIV)

**WASHINGTON STEVEN REV** (205)875-9108
1900 Range St Selma AL 36703-2933 • swashington@zebra.net • SO • SP • Trinity Selma AL • (205)874-8404 • (CQ 1982)

**WASMUTH JAMES S REV** (218)375-3781
PO Box 98 Callaway MN 56521-0098 • MNN • SP • Immanuel Callaway MN* • (218)375-2786 • (FW 1998 MDIV)

**WASSMAN DARWIN D REV** (308)352-4565
RFD 1 Box 289 Ogallala NE 69153-9801 • NEB • EM • * • (SL 1963 MST)

**WATFORD TROY SCOTT REV** (828)464-5813
2440 Emmanuel Church Rd Conover NC 28613 • SE • SP • Immanuel Conover NC • (828)464-5813 • (CQ 1999)

**WATKINS ANDREW C REV** (850)683-9690
207 Walker Cir W Crestview FL 32539-8339 • pastoroslc@cfi.net • SO • SP • Our Savior Crestview FL • (850)682-3154 • (SL 1998 MDIV)

**WATKINS LINDSAY W REV** (515)432-9749
527 S Marshall St Boone IA 50036-5110 • IW • Sn/Adm • Trinity Boone IA • (515)432-5140 • (SL 1979 MDIV DMIN)

**WATSON CHRISTOPHER J REV** (314)469-7630
12224 Country Wood Ct Maryland Heights MO 63043 • dctalkfan99@yahoo.com • MO • Assoc • King Of Kings Chesterfield MO • (314)469-2224 • (SL 1997 MDIV)

**WATSON EDWARD L REV** (314)355-6719
12028 Rosevalley Ln Saint Louis MO 63138-1305 • MO • Missouri Saint Louis MO • (314)317-4550 • (CQ 1984)

**WATSON JAMES C REV** (706)689-5044
Installation Chaplain Office Fort Drum NY 13602 • chapwat@aol.com • FG • M Chap • Florida-Georgia Orlando FL • (SL 1981 MS MDIV)

**WATSON JAY WILLIAM REV** (785)331-3890
2925 Kensington Rd Lawrence KS 66046 • rlc@lawrence.ixks.com • KS • SP • Redeemer Lawrence KS • (785)843-8181 • (FW 1995 MDIV JD)

**WATSON JOSEPH M REV** (830)257-6747
C/O Hosanna Lutheran Church 134 Camp Meeting Rd Kerrville TX 78028 • watson@omniglobal.net • TX • SP • Hosanna Kerrville TX • (830)257-6767 • (SL 1996 MS MDIV)

**WATSON KENNETH ROBERT REV** (817)599-9306
1419 Shadow Run Weatherford TX 76086-3955 • TX • SP • Trinity Weatherford TX • (817)613-1939 • (SL 1994 MST MDIV)

**WATSON RICHARD E REV** (618)529-3537
517 N Almond St Carbondale IL 62901-1305 • SI • EM • (CQ 1987 MS PHD)

**WAYNICK THOMAS C REV** (337)537-2045
5429 B Seay St Fort Polk LA 71459 • tomdianew@wnonline.net • TX • M Chap • Texas Austin TX • (FW 1982 MS MDIV)

**WEANDER KENNETH LEE JR. REV** (402)379-4448
513 Valley Rd Norfolk NE 68701-3243 • pastorlee@oursav.org • NEB • Assoc • Our Savior Norfolk NE • (402)371-9005 • (SL 1994 MDIV)

**WEBB JEFFREY N REV** (518)758-1891
162 County Route 26A Stuyvesant NY 12173-2411 • webb@berk.com • AT • SP • St John Stuyvesant NY* • (518)758-1891 • (SL 1992 MDIV)

**WEBER CHARLES W REV**
PO Box 144 Altenburg MO 63732-0144 • MO • SP • Immanuel Altenburg MO • (573)824-5636 • (SL 1993 MDIV)

**WEBER DAVID C REV** (319)927-3011
114 Guetzko Court Manchester IA 52057-1325 • rev.dave-osl@juno.com • IE • SP • Our Savior Manchester IA • (319)927-4860 • (SL 1991 MDIV)

**WEBER DAVID J REV** (906)482-2212
307 Montezuma St Hancock MI 49930-2024 • djweber@up.net • NW • SP • SS Peter&Paul Hancock MI • (906)482-4750 • (SL 1979 MDIV)

**WEBER DAVID K REV** (219)548-3259
602 Roosevelt Dr Valparaiso IN 46383 • dweber@valpo.edu • IN • Indiana Fort Wayne IN • (FW 1982 MDIV MA PHD)

**WEBER EDMUND J REV** (512)565-6149
1075 Rio Rico Rd Apt 6 Mercedes TX 78570-4517 • TX • D Miss • Mision Emanuel Mercedes TX • (512)565-4678 • (FW 1990 MDIV)

**WEBER ERHARDT P REV** (503)697-7360
9 Churchill Downs St Lake Oswego OR 97035-1419 • epnw@aol.com • NOW • EM • (SL 1941 MDIV MA STD)

**WEBER GLENN A REV** (915)599-2613
3225 Matagorda St El Paso TX 79936-1807 • sweber370@aol.com • RM • SP • Our Savior El Paso TX • (915)591-9311 • (SL 1970 STM)

**WEBER JAMES E REV** (231)264-8720
301 Lamoreaux Dr Elk Rapids MI 49629-9737 • MI • SP • Grace Elk Rapids MI • (231)264-5312 • (CQ 1998)

**WEBER KARL A REV** (217)429-5808
1952 E Johns Ave Decatur IL 62521-3105 • karlweber@juno.com • CI • SP • Trinity Decatur IL • (217)422-3630 • (FW 1991 MDIV)

**WEBER PAUL A IV REV** (419)592-5671
1005 Lynne Ave Napoleon OH 43545-1219 • OH • EM • (SL 1952)

**WEBER PAUL A REV** (906)226-6195
518 Forest Park Dr Marquette MI 49855-4404 • RLutheranC@aol.com • NW • Sn/Adm • Redeemer Marquette MI • (906)228-9883 • (SL 1973 MDIV)

**WEBER PAUL M REV** (618)833-4765
402 Walton St Anna IL 62906-1251 • phweber@shawneelink.com • SI • SP • Trinity Anna IL • (618)833-2475 • (FW 1997 MDIV)

**WEBER ROBERT L REV** (360)574-6095
1715 NW 91st Cir Vancouver WA 98665-6747 • NOW • EM • (SL 1955)

**WEBERN WOLFGANG M REV** (314)428-5478
3012 Georgetown Farm Ct Saint Ann MO 63074 • weberng@cs.com • MO • EM • (SPR 1964)

**WEBSTER JAMES D REV** (208)464-1044
HC64 Box 46A Pierce IA 83546 • IE • 06/2000 • (FW 1987 MDIV)

**WEBSTER STANLEY D REV** (518)828-9514
8 Storm Avenue Hudson NY 12534-2633 • AT • 04/2000 • (CQ 1988)

**WEDERGREN ROBERT B REV** (409)938-1742
2706 John Dr La Marque TX 77568-3802 • wedergren1e@aol.com • TX • EM • (SPR 1956)

**WEDIG CHARLES E REV** (707)464-2465
1752 Parkway Dr Crescent City CA 95531-8518 • CNH • EM • (SL 1940)

**WEEDON WILLIAM C REV** (618)633-2502
6969 W Frontage Rd Worden IL 62097-2431 • wmweedon@madisontelco.com • SI • SP • St Paul Hamel IL • (618)633-2209 • (SL 1986 MDIV STM)

**WEEKS DAVID L REV** (412)751-2754
1201 Schweitzer Rd Mc Keesport PA 15135-2017 • revdlw@aol.com • EA • D Ex/S • Eastern Williamsville NY • (716)634-5111 • (FW 1980 MDIV)

**WEEMAN RICHARD D REV** (605)779-5181
C/O Zion Luth Church PO Box 204 Delmont SD 57330-0204 • SD • SP • Zion Delmont SD* • (605)779-5181 • (FW 1990 MDIV)

**WEERTS LESLIE A DR** (501)922-5905
3 Encantado Way Hot Springs AR 71909-7406 • MDS • SP • Faith Hot Springs Village AR • (501)922-5700 • (SL 1968 MDIV)

**WEERTS MILAN G DR** (407)469-2830
15749 County Road 455 Montverde FL 34756-3775 • mweerts@digital.net • FG • O Sp Min • Florida-Georgia Orlando FL • (SL 1961 MDIV DMIN)

**WEGENER KENNETH W REV** (309)853-9953
716 Henry St Kewanee IL 61443-2852 • kwweg@juno.com • CI • EM • (SL 1958)

**WEGENER MERLEN F REV** (765)446-8659
3917 Peters Mill Dr Lafayette IN 47905 • pastorwegener@stjameslaf.org • IN • EM • (SL 1964 MDIV)

**WEGENER RALPH A REV** (503)359-4635
2822 15th Pl Forest Grove OR 97116-3108 • brwegener@juno.com • NOW • EM • (SL 1941)

**WEGENER THOMAS C REV** (319)236-1065
3310 W Ridge Dr Waterloo IA 50701-4648 • IE • SP • Faith Waterloo IA • (319)236-1771 • (SPR 1967 MDIV)

**WEGNER HAROLD G REV** (763)754-5468
12191 Grouse St NW Unit 401 Coon Rapids MN 55448-1996 • hvwegner@juno.com • MNS • EM • (SL 1981 MDIV)

**WEGNER MARK ALLAN REV**
PO Box 5492 Ketchikan AK 99501-0492 • NOW • 06/1994 06/2000 • (SL 1982 MDIV MS)

**WEGNER PETER C REV** (515)223-9209
612 45th St W Des Moines IA 50265-3819 • IW • SP • Peace Des Moines IA • (515)285-3769 • (SL 1972 MDIV)

**WEGRZYN DANIEL J REV**
6107 Sunderland Dr Cleveland OH 44129-4627 • OH • Sn/Adm • Bethany Parma OH • (440)884-1230 • (SL 1989 MDIV)

**WEHLING ANDREW ALAN REV**
912 N Calhoun Liberal KS 67901 • revwehling@juno.com • KS • SP • Grace Liberal KS • (316)624-5900 • (SL 1993 MDIV)

**WEHMEIER DANIEL LEE REV** (203)744-4826
10 Sharon Ct Bethel CT 06801-2308 • danwehmeier@juno.com • NE • Sn/Adm • Immanuel Danbury CT • (203)748-3320 • (SL 1993 MDIV)

**WEHMEIER WALDEMAR W REV** (979)849-1592
2 Lapaloma St Angleton TX 77515-2724 • TX • EM • (SL 1959 THD)

**WEHMEIER WALTER J REV** (405)624-1904
1710 Briarwood Dr Stillwater OK 74075-2944 • OK • EM • (SL 1953 MDIV)

**WEHRMEISTER ARTHUR H REV** (317)885-7168
8165 Ehlerbrook Rd Indianapolis IN 46237-9789 • awehrmeisterclc@yahoo.com • IN • Sn/Adm • Calvary Indianapolis IN • (317)783-2000 • (CQ 1980 MDIV)

**WEHRSPANN DAN T REV** (503)649-2330
8124 SW 168th Ave Beaverton OR 97007 • danner@teleport.com • NOW • SP • Prince Of Peace Portland OR • (503)645-1211 • (SPR 1975 MDIV)

**WEHRSPANN LEO E REV**
1722 Martin Ln Apt 205 Saint Louis MO 63138-1747 • lewehr@earthlink.net • SO • EM • (SPR 1951 MAR MDIV)

**WEIBEL DEAN J REV** (612)473-0171
215 Barry Ave S Apt 122 Wayzata MN 55391-1645 • MNS • EM • (FW 1981 MAR)

**WEIDLER RONALD W REV** (630)761-8830
1073 Ponca Dr Batavia IL 60510-1145 • NI • SP • Immanuel Batavia IL • (630)879-7163 • (SPR 1976 MDIV)

**WEIDMAYER ROBERT CARL REV**
1650 Gentian Dr SE Kentwood MI 49508-6404 • revbob@spacestar.net • EN • SP • Grace Wyoming MI • (616)534-0805 • (SL 1996 MDIV)

**WEIDNER ARTHUR P REV** (701)232-1516
C/O Grace Luth Church 821 5th Ave S Fargo ND 58103-1841 • ND • SP • Grace Fargo ND • (701)232-1516 • (SPR 1967)

**WEIER GARY W REV** (601)896-9363
34 Greenbriar Dr Gulfport MS 39507-4215 • gweier@juno.com • SO • SP • Holy Trinity Gulfport MS • (601)896-5878 • (SL 1969 MDIV MCED)

**WEIKART ROBERT C REV**
1840 NE 41st St Pompano Beach FL 33064-6071 • FG • SP • Hope Pompano Beach FL • (954)942-2570 • (SPR 1969 MA DMIN)

**WEINHOLD RALPH REV** (206)301-0130
2601 W Howe St Seattle WA 98199-4320 • jeanandralphweinhold@home.com • NOW • EM • (SL 1951 MA MA)

**WEINHOLD ROBERT J REV** (602)894-6578
1014 E Balboa Cir Tempe AZ 85282-3964 • EN • EM • (SL 1955)

**WEINHOLD ROBERT W REV** (319)582-1217
2796 Hickory Hill St Dubuque IA 52001-1539 • pastorweinhold@juno.com • IE • SP • St Paul Dubuque IA • (319)556-7636 • (SL 1982 MDIV MSW)

**WEINHOLD TERRY REV** (816)279-2292
6002 Palamino Rd Saint Joseph MO 64505-9368 • debtwein@ponyexpress.net • MO • Sn/Adm • St Paul Saint Joseph MO • (816)279-1110 • (SL 1977 MDIV)

**WEINKAUF RANDALL L REV** (671)477-4578
C/O Lutheran Church Of Guam 787 W Marine Dr Agana GU 96910-4997 • weinkauf@ite.net • MO • S Miss • Missouri Saint Louis MO • (314)317-4550 • (SL 1981 MDIV)

**WEINRICH CHARLES A REV** (414)545-4333
3849 S Marcy St Milwaukee WI 53220-1836 • charles.weinrich@vmp.org • EN • Inst C • English Farmington MI • (SL 1967 MDIV)

**WEINRICH RALPH A REV** (706)896-1253
1037 Barbara Ln Hiawassee GA 30546-2901 • rev1@whitelion.net • FG • EM • (SPR 1962)

**WEINRICH WILLIAM C REV** (219)637-5202
11421 Trails North Dr Fort Wayne IN 46845-1314 • wmwein@aol.com • IN • SHS/C • Indiana Fort Wayne IN • (SL 1972 MDIV THD)

**WEIS CARL W REV** (616)657-7888
35284 51st Ave Paw Paw MI 49079-9657 • cwweis@trinitylutheran.com • MI • Sn/Adm • Trinity Paw Paw MI • (616)657-4840 • (SL 1985 MDIV)

**WEIS EARL E REV** (501)884-6257
PO Box 1325 Fairfield Bay AR 72088-1325 • earllois@hypertech.net • MDS • EM • (SL 1945 MDIV)

**WEIS JAMES M REV** (217)787-0867
2048 Briarcliff Dr Springfield IL 62704-4126 • CI • EM • (SL 1961 MDIV)

**WEISE ROBERT W REV** (618)656-3853
224 Beldon Dr Edwardsville IL 62025 • weiser@csl.edu • MO • SHS/C • Missouri Saint Louis MO • (314)317-4550 • (SL 1982 MDIV PHD)

**WEISE RUSSELL J REV**
C/O St John Lutheran Church 2727 N Union St Decatur IL 62526-3247 • CI • Sn/Adm • St John Decatur IL • (217)875-3656 • (CQ 1982 DMIN)

**WEISENBORN FREDERICK C REV** (660)463-2880
602 NW 8th St Concordia MO 64020-9784 • fcweisenborn@almanet.net • MO • EM • (SPR 1954)

**WEISENBORN PAUL C REV** (573)546-1451
358 Eidson Ct Ironton MO 63650 • revy2born@mail.tigernet.gen.mo.us • MO • SP • St Paul Ironton MO • (573)546-2171 • (FW 1997 MDIV)

**WEISER DELTON R REV** (512)252-9387
104 Redwood Ln Pflugerville TX 78660 • TX • D Miss • Texas Austin TX • (SL 1991 MDIV)

**WEISHAUPT THEODORE F REV**
70119 Memphis Rd Wiota IA 50274-8745 • IW • SP • First Wiota IA • (712)774-5787 • (CQ 1995 MDIV)

**WEISHOFF ROBERT LEE REV** (406)566-2723
PO Box 553 Stanford MT 59479-0553 • MT • SP • Trinity Stanford MT* • (406)566-2723 • (CQ 1990 MDIV)

**WEISS DAVID E REV** (616)445-3950
61290 Mary Lou Ln Cassopolis MI 49031-9703 • stpaul@beantalk.net • MI • Sn/Adm • St Paul Cassopolis MI • (616)445-3950 • (SL 1993 MDIV)

**WEISS DONALD E REV** (419)693-9662
4125 Pickle Rd Oregon OH 43616-4135 • dewpop@aol.com • OH • SP • Prince Peace Oregon OH • (419)691-9407 • (SPR 1973 MDIV)

**WEISS DONALD P REV** (414)355-8113
8744 W Magnolia St Milwaukee WI 53224-4024 • dpweiss@execpc.com • SW • Sn/Adm • St Peter-Immanuel Milwaukee WI • (414)353-6800 • (SL 1973 MDIV)

**WEIST JAMES DONALD REV** (440)543-5593
8375 Lucerne Dr Chagrin Falls OH 44023 • msujim@yahoo.com • FG • S Miss • Florida-Georgia Orlando FL • (FW 1997 MDIV)

**WELCH DANIEL J REV** (402)634-2953
PO Box 48 Meadow Grove NE 68752 • dwelch@ncfcomm.com • NEB • SP • St Matthew Meadow Grove NE* • (402)634-2933 • (SL 1998 MDIV)

**WELCH HOWARD G REV** (334)949-6242
PO Box 171 Bon Secour AL 36511-0171 • SO • EM • * • (SPR 1951)

**WELDON JOHN H REV** (412)731-3068
230 Dorothy Dr Pittsburgh PA 15235 • EA • SP • Epiphany Penn Hills PA • (412)241-1313 • (SL 1971 MDIV MA)

**WELGE JOHN W REV** (330)677-5836
4574 Chatwood Dr Stow OH 44224-1956 • OH • Asst • Gloria Dei Hudson OH • (330)650-6550 • (SPR 1972 MDIV)

**WELLER ROBERT DENNIS JR. REV**
C/O Shepherd Of The Valley LC 1281 Redmond Ave San Jose CA 95120-2747 • CNH • SP • Shep Of Valley San Jose CA • (408)997-4848 • (FW 1994 MDIV)

**WELLHOUSEN MERLIN R REV** (615)595-1990
2894 Stewart Campbell Point Thompson Station TN 37179 • lmwell@bellsouth.net • MDS • 09/1999 • (SL 1985 MDIV)

**WELLMAN KEITH B REV** (308)394-5562
RR 2 Box 37 Wauneta NE 69045 • byron@bwtelcom.net • NEB • SP • St Paul Wauneta NE • (308)394-5562 • (SL 1974 MDIV)

**WELLNITZ KARL ARTHUR REV** (708)946-2287
1417 W Church Rd Beecher IL 60401-3425 • NI • SP • St Paul Beecher IL • (708)946-2050 • (FW 1992 MDIV)

**WELLS JAMES L REV** (817)246-5919
740 Burlington Ave Fort Worth TX 76108-4556 • jlwells@flash.net • TX • 05/1997 05/2000 • (SL 1979 MDIV)

**WELMER MICHAEL F REV** (713)896-1773
C/O Epiphany Luth Church 8101 Senate St Houston TX 77040-1277 • mwelmer@aol • TX • Sn/Adm • Epiphany Houston TX • (713)896-1773 • (SPR 1973 MDIV)

**WELSH RONALD C REV** (317)595-8644
8640 Lantern Farms Dr Fishers IN 46038-1055 • IN • Inst C • Indiana Fort Wayne IN • (SPR 1969)

**WENCK CARL R REV** (615)904-2315
598 Foxfire Ct Murfreesboro TN 37129 • MDS • Sn/Adm • Grace Murfreesboro TN • (615)893-0338 • (FW 1981 MDIV)

**WENDE JOHN DAVID REV** (651)228-0524
849 Armstrong Ave Saint Paul MN 55102-3815 • golfmantom@earthlink.net • MNS • SP • St Peter Saint Paul MN • (651)228-1482 • (SPR 1970 MDIV)

**WENDEL RUDY REV** (830)997-8893
109 W Nimitz Fredericksburg TX 78624 • TX • EM • (WBS 1953 MDIV MA)

**WENDLAND LELAND J REV** (360)604-9912
3205 SE 153rd Ave Vancouver WA 98683-5142 • NOW • EM • (SL 1957)

**WENDLER HARLAN C REV** (417)886-1917
3942 S Gatlin Ct Springfield MO 65807-5368 • dwendler@juno.com • MO • EM • (SL 1946 MDIV STM)

**WENDORF KENTON G REV** (440)354-0296
7067 Sandpiper Ct Painesville OH 44077-2143 • pkent508@aol.com • OH • Sn/Adm • Zion Painesville OH • (440)357-5174 • (CQ 1979)

**WENDT ERNEST C REV** (517)883-3524
9641 Bach Rd Sebewaing MI 48759-9566 • MI • SP • St Peter Sebewaing MI • (517)883-3524 • (CQ 1986 MAR MED)

**WENDT HAROLD N DR** (612)828-6005
8268 Kingslee Rd Bloomington MN 55438-1254 • crosswaysi@aol.com • MNS • Asst • Cross View Edina MN • (952)941-1094 • (CQ 1968 STM LITTD)

**WENDT KEVIN M REV** (636)464-6328
1416 Appleton Ct Arnold MO 63010 • kevnjenwendt@sprynet.com • MO • Asst • Abiding Savior Saint Louis MO • (314)894-9703 • (SL 1993 MDIV)

**WENDT VERNON E JR. DR** (310)837-6218
10751 Rose Ave Apt 108 Los Angeles CA 90034 • vernwendt@aol.com • EN • D Miss • Pacific Southwest Irvine CA • (949)854-3232 • (FW 1990 MDIV DMISS)

**WENDZEL LINDEN B REV** (515)789-4290
PO Box 127 Dexter IA 50070-0127 • IW • SP • Zion Dexter IA • (515)789-4295 • (FW 1977 MDIV)

**WENGER ERIC R REV** (920)831-0931
1003 W Harris St Appleton WI 54914-3857 • ewenger@shepherdhills.org • NW • Assoc • Shepherd Hills Greenville WI • (920)757-5722 • (SL 1997 MDIV)

**WENGER MARK P REV** (816)690-5616
822 SE 15th St Oak Grove MO 64075-9556 • MO • SP • Shep Of Valley Oak Grove MO • (816)690-4020 • (SL 1981 MDIV)

**WENGER NORMAN E REV** (605)835-9176
1117 Spencer Ave Gregory SD 57533-1150 • SD • EM • (CQ 1977)

**WENGER TIMOTHY E REV** (715)423-7821
2310 11th St S Wisconsin Rapids WI 54494-6305 • stlukesl@tznet.com • NW • Sn/Adm • St Luke Wisconsin Rapids WI • (715)423-5990 • (SL 1970 MDIV STM DMIN)

**WENIG THOMAS D REV** (812)476-9991
229 Plaza Evansville IN 47714 • tdwenig@earthlink.com • IN • SP • Our Redeemer Evansville IN • (812)476-9991 • (SL 1991 MDIV)

**WENK STEPHEN B REV** (608)244-9272
1661 Delaware Blvd Madison WI 53704-1861 • sb.wenk@hosp.wisc.edu • SW • Inst C • South Wisconsin Milwaukee WI • (414)464-8100 • (SL 1983 MDIV)

**WENKER KEVIN L REV**
15127 N 86th Dr Peoria AZ 85381-3743 • NI • SP • St Martini Chicago IL • (773)776-7610 • (SPR 1976 MDIV)

**WENNDT THOMAS R REV** (309)348-3496
13441 Townline Rd Green Valley IL 61534-9216 • trwenndt@dpc.net • CI • SP • St John Green Valley IL • (309)348-3180 • (FW 1988 MDIV)

**WENSKAY LEE C REV** (517)453-2381
7361 Kilmanagh Rd Pigeon MI 48755 • MI • SP • St Paul Pigeon MI • (517)453-2271 • (FW 2000 MDIV)

**WENTHE DEAN ORRIN REV** (219)483-7256
1 Coverdale Dr Fort Wayne IN 46825-4928 • wenthe@ctsfw.edu • IN • SHS/C • Indiana Fort Wayne IN • (SL 1971 MDIV MA MTH PHD)

**WENTZEL ERNEST F REV** (618)344-8205
99 Westmoreland St Collinsville IL 62234-2957 • SI • EM • (SL 1953 MA)

**WENTZEL WAYNE H REV** (810)695-8613
7040 Mancour Dr Grand Blanc MI 48439-7402 • whwentz@aol.com • MI • Sn/Adm • Faith Grand Blanc MI • (810)694-9351 • (FW 1977 MDIV MS DMIN)

**WENZ PAUL GEORGE REV** (605)668-0496
1807 College St Yankton SD 57078-2217 • paulwenz@netscape.net • SD • Asst • St John Yankton SD • (605)665-7337 • (SL 1993 MDIV STM)

**WENZEL ALSEN K REV** (517)831-9140
4733 West Stanton Rd Stanton MI 48888-9747 • pilotwen@pathwaynet.com • MI • SP • Hope Stanton MI • (517)831-5594 • (SL 1998 MDIV)

**WENZEL ELMER W REV** (360)653-7709
5913 74th Ave NE Marysville WA 98270-8879 • NOW • EM • (SL 1956)

**WENZEL MARK ARMEN REV** (920)746-1625
1557 Michigan St Sturgeon Bay WI 54235 • mjwenzel@usa.net • NW • SP • Prince Peace Sturgeon Bay WI • (920)743-7750 • (SL 1996 MDIV)

**WENZEL MARTIN H REV** (701)228-3688
775 85th St NE Willow City ND 58384-9795 • ND • EM • (SL 1943)

**WENZELBURGER MARK E REV** (316)724-6680
109 W St John Girard KS 66743-1226 • mkmkwenz@ckt.net • KS • SP • Trinity Girard KS • (316)724-8895 • (SL 1998 MDIV MS)

**WERDIN GREGORY G REV** (505)275-0799
3709 Valerie Pl NE Albuquerque NM 87111-4030 • revrup@uswest.net • RM • SP • Christ Albuquerque NM • (505)884-3876 • (SPR 1976 MDIV)

**WERFELMANN ARTHUR H REV** (509)547-0683
2704 W Henry St Pasco WA 99301-3913 • NOW • SP • Trinity Pasco WA* • (509)547-3466 • (CQ 1984)

**WERFELMANN THEODORE REV** (253)874-2517
5307 Nathan Loop SE Auburn WA 98092 • NOW • SP • Light Of Christ Federal Way WA • (253)874-2517 • (SL 1976 MDIV)

**WERK ALLEN A REV** (716)344-0219
24 Park Ave Batavia NY 14020-2023 • werkasap@iinc.com • EA • SP • St Paul Batavia NY • (716)343-0488 • (SL 1982 MDIV)

**WERLING GARY W REV** (402)332-3922
425 Devonshire Dr Gretna NE 68028-4517 • gwwerling@yahoo.com • NEB • SP • Good Shepherd Gretna NE • (402)332-3345 • (FW 1979 MDIV)

**WERLING HENRY F REV** (651)490-1496
2976 W Owasso Blvd Saint Paul MN 55113-2159 • MNS • EM • (SL 1935 MDIV MA PHD)

**WERLY DAVID C REV**
PO Box 525 Chenango Bridge NY 13745 • EA • SP • Holy Trinity Chenango Bridge NY • (607)648-8104 • (FW 1999 MDIV)

**WERNECKE JOHN W REV** (517)839-0395
2514 Abbott Rd Apt T-1 Midland MI 48642 • pastor-john@writeme.com • MI • 12/1999 • (FW 1985 MDIV)

**WERNER DAVID W REV** (219)485-3586
4517 E Shenandoah Cir Fort Wayne IN 46835-4416 • IN • 09/1985 09/1999 • (CQ 1978)

**WERNER JOHN T P REV** (605)825-4270
42654 272nd St Emery SD 57332-5306 • johnwerner@basec.net • SD • SP • St Peter Emery SD* • (605)825-4222 • (SPR 1970 MDIV)

**WERNER JOSEPH G REV** (507)433-5883
103 21st St NW Austin MN 55912-4653 • MNS • EM • * • (SPR 1942)

**WERNER KEVIN L REV** (507)945-8102
401 5th Ave Round Lake MN 56167-9757 • kwerner@rconnect.com • MNS • SP • Bethel Round Lake MN • (507)945-8102 • (FW 1991 MDIV)

**WERNER PAUL G REV** (810)220-0307
368 Woodlake Dr Brighton MI 48116-2061 • shepherd@ismi.net • MI • Sn/Adm • Shep Lakes Brighton MI • (810)227-5099 • (SL 1987 MDIV)

**WERNING WALDO J REV** (262)691-2303
N34 W23109 Circle Rdg Rd #101 Pewaukee WI 53072 • rcwern1@aol.com • SW • EM • (SL 1945 MDIV DD)

**WERTH ALAN R REV** (701)642-5723
402 3rd Ave N Wahpeton ND 58075-4421 • immanuel@rrt.net • ND • SP • Immanuel Wahpeton ND • (701)642-6910 • (FW 1993 MDIV)

**WERTH CHARLES E REV** (920)925-3506
W4445 Smith Rd Watertown WI 53098-4664 • cewwi@execpc.com • EN • 08/1997 08/2000 • (SL 1979 MDIV)

**WERTH LUTHER A REV** (734)464-9292
35698 Vargo St Livonia MI 48152-2941 • lutherwerth@aol.com • MI • Sn/Adm • Christ Our Savior Livonia MI • (734)522-6830 • (SL 1965 MDIV)

**WERTZ RICHARD P REV** (708)410-1569
520 Andy Dr Melrose Park IL 60160 • crfwertzd@curf.edu • NI • SHS/C • Northern Illinois Hillside IL • (SPR 1973 MAR MDIV MBA)

**WESCOATT MARK ALLEN REV** (580)338-2563
1701 N Oklahoma St Guymon OK 73942-2601 • wescoatt@ptsi.net • OK • SP • Trinity Guymon OK • (580)338-3820 • (FW 1991 MDIV)

**WESELOH MELVIN L REV** (217)425-5753
109 Fenway Dr Decatur IL 62521-5609 • revpepsimel@aol.com • CI • EM • (SL 1957)

**WESEMANN KENNETH R DR** (219)452-2188
C/O Concordia Theo Seminary 6600 N Clinton St Fort Wayne IN 46825-4916 • revkrw@aol.com • IN • SHS/C • Indiana Fort Wayne IN • (SL 1985 MDIV MS PHD)

**WESEMANN TIMOTHY P REV** (314)631-4788
4647 Weber Terrace Ct Saint Louis MO 63123-4642 • tpwesemann@aol.com • MO • 05/2000 • (SL 1989 MDIV)

**WESENBERG HENRY C REV** (517)795-9399
25 Elmwood Rd Fostoria MI 48435 • MI • SP • Nw Life Christ North Branch MI • (810)688-2747 • (SPR 1965 MDIV)

**WESENER DONALD O REV** (715)423-3167
1031 18th Ave S Wisconsin Rapids WI 54495-3922 • revwsnr@webtv.net • NW • EM • (SL 1956)

**WESOLIK LARRY F REV** (216)899-7275
1703 Settlers Reserve Way Westlake OH 44145-2044 • OH • Sn/Adm • St Paul Westlake OH • (440)835-3050 • (SPR 1970 MDIV)

**WESSEL JONATHAN A REV** (715)345-9669
1650 Clark St - Apt 4 Stevens Point WI 54481-3042 • padrejon88@voyager.net • NW • Assoc • St Paul Stevens Point WI • (715)344-5664 • (FW 1988 MDIV)

**WESSEL KENNETH H REV**
1503 Cowling Bay Rd Neenah WI 54956-9720 • FG • EM • (SL 1956 MDIV)

**WESSEL LOEL A REV** (763)494-8528
C/O St John Lutheran Church 9141 County Road 101 N Maple Grove MN 55311-1302 • MNS • Assoc • St John Maple Grove MN • (763)420-2426 • (FW 1993 MDIV)

**WESSELSCHMIDT QUENTIN F DR** (636)532-1993
444 Eatherton Valley Rd Chesterfield MO 63005 • MO • SHS/C • Missouri Saint Louis MO • (314)317-4550 • (SL 1963 MDIV MA PHD)

**WESSLER ARNOLD A REV** (303)773-3711
7886 S University Way Littleton CO 80122-3300 • RM • EM • (SL 1943 MDIV)

**WESSLER RAYMOND W REV** (602)566-6333
10134 W Mohawk Ln Apt 1024 Peoria AZ 85382-2251 • PSW • EM • (SPR 1961)

**WESSLING EDWARD W REV** (520)684-2368
610 N Madison St Wickenburg AZ 85390-1299 • PSW • EM • (SL 1949 STM MA)

**WESSLING MARK REV** (305)885-0776
215 Lenape Dr Miami Springs FL 33166-5118 • FG • SP • Faith Hialeah FL • (305)888-6706 • (SL 1981 MDIV)

**WESSON JIM R REV** (704)896-2493
7602 Mariner Cove Dr Cornelius NC 28031-8658 • SE • EM • (SL 1963 MST)

**WEST DONALD E REV** (507)545-2158
234 Carolann St Eyota MN 55934-9722 • MNS • EM • (SPR 1965)

**WESTAD ROBERT C REV** (605)882-1171
1109 N Broadway Watertown SD 57201-1437 • SD • SP • Mount Olive Watertown SD • (605)886-5671 • (SL 1965 MDIV DMIN)

**WESTBY CHARLES W REV** (970)490-2002
1919 Winterberry Way Unit C Fort Collins CO 80526-1954 • KS • 07/1997 07/1999 • (CQ 1992 MDIV)

**WESTCOTT EDWARD A JR. REV** (623)933-6037
11237 N 110th Dr Sun City AZ 85351-4014 • redjean@prodigy.net • PSW • EM • (SPR 1947 MDIV DD)

**WESTERGREN KEVIN T REV** (512)459-1500
C/O Redeemer Luth Church 1500 W Anderson Ln Austin TX 78757-1453 • pastor@redeemer.net • TX • Assoc • Redeemer Austin TX • (512)459-1500 • (SL 1987 MDIV)

**WESTERLUND PAUL L REV** (612)926-9359
5724 Drew Ave S Minneapolis MN 55410-2348 • MNS • EM • (SL 1973 MA MA)

**WESTERMANN TED D DR**
6183 Forest Villas Cir Fort Myers FL 33908 • IN • EM • (SL 1953 PHD)

**WESTHAFER JOHN A REV** (209)772-0950
5144 Treosti Pl # 485 Valley Springs CA 95252-9138 • CNH • SP • The Divide Georgetown CA • (530)333-2633 • (SL 1985 MDIV)

**WESTON ROBERT W REV** (303)663-8808
1032 Snow Lily Ct Castle Rock CO 80104-8275 • RM • 08/1982 08/2000 • (SPR 1963 MDIV MA)

**WESTPHAL LEROY R REV** (517)839-9780
3208 Fernside Street Midland MI 48642-4084 • MI • EM • (SL 1958)

**WESTRA JOHN REV** (616)394-4784
66 W 31st St Holland MI 49423-5025 • westra@macatawa.com • MI • Sn/Adm • Zion Holland MI • (616)392-7151 • (SPR 1975 MDIV)

**WETMORE DAVID L REV** (507)632-4596
302 West Main St PO Box 347 Ceylon MN 56121 • MNS • SP • Our Savior Ceylon MN* • (507)632-4596 • (FW 1999 MDIV)

**WETZEL LOUIS M REV** (360)668-4387
17822 87th Ave SE Snohomish WA 98296-4817 • NOW • EM • * • (SL 1929)

**WETZEL OLIVER H REV** (847)782-1407
37850 Red Oak Terrace Wadsworth IL 60083 • ohwetzel@aol.com • NI • EM • * • (SL 1956)

**WETZEL RALPH M JR. DR** (219)493-3695
4310 Ara Dr PO Box 286 Woodburn IN 46797-9588 • suscaro/outwetz8@aol.com • IN • 11/1988 11/1999 • * • (SPR 1964 STM MDIV DMIN)

**WETZSTEIN JAMES A REV** (219)938-9069
C/O Our Savior Lutheran Church 1150 W 49th Ave Gary IN 46408 • wetzsteins@aol.com • IN • SP • Our Saviour Gary IN • (219)887-5031 • (SL 1989 MDIV)

**WETZSTEIN W H REV** (281)251-2008
12810 Bowing Oaks Dr Cypress TX 77429-2045 • EN • EM • (SPR 1941 MDIV)

**WETZSTEIN WERNER F REV** (712)644-3153
C/O Zion Luth Church 216 N 3rd Ave Logan IA 51546-1310 • IW • EM • (SPR 1962)

**WHEELER JAY R REV** (515)342-6297
106 E View Pl Osceola IA 50213-1300 • IW • SP • Immanuel Osceola IA • (515)342-3121 • (FW 1983 MDIV)

**WHEELER STEVEN JAMES REV** (303)238-7676
C/O Bethlehem Luth Church 2100 Wadsworth Blvd Lakewood CO 80215-2007 • swheeler@bethluth.net • RM • Assoc • Bethlehem Lakewood CO • (303)238-7676 • (SL 1995 MDIV)

**WHEELHOUSE PAUL ALLEN REV**
1776 SE 178 Ave Silver Springs FL 34488-6152 • pwheel2@juno.com • EN • SP • Forest Silver Springs FL • (352)625-8700 • (SL 1994 MDIV)

**WHITBY KRISTOPHER R REV** (904)419-6125
2478 Whispering Woods Blvd Apt Unit 3 Jacksonville FL 32246-9728 • FG • SP • Guardian Jacksonville FL • (904)268-5816 • (SL 1996 MDIV)

**WHITE DONALD E REV** (715)675-0316
3627 6th St Apt 104 Wausau WI 54403 • NW • EM • (CQ 1983 MS)

**WHITE DONALD RAY REV** (785)885-4821
C/O Peace Luth Church PO Box 292 Natoma KS 67651-0292 • revdon@ruraltel.net • KS • SP • Peace Natoma KS • (785)885-4718 • (SL 1991 MDIV)

**WHITE HARRY W REV** (517)624-9263
10787 Rose Ln PO Box 248 Birch Run MI 48415 • MI • EM • (SPR 1960)

**WHITE LAURENCE L REV** (713)686-5928
1008 Richelieu Ln Houston TX 77018-2018 • TX • Sn/Adm • Our Savior Houston TX • (713)290-9087 • (SPR 1974 MDIV DD)

**WHITECOTTON HOWARD III REV** (317)862-4833
2107 S Post Rd Indianapolis IN 46239-9338 • derstift@hotmail.com • IN • SP • St Mark Pendleton IN • (765)778-3201 • (FW 1987 MDIV)

**WHITED CHARLES E JR. REV** (716)334-1392
C/O Pinnacle Luth Church 250 Pinnacle Rd Rochester NY 14623 • revwhited@juno.com • EA • Sn/Adm • Pinnacle Rochester NY • (716)334-1392 • (SL 1993 MDIV)

**WHITFIELD ALEXANDER REV** (605)338-5226
C/O Zion Lutheran Church 1400 S Duluth Ave Sioux Falls SD 57105 • c1tracy@yahoo.com • SD • Assoc • Zion Sioux Falls SD • (605)338-5226 • (SL 1997 MDIV)

**WHITSETT MARK D REV** (765)649-9952
3143 Greenbriar Rd Anderson IN 46011-2301 • whitsemd@indy.net • IN • Sn/Adm • Christ Anderson IN • (765)642-2154 • (SL 1979 MDIV)

**WHITSON CRAIG E REV** (281)255-6278
28211 Camille Dr Tomball TX 77375-4053 • cwhitson@salem4u.com • TX • Assoc • Salem Tomball TX • (281)351-8223 • (SL 1984 MA MDIV)

**WHITTAKER MARK C REV** (616)353-0487
C/O Trinity Lutheran Church 721 Pine St Paw Paw MI 49079-1248 • markjodi@surfree.com • MI • Assoc • Trinity Paw Paw MI • (616)657-4840 • (SL 1984 MDIV)

**WHITTLE BRIAN C REV** (417)345-5710
805 N Hickory St Buffalo MO 65622-9443 • whittle@todays-tech.com • MO • SP • Hope Hermitage MO* • (417)745-2117 • (SL 1998 MST MDIV)

**WHYBREW KENE A REV**
C/O Zion Lutheran Church 190 Concordia Dr Chebanse IL 60922-9761 • pkaw@stewstras.net • NI • Hope Hermitage MO • (417)745-2117 • (FW 1990 MDIV)

**WICHER CHRIS C REV**
150 Unionvale Cheektowaga NY 14225 • ccwicher@aol.com • EA • SP • St Luke Cheektowaga NY • (716)633-6752 • (SL 1982 MDIV MST DMIN)

**WICHNER ERWIN REV** (206)681-4825
668 NE Alexis Hillsboro OR 97124 • NOW • SP • Zion Hillsboro OR • (503)640-8914 • (SPR 1968 MA)

**WICKERT GARRY E REV** (219)866-8894
725 E Emilie St Rensselaer IN 47978-2902 • gmwickert@netnitco.net • IN • SP • St Luke Rensselaer IN • (219)866-7681 • (FW 1986 MDIV)

**WIDGER DONAL C REV**
Cross Of Christ Lutheran Ch 1840 S 75 E Bountiful UT 84010-5544 • RM • SP • Cross Christ Bountiful UT • (801)295-7677 • (SL 2000 MDIV)

**WIDMANN ELMER H REV** (319)396-1207
5310 Midway Dr NW Cedar Rapids IA 52405-3348 • IE • EM • (SL 1926)

**WIDMANN RICHARD W REV** (619)287-3882
7264 Conestoga Pl San Diego CA 92120-1820 • PSW • EM • (SPR 1958 MA)

**WIEBEL EDWIN H REV** (407)366-3622
2084 Catbird Ct Oviedo FL 32765-8539 • FG • EM • (SL 1944 MDIV)

**WIEBEL JAMES R REV** (407)277-3945
C/O Prince Of Peace Luth Ch 1515 S Semoran Blvd Orlando FL 32807-2919 • churchpop@aol.com • FG • Sn/Adm • Prince Of Peace Orlando FL • (407)277-3945 • (SL 1971 MDIV STM)

**WIEBOLD RAYMOND E REV**
1803 Willow Dr Hudson WI 54016-1457 • MNS • Assoc • Trinity Hudson WI • (715)386-9313 • (SL 1973 MDIV)

**WIECHMANN HELMUT H REV** (703)569-2434
7442 Spring Village Dr Springfield VA 22150-4446 • SE • EM • (SPR 1930)

**WIECHMANN RALPH E REV** (703)818-3487
13825 S Springs Dr Clifton VA 20124-2451 • revralph@erols.com • SE • Assoc • Prince Of Peace Springfield VA • (703)451-5855 • (SL 1962 MDIV)

**WIED HENRY C SR. REV** (979)242-5086
704 Frio St Winchester TX 78945-5235 • TX • SP • St Michael Winchester TX • (979)242-3444 • (FW 1993 MDIV)

**WIEGAND ADAM C REV** (518)583-0510
10 Judys Way Saratoga Springs NY 12866 • AT • Assoc • St Paul Saratoga Springs NY • (518)584-0904 • (SL 1996 MDIV)

**WIEGERT PAUL H REV** (715)268-2806
610 Keller Ave S Amery WI 54001-1252 • rlcpo@spaceston.net • NW • SP • Redeemer Amery WI • (715)268-7283 • (CQ 1979 MA)

**WIEGERT RAYMOND P REV** (406)549-2705
4007 Lincoln Rd Missoula MT 59802-3089 • ray³wiegert@prodigy.net • MT • SP • Messiah Missoula MT • (406)549-9222 • (SPR 1959 MDIV)

**WIERSCHKE ALLAN DIDRIK REV** (218)835-7309
PO Box 219 Blackduck MN 56630-0219 • MNN • SP • Holy Trinity Blackduck MN • (218)835-4423 • (FW 1994 MDIV)

**WIESE JAMES LORENZ REV** (816)453-1303
1110 NE Parvin Rd #205 Kansas City MO 64116 • wiese@speedchoice.com • MO • 01/2000 • (SL 1961 MDIV MA)

**WIESE JAMES M REV** (413)527-3486
7 Clark St Easthampton MA 01027 • NE • 09/1999 • (FW 1988 MDIV)

**WIESE RONALD JAMES REV** (901)454-1170
3276 N Waynoka Cir Memphis TN 38111-3616 • rjwiese@aol.com • MDS • Sn/Adm • Trinity Memphis TN • (901)525-1056 • (SL 1969 MDIV DMIN)

**WIESNER DAVID E REV** (314)892-3477
723 Woodward Dr Saint Louis MO 63125-5128 • MO • EM • (CQ 1985 MS PHD)

**WIESNER MARK D REV** (618)632-9987
1567 Sinking Springs Dr O Fallon IL 62269-6658 • MDwiesner@aol.com • SI • 07/1999 • (SL 1984 MDIV MS)

**WIEST STEPHEN R REV** (414)332-5641
4420 N Cramer Milwaukee WI 53211-1602 • SW • 08/1997 08/2000 • (FW 1986 MDIV)

**WIETING KENNETH W REV** (414)964-6250
2118 E Shorewood Blvd Shorewood WI 53211-2559 • lutherm@execpc.com • SW • SP • Luther Memorial Milwaukee WI • (414)332-5732 • (SL 1982 MDIV)

**WIGGINS JAMES SR. REV** (334)264-1797
3365 Southmont Dr Montgomery AL 36105-1729 • SO • EM • (GB 1959)

**WIGGINS JAMES JR. REV** (202)398-5503
C/O Peace Lutheran Church 15 49th Pl NE Washington DC 20019-5302 • revjwjr@aol.com • SE • SP • Peace Washington DC • (202)398-5503 • (FW 1986 MDIV)

**WIGGINS STEPHEN A SR. REV** (616)248-4041
2604 Union Ave SE Grand Rapids MI 49507-3547 • redeemerlutherangr@prodigy.net • MI • SP • Redeemer Grand Rapids MI • (616)452-1529 • (FW 1988 MDIV)

**WIIST DAVID E REV** (608)779-0572
812 14 Ave N Onalaska WI 54650-2413 • SW • Assoc • Shepherd Hills Onalaska WI • (608)783-0330 • (SL 1997 MDIV)

**WIKSTROM MARK J REV** (559)896-8709
1178 Mill St Selma CA 93662 • wikstrom@jps.net • CNH • SP • Our Savior Caruthers CA • (559)864-3008 • (CQ 1997 MDIV DMIN)

**WILBER JAMES G REV** (810)232-4223
2061 W Maple Ave Flint MI 48507-3501 • jgwmi@aol.com • MI • SP • Peace Flint MI • (810)234-2423 • (SPR 1972 MDIV)

**WILCKEN ROBERT S REV** (715)669-5424
202 E Rusch St PO Box 134 Thorp WI 54771-9219 • pastorob@discover-net.net • NW • SP • St Paul Thorp WI* • (715)669-5608 • (SPR 1963 MDIV)

**WILD F WILLIAM REV**
PO Box 1030 New Britain CT 06050-1030 • NE • EM • * • (SPR 1939)

**WILDAUER LEONARD PAUL REV**
Saint Paul Lutheran Church PO Box 395 Bonduel WI 54107-0395 • NW • Assoc • St Paul Bonduel WI • (715)758-8559 • (FW 1995 MDIV MS)

**WILDERMUTH DARYL C REV** (253)848-1491
9122 118th St E Puyallup WA 98373-3820 • NOW • SP • Our Savior Tacoma WA • (253)531-2112 • (SL 1957 MDIV)

**WILDERMUTH DENNIS J REV** (360)371-7365
PO Box 1646 Blaine WA 98231-1646 • NOW • IndC P • Northwest Portland OR • (SL 1972 MDIV)

**WILDGRUBE ERICH H REV** (215)646-4418
6026 Butler Pike Blue Bell PA 19422-2603 • EN • EM • (SL 1949 MDIV MA STM)

**WILDGRUBE PAUL F G REV** (518)374-1003
829 Northumberland Dr Schenectady NY 12309-4900 • pfgwildgrube@juno.com • AT • Sn/Adm • Zion Schenectady NY • (518)374-1811 • (SL 1960 MDIV)

**WILDNER CHARLES L REV** (301)233-3357
1932 Wilkens Ave Baltimore MD 21223-3444 • SE • SP • St Thomas Baltimore MD • (410)947-7258 • (FW 1980)

**WILEY DON C REV** (909)875-8545
1032 S Fillmore Ave Rialto CA 92376-7580 • wileyfamily@prodigy.net • PSW • SP • St John Colton CA • (909)825-2395 • (FW 1992 MDIV)

**WILEY TERRY WILLIAM REV** (307)324-7710
1305 Ritter St Rawlins WY 82301-4439 • kidwiley@hotmail.com • WY • SP • Christ Rawlins WY • (307)324-4168 • (SL 1993 MDIV)

**WILHELMSEN DANA REV** (820)282-3262
390 Dry Creek Rd Sedona AZ 86336-4332 • pneuagex@sedona.net • PSW • SP • Rock of Ages Sedona AZ • (520)282-4091 • (FW 1992 MDIV)

**WILK JAMES L REV** (952)442-2558
10020 Highway 284 Waconia MN 55387-9571 • MNS • EM • (SL 1958)

**WILK MAX W REV** (719)687-4268
2150 Valley View Dr Woodland Park CO 80863-8375 • NJ • EM • (SL 1960)

**WILKE DONALD C DR** (414)728-8234
404 W Geneva Delavan WI 53115-1006 • wilke@pensys.com • SW • EM • (SPR 1954)

**WILKE DONALD L REV** (320)252-1344
2034 Highview Dr Sauk Rapids MN 56379 • dwilke1@bsm1.org • MNN • Inst C • Minnesota North Brainerd MN • (SL 1978 MDIV)

**WILKE RAY S REV** (402)371-3076
84607 Hadar Rd Norfolk NE 68701-9801 • NEB • Sn/Adm • Grace Norfolk NE • (402)371-1044 • (SPR 1970)

**WILKE WAYNE W DR** (734)663-5721
4084 Boulder Pond Dr Ann Arbor MI 48108-8597 • wilkew@ccaa.edu • MI • SHS/C • Michigan Ann Arbor MI • (SL 1974 MDIV STM PHD)

**WILKEN TODD A REV** (618)939-9064
1437 Jamie Ln Waterloo IL 62298 • twilken@htc.net • SI • D Ex/S • Southern Illinois Belleville IL • (SL 1990 MDIV)

**WILKENS JAMES D REV** (402)553-1979
4905 California St Apt 14 Omaha NE 68132-2443 • NEB • 08/1999 • (SL 1961 MDIV)

**WILKENS MARK C REV** (216)520-3993
6709 Brecksville Rd Independence OH 44131-4833 • wilkens@access1.net • OH • Asst • Concordia Independence OH • (216)524-2188 • (SL 1994 MDIV)

**WILKEY MICKEY D REV** (417)546-2246
150 Sunken Forrest Dr #3-134 Forsyth MO 65653-8121 • doc2792@hotmail.com • MO • SP • Shepherd/Lakes Forsyth MO • (417)546-2246 • (FW 1983 MDIV)

**WILKIE DANA MARK REV** (417)767-4147
C/O Zion Luth Church 438 South Diggins Main St Seymour MO 65746 • dwilkie595@aol.com • MO • SP • Zion Seymour MO • (417)767-4019 • (FW 1995 MDIV)

**WILKIE RICHARD L REV** (507)334-4225
1305 Highland Pl Faribault MN 55021-6603 • MNS • Sn/Adm • Peace Faribault MN • (507)334-9610 • (CQ 1985 MA)

**WILKIE WESLEY H REV** (708)386-3744
605 S Scoville Ave Oak Park IL 60304-1405 • wwilkie@megsinet.net • NI • SHS/C • Northern Illinois Hillside IL • (SL 1964 MDIV)

**WILL THEODORE W JR. REV** (360)256-0753
10104 NE 14th Cir Vancouver WA 98664-3008 • twwill@home.com • NOW • Assoc • Memorial Vancouver WA • (360)695-7501 • (SL 1973 MDIV)

**WILLADSEN TOM P REV** (601)749-4452
154 Tennyson Cove Picayune MS 39466 • SO • SP • St Paul Picayune MS • (601)798-4586 • (SL 1975 MDIV)

**WILLE EUGENE E REV** (815)544-2631
910 E 5th St Belvidere IL 61008-4544 • NI • Assoc • Immanuel Belvidere IL • (815)544-8058 • (SL 1959 MDIV)

**WILLE JOHN C REV** (608)372-6509
1428 Jason Ave Tomah WI 54660-3258 • goodshep@mwt.net • SW • SP • Good Shepherd Tomah WI • (608)374-2444 • (CQ 1984 MDIV MDIV)

**WILLE JULIUS G REV** (870)436-5606
363 MC 2086 Peel AR 72668 • MO • EM • (CQ 1982)

**WILLE WARREN H REV** (970)493-5763
2301 Limousine Ct Fort Collins CO 80526-1428 • warren.wille@juno.com • RM • EM • (SPR 1950)

**WILLIAMS BYRON RAY SR. REV** (504)366-5180
225 Wright Ave Apt C Terrytown LA 70056-2684 • pastorbrw@aol.com • SO • SP • Trinity New Orleans LA • (504)945-4447 • (CQ 1996)

**WILLIAMS D GEORG REV** (402)387-2743
RR 1 Box 125B Ainsworth NE 69210-9700 • georgw01@nol.org • NEB • SP • Zion Ainsworth NE • (402)387-1512 • (FW 1977 MDIV STM PHD)

**WILLIAMS DANIEL RAUL REV** (210)653-6020
12518 Sandpiper Dr San Antonio TX 78233-2734 • NOW • EM • (CQ 1994)

**WILLIAMS DONALD H REV** (219)464-4466
4103 Lancaster Dr Valparaiso IN 46383-1932 • dhw@immanuel.put.k12.in.us • IN • Sn/Adm • Immanuel Valparaiso IN • (219)462-8207 • (SL 1966 MDIV)

**WILLIAMS DONN P REV** (713)957-4435
5427 Bent Bough Ln Houston TX 77088-5501 • williamsix@juno.com • TX • SP • Bethany Houston TX • (713)695-2933 • (SL 1981 MDIV)

**WILLIAMS EDWARD R REV** (352)365-2508
147 Jacaranda Dr Leesburg FL 34748-8839 • FG • EM • (CQ 1948 MS MST)

**WILLIAMS EDWIN REV**
5068 S 105th St Omaha NE 68127 • IW • EM • (SL 1961 MDIV)

**WILLIAMS GARY C REV** (616)473-2744
11170 Old US 315 Berrien Springs MI 49103 • CHWilliams@aol.com • MI • Assoc • Trinity Berrien Springs MI • (616)473-1811 • (FW 1983 MA)

**WILLIAMS GUILLAUME J S REV** (580)254-3382
1306 Oak Ave Woodward OK 73801-4418 • revhardheaded@geocities.com • OK • SP • Trinity Woodward OK • (580)256-2524 • (SL 1995 MDIV)

**WILLIAMS HERMAN J REV** (503)434-6129
1037 NE 28Th St Mc Minnville OR 97128-2211 • prwms³777@yahoo.com • NOW • Sn/Adm • Peace Chehalis WA • (360)748-4108 • (CQ 1985)

**WILLIAMS JEFFREY BAXTER REV**
C/O Concordia University 12800 N Lake Shore Dr Mequon WI 53097-2402 • cfiaime@mpks.net • SW • Peace Chehalis WA • (360)748-4108 • (FW 1992 MDIV)

**WILLIAMS RONALD E REV** (619)226-8646
4478 Pescadero Ave San Diego CA 92107-3629 • PSW • EM • (CQ 1968 STM MDIV DD)

**WILLIAMS S T JR. REV** (402)486-0474
4015 S 30th St Lincoln NE 68506 • stwilliams@christlutheranchurch.org • NEB • Assoc • Christ Lincoln NE • (402)483-7774 • (FW 1993 MDIV)

**WILLIAMS STEVEN A** (402)563-0863
#96 Cottonwood Dr Columbus NE 68601 • NEB • Asst • Peace Columbus NE • (402)564-8311 • (FW 2000 MDIV)

**WILLIAMSON GREGORY K REV** (910)868-2412
3451 Sugar Cane Cir Fayettsville NC 28303-4635 • usachaplain@mail.faynet.com • RM • M Chap • Rocky Mountain Aurora CO • (SL 1983 MDIV)

**WILLIAMSON GREGORY R REV** (847)690-9987
465 Florian Dr Des Plaines IL 60016-5756 • geearew@home.com • NI • Assoc • St Andrews Park Ridge IL • (847)823-6656 • (FW 1983 MDIV)

**WILLIAMSON KENNETH L REV** (517)584-2080
PO Box 521 Carson City MI 48811-0521 • klw@mvcc.com • MI • SP • Calvary Carson City MI • (517)584-6068 • (SL 1994 MDIV)

**WILLIG MARK S REV** (618)826-2664
934 William St Chester IL 62233-1737 • muknpuca@midwest.net • SI • Sn/Adm • St John Chester IL • (618)826-3545 • (SL 1981 MDIV)

**WILLMANN VICTOR D REV** (407)831-5348
2165 Hunterfield Rd Maitland FL 32751-3551 • vpwillmann@aol.com • FG • Sn/Adm • Ascension Casselberry FL • (407)831-7788 • (SL 1971 MDIV)

**WILLSON WILLIAM C REV** (716)268-5326
5761 Corbin Hill Rd Scio NY 14880 • kb3wl@infoblvd.net • EA • 12/1999 • (SPR 1973 MDIV)

**WILLWEBER LLOYD HENRY REV** (206)364-7613
1136 N 115th St Apt A102 Seattle WA 98133-8358 • LWillweber@aol.com • NOW • SP • Zion Seattle WA • (206)782-6734 • (CQ 1996)

**WILLWEBER PAUL LUTHER REV** (619)582-2306
6836 Easton Ct San Diego CA 92120-2909 • pswillweber@juno.com • PSW • SP • Prince Peace San Diego CA • (619)583-1436 • (SL 1995 MDIV)

**WILLWEBER STEPHEN KARL REV** (209)956-2057
5307 Barbados Cir Stockton CA 95210 • swillweber@juno.com • CNH • SP • Immanuel Stockton CA • (209)465-8383 • (SL 1998 MDIV)

**WILMAN JOHN A REV** (715)986-4920
Box 32 Turtle Lake WI 54889-0032 • NW • SP • Zion Turtle Lake WI* • (715)986-4927 • (FW 1999 MDIV)

**WILMOT TIMOTHY BRENT REV** (406)254-9428
36 Nimitz Dr Billings MT 59101-4658 • MT • SP • Christ King Billings MT • (406)252-9250 • (SL 1995 MDIV)

**WILSHEK DAVID E REV** (210)691-5047
11020 Huebner Oaks Apt 814 San Antonio TX 78230 • SI • M Chap • Southern Illinois Belleville IL • (SL 1984 MDIV MA)

**WILSON JAMES D REV** (406)846-1713
1220 Arizona St Deer Lodge MT 59722-2053 • hayakawa@in-tch.com • MT • SP • Redeemer Anaconda MT* • (406)846-1713 • (SL 1988 MDIV)

**WILSON JIMMIE REV** (314)652-3678
4574 Evans Ave Saint Louis MO 63113-2314 • MO • 03/1988 03/2000 • * • (CQ 1984)

**WILSON KEVIN ALAN REV** (913)651-5913
2608 S 16th Ter Leavenworth KS 66048-4127 • qwilso@hotmail.com • KS • Sn/Adm • Trinity Leavenworth KS • (913)682-7474 • (SL 1992 MDIV)

**WILSON RICHARD G REV** (517)864-3489
C/O Trinity Luth Church 5034 Bay City Forestville Rd Minden City MI 48456-9769 • trinity@hbch.com • MI • SP • Trinity Minden City MI • (517)864-3745 • (FW 1990 MDIV)

**WILSON ROBERT HAROLD REV** (785)526-7416
C/O Bethlehem Lutheran Church RR 2 Box 53 Sylvan Grove KS 67481-9408 • taina@midusa.net • KS • SP • Bethlehem Sylvan Grove KS • (913)526-7766 • (SL 1996 MDIV)

**WILSON STEVEN D REV** (507)764-3556
317 S Main St Sherburn MN 56171 • sbwinmn@juno.com • MNS • SP • St John Sherburn MN • (507)764-5312 • (FW 1989 MDIV)

**WILTENBURG ROBERT E REV** (732)271-2921
186 Driscoll Ct Somerset NJ 08873-6405 • NJ • EM • (SL 1945 MDIV)

**WILTENBURG WILLIAM J REV**
14 Heritage Way Bellingham MA 02019 • NE • EM • (SL 1942 MDIV)

**WIND ROBERT H REV** (804)379-4565
11216 Lady Slipper Ln Richmond VA 23236-2444 • SE • EM • (SL 1951)

**WINDISCH-GRAETZ A F FUERST REV** (773)755-1637
C/O Concordia Luth Church 2645 W Belmont Ave Chicago IL 60618-5912 • awindischg@aol.com • NI • Sn/Adm • Concordia Chicago IL • (773)588-4040 • (SPR 1963 MDIV)

**WINDSOR THOMAS J REV** (808)941-8576
1629 Wilder Ave Apt 704 Honolulu HI 96822 • twindsor@worldnet.att.net • CNH • Sn/Adm • Our Redeemer Honolulu HI • (808)946-4223 • (SL 1968 MDIV)

**WINGFIELD ALBERT B REV** (219)452-2100
C/O Concordia Theo Seminary 6600 N Clinton St Fort Wayne IN 46825-4916 • IN • SHS/C • Indiana Fort Wayne IN • (CQ 1983 MED)

**WINK THOMAS R REV** (262)367-0067
718 Cameron Cir Hartland WI 53029-2509 • winker@execpc.com • SW • SP • Shepherd Hills Pewaukee WI • (414)691-0700 • (SL 1976 MDIV)

**WINKEL RANDY REV** (941)493-5102
C/O Lakeside Luth Church 2401 Tamiami Trl S Venice FL 34293-5000 • rwinkel614@aol.com • FG • SP • Lakeside Venice FL • (941)493-5102 • (CQ 1981 STM DMIN)

**WINKELMAN MICHAEL L REV** (815)772-3386
C/O St Peter Luth Church 601 N Jackson St Morrison IL 61270-3007 • stpeters@sanasys.com • NI • SP • St Peter Morrison IL • (815)772-3386 • (SL 1972 MDIV)

**WINKELMAN VICTOR L REV** (936)646-6392
Rev Victor L Winkelman PO Box 1163 Livingston TX 77351-1163 • revwink@livingston.net • TX • SP • Trinity Livingston TX • (936)327-3239 • (FW 1987 MDIV)

**WINKER ELDON K REV** (314)846-5246
5648 Briarwood Estates Dr Saint Louis MO 63129-6024 • MO • SP • Epiphany Saint Louis MO • (314)752-7065 • (SL 1969 MDIV)

**WINKLER WILBERT D REV** (810)598-4254
51201 Elly Dr Chesterfield MI 48051-1965 • MI • EM • (SL 1942)

**WINNINGHAM DAVID C REV** (734)669-0519
2971 Green Valley Dr Ann Arbor MI 48103 • dcwinningham@hotmail.com • MI • Tchr • LHS North Macomb MI • (810)781-9151 • (SL 1977 MDIV)

**WINNINGHAM PAUL R REV** (573)788-2342
PO Box 105 Uniontown MO 63783-0105 • winn7@midwest.com • MO • SP • Grace Uniontown MO* • (573)788-2342 • (SL 1990 MDIV)

**WINSOR JAMES REV** (303)421-5872
8230 Jay Ct Arvada CO 80003-1730 • orthoprax@juno.com • RM • SP • Risen Christ Arvada CO • (303)421-5872 • (FW 1985 MDIV)

**WINTER CLIFFORD A REV** (316)942-5811
114 Vantage View Cir Wichita KS 67212-3310 • standrews@feist.com • KS • SP • St Andrew Wichita KS • (316)838-0944 • (SL 1965 MDIV STM DMIN)

**WINTER DAVID W REV** (612)467-3978
17495 134th St Hamburg MN 55339 • MNS • Sn/Adm • St John Young America MN • (612)467-2740 • (FW 1984 MDIV)

**WINTER FRANK E REV** (970)221-3568
998 Mt Champion Dr Livermore CO 80536 • frankncarla@juno.com • RM • EM • (SL 1961 MDIV)

**WINTER FRANK E REV** (970)223-2770
3112 Colony Dr Fort Collins CO 80526-2749 • chipjami@juno.com • RM • SP • Peace W Christ Fort Collins CO • (970)226-4721 • (SL 1988 MDIV)

**WINTER HAROLD F REV** (715)356-7724
300 Brandy Point Dr Unit 14 Arbor Vitae WI 54568-9551 • NW • EM • (SPR 1944)

**WINTER LINCOLN C REV** (773)561-8391
5950 N Magnolia Ave Chicago IL 60660-3317 • lctdwint@enteract.com • EN • SP • Bethany Chicago IL • (773)561-9159 • (FW 1998 MDIV)

**WINTER WILLIAM C REV** (517)366-4908
302 Kimberly Dr Prudenville MI 48651-9740 • winterhaus@voyager.net • MI • SP • St John Houghton Lake MI • (517)366-5164 • (SL 1973 MDIV)

**WINTERFELDT JONATHAN CARL REV** (618)337-6734
2300 Jerome Ln Cahokia IL 62206-2602 • jwinterfel@aol.com • SI • SP • Mount Calvary Cahokia IL • (618)337-9107 • (SL 1998 MDIV)

**WINTERHOFF WARREN REV** (518)439-6217
111 Elm Ave Delmar NY 12054-9762 • blutheran@juno.com • AT • SP • Bethlehem Delmar NY • (518)439-4328 • (SPR 1969 MDIV)

**WINTERROWD DONALD H REV** (515)272-4243
PO Box 304 Swea City IA 50590-0304 • IW • SP • Our Savior Swea City IA • (515)272-4713 • (SL 1963 MDIV)

**WINTERS RAYMOND F JR. REV** (804)971-1141
2770 Gelletly Rd Charlottesville VA 22902 • de-rev@juno.com • SE • 02/1999 • (FW 1979 MDIV)

**WINTERS WALTER A DR** (314)353-6925
7000 Hampton Ave Saint Louis MO 63109-3923 • winters@attglobal.net • MO • Our Savior Swea City IA • (515)272-4713 • (SL 1975 MA JD)

**WINTERSTEIN GEORGE REV** (949)586-8660
116 Via Estrada Unit A Laguna Woods CA 92653-4015 • PSW • EM • (SL 1932 MDIV)

**WINTERSTEIN PAUL E REV** (206)937-6590
C/O Calvary Lutheran Church 3420 SW Cloverdale St Seattle WA 98126-3761 • calvarylutheran@juno.com • NOW • SP • Calvary Seattle WA • (206)937-6590 • (SL 1967 MDIV)

**WIPPERMAN STEPHEN K REV** (715)359-3373
4301 Peppermint Ln Wausau WI 54401-9263 • stevew@dwave.net • NW • Sn/Adm • Christ Wausau WI • (715)848-2040 • (SL 1978 MDIV)

**WIPPICH DE LLOYD D REV** (612)537-3296
4057 Quail Ave N Robbinsdale MN 55422-1712 • MNS • SP • Trinity First Minneapolis MN • (612)870-9487 • (SPR 1962 MDIV)

**WIPPICH ELLSWORTH R REV** (218)342-3632
PO Box 146 Vergas MN 56587-0146 • MNN • EM • (SPR 1971 MDIV)

**WIPPICH FRED J JR. REV** (417)546-3273
PO Box 517 Forsyth MO 65653-0517 • MO • EM • (SL 1956 MDIV MA)

**WIRSING THOMAS C REV** (309)454-2015
1402 Henry St Normal IL 61761-4857 • tow1@trinluth.org • CI • Sn/Adm • Trinity Bloomington IL • (309)828-6265 • (SL 1979 MDIV)

**WIRTZ NICHOLAS DONALD REV** (909)923-9645
2619 Dover Pl Ontario CA 91761-7328 • RevNWirtz@CS.com • EN • SP • Highland Park Los Angeles CA • (323)255-0309 • (FW 1994 MDIV)

**WISCH JOHN K REV** (440)461-0981
6593 Indiana Ave Cleveland OH 44124-1926 • EN • EM • (SL 1958 MSW)

**WISE KENNETH M REV** (219)493-9180
2009 Dublin Ct Fort Wayne IN 46815-8724 • pastorken@concordiachurch.org • IN • Assoc • Concordia Fort Wayne IN • (219)422-2429 • (SL 1988 MDIV)

**WISE RODNEY A REV** (314)427-3444
3414 Taylor Ave Bridgeton MO 63044 • redeemer@primary.net • MO • SP • Our Redeemer Overland MO • (314)427-3444 • (SL 1999 MDIV JD)

**WISE WILLIAM G REV**
341 Skyler Run Destin FL 32541-2126 • wiseservnt@aol.com • SO • 08/1998 08/2000 • (SPR 1970 MDIV)

**WISMAR ADOLPH H JR. DR** (617)472-8394
8 Ellington Rd Quincy MA 02170-1906 • a.wismar@ultranet.com • NE • Sn/Adm • Wollaston Quincy MA • (617)773-5482 • (SL 1969 MDIV DMIN)

**WISMAR GREGORY J REV** (203)426-0651
81 Mount Pleasant Rd Newtown CT 06470-1545 • wismar@prodigy.net • NE • SP • Christ King Newtown CT • (203)426-6300 • (SL 1971 MS MDIV DMIN)

**WISROTH LEE A REV** (307)326-8862
C/O Platte Valley Luth Ch PO Box 385 Saratoga WY 82331-0385 • wizzy@union-tel.com • WY • SP • Platte Valley Saratoga WY* • (307)326-5449 • (FW 1983 MDIV)

**WITSCHY EMIL A REV** (203)268-1722
6025 Main St Trumbull CT 06611 • wits.end@worldnet.att.net • NE • SP • Holy Cross Trumbull CT • (203)268-7555 • (SL 1981 MDIV)

**WITT AARON M** (402)645-8218
316 S 10th Wymore NE 68466 • NEB • SP • St Peter Wymore NE • (402)645-8215 • (SL 2000 MDIV)

**WITT JAMES E** (402)756-2901
309 N Pine - PO Box 505 Blue Hill NE 68930 • jbwitt@gtmc.net • NEB • SP • Trinity Blue Hill NE • (402)756-2102 • (SL 2000)

**WITT LYNN F REV** (810)752-0115
70290 White Tail Ln Romeo MI 48065-4452 • witt@ees.eesc.com • MI • SP • Grace Fellowsh Romeo MI • (810)752-9800 • (FW 1991 MDIV)

**WITT MELVIN E REV** (314)892-2951
5310 Warmwinds Ct Saint Louis MO 63129-3013 • MO • EM • (SL 1952 MDIV DLITT DLITT)

**WITTE CLARENCE R REV** (618)758-3049
10681 Boyd Rd Coulterville IL 62237-1101 • crwitte@egyptian.net • SI • EM • (SL 1945 MDIV)

**WITTE HENRY F REV** (091)
C/O Jet Cargo Intnl M 182 PO Box 20010 Miami FL 33102-0010 • IN • S Miss • Indiana Fort Wayne IN • (FW 1979 MDIV)

**WITTEN DAVID M REV** (859)236-2970
839 Hilltop Rd Danville KY 40422-1140 • davidoslc@searnet.com • IN • SP • Our Savior Danville KY • (859)236-2970 • (FW 1981 MDIV)

**WITTENBERGER DENIS J REV** (419)756-1847
1146 Yorkwood Rd Mansfield OH 44907 • OH • SP • Faith Mansfield OH • (419)756-4665 • (CQ 1983 MS)

**WITTENBURG KENNETH K REV** (218)732-5441
35547 Dinner Lake Loop Park Rapids MN 56470 • MNN • EM • (SPR 1952 MGC)

**WITTLER ROBERT C REV** (904)673-1625
111 S Atlantic Ave Apt 1101 Ormond Beach FL 32176-6609 • FG • EM • (CQ 1995 MDIV)

**WITTMAIER GERALD L REV** (573)364-3184
1811 Meadow Ct Rolla MO 65401-3717 • redeemer@rollanet.org • MO • SP • Redeemer Rolla MO • (573)364-7071 • (SPR 1971 MDIV)

**WITTMAYER GARLAND R REV** (414)962-7858
6029 N Santa Monica Blvd Milwaukee WI 53217-4660 • SW • SP • Our Savior Whitefish Bay WI • (414)332-4458 • (SL 1963 MDIV)

**WITTO LAWRENCE E REV** (313)532-3688
14013 Farley Redford MI 48239-2828 • MI • Sn/Adm • Hosanna-Tabor Redford MI • (313)937-2424 • (SL 1963 MDIV)

**WITTROCK THEODORE REV** (914)232-3457
99 Harris Rd Katonah NY 10536-2306 • AT • EM • (SL 1946)

**WOBROCK DAVID EDWARD REV** (415)383-8681
205 Tennessee Valley Rd Mill Valley CA 94941 • CNH • SP • Peace Mill Valley CA • (415)388-2065 • (SL 1973 MDIV)

**WOBROCK ROBERT E REV** (559)539-3550
33663 Globe Dr Springville CA 93265-9721 • PSW • EM • (SL 1957)

**WODTKE NORBERT R REV** (785)266-7658
2628 SE Minnesota Ave Topeka KS 66605-1642 • MJW2628@aol.com • KS • EM • (SL 1954 MDIV)

**WOEBBEKING PAUL S REV** (507)831-5615
769 16th St Windom MN 56101-1150 • pswebbs@rconnect.com • MNS • SP • Our Savior Windom MN • (507)831-3522 • (SL 1979 MDIV)

**WOELMER JAMES D REV** (402)454-2823 C/O St John Luth Church 82660 547 Ave Madison NE 68748-6141 • jwoelmer@aol.com • NEB • SP • St John Madison NE • (402)454-2823 • (FW 1990 MDIV MSFLM)

**WOELMER RICHARD L REV** (812)333-0624 1112 Chaseway Ct Bloomington IN 47401-8173 • rwoelmer@indiana.edu • IN • Cmp P • University Bloomington IN • (812)336-5387 • (FW 1988 MDIV)

**WOELZLEIN ALLEN J REV** (785)366-7386 C/O St John Luth Church 2126 Highway 4 Herington KS 67449-8705 • KS • SP • St John Herington KS* • (785)366-7386 • (SPR 1976 MDIV)

**WOERTH WARREN R REV** (636)467-3717 2025 El Lago Dr Arnold MO 63010-4113 • MO • SP • Good Shepherd Arnold MO • (636)296-1292 • (FW 1979 MDIV)

**WOHLERS RICHARD L REV** (414)377-7852 449 Green Bay Rd Cedarburg WI 53012-9123 • wohlers@execpc.com • SW • SHS/C • South Wisconsin Milwaukee WI • (414)464-8100 • (SL 1968 MLS MDIV)

**WOHLETZ ROGER C REV** (505)856-6197 Faith In Christ 1750 Faith Ct NE Albuquerque NM 87112-4630 • RM • SP • Faith Christ Albuquerque NM • (505)292-5673 • (SL 1998 MDIV)

**WOHLFEIL JEROME V REV** (208)587-4130 1145 N 7th E Mountain Home ID 83647-2037 • NOW • SP • Faith Mountain Home ID • (208)587-4127 • (SL 1962 MDIV)

**WOHLRABE JOHN C JR. DR** USS Blue Ridge (LCC 19) FPO AP 96628-3300 • chaps@blue-ridge.navy.mil • MO • M Chap • Missouri Saint Louis MO • (314)317-4550 • (SL 1982 STM THD)

**WOLBRECHT THOMAS P REV** (501)217-9373 12810 Misty Creek Dr Little Rock AR 72211 • tcwolbrecht@aristolle.net • MDS • Tchr • Grace Little Rock AR • (501)663-3631 • (SL 1970 MSED MDIV DED)

**WOLF BLAKE G REV** (314)846-0144 3016 Cross View Est Saint Louis MO 63129-6424 • blwo@prodigy.net • MO • Asst • Christ Memorial Saint Louis MO • (314)631-0304 • (SL 1977 MDIV)

**WOLF ERHARD W REV** (417)725-8023 401 Niangua Dr Nixa MO 65714-8158 • MO • EM • (SPR 1964 MDIV)

**WOLF GARY C REV** (785)524-4046 C/O St Paul Lutheran Church Rt 2 Box 40 Lincoln KS 67455-9521 • gswolf@nckcn.com • KS • SP • St Paul Lincoln KS • (913)524-4046 • (SL 1982 MDIV)

**WOLF LESTER AUGUST REV** (336)924-6061 2710 Speas Rd Winston Salem NC 27106-2309 • SE • EM • (SL 1942)

**WOLF PHILIP B REV** (660)598-6215 C/O Zion Lutheran Church RR 1 Box 31A Rockville MO 64780-9022 • mrchurch@juno.com • MO • SP • Zion Rockville MO • (660)598-6215 • (SL 1986 MDIV)

**WOLFE EDWARD K REV** (618)288-9916 43 Summit Ave Glen Carbon IL 62034-1411 • ewolfe@empowering.com • SI • SP • St James Glen Carbon IL • (618)288-6120 • (SL 1972 MDIV)

**WOLFF MICHAEL D REV** (316)326-6571 711 N F St Wellington KS 67152 • mdwolff@juno.com • KS • SP • Calvary Wellington KS • (316)326-7715 • (SL 1989 MDIV)

**WOLFF PAUL A REV** (248)827-1550 27500 Franklin Rd Apt 315 Southfield MI 48034-2322 • pawolff@aol.com • MI • SP • St Timothy Detroit MI • (313)535-1970 • (SL 1996 MDIV)

**WOLFF ROBERT P REV** (909)628-6827 11869 Monte Vista Ave Chino CA 91710-1739 • PSW • EM • (SPR 1958)

**WOLFGRAM LESTER JEROME REV** 4601 Rolling Ridge Rd Bismarck ND 58501-8037 • revles@uswest.net • ND • SP • Shep Valley Bismarck ND • (701)258-4231 • (SL 1992 MDIV)

**WOLFRAM JAMES T REV** (712)336-2475 3304 Center Lake Dr Spirit Lake IA 51360-7274 • IW • EM • (SL 1948)

**WOLFRAM MICHAEL C REV** (712)943-5786 PO Box 36 Sergeant Bluff IA 51054-0036 • mcwolfram@aol.com • IW • SP • Shepherd Peace Sergeant Bluff IA • (712)943-4502 • (FW 1977 MDIV)

**WOLFRAM RICHARD J REV** (734)394-0201 39903 Deepwood St Canton MI 48188-1531 • wolfram@concentric.net • MI • D Ex/S • Michigan Ann Arbor MI • (SL 1982 MDIV DMIN)

**WOLKA ALLEN D REV** 350 Shannon Dr Chillicothe OH 45601-2112 • allwolka@bright.net • OH • SP • Our Savior Chillicothe OH • (614)775-2470 • (SL 1988 MDIV)

**WOLKENHAUER RICHARD H REV** (925)825-3436 4408 Smoke Tree Ct Concord CA 94521-4323 • rwolky@aol.com • CNH • EM • (SL 1957)

**WOLLBERG JEFFREY N REV** 16 Landmark Dr Lawton OK 73501 • wollbergj@hotmail.com • NEB • M Chap • Nebraska Seward NE • (FW 1989 MDIV)

**WOLLENBURG ALAN J REV** (573)471-7011 104 Linda Dr Sikeston MO 63801 • ajwrev@yahoo.com • MO • SP • Concordia Sikeston MO • (573)471-5842 • (SL 1979 MDIV)

**WOLLENBURG DAVID WM REV** (931)707-5684 331 Laurel Cir Crossville TN 38555 • dwollenburg@tnaccess.com • MDS • SP • Shepherd Hills Crossville TN • (931)484-3461 • (SL 1971 MDIV STM)

**WOLLENBURG GEORGE F REV** (406)252-4232 4221 Clevenger Ave Billings MT 59101-5006 • MT • DP • Montana Billings MT • (SL 1955 MDIV DD)

**WOLLENBURG WILLIAM J REV** (512)301-8735 9106 La Fauna Vw Austin TX 78737-3027 • TX • EM • (SL 1944)

**WOLLMAN MICHAEL W REV** (301)592-8100 C/O St Paul Luth Church 12028 Jerusalem Rd Kingsville MD 21087-1146 • SE • Sn/Adm • St Paul Kingsville MD • (410)592-8100 • (FW 1990 MDIV)

**WOLTEMATH DOUGLAS M REV** (402)362-6245 1211 Pennsylvania Ave York NE 68467-2209 • wokado@inetnebr.com • NEB • Assoc • Emmanuel York NE • (402)362-3655 • (CQ 1999 MA)

**WOLTER DEREK M REV** (262)268-7063 409 W Foster St Port Washington WI 53074 • dalinmilw@aol.com • SW • Asst • St John Port Washington WI • (414)284-2131 • (FW 1989 MDIV)

**WOLTER ROBERT W REV** (909)797-3226 35450 Balsa St Yucaipa CA 92399-9414 • buckywol@aol.com • PSW • EM • (SL 1953 MA)

**WOLTERS MELVIN R REV** (208)324-7026 449 S 300 W Jerome ID 83338-6050 • NOW • EM • (SPR 1967)

**WOLTERS MICHAEL D REV** (218)342-2014 RR 1 Box 39A Vergas MN 56587 • MNN • SP • St Paul Vergas MN* • (218)342-2379 • (SL 1987 MDIV)

**WOMER WILLIAM B REV** (770)503-0843 7184 Ironwood Dr Gainesville GA 30507 • wwomer@mindspring.com • FG • SP • Good Shepherd Gainesville GA • (770)532-2428 • (CQ 1982 MAR)

**WONDERLY DANIEL A REV** (810)743-2747 4340 Chicory Ln Burton MI 48519-1221 • MI • SP • Pilgrim Burton MI • (810)744-1188 • (FW 1985 MDIV)

**WONG HENRY B REV** (541)942-2486 1661 N Pacific Hwy 21 Cottage Grove OR 97424 • NOW • EM • (SPR 1960)

**WONNACOTT JAMES M REV** (515)573-4698 1117 S 27th St Fort Dodge IA 50501-6312 • IW • Iowa West Fort Dodge IA • (SL 1982 MDIV)

**WONNACOTT NEIL K REV** (219)546-4181 126 E South St Bremen IN 46506-1331 • ncwonna@skyenet.net • IN • Asst • St Paul Bremen IN • (219)546-2332 • (FW 1993 MDIV)

**WOO DANIEL K REV** (650)737-0929 89 Shelbourne Ave Daly City CA 94015 • CNH • Asst • Hope Daly City CA • (650)991-4673 • (SL 1998 MDIV)

**WOOD DAVID A REV** (414)481-8480 3320 S Whitnall Ave Milwaukee WI 53207-2751 • dawood@execpc.com • SW • SP • Chapel Cross Milwaukee WI • (414)481-1880 • (SL 1968 MDIV)

**WOOD ERIC R REV** 942 Fairman Dr Manhattan KS 66503 • KS • Assoc • St Luke Manhattan KS • (785)539-2604 • (SL 2000 MDIV)

**WOOD FREDERICK J REV** (515)423-2026 1025 11th St NE Mason City IA 50401-1455 • IE • Sn/Adm • Bethlehem Mason City IA • (515)423-0438 • (SPR 1971)

**WOOD MARK A REV** C/O Immanuel Luth Church 2913 S John Moore Rd Brandon FL 33511-7139 • FG • Assoc • Immanuel Brandon FL • (813)689-1787 • (FW 2000 MDIV)

**WOOD OTTO LANE REV** 1100 W Grace St Richmond VA 23220-3613 • SE • Assoc • Bethlehem Richmond VA • (804)353-4413 • (SL 1997 MDIV)

**WOODRING DANIEL H REV** St Paul Lutheran Church PO Box 766 Niles MI 49120 • MI • Assoc • St Paul Niles MI* • (616)683-0771 • (FW 1996 MDIV)

**WOODS MATTHEW B REV** (219)946-7942 801 S Market Winamac IN 46996-1548 • IN • SP • St Luke Winamac IN • (219)946-3501 • (SL 1996 MDIV)

**WOODS ROBERT A REV** (309)949-2517 C/O St John Luth Church 8948 N 1900th Ave Geneseo IL 61254-8941 • revwoods@netexpress.net • CI • SP • St John Geneseo IL • (309)949-2516 • (FW 1985 MDIV)

**WOODS V POWELL REV** (216)963-6302 10350 Hanford Ln Twinsburg OH 44087-1471 • OH • Sn/Adm • Our Redeemer Solon OH • (440)248-4066 • (CQ 1994 MA MA)

**WOODWORTH HAROLD G REV** C/O St John Lutheran Church 2001 Hardy St Hattiesburg MS 39401-4919 • padre@fgi.net • SO • EM • (SPR 1958 MA MDIV DMIN)

**WOODYARD DEVON WAYNE REV** 5409 S Stoneborough Wichita KS 67217 • KS • Assoc • Bethany Wichita KS • (316)265-7415 • (SL 2000 MDIV)

**WOOLERY WAYNE N REV** (618)262-8511 1504 N Cherry St Mount Carmel IL 62863-1855 • SI • SP • Hope Mount Carmel IL • (618)262-7373 • (CQ 1992 MSED MAR)

**WOOLSEY BILL R REV** (281)646-9145 1146 Dominion Katy TX 77450 • srpastor@crosspt.org • TX • SP • Crosspoint Katy TX • (281)398-6464 • (SL 1987 MDIV)

**WOOLSEY DAVID C REV** (787)841-8378 San Antonio Gardens #205 Ponca PR 00731 • IN • S Miss • Indiana Fort Wayne IN • (SL 1998 MDIV)

**WOOTTON DANIEL REV** (909)679-8363 29042 Pebble Beach Dr Sun City CA 92586-2833 • PSW • EM • (SPR 1961 MDIV)

**WOOTTON GLENN E REV** C/O St Johns Lutheran Church 114 2nd St Aliceville KS 66093-7108 • emerson51@aol.com • KS • 02/1992 02/2000 • (SL 1982 MDIV)

**WORDELL KARL A REV** (920)756-2776 121 Monroe Brillion WI 54110 • kwordell@juno.com • SW • EM • (FW 1984)

**WORRAL BERNARD M REV** (701)293-0905 2814 Hickory St NE Fargo ND 58102-1715 • bworral@cableone.net • ND • Assoc • Immanuel Fargo ND • (701)293-7979 • (SL 1986 MDIV)

**WOTTRICH PHILIP CHARLES REV** (601)693-1879 C/O Trinity Lutheran Church PO Box 3460 Meridian MS 39303-3460 • pastorwott@aol.com • SO • SP • Trinity Meridian MS • (601)483-5457 • (SL 1992 MDIV)

**WRAALSTAD ORLIN REV** (760)326-6220 1501 Lillyhill Dr #63 Needles CA 92363-3434 • PSW • EM • (CQ 1987)

**WREDE WILLIAM F** C/O Atlantic District Office 171 White Plains Rd Bronxville NY 10708-1923 • AT • Df Min • St Mark Deaf New York NY* • (718)478-2108 • (SL 2000 MDIV)

**WRIGHT ARTHUR F REV** (808)883-3645 68-1823 Ho oko St PO Box 38-4629 Waikoloa HI 96738 • arthurfwright@aol.com • CNH • SP • Waikoloa Waikoloa HI • (808)883-9255 • (SPR 1955 MA MS)

**WRIGHT GARY A REV** (309)496-2614 17618 Hubbard Rd East Moline IL 61244 • wright³gary@hotmail.com • CI • SP • Zion East Moline IL • (309)496-2186 • (FW 1987 MDIV)

**WRIGHT JAMES F REV** (217)359-7869 2106 Branch Rd Champaign IL 61821-6350 • jwright@stjohn-lcms.org • CI • Assoc • St John Champaign IL • (217)359-1123 • (SL 1988 MDIV)

**WRIGHT KARL F REV** (719)589-3095 703 Douglas Dr Alamosa CO 81101-2020 • wrigksen@fone.net • RM • SP • Trinity Alamosa CO • (719)589-4611 • (SL 1987 MDIV)

**WUDY ROBERT O REV** (520)763-3761 1544 Central Ave Bullhead City AZ 86442-8009 • PSW • EM • (SL 1945 PHD)

**WUENSCHE ALBERT REV** (915)947-7542 4117 Shefflera Dr San Angelo TX 76904-4573 • TX • EM • (SPR 1963)

**WUENSCHE REINHARD H REV** (512)926-4950 7404 Bucknell Dr Austin TX 78723-1634 • wuensche@texas.net • TX • EM • (SL 1937 MA)

**WUENSCHE REINHARD H REV** (409)438-8404 111 Sumac Rd Huntsville TX 77340-8944 • TX • Sn/Adm • Faith Huntsville TX • (409)295-5298 • (SPR 1975 MDIV)

**WUERFFEL JON L REV** 713 6th St Destin FL 32541-1902 • SO • M Chap • Southern New Orleans LA • (SL 1972 PHD)

**WUERFFEL THEODORE L REV** 19520 Evanston Ave N Shoreline WA 98133 • wuerffelt@sprintmail.com • NOW • Cmp P • Agape Seattle WA • (206)634-3370 • (SL 1972 MA MA)

**WUERTZ JEFFREY G REV** (336)992-3023 917 George Place Dr Kernersville NC 27284-2349 • SE • SP • Fountain Life Kernersville NC • (336)993-4447 • (SL 1992 MDIV)

**WUGGAZER DUANE T REV** (248)644-6669 3075 Fairgrove Terr Rochester Hills MI 48309 • MI • EM • (SL 1959 MDIV)

**WULF CRAIG M REV** (509)328-9090 PO Box 18763 Spokane WA 99228 • NOW • SP • Hope Greenacres WA • (509)924-1630 • (FW 1980 MDIV)

**WUNDERLICH LEWIS H REV** (254)857-3674 323 Woodard Ln Bruceville TX 76630-3274 • TX • EM • (SL 1959)

**WUNROW DONALD N REV** (219)489-6247 7912 Weymouth Ct Fort Wayne IN 46825-3533 • IN • EM • (SL 1967 STM)

**WUNROW GERALD B REV** (651)738-3046 625 Winthrop St N Saint Paul MN 55119-3939 • wunrowgb@uswest.net • MNS • EM • (SL 1956 MDIV)

**WURDEMAN GLEN D REV** (605)232-0433 PO Box 1902 North Sioux City SD 57049-5044 • SD • SP • Holy Cross North Sioux City SD • (605)232-9117 • (SL 1990 MDIV MS)

**WURM WILLIAM C REV** (920)467-8612 N 6771 Charter Rd Sheboygan WI 53083 • revsons@bytehead.com • SW • EM • (SPR 1967)

**WURST ROBERT WALTER JR. REV** (812)479-7753 6817 Kolb Dr Evansville IN 47715-8405 • loehe@sigecom.net • IN • SP • Our Saviour Evansville IN • (812)476-8707 • (FW 1995 MDIV)

**WURSTER DANIEL A REV** (406)677-2181 1655 Air Port Rd PO Box 310 Seeley Lake MT 59868-0869 • pastordan@blackfoot.net • MT • SP • Holy Cross Seeley Lake MT* • (406)677-2281 • (SL 1973 MDIV)

**WURSTER DAVID F C REV** (716)434-6560 C/O Immanuel Luth Church 7147 Ridge Rd Lockport NY 14094-9457 • dfcrew2@juno.com • EA • SP • Immanuel Lockport NY • (716)434-0521 • (SL 1969 STM PHD)

**WYCKOFF J KEVIN REV** (618)544-8679 806 S Franklin St Robinson IL 62454-2328 • jkevinw@midwest.net • CI • SP • Our Savior Lawrenceville IL* • (618)943-6680 • (SL 1995 MDIV)

**WYNEKEN ALAN A REV** (619)421-3016 355 Canyon Ridge Dr Bonita CA 91902-4261 • judyalan@juno.com • PSW • Sn/Adm • Pilgrim Chula Vista CA • (619)422-0492 • (SL 1961 MDIV MST DMIN)

**WYNEKEN GERALD E REV** (415)884-2268 250 Pelican Ln Novato CA 94949-6696 • gwyn@cmc.net • CNH • EM • (SL 1958 MDIV MS)

**WYNEKEN KARL H REV** (559)439-8530 6289 N Colonial Ave Fresno CA 93704-1437 • wyneken@msn.com • CNH • EM • (SL 1962 MDIV STM)

**WYNEKEN KENNETH M REV** (425)255-2925 4516 NE 21st Pl Renton WA 98059 • pastorken@king-of-kings.org • NOW • SP • King Of Kings Renton WA • (425)226-1480 • (SL 1971 MDIV)

**WYPPICH RAYMOND W REV** (610)543-5323 307 Gleaves Rd Springfield PA 19064-2101 • EN • EM • (SL 1957 MDIV MTH)

**WYSSMANN GENE A REV** (417)725-1047 1807 Quail Ln Nixa MO 65714-9441 • MO • Missouri Saint Louis MO • (314)317-4550 • (FW 1978 MDIV)

**WYSSMANN KEVIN L REV** (480)892-8139
608 S Riata St Gilbert AZ 85296-2928 • PSW • SP • Christ Greenfld Gilbert AZ • (480)892-8314 • (SL 1982 MDIV)

**WYSSMANN ROBERT W REV**
646 W Katella St Springfield MO 65807-4508 • MO • EM • (SPR 1954)

## Y

**YAHR TERRY L REV**
7020 Valley Brook Dr Charleston WV 25312 • OH • Asst • Redeemer South Charleston WV • (304)744-6251 • (CQ 2000)

**YANG PHILIP N REV** (201)963-8503
222 Christopher Columbus Dr Jersey City NJ 07302-3434 • AT • EM • (CQ 1964 STM)

**YANG ZONG HOUA REV** (517)337-1052
3234 Biber St East Lansing MI 48823-1524 • MI • O Miss • Our Savior Lansing MI • (517)882-8665 • (CQ 1993 MDIV)

**YANKE PAUL A REV** (517)248-3005
10645 S Sheridan Rd Fenwick MI 48834-2659 • MI • SP • St John Ionia MI • (616)527-1250 • (FW 1999)

**YARRINGTON DAVID L REV** (732)855-0580
57 Heritage Ln Fords NJ 08863-1464 • NJ • SP • Our Redeemer Fords NJ • (732)738-7470 • (SL 1963 MDIV)

**YASPELKIS BENEDICT B JR. DR** (805)647-2644
624 Montgomery Ave Ventura CA 93004-2120 • PSW • Sn/Adm • Grace Ventura CA • (805)642-2267 • (SPR 1963 MDIV PHD)

**YATES ALVEY A REV** (915)759-6747
9301 Diana Dr El Paso TX 79924-6412 • RM • SP • Grace El Paso TX • (915)755-1322 • (FW 1984 MDIV)

**YATES MARK B REV** (800)321-5824
Ravenrock Outdoor Ministries PO Box 136 Sabillasville MD 21780-0136 • ravenrock@innernet.net • SE • O Sp Min • Southeastern Alexandria VA • (FW 1980 MDIV MMFC)

**YATES WILLIAM T REV** (317)889-8064
11 N Serenity Way Greenwood IN 46142-8423 • wyates@iquest.net • IN • Assoc • Calvary Indianapolis IN • (317)783-2000 • (SL 1982 MDIV STM)

**YEADON TIMOTHY R REV** (860)379-0860
37 Prospect St New Hartford CT 06057-2223 • popetim@compsol.net • NE • SP • St Paul New Hartford CT • (860)379-3172 • (SL 1985 MDIV)

**YIP TIMOTHY K REV**
Life Lutheran Church On Shun St Yuen Long HONG KONG • timyip@hkstar.com • CNH • 06/1997 06/2000 • (FW 1982 MDIV MST)

**YOAKUM KEVIN LEE REV** (405)741-5249
208 Oak Tree Ln Midwest City OK 73130-3533 • ky96@earthlink.net • OK • Asst • Good Shepherd Midwest City OK • (405)732-2585 • (SL 1998 MDIV)

**YOHANNES ZERIT O REV**
PO Box 2659 Asmara Eritrea EAST AFRICA • EN • S Miss • English Farmington MI • (CQ 1990)

**YONKER WILLIAM P REV**
460 Tartans Dr West Dundee IL 60118-3301 • revbynkr44@aol.com • NI • Sn/Adm • Immanuel Dundee IL • (847)428-4477 • (SL 1986 MDIV)

**YOPS BRADLEY J REV** (810)341-9678
1214 Maxine St Flint MI 48503-5371 • MI • SP • New Life Comm Flint MI • (810)239-7127 • (FW 1984 MDIV)

**YOUNCE LORING REV** (334)874-4912
C/O Concordia College 1804 Green St Selma AL 36701 • SO • 08/1999 • (SL 1960 MLS MDIV)

**YOUNG ALVIN P REV** (805)522-7782
2047 Potter Ave Simi Valley CA 93065-2442 • airrev@aol • PSW • SP • Trinity Simi Valley CA • (805)526-2429 • (SL 1964 STM MDIV)

**YOUNG DALE G REV** (701)642-5434
1205 11th St N Apt 4 Wahpeton ND 58075-5021 • dgy@nnt.net • ND • EM • (SL 1955)

**YOUNG DAVID R REV** (716)833-4898
255 Glenhurst Rd Tonawanda NY 14150-7519 • EA • EM • (SL 1961 STM)

**YOUNG GREGORY S REV** (559)222-2320
C/O Peace Luth Church 4672 N Cedar Ave Fresno CA 93726-1001 • CNH • SP • Peace Fresno CA • (559)222-2320 • (SL 1982 MDIV MS MS)

**YOUNG JAMES P REV** (760)743-3356
2023 Via Alexandra Escondido CA 92026-3303 • pastorjimy@home.com • PSW • SP • Grace Escondido CA • (760)745-0831 • (CQ 1979)

**YOUNG JOHN MICHAEL REV** (210)967-0686
15131 Kamary Ln San Antonio TX 78247-5425 • revjmyoung@freewwweb.com • TX • Asst • King Of Kings San Antonio TX • (210)656-6508 • (SL 1996 MDIV)

**YOUNG KENNETH R REV** (618)826-5012
637 White Oak Dr Chester IL 62233-2735 • kenryoung99@yahoo.com • SI • EM • (SL 1955 MSW MDIV)

**YOUNG PAUL V REV**
172 W Saginaw Rd Sanford MI 48657 • MI • SP • St Paul Sanford MI • (517)687-2209 • (FW 1988 MDIV)

**YOUNG PHILIP H REV** (912)882-9431
102 Craig Way St Marys GA 31558-2927 • FG • SP • Holy Trinity Kingsland GA • (912)729-6085 • (SL 1998 MDIV)

**YOUNG RONALD L REV** (248)288-0368
498 Shenandoah Clawson MI 48017-1300 • revrun@home.com • MI • Assoc • Our Shepherd Birmingham MI • (248)646-6100 • (FW 1981 MDIV)

**YOUNG RUFUS L REV** (918)749-7554
PO Box 521007 Tulsa OK 74152-1007 • OK • EM • (SPR 1945)

**YOUNG VICTOR P REV** (319)422-8833
244 S Walnut St West Union IA 52175 • vpyoung@trxinc.com • IE • SP • Good Shepherd West Union IA • (319)422-3393 • (FW 1982 MDIV)

**YOUNG VIRTUS E REV** (509)328-7517
3731 W Indian Trl Rd Spokane WA 99208-4735 • NOW • EM • (SL 1959)

**YOUNGDALE RONALD A REV** (209)667-5494
4246 Piro Ct Turlock CA 95382-0292 • prayou@thevision.net • CNH • Sn/Adm • Good Shepherd Turlock CA • (209)667-7712 • (SL 1981)

**YOUNGER MELVIN F REV** (513)233-5222
4949 Bath Rd Dayton OH 45424-1756 • mygolf@earthlink.net • OH • EM • (SL 1962 MDIV MA)

**YOUNT ROBERT E REV** (309)944-4108
727 Hummingbird Ct Geneseo IL 61254-1157 • CI • EM • (SPR 1967)

**YUNGHANS CHARLES E REV** (507)281-5573
402 31st St NE Apt 103 Rochester MN 55906-3459 • IE • 09/1979 09/1999 • (SL 1973 MDIV STM MA MA)

**YUNGHANS ERNEST E DR** (507)281-5573
402 31st St NE Apt 103 Rochester MN 55906-3459 • IE • EM • (CQ 1979 MA DED)

**YUNGMANN RONALD R REV** (507)853-4477
RR 3 Box 113 Lakefield MN 56150-9332 • yungmann@rconnect.com • MNS • SP • St Paul Lakefield MN* • (507)853-4512 • (FW 1977 MDIV)

**YUNKER ARTHUR D REV** (504)943-8395
815 Port St New Orleans LA 70117 • SO • SP • St Paul New Orleans LA • (504)945-3741 • (SL 1972 MDIV)

## Z

**ZABEL RICHARD LEE REV** (316)685-6781
C/O Grace Lutheran Church 3310 East Pawnee Wichita KS 67218 • rzgrace@juno.com • KS • SP • Grace Wichita KS • (316)685-6781 • (SL 1973 MDIV MS)

**ZABEL WILLIAM E REV** (773)763-0683
6458 N Oketo Ave Chicago IL 60631-1542 • pipza@aol.com • NI • 09/1994 09/1999 • (SL 1976 MDIV)

**ZABELL PHILIP W REV**
C/O St Paul Lutheran Church PO Box 229 Artois CA 95913-0229 • pzcard@hotmail.com • CNH • SP • St Paul Artois CA* • (916)934-7470 • (SL 1972 MDIV)

**ZABROCKI LEE H REV** (231)592-1246
15274 Mc Kinley Rd Big Rapids MI 49307 • zabrocki@tucker-usa.com • MI • Sn/Adm • St Peter Big Rapids MI • (231)796-6684 • (SPR 1970 MDIV)

**ZACHARIAS EDWARD H P REV** (216)676-0543
4569 W 156th St Cleveland OH 44135-2762 • OH • EM • (SPR 1956)

**ZACHARIAS ERIC L REV** (952)466-2123
14725 County Road 153 Cologne MN 55322-9143 • revez123.juno.com • MNS • SP • Zion Cologne MN • (612)466-3379 • (SL 1987 MDIV MA)

**ZACHRICH DAVID R DR** (330)633-5350
149 Parker Ln Tallmadge OH 44278-2522 • tallmadgeluthchurch@juno.com • OH • SP • Tallmadge Tallmadge OH • (330)633-4775 • (SPR 1975 MDIV DMIN)

**ZADEIK PETER A REV** (847)956-1263
1708 W Catalpa Ln Mt Prospect IL 60056-4559 • NI • SP • Northern Illinois Hillside IL • (SL 1958 MDIV MA)

**ZAGEL BRUCE R REV** (503)982-0194
791 S Settlmeir Ave Woodburn OR 97071-5505 • zagel@open.org • NOW • SP • Hope Woodburn OR • (503)981-0400 • (SL 1985 MDIV)

**ZAGEL RICHARD C REV** (509)326-3747
3620 W Beacon Ave Spokane WA 99208-4704 • NOW • EM • (SPR 1947)

**ZAGORE ROBERT M REV** (616)683-5774
1310 Sycamore St Niles MI 49120-2033 • pastor@stpaullutheran.org • MI • Sn/Adm • St Paul Niles MI • (616)683-0771 • (FW 1990 MDIV)

**ZAHN CARLETON E REV** (763)536-9115
8800 45th Ave N New Hope MN 55428-4705 • MNS • SP • Peace Robbinsdale MN • (763)533-0570 • (SL 1964 MDIV)

**ZAHRTE CARL E REV** (941)394-5976
1006 Mainsail #222 Naples FL 34114 • OH • EM • (SL 1954 STM)

**ZAHRTE JOHN C REV** (612)470-9477
23210 Park St Excelsior MN 55331-3144 • pz4jc@aol.com • MNS • SP • Our Savior Excelsior MN • (952)474-5181 • (SL 1988 MDIV)

**ZANDER GLENN R REV** (503)624-6186
10925 SW 108th Ave Tigard OR 97223-4211 • forgivn@agora.rdrop.com • NOW • SP • Good Shepherd Portland OR • (503)244-4558 • (SL 1975 MDIV)

**ZANDT DAVID K** (715)355-9641
5210 Linda St Schoefield WI 54476 • NW • Assoc • Mount Olive Weston WI • (715)359-5546 • (SL 2000 MDIV)

**ZASTROW WILLIAM F REV** (573)459-6432
9100 Highway Yy Leslie MO 63056-1101 • rungelgfidnet.com • MO • SP • Ebenezer Leslie MO • (573)459-6432 • (SL 1986 MDIV)

**ZECHIEL TIM BRIAN REV** (419)495-2398
17396 Schumm Rd Willshire OH 45898-9837 • zechiel5@juno.com • OH • SP • Zion Willshire OH • (419)495-2398 • (FW 1995 MDIV)

**ZECKZER SCOTT A REV** (219)493-2143
8726 Greenmeadow Dr New Haven IN 46774-1825 • dsz@juno.com • IN • Assoc • Emanuel New Haven IN • (219)749-2163 • (FW 1996 MDIV)

**ZEEB OTTO T REV** (732)657-2810
775 Liverpool Cir # B Lakehurst NJ 08733-5255 • NJ • EM • (SPR 1947)

**ZEHNDER GEORGE P REV** (712)239-3682
2426 Mohawk Dr Sioux City IA 51104-1544 • 24240gzehn@aol.com • IW • Assoc • St Paul Sioux City IA • (712)252-0338 • (FW 1984 MDIV)

**ZEHNDER JON HENRY GEYER REV** (941)334-3181
1470 Grace Ave Fort Myers FL 33901-6831 • jzehnder@sml.org • FG • SP • St Michael Fort Myers FL • (941)939-4711 • (SL 1982 MDIV)

**ZEHNDER MARK P REV** (402)333-9886
14909 Dorcas Cir Omaha NE 68144-2033 • mark@kingofkingsomaha.org • NEB • Sn/Adm • King Of Kings Omaha NE • (402)333-6464 • (SL 1981 MDIV DMIN)

**ZEHNDER MICHAEL J REV** (480)558-3331
1718 W Campbell Ave Gilbert AZ 85233-4018 • mjzehnder@aol.com • PSW • 12/1997 12/1999 • (CQ 1993 MCMU MA)

**ZEHNDER RONALD R REV** (734)483-7748
5788 Merritt Rd Ypsilanti MI 48197-6602 • razehnder@aol.com • MI • EM • (SL 1953)

**ZEHNDER THOMAS R REV** (757)564-1184
2505 Burrows Ct Williamsburg VA 23185 • tomrz@aol.com • SE • SP • King of Glory Williamsburg VA • (757)258-9701 • (SL 1961 MDIV LLD)

**ZEIGE WILLIAM C REV** (218)326-9560
504 NE 4th Ave Grand Rapids MN 55744-2820 • wzeige@grandnet.com • MNN • SP • Our Redeemer Cohasset MN • (218)328-5165 • (SL 1973 MDIV)

**ZEILE ERHARD A REV** (920)823-2414
6586 State Highway 57 Baileys Harbor WI 54202-9101 • johnzee@itol.com • NI • EM • (SL 1948 MA MA)

**ZEILE JOHN C REV** (310)831-0848
C/O Christ Lutheran Church 28850 S Western Ave Rancho Palos Verdes CA 90275-0803 • jzeile@clschool.org • PSW • SP • Christ Rancho Palos Verdes CA • (310)831-0848 • (SL 1971 STM)

**ZEILE RICHARD A REV** (313)532-1146
16800 Plainview Ave Detroit MI 48219-3363 • frzeile@juno.com • MI • Assoc • Redford Detroit MI • (313)535-3733 • (FW 1986 MDIV MA MTH EDS)

**ZEILE THEODORE A REV** (810)732-8565
3507 Mackin Rd Flint MI 48504-3260 • MI • EM • (SL 1937 DD)

**ZEILE WALTER L REV** (941)481-1418
10100 Cypress Cove Dr #458 Fort Myers FL 33908 • NJ • EM • (SL 1945 MDIV LLD)

**ZELLER THOMAS A REV** (218)528-4555
29976 County Rd 3 Badger MN 56714 • MNN • D Miss • Minnesota North Brainerd MN • (FW 1986 MDIV)

**ZELLERS KEVIN C REV** (701)282-6473
125 10th Ave E West Fargo ND 58078-3025 • kczellers@juno.com • ND • Assoc • St Andrew West Fargo ND • (701)282-4195 • (FW 1991 MDIV)

**ZELLMER JOHN WILLIAM REV** (847)356-1710
C/O Good Shepherd Luth Ch 25100 W Grand Ave Lake Villa IL 60046-9704 • zelljw@hotmail.com • NI • SP • Good Shepherd Lake Villa IL • (847)356-5158 • (SPR 1973 MDIV)

**ZELT THOMAS J REV** (510)429-1905
4115 Sedge St Fremont CA 94555-1153 • tzelt@aol.com • CNH • Sn/Adm • Prince Peace Fremont CA • (510)793-3366 • (SL 1984 MDIV)

**ZERBE ROY M REV** (219)764-4617
6078 Mulberry Ave Portage IN 46368-3102 • rhzerbe@excelonline.com • IN • SP • St Peter Portage IN • (219)762-2673 • (SPR 1973 MDIV)

**ZERSEN DAVID REV** (512)452-7661
C/O Concordia Univ at Austin 3400 N I H 35 Austin TX 78705-2702 • zersen@concordia.edu • TX • SHS/C • Texas Austin TX • (SPR 1964 MDIV MA DMIN DED)

**ZICK ROBERT C REV** (414)692-9908
134 Edmaro St Fredonia WI 53021-9413 • rczick@yahoo.com • SW • SP • St John Fredonia WI • (414)692-2734 • (FW 1979 MST)

**ZIEGLER ARTHUR H REV** (216)941-0051
16405 Valleyview Ave Cleveland OH 44135-4319 • OH • EM • (SL 1935 LHS)

**ZIEGLER ERIC R REV** (973)471-3208
52 Mayflower St Clifton NJ 07013-2555 • ezieg44001@aol.com • NJ • P Df • San Pablo West New York NJ* • (201)348-0004 • (FW 1991 MDIV)

**ZIEGLER KARL P REV** (308)687-6437
1653 Worms Rd St Libory NE 68872-2906 • ziegworms@juno.com • NEB • SP • Zion Saint Libory NE • (308)687-6314 • (CQ 1994 MS)

**ZIEGLER LARRY E REV** (303)688-5986
202 Elm Ave Castle Rock CO 80104-2308 • zlckem@aol.com • RM • SP • Mount Zion Castle Rock CO* • (303)688-9550 • (SPR 1973 MDIV)

**ZIEGLER PAUL A REV** (970)867-5801
433 Gayle St Fort Morgan CO 80701-3920 • RM • 12/1993 • * • (FW 1990 MDIV)

**ZIEGLER ROBERT M REV** (913)367-2056
818 N 6th St Atchison KS 66002-1830 • KS • SP • Trinity Atchison KS • (913)367-2837 • (SL 1959 MDIV)

**ZIEHR DAVID WILLIAM REV**
C/O Saint Paul Lutheran Church 8436 Kraft Ave SE Caledonia MI 49316-9718 • dzmaczero@aol.com • MI • Trinity Atchison KS • (913)367-2837 • (SL 1992 MDIV)

**ZIEHR RICHARD O REV** (850)862-2630
803 Bradford Dr Ft Walton Bch FL 32547-3208 • elahar@aol.com • SO • EM • (SL 1956 MDIV)

**ZIEKERT WILFRED L REV** (417)334-7261
201 American Way Branson MO 65616-9123 • MO • EM • (SPR 1955)

**ZIELKE KENNETH E REV** (517)238-2188
4051 Wayne Bch Coldwater MI 49036-8509 • MI • EM • (SL 1962 MTH)

**ZIELKE WILBUR W REV** (715)834-2678
1122 Florence Ave Eau Claire WI 54703-5720 • NW • EM • (SL 1950 MDIV)

**ZIEROTH GARY W REV** (410)420-2454
713 Fox Bow Dr Bel Air MD 21014 • garyzieroth@juno.com • SE • Assoc • St Paul Kingsville MD • (410)592-8100 • (FW 1990 MDIV)

**ZIETLOW HAROLD H REV** (219)484-6941
2104 Parkland Dr Fort Wayne IN 46825-3929 • IN • SHS/C • Indiana Fort Wayne IN • (CPS 1951 MA PHD)

**ZILL MARCUS T REV** (307)742-1628
1656 Coughlin St Laramie WY 82072-2386 • tedeumlaudamus@juno.com • WY • SP • St Andrew Laramie WY • (307)745-5892 • (FW 1996 MDIV)

**ZILLINGER GREGORY A REV**
2095 Hwy 31 Hannover ND 58563 • ND • SP • St Peter Hannover ND • (701)794-8705 • (SL 2000 MDIV)

**ZILZ MELVIN L REV** (219)484-5735
1704 Frenchmans Xing Fort Wayne IN 46825-5903 • mzilz@aol.com • IN • SHS/C • Indiana Fort Wayne IN • (CQ 1978 MS MA PHD)

**ZIMBRICK EDWARD C REV** (509)244-0137
1210 N Christensen Rd Medical Lake WA 99022-9693 • PSW • EM • (SL 1958 MA)

**ZIMDARS DAVID H REV** (608)757-2688
1901 Kellogg Ave Janesville WI 53546-3906 • logon2logos@aol.com • SW • SP • Our Savior Janesville WI* • (608)754-8448 • (SPR 1976 MDIV)

**ZIMMER GILES REV** (507)528-2643
C/O St John Luth Church 4489 SE 84 Ave Claremont MN 55924-4532 • gzpz@clear.lakes.com • MNS • SP • St John Claremont MN • (507)528-2643 • (SL 1989 PHD)

**ZIMMERMAN DARRELL W REV** (314)822-3539
13259 Bonroyal Dr Des Peres MO 63131-1904 • mtcalvary@primary.net • MO • SP • Mount Calvary Brentwood MO • (314)968-2360 • (SL 1982 MDIV)

**ZIMMERMAN DAVID-PAUL REV** (425)226-4089
7003 S 132nd St Seattle WA 98178-5028 • DavPauZim@msn.com • NOW • SP • Amazing Grace Seattle WA • (206)723-5526 • (FW 1988 MDIV DMIN)

**ZIMMERMAN EARL J REV** (785)242-1429
1636 S Apple Ln Ottawa KS 66067-3713 • KS • EM • (SL 1953 MDIV)

**ZIMMERMAN FRANK W REV** (309)963-4825
PO Box 545 Danvers IL 61732-0545 • fwz@frontiernet.net • CI • SP • Zion Danvers IL* • (309)963-4825 • (FW 1992 MDIV MA)

**ZIMMERMAN JAMES G REV** (618)667-3326
14 Sandstone Troy IL 62294 • jzimmer555@aol.com • SI • SP • St Paul Troy IL • (618)667-6681 • (SL 1986 MDIV)

**ZIMMERMAN LEON E REV** (308)745-0884
PO Box 501 Loup City NE 68853-0501 • NEB • EM • (CQ 1993 MDIV)

**ZIMMERMAN MARK E REV** (231)798-2197
C/O St Mark Lutheran Church 4475 Henry St Muskegon MI 49441-4927 • revmez@aol.com • MI • SP • St Mark Muskegon MI • (231)798-2197 • (SPR 1972 MA MDIV)

**ZIMMERMAN PAUL A REV** (231)922-0523
2798 Princeton Dr Traverse City MI 49684-9131 • MI • EM • (SL 1944 MA PHD DD LLD)

**ZIMMERMAN RUSSELL REV**
15277 Burr St Taylor MI 48180-5190 • MI • 12/1994 12/1999 • (SPR 1975 MDIV)

**ZIMMERMAN THEODORE B REV** (415)665-4043
2353 Funston Ave San Francisco CA 94116-1948 • revtbz@aol.com • CNH • Sn/Adm • Zion San Francisco CA • (415)221-7500 • (SL 1967 MDIV)

**ZIMMERMAN THOMAS P REV** (231)228-2303
1931 E Swanson Trl Cedar MI 49621-9778 • tpzimm@aol.com • MI • SP • St Paul Cedar MI • (231)228-6888 • (CQ 1984 MA)

**ZIMMERMANN B CHRISTIAN REV** (208)634-6900
Box 121 Bogie Dr Cascade ID 83611-0121 • NOW • EM • (SL 1980 MDIV MDIV)

**ZIMMERMANN BRUCE L REV**
C/O St John Luth Church 806 S Washington Wellsburg IA 50680-0564 • IE • SP • St John Wellsburg IA* • (515)869-3838 • (SL 1968 MDIV)

**ZIMMERMANN ELWOOD H REV** (219)486-8849
6432 Stony Brook Dr Fort Wayne IN 46835-2381 • ehzbjz@juno.com • IN • EM • * • (SL 1944 DD)

**ZIMMERMANN FRED T REV** (715)524-2894
325 S Andrews St Shawano WI 54166-2405 • NW • Assoc • St James Shawano WI • (715)524-4815 • (SL 1978 MDIV)

**ZIMMERMANN JAMES WAYNE REV**
3434 Windham Cir Stockton CA 95209-1135 • soquelzimm@juno.com • CNH • EM • (SL 1960 MDIV)

**ZIMMERMANN JOHN C REV** (515)858-2549
914 11th St Eldora IA 50627-1338 • IE • EM • (SL 1937 MDIV DD)

**ZIMMERMANN LAWRENCE J DR** (757)430-4113
2301 Barnsley Ct Virginia Beach VA 23456-7845 • ljzimm0521@cs.com • SE • SP • Christ Norfolk VA • (757)853-5655 • (SPR 1975 STM DMIN)

**ZIMMERMANN PAUL S REV**
C/O St Peter Lutheran Church 2400 Oxford Way Lodi CA 95242-2854 • pastorz@inreach.com • CNH • Sn/Adm • St Peter Lodi CA • (209)333-2223 • (FW 1987 MDIV)

**ZIMMERMANN TIMOTHY J REV** (319)339-1673
3110 Alpine Ct Iowa City IA 52245-5400 • zimmermn@ourredeemer.org • IE • Sn/Adm • Our Redeemer Iowa City IA • (319)338-5626 • (SL 1970)

**ZINKOWICH JAMES R REV** (440)357-1713
69 Wonderlust Ct Painesville OH 44077-5262 • OH • Assoc • Zion Painesville OH • (440)357-5174 • (SPR 1969 MA)

**ZIPAY JOEL S REV** (219)733-9475
C/O St John Luth Church 15496 S 900 W Wanatah IN 46390-9614 • IN • SP • St John Wanatah IN* • (219)733-9475 • (SL 1988 MD)

**ZIPAY NICHOLAS REV** (440)324-4707
340 49th St Elyria OH 44035-2412 • EN • EM • * • (SPR 1954 MDIV)

**ZIRBEL FRANK J REV** (870)743-1617
3917A Sansing Hollow Rd Harrison AR 72601-9213 • MDS • EM • * • (SL 1960 MDIV)

**ZIRKLE JAMES C REV** (509)249-0994
914 S 9th Ave Yakima WA 98902 • NOW • 04/2000 • * • (FW 1983 MDIV)

**ZIRPEL DAVID N REV** (314)732-4880
654 E Pine Bourbon MO 65441 • zirpel@fidnet.com • MO • SP • Concordia Bourbon MO • (573)732-4477 • (SL 1991 MDIV)

**ZIRZOW WAYNE H REV** (517)448-6026
204 N Church St Hudson MI 49247-1014 • wzirz@tc3net.com • MI • Inst C • Michigan Ann Arbor MI • (SL 1968 MDIV)

**ZMIJEWSKI EMIL REV** (712)668-2824
PO Box 237 Odebolt IA 51458-0237 • IW • EM • (CQ 1967)

**ZOBEL JASON W REV** (815)458-9456
178 Oak St Braidwood IL 60408 • NI • D Miss • Shep Of Peace Braidwood IL • (815)458-9445 • (SL 1997 MDIV)

**ZOEBL GEORGE T REV** (614)863-8929
7037 Nocturne Rd E Reynoldsburg OH 43068-1769 • OH • SP • Bethany Columbus OH • (614)866-7755 • (FW 1981 MDIV DMIN)

**ZOELLER KENNETH H REV** (406)651-2064
4403 Palisades Park Dr Billings MT 59106-1342 • MT • Assoc • Mount Olive Billings MT • (406)656-6687 • (FW 1999 MDIV)

**ZOLLER ALBERT P REV** (716)392-2121
120 Gorton Ave Hilton NY 14468-1221 • EA • SP • St Paul Hilton NY • (716)392-4000 • (SPR 1966 MA)

**ZORN KENNETH LLOYD REV** (519)894-6462
24 Midland Dr Apt 707 Kitchener ON N2A 2A8 CANADA • EN • EM • (SL 1956 MDIV)

**ZSCHIEGNER ARTHUR H REV** (219)432-1945
2420 Covington Pointe Cv Fort Wayne IN 46804 • zschieg@christcom.net • IN • EM • (SL 1956)

**ZSCHIEGNER MAX C E REV** (618)288-2588
26 Evergreen Ln Glen Carbon IL 62034 • SI • EM • (SL 1948)

**ZUBERBIER ORLAN G REV** (715)248-7100
1146 County Road H New Richmond WI 54017-6125 • ogzubie@frontiernet.net • NW • EM • (SPR 1962 MDIV)

**ZUCKER TYGE C REV** (608)985-7412
C/O St Paul Lutheran Church PO Box 140 La Valle WI 53941-0140 • tdzuke@jvlnet.com • SW • SP • Zion La Valle WI* • (608)985-7477 • (SL 1997 MDIV)

**ZUHN DONALD W REV** (651)481-1738
122 E Demont Ave #360 Little Canada MN 55117 • donzuhn@aol.com • MNS • EM • * • (SL 1966 MDIV)

**ZUP LANNY R REV** (419)636-5506
204 Illinois Dr Bryan OH 43506-8950 • lbzup@bright.net • OH • EM • * • (SL 1960 MDIV MA)

**ZUTZ ALFRED E REV** (707)864-3053
3996 Green Valley Rd Suisun City CA 94585-1470 • CNH • EM • * • (SPR 1968)

**ZWEMKE MICHAEL G REV** (912)446-1185
2903 Stonewater Dr Albany GA 31707-6221 • FG • SP • Trinity Albany GA • (912)436-5272 • (SL 1999 MDIV)

**ZWERNEMANN JAMES C DR** (914)337-8299
51 Edgewood Ln Bronxville NY 10708-1945 • pastaz1@aol.com • AT • Sn/Adm • The Village Bronxville NY • (914)337-0207 • (SL 1964 MDIV STM DMIN)

**ZWONITZER RODNEY E REV** (313)561-8404
22845 Wellington St Dearborn MI 48124-1059 • rodboomboom@msn.com • MI • Sn/Adm • Emmanuel Dearborn MI • (313)565-4002 • (SL 1988 MDIV)

**ZYSKOWSKI STANLEY J JR. REV** (847)945-0327
701 Westgate Deerfield IL 60015 • szyskow999@aol.com • EN • SP • Our Savior Chicago IL • (773)631-1100 • (FW 1979 MDIV MS PHD)

### V

**VON WERDER PAUL WILLIAM REV** (407)282-9266
11165 Sylvan Pond Cir Orlando FL 32825 • paul@hopeoforlando.org • FG • SP • Hope Orlando FL • (407)657-4556 • (SL 1994 MDIV)

# MINISTERS OF RELIGION—COMMISSIONED

Corrected to October 18, 2000

Individuals on this listing were on the official commissioned member roster of the Synod as of the above date, i.e., held membership in the Synod in conformity with Articles V and VI of the Constitution of The Lutheran Church–Missouri Synod.

Qualified individuals who are not listed should contact their respective district president.

Any congregation or other calling entity must contact the appropriate district president to find out whether an individual whose name is listed in this section is currently eligible for a call or service in the church.

The listing that follows is divided into six sections. Section A: Teachers; Section B: Directors of Christian Education; Section C: Deaconesses; Section D: Directors of Christian Outreach; Section E: Lay Ministers; Section F: Parish Assistant.

Commissioned Minister records are formatted in the following order:

Name, previous name, phone number, mailing address, e-mail, district, position held, where serving, an asterisk (*) indicates that he/she is serving in more positions, or status EM or CAND (See NOTE), office phone number

An asterisk (*) behind a name, indicates that the individual is qualified to be listed under Teachers and Directors of Christian Education. If a plus (+) appears behind a name, this indicates the individual is qualified to be listed under Teachers, Directors of Christian Education, and Directors of Christian Outreach. **The position the individual is serving will determine in which section the individual will be listed.**

In parenthesis: (Rostering Entity, Year of graduation or colloquy, and graduate degrees).

NOTE: If a minister is on Candidate status, the month and year such status was granted will appear in place of position held. Those individuals whose CAND status was extended one additional year by the Council of Presidents (Handbook, Bylaw 2.19) will be listed with two dates, the initial month and year candidate status was granted and the month and year on which the one-year extension was given.

## KEY TO ABBREVIATIONS

Candidate (CAND) =a minister who is not currently performing the duties of any of the offices of ministry specified in Bylaw 2.15, and is eligible to do so.

Emeritus (EM)=retired.

### Rostering Entity

A=Addison
AA=Ann Arbor
AU=Austin
BR=Bronxville
HIT=Hispanic Inst of Theology
IV=Irvine
M=Mankato
MQ=Mequon (formerly Milwaukee)
MW=Milwaukee
NU=New Ulm
PA=Porto Alegre
PO=Portland
RF=River Forest
S=Seward
SP=St. Paul
*V=Valparaiso—Certified
VB=Villa Ballester
WN=Winfield
CQ=Colloquized

### Missouri Synod District

AT=Atlantic
CNH=Calif.-Nev.-Hawai
CI=Central Illinois
EA=Eastern
EN=English
FG=Florida-Georgia
IN=Indiana
IE=Iowa East
IW=Iowa West
KS=Kansas
MI=Michigan
MDS=Mid-South
MNN=Minnesota North
MNS=Minnesota South
MO=Missouri
MT=Montana
NE=New England
NEB=Nebraska
ND=North Dakota
NJ=New Jersey
NW=North Wisconsin
NI=Northern Illinois
NOW=Northwest
OH=Ohio
OK=Oklahoma
PSW=Pacific Southwest
RM=Rocky Mountain
S=SELC District
SD=South Dakota
SE=Southeastern
SI=Southern Illinois
SO=Southern
SW=South Wisconsin
TX=Texas
WY=Wyoming

### Position Titles

Aux=Auxiliary Ministry
CCRA=Cooperative Church Related Agency
D Ex/S=District Executive or Staff
Df Min=Deaf Missionary
END=Endorsed by Synod
HS/C=Synod HS/College/Univ/Seminary
Inst C=Institutional Chaplain
LHS=Lutheran High School Faculty or Staff
M Chap=Military Chaplain/Dir of Rel Ed
Mem C=Serving a Member Congregation
NMem C=Serving a Non-Member Congregation
O Miss=Other Missionary
O Sp Min=Other Special Ministry
P O EL=Principal Only Elementary
PO HS=Principal Only High School
RSO=Recognized Service Organization
S Ex/S=Synodical Executive or Staff
S HS/C=Synodical High School/College/Univ/Seminary
S Miss=Synodical Missionary
Sp S=Special School or Spec Lutheran Classes
T PS O=Teacher in a Pre-School Only
T EL=Teacher Elementary
T P EL=Teacher/Principal Elementary

# Section A
# Certified Teachers

### A

**AADSEN LORI ANN** (281)480-7316
15811 River Birch Way Houston TX 77059-4075 • lori-aadsen@ghg.net • TX • S Ex/S • Texas Austin TX • (CQ 1997 MED)

**ABBOTT PHILLIP G** (972)235-3415
530 Wentworth Dr Richardson TX 75081-5620 • abbottg.lshd@usa.net • TX • Tchr • Lutheran HS of Dalla Dallas TX • (214)349-8912 • (CQ 1985)

**ABBUHL NANCY J** (918)834-3813
6604 E 19th St Apt A Tulsa OK 74112 • OK • Tchr • Tulsa Tulsa OK • (918)834-3813 • (S 1994)

**ABEGGLEN STEFFANI MARIE** (405)616-5255
8140 Weyland Ct Apt A Tinker AFB OK 73145-4447 • rocman3@ilinkusa.net • OK • Tchr • Trinity Norman OK • (405)321-3443 • (S 1998)

**ABEL JOAN K** (507)235-3418
625 W Interlaken Rd Fairmont MN 56031 • MNS • Tchr • St Pauls Fairmont MN • (507)238-9492 • (SP 1981)

**ABERNATHY JOHN F*** (970)565-8248
509 N Market St Cortez CO 81321-2149 • RM • 08/1999 • (S 1988)

**ABRESCH MARK T** (770)304-1710
120 Lullwater Dr Sharpsburg GA 30277 • mabresch@charter.net • FG • Tchr • St Paul Peachtree City GA • (770)487-0339 • (S 1982)

**ABRESCH VERA K** (517)839-7241
C/O St Paul Lutheran Church 402 S Ballenger Hwy Flint MI 48532-3600 • vabr@tm.net • MI • Tchr • St Paul Flint MI • (810)239-6200 • (S 1991)

**ACCOLA MELANIE ANN** (440)777-3201
23955 Smith Ave Westlake OH 44145 • mschull@hotmail.com • OH • Tchr • St Paul Westlake OH • (440)835-3051 • (SP 1994)

**ACETO ALFRED A JR.** (813)324-5854
706 Lake Eloise Place Dr Winter Haven FL 33884-3400 • FG • Tchr • Grace Winter Haven FL • (863)293-8447 • (RF 1969)

**ACHTERBERG KATHLEEN R** (512)837-0051
12503 Terra Nova Ln Austin TX 78727-5163 • kraberg@prismnet.com • TX • Mem C • St Paul Austin TX • (512)472-8301 • (S 1970 MCMU)

**ACHTERBERG ROBERT A** (512)837-0051
12503 Terra Nova Ln Austin TX 78727-5163 • TX • SHS/C • Texas Austin TX • (S 1970 MCMU)

**ACKMANN JAMES** (219)486-1828
4008 Willshire Estates Dr Fort Wayne IN 46815-5335 • IN • EM • (RF 1953 MED)

**ACORD DEANNA L** (319)396-8960
2614 29th St SW Cedar Rapids IA 52404-3219 • IE • Tchr • Trinity Cedar Rapids IA • (319)362-6952 • (SP 1965)

**ADAMS ANDREA K** (808)485-8077
98-288 Kaonohi #1803 Aiea HI 96701 • aadams69@hotmail.com • CNH • Tchr • Our Savior Aiea HI • (808)488-0000 • (MQ 1998)

**ADAMS CURTIS W** (262)367-2565
613 Renson Rd Hartland WI 53029-1819 • curjoy@execpc.com • SW • Mem C • Divine Redeemer Hartland WI • (414)367-8400 • (S 1972 MED)

**ADAMS DONALD W** (217)222-7497
2710 Kentucky Rd Quincy IL 62301-4478 • dwadams@accessus.net • CI • P/Tchr • St James Quincy IL • (217)222-8447 • (RF 1961 MA)

**ADAMS FORREST E** (510)278-9640
18043 Robscott Ave Hayward CA 94541-2241 • trees510@aol • CNH • Prin • Calvary San Lorenzo CA • (510)278-2598 • (S 1968 MED)

**ADAMS JOYCE ANN** (414)367-2565
613 Renson Rd Hartland WI 53029-1819 • SW • Tchr • Divine Redeemer Hartland WI • (414)367-8400 • (S 1972)

**ADAMS KATHLEEN ANN** (414)242-0679
11823 N Church Pl 109W Mequon WI 53097-2801 • SW • Tchr • Trinity Mequon WI • (414)242-2045 • (MQ 1985)

**ADAMS RICHARD J** (414)242-0679
11823 N Church Pl 109W Mequon WI 53097-2801 • SW • Mem C • Trinity Mequon WI • (262)242-2045 • (MQ 1984 MS)

**ADAMS ROBYN L**
332 W Oak St Seymour IN 47274-2974 • MO • Tchr • Missouri Saint Louis MO • (314)317-4550 • (AA 1996)

**ADAMS WALTER F** (612)937-1117
8438 Morgan Ln Eden Prairie MN 55347-1621 • MNS • Tchr • Luth HS Of Greater M Bloomington MN • (612)854-0224 • (S 1971 MA)

**ADLER BARBARA JEAN** (313)663-8489
1404 Coventry Square Dr Ann Arbor MI 48103-6311 • adlerb@ccaa.edu • MI • SHS/C • Michigan Ann Arbor MI • (CQ 1984 MA PHD)

**ADLER CLINTON J**
W54N280 Van Buren Dr Cedarburg WI 53012-2809 • SW • Tchr • St Paul Grafton WI • (414)377-4659 • (RF 1993)

**ADLER DENISE LYNN** (703)920-1552
975 S Taylor St Arlington VA 22204-3020 • brent.adler@cwix.com • SE • Tchr • Our Savior Arlington VA • (703)892-4846 • (MQ 1996)

**ADLER KIRSTEN M**
W54N280 Van Buren Dr Cedarburg WI 53012-2809 • NI • 11/1999 • (RF 1990)

**ADLER RICHARD W** (314)353-4505
5436 Holly Hills Ave Saint Louis MO 63109-3547 • MO • EM • (RF 1962)

**AFFELDT-BOETCHER DENISE E*** (218)281-1108
1108 Groveland Crookston MN 56716 • MNN • 04/2000 • (SP 1981)

**AGNER RICHELLE LYN**
224 SE Saint Lucie Blvd #30 Stuart FL 34996-1315 • FG • 09/1998 • (AA 1995)

**AGNEW ELIZABETH A** (410)729-8793
317 Watermill Ct Millersville MD 21108 • agnewteach@aol.com • SE • 11/1999 • (S 1985)

**AHLBRAND SHIRLEY H** (317)546-1636
5351 Hawthorne Dr Indianapolis IN 46226-1615 • IN • Tchr • Trinity Indianapolis IN • (317)897-0243 • (RF 1960 MS)

**AHLERS ARLEN G** (402)329-6574
523 W Elkhorn St Pierce NE 68767 • pswarlen@aol.com • PSW • EM • (S 1958 MSED)

**AHLERS ERICH R** (713)956-9467
4000 W 34th St Apt 25 Houston TX 77092 • TX • Tchr • LHS North Houston TX • (713)880-3131 • (MQ 1998)

**AHLES PAMELA SARAH** (949)461-0828
21442 Lake Forest Dr Apt F Lake Forest CA 92630 • PAvolleyball@hotmail.com • PSW • Tchr • Abiding Savior Lake Forest CA • (949)830-1461 • (RF 1990 MED)

**AHLMAN LILLIAN A** (952)938-1593
12817 Hideaway Trl Minnetonka MN 55305-5021 • donahl@megsinet.net • MNS • Tchr • Mount Hope-Redemptio Bloomington MN • (612)881-0036 • (SP 1968)

**AHLSCHWEDE GORDON E** (909)986-1958
127 E Harvard Pl Ontario CA 91764-2701 • PSW • P/Tchr • Redeemer Ontario CA • (909)986-6510 • (S 1964 MA)

**AHO TIMOTHY J** (303)663-6384
924 21st St SW Loveland CO 80537-7006 • RM • Tchr • Immanuel Loveland CO • (970)667-7606 • (SP 1975)

**AHRENS FRANK W** (305)475-2865
11943 SW 11th Ct Davie FL 33325-3841 • fahrens925@webmail.bellsouth.net • FG • Tchr • Faith Fort Lauderdale FL • (954)581-2918 • (RF 1972 MA)

**AHRENS LINDA A** (402)463-0362
1395 S Wabash Ave Hastings NE 68901-7068 • NEB • Tchr • Zion Hastings NE • (402)462-5012 • (S 1990)

**ALBERDA JOHN**
140 Cedar Rd East Northport NY 11731-4633 • AT • Tchr • Long Island Brookville NY • (516)626-1700 • (RF 1969 MA)

**ALBERS DEBORAH M** (813)643-1767
2420 Buckhorn Run Dr Valrico FL 33594-5764 • dm³albers@hotmail.com • FG • Tchr • Immanuel Brandon FL • (813)685-1978 • (RF 1980)

**ALBERS GEORGE A** (217)463-3526
61 Concordia Dr Paris IL 61944-2378 • CI • EM • (RF 1934 MA)

**ALBERS MICHAEL** (314)631-9240
9718 Lenor Dr Saint Louis MO 63123-4010 • albersm@slu.edu • MO • Tchr • LHS South Saint Louis MO • (314)631-1400 • (S 1972 MS)

**ALBERS OSCAR H** (219)484-2994
3008 Glencairn Dr Fort Wayne IN 46815-6718 • IN • EM • (RF 1938 MA)

**ALBERS PAUL A** (303)659-9030
286 S 13th Ave Brighton CO 80601-2229 • paul.albers@rm.lcms.org • RM • LHS South Saint Louis MO • (RF 1984 MA)

**ALBERT JANINE M** (219)547-4171
7030 N 450 W Decatur IN 46733 • IN • 08/1995 08/2000 • (AA 1985 MA)

**ALBERT RAYMOND A** (708)484-8225
6946 30th St Berwyn IL 60402-2958 • NI • EM • (RF 1956)

**ALBERTIN DANIEL A** (219)486-3492
8225 Meadow Hills Dr Fort Wayne IN 46835-4738 • IN • Tchr • Holy Cross Fort Wayne IN • (219)483-3173 • (S 1974 MS)

**ALBERTIN PAUL L** (219)347-1877
544 Warren Ct Kendallville IN 46755 • IN • Tchr • St John Kendallville IN • (219)347-2444 • (S 1976 MA)

**ALBIN DEE-EDDA LYNN** (734)454-9068
7008 Harvard Ln Canton MI 48187-2504 • MI • 06/2000 • (AA 1984)

**ALBRECHT CARRIE M** (847)885-3350
St Peter Lutheran Church 208 E Schaumburg Rd Schaumburg IL 60194-3517 • NI • Tchr • St Peter Schaumburg IL • (847)885-3350 • (RF 1995)

**ALBRECHT DANIEL R** (815)547-7503
424 W Boone St Belvidere IL 61008-3131 • NI • Tchr • Immanuel Belvidere IL • (815)547-5346 • (RF 1983 MCMU)

**ALBRECHT KIMBERLY ANN** (248)651-7091
221 Lonesome Oak Dr Rochester MI 48306-2835 • afunkim@aol.com • MI • Tchr • Special Ed Ministrie Detroit MI • (313)368-1220 • (AA 1994)

**ALBRECHT LOIS E** (303)466-6385
1005 Ash St Broomfield CO 80020-1215 • RM • EM • (S 1953)

**ALBRIGHT JANICE M** (414)637-7011
1813 Tiffany Dr Racine WI 53402-1795 • SW • P/Tchr • St John Racine WI • (414)633-2758 • (RF 1958)

**ALEXANDER JAMES L** (309)263-0610
430 N Bauman Morton IL 61550 • alexanderjames@hotmail.com • CI • Tchr • Bethel Morton IL • (309)266-6592 • (S 1969 MA)

**ALEXANDER JOY L** (714)832-0887
14371 Wildeve Ln Tustin CA 92780-5723 • alexander@cui.edu • PSW • SHS/C • Pacific Southwest Irvine CA • (949)854-3232 • (IV 1989)

**ALEXANDER ROBERT MICHAEL**
4100 S Phoenix Rd Columbia MO 65202-4172 • MO • EM • (CQ 1993)

**ALLE BONNIE JO** (415)530-7909
C/O Zion Lutheran School 5201 Park Blvd Piedmont CA 94611-3328 • CNH • Tchr • Zion Piedmont CA • (510)530-4213 • (RF 1982)

**ALLEN DEBRA J DR** (512)252-0717
16221 Edgemere Dr Pflugerville TX 78660-2102 • allend@concordia.edu • TX • SHS/C • Texas Austin TX • (CQ 1995)

**ALLEN JEFFREY A** (541)461-8551
310 Dublin Ave Eugene OR 97404 • NOW • Tchr • Life Eugene OR • (541)342-5433 • (S 1979 MSED)

**ALLEN RONALD M DR** (734)668-7593
475 Pine Brae St Ann Arbor MI 48105-2743 • allenr@ccaa.edu • MI • SHS/C • Michigan Ann Arbor MI • (RF 1972 MS MS PHD)

**ALLENSWORTH EVELYN** (701)352-0352
1438 Fernwood Dr Grafton ND 58237 • eve@polarcomm.com • ND • Tchr • North Dakota Fargo ND • (SP 1989)

**ALLES BRAD A** (414)760-2411
9710 W Kaul Ave Milwaukee WI 53225-1623 • balles@execpc.com • SW • Tchr • Milwaukee LHS Milwaukee WI • (414)461-6000 • (S 1987 MA)

**ALLMAN RICHARD K**
3851 S Desert Lake Dr Tucson AZ 85730-5716 • PSW • EM • (RF 1978)

**ALLMON RICHARD L** (708)787-1206
110 E George Bensenville IL 60106 • crfallmonrl@curf.edu • NI • SHS/C • Northern Illinois Hillside IL • (RF 1973 MED MS)

**ALLMON STEVEN A** (214)341-9688
10907 Villa Haven Dr Dallas TX 75238-2940 • sallmon5@aol.com • TX • Tchr • Lutheran HS of Dalla Dallas TX • (214)349-8912 • (RF 1972 MED)

**ALLOR CINDY ANN** (708)787-9303
6N451 Cedar Ave Wood Dale IL 60191-1426 • callor@aol.com • NI • Tchr • Immanuel Des Plaines IL • (847)390-0990 • (RF 1984 MA)

**ALLWARDT BARBARA L**
N8688 North Rd Ixonia WI 53036-9713 • SW • Tchr • St Paul Oconomowoc WI • (262)567-5001 • (S 1973)

**ALMS NATASHA A** (314)845-2737
5028 Clayridge Apt 205 St Louis MO 63129 • MO • Tchr • Luth Association Saint Louis MO • (314)268-1234 • (S 1998)

**ALSIN KRISTINE** (913)268-1162
7138 Caenen St Shawnee KS 66216-3606 • KS • Tchr • Hope Shawnee KS • (913)631-6940 • (CQ 1994)

**ALTEVOGT LESTER L** (517)642-2788
14815 Boynton Ln Hemlock MI 48626-9701 • MI • P/Tchr • St Peter Hemlock MI • (517)642-5659 • (S 1968 MS EDS)

**ALTEVOGT ORVILLE C** (913)765-3461
PO Box 368 Alma KS 66401-0368 • KS • P/Tchr • St John Alma KS • (785)765-3914 • (S 1971 MED MEAD)

**ALTHAGE RICHARD A**
C/O Salem Lutheran Church 418 4th St Gretna LA 70053-5317 • SO • St John Alma KS • (S 1965 MED)

**ALTHOUSE J STANTON** (804)353-6078
3004 Seminary Ave Richmond VA 23227-4810 • SE • EM • (CQ 1955 MA)

**ALTIS MARVIN R** (715)423-2982
3221 44th St S Wisconsin Rapids WI 54494 • mcaltis@juno.com • NW • Tchr • Immanuel Wisconsin Rapids WI • (715)423-0272 • (RF 1978 MCMU)

**ALTMAN GARY DAVID** (818)362-9223
545 Orange Grove Ave San Fernando CA 91340-1941 • PSW • Tchr • First LHS Sylmar CA • (818)362-9223 • (PO 1996 MA)

**ALVIANI CYNTHIA D*** (715)685-9877
518 18th Ave W Ashland WI 54806-1143 • dcemom@ncis.net • ND • 09/1995 09/1997 • (RF 1982)

**ALWARDT MICHAEL DAVID** (618)344-4731
#1 Aspen Cir Collinsville IL 62234 • SI • Tchr • Metro-East LHS Edwardsville IL • (618)656-0043 • (MQ 2000)

**ALYEA-BROOKS ELIZABETH F** (281)353-4581
3210 Haydee Spring TX 77388 • TX • Tchr • Trinity Spring TX • (281)376-5810 • (AU 1982)

**AMBROSE JUDYE A** (724)352-2089
425 Bicker Rd Cabot PA 16023 • EN • Tchr • Redeemer Oakmont PA • (412)828-9323 • (BR 1999)

**AMEY BETTY** (316)744-3653
4170 N Parkwood Wichita KS 67220 • KS • Tchr • Holy Cross Wichita KS • (316)684-4431 • (S 1968 MSED)

**AMLING ALBERT J III** (414)502-3929
N106W16272 Fieldstone Pass Germantown WI 53022 • aamling@hcl.org • EN • Tchr • Hales Corners Hales Corners WI • (414)529-6701 • (S 1981 MS)

**AMPT KIMBER LYNN** (812)926-4729
5920 Melody Ln Aurora IN 47001-1750 • IN • Tchr • St John Aurora IN • (812)926-2656 • (SP 1989)

**AMT PHILIP M** (219)482-6516
3402 Kirkland Ave Fort Wayne IN 46805-1557 • psja1@aol.com • IN • Tchr • Bethlehem Fort Wayne IN • (219)456-3587 • (RF 1969 MED)

**ANDERMANN ROSEMARY SUE** (314)278-3277
#3 Windstream Ct St Peters MO 63376-4045 • MO • Tchr • Zion Harvester MO • (314)441-7424 • (RF 1984)

**ANDERS BRIAN L*** (313)532-4290
16121 Wormer St Detroit MI 48219-3625 • MI • Tchr • Trinity Clinton Township MI • (810)468-8511 • (S 1984)

**ANDERS KAREN LYNN** (618)344-3620
478 S Mulberry Rd Collinsville IL 62234-6320 • SI • 06/1990 06/2000 • (S 1979 MS)

**ANDERSEN AMELIA E** (718)461-1575
65-44 165th St Flushing NY 11365-1930 • AT • Tchr • Flushing & Bayside Flushing NY • (718)229-5262 • (S 1988)

**ANDERSEN CYNTHIA L**
4608 Acorn Ln NW Rochester MN 55901-7798 • FG • 10/1995 10/1999 • (CQ 1988)

**ANDERSEN KATHY S**
2844 Sissel Rd Lincoln NE 68516-1401 • NEB • 10/1998 • (S 1989)

**ANDERSEN LARRY A** (218)828-2082
4050 Ashdale Ln Baxter MN 56425 • MNN • P/Tchr • Family Of Christ Baxter MN • (218)829-9020 • (S 1979 MA MED)

**ANDERSEN RHONDA JOY** (218)828-2082
4050 Ashdale Ln Baxter MN 56425 • landersen@brainerd.net • MNN • Tchr • Family Of Christ Baxter MN • (218)829-9020 • (SP 1986)

**ANDERSON ANN MARIE** (308)832-2764
606 East 1st St Minden NE 68959-1704 • NEB • Tchr • Zion Hastings NE • (402)462-5012 • (S 1996)

**ANDERSON BRADLEY RAY** (618)343-0050
806 Indiana Collinsville IL 62234 • anderbk@stlnet.com • SI • Tchr • Holy Cross Collinsville IL • (618)344-3145 • (AA 1998)

**ANDERSON BRITT S** (310)442-9120
1326 Centinela Ave Apt 9 Los Angeles CA 90025 • PSW • Tchr • Pilgrim Santa Monica CA • (310)829-2239 • (IV 1998)

**ANDERSON DOROTHY I** (952)473-6090
3803 Dartmouth Dr Minnetonka MN 55345-1712 • dwandy62@aol.com • MNS • Tchr • Our Savior Excelsior MN • (612)474-9710 • (RF 1962)

**ANDERSON ELIZABETH MARIE**
11009 E 3rd Ave Apt 70 Spokane WA 99206-5294 • NOW • 08/1998 08/2000 • (PO 1995)

**ANDERSON ELOISE MARIE** (559)535-5136
10313 Road 256 Terra Bella CA 93270-9722 • CNH • Tchr • Zion Terra Bella CA • (559)535-4346 • (S 1970)

**ANDERSON G PETER** (208)467-2374
1506 E Nebraska Nampa ID 83686 • NOW • Tchr • Zion Nampa ID • (208)466-6746 • (S 1976 MA)

**ANDERSON HOLLY K**
C/O Golden Valley Chld Care Ct 5501 Glenwood Ave Golden Valley MN 55422-5070 • MNS • Tchr • Golden Valley Golden Valley MN • (763)544-2810 • (CQ 1997)

**ANDERSON JANET ANN** (630)833-2795
24 W Adams St Villa Park IL 60181-3105 • augviking@aol.com • NI • Tchr • St John Lombard IL • (630)629-2515 • (S 1973)

**ANDERSON JEAN E** (208)467-2374
1506 E Nebraska Nampa ID 83686 • NOW • Tchr • Zion Nampa ID • (208)466-6746 • (S 1976 MA)

**ANDERSON JENNIFER LYNN** (402)643-6628
316 N 6th St Apt #3 Seward NE 68434-1758 • janderson@seward.cune.edu • NEB • SHS/C • Nebraska Seward NE • (S 1997)

**ANDERSON JOHN A** (712)542-5652
623 1/2 W Clark St Clarinda IA 51632 • FG • 02/2000 • (S 1980 MA)

**ANDERSON KATHLEEN E** (618)343-0050
806 Indiana Ave Collinsville IL 62234-4516 • anderbk@stlnet.com • SI • Tchr • Metro-East LHS Edwardsville IL • (618)656-0043 • (AA 1998)

**ANDERSON KIMBERLY K** (660)829-4902
915 S Carr Ave Sedalia MO 65301-5345 • jasonkim@iland.net • MO • Tchr • St Paul Sedalia MO • (816)826-1925 • (S 1997)

**ANDERSON LAURIE S** (307)638-1629
653 Vista Ln Cheyenne WY 82009 • WY • Tchr • Our Savior Cheyenne WY • (307)632-2580 • (RF 1984)

**ANDERSON LINDA LORRAINE** (770)632-9164
409 Hampton Grn Peachtree City GA 30269-2712 • chadolfan@mindspring.com • FG • Tchr • St Paul Peachtree City GA • (770)486-3545 • (RF 1970 MA)

**ANDERSON LISA M** (517)652-3119
8720 S Gera Rd Birch Run MI 48415-9225 • MI • Tchr • St Lorenz Frankenmuth MI • (517)652-6141 • (SP 1977)

**ANDERSON MARGARET L** (515)241-6411
Iowa Methodist Medical Center 1200 Pleasant St Des Moines IA 50309-1453 • seelsorge@yahoo.com • OH • 05/1997 05/2000 • (RF 1971 MAR MAT)

**ANDERSON MARY JANE** (714)774-0993
2320 Virazon Dr La Habra Heights CA 90631 • PSW • Tchr • Prince Of Peace Anaheim CA • (714)774-0993 • (S 1982)

**ANDERSON ROBERT C** (414)578-0722
C/O Trinity Lutheran Church 10729 W Freistadt Rd Mequon WI 53097-2503 • SW • Tchr • Trinity Mequon WI • (262)242-2045 • (RF 1978 MSED)

**ANDERSON RUTH A**
6217 Mid Rivers Mall Dr #107 Saint Charles MO 63304-1102 • MO • Tchr • Zion Harvester MO • (314)441-7424 • (S 1995)

**ANDERSON STEPHEN L** (818)344-2566
18645 Hatteras #120 Tarzana CA 91356 • PSW • Tchr • Trinity Jr/Sr High S Reseda CA • (818)342-7855 • (PO 1995)

**ANDERSON STEVEN M** (414)251-3581
W161N11064 Meadow Dr Germantown WI 53022-5610 • SW • Prin • Grace Menomonee Falls WI • (414)251-7140 • (RF 1975 MAD)

**ANDERSON TERESA LYN** (414)541-2246
2167 N 71st St St #A Milwaukee WI 53213-1801 • SW • Tchr • Elm Grove Elm Grove WI • (262)797-2970 • (S 1985)

**ANDREAS SHERRI L** (209)897-2354
5988B Avenue 360 Kingsburg CA 93631-8800 • CNH • Tchr • Grace Visalia CA • (559)734-7694 • (RF 1985)

**ANDREASEN DENNIS C**
6730 Elmore Woods Ln Memphis TN 38134 • MDS • Tchr • Immanuel Memphis TN • (901)373-4486 • (S 1963 MA)

**ANDREWS JANET** (617)769-9532
64 Green St Medfield MA 02052-1713 • NE • 10/1994 10/1999 • (BR 1984)

**ANDREWS VALINDA GAIL** (913)849-3343
RR 2 Paola KS 66071-9802 • KS • 12/1996 12/1998 • (S 1973)

**ANDRICH JANIE L** (310)833-8571
966 W Bloomwood Rd San Pedro CA 90731-1223 • andrich5@prodigy.net • PSW • P/Tchr • Trinity Whittier CA • (562)699-7431 • (CQ 1993 MA)

**ANENSON RONALD D** (612)657-2580
521 Rustic Rd Mayer MN 55360-9605 • MNS • Tchr • Trinity Waconia MN • (952)442-4165 • (SP 1983)

**ANGELL PAUL MARK** (801)562-5338
9096 S Peach Blossom Dr Salt Lake City UT 84094 • mangell@redeemer-slc.org • RM • Tchr • Redeemer Salt Lake City UT • (801)487-6283 • (S 1974 MSED)

**ANGER ELLEN MARIE** (920)994-8230
203 Milwaukee St Adell WI 53001 • eanger@hotmail.com • SW • Tchr • Emmanuel Adell WI • (920)994-9005 • (MQ 1996)

**ANGOTT DONNA L** (313)254-2430
48887 Golden Oaks Ln Utica MI 48317-2618 • MI • Tchr • Trinity Utica MI • (810)731-4490 • (CQ 1978 MA)

**ANKERBERG ERIK P** (313)724-8096
21514 Francis St Dearborn MI 48124-2905 • ankere@ccaa.edu • MI • SHS/C • Michigan Ann Arbor MI • (RF 1992 MA)

**ANKLAM ELIZABETH K** (715)842-3001
1202 Washington St Wausau WI 54403-5676 • NW • Tchr • Trinity Wausau WI • (715)848-0166 • (MQ 1989 MED)

**ANNAS MICHELLE LUANN** (810)229-7535
10543 Lafollette Dr Brighton MI 48116-9623 • EN • Tchr • Child Of Christ Hartland MI • (248)887-3836 • (AA 1984)

**ANTHONY JILL** (440)458-8605
18 Waterfall Dr Grafton OH 44044-1520 • docantony@aol.com • S • 08/1991 08/2000 • (RF 1968 MED PHD)

**APPOLD PATRICE M** (661)663-7423
3823 Park View Dr Bakersfield CA 93311 • pmappold@ev1.net • CNH • Tchr • St John Bakersfield CA • (661)834-1412 • (AA 1983)

**APPOLD PAUL C**
8 D Founders Way Saint Louis MO 63105 • pacap5@juno.com • MI • 05/1997 05/2000 • (AA 1984 MED)

**APSE AMY L** (817)465-6225
1815 Greenbend Dr Arlington TX 76018 • TX • Tchr • Christ Our Savior Coppell TX • (972)393-7074 • (AU 1999)

**ARBEITER ARLIN A** (863)293-8156
19 Lake Link Dr SE Winter Haven FL 33884-1043 • arlin@gate.net • FG • Tchr • Grace Winter Haven FL • (941)293-9744 • (RF 1966 MA)

**ARING ELIZABETH R** (217)245-8573
13 Trussell Rd Jacksonville IL 62650 • laring@fgi.net • CI • Tchr • Salem Jacksonville IL • (217)243-3419 • (RF 1980)

**ARLDT JUDITH L** (512)451-7646
7709 Creston Ln Austin TX 78752-1328 • TX • EM • (AU 1985)

**ARMAO ROBERT W**
826-6 Ridgewood Dr Fort Wayne IN 46805 • midnightclear1@hotmail.com • IN • Tchr • Indiana Fort Wayne IN • (S 1981 MA)

**ARMAO RUTH A**
826-6 Ridgewood Dr Fort Wayne IN 46805 • raharmao@hotmail.com • IN • Tchr • Wyneken Memorial Decatur IN • (219)639-6177 • (S 1982)

**ARMBRECHT ANDY P** (319)668-1562
2677 230th St Williamsburg IA 52361-8602 • IE • Tchr • Lutheran Interparish Williamsburg IA • (319)668-1711 • (S 1989)

**ARMBRECHT DEANNA JEAN** (319)824-3556
20258 P Ave Grundy Center IA 50638-8559 • IE • 06/1994 06/2000 • (MQ 1991)

**ARMBRECHT DONNA JOY** (319)668-1562
2677 230th St Williamsburg IA 52361-8602 • IE • 06/1996 06/2000 • (S 1991)

**ARMBRECHT EDITH G**
1511 Fremont St Marshalltown IA 50158-5480 • IE • 06/1998 • (RF 1988)

**ARMBRUSTER DEBORAH A** (314)394-9892
1449 Palisades Wildwood MO 63021 • MO • Tchr • St Mark Eureka MO • (636)938-4432 • (S 1978 MED)

**ARMBRUSTER EARL A*** (517)346-7512
4095 M 30 West Branch MI 48661-9143 • lukester@mail.com • MI • 07/2000 • (SP 1980)

**ARMSTRONG SANDRA A** (308)384-9645
3425 Graham Ave Grand Island NE 68803-6526 • NEB • Tchr • Trinity Grand Island NE • (308)382-5274 • (CQ 1993)

**ARNDT ANN L** (816)833-0957
400 Kirk Ave Independence MO 64050-1614 • MO • Prin • Messiah Independence MO • (816)254-9409 • (S 1970)

**ARNDT JACQUELYN** (515)579-6159
1816 Indigo Ave Latimer IA 50452-7535 • kjarndt@hotmail.com • IE • Tchr • St Paul Latimer IA • (515)579-6046 • (S 1994)

**ARNDT JOHN E*** (816)833-0957
400 Kirk Ave Independence MO 64050-1614 • MO • Tchr • Messiah Independence MO • (816)254-9409 • (S 1966)

**ARNDT RICHARD E** (708)946-3066
141 W Eagle Lake Rd Beecher IL 60401 • reamac@chicago.avenew.com • NI • Tchr • Zion Beecher IL • (708)946-2272 • (RF 1992)

**ARNDT SHARON LYNN** (219)763-9985
2130 Pennsylvania St Portage IN 46368-2422 • cubrich6@gte.net • IN • Tchr • Our Saviour Gary IN • (219)887-5031 • (RF 1994)

**ARNETT BEVERLY LUCILLE** (619)728-3940
4107 Cypress Island Ct Fallbrook CA 92028-4909 • PSW • Tchr • Zion Fallbrook CA • (760)723-3500 • (RF 1965 MSED)

**ARNHOLT PHILIP J** (414)241-4419
10910 N San Marino Dr Mequon WI 53092-5850 • philip.arnholt@cuw.edu • SW • SHS/C • South Wisconsin Milwaukee WI • (414)464-8100 • (MW 1982 MSED PHD)

**ARNHOLT WILLIAM H** (216)884-2128
4610 Pershing Ave Cleveland OH 44134-2320 • OH • EM • (RF 1955)

**ARNHOLZ DONALD R** (813)995-0440
3437 Shore Ct Land O Lakes FL 34639-6608 • dsarnholz@aol.com • FG • Tchr • Peace Fort Lauderdale FL • (954)772-8010 • (RF 1964 MA)

**ARNOLD BARBARA ANN** (319)372-0385
101 23rd St Fort Madison IA 52627 • OK • Tchr • First Ponca City OK • (580)762-1111 • (WN 1954)

**ARNOLD LARRY J** (571)684-0431
3334 W Fisher Bay City MI 48706 • EN • Tchr • Child Of Christ Hartland MI • (248)887-3836 • (AA 1992)

**ARNOLD LAWRELL D**
PO Box 288 Brooklyn NY 11236 • enchemade@aol.com • AT • Tchr • Grace Queens Village NY • (718)465-1010 • (BR 1995)

**ARNOLD RICHARD J**
6804 Casselberry Ct Saint Louis MO 63123-3241 • MO • Tchr • LHS South Saint Louis MO • (314)631-1400 • (S 1968 MA)

**ARNOLD STEVEN F*** (651)486-7372
563 Sextant Ave W Saint Paul MN 55113-3400 • sarnold@csp.edu • EN • SHS/C • English Farmington MI • (S 1970 MA EDD)

**ARONE KRISTEN** (914)337-0207
400 Broadway Hastings NY 10706 • AT • Tchr • The Village Bronxville NY • (914)337-0207 • (BR 1993)

**ARONSON DEVIE S** (402)727-1541
2149 1/2 N D St Fremont NE 68025-2613 • NEB • Tchr • Trinity Fremont NE • (402)721-5959 • (S 1976)

**ARP WOODROW A**
9606 Chukar Cir Austin TX 78758-6252 • TX • S Miss • Texas Austin TX • (S 1965 MA)

**ARRICK MARY SUE** (517)552-0547
1317 Maple Leaf Ln Howell MI 48843-8379 • Arrich@voyager.net • MI • 09/2000 • (AA 1988)

**ARTHURTON MELISSA**
C/O Our Savior Luth Church 1601 W Holmes Rd Lansing MI 48910-4394 • MI • Tchr • Our Savior Lansing MI • (517)882-8665 • (AA 1996)

**ASCHBRENNER HENRY J** (714)854-8002
209 N Avenida Veracruz Anaheim CA 92808-1022 • PSW • SHS/C • Pacific Southwest Irvine CA • (949)854-3232 • (S 1960 MA)

**ASCHE NANCY D** (801)261-0725
3962 S 1040 E Salt Lake City UT 84124-1127 • n.asche@worldnet.att.net • RM • Tchr • Salt Lake LHS Salt Lake City UT • (801)266-6676 • (S 1984)

**ASCHEMEIER SUSAN K** (419)267-5585
1800 Walnut Grove Rd Defiance OH 43512-9161 • OH • Tchr • St Paul Napoleon OH • (419)592-5536 • (RF 1975)

**ASH MARGARET R** (208)528-6031
3241 Wexford Cir Idaho Falls ID 83404 • mrash@srv.net • NOW • Prin • Hope Idaho Falls ID • (208)529-8080 • (RF 1970 MED)

**ASH RANDALL W** (952)941-3173
7432 W 103rd St Bloomington MN 55438-2173 • rash21752@aol.com • MNS • Prin • Luth HS Of Greater M Bloomington MN • (612)854-0224 • (RF 1975 MED)

**ASH WILLIAM N*** (208)528-6031
3241 Wexford Cir Idaho Falls ID 83404 • NOW • 06/1997 06/2000 • (RF 1967 MA)

**ASHBY LISA ANN** (402)643-4100
419 N 7th St Seward NE 68434-1721 • lashby@seward.ccsn.edu • NEB • SHS/C • Nebraska Seward NE • (S 1987 MA PHD)

**ASHCRAFT JOHN ROBERT** (954)916-9354
C/O Faith Lutheran Church 1161 SW 30th Ave Fort Lauderdale FL 33312-2856 • FG • 07/1996 07/1998 • (RF 1994)

**ASHFORD JULIE LYN** (405)733-1519
1326 Damron Dr Midwest City OK 73110-1404 • OK • Tchr • Good Shepherd Midwest City OK • (405)732-2585 • (S 1990)

**ASMUS DANIEL MARK** (612)659-0796
1689 Ashland Ave Saint Paul MN 55104-6158 • MNS • SHS/C • Minnesota South Burnsville MN • (SP 1989)

**ASMUS EUNICE E** (612)237-2082
28241 505th Ave Winthrop MN 55396 • MNS • EM • (S 1960)

**ASPLIN LAURA D** (402)643-2786
438 Grand Ave Seward NE 68434-1616 • NEB • Tchr • St John Seward NE • (402)643-4535 • (S 1991)

**ATKINSON KEITH** (414)463-4727
4632 N Houston Ave Milwaukee WI 53218-4559 • atkinson@aero.net • SW • Prin • Pilgrim Wauwatosa WI • (414)476-0736 • (PO 1981 MED)

**ATTENBERGER DAVID FRANK** (313)773-1862
30555 Park St Roseville MI 48066-1393 • MI • Tchr • St Peter Eastpointe MI • (810)771-2809 • (RF 1973 MA)

**AU BUCHON BARBARA ANN** (313)241-5526
5020 Kay Dr Monroe MI 48161-3658 • revaubuchon@earthlink.net • MI • Tchr • Trinity Monroe MI • (734)241-1160 • (RF 1968)

**AUFDEMBERGE CAROL** (972)377-3604
9339 Homestead Ln Frisco TX 75034 • TX • Tchr • Prince Peace Carrollton TX • (972)447-9887 • (S 1969 MSED)

**AUFDEMBERGE ERWIN J** (810)949-2961
23805 24 Mile Rd Macomb MI 48042-3304 • MI • EM • (S 1957 MMU)

**AUFDEMBERGE RICHARD O**
1275 W Braewood Ave Highlands Ranch CO 80126-5674 • RM • EM • (S 1958 MA)

**AUFDEMBERGE THEODORE P** (734)426-4916
9020 Gross Rd Dexter MI 48130-9422 • MI • EM • (S 1956 MA PHD)

**AUGER ROBERT G*** (813)657-4025
616 Talwood Cir Apt E Brandon FL 33510 • rmauger@prodigy.net • FG • Tchr • Immanuel Brandon FL • (813)689-1787 • (SP 1984)

**AUMANN JAMES C** (414)423-6472
7317 Edgemont Ave Greendale WI 53129-1611 • SW • Tchr • Martin LHS Greendale WI • (414)421-4000 • (RF 1982)

**AUMICK JAMES T** (219)749-4445
1115 Canal St New Haven IN 46774-1239 • IN • Tchr • Central New Haven IN • (219)493-2502 • (RF 1983 MS)

**AURICH DEAN R** (952)657-2586
15015 County Road 30 Mayer MN 55360-9691 • MNS • Tchr • Lutheran High Mayer MN • (612)657-2251 • (S 1979)

**AURICH JOHN B** (612)741-2286
2684 Brittany Ln Woodbury MN 55125-3017 • jaurich@stpeter.pvt.k12.mn.us • MNS • Prin • St Peter Edina MN • (612)927-8400 • (S 1976 MA)

**AURICH MICHAEL A** (612)739-8070
14 Nelson St Saint Paul MN 55119-4632 • maurich@mail.concordia-academy.pvt.k12.mn.us • MNS • Tchr • Concordia Academy Roseville MN • (612)484-8429 • (S 1976 MA)

**AWE NANETTE** (815)254-2340
24854 Jordan Ln Plainfield IL 60544-7465 • NI • 04/1997 • (S 1975)

**AXTELL VIRGINIA D** (210)666-5560
6103 Ashley Springs San Antonio TX 78244-2113 • TX • Tchr • Shepherd Of The Hill San Antonio TX • (210)614-3741 • (AU 1982)

## B

**BAACK JOLEEN G** (812)373-0504
1001 Sycamore St Columbus IN 47201-6267 • jobaack@juno.com • IN • Tchr • St Peter Columbus IN • (812)372-5266 • (S 1987 MS)

**BAACK LARRY D** (812)372-3291
5561 E Forster Ave Columbus IN 47201-4902 • IN • Tchr • St Peter Columbus IN • (812)372-5266 • (S 1962 MED MPE)

**BAACKE BRUCE M** (713)328-1076
15915 Castaway Ct Crosby TX 77532-5533 • bbaacke@ix.netcom.com • TX • Tchr • Lutheran South Acade Houston TX • (281)464-8299 • (S 1970 MED)

**BAACKE DEBORAH J** (281)993-9532
4711 Cavern Dr Friendswood TX 77546-3151 • dbaacke@hotmail.com • TX • Tchr • Lutheran South Acade Houston TX • (281)464-9320 • (S 1973 MED)

**BAARCK STEPHANIE L**
410 Trinklein St Frankenmuth MI 48734-1518 • sbaarck@stlorenz.com • MI • Tchr • St Lorenz Frankenmuth MI • (517)652-6141 • (RF 1990)

**BAARS MARILYN J** (608)592-7591
N1482 Sunset Dr Lodi WI 53555-9442 • SW • Tchr • St John Portage WI • (608)742-4222 • (RF 1969)

**BAASE LINDA L** (773)792-8319
7715 W Farragut Ave Chicago IL 60656-1625 • lindabaase@aol.com • EN • Tchr • Bethesda Chicago IL • (312)743-0800 • (RF 1971 MA)

**BABBITT SHELLEY R**
1728 Vintage Dr Denton TX 76210-3073 • TX • Tchr • Salem Tomball TX • (281)351-8122 • (IV 1997)

**BABCHAK ELIZABETH A** (573)335-0857
1236 W Cape Rock Dr Apt 42 Cape Girardeau MO 63701-2642 • MO • Tchr • Trinity Cape Girardeau MO • (573)334-1068 • (RF 1976 MA)

**BACH LISA ANN** (810)793-1511
4193 Sundowner Ln Columbiaville MI 48421 • MI • 09/2000 • (AA 1989 MAT)

**BACHERT ZINA M** (708)946-2963
PO Box 593 Beecher IL 60401-0593 • gkatz593@aol.com • NI • Tchr • Zion Beecher IL • (708)946-2272 • (RF 1986)

**BACHMANN CHARLENE K** (618)493-7596
270 N Main PO Box 192 Hoyleton IL 62803-0192 • SI • Tchr • Trinity Hoyleton IL • (618)493-7754 • (S 1980)

**BACHMANN RAYMOND E** (812)358-4461
1025 W Spring St Brownstown IN 47220-1038 • IN • Tchr • Central Brownstown IN • (812)358-2512 • (RF 1956 MS)

**BACIC FRANCES MARIE** (734)955-6549
15217 Spruce Ct Romulus MI 48174 • MI • Tchr • St John New Boston MI • (734)654-6366 • (AA 1993)

**BACK LEAH K**
15851 Pasadena #H 4 Tustin CA 92780 • LeahBack@aol.com • PSW • Tchr • Christ Costa Mesa CA • (949)548-6866 • (S 1998 MED)

**BACKS DIANE K** (618)824-6492
1497 Grouse Rd Venedy IL 62214-1011 • cdkbacks@egyptian.net • SI • Tchr • Trinity-St John Nashville IL • (618)327-8561 • (RF 1983)

**BACON HAROLD L** (810)364-8522
800 5th Street Marysville MI 48040 • MI • Prin • Trinity Port Huron MI • (810)984-2501 • (RF 1965 MA)

**BADCIONG RUTH E DR** (507)454-4418
1419 Homer Rd Winona MN 55987 • badciong@hbci.com • NOW • SHS/C • Northwest Portland OR • (MQ 1987 MED DED)

**BADE BARBARA L** (760)806-3920
739 Bel Air Dr Vista CA 92084 • wlb7939@home.com • PSW • Tchr • Faith Vista CA • (760)724-7700 • (S 1963)

**BADE WILLIAM D** (217)698-9208
1033 S Grand Ave W Springfield IL 62704-3550 • bade@eosinc.com • CI • Tchr • Central Illinois Springfield IL • (S 1983 MA)

**BADE WILLIAM L** (760)806-3920
739 Bel Air Dr Vista CA 92084 • wlb7939@home.com • PSW • Tchr • Faith Vista CA • (760)724-7700 • (S 1963 MMU)

**BADEN MARIAN J DR** (714)974-8928
1796 N Shattuck Pl Orange CA 92865-4639 • paradox59@earthlink.net • PSW • EM • (S 1959 MED PHD)

**BADEN ROBERT C DR** (714)974-8928
1796 N Shattuck Pl Orange CA 92865-4639 • paradox59@earthlink.com • PSW • EM • (S 1958 MA PHD)

**BADEN THOMAS W** (915)942-9275
3217 Cumberland Dr San Angelo TX 76904-6001 • tbaden@aol.com • TX • Tchr • Trinity San Angelo TX • (915)947-1275 • (S 1962 MED)

**BADER JOANNE E** (314)946-6219
2061 Beau Ct Saint Charles MO 63303-5963 • MO • Prin • Immanuel Saint Charles MO • (636)946-0051 • (RF 1958 MA)

**BADER JUDITH J** (818)878-9130
3815 Orchid Ln # A Calabasas CA 91302 • teddyandfamily@msn.com • PSW • Tchr • Our Savior First Granada Hills CA • (818)363-9505 • (S 1978)

**BAERENKLAU JAMES C**
159 Elmhurst Ave Elmhurst IL 60126 • NI • Tchr • Immanuel Elmhurst IL • (630)832-1649 • (RF 1990)

**BAERWOLF PAUL R**
225 Washington Ave Chuluota FL 32766-8602 • S • Tchr • St Luke Oviedo FL • (407)365-3228 • (AA 1992)

**BAGANZ CHAD DAVID** (262)681-2343
3548 Douglas Ave Apt 105 Racine WI 53402 • cdbaganz@hotmail.com • SW • Tchr • St John Racine WI • (262)637-7011 • (RF 1996)

**BAGANZ MARK J** (414)681-2600
1208 Carlton Dr Racine WI 53402-3312 • SW • Prin • Trinity Racine WI • (414)632-1766 • (RF 1965 MA)

**BAGANZ RANDAL D** (414)764-6555
2830 E Emily Ave Oak Creek WI 53154-3418 • SW • Prin • Lutheran High School Racine WI • (414)637-6538 • (RF 1972 MA)

**BAGBY KATHRYN L** (616)471-7521
8780 S Bluffview Dr Berrien Springs MI 49103 • MI • Tchr • Immanuel Bridgman MI • (616)465-6031 • (RF 1982)

**BAGBY TIMOTHY D** (616)471-7521
8780 S Bluffview Dr Berrien Springs MI 49103 • MI • Prin • Trinity Berrien Springs MI • (616)473-1811 • (RF 1983)

**BAGINSKI JOHN C**
504 N James Steeleville IL 62288 • jbaginski@lhsa.net • SI • Prin • St Mark Steeleville IL • (618)965-3838 • (RF 1969)

**BAHN KAREN E** (715)384-7968
300 N Adams Ave Marshfield WI 54449-1708 • dbahn@commplusis.net • NW • Tchr • Trinity Athens WI • (715)257-7559 • (MQ 1988 MS)

**BAHN NICOLE MARIE** (817)496-5455
6051 Bridge St #6045B Fort Worth TX 76112 • mdbahn@earthlink.net • TX • SHS/C • St Timothy Grand Prairie TX • (817)557-9411 • (S 1998)

**BAHN SHERLYN J** (651)686-2937
1120 Gabbert Cir Eagan MN 55123-1844 • MNS • Tchr • Trinity Lone Oak Eagan MN • (651)454-1139 • (SP 1994)

**BAHR DAVID M** (219)486-2039
7315 Silverthorn Run Fort Wayne IN 46835-1842 • davidbahr@juno.com • IN • Tchr • Concordia LHS Fort Wayne IN • (219)483-1102 • (RF 1987 MED)

**BAHR DONALD G** (314)867-3442
1245 Nectar Dr Saint Louis MO 63137-2246 • MO • Tchr • River Roads Saint Louis MO • (314)388-0300 • (S 1977 MSED)

**BAHR JANET L** (219)486-2039
7315 Silverthorn Run Fort Wayne IN 46835-1842 • janetbahr@juno.com • IN • Tchr • Indiana Fort Wayne IN • (RF 1987)

**BAHR JOEL M** (440)442-8151
1404 Henning Dr Lyndhurst OH 44124-2421 • OH • Tchr • St John South Euclid OH • (216)381-8595 • (BR 1977)

**BAHR KENNETH E** (262)255-4643
W158N9752 Broadleaf Ln Germantown WI 53022-5119 • SW • EM • (RF 1956 MED)

**BAHR MARK M** (262)966-7660
N57W33056 Cedar Bay Ct Nashotah WI 53058-9542 • mbahr@execpc.com • SW • Prin • Lake Country Hartland WI • (262)461-6000 • (RF 1982 MA)

**BAHR PAUL M** (414)462-6789
9515 W Palmetto Ave Wauwatosa WI 53222-1557 • SW • Prin • Milwaukee LHS Milwaukee WI • (414)461-6000 • (RF 1973 MEDADM)

**BAILEY ANDREW D** (231)832-2847
124 W Todd Ave Reed City MI 49677-1124 • abailey657@hotmail.com • MI • P/Tchr • Trinity Reed City MI • (616)832-5186 • (S 1979 MAR MA)

**BAILEY BONNIE JEAN**
52 Hather Glen Ct Crossville TN 38558-6437 • MI • EM • (CQ 1986)

**BAILEY ENITH C** (608)254-7793
N9458 Pine Valley Ln Wisconsin Dells WI 53965-8702 • SW • Tchr • Trinity Wisconsin Dells WI • (608)253-3241 • (SP 1969)

**BAILEY LINDA MARIE** (630)434-8765
1000 Division St Lisle IL 60532 • linda.bailey@trinitylisle.org • NI • Tchr • Trinity Lisle IL • (630)964-1272 • (SP 1983 MED)

**BAILEY PAMELA LYNN** (407)207-4720
7944 Pine Crossings Cir #228 Orlando FL 32807 • scheer33bailey@hotmail.com • FG • Tchr • Orlando Lutheran Aca Orlando FL • (407)275-7750 • (AA 1998)

**BAIRD BARBARA K** (608)253-7933
4035 9th Ave Wisconsin Dells WI 53965-8668 • SW • Tchr • Trinity Wisconsin Dells WI • (608)253-3241 • (S 1969 MS)

**BAISCH EVELYN JEAN** (309)822-8812
77 S Riverview Dr East Peoria IL 61611-9644 • garbanzo77@juno.com • CI • 08/1990 08/2000 • (RF 1969)

**BAJUS LUTHER J II** (920)457-9519
3210 S 11th Pl Sheboygan WI 53081-6932 • mn2wi713@excel.net • SW • Tchr • Bethlehem Sheboygan WI • (920)452-5071 • (RF 1977)

**BAKALYAR JUDITH ANN** (562)926-1752
17914 Gerritt Pl Cerritos CA 90703-8939 • PSW • Tchr • Zion Anaheim CA • (714)535-3600 • (RF 1969)

**BAKER KEVIN CLAYTON** (972)731-8144
4028 Sendero Trl Plano TX 75024 • kbaker@popcs.net • TX • Messiah Charlotte NC • (S 1986 MED)

**BAKER PAUL** (417)877-0248
2726 S Williams Ave Springfield MO 65807 • pajlbaker@aol.com • MO • Prin • Springfield Springfield MO • (417)883-5717 • (S 1973 MS)

**BAKER RACHEL PENELOPE** (314)505-7656
Fritz 3A W 801 De Mun Ave St Louis MO 63105 • SI • Tchr • Zion Belleville IL • (618)234-0275 • (S 1998)

**BAKER SUSAN GALE** (616)982-4252
1201 Mohawk Ln Saint Joseph MI 49085-1753 • sbaker@remcll.k12.mi.us • MI • Tchr • Trinity Saint Joseph MI • (616)983-3056 • (S 1974 MA)

**BALBACH MARTHA L**
1313 Joliet St Aurora CO 80010-3437 • RM • Tchr • St Andrew Denver CO • (303)371-7014 • (RF 1967 MED)

**BALDWIN ALICE FAY** (719)269-1236
2511 Pear St Canon City CO 81212-2667 • mommynet@aol.com • RM • 12/1999 • (S 1965 MA)

**BALDWIN LANA M** (813)752-8948
4510 Platt Rd Plant City FL 33565-3868 • FG • Tchr • Hope Plant City FL • (813)752-4621 • (S 1969)

**BALKE WILLIAM H** (503)666-3858
515 SW 7th St Gresham OR 97080-9478 • billb@cu-portland.edu • NOW • SHS/C • Northwest Portland OR • (S 1959 MSED)

**BALL CAROL MARIE** (630)325-2407
9035 Skyline Dr Hinsdale IL 60521-6252 • iteech34@juno.com • NI • Tchr • Trinity Burr Ridge IL • (708)839-1444 • (CQ 1997)

**BALSTERS SANDRA M** (618)377-9077
905 S Moreland Rd Bethalto IL 62010-2111 • SI • Tchr • Zion Bethalto IL • (618)377-5507 • (S 1975 MSED)

**BALZER JO ANN** (616)651-1418
901 Canterbury Dr Sturgis MI 49091-9021 • MI • Tchr • Trinity Sturgis MI • (616)651-4245 • (AA 1984)

**BALZUM MARY J** (612)467-3713
101 1st Ave SW Young America MN 55397-9203 • MNS • Tchr • St Johns Young America MN • (612)467-3461 • (SP 1974)

**BAMESBERGER JOANN** (402)464-0040
2507 Dorothy Dr Lincoln NE 68507-2928 • NEB • Tchr • Trinity Lincoln NE • (402)466-1800 • (CQ 1985)

**BANDELOW DENISE E** (217)624-2308
10499 Mansion Rd Loami IL 62661-3203 • CI • Tchr • Concordia Springfield IL • (217)529-3307 • (RF 1976)

**BANGERT ARTHUR M** (402)643-3822
457 Bader Ave Seward NE 68434-1125 • NEB • EM • (S 1942 MED)

**BANGERT DAVID J** (414)422-0298
W154S7935 Foxboro Ct Muskego WI 53150-7731 • martylu@execpc.com • SW • Tchr • Martin LHS Greendale WI • (414)421-4000 • (RF 1978 MA)

**BANGERT JEAN M** (414)422-0298
W154S7935 Foxboro Ct Muskego WI 53150-7731 • martylv@execpc.com • EN • Tchr • Hales Corners Hales Corners WI • (414)529-6701 • (RF 1978)

**BANGERT SANDRA JEAN** (402)643-6340
1542 Plainview Ave Seward NE 68434-1134 • NEB • 08/2000 • (S 1982 MED)

**BANHOLZER EILEEN J** (208)326-5303
2020 E 3550 N Filer ID 83328-5628 • NOW • EM • (S 1964)

**BANKS FONYA TRINETTE**
5758 Saloma Ave Saint Louis MO 63120 • MO • Tchr • St Matthew Saint Louis MO • (314)261-7708 • (RF 1995)

**BANKS LAURA L** (812)314-0833
2335 Charleston Pl Apt #69 Columbus IN 47203 • banlau_0610@yahoo.com • IN • Tchr • St Peter Columbus IN • (812)372-5266 • (RF 1998)

**BANKSTON SHERON** (301)884-4570
13690 Charles St Charlotte Hall MD 20622 • SE • Tchr • Grace LA Plata MD • (301)932-0963 • (S 1981 MA)

**BANNING BENJAMIN D** (262)637-9806
1839 1/2 Green St Racine WI 53402 • SW • Tchr • Lutheran High School Racine WI • (414)637-6538 • (MQ 2000)

**BANUELOS AMY E** (714)643-0352
11 Southside Ct Aliso Viejo CA 92656-4278 • PSW • Tchr • Shepherd Of Peace Irvine CA • (949)786-3997 • (IV 1991)

**BANWART RANDOLPH J** (828)464-2814
1141 Hefner Dr Conover NC 28613-8968 • dihrdcub@hotmail.com • SE • Tchr • Concordia Conover NC • (828)464-3011 • (RF 1966)

**BARCKHOLTZ MARGARET L** (661)946-6806
2640 Harmony Way Lancaster CA 93535-5690 • margeb@qnet.com • PSW • Tchr • Grace Lancaster CA • (805)948-1018 • (RF 1962)

**BARCKHOLTZ WENDY D** (760)934-4223
PO Box 841 Mammoth Lakes CA 93546-0841 • mllutheran@qnet.com • PSW • 10/1994 10/1999 • (S 1990)

**BARDELEBEN ALAN*** (217)425-8733
2423 W Forest Ave Decatur IL 62522-2672 • CI • Tchr • Lutheran School Asso Decatur IL • (217)233-2001 • (RF 1982 MS)

**BARGEN CHRISTINE A** (314)940-9005
3286 Principia Ave Saint Charles MO 63301-5721 • MO • Tchr • Immanuel Saint Charles MO • (636)946-0051 • (S 1976 MS)

**BARKHAU ALVIN L** (847)823-3092
1711 Norman Blvd Park Ridge IL 60068-3850 • NI • Tchr • St Paul Skokie IL • (847)673-5030 • (RF 1958 MA)

**BARKLAGE CAROL ELIZABETH** (916)725-6358
6635 Sylvan Rd - Apt 528 Citrus Heights CA 95610 • CNH • Mem C • Faith Fair Oaks CA • (916)961-4252 • (S 1979)

**BARLAU MARTIN W** (970)667-9591
2229 Scotch Pine Ct Loveland CO 80538-3924 • mbarlau@juno.com • RM • Rocky Mountain Aurora CO* • (S 1957 MSED)

**BARNES AUDREY J** (913)849-3804
35330 Block Rd Paola KS 66071-7299 • KS • Rocky Mountain Aurora CO • (S 1970 MA)

**BARNES HOLLY MICHELLE** (713)784-8044
2301 Lazy Hollow #485A Houston TX 77063 • hollymichellebarnes@yahoo.com • TX • Tchr • Memorial Houston TX • (713)782-4022 • (S 1999)

**BARNES PAUL M** (719)850-1907
301 Faraday St Monte Vista CO 81144-1616 • stpeters@amigo.net • RM • Tchr • St Peter Monte Vista CO • (719)852-5449 • (WN 1984 MA)

**BARNES RICHARD M** (901)757-3815
7606 Dexter Run Cir Cordova TN 38018-8754 • MDS • Tchr • Immanuel Memphis TN • (901)388-0205 • (SP 1978)

**BARNES ROBERT D** (949)786-7467
4 Silkberry Irvine CA 92614-7480 • robert.barnes@cui.edu • PSW • EM • (S 1957 MBA)

**BARNES ROBERT E** (612)888-0905
1400 E 99th St Bloomington MN 55425-2609 • MNS • EM • (CQ 1959 MED)

**BARNHART JACCI SUZANNE** (817)354-0410
3911 Kirby Dr Apt 915 Fort Worth TX 76155 • TX • Tchr • Grace Arlington TX • (817)274-1626 • (AU 2000)

**BARNHOUSE KRISTA KAY** (402)327-0201
4620 Van Dorn Lincoln NE 68506-2560 • kbarnho@lps.com • NEB • Tchr • Faith Lincoln NE • (402)466-6861 • (S 1995)

**BARNINGHAM NOLA L** (208)756-4630
Rt 1 Box 80 Salmon ID 83467 • n1682096@salmoninternet.net • NOW • 08/1988 08/2000 • (PO 1981)

**BARONE KATHLEEN JEAN** (714)687-1789
1181 S Sunkist #14 Anaheim CA 92806-5438 • kathwean@aol.com • PSW • Tchr • Pilgrim Santa Monica CA • (310)829-2239 • (S 1995)

**BARR ANDREW K** (815)439-5930
1814 Olde Mill Rd Plainfield IL 60544 • NI • EM • (RF 1962 MAD)

**BARR KATHLEEN ELAINE** (678)817-9278
100 Knight Way Apt 1205 Fayetteville GA 30214-1798 • kbarr@mindspring.com • FG • Tchr • St Paul Peachtree City GA • (770)486-3545 • (S 1986 MED)

**BARRICK SHARON RUTH** (847)985-5221
1934 Weston Ln Schaumburg IL 60193 • NI • Tchr • St Peter Schaumburg IL • (847)885-7636 • (RF 1979 MA)

**BARRIE PAMELA** (517)742-4049
22680 Cohoon Rd Hillman MI 49746 • MI • Tchr • Immanuel Alpena MI • (517)354-3443 • (S 1975)

**BARROW JERRI-JAYNE**
21-12 123 St College Point NY 11356 • AT • 09/1999 • (BR 1983)

**BARTELL MARVIN H** (708)456-4986
1704 N 77th Ave Elmwood Park IL 60707-4107 • bartellm@curf.edu • NI • SHS/C • Northern Illinois Hillside IL • (RF 1961 MS PHD)

**BARTELS JACK D** (301)464-8013
6601 Alexis Dr Bowie MD 20720-4716 • SE • Prin • Ascension Landover Hills MD • (301)577-0500 • (S 1966 MED)

**BARTELS JUDY K** (402)243-2316
RR 1 Box 125 Tobias NE 68453-9730 • NEB • P/Tchr • Zion Tobias NE • (402)243-2354 • (S 1971 MED)

**BARTELS KATHY L** (785)234-3154
701 Roosevelt Topeka KS 66604 • KS • Tchr • Topeka Topeka KS • (785)357-0382 • (S 1990 MED)

**BARTELS KEVIN W** (314)547-2698
326 S Spring St Apt D Perryville MO 63775-2632 • MO • Tchr • Immanuel Perryville MO • (573)547-6161 • (RF 1982)

**BARTELS RENEE L**
306 Oak Dr Young America MN 55397-9208 • MNS • Tchr • St Johns Young America MN • (612)467-3461 • (SP 1982)

**BARTELS WALTER O** (505)268-1241
1719 Vassar Dr NE Albuquerque NM 87106-2539 • RM • EM • (S 1942 MA)

**BARTELT HEATHER RAE**
C/O St John Lutheran Church 1915 SE Lake Weir Rd Ocala FL 34471-5498 • FG • Tchr • St John Ocala FL • (352)629-1794 • (MQ 2000)

**BARTELT JENISE J** (405)263-7704
519 W Colorado St Okarche OK 73762-9415 • OK • Tchr • St John Okarche OK • (405)263-4488 • (S 1992)

**BARTELT KRISTINE SUE** (847)426-7925
132 N Wisconsin St Carpentersvle IL 60110-2001 • NI • Tchr • Immanuel Dundee IL • (847)428-1010 • (RF 1986)

**BARTHEL CATHY L**
621 3rd Ave Rear Cheasapeake OH 45619-1038 • CI • Tchr • St John Buckley IL • (217)394-2444 • (AA 1994)

**BARTHOLOMEW DIANA LYNN** (414)329-3086
2335 S 56th St West Allis WI 53219 • mbart@milwpc.com • EN • Tchr • Hales Corners Hales Corners WI • (414)529-6701 • (MQ 1986)

**BARTZSCH DAINA MAE** (602)867-0332
15842 N 6th Pl Phoenix AZ 85022 • barchwoman@aol.com • PSW • Tchr • Christ Redeemer Phoenix AZ • (623)934-3286 • (BR 1985)

**BARWA WILLIAM H** (414)327-7300
W323S7771 Cherry Ln Mukwonago WI 53149-9340 • SW • Tchr • Martin LHS Greendale WI • (414)421-4000 • (S 1979)

**BARZ DANIEL S** (616)428-8065
5648 E Mohican Dr Stevensville MI 49127-9643 • dbarz@remcll.k12.mi.us • MI • 09/1998 • (S 1976 MCRT)

**BARZ JONATHAN M DR** (708)209-1245
1115 Bonnie Brae River Forest IL 60305 • crfbarzjm@curf.edu • NI • SHS/C • Northern Illinois Hillside IL • (S 1982 MA PHD)

**BASCHAL ELYSE MARIE** (414)619-9980
913 Perry Ave Racine WI 53406 • SW • 01/2000 • (CQ 1978)

**BASS JANICE L** (402)371-7717
1806 College View Dr Norfolk NE 68701-2172 • jbass@christlutherannorfolk.org • NEB • Tchr • Christ Norfolk NE • (402)371-5536 • (S 1973)

**BASS JENNIFER LYNN** (206)364-7761
12532 35th Ave NE Apt B301 Seattle WA 98125-4554 • jlbass@spu.edu • NOW • 03/1997 03/2000 • (S 1993 MEDSC)

**BASSETT LEONARD E DR** (402)646-2188
1254 Rainbow Ave Seward NE 68434-1324 • lbassett@seward.cune.edu • NEB • SHS/C • Nebraska Seward NE • (S 1986 MED PHD)

**BASSETT MOLLY L** (402)465-4745
5319 Walker Ave Lincoln NE 68504-2966 • bassetthome@juno.com • NEB • 06/1997 06/2000 • (S 1995)

**BASSETT NATHAN C** (402)465-4745
5319 Walker Ave Lincoln NE 68504-2966 • NEB • Tchr • Lincoln Luth Jr/Sr H Lincoln NE • (402)467-5404 • (S 1993 MA)

**BASSUENER JENNIFER A** (815)568-9081
605 James Ct Marengo IL 60152-2211 • bassuen@mc.net • NI • Tchr • Zion Marengo IL • (815)568-5156 • (MQ 1990)

**BATCHELOR JAMES** (319)732-2893
1421 Trail Ave Wilton IA 52778-9312 • IE • EM • (CQ 1964 MNS)

**BATES JANICE A** (612)473-5356
5808 Brook Dr Edina MN 55439-1339 • jraffers@aol.com • MNS • Tchr • Redeemer Wayzata MN • (612)473-5356 • (SP 1987)

**BATHJE ARNOLD A**
3919 Cherry Hills Pl Traverse Ctiy MI 49684 • MI • EM • (RF 1949 MA)

**BATTERMAN-SMITH MARY B**
6113 Downing St Greendale WI 53129-2221 • mbbs@execpc.com • EN • Redeemer Wayzata MN • (SP 1979 MS)

**BATTERMANN WILLIAM E** (510)526-3912
24 San Carlos Ave El Cerrito CA 94530-4147 • CNH • EM • (S 1966)

**BATTLE JOE-LEN** (407)469-2837
C/O Woodlands Luth Ministry 15749 County Road 455 Montverde FL 34756-3775 • FG • O Sp Min • Florida-Georgia Orlando FL • (RF 1963)

**BAUDER JENNIFER L**
748 Lippert Ln Glendale Heights IL 60139-2977 • NI • 08/1999 • (RF 1995)

**BAUDER KAREN F** (847)392-8590
1200 N Sycamore Ln Mt Prospect IL 60056-1540 • karenbauder@ilcp.org • NI • Tchr • Immanuel Palatine IL • (847)359-1936 • (S 1964 MA)

**BAUDER TERRI J** (802)763-2997
120 Tortolano Rd South Royalton VT 05068-0843 • terri_bauder@hotmail.com • NE • 09/1999 • (SP 1981)

**BAUER ARLIN J** (660)674-2208
PO Box 214 Alma MO 64001-0214 • arlinbauer@hotmail.com • MO • Prin • Trinity Alma MO • (660)674-2376 • (S 1966 MS)

**BAUER DONALD W** (602)267-0741
2401 N 39th Pl Phoenix AZ 85008-2239 • EN • EM • (RF 1954 MS)

**BAUER JENNIFER L** (847)692-7159
1510 Good Ave Park Ridge IL 60068-1418 • NI • 01/1996 02/2000 • (CQ 1988)

**BAUER JUDITH ELAINE** (219)432-7620
11323 Bittersweet Creek Run Fort Wayne IN 46804-8207 • IN • Tchr • Christ Child Fort Wayne IN • (219)452-2240 • (RF 1968)

**BAUER NANCY K** (517)686-5239
1830 Delta Rd Bay City MI 48706-9768 • MI • Tchr • St John Bay City MI • (517)686-0176 • (RF 1972)

**BAUER PETER W*** (320)762-2515
5721 Mud Lake Ln SW Alexandria MN 56308-6304 • jaybriar@rea-alp.com • MNN • Tchr • Zion Alexandria MN • (320)763-4842 • (RF 1966 MSEDADM)

**BAUER VIVIAN V** (707)765-0946
C/O Trinity Luth Church 333 Woodland Ave San Rafael CA 94901 • trinityforkids@aol.com • CNH • Tchr • Trinity San Rafael CA • (415)454-4135 • (S 1988)

**BAUGHAM CAROL ELAINE**
101 Chanticlair Dr Yorktown VA 23693 • SE • Tchr • Emmanuel Hampton VA • (757)723-8782 • (SP 1966)

**BAUGHMAN KRISTINA LYNN** (317)786-6869
5466 Sleet Dr Indianapolis IN 46237 • luthvolley@aol.com • IN • Tchr • Zion New Palestine IN • (317)861-4210 • (MQ 1996)

**BAUGHMAN TERRY ALAN** (317)786-6869
5466 Sleet Dr Indianapolis IN 46237 • luthvolley@aol.com • IN • Tchr • LHS Of Indianapolis Indianapolis IN • (317)787-5474 • (MQ 1992)

**BAUMAN MICHELLE A** (517)492-9889
3512 Ferndale Dr #104 Fort Wayne IN 46815-8632 • lmdbauman@aol.com • IN • Tchr • Holy Cross Fort Wayne IN • (219)483-3173 • (S 1998)

**BAUMANN GREGORY J** (612)543-2310
PO Box 492 Howard Lake MN 55349-0492 • MNS • Tchr • St James Howard Lake MN • (320)543-2630 • (S 1983)

**BAUMANN KENNETH E** (608)524-8503
1350 N Dewey Ave Reedsburg WI 53959-1029 • kbaumann@mwt.net • SW • Tchr • St Peter Reedsburg WI • (608)524-4066 • (SP 1969 MED)

**BAUMBACH MARK HARLAN** (314)772-4474
C/O Messiah Lutheran Church 2846 S Grand Blvd Saint Louis MO 63118-1033 • SI • 08/1996 08/1999 • (RF 1995)

**BAUMGARN CAROL** (612)753-2451
23926 Nightingale St NW Saint Francis MN 55070-9648 • MNS • Tchr • Trinity Saint Francis MN • (612)753-1234 • (S 1964)

**BAUMGART EDGAR R** (812)952-3853
6585 Rainsplitter Ln NE Lanesville IN 47136-8329 • IN • EM • (RF 1958)

**BAUMGARTEL ENNIS J** (909)659-5388
PO Box 7596 Victorville CA 92392 • PSW • P/Tchr • Zion Victorville CA • (760)243-3074 • (RF 1973)

**BAUMGARTEL JONATHAN**
14161 E Jewell Apt 204 Aurora CO 80012 • RM • Tchr • Peace Aurora CO • (303)766-7116 • (S 1996)

**BAUMGARTEL MARK WILLIAM** (734)397-1569
1576 Rustic Ridge Canton MI 48188-1247 • baumgartelmh@excite.com • MI • EM • (S 1961 MED)

**BAXTER JULIANNA M**
W6475 Greenville Dr Greenville WI 54942 • mollycat@execpc.com • NW • Mem C • Shepherd Hills Greenville WI • (920)757-5722 • (SP 1974 MSCT)

**BAYER LESTER R** (512)345-5234
4004 Madrid Cv Austin TX 78759-5058 • TX • EM • (RF 1946 MA DED LITTD)

**BAYER ROXANNE M**
504 E Columbia St Litchfield IL 62056-2320 • SI • Tchr • Zion Litchfield IL • (217)324-2033 • (S 1985 MED)

**BEALE NAOMI J** (317)628-0222
813 White Tail Ct Greentown IN 46936-9628 • tnllj@bigfoot.com • IN • Tchr • Redeemer Kokomo IN • (765)864-6466 • (MQ 1987)

**BEARDSLEY RONALD L**
510 S 3rd St Brighton MI 48116-1417 • MI • EM • (S 1958 MSED)

**BEATY KAREN A** (636)947-7441
1670 Deergrass Dr Saint Charles MO 63303-4613 • MO • Tchr • Zion Harvester MO • (314)441-7424 • (S 1972 MED)

**BEAUDOIN JAMES MICHAEL** (714)771-4284
801 E Trenton Ave Orange CA 92867-3729 • PSW • Prin • St Paul Orange CA • (714)921-3188 • (S 1982 MUED MA)

**BECCUE MARILYNN R** (760)735-9319
1912 Bear Valley Oaks Rd Escondido CA 92025-6300 • marilynn@beccue.com • PSW • Pacific Southwest Irvine CA • (949)854-3232 • (RF 1957 MA)

**BECERRA KIM L**
211 Enchanted Pkwy Manchester MO 63021 • MO • 02/2000 • (S 1994)

**BECK ARTHUR A**
101 Albion Ave Apt 305 Fairmont MN 56031-2101 • MNS • EM • (S 1954)

**BECK DAWN E** (402)470-0200
5021 W Elba Lincoln NE 68524 • dbeck@lps.org • NEB • Tchr • Messiah Lincoln NE • (402)489-3024 • (S 1995)

**BECK ROBERTA Y** (208)423-6818
3415 E 3500 N Kimberly ID 83341 • NOW • Tchr • Immanuel Twin Falls ID • (208)733-7820 • (S 1979)

**BECK THEODORE A** (402)643-4012
1040 Plainview Ave Seward NE 68434-1343 • NEB • EM • (RF 1950 MMU PHD)

**BECKEN LINDA M** (715)386-9531
219 Liberty St Hudson WI 54016-1966 • MNS • Tchr • Trinity Hudson WI • (715)386-9349 • (RF 1972 MA)

**BECKENDORF LEON E** (312)857-7098
808 S Kensington Dr Appleton WI 54915-6110 • NI • EM • (RF 1957 MA)

**BECKER ALVINA** (417)890-9189
3612 W Birchwood Pl Springfield MO 65807-0981 • MO • 08/1994 • (S 1974)

**BECKER AMY S** (773)427-7954
4310 N Menard Chicago IL 60634 • NI • SHS/C • Northern Illinois Hillside IL • (RF 1999)

**BECKER ANGELA J**
336 Arthur Neu Dr Carroll IA 51401-3225 • tabecker@netins.net • IW • 07/1999 • (S 1994)

**BECKER BRIAN J**
4310 N Menard Chicago IL 60634 • cejla-elf@hotmail.com • NI • SHS/C • Northern Illinois Hillside IL • (RF 1998)

**BECKER CENA C** (847)836-0780
202 S River St East Dundee IL 60118 • cburdeen@aol.com • NI • Tchr • Immanuel Dundee IL • (847)428-4477 • (RF 1996)

**BECKER CONNIE S** (501)227-8978
301 Santa Fe Trl Little Rock AR 72205-2205 • darrel-conbecker@worldnet.att.net • MDS • Tchr • Christ Little Rock AR • (501)663-5212 • (S 1970)

**BECKER DENICE E** (612)689-5689
928 Dellwood St S Cambridge MN 55008-2123 • MNN • 06/1999 • (SP 1977)

**BECKER ELMER H** (708)754-1207
240 Constance Ln Chicago Heights IL 60411-1724 • NI • EM • (S 1941)

**BECKER ESTHER R** (417)235-3019
215 N Main Freistatt MO 65654-9999 • MO • 09/1990 09/1999 • (S 1972 MED)

**BECKER GERHARDT C** (708)366-1219
612 Hannah Ave Forest Park IL 60130-1911 • NI • EM • (RF 1939 MMU)

**BECKER GREGORY N** (920)467-4967
6803 Sunset Rd Kohler WI 53044-1019 • gbecker@powercom.net • SW • Tchr • Trinity Sheboygan WI • (920)458-8248 • (RF 1982 MS)

**BECKER HARLAN H** (920)485-4195
178 S Wind Trl Horicon WI 53032-1220 • hbecker@powercom.net • SW • EM • (S 1953 MA)

**BECKER HERBERT H** (262)251-2897
W150N8213 Norman Dr Menomonee Falls WI 53051-3832 • beckerhh@execpc.com • SW • EM • (RF 1958 MED)

**BECKER JOEL C** (336)922-3316
2914 Pioneer Trl Winston Salem NC 27106-2227 • SE • Tchr • St John Winston-Salem NC • (336)725-1651 • (RF 1965)

**BECKER JOY KYRIA**
449 CMR 421 APO AE 09056-0449 • SE • 06/1999 • (BR 1994)

**BECKER JULIANNE M** (414)377-5997
N72W5321 Georgetown Dr Cedarburg WI 53012-1527 • jillbecker@hotmail.com • SW • Tchr • First Immanuel Cedarburg WI • (262)377-6610 • (CQ 1985 MED)

**BECKER KENNETH J** (847)428-4477
178 Hilltop Dr Lk In The Hls IL 60102-3306 • NI • Tchr • Immanuel Dundee IL • (847)428-1010 • (RF 1968 MA)

**BECKER KEVIN JOHN** (847)836-0780
202 S River St East Dundee IL 60118 • becker13@goplay.com • NI • Tchr • Immanuel Crystal Lake IL • (815)459-1444 • (RF 1996)

**BECKER KRISTIN ANN** (314)729-1332
8618 Villa Crest Dr Saint Louis MO 63126 • dceskater@aol.com • MO • Tchr • Missouri Saint Louis MO • (314)317-4550 • (RF 1998)

**BECKER LARRY D** (618)222-1965
220 Lake Stratford Dr Fairview Heights IL 62208 • SI • EM • (S 1958 MSED)

**BECKER MARY LEE** (312)434-8875
6512 Pine Trail Ln Unit 1 Tinley Park IL 60477-5013 • mbecker663 • EN • EM • (RF 1978 MA)

**BECKER MARY** (319)365-5290
3647 Cottage Grove Ave SE Cedar Rapids IA 52403-1612 • IE • Tchr • Trinity Cedar Rapids IA • (319)362-6952 • (S 1974)

**BECKER MICHAEL DAVID** (210)699-8593
7607 Stone Crop Ln San Antonio TX 78249-2538 • TX • Tchr • LHS Of San Antonio San Antonio TX • (210)733-7771 • (RF 1983)

**BECKER MICHAEL R** (440)734-1005
5250 Columbia Rd Apt 726 North Olmsted OH 44070 • mbecker@lutheranwest.com • OH • Tchr • LHS West Rocky River OH • (440)333-1660 • (S 1978)

**BECKER TIMOTHY JON** (219)477-6790
2320 Chicago St Apt 203 Valparaiso IN 46383 • IN • Tchr • Immanuel Valparaiso IN • (219)462-8207 • (RF 1994)

**BECKER WILLIAM FESTUS** (618)282-2958
608 Catherine Dr Red Bud IL 62278-1335 • SI • Tchr • St John Red Bud IL • (618)282-3873 • (RF 1994)

**BECKLER JUDITH K** (308)381-1639
121 W 23rd St Grand Island NE 68801-2336 • NEB • Tchr • Trinity Grand Island NE • (308)382-5274 • (CQ 1995)

**BECKLER ROBERT W** (316)744-2959
2548 N Fox Run Ct Wichita KS 67226-3606 • KS • Tchr • Holy Cross Wichita KS • (316)684-5201 • (WN 1983)

**BECKMAN GARY L** (417)882-6362
3305 W Meadowlark St Springfield MO 65810-1930 • gary-beckman@webtv.net • MO • Tchr • Springfield Springfield MO • (417)883-5717 • (S 1972 MS)

**BECKMAN JANINE A** (847)247-0405
821 Dunhill Ct Gurnee IL 60031 • NI • Tchr • St Philip Chicago IL • (773)561-9830 • (RF 1991)

**BECKMAN KATHERINE SUE** (616)756-7463
19104 S Three Oaks Rd Three Oaks MI 49128-9511 • MI • P/Tchr • Trinity Sawyer MI • (616)426-3151 • (RF 1974)

**BECKMAN LORETTA E** (636)227-4459
605 Showplace Ct Ballwin MO 63021-6231 • MO • Tchr • St Mark Eureka MO • (636)938-4432 • (S 1968 MED)

**BECKMAN RONALD C** (636)227-4459
605 Showplace Ct Ballwin MO 63021-6231 • MO • Tchr • St John Ellisville MO • (314)394-4100 • (CQ 1969 MA)

**BECKMANN LUCINDA** (402)475-1329
3425 L St Lincoln NE 68510-3357 • NEB • EM • (S 1949 MED)

**BECKMANN ROBERT T** (508)761-9205
92 Laurier Ave Attleboro MA 02703-7618 • NE • EM • (RF 1955 MED)

**BECKMANN THEODORE J** (407)365-2678
1540 Chipmunk Ln Oviedo FL 32765-8666 • FG • EM • (S 1929)

**BEECHER ESTHER**
2099 Bayview Dr Fort Wayne IN 46815 • IN • EM • (RF 1975)

**BEERMAN JOHN** (660)463-2752
305 S Orange Box 364 Concordia MO 64020-0364 • MO • SHS/C • Missouri Saint Louis MO • (314)317-4550 • (S 1971 MSED)

**BEERY BRENDA J** (702)395-5238
3673 Ian Thomas St #106 Las Vegas NV 89129 • PSW • Tchr • Pacific Southwest Irvine CA • (949)854-3232 • (S 1996)

**BEETHE IVAN R** (810)323-0383
51231 Sunny Hill Dr Shelby Township MI 48316-4547 • irbeethe@juno.com • MI • Mem C • St Peter Macomb MI • (810)781-3434 • (S 1976 MED)

**BEETHE RHONDA J** (402)537-9977
621 Fenwick Dr #30 Papillion NE 68046-5715 • NEB • Tchr • First Papillion NE • (402)339-1178 • (S 1987)

**BEGLEY JANET L**
11751 New London Gravel Rd Hannibal MO 63401-7676 • EN • Tchr • St John Hannibal MO • (573)221-0215 • (S 1983)

**BEHLING MARK** (314)842-1029
7127 Fernbrook Dr Saint Louis MO 63123-2307 • MO • Tchr • LHS South Saint Louis MO • (314)631-1400 • (RF 1973)

**BEHM CONSTANCE R** (616)842-6518
17864 Comstock St Grand Haven MI 49417-9361 • kcdsbeh@aol.com • MI • Tchr • St John Grand Haven MI • (616)842-0260 • (SP 1969)

**BEHMER ARLENE M** (501)329-1175
30 Christina Way Conway AR 72032 • behmerand@earthlink.net • MDS • EM • (RF 1972)

**BEHMLANDER TODD G**
22767 Firwood Ave Eastpointe MI 48021-3508 • MI • Prin • St Peter Eastpointe MI • (810)771-2809 • (AA 1984 MA)

**BEHNKE ELAINE** (708)849-2408
14532 S Lowe Ave Riverdale IL 60827-2626 • NI • Tchr • St Paul Dolton IL • (708)849-6929 • (RF 1965)

**BEHNKE ELMER F**
C/O Evangelical Home 440 Russell St Saline MI 48176-1198 • MI • EM • (RF 1933)

**BEHNKE FRED H** (312)849-2408
14532 S Lowe Ave Riverdale IL 60627-2626 • fbehnke@enc.k12.il.us • NI • P/Tchr • St John LA Grange IL • (708)354-1690 • (RF 1965 MA)

**BEHNKE JOHN A DR** (414)243-4240
5310 Sandy Beach Ln Belgium WI 53004-9731 • SW • SHS/C • South Wisconsin Milwaukee WI • (414)464-8100 • (RF 1974 MMU DMU)

**BEHNKE KATHRYN E*** (319)279-3282
2742 260th St Readlyn IA 50668-9618 • dktsaj@netins.net • IE • Tchr • Community Readlyn IA • (319)279-3968 • (SP 1968)

**BEHNKEN DONNA D** (256)881-6659
305 Chateau Dr SW Huntsville AL 35801-3407 • ddbehn@juno.com • SO • Tchr • Grace Huntsville AL • (256)881-0553 • (RF 1969 MED)

**BEHNKEN PHYLLIS IRENE** (907)345-3758
1401 Helen Dr Anchorage AK 99515-3833 • NOW • Tchr • Anchor Anchorage AK • (907)522-3636 • (S 1967)

**BEHREND ELISABETH A** (214)270-9240
11447 Glen Cross Dr Dallas TX 75228-1932 • txlisbeth@aol.com • TX • Tchr • Zion Dallas TX • (214)363-1630 • (S 1963 MS)

**BEHRENDT HOWARD L** (860)621-7973
PO Box 842 Southington CT 06489-0842 • NE • EM • (RF 1952 MED)

**BEHRENDT LINDA SUSAN*** (734)995-7346
2736 Beacon Hl Ann Arbor MI 48104-6502 • behrel@ccaa.edu • MI • SHS/C • Michigan Ann Arbor MI • (RF 1980 MS)

**BEHRENDT MARY L** (414)962-2968
3554 N Cramer St Milwaukee WI 53211-2505 • SW • 08/1998 08/2000 • (RF 1978)

**BEHRENS CALVIN MARVIN** (317)882-0834
886 W Cutsinger Rd Greenwood IN 46143 • IN • Tchr • LHS Of Indianapolis Indianapolis IN • (317)787-5474 • (RF 1973 MA)

**BEHRENS FLOYD F** (863)325-8707
152 Chaucer Ln SE Winter Haven FL 33884-2303 • FG • EM • (S 1954 MA EDD)

**BEHRENS GARY E** (415)366-5101
1912 Goodwin Ave Redwood City CA 94061-2605 • gbehrens@ricochet.net • CNH • P/Tchr • Redeemer Redwood City CA • (650)366-3466 • (S 1957 MA)

**BEHRENS MATTHEW** (831)336-2236
Mt Cross Luth Camp PO Box 387 Felton CA 95018 • matt@mtcross.org • CNH • Calif/Nevada/Hawaii San Francisco CA • (415)468-2336 • (S 1999)
**BEHRENS RALPH M** (703)548-3446
2705 Sycamore St Alexandria VA 22305-1809 • loralbeh@sourcenet.com • SE • EM • (RF 1946)
**BEIERWALTES RUTH E** (708)343-2469
513 N 4th Ave Maywood IL 60153-1121 • NI • Tchr • St Paul Melrose Park IL • (708)343-5000 • (RF 1962 MA)
**BEIJER KELLIE DELORES** (303)789-9281
2709 S Logan St Englewood CO 80110 • RM • Tchr • St John Denver CO • (303)733-3777 • (S 1995)
**BEIKMANN DAVID R** (515)225-3259
1624 19th St West Des Moines IA 50265 • IW • Tchr • MT Olive Des Moines IA • (515)277-0247 • (S 1999)
**BEIKMANN MILDRED L** (256)650-5391
1112 Joshua Dr SE Huntsville AL 35803-2322 • SO • EM • (S 1951)
**BEISE MELISSA**
920 Feltl Ct Apt 243 Minnetonka MN 55343-7988 • MNS • Tchr • Trinity Waconia MN • (952)442-4165 • (SP 1999)
**BEISEL MATTHEW STEFAN** (501)954-8033
305 Brookpark Dr Little Rock AR 72205 • mattbeisel@hotmail.com • MDS • 06/1995 06/2000 • (S 1992 MSSED)
**BEISERT DEBORAH K** (409)542-5424
RR 1 Box 298A Giddings TX 78942-9725 • TX • Tchr • St John Giddings TX • (512)253-6358 • (S 1977)
**BELITZ LARRY F** (605)745-3902
HC 52 Box 176 Hot Springs SD 57747-9609 • SD • O Sp Min • South Dakota Sioux Falls SD • (RF 1965)
**BELL JILL ROBIN** (920)387-1213
920 Mayer Ln Mayville WI 53050-1432 • belljill@hotmail.com • SW • Tchr • St John Mayville WI • (920)387-4310 • (RF 1986)
**BELL JUANITA H** (305)378-6311
14030 Madison St Miami FL 33176-6324 • FG • 06/1999 • (S 1969)
**BELL LONNIE MARIE** (507)252-5073
212 42nd Ave NW Rochester MN 55901-7531 • MNS • Tchr • Rochester Central Rochester MN • (507)289-3267 • (SP 1995)
**BELL SCOTT WILLIAM** (920)387-1213
920 Mayer Ln Mayville WI 53050-1432 • sbflyer@internetwis.com • SW • Prin • St John Mayville WI • (920)387-4310 • (RF 1985 MA)
**BELLHORN E L** (407)365-3186
1544 Chipmunk Ln Oviedo FL 32765-8666 • S • EM • (RF 1938 MS)
**BELLI MARK J**
C/O Holy Ghost Lutheran Sch 6630 Luther St Niagra Falls NY 14304-2011 • EA • St John Mayville WI • (MQ 1990)
**BELLIN SHARON L** (262)632-4102
2601 Ole Davidson Rd Racine WI 53405-1440 • wsbellin@execpc.com • SW • Tchr • Concordia Racine WI • (262)554-1659 • (S 1973)
**BELLIN WILLARD H** (262)632-4102
2601 Ole Davidson Rd Racine WI 53405-1440 • wsbellin@execpc.com • SW • P/Tchr • Concordia Racine WI • (262)554-1659 • (RF 1966 MS)
**BELT KELLI LOUISE** (512)990-8118
13715 Greinert Dr Pflugerville TX 78660 • TX • Tchr • St Paul Austin TX • (512)472-8301 • (AU 1997)
**BELTRAN ALICE ANN** (916)967-1876
5026 Dewey Dr Fair Oaks CA 95628-4204 • CNH • Tchr • Faith Fair Oaks CA • (916)961-4253 • (CQ 1983)
**BELTRAN CHERYL**
6635 Sylvan Rd #127 Citrus Heights CA 95610 • CNH • Tchr • Town & Country Sacramento CA • (916)481-2542 • (PO 1997)
**BENDER EDGAR L** (734)285-3390
2469 17th St Wyandotte MI 48192-4419 • MI • EM • (RF 1957 MED)
**BENDER MARK L** (636)230-0099
1101 Wrought Iron Ln Manchester MO 63011-4345 • MO • Mem C • St Paul Saint Louis MO • (314)822-0447 • (RF 1974 MCMU)
**BENDER MICHAEL H** (517)652-2486
11109 N Evergreen Rd Birch Run MI 48415-9712 • mbender@stlorenz.org • MI • Tchr • St Lorenz Frankenmuth MI • (517)652-6141 • (RF 1987)
**BENECKE EMILY ELIZABETH** (720)748-7765
10700 E Dartmouth Ave # J 204 Aurora CO 80014 • RM • Tchr • Peace Aurora CO • (303)766-7116 • (RF 1999)
**BENECKE VERA L** (815)568-5370
4506 Thorne Rd Marengo IL 60152-9295 • NI • Tchr • Zion Marengo IL • (815)568-5156 • (S 1965)
**BENEDUM CHARLES E**
C/O Concordia Univ Wisconsin 12800 N Lake Shore Dr Mequon WI 53097-2402 • rbenedum@excel.net • SW • SHS/C • South Wisconsin Milwaukee WI • (414)464-8100 • (RF 1969 MEAD)
**BENEDUM KATHRYN LYNN** (504)393-1424
1784 Carol Sue Ave #14E Gretna LA 70056 • SO • Tchr • Salem Gretna LA • (504)367-5126 • (MQ 1998)
**BENKENDORF RODNEY A**
1505 Collins Ave Saint Louis MO 63117-2114 • TX • 10/1998 • (S 1991)
**BENNE B J**
PO Box 6201 Orange CA 92863-6201 • PSW • Tchr • Immanuel Orange CA • (714)538-2374 • (S 1987)
**BENNETT ROBERT E**
RR 1 Box 31 Rockville MO 64780-9022 • MO • P/Tchr • Zion Rockville MO • (660)598-6213 • (S 1973)
**BENNING CARL D** (618)349-6429
RR 1 Box 137 Shobonier IL 62885-9725 • cbenning@csuol.com • CI • P/Tchr • Altamont Altamont IL • (618)483-6428 • (S 1975 MS)
**BENNING CATHLEEN M** (217)793-8765
325 Cartwright Dr Springfield IL 62704-1205 • ben5ing@fgi.net • CI • Tchr • Our Savior's Springfield IL • (217)546-4531 • (RF 1970)
**BENNING EVELYN M** (317)839-7401
4523 E County Road 200 S Avon IN 46123-8807 • evecarl@indy.net • IN • Tchr • LHS Of Indianapolis Indianapolis IN • (317)787-5474 • (RF 1963 MA)
**BENNING KAREN L** (618)349-6429
RR 1 Box 137 Shobonier IL 62885-9725 • cbenning@csuol.com • CI • Tchr • St Peter Saint Peter IL • (618)349-8888 • (S 1975)
**BENNING RUSSELL D** (217)793-8765
325 Cartwright Dr Springfield IL 62704-1205 • ben5ing@fgi.net • CI • Tchr • Trinity Springfield IL • (217)787-2323 • (S 1968 MMED)
**BENSON GENE A**
C/O Lutheran South Academy 12555 Ryewater Dr Houston TX 77089-6625 • TX • Tchr • Lutheran South Acade Houston TX • (281)464-8299 • (S 1986)
**BENSON KATRINA E** (815)544-8058
1912 S Trainer Rd Rockford IL 61108 • NI • Tchr • Immanuel Belvidere IL • (815)547-5346 • (RF 1997)
**BENSON RANDI LYN P** (417)889-3750
5572 S Burrows Ave Springfield MO 65810-2046 • tomrandi@aol.com • MO • 08/1995 08/2000 • (WN 1984 MA)
**BENSON RONALD J*** (402)564-8311
1410 9th St Columbus NE 68601 • NEB • 08/1998 08/2000 • (S 1981)
**BENSON STEPHEN E** (630)761-1667
111 S River St Batavia IL 60510 • NI • Tchr • Grace Chicago IL • (773)762-1234 • (RF 1994)
**BENTON KAREN SUE** (314)424-2389
3705 Gordon Ave Saint Louis MO 63114-4059 • MO • Tchr • Our Redeemer Overland MO • (314)427-3462 • (CQ 1993 MA)
**BENTZ TERRI LYNN** (612)226-5689
6050 135th St W Savage MN 55378 • toddandterri@imajis.com • MNS • Tchr • Trinity First Minneapolis MN • (612)870-9487 • (S 1990)
**BENTZ TODD ALLEN** (612)226-5689
6050 135th St W Savage MN 55378 • toddandterri@imajis.com • MNS • Tchr • Minnesota South Burnsville MN • (S 1990)
**BERDIS JUANITA MARY** (630)736-0567
1183 Parkview Ct Carol Stream IL 60188-6085 • jmb@amerilink.net • NI • Tchr • Trinity Roselle IL • (630)894-3263 • (RF 1976)
**BERENTSEN KURTIS GEORGE** (503)280-8511
Concordia University 2811 NE Holman St Portland OR 97211-6067 • kberentsen@cu-portland.edu • NOW • SHS/C • Northwest Portland OR • (CQ 1996 MA)
**BERG ALAN M** (773)334-0907
5919 N Fairfield Ave Chicago IL 60659-3907 • beatle1617@aol.com • NI • Tchr • St John Chicago IL • (773)736-1112 • (RF 1983 MA)
**BERG ANDREW J** (952)353-8044
PO Box 92 New Germany MN 55367-0092 • taterberg@sprynet.com • MNS • Tchr • Lutheran High Mayer MN • (612)657-2251 • (RF 1994)
**BERG DEBORAH G** (708)323-5844
17 W 170 Hillside Ln Hinsdale IL 60521-6030 • NI • Tchr • Zion Hinsdale IL • (630)323-0045 • (RF 1986)
**BERG JAMES N** (414)462-5871
4645 N 103rd St Wauwatosa WI 53225-4603 • SW • Tchr • Our Redeemer Wauwatosa WI • (414)258-4558 • (S 1964)
**BERGAN LINDA JO** (612)474-8252
3241 Tanadoona Dr Excelsior MN 55331-8048 • lbergan@excite.com • MNS • Tchr • Our Savior Excelsior MN • (612)474-9710 • (SP 1983)
**BERGANT DAVID F** (517)792-5835
5582 Lessandro St Saginaw MI 48603-3626 • kingwens@aol.com • MI • Tchr • Bethlehem Saginaw MI • (517)755-1146 • (RF 1966)
**BERGANT VIRGINIA A** (517)792-5835
5582 Lessandro St Saginaw MI 48603-3626 • kingwens@aol.com • MI • Tchr • Bethlehem Saginaw MI • (517)755-1146 • (RF 1966)
**BERGDOLT KARL J** (308)389-4402
118 E 10th St Grand Island NE 68801-3918 • triluth@computer-concepts.com • NEB • Tchr • Trinity Grand Island NE • (308)382-5274 • (S 1988)
**BERGDOLT KATHERINE MARY** (314)653-1726
12884 Fox Haven Dr Florissant MO 63033-4810 • bergdolt@slu.edu • MO • 01/1999 • (S 1992)
**BERGDOLT KURT PAUL** (314)653-1726
12884 Fox Haven Dr Florissant MO 63033-4810 • bergdolt@slu.edu • MO • Tchr • Lutheran North Saint Louis MO • (314)389-3100 • (S 1992 MSED)
**BERGELIN DAWN B** (715)845-5126
112 1/2 N 36th Ave Wausau WI 54401 • NW • Tchr • Trinity Wausau WI • (715)842-0769 • (MQ 1999)
**BERGELIN DIANNA LYNN** (618)346-4543
192 Sky Line View Dr Collinsville IL 62234 • SI • Tchr • Good Shepherd Collinsville IL • (618)344-3151 • (MQ 1998)
**BERGER DAVID O** (314)997-6911
800 Berry Hill Dr Olivette MO 63132-3502 • bergerd@csl.edu • MO • SHS/C • Missouri Saint Louis MO • (314)317-4550 • (RF 1962 MA MLS)
**BERGKOETTER MOLLY ANN** (248)394-1125
8018 Sugarloaf Trl Clarkston MI 48348-3748 • MI • Tchr • St Stephen Waterford MI • (248)673-5906 • (CQ 1993)
**BERGMAN ANN M** (509)662-9760
1410 Millerdale Ave Wenatchee WA 98801-3115 • tberg@televar.com • NOW • Tchr • St Paul Wenatchee WA • (509)662-3659 • (RF 1973 MED)
**BERGMAN DELIA** (231)723-5712
445 8th St Manistee MI 49660-1846 • MI • EM • (RF 1973)
**BERGMAN FRED E** (714)997-2785
570 N Cambridge St Orange CA 92867-6838 • PSW • EM • (RF 1950)
**BERGMAN HENRY W** (231)723-5712
445 8th St Manistee MI 49660-1846 • MI • EM • (RF 1951 MA)
**BERGMAN MARY B** (248)547-4798
706 E 6th St Royal Oak MI 48067-2804 • marybergman@earthlink.net • MI • Tchr • St Paul Royal Oak MI • (248)546-6555 • (S 1972)
**BERGMAN PAUL RICHARD** (509)662-9760
1410 Millerdale Ave Wenatchee WA 98801-3115 • NOW • Prin • St Paul Wenatchee WA • (509)662-3659 • (RF 1973)
**BERGMANN MAUREEN J** (763)753-3001
23102 Kerry St NW Saint Francis MN 55070-8730 • momdad70@hotmail.com • MNS • Tchr • Trinity Saint Francis MN • (612)753-1234 • (SP 1968)
**BERGMANN PETER ALLEN** (763)753-3001
23102 Kerry St NW Saint Francis MN 55070-8730 • MNS • Tchr • Trinity Saint Francis MN • (612)753-1234 • (SP 1968)
**BERGT CAROLYN S** (314)845-9138
3684 Lemay Woods Dr Saint Louis MO 63129-2238 • MO • S Ex/S • Missouri Saint Louis MO • (314)317-4550 • (S 1967 MA)
**BERGT GERALD A** (507)238-4035
622 Washington Ave Fairmont MN 56031-4356 • splfm2@hotmail.com • MNS • P/Tchr • St Pauls Fairmont MN • (507)238-9492 • (S 1969 MS)
**BERGT HAROLD M** (507)238-4003
1358 Oak Beach Dr Fairmont MN 56031-3105 • NEB • EM • (S 1941 MED)
**BERGT PAULINE C** (507)238-4035
622 Washington Ave Fairmont MN 56031-4356 • mdfmn@juno.com • MNS • 02/1997 02/2000 • (S 1970)
**BERGT RICHARD D** (217)546-9323
2512 Lindbergh Blvd Springfield IL 62704-5571 • CI • Tchr • Our Savior's Springfield IL • (217)546-4531 • (S 1973)
**BERGT SHARON R** (217)546-9323
2512 Lindbergh Blvd Springfield IL 62704-5571 • CI • 11/1995 11/2000 • (RF 1975 MA)
**BERINGER CHRISTINE A**
7244 Feather Run Cir Indianapolis IN 46237 • IN • Tchr • Calvary Indianapolis IN • (317)783-2000 • (RF 1984)
**BERINGER DANIEL W** (517)883-3824
39 S Miller St Sebewaing MI 48759-1333 • MI • Tchr • Immanuel Sebewaing MI • (517)883-3050 • (RF 1971 MA)
**BERINGER DAVID C** (317)883-2198
7244 Feather Run Cir Indianapolis IN 46237 • david³beringer@cuw.edu • IN • Prin • LHS Of Indianapolis Indianapolis IN • (317)787-5474 • (RF 1984)
**BERINGER GLORIA L** (517)883-3824
39 S Miller St Sebewaing MI 48759-1333 • MI • Tchr • Immanuel Sebewaing MI • (517)883-3050 • (RF 1971)
**BERKESCH MARY ANN** (219)495-4040
215 Deborah Dr Fremont IN 46737 • inberk@gte.net • EN • 07/1987 07/2000 • (RF 1977 MA)
**BERLINSKI DONALD W** (303)337-8853
13943 E Arkansas Dr Aurora CO 80012-5570 • berlinskidw@juno.com • RM • EM • (RF 1956 MAR MA)
**BERNARDINI KATE L** (216)441-5694
4804 E 85th St Garfield Heights OH 44125-2008 • OH • Tchr • St John Garfield Heights OH • (216)587-4222 • (RF 1990)
**BERNARDS EMILY E**
7927 E Quinn Dr Anaheim CA 92808-1510 • PSW • Tchr • Christ Fullerton CA • (714)870-7460 • (IV 1996)
**BERNDT BETTY E**
PO Box 238 Saginaw MO 65865-0238 • MO • Tchr • Martin Luther Joplin MO • (417)624-1403 • (S 1991)
**BERNDT CLARENCE F** (636)305-0329
1042 Winter Park Dr Fenton MO 63026-5689 • MO • CCRA • Missouri Saint Louis MO • (314)317-4550 • (RF 1961 MA MED)
**BERNDT ROSALIE S** (636)305-0329
1042 Winter Park Dr Fenton MO 63026-5689 • MO • Tchr • St John Arnold MO • (314)464-0096 • (S 1965)
**BERNER MARDELL E** (208)378-8793
10066 W Java Ct Boise ID 83704-6776 • CNH • EM • (S 1948)
**BERNHARD MELVIN G** (850)650-1566
358 Evergreen Pl Destin FL 32541-2237 • SI • EM • (RF 1940 MSED)
**BERNHARDT AMY ELIZABETH** (314)447-4651
3009 Plum Creek Dr Saint Charles MO 63303-1201 • MO • Tchr • Zion Saint Charles MO • (636)441-7425 • (RF 1994)
**BERNHARDT BEVERLY LORAINE** (817)361-7694
5009 Overton Ridge Cir # 724 Fort Worth TX 76132-1927 • Boysenberry1@msn.com • TX • Tchr • Redeemer Fort Worth TX • (817)560-0030 • (S 1968)
**BERNHARDT DAVID H** (217)793-5350
4001 Guilford Dr Springfield IL 62707-8040 • dbern37@aol.com • CI • Central Illinois Springfield IL* • (RF 1960 MSED)
**BERNHARDT EDYTHE E** (217)793-5350
4001 Guilford Dr Springfield IL 62707-8040 • dbern37@aol.com • CI • Tchr • Our Savior's Springfield IL • (217)546-4531 • (RF 1960 MSED)
**BERNHARDT JONATHAN DAVID** (314)447-4651
3009 Plum Creek Dr Saint Charles MO 63303-1201 • jdbernhardt@yahoo.com • MO • Tchr • Missouri Saint Louis MO • (314)317-4550 • (RF 1994 MED)

**BERNI KATHY ANN** (626)287-0968
1690 Walworth Ave Pasadena CA 91104-2329 • kberni@aol.com • PSW • Tchr • First Temple City CA • (626)287-0968 • (RF 1974)

**BERNS NANCY ELLEN** (313)241-7517
1788 Riverside Dr Monroe MI 48162-3244 • MI • Tchr • Trinity Monroe MI • (734)241-1160 • (RF 1971)

**BERNTHAL EDWARD H*** (920)324-4892
1013 Rock Ave Waupun WI 53963-1219 • SW • EM • (RF 1946 MED)

**BERREY BONNIE LOUISE** (515)477-8222
1717 Jessup Ave Albion IA 50005-9628 • IE • Tchr • Clemons Clemons IA • (515)477-8263 • (CQ 1989)

**BERRY JEROME G** (409)366-2389
Rt 2 Box 101 Giddings TX 78942 • TX • 11/1999 • (S 1967 MED)

**BERRY KAY S** (319)322-0620
2418 Wilkes Ave Davenport IA 52804-2349 • jkberry79@yahoo.com • IE • Tchr • Trinity Davenport IA • (319)322-5224 • (RF 1974 MS)

**BERRY PEGGY DELORES** (281)446-5612
7118 Foxway Ln Humble TX 77338-1625 • lllc@lambofgod.net • TX • Tchr • Little Lamb Humble TX • (281)446-5262 • (S 1965)

**BERSIE MARK B** (312)736-4742
4027 N Mc Vicker Ave Chicago IL 60634-1601 • NI • Tchr • St Paul Chicago IL • (773)378-6644 • (RF 1978)

**BERSON SUSAN DIANNE** (307)687-7437
610 Clarion Dr Gillette WY 82718 • WY • Tchr • Trinity Gillette WY • (307)682-4886 • (SP 1977)

**BERTERMANN RENA** (509)667-0582
1400 Central Ave #503 Wenatchee WA 98801 • NOW • P/Tchr • St Paul Wenatchee WA • (509)662-3659 • (PO 1995)

**BERTHOLD ANN L** (517)663-7176
5695 Durfee Rd Eaton Rapids MI 48827-8912 • MI • 12/1995 12/1999 • (CQ 1986 MA)

**BERTHOLD EDWARD K** (517)663-7176
5695 Durfee Rd Eaton Rapids MI 48827-8912 • MI • 09/1989 09/1999 • (RF 1958 MA)

**BERTRAND ELIZABETH**
C/O Pilgrim Lutheran Church 8601 Chimney Rock Houston TX 77096 • TX • Tchr • Pilgrim Houston TX • (713)666-3693 • (MQ 2000)

**BESEL ROSS E** (208)232-0206
952 E Lewis Pocatello ID 83201-5363 • rbesel@gracepocid.org • NOW • Tchr • Grace Pocatello ID • (208)237-4142 • (PO 1985)

**BESSERT KARLA M**
2044 N 113th St Milwaukee WI 53226-2210 • bhbessert@asapnet.net • SW • Tchr • Elm Grove Elm Grove WI • (262)797-2970 • (S 1978)

**BESSERT MICHAEL** (402)327-9264
842 Foxcroft Ct #152 Lincoln NE 68510 • Bessert@aol.com • NI • 08/1999 • (S 1992)

**BESSERT WILLIAM H** (262)548-3697
1700 S Craftsman #B New Berlin WI 53146 • bgbessert@aol.com • SW • EM • (S 1967 MAD)

**BETHKE PAUL H** (253)845-8199
11510 126th Avenue Ct E Puyallup WA 98374-5075 • mpb453@integrityol.com • NOW • P/Tchr • Concordia Tacoma WA • (253)475-9513 • (S 1973 MAT)

**BETHKE SUSAN** (510)690-0238
23401 Mona Marie Ct Hayward CA 94541-3572 • suwib@aol.com • CNH • Tchr • Grace San Mateo CA • (650)345-9082 • (RF 1980)

**BETHKE WILLIAM R** (510)690-0238
23401 Mona Marie Ct Hayward CA 94541-3572 • suwib@aol.com • CNH • Tchr • Grace San Mateo CA • (650)345-9082 • (RF 1967)

**BETTS BRIAN JOHN** (715)435-3660
6606 Lundberg Rd Wisconsin Rapids WI 54495-8879 • NW • Tchr • Immanuel Wisconsin Rapids WI • (715)423-0272 • (SP 1992)

**BEUSCHLEIN MARTHA I** (541)312-2346
60061 Cheyene Rd Bend OR 97702 • martibeusc@aol.com • NOW • EM • (RF 1978)

**BEVER DAVID P**
9424 Summer Rain Dr Las Vegas NV 89134 • PSW • Immanuel Wisconsin Rapids WI • (S 1973 MA)

**BEVERIDGE SHIRLEY A** (312)343-3082
619 N 6th Ave Maywood IL 60153 • NI • Tchr • Walther LHS Melrose Park IL • (708)344-0404 • (RF 1971)

**BEVERSDORF ANDREA JOYCE** (402)724-2194
PO Box 95 Mc Cool NE 68401-0095 • NEB • Tchr • Emmanuel York NE • (402)362-6575 • (S 1970)

**BEVERSDORF BONNIE J** (724)352-0108
329 Hannahstown Rd Cabot PA 16023-2203 • jim42bon@pgh.net • EA • 07/1997 07/2000 • (RF 1966 MA)

**BEVERSDORF JANET**
W8499 County Rd M Shawano WI 54166 • NW • Tchr • St James Shawano WI • (715)524-4815 • (SP 1976)

**BEVERSDORF RALPH W** (715)524-3006
W8499 County Road M Shawano WI 54166-6201 • immchrist@ez-net.com • NW • Tchr • St Paul Bonduel WI • (715)758-8559 • (SP 1977)

**BEVERSDORF RICHARD A** (402)724-2194
PO Box 95 Mc Cool Junction NE 68401-0095 • NEB • Tchr • Emmanuel York NE • (402)362-6575 • (S 1968 MED)

**BEVIRT CATHY JEAN** (618)345-3904
490 S Mulberry Collinsville IL 62234-6320 • cbevirt@hotmail.com • SI • Tchr • Holy Cross Collinsville IL • (618)344-3145 • (RF 1986)

**BEYER ANNA MARIE**
1360 W Capitol Ave Apt 141 San Pedro CA 90732-5032 • PSW • Tchr • Christ Rancho Palos Verdes CA • (310)831-0848 • (SP 1983)

**BEYER BEVERLY J** (805)983-0094
1820 Holly Ave Oxnard CA 93030-6233 • PSW • Tchr • St John Oxnard CA • (805)983-0330 • (BR 1976)

**BEYER GARY A** (714)288-4406
154 S Shaffer St Orange CA 92866-1609 • gbeyer@ix.netcom.com • PSW • Prin • St John Orange CA • (714)288-4406 • (RF 1969 MS)

**BEYER MARILYN A** (734)668-7951
3014 Lexington Dr Ann Arbor MI 48105-1481 • beyerm@ccaa.edu • MI • EM • (RF 1960 MA)

**BEYER NORMAN C** (661)940-8020
45520 13th St W Lancaster CA 93534-1781 • ncbeyer@juno.com • PSW • EM • (RF 1953 MA)

**BIAR CYNTHIA LOUISE** (602)396-5232
4150 E Aspen Ave Mesa AZ 85206-1121 • EN • Tchr • Christ Phoenix AZ • (602)957-7010 • (S 1973)

**BIAR KRISTINE RUTH**
504 Elm Bastrop TX 78602 • TX • Tchr • Immanuel Giddings TX • (409)542-3319 • (S 1992)

**BICKEL DAVID W**
C/O Hong Kong Intl School 23 South Bay Close Repulse Bay HONG KONG • dbickel@hs.hkis.edu.hk • SW • S Miss • South Wisconsin Milwaukee WI • (414)464-8100 • (S 1972 MA)

**BICKEL ELAINE C** (517)871-4659
4827 Center St Millington MI 48746-9666 • elainebickel@juno.com • MI • P/Tchr • St Paul Millington MI • (517)871-4581 • (RF 1970 MA)

**BICKEL ERIC J**
47780 Pinecrese Shelby Twp MI 48317-2854 • MI • Tchr • Peace Shelby Township MI • (810)731-4120 • (S 1992)

**BICKEL EUGENE M*** (314)962-2606
8601 Henrietta Ave Saint Louis MO 63144-2410 • MO • EM • (S 1958 MA)

**BICKEL HOWARD E**
1814 Saint George Ln Janesville WI 53545-0687 • NW • EM • (RF 1945)

**BICKEL KAREN E** 2
2206 Worthington Dr Valparaiso IN 46383-3254 • IN • Tchr • Immanuel Valparaiso IN • (219)462-8207 • (RF 1969 MED)

**BICKEL MARTHA R** (410)661-1028
1805 Cromwood Rd Baltimore MD 21234-2701 • SE • Tchr • Baltimore LHS Baltimore MD • (410)825-2323 • (S 1970)

**BICKEL NATHAN** (414)632-7657
1423 Arthur Ave Racine WI 53405-3325 • bickelnate@juno.com • SW • Tchr • Lutheran High School Racine WI • (414)637-6538 • (RF 1981)

**BICKEL PHILIP G** (219)462-2030
2206 Worthington Dr Valparaiso IN 46383-3254 • IN • Tchr • Immanuel Valparaiso IN • (219)462-8207 • (RF 1969 MA)

**BICKEL RANDALL J** (313)283-1937
18735 Valade St Riverview MI 48192-4520 • MI • Tchr • Christ The King Southgate MI • (734)285-9697 • (AA 1986)

**BICKMEIER STEPHANIE CAROL** (517)642-6535
15534 Evergreen East Pointe MI 48021-1614 • stecie@prodigy.net • MI • Tchr • Trinity Clinton Township MI • (810)463-2921 • (RF 1999)

**BIDDLE JEREMY** (815)873-1411
5049 Linden Rd Apt 6105 Rockford IL 61109 • NI • SHS/C • Northern Illinois Hillside IL • (S 1998)

**BIEDINGER BRUCE R** (210)520-6856
7311 Yakima Dr San Antonio TX 78250-5248 • TX • Tchr • LHS Of San Antonio San Antonio TX • (210)733-7771 • (RF 1985 MA)

**BIELEFELDT ANGIE K** (281)583-5816
3439 Kennonview Dr Houston TX 77068-1314 • TX • Tchr • Trinity Spring TX • (281)376-5810 • (S 1963)

**BIELEFELDT TERESA K** (817)261-9848
603 Andrews St Arlington TX 76011-4810 • TX • Tchr • St Paul Fort Worth TX • (817)332-4563 • (RF 1980 MED)

**BIERBAUM DEANNA JOYCE**
4200 Horizon North Pkwy #1115 Dallas TX 75287-2819 • TX • St Paul Fort Worth TX • (S 1996)

**BIERBAUM EDWARD W** (785)692-4542
1509 3rd Rd Palmer KS 66962-8905 • debier@bluevalley.net • KS • P/Tchr • Linn Association Linn KS • (785)348-5792 • (S 1966 MED MED)

**BIERBAUM PAMELA KAY** (612)467-3868
117 Hill St Norwood MN 55368-9748 • tpbierbaum@aol.com • MNS • Tchr • Lutheran High Mayer MN • (612)657-2251 • (SP 1989)

**BIERBAUM TIMOTHY M** (952)467-3868
117 Hill St Norwood MN 55368-9748 • tpbierbaum@aol.com • MNS • Tchr • Lutheran High Mayer MN • (612)657-2251 • (S 1992)

**BIERLEIN BETH N** (708)343-7448
C/O St Pauls Luth High School 1025 Lake St Melrose Park IL 60160 • mrsbierlein@yahoo.com • NI • Tchr • St Paul Melrose Park IL • (708)343-1000 • (RF 1996)

**BIERLEIN KIMBERLY K** (352)589-2563
2702 Lakewood Ln Eustis FL 32726-7003 • FG • Tchr • Faith Eustis FL • (352)589-5683 • (RF 1982)

**BIERLEIN LEON C** (847)695-5104
1630 Alison Dr Elgin IL 60123-5905 • shepherd@foxvalley.net • NI • Prin • Good Shepherd Elgin IL • (847)741-7795 • (RF 1964 MA)

**BIERLEIN MARY B** (517)652-8654
10605 King Rd Frankenmuth MI 48734-9749 • MI • Tchr • St Lorenz Frankenmuth MI • (517)652-6141 • (CQ 1993 MA)

**BIERLING ANNE M** (818)363-3763
11756 Doral Ave Northridge CA 91326-1219 • PSW • 06/1997 06/2000 • (S 1989 MA)

**BIERMANN HEATHER L** (440)884-0186
3327 Park Dr Parma OH 44134-4644 • tabiermann@juno.com • S • Tchr • St Mark Cleveland OH • (216)749-3545 • (RF 1995)

**BIERMANN-MILLER KAREN LYNN** (815)496-9639
4371 E 2925th Rd Sheridan IL 60551-9606 • NI • Tchr • Cross Yorkville IL • (630)553-7335 • (SP 1987 MSED)

**BIERWAGEN SHERRY A** (636)296-1471
419 Bluffview Hts Arnold MO 63010-1454 • MO • Mem C • Peace Saint Louis MO • (314)892-5610 • (S 1957)

**BIESENDORFER LYNETTE K**
5626 Providence Place Dr Saint Louis MO 63129-7240 • MO • Tchr • Salem Affton MO • (314)353-9242 • (RF 1978)

**BIESENDORFER ROBERT J**
5626 Providence Place Dr Saint Louis MO 63129-7240 • MO • Prin • Salem Affton MO • (314)352-4454 • (RF 1979 MA)

**BILLOTTE PAMELA A** (217)529-8861
3219 Sherman St Springfield IL 62703-4850 • CI • Tchr • Concordia Springfield IL • (217)529-3307 • (S 1967)

**BIMLER KIMBERLY ANN** (847)741-4725
777 Sundown Rd South Elgin IL 60177 • NI • Tchr • St John Elgin IL • (847)741-7633 • (RF 1990)

**BIMLER REBECCA ELAINE**
8693 Buffett Pkwy Fishers IN 46038-3566 • IN • Tchr • Holy Cross Indianapolis IN • (317)823-5801 • (S 1985 MED)

**BIRD TERRY LYN** (913)334-7491
6900 Cleveland Ave Kansas City KS 66109-1808 • KS • P/Tchr • Grace Kansas City KS • (913)281-1621 • (S 1977 MED)

**BIRD THOMAS G** (412)487-2835
124 Homer Pl Pittsburgh PA 15223-1017 • EA • 07/1995 07/1997 • (BR 1979 MSED)

**BIRNBAUM DAVID CHARLES** (972)230-0930
1046 Barton Rd Glenn Heights TX 75154 • teacherbirnbaum@hotmail.com • TX • Tchr • Cross Of Christ De Soto TX • (972)223-9586 • (AU 1990 MAD)

**BIRNER SANDRA J**
C/O Christ Community Luth Sch 777 Mooring Line Dr Naples FL 34103 • FG • Tchr • Christ Community Naples FL • (941)430-2655 • (BR 1983)

**BIRNSTEIN KARL D** (503)668-5972
36280 Dubarko Rd Sandy OR 97055 • kbirnstein@aol.com • NOW • Prin • Portland Portland OR • (503)667-3199 • (S 1970 MA)

**BISCHOFF BEVERLY** (602)941-2449
6029 E Mariposa St Scottsdale AZ 85251-1935 • EN • Tchr • Christ Phoenix AZ • (602)957-7010 • (CQ 1995)

**BISHOP GARY L** (616)846-3862
1625 Moreland St Grand Haven MI 49417-2831 • gmbishop@i2k.com • MI • 10/1999 • (RF 1967 MA)

**BISHOP MARY J** (616)846-3862
1625 Moreland St Grand Haven MI 49417-2831 • gmbishop@i2k • MI • Tchr • St John Grand Haven MI • (616)842-0260 • (RF 1967 MED)

**BISHOP NATALIE DAWN** (503)491-9591
1940 SW Cerise Way Troutdale OR 97060 • NOW • 04/2000 • (PO 1990)

**BISHOP PAULETTE** (573)756-1612
506 W Liberty St Farmington MO 63640-1910 • MO • Tchr • St Paul Farmington MO • (573)756-5147 • (RF 1964 MED)

**BISHOP RITA L** (217)423-5041
2654 S 35th St Decatur IL 62521-4911 • CI • Tchr • Lutheran School Asso Decatur IL • (217)233-2001 • (RF 1976 MS)

**BISPING JERALD L** (912)988-1432
931 Forest Ave Perry GA 31069 • jbisping@hotmail.com • FG • Mem C • Mount Calvary Warner Robins GA • (912)922-1418 • (S 1964)

**BITTER DENISE A** (785)232-0962
2414 SE Alexander Dr Topeka KS 66605-1856 • denbitter@bigfoot.com • KS • Tchr • Topeka Topeka KS • (785)357-0382 • (S 1971 MA)

**BITTNER CAROL S** (219)724-9713
8550 NW Winchester Rd Decatur IN 46733-8831 • IN • Tchr • Zion Decatur IN • (219)728-9995 • (RF 1964 MS)

**BITTNER ELDOR W** (504)367-3062
2101 Manhattan Blvd Apt D-207 Harvey LA 70058-3459 • NW • EM • (RF 1948)

**BIVENS DEBRA JO** (618)233-3355
6942 Roachtown Rd Millstadt IL 62260-3318 • SI • 07/2000 • (CQ 1995)

**BJORKLUND BELINDA KAY** (708)594-7924
5432 S 73rd Ave Summit Argo IL 60501-1116 • dbjorklu@flash.net • NI • Tchr • Grace Chicago IL • (773)762-1234 • (RF 1987)

**BLACK DAVID W** (317)888-8922
611 Daffon Dr Indianapolis IN 46227-2764 • dwblack@in.net • IN • Tchr • Calvary Indianapolis IN • (317)783-2305 • (MQ 1988 MA)

**BLACK KENNETH W** (630)529-9383
530 Pinecroft Dr Roselle IL 60172-2537 • kenmar@interaccess.com • NI • Mem C • Trinity Roselle IL • (630)894-3263 • (RF 1958 MA)

**BLACK SARAH LOUISE** (817)337-1982
901 Meadow Cir N Keller TX 76248 • chickiemonkey7@yahoo.com • TX • Tchr • Crown of Life Colleyville TX • (817)421-5683 • (AU 1994)

**BLACKWELL RUTH** (301)638-3481
6014-6 New Forest Ct Waldorf MD 20603 • ruthblackwell@hotmail.com • SE • Prin • Grace LA Plata MD • (301)932-0963 • (BR 1992)

**BLACKWOOD DEBRA LOUISE** (407)228-0111
2510 Peel Ave Orlando FL 32806-5050 • dblackwd@prodigy.net • FG • Tchr • Trinity Orlando FL • (407)843-4896 • (SP 1993)

**BLACKWOOD JENNIFER M**
728 Bryn Mawr St Orlando FL 32804 • grosswood@mindspring.com • FG • Tchr • Trinity Orlando FL • (407)843-4896 • (BR 1994)

**BLAILE JANE E** (314)822-7774
5524 Walsh St Saint Louis MO 63109-2861 • jblaile@networkusa.net • MO • Tchr • Christ Community Kirkwood MO • (314)822-7774 • (CQ 1998)

**BLAKE KENNETH W III** (608)524-9992
507 Clark St Reedsburg WI 53959 • kwblakeiii@hotmail.com • SW • Mem C • St Peter Reedsburg WI • (608)524-4512 • (MQ 1993)

**BLAKE MARY ANN** (630)852-0232
6728 Woodridge Dr Woodridge IL 60517-1914 • ni³blakema@ni.lcms.org • NI • Tchr • Trinity Lisle IL • (630)964-1272 • (RF 1968)

**BLAKE SHARON E** (810)392-2694
78101 M-19 Richmond MI 48062-3003 • MI • Tchr • Trinity Port Huron MI • (810)984-2501 • (RF 1964)

**BLAKLEY SARAH**
Immanuel Lutheran Church 5701 Loch Raven Blvd Baltimore MD 21239 • SE • Tchr • Immanuel Baltimore MD • (410)435-6861 • (S 1999)

**BLANCO MIRIAM K** (914)779-3758
8 Concordia Pl Bronxville NY 10708-1998 • AT • 02/2000 • (BR 1977 MS)

**BLANK JONATHAN H** (509)735-1880
3611 W 9th Ave Kennewick WA 99336-4402 • jonathan³h³blank@yahoo.com • NOW • Tchr • Bethlehem Kennewick WA • (509)582-5624 • (RF 1989 MED)

**BLANK KATHLEEN D**
RR 1 Box 87A Nicollet MN 56074-9624 • MNS • Tchr • Immanuel Courtland MN • (507)359-2534 • (SP 1967)

**BLANK NORMA LOUISE*** (510)278-4436
1645 Via Ventana San Lorenzo CA 94580-2043 • nblank@worldnet.att.net • CNH • Tchr • Calvary San Lorenzo CA • (510)278-2598 • (RF 1966)

**BLANK STEPHEN MICHAEL** (209)722-3340
1443 E 21st #8 Merced CA 95340 • blank@cyberlynk.com • CNH • Tchr • St Paul Merced CA • (209)383-3302 • (RF 1998)

**BLANKE MARK STEPHEN*** (402)643-4278
1142 Eastridge Dr Seward NE 68434-1330 • mblanke@seward.cune.edu • NEB • SHS/C • Nebraska Seward NE • (S 1982 MS MA)

**BLASE MARIE L** (203)521-2682
94 Meadowbrook Rd W Hartford CT 06107-2532 • NE • Tchr • Immanuel Bristol CT • (860)583-5631 • (S 1968)

**BLATT RICHARD H** (773)784-5844
5810 N Fairfield Ave Chicago IL 60659-3906 • NI • P/Tchr • St Philip Chicago IL • (773)561-9830 • (RF 1960 MED)

**BLAU DEBORAH D** (714)538-5002
390 1/2 N Shaffer St Orange CA 92866-1114 • PSW • Tchr • Shepherd Of Peace Irvine CA • (949)786-3997 • (CQ 1986 MA)

**BLAZEK KRISTA J**
504 Brightwood Pl Apt B3 Louisville KY 40207-4188 • IN • Tchr • Our Savior Louisville KY • (502)426-0864 • (RF 1988)

**BLAZEK ROBERT A** (317)885-9426
4463 Silver Springs Dr Greenwood IN 46142-9622 • blazer@tcon.net • IN • Mem C • Calvary Indianapolis IN • (317)783-2000 • (RF 1964)

**BLAZEK ROSALYN J** (317)885-9426
4463 Silver Springs Dr Greenwood IN 46142-9622 • blazer@tcon.net • IN • Tchr • Calvary Indianapolis IN • (317)783-2305 • (RF 1964 MS)

**BLEEKE FRED A** (314)862-7944
200 S Brentwood Blvd Apt 13B Clayton MO 63105-1618 • MO • Missouri Saint Louis MO • (314)317-4550 • (RF 1967 MA)

**BLEEKE JOHN H** (414)637-4533
1410 Spring Valley Dr Racine WI 53405-1635 • SW • EM • (RF 1952 MED)

**BLEEKE MARGARET L** (334)858-2657
315 E 5th Ave Florala AL 36442-1643 • SO • EM • (RF 1960)

**BLEEKE RALPH J**
315 E 5th Ave Florala AL 36442-1643 • SO • EM • (RF 1960 MED)

**BLEKE LOIS E** (407)392-6171
918 SW 9th Street Cir Apt 104 Boca Raton FL 33486-5274 • FG • 07/1996 07/2000 • (RF 1974)

**BLEKE RENEE S** (219)447-2695
7519 Ensign Ct Fort Wayne IN 46816-2751 • IN • Tchr • Bethlehem Fort Wayne IN • (219)456-3587 • (S 1984 MA)

**BLEKE WALTER F** (517)652-4369
255 Mayer Rd Frankenmuth MI 48734-1345 • MI • EM • (RF 1936 MA)

**BLIESE ELIZABETH DOROTHY**
2512 W Bridge St Milwaukee WI 53221-4961 • SW • EM • (RF 1981)

**BLIESE SUSAN E** (330)455-4387
1931 Rowland Ave NE Canton OH 44714 • OH • Tchr • Zion Akron OH • (330)253-3136 • (AA 1992)

**BLINN KRISTEN K** (847)352-8189
2400 Fabish Ct Schaumburg IL 60193 • NI • Tchr • St Peter Schaumburg IL • (847)885-7636 • (RF 1997)

**BLISS DAVID A*** (254)420-2443
237 Bonham Dr Hewitt TX 76643 • dbliss@prodigy.net • TX • P/Tchr • Trinity Waco TX • (817)772-4225 • (S 1979 MA)

**BLOCK DENISE RENEE** (319)390-3563
3929 21st Ave Pl SW #1 Cedar Rapids IA 52404 • tdb1095@cedar-rapids.net • IE • Tchr • Central Newhall IA • (319)223-5271 • (S 1996)

**BLOCK E CHANDLER**
1010 La Terraza Cir Apt 308 Corona CA 92879-7992 • PSW • Tchr • Abiding Savior Lake Forest CA • (949)830-1461 • (IV 1998)

**BLOCK GREGORY E** (815)436-1627
2023 Watertower Pl Joliet IL 60435-0825 • NI • Tchr • Salem Blue Island IL • (708)388-6175 • (RF 1978 MA)

**BLOCK JAMES**
1401 W John St #C Bay City MI 48706-2900 • MI • Tchr • Zion Bay City MI • (517)893-5793 • (AA 1998)

**BLOCK JASON R** (303)789-9124
3916 S Pearl St Englewood CO 80110-4736 • jblock2525@aol.com • RM • Tchr • Denver Lutheran High Denver CO • (303)934-2345 • (MQ 1993 MA)

**BLOCK MARAJEAN A** (815)436-6380
23726 Pondview Dr Plainfield IL 60544 • rblock5555@aol.com • NI • Tchr • Zion Naperville IL • (630)904-1124 • (RF 1967)

**BLOCK MARLENE V** (402)643-3324
1261 N 1st St Seward NE 68434-1224 • NEB • SHS/C • Nebraska Seward NE • (CQ 1991)

**BLOCK MELVIN W** (708)366-3151
620 Beloit Ave Forest Park IL 60130-1908 • mel-block@walther.com • NI • Tchr • Walther LHS Melrose Park IL • (708)344-0404 • (RF 1961 MED)

**BLOCK RICHARD A** (815)436-6380
23726 Pondview Dr Plainfield IL 60544 • rblock5555@aol.com • NI • Walther LHS Melrose Park IL • (RF 1968 MA)

**BLOCK RICHARD W** (612)454-7898
3370 Rolling Hills Dr Eagan MN 55121-2345 • MNS • Tchr • Trin Lone Oak Eagan MN • (651)454-7235 • (SP 1978 MED)

**BLOCK SANDRA K** (612)454-7898
3370 Rolling Hills Dr Eagan MN 55121-2345 • blockflock@prodigy.net • MNS • Tchr • Trinity Lone Oak Eagan MN • (651)454-1139 • (SP 1979 MED)

**BLOCKER HOLLY B**
Zion Lutheran Church PO Box 259 Oconto WI 54153-0259 • NW • Tchr • LHS Assoc Of NE Wisc Green Bay WI • (920)469-6810 • (S 1983 MA)

**BLOMENBERG GILBERT P** (402)643-3562
345 N 2nd St Seward NE 68434-1807 • NEB • EM • (RF 1940 MED)

**BLOMKER JOYCE D** (320)235-9008
410 30th St NW Apt 101 Willmar MN 56201-2347 • MNN • 03/1999 • (RF 1979 MS)

**BLOMQUIST BARRY E** (616)942-8692
1820 Rowland Ave SE Grand Rapids MI 49546-4329 • bblom@maindex.com • MI • P/Tchr • Our Savior Grand Rapids MI • (616)949-0710 • (SP 1971 MA)

**BLUHM DON G** (715)848-5265
3011 Glendale Ave Wausau WI 54401-4021 • NW • Tchr • Trinity Wausau WI • (715)848-0166 • (S 1970 MA)

**BLUHM GERALD A** (319)232-6105
1036 Newton St Waterloo IA 50703 • IE • EM • (RF 1967 MA)

**BLUM ARTHUR P** (708)946-6477
PO Box 391 Beecher IL 60401-0391 • NI • EM • (RF 1962 MA)

**BLUMA GEORGE W** (402)478-4988
432 N 7th St Arlington NE 68002-4002 • NEB • EM • (S 1935)

**BLUME KATHRYN L** (626)444-0497
5607 Santa Anita Ave #15 Temple City CA 91780 • kblume9204@aol.com • PSW • Tchr • First Temple City CA • (626)287-0968 • (S 1980)

**BOARDMAN RALPH H** (708)474-2519
2025 178th St Lansing IL 60438-1701 • NI • EM • (RF 1949 MA)

**BOATMAN AMY GALE** (713)643-9667
7045 Ashburn St Houston TX 77061-2609 • boatman206@aol.com • TX • Tchr • Lutheran South Acade Houston TX • (281)464-8299 • (S 1994)

**BOBB BARRY L DR** (314)631-1517
9806 Tiffany Square Pkwy Saint Louis MO 63123-6264 • blbobb@cphnet.org • MO • CCRA • Missouri Saint Louis MO • (314)317-4550 • (RF 1973 MMU)

**BOBO SHANNON MARIE** (916)972-8407
2874 Westwood Ln #6 Carmichael CA 95608 • shannon³bobo@hotmail.com • CNH • Tchr • Sacramento Lutheran Sacramento CA • (916)978-2720 • (AU 1999)

**BOBURKA CARL M**
319 Wood Rd Rockford IL 61114 • NI • Tchr • Luther Academy Rockford IL • (815)877-9551 • (RF 1975 MED)

**BOBZIN JOHN C** (660)463-7586
PO Box 358 Concordia MO 64020-0358 • MO • SHS/C • Missouri Saint Louis MO • (314)317-4550 • (S 1965 MS)

**BOCKELMAN BYRON B** (515)255-8387
6220 Dawson Dr Des Moines IA 50322-5015 • IW • P/Tchr • Mount Olive Des Moines IA • (515)277-8349 • (S 1957 MS)

**BOCKELMAN JAMES E** (402)643-6853
707 N 5th St Seward NE 68434-1519 • jbockelman@seward.cune.edu • NEB • SHS/C • Nebraska Seward NE • (S 1989 MFA)

**BOCKELMAN KATIE LYNN** (402)476-9676
1501 Hilltop Rd Apt LL08 Lincoln NE 68521 • klbockelman@hotmail.com • NEB • Tchr • Nebraska Seward NE • (S 1992)

**BOCKELMAN REBECCA M** (573)243-6482
183 Hillside Dr Jackson MO 63755 • rebeccamangels@hotmail.com • MO • Tchr • St Paul Jackson MO • (573)243-5360 • (S 1997)

**BOCKELMANN LOUISE ANN** (708)946-6026
1416 W County Line Rd Beecher IL 60401-3435 • NI • Tchr • Zion Beecher IL • (708)946-2272 • (RF 1970 MA)

**BODE JAMES T** (714)639-6738
530 E Lomita Ave Orange CA 92867-6848 • PSW • EM • (S 1957)

**BODE JOEL**
6319 Elm Grove Rd Spring TX 77389 • TX • 09/1999 • (MQ 1983)

**BODE RICHARD L** (414)632-2506
1025 Hayes Ave Racine WI 53405-2551 • bode@execpc.com • SW • EM • (S 1955 MAR)

**BODIN KATHY D** (915)595-5482
3702 Tarawood Ct Spring TX 77388-4199 • TX • Tchr • Zion Tomball TX • (281)351-5757 • (RF 1979)

**BODLING LINDA M** (336)766-2947
1760 Harper Spring Dr Clemmons NC 27012-7417 • lmbodling@aol.com • SE • Tchr • St John Winston-Salem NC • (336)725-1651 • (BR 1979 MED)

**BODLING PAUL F III** (336)766-2947
1760 Harper Spring Dr Clemmons NC 27012-7417 • pfbodling@aol.com • SE • Tchr • St John Winston-Salem NC • (336)725-1651 • (BR 1989)

**BOEDER CURTIS I** (208)465-0858
1918 Glen View Dr Nampa ID 83686-7225 • NOW • 08/1998 08/2000 • (S 1977 MED)

**BOEHLKE CHRISTINE M** (216)945-8074
448 Grove Ave Cuyahoga Falls OH 44221-2247 • OH • Tchr • Redeemer Cuyahoga Falls OH • (330)923-1280 • (RF 1990)

**BOEHLKE JEFFREY K** (320)485-3317
139 West Gate Dr Winstead MN 55395 • MNS • P/Tchr • St Paul-St Peter Watertown MN • (612)955-1419 • (RF 1992)

**BOEHLKE KEITH W** (314)647-5245
2637 Roseland Ter Saint Louis MO 63143-2303 • kboehlke@stlnet.com • MO • P/Tchr • Holy Cross Saint Louis MO • (314)771-9521 • (S 1971 MED)

**BOEHLKE MICHELE RAE** (320)485-3317
139 West Gate Dr Winstead MN 55395 • MNS • Tchr • St James Howard Lake MN • (320)543-2766 • (SP 1987)

**BOEHM JERRY R** (517)792-8327
480 Somerset Rd Saginaw MI 48603-6218 • MI • Tchr • Valley Saginaw MI • (517)790-1676 • (CQ 1986 MA MED)

**BOEHME CAROLYN K** (262)253-4808
N91W17546 Saint Regis Dr Menomonee Falls WI 53051-1922 • SW • Tchr • Our Redeemer Wauwatosa WI • (414)258-4558 • (RF 1969 MA)

**BOEHME JOYCE A** (217)787-5415
8342 Bomke Rd Pleasant Plains IL 62677-9412 • CI • Tchr • Our Savior's Springfield IL • (217)546-4531 • (CQ 1995 MED)

**BOEHMER JUDY L** (660)674-2319
101 W 4th Alma MO 64001 • 1682jlm@almanet.net • MO • Tchr • Trinity Alma MO • (660)674-2444 • (S 1973)

**BOEHNE BRUCE K** (712)448-2905
PO Box 389 Paullina IA 51046-0389 • zsschool@pionet.net • IW • P/Tchr • Zion-St John Paullina IA • (712)448-3915 • (CQ 1995 MA)

**BOEHNE RUTH E** (618)493-7709
21324 Sycamore Rd Hoyleton IL 62803-1202 • SI • Tchr • Trinity Hoffman IL • (618)495-2246 • (RF 1973)

**BOEHNKE ANNETTE C** (972)221-0547
1334 Edmonton Dr Lewisville TX 75077 • TX • Tchr • Lamb Of God Flower Mound TX • (972)539-5200 • (SP 1977)

**BOENKER MARY JANE** (630)307-0120
332 Lakemont Ct Bloomingdale IL 60108-1387 • mjboenker@ameritech.net • NI • Tchr • Trinity Roselle IL • (630)894-3263 • (S 1963)

**BOERGER CRYSTAL LOUISE**
10461 Streng Rd Milford Center OH 43045-9718 • cboerger@usa.net • SI • 07/2000 • (RF 1994)

**BOERGER FRED L** (308)345-7321
810 E 3rd St Mc Cook NE 69001-3226 • NEB • EM • (S 1952 MA)

**BOERGER KAREN M** (317)861-5210
3915 S Creekside Dr New Palestine IN 46163-9547 • IN • Tchr • Zion New Palestine IN • (317)861-4210 • (S 1966)

**BOERGER KENNETH M** (216)267-1163
19609 Marwood Ave Cleveland OH 44135-1025 • ksboerger@aol.com • OH • Prin • Bethany Parma OH • (440)884-1010 • (S 1972 MA)

**BOERGER MARK A** (317)861-5210
3915 S Creekside Dr New Palestine IN 46163-9547 • IN • Tchr • Trinity Indianapolis IN • (317)897-0243 • (S 1966 MA)

**BOERGER SUSAN J** (216)267-1163
19609 Marwood Ave Cleveland OH 44135-1025 • ksboerger@aol.com • OH • Tchr • Bethany Parma OH • (440)884-1010 • (S 1973)

**BOETEL ROBERT C** (219)462-5457
1207 Monticello Park Dr Valparaiso IN 46383-4019 • IN • Tchr • Immanuel Valparaiso IN • (219)462-8207 • (S 1958 MA)

**BOETTCHER ARDELLA A** (815)547-5430
1015 E 4th St Belvidere IL 61008-4535 • NI • EM • (RF 1967)

**BOETTCHER JOEL W** (816)796-6916
812 Mohican Dr Independence MO 64056-2196 • jboettcher@lhskc.com • MO • Tchr • Kansas City LHS Kansas City MO • (816)241-5478 • (AA 1983 MLS)

**BOETTCHER LOUIS**
1870 W 4th St Winona MN 55987-1802 • MNS • EM • (RF 1954)

**BOETTCHER MYRON D** (402)643-2850
1337 Kolterman Ave Apt 07 Seward NE 68434-1358 • mboettcher@seward.cune.edu • NEB • SHS/C • Nebraska Seward NE • (S 1965 MSLS)

**BOETTCHER PAUL J**
1019 Grove St Menasha WI 54952 • pjboettc@cyberhighway.net • SW • Tchr • Trinity Menasha WI • (920)722-2662 • (S 1986)

**BOETTNER MARTIN R** (203)223-7829
16 Buell St New Britain CT 06051-3402 • NE • P/Tchr • St Matthew New Britain CT • (860)223-7829 • (RF 1974)

**BOGGESS STEVE D** (515)266-8231
4112 Hull Ave Des Moines IA 50317-5560 • stboggess@hotmail.com • IW • Mem C • Hope Des Moines IA • (515)265-2057 • (S 1982 MSED)

**BOHL NOREEN FAYE** (712)859-3117
3734 280th St Graettinger IA 51342 • IW • Tchr • Iowa Great Lakes Spencer IA • (712)262-1187 • (S 1972)

**BOHLER DONALD M** (314)638-9350
7821 Wilmar Pl Saint Louis MO 63123-7740 • dmbohler@postnet.com • MO • EM • (RF 1961)

**BOHLMANN ARLEEN** (937)325-5120
3120 E Leffel Ln Springfield OH 45505-4528 • gaagape@yahoo.com • OH • 05/1986 05/2000 • (RF 1962 MED)

**BOHLMANN DEBORAH ANN** (580)338-3820
1212 N Crumley Guymon OK 73942-3643 • OK • Tchr • Trinity Guymon OK • (580)338-6000 • (SP 1977)

**BOHLMANN DEREK G**
440 N Martha St Lombard IL 60148-1718 • NI • Tchr • St Peter Schaumburg IL • (847)885-3350 • (S 1991)

**BOHMANN KARI SUE** (414)543-4748
2555 S 94th St West Allis WI 53227-2333 • SW • Tchr • Mount Olive Milwaukee WI • (414)774-2113 • (MQ 1988)

**BOHNET KATHLEEN K** (618)345-5086
70 Oakwood Ct Collinsville IL 62234-5806 • SI • Tchr • Good Shepherd Collinsville IL • (618)344-3153 • (S 1962 MSED)

**BOHNET SIGMUND** (618)345-5086
70 Oakwood Ct Collinsville IL 62234-5806 • SI • Prin • Metro-East LHS Edwardsville IL • (618)656-0043 • (S 1961 MSED EDS)

**BOHNING ROY W** (314)733-0663
3626 S Jefferson Ave Saint Louis MO 63118-3926 • bohningrw@postnet.com • MO • Prin • Immanuel Wentzville MO • (636)327-4416 • (S 1976 MA)

**BOHOT KIM LIEN** (281)477-7810
9522 Walnut Glen Houston TX 77064 • jkbohot@aol.com • TX • Tchr • Memorial Houston TX • (713)782-4022 • (AU 1995)

**BOLDT BARBARA L** (414)567-0034
W117 Vista Dr Oconomowoc WI 53066-2061 • SW • 08/1999 • (RF 1968)

**BOLDT DENNIS H** (972)723-6570
2220 Cypress Ct Midlothian TX 76065 • TX • Prin • Cross Of Christ De Soto TX • (972)223-9586 • (RF 1964 MSED MS)

**BOLDT FREDERICK F** (414)567-0034
W117 Vista Dr Oconomowoc WI 53066-2061 • ffboldt@execpc.com • SW • Tchr • St Paul Oconomowoc WI • (262)567-5001 • (RF 1968 MA)

**BOLDT H JAMES DR** (248)601-0838
1280 Washington Rd Rochester MI 48306 • jboldt@stjohnrochester.org • MI • Prin • St John Rochester MI • (248)652-8830 • (RF 1961 MS LLD)

**BOLDT HAROLD DAVID** (770)599-0354
7 Joy Springs Dr Senoia GA 30276 • FG • Tchr • St Paul Peachtree City GA • (770)486-3545 • (MQ 1992)

**BOLDT JEAN L** (972)723-6570
2220 Cypress Ct Midlothian TX 76065 • TX • Tchr • Cross Of Christ De Soto TX • (972)223-9586 • (CQ 1997)

**BOLDT JOHN PHILIP** (313)242-3393
15385 Eastwood St Apt 3B Monroe MI 48161-5420 • MI • Tchr • Trinity Monroe MI • (734)241-1160 • (S 1978)

**BOLL CAROLINE A** (507)765-5289
401 Winona St NW Preston MN 55965 • MNS • Tchr • St John Wykoff MN • (507)352-2296 • (S 1961)

**BOLL DAVID R** (651)778-8874
1585 Nebraska Ave E Saint Paul MN 55106-1520 • dboll@mail.concordia-academy.pvt.k12.mn.us • MNS • Tchr • Concordia Academy Roseville MN • (612)484-8429 • (S 1987)

**BOLL DOLORES ANN** (651)778-8874
1585 Nebraska Ave E St Paul MN 55106-1520 • MNS • 12/1999 • (S 1987)

**BOLL JOHN V** (507)765-5289
401 Winona St NW Preston MN 55965 • MNS • P/Tchr • St John Wykoff MN • (507)352-2296 • (S 1962 MED)

**BOLLAND KATHERINE** (214)348-4567
9602 Orchard Hl Dallas TX 75243-8014 • TX • EM • (S 1955)

**BOLLAND LINDA L** (907)731-9891
2132 Lake Forest Cir Pagosa Springs CO 81147-8835 • RM • Tchr • Our Savior Pagosa Springs CO • (970)731-4668 • (S 1969)

**BOLLMANN BRET** (215)547-5507
107 Fieldstone Rd Levittown PA 19056-1918 • macbret@earthlink.net • EA • Prin • Hope Levittown PA • (215)946-3467 • (S 1970 MA)

**BOLT JEANINE L** (719)560-9737
991 W Stallion Dr Pueblo West CO 81007-1931 • RM • 11/1997 11/1999 • (S 1978)

**BOLT LOUISE R** (630)983-3058
1620 E Bailey Rd Naperville IL 60565-1744 • NI • Tchr • Bethany Naperville IL • (630)355-6607 • (RF 1970)

**BOLT R KIRK** (630)983-3058
1620 E Bailey Rd Naperville IL 60565-1744 • NI • Tchr • Bethany Naperville IL • (630)355-6607 • (RF 1970 MA)

**BOLT RACHEL K** (703)751-3357
225 S Whiting St #312 Alexandria VA 22304 • SE • Tchr • Our Savior Arlington VA • (703)892-4846 • (MQ 1998)

**BOLTER HEIDI L** (612)854-8867
8680 Old Cedar Ave S Apt 209 Bloomington MN 55425-2032 • MNS • Tchr • Cross View Edina MN • (612)941-0009 • (SP 1996)

**BOLZMAN JEFFREY K** (517)871-4863
4861 Main St Millington MI 48746-9671 • jbolzman@juno.com • MI • 09/1999 • (S 1982 MA)

**BONITZ WILLIAM C** (317)359-0832
6610 Southeastern Ave Indianapolis IN 46203-5834 • IN • EM • (RF 1955 MA MED)

**BONK EUGENE J**
C/O Grace Lutheran Church 643 W 13th Ave Escondido CA 92025-5620 • PSW • Mem C • Grace Escondido CA • (760)745-0831 • (S 1981)

**BONNER SUSAN KAY** (623)877-3419
11528 W Rosewood Dr Avondale AZ 85323 • PSW • Tchr • Christ Redeemer Phoenix AZ • (623)934-3286 • (S 1965)

**BOOR JOHN M**
C/O Trinity Lutheran Church 6850 159th St Tinley Park IL 60477-1629 • NI • Tchr • Trinity Tinley Park IL • (708)532-3529 • (RF 1975)

**BOOS MANFRED B DR** (708)848-3791
1018 Home Ave Oak Park IL 60304-1835 • crfboosmb@curf.edu • NI • SHS/C • Northern Illinois Hillside IL • (RF 1970 MTM MED MPHIL PHD)

**BOOS SHARON ANN** (708)848-3791
1018 Home Ave Oak Park IL 60304-1835 • s3boos@hotmail.com • NI • Tchr • St Paul Melrose Park IL • (708)343-5000 • (RF 1970 MSLS)

**BOOTS CYNTHIA F** (231)972-5530
12040 Cape Breton Stanwood MI 49346 • MI • EM • (RF 1964)

**BOOZIKEE KEVIN T** (320)864-2729
1427 Greeley Ave North Glencoe MN 55336-1347 • kboozikee@hotmail.com • MNS • Tchr • Lutheran High Mayer MN • (612)657-2251 • (S 1991 MEED)

**BOPP ANNE E** (208)238-0648
534 Brent St Pocatello ID 83201-7030 • NOW • Tchr • Grace Pocatello ID • (208)237-4142 • (PO 1986 MED)

**BORCHARDT DIANE M** (612)423-4905
13969 Edenwood Ct Apple Valley MN 55124-9241 • borchardt@luther.csp.edu • MNS • SHS/C • Minnesota South Burnsville MN • (SP 1976)

**BORCHARDT EDWIN J*** (218)583-2825
PO Box 461 Henning MN 56551-0461 • MNN • 05/1993 05/2000 • (S 1987)

**BORCHARDT MELVIN A*** (303)255-9795
C/O Gethsemane Lutheran Church 10675 Washington St Northglenn CO 80233-4101 • RM • EM • (RF 1957)

**BORCHERDING DAVID F** (816)461-5849
16220 E Elm St Independence MO 64050 • borcherding96@yahoo.com • MO • Minnesota South Burnsville MN • (S 1990 MBA)

**BORCHERDING GORDON L** (312)577-9398
116 S Albert St Mount Prospect IL 60056-3404 • NI • EM • (RF 1958 MGC)

**BORCHERDING WILLIAM** (504)366-3948
1331 Shirley Dr New Orleans LA 70114-2907 • SO • EM • (S 1928)

**BORCHIN JANE** (908)233-2328
221 Cowperthwaite Pl Westfield NJ 07090-4015 • NJ • Tchr • Redeemer Westfield NJ • (908)232-1592 • (RF 1971)

**BORCHIN ROGER G** (908)233-2328
221 Cowperthwaite Pl Westfield NJ 07090-4015 • NJ • Prin • Redeemer Westfield NJ • (908)232-1592 • (RF 1965 MA)

**BORDEAUX BETTY JEAN** (314)631-9932
9901 Affton Pl Saint Louis MO 63123-4305 • MO • Tchr • Abiding Savior Saint Louis County MO • (314)894-9703 • (RF 1968 MA)

**BORDEAUX JOSEPH A DR** (314)631-9932
9901 Affton Pl Saint Louis MO 63123-4305 • jbwls@stlnet.com • MO • Prin • Washington Saint Louis County MO • (314)892-4408 • (CQ 1972 MED PHD)

**BORDELEAU EILEEN** (414)869-2540
472 Rose Hill Dr Oneida WI 54155-9024 • bord@netnet.net • NW • Tchr • Pilgrim Green Bay WI • (920)494-6530 • (S 1975)

**BORG BRUCE T** (516)938-5829
74 6th St Hicksville NY 11801-5418 • cbborg@msn.com • AT • Tchr • St John College Point NY • (718)463-4790 • (BR 1976 MMU)

**BORG STEVEN E** (561)734-1639
172 SE 28th Ct Boynton Beach FL 33435-7613 • FG • Tchr • Trinity Delray Beach FL • (561)276-8458 • (RF 1976)

**BORGERS KAREN J** (815)889-5223
116 S Woodworth Milford IL 60953 • NI • Tchr • St Paul Milford IL • (815)889-4209 • (RF 1969)

**BORGSTEDE SARA**
207 E John St Alexandria IN 46001-2025 • KS • Tchr • St Paul Leavenworth KS • (913)682-0387 • (MQ 1994)

**BORIS JENNIFER R** (419)395-1344
29141 Steinmaier Rd Defiance OH 43512-8969 • OH • Tchr • St John Defiance OH • (419)782-1751 • (MQ 1994)

**BORIS SCOTT W** (419)395-1344
29141 Steinmaier Rd Defiance OH 43512-8969 • OH • Tchr • St John Defiance OH • (419)782-1751 • (MQ 1995)

**BORK MARILYN J** (816)587-8395
5216 NW Walden Dr Kansas City MO 64151-2648 • rmkabork@gateway.net • MO • Tchr • Holy Cross Kansas City MO • (816)453-7211 • (S 1970)

**BORK RONALD D DR** (816)587-8395
5216 NW Walden Dr Kansas City MO 64151-2648 • rmkabork@gateway.net • MO • Prin • Holy Cross Kansas City MO • (816)453-7211 • (S 1970 MED DED)

**BORKENHAGEN JENNIFER**
C/O Zion Lutheran School 7515 269th Ave NW Saint Francis MN 55070 • MNN • Tchr • Zion Saint Francis MN • (612)856-2099 • (S 2000)

**BORKENHAGEN MARTIN H** (408)253-4390
1011 Johnson Ave San Jose CA 95129-3127 • elliebork@cs.com • CNH • EM • (RF 1945 MA)

**BORKEY CAROLINE C** (817)573-7023
6850 Headquarters Cir Granbury TX 76049-4548 • TX • Tchr • Grace Arlington TX • (817)274-1654 • (RF 1973)

**BORTZ TODD ERIC** (407)384-6741
12716 Woodbury Glen Dr Orlando FL 32828-5921 • FG • Tchr • Orlando Lutheran Aca Orlando FL • (407)275-7750 • (RF 1993)

**BOSSALLER CINDY KAY** (636)390-2285
59 Durham Dr Washington MO 63090-2930 • MO • 09/1996 09/1999 • (RF 1984)

**BOSSEN NORMA** (206)536-7009
11328 22nd Ave E Tacoma WA 98445-3777 • NOW • Tchr • Concordia Tacoma WA • (253)475-9513 • (PO 1985)

**BOSTON VICKI L** (618)344-6038
2035 Greenbrier Dr Collinsville IL 62234-5272 • SI • Tchr • Holy Cross Collinsville IL • (618)344-3145 • (S 1975)

**BOTTCHER RONALD R** (618)282-6471
10229 S Prairie Rd Red Bud IL 62278-4611 • SI • P/Tchr • Trinity Red Bud IL • (618)282-2881 • (S 1969)

**BOTTRELL SANDRA B** (217)498-7847
100 Deer Creek Rd Rochester IL 62563-9220 • CI • Tchr • Trinity Springfield IL • (217)787-2323 • (CQ 1983)

**BOUMA MARI-BETH** (616)261-2955
4290 Thorndyke Ave SW Wyoming MI 49548-3029 • MI • Tchr • Immanuel Grand Rapids MI • (616)363-0505 • (RF 1982)

**BOURGEOIS JANIS KAY** (618)493-6305
186 N Main St Hoyleton IL 62803-2002 • SI • Tchr • Trinity Hoyleton IL • (618)493-7754 • (SP 1978)

**BOURLAND F MIRANDA** (303)469-2049
C/O Beautiful Savior Lutheran PO Box 8 Broomfield CO 80038-0008 • RM • Tchr • Beaut Savior Broomfield CO • (303)469-1785 • (S 1995)

**BOURNE SARAH K*** (415)379-9322
847A 32nd Ave San Francisco CA 94121 • saraib@juno.com • CNH • Tchr • Zion San Francisco CA • (415)221-7500 • (IV 1997)

**BOURRET BONNIE L** (308)879-4532
4470 Rd 89 Potter NE 69156-6637 • tbour@juno.com • WY • 06/1986 06/2000 • (S 1981)

**BOUTAN TONDA M** (630)690-0057
199 Arapahoe Trl Carol Stream IL 60188-1731 • NI • Tchr • St John Wheaton IL • (630)668-0701 • (CQ 1984)

**BOWDEN SUE ANN** (320)763-4842
300 Lake St Alexandria MN 56308 • sabowden@aol.com • MNN • P/Tchr • Zion Alexandria MN • (320)763-4842 • (CQ 1986 MA)

**BOWDITCH BARBARA H** (808)234-0225
45-537 Alokahi Pl Kaneohe HI 96744 • CNH • Tchr • St Mark Kaneohe HI • (808)247-4565 • (AA 1985)

**BOWEN CAROL LYNN**
16409 Currie Rd #103 Monroe WA 98272 • NOW • Tchr • Little Doves Monroe WA • (206)794-7230 • (AU 1998)

**BOWER EDWARD R** (314)227-2623
729 Oak Meadows Ct Ballwin MO 63021-6143 • edbower@slcas.com • MO • Prin • Salem Affton MO • (314)353-9242 • (RF 1975 MA)

**BOWER KRISTINE E** (303)466-1311
1135 Ash St Broomfield CO 80020 • mkkbower13@cs.com • RM • Tchr • Beautiful Savior Broomfield CO • (303)469-2049 • (IV 1994)

**BOWLINE MELANIE SUSAN**
5652 Gazebo Way Las Vegas NV 89122-2673 • PSW • Tchr • Faith LHS Las Vegas NV • (702)804-4400 • (S 1994)

**BOYD ELIZABETH ANN** (760)746-4125
1047 Park Hill Dr Escondido CA 92025 • ebuboyd@home.com • PSW • 05/1994 05/1999 • (IV 1990)

**BOYD HEIDI ANNAKAY** (562)945-9301
6237 Bright Ave Whittier CA 90601 • PSW • Tchr • Emmaus Alhambra CA • (626)289-3664 • (BR 1996)

**BOYD JASON SCOTT** (702)233-5586
350 S Durango #224 Las Vegas NV 89128 • PSW • Tchr • Faith LHS Las Vegas NV • (702)804-4400 • (S 1998)

**BOYD ROBERT C**
6915 Mowhawa Dr Ft Wayne IN 46815 • IN • Prin • Concordia Fort Wayne IN • (219)422-2429 • (CQ 1982 MA)

**BOYD TERRY LYNN**
1246 County Road 140 Ledbetter TX 78946-7102 • TX • Tchr • Immanuel Giddings TX • (409)542-3319 • (AU 1991)

**BOYE JANET K** (319)445-7865
4410 Cedar St Davenport IA 52806 • IE • Prin • Christ Bettendorf IA • (319)391-2190 • (S 1975 MED)

**BOYE VICKI L DR** (402)643-3167
1744 Eastridge Ave Seward NE 68434-1144 • vboye@seward.cune.edu • NEB • SHS/C • Nebraska Seward NE • (S 1982 MSED PHD)

**BOYER DEBORAH KAY** (636)922-3852
16 Trappers Way Saint Charles MO 63303-6216 • MO • Tchr • Immanuel Saint Charles MO • (636)946-0051 • (CQ 1998)

**BOYLE KIMBERLY K** (402)563-3483
5270 Navajo Ave Columbus NE 68601-8248 • NEB • Tchr • Immanuel Columbus NE • (402)564-8423 • (S 1980 MA)

**BRAATEN REBECCA L** (406)257-0750
275 Bald Rock Rd Kalispell MT 59901-7041 • MT • Tchr • Trinity Kalispell MT • (406)257-6716 • (PO 1982)

**BRAATZ RUTH E** (608)755-1724
2519 Lilac Ln Janesville WI 53545-1356 • SW • EM • (RF 1960)

**BRACKENSICK JAMES R** (630)969-7341
4106 N Park St Westmont IL 60559-1329 • NI • EM • (S 1962 MA)

**BRACKMAN BARBARA J** (618)635-8394
1301 S Hackman Staunton IL 62088-1736 • SI • Tchr • Zion Staunton IL • (618)635-3060 • (CQ 1998)

**BRACKMAN DIANE M** (708)474-1943
17844 Oakwood Ave Lansing IL 60438-1934 • NI • Tchr • Trinity Lansing IL • (708)474-7997 • (RF 1985)

**BRACKMAN JAMES E** (314)447-3376
45 Little Creek Ln Saint Charles MO 63304-7402 • jb004@mail.win.org • MO • EM • (S 1961 MA)

**BRACKMAN JANA M** (314)638-5851
3911 Comstock Dr Saint Louis MO 63123-7760 • MO • 10/1994 10/1999 • (S 1989)

**BRACKMAN TIMOTHY J** (314)638-5851
3911 Comstock Dr Saint Louis MO 63123-7760 • s1025820@admiral.umsl.edu • MO • Tchr • Lutheran North Saint Louis MO • (314)389-3100 • (S 1989)

**BRACKNEY MARTHA MARIE** (972)578-4722
637 Middle Cove Dr Plano TX 75023-4803 • mmbrack@airmail.net • TX • Tchr • Faith Plano TX • (972)423-7448 • (S 1995)

**BRADLEY ALBERT M** (713)943-2531
2914 Peach Ln Pasadena TX 77502-5418 • TX • Tchr • Zion Pasadena TX • (713)473-1789 • (S 1972)

**BRADLEY CAROL J** (713)943-2531
2914 Peach Ln Pasadena TX 77502-5418 • TX • Tchr • Zion Pasadena TX • (713)473-1789 • (S 1968)

**BRADLEY RICK JEFFREY** (760)921-6444
460 Holley Ln Blythe CA 92225 • rbrad78622@aol.com • PSW • 08/1996 08/2000 • (S 1970 MED)

**BRADSHAW JOANNA D** (785)273-5175
1940 SW Stone Ave Topeka KS 66604-3353 • KS • Tchr • Topeka Topeka KS • (785)357-0382 • (S 1981)

**BRADSHAW MAXINE A** (979)366-2385
RR 2 Box 54A Giddings TX 78942-9802 • TX • Tchr • St John Giddings TX • (512)253-6358 • (AU 1992)

**BRADTMUELLER DEBRA ANN** (704)465-5972
10 Maple Ct Newton NC 28658-4105 • SE • Tchr • St Stephen Hickory NC • (828)256-2166 • (RF 1992)

**BRADY TIA M**
7227 Hwy 290E #4306 Austin TX 78723 • TX • Tchr • Hope Austin TX • (512)926-0003 • (AU 1998)

**BRAGENZER DEBORAH L** (616)348-2024
1197 Woodland Dr Petoskey MI 49770-9714 • pbragen@freewaynet • MI • Mem C • Zion Petoskey MI • (231)347-3438 • (AA 1983)

**BRAKENHOFF NANCY A** (217)324-5686
1104 N Harrison St Litchfield IL 62056-1306 • SI • Tchr • Zion Litchfield IL • (217)324-2033 • (RF 1984)

**BRAMSTADT LOIS ANN** (219)661-0498
223 Wood St Crown Point IN 46307 • IN • St Paul Coffeyville KS • (RF 1983 MA)

**BRAND ALISON M** (417)869-7123
757 S Weller Ave Springfield MO 65802-3344 • MO • 11/1993 11/1999 • (S 1989)

**BRAND GREGORY D** (507)453-0332
517 E 10th St Winona MN 55987-4347 • gbrand@tvsw.org • MNS • Tchr • St Martins Winona MN • (507)452-6056 • (SP 1986)

**BRAND SUSAN LYNN** (616)933-7112
1030 Centre St Traverse City MI 49686 • tsbrand@aol.com • MI • Tchr • Trinity Traverse City MI • (231)946-2720 • (RF 1989)

**BRANDENBURG DARCY LYNN**
4944 W Berenice Chicago IL 60641 • NI • Tchr • St Philip Chicago IL • (773)561-9830 • (RF 1997)

**BRANDENBURGER COREY JAMES** (713)802-0531
733 W 43rd St Houston TX 77018 • TX • Tchr • Trinity-Messiah Houston TX* • (713)224-7265 • (SP 1997)

**BRANDENBURGER MELISSA JUNE** (713)694-2301
733 W 43rd St Houston TX 77018-4401 • cmjb1219@earthlink.net • TX • Tchr • St Mark Houston TX • (713)468-2623 • (SP 1996)

**BRANDHORST RONALD L** (303)986-7809
3633 S Sheridan Blvd Apt 21 Lakewood CO 80235-2909 • RM • Tchr • Denver Lutheran High Denver CO • (303)934-2345 • (S 1966 MA)

**BRANDON KATHERINE JANE** (734)439-3041
510 Ideal St Milan MI 48160-1415 • smabrandj@ccaa.edu • MI • Tchr • Emmanuel Dearborn MI • (313)561-6265 • (S 1972 MA)

**BRANDON KEVIN J** (734)439-3041
510 Ideal St Milan MI 48160-1415 • brandonk@ccaa.edu • MI • SHS/C • Michigan Ann Arbor MI • (CQ 1983 MA)

**BRANDT DAVID R** (219)836-5482
7639 State Line Ave Munster IN 46321-1045 • IN • Tchr • St Paul Munster IN • (219)836-6270 • (RF 1954)

**BRANDT DWAINE C** (503)284-1258
6326 NE 31st Ave Portland OR 97211-6621 • NOW • EM • (CQ 1966 MA PHD)

**BRANDT GILBERT H** (317)787-5715
957 E Cragmont Dr Indianapolis IN 46227-2114 • IN • Tchr • Calvary Indianapolis IN • (317)783-2305 • (RF 1967 MA)

**BRANDT JOHN E** (810)463-5183
1419 Warrington St Mount Clemens MI 48043-3012 • jbrandt@lhsa.com • MI • Tchr • LHS North Macomb MI • (810)781-9151 • (AA 1985 MED)

**BRANDT JOHN M** (517)799-0201
4829 Thornehurst Pl Saginaw MI 48603-3846 • brandtj@svol.org • MI • Tchr • Valley Saginaw MI • (517)790-1676 • (RF 1977 MAT)

**BRANDT LILLIAN C** (308)384-6373
2223 W 11th St Grand Island NE 68803-3621 • NEB • Tchr • Trinity Grand Island NE • (308)382-5274 • (S 1961 MED)

**BRANDT MARVIN J DR**
4616 N Dawn Dr Peoria IL 61614 • mjb839@aol.com • CI • EM • (RF 1952 MED EDS LLD)

**BRANDT MICHAEL B** (317)783-2964
5544 Meckes Ln Indianapolis IN 46237-2338 • IN • Tchr • LHS Of Indianapolis Indianapolis IN • (317)787-5474 • (S 1990 MED)

**BRANDT NADINE M** (636)724-5828
16 Ashbourne Way Saint Charles MO 63301-5512 • MO • Tchr • Immanuel Saint Charles MO • (636)946-0051 • (S 1964)

**BRANDT PAMELA J** (660)826-6608
31695 Hwy 65 Sedalia MO 65301 • MO • 04/2000 • (S 1983 MSPED)

**BRANDT PAUL M** (480)860-1188
9590 E Shea Blvd Scottsdale AZ 85260-6724 • pmbrandt@hotmail.com • PSW • Immanuel Saint Charles MO • (RF 1979 MA)

**BRANDT ROBERT W** (417)235-0357
112 E 3rd St Freistatt MO 65654 • MO • EM • (S 1960 MS)

**BRANDT SHIRLEY M** (417)235-0357
112 E 3rd St Freistatt MO 65654 • MO • EM • (S 1958)

**BRANDT STEPHANIE N**
932 Oakview Dr Roseburg OR 97470-9578 • plbrandt@juno.com • NOW • 06/1994 06/1999 • (S 1989 MS)

**BRANDT SUSAN R** (517)799-0201
4829 Thornehurst Pl Saginaw MI 48603-3846 • brandtj@svol.org • MI • Tchr • Bethlehem Saginaw MI • (517)755-1146 • (RF 1977 MLS)

**BRANNAN CAROL ANN** (314)631-3140
9911 Lakeford Ln Affton MO 63123-6231 • cabrannan@aol.com • MO • Tchr • Christ Community Kirkwood MO • (314)822-7774 • (SP 1971 MAT)

**BRASE ALICE ANN** (507)278-3589
RR 2 Box 62 Good Thunder MN 56037-9631 • MNS • P/Tchr • St Johns Good Thunder MN • (507)278-3635 • (SP 1978)

**BRASE WALTER G** (970)667-8914
2117 Agate Ct Loveland CO 80538-3690 • RM • EM • (S 1928)

**BRASHER KRISTINA LYNN** (417)886-6698
2427 S Westwood Ave Springfield MO 65807-3372 • kbrasher@pcis.net • MO • Tchr • Springfield Springfield MO • (417)883-5717 • (S 1994)

**BRASSIE ALICE MARGARET** (636)458-9078
2313 Winegarden Ct Wildwood MO 63011-1808 • MO • Tchr • St John Ellisville MO • (314)394-4100 • (S 1969)

**BRAUER BRIAN** (414)502-0454
N103W15923 Founders Ln Germantown WI 53022-4857 • SW • Tchr • Grace Menomonee Falls WI • (414)251-7140 • (MQ 1997)

**BRAUER ETHAN R** (313)533-8959
18680 Winston St Detroit MI 48219-3050 • MI • EM • (OTHER 1955 MA)

**BRAUER FRIEDRICH E** (218)763-3568
18614 Woodlake Blvd Fifty Lakes MN 56448 • MNN • EM • (RF 1949 MMU DMU)

**BRAUER JENNIFER** (217)399-2747
PO Box 436 Buckley IL 60918-0436 • wrennep@yahoo.com • CI • Tchr • St John Onarga IL • (815)457-2909 • (AA 1999)

**BRAUER NORMAN P** (916)967-0657
5500 Wildwood Way Citrus Heights CA 95610-7530 • bxnbrauer@hotmail.com • CNH • Prin • Sacramento Lutheran Sacramento CA • (916)978-2720 • (S 1967 MED)

**BRAUER PAUL A** (509)452-4542
1212 S 33rd Ave Yakima WA 98902-4921 • SI • EM • (RF 1924)

**BRAUER PAUL G** (573)486-2175
1314 Washington St Hermann MO 65041-1525 • MO • EM • (RF 1949 MED)

**BRAUER ROBERT DAVID** (402)534-3406
625 Indiana Utica NE 68456-6090 • sp34117@navix.net • NEB • P/Tchr • St Paul Utica NE • (402)534-2121 • (S 1979 MA)

**BRAUN BRUCE NEAL** (734)728-8539
2061 W Williams Cir Westland MI 48186 • braunbn@mc.lcms.org • MI • Michigan Ann Arbor MI • (RF 1978 MAT)

**BRAUN CAROLE JEAN** (414)781-1494
15780 Vernon Dr Brookfield WI 53005-2237 • SW • Tchr • Elm Grove Elm Grove WI • (262)797-2970 • (CQ 1990)

**BRAUN DOUGLAS J** (303)469-6918
1040 E 10th Ave #212 Broomfield CO 80020 • rabbonl1@yahoo.com • RM • Tchr • North Lutheran Broomfield CO • (720)887-9031 • (RF 1995)

**BRAUN GREGG A**
3710 Cheyenne Round Rock TX 78664 • braungregg@aol.com • TX • North Lutheran Broomfield CO • (RF 1973 MA)

**BRAUN JAMES R** (920)485-3231
N5776 W Horseshoe Rd Horicon WI 53032-9722 • arnie@powercom.net • SW • P/Tchr • St Stephen Horicon WI • (920)485-6687 • (SP 1971)

**BRAUN JOANNA CHRISTINE** (612)484-5871
1054 Lovell Ave Roseville MN 55113-4419 • jbraun@mail.concordia-academy.pvt.k12.mn.us • MNS • Tchr • Mount Hope-Redemptio Bloomington MN • (612)881-0036 • (SP 1994)

**BRAUN ROSEMARY ANN** (651)483-3157
2975 Highpointe Curve Roseville MN 55113 • braun@csp.edu • MNS • SHS/C • Minnesota South Burnsville MN • (RF 1966)

**BRAUN RUTH E**
1809 N 121st St Apt 102 Omaha NE 68154-4389 • TX • EM • (S 1958 MED)

**BRAUN THEODORE T** (219)625-3477
8623 Yellow River Rd Fort Wayne IN 46818-9728 • EN • EM • (RF 1966 MS)

**BRAUTNICK JANICE M** (248)651-4185
1428 N Fairview Ln Rochester Hills MI 48306-4134 • jhbrautnick@home.com • MI • Tchr • St John Rochester MI • (248)652-8830 • (SP 1965 MAT)

**BRAY MERLIN L** (219)462-4914
1403 Fairlane Dr Valparaiso IN 46383-3644 • mert@netnitco.net • IN • EM • (RF 1954 MA)

**BRAZEAL GERALDINE** (773)536-1984
C/O Christ The King Luth Churc 3701 S Lake Park Ave Chicago IL 60653-2012 • mrsgb@earthlink.net • NI • P/Tchr • Christ King Chicago IL • (773)536-1984 • (RF 1970)

**BRAZELTON WILLIAM T JR.** (847)437-2782
450 Sandy Ln Des Plaines IL 60016-2639 • EN • Tchr • Our Savior Chicago IL • (773)631-1606 • (RF 1995)

**BRAZGEL GREGORY S** (440)356-8805
20073 Bonnie Bank Blvd Rocky River OH 44116-4116 • brazrn@yahoo.com • OH • Tchr • Ohio Olmsted Falls OH • (MQ 1998)

**BRDA ELLEN J** (504)391-1079
5161 Carlisle Ct New Orleans LA 70131 • brda@salemlutheranschool.com • SO • Tchr • Salem Gretna LA • (504)367-5144 • (CQ 1986 MMU)

**BRECHT SUSAN M** (517)738-6435
PO Box 569 Port Austin MI 48467 • jbrecht@avci.net • MI • 12/1999 • (S 1986)

**BREDEHOEFT GLORIA JEAN** (317)299-3811
5351 Deer Creek Dr Indianapolis IN 46254-3559 • wgbredeh@iquest.net • IN • Tchr • Trinity Indianapolis IN • (317)897-0243 • (S 1972 MS)

**BREDEHOEFT DAVID PAUL** (630)530-4045
241 Michigan St Elmhurst IL 60126-2735 • dlbae@juno.com • NI • Tchr • Immanuel Elmhurst IL • (630)832-9302 • (S 1970)

**BREDEHOFT DOROTHY R** (409)836-4094
1407 S Jackson St # A Brenham TX 77833-4533 • TX • Tchr • Grace Brenham TX • (409)836-2030 • (S 1973)

**BREDEHOFT GEORGE W** (503)293-6151
3733 SW Canby St Portland OR 97219-1540 • NOW • Tchr • Pilgrim Beaverton OR • (503)644-8697 • (S 1976 MED)

**BREDEHOFT JOHN C**
Our Redeemer Luth Church 1404 University Ave Honolulu HI 96822-2414 • CNH • Prin • Our Redeemer Honolulu HI • (808)946-4223 • (S 1970 MA)

**BREDEHOFT JUDITH LOUISE** (909)981-3457
2067 Katrina Way Upland CA 91784-7985 • PSW • Tchr • Pacific Southwest Irvine CA • (949)854-3232 • (RF 1962)

**BREDEHOFT SUSAN L** (909)988-9680
661 W Yale St Ontario CA 91762-1918 • PSW • Tchr • First Fontana CA • (909)823-3457 • (RF 1987)

**BREDEHOFT THOMAS A** (714)538-2351
331 S Greengrove Dr Orange CA 92866-2418 • PSW • Mem C • St Paul Orange CA • (714)637-2640 • (RF 1982)

**BREDEHOFT WILLIS W** (714)771-0446
374 S California St Orange CA 92866-2406 • PSW • EM • (S 1939 MA)

**BREDOW GORDON J** (636)279-6986
213 Laurelwood Dr Saint Peters MO 63376-1241 • MO • Tchr • LHS St Charles Saint Peters MO • (636)928-5100 • (S 1964 MED)

**BREHM PAUL A**
189 Duranzo Aisle Irvine CA 92606-8358 • PSW • Tchr • Prince Of Peace Anaheim CA • (714)774-0993 • (IV 1988 MS)

**BREIDERT DENNIS D** (303)233-9418
7080 W 34th Pl Wheat Ridge CO 80033-6310 • dbreidert@blm.net • RM • Tchr • Bethlehem Lakewood CO • (303)233-0401 • (S 1970 MA)

**BREININGER TERRY** (219)486-3932
1225 Vance Ave Fort Wayne IN 46815 • IN • Indiana Fort Wayne IN • (RF 1971 MAR)

**BREITBARTH JONATHAN**
Concordia University 275 N Syndicate Saint Paul MN 55104 • MNS • SHS/C • Minnesota South Burnsville MN • (SP 1999)

**BREITE MARY M** (501)455-4947
4 Lemoncrest Pl Little Rock AR 72209-5661 • MDS • Tchr • Christ Little Rock AR • (501)663-5212 • (S 1975 MA)

**BREITWISCH JOHN A** (715)539-9831
906 Adams St Merrill WI 54452 • breitwisch@worldnet.att.net • NW • Tchr • St John Merrill WI • (715)536-4722 • (MQ 1993)

**BREITWISCH RUTHANN LOIS** (715)539-9831
906 Adams St Merrill WI 54452 • NW • Tchr • St John Merrill WI • (715)536-7264 • (MQ 1993)

**BREMER ALVIN L** (219)462-8207
1602 Sanibel Ct Valparaiso IN 46383-3882 • lynn.bremer@immanuel.pvt.k12.in.us • IN • Prin • Immanuel Valparaiso IN • (219)462-8207 • (S 1967 MSED)

**BREMER DAVID A** (517)224-4665
8982 Church Rd Saint Johns MI 48879-9230 • lcmsbremd@abraham.ccaa.edu • MI • P/Tchr • St Peter Saint Johns MI • (517)224-3113 • (RF 1972)

**BREMER JANET L** (319)391-6320
2237 W Columbia Ave Davenport IA 52804-1549 • jlbphred@hotmail.com • IE • Tchr • Trinity Davenport IA • (319)322-5224 • (RF 1977)

**BREMER JOHN A** (319)391-6320
2237 W Columbia Ave Davenport IA 52804-1549 • IE • Tchr • Trinity Davenport IA • (319)322-5224 • (RF 1975)

**BREMER SHEILA KAY** (503)281-2026
6315 NE 27th Ave Portland OR 97211 • NOW • Tchr • St Michael Portland OR • (503)282-0000 • (PO 1988)

**BREMER VALERIE** (972)266-8607
620 W Westchester Pkwy #13207 Grand Prairie TX 75052-3290 • TX • Tchr • St Timothy Houston TX • (281)469-2457 • (S 1997)

**BRENNAN JAN L** (281)370-9675
18523 Mellowgrove Ln Spring TX 77379 • sjblucru@ev1.net • TX • Tchr • Concordia LHS Tomball TX • (281)351-2547 • (S 1991)

**BRENNAN STEPHEN M** (281)370-9675
18523 Mellowgrove Ln Spring TX 77379 • sjblucru@ev1.net • TX • Tchr • Trinity Spring TX • (281)376-5810 • (S 1989)

**BRENNAN TAMI WYNETTE** (310)838-5281
3670 Glendon Ave Apt 235 Los Angeles CA 90034-6244 • PSW • Tchr • South Bay HS-Torranc Torrance CA • (310)530-1231 • (S 1994)

**BRENNER RENEE C** (734)721-2709
35910 John R Wayne MI 48184 • spanishtchr@yahoo.com • MI • Tchr • LHS Westland Westland MI • (734)422-2090 • (AA 1996)

**BRENNER WALTER M** (602)864-8018
C/O W J Flesner 902 W Rovey Ave Phoenix AZ 85013 • FG • EM • (RF 1926)

**BRENT HEIDI L**
175 E Homestead Rd Apt 17 Sunnyvale CA 94087-4639 • CNH • 06/2000 • (MQ 1985 MA)

**BRESE SUSAN E** (716)694-5681
145 Lorelee Dr Tonawanda NY 14150-4326 • jbrese@aol.com • EA • Tchr • Trinity West Seneca NY • (716)674-9188 • (RF 1964 MA)

**BRESEMANN LINDA G**
623 Franconian Dr E Frankenmuth MI 48734-1005 • MI • Tchr • St Lorenz Frankenmuth MI • (517)652-6141 • (RF 1969 MED)

**BRESEMANN PERRY**
623 Franconian Dr E Frankenmuth MI 48734-1005 • pab@stlorenz.org • MI • Prin • St Lorenz Frankenmuth MI • (517)652-6141 • (RF 1970 MA)

**BRETTMANN LINDA** (402)643-4609
705 Bader Ave Seward NE 68434-1199 • NEB • Tchr • St John Seward NE • (402)643-4535 • (S 1970)

**BREWER AMY LA MAE** (808)487-7276
98-500 Koauka Loop #18K Aiea HI 96701 • CNH • Tchr • Our Savior Aiea HI • (808)488-0000 • (PO 1998)

**BREWER PAMELA ANN**
517 Wyss Ridge Dr Fort Wayne IN 46819 • IN • Tchr • Unity Fort Wayne IN • (219)744-0459 • (S 1985)

**BREWNER LINDA S** (630)879-5233
1347 Brandywine Cir Batavia IL 60510-3517 • trialbunch@aol.com • NI • Tchr • Immanuel Batavia IL • (630)406-0157 • (RF 1973 MA)

**BREYTUNG BARBARA A** (262)728-8858
333 W Wisconsin St Delavan WI 53115-1659 • bbreytung@orlcs.org • SW • Tchr • Our Redeemer Delavan WI • (262)728-6589 • (S 1975 MSED)

**BREYTUNG JAMES S** (414)728-6589
333 W Wisconsin St Delavan WI 53115-1659 • jbreytung@orlcs.org • SW • Prin • Our Redeemer Delavan WI • (262)728-4266 • (S 1975 MED)

**BRIESCHKE MARTIN A** (419)782-9355
100 Monterey Rd Defiance OH 43512 • OH • Prin • St John Defiance OH • (419)782-1751 • (S 1970 MED)

**BRIGGS SCOTT NELSON** (904)738-5642
217 Elmwood Ave De Land FL 32724 • MI • Tchr • Immanuel Macomb MI • (810)286-7076 • (AA 1983)

**BRIGHTMAN JOELLEN** (515)576-0772
2740 22nd Ave N Fort Dodge IA 50501-7324 • IW • Tchr • St Paul Fort Dodge IA • (515)955-7208 • (S 1975)

**BRILL GERALDINE A** (303)660-6584
2013 Vineyard Dr Castle Rock CO 80104 • RM • Rocky Mountain Aurora CO • (RF 2000)

**BRILL PAUL G*** (303)660-6584
3013 Vineyard Dr Castle Rock CO 80104-2349 • RM • EM • (S 1953 MED)

**BRINGEWATT DEBORRAH J** (402)563-4185
215 S Calle Columbo Columbus NE 68601-2787 • dbbringew@gilligan.esu7.k12.ne.us • NEB • 02/1990 02/2000 • (S 1974)

**BRINK MARK A** (407)299-1161
8535 Snowfire Dr Orlando FL 32818-5675 • mabrinkfg@cs.com • FG • Florida-Georgia Orlando FL • (RF 1975)

**BRINKLEY RICHARD** (219)622-9194
8242 N 450 E Ossian IN 46777-9638 • IN • Tchr • Bethlehem Ossian IN • (219)597-7366 • (RF 1972 MED MCMU)

**BRINKMAN ANNETTE D** (816)668-2139
PO Box 91 Cole Camp MO 65325-0091 • MO • Tchr • Lutheran School Asso Cole Camp MO • (660)668-4614 • (S 1992)

**BRINKMAN LIANE KYLE**
St Marks Lutheran Church 500 Meramec Blvd Eureka MO 63025-1147 • TheBrinkmans@bigfoot.com • MO • Lutheran School Asso Cole Camp MO • (SP 1997)

**BRISBIN RAE L** (612)441-7549
13419 Island View Dr Elk River MN 55330-1125 • MNS • Tchr • St John Elk River MN • (612)441-6616 • (S 1977)

**BRISTOL NANCY E** (714)599-5350
1668 Grasscreek Dr San Dimas CA 91773-1314 • PSW • Tchr • Hope Glendora CA • (626)335-5315 • (S 1968)

**BRITTAIN THOMAS W** (602)222-8522
1108 E Ocotillo Rd Phoenix AZ 85014-1055 • EN • Tchr • Christ Phoenix AZ • (602)957-7010 • (CQ 1995)

**BRITTON JOHN W** 011-675-547-1235
Highland International School PO Box 363 Papua NEW GUINEA • claudia@maf.org • RM • S Miss • Rocky Mountain Aurora CO • (RF 1982)

**BROCKBERG HAROLD F DR** (320)763-5679
1456 Brophy Park Rd NW Alexandria MN 56308-8102 • MNN • EM • (S 1952 MS DED)

**BROCKBERG KEVIN H** (248)828-3565
5175 Shrewsbury Ln Troy MI 48098 • brockberg@worldnet.att.net • MI • Prin • Our Shepherd Birmingham MI • (248)645-0551 • (RF 1978 MA)

**BROCKDORF JEANETTE E** (414)463-3326
5867 N 71st St Milwaukee WI 53218-1819 • SW • EM • (RF 1952)

**BROCKHOFF MARIAN F** (502)241-4435
7311 Lark Rd Crestwood KY 40014-9451 • IN • Tchr • Our Savior Louisville KY • (502)426-0864 • (S 1961 MAD)

**BROCKMEIER RUSSEL LEE** (801)352-9846
860 E Chariot Dr Sandy UT 84094 • RM • Prin • Redeemer Salt Lake City UT • (801)487-6283 • (S 1978)

**BROD CHARLES W** (708)366-7731
628 Elgin Ave Forest Park IL 60130-1925 • cbrod@enc.k12.il.us • NI • Tchr • St John Forest Park IL • (708)366-2764 • (RF 1964 MA)

**BROFFORD ERIC MICHAEL** (612)929-6691
2900 Maryland Ave S St Louis Park MN 55426 • MNS • Tchr • Redeemer Wayzata MN • (612)473-5356 • (RF 1988 MA)

**BROGAARD JO NETTE L** (320)846-0984
6158 County Road 11 NW Alexandria MN 56308-8064 • MNN • Tchr • Zion Alexandria MN • (320)763-4842 • (SP 1970)

**BROKER FLOYD H** (414)261-1561
1141 Hus Dr Apt 303 Watertown WI 53098-3259 • SW • EM • (NU 1934 MA)

**BRONDOS MARILYN A**
Zion Lutheran Church 2113 S Hanna Fort Wayne IN 46803 • mabron@aol.com • IN • Tchr • Zion Fort Wayne IN • (219)744-1389 • (S 1981)

**BROOK NICHOLE F** (414)662-0270
28800 Cardinal Ct Waterford WI 53185-1189 • SW • Tchr • St Paul West Allis WI • (414)541-6251 • (RF 1996)

**BROOKENS KAREN M** (241)319-7898
9569 Dixie Ln Dallas TX 75228-3738 • elpenguino@aol.com • TX • Tchr • Zion Dallas TX • (214)363-1630 • (S 1988)

**BROOKS DAVID G** (402)643-4382
511 Grand Ave Seward NE 68434-1617 • NEB • SHS/C • Nebraska Seward NE • (S 1991)

**BROSE MARY ELEANORE** (425)277-6635
9915 126th Ave SE Renton WA 98056-2474 • marybrose@worldnet.att.net • NOW • Tchr • King Of Kings Renton WA • (206)255-8520 • (RF 1965)

**BROSZ KEITH E** (907)344-9903
7337 Foxridge Cir # 2 Anchorage AK 99518-2710 • kbanchor@aol.com • NOW • Prin • Anchor Anchorage AK • (907)522-3636 • (S 1971 MED)

**BROTT CAROLYN M**
1201 High St Beatrice NE 68310-3134 • NEB • Tchr • St Paul Beatrice NE • (402)223-3414 • (S 1977)

**BROTT EUGENE C** (402)643-3993
1127 N 5th St Seward NE 68434-1238 • gbrott@seward.cune.edu • NEB • EM • (RF 1955 MA DED)

**BROTT PAUL RAYMOND** (206)932-1415
4104 SW Holly St Seattle WA 98136-1851 • NOW • Prin • Hope Seattle WA • (206)935-8500 • (S 1956)

**BROUCH GRETCHEN ANN** (508)478-0094
7 Madison Ave Milford MA 01757-2219 • dgbrouch@juno.com • NE • 07/1998 07/2000 • (RF 1990 MSED)

**BROWER MARK T** (402)652-8115
421 E 7th St PO Box 171 North Bend NE 68649-0171 • NEB • 09/1998 • (CQ 1996)

**BROWN AIMEE CLAIRE** (715)627-0112
503 1/2 Lincoln St Antigo WI 54409-1470 • aclaireb74@hotmail.com • NW • Tchr • Peace Antigo WI • (715)623-2209 • (MQ 1996)

**BROWN BARBARA J** (516)623-5826
583 Ashland Ave Baldwin NY 11510-2624 • AT • Tchr • Nassau Lutheran Scho Mineola NY • (516)746-2004 • (BR 1984)

**BROWN CHERYL A** (330)794-4301
386 Ellen Ave Akron OH 44305-3921 • OH • Tchr • Zion Akron OH • (330)253-3136 • (AA 1986)

**BROWN CYNTHIA A** (517)479-3889
503 School St Harbor Beach MI 48441-1130 • hbbrownl@aol.com • MI • P/Tchr • Zion Harbor Beach MI • (517)479-3615 • (RF 1980)

**BROWN DAVID C*** (313)388-9440
6860 Mayfair St Taylor MI 48180-1977 • MI • Tchr • LHS Westland Westland MI • (734)422-2090 • (S 1981 MA)

**BROWN GAIL L** (712)276-6579
4316 Lincoln Way Sioux City IA 51106-4302 • IW • Tchr • St Paul Sioux City IA • (712)258-6325 • (S 1972)

**BROWN IRENE LUCINDA** (573)769-3416
325 S Home St Palmyra MO 63461-1715 • MO • 05/2000 • (S 1992)

**BROWN JODY RAE** (913)294-4926
1002 N Pearl St Paola KS 66071-1142 • KS • Tchr • Trinity Paola KS • (913)849-3344 • (S 1974)

**BROWN LARRY G** (314)849-5286
9832 Sunset Greens Dr Saint Louis MO 63127-1549 • MO • Tchr • Christ Community Kirkwood MO • (314)822-7774 • (S 1965 MED)

**BROWN LYNNETTE R** (970)667-4506
2355 Greeley Dr #5 Loveland CO 80538 • RM • Tchr • Immanuel Loveland CO • (970)667-4506 • (S 1982)

**BROWN MARCUS V**
C/O Concordia Lutheran School 202 E 56th St Tacoma WA 98404-1236 • NOW • Tchr • Concordia Tacoma WA • (253)475-9513 • (PO 1995)

**BROWN MARY KAY** (414)442-2597
9300 W Auer Ave Milwaukee WI 53222-3531 • SW • Tchr • Pilgrim Wauwatosa WI • (414)476-0736 • (S 1980)

**BROWN SHIRLEY ANNE** (714)986-5424
1527 N Granite Ave Ontario CA 91762-1236 • PSW • EM • (RF 1960)

**BROWN SUSAN LEIMER** (609)620-1444
161 Franklin Corner Rd # E-7 Lawrenceville NJ 08648-2511 • brownch1@juno.com • EA • Tchr • Hope Levittown PA • (215)946-3467 • (S 1988 MMU)

**BROWNING KRISTEN LOUISE** (501)223-0347
55 Belmont Dr Little Rock AR 72204-3501 • MDS • Tchr • Christ Little Rock AR • (501)663-5232 • (S 1996)

**BROWNING SCOTT D** (501)223-0347
55 Belmont Dr Little Rock AR 72204-3501 • MDS • Tchr • Christ Little Rock AR • (501)663-5212 • (S 1996)

**BROYLES BOBBY D** (808)621-5687
143 Makaweo Ave Wahiawa HI 96786 • CNH • Tchr • Trinity Wahiawa HI • (808)621-6033 • (S 1981 MSED)

**BRUDEEN CENA C**
178 Hilltop Dr Lake in the Hills IL 60102-3306 • NI • Tchr • St Luke Itasca IL • (630)773-0396 • (RF 1995)

**BRUDI DANIEL P** (708)841-7296
14430 Chicago Rd Dolton IL 60419-1712 • dbrudi@kiwi.dep.anl.gov • NI • Tchr • Luther East Lansing IL • (708)895-8441 • (RF 1996)

**BRUEGGEMANN KAREN B** (262)375-1921
738 Lancaster Ct Grafton WI 53024-9536 • brug@execpc.com • SW • Tchr • St Paul Grafton WI • (414)377-4659 • (RF 1982)

**BRUEGGEMANN MILTON R** (913)268-5528
12507 W 74th St Shawnee KS 66216-3679 • mrb@hopelutheran.org • KS • Prin • Hope Shawnee KS • (913)631-6940 • (S 1969 MAT)

**BRUENGER A KENNETH** (313)532-5109
12856 Fenton Detroit MI 48239-2604 • MI • EM • (S 1952 MCMU)

**BRUENGER ADAM J**
3227 Alden Pond Ln Eagan MN 55122 • MNS • Tchr • Luth HS Of Greater M Bloomington MN • (612)854-0224 • (S 1994)

**BRUENGER JENNIFER L**
3227 Alden Pond Ln Eagan MN 55122 • MNS • Tchr • Redeemer Wayzata MN • (612)473-5356 • (S 1994)

**BRUENGER MARILYN J** (785)632-3465
2220 8th St Clay Center KS 67432 • KS • Tchr • Immanuel Junction City KS • (785)238-5921 • (S 1965)

**BRUENING FAYLEEN M** (314)335-3398
1953 Dixie Blvd Cape Girardeau MO 63701-2281 • MO • Tchr • Trinity Cape Girardeau MO • (573)334-1068 • (S 1972)

**BRUENING JOHN S** (262)639-8315
1217 William St Racine WI 53402-4157 • jsbrue@hotmail.com • SW • Tchr • Lutheran High School Racine WI • (414)637-6538 • (RF 1981)

**BRUESEHOFF ALBERT W** (920)452-5602
708 N 15th St Sheboygan WI 53081-3818 • EN • EM • (NU 1945 MS)

**BRUGGEMANN-WONG CHARLENE E** (415)588-2701
1016 Crestview Dr Millbrae CA 94030-1035 • EN • EM • (CQ 1987 MA)

**BRUGMAN JANET LOUISE** (281)379-5725
17103 Wunder Hill Dr Spring TX 77379-4583 • TX • Tchr • Trinity Spring TX • (281)376-5810 • (CQ 1995)

**BRUHN PAUL R DR** (216)382-1461
3433 Woodridge Rd Cleveland OH 44121-1531 • OH • Prin • Lutheran High School Cleveland Heights OH • (216)382-6100 • (S 1978 MED PHD)

**BRUMMER MARY L** (217)735-1838
925 Primm Rd Apt 208 Lincoln IL 62656-3177 • CI • EM • (RF 1956 MA)

**BRUMMER ROCHELLE M** (402)476-7151
5055 Constitution Ave Lincoln NE 68521-1114 • NEB • Tchr • Messiah Lincoln NE • (402)489-3024 • (S 1982)

**BRUMMET FAITH M** (219)264-3254
51883 Woodview Way Elkhart IN 46514-9104 • faith0405@aol.com • IN • 07/1999 • (RF 1990)

**BRUMMET LARRY E** (219)264-3254
51883 Woodview Way Elkhart IN 46514-9104 • IN • Tchr • Trinity Elkhart IN • (219)522-1491 • (RF 1990)

**BRUNDAGE CHRISTA L**
1209 S Main St Red Bud IL 62278-1350 • NI • 08/1999 • (RF 1990)

**BRUNE PAMELA J** (219)747-0428
9636 Shoals Dr Fort Wayne IN 46819-2650 • brune1254@aol.com • IN • Tchr • Unity Fort Wayne IN • (219)744-0459 • (RF 1976)

**BRUNE RICHARD F** (213)747-0428
9636 Shoals Dr Fort Wayne IN 46819-2650 • brune1254@aol.com • IN • P/Tchr • Unity Fort Wayne IN • (219)744-0459 • (S 1976 MA MA)

**BRUNETTE JANET** (352)357-7097
2711 Bayview Dr Eustis FL 37226-6960 • FG • EM • (S 1967)

**BRUNIG RUTH A** (281)443-6043
16707 Rock West Dr Houston TX 77073-6301 • TX • Tchr • Zion Pasadena TX • (713)473-1789 • (S 1972)

**BRUNK DONNA J** (810)677-9421
8276 Ashton Ct Washington MI 48094 • MI • Tchr • Trinity Utica MI • (810)731-4490 • (S 1975 MA)

**BRUNS LORALEE L** (219)322-8640
126 Lexington Dr Dyer IN 46311-1316 • NI • Tchr • Zion Beecher IL • (708)946-2272 • (S 1972)

**BRUNWORTH GERALD C DR** (972)496-0632
518 Baltusrol Cir Garland TX 75044-5057 • gbrunworth@home.com • TX • Tchr • Lutheran HS of Dalla Dallas TX • (214)349-8912 • (RF 1960 MA DED)

**BRUTCHER JUNE ELVA** (317)784-8235
87 N 13th Ave Beech Grove IN 46107-1523 • IN • Tchr • Emmaus Indianapolis IN • (317)632-1486 • (S 1960 MS)

**BRUTLAG CAROL A** (218)385-2163
RR 3 Box 151 New York Mills MN 56567-9543 • mbrutlag@wcta.net • MNN • EM • (RF 1956 MS MED)

**BRUTLAG J DALE** (773)622-6247
3108 N New England Ave Chicago IL 60634-4620 • brutlajd@crf.cuis.edu • NI • SHS/C • Northern Illinois Hillside IL • (RF 1963 MA MS)

**BRUTLAG MARLIN J** (218)385-2163
RR 3 Box 151 New York Mills MN 56567-9543 • mbrutlag@wcta.net • MNN • EM • (RF 1956 MED)

**BRYANT ANN AMMONS**
2115 Cactus Ct #4 Walnut Creek CA 94595-2526 • EN • EM • (CQ 1987)

**BRYANT ELAINE RUTH DR** (636)227-7419
846 Woodside Trails Dr Ballwin MO 63021-6187 • MO • S Ex/S • Missouri Saint Louis MO • (314)317-4550 • (RF 1964 MS JD)

**BRYANT JANICE LOU** (217)423-5933
222 N 16th St Decatur IL 62521-2017 • jan3bryant@yahoo.com • CI • Tchr • Lutheran School Asso Decatur IL • (217)233-2001 • (RF 1966 MA)

**BUBLITZ DONALD R** (715)526-5315
811 Oak St Shawano WI 54166-2031 • NW • EM • (RF 1958 MA)

**BUCHHEIMER PAUL DAVID** (281)856-8476
17111 Crown Meadow Ct Houston TX 77095-4320 • ppbuch@flash.net • TX • Prin • St Mark Houston TX • (713)468-2623 • (RF 1968 MS)

**BUCHHEIMER PEGGY A** (281)856-8476
17111 Crown Meadow Ct Houston TX 77095 • ppbuch@flash.net • TX • Tchr • St Mark Houston TX • (713)468-2623 • (RF 1968)

**BUCHHOLZ DAVID A** (816)674-2666
213 W 3rd St PO Box 47 Alma MO 64001-0047 • MO • Tchr • Trinity Alma MO • (660)674-2444 • (S 1978 MED)

**BUCHHOLZ MARGARET L** (715)758-8715
511 E Green Bay St Bonduel WI 54107-9266 • NW • Tchr • St Paul Bonduel WI • (715)758-8532 • (SP 1975)

**BUCHHORN ALICE LANELL** (254)527-3712
13520 FM 487 Bartlett TX 76511 • TX • EM • (AU 1988)

**BUCHINGER DANIEL C** (815)547-5291
1120 Luther Ave Belvidere IL 61008-4593 • dbuchinger@aol • NI • Tchr • Immanuel Belvidere IL • (815)547-5346 • (S 1975 MA)

**BUCHINGER LORI ANN** (517)652-2722
411 Heine St Frankenmuth MI 48734-1505 • slsrsbuc@concentric.net • MI • Tchr • St Paul Millington MI • (517)871-4581 • (S 1976 MA)

**BUCHINGER STEVEN L** (517)652-2722
411 Heine St Frankenmuth MI 48734-1505 • s.buchinger@stlorenz.org • MI • Tchr • St Lorenz Frankenmuth MI • (517)652-6141 • (S 1976 MA)

**BUCK JANE E** (262)827-0534
2765 Arbor Dr Brookfield WI 53005-3868 • SW • Tchr • Northwest Milwaukee WI • (414)463-4040 • (RF 1963)

**BUCK KAREN** (402)643-3093
1132 N 2nd St Seward NE 68434-1231 • ksb5048@seward.cune.edu • NEB • Tchr • St John Seward NE • (402)643-4535 • (RF 1965 MSMU MED)

**BUCK ROGER L** (920)459-7080
1815 N 4th St Sheboygan WI 53081-2825 • SW • Mem C • Trinity Sheboygan WI • (920)458-8246 • (S 1973)

**BUCK THOMAS M DR** (262)827-0534
2765 Arbor Dr Brookfield WI 53005-3868 • tmb@execpc.com • SW • Tchr • Martin LHS Greendale WI • (414)421-4000 • (RF 1964 MS PHD)

**BUCKLEY SARA LYNN** (618)377-6237
121 Walnut Ridge Bethalto IL 62010 • SI • Tchr • Zion Bethalto IL • (618)377-8314 • (CQ 2000)

**BUDE CATHERINE** (314)892-7035
4928 Sabre Ct Saint Louis MO 63128-3446 • MO • Tchr • Word Of Life Saint Louis MO • (314)832-1244 • (RF 1963 MED)

**BUDE CLEO** (314)353-6985
5721 Itaska St Saint Louis MO 63109-2835 • MO • EM • (RF 1962)

**BUECKMAN BLAIR K** (314)349-1722
734 Wagon Ridge Dr Fenton MO 63026-3304 • MO • Tchr • Our Savior Fenton MO • (314)343-7511 • (S 1975)

**BUEHRING CYRA M** (805)653-2585
152 N Crimea St Ventura CA 93001-2133 • PSW • Tchr • Grace Ventura CA • (805)642-5424 • (IV 1987)

**BUELTMANN KEITH A** (618)659-1969
610 Yale Ave Edwardsville IL 62025-1764 • buzyb@freewwweb.com • SI • Tchr • Trinity Edwardsville IL • (618)656-2918 • (RF 1990)

**BUELTMANN KURTIS ALFRED** (920)622-4812
W5480 S Round Lake Rd Wild Rose WI 54984-9034 • luwisomo@vbe.com • SW • O Sp Min • Nebraska Seward NE • (RF 1994)

**BUERCK BRAD J**
1516 Marbella Apt 6 St Louis MO 63138 • MO • Tchr • Grace Chapel Saint Louis MO • (314)868-3232 • (S 2000)

**BUERGER JANE R** (914)337-7975
228 Midland Ave Tuckahoe NY 10707-4308 • jrb@concordia-ny.edu • AT • SHS/C • Atlantic Bronxville NY • (914)337-5700 • (CQ 1987 MED PHD)

**BUESCHER BARBARA A** (515)278-9482
7612 Horton Ave Urbandale IA 50322-2573 • mbuescher@aol.com • IW • P/Tchr • MT Olive Des Moines IA • (515)277-0247 • (S 1974 MA MED)

**BUESCHER HERBERT F** (713)320-2946
6427 Willow Pine Dr Spring TX 77379-6467 • TX • EM • (RF 1918)

**BUESING RICHARD G** (313)449-2847
301 Lillian Whitmore Lake MI 48189-9533 • buesir@ccaa.edu • MI • SHS/C • Michigan Ann Arbor MI • (S 1962 MSLS)

**BUETER ARTHUR L** (920)452-2905
2902 S 22nd St Sheboygan WI 53081-6514 • SW • EM • (RF 1941)

**BUETOW PAUL E** (314)835-9445
46 Orchard Ln Kirkwood MO 63122-6945 • lancerprin@hotmail.com • MO • Prin • LHS South Saint Louis MO • (314)631-1400 • (CQ 1986 MA)

**BUETTNER RICHARD E** (253)473-5848
7632 Tacoma Ave S Tacoma WA 98408-5928 • NOW • Tchr • Concordia Tacoma WA • (253)475-9513 • (SP 1967 MA)

**BUFFINGTON LINDA G** (210)497-0776
1539 Crescent Glen San Antonio TX 78258 • TX • Tchr • Concordia San Antonio TX • (210)479-1477 • (MQ 2000)

**BUHMAN JEANA MARIE** (402)564-1280
33359 126th Ave Columbus NE 68601-9770 • NEB • 06/1999 • (S 1989)

**BUHRANDT TAMMY LYNN** (920)842-9875
9391 Wiscobee Ln Suring WI 54174-9542 • NW • Tchr • St John Suring WI • (920)842-4443 • (MQ 1991)

**BUHRKE LYNN D** (847)359-8830
4500 Sundance Ct Hoffman Estates IL 60195-1117 • NI • Tchr • Immanuel Palatine IL • (847)359-1936 • (RF 1968 MA)

**BULL BERNARD D**
10621 W Hampton Ave Milwaukee WI 53225 • christalone@juno.com • SW • Tchr • Milwaukee LHS Milwaukee WI • (414)461-6000 • (MQ 1994)

**BULL JOYANNA**
10621 W Hampton Ave Milwaukee WI 53225 • SW • Tchr • Grace Menomonee Falls WI • (262)251-0670 • (MQ 1996)

**BULS LINDA J**
26240 Silver Cloud Dr San Antonio TX 78258-5806 • PSW • Tchr • Bethany Long Beach CA • (562)421-4711 • (S 1965)

**BULTEMEYER DANIEL P** (219)492-2292
6628 Rockingham Dr Fort Wayne IN 46835 • IN • Tchr • St Peter Fort Wayne IN • (219)749-5811 • (RF 1988)

**BULTEMEYER RICHARD L*** (941)729-0399
87 Whipporwill Ct Ellenton FL 34222-4246 • rlrab@cs.com • FG • EM • (RF 1960 MA)

**BUMGARNER MAUREEN H** (612)763-5355
2501 Sara Ave Alexandria MN 56308-8572 • MNN • Tchr • Zion Alexandria MN • (320)763-4842 • (SP 1970)

**BUNCE KAREN LEE** (714)848-7310
6401 Warner Ave Apt 507 Huntington Beach CA 92647 • PSW • Tchr • Good Shepherd Downey CA • (562)803-4918 • (IV 1997)

**BUNDERMAN JULIE**
2200 Ashland Ave #3 Racine WI 53403 • SW • Tchr • Lutheran High School Racine WI • (414)637-6538 • (S 2000)

**BUNDSCHUH ANNETTE ROCHELLE** (716)227-7793
58 Blue Birch Dr Rochester NY 14612-6004 • EA • Tchr • St Paul Hilton NY • (716)392-4000 • (AA 1984 MSED)

**BUNGE HAROLD O** (734)457-6587
4601 Bluebush Rd Monroe MI 48162-9488 • MI • EM • (RF 1950 MED)

**BUNKE JAMES E*** (517)883-2539
31 Auch St Sebewaing MI 48759-1603 • MI • Tchr • Immanuel Sebewaing MI • (517)883-3050 • (RF 1978 MA)

**BUNKELMAN JAMES OWEN** (313)243-5180
852 Kings Park Rd Monroe MI 48161-9764 • MI • Tchr • Trinity Monroe MI • (734)241-1160 • (CQ 1984)

**BUNNETT JANE** (402)362-6694
4 Belmont Dr York NE 68467-2008 • NEB • Tchr • St John Waco NE • (402)728-5244 • (S 1964)

**BUNNOW MARY BETH** (414)255-1913
W226N8304 Friess Pl Sussex WI 53089-1604 • SW • Tchr • Immanuel Brookfield WI • (262)781-7140 • (MQ 1990)

**BUNTE MARIA LYN** (708)754-7853
1140 Wallace Ct Chicago Heights IL 60411-2635 • NI • Tchr • St Paul Chicago Heights IL • (708)754-4492 • (RF 1977 MA)

**BURANDT SHELAH J** (612)442-4216
1340 Waconia Pkwy S Waconia MN 55387-9678 • MNS • Tchr • Trinity Waconia MN • (952)442-4165 • (SP 1994)

**BURBRINK SANDRA L** (812)522-7666
508 E 14th St Seymour IN 47274-1149 • IN • Tchr • Immanuel Seymour IN • (812)522-1301 • (S 1973 MED)

**BURCH MARY J** (217)523-3738
639 S Glenwood Ave Springfield IL 62704-2440 • CI • Tchr • LHS Springfield IL • (217)546-6363 • (S 1978 MA)

**BURDICK BRENDA RUTH** (281)370-6337
14203 Lakewood Forest Dr Houston TX 77070-2525 • TX • Tchr • Trinity Klein TX • (281)376-5773 • (CQ 1998)

**BURFORD SANDRA L** (314)965-6079
622 Cleveland Ave Kirkwood MO 63122 • MO • Tchr • Salem Affton MO • (314)353-9242 • (RF 1968)

**BURGDORF EDITH A** (636)942-2500
3456 Judith Ridge Rd Imperial MO 63052-3910 • MO • EM • (S 1955)

**BURGDORF SUSAN L** (314)894-5613
2573 Grayland Walk Saint Louis MO 63129-3309 • MO • Tchr • St John Saint Louis MO • (314)773-0784 • (S 1982)

**BURGER H EUGENE** (219)482-2287
2703 Bosworth Dr Fort Wayne IN 46805-3030 • IN • EM • (RF 1942 MED)

**BURGER ROBERT L**
3270 Applegate Ln Brookfield WI 53005-3022 • SW • Tchr • Our Redeemer Wauwatosa WI • (414)258-4558 • (S 1964 MED)

**BURGER RONALD G** (317)784-9023
3417 Brunswick Ave Indianapolis IN 46227-8756 • rburger@juno.com • IN • Tchr • St John Indianapolis IN • (317)352-9196 • (CQ 1986 MSED)

**BURGER ROSALIND A** (501)996-2154
PO Box 425 Greenwood AR 72936-0425 • MDS • 08/1990 08/2000 • (RF 1974)

**BURGER STEPHEN F** (810)629-3843
7292 Denton Hill Rd Fenton MI 48430-9480 • EN • Tchr • Child Of Christ Hartland MI • (248)887-3836 • (S 1975 MSED)

**BURGESS CRYSTAL DAWN** (815)697-2560
261 1st South St Chebanse IL 60922 • NI • Tchr • Zion Chebanse IL • (815)697-2212 • (S 1997)

**BURGESS DAVID S** (414)421-6985
5720 W Allwood Dr Franklin WI 53132-9245 • SW • Tchr • Martin LHS Greendale WI • (414)421-4000 • (RF 1980 MA)

**BURGESS ROBERT M** (810)997-3510
45528 Louise Ct Utica MI 48317-5781 • MI • Tchr • Trinity Utica MI • (810)731-4490 • (RF 1984)

**BURGESS SUSAN G** (414)421-6985
5720 W Allwood Dr Franklin WI 53132-9245 • SW • 06/1987 06/2000 • (RF 1980)

**BURGHARD GRACE L** (210)655-7719
3118 John Glenn Dr San Antonio TX 78217-4011 • TX • Tchr • Concordia San Antonio TX • (210)479-1477 • (CQ 1995)

**BURK RHONDA C** (402)243-2395
2249 County Rd 400 Tobias NE 68453 • rcburk@alltel.net • EA • 06/1994 • (S 1988)

**BURKART JEFFREY E** (651)484-7722
433 Irene Ct Roseville MN 55113-3520 • burkart@luther.csp.edu • MNS • SHS/C • Minnesota South Burnsville MN • (RF 1971 MA PHD)

**BURKART MARTHA** (651)484-7722
433 Irene Ct Roseville MN 55113-3520 • mburkart@luther.csp.edu • MNS • SHS/C • Minnesota South Burnsville MN • (RF 1971)

**BURKE KIMBERLY K**
6254 E Northfield Ave Anaheim CA 92807-2342 • PSW • Mem C • Trinity Santa Ana CA • (714)542-0784 • (S 1985)

**BURKE SUSAN** (602)971-4560
2501 E Yucca St Phoenix AZ 85028-2556 • prkybrky@aol.com • EN • Tchr • Christ Phoenix AZ • (602)957-7010 • (CQ 1995)

**BURKEE JEFFREY R** (313)359-3517
24057 Andover Dr Dearborn Heights MI 48125-1901 • stmatthew105256.2073@compuserve.com • MI • Prin • St Matthew Westland MI • (734)425-0261 • (RF 1981)

**BURKEE JOHN G**
8536 W Arthur Pl Milwaukee WI 53227-2523 • SW • Tchr • St Paul West Allis WI • (414)541-6251 • (MW 1982 MA)

**BURMEISTER JANET M** (847)622-8803
645 Lancaster Cir Elgin IL 60123 • janbur@aol.com • NI • Prin • Northern Illinois Hillside IL • (RF 1980 MA)

**BURMEISTER SYLVIA A** (507)776-3827
10293 473 Ave Truman MN 56088-9331 • MNS • Tchr • St Paul Truman MN • (507)776-6541 • (SP 1968)

**BURMESTER ELLEN J** (707)252-8606
1150 La Homa Dr # B Napa CA 94558-3009 • CNH • Tchr • St John Napa CA • (707)226-7970 • (SP 1975)

**BURNETT JENNIFER JOAN** (714)532-1462
2605 E Rose Ave Orange CA 92867-7349 • camptimekazia@hotmail.com • PSW • Tchr • Salem Orange CA • (714)639-1946 • (CQ 1996)

**BURNS KIMBERLY K** (651)388-1379
4813 Mill Rd Red Wing MN 55066-9421 • MNS • Tchr • Concordia Red Wing MN • (651)388-5447 • (WN 1985)

**BUROW PETER**
C/O Lutheran High School 8494 Stults Rd Dallas TX 75234 • TX • Tchr • Lutheran HS of Dalla Dallas TX • (214)349-8912 • (AU 2000)

**BURRIGHT GEORGE DOUG*** (501)452-4996
803 I Cir Barling AR 72923-1993 • MDS • EM • (S 1977 MED)

**BURROUGHS DANIEL R** (314)287-9196
3243 Rosedale Dr Arnold MO 63010-3757 • burroughs@lcms.org • MO • S Ex/S • Missouri Saint Louis MO • (314)317-4550 • (RF 1971 MA)

**BURROUGHS DOROTHY PRALLE** (713)681-8023
1138 Danbury Rd Houston TX 77055-6829 • dburroughs@academicplanet.com • TX • Tchr • LHS North Houston TX • (713)880-3131 • (RF 1975 MMU)

**BURTNER CAROL A** (714)879-3764
721 Harmony Ln Fullerton CA 92831-1865 • PSW • EM • (RF 1958)

**BUSACKER WILLIAM P** (262)375-3607
132 W Juniper Dr Grafton WI 53024-2234 • wsbusacker@milwpc.com • SW • Tchr • St Paul Grafton WI • (414)377-4659 • (S 1975)

**BUSCH EDNA F** (516)935-4688
14 Barrister Rd Levittown NY 11756-4319 • AT • Tchr • Trinity Hicksville NY • (516)931-2211 • (BR 1982)

**BUSCH JOAN L** (918)456-3974
1207 E Normal St Tahlequah OK 74464-3329 • OK • 06/1989 09/1999 • (RF 1979)

**BUSCH JOHN E** (918)456-3974
1207 E Normal St Tahlequah OK 74464-3326 • OK • O Sp Min • Oklahoma Tulsa OK • (CQ 1986)

**BUSCH MICHAEL J** (516)935-4688
14 Barrister Rd Levittown NY 11756-4319 • AT • Tchr • Trinity Hicksville NY • (516)931-2211 • (BR 1982)

**BUSCHENA WENDY L** (507)425-2649
2140 41st St Fulda MN 56131 • MNS • Tchr • St Paul Fulda MN • (507)425-2169 • (S 1981)

**BUSER SHIRLEY** (817)773-0605
3114 Shady Hill Dr Temple TX 76502-1343 • TX • Tchr • Immanuel Temple TX • (254)773-9485 • (S 1965)

**BUSHUR ANN JOLENE** (423)281-8606
1146 Whitesburg Dr Knoxville TN 37918 • MDS • Tchr • First Knoxville TN • (423)524-0308 • (RF 1986)

**BUSS JANICE L** (812)342-4645
16200 S 300 W Columbus IN 47201-9357 • IN • P/Tchr • White Creek Columbus IN • (812)342-6832 • (RF 1975 MED)

**BUSS MARK A** (812)342-4645
16200 S 300 W Columbus IN 47201-9357 • IN • Tchr • St Peter Columbus IN • (812)372-5266 • (RF 1974 MA)

**BUSSE DALE A** (330)724-2583
2209 Pamer Dr Akron OH 44319-1311 • dlb.godwithus@juno.com • IN • EM • (RF 1957 MED)

**BUSSE KURT ALAN** (309)663-5745
1218 Bancroft Dr Bloomington IL 61704-3680 • kab1@trinluth.org • CI • Tchr • Trinity Bloomington IL • (309)829-7513 • (S 1983 MA)

**BUSSE ROBERT L** (708)771-8190
140 Marengo Ave Apt 301 Forest Park IL 60130-1316 • NI • EM • (CQ 1960)

**BUSSEAU CRAIG R** (626)339-5243
4403 N Larkin Dr Covina CA 91722-3238 • PSW • Tchr • St John Covina CA • (626)915-2122 • (S 1980)

**BUTEYN BRIAN PHILIP** (701)271-8139
2437 W Country Club Dr - Apt 4 Fargo ND 58103 • ND • Tchr • Grace Fargo ND • (701)232-1516 • (S 1995)

**BUTH KENNETH M** (941)382-1139
2734 Orange Grove Dr Sebring FL 33870-2334 • FG • Tchr • Faith Sebring FL • (941)385-0406 • (S 1973)

**BUTLER JUDY A** (847)622-9506
1469 Meyer St Apt 3 Elgin IL 60123-7052 • NI • Tchr • Fox Valley Academy Elgin IL • (847)468-8207 • (RF 1986)

**BUTTERFIELD MICHAEL WAYNE** (512)250-9507
8009 Buckshot Trl Austin TX 78729-7322 • TX • SHS/C • Texas Austin TX • (CQ 1995 MS)

**BUTTS LU JUANA R** (708)209-3492
1111 Bonnie Brae Pl # 1-W River Forest IL 60305 • crfbuttsl@crf.cuis.edu • NI • SHS/C • Northern Illinois Hillside IL • (CQ 1997 MA EDS EDD)

**BUTZ THOMAS C** (949)458-3738
22446 Bywater Rd Lake Forest CA 92630-3010 • pswbutztc@aol.com • PSW • Pacific Southwest Irvine CA • (949)854-3232 • (CQ 1993 MA)

**BUUCK DARLENE L** (219)347-5950
209 Prestwick Dr Kendallville IN 46755-2972 • IN • Tchr • St John Kendallville IN • (219)347-2444 • (SP 1981)

**BUUCK DONALD G** (219)923-8365
3127 Maple Dr Highland IN 46322-1248 • NI • Tchr • Luther East Lansing IL • (708)895-8441 • (RF 1966)

**BUUCK PAUL A** (219)347-5950
209 Prestwick Dr Kendallville IN 46755-2972 • IN • Tchr • St John Kendallville IN • (219)347-2444 • (SP 1983)

**BUUCK STEVEN JEFFREY DR** (810)677-9766
19138 Pinecone Dr Macomb MI 48042-4213 • sbuuck@lhsa.com • MI • Prin • LHS North Macomb MI • (810)781-9151 • (MQ 1985 MS PHD)

## C

**CAGE SARA K** (405)721-1288
10716 N Council Rd Apt 9 Oklahoma City OK 73162 • TX • Tchr • St Mark Houston TX • (713)468-2623 • (MQ 1999)

**CAHILL CHERYL L** (210)699-8049
7210 Autumn Park San Antonio TX 78249-4271 • ccahill1@hotmail.com • TX • 08/1998 08/2000 • (RF 1981)

**CAHILL ROBERT ALAN SR.** (210)699-8049
7210 Autumn Park San Antonio TX 78249-4271 • Bobc@concordia-satx.com • TX • Tchr • Concordia San Antonio TX • (210)479-1477 • (RF 1981)

**CAIN PATRICIA A** (320)554-2161
PO Box 36 Villard MN 56385-0036 • MNS • Tchr • St Paul Pipestone MN • (507)825-2142 • (SP 1969)

**CALABRESE DEBORAH L** (630)860-9146
166 E Potter St Wood Dale IL 60191 • NI • Northern Illinois Hillside IL • (RF 1979 MA)

**CALHOUN RICHARD** (708)209-3034
671 Winston Dr Melrose Park IL 60160 • calhourc@crf.cuis.edu • NI • SHS/C • Northern Illinois Hillside IL • (RF 1966 MS PHD)

**CALLAHAN CHERYL M** (718)417-5831
6218 80th Ave Glendale NY 11385-6839 • AT • Mem C • Redeemer Glendale NY • (718)456-5292 • (BR 1987)

**CALLIES BERNHARD J** (313)841-0107
9125 Falcon St Detroit MI 48209-1707 • MI • EM • (RF 1951 MED)

**CALLIHAN JUANITA L** (281)357-8694
13543 Country Cir Tomball TX 77375-3058 • TX • Tchr • Our Savior Houston TX • (713)290-8277 • (AU 1989)

**CALVIN MATTHEW KENT** (708)562-5580
7325 Woodward Ave Apt 205 Woodridge IL 60517 • NI • Tchr • Immanuel Hillside IL • (708)562-5580 • (S 1999)

**CAMBERG TERRY N** (916)682-7857
119 American Way Vacaville CA 95687 • MrCee42@aol.com • CNH • P/Tchr • Trinity Fairfield CA • (707)435-1123 • (S 1968)

**CAMPBELL ELIZABETH A** (319)285-7379
804 W Sheridan Dr Eldridge IA 52748-1561 • IE • Tchr • Trinity Davenport IA • (319)323-8001 • (S 1982)

**CAMPBELL GARY H** (517)799-8528
4338 S Wayside Dr Saginaw MI 48603-3060 • vegcam@concentric.net • MI • Tchr • Peace Saginaw MI • (517)792-2581 • (RF 1970 MA)

**CAMPBELL KATHERINE** (210)732-1371
1721 Santa Barbara San Antonio TX 78201 • TX • Tchr • Redeemer San Antonio TX • (210)735-9903 • (AU 1998)

**CANNATA CHRISTINE** (708)474-4208
3454 Lake St Apt 3 Lansing IL 60438-2366 • NI • Tchr • St John Lansing IL • (708)895-9280 • (RF 1997)

**CAPDEVILLE ROY M*** (512)869-1956
5951 FM 1105 Georgetown TX 78626-9792 • rmcap@texas.net • TX • Tchr • Zion Georgetown TX • (512)863-5345 • (RF 1968 MED)

**CAPOUCH JUDITH R** (847)394-4690
224 E Kerry Brook Ln Arlington Hts IL 60004-2199 • eacapouch@aol.com • NI • Tchr • St Peter Arlington Heights IL • (847)253-6638 • (RF 1964 MED)

**CAPPA SUSAN DEE** (708)354-1524
6510 Conrad Ave Hodgkins IL 60525-7612 • NI • Tchr • St John Lombard IL • (630)629-2515 • (RF 1989)

**CARIKER GRETCHEN D** (714)639-4641
1026 E Palmyra Ave Orange CA 92866-2423 • PSW • Tchr • St John Orange CA • (714)288-4406 • (S 1979)

**CARIO WILLIAM DR** (414)449-0808
3863 N 55th St Milwaukee WI 53216-2209 • william.cario@cuw.edu • SW • SHS/C • South Wisconsin Milwaukee WI • (414)464-8100 • (RF 1978 PHD)

**CARLOVE PATRICK A** (512)775-7452
3216 Arroyo Bluff Round Rock TX 78664 • TX • St Stephanus Saint Paul MN • (MQ 1991 MA)

**CARLSEN CHRISTINA**
186 Ashfield Ct Bloomingdale IL 60108 • tomussg@msn.com • NI • Tchr • St John Lombard IL • (630)629-2515 • (CQ 1997)

**CARLSON BRUCE J** (914)744-2969
26 Chapel Ct Pine Bush NY 12566-6227 • AT • Mem C • Trinity Walden NY • (845)778-7119 • (RF 1970)

**CARLSON DONNA MARIE**
365 Long Hill Ave Shelton CT 06484-5502 • NE • Tchr • Immanuel Bristol CT • (860)583-5649 • (BR 1996)

**CARLSON JAMES A** (314)723-2236
2020 Sibley St Saint Charles MO 63301-1630 • MO • Tchr • Immanuel Saint Charles MO • (636)946-0051 • (S 1970)

**CARLSON KAREN J** (309)797-7944
1173 34th St Moline IL 61265-2368 • IE • Tchr • Trinity Davenport IA • (319)322-5224 • (RF 1980)

**CARLSON LINDA JOYCE** (615)662-8742
204 Still Water Cir Nashville TN 37221-4042 • Linda.Carlson@home.com • MDS • 08/2000 • (RF 1984 MA)

**CARLSON NANCY G** (914)744-2969
26 Chapel Circle Ct Pine Bush NY 12566-6227 • AT • Tchr • Trinity Walden NY • (845)778-7119 • (RF 1969 MS)

**CARLSON SANDRA L** (313)978-2227
38777 Monterey Dr Sterling Heights MI 48312-1353 • MI • Tchr • Trinity Utica MI • (810)731-4490 • (CQ 1979 MA)

**CARLTON JANET** (941)992-3400
22632 Fountain Lakes Blvd Estero FL 33928-2328 • FG • 10/1991 10/1999 • (RF 1975)

**CARNEHL JANET E** (847)359-7732
25 N Linden Ave Palatine IL 60067-5435 • NI • Tchr • St Peter Arlington Heights IL • (847)253-6638 • (RF 1976 MA)

**CARNEY DONNA** (716)434-0174
7064 Northview Dr Lockport NY 14094-5335 • carney5@wzrd.com • EA • 07/1995 • (BR 1984)

**CARNEY KELLY J** (219)489-2350
11324 Oxnard Ct Ft Wayne IN 46845-2010 • bkcarney@worldnet.att.net • IN • Tchr • Emmaus Fort Wayne IN • (219)456-4573 • (BR 1995)

**CARNOALI JEAN C**
1509 N Y Rd Hampton NE 68843-3517 • NEB • Tchr • Zion Hampton NE • (402)725-3320 • (S 1989)

**CAROTHERS CHERYL L** (812)376-0053
3114 29th St Columbus IN 47203 • IN • Tchr • St Peter Columbus IN • (812)372-5266 • (AA 1994)

**CARPENTER AARON LOUIS** (281)489-6605
5402 Pregeant Pearland TX 77584-9642 • TX • Tchr • LHS North Houston TX • (713)880-3131 • (MQ 1996)

**CARPENTER ROBERT M** (504)367-7187
2620 Jupiter St Harvey LA 70058-2918 • SO • 06/1996 06/2000 • (RF 1959 MA)

**CARPENTER SHIRLEY A**
200 Dorothy St - Apt B2 East Pittsburgh PA 15112 • eco6olec@aol.com • EA • Prin • Christ Pittsburgh PA • (412)271-7173 • (RF 1960)

**CARR ELAINE D** (727)524-4502
2591 Keene Park Dr Largo FL 33771-1819 • libbycarr@ij.net • FG • Tchr • First Clearwater FL • (727)461-3444 • (RF 1980 MA)

**CARRIER LORI JEAN** (708)788-6554
3421 Wenonah Ave Berwyn IL 60402-3349 • pjsc@prodigy.net • NI • Prin • Messiah Chicago IL • (773)725-8903 • (S 1979)

**CARROLL DOROTHY M** (231)796-8522
18170 Woodland Dr Big Rapids MI 49307-9734 • carroll@net-port.com • MI • EM • (RF 1972)

**CARSON WENDE JEAN** (402)529-6899
998 6th Rd Wisner NE 68791-3021 • NEB • P/Tchr • Zion St John Wisner NE • (402)529-3348 • (S 1978)

**CARTER DEBRA S** (303)750-2440
1676 S Tucson St Aurora CO 80012 • deb-carter@usa.net • RM • 04/1999 • (S 1977)

**CARTER GAIL ROANE** (314)846-7473
6240 Kings Ferry Pl Saint Louis MO 63129-5044 • cartergr@aol.com • MO • EM • (RF 1962 MS)

**CARTER JEANETTE N**
C/O Lutheran HS North 5401 Lucas and Hunt Rd Saint Louis MO 63121-1599 • MO • Zion St John Wisner NE • (S 1997)

**CARVER GAIL B** (507)334-0656
709 Valley View Rd Faribault MN 55021-5741 • MNS • Tchr • Faribault Faribault MN • (507)334-7982 • (SP 1979)

**CASCIONE VIRGINIA HELENE** (810)294-1988
31011 Greater Mac Ave St Clair Shrs MI 48082-1446 • MI • Tchr • Redeemer St Clair Shrs MI • (313)294-0640 • (S 1969)

**CASHMER CAROL L** (313)281-3773
13690 Argyle St Southgate MI 48195-1929 • MI • Tchr • Christ The King Southgate MI • (734)285-9697 • (RF 1983 MA MA)

**CASPERSEN CAROL ANN** (307)637-4947
5131 Bowie Dr Cheyenne WY 82009-4936 • WY • Tchr • Trinity Cheyenne WY • (307)635-2802 • (S 1967)

**CASS THERESE R** (303)678-1647
3581 Larkspur Cir Longmont CO 80503-7584 • RM • 09/1999 • (S 1990)

**CASSELMAN LYNN ROSA**
150 W Warren St Trlr 63 Peru IN 46970-2759 • IN • Tchr • St John Peru IN • (765)473-6659 • (RF 1984)

**CASSENS LAURA L**
RR 1 Box 4 Canistota SD 57012 • SD • 05/1999 • (S 1996)

**CASSIDY SHAWN C**
1422 E Quincy Orange CA 92867 • PSW • Tchr • Lutheran HS/Orange C Orange CA • (714)998-5151 • (MQ 1993)

**CASTENS CHRISTINE MARIE**
1400 Elm St New Haven IN 46774 • IN • Tchr • Emanuel New Haven IN • (219)749-2163 • (S 1999)

**CASTENS JENNIFER DENISE**
13613 Tastad Rd Arlington WA 98223 • jkcastens@juno.com • NOW • Tchr • Zion Everett WA • (425)334-5064 • (SP 1995)

**CASTENS NEAL C** (316)687-5724
Holy Cross Luth School 600 N Greenwich Rd Wichita KS 67206 • KS • Tchr • Holy Cross Wichita KS • (316)684-4431 • (S 1971)

**CATTAU CURT W** (714)921-8764
2698 Sylvan Cr Orange CA 92865-2121 • curt.cattau@cui.edu • PSW • SHS/C • Pacific Southwest Irvine CA • (949)854-3232 • (S 1973 MS)

**CATTAU ROLLIN C** (713)682-3549
5915 Autumn Forest Dr Houston TX 77092-2307 • TX • EM • (S 1954 MA)

**CATTAU RUTH ANN** (714)921-8764
2698 Sylvan Cr Orange CA 92865-2121 • PSW • Tchr • St Paul Orange CA • (714)921-3188 • (S 1972)

**CECIL TIMOTHY VERDUN** (414)367-7575
N28W29860 Oakwood Grove Rd Pewaukee WI 53072-4227 • SW • Tchr • Immanuel Brookfield WI • (262)781-7140 • (MQ 1993)

**CEPLECHA PAULA** (517)689-5278
2862 E Bombay Rd Midland MI 48642-7381 • MI • Tchr • St John Midland MI • (517)835-7041 • (AA 1987 MED)

**CHABOT ANGELA R** (618)659-2323
1 Burton Pl Edwardsville IL 62025-1722 • SI • Tchr • Good Shepherd Collinsville IL • (618)344-3151 • (S 1997)

**CHAMPLIN CINDY M** (208)736-0359
3775 N 3300 E Kimberly ID 83341 • NOW • Tchr • Immanuel Twin Falls ID • (208)733-7820 • (PO 1981)

**CHANDLER CAROL A** (214)343-0880
9959 Adleta Blvd Apt 1123 Dallas TX 75243-8127 • cachan@flash.net • TX • Tchr • Zion Dallas TX • (214)363-1630 • (AU 1984 MED)

**CHANDLER F WILLIAM** (308)384-3312
205 W 21st St Grand Island NE 68801-2372 • NEB • Prin • Trinity Grand Island NE • (308)382-5274 • (RF 1959 MNS)

**CHANDLER TAMI LYNN**
2458 N 42nd Rd Sheridan IL 60551-9770 • NI • Tchr • Cross Yorkville IL • (630)553-7861 • (S 1990)

**CHANEY CARIN K** (612)263-8906
19804 202nd Ave Big Lake MN 55309-9354 • MNS • Tchr • St James Howard Lake MN • (320)543-2630 • (SP 1969)

**CHAPIN KATHRYNE ANN** (314)947-9138
2773 Red Cedar Parc Dr O Fallon MO 63366-6609 • MO • Tchr • Trinity Saint Charles MO • (636)250-3654 • (S 1996)

**CHAPMAN LISA A** (810)619-9586
5298 Church Hill Dr Troy MI 48098-3422 • MI • Tchr • St Paul Royal Oak MI • (248)546-6555 • (S 1979 MA)

**CHARPENTIER KEVIN MICHAEL** (630)629-5783
2015 S Finley Rd Apt #502 Lombard IL 60148-4848 • kevin-charpentier@walther.com • NI • Tchr • Walther LHS Melrose Park IL • (708)344-0404 • (MQ 1997)

**CHELLEW DEBORAH S**
C/O Christ Memorial Luth PS 2833 Raritan Rd Madison WI 53711 • SW • Tchr • Christ Madison WI • (608)271-2811 • (SP 1983)

**CHENEY MARK ROBERT** (702)256-9158
3357 Kylemore St #103 Las Vegas NV 89129 • mark³cheney@hotmail.com • PSW • Tchr • Faith LHS Las Vegas NV • (702)804-4400 • (S 1999)

**CHESLOCK BETH ANNE*** (414)430-8719
2323B S Webster Ave Green Bay WI 54301-2123 • NW • Tchr • Zion Greenleaf WI • (920)864-2463 • (RF 1997)

**CHILES JILL**
1411 Elmwood Ave Berwyn IL 60402 • NI • Tchr • Grace Chicago IL • (773)762-1234 • (S 1999)

**CHILES ROSS**
3514 Odlum Point Ln North Las Vegas NV 89032-0506 • NI • Tchr • Grace Chicago IL • (773)762-1234 • (S 1999)

**CHILMAN JOHN** (612)789-4813
1004 45th Ave NE Columbia Heights MN 55421 • jchilman@mail.concordia-academy.pvt.k12.mn.us • MNS • Tchr • Concordia Academy Roseville MN • (612)484-8429 • (SP 1992)

**CHISM DE ANN CECILIA**
1592 NW Angeline Ct Gresham OR 97030-4896 • NOW • Tchr • Portland Portland OR • (503)667-3199 • (PO 1996)

**CHITTICK CARI A**
22161 Caminito Laureles Laguna Hills CA 92653-1191 • PSW • Tchr • Abiding Savior Lake Forest CA • (949)830-1460 • (S 1995)

**CHOKSI PAMELA L**
7258 W James Ln Monee IL 60449-8811 • NI • 10/2000 • (S 1991)

**CHOLCHER NORMA JEAN** (501)782-5788
2119 Churchill Rd Fort Smith AR 72904-6205 • ncholcher@hotmail.com • MDS • EM • (S 1961)

**CHORLEY CAROL A** (407)871-2522
2458 SW Hinchman St Port Saint Lucie FL 34984-5071 • FG • Tchr • Redeemer Stuart FL • (561)286-0932 • (SP 1983)

**CHOROBA KATHERINE J** (810)750-2015
6140 Mc Guire Rd Fenton MI 48430 • MI • Tchr • St Paul Lapeer MI • (810)664-0046 • (RF 1980)

**CHOW TERRY S**
1317 Mandarin Ln Duarte CA 91010 • PSW • Tchr • Zion Glendale CA • (818)243-3119 • (RF 1977)

**CHRISTENSEN NEAL RAY** (801)262-7862
3973 S 900 E Apt 47 Salt Lake City UT 84124-1144 • nrcraul@aol.com • RM • 06/1999 • (MQ 1995)

**CHRISTENSEN STEPHANIE L*** (708)260-9215
917 E Indiana St Wheaton IL 60187-5642 • NI • 07/1999 • (CQ 1988 MS)

**CHRISTIAN BRENDA S** (605)394-7760
4550 S Hwy 16 Rapid City SD 57701 • SD • Tchr • Zion Rapid City SD • (605)342-5749 • (SP 1998)

**CHRISTIAN CARL F DR** (503)669-8805
1150 SW Chastain Dr Gresham OR 97080-6607 • cjchris@teleport.com • NOW • SHS/C • Northwest Portland OR • (RF 1953 MSED DED)

**CHRISTIAN DEBORAH L** (219)639-3293
12912 Franke Rd Monroeville IN 46773-9559 • IN • 11/1985 05/1997 • (S 1982)

**CHRISTIAN DEBORAH RUTH** (713)680-9232
1127 Lehman Houston TX 77018 • bomeme@aol.com • TX • Tchr • Texas Austin TX • (RF 1980 MED)

**CHRISTIAN DONALD A** (713)680-9232
1127 Lehman Houston TX 77018 • bomeme@aol.com • TX • Tchr • Texas Austin TX • (RF 1981 MMU)

**CHRISTIAN ERICA LYNNE** (636)441-6838
2102 Woodridge Dr St Peters MO 63376 • echristian@lhssc.org • MO • Tchr • LHS St Charles Saint Peters MO • (636)928-5100 • (SP 1998)

**CHRISTIAN JUDITH ANNE** (314)771-7372
1307 Sidney St Saint Louis MO 63104-4314 • MO • S Ex/S • Missouri Saint Louis MO • (314)317-4550 • (RF 1969 MA)

**CHRISTIAN ROBERT E** (206)935-4801
4618 SW Othello St Seattle WA 98136-2023 • NOW • EM • (RF 1949 MA)

**CHRISTIAN ROBERT J** (810)463-4735
130 S Highland Mount Clemens MI 48043-2142 • bchristian@immlutheran.org • MI • P/Tchr • Immanuel Macomb MI • (810)286-7076 • (RF 1975 MED)

**CHRISTIANSAN DEANNA J E**
28850 S Western Ave Rancho Palos Verdes CA 90275 • PSW • Tchr • Christ Rancho Palos Verdes CA • (310)831-0848 • (IV 1998)

**CHRISTIANSEN ALFRED O** (517)781-1298
945 Kennely Rd Apt 146 Saginaw MI 48609-6780 • alrene@cris.com • MI • EM • (S 1950)

**CHRISTIE LORETTA K** (719)528-5056
2824 Boxwood Pl Colorado Springs CO 80920-4019 • RM • Tchr • Shep Springs Colorado Springs CO • (719)598-7446 • (S 1976)

**CHRISTMAN JOHN T** (402)379-7942
400 S 6th St Norfolk NE 68701 • NEB • Tchr • Lutheran High Northe Norfolk NE • (402)379-3040 • (S 1999)

**CHRISTMAN KIMBERLIE DI ANN** (949)951-0112
23321 Caminito Andreta Laguna Hills CA 92653-1602 • PSW • Tchr • Abiding Savior Lake Forest CA • (949)830-1460 • (IV 1997)

**CHRISTMAN NATHANIEL** (949)951-0112
23321 Caminito Andreta Laguna Hills CA 92653-1602 • birdmannat@hotmail.com • PSW • Tchr • Abiding Savior Lake Forest CA • (949)830-1461 • (IV 1996)

**CHRISTMAN THOMAS P** (405)737-8289
808 Timber Ridge Rd Midwest City OK 73130-4326 • mchrist721@aol.com • OK • Oklahoma Tulsa OK* • (S 1970 MSED)

**CHRYSAM CYNTHIA S** (410)836-9623
322 E Jarrettsville Rd Forest Hill MD 21050-1608 • SE • Tchr • Baltimore LHS Baltimore MD • (410)825-2323 • (AA 1987 MED)

**CHRZAN BETH E** (323)849-4489
1142 N Ontario St Burbank CA 91505-2315 • chrzan@juno.com • PSW • Tchr • First Burbank CA • (818)848-3076 • (S 1977)

**CHUHRAN KYLE BRYAN**
C/O Baltimore Lutheran School 1145 Concordia Dr Towson MD 21286 • SE • Tchr • Baltimore LHS Baltimore MD • (410)825-2323 • (AA 1987)

**CHURCH CANDACE L** (954)522-7147
17 SW 11th Ct Fort Lauderdale FL 33315-1240 • FG • Tchr • Lutheran Central Sch Fort Lauderdale FL • (305)463-7471 • (S 1978)

**CHURCH SUSAN KAY** (281)370-4646
17306 Autumn Oak Ct Spring TX 77379 • TX • Tchr • Trinity Spring TX • (281)376-5810 • (CQ 1998)

**CHUTE SOPHIA R**
PSC 566 Box 497 FPO AP 96386 • raenna@yahoo.com • PSW • Tchr • Pilgrim Santa Monica CA • (310)829-4113 • (IV 1997)

**CISEWSKI LISA MARIE** (320)234-6229
725 Ridge Ave NE Apt 201 Hutchinson MN 55350-1273 • lmclsc@hutchtel.nt • MNS • Tchr • Our Saviors Hutchinson MN • (320)587-3318 • (SP 1997)

**CLAASSEN WALTER B** (312)741-5289
860 Cookane Ave Elgin IL 60120-8530 • NI • EM • (RF 1960)

**CLAKLEY-JONAS KAREN E** (818)609-9584
18755 Runnymede St Reseda CA 91335-2765 • PSW • Tchr • Trinity Jr/Sr High S Reseda CA • (818)342-7855 • (S 1979 MED)

**CLANCY EUNICE Y** (205)432-3927
1208 Cottrell St Mobile AL 36605-4721 • SO • Tchr • Mount Calvary Mobile AL • (205)471-4200 • (CQ 1984)

**CLAPP JILL**
862 Carlisle Way Sunnyvale CA 94087-3602 • lofiluther@aol.com • CNH • Tchr • Redeemer Redwood City CA • (650)366-5892 • (IV 1989)

**CLARIDGE ANITA LYN** (210)402-7331
3630 Ridge Cluster San Antonio TX 78247-3422 • TX • Tchr • LHS Of San Antonio San Antonio TX • (210)733-7771 • (AU 1998)

**CLARK DENNIS W** (810)324-2877
7437 Imlay City Rd North Street MI 48049-2810 • MI • Tchr • Trinity Port Huron MI • (810)984-2501 • (RF 1982)

**CLARK GAIL ANN** (314)225-5852
10 Gentle Ct Fenton MO 63026-2745 • MO • Tchr • Our Savior Fenton MO • (314)343-7511 • (CQ 1993)

**CLARK KATHERINE A** (812)524-0597
332 W Oak Seymour IN 47274 • kclark318@hotmail.com • MO • Mem C • St Paul Saint Louis MO • (314)822-0447 • (SP 1997 MA)

**CLARK LORI DONIELLE** (810)498-9633
15755 Camden Grosse Pointe MI 48021 • MI • 06/1999 • (AA 1992)

**CLARK MARY E** (313)272-8992
13546 Abington Ave Detroit MI 48227-1328 • MI • Tchr • Detroit Urban Detroit MI • (313)582-9900 • (RF 1974 MED)

**CLARK PENNY SUE** (808)836-4855
807 Peltier Ave Honolulu HI 96818 • penshni@aol.com • CNH • Tchr • Trinity Wahiawa HI • (808)621-6033 • (MQ 1997)

**CLARK RACHEL JOY**
C/O Cross of Calvary 4327 Elvis Presley Blvd Memphis TN 38116-6405 • MDS • Tchr • Cross/Calvary Memphis TN • (901)396-5566 • (SEL )

**CLARK STANLEY H** (507)287-0593
1901 26 Ave NW Apt 23 Rochester MN 55901 • stansue@bellsouth.net • MNS • Tchr • Rochester Central Rochester MN • (507)289-3267 • (SP 1971)

**CLARK SUSAN**
1901 26th Ave NW Apt 23 Rochester MN 55901 • stansue@bellsouth.net • MNS • 07/2000 • (SP 1970 MA)

**CLARK TINA MICHELLE** (217)355-9197
1501 W University Ave Champaign IL 61821-3132 • TinaClarkl@aol.com • CI • 09/1998 • (IV 1992)

**CLARKSON JULENE MARIE** (402)454-3780
101 Fairview Dr Madison NE 68748-6005 • NEB • 09/1997 09/1999 • (CQ 1995)

**CLARKSON LESA M** (651)641-8220
1230 Concordia Ave Saint Paul MN 55104-5444 • clarkson@luther.csp.edu • MNS • SHS/C • Minnesota South Burnsville MN • (S 1980 MA)

**CLASEN NORMAN L** (214)348-5449
9338 Whittenburg Gate Dallas TX 75243-6528 • TX • EM • (S 1955)

**CLAUGHERTY DARLENE J** (651)738-0407
503 Guthrie Ave N Oakdale MN 55128-6712 • MNS • Tchr • East St Paul Saint Paul MN • (612)774-2030 • (SP 1967)

**CLAUS KENNETH F** (812)471-8619
1730 Dianne Ave Evansville IN 47714-5423 • kfcdmoc@juno.com • IN • Tchr • Evansville Evansville IN • (812)424-7252 • (S 1961 MA MED)

**CLAUS LORI V** (217)546-4371
515 Illini Ct Springfield IL 62704-1709 • CI • Tchr • Our Savior's Springfield IL • (217)546-4531 • (AA 1986)

**CLAUS RICHARD J** (708)429-6273
17631 66th Ct Tinley Park IL 60477-4021 • mrclausg7@aol.com • NI • Tchr • Trinity Tinley Park IL • (708)532-3529 • (RF 1966 MA)

**CLAUSEN KAREN A** (402)534-5581
650 Indiana Ave Utica NE 68456-6093 • NEB • Tchr • St John Waco NE • (402)728-5244 • (S 1964)

**CLAUSEN STEPHEN W** (409)542-5369
738 Edgewood Ave Giddings TX 78942-4425 • swclausen@bluebon.net • TX • 07/1993 07/2000 • (S 1977 MED)

**CLAUSEN VERNON M** (830)931-3388
455 County Road 385 San Antonio TX 78253-6823 • vclausen@juno.com • TX • EM • (S 1959)

**CLAVIR KENNETH ROBERT**
14 Las Cruces Rcho Santa Margarita CA 92688-2853 • kclavir@cui.edu • PSW • SHS/C • Pacific Southwest Irvine CA • (949)854-3232 • (IV 1994)

**CLAXTON CELINDA M** (703)768-7041
2604 Stone Hedge Dr Alexandria VA 22306-2454 • cindyclax@erols.com • SE • P/Tchr • Immanuel Alexandria VA • (703)549-7323 • (CQ 1985 MA)

**CLAYTON LORI JEAN** (309)647-5431
138 Pecan St Canton IL 61520 • SI • 07/2000 • (RF 1995)

**CLEAR BERLYN ANN** (307)436-8290
PO Box 1571 Glenrock WY 82637-1571 • gbclear@pld.com • KS • 07/1997 • (S 1988)

**CLEGG ROBERT J** (314)831-5226
3030 Hampshire Dr Florissant MO 63033-1424 • EN • S Ex/S • English Farmington MI • (RF 1960)

**CLELAND MARLENE MARIE** (602)956-0720
3860 N 30th St Phoenix AZ 85016-6960 • EN • Tchr • Christ Phoenix AZ • (602)957-7010 • (RF 1964 MED)

**CLEMENS JENNIFER KAY**
8065 N 51st St Brown Deer WI 53223 • SW • Tchr • Christ Phoenix AZ • (MQ 1995)

**CLEMENT LAVETA M** (712)542-4055
1858 T Ave Clarinda IA 51632-9804 • IW • Tchr • Clarinda Clarinda IA • (712)542-3657 • (S 1984)

**CLEMENTS WAYNE E*** (636)239-6376
4 Eleanor Dr Washington MO 63090-3904 • clements@midwestis.net • MO • Prin • Immanuel Washington MO • (314)239-1636 • (S 1964 MA)

**CLINARD RANDALL R** (414)783-5820
4420 N 144th St Brookfield WI 53005-1604 • rclinmch@exexpc.com • SW • Tchr • Milwaukee LHS Milwaukee WI • (414)461-6000 • (RF 1969 MLS)

**CLINE LISA JANENE** (520)544-2578
3048 W Monmouth St Tucson AZ 85742 • prek@faith-lutheran.org • EN • Tchr • Faith Tucson AZ • (520)881-0670 • (MQ 1994)

**CLINE THOMAS LOUIS** (520)520-2578
3048 W Monmouth St Tucson AZ 85742 • grade5@faith-lutheran.org • EN • Tchr • Faith Tucson AZ • (520)881-0670 • (WN 1982)

**CLINKENBEARD SANDRA K** (979)251-7870
1108 Apache Dr Brenham TX 77833-5730 • TX • Tchr • Grace Brenham TX • (979)836-3475 • (S 1976)

**CLITTY CYNTHIA S** (612)255-9473
1310 5th Ave N Sauk Rapids MN 56379-2240 • MNN • Tchr • Trinity Sauk Rapids MN • (320)251-1477 • (S 1979)

**CLOETER AMY M**
2472 Lake In The Woods #964 Ypsilanti MI 48198 • MI • Tchr • St Paul Ann Arbor MI • (734)665-9117 • (S 2000)

**CLOETER CHRISTINE A** (715)823-5323
W8287 Cloverleaf Lake Rd Clintonville WI 54929-8514 • chrisc@hotmail.com • NW • Tchr • St Martin Clintonville WI • (715)823-6538 • (S 1980)

**CLOETER HUBERT V** (507)334-2346
1308 Summer Ln Faribault MN 55021-6923 • MNS • EM • (S 1952 MMU)

**CLOETER ROBERT C** (507)689-4502
RR 1 Box 147 Winona MN 55987-9788 • MNS • Mem C • St Martin Winona MN • (507)452-8879 • (SP 1977)

**CLOETER TIMOTHY J** (518)346-6466
1906 Cambridge Manor Dr Scotia NY 12302-2443 • timcloeter@aol.com • AT • 09/1991 09/1999 • (S 1987 MMU)

**CLOETER WALDO H** (661)251-8184
26316 Green Terrace Dr Santa Clarita CA 91321-1325 • walbet@aol.com • PSW • EM • (S 1948 MA)

**CLONKEY ELIZABETH MARIE**
S76W16906 Gregory Dr - Unit E Muskego WI 53150 • emclonkey@yahoo.com • SW • Tchr • Good Shepherd East Troy WI • (414)642-3310 • (SP 1995)

**CLOW KAY J** (812)522-4520
1822 E 950 S Columbus IN 47201-9218 • IN • Tchr • White Creek Columbus IN • (812)342-6832 • (RF 1971 MS)

**CLUPPERT ELIZABETH A** (314)579-1905
12369 Duneden #102 Saint Louis MO 63146 • MO • White Creek Columbus IN • (SP 1998)

**CLUVER DANIEL D** (815)622-9266
25436 Front St Sterling IL 61081 • NI • P/Tchr • Christ Sterling IL • (815)625-3800 • (S 1973 MA)

**CLUVER ELLEN S** (815)622-9266
25436 Front St Sterling IL 61081 • NI • Tchr • Christ Sterling IL • (815)625-3800 • (S 1973 MA)

**CLYMER JANICE S** (719)260-8252
5290 Sevenoaks Dr Colorado Springs CO 80919-5405 • RM • Tchr • Rock Of Ages Colorado Springs CO • (719)632-9491 • (MQ 1986)

**COBURN WAYNE E** (612)757-3720
14440 Quinn Dr NW Anoka MN 55304-3327 • MNS • Tchr • Prince Of Peace Spring Lake Park MN • (612)786-1755 • (SP 1972)

**COCHRAN WILLIAM DAVID** (636)861-0433
1430 Whispering Crk Dr Ballwin MO 63021-8424 • cochraned@aol.com • MO • Prin • Christ Community Kirkwood MO • (314)822-7774 • (S 1968 MSED)

**COE JAMES F** (727)530-7928
1444 Stewart Blvd Clearwater FL 33764-2809 • FG • Tchr • First Clearwater FL • (727)461-3444 • (S 1977 MA MA)

**COE SHARON K** (727)530-7928
1444 Stewart Blvd Clearwater FL 33764-2809 • FG • Tchr • First Clearwater FL • (727)461-3444 • (S 1977 MA)

**COERBER TECKLA RUTH** (901)377-2237
5836 Third Cove Apt #6 Memphis TN 38134 • MDS • Tchr • Christ King Memphis TN • (901)682-8404 • (S 2000)

**COHRS ARLENE R** (314)416-7205
10916 Arctic Dr Saint Louis MO 63123-7006 • teachercohrs@hotmail.com • MO • Tchr • St Luke Saint Louis MO • (314)832-0118 • (RF 1970 MED)

**COHRS RICHARD P** (314)416-7205
10916 Arctic Dr St Louis MO 63123-7006 • lllcohrsrp@lhm.org • MO • St Luke Saint Louis MO • (RF 1971 MED)

**COHRS TROY RICHARD**
13125 50th St Watertown MN 55388-8329 • MNS • 06/1996 06/2000 • (SP 1992)

**COLBA FRANK H** (314)839-8772
3957 Grand National Dr Florissant MO 63034-3463 • MO • EM • (RF 1941 MA)

**COLE SHARON LYNN**
2317 Maplewood Dr Gastonia NC 28052-9409 • EA • Tchr • St John Hamlin NY • (716)964-2550 • (CQ 1997 MS)

**COLEMAN HEATHER RUEHLE**
7562 Daisy Shelby Twsp MI 48317 • MI • Tchr • Immanuel Macomb MI • (810)286-4231 • (RF 1999)

**COLEMAN LINDA F**
6200 Woodward Ave Birmingham AL 35228 • SO • Tchr • Zion Bessemer AL • (205)425-2091 • (S 1972)

**COLLEVER DALLAS W** (817)831-3244
PO Box 7387 Fort Worth TX 76111-0387 • TX • Mem C • St Paul Fort Worth TX • (817)332-2281 • (RF 1959 MED)

**COLLINS MARY LYNN** (320)732-3394
Rt 4 Box 420 Long Prairie MN 56347 • MNN • Tchr • Trinity Long Prairie MN • (320)732-2238 • (SP 1976)

**COLONEY JODY LYNN** (716)663-0091
214 Duffern Dr Rochester NY 14616 • EA • 06/1995 • (AA 1989 MA)

**COLROSS RUTH A** (410)969-1918
8142 Windmill Ct Severn MD 21144-2311 • rcolr@stpauls-lutheran.org • SE • Prin • St Paul Glen Burnie MD • (410)766-5790 • (S 1971 MED)

**COLVIN EDWARD D** (516)588-6581
4 Park St Centereach NY 11720-3853 • AT • 07/1994 07/1997 • (RF 1974 MA)

**COLVIN MICHELLE** (516)588-6581
4 Park St Centereach NY 11720-3853 • AT • 07/1994 07/1997 • (BR 1975)

**COLYER KENNETH R** (209)952-6250
7008 Germanna Ct Stockton CA 95219-3117 • CNH • Tchr • Trinity Stockton CA • (209)464-0895 • (SP 1974)

**COMBS JANICE A** (812)522-7878
809 W 8th St Seymour IN 47274-1473 • IN • 01/1996 02/2000 • (S 1978 MA EDS DED)

**COMER CHERYL KAY** (409)291-6751
1210 Cresthill St Huntsville TX 77340-6733 • TX • Tchr • Faith Huntsville TX • (409)291-1706 • (AU 1997)

**COMOTTO MARILYN** (713)729-9762
11015 Atwell Dr Houston TX 77096-6129 • TX • Tchr • Pilgrim Houston TX • (713)666-3706 • (S 1961)

**COMPTON ANNE M**
960 Northgate Ave Waynesboro VA 22980-3456 • OK • Tchr • First Ponca City OK • (580)762-1111 • (WN 1985 MMU)

**CONDON CONNIE C** (515)483-2022
PO Box 514 State Center IA 50247-0514 • IE • Tchr • Clemons Clemons IA • (515)477-8263 • (S 1987)

**CONEYBEER KRISTINE O** (317)862-3118
8256 S Franklin Rd Indianapolis IN 46259-9632 • coneybeer@tcon.net • IN • Tchr • LHS Of Indianapolis Indianapolis IN • (317)787-5474 • (CQ 1985 MS)

**CONGER NORENE J** (313)885-7238
633 S Higbie Pl Grosse Pointe MI 48236-2417 • MI • Tchr • St Thomas Eastpointe MI • (810)772-3370 • (SP 1973)

**CONIGLIO STEVEN LEE** (307)987-2094
502 E Park Ave Riverton WY 82501 • WY • Tchr • Trinity Riverton WY • (307)857-5710 • (AU 1997)

**CONNER LOIS J** (309)692-6427
6620 N Brookwood Ln Peoria IL 61614 • CI • Tchr • Good Shepherd Pekin IL • (309)347-2020 • (RF 1975)

**CONNICK SHARON J** (209)545-3042
5209 Bora Ct Salida CA 95368 • jcscac@aol.com • CNH • Tchr • Grace Modesto CA • (209)529-1800 • (S 1986)

**CONNOLLY KAREN** (516)676-4517
49 Grove St Glenwood Landing NY 11547 • AT • Tchr • Our Saviour Bronx NY • (718)792-5665 • (BR 1991 MS)

**CONNORS ADAM S**
8507 B Titchfield Ct Saint Louis MO 63123 • MO • Tchr • LHS South Saint Louis MO • (314)631-1400 • (S 1996)

**CONOVER CHARLES W** (314)842-3297
9324 Werkdale Dr Saint Louis MO 63126-3031 • MO • Prin • Word Of Life Saint Louis MO • (314)832-1244 • (S 1967 MCRT)

**CONRAD JOHN A SR.** (920)387-5549
424 Dayton St Mayville WI 53050-1111 • jconrad@stjohns-lcms.org • SW • Tchr • St John Mayville WI • (920)387-4310 • (S 1977 MS)

**CONSOLINO JEANINE E** (314)892-6170
2211 Apple Bud Ln Saint Louis MO 63125-3102 • MO • Tchr • Hope Saint Louis MO • (314)832-1850 • (S 1973 MA)

**CONTRERAS ANDREW J** (810)727-7344
8910 Bartel Rd Columbus MI 48063-4302 • MI • Tchr • St Peter Richmond MI • (810)727-9080 • (S 1991 MAT)

**CONTRERAS KATIE JEANNE** (810)727-7344
8910 Bartel Rd Columbus MI 48063-4302 • MI • Tchr • St Peter Richmond MI • (810)727-9080 • (S 1991)

**CONVERSET MICHELLE L** (219)637-8873
1531 Greentree Ct Fort Wayne IN 46845-9766 • converset@aol.com • IN • Tchr • Concordia LHS Fort Wayne IN • (219)483-1102 • (S 1988)

**COOK BARBARA L** (402)727-9673
410 E 9th Fremont NE 68025-3784 • NEB • Tchr • Trinity Fremont NE • (402)721-5959 • (S 1971)

**COOK CARLA JEAN** (608)755-9809
610 N Ringold St Janesville WI 53545-2557 • ccook@ticon.net • SW • Tchr • St Paul Janesville WI • (608)754-4471 • (RF 1991)

**COOK DAVID ALVIN** (651)484-9206
1975 Oxford St N Roseville MN 55113-6472 • MNS • Tchr • King Of Kings Roseville MN • (651)484-9206 • (S 1975 MS)

**COOK EDWARD C** (618)288-5473
48 Foreman Dr Glen Carbon IL 62034-1308 • SI • Tchr • Trinity Edwardsville IL • (618)656-7002 • (CQ 1994)

**COOK JOANNE M** (209)732-1993
2829 E Valley Oaks Dr Visalia CA 93292-6779 • CNH • Tchr • Grace Visalia CA • (559)734-7694 • (BR 1989)

**COOK JUNE M**
C/O Trinity Lutheran Church 6850 159th St Tinley Park IL 60477 • NI • Tchr • Trinity Tinley Park IL • (708)532-9395 • (SP 1985)

**COOK KATHY M** (402)371-0741
2005 Clark St Norfolk NE 68701-2354 • dcook@cereal.nefcomm.com • NEB • Tchr • Christ Norfolk NE • (402)371-5536 • (S 1965)

**COOK KEVIN T** (914)779-5371
4 Concordia Pl Bronxville NY 10708-1802 • ktc@concordia-ny.edu • AT • SHS/C • Atlantic Bronxville NY • (914)337-5700 • (BR 1976 MS)

**COOK PAMELA J**
1201 Fairhaven Ave #209 Santa Ana CA 92705-6767 • pcook@lutheranschool.org • PSW • Tchr • St John Orange CA • (714)288-4400 • (S 1972 MED)

**COOK PRISCILLA** (703)683-0311
23 W Wyatt Ave Alexandria VA 22301-1553 • SE • EM • (RF 1955)

**COOK SUSAN E** (303)922-2721
909 S Saulsbury St Lakewood CO 80226-4513 • RM • Tchr • Univ Hills Denver CO • (303)759-0161 • (S 1981)

**COOKS JOYCE M** (314)231-6053
2236 Warren St Saint Louis MO 63106-2441 • MO • Tchr • St Matthew Saint Louis MO • (314)261-7765 • (CQ 1983)

**COOKSEY ROBERT L** (605)371-3148
4301 E 38th St Sioux Falls SD 57103-6567 • rdcooks@dtgnet.com • SD • Prin • Sioux Falls Sioux Falls SD • (605)335-1923 • (S 1984 MED MA MA)

**COONS KEVIN W** (410)663-4248
2903-E Cold Stream Way Baltimore MD 21234 • SE • Tchr • Baltimore LHS Baltimore MD • (410)825-2323 • (BR 2000)

**COOPER CAROLYN M** (281)255-8342
21226 Farm Rd #2920 Hockley TX 77447 • TX • Tchr • Trinity Spring TX • (281)376-5810 • (S 1973 MA)

**COOPER DALE E** (281)255-8342
21226 FM 2920 Rd Hockley TX 77447-9343 • TX • Prin • Concordia LHS Tomball TX • (281)351-2547 • (S 1972 MED)

**COOPER JENNIFER LOUISE**
477 Hidden Valley Rd Clinton TN 37716-5835 • js2405@aolcom • MDS • Tchr • First Knoxville TN • (423)524-0308 • (S 1995 MS)

**COPE LAVELL J** (513)662-7258
2661 Leda Ct Cincinnati OH 45211-7204 • OH • Tchr • Grace Cincinnati OH • (513)661-8467 • (RF 1970)

**COPPERSMITH DONNA J** (760)321-9343
24 Lincoln Place Rancho Mirage CA 92270 • PSW • 05/1994 05/2000 • (RF 1972 MA)

**CORDANI SHARON DI ANN** (217)324-4657
29 Birchwood Rd Litchfield IL 62056-1701 • SI • Tchr • Zion Litchfield IL • (217)324-3166 • (CQ 1997)

**CORDES NANCY A** (630)420-2039
1728 Atwood Cir Naperville IL 60565-6745 • NI • Tchr • St John LA Grange IL • (708)354-1690 • (RF 1961)

**CORDES ROY W** (815)939-3559
1108 S 6th Ave Kankakee IL 60901-4840 • NI • EM • (RF 1965)

**CORDOVA CONNIE L** (303)421-4729
7300 Tabor St Arvada CO 80005-3226 • RM • Tchr • Emmaus Denver CO • (303)433-3303 • (RF 1975)

**CORDT VICTORIA J**
2345 Crestlake Dr Rockwall TX 75087 • TX • Mem C • Tree Of Life Garland TX • (972)226-6086 • (S 1979)

**CORNETT RONALD C** (402)371-8092
316 Aspen Dr Norfolk NE 68701-6907 • NEB • Tchr • St John Battle Creek NE • (402)675-3605 • (S 1962)

**CORNWELL KATHRYN M** (904)433-2046
28 Hillbrook Way Pensacola FL 32503-2850 • SO • Tchr • Redeemer Warrington FL • (850)455-0330 • (RF 1962)

**COSTENARO LORILEE** (219)365-4612
8713 Lantern Dr Saint John IN 46373 • NI • Tchr • St John Lansing IL • (708)895-9280 • (RF 1975)

**COSTLEY DOROTHY CAROLINE**
35 Isabella St Holyoke MA 01040 • NE • Tchr • First Holyoke MA • (413)534-7071 • (S 2000)

**COTTER JENNIFER ANNE**
PO Box 308 Clifton IL 60927 • NI • Tchr • Zion Chebanse IL • (815)697-2212 • (RF 1999)

**COUCHMAN BARBARA G** (212)430-0913
1651 Williamsbridge Rd # 1E Bronx NY 10461-6249 • AT • Tchr • Our Saviour Bronx NY • (718)792-5665 • (BR 1975 MSED)

**COUFAL LORI L** (402)571-5797
6154 Jaynes St Omaha NE 68104-1659 • NEB • Tchr • Mount Calvary Omaha NE • (402)551-7020 • (S 1995)

**COURTNEY ANGELA N** (509)627-6407
184 Edgewood Dr Richland WA 99352-8509 • NOW • Tchr • Bethlehem Kennewick WA • (509)582-5624 • (S 1967 MA)

**COURVOISIER ELINOR L** (949)646-1832
804 Congress St Costa Mesa CA 92627-3338 • PSW • Tchr • Christ Costa Mesa CA • (949)548-6866 • (RF 1971 MA)

**COUSER THOMAS D*** (972)484-7080
2921 Meadow Green Dr Farmers Branch TX 75234-4948 • tcouser@usa.net • TX • Tchr • Lutheran HS of Dalla Dallas TX • (214)349-8912 • (RF 1969 MED)

**COVELL MARY ARLENE** (616)946-5478
826 Pine Grove Ave Traverse City MI 49686-3657 • MI • Tchr • Trinity Traverse City MI • (231)946-2720 • (CQ 1994)

**COVERSTON LINDA LOU** (301)422-7323
6719 Knollbrook Dr Hyattsville MD 20783-3037 • SE • Tchr • Concordia Hyattsville MD • (301)927-0266 • (S 1968)

**COWAN BETH A** (231)755-4322
1296 W Dale Ave Muskegon MI 49441-2251 • MI • Tchr • West Shore Muskegon MI • (616)755-1048 • (AA 1984 MA)

**COWAN MARY T** (217)394-2632
PO Box 348 Buckley IL 60918-0348 • CI • Tchr • St John Buckley IL • (217)394-2422 • (RF 1988)

**COWEN RACHEL LYNN** (504)365-8359
2620 Jupiter St Harvey LA 70058 • SO • Tchr • Atonement Metairie LA • (504)887-3980 • (RF 1986)

**COX BRENDA KAY**
1140 Overden Pl Pomona CA 91766-1124 • PSW • Tchr • Mount Calvary Diamond Bar CA • (909)861-2740 • (SP 1989)

**COX BRENDA R** (612)479-3312
5024 Perkinsville Rd Maple Plain MN 55359 • MNS • Tchr • St Paul-St Peter Watertown MN • (612)955-1419 • (SP 1990)

**COX JANELL D** (480)926-9286
1017 N Saint Elena St Gilbert AZ 85234-3596 • coxt@uswest.net • PSW • Tchr • Christ Greenfield Gilbert AZ • (480)892-8521 • (MQ 1987)

**COX JOHN E**
140 Overden Pl Pomona CA 91766-1124 • PSW • Tchr • Mount Calvary Diamond Bar CA • (909)861-2740 • (MQ 1988)

**COX LORI LYNN** (734)398-5748
1590 Le Blanc Lincoln Park MI 48146 • MI • Tchr • Trinity Wyandotte MI • (734)282-5896 • (AA 1996)

**COX LYNN M** (262)821-5761
1260 Greenway Ter Apt 4 Brookfield WI 53005-6920 • lweerts@juno.com • SW • Tchr • Pilgrim Wauwatosa WI • (414)476-0735 • (MQ 1998)

**COXEY WENDY C** (219)633-9942
2973 Dogwood Ct PO Box 117 Bremen IN 46506-0117 • IN • Tchr • Redeemer Warsaw IN • (219)267-5656 • (MW 1980)

**CRABBS CHERYL L** (303)682-2939
157 Donovan Ct Longmont CO 80501-4769 • RM • Prin • Mount Zion Boulder CO • (303)443-4151 • (S 1985 MA)

**CRAIG KENNETH L** (716)693-1373
244 Rumbold Ave N Tonawanda NY 14120-4752 • kcraig1125@aol.com • EA • Tchr • St Mark North Tonawanda NY • (716)693-3715 • (BR 1986)

**CRAM BEVERLY JEAN** (402)486-3449
6936 Halsey Ct Lincoln NE 68516 • bjcram@mailcity.com • NEB • Tchr • Messiah Lincoln NE • (402)489-3024 • (CQ 1999 MSED)

**CRAMER JOAN MARIE** (720)886-0914
3367 S Uravan Way #306 Aurora CO 80013 • curfgrad99@hotmail.com • RM • Tchr • Lutheran HS Rockies Parker CO • (303)841-5551 • (RF 1999)

**CRASS CANDACE**
1114 W Riverview Dr Glendale WI 53209 • SW • Tchr • St John Glendale WI • (414)352-4150 • (MQ 1992)

**CRAVEN JAMES A** (352)620-9197
509 SE 19th St Ocala FL 34471-5326 • jcraven2praxis.net • FG • Tchr • St John Ocala FL • (352)629-1794 • (RF 1975 MA)

**CRAVEN KATHRYN E** (352)620-9197
509 SE 19th St Ocala FL 34471-5326 • FG • Tchr • St John Ocala FL • (352)629-1794 • (RF 1974)

**CRAVEN STEPHANIE S** (708)544-2531
4341 Butterfield Rd - Apt 2 Hillside IL 60162 • NI • Tchr • Immanuel Elmhurst IL • (630)832-1649 • (RF 1999)

**CRIMMINS RUTH E**
404 Melrose Dr Barrington IL 60010-1249 • NI • Tchr • Immanuel Palatine IL • (847)359-1936 • (RF 1987)

**CRISLER PAUL G** (314)846-7336
2608 Storm Lake Dr Saint Louis MO 63129-5430 • crislerp@slu.edu • MO • Prin • Lutheran North Saint Louis MO • (314)389-3100 • (RF 1960 MED)

**CROLIUS MICHELLE K** (815)468-7360
228 E 3rd St Manteno IL 60950-1310 • NI • 11/1999 • (SP 1986)

**CRONAUER SHIRLEY JEAN** (317)272-4520
1843 Thistle Ct Avon IN 46123 • tcronauer@iquest.net • IN • Tchr • Our Shepherd Indianapolis IN • (317)271-9103 • (S 1986)

**CROSMER JESSE** (727)344-2500
5896 27th Ave N Saint Petersburg FL 33710-3367 • jecrosmer@aol.com • FG • Prin • Our Savior Saint Petersburg FL • (727)344-1026 • (RF 1980 MED)

**CROUCHER DOUGLAS EARL**
C/O Bethlehem Lutheran Church 2100 Wadsworth Blvd Lakewood CO 80215-2007 • RM • Tchr • Bethlehem Lakewood CO • (303)238-7676 • (AA 1986)

**CROUSE KAREN S** (618)532-3545
15 Arline Dr Centralia IL 62801-4405 • rkcrouse@isbe.accessus.net • SI • Tchr • Trinity Centralia IL • (618)532-5434 • (RF 1970 MS)

**CROUSE RICHARD A** (618)532-3545
15 Arline Dr Centralia IL 62801-4405 • rkcrouse@isbe.accessus.net • SI • EM • (S 1965 MS)

**CROW JOAN PAEZ** (303)679-9603
31371 Shadow Mountain Dr Conifer CO 80433 • starcars@worldnet.att.net • RM • 08/1997 • (RF 1973)

**CROWE ELIZABETH M** (718)470-6202
120-20 Riviera Ct # 22A College Point NY 11356-1100 • AT • Prin • Martin Luther Maspeth NY • (718)894-4000 • (RF 1974 MA)

**CROWN MARY JO** (612)831-5395
5101 W 92nd St Bloomington MN 55437-1820 • MNS • Tchr • St Michael Bloomington MN • (612)831-5276 • (SP 1967)

**CRUISE JAMES R** (352)589-2732
507 Firewood Ave Eustis FL 32726-5631 • jrcruise@aol.com • FG • Tchr • Faith Eustis FL • (352)589-5683 • (RF 1969 MA)

**CULLEN CHRISTINE** (503)642-1198
5545 SW 191st Ct Aloha OR 97007-2953 • jcullen@cu-portland.edu • NOW • Tchr • St Paul Sherwood OR • (503)625-6648 • (RF 1973)

**CULLEN GUELDA ELAINE** (281)298-1769
79 Woodhaven Wood Dr The Woodlands TX 77380-3972 • mmcullen@wt.net • TX • Mem C • Trinity Klein TX • (281)376-5773 • (CQ 1994 MSED)

**CULLI HEATHER M**
11914 W Rio St Milwaukee WI 53225 • SW • Tchr • Elm Grove Elm Grove WI • (262)797-2970 • (RF 1996)

**CULLINGS JERIL LYN**
2432 NW Ava Ave Gresham OR 97030 • NOW • SHS/C • Northwest Portland OR • (S 1986)

**CUMMING BRENDA LYNN** (972)235-2391
2115 Drake Dr Richardson TX 75081 • brendacumming@hotmail.com • TX • Tchr • Faith Plano TX • (972)423-7447 • (CQ 1997)

**CUMMINS LEANN JEANETTE** (612)420-2317
9245 Cherry Ln Hamel MN 55340-9335 • MNS • Tchr • St John Maple Grove MN • (612)420-2426 • (SP 1966 MA)
**CUNNINGHAM JUDITH E** (217)523-0227
3036 Buena Vista Dr Springfield IL 62707-6900 • CI • EM • (RF 1963)
**CUNNINGHAM LYNN M** (405)737-5208
124 W Silver Meadow Dr Midwest City OK 73110-4139 • jeffcll@swbell.com • OK • Tchr • Good Shepherd Midwest City OK • (405)732-0070 • (SP 1987)
**CURRY CHRIS W**
PO Box 311 Oakridge OR 97463-0311 • NOW • 07/1996 07/2000 • (PO 1982)
**CUSTER MARTHA L** (216)475-8013
15509 Wingate Rd Maple Heights OH 44137-3728 • mcuster364@aol.com • OH • Tchr • St John South Euclid OH • (216)381-1513 • (S 1987 MMU)
**CUTLER JOANN L** (402)646-2001
603 S Evergreen Dr Seward NE 68434 • mjlbrj@juno.com • OK • 08/1986 08/2000 • (S 1985)
**CUTTRISS RACHEL L** (217)546-8473
1948 S Douglas Ave Springfield IL 62704-3524 • CI • Tchr • LHS Springfield IL • (217)546-6363 • (S 1989 MS)
**CYPHER ALAN J** (205)772-8127
902 Highland Dr Madison AL 35758-8484 • A.Cypher@usa.net • SO • Tchr • Grace Huntsville AL • (256)881-0553 • (RF 1977 MS)
**CYPHER HARRY J III** (714)638-0114
1577 W Wakefield Ave Anaheim CA 92802-3932 • PSW • P/Tchr • Good Shepherd Inglewood CA • (310)671-0427 • (RF 1975 MA)
**CZAJKOWSKI DENISE** (618)327-3331
347 E Walnut St Nashville IL 62263-1722 • SI • 07/1994 07/2000 • (RF 1985)
**CZAPLEWSKI SARAH RUTH** (954)202-7345
1621 NE 56th St Fort Lauderdale FL 33334 • czapled@concentric.net • FG • 08/1997 08/2000 • (RF 1987)
**CZECH RICHARD D** (715)257-9167
1470 Hill Rd Athens WI 54411-9506 • NW • EM • (RF 1955)
**CZIOK KATHLEEN M** (701)235-8766
1641 3rd Ave S Fargo ND 58103-1515 • ND • Tchr • Grace Fargo ND • (701)232-7747 • (SP 1979)

## D

**D ORAZIO JOSETTE MICHELE** (626)795-0915
241 N Wilson Ave Pasadena CA 91106 • jnadeau@foothillchristian.org • PSW • Tchr • Emmaus Alhambra CA • (626)289-3664 • (S 1994)
**DAAKE JENNIFER R** (219)661-0979
31 Walnut Pkwy Crown Point IN 46307 • NI • Tchr • Luther East Lansing IL • (708)895-8441 • (S 1996)
**DABERKOW EVELYN M** (719)561-8620
1739 Stone Ave Pueblo CO 81004-3336 • RM • Tchr • Trinity Pueblo CO • (719)542-1864 • (S 1972)
**DAENZER CHARLES G** (219)672-3915
7908 Amber Rd Fort Wayne IN 46814-9774 • cdaenzer@fwi.com • EN • P/Tchr • Emmanuel-St Michael Fort Wayne IN • (219)422-6712 • (RF 1965 MS)
**DAENZER GILBERT H** (402)643-4749
540 E Hillcrest Dr Seward NE 68434-1340 • gdaenzer@seward.cune.edu • NEB • EM • (RF 1952 MA)
**DAENZER KATHERINE L** (313)468-7827
52 Miller St Mount Clemens MI 48043-2224 • daenzer@rust.net • MI • Tchr • St Peter Macomb MI • (810)781-9296 • (S 1976 MA)
**DAGEL JULIE KAY** (402)451-0886
7509 Northridge Dr Omaha NE 68112-2528 • NEB • Tchr • St Paul Omaha NE • (402)451-2865 • (S 1978)
**DAGER JANICE E** (410)592-2177
12912 Fork Rd Baldwin MD 21013-9345 • jedager@juno.com • SE • Tchr • St Paul Kingsville MD • (410)592-8100 • (RF 1971)
**DAHL LUKE A**
PO Box 607 Howard Lake MN 55349 • ldahli@hotmail.com • MNS • Tchr • St James Howard Lake MN • (320)543-2766 • (SP 1995)
**DAHL VALERIE A**
45 Martens Blvd San Rafael CA 94901-5028 • CNH • Tchr • Trinity San Rafael CA • (415)453-4526 • (S 1984)
**DAHLHAUSER MARY L** (402)721-1786
2050 Hazel St Fremont NE 68025-2748 • NEB • Tchr • Trinity Fremont NE • (402)721-5959 • (S 1975)
**DAHLKE BETTY LOUISE** (256)775-6255
1559 Lakeview Dr NW Cullman AL 35055-2313 • SO • EM • (RF 1962)
**DAHLKE DOROTHY HILDA** (517)652-6883
644 Franconian Dr E Frankenmuth MI 48734-1006 • MI • Tchr • St Lorenz Frankenmuth MI • (517)652-6141 • (SP 1966 MED)
**DAHM JANET A** (262)567-4415
1194 Dorchester Dr Oconomowoc WI 53066-4408 • SW • Tchr • Divine Redeemer Hartland WI • (414)367-8400 • (RF 1964)
**DAHM JOHN W** (262)567-4415
1194 Dorchester Dr Oconomowoc WI 53066-4408 • SW • Tchr • St Paul Oconomowoc WI • (262)567-5001 • (S 1967)
**DAHMS SARA E**
6915 Bentley Ave Darien IL 60561-4060 • crfdahmsse@crf.cuis.edu • NI • SHS/C • Northern Illinois Hillside IL • (RF 1986 MA)
**DAHN JENNIFER M**
333 E Jackson Marengo IL 60152 • NI • Tchr • Immanuel Crystal Lake IL • (815)459-1441 • (RF 2000)
**DAHN JULIE ANNE** (314)968-1398
1351-C Mc Cutcheon Rd Saint Louis MO 63144 • mjdahn@juno.com • SI • Tchr • Good Shepherd Collinsville IL • (618)344-3151 • (RF 1997)
**DAHN MARY L** (810)228-3998
39605 Chaffer Dr Clinton Township MI 48038-2623 • MI • Tchr • St Luke Clinton Township MI • (810)791-1151 • (AA 1982 MAT)
**DAHN MICHAEL R** (815)568-0306
333 E Jackson St Apt 2E Marengo IL 60152-3117 • NI • Tchr • Zion Marengo IL • (815)568-5156 • (RF 1999)
**DAIL CHRISTINE MARIE**
1726 Cason Trl Murfreesboro TN 37128-5032 • MO • Tchr • Trinity Saint Louis MO • (314)621-0228 • (MQ 1996)
**DALEY JEFFREY D DR** (512)339-4880
610 Don Hovy Dr Valparaiso IN 46383 • daleyj@concordia.edu • IN • Trinity Saint Louis MO • (RF 1966 MED PHD)
**DALEY SHEILA R** (262)650-9265
2114B Mac Arthur Rd Waukesha WI 53188 • SW • Tchr • Elm Grove Elm Grove WI • (262)797-2970 • (RF 1974 MED)
**DALLMANN LA VERNE M** (248)689-9333
4115 Washington Crescent Dr Troy MI 48098 • MI • Tchr • Michigan Ann Arbor MI • (CQ 1998)
**DALPINI SHARON N** (630)851-6080
1585 Kaimy Ct Aurora IL 60504-7538 • NI • Tchr • Immanuel Batavia IL • (630)406-0157 • (S 1978)
**DAMERY DOROTHY A** (217)875-4956
200 Hickory Point Ct Forsyth IL 62535-9707 • dodamery@aol.com • CI • Tchr • Lutheran School Asso Decatur IL • (217)233-2001 • (CQ 1993)
**DAMMAN SANDRA KAY** (419)598-8855
16 - 478 V Rt 1 Napoleon OH 43545 • brookedamman@hotmail.com • OH • Tchr • St John Napoleon OH • (419)598-8702 • (CQ 1992 MED)
**DAMMANN DEAN W DR** (714)544-7169
14772 Briarcliff Pl Tustin CA 92780-6639 • deand12@aol.com • PSW • EM • (S 1952 MED LITTD)
**DANIEL CATHERINE SUE**
771 Aster St #177 Oxnard CA 93030 • PSW • Tchr • St John Oxnard CA • (805)983-0330 • (S 1999)
**DANIELL SHERI L**
C/O Emmanuel Lutheran Church 800 S Militay St Dearborn MI 48124 • MI • Tchr • Emmanuel Dearborn MI • (313)565-4002 • (AA 1992)
**DANKENBRING DAVID A** (216)227-0807
2200 Concord Dr Cleveland OH 44107-5375 • ddank5@flash.net • OH • Tchr • St Paul Lakewood OH • (216)521-5610 • (S 1977)
**DANKENBRING ELIZABETH ANNE** (402)768-6461
1145 Olive Ave Hebron NE 68370-1733 • NEB • Tchr • Deshler Lutheran Sch Deshler NE • (402)365-7858 • (S 1986)
**DANLEY SUSAN KATHERINE** (217)352-5540
3808 Clubhouse Dr Champaign IL 61821-9769 • CI • 06/1998 06/2000 • (CQ 1993 MA)
**DANNER CHRISTOPHER B** (815)943-7678
1412 - 9th St Harvard IL 60033-3686 • NI • Tchr • Zion Marengo IL • (815)568-6564 • (RF 1996)
**DANZ SHIRLEY M** (517)754-1034
8860 E Washington Rd Saginaw MI 48601-9690 • sdanz@stlorenz.org • MI • Tchr • St Lorenz Frankenmuth MI • (517)652-6141 • (RF 1963 MED)
**DAPELO MATTHEW C** (414)332-2955
2411 N Cramer St Milwaukee WI 53211 • SW • Tchr • St Peter-Immanuel Milwaukee WI • (414)353-6800 • (S 1999)
**DARDEEN PHYLLIS JOAN** (812)423-1912
1704 Russell Ave Evansville IN 47720-8235 • IN • Tchr • Trinity Evansville IN • (812)867-5279 • (RF 1962 MS)
**DARLING BRAD DAVIS** (714)635-7105
408 N Janss St Anaheim CA 92805-2527 • PSW • Tchr • Zion Anaheim CA • (714)535-3600 • (IV 1996 MED)
**DARROHN AMBER MAE** (402)476-8424
1515 Hilltop Rd Apt 103 Lincoln NE 68521-7406 • adarrohn@lps.org • NEB • Tchr • Trinity Lincoln NE • (402)466-1800 • (S 1999)
**DART ANNE L** (217)787-9186
1115 Rantoul Springfield IL 62704 • ald@usiw.net • CI • Tchr • Concordia Springfield IL • (217)529-3307 • (S 1962 MSED)
**DART JASON S** (314)382-2124
7322 Burrwood Dr Apt B Saint Louis MO 63121-1522 • jdart@usiw.net • NEB • 06/2000 • (S 1998)
**DARTMANN SHELLEY K** (402)592-2336
11074 V St Omaha NE 68137-3714 • jsdartmann@juno.com • NEB • Tchr • Abundant Life Omaha NE • (402)592-8005 • (S 1989)
**DATHE LOREN J*** (219)622-6830
604 Countryside Dr Ossian IN 46777-9395 • IN • 06/1998 06/2000 • (S 1984 MA)
**DAUGHERTY LAURA JO** (314)281-2223
6404 High Meadow Dr O Fallon MO 63366-7825 • teachpeljd@aol.com • MO • Tchr • Immanuel Wentzville MO • (636)327-4416 • (RF 1985)
**DAUGHERTY TAMARA S** (352)840-0610
1547 SE 27th St Apt F Ocala FL 34471-6062 • FG • Tchr • St John Ocala FL • (352)629-1794 • (S 1990)
**DAUTENHAHN ELMER H** (636)464-1765
3750 Paulina Dr Arnold MO 63010-4227 • MO • EM • (RF 1945 MED)
**DAVIDSMEYER DIANN R** (812)372-1397
1943 Chandler Ln Columbus IN 47203-4014 • IN • Tchr • St Peter Columbus IN • (812)372-5266 • (S 1973 MS)
**DAVIS CHRISTINE SANDRA** (219)471-8067
1409 Sycamore Dr Fort Wayne IN 46825-4730 • wdjd4us.@juno.com • IN • Tchr • St John Monroeville IN • (219)639-6404 • (PO 1994)
**DAVIS DARLENE B** (402)371-9659
83479 556th Ave Norfolk NE 68701-1521 • jtdne@kdsi.net • NEB • Tchr • Christ Norfolk NE • (402)371-5536 • (S 1964)
**DAVIS JEFFREY MICHAEL** (248)879-3880
1061 Woodside Trail Dr # 52B Troy MI 48098-1321 • jdavis@lhsa.lhnw.com • MI • Tchr • LHS Northwest Rochester Hills MI • (810)852-6677 • (AA 1993)
**DAVIS KATHRYN RUTH** (734)379-5277
30172 Dover St Flat Rock MI 48134-1447 • MI • Tchr • St John New Boston MI • (734)654-6366 • (RF 1977)
**DAVIS MARK A**
2222 N Santiago Orange CA 92867 • aaron@doitnow.com • PSW • S Ex/S • Pacific Southwest Irvine CA • (949)854-3232 • (S 1981)
**DAVIS SHELLY** (801)272-3595
5860 S 1900 E Salt Lake City UT 84121-1354 • RM • Tchr • Salt Lake LHS Salt Lake City UT • (801)266-6676 • (AA 1990)
**DAVIS SHIRLEY A** (219)745-6807
4030 Weisser Park Ave Fort Wayne IN 46806-1815 • Shirley³Davis@juno.com • IN • Tchr • Bethlehem Fort Wayne IN • (219)456-3587 • (RF 1971 MS)
**DAVIS SHIRLEY ANN** (210)822-3263
118 Abiso Ave San Antonio TX 78209-5102 • TX • Tchr • Concordia San Antonio TX • (210)479-1477 • (CQ 1995)
**DAVIS TERRY M** (810)949-9261
23775 24 Mile Rd Macomb MI 48042-3303 • MI • Prin • St Peter Macomb MI • (810)781-9296 • (RF 1968 MA)
**DAVITT JILL MAXINE** (503)848-8483
18633 SW Mapleoak Ln #47 Aloha OR 97006 • NOW • Tchr • Pilgrim Beaverton OR • (503)644-8697 • (PO 1993)
**DAWURSK GLEN E** (715)675-5436
4009 Carl St Wausau WI 54403-2287 • glend@dwave.net • NW • Tchr • Trinity Wausau WI • (715)842-0769 • (S 1982)
**DE BERARD MARY IONE** (970)241-0990
515 Santa Clara Ave Grand Junction CO 81503-4803 • RM • Tchr • Messiah Grand Junction CO • (970)245-2838 • (S 1962)
**DE BLOCK LYDIA**
2776 Eastview Saskatoon SK 57J 3H5 CANADA • CNH • Tchr • St Peter Lodi CA • (209)333-2225 • (SP 1986)
**DE BOARD CHRISTINA KAY** (618)532-6930
529 W 2nd St Centralia IL 62801-3428 • deboard@isbe.accessus.net • SI • Tchr • Trinity Centralia IL • (618)532-5434 • (RF 1990)
**DE BOER KRISTINE K** (678)560-0347
2582 Morgan Lake Dr Marietta GA 30066 • kkdeboer@hotmail.com • FG • Tchr • Faith Marietta GA • (770)973-8877 • (S 1986)
**DE HART WILLIAM C** (812)477-7648
5021 Shoreline Ter Evansville IN 47715-7650 • IN • Tchr • Our Redeemer Evansville IN • (812)476-9991 • (MQ 1997)
**DE LA CERDA TERRI AYNNE** (713)721-3537
4414 Osby Dr Houston TX 77096 • TX • Tchr • Bethany Houston TX • (713)695-2933 • (AU 1996)
**DE LAET BRIAN D**
Azabu Chuo Building 607 2-9-8 Azabu Juban Minato-Ku Tokyo 106 JAPAN • NEB • S Miss • Nebraska Seward NE • (S 1986)
**DE LAGE DEBORAH LYNN** (313)561-3504
21711 Francis St Dearborn MI 48124-2933 • dldelage@hotmail.com • MI • Tchr • Christ The King Southgate MI • (734)285-9697 • (RF 1975)
**DE LELLIS JENNIFER MICHELLE** (253)573-9058
3202 S Mason Ave #N201 Tacoma WA 98409 • NOW • 07/1999 • (S 1998)
**DE MAIO VIRGINIA C** (301)464-1237
6212 Gideon St Bowie MD 20720-3864 • SE • Tchr • Ascension Landover Hills MD • (301)577-0500 • (BR 1978 MED)
**DE MEYERE ROGER**
52348 Walnut Dr Chesterfield MI 48047-4548 • MI • Tchr • Special Ed Ministrie Detroit MI • (313)368-1220 • (RF 1970 MSW)
**DE PEW MARY** (812)876-8472
6501 Rhinestone Dr Ellettsville IN 47429-9695 • IN • 09/1998 • (RF 1965)
**DE REMER MARK ALAN** (503)761-8054
8019 SE 141st Ave Portland OR 97236 • NOW • SHS/C • Northwest Portland OR • (CQ 1994 MA MBA MA)
**DE SIMPELARE SUSAN M** (330)677-9956
388 Adamle Dr Kent OH 44240-2010 • OH • Tchr • Redeemer Cuyahoga Falls OH • (330)923-1280 • (AA 1991)
**DE VRIES HENRY A** (516)935-0290
36 Raymond St Hicksville NY 11801-4332 • AT • Tchr • Trinity Hicksville NY • (516)931-2211 • (CQ 1998)
**DE WERFF KAROL K** (217)563-2856
17255 N 21st Ave Nokomis IL 62075-3606 • SI • Tchr • St Paul Nokomis IL • (217)563-2487 • (RF 1980)
**DE WITT RICHARD** (847)895-8975
1031 Lighthouse Dr Schaumburg IL 60193 • rgdewitt@yahoo.com • NI • Tchr • Immanuel Palatine IL • (847)359-1549 • (CQ 1999 MS)
**DE LA MOTTE HEIDI R**
5812 N Walnut Rd Turlock CA 95382 • delamotteh@aol.com • CNH • 07/2000 • (IV 1993 MA)
**DEADMOND JANA S** (618)483-9430
308 S 4th St Altamont IL 62411-1118 • jsdeadmond@yahoo.com • CI • Tchr • Altamont Altamont IL • (618)483-6428 • (CQ 1996)
**DEAN BRENDA KAY** (219)365-5165
9390 Northcote Ave Saint John IN 46373-9501 • mbd324@cs.com • IN • 11/1999 • (RF 1986)
**DEAN SHANNON MICHELLE** (210)682-7268
9206 Valley Dale San Antonio TX 78250 • TX • Tchr • Shepherd Of The Hill San Antonio TX • (210)614-3741 • (AU 1994)

**DEARDOFF LAURA R**
9333 N 156th St Bennington NE 68007-2105 • NEB • Tchr • Zion Omaha NE • (402)731-1418 • (WN 1985 MS)

**DEAVER SARAH GINA** (206)525-7407
PO Box 2086 Kirkland WA 98083-2086 • NOW • Tchr • Concordia Seattle WA • (206)525-7407 • (S 1999)

**DEBRICK BARBARA J** 402)470-3389
3727 NW 50th Lincoln NE 68524 • NEB • 09/1999 • (S 1970)

**DEBRICK MARC W** (636)447-7909
1131 Claycrest Cir Saint Charles MO 63304 • mdebrick@aol.com • MO • Prin • Zion Harvester MO • (314)441-7424 • (WN 1984 MS)

**DECHEIM SANDRA**
PO Box 595 Hartland MI 48353-0595 • MI • Tchr • St Paul Northville MI • (248)349-3146 • (RF 1963)

**DECKER ELIZABETH D** (612)368-3279
1725 White Oak Dr Chaska MN 55318-1444 • MNS • Tchr • St John Chaska MN • (612)448-2433 • (RF 1983)

**DEDE ALBERT W** (920)261-4631
221 Margaret St Watertown WI 53098-2114 • SW • EM • (RF 1947)

**DEDOR RHONDA L** (319)422-5915
701 Jefferson St West Union IA 52175 • IE • Tchr • Open Arms West Union IA • (319)422-3393 • (S 1976 MCMU)

**DEETER CHRISTOPHER L** (402)643-4442
741 N 3rd St Seward NE 68434 • NEB • SHS/C • Nebraska Seward NE • (S 1986 MSED)

**DEHNE JOHN A** (209)832-1337
61 W Deerwood Ln Tracy CA 95376-2927 • CNH • Tchr • St Paul Tracy CA • (209)835-7438 • (RF 1995)

**DEHNE KATHERINE A**
417 Plum St Collinsville IL 62234-3345 • SI • Tchr • Holy Cross Collinsville IL • (618)344-3145 • (RF 1992)

**DEHNING MERVIN WAINE** (956)687-4879
413 W Hibiscus Ave Mc Allen TX 78501-1820 • stpaulmca@juno.com • TX • Tchr • St Paul Mc Allen TX • (956)682-2201 • (S 1980)

**DEINERT MARILYN A** (909)658-0459
1790 E Campus Way Hemet CA 92544-3123 • mdeinert@hotmail.com • PSW • Tchr • St John Hemet CA • (909)652-5909 • (CQ 1989 MS)

**DEIST CARRIE S** (281)286-8514
15800 Hwy 3 Apt 522 Webster TX 77598 • TX • Tchr • Lutheran South Acade Houston TX • (281)464-8299 • (S 2000)

**DEITZ LORI JEAN**
PO Box 158 Butternut WI 54514-0158 • NW • 08/1999 • (MQ 1989)

**DELLAR FRANCES ANN** (847)823-1777
1301 W Touhy Ave Apt 211 Park Ridge IL 60068-3162 • conlutsch@juno.com • NI • Tchr • Concord Addison IL • (630)543-6404 • (S 1971)

**DELLINGER CAROL C** (614)873-5542
16750 Middleburg-Plain City Rd Marysville OH 43040 • carolde@attglobal.net • OH • Tchr • St Paul Milford Center OH • (937)349-5939 • (S 1970)

**DELMOTTE KAREN M** (810)786-6908
51528 Shadywood Dr Macomb MI 48042-4293 • kadelmotte@hotmail.com • MI • Tchr • Trinity Utica MI • (810)731-4490 • (AA 1984)

**DELVENTHAL WAYNE H** (808)637-9295
PO Box 633 Waialua HI 96791-0633 • waynelaine@hawaii.rr.com • CNH • EM • (S 1951 MSED)

**DEMBECK DAVID E** (810)954-9041
66 Moross St Mount Clemens MI 48043-2210 • vdembeck@juno.com • MI • Tchr • St Peter Macomb MI • (810)781-9296 • (S 1974 MA)

**DEMSKE ROBERT M** (812)522-1466
1021 Gaiser Dr Seymour IN 47274-3154 • IN • EM • (RF 1940 MA)

**DENNEY REBECCA RUTH** (913)680-0671
1707 Remington Ct Leavenworth KS 66048-5340 • rdenney@kc.rr.com • KS • Tchr • St Paul Leavenworth KS • (913)682-5553 • (AU 1992)

**DENOW DENNIS** (909)338-5458
PO Box 2410 Crestline CA 92325-2410 • denowdk@cci.christ.edu • PSW • SHS/C • Pacific Southwest Irvine CA • (949)854-3232 • (RF 1970 MED)

**DENZLER DOUGLAS M**
152 Mill Rd Waconia MN 55387 • denzler@micron.net • MNS • 06/2000 • (S 1995)

**DETERDING PATRICIA MARIE** (314)505-7733
15C Founders Way Saint Louis MO 63105 • MO • Tchr • St John Saint Louis MO • (314)773-0126 • (SP 1999)

**DETERLING LILLIAN M** (214)348-8135
11114 Scotsmeadow Dr Dallas TX 75218-1358 • TX • EM • (RF 1955)

**DETMER MARGARET A** (402)663-4303
1491 Co Rd 30 Weston NE 68070-4038 • MO • Tchr • Missouri Saint Louis MO • (314)317-4550 • (S 1994)

**DETTMAN KELLI S**
Holy Cross Luth Church 650 NE 135th St North Miami FL 33161-7519 • FG • Tchr • Holy Cross North Miami FL • (305)893-0851 • (BR 1994)

**DEUTSCH CATHLYN M** (218)251-1076
17007 Camberwell Green Ln Houston TX 77070-1815 • TX • Tchr • Trinity Spring TX • (281)376-5810 • (S 1974)

**DEVINE RITA JO** (217)787-3241
3125 Temple Dr Springfield IL 62704-5424 • chem3tchr@juno.com • CI • Tchr • LHS Springfield IL • (217)546-6363 • (S 1981)

**DEXHEIMER LARRY J** (352)351-8539
2152 SE 7th Ter Ocala FL 34471-5368 • ldex@aol.com • FG • Tchr • St John LHS Ocala FL • (352)622-7275 • (S 1967)

**DHYNE JAMES T**
25 North Rd Bronxville NY 10708 • AT • Tchr • The Village Bronxville NY • (914)337-0207 • (S 1972 MA)

**DIAZ JOSE J**
2121 N Jones Blvd Bldg 3 #132 Las Vegas NV 89108 • PSW • Tchr • Faith LHS Las Vegas NV • (702)804-4400 • (RF 1999)

**DIAZ LINDA K** (210)616-0385
6135 Feather Nest Ln San Antonio TX 78233 • TX • Tchr • Shepherd Of The Hill San Antonio TX • (210)614-3741 • (AU 1994)

**DIBOS WAYNE W** (702)648-3261
6521 Starcrest Dr Las Vegas NV 89108-2713 • PSW • Tchr • First Good Shepherd Las Vegas NV • (702)382-8610 • (S 1979)

**DICKE MARK LOWELL** (281)482-1583
2701 W Bay Area Blvd #2714 Webster TX 77598 • chmld@aol.com • TX • Tchr • Lutheran South Acade Houston TX • (281)464-8299 • (SP 1990)

**DICKERSON AARON L** (901)332-3858
C/O Cross Of Calvary 4327 Elvis Presley Blvd Memphis TN 38116-6405 • MDS • Prin • Cross Of Calvary Memphis TN • (901)396-5566 • (S 1982)

**DICKERSON JOE B DR** (818)951-5810
7741 Apperson St Tujunga CA 91042-2110 • jdicker452@aol.com • PSW • Tchr • Ascension Torrance CA • (310)793-0071 • (CQ 1989 MED EDD)

**DICKERSON ROBERT E**
13156 Carter St Overland Park KS 66213-4654 • MO • Tchr • Calvary Kansas City MO • (816)444-6908 • (RF 1974)

**DICKHUDT ROBERT J** (313)837-2280
15320 Glastonbury Ave Detroit MI 48223-2211 • b-datdetwluv@juno.com • MI • EM • (S 1958 MA MA)

**DICKHUDT STEVEN T** (612)484-3883
730 County Road B2 W Roseville MN 55113-3422 • MNS • Tchr • Concordia Academy Roseville MN • (612)484-8429 • (SP 1975)

**DICKINSON MELINDA S** (616)941-4232
1018 Randolph St Traverse City MI 49684-2121 • MI • Tchr • Trinity Traverse City MI • (231)946-2720 • (S 1976)

**DIECKHOFF BILL D**
4412 Saint James Pl Wichita KS 67226-1432 • KS • Prin • Holy Cross Wichita KS • (316)684-4431 • (S 1960 MA)

**DIECKHOFF BRENT W** (316)618-9045
101 S Battin Wichita KS 67208 • btdcough@showme.net • KS • P/Tchr • Holy Cross Wichita KS • (316)684-4431 • (S 1990)

**DIEHL JUDY** (408)247-3075
2353 Pauline Dr San Jose CA 95124-1039 • CNH • 11/1999 • (RF 1968)

**DIELMANN MARILYN K** (714)939-8661
1910 W Palmyra #100 Orange CA 92868-3756 • PSW • Tchr • St Paul Orange CA • (714)921-3188 • (RF 1970)

**DIEPENBROCK RAY LEE** (507)776-8316
218 N 2nd Ave E Truman MN 56088 • raynina@frontiernet.net • MNS • P/Tchr • St Paul Truman MN • (507)776-6541 • (S 1964 MA)

**DIERDORF NANCY C** (612)475-3006
2110 Urbandale Ln N Plymouth MN 55447-2030 • MNS • 10/1999 • (S 1974 MSED)

**DIERKER WILMA M** (310)677-7653
1145 Walnut St Inglewood CA 90301-3835 • PSW • EM • (S 1942)

**DIERKS DAVID J** (219)728-5123
320 N 5th Decatur IN 46733 • IN • Prin • Zion Decatur IN • (219)547-4248 • (S 1975 MA)

**DIERKS EUGENE D** (507)436-5262
PO Box 21 Northrop MN 56075-0021 • MNS • P/Tchr • St James Northrop MN • (507)436-5289 • (SP 1971 MSED)

**DIERKS JULIE A** (612)864-3647
1425 Knight Ave N Glencoe MN 55336-1537 • jules3ad@hotmail.com • MNS • Tchr • Trinity Waconia MN • (952)442-4165 • (SP 1981)

**DIERKS KEVIN GENE** (972)761-0548
1221 Northlake Dr Richardson TX 75080 • TX • Tchr • Zion Dallas TX • (214)363-1630 • (MQ 1994 MA)

**DIERKS MARKHAM W** (612)864-3647
1425 Knight Ave N Glencoe MN 55336-1537 • MNS • Tchr • First Glencoe MN • (320)864-3317 • (SP 1985)

**DIERKS WERNER E** (219)493-3642
7609 Preakness Cv Fort Wayne IN 46815-8705 • IN • EM • (RF 1944 MS)

**DIETERS TROY F**
PO Box 6941 Colorado Springs CO 80934-6941 • RM • Tchr • Rock Of Ages Colorado Springs CO • (719)632-9394 • (S 1993)

**DIETRICH BRIAN R** (805)527-6039
5781 Pittman St Simi Valley CA 93063-3560 • brdietrich@aol.com • PSW • Prin • Good Shepherd Simi Valley CA • (805)526-2482 • (S 1965 MA)

**DIETRICH CLIFFORD A** (219)486-8881
6014 Andro Run Fort Wayne IN 46815-8425 • cliff.dietrich@in.lcms.org • IN • Tchr • Assoc For Elementary Fort Wayne IN • (219)422-9662 • (RF 1958 MA EDS)

**DIETRICH JENNIFER LYNN** (517)652-2158
2141 Maple Rd Saginaw MI 48601 • jdplaid@juno.com • MI • Tchr • St Michael Richville MI • (517)868-4791 • (AA 1997)

**DIETRICH JULIE L** (812)378-4743
3664 Greenbriar Dr Columbus IN 47203-2540 • IN • Tchr • St Peter Columbus IN • (812)342-4921 • (RF 1987)

**DIETRICH SARAH G** (909)736-9876
784 Donatello Dr Corona CA 92882 • PSW • Tchr • St Paul Orange CA • (714)921-3188 • (IV 1996)

**DIETRICH TREVOR ROY** (909)736-9876
784 Donatello Dr Corona CA 92882 • PSW • Tchr • St Paul Orange CA • (714)637-2640 • (IV 1997)

**DIETZ JAMES C** (414)762-7558
3100 E James Dr Oak Creek WI 53154-6536 • SW • Tchr • Martin LHS Greendale WI • (414)421-4000 • (S 1974 MED)

**DIFATTA DAVID C** (810)758-3125
22593 Cunningham Ave Warren MI 48091-2576 • MI • Tchr • Peace Warren MI • (810)751-8010 • (S 1971)

**DIFATTA REBECCA LYNNE** (810)758-3125
22593 Cunningham Warren MI 48091 • MI • Tchr • Christ King Southgate MI • (734)285-9695 • (AA 2000)

**DIGGS REBECCA L**
1801 Mississippi Jefferson City MO 65101-2368 • MO • Tchr • Trinity Jefferson City MO • (573)636-6750 • (S 1998)

**DILLAHAY KATHLEEN M** (314)788-2519
PO Box 19 Uniontown MO 63783-0019 • MO • Tchr • Immanuel Perryville MO • (573)547-8317 • (CO 1973 MA)

**DILLON DEBRA JOY** (913)831-7508
5012 Broadmoor #191 Mission KS 66202 • dillontimm@juno.com • KS • Immanuel Perryville MO • (MQ 1994)

**DILLON WENDY JOY** (505)271-1685
3304 Candlelight Dr NE Albuquerque NM 87111-5011 • rdillon@eudoramail.com • RM • Tchr • Christ Albuquerque NM • (505)884-3876 • (S 1986)

**DIMMEL-SCHULTZ MARCIA KAY** (507)234-5632
203 Prairie Ln Janesville MN 56048-9366 • jmschult@frontiernet.net • MNS • Tchr • Trinity Janesville MN • (507)231-6646 • (SP 1972)

**DINDA LAURA J** (512)836-8456
1103 E Applegate Dr Austin TX 78753-4005 • TX • Mem C • Redeemer Austin TX • (512)459-1500 • (SP 1964)

**DINGER RALPH E** (623)933-7209
12432 N Augusta Dr Sun City AZ 85351-3354 • PSW • EM • (S 1950 MED)

**DIPPEL LISA K*** (217)394-2575
412 N Pine St PO Box 182 Buckley IL 60918-0182 • ladippel@illicom.net • CI • P/Tchr • St John Buckley IL • (217)394-2422 • (RF 1982 MSED)

**DIRKS DENNIS J** (209)836-0313
650 Petrig St Tracy CA 95376 • CNH • Prin • Our Savior Livermore CA • (925)447-1246 • (SP 1971 MS)

**DIRKS KEITH R** (402)435-6684
1931 Hartley St Lincoln NE 68521-1734 • NEB • Tchr • Trinity Lincoln NE • (402)466-1800 • (S 1978 MA)

**DITTMAN JAMES B** (414)321-0030
2218 S 79th St West Allis WI 53219-1706 • jdittman@execpc.com • SW • Tchr • St Paul West Allis WI • (414)541-6251 • (MQ 1984)

**DITTMAN MARY KAY** (810)727-1629
68354 Rosewood Ln Richmond MI 48062-1460 • MI • Tchr • St Peter Richmond MI • (810)727-9080 • (AA 1985)

**DITTMAR BARBARA** (203)270-9124
C/O Immanuel Lutheran School 35 Foster St Danbury CT 06810-7836 • NE • Tchr • Immanuel Danbury CT • (203)748-7823 • (BR 1980)

**DITTMAR GARY D**
3835 West 213th St Fairview Park OH 44126 • OH • Prin • Lakewood Lakewood OH • (216)221-6941 • (S 1975 MS)

**DITTMER EMILY**
6236 Oakland 3N Saint Louis MO 63139 • MO • Tchr • Christ Community Kirkwood MO • (314)822-7774 • (S 1998)

**DITTMER JOEL T** (972)395-0752
4107 Province Dr Carrollton TX 75007-1639 • jtditt@popcs.net • TX • 01/2000 • (AU 1987 MA)

**DITTMER OMAR H** (941)646-5968
1622 Monterey Ln Lakeland FL 33813-2331 • godittmer@aol.com • FG • EM • (S 1954 MA)

**DIXON TERESA DIANE** (773)651-9045
8336 S May St #2 Chicago IL 60620-3113 • NI • Tchr • Bethel Chicago IL • (773)252-1104 • (RF 1992)

**DOBBERFUHL ALMA M** (608)754-0396
2707 N Lexington Dr Apt 316 Janesville WI 53545-0341 • SW • EM • (RF 1943 MLS)

**DOBBERFUHL MARJORIE LEE** (262)781-3771
17510 Bedford Dr Brookfield WI 53045-1300 • tomdobberfuhl@aol.com • SW • Tchr • Our Redeemer Wauwatosa WI • (414)258-4558 • (RF 1970 MA)

**DOBBERFUHL WALTER F** (414)258-8053
2516 N 66th St Wauwatosa WI 53213-1435 • SW • EM • (RF 1943 MA)

**DOBBERSTEIN MARY ESTHER** (715)526-5732
N3060 River Dr Shawano WI 54166-4243 • dobberl@frontiernet.net • NW • Tchr • St James Shawano WI • (715)524-4213 • (SP 1969)

**DOBBERTIEN GLENDA LYNN** (308)284-0947
409 E 9th St Ogallala NE 69153 • revddobb@yahoo.com • NEB • Tchr • St Paul Ogallala NE • (308)284-2944 • (S 1966)

**DOBBINS KATHERINE** (817)263-5108
7717 Grassland Dr Fort Worth TX 76133-7923 • TX • Tchr • St Paul Fort Worth TX • (817)332-2281 • (WN 1985)

**DOBLER LORI A** (818)364-1455
14344 Foothill Blvd Unit 506 Sylmar CA 91342-7563 • PSW • Tchr • Los Angeles Junior/S Sylmar CA • (818)362-5861 • (RF 1983 MA)

**DOBLER STAN R** (818)364-1455
14344 Foothill Blvd Unit 506 Sylmar CA 91342-7563 • PSW • Tchr • Los Angeles Junior/S Sylmar CA • (818)362-5861 • (S 1977)

**DOCKERY DANIEL L** (616)941-8428
3100 Silver Farms Ln Traverse City MI 49684-8281 • DLDockery@aol.com • MI • Tchr • Trinity Traverse City MI • (231)946-2720 • (RF 1971 MSW)

**DODIC ERIN L** (512)989-1125
2323 Wells Branch Pkwy B203 Austin TX 78728 • TX • Tchr • Redeemer Austin TX • (512)451-6478 • (AU 1998)

**DODSON KRISTEN L** (734)326-2824
3605 Hannan Apt 307 Wayne MI 48184 • A25151@aol.com • MI • Tchr • Detroit Urban Detroit MI • (313)582-9900 • (AA 1996)

**DOEBLER DAVID G**
16260 Fairmount Dr Detroit MI 48205-1452 • MI • Tchr • Michigan Ann Arbor MI • (RF 1988)

**DOEBLER LYNDA** (248)651-9226
828 Miller Ave Rochester MI 48307-1609 • MI • EM • (S 1973 MAT)

**DOEDERLEIN-WYANT KAREN ANN** (941)676-7300
5018 Avon St Lake Wales FL 33853-8751 • FG • P/Tchr • Lake Wales Lake Wales FL • (863)676-4715 • (RF 1979 MAT)

**DOEHRMANN LOREN** (812)867-2632
12885 Tibarand Rd Evansville IN 47725 • janlorend@aol.com • IN • EM • (S 1951 MA)

**DOEHRMANN LYNNE** (319)668-2837
PO Box 445 Williamsburg IA 52361-0445 • IE • Tchr • Lutheran Interparish Williamsburg IA • (319)668-1711 • (S 1991)

**DOELL LORRAINE K**
406A E Park St Bonduel WI 54107 • NW • Tchr • St Paul Bonduel WI • (715)758-8559 • (MQ 1987)

**DOELLING MICHELLE LYNN**
112 Westscott Dr #A Madison AL 35758-1964 • SO • Tchr • Grace Huntsville AL • (256)881-0553 • (S 1999)

**DOELLINGER DOUGLAS** (717)227-0571
13322 Spice Ln New Freedom PA 17349-9125 • dddoel@nfde.net • SE • Tchr • Southeastern Alexandria VA • (RF 1978 MA)

**DOEPKE KONRAD H**
3084 Sunlight Ln Conover WI 54519-9541 • SW • EM • (RF 1957 MA)

**DOEPNER MARK D** (219)747-9723
2115 Saint Louis Ave Fort Wayne IN 46819-2028 • nate7791@aol.com • IN • Tchr • Unity Fort Wayne IN • (219)744-0459 • (RF 1976 MS)

**DOEPNER SUE ANN E** (219)747-9723
2115 Saint Louis Ave Fort Wayne IN 46819-2028 • suedoepner@aol.com • IN • Tchr • Mount Calvary Fort Wayne IN • (219)747-4121 • (RF 1977)

**DOERING RACHEL J** (501)374-8980
414 E 6th St Apt G Little Rock AR 72202-2582 • rjdoering@att.net • MDS • Tchr • Christ Little Rock AR • (501)663-5212 • (S 1995 MED)

**DOERING RUTH E** (409)542-2688
427 N Leon St Giddings TX 78942-2637 • TX • EM • (RF 1947)

**DOERING SANDRA K DR** (512)365-8021
1301 Sagewood Dr Taylor TX 76574-7010 • sdoering@aol.com • TX • SHS/C • Texas Austin TX • (RF 1971 MED DED)

**DOERING WILLARD E*** (417)887-7115
1715 E Briar St Springfield MO 65804-7756 • MO • EM • (RF 1952)

**DOERING WILLIAM O** (580)762-8284
1038 N 3rd St Ponca City OK 74601-2649 • djdwod@poncacity.net • OK • EM • (RF 1952 MS)

**DOERR PAUL A** (414)327-6894
2945 S 45th St Milwaukee WI 53219-3413 • SW • Tchr • Martin LHS Greendale WI • (414)421-4000 • (S 1980 MS)

**DOHRING MARGARETE** (360)427-0925
224 W D St Shelton WA 98584-3022 • NOW • Tchr • Mount Olive Shelton WA • (360)427-3165 • (PO 1984 MED)

**DOHRMANN AARON C** (517)868-4055
1684 Meridian Reese MI 48757 • MI • EM • (RF 1953 MA)

**DOHRMANN JANE M** (517)868-3588
2213 S Van Buren Rd Reese MI 48757-9202 • nnamrhod@aol.com • MI • Tchr • Trinity Reese MI • (517)868-4501 • (RF 1976)

**DOLAK E DAVID DR** (402)643-2493
1407 N 1st St Seward NE 68434-1013 • ddolak@seward.cune.edu • NEB • SHS/C • Nebraska Seward NE • (S 1964 MS MA DED)

**DOLDE DONOVAN JOHN**
921 Hillgrove Ln Auburndale FL 33823-3602 • siestakeydjd@hotmail.com • FG • Tchr • Grace Winter Haven FL • (941)293-9744 • (RF 1995)

**DOLDE MARK DAVID** (219)483-4135
3315 Collegiate Ct Fort Wayne IN 46805 • IN • Tchr • Concordia LHS Fort Wayne IN • (219)483-1102 • (RF 1994)

**DOLLASE TINA MARIE** (303)637-9323
63 S 22nd Ave Apt D-4 Brighton CO 80601-2536 • tdteach@aol.com • RM • Tchr • Zion Brighton CO • (303)659-3443 • (CQ 1998)

**DOMBKOWSKI AMY MARIE** (765)742-6418
811 S 9th St Lafayette IN 47905 • jdom49@peoplepc.com • IN • Tchr • St James Lafayette IN • (765)742-6464 • (CQ 1999)

**DOMEIER SUE ANN** (312)462-9375
25W689 Mac Arthur Ave Carol Stream IL 60188-4560 • NI • Tchr • St John Wheaton IL • (630)668-0701 • (RF 1977 MA)

**DOMKE KRISTIN MARIE** (727)866-6747
5465 21st Way S #1007 Saint Petersburg FL 33712 • FG • Tchr • Grace Saint Petersburg FL • (727)527-6213 • (SP 1995)

**DOMMER TIMOTHY A** (281)351-7072
14127 Pollux Ct Tomball TX 77375-2303 • TX • Mem C • Salem Tomball TX • (281)351-8223 • (S 1971)

**DOMROESE KENNETH A** (708)386-1687
712 N Kenilworth Ave Oak Park IL 60302-1517 • NI • EM • (RF 1955 PHD)

**DOMSCH CHRISTOPHER L** (816)781-1966
1955 S La Frenz Rd Liberty MO 64068-8358 • cdomsch@lhskc.com • MO • Tchr • Kansas City LHS Kansas City MO • (816)241-5478 • (S 1972)

**DONAL KARYN MARIE** (248)442-9260
20862 Kenwood Farmington Hills MI 48336-5534 • MI • Tchr • St Paul Farmington Hills MI • (248)474-2488 • (AA 1993)

**DONLON LYNEE M** (703)751-3357
225 S Whiting St #312 Alexandria VA 22304 • lmdonlon@webtv.net • SE • Tchr • Our Savior Arlington VA • (703)892-4846 • (BR 1991)

**DONNAY LINDA JEAN** (612)864-4159
1604 Birch Ave N Glencoe MN 55336-1150 • MNS • Tchr • First Glencoe MN • (320)864-3317 • (SP 1986 MS)

**DOPKE ROBERT A** (262)542-5222
2706 Darrell Dr Waukesha WI 53188-2027 • radopke@aol.com • SW • Tchr • Pilgrim Wauwatosa WI • (414)476-0736 • (RF 1979)

**DOPP SHERRY E** (517)782-3573
3685 W Primilia Ln Jackson MI 49201 • sdopp44@cs.com • MI • Tchr • Trinity Jackson MI • (517)750-2105 • (SP 1978 MA)

**DOREMUS PENELOPE REBECCA** (605)361-1263
6605 W Cheyenne Dr Sioux Falls SD 57106-1649 • SD • Tchr • Sioux Falls Sioux Falls SD • (605)335-1923 • (S 1992)

**DORING LOIS R** (973)347-3293
28 Musconetcong Ave Stanhope NJ 07874-2936 • NJ • Tchr • Our Savior Stanhope NJ • (201)347-1818 • (RF 1957)

**DORLAC BARBARA** (561)477-7081
9328 Sable Ridge Cir Apt C Boca Raton FL 33428-1446 • FG • Tchr • St Paul Boca Raton FL • (561)395-8548 • (RF 1970)

**DORN RICHARD J** (612)467-2428
PO Box 62 Norwood MN 55368-0062 • MNS • Tchr • Lutheran High Mayer MN • (612)657-2251 • (RF 1962 MED)

**DOROW SUSAN E**
15 Squaw Ct Warrenton MO 63383-7039 • MO • Tchr • Immanuel Wentzville MO • (636)327-4416 • (AA 1985)

**DORRE ADRIENNE T**
334 N Terrace Ave Mount Vernon NY 10550 • AT • 09/1999 • (BR 1990)

**DOSIEN ROBERT P** (618)259-6186
221 Riverwoods Cv East Alton IL 62024-1620 • SI • EM • (RF 1947 MA)

**DOUGHERTY WILLIAM D**
2023 Hwy B Perryville MO 63775-9101 • MO • EM • (S 1958 MA)

**DOWDING ROBERT E**
3522 SW 112th St Seattle WA 98146-1610 • NOW • Tchr • Seattle LHS Seattle WA • (206)937-7722 • (S 1970 MA MPE)

**DOYLE BARBARA E**
3240 Luther Rd Saginaw MI 48603-3215 • MI • Tchr • Valley Saginaw MI • (517)790-1676 • (MQ 1995)

**DOYLE FAITH J** (219)269-2150
1967 Chapman Lake Dr Warsaw IN 46582-7839 • adoyle@kconline.com • IN • Tchr • Redeemer Warsaw IN • (219)267-5656 • (MQ 1992)

**DOYLE LORI BETH**
2706 Badger Glen Pl Ontario CA 91761-0120 • PSW • Tchr • Lutheran High School La Verne CA • (909)593-4494 • (IV 1998)

**DOYLE THOMAS J DR** (949)643-0901
4 Shady Nook Aliso Viejo CA 92656-4231 • doyletj@cui.edu • PSW • SHS/C • Pacific Southwest Irvine CA • (949)854-3232 • (RF 1975 MS DED EDS)

**DRAEGER LINDA M** (818)994-3154
1830 Rory Ln Unit 6 Simi Valley CA 93063-4366 • PSW • Tchr • First Van Nuys CA • (818)786-3002 • (RF 1970 MA)

**DRAKE ALLISON M**
27010 Southwestern Redford MI 48239-2366 • MI • Tchr • Detroit Urban Detroit MI • (313)582-9900 • (AA 1987)

**DRAKE KRISTIN RENEE** (847)358-7648
139 E Heatherlea Dr Palatine IL 60067 • bkdrake99@juno.com • NI • Tchr • St Peter Arlington Heights IL • (847)253-6638 • (RF 1999)

**DRAVES THOMAS** (313)484-0660
1239 Rue Deauville Blvd Ypsilanti MI 48198-7545 • MI • Tchr • St Paul Ann Arbor MI • (734)665-0604 • (RF 1980 MSSED)

**DREES EMILY A** (512)835-7409
3401 Parmer Ln W #422 Austin TX 78727 • emmilita@juno.com • TX • Tchr • Trinity Waco TX • (254)772-7840 • (AU 1997)

**DREES JENNIFER R**
PO Box 148 Salix IA 51052-0148 • CI • Tchr • Concordia Peoria IL • (309)691-8921 • (SP 1996)

**DREESSEN CHARLES R** (636)349-4416
211 Laverne Dr Fenton MO 63026-4415 • MO • Tchr • Christ Community Kirkwood MO • (314)822-7774 • (RF 1972 MS)

**DREFKE GARY LESTER** (402)371-4489
2612 Crestview Rd Norfolk NE 68701 • NEB • Tchr • Christ Norfolk NE • (402)371-5536 • (S 1966 MA)

**DRENNON TERESA A** (210)558-9897
11210 Spring Crest St San Antonio TX 78249-2676 • TX • Tchr • Redeemer San Antonio TX • (210)735-9903 • (S 1980)

**DRESSER GARY J**
3651 Hollow Trail Ct Palm Harbor FL 34684 • FG • Prin • Grace Saint Petersburg FL • (727)527-1168 • (BR 1979 MA)

**DRESSLER DERWIN J** (206)473-2971
8023 A St S Tacoma WA 98408-5802 • NOW • Tchr • Concordia Tacoma WA • (253)475-9513 • (PO 1980)

**DRESSLER LINDA** (636)488-5808
308 E Booneslick Rd Jonesburg MO 63351-9769 • sdrev@jonesburg.net • MO • 10/1993 10/1999 • (RF 1975)

**DRESSLER RONALD L** (517)781-8980
2362 Manchester Dr Saginaw MI 48609 • MI • Prin • Bethlehem Saginaw MI • (517)755-1146 • (RF 1971 MA)

**DREVLOW HENRY J** (714)774-8146
2222 E Lizbeth Anaheim CA 92806 • renedrev@aol.com • PSW • Tchr • Zion Anaheim CA • (714)535-3600 • (RF 1963 MED)

**DREW LYNNE S**
320 Ridgelake Dr Metairie LA 70001-5316 • SO • Tchr • Trinity Baton Rouge LA • (225)272-3110 • (AA 1988)

**DREWS MARK ROGER**
801 De Mun Ave Saint Louis MO 63105-3168 • maro2065@email.msn.com • MO • 04/1999 • (SP 1988)

**DREWS NATALIE LOIS** (703)339-1266
7738 Effingham Sq Alexandria VA 22315-5918 • drews4@juno.com • SE • Tchr • Our Savior Arlington VA • (703)892-4846 • (RF 1968)

**DREWS RONALD S**
7584 Ashlar Ct Canal Winchester OH 43110 • OH • 06/1999 • (S 1976)

**DREYER DEBRA JO** (515)955-5508
2242 140th St Fort Dodge IA 50501-8514 • IW • Tchr • St Paul Fort Dodge IA • (515)955-7208 • (CQ 1993)

**DRIEMEIER CINDE L** (618)235-2925
500 Leawood Dr Swansea IL 62226-1925 • SI • 09/1983 09/1999 • (RF 1977)

**DRIER MARVIN D**
3091 W 750 N Decatur IN 46733-8868 • IN • Tchr • Wyneken Memorial Decatur IN • (219)639-6177 • (AA 1984)

**DRIESSNER JOHNNIE RAY DR** (503)667-2737
674 SW 7th St Gresham OR 97080-5371 • johnd@cu-portland.edu • NOW • SHS/C • Northwest Portland OR • (S 1978 DED)

**DRILLER CATHY ANN** (719)599-4675
5220 Park Vista Blvd Colorado Springs CO 80918-2447 • RM • Tchr • Immanuel Colorado Springs CO • (719)636-3681 • (S 1977 MA)

**DRINAN LORI JEAN**
2622 Chapel Dr E Saginaw MI 48603-2803 • MI • Tchr • Peace Saginaw MI • (517)792-2581 • (RF 1983)

**DRISKILL WILLIAM C DR** (512)486-1127
3400 N I H 35 Austin TX 78705-2702 • driskill@concordia.edu • TX • SHS/C • Texas Austin TX • (RF 1964 MA PHD)

**DROEGE ELEANOR** (301)422-2316
6710 W Park Dr Hyattsville MD 20782-1727 • SE • EM • (RF 1954 MED)

**DROEGE RALPH E DR** (812)667-6498
6879 State Rd 62 Dillsboro IN 47018-9143 • rdroege@scidata.com • IN • EM • (RF 1953 MED EDD LLD)

**DROEGEMUELLER KIM MARIE** (409)542-6208
RR 1 Box 164 Giddings TX 78942-9714 • TX • Tchr • St Paul Giddings TX • (409)366-2218 • (S 1998)

**DROEGEMUELLER SUSAN ELAINE** (956)565-6325
630 Moon Lake Dr N Weslaco TX 78596 • TX • Tchr • St Paul Harlingen TX • (956)423-3924 • (RF 1996)

**DROEGEMUELLER WILMA A** (217)792-3359
219 E Cooke St Mount Pulaski IL 62548-1209 • drgmller43@juno.com • CI • Tchr • Zion Mount Pulaski IL • (217)792-5715 • (S 1965)

**DROOGSMA RUTH E** (612)315-4798
7825 N College Park Dr Brooklyn Park MN 55445-2444 • MNS • Tchr • St John Maple Grove MN • (612)420-2426 • (SP 1984)

**DRUMM DEBORAH K** (954)925-7825
2910 Pierce St Apt 202 Hollywood FL 33020-3864 • FG • Tchr • St Mark Hollywood FL • (954)922-7572 • (RF 1974)

**DUBBERKE ROBERT DALE*** (815)455-0470
463 Brook Dr Crystal Lake IL 60014 • coachd@owc.net • NI • Tchr • Immanuel Crystal Lake IL • (815)459-1444 • (S 1988)

**DUBBERKE SHERI J** (815)455-0470
463 Brook Dr Crystal Lake IL 60014 • coachd@owc.net • NI • Tchr • Immanuel Crystal Lake IL • (815)459-1444 • (S 1988)

**DUBE BEVERLY J** (512)821-3222
12166 Metric Blvd #149 Austin TX 78758 • storyteller@flashmail.com • TX • Tchr • Our Savior Austin TX • (512)836-9600 • (S 1968)

**DUBKE DARWIN C** (517)868-4988
3352 S Van Buren PO Box 26 Richville MI 48758-0026 • dar.dubke@juno.com • MI • EM • (RF 1959 MA)

**DUBKE LISA MARIE** (317)342-2004
2201 N Raceway Rd Indianapolis IN 46234 • jon.dubke@worldnet.att.net • IN • Tchr • Prince of Peace Martinsville IN • (317)342-2004 • (RF 1993 MA)

**DUCHOW CAROLYN** (414)421-4939
5673 Oxford Dr Greendale WI 53129-2560 • EN • 08/1997 • (S 1963 MSED)

**DUCHOW MARTIN C** (414)421-4939
5673 Oxford Dr Greendale WI 53129-2560 • martin.duchow@cuw.edu • SW • SHS/C • South Wisconsin Milwaukee WI • (414)464-8100 • (S 1964 MA EDD)

**DUDEK LORI J**
712 College Ave Howards Grove WI 53083-1207 • SW • Tchr • Lutheran HS Sheboygan WI • (920)452-3323 • (MQ 1993)

**DUDERSTADT LORNA** (423)553-9772
710 Astor Ln Chattanooga TN 37412-2507 • lduderstad@aol.com • MDS • Tchr • Lutheran Chattanooga TN • (423)622-3755 • (S 1970 MS MED)

**DUECK DANIEL** (714)540-9027
1555 Mesa Verde Dr E Apt 15E Costa Mesa CA 92626-5148 • PSW • Tchr • Christ Costa Mesa CA • (949)548-6866 • (S 1998)

**DUECK ERIN LYNN**
1555 Mesa Verde Dr E Apt 15E Costa Mesa CA 92626-5148 • PSW • Tchr • Christ Costa Mesa CA • (949)548-6866 • (S 1996)

**DUECK-STUEBER DENISE ANNE** (801)954-8310
3844 Grasmere Ln Salt Lake City UT 84119-6273 • stueberslc@aol.com • RM • Tchr • Grace Sandy UT • (801)572-6375 • (S 1995)

**DUEKER KAREN LYN** (909)927-2489
42216 Ferguson Dr Hemet CA 92544-6427 • PSW • Tchr • St John Hemet CA • (909)652-5909 • (IV 1985)

**DUENSING BEVERLY A** (402)228-3180
1818 Summit St Beatrice NE 68310-2565 • NEB • Tchr • St Paul Beatrice NE • (402)223-3414 • (S 1970)

**DUENSING DON W** (217)787-3473
930 Flossmore Dr # 6 Springfield IL 62707-6129 • CI • Tchr • LHS Springfield IL • (217)546-6363 • (S 1992)

**DUENSING ELDEN F** (402)643-6324
1320 N 1st St Seward NE 68434-1227 • NEB • EM • (S 1953 MED PHD)

**DUENSING LONNIE G** (402)228-3180
1818 Summit St Beatrice NE 68310-2565 • NEB • P/Tchr • St Paul Beatrice NE • (402)223-3414 • (S 1970 MED)

**DUENSING MELISSA A** (713)463-8607
10318 Richmond Hill Dr Houston TX 77041 • TX • Tchr • Texas Austin TX • (S 1999)

**DUENSING PAUL S** (303)795-7412
4001 W Rutgers Pl Denver CO 80236-3511 • RM • Tchr • Lutheran HS Rockies Parker CO • (303)841-5551 • (S 1977)

**DUERR PHILIP G** (714)288-8813
2537 E Collins Ave Orange CA 92867-6209 • PSW • Tchr • Salem Orange CA • (714)639-1946 • (IV 1988 MEAD)

**DUFF ALEXANDER L**
1910 Pemberton Dr Fort Wayne IN 46805 • NI • Tchr • St Peter Schaumburg IL • (847)885-3350 • (RF 1981)

**DUFF SHERYL K** (630)690-1201
1617 E Willow Wheaton IL 60187 • NI • Tchr • St John Wheaton IL • (630)668-0701 • (RF 1983 MSED)

**DUFFY COLLEEN D** (651)686-5634
4033 Northview Ter Eagan MN 55123-1555 • S • 04/1999 • (SP 1990)

**DUFFY JULIE ANN** (303)781-3638
3735 S Delaware St Englewood CO 80110-3533 • RM • Tchr • Shepherd Of The Hill Littleton CO • (303)798-0711 • (S 1988)

**DUFRESNE ELISA RUTH**
24576 Westhaven Ct Murrieta CA 92562-3840 • PSW • Tchr • Grace San Diego CA • (619)299-2890 • (IV 1992)

**DUITSMAN DONALD L** (402)466-9232
7024 Eagle Dr Lincoln NE 68507-2146 • NEB • Tchr • Lincoln Luth Jr/Sr H Lincoln NE • (402)467-5404 • (S 1969 MED)

**DUITSMAN JOYCE E** (913)367-7236
713 Mound St Atchison KS 66002-1852 • KS • Tchr • Trinity Atchison KS • (913)367-4763 • (S 1974)

**DULAS JAMES EDWARD**
720 Ivanhoe Dr Watertown MN 55388 • MNS • Tchr • Lutheran High Mayer MN • (612)657-2251 • (RF 1991)

**DUMAR JOHN E** (810)469-8753
115 Moross St Mount Clemens MI 48043-2242 • jdumar@lhsa.com • MI • Tchr • LHS North Macomb MI • (810)781-9151 • (S 1982 MED)

**DUMKE JANE LYNN** (513)941-0963
2831 Hocking Dr Cincinnati OH 45233-4226 • OH • Tchr • Grace Cincinnati OH • (513)661-8467 • (RF 1965)

**DUMLER MARVIN J** (303)667-1532
1710 Agate Ct Loveland CO 80538-3710 • RM • EM • (CQ 1960 MS DED)

**DUNCAN SANDRA JANE** (317)783-3726
2927 E Berwyn St Indianapolis IN 46203-5506 • IN • Tchr • Emmaus Indianapolis IN • (317)632-1486 • (RF 1974)

**DUNDEK HILARY J** (630)910-4240
8433 Mending Wall Dr Woodridge IL 60517 • NI • Tchr • Gloria Dei Chicago IL • (773)581-5259 • (S 1976)

**DUNGAN REBEKAH**
101 1st St Fayetteville NY 13066-1213 • EA • 08/1984 08/1998 • (BR 1982)

**DUNK CARL C** (915)944-8753
2819 Lindenwood Dr San Angelo TX 76904-6147 • TX • Prin • Trinity San Angelo TX • (915)947-1275 • (S 1959 MED)

**DUNK DELORIS E** (612)753-4474
885 227th Ave NW Bethel MN 55005-9535 • MNS • Tchr • Trinity Saint Francis MN • (612)753-1234 • (RF 1966 MED)

**DUNK WILLIAM F** (612)753-4474
885 227th Ave NW Bethel MN 55005-9535 • MNS • P/Tchr • Trinity Saint Francis MN • (612)753-1234 • (S 1966 MED)

**DUNKER DORCAS M** (810)765-8652
545 Shady Ln East China MI 48054 • MI • Tchr • St Peter Richmond MI • (810)727-9693 • (S 1979 MS)

**DUNKER SANDEE S** (815)568-5596
333 Jackson St Lower Marengo IL 60152-3117 • NI • Tchr • Zion Marengo IL • (815)568-5156 • (RF 1979 MA)

**DUNKLAU CAROL SUE** (402)664-3128
901 Howard St Scribner NE 68057-3031 • NEB • Tchr • Trinity Fremont NE • (402)721-5959 • (S 1988)

**DUNKLAU EDWARD H** (810)247-5329
16034 Haverhill Dr Macomb MI 48044-1946 • dunklauelcs@juno.com • MI • Tchr • LHS North Macomb MI • (810)781-9151 • (S 1970 MA)

**DUNKLAU ESTHER MAY** (810)566-6243
13900 Lakeside Bld N B124 Shelby Township MI 48315-6046 • MI • EM • (WN 1940)

**DUNKLAU HAROLD H** (810)566-6243
13900 Lakeside Blvd N B124 Shelby Township MI 48315-6046 • MI • EM • (S 1934)

**DUNKLAU JOYCE E** (402)478-4118
21748 County Rd P32 Arlington NE 68002-5653 • NEB • Tchr • St Paul Arlington NE • (402)478-4278 • (S 1983)

**DUNKLAU LINDA J** (810)247-5329
16034 Haverhill Dr Macomb MI 48044-1946 • dunklauelcs@juno.com • MI • Tchr • St Peter Macomb MI • (810)781-9296 • (S 1970 MA)

**DUNNING KEVIN M**
2236 Juniper Berry Dr Las Vegas NV 89117 • kevindunning@thoughtport.com • PSW • Tchr • Faith LHS Las Vegas NV • (702)804-4400 • (RF 1978 MA)

**DUNSMORE DAVID MARK** (248)682-1792
28 Camley St Waterford MI 48328-3200 • MI • Tchr • St Stephen Waterford MI • (248)673-5906 • (AA 1984)

**DUNWELL ERIN LEE**
24900 W Linda Ln Naperville IL 60564-5812 • NI • Tchr • St Paul Mount Prospect IL • (847)255-0332 • (RF 1992)

**DUPORT REBECCA HIRSCH**
3250B Cumberland Trace Rd Bowling Green KY 42103 • dce@htlc-bg.org • MDS • Mem C • Holy Trinity Bowling Green KY • (270)843-9595 • (IV 1998)

**DURHAM RICHARD E** (410)747-9291
6 Sweetgum Ct Catonsville MD 21228-5873 • SE • Tchr • Emmanuel Baltimore MD • (410)744-0015 • (RF 1973 MMU)

**DURHEIM MICHELLE R** (405)263-4736
308 S 4th Okarche OK 73762-9125 • EA • Tchr • Trinity West Seneca NY • (716)674-9188 • (S 1997)

**DURKEE KAY A** (217)876-8041
591 Shadow Dr Decatur IL 62526-1167 • kdurkee@webmart.net • CI • 09/1998 • (CQ 1994)

**DURR MARNA A** (319)668-2991
2671 K Ave Williamsburg IA 52361-8516 • IE • Tchr • Lutheran Interparish Williamsburg IA • (319)668-1711 • (SP 1974)

**DURST CHRISTINE MAE**
202 Clearwood Ct Saint Peters MO 63376-4689 • MO • Tchr • Lutheran North Saint Louis MO • (314)389-3100 • (RF 1981 MED)

**DUTCHER ALAN J** (612)758-6755
504 1st Ave NW New Prague MN 56071-1405 • MNS • Tchr • St Johns Chaska MN • (612)448-2526 • (S 1987)

**DUTTON KAREN** (216)341-4884
10112 Russell Ave Cleveland OH 44125-1615 • duttonk@oh.lcms.org • OH • Tchr • St John Garfield Heights OH • (216)587-4222 • (RF 1975)

**DWYER GARNET PATRICIA** (660)598-2904
RR 1 Box 106 Rockville MO 64780-9057 • MO • 05/2000 • (RF 1963)

**DYBWAD DAVID B**
7327 58th St Ct W #102 University Place WA 98467 • dldybwad@aol.com • NOW • St John Garfield Heights OH • (S 1972 MED)

**DYBWAD LINDA E**
7327 58th St Ct W #102 University Place WA 98467 • dldybwad@aol.com • NOW • Tchr • Concordia Tacoma WA • (253)475-9513 • (S 1972)

**DYKES JOYCE LOUISE** (210)491-0128
14307 Walmer St San Antonio TX 78247-3734 • TX • Tchr • Concordia San Antonio TX • (210)479-1477 • (CQ 1997)

**DYKSTRA SHARON L** (715)421-3399
1220 20th Pl Wisconsin Rapids WI 54494-5490 • NW • Tchr • Immanuel Wisconsin Rapids WI • (715)423-0272 • (RF 1984)

**DYNNESON DONALD** (402)643-4486
1483 252nd Seward NE 68434-8045 • ddynneson@seward.ccsn.edu • NEB • SHS/C • Nebraska Seward NE • (CQ 1978 MA MFA)

**DYNNESON LANE A**
304 W Washington Jackson MO 63755 • MO • Tchr • Trinity Cape Girardeau MO • (573)334-1068 • (S 1995)

**DYNNESON MICHELLE RENEE** (573)243-6339
304 W Washington St Jackson MO 63755-1860 • MO • Tchr • St Paul Jackson MO • (573)243-2236 • (S 1995)

**DYSLIN ELAINE CAROL** (303)422-3972
4025 Jay St Wheat Ridge CO 80033-5018 • dyslin@colorado.edu • RM • Tchr • Beautiful Savior Broomfield CO • (303)469-1785 • (S 1999)

**DZELZKALNS STACY** (352)690-9521
1547 SE 27th St Apt H Ocala FL 34471-6062 • FG • Tchr • St John Ocala FL • (352)622-7275 • (RF 1994)

**DZURICK ZACHARY M**
3028 West 100th St Cleveland OH 44111-1827 • EN • 05/1999 • (AA 1995)

## E

**EARLEY KAREN L** (517)642-8317
2820 N Raucholz Rd Hemlock MI 48626-9680 • kle291@aol.com • MI • Tchr • St Peter Hemlock MI • (517)642-5659 • (RF 1976)

**EASLEY JACQUELINE L**
1205 Macintosh Wauconda IL 60084 • crfeasleyjl@crf.cuis.edu • NI • SHS/C • Northern Illinois Hillside IL • (RF 1989 MA)

**EASTIN NOEL C** (410)663-7307
1728 Aberdeen Rd Baltimore MD 21234 • SE • Tchr • Baltimore LHS Baltimore MD • (410)825-2323 • (RF 1999)

**EASTON CINDEE SUE** (561)364-0227
5041 Brian Blvd Boynton Beach FL 33437 • eastoncindee@hotmail.com • FG • 07/1999 • (RF 1982 MED)

**EATHERTON LOIS C** (214)553-9553
9254 Forest Ln #1005 Dallas TX 75243 • MI • Tchr • Trinity Saint Joseph MI • (616)983-3056 • (S 1996)

**EATHERTON SAMUEL JAMES** (214)553-9553
9254 Forest Ln #1005 Dallas TX 75243 • TX • Trinity Saint Joseph MI • (S 1996)

**EATON CYNTHIA A** (417)782-7521
2124 New Jersey Ave Joplin MO 64804-1148 • MO • 01/1996 02/2000 • (MQ 1992)

**EATON GWENDOLYN R** (303)480-1901
2323 W 30th Ave #4 Denver CO 80211 • RM • Tchr • Gethsemane Northglenn CO • (303)451-6908 • (IV 1988)

**EBBERS SUSAN M** (510)447-2423
870 S G St Livermore CA 94550-4661 • sebbers@pacbell.net • CNH • 11/1999 • (MQ 1983 MA)

**EBEL ANNE MARIE** (810)468-2461
1430 Burlington Dr Mount Clemens MI 48043 • aebel@lhsa.com • MI • 06/1999 • (RF 1988 MA)

**EBEL ERIKA J**
208 Princeton Dr Costa Mesa CA 92626-6125 • PSW • 06/1998 • (IV 1997)

**EBEL KELLY**
812 Stanislaus Cir Claremont CA 91711 • PSW • Tchr • Zion Anaheim CA • (714)535-1169 • (IV 1994)

**EBEL KENNETH K** (714)854-2785
35 Rocky Knls Irvine CA 92612-3258 • ebelkk@cui.edu • PSW • SHS/C • Pacific Southwest Irvine CA • (949)854-3232 • (S 1968 MSCT DART)

**EBEL NANCY** (406)265-2115
1000 11th Ave Havre MT 59501-4630 • MT • 09/1997 09/1999 • (S 1966 MA)

**EBEL PAUL O** (213)831-0993
315 N Malgren Ave San Pedro CA 90732-2715 • PSW • EM • (S 1937 MA LLD)

**EBEL WILLIAM H DR** (218)534-3571
22699 Cedar Shores Dr Aitkin MN 56431 • ebelcab@emily.net • MNN • EM • (S 1957 MSED)

**EBEL WILLIAM H**
1430 Burlington Dr Mount Clemens MI 48043-6565 • webel@lhsa.com • MI • Tchr • LHS North Macomb MI • (810)781-9151 • (MQ 1987)

**EBELING DAVID G DR** (812)339-6503
1724 E Windsor Dr Bloomington IN 47401-6762 • ebeling@cphnet.org • IN • CCRA • Indiana Fort Wayne IN • (RF 1963 MSED EDD)

**EBELING PATRICIA A** (608)756-1459
1814 Saint George Ln Janesville WI 53545-0687 • SW • Tchr • St Paul Janesville WI • (608)754-4471 • (RF 1970)

**EBELING TIMOTHY J** (608)756-1459
1814 Saint George Ln Janesville WI 53545-0687 • SW • Tchr • St Paul Janesville WI • (608)754-4471 • (RF 1970 MEPD)

**EBENDICK TIMOTHY J** (313)255-2805
16110 W Parkway St Detroit MI 48219-3766 • MI • Tchr • Hosanna-Tabor Redford MI • (313)937-2424 • (S 1972 MS)

**EBERHARD BERNICE M** (303)659-5403
312 S 22nd Ave Brighton CO 80601-2530 • lce4lcef@juno.com • RM • EM • (S 1946)

**EBERHARD LOUIS C** (303)659-5403
312 S 22nd Ave Brighton CO 80601-2530 • lce4lcef@juno.com • RM • EM • (S 1946 MA)

**EBERHARDT MARY E** (262)377-6174
1826 17th Ave Grafton WI 53024 • mary.eberhardt@cuw.edu • SW • SHS/C • South Wisconsin Milwaukee WI • (414)464-8100 • (RF 1970 MA)

**EBERLE AMANDA B** (208)235-6253
30 Creighton St Pocatello ID 83201-3456 • aeberle@gracepocid.org • NOW • Tchr • Grace Pocatello ID • (208)237-4142 • (S 1994)

**EBERS CYNTHIA K** (660)463-7765
212 E 10th St Ter Concordia MO 64020-9400 • MO • Tchr • St Paul Concordia MO • (660)463-7654 • (S 1975)

**EBERS JIM LEE** (660)463-7765
212 E 10th Street Ter Concordia MO 64020-9400 • MO • Tchr • St Paul Concordia MO • (660)463-7654 • (S 1979)

**EBERT DOROTHY L** (407)359-0185
2142 Goldfinch Ct Oviedo FL 32765-5207 • FG • EM • (RF 1955 MA)

**EBERT ERNEST R** (847)437-1829
510 Oak St Elk Grove Vlg IL 60007-4210 • NI • EM • (RF 1943 MS)

**EBERT JANANE F** (303)789-1124
4089 S Acoma St Englewood CO 80110-4622 • janebert@juno.com • RM • 10/1999 • (S 1967)

**EBERTS ROSANNE** (832)593-0295
6656 Montauk Dr Houston TX 77084 • TX • Tchr • St Mark Houston TX • (713)468-2623 • (S 1985)

**EBEST JO C** (314)961-6595
8866 Sturdy Dr Saint Louis MO 63126-2326 • jcse@mciworld.com • MO • Tchr • Christ Community Kirkwood MO • (314)822-7774 • (CQ 1998 MA)

**EBKE HAROLD D** (618)466-0608
5130 Riverwood Dr Godfrey IL 62035-1411 • SI • P/Tchr • Faith Godfrey IL • (618)466-9153 • (S 1962)

**ECKELS PATRICIA LYNN**
C/O St John Luth Church 510 N Wilson Ave Oberlin KS 67749 • KS • 07/1996 • (S 1994)

**ECKERT CONNIE MAE** (402)529-3225
83125 576th Ave Pilger NE 68768 • NEB • Tchr • Zion St John Wisner NE • (402)529-3348 • (SP 1979)

**ECKERT DOROTHEA CHARLOTTE** (956)428-4069
815 N 21st St Harlingen TX 78550-5115 • raeckert@acnet.net • TX • Tchr • St Paul Harlingen TX • (956)423-3926 • (RF 1966 MA)

**ECKERT JUDITH ANN** (262)797-9300
765 Summit Dr Waukesha WI 53186 • SW • Tchr • Gospel Milwaukee WI • (414)372-5159 • (S 1968 MA)

**ECKERT KENNETH L** (314)429-6530
9120 Brownridge Dr Overland MO 63114-5626 • MO • Tchr • Immanuel Olivette MO • (314)993-5004 • (S 1965 MA)

**ECKERT LINN W** (217)496-2665
512 Radford Dr Sherman IL 62684 • CI • Tchr • Immanuel Springfield IL • (217)528-5232 • (S 1970 MA)
**ECKERT LOIS C** (618)785-2344
PO Box 162 Baldwin IL 62217-0162 • leenlois@egyptian.net • SI • Tchr • Trinity Red Bud IL • (618)282-2881 • (RF 1962 MA)
**ECKERT LORRAINE R** (616)927-6083
535 Lynwood Benton Harbor MI 49022-6932 • MI • EM • (RF 1958 MA)
**ECKERT MICHELE K** (217)496-2665
512 Radford Dr Sherman IL 62684 • CI • Tchr • Immanuel Springfield IL • (217)528-5232 • (S 1978)
**ECKERT ROBERT** (414)797-9300
765 Summit Dr Waukesha WI 53186-2316 • SW • EM • (RF 1972)
**ECKERT RODNEY A** (956)428-4069
815 N 21st St Harlingen TX 78550-5115 • raeckert@acnet.net • TX • Tchr • St Paul Harlingen TX • (956)423-3926 • (RF 1966 MA)
**ECKHARDT RAYMOND C** (612)943-0934
7401 W 101st St Apt 202 Bloomington MN 55438-2506 • MNS • EM • (RF 1932)
**ECKHOFF DEBRA SUE*** (573)377-4177
PO Box 197 Stover MO 65078-0370 • MO • Tchr • St Paul Stover MO • (573)377-2690 • (S 1990)
**ECKSTORM KAY E**
732 Avondale St Bay City MI 48708-5587 • MI • Tchr • Faith Bay City MI • (517)684-3448 • (AA 1983)
**EDEN ELLEN** (618)888-2408
5559 Seiler Rd Dorsey IL 62021-1705 • eceden@madisontelco.com • SI • Tchr • Metro-East LHS Edwardsville IL • (618)656-0043 • (CQ 1997)
**EDENFIELD MARILYN J** (734)479-6337
19545 Wherle Dr Riverview MI 48192-8533 • medenfield@juno.com • MI • Tchr • Christ The King Southgate MI • (734)285-9697 • (RF 1968 MAT)
**EDGE ALEEN DEGLER** (913)631-4276
6614 Garnett Dr Shawnee KS 66203-3324 • KS • Tchr • Hope Shawnee KS • (913)631-6940 • (SP 1979)
**EDMISON GORDON D** (612)353-2514
17680 53rd St New Germany MN 55367-9315 • weglaad@aol.com • MNS • Tchr • St Mark-St John New Germany MN • (612)353-2464 • (S 1985 MS)
**EGGEBRECHT DAVID W** (414)527-2736
4705 N Parkside Dr Milwaukee WI 53225-4438 • SW • SHS/C • South Wisconsin Milwaukee WI • (414)464-8100 • (RF 1960 MA PHD)
**EGGEBRECHT PAUL ARTHUR** (419)592-6812
730 Strong St Napoleon OH 43545-1461 • pseggs@henry-net.com • OH • Tchr • St Paul Napoleon OH • (419)592-5536 • (RF 1987)
**EGGERDING ROLAND F** (314)351-2131
5904 Apple Valley Dr Saint Louis MO 63123-2702 • MO • EM • (RF 1945 MS)
**EGGERDING THOMAS M** (818)340-6079
24425 Woolsey Canyon Rd Spce44 West Hills CA 91304 • EN • Tchr • Chapel Cross Mission Hills CA • (818)892-8490 • (RF 1964)
**EGGERLING REINHARD M** (317)247-0282
3230 Lupine Dr Indianapolis IN 46224-2022 • IN • EM • (S 1938)
**EGGERMAN KIMBERLY A** (618)594-8007
12635 Corey Rd Carlyle IL 62231-2831 • kimike@isbe.accessus.net • SI • Tchr • Trinity Hoffman IL • (618)495-2246 • (RF 1984)
**EGGERS DAVID E** (314)427-5147
3314 Saint Joachim Ln Saint Ann MO 63074-3511 • MO • Tchr • River Roads Saint Louis MO • (314)388-0300 • (S 1971)
**EGGERS MARK FREDRIC** (314)842-0510
9836 Emil Ave Saint Louis MO 63126-3207 • prinmfe@i1.net • MO • P/Tchr • Christ Community Kirkwood MO • (314)822-7774 • (CQ 1998 MA)
**EGGERS MILTON H** (805)492-4206
736 San Martin Pl Thousand Oaks CA 91360-1322 • PSW • EM • (RF 1945)
**EGGERS NORMAN A** (812)522-8489
1803 N Ewing St Seymour IN 47274-1126 • IN • Tchr • Immanuel Seymour IN • (812)522-1301 • (RF 1970 MS)
**EGGERS WILBERT G** (660)463-2781
Good Shepherd Village Concordia MO 64020 • MO • EM • (S 1940)
**EGGERSTEDT KIM L** (715)524-3999
410 S Sawyer St Shawano WI 54166-2928 • kg8870@ezwebtech.com • NW • Prin • St James Shawano WI • (715)524-4213 • (RF 1968 MA)
**EGGERT JEANETTE G**
5020 NE 32nd Ave Apt 3 Portland OR 97211-6067 • NOW • SHS/C • Northwest Portland OR • (RF 1975 MA)
**EGGERT JOHN R DR** (651)298-1041
657 Laurel Ave Saint Paul MN 55104-7105 • eggert@csp.edu • MNS • SHS/C • Minnesota South Burnsville MN • (S 1968 MMU DMU)
**EGGERT PAUL W**
1824 Laurence Ct Clearwater FL 33764-6617 • FG • Prin • First Clearwater FL • (727)447-4504 • (RF 1973 MA)
**EGGOLD JOSHUA MICHAEL**
Saint John Luth Church 1915 SE Lake Weir Rd Ocala FL 34471-5424 • FG • Tchr • St John Ocala FL • (352)629-1794 • (S 1994)
**EGGOLD ROBERT L** (785)232-9708
2532 SE Peck Rd Topeka KS 66605-1943 • KS • EM • (RF 1951 MED)
**EGGOLD STEPHEN F** (314)282-2924
1212 Walnut Dr Arnold MO 63010-1321 • MO • Tchr • LHS South Saint Louis MO • (314)631-1400 • (S 1984 MA)
**EGGOLD THOMAS A** (219)423-9694
C/O Emmanuel Lutheran PS 917 W Jefferson Blvd Fort Wayne IN 46808-4007 • IN • Mem C • Emmanuel Fort Wayne IN • (219)423-1369 • (S 1992)
**EHLERS HEIDI S**
Merced CA 95348 • ehlers@cyberlynk.com • CNH • Tchr • St Paul Merced CA • (209)383-3302 • (IV 1998)
**EHLERS JANA L** (816)836-5914
1602B S Harris St Independence MO 64052 • MO • Tchr • Messiah Independence MO • (816)254-9405 • (S 1997)
**EHLERS JANE L** (208)825-5035
875 S 950 E Eden ID 83325-5027 • NOW • 08/1994 08/2000 • (S 1988)
**EHLERS KATHRYN M** (320)864-4186
16659 411 Ave Glencoe MN 55336 • kjehlers@xtratyme.com • MNS • Tchr • First Glencoe MN • (320)864-3317 • (SP 1969)
**EHLERS VIOLA** (712)732-4203
701 E 12th St Storm Lake IA 50588-1983 • IW • EM • (S 1949 MMU)
**EHLERT LORNA MAE** (920)485-4032
504 N Cedar St Horicon WI 53032-1041 • SW • Tchr • St Stephen Horicon WI • (920)485-6687 • (RF 1972 MA)
**EICHERT CAROL** (852)2-813-7295
1A Scenic View 1 Red Hill Rd Tai Tam HONG KONG • ceichert@hkis.edu.hk • NI • S Miss • Northern Illinois Hillside IL • (RF 1977 MA)
**EICHERT LAWRENCE R** (852)2-813-7295
1A Scenic View 1 Red Hill Rd Tai Tam HONG KONG • leichert@hs.hkis.edu.hk • NI • S Miss • Northern Illinois Hillside IL • (RF 1966 MA)
**EICHHORN ARTHUR DAVID** (314)645-0730
7116 Mardel Ave Saint Louis MO 63109-1123 • arthur.eichhorn@mciworld.com • MO • Mem C • Timothy Saint Louis MO • (314)781-8673 • (RF 1975 MA MAT DED)
**EICHINGER DIANE J** (517)892-4277
1703 Raymond St Bay City MI 48706-5256 • MI • Tchr • Zion Bay City MI • (517)893-5793 • (S 1970 MA)
**EICHINGER KENNETH R** (219)546-4607
415 S Montgomery St Bremen IN 46506-1656 • keiching@iusb.edu • IN • Tchr • St Paul Bremen IN • (219)546-2790 • (S 1973 MS)
**EICHOLTZ DONALD G** (407)365-6015
1002 Gammage Pt Oviedo FL 32765-7069 • S • EM • (RF 1955 MS)
**EICHSTAEDT ESTHER** (312)754-7394
181 W Maple Dr Chicago Heights IL 60411-2122 • NI • EM • (RF 1945)
**EICHSTAEDT PAULINE E** (414)494-8132
1627 Kennedy Dr Green Bay WI 54304-2951 • NW • Tchr • Pilgrim Green Bay WI • (920)494-6530 • (RF 1964)
**EICKEMEYER LYNNETTE** (713)681-2373
5031 Oak Shadows Dr Houston TX 77091-4529 • lynneickemeyer@hotmail.com • TX • Tchr • LHS North Houston TX • (713)880-3131 • (RF 1977 MED)
**EICKMANN AMY T** (313)274-2377
20601 Carlysle Dearborn MI 48124 • aeickmann@lhsa.com • MI • Tchr • LHS Westland Westland MI • (734)422-2090 • (MQ 1988 MED)
**EICKMANN NATHAN A*** (303)973-4572
5357 W Fremont Pl Littleton CO 80128-4979 • eickmana@csn.net • RM • EM • (S 1956 MMU)
**EICKMEIER HANS W** (308)395-9627
3205 W Strolley Pk Rd #140 Grand Island NE 68801 • NEB • Tchr • Trinity Grand Island NE • (308)382-5274 • (S 1999)
**EICKMEYER KENNETH F** (517)686-0526
3390 Sherwood St Saginaw MI 48603-2021 • MI • EM • (RF 1956)
**EICKSTEAD F TIMOTHY** (210)695-9006
10235 Whip O Will Way Helotes TX 78023-3507 • timeick@aol.com • TX • Prin • Shepherd Of The Hill San Antonio TX • (210)614-3741 • (RF 1980 MA)
**EIFERT JAMES M** (713)688-4221
5401 Nine Lee Ln Houston TX 77092 • eifertjk@aol.com • TX • Tchr • Our Savior Houston TX • (713)290-9087 • (AU 1992)
**EIFERT JONATHAN D** (920)803-8145
1707 Carmen Ave Sheboygan WI 53081-7527 • eifert@trinitysheboygan.org • SW • Tchr • Trinity Sheboygan WI • (920)458-8248 • (RF 1988 MMU)
**EIFERT MARTIN E** (512)251-6403
603 Candleberry Cir Pflugerville TX 78660-4335 • TX • EM • (CQ 1952)
**EIFERT MARY M** (920)803-8145
1707 Carmen Ave Sheboygan WI 53081-7527 • mjeifert@aol.com • SW • 11/1995 11/1999 • (RF 1988)
**EIGENFELD JANICE R** (847)824-7400
674 E Algonquin Rd Des Plaines IL 60016-6250 • norskjan@aol.com • NI • Tchr • Immanuel Des Plaines IL • (847)390-0990 • (RF 1975)
**EILERS CHRISTINE** (808)488-4578
C/O Our Savior Lutheran School 98-1098 Moanalua Rd Aiea HI 96701-4617 • CNH • 06/2000 • (SP 1977)
**EINEM RANDY H**
Trinity Lutheran Church 800 Houston Ave Houston TX 77007-7710 • TX • Prin • Trinity Houston TX • (713)224-0684 • (S 1976 MS)
**EINSPAHR BYRON BYRDELL** (727)323-3183
3618 16th Ave N Saint Petersburg FL 33713-5342 • FG • Tchr • Grace Saint Petersburg FL • (727)527-6213 • (S 1972)
**EINSPAHR DONNA M**
PO Box 520594 Salt Lake City UT 81406 • RM • Tchr • Redeemer Salt Lake City UT • (801)467-4352 • (PO 1990)
**EINSPAHR GLENN C** (402)643-3125
430 N 1st St Seward NE 68434-1804 • NEB • EM • (S 1947 MA DED)
**EINSPAHR KARLA M** (281)484-6913
11150 Beamer Rd Apt 312 Houston TX 77089-2335 • TX • Tchr • Lutheran South Acade Houston TX • (281)464-8299 • (S 1985)
**EINSPAHR KELVIN W** (816)455-9210
1901 NE 55th Ter Kansas City MO 64118-5609 • keinspahr@lhskc.com • MO • Tchr • Kansas City LHS Kansas City MO • (816)241-5478 • (S 1978)
**EINSPAHR KENT DR** (402)643-6305
722 N 5th St Seward NE 68434-1520 • eins@seward.cune.edu • NEB • SHS/C • Nebraska Seward NE • (S 1979 MS PHD)
**EINSPAHR KIRK D** (660)463-1021
317 College Dr Concordia MO 64020 • kdeins@yahoo.com • MO • SHS/C • Missouri Saint Louis MO • (314)317-4550 • (PO 1984 MS)
**EINSPAHR MARIE E** (402)643-4069
1747 Edgewood Ln Seward NE 68434-1192 • NEB • EM • (S 1978 MSED)
**EISCHER MARK W** (314)487-5975
5619 Gumtree Ct Saint Louis MO 63129-2262 • lleischemw@lhm.org • MO • Missouri Saint Louis MO • (RF 1976)
**EISELE DOUGLAS J** (801)969-2784
2069 Happiness Dr West Jordan UT 84084-1303 • RM • Tchr • Christ Murray UT • (801)262-4354 • (S 1982 MS)
**EISENBRAUN JOEL ALAN** (281)379-2914
6503 Knollview Dr Spring TX 77389-3649 • braun4@aol.com • TX • Tchr • Trinity Spring TX • (281)376-5810 • (CQ 1998)
**EISENBRAUN KATHRYN ANN** (812)372-7083
3106 16th Street Columbus IN 47201-5555 • eisenbrp@juno.com • IN • Tchr • St Peter Columbus IN • (812)372-1571 • (S 1963)
**EISENBRAUN PAUL G** (812)372-7083
3106 16th St Columbus IN 47201-5555 • eisenbrp@juno.com • IN • EM • (S 1963 MSED)
**EISENHOWER DOROTHY M** (623)975-7135
13152 W Market St Surprise AZ 85374-5234 • maggie13152@webtv.net • PSW • EM • (RF 1961)
**EISENMAN BARBARA M** (313)274-1646
22209 Edison Dearborn MI 48124 • tchrbarbe@aol.com • MI • Tchr • Guardian Dearborn MI • (313)274-3665 • (RF 1977 MA)
**EISING CHRISTINA E** (313)545-8349
807 N Washington Ave Royal Oak MI 48067-1737 • MI • Tchr • St Paul Royal Oak MI • (248)541-0613 • (AA 1986)
**EISMAN CARL S** (414)425-9652
5315 S Balboa Dr New Berlin WI 53151-8111 • SW • Prin • Martin LHS Greendale WI • (414)421-4000 • (RF 1966 MA MS)
**EISMAN JERRY M** (517)835-9892
2261 E Gordonville Rd Midland MI 48640 • MI • P/Tchr • St John Midland MI • (517)835-7041 • (RF 1978)
**EISMAN KATHLEEN S** (517)835-9892
2261 E Gordonville Rd Midland MI 48640 • MI • Tchr • St Peter Hemlock MI • (517)642-5659 • (RF 1970)
**ELDER GLORIA A** (312)748-2741
22509 Mission Dr Richton Park IL 60471-1618 • NI • Tchr • Trinity Tinley Park IL • (708)532-9395 • (CQ 1986)
**ELFMAN DAVID** (714)354-9896
10525 Stover Ave Riverside CA 92505-2057 • elfrnan@lhsoc.org • PSW • Tchr • Lutheran HS/Orange C Orange CA • (714)998-5151 • (S 1968 MED)
**ELKINS CHARLOTTE D** (812)523-1487
3050 E 850 S Columbus IN 47201-9208 • IN • Tchr • Immanuel Seymour IN • (812)522-1301 • (AA 1984 MED)
**ELLEFSON JAMES E** (630)887-7803
205 S Vine St Hinsdale IL 60521-4041 • jellef@concentric.net • NI • P/Tchr • Zion Hinsdale IL • (630)323-0045 • (CQ 1978 MA)
**ELLIOTT DAVID W** (303)671-9764
10025 E Girard Ave BLDG 27 #112 Denver CO 80231 • davo19@aol.com • RM • Tchr • Denver Lutheran High Denver CO • (303)934-2345 • (IV 1993)
**ELLIOTT SAMMYE L** (314)364-8896
11752 State Route BB Rolla MO 65401-7774 • MO • Tchr • Rolla Lutheran Schoo Rolla MO • (314)364-3915 • (SP 1988 MA)
**ELLIOTT SUZANNE KATHLEEN** (406)755-0130
1221 8th Ave E Kalispell MT 59901 • MT • Tchr • Trinity Kalispell MT • (406)257-5683 • (S 1993)
**ELLIS PHYLLIS J** (507)235-8397
RR 1 Box 605 Fairmont MN 56031-9600 • MNS • 11/1995 11/1999 • (RF 1980 MA)
**ELLWEIN KENNETH L** (714)838-8991
2311 Caper Tree Dr Tustin CA 92780-7114 • PSW • Tchr • Lutheran HS/Orange C Orange CA • (714)998-5151 • (RF 1965 MS LLD)
**ELLWEIN LISA J** (714)288-4400
898 Fawnwood Ln Orange CA 92869 • clellwein@aol.com • PSW • Tchr • St John Orange CA • (714)288-4406 • (S 1987 MSED)
**ELMHORST BRIAN DAVID** (920)387-1419
N8076 Cty AY Mayville WI 53050 • belmhorst@hotmail.com • SW • P/Tchr • Immanuel Mayville WI • (920)387-2158 • (MQ 1998)
**ELMSHAEUSER ORVILLE L** (319)732-3175
906 Maurer St Wilton IA 52778-9523 • IE • 01/1994 01/1996 • (S 1955 MSED)
**ELSAS SANDRA LOU** (309)266-7517
621 E Harrison St Morton IL 61550-1701 • CI • Tchr • Bethel Morton IL • (309)266-6592 • (CQ 1993)
**ELSE DULCEY J** (907)789-5463
C/O Faith Lutheran Church 2500 Sunset Dr Juneau AK 99801-9371 • NOW • 07/1995 07/2000 • (MQ 1990)
**ELSNER JAMES L*** (507)453-0312
2521 Clara Ave Fort Wayne IN 46805-3825 • jimelsner@juno.com • EN • 04/1999 • (S 1973 MED)

**ELVERS THERESA A** (414)760-1792
6654 N 85th St Milwaukee WI 53224-5414 • melvers@execpc.com • SW • Tchr • Christ The Life Waukesha WI • (262)547-1817 • (MQ 1993)

**EMAN MICHAEL L** (303)439-2575
10259 Garrison St Broomfield CO 80021-3883 • RM • Tchr • Denver Lutheran High Denver CO • (303)934-2345 • (S 1975 MS)

**EMBREE KAREN** (219)375-3678
3893 W 900 S Warren IN 46792 • IN • Tchr • St John Monroeville IN • (219)639-6404 • (RF 1971 MS)

**EMBRETSON ANGELA R**
855 Victoria Ave Venice CA 90291-3931 • PSW • Tchr • First Venice CA • (310)823-9367 • (S 1990)

**EMERY GLEN A** (402)563-1847
420 120th Lane NW Coon Rapids MN 55433 • gemery@gilligan.esu7.k12.ne.us • MNS • P/Tchr • Prince Of Peace Spring Lake Park MN • (763)786-1706 • (MQ 1983)

**ENDERLE JANETTE WANDA** (773)767-0808
4125 W 59th St Chicago IL 60629-4909 • janners14@aol.com • NI • Tchr • Gloria Dei Chicago IL • (773)581-5259 • (RF 1994)

**ENDERLE PAUL** (708)422-9476
5024 W 109th St Oak Lawn IL 60453-5169 • NI • Tchr • Luther HS South Chicago IL • (773)737-1416 • (RF 1992 MA)

**ENDORF ANN FRANCES** (952)432-8002
13376 Eveleth Way Apple Valley MN 55124-8050 • aendorf@isd.net • S • 12/1999 • (S 1987)

**ENDORF GAIL N** (717)698-7904
236 The Hideout Lake Ariel PA 18436-9769 • AT • 09/1999 • (BR 1977)

**ENDORF TRACY MAE** (402)346-2373
3863 Dewey Ave Omaha NE 68105 • trmhinz@yahoo.com • KS • Tchr • Linn Association Linn KS • (785)348-5792 • (S 1996)

**ENDORF WELDON W** (717)698-7904
236 The Hideout Lake Ariel PA 18436-9769 • AT • EM • (S 1955 MSED)

**ENGE HEIDI ANNE**
320 San Miguel Ave San Mateo CA 94403-2958 • CNH • Tchr • Grace San Mateo CA • (650)345-9082 • (IV 1990)

**ENGE JENNIFER ANN** (517)497-9144
6425 Mackinaw Rd Saginaw MI 48604 • engej@earthlink.net • MI • 09/2000 • (RF 1993)

**ENGEBRECHT FRANKLIN E** (219)636-3614
3462 N Skinner Lake Dr W Albion IN 46701-9741 • IN • EM • (RF 1953 MA)

**ENGEBRECHT NORBERT R** (414)464-3876
4451 N Houston Ave Milwaukee WI 53218-4553 • SW • EM • (RF 1943 MED)

**ENGEL ELIZABETH** (216)651-6863
3025 W 101st St Cleveland OH 44111-1833 • OH • Tchr • St Thomas Rocky River OH • (440)331-2680 • (RF 1974)

**ENGELAGE ELIZABETH KAREN** (618)377-1867
513 Short St Bethalto IL 62010-1474 • beth@ezl.com • SI • Tchr • Zion Bethalto IL • (618)377-5507 • (RF 1994)

**ENGELBART DARIN SCOTT** (602)331-8982
2220 W Mission Ln Apt 2159 Phoenix AZ 85021-5808 • engelbart@juno.com • PSW • 06/1999 • (S 1996)

**ENGELBRECHT ALLEN W** (573)635-2348
2626 Saint Louis Rd Jefferson City MO 65101-4454 • MO • EM • (RF 1958)

**ENGELBRECHT JOHN M** (660)463-7621
202 Sunset Hills Dr Concordia MO 64020-9710 • jengelbrecht@galaxyispc.com • MO • SHS/C • Missouri Saint Louis MO • (314)317-4550 • (S 1975 MED)

**ENGELBRECHT THEODORE** (314)505-7746
23 C Founders Way Saint Louis MO 63105 • NOW • S Miss • Northwest Portland OR • (BR 1979 MA)

**ENGELBY PAUL JEROME** (507)235-8173
1530 Lucia Ave Fairmont MN 56031-1581 • MNS • Tchr • St Pauls Fairmont MN • (507)238-9492 • (MQ 1992)

**ENGELHARD CYNTHIA MARIE** (517)674-2766
5789 Clark Rd Unionville MI 48767-9727 • enge5@avci.net • MI • Tchr • St Paul Unionville MI • (517)674-8681 • (CQ 1997 MA)

**ENGELHARDT SANDRA KAY** (507)523-2391
PO Box 81 Lewiston MN 55952-0081 • MNS • Tchr • Immanuel Lewiston MN • (507)523-3143 • (SP 1975)

**ENTZENBERGER KATHRYN S** (210)479-8576
2939 Green Run Ln San Antonio TX 78231-1612 • kathye@concordia-satx.com • TX • Tchr • Concordia San Antonio TX • (210)479-1477 • (RF 1987)

**EPPERSON LINDA-MARIE** (310)314-4049
1030 Bay St #3 Santa Monica CA 90405 • msepperson@aol.com • PSW • Tchr • Pilgrim Santa Monica CA • (310)829-2239 • (RF 1971 MCMU MMU)

**ERBER GLENN R** (517)750-3388
3809 Westchester Blvd Jackson MI 49203-1117 • MI • EM • (S 1954 MED)

**ERDMAN ALICIA CONSTANCE** (309)682-4865
3012 W Brookside Dr Peoria IL 61615-4012 • CI • Tchr • Concordia Peoria IL • (309)691-8921 • (RF 1991)

**ERDMAN DANIEL D** (507)359-4575
RR 1 Box 40 Courtland MN 56021-9701 • ils@newulmtel.net • MNS • Tchr • Immanuel Courtland MN • (507)359-2528 • (SP 1983)

**ERDMAN JERALD SCOTT**
7677 Bramell Detroit MI 48239 • MI • Tchr • Detroit Urban Detroit MI • (313)582-9900 • (MQ 1996)

**ERDMAN JONATHAN A** (517)871-9372
4849 Swaffer Rd Millington MI 48746-9115 • MI • Tchr • St Paul Millington MI • (517)871-4581 • (AA 1985)

**ERDMAN MARVIN R** (507)632-4276
1666 40th St Ceylon MN 56121-9719 • MNS • EM • (S 1957)

**ERDMAN SUSAN L** (507)359-4575
RR 1 Box 40 Courtland MN 56021-9701 • ils@newulmtel.net • MNS • Tchr • Immanuel Courtland MN • (507)359-2534 • (SP 1984)

**ERDMANN DENISE ELIZABETH** (317)862-4240
6030 S Routiers Ave Indianapolis IN 46259 • IN • Tchr • Trinity Indianapolis IN • (317)897-0243 • (RF 1990)

**ERFOURTH LEE E** (517)787-3155
742 Woodlawn Jackson MI 49203 • MI • Tchr • Trinity Jackson MI • (517)750-2105 • (RF 1979)

**ERGER LYNNE M** (406)256-1639
1180 Amendment Cir Billings MT 59105-5702 • lynne43713@aol.com • MT • Tchr • Trinity Billings MT • (406)656-1021 • (S 1976)

**ERICKSON MARGIE A** (402)372-2549
1111 N Lincoln West Point NE 68788 • NEB • Tchr • St Paul West Point NE • (402)372-2355 • (S 1975)

**ERICKSON MEGAN LOUISE**
C/O St Paul Lutheran Church 1025 Lake St Melrose Park IL 60160-4150 • NI • Tchr • St Paul Melrose Park IL • (708)343-1000 • (IV 2000)

**ERIKSEN JOHN**
9 Tailor Sq O Fallon MO 63366-7319 • MO • Tchr • Zion Harvester MO • (314)441-7424 • (S 1995)

**ERIKSEN LAURIE BETH** (636)980-3470
9 Tailor Square O Fallon MO 63366-7319 • MO • Tchr • Zion Harvester MO • (314)441-7424 • (S 1996)

**ERJAVEC LINDA L** (708)671-1677
3725 N Sarah St Schiller Park IL 60176 • NI • Tchr • Bethlehem River Grove IL • (708)456-8786 • (RF 1975 SPMU)

**ERKE ALAN F** (708)849-0684
204 E 141 Pl Dolton IL 60419-1106 • NI • Tchr • Luther East Lansing IL • (708)895-8441 • (RF 1971 MED)

**ERKE LYNN ELLEN** (708)849-0684
204 E 141st Pl Dolton IL 60419-1106 • NI • Tchr • St Paul Dolton IL • (708)849-3225 • (RF 1971)

**ERMELING BRADLEY A**
206 Keyaki Garden 147 Bonsai Cho Omiya Shi Saitama330 JAPAN • PSW • S Miss • Pacific Southwest Irvine CA • (949)854-3232 • (IV 1992)

**ERMELING LYNDSAY K**
535 S Ranch View Cir #74 Anaheim Hills CA 92807 • PSW • Tchr • Lutheran HS/Orange C Orange CA • (714)998-5151 • (IV 1998)

**ERNST CYNTHIA S** (616)429-7494
1655 Sun Prairie Dr Saint Joseph MI 49085-9431 • math-mom@prodigy.net • MI • Tchr • Trinity Saint Joseph MI • (616)983-3056 • (S 1975 MS)

**ERNST SUSAN J**
12243 N Farmdale Rd Mequon WI 53097-2610 • SW • Tchr • Trinity Mequon WI • (414)242-2045 • (S 1974)

**ERNST THOMAS J** (314)227-8424
1536 Patterson Ln Manchester MO 63021-8071 • ternst@stpauls.org • MO • Tchr • St Paul Des Peres MO • (314)822-2771 • (S 1975 MED)

**ERNST TIMOTHY L** (616)429-7494
1655 Sun Prairie Dr Saint Joseph MI 49085-9431 • math-mom@prodigy.net • MI • Tchr • Trinity Saint Joseph MI • (616)983-3056 • (S 1975 MS)

**ERNSTMEYER CRAIG ALLEN** (402)466-6910
5331 Aylesworth Ave Lincoln NE 68507 • NEB • Tchr • Lincoln Luth Jr/Sr H Lincoln NE • (402)467-5404 • (S 1996)

**ERNSTMEYER REBECCA A** (402)421-8547
11805 S 5th St Roca NE 68430 • NEB • Tchr • Nebraska Seward NE • (S 1998)

**ERNSTMEYER SCOTT JASON** (402)488-5176
5509 Franklin St Lincoln NE 68506 • NEB • Tchr • Lincoln Luth Jr/Sr H Lincoln NE • (402)467-5404 • (S 1997)

**ESALA KEITH M** (612)773-9259
1745 Lark Ave Maplewood MN 55109-2622 • MNS • Tchr • Concordia Academy Roseville MN • (612)484-8429 • (SP 1976 MMU)

**ESCHMANN JOHANNA FAITH** (863)647-4126
131 Heartland Blvd Mulberry FL 33860 • jeschmann@hotmail.com • FG • Tchr • St Paul Lakeland FL • (863)644-7710 • (S 1991)

**ESCHMANN PAUL D**
1812 Lessur St Saginaw MI 48603 • pemann@juno.com • MI • Tchr • Michigan Ann Arbor MI • (S 1995)

**ESKILSON EDWARD W** (209)734-6353
1215 W Mary Ave Visalia CA 93277-6362 • CNH • Mem C • Grace Visalia CA • (559)734-7694 • (RF 1962)

**ESSIG JAMES P** (954)961-9353
4800 Garfield St Hollywood FL 33021-5228 • diannejim@mindspring.com • FG • Prin • St Mark Hollywood FL • (954)922-7572 • (RF 1974 MED)

**ESSLINGER LYNETTE ESTHER** (219)456-7144
2921 Plaza Dr Fort Wayne IN 46806-1310 • IN • Tchr • Bethlehem Fort Wayne IN • (219)456-3587 • (RF 1964)

**ESTERLINE WENDY K** (812)473-2479
2724 C Corona Dr Evansville IN 47715 • IN • Tchr • Evansville Evansville IN • (812)424-7252 • (AA 1995)

**ESTRADA HEATHER KRUMBEIN** (503)254-0286
8125 SE Morrison St Portland OR 97215-2333 • akrum@uswest.net • NOW • Tchr • Trinity Portland OR • (503)288-6403 • (PO 1997)

**ETTNER SUSAN KAY** (815)568-6536
20015 Harmony Rd Marengo IL 60152-8116 • NI • Tchr • Zion Marengo IL • (815)568-5156 • (RF 1972)

**EUKEN PHILIP L** (719)495-0828
12045 Greentree Rd Black Forest CO 80908 • RM • Tchr • Immanuel Colorado Springs CO • (719)636-3681 • (IV 1985)

**EVANS CLIFFORD H** (805)647-2232
1341 Phelps Ave Ventura CA 93004 • PSW • Prin • Grace Ventura CA • (805)642-5424 • (S 1969 MED)

**EVANS EVELYN L**
3056 S Glenway Dr Bay City MI 48706-2358 • MI • Tchr • Faith Bay City MI • (517)684-3448 • (S 1968)

**EVANS FAITH**
7027 Oak Glen Dr Hughesville MD 20637 • bfrevans@bellatlantic.net • SE • 07/1999 • (S 1972 MED)

**EVANS LEE ANN** (612)472-2151
5200 Bartlett Blvd Mound MN 55364-1748 • eagle³crest@msn.com • MNS • Tchr • Zion Mayer MN • (612)657-2339 • (SP 1981)

**EVANS SUSAN K** (805)647-2232
1341 Phelps Ave Ventura CA 93004 • PSW • Tchr • Grace Ventura CA • (805)642-5424 • (S 1969)

**EVENSEN GEORGE H** (916)536-1535
4691 Oak Twig Way Carmichael CA 95608-1179 • CNH • P/Tchr • Faith Fair Oaks CA • (916)961-4253 • (S 1978 MED)

**EVERS CRIS D** (407)384-8822
6025 Windhover Dr Orlando FL 32819-7529 • SW • 07/1996 07/1998 • (RF 1987)

**EVERT CATHERINE L**
12622 Orchard Summit Dr Sugar Land TX 77478-7363 • iloveteach@yahoo.com • TX • Tchr • Faith Sugar Land TX • (281)242-4453 • (AU 1984)

**EVERTS CARL H DR** (402)643-3491
1664 Plainview Ave Seward NE 68434-1171 • NEB • EM • (S 1953 MA DED)

**EVERTS ERIC NATHAN**
1525 Wisconsin Ave #10 Grafton WI 53024 • SW • Tchr • First Immanuel Cedarburg WI • (262)377-6610 • (MQ 1998)

**EWALD GENE K** (205)739-9341
1010 Avenue J SE Cullman AL 35055-3876 • cdgkewald@yahoo.com • SO • P/Tchr • St Paul Cullman AL • (205)734-6580 • (RF 1966)

**EWALD WENDY MARIE** (612)535-8373
6073 Xylon Ave N New Hope MN 55428-2743 • MNS • P/Tchr • Golden Valley Golden Valley MN • (763)544-0590 • (SP 1979)

**EWALD WILLIAM M** (708)848-3206
1000 N Harvey Ave Oak Park IL 60302-1452 • crfewald@curf.edu • NI • SHS/C • Northern Illinois Hillside IL • (RF 1965 MBA MA)

**EWELL TIMOTHY J** (810)726-2450
46175 Sterritt St Utica MI 48317-5840 • MI • Mem C • Trinity Utica MI • (810)731-4490 • (RF 1984)

**EWEN PATRICIA**
17803 E Tennessee Ave Aurora CO 80017-3343 • RM • Tchr • Trinity Franktown CO • (303)841-4660 • (IV 1997)

**EXNER CAROL ANN** (502)425-4457
1506 Cadet Ct Louisville KY 40222 • TX • Tchr • Salem Tomball TX • (281)351-8122 • (SP 1985)

**EXNER JEFFREY LEE** (502)425-4457
1506 Cadet Ct Louisville KY 40222-3940 • TX • Tchr • Salem Tomball TX • (281)351-8223 • (SP 1985 MA)

**EYERLY RICHARD A** (507)238-1802
443 Lake Park Blvd Fairmont MN 56031-2137 • MNS • Tchr • St Pauls Fairmont MN • (507)238-9492 • (CQ 1972 MA)

**EYSTER TIMOTHY K** (815)935-2914
1298 S 5th Ave Kankakee IL 60901-4822 • NI • Tchr • St Paul Kankakee IL • (815)932-3241 • (RF 1983)

**EZELL CHARLOTTE ANN** (757)766-2712
121 Ivy Arch Yorktown VA 23693 • SE • Mem C • Resurrection Newport News VA • (757)596-5808 • (BR 1975)

## F

**FABBRO RUTH H** (810)598-0398
25623 Brumar St Chesterfield MI 48051-1914 • MI • Tchr • LHS North Macomb MI • (810)781-9151 • (BR 1986 MA)

**FABRY KRISTIN K** (660)463-3158
901 Orange St PO Box 924 Concordia MO 64020-0924 • MO • 02/1994 02/2000 • (S 1976)

**FABRY TIMOTHY J** (660)463-3158
PO Box 924 Concordia MO 64020-0924 • tjfabry@yahoo.com • MO • SHS/C • Missouri Saint Louis MO • (314)317-4550 • (RF 1974 MSED)

**FACKLER LISA MARIE** (314)524-3258
85 Du Bourg Ln Florissant MO 63031-8442 • MO • Tchr • Hope Saint Ann MO • (314)429-3808 • (RF 1992)

**FAGA BARRY** (708)697-6177
832 Augusta Ave Elgin IL 60120-2926 • NI • Tchr • Immanuel Dundee IL • (847)428-1010 • (S 1970 MS)

**FAGA SHELLY S** (847)697-7536
832 Augusta Ave Elgin IL 60120-2926 • NI • Tchr • Immanuel Dundee IL • (847)428-1010 • (RF 1993)

**FAHLSING GLORIA D** (810)732-1842
1192 Normandy Terrace Dr Flint MI 48532-3550 • MI • Tchr • St Paul Flint MI • (810)239-6733 • (RF 1982 MA)

**FAHR JULIE KAY** (402)365-4245
PO Box 69 Deshler NE 68340-0069 • jfahr@gpcom.net • NEB • Tchr • St Peter Davenport NE • (402)364-2182 • (S 1989)

**FAHRMANN MARILYN** (515)692-3504
248 160th St Alexander IA 50420-8014 • IE • Tchr • St Paul Latimer IA • (515)579-6046 • (CQ 1984)

**FAHSHOLZ BARBARA** (912)888-9261
3516 Wexford Dr Albany GA 31707-2022 • FG • 03/1992 03/2000 • (RF 1966 MAR)

**FAIR DIANA K** (219)482-3845
2810 Farnsworth Dr Fort Wayne IN 46805-3118 • IN • Tchr • Concordia Fort Wayne IN • (219)422-2429 • (RF 1967 MA)

**FALCONE GARRY K** (636)932-0938
2005 Finley # 1007 Lombard IL 60148 • NI • Prin • Concord Addison IL • (630)543-6404 • (RF 1975 MA)

**FALK SUZANNE R** (310)979-9034
823 S Bundy Dr West Los Angeles CA 90049 • tscottfalk@msn.com • PSW • Prin • Pilgrim Santa Monica CA • (310)829-2239 • (RF 1992)

**FALKENSTERN EUGENE** (219)485-1484
4928 Willow Brook Dr Fort Wayne IN 46835-1576 • IN • EM • (RF 1961 MA)

**FALKNER DAVID ALLEN** (504)488-6641
3441 Gentilly Blvd New Orleans LA 70122-4933 • SO • Prin • St John New Orleans LA • (504)488-6641 • (CQ 1986 MA PHD)

**FALLERT BARBARA GERTRUDE** (651)779-8063
1448 Mc Knight Rd N Maplewood MN 55119-3192 • MNS • Prin • East St Paul Saint Paul MN • (612)774-2030 • (SP 1965)

**FANARA ANNETTE RENEE** (718)746-7181
150-26 19th Ave Whitestone NY 11357-3129 • tga2522@aol.com • AT • Tchr • Martin Luther Maspeth NY • (718)894-4000 • (RF 1980)

**FANGMANN DENNIS D** (801)571-5903
11276 Windy Peak Ridge Dr Sandy UT 84094-5427 • dennis.fangmann@glcs-lcms.org • RM • P/Tchr • Zion Brighton CO • (303)659-2339 • (S 1978 MSED)

**FARK SANDRA J** (618)687-2160
1 Scenic View Ln Murphysboro IL 62966 • SI • 02/1998 02/2000 • (RF 1975 MED)

**FARK TERRY G** (618)687-2160
1 Scenic View Ln Murphysboro IL 62966-4755 • SI • P/Tchr • Immanuel Murphysboro IL • (618)687-3917 • (RF 1974 MA)

**FARMER JENNIFER JOY** (714)637-8988
1189 N Shattuck St #C Orange CA 92867-5007 • jilliann@mindspring.com • PSW • Tchr • Hephatha Anaheim CA • (714)637-4022 • (IV 1992)

**FARMER VICKIE L** (217)793-1406
2304 Lombard Ave Springfield IL 62704-4253 • vfarmer@springnet2.com • CI • Tchr • Our Savior's Springfield IL • (217)546-4531 • (S 1975)

**FARQUHARSON DIANE RENEE** (405)288-6188
2460 Goldsby Dr Goldsby OK 73093 • dfarq@juno.com • TX • Tchr • Cross Of Christ De Soto TX • (972)223-9586 • (AU 1996)

**FARRAND THOMAS J** (616)429-5907
4850 S Cedar Trl Stevensville MI 49127-9102 • tfarrand@hotmail.com • MI • Tchr • Christ Stevensville MI • (616)429-7111 • (RF 1979 MA)

**FARRELL MYRA A** (618)656-3526
5975 Eaton Ln Edwardsville IL 62025-6251 • myfarrell@iw.edwpub.com • SI • 07/1993 07/2000 • (RF 1977 MSED)

**FASSHAUER KENNETH E** (630)690-6699
1720 Trent Ct Wheaton IL 60187-7726 • NI • Tchr • St John Wheaton IL • (630)668-0701 • (RF 1970 MA)

**FAST CARLA** (618)763-4663
206 W Jacob Rd Jacob IL 62950-2720 • MNS • 06/2000 • (AU 1983)

**FASZHOLZ EUGENE R** (402)643-4662
1967 N Columbia Ave Seward NE 68434-9756 • SW • EM • (S 1958 MED)

**FASZHOLZ GARY WILLIAM**
52526 Fawn Dr Macomb MI 48042-3488 • MI • Tchr • LHS North Macomb MI • (810)781-9151 • (S 1976)

**FAWCETT CAROL JEAN** (216)398-8208
708 W Schaaf Rd Cleveland OH 44109-4639 • OH • Tchr • Luther Memorial Cleveland OH • (216)631-3640 • (RF 1958)

**FECHIK CAROL ANN** (616)624-1457
223 Adams St Lawton MI 49065 • cafechik@aol.com • MI • Tchr • Trinity Paw Paw MI • (616)657-4840 • (RF 1972)

**FECHNER ERWIN W** (517)781-3821
10247 Frost Rd Freeland MI 48623-8850 • MI • EM • (RF 1940 MED)

**FECHNER ROSEMARIE** (708)692-7824
160 E Lahon St Park Ridge IL 60068-2742 • NI • Tchr • St Andrew Park Ridge IL • (847)823-9308 • (RF 1974)

**FEDERWITZ DAVID M** (815)226-0684
363 Gramerey Apt #4 Rockford IL 61107 • NI • SHS/C • Northern Illinois Hillside IL • (MQ 1999)

**FEDERWITZ REBECCA ANN**
C/O Lutheran Bible Translator Box 2050 Aurora IL 60507 • beccafed@juno.com • MDS • 07/1999 • (S 1995)

**FEDERWITZ VIRGINIA CLARA** (715)823-3280
N10048 Buelow Rd Clintonville WI 54929-9790 • federw@frontiernet.net • NW • Tchr • St Martin Clintonville WI • (715)823-6538 • (S 1971)

**FEEK AMY S** (612)368-7435
1108 Village Rd Apt 16A Chaska MN 55318-1334 • MNS • Tchr • St Johns Chaska MN • (612)448-2526 • (S 1994 MA)

**FEHLHAFER BETTY J**
400 Colorado St Utica NE 68456-6057 • NEB • Tchr • St Paul Utica NE • (402)534-2121 • (S 1966)

**FEHLHAFER STANLEY O** (402)786-5571
15700 Havelock Ave Lincoln NE 68527-9712 • sf00412@alltel.net • NEB • P/Tchr • Messiah Lincoln NE • (402)489-3024 • (S 1966 MED)

**FEHLHAFER SUSAN G**
320 N 7th St Leavenworth KS 66048-1933 • KS • Tchr • St Paul Leavenworth KS • (913)682-0387 • (S 1987)

**FEHN KELLEY JEAN** (517)642-5133
16221 E Tittabawassee Rd Hemlock MI 48626-9654 • MI • Tchr • St Peter Hemlock MI • (517)642-8188 • (AA 1993)

**FEHN LYNN A** (517)642-3631
3216 Pruess Rd Hemlock MI 48626-9415 • MI • Tchr • St Peter Hemlock MI • (517)642-5659 • (AA 1993)

**FEHRS TROY A** (440)331-5005
20128 Bonnie Bank Blvd Rocky River OH 44116-4119 • OH • SHS/C • Ohio Olmsted Falls OH • (S 1989)

**FELDERMAN CAROL SUE**
DISA Europe Unit 30403 Box #209 APO AE 09131 • csf3daytona@yahoo.com • FG • P/Tchr • Trinity Holly Hill FL • (904)255-7580 • (S 1979 MED)

**FELDMAN PATSY RUTH** (713)255-2208
312 High St Tomball TX 77375-4220 • TX • Tchr • Zion Tomball TX • (713)255-6203 • (S 1965)

**FELICE JUDY ANN** (216)779-7883
4363 W 226th St Fairview Park OH 44126-1828 • OH • Tchr • St Thomas Rocky River OH • (440)331-4426 • (RF 1970)

**FELLWOCK GERALDINE R** (626)309-9067
5936 1/4 Camellia Ave Temple City CA 91780-2001 • PSW • Prin • First Temple City CA • (626)287-0968 • (SP 1979)

**FELTEN DANIEL K** (636)922-0844
507 Summerwood Ct Saint Peters MO 63376-4693 • MO • Tchr • Zion Harvester MO • (314)441-7424 • (S 1975 MED)

**FELTEN DANIEL L** (517)652-4561
642 Gruber St Apt B5 Frankenmuth MI 48734 • MI • Tchr • Faith Bridgeport MI • (517)777-2600 • (RF 1999)

**FELTEN JOHN C** (216)226-7516
2178 Concord Dr Lakewood OH 44107-5374 • OH • Tchr • LHS West Rocky River OH • (440)333-1660 • (RF 1963 MED)

**FELTEN JOLYN RAE** (810)412-1016
15820 Lakeside Vlg Dr #101 Clinton Township MI 48038-6124 • jdaenzer@juno.com • MI • Tchr • Trinity Utica MI • (810)731-4490 • (AA 1997)

**FELTEN MARK G** (810)783-7922
113 High St Mount Clemens MI 48043-1785 • mfelten@lhsa.com • MI • Tchr • LHS North Macomb MI • (810)781-9151 • (AA 1996)

**FELTEN PAMELA SUE** (440)930-5303
142 Forest Blvd Avon Lake OH 44012 • OH • 06/1999 • (AA 1991)

**FELTEN SCOTT ANDREW** (440)930-5303
142 Forest Blvd Avon Lake OH 44012 • OH • Tchr • St Paul Westlake OH • (440)835-3050 • (AA 1993)

**FELTS FLORIAN L** (715)754-4856
102B Riverview Dr Marion WI 54950 • NW • EM • (RF 1963 MA)

**FENDRICK DAWN L** (515)576-7994
507 North 12th St Fort Dodge IA 50501 • IW • Tchr • St Paul Fort Dodge IA • (515)955-7208 • (S 1997)

**FENNER MARGARET** (812)372-7322
3305 30th St Columbus IN 47203-2624 • IN • EM • (RF 1971 MED)

**FENRICK MARK O** (608)754-1260
752 Logan St Janesville WI 53545 • jamfen@ticon.net • SW • Tchr • St Paul Janesville WI • (608)754-4471 • (MQ 1995)

**FENSKE JAMES** (216)835-8512
28640 Bassett Rd Westlake OH 44145-2915 • OH • Tchr • LHS West Rocky River OH • (440)333-1660 • (RF 1970)

**FENSKE SANDRA L** (414)452-4539
1420 N 17th St Sheboygan WI 53081-3275 • SW • Tchr • Trinity Sheboygan WI • (920)458-8248 • (RF 1963)

**FENSTERMAKER MARSHA** (513)733-5998
4212 Fox Hollow Dr Cincinnati OH 45241-2941 • OH • Tchr • Our Redeemer Maineville OH • (513)697-7335 • (S 1979)

**FERBER DENISE M** (636)978-2195
1934 Nightingale Ct Saint Paul MO 63366 • dferber@immanuelluth.org • MO • Tchr • Immanuel Saint Charles MO • (636)946-0051 • (RF 1980 MA)

**FERG JENNIFER JAYNE**
C/O Zion Lutheran Church 222 N East St Anaheim CA 92805-3317 • PSW • Tchr • Zion Anaheim CA • (714)535-1169 • (IV 1990)

**FERGUSON CARL J**
144 S Martha St Lombard IL 60148-2614 • NI • P/Tchr • Bethlehem River Grove IL • (708)453-1113 • (RF 1981 MA)

**FERGUSON JENNIFER JEAN**
1230 Fieldcrest Dr Rockford IL 61108-4166 • jjferguson@worldnet.att.net • NI • Tchr • Grace Chicago IL • (773)762-1234 • (AU 1995)

**FERGUSON SUSAN L**
7110 16th Ave Kenosha WI 53143-5332 • SW • 12/1998 12/2000 • (S 1994)

**FERREBEE DUANE R** (815)935-5503
1057 W Hawkins St Kankakee IL 60901-4613 • NI • Tchr • St Paul Kankakee IL • (815)932-3241 • (RF 1975)

**FERRELL LOUISE A** (714)281-8625
270 S Old Bridge Rd Anaheim CA 92808-1325 • louiseferrell@aol.com • PSW • 02/1999 • (CQ 1995)

**FERRELL REBECCA A** (216)934-1170
5316 Oakwood Dr Sheffield OH 44054-2405 • pbferrel@apk.net • OH • Tchr • St Paul Westlake OH • (440)835-3051 • (RF 1979 MA)

**FERRERO JANET L** (217)563-7664
301 N Vine St Nokomis IL 62075-1248 • SI • 09/1990 09/1997 • (RF 1989)

**FERRIN RICHARD L** (805)527-4295
3053 Springfield St Simi Valley CA 93063-1612 • rwferrin@earthlink.net • PSW • Tchr • Good Shepherd Simi Valley CA • (805)526-2482 • (S 1973)

**FERRIN WANDA JEAN** (805)527-4295
3053 N Springfield St Simi Valley CA 93063 • rwferrin@earthlink.net • PSW • Mem C • Trinity Simi Valley CA • (805)526-2429 • (S 1973)

**FESTA DIANNE L** (256)880-6557
2536 Clovis Rd SW Huntsville AL 35803-3521 • SO • 05/1999 • (RF 1967)

**FETT APRIL ANN**
3738 Glen Oaks Blvd #39 Sioux City IA 51104 • IW • Tchr • St Paul Sioux City IA • (712)252-0338 • (S 1999)

**FETT BRENDA*** (724)352-2112
116 W Water St Saxonburg PA 16056-9524 • EA • Tchr • St Luke Cabot PA • (412)352-2221 • (S 1982)

**FIALA MAXINE** (402)643-2849
411 N Columbia Ave Seward NE 68434-1601 • mmf5678@seward.cune.edu • NEB • Tchr • St John Seward NE • (402)643-4535 • (S 1970 MA)

**FIALA R JONATHAN** (314)225-8538
462 Xavier Ct Valley Park MO 63088-2323 • jfiala@stlnet.com • MO • Tchr • Our Savior Fenton MO • (314)343-7511 • (S 1989)

**FIALA ROBERT D DR** (402)643-2849
411 N Columbia Ave Seward NE 68434-1601 • rfiala@seward.cune.edu • NEB • SHS/C • Nebraska Seward NE • (S 1960 MA PHD)

**FIBIGER MARY ELLEN** (817)361-0561
2304 Whispering Ct Fort Worth TX 76133 • maryfibiger@mail.com • TX • Tchr • Grace Arlington TX • (817)274-1626 • (MQ 1993)

**FICHTNER ALLEN G** (414)632-5661
125 Crab Tree Ln Racine WI 53406-3620 • SW • EM • (S 1954 MED)

**FICHTNER L JOE** (708)450-9306
752 Worcester Ave Westchester IL 60154 • jkafich@aol.com • NI • Tchr • Bethel Chicago IL • (773)252-1104 • (S 1975)

**FICK DORENE P** (914)793-2356
118 Sagamore Rd # 1 Tuckahoe NY 10707-4008 • AT • 09/1999 • (BR 1992 MSW)

**FICK ELAINE CAROL** (815)568-6953
1012 N State St Marengo IL 60152-2264 • poplchurchmfwpreschool@juno.com • NI • Tchr • My Fathers World Crystal Lake IL • (815)455-3200 • (MQ 1989)

**FICK JEFFREY A** (515)275-3101
619 W Locust Ogden IA 50212-0759 • IW • P/Tchr • Trinity Boone IA • (515)432-5140 • (RF 1982)

**FICK KENNETH W** (262)681-0414
2425 Catherine Dr Racine WI 53402-1605 • SW • Tchr • Trinity Racine WI • (414)632-1766 • (S 1974)

**FICK MARSHA L** (561)964-8872
2684 Worcester Rd Lantana FL 33462-3870 • mlfdon93@aol.com • FG • Tchr • St Paul Boca Raton FL • (561)395-8548 • (RF 1971)

**FICK PATRICIA A**
831 Via Felicidad Vista CA 92084 • peacelemay@aol.com • PSW • St Paul Boca Raton FL • (S 1984 MPED)

**FICK REBECCA SUSANNE** (262)681-0414
2425 Catherine Dr Racine WI 53402-1605 • SW • Tchr • Trinity Racine WI • (414)632-1766 • (S 1974 MA)

**FIEDLER EUGENE K** (414)496-0849
2966 Sandia Dr Green Bay WI 54313-1423 • NW • EM • (RF 1958 MA)

**FIEDLER LEONARD V** (314)892-4884
4920 Dorsie Dr Saint Louis MO 63128-1810 • MO • SHS/C • Missouri Saint Louis MO • (314)317-4550 • (S 1967 MED)

**FIELDS PAM M**
10702 E Bogart Ave Mesa AZ 85208-8768 • EN • Tchr • Hales Corners Hales Corners WI • (414)529-6700 • (RF 1986)

**FIELITZ JANE L** (810)286-0689
39896 Rager Ct Clinton Township MI 48038-3095 • MI • Tchr • St Luke Clinton Township MI • (810)791-1151 • (S 1985)

**FIENE SHERYL ANN** (217)463-2117
2 Currey Dr Paris IL 61944 • 1234@comwares.net • CI • Mem C • Grace Paris IL • (217)466-1215 • (SP 1968)

**FILLMORE LAVERNE C**
2283 Waits Rd Owego NY 13827-6323 • EA • 06/1996 • (CQ 1986)

**FILTER MICHAEL R** (217)787-9029
3025 S Lincoln Ave Springfield IL 62704-4951 • CI • Tchr • LHS Springfield IL • (217)546-6363 • (RF 1982 MA)

**FINGERLING DANIEL R**
2909 E Weaver Pl Littleton CO 80121 • RM • S Miss • Rocky Mountain Aurora CO • (S 1993)

**FINK KARL J*** (562)420-5603
5390 E Canton St Long Beach CA 90815 • kfink@lalc.k12.ca.us • PSW • Tchr • Bethany Long Beach CA • (562)420-7783 • (S 1983 MED)

**FINK KRISTIN KAY**
3421 E Salisbury Cir Orange CA 92869-2592 • PSW • Tchr • Christ Fullerton CA • (714)870-7460 • (IV 1992)

**FINK MARY E** (562)420-5603
5390 Canton St Long Beach CA 90815 • PSW • Tchr • Bethany Long Beach CA • (562)420-7783 • (S 1983 MED)

**FINK NANCY J** (314)756-7674
6043 Highway 32 Farmington MO 63640-8729 • MO • Tchr • St Paul Farmington MO • (573)756-7872 • (S 1979)

**FINK ROBERT JEFFREY** (310)373-3030
17636 3/4 Virginia Ave Bellflower CA 90706 • PSW • Mem C • Ascension Torrance CA • (310)793-0071 • (S 1981)

**FINKE CHARLES W** (262)377-6218
1460 County Road C Grafton WI 53024-9739 • SW • SHS/C • South Wisconsin Milwaukee WI • (414)464-8100 • (RF 1958 MS MA)

**FINKE JULIE ANN** (817)861-3919
1705 Homedale Dr Apt 1701 Fort Worth TX 76112-3651 • TX • Tchr • Grace Arlington TX • (817)274-1654 • (RF 1990)

**FINKEL LINDA LEE** (313)263-5465
47116 Blueridge Dr Macomb MI 48044-2730 • MI • Tchr • St Paul Sterling Heights MI • (810)247-4427 • (S 1984)

**FINLEY MARGARET ANN** (415)731-4808
135 San Rafael Way San Francisco CA 94127-1919 • EN • Tchr • West Portal San Francisco CA • (415)665-6330 • (CQ 1987 MA)

**FINNEGAN PETER C** (708)383-2780
441 S Taylor Ave # 3C Oak Park IL 60302-4361 • petespin@mcs.net • NI • Tchr • Walther LHS Melrose Park IL • (708)344-0404 • (RF 1995)

**FIRNHABER HUBERT O***
1316 S 261st Pl Des Moines WA 98198 • NOW • EM • (S 1954 MED)

**FISCHER CHARLES E** (703)354-0176
7303 Elgar St Springfield VA 22151-3133 • SE • P/Tchr • Our Savior Arlington VA • (703)892-4846 • (RF 1965 MA)

**FISCHER CURTIS E** (308)385-4772
1726 Garland St Grand Island IL 68802 • curtone@go.com • NEB • Prin • Heartland Luth HS Grand Island NE • (308)381-7415 • (S 1969 MS)

**FISCHER DANIEL D** (852)28121568
C-4 South Bay Villas 4 South Bay Close Repulse Bay HONG KONG • dfischer@iawhk.com • PSW • S Miss • Pacific Southwest Irvine CA • (949)854-3232 • (S 1973 MA)

**FISCHER DENNIS** (517)652-8394
434 W Tuscola St Frankenmuth MI 48734-1551 • denfisch@juno.com • MI • Tchr • St Michael Richville MI • (517)868-4809 • (S 1970 MED)

**FISCHER FRANKLIN J** (360)437-6424
PO Box 65294 Port Ludlow WA 98365-0294 • NOW • EM • (S 1960 MED)

**FISCHER JERALYN S** (612)689-3703
32068 Lever St NE Cambridge MN 55008-6712 • MNN • 11/1998 • (S 1973)

**FISCHER JUNIOR P** (812)882-7079
1320 Upper 11th St Vincennes IN 47591-3338 • IN • EM • (S 1952 MS)

**FISCHER KAREN E** (810)296-9890
31215 Regal Dr Warren MI 48093-7336 • fischer-ak@juno.com • MI • Tchr • St Peter Macomb MI • (810)781-9296 • (CQ 1994)

**FISCHER KAREN KAY** (810)625-8565
5625 Wembly Ct Clarkston MI 48346-3062 • MI • Tchr • St Stephen Waterford MI • (248)673-6621 • (RF 1975)

**FISCHER MICHAEL N** (602)706-5119
3712 E Summerhaven Dr Phoenix AZ 85044-4532 • 103063.1114@compuserve.com • PSW • S Ex/S • Pacific Southwest Irvine CA • (949)854-3232 • (S 1975 MA)

**FISCHER ROBERT** (352)687-1592
9 Silver Ter Ocala FL 34472-2305 • FG • Tchr • St John Ocala FL • (352)622-7275 • (S 1973)

**FISCHER SHERI LYNN** (817)254-3560
4050 Fischer Rd Bartlett TX 76511-4024 • TX • Tchr • St Paul Thorndale TX • (512)898-2711 • (S 1993)

**FISCHER TRINA M** (713)827-8664
9310 Rosstown Way Houston TX 77080-7416 • TX • Tchr • St Mark Houston TX • (713)468-2623 • (S 1965)

**FISCHER WILLIAM C** (312)736-7318
3525 N Neva Ave Chicago IL 60634-3632 • NI • EM • (RF 1951 MED)

**FISCHL MARY JO** (916)725-0336
7811 Casa Bella Way Citrus Heights CA 95610-3923 • CNH • Tchr • Faith Fair Oaks CA • (916)961-4252 • (SP 1972)

**FISH CAROLYN ANN**
6605 Clayton Ave #413 Saint Louis MO 63139 • MO • Tchr • St Paul Saint Louis MO • (314)822-0447 • (RF 1969)

**FISH CYNTHIA A**
632 Sonya Dr Boonville MO 65233-1862 • dfish@undata.com • MO • Tchr • Zion Bunceton MO • (816)838-6428 • (RF 1983 MED)

**FISH DALE WALTON** (248)349-7558
40557 Heatherbrook Ln Novi MI 48375-4439 • MI • P/Tchr • Bethlehem Roseville MI • (810)777-9130 • (CQ 1978 MED)

**FISH JACK D**
6605 Clayton Ave Apt 413 Saint Louis MO 63139-3362 • SW • 08/1999 • (RF 1969 MA)

**FISHER JANET L** (773)775-6285
8300 W Summerdale Ave Chicago IL 60656-1449 • crffisherjl@crf.cuis.edu • NI • SHS/C • Northern Illinois Hillside IL • (RF 1976 MS)

**FISHER KATHERINE J** (423)490-0269
804 Harris Ln Chattanooga TN 37412-4114 • MDS • Tchr • Lutheran Chattanooga TN • (615)622-3755 • (RF 1977 MED)

**FISHER KATHRYN ANN** (757)930-0565
149 Milstead Rd Newport News VA 23606-1117 • SE • Tchr • Emmanuel Hampton VA • (757)723-8782 • (BR 1979)

**FISHER REBECCA LYNN** (402)477-3616
1618 S 20th St Lincoln NE 68502-2609 • rfisher@seward.cune.edu • NEB • SHS/C • Nebraska Seward NE • (S 1985 MA)

**FISK A CLIFFORD** (920)261-3119
866 Brentwood Ln Watertown WI 53094-6002 • SW • South Wisconsin Milwaukee WI • (414)464-8100 • (RF 1963)

**FISK DALE** (619)461-3315
4355 Summit Dr La Mesa CA 91941-7842 • PSW • Mem C • Christ La Mesa CA • (619)462-5211 • (RF 1963 MSMU)

**FISK HAROLD TALMAGE III** (217)789-2527
504 W Edwards St # 1 C Springfield IL 62704-1920 • trey@springnet1.com • CI • Tchr • LHS Springfield IL • (217)546-6363 • (RF 1994)

**FISK KATRINA A** (213)398-9275
168 Taylor St Manistee MI 49660-1252 • MI • Tchr • Trinity Manistee MI • (616)723-8700 • (RF 1984)

**FITCH RICK J*** (219)935-3536
5648 N Old US Highway 31 Rochester IN 46975-8324 • IN • 01/1999 • (RF 1982)

**FITZ HENRY WENDY SUE** (541)504-4231
1922 SW Reindeer Ave #A Redmond OR 97756 • wfitzhenry@hotmail.com • NOW • Tchr • Trinity Bend OR • (541)382-1832 • (SP 1995)

**FITZ PATRICK DAVID** (410)931-2588
11 Ratna Ct Baltimore MD 21236-2144 • SE • Tchr • Calvary Baltimore MD • (410)426-4301 • (S 1973 MED)

**FITZGERALD LUCAS MICHAEL** (949)854-6727
3926 S Flower Santa Ana CA 92707 • PSW • Tchr • South Bay HS-Torranc Torrance CA • (310)530-1231 • (IV 1998)

**FITZNER CYNTHIA E** (507)776-3226
234 N Central Ave Truman MN 56088-1002 • MNS • Tchr • St Paul Truman MN • (507)776-6541 • (SP 1978)

**FLACHSBART WALTER J** (510)933-8548
1580 Geary Rd Apt 277 Walnut Creek CA 94596-2745 • CI • EM • (RF 1929)

**FLAISCHAKER DONNA L** (708)349-8510
11604 Kaup Ln Orland Park IL 60467-6864 • NI • Tchr • Hope Chicago IL • (773)776-7816 • (RF 1983)

**FLAMMANN CHRISTINE M** (716)388-9658
19 Edenfield Rd Penfield NY 14526-1975 • cmfdel@rochester.rr.com • EA • Tchr • Faith Rochester NY • (716)385-2360 • (BR 1978)

**FLANDERMEYER CHRISTINE L** (636)925-0126
3010 Sherwood Ln Saint Charles MO 63301-0723 • mflandermeyer@earthlink.net • MO • 02/1992 02/2000 • (S 1974)

**FLANDERMEYER MICHAEL D** (314)925-0126
3010 Sherwood Ln Saint Charles MO 63301-0723 • mflandermeyer@lhssc.org • MO • Tchr • LHS St Charles Saint Peters MO • (636)928-5100 • (S 1975 MMU)

**FLANDERMEYER ROGER H** (708)456-3220
7925 W Cortland Pkwy Elmwood Park IL 60707-3525 • crfflanderh@curf.edu • NI • SHS/C • Northern Illinois Hillside IL • (CQ 1982 MA DPH)

**FLANDERMEYER WILFRED W** (708)647-0744
4211 W 83rd St Country Club Hills IL 60478 • wflander@intelnet.net.gt • NI • P/Tchr • St John Country Club Hills IL • (708)798-4131 • (S 1966 MED)

**FLANDERS JANELLE A** (417)887-4569
3124 E Swallow St Springfield MO 65804-6659 • flanders@rss.net • MO • Tchr • Springfield Springfield MO • (417)883-5717 • (S 1989)

**FLEER LAVONNE L** (402)329-6755
RR 1 Box 209 Pierce NE 68767-9304 • NEB • 06/1994 06/2000 • (S 1977)

**FLEGLER BRENDA KAY** (770)632-5776
25 Olympia PT Newnan GA 30265-3303 • bkf450ptga@aol.com • FG • Tchr • St Paul Peachtree City GA • (770)486-3545 • (S 1971 MED)

**FLEMING RUTH A** (309)682-2891
3021 W Wardcliffe Peoria IL 61604 • df3021@aol.com • CI • Tchr • Good Shepherd Pekin IL • (309)347-2020 • (RF 1967)

**FLENTGEN ANNE M** (718)894-4000
60-02 Maspeth Ave # 17 Maspeth NY 11378-2712 • AT • Tchr • Atlantic Bronxville NY • (914)337-5700 • (S 1989)

**FLESCH ROBERT W** (407)365-6670
1032 Beckstrom Dr Oviedo FL 32765-5914 • amfree1@aol.com • S • EM • (S 1965 MED)

**FLETT DOUGLAS A**
304 E Schaumburg Rd Schaumburg IL 60194-3515 • NI • Tchr • St Peter Schaumburg IL • (847)885-7636 • (RF 1971)

**FLETT MARY E** (310)644-6057
4602 Broadway Hawthorne CA 90250-3608 • PSW • Tchr • South Bay LHS Inglewood CA • (310)672-1101 • (RF 1978 MUED)

**FLICKER GAYLORD E** (208)237-2467
2614 Faye Ln Pocatello ID 83201-1916 • geflicker@aol.com • NOW • Mem C • Grace Pocatello ID • (208)237-0467 • (S 1974 MAD)

**FLIEGE JUDITH B** (217)787-9011
2188 Winch Rd Springfield IL 62707-7751 • sfliege@aol.com • CI • Tchr • Trinity Springfield IL • (217)787-2323 • (CQ 1986 MA)

**FLIEGE LAURA L** (217)753-2308
208 E Black Ave Springfield IL 62702-2613 • CI • Tchr • Trinity Springfield IL • (217)787-2323 • (RF 1976 MCMU)

**FLOETKE JAY W** (913)651-2764
710 Miami St Leavenworth KS 66048-1856 • KS • Prin • St Paul Leavenworth KS • (913)682-5553 • (S 1970 MED)

**FLOETKE KAMELA S**
207 W Van Emmon Yorkville IL 60560 • NI • Tchr • Cross Yorkville IL • (630)553-7861 • (S 1998)

**FLOETKE KARL D** (941)619-7218
5803 Buck Run Dr Lakeland FL 33811 • kfloetke@aol.com • FG • Prin • St Paul Lakeland FL • (941)644-7710 • (S 1972 MED)

**FLOETKE PAMELA B** (913)651-2764
710 Miami St Leavenworth KS 66048-1856 • KS • Tchr • St Paul Leavenworth KS • (913)682-5553 • (S 1971)

**FLORES DE APODACA LUCILLE** (714)744-6038
9742 Willow Glenn Cir Santa Ana CA 92705 • luciflores@home.com • PSW • Tchr • Salem Orange CA • (714)633-2366 • (CQ 1999)

**FLORINE DAVID A** (812)378-4907
5645 E Fountain Way Columbus IN 47201-8271 • dflorine@stpeters-columbus.org • IN • Prin • St Peter Columbus IN • (812)372-5266 • (RF 1978 MSED)

**FLORIP EUNICE E** (616)458-9516
1310 Cranbrook Ter NE Grand Rapids MI 49505-5781 • MI • EM • (RF 1956 MA)

**FLOYD DEBRA LYN** (217)222-3138
827 Harrison Quincy IL 62301 • CI • Tchr • St James Quincy IL • (217)222-8447 • (S 1986 MA)

**FLUEGEL DOYLE WAYNE**
917 Hudson Dr Garland TX 75043-5333 • TX • Tchr • Lutheran HS of Dalla Dallas TX • (214)349-8912 • (CQ 1995)

**FLUEGEL ELIZABETH A** (703)379-4167
1734 Kingsgate Ct Unit 302 Alexandria VA 22302-2255 • SE • S Ex/S • Southeastern Alexandria VA • (RF 1977 MA)

**FLUEGGE CHRISTIANE FAYE** (760)291-0210
301 W Vermont Ave #125 Escondido CA 92025 • PSW • Tchr • Grace Escondido CA • (760)745-0831 • (S 1999)

**FLUEGGE KATHLEEN M** (219)485-9010
2504 Silver Wolf Trl Fort Wayne IN 46815-8582 • IN • Tchr • Holy Cross Fort Wayne IN • (219)483-3173 • (RF 1976 MA)

**FLYNN ALAN J**
C/O Messiah Lutheran Church PO Box 7190 Citrus Heights CA 95621-7190 • CNH • 09/1998 • (RF 1973 MED)

**FLYNN DANIEL J**
7580 Webster Church Rd Whitmore Lake Ann Arbor MI 48189 • flynnd@ccaa.edu • MI • SHS/C • Michigan Ann Arbor MI • (S 1977 MED)

**FLYNN MICHAEL D** (651)639-1221
1425 Arden Oaks Dr Arden Hills MN 55112-6956 • MNS • SHS/C • Minnesota South Burnsville MN • (SP 1975)

**FOARD JULIA MAE**
115 E 73rd St Chicago IL 60619 • NI • Tchr • Saint Paul Chicago IL • (773)721-1438 • (GB 1937 MA)

**FODE RONALD A** (708)636-1542
9156 S Sawyer Ave Evergreen Park IL 60805-1640 • NI • Tchr • Saint Paul Chicago IL • (RF 1964 MMU)

**FOERSTER JUDY ELLEN** (716)662-2646
4523 S Buffalo Orchard Park NY 14127 • EA • 07/1999 • (S 1971 MA)

**FOERSTER ROBERT C** (716)634-5111
4523 S Buffalo St Orchard Park NY 14127 • foerster6@aol.com • EA • Eastern Williamsville NY • (716)634-5111 • (S 1971 MA)

**FOGO R SCOTT**
2073 Seahurst Las Vegas NV 89122 • PSW • Tchr • Faith LHS Las Vegas NV • (702)804-4400 • (IV 1996)

**FOLKERTS DEBORAH K** (310)539-7895
22555 Nadine Cir Apt 126 Torrance CA 90505-2724 • PSW • Mem C • Ascension Torrance CA • (310)793-0071 • (S 1995)

**FONT MICHAEL ALAN** (219)264-9847
27350 Bittersweet Ln Elkhart IN 46514-8203 • mike@trinityl.org • IN • Tchr • Trinity Elkhart IN • (219)522-1491 • (RF 1993 MEAD)

**FOOTE HENRY C** (716)731-9601
2499 Niagara Rd Niagara Falls NY 14304-2018 • EA • Tchr • St John North Tonawanda NY • (716)693-9677 • (BR 1983)

**FOOTE KAREN A** (716)731-9601
2499 Niagara Rd Niagara Falls NY 14304-2018 • EA • Tchr • St John North Tonawanda NY • (716)693-9677 • (BR 1983 MA)

**FORD DOROTHEA M** (727)442-3426
1457 Norwood Ave Clearwater FL 33756-2456 • FG • EM • (RF 1973)

**FORD LOIS JEAN** (352)324-2640
703 S Lakeshore Blvd Howey in the Hills FL 34737-3903 • fordplace@aol.com • FG • Tchr • Faith Eustis FL • (352)589-5683 • (BR 1975)

**FOREMAN JANISE M** (313)697-2096
10942 Buchanan St Belleville MI 48111-3454 • MI • Tchr • Emmanuel Dearborn MI • (313)561-6265 • (S 1982)

**FORKE BRIAN** (414)353-7431
6304 N 119th St Milwaukee WI 53225-1117 • SW • Tchr • Milwaukee LHS Milwaukee WI • (414)461-6000 • (S 1985)

**FORKE DONNA J** (402)643-4059
1038 N 8th St Seward NE 68434-1212 • NEB • Tchr • St John Seward NE • (402)643-4535 • (S 1975 MED)

**FORKE MARLEE ANN** (715)833-9067
2022 E Lexington Blvd Eau Claire WI 54701-6734 • NW • 06/1989 03/2000 • (S 1984)

**FORSHEE MARLENE J** (920)994-2433
128 Park St Adell WI 53001 • mforshee@yzkids.com • SW • Tchr • St John Random Lake WI • (920)994-9190 • (MQ 1988)

**FORTKAMP ELIZABETH ANN**
642 Gruber Apt D3 Frankenmuth MI 48734 • MI • Tchr • St Lorenz Frankenmuth MI • (517)652-6141 • (S 1999)

**FOSSE BETH SUSANNE** (319)393-6691
3700 Northwood Dr NE Cedar Rapids IA 52402-2733 • kbfosse@aol.com • IE • 07/1998 07/2000 • (RF 1992)

**FOSTER CARMEN M** (309)935-6684
5-4 S State St Annawan IL 61234-9777 • cfoster68@hotmail.com • CI • Tchr • St Paul Kewanee IL • (309)852-2421 • (RF 1990)

**FOSTER JEANETTE MARILYN** (414)452-3147
1401 Carmen Ave Sheboygan WI 53081-7521 • SW • Tchr • Trinity Sheboygan WI • (920)458-8248 • (CQ 1996)

**FOUNTAIN JOSEPH C** (320)864-3763
102 Desoto Ave N Glencoe MN 55336-3003 • fountain@hutchtel.net • MNS • Tchr • First Glencoe MN • (320)864-3317 • (SP 1968)

**FOUST GLADYS A** (407)889-5958
6430 Lakeville Rd Orlando FL 32818-8817 • S • Tchr • St Luke Oviedo FL • (407)365-3228 • (RF 1974)

**FOWLER ELEANOR L** (303)948-9519
12205 W Temple Dr Morrison CO 80465-1735 • efowler@bethluth.net • RM • Tchr • Bethlehem Lakewood CO • (303)238-7676 • (RF 1981 MA)

**FOWLER KATRINA MARIE** (630)307-8028
1171 W Bryn Manr Ave Roselle IL 60172-2670 • NI • Tchr • Immanuel Palatine IL • (847)359-1936 • (RF 1999)

**FOWLS ROBERT W** (541)382-1850
2511 NE Ravenwood Bend OR 97701 • bfowls@bendcable.com • NOW • Prin • Trinity Bend OR • (541)382-1832 • (RF 1974 MA)

**FOX DOUGLAS D**
PO Box 150 Downsville NY 13755-0150 • dougfox@aol.com • TX • Tchr • Texas Austin TX • (RF 1975 MA)

**FOX GEORGE G** (714)226-0905
3156 W Bridgeport Ave Anaheim CA 92804-1702 • PSW • Tchr • Holy Cross Cypress CA • (714)527-7928 • (RF 1971)

**FOX STARLAYNE G** (714)226-0905
3156 W Bridgeport Ave Anaheim CA 92804-1702 • foxes456@aol.com • PSW • Tchr • Holy Cross Cypress CA • (714)527-7928 • (RF 1971)

**FOXE GARY W** (262)246-8233
W240N6532 Ash St Sussex WI 53089-3016 • SW • Mem C • Brookfield Brookfield WI • (262)783-4270 • (RF 1974 MCMU)

**FRAHM TIMOTHY R**
8303 Timber Cabin San Antonio TX 78250-4260 • TX • Tchr • Shepherd Of The Hill San Antonio TX • (210)614-3741 • (AU 1995)

**FRANCK DONNA JEAN** (847)253-8019
1315 E Ironwood Dr Mt Prospect IL 60056-1441 • NI • Tchr • St Paul Mount Prospect IL • (847)255-6733 • (RF 1972 MED)

**FRANK ANN M** (636)464-0075
3529 Jeffco Blvd Arnold MO 63010 • MO • St Paul Mount Prospect IL • (S 1971 MS)

**FRANK ANNA MARIE**
10501 E Bloomington Freewy#214 Bloomington MN 55420 • S • Tchr • Open Arms Bloomington MN • (612)888-5116 • (S 1999)

**FRANK DAVID J** (816)224-3262
808 SW Stonehenge Dr Blue Springs MO 64015 • davefrank@compuserve.com • MO • Mem C • Timothy Blue Springs MO • (816)228-5300 • (S 1975)

**FRANK DONALD D** (319)296-2732
877 Juniper Dr Waterloo IA 50702-4630 • IE • 01/1987 01/2000 • (S 1959 MS)

**FRANK GEORGE C** (517)792-4726
2416 N Woodbridge St Saginaw MI 48602-5256 • MI • Tchr • Bethlehem Saginaw MI • (517)755-1146 • (RF 1964 MCMU)

**FRANK GLENN W** (715)536-4274
1003 Madison St Merrill WI 54452-3031 • NW • Tchr • Trinity Merrill WI • (715)536-7501 • (S 1966 MA)

**FRANK JOHN R** (314)305-8286
17 Keystone Ct Fenton MO 63026-4883 • MO • Mem C • Resurrection Saint Louis MO • (314)843-6633 • (S 1969 MCMU)

**FRANK JON D** (517)791-5003
3600 Barnard Rd Saginaw MI 48603-2509 • getfritzed@hotmail.com • MI • Tchr • Valley Saginaw MI • (517)790-1676 • (S 1992)

**FRANK MARGARET ANN** (512)251-2526
2106 Haas Ln Austin TX 78728-6844 • TX • Tchr • Our Savior Austin TX • (512)836-9600 • (S 1975)

**FRANK REBECCA JANE** (785)765-3815
PO Box 361 Alma KS 66401-0361 • becky³frank@yahoo.com • KS • Tchr • St John Alma KS • (785)765-3914 • (S 1987)

**FRANK REINHOLD E** (219)749-9817
3220 Marias Dr Fort Wayne IN 46815-6324 • IN • Tchr • Bethlehem Fort Wayne IN • (219)456-3587 • (RF 1971 MS)

**FRANK SHERRY J** (319)296-2732
877 Juniper Dr Waterloo IA 50702-4630 • sf12599@cedarnet.org • IE • Tchr • Immanuel Waterloo IA • (319)233-3967 • (CQ 1986 LITTD)

**FRANK SUSAN FAYE** (904)672-3612
18 Southern Trace Blvd Ormond Beach FL 32174-1817 • tedsuefrank@msn.com • FG • Tchr • Trinity Holly Hill FL • (904)255-7580 • (RF 1968)

**FRANK TED A** (904)672-3612
18 Southern Trace Blvd Ormond Beach FL 32174 • tedsuefrank@msn.com • FG • Prin • Trinity Holly Hill FL • (904)255-7580 • (RF 1968 MA)

**FRANK WARREN G**
C/O Washington Lutheran School 4474 Butler Hill Rd Saint Louis MO 63128-3635 • MO • Trinity Holly Hill FL • (S 1970 MSED)

**FRANKE GINA GAYLE**
5907 Eckhert Rd #223 II San Antonio TX 78240 • gina30girl@yahoo.com • TX • Tchr • Redeemer San Antonio TX • (210)732-4112 • (AU 1992 MED)

**FRANKE NANCY L** (812)523-1710
2067 Creekside Dr Seymour IN 47274 • diggernancfranke@juno.com • IN • 06/1993 06/2000 • (RF 1990)

**FRANKE SANDRA R** (812)522-7517
9309 E 100 N Seymour IN 47274 • frankefarm@juno.com • IN • 09/1995 09/1999 • (RF 1984 MS)

**FRANZ TIMOTHY S** (414)327-6617
4141 S 60th St Apt 20 Greenfield WI 53220-3105 • SW • Tchr • Martin LHS Greendale WI • (414)421-4000 • (S 1980)

**FRANZEN ARLYN D** (217)787-5440
1212 S Grand Ave W Apt 211 Springfield IL 62704-3574 • CI • Tchr • Our Savior's Springfield IL • (217)546-4531 • (S 1962 MA)

**FRANZEN KIMBERLY D** (402)564-1508
2918 32nd St Columbus NE 68601-1750 • NEB • Tchr • Immanuel Columbus NE • (402)564-8423 • (CQ 1998)

**FRAZIER HOWARD KIRBY**
1002 Allison St Brenham TX 77833-5857 • TX • Tchr • Grace Brenham TX • (979)836-3475 • (AU 1988)

**FREDENBURG MARTHA ANN** (713)849-0285
9634 Lark Meadow Dr Houston TX 77040-3916 • AFredenbrg@aol.com • TX • Tchr • Memorial Houston TX • (713)782-4022 • (CQ 1990)

**FREDERICKSEN GARY J** (718)428-6676
213-50 36th Ave Bayside NY 11361-1547 • AT • Tchr • Martin Luther Maspeth NY • (718)894-4000 • (CQ 1993)

**FREDERICKSEN HEATHER J**
1010 Maurer St Wilton IA 52778-9563 • IE • Tchr • Zion Wilton IA • (319)732-2912 • (BR 1987)

**FREDERICKSEN LYNNETTE** (414)694-3534
10425 50th Ave Pleasant Prairie WI 53158-3400 • lfreder@execpc.com • SW • Tchr • Lutheran High School Racine WI • (414)637-6538 • (MQ 1995)

**FREDERICKSON SHARON K** (507)534-4160
407 8th St SW Plainview MN 55964-1105 • MNS • Tchr • Immanuel Plainview MN • (507)534-2108 • (SP 1974)

**FREDERIKSEN DIANA LOUISE** (708)834-3892
634 S Hawthorne Ave Elmhurst IL 60126-4243 • NI • Tchr • Immanuel Elmhurst IL • (630)832-9302 • (RF 1961)

**FREDRICH PETER D** (517)662-2327
209 Ruth St Auburn MI 48611-9463 • pcfredri@concentric.net • MI • P/Tchr • Grace Auburn MI • (517)662-4791 • (S 1975)

**FREEL DEBRA S** (913)286-2608
3015 N Kansas Ave Topeka KS 66617-1456 • KS • Tchr • Topeka Topeka KS • (785)357-0382 • (CQ 1979)

**FREEMAN ALAN L** (410)663-1145
19 Oak Sylvan Way Baltimore MD 21236 • alan0@erols.com • SE • Tchr • Baltimore LHS Baltimore MD • (410)825-2323 • (CQ 1995)

**FREEMAN LISA M** (847)803-5493
1710 N Beech Rd Mt Prospect IL 60056-1602 • NI • 08/1999 • (S 1985 MA)

**FREESE JAMES W** (414)442-3645
3222 N 49th St Milwaukee WI 53216-3204 • freesej@aol.com • SW • SHS/C • South Wisconsin Milwaukee WI • (414)464-8100 • (RF 1978 MCMU)

**FREIDENBERGER KAREN L** (970)867-6808
732 Carol St Fort Morgan CO 80701-3516 • fredf@twol.com • RM • Tchr • Trinity Fort Morgan CO • (970)867-4931 • (S 1976)

**FREITAG GENE R** (810)773-5059
23708 Petersburg Ave Eastpointe MI 48021-3402 • gfreitag@lhsa.com • MI • Tchr • LHS North Macomb MI • (810)781-9151 • (S 1967 MSLS MHST)

**FREMDER LINDA K** (219)563-3408
541 Bond St Wabash IN 46992-2107 • IN • 09/1996 09/1999 • (S 1969 MSED)

**FRENK ELLEN LOUISE** (815)459-6499
237 Edgewater Dr Crystal Lake IL 60014-5170 • NI • Tchr • Immanuel Crystal Lake IL • (815)459-1444 • (RF 1988)

**FRERICHS BRENDA M** (541)888-2698
2312 N Green Valley Pkwy # 713 Henderson NV 89014 • NOW • 12/1998 • (PO 1998)

**FRERICHS DEBORAH E** (541)850-6651
5507 Bel Aire Dr Klamath Falls OR 97603 • pfrerich@kfall.net • NOW • Tchr • Little Lambs Klamath Falls OR • (541)882-9552 • (RF 1995)

**FRERICHS TAMMY JO**
2120 E 100 S Saint George UT 84790-1578 • NOW • Tchr • Forest Hills Cornelius OR • (503)359-4853 • (PO 1991)

**FRERKING JAMES V**
14780 Diamond View Dr Pioneer CA 95666-9217 • frerking@noahslanding.com • CNH • 08/1998 08/2000 • (SP 1978 MED)

**FRERKING LOIS A** (413)532-4272
39 Belvidere Ave Holyoke MA 01040 • lfrerking@hotmail.com • NE • P/Tchr • First Holyoke MA • (413)532-4272 • (S 1974 MA)

**FRERKING NATHAN D** (281)370-1082
8318 Autumn Willow Dr Tomball TX 77375-2811 • nfrerking@ev1.net • TX • Tchr • Trinity Spring TX • (281)376-5810 • (S 1991)

**FRERKING PATRICK D**
C/O Rev Craig Molitoris China Min Team 12 Wiltshire Rd Kowloon Tong HONG KONG • frerking@hs.hkis.edu.hk • NOW • S Miss • Northwest Portland OR • (S 1987 MED)

**FRESE ARTHUR E** (415)469-9099
1275 Monterey Blvd San Francisco CA 94127-2507 • EN • Tchr • West Portal San Francisco CA • (415)665-6330 • (S 1962 MA)

**FRESE LELAND G** (408)253-3216
20040 Rodrigues Ave Apt D Cupertino CA 95014-3142 • CNH • Tchr • School Of Our Savior Cupertino CA • (408)252-0250 • (S 1959)

**FRESE PAUL M** (312)620-5434
426 S Lewis Ave Lombard IL 60148-2937 • NI • Mem C • Zion Hinsdale IL • (630)323-0384 • (S 1963)

**FREUDENBERG HOWARD THOMAS** (815)227-1138
1904 Spring Brook Ave Rockford IL 61107-1544 • NI • Tchr • Luther Academy Rockford IL • (815)877-9551 • (S 1979)

**FREUDENBERG KAREN JOAN** (815)227-1138
1904 Spring Brook Ave Rockford IL 61107-1544 • kfreudberg@aol.com • NI • Tchr • Luther Academy Rockford IL • (815)877-9551 • (PO 1983)

**FREUDENBURG CURTIS C** (517)893-1062
1903 S Kiesel St Bay City MI 48706-5243 • MI • Tchr • Zion Bay City MI • (517)893-5793 • (S 1960 MED)

**FREUDENBURG DON L** (845)783-0852
29 Dorothy Dr Monroe NY 10950-4307 • dfreud@stpaulmonroeny.org • AT • Mem C • St Paul Monroe NY • (845)782-5600 • (S 1961 MA)

**FREUDENBURG JOAN K** (309)691-5022
5118 N Merrimac Ave Peoria IL 61614-4658 • CI • EM • (S 1957)

**FREUDENBURG KATHRYN ANN** (507)282-4162
2512 9th Ave NW Rochester MN 55901-2309 • kafreudenburg@rcls.net • MNS • Tchr • Rochester Central Rochester MN • (507)289-3267 • (SP 1968)

**FREUDENBURG VICTOR E** (407)277-4903
532 Pinar Dr Orlando FL 32825-7818 • FG • EM • (S 1949 MA)

**FREUND JOYCE E** (660)463-3163
RR 3 Box 183 Concordia MO 64020-9504 • MO • Tchr • St Paul Stover MO • (573)377-2690 • (S 1989)

**FREYMARK ROBERT C** (414)355-7587
6471 W Goodrich Ln Brown Deer WI 53223 • rfreymark@aol.com • SW • South Wisconsin Milwaukee WI • (414)464-8100 • (S 1968 MED)

**FRICK DEAN D** (303)637-0349
2632 Cherry Cir Brighton CO 80601-3458 • RM • Tchr • Zion Brighton CO • (303)659-3443 • (SP 1991)

**FRICK KARL G** (219)493-6360
2103 Skyhawk Dr Fort Wayne IN 46815-7758 • IN • Tchr • St Peter Fort Wayne IN • (219)749-5811 • (RF 1975 MED)

**FRICK KRISTEN SUE** (920)845-9238
PO Box 275 Luxemburg WI 54217 • deerwh@netscape.net • NW • P/Tchr • St Paul Luxemburg WI • (920)845-2095 • (MQ 1992)

**FRICKE JOHN M** (734)971-5463
3150 Fernwood Ave Ann Arbor MI 48108-1956 • MI • EM • (S 1966 MAT PHD)

**FRICKE RAYMOND W** (972)492-4288
3121 Fairgate Dr Carrollton TX 75007-3953 • TX • EM • (RF 1955 MA)

**FRIDLEY SANDRA KAY** (314)447-7283
1611 Whitehirst Manor Dr Saint Charles MO 63304-5597 • MO • Tchr • Zion Harvester MO • (314)441-7424 • (S 1969 MED)

**FRIEDRICH CHRISTEN LOUISE*** (309)348-3568
11510 Friedrich Rd Green Valley IL 61534-9584 • friedrich@heart.net • CI • 11/1998 • (RF 1985)

**FRIEDRICH EUGENE T** (219)749-5518
7726 Maysville Rd Fort Wayne IN 46815-8029 • friedrich1@juno.com • IN • Prin • St Peter Fort Wayne IN • (219)749-5811 • (RF 1966 MSED)

**FRIEDRICH LAURIE A** (402)643-4380
503 Bader Ave Seward NE 68434-1127 • lfriedrich@seward.cune.edu • NEB • SHS/C • Nebraska Seward NE • (SP 1980 MS)

**FRIEDRICH RONALD H** (720)685-3009
525 Badger Creek Dr Brighton CO 80601 • friedu2@isbe.accessus.net • RM • Prin • Zion Brighton CO • (303)659-2339 • (S 1970 MA)

**FRIEDRICH RONALD P** (661)272-0231
2049 Clearwater Ave Palmdale CA 93551-4118 • PSW • Tchr • First Van Nuys CA • (818)786-3002 • (RF 1969)

**FRIEDRICHS FREDERICK** (619)558-1735
3919 Kenosha Ave San Diego CA 92117-5305 • PSW • Tchr • St Paul San Diego CA • (619)272-6363 • (S 1982)

**FRIELING DELVIN R**
146 Narrows Loop #2176 Waleska GA 33813-3705 • FG • Tchr • St Paul Lakeland FL • (941)644-7710 • (S 1969)

**FRIELING GARY M** (972)517-8072
6200 Allegheny Trl Plano TX 75023-4408 • TX • Tchr • Our Redeemer Dallas TX • (214)368-1465 • (S 1970)

**FRIELING KURT F** (972)943-9468
2905 Mulberry Ln Plano TX 75074 • TX • Tchr • Lutheran HS of Dalla Dallas TX • (214)349-8912 • (AU 1998)

**FRIESENHAHN JUDITH L** (210)690-0757
8714 Wellesley Manor Dr San Antonio TX 78240-2116 • TX • Tchr • Shepherd Hills San Antonio TX • (210)614-3742 • (RF 1982 MA)

**FRILLMANN EDNA M** (717)226-8825
HC 1 Hawley PA 18428-9552 • AT • EM • (RF 1950)

**FRINGER EILEEN E** (763)780-5341
1102 97th Ln NE Blaine MN 55434-3556 • lfringer@pclink.com • MNS • Tchr • King Of Kings Roseville MN • (651)484-9206 • (SP 1967)

**FRITSCH KREGG C** (972)418-9182
2408 Via Bonita Carrollton TX 75006-4506 • TX • Tchr • Holy Cross Dallas TX • (214)358-4396 • (AA 1987 MA)

**FRITSCHE RONALD W**
2405 Progress Dr Brenham TX 77833-5531 • TX • P/Tchr • Grace Brenham TX • (409)836-2030 • (RF 1976 MED)

**FRITZ ANDREW S** (847)359-4628
103 S Plum Grove Rd Palatine IL 60067-6244 • NI • Tchr • St Peter Arlington Heights IL • (847)253-6638 • (AA 1993)

**FRITZ ANN R** (219)744-4074
429 Englewood Ct Fort Wayne IN 46807-2018 • IN • Tchr • St Paul Fort Wayne IN • (219)424-0049 • (RF 1981)

**FRITZ BEVERLY ANN** (317)786-7618
6320 Meridian Woods Blvd Indianapolis IN 46217-3850 • emmaus@inct.net • IN • Tchr • Emmaus Indianapolis IN • (317)632-1486 • (RF 1965)

**FRITZ ELMER E** (612)467-2844
9625 Zebra Ave Young America MN 55397-9417 • MNS • EM • (RF 1952)

**FRITZ ESTELLA** (417)623-5589
820 S Moffet Ave Joplin MO 64801-4321 • MO • EM • (WN 1945 MS)

**FRITZ GARY A** (612)486-9123
5887 Hodgson Rd Shoreview MN 55126 • bjsded@aol.com • MNS • Tchr • Concordia Academy Roseville MN • (612)484-8429 • (SP 1988)

**FRITZ KAREN D** (715)675-2132
4800 N 32nd Ave Wausau WI 54401-8308 • NW • Tchr • St John Merrill WI • (715)536-7264 • (SP 1989)

**FRITZ SHARLYN SUE** (713)778-9033
5763 Birdwood Rd Houston TX 77096-2108 • fritzrr@flash.net • TX • Tchr • Pilgrim Houston TX • (713)666-3706 • (S 1966 MS)

**FRITZ ZELMA ETHEL** (815)338-4589
13210 Perkins Rd Woodstock IL 60098-7379 • NI • Tchr • Immanuel Crystal Lake IL • (815)459-1444 • (RF 1982)

**FROBEL DAVID P** (248)681-4840
2987 Muirwood Ct Waterford MI 48329-2396 • MI • Tchr • St John Rochester MI • (248)652-8830 • (AA 1986)

**FROEHLICH JUDITH A** (414)462-5510
9502 W Ruby Ave Wauwatosa WI 53225 • NE • Tchr • Immanuel Danbury CT • (203)748-3320 • (RF 1952)

**FROMM CLAY M** (414)329-9216
5309 W Oklahoma Ave Milwaukee WI 53219 • clfromm@execpc.com • SW • Tchr • Oklahoma Avenue Milwaukee WI • (414)543-3580 • (CQ 1999)

**FROMM LA RAE L** (414)329-9216
5309 W Oklahoma Ave Milwaukee WI 53219 • clfromm@execpc.com • SW • Tchr • Oklahoma Avenue Milwaukee WI • (414)543-3580 • (CQ 1999)

**FROMME MELINDA G** (512)285-3421
612 Cardinal Elgin TX 78621 • TX • Tchr • Redeemer Austin TX • (512)451-6478 • (AU 1997)

**FRUEND ELIZABETH LEAH** (314)397-3764
303 Green Haven Dr Saint Peters MO 63376-1991 • MO • Tchr • LHS St Charles Saint Peters MO • (636)928-5100 • (MQ 1992)

**FRUSCO DIANE I** (201)381-0873
288 Watchung Ave North Plainfield NJ 07060-4041 • NJ • Tchr • Redeemer Westfield NJ • (908)232-1592 • (BR 1984)

**FRUSH SHAWN M** (219)269-2699
406 N Maple Ave Warsaw IN 46580-3424 • IN • Tchr • Redeemer Warsaw IN • (219)267-5656 • (RF 1985)

**FRUSTI KATHLEEN H** (517)784-6791
3373 Eastlane St Jackson MI 49203-5055 • MI • Tchr • Trinity Jackson MI • (517)750-2105 • (S 1981 MED)

**FRUSTI PHILIP JOHN**
3260 S 850 W San Pierre IN 46374 • IN • Tchr • St Peter North Judson IN • (219)896-2025 • (AA 1983)

**FRUSTI TIMOTHY MARK** (517)784-6791
3373 Eastlane St Jackson MI 49203-5055 • frustt@ccaa.edu • MI • SHS/C • Michigan Ann Arbor MI • (SP 1977 MA)

**FRY LORI S**
E7766 North Ave Lyndon Station WI 53944-9605 • SW • Tchr • St Peter Reedsburg WI • (608)524-4066 • (RF 1985)

**FRY TIMOTHY K** (972)494-4384
1920 Cobblestone Ln Garland TX 75042-4652 • TX • Tchr • Lutheran HS of Dalla Dallas TX • (214)349-8912 • (S 1988 MS)

**FRYAR JANE L** (314)846-8528
6500 Towne Woods Dr Saint Louis MO 63129-4522 • MO • S Ex/S • Missouri Saint Louis MO • (314)317-4550 • (S 1972 MAT)

**FRYMAN SHARON MARIE** (901)373-9795
4349 Manor Haven Dr Memphis TN 38128-3222 • MDS • 06/1996 • (RF 1991)

**FUCHS ARTHUR H** (612)467-3466
24 1st Ave SW Young America MN 55397-9200 • MNS • EM • (S 1949 MED)

**FUCHS JUDITH M** (210)641-1520
11603 Spring Crest Dr San Antonio TX 78249 • judimf@yahoo.com • TX • Tchr • LHS Of San Antonio San Antonio TX • (210)733-7771 • (CQ 1997 MS MA)

**FUCHS KAREN G** (507)334-1954
1619 Greenwood Pl Faribault MN 55021-6786 • MNS • Tchr • Faribault Faribault MN • (507)334-7982 • (SP 1972)

**FUCHS STEVEN M** (216)333-8975
562 Humiston Dr Bay Village OH 44140-3018 • OH • Tchr • LHS West Rocky River OH • (440)333-1660 • (S 1979 MA)

**FUERSTENAU JEANNINE L** (414)481-5775
3270 S Logan Ave Bay View WI 53207-2856 • rfuerst@execpc.com • SW • Tchr • Concordia Racine WI • (262)554-1659 • (MQ 1986)

**FUESSEL SUSAN** (915)651-9555
4077 Commissioners Ln San Angelo TX 76905-7557 • TX • Tchr • Trinity San Angelo TX • (915)947-1275 • (RF 1970)

**FUHRMANN GERALD W** (914)245-4172
197 Granite Springs Rd Yorktown Heights NY 10598-3305 • AT • SHS/C • Atlantic Bronxville NY • (914)337-5700 • (S 1965 MS)

**FULLINGTON MICHAEL** (262)375-0335
1603 River Ln Grafton WI 53024 • fullhouse2000@ameritech.net • FG • 08/2000 • (MQ 1998)

**FULMER MARSHA J**
17 D Founders Way St Louis MO 63105 • MO • Tchr • Salem Affton MO • (314)352-4454 • (RF 1982)

**FUNCK LYNNE S** (410)661-1763
3201 Hiss Ave Baltimore MD 21234 • signdovesf@aol.com • SE • 03/1984 03/2000 • (RF 1968 MA)

**FUNK BETTY M** (216)481-8845
17917 E Park Dr Cleveland OH 44119-2013 • OH • 08/1991 08/2000 • (RF 1973)

## G

**GABLE DONNA J** (901)387-0306
3350 Pembroke Ellis Cv Memphis TN 38133-3870 • MDS • Tchr • Christ The King Memphis TN • (901)682-8405 • (RF 1959)

**GABLE GARY G** (425)277-1303
1108 Tacoma Ave NE Renton WA 98056-3539 • gggab@king-of-kings.org • NOW • Mem C • King Of Kings Renton WA • (425)226-1480 • (S 1962 MA)

**GABLER FRANK H** (414)282-0928
3735 W Loomis Rd Greenfield WI 53221-1054 • SW • Tchr • Martin LHS Greendale WI • (414)421-4000 • (RF 1965 MSED)

**GABRIEL SHARON K** (217)525-3568
4120 Cessna Ln Springfield IL 62707-3510 • sharonkg@famvid.com • CI • 02/1995 02/2000 • (RF 1977 MSED)

**GADBURY ANDREA MICHELE** (909)361-4415
6364 Brian Cir Riverside CA 92509-0153 • agadbury@hotmail.com • PSW • Tchr • Mount Calvary Diamond Bar CA • (909)861-2740 • (PO 1993 MA)

**GADE DONALD E** (573)406-1530
20 Village Rd Hannibal MO 63401-6849 • dgade@gar.ivy.tec.in.us • EN • P/Tchr • St John Hannibal MO • (573)221-0215 • (S 1960 MA)

**GADE WILLIAM EUGENE**
1154 S 8th Kankakee IL 60901 • NI • Mem C • Immanuel Dundee IL • (847)428-4477 • (CQ 1983)

**GAEDE RICHARD H** (713)473-0715
1207 Rebecca Dr Pasadena TX 77506-5120 • TX • EM • (S 1959)

**GAEDE VALERIE L** (630)231-1986
555 Elite Ave West Chicago IL 60185-2111 • NI • Tchr • St John Wheaton IL • (630)668-0701 • (S 1979)

**GAGAN PATRICK S** (562)429-1538
4229 Iroquois Ave Lakewood CA 90713-3211 • psgag@earthlink.net • PSW • P/Tchr • Concordia Cerritos CA • (562)926-2491 • (S 1978)

**GALEK LINDA L** (773)286-3385
6530 W Irving Park Rd # 208 Chicago IL 60634-2461 • NI • Tchr • Luther HS North Chicago IL • (773)286-3600 • (RF 1974 MA)

**GALEN BETTY JEAN** (402)643-6191
1206 Sunrise Dr Seward NE 68434-1355 • NEB • SHS/C • Nebraska Seward NE • (RF 1959 MMU)

**GALL MICHAEL JOHN** (301)754-3711
2104 Dexter Ave #102 Silver Spring MD 20902-5039 • SE • Tchr • Calvary Silver Spring MD • (301)589-4001 • (RF 1994)

**GALLERT FREDERICK D**
150 N Patterson Rd Wayland MI 49348-9338 • MI • Tchr • Our Savior Grand Rapids MI • (616)949-0710 • (S 1975 MA MED)

**GALLMANN GRACE M** (909)737-3154
1189 Miller Cir Corona CA 91720-3814 • PSW • Tchr • Salem Orange CA • (714)639-1946 • (IV 1985)

**GALLMEIER EDWARD C** (713)849-0010
7211 Majestic Oaks Dr Houston TX 77040-3919 • TX • EM • (S 1962)

**GALLMEIER ELIZABETH A** (713)849-0010
7211 Majestic Oaks Dr Houston TX 77040-3919 • TX • EM • (S 1962)

**GALLUP KATHLEEN M** (815)226-0834
3507 Greenwood Ave S Rockford IL 61107-4817 • k3gallup@hotmail.com • NI • Tchr • Luther Academy Rockford IL • (815)877-9551 • (RF 1972 MA)

**GANDT KARL O** (630)941-7681
312 Highview Ave Elmhurst IL 60126-2222 • NI • EM • (RF 1945 MLS MED)

**GANSWINDT PAMELA KAY** (262)691-2658
1352 Meadowcreek Dr Apt B Pewaukee WI 53072-5626 • SW • Tchr • Elm Grove Elm Grove WI • (262)797-2970 • (CQ 1994)

**GARBE CAROLE JEAN** (626)796-2576
65 Malcolm Dr Pasadena CA 91105 • PSW • Tchr • Zion Glendale CA • (818)243-3119 • (CQ 1998)

**GARBER DARLA RAE** (402)562-8243
3031 21st St Columbus NE 68601 • NEB • Tchr • Immanuel Columbus NE • (402)564-8423 • (S 1983 MA)

**GARBISCH WANDA J** (616)489-5320
1228 Glades Dr Altoona WI 54720 • NW • 09/1998 • (SP 1979)

**GARCHOW CHRISTINE LEE** (608)756-0814
603 E Court St Janesville WI 53545 • garchow@aol.com • SW • Tchr • St Paul Janesville WI • (608)754-4471 • (S 1974 MED)

**GARCIA JORGE E** (714)255-8615
1336 Ponderosa Ave Fullerton CA 92835-2035 • jorgeeg@aol.com • PSW • 04/1999 • (CQ 1993 MED)

**GARDELS ANN M** (785)223-0934
430 Skyline Dr Apt 7 Junction City KS 66441-3866 • teacher1@oz-online.net • KS • Tchr • Immanuel Junction City KS • (785)238-5921 • (S 1991 MED)

**GARDINER LINDA L** (714)966-9025
3291 Arizona Ln Costa Mesa CA 92626-2010 • PSW • Tchr • Christ Costa Mesa CA • (949)548-6866 • (RF 1961 MED)

**GARLAND JULIE ANN** (210)497-6311
22311 Madison Park San Antonio TX 78258-2528 • TX • 01/1999 • (S 1991)

**GARLOCK REBECCA** (414)369-3802
4719 Vista Park Ct #5 Nashotah WI 53058 • SW • Tchr • Martin LHS Greendale WI • (414)421-4000 • (RF 1997)

**GARMAN CAROLYN A** (507)278-3818
17316 553 Ave Good Thunder MN 56037-9725 • MNS • Tchr • St Johns Good Thunder MN • (507)278-3635 • (SP 1972)

**GARMATZ MARGARET PAULA** (636)227-7558
1308 Turtle Cv Ballwin MO 63011-4249 • MO • 09/1996 09/1999 • (S 1963)

**GARMATZ ROBERT W** (636)227-7558
1308 Turtle Cv Ballwin MO 63011-4249 • MO • EM • (S 1941 MED)

**GARRABRANT RACHEL ANN** (248)334-1303
2612 Crofthill Dr Auburn Hills MI 48326 • MI • Tchr • Our Shepherd Birmingham MI • (248)646-6100 • (AA 1998)

**GARRABRANT STEVEN AUSTIN** (248)334-1303
2612 Crofthill Dr Auburn Hills MI 48326 • MI • Tchr • LHS North Macomb MI • (810)781-9151 • (AA 1998)

**GARRETT ETHEL M** (414)938-0339
14720 W Fenway Dr New Berlin WI 53151-6768 • ethelm37@aol.com • NI • EM • (RF 1975)

**GARRETT SHERI L** (219)836-5231
231 Lawndale Dr Munster IN 46321-2104 • NI • Tchr • Trinity Lansing IL • (708)474-8539 • (RF 1970)

**GARRISON JAMES M** (314)629-0071
466 Lakeshore Dr Saint Clair MO 63077-2107 • garrison@usmo.com • MO • EM • (RF 1954 MA PHD)

**GARROW LYNN C**
N108W15316 Bel Aire Ln Germantown WI 53022-4277 • SW • Tchr • Northwest Milwaukee WI • (414)463-4040 • (RF 1984)

**GARSKE HERBERT E** (734)434-5175
3904 Cloverlawn Ave Ypsilanti MI 48197-8611 • MI • EM • (RF 1942 MMU MA)

**GARVEY BARBARA A** (314)869-9547
147 Green Acres Rd Saint Louis MO 63137-1813 • gclutheran@stlnet.com • MO • Tchr • Grace Chapel Bellefontaine Nbrs MO • (314)867-6564 • (CQ 1992 MED)

**GARVUE ERIC** (217)787-0032
42 Horseshoe Dr Springfield IL 62702-1560 • CI • Tchr • Central Illinois Springfield IL • (MQ 1993)

**GARVUE KIMBERLY LYNN** (217)698-2949
2200 Lexington #3 Springfield WI 62704 • ekgarvue@aol.com • CI • Tchr • Our Savior's Springfield IL • (217)546-4531 • (MQ 1993)

**GARY SUSAN D** (210)533-2833
122 Panama Ave San Antonio TX 78210-1608 • TX • Tchr • Shepherd Of The Hill San Antonio TX • (210)614-3741 • (RF 1985)

**GASAU WILLIAM L** (660)463-7830
404 Faculty Ln Concordia MO 64020 • MO • SHS/C • Missouri Saint Louis MO • (314)317-4550 • (S 1968 MED)

**GAST CAROLYN RUTH** (810)731-6475
49123 Driftwood Dr Shelby Twp MI 48317-1743 • MI • Tchr • Trinity Utica MI • (810)731-4490 • (RF 1966 MA)

**GAST FREDERICK J** (313)731-6475
49123 Driftwood Dr Shelby Twp MI 48317-1743 • MI • Tchr • Peace Shelby Township MI • (810)731-4120 • (CQ 1969 MA)

**GAST RANDAL C** (443)512-0746
2964 Dumbarton Dr Abingdon MD 21009 • rgast@lhsa.com • SE • Prin • Baltimore LHS Baltimore MD • (410)825-2323 • (S 1979 MA)

**GAST WARREN E** (312)281-2613
2026 W Bradley Pl Chicago IL 60618-4908 • NI • P/Tchr • St James Chicago IL • (773)525-4990 • (RF 1975 MA)

**GASTEINER NANCY L** (630)773-8220
1150 Granville Ave Itasca IL 60143-2822 • NI • Tchr • Trinity Roselle IL • (630)894-3263 • (RF 1973)

**GASTLER GREGORY LEO** (314)832-7696
6712 Alexander St Saint Louis MO 63116-2802 • greg.gastler@cph.org • MO • CCRA • Missouri Saint Louis MO • (314)317-4550 • (RF 1986 MCMU)

**GASTLER O BERNARD** (512)929-3391
8604 Karling Dr Austin TX 78724-1802 • TX • EM • (S 1953 MMU PHD)

**GASTLER SUSAN** (412)351-6030
5 3rd St Rankin PA 15104-1143 • susangastler@hotmail.com • EA • Tchr • Christ Pittsburgh PA • (412)271-7173 • (S 1994)

**GATH EDYTHE MARIE** (716)694-6825
572 Ward Rd North Tonawanda NY 14120-1743 • emgrpg636@aol.com • EA • Tchr • St John North Tonawanda NY • (716)693-9677 • (CQ 1998)

**GATLIN CARLEE**
5601 Hanley Rd Tampa FL 33634 • FG • Tchr • Concordia Tampa FL • (813)806-9199 • (S 1999)

**GATZKE LAURA A**
12249 Dunbar Cir S Indianapolis IN 46229-3263 • IN • Tchr • Zion New Palestine IN • (317)861-4210 • (RF 1998)

**GAUDINEER ELIZABETH M** (612)934-4213
8941 Knollwood Dr Eden Prairie MN 55347-1723 • MNS • Tchr • St Peter Edina MN • (612)927-8400 • (SP 1967)

**GAUGER ANDREA JEAN** (847)825-2718
1104 S Vine Ave Park Ridge IL 60068-4824 • ajgauger@aol.com • NI • Tchr • Luther HS North Chicago IL • (773)286-3600 • (RF 1961 MAT)

**GAUNT MICAH RILEY** (713)956-5204
1000 Westview Houston TX 77055 • TX • Tchr • LHS North Houston TX • (713)880-3131 • (S 2000)

**GEACH T JAMES**
8259 Garden Ct Alta Loma CA 91701-3132 • PSW • Tchr • Lutheran High School La Verne CA • (909)593-4494 • (CQ 1997 MA)

**GEBHARDT CHARLES E**
2415 Westside Ave Norfolk NE 68701 • NEB • Tchr • Lutheran High Northe Norfolk NE • (402)379-3040 • (S 1992 MED)

**GEBHARDT DEBORAH ESTHER** (402)379-8676
2415 Westside Ave Norfolk NE 68701 • NEB • Tchr • Christ Norfolk NE • (402)371-5536 • (S 1993)

**GEBHARDT GRETCHEN S** (712)678-3618
C/O St John Luth Church PO Box 73 Charter Oak IA 51439-0073 • gsgeb@frontiernet.net • IW • 01/1997 01/2000 • (S 1975 MA)

**GEDDES ASHLEIGH**
609 Exchange St - #4 North Bend OR 97459 • NOW • Tchr • Christ Coos Bay OR • (541)267-3851 • (CQ 2000)

**GEER JULIE LYNN** (216)749-3545
Saint Mark Luth Church 4464 Pearl Rd Cleveland OH 44109 • neatduck@hotmail.com • OH • Tchr • St Mark Cleveland OH • (216)749-3545 • (AA 1997)

**GEER WESLEY ALLEN** (216)587-6748
11509 Tonsing Rd Garfield Heights OH 44125 • wjgeer@earthlink.net • OH • Tchr • Ohio Olmsted Falls OH • (AA 1997)

**GEFEKE LAWRENCE** (810)775-1624
21739 Trombly St St Clair Shrs MI 48080-3977 • MI • EM • (RF 1939 MSED)

**GEHEB THEODORE O** (248)258-5760
32889 Bassett Woods Ct Beverly Hills MI 48025-2764 • mtgeheb@aol.com • EN • English Farmington MI • (CQ 1965 MED)

**GEHL DUANE H** (507)468-2275
12850 Town Ave Dundee MN 56131 • RM • 05/1990 05/2000 • (S 1964 MED)

**GEHNER NORMA JEAN** (217)999-7494
22805 Monke Road Mount Olive IL 62069-3121 • SI • Tchr • Zion Litchfield IL • (217)324-3166 • (S 1968)

**GEHRING IRENE H** (206)937-9180
2722 Garlough Ave SW Seattle WA 98116-2929 • dgehr5803@aol.com • NOW • Tchr • Hope Seattle WA • (206)935-8500 • (RF 1961)

**GEHRING MARY** (602)483-9342
8313 E Citrus Way Scottsdale AZ 85250-5602 • EN • Tchr • Christ Phoenix AZ • (602)957-7010 • (CQ 1995 MS)

**GEHRKE AMY C** (805)238-9232
C/O Trinity Luth School 940 Creston Rd Paso Robles CA 93446-3002 • amygehrke@juno.com • CNH • Tchr • Trinity Paso Robles CA • (805)238-0335 • (PO 1996)

**GEHRKE DANIEL E** (303)771-7347
9481 Vance Ct Broomfield CO 80021-4839 • RM • Tchr • Denver Lutheran High Denver CO • (303)934-2345 • (MQ 1995)

**GEHRKE DENNIS E** (847)870-9512
936 Thornton Ln Buffalo Grove IL 60089-4234 • gehrkede@concentric.net • NI • Prin • St Peter Arlington Heights IL • (847)253-6638 • (SP 1970 MA)

**GEHRKE DOROTHY J** (847)870-9512
936 Thornton Ln Buffalo Grove IL 60089-4234 • NI • Tchr • St Peter Arlington Heights IL • (847)253-6638 • (SP 1970 MA)

**GEHRS KATHLEEN A** (517)652-2723
400 Sunburst Dr Frankenmuth MI 48734-1241 • MI • Tchr • St Lorenz Frankenmuth MI • (517)652-6141 • (RF 1973)

**GEHRS MARTIN C** (517)652-8438
641 W Schleier St Apt C-2 Frankenmuth MI 48734-1082 • MI • EM • (RF 1941)

**GEHRS PAULINE A** (773)375-2664
10316 S Avenue H Chicago IL 60617-6050 • NI • P/Tchr • Bethlehem Chicago IL • (773)768-0441 • (RF 1969)

**GEIDEL AMANDA BETH** (402)646-2215
1006 Seward St Seward NE 68434-1919 • ageidel@seward.cune.edu • NEB • 08/2000 • (S 1996 MA)

**GEIDEL DAVID O** (970)667-9522
1322 E Broadmoor Dr Loveland CO 80537-4469 • RM • P/Tchr • Immanuel Loveland CO • (970)667-7606 • (S 1972 MS)

**GEIDEL JEREMY THOMAS** (402)646-2215
246 Plum Creek Seward NE 68434 • jgeidel@seward.cune.edu • NEB • SHS/C • Nebraska Seward NE • (S 1996 MEDADM)

**GEIER GARY L** (414)327-8648
9182 W Waterford Sq S Milwaukee WI 53228-2200 • garyg725@execpc.com • SW • SHS/C • South Wisconsin Milwaukee WI • (414)464-8100 • (RF 1966)

**GEIGER RUTH ANN** (937)644-8749
12891 Brown Moder Rd Marysville OH 43040-9513 • OH • Tchr • St John Marysville OH • (937)644-5540 • (S 1970)

**GEIL JEAN R** (248)652-7098
1221 Miniature Ct Rochester Hills MI 48307-3093 • MI • EM • (RF 1964 MAT)

**GEISINGER DONALD W** (619)698-6045
9282 Golondrina Dr La Mesa CA 91941-5646 • PSW • Tchr • Christ La Mesa CA • (619)462-5211 • (S 1963)

**GEISLER CAROL A** (310)326-3975
22317 Ladeene Ave Torrance CA 90505 • PSW • Prin • Ascension Torrance CA • (310)371-3531 • (S 1975 MAD)

**GEISLER DAWN LEE**
637 Saraina Ln New Whiteland IN 46184-1823 • IN • 06/1999 • (AA 1996)

**GEISLER GEORGE H**
622 E Riverdale Ave Orange CA 92865 • PSW • Tchr • Faith Whittier CA • (562)941-0245 • (CQ 1986 MA)

**GEISLER HERBERT G JR. DR** (949)581-2735
24352 Falcon St Lake Forest CA 92630-1820 • geislerh@cui.edu • PSW • SHS/C • Pacific Southwest Irvine CA • (949)854-3232 • (RF 1971 MED PHD)

**GEISLER RUTH E** (949)425-8325
33 Coronado Cay Aliso Viejo CA 92656 • ruth³geisler@hotmail.com • PSW • Tchr • Abiding Savior Lake Forest CA • (949)830-1460 • (S 1970 MA)

**GEISLER STEVEN J** (317)786-5721
6813 Valley Forge Ln Indianapolis IN 46237-9624 • IN • Tchr • Indiana Fort Wayne IN • (S 1987 MA)

**GEISTFELD CHRISTINE KAY** (507)776-2452
2491 160th Ave Truman MN 56088 • MNS • Tchr • St Paul Truman MN • (507)776-6541 • (S 1992)

**GELHAUSEN ALBERT F** (810)664-4093
440 Lincoln St Lapeer MI 48446-1846 • mayoral@aol.com • MI • EM • (RF 1956 MA)

**GELLER AMY SUZANNE** (219)492-2638
9011 St Joe Rd Fort Wayne IN 46835 • IN • Tchr • Sub Bethlehem Fort Wayne IN • (219)484-7873 • (RF 2000)

**GEMAEHLICH MARGARET M** (307)635-8129
3011 Foothills Rd Cheyenne WY 82009-4543 • WY • 04/1991 04/1997 • (RF 1970)

**GEMMER DAVID P** (219)281-2757
712 State Road 327 Corunna IN 46730-9753 • IN • EM • (RF 1952 MA MA)

**GENGLER CONSTANCE C** (517)662-7088
1625 Wilder Rd Auburn MI 48611-9530 • jocog@juno.com • MI • Tchr • Grace Auburn MI • (517)662-4791 • (RF 1970)

**GENIG DENNIS K DR** (313)282-2813
14123 Cranbrook St Riverview MI 48192-7527 • dmgenig@home.com • MI • 09/1999 • (RF 1974 MED DED)

**GENRICH LEEANN E** (402)228-1357
322 N 21st St Beatrice NE 68310-3321 • NEB • Tchr • St Paul Beatrice NE • (402)223-3414 • (S 1963)

**GENTER HELEN L** (913)682-6434
724 W 7th St Leavenworth KS 66048-6003 • hlgenter@lvnworth.com • KS • Tchr • St Paul Leavenworth KS • (913)682-5553 • (RF 1965)

**GENTHNER CLINTON FORREST**
8140 Parks Dr Apt H 8 Spring Arbor MI 49283-9720 • MI • Tchr • Trinity Jackson MI • (517)784-3135 • (AA 1995)

**GENTRY VERLEEN F** (308)236-9127
1407 W 35th St Kearney NE 68845-2743 • NEB • Tchr • Zion Kearney NE • (308)234-3410 • (S 1963)

**GEORGE CONNIE MARIE** (219)464-7573
1308 Monticello Park Dr Valparaiso IN 46383-4022 • IN • Tchr • Immanuel Valparaiso IN • (219)462-8207 • (RF 1990 MMU)

**GEORGE DIANE KAY**
C/O Saint Paul Lutheran 1635 Chester Dr Tracy CA 95376-2927 • CNH • Immanuel Valparaiso IN • (RF 1973)

**GEORGE PATRICIA S** (925)680-2512
8135 Camelback Pl Pleasant Hill CA 94523-1218 • EN • Tchr • West Portal San Francisco CA • (415)661-0242 • (CQ 1987)

**GEORGE VIJAYASEKARAN**
163 White Plains Rd Bronxville NY 10708 • AT • SHS/C • Atlantic Bronxville NY • (914)337-5700 • (RF 1974 MA)

**GEORGI MARY ELLEN** (440)934-3424
36451 N Reserve Cir Avon OH 44011-2821 • OH • Tchr • Bethany Parma OH • (440)884-1230 • (RF 1967)

**GERARD DANA S** (713)290-9448
5502 Oak Trail Houston TX 77091 • TX • Tchr • LHS North Houston TX • (713)880-3131 • (S 1985 MED)

**GERARD LANCE D** (713)893-1121
6723 Greenvale Ln Houston TX 77066-3826 • TX • Mem C • Our Savior Houston TX • (713)290-9087 • (S 1986)

**GERBER GLENN D** (314)631-2319
10211 Concord Valley Ct Saint Louis MO 63123-6277 • MO • 11/1995 11/1999 • (RF 1974 MS)

**GERBER JOAN C** (619)420-2055
694 Myra Ave Chula Vista CA 91910-6230 • joancg@home.com • PSW • Tchr • Pilgrim Chula Vista CA • (619)420-6233 • (S 1972)

**GERBER JUDITH LYNNE** (314)631-2319
10211 Concord Valley Ct Saint Louis MO 63123-6277 • MO • Tchr • Webster Gardens Webster Groves MO • (314)961-5275 • (RF 1975 MAT)

**GERDES DREW D** (417)890-9391
219 E Montclair St Apt 3A Springfield MO 65807-7930 • MO • Tchr • Redeemer Springfield MO • (417)881-5470 • (SP 2000)

**GERDES KATHERINE M**
PO Box 56 Granite OK 73547 • kgerdesmom@aol.com • MI • EM • (RF 1962)

**GERDS FREDRICK** (248)549-3642
4614 Hampton Blvd Royal Oak MI 48073-1618 • fmgerds@gateway.net • MI • Tchr • Our Shepherd Birmingham MI • (248)645-0551 • (RF 1964 MA)

**GERDTS TERRY L** (660)463-2877
PO Box 877 Concordia MO 64020-0877 • MO • Missouri Saint Louis MO • (314)317-4550 • (S 1968 MS)

**GERES THEONE P** (805)584-9361
2063 Sheridan Ct Simi Valley CA 93065-2444 • PSW • Tchr • Good Shepherd Simi Valley CA • (805)526-2482 • (S 1973 MA)

**GERHARDT ELSIE A** (414)334-2987
1028 Chestnut St West Bend WI 53095-3127 • SW • Mem C • St John West Bend WI • (262)334-4901 • (RF 1957 MS SPRD)

**GERKEN BEVERLY J**
C/O St Paul Luth School 27981 Detroit Rd Westlake OH 44145 • OH • Tchr • St Paul Westlake OH • (440)835-3051 • (S 1977 MA)

**GERLACH JOHN W** (734)542-0480
17939 Woodside Livonia MI 48152-2760 • MI • Tchr • LHS Westland Westland MI • (734)422-2090 • (S 1968 MA)

**GERLACH LUCAS J** (303)202-6921
2468 Gray St Edgewater CO 80214-1141 • Lucas.michelle@juno.com • RM • Tchr • Bethlehem Lakewood CO • (303)233-0401 • (S 1996)

**GERLACH PAUL C** (716)692-8974
821 Ohio St N Tonawanda NY 14120-1972 • pgerlach@buffnet.net • EA • P/Tchr • St Paul North Tonawanda NY • (716)692-3255 • (RF 1962 MSED)

**GERLACH ROBIN K** (512)310-1986
3928 Katzman Dr Austin TX 78728-3525 • TX • Tchr • Redeemer Austin TX • (512)459-1500 • (S 1978 MMU)

**GERLACH ROXANNE** (920)625-3296
423 S Schulyer Neosho WI 53059 • SW • Tchr • St Paul Oconomowoc WI • (262)567-5001 • (CQ 1991 MA)

**GERLACH-PULLMANN KAREN L**
Trinity Luth Church 1034 NE 11th St Bend OR 97701-4402 • MT • Tchr • Trinity Kalispell MT • (406)257-5683 • (RF 1981 MED)

**GERMANN KENNETH R** (972)509-8008
2209 Covered Wagon Plano TX 75074-2757 • cageycougar@juno.com • TX • Tchr • Faith Plano TX • (972)423-7447 • (RF 1965 MS EDS)

**GERMEROTH PAUL L** (734)455-6262
8232 Sandpiper Dr Canton MI 48187-1738 • MI • EM • (S 1951)

**GERNANT RENEA B** (402)643-4100
419 N 7th St Seward NE 68434 • rgernant@seward.ccsn.edu • NEB • SHS/C • Nebraska Seward NE • (S 1988 MA PHD)

**GERNDT DONNA M** (262)392-2079
W314S6210 Dable Rd Mukwonago WI 53149-9736 • ggerndt@execpc.com • SW • Tchr • St Paul Oconomowoc WI • (262)567-5001 • (SP 1970)

**GERSMEHL HEROLD C** (219)485-6729
4636 Tamarack Dr Fort Wayne IN 46835-3452 • IN • EM • (RF 1936 MA)

**GERSMEHL LIENHARD W** (608)754-7053
1901 Kensington St Janesville WI 53546-5749 • SW • EM • (RF 1934)

**GERTH YVONNE M** (414)475-7113
2327 N 101St St Wauwatosa WI 53226-1631 • SW • Tchr • Our Redeemer Wauwatosa WI • (414)258-4558 • (S 1971 MA)

**GERY MARGIT R** (216)722-8973
6340 Branch Rd Medina OH 44256-8943 • OH • Tchr • St Mark Brunswick OH • (330)225-4395 • (RF 1970)

**GESCH DAVID S** (612)472-5508
2459 Chateau Ln Mound MN 55364-1752 • MNS • Tchr • Redeemer Wayzata MN • (612)473-5356 • (S 1985)

**GESCH JOEL TODD** (216)934-5180
2560 Barkwood Dr Sheffield Lake OH 44054-2461 • OH • Tchr • LHS West Rocky River OH • (440)333-1660 • (S 1977 MED)

**GESCH RONALD D DR** (816)584-5278
1304 Olive St Higginsville MO 64037-1234 • rdgesch@ctcis.net • MO • Tchr • Immanuel Higginsville MO • (660)584-2854 • (S 1971)

**GESKE LAURA RUTH** (785)765-3620
315 Main PO Box 83 Mc Farland KS 66501-0083 • jlgeske@kansas.net • KS • Tchr • Topeka Topeka KS • (785)357-0382 • (S 1995)

**GESTRICH KRISTEN M** (608)756-0527
444 Douglas St Janesville WI 53545 • SW • Tchr • St Paul Janesville WI • (608)754-4471 • (CQ 2000)

**GETBEHEAD NANCY J** (716)392-7962
16 Peach Blossom Rd N Hilton NY 14468-1016 • EA • Tchr • St Paul Hilton NY • (716)392-4000 • (BR 1990 MA)

**GETZLAFF DENNIS L** (651)459-3333
8231 Janero Ave S Cottage Grove MN 55016-3447 • getzlaff@csp.edu • MNS • SHS/C • Minnesota South Burnsville MN • (S 1973 MA)

**GEUDER ALAN B** (505)294-5507
2531 Claremont Ct NE Albuquerque NM 87112-2006 • RM • Tchr • Immanuel Albuquerque NM • (505)243-2589 • (RF 1961 EDS)

**GEURINK BRENDA RENEE**
Mt Olive Lutheran Church 5625 Franklin Ave Des Moines IA 50310-1031 • IW • Tchr • Mount Olive Des Moines IA • (515)277-8349 • (S 1996)

**GEWIRZ BETSY A** (707)255-8498
2452 Cabernet St Napa CA 94558-2503 • CNH • Tchr • St John Napa CA • (707)226-7970 • (S 1974)

**GEYE CYNTHIA ANNE** (708)426-2313
823 Bannock Rd East Dundee IL 60118-1630 • steve³geye@msn.com • NI • Tchr • Immanuel Dundee IL • (847)428-1010 • (RF 1984)

**GEYER STEPHEN HAROLD** (248)634-0211
8971 Eaton Rd Davisburg MI 48350-1517 • MI • Tchr • St Stephen Waterford MI • (248)673-5906 • (S 1974)

**GEYER THOMAS W** (817)441-1534
160 Lakeview Dr Aledo TX 76008-3984 • TX • Prin • St Paul Fort Worth TX • (817)332-2281 • (RF 1982 MA)

**GEYSER PAIGE W** (972)422-4080
2200 Molly Ln Plano TX 75074-3577 • geyserclifford@msn.com • TX • Tchr • Faith Plano TX • (972)423-7447 • (CQ 1999)

**GIANNOTTA CARLO BRUNO** (708)484-1323
3133S Highland Ave Berwyn IL 60402-3513 • cgiannotta@aol.com • NI • Prin • Grace Chicago IL • (773)762-1234 • (RF 1995)

**GIANNOTTA JILL MARIE** (708)484-1323
3133S Highland Ave Berwyn IL 60402-3513 • cgiannotta@aol.com • NI • Tchr • Grace Chicago IL • (773)762-1234 • (RF 1994)

**GIBBONS LANA R** (815)568-7835
3014 Deerpass Rd Marengo IL 60152-8007 • NI • Tchr • Zion Marengo IL • (815)568-6564 • (RF 1976)

**GIBSON DEBRA SUE** (248)922-3759
5849 Deepwood Ct Clarkston MI 48346-3617 • MI • Tchr • St Stephen Waterford MI • (248)673-6621 • (AA 1983)

**GIBSON LISETTE L** (517)667-0852
6034 WS Saginaw Rd Bay City MI 48706 • MI • Tchr • St Paul Bay City MI • (517)684-4450 • (RF 1967 MA)

**GIELAROWSKI KATHRYN ANN** (412)746-6794
303 W Grant St Houston PA 15342-1409 • katie@tallysoft.com • EA • 06/1996 • (BR 1992)

**GIERACH DOREEN G** (810)226-1376
50144 Riverside Dr Macomb MI 48044 • MI • 03/1997 03/2000 • (RF 1978 MA)

**GIERACH RAYMOND C** (810)226-1376
50144 Riverside Dr Maomb Township MI 48044 • rgierach@familyconnect.com • MI • Tchr • LHS North Macomb MI • (810)781-9151 • (RF 1976 MED)

**GIERKE JULIE ANNE**
9937 S Cicero Ave Apt 102 Oak Lawn IL 60453-4062 • NI • Tchr • Luther HS South Chicago IL • (773)737-1416 • (S 1993 MLS)

**GIESCHEN CHRISTOPHER J** (219)485-9675
3605 Walden Run Fort Wayne IN 46815-6171 • dila5@juno.com • IN • Tchr • Concordia LHS Fort Wayne IN • (219)483-1102 • (RF 1977 MS)

**GIESCHEN ROSELYN M** (708)524-0574
1120 Superior St Oak Park IL 60302-1824 • NI • EM • (RF 1967)

**GIESCHEN THOMAS E** (708)524-0574
1120 Superior St Oak Park IL 60302-1824 • crfgieschte.crf.cuis.edu • NI • SHS/C • Northern Illinois Hillside IL • (RF 1952 MMU DMU)

**GIESCHEN TIMOTHY J** (313)730-0779
245 S Denwood St Dearborn MI 48124-1380 • tgieschen@lhsa.com • MI • Tchr • LHS Westland Westland MI • (734)422-2090 • (RF 1982 MED)

**GIESE ESTHER M**
2225 E 14 Mile Road Birmingham MI 48009 • MI • Tchr • Our Shepherd Birmingham MI • (248)646-6100 • (AA 1995)

**GIESE MARY A** (216)226-3392
14629 Leonard Ave Lakewood OH 44107-5928 • OH • Tchr • Lakewood Lakewood OH • (216)221-6941 • (RF 1969)

**GIESEKE RICHARD W** (314)317-4152
835 Kentridge Ct Manchester MO 63021-7568 • richard.gieseke@lhm.com • MO • Tchr • St Paul Des Peres MO • (314)822-2771 • (RF 1974 MCMU)

**GIESEKE RUTHANN L** (314)846-0765
2720 Cripple Creek Dr Saint Louis MO 63129-4956 • rlgieseke@aol.com • MO • Tchr • Green Park Lemay MO • (314)544-4248 • (RF 1978 MMU)

**GIESSELMANN DARRYL L** (952)353-2346
120 Jefferson Ave N New Germany MN 55367 • MNS • Tchr • St Mark-St John New Germany MN • (612)353-2464 • (S 1971)

**GIESSELMANN DUANE L** (573)756-2249
PO Box 101 Doe Run MO 63637-0101 • MO • P/Tchr • St Paul Farmington MO • (573)756-5147 • (S 1969 MA)

**GIESSELMANN RUPERT E**
10135 Midland Blvd Saint Louis MO 63114-1536 • MO • EM • (S 1952 MED)

**GIFF LORAYNE PERNELLE** (507)825-5539
318 4th St SW Pipestone MN 56164-1504 • inlgiff@rconnect.com • MNS • 08/1994 08/2000 • (RF 1966 MS)

**GIFFORD CHARLES J SR.**
125 N Main St PO Box 57 Hoyleton IL 62803 • gbtrout@yahoo.com • SI • P/Tchr • Trinity Hoyleton IL • (618)493-6226 • (RF 1984)

**GIFFORD TERESA L** (785)562-4007
125 N Main St Hoyleton IL 62803 • dynomom@yahoo.com • KS • Tchr • Good Shepherd Marysville KS • (785)562-3181 • (RF 1983)

**GIGUERE NORMAN W** (410)747-1619
6003 Keithmont Ct Baltimore MD 21228-2724 • SE • Prin • St Paul Catonsville MD • (410)747-1924 • (RF 1965 MS)

**GIHRING BARBARA J** (360)692-7350
1428 NW Selbo Rd Bremerton WA 98311-9021 • NOW • Tchr • Peace Bremerton WA • (360)373-2116 • (S 1974 MEAD)

**GIHRING DIANE ARTHURS** (714)744-0326
149 N Citrus St Orange CA 92868 • gihring@lhsoc. • PSW • Tchr • Lutheran HS/Orange C Orange CA • (714)998-5151 • (IV 1993)

**GILBERT CHERYL E** (970)669-7914
2224 S Del Norte Dr Loveland CO 80537-3711 • RM • Tchr • Immanuel Loveland CO • (970)667-7606 • (S 1990)

**GILES DONNA L** (262)884-4401
8708 Fox Haven Chase Sturtevant WI 53177 • SW • Tchr • Holy Cross Racine WI • (262)554-7010 • (RF 1969)

**GILL VICKIE** (801)467-7856
PO Box 520071 Salt Lake City UT 84152-0071 • RM • Tchr • Christ Murray UT • (801)262-4354 • (PO 1984)

**GILLAM JENNIFER LEE**
Crown of Life Luth Chuch 6605 Pleasant Run Rd Colleyville TX 76034 • gllmjn@aol.com • TX • Tchr • Crown of Life Colleyville TX • (817)421-5683 • (RF 1991 MA)

**GILLAM LINDA A** (308)826-4403
Trinity Luth Church PO Box 157 Amherst NE 68812-0157 • jgillam@nebi.com • NEB • 03/2000 • (S 1974 MED)

**GILLES RACHEL BETH** (715)257-7114
520 Elm St Athens WI 54411-9761 • NW • Tchr • Trinity Athens WI • (715)257-7559 • (MQ 1994)

**GILLILAND CHRISTINE MARIE** (314)832-3458
7833 Adkins Ave Saint Louis MO 63123-7701 • MO • Tchr • Hope Saint Louis MO • (314)352-0014 • (S 1994)

**GILLINGHAM DONALD E** (312)344-5562
410 N 3rd Ave Maywood IL 60153-1114 • NI • Tchr • Walther LHS Melrose Park IL • (708)344-0404 • (RF 1976)

**GILSON LAURA MARIE**
600 W Burr Oak St Centreville MI 49032-9781 • IN • 11/1996 11/1999 • (AA 1989)

**GINGERICH KATHLEEN L** (515)251-4676
3842 52nd St Des Moines IA 50310-1816 • rebeldog9@aol.com • IW • Tchr • Shepherds Flock West Des Moines IA • (515)225-1623 • (SP 1989)

**GIOE CHRISTOPHER M** (517)652-3178
564 Franconian Dr E Frankenmuth MI 48734-1004 • cgioe@stlorenz.org • MI • Tchr • St Lorenz Frankenmuth MI • (517)652-6141 • (RF 1970 MA)

**GIOE LOUISE E** (517)652-3178
564 Franconian Dr E Frankenmuth MI 48734-1004 • lgioe@stlorenz.org • MI • Tchr • St Lorenz Frankenmuth MI • (517)652-6141 • (RF 1970)

**GIORDANO JONATHON** (618)288-8813
804 Village Dr Glen Carbon IL 62034-2730 • giowop@apci.net • SI • Tchr • Metro-East LHS Edwardsville IL • (618)656-0043 • (RF 1995)

**GIORDANO LOIS L** (262)375-9223
W64N362 Madison Ave Cedarburg WI 53012-2331 • tlgiordano@milwpc.com • SW • 07/1992 07/2000 • (RF 1970 MA)

**GIORDANO THOMAS A** (262)375-9223
W64N362 Madison Ave Cedarburg WI 53012-2331 • tlgiordano@milwpc.com • SW • Tchr • First Immanuel Cedarburg WI • (262)377-6610 • (RF 1968 MA)

**GLADSTONE JAMES HOYT** (317)575-0899
15009 Windmill Cir Carmel IN 46033-9075 • gladrocks@aol.com • IN • Mem C • Carmel Carmel IN • (317)814-4252 • (RF 1970)

**GLAESEMAN KARI LEA** (801)567-9024
139W Inglenook Dr Apt 2420 Midvale UT 84047 • RM • Tchr • Christ Murray UT • (801)266-8714 • (SP 1998)

**GLAESER KRISTY L** (619)279-9720
9689 Stonecrest Blvd San Diego CA 92123-5414 • PSW • Tchr • Christ La Mesa CA • (619)462-5211 • (SP 1983 MA)

**GLAESS HERMAN L DR** (402)643-4193
2614 E Seward Rd Seward NE 68434-8032 • hglaess@usa.net • NEB • EM • (RF 1948 MED DED)

**GLANDORF BRENDA K** (815)235-8197
1618 Karcher Ct Freeport IL 61032-9738 • NI • Tchr • St John Elgin IL • (847)741-0814 • (CQ 1986)

**GLANDORF STEVEN P** (970)949-7955
PO Box 965 Avon CO 81620-0965 • steveng@lutheranhigh.orange.ca.us • RM • Tchr • Vail Christian Edwards CO • (970)926-3015 • (S 1980 MA)

**GLANVILLE KRISTINA**
517 Roxbury Dr Lake Orion MI 48359-1895 • MI • Tchr • St John Rochester MI • (248)652-8830 • (S 1983)

**GLANZER ELLEN E** (402)371-1907
2310 Belmont Dr Norfolk NE 68701-2337 • NEB • EM • (S 1974)

**GLANZER JOHN H** (801)566-5464
9180 Scirlein Dr Sandy UT 84094-3013 • RM • Tchr • Grace Sandy UT • (801)572-3793 • (S 1990)

**GLANZER STEPHANIE E** (801)255-3857
7910 S Candlestick Ln #209 Midvale UT 84047-5214 • sglanzer@glcs-lems.org • RM • Tchr • Grace Sandy UT • (801)572-3793 • (S 1998)

**GLASGOW DIANE M** (316)221-3860
1412 E 14th Ave Winfield KS 67156-4608 • davidg@horizon.hit.net • KS • Tchr • Trinity Winfield KS • (316)221-1820 • (S 1975 MED)

**GLASKEY LYLA JO** (660)826-3347
621 W Seventh Sedalia MO 65301 • MO • Tchr • Trinity Cole Camp MO • (816)668-2364 • (S 1997)

**GLASNAPP SUSAN M**
2905 Hampton Cir E Delray Beach FL 33445-7126 • FG • Tchr • St Paul Boca Raton FL • (561)395-8548 • (CQ 1997)

**GLASSER PEGGY E** (412)833-6673
601 Glenrock Dr Bethel Park PA 15102-1435 • tomandpeg@aol.com • EA • 07/1987 07/2000 • (BR 1978)

**GLAWE JOEL MARTIN** (414)485-4042
414 Lynn St Horicon WI 53032-1134 • SW • Tchr • St Stephen Horicon WI • (920)485-6687 • (RF 1973)

**GLEDHILL ERIC A**
259 S Westlawn Dr Midland MI 48640-7802 • bioman@en.com • MI • Mem C • Messiah Midland MI • (517)835-7143 • (AA 1990)

**GLEDHILL KRISTIN A**
259 S Westlawn Dr Midland MI 48640-7802 • OH • Tchr • St Mark Brunswick OH • (330)225-3110 • (AA 1990)

**GLEDHILL STEPHANIE**
20440 Pullingbrook #440 Livonia MI 48152 • MI • Tchr • Detroit Urban Detroit MI • (313)582-9900 • (AA 1999)

**GLEITZ DIANE J** (270)234-1703
150 Ridgeway Dr E Elizabethtown KY 42701-9739 • gleitzmd@juno.com • IN • 06/1999 • (RF 1981 MA)

**GLENN LEANNE LYNELLE** (801)397-0765
C/O Cross of Christ Luth Ch 1840 S 75 E Bountiful UT 84010 • crossofchrist-utah@juno.com • RM • 01/1999 • (S 1995)

**GLENN ERICKSON BRENDA DIANNE** (407)737-2745
7651 Rio Pinar Lakes Blvd Orlando FL 32822 • bglennerickson@prodigy.net • FG • Tchr • Florida-Georgia Orlando FL • (S 1995)

**GLESSING MARLENE K** (612)543-3707
11573 78th St SW Howard Lake MN 55349-5319 • MNS • Tchr • St James Howard Lake MN • (320)543-2630 • (SP 1978)

**GLIENKE DAVID H** (512)832-8873
9712 Halifax Dr Austin TX 78753-4621 • TX • P/Tchr • Hope Austin TX • (512)926-0003 • (S 1975 MED)

**GLINES JACKIE LYNN** (402)325-9188
2318 N 74th Lincoln NE 68507 • jglines@aol.com • NEB • Tchr • Messiah Lincoln NE • (402)489-3024 • (S 1995)

**GLINSMANN ERVIN E** (319)434-3167
Luzerne IA 52257 • IE • EM • (S 1952 MS)

**GLOCK STEPHEN L** (510)792-9956
37423 Stonewood Dr Fremont CA 94536-6651 • CNH • Tchr • Prince Of Peace Fremont CA • (510)797-8186 • (S 1966)

**GLOTZHOBER ALYCE KAY** (313)277-3857
1751 N Rosevere Ave Dearborn MI 48128-1242 • MI • EM • (RF 1952 MA)

**GLOVER MARTHA**
7 Scarsdale Manor Ct Saint Charles MO 63303-3158 • MO • Tchr • Zion Harvester MO • (314)441-7424 • (RF 1972 MA)

**GLOWINSKI MICHAEL A** (954)785-3723
2865 NE 12th Ave Pompano Beach FL 33064 • FG • Tchr • Peace Fort Lauderdale FL • (954)772-8010 • (RF 2000)

**GNAGY SUSAN C** (303)237-9759
2120 Vance St Lakewood CO 80215-2137 • RM • Tchr • Bethlehem Lakewood CO • (303)233-0401 • (S 1978)

**GNAM JANET SUE** (623)556-0834
13316 W Port Au Prince Ln Surprise AZ 85374 • otenaj@aol.com • PSW • Tchr • Christ Redeemer Phoenix AZ • (623)934-3286 • (S 1994)

**GNAN PAUL WILLIAM** (414)535-1469
10904 W Derby Ave Wauwatosa WI 53225 • SW • Tchr • South Wisconsin Milwaukee WI • (414)464-8100 • (MQ 1990)

**GNAN PETER DAVID** (414)692-6361
239 Saint Rose Ave Fredonia WI 53021-9479 • pgnan@bachcuw.edu • SW • SHS/C • South Wisconsin Milwaukee WI • (414)464-8100 • (MQ 1992 MED)

**GNATZIG LINDA MARY** (402)827-3171
11208 Franklin Plaza #1121 Omaha NE 68154 • momy2all@aol.com • NEB • Tchr • Bread Of Life Omaha NE • (402)391-3505 • (RF 1977)

**GNEWUCH CYNTHIA ANN** (843)361-0568
810 Arbor Ln North Myrtle Beach SC 29582 • cgnewuch@aol.com • SE • 12/1996 12/1999 • (RF 1986 MA)

**GNEWUCH MINNIE MATHILDA DR** (708)366-0638
7712 Monroe St Forest Park IL 60130-1725 • NI • Tchr • St John Forest Park IL • (708)366-2764 • (CQ 1995 MA EDD)

**GODBOLD ELLEN EILEEN** (616)554-5792
7455 Carpet Rose Dr SE Caledonia MI 49316 • pgod63@yahoo.com • MI • Tchr • Immanuel Grand Rapids MI • (616)363-0505 • (RF 1993)

**GODEMANN DAWN RENAE** (402)563-9131
3805 27th St Apt 26 Columbus NE 68601-2229 • NEB • Tchr • Immanuel Columbus NE • (402)564-8423 • (S 1998)

**GODWIN LEANN TRACY**
C/O Christ Our Savior Luth Ch 140 Heartz Rd Coppell TX 75019 • TX • Tchr • Christ Our Savior Coppell TX • (972)393-7074 • (AU 1995)

**GOECKER LOWELL R** (713)939-1730
2747 Kismet Ln Houston TX 77043-1720 • lgoecker@aol.com • TX • Tchr • Lutheran South Acade Houston TX • (281)464-8299 • (S 1967 MSED)

**GOECKER REBECCA ANN** (812)358-9044
308 W Walnut Brownstown IN 47220-1841 • gvrassoc@hsonline.net • IN • Tchr • Immanuel Seymour IN • (812)522-1301 • (RF 1990)

**GOEDECKE KEITH D** (713)259-9329
7506 Ramblewood Dr Magnolia TX 77355-2226 • TX • Tchr • Trinity Spring TX • (281)376-5810 • (AU 1982)

**GOEGLEIN DELOY D** (303)233-5979
11239 W 27th Ave Lakewood CO 80215-7106 • ddgbellman@aol.com • RM • Tchr • Bethlehem Lakewood CO • (303)238-7676 • (RF 1962)

**GOEGLEIN ERIC W** (816)942-2964
11224 Grand Ave Kansas City MO 64114-5405 • egoeglein@calvarykc.com • MO • Prin • Calvary Kansas City MO • (816)444-5517 • (S 1975 EDS)

**GOEHNER JANICE E** (410)838-1694
715 Mayton Ct Bel Air MD 21014-5315 • jliz57@aol.com • SE • Tchr • St Paul Kingsville MD • (410)592-8100 • (BR 1979)

**GOEHNER LOREN H** (410)638-0871
709 Foothill Rd Bel Air MD 21014-5352 • lhg31@aol.com • SE • EM • (S 1957 MED)

**GOEHRING THEOPHIL M** (714)845-7268
40602 Brookside Ave Cherry Valley CA 92223-5530 • PSW • EM • (RF 1933 MA)

**GOEKE JOHN A** (512)261-9624
720 Rolling Green Dr Austin TX 78734-5227 • jag7900@aol.com • TX • Texas Austin TX • (S 1962)

**GOEMAN MARILYN H** (414)377-1691
1057 8th Ave Grafton WI 53024-1813 • SW • EM • (RF 1958)

**GOERES GLENN WILLIAM**
755 Terrace Dr Elm Grove WI 53122 • ggoeres@juno.com • SW • Prin • Elm Grove Elm Grove WI • (262)797-2970 • (RF 1972 MA)

**GOERES RHONDA J** (262)938-3198
755 Terrace Dr Elm Grove WI 53122 • ggoeres@juno.com • SW • Tchr • St Peter-Immanuel Milwaukee WI • (414)353-6800 • (RF 1972)

**GOETZ BETTY J** (785)273-0613
1918 SW Arrowhead Rd Topeka KS 66604-3725 • KS • Tchr • Topeka Topeka KS • (785)357-0382 • (SP 1966)

**GOETZ JOHN D** (612)972-2270
315 1st St Delano MN 55328-9768 • goetzwho@aol.com • MNS • Tchr • Lutheran High Mayer MN • (612)657-2251 • (SP 1992)

**GOETZ LOIS A** (313)294-8137
13748 Adams Ave Warren MI 48093-1426 • MI • Tchr • St Luke Clinton Township MI • (810)791-1151 • (RF 1974)

**GOHDE PAUL F** (414)453-6775
1260 N 85th St Wauwatosa WI 53226-3201 • SW • Tchr • Immanuel Brookfield WI • (414)781-4135 • (CQ 1985)

**GOING GLENN W** (801)266-6676
1118 E 1700 S Salt Lake City UT 84105-3522 • RM • Tchr • Salt Lake LHS Salt Lake City UT • (801)266-6676 • (S 1976 MED)

**GOING PAMELA JEAN** (952)873-5591
712 Shannon Cir Belle Plaine MN 56011 • MNS • Tchr • St John Chaska MN • (612)448-2433 • (SP 1988)

**GOLCHERT KENT R** (314)824-5934
10177 Hwy C Frohna MO 63748-9701 • ktgolch@showme.net • MO • Prin • Concordia Frohna MO • (573)824-5218 • (S 1974 MA)

**GOLDBECK MAXINE E**
1236 E Collins Ave Orange CA 92867-5838 • PSW • EM • (RF 1947 MA)

**GOLDEN J ROBERT** (559)733-3855
1609 S Peppertree Ct Visalia CA 93277 • bbwgoldn@sosinet.net • CNH • EM • (RF 1958)

**GOLDENSTERN CLARENCE E** (815)697-2462
266 W 1st South St Chebanse IL 60922-9625 • NI • EM • (RF 1950 MA)

**GOLDGRABE EUNICE DR** (402)643-3814
1807 N Columbia Ave Seward NE 68434-9730 • egoldgrabe@seward.ccsn.edu • NEB • SHS/C • Nebraska Seward NE • (S 1966 MA DART)

**GOLL JANET L** (405)762-7749
1101 N Ash St Ponca City OK 74601-2204 • OK • Tchr • First Ponca City OK • (580)762-4243 • (S 1972)

**GOLNICK MERLE G DR** (228)875-7394
108 Water Oaks Cv Ocean Springs MS 39564-8556 • merle@datasync.com • SO • EM • (RF 1951 MA MA LLD)

**GOLNITZ ROBERT M** (320)732-3797
RR 4 Box 419 Long Prairie MN 56347 • MNN • Tchr • Trinity Long Prairie MN • (320)732-2238 • (S 1962 MAR)

**GOLTERMANN VICKY L** (815)547-4443
1018 E 2nd St Belvidere IL 61008-4520 • NI • Tchr • Immanuel Belvidere IL • (815)544-8058 • (RF 1988)

**GOLTL DEBORAH A** (316)722-3691
12714 Taft St Wichita KS 67235-8434 • sgoltl@dtc.net • KS • 06/1991 06/1999 • (S 1989)

**GOLZ LESTER P** (618)656-6606
229 Adams St Edwardsville IL 62025-1807 • SI • EM • (RF 1950 MED)

**GOMES DOMINGO GARY** (702)243-7270
8703 Harwich Ave Las Vegas NV 89129 • PSW • Tchr • Mountain View Las Vegas NV • (702)360-8290 • (IV 1999)

**GOMEZ CARLOS A** (319)279-3654
103 E Ridge St Readlyn IA 50668 • jefe@netins.net • IE • Prin • Immanuel Waterloo IA • (319)233-3967 • (SP 1978 MED)

**GOMEZ LINDA JOYCE** (319)279-3654
103 East Ridge St Readlyn IA 50668 • jefe@netins.net • IE • Tchr • Immanuel Waterloo IA • (319)233-3967 • (SP 1971)

**GONZALES STEPHAN P**
1705 Independence Jefferson City MO 65109-5641 • MO • Tchr • Trinity Jefferson City MO • (573)636-7807 • (WN 1983)

**GOODE GAIL LYNNE** (254)867-1312
1102 1/2 Lewis Waco TX 76705 • TX • Tchr • Trinity Waco TX • (817)772-4225 • (CQ 1994)

**GOODSON LAURA N** (573)517-0774
997 Hwy U Perryville MO 63775 • MO • Tchr • Salem Farrar MO • (573)824-5728 • (S 1996)

**GORCYCA REBECCA A**
St James Luth Church 2046 N Fremont St Chicago IL 60614-4312 • NI • Tchr • St James Chicago IL • (773)525-4990 • (RF 1998)

**GORDENIER KAREN L** (909)696-2183
39518 Country Mill Rd Murrieta CA 92562-3108 • jkr.zoo@gateway.net • PSW • Tchr • Zion Fallbrook CA • (760)728-8288 • (IV 1988)

**GORDON TAMMY LOUISE** (310)670-7270
8600 Emerson Ave Apt 205 Los Angeles CA 90045-6712 • tlgordon@juno.com • PSW • Tchr • First Venice CA • (310)823-9367 • (S 1991)

**GOSCH DENISE ANN** (941)644-1378
102 Imperial Southgate Villas Lakeland FL 33803-5602 • FG • Tchr • St Paul Lakeland FL • (941)644-7710 • (S 1988)

**GOTSCH MARILYN** (708)771-8171
604 Beloit Ave Forest Park IL 60130-1908 • NI • EM • (RF 1968 MED)

**GOTTSCHALK ANN C** (708)354-5956
744 S Catherine Ave La Grange IL 60525-2827 • NI • Tchr • St John LA Grange IL • (708)354-1690 • (CQ 1995 MA)

**GOTTSCHALK ARDELLE D**
6245 Stevens Ave S Richfield MN 55423 • MNS • Tchr • Mount Calvary Richfield MN • (612)866-5405 • (RF 1964)

**GOTTSCHALK DANIEL L**
8001 Westwood Dr Fort Wayne IN 46818-9652 • IN • Tchr • Sub Bethlehem Fort Wayne IN • (219)484-7873 • (RF 1990)

**GOTTSCHALK JANET C** (516)679-9365
1082 Bellmore Rd North Bellmore NY 11710-3719 • AT • Tchr • Calvary East Meadow NY • (516)520-4067 • (RF 1970 MA)

**GOTTSCHALK JOHN R**
6245 Stevens Ave S Richfield MN 55423 • MNS • Tchr • Mount Calvary Richfield MN • (612)869-9441 • (RF 1966 MA)

**GOTTSCHALK RICHARD ERWIN** (414)543-7678
3130 S 54th St Milwaukee WI 53219-4419 • mrg@aero.net • SW • P/Tchr • Oklahoma Avenue Milwaukee WI • (414)543-3580 • (SP 1967 MA)

**GOTTSCHALK ROGER A** (414)543-9714
2461 S 73rd St West Allis WI 53219-1807 • SW • Tchr • St Paul West Allis WI • (414)541-6251 • (RF 1966 MAT)

**GOVE RICHARD G** (660)463-2556
316 S College Dr PO Box 521 Concordia MO 64020 • rggove@almanet.net • MO • SHS/C • Missouri Saint Louis MO • (314)317-4550 • (RF 1964 MED)

**GOWEN NANCY E** (808)488-0664
98-325 Koauka St Aiea HI 96701-4433 • oslc@aloha.net • CNH • 08/1990 08/2000 • (S 1983)

**GRAB DAVID A** (708)957-2967
1349 Jeffery Dr Homewood IL 60430-4041 • grabd@flash.net • NI • 08/2000 • (S 1969)

**GRABAU HERBERT E** (402)488-0675
621 S Cotner Blvd Lincoln NE 68510-3902 • hegrabau@navix.net • NEB • EM • (S 1945 MS)

**GRABENHOFER KAETHE KAROLA**
N44 W6010 Hamilton Rd Cedarburg WI 53012 • grabenhofer@grafton.net • SW • Tchr • First Immanuel Cedarburg WI • (262)377-6610 • (MQ 1993)

**GRABOWSKI LOUANN** (312)696-2823
432 S Cumberland Ave Park Ridge IL 60068-4672 • NI • Tchr • St Andrew Park Ridge IL • (847)823-9308 • (RF 1963)

**GRAEFE JOSEPH A** (573)243-9757
650 Strawberry Ln Jackson MO 63755-1108 • MO • Tchr • St Paul Jackson MO • (573)243-5360 • (MQ 1985)

**GRAF DEBRA S** (262)306-8602
3314 Windsor Pl West Bend WI 53090 • SW • 08/1997 08/2000 • (S 1975)

**GRAF DUANE S** (414)543-8808
9410 W Waterford Ave Greenfield WI 53228-2171 • SW • Prin • St Paul West Allis WI • (414)541-6251 • (SP 1971 MA)

**GRAF JENNIFER SUE** (847)640-9551
1225 S Chestnut Ave Arlington Hts IL 60005-3105 • NI • Tchr • St Paul Chicago IL • (708)867-5044 • (RF 1981 MED)

**GRAF LYNNE M** (402)563-2699
1759 29th Ave Columbus NE 68601-4339 • lgraf@gilligan.esu7.k12.ne.us • NEB • Tchr • Immanuel Columbus NE • (402)564-8423 • (S 1984)

**GRAF PATRICIA S** (414)543-6579
2634 S 99th St West Allis WI 53227-2614 • SW • Tchr • St Paul West Allis WI • (414)541-6251 • (MQ 1991)

**GRAF SUSAN R** (414)543-8808
9410 W Waterford Ave Greenfield WI 53228-2171 • SW • Tchr • St Paul West Allis WI • (414)541-6251 • (RF 1971 MA)

**GRAF WARREN R***
3314 Windsor Pl West Bend WI 53090 • SW • Tchr • St John West Bend WI • (262)334-4901 • (S 1975)

**GRAGE GLENN G*** (313)287-3866
13010 Princeton St Apt 6 Taylor MI 48180-4582 • MI • Tchr • St John Taylor MI • (734)287-3866 • (RF 1978 MA)

**GRAHAM JULIE ANN*** (630)307-3556
8 E Hattendorf #4 Roselle IL 60172 • gagraham@email.msn.com • NI • Tchr • St Paul Mount Prospect IL • (847)255-0332 • (RF 1988)

**GRAHAM MICHAEL A*** (817)927-3331
2234 Lipscomb St Fort Worth TX 76110-2049 • teachermg@aol.com • TX • Tchr • St Paul Fort Worth TX • (817)332-4563 • (RF 1978)

**GRAME LLONDA JO**
4448 SE 105th St Berryton KS 66409-9645 • MO • Tchr • Messiah Independence MO • (816)254-9405 • (S 1994)

**GRAMENZ CAROLYN S** (618)965-3514
4942 Ballpark Rd Steeleville IL 62288-2825 • SI • Tchr • St Mark Steeleville IL • (618)965-3838 • (S 1979)

**GRAMENZ KAREN M** (618)965-9455
5019 Ballpark Rd Steeleville IL 62288-2825 • SI • Tchr • St Mark Steeleville IL • (618)965-3192 • (SP 1980)

**GRAMS SUSAN E**
1231 Middlefield Rd Palo Alto CA 94301 • ripkes@aol.com • IN • Tchr • Central New Haven IN • (219)493-2502 • (AA 1997)

**GRAMZOW WILLIAM K IV** (248)981-6368
510 Highland Ave #175 Milford MI 48381-1516 • cocls20@tir.com • EN • Tchr • Child Of Christ Hartland MI • (248)887-3836 • (RF 1986 MCMU)

**GRANDSTAFF MELINDA K** (402)656-5775
PO Box 181 Plymouth NE 68424 • NEB • Tchr • St Paul Beatrice NE • (402)223-3414 • (S 1989)

**GRANGER RALPH F** (618)826-2152
205 Ridge Dr Chester IL 62233-1820 • mardell@midwest.net • SI • 06/1992 06/2000 • (RF 1957 MA)

**GRANHOLM KATHLEEN E** (630)892-9088
32 Pasadena Oswego IL 60543 • NI • Tchr • St Paul Aurora IL • (630)820-3457 • (RF 1972)

**GRANLEY BRENDA S** (414)545-0962
3870 S 54th St Milwaukee WI 53220 • granley@juno.com • EN • 11/1999 • (S 1980)

**GRANLEY RUSSELL J** (414)545-0962
3870 S 54th St Milwaukee WI 53220 • granley@juno.com • SW • Tchr • St Martini Milwaukee WI • (414)645-4094 • (RF 1976)

**GRANNIS GLENNA GENE**
2811 Wane Ln Fort Wayne IN 46808 • (wanelanetrane@msn.com • IN • Tchr • Trinity Fort Wayne IN • (219)447-2411 • (S 1970 MSED)

**GRANT DANNA M***
222 S Bench St Galena IL 61036-2204 • NI • EM • (RF 1987)

**GRAPATIN EDWARD R** (773)736-9584
4310 N Menard Ave Chicago IL 60634-1720 • NI • EM • (RF 1962 MED)

**GRAPATIN WENDY S** (414)375-0935
N82W6754 Fair St Cedarburg WI 53012-1139 • wendy.grapatin@cuw.edu • SW • SHS/C • South Wisconsin Milwaukee WI • (414)464-8100 • (MQ 1989)

**GRASMICK DENNIS L** (952)448-2156
1531 Sunshine Cir Chaska MN 55318-1727 • MNS • 01/1999 • (RF 1976 MED)

**GRASS JOHN P** (715)845-2563
1310 Pine St Wausau WI 54401-4249 • NW • Tchr • Trinity Wausau WI • (715)848-0166 • (RF 1969 MS)

**GRASS LARRY E** (660)463-7686
PO Box 139 Emma MO 65327-0139 • MO • Tchr • St Paul Concordia MO • (660)463-7654 • (S 1974)

**GRASS PETER J** (414)466-7662
827 Parkside Dr Wheaton IL 60187-3669 • NI • Tchr • St John Wheaton IL • (630)668-0701 • (S 1974 MS)

**GRASSE KELLI L** (920)208-4722
2214 Superior Ave #2 Sheboygan WI 53081-2159 • snyder@lutheranhigh.com • SW • Tchr • Lutheran HS Sheboygan WI • (920)452-3323 • (MQ 1996)

**GRASZ DUANE F** (719)570-9518
5016 Raindrop Cir S Colorado Springs CO 80917-3244 • RM • Tchr • Immanuel Colorado Springs CO • (719)636-3681 • (S 1962 MSED)

**GRASZ MICHAEL J** (562)866-9887
5812 Hazelbrook Ave Lakewood CA 90712-1132 • huskrmg@aol.com • PSW • Tchr • South Bay LHS Inglewood CA • (310)672-1101 • (S 1989 MA)

**GRASZ TANYA MALENA** (562)866-9887
5812 Hazelbrook Ave Lakewood CA 90712 • huskrmg@aol.com • PSW • Tchr • South Bay HS-Torranc Torrance CA • (310)530-1231 • (IV 1992)

**GRATZ KATHRYN M*** (507)238-2975
1115 240th Ave Fairmont MN 56031-9542 • MNS • Tchr • St Pauls Fairmont MN • (507)238-9492 • (S 1985)

**GRAUDIN PETER J** (612)467-2260
22 Trilane Dr Young America MN 55397-9603 • pgraudin@aol.com • MNS • Tchr • Trinity Waconia MN • (952)442-4165 • (S 1979)

**GRAVES CANDACE ANN** (501)452-1705
9801 Meandering Way #39 Fort Smith AR 72903 • candace-g@hotmail.com • MDS • Tchr • First Fort Smith AR • (501)785-2886 • (S 1999)

**GRAVES JEAN E**
1138 S Luther Ave Lombard IL 60148-4127 • NI • Tchr • Trinity Lombard IL • (630)627-5601 • (RF 1968)

**GRAY CONSTANCE** (314)939-3724
312 Whispering Woods Dr Saint Charles MO 63304-6784 • MO • Tchr • Zion Saint Charles MO • (636)441-7425 • (RF 1989)

**GRAY JANNIECE** (402)362-7560
1002 Road 10 York NE 68467-9713 • NEB • Tchr • Emmanuel York NE • (402)362-6575 • (S 1976 MA)

**GRAY JOHN MARK** (314)939-3724
312 Whispering Woods Dr Saint Charles MO 63304-6784 • MO • Tchr • Zion Saint Charles MO • (636)441-7425 • (RF 1992)

**GRAYS JEAN M** (313)491-0967
5044 Oakman Blvd Detroit MI 48204-2671 • jogrys@gateway.net • MI • Tchr • St John Detroit MI • (313)933-8928 • (SP 1978)

**GREBASCH DOUGLAS H** (847)695-9603
207 W Montrey Elmhurst IL 60126-3006 • NI • Prin • St Paul Melrose Park IL • (708)343-1000 • (S 1969 MA)

**GREBASCH GAIL E**
207 Monterey Ave Elmhurst IL 60126-3006 • dggrebasch@aol.com • NI • Tchr • St Peter Schaumburg IL • (847)885-7636 • (RF 1976)

**GREDER GARY L** (602)971-4769
4327 E Meadow Rd Phoenix AZ 85032 • EN • Tchr • Christ Phoenix AZ • (602)957-7010 • (S 1980)

**GREEN DANNY L** (630)766-1418
861 S Church Rd Bensenville IL 60106-2904 • laup@gateway.net • NI • Tchr • Zion Bensenville IL • (630)766-1039 • (RF 1988)

**GREEN SHEILA M** (248)656-8984
53774 Regency Hills Ct Shelby Township MI 48316-2047 • MI • Tchr • St John Fraser MI • (810)294-8740 • (S 1972 MA)

**GREENWALD CELIA JANE** (619)728-2594
1652 Pala Lake Dr Fallbrook CA 92028-4911 • PSW • Tchr • Zion Fallbrook CA • (760)723-3500 • (CQ 1996)

**GREENWALD LINDA LEE** (281)498-1264
12530 Chessington Dr Houston TX 77031-3305 • music8232@aol.com • TX • Mem C • St Philip Houston TX • (713)771-8907 • (CQ 1998)

**GREER REBECCA** (817)431-3589
696 Chisolm Trl Keller TX 76248-4969 • bgreer@crownoflife.org • TX • Tchr • Crown Of Life Colleyville TX • (817)421-5683 • (CQ 1994)

**GREER THERESA** (313)397-0565
43188 Lancelot Dr Canton MI 48188-1919 • tmir@wwnet.com • MI • Tchr • St Michael Wayne MI • (734)728-3315 • (AA 1993 MA)

**GREGORY DAHLAS A** (630)231-0077
122 W Hazel St West Chicago IL 60185-3375 • NI • Tchr • Trinity West Chicago IL • (708)231-5849 • (RF 1972)

**GREIMANN STEVEN P** (214)613-1945
4111 Coryell Way Mesquite TX 75150-2813 • TX • Tchr • Lutheran HS of Dalla Dallas TX • (214)349-8912 • (S 1979 MED)

**GREIN DENISE F** (402)748-3806
RR 1 Box 305 Osmond NE 68765-9659 • NEB • 09/1997 09/1999 • (S 1977 MED)

**GREIN LINDA L** (303)659-2788
15201 WCR #2 Brighton CO 80603 • RM • Tchr • Zion Brighton CO • (303)659-3443 • (S 1979)

**GREINKE ANN M**
1805 Roswell Rd Apt 29S Marietta GA 30062-3946 • FG • Tchr • First Clearwater FL • (727)461-3444 • (RF 1979)

**GREINKE RALPH G** (414)443-0484
2442 N Le Feber Ave Wauwatosa WI 53213-1220 • greinke2@execpc.com • SW • EM • (RF 1960 MA)

**GRELK MARGARET C** (414)821-5156
2270 S Lombardy Ln New Berlin WI 53151-2474 • SW • Tchr • Elm Grove Elm Grove WI • (262)797-2970 • (RF 1977)

**GREMEL BRUCE** (248)969-1113
1615 W Leonard Rd Leonard MI 48367-1633 • bgremel@yahoo.com • MI • Mem C • St John Rochester MI • (248)652-8830 • (RF 1967 MAT)

**GREMEL DARLA J** (602)745-0049
7034 E Kenyon Dr Tucson AZ 85710-4824 • PSW • Tchr • Fountain Of Life Tucson AZ • (520)747-1213 • (S 1980 MA)

**GREMMER ELIZABETH** (512)490-3238
4006 Knoll Bnd San Antonio TX 78247-2124 • TX • Tchr • Concordia San Antonio TX • (210)479-1477 • (S 1975)

**GRESE SUSAN J** (734)663-4047
1512 Charlton St Ann Arbor MI 48103-4168 • MI • Tchr • St Paul Ann Arbor MI • (734)665-0604 • (RF 1972 MA)

**GRESENS RONALD J** (708)335-0193
3604 Wellington Ct Hazel Crest IL 60429-1528 • ron4stpaul@aol.com • NI • Tchr • St Paul Dolton IL • (708)849-3225 • (RF 1957 MA)

**GRESENS WALTER F** (810)603-2164
12453 Pagels Dr Grand Blanc MI 48439 • wgresens@sun.tir.com • MI • Mem C • Faith Grand Blanc MI • (810)694-9351 • (RF 1959)

**GRESENS WILMER E** (715)842-8058
H8051 County Road J Wausau WI 54403-9637 • NW • EM • (CQ 1942)

**GRESETH KARI M** (319)359-3999
3505 Jersey Ridge Rd #718 Davenport IA 52807 • IE • Tchr • Trinity Davenport IA • (319)322-5224 • (S 1999)

**GREVE DEJE KATHLEEN** (402)556-4403
6641 Lafayette Ave Omaha NE 68132-1147 • lovespasta@juno.com • NEB • Tchr • St Mark Omaha NE • (402)391-6148 • (MQ 1992 MA)

**GREVE DONALD G** (440)331-3521
4314 Grannis Rd Fairview Park OH 44126-1530 • dggreve@aol.com • OH • Tchr • Ohio Olmsted Falls OH • (RF 1953 MA)

**GREWE EDWIN A** (757)258-9433
504 Musket Dr Williamsburg VA 23185-5326 • SE • EM • (RF 1953)

**GREWE MARK JEFFREY** (217)222-1937
1507 Quail Creek Dr Quincy IL 62301 • CI • Prin • St James Quincy IL • (217)222-8447 • (RF 1981 MA)

**GREWE RALPH A** (219)486-2240
3914 Shannon Dr Fort Wayne IN 46835-2153 • parteetyme@juno.com • IN • EM • (RF 1958 MED)

**GRICE RICHARD THOMAS** (303)683-5690
3 W Sylvestor Pl Highlands Ranch CO 80129 • doliver88@aol.com • RM • EM • (S 1960 MED)

**GRIEDL MARY SUE** (713)251-4372
9214 Bayou Bluff Dr Spring TX 77379-4423 • TX • Tchr • Trinity Spring TX • (281)376-5810 • (CQ 1994 MA)

**GRIESSE YVONNE R**
695 Park Ln Monroe WA 98272 • NOW • P/Tchr • Zion Snohomish WA • (360)568-2700 • (S 1979)

**GRIFFIN MICHELLE LYNN** (972)939-1588
2027 Stradivarius Ln Carrollton TX 75007 • TX • Tchr • Prince Of Peace Carrollton TX • (972)447-9887 • (AU 1986 MA)

**GRIFFIN PETER W** (208)237-8119
2386 Gooding St Pocatello ID 83201-1813 • pgriffin@gracepocid.org • NOW • Tchr • Grace Pocatello ID • (208)237-4142 • (SP 1980)

**GRIFFIN SHIRLEY A**
17730 Pheasant Ln Country Clubs Hill IL 60478-4984 • NI • Tchr • Zion Matteson IL • (708)747-7490 • (BR 1975)

**GRIFFITH BILLIE J** (956)423-7985
2021 Theresa St Harlingen TX 78550-5130 • TX • Tchr • St Paul Harlingen TX • (956)423-3926 • (CQ 1997)

**GRIFFITH WILLIAM E** (913)651-1480
1940 Pottawatomie St Leavenworth KS 66048-1657 • KS • Tchr • St Paul Leavenworth KS • (913)682-0387 • (S 1984)

**GRIM REBECCA R** (517)479-3174
236 N 2nd St Harbor Beach MI 48441 • MI • Tchr • Zion Harbor Beach MI • (517)479-3615 • (RF 1990)

**GRIM STEPHEN M** (219)486-6203
7115 Bradford Dr Fort Wayne IN 46835-1522 • IN • Tchr • Concordia Fort Wayne IN • (219)426-9922 • (RF 1985)

**GRIMALDO IRMA**
Jehovan-El Buen Pastor Luthera 3740 W Belden Ave Chicago IL 60647-2348 • NI • Tchr • Jehovah-El Buen Past Chicago IL • (773)342-5854 • (RF 1981)

**GRIMM ELLEN K** (616)744-3408
1835 Riegler Rd Muskegon MI 49445-1631 • grimmb936@cs.com • MI • Tchr • Good Shepherd Montague MI • (616)894-8471 • (RF 1976)

**GRIMM KAREN M**
PO Box 2083 Orlando FL 32802-2083 • S • Tchr • Good Shepherd Montague MI • (S 1987)

**GRIMM PEGGY L** (319)664-3038
2976 KK Ave North English IA 52316 • IE • Tchr • Lutheran Interparish Williamsburg IA • (319)668-1711 • (S 1978)

**GRIMM WILLIAM I*** (715)275-3270
N9304 N Shore Rd Summit Lake WI 54485-9729 • NW • 01/1992 01/2000 • (V 1965)

**GRIMPO RONALD D** (517)868-3106
1874 Rhodes St Reese MI 48757-9553 • MI • 09/1998 • (S 1973 MA)

**GRIMSLEY JOELLE MARIE**
15655 70th St Mayer MN 55360 • MNS • Tchr • Lutheran High Mayer MN • (612)657-2251 • (SP 1989)

**GRISSETT ROSE ANN** (512)892-5330
5405 Honey Dew Ter Austin TX 78749-1278 • TX • Tchr • St Paul Austin TX • (512)472-3313 • (RF 1965 MED)

**GRISWOLD RENE A** (952)938-6478
7425 W Lake St Saint Louis Park MN 55426-4322 • MNS • Tchr • St Peter Edina MN • (612)927-8400 • (SP 1978)

**GROBELNY CHERYL ANN** (810)997-2443
5615 Althea Shelby Township MI 48316-4223 • cgrobelny@lhsa.com • MI • Tchr • LHS North Macomb MI • (810)781-9151 • (S 1981 MS MED)

**GROEPER ROBIN F** (314)282-3759
2159 Santa Fe Cir Arnold MO 63010-5215 • MO • Mem C • Christ Memorial Saint Louis MO • (314)631-0304 • (CQ 1996)

**GROERICH DEBORAH J** (314)638-6012
9915 Wolff Dr Saint Louis MO 63123-6209 • MO • Tchr • Salem Affton MO • (314)353-9242 • (S 1979)

**GROESCHEL GAIL ELAINE** (713)862-1842
1838 Widdicomb Ct Houston TX 77008-1242 • TX • EM • (RF 1963)

**GROLL DAVID H** (517)770-4938
12840 Tamarack Dr Burt MI 48417-9418 • dgroll@worldnet.att.net • MI • EM • (RF 1961)

**GRONAU JANE M** (712)675-4347
C/O St John Lutheran School RR 1 Box 112 Columbus NE 68601-9749 • NEB • P/Tchr • St John Columbus NE • (402)285-0335 • (S 1966)

**GRONEWOLD HAROLD W** (708)895-3387
2957 192nd St Lansing IL 60438-3719 • halmargron@aol.com • NI • EM • (RF 1960)

**GRONEWOLD WILBUR E** (708)946-3259
PO Box 423 Beecher IL 60401-0423 • NI • EM • (RF 1949 MA)

**GROPPE EVA E** (262)377-4321
1538 Green Valley Rd Grafton WI 53024-1004 • SW • Tchr • St Paul Grafton WI • (414)377-4659 • (MW 1983)

**GROSS LARRY E** (503)282-6114
5740 NE Emerson St Portland OR 97218-2406 • NOW • SHS/C • Northwest Portland OR • (CQ 1990 MSCT)

**GROSS LISABETH KAY** (714)283-3368
5809 E Paseo De Leon Anaheim CA 92807-3934 • lgross@stpaulsorg.org • PSW • Tchr • St Paul Orange CA • (714)921-3188 • (RF 1980)

**GROSSHEIDER NELSON L** (314)353-5264
5837 Robert Ave Saint Louis MO 63109-3861 • MO • Tchr • Salem Affton MO • (314)353-9242 • (RF 1971)

**GROTELUESCHEN DANIEL R** (317)898-1281
900 N Fenton Ave Indianapolis IN 46219-5404 • IN • P/Tchr • Zion New Palestine IN • (317)861-4210 • (RF 1964)

**GROTELUESCHEN DAVID P** (317)861-4804
5634 High Acres North Ct New Palestine IN 46163-9726 • IN • Tchr • LHS Of Indianapolis Indianapolis IN • (317)787-5474 • (RF 1966)

**GROTELUESCHEN JUDITH LYNN** (317)861-4804
5634 High Acres North Ct New Palestine IN 46163-9726 • judycsa@aol.com • IN • EM • (RF 1966)

**GROTELUESCHEN LAURIE** (708)344-6595
726 Franklin Ave River Forest IL 60305-1724 • NI • Tchr • St Andrews Park Ridge IL • (847)823-6656 • (RF 1985)

**GROTELUESCHEN LESLEY ANNE** (317)898-1281
900 N Fenton Ave Indianapolis IN 46219-5404 • IN • Tchr • St John Indianapolis IN • (317)352-9196 • (RF 1964 MS)

**GROTELUESCHEN PAUL G** (708)366-7608
604 Ashland Ave River Forest IL 60305-1827 • 107767.2067@compuserve.com • NI • EM • (RF 1950 MA)

**GROTELUESCHEN TIMOTHY L** (618)495-9001
PO Box 414 Hoffman IL 62250 • SI • Tchr • Trinity Hoffman IL • (618)495-2246 • (RF 1994)

**GROTH PAUL W** (765)447-6762
90 Elkton Ct Lafayette IN 47905-4018 • IN • Tchr • St James Lafayette IN • (765)742-6464 • (RF 1970)

**GROTH ROBERT W** (317)787-6630
1015 Southwood Dr Indianapolis IN 46227-2235 • IN • Tchr • Emmaus Indianapolis IN • (317)632-1486 • (S 1978 MA)

**GROTHAUS LARRY H** (402)643-3578
120 Hillcrest Dr Seward NE 68434-2820 • lgrothaus@seward.cune.edu • NEB • EM • (RF 1954 MA PHD)

**GROTHAUS PETER D** (310)490-0286
4568 Falcon Ave Long Beach CA 90807-1815 • PSW • Tchr • Bethany Long Beach CA • (562)420-7783 • (S 1985)

**GROTHAUS TIMOTHY A** (248)651-8986
1187 Burgoyne Blvd Rochester Hills MI 48307-2505 • MI • Tchr • St John Rochester MI • (248)652-8830 • (S 1980)

**GROVER ALISON ANNE** (618)656-5766
6823 Deer Crk Edwardsville IL 62025-3060 • SI • Tchr • Trinity Edwardsville IL • (618)656-7002 • (CQ 1996)

**GRUBB CRISLYN R** (561)225-8090
2467 NE 17th Ct Jensen Beach FL 34957 • crgrubb@yahoo.com • FG • Tchr • Redeemer Stuart FL • (561)286-0932 • (S 1996)

**GRUBE EDWARD C** (630)543-3493
19W020 Oak St Addison IL 60101-2405 • egrube@aol.com • NI • Prin • Concord Addison IL • (630)543-6404 • (RF 1970 MA)

**GRUBE RENEE L** (630)543-3493
19W020 Oak St Addison IL 60101-2405 • egrube@aol.com • NI • Tchr • St Paul Addison IL • (630)543-6909 • (RF 1973)

**GRUBEN KATHRYN ANNE** (319)322-8565
1115 E High St Davenport IA 52803-3112 • IE • Tchr • Trinity Davenport IA • (319)323-8001 • (RF 1990)

**GRUBER KATHRYN ANNA** (608)362-5714
807 W Big Hill Rd Beloit WI 53511-8604 • SW • EM • (S 1965)

**GRUBER MIRIAM** (501)513-2451
1839 Tyler St Apt 3 Conway AR 72032 • mrg2099@hotmail.com • MDS • Tchr • Christ Little Rock AR • (501)663-5212 • (S 1999)

**GRUEBER DAVID JOHN** (517)652-9779
4225 Maple Rd Frankenmuth MI 48734 • MI • Tchr • Valley Saginaw MI • (517)790-1676 • (CQ 1997)

**GRUEBER SUSAN E** (517)652-9779
4225 Maple Rd Frankenmuth MI 48734-9115 • MI • Tchr • Immanuel Saginaw MI • (517)754-4285 • (S 1966 MA)

**GRUEL JONATHAN L** (310)422-9935
6550 Orange Ave Apt 2 Long Beach CA 90805-2432 • PSW • 08/1996 08/2000 • (S 1978)

**GRUENBAUM LUTHER P** (314)869-6358
9985 Lochiel Ln Saint Louis MO 63137-1836 • MO • EM • (RF 1939 MSW)

**GRUENDLER CARL G** (708)345-1756
1602 9th Ave Melrose Park IL 60160-2207 • EN • EM • (RF 1953 MED)

**GRUENWALD BEVERLY ANN** (314)839-1043
1470 Ascot Ter Florissant MO 63033-3121 • gruenwald@stlnet.com • MO • Tchr • Grace Chapel Bellefontaine Nbrs MO • (314)867-6564 • (RF 1984 MA)

**GRUENWALD CATHERINE J**
82 N End House Fitzjames Ave London 2140RX ENGLAND • NI • 08/1999 • (RF 1988 MA)

**GRUETZMACHER GENE E** (414)786-1284
18295 Milwaukee Ave Brookfield WI 53045-3406 • SW • Tchr • Northwest Milwaukee WI • (414)463-4040 • (RF 1963)

**GRUETZMACHER HEIDI** (414)695-4039
967 Quinlan Dr Unit A Pewaukee WI 53072-1869 • SW • Tchr • Divine Redeemer Hartland WI • (414)367-8400 • (MQ 1995)

**GRUETZMACHER PAUL M** (414)786-1284
18295 Milwaukee Ave Brookfield WI 53045-3406 • SW • Tchr • Elm Grove Elm Grove WI • (262)797-2970 • (RF 1962 MS)

**GRUNDMANN IONA L**
1200 32nd St South #87 Great Falls MT 59405-5343 • MT • 06/1999 • (S 1970 MED)

**GRUNDT CAROLYN J**
327 Vernon St San Francisco CA 94132-2713 • cgrundt@earthlink.net • CNH • Prin • Zion San Francisco CA • (415)221-7500 • (RF 1983 MAD)

**GRUNOW KARIN B** (503)762-4303
11709 SE Flavel St Portland OR 97266-5979 • grunowk@aol.com • NOW • Tchr • Trinity Portland OR • (503)288-6403 • (RF 1975)

**GRUNOW THOMAS P** (503)762-4302
11709 SE Flavel St Portland OR 97266-5979 • lfalsc@aol.com • NOW • 01/1995 01/1999 • (RF 1975 MED)

**GRUNST NATHANIEL M** (312)299-1589
1329 Wicke Ave Des Plaines IL 60018-1708 • NI • Tchr • Luther HS North Chicago IL • (773)286-3600 • (RF 1961 MA)

**GRUNWALD KAREN W** (715)524-2995
1127 S Weed St Shawano WI 54166-3241 • punk13@ezwebtech.com • NW • Tchr • St James Shawano WI • (715)524-4213 • (SP 1967)

**GRUPE ELIZABETH F** (810)566-1525
49133 Conway Ct Shelby Twp MI 48315-3916 • MI • Tchr • Trinity Utica MI • (810)731-4490 • (S 1962)

**GRUPE LARRY R** (810)566-1525
49133 Conway Ct Utica MI 48315-3916 • llgrupe@worldnet.att.net • MI • Mem C • Trinity Utica MI • (810)731-4490 • (S 1962 MA)

**GRUPE MICHAEL J** (314)721-4159
2336 Rockdale Ave Saint Louis MO 63121-4741 • mgrupe@info.csd.org • MO • Tchr • Lutheran North Saint Louis MO • (314)389-3100 • (S 1976 MED MS)

**GSELL KARA LEE**
12600 Braddock Dr #C124 Los Angeles CA 90066-6735 • PSW • Tchr • Pilgrim Santa Monica CA • (310)829-2239 • (PO 1999)

**GUAGLIARDO JOSEPH A**
C/O Zion Lutheran Church 7401 Winkler Rd Fort Myers FL 33919 • joegosl@aol.com • FG • Mem C • Zion Fort Myers FL • (941)481-4040 • (CQ 1999)

**GUBANYI JOSEPH** (402)643-3989
210 Hillcrest Seward NE 68434 • NEB • SHS/C • Nebraska Seward NE • (S 1972 MS)

**GUDA JANET** (216)333-6625
2935 Hampton Rd Rocky River OH 44116-2552 • jguda@kent.edu • OH • 07/1981 10/1999 • (RF 1961)

**GUDE MARY A** (618)377-6246
5221 Loop Rd Dorsey IL 62021-1103 • SI • Tchr • Trinity Edwardsville IL • (618)656-7002 • (RF 1965)

**GUEBERT JANEL SUE** (618)493-6220
146 N Main PO Box 21 Hoyleton IL 62803-0021 • SI • Tchr • Trinity Hoyleton IL • (618)493-7754 • (S 1992)

**GUEBERT LOIS** (219)486-6629
3426 Walden Run Fort Wayne IN 46815-6168 • cogueber@ash.palni.edu • IN • SHS/C • Indiana Fort Wayne IN • (RF 1974 MLS)

**GUELZOW ERIN RUTH**
Holy Cross Lutheran Church 760 N Sun Dr Lake Mary FL 32746-2507 • S • Indiana Fort Wayne IN • (RF 1997)

**GUELZOW JONATHAN P** (828)324-9575
1010 38th Ave NE Hickory NC 28601-7466 • SE • P/Tchr • St Stephen Hickory NC • (828)256-2166 • (RF 1968 MS)

**GUELZOW STEPHANIE J** (336)760-3074
122 Cedar Cove Ln Winston Salem NC 27104-4402 • SE • Tchr • St John Winston-Salem NC • (336)725-1651 • (RF 1994 MED)

**GUENTHER DOUGLAS D** (517)792-4506
2359 Linda St Saginaw MI 48603-4126 • MI • Tchr • Michigan Ann Arbor MI • (AA 1983 MA)

**GUENTHER MARLA LYNNE** (763)753-3606
21475 Ibis St NW Cedar MN 55011 • MNS • Tchr • Olive Branch Coon Rapids MN • (612)755-2707 • (SP 1997)

**GUENTHER SCOTT A** (248)652-9466
4401 N Adams Rd Rochester MI 48306-1409 • thespiderman@geocities.com • MI • Tchr • LHS Northwest Rochester Hills MI • (810)852-6677 • (AA 1985 MS)

**GUENTHER VERNON C**
660 Meadow Ln Frankenmuth MI 48734-9306 • IN • EM • (S 1950 MSED MMU)

**GUGEL ROBERT A** (714)637-2292
5121 E Henley Pl Unit F Orange CA 92867 • PSW • Prin • Hope Glendora CA • (626)335-5315 • (RF 1966 MA)

**GUGEL RUTH E** (810)254-1981
45526 Remer Ct Utica MI 48317 • MI • 02/2000 • (S 1966 MED)

**GUIDERA GEORGE A DR*** (651)633-6406
2978 Pascal St Roseville MN 55113-1644 • guidera@csp.edu • MNS • SHS/C • Minnesota South Burnsville MN • (RF 1969 MA EDD)

**GUILFORD HOLLY LEIGH** (402)464-8462
5802 Saint Paul Ave Lincoln NE 68507-2364 • hollyguilford@juno.com • NEB • 08/1996 • (S 1995)

**GUILFORD THOMAS K** (402)464-8462
5802 St Paul Ave Lincoln NE 68507 • tomguilford@juno.com • NEB • Tchr • Lincoln Luth Jr/Sr H Lincoln NE • (402)467-5404 • (S 1992)

**GULBRANDSEN SONJA E** (630)226-9707
5 I Fernwood Dr Bolingbrook IL 60440 • NI • Tchr • Trinity Burr Ridge IL • (708)839-1200 • (S 1993)

**GULDENSTEIN PAUL** (217)875-0271
3777 N Ashley Ct Decatur IL 62526-1291 • rdgstrat@aol.com • CI • Tchr • Lutheran School Asso Decatur IL • (217)233-2001 • (S 1968 MA)

**GULLEN LINDA S** (402)372-5122
38 Edgewood Ln N Centralia IL 62801-3707 • SI • Tchr • Trinity Centralia IL • (618)532-5434 • (S 1975)

**GUMMELT MICHAEL W** (818)701-3070
19851 Citronia St Chatsworth CA 91311-5602 • gummelt@pacbell.net • PSW • Tchr • Los Angeles Junior/S Sylmar CA • (818)362-5861 • (S 1979)

**GUMTOW WILLIAM A** (713)697-5408
505 Sunnyside St Houston TX 77076-3124 • TX • Tchr • Immanuel Houston TX • (713)861-8787 • (S 1972)

**GUNDELACH MARY** (415)366-0230
116 Stockbridge Ave Atherton CA 94027-3915 • CNH • EM • (S 1960)

**GUNDELL ARTHUR**
46-090 Puulena St Apt 1316 Kaneohe HI 96744-3757 • CNH • Prin • LHS Of Hawaii Honolulu HI • (808)949-5302 • (S 1968 MS)

**GUNDELL KATIE L** (710)731-9386
6777 Nash Rd North Tonawanda NY 14120-1231 • EA • Tchr • St John North Tonawanda NY • (716)693-9677 • (BR 1996)

**GUNDELL KEVIN**
6777 Nash Rd North Tonawanda NY 14210 • EA • Tchr • Holy Ghost Niagara Falls NY • (716)731-3030 • (BR 1998)

**GUNDLACH KENNETH L** (920)451-7060
4020 S 15th St Sheboygan WI 53081-7506 • kgundlach@juno.com • SW • Prin • Bethlehem Sheboygan WI • (920)452-5071 • (RF 1966 MED)

**GURGEL TIFFANY** (630)852-6471
257 W 157th St Westmont IL 60559 • tiffg98@hotmail.com • NI • Tchr • Trinity Tinley Park IL • (708)532-3529 • (MQ 1998)

**GUSE ANNE MARIE** (651)489-8703
44 W Arlington Apt 202 St Paul MN 55117 • MNS • Tchr • East St Paul Saint Paul MN • (612)774-2030 • (SP 2000)

**GUSE EARL W C** (262)306-9725
2122 Willowbrook Dr West Bend WI 53090-1780 • SW • P/Tchr • St John West Bend WI • (414)334-3077 • (S 1988 MED)

**GUSE' PAUL BRENT** (734)729-4959
38529 Cherry Hill Rd Westland MI 48186-3264 • MI • Tchr • Michigan Ann Arbor MI • (AA 1987)

**GUST CLARA F** (517)428-4845
7364 Dobson Rd Port Hope MI 48468 • MI • Tchr • St John Port Hope MI • (517)428-4140 • (S 1986)

**GUSTAFSON KAREN B**
9403 Willow Ln Mokena IL 60448-9322 • NI • Tchr • Trinity Tinley Park IL • (708)532-9395 • (RF 1981)

**GUTEKUNST NYLA H** (504)893-6865
1215 W Magnolia St Covington LA 70433-1838 • SO • 09/1986 09/1999 • (S 1979)

**GUTENKUNST GARY A**
Lutheran High School East 20100 Kelly Rd Harper Woods MI 48225-1282 • MI • Holy Trinity Covington LA • (S 1981)

**GUTHMAN DELORES JOAN** (715)229-4156
433 S 5th Ave Owen WI 54460-9750 • NW • Mem C • Zion Colby WI • (715)223-2166 • (SP 1970)

**GUTWEIN MANFRED** (630)859-8245
345 S Commonwealth Ave Aurora IL 60506-4845 • NI • Tchr • Trinity Lombard IL • (630)629-8765 • (S 1978 MA)

**GUTWEIN SUSAN MARIE** (630)859-8245
345 S Commonwealth Ave Aurora IL 60506 • NI • Tchr • Immanuel Batavia IL • (630)879-7163 • (S 1978)

**GUTZLER MARK D** (262)598-0997
3027 Meyer Ct - #4 Racine WI 53406 • SW • Tchr • Concordia Racine WI • (262)554-1659 • (RF 1971)

**GUTZLER MATTHEW MICHAEL**
17 S Elm St Mt Prospect IL 60056 • NI • Tchr • St Paul Mount Prospect IL • (847)255-0332 • (SP 1996)

**GYNTHER J STUART** (805)985-7693
3080 Jacktar Ave Oxnard CA 93035-3236 • PSW • Tchr • St John Oxnard CA • (805)983-0330 • (PO 1992)

**GYURNEK SANDRA D** (419)784-4911
518 Jefferson Ave Defiance OH 43512-2612 • OH • Tchr • St John Defiance OH • (419)782-1751 • (S 1975)

## H

**HAACK LOREN F** (714)635-6016
625 S Boxwood St Anaheim CA 92802-1454 • PSW • P/Tchr • Prince Of Peace Anaheim CA • (714)774-0993 • (RF 1969 MA)

**HAAG ROBERT J** (314)832-3863
4670 Idaho Ave Saint Louis MO 63111-1403 • MO • P/Tchr • St Luke Saint Louis MO • (314)832-0118 • (RF 1961)

**HAAK ARMAND L** (314)925-1274
433 Nantucket Dr Saint Charles MO 63301-1223 • ahaak01amail.win.org • MO • Tchr • LHS St Charles Saint Peters MO • (636)928-5100 • (S 1975 MSCT)

**HAAK CAROL L**
5320 Rockwell Indianapolis IN 46237 • IN • Tchr • Calvary Indianapolis IN • (317)783-2000 • (S 1970)

**HAAK CHARLES E** (312)927-7280
4446 S Trumbull Ave Chicago IL 60632-3534 • NI • Tchr • St Paul Melrose Park IL • (708)343-5000 • (RF 1971 MA)

**HAAK DIANE V** (941)278-1357
7132 Penner Ln Apt 28 Fort Myers FL 33907-7700 • FG • Tchr • St Michael Fort Myers FL • (941)939-1218 • (S 1968)

**HAAK LISA JEANNE** (708)850-9492
447 Burlington Ave Apt #4 Clarendon Hills IL 60514-1161 • ljhaak@juno.com • NI • Tchr • Trinity Burr Ridge IL • (708)839-1444 • (AA 1985 MA)

**HAAK SALLY C** (812)376-3765
3819 Lantern Ln Columbus IN 47203-2914 • haak@hsonline.net • IN • 06/1998 06/2000 • (RF 1986)

**HAAKE DALE L** (515)576-8471
2905 21st Ave N Fort Dodge IA 50501-7339 • IW • EM • (S 1959)

**HAAKE DONALD L** (636)327-6919
1172 Wilmer Rd Wentzville MO 63385-4412 • MO • EM • (S 1972)

**HAAKE JEAN C** (314)352-8385
6020 Savio Dr Saint Louis MO 63123-2761 • MO • EM • (RF 1958)

**HAAKE JEAN MARIE** (515)576-8471
2905 21st Ave N Fort Dodge IA 50501 • IW • Tchr • St Paul Fort Dodge IA • (515)955-7208 • (S 1986)

**HAAR BARBARA L** (410)944-0167
1705 Chesterton Rd Baltimore MD 21244-1701 • blhaar@aol.com • SE • Mem C • St Paul Catonsville MD • (410)747-1897 • (S 1983)

**HAAR STEVEN J** (410)944-0167
1705 Chesterton Rd Baltimore MD 21244-1701 • sjhaar@aol.com • SE • Tchr • Baltimore LHS Baltimore MD • (410)825-2323 • (S 1983)

**HAAS DE ANN L** (515)278-2554
3904 48th Pl Des Moines IA 50310-2703 • haas.deann@gd-lc.org • IW • Mem C • Gloria Dei Urbandale IA • (515)276-1700 • (S 1985)

**HAAS JANE** (314)282-8295
1327 Libra Dr Arnold MO 63010-3008 • MO • S Ex/S • Missouri Saint Louis MO • (314)317-4550 • (S 1969)

**HAAS WALTER D** (414)761-2270
1800 W Mangold Ave Milwaukee WI 53221-5063 • SW • EM • (RF 1954 MED)

**HAASE LORILY** (913)342-7290
C/O Grace Lutheran Church 3333 Wood Ave Kansas City KS 66102-2137 • KS • Tchr • Grace Kansas City KS • (913)281-1621 • (S 1997)

**HAASE PAMELA SUE** (217)352-6008
3306 Roxford Dr Champaign IL 61822 • haase@c-u.net • CI • Tchr • St John Champaign IL • (217)359-1714 • (S 1972)

**HAASE PEGGY L** (310)519-3930
1043 S Walker Ave San Pedro CA 90731 • phaase@olschool.org • PSW • Tchr • Christ Rancho Palos Verdes CA • (310)831-0848 • (RF 1974)

**HABECK JENNIFER L** (303)771-7523
3561 S Quebec St Denver CO 80237-1334 • jhabeck@aismis.com • RM • Tchr • Peace W Christ Aurora CO • (303)693-5618 • (S 1978)

**HABEDANK CAROLYN M** (716)674-7414
156 Reserve Rd West Seneca NY 14224 • EA • Tchr • Trinity West Seneca NY • (716)674-5353 • (RF 1968 MSED)

**HABEDANK RONALD R** (716)674-7414
156 Reserve Rd West Seneca NY 14224 • EA • Mem C • Trinity West Seneca NY • (716)674-9188 • (RF 1969 MSED)

**HABERHERN DENNIS M** (216)230-2434
10127 Jamestown Dr North Royalton OH 44133-3316 • dhaberhern@lutheranwest.com • OH • Tchr • LHS West Rocky River OH • (440)333-1660 • (S 1970 MS)

**HABERHERN JEAN A** (216)230-2434
10127 Jamestown Dr North Royalton OH 44133-3316 • jhaberhern@lutheranwest.com • OH • Tchr • LHS West Rocky River OH • (440)333-1660 • (S 1970 MLS)

**HABERKAMP SHARON R** (320)587-6185
907 Dale St SW Apt 334 Hutchinson MN 55350-3077 • MNS • P/Tchr • Our Saviors Hutchinson MN • (320)587-3318 • (RF 1970)

**HACKBARTH MICHAEL R** (414)282-1310
4909 W Edgerton Ave #211 Greenfield WI 53220 • SW • Tchr • Martin LHS Greendale WI • (414)421-4000 • (MQ 1999)

**HACKBARTH RICHARD O E** (616)429-5376
4670 Beechnut Dr Saint Joseph MI 49085-9373 • rhackbar@remc11.k12.mi.us • MI • Prin • Trinity Saint Joseph MI • (616)983-3056 • (S 1968 MA)

**HACKELBERG HOLLY R** (630)323-5909
21 Gilbert Ave Clarendon Hills IL 60514-1139 • NI • Tchr • St John LA Grange IL • (708)354-1690 • (RF 1982 MED)

**HADDON AMY ANN** (248)853-7642
2880 S Livernois Rd Rochester Hills MI 48307 • MI • Tchr • Our Shepherd Birmingham MI • (248)645-0551 • (AA 1994)

**HADLE JOANNA BEA*** (913)783-4510
23289 W 239th St Paola KS 66071-5580 • hadle.farm@juno.com • KS • 07/1989 07/1999 • (S 1986)

**HAEGELE DENNIS F** (810)731-5580
5621 Montgomery Shelby Twp MI 48316-4108 • MI • Tchr • Michigan Ann Arbor MI • (RF 1969 MA)

**HAERTLING CLINTON O** (573)547-9138
1195 PCR 510 Perryville MO 63775 • MO • Tchr • Immanuel Perryville MO • (573)547-6161 • (RF 1962 MED)

**HAERTLING LLOYD W** (314)894-2329
4966 Brockwood Dr Saint Louis MO 63128-2720 • lhaert@webtv.net • MO • EM • (RF 1955 MSED)

**HAERTLING VELDA F** (573)547-5054
4243 PCR 210 Perryville MO 63775 • vhaertling@perryville.k12.mo.us • MO • Tchr • Immanuel Perryville MO • (573)547-8317 • (RF 1968 MA MEAD)

**HAFEMAN NORMAN H** (262)637-2108
5413 Norman St Racine WI 53406-1948 • SW • EM • (CQ 1963 MED)

**HAFEMANN CRAIG A**
5853 S Kurtz Rd Hales Corners WI 53130-1744 • SW • Tchr • South Wisconsin Milwaukee WI • (414)464-8100 • (MQ 1992)

**HAFER MARSHA J** (714)997-9915
374 N Lincoln St Orange CA 92866-1209 • mjhafer@yahoo.com • PSW • Tchr • St John Orange CA • (714)288-4406 • (IV 1983 MS)

**HAGEMAN ELLEN L** (808)623-4260
95-2043 Waikalani Pl #302-A Mililani HI 96789-3445 • CNH • 09/1997 • (RF 1964)

**HAGEMEIER JONETTA E**
404 Marlborough Ave Beatrice NE 68310-4852 • NEB • Tchr • St Paul Beatrice NE • (402)223-3414 • (CQ 1996)

**HAGEN JEAN MERRILL**
6609 N Rustic Oak Ct Peoria IL 61614-2344 • CI • Tchr • St John Champaign IL • (217)359-1123 • (CQ 1986 MS)

**HAGEN M ALLEN** (253)848-5017
2606 38th Ave SE Puyallup WA 98374-1941 • athagen@aol.com • NOW • Tchr • Concordia Tacoma WA • (253)475-9513 • (S 1975 MED)

**HAGENLOCHER AENNE E** (707)578-6137
4747 Woodview Dr Santa Rosa CA 95405-8754 • aenneh@cs.com • CNH • Tchr • St Luke Santa Rosa CA • (707)545-0526 • (CQ 1996)

**HAGENMUELLER ELAINE** (815)568-0648
1006 Jacquelyn Ct Marengo IL 60152-3090 • NI • EM • (RF 1978)

**HAGENMUELLER ERNEST H** (815)568-0648
1006 Jacquelyn Ct Marengo IL 60152-3090 • ehagenmu@mc.net • NI • EM • (RF 1952 MA)

**HAGENOW ERIC MARTIN** (517)642-8884
2323 N Raucholz Rd Hemlock MI 48626-9461 • MI • Tchr • St Peter Hemlock MI • (517)642-5659 • (AA 1996)

**HAGENOW MARGARET ANN** (517)642-8884
2323 N Raucholz Rd Hemlock MI 48626-9461 • MI • Tchr • St Peter Hemlock MI • (517)642-5659 • (CQ 1996)

**HAHN CAROL A**
6241 Thousand Oaks Dr Lakeland FL 33813 • FG • Tchr • St Paul Lakeland FL • (863)644-7710 • (S 1966)

**HAHN CHRISTOPHER J** (972)394-1810
2004 Stradivarius Ln Carrollton TX 75007-2215 • chahn@popcs.net • TX • Tchr • Prince Of Peace Carrollton TX • (972)447-9887 • (SP 1990)

**HAHN DAVID M** (516)626-2872
131 Brookville Rd Glen Head NY 11545-3329 • AT • Prin • Long Island Brookville NY • (516)626-1700 • (RF 1975 MED PHD)

**HAHN HEATHER L**
4706 Main St Apt A Lisle IL 60532 • NI • Tchr • St John Wheaton IL • (630)668-0701 • (RF 1998)

**HAHN JEFFREY S** (630)553-6903
510 W Washington Yorkville IL 60560-1540 • jphahn1@juno.com • NI • Tchr • Cross Yorkville IL • (630)553-7861 • (AA 1989)

**HAHN KATHLEEN M** (715)536-1073
1700 E 12th St Merrill WI 54452-3174 • thomhn@dwave.net • NW • Tchr • St John Merrill WI • (715)536-7264 • (S 1978)

**HAHN LANA J** (815)254-8265
11357 S Churchill Dr Plainfield IL 60544 • NI • Tchr • Bethany Naperville IL • (630)355-6607 • (CQ 1997)

**HAHN MELISSA V** (214)942-4717
2012 W Colorado Blvd Dallas TX 75208-3029 • TX • 04/2000 • (S 1987)

**HAHN RICK E** (815)639-9179
5910 Old Millstone Rd Rockford IL 61114-5527 • NI • P/Tchr • Concordia Machesney Park IL • (815)633-6450 • (RF 1974)

**HAHN THOMAS M** (715)536-1073
1700 E 12th St Merrill WI 54452-3174 • thomhn@dwave.net • NW • Tchr • St John Merrill WI • (715)536-4722 • (S 1980)

**HAIGHT LAURA M** (805)945-2355
23741 Port Royal Ct Tehachapi CA 93561-8585 • PSW • 10/1994 10/1997 • (S 1979 MA)

**HAIST AMY M** (316)442-0353
7952 322nd Rd Arkansas City KS 67005-9139 • mhaist@hit.net • KS • Tchr • Trinity Winfield KS • (316)221-1820 • (WN 1984)

**HALE ANGELA MARY**
C/O Mount Hope-Redemption LS 927 E Old Shakopee Rd Bloomington MN 55420-4599 • MNS • 08/1999 • (IV 1998)

**HALEY MANUEL RICHARD** (312)217-5283
8025 Nola Ave Saint Louis MO 63114-5325 • haleymanuel@hotmail.com • MO • 12/1998 • (RF 1996)

**HALFMANN WALTER K** (517)793-7489
5950 Willowbrook Dr Saginaw MI 48603-5487 • merwillow@aol.com • MI • P/Tchr • Holy Cross Saginaw MI • (517)793-9795 • (S 1968 MED)

**HALKA ELLEN**
C/O Trinity Luthran Ch 40 W Nicholai St Hicksville NY 11801 • AT • Tchr • Trinity Hicksville NY • (516)931-2225 • (BR 1990 MS)

**HALL BELINDA**
755 E Bellville Giddings TX 78942 • TX • Tchr • Immanuel Giddings TX • (409)542-3319 • (S 1994)
**HALL CARL G** (734)457-0934
3678 Gruber Rd Monroe MI 48162-9455 • MI • P/Tchr • Holy Ghost Monroe MI • (734)242-0509 • (S 1972 MED)
**HALL FREDDIE JO ANN** (713)686-4601
2118 Althea Dr Houston TX 77018 • TX • Tchr • Concordia LHS Tomball TX • (281)351-2547 • (S 1998)
**HALL GEORGE R JR.** (301)474-0555
6605 Ian St New Carrollton MD 20784-3629 • kangarookrew@hotmail.com • SE • Tchr • Concordia Hyattsville MD • (301)927-0266 • (RF 1970 MED)
**HALL STEVEN L** (630)268-9522
224 W Ethel Ave Lombard IL 60148-3330 • NI • Tchr • St John Lombard IL • (630)629-2515 • (RF 1985)
**HALLIEN AARON M** (636)239-4971
1182 Jefferson St Apt 5 Washington MO 63090-4439 • MO • Tchr • Immanuel Washington MO • (314)239-1636 • (RF 1999)
**HALTER CLIFFORD A** (313)562-6457
7762 Rosemary St Dearborn Heights MI 48127-1657 • MI • EM • (RF 1952 MMU)
**HALTER KAREN A** (213)343-4573
318 N 2nd Ave Maywood IL 60153-1612 • NI • Tchr • St John Chicago IL • (773)736-1112 • (RF 1978)
**HALTER LOIS ANN** (314)892-4408
C/O Washington Lutheran School 4474 Butler Hill Rd Saint Louis MO 63128-3635 • lhalter@stlnet.com • MO • Tchr • Washington Saint Louis County MO • (314)892-4408 • (RF 1976)
**HALVORSON PETER JOHN** (619)656-0135
1738 Elmhurst St Chula Vista CA 91913-2613 • PSW • Prin • Pilgrim Chula Vista CA • (619)420-6233 • (RF 1969 MED)
**HAMANN JANINE ANNE** (262)377-9291
W65 N367 Westlawn Ave Cedarburg WI 53012 • SW • Tchr • First Immanuel Cedarburg WI • (262)377-6610 • (MQ 1998)
**HAMBAUM PATRICIA SUE** (517)868-4990
9471 W Saginaw Rd Richville MI 48758 • MHambaum@aol.com • MI • Tchr • St John Taylor MI • (734)287-2080 • (RF 1992)
**HAMBRIDGE LES**
1420 S Randolph St Arlington VA 22204-4011 • SE • Tchr • Our Savior Arlington VA • (703)892-4846 • (IV 1982)
**HAMBURG DIANA KAYE*** (580)336-9402
1305 Rose Ter Perry OK 73077-2018 • OK • Tchr • Christ Perry OK • (580)336-2347 • (WN 1971)
**HAMER JENNIFER L** (813)643-4692
1815 Princeton Lks Dr Apt 704 Brandon FL 33511-2024 • FG • Tchr • Immanuel Brandon FL • (813)685-1978 • (AA 1995)
**HAMMES DEBRA L** (708)865-2498
2101 Norfolk Ave Westchester IL 60154 • hammesdeb@juno.com • NI • Tchr • Trinity Burr Ridge IL • (708)839-1444 • (RF 1988)
**HAMMES NEIL R** (708)865-2498
2101 Norfolk Ave Westchester IL 60154 • neilham@juno.com • NI • Tchr • Trinity Burr Ridge IL • (708)839-1444 • (RF 1980 MA)
**HAMMON CHERRY A** (210)696-5157
4330 Millstead St San Antonio TX 78230-1627 • TX • EM • (S 1962)
**HAMMON JOHN F** (419)599-2248
915 Clairmont Ave Napoleon OH 43545-1238 • hamneggs@mail.bright.net • OH • Tchr • St Paul Napoleon OH • (419)592-5536 • (RF 1972)
**HAMMONS CYNTHIA J** (901)213-4958
7068 Rose Trail Dr Memphis TN 38133 • MDS • Tchr • Immanuel Memphis TN • (901)373-4486 • (RF 1984 MA)
**HAMPTON SANDRA E** (281)251-7817
6615 Saffron Hills Dr Spring TX 77379-7516 • TX • Tchr • Trinity Spring TX • (281)376-5810 • (IV 1986)
**HAMRE RACHAEL ELIZABETH** (254)933-2859
135 E 13th Ave Belton TX 76513 • z³rachael³hamre@hotmail.com • TX • Tchr • Zion Georgetown TX • (512)863-3065 • (S 1996)
**HAMRICK MARY E** (618)344-3564
230 South St Collinsville IL 62234 • SI • Tchr • Holy Cross Collinsville IL • (618)344-3145 • (RF 1988)
**HAMRICK ROY A*** (618)344-3564
230 South St Collinsville IL 62234 • MI • 06/1999 • (RF 1984)
**HAND MARSHA JOY**
1381 Arbor St Monroe MI 48162-3019 • MI • Tchr • Trinity Monroe MI • (734)241-1160 • (AA 1988)
**HANDRICH JAMES A**
8 A Scenic View 1 Red Hill Rd Tai Tam HONG KONG • jhandrich@admin.hkis.edu.hk • AT • S Miss • Atlantic Bronxville NY • (914)337-5700 • (RF 1966 MS MA)
**HANDRICK HEIDI Y** (713)690-6009
2834 Kismet Houston TX 77043 • TX • Tchr • St Mark Houston TX • (713)468-2623 • (AU 1999)
**HANDY DENA MARIE** (410)695-0736
8715 Thornbrook Dr Odenton MD 21113-3409 • pndhandy@maranatha.net • SE • Tchr • Pilgrim Baltimore MD • (410)484-6692 • (BR 1995)
**HANDY REBECCA LYNN** (414)789-9047
3035 S Fountain Sq Blvd #102 New Berlin WI 53151-8906 • SW • Tchr • Martin LHS Greendale WI • (414)421-4000 • (RF 1990 MED)
**HANEBUTT RICHARD C** (765)864-0736
1705 John D Dr Kokomo IN 40902 • IN • Prin • Redeemer Kokomo IN • (765)864-6466 • (RF 1974 MS EDS)
**HANKE ELSIE C** (616)465-6520
9807 Jericho Rd Bridgman MI 49106-9740 • MI • EM • (WN 1957 MA)
**HANKEL DONALD W** (317)861-8016
6169 W Deer Run Dr New Palestine IN 46163-9592 • IN • EM • (RF 1954 MED)
**HANN ARTHUR L** (847)608-1201
69 Melbrooke Rd Elgin IL 60123-1630 • NI • EM • (RF 1944 MA)
**HANNA THOMAS WAYNE** (561)689-3425
1504 Maplewood Dr West Palm Beach FL 33415-1476 • FG • Mem C • Our Savior Lake Worth FL • (561)582-4430 • (SP 1999)
**HANS SARA RUTH**
2961 N 73rd St Milwaukee WI 53210-1066 • SW • Tchr • Our Redeemer Wauwatosa WI • (414)258-4558 • (S 1997)
**HANSEN DARREN D** (661)538-9917
37865 Cabana Pl Palmdale CA 93550-2448 • PSW • Tchr • First LHS Sylmar CA • (818)362-9223 • (S 1987)
**HANSEN DEAN R** (704)256-3856
1732 Poe Cir Hickory NC 28601-9318 • deanhansen@twave.net • SE • Tchr • St Stephen Hickory NC • (828)256-9865 • (S 1973 MS)
**HANSEN KAREN RAE** (414)864-2823
6708 Deuster Rd Apt 7 Greenleaf WI 54126-9111 • NW • Tchr • Zion Of Wayside Greenleaf WI • (414)864-2468 • (MQ 1995)
**HANSEN KELLY ANNE** (949)458-9357
26471 Elmcrest Way Lake Forest CA 92630-6563 • PSW • 02/1999 • (IV 1991)
**HANSEN LORI VERREE** (805)538-9917
37865 Cabana Pl Palmdale CA 93550-2448 • PSW • Tchr • First LHS Sylmar CA • (818)362-9223 • (S 1988)
**HANSEN TIM MARK** (613)343-0367
404 C Hesperia Collinsville IL 62234 • hansens@netexpress.net • SI • Tchr • Holy Cross Collinsville IL • (618)344-3145 • (IV 1983)
**HANSSEN MELBA J** (630)250-0401
392 Bay Dr Itasca IL 60143 • mhanssen@aol.com • NI • 07/1999 • (RF 1963 MA EDS EDD)
**HANTULA BRENDA M***
17 El Balazo Rancho Santa Margari CA 92688-4115 • PSW • Tchr • Abiding Savior Lake Forest CA • (949)830-1461 • (PO 1984)
**HANUSA LOIS MARIE** (712)325-4378
518 Elliott St Council Bluffs IA 51503-0202 • IW • Tchr • Trinity Interparish Council Bluffs IA • (712)322-3294 • (S 1975 MED)
**HAPKE GERALD D** (219)447-9437
9019 Hartzell Rd Fort Wayne IN 46816 • jhapke@holycrossfw.org • IN • 11/1997 11/1999 • (RF 1964 MS)
**HARBIG RACHEL ANN** (612)763-9423
1407 N McKay Ave NE Alexandria MN 56308-7539 • MNN • Tchr • Zion Alexandria MN • (320)763-4842 • (SP 1986)
**HARBKE JAMES M** (847)253-4839
4107 Owl Dr Rolling Mdws IL 60008-2512 • jblk4@aol.com • EN • Mem C • Faith Arlington Hts IL • (847)253-4839 • (RF 1970)
**HARDER SCOTT D** (847)669-1467
190 Bridlewood Cir Lk In The Hls IL 60102-5857 • aharder@d211.org • MO • Tchr • Missouri Saint Louis MO • (314)317-4550 • (RF 1990)
**HARDIES MICHAEL ALLEN** (561)395-1358
149 NW 8th Boca Raton FL 33432-2627 • mhardk@aol.com • FG • Mem C • St Paul Boca Raton FL • (561)395-0433 • (RF 1994)
**HARDIN BETH ANN** (910)725-1651
4136 Greenmead Rd Winston Salem NC 27106-2916 • SE • Tchr • St John Winston-Salem NC • (336)725-1651 • (RF 1982)
**HARDT JAMES WALTER** (414)334-9649
602 S Indiana Ave West Bend WI 53095-4028 • SW • Tchr • St John West Bend WI • (414)334-3077 • (S 1974)
**HARDT KELLY** (618)346-5641
16 A Holloway Ct Collinsville IL 62234 • deackelly@aol.com • SI • Mem C • Holy Cross Collinsville IL • (618)344-3145 • (RF 2000)
**HARDY TIMOTHY DANIEL**
44488 Bayview Ave Apt 15312 Clinton Twp MI 48038-7033 • MI • Tchr • LHS North Macomb MI • (810)781-9151 • (RF 1995)
**HARGER STEVEN K** (715)627-2987
502 Deleglise St Antigo WI 54409-1448 • sharger@antigopro.net • NW • Tchr • Peace Antigo WI • (715)623-2209 • (RF 1988)
**HARKINS RICHARD R** (217)487-7128
4124 Camp CILCA Rd Cantrall IL 62625-8764 • camp@cilca.org • CI • O Sp Min • Central Illinois Springfield IL • (RF 1986)
**HARKS THEO E** (620)892-2999
N4939 Hillwind Rd Plymouth WI 53073-4033 • harkste@dotnet.com • SW • 09/1998 • (SP 1967)
**HARM MARY** (618)533-7790
524 E Broadway Centralia IL 62801 • SI • Tchr • Trinity Centralia IL • (618)532-2614 • (RF 1973)
**HARMAN ANTHONY C** (206)535-9467
4701 144th St E Tacoma WA 98446-4137 • NOW • Tchr • Concordia Tacoma WA • (253)475-9513 • (S 1982 MED)
**HARMAN GREGORY E** (602)787-8399
4546 E Sunnyside Ln Phoenix AZ 85032 • gharman@cclphoenix.org • EN • P/Tchr • Christ Phoenix AZ • (602)957-7010 • (S 1983 MED)
**HARMAN RONALD V** (602)267-7740
2414 N 39th Pl Phoenix AZ 85008-2240 • ronaldharman@earthlink.net • EN • EM • (RF 1955 MED)
**HARMAN TAMARA LYNN** (520)317-0560
2242 E San Marcos Dr Yuma AZ 85365-3219 • PSW • Tchr • Yuma Yuma AZ • (520)726-8410 • (S 1985)
**HARMENING DUANE JOHN** (651)489-1283
1189 Ruggles Ave Roseville MN 55113-6120 • MNS • EM • (S 1955 MED)
**HARMON JENNIFER MARIE** (210)979-7137
1401 Patricia #1205 San Antonio TX 78213 • jenniferh@concordia-satx.com • TX • Tchr • Concordia San Antonio TX • (210)479-1477 • (AU 1998)
**HARMS HELMUTH H** (618)532-5935
2 Redwood Dr Centralia IL 62801-4408 • SI • EM • (S 1955 MS)
**HARMS HILLARD H** (414)332-9543
410 W Hampton Ave #201 Milwaukee WI 53217 • SW • 02/2000 • (SP 1969)
**HARMS MARTHA JANE** (937)642-9924
12741 State Route 736 Marysville OH 43040-9056 • OH • Tchr • St John Marysville OH • (937)644-5540 • (RF 1982 MS)
**HARP JENNIFER**
8682 21 Mile Rd Utica MI 48317-3408 • IN • Tchr • St Paul Munster IN • (219)836-6270 • (RF 1994)
**HARPER LISA F** (314)965-7702
912 Chelsea Ave Saint Louis MO 63122-3213 • MO • Tchr • Hope Saint Louis MO • (314)832-1850 • (RF 1991)
**HARPER PATTI JO**
6423 Read St Omaha NE 68152-2236 • MO • Tchr • Green Park Lemay MO • (314)544-4248 • (S 1985)
**HARRIES CYNTHIA L** (816)833-4872
2131 S Norwood Ave Independence MO 64052-3640 • MO • Tchr • Messiah Independence MO • (816)254-9409 • (S 1975)
**HARRIES DANIEL L** (308)381-8142
118 Centennial Dr Grand Island NE 68801-2307 • NEB • 05/1998 05/2000 • (S 1969 MS)
**HARRIMAN RHONDA J**
31 Wetmore St Keene NH 03431-3911 • CNH • Tchr • Good Shepherd Honolulu HI • (808)523-2927 • (BR 1994)
**HARRIS CHRISTINE** (301)468-7371
12317 Village Square Ter #302 Rockville MD 20852-1943 • SE • Tchr • Calvary Silver Spring MD • (301)589-4001 • (BR 1996)
**HARRIS LINDA CAROL** (217)546-2924
3501 Bluff Rd Springfield IL 62707-7954 • CI • Tchr • LHS Springfield IL • (217)546-6363 • (CQ 1986)
**HARRIS MARGARET L** (281)320-8962
22402 Mosswillow Ln Tomball TX 77375-2834 • bharris@pdq.net • TX • Tchr • Concordia LHS Tomball TX • (281)351-2547 • (SP 1975 MED)
**HARRIS RACHEL M** (810)226-1911
42430 Clinton Pl Dr Clinton Twp MI 48038 • goodgoofy2@cs.com • MI • Tchr • LHS North Macomb MI • (810)781-9151 • (AA 1999)
**HARRIS VALERIE J**
14140 Merriweather St #213 Sterling Heights MI 48312-2482 • MI • Tchr • Trinity Utica MI • (810)731-4490 • (RF 1982 MAT)
**HARRISON JOHN B** (219)736-8281
6932 Hawk Dr Schererville IN 46375-4456 • NI • 08/2000 • (RF 1988)
**HART AMY BETH** (425)821-2793
12429 NE 141st Pl Kirkland WA 98034 • NOW • 04/1998 04/2000 • (S 1992)
**HART CHARLES M** (303)659-4954
287 S 13th Ave Brighton CO 80601-2228 • RM • Tchr • Zion Brighton CO • (303)659-3443 • (S 1984)
**HART GAIL A** (708)873-9159
14122 Timothy Dr Orland Park IL 60462-2242 • NI • 12/1999 • (CQ 1993 MA)
**HART JENNIFER K** (612)894-3724
3301 W 132nd St Burnsville MN 55337-1878 • hartfamily@uswest.net • MNS • Tchr • St Paul Prior Lake MN • (612)447-2117 • (S 1977)
**HART LEROY J** (763)383-0940
14913 45th Ave N Plymouth MN 55446-3415 • theharts@pclink.com • SW • EM • (CQ 1953 MSED)
**HART REGINA A** (626)281-7517
1832 S 9th St Alhambra CA 91803-3427 • PSW • Tchr • Emmaus Alhambra CA • (626)289-3664 • (SP 1964 MA)
**HARTFIELD KATHRYN JEAN**
1915 S State St Saint Joseph MI 49085 • hartfld@erols.com • MI • Tchr • Trinity Saint Joseph MI • (616)983-3056 • (RF 1995)
**HARTHUN KIM R** (941)619-7954
6328 Sweetwater Dr E Lakeland FL 33811-1920 • FG • Tchr • St Paul Lakeland FL • (941)644-7710 • (S 1973 MS)
**HARTING WALTER F** (313)426-8511
3595 Forshee Ln Dexter MI 48130-8533 • MI • EM • (RF 1943 MED)
**HARTKE NATHAN CARL** (810)447-1225
7051 Wise Ave Saint Louis MO 48089 • MI • Tchr • LHS East Harper Woods MI • (313)371-8750 • (AA 1999)
**HARTKOPF WALTER H** (415)589-3205
1147 Fairmont Dr San Bruno CA 94066-2719 • CNH • EM • (RF 1937 MA LLD)
**HARTMAN DAVID A** (715)848-4160
2206 Falcon Ave Wausau WI 54401-6210 • NW • P/Tchr • Trinity Wausau WI • (715)848-0166 • (S 1969 MA)
**HARTMAN ELISA J** (715)675-6617
1516 Pearson St Wausau WI 54401 • NW • Tchr • Trinity Wausau WI • (715)848-0166 • (MQ 1995)
**HARTMAN KENNETH W** (573)635-5104
1729 Greenridge Ct Jefferson City MO 65101 • MO • Prin • Trinity Jefferson City MO • (573)636-7807 • (RF 1973 MED)
**HARTMAN LORNA JEAN** (419)782-7465
1113 Emory St Defiance OH 43512-2906 • OH • Tchr • St John Defiance OH • (419)782-1751 • (RF 1971 MSED)

**HARTMAN PATRICIA A** (716)627-9836
95 Waterview Pkwy Hamburg NY 14075-1835 • www.pathartman@msn.com • EA • Tchr • Trinity West Seneca NY • (716)674-5353 • (S 1968 MSED)

**HARTMAN SHERYL J** (765)459-5147
4332 N 700 W Kokomo IN 46901-9671 • rowrunner@aol.com • IN • 06/1996 06/2000 • (RF 1984 MS)

**HARTMANN DALE W** (714)639-5863
2400 E Palm Ave Orange CA 92867-7825 • PSW • SHS/C • Pacific Southwest Irvine CA • (949)854-3232 • (S 1954 MA)

**HARTMANN DEIDRE JUNE** (501)227-2056
501 Napa Valley Dr #303 Little Rock AR 72211 • MDS • Tchr • Christ Little Rock AR • (501)663-5212 • (S 1995)

**HARTMANN DELLA** (402)643-3084
111 Plum Creek Ln Seward NE 68434-2215 • NEB • EM • (S 1951)

**HARTMANN DENNIS RANDALL** (501)227-2056
501 Napa Valley Dr #303 Little Rock AR 72211 • MDS • Tchr • Christ Little Rock AR • (501)663-5232 • (S 1995)

**HARTMANN ESTHER** (314)334-4250
1339 Karen Dr Cape Girardeau MO 63701-3710 • MO • Tchr • Trinity Cape Girardeau MO • (573)334-1068 • (S 1960)

**HARTMANN MELISSA ANN**
435 S Clay Ave Apt 6 Kirkwood MO 63122-5836 • MO • Tchr • Immanuel Olivette MO • (314)993-5004 • (S 1998)

**HARTMANN RICHARD P** (402)643-4533
2519 Fletcher Rd Seward NE 68434-8101 • NEB • EM • (S 1960 MA)

**HARTMANN ROBERT T** (314)334-4250
1339 Karen Dr Cape Girardeau MO 63701-3710 • MO • EM • (S 1954 MSED)

**HARTMANN ROYCE RAY** (313)532-8252
17220 Gaylord Redford MI 48240-2312 • rhart6692@aol.com • MI • Tchr • St Matthew Walled Lake MI • (248)624-7677 • (AA 1991 MA)

**HARTWIG SANDRA LYNN** (630)543-2651
348 W Myrick Ave Addison IL 60101-3521 • NI • Tchr • St Paul Addison IL • (630)543-6909 • (RF 1972)

**HARVEY KIMBERLY S** (215)946-3352
32 Inkberry Rd Levittown PA 19057-2218 • kharv@philly.infi.net • EA • Tchr • Hope Levittown PA • (215)946-3467 • (BR 1989 MEDSC)

**HASEMAN IRMA L** (708)255-6294
824 N Kaspar Ave Arlington Hts IL 60004-5326 • NI • EM • (RF 1966)

**HASHIMOTO CYNTHIA LYNN** (909)279-6682
12700 Carnation St Corona CA 92880 • chriscindi@earthlink.net • PSW • Tchr • Loving Savior Chino Hills CA • (909)597-2358 • (SP 1992)

**HASKO JOYCE** (262)554-1431
2815 Oregon St Racine WI 53405-4327 • wrh2815@rli-net.net • S • EM • (SP 1977)

**HASS CHRISTOPHER A** (440)892-8735
24209 Russell Rd Bay Village OH 44140-2848 • chass@mediaone.net • OH • 12/1998 • (SP 1977 MA)

**HASS DONNA M** (913)246-0336
4650 NW Brickyard Rd Topeka KS 66618-3301 • KS • Tchr • Topeka Topeka KS • (785)357-0382 • (S 1960)

**HASS KENNETH E** (810)392-3640
758 Memphis Ridge Rd Memphis MI 48041-3822 • eehass@oakland.edu • MI • Tchr • St Peter Richmond MI • (810)727-9080 • (S 1972 MA)

**HASS VERNON F** (913)246-0336
4650 NW Brickyard Rd Topeka KS 66618-3301 • KS • EM • (S 1953)

**HASSELBRING SUE A**
C/O Bible Society PO Box 251 Gaborone BOTSWANA • SI • Southern Illinois Belleville IL • (RF 1986 MS)

**HASSELDAHL CYNTHIA L** (402)365-7282
PO Box 266 Deshler NE 68340-0266 • moderow@yahoo.com • NEB • Tchr • Deshler Deshler NE • (402)365-7858 • (S 1980)

**HASSELDAHL GREGORY C** (402)365-7282
PO Box 266 Deshler NE 68340-0266 • NEB • P/Tchr • Deshler Deshler NE • (402)365-7858 • (S 1981 MS)

**HASSTEDT FREDERICK O** (618)277-3236
348 Roanoke Dr Belleville IL 62221-5724 • SI • Tchr • Zion Belleville IL • (618)233-2299 • (S 1977)

**HASZ BARBARA J** (901)423-5383
380 Henderson Rd Jackson TN 38305-9558 • lushorse@aol.com • MDS • Tchr • Concordia Jackson TN • (901)668-0757 • (RF 1962)

**HASZ DENESE** (618)495-2239
PO Box 154 Hoffman IL 62250 • SI • Tchr • Trinity Hoffman IL • (618)495-2246 • (S 1988)

**HAUCH JAMES E** (815)332-4679
8724 Centaur Dr Belvidere IL 61008-8722 • NI • Tchr • Immanuel Belvidere IL • (815)547-5346 • (RF 1962 MED)

**HAUCH ROBERT** (707)253-7441
2914 Soscol Ave Apt 14 Napa CA 94558-6423 • CNH • Tchr • St John Napa CA • (707)226-7970 • (RF 1972)

**HAUER RAYMOND P** (256)881-0553
11247 Springwood Dr Huntsville AL 35803 • rhauer@ro.com • SO • Prin • Grace Huntsville AL • (256)881-0553 • (S 1965 MA)

**HAUER WALTER O** (847)358-6656
909 E Kenilworth Ave Apt 416 Palatine IL 60067-1534 • EN • EM • (RF 1959)

**HAUG-OWSLEY DONATA R**
1904 Bono Rd New Albany IN 47150-4608 • IN • Tchr • St John Lanesville IN • (812)952-3711 • (RF 1961)

**HAUN MONTE R**
16481 Cove Landing Ct Wildwood MO 63040-1562 • MO • Tchr • St John Ellisville MO • (314)394-4100 • (RF 1983 MA)

**HAUPT LINDA** (732)257-6557
295 Summerhill Rd East Brunswick NJ 08816-4201 • NJ • 09/1985 09/1999 • (RF 1968)

**HAUPT SARAH E** (770)486-1369
450 S Peachtree Pkwy #R302 Peachtree City IL 30269 • Seliz76@aol.com • FG • Tchr • St Paul Peachtree City GA • (770)486-3545 • (RF 1999)

**HAUSCH LINDA I** (208)938-0752
398 N Sierra View Way Eagle ID 83616-4600 • lhausch@juno.com • NOW • 08/1992 08/2000 • (S 1969)

**HAUSER ANDREA MICHELLE** (281)599-8480
2007 Highland Bay Ct Katy TX 77450-6674 • dahausers@msn.com • CI • Tchr • Good Shepherd Pekin IL • (309)347-2020 • (RF 1996)

**HAUSER DELORES A** (412)341-4532
813 Alden Dr Pittsburgh PA 15220-1008 • hauserri@aol.com • EA • EM • (S 1957)

**HAUSER RONALD L** (517)893-2702
1172 N Pine St Essexville MI 48732-1930 • MI • EM • (RF 1954 MED MCMU)

**HAUSLER EUNICE A** (618)478-5762
15611 State Rt 127 Hoyleton IL 62803 • rayhausl@accessus.net • SI • EM • (RF 1956)

**HAUTER DONNA R** (806)359-6984
5516 Randolph Rd Amarillo TX 79106-5019 • TX • Tchr • Trinity Amarillo TX • (806)352-5620 • (SP 1975)

**HAVEKOST JEFFREY** (303)368-9281
3297 S Emporia Ct Denver CO 80231-4738 • jhavekost@bethluth.net • RM • Tchr • Bethlehem Lakewood CO • (303)233-0401 • (S 1972)

**HAVERA BEVERLY A** (616)663-2309
26357 Acorn St Edwardsburg MI 49112-9108 • IN • EM • (SP 1965)

**HAVERS BRENDA E** (810)254-8572
44009 Donley Dr Sterling Heights MI 48314-2637 • MI • Tchr • Trinity Utica MI • (810)731-4490 • (AA 1985 MA)

**HAVRILCSAK LAURA ANN** (810)772-6335
15094 Eldorado Ter Warren MI 48093 • MI • Tchr • St John Fraser MI • (810)293-0333 • (AA 1982)

**HAWLEY CYNTHIA ANN**
2823 Alvarado Sq #1 Baltimore MD 21234-7601 • SE • Tchr • Immanuel Baltimore MD • (410)435-6961 • (S 1986)

**HAWLEY ROBERT E** (714)633-4601
C/O St John Lutheran School 154 S Shaffer St Orange CA 92866-1609 • PSW • Tchr • St John Orange CA • (714)288-4400 • (IV 1984)

**HAWTHORNE NANCY JEAN** (805)527-0764
1532 Arabian St Simi Valley CA 93065-3365 • PSW • Tchr • Trinity Simi Valley CA • (805)526-2429 • (S 1977 MA)

**HAY DONNA D** (810)227-5849
10616 Villa Dr Brighton MI 48114 • EN • Tchr • Child Of Christ Hartland MI • (248)887-3836 • (S 1965)

**HAYES H ROBERT** (708)344-2259
409 N 3rd Ave Maywood IL 60153-1113 • hayeshr@curf.edu • NI • SHS/C • Northern Illinois Hillside IL • (CQ 1974 MA MA PHD)

**HAYES HENRY L** (206)845-1177
8818 121st St E Puyallup WA 98373-7914 • NOW • Prin • Concordia Tacoma WA • (253)475-9513 • (S 1970)

**HAYNES COLEEN RENEE** (503)304-9391
3295 Jack St N Keizer OR 97303-6029 • NOW • Tchr • Concordia Salem OR • (503)393-7188 • (S 1992)

**HAYNES TRAVIS M** (714)671-4181
3214 Stonewood Ct Fullerton CA 92835-2330 • tshaynes@earthlink.net • PSW • Tchr • Zion Anaheim CA • (714)535-3600 • (IV 1995 MED)

**HAYWARD JANET K** (219)493-6678
1220 Canal St New Haven IN 46774 • jkhayward@aol.com • IN • Tchr • Central New Haven IN • (219)493-2502 • (CQ 1996)

**HAZELBERG FAYE MARIE** (920)387-0315
W2236 Elm Dr Mayville WI 53050-2040 • SW • Tchr • St John Mayville WI • (920)387-4310 • (MQ 1994)

**HEADAPOHL VIRGINIA A** (313)522-4576
31478 Rosslyn Ave Garden City MI 48135-1344 • MI • Tchr • LHS Westland Westland MI • (734)422-2090 • (CQ 1995)

**HEARD VICKI LYNN** (573)547-9318
510 Edgemont Blvd Perryville MO 63775-2420 • wmheard@midwest.com • MO • Tchr • Immanuel Perryville MO • (573)547-8317 • (S 1996)

**HEATH MARY BETH** (713)370-2313
11727 Primwood Dr Houston TX 77070-2537 • TX • Tchr • LHS North Houston TX • (713)880-3131 • (S 1974)

**HEBEL HARRY GERHARD** (949)348-2385
26926 Recodo Ln Mission Viejo CA 92691-6005 • harry³hebel@hotmail.com • PSW • Prin • Abiding Savior Lake Forest CA • (949)830-1461 • (S 1966 MS)

**HEBEL KAREN E** (415)530-0877
4106 Patterson Ave Oakland CA 94619-1557 • karehebel@aol.com • CNH • Tchr • Trinity Walnut Creek CA • (925)935-3360 • (S 1971)

**HECK EDWIN G** (805)499-4258
891 La Grange Ave Newbury Park CA 91320-5310 • PSW • Tchr • St John Oxnard CA • (805)983-0330 • (S 1973)

**HECK ZONNA L** (616)796-0405
318 Sanborn Ave Big Rapids MI 49307-1740 • MI • Tchr • St Peter Big Rapids MI • (231)796-8782 • (RF 1981 MA)

**HECKLER SANDRA L** (414)251-9626
N91W17626 Saint Regis Dr Menomonee Falls WI 53051-1977 • SW • Tchr • Grace Menomonee Falls WI • (414)251-7140 • (CQ 1996 MSED)

**HECKMAN ROBERT G** (626)286-3049
5212 N Burton Ave San Gabriel CA 91776-2014 • PSW • EM • (S 1959)

**HECKSEL SHANNON** (952)832-9481
3901 Heritage Hills Dr Bloomington MN 55437 • MNS • Tchr • Luth HS Of Greater M Bloomington MN • (612)854-0224 • (SP 2000)

**HECKSEL SHAWN RYAN** (612)682-6644
1500 Anderson Ave #203 Buffalo MN 55313 • thehex@excite.com • MNS • Mem C • St John Buffalo MN • (763)682-1883 • (SP 1997)

**HEDEMANN PHILIP E**
2819 N 67th St Milwaukee WI 53210 • phedemann@juno.com • SW • Tchr • St John Glendale WI • (414)352-4150 • (S 1968)

**HEDRICK FRANKLIN J** (309)793-1489
2513 35th Ave Rock Island IL 61201 • fjhedrick@excite.com • CI • Tchr • Immanuel Rock Island IL • (309)788-8242 • (RF 1988 MA)

**HEERBOTH CHRISTINE R** (314)968-0691
922 Coffey Dr Saint Louis MO 63126-1314 • MO • Tchr • Christ Community Kirkwood MO • (314)822-7774 • (RF 1972)

**HEEREN LYNELLE M** (413)536-2599
2 Harrison Ave Holyoke MA 01040-3531 • NE • Tchr • First Holyoke MA • (413)532-4272 • (SP 1981)

**HEEREN SUSAN A** (712)448-2275
5422 420th St Paullina IA 51046 • IW • Tchr • Zion Paullina IA • (712)448-3910 • (RF 1992)

**HEFFELFINGER MARK L** (414)475-0238
159 N 73rd St Milwaukee WI 53213-3670 • SW • Prin • Lutheran HS Sheboygan WI • (920)452-3323 • (RF 1968 MA)

**HEIBEL DANIEL R** (402)488-2812
7340 Englewood Dr Lincoln NE 68510-4223 • NEB • EM • (S 1958 MED)

**HEIBEL MATTHEW S** (217)428-1046
5221 Melwood Ct Decatur IL 62521 • mheibel³2000@yahoo.com • CI • Prin • Lutheran School Asso Decatur IL • (217)233-2001 • (S 1984 MED)

**HEIDE WILLIAM J** (714)283-1951
2538 E Lakeside Ave Orange CA 92867-8405 • bill@stjohnsorange.org • PSW • Mem C • St John Orange CA • (714)288-4400 • (RF 1973 MMU)

**HEIDEMAN HARLAN G** (812)375-1407
2000 Jolinda Dr Columbus IN 47203-3555 • IN • EM • (RF 1956 MA)

**HEIDEMAN JULIE K** (317)841-9514
9420 Goodway Ct Indianapolis IN 46256-1822 • IN • Tchr • Holy Cross Indianapolis IN • (317)826-1234 • (RF 1989)

**HEIDEN TERESA L** (208)235-9778
1507 Northridge Dr - #20 Pocatello ID 83201 • NOW • Tchr • Grace Pocatello ID • (208)237-0467 • (MQ 2000)

**HEIDER JOANNE W** (308)382-5840
315 W 18th St Grand Island NE 68801-2309 • NEB • EM • (S 1983 MA)

**HEIDER LOUIS H** (402)451-1091
4850 Grand Ave Omaha NE 68104-2341 • NEB • EM • (S 1935 MSW)

**HEIDER WENDY E** (308)382-1034
4148 Springview Dr Grand Island NE 68803-6505 • NEB • Tchr • Trinity Grand Island NE • (308)382-5274 • (S 1974)

**HEIDLAUF JOANNE V** (773)725-0753
5014 W Gunnison St Apt 2 Chicago IL 60630-2311 • NI • Tchr • St Paul Skokie IL • (847)673-5030 • (RF 1965)

**HEIDLE SUE ANN** (513)576-0286
1280 Eagle Ridge Dr Milford OH 45150-9613 • OH • Tchr • St Paul Cincinnati OH • (513)271-4147 • (AA 1986 MA)

**HEIDLOFF DAVID N** (309)663-9159
917 S Mercer Ave Bloomington IL 61701-7132 • CI • EM • (RF 1953 MS)

**HEIDLOFF LINDA S** (309)827-0713
802 S Morris Ave Bloomington IL 61701-4843 • CI • Tchr • Trinity Bloomington IL • (309)829-7513 • (RF 1977)

**HEIDORN CAROLINE** (402)534-4191
PO Box 157 Utica NE 68456-0157 • NEB • EM • (S 1973)

**HEIDORN DOROTHY H** (815)683-2448
409 Main St PO Box 284 Crescent City IL 60928-0284 • IN • EM • (RF 1976 MED)

**HEIDORN PAUL E** (402)534-4191
PO Box 157 Utica NE 68456-0157 • NEB • EM • (RF 1954)

**HEIEN DAVID** (309)682-0827
3545 W Saymore Ln Peoria IL 61615-3941 • CI • Tchr • Concordia Peoria IL • (309)691-8921 • (S 1970 MA)

**HEIL JOHN OMER** (815)935-2546
3093 Lowe Rd Kankakee IL 60901-6027 • NI • Tchr • St Paul Kankakee IL • (815)932-3241 • (RF 1978 MS)

**HEILMAN DEBORAH E** (352)589-2563
2702 Lakewood Ln Eustis FL 32726-7003 • FG • Tchr • Faith Eustis FL • (352)589-5683 • (S 1979)

**HEILMAN RICHARD A** (410)666-2806
10312 Greenside Dr Hunt Valley MD 21030 • SE • EM • (S 1952)

**HEILMAN RUTH ANN** (410)938-2282
1304 Mc Pherson Ct Lutherville MD 21093-5508 • heilmanjr@prodigy.net • SE • Prin • Calvary Baltimore MD • (410)426-4302 • (RF 1985 MED)

**HEILMANN DONALD J**
8911 Harper Point Dr Apt D Cincinnati OH 45249-2632 • OH • Tchr • Our Redeemer Maineville OH • (513)697-7335 • (S 1960)

**HEIMLICH CARRIE M**
8301 W Charleston Blvd #209 Las Vegas NV 89117 • PSW • Tchr • Faith LHS Las Vegas NV • (702)804-4400 • (RF 1997)

**HEIMLICH LYNN E**
St Paul Luth Church 2001 Old Frederick Rd Catonsville MD 21228 • SE • Tchr • St Paul Catonsville MD • (410)747-1924 • (AA 1990)

**HEIMSOTH BARBARA R** (414)545-6618
2208 S 83rd St West Allis WI 53219-1741 • SW • Tchr • St Paul West Allis WI • (414)541-6251 • (S 1980)

**HEIMSOTH CARLA EVELYN** (847)259-2750
711 W Gettysburg Dr Arlington Hts IL 60004-3001 • NI • EM • (CQ 1987)

**HEIMSOTH ELROY L** (573)243-0092
1227 Ashbury Ct Jackson MO 63755-1005 • eheimsoth@prodigy.net • MO • EM • (RF 1953)

**HEIMSOTH GERALD V** (414)545-6618
2208 S 83rd St West Allis WI 53219-1741 • SW • 02/2000 • (RF 1971)

**HEIMSOTH HEATHER** (501)835-1017
Hope Lutheran Church 1904 Mc Arthur Dr Jacksonville AR 72076-3728 • hdhtech@flash.net • MDS • Tchr • Hope Jacksonville AR • (501)982-1333 • (S 1998)

**HEIMSOTH ORLYN A** (660)463-7714
PO Box 14A Concordia MO 64020-0014 • MO • Prin • St Paul Concordia MO • (660)463-7654 • (RF 1969 MSED)

**HEIN GAIL ELAINE** (970)493-1889
1509 Haymarket St Fort Collins CO 80526 • heinsite@bwn.net • RM • Tchr • Immanuel Loveland CO • (970)667-4506 • (PO 1982)

**HEIN MARTIN A** (402)464-9121
7000 Gladstone St Lincoln NE 68507-2156 • martyhein@hotmail.com • NEB • Tchr • Messiah Lincoln NE • (402)489-3024 • (S 1984 MSED)

**HEIN SHELLEY R** (715)723-6896
13276 35th Ave Chippewa Falls WI 54729-7356 • heinss@hotmail.com • NW • 12/1996 12/1999 • (SP 1991)

**HEIN SUSAN DIANE** (219)471-2548
1109 Lynn Ave Fort Wayne IN 46805-3549 • EN • 07/1997 07/2000 • (RF 1987 MS)

**HEINE GILBERT R** (307)674-5393
1440 Champion Dr Sheridan WY 82801 • gheine@wyoming.com • NEB • EM • (S 1950)

**HEINE MELINDA K** (307)674-9196
910 Idaho Sheridan WY 82801 • WY • 09/1994 09/1999 • (S 1979)

**HEINECKE NORMA FRIEDA** (714)772-7835
2324 E Ward Ter Anaheim CA 92806-3657 • PSW • Tchr • Zion Anaheim CA • (714)535-3600 • (RF 1955)

**HEINEMANN BRIAN W** (734)747-8089
412 Pine Brae St Ann Arbor MI 48105-2723 • heineb@ccaa.edu • MI • SHS/C • Michigan Ann Arbor MI • (S 1972 MED)

**HEINEMANN CHARLES EDWARD** (352)357-7006
119 Burrel Rd Eustis FL 32726-2511 • heinemannc@aol.com • FG • Prin • Faith Eustis FL • (352)589-5683 • (RF 1970 MED)

**HEINEMANN DOREEN L**
C/O Trinity Lutheran School 3112 W Broadway Council Bluffs IA 51501-3310 • dheinemann@ne.freei.net • IW • 12/1999 • (S 1970 MED)

**HEINERT KARLA SUE** (313)380-0361
44620 N Hills Dr # B-26 Northville MI 48167-2156 • MI • Tchr • St Stephen Waterford MI • (248)673-5906 • (AA 1990)

**HEINICKE MIRIAM RACHEL** (714)637-3899
705 E Heim Ave Orange CA 92865-2813 • mirken123@mail.msn.com • PSW • Tchr • Lutheran HS/Orange C Orange CA • (714)998-5151 • (IV 1990 MA)

**HEINICKE THEODORE G** (651)552-9328
5905 Bradbury Ct Inver Grove Heights MN 55076 • tedheinicke@hotmail.com • MNS • EM • (S 1947)

**HEINICKE WILLIAM F** (970)882-3293
17580 Rd 26 Dolores CO 81323 • heinicke@frontier.net • RM • O Sp Min • Rocky Mountain Aurora CO • (S 1953 MA DED)

**HEINITZ JAN M DR** (262)238-0754
417 Madero Dr Thiensville WI 53092-1444 • jan.heinitz@cuw.edu • SW • SHS/C • South Wisconsin Milwaukee WI • (414)464-8100 • (S 1976 PHD)

**HEINITZ JOHN R** (510)569-9594
3926 Delmont Ave Oakland CA 94605-2233 • CNH • Tchr • Zion Piedmont CA • (510)530-7909 • (S 1980 MS)

**HEINITZ LINDSEY** (707)745-2849
103 White Chapel Dr Benicia CA 94510 • CNH • Tchr • Zion Piedmont CA • (510)530-4213 • (IV 2000)

**HEINS ERIC J** (313)593-4887
6814 Heyden St Detroit MI 48228-4934 • MI • Tchr • Guardian Dearborn MI • (313)274-3665 • (S 1977)

**HEINSEN BARBARA SUE** (319)390-0662
2720 Johnson Ave NW Apt 307 Cedar Rapids IA 52405 • IE • Tchr • Trinity Cedar Rapids IA • (319)362-6952 • (CQ 1997)

**HEINTZ MARILYN J** (708)349-1547
14143 W 84th Ave Orland Park IL 60462-2371 • NI • EM • (RF 1971 MED)

**HEINTZE PAUL N** (219)356-7288
750 Dimond St Apt 11 Huntington IN 46750-1916 • IN • EM • (RF 1961)

**HEINZ EDWARD C** (201)666-2760
405 Fairview Ave Westwood NJ 07675-1615 • heinzbjed@aol.com • NJ • 08/1994 08/1999 • (RF 1963 MED)

**HEINZ FRANCIE A** (630)894-9524
300 Crestwood Dr Roselle IL 60172-3019 • mikenfran@juno.com • NI • Tchr • Trinity Roselle IL • (630)894-3263 • (S 1972)

**HEINZ KRISTI R** (812)952-1903
1440 St Johns Church Rd NE Lanesville IN 47136-8536 • revstamp@aol.com • NI • Tchr • St John Algonquin IL • (847)658-9300 • (RF 1989)

**HEINZ SHAR R** (208)326-4480
2050 E 3500 N Filer ID 83328-5638 • NOW • Tchr • Clover Trinity Buhl ID • (208)326-5198 • (S 1977 MED)

**HEINZ SUZANNE** (618)637-2109
11426 Libbra Rd New Douglas IL 62074-1912 • SI • Tchr • Metro-East LHS Edwardsville IL • (618)656-0043 • (CQ 2000)

**HEINZE FREDERICK C** (256)462-3864
1620 County Road 1069 Vinemont AL 35179-7494 • SO • Tchr • St Paul Cullman AL • (205)734-6580 • (S 1970)

**HEINZE HAZEL B** (256)462-3864
1620 County Road 1069 Vinemont AL 35179-7494 • SO • Tchr • St Paul Cullman AL • (205)734-6580 • (S 1966)

**HEINZE MICHAEL E** (708)398-2660
101 N Maple St Mt Prospect IL 60056-2525 • NI • Tchr • St Paul Chicago IL • (708)867-5044 • (RF 1982 MA)

**HEISLEN SARAH CHRISTINE** (972)479-0482
530 Buckingham #727 Richardson TX 75081 • TX • Tchr • Lutheran HS of Dalla Dallas TX • (214)349-8912 • (S 1994)

**HEISSENBUETTEL BRENDA MARIE** (313)282-5726
441 Bondie St Wyandotte MI 48192-2614 • buettel31@aol.com • MI • Mem C • Trinity Wyandotte MI • (734)282-5877 • (RF 1987 MA)

**HEISSENBUETTEL MONICA MARIE** (734)692-3137
2500 W Jefferson Ave Trenton MI 48183-2710 • MI • 08/1999 • (AA 1991)

**HEITMANN CHERYL M** (615)453-6809
1377 Eastover Rd Lebanon TN 37090 • NI • Tchr • Divine Shepherd Bolingbrook IL • (708)759-5300 • (RF 1968)

**HEITSCHMIDT KATHERINE S** (303)659-2698
685 S 14th Ave Brighton CO 80601-3372 • RM • Tchr • Zion Brighton CO • (303)659-3443 • (S 1971)

**HELD DAVID P DR** (402)643-6330
372 Shannon Rd Seward NE 68434-1118 • dheld@seward.cune.edu • NEB • SHS/C • Nebraska Seward NE • (S 1960 MA DMA)

**HELD LISA MARIE**
18065 Apple Rdg Apt 3534 Dallas TX 75287-4547 • lisaheld@juno.com • TX • Tchr • Holy Cross Dallas TX • (214)358-4396 • (S 1995)

**HELD MICHAEL** (713)932-0581
9130 Rangely Dr Houston TX 77055-4511 • jheld@flash.net • TX • Tchr • Trinity Houston TX • (713)224-0684 • (S 1966 MMU)

**HELDMAN SANDRA JOANNE** (330)273-3218
204 Westchester Dr Brunswick OH 44212-1561 • OH • Tchr • St Mark Brunswick OH • (330)225-4395 • (RF 1965)

**HELDT AMY LOUISE** (970)346-0110
24222 WCR 70 Eaton CO 80615-9515 • RM • Tchr • Gloria Christi Greeley CO • (970)353-2554 • (S 1996)

**HELGE ERICH E DR** (505)897-5974
7600 Rio Penasco Ct NW Albuquerque NM 87120-5315 • ededem@aol.com • RM • EM • (RF 1952 MA DED)

**HELLAND RACHEL ERIN** (308)382-9583
718 Hedde Apt 5 Grand Island NE 68801 • NEB • Tchr • Trinity Grand Island NE • (308)382-5274 • (S 1999)

**HELLBUSCH MAYNARD MARTIN**
C/O Saint John Lutheran Church 1000 Bluff St Beloit WI 53511-5167 • SW • P/Tchr • St John Beloit WI • (608)365-7838 • (S 1961 MAT)

**HELLER RUTH A**
1554 Foeller Dr Green Bay WI 54302 • ruthann74@freewwweb.com • NW • Tchr • LHS Assoc Of NE Wisc Green Bay WI • (920)469-6810 • (IV 1996)

**HELLMERS TINA M** (504)486-6114
6069 Vicksburg St New Orleans LA 70124-2951 • horenkamp@eschoolhouse.net • SO • Tchr • Atonement Metairie LA • (504)887-0225 • (S 1984)

**HELLWIG CYNTHIA D** (319)386-9404
1517 W 46th Pl Davenport IA 52806-3614 • IE • Tchr • Trinity Davenport IA • (319)322-5224 • (RF 1974 MSED MA)

**HELMCHEN LIANE BRIGITTE** (305)885-1232
937 Hunting Lodge Dr Miami Springs FL 33166-5751 • FG • 11/1998 • (RF 1994)

**HELMER REBECCA JEAN** (281)516-9636
1000 Hicks St Apt 911 Tomball TX 77375 • TX • Tchr • Concordia LHS Tomball TX • (281)351-2547 • (S 1998)

**HELMER THEODORE N** (316)686-1190
401 S Clifton Ave Wichita KS 67218-1106 • htchelmer@aol.com • KS • Tchr • Holy Cross Wichita KS • (316)684-4431 • (S 1967 MA)

**HELMICK DONNA J** (309)565-4506
1614 N Conn Rd Hanna City IL 61536-9609 • donna@wibscockers.com • CI • EM • (RF 1963)

**HELMING SCOTT B** (708)895-6523
18340 Oakwood Ave Lansing IL 60438-2906 • sbhelming@aol.com • NI • P/Tchr • Trinity Lansing IL • (708)474-8539 • (BR 1975 MSED)

**HELMKAMP BARBARA** (618)377-8254
215 Lakeside Dr Bethalto IL 62010-2011 • SI • Tchr • Zion Bethalto IL • (618)377-5507 • (S 1969)

**HELMKAMP KARL** (314)838-2639
1355 Nashua Dr Florissant MO 63033-2232 • MO • EM • (RF 1934 MA)

**HELMKAMP ROBERT K DR** (303)715-3506
480 S Marion Pkwy # 803-A Denver CO 80209-2589 • st³johns@juno.com • RM • P/Tchr • St John Denver CO • (303)733-3777 • (RF 1964 MED EDD)

**HELMKE RICHARD A** (630)628-1396
949 Surrey Rd Addison IL 60101-1193 • helmke@curf.edu • NI • SHS/C • Northern Illinois Hillside IL • (RF 1970 MCS)

**HELMLING VICKI J** (708)386-4513
835 N Lombard Ave Oak Park IL 60302-1430 • EN • Tchr • Christ English Chicago IL • (773)637-4800 • (RF 1978)

**HELMREICH CHRISTINE AMELIA** (810)987-4329
1226 Young St Port Huron MI 48060-4310 • MI • Tchr • Trinity Port Huron MI • (810)984-2501 • (S 1972 MA)

**HELMREICH EMILY LOUISE** (248)685-9290
400 Lawrence Dr Milford MI 48381-3140 • EN • Tchr • Child Of Christ Hartland MI • (248)887-3836 • (CQ 2000 MS)

**HELMREICH HARRY JAY** (231)276-9594
1789 Fairfield Dr Grawn MI 49637-9601 • bhelmreich@northlink.net • MI • Tchr • Trinity Traverse City MI • (231)946-2720 • (RF 1980 MA)

**HELMS CAROL M** (512)250-1031
11300 Songbird Cv Austin TX 78750-1323 • dhelms@austin.rr.com • TX • Tchr • Our Savior Austin TX • (512)836-9600 • (S 1968)

**HELPAP THOMAS E** (920)596-2641
N5905 Summit Ln Manawa WI 54949-8749 • NW • P/Tchr • St Paul Manawa WI • (920)596-2815 • (RF 1971)

**HEMLER ARTHUR G** (847)429-1854
1042 Polly Ct Elgin IL 60120 • NI • Prin • St John Elgin IL • (847)741-7633 • (RF 1964 MED)

**HEMLER HEATHER ANNE** (314)997-5670
975 J Rue de la Banque # J Creve Coeur MO 63141-5106 • hemler@hotmail.com • MO • Tchr • St Paul Saint Louis MO • (314)822-0447 • (RF 1996)

**HEMMANN OLIVER R** (708)366-1104
612 Beloit Ave Forest Park IL 60130-1908 • NI • Tchr • St Paul Melrose Park IL • (708)343-5000 • (S 1979 MA)

**HEMME MATHILDA A** (206)937-7722
9203 11th Ave SW Seattle WA 98106-2905 • mathemme@juno.com • NOW • Tchr • Seattle LHS Seattle WA • (206)937-7722 • (S 1966)

**HEMMEN ROSELLA K** (303)669-5543
2104 S Arthur Ave Loveland CO 80537-7360 • RM • Tchr • Immanuel Loveland CO • (970)667-7606 • (S 1971)

**HEMMINGHAUS HENRY G** (516)568-2814
436 Seward St Seward NE 68434-2129 • AT • Tchr • Atlantic Bronxville NY • (914)337-5700 • (S 1987)

**HEMMINGS JENNY R** (714)633-9218
216 S Clark Orange CA 92868 • hemmer1@aol.com • PSW • Tchr • Prince Of Peace Anaheim CA • (714)774-0993 • (S 1994)

**HEMPEL DONN F** (708)442-1505
8011 Salisbury Ave Lyons IL 60534-1114 • NI • Tchr • Immanuel Hillside IL • (708)562-5580 • (RF 1976)

**HEMPEL RUTH R**
28604 Sunnydale St Livonia MI 48154-3330 • MI • Tchr • Mt Hope Allen Park MI • (313)565-9140 • (RF 1976)

**HEMPHILL LISHELLE LEIGH**
723 Sunward SW Albuquerque NM 87121-9465 • RM • Tchr • Christ Albuquerque NM • (505)884-3876 • (S 1993)

**HENCYE LAWRENCE K** (219)485-9399
3409 Merrimack Pl Fort Wayne IN 46815-8412 • IN • Mem C • Holy Cross Fort Wayne IN • (219)483-3173 • (S 1972 MA)

**HENDERSHOT DIANA ANN** (716)392-4000
163 Haskins Ln S Hilton NY 14468-9003 • dianahendershot@hotmail.com • EA • Tchr • St Paul Hilton NY • (716)392-4000 • (CQ 1997 MED)

**HENDRICKS JANELLE R**
54 Steeplechase Dr Saint Peters MO 63376-1338 • MO • Tchr • Zion Saint Charles MO • (636)441-7425 • (S 1998)

**HENDRICKS STEVAN L**
54 Steeplechase Dr Saint Peters MO 63376-1338 • MO • Tchr • LHS St Charles Saint Peters MO • (636)928-5100 • (S 1998)

**HENDRICKSEN DONALD H** (219)749-0530
5406 Forest Ave Fort Wayne IN 46815-7463 • IN • EM • (RF 1952 MA MED)

**HENDRICKSON EUNICE M** (979)884-0200
1667 CR 130 Ledbetter TX 78946-7001 • TX • Tchr • Immanuel Giddings TX • (409)542-3319 • (S 1969)

**HENDRICKSON LISA**
25897 C Chippendale Ct Roseville MI 48066 • MI • Tchr • St Thomas Eastpointe MI • (810)772-3370 • (RF 2000)

**HENDRICKSON MARY B** (309)944-3378
108 Sherwood Dr Geneseo IL 61254-9147 • mbhnc40@tcpl.com • CI • 07/1988 07/2000 • (RF 1981 MA)

**HENDRIKSON KEVIN J** (608)524-9953
1430 Gavin Ct Reedsburg WI 53959-2220 • khen-wwjd@juno.com • SW • Tchr • St Peter Reedsburg WI • (608)524-4512 • (MQ 1994)

**HENDRYX SHERYL D** (815)226-1006
2815 Kentwood Pkwy Rockford IL 61109-2725 • hendryx5@earthlink.net • NI • Tchr • St Paul Rockford IL • (815)965-3335 • (RF 1985)

**HENKE CHAD R**
5614 Sheraton Oaks Houston TX 77091 • TX • Tchr • Pilgrim Houston TX • (713)666-3706 • (AU 1999)

**HENKE STEPHEN M** (713)686-6834
5614 Sheraton Oaks Dr Houston TX 77091-1306 • TX • Prin • Our Savior Houston TX • (713)290-8277 • (RF 1966 MED)

**HENKELL JOE D** (760)631-2252
1097 La Tortuga Vista CA 92083 • jhenkvista@aol.com • PSW • P/Tchr • Faith Vista CA • (760)724-7700 • (RF 1967 MA)

**HENKELL KELLY ERIN** (805)499-3657
1115 Amberton Ln Newbury Park CA 91320 • henkhouse@aol.com • PSW • 07/1994 07/2000 • (IV 1993)

**HENKELMAN TIMOTHY ALLEN** (618)258-0395
205 2nd St NW PO Box 137 Mayer MN 55360-0137 • henk@prodigy.net • MNS • Tchr • Zion Mayer MN • 245 • (SP 1986)

**HENKES MICHAEL** (801)568-9487
331 Chad Heights Ln Midvale UT 84047-5718 • mhenkes@aros.net • RM • Tchr • Redeemer Salt Lake City UT • (801)487-6283 • (S 1975 MA)

**HENN CAROLYN MARIE** (410)833-0970
422 Deacon Brook Cir Reisterstown MD 21136-2229 • SE • 08/1997 08/2000 • (RF 1968 MA)

**HENN THEODORE L**
422 Deacon Brook Cir Reisterstown MD 21136-2229 • SE • Tchr • Southeastern Alexandria VA • (RF 1966)

**HENNIES HOPE MARIE**
Zion Lutheran School 4550 S Highway 16 Rapid City SD 57701-8913 • SD • Tchr • Zion Rapid City SD • (605)342-5749 • (S 1999)

**HENNIG DENISE KAY** (618)888-2356
7187 Renken Rd Dorsey IL 62021-1803 • pjdjajm@juno.com • SI • 06/1991 06/2000 • (S 1985)

**HENNIG JOSEPH F** (208)733-4724
633 Falls Ave W Twin Falls ID 83301-3632 • jfbahennig@juno.com • NOW • EM • (S 1956 MS)

**HENNIG SHARON F** (717)244-3089
365 S Park St Dallastown PA 17313-9735 • SE • Tchr • St John York PA • (717)755-4779 • (S 1965)

**HENNING DAVID W** (414)545-0065
3975 S 84th St #7 Greenfield WI 53228-2338 • duhenning@webtv.net • SW • Tchr • Northwest Milwaukee WI • (414)463-4040 • (RF 1973 MS)

**HENNING GAIL** (817)244-7741
6728 Cool Meadow Dr Fort Worth TX 76132-1153 • TX • Tchr • St Paul Fort Worth TX • (817)332-4563 • (CQ 1998)

**HENNING JAMES C** (715)384-6679
905 W 8th St Marshfield WI 54449-3516 • henningj@tznet.com • NW • P/Tchr • Immanuel Marshfield WI • (715)384-5121 • (S 1969 MED)

**HENRICKSEN GARY W** (805)981-1911
741 Nandina Ct Oxnard CA 93030 • ghenricksen@stjohns.pvt.k12.ca.us • PSW • Tchr • St John Oxnard CA • (805)983-0330 • (S 1980 MMU)

**HENRY DEBORAH S** (972)274-0492
211 Marsha Ln De Soto TX 75115 • dhenry1019@aol.com • TX • Tchr • Cross Of Christ De Soto TX • (972)223-9586 • (S 1975)

**HENRY DEBORAH** (512)285-4373
817A Lexington Rd Elgin TX 78621-1249 • TX • Tchr • Hope Austin TX • (512)926-0003 • (S 1971)

**HENRY LYNN E** (612)824-4881
4206 Harriet Ave Minneapolis MN 55409-1836 • lhenry@concordia-academy.pvt.k12.mn.us • MNS • Tchr • Concordia Academy Roseville MN • (612)484-8429 • (S 1978 MED)

**HENSCHEN DANIEL R** (217)529-7347
34 Carole Rd Springfield IL 62707-9466 • henschen@eosinc.com • CI • P/Tchr • Concordia Springfield IL • (217)529-3307 • (S 1973 MS)

**HENSCHEN RONALD J** (618)656-4333
1209 Richetta Dr Edwardsville IL 62025-4211 • ronh³50@yahoo.com • SI • Tchr • Metro-East LHS Edwardsville IL • (618)656-0043 • (S 1972 MS)

**HENSLEY DOUGLAS D** (562)867-2363
9530 Alondra Blvd Spc 25 Bellflower CA 90706-3581 • dhensley13f31@yahoo.com • PSW • Prin • Bethany Long Beach CA • (562)420-7783 • (RF 1964)

**HENSON KARIN R** (618)942-2890
605 Indian Hill Dr Herrin IL 62948 • SI • 06/1992 06/2000 • (S 1989)

**HENTE BRENDA J** (314)427-3124
3226 Saint Joachim Ln Saint Ann MO 63074-3509 • MO • Tchr • Immanuel Olivette MO • (314)993-5004 • (RF 1987)

**HENTSCHER ROBERT C** (828)466-0410
1005 E 24th St Newton NC 28658-1924 • SE • EM • (RF 1950 MED)

**HENTZEN DAVID A**
11884 W 56th Dr Arvada CO 80002 • RM • Tchr • St John Denver CO • (303)733-3777 • (S 1998)

**HENTZEN PATSY A** (208)523-6423
2381 Richards Ave Idaho Falls ID 83404-6334 • NOW • Tchr • Hope Idaho Falls ID • (208)529-8080 • (S 1963)

**HENWOOD JANE D**
6724 Chirco Shelby Township MI 48316-3416 • MI • Tchr • Trinity Utica MI • (810)731-4490 • (RF 1967 MA)

**HEPBURN AMY BETH**
157 Sierra Pass Dr Schaumburg IL 60194-4975 • NI • Tchr • Gloria Dei Chicago IL • (773)767-2771 • (RF 1991)

**HEPBURN JOYCE ANDREA** (708)350-1573
117 E Potter St Wood Dale IL 60191-2025 • NI • Tchr • Immanuel Elmhurst IL • (630)832-9302 • (RF 1967)

**HERBRICH BEN T**
21815 Stewart Rd Queens Village NY 11427-1107 • mlutherhs@aol.com • AT • Tchr • Martin Luther Maspeth NY • (718)894-4000 • (S 1964 MA)

**HERBST H ALLEN DR** (636)281-1133
1701 Western Pines Ct O Fallon MO 63366 • RM • Rocky Mountain Aurora CO • (RF 1959 MMU MA PHD)

**HERBST KATHRYN ANN** (262)784-9575
1155 Jewel St Brookfield WI 53005-7010 • normkathy@milwpc.com • SW • Tchr • Pilgrim Wauwatosa WI • (414)476-0736 • (S 1966)

**HEREN ANDREW S*** (715)831-9236
3542 Hester St Eau Claire WI 54701-7701 • Rcktnut007@aol.com • NW • Tchr • Eau Claire Eau Claire WI • (715)835-9314 • (RF 1987)

**HERETH LYNNE A** (360)568-2805
11930 Springhetti Rd Snohomish WA 98296-8220 • springherd2@cs.com • NOW • Tchr • Zion Everett WA • (425)334-5064 • (CQ 1986 MED)

**HERGENRADER CHRISTINA L** (281)218-7944
2341 Ramada Houston TX 77043 • mikeandtin@aol.com • TX • Tchr • Lutheran South Acade Houston TX • (281)464-8299 • (S 1996)

**HERING RUTH ANN** (414)458-9006
2305 N 29th St Sheboygan WI 53083-4404 • SW • Tchr • Trinity Sheboygan WI • (920)458-8248 • (RF 1971)

**HERKA CATHERINE M**
2500 W College Ave Milwaukee WI 53221-4938 • SW • Tchr • Christ Memorial Milwaukee WI • (414)461-3371 • (MQ 1986)

**HERLIEN JILL** (630)858-7219
22 W 364 Mc Carron Rd Glen Ellyn IL 60137 • NI • Tchr • St James Chicago IL • (773)525-4990 • (RF 1998)

**HERMAN CAROL S** (219)749-4433
1409 S Park Dr New Haven IN 46774 • csherman@hotmail.com • IN • Tchr • Central New Haven IN • (219)493-2502 • (CQ 1996 MS)

**HERMAN DEBRA J** (630)351-8805
640 Walnut Oaks Dr Roselle IL 60172-2200 • office@trinityroselle • NI • Mem C • Trinity Roselle IL • (630)894-3263 • (RF 1977)

**HERMAN LINDA RUTH**
18010 128th Pl SE Snohomish WA 98290-8628 • NOW • Tchr • Little Doves Monroe WA • (206)794-7230 • (S 1981 MA)

**HERMAN RICHARD E** (630)351-8805
640 Walnut Oaks Dr Roselle IL 60172-2200 • wrmhermanre@wheatridge.org • NI • CCRA • Northern Illinois Hillside IL • (RF 1974 MED EDS LLD)

**HERMAN SANDRA K** (219)749-9842
1321 Landin Rd New Haven IN 46774 • IN • Tchr • Central New Haven IN • (219)493-2502 • (S 1969 MA)

**HERMANN ALFRED L** (708)338-0155
360 Andy Dr Melrose Park IL 60160-2515 • NI • SHS/C • Northern Illinois Hillside IL • (RF 1964 MED)

**HERMANN DONALD F** (847)253-0975
908 N Chestnut Ave Arlington Hts IL 60004-5549 • NI • EM • (S 1951 MMU)

**HERMANN HENRY H** (414)771-1211
2816 N 71st St Milwaukee WI 53210-1157 • SW • EM • (RF 1956)

**HERMANN HENRY K** (970)523-8123
577 W Conestoga Cir Grand Junction CO 81504 • RM • EM • (RF 1959 MA)

**HERMANN RANDI S** (313)379-5431
32162 Covington St Rockwood MI 48173-9652 • MI • Tchr • Christ The King Southgate MI • (734)285-9697 • (S 1977)

**HERRE NORMA E** (317)862-4253
7110 Bel Moore Cir Indianapolis IN 46259 • IN • Tchr • St John Indianapolis IN • (317)352-9196 • (S 1968 MS)

**HERRING LOUIS B** (219)896-2434
202 E Weninger St North Judson IN 46366-1430 • IN • EM • (RF 1959 MS MSED)

**HERRING PAUL MICHAEL** (308)385-2961
121 W 14th St Grand Island NE 68801-3847 • NEB • 06/1998 06/2000 • (S 1993)

**HERRMANN CRAIG G** (212)931-4682
C/O Our Saviour Luth Church 1734 Williamsbridge Rd Bronx NY 10461-6204 • AT • Tchr • Our Saviour Bronx NY • (718)792-5665 • (SP 1989)

**HERRMANN JONATHAN**
15796 Flamingo Dr Fontana CA 92337 • PSW • Tchr • Redeemer Ontario CA • (909)986-6510 • (S 1991)

**HERRMANN JULIE A** (612)466-2003
2015 Parkside St Cologne MN 55322-9099 • MNS • Tchr • St Johns Chaska MN • (612)448-2526 • (MQ 1996)

**HERRMANN LORRIE L**
15796 Flamingo Dr Fontana CA 92337 • PSW • Tchr • First Fontana CA • (909)823-3457 • (S 1993)

**HERRMANN ROBERT L** (414)892-2271
315 N Stafford St Plymouth WI 53073-1242 • SW • EM • (RF 1955 MA)

**HERRON BARBARA** (954)981-4850
5790 Stirling Rd Apt 208 Hollywood FL 33021-1544 • FG • Tchr • Gloria Dei Davie FL • (954)475-0683 • (CQ 1999)

**HERRON LAUREL M** (330)940-2574
406 Van Buren Ave Cuyahoga Falls OH 44221 • OH • Tchr • Redeemer Cuyahoga Falls OH • (330)923-1280 • (AA 1999)

**HERTEL DELORES L** (847)934-6266
629 W Hill Rd Palatine IL 60067-2011 • NI • Tchr • Immanuel Palatine IL • (847)359-1936 • (RF 1961 MA)

**HERTNEKY MARGARET L** (262)567-5571
906 York Imperial Dr Oconomowoc WI 53066-3444 • SW • Tchr • St Paul Oconomowoc WI • (262)567-5001 • (RF 1979)

**HERZFELD GENIECE V**
408 S Lawrence St Mobile AL 36603-1818 • SO • EM • (RF 1982)

**HERZOG ARTHUR O** (417)358-3850
1104 Lillie Dr Carthage MO 64836 • MO • EM • (RF 1944 MED)

**HERZOG GUENTHER K** (219)749-9719
8408 Hasta Ct Fort Wayne IN 46815-8770 • IN • EM • (RF 1950 MS LLD)

**HERZOG JANET S** (708)705-1727
937 N Williams Dr Palatine IL 60067-4054 • NI • Tchr • St Peter Arlington Heights IL • (847)253-6638 • (RF 1974 MA)

**HERZOG PHILLIP G** (414)764-1739
621 E Mary Ln Oak Creek WI 53154-6486 • psherzog@gateway.net • SW • Tchr • Martin LHS Greendale WI • (414)421-4000 • (RF 1974 MA)

**HESCHKE RICHARD J** (914)237-3443
811 Bronx River Rd Apt 6E Bronxville NY 10708-7019 • AT • SHS/C • Atlantic Bronxville NY • (914)337-5700 • (RF 1961 MMU DMU)

**HESS ANNE L** (208)667-2869
2525 S Greenferry Ceour d Alene ID 83814-7605 • NOW • 02/2000 • (S 1978 MA)

**HESS JO ANN** (815)933-6563
1507 E Armour Rd Bourbonnais IL 60914-4487 • NI • Tchr • St John Country Club Hills IL • (708)799-7491 • (RF 1979)

**HESS MARK*** (815)933-6563
1507 E Armour Rd Bourbonnais IL 60914-4487 • mhess@stpaulslutheran.net • NI • Tchr • St Paul Kankakee IL • (815)932-3241 • (S 1980)

**HESSE BONNIE J** (314)638-8562
818 Summer Meadow Ct St Louis MO 63125-3232 • MO • Tchr • St Paul Des Peres MO • (314)822-2771 • (RF 1973)

**HESSE MERLENE J** (513)598-4899
5682 Boomer Rd Cincinnati OH 45247 • OH • Tchr • Grace Cincinnati OH • (513)661-8467 • (SP 1990)

**HESSE WAYNE** (314)638-8562
818 Summer Meadow Ct Saint Louis MO 63125-3232 • MO • Tchr • Green Park Lemay MO • (314)544-4248 • (RF 1976 MAT)

**HESSLER DOROTHY** (415)364-8424
956 Round Hill Rd Redwood City CA 94061-1135 • CNH • Tchr • Redeemer Redwood City CA • (650)366-5892 • (RF 1960 MA)

**HESSLER EDWARD A** (920)485-4935
408 Rich St Horicon WI 53032-1625 • SW • 09/1996 09/1999 • (RF 1964 MA)

**HESTERMAN PHILLIP K** (308)382-8819
641 Martin Ave Grand Island NE 68801 • phesterman@ginetworks.com • NEB • Tchr • Trinity Grand Island NE • (308)382-5274 • (S 1984 MCMU MAT)

**HETHERINGTON KIMBERLY A** (502)423-8132
1403 Cadet Ct Louisville KY 40222 • gkriemg@aol.com • IN • Tchr • Our Savior Louisville KY • (502)426-0864 • (RF 1992)

**HETZ ELLEN M** (314)832-6428
6428 Printz Ct Saint Louis MO 63116-1134 • MO • Tchr • Word Of Life Saint Louis MO • (314)832-1244 • (RF 1962)

**HETZ PATRICIA JEAN** (314)631-4586
613 Sandra Ct St Louis MO 63125-1139 • pjhteach1@msn.com • MO • Tchr • St John Arnold MO • (636)464-7303 • (RF 1976 MAT)

**HETZNER JACQUELYN L** (708)991-6625
123 S Brockway St Palatine IL 60067-6125 • NI • Tchr • Immanuel Palatine IL • (847)359-1936 • (RF 1978 MED)

**HEUBLEIN METTA F** (810)234-4943
602 S Lynch Ave Flint MI 48503-2240 • mheublein@hotmail.com • MI • Tchr • St Paul Flint MI • (810)239-6733 • (RF 1974 MA)

**HEUBLEIN ROBERT R*** (810)234-4943
602 S Lynch Ave Flint MI 48503-2240 • rheublein@mr-h.com • MI • Tchr • St Paul Flint MI • (810)239-6733 • (RF 1976 MA)

**HEUER AMY J**
12 E Ave A Melbourne FL 32901-1391 • FG • Mem C • Redeemer Melbourne FL • (321)723-4152 • (S 2000)

**HEUTON EUGENE W** (612)646-1323
1236 Marshall Ave Saint Paul MN 55104-6435 • ewheut@aol.com • MNS • Tchr • Central Saint Paul MN • (651)645-8649 • (SP 1979)

**HEYNIGER KRISTEN MARIE** (734)676-8712
5323 Lathrop St Trenton MI 48183-4724 • MI • Tchr • St John New Boston MI • (734)654-6366 • (AA 1990)

**HICKS STEVEN B**
143-16 Barclay Ave Apt 5A Flushing NY 11355 • AT • Tchr • Martin Luther Maspeth NY • (718)894-4000 • (BR 1983)

**HIEBER JANICE M** (219)493-8714
3211 Devereux Dr Fort Wayne IN 46815-6574 • IN • Tchr • St Peter Fort Wayne IN • (219)749-5811 • (S 1973 MS MS)

**HIEGEL CONNIE J** (308)389-4551
404 E 19th St Grand Island NE 68801-2447 • NEB • Tchr • Trinity Grand Island NE • (308)382-5274 • (S 1989)

**HIEGEL JACK L** (502)485-0950
1930 Rutherford Ave Louisville KY 40205 • IN • Tchr • Our Savior Louisville KY • (502)426-0864 • (S 1983 MED)

**HIEGEL LINDA GAIL** (219)485-0224
5304 Stonehedge Blvd Apt 2 Ft Wayne IN 46835 • IN • 04/2000 • (S 1978 MS)

**HIEGEL THOMAS A** (219)639-6064
826 Kensington Blvd Fort Wayne IN 46805-5310 • IN • 06/1999 • (S 1978 MS)

**HIGHFILL VICKIE L** (213)721-7141
1905 Millis St Montebello CA 90640-4533 • PSW • Tchr • Immanuel First West Covina CA • (818)919-1530 • (CQ 1979)

**HIGHT PAMELA J** (512)930-4898
1965 FM 972 Georgetown TX 78626-9786 • TX • Tchr • Zion Georgetown TX • (512)863-5345 • (S 1977)

**HIGHT STEVEN R** (714)974-4567
2064 N Cleveland St Orange CA 92865-3827 • srhight@aol.com • PSW • Tchr • St Paul Orange CA • (714)921-3188 • (S 1983)

**HILCHEN LEANN MARIE**
10250 SW School St Tigard OR 97223-5105 • NOW • Tchr • Pilgrim Beaverton OR • (503)644-4656 • (S 1990)

**HILDEBRAND ALICE MAE** (314)447-3969
226 Cedar Grove Dr Saint Charles MO 63304-7378 • MO • Tchr • Zion Saint Charles MO • (636)441-7425 • (RF 1974)

**HILDEBRAND DANIELLE SUSAN** (810)226-4013
17637 Kingsbrooke Cir # 104 Clinton Township MI 48038 • hildebrand.d@macomb.cc.mi.us • NI • 07/1999 • (RF 1995)

**HILDEBRAND KEVIN J** (810)226-4013
17899 Costello Clinton Township MI 48038-3788 • kjhilde@aol.com • MI • Tchr • St Luke Clinton Township MI • (810)791-1151 • (RF 1995 MMU)

**HILDEBRAND LAURA ANN**
217 Carol Ave Niles MI 49120 • gigerla@aol.com • MI • Tchr • Trinity Berrien Springs MI • (616)473-1811 • (AA 1996)

**HILDEBRAND PAUL D** (815)286-7396
14549 US Highway 30 Hinckley IL 60520-6179 • NI • Tchr • Emmanuel Aurora IL • (630)851-2200 • (RF 1985)

**HILDNER VICTOR** (708)524-1966
846 N Cuyler Ave Oak Park IL 60302-1408 • EN • EM • (CQ 1943 MMU DMU)

**HILGENDORF DUANE H** (414)376-8949
W59N973 Essex Dr Cedarburg WI 53012-1439 • duane.hilgendorf@cuw.edu • SW • SHS/C • South Wisconsin Milwaukee WI • (414)464-8100 • (S 1974 MED)

**HILGENDORF MARY** (414)376-8949
W59N973 Essex Dr Cedarburg WI 53012-1439 • mhilgend@bach.cuw.edu • SW • SHS/C • South Wisconsin Milwaukee WI • (414)464-8100 • (S 1973 MED)

**HILGENDORF RICHARD**
8015 US Highway 285 S Alamosa CO 81101-9702 • CNH • Mem C • All Nations Christia Bakersfield CA • (661)397-4322 • (RF 1962 MA)

**HILGENDORF THOMAS C DR** (512)990-8376
17915 Holderness Ln Pflugerville TX 78660-5128 • thilgen@aol.com • TX • SHS/C • Texas Austin TX • (S 1975 MED PHD)

**HILGENDORF WILLIAM A** (920)426-0476
1630 E Murdock Ave Oshkosh WI 54901-2530 • billbert@vbe.com • SW • Tchr • Trinity Oshkosh WI • (920)235-1730 • (S 1972 MA)

**HILGER LORI LYN** (815)462-4282
1010 School Gate Rd New Lenox IL 60451-2681 • llh94@aol.com • NI • Tchr • Trinity Tinley Park IL • (708)532-3529 • (RF 1980)

**HILGER RONALD OTTO** (630)834-8413
311 Clinton Elmhurst IL 60126 • NI • Tchr • Immanuel Glenview IL • (847)724-1034 • (RF 2000)

**HILK MIRIAM R** (612)442-5277
7025 County Road 10 N Waconia MN 55387-9644 • MNS • Tchr • Trinity Waconia MN • (952)442-4165 • (SP 1974)

**HILK RONALD J** (612)442-5277
7025 County Road 10 N Waconia MN 55387-9644 • MNS • Tchr • Lutheran High Mayer MN • (612)657-2251 • (SP 1973 MS)

**HILKEN JOHN CHARLES** (734)243-2015
1020 Donnalee St Monroe MI 48162-5118 • jchilken@foxberry.net • MI • Prin • Trinity Monroe MI • (734)241-1160 • (RF 1978 MA)

**HILKER DIANA K** (308)493-5628
PO Box 83 Holbrook NE 68948 • RM • Tchr • University Hills Denver CO • (303)759-5363 • (S 1998)

**HILL KENNETH S** (920)922-5130
C/O Hope Lutheran Church 260 Vincent St Fond du Lac WI 54935-5331 • SW • Mem C • Hope Fond Du Lac WI • (920)922-5130 • (RF 1978 MA)

**HILLEMAN JEANINE** (314)646-1274
7108 Horner Ave Apt C 8 Richmond Heights MO 63117 • MO • Hope Fond Du Lac WI • (S 1993 MA)

**HILLERT RICHARD W DR** (708)681-5598
1620 Clay Ct Melrose Park IL 60160-2419 • rwhillert@aol.com • NI • EM • (RF 1951 MMU DMU LITTD)

**HILLMAN VELMA L** (308)382-2607
4703 E US Highway 30 Grand Island NE 68801-9431 • NEB • EM • (CQ 1997)

**HILLMANN PAUL L** (559)535-5103
26002 Avenue 100 Terra Bella CA 93270-9698 • CNH • EM • (S 1947)

**HILSABECK JANET E** (810)792-1179
36348 Egan St Clinton Township MI 48035-4421 • MI • Tchr • St Luke Clinton Township MI • (810)791-1151 • (AA 1982)

**HILST HELEN M** (415)751-4609
445 9th Ave San Francisco CA 94118-2912 • CNH • EM • (RF 1965 MA)

**HIMMLER GARY W** (281)999-2976
4730 Kipper Cir Pasadena TX 77505 • TX • Tchr • Lutheran South Acade Houston TX • (281)464-8299 • (S 1981 MED)

**HIMMLER MARVIN M** (313)731-7357
48703 Bluebird Dr Utica MI 48317-2328 • MI • EM • (RF 1955)

**HINCK DIANE E** (815)568-4423
633 W Prairie St Marengo IL 60152-2144 • hinck@mc.net • NI • Tchr • Zion Marengo IL • (815)568-5156 • (RF 1986 MA)

**HINCK JAMIE**
C/O Our Savior Luth Church PO Box 925188 Houston TX 77292-5188 • TX • Tchr • Our Savior Houston TX • (713)290-9087 • (RF 2000)

**HINCK JOHN T** (313)525-0766
41950 Trent Ct Canton MI 48188 • MI • Tchr • Christ Good Shepherd Canton MI • (734)981-0286 • (S 1974 MED)

**HINCK SANDRA S** (660)463-2823
27231 Hwy AA Concordia MO 64020-9609 • MO • Tchr • St Paul Concordia MO • (660)463-7654 • (RF 1978)

**HINDENACH DEANNA J** (616)657-4987
211 W North St Paw Paw MI 49079-0011 • trinityschool@trinitylutheran.com • MI • Tchr • Trinity Paw Paw MI • (616)657-4840 • (CQ 1998)

**HINES MARY M** (219)483-1487
903 Elnora Dr Fort Wayne IN 46825-4529 • trinitysk@aol.com • IN • Tchr • Trinity Fort Wayne IN • (219)426-4292 • (RF 1975 MED)

**HINES MICHELLE** (714)525-1931
2249 Ardemore Dr Fullerton CA 92833 • PSW • Tchr • Christ Fullerton CA • (714)870-7460 • (IV 1998)

**HINGST DUANE E** (314)567-1325
1053 Wappapello Ln Saint Louis MO 63146-5140 • hingstdm@worldnet.att.net • MO • EM • (RF 1953 MED)

**HINK PAUL H** (216)731-2124
705 E 258th St Euclid OH 44132-2211 • EN • EM • (RF 1961)

**HINKLE DAVID** (618)377-5507
C/O Zion Lutheran School 625 Church Dr Bethalto IL 62010-1830 • zionhinkle@ezl.com • SI • Tchr • Zion Bethalto IL • (618)377-8314 • (S 1984)

**HINRICHS EDMUND C** (507)235-5874
500 Albion Ave Fairmont MN 56031-2108 • MNS • EM • (RF 1952 MSED)

**HINRICHS SARAH LYNN** (727)559-0885
200 Country Club Dr - Apt 1002 Largo FL 33771 • FG • Tchr • First Clearwater FL • (727)447-4504 • (UNKNWN 1999)

**HINRICHS VANCE H DR** (402)488-4233
3431 Crown Pointe Rd Lincoln NE 68506-4151 • vhhcph@juno.com • NEB • EM • (S 1953 MA DED)

**HINTZ EARL E** (718)849-6853
88-39 82nd Ave Glendale NY 11385-7811 • AT • Tchr • St John Glendale NY • (718)441-2120 • (RF 1956)

**HINTZ GARY H** (713)462-0885
3622 Millspring Dr Houston TX 77080-1427 • TX • Tchr • Our Savior Houston TX • (713)290-8277 • (S 1960)

**HINTZE GRETCHEN ELIZABETH** (314)544-7685
9139 A Paul Revere Dr Affton MO 63123 • MO • Our Savior Houston TX • (MQ 1998)

**HINTZMAN REBEKAH L**
56 Meadows Dr Pagosa Springs CO 81147 • RM • Tchr • Our Savior Pagosa Springs CO • (970)731-4668 • (S 2000)

**HINZ AMY M** (540)373-5378
15 Osprey Ln Fredericksburg VA 22405-3481 • ahinz@mail.acps.k12.va.us • SE • Tchr • Prince Of Peace Springfield VA • (703)451-5855 • (BR 1990)

**HINZ ANN M** (630)964-4267
1716 Janet St Downers Grove IL 60515-1841 • daze87@hotmail.com • NI • Tchr • St John Lombard IL • (630)629-2515 • (RF 1982 MCMU)

**HINZ KENNETH E** (217)429-3470
166 S Elder Ln Decatur IL 62522-1845 • CI • Tchr • Lutheran School Asso Decatur IL • (217)233-2001 • (RF 1963 MED)

**HINZ WILLIAM VERN DR** (512)990-2158
606 Dartmouth Cv Pflugerville TX 78660 • wvhinz@aol.com • TX • Texas Austin TX • (RF 1978 MA EDD)

**HINZE ADELE L** (815)933-1397
252 Tomagene Dr Bournonnais IL 60914 • iteach31st@hotmail.com • NI • Tchr • St Paul Kankakee IL • (815)932-3241 • (RF 1977)

**HINZE NEAL T** (262)512-1627
N112W13102 Mequon Rd Germantown WI 53022 • hnz3@execp.com • SW • Mem C • Grace Menomonee Falls WI • (262)251-0670 • (MQ 1987 MA)

**HIPENBECKER STEVEN M** (414)475-9012
12220 W Ripley Ave Wauwatosa WI 53226-3828 • NI • Tchr • Concordia Machesney Park IL • (815)633-6450 • (MQ 1999)

**HIPENBECKER TIMOTHY J** (303)255-9795
C/O Lutheran HS of the Rockies 10423 S Parker Rd Parker CO 80134 • trjhips@aol.com • RM • Tchr • Lutheran HS Rockies Parker CO • (303)841-5551 • (MQ 1988 MBA)

**HIPPLE ERIC CHRISTIAN** (618)659-9675
1118 Jacquelyn Ct Maryville IL 62062 • bandmanech@aol.com • SI • Tchr • Metro-East LHS Edwardsville IL • (618)656-0043 • (RF 1996)

**HIRSCH BRADLEY W*** (707)464-7935
1126 California St Crescent City CA 95531-2240 • hirschfam@telis.org • CNH • 08/2000 • (S 1974 MA)

**HIRSCH LISA L** (320)543-2724
816 12th Ave PO Box 313 Howard Lake MN 55349-0313 • leeze@hutchtel.net • MNS • Tchr • St James Howard Lake MN • (320)543-2630 • (SP 1993)

**HISKE BEVERLY G** (410)893-1245
608 Churchill Rd Apt M Bel Air MD 21014-4254 • SE • Tchr • Immanuel Baltimore MD • (410)435-6961 • (RF 1962)

**HISKEY WILLIAM R** (712)262-2476
First English Lutheran Church 23 E 10th St Spencer IA 51301-4317 • brhiskey@qhotmail.com • IW • Mem C • First English Spencer IA • (712)262-5598 • (S 1987)

**HITZEMAN JACQUELINE A** (219)485-6386
3890 Buesching Dr Fort Wayne IN 46815-4802 • IN • Tchr • Holy Cross Fort Wayne IN • (219)483-3173 • (RF 1970)

**HITZEMANN ERHARDT W** (517)893-7358
404 W Osage St Bay City MI 48706-5251 • MI • EM • (RF 1924 MMU)

**HJERSTEDT KIM**
799 Grandview Dr Crystal Lake IL 60014-7367 • NI • Tchr • Immanuel Crystal Lake IL • (815)459-1441 • (RF 1983)

**HOBACK BARBARA A** (952)467-2246
114 Trilane Dr Young America MN 55397-9605 • bahoback@hotmail.com • MNS • Tchr • Lutheran High Mayer MN • (612)657-2251 • (S 1980)

**HOBBS NANCY JANE** (714)535-6456
2250 E South Redwood Dr Anaheim CA 92806 • seannancy@aol.com • PSW • Tchr • Mount Calvary Diamond Bar CA • (909)861-2740 • (IV 1993)

**HOBBY JENNIFER LEE**
2426 Buckhurst Run Fort Wayne IN 46815-8507 • rhobby6172@aol.com • IN • Tchr • Emmanuel-St Michael Fort Wayne IN • (219)422-6712 • (RF 1987 MS)

**HOBUS DAVID A** (406)755-7890
771 Kookoosint Trl Kalispell MT 59901-7400 • MT • Prin • Trinity Kalispell MT • (406)257-6716 • (S 1977 MED)

**HOCH ARTHUR G** (517)356-2467
176 Parker Ave Alpena MI 49707-1414 • arthoch@freeway.net • MI • Tchr • Immanuel Alpena MI • (517)354-4805 • (SP 1971)

**HOCH JUDITH L** (517)356-2467
176 Parker Ave Alpena MI 49707-1414 • MI • Tchr • Immanuel Alpena MI • (517)354-4805 • (SP 1991)

**HOCH ROBERT M** (810)949-6263
25795 Lord Dr Chesterfield MI 48051-3229 • MI • Prin • St Peter Macomb MI • (810)781-9296 • (SP 1976 MAT)

**HOCHTHANNER KELLY A** (313)581-4618
5253 Argyle Dearborn MI 48126 • MI • Tchr • Atonement Dearborn MI • (313)581-2525 • (AA 1995)

**HOCK KRISTINE L** (303)420-8602
5627 Taft Ct Arvada CO 80002-1405 • RM • Tchr • Bethlehem Lakewood CO • (303)233-0401 • (S 1978 MA)

**HOCKEMEYER PHYLLIS A** (219)749-0896
8412 Newfield Dr Fort Wayne IN 46815-8033 • phockem@aol.com • IN • Tchr • Emmanuel-St Michael Fort Wayne IN • (219)422-6712 • (RF 1981 MS)

**HODGE SUSAN M** (314)432-2809
1043 Orchard Lakes Dr Saint Louis MO 63146-5128 • suhodg@postnet.com • MO • Tchr • Salem Florissant MO • (314)741-6781 • (S 1969 MED)

**HODGSON CAROL I** (913)262-2310
4111 Elledge Dr Roeland Park KS 66205-1359 • KS • 12/1994 12/1998 • (S 1979 MA)

**HODGSON WILLIAM E JR.** (602)956-8507
3301 E Turney Ave Phoenix AZ 85018-3925 • bhodgson@cclphoenix.org • EN • Tchr • Christ Phoenix AZ • (602)957-7010 • (S 1972 MED)

**HOEFT JAMES M** (734)326-9365
38710 Covington Dr Wayne MI 48184 • rjhoeft99@netscape.net • MI • Tchr • Hosanna-Tabor Redford MI • (313)937-2424 • (AA 1999)

**HOEFT KAREN R** (734)326-9365
38710 Covington Dr Wayne MI 48184-1086 • kruthoz@aol.com • MI • Tchr • St Michael Wayne MI • (734)728-3315 • (CQ 1993)

**HOEFT REBEKAH J** (734)326-9365
38710 Covington Dr Wayme MI 48184 • rjhoeft99@netscape.net • MI • Tchr • Hosanna-Tabor Redford MI • (313)937-2424 • (AA 1998)

**HOEFT STACY J** (313)937-4089
11421 Arnold Redford MI 48239 • dshoeft@hotmail.com • MI • Tchr • Hosanna-Tabor Redford MI • (313)937-2424 • (MQ 1996)

**HOEHNE EMIL E** (314)821-0157
337 Crest Ave Kirkwood MO 63122-5642 • MO • EM • (RF 1953 MAR)

**HOEHNE MATTHEW J** (847)991-1492
503 S Benton St Palatine IL 60067-6905 • mhoehne@pop-lcms.org • NI • Mem C • Prince Peace Palatine IL • (847)359-3451 • (RF 1992 MCMU)

**HOELTER STEPHEN W** (312)421-3130
30517 Minton Livonia MI 48150-2938 • MI • Tchr • St Paul Farmington Hills MI • (248)474-2488 • (S 1972 MMU)

**HOENER JANET L** (303)973-6714
7277 S Allison Way Littleton CO 80128 • jschmidt@power-online.net • RM • Tchr • Denver Lutheran High Denver CO • (303)934-2345 • (S 1975 MA)

**HOEPPNER BETH A** 852-2812-6544
74 D Repulse Bay Rd Repulse Bay HONG KONG • bhoeppner@hkis.edu.hk • NOW • 09/1990 09/1999 • (RF 1970 MS)

**HOEPPNER DAVID A** (852)812-6544
74 D Repulse Bay Rd Repulse Bay HONG KONG • dhoeppner@hkis.edu.hk • NOW • S Miss • Northwest Portland OR • (RF 1970 MS)

**HOERAUF KAREN F** (810)247-5177
15134 Congress Dr Sterling Heights MI 48313-4423 • MI • Tchr • St John Fraser MI • (810)294-8740 • (S 1973 MED)

**HOERAUF NORMAN A** (410)586-9734
5520 Wells Cove Dr Saint Leonard MD 20685-3015 • nhoerauf@chesapeake.net • SE • EM • (RF 1953 MA)

**HOFFER ANGIE N** (310)442-9120
1326 Centinela Ave Apt 9 Los Angeles CA 90025 • PSW • Tchr • Pilgrim Santa Monica CA • (310)829-2239 • (PO 1998)

**HOFFERT CORINNE**
9123 Uppercove Cir Houston TX 77064-7012 • choffert@oslschool.org • TX • Tchr • Our Savior Houston TX • (713)290-8277 • (RF 1975 MS)

**HOFFERT ERICK K** (281)897-0031
9123 Uppercove Cir Houston TX 77064-7012 • rhoffert@rae.katy.isd.tenet.edu • TX • 11/1996 11/1999 • (RF 1975)

**HOFFMAN HENRY R II** (414)464-2013
9626 W Metcalf Pl Milwaukee WI 53222 • hoffmanlclhs@worldnet.att.net • SW • Tchr • South Wisconsin Milwaukee WI • (414)464-8100 • (RF 1996)

**HOFFMAN JOHN LOUIS DR**
C/O Concordia University 1530 Concordia West Irvine CA 92612-3299 • john.hoffman@cui.edu • PSW • SHS/C • Pacific Southwest Irvine CA • (949)854-3232 • (S 1994 MA PHD)

**HOFFMAN LADONNA RUTH** (708)452-8366
2001 N 74th Ct Elmwood Park IL 60707-3111 • NI • P/Tchr • Our Saviour Chicago IL • (773)736-1157 • (RF 1970)

**HOFFMAN LANCE C** (219)749-4856
4017 Thorton Dr Fort Wayne IN 46815-7658 • IN • Tchr • Concordia LHS Fort Wayne IN • (219)483-1102 • (MQ 1990)

**HOFFMAN MARY ANN** (760)375-7444
731 N Sanders St Ridgecrest CA 93555-3527 • PSW • Prin • Ridgecrest Ridgecrest CA • (760)375-9121 • (S 1965)

**HOFFMAN NANCY L**
522 S 1st Ave Wausau WI 54401 • NW • Tchr • Trinity Wausau WI • (715)848-0166 • (SP 1977)

**HOFFMAN PATRICIA ANN DR** (714)559-4856
77 Foxhollow Irvine CA 92614-7965 • hoffmapa@cui.edu • PSW • SHS/C • Pacific Southwest Irvine CA • (949)854-3232 • (RF 1976 MED PHD)

**HOFFMAN SANDRA E** (503)645-6414
20840 NW Wapinitia Pl Portland OR 97229-1032 • soffman@ipns.com • NOW • Tchr • Forest Hills Cornelius OR • (503)359-4853 • (S 1974)

**HOFFMAN SARAH R**
353 SE 43rd Ave Hillsboro OR 97123-5909 • NOW • Tchr • Forest Hills Cornelius OR • (503)359-4853 • (PO 1982)

**HOFFMAN SUSAN L**
C/O St Luke Lutheran Church 13552 Goldencrest St Westminster CA 92683-3119 • PSW • Tchr • St Luke Westminster CA • (714)893-8074 • (S 1979)

**HOFFMANN DEBORAH A** (206)439-0804
219 S 156th St # 215 Burien WA 98148 • NOW • Tchr • Pilgrim Bellevue WA • (425)454-1162 • (PO 1983)

**HOFFMANN ELAINE D**
C/O Peace Lutheran Church 218 S Bloomington St Greencastle IN 46135-1733 • IN • Mem C • Peace Greencastle IN • (765)653-6995 • (RF 1964)

**HOFFMANN LINDA L** (262)786-1203
20835 Brook Park Ct Brookfield WI 53045-4645 • SW • Tchr • Elm Grove Elm Grove WI • (262)797-2970 • (CQ 1994)

**HOFFMANN RONALD A** (630)584-7782
913 S 7th St Saint Charles IL 60174-3945 • NI • EM • (S 1956 MA)

**HOFFMANN SHAWN M**
103 S Towanda #6 Normal IL 61761 • CI • Tchr • Trinity Bloomington IL • (309)829-7513 • (RF 1995)

**HOFFMANN SUSAN MICHELLE** (309)828-4006
2005 Tracy Dr #4 Bloomington IL 61704 • smh2@trinluth.org • CI • Tchr • Trinity Bloomington IL • (309)829-7513 • (RF 1997)

**HOFFMANN WILLIAM A** (312)895-4249
18452 Roy St Lansing IL 60438-3234 • IN • EM • (RF 1954 MA)

**HOFFSCHNEIDER BONNIE JEAN** (805)983-1115
609 Holly Ave Oxnard CA 93030-1933 • PSW • Tchr • St John Oxnard CA • (805)983-0330 • (MQ 1986)

**HOFFSCHNEIDER GERTRUDE** (805)271-0356
5321 Barrymore Dr Oxnard CA 93033-8535 • PSW • EM • (S 1953 MA)

**HOFFSCHNEIDER JOEL T**
C/O Concordia Lutheran 4245 Lake Ave Fort Wayne IN 46815-7219 • IN • Tchr • Concordia Fort Wayne IN • (219)422-2429 • (RF 1988)

**HOFFSCHNEIDER LARRY E** (972)416-5218
2218 Cedar Cir Carrollton TX 75006-1913 • lhoffschneider@compuserve.com • TX • Prin • Holy Cross Dallas TX • (214)358-4396 • (RF 1966 MED)

**HOFFSCHNEIDER NANCY M** (972)416-5218
2218 Cedar Cir Carrollton TX 75006-1913 • TX • Tchr • Holy Cross Dallas TX • (214)358-4396 • (S 1968 MED)

**HOFFSCHNEIDER STEVEN L** (972)625-5061
4829 Arbor Glen Rd The Colony TX 75056 • shoff@popcs.net • TX • Tchr • Prince Of Peace Carrollton TX • (972)447-9887 • (S 1991 MED)

**HOFMAN AMY R** (785)562-2046
1704 Jenkins St Marysville KS 66508-1348 • KS • Tchr • Good Shepherd Marysville KS • (785)562-3181 • (SP 1973)

**HOFMAN MARK D** (314)832-1476
8530 Elgin Ave St Louis MO 63123-3629 • hofmanm@csl.edu • MO • SHS/C • Missouri Saint Louis MO • (314)317-4550 • (S 1993)

**HOFMAN SUE E** (954)966-3739
1904 N 39th Ave Hollywood FL 33021-4841 • FG • Tchr • St Mark Hollywood FL • (954)922-7572 • (S 1965)

**HOFMAN WILLIAM W** (402)643-9510
314 N 4th St #4 Seward NE 68434-1820 • NEB • SHS/C • Nebraska Seward NE • (S 1998)

**HOFMANN SANDRA E** (201)664-7667
645 Ridgewood Rd Washington Tp NJ 07675-4956 • NJ • Tchr • Zion Westwood NJ • (201)664-8060 • (RF 1969)

**HOFMEISTER KURT R** (517)671-0053
3389 Brentway Dr Bay City MI 48706-3323 • MI • Tchr • Valley Saginaw MI • (517)790-1676 • (CQ 1994)

**HOFT BETHANY CHRISTINE** (618)343-1815
816 Westwood Village Maryville IL 62062 • petros8@juno.com • SI • Tchr • Southern Illinois Belleville IL • (MQ 1997)

**HOGAN DIANE S**
1308 Fordham Ct Bel Air MD 21014-2006 • SE • Tchr • St Paul Kingsville MD • (410)592-8100 • (RF 1982)

**HOGAN KIMBERLY ANN**
2110 W Arthur Ave #2 Chicago IL 60645-5502 • EN • Tchr • Bethesda Chicago IL • (312)743-0800 • (RF 1990)

**HOGER CHARLES E** (714)637-8094
5344 E Gerda Dr Anaheim CA 92807-3111 • cehoger@earthlink.net • PSW • EM • (RF 1952 MA MS PHD)

**HOHENSTEIN REBECCA A** (314)349-0765
725 Settlers Rd Fenton MO 63026 • MO • Tchr • St Paul Saint Louis MO • (314)822-0447 • (RF 1978)

**HOHLE GWENDOLYN L** (314)822-2960
8739 Gayle Ave Saint Louis MO 63126-1810 • hohle@parabdicvideo.com • MO • Mem C • Concordia Kirkwood MO • (314)822-7772 • (AU 1983)

**HOHLE R LEROY** (409)540-3906
608 Edgewood Ave Giddings TX 78942 • TX • EM • (S 1954 MED)

**HOHLFELD ELIZABETH** (309)686-0769
820 W Purtscher Dr Peoria IL 61614-7011 • CI • Tchr • Concordia Peoria IL • (309)691-8921 • (S 1965)

**HOHNBAUM JAMES M** (817)469-9846
2009 Ford St Arlington TX 76013-4929 • TX • Prin • Grace Arlington TX • (817)274-1654 • (S 1968 MA)

**HOHNSTADT REBECCA S**
11921 N Granville Rd Mequon WI 53097 • rebeck64@aol.com • SW • Mem C • Trinity Mequon WI • (414)242-2045 • (AA 1986)

**HOHNSTADT SHARI R** (810)786-0925
55147 Belle Rose Dr Shelby Twp MI 48316-5202 • sharidan@tir.com • MI • Tchr • Michigan Ann Arbor MI • (S 1983)

**HOJNACKI JOAN DOROTHY** (414)545-1529
3326 S 93rd St Milwaukee WI 53227-4307 • honjon3326@msn.com • SW • Tchr • Blessed Savior New Berlin WI • (414)786-6465 • (SP 1980)

**HOLDEMAN JEAN A** (909)277-1828
22905 Copper Ridge Dr Corona CA 92883-9163 • PSW • Tchr • Mount Calvary Diamond Bar CA • (909)861-2740 • (SP 1984 MA)

**HOLL MARY K** (949)786-5430
9 Marigold Irvine CA 92614-5471 • holl@cui.edu • PSW • SHS/C • Pacific Southwest Irvine CA • (949)854-3232 • (RF 1980 MA EDD)

**HOLLATZ JACOB D** (651)365-6319
3921 N Valley View #302 Eagan MN 55122 • MNS • Tchr • Trin Lone Oak Eagan MN • (651)454-7235 • (SP 2000)

**HOLLE MARY K** (717)993-0008
10 Firebox Ct Stewartstown PA 17363-8313 • marylieske@hotmail.com • SE • 10/1993 10/1997 • (BR 1986)

**HOLLENBECK DIANE RUTH** (303)592-1882
6288 Vance Sst Arvada CO 80003-4832 • RM • 06/1999 • (S 1986)

**HOLLENBECK MARK**
6288 Vance St Arvada CO 80003-4832 • RM • Tchr • Denver Lutheran High Denver CO • (303)934-2345 • (IV 1999)

**HOLLER NORA M** (708)627-1194
601 E Sunset Ave Lombard IL 60148-1862 • NI • Tchr • St John Lombard IL • (630)629-2515 • (RF 1980)

**HOLLIDAY CYNTHIA R** (352)629-0297
1537 SE 27th St Apt G Ocala FL 34471 • dcholliday@hitter.net • FG • Tchr • St John Ocala FL • (352)629-1794 • (RF 1997)

**HOLLIDAY ROBERT D** (314)487-0570
10807 Atterbury Dr Saint Louis MO 63123-7119 • MO • Tchr • LHS South Saint Louis MO • (314)631-1400 • (CQ 1973 MS)

**HOLLRAH DEANNA S** (810)469-0168
294 Jones Mt Clemens MI 48043 • MI • Tchr • Trinity Clinton Township MI • (810)468-8511 • (S 1968 MED)

**HOLLRAH DEBBIE L** (203)798-9426
19 Beechwood Dr Danbury CT 06810-7005 • dhollrah@juno.com • NE • 11/1995 11/1999 • (BR 1985 MS)

**HOLLRAH JOYCE E** (636)394-2625
149 Cumberland Park Ct Apt H Ballwin MO 63011-3058 • jhollrah@stpaulsdesperes.org • MO • Tchr • St Paul Des Peres MO • (314)822-2771 • (RF 1960)

**HOLMES DENNIS L** (209)334-4087
1818 Colette St Lodi CA 95242-2501 • dlholmes@softcom.net • CNH • 08/1999 • (S 1974)

**HOLMES VIRGINIA MARALYN** (954)428-7305
4730 NW 75th St Coconut Creek FL 33073 • beachnote@aol.com • FG • Mem C • Peace Fort Lauderdale FL • (954)772-8010 • (S 1975)

**HOLMQUIST ERIN R**
1229 Wisteria Dr SE Olympia WA 98513-6657 • NOW • Tchr • Faith Lacey WA • (360)491-1733 • (PO 1985)

**HOLMQUIST JOELLE MARIE** (208)528-8903
2197 Meppen Dr Idaho Falls ID 83401 • jrehberg@hotmail.com • NOW • Tchr • Hope Idaho Falls ID • (208)529-8080 • (MQ 1996)

**HOLSCHEN CARL DR** (314)355-8148
6635 Mignon Dr Florissant MO 63033-5031 • holschcc@slu.edu • MO • Tchr • Lutheran North Saint Louis MO • (314)389-3100 • (RF 1970 MS EDD)

**HOLSCHEN HOWARD H** (314)353-3233
6373 Bancroft Ave Saint Louis MO 63109-2249 • hopeluth@stlnet.com • MO • Prin • Hope Saint Louis MO • (314)832-1850 • (RF 1964 MAT)

**HOLSCHEN JUDITH A** (314)353-3233
6373 Bancroft Ave Saint Louis MO 63109-2249 • jholsc@aol.com • MO • Tchr • Hope Saint Louis MO • (314)832-1850 • (RF 1981 MAT)

**HOLST LARRY RICHARD** (816)795-6015
18209 E 25th Ter Independence MO 64057 • MO • Tchr • Messiah Independence MO • (816)254-9409 • (S 1968 MA)

**HOLSTE CYNTHIA KAYE** (423)637-1940
3100 E Towne Mall Cir Apt D238 Knoxville TN 37924-2039 • tcholste@mindspring.com • MDS • Tchr • First Knoxville TN • (423)524-0308 • (S 1995)

**HOLSTE HERMAN M DR** (517)269-6846
1686 N Pinnebog Rd Elkton MI 48731-9778 • hbholste@bau-net.com • MI • EM • (S 1951 MS PHD)

**HOLSTE KENNETH E** (406)257-4374
375 Third Ave W N Kalispell MT 59901 • MT • Tchr • Trinity Kalispell MT • (406)257-6716 • (S 1969 MED)

**HOLSTE RICHARD W** (319)233-7052
1405 Oregon St Waterloo IA 50702 • IE • Tchr • Immanuel Waterloo IA • (319)233-7052 • (S 1982)

**HOLSTE ROBERT W** (812)426-1568
1262 Sheffield Dr Evansville IN 47710-3858 • IN • EM • (S 1954 MA)

**HOLSTE TIMOTHY JAMES** (423)637-1940
3100 E Towne Mall Cir Apt D238 Knoxville TN 37924-2039 • tcholste@mindspring.com • MDS • Tchr • First Knoxville TN • (423)524-0308 • (S 1994)

**HOLSTEIN HERTHA** (708)383-3592
926 Wisconsin Ave Oak Park IL 60304-1859 • NI • EM • (RF 1961 MA)

**HOLSTEN LLOYD E** (210)474-0123
142 Fontaine Heights Rd Benton KY 42025-6207 • MO • EM • (S 1961 MED)

**HOLT DANIEL V** (650)877-1578
2860 Tipperary Ave South San Francisco CA 94080-5360 • EN • Tchr • West Portal San Francisco CA • (415)665-6330 • (RF 1985 MED)

**HOLT JEFFREY S** (920)458-0924
1123 Bell Ave Sheboygan WI 53083-4850 • holt@lutheranhigh.com • SW • Tchr • Lutheran HS Sheboygan WI • (920)452-3323 • (MQ 1995)

**HOLTAN ALICE M** (708)965-3744
7101 Foster St Morton Grove IL 60053-1215 • NI • EM • (RF 1961)

**HOLTEN BEN H** (507)246-5183
RR 2 Box 159 Nicollet MN 56074-9751 • MNS • Tchr • Immanuel Courtland MN • (507)359-2534 • (SP 1986)

**HOLTHUS ALLEN D***
C/O St Marks Lutheran Church PO Box 69 New Germany MN 55367-0069 • MNS • 05/1998 05/2000 • (SP 1967 MA)

**HOLTHUS TERRY W** (402)643-3850
54 Lincoln St Seward NE 68434-1559 • NEB • Tchr • St John Seward NE • (402)643-4535 • (S 1976 MED)

**HOLTMEIER JOHN F** (612)442-5896
300 E 1st St Waconia MN 55387-1530 • MNS • 01/2000 • (S 1966 MA MS)

**HOLTMEIER MICHAEL G** (314)970-3481
1268 Poseidon Ct Saint Peters MO 63376-5229 • MO • 03/1989 03/2000 • (S 1980 MAR MA)

**HOLTMEIER RONALD G** (314)561-1150
9 Fox Wood Dr O Fallon MO 63366-6429 • MO • EM • (CQ 1967)

**HOLTZ CARLA M** (217)868-5810
15433 N Siemer Rd Effingham IL 62401 • CI • Mem C • St John Effingham IL • (217)342-4334 • (CQ 1997)

**HOLTZ ROBERT E** (651)484-8832
668 Overlook Dr Roseville MN 55113-2177 • holtz@csp.edu • MNS • EM • (S 1955 MA DED)

**HOLTZEN LEE ROY DR** (402)643-6037
540 Bader Ave Seward NE 68434-1128 • lholtzen@alltel.net • NEB • EM • (S 1952 MED PHD)

**HOLTZEN MARY KATHERINE** (734)457-2583
207 Crampton Dr Monroe MI 48162-3515 • holtzen@foxberry.net • MI • Tchr • Trinity Monroe MI • (734)241-1160 • (AA 1988 MA)

**HOLTZEN MILTON P** (402)768-7102
642 N 6th St Hebron NE 68370-1009 • NEB • EM • (S 1944)

**HOLTZEN RICHARD OTTO** (734)457-2583
207 Crampton Dr Monroe MI 48162-3515 • holtzen@foxberry.net • MI • Tchr • Trinity Monroe MI • (734)241-1160 • (S 1983)

**HOLZERLAND ARNOLD W** (573)732-5776
PO Box 218 Bourbon MO 65441-0218 • MO • EM • (S 1977)

**HOLZERLAND BARBARA A** (573)732-5776
PO Box 218 Bourbon MO 65441-0218 • MO • EM • (S 1960)

**HOLZHEIMER ALLEN JEROME II**
1622 N 27th Pl Sheboygan WI 53081 • SW • P/Tchr • Immanuel Sheboygan WI • (920)452-7266 • (MQ 1993)

**HOMAN LYDIA** (618)826-2473
120 Clifford Dr Chester IL 62233-2833 • SI • EM • (S 1972)

**HOMP MICHELLE DIANN** (402)643-4423
1210 Eastridge Seward NE 68434 • mhomp@seward.ccsn.edu • NEB • SHS/C • Nebraska Seward NE • (S 1991 MS PHD)

**HONIG LUCY B** (402)761-3525
1281 210th Seward NE 68434-8093 • EN • EM • (S 1984)

**HONIG MARTIN L** (402)761-3525
1281 210th Seward NE 68434 • NI • EM • (S 1962)

**HONOREE CHERYL C** (504)652-7379
7 Fagot Loop La Place LA 70068-5427 • SO • Tchr • Faith Harahan LA • (504)737-9554 • (RF 1980)

**HONOREE CHERYL L** (412)271-4983
141 Sumner Ave Pittsburgh PA 15221 • EA • Tchr • Christ Pittsburgh PA • (412)271-7173 • (S 1981)

**HOOD KIMBERLY L** (206)243-0410
11616 23rd Ave SW Seattle WA 98146-2503 • NOW • Tchr • Hope Seattle WA • (206)935-8500 • (IV 1988 MED)

**HOOLAHAN CONNIE E**
1840 Scobee Ave SW Decatur AL 35603 • FG • 10/1999 • (RF 1989)

**HOOPER DEBORAH L** (626)335-1977
832 E Ada Ave Glendora CA 91741-3645 • PSW • Tchr • Hope Glendora CA • (626)335-5315 • (CQ 1997 MS)

**HOOPER MARY E** (619)656-9025
376 Canyon Ridge Dr Bonita CA 91902-4263 • PSW • Tchr • Pilgrim Chula Vista CA • (619)420-6233 • (CQ 1993 MED)

**HOOPER SUSAN L** (810)232-1299
3633 Brentwood Flint MI 48503-2343 • rsjchoop@tir.com • MI • 02/1997 02/2000 • (S 1973)

**HOPFENSPERGER EMILY ANNE** (773)728-6218
2819 W Summerdale Chicago IL 60625 • NI • Tchr • St Philip Chicago IL • (773)493-3865 • (RF 2000)

**HOPFENSPERGER NICK AARON** (773)728-6218
2819 W Summerdale Chicago IL 60625 • NI • Tchr • St Philip Chicago IL • (773)493-3865 • (RF 2000)

**HOPKINS SOFIA KOVALENKO** (573)636-2604
1015 Roseridge Cir Jefferson City MO 65101-3639 • skovalenko@aol.com • MO • Tchr • Trinity Jefferson City MO • (573)636-7807 • (CQ 1996 MA)

**HOPKINS TAMMY A**
3950 W 77th Pl #11 Merrillville IN 46410 • IN • Tchr • St Paul Munster IN • (219)836-6270 • (MQ 1993)

**HOPKIRK PAMELA J** (714)835-7294
1509 N Hathaway St Santa Ana CA 92701-2632 • hopkirks@home.com • PSW • Tchr • St John Orange CA • (714)288-4406 • (CQ 1993 MA)

**HOPMANN ROBERT P** (623)915-2883
6540 W Butler Dr Glendale AZ 85302-4313 • NI • EM • (S 1952 MA LITTD)

**HOPP JERRY L** (517)686-2767
6104 W S Saginaw Rd Bay City MI 48706 • MI • P/Tchr • St Paul Bay City MI • (517)684-4450 • (RF 1965 MA)

**HOPPE CARL E** (708)396-2935
2136 W 121st Pl Blue Island IL 60406-1402 • EN • Tchr • Grace English Chicago IL • (773)637-2250 • (RF 1975)

**HOPPER MARILYN** (219)626-2787
10428 E County Road 450 S Walton IN 46994-9039 • IN • Tchr • St John Peru IN • (765)473-6659 • (SP 1967 MS)

**HOPPMANN NORMAN G** (402)563-0438
3910 87th St Columbus NE 68601-8012 • nghoppm@megavision.com • NEB • EM • (S 1960 MED)

**HORAK JOHN BOHDAN** (810)731-8069
7622 Jeanette Dr Shelby Township MI 48317 • MI • Tchr • Trinity Utica MI • (810)731-4490 • (S 1983 MMU)

**HORKEY MARSHA B** (402)494-7680
513 E 39th St South Sioux City NE 68776-3447 • NEB • 07/1999 • (SP 1978 MED)

**HORN JANE ELIZABETH**
10109 Zenith Rd Bloomington MN 55431-2738 • MNS • Mem C • St Michael Bloomington MN • (952)831-5276 • (SP 1973)

**HORN LESLEY ANN** (512)453-2765
7210 Hardy Dr #A Austin TX 78757-2207 • lesann70@hotmail.com • TX • Tchr • Redeemer Austin TX • (512)459-1500 • (AU 1994)

**HORNE LAURIE A** (414)427-9242
11120 W Grange Ave Hales Corners WI 53130-1230 • EN • Mem C • Hales Corners Hales Corners WI • (414)529-6700 • (MQ 1988)

**HORRIGAN KAREN JANE** (913)236-8184
5130 W 72nd Ter Prairie Village KS 66208-2419 • mkhorrigan@dellnet.com • KS • 04/1996 04/1999 • (WN 1985)

**HORST LEROY A** (303)371-3557
4800 Quentin St Denver CO 80239-4443 • RM • EM • (S 1960 MA)

**HORTON NANCY LOUISE** (254)527-4212
PO Box 5 Schwertner TX 76573-0005 • jnhorton@juno.com • TX • Tchr • St Paul Thorndale TX • (512)898-2711 • (AU 1982)

**HORVATH KARA MARIE** (618)343-1708
402C N Hesperia Collinsville IL 62234 • SI • Tchr • Holy Cross Collinsville IL • (618)344-3145 • (MQ 1999)

**HORVATH KENNETH E** (636)296-1373
3273 Rosedale Dr Arnold MO 63010-3757 • khorvath76@hotmail.com • MO • Tchr • Green Park Lemay MO • (314)544-4248 • (S 1976 MAT)

**HORVATH TERA DEANNE** (815)229-1521
1512 14th St #1 Rockford IL 61104-5541 • terahorv@aol.com • NI • Tchr • St Paul Rockford IL • (815)965-3335 • (MQ 1997)

**HOSMON MICHELE M**
4412 Stringtown Rd Evansville IN 47711-2276 • IN • Tchr • Evansville Evansville IN • (812)424-7252 • (S 1976)

**HOTZ LEROY F** (626)919-4678
1045 E Cameron Ave West Covina CA 91790-3848 • bobbe3@juno.com • PSW • EM • (S 1954 MA)

**HOUSE DAVID A** (254)939-3412
1503 North Beal Belton TX 76513 • TX • Prin • Grace Killeen TX • (254)634-4424 • (AU 1987)

**HOUSE JAMES L** (636)938-9225
193 Walden Dr Eureka MO 63025-1128 • jhouse@stmarkseureka.org • MO • P/Tchr • St Mark Eureka MO • (636)938-4432 • (S 1979 MS)

**HOUSE JOSEPH A** (330)923-4216
2230 16th St Cuyahoga Falls OH 44223-1934 • OH • EM • (S 1955 MED)

**HOUSE ROBERT L** (210)681-8800
9302 Bianca St San Antonio TX 78250-2540 • TX • EM • (RF 1954)

**HOUSEHOLDER CAROL A** (970)674-0551
455 Pelican Cove Windsor CO 80550 • PSW • Tchr • Fountain Life Tucson AZ • (520)747-1213 • (S 1962 MA MS)

**HOVEY DANIEL R** (414)268-0904
120 E Woodruff St Port Washington WI 53074 • dhovey@pwsb.com • SW • Tchr • Trinity Mequon WI • (414)242-2045 • (MQ 1998)

**HOWARD KAREN J** (920)451-7061
1632 Ohio Ave Sheboygan WI 53081-6619 • SW • Tchr • Trinity Sheboygan WI • (920)458-8248 • (RF 1975)

**HOWARD KAY H** (812)376-7871
1162 Kevin Dr Apt 2D Columbus IN 47201-6187 • kyhoward@seidata.com • IN • Tchr • St Peter Columbus IN • (812)372-5266 • (RF 1979)

**HOWARD KENNETH D** (920)451-7061
1632 Ohio Ave Sheboygan WI 53081-6619 • SW • Tchr • Trinity Sheboygan WI • (920)458-8248 • (RF 1975 MA)

**HOWARD NANCY JOYCE** (714)991-5546
2220 E Nura Ave Anaheim CA 92806-4632 • PSW • Tchr • Prince Of Peace Anaheim CA • (714)774-0993 • (S 1973)

**HOWARD TERESA L**
515 John Muir Dr #A517 San Francisco CA 94132 • EN • Trinity Toledo OH • (S 1994)

**HOWELL JEFFREY PAUL** (708)889-1867
17340 Greenbay Ave Lansing IL 60438-1336 • jho3982871@aol.com • NI • P/Tchr • Zion Chicago IL • (773)928-3530 • (S 1988)

**HOWELL VICKI LYNN** (715)926-5025
551 W Main St Mondovi WI 54755 • vlh@marten.com • MNS • 05/1999 • (SP 1992)

**HOWER CAROL D** (314)451-5471
230 Killarney Ln Pacific MO 63069-2469 • chower@stjohnsellisville.org • MO • Tchr • St John Ellisville MO • (314)394-4100 • (RF 1974)

**HOY HEATHER I** (630)782-0958
433 N Third Ave Villa Park IL 60181 • heather³hoy@walther.com • NI • Tchr • Walther LHS Melrose Park IL • (708)344-0404 • (RF 1996)

**HOY LYNN C** (815)464-0736
705 Vermont Rd W Frankfort IL 60423-1217 • lh125@prodigy.net • NI • Tchr • St Paul Chicago Heights IL • (708)754-4492 • (RF 1968 MA)

**HOYE ALLEN C** (920)853-3913
54 N 3rd St Hilbert WI 54129 • SW • P/Tchr • St Peter Hilbert WI • (920)853-3851 • (RF 1970)

**HOYER DEXTER C** (319)390-4111
4630 Pearl Ave NW Cedar Rapids IA 52405 • dchatrcs@juno.com • IE • Prin • Trinity Cedar Rapids IA • (319)366-1569 • (S 1969 MS)

**HOYER RACHEL C** (636)861-0958
1831 Strawberry Ridge Dr Ballwin MO 63021-7775 • rachel@thehoyers.com • MO • 12/1999 • (S 1987 MA)

**HOYT ADELE M** (714)978-3340
2100 W Palmyra Ave Apt 50 Orange CA 92868-3744 • PSW • Tchr • St John Orange CA • (714)288-4406 • (S 1968)

**HOYT SHELLY DIANE** (210)685-9228
5100 USAA Blvd #2001 San Antonio TX 78240 • TX • Tchr • Shepherd Of The Hill San Antonio TX • (210)614-3741 • (AU 1999)

**HOYUM JERRY LEE** (972)406-4811
12247 Cox Ln Dallas TX 75234 • jhoyum@flash.net • TX • Tchr • Holy Cross Dallas TX • (214)358-4396 • (S 1985)

**HOYUM LYNETTE M**
12247 Cox Ln Dallas TX 75234 • jhoyum@flash.net • TX • Tchr • Holy Cross Dallas TX • (214)358-4396 • (S 1981)

**HRDLICKA LEROY A** (630)495-1056
2S631 Gray Ave Lombard IL 60148-5140 • NI • Tchr • St John Wheaton IL • (630)668-0701 • (RF 1969 MA)

**HRDLICKA RHONDA** (515)628-8718
1429 Hazel St Pella IA 50219-1001 • IE • 04/1990 04/2000 • (SP 1985)

**HU ANNA YING NA**
Concordia Intern Sch Shanghai Jinquiao Plot S2 Huang Yang Rd Pudong Shanghai 201206 CHINA • EN • Tchr • West Portal San Francisco CA • (415)661-0242 • (RF 1980 MA)

**HUANG CYNTHIA** (415)668-1065
523-6th Ave San Francisco CA 94118 • EN • Tchr • West Portal San Francisco CA • (415)665-6330 • (IV 1998)

**HUBACEK CAROL L** (219)865-6054
1845 Robinhood Blvd Schererville IN 46375-1825 • burly@netnitco.net • IN • Prin • Trinity Crown Point IN • (219)663-1586 • (RF 1970 MS)

**HUBACH RILEY** (918)274-0279
8722 N 121st E Ave Owasso OK 74055 • lightyear36@yahoo.com • NEB • Tchr • Trinity Fremont NE • (402)721-5959 • (S 1998)

**HUBACH TIMOTHY P**
650 Voiles Pl Brighton CO 80601 • reddirt@infowest.com • RM • Tchr • Zion Brighton CO • (303)659-2339 • (S 1970)

**HUBBARD TERRY L** (920)893-5114
106 Evergreen Rd Plymouth WI 53073-4137 • tdthub@aol.com • SW • Prin • St John Plymouth WI • (920)893-3071 • (SP 1971 MS)

**HUBER NORBERT A** (310)675-4017
13919 Eucalyptus Ave Hawthorne CA 90250-6825 • hhuber.telis • PSW • 08/1998 08/2000 • (CQ 1984 MA)

**HUBMEIER BRUCE N** (734)281-0784
18143 Mulberry St Riverview MI 48192-7628 • hubmeier@home.com • MI • Mem C • St Paul Trenton MI • (734)676-1565 • (RF 1968)

**HUBMEIER LINDA E** (313)281-0784
18143 Mulberry St Riverview MI 48192-7628 • hubmeier@home.com • MI • Tchr • Christ The King Southgate MI • (734)285-9697 • (RF 1969)

**HUBNER PATRICIA J** (765)893-4630
10577 W State Rd 28 West Lebanon IN 47991-8064 • (Hellwege) • CI • Tchr • Danville Danville IL • (217)442-5036 • (S 1967 MSED)

**HUDNALL GAIL A**
1140 W Lark Dr Chandler AZ 85248-2500 • PSW • Tchr • Christ Greenfield Gilbert AZ • (480)892-8521 • (CQ 1984)

**HUDSON ANNEKE OLIVIA** (314)991-8686
54 Roan Ln Saint Louis MO 63124-1480 • SI • Tchr • Good Shepherd Collinsville IL • (618)344-3153 • (RF 1999)

**HUEBNER LELAND DALE** (402)477-6170
5330 NW 4th Lincoln NE 68521 • NEB • Prin • Trinity Lincoln NE • (402)466-1800 • (S 1970 MED)

**HUEBNER TODD ALAN** (516)625-6904
C/O Long Island Luth Jr/Sr HS 131 Brookville Rd Glen Head NY 11545-3329 • toddalan68@hotmail.com • AT • SHS/C • Atlantic Bronxville NY • (914)337-5700 • (MQ 1990)

**HUEBSCHMAN RAYMOND DR*** (402)643-4444
520 Bader Ave Seward NE 68434-1128 • rhuebschman@seward.cune.edu • NEB • SHS/C • Nebraska Seward NE • (S 1963 MA EDD)

**HUEBSCHMAN TIMOTHY PAUL** (920)892-6780
216 Division St Plymouth WI 53073-1839 • thuebschman@hotmail.com • SW • Mem C • St John Plymouth WI • (920)893-3071 • (S 1989)

**HUEHN BARBARA J**
2-I Winesap Ct Baltimore MD 21228 • hueinn@aol.com • SE • Tchr • St Paul Catonsville MD • (410)747-1897 • (RF 1974 MED)

**HUELLER DANIEL C**
316 S St Charles Ave Joplin MO 64801-1826 • MO • Tchr • Martin Luther Joplin MO • (417)624-1403 • (MQ 1993)

**HUELSMAN STEPHANIE KAREN**
748 Debra Dr Des Plaines IL 60016 • NI • Tchr • The Ark Highland Park IL • (847)831-2224 • (RF 1994)

**HUELSNITZ INGRID M** (507)835-3337
39510 Reeds Lake Rd Waseca MN 56093-4115 • MNS • Tchr • Trinity Janesville MN • (507)231-6646 • (S 1987)

**HUEMOELLER KRISTIN**
2731 San Leandro Blvd #102 San Leandro CA 94578 • CNH • Tchr • Calvary San Lorenzo CA • (510)278-2598 • (IV 1998)

**HUFFORD AMY JOY** (630)681-8028
0N631 Knollwood Dr Wheaton IL 60187 • NI • Tchr • St John Wheaton IL • (630)668-0701 • (RF 1990)

**HUGHES DONITA G** (402)643-2619
444 Locust Ave # 1 Seward NE 68434-1632 • dgh2129@seward.cusn.edu • NEB • Tchr • St John Seward NE • (402)643-4535 • (S 1973 MA)

**HUGHES JUDITH DARLENE** (248)356-2214
26245 W 9 Mile Rd Southfield MI 48034-3405 • teaisgood@webtv.net • MI • Tchr • St Michael Wayne MI • (734)728-3315 • (RF 1965)

**HUGHES KATHRYN MYRA** (203)849-3289
46 Silvermine Ave Norwalk CT 06850-2008 • S • Tchr • St Paul Westport CT • (203)227-7920 • (S 1990)

**HUGHES KIMBERLY E**
1005 Ridgewood Dr #2 Fort Wayne IN 46805-5735 • IN • Tchr • Zion Fort Wayne IN • (219)744-1389 • (MQ 1986)

**HUGHEY LOIS EILEEN** (503)690-3162
15868 NW West Union Rd #46 Portland OR 97229 • davelois@earthlink.net • NOW • Tchr • Pilgrim Beaverton OR • (503)644-4656 • (PO 1992)

**HUHNER MARGARET** (253)912-9408
6445 A Cooper Dr Ft Lewis WA 98433 • gscrazy@juno.com • NOW • 05/1987 05/2000 • (S 1984)

**HULL DEBRA A** (863)647-0901
317 Hillside Dr Lakeland FL 33803-5126 • FG • 10/1997 10/1999 • (RF 1987)

**HULL DEON L*** (863)647-0901
317 Hillside Dr Lakeland FL 33803-5126 • FG • 07/1999 • (RF 1988)

**HULL RENEE N** (312)598-7605
15456 Alameda Ave Oak Forest IL 60452-1808 • NI • Tchr • St Paul Oak Lawn IL • (708)423-1040 • (RF 1982)

**HUMMEL CLIFFORD W** (716)693-5611
514 Duane Dr N Tonawanda NY 14120-4140 • EA • Prin • St Matthew North Tonawanda NY • (716)692-6862 • (RF 1970 MS)

**HUMMEL RUTH** (760)746-5945
2166 Shadetree Ln Escondido CA 92029-5305 • rshummel@home.com • PSW • EM • (RF 1951 MED MAR)

**HUMPHREY ROXANE M** (714)538-3901
2517 N Hathaway St Santa Ana CA 92705-6731 • humphrey@lanset.com • PSW • Tchr • Holy Trinity Hacienda Heights CA • (626)333-9017 • (SP 1992 MA)

**HUNSLEY DIANE S** (217)735-1005
1281 Richland Ave Lincoln IL 62656-1250 • CI • Tchr • Zion Mount Pulaski IL • (217)792-5965 • (RF 1984)

**HUNT EDITH J** (580)765-9872
5250 N Union St Ponca City OK 74601-1069 • OK • Tchr • First Ponca City OK • (580)762-4243 • (S 1967 MS)

**HUNT G WARREN** (314)832-9063
5234 Neosho St Saint Louis MO 63109-2967 • g-meister@usa.net • MO • Tchr • Hope Saint Louis MO • (314)832-1850 • (RF 1993)

**HUNTER JANET M** (219)281-2688
347 County Road 20 Corunna IN 46730-9766 • IN • Tchr • St John Kendallville IN • (219)347-2444 • (RF 1968 MED)

**HUNTINGTON JEFFREY DENNIS** (813)707-5745
1108 Woodlawn Ave Plant City FL 33566 • jhuntin1@tampabay.rr.com • FG • Tchr • Hope Plant City FL • (813)752-4621 • (MQ 1997)

**HURD JAMES** (517)799-0413
203 S Andre St Saginaw MI 48602-2519 • MI • Tchr • Holy Cross Saginaw MI • (517)793-9795 • (S 1970)

**HURD LORAINE K** (517)799-0413
203 S Andre St Saginaw MI 48602-2519 • MI • Tchr • Holy Cross Saginaw MI • (517)793-9795 • (S 1970)

**HURLEY TAMMY KAY** (952)287-8151
3647 Washburn Ave N Minneapolis MN 55412 • OH • 06/2000 • (SP 1990)

**HURST DOREEN L** (440)842-8332
5903 Westlake Ave Parma OH 44129-2344 • EN • Tchr • West Park Cleveland OH • (216)941-2770 • (RF 1989)

**HURST JAMES W** (440)842-8332
5903 Westlake Ave Parma OH 44129-2344 • S • Tchr • Calvary Parma OH • (440)845-0070 • (RF 1990)

**HURST NANCY LYNETTE** (806)359-3931
6101 Calumet Rd Amarillo TX 79106-3513 • TX • Tchr • Trinity Amarillo TX • (806)352-5620 • (S 1987)

**HURST RACHEL ANNE**
248 E Southwest Pkwy #423 Lewisville TX 75067-8704 • TX • Tchr • Christ Our Savior Coppell TX • (972)393-7074 • (AU 1995)

**HURTGAM JODIE B** (716)392-6692
Village II Drive 200C Hilton NY 14468 • EA • Tchr • St Paul Hilton NY • (716)392-4000 • (BR 1998)

**HURTTGAM SUSAN LYN** (313)263-3278
47652 Lexington Dr Macomb MI 48044-2654 • MI • Tchr • Immanuel Macomb MI • (810)286-4231 • (S 1973 MS)

**HUSBERG WILLIAM A** (612)864-4479
711 9th St E Glencoe MN 55336-2914 • mbsm711@hutchtel.net • MNS • Tchr • First Glencoe MN • (320)864-3317 • (SP 1969)

**HUSCHER CHRISTIAN F**
756 S Walnut Ave San Dimas CA 91773-3658 • PSW • Mem C • Gethsemane Riverside CA • (909)684-6446 • (IV 1985)

**HUSKE MICHELE LEANN** (317)915-1498
12048 Wesley Ct Fischers IN 46038 • micster@webtv.net • IN • Tchr • Calvary Indianapolis IN • (317)783-2305 • (RF 1993)
**HUTT JUDY LYNN** (818)362-7324
27749 Crookshank Dr Saugus CA 91350-1378 • PSW • Tchr • Our Savior First Granada Hills CA • (818)363-9505 • (PO 1984)
**HUTTER JAMES E** (502)493-8139
8705 Tranquil Valley Ln Louisville KY 40299-1337 • jeiehutter@aol.com • IN • Prin • Our Savior Louisville KY • (502)426-1130 • (S 1961 MSED)
**HUTTON WILLIAM P**
1611 Lawnel Muskegon MI 49441 • MI • Mem C • Trinity Muskegon MI • (616)755-1292 • (RF 1983)
**HYLLESTED JASON F** (407)365-3228
C/O St Luke Lutheran Church 2021 W State Road 426 Oviedo FL 32765-8524 • S • Tchr • St Luke Oviedo FL • (407)365-3408 • (SP 1994)
**HYNOUS TERRY A** (713)363-1677
36 N Mossrock Rd The Woodlands TX 77380-1846 • TX • Tchr • LHS North Houston TX • (713)880-3131 • (RF 1965 MA)
**HYSLOP DORA J** (517)652-8726
11240 S Evergreen Birch Run MI 48415 • hyslopscottdora@juno.com • MI • Tchr • St Lorenz Frankenmuth MI • (517)652-6141 • (RF 1991)

## I

**ICKSTADT KATHLEEN L** (219)464-0374
1754 Wildcat Ct Valparaiso IN 46385-6141 • IN • Tchr • Trinity Crown Point IN • (219)663-1586 • (RF 1982 MMU)
**ICKSTADT WILLIAM M** (219)464-0374
1754 Wildcat Ct Valparaiso IN 46385 • bill.ickstadt@immanuel.pvt.k12.in.us • IN • Mem C • Immanuel Valparaiso IN • (219)462-8207 • (RF 1981 MCMU MBA)
**IEHL SANDRA S** (618)344-3216
138 Helen Pl Collinsville IL 62234-1463 • iehlstamp@aol.com • SI • Tchr • Holy Cross Collinsville IL • (618)344-3145 • (CQ 1988 MED)
**IGOE REBECCA ANN** (410)768-5278
140 Pointer Cir Glen Burnie MD 21061-6201 • SE • Tchr • St Paul Glen Burnie MD • (410)766-5790 • (RF 1970 MSED)
**IHSSEN WILLIAM F** (219)447-0227
5029 Yorkshire Dr Fort Wayne IN 46806-3551 • bihssen@juneau.com • IN • EM • (RF 1969 MA MA)
**ILLIAN JACQUELINE L** (763)767-2239
11738 3rd St Apt 304 Blaine MN 55434 • illiteach@hotmail.com • MNS • Tchr • Prince Of Peace Spring Lake Park MN • (612)786-1755 • (SP 1995)
**ILTEN KARLA NADINE** (708)456-4651
9735 Sumac Rd Apt 417 Des Plaines IL 60016 • NI • Tchr • St Paul Chicago IL • (708)867-5044 • (CQ 1995)
**ILTEN STEVEN R**
21519 N Tangle Creek Ln Spring TX 77388 • TX • Tchr • Concordia LHS Tomball TX • (281)351-2547 • (IV 1986 MA)
**IMES KIM ROSE**
1215 E 1st St Long Beach CA 90802-5707 • PSW • Tchr • Bethany Long Beach CA • (562)420-7783 • (RF 1978)
**IMLAH PETER R**
333 W Pleasant Hill Blvd Palatine IL 60067-6851 • NI • Mem C • Immanuel Palatine IL • (847)359-1549 • (RF 1988)
**INGLIS KATHERINE ELIZABETH** (281)334-2452
3045 Marina Bay Dr #11110 League City TX 77573 • TX • Tchr • Texas Austin TX • (AU 1998)
**INGWERSEN DAVID J***
2584 Big Buck Ln Lapeer MI 48446 • ingwerse@execpc.com • MI • P/Tchr • St Paul Lapeer MI • (810)664-6653 • (SP 1975 MS)
**INKINEN PAMELA J** (312)742-3665
1325 Algonquin Dr Elgin IL 60120-2321 • NI • Tchr • Immanuel Dundee IL • (847)428-1010 • (RF 1979 MA)
**INKROTT SUSAN**
2406 Carlisle Pl Sarasota FL 34231-7014 • inkrots@mail.firn.edu • FG • Tchr • St John Ocala FL • (352)622-7275 • (AU 1995)
**INSERRA CAROLYN M** (618)637-2506
719 W 5th St Staunton IL 62088 • SI • Tchr • Zion Staunton IL • (618)635-3060 • (CQ 1996)
**IRISH MARY E** (414)783-9921
14130 Lilly Heights Dr Brookfield WI 53005-1135 • mirish@execpc.com • SW • Tchr • Our Redeemer Wauwatosa WI • (414)258-4558 • (RF 1975 MEDSD)
**IRWIN DAVID WAYNE** (314)741-8826
St Paul Luth Church 106 N Border St Troy IL 62294-1137 • ddirwin@epconline.com • SI • Prin • St Paul Troy IL • (618)667-6681 • (S 1971 MA)
**IRWIN DEBORAH A** (314)741-8826
1851 Roseview Ln Saint Louis MO 63138-1240 • MO • Tchr • Grace Chapel Bellefontaine Nbrs MO • (314)867-6564 • (S 1971)
**IRWIN KAY M**
6926 Washington Pike Knoxville TN 37918 • greenmoose@msn.com • MDS • Tchr • First Knoxville TN • (423)524-0366 • (RF 1980)
**ISAAC TONYA G** (402)496-9273
9630 Boyd Cir Omaha NE 68134-3869 • NEB • Tchr • St Paul Omaha NE • (402)451-2865 • (S 1996)
**ISELER JANET ANN** (313)724-0795
430 Tobin Dr Canterbury Woods Apt 208 Inkster MI 48141-3555 • MI • Tchr • Atonement Dearborn MI • (313)581-2525 • (RF 1967)
**ISHAM JO ANN** (217)787-8660
2621 Lemont Dr Springfield IL 62704-1117 • CI • 06/2000 • (RF 1994)
**IVERSON JENA L** (320)864-4345
1320 Greeley Ave N Glencoe MN 55336-1342 • noelynn94@ll.net • MNS • 06/1994 06/2000 • (MQ 1990 MA)
**IYASSU ZEREZGHI**
7845 Keystone Ave Skokie IL 60076-3611 • NI • Tchr • Luther HS South Chicago IL • (773)737-1416 • (S 1979)

## J

**JABS JOAN IDA** (920)458-8512
6502 S Business Dr Sheboygan WI 53081-8988 • IE • Tchr • Central Newhall IA • (319)223-5271 • (SP 1976)
**JACK DANIEL B** (517)354-5699
4854 Haken Rd Alpena MI 49707-9707 • MI • 10/1999 • (RF 1977 MAD)
**JACKE ROBERT J**
10305 NE 9th St Vancouver WA 98664-3869 • bjacke@cu-portland.edu • NOW • EM • (RF 1961 MA)
**JACKLIN ROBERT MATTHEW** (314)625-4713
621 Bent Oak Dr Lake St Louis MO 63367 • MO • Tchr • Immanuel Wentzville MO • (636)327-4416 • (RF 1998)
**JACKSON LINDA J** (314)843-3224
10761 Willinda Dr Saint Louis MO 63123-6031 • MO • Tchr • Immanuel Olivette MO • (314)993-5004 • (S 1985)
**JACKSON RHONDA L** (504)737-7897
8105 Barocco Dr Harahan LA 70123-4418 • pauljack@bellsouth.net • SO • Tchr • Atonement Metairie LA • (504)887-3980 • (S 1974)
**JACKSON TERI L** (414)375-4862
10480 Highlawn Ct Cedarburg WI 53012-9321 • SW • Tchr • First Immanuel Cedarburg WI • (262)377-6610 • (MQ 1985)
**JACOB DOROTHEA B** (281)655-8015
16115 Willowpark Dr Tomball TX 77375 • MDS • EM • (RF 1957 MED MED)
**JACOB NORMA B** (913)321-8023
3404 Oakland Ave Kansas City KS 66102-2334 • KS • EM • (S 1960 MS)
**JACOBITZ LISA MICHELLE** (660)674-2440
PO Box 213 Alma MO 64001-0213 • ljacobitz@almanet.net • MO • Tchr • Trinity Alma MO • (660)674-2444 • (S 1996)
**JACOBSEN JOAN R** (415)359-4208
424 Bally Way Pacifica CA 94044-1489 • CNH • Tchr • Zion San Francisco CA • (415)221-7500 • (S 1964 MS)
**JACOBSEN JOHN C** (650)359-4208
424 Bally Way Pacifica CA 94044-1489 • jcjacobsen@zionlutheranchurch.org • CNH • Tchr • Zion San Francisco CA • (415)221-7500 • (S 1965 MSED)
**JACOBSEN LYNNE M** (608)752-2447
1107 Morningside Dr Janesville WI 53546-1625 • SW • Tchr • St Paul Janesville WI • (608)754-4471 • (RF 1977 MSED)
**JACOBSON DENNIS M** (313)641-7340
8022 Mc Connell Ave Los Angeles CA 90045-2716 • jacobson86@aol.com • PSW • Tchr • First Venice CA • (310)823-9367 • (S 1981)
**JACOBSON KAY** (847)464-4267
42W827 Robin Ln Hampshire IL 60140-8830 • NI • Tchr • St John Elgin IL • (847)741-7633 • (RF 1966 MED)
**JACOBSON SHANNON**
3862 Loma Alta Dr San Diego CA 92115 • PSW • Tchr • Grace San Diego CA • (619)299-2890 • (IV 1997)
**JACOBY DOUGLAS J**
412 Thomas Dr Port Washington WI 53074 • SW • P/Tchr • St John Glendale WI • (414)352-4150 • (MQ 1987 MS)
**JACQUES KRISTA E** (810)598-0498
49161 Morning Glory Dr Macomb MI 48044-1838 • MI • Tchr • Immanuel Macomb MI • (810)286-7076 • (RF 1982 MA)
**JADUSINGH KARIN M**
4902 Deer Point Dr Spring TX 77389-3906 • karinb@texas.net • TX • Tchr • LHS North Houston TX • (713)880-3131 • (S 1990)
**JAECH RENATA ANNA**
17518 151st Ave SE #2-11 Renton WA 98058-8795 • NOW • Tchr • Pilgrim Bellevue WA • (425)454-4790 • (PO 1989)
**JAEGER CHRISTINE R** (414)541-9027
3966 S 43rd St Greenfield WI 53220-2751 • EN • 07/1992 07/2000 • (MQ 1989)
**JAEGER LORI A** (562)799-0704
8371 E Blithedale St Long Beach CA 90808-3301 • PSW • Tchr • Bethany Long Beach CA • (562)420-7783 • (RF 1986 MA)
**JAEGER TIMOTHY PAUL*** (562)799-0704
8371 E Blithedale St Long Beach CA 90808-3301 • PSW • SHS/C • Pacific Southwest Irvine CA • (949)854-3232 • (RF 1986 MA)
**JAENKE JANE E** (715)831-1358
510 Garden St Eau Claire WI 54703-1452 • jaenkej@yahoo.com • NW • Tchr • Eau Claire Eau Claire WI • (715)835-9314 • (SP 1989)
**JAGELS HAROLD E** (636)462-8709
674 Mennemeyer Rd Troy MO 63379 • EN • EM • (S 1941 MED MMU)
**JAHNKE STEVEN M** (512)733-1413
1431 Thibodeaux Dr Round Rock TX 78664 • iamtaz1@aol.com • TX • Tchr • Redeemer Austin TX • (512)451-6478 • (AU 1995)
**JAHNKE SUSAN R** (701)281-9367
325 Cherry Ct West Fargo ND 58078-2923 • chjahnke@aol.com • ND • Tchr • Grace Fargo ND • (701)232-7747 • (SP 1986)
**JAHR MARSHA K** (320)328-5325
25673 381st Ave Arlington MN 55307-9781 • MNS • Tchr • Noahs Ark Brownton MN • (612)328-5325 • (S 1984)
**JAHR RACHEL R** (612)770-3690
2373 Oak Ln White Bear Lake MN 55110-5563 • MNS • Tchr • Central Saint Paul MN • (651)645-8649 • (S 1983)
**JAKUBCIN CAROLINE M** (305)365-5927
2000 W State Road 426 Oviedo FL 32765-8825 • S • Tchr • St Luke Oviedo FL • (407)365-3228 • (RF 1969)
**JALAS DARIN D** (402)643-2793
1239 N Sunrise Seward NE 68434-1354 • djalasda@seward.cune.edu • NEB • 12/1998 • (S 1996)
**JALAS DEANNA DENISE** (402)643-2793
1239 N Sunrise Seward NE 68434-1354 • dee@seward.cune.edu • NEB • SHS/C • Nebraska Seward NE • (S 1996)
**JAMES PATRICIA R** (219)493-7910
1003 Daly Dr New Haven IN 46774-1811 • IN • Tchr • Central New Haven IN • (219)493-2502 • (S 1973 MS)
**JAMISION BEVERLY S** (816)737-5444
7702 Crescent Ave Raytown MO 64138-1658 • MO • Tchr • Calvary Kansas City MO • (816)444-5517 • (S 1980 MRD MA)
**JAMMER BONNIE M** (517)662-6820
1760 11 Mile Rd Auburn MI 48611-9731 • MI • Tchr • Zion Auburn MI • (517)662-4264 • (S 1979)
**JANETZKE BRUCE D** (303)659-5231
111 S 14th Avenue Dr Brighton CO 80601-2303 • RM • Tchr • Zion Brighton CO • (303)659-3443 • (RF 1965)
**JANETZKE EDMUND W** (219)485-9850
5715 Meadowbrook Dr Fort Wayne IN 46835-3346 • IN • EM • (RF 1934 MSED)
**JANISKO DAVID A** (828)645-2060
106 Forest Knoll Pl Weaverville NC 28787 • SE • Prin • Emmanuel Asheville NC • (828)252-1795 • (RF 1963 MA)
**JANISKO SHIRLEY R** (904)621-1691
3475 W Woodthrush St Lecanto FL 34461-8555 • FG • Tchr • Faith Eustis FL • (352)589-5433 • (RF 1958 MED)
**JANKE LAURA THERESE**
4915 Greenway Dr North Little Rock AR 72116-6813 • MDS • Tchr • Hope Jacksonville AR • (501)982-1333 • (S 1998)
**JANKO DENNIS L** (301)805-1936
12003 Backus Dr Bowie MD 20720-4467 • SE • Prin • Concordia Hyattsville MD • (301)927-0266 • (RF 1960 MED)
**JANSSEN F ARLENE** (530)722-0320
2100 Deerfield Ave Redding CA 96002-0434 • CNH • EM • (CQ 1986)
**JANSSEN GERALD H** (530)722-0320
2100 Deerfield Ave Redding CA 96002-0434 • CNH • EM • (RF 1959 MA)
**JANSSEN LELAND L** (314)432-4514
12179 Lake Placid Dr Saint Louis MO 63146-5112 • MO • EM • (RF 1957)
**JANSSEN LISA MARIE** (218)281-5270
111 W Loring St Apt 3 Crookston MN 56716-1938 • MNN • Tchr • Our Savior Crookston MN • (218)281-5191 • (SP 1994)
**JANSSEN RICHARD W** (618)826-2683
518 W German St Chester IL 62233-1327 • SI • 09/2000 • (S 1967)
**JANSSEN SHARON R** (217)287-1086
325 N 1250 East Rd Morrisonville IL 62546-6523 • ejanssen@chipsnet.com • SI • Tchr • St Paul Nokomis IL • (217)563-8670 • (CQ 1993)
**JANUS LISA ANN** (414)644-8026
4435 Birdie Cir Slinger WI 53086-9722 • EN • Tchr • Prince Of Peace Menomonee Falls WI • (414)251-3360 • (MQ 1986)
**JANZOW JOHN F** (520)722-2412
8822 E 5th St Tucson AZ 85710-3040 • jojanzowata@aol.com • PSW • EM • (RF 1952 MA MA)
**JANZOW LUDWIG E** (415)483-1056
790 Joaquin Ave San Leandro CA 94577-5115 • CNH • EM • (S 1933)
**JARABAK EMILY K** (773)871-3807
3950 N Lake Shore Dr #2221D Chicago IL 60613 • tching76@aol.com • NI • Tchr • St James Chicago IL • (773)525-4990 • (RF 1998)
**JARDIM SUSAN J** (818)831-1844
17205 Donmetz St Granada Hills CA 91344-4126 • PSW • Tchr • Our Redeemer Winnetka CA • (818)341-3460 • (CQ 1995)
**JAROCKI KAREN K** (520)342-9466
12606 E Brenda Dr Yuma AZ 85367 • PSW • 04/2000 • (S 1980)
**JASBERG TRACEY** (516)932-3476
97 W Nicholai St Hicksville NY 11801-3825 • traceyjasberg@juno.com • AT • Tchr • Trinity Hicksville NY • (516)931-2225 • (BR 1996)
**JAUSS LANETT S** (816)584-6677
109 E 12th St Higginsville MO 64037-1116 • lsjauss@ctcis.net • MO • 02/1994 02/2000 • (S 1980 MAT)
**JEDELE CHARLES E** (303)569-0271
PO Box 475 Silver Plume CO 80476-0475 • RM • EM • (S 1959 MS)
**JEDELE PAULINE ANN** (303)569-0271
PO Box 475 Silver Plume CO 80476-0475 • RM • EM • (WN 1956)
**JEFFERIES DOROTHY ROSA** (303)755-9475
2998 S Verbena Way Denver CO 80231-4219 • RM • Tchr • St John Denver CO • (303)733-3777 • (CQ 1999 MA)
**JEFFRIES RUTH L** (816)882-8160
2441 Pioneer St Boonville MO 65233-2762 • MO • Tchr • Zion Bunceton MO • (816)838-6428 • (RF 1967)
**JELNECK RUTH ANN** (219)942-2522
909 E 8th St Hobart IN 46342-5217 • IN • Tchr • Trinity Hobart IN • (219)942-3147 • (SP 1974 MMU)
**JENKINS JULIUS** (205)874-5708
1804 Green St Selma AL 36703-3323 • SO • SHS/C • Southern New Orleans LA • (S 1968 MED MED PHD)

**JENKS ALBERT N** (608)365-6063
1914 Grant St Beloit WI 53511-2836 • SW • EM • (S 1957 MAT)

**JENKS AMY DORETTA** (952)912-9868
335 17th Ave N #2 Hopkins MN 55343 • newyork³nanny@yahoo.com • MNS • Tchr • Bethlehem Minnetonka MN • (612)934-5959 • (SP 1997)

**JENNINGS CHARLES A** (254)526-9692
2905 Tortoise Ln Killeen TX 76542-2630 • TX • EM • (RF 1960 MED)

**JENNINGS JENNIFER LYNN** (206)568-8280
1210 10th Ave E Seattle WA 98102 • NOW • Tchr • Concordia Seattle WA • (206)525-7407 • (IV 1993)

**JENNINGS MATTHEW HAMILTON** (206)568-8280
1210 10th Ave E Seattle WA 98102 • NOW • Tchr • Concordia Seattle WA • (206)525-7407 • (IV 1994)

**JENNINGS SUSAN MARIE** (562)429-5722
3712 Allred St Lakewood CA 90712-3527 • PSW • Tchr • Concordia Cerritos CA • (562)926-2491 • (IV 1992)

**JENSEN DANIEL LEONARD** (262)681-8694
143 Lakefield Ct Racine WI 53402-3102 • SW • Tchr • South Wisconsin Milwaukee WI • (414)464-8100 • (S 1975 MED)

**JENSEN WAYNE E DR** (414)527-6704
4653 N 92nd St Milwaukee WI 53225 • SW • Tchr • Milwaukee LHS Milwaukee WI • (414)461-6000 • (CQ 1999 MEPD EDD)

**JENSON KRISTIN MARIE** (303)424-9131
9131 W 79th Pl Arvada CO 80005 • kjenson@gateway.net • RM • Tchr • Mount Hope Boulder CO • (303)499-9800 • (S 1995)

**JERABEK PAULINE M** (715)823-2593
PO Box 197 Embarrass WI 54933 • pjerabek@frontiernet.net • NE • 06/1993 06/2000 • (RF 1985)

**JERKE VICTORIA LYN** (650)967-8626
330 Franklin St Mountain View CA 94041 • vjerke@hotmail.com • CNH • Prin • St Paul Mountain View CA • (650)967-0666 • (S 1998)

**JESERITZ LAURA** (713)690-3655
5801 Hollister Houston TX 77040 • TX • Tchr • Our Savior Houston TX • (713)290-9087 • (MQ 2000)

**JESGARZ FREDERICK K** (616)723-6987
384 Piney Rd Manistee MI 49660-9151 • MI • Tchr • Trinity Manistee MI • (231)723-5149 • (RF 1984)

**JESGARZ SHERRI LYNN** (217)774-5900
RR 1 Box 211D Shelbyville IL 62565-9701 • spjz94@stewstras.net • CI • Tchr • Trinity Stewardson IL • (217)682-3881 • (S 1992)

**JESKE JOANNE R** (314)772-0402
4061 Wyoming St Saint Louis MO 63116-3919 • puddy@nothnbut.net • MO • Tchr • Messiah Saint Louis MO • (314)771-7716 • (S 1974)

**JESSEN CAROL JEAN** (630)893-4547
43 W Hattendorf Ave Roselle IL 60172-1114 • NI • Tchr • Our Savior Carol Stream IL • (630)830-4851 • (S 1968)

**JIEDE EDWIN A** (407)366-9543
2116 Toucan Ct Oviedo FL 32765-5210 • FG • EM • (RF 1935 MSED MA)

**JIPP ALICIA M** (812)473-5438
4515 Bellemeade Evansville IN 47714-0619 • jippam@juno.com • IN • Tchr • Evansville Evansville IN • (812)424-7252 • (RF 1997)

**JIPP ANDREW W**
210 W Rainbow Ridge Apt 1202 Oak Creek WI 53154 • SW • Tchr • Grace Oak Creek WI • (414)762-8990 • (S 1999)

**JIPP KIMBERLY ANN** (402)753-9257
210 W Rainbow Ridge #1202 Oak Creek WI 53154 • NEB • Tchr • Northwest Milwaukee WI • (414)463-4040 • (S 1999)

**JITER JERRY LEE** (715)623-7254
214 Lincoln St Antigo WI 54409-1344 • NW • Tchr • Peace Antigo WI • (715)623-2209 • (CQ 1980 MSED)

**JOBE DELORES** (262)255-5251
N102W17488 Lone Oaks Dr Germantown WI 53022-4683 • jolade@aol.com • SW • Tchr • Grace Menomonee Falls WI • (414)251-7140 • (S 1966)

**JOBST DWAYNE D*** (262)781-3683
N53 W14345 Aberdeen Dr Menomonee Falls WI 53051 • SW • Tchr • South Wisconsin Milwaukee WI • (414)464-8100 • (SP 1975 MA MA)

**JOCUS JOANNE** (908)238-2494
66 Main St Sayreville NJ 08872-1564 • NJ • Tchr • Redeemer Westfield NJ • (908)232-1517 • (BR 1985)

**JOERZ LORI LEE** (516)654-3387
31 Pine Neck Ave Patchoque NY 11772-5765 • AT • Tchr • Emanuel Patchogue NY • (516)758-2250 • (BR 1989 MA)

**JOHANN KRISTIN LOUISE** (812)473-5438
4515 Bellemeade Evansville IN 47714-0619 • IN • Tchr • Evansville Evansville IN • (812)424-7252 • (S 1997)

**JOHNSON AMY BETH** (651)686-5995
4362 Golden Meadow Ct Eagan MN 55123 • ajohnson@tsilink.net • MNS • S Ex/S • Mount Hope-Redemptio Bloomington MN • (612)881-0036 • (CQ 1997 MA)

**JOHNSON ANDREA C** (712)263-3990
1311 2nd Ave N Denison IA 51442-1844 • IW • Tchr • Zion Denison IA • (712)263-4766 • (S 1993)

**JOHNSON ANDREA L** (810)227-9615
3150 Old Orchard Dr Brighton MI 48114-8115 • EN • Tchr • Child Of Christ Hartland MI • (248)887-3836 • (RF 1973 MA)

**JOHNSON ANGELA DENISE** (719)210-1097
1750 Blackfoot Trl Woodland Park CO 80863 • missbardonner@hotmail.com • FG • Tchr • St John Ocala FL • (352)629-1794 • (RF 1999)

**JOHNSON ARDITH** (406)656-2544
PO Box 20375 Billings MT 59104-0375 • MT • Tchr • Trinity Billings MT • (406)656-1021 • (SP 1965)

**JOHNSON BARBARA** (219)749-5636
1033 Park Ave New Haven IN 46774-1615 • IN • 06/1997 06/2000 • (S 1970 MA MED)

**JOHNSON BETTY KATHLEEN** (770)432-1709
125 Walton Way SE Smyrna GA 30082-3849 • FG • Tchr • Christ East Point GA • (404)767-2892 • (RF 1970)

**JOHNSON CAROL RUTH** (908)738-3842
66 Corey St Fords NJ 08863-2057 • NJ • 12/1995 12/1999 • (RF 1978)

**JOHNSON CHRISTINE A** (313)777-3834
27102 Maywood St Roseville MI 48066-3017 • MI • Tchr • St Peter Eastpointe MI • (810)776-1663 • (S 1975)

**JOHNSON CHRISTINE**
N111W16328 Catskill Ln Germantown WI 53022-4019 • IE • 09/1997 • (RF 1997)

**JOHNSON CINDY R**
10226 Eagle Blf San Antonio TX 78240-3558 • TX • Tchr • Shepherd Of The Hill San Antonio TX • (210)614-3741 • (AU 1985)

**JOHNSON DANNY C** (219)749-5636
1033 Park Ave New Haven IN 46774-1615 • dannyc@ctlnet.com • IN • Tchr • Concordia LHS Fort Wayne IN • (219)483-1102 • (S 1970)

**JOHNSON DEBORAH L** (847)296-2729
8937 Robin Dr Des Plaines IL 60016-5412 • NI • Tchr • St Paul Chicago IL • (708)867-5044 • (RF 1985)

**JOHNSON EVELYN** (407)383-2169
1690 Carriage Dr Titusville FL 32796 • FG • 06/1990 06/2000 • (RF 1968 MA)

**JOHNSON JAMES JOHN** (281)251-0814
16414 Stuebner Airline Rd#505 Spring TX 77379-7366 • TX • Tchr • Concordia LHS Tomball TX • (281)351-2547 • (MQ 1997)

**JOHNSON JILL K** (612)261-0389
11225 Julia Ln Becker MN 55308 • MNN • 06/1987 06/2000 • (SP 1983)

**JOHNSON KAREN M**
4512 Driving Range Rd Corona CA 92883-0664 • PSW • Tchr • Loving Savior Chino Hills CA • (909)597-4668 • (S 1962)

**JOHNSON KARIN K** (414)353-9569
6572 N 81st St Milwaukee WI 53223 • SW • Tchr • St Peter-Immanuel Milwaukee WI • (414)353-6800 • (MQ 1987)

**JOHNSON KEITH R** (512)980-3726
3126 Charter Corpus Christi TX 78414 • kjohnson@clearsource.net • TX • 04/1998 04/2000 • (AU 1991 MED)

**JOHNSON KRAIG CARROLL**
14273 Briarfield Ln Grand Haven MI 49417-9791 • MI • P/Tchr • St John Grand Haven MI • (616)842-4510 • (SP 1971 MA)

**JOHNSON LESLEE L** (312)286-3188
4141 N Parkside Ave Chicago IL 60634-1824 • johnsonglm1@aol.com • NI • Tchr • St John Chicago IL • (773)736-1196 • (S 1976)

**JOHNSON LINDA E** (708)544-3864
5430 Bohlander Berkeley IL 60163 • lineljohns@aol.com • NI • Tchr • St John Forest Park IL • (708)366-2764 • (RF 1977 MA)

**JOHNSON LYNDA P**
7610 Williams Ave Saint Louis MO 63143-1222 • MO • Tchr • Washington Saint Louis County MO • (314)892-4408 • (SP 1983)

**JOHNSON MARGARET R** (414)728-0538
1506 Delavan Club Dr Delavan WI 53115 • NI • EM • (RF 1981 MA MA)

**JOHNSON MARY L** (313)885-7126
3460 Kensington Ave Detroit MI 48224-2724 • mljohnson4592@netscape.net • MI • Prin • Bethany Detroit MI • (313)885-0180 • (RF 1980 MED)

**JOHNSON MELISSA LYNN** (708)583-9427
2130 N 75th Ct Elmwood Park IL 60707-3001 • mljteacher@aol.com • NI • Tchr • St Paul Melrose Park IL • (708)343-5000 • (RF 1996 MA)

**JOHNSON MELODY ANN** (406)844-2444
PO Box 824 Lakeside MT 59922-0824 • dudley@digisys.net • MT • Tchr • Trinity Kalispell MT • (406)257-6716 • (S 1969)

**JOHNSON MYRENE K** (580)338-2356
PO Box 387 Guymon OK 73942-0387 • OK • Tchr • Trinity Guymon OK • (580)338-6000 • (S 1975)

**JOHNSON PAMELA ANNE** (630)830-4319
621 Arnold Ave Streamwood IL 60107-3079 • NI • Tchr • St Peter Schaumburg IL • (847)885-7636 • (RF 1975 MA)

**JOHNSON PAMELA D** (317)862-1408
6051 S Eaton Ave Indianapolis IN 46259-1300 • ppphea@aol.com • IN • Tchr • St John Indianapolis IN • (317)352-9196 • (RF 1976 MA)

**JOHNSON PAUL W** (317)862-1408
6051 S Eaton Ave Indianapolis IN 46259-1300 • packrteach@aol.com • IN • Tchr • LHS Of Indianapolis Indianapolis IN • (317)787-5474 • (RF 1977 MMU)

**JOHNSON PENNY J** (248)652-8775
1779 Charm Ct Rochester Hills MI 48306 • pjohnson@lhsa.com • MI • Tchr • LHS North Macomb MI • (810)781-9151 • (AA 1999)

**JOHNSON RICHARD J** (734)481-0373
2277 S Grove #322 Ypsilanti MI 48198 • MI • 07/1999 • (RF 1967 MED)

**JOHNSON ROBERT D** (815)455-5223
336 Poplar St Crystal Lake IL 60014-4411 • rjohnson@mc.net • NI • Tchr • Immanuel Crystal Lake IL • (815)459-1444 • (SP 1988 MA)

**JOHNSON ROSS E** (419)826-4131
4150 County Road 2 Swanton OH 43558-9758 • OH • Prin • St John Napoleon OH • (419)598-8702 • (RF 1971 MA MED)

**JOHNSON SCOTT R** (715)536-4388
2006 Water St Merrill WI 54452-2172 • scojohn@aol.com • NW • Tchr • Trinity Merrill WI • (715)536-7501 • (SP 1995)

**JOHNSON SHARON A** (402)734-4614
1516 Jefferson St Omaha NE 68107-4330 • arj2@ix.netcom.com • NEB • Tchr • St Paul Omaha NE • (402)451-2865 • (S 1964)

**JOHNSON SHERRIN K**
24360 Jacarte Dr Murrieta CA 92562-4007 • PSW • Tchr • St Paul Orange CA • (714)637-2640 • (IV 1986 MS)

**JOHNSON STEPHEN P** (763)535-2494
4730 Xenia Ave N Crystal MN 55429-3525 • steveo236@juno.com • MNS • Tchr • St John Maple Grove MN • (612)420-2426 • (RF 1996)

**JOHNSTON CHRISTOPHER J** (708)452-1996
5102 N Leonard Dr Apt 1B Norridge IL 60706-2607 • cjj76@hotmail.com • NI • Tchr • St Paul Chicago IL • (708)867-5044 • (RF 1998)

**JOHNSTON DIANE M** (818)842-2271
639 E Olive Ave Apt 4 Burbank CA 91501-2141 • PSW • Tchr • Zion Glendale CA • (818)243-3119 • (SP 1983)

**JOHNSTON HELEN LOUISE** (314)364-3043
603 Salem Ave Rolla MO 65401-3410 • MO • Tchr • Rolla Lutheran Schoo Rolla MO • (314)364-3915 • (RF 1968 MED)

**JOHNSTON JANICE M** (920)830-3448
37 Olde Paltzer Ln Appleton WI 54913 • SW • Tchr • Trinity Menasha WI • (920)722-2662 • (RF 1971)

**JOHNSTON SUSAN M** (504)340-5575
406 20th St Apt 14 Gretna LA 70053 • SO • 09/1999 • (CQ 1974)

**JONAS LAUREL M** (608)981-2167
W8095 Grouse Rd Portage WI 53901-9308 • jonas@jvlnet.com • SW • Tchr • Trinity Wisconsin Dells WI • (608)253-3241 • (SP 1980)

**JONES CATHY J** (630)922-0398
2815 Fairhauser Ct Naperville IL 60564-5859 • troubles@execpc.com • NI • 10/1998 • (S 1973)

**JONES DAVID W** (920)434-6051
800 Patriot Pl Green Bay WI 54313-6835 • NW • Tchr • Pilgrim Green Bay WI • (920)494-6530 • (CQ 1986)

**JONES JENNIFER R** (704)465-3493
1941 Kings Grant Dr Newton NC 28658-9158 • SE • Tchr • St Stephen Hickory NC • (828)256-2166 • (RF 1994)

**JONES JUANITA** (205)457-3920
2722 Harper Ave Mobile AL 36617-1812 • SO • Tchr • Trinity Mobile AL • (334)456-7960 • (S 1979)

**JONES KAREN BETH** (313)397-8375
47774 Pavillon Rd Canton MI 48188-6288 • MI • Tchr • Detroit Urban Detroit MI • (313)582-9900 • (AA 1994)

**JONES KATHRYN L** (651)456-5891
2988 Pilot Knob Rd Eagan MN 55121-1122 • MNS • Tchr • Redemption Bloomington MN • (952)881-0035 • (SP 1980 MED)

**JONES KIMBERLY D** (775)629-1115
6400 Gerre Ln Stagecoach NV 89429 • kkuntz@aol.com • CNH • Tchr • Bethlehem Carson City NV • (775)882-5252 • (IV 1987)

**JONES LEAH MARIE**
561 Yorkshire #99 Rochester Hills MI 48307 • MI • Tchr • St John Rochester MI • (248)652-8830 • (CQ 2000)

**JONES LORNE E** (503)992-0140
Forest Hills Luth School 4221 SW Golf Course Rd Cornelius OR 97113-6017 • NOW • Tchr • Forest Hills Cornelius OR • (503)359-4853 • (S 1967)

**JONES MARILYN SUE** (515)279-7660
1910 Merklin Way Des Moines IA 50310-1036 • mjones2629@aol.com • IW • 08/2000 • (S 1971)

**JONES MARY ANN** (815)568-7432
1012 Jacquelyn Ct Marengo IL 60152-3090 • jones5@mc.net • NI • Tchr • Zion Marengo IL • (815)568-5156 • (S 1975)

**JONES MICHELLE ELIZABETH** (734)455-3776
42560 Postiff Apt 1 Plymouth MI 48170 • amj71198@hotmail.com • MI • Tchr • St Paul Northville MI • (248)349-3140 • (AA 1999)

**JONES NANCY M** (219)493-2117
1550 Dundee Dr New Haven IN 46774-2216 • nanjns3j@gateway.net • IN • Tchr • Central New Haven IN • (219)493-2502 • (RF 1969 MS)

**JONES SHARON ANN** (281)992-0195
17015 Stone Stile Dr Friendswood TX 77546-2627 • sawjones@flash.net • TX • Tchr • Texas Austin TX • (S 1970 MCMU)

**JOPP JILL MARIE** (612)886-0099
8218 Sheridan Ave S Bloomington MN 55431-1646 • MNS • Tchr • Christ Eagan MN • (651)454-4091 • (SP 1997)

**JOPP KEITH R** (316)542-3527
PO Box 278 Cheney KS 67025-0278 • KS • P/Tchr • St Paul Cheney KS • (316)542-3584 • (S 1965 MED MED)

**JOPP TRACY MARIE** (952)657-2138
14935 50th St Mayer MN 55360 • MNS • Tchr • Cross View Edina MN • (952)941-1094 • (SPR 1999)

**JORDAN JENNY L** (714)556-2396
2210 W Moore Ave Santa Ana CA 92704-6639 • PSW • Tchr • Christ Costa Mesa CA • (949)548-6866 • (S 1980 MED)

**JORDAN SHARON BETH** (734)941-0029
18301 Aspen Trl Brownstown MI 48174 • MI • Tchr • Christ King Southgate MI • (734)285-9695 • (AA 2000)

**JORDING DAVID C** (414)722-4950
1024 Grove St Menasha WI 54952-1924 • jord@athenet.net • SW • Prin • Trinity Menasha WI • (920)725-1715 • (RF 1966 MA)

**JOST SYLVIA M** (314)869-1736
160 Green Acres Rd Saint Louis MO 63137-1812 • MO • Tchr • Grace Chapel Bellefontaine Nbrs MO • (314)867-6564 • (S 1966)

**JOSTES RICHARD A** (402)643-3399
804 S 5th St Norfolk NE 68701 • rjostes@alltel.net • NEB • Grace Chapel Bellefontaine Nbrs MO • (S 1973 MA)

**JOYCE MARK L** (313)973-8613
2775 Oakdale Dr Ann Arbor MI 48108-1266 • joycem@ccaa.edu • MI • SHS/C • Michigan Ann Arbor MI • (S 1970 MSED DED)

**JUD CAROLYN R** (217)243-2040
415 W Beecher Ave Jacksonville IL 62650-2440 • CI • Tchr • Salem Jacksonville IL • (217)243-3419 • (CQ 1998 MLS)

**JUDGE THERESA M**
1713 Braemore Ct Kernersville NC 27284-8617 • judgnot@aol.com • SE • 07/1989 07/1999 • (BR 1980)

**JUERGENSEN JAMES D** (414)462-2560
4476 N 89th St Milwaukee WI 53225 • SW • Tchr • South Wisconsin Milwaukee WI • (414)464-8100 • (MQ 1993)

**JUERGENSEN JAMES J DR** (414)438-0204
8025 W Fiebrantz Ave Milwaukee WI 53222-1925 • james.juergensen@cuw.edu • SW • SHS/C • South Wisconsin Milwaukee WI • (414)464-8100 • (S 1962 MA MS PHD)

**JUERGENSEN MARTIN F** (913)273-4312
4833 SW 18th St Topeka KS 66604-3520 • KS • EM • (S 1935)

**JUERGENSEN STEPHANIE LYNN**
4476 N 89th St Milwaukee WI 53225 • SW • 07/1999 • (MQ 1996)

**JUNG ANN M** (817)788-0659
6865 Dogwood Ct N Richlnd Hls TX 76180-2050 • TX • Tchr • Crown Of Life Colleyville TX • (817)421-5683 • (RF 1977 MA)

**JUNG CHARLENE E** (219)493-4270
2240 Cimarron Pass Fort Wayne IN 46815-7731 • larryjung@aol.com • IN • Tchr • Emmanuel-St Michael Fort Wayne IN • (219)422-6712 • (RF 1971 MS)

**JUNGKUNTZ MARTIN K** (314)921-0092
2115 E Humes Ln Florissant MO 63033-1716 • EN • EM • (RF 1961 MED)

**JUNGKUNTZ SANDRA S** (847)843-7345
302 E Schaumburg Rd Schaumburg IL 60194-3515 • NI • Tchr • St Peter Schaumburg IL • (847)885-7636 • (RF 1990 MA)

**JUNGKUNTZ VICTOR P*** (920)262-0486
918 N Water St Watertown WI 53098-1822 • SW • EM • (RF 1951 MA)

**JUNKIN DANIEL E**
W233N6245 Deyer Dr Sussex WI 53089-3813 • djunkin@execpc.com • SI • Tchr • St John Chester IL • (618)826-3545 • (MQ 1992)

**JUNOD MONICA LYNN** (214)221-7020
201 W Southwest Pkwy Apt 7201 Lewisville TX 75067-7710 • mljunod@gte.net • TX • Tchr • Christ Our Savior Coppell TX • (972)393-7074 • (AU 1995)

**JURGENSEN JENNIFER** (507)292-0439
1225 Cascade St NW Rochester MN 55901 • gltimm@yahoo.com • MNS • Tchr • Rochester Central Rochester MN • (507)289-3267 • (SP 1996)

**JURSS JASON B** (262)677-3407
W201 N16300 Ash Dr Jackson WI 53037 • SW • Tchr • South Wisconsin Milwaukee WI • (414)464-8100 • (RF 1995)

**JURSS JEFFREY A** (414)458-6552
1726 Terry Andrae Ave Sheboygan WI 53081-8810 • jurss@lutheranhigh.com • SW • Tchr • South Wisconsin Milwaukee WI • (414)464-8100 • (RF 1989)

**JUST DARREL D**
2221 E Lincoln Dr Phoenix AZ 85016-1145 • PSW • Tchr • Gethsemane Tempe AZ • (480)839-0906 • (RF 1969)

**JUSTICE DONALD C** (313)882-2441
20476 Mc Cormick St Detroit MI 48224-1273 • djustice@lhsa.com • MI • Tchr • LHS East Harper Woods MI • (313)371-8750 • (S 1996)

**JUSZCZAK SHERILYN D** (360)692-0575
7475 Woodridge Ln NW Bremerton WA 98311-8929 • johnsheri@prodigy.net • NOW • Tchr • Peace Bremerton WA • (360)373-2116 • (PO 1982)

## K

**KAAZ RAYMOND EDWARD** (618)282-6685
515 E S 2nd St Red Bud IL 62278 • ctrytchr@hotmail.com • SI • Tchr • St John Red Bud IL • (618)282-3873 • (RF 1977 MED)

**KACZMAR DEBORAH J*** (847)680-7871
29845 N Forest Lake Ln Libertyville IL 60048-2468 • sndkaz@aol.com • NI • 08/1997 • (RF 1987)

**KADDATZ JILL ANN** (414)774-1644
1218 S 58th St West Allis WI 53214-3313 • SW • Tchr • Our Redeemer Wauwatosa WI • (414)258-4558 • (MQ 1985 MA)

**KADERA DEBORAH L**
7863 Jayseel St Sunland CA 91040-2511 • contryclwn@aol.com • PSW • 06/1998 • (S 1991)

**KAELBERER CHARITY ANN**
Valley Luth High School 3560 Mc Carty Saginaw MI 48603 • MI • 07/1999 • (S 1996)

**KAELBERER EDWARD B** (719)269-1783
3304 Skyline Loop Canon City CO 81212 • RM • EM • (S 1955 MMU)

**KAELBERER JAY A**
Valley Luth High School 3560 Mc Carty Saginaw MI 48603 • MI • Tchr • Michigan Ann Arbor MI • (S 1997)

**KAELBERER JEROME T** (507)776-6487
RR 2 Truman MN 56088-9803 • MNS • P/Tchr • St John Saint James MN • (507)375-3433 • (S 1961)

**KAELBERER KENT J** (414)760-9087
11823 W Bobolink Ave Milwaukee WI 53225-2216 • SW • Tchr • Immanuel Brookfield WI • (414)781-4135 • (MQ 1992)

**KAELBERER MARY LOU** (303)750-7541
9831 E Cornell Ave Denver CO 80231-4702 • wkaelberer@uswest.net • RM • Tchr • St John Denver CO • (303)733-3777 • (SP 1969)

**KAES JANE MARIE** (208)733-6963
395 Dubois Ave Twin Falls ID 83301-4614 • NOW • EM • (RF 1959)

**KAESTNER DOROTHY A** (636)273-5268
1648 Timber Hollow Dr Wildwood MO 63011-1978 • dorothy.kaestner@lfnd.org • MO • S Ex/S • Missouri Saint Louis MO • (314)317-4550 • (RF 1969 MS MLS)

**KAHL LYNN M** (708)485-0204
4124 Maple Ave Brookfield IL 60513-1916 • lkahl@mcsv.com • NI • Tchr • St John LA Grange IL • (708)354-1690 • (RF 1972 MA)

**KAHLER MICHEAL L** (314)561-8999
60 Normandy Dr Lake Saint Louis MO 63367-1501 • MO • 11/1983 11/1998 • (S 1975)

**KAHLFELDT ALBERT L** (414)827-0415
16345 W Melody Dr New Berlin WI 53151-9245 • NI • Northern Illinois Hillside IL • (RF 1969)

**KAHLFELDT CARL L** (847)965-1507
8248 W Lyons St Niles IL 60714-1336 • NI • Northern Illinois Hillside IL • (RF 1965 MSED MED)

**KAISER DAVID ALLEN** (810)653-4333
9133 Chatwell Club Dr - #2 Davison MI 48423-2878 • MI • Tchr • St Paul Millington MI • (517)871-4581 • (AA 1997)

**KAISER ERIKA JOY** (810)653-4333
9133 Chatwell Club Dr - #2 Davison MI 48423-2874 • MI • Tchr • St Paul Millington MI • (517)871-4581 • (AA 1998)

**KAISER GEORGE J** (419)784-0706
211 Wilson St Defiance OH 43512-1441 • OH • 02/1999 • (RF 1969 MA)

**KAISER ROY G** (248)651-8621
370 Maplehill Rd Rochester Hills MI 48306-4315 • roykaiser@compuserve.com • MI • EM • (RF 1954 MED EDS DED)

**KALAL THOMAS C** (708)345-6806
417 N 7th Ave Maywood IL 60153-1154 • neiffl@aol.com • NI • Tchr • St John Forest Park IL • (708)366-2764 • (RF 1985)

**KALCHBRENNER SUSAN K** (414)453-2054
359 N 63rd St Milwaukee WI 53213-4138 • SW • Tchr • Zion Menomonee Falls WI • (414)781-7437 • (S 1973)

**KALMES MICHAEL W** (734)572-0185
5771 Dartmouth Ct Ypsilanti MI 48197-9039 • kalmesm@ccaa.edu • MI • SHS/C • Michigan Ann Arbor MI • (S 1971 MED)

**KALOUS KEITH L** (414)781-1031
W144N4937 Stone Dr Menomonee Falls WI 53051-6953 • SW • Tchr • Milwaukee LHS Milwaukee WI • (414)461-6000 • (RF 1978 MCOUN)

**KALOUS KEVIN R** (708)854-7619
331 Briarwood Ln Algonquin IL 60102-1984 • NI • Tchr • St Paul Milford IL • (815)889-4569 • (RF 1985 MA)

**KAMIN ROBIN R** (630)887-1626
529 W 58th Pl Hinsdale IL 60521 • NI • 08/1999 • (RF 1974)

**KAMM-DOOLEY SUZETTE** (503)249-0506
4410 NE Ainsworth St Portland OR 97218-1328 • sjkamm@aol.com • NOW • Tchr • Trinity Portland OR • (503)288-6403 • (CQ 1984 MA)

**KAMMAN REBECCA ANN** (502)254-1308
501 Hillrose Dr Louisville KY 40243 • srkamma@aol.com • IN • Tchr • Our Savior Louisville KY • (502)426-0864 • (S 1990 MA)

**KAMMAN SCOTT R** (502)254-1308
501 Hillrose Dr Louisville KY 40243-1926 • srkamma@aol.com • IN • Tchr • Our Savior Louisville KY • (502)426-0864 • (AA 1987 MMU)

**KAMMERLOHR WILLIAM A** (217)525-0805
3509 Angelo Springfield IL 62707-7409 • CI • Tchr • LHS Springfield IL • (217)546-6363 • (S 1974)

**KAMMEYER LAUREL E** (660)463-7354
1204 Maple St Concordia MO 64020-9355 • MO • Tchr • St Paul Concordia MO • (660)463-7654 • (MW 1969 MS)

**KAMMRATH WILLIAM H** (708)452-0423
1900 N 73rd Ave Elmwood Park IL 60707 • NI • SHS/C • Northern Illinois Hillside IL • (RF 1964 MBA MA PHD)

**KAMPRATH CHRISTOPHER M**
St Martins Luth School 253 Liberty St Winona MN 55987-3799 • ckamprat@tvsw • MNS • Tchr • St Martins Winona MN • (507)452-6056 • (S 1997)

**KAMPRATH ELIZABETH IDA** (920)734-3039
1431 Linda Ave Menasha WI 54952-1622 • SW • Tchr • Trinity Menasha WI • (920)725-1715 • (SP 1968)

**KAMPRATH FREDRIC W** (407)392-6140
481 NW 11th Ave Boca Raton FL 33486-3460 • FG • Tchr • St Paul Boca Raton FL • (561)395-8548 • (S 1958 MAT)

**KAMPRATH HOLLY C** (402)421-1965
5801 Doe Cir Lincoln NE 68516-9333 • NEB • Tchr • Faith Lincoln NE • (402)466-6861 • (S 1980 MA)

**KAMPRATH JAMES E** (901)396-3335
1369 N Faronia Sq Memphis TN 38116-6510 • jimkamprath@msn.com • MDS • Tchr • Cross/Calvary Memphis TN • (901)396-5566 • (S 1970 MSED)

**KAMPRATH LEI LANI E** (561)392-6140
481 NW 11th Ave Boca Raton FL 33486 • FG • EM • (S 1959)

**KAMPRATH PAULETTE G** (901)396-3335
1369 N Faronia Sq Memphis TN 38116-6510 • jimkamprath@msn.com • MDS • Tchr • Cross/Calvary Memphis TN • (901)396-5566 • (S 1969 MS)

**KAMPRATH RONALD P** (920)208-1296
2517 N 6th St Sheboygan WI 53083-4962 • SW • Tchr • St Paul Sheboygan WI • (920)452-6882 • (S 1965 MA)

**KAMPRATH THOMAS E**
1637 SW 37th Ter Apt 119 Topeka KS 66609-2118 • KS • Tchr • Topeka Topeka KS • (785)357-0382 • (S 1998)

**KAMPRATH VICTOR M**
3203 Parnell Ave Fort Wayne IN 46805 • IN • EM • (RF 1937 MS)

**KAMPRATH WALDEMAR R** (206)522-8304
2516 NE 91st St Seattle WA 98115-3466 • NOW • EM • (S 1937)

**KAMPS SALLIE JO** (715)536-3243
604 Hollywood Dr #1 Merrill WI 54452 • NW • Tchr • Trinity Merrill WI • (715)536-7501 • (RF 1981)

**KAMPSCHNEIDER YVETTE** (215)741-2048
530 Main St Hulmeville PA 19047-5820 • EA • Tchr • Hope Levittown PA • (215)946-3467 • (S 1994)

**KAMRATH ANGELA SUE**
2300 Timberline Dr Apt 281 Grapevine TX 76051 • TX • Tchr • Crown of Life Colleyville TX • (817)421-5683 • (MQ 1999)

**KANE DEBRA LYNN** (419)782-7598
1322 Heatherdowns Dr Defiance OH 43512 • OH • 03/1999 • (CQ 1993 MAT)

**KANE EWALD** (216)871-1654
403 Canterbury Rd Bay Village OH 44140-2408 • OH • Ohio Olmsted Falls OH* • (RF 1957 MED PHD LLD)

**KANGAS LEAH JEAN** (262)695-2339
340 Morris St Apt 13 Pewaukee WI 53072-4665 • SW • Tchr • Divine Redeemer Hartland WI • (414)367-8400 • (MQ 1995)

**KANGAS SEAN**
435 San Vicente Blvd Apt M Santa Monica CA 90402-1733 • PSW • Tchr • Pilgrim Santa Monica CA • (310)829-4113 • (PO 1997)

**KANNENWISCHER HORST**
C/O First Lutheran Church 1101 N 4th St Ponca City OK 74601-2724 • hpkannen@fullnet.net • OK • Tchr • First Ponca City OK • (580)762-1111 • (AA 1987)

**KANNENWISCHER MARK** (614)891-8395
510 Susan Ave Westerville OH 43081 • mslkannen@aol.com • OH • 06/1999 • (AA 1998)

**KANNING MARCEIL E** (219)483-3003
4408 Karen Ave Fort Wayne IN 46815-6939 • IN • EM • (RF 1954 MS)

**KAPELKE PATRICIA ANN** (414)338-9630
153 E Washington St West Bend WI 53095-2571 • jkapelke@aol.com • SW • Tchr • St Paul Grafton WI • (262)377-4659 • (MQ 1993)

**KARCHER TROY ALLEN** (281)364-7526
15 Grey Birch Pl The Woodlands TX 77381 • TX • Tchr • Lutheran South Acade Houston TX • (281)464-9320 • (S 1995)

**KARCHER WAYNE** (281)364-7526
15 Grey Birch Pl The Woodlands TX 77381-4625 • karch1197.@msn.com • TX • EM • (S 1968)

**KARGES LONNIE R*** (702)246-7757
171 Six Mile Canyon Rd Dayton NV 89403-8003 • CNH • Tchr • Bethlehem Carson City NV • (775)882-5252 • (S 1982 MED)

**KARLE DELORIS** (708)259-5681
542 S Evergreen Ave Arlington Hts IL 60005-1920 • NI • EM • (RF 1961 MS)

**KARLIN DANIEL W** (810)997-0575
13091 Independence Ave Shelby Township MI 48315-4724 • tontotis@hotmail.com • MI • Mem C • Trinity Utica MI • (810)731-4490 • (S 1972)

**KARNER DALE F** (314)894-4693
2775 Clager Dr Saint Louis MO 63125-4013 • dkarnerstj@postnet.com • MO • P/Tchr • St John Saint Louis MO • (314)773-0784 • (S 1972 MED)

**KARPINSKY KRISTIN S** (702)360-8668
9501 W Sahara Ave Apt 2222 Las Vegas NV 89117-5333 • kkarpinsky@hotmail.com • PSW • Tchr • Faith LHS Las Vegas NV • (702)804-4400 • (MQ 1994)

**KARPINSKY ROY D** (414)634-6370
1703 Chatham St Racine WI 53402-4906 • the5ks@execpc.com • SW • Tchr • St John Racine WI • (414)633-2758 • (RF 1967)

**KARSTEN BEVERLY M** (517)356-9593
1600 Lakeview Dr Alpena MI 49707-4324 • MI • Tchr • Immanuel Alpena MI • (517)354-4805 • (RF 1974)

**KARSTEN KYLE L** (810)566-8835
13754 Hillsdale Dr Sterling Heights MI 48313-3533 • kkarsten@lhsa.com • MI • Tchr • LHS North Macomb MI • (810)781-9151 • (S 1992 MAD)

**KASCHINSKE ERIC JAMES** (219)493-4166
7713 Placer Run Fort Wayne IN 46815-8241 • schinskes@juno.com • IN • Tchr • Concordia LHS Fort Wayne IN • (219)483-1102 • (RF 1996)

**KASCHINSKE KENNETH A** (517)793-3607
4850 Hanover Dr Saginaw MI 48603-2921 • MI • Prin • Peace Saginaw MI • (517)792-2581 • (RF 1967 MED)

**KASPER DEBORAH L** (810)786-0255
13011 27 Mile Rd Washington MI 48094 • RobKasper@juno.com • MI • Tchr • St Peter Macomb MI • (810)781-9296 • (SP 1985)

**KASSEL ROBERT G** (618)483-5132
20 Fairlane Cir Altamont IL 62411-1704 • CI • P/Tchr • Altamont Altamont IL • (618)483-6428 • (RF 1963 MA)

**KASSL LINDA M**
1410 Dallas St Bloomington IL 61704-2322 • CI • Tchr • Trinity Bloomington IL • (309)828-6265 • (RF 1981)

**KASTEN ROBERT R** (734)995-7343
3084 River Meadow Cir Canton MI 48188 • kaster@ccaa.edu • MI • SHS/C • Michigan Ann Arbor MI • (RF 1968 MS)

**KASTEN RONALD L** (520)648-5375
735 W Calle Del Ensalmo Green Valley AZ 85614-2801 • EN • Mem C • Risen Savior Green Valley AZ • (520)625-2612 • (RF 1958 MEAD)

**KASTEN SANDRA LEE** (414)452-5071
3317 S 18th St Sheboygan WI 53081-6624 • ejohnson@excel.net • SW • Tchr • Bethlehem Sheboygan WI • (920)452-5071 • (RF 1975)

**KASTENS ALICE C** (314)892-0888
5101 Kings Park Dr Saint Louis MO 63129-3353 • dakastens@aol.com • SI • Tchr • St John Red Bud IL • (618)282-3873 • (CQ 1998 MS)

**KASTING MELANIE S** (702)360-8668
9501 W Sahara #2222 Las Vegas NV 89117-5333 • mskasting@hotmail.com • PSW • Tchr • Faith LHS Las Vegas NV • (702)804-4400 • (SP 1998)

**KATZ DIANE L** (708)717-6489
112 Quail Hollow Ct Naperville IL 60540-4832 • NI • Tchr • St Paul Aurora IL • (630)820-3457 • (RF 1980 MA)

**KATZENBERGER STEPHANIE MARIE** (708)660-1650
420 S Kenilworth #6 Oak Park IL 60302 • NI • Tchr • Walther LHS Melrose Park IL • (708)344-0404 • (RF 1999)

**KAUFFELD FRED A** (608)273-9492
5606 Hammersley Rd Madison WI 53711-3408 • MNS • EM • (S 1932 MED)

**KAUFMANN REBECCA CHRISTINE** (423)652-0550
6038 Old Jonesboro Rd Bristol TN 37620-3057 • MDS • 05/1996 05/2000 • (RF 1974)

**KAUN CHARLES R** (507)352-4100
328 S Line St PO Box 248 Wykoff MN 55990-0248 • ckaun@hmtel.com • MNS • EM • (RF 1956)

**KAUN ROBERT W** (414)421-9050
5770 Eldon St Greendale WI 53129-1632 • SW • Tchr • Our Father Greenfield WI • (414)282-8220 • (MW 1980 MED)

**KECK NADINE MARIE** (612)871-4003
2323 Clinton Ave S #104 Minneapolis MN 55404-3661 • MNS • Tchr • Trinity First Minneapolis MN • (612)871-2353 • (S 1988)

**KECK ROBERT A** (410)832-5458
807 Hillen Rd Towson MD 21286 • SE • Tchr • Baltimore LHS Baltimore MD • (410)825-2323 • (BR 1976 MS)

**KEDAITIS TRICIA LEIGH** (708)534-6316
26229 Cherry Ln Monee IL 60449 • georgtrica@aol.com • NI • Tchr • St Paul Dolton IL • (708)849-3225 • (SP 1991)

**KEENAN SARA ELIZABETH** (909)920-3439
PO Box 812 Mt Baldy CA 91759-0812 • PSW • Tchr • Redeemer Ontario CA • (909)986-6510 • (IV 1988)

**KEHR MARK A*** (504)649-4583
1003 Janette Ct Slidell LA 70461 • SO • Prin • Prince Of Peace New Orleans LA • (504)242-4348 • (S 1972 MED)

**KEHR SARA M** (727)576-5232
190 112th Ave N #1305 St Petersburg NY 33716 • FG • Tchr • Grace Saint Petersburg FL • (727)527-6213 • (BR 1999)

**KEHR SARAH M** (562)997-0602
268 E San Antonio Dr Long Beach CA 90807 • PSW • Grace Saint Petersburg FL • (BR 1999)

**KEILIG BECKY L**
1006 Grand Ave Ravenna NE 68869-1016 • NEB • Tchr • Trinity Fremont NE • (402)721-5536 • (CQ 1997)

**KEILMAN AMY RENAY** (915)223-0962
2901 Sunset Dr #39F San Angelo TX 76904 • TX • Tchr • Trinity San Angelo TX • (915)944-8660 • (AU 2000)

**KEILMAN TAMARA SUE** (915)947-3126
3140 Sunset Dr San Angelo TX 76904-7154 • tsgk98@aol.com • TX • Tchr • Trinity San Angelo TX • (915)944-8660 • (AA 1993)

**KEINATH KAY A** (517)823-3789
6575 W Frankenmuth Vassar MI 48768-9420 • rkeinath@wolvtds.net • MI • Tchr • St Paul Millington MI • (517)871-4581 • (CQ 1993)

**KEIPER CHRISTA FAITH**
103 Batts Bryan TX 77803-4965 • TX • 06/1999 • (RF 1995)

**KEIPER GERTRUDE M** (512)291-9997
2915 Windcliff Way Austin TX 78748 • keiperg@austin.concordia.edu • TX • SHS/C • Texas Austin TX • (CQ 1989 DED)

**KEIPER PAUL E**
103 Batts St Bryan TX 77803-4965 • TX • 06/1999 • (MQ 1987)

**KEIPER VAL H DR** (414)964-8012
5413 N Navajo Ave Glendale WI 53217-5038 • val.keiper@cuw.edu • SW • SHS/C • South Wisconsin Milwaukee WI • (414)464-8100 • (PO 1980 MS PHD)

**KEISER LAWRENCE** (714)538-7916
359 N Maplewood St Orange CA 92866-1214 • PSW • EM • (S 1953 MED MED)

**KEISER PAMELA MARIE** (415)363-8732
464 Clinton St Apt 211 Redwood City CA 94062-1004 • EN • Tchr • West Portal San Francisco CA • (415)665-6330 • (S 1979)

**KELDERMAN LAVERNE I** (319)984-5065
108 Hidden Meadow Ln Denver IA 50622-1055 • IE • Tchr • Immanuel Waterloo IA • (319)233-3967 • (SP 1972)

**KELL DELMAR A** (517)835-9928
3301 Boston St Midland MI 48642-3676 • MI • EM • (RF 1962 MA)

**KELL DONALD L** (916)434-0759
1236 Secret Lake Loop Lincoln CA 95648 • donkell@psyber.com • MI • EM • (RF 1953 MA LLD)

**KELL ELTA L** (715)623-2298
126 Virginia St Antigo WI 54409-2664 • NW • EM • (RF 1977)

**KELL JEREMY JAMES** (920)892-8153
734 Summit St Plymouth WI 53073 • SW • Tchr • St Paul Grafton WI • (262)377-4659 • (MQ 1998)

**KELL LUTHER P** (810)340-9697
1600 Taylor Rd Auburn Hills MI 48326-1564 • MI • P/Tchr • St Paul Sterling Heights MI • (810)247-4427 • (SP 1971)

**KELL MARY L** (517)835-9928
3301 Boston St Midland MI 48642-3676 • MI • Tchr • St John Midland MI • (517)835-7041 • (RF 1963 MA)

**KELLAR ROBERT J** (561)498-3733
5095 Beechwood Rd Delray Beach FL 33484 • rkellar007@hotmail.com • FG • 11/1999 • (RF 1989 MED)

**KELLER JAMES N** (219)456-3268
2829 S Harrison St Fort Wayne IN 46807 • magisterjk@juno.com • CNH • 07/1998 07/2000 • (RF 1987)

**KELLER JENNIFER MARIE** (708)209-3099
485 Gregory Ave Apt 2D Glendale Heights IL 60139 • crfkellerjm@curf.edu • NI • SHS/C • Northern Illinois Hillside IL • (S 1996 MA)

**KELLER JILL D** (972)712-1790
7680 King Arthur Rd Frisco TX 75035-7103 • TX • Tchr • Prince Of Peace Carrollton TX • (972)447-9887 • (AU 1996)

**KELLER KATHY JO**
4944 Stengel Ave Toledo OH 43614-5259 • OH • Tchr • Trinity Toledo OH • (419)385-2651 • (RF 1982)

**KELLER STEPHANIE L** (815)477-3212
1733 Il Route 176 Crystal Lake IL 60014-2253 • NI • Tchr • St Peter Arlington Heights IL • (847)253-6638 • (RF 1987 MA)

**KELLERMAN DAVID M** (414)871-0171
3261 N 89th St Milwaukee WI 53222-3607 • SW • Prin • Northwest Milwaukee WI • (414)463-4040 • (SP 1977)

**KELLING STEPHANIE R** (414)549-2150
1908 Avalon Dr Waukesha WI 53186-2802 • SW • Tchr • St Paul Oconomowoc WI • (262)567-5001 • (S 1976)

**KELLY BETTY L** (813)884-4894
7204 Beasley Rd Tampa FL 33615-2102 • chapkelly@juno.com • FG • EM • (RF 1964 MA)

**KELM DIANNE F** (314)937-4264
103 Crystal Meadow Dr Crystal City MO 63019-1346 • kelm7@postnet.com • MO • Tchr • St John Arnold MO • (636)464-7303 • (SP 1977)

**KELM GEORGE G** (847)394-4786
361 S Jewel Ct Palatine IL 60067-1526 • NI • Tchr • St Peter Arlington Heights IL • (847)253-6638 • (SP 1971)

**KELSO DANIELLE C** (714)639-7954
2408 E Adams Ave Orange CA 92867-6108 • ddctkelso@aol.com • PSW • Tchr • Salem Orange CA • (714)639-1946 • (IV 1988 MED)

**KELSO DARREN L** (714)639-7954
2408 E Adams Ave Orange CA 92867-6108 • PSW • Tchr • Salem Orange CA • (714)639-1946 • (IV 1986)

**KELZER DEBRA SUSAN** (612)657-2316
6785 Quartz Ave Mayer MN 55360 • MNS • P/Tchr • Zion Mayer MN • (612)657-2339 • (SP 1982 MA)

**KEMBEL SHARON ANN** (970)867-5122
17557 County Rd V Fort Morgan CO 80701-9221 • RM • Tchr • Trinity Fort Morgan CO • (970)867-4931 • (RF 1969 MA)

**KEMNITZ DETLEF K** (713)686-5814
5631 Sheraton Oaks Dr Houston TX 77091-1305 • detlef@hotmail.com • TX • Tchr • LHS North Houston TX • (713)880-3131 • (S 1983 MED)

**KEMNITZ DIRK** (713)686-4955
946 Del Norte St Houston TX 77018 • scigolf@aol.com • TX • Tchr • Our Savior Houston TX • (713)290-8277 • (S 1982 MSED)

**KEMPF ANNA M** (714)516-2746
5710 E Valencia Dr Orange CA 92869-1450 • annak@lutheranhigh.orange.ca.u.s. • PSW • Tchr • Lutheran HS/Orange C Orange CA • (714)998-5151 • (IV 1986)

**KEMPF MARK J*** (714)516-2746
5710 E Valencia Dr Orange CA 92869-1450 • markk@lutheranhigh.orange.ca.us • PSW • Tchr • Lutheran HS/Orange C Orange CA • (714)998-5151 • (IV 1986 MA)

**KEMPFF ELNA MARIE** (616)428-9887
3366 Coventry Ct Saint Joseph MI 49085 • MI • EM • (RF 1957 MA)

**KEMPFF MARK N** (582)977-1176
PO Box 25255 Miami FL 33102-5255 • NOW • S Miss • Northwest Portland OR • (S 1974 MS)

**KENNEDY DONNA M** (718)539-6511
22-15 127th St College Point NY 11356-2717 • AT • Tchr • St John College Point NY • (718)463-4790 • (BR 1980 MS)

**KENNEDY SUSAN Q** (301)699-9855
5732 39th Ave Hyattsville MD 20781-1715 • SE • Tchr • Ascension Landover Hills MD • (301)577-0500 • (BR 1987)

**KENNELL CHARLES** (414)354-6810
6336 W Donges Ln Brown Deer WI 53223-1237 • SW • Tchr • St John Glendale WI • (414)352-4150 • (S 1965 MED)

**KENNISTON RITA FRANCES** (541)389-0650
21035 Azalia Ave Bend OR 97702-2441 • NOW • Tchr • Trinity Bend OR • (541)382-1850 • (CQ 1990)

**KENNY DONNA MARIE** (412)487-4584
2900 Cavey Crest Cir Allison Park PA 15101-2504 • EA • Tchr • First Pittsburgh PA • (412)782-2772 • (RF 1969)

**KENOW HAROLD R** (651)776-6648
1364 Bush Ave Saint Paul MN 55106-4114 • MNS • EM • (RF 1953)

**KENOW PETER D*** (402)643-2768
945 N 3rd St Seward NE 68434-1511 • pkenow@seward.ccsn.edu • NEB • SHS/C • Nebraska Seward NE • (S 1988)

**KERCHER ELAINE B** (714)772-9179
1585 W Beacon Ave Anaheim CA 92802-1313 • PSW • Tchr • Prince Of Peace Anaheim CA • (714)774-0993 • (RF 1961)

**KERN AARON F**
4429 Grant St PO Box 1613 Bridgeport MI 48722-1613 • MI • Tchr • St Lorenz Frankenmuth MI • (517)652-6141 • (RF 1996)

**KERN BECKY SUE** (406)755-5144
326 Harrison Blvd Kalispell MT 59901-2625 • MT • Tchr • Trinity Kalispell MT • (406)257-6716 • (S 1978)

**KERN BONNIE LOU** (517)652-9445
3839 S Block Rd Frankenmuth MI 48734-9134 • MI • Tchr • St Michael Richville MI • (517)868-4809 • (RF 1969)

**KERN DENNIS L** (616)429-4979
1159 Adams Dr Saint Joseph MI 49085-9732 • MI • Tchr • Christ Stevensville MI • (616)429-7111 • (S 1972 MRD)

**KERN EDWARD A** (812)523-8554
210 Vehslage Rd Seymour IN 47274-2230 • ekern@hsonline.net • IN • Tchr • St John Seymour IN • (812)523-3131 • (RF 1964 MA)

**KERN HEIDI SUE** (517)868-4807
3510 Tressla Rd Reese MI 48757 • hkern@stlorenz.org • MI • Tchr • St Lorenz Frankenmuth MI • (517)652-6141 • (AA 1991)

**KERN JOAN MARIE** (616)429-4979
1159 Adams Dr Saint Joseph MI 49085-9732 • MI • Tchr • Christ Stevensville MI • (616)429-7111 • (S 1972)

**KERN KENT L** (517)868-4807
3510 Tressla Rd Reese MI 48757 • kernk@svol.org • MI • P/Tchr • Trinity Reese MI • (517)868-4501 • (AA 1990 MED)

**KERN KIMBERLY LYNN** (248)269-0237
1285 Kirts Blvd Apt 42 Troy MI 48084 • kernkl@gateway.net • MI • Tchr • Our Shepherd Birmingham MI • (248)645-0551 • (AA 1987 MA)

**KERN LORETTA L** (517)652-8579
236 Cherry St Frankenmuth MI 48734-1705 • MI • EM • (RF 1964 MA)

**KERN STUART C** (517)868-4026
843 N Block Rd Reese MI 48757-9308 • MI • Tchr • Immanuel Saginaw MI • (517)754-4285 • (RF 1966)

**KERNKAMP LYNN M** (561)218-6353
9282 Ketay Cir Boca Raton FL 33428-1516 • lkernkamp@aol.com • FG • Tchr • St Paul Boca Raton FL • (561)395-0433 • (RF 1970 MA)

**KERR HOMER U** (317)862-3690
4257 Wanamaker Dr Indianapolis IN 46239-1633 • rk1950@aol.com • IN • Prin • St John Indianapolis IN • (317)352-9196 • (CQ 1986 MED)

**KERRINS MELIA R**
994 Cottonwood Ln Larkspur CO 80118 • RM • 10/1998 • (IV 1992)

**KERSTEN CHERIE L**
C/O St Matthew Lutheran Church PO Box 297 Nortonville KS 66060-0297 • KS • 07/1991 07/1999 • (S 1988)

**KERSTEN HENRY O** (219)485-2266
6303 Pawawna Dr Fort Wayne IN 46815-6375 • IN • EM • (S 1939 MED)

**KERSTEN JAYNE E** (630)553-2975
111A Colonial Pkwy Yorkville IL 60560 • jaynekl@ameritech.net • NI • Tchr • St Luke Montgomery IL • (630)892-9309 • (RF 1972)

**KERSTEN JOHN V JR.** (314)868-4165
1935 Keelen Dr Saint Louis MO 63136-3337 • jkersten@stl.com • MO • Tchr • Lutheran North Saint Louis MO • (314)389-3100 • (S 1977 MS)

**KERSTEN LOIS M** (636)464-9760
1960 Parkton West Dr Barnhart MO 63012-1239 • MO • Tchr • St John Arnold MO • (636)464-7303 • (S 1964)

**KERSTEN ROBERT A** (630)553-2975
111 A Colonial Pkwy Yorkville IL 60560 • jaynekl@ameritech.net • NI • Tchr • Zion Matteson IL • (708)747-7490 • (SP 1972)

**KERSTEN WILLIAM C** (310)437-5538
1213 E 1st St Long Beach CA 90802-5707 • PSW • Tchr • First Long Beach CA • (562)437-8532 • (RF 1973)

**KESAR MICHAEL L** (402)571-8272
8525 Pratt Omaha NE 68134 • mkesar@st-mark.org • NEB • Mem C • St Mark Omaha NE • (402)391-6148 • (AA 1983 MMU)

**KESEMAN BRENT ALLEN** (208)734-4698
311 Ash St Twin Falls ID 83301-7235 • NOW • 10/1997 • (S 1991)

**KESKE RICHARD PAUL** (815)874-7499
5575 Skywood Ter Rockford IL 61109-3548 • NI • P/Tchr • St Paul Rockford IL • (815)965-3335 • (RF 1968 MA)

**KESSLER STEPHANIE NICOLE** (608)742-3218
122 W Cook St Apt A Portage WI 53901 • SW • Tchr • St John Portage WI • (608)742-2387 • (BR 1997)

**KESTER BRENDA ANN** (920)446-3178
N205 Kester Rd Fremont WI 54940-9402 • SW • Tchr • Grace Omro WI • (920)685-2621 • (MQ 1986)

**KETCHER RONALD LORENZ** (612)467-2596
515 W Elm St Norwood MN 55368-9776 • MNS • Tchr • Zion Mayer MN • (612)657-2339 • (SP 1983)

**KETTLER LUCINDA C** (913)849-3367
21370 W 335th St Paola KS 66071-6217 • KS • Tchr • Trinity Paola KS • (913)849-3343 • (S 1980)

**KETTNER WARREN W** (303)935-2969
3246 S Wolff St Denver CO 80236-3803 • RM • EM • (CQ 1963)

**KEUER EDWARD J** (903)561-7581
17956 S Shore Dr Flint TX 75762-9302 • TX • EM • (RF 1944 MED PHD)

**KEUP ALLAN L** (217)789-9112
518 S Glenwood Ave Springfield IL 62704-1842 • alkeup@aol.com • CI • 01/1988 01/2000 • (RF 1966 MCMU MED)

**KEUP JOEL A** (217)394-2421
103 S Third St PO Box 358 Buckley IL 60918-0358 • jnkeup@illicom.net • CI • Tchr • Central Illinois Springfield IL • (RF 1997)

**KEUP KAREN L** (517)777-8321
5115 Sheridan Rd Saginaw MI 48601-9304 • MI • Tchr • Trinity Reese MI • (517)868-4501 • (RF 1990)

**KEUP NATALIE DIANE** (217)394-2421
PO Box 358 Buckley IL 60918-0358 • jnkeup@illicom.net • CI • Tchr • Christ Lhs Buckley IL • (217)394-2547 • (RF 1995)

**KEUP RONALD W** (517)777-8321
5115 Sheridan Rd Saginaw MI 48601-9304 • kvkeup@juno.com • MI • Tchr • Trinity Reese MI • (517)868-4501 • (RF 1971)

**KEYNE LISA K DR*** (503)335-0720
3614 NE Holman St Portland OR 97211-7802 • lkeyne@cu-portland.edu • NOW • SHS/C • Northwest Portland OR • (SP 1981 MPAD PHD)

**KEYNE-MICHAELS LYNN** (360)546-5906
11118 NW 6th Ave Vancouver WA 98685 • lkeyne-michaels@cu-portland.edu • NOW • SHS/C • Northwest Portland OR • (S 1978 MSED)

**KEYS CAROLYN R** (281)590-1859
4726 Sandydale Ln Houston TX 77039-3606 • TX • Tchr • Memorial Houston TX • (713)782-4022 • (S 1973 MED)

**KIBLER WILLIAM** (480)969-4561
151 E 1st St #147 Mesa AZ 85201 • kiblerelves@prodigy.net • AT • Tchr • Atlantic Bronxville NY • (914)337-5700 • (MQ 1994 MED)

**KIEHL KAREN KATHLEEN** (623)435-8218
10232 N 56th Ave Glendale AZ 85302 • PSW • Tchr • Christian Phoenix AZ • (602)934-5896 • (S 1967)

**KIEHL PETER JAMES**
1575 Pal Dr Apt R 9 Vista CA 92084-3532 • PSW • Tchr • Faith Vista CA • (760)724-7700 • (S 1997)

**KIEL JANICE R** (812)392-2797
St Peter Lutheran Church 719 5th St Columbus IN 47201 • jrkjdw@msn.com • IN • Indiana Fort Wayne IN • (RF 1986 MA)

**KIESCHNICK GLEN** (512)331-7583
12309 Bent Cedar Cv Austin TX 78750-1027 • TX • Prin • Redeemer Austin TX • (512)451-6478 • (S 1973 MED)

**KIESCHNICK HAROLD C** (504)244-7406
4617 Knight Dr New Orleans LA 70127-3327 • kiesch@aol.com • SO • EM • (RF 1958 MA)

**KIESCHNICK HENRIETTA** (504)244-7406
4617 Knight Dr New Orleans LA 70127-3327 • SO • EM • (RF 1958)

**KIESCHNICK OSCAR L**
16950 Page Ave Hazel Crest IL 60429-1426 • NI • Tchr • Northern Illinois Hillside IL • (S 1964)

**KIESEL RICHARD C** (305)962-0332
C/O St Mark Lutheran Church 502 N 28th Ave Hollywood FL 33020-3811 • FG • Tchr • St Mark Hollywood FL • (954)922-7572 • (RF 1972)

**KIESER STEPHEN WAYNE** (972)429-9527
3612 Parker Rd Wylie TX 75098 • TX • Prin • Faith Plano TX • (972)423-7448 • (AA 1993 MA)

**KIESS KIMBERLY SUE** (219)724-3150
12825 S County Line Rd E Decatur IN 46733-9621 • IN • 06/1999 • (CQ 1996)

**KIETZMAN CAROL DIANE** (612)754-0277
11211 Zion St NW Coon Rapids MN 55433-3526 • MNS • Tchr • Prince Of Peace Spring Lake Park MN • (612)786-1755 • (SP 1985)

**KIETZMAN CYNTHIA BETH**
615 W 4th St Red Wing MN 55066-2413 • MNS • Tchr • Concordia Red Wing MN • (651)388-5447 • (SP 1995)

**KIETZMAN JANNA K** (218)281-3177
311 Crescent Ave Crookston MN 56716-2328 • MNN • P/Tchr • Our Savior Crookston MN • (218)281-5191 • (SP 1984)

**KILIAN NATHAN RICHARD** (760)945-4506
831 Via Felicidad Vista CA 92084 • PSW • 07/1997 • (IV 1993)

**KILLIAN LISA M** (847)658-5251
427 S Hubbard St Algonquin IL 60102-2812 • NI • Tchr • St John Algonquin IL • (847)658-9311 • (RF 1987)

**KILPS LORI L**
3504 Pierce Ct Two Rivers WI 54241-1858 • SW • Tchr • Good Shepherd Two Rivers WI • (920)793-1716 • (RF 1978)

**KIMBLE DANIEL F** (612)467-3581
303 4th Ave SW Young America MN 55397-9263 • MNS • Tchr • St Johns Young America MN • (612)467-3461 • (RF 1972)

**KIMMEL BETH J** (248)391-4634
3961 Morgan Rd Orion Twp MI 48359-1948 • kimmelclan@hotmail.com • MI • Mem C • Living Word Rochester MI • (248)651-5316 • (RF 1985)

**KIMMEL SHARON K** (716)637-5638
2227 Sweden Walker Rd Hilton NY 14468-9730 • stskim@yahoo.com • EA • Tchr • St Paul Hilton NY • (716)392-4000 • (CQ 1997 MAD MA)

**KIMMINAU ELIZABETH K**
7045 W 63rd Pl Chicago IL 60638 • NI • Tchr • Gloria Dei Chicago IL • (773)581-5259 • (RF 1987)

**KIMSAL RONALD F*** (313)329-6330
990 N 2nd St Apt 2 Saint Clair MI 48079-4290 • MI • EM • (RF 1965 MED)

**KINAS HAROLD A** (414)527-3906
4078 N 84th St Milwaukee WI 53222-1812 • hakinas@coollink.net • NW • EM • (RF 1948 MED)

**KING DOROTHY LOUISE** (314)355-0457
11747 Prigge Meadows Dr Saint Louis MO 63138-3662 • MO • Tchr • Immanuel Saint Charles MO • (636)946-0051 • (RF 1969)

**KING JENNIFER ANNE** (512)260-2954
1226 Brashear Ln Cedar Park TX 78613-6852 • TX • Tchr • Redeemer Austin TX • (512)451-6478 • (AU 1997)

**KING JUDITH H** (612)421-2087
11969 Utah Ave N Champlin MN 55316-2347 • MNS • Tchr • St John Elk River MN • (612)441-6616 • (SP 1977)

**KING JUDITH I** (310)638-1967
19116 Caney Ave Carson CA 90746-2411 • rjteachkings@cs.com • PSW • Tchr • St Paul Garden Grove CA • (714)534-6320 • (S 1971 MCOUN)

**KING LINDA LEE** (630)907-0332
C/O Immanuel Lutheran Church 2317 S Wolf Rd Hillside IL 60162-2211 • NI • Prin • Immanuel Hillside IL • (708)562-5590 • (CQ 1996)

**KING ROBERT A** (310)638-1967
19116 Caney Ave Carson CA 90746-2411 • rjteachkings@cs.com • PSW • Tchr • St Paul Garden Grove CA • (714)534-6320 • (S 1972 MSED)

**KING ROSS E** (219)456-1134
9416 Stagecoach Dr Fort Wayne IN 46804 • IN • Prin • Emmaus Fort Wayne IN • (219)456-4573 • (CQ 1980 MA)

**KING TAMI L**
2338 S 79th St West Allis WI 53219 • SW • 08/2000 • (RF 1998)

**KING TAMMY LYNN** (334)457-3940
2709 Harper Ave Mobile AL 36617-1840 • SO • Tchr • Trinity Mobile AL • (334)456-7960 • (SEL 1996)

**KING THOMAS A III**
2338 S 79th St West Allis WI 53219 • SW • Tchr • Milwaukee LHS Milwaukee WI • (414)461-6000 • (RF 1998)

**KING THOMAS A JR.** (314)355-0457
11747 Prigge Meadows Dr Saint Louis MO 63138-3662 • dotom@epconline.com • MO • Tchr • Immanuel Saint Charles MO • (636)946-2656 • (RF 1968 MAT)

**KINGSTON GAYLE M** (602)893-8352
3701 E Nambe Ct Phoenix AZ 85044-3874 • jerry.kingston@asu.edu • PSW • Tchr • Gethsemane Tempe AZ • (480)839-0906 • (CQ 1989)

**KINWORTHY JOHN C DR** (402)643-2592
714 N 1st St Seward NE 68434-1502 • jkinworthy@seward.cune.edu • NEB • SHS/C • Nebraska Seward NE • (RF 1963 MA PHD)

**KIPP ANITA E** (314)894-3019
1113 Victory Dr Saint Louis MO 63125-4638 • MO • Tchr • Salem Affton MO • (314)353-9242 • (S 1977)

**KIRBY JEAN C** (214)596-1150
1521 Cherbourg Dr Plano TX 75075-2276 • TX • Tchr • Faith Plano TX • (972)423-7448 • (S 1968)

**KIRBY KATHRYN J** (217)682-5429
PO Box 443 Stewardson IL 62463-0443 • CI • Tchr • Trinity Stewardson IL • (217)682-3881 • (S 1984)

**KIRCH GLEN W** (303)934-4084
1693 S Knox Ct Denver CO 80219-4526 • RM • EM • (S 1960)

**KIRCHENBERG MARK R** (231)723-3373
433 2nd St Manistee MI 49660-1541 • mkirchen@edcen.ehhs.cmich.edu • MI • Tchr • Trinity Manistee MI • (616)723-8700 • (RF 1976 MCMU)

**KIRCHENBERG RALPH J** (708)345-9353
1000 N 2nd Ave Maywood IL 60153-1011 • NI • SHS/C • Northern Illinois Hillside IL • (RF 1955 MS)

**KIRCHHOFF DAVID W** (810)736-4694
5033 Daly Blvd Flint MI 48506 • davidk72@hotmail.com • MI • Tchr • St Mark Flint MI • (810)736-6910 • (RF 1995)

**KIRCHHOFF SUSAN KAYE** (810)736-4694
5033 Daly Blvd Flint MI 48506 • daveandsue91@aol.com • MI • Tchr • St Mark Flint MI • (810)736-6910 • (RF 1995)

**KIRCHHOFF W JAMES DR** (630)420-1263
505 Tupelo Dr Naperville IL 60540-7831 • ni³kirchhwj@ni.lcms.org • NI • Northern Illinois Hillside IL* • (RF 1957 MA DED)

**KIRCHNER CHERYL N** (612)894-8781
11209 Lewis Ct Burnsville MN 55337-3219 • MNS • Tchr • St Peter Edina MN • (612)927-8400 • (SP 1985)

**KIRCHNER JOHN A** (612)894-8781
11209 Lewis Ct Burnsville MN 55337-3219 • MNS • Tchr • St Peter Edina MN • (612)927-8400 • (RF 1985)

**KIRCHNER PEGGY JEAN** (956)687-1974
108 E Lark Ave Mc Allen TX 78504-2013 • TX • Tchr • St Paul Mc Allen TX • (956)682-2201 • (S 1968 MA)

**KIRIN WENDY J** (863)324-7891
129 Lake Otis Rd Winter Haven FL 33884-1061 • rmkirin@juno.com • FG • Tchr • Grace Winter Haven FL • (941)293-9744 • (RF 1983)

**KIRK PAUL MARTIN** (630)830-6899
2045 Camden Ln Hanover Park IL 60103 • kirk@stjohnwheaton.pvt.k12.il.us • NI • Tchr • St John Wheaton IL • (630)668-0701 • (RF 1997)

**KIRKENDOLL CHERYL RENEE** (913)651-5961
773 Pottawatomie St Leavenworth KS 66048-1873 • thekrkndls@juno.com • KS • Tchr • St Paul Leavenworth KS • (913)682-5553 • (S 1993)

**KIRKSEY DAISY B** (205)456-6578
639 Summerville St Mobile AL 36617-2525 • SO • P/Tchr • Faith Mobile AL • (834)471-1629 • (S 1983)

**KIRSCH ROGER A** (312)893-5312
275 Thrasher St Bloomingdale IL 60108-1370 • NI • Tchr • St Peter Schaumburg IL • (847)885-7636 • (RF 1971 MA)

**KIRSCHENMANN JANE ANN** (605)343-2399
623 Sage Ave Rapid City SD 57701-7570 • SD • Tchr • Zion Rapid City SD • (605)342-5749 • (SP 1971)

**KIRST DONNA JEAN** (618)344-4095
370 Skyline View Dr Collinsville IL 62234-6036 • SI • Tchr • Holy Cross Collinsville IL • (618)344-3145 • (RF 1983)

**KIRST KATHLEEN L** (414)458-8890
3209 Silver Leaf Ln Sheboygan WI 53083-2740 • SW • Tchr • Trinity Sheboygan WI • (920)458-8248 • (SP 1970)

**KISCHNICK REBECCA ANN** (812)949-9014
2463 Birch Dr Clarksville IN 47129-1286 • IN • 10/1993 10/1999 • (RF 1977 MA)

**KISON CONNIE L** (262)377-5670
10017 Flagstone Dr Cedarburg WI 53012-8822 • SW • Tchr • First Immanuel Cedarburg WI • (262)377-6610 • (RF 1975)

**KITASHIMA ROBBIN R** (303)458-7217
4900 W 30th Ave Denver CO 80212 • RM • Tchr • Bethlehem Lakewood CO • (303)238-7676 • (CQ 1999)

**KITTEL WALTER J** (941)939-5766
1263 Sunbury Dr Fort Myers FL 33901-8738 • FG • EM • (RF 1953)

**KITZING KAREN ELIZABETH** (308)745-0808
PO Box 100 Loup City NE 68853 • NEB • 06/2000 • (S 1996)

**KITZMAN LAURA ANNE**
1111 Minda Ct Walled Lake MI 48390-2553 • MI • Tchr • St Matthew Walled Lake MI • (248)624-7677 • (AA 1986)

**KLAAS JOAN E** (920)734-1612
1925 N Eugene St Appleton WI 54914-2422 • NW • P/Tchr • Celebration Appleton WI • (920)734-8218 • (RF 1969)

**KLADE JEFFREY H** (405)263-7457
RR 4 Box 83A Okarche OK 73762-9336 • OK • P/Tchr • St John Okarche OK • (405)263-4488 • (S 1981)

**KLAGES KENNETH J** (517)792-2688
4263 Kirkwood Dr Saginaw MI 48603-5834 • MI • Mem C • Peace Saginaw MI • (RF 1967)

**KLAHSEN JANE A** (612)443-1992
8585 Rhoy St Victoria MN 55386 • MNS • Tchr • Redeemer Wayzata MN • (612)473-5356 • (CQ 1998)

**KLAMMER JANE L** 011-852-2813-7154
5A Scenic View 1 Red Hill Rd Tai Tam HONG KONG • jklammer@hkis.edu.hk • NI • S Miss • Northern Illinois Hillside IL • (S 1981 MS)

**KLAMMER JOEL R** 011-852-2813-7154
5A Scenic View 1 Red Hill Rd Tai Tam HONG KONG • klammer@hkis.edu.hk • NI • S Miss • Northern Illinois Hillside IL • (AA 1985 MA)

**KLAMMER WERNER C**
446 Church St Seward NE 68434-6005 • NEB • EM • (RF 1946 MS)

**KLATT CORRIE L**
2492 Dublin Dr Carrollton TX 75006-2638 • TX • 04/1997 04/2000 • (IV 1990)

**KLATT RICHARD E** (801)565-3631
17155 Parktrail Dr Monument CO 80132 • RKlatt@uswest.net • RM • EM • (RF 1960 MA)

**KLAUS KURT R P**
14050 Newcomb Ave Orlando FL 32826 • FG • Tchr • Orlando Lutheran Aca Orlando FL • (407)275-7750 • (MQ 1998)

**KLAUSMEIER CAROLINE L** (248)335-5261
3321 Devon Brook Dr Bloomfield Hills MI 48302-1430 • hcklausmeier@earthlink.net • MI • Tchr • Our Shepherd Birmingham MI • (248)645-0551 • (RF 1955 MED)

**KLAUSTERMEIER JEREMY ROGER** (573)221-0615
C/O St John Lutheran Church 1201 Lyon St Hannibal MO 63401-4115 • CI • 08/1999 • (MQ 1993)

**KLAWITER JAMES F** (909)927-8827
44225 Alsace Ln Hemet CA 92544-9105 • klaw@koan.com • PSW • EM • (RF 1957 MA)

**KLEBA DALE J** (414)367-9029
912 Manchester Ct Hartland WI 53029-2705 • SW • Tchr • Divine Redeemer Hartland WI • (414)367-8400 • (SP 1974 MA)

**KLEBER SUSAN K** (316)682-5104
9422 Parkmont Dr Wichita KS 67207-6628 • cookieelf@aol.com • KS • P/Tchr • Bethany Wichita KS • (316)265-7415 • (S 1975 MED)

**KLECKNER ERIC MICHAEL** (618)243-5501
604 S Hanover St Okawville IL 62271 • erklec@juno.com • SI • P/Tchr • Immanuel Okawville IL • (618)243-6215 • (RF 1995)

**KLECKNER KIMBERLY A** (419)298-2594
1018 Cicero Rd Edgerton OH 43517-9514 • kakleck@saa.net • OH • 08/1985 08/2000 • (RF 1979 MS)

**KLECKNER PAMELA SUE** (618)243-5501
604 S Hanover St Okawville IL 62271 • erklec@juno.com • SI • Tchr • Immanuel Okawville IL • (618)243-6215 • (RF 1995)

**KLEIMOLA DAVID A** (507)234-6268
511 N Main St Janesville MN 56048-9794 • dak51@evdoramail.com • MNS • P/Tchr • Trinity Janesville MN • (507)231-6646 • (S 1973)

**KLEIN BRADLEY JAY** (918)445-0763
6112 S Waco Ave Tulsa OK 74132-1900 • OK • Mem C • Our Savior Tulsa OK • (918)836-3752 • (RF 1987)

**KLEIN BRYAN PAUL**
5054 Cherry View Dr West Valley City UT 84120 • brymir@bellsouth.net • RM • Tchr • Christ Murray UT • (801)262-4354 • (S 1981)

**KLEIN CHARLES** (415)752-9451
461 9th Ave San Francisco CA 94118-2912 • CNH • Tchr • Zion San Francisco CA • (415)221-7500 • (S 1963)

**KLEIN CHERYL M** (580)362-2827
6501 N W St Newkirk OK 74647 • OK • Tchr • First Ponca City OK • (580)762-4243 • (S 1970)

**KLEIN DAVE R** (618)545-0150
11 Edgewood Ln N Centralia IL 62801 • dkjjl@juno.com • SI • Prin • Trinity Centralia IL • (618)532-2614 • (S 1984 MSED)

**KLEIN DONALD E** (815)633-2807
725 Sheridan Dr Loves Park IL 61111-4640 • NI • Tchr • Concordia Machesney Park IL • (815)633-6450 • (RF 1965)

**KLEIN DORIS J** (707)253-8625
2516 Grove Ave Napa CA 94558-4415 • dklein@i-cafe.net • CNH • Tchr • St John Napa CA • (707)226-7970 • (S 1971)

**KLEIN HAROLD W** (573)896-5349
133 Manview Ln Holts Summit MO 65043-1119 • MO • EM • (RF 1955 MED)

**KLEIN KAREN K** (847)658-1386
401 Village Creek Dr Lake in the Hills IL 60156-4810 • karlotta323@yahoo.com • NI • Tchr • Good Shepherd Elgin IL • (847)741-7788 • (RF 1999)

**KLEIN LINDA G** (815)633-2807
725 Sheridan Dr Loves Park IL 61111-4640 • NI • EM • (RF 1966)

**KLEIN LOIS JOYCE**
2610 Monroe St Hollywood FL 33020 • FG • Tchr • St Mark Hollywood FL • (954)922-7568 • (S 1969 MS)

**KLEIN MIRIAM K**
5054 Cherry View Dr West Valley City UT 84120 • brymir@bellsouth.net • RM • Tchr • Christ Murray UT • (801)262-4354 • (S 1987)

**KLEIN PAULA C** (618)277-0128
217 Clearwater Dr Belleville IL 62220-2968 • SI • Tchr • Zion Belleville IL • (618)234-0275 • (CQ 1996)

**KLEIN SHARON L** (773)283-1709
2951 N Lowell Ave Chicago IL 60641-5353 • NI • Tchr • St John Chicago IL • (773)736-1196 • (RF 1972)

**KLEIN SUSAN JOAN** (909)689-6656
2972 Joshua Tree Rd Riverside CA 92503-5632 • PSW • Tchr • Grace Corona CA • (909)737-2187 • (S 1970)

**KLEINE RACHEAL A**
8381 Constitution Bldg 1 Apt 202 Sterling Heights MI 48313 • kleinera@mailcity.com • MI • Tchr • LHS North Macomb MI • (810)781-9151 • (RF 2000)

**KLEINERT KARL R** (281)397-7830
15127 Morning Pine Houston TX 77068 • TX • Tchr • St Mark Houston TX • (713)468-2623 • (AU 1999)

**KLEINERT KRISTIN JOY** (281)397-7830
15127 Morning Pine Houston TX 77068 • TX • Tchr • St Mark Houston TX • (713)468-2623 • (AU 1999)

**KLEINSASSER VICKIE L** (303)347-0188
7817 S Windermere Cir Littleton CO 80120-4467 • RM • Tchr • University Hills Denver CO • (303)759-5363 • (SP 1983)

**KLEINSCHMIDT MARLENE A** (219)485-0057
9526 Mound Creek Cv Fort Wayne IN 46835-9490 • IN • EM • (RF 1960 MSED)

**KLEINSCHMIDT WILBUR H** (715)526-6292
321 S Andrews St Shawano WI 54166-2405 • NW • Mem C • St James Shawano WI • (715)524-4815 • (RF 1952 MA)

**KLEKAMP PATRICIA ANN** (972)918-0848
1842 Place 1 Ln Garland TX 75042-4560 • pklhsd@aol.com • TX • Prin • Lutheran HS of Dalla Dallas TX • (214)349-8912 • (CQ 1985 MA)

**KLEMENT ALICE M** (210)342-9304
3235 Castledale St San Antonio TX 78230-3901 • shlcschool@aol.com • TX • Mem C • Shepherd Hills San Antonio TX • (210)614-3742 • (SP 1969 MA)

**KLEMM KARRI LYN** (561)278-8505
1230 Delray Lakes Dr Delray Beach FL 33444 • rkklemm@compuserve.com • FG • Tchr • Trinity Delray Beach FL • (561)276-8458 • (BR 1985)

**KLEMM LOWELL E** (630)906-9544
1919 Kenilworth Pl Aurora IL 60506-5249 • NI • P/Tchr • Immanuel Des Plaines IL • (847)390-0990 • (RF 1963 MA)

**KLEMP GARRETH** (414)242-6052
11856 N Church Pl 109W Mequon WI 53097-2800 • SW • Tchr • Trinity Mequon WI • (262)242-2045 • (RF 1967 MS)

**KLEMP KYLE**
1611 California Ave Wahiawa HI 96789 • CNH • Tchr • Trinity Wahiawa HI • (808)621-6033 • (MQ 1999)

**KLEMP PETER S** (507)252-9533
710 Zumbro Dr NW Rochester MN 55901-2379 • MNS • Tchr • Rochester Central Rochester MN • (507)289-3267 • (SP 1992)

**KLEMZ HARLAN H***
415 S Watertown St Waupun WI 53963-2143 • SW • EM • (S 1958 MS)

**KLENKE LUTHER** (402)643-4886
184 E Seward St Seward NE 68434-2220 • NEB • SHS/C • Nebraska Seward NE • (S 1968)

**KLENKE REBECCA A** (219)639-3212
92 W Honeysuckle Ln Decatur IN 46733-7421 • IN • Tchr • Wyneken Memorial Decatur IN • (219)639-6177 • (SP 1976)

**KLENZ TAMMY** (414)445-7242
3414 N 78th St Milwaukee WI 53222 • gimmiemail@aol.com • SW • Tchr • Mount Calvary Milwaukee WI • (414)873-3466 • (MQ 1990)

**KLEPACKI NINA LEANNE**
440 Timber Ridge Cir Derby KS 67037 • KS • Tchr • Hope Shawnee KS • (913)631-6940 • (S 2000)

**KLETKE DALE BRUCE** (913)238-5921
9029 Grandview Dr Overland Park KS 66212-3857 • dbkletke@jc.net • MO • P/Tchr • Calvary Kansas City MO • (816)444-6908 • (WN 1985 MED)

**KLINGELHOFER CAROL** (847)803-9791
65 N 7th Ave Des Plaines IL 60016-2323 • NI • Tchr • St Paul Mount Prospect IL • (847)255-6733 • (RF 1967 MED)

**KLINKENBERG KAY M** (714)693-3615
5375 Via De La Zorra Yorba Linda CA 92887-3535 • kkay55@aol.com • PSW • Tchr • St John Orange CA • (714)288-4400 • (RF 1962 MED)

**KLINTWORTH KATHRYN G**
318 Willis Rd Saline MI 48176-1597 • MI • SHS/C • Michigan Ann Arbor MI • (RF 1961)

**KLIPFEL SANNA L** (209)383-5231
2049 Kimberly Ave Merced CA 95340-1721 • sklipfez@cyberlynk.com • CNH • Prin • St Paul Merced CA • (209)383-3302 • (S 1974 MA)

**KLITZING GAYLE L** (618)235-7190
204 Susan Dr Albers IL 62215 • SI • Tchr • Zion Belleville IL • (618)234-0275 • (S 1980)

**KLITZING MARK A** (949)852-0119
8 Cosenza Irvine CA 92614-5344 • PSW • Tchr • Christ Costa Mesa CA • (949)548-6866 • (S 1979 MA)

**KLITZING RACHEL** (949)852-0119
8 Cosenza Irvine CA 92614-5344 • pswrachel@aol.com • PSW • Pacific Southwest Irvine CA • (949)854-3232 • (S 1979 MA)

**KLOCKE ELAINE L** (612)906-1340
8312 Suffolk Dr Chanhassen MN 55317-8706 • MNS • EM • (S 1965)

**KLOCKZIEM GLORIA** (863)644-0367
6329 Butternut Dr Lakeland FL 33813-4628 • glooooria@aol.com • FG • Mem C • St Paul Lakeland FL • (863)644-7710 • (SP 1970)

**KLOESS GARY M** (847)696-4672
254 N Northwest Hwy Park Ridge IL 60068-3353 • NI • Tchr • St Andrew Park Ridge IL • (847)823-9308 • (RF 1975 MA)

**KLOHA GLENN E** (216)941-6157
16309 Pearldale Ave Cleveland OH 44135-4425 • gkloha@oh.verio.com • EN • Prin • West Park Cleveland OH • (216)941-2770 • (RF 1967 MA)

**KLOPKE JULIE STREIT** (847)797-8535
627 E Dundee Rd Arlington Hts IL 60004-1541 • jsklopke@aol.com • NI • Tchr • St Peter Arlington Heights IL • (847)253-6638 • (RF 1982)

**KLOSS SANDRA** (954)252-1947
5761 SW 127th Ave Fort Lauderdale FL 33330 • FG • P/Tchr • St Matthew Miami FL • (305)642-2860 • (MQ 1991)

**KLOTZ DEBRA A** (313)673-6575
2500 Mann Rd Lot 287 Clarkston MI 48346-4288 • MI • Tchr • St Paul Royal Oak MI • (248)546-6555 • (RF 1976)

**KLOTZ JOY CAROL** (414)578-2617
3870 N 78th St Milwaukee WI 53222-3099 • SW • Tchr • Martin LHS Greendale WI • (414)421-4000 • (RF 1992 MED MA)

**KLOTZ VERNER** (312)953-9360
122 W Greenfield Ave Lombard IL 60148-1604 • crfklotzvh@curf.edu • NI • SHS/C • Northern Illinois Hillside IL • (RF 1968 MED MS)

**KLUENDER SELMA** (317)271-7268
7854 Maureen Ter Indianapolis IN 46214-2405 • IN • P/Tchr • Our Shepherd Indianapolis IN • (317)271-9103 • (RF 1987)

**KLUG DAVID H** (616)755-1722
517 Tournament Cir Muskegon MI 49441 • MI • P/Tchr • West Shore Muskegon MI • (616)755-1048 • (CQ 1981)

**KLUG JAMES** (217)793-8287
404 Five Forks Dr Springfield IL 62707-8299 • CI • Tchr • Central Illinois Springfield IL • (S 1969 MA)

**KLUG JOSHUA AARON** (703)486-3562
3856 Columbia Pike #13 Arlington VA 22204-4135 • jklug@prodigy.net • SE • Tchr • Our Savior Arlington VA • (703)892-4846 • (MQ 1998)

**KLUG KAY E** (715)536-9661
409 Taylor St Merrill WI 54452 • NW • Tchr • St John Merrill WI • (715)536-7264 • (RF 1973)

**KLUG SARAH LYN** (703)486-3562
3856 Columbia Pike #13 Arlington VA 22204-4135 • jklug@prodigy.net • SE • Tchr • Our Savior Arlington VA • (703)892-4846 • (MQ 1998)

**KLUG ZACHARY ADAM**
C/O Lutheran HS South 9515 Tesson Ferry Rd Saint Louis MO 63121-1599 • MO • Our Savior Arlington VA • (RF 1999)

**KLUGE DAVID A** (410)444-6016
2613 Chesley Ave Baltimore MD 21234-7507 • dmkluge@aol.com • SE • Tchr • Southeastern Alexandria VA • (RF 1957 MA)

**KLUMB DEBORAH L** (360)456-0428
935 Oakcrest Dr SE Lacey WA 98503-1842 • 96greenphantom@home.com • NOW • Tchr • Faith Lacey WA • (360)491-1733 • (S 1976 MED)

**KLUTH CAROL M** (512)218-1732
2508 Plantation Dr Round Rock TX 78681-2609 • TX • Tchr • Hope Austin TX • (512)926-8574 • (SP 1973 MED)

**KLUTMAN LAURIE LYNN**
4485 Lucas Dr SW Grandville MI 49418-2220 • RM • Tchr • Redeemer Salt Lake City UT • (801)487-6283 • (SP 1995)

**KNAACK RUTH E**
131 W 11th St Apt 9 Gibbon MN 55335-9622 • MNS • Redeemer Salt Lake City UT • (SP 1973)

**KNAGGS WILLIAM H** (216)327-6032
5726 Paula Blvd North Ridgeville OH 44039-1758 • OH • Tchr • St Paul Westlake OH • (440)835-3050 • (S 1960 MED)

**KNAPP ANDREW O** (303)986-8063
9481 Vance Ct Broomfield CO 80021-4839 • RM • Tchr • Denver Lutheran High Denver CO • (303)934-2345 • (S 1995)

**KNAPP GAYLE L** (413)527-8806
39 Cook Rd Southampton MA 01073 • NE • Tchr • First Holyoke MA • (413)532-4272 • (RF 1977)

**KNAPP JEFFERY W**
2224 Atkin Ave Salt Lake City CO 84109-1906 • RM • Tchr • Redeemer Salt Lake City UT • (801)467-4352 • (S 1991)

**KNAPP RONALD F** (501)927-3546
C/O Salem Lutheran Church 1800 W Emma Ave Springdale AR 72762 • rknapp751@earthlink.net • MDS • 07/1997 07/2000 • (S 1966 MED)

**KNAUFT CHRISTINE J** (708)705-9129
1010 N Sterling Ave Apt 102 Palatine IL 60067-1971 • NI • Tchr • St Matthew Lake Zurich IL • (847)438-6103 • (RF 1988)

**KNAUFT PAUL D** (708)474-7894
19140 Greenbay Ave Lansing IL 60438 • NI • EM • (RF 1955)

**KNAUFT RAYMOND H** (760)471-5203
807 River Run Cir San Marcos CA 92069 • PSW • EM • (RF 1951)

**KNEA DONALD L** (612)467-2196
205 Washington St Young America MN 55397-9243 • MNS • 09/1999 • (SP 1969 MSCT)

**KNEA HEATHER** (708)895-8441
2044 Porte Delcau Ct #202 Highland IN 46322-2384 • NI • Tchr • Luther East Lansing IL • (708)895-8441 • (S 1996)

**KNEA KATHERINE E** (765)477-9842
1017 Stoneripple Ct Lafayette IN 47909 • IN • Tchr • St James Lafayette IN • (765)742-6464 • (SP 1968)

**KNEA LINDA A** (612)467-2196
205 Washington Street Young America MN 55397-9243 • MNS • Tchr • St John Young America MN • (612)467-2740 • (SP 1969)

**KNEA MARIANA E** (847)394-8632
1705 W Fremont St Arlington Heights IL 60005-1107 • mknea@hotmail.com • NI • Tchr • St Peter Arlington Heights IL • (847)253-6638 • (RF 1992)

**KNEA WILLIAM EARL** (765)477-9842
1017 Stoneripple Ct Lafayette IN 47909-7266 • billk@stjameslaf.org • IN • Prin • St James Lafayette IN • (765)742-6464 • (SP 1968 MA)

**KNIGHT NANCY J** (619)789-4804
2038 Walnut St Ramona CA 92065-1760 • PSW • Tchr • Grace Escondido CA • (760)747-3029 • (S 1971)

**KNIGHT VALERIE RUTH** (618)282-8252
6294 Griggs Rd Red Bud IL 62278 • vknight@randolph.k12.il.us • SI • Tchr • Trinity Red Bud IL • (618)282-2881 • (S 1998)

**KNIPPA ALICIA ELAINE** (254)675-2459
302 N Avenue R Clifton TX 76634-1250 • immanuel@htcomp.net • TX • 06/1998 06/2000 • (AU 1988)

**KNIPPENBERG KIMBERLY M** (317)357-9356
1333 Mutz Dr Indianapolis IN 46229-2248 • IN • Tchr • Zion New Palestine IN • (317)861-4210 • (RF 1989)

**KNITTEL JAMES L** (206)938-0782
4845 40th Ave SW Seattle WA 98116-4505 • NOW • Tchr • Hope Seattle WA • (206)935-8500 • (S 1963 MED)

**KNITTER SUSAN K** (847)584-2777
827 S Springinsguth Rd Schaumburg IL 60193-3329 • knitfour@aol.com • NI • Tchr • Trinity Roselle IL • (630)894-3263 • (RF 1981)

**KNOEDLER ROBERT H** (209)368-9820
208 Palomar Dr Lodi CA 95242-2612 • CNH • Tchr • St Peter Lodi CA • (209)333-2225 • (RF 1961 MA)

**KNOEDLER WALTER G** (714)557-6947
38960 Calle Hermosa Apt 9 Murrieta CA 92563-6005 • PSW • Tchr • Lutheran HS/Orange C Orange CA • (714)998-5151 • (RF 1965)

**KNOEPFEL JAMES B**
1307 16th Ave Kearney NE 68845 • NEB • P/Tchr • Zion Kearney NE • (308)234-3410 • (S 1987 MAD)

**KNOEPFEL LISA C**
1307 16th Ave Kearney NE 68845 • NEB • Tchr • Zion Kearney NE • (308)234-3410 • (S 1987)

**KNOKE DIANE** (813)544-4707
7840 Sundown Dr N Saint Petersburg FL 33709-1254 • FG • 10/1993 10/1999 • (RF 1968 MA)

**KNOLL LOIS E** (262)338-0809
901 Decker Dr West Bend WI 53090-2342 • SW • Tchr • St John West Bend WI • (414)334-3077 • (RF 1968)

**KNOLL MARTIN A** (262)338-0809
901 Decker Dr West Bend WI 53090-2342 • SW • Tchr • St John West Bend WI • (414)334-3077 • (RF 1969)

**KNOP MARGARET E** (618)826-3686
1415 Allendale Blvd Chester IL 62233-1321 • SI • Tchr • St John Chester IL • (618)826-4345 • (S 1979)

**KNOPF LINDA A** (219)485-9164
6324 Drakes Bay Run Fort Wayne IN 46835-9614 • knopfd@aol.com • IN • Tchr • St Paul Fort Wayne IN • (219)423-2496 • (RF 1959 MSED)

**KNOPP ALLEN M** (313)777-5914
17900 Glendale St Apt 6B Roseville MI 48066-3476 • MI • EM • (RF 1955 MA)

**KNORP BRENDAN D** (734)595-6680
35620 Chestnut St Wayne MI 48184-1160 • bknorp@lhsa.com • MI • Tchr • LHS Westland Westland MI • (734)422-2090 • (AA 1997)

**KNORR KARL W**
Concordia University Wisconsin 12800 N Lake Shore Dr Mequon WI 53097-2402 • SW • SHS/C • South Wisconsin Milwaukee WI • (414)464-8100 • (RF 1985 MA)

**KNORR WILLIAM H** (414)771-7837
2419 N 65th St Wauwatosa WI 53213-1428 • SW • EM • (RF 1952 MA)

**KNOSHER BRUCE A** (708)931-9505
308 N Worth Ave Elgin IL 60123-3449 • knosher@megsinet.net • NI • Tchr • Good Shepherd Elgin IL • (847)741-7795 • (RF 1977 MA)

**KNOTTS RICHARD E JR.** (734)975-9121
3135 Hawks Ann Arbor MI 48108 • knottr@ccaa.edu • MI • SHS/C • Michigan Ann Arbor MI • (AA 1984 MA)

**KNOX WENDY ANN** (314)487-0514
4120 O Bannon Rd Apt 7 Saint Louis MO 63129-1125 • wendy3knox@hotmail.com • MO • Tchr • Green Park Lemay MO • (314)544-4248 • (RF 1995)

**KNUDSEN KRISTIE J** (810)233-7365
3369 Barnes Rd Millington MI 48746-9028 • s.k.jjj@juno.com • MI • Tchr • St Paul Millington MI • (517)871-4581 • (S 1981)

**KNUDSON ELLA R** (904)871-0561
139 H L Sudduth Dr Panama City FL 32404-7917 • SO • Tchr • Good Shepherd Panama City FL • (850)871-6311 • (S 1964)

**KNUDTEN GEORGE V** (219)485-2120
6205 Graysford Pl Fort Wayne IN 46835-4721 • mytss@juno.com • IN • EM • (S 1958 MS)

**KNUEPPEL CAROL L** (219)625-4607
4422 Darnley Ct Fort Wayne IN 46804-9793 • IN • Tchr • Indiana Fort Wayne IN • (S 1966)

**KNUEPPEL HENRY P** (847)692-4563
1233 Grove Ave Park Ridge IL 60068-5515 • NI • EM • (S 1952 MA)

**KNURR KATHLEEN P** (520)456-0399
28280 Rain Valley Loop Rd HC 1 Box 703 Elgin AZ 85611 • kurtsmouse@hotmail.com • NI • 04/1999 • (S 1996)

**KNUTH FRED F** (616)429-5163
2876 Kim St Saint Joseph MI 49085-3329 • MI • Tchr • Christ Stevensville MI • (616)429-7111 • (S 1964 MA MA)

**KNUTH SARA A**
2945 Red Fox Run #203 Portage WI 53901 • SW • Tchr • St John Portage WI • (608)742-2387 • (MQ 2000)

**KNUTSON FRANCESCA L** (561)496-3283
4812 S Lee Rd Delray Beach FL 33445 • jfknutson@worldnet.att.net • FG • Tchr • Trinity Delray Beach FL • (561)276-8458 • (RF 1984)

**KNUTSON JEFFREY R** (561)496-3283
4812 S Lee Rd Delray Beach FL 33445 • jfknutson@worldnet.att.net • FG • Tchr • Trinity Delray Beach FL • (561)276-8458 • (RF 1986)

**KOBOLDT MARY ELLEN** (517)752-8532
2918 E Anita Dr Saginaw MI 48601-9238 • MI • Tchr • Peace Saginaw MI • (517)792-2581 • (AA 1986)

**KOCAB SANDRA K** (517)694-4909
5520 Kay North Apt 6 Lansing MI 48911-3870 • MI • Tchr • Trinity Lansing MI • (517)372-3003 • (S 1975)

**KOCH BEVERLY J** (248)852-1048
120 Eastlawn Dr Rochester Hills MI 48307-5321 • MI • Tchr • St John Rochester MI • (248)652-8830 • (S 1978 MA)

**KOCH GENE E** (219)745-0159
1311 W Branning Ave Fort Wayne IN 46807-2106 • IN • Tchr • Unity Fort Wayne IN • (219)744-0459 • (RF 1979 MA)

**KOCH KAREN L** (612)434-5949
24011 Fillmore St NE Bethel MN 55005-9753 • MNS • Tchr • Trinity Saint Francis MN • (612)753-1234 • (S 1975)

**KOCH KENNETH C** (612)434-5949
24011 Fillmore St NE Bethel MN 55005-9753 • MNS • Tchr • Trinity Saint Francis MN • (612)753-1234 • (S 1975)

**KOCH LINDA CAROL** (502)426-2720
4309 Windy Oaks Rd Louisville KY 40241-1743 • IN • 09/1995 09/1999 • (RF 1980)

**KOCH NEAL S** (402)534-2133
PO Box 456 Utica NE 68456-0456 • NEB • Nebraska Seward NE • (S 1972 MA)

**KOCH SHERRY LYNN**
1104 Saint Paul Dr Merrill WI 54452-3046 • NW • 08/1995 08/2000 • (RF 1987)

**KOCH SHIRLENE L** (616)983-2475
2403 Lakeview Ave Saint Joseph MI 49085-1813 • kochshirlene@hotmail.com • MI • Tchr • Trinity Saint Joseph MI • (616)983-3056 • (S 1972 MA)

**KOCH VERNON C** (860)584-0078
154 Meadow St Bristol CT 06010-5730 • vkoch@snet.net • NE • Tchr • Immanuel Bristol CT • (860)583-5631 • (RF 1961 MS)

**KOCH WILLIAM** (608)355-9652
852 Iroquois Cir Baraboo WI 53913 • SW • EM • (RF 1957 MSED)

**KOEBERT JAY WILLIAM** (262)502-9566
W168N10338 Wildrose Ln Germantown WI 53022-4796 • SW • Tchr • Milwaukee LHS Milwaukee WI • (414)461-6000 • (S 1987)

**KOEHLER DEBRA G** (630)668-3884
1489C Woodcutter Ln Apt C Wheaton IL 60187 • NI • Tchr • St John Lombard IL • (630)629-2515 • (RF 1982 MA)

**KOEHLER ELIZABETH ANN**
16857 San Fernando Mission Blv #13 Granada Hills CA 91344-4217 • PSW • Tchr • Pacific Southwest Irvine CA • (949)854-3232 • (RF 1995)

**KOEHLER HENRY E** (630)833-1647
213 Michigan Elmhurst IL 60126 • hankkoehler@hotmail.com • NI • Tchr • Immanuel Elmhurst IL • (630)832-9302 • (RF 1964 MA)

**KOEHLER PAUL E** (507)534-3943
430 2nd St NE Plainview MN 55964-1426 • MNS • Tchr • Immanuel Plainview MN • (507)534-2108 • (RF 1991)

**KOEHLERT KAREN K** (219)490-8241
3218 Victor Ln Fort Wayne IN 46805-2030 • princl@aol.com • IN • Tchr • Zion Fort Wayne IN • (219)744-1389 • (MQ 1987)

**KOEHLERT MARILYN E** (847)426-7452
201 King St East Dundee IL 60118-2407 • NI • Tchr • Immanuel Dundee IL • (847)428-1010 • (RF 1976)

**KOEHLINGER MARK R** (219)484-6352
5225 Stonecreek Trl Fort Wayne IN 46825-5962 • mkoehlinger@aol.com • IN • Tchr • Holy Cross Fort Wayne IN • (219)483-3173 • (S 1983)

**KOEHNE WILLIAM A** (708)771-1939
1135 Nichols Ln Maywood IL 60153-1079 • NI • Tchr • Walther LHS Melrose Park IL • (708)344-0404 • (RF 1991)

**KOEHNEKE KAREN L** (616)983-4701
1219 Lake Blvd Saint Joseph MI 49085-1577 • MI • Tchr • Trinity Saint Joseph MI • (616)983-3056 • (RF 1978 MED)

**KOEHNKE PAUL E** (714)633-5287
929 E Chalynn Ave Orange CA 92866-2801 • PSW • EM • (S 1953)

**KOEHNKE PHILLIP C**
820 Autumn Ln Corona CA 91719-8325 • PSW • Tchr • St John Orange CA • (714)288-4406 • (S 1989)

**KOEHNLEIN LORNA K** (816)436-2398
1216 NW 73rd Ter Kansas City MO 64118-8381 • MO • Tchr • Timothy Blue Springs MO • (816)228-5300 • (CQ 1996)

**KOELLER RENEE L**
PO Box 261758 Littleton CO 80163-1758 • RM • Tchr • Trinity Franktown CO • (303)841-8620 • (S 1983)

**KOELPER LAWRENCE R***
1619 Lakewood Dr Fort Wayne IN 46819 • IN • Tchr • St Paul Fort Wayne IN • (219)423-2496 • (RF 1987 MA)

**KOENEMANN DARIN D** (734)287-2859
12545 Pine St Taylor MI 48180 • koened@juno.com • MI • Tchr • St John Taylor MI • (734)287-2080 • (AA 1999)

**KOENEMANN JULIE A** (562)691-9357
550-A Ridgeway Ln La Habra CA 90631-4454 • faithwildcat@earthlink.net • PSW • Tchr • Faith Whittier CA • (562)941-0245 • (CQ 1980 MED)

**KOENEN GENELLE L** (515)432-5763
601 S Boone Boone IA 50036 • dgkoenen@willinet.net • IW • Tchr • Trinity Boone IA • (515)432-5140 • (S 1980)

**KOENIG ANDREA DAWN** (319)441-0023
3515 Jersey Ridge Rd Apt 403 Davenport IA 52807 • andikoenig@hotmail.com • IE • Tchr • Trinity Davenport IA • (319)322-5224 • (RF 1997)

**KOENIG CAROL J** (636)928-4465
100 Barleystone Dr Saint Charles MO 63304-6803 • vaa213@aol.com • MO • Tchr • Zion Harvester MO • (314)441-7424 • (RF 1974 MA)

**KOENIG DAVID L** (512)836-3434
11709 Drayton Dr Austin TX 78758-3809 • TX • EM • (S 1961 MED)

**KOENIG DAVID P** (219)485-4095
6426 Post Brook Ln Fort Wayne IN 46835 • dpkoenig43@aol.com • IN • Tchr • Concordia LHS Fort Wayne IN • (219)483-1102 • (BR 1976 MA)

**KOENIG MATTHEW LEE**
1915 Cole Dr Jefferson City MO 65101 • MO • Tchr • Trinity Jefferson City MO • (573)636-7807 • (RF 1994)

**KOENIG REBECCA ANN**
1200 Dallas Dr Apt 2124 Denton TX 76205-5175 • TX • 02/1998 02/2000 • (AU 1985)

**KOENIG ROBYN J** (573)824-5157
26S PCR 328 Farrar MO 63746 • trkoenig@excite.com • MO • Tchr • Salem Farrar MO • (573)824-5472 • (S 1993)

**KOEPKE ALAN R** (636)225-5975
907 Grove Hill Ct Fenton MO 63026-7001 • MO • Salem Farrar MO • (S 1975 MS)

**KOEPKE EDGAR A** (414)781-9634
W153N5210 Plaza Dr Menomonee Falls WI 53051-6729 • SW • EM • (RF 1944)

**KOEPKE JOEL L** (262)681-1012
1021 Florence Ave Racine WI 53402-3917 • SW • Tchr • Trinity Racine WI • (414)632-1766 • (RF 1970 MAT)

**KOEPKE MARLENE E** (262)681-1012
1021 Florence Ave Racine WI 53402-3917 • SW • Tchr • Trinity Racine WI • (414)632-1766 • (S 1974)

**KOEPKE ROGER A** (314)428-3416
8616 Belhaven Dr Saint Louis MO 63114-4429 • MO • Tchr • Our Redeemer Overland MO • (314)427-3444 • (S 1960)

**KOERITZ HEIDI SUE** (507)436-5557
PO Box 84 Northrop MN 56075 • MNS • Tchr • St James Northrop MN • (507)436-5289 • (S 1983)

**KOERNER WILLIAM STEVEN** (812)522-6224
934 Wendemere Dr Seymour IN 47274-2706 • IN • Tchr • Immanuel Seymour IN • (812)522-3118 • (RF 1971 MED)

**KOERSCHEN JAMES M DR** (734)663-8280
435 Pine Brae St Ann Arbor MI 48105-2743 • koersj@ccaa.edu • MI • SHS/C • Michigan Ann Arbor MI • (S 1968 MMU PHD)

**KOERSCHEN JOEL**
2681 Kensington Way Stockton CA 95204-5140 • jokor@pacbell.net • CNH • Calif/Nevada/Hawaii San Francisco CA • (415)468-2336 • (SP 1971 MA)

**KOESTER ELMER B** (515)961-0859
1203 N E St Apt 2002 Indianola IA 50125 • IE • EM • (RF 1929)

**KOESTER SANDRA L** (504)945-9918
2219 Saint Denis St New Orleans LA 70122-4566 • SO • Tchr • St Paul New Orleans LA • (504)947-1773 • (S 1979)

**KOESTER SARAH LOUISE** (618)282-4265
9400 S Prairie Rd Red Bud IL 62278-4910 • SI • 08/1996 08/2000 • (S 1991)

**KOFFARNUS DALLAS LEE** (573)496-3099
1813 Honey Creek Rd Jefferson City MO 65101-9462 • ddmast@socket.net • MO • P/Tchr • Immanuel Jefferson City MO • (573)496-3451 • (SP 1973)

**KOGELMANN GERALD F**
1215 W 7th Ave Fort Morgan CO 80701 • RM • P/Tchr • Trinity Fort Morgan CO • (970)867-4931 • (RF 1964)

**KOGLER HENRY J** (734)246-3187
13690 Phelps St Southgate MI 48195-1924 • henry@ctk-church.org • MI • Mem C • Christ King Southgate MI • (734)285-9695 • (RF 1973 MCMU)

**KOGUTKIEWICZ CHAD A**
5813 S 112th St Hales Corners WI 53130 • EN • Tchr • Hales Corners Hales Corners WI • (414)529-6701 • (MQ 1998)

**KOHLER GREGORY P** (920)994-8444
W5415 Hwy SS Random Lake WI 53075 • kidz2473@yahoo.com • SW • Tchr • Emmanuel Adell WI • (920)994-9005 • (MQ 1996)

**KOHLMEIER JAMES N** (414)453-0665
1828 N 55th St Milwaukee WI 53208-1666 • SW • Tchr • Our Redeemer Wauwatosa WI • (414)258-4558 • (AA 1992)

**KOHLMEIER JONATHAN W** (402)643-9489
131 E Moffitt Seward NE 68434 • jwk3413@seward.cune.edu • NEB • Tchr • St John Seward NE • (402)643-2983 • (S 1995)

**KOHLMEIER SARA J** (414)329-1640
2239 S 106th St Milwaukee WI 53227-1215 • skohlmeier@egl.org • SW • Tchr • Elm Grove Elm Grove WI • (262)797-2970 • (RF 1984)

**KOHLS CRAIG V** (612)864-4628
1031 14th St E Glencoe MN 55336-1547 • MNS • Tchr • First Glencoe MN • (320)864-3317 • (S 1971)

**KOHLS JEFFREY J** (417)823-7253
1953 E Swallow St Springfield MO 65804-4321 • djkohls@juno.com • MO • Tchr • Springfield Springfield MO • (417)883-5717 • (S 1985 MS)

**KOHLWEY MARTIN R** (402)646-2219
564 E Pinewood Ave Seward NE 68434-1152 • NEB • SHS/C • Nebraska Seward NE • (S 1983 MA)

**KOHN COURTNEY J** (414)376-9149
N89W6846 Evergreen Ct Apt #202 Cedarburg WI 53012-1182 • SW • Tchr • First Immanuel Cedarburg WI • (262)377-6610 • (MQ 1997)

**KOHRS JONATHAN A** (847)205-7802
2536 Oak Ave Northbrook IL 60062 • NI • Mem C • Grace Northbrook IL • (847)498-3060 • (RF 1985 MCMU)

**KOHRS RALPH L** (262)790-1398
3360 Bermuda Blvd Brookfield WI 53045-2661 • SW • Tchr • Mount Olive Milwaukee WI • (414)774-2113 • (RF 1958)

**KOHRS STEPHEN A** (262)821-5139
15020 W Harcove Dr New Berlin WI 53151-5730 • sakohrs@hotmail.com • SW • Tchr • Milwaukee LHS Milwaukee WI • (414)461-6000 • (RF 1983 MEPD)

**KOHTZ ROGER O** (313)581-5364
7645 Ternes St Dearborn MI 48126-1017 • MI • EM • (S 1956 MS)

**KOHTZ VIRGINIA** (402)643-2727
1151 Fairlane Ave Seward NE 68434-1311 • NEB • Tchr • St John Seward NE • (402)643-4535 • (S 1961 MA)

**KOKEL JOYCE L** (281)251-1196
6126 Northway Dr Spring TX 77389-3771 • TX • Tchr • Salem Tomball TX • (281)351-8122 • (RF 1968 MED)

**KOKEL SYLVIA JEAN** (512)281-5126
15602 Giese Ln Manor TX 78653-3701 • TX • Tchr • Hope Austin TX • (512)926-0003 • (S 1971)

**KOLANDER EUGENE E** (920)794-8841
1510 Blue Heron Dr Two Rivers WI 54241-1761 • ekolander@lsol.net • SW • EM • (S 1958 MSCT MED)

**KOLANDER KEVIN** (414)677-4895
W196N16581 Hawthorn Dr Jackson WI 53037-9556 • SW • Tchr • First Immanuel Cedarburg WI • (262)377-6610 • (S 1984 MS)

**KOLB ARLENE C** (810)689-4664
36314 Park Place Dr Sterling Hts MI 48310-4217 • MI • Mem C • Faith Troy MI • (248)689-4664 • (RF 1969 MCMU)

**KOLB KATHY S** (414)744-7781
2025 E Leroy Ave Saint Francis WI 53235-4605 • SW • Tchr • St Peter Milwaukee WI • (414)353-6800 • (S 1974)

**KOLB KRISTIE SUE** (314)505-7651
801 De Mun Ave Saint Louis MO 63105-3168 • MO • Tchr • Missouri Saint Louis MO • (314)317-4550 • (S 1995)

**KOLB THOMAS W** (410)817-4072
12030 Jerusalem Rd Kingsville MD 21087-1146 • tkolb1@juno.com • SE • Prin • St Paul Kingsville MD • (410)592-8100 • (CQ 1999)

**KOLBERG DEBORAH L** (616)842-7151
17445 Beechill Dr Grand Haven MI 49417-8840 • ddkolberg@yahoo.com • MI • Tchr • St John Grand Haven MI • (616)842-0260 • (RF 1977)

**KOLESAR TANYA** (414)632-5557
1348 Indiana St Racine WI 53405 • SW • Tchr • Good Shepherd Pleasant Prairie WI • (414)694-4405 • (MQ 1998)

**KOLLMANN MARCIA E** (914)337-7554
46 Rose Ave Eastchester NY 10709-3706 • AT • 11/1982 09/1999 • (BR 1977 MMU)

**KOLLMORGEN PAUL G** (414)264-5456
C/O Lutheran High School Assoc 5201 S 76th St Greendale WI 53129-1117 • paulkoll@execpc.com • SW • Tchr • South Wisconsin Milwaukee WI • (414)464-8100 • (S 1994)

**KOLLMORGEN REBECCA JANE** (419)861-7141
102 Leander Dr Toledo OH 43615 • rkollmorgen@trinity.pvt.k12.oh.us • FG • 02/2000 • (S 1987)

**KOLLMORGEN REX T***
1814 Smith Rd Temperance MI 48182 • EN • EM • (S 1959 MAR)

**KOLLMORGEN SANDRA J** (734)874-6585
1814 Smith Rd Temperance MI 48182 • EN • 09/1998 • (S 1960)

**KOLLMORGEN TIMOTHY ALAN** (419)861-7141
102 Leander Dr Toledo OH 43615 • tkollmorgen@trinity.pvt.k12.oh.us • OH • Tchr • Trinity Toledo OH • (419)385-2301 • (S 1988)

**KOLUMBAN ROBIN LYNN** (360)491-5921
8824 Steilacoom Rd SE Olympia WA 98513 • meekorl@juno.com • NOW • Tchr • Faith Lacey WA • (360)491-1733 • (PO 1992 MED)

**KOLVITZ LAURLEI L** (708)344-7015
1402 N 14th Ave Melrose Park IL 60160-3430 • EN • Tchr • Bethesda Chicago IL • (312)743-0800 • (RF 1993)

**KOLZOW JANET L** (847)741-5478
725 Morgan St Elgin IL 60123-7441 • NI • Tchr • Good Shepherd Elgin IL • (847)741-7795 • (S 1976)

**KONKEL LYNNETTE S** (734)246-4390
12839 Rosedale St Southgate MI 48195-1022 • MI • Tchr • Christ The King Southgate MI • (734)285-9697 • (S 1982 MED MA)

**KOOI PATTI J**
642 Pennoyer Ave Grand Haven MI 49417-1849 • MI • Tchr • St John Grand Haven MI • (616)842-0260 • (RF 1978)

**KOOPMAN DAVID L** (636)305-1387
13267 Wintergreen Est Dr Fenton MO 63026-4066 • dkoopman@stpaulsdesperes.org • MO • Prin • St Paul Des Peres MO • (314)822-2771 • (S 1970 MED)

**KOOPMAN KARLEEN J**
2827 Stein Blvd Eau Claire WI 54701-6284 • NW • Tchr • Eau Claire Eau Claire WI • (715)835-9314 • (SP 1987)

**KOOSMAN HOWARD E** (314)994-0987
58 Decorah Dr Saint Louis MO 63146-4849 • MO • Prin • Immanuel Olivette MO • (314)993-5004 • (SP 1969 MED)

**KOPLIN JOYCE ELLEN** (815)568-6386
1209 N Hale St Marengo IL 60152-2350 • NI • Tchr • Zion Marengo IL • (815)568-5156 • (RF 1968)

**KOPPENHAFER DEBRA ANN** (303)646-5876
35149 Cherokee Trl Elizabeth CO 80107-8455 • cdkoppenha@aol.com • RM • Tchr • Trinity Franktown CO • (303)841-4660 • (S 1982)

**KOPPLIN ELAINE A** (618)483-5499
16 Lincoln Dr Altamont IL 62411-1706 • dekopplin7@aol.com • CI • Tchr • Altamont Altamont IL • (618)483-6428 • (RF 1989 MA)

**KOREN DONNA L** (319)472-3839
1009 1st Ave Vinton IA 52349 • korens@fyiowa.infi.net • IE • 06/2000 • (RF 1980 MA)

**KOREN JOHN** (319)472-3839
1009 1st Ave Vinton IA 52349 • korens@fyiowa.infi.net • IE • 06/2000 • (RF 1976 MA)

**KORFF LYNN J** (847)255-9514
2630 Northampton Dr Apt C1 Rolling Meadows IL 60008-4351 • lynn³korff@thoughtport.com • NI • Tchr • Walther LHS Melrose Park IL • (708)344-0404 • (RF 1985 MA)

**KORNTHEUER MARK A** (708)344-5277
706 N 2nd Ave Maywood IL 60153-1005 • broncotennis@juno.com • NI • Tchr • Walther LHS Melrose Park IL • (708)344-0404 • (RF 1974 MA)

**KOROMHAS KAREN LUISE** (973)279-2137
17 Hemlock St Paterson NJ 07503-2646 • kkoromhas@earthlink.net • NJ • Mem C • Bethlehem Ridgewood NJ • (201)444-3600 • (BR 1975 MA)

**KORTE DON W JR.**
2324 W Chestnut Rd Mequon WI 53092 • SW • SHS/C • South Wisconsin Milwaukee WI • (414)464-8100 • (CQ 2000)

**KORTE MARY H**
2324 W Chestnut Rd Mequon WI 53092 • SW • SHS/C • South Wisconsin Milwaukee WI • (414)464-8100 • (CQ 2000)

**KORTE SARA J** (810)714-3031
12331 St Andrews Way Fenton MI 48430 • EN • Tchr • Child Of Christ Hartland MI • (248)887-3836 • (AA 1986 MA)

**KORTZE DONALD E** (815)633-8530
4712 Pepper Dr Rockford IL 61114-5342 • NI • Prin • Luther Academy Rockford IL • (815)877-9551 • (S 1982 MED)

**KOSBERG AMANDA L** (480)833-9351
1010 N Stapley #119 Mesa AZ 85203 • PSW • Tchr • St Luke Mesa AZ • (480)969-3848 • (S 1999)

**KOSCHE KENNETH T** (414)354-4584
4407 W Dunwood Rd Brown Deer WI 53223-4427 • kenneth.kosche@cuw.edu • SW • SHS/C • South Wisconsin Milwaukee WI • (414)464-8100 • (CQ 1986 MS DMA)

**KOSCHMANN EDWARD G** (216)398-0484
9941 Shady Ln Brooklyn OH 44144-3010 • enjay@mail.bcpl.md.us • OH • EM • (RF 1940 MA)

**KOSCHMANN MARK E** (219)749-2967
6909 Mowhawa Dr Fort Wayne IN 46815 • mekosch@aol.com • IN • Tchr • Concordia Fort Wayne IN • (219)426-9922 • (S 1976 MED)

**KOSCIK ANNETTE E** (216)639-1881
9518 Graystone Ln Mentor OH 44060-4538 • slimjim@ncweb.com • OH • Tchr • Our Shepherd Painesville OH • (440)357-7776 • (S 1972)

**KOSCIK JAMES R** (216)639-1881
9518 Graystone Ln Mentor OH 44060-4538 • slimjim@ncweb.com • OH • Tchr • Our Shepherd Painesville OH • (440)357-7776 • (S 1971 MS)

**KOSINSKY JOHN P**
9800 Fenwick Ft Smith AR 72908 • barbandjohn@worldnet.att.net • MDS • Prin • First Fort Smith AR • (501)452-5330 • (RF 1964 MA MS)

**KOSLAN CAROLYN S** (409)542-3581
PO Box 448 Giddings TX 78942-0448 • TX • Tchr • Immanuel Giddings TX • (409)542-3319 • (S 1977)

**KOSMALA DIANE L** (414)554-7762
3407 Monarch Dr Racine WI 53406 • SW • Tchr • Concordia Racine WI • (262)554-1659 • (S 1976)

**KOSMAN PAUL K** (616)651-2386
605 Parkside Dr Sturgis MI 49091 • pkosman@kresanet.org • MI • P/Tchr • Trinity Sturgis MI • (616)651-4245 • (RF 1983)

**KOSMATKA BRUCE J DR** (810)731-4942
7211 Yorktown Ln Shelby Township MI 48317-4272 • justbkos@netexp.com • MI • Prin • Trinity Utica MI • (810)731-4490 • (RF 1964 MSED LITTD)

**KOSTUSH ELAINE**
1011 S Town And River Dr Fort Myers FL 33919-6118 • NI • EM • (RF 1968 MA)

**KOTTWITZ ROGER L** (808)572-3712
2668 Iolani St Makawao HI 96768-8733 • CNH • Tchr • Emmanuel Kahului HI • (808)877-3037 • (S 1961)

**KOVACH JILL MARIE** (952)921-9796
4480 Parklawn Ave S #107 Edina MN 55435 • MNS • Tchr • Mount Calvary Richfield MN • (612)866-5405 • (CQ 2000)

**KOWALKE JULIE A**
8851 Janis Shelby Twp MI 48317 • MI • Tchr • Trinity Utica MI • (810)731-4490 • (SP 1989)

**KRAASE PEGGY A** (262)306-0904
3300 Mediterranean Ave West Bend WI 53090-8419 • peggyak@dotplanet.com • SW • Tchr • St John West Bend WI • (414)334-3077 • (SP 1981)

**KRAATZ RONALD A** (847)795-8909
842 Lee St Des Plaines IL 60016 • NI • Mem C • Immanuel Des Plaines IL • (847)824-3652 • (S 1973)

**KRAAYENBRINK SALLY J** (515)576-0417
1912 N 30th Ct Fort Dodge IA 50501-7861 • IW • P/Tchr • St Paul Fort Dodge IA • (515)955-7208 • (S 1983 MED)

**KRABBENHOFT ELOIESE** (512)447-4525
5808 Breezewood Dr Austin TX 78745-4088 • TX • 12/1998 • (S 1969 MA)

**KRACH GEORGE M** (231)775-5910
108 Forest Lawn Dr Cadillac MI 49601-9734 • MI • EM • (RF 1953 MA)

**KRACH MARY L** (626)284-2812
1832 S Marguerita Ave Alhambra CA 91803-3150 • mkrach@earthlink.net • PSW • Tchr • Emmaus Alhambra CA • (626)289-3664 • (S 1968 MA)

**KRAEMER KENNETH L** (219)484-0023
3215 Chancellor Dr Fort Wayne IN 46815-5927 • IN • EM • (RF 1943 MA)

**KRAFFT ARTHUR E** (262)253-0726
N82W14115 Lilly Ct Menomonee Falls WI 53051-3937 • SW • EM • (RF 1948 MS)

**KRAFFT JAMES E** (702)641-9599
2746 Wentworth Cir Las Vegas NV 89122-2712 • PSW • P/Tchr • First Good Shepherd Las Vegas NV • (702)382-8610 • (RF 1959)

**KRAFT GLENN O SR. DR** (262)549-0521
1929 A Springbrook N Waukesha WI 53186-1222 • svk81256@aol.com • SW • 01/1999 • (S 1955 MA DED)

**KRAFT JUNE E** (410)817-9043
13514 Blenheim Rd N Phoenix MD 21131-2128 • billjune95@hotmail.com • SE • EM • (RF 1982)

**KRAGE HARVEY W** (517)523-3252
9200 E Beecher Rd Pittsford MI 49271-9642 • MI • EM • (RF 1929)

**KRAKAT ROY H** (410)665-4254
7158 Fairbrook Rd Baltimore MD 21244-2318 • SE • Tchr • Southeastern Alexandria VA • (AA 1990)

**KRALIK CHUCK WADE**
2610 Indiana Joplin MO 64804 • MO • Tchr • Martin Luther Joplin MO • (417)624-1403 • (S 1997)

**KRALL JAYSON S** (920)893-5533
108 N Park Pl Plymouth WI 53073-1618 • SW • Tchr • St John Plymouth WI • (920)893-5114 • (S 1979)

**KRAMER CARLA J** (573)445-5920
5550 W Hatton Chapel Rd Columbia MO 65202-7817 • ckramer@coin.org • MO • Tchr • Trinity Columbia MO • (573)445-2112 • (S 1976)

**KRAMER CHARLES E** (419)822-4885
5284 County Road 6 Delta OH 43515-9648 • patcharl@powersupply.net • OH • 06/1999 • (S 1973 MED)

**KRAMER CONNIE L** (319)233-6461
2507 Baltimore St Waterloo IA 50702-5103 • IE • Tchr • Immanuel Waterloo IA • (319)233-3967 • (CQ 1986)

**KRAMER FREDERICK D** (503)280-0358
6102 NE 28th Ave Portland OR 97211-6028 • fkramer@cu-portland.edu • NOW • EM • (RF 1949 MA PHD LLD)

**KRAMER JANE E** (516)433-8315
45 Bobwhite Ln Hicksville NY 11801-4520 • AT • Tchr • Trinity Hicksville NY • (516)931-2211 • (RF 1961)

**KRAMER KIRSTEN JOY**
521 Beloit St Apt 7 Delavan WI 53115-1570 • SW • Tchr • Our Redeemer Delavan WI • (262)728-6589 • (RF 1991)

**KRAMER KOURTNEY PAIGE** (414)512-2977
775C Cheyenne Ave Unit C Grafton WI 53024-1641 • SW • Tchr • First Immanuel Cedarburg WI • (262)377-6610 • (MQ 1997)

**KRAMER LLEWELLYN J** (414)497-2235
428 Echo Hill Dr Green Bay WI 54302 • NW • Tchr • Redeemer Green Bay WI • (920)499-1033 • (SP 1982)

**KRAMER MARILYN MARIE** (208)655-4306
2664N 2800E Twin Falls ID 83301 • NOW • Tchr • Immanuel Twin Falls ID • (208)733-7820 • (S 1968)

**KRAMER MICHAEL W** (573)445-5920
5550 W Hatton Chapel Rd Columbia MO 65202-7817 • kramerm@missouri.edu • MO • 08/1991 08/2000 • (S 1976 MA PHD)

**KRAMER PATRICIA A** (419)822-4885
5284 County Road 6 Delta OH 43515-9648 • patcharl@powersupply.net • OH • Tchr • St Paul Napoleon OH • (419)592-5536 • (S 1972 MED)

**KRAMER ROY E** (651)484-8643
3979 Victoria St N Shoreview MN 55126-2943 • MNS • SHS/C • Minnesota South Burnsville MN • (RF 1956 MA)

**KRAMER STANLEY J** (516)433-8315
45 Bobwhite Ln Hicksville NY 11801-4520 • AT • Tchr • Trinity Hicksville NY • (516)931-2211 • (RF 1962 MA)

**KRAMER SYBIL J** (847)202-8239
865 E Carriage Ln Apt 2 Palatine IL 60074-1888 • NI • Tchr • St Peter Arlington Heights IL • (847)253-6638 • (S 1969 MPD)

**KRAMER WAYNE C DR** (281)464-2441
2114 Birdie Ct Pearland TX 77581 • wckramer@hotmail.com • TX • Prin • Lutheran South Acade Houston TX • (281)464-8299 • (S 1972 MED EDD)

**KRANZ BONNIE J** (419)385-4894
2944 Lutaway Dr Toledo OH 43614-5431 • OH • Tchr • Trinity Toledo OH • (419)385-2301 • (RF 1972)

**KRANZ LESLIE J** (312)798-3729
18105 Loomis Ave Homewood IL 60430-2406 • NI • Tchr • St Paul Chicago Heights IL • (708)754-4492 • (RF 1976)

**KRASS KATHLEEN G** (516)931-2702
157 W Nicholai St Hicksville NY 11801-3827 • cdkk665170@aol.com • AT • Tchr • Trinity Hicksville NY • (516)931-2211 • (RF 1968 MA)

**KRASS ROBERT J** (516)931-2702
157 W Nicholai St Hicksville NY 11801-3827 • rkrass7300@aol.com • AT • Tchr • Chapel Redeemer Flushing NY • (718)465-4236 • (BR 1978 MS)

**KRATZ DEAN E** (810)749-5812
54777 Foss Rd Macomb MI 48042-2505 • dkratz@lhsa.com • MI • Tchr • LHS North Macomb MI • (810)781-9151 • (S 1973 MMU)

**KRATZ DONALD L** (847)632-0626
1118 N Dryden Ave Arlington Hts IL 60004-4919 • NI • P/Tchr • St John Mount Prospect IL • (847)593-7670 • (RF 1972 MA)

**KRATZ ROBYN M** (515)576-6063
301 S 10th St Apt 20 Fort Dodge IA 50501 • IW • Tchr • St Paul Fort Dodge IA • (515)955-7208 • (MQ 1988)

**KRATZER DOROTHY** (785)765-3637
324 Iowa St Alma KS 66401-9701 • KS • EM • (S 1974 MED)

**KRATZER MICHAEL J** (314)869-8858
10408 Gardo Ct Saint Louis MO 63137-3525 • kratzerm@slu.edu • MO • Tchr • Lutheran North Saint Louis MO • (314)389-3100 • (RF 1975 MED)

**KRAUSE ALAN** (517)627-8569
11068 Broadbent Rd Lansing MI 48917-9627 • MI • Prin • Our Savior Lansing MI • (517)882-3550 • (RF 1964 MS)

**KRAUSE ALICE**
1301 Saint Hilaire Rd Yakima WA 98901-8098 • NOW • EM • (PO 1987)

**KRAUSE BARBARA J** (214)783-8619
805 Hillsdale Dr Richardson TX 75081-5231 • TX • Tchr • Zion Dallas TX • (214)363-1630 • (SP 1973)

**KRAUSE BETH E** (517)699-8559
4580 Doncaster Ave Holt MI 48842-2000 • bkrause@oursaviorchurch.org • MI • Tchr • Our Savior Lansing MI • (517)882-3550 • (S 1976)

**KRAUSE BRADLEY R** (214)661-3903
305 Shady Timbers Ln Murphy TX 75094-3535 • brkrause@aol.com • TX • Tchr • Lutheran HS of Dalla Dallas TX • (214)349-8912 • (S 1986 MED)

**KRAUSE BRENDA D** (719)481-0796
1805 Chapel Hills Dr Colorado Springs CO 80920 • RM • 08/1998 08/2000 • (S 1984)

**KRAUSE BRENDA KAY** (765)742-6464
3608 N Driftwood Dr #100 Lafayette IN 47905-6075 • brendak@stjameslaf.org • IN • Tchr • St James Lafayette IN • (765)742-6464 • (S 1998)

**KRAUSE DAVID L** (517)792-2978
1824 Glendale Ave Saginaw MI 48603-4056 • MI • EM • (RF 1963 MA EDS)

**KRAUSE EDWARD B**
120 E Wilson Norwood MN 55368 • MNS • EM • (RF 1940 MA)

**KRAUSE JAY A DR** (512)249-6366
7902 Cahill Dr Austin TX 78729 • krausej@concordia.edu • TX • SHS/C • Texas Austin TX • (S 1983 MS PHD)

**KRAUSE JERALD A** (262)781-2787
18305 Ashlea Dr Brookfield WI 53045-7401 • belzebabe@aol.com • SW • Tchr • Pilgrim Wauwatosa WI • (414)476-0736 • (S 1974)

**KRAUSE KRISTINE A** (512)249-6366
7902 Cahill Dr Austin TX 78729 • TX • Tchr • Redeemer Austin TX • (512)459-1500 • (S 1984)

**KRAUSE LAUREL A** (414)899-3301
6123 Klaus Lake Rd Gillett WI 54124-9339 • NW • Tchr • St John Suring WI • (920)842-4443 • (RF 1984)

**KRAUSE MADGE R**
1501 Lillyhill Dr #52 Needles CA 92363-3434 • PSW • Tchr • First Temple City CA • (626)287-0968 • (S 1962)

**KRAUSE PAMELA S** (409)366-2456
Rt 1 Box 74 B Giddings TX 78942-9702 • TX • Tchr • St Paul Giddings TX • (409)366-2218 • (S 1982)

**KRAUSE ROY C** (941)369-8696
215 Edward Ave Lehigh Acres FL 33972-5413 • FG • EM • (RF 1938 MSED PHD)

**KRAUSE RUSTI W**
31204 Village Green Ct Warrenville IL 60555-5918 • NI • Tchr • Zion Matteson IL • (708)747-7490 • (RF 1996)

**KRAUSE SANDRA L** (517)792-2978
1824 Glendale Ave Saginaw MI 48603-4056 • MI • Tchr • Peace Saginaw MI • (517)792-2581 • (AA 1987)

**KRAUSE STEVEN JON** (414)536-1355
4325 N 87th St Milwaukee WI 53222-1799 • skrause@stritch.edu • SW • Tchr • Milwaukee LHS Milwaukee WI • (414)461-6000 • (MQ 1986 MS)

**KRAUSE WILBERT E** (214)363-6697
4829 Abrams Rd Dallas TX 75214-2210 • TX • EM • (RF 1943 MA)

**KRECKLOW RUSSELL CONRAD** (520)825-4695
2250 E Indian Town Way Tucson AZ 85737-4727 • EN • EM • (S 1956 MAD)

**KREGER SHEILA MARIE** (507)333-9690
2127 16th St NW Faribault MN 55021-2812 • kckreger@rconnect.com • MNS • 06/2000 • (S 1973)

**KREISS PAUL T** (312)383-8746
326 N Ridgeland Ave Oak Park IL 60302-2325 • NI • EM • (RF 1952 MED PHD)

**KREISS SARA LYN** (708)848-8737
7346 W Lake St River Forest IL 60305 • sarakreiss@cs.com • NI • SHS/C • Northern Illinois Hillside IL • (RF 1987 MA)

**KREMER JAMES G** (219)749-0160
1340 Canal St New Haven IN 46774-1507 • kremer1340@aol.com • IN • Tchr • Central New Haven IN • (219)493-2502 • (RF 1965 MA)

**KREMPLER JEFFREY E** (407)392-5027
1480 NW 12th Way Boca Raton FL 33486-1221 • FG • Prin • St Paul Boca Raton FL • (561)395-8548 • (BR 1975 MED PHD)

**KRENNING CAROLINE M**
432 S Clay #6 Kirkwood MO 63122 • MO • St Paul Boca Raton FL • (S 1997)

**KRENNING MARGUERITE M** (314)872-8716
14 Graeler Dr Saint Louis MO 63146-4953 • MO • Tchr • Immanuel Olivette MO • (314)993-5004 • (S 1958)

**KRENTZ REBECCA JEAN** (512)819-9575
103 Parque Vista Dr Georgetown TX 78626 • TX • Mem C • Faith Georgetown TX • (512)863-7332 • (S 1971)

**KRENZ STACIE LYNN**
222 E Lake Ave Fulda MN 56131 • krenzstac@hotmail.com • MNS • Tchr • St Paul Fulda MN • (507)425-2169 • (S 1994)

**KRENZKE BETTE J**
Concordia Int Schl Shanghai Plot S2 Huang Yang Rd JinQiao 201206 CHINA • bettek@ciss.com.cn • NI • S Miss • Northern Illinois Hillside IL • (RF 1966 MS EDD)

**KRENZKE THOMAS A** (414)466-1793
8922 W Hope Ave Milwaukee WI 53222-1744 • thomas.krenzke@cuw.edu • SW • SHS/C • South Wisconsin Milwaukee WI • (414)464-8100 • (CQ 1975 MLS MA)

**KRENZKE TIMOTHY L**
Concordia Inter Sch Shanghai Plot S2 Huang Yang Rd JinQiao Pudong Shanghai 201206 CHINA • NI • S Miss • Northern Illinois Hillside IL • (RF 1966 MS PHD)

**KREPSKY RICHARD D** (313)730-5096
3758 Heritage Pkwy Dearborn MI 48124-3178 • MI • EM • (CQ 1969)

**KRESSIN DEBORAH KIRSTEN** (909)677-3540
39191 Foxglove Cir Murrieta CA 92563-5364 • PSW • Tchr • Zion Fallbrook CA • (760)723-3500 • (S 1977)

**KRESSIN HEIDI C** (713)283-8726
9600 Glenfield Ct Apt 207 Houston TX 77096 • TX • Tchr • Pilgrim Houston TX • (713)666-3706 • (MQ 1999)

**KRETZMANN DAVID C** (916)482-6439
4265 Carle Ln Sacramento CA 95841-4123 • CNH • Tchr • Sacramento Lutheran Sacramento CA • (916)978-2720 • (PO 1980)

**KRETZMANN NATHAN O** (281)257-1117
8307 Amurwood Dr Tomball TX 77375-2808 • nkretzmann@salem4u.com • TX • Tchr • Salem Tomball TX • (281)351-8223 • (IV 1985 MED)

**KRETZMANN NORMA JEAN** (314)849-6585
8952 Lindenhurst Dr St Louis MO 63126-2403 • TX • 06/2000 • (CQ 1998 MA)

**KRETZSCHMAR TRACEY DEBORAH** (410)882-1613
5 Skylark Ct Apt E Baltimore MD 21234-2050 • tracekretz@aol.com • SE • Tchr • Calvary Baltimore MD • (410)426-4302 • (BR 1997)

**KRIEGER MARY KATHRYN**
8207 Citrus Chase Dr Orlando FL 32836-5328 • kkrieger@harcourtbrace.com • MO • CCRA • Missouri Saint Louis MO • (314)317-4550 • (RF 1971 MED)

**KRIEGER RANDY JON** (602)765-0614
3902 E Paradise Dr Phoenix AZ 85028 • EN • Tchr • Valley LHS Associati Phoenix AZ • (602)230-1600 • (S 1982 MA)

**KRIEGER RUTH A** (616)471-4729
201 S Mechanic St Berrien Springs MI 49103-1138 • MI • Tchr • Trinity Berrien Springs MI • (616)473-1811 • (RF 1982 MA)

**KRIEGER SUSAN L** (602)765-0614
3902 E Paradise Dr Phoenix AZ 85028-1430 • EN • Tchr • Christ Phoenix AZ • (602)957-7010 • (S 1982)

**KRIER CHRISTINE** (847)965-8649
9000 Marmora Morton Grove IL 60053 • EN • Tchr • Bethesda Chicago IL • (312)743-0800 • (RF 1997)

**KRINGEL DOROTHY ANN** (302)736-0744
770 Oak Dr Dover DE 19904-4342 • artk770@aol.com • SE • Tchr • St John Dover DE • (302)734-1211 • (S 1968)

**KRINKE ARLEN D** (612)441-4589
13484 190th Ave NW Elk River MN 55330-1177 • mkrinke@sprintmail.com • MNS • P/Tchr • St John Elk River MN • (612)441-6616 • (SP 1968 MA)

**KROEGER JANICE** (314)351-4451
7124 Marwinette Ave Saint Louis MO 63116-3036 • MO • EM • (S 1968 MAT)

**KROEMER CHRISTINA RENEE** (618)656-3638
1208 Grant Dr Edwardsville IL 62025-2442 • SI • Tchr • Trinity Edwardsville IL • (618)656-7002 • (S 1991)

**KROEMER JEFFREY JAMES** (618)656-3638
1208 Grant Dr Edwardsville IL 62025-2442 • kroemer@plantnet.com • SI • Tchr • Trinity Edwardsville IL • (618)656-7002 • (S 1989 MA)

**KROEMER KAREN JEAN** (319)363-3349
1424 25th St SE Cedar Rapids IA 52403-3442 • IE • Tchr • Trinity Cedar Rapids IA • (319)362-6952 • (CQ 1987)

**KROFT DAVID** (512)445-0035
2600 Coatbridge Dr Austin TX 78745-3424 • TX • SHS/C • Texas Austin TX • (S 1970 MFA)

**KROFT SUSAN T** (512)445-0035
2600 Coatbridge Dr Austin TX 78745-3424 • TX • Tchr • St Paul Austin TX • (512)472-8301 • (S 1971 MED)

**KROGSTAD WARREN D**
22922 Via Nuez Mission Viejo CA 92691-2590 • PSW • Mem C • St Paul Orange CA • (714)637-2640 • (S 1977 MSED)

**KROHE KATHRYN LYNN** (320)229-1158
419 33rd Ave N Apt 108 Saint Cloud MN 56303 • klkrohe@hotmail.com • MNN • 04/2000 • (RF 1997)

**KROHE LOIS ANN** (870)932-3505
1404 Links Cir #3 Jonesboro AR 72404 • lak456@aol.com • MDS • P/Tchr • Zion Waldenburg AR • (870)579-2276 • (RF 1973)

**KROHE SUSAN JO** (309)353-9534
918 Margaret Pekin IL 61554 • CI • Tchr • Good Shepherd Pekin IL • (309)347-2020 • (S 1998)

**KROHSE KENNETH C** (630)495-4313
1008 E Roosevelt Rd Lombard IL 60148-4143 • kmkrohse@concentric.com • NI • P/Tchr • Trinity Lombard IL • (630)627-5601 • (CQ 1981 MA)

**KROHSE RONALD D** (217)488-6135
6765E Gibson St New Berlin IL 62670-4511 • CI • P/Tchr • St John New Berlin IL • (217)488-3190 • (RF 1968)

**KROLL DAVID LEE**
5848 4th Ave S St Petersburg FL 33707 • krolldl@aol.com • FG • Tchr • Our Savior Saint Petersburg FL • (727)344-2684 • (RF 1996)

**KROLL JAMES W** (608)756-2286
608 S Academy St Janesville WI 53545-5134 • kroll@spsflames.k12.wl.us • SW • Tchr • St Paul Janesville WI • (608)754-4471 • (RF 1978)

**KROLL MARY LOU** (312)986-8154
259 S Prospect Ave Clarendon Hills IL 60514 • NI • Tchr • Zion Hinsdale IL • (630)323-0384 • (RF 1976)

**KROLL RENEE LYNN** (727)343-5481
5848 4th Ave S St Petersburg FL 33707-1714 • kinderkrol@aol.com • FG • Tchr • Our Savior Saint Petersburg FL • (727)344-1026 • (RF 1999)

**KROLL SHARON JOY** (414)228-9081
7523 N 41st St Milwaukee WI 53209-1912 • sjkroll@worldnet.att.net • SW • Tchr • Nazareth Milwaukee WI • (414)354-6601 • (RF 1969)

**KROLL SHELLEY LYNN** (608)756-2286
608 S Academy St Janesville WI 53545-5134 • elmon608@aol.com • SW • Tchr • St John Beloit WI • (608)362-8595 • (MQ 1986)

**KROMMINGA GREGORY P** (507)334-4734
1667 Buckingham Path Faribault MN 55021 • MNS • Prin • Faribault Faribault MN • (507)334-7982 • (SP 1979)

**KROMMINGA JOYCE M**
1667 Buckingham Path Faribault MN 55021 • MNS • Tchr • Faribault Faribault MN • (507)334-7982 • (SP 1979)

**KROMMINGA KEVIN K** (714)639-5923
2845 E Oakmont Ave Orange CA 92867-7338 • kevink@lutheranhigh.orange.ca.us • PSW • Tchr • Lutheran HS/Orange C Orange CA • (714)998-5151 • (S 1989)

**KROMMINGA REBECCA KAY** (602)971-4769
2845 E Oakmont Ave Orange CA 92867-7338 • PSW • Tchr • Lutheran HS/Orange C Orange CA • (714)998-5151 • (S 1990 MA)

**KROMPHARDT WILBUR F** (716)695-8510
7229 Winbert Dr North Tonawanda NY 14120-1450 • EA • EM • (RF 1953 MED)

**KRONE JAMES R** (708)985-2204
16996 Gary Ln Livonia MI 48152 • lsem@curf.edu • NI • Tchr • Special Educ Ministr River Forest IL • (708)209-3344 • (RF 1981 MSED)

**KRONE SHIRLEY M** (313)881-4012
5900 Bluehill St Detroit MI 48224-2018 • skrone@mindspring.com • MI • Tchr • Mt Calvary Detroit MI • (313)527-3366 • (S 1969 MA)

**KRONE TONI L** (440)322-5497
7557 Root Rd North Ridgeville OH 44039-4007 • EN • Tchr • Grace Elyria OH • (216)322-5497 • (RF 1973)

**KRONE WALTER K** (313)881-4012
5900 Bluehill St Detroit MI 48224-2018 • mtcal@voyager.net • MI • P/Tchr • Mt Calvary Detroit MI • (313)527-3366 • (RF 1966 MA)

**KROOHN DAWN C** (612)971-8662
4230 Hampshire Ave N Crystal MN 55428 • dckroohn@juno.com • MNS • Tchr • St John Maple Grove MN • (612)420-2426 • (SP 1997)

**KROTZ KAREN ELISABETH** (217)942-3025
RR 1 Box 73 Carrollton IL 62016-9733 • SI • 08/1993 • (RF 1983)

**KRUBSACK DAVID H** (414)321-8574
2960 S 96th St West Allis WI 53227-3618 • SW • EM • (RF 1958 MMU MA)

**KRUEGER EDWARD F** (217)787-3001
2801 Montaluma Dr #114 Springfield IL 62704 • pkykrug@warpnet.net • CI • EM • * • (RF 1946 MED)

**KRUEGER FREDERIC R**
202 Hickory Ln Lincoln IL 62656 • zlslinc@abelink.com • CI • P/Tchr • Zion Lincoln IL • (217)732-3946 • (S 1966 MA)

**KRUEGER GEORGE P** (217)546-8305
1333 Johnson Ln Springfield IL 62702-2270 • gpkrueger@aol.com • CI • EM • (RF 1955 MED)

**KRUEGER JAMES F** (314)968-4864
8801 Eager Rd Apt A Saint Louis MO 63144 • revjfk@hotmail.com • NEB • 09/1999 • (S 1989)

**KRUEGER JUANITA L** (701)667-7165
1000 25th St SE Mandan ND 58554 • angelbear77@yahoo.com • ND • Tchr • Martin Luther Bismarck ND • (701)224-9070 • (SP 1982 MED)

**KRUEGER KURT J DR** (714)921-9392
2684 N Dell St Orange CA 92865-2110 • krueger@cui.edu • PSW • SHS/C • Pacific Southwest Irvine CA • (949)854-3232 • (CQ 1971 MA MAT PHD)

**KRUEGER MICHAEL DAVID** (618)288-3080
116 Ridge Maryville IL 62062 • mdkrueger@hotmail.com • SI • Tchr • Good Shepherd Collinsville IL • (618)344-3153 • (S 1991)

**KRUEGER PAUL H** (920)459-8049
319 Michigan Ave Sheboygan WI 53081-3556 • SW • Tchr • Trinity Sheboygan WI • (920)458-8248 • (S 1975 MED)

**KRUEGER RENEE KRISTINE**
C/O Zion Lutheran School 3866 Harvester Rd Harvester MO 63304-2825 • MO • Trinity Sheboygan WI • (S 1996)

**KRUEGER ROSS LORAIN** (319)223-7421
110 A Ave PO Box 352 Newhall IA 52315 • kruegerred@aol.com • IE • Tchr • Central Newhall IA • (319)223-5271 • (S 1999)

**KRUEGER SCOTT HERMAN**
117 James St Beaver Dam WI 53916-2501 • y • SW • Tchr • Bethesda Home Watertown WI • (414)261-3050 • (S 1997)

**KRUEGER SHARON R** (651)645-2685
186 Syndicate St N Saint Paul MN 55104-6437 • krueger@csp.edu • MNS • SHS/C • Minnesota South Burnsville MN • (S 1977 MSED)

**KRUEGER VERA I** (303)452-3192
12457 Columbine Ct Denver CO 80241-2739 • RM • EM • (S 1966)

**KRUEGER WALTER E DR** (503)492-0891
1585 SW Willowbrook Ave Gresham OR 97080-9642 • wkrueger@teleport.com • NOW • Tchr • Portland Portland OR • (503)667-3199 • (RF 1968 MMU DMU)

**KRUEGER WILLIAM G** (309)353-7290
231 Maple Park Dr Pekin IL 61554-2527 • CI • Mem C • St John Green Valley IL • (309)348-3180 • (S 1961 MED)

**KRUG ELIZABETH A** (262)752-0946
5412 Langdale Dr Racine WI 53402 • lisakrug@earthlink.net • SW • Tchr • Lutheran High School Racine WI • (414)637-6538 • (RF 1997)

**KRUGER RICHARD J** (812)378-9276
7603 S Artesian Dr Columbus IN 47201-9678 • IN • Tchr • St Peter Columbus IN • (812)372-5266 • (RF 1964)

**KRUGER ROBERT L F*** (216)382-3655
2015 Waycross Ave Akron OH 44320-1550 • OH • Tchr • Zion Akron OH • (330)253-3136 • (RF 1984)

**KRUICHAK LU WAYNE KAY** (941)314-9872
423 Lime St Sebring FL 33870 • FG • Tchr • Faith Sebring FL • (941)385-0406 • (SP 1995)

**KRUMDIECK GARY A** (509)663-8580
505 Marjo St Wenatchee WA 98801-3546 • NOW • Tchr • St Paul Wenatchee WA • (509)662-3659 • (PO 1981)

**KRUMLAND RICK** (573)364-8599
6 Frost Dr Rolla MO 65402-3906 • MO • P/Tchr • Rolla Rolla MO • (573)364-3915 • (S 1971 MED)

**KRUPSKI JAMES F** (317)894-8903
10611 E Creekside Woods Dr Indianapolis IN 46239 • krupskij@aol.com • IN • Prin • Zion New Palestine IN • (317)861-4210 • (RF 1982 MSED)

**KRUPSKI JUDITH K**
1651 S Juniper Apt 167 Escondido CA 92025-6134 • PSW • Tchr • Grace Escondido CA • (760)745-0831 • (RF 1964 MA)

**KRUPSKY HAROLD K**
37780 Jefferson Ave Harrison Twp MI 48045-2697 • MI • Mem C • Faith Troy MI • (248)689-4664 • (RF 1971 MED)

**KRUSE BARBARA L** (630)443-9322
61 Hunt Club Dr # 10 Saint Charles IL 60174-4701 • NI • Tchr • Immanuel Dundee IL • (847)428-4477 • (RF 1967 MS MSED)

**KRUSE DARYL M** (815)562-7746
1213 Pickwick Dr Rochelle IL 61068 • dpkruse@rochelle.net • NI • P/Tchr • St Paul Rochelle IL • (815)562-6323 • (RF 1979 MEDADM)

**KRUSE DONALD W**
2955 Newton St Apt A Denver CO 80211-3645 • RM • 12/1996 12/1999 • (RF 1973 MA)

**KRUSE DONNA** (708)366-0959
132 Rockford Ave Forest Park IL 60130-1220 • NI • EM • (RF 1960)

**KRUSE LAURA MARIE** (818)841-6415
621 E Magnolia Blvd Apt A Burbank CA 91501 • PSW • Tchr • First Burbank CA • (818)848-3076 • (SP 1995)

**KRUSE ROBIN FAITH*** (320)587-5440
60436 120th St Hutchinson MN 55350 • MNS • Tchr • St Johns Hutchinson MN • (320)587-4851 • (S 1990)

**KRUSE SHERYL M** (785)337-2308
3024 24th Rd Hanover KS 66945-8899 • KS • Tchr • Immanuel Bremen KS • (785)337-2472 • (S 1971)

**KRUSE STANLEY E** (541)322-0481
2656 NW Strath Way Bend OR 97701 • kruse@bend.com • RM • Tchr • Vail Christian Edwards CO • (970)926-3015 • (RF 1987 MA)

**KRUTZ CHARLES H** (402)643-3464
RR 1 Seward NE 68434-9801 • NEB • EM • (S 1954 MMU)

**KRZESINKSI MARJORIE** (913)422-2037
730 S 9th St Edwardsville KS 66111-1336 • itsze@aol.com • KS • Tchr • Hope Shawnee KS • (913)631-6940 • (S 1985)

**KUBALL DANIEL CARL** (612)571-4920
501 67th Ave NE Fridley MN 55432-4411 • djkuball@juno.com • MNS • P/Tchr • King Of Kings Roseville MN • (651)484-9206 • (SP 1992 MED)

**KUBE LISA JOAN**
9535 S Utica Ave Evergreen Park IL 60805-2639 • NI • Tchr • Luther HS South Chicago IL • (773)737-1416 • (SP 1990)

**KUBE RICHARD W** (253)638-6772
14901 SE 272nd 0-2 Kent WA 98042 • rickube@uswest.net • NOW • Prin • Northwest Portland OR • (SP 1972 MED)

**KUCHENBECKER RANDALL D**
C/O Saint Peter Lutheran Sch 2400 Oxford Way Lodi CA 95242-2854 • rdkteacher@aol.com • CNH • Tchr • St Peter Lodi CA • (209)333-2223 • (S 1970)

**KUCHLER DORIS K** (262)679-3684
5935 S Aberdeen Dr New Berlin WI 53146-5202 • jkuchler@execpc.com • EN • Tchr • Little Lambs Of Peac New Berlin WI • (414)679-1441 • (RF 1983)

**KUCK GLEN** (773)889-6518
2639 N Meade Ave Chicago IL 60639-1117 • clkuck@aol.com • NI • P/Tchr • St Paul Chicago IL • (773)378-6644 • (RF 1972 MA)

**KUCK WILLIAM E** (407)282-2800
13613 Lakes Way Orlando FL 32828 • FG • St Paul Chicago IL • (RF 1969)

**KUEBLER EUGENE C**
5181 Oakbrook Ct Saginaw MI 48603-8705 • MI • S Ex/S • Michigan Ann Arbor MI • (S 1972)

**KUECK JANICE M** (972)578-9412
1416 Glenwood Ln Plano TX 75074-2402 • djkueck@hotmail.com • TX • Tchr • Faith Plano TX • (972)423-7448 • (S 1967)

**KUEFNER MARLA R** (650)361-1583
1631 Kansas Redwood City CA 94061 • mkuefner@home.com • CNH • Tchr • Redeemer Redwood City CA • (650)366-3466 • (S 1977 MA)

**KUEGELE AMY E** (818)342-0949
19134 Delano St Reseda CA 91335 • PSW • Tchr • Trinity Jr/Sr High S Reseda CA • (818)342-7855 • (AU 1997)

**KUEHL MARY L**
4045 Brook Ln Brookfield WI 53005-1467 • SW • Tchr • Elm Grove Elm Grove WI • (262)797-2970 • (CQ 1988)

**KUEKER LINDA C** (708)394-1798
4203 N Harvard Ave Arlington Hts IL 60004-7904 • NI • Tchr • St Peter Arlington Heights IL • (847)253-6638 • (RF 1975)

**KUERSCHNER EDWIN FRED** (612)467-4673
402 Colonial Cir Norwd Young America MN 55397-9236 • MNS • P/Tchr • St John Young America MN • (612)467-2740 • (SP 1982)

**KUERSCHNER JOHN P** (941)594-7644
2505 Citrus Lake Dr Naples FL 34109 • JKuers2811@aol.com • FG • Prin • Christ Community Naples FL • (941)430-2655 • (RF 1966 MA)

**KUERSCHNER SHIRLEY A** (941)594-7644
2505 Citrus Lake Dr Naples FL 34109 • JKuers2811@aol.com • FG • Tchr • Christ Commuinity Naples FL • (941)430-2655 • (SP 1971)

**KUERSCHNER VERNON C** (630)833-9695
261 Illinois St Elmhurst IL 60126-2448 • vck³ils@hotmail.com • NI • Prin • Immanuel Elmhurst IL • (630)832-9302 • (RF 1961 MA)

**KUGLER COLLEEN** (616)426-4741
3856 W Warren Woods Rd Three Oaks MI 49128-9536 • MI • Tchr • Trinity Sawyer MI • (616)426-3151 • (S 1972)

**KUH ELAINE LOUISE** (815)469-5299
837 Overlook Ct E Frankfort IL 60423-1036 • NI • EM • (RF 1959)

**KUHL DEANNE I** (941)755-6639
3404 27th St W Bradenton FL 34205-3623 • FG • 12/1994 12/1999 • (RF 1974)

**KUHL LINDA L** (770)486-3545
25 Olympia PT Newnan GA 30265-3303 • llk450pcht@aol.com • FG • Tchr • St Paul Peachtree City GA • (770)486-3545 • (S 1971 MA)

**KUHLMAN DAVID W**
78 W Los Arboles Tempe AZ 85284-2227 • david³kuhlman@walther.com • NI • Tchr • Northern Illinois Hillside IL • (RF 1963 MED)

**KUHLMAN ROBERT P** (612)926-9483
5509 Beard Ct Edina MN 55410-2315 • MNS • Tchr • Luth HS Of Greater M Bloomington MN • (612)854-0224 • (S 1974)

**KUHLMANN BRENT S** (314)946-8516
2524 Westport Ln Saint Charles MO 63301-4759 • MO • Tchr • Immanuel Saint Charles MO • (636)946-2656 • (S 1977 MA)

**KUHLMANN BRICE E** (979)542-9254
1109 P R 1141 Giddings TX 78942-9749 • bkuhlmann@bluebon.net • TX • EM • (S 1957)

**KUHLMANN DOUGLAS J** (402)467-5404
1100 N 56th St Lincoln NE 68504 • dkuhlmann@n2espanol.com • NEB • Tchr • Lincoln Luth Jr/Sr H Lincoln NE • (402)467-5404 • (S 1998)

**KUHLMANN ELOISE S** (806)383-7700
325 Fairlane St Amarillo TX 79108-4215 • rek68@aol.com • TX • Tchr • Trinity Amarillo TX • (806)352-5620 • (S 1967 MED)

**KUHLMANN LINDA J** (503)667-3014
18169 SE Richey Rd Portland OR 97236-5116 • jlk7727@teleport.com • NOW • Tchr • Trinity Portland OR • (503)288-6403 • (S 1972 MAT)

**KUHLMANN TRISHA LYNN** (317)781-9336
3008 El Lago N Dr - #A Indianapolis IN 46227 • IN • Tchr • Calvary Indianapolis IN • (317)783-2000 • (S 1993)

**KUHN KATHLEEN R** (402)246-3025
RR 1 Box 78 Platte Center NE 68653-9746 • NEB • Tchr • Immanuel Columbus NE • (402)564-8423 • (SP 1966)

**KUHN WILLIAM F** (402)643-6875
947 N 12th St Seward NE 68434-1403 • wkuhn@seward.cune.edu • NEB • SHS/C • Nebraska Seward NE • (RF 1977 MMU)

**KUHNERT SUSAN E** (630)964-3954
7421 Blackburn Ave Apt 102 Downers Grove IL 60516-4160 • NI • 12/1995 12/1999 • (CQ 1987)

**KUKER GERALD W** (708)839-4851
8148 Nueport Dr Willow Springs IL 60480 • gkuker@enc.k12.il.us • NI • Tchr • St John LA Grange IL • (708)354-1690 • (RF 1967 MCMU)

**KULAT DIANE L** (630)971-0118
6418 Bradley Dr Woodridge IL 60517-1233 • NI • P/Tchr • Trinity Lisle IL • (630)964-1276 • (RF 1972 MA)

**KULAT TERRY L** (630)971-0118
6418 Bradley Dr Woodridge IL 60517-1233 • NI • Northern Illinois Hillside IL • (RF 1972 MA)

**KUNDINGER DEBRA JEAN** (517)883-3949
9543 Kilmanagh Rd Sebewaing MI 48759-9742 • MI • P/Tchr • St John Sebewaing MI • (517)883-2279 • (AA 1986)

**KUNERT CHARLES J** (503)677-8929
18620 SE Tibbetts Ct Gresham OR 97030-6205 • ckunert@cu-portland.edu • NOW • SHS/C • Northwest Portland OR • (S 1969 MS PHD)

**KUNERT NANCY ANNE** (503)669-2911
1017 SW 4th St Gresham OR 97080-5307 • kunato@ix.netcom.com • NOW • Tchr • Portland Portland OR • (503)667-3199 • (RF 1962 MA)

**KUNKEL JESSE H** (660)463-7762
404 Leona St Concordia MO 64020-9654 • MO • EM • (S 1956 MED)

**KUNKEL RUTH MARIE E** (816)525-5768
1601 NE Ball Dr Lees Summit MO 64063 • MO • Tchr • Calvary Kansas City MO • (816)444-6908 • (S 1984)

**KUNST RICHARD O** (215)788-5117
145 Otter St Bristol PA 19007-3607 • EA • Tchr • Hope Levittown PA • (215)946-3467 • (CQ 1995)

**KUNTZ CYNTHIA G**
2430 Sims Ave Saint Louis MO 63114-3207 • MO • Tchr • Our Redeemer Overland MO • (314)427-3462 • (S 1987)

**KUNZ DORIS ELIZABETH** (281)538-4795
405 Seaborough Ln League City TX 77573 • clkunz@juno.com • TX • 07/1998 07/2000 • (RF 1962)

**KUNZ MARSHALL F** (651)228-0119
966 Ashland Ave Saint Paul MN 55104 • MNS • 07/1999 • (SP 1971 MA)

**KUNZ REYNOLD W** (281)556-8521
15818 Crystal Grove Dr Houston TX 77082-1420 • TX • EM • (RF 1956 MED)

**KUNZ SUSAN M** (708)482-9040
416 S Ashland Ave La Grange IL 60525-6310 • skunz@enc.k12.il.us • NI • Tchr • St John LA Grange IL • (708)354-1690 • (RF 1974)

**KUPSKY JOHN A** (715)675-2461
624 Broken Arrow Rd Wausau WI 54401-2167 • jekupsky@wave.net • NW • EM • (RF 1964)

**KUREK STEPHEN** (708)445-8665
222 N Marion St Oak Park IL 60302-1968 • 1hsnkureksc@crf.cuis.edu • NI • Tchr • Luther HS North Chicago IL • (773)286-3600 • (RF 1970 MA)

**KURIO NANCY ANN** (512)255-4150
4100 Mc Neil Dr Austin TX 78727-1116 • TX • 08/1999 • (CQ 1993)

**KURKA GERALD E**
728 Cumberland Dr Saint Louis MO 63125-2516 • MO • Tchr • Holy Cross Saint Louis MO • (314)771-9521 • (S 1980)

**KURKA MARGIE**
728 Cumberland Dr Saint Louis MO 63125-2516 • MO • 03/1988 03/2000 • (S 1981)

**KURTH BARBARA T** (262)252-4573
N56W15891 Scott Ln Menomonee Falls WI 53051-5727 • SW • EM • (RF 1958 MA)

**KURTH ELIZABETH F** (773)736-9465
6145 W Grace St Chicago IL 60634-2549 • NI • P/Tchr • Bethel Chicago IL • (773)252-1104 • (RF 1975 MED)

**KURTH FLORENCE M** (612)881-7583
8506 2nd Ave S Bloomington MN 55420-2342 • MNS • EM • (OTHER 1936 MA)

**KURTH FREDERICK A** (262)252-4573
N56W15891 Scott Ln Menomonee Falls WI 53051-5727 • SW • EM • (RF 1960)

**KURTH LYLE J*** (847)742-2454
923 Scott Dr Elgin IL 60123-2026 • NI • EM • (S 1954 MS DED)

**KURTH RUTH J DR** (708)452-8342
1733 N 74th Ct Elmwood Park IL 60707-4225 • crfkurthrj@crf.cuis.edu • NI • SHS/C • Northern Illinois Hillside IL • (RF 1962 MS PHD)

**KURTH TIMOTHY J**
1165 Greensfield Dr Naperville IL 60563-3337 • peaceguys@aol.com • NI • Mem C • Peace Lombard IL • (630)627-1101 • (RF 1981 MA)

**KURTZ NANCY** (313)671-9354
25489 Montebello Ct Woodhaven MI 48183-4324 • MI • Mem C • Community Flat Rock MI • (734)782-0563 • (AA 1984 MA)

**KURTZ NEAL I** (402)329-4147
609 E Florence St Pierce NE 68767 • nkurtz@ptcnet.net • NEB • P/Tchr • Zion Pierce NE • (402)329-4658 • (S 1971 MS)

**KUSCH DAVID S** (219)486-9543
4206 Tamarack Dr Fort Wayne IN 46835 • davidkusch@aol.com • IN • Tchr • Concordia LHS Fort Wayne IN • (219)483-1102 • (AA 1984)

**KUSCHMANN HELMUT P** (313)247-5299
47635 Goldridge Ln Macomb MI 48044-2418 • MI • Tchr • Trinity Utica MI • (810)731-4490 • (RF 1966 MAT)

**KUSCHMANN MARGIE A** (313)247-5299
47635 Goldridge Ln Macomb MI 48044-2418 • mkuschmann@lhsa.net • MI • Tchr • LHS North Macomb MI • (810)781-9151 • (RF 1966 MAT)

**KUSCHNEREIT GARY J** (405)733-8921
1402 Magnolia Ln Midwest City OK 73110-4820 • luteaprin@aol.com • OK • P/Tchr • Good Shepherd Midwest City OK • (405)732-2585 • (S 1972 MA MS)

**KUSESKE THOMAS E** (651)774-7045
652 McLean Ave Saint Paul MN 55106-6311 • tc1kuseske@aol.com • MNS • Tchr • Concordia Academy Roseville MN • (612)484-8429 • (SP 1968 MAT)

**KUSKE EUGENE C** (517)652-9806
649 Willow Ln Frankenmuth MI 48734-1441 • eckuske@worldnet.att.net • MI • EM • (S 1956)

**KUSKE KEVIN E** (920)662-0411
2405 Wildwood Dr Green Bay WI 54302 • NW • P/Tchr • Redeemer Green Bay WI • (920)499-1033 • (S 1983 MED)

**KUSKE MARY E** (517)652-9806
649 Willow Ln Frankenmuth MI 48734-1441 • eckuske@worldnet.att.net • MI • EM • (RF 1954 MA)

**KUSKE WILMER G** (828)258-2449
22 American Way Asheville NC 28806-1803 • SE • EM • (RF 1953)

**KUSMIK CORNELL J** (216)237-8416
901 Tollis Pkwy Broadview Hts OH 44147-1818 • NI • EM • (CQ 1959)

**KUSSEROW MARY LOU** (517)784-5070
2018 Jeffrey Ct Jackson MI 49203-3826 • MI • Tchr • Trinity Jackson MI • (517)750-2105 • (SP 1970)

**KUSSEROW THOMAS E** (517)784-5070
2018 Jeffrey Ct Jackson MI 49203-3826 • MI • Tchr • Trinity Jackson MI • (517)750-2105 • (SP 1971 MA)

**KUTZ DORIS MARIE** (612)763-5394
1103 Eckert St NW Alexandria MN 56308-4967 • MNN • Tchr • Zion Alexandria MN • (320)763-4842 • (S 1979)

**KUTZ JOHN C** (810)792-3524
35737 Lucerne St Clinton Twp MI 48035-2746 • jkutz@stlukemi.org • MI • Prin • St Luke Clinton Township MI • (810)791-1151 • (S 1970 MED)

## L

**L HEUREUX BRIAN T**
418 S Clark Lyons KS 67554 • OH • 07/2000 • (S 1996)

**L HEUREUX KATHYRINE RENEE** (402)643-9420
C/O Central Lutheran School PO Box 190 Newhall IA 52315-0190 • mh00114@nvix.net • IE • Tchr • Central Newhall IA • (319)223-5271 • (S 1997)

**L HEUREUX MARK JUSTIN**
C/OCentral Luth School PO Box 190 Newhall IA 52315-0190 • mh00414@navix.net • IE • Prin • Central Newhall IA • (319)223-5271 • (S 1997)

**L HEUREUX MICHAEL L**
6615 Pawawna Dr Fort Wayne IN 46815-6339 • IN • Tchr • Bethlehem Fort Wayne IN • (219)456-3587 • (RF 1992)

**LA CROIX SUSAN M** (219)493-0278
6205 Landover Pl Fort Wayne IN 46815-7647 • IN • Tchr • Holy Cross Fort Wayne IN • (219)483-3173 • (RF 1985)

**LA CROIX TIMOTHY C** (219)493-0278
6205 Landover Pl Fort Wayne IN 46815-7647 • IN • Tchr • Concordia LHS Fort Wayne IN • (219)483-1102 • (RF 1985 MMU)

**LAABS BARBARA RUTH**
216 Mc Leod Ave N Plato MN 55370 • MNS • Tchr • St Paul-St Peter Watertown MN • (612)955-1419 • (SP 1983)

**LAABS CHARLES W DR** (708)345-2217
615 N 2nd Ave Maywood IL 60153-1111 • crflaabscwcrf.cuis.edu • NI • EM • (RF 1951 MA DED)

**LAABS JONATHAN C DR** (630)671-0306
116 Cambrian Ct Roselle IL 60172 • laabsje@curf.edu • NI • Northern Illinois Hillside IL • (RF 1977 MA DED)

**LAABS JUNE M** (630)671-0306
116 Cambrian Ct Roselle IL 60172 • laabsjc@crf.cuis.edu • NI • 11/1999 10/1999 • (S 1975 MSW MAT)

**LAATSCH JOEL M** (813)752-6024
4207 Thackery Way Plant City FL 33567-7297 • joel-angela-laatsch@io124.com • FG • Tchr • Hope Plant City FL • (813)752-4622 • (S 1996 MA)

**LAATSCH SARAH A** (920)739-9972
2201 W Pershing St - Apt #3 Appleton WI 54914 • NW • Tchr • Celebration Appleton WI • (920)734-7779 • (MW 2000)

**LABBUS PAUL** (715)536-3048
1005 Monroe St Merrill WI 54452-3033 • NW • Prin • Trinity Merrill WI • (715)536-5482 • (SP 1972 MEPD)

**LACEY HOWARD WAYNE** (512)339-6724
4606 Adelphi Ln Austin TX 78727-5210 • laceyh@concordia.edu • TX • SHS/C • Texas Austin TX • (CQ 1992 MBA DBA)

**LACEY MICHAEL W** (504)889-7084
3801 N Woodlawn Ave Metairie LA 70006-2835 • mwl004@lfn.org • SO • Tchr • Atonement Metairie LA • (504)887-3980 • (AU 1986 MS)

**LADD MARCIA A** (314)961-5430
9129 Desmond Drd Saint Louis MO 63126-2807 • MO • Tchr • Christ Community Kirkwood MO • (314)822-7774 • (CQ 1998 MA)

**LADENDORF GENE W** (972)377-7379
9816 Presthope Dr Frisco TX 75035-5270 • gwl@ourredeemer-dallas.org • TX • Prin • Our Redeemer Dallas TX • (214)368-1371 • (SP 1966 MSED)

**LADENDORF JANICE F** (972)377-7379
9816 Presthope Dr Frisco TX 75035-5270 • genejanl@earthlink.net • TX • Tchr • Prince Of Peace Carrollton TX • (972)447-9887 • (SP 1966 MS)

**LADWIG BARBARA-EM** (847)741-8455
730 Cooper Ave Elgin IL 60120-3104 • NI • Tchr • St John Elgin IL • (847)741-0814 • (CQ 1994)

**LAEDER KAREN SUE**
8181 Greenfield Rd Detroit MI 48228-2220 • MI • Tchr • Detroit Urban Detroit MI • (313)582-9900 • (AA 1994)

**LAEDER LEROY D** (517)631-3758
1320 George St Midland MI 48640-5425 • MI • EM • (RF 1953 MED EDS DED)

**LAESCH ROGER C** (414)464-4702
4503 N 106th St Milwaukee WI 53225-4518 • rlaesch@milwpc.com • SW • EM • (RF 1957 MS)

**LAESCH RUTH A** (813)689-1787
C/O Immanuel Lutheran Church 2913 John Moore Rd Brandon FL 33511-7139 • FG • Tchr • Immanuel Brandon FL • (813)689-1787 • (RF 1986)

**LAESCH WILLIAM J** (402)844-3697
928 S 16th St Norfolk NE 68701 • SW • 08/2000 • (CQ 1976 MMU)

**LAFRENTZ LOUISE JANE** (605)331-4404
3604 E 15th St Sioux Falls SD 57103-2908 • SD • Tchr • Sioux Falls Sioux Falls SD • (605)335-1923 • (S 1967)

**LAFRENTZ RANDALL** (219)447-1149
7620 Ensign Ct Fort Wayne IN 46816-2754 • IN • Tchr • St John Monroeville IN • (219)639-6404 • (S 1973)

**LAGERLEF DONNA K** (907)349-2711
9777 Reliance Dr Anchorage AK 99507 • donnakay@gci.net • NOW • Tchr • Anchor Anchorage AK • (907)522-3636 • (WN 1986)

**LAHN TRACY L**
222 N Muller St Apt 23 Anaheim CA 92801-5457 • PSW • Tchr • First Monrovia CA • (626)357-3596 • (IV 1999)

**LAIL CHERYL L** (636)278-8519
39 Countrywood Dr Saint Peters MO 63376-1232 • MO • Tchr • Zion Harvester MO • (314)441-7424 • (RF 1976)

**LAIL CHRISTOPHER J** (636)278-8519
39 Countrywood Dr Saint Peters MO 63376-1232 • clail01@mail.win.org • MO • Tchr • LHS St Charles Saint Peters MO • (636)928-5100 • (S 1974 MS)

**LAKE SHIRLEY ANN** (301)249-7132
15604 Peyton Ct Bowie MD 20716-1682 • SE • Tchr • Concordia Hyattsville MD • (301)927-0266 • (RF 1967 MA)

**LAMB CAROLYN L**
409 W 3rd Littlefield TX 79339 • ricalamb@juno.com • TX • 06/1991 06/2000 • (AU 1990)

**LAMB KENNETH A** (619)469-9267
10350 Fairhill Dr Spring Valley CA 91977-5408 • PSW • EM • (RF 1955)

**LAMBERT DEBRA R** (812)522-4320
212 Church Ave Seymour IN 47274-3624 • IN • Tchr • Immanuel Seymour IN • (812)522-1301 • (RF 1976 MS)

**LAMBERT TIMOTHY** (909)599-5724
812 Stanislaus Cir Claremont CA 91711-2900 • PSW • Tchr • Trinity Whittier CA • (562)699-7431 • (PO 1997)

**LAMBERTY ANTONETTE MARIE** (312)763-0441
6243 W Peterson Ave Chicago IL 60646-4616 • lamberty@gateway.net • EN • 07/1998 07/2000 • (RF 1991)

**LAMBRECHT JEFFREY A** (718)326-0386
Concordia Seminary 801 De Mun Ave Saint Louis MO 63105 • NW • 06/1999 • (MQ 1997)

**LAMBRECHT JO ANN** (402)489-1503
339 S 48th St Lincoln NE 68510-1831 • jalambecht@navix.net • NEB • Tchr • Christ Lincoln NE • (402)483-7774 • (S 1968 MA)

**LAMPE DIANN V**
12670 Bayshore Dr Florissant MO 63033 • MO • Tchr • River Roads Saint Louis MO • (314)388-0300 • (SP 1965)

**LAMS E THEODORE** (312)485-3474
4211 Arthur Ave Brookfield IL 60513-1913 • NI • P/Tchr • St Paul Brookfield IL • (708)485-0650 • (RF 1965 MMU)

**LAMSFUSS KRISTEN** (830)379-5341
465 Journeys End Seguin TX 78155-0526 • TX • Tchr • Grace Seguin TX • (830)379-1690 • (S 1974 MED)

**LAND JULIE ANNE** (812)522-2534
700 Ardenlee Parkway Peachtree City GA 30269 • FG • Tchr • St Paul Peachtree City GA • (770)487-0339 • (RF 1986)

**LANDES ELBERT**
442 Dutton Dr Pagosa Springs CO 81147 • RM • P/Tchr • Our Savior Pagosa Springs CO • (970)731-4668 • (RF 1970)

**LANDFRIED ELIZABETH A** (512)836-6280
11006 Sage Hollow Dr Austin TX 78758-4235 • TX • Tchr • Redeemer Austin TX • (512)451-6478 • (S 1975)

**LANDGRAF AMY LEE**
18411 Hatteras St Apt 115 Tarzana CA 91356-1962 • amylee3@hotmail.com • PSW • Tchr • Our Redeemer Canoga Park CA • (818)700-0390 • (RF 1994)

**LANDGRAVE AARON MARTIN** (708)784-9288
5901 S Franklin Ave La Grange IL 60525 • shermnike@hotmail.com • NI • Prin • St Paul Oak Lawn IL • (847)423-1058 • (RF 1985 MED)

**LANDGRAVE ADRIENNE A** (708)784-9288
5901 S Franklin Ave La Grange IL 60525 • shermanl@hotmail.com • NI • Tchr • Immanuel Hillside IL • (708)562-5590 • (RF 1986)

**LANDON BETH D**
1640 S Iris Way Lakewood CO 80232 • bdaenzerlandon@hotmail.com • RM • Tchr • Bethlehem Lakewood CO • (303)238-7676 • (S 1977 MA)

**LANDRAM KAREN MARIE** (714)979-6322
2466 Fairbrook Way Costa Mesa CA 92626-6573 • PSW • 03/1997 03/2000 • (IV 1995)

**LANDSKROENER ELLEN ANN** (317)271-9103
9101 W 10th St Indianapolis IN 46234 • jimandellen@hotmail.com • MI • Tchr • St John Rochester MI • (248)652-8830 • (AA 1992 MA)

**LANDSKROENER JAMES A**
1921 Wayfield Dr Avon IN 46123 • jimandellen@hotmail.com • IN • P/Tchr • Our Shepherd Indianapolis IN • (317)271-9103 • (S 1991 MED)

**LANDSKROENER JOEL P** (812)524-8380
721 Sycamore Rd Seymour IN 47274 • joelpl@hotmail.com • IN • Tchr • Trinity Lutheran Hig Seymour IN • (812)524-8547 • (S 1983 MA)

**LANDSKROENER NATHAN L** (702)432-1002
1877 Blue Ribbon Dr Las Vegas NV 89142-0740 • PSW • Tchr • First Good Shepherd Las Vegas NV • (702)382-8610 • (S 1980 MA)

**LANE DAVID M** (612)442-5978
9350 Morgan Ln Cologne MN 55322-9086 • MNS • Tchr • Lutheran High Mayer MN • (612)657-2251 • (CQ 1985)

**LANG EMMA J** (561)278-9346
709 Birdie Ct Delray Beach FL 33445-8736 • jlang@flinet.com • FG • Tchr • Trinity Delray Beach FL • (561)276-8458 • (RF 1968)

**LANG KERRI ANN** (402)476-4191
6151 NW 2nd Cir Apt 201 Lincoln NE 68521-4422 • kerri.lang@mailcity.com • MO • Tchr • Missouri Saint Louis MO • (314)317-4550 • (S 1998)

**LANG MARY A** (502)459-1124
2545 Dundee Rd Louisville KY 40205-2415 • IN • 10/1989 10/1999 • (S 1978 MA)

**LANG PHILIP W** (310)514-1099
1446 Brett Pl Apt 36 San Pedro CA 90732-5108 • tchrslang@aol.com • PSW • Tchr • Christ Rancho Palos Verdes CA • (310)831-0848 • (S 1969 MSED)

**LANGBEHN MARCIA L** (503)357-7613
2716 Strasburg Dr Forest Grove OR 97116 • NOW • Tchr • Bethlehem Aloha OR • (503)649-3380 • (S 1975)

**LANGE DEBRA KAY** (618)327-4878
426 E Alton St Nashville IL 62263-1886 • tdlange@midwest.com • SI • Tchr • St John Nashville IL • (618)478-5544 • (CQ 1994)

**LANGE JANICE A** (618)327-3115
682 W Saint Louis St Nashville IL 62263-1209 • sjblange@accessus.net • SI • Tchr • Trinity Nashville IL • (618)327-3311 • (RF 1980)

**LANGE LOIS C** (512)459-6091
5006 Shoal Creek Blvd Austin TX 78756-2524 • TX • Tchr • St Paul Austin TX • (512)472-3313 • (RF 1962 MED)

**LANGE LORI LEE** (714)890-3710
5381 Holland Ave Garden Grove CA 92845-1530 • PSW • 05/1997 05/2000 • (S 1990)

**LANGE PAUL W** (219)462-7382
2304 Linden Dr Valparaiso IN 46383-2333 • IN • EM • (RF 1927 MA PHD LLD)

**LANGE REBECCA ANNE** (817)852-0943
6130 Newton Dr Apt 4306 Fort Worth TX 76132-5305 • ralange@hotmail.com • TX • Tchr • St Paul Fort Worth TX • (817)332-2281 • (CQ 1996)

**LANGE ROBERT EARL** (402)734-7306
2614 E St Omaha NE 68107-1626 • NEB • P/Tchr • Mount Calvary Omaha NE • (402)551-7020 • (S 1972 MS)

**LANGE RUTH**
3134 N 82nd St Milwaukee WI 53222-3837 • SW • Tchr • Mount Olive Milwaukee WI • (414)774-2113 • (RF 1959)

**LANGEFELD RICHARD ALAN** (314)868-4516
10125 Elba Ln Saint Louis MO 63137-2931 • MO • Tchr • Lutheran North Saint Louis MO • (314)389-3100 • (S 1974)

**LANGFIELD TAMMY LYNN** (262)375-6919
292 N Port Washington Rd Grafton WI 53024-9767 • SW • Tchr • St John Glendale WI • (414)352-4150 • (RF 1986)

**LANGREHR LYNN** (618)282-3481
918 Monroe St Red Bud IL 62278-1357 • SI • Tchr • St John Red Bud IL • (618)282-3873 • (S 1976)

**LANGSTON ERIN JOSEPH**
Trinity Lutheran Church 940 Creston Rd Paso Robles CA 93446-3002 • CNH • Tchr • Trinity Paso Robles CA • (805)238-0335 • (PO 1994)

**LANNING CHANTAL M** (810)695-3217
3474 E Cook Rd Grand Blanc MI 48439-8014 • lannings2@aol.com • MI • Tchr • St Paul Flint MI • (810)239-6733 • (RF 1993)

**LANNING JOYCE ANN** (248)969-0410
4201 Curtis Rd Leonard MI 48367-1605 • MI • Tchr • St Trinity Clarkston MI • (810)620-6154 • (CQ 1998)

**LAPPE DUSTIN**
960 N Gilbert Rd Apt 124 Gilbert AZ 85234-3320 • MO • 09/1998 • (S 1997)

**LAPSLEY RAMONA ANN** (719)685-3717
One Delaware Rd Manitou Springs CO 80829-2205 • rlapsley@ffc8.k12.co.us • RM • 09/1992 09/1999 • (S 1986 MSED)

**LARAIA LORI A**
4711 Yender #2B Lisle IL 60532 • NI • Tchr • St John Wheaton IL • (630)668-0701 • (RF 1996)

**LAREVA NANCY R** (714)997-7397
363 N Fern St Orange CA 92867-7806 • nlareva@aol.com • PSW • Tchr • St Paul Orange CA • (714)637-2640 • (RF 1966 MA)

**LARK DEVON H** (612)738-8150
2168 Falcon Ave Saint Paul MN 55119-5036 • dlark@mail.concordia-academy.k12.pvt.mn.us • MNS • Tchr • Concordia Academy Roseville MN • (612)484-8429 • (S 1969 MAT)

**LARK PETER J** (352)629-1794
St John Lutheran Church 1915 SE Lake Weir Rd Ocala FL 34471-5424 • FG • Tchr • St John Ocala FL • (352)629-1794 • (RF 1999)

**LARRABEE LINDA E** (303)280-1639
11916 Monroe St Thornton CO 80233-1651 • RM • Tchr • Gethsemane Northglenn CO • (303)451-6908 • (S 1975)

**LARRABEE LOREN L** (303)427-5574
6305 Tennyson St Arvada CO 80003-6707 • llarrabee@usa.net • RM • Tchr • Denver Lutheran High Denver CO • (303)934-2345 • (S 1976 MSED)

**LARRABEE LU ANN E** (303)794-9353
6884 S Broadway Littleton CO 80122-1010 • luann@ecentral.com • RM • Tchr • Shepherd Of The Hill Littleton CO • (303)798-0711 • (S 1979 MSED)

**LARSEN MELISSA E** (281)448-4643
4444 Victory Dr #1106 Houston TX 77088 • pmlarsen@juno.com • TX • Tchr • St Mark Houston TX • (713)468-2623 • (S 1991 MED)

**LARSEN NANCY KAYE** (414)494-3567
958 La Croix Ave Green Bay WI 54304-4424 • NW • 04/1997 04/2000 • (RF 1986)

**LARSEN SARA NATALIE** (979(540-2182
353 E Houston Giddings TX 78942 • TX • Tchr • Zion Tomball TX • (713)255-6203 • (S 1998)

**LARSON DOUGLAS KEITH** (507)776-3101
206 E Ciro Truman MN 56088 • MNN • 02/2000 • (SP 1976)

**LARSON KATHERINE**
2719 Delowe Dr East Point GA 30344-2303 • FG • Tchr • Christ East Point GA • (404)767-2892 • (S 1997)

**LARSON LISA LYNN**
18308 E Dickenson Pl Aurora CO 80013-5912 • RM • Christ East Point GA • (CQ 1999)

**LARSON TAMMY L** (612)732-3582
125 Central Ave #2 Long Prairie MN 56347-1336 • MNN • Tchr • Trinity Long Prairie MN • (320)732-2238 • (SP 1988)

**LASSANSKE ROLAND R DR** (805)544-9274
4940 Caballeros Ave San Luis Obispo CA 93401-7975 • CNH • EM • (RF 1941 MA PHD)

**LASSEIGNE DIANE E** (618)288-3209
32 Windermere Dr Glen Carbon IL 62034-1477 • laseigne@juno.com • SI • Tchr • Trinity Edwardsville IL • (618)656-7002 • (WN 1984)

**LASTUSKY MYRNA MARIE** (414)451-4723
3720 10th St Sheboygan WI 53081 • lastusky@lutheranhigh.com • SW • Tchr • Lutheran HS Sheboygan WI • (920)452-3323 • (S 1993)

**LATZKE HENRY R** (708)345-6685
1104 N 10th Ave Melrose Park IL 60160-3504 • crflatzkehr@curf.edu • NI • EM • (RF 1956 MS DED)

**LATZKE LAURA L** (708)345-6685
1104 N 10th Ave Melrose Park IL 60160-3504 • crflatzkehr@curf.edu • NI • EM • (RF 1966 MS)

**LAUBENSTEIN JOAN L** (602)954-6570
4821 N 28th Pl Phoenix AZ 85016-4804 • joanlaubenstein@yahoo.com • EN • Tchr • Christ Phoenix AZ • (602)957-7010 • (S 1973 MA)

**LAUBENSTEIN LARRY P** (660)463-7831
314 College Dr PO Box 719 Concordia MO 64020-0719 • MO • SHS/C • Missouri Saint Louis MO • (314)317-4550 • (S 1970 MED)

**LAUBENSTEIN LEONARD P** (303)985-2094
1778 S Cody St Lakewood CO 80232-6613 • RM • EM • (RF 1942)

**LAUBSCH JENNIFER M** (419)591-1498
740 Trail Dr Apt 13 Napoleon OH 43545 • OH • Tchr • St Paul Napoleon OH • (419)592-5536 • (RF 1999)

**LAUBSCH TERRY J** (517)652-6885
9440 Junction Rd Frankenmuth MI 48734-9577 • MI • Tchr • St Lorenz Frankenmuth MI • (517)652-6141 • (RF 1968)

**LAUCKNER EDIE H** (810)694-5979
2243 Rollins St Grand Blanc MI 48439-4352 • jtleml@aol.com • MI • Tchr • St Paul Flint MI • (810)239-6733 • (SP 1968 MAT)

**LAUFER EDITH MARIE** (618)458-7177
C/O Holy Cross Lutheran Church PO Box 7 Renault IL 62279-0007 • rlaufer@htc.net • SI • 09/1994 09/1999 • (WN 1982)

**LAUGHLIN WILLIAM M** (561)287-4676
950 Colorado Ave #C-23 Stuart FL 34994-3758 • FG • 08/1996 08/2000 • (RF 1990)

**LAURENTE MARVIN L** (775)882-5252
600 W Long St Carson City NV 89703-2935 • marvnkaren@aol.com • CNH • P/Tchr • Bethlehem Carson City NV • (775)882-5252 • (RF 1962 MA)

**LAUX LINDA L**
726 Meadows Dr Marysville OH 43040-8688 • OH • Tchr • St John Marysville OH • (937)644-5540 • (AA 1995)

**LAUX LORI** (412)823-1244
2502 Hyer Ave Apt 52F North Versailles PA 15137 • lllaux³goblue@hotmail.com • EA • Mem C • Christ Pittsburgh PA • (412)271-7173 • (AA 1991 MA)

**LAVRENZ RUTH H** (319)362-6952
325 Murray Dr SW Cedar Rapids IA 52404-1845 • IE • Tchr • Trinity Cedar Rapids IA • (319)362-6952 • (S 1979)

**LAWIN PRISCILLA DR** (402)643-4383
1811 N Columbia Ave Seward NE 68434-9730 • plawin@seward.cune.edu • NEB • SHS/C • Nebraska Seward NE • (S 1963 MED DED)

**LAWIN TANYA** (815)459-1462
11 W Acorn Lane Apt 1D Lake in the Hills IL 60102 • NI • Tchr • Immanuel Crystal Lake IL • (815)459-1444 • (BR 1990)

**LAWRENCE GLORIA M** (216)899-5137
27910 Knickerbocker Rd Bay Village OH 44140-2151 • pwrengserv@ameritech.net • OH • Tchr • St Paul Westlake OH • (440)835-3051 • (RF 1974)

**LAWRENZ DENISE LYNN** (870)698-9739
75 Morris Rd #A Batesville AR 72501-9612 • clawrenz@juno.com • MDS • Tchr • Hope Batesville AR • (870)793-3078 • (S 1996)

**LAWSON HERMAN E** (707)253-8711
1330 Darling St Napa CA 94558-1911 • helawson@napanet.net • CNH • Prin • St John Napa CA • (707)226-7970 • (S 1972 MED)

**LAWSON SANDRA MAE** (707)253-8711
1330 Darling St Napa CA 94558-1911 • helawson@napanet.net • CNH • Tchr • St John Napa CA • (707)226-7970 • (S 1972)

**LAZARUS PHYLLENE DARNELL** (847)438-8446
707 Edelweiss Dr Lake Zurich IL 60047-2492 • NI • Tchr • St Matthew Lake Zurich IL • (847)438-6103 • (CQ 1991)

**LE BEAU EDWARD W** (219)486-5053
C/O Concordia Luth High School 1601 Saint Joe River Dr Fort Wayne IN 46805-1433 • jeere@msn.com • IN • Tchr • Indiana Fort Wayne IN • (S 1965 MA)

**LE BEAU LU ANN MARIE**
2990 N Millden Rd Avon Park FL 33825 • luann-lebeau@yahoo.com • IN • Tchr • Woodburn Woodburn IN • (219)632-5493 • (RF 1990)

**LE BLANC CHRISTOPHER JAY**
C/O Salem Lutheran Church 418 4th St Gretna LA 70053-5317 • SO • Tchr • Salem Gretna LA • (504)367-5144 • (MQ 1996)

**LE CLERE BRUCE A** (612)467-3715
714 W Elm St Norwood MN 55368-9737 • MNS • Prin • Lutheran High Mayer MN • (612)657-2251 • (S 1985)

**LEANNAIS KIMBERLY DAWN** (414)774-8810
457 S 74th St Milwaukee WI 53214-1512 • dkleannais@juno.com • SW • 08/2000 • (RF 1997)

**LEAPALDT REUBEN L**
20250 SW Johnson St Aloha OR 97006 • NOW • EM • (RF 1953)

**LEAPLEY KURT ALLEN**
1700 S Craftsman New Berlin WI 53146 • NI • Tchr • St Paul Mount Prospect IL • (847)255-6733 • (S 1986)

**LEAPLEY MARGARET S**
1700 S Craftsman New Berlin WI 53146 • NI • Tchr • St Paul Mount Prospect IL • (847)255-0332 • (S 1986)

**LEATZOW EDWARD A** (231)780-4234
1962 Spencer Dr Muskegon MI 49441-4538 • ealeatzow@aol.com • MI • Tchr • Trinity Muskegon MI • (616)755-1292 • (SP 1968 MA)

**LEBECK SANDRA IRENE** (815)432-2506
843 E Locust St Watseka IL 60970-1816 • NI • Tchr • St Paul Milford IL • (815)889-4569 • (S 1981)

**LEBRECHT LARRY G** (714)529-5746
1981 Chevy Chase Brea CA 92821 • llebrecht@aol.com • PSW • Prin • Christ Fullerton CA • (714)870-7460 • (S 1965 MA)

**LEBRECHT RICHARD** (714)974-9486
2754 N Galley St Orange CA 92865-2423 • PSW • Tchr • St Paul Orange CA • (714)921-3188 • (S 1970 MA)

**LECKBAND KRISTIN KAY** (402)329-4262
RR 2 Box 544 Foster NE 68737 • schleckorgan@juno.com • RM • 05/1998 05/2000 • (S 1994)

**LECKBAND LOIS E** (402)371-6459
1606 Skyline Dr Norfolk NE 68701-2666 • lois49436@aol.com • NEB • Tchr • Christ Norfolk NE • (402)371-5536 • (RF 1977)

**LECKBAND PAUL R** (402)371-6459
1606 Skyline Dr Norfolk NE 68701 • luthhigh@ncfcomm.com • NEB • Prin • Lutheran High Northe Norfolk NE • (402)379-3040 • (S 1975 MS)

**LECKBAND VIRGIL E** (660)463-7546
406 Gordon St # 16 Concordia MO 64020-9673 • MO • EM • (S 1950 MSED)

**LEDBETTER BOBBIE ANN** (281)485-7955
PO Box 788 Pearland TX 77588-0788 • TX • Tchr • Mount Olive Houston TX • (713)922-5673 • (S 1975)

**LEDEBUHR JAMES A**
500 Millstone Dr Belleville IL 62221-5828 • SI • Tchr • Zion Belleville IL • (618)234-0275 • (RF 1992 MPE)

**LEDIC JEAN BETH**
Messiah Luth Church 2305 Camino Tassajara Danville CA 94526-4402 • EN • 06/1999 • (RF 1978)

**LEE JAMES C**
C/O St Paul Lutheran Church 5433 Madison Rd Cincinnati OH 45227-1507 • OH • 01/1999 • (PO 1981)

**LEE KAREN H** (218)338-5351
609 S Douglas Ave PO Box 66 Parkers Prairie MN 56361-0066 • k3lee@mail.ppps.fed.k12.mn.us • MNN • 09/1990 09/1999 • (SP 1986)

**LEE NANCY A** (708)851-1534
3053 Winchester Ct W Aurora IL 60504-8958 • teacher689@cs.com • NI • Tchr • Cross Yorkville IL • (630)553-7861 • (RF 1977)

**LEECH WILLIAM ALAN** (308)532-0166
103 N Mc Cabe Ave North Platte NE 69101-5758 • bleech@kdsi.net • NEB • P/Tchr • Our Redeemer North Platte NE • (308)532-6421 • (S 1973 MA)

**LEELAND CARLENE L** (608)355-6477
710 Bascom Hill Dr Baraboo WI 53913 • SW • Tchr • St John Portage WI • (608)742-4222 • (SP 1968)

**LEEPER KARMEN K** (219)546-3310
2839 2B Rd Bremen IN 46506-9048 • IN • Tchr • St Paul Bremen IN • (219)546-2790 • (AA 1989)

**LEET JANET B** (314)394-1790
302 Twinview Ter Manchester MO 63011-4361 • MO • P/Tchr • Christ Community Kirkwood MO • (314)822-7774 • (CQ 1998 MED)

**LEGER SANDRA K** (713)812-1739
6401 Deihl Rd #405 Houston TX 77092-1318 • TX • Tchr • Our Savior Houston TX • (713)290-9087 • (AU 1984)

**LEGGE JEAN L** (901)761-6158
5072 Alrose Ave Memphis TN 38117-5802 • jklegge@yahoo.com • MDS • Tchr • Christ The King Memphis TN • (901)682-8405 • (SP 1973 MED)

**LEHENBAUER BECKY A**
884 Benchwood Dr Winter Springs FL 32708 • bal@teacher.com • S • Tchr • St Luke Oviedo FL • (407)365-3408 • (S 1986)

**LEHENBAUER RENEE E** (502)921-2443
471 Peaceful Way Shepherdsville KY 40165-7849 • jlky@juno.com • IN • 07/1991 07/2000 • (S 1980)

**LEHENBAUER STEVEN L**
884 Benchwood Dr Winter Springs FL 32708 • steve.becky@baptized.com • S • Tchr • St Luke Oviedo FL • (407)365-3408 • (S 1985)

**LEHL ELLA LOUISE**
2761 Taft St Apt 301 Hollywood FL 33020 • FG • Tchr • St Mark Hollywood FL • (954)922-7572 • (S 1966)

**LEHMAN ARRON L**
911 W Crestview Ct Crown Point IN 46307-4828 • yipeekia@hmtel.com • IN • Tchr • Trinity Crown Point IN • (219)663-1586 • (S 1994)

**LEHMAN JANET R** (920)387-4745
245 Hyland Trl Mayville WI 53050-1340 • SW • Tchr • St John Mayville WI • (920)387-4310 • (RF 1974)

**LEHMAN MICHELLE A** (507)775-6325
200 7th St NW Byron MN 55920-1344 • MNS • Tchr • Rochester Central Rochester MN • (507)289-3267 • (S 1992)

**LEHMANN ARLO V** (316)587-3309
C/O Zion Lutheran Church PO Box 415 Claflin KS 67525-0415 • KS • Mem C • Zion Claflin KS • (316)587-3698 • (S 1962 MRE)

**LEHMANN CHARLES R**
C/O Luther East High School PO Box 404 Lansing IL 60438-0404 • NI • Tchr • Luther East Lansing IL • (708)895-8441 • (S 1999)

**LEHMANN JUDITH E** (660)463-7181
201 West St Concordia MO 64020-9644 • MO • Tchr • Holy Cross Emma MO • (660)463-2553 • (S 1960)

**LEHMANN ROBERT A*** (660)463-7181
201 West St Concordia MO 64020-9644 • MO • EM • (S 1959 MA MSED)

**LEHRKE DALE A** (440)353-9517
7191 Kenssington Dr North Ridgeville OH 44039-3199 • OH • Tchr • St Paul Westlake OH • (440)835-3051 • (RF 1984 MA)

**LEHRKE GEORGE J** (715)758-8591
N4539 State Hwy 117 Bonduel WI 54107-8813 • NW • EM • (RF 1959)

**LEIBIG REBECCA A** (870)673-1003
1105 S Grand St Stuttgart AR 72160-5347 • MDS • Tchr • St John Stuttgart AR • (870)673-7096 • (RF 1968)

**LEIDECKER KARLA JEAN** (810)775-2596
15315 Evergreen Eastpointe MI 48021 • MI • Tchr • St Peter Eastpointe MI • (810)776-1663 • (AA 1998)

**LEIDECKER SHIRLEY ANN** (810)727-9757
9187 Springborn Rd Casco MI 48064-3609 • MI • Tchr • Immanuel Macomb MI • (810)286-7076 • (RF 1966 MA)

**LEIDICH ROY E** (810)465-5475
22800 Stair St Clinton Twp MI 48036-2747 • MI • Tchr • St Thomas Eastpointe MI • (810)772-3372 • (RF 1968)

**LEIMBACH JASON ANDREW**
809 Manes Ct Lincoln NE 68505-2021 • FG • 09/1998 • (S 1996)

**LEIMBACH STACY CHRISTINE** (770)631-8087
809 Manes Ct Lincoln NE 68505-2021 • NEB • Tchr • Trinity Lincoln NE • (402)466-1800 • (S 1996)

**LEIMBACH WILLIAM W** (713)473-5447
2215 Walnut Ln Pasadena TX 77502-4044 • bcleimbach@aol.com • TX • EM • (RF 1955 MA)

**LEIMER ANN ELIZABETH**
4302 Mesa View Ln Fort Collins CO 80526-3376 • RM • Trinity Lincoln NE • (S 1996)

**LEIMER DAVID JOHN**
4302 Mesa View Ln Fort Collins CO 80526-3376 • RM • Trinity Lincoln NE • (BR 1991)

**LEIMER HAROLD A** (314)739-5890
3751 Vincentian Ln Bridgeton MO 63044-3518 • harleim@aol.com • MO • EM • (S 1933 MA)

**LEIMER JOHN F** (816)941-3532
306 W 109th St Kansas City MO 64114-1945 • jleimer@calvarykc.com • MO • Tchr • Calvary Kansas City MO • (816)444-5517 • (RF 1967 MSED)

**LEIMER WALTER B** (402)675-7461
PO Box 393 Battle Creek NE 68715-0393 • NEB • EM • (S 1937 MED)

**LEIN JANE W**
4489 Lyndenwood Cir Highlands Ranch CO 80126 • RM • Tchr • Shepherd Hills Littleton CO • (303)798-0711 • (CQ 1999)

**LEINBERGER DAVID W** (810)781-5434
53225 Venus Dr Shelby Twp MI 48316-2359 • dlein38@bignet.net • MI • Tchr • LHS North Macomb MI • (810)781-9151 • (RF 1961 MAT)

**LEINBERGER TIMOTHY** (352)620-2732
C/O Saint John Luth School 1915 SE Lake Weir Rd Ocala FL 34471-5424 • tleinbel102@aol.com • FG • Tchr • St John Ocala FL • (352)622-7275 • (RF 1997)

**LEININGER RACHEL M** 44-1223-362089
31 Benson St Cambridge Cambridgeshire CB4 3QJ UNITED KINGDOM • rachell@uk.amgen.com • TX • 08/1996 08/2000 • (RF 1993)

**LEININGER ROBERT W** (612)641-8249
457 Sextant Ave Saint Paul MN 55113-3530 • MNS • SHS/C • Minnesota South Burnsville MN • (CQ 1969 MMU MFA)

**LEISSINGER MARILYN JO** (504)737-9554
4616 Clearlake Dr Metairie LA 70006-2222 • SO • P/Tchr • Faith Harahan LA • (504)737-9554 • (S 1969 MED)

**LEISTICO LAURENE ELAINE** (209)388-0290
367 Collins Dr #1 Merced CA 95348 • leistico@yahoo.com • CNH • Tchr • St Paul Merced CA • (209)383-3302 • (IV 1999)

**LEITNER GEORGE W** (512)252-9599
1524 Emperor Ct Round Rock TX 78664 • leitner@ecpl.com • TX • Prin • Our Savior Austin TX • (512)836-9600 • (AU 1982 MS)

**LEITNER LINDA D** (512)252-9599
1524 Emperor Ct Round Rock TX 78664 • leitner@ecpi.com • TX • Tchr • Our Savior Austin TX • (512)836-9600 • (S 1973)

**LEITZ ADOLPH H** (941)597-7392
520 Nottingham Dr Naples FL 34109-1616 • MI • EM • (RF 1933)

**LEITZKE MARTIN W** (920)485-2351
808 E Walnut St Horicon WI 53032-1226 • SW • EM • (NU 1943 MA MA)

**LELLE JOHN B** (440)639-0973
1120 Dartmouth Dr Painesville OH 44077-5288 • jblelle@oh.verio.com • OH • P/Tchr • Our Shepherd Painesville OH • (440)357-7776 • (S 1970 MED)

**LELLE WILBERTA J** (440)639-0973
1120 Dartmouth Dr Painesville OH 44077-5288 • blelle@hotmail.com • OH • Tchr • Our Shepherd Painesville OH • (440)357-7776 • (S 1970)

**LEMANSKI JUDITH E** (216)781-9512
2928 Scranton Rd Cleveland OH 44113-5322 • jlemanski@juno.com • OH • 01/1993 01/2000 • (AA 1985)

**LEMKE CYNTHIA M** (402)643-4210
305 Grand Ave Seward NE 68434-1613 • cml6294@seward.cune.edu • NEB • Tchr • St John Seward NE • (402)643-4535 • (S 1976 MED)

**LEMKE GEORGE F** (313)549-5208
4146 Normandy Rd Royal Oak MI 48073-6368 • MI • Tchr • LHS East Harper Woods MI • (313)371-8750 • (RF 1966 MA)

**LEMKE JANE ELLEN** (734)241-0639
415 Laurel Dr Monroe MI 48161-5766 • MI • Tchr • Trinity Monroe MI • (734)241-1160 • (S 1971)

**LEMKE KATHLEEN LYNN** (414)853-3331
745 River View Rd Hilbert WI 54129 • SW • Tchr • Trinity Hilbert WI • (920)853-3134 • (MQ 1993)

**LEMKE LINDA M** (715)839-8837
2130 Sunray Cir Eau Claire WI 54703-5849 • NW • Tchr • Eau Claire Eau Claire WI • (715)835-9314 • (S 1973)

**LEMKE MARK A DR** (402)643-4210
305 Grand Ave Seward NE 68434-1613 • mlemke@seward.cune.edu • NEB • SHS/C • Nebraska Seward NE • (S 1976 MED EDD)

**LENGHART SUSAN M**
1916 Glen Iris Dr Commerce Twp MI 48382-2105 • MI • Tchr • St Matthew Walled Lake MI • (248)624-7677 • (CQ 1988)

**LENTSCH THOMAS B JR.** (410)747-2256
6200 Lakemont Ct Catonsville MD 21228-1248 • SE • Tchr • Baltimore LHS Baltimore MD • (410)825-2323 • (S 1970)

**LENZ RODNEY G** (319)446-7029
421 1st St Atkins IA 52206-9755 • IE • 09/1994 09/1999 • (SP 1979 MA)

**LENZ TINA MARIE** (319)446-7029
421 1st St Atkins IA 52206-9755 • IE • 06/1998 • (SP 1979)

**LEONARD CHRISTINE R** (610)683-7545
591 College Garden Dr Kutztown PA 19530-1011 • cleonard@talon.net • S • Tchr • Concordia Bethlehem PA* • (610)691-7625 • (RF 1981)

**LEONARD JONATHAN T** (503)761-5552
2146 SE 178th Pl Portland OR 97233-3224 • NOW • SHS/C • Northwest Portland OR • (RF 1979 MS PHD)

**LEONARD THOMAS** (414)677-4267
N168W21700 Main St Lot 243 Jackson WI 53037-9305 • tlednard@bach.cuw.edu • SW • EM • (CQ 1966 PHD)

**LEONHARDT JANELLE M**
395 S Xapary St Aurora CO 80012-2463 • RM • Tchr • Redeemer Denver CO • (303)934-5447 • (S 1978 MA)

**LERCH KATHLEEN P** (909)279-6769
1327 Pajero Dr Corona CA 92882-4502 • lrchwoman@aol.com • PSW • Tchr • Holy Cross Cypress CA • (714)527-7928 • (IV 1988)

**LERRET BRIAN W**
2645 N 65th St Wauwatosa WI 53213 • SW • Tchr • Mount Olive Milwaukee WI • (414)774-2113 • (MQ 1998)

**LESSNER AIMEE L**
894 Mackinaw Ave Calumet City IL 60409-4413 • IN • 06/1999 • (RF 1996)

**LESTINA EMMA LOUISE** (818)249-2060
5105 Cloud Ave La Crescenta CA 91214 • duncan@ktb.net • PSW • Tchr • Emmaus Alhambra CA • (626)289-3664 • (RF 1973)

**LEUPOLD PATRICK H** (309)664-0677
22 Aberdeen Way Bloomington IL 61704-8116 • phl1@trinluth.org • CI • Prin • Trinity Bloomington IL • (309)829-7513 • (S 1979 MA)

**LEUTHAUSER TRUMAN W** (303)639-3238
1625 S Birch Apt 602 Denver CO 80222 • RM • EM • (S 1939)

**LEVENHAGEN AMY DAWN** (773)625-2849
5121 N East River Rd #1K Chicago IL 60656 • leve0932@cs.com • NI • Tchr • St Andrew Park Ridge IL • (847)823-9308 • (RF 1998)

**LEVENHAGEN WILLIAM A** (407)658-1437
7805 Captain Morgan Blvd Orlando FL 32822-6962 • NI • EM • (RF 1955 MS EDS)

**LEWANDOWSKI HEATHER J** (708)474-1442
18181 S Clyde Ave Lansing IL 60438 • IN • Tchr • St Paul Munster IN • (219)836-6270 • (RF 2000)

**LEWER STEVEN F** (317)894-8433
12216 Dunbar Ct Indianapolis IN 46229-3213 • slewer@inct.net • IN • Tchr • LHS Of Indianapolis Indianapolis IN • (317)787-5474 • (S 1985 MS)

**LEWIS CHRISTOPHER ALLEN**
4029 Mc Clain Way #41 Carmichael CA 95608 • CNH • Tchr • Sacramento Lutheran Sacramento CA • (916)978-2720 • (S 1996)

**LEWIS ELLEN KAY** (626)851-8682
Emmaus Lutheran Church 840 S Almansor St Alhamabra CA 91801-4538 • ellnnbr@aol.com • PSW • Tchr • Emmaus Alhambra CA • (626)289-3664 • (S 1985)

**LEWIS INGRID E** (216)691-0675
880 Stuart Dr South Euclid OH 44121 • OH • Tchr • St John South Euclid OH • (216)381-1513 • (RF 1986)

**LEWIS LORI J** (262)644-1521
522 Oak Ter Slinger WI 53086 • SW • Tchr • Trinity Mequon WI • (262)242-2045 • (AA 1989 MA)

**LEWIS MILDRED C** (520)742-5861
2900 W Greenridge Pl Tucson AZ 85741-3004 • EN • Tchr • Faith Tucson AZ • (520)881-0670 • (CQ 1995)

**LEWIS SUSAN L** (847)827-4158
366 Alles Ave Des Plaines IL 60016-4420 • sllewis@sprintmail.com • NI • Tchr • Special Educ Ministr River Forest IL • (708)209-3344 • (RF 1971 MA)

**LEWIS TIMOTHY B** (216)731-6654
C/O Lutheran High School East 3565 Mayfield Rd Cleveland Hts OH 44118-1401 • OH • Tchr • Ohio Olmsted Falls OH • (RF 1987)

**LEYVA COLLEEN A** (828)684-5440
36 Meadow Cir Arden NC 28704-9501 • cleyva@home.com • SE • Tchr • Emmanuel Asheville NC • (828)252-1795 • (RF 1984 MED)

**LIBHART REBECCA ANN** (316)938-2500
1225 3rd Rd Chase KS 67524-9448 • KS • 08/1997 08/1999 • (S 1996)

**LIBKA ROBERT J** (708)343-6013
805 N 6th Ave Maywood IL 60153-1046 • adistudent@aol.com • NI • Tchr • Fox Valley Academy Elgin IL • (847)468-8207 • (RF 1975 MED MED)

**LIBRIZZI KATHRYN A** (414)771-7649
2117 S 96th St Milwaukee WI 53227-1426 • SW • Tchr • Mount Olive Milwaukee WI • (414)774-2113 • (MQ 1992)

**LIEB TRINA K** (501)280-0151
1901 Shumate Dr Little Rock AR 72212-3861 • dlieb@aristotle.net • MDS • Tchr • Christ Little Rock AR • (501)663-5212 • (AU 1993 MED)

**LIEBENOW HERBERT W** (414)464-0958
4728 N 74th St Milwaukee WI 53218-4715 • SW • EM • (RF 1954 MED)

**LIEBMANN CAROLYN MARIE** (219)441-0728
6701 S Anthony Blvd #R207 Fort Wayne IN 46816-2012 • IN • EM • (RF 1953 MA)

**LIEBMANN LAURA**
126 Glenview Inn Rd Glen Carbon IL 62034-1410 • SI • Tchr • Metro-East LHS Edwardsville IL • (618)656-0043 • (S 1996)

**LIEBMANN MARTIN W** (816)921-4605
3009 S Norton Ave Independence MO 64052-3185 • MO • Tchr • Kansas City LHS Kansas City MO • (816)241-5478 • (S 1991)

**LIEBMANN MELANIE**
227 E Market St Havana IL 62644-1407 • FG • Tchr • Faith Eustis FL • (352)589-5683 • (S 1997)

**LIEDER CHARLES H**
24744 Old Church Rd Red Wing MN 55066 • MNS • Prin • Concordia-Immanuel Red Wing MN • (612)388-3839 • (RF 1971 MED)

**LIEDER ELAINE T** (651)388-9369
24744 Old Church Rd Red Wing MN 55066 • chlieder@win.bright.net • MNS • Tchr • Concordia-Immanuel Red Wing MN • (612)388-3839 • (RF 1972 MED)

**LIENAU JANE ELIZABETH** (313)278-7351
731 Sandra Ct Dearborn Heights MI 48127-4137 • MI • Tchr • LHS Westland Westland MI • (734)422-2090 • (CQ 1995 MA)

**LIENEMANN HEATHER A** (612)808-7462
12570 Portland Ave S #305 Burnsville MN 55337 • MNS • Tchr • Bethlehem Minnetonka MN • (612)934-5959 • (SP 1995)

**LIESCHEIDT BETTY ANN** (636)391-8344
1106 Westrun Dr Ballwin MO 63021-6106 • MO • Tchr • St John Ellisville MO • (314)394-4100 • (RF 1969)

**LIESCHEIDT RICHARD H** (718)720-8276
40 S Greenleaf Ave Staten Island NY 10314-2429 • AT • Prin • St John Staten Island NY • (718)761-1858 • (RF 1959)

**LIESE LLOYD D** (630)985-3387
7655 Woodview Dr Woodridge IL 60517-2703 • NI • EM • (RF 1959 MA MMU)

**LIESE MARC T** (440)884-7206
3212 Priscilla Ave Parma OH 44134-4235 • mliese.bls@iol13.com • OH • Tchr • Bethany Parma OH • (440)884-1010 • (RF 1982)

**LIESE MATTHEW P**
11200 Appleton Dr Cleveland OH 44130-4456 • OH • Tchr • St Thomas Rocky River OH • (440)331-4426 • (RF 1996)

**LIESE STACEY L*** (309)446-3436
PO Box 297 Brimfield IL 61517-0297 • CI • 07/1995 07/2000 • (RF 1987)

**LIETKE EDWARD C**
11613 SE 7th St Apt 265 Vancouver WA 98683-5254 • NOW • EM • (RF 1938 MED DED)

**LIETZ BRENDA L** (330)929-9509
2321 Iota Ave Cuyahoga Falls OH 44223-1005 • lietz@juno.com • OH • 09/1998 • (S 1973)

**LIETZ FRED E** (407)365-5437
2091 Catbird Ct Oviedo FL 32765-8540 • frdltz16@aol.com • FG • EM • (RF 1939 LLD)

**LILIENTHAL SUE ANN** (715)341-0873
1511 Dennis Dr Plover WI 54467-2320 • NW • Tchr • St Paul Stevens Point WI • (715)344-5660 • (MQ 1991 MA)

**LILLICH DENNIS M** (330)833-5752
3523 Bailey Rd NW Massillon OH 44646-3684 • S • 08/1993 08/2000 • (S 1973)

**LIMBACK JANE L** (913)642-0611
7633 Mackey St Overland Park KS 66204-2653 • thefigtree@juno.com • KS • Tchr • Hope Shawnee KS • (913)631-6940 • (S 1984 MED)

**LIMBACK KELLEY M**
1908 Ruger Ct Saint Charles MO 63303 • MO • Tchr • LHS St Charles Saint Peters MO • (636)928-5100 • (S 2000)

**LIMMEL FRED B** (612)470-7975
C/O Our Savior Lutheran Church 23290 Highway 7 Excelsior MN 55331-3139 • MNS • P/Tchr • Our Savior Excelsior MN • (612)474-9710 • (S 1985)

**LIMMEL TAMARA J** (612)470-7975
C/O Our Savior Lutheran Church 23290 Highway 7 Excelsior MN 55331-3139 • MNS • Tchr • Our Savior Excelsior MN • (612)474-9710 • (S 1984)

**LIMMER ANDREW J** (414)423-8439
6029 Middleton Ct S Greendale WI 53129-1357 • limphys@juno.com • SW • Tchr • Martin LHS Greendale WI • (414)421-4000 • (S 1987 MS)

**LINCOLN CYNTHIA A** (810)294-5374
31719 Courtland St St Clair Shrs MI 48082-1227 • MI • Tchr • Special Ed Ministrie Detroit MI • (313)368-1220 • (CQ 1977)

**LIND CHARLES E** (314)544-4371
821 Shady Ridge Ct Saint Louis MO 63125-3231 • bertlind@postnet.com • MO • Tchr • Green Park Lemay MO • (314)544-4248 • (RF 1960 MAT)

**LINDAU REBECCA E** (210)681-7227
5011 Glen Ridge #U20 San Antonio TX 78229 • blindau@ezl.com • TX • Green Park Lemay MO • (MQ 1994)

**LINDEMAN ALISE A** (303)425-0403
6424 W 82nd Dr Arvada CO 80003-1720 • RM • 06/1990 06/2000 • (S 1981)

**LINDEMAN LOIS E** (414)628-7395
1380 Homestead Ct Hubertus WI 53033-9433 • EN • Tchr • Hales Corners Hales Corners WI • (414)529-6701 • (S 1971)

**LINDEMAN MARILYN K** (847)824-6357
1012 Clark Ln Des Plaines IL 60016-6008 • marilind2@juno.com • NI • EM • (RF 1971 MED)

**LINDEMANN EMIL R** (847)824-6357
1012 Clark Ln Des Plaines IL 60016-6008 • NEB • EM • (S 1922)

**LINDEMANN SHARON** (920)485-0467
709 Karen Lane Horicon WI 53032-1590 • SW • Tchr • St Stephen Horicon WI • (920)485-6687 • (MQ 1996)

**LINDEN ROBERT E** (253)845-0061
12326 132nd Ave E Puyallup WA 98374-2958 • bobwa@worldnet.att.net • NOW • 08/1986 08/2000 • (RF 1973 MED)

**LINDENFELSER LYNN MARIE** (734)284-0237
1833 Cora Wyandotte MI 48192 • MI • Tchr • Trinity Wyandotte MI • (734)282-5896 • (AA 1999)

**LINDGREN FREDERICK** (414)466-8071
3950 N 65th St Milwaukee WI 53216 • lindgren@execpc.com • SW • Tchr • Gospel Milwaukee WI • (414)562-1890 • (RF 1975 MA)

**LINDGREN JOANNE L** (414)466-8071
3950 N 65th St Milwaukee WI 53216-2116 • lindgren@execpc.com • SW • Tchr • Christ Memorial Milwaukee WI • (414)461-3371 • (S 1973)

**LINDQUIST JULIE A** (714)577-0457
230 E Chapman Ave Apt 22 Placentia CA 92870-4648 • PSW • Tchr • Zion Anaheim CA • (714)535-3600 • (IV 1992 MSED)

**LINDSEY DEAN JAY JR.**
110 Portland Terrace Collinsville IL 62234 • jaynjodi@stlnet.com • SI • Tchr • Metro-East LHS Edwardsville IL • (618)656-0043 • (MQ 1991)

**LINDSEY JODI E**
110 Portland Ter Collinsville IL 62234 • jaynjodi@stlnet.com • SI • Tchr • Holy Cross Collinsville IL • (618)344-3145 • (MQ 1991)

**LINEBERGER DAVID F** (214)517-0514
7701 Iola Dr Plano TX 75025-2820 • TX • Mem C • Messiah Richardson TX • (972)234-6972 • (RF 1968)

**LINEBRINK MICHAEL G**
607 Institute Valparaiso IN 46383-4950 • michael.linebrink@valpo.edu • IN • END • Indiana Fort Wayne IN • (RF 1970 MED)

**LININGER DAVID I** (417)993-0173
RR 2 Box 33E Urbana MO 65767-9802 • djlinin@todays-tech.com • MO • SHS/C • Missouri Saint Louis MO • (314)317-4550 • (S 1971 MS)

**LININGER JO ANN** (417)993-0173
Rt 2 Box 33E Urbana MO 65767-9802 • dilininger@vaxl.rain.gen.mo.us • MO • Tchr • Immanuel Higginsville MO • (660)584-3541 • (CQ 1986 MED)

**LINK ALLEN**
14B International Tower 23 South Bay Close Repulse Bay HONG KONG • MDS • S Miss • Mid-South Cordova TN • (S 1972)

**LINKUGEL GARY L** (713)477-6514
2013 Cleveland St Pasadena TX 77502-3801 • TX • Tchr • Zion Pasadena TX • (713)473-1789 • (S 1971)

**LINNELL LINDSEY A** (972)316-7533
Christ Our Savior Luth Church 140 Heartz Rd Coppell TX 75019 • lalsmiles@aol.com • TX • Tchr • Christ Our Savior Coppell TX • (972)393-7074 • (AU 1999)

**LINNEMANN ARTHUR L** (503)256-3519
2820 NE 92nd Ave Portland OR 97220-5365 • artlinnem@aol.com • NOW • EM • (RF 1952 MED LITTD)

**LINNEMANN VERNETTE M** (503)256-3519
2820 NE 92nd Ave Portland OR 97220-5365 • artlinnem@aol.com • NOW • EM • (RF 1981)

**LIPKA NANCY J**
827 Phillips LN Seymour IN 47274-3019 • IN • Tchr • Zion Seymour IN • (812)522-1089 • (S 1978)

**LIPKE ALAN K** (314)243-8903
630 Strawberry Ln Jackson MO 63755-1108 • aklipke@hotmail.com • MO • P/Tchr • St Paul Jackson MO • (573)243-5360 • (RF 1964 MA)

**LISIUS CARL H** (708)687-6864
15422 Ridgeland Ave Oak Forest IL 60452-1621 • NI • Tchr • Trinity Tinley Park IL • (708)532-3529 • (RF 1970 MA)

**LISIUS CHARLOTTE MAE** (708)687-6864
15422 Ridgeland Ave Oak Forest IL 60452-1621 • NI • Tchr • Zion Matteson IL • (708)747-7490 • (RF 1970)

**LIST DAVID F**
C/O St Johns Lutheran Church 330 Lambrecht St Beemer NE 68716-4213 • NEB • 09/1998 • (S 1975 MA)

**LIST PATSY L** (636)938-9139
305 Wallach Dr Eureka MO 63025-2111 • bobpatlist@aol.com • MO • Tchr • St John Ellisville MO • (314)394-4100 • (RF 1967 MA)

**LIST ROSE** (517)652-8978
222 Trinklein St Frankenmuth MI 48734-1553 • MI • EM • (RF 1967)

**LIST VICKY L** (517)652-3116
728 Heine Frankenmuth MI 48734-1425 • MI • Tchr • St Lorenz Frankenmuth MI • (517)652-6141 • (RF 1982)

**LITTLE LYNN**
W61 N947 Glenwood Dr Cedarburg WI 53012 • SW • SHS/C • South Wisconsin Milwaukee WI • (414)464-8100 • (CQ 1997 MMU)

**LIVINGSTON JANET L** (308)534-5021
67 Maplewood Cir North Platte NE 69101-4478 • NEB • Tchr • Our Redeemer North Platte NE • (308)532-6421 • (S 1976)

**LIVO GILBERT R** (314)926-8521
2945 Oetting Dr Saint Charles MO 63303-6034 • MO • Prin • Hope Saint Ann MO • (314)429-0988 • (S 1971 MED)

**LIZOTTE RICHARD L** (718)626-6750
25-14 38th St FL 2 Astoria NY 11103-4224 • AT • Tchr • Martin Luther Maspeth NY • (718)894-4000 • (PO 1991)

**LOCHHEAD TIMOTHY J** (618)826-5965
416 Riverview Chester IL 62233 • SI • 11/1997 11/1999 • (RF 1983)

**LOCHHEAD WENDY L** (618)826-5965
416 Riverview Blvd Chester IL 62233-1827 • SI • Tchr • Christ Jacob IL • (618)763-4663 • (RF 1984 MS)

**LOCHMANN NANCY J** (618)344-3150
127 E Country Ln Collinsville IL 62234-4802 • nancylochmann@juno.com • SI • Tchr • Holy Cross Collinsville IL • (618)344-3145 • (S 1975 MS)

**LOCHMANN WILLIAM JAMES** (618)344-3150
127 E Country Ln Collinsville IL 62234-4802 • SI • Tchr • Holy Cross Collinsville IL • (618)344-3145 • (S 1975 MED)

**LOCKE ANDREW G** (630)587-4464
149 St Germain Pl Saint Charles IL 60175 • locke.andrew@luthbro.com • NI • 03/2000 • (MQ 1989 MS)

**LOCKE GEORGE M DR** (737)913-5335
491 Pine Brae St Ann Arbor MI 48105-2743 • mc³lockegm@mc.lcms.org • MI • Michigan Ann Arbor MI* • (S 1962 MED LLD)

**LOCKHART CAROL ELLEN**
9402 Canfield La Habra CA 90631 • PSW • Tchr • Faith Whittier CA • (562)941-0245 • (S 1967)

**LOCKHART JOHN WESLEY**
9402 Canfield Dr La Habra CA 90631-2448 • PSW • P/Tchr • Faith Whittier CA • (562)941-0245 • (S 1967)

**LOCKLAIR GARY H** (414)357-6226
10042 W Tower Ave Milwaukee WI 53224-2959 • locklair@cuw.edu • SW • SHS/C • South Wisconsin Milwaukee WI • (414)464-8100 • (CQ 1988 MCS)

**LOEB FLORA E** (573)437-3801
301 N 1st St Owensville MO 65066-1362 • MI • EM • (RF 1949 MA)

**LOEFFLER ESTHER M** (314)250-3172
5016 Blase Station Rd Saint Charles MO 63301-6314 • MO • P/Tchr • Trinity Saint Charles MO • (636)250-3654 • (RF 1985)

**LOESCH CAROL J** (319)378-4110
240 15th Ave Court Hiawatha IA 52233 • IE • EM • (S 1984)

**LOESEL ALLEN H** (314)946-8366
2824 Birch Tree Dr Saint Charles MO 63301-1235 • MO • Tchr • Immanuel Saint Charles MO • (636)946-0051 • (S 1973 MCMU)

**LOESEL ALVIN E** (847)392-3604
926 N Princeton Ave Arlington Hts IL 60004-5206 • NI • EM • (RF 1952 MA)

**LOEWE GILBERT C**
237 Milburn Crete IL 60417 • NI • Prin • St Paul Chicago Heights IL • (708)754-4493 • (RF 1977)

**LOFINK KAREN LOUISE** (714)538-0534
752 N Milford Orange CA 92867 • PSW • Tchr • St John Orange CA • (714)288-4400 • (S 1992)

**LOFINK MARK C** (714)538-0534
752 N Milford St Orange CA 92867-7220 • PSW • Tchr • Hephatha Anaheim CA • (714)637-4022 • (IV 1995)

**LOHMEYER JAN W**
Memorial Lutheran Church 5800 Westheimer Rd Houston TX 77057-5617 • TX • Prin • Memorial Houston TX • (713)782-6079 • (S 1971 MED)

**LOHMEYER LISA G** (812)342-7975
9785 S State Rd 58 Columbus IN 47201-8519 • jlohmeye@hsonline.net • IN • Mem C • St Peter Columbus IN • (812)372-1571 • (RF 1979 MA)

**LOHMEYER MILTON GARY** (210)497-0475
1306 Durbin Way San Antonio TX 78258 • garyl@concordia-satx.com • TX • Mem C • Concordia San Antonio TX • (210)479-1477 • (S 1963)

**LOHMEYER RUTH E** (573)875-4100
4303 Melrose Dr Columbia MO 65203-6059 • MO • 09/1991 09/1999 • (WN 1983 MED)

**LOLL KARI L**
1512 E Orange Grove Ave Orange CA 92867-7056 • PSW • Tchr • Pilgrim Santa Monica CA • (310)829-4113 • (SP 1996)

**LOMBARD MILO D** (314)741-2739
12810 Verwood Dr Florissant MO 63033-4823 • mil706@cs.com • EN • Tchr • Chapel Cross Saint Louis MO • (314)741-3737 • (RF 1961 MMU)

**LONG MARCHETA** (402)675-1601
PO Box 388 Battle Creek NE 68715-0388 • NEB • Tchr • St John Battle Creek NE • (402)675-3605 • (S 1963)

**LONGHAUSER DONNA** (316)686-3190
1107 N Pershing St Wichita KS 67208-2829 • KS • Tchr • Holy Cross Wichita KS • (316)684-4431 • (RF 1974)

**LONGMIRE DUANE L** (419)592-8221
1055 Lynne Ave Napoleon OH 43545-1219 • longmire@bright.net • OH • Tchr • St Paul Napoleon OH • (419)592-5536 • (SP 1980)

**LONGMIRE KARI L** (419)592-8221
1055 Lynne Ave Napoleon OH 43545-1219 • longmire@bright.net • OH • 09/1988 09/1999 • (RF 1980)

**LONGMIRE KENNY L** (414)497-9462
2057 S Ridge Rd Green Bay WI 54304-4126 • NW • Prin • Pilgrim Green Bay WI • (920)494-6530 • (SP 1974 MS)

**LOOKER MARK S** (313)665-9395
4090 Geddes Rd Ann Arbor MI 48105-2750 • lookerm@ccaa.edu • MI • SHS/C • Michigan Ann Arbor MI • (RF 1973 MA PHD)

**LOOKER PAUL J** (810)254-8615
43078 Hartwick Dr Sterling Heights MI 48313-1924 • MI • Prin • LHS Northwest Rochester Hills MI • (810)852-6677 • (AA 1983 MA)

**LOOMANS DALE C** (608)524-2735
S2504A Horkan Rd Reedsburg WI 53959-9708 • SW • EM • (RF 1961)

**LOOMANS KEITH A** (512)926-2378
7401 Charlton Dr Austin TX 78723-1637 • kal7900@aol.com • TX • EM • (RF 1954 MA LLD)

**LOOMANS LOWELL A** (636)947-9902
1153 Fordyce Ct Saint Charles MO 63303-4019 • MO • EM • (RF 1958)

**LOOMANS TED PAUL** (406)259-6133
511 13th St W Billings MT 59102-5207 • MT • Tchr • Trinity Billings MT • (406)656-1021 • (MQ 1995)

**LOONTJER GARY L** (402)483-0037
610 Glenhaven Dr Lincoln NE 68505-2547 • gloontj@lps.org • NEB • Tchr • Lincoln Luth Jr/Sr H Lincoln NE • (402)467-5404 • (S 1975 MED)

**LOONTJER JACQUELINE L** (816)333-3693
602 W 91st Ter Kansas City MO 64114-3559 • nateman@worldnet.att.net • MO • Tchr • Calvary Kansas City MO • (816)444-5517 • (S 1969)

**LOPEZ SUSAN W** (815)695-9469
PO Box 566 Newark IL 60541-0566 • lopezsw@juno.com • NI • P/Tchr • Cross Yorkville IL • (630)553-7861 • (SP 1975)

**LOPPNOW AMY S** (219)471-5352
5016 S Camden Dr Fort Wayne IN 46825-5514 • IN • Tchr • Suburban Bethlehem Fort Wayne IN • (219)483-9371 • (AA 1990)

**LORENTZ DEBORAH A** (215)547-1951
58 Jonquil Ln Levittown PA 19055-2306 • EA • Tchr • Hope Levittown PA • (215)946-3467 • (SP 1980)

**LORENZ DAVID E** (630)773-0013
111 Millers Crossing Itasca IL 60143-2831 • NI • Tchr • St Luke Itasca IL • (630)773-0509 • (RF 1966 MA)

**LORENZ DONALD W** (503)693-3629
3779 SE Pipers Dr Hillsboro OR 97123-8617 • dlorenz502@aol.com • NOW • EM • (RF 1947 MED)

**LORENZ JILL IRENE**
4261 Carnwath Rd Tallahassee FL 32303 • FG • Tchr • Epiphany Tallahassee FL • (904)385-9822 • (BR 1996)

**LORENZ LINDA** (314)824-5600
100 PCR 328 Farrar MO 63746 • MO • Tchr • Salem Farrar MO • (573)824-5472 • (S 1984)

**LORENZ NANCY DOREEN** (312)736-8081
4900 N Lester Ave Apt 5 Chicago IL 60630-2163 • NI • Tchr • Immanuel Palatine IL • (847)359-1936 • (RF 1972 MA)

**LORENZ THOMAS** (847)934-9118
1365A N Sterling Ave Apt 203 Palatine IL 60067-8404 • NI • Tchr • Immanuel Palatine IL • (847)359-1936 • (RF 1971)

**LOSEE ANNE E** (914)969-4406
21 Clayton Pl Yonkers NY 10704-2711 • AT • Prin • St Mark Yonkers NY • (914)237-4944 • (CQ 1993 MAT)

**LOSEKE MARY ALICE** (503)626-5310
14155 SW Barlow Rd Beaverton OR 97008-5549 • NOW • Tchr • Pilgrim Beaverton OR • (503)644-8697 • (S 1975 MED)

**LOSEY VIRGIL L** (719)596-4055
2117 Wynkoop Dr Colorado Springs CO 80909-1444 • RM • 04/2000 • (S 1966)

**LOSSER LORI K** (801)944-9344
8433 Kings Hill Dr Salt Lake City UT 84121-6017 • RM • 04/2000 • (S 1988)

**LOTHIAN JOAN CAROL** (714)962-3573
21372 Brookhurst St Apt 728 Huntington Beach CA 92646-7316 • PSW • Tchr • Lutheran HS/Orange C Orange CA • (714)998-5151 • (CQ 1993 MA)

**LOTT LORI A** (913)651-7592
201 Sheldon St Leavenworth KS 66048-1794 • KS • Tchr • St Paul Leavenworth KS • (913)682-5553 • (S 1987)

**LOTZ JENNIFER LYNNE** (901)756-7589
4315 Whispering Bend Cv N Memphis TN 38125-3270 • mwlotz@worldnet.att.net • MDS • Tchr • Christ The King Memphis TN • (901)682-8405 • (S 1993 MED)

**LOUDEN SANDRA J** (810)632-5768
1626 Hartland Woods Dr Howell MI 48843-9044 • EN • EM • (CQ 1986)

**LOUIE KAREN SHUET-KING** (808)585-8532
625 E Kunawai Ln Honolulu HI 96817 • karenlouie@cs.com • CNH • Tchr • Good Shepherd Honolulu HI • (808)533-3088 • (PO 1993)

**LOVE DIANE K**
102 S Railway St Mascoutah IL 62258-1934 • SI • 11/1998 12/1997 • (RF 1992)

**LOVELESS MICHAEL P** (414)774-4972
709 S 57th St West Allis WI 53214-3332 • mpwl@execpc.com • SW • Tchr • Martin LHS Greendale WI • (414)421-4000 • (S 1989 MED)

**LOVERCHECK NANCY LOU**
3013 Market St Hannibal MO 63401-5738 • MO • Tchr • Zion Palmyra MO • (573)769-2739 • (S 1996)

**LOVHAUG BRENDA ANN** (612)566-1635
6741 Brunswick Ave N Brooklyn Park MN 55429-1594 • lovhaugbpmn@aol.com • MNS • Tchr • Golden Valley Golden Valley MN • (763)544-0590 • (SP 1990)

**LOVIG DEAN S**
306 East Wea Paola KS 66071 • KS • 06/1993 06/1999 • (S 1968 MAD)

**LOVITSCH LISA**
27W161 Mack Rd Wheaton IL 60187-6003 • NI • Tchr • Trinity Roselle IL • (630)894-3263 • (S 1990 MED)

**LOWE JEREMY**
10757 Lemon Ave Apt 1317 Alta Loma CA 91737-6948 • PSW • Trinity Roselle IL • (CQ 1999)

**LOWE RANDY D** (612)483-4612
883 Colleen Ave Shoreview MN 55126-6401 • rl2400ndal@aol.com • MNS • Tchr • Concordia Academy Roseville MN • (612)484-8429 • (RF 1971 MA)

**LUA ANDREA L** (818)348-5714
6032 Larkellen Ct Agoura CA 91301-1114 • PSW • Tchr • Canoga Park Canoga Park CA • (818)348-5714 • (S 1977)

**LUBBEN WILLIAM H**
1024 Glenford Ct St Louis MO 63122-6929 • MO • Mem C • Glendale Saint Louis MO • (314)966-3220 • (RF 1970)

**LUBKER DEBRA ANN** (402)558-5717
14615 Echo Hills Dr Omaha NE 68138-6427 • NEB • Tchr • Mount Calvary Omaha NE • (402)551-0244 • (S 1988)

**LUBS CHRISTINE MICHELLE** (310)322-5342
409 Bungalow Dr El Segundo CA 90245-4044 • PSW • Tchr • Circle Of Love Manhattan Beach CA • (310)546-2318 • (S 1988)

**LUCARELLI CATHIE L** (216)238-2735
18405 Admiralty Dr Strongsville OH 44136-7019 • OH • Tchr • St Mark Brunswick OH • (330)225-4395 • (RF 1972 MED)

**LUCAS CINDY LEE** (313)242-9835
136 Arbor St Monroe MI 48162-2509 • MI • Tchr • Trinity Monroe MI • (734)241-1160 • (S 1978 MA)

**LUCAS MARK C*** (206)888-3766
38575 Newton St #23 PO Box 155 Snoqualmie WA 98065-0155 • NOW • Tchr • Zion Everett WA • (425)334-5064 • (RF 1974 MS)

**LUCAS NATHANAEL P** (619)464-3020
8041 Fairview Ave La Mesa CA 91941-6449 • nlucas@home • PSW • Tchr • Pilgrim Chula Vista CA • (619)420-6233 • (S 1959)

**LUCAS PRISCILLA ERNESTINE** (956)682-7630
1112 Martin Ave Mc Allen TX 78504-3260 • TX • Tchr • St Paul Mc Allen TX • (956)682-2201 • (CQ 1997 MED)

**LUCAS WILLIAM E** (314)892-5046
9650 Carrimae Crestwood MO 63126-2018 • MO • Tchr • Concordia Middle Saint Louis MO • (314)865-1144 • (CQ 1998)

**LUCE RONALD E** (402)534-3403
195 1st St Utica NE 68456 • rl43212@navix.net • NEB • Tchr • St Paul Utica NE • (402)534-2121 • (S 1980 MED)

**LUCHT DARLEEN JEAN** (626)333-4765
3250 Pozo Dr Hacienda Heights CA 91745 • DLuchty@aol.com • PSW • Tchr • Holy Trinity Hacienda Heights CA • (626)961-2070 • (CQ 1996)

**LUCHT WAYNE E** (708)386-0820
733 Woodbine Ave Oak Park IL 60302-1512 • crfluchtwe@curf.edu • NI • EM • (RF 1948 MED PHD)

**LUDKE ALISON**
C/O Hope Luth School 1041 E Foothill Blvd Glendora CA 91741 • PSW • Holy Trinity Hacienda Heights CA • (PO 1999)

**LUDTKE ALVIN L** (562)923-4232
7330 Quill Dr Unit 58 Downey CA 90242-2027 • aludtke@hotmail.com • PSW • Tchr • Los Angeles Junior/S Sylmar CA • (818)362-5861 • (CQ 1985 MA)

**LUDWIG ARNOLD J** (712)297-8071
712 Tonawanda St Rockwell City IA 50579-2022 • IW • EM • (S 1933)

**LUDWIG KATHERINE ANNE** (828)324-7879
1974 12th Street Pl NE Hickory NC 28601-1649 • ludwig@lrc.edu • SE • 12/1993 12/1999 • (RF 1961)

**LUDWIG WILLIAM E** (406)257-2477
594 4th Ave West N Kalispell MT 59901-3620 • MT • EM • (S 1956 MA)

**LUEBBE KAREN F** (513)523-4340
1210 Dana Dr Oxford OH 45056-2556 • OH • Tchr • Grace Cincinnati OH • (513)661-5166 • (S 1962 MSED)

**LUEBBE RANELLE J** (402)478-5557
455 N 6th St PO Box 112 Arlington NE 68002 • ran.luebbe@juno.com • NEB • Tchr • St Paul Arlington NE • (402)478-4278 • (S 1999)

**LUEBKE MARTIN F** (314)741-5585
6507 Dolphin Cir E Florissant MO 63033-4756 • MO • EM • (RF 1938 MA PHD)

**LUECK JOHN W** (415)755-8312
134 San Diego Ave Daly City CA 94014-1037 • CNH • Tchr • Zion San Francisco CA • (415)221-7500 • (RF 1971 MA)

**LUECKE AUDREY LEE** (708)534-5088
25642 S Linden Ave Monee IL 60449 • NI • 11/1999 • (RF 1988)

**LUECKE RITA V** (612)467-3462
410 4th Ave SW Young America MN 55397-9235 • MNS • Tchr • St Johns Young America MN • (612)467-3461 • (SP 1971)

**LUECKE ROBERT K** (612)467-3462
410 4th Ave SW Young America MN 55397-9235 • MNS • Tchr • Lutheran High Mayer MN • (612)657-2251 • (SP 1971 MA)

**LUEDDERS ARTHUR F** (870)257-2435
55 Cheyenne Dr Cherokee Village AR 72529-2112 • marlued@juno.com • SI • EM • (S 1951 MED)

**LUEDDERS LARRY A** (618)965-9283
11355 Oak Terrace Dr Steeleville IL 62288 • SI • Tchr • St Mark Steeleville IL • (618)965-3838 • (S 1972)

**LUEDEMANN SHERI ELLEN**
C/O Baltimore Lutheran School 1145 Concordia Dr Towson MD 21286-1714 • bartjl@juno.com • SE • Tchr • Baltimore LHS Baltimore MD • (410)825-2323 • (S 1996)

**LUEDERS KIMBERLY ANN** (616)471-4810
1610 E Shawnee Rd Berrien Springs MI 49103-9754 • MI • Tchr • Trinity Berrien Springs MI • (616)473-1811 • (RF 1988)

**LUEDTKE JANET A**
Concordia Intern Sch Shanghai Jinqiao Plot S2 Huang Yang Rd Pudong Shanghai 201206 CHINA • SO • Tchr • Southern New Orleans LA • (RF 1968 MED)

**LUEDTKE MARILYN N** (219)422-5830
1601 Hobson Rd Fort Wayne IN 46805-4804 • IN • Tchr • Zion Fort Wayne IN • (219)744-1389 • (SP 1970)

**LUEDTKE TODD NORMAN**
Concordia Intern Sch Shanghai Jinquiao Plot S2 Huang Yang Rd Pudong Shanghai 201206 CHINA • SO • Tchr • Southern New Orleans LA • (RF 1969 MA PHD)

**LUEDTKE WILLIAM E** (423)855-1505
9002 Kesler Ln Chattanooga TN 37421 • wel@lutheranschool.net • MDS • Prin • Lutheran Chattanooga TN • (423)622-3755 • (RF 1971 MSED)

**LUEHMANN LLOYD L** (507)437-7619
600 25th St SW Austin MN 55912 • MNS • P/Tchr • Holy Cross Austin MN • (507)433-7844 • (S 1964 MA MA)

**LUEHRS IRENE** (402)223-2782
508 S 10th St Beatrice NE 68310-4525 • NEB • EM • (S 1972)

**LUEHRS MARJORIE L** (510)278-9059
17348 Via Encinas San Lorenzo CA 94580-2913 • ericlouis@aol.com • CNH • Tchr • Calvary San Lorenzo CA • (510)278-2598 • (S 1974)

**LUEPKE DONALD M** (219)485-3274
3877 David Ln Fort Wayne IN 46815-4917 • donluepke@juno.com • IN • Tchr • Concordia LHS Fort Wayne IN • (219)483-1102 • (CQ 1967 MS MS)

**LUEPKE ELDOR G** (314)631-1383
4479 Cayuga Dr Affton MO 63123-6653 • MO • EM • (RF 1937 MED)

**LUEPKE JAMES E** (219)484-3732
3630 Dover Dr Fort Wayne IN 46805-3045 • IN • Tchr • Holy Cross Fort Wayne IN • (219)483-3173 • (S 1973 MED)

**LUERSSEN HOLLY ANN** (715)623-3110
129 S Sunset Dr Antigo WI 54409-1050 • NW • Tchr • Peace Antigo WI • (715)623-2200 • (MQ 1994)

**LUETJE ANITA M**
St John Luth Church 305 Circle Ave Forest Park IL 60130-1609 • NI • Tchr • St John Forest Park IL • (708)366-2764 • (RF 1983)

**LUHRING ROBERT W*** (509)332-6665
NW 1445 Douglas Pullman WA 99163-3321 • NOW • 02/1998 02/2000 • (S 1964 MED)

**LUKE AMY L**
2505 Westminster Dr Valparaiso IN 46385 • IN • 11/1999 • (RF 1982)

**LUKSHA DALE W** (847)967-6852
5311 Carol St Skokie IL 60077-2002 • NI • P/Tchr • St Paul Skokie IL • (847)673-5030 • (RF 1974 MED)

**LUND KEITH R** (903)786-9005
77 Cooper Ln Pottsboro TX 75076-6058 • lomt@texoma.net • TX • O Sp Min • Texas Austin TX • (S 1976)

**LUNSFORD AMY JO** (281)242-8833
13838 Vinehill Dr Sugar Land TX 77478-2404 • TX • Tchr • Pilgrim Houston TX • (713)666-3706 • (AU 1987)

**LUNZ ROBERT G** (281)482-0474
218 W Castle Harbour Dr Friendswood TX 77546-5618 • TX • EM • (RF 1954 MA)

**LUPTAK ANDREW J** (414)781-6655
N54W14381 Vera Ln Menomonee Falls WI 53051-5820 • SW • SHS/C • South Wisconsin Milwaukee WI • (414)464-8100 • (S 1966 MS PHD)

**LUTRINGER ALVIN EUGENE** (507)534-2349
415 6th Ave NE Plainview MN 55964-1470 • MNS • P/Tchr • Immanuel Plainview MN • (507)534-2108 • (S 1973 MA)

**LUTZ ALAN O**
2690 N River Trail Rd Orange CA 92865-2013 • PSW • Tchr • St Paul Orange CA • (714)921-3188 • (S 1973 MA)

**LUTZ DAVID A** (203)743-5190
5 Valley View Dr Danbury CT 06810-7019 • NE • Tchr • Immanuel Danbury CT • (203)748-3320 • (S 1968 MS)

**LUTZ DAVID D** (660)668-4699
602 S Blakey Cole Camp MO 65325 • MO • Tchr • Lutheran School Asso Cole Camp MO • (660)668-4614 • (CQ 1996)

**LUTZ NANCY ANN** (203)743-5190
5 Valley View Dr Danbury CT 06810-7019 • NE • Tchr • Immanuel Danbury CT • (203)748-7823 • (S 1968)

**LUTZ NINA L**
2690 N River Trail Rd Orange CA 92865 • ninal97@aol.com • PSW • 09/1993 09/1999 • (RF 1976)

**LUTZ ROBERT KARL** (218)281-7279
RR 1 Box 102 Crookston MN 56716-9773 • MNN • Tchr • Our Savior Crookston MN • (218)281-5191 • (SP 1983)

**LUTZE SONYA SUE**
505 W Dearborn Plano IL 60545 • NI • Tchr • St Luke Montgomery IL • (630)892-9309 • (S 1996)

**LUTZINGER NORMA J**
3377 N 150th Dr Goodyear AZ 85338-8529 • CNH • EM • (RF 1956)

**LYNCH JAMES R** (360)568-0773
108 16th St Snohomish MI 98290-1907 • Jrizls@juno.com • NOW • Prin • Zion Everett WA • (425)334-5064 • (S 1970)

**LYNN KAREN L**
2010 S Ingram Mill Rd Apt F 6 Springfield MO 65804 • MO • Tchr • Redeemer Springfield MO • (417)881-5470 • (RF 1974)

**LYON GINA**
5201 Park Blvd Piedmont CA 94611 • CNH • Tchr • Zion Piedmont CA • (510)530-7909 • (PO 1997)

**LYON KAREN D**
1033 SE Cobb St Roseburg OR 97470-4833 • PSW • Tchr • Faith Whittier CA • (562)941-0245 • (SP 1990 MA)

**LYONS EILEEN S** (512)990-1944
401 Pleasant Valley Dr Pflugerville TX 78660-2624 • TX • Tchr • Redeemer Austin TX • (512)451-6478 • (RF 1975)

**LYSEN CYNTHIA E** (206)935-9395
3046 SW Avalon Way Apt F Seattle WA 98126-2671 • NOW • Tchr • Seattle LHS Seattle WA • (206)937-7722 • (S 1990)

## M

**MAAS JOHN H** (816)452-9097
5740 NE Wilson Blvd Kansas City MO 64118-5245 • jomaas@mwis.net • MO • Tchr • Holy Cross Kansas City MO • (816)453-7211 • (S 1981)

**MAAS JULIE ANN** (402)329-4082
527 E Florence St Pierce NE 68767-1608 • zionjam@ptcnet.net • NEB • Tchr • Zion Pierce NE • (402)329-4658 • (S 1977 MA)

**MAAS MYRA A** (317)356-8126
7745 Lola Ct Indianapolis IN 46219-3819 • IN • EM • (RF 1945 MS)

**MAAS NANCY L** (816)452-9097
5740 NE Wilson Blvd Kansas City MO 64118-5245 • nmaas@mwis.net • MO • Tchr • Holy Cross Kansas City MO • (816)453-7211 • (S 1980)

**MAAS RICHARD E** (262)255-1862
N93W15358 Hillside Ln Menomonee Falls WI 53051-1529 • rcmaas@juno.com • SW • EM • (RF 1950 MED)

**MAAS RUTH ELLEN** (713)868-3980
845 Beverly St Apt 8 Houston TX 77007-1741 • rem90rose@aol.com • TX • Tchr • Pilgrim Houston TX • (713)666-3706 • (RF 1981)

**MAAS TERRY P**
1057 E Whitcomb Ave Glendora CA 91741 • PSW • Tchr • First Monrovia CA • (626)357-3596 • (S 1972)

**MAC KAIN CHERYL L**
2453 Spring St Apt 3706 Woodridge IL 60517-4215 • OH • 06/1999 • (IV 1991)

**MAC KENZIE ELIZABETH IRENE** (248)601-3277
1429 Oakridge Rochester Hills MI 48307 • MI • Tchr • LHS Northwest Rochester Hills MI • (810)852-6677 • (RF 1999)

**MACEJKOVIC MICHAEL C** (414)377-6433
W62N359 Hanover Ave Cedarburg WI 53012-2305 • EN • Tchr • Hales Corners Hales Corners WI • (414)529-6701 • (MQ 1988)

**MACHEMER MELVIN A** (810)774-3419
24502 Grove Ave Eastpointe MI 48021-1031 • mmachemer@lhsa.net • MI • Tchr • LHS East Harper Woods MI • (313)371-8750 • (RF 1981 MMU)

**MACK MARTIN M** (507)288-7269
5612 26th Ave NW Rochester MN 55901-0105 • MNS • Tchr • Rochester Central Rochester MN • (507)289-3267 • (S 1968)

**MACKE ERIC JEFFREY** (727)595-6252
12800 Vonn Rd Apt #8451 Largo FL 33774 • FG • Tchr • Grace Saint Petersburg FL • (727)527-6213 • (BR 1999)

**MACKE THOMAS E** (573)335-6055
2412 Lynnwood Dr Cape Girardeau MO 63701-2344 • MO • EM • (RF 1957 MED)

**MACKENTHUN KATHERINE M**
1333 Dunsmore Dr Waconia MN 55387-1256 • MNS • Tchr • Emanuel Hamburg MN • (612)467-2780 • (RF 1980)

**MACKIE DEBRA J** (630)766-8941
420 S Addison St Bensenville IL 60106-2635 • NI • Tchr • St John Chicago IL • (773)736-1196 • (RF 1976)

**MACKIE JAMES D** (402)643-4858
1263 Eastridge Dr Seward NE 68434-1331 • jmackie@alltel.net • NEB • EM • (S 1981 MMU)

**MACY JOHN A**
C/O Good Shepherd Association 206 S 17th St Marysville KS 66508-1750 • jmacy@stpaullcms.org • KS • St John Chicago IL • (SP 1970 MED)

**MADDEN BETTYJEAN** (518)767-3647
5 Van Rensselaer Way Glenmont NY 12077-3639 • AT • Tchr • Our Savior Albany NY • (518)459-2248 • (S 1962)

**MADDICK MELANIE K** (515)477-8389
1244A 190th St State Center IA 50247-9609 • IE • Tchr • Clemons Clemons IA • (515)477-8263 • (RF 1981)

**MADDOCK JAMES**
1345 Cottonwood Ct Corona CA 91719 • CNH • Tchr • Faith Fair Oaks CA • (916)961-4252 • (IV 1999)

**MADDUX PAULA** (817)478-7162
1246 Elmbrook Dr Kennedale TX 76060 • TX • Tchr • St Paul Fort Worth TX • (817)332-4563 • (CQ 1998)

**MADIGAN SUSAN H** (718)792-5665
C/O Our Savior Lutheran Church 1734 Williamsbridge Rd Bronx NY 10461-6204 • AT • Tchr • Our Saviour Bronx NY • (718)792-5665 • (RF 1986)

**MAERTZ BETTYANN** (516)928-9664
383 Pipe Stave Hollow Rd Mount Sinai NY 11766 • AT • Tchr • Emanuel Patchogue NY • (516)758-2250 • (CQ 1989 MS)

**MAFFIN DANIEL FRANK** (941)299-1698
215 9th St SE Winter Haven FL 33880-3112 • FG • Tchr • Grace Winter Haven FL • (941)293-9744 • (S 1991)

**MAGNUS DAN** (417)887-4239
1101 W Westview St Springfield MO 65807-4651 • dm7025@earthlink.net • MO • 04/1987 04/2000 • (S 1973)

**MAGNUS MARY K** (417)887-4239
1101 W Westview St Springfield MO 65807-4651 • mkmagnus@pcis.net • MO • Tchr • Springfield Springfield MO • (417)883-5717 • (S 1974 MSED)

**MAGNUS-DUITSMAN JENNIFER ANN** (952)886-3898
300 W 96th St #2G Bloomington MN 55420 • jennifer.duitsman@lutheranhighschool.com • MNS • Tchr • Minnesota South Burnsville MN • (S 1999)

**MAGNUSON JULIE E**
3737 Taft Ave Chino CA 91710-1553 • PSW • Tchr • Immanuel West Covina CA • (626)919-1072 • (IV 1985)

**MAHER M VALAINA** (716)242-0751
73 Boardman St Apt 2 Rochester NY 14607-3805 • EA • Tchr • St John Hamlin NY • (716)964-2550 • (RF 1973 MED)

**MAHLER H JAMES** (954)984-8210
2206 S Cypress Bend Dr Apt 502 Pompano Beach FL 33069-4437 • FG • Tchr • Peace Fort Lauderdale FL • (954)772-8010 • (SP 1995 MED)

**MAHLER RICHARD J**
1641 Harvard Rd Berkley MI 48072-1985 • MI • Mem C • St Paul Royal Oak MI • (248)541-0613 • (S 1969)

**MAHNKE GLENN R** (815)568-5824
514 W Washington St Marengo IL 60152 • dommzion@mc.net • NI • Mem C • Zion Marengo IL • (815)568-6564 • (RF 1969 MMU)

**MAHNKEN CAROL A** (636)946-9222
2801 Cherokee Ln Saint Charles MO 63301-0601 • cmahnken@immanueluth.org • MO • Tchr • Immanuel Saint Charles MO • (636)946-0051 • (S 1972)

**MAIN PATRICIA ANNE**
Concordia Lutheran School 3799 E West Hwy Hyattsville MD 20782 • main3@dpc.net • SE • Tchr • Concordia Hyattsville MD • (301)927-0266 • (BR 1999)

**MAJEWSKI MICHAEL MARLON** (714)363-5354
42149 Rubicon Circle Temecula CA 92591 • PSW • Tchr • Zion Fallbrook CA • (760)723-3500 • (IV 1993)

**MAJOR CYNTHIA C** (313)928-0094
10995 Dixie Hwy Birch Run MI 48415 • MI • Tchr • Michigan Ann Arbor MI • (RF 1986)

**MAKEY BRIAN S** (716)675-0047
6184 Lake Ave Orchard Park NY 14127 • bmky@juno.com • EA • Prin • Trinity West Seneca NY • (716)674-5353 • (BR 1980 MED)

**MAKEY ELLEN S** (716)675-0047
6184 Lake Rd Orchard Park NY 14127 • MI • 04/1999 • (BR 1980)

**MALCHOW JOY G**
13905 Jennifer Rd Omaha NE 68138 • NEB • 06/1999 • (S 1989)

**MALENKE NORBERT J** (630)322-9955
5438 Burr Oak Rd #307 Lisle IL 60532 • NI • Mem C • Trinity Lisle IL • (630)964-1272 • (S 1972)

**MALLEGNI GRETCHEN** (815)568-5766
24408 Grange Rd Marengo IL 60152-9577 • NI • Tchr • Zion Marengo IL • (815)568-6564 • (S 1982)

**MALLORY BETHANY ANN** (818)832-8014
16857 San Fernando Mssn Blvd Unit 13 Granada Hills CA 91344-4217 • mal25@aol.com • PSW • Tchr • Los Angeles Junior/S Sylmar CA • (818)362-5861 • (S 1993)

**MALLORY THEORDORE J**
PO Box 75 Charter Oak IA 51439-0075 • tjmallory@hotmail.com • PSW • Tchr • Los Angeles Junior/S Sylmar CA • (818)362-5861 • (S 1993)

**MALM ERIK** (281)251-5166
6503 Knollview Dr Spring TX 77389 • TX • Tchr • Concordia LHS Tomball TX • (281)351-2547 • (MQ 2000)

**MALO KANE JASON**
1037 1st Ave S Apt 2E Fort Dodge IA 50501 • IW • Tchr • St Paul Fort Dodge IA • (515)955-7285 • (SP 1999)

**MALONE DENNIS L DR**
41/5 Soi Sailom Phahol Yothin Samsennai Phayathai Bangkok 10400 THAILAND • MO • 09/1975 09/1999 • (RF 1964 MA PHD)

**MALONE VETA BONITA** (213)581-0873
2652 1/2 Broadway Huntington Park CA 90255-6346 • PSW • Tchr • St Paul Orange CA • (714)921-3188 • (S 1983)

**MALONE WALTER D** (785)271-2856
3318 SW Lakeside Dr Topeka KS 66614-3313 • KS • Tchr • Topeka Topeka KS • (785)357-0382 • (S 1969)

**MALUCKY MARALYN B** (818)284-4689
8223 Sheffield Rd San Gabriel CA 91775 • PSW • Tchr • Emmaus Alhambra CA • (626)289-3664 • (S 1961 MA)

**MALY LONN DAVID** (651)772-2204
1634 Margaret St Saint Paul MN 55106-4902 • maly@csp.edu • MNS • SHS/C • Minnesota South Burnsville MN • (SP 1981 MSED)

**MALZAHN ELLEN M** (817)421-3296
1916 Fair Field Dr Grapevine TX 76051-7100 • TX • P/Tchr • Crown Of Life Colleyville TX • (817)421-5683 • (S 1971 MED)

**MALZAHN ROBERT W DR** (817)421-3296
1916 Fair Field Dr Grapevine TX 76051-7100 • TX • Prin • St Timothy Grand Prairie TX • (817)557-9411 • (S 1971 MED MED EDD)

**MANGELS ANNE** (314)842-1389
9042 Crestmoor Dr Saint Louis MO 63126-2906 • MO • Tchr • Hope Saint Louis MO • (314)832-1850 • (RF 1965 MED)

**MANGELS HERSEY G** (812)522-6926
241 Marshall Dr Seymour IN 47274-3651 • IN • Tchr • Immanuel Seymour IN • (812)522-1301 • (S 1958 MA MED)

**MANGELS KENNETH E DR** (714)998-2603
1219 E Ensign Cir Orange CA 92865-2911 • mangels@cui.edu • PSW • SHS/C • Pacific Southwest Irvine CA • (949)854-3232 • (S 1968 MAT PHD)

**MANGIERI GESINE E** (561)374-9156
4570B Rosewood Tree Ct Boynton Beach FL 33436-3610 • FG • 06/1999 • (RF 1963 MA)

**MANKE THERESA L** (414)634-7285
2800 Douglas Ave Racine WI 53402-4116 • SW • 10/1994 10/1999 • (AA 1989)

**MANKIEWICZ DEBORAH VOSS** (708)788-1836
1808 Clinton Ave Berwyn IL 60402-1609 • NI • Tchr • Grace Chicago IL • (773)762-1234 • (RF 1987 MED)

**MANLEY JOAN** (215)946-3374
11 Steeplebush Rd Levittown PA 19056-2218 • EA • Tchr • Hope Levittown PA • (215)946-3467 • (CQ 1988)

**MANN DARIA E** (303)477-5812
4765 Eliot St Denver CO 80211-1125 • daria@oafc.org • RM • Tchr • Faith Denver CO • (303)455-5878 • (S 1989)

**MANN KEVIN DENNIS** (254)774-9247
4818 Silverwood Ct Temple TX 76502 • mmudmann@aol.com • TX • Tchr • Immanuel Temple TX • (254)773-3898 • (RF 1998)

**MANN NANCY LOUISE** (503)253-9249
1051 NE 113th Ave Portland OR 97220-2211 • NOW • Tchr • Trinity Portland OR • (503)288-6403 • (SP 1972)

**MANNIGEL DAVID R** (402)643-2581
729 Cory Dr Seward NE 68434-1186 • NEB • P/Tchr • St John Seward NE • (402)643-4535 • (S 1967 MED)

**MANNIGEL REBECCA K**
10406 Fort Plaza #12 Omaha NE 68134 • NEB • Tchr • St Paul Omaha NE • (402)451-2865 • (S 1998)

**MANNIGEL TIMOTHY**
1858 River Run Trail Apt A Fort Wayne IN 46825-5987 • IN • Tchr • Concordia LHS Fort Wayne IN • (219)483-1102 • (S 1997)

**MANNING RAKOW CHRISTINE M** (630)293-0564
552 Claremont Ave West Chicago IL 60185-2108 • NI • Tchr • Our Savior Carol Stream IL • (630)830-4833 • (RF 1966)

**MANNION JOSEPH C** (503)698-6435
12999 SE 137th Dr Clackamas OR 97015-8395 • NOW • SHS/C • Northwest Portland OR • (RF 1973 MED DED)

**MANS LISA ANN** (847)669-8101
301 Warwick Ln Lake In The Hills IL 60156 • NI • Tchr • Immanuel Crystal Lake IL • (815)459-1444 • (RF 1999)

**MANSK DANIEL J** (715)845-7944
316 N 7th Ave Wausau WI 54401-4315 • NW • Tchr • Trinity Wausau WI • (715)848-0166 • (SP 1975 MAT)

**MANTHEI GAYLE E**
C/O Our Savior Lutheran Church 22511 West Main St Armada MI 48005-3207 • OH • Prin • St Mark Brunswick OH* • (330)225-4395 • (RF 1964 MED)

**MANTHEI GREGORY WAYNE**
4421 Hunt Club Dr Ypsilanti MI 48197 • MI • Tchr • St John New Boston MI • (734)654-6366 • (AA 1991)

**MARA RODNEY J*** (209)472-9163
4516 Romano Dr Stockton CA 95207-6639 • rjmara@mediaone.net • CNH • P/Tchr • Trinity Stockton CA • (209)464-0895 • (S 1979 MED MA)

**MARCH JOHN D** (518)482-6967
31 Lily St Albany NY 12205-3537 • mrmarch@compuserve.com • AT • Tchr • Our Savior Albany NY • (518)459-2273 • (AA 1997)

**MARCHESE RUTH ALANE*** (414)695-1963
580 Foxtail Dr #202 Pewaukee WI 53072-2494 • EN • 07/1995 07/2000 • (RF 1992 MMU)

**MARCINIAK TRUDY** (312)485-3151
3621 Park Ave Brookfield IL 60513-1540 • NI • Tchr • St Paul Brookfield IL • (708)485-0650 • (RF 1980)

**MARCINKOWSKI SUSAN** (708)423-7083
10818 S Komensky Oak Lawn IL 60453 • NI • 08/2000 • (RF 1974)

**MARCSISAK THOMAS A** (612)442-4679
1701 Park Point Rd Waconia MN 55387-1540 • MNS • Tchr • Zion Cologne MN • (612)466-3379 • (SP 1981)

**MAREE PATRICIA J** (573)788-2132
9850 S Hwy 61 Perryville MO 63775-6222 • MO • Tchr • Immanuel Perryville MO • (573)547-8317 • (CQ 1991)

**MARENO CARRIE**
21880 Foxhaven Run Waukesha WI 53126 • SW • Tchr • Elm Grove Elm Grove WI • (262)797-2970 • (MQ 1996)

**MARGRETT DEBORAH ANNE** (414)871-3298
6656 W Locust St Milwaukee WI 53210-1256 • SW • Tchr • Elm Grove Elm Grove WI • (262)797-2970 • (RF 1990)

**MARINKO PAUL BRIAN**
6108 Ranger Trl Fort Wayne IN 46835 • marinkop@aol.com • IN • Tchr • St Paul Fort Wayne IN • (219)424-0049 • (RF 1986 MED)

**MARINO CORINNE MARIE**
23267 Scotch Pine Ct California MD 20619-6118 • johncm@erols.com • SE • Tchr • Our Savior Arlington VA • (703)892-4846 • (BR 1994 MED)

**MARINO QUENTIN M** (313)663-3865
3180 Bolgos Cir Ann Arbor MI 48105-1564 • carjanmar@juno.com • MI • EM • (CQ 1963 MMU)

**MARKIN KAREN J** (852)2899-0947
C3 Tai Tam Gardens 700 Tai Tam Reservoir Rd Tai Tam HONG KONG • kmarkin@hkis.edu.hk • PSW • 07/1996 07/2000 • (S 1984 MED)

**MARKS JOHN B** (219)486-7400
9609 Hidden Village Pl Fort Wayne IN 46835-9348 • jbmarks05@hotmail.com • IN • Tchr • Concordia LHS Fort Wayne IN • (219)483-1102 • (CQ 1970)

**MARKS KATHY ANN** (815)395-1974
311 Bienterra Trl Apt 9 Rockford IL 61107-5873 • kamarks1@juno.com • NI • 09/1994 09/1999 • (CQ 1985)

**MARKS SUSAN E** (908)889-9136
8 Mac Lennan Pl Fanwood NJ 07023-1713 • teaforsue@hotmail.com • NJ • Tchr • Redeemer Westfield NJ • (908)232-1592 • (BR 1975)

**MARKWORTH ALFRED E** (414)461-6504
8869 W Appleton Apt 2 Milwaukee WI 53225-4200 • aliphint@gateway.net • SW • P/Tchr • Gospel Milwaukee WI • (414)372-5159 • (S 1963)

**MARKWORTH DOUGLAS W** (773)205-1907
5330 W Belle Plaine Ave Chicago IL 60641-1336 • markworths@juno.com • NI • Tchr • Luther HS North Chicago IL • (773)286-3600 • (S 1977 MA)

**MARKWORTH JOAN L** (773)205-1907
5330 W Belle Plaine Ave Chicago IL 60641-1336 • markworths@juno.com • EN • Tchr • Bethesda Chicago IL • (312)743-0800 • (S 1977)

**MARKWORTH SHARON ANN** (419)826-8503
2830 Oak Grove Pl Toledo OH 43613-3353 • OH • Tchr • Trinity Toledo OH • (419)385-2651 • (RF 1983)

**MARLATT KRISTINE M** (801)553-8901
1381 E Ridgemark Dr Sandy UT 84092-2916 • jmarlatt@bitcorp.net • RM • 07/1999 • (BR 1987 MA)

**MARNHOLTZ LAURA M** (715)536-8492
1105 E 3rd St Merrill WI 54452-9998 • NW • Tchr • Trinity Merrill WI • (715)536-7501 • (RF 1985 MED)

**MAROHN VIRGINIA ANN** (630)325-5166
442 Naperville Rd Clarendon Hills IL 60514-2815 • NI • Mem C • St John La Grange IL • (708)354-1690 • (RF 1958)

**MAROLF SHIRLEY** (319)391-3019
2838 Kelling St Davenport IA 52804-1552 • IE • EM • (RF 1967)

**MARONEY AMBER MELANIE** (512)899-1098
7221 Lamb Rd San Antonio TX 78240 • TX • Tchr • Mount Olive Austin TX • (512)288-2370 • (AU 1995)

**MAROSE DAVID**
1700 S Craftsman Dr New Berlin WI 53146 • dpmarose@aol.com • SW • Tchr • Elm Grove Elm Grove WI • (262)797-2970 • (S 1982)

**MAROSE NATALIE S** (952)881-1306
9301 11th Ave S Bloomington MN 55420-3927 • MNS • 01/1994 01/2000 • (S 1987)

**MAROSZEK GINA M** (715)675-7578
2702 N 96th Ave Wausau WI 54401-9757 • dwayne27@aol.com • NW • Tchr • Trinity Wausau WI • (715)848-0166 • (MQ 1985 MA)

**MAROTZKE JUDY L** (618)282-2105
10201 State Route 3 Apt B Red Bud IL 62278-4452 • SI • Tchr • Trinity Red Bud IL • (618)282-2881 • (S 1984)

**MAROTZKE RYAN K** (281)983-5362
5723 Greencraig Dr Houston TX 77035 • TX • 11/1996 11/1999 • (S 1991)

**MARQUARDT LEONARD M** (708)532-4138
6811 157th Pl Tinley Park IL 60477-1056 • NI • EM • (RF 1950 MS)

**MARQUARDT PAUL J** (909)396-9925
637 Big Falls Dr Diamond Bar CA 91765 • pmarquardt@hotmail.com • PSW • Prin • Mount Calvary Diamond Bar CA • (909)861-2740 • (IV 1990 MEAD)

**MARQUARDT ROMAINE J** (414)761-1356
2512 W Lindenwood Ave Oak Creek WI 53154-1069 • SW • EM • (RF 1974)

**MARQUARDT-SMITH JUDY L** (815)455-4607
9309 Route 14 Woodstock IL 60098 • NI • Tchr • Immanuel Crystal Lake IL • (815)459-1441 • (CQ 1999)

**MARRIOTT CATHERINE C** (262)542-2645
W225S3626 Foxcroft Ln Waukesha WI 53189-8008 • armarriott@juno.com • SW • Tchr • Christ the Life Waukesha WI • (414)547-1817 • (MW 1980 MED)

**MARSCH CHERYL**
8500 W Beloit Rd West Allis WI 53227-3710 • SW • Tchr • St Paul West Allis WI • (414)541-6250 • (RF 1971)

**MARSCHEL MARY RUTH** (314)433-5627
1679 N Highway 47 Marthasville MO 63357-2703 • MO • Tchr • Immanuel Washington MO • (314)239-1636 • (S 1965)

**MARSH KEITH ARTHUR** (561)219-8139
323 Ridge Ln Stuart FL 34994-7127 • The³Marshes@hotmail.com • FG • Tchr • Redeemer Stuart FL • (561)286-0932 • (S 1973)

**MARSHALL ELIZABETH M**
1115 N 8th Ave Maywood IL 60153-1071 • marshale@inw.net • IE • 07/2000 • (SP 1985)

**MARSHALL GWEN E** (303)986-4143
2101 S Depew St Apt 14 Denver CO 80227-3640 • RM • Tchr • Trinity Denver CO • (303)934-6160 • (WN 1982 MA)

**MARSHALL JENNIFER L** (818)243-8139
357 W Milford St Apt 1 Glendale CA 91203-2030 • PSW • 07/1998 • (IV 1988)

**MARSHALL LINDA Z** (573)635-8071
1313 Moreland Ave Jefferson City MO 65101-3734 • MO • Tchr • Trinity Jefferson City MO • (573)636-6750 • (CQ 1985)

**MARSHALL PATRICIA L** (419)782-1306
805 Kentner St Defiance OH 43512-2053 • OH • Tchr • St John Defiance OH • (419)782-1751 • (S 1970)

**MARTCHENKE WILLIAM C** (651)698-3580
1322 Alton St #222 Saint Paul MN 55116 • bill.martchenke@lutheranhighschool.com • MNS • Tchr • Luth HS Of Greater M Bloomington MN • (612)854-0224 • (SP 1993)

**MARTEN CARYN L** (312)530-0414
675 Fairview Elmhurst IL 60126 • NI • Tchr • Immanuel Elmhurst IL • (630)832-9302 • (RF 1985)

**MARTEN DENNIS L** (316)331-3855
2220 Kelly Ln Independence KS 67301 • dennismarten@cs.com • KS • Tchr • Zion Independence KS • (316)332-3300 • (S 1998)

**MARTEN DONALD E** (847)965-6255
8527 N Ozark Ave Niles IL 60714-1941 • NI • EM • (RF 1955)

**MARTEN MILTON E DR** (812)332-4233
3501 E Longview Ave Bloomington IN 47408-4314 • IN • EM • (RF 1937 MA PHD)

**MARTEN WILBERT C** (414)463-4082
9606 W Palmetto Ave Wauwatosa WI 53222-1448 • SW • EM • (RF 1934 MSED)

**MARTENS EDMUND R** (402)477-5460
5440 W Chancery Rd Lincoln NE 68521-5360 • em05427@navix.net • NEB • EM • (S 1949 MMU)

**MARTENS FRANKLIN C REV** (507)453-0312
1480 48th Ave Winona MN 55987-6117 • fmartens@tvsw.org • MNS • EM • (CQ 1960)

**MARTENS GINA RENAE** (660)463-1337
26273 Duensing Rd Concordia MO 64020 • MO • Tchr • Holy Cross Emma MO • (660)463-2553 • (S 1992)

**MARTENS MELANIE M** (573)339-1936
623 Sycamore Cir Apt 4 Cape Girardeau MO 63701-8201 • melmar@clas.net • MO • Tchr • Trinity Cape Girardeau MO • (573)334-1068 • (S 1981)

**MARTENS SEAN PAUL** (402)643-6523
1241 Plainview Ave Seward NE 68434-1346 • spm7546@seward.ccsn.edu • NEB • Tchr • St John Seward NE • (402)643-4535 • (S 1991)

**MARTH MARLIN J** (816)584-6415
619 W 29th St Higginsville MO 64037-1817 • MO • P/Tchr • Immanuel Higginsville MO • (660)584-2854 • (CQ 1993 MA)

**MARTIN DOUGLAS P** (815)397-0793
3306 Buckingham Dr Rockford IL 61107-2006 • NI • Tchr • Luther Academy Rockford IL • (815)877-9551 • (S 1983 MED)

**MARTIN FRED D** (847)526-7658
426 Foster Rd Wauconda IL 60084-1508 • NI • EM • (RF 1954)

**MARTIN JOY** (920)336-0448
410 Rockland Rd De Pere WI 54115 • NW • Tchr • Zion Of Wayside Greenleaf WI • (414)864-2468 • (RF 1970)

**MARTIN JULIANA E**
C/O Redeemer Lutheran Church 2626 Liberty Blvd South Gate CA 90280-2004 • PSW • Tchr • Redeemer South Gate CA • (323)588-0934 • (AA 1986)

**MARTIN KATHY A** (517)892-4963
1801 Loretta Cir Essexville MI 48732-9408 • MI • Tchr • Zion Bay City MI • (517)893-5793 • (S 1976)

**MARTIN KEITH DALE** (219)728-9225
10877 N 100 E Decatur IN 46733-8405 • sleepingzeke@decaturnet.com • IN • P/Tchr • St Peter-Immanuel Decatur IN • (219)623-6115 • (CQ 1989 MA)

**MARTIN KERRY JAMES** (303)450-2566
13013 Birch Dr Thornton CO 80241-3718 • RM • Tchr • Redeemer Denver CO • (303)934-0422 • (RF 1978)

**MARTIN LYN**
2673 N Harding Blvd Milwaukee WI 53226-1609 • SW • Tchr • Mount Olive Milwaukee WI • (414)774-2113 • (S 1971)

**MARTIN MARGO M** (317)247-1135
2009 Fullerton Dr Indianapolis IN 46214-3380 • mmm³46214@yahoo.com • IN • Tchr • Our Shepherd Indianapolis IN • (317)271-9103 • (RF 1971)

**MARTIN WALTER W** (708)771-8300
730 William St River Forest IL 60305-1926 • NI • EM • (RF 1952 MA MA)

**MARTING EILEEN M** (760)741-3864
336 Whippoorwill Gln Escondido CA 92026-1460 • emarting@msn.com • PSW • Tchr • Grace Escondido CA • (760)747-3029 • (IV 1987)

**MARTON KENNETH R** (414)527-0746
4109 N 88th St Milwaukee WI 53222-1716 • kbiggdoggwisc@aol.com • SW • Tchr • Christ Memorial Milwaukee WI • (414)461-3371 • (RF 1978)

**MARTS JENNIFER LEIGH** (254)751-9036
300 Brooks Ln Waco TX 67605-1509 • lermarts@hotmail.com • TX • Tchr • Trinity Waco TX • (254)772-7840 • (S 1996)

**MARTY GERALD H**
2471 Marigold Way Corona CA 91719-3691 • PSW • Tchr • Pacific Southwest Irvine CA • (949)854-3232 • (S 1959 MS)

**MARTY LARRY D** (314)947-4652
1300 Country Club Rd Saint Charles MO 63303-3309 • lmarty@mail.win.org • MO • Tchr • LHS St Charles Saint Peters MO • (636)928-5100 • (S 1972 MS MA)

**MARTY MARGARET K**
2471 Marigold Way Corona CA 91719-3491 • PSW • Tchr • Zion Anaheim CA • (714)535-3600 • (S 1960)

**MARTY ROBERT E SR.** (916)424-3984
7416 Rio Mondego Dr Sacramento CA 95831-4635 • CNH • EM • (S 1955 MA)

**MARUT JANICE B** (817)478-2304
3629 Lake Tahoe Dr Arlington TX 76016-3521 • jmarut@flash.net • TX • Tchr • St Paul Fort Worth TX • (817)332-4563 • (CQ 1998)

**MARXHAUSEN BENJAMIN W DR** (402)483-7661
5411 La Salle St Lincoln NE 68516 • NEB • EM • (S 1958 MA LLD)

**MARXHAUSEN GARY P**
671 E Hickory Ct Sebewaing MI 48759-1421 • mwarrior@avci.net • MI • P/Tchr • Immanuel Sebewaing MI • (517)883-3050 • (SP 1971 MS)

**MARXHAUSEN KIM D** (402)466-8248
6211 Glendale Rd Lincoln NE 68505-1646 • kmarxha@lps.org • NEB • Tchr • Faith Lincoln NE • (402)466-6861 • (S 1981 MA)

**MARXHAUSEN REINHOLD P** (402)643-3248
PO Box 271 Seward NE 68434-0271 • NEB • EM • (S 1957 MFA)

**MASAT KRISTA LYNN** (402)842-3185
RR 1 Box 153 Brunswick NE 68720-9783 • NEB • Tchr • Zion Plainview NE • (402)582-3312 • (S 1987)

**MASCHKE SAMUEL R** (203)532-1220
102 Pine St Greenwich CT 06830 • AT • Tchr • Chapel Bronxville NY • (914)337-3202 • (RF 1974)

**MASENGARB DAVID G** (262)633-4554
206 Virginia St Racine WI 53405 • rlhs@execpc.com • SW • Tchr • Lutheran High School Racine WI • (414)637-6538 • (RF 1969)

**MASENGARB VIRGINIA R** (262)633-4554
206 Virginia St Racine WI 53405 • vmasengarb@hotmail.com • SW • 08/2000 • (RF 1969)

**MASER CAROL A** (320)384-0950
211 Sunrise Dr PO Box 373 Medford MN 55049-0373 • dcmaser@rconnect.com • MNN • 08/1994 08/2000 • (SP 1989)

**MASER GAIL R** (651)688-6426
688 Stonewood Rd Eagan MN 55123-1323 • grmqueen@aol.com • MNS • Tchr • Trinity Lone Oak Eagan MN • (651)454-1139 • (SP 1978)

**MASER M DANIEL** (507)446-8191
211 Sunrise Dr PO Box 373 Medford MN 55049-0373 • dcmaser@rconnect.com • MNN • 08/1994 08/2000 • (SP 1990)

**MASHEIMER JILL ANN** (708)484-1074
1239 East Ave Berwyn IL 60402-1004 • jmasheimer@kiwi.dep.anl.gov • NI • Tchr • St Luke Itasca IL • (630)773-0509 • (RF 1996 MED)

**MASKE RICHARD JOHN** (262)373-0183
W141N4979 Somerset Dr Menomonee Falls WI 53051-6981 • maske@execpc.com • SW • Tchr • Zion Menomonee Falls WI • (414)781-7437 • (S 1971)

**MASON SHARON L** (773)471-2424
8230 S Whipple St Chicago IL 60652-3446 • NI • Tchr • Luther HS South Chicago IL • (773)737-1416 • (RF 1979 MMU MA)

**MASSEY BRADLEY R** (734)483-4341
5956 Willowbridge Rd Ypsilanti MI 48197-7133 • MI • Tchr • St Paul Ann Arbor MI • (734)665-0604 • (AA 1987 MS)

**MASSMANN JANICE CAROL** (949)476-0770
15 Las Cruces Irvine CA 92614 • PSW • SHS/C • Pacific Southwest Irvine CA • (949)854-3232 • (S 1969 MA)

**MASSMANN PAUL F** (949)476-0770
15 Las Cruces Irvine CA 92614-5300 • massmann@cui.edu • PSW • SHS/C • Pacific Southwest Irvine CA • (949)854-3232 • (S 1968 MA)

**MASTERS WILLIAM L JR.** (402)634-2525
53733 836 Rd Meadow Grove NE 68752-4101 • NEB • Tchr • St John Battle Creek NE • (402)675-3605 • (S 1979)

**MATERN JANE E**
C/O Queens Lutheran School 3120 37th St Long Island City NY 11103-3933 • AT • Tchr • Queens Long Island City NY • (718)721-4313 • (BR 1982)

**MATERN JOHN H** (757)599-3233
5 Corbin Dr Newport News VA 23606-2901 • jhmatern@aol.com • AT • EM • (CQ 1955 MSED)

**MATHERS RICHARD C** (702)737-5062
2117 Alhambra Cir Las Vegas NV 89104-2910 • PSW • Tchr • Pacific Southwest Irvine CA • (949)854-3232 • (RF 1974 MA)

**MATHEWS CRAIG A*** (715)720-7656
1130 Weatheridge Rd #2 Chippewa Falls WI 54729 • NEB • 08/1998 08/2000 • (SP 1977 MED)

**MATHEWS EUNICE F** (715)720-7656
1130 Weatheridge Rd Chippewa Falls WI 54729 • NEB • Tchr • St Paul Omaha NE • (402)451-2865 • (SP 1977)

**MATHEWS KRISTEN K** (618)234-0874
6 Second Fairway Ct Belleville IL 62220 • SI • 12/1995 12/1999 • (RF 1987)

**MATHIAS CONNIE J** (618)483-6975
9622 N First St Altamont IL 62411-9519 • CI • Tchr • Altamont Altamont IL • (618)483-6428 • (CQ 1996)

**MATHIOWETZ BARBARA E** (619)588-8642
1834 Brabham St El Cajon CA 92019-4103 • PSW • Tchr • Christ La Mesa CA • (619)462-5211 • (CQ 1996)

**MATTER EUNICE J** (414)633-0798
4026 17th St Racine WI 53405-3711 • SW • 06/1995 06/2000 • (S 1982)

**MATTES SCOTT W**
1333 Barry #7 Los Angeles CA 90025 • PSW • Tchr • Pilgrim Santa Monica CA • (310)829-2239 • (S 1996)

**MATTHEES BARBARA JEAN** (507)235-6021
132 Linden Dr Fairmont MN 56031-2179 • MNS • Tchr • St Pauls Fairmont MN • (507)238-9492 • (SP 1970)

**MATTHEWS FRANCES ANNETTE** (504)244-0508
10906 S Hardy St New Orleans LA 70127-2805 • rdcuers@aol.com • SO • 08/2000 • (CQ 1995 MSED)

**MATTHEWS KAY L** (708)749-8899
3138 Home Ave Berwyn IL 60402-2910 • lambsteacher@hotmail.com • EN • Tchr • Concordia Little Lam Berwyn IL • (708)795-7563 • (RF 1968)

**MATTHEWS LARRY A DR** (402)643-2093
1260 Eastridge Dr Seward NE 68434-1332 • NEB • SHS/C • Nebraska Seward NE • (S 1958 MS PHD)

**MATTHEWS LISA JANEEN** (909)622-0304
230 E Pasadena St Pomona CA 91767-4706 • PSW • Tchr • Pacific Southwest Irvine CA • (949)854-3232 • (AA 1995)

**MATTHEWS SANDRA H** (828)466-0472
203 5th Street Pl NE Conover NC 28613-1626 • sdm11155@aol.com • SE • Tchr • St Stephen Hickory NC • (828)256-2166 • (RF 1977)

**MATTHIAS DONLEY D** (708)394-2224
704 S Dryden Pl Arlington Hts IL 60005-2764 • NI • EM • (S 1958 MA)

**MATTHIAS JOHN W** (313)792-9588
718 N Vernon Dearborn MI 48128-2501 • lcmattj@ccaa.edu • MI • Tchr • Guardian Dearborn MI • (313)274-3665 • (RF 1993 MCMU)

**MATTHYS JENNIFER NICOLE** (512)252-0630
14000 Renaissance Ct #3088 Austin TX 78728 • matthysj@aol.com • TX • Tchr • Hope Austin TX • (512)926-0003 • (AU 1992)

**MATTHYS NAOMI R** (254)547-1824
503 Yucca Dr Copperas Cove TX 76522-3021 • matthys@dashlink.com • TX • Tchr • Grace Killeen TX • (254)634-4424 • (S 1973)

**MATTICE KAILE**
2318 Arkwright Ln Knoxville TN 37921-7408 • MDS • Tchr • First Knoxville TN • (423)524-0308 • (S 1994)

**MATTOON JANETTE D**
St Paul Lutheran Church 901 E Heim Ave Orange CA 92865-2817 • PSW • Tchr • St Paul Orange CA • (714)921-3188 • (IV 1988 MA)

**MATTSFIELD MICHELLE L** (618)466-3448
5310 Godfrey Rd Apt #16 Godfrey IL 62035 • tchrsrgr8@aol.com • SI • Tchr • Faith Godfrey IL • (618)466-9153 • (S 1996)

**MATZKE SALLY L** (616)429-1545
3314 Lincoln Ave Saint Joseph MI 49085-3703 • MI • Tchr • Trinity Saint Joseph MI • (616)983-3056 • (RF 1971 MA)

**MATZKE SUSAN M** (330)995-2658
475 Sycamore Ln Apt 207 Aurora OH 44202-7648 • charis30@juno.com • IN • Tchr • Trinity Crown Point IN • (219)663-1578 • (RF 1994)

**MAU AARON JOEL BRANDON** (602)335-1627
7121 N 22nd Dr Phoenix AZ 85021 • PSW • Tchr • Martin Luther Phoenix AZ • (602)248-0656 • (MQ 1995)

**MAU DELMER J** (713)681-4177
6123 Autumn Forest Dr Houston TX 77092-2311 • TX • Tchr • Immanuel Houston TX • (713)861-8787 • (SP 1968 MA)

**MAU JACQUELINE J** (713)681-4177
6123 Autumn Forest Dr Houston TX 77092-2311 • TX • Tchr • Immanuel Houston TX • (713)861-8787 • (SP 1968)

**MAU RITA J** (847)391-9284
1780 E Algonquin Rd Des Plaines IL 60016 • maushaus@juno.com • NI • Tchr • Immanuel Glenview IL • (847)724-1034 • (S 1972)

**MAUCH JEANNINE A** (402)582-3827
PO Box 218 Plainview NE 68769-0218 • NEB • Tchr • Zion Plainview NE • (402)582-3312 • (S 1966 MED)

**MAUE ANGELA L** (636)397-3275
2 Hope Ct St Peters MO 63376 • MO • 04/2000 • (RF 1985)

**MAURER DIANE B** (314)928-6333
1221 Colby Dr St. Peters MO 63376-5514 • MO • Tchr • Immanuel Saint Charles MO • (636)946-0051 • (RF 1974 MA)

**MAURER MARION V** (520)782-6610
669 S Avenue B Yuma AZ 85364-2751 • PSW • EM • (RF 1947 MA)

**MAURER MARY D** (503)389-2157
20344 Rae Rd Bend OR 97702-2773 • mmaurer@bendcable.com • NOW • Tchr • Trinity Bend OR • (541)382-1850 • (S 1977)

**MAXEY DEBORAH S** (419)784-3075
1528 Mayo Dr Defiance OH 43512-3320 • OH • Tchr • St John Defiance OH • (419)782-1751 • (S 1984)

**MAXSON STEPHANIE C** (219)432-6312
8824 Dunmore Ln Fort Wayne IN 46804 • tsmaxson@aol.com • EN • 08/1999 • (RF 1994 MED)

**MAXWELL DERYL R JR.** (714)579-7521
2336 N Bedford Dr Fullerton CA 92831-1506 • dmaxwell@clcs-brea.com • PSW • Prin • Christ Fullerton CA • (714)870-7460 • (S 1984 MA)

**MAXWELL SUSAN J** (714)579-7521
2336 Bedford Dr Fullerton CA 92831-1506 • PSW • Tchr • Christ Fullerton CA • (714)870-7460 • (S 1984 MS)

**MAY SHARON L** (360)435-9148
6701 Oakwood Pl Arlington WA 98223-7406 • mayjoshar@aol.com • NOW • Tchr • Zion Everett WA • (425)334-5064 • (CQ 1987)

**MAYCROFT LESLIE ANNE** (952)884-2673
5108 W 108th St Bloomington MN 55437 • lamaycroft@aol.com • MNS • 02/2000 • (SP 1974 MA)

**MAYER DIANE KAY** (509)783-5076
2500 S Harrison Pl Kennewick WA 99337-1960 • FG • Tchr • Grace Saint Petersburg FL • (727)527-1168 • (RF 1969)

**MAYER HEIDI MARIE** (718)324-8977
4216 Oneida Ave Apt 1C Bronx NY 10470-2137 • hmm1213@aol.com • AT • Tchr • St Mark Yonkers NY • (914)237-4944 • (BR 1993 MED)

**MAYHEW JOHN ROBERT** (618)345-1405
2709 Sandstone Dr Maryville IL 62062-6401 • SI • Tchr • Good Shepherd Collinsville IL • (618)344-3153 • (RF 1979 MS)

**MAYO CATHERINE MARIE** (513)923-1557
3462 Statewood Dr Cincinnati OH 45251-2381 • OH • Tchr • Concordia Cincinnati OH • (513)861-9568 • (S 1974)

**MAYO MICHAEL A** (513)861-9552
3462 Statewood Dr Cincinnati OH 45251-2381 • OH • Tchr • Concordia Cincinnati OH • (513)861-9568 • (S 1974)

**MAZUR TAMMY EVA MARIE** (248)280-2703
2110 W 14 Mile Rd Apt 103 Royal Oak MI 48073-1438 • t.e.mazur@worldnet.att.net • MI • Tchr • Our Shepherd Birmingham MI • (248)645-0551 • (RF 1997)

**MC ANALLY MARJIE R** (313)942-1808
37280 Mc Bride St Romulus MI 48174-3976 • MI • 09/1999 • (AA 1984)

**MC ARTHUR LINDA**
4727 Rivertree Spring TX 77388 • TX • 09/1999 • (S 1984)

**MC BRIDE MARIE C** (309)452-4714
11 Robinwood Dr Normal IL 61761-4037 • CI • 06/1991 06/2000 • (RF 1964)

**MC CAIN JEAN ANNA** (517)792-7309
5177 Narcissus Dr Saginaw MI 48603-1147 • MI • EM • (RF 1955)

**MC CAIN LYNN C**
622 Clear Creek Ct Ballwin MO 63021-6221 • MO • 09/1990 09/2000 • (RF 1983 MED)

**MC CAMANT DIANE** (817)249-6577
1004 Duane St Fort Worth TX 76126 • cowtown6@swbell.net • TX • Tchr • St Paul Fort Worth TX • (817)332-4563 • (CQ 1998)

**MC CANN TIMOTHY E** (714)283-2840
231 N Cambridge St Orange CA 92866 • PSW • Tchr • St Paul Orange CA • (714)921-3188 • (CQ 1998)

**MC CARTY EUNICE J** (308)384-7531
4067 W Capital Ave Grand Island NE 68803-1117 • lmccarty@gionline.net • NEB • Tchr • Trinity Grand Island NE • (308)382-5274 • (S 1978)

**MC CARTY NANCYANN GLADYS**
400 W Main St Belle Plaine MN 56011-1433 • MNS • Tchr • St Paul Prior Lake MN • (612)447-2117 • (SP 1980)

**MC CLAIN LEANN E** (979)242-5097
107 Tomahawk Ln La Grange TX 78945-5337 • bachmus@cvtv.net • TX • Tchr • Immanuel Giddings TX • (409)542-3319 • (S 1976)

**MC CLAIN MARK A** (409)242-5097
107 Tomahawk Ln La Grange TX 78945-5337 • bachmus@cvtv.net • TX • P/Tchr • St Paul Giddings TX • (409)366-2218 • (S 1976 MED)

**MC CLARY RICHARD W** (714)639-5964
1148 E Trenton Ave Orange CA 92867-3806 • rmcclary@socal.rr.com • PSW • Tchr • Hephatha Anaheim CA • (714)637-4022 • (S 1961)

**MC CLATCHEY RITA I** (248)398-7171
28690 Diesing Dr Madison Heights MI 48071-4537 • MI • Tchr • St Paul Royal Oak MI • (248)546-6555 • (RF 1974)

**MC CLELLAN JAMES R** (920)468-3128
116 S Platten St Green Bay WI 54303-1935 • NW • Tchr • LHS Assoc Of NE Wisc Green Bay WI • (920)469-6810 • (MQ 1993)

**MC CLELLAND KAREN K** (517)734-3225
338 W Michigan Ave Rogers City MI 49779 • kkm³teacher@hotmail.com • MI • Tchr • St John Rogers City MI • (517)734-4522 • (AA 1986 MA)

**MC CLINTOCK LAURIE JO** (618)327-8537
836 S Moore St Nashville IL 62263-1525 • lauriejo922@aol.com • SI • Tchr • Trinity Nashville IL • (618)327-3311 • (RF 1981)

**MC CLURE ELIZABETH ANN** (916)927-8237
920 San Juan Rd Sacramento CA 95834-2211 • MDS • 12/1995 12/1997 • (AA 1986)

**MC CLURE JOYCE ANN** (256)883-9987
10324 Picadilly Ln SW Huntsville AL 35803-2034 • jmcclur3@bellsouth.net • SO • Tchr • Grace Huntsville AL • (256)881-0553 • (S 1968)

**MC CLURE MARILYN R** (520)881-2252
2012 E Monte Vista Dr Tucson AZ 85719-2874 • EN • 08/1988 08/2000 • (RF 1967 MA)

**MC COLLISTER DAVID P** (636)949-2804
6 Archer Cir Saint Charles MO 63301-1201 • MO • Tchr • Lutheran North Saint Louis MO • (314)389-3100 • (S 1967 MA)

**MC COLLOR REBEKAH LYNN** (715)421-1428
3211 Franklin St Apt 313 Wisconsin Rapids WI 54494-6056 • NW • Tchr • Immanuel Wisconsin Rapids WI • (715)423-0272 • (RF 1997)

**MC COMAS BARBARA L** (913)233-7293
736 SW Wayne Ave Topeka KS 66606-1753 • KS • Tchr • Topeka Topeka KS • (785)357-0382 • (RF 1967)

**MC COY MARGARET M**
712 Alma St Laurel NE 68745-1712 • NEB • Tchr • Zion Plainview NE • (402)582-3312 • (S 1981)

**MC DANIEL CAROL R** (714)826-0471
9565 Normandy Way Cypress CA 90630 • mcdaniel@cui.edu • PSW • Mem C • Bethany Long Beach CA • (562)421-4711 • (S 1983 MMU)

**MC DANIEL GARY R** (714)826-0471
9565 Normandy Way Cypress CA 90630 • mcdaniel@cui.edu • PSW • SHS/C • Pacific Southwest Irvine CA • (949)854-3232 • (S 1983 MA)

**MC DANIEL JOYCE ANN** (636)467-5764
3548 Swan Cir S Arnold MO 63010 • MO • Tchr • St John Arnold MO • (636)464-7303 • (RF 1986)

**MC DERMOTT MICHAEL S** (216)228-1643
12520 Edgewater Dr Apt 1602 Lakewood OH 44107-1608 • EN • Tchr • Holy Cross Cleveland OH • (216)252-2348 • (S 1977)

**MC DONALD DEBORAH M** (313)538-2183
14844 Inkster Rd Redford Township MI 48239-3015 • dmcdonald@lhsa.net • MI • Tchr • St Paul Farmington Hills MI • (248)474-2488 • (RF 1976)

**MC DONALD IAN K** (313)538-2183
14844 Inkster Rd Redford Twp MI 48239-3015 • imcdonald@lhsa.com • MI • Tchr • Fox Valley Academy Elgin IL • (847)468-8207 • (RF 1973 MA)

**MC DONALD SHARON MARIE** (972)775-1317
2241 Cottonwood Ct Midlothian TX 76065 • smac1@airmail.net • TX • Tchr • Cross Of Christ De Soto TX • (972)223-9586 • (S 1986)

**MC DOWELL CAROL** (210)639-4344
PO Box 83 Kingsbury TX 78638-0083 • TX • P/Tchr • Cross New Braunfels TX • (830)625-3969 • (S 1986)

**MC DOWELL ROBERT R*** (830)639-4344
113 S River St Ste 100 Sequin TX 78155-5740 • mcdower1@fld.aal.org • TX • 04/1996 04/2000 • (S 1982)

**MC FALL KATHLEEN ANN** (517)734-3769
1230 Heythaler Hwy Rogers City MI 49779 • mcfall@freeway.net • MI • P/Tchr • St John Rogers City MI • (517)734-3580 • (SP 1975)

**MC FARLAND LISA ANN** (218)789-7427
PO Box 181 Sabin MN 56580-0181 • ND • Tchr • Grace Fargo ND • (701)232-7747 • (S 1997)

**MC FARLIN JERRY A** (708)331-5293
16210 Springfield Ave Markham IL 60426-4449 • NI • Tchr • St Paul Oak Lawn IL • (847)423-1058 • (S 1971 MA)

**MC FARLIN VICKIE** (708)331-5293
16210 Springfield Ave Markham IL 60426-4449 • NI • Tchr • St Paul Oak Lawn IL • (847)423-1058 • (S 1971)

**MC FERRAN PEGGY JANETTE** (314)296-4655
3222 E Romaine Creek Rd Imperial MO 63052-1002 • MO • Tchr • Salem Affton MO • (314)353-9242 • (CQ 1992)

**MC GHEE D MICHAEL** (419)782-3533
22711 Garman Rd Defiance OH 43512-9089 • hondomc@defnet.com • OH • Tchr • St John Defiance OH • (419)782-1751 • (RF 1966 MA MA)

**MC GHEE JANICE L** (419)782-3533
22711 Garman Rd Defiance OH 43512-9089 • hondomc@defnet.com • OH • Tchr • St John Defiance OH • (419)782-1751 • (RF 1981)

**MC GHEE THOMAS E** (314)631-0854
9220 Dana Dale Ct Saint Louis MO 63123-5605 • SI • 10/1989 10/1999 • (RF 1962 MED)

**MC KEE TERRY L** (352)683-5252
1445 Escobar Ave Spring Hill FL 34608-5927 • FG • Mem C • Christ Brooksville FL • (352)796-8331 • (CQ 2000)

**MC KIM GALE F** (310)832-8161
28119 Pontevedra Dr Rncho Pls Vrd CA 90275-1239 • jmckim@laedu.lalc.k12.ca.us • PSW • Tchr • Christ Rancho Palos Verdes CA • (310)831-0848 • (RF 1972 MA)

**MC KINNEY ELAINE C** (501)452-4642
5414 Collins Ln Fort Smith AR 72904-7461 • emck307@hotmail.com • MDS • Tchr • First Fort Smith AR • (501)785-2886 • (S 1969)

**MC KINNON MARGARET L**
202 Westview St Collinsville IL 62234-3772 • SI • Tchr • St Paul Troy IL • (618)667-6681 • (CQ 1988)

**MC KOWN KONNIE JO** (706)861-4056
46 Patricia Cir Ringgold GA 30736-8251 • lkegjm@aol.com • MDS • Tchr • Lutheran Chattanooga TN • (615)622-3755 • (S 1988)

**MC LAIN MARGARET BERNICE** (919)765-9546
2940 Burlwood Dr Winston Salem NC 27103-6208 • SE • Tchr • St John Winston Salem NC • (336)725-1651 • (SP 1975)

**MC LAIN MICHAEL W** (972)680-1383
1503 Reston Dr Richardson TX 75081-2653 • mclain15@hotmail.com • TX • Tchr • Lutheran HS of Dalla Dallas TX • (214)349-8912 • (AU 1998)

**MC LAUGHLIN CANDACE JO** (219)845-4207
7022 White Oak Ave Hammond IN 46324-2137 • NI • 07/2000 • (RF 1982)

**MC LEOD SANDRA A** (614)773-9235
1355 Western Ave Apt 20 Chillicothe OH 45601-1110 • OH • 09/1994 • (S 1976)

**MC LOUGHLIN JANET M**
1357 Stonetree Dr Troy MI 48083-5352 • MI • Tchr • Our Shepherd Birmingham MI • (248)645-0551 • (AA 1984)

**MC LOUGHLIN MARK EDWARD** (248)597-3976
1357 Stonetree Troy MI 48083-5352 • mmcloughlin@lhsa.com • MI • Tchr • LHS Northwest Rochester Hills MI • (810)852-6677 • (AA 1987 MA)

**MC MAHON BARBARA H** (217)287-7447
624 S Clay St Taylorville IL 62568-2524 • CI • Tchr • Trinity Springfield IL • (217)522-8151 • (S 1969 MA)

**MC NABB SALLY A** (501)227-7928
12011 Shawnee Forest Dr Little Rock AR 72212-2325 • MDS • Tchr • Christ Little Rock AR • (501)663-5212 • (S 1974)

**MC NALLY BRIAN DOUGLAS** (810)293-9497
1064 Country Club Dr St Clair Shrs MI 48082-2941 • brianmcnally@ameritech.net • MI • Tchr • Mount Calvary Detroit MI • (313)527-3366 • (S 1972)

**MC NAMAR TERRIA** (503)753-8335
5641 SW Bluestem Pl Corvallis OR 97333-1355 • NOW • Tchr • Zion Corvallis OR • (541)753-7503 • (PO 1982)

**MC NEELEY MARK** (313)776-8471
15611 Camden Ave Eastpointe MI 48021-1681 • MI • Tchr • St Peter Eastpointe MI • (810)776-1663 • (RF 1968 MA)

**MC NEIL DAVID A**
910 Colony Dr Saline MI 48176-1039 • MI • Mem C • Christ King Saline MI • (734)429-9200 • (S 1986)

**MC PEEK LYNN E** (503)661-4841
1127 NE 27th St Gresham OR 97030-3031 • saminex@aol.com • NOW • 08/1988 08/2000 • (RF 1976)

**MC PHERSON DEBI** (870)673-4778
205 W Hastings St Stuttgart AR 72160-6654 • admcpherson@hotmail.com • MDS • Tchr • St John Stuttgart AR • (870)673-7096 • (SP 1979)

**MC PHERSON NORMAN** (616)429-6493
825 Ansley Dr Saint Joseph MI 49085-3670 • parished@parrett.net • MI • Mem C • Trinity Saint Joseph MI • (616)983-5000 • (S 1970 MED)

**MC QUEEN CARLA** (517)642-8829
14540 Frost Rd Hemlock MI 48626-9444 • MI • Tchr • St Peter Hemlock MI • (517)642-8188 • (S 1974)

**MC REYNOLDS RUTH J** (518)494-7689
PO Box 51 Pottersville NY 12860-0051 • mcrfam@netheaven.com • AT • 05/1995 05/1997 • (BR 1979)

**MDLULI SAMUEL** (334)874-6025
1216 9th Ave PO Box 1193 Selma AL 36701 • FG • Tchr • Christ East Point GA • (404)767-2892 • (SEL 2000)

**MEAD KAREN MARIE**
4105 Garfield Ave Lot 41 Loveland CO 80538-8405 • RM • Tchr • Immanuel Loveland CO • (970)667-4506 • (S 1993)

**MEADOR JILL MARIE**
E7263 Star Rd Aniwa WI 54408-9622 • NW • 12/1995 12/1999 • (MQ 1991)

**MEADOWS SHARON L** (702)642-3413
3854 Tatiana St Las Vegas NV 89115-2405 • PSW • Tchr • Redeemer Las Vegas NV • (702)642-6144 • (RF 1965 MA)

**MEARLING STEPHEN R** (812)477-3071
5307 Cunningham Dr Evansville IN 47711-2416 • IN • P/Tchr • Trinity Evansville IN • (812)867-5279 • (RF 1971 MED)

**MEDBERY CHRISTINA ANN**
2323 Bellwood Dr Trlr 200 Grand Island NE 68801-6207 • NEB • Tchr • St Paul Ogallala NE • (308)284-2944 • (S 1996)

**MEDER KAREN A** (330)644-7493
354 Cheshire Rd Akron OH 44319-3816 • OH • Tchr • Zion Akron OH • (330)253-3137 • (RF 1972)

**MEEHL MARK W DR** (402)643-6652
628 N 2nd St Seward NE 68434-1504 • mmeehl@seward.cune.edu • NEB • SHS/C • Nebraska Seward NE • (S 1979 MA PHD)

**MEEK CYNTHIA G** (512)345-5188
5713 Sam Houston Cir Austin TX 78731 • cmeek@redeemer.net • TX • Tchr • Redeemer Austin TX • (512)459-1500 • (S 1970)

**MEEKS CAROL A** (954)748-4654
2010 Sunset Strip Sunrise FL 33313-2948 • rmeeks2@ix.netcom.com • FG • Tchr • Trinity Fort Lauderdale FL • (954)463-7471 • (RF 1966)

**MEERS DIANA DOLORES** (314)947-8028
2901 Blanchette Dr Saint Charles MO 63301-0762 • MO • Tchr • Immanuel Saint Charles MO • (636)946-0051 • (CQ 1998)

**MEERSTEIN MARK W** (920)435-0853
1830 Juneberry Dr Green Bay WI 54311-6548 • NW • Tchr • LHS Assoc Of NE Wisc Green Bay WI • (920)469-6810 • (MQ 1991)

**MEGOWN DALE KEVIN** (608)745-4988
124 E Marion St Portage WI 53901 • SW • Tchr • St John Portage WI • (608)742-2387 • (SP 1985)

**MEHL KATHRYN L** (314)671-0006
6425 Highway MM House Springs MO 63051-2323 • MO • Tchr • Salem Affton MO • (314)353-9242 • (S 1972 MA)

**MEHNER MIRIAM** (303)355-9045
1235 Ivy St Denver CO 80220-2641 • RM • 06/1999 • (RF 1961)

**MEIER ELISABETH E** (650)592-7532
1319 Geneva Ave San Carlos CA 94070-4820 • rpm1meier@aol.com • CNH • Tchr • Grace San Mateo CA • (650)345-9082 • (RF 1977)

**MEIER FREDERICK A** (262)251-9017
W141N8314 Merrimac Dr Menomonee Falls WI 53051-3947 • SW • EM • (RF 1949 MMU)

**MEIER LESTER T**
115 S Queensbury St Anaheim CA 92806-3818 • PSW • Tchr • St John Orange CA • (714)288-4406 • (S 1984)

**MEIER MARJORIE A** (407)365-7521
2128 Sunbird Ct Oviedo FL 32765-5208 • FG • EM • (RF 1952 MMU MLS AMD)

**MEIER MATTHEW C** (847)788-0097
2905 Thrush Ln Rolling Meadows IL 60008 • c3mmeier@aol.com • NI • Prin • St Paul Mount Prospect IL • (847)255-0332 • (RF 1990 MS)

**MEIER MAUREEN E** (360)452-4879
1120 E 8th St Port Angeles WA 98362-6629 • mmeier@olypen.com • NOW • Tchr • St Matthew Port Angeles WA • (360)457-4122 • (RF 1969)

**MEIER PAULA K** (816)455-0273
5345 N Woodland Ave Kansas City MO 64118-5702 • MO • Tchr • Holy Cross Kansas City MO • (816)453-7211 • (CQ 1981)

**MEIER ROBERT J DR** (914)779-7701
15 Winslow Cir Tuckahoe NY 10707-3710 • rjm@concordia-ny.edu • AT • SHS/C • Atlantic Bronxville NY • (914)337-5700 • (RF 1955 MS MS DED)

**MEIER ROBERT P** (650)592-7532
1319 Geneva Ave San Carlos CA 94070-4820 • rpm1meier@aol.com • CNH • P/Tchr • Grace San Mateo CA • (650)345-9082 • (RF 1976)

**MEIER ROGER EDWARD** (810)791-8514
35431 Hickory Woods Dr Apt 8 Clinton Twp MI 48035-5145 • rogermeier@go.com • MI • Tchr • Trinity Clinton Township MI • (810)468-8511 • (MQ 1994)

**MEIER ROSALIE A** (414)255-1276
N76W14573 Fairfield Ct Menomonee Falls WI 53051-4359 • SW • Tchr • St Paul Grafton WI • (414)377-4659 • (S 1982)

**MEINEKE DAVID A** (719)475-7379
1313 Wilbur Cir Colorado Springs CO 80909-3133 • RM • P/Tchr • Redeemer Colorado Springs CO • (719)633-7600 • (RF 1977 MA)

**MEINERT JILL M** (308)687-6069
1646 Worms Rd Saint Libory NE 68872-2906 • zlsworms@kdsi.net • NEB • Tchr • Zion Saint Libory NE • (308)687-6486 • (S 1996)

**MEINZEN PHILIP E** (262)243-2617
C/O Concordia Univ Wisconsin 12800 N Lake Shore Dr Mequon WI 53097-2402 • philip.meinzen@cuw.edu • SW • SHS/C • South Wisconsin Milwaukee WI • (414)464-8100 • (S 1977 MSED)

**MEINZEN W JOHN** (219)424-8551
631 Lawton Pl Fort Wayne IN 46805-4129 • IN • EM • (CQ 1958 MS)

**MEISINGER ARDEL** (336)765-2942
3110 Shannon Dr Winston-Salem NC 27106-3648 • ardle4949@aol.com • SE • P/Tchr • St John Winston-Salem NC • (336)725-1651 • (S 1971 MAD)

**MEISSNER DOUGLAS**
10615 Penn Dr Indianapolis IN 46280 • IN • Tchr • Trinity Indianapolis IN • (317)897-0243 • (BR 1998)

**MEISSNER GRETCHEN ANNE** (716)649-2662
62 Saint Marys Pl Hamburg NY 14075-5234 • gretcham@aol.com • EA • 07/1997 07/2000 • (BR 1992)

**MEISSNER H DOUGLAS**
10615 Penn Dr Indianapolis IN 46280 • IN • Tchr • Trinity Indianapolis IN • (317)897-0243 • (BR 1998)

**MEISSNER HERBERT W** (716)693-2374
6964 Ward Rd North Tonawanda NY 14120-1413 • EA • P/Tchr • St John North Tonawanda NY • (716)693-9677 • (RF 1968 MA)

**MEISSNER LAURENCE DR** (512)759-3391
450 Spring Valley St Hutto TX 78634 • meissnerl@concordia.edu • TX • SHS/C • Texas Austin TX • (S 1968 MS PHD)

**MELCHER CYNTHIA A** (512)898-2815
PO Box 455 Thorndale TX 76577-0455 • melcherc@ad.com • TX • Tchr • St Paul Thorndale TX • (512)898-2711 • (S 1977)

**MELDE ROBERT H JR.** (952)432-4165
8110 170th St West Lakeville MN 55044 • robert.melde@lutheranhighschool.com • MNS • Tchr • Luth HS Of Greater M Bloomington MN • (612)854-0224 • (S 1998 MED)

**MELENDEZ ANDREW A*** (660)882-5714
502 Poplar St Boonville MO 65233-1770 • MO • EM • (RF 1959 MA)

**MELENDEZ BRIAN A** (612)861-5745
7134 James Ave S Richfield MN 55423 • melendba@spacestar.net • MNS • Tchr • Luth HS Of Greater M Bloomington MN • (612)854-0224 • (RF 1990)

**MELERINE ROXANNE** (314)644-1386
1341 Highland Ter Saint Louis MO 63117 • MDS • 01/1999 • (AU 1998)

**MELILLO LORI ANN** (301)233-0779
178 Opal Ave Westminster MD 21157-6632 • SE • Tchr • Emmanuel Baltimore MD • (410)744-0015 • (BR 1980)

**MELLENDORF CRAIG** (262)789-9081
965 S Post Rd Brookfield WI 53005-6829 • cemel@execpc.com • SW • Tchr • Martin LHS Greendale WI • (414)421-4000 • (S 1981 MED)

**MENDEZ EDWARD W** (714)505-4148
9 Alassio Irvine CA 92620-2569 • mendezbw@cui.edu • PSW • SHS/C • Pacific Southwest Irvine CA • (949)854-3232 • (CQ 1996 MA PHD)

**MENKE STEVEN A** (512)990-8727
1607 Middleway Rd Pflugerville TX 78660-4399 • TX • Tchr • St Paul Austin TX • (512)472-3313 • (RF 1981 MA)

**MENKE THOMAS O** (512)990-7365
703 W Custers Creek Bnd Pflugerville TX 78660-4739 • TX • Tchr • Our Savior Austin TX • (512)836-9600 • (S 1982)

**MENNICKE SALLY J**
C/O Saint John Lutheran Church 1915 SE Lake Weir Rd Ocala FL 34471-5424 • FG • Tchr • St John Ocala FL • (352)622-7275 • (SP 1995)

**MENNICKE STEVEN T** (352)690-1623
2101 SE 10th Ct Ocala FL 34471-5461 • FG • Tchr • Florida-Georgia Orlando FL • (SP 1984)

**MENZEL KATHLEEN BETH** (817)249-5855
1609 S Timber Ct Fort Worth TX 76126-3911 • TX • Tchr • St Paul Fort Worth TX • (817)332-4563 • (S 1975 MED)

**MENZEL LORNA R** (504)461-8658
4210 Saint Elizabeth Dr Kenner LA 70065-1645 • lormenz@aol.com • SO • Tchr • Atonement Metairie LA • (504)887-3980 • (S 1971 MED)

**MERCIER GARY L** (262)377-0779
749 Homestead Trl Grafton WI 53024-1160 • SW • Tchr • St Paul Grafton WI • (414)377-4659 • (RF 1969 MA)

**MERKORD DEBORAH ANNE** (210)497-7836
24819 Shining Arrow San Antonio TX 78258-2745 • landeb3@gateway.net • TX • Tchr • Concordia San Antonio TX • (210)479-1477 • (S 1977)

**MERKORD LANNY DEAN** (210)497-7836
24819 Shining Arrow San Antonio TX 78258-2745 • landeb3@gateway.net • TX • Tchr • LHS Of San Antonio San Antonio TX • (210)733-7771 • (S 1977)

**MERRILL RANDOLPH M** (573)760-0305
409 Potosi St Farmington MO 63640-2403 • rmerrill@jcn1.com • MO • Prin • St Paul Farmington MO • (573)756-5147 • (S 1971)

**MERRITT GARY E** (816)632-8805
516 N Mead St Cameron MO 64429 • garymerritt@webtv.com • KS • 09/1998 • (S 1967 MA)

**MERRITT ROBERT A** (602)224-0828
2838 E Highland Ave Phoenix AZ 85016-4937 • EN • Tchr • Christ Phoenix AZ • (602)957-7010 • (S 1970 MED)

**MERRITT RONNIE G** (417)869-9573
7040 W Lone Oak St Springfield MO 65803-8710 • MO • 08/1998 08/2000 • (RF 1964 MA)

**MERRITT TIMOTHY M** (410)551-8695
7738 Acrocomia Dr Hanover MD 21076-1675 • SE • Tchr • Emmanuel Baltimore MD • (410)744-0016 • (BR 1981)

**MERRITT TIMOTHY TODD** (972)881-4324
1922 R Ave Plano TX 75074-5017 • TX • Tchr • Faith Plano TX • (972)423-7448 • (IV 1994)

**MERSIOVSKY JEAN M** (512)863-6418
PO Box 502 Walburg TX 78673-0502 • TX • Tchr • Zion Georgetown TX • (512)863-5345 • (SP 1971)

**MERTENS BARBARA JEAN** (303)682-1558
815 6th Ave Apt 10 Longmont CO 80501-4949 • RM • Tchr • Messiah Longmont CO • (303)776-2573 • (S 1993)

**MERTENS BRUCE ALLAN**
210 W 4th St Janesville MN 56048 • MNS • Tchr • Trinity Janesville MN • (507)231-5189 • (S 1995)

**MERTINS LINDY RENEE** (602)861-3834
2220 W Mission Ln Apt # 2159 Phoenix AZ 85021-5808 • lmertins@cbrichardellis.com • PSW • 03/1997 • (S 1995)

**MERTINS STACY M** (602)938-2111
14221 N 51st Ave #3107 Glendale AZ 85306 • smmertins@juno.com • PSW • Tchr • Christian Phoenix AZ • (602)934-5896 • (S 1994)

**MERTZ DARRYL H** (815)633-6931
1035 Luanna Dr Rockford IL 61103-8705 • darmar@hughestech.net • NI • Tchr • Luther Academy Rockford IL • (815)877-9551 • (RF 1984)

**MERTZ PAULA M** (314)731-1543
233 C Chapel Ridge Hazelwood MO 63042-2625 • pmmblues@hotmail.com • MO • Tchr • Immanuel Olivette MO • (314)993-5004 • (S 1991 MED)

**MERZ KATHY M** (618)867-2627
506 Cambridge Dr De Soto IL 62924-1014 • kmmerz@hotmail.com • SI • Tchr • Immanuel Murphysboro IL • (618)687-3917 • (S 1971)

**MERZ MARTIN C** (517)643-7443
4084 S Badour Rd Merrill MI 48637-9311 • MI • EM • (RF 1941)

**MESECK JULIE ANNE** (402)731-1923
4829 Holmes St Apt 220 Omaha NE 68117-2054 • NEB • Tchr • Zion Omaha NE • (402)731-1418 • (S 1968)

**MESEKE STEVEN D** (810)468-0453
37228 Ingleside St Clinton Township MI 48036-2615 • smeseke@lhsa.com • MI • Tchr • Michigan Ann Arbor MI • (RF 1975 MS MED)

**MESSER LA VAUN M** (541)754-1514
3253 NW Harrison Blvd Corvallis OR 97330-5002 • dlmesser@proaxis.com • NOW • Tchr • Zion Corvallis OR • (541)753-7503 • (RF 1971)

**MESSERSCHMIDT EDNA** (847)679-2760
9221 Drake Ave Evanston IL 60203-1651 • NI • Tchr • St Philip Chicago IL • (773)561-9830 • (RF 1946 MA)

**MESSICK TIMOTHY A** 852-2812-0048
C12 South Bay Villa 4 South Bay Close Repulse Bay HONG KONG • tmessick@hkis.edu.hk • NOW • S Miss • Northwest Portland OR • (PO 1981 MED)

**MESSMANN RACHEL LOUISE** (219)745-3218
4530 S Calhoun St Fort Wayne IN 46807 • rlmessmann@aol.com • IN • Tchr • Zion Fort Wayne IN • (219)744-1389 • (MQ 1996)

**MESTER KIM MARIE** (319)391-3889
4724 N Ripley St Davenport IA 52806-4126 • k3mester@hotmail.com • IE • Tchr • Trinity Davenport IA • (319)322-5224 • (S 1995)

**MESTER RANDALL EARL** (319)391-3889
4724 N Ripley St Davenport IA 52806-4126 • IE • Tchr • Trinity Davenport IA • (319)323-8001 • (S 1994)

**METTENBRINK ELLEN L**
4411 Colfax Cir Lincoln NE 68504-1628 • NE • 09/1994 09/1999 • (S 1991 MED)

**METZGER MICHELLE RENEE** (402)465-5438
7100 N Adams St Apt 14 Lincoln NE 68507 • NEB • Tchr • Lincoln Luth Jr/Sr H Lincoln NE • (402)467-5404 • (S 1993)

**MEWS AMY LOUISE** (219)436-3154
4019 Aboite Lake Dr Fort Wayne IN 46804-3909 • amews@juno.com • IN • 06/2000 • (SP 1977)

**MEWS GARY R** (219)436-3154
4019 Aboite Lake Dr Fort Wayne IN 46804-3909 • grmews@cs.com • IN • Tchr • Suburban Bethlehem Fort Wayne IN • (219)483-9371 • (SP 1996)

**MEYER ALAN J** (314)343-4519
1803 Rutger St Saint Louis MO 63104-2943 • meyeraj@lcms.org • MO • S Ex/S • Missouri Saint Louis MO • (314)317-4550 • (S 1971 MS)

**MEYER ARLEN L** (402)643-2848
719 N Columbia Ave Seward NE 68434-1554 • alm2129@seward.cune.edu • NEB • Tchr • St John Seward NE • (402)643-4535 • (S 1959 MED)

**MEYER ARLENE SUE** (708)345-1705
1214 N 15th Ave Melrose Park IL 60160-3406 • NI • Tchr • Immanuel Hillside IL • (708)562-5580 • (RF 1978)

**MEYER CAROL J** (319)655-7304
2647 G Ave Ladora IA 52251-7549 • IE • Tchr • Lutheran Interparish Williamsburg IA • (319)668-1711 • (RF 1980)

**MEYER CHARLOTTE H** (714)538-5001
661 N Buttonbush Trl Orange CA 92869-2414 • PSW • Prin • Salem Orange CA • (714)639-1946 • (S 1959 MCOUN MRD MCOUN)

**MEYER CHRISTINE A** (512)302-9961
1020 E 45th St - #205 Austin TX 78751 • TX • Tchr • St Paul Austin TX • (512)472-3313 • (AU 2000)

**MEYER COURTNEY A** (402)643-4774
1680 Edgewood Ln Seward NE 68434-1190 • NEB • SHS/C • Nebraska Seward NE • (S 1965 MA)

**MEYER DAVID J** (517)354-5864
1115 Merchant St Alpena MI 49707-2147 • djhkmyr@freeway.net • MI • EM • (RF 1956 MA)

**MEYER DAVID J** (847)844-9733
161 Linden Ave Apt # 4 East Dundee IL 60118 • NI • Tchr • Immanuel Dundee IL • (847)428-4477 • (S 1995)

**MEYER DAVID ROBERT** (206)938-4070
7711 26th Ave SW Seattle WA 98106 • NOW • Tchr • Hope Seattle WA • (206)935-8500 • (PO 1989)

**MEYER DORIS M** (210)614-5361
4212 Medical Dr #1401 San Antonio TX 78229-2157 • TX • Mem C • Trinity Corpus Christi TX • (361)884-4041 • (S 1953 MED)

**MEYER ELMER G** (317)898-6488
8114 Shibler Dr Indianapolis IN 46219-1332 • IN • EM • (RF 1932 MS)

**MEYER EUNICE A** (972)394-1180
1945 Sussex Dr Carrollton TX 75007-2409 • TX • Tchr • Prince Of Peace Carrollton TX • (972)447-9887 • (S 1979)

**MEYER FRED G** (708)409-0693
10700 W Cermak Rd Apt 1 Westchester IL 60154-5231 • NI • EM • (RF 1933 MA)

**MEYER FREDERICK A DR** (314)968-2030
450 Brownbert Ln Saint Louis MO 63119-1324 • MO • EM • (RF 1944 MA PHD)

**MEYER GERHARDT M DR** (360)357-1888
758 Victoria St Costa Mesa CA 92627 • gemgm@aol.com • PSW • Prince Of Peace Carrollton TX • (RF 1963 MA DED)

**MEYER GERHARDT V** (651)484-9616
4285 Virginia Ave Saint Paul MN 55126-2382 • lmeyer@csp.edu • MNS • EM • (S 1947 MS DED)

**MEYER HEATHER N** (303)465-9349
10211 Ura Ln #7-101 Thornton CO 80260 • sahmeyer@yahoo.com • RM • Tchr • Emmaus Denver CO • (303)433-3303 • (S 1997)

**MEYER HERMAN W** (314)892-6908
5012 Cold Springs Ln Saint Louis MO 63128-1803 • pkmeyer@postnet.com • MO • EM • (CQ 1966 MS)

**MEYER JANET C** (512)863-9794
5901 FM 1105 Georgetown TX 78626-9792 • TX • Tchr • Zion Georgetown TX • (512)863-5345 • (S 1968)

**MEYER JENNIFER MARIE** (863)686-5023
321 Imperial Blvd #160P Lakeland FL 33803-4665 • FG • Tchr • St Paul Lakeland FL • (941)644-7710 • (AU 1999)

**MEYER JOANNE C** (203)268-2080
54 Salem Rd Trumbull CT 06611-1224 • delsmeyer@prodigy.net • NE • 11/1995 11/1998 • (RF 1959)

**MEYER JUDITH ANN** (925)924-1317
5740 Belleza Dr Pleasanton CA 94588 • Bakmeyer@aol.com • CNH • P/Tchr • Prince Of Peace Fremont CA • (510)797-8186 • (S 1961)

**MEYER JULIET L** (970)669-5108
1835 Abbey Ct Loveland CO 80538-4352 • mjcr@juno.com • RM • Tchr • Immanuel Loveland CO • (970)667-7606 • (WN 1983)

**MEYER KAREN K** (317)787-0982
2245 Cardinal Dr Indianapolis IN 46227-9503 • IN • P/Tchr • Prince Peace Martinsville IN • (317)342-2004 • (SP 1966 MSED)

**MEYER KARL F** (716)964-7492
2268 Church Rd Hamlin NY 14464-9749 • kfmyr@frontiernet.net • EA • P/Tchr • St John Hamlin NY • (716)964-2550 • (S 1969 MED)

**MEYER KAY E** (214)696-9462
10702 Stone Canyon Rd Apt 228 Dallas TX 75230-5920 • kaymeyer@usa.net • TX • Tchr • Lutheran HS of Dalla Dallas TX • (214)349-8912 • (S 1988 MED)

**MEYER KEVIN E**
709 Karen Ln Horicon WI 53032-1006 • SW • Tchr • St Stephen Horicon WI • (920)485-6687 • (SP 1988)

**MEYER LAURA M** (936)546-7102
207 Pecan Dr Crockett TX 75835 • MO • Tchr • St John Arnold MO • (314)464-0096 • (AU 1996)

**MEYER LOMA R** (651)484-9616
4285 Virginia Ave Saint Paul MN 55126-2382 • lmeyer@csp.edu • MNS • EM • (CQ 1978 MS DED PHD LLD)

**MEYER MARDELLE M** (618)466-3757
7705 Redbird Ln Godfrey IL 62035-2353 • SI • Tchr • Faith Godfrey IL • (618)466-9153 • (SP 1986)

**MEYER MARGARET E** (618)277-8728
405 Windrift Dr Belleville IL 62221 • SI • Tchr • Zion Belleville IL • (618)233-2299 • (CQ 1996)

**MEYER MARY L** (502)429-0055
7519 Greenlawn Louisville KY 40242 • oslcmeyer@aol.com • IN • Prin • Our Savior Louisville KY • (502)426-0864 • (RF 1972 MED)

**MEYER MERLE J** (504)366-8405
652 Oakwood Dr Gretna LA 70056-2933 • SO • Tchr • Salem Gretna LA • (504)367-5144 • (S 1969)

**MEYER MICHAEL J**
Walther Luth High School 900 Chicago Ave Melrose Park IL 60160 • mjmeyer@hs.hkis.edu.hk • NI • Tchr • Northern Illinois Hillside IL • (RF 1965 MA PHD)

**MEYER NEIL H F JR.** (619)258-7337
11028 Collinwood Dr Santee CA 92071-3105 • nhfmjr@aol.com • PSW • Tchr • Pacific Southwest Irvine CA • (949)854-3232 • (CQ 1984 MED)

**MEYER PAULA SUE**
C/O Trinity Lutheran Church 2260 Red Cliff Dr Saint George UT 84790-8153 • RM • Tchr • Trinity St George UT • (435)628-1850 • (SP 1990)

**MEYER PETER JOHN** (219)441-9559
7205 S Hanna Fort Wayne IN 46816 • pjmeyer@fwi.com • IN • Prin • St John Monroeville IN • (219)639-6404 • (RF 1988 MED)

**MEYER REBEKAH ANN** (414)752-0428
2914 1/2 N Main St Racine WI 53402-4204 • SW • Tchr • St John Racine WI • (414)633-2758 • (SP 1994)

**MEYER RICHARD A** (716)694-1861
52 Brundage Ave N Tonawanda NY 14120-1704 • EA • Tchr • St Matthew North Tonawanda NY • (716)692-6862 • (RF 1961 MA)

**MEYER ROGENE GAIL** (208)326-5379
3527 N 2200 E Filer ID 83328-5679 • NOW • Tchr • Clover Trinity Buhl ID • (208)326-5198 • (CQ 1980)

**MEYER RUTH L** (314)968-2030
450 Brownbert Ln Saint Louis MO 63119-1324 • MO • EM • (RF 1945)

**MEYER SETH** (303)469-1785
10211 Ura Lane Thornton CO 80211-6357 • RM • Tchr • Beautiful Savior Broomfield CO • (303)469-2049 • (S 1996)

**MEYER SHIRLEY ANN** (310)833-5660
28004 S Western Ave Unit 319 San Pedro CA 90732-1273 • shirleymeyer@usa.net • PSW • Tchr • Christ Rancho Palos Verdes CA • (310)831-0848 • (S 1965 MED)

**MEYER STACEY L** (402)721-1165
449 E 3rd St Fremont NE 68025 • NEB • Tchr • Trinity Fremont NE • (402)721-5959 • (S 1993)

**MEYER STEPHANIE A** (541)617-1325
1242 NW Elliot Ct Bend OR 97701-5408 • meyerws@bendnet.com • NOW • 07/1990 07/2000 • (S 1984)

**MEYER SUSAN EILEEN** (517)872-1847
4283 Maple St Cass City MI 48726 • MI • Tchr • Zion Harbor Beach MI • (517)479-3615 • (RF 1972)

**MEYER THEODORE H** (219)493-1362
1520 N Park Dr New Haven IN 46774-1720 • IN • EM • (RF 1947)

**MEYER WENDELL N** (262)644-5703
519 Oakview Dr Slinger WI 53086-9593 • SW • EM • (RF 1945 MED)

**MEYER WILFRED**
303 Chestnut St Lockwood MO 65682-9631 • mr.meyer@sedaliastpauls.org • MO • P/Tchr • Immanuel Lockwood MO • (417)232-4530 • (S 1965 MA)

**MEYER WILLIAM C** (402)721-5536
2125 N Main St Fremont NE 68025-2615 • NEB • Prin • Trinity Fremont NE • (402)721-5959 • (S 1980 MED)

**MEYERHOFER NANCY LYNN** (716)693-7253
56 Zimmerman St North Tonawanda NY 14120-4708 • EA • Tchr • St Matthew North Tonawanda NY • (716)692-6862 • (BR 1975)

**MEYERMANN ARMIN W** (314)756-4948
206 Laura St Farmington MO 63640-2826 • MO • EM • (RF 1945 MA)

**MEYERS ANITA G** (616)942-2793
2427 Santigo Ave SE Grand Rapids MI 49546-6740 • MI • Tchr • Our Savior Grand Rapids MI • (616)949-0710 • (RF 1960 MA)

**MEYERS HEIDI** (708)209-3400
4807 Marston Dr Fort Wayne IN 46825 • IN • Tchr • Concordia Fort Wayne IN • (219)426-9922 • (RF 1977 MA)

**MEYERS JAMES H**
4708 Marston Dr Fort wayne IN 46825-5612 • EN • 06/1994 06/2000 • (RF 1986 MA)

**MEYERS LISA H** (517)790-2871
2621 Hemmeter Rd Saginaw MI 48603-3023 • MI • Tchr • Valley Saginaw MI • (517)790-1676 • (S 1987 MAT)

**MEYR CHRISTINE ANN** (314)428-7072
10809 Waycroft Dr Saint Louis MO 63114-1821 • MO • Tchr • Immanuel Olivette MO • (314)993-5004 • (S 1992 MED)

**MEYR DELVIN G** (573)334-9239
1835 Nieman Dr Cape Girardeau MO 63701-2947 • MO • Tchr • Trinity Cape Girardeau MO • (573)334-1068 • (S 1966 MED)

**MEYR DOROTHY R** (573)334-9239
1835 Niemann Dr Cape Girardeau MO 63701-2947 • MO • Tchr • Trinity Cape Girardeau MO • (573)334-1068 • (S 1964)

**MICHAEL PATRICIA M** (616)471-1761
8855 Maplewood Dr Berrien Springs MI 49103-1420 • PM8855@aol.com • MI • Tchr • Trinity Berrien Springs MI • (616)473-1811 • (RF 1968)

**MICHALK DAWN ANNETTE**
1410 Ashley Dr Nolanville TX 76559-4503 • TX • Tchr • Grace Killeen TX • (254)634-4424 • (AU 1996)

**MICHALK MELISSA ANN** (813)681-5992
10514 Salisbury St Riverview FL 33569 • mmichal1@tampabay.rr.com • FG • 08/1998 08/2000 • (AU 1996)

**MICHALK TERRI S** (254)547-3495
905B North Dr Copperas Cove TX 76522 • TX • Tchr • Grace Killeen TX • (254)634-4424 • (AU 1998)

**MICHEL KAROLE ANN** (406)652-2048
2805 Lewis Ave Billings MT 59102-3718 • MT • 06/1984 06/1999 • (S 1982 MA)

**MICHEL SUSAN JANE** (715)675-7143
1608 Woodland Ridge Rd Wausau WI 54403 • gsmichel@worldnet.att.net • NW • 11/1998 • (RF 1993)

**MICHELS BETTY J** (414)353-5370
6333 W Boehlke Ave Milwaukee WI 53223-5412 • SW • 08/2000 • (S 1965)

**MICHELS GERALD L** (414)353-5370
6333 W Boehlke Ave Milwaukee WI 53223-5412 • SW • Tchr • St Peter Milwaukee WI • (414)353-6800 • (S 1968 MA)

**MICKLEY RALPH E** (309)353-9529
2409 Montecello Ct Pekin IL 61554 • rmickley@bitwisesystems.com • CI • P/Tchr • Good Shepherd Pekin IL • (309)347-2020 • (RF 1968 MA)

**MIDDAUGH BARBARA A** (219)546-4869
305 S Liberty Dr Bremen IN 46506-1248 • IN • Tchr • St Paul Bremen IN • (219)546-2790 • (RF 1973 MS)

**MIDDELDORF CARL W** (810)776-5818
15105 Charles R Ave Eastpointe MI 48021-1550 • oldmid@aol.com • MI • EM • (RF 1948 MS)

**MIDDLETON MARY P** (973)770-0667
46 Condict Rd Landing NJ 07850-1643 • rcmidd@cybernex.net • NJ • 04/1998 04/2000 • (BR 1980)

**MIELKE DOLORES** (402)643-3262
228 Hillcrest Ct Seward NE 68434-1253 • NEB • EM • (RF 1951 MA)

**MIELKE JON A** (414)377-6610
W76N7182 Linden St Cedarburg WI 53012 • SW • P/Tchr • First Immanuel Cedarburg WI • (262)377-6610 • (RF 1979 MA)

**MIELKE JUDY M** (414)377-9569
N76W7182 Linden St Cedarburg WI 53012-1116 • SW • Tchr • First Immanuel Cedarburg WI • (262)377-6610 • (RF 1979)

**MIELKE KAREN J** (847)358-4429
833 E Kings Row #4 Palatine IL 60074-1874 • NI • Tchr • St Peter Arlington Heights IL • (847)253-6638 • (RF 1970 MA)

**MIELKE SHELLEY LYN** (219)293-1481
1901 Aspin Dr Elkhart IN 46514-1401 • MO • Tchr • St John Arnold MO • (314)464-0096 • (RF 1995)

**MIEROW DOUGLAS A**
C/O Cannon Valley Luth HS 406 W Franklin Morristown MN 55052-0346 • MNS • Tchr • Cannon Valley LHS Morristown MN • (507)685-2636 • (SP 1971)

**MIEROW JOHN E** (414)536-9626
3847 N 101st St Wauwatosa WI 53222-2310 • ofls@aol.com • SW • P/Tchr • Our Father Greenfield WI • (414)282-7500 • (S 1975 MS)

**MIESNER SUSAN B** (817)921-9765
2513 Highview Ter Fort Worth TX 76109-1037 • TX • Tchr • St Paul Fort Worth TX • (817)332-4563 • (S 1974)

**MIESNER TIMOTHY G** (817)921-9765
2513 Highview Ter Fort Worth TX 76109-1037 • miesner5@flash.net • TX • Mem C • St Paul Fort Worth TX • (817)332-2281 • (S 1974 MED)

**MIESSLER MARK L** (850)784-3014
4905 S Lakewood Dr Panama City FL 32404 • SO • Prin • Good Shepherd Panama City FL • (850)871-6311 • (RF 1986)

**MIESSLER MERWYN L** (979)836-6975
1703 Westwind Brenham TX 77833-4757 • mndmiessler@webtv.net • TX • Tchr • Grace Brenham TX • (409)836-2030 • (RF 1961 MMU)

**MIETZNER REBECCA ANN** (920)954-0254
434 Apple Creek Rd Appleton WI 54913 • dmietzner@aol.com • NW • 03/1993 03/2000 • (RF 1979)

**MIHM SUSAN VICTORIA** (217)355-5024
3305 Timberline Dr Champaign IL 61821-1836 • CI • Tchr • St John Champaign IL • (217)359-1714 • (RF 1988)

**MIKESELL DONNA LEE** (309)829-9848
1315 E Washington St Bloomington IL 61701-4228 • dmikesel@gte.net • CI • Tchr • Trinity Bloomington IL • (309)829-7513 • (CQ 1992)

**MILAM MARCIA A** (513)271-2214
3820 Miami Rd #3 Cincinnati OH 45227-4339 • marciaam@aol.com • OH • Tchr • St Paul Cincinnati OH • (513)271-8266 • (MQ 1997)

**MILAS MARTHA JANE** (217)359-5630
1109 Foothill Dr Champaign IL 61821 • mmilas@prairienet.org • CI • Tchr • St John Champaign IL • (217)359-1714 • (RF 1979)

**MILBRATH JUDITH L** (414)466-1302
4152 Glenway St Wauwatosa WI 53222-1116 • mmilbrat@execpc.com • SW • Tchr • Northwest Milwaukee WI • (414)463-4040 • (RF 1969)

**MILDRED ERIKA E**
2331 St Marks Way Sacramento CA 95864 • CNH • Tchr • Calif/Nevada/Hawaii San Francisco CA • (415)468-2336 • (RF 1999)

**MILES BARBARA A** (716)694-5838
1124 Niagara Falls Blvd North Tonawanda NY 14120-1224 • EA • Tchr • St John North Tonawanda NY • (716)693-9677 • (CQ 1997 MS)

**MILES ROBERT G** (517)892-6635
705 Park Ave Bay City MI 48708-6861 • rmiles@lcfsmi.org • MI • Michigan Ann Arbor MI • (RF 1965 MS)

**MILES SHARON R** (503)289-5357
7313 N Washburne Ave Portland OR 97217-5859 • snoopy1@teleport.com • NOW • Tchr • Trinity Portland OR • (503)288-6403 • (RF 1968)

**MILITELLO BRITTNEY A** (708)583-2082
2516 N Wood St River Grove IL 60171-1615 • mili@worldskyline.com • NI • Tchr • Bethlehem River Grove IL • (708)456-8786 • (RF 1993)

**MILLER BARBARA L** (414)771-4245
2252 N 104th St Wauwatosa WI 53226-2422 • SW • Tchr • Zion Menomonee Falls WI • (414)781-7437 • (RF 1987)

**MILLER CAROLINE LOUISE** (262)637-9547
3716 Washington Ave #1 Racine WI 53405 • SW • Tchr • Concordia Racine WI • (262)554-1659 • (MQ 1999)

**MILLER CARRIE LYNN** (414)771-4245
2252 N 104th St Wauwatosa WI 53226-2422 • clmdopey@aol.com • SW • Tchr • Mount Calvary Milwaukee WI • (414)873-3466 • (MQ 1996)

**MILLER CHRISTINE E** 219-226-0226
1233 W 95th Ave Crown Point IN 46307-6255 • pepsiamigo@aol.com • IN • Tchr • Trinity Crown Point IN • (219)663-1586 • (RF 1996)

**MILLER CHRISTOPHER JAMES**
2929 Columbia Rd Westlake OH 44145 • OH • Tchr • LHS West Rocky River OH • (440)333-1660 • (CQ 1998)

**MILLER CINDY** (210)647-7313
6327 Maverick Oak Dr San Antonio TX 78240-2672 • TX • Tchr • Shepherd Hills San Antonio TX • (210)614-3742 • (AU 1982)

**MILLER CORWIN L** (303)241-5860
1515 N 18th St Grand Jct CO 81501-6601 • RM • Tchr • Messiah Grand Junction CO • (970)245-2838 • (S 1975 MA MED)

**MILLER DEBORAH L** (219)639-6480
11827 Hoagland Rd Hoagland IN 46745-9554 • IN • Tchr • Concordia Fort Wayne IN • (219)422-2429 • (S 1974)

**MILLER DUANE E** (414)461-0639
4243 N 63rd St Milwaukee WI 53216-1242 • demiller@execpc.com • SW • P/Tchr • Mount Calvary Milwaukee WI • (414)873-3466 • (S 1970 MA)

**MILLER EUNICE A** (219)465-7458
1504 Del Vista Dr Valparaiso IN 46385 • IN • Tchr • Immanuel Valparaiso IN • (219)462-8207 • (RF 1964 MED)

**MILLER GRACE E** (303)221-6052
4982 S Ulster St #602 Denver CO 80237 • dale.l.miller@worldnet.att.net • RM • Tchr • Shepherd Hills Littleton CO • (303)798-0711 • (RF 1962)

**MILLER HERMAN F**
4309 SE First Ave Cape Coral FL 33904 • MI • EM • (RF 1940 MA)

**MILLER JAMES L** (414)453-4576
2746 N 83rd St Milwaukee WI 53222-4820 • imcman@execpc.com • SW • Tchr • Martin LHS Greendale WI • (414)421-4000 • (SP 1971 MA MS)

**MILLER JAMES M** (636)349-2931
1806 Colina Tierra Ln Fenton MO 63026-6316 • MO • S Ex/S • Missouri Saint Louis MO • (314)317-4550 • (S 1974)

**MILLER JANE ANN** (630)551-1845
2100 Light Rd Apt 205 Oswego IL 60543-9362 • teach17@ix.netcom.com • NI • Tchr • St Paul Aurora IL • (630)820-3457 • (CQ 1986)

**MILLER JANE R** (757)857-4846
3736 Henrico St Norfolk VA 23513-4123 • SE • Tchr • Trinity Norfolk VA • (757)489-2732 • (RF 1959)

**MILLER JASON THOMAS** (773)799-2139
8814 N Grace Niles IL 60714 • NI • Tchr • St Philip Chicago IL • (773)561-9830 • (MQ 1997)

**MILLER JENNIFER ANNE** (314)781-5835
7380 Dale Apt 3 Richmond Heights MO 63117-2262 • oczepek@yahoo.com • MO • Tchr • Grace Chapel Bellefontaine Nbrs MO • (314)867-6564 • (AA 1998)

**MILLER JOANNE MARGARET** (231)592-4986
21545 University Dr Big Rapids MI 49307 • jimjo@net-port.com • MI • Tchr • St Peter Big Rapids MI • (231)796-6684 • (AA 1988 MED)

**MILLER JOHN WALTER**
2108 Crimson Oaks Ct Saint Louis MO 63129-4371 • jmjazz@worldnet.att.net • MO • Tchr • LHS South Saint Louis MO • (314)631-1400 • (RF 1976 MMU)

**MILLER JULIA A** (801)776-4616
2576 W 4850 S Roy UT 84067-1720 • RM • Tchr • St Paul Ogden UT • (801)392-6368 • (SP 1981)

**MILLER KRISTIN ANN** (216)254-3508
7296 Callow Rd Leroy OH 44077 • OH • Tchr • Our Shepherd Painesville OH • (440)357-7776 • (RF 1990)

**MILLER LA MAR JR.** (310)946-5219
13644 Allegan St Whittier CA 90605-3423 • PSW • Prin • Holy Cross Cypress CA • (714)527-7225 • (S 1978 MA)

**MILLER LAWREN L** (925)846-1248
4547 El Dorado Ct Pleasanton CA 94566-4636 • cooter@home.com • CNH • Prin • Our Savior Livermore CA • (925)447-2082 • (S 1973 MS)

**MILLER LESLIE J** (314)467-2308
1793 Woodwind Dr Imperial MO 63052-1561 • MO • Tchr • St John Arnold MO • (314)464-0096 • (S 1974 MED)

**MILLER LINDA E** (512)647-0238
5900 Wurzbach Rd Apt 108 San Antonio TX 78238-1721 • TX • Tchr • Shepherd Of The Hill San Antonio TX • (210)614-3741 • (RF 1982)

**MILLER LISA MARIE** (651)766-5163
961 E Cty Rd D#104 Varneis Hts MN 55109 • MNS • Tchr • S Shore Trinity White Bear Lake MN • (612)429-4293 • (SP 1995)

**MILLER LLOYD L** (316)221-9189
501 College St Winfield KS 67156-2417 • KS • EM • (CQ 1967 MS)

**MILLER MICHAEL A** (210)647-7313
6327 Maverick Oak Dr San Antonio TX 78240-2672 • mamiller98@yahoo.com • TX • Prin • LHS Of San Antonio San Antonio TX • (210)733-7771 • (CQ 1997 MSED)

**MILLER NIKELLE MARIE**
2055 Stonefield Dr Glendale Heights IL 60139-1865 • dnzmiller3@aol.com • NI • Tchr • Walther LHS Melrose Park IL • (708)344-0404 • (RF 1995)

**MILLER NORMAN R** (920)749-4992
1707 S Nicolet Rd Apt 7 Appleton WI 54915-7543 • normanmiller@aal.org • PSW • 09/1995 09/1997 • (S 1962 MED)

**MILLER PAMELA S** (636)467-2308
1793 Woodwind Dr Imperial MO 63052-1561 • milltownteach@altavista.net • MO • 11/1998 • (S 1974)

**MILLER PAUL M** (618)635-2964
218 W Mill St Staunton IL 62088-1825 • zionstau@midwest.net • SI • P/Tchr • Zion Staunton IL • (618)635-3060 • (CQ 1978 MA)

**MILLER PAULINE RUTH** (281)255-8735
30931 Ulrich Rd Tomball TX 77375-2904 • TX • Tchr • Salem Tomball TX • (281)351-8122 • (S 1962 MRE)

**MILLER PERRY M** (281)257-2721
8227 Amurwood Dr Tomball TX 77375-2809 • perrycubmiller@hotmail.com • TX • Tchr • Salem Tomball TX • (281)351-8122 • (IV 1989)

**MILLER RACHEL E** (618)473-2641
9441 Trappers Creek Dr Red Bud IL 62278-3361 • SI • Tchr • Good Shepherd Collinsville IL • (618)344-3151 • (RF 1988)

**MILLER RICHARD J** (312)286-4211
5720 W Sunnyside Ave Chicago IL 60630-3337 • NI • SHS/C • Northern Illinois Hillside IL • (RF 1966 MS)

**MILLER SHERYL J** (636)349-2931
1806 Colina Tierra Ln Fenton MO 63026-6316 • MO • Tchr • Our Savior Fenton MO • (314)343-7511 • (S 1974)

**MILLER TAMMY L** (248)674-4958
3923 Reseda Rd Waterford MI 48329-2558 • MI • Mem C • St Stephen Waterford MI • (248)673-6621 • (AA 1986)

**MILLER TERRY W** (801)776-4616
2576 W 4850 S Roy UT 84067-1720 • RM • Tchr • St Paul Ogden UT • (801)392-2912 • (SP 1980)

**MILLEVILLE JUDY A** (618)483-5308
3512 E 900th Ave Altamont IL 62411 • CI • Tchr • Altamont Altamont IL • (618)483-6428 • (CQ 1996)

**MILLS ELAINE E** (650)875-7754
1126 Cherry Ave #89 San Bruno CA 94066 • EN • Tchr • West Portal San Francisco CA • (415)665-6330 • (CQ 1994)

**MILNIKEL BRIAN KEITH** (630)295-8215
317 Catalpa Ave Roselle IL 60172 • bmilnikel@amerilink.net • NI • Mem C • Trinity Roselle IL • (630)894-3263 • (AA 1987 MA)

**MILNIKEL JENIFER J** (616)429-0475
2837 Washington Ave Saint Joseph MI 49085-3132 • jmilnike@prodigy.net • MI • Tchr • Trinity Saint Joseph MI • (616)983-3056 • (SP 1973 MA)

**MILOSCH DANIEL P** (907)337-1541
401 Capricorn Cir Anchorage AK 99508-2570 • NOW • Tchr • Anchor Anchorage AK • (907)522-3636 • (RF 1974 MA)

**MILZ AMY E**
370 Woodside Ct Apt 34 Rochester Hills MI 48307-4176 • MI • Tchr • St John Rochester MI • (248)652-8830 • (AA 1987)

**MILZ CHARLENE K** (209)369-1495
446 Madrone Ct Lodi CA 95242 • ramanamaz@aol.com • CNH • Tchr • Prince Peace Fremont CA • (510)793-3366 • (CQ 1983)

**MILZ NORMAN W** (209)369-1495
446 Madrone Ct Lodi CA 95242 • ramanama@aol.com • CNH • Mem C • St Peter Lodi CA • (209)333-2223 • (S 1975 MMU)

**MINDA KEITH A** (517)799-3308
2606 Blackmore St Saginaw MI 48602-3552 • MI • Tchr • Peace Saginaw MI • (517)792-2581 • (S 1976 MED)

**MINNER BOBBY B** (925)709-2889
2004 Rapallo Way Bay Point CA 94565 • CNH • P/Tchr • First Concord CA • (925)671-9717 • (S 1972 MEAD)

**MINNICK DEBORAH E** (708)506-9196
207 Monterey Elmhurst IL 60126 • deborahem@aol.com • NI • Tchr • St Peter Schaumburg IL • (847)885-7636 • (RF 1975)

**MIRANDA TRACY O**
1994 Somerset Dr Romeoville IL 60446 • NI • Tchr • St John Forest Park IL • (708)366-3226 • (SP 1995)

**MIRLY LISA LYNNE*** (573)243-6182
602 Randy Dr Jackson MO 63755-1272 • SI • Tchr • St John Chester IL • (618)826-3545 • (RF 1985)

**MIRLY TIMOTHY S** (314)243-6182
602 Randy Dr Jackson MO 63755-1272 • spscc@ldd.net • MO • Mem C • St Paul Jackson MO • (573)243-2236 • (RF 1987)

**MISCHNICK MARJORIE E** (715)877-2046
E19775 State Rd # 27 Fall Creek WI 54742-5200 • markmarj1@juno.com • NW • 07/1997 • (S 1972)

**MISCHNICK WALTER T** (813)672-8739
10314 Ashley Oaks Dr Riverview FL 33569-8842 • lead1221@prodigy.net • FG • Prin • Immanuel Brandon FL • (813)685-1978 • (RF 1972 MA)

**MISKE SHIRLEY J DR** (651)415-9715
2838 Lakeview Ave Saint Paul MN 55113-2033 • shirleym@minn.net • SI • 09/1997 09/1999 • (RF 1976 MA PHD)

**MISKIMEN BETHANY ANN** (217)268-4814
904 W Seminary St Onarga IL 60955-1401 • miski@n2.com • CI • Tchr • St John Buckley IL • (217)394-2422 • (MQ 1994)

**MISKIMEN DAVID MATTHEW** (217)394-2547
904 W Seminary Ave Onarga IL 60955 • miski@n2.com • CI • Tchr • Christ Lhs Buckley IL • (217)394-2547 • (MQ 1994)

**MISKIMEN GRACE V** (414)438-0711
3534 N 78th St Milwaukee WI 53222-3014 • EN • Tchr • Hales Corners Hales Corners WI • (414)529-6700 • (S 1962)

**MISKIMEN HARVEY D** (414)438-0711
3534 N 78th St Milwaukee WI 53222-3014 • miskco@msn.com • SW • Tchr • Immanuel Brookfield WI • (414)781-4135 • (S 1962)

**MITCHELL JOEL DANIEL** (713)773-3729
6500 Harbor Town Dr Apt 3211 Houston TX 77036-4059 • jdmitch@flash.net • TX • Tchr • Pilgrim Houston TX • (713)666-3706 • (AU 1995)

**MITTEIS KELLY GENE** (618)346-1103
403 South St Collinsville IL 62234-2621 • SI • 08/1999 • (S 1978)

**MITTEIS MARY ANN** (618)346-1103
403 South St Collinsville IL 62234-2621 • SI • Tchr • Holy Cross Collinsville IL • (618)344-3145 • (IV 1985)

**MITTELSTAEDT SUSAN ANN** (219)747-4478
2005 Woodhaven Dr Apt 5 Fort Wayne IN 46819-1042 • IN • Tchr • Mount Calvary Fort Wayne IN • (219)747-4121 • (S 1977 MED)

**MOBLEY PAMELA G** (407)277-4080
11059 Fairhaven Way Orlando FL 32825-7111 • pgmobley@prodigy.net • FG • Tchr • Orlando Lutheran Aca Orlando FL • (407)275-7750 • (S 1973)

**MOCK HERBERT J** (513)644-0112
17780 Timber Ln Marysville OH 43040-9017 • OH • P/Tchr • St John Marysville OH • (937)644-5540 • (SP 1970 MA)

**MOCKLER GAYE L** (805)238-0335
C/O Trinity Lutheran Church 940 Creston Rd Paso Robles CA 93446-3002 • CNH • Tchr • Trinity Paso Robles CA • (805)238-0335 • (S 1986)

**MODEROW LEROY E** (708)543-9433
26 N School St Addison IL 60101-3548 • leemod@aol.com • NI • EM • (S 1943)

**MOE JANICE RUTH** (218)624-9310
314 N 43rd Ave W Duluth MN 55807 • duluthmoe@aol.com • MNN • 07/2000 • (SP 1986)

**MOEDE DOROTHY J** (920)842-2682
10638 S Branch Rd Suring WI 54174-9734 • NW • Tchr • St Paul Bonduel WI • (715)758-8532 • (S 1980)

**MOEHLE SHARILYN ROSE** (618)633-2413
9143 Trio Ln Edwardsville IL 62025 • SI • Tchr • Zion Staunton IL • (618)635-3060 • (RF 1966 MA)

**MOEHLENKAMP MARILYN** (708)453-2654
2817 N 73rd Ave Elmwood Park IL 60707-1516 • NI • SHS/C • Northern Illinois Hillside IL • (S 1969 MSCT PHD)

**MOEHRING DAVID PAUL** (440)835-8651
2035 Salem Parkway Westlake OH 44145-3350 • dmoehring@netzero.net • OH • P/Tchr • St Thomas Rocky River OH • (440)331-4426 • (RF 1973 MED MED)

**MOEHRING JUDITH A** (219)724-7552
1034 E 1100 N Decatur IN 46733-8407 • IN • Tchr • Bethlehem Ossian IN • (219)597-7366 • (RF 1978)

**MOEHRING MARY M** (440)835-8651
2035 Salem Pkwy Westlake OH 44145-3350 • OH • 09/1998 • (S 1974 MAT)

**MOELLER AMY L** (630)351-5322
520 Dover Dr Roselle IL 60172-2611 • moellera@trinityroselle.com • NI • Tchr • Trinity Roselle IL • (630)894-3263 • (RF 1978 MA)

**MOELLER BONNIE JEAN** (503)357-5149
4018 19th Ave Forest Grove OR 97116-2204 • loubon@aracnet.com • NOW • Tchr • Forest Hills Cornelius OR • (503)359-4853 • (S 1991)

**MOELLER JANET KAY** (515)432-8558
404 11th St Boone IA 50036-2015 • IW • Tchr • Trinity Boone IA • (515)432-6912 • (RF 1975)

**MOELLER JANET KRISTIN** (503)656-5975
PO Box 725 Gladstone OR 97027-0725 • teacher@teleport.com • NOW • 08/1997 08/2000 • (PO 1993 MSED)

**MOELLER LESLIE A** (813)752-4621
1432 Plantation Cir #1915 Plant City FL 33567 • FG • Tchr • Hope Plant City FL • (813)752-4622 • (MQ 1997)

**MOELLER MARCY JEAN** (619)660-9698
10635 Itzamna Rd La Mesa CA 91941-7113 • PSW • Tchr • Christ La Mesa CA • (619)462-5211 • (S 1968 MA)

**MOELLER RANDALL J** (636)349-9458
842 San Sebastian Dr Fenton MO 63026-3035 • rmoe854182@aol.com • MO • Our Savior Fenton MO • (636)343-2192 • (RF 1974 MAT)

**MOELLERING DIANNE** (219)483-3281
4318 Lynwood Ct Fort Wayne IN 46815-6965 • dmoellering@chnet.com • IN • Tchr • Concordia LHS Fort Wayne IN • (219)483-1102 • (S 1972 MED)

**MOELLERING THOMAS P** (219)483-3281
4318 Lynwood Ct Fort Wayne IN 46815-6965 • IN • Tchr • Central New Haven IN • (219)493-2502 • (S 1972)

**MOERBE SUSAN LYNN** (361)584-2064
803 E Henderson St Bishop TX 78343-2907 • TX • P/Tchr • St Paul Bishop TX • (512)584-2778 • (S 1974 MED)

**MOERER LUCILLE P**
1260 Marseille Ct Rochester Hills MI 48307-3035 • MI • Tchr • St John Rochester MI • (248)652-8830 • (S 1970 MA)

**MOERMOND ELIZABETH JULIE**
6211 High Country Dr NE Cedar Rapids IA 52411-7719 • IN • Tchr • Zion Fort Wayne IN • (219)744-1389 • (MQ 1997)

**MOESCH JASON ROGER** (414)466-8568
5122 N 106th St Milwaukee WI 53225-3929 • SW • Tchr • Milwaukee LHS Milwaukee WI • (414)461-6000 • (MQ 1993)

**MOHLENHOFF RICHARD W** (810)465-2645
37893 Rosedale Dr Clinton Twp MI 48036-2296 • MI • Tchr • Bethlehem Roseville MI • (810)777-9130 • (RF 1960 MA)

**MOHLENHOFF WILLIAM H** (517)782-1888
1111 Park Rd Jackson MI 49203-5066 • MI • Tchr • Trinity Jackson MI • (517)750-2105 • (RF 1967 MS)

**MOHLER DAVID G** (712)263-4144
The Park Motel 803 4th Ave S Apt 45 Denison IA 51442 • IW • Tchr • Zion Denison IA • (712)263-4766 • (RF 1963)

**MOHR LYNN C** (909)737-5279
403 Termino St Corona CA 92879-1129 • PSW • Tchr • Grace Corona CA • (909)737-2187 • (S 1963)

**MOHR RENITA A** (217)224-2124
2629 Rogers Ct Quincy IL 62301-6356 • drmamam4@adams.net • CI • Tchr • St James Quincy IL • (217)222-8447 • (RF 1983)

**MOHR RHONDA J*** (712)653-2887
904 Nishnabotna Dr Manning IA 51455 • IW • P/Tchr • Zion Denison IA • (712)263-2235 • (S 1986)

**MOILANEN KAREN K** (517)787-2274
2012 Forest Park Dr Jackson MI 49201-8306 • moilanen@dmci.net • MI • Tchr • Trinity Jackson MI • (517)750-2105 • (CQ 1999)

**MOLDENHAUER DONNA L** (217)438-3872
415 Pine View Dr Auburn IL 62615 • CI • Tchr • St James Quincy IL • (217)222-8447 • (RF 1995)

**MOLDENHAUER HERBERT C** (810)772-5627
15551 N Park Ave Eastpointe MI 48021-1630 • MI • EM • (RF 1945 MA LLD)

**MOLIN DOUGLAS C** (504)764-4350
408 Longwood Dr Destrehan LA 70047 • dmolin@alcs.org • SO • Prin • Atonement Metairie LA • (504)887-0225 • (SP 1982 MA)

**MOLL MARION C** (860)589-0897
65 Ridgecrest Ln Bristol CT 06010-2910 • marion.moll@snet.net • NE • Tchr • Immanuel Bristol CT • (860)583-5631 • (S 1967 MA MS)

**MOLL PATRICIA J** (860)589-0897
65 Ridgecrest Ln Bristol CT 06010-2910 • NE • Tchr • Immanuel Bristol CT • (860)583-5631 • (S 1967)

**MONDRAGON VIRGINIA I** (310)548-4583
28605 Vista Madera Rancho Palos Verdes CA 90275-0866 • PSW • Tchr • Christ Rancho Palos Verdes CA • (310)831-0848 • (S 1975 MED)

**MONFRE SUSAN E** (414)427-9120
14225 W North Oak Blvd New Berlin WI 53151-7469 • EN • Tchr • Hales Corners Hales Corners WI • (414)529-6700 • (RF 1979)

**MONROE AMY**
C/O Saint Peter Lutheran 208 E Schaumburg Rd Schaumburg IL 60194-3517 • NI • Tchr • St Peter Schaumburg IL • (847)885-3350 • (RF 2000)

**MONROE KELLY MARIE** (313)773-7781
30210 Gloria St St Clair Shores MI 48082-1685 • MI • 06/1999 • (AA 1990)

**MONSON BETTY L** (970)352-2648
3837 8th St Greeley CO 80634-1527 • gmonson@netzero.net • RM • Tchr • Trinity Greeley CO • (970)330-1203 • (S 1973)

**MONSON KATHRYN P** (507)834-6356
63885 290th St PO Box 497 Gibbon MN 55335-0497 • MNS • 08/2000 • (S 1972)

**MONTAG MARY JEAN** (412)352-9235
139 Keck Rd Sarver PA 16055-8512 • EA • Tchr • St Luke Cabot PA • (412)352-2221 • (RF 1972)

**MOODIE KEITH E** (801)266-9793
557 Virginia St Murray UT 84107 • RM • Tchr • Christ Murray UT • (801)262-4354 • (S 1977)

**MOODY CARL A** (408)257-1807
1087 Avondale St San Jose CA 95129-2804 • CNH • P/Tchr • School Of Our Savior Cupertino CA • (408)252-0250 • (S 1968)

**MOODY JANE AUGUSTA** (978)887-9171
11 Andrews Farm Rd Boxford MA 01921-2652 • jane³moody@harvard.edu • NE • 06/1989 02/2000 • (RF 1961 MA)

**MOODY JENNIFER C** (703)960-4266
5614 Hill Ct Alexandria VA 22303 • AT • Tchr • Chapel Redeemer Flushing NY • (718)465-4236 • (BR 1989)

**MOODY WANDA EILEEN** (210)657-4201
10327 Luzon Dr San Antonio TX 78217-3917 • TX • Tchr • Concordia San Antonio TX • (210)479-1477 • (CQ 1995)

**MOON RODNEY C** (715)823-5686
119 Bellevue St Embarrass WI 54933 • NW • Tchr • St Martin Clintonville WI • (715)823-6538 • (MQ 1987)

**MOONEY TERRY M** (309)697-2514
11 Stahl Pl Bartonville IL 61607-1868 • CI • P/Tchr • Christ Peoria IL • (309)637-1512 • (S 1978 MSED)

**MOORE BONNIE KAY** (806)354-9463
7311 Calumet Pl Amarillo TX 79121-1401 • TX • Tchr • Trinity Amarillo TX • (806)352-5620 • (AU 1988)

**MOORE DAWN MARIE** (920)687-0943
W2531 Block Rd Appleton WI 54915-9471 • NW • 08/1996 08/2000 • (MQ 1994)

**MOORE GEORGE T**
3111 Hillside Dr Burlingame CA 94010-5911 • EN • Tchr • West Portal San Francisco CA • (415)665-6330 • (RF 1978)

**MOORE KATHERINE L**
10574 Sunland Blvd Apt 7 Sunland CA 91040-1960 • PSW • Tchr • Our Savior First Granada Hills CA • (818)368-0892 • (SP 1983)

**MOORE KATHLEEN DOROTHY** (715)834-4028
413 Twin Oak Altoona WI 54720 • NW • Mem C • St Matthew Eau Claire WI • (715)834-4028 • (SP 1981 MED)

**MOORE KIMBERLY A**
Calvary Luth Church 6111 Shelby St Indianapolis IN 46227-4879 • IN • Tchr • Calvary Indianapolis IN • (317)783-2305 • (S 1985)

**MOORE KRISTA R** (503)249-1597
6636 NE 27th Ave Portland OR 97211-6071 • moorzy6@hotmail.com • PSW • 05/2000 • (PO 1996)

**MOORE LINDA M** (309)266-9409
545 Taylor St Morton IL 61550-1763 • lmcmc@mtco.com • CI • Tchr • Bethel Morton IL • (309)266-6592 • (S 1974)

**MOORE LISA M**
C/O Holy Cross Lutheran 304 South St Collinsville IL 62234 • lrmoore856@aol.com • SI • Tchr • Holy Cross Collinsville IL • (618)344-3145 • (RF 1978)

**MOORE NORMA L*** (901)661-0138
164 Channing Way Jackson TN 38305-1747 • EN • 04/1992 06/2000 • (S 1964 MLS)

**MOORE PAMELA J** (562)946-0660
12914 Biola Ave La Mirada CA 90638-2103 • ermoore@prodigy.net • PSW • Tchr • Zion Glendale CA • (818)243-3119 • (IV 1988)

**MOORE DURKIN MARY T** (262)532-0259
W169 N8924 Hoyt Dr Apt 3 Menomonee Falls WI 53051-2052 • durkins975@prodijy.net • SW • Tchr • Trinity Mequon WI • (262)242-2045 • (RF 1998)

**MOORMAN COLLEEN** (501)312-9790
11404 Hickory Hill Rd Little Rock AR 72211 • MDS • Tchr • Grace Little Rock AR • (501)663-3631 • (CQ 1999)

**MORAN MARK A** (920)989-2205
PO Box 114 Forest Junction WI 54123-0114 • bugsymoran@yahoo.com • NW • P/Tchr • Zion Of Wayside Greenleaf WI • (414)864-2468 • (MQ 1987)

**MORAVEC ALAN M** (312)767-1034
3728 W 82nd Pl Chicago IL 60652-2408 • katmora@aol.com • NI • Tchr • Luther HS South Chicago IL • (773)737-1416 • (S 1986 MA)

**MORAVEC KATHLEEN M** (773)767-1034
3728 W 82nd Pl Chicago IL 60652-2408 • katmora@aol.com • NI • Tchr • St Paul Oak Lawn IL • (708)423-1040 • (RF 1979)

**MORENO LISA MARIE**
C/O Pilgrim Lutheran Church 497 E St Chula Vista CA 92010-2445 • PSW • St Paul Oak Lawn IL • (S 1989)

**MORGAN AMY COLLEEN** (217)522-3454
2604 S Lowell Ave Springfield IL 62704-5116 • CI • Tchr • Our Savior's Springfield IL • (217)546-4531 • (RF 1996)

**MORGAN BEATRICE B** (305)893-9011
132 Almond Rd Ocala FL 34472-8636 • FG • 09/1998 • (RF 1990)

**MORGENTHALER SHIRLEY K DR** (708)246-2759
512 Rugeley Rd Western Springs IL 60558-1959 • morgensk@crf.cuis.edu • NI • SHS/C • Northern Illinois Hillside IL • (RF 1959 MED PHD)

**MORIARITY LINDA R** (602)846-9558
3608 E Renee Dr Phoenix AZ 85024-6358 • PSW • 09/1999 • (RF 1970 MA)

**MORITZ JOEL WILLIAM**
618 Ferdinand Ave Apt #1 Forest Park IL 60130 • NI • SHS/C • Northern Illinois Hillside IL • (RF 1996)

**MORITZ LORELLE R** (309)676-4609
1111 W Brookforest Peoria IL 61615-1077 • CI • 04/2000 • (RF 1968)

**MORKERT CHRISTOPHER ALAN** (630)553-1210
404 W Van Emmon St Yorkville IL 60560-1454 • NI • Tchr • Cross Yorkville IL • (630)553-7861 • (RF 1992)

**MORKERT DAVID L** (423)499-9759
6804 Cedar Wood Ct Chattanooga TN 37412-4057 • dmorkert@aol.com • MDS • Tchr • Lutheran Chattanooga TN • (423)622-3755 • (S 1964)

**MORKERT MICHAEL D**
724 N Sherman St Aurora IL 60505 • NI • Tchr • St Paul Aurora IL • (630)820-3450 • (S 1973 MA MMU)

**MORNER DONALD E** (714)544-6367
1281 Mitchell Ave Tustin CA 92780-5744 • PSW • EM • (S 1956 MAR MAR)

**MORNER LEAH M** (714)771-2117
921 Grovemont St Santa Ana CA 92706-2045 • morner@juno.com • PSW • Tchr • Prince Of Peace Anaheim CA • (714)774-0993 • (IV 1986)

**MORNER TIMOTHY S** (714)771-2117
921 Grovemont St Santa Ana CA 92706-2045 • morner@juno.com • PSW • Tchr • Trinity Santa Ana CA • (714)543-0341 • (IV 1987 MED)

**MORO MARTIN LOUIS III** (734)722-0431
37729 Hillcrest Dr Wayne MI 48184-1055 • MI • Tchr • Detroit Urban Detroit MI • (313)582-9900 • (S 1981 MSED)

**MORRIS CHRISTINE M** (817)481-3272
2930 Creekwood Dr S Grapevine TX 76051-5664 • srmorris@sprynet.com • TX • Tchr • Lutheran HS of Dalla Dallas TX • (214)349-8912 • (S 1988)

**MORRIS WENDY E** (770)920-8425
3488 Willow Tree Cir Douglasville GA 30135-2994 • stlrams3@aol.com • FG • Tchr • Christ East Point GA • (404)767-2892 • (RF 1989 MA)

**MORRISON BARBARA J** (217)394-2373
PO Box 234 Buckley IL 60918-0234 • CI • Tchr • St John Buckley IL • (217)394-2422 • (CQ 1997)

**MORRISON FAITH ANN** (214)827-7812
C/O Zion Lutheran School 6121 E Lovers Ln Dallas TX 75214-2088 • TX • Tchr • Zion Dallas TX • (214)363-1630 • (RF 1972)

**MORRISON JANET L** (216)884-7730
3385 Sunhaven Oval Parma OH 44134-5836 • OH • Tchr • Bethany Parma OH • (440)884-1010 • (RF 1977)

**MORRISON JUDY E**
10586 Talisman Dr Noblesville IN 46060-7623 • IN • Tchr • Calvary Indianapolis IN • (317)783-2305 • (RF 1984)

**MORRISON LAURA J** (314)352-7598
6637 Lansdowne Ave Saint Louis MO 63109-2009 • S • Tchr • St Lucas Saint Louis MO • (314)351-2628 • (MW 1987)

**MORRISSEY ERIK S**
15902 Hwy 3 #228 Webster TX 77598 • TX • Tchr • Our Savior Houston TX • (713)290-9087 • (S 1995)

**MORROW VICKI**
8922 Fleetwing Ave Los Angeles CA 90045-4122 • PSW • Tchr • Ascension Torrance CA • (310)793-0071 • (RF 1976 MA)

**MORSCHEN STEPHANIE C** (612)442-4750
13180 County Rd 32 Cologne MN 55322 • MNS • 09/1997 • (S 1988)

**MORTENSEN GAYLE E*** (218)828-4007
3300 Dalmar Dr N Brainerd MN 56401-7742 • mgkemort@brainerd.net • MNN • 06/1989 • (SP 1985)

**MORTON BARBARA**
52 Greenbough Irvine CA 92614-5475 • PSW • SHS/C • Pacific Southwest Irvine CA • (949)854-3232 • (RF 1967 MED PHD)

**MORTON CHRISTINA M**
25805 Marguerite Pkw #101 Mission Viejo CA 92692 • PSW • Tchr • Abiding Savior Lake Forest CA • (949)830-1460 • (IV 1998)

**MORTON KIMBERLY LOUISE** (253)473-5649
7018 E Homestead Tacoma WA 98404-5012 • norwstr@hotmail.com • FG • Tchr • Trinity Fort Lauderdale FL • (954)463-7471 • (PO 1996)

**MORTON LINDA J** (714)995-5784
242 Crawford Canyon Rd #20 Orange CA 92869-3184 • PSW • Tchr • Trinity Santa Ana CA • (714)543-0341 • (S 1973)

**MORTON REBECCA**
62 Hege Ave - Apt 2 Columbus IN 47201 • IN • Tchr • St Peter Columbus IN • (812)342-4921 • (MQ 1999)

**MOSEMANN RUSSELL J DR**
333 Locust Ave Seward NE 68434-1629 • mose@seward.cune.edu • NEB • SHS/C • Nebraska Seward NE • (S 1984 MS PHD)

**MOSER CARL J DR** (636)946-9866
3601 Runnymede Dr Saint Charles MO 63301-4509 • MO • S Ex/S • Missouri Saint Louis MO • (314)317-4550 • (CQ 1964 MA DED)

**MOSES CLARENCE M** (216)885-4604
6924 Day Dr Parma OH 44129-5441 • OH • EM • (S 1951)

**MOSES DEBRA L** (216)748-3857
8838 Harris Dr North Ridgeville OH 44039-4424 • OH • Tchr • LHS West Rocky River OH • (440)333-1660 • (RF 1983)

**MOSES LORI J** (719)380-8175
1201 Wooten Rd Colorado Springs CO 80915 • dcemoses@msn.com • RM • 09/1995 09/1999 • (IV 1992)

**MOSES VICTORIA P** (210)684-4403
5401 King Albert St San Antonio TX 78229-5236 • TX • Tchr • Redeemer San Antonio TX • (210)735-9903 • (AU 1993)

**MOSHER WILLIAM WATSON** (413)665-9010
52 River Rd #18 Sunderland MA 01375 • workscited@juno.com • NE • Tchr • First Holyoke MA • (413)532-4272 • (S 1996)

**MOSSBARGER CATHY L** (409)849-9256
24 N Kaysie Angleton TX 77515 • TX • Tchr • Immanuel Houston TX • (713)864-2651 • (AU 1985)

**MOTZKUS KYLE**
517 N Ann St Thor IA 50591-5005 • IW • Tchr • St Paul Fort Dodge IA • (515)955-7208 • (MQ 1987)

**MOULDS RUSSELL G DR** (402)643-3672
441 N 3rd St Seward NE 68434-1815 • rmoulds@seward.cune.edu • NEB • SHS/C • Nebraska Seward NE • (S 1976 MS PHD)

**MOUNTFORD MARY J** (713)465-5551
1470 Springrock Ln N I Houston TX 77055 • mmount@stmarkhouston.org • TX • Tchr • St Mark Houston TX • (713)468-2623 • (S 1971)

**MOUNTFORD METFORD E** (281)463-0495
1515 Hillendahl Blvd Houston TX 77055-3411 • TX • Mem C • St Mark Houston TX • (713)468-2623 • (S 1971 SPMU)

**MOUREY DEBRA J**
2507 S Lees Summit Rd Independence MO 64055-1938 • MO • Tchr • Messiah Independence MO • (816)254-9409 • (S 1984)

**MOWERY RUTH C**
7945 Brentwood Rd Mentor OH 44060-5505 • KS • Tchr • Grace Kansas City KS • (913)281-1621 • (AA 1992)

**MOYER JEAN ELLEN** (562)929-8144
14523 S Flatbush Ave Norwalk CA 90650-3444 • PSW • Tchr • Bethany Long Beach CA • (562)421-4711 • (IV 1991 MED)

**MOZA PAULETTE J** (708)526-1502
910 Highland Ave Wauconda IL 60084-1516 • NI • Tchr • St Matthew Lake Zurich IL • (847)438-6103 • (RF 1970)

**MROSKO GARY L** (515)357-5553
507 18th St W Clear Lake IA 50428-1210 • IE • 12/1984 12/1999 • (RF 1963 MED)

**MUCK RUTH E** (716)695-2835
3455 Stevenson Ct North Tonawanda NY 14120-9721 • drlmuck@aol.com • EA • Tchr • St Peter Lockport NY • (716)433-9013 • (S 1970 MA MA)

**MUCK SUSAN KAY** (517)265-7973
2349 Sword Hwy Adrian MI 49221-9709 • MI • Tchr • St John Adrian MI • (517)265-6998 • (RF 1968)

**MUEHL MARK P** (812)523-1181
2175 N Lakeview Dr Seymour IN 47274-9288 • IN • Prin • Immanuel Seymour IN • (812)522-1301 • (RF 1984 MA)

**MUEHL PAUL H**
C/O Danville Luth School 1930 N Bowman Ave Rd Danville IL 61832 • CI • EM • (S 1957 MED)

**MUEHL WALTER C** (317)791-6232
5431 Kim Way Apt 2 Indianapolis IN 46237 • IN • EM • (RF 1936)

**MUELLER ALBERT F** (610)279-9028
405 Beacon Hill Ln Plymouth Meeting PA 19462 • EN • EM • (S 1932)

**MUELLER ANDREW D** (630)953-2316
1 S 151 Ingersoll Ln Villa Park IL 60181 • AnCMllr@aol.com • NI • Tchr • Northern Illinois Hillside IL • (RF 1994)

**MUELLER BERNADETTE**
3036 N 27th St Sheboygan WI 53083-2755 • SW • 12/1999 • (MQ 1998)

**MUELLER BONNIE JEAN** (518)767-2131
PO Box 55 Selkirk NY 12158 • stlmueller@aol.com • AT • 08/1995 08/2000 • (RF 1989)

**MUELLER CAROL R** (402)330-4786
17277 Pine St Omaha NE 68130-1125 • crmueller@yahoo.com • NEB • P/Tchr • Abundant Life Omaha NE • (402)592-8005 • (RF 1979)

**MUELLER CHRISTINE LYNN** (630)953-2316
1S151 Ingersoll Ln Villa Park IL 60181 • AnCMllr@aol.com • NI • Tchr • St Paul Melrose Park IL • (708)343-1000 • (RF 1995)

**MUELLER DAVID J** (713)251-9321
9706 Ballin David Dr Spring TX 77379-3803 • TX • Tchr • Trinity Spring TX • (281)376-5810 • (S 1978)

**MUELLER DAVID W*** (402)330-4786
17277 Pine St Omaha NE 68130-1125 • dwmueller@yahoo.com • NEB • Prin • Abundant Life Omaha NE • (402)592-8005 • (RF 1980 MED)

**MUELLER DAWN M** (314)416-9664
4456 Butler Hill Rd Saint Louis MO 63128-3610 • MO • Tchr • Washington Saint Louis County MO • (314)892-4408 • (S 1992)

**MUELLER DELBERT W DR** (708)343-8321
1141 Nichols Ln Maywood IL 60153-1079 • NI • EM • (RF 1951 MA PHD)

**MUELLER DELORES** (314)839-2043
15554 Chaste St Florissant MO 63034-2171 • MO • EM • (RF 1977)

**MUELLER DONNA K** (713)251-9321
9706 Ballin David Dr Spring TX 77379-3803 • TX • Tchr • Trinity Spring TX • (281)376-5810 • (S 1981)

**MUELLER EDWARD H**
Eglise Evan Luth du Cameroun B P 111 Ngadundere Cameroun WEST AFRICA • PSW • O Sp Min • Pacific Southwest Irvine CA • (949)854-3232 • (S 1959 MED MED)

**MUELLER ERICH P** (314)839-2043
15554 Chaste St Florissant MO 63034-2171 • MO • EM • (RF 1954 MA)

**MUELLER GENE MARIE** (210)399-5490
El Camino Real Box 68 San Benito TX 78586 • TX • Tchr • St Paul Harlingen TX • (956)423-3926 • (S 1980)

**MUELLER GLENN F** (402)727-1796
1924 Phelps Ave Fremont NE 68025-4427 • NEB • EM • (RF 1955 MMU)

**MUELLER GORDON P** (314)264-1178
411 N Lincoln St Scott City MO 63780-1535 • MO • EM • (RF 1955)

**MUELLER JAMES E**
3755 N Gunnison Dr Tucson AZ 85749-9474 • PSW • Prin • Fountain Of Life Tucson AZ • (520)747-1213 • (S 1987 MED)

**MUELLER JILL N** (308)762-9208
1042 Duncan Ave Alliance NE 69301-2630 • rmueller@premaonline.com • WY • 06/1996 06/2000 • (S 1987)

**MUELLER JOANN** (414)462-5996
5313 N 73rd St Milwaukee WI 53218-2824 • SW • Tchr • Grace Menomonee Falls WI • (414)251-7140 • (RF 1969 MEPD)

**MUELLER JOEL R** (414)462-5996
5313 N 73rd St Milwaukee WI 53218-2824 • SW • EM • (SP 1969 MA)

**MUELLER JOHN G** (219)485-9230
5624 N Brookwood Dr Fort Wayne IN 46835-3357 • jmueller@holycrossfw.org • IN • Tchr • Holy Cross Fort Wayne IN • (219)483-3173 • (RF 1961 MA)

**MUELLER JOHN L** (414)466-2253
9825 W Palmetto Ave Wauwatosa WI 53222-1450 • SW • EM • (RF 1956 MED)

**MUELLER JONATHAN ROBERT** (630)668-0313
1709 N President Wheaton IL 60187 • mueller@stjohnwheaton.org • NI • Mem C • St John Wheaton IL • (630)668-0701 • (S 1987 MMU)

**MUELLER KATHLEEN M** (330)773-5752
534 E Wilbeth Rd Akron OH 44301-2349 • OH • Tchr • Redeemer Cuyahoga Falls OH • (330)923-1280 • (S 1972 MED)

**MUELLER KIRK H** (314)385-9277
4543 Nadine Ct Saint Louis MO 63121-2611 • kirkhmueller@hotmail.com • MO • Tchr • Lutheran North Saint Louis MO • (314)389-3100 • (S 1975 MED)

**MUELLER LAURA L** (636)273-5394
16063 Sandalwood Creek Wildwood MO 63038 • lmueller@stjohnsellisville.org • MO • Mem C • St John Ellisville MO • (314)394-4100 • (S 1984)

**MUELLER LYNN R** (618)344-5321
511 E Perry St Maryville IL 62062-2005 • SI • Tchr • Zion Belleville IL • (618)234-0275 • (S 1967)

**MUELLER MARK S** (319)364-3395
1430 A Ave NW Cedar Rapids IA 52405-4834 • IE • Tchr • Trinity Cedar Rapids IA • (319)362-6952 • (S 1979)

**MUELLER MARLENE** (517)883-2295
456 S 5th St Sebewaing MI 48759-1559 • MI • EM • (S 1955)

**MUELLER MARTIN B*** (713)697-6200
1008 Lindale St Houston TX 77022-5644 • TX • EM • (RF 1948 MED)

**MUELLER MARY A** (402)727-1796
1924 Phelps Ave Fremont NE 68025-4427 • NEB • EM • (RF 1971 MED)

**MUELLER MARY M** (314)423-0685
8604 Ardelia Ave Saint Louis MO 63114-4408 • garymarymueller@aol.com • MO • Tchr • Our Redeemer Overland MO • (314)427-3462 • (RF 1967)

**MUELLER PAMELA J** (630)820-2811
87 Cammeron Ct Aurora IL 60504 • pmueller@kiwi.dep.anl.gov • NI • Tchr • Bethany Naperville IL • (630)355-2198 • (RF 1974 MED)

**MUELLER PAULA K*** (602)654-6714
5345 E Mc Lellan #37 Mesa AZ 85205 • EN • Tchr • Christ Phoenix AZ • (602)957-7010 • (S 1976)

**MUELLER RALPH P** (715)526-5218
121 S Hamlin St Shawano WI 54166-2507 • vikesfan@frontiernet.net • NW • Tchr • St James Shawano WI • (715)524-4213 • (SP 1968)

**MUELLER ROBERT K**
1011 S Thomas Rd Saginaw MI 48609-9570 • MI • Tchr • Peace Saginaw MI • (517)792-2581 • (AA 1984)

**MUELLER ROBERT P** (715)536-7082
906 E 3rd St Merrill WI 54452-2526 • eagle@dwave.net • NW • P/Tchr • St John Merrill WI • (715)536-7264 • (RF 1969 MS)

**MUELLER ROLAND M** (316)221-4306
1616 E 20th Ave Winfield KS 67156 • PSW • EM • (RF 1951 MA PHD)

**MUELLER ROXANNA P** (920)459-7294
2515 N 8th St Sheboygan WI 53083-4919 • rdmrdm@compuserve.com • SW • Tchr • St Paul Sheboygan WI • (920)452-6882 • (RF 1967 MSED)

**MUELLER RUBY L** (713)697-6200
1008 Lindale St Houston TX 77022-5644 • TX • EM • (WN 1947)

**MUELLER STEPHANIE J** (317)881-1112
4712 Auburn Ford Greenwood IN 46142-9201 • IN • Tchr • Calvary Indianapolis IN • (317)783-2000 • (S 1990)

**MUELLER SUSAN KAY** (405)762-5139
604 Park St Pawnee OK 74058-4509 • OK • Tchr • First Ponca City OK • (580)762-1111 • (S 1988)

**MUELLER THOMAS P** (817)292-6333
6721 Audubon Trl Fort Worth TX 76132 • TX • 02/1999 • (S 1967 MS)

**MUELLER VICTORIA L** (513)561-1660
5421 Madison Rd Cincinnati OH 45227 • vmueller6@juno.com • OH • Mem C • St Paul Cincinnati OH • (513)271-4147 • (MQ 1997)

**MUELLER WALTER M** (219)639-6691
14434 Minnich Rd Hoagland IN 46745-9793 • IN • EM • (RF 1933)

**MUELLER WALTER O*** (810)798-3663
79855 Mc Fadden Rd Armada MI 48005-1010 • MI • 06/1998 06/2000 • (S 1981)

**MUELLER WILBERT C** (414)334-5996
5459 Village Dr West Bend WI 53095-9220 • SW • EM • (NU 1941 MS)

**MUELLER-ROEBKE JENNY M** (402)643-3013
934 N 11th St Seward NE 68434-1402 • NEB • SHS/C • Nebraska Seward NE • (S 1973 MED PHD)

**MUHL CAROL M** (810)736-7973
4290 Bob White Dr Flint MI 48506-1705 • MI • 06/1999 • (RF 1968)

**MUHLENBRUCK MARVIN R** (913)886-2354
20236 Nemaha Rd Nortonville KS 66060 • nortonville2@juno.com • KS • EM • (RF 1966)

**MUINCH LINDA CHRISTINE** (660)463-7592
214 NW 8th St Concordia MO 64020 • MO • Tchr • St Paul Concordia MO • (660)463-7654 • (CQ 1992)

**MULDER AUDRA C**
2105 - 33rd St - Aprt 108 Lubbock TX 79411-1745 • TX • Tchr • St Paul Mc Allen TX • (956)682-2201 • (S 1995)

**MULL LISA R** (210)680-7134
5011 Glen Ridge Dr Apt P-14 San Antonio TX 78229 • IN • Tchr • St Peter Columbus IN • (812)372-5266 • (RF 1987 MSED)

**MULSO SARA KATHLEEN** (612)646-5699
1280 Marshall Ave St Paul MN 55104 • S • 08/1999 • (SP 1997)

**MUNDT ALLEN F** (219)436-9557
3720 Winterfield Run Fort Wayne IN 46804-2661 • IN • Tchr • Emmaus Fort Wayne IN • (219)456-4573 • (S 1966 MS)

**MUNDT ANGELA MARIE** (816)690-5696
302 SW 24th Ter Oak Grove MO 64075 • MO • Tchr • Messiah Independence MO • (816)254-9409 • (S 1997)

**MUNDT KATHLEEN M** (517)642-8346
199 Norbert Ln Hemlock MI 48626-9708 • MI • 07/2000 • (RF 1968)

**MUNDT SARAH LYNN** (812)358-2512
416 N Poplar St Apt B Seymour IN 47274-1557 • IN • Tchr • Central Brownstown IN • (812)358-2512 • (S 1998)

**MUNOZ ARIEL WENZ**
23 - 24 123 St College Point NY 11356 • AT • Tchr • St John College Point NY • (S 2000)

**MUNSTER MERVIN D** (541)758-3027
972 NW Cypress Corvallis OR 97330 • NOW • Tchr • Zion Corvallis OR • (541)753-7503 • (S 1970)

**MURKEN MATTHEW P**
5700 Ely Rd Cedar Rapids IA 52404 • IE • Tchr • Trinity Cedar Rapids IA • (319)366-1569 • (S 2000)

**MURPHY CHRISTOPHER LEE** (219)489-4699
1309 Big Horn Pl Fort Wayne IN 46825-3420 • murph2459@aol.com • IN • Tchr • Emmanuel-St Michael Fort Wayne IN • (219)422-6712 • (RF 1985 MS)

**MURPHY DEANNA M** (217)429-9115
94 N Country Club Rd Decatur IL 62521-4171 • CI • Tchr • Lutheran School Asso Decatur IL • (217)233-2001 • (CQ 1993)

**MURPHY NANCY A** (920)592-0354
1065 Schanock Dr Green Bay WI 54303 • NW • Tchr • Redeemer Green Bay WI • (920)499-1033 • (RF 1989)

**MURRAY CYNTHIA LYNN**
C/O Mid South District 823 Exocet Suite 102 Cordova TN 38018-2267 • MDS • 07/1998 • (S 1995)

**MUSELLA MIRIAM LOUISE** (909)622-2914
1615 Juniper Ridge Pomona CA 91766 • himusella@aol.com • PSW • Tchr • Mount Calvary Diamond Bar CA • (909)861-2740 • (S 1979)

**MUSFELDT JAY N*** (503)378-0179
563 Tierra Dr NE Salem OR 97301 • NOW • Prin • Zion Corvallis OR • (541)757-0946 • (S 1963)

**MUTH JANET J**
C/O Memorial Lutheran Church 5800 Westheimer Rd Houston TX 77057-5617 • TX • Mount Olive Folsom CA • (PO 1985)

**MUTH TIMOTHY D** (920)208-3563
3802 S 14th St Sheboygan WI 53081 • SW • Tchr • South Wisconsin Milwaukee WI • (414)464-8100 • (MQ 1990 MA)

**MUTHER CINDY B** (920)662-1308
3561 Spring Green Rd Green Bay WI 54313-7569 • c-b-muther@juno.com • NW • Tchr • St Paul Bonduel WI • (715)758-8559 • (S 1977)

**MUTHER JULIA E** (815)227-0356
919 Luther Ave Rockford IL 61107-3415 • NI • 09/2000 • (S 1983)

**MUTHER PAMELA J** (414)338-9435
915 E Kilbourn Ave West Bend WI 53095-4221 • SW • Tchr • St John West Bend WI • (414)334-3077 • (S 1976)

**MUTHER TIMOTHY A** (815)227-0356
919 Luther Ave Rockford IL 61107-3415 • NI • Tchr • Luther Academy Rockford IL • (815)877-9551 • (S 1984 MSED)

**MUZIKA JENNIFER LEIGH** (407)445-0308
5164 Chesapeake Ave Orlando FL 32808-1613 • j3muzika@gateway.net • FG • 11/1996 11/1998 • (AA 1996)

**MYCOCK CAROL L** (830)816-9122
32345 IH 10 W Boerne TX 78006-9240 • TX • Tchr • Shepherd Of The Hill San Antonio TX • (210)614-3741 • (S 1973)

**MYER MARIE T**
566 Bay Dale Ct Arnold MD 21012-2352 • SE • 06/1999 • (BR 1980 MED)

**MYERS CINDY LYNN** (402)947-2066
715 1st St Friend NE 68359 • NEB • Tchr • Zion Tobias NE • (402)243-2354 • (S 1997)

**MYERS ELIZABETH D** (847)427-9380
1520 W Dempster Apt 105 Mount Prospect IL 60056 • elizabeth300@home.com • NI • P/Tchr • St John Mount Prospect IL • (847)593-7670 • (SP 1981 MA)

**MYERS MELISSA E** (925)280-1052
190 Cleaveland Rd @20 Pleasant Hill CA 94523 • davidmel@earthlink.net • CNH • Tchr • Prince Peace Fremont CA • (510)793-3366 • (CQ 1992)

**MYERS MICHAEL JOHN**
324 North Ave Apt 4 Mount Clemens MI 48043-1791 • MI • 09/1999 • (CQ 1998)

**MYERS PAULA MAY** (313)984-8872
3279 Krafft Rd Fort Gratiot MI 48059-3827 • MI • Tchr • Trinity Port Huron MI • (810)984-2501 • (AA 1987)

**MYTAS LOIS MARIE** (715)623-6522
205 E 9th Ave Antigo WI 54409-2636 • NW • Tchr • Peace Antigo WI • (715)623-2200 • (S 1975)

## N

**NAATZ THOMAS J** (205)883-5291
15122 Balsam Dr SE Huntsville AL 35803-2376 • tnaatz@juno.com • SO • Tchr • Grace Huntsville AL • (256)881-0553 • (S 1974)

**NABER DARRELL H** (616)887-5044
303 Blake St Sparta MI 49345-1405 • MI • EM • (S 1946 MED)

**NABER LYNETTE I** (402)362-6446
2035 Nebraska Ave York NE 68467-1130 • gn25845@navix.net • NEB • Tchr • Emmanuel York NE • (402)362-6575 • (S 1969)

**NAFZGER CARROLL W** (708)469-5435
380 Grandview Ave Glen Ellyn IL 60137-5246 • NI • Northern Illinois Hillside IL • (S 1963 MSW)

**NAGEL CHARLES**
623 N Jefferson St Ionia MI 48846-1230 • MI • Northern Illinois Hillside IL • (AA 1999)

**NAGEL MATTHEW C**
3540 Oreana Ave Las Vegas NV 89120-2021 • PSW • Tchr • Faith LHS Las Vegas NV • (702)804-4400 • (S 1987 MED)

**NAGY KRISTA F**
2728 Delgar St Pittsburgh PA 15214-2804 • EA • Prin • St Matthew Pittsburgh PA • (412)321-6662 • (RF 1989)

**NAHNSEN THOMAS F** (217)487-7532
5386 Irwin Bridge Rd Pleasant Plains IL 62677-3913 • CI • EM • (RF 1955 MSED)

**NALE CHARLOTTE W** (510)443-1018
814 Orion Way Livermore CA 94550-6332 • CNH • Tchr • St Philip Dublin CA • (925)828-2117 • (RF 1980)

**NALEIEHA MICHAEL M** (512)837-0685
11611 Parkfield Dr Austin TX 78758-3739 • TX • Mem C • Redeemer Austin TX • (512)459-1500 • (RF 1973)

**NAPIER DAWN L** (757)851-3278
302 Gaines Mill Ln Hampton VA 23669-1427 • pnap2000@aol.com • SE • Prin • Emmanuel Hampton VA • (757)723-8782 • (BR 1977 MED)

**NASH PATRICIA LYNN** (616)476-9533
59489 Kirk Lake Rd Vandalia MI 49095 • MI • 09/2000 • (AA 1984)

**NATZ DEBRA J** (608)754-0232
2338 Garden Dr Janesville WI 53546 • debranatz@hotmail.com • SW • Tchr • St Paul Janesville WI • (608)754-4471 • (CQ 2000)

**NATZKE CONNIE K** (507)433-2974
1401 10th St NW Austin MN 55912-1875 • wjnatzke@wolf.co.net • MNS • Tchr • Holy Cross Austin MN • (507)433-7844 • (S 1966)

**NAUMANN TAMMI JILL** (956)412-2503
4402 Glasscock Ave #214 Harlingen TX 78550-9212 • TX • 11/1997 11/1999 • (BR 1983 MA)

**NAVARRO ALBERT M** (847)426-2886
309 S Second St West Dundee IL 60118 • acnavarro1@juno.com • NI • Tchr • Christ Sterling IL • (815)625-3800 • (RF 1993)

**NAVURSKIS MIRIAM E** (314)781-8421
2026 Bellevue Apt 1 D Saint Louis MO 63143 • SI • Tchr • Zion Belleville IL • (618)233-2299 • (MQ 1999)

**NCUBE PHYLLIS** (504)248-3039
6844 Seagull Ln #G New Orleans LA 70126 • jpns4@gateway.net • SO • Tchr • Prince Of Peace New Orleans LA • (504)242-4348 • (SEL 1998)

**NEBEL CINDY FAY** (618)493-6226
PO Box 176 Hoyleton IL 62803-0176 • SI • 06/1991 • (RF 1986)

**NEBEL MARK C** (314)839-8627
2660 N Waterford Dr Florissant MO 63033-2522 • MO • Tchr • Salem Florissant MO • (314)741-8220 • (S 1975 MAT)

**NEBEN ELDON J** (714)538-5684
414 N Swidler St Orange CA 92869-2829 • nobbyn@aol.com • PSW • EM • (S 1957 MA)

**NEBEN JULIE MELISSA** (909)898-9402
1447 Roadrunner Dr Corona CA 92881 • jmn4edu@aol.com. • PSW • Tchr • Pacific Southwest Irvine CA • (949)854-3232 • (CQ 1996 MMU MA)

**NEBEN WILBUR C** (805)547-9240
1359 Avalon St San Luis Obispo CA 93405-4901 • wilbneben@aol.com • CNH • EM • (S 1949 MA)

**NEEDHAM BRENDA RENE** (810)288-1557
3032 Benjamin Ave Royal Oak MI 48073-3089 • MI • Tchr • Our Shepherd Birmingham MI • (248)645-0551 • (AA 1992)

**NEHLS ROSEMARY** (520)578-7379
1941 S Flying Q Ln Tucson AZ 85713-6794 • EN • Tchr • Faith Tucson AZ • (520)881-0670 • (RF 1966)

**NEHLS WILLIAM ALLEN** (520)578-7379
1941 S Flying Q Ln Tucson AZ 85713-6794 • billrosenehls@aol.com • EN • P/Tchr • Faith Tucson AZ • (520)881-0670 • (RF 1965 MA)

**NEHRENZ SHEILA KAE** (219)436-5467
4620 Williamsburg Ct Fort Wayne IN 46804-4009 • IN • Tchr • Unity Fort Wayne IN • (219)744-0459 • (RF 1979)

**NEHRING CHARLES G** (414)494-0227
1237 Reed St Green Bay WI 54303-3024 • NW • EM • (RF 1959 MED)

**NEHRT REBECCA L** (812)358-5410
C/O Lutheran Central School 415 N Elm St Brownstown IN 47220-1309 • IN • Tchr • Central Brownstown IN • (812)358-2512 • (RF 1983)

**NEIDHOLD EUNICE P** (509)328-9521
6602 N Jefferson St Spokane WA 99208-4236 • fneidhold@earthlink.net • NOW • EM • (S 1958)

**NEIDHOLD GAIL M**
6624 N Elizabeth St Spokane WA 99208-3809 • NOW • Tchr • Concordia Tacoma WA • (253)475-9513 • (PO 1984)

**NEIDIGK MATTHEW W** (810)781-9151
45074 Deshon Utica MI 48317 • MI • Tchr • Michigan Ann Arbor MI • (MQ 1997)

**NEITSCH HOWARD W** (863)422-2820
2800 W Lake Hamilton Dr Winter Haven FL 33881-9206 • FG • Tchr • Grace Winter Haven FL • (941)293-9744 • (RF 1971)

**NELSON BECKY J** (314)939-3082
2738 16th Ave Forest Grove OR 97116-3116 • sraedeke@aol.com • NOW • 06/1999 • (SP 1983)

**NELSON BRENDA J** (507)281-5103
2121 50th St NW Rochester MN 55901 • MNS • 04/2000 • (S 1993 MED)

**NELSON CHRISTOPHER CARL** (414)294-3305
2531 S Graham St Milwaukee WI 53207 • neleez@usa.net • EN • Tchr • Hales Corners Hales Corners WI • (414)529-6701 • (MQ 1994)

**NELSON COREY ALLEN** (507)281-5103
2121 50th St NW Rochester MN 55901 • gocubs2000@aol.com • MNS • Tchr • Rochester Central Rochester MN • (507)289-3267 • (S 1993 MA)

**NELSON FREDERICK C** (414)445-9127
3203 N 94th St Milwaukee WI 53222-3518 • SW • Tchr • Martin LHS Greendale WI • (414)421-4000 • (CQ 1984 MS)

**NELSON GARY RICHARD** (734)671-5170
3237 John R St Trenton MI 48183-3627 • grnelson@metroshores.net • MI • Tchr • St John New Boston MI • (734)654-6366 • (RF 1981 MA)

**NELSON GERALDINE** (517)354-2506
3674 Bloom Rd Alpena MI 49707-8957 • snelson@northland.lib.mi.us • MI • Tchr • Immanuel Alpena MI • (517)354-4805 • (S 1970)

**NELSON KRISTINA LYNN** (608)758-9944
1231 E Holmes St Janesville WI 53545-4124 • ttn9767@juno.com • MO • 07/2000 • (AU 1995)

**NELSON MELISSA ANN** (208)238-8390
534 Michael Ave Pocatello ID 83201 • NOW • 08/1994 08/2000 • (PO 1991)

**NELSON MICHAEL TED**
10498 Fountain Lake Dr Apt 835 Stafford TX 77477-3764 • TX • Tchr • Memorial Houston TX • (713)782-4022 • (RF 1970)

**NELSON PAULA B** (314)638-7131
9826 Affton View Ct Saint Louis MO 63123-6273 • kandomo@aol.com • MO • Tchr • Green Park Lemay MO • (314)544-4248 • (S 1969 MEAD MED)

**NELSON ROBERTA L DR** (402)643-6526
302 E Hillcrest Dr Seward NE 68434-1338 • rnelson@seward.cune.edu • NEB • SHS/C • Nebraska Seward NE • (RF 1963 MA PHD)

**NELSON SANDRA JEAN** (913)962-2461
6630 Long St Shawnee KS 66216-2542 • KS • Tchr • Hope Shawnee KS • (913)631-6940 • (CQ 1993)

**NELSON SCOTT D** (503)359-1168
2738 16th Ave Forest Grove OR 97116-3116 • brlymkgit@aol.com • NOW • Tchr • Forest Hills Cornelius OR • (503)359-4853 • (S 1983)

**NELSON WAYNE R**
506 S 21st St Bellville IL 62226-7529 • SI • Tchr • St John Nashville IL • (618)478-5544 • (MQ 1984)

**NELSON WENDY MARIE**
312 Elm St Apt # Batavia IL 60510 • NI • Tchr • Immanuel Batavia IL • (630)406-0157 • (RF 1997)

**NEMETH GRACE M** (310)697-2045
1234 Solejar Dr Whittier CA 90603-1713 • PSW • Tchr • Faith Whittier CA • (562)941-0245 • (RF 1960)

**NERGER MARTINA N** (314)752-7991
6238 Nottingham Ave #2E Saint Louis MO 63019 • martina.n@mciworld.com • MO • Mem C • Hope Saint Louis MO • (314)352-0014 • (RF 1999)

**NETHERTON DANA JOY** (501)785-4672
415 Lecta Ave Fort Smith AR 72901-3513 • dnether179@aol.com • MDS • Tchr • First Fort Smith AR • (501)452-5330 • (S 1994)

**NETHERTON KAREN ANN** (713)849-4648
13410 Canaan Bridge Houston TX 77041 • knethert@hal-pc.org • TX • Tchr • St Mark Houston TX • (713)468-2623 • (RF 1965 MSED)

**NETTLING KATHY M** (913)492-7909
11585 S Chestnut St Olathe KS 66061-8789 • KS • 02/1993 10/1995 • (RF 1978 MED)

**NETTNIN KATHLEEN LOUISE** (716)964-8703
1739 Apple Hollow Ln Hamlin NY 14464-9504 • EA • Tchr • St John Hamlin NY • (716)964-2550 • (BR 1977)

**NEU CORAL L** (616)887-1052
126 Ida Red Ave #203 Sparta MI 49345 • MI • Tchr • Trinity Conklin MI • (616)899-2152 • (S 1974 MAT)

**NEUENFELDT JANE D** (612)323-1807
1720 West Ln Anoka MN 55303-1923 • MNS • Tchr • Mount Olive Anoka MN • (763)421-3223 • (SP 1975)

**NEUMAN DENISE L** (414)376-1587
W67N421 Grant Ave Cedarburg WI 53012-2303 • SW • Tchr • First Immanuel Cedarburg WI • (262)377-6610 • (RF 1977)

**NEUMANN AMY LYNN** (630)279-2293
313 S West Ave Apt. E Elmhurst IL 60126-3040 • crfneumanal@curf.edu • NI • SHS/C • Northern Illinois Hillside IL • (RF 1994 MA)

**NEUMANN JAMES A** (310)831-5111
1410 Brett Pl Unit 131 San Pedro CA 90732-5075 • PSW • Prin • Christ Rancho Palos Verdes CA • (310)831-0848 • (RF 1961 MA)

**NEUMANN KARLA RAE** (734)728-4711
28615 Hanover Blvd Westland MI 48186-6892 • iteachps@aol.com • MI • 01/2000 • (S 1977 MA)

**NEUMANN KATHERINE F** (847)945-7530
28 Dukes Ln Lincolnshire IL 60069 • NI • Tchr • St Matthew Lake Zurich IL • (847)438-7709 • (RF 1966)

**NEUMANN KIM** (313)728-4711
PO Box 490 Hamburg MI 48139-0490 • MI • 11/1984 11/1999 • (S 1980 MSED)

**NEUMEYER DENNIS K** (517)752-4599
2260 S Portsmouth Rd Saginaw MI 48601-9420 • trost2260@prodigy.net • MI • P/Tchr • Immanuel Saginaw MI • (517)754-4285 • (RF 1968 MED)

**NEUMEYER JOEL KEITH** (810)463-6827
113 High St Mount Clemens MI 48043 • MI • Tchr • St Luke Clinton Township MI • (810)791-1151 • (AA 1996)

**NEUMEYER KAREN BETH** (248)693-3186
2295 Cole Rd Lake Orion MI 48362-2109 • neuby@juno.com • MI • Tchr • St Stephen Waterford MI • (248)673-6621 • (AA 1986)

**NEUMEYER MARSHA J** (517)752-4599
2260 S Portsmouth Rd Saginaw MI 48601-9420 • trost2260@prodigy.net • MI • Tchr • Immanuel Saginaw MI • (517)754-4285 • (RF 1968 MED)

**NEUMEYER ROSALIE ANN** (712)542-2591
921 S 19th St Clarinda IA 51632 • IW • Tchr • Clarinda Clarinda IA • (712)542-3657 • (S 1969)

**NEUMEYER SCOTT RICHARD**
10425 Gratiot Rd Saginaw MI 48609-9636 • scotthoops11@hotmail.com • MI • Tchr • St Peter Hemlock MI • (517)642-5659 • (AA 1994)

**NEUMEYER WILLIAM** (219)490-7533
1008 Oak Branch Ct Fort Wayne IN 46845-1039 • drxtv@aol.com • IN • Tchr • Concordia LHS Fort Wayne IN • (219)483-1102 • (S 1973 MS)

**NEUNABER JOHN H** (618)656-3157
667 Notre Dame Ave Edwardsville IL 62025-2626 • SI • Tchr • Trinity Edwardsville IL • (618)656-7002 • (RF 1962 MED)

**NEWARD DONNA RUTH** (801)568-6877
1932 Stalbridge Cir Sandy UT 84093-7050 • RM • Tchr • Grace Sandy UT • (801)572-3793 • (RF 1961)

**NEWKIRK JENNIFER ELIZABETH** (608)754-2051
2305 Holiday Dr #4 Janesville WI 53545 • jennnewkirk@hotmail.com • SW • Tchr • St Paul Janesville WI • (608)754-4471 • (SP 1999)

**NEWKIRK RABEL F** (812)523-2362
1149 Cottage Cir Seymour IN 47274-4702 • IN • EM • (RF 1950 MA)

**NEWMAN MARK P** (281)477-9938
10325 Cypresswood Dr #1417 Houston TX 77070 • TX • Tchr • Texas Austin TX • (MQ 1996)

**NEWTON DAVID MICHAEL** (707)224-2473
2572 Greenwood Ct Napa CA 94558-4413 • CNH • Tchr • St John Napa CA • (707)226-7970 • (CQ 1986)

**NEWTON ROSELYN** (206)363-2534
3712 NE 188th St Seattle WA 98155-2740 • NOW • Tchr • Concordia Seattle WA • (206)525-7407 • (S 1969)

**NGUYEN BRENDA**
St Paul Lutheran School 13082 Bowen St Garden Grove CA 92843-1092 • PSW • Tchr • St Paul Garden Grove CA • (714)534-6320 • (IV 1998)

**NICHOLS MARY L** (219)672-3334
6309 Southampton Ct Fort Wayne IN 46804 • PSW • Tchr • Shepherd Peace Irvine CA • (949)786-3326 • (RF 1960)

**NICHOLSON GWENDOLYN**
N8116 La Salle Cir Oconomowoc WI 53066-5512 • SW • Tchr • St Paul Oconomowoc WI • (414)567-5001 • (RF 1961)

**NICKEL KIRSTEN L** (414)762-4682
10403 S Chicago Rd Oak Creek WI 53154-6603 • SW • 01/1992 01/1999 • (AA 1986)

**NICKEL PAUL E** (502)458-7826
3331 Frontier Trl Louisville KY 40220-2609 • penickel@aol.com • IN • Mem C • Our Savior Louisville KY • (502)426-1130 • (RF 1970)

**NICKEL PAUL G** (314)843-0885
10575 Larkspur Dr Saint Louis MO 63123-5009 • MO • EM • (RF 1944 MSED)

**NICKEL SCOTT G** (414)762-4682
10403 S Chicago Rd Oak Creek WI 53154-6603 • SW • Tchr • Martin LHS Greendale WI • (414)421-4000 • (AA 1986 MED)

**NIEBERGALL CAROL** (651)653-9734
5745 Meadowview Dr White Bear Lake MN 55110-2289 • whbearlk@pclink.com • MNS • EM • (RF 1962 MSED)

**NIEBERGALL DONALD L** (419)598-8251
U-014 Rd 16 Rt 1 Napoleon OH 43545 • kan@henry-net.com • OH • EM • (S 1958)

**NIEBERGALL WILLIAM A DR** (651)653-9734
5745 Meadowview Dr White Bear Lake MN 55110-2289 • whbearlk@pclink.com • MNS • EM • (S 1957 MA MS DED EDS)

**NIEBLING GERALD L** (402)534-2092
100 Iowa Utica NE 68456-6065 • NEB • EM • (S 1982)

**NIEBUHR JOEL A** (702)645-7429
5601 Mare Way Las Vegas NV 89108-4139 • PSW • Tchr • Pacific Southwest Irvine CA • (949)854-3232 • (S 1983)

**NIEDNER NORMA LEE**
11578 Hemlock Overland Park KS 66210 • KS • Prin • Bethany Shawnee Mission KS • (913)648-2228 • (S 1960)

**NIELSEN ALLAN C** (626)858-9648
283 E Benwood St Covina CA 91722 • PSW • Tchr • Emmaus Alhambra CA • (626)289-3664 • (RF 1965)

**NIELSEN GEORGE R** (605)394-0289
1132 Enchantment Rd Rapid City SD 57701 • gnie857317@aol.com • NI • EM • (S 1954 MA PHD)

**NIELSEN MICHELLE RENEE** (517)652-9755
641 W Schleier Apt A 7 Frankenmuth MI 48734 • mnielsen@stlorenz.org • MI • Tchr • St Lorenz Frankenmuth MI • (517)652-6141 • (S 1999)

**NIELSEN WILLIAM H** (636)447-1964
600 Breeze Park Dr # 2 Saint Charles MO 63304-9142 • TX • EM • (S 1920)

**NIEMAN ANNA E** (810)778-1776
30504 Utica Rd Roseville MI 48066-1585 • MI • EM • (S 1957 MS MA)

**NIEMAN DALE W** (810)784-8041
23055 Irwin Rd Armada Twp MI 48005-2104 • MI • P/Tchr • Our Saviour Armada MI • (810)784-9088 • (SP 1981 MA)

**NIEMAN LENORE** (810)796-2083
6090 Ada Van Dr Dryden MI 48428-9751 • MI • Tchr • LHS North Macomb MI • (810)781-9151 • (CQ 1998)

**NIEMAN MATTHEW W** (812)342-4160
14000 W Poplar Ct Seymour IN 47274 • immanuel@hsonline.net • IN • Mem C • Immanuel Seymour IN • (812)522-3118 • (RF 1994)

**NIEMANN CAROL SUE** (217)356-4146
2605 Cherry Creek Rd Champaign IL 61822-7960 • CI • Tchr • St John Champaign IL • (217)359-1714 • (RF 1972)

**NIEMANN CLAUDIA** (518)372-6185
6 Greenlawn Ct Schenectady NY 12304-4558 • AT • Tchr • Our Savior Albany NY • (518)459-2273 • (RF 1962 MA)

**NIEMANN CRYSTAL ILENE** (309)829-9142
502 Fox Hill Cir Apt H Bloomington IL 61701-6395 • cin1@trinluth.org • CI • Tchr • Trinity Bloomington IL • (309)829-7513 • (RF 1995)

**NIEMANN RANDY LYNN** (217)356-4146
2605 Cherry Creek Rd Champaign IL 61822-7960 • CI • Tchr • St John Champaign IL • (217)359-1714 • (RF 1972 MS)

**NIEMEYER ARTHUR E** (219)424-6221
1219 California Ave Fort Wayne IN 46805-5017 • IN • EM • (RF 1926)

**NIEMEYER CATHERINE A** (402)466-4291
5820 Saint Paul Ave Lincoln NE 68507-2364 • NEB • Tchr • Faith Lincoln NE • (402)466-6861 • (CQ 1987)

**NIERMAN JOANNE** (314)968-7213
7594 Watson Rd #212 Saint Louis MO 63119 • MO • Tchr • Concordia Middle Saint Louis MO • (314)865-1144 • (S 1999)

**NIERMEIER ARTHUR H** (683)676-6455
2700 N US Hwy 27 Lot 95 Lake Wales FL 33853-7874 • artniermeier@hotmail.com • FG • 07/1999 • (S 1965 MA MS)

**NIETING KATHRYN A** (501)452-7319
1122 N Waldron Rd Fort Smith AR 72904-7316 • MDS • Tchr • First Fort Smith AR • (501)452-5330 • (S 1977)

**NIETING ROBERT E** (414)771-2709
8909 Stickney Ave Wauwatosa WI 53226-2736 • SW • EM • (S 1942 MA)

**NIEWALD PAMELA JO** (314)878-0716
2179 Seven Pines Dr Creve Coeur MO 63146-2215 • MO • Tchr • Immanuel Olivette MO • (314)993-5004 • (CQ 1994)

**NIGHTLINGER CATHY JO** (517)652-6063
23 Wilshire Dr Frankenmuth MI 48734-1331 • MI • Tchr • St Lorenz Frankenmuth MI • (517)652-6141 • (S 1963)

**NIHISER JANE ANN** (517)856-3013
9130 Point Charity Dr Pigeon MI 48755 • EN • Tchr • St Michael Fort Wayne IN • (219)432-2033 • (S 1977 MA)

**NIMTZ FAITH D** (214)223-3565
437 Raintree Cir De Soto TX 75115-7522 • TX • Tchr • Cross Of Christ De Soto TX • (972)223-9586 • (AU 1982)

**NIMTZ MARK A** (248)524-1619
1127 Shadow Dr Troy MI 48098 • mnimtz@home.com • MI • Mem C • Our Shepherd Birmingham MI • (248)646-6100 • (S 1981 MSFLM MAT)

**NIMTZ WENDY E**
1127 Shadow Dr Troy MI 48098-1779 • mnimtz@home.com • MI • 04/2000 • (SP 1988)

**NISKA HEIDI ANN** (810)231-3399
190 Newcastle Ln Whitmore Lake MI 48189-9033 • MI • Tchr • Shepherd Of The Lake Brighton MI • (810)227-6473 • (AA 1993)

**NISS MURIEL D** (847)426-8040
147 Bannock Ct East Dundee IL 60118-1626 • NI • Tchr • Immanuel Dundee IL • (847)428-1010 • (RF 1987)

**NISSEN AMY JOANNE** (310)420-7783
268 E San Antonio Dr Long Beach CA 90807 • PSW • Tchr • Bethany Long Beach CA • (562)420-7783 • (S 1996)

**NITSCHKE FREDERIC A** (507)289-7119
1822 38th St NW Rochester MN 55901-0555 • fritznitch@prodigy.net • MNS • EM • (S 1946 MA)

**NITZ RALPH E** (217)529-5073
2325 Queensway Rd Springfield IL 62703-5023 • rnitz@family-net.net • CI • Prin • LHS Springfield IL • (217)546-6363 • (S 1966 MGEO MED)

**NITZ TODD ERIC** (214)341-6352
8600 Coppertowne Ln Apt 1002 Dallas TX 75243-8047 • toddnitz@usa.net • TX • Tchr • Lutheran HS of Dalla Dallas TX • (214)349-8912 • (MQ 1991 MA)

**NIXON JOANN M** (214)493-6344
7109 Elkhorn Dr Fort Wayne IN 46815 • nixons@iname.com • IN • 09/1999 • (RF 1971 MED)

**NOACK BONNIE B** (972)780-9204
7315 Long Canyon Trl Dallas TX 75249 • TX • Mem C • Cross Christ De Soto TX • (972)223-9340 • (S 1966)

**NOACK DALTON J** 233-51-27402
PO Box 3536 Kumasi Ghana WEST AFRICA • djnoack@africaonline.com.gh • TX • S Miss • Texas Austin TX • (S 1959 MA)

**NOACK KRISTIN M**
Lutheran HS Of Dallas 8494 Stults Rd Dallas TX 75243-4006 • TX • Tchr • Lutheran HS of Dalla Dallas TX • (214)349-8912 • (S 1998)

**NOBIS LLOYD B** (517)652-9039
1005 W Tuscola Frankenmuth MI 48734-9201 • lnobis@stlorenz.org • MI • Tchr • St Lorenz Frankenmuth MI • (517)652-6141 • (RF 1970)

**NOBIS SHARON**
11020 E Betony Dr Scottsdale AZ 85259 • EN • Tchr • Christ Phoenix AZ • (602)957-7010 • (RF 1966)

**NOBLE KRISTEN LEE** (847)253-7381
2305 Martin Ln Rolling Meadows IL 60008 • NI • Tchr • St Peter Schaumburg IL • (847)885-7636 • (RF 1995)

**NOBLE SANDRA J** (847)253-7381
2305 Martin Ln Rolling Mdws IL 60008-2749 • NI • Tchr • St Peter Arlington Heights IL • (847)253-6638 • (RF 1968 MA)

**NOCELLA LARRY A JR.** (517)893-6178
1000 Garfield Ave Bay City MI 48708-7176 • lalsnfamily@netzero.net • MI • Tchr • Immanuel Bay City MI • (517)893-8521 • (AA 1991)

**NOEL CYNTHIA L** (909)272-0344
2016 Maywood Cir Corona CA 92881-7456 • PSW • Tchr • Grace Corona CA • (909)737-3217 • (S 1973)

**NOENNIG MARK T** (218)789-7868
120 2nd St S Sabin MN 56580-4119 • dcemark@netzero.net • MNN • Mem C • Trinity Sabin MN • (218)789-7259 • (S 1978)

**NOENNIG RACHEL M** (612)856-2936
26655 120th St Zimmerman MN 55398 • MNN • Tchr • Zion Saint Francis MN • (612)856-2099 • (SP 1999)

**NOFFKE CHRISTINE A** (630)527-8309
1755 Iona Naperville IL 60565 • NI • 11/1998 • (RF 1980)

**NOFFZE DENISE JANET**
C/O Denver Lutheran HS 3201 W Arizona Ave Denver CO 80219-3941 • RM • Tchr • Denver Lutheran High Denver CO • (303)934-2345 • (AA 1983)

**NOLL TERRY E** (216)333-0872
21382 Maplewood Ave Rocky River OH 44116-1246 • OH • Tchr • St Thomas Rocky River OH • (440)331-4426 • (CQ 1990 MED)

**NORBY HANNE E**
7371 Viar Ave San Diego CA 92120-1927 • sdnative08@hotmail.com • PSW • Tchr • Pacific Southwest Irvine CA • (949)854-3232 • (MQ 1993 MA)

**NORD LOIS A**
236 Johnson Ave NW Cedar Rapids IA 52405-4862 • IE • Tchr • Trinity Cedar Rapids IA • (319)362-6952 • (RF 1972 MA)

**NORDBROCK EDGAR E** (708)335-4979
17400 S Keazie Ave Apt 319 Hazel Creek IL 60429 • pgno142@tenet.edu • NI • EM • (RF 1937)

**NORDBROCK JANICE A** (602)843-2553
3827 W Phelps Rd Phoenix AZ 85053-2858 • vicki.n@juno.com • PSW • Tchr • Christ Redeemer Phoenix AZ • (623)934-3286 • (RF 1982 MA)

**NORDEEN MARY** (718)387-5594
159 Maujer St Brooklyn NY 11206-1220 • AT • Tchr • St Mark Brooklyn NY • (718)453-4040 • (RF 1966 MAR)

**NORDHAUSEN JOANNE R** (716)392-5160
35 Peach Blossom Rd N Hilton NY 14468-1000 • EA • Prin • St Paul Hilton NY • (716)392-4000 • (RF 1974 MS)

**NORDLING PHILIP J** (281)895-8908
100 Hollow Tree St #2126 Houston TX 77090 • pnordling@pdq.net • TX • Tchr • Concordia LHS Tomball TX • (281)351-2547 • (S 1994)

**NORDMEYER KEITH** (602)783-4021
1745 S Athens Ave Yuma AZ 85364-5011 • PSW • Tchr • Christ Yuma AZ • (520)726-0773 • (SP 1973)

**NORDMEYER RICHARD CLEO** (815)697-2605
PO Box 96 Chebanse IL 60922-0096 • rnord@dlogue.net • NI • Prin • St Paul Kankakee IL • (815)932-3241 • (RF 1973 MED)

**NORTHROP TIMOTHY F C** (626)967-2225
1621 E Ruddock St Covina CA 91724-2843 • timnorthrop@netzero.net • PSW • 08/1998 08/2000 • (RF 1982 MA)

**NORTON GARY P**
8106 Vista Dr La Mesa CA 91941 • PSW • S Ex/S • Pacific Southwest Irvine CA • (949)854-3232 • (S 1963 MA)

**NORTON JUDITH L**
91-679 Ft Weaver Rd Ewa Beach HI 96706 • NOW • 07/1998 07/2000 • (S 1961)

**NORTON KENNETH J** (206)243-5813
Concordia Luth School 7040 36th Ave NE Seattle WA 98115-5966 • 73512.125@compuserve.com • NOW • Prin • Concordia Seattle WA • (206)525-7407 • (S 1959 MED)

**NORTON MARY** (253)839-7176
PO Box 54236 Redondo WA 98054 • jnorto@aol.com • NOW • Tchr • Hope Seattle WA • (206)935-8500 • (PO 1984)

**NOTTINGHAM KIM L** (708)493-2681
1301 N Irving Ave Berkeley IL 60163 • nottinghamkim@excite.com • NI • Tchr • Immanuel Elmhurst IL • (630)832-1649 • (RF 1982)

**NOVAK CHARLES J JR.** (847)724-7831
1520 Executive Ln Glenview IL 60025-1536 • qqqcadmium@aol.com • EN • P/Tchr • Our Savior Chicago IL • (773)631-1100 • (CQ 1981 MA)

**NOVAK JAN A** (360)691-3372
13313 74th St NE Lake Stevens WA 98258-9656 • NOW • Tchr • Zion Everett WA • (425)334-5064 • (IV 1988)

**NOVAK JULIE M** (734)528-1917
105 Edison St Ypsilanti MI 48197-4317 • jnovak@stpaul.k12.mi.us • MI • Tchr • St Paul Ann Arbor MI • (734)665-0604 • (RF 1986)

**NOVAK MARI-JANE G** (360)691-3372
13313 74th St NE Lake Stevens WA 98258-9656 • mj-jannovak@juno.com • NOW • Tchr • Zion Everett WA • (425)334-5064 • (CQ 1987)

**NOVAK THELMA A** (410)638-6644
803 Kilber Ct Bel Air MD 21014-5362 • SE • Tchr • St Paul Kingsville MD • (410)592-8100 • (BR 1977)

**NOVOTNY SHELLEY S** (612)484-8429
PO Box 131871 Saint Paul MN 55113-0021 • MNS • Tchr • Concordia Academy Roseville MN • (612)484-8429 • (SP 1991)

**NOVY ANDREW J** (561)499-5856
5212 Adams Rd Delray Beach FL 33484-8104 • anovy@trinitydelray.org • FG • Prin • Trinity Delray Beach FL • (561)276-8458 • (WN 1984 MED)

**NOVY JAMES R**
1465 Wheaton Memphis TN 38117 • MDS • Tchr • Christ The King Memphis TN • (901)682-8405 • (S 1991)

**NOWICKI MICHAEL W** (407)699-6931
985 Willow Run Ln Winter Springs FL 32708-4950 • smnow@mpinet.net • FG • 01/2000 • (MW 1983)

**NOWICKI SARAH E**
985 Willow Run Ln Winter Springs FL 32708-4950 • smnow@mpinet.net • S • Tchr • St Luke Oviedo FL • (407)365-3228 • (MW 1982)

**NUECHTERLEIN HERBERT** (219)744-5786
1011 W Oakdale Dr Fort Wayne IN 46807-1745 • j.nuech@aol.com • IN • EM • (CQ 1969 MMU PHD)

**NUERGE MARY K** (412)869-1936
675 Moonridge Dr Freedom PA 15042-2633 • EA • Tchr • Prince Peace Freedom PA • (724)728-3881 • (SP 1970)

**NUN SANDRA J** (512)834-1613
11803 Oak Trl Austin TX 78753-2318 • TX • Tchr • Redeemer Austin TX • (512)451-6478 • (RF 1971)

**NUNNALLY WILMA JEANE**
PO Box 7533 Chandler AZ 85246-7533 • PSW • Tchr • Gethsemane Tempe AZ • (480)839-0906 • (CQ 1989)

**NUOFFER MARCELLE D**
13253 Tripoli Ave Sylmar CA 91342 • PSW • Tchr • First LHS Sylmar CA • (818)362-9223 • (IV 1995)

**NUTT ELIZABETH ANNE**
5252 Bonita Ave Saint Louis MO 63109-3729 • MO • Tchr • St Mark Eureka MO* • (636)938-4432 • (RF 1998)

**NUTTMANN QUENTIN T**
9119 Lucia Dr Affton MO 63123-4509 • SI • Tchr • Metro-East LHS Edwardsville IL • (618)656-0043 • (S 1997)

**NYBERG STEPHANIE**
C/O Living Savior Lutheran PS 5500 Ox Rd Fairfax Station VA 22039-1020 • SE • Mem C • Living Savior Fairfax Station VA • (703)352-4208 • (RF 1999)

**NYEN DUANE M** (435)656-5172
2921 Box Elder Cir Saint George UT 84790-6903 • smudgeny@aol.com • RM • Tchr • Redeemer Salt Lake City UT • (801)467-4352 • (S 1988)

**NYSTUEN SARA L**
2425 Larpenteur Ave East #107 Maplewood MN 55109 • MNS • Tchr • Minnesota South Burnsville MN • (SP 1991)

## O

**O BOYLE SHARILYN M** (313)532-3062
3066 Helena Dr Troy MI 48083-5016 • MI • Tchr • Our Shepherd Birmingham MI • (248)645-0551 • (AA 1986)

**O BRIEN KAREN M**
1164 W Mulberry Ln Highlands Ranch CO 80126-6263 • RM • Tchr • Denver Lutheran High Denver CO • (303)934-2345 • (S 1987)

**O BRIEN KENNETH WYNN**
C/O Redeemer Lutheran School 1955 E Stratford Ave Salt Lake City UT 84106-4151 • RM • 01/1999 • (S 1989)

**O BRIEN LISA A** (801)364-4874
1320 Atkin Ave Salt Lake City UT 84106-3115 • lisaobrien@juno.com • RM • Tchr • St John Salt Lake City UT • (801)364-4874 • (S 1997)

**O CONNOR DAWN K** (262)334-7854
3137 Kristine Ln West Bend WI 53090-8649 • SW • Tchr • St John West Bend WI • (414)334-3077 • (RF 1966)

**O CONNOR KARI ANN** (415)452-8563
162 Beverly St San Francisco CA 94132 • tchrkari@aol.com • EN • Tchr • West Portal San Francisco CA • (415)665-6330 • (PO 1999)

**O CONNOR KATHLEEN** (847)695-1507
2000 Muirfield Cir Elgin IL 60123 • NI • Tchr • Northern Illinois Hillside IL • (CQ 1997 MS EDS)

**O HARA CINDY LOU** (216)252-5043
3566 W 146th St Cleveland OH 44111-3109 • tcofam@juno.com • OH • 10/1989 10/1999 • (RF 1985)

**O HARA THOMAS** (216)252-5043
3566 W 146th St Cleveland OH 44111-3109 • tcofam@juno.com • OH • 06/1999 • (RF 1985)

**O KEEFE RUTH ELAINE** (209)368-2090
1716 Reisling Dr Lodi CA 95240-6113 • CNH • Tchr • St Peter Lodi CA • (209)333-2225 • (S 1968)

**O LEARY MICHAEL LIND JR.** (630)295-9368
57 E Hattendorf Ave #213 Roselle IL 60172 • crfolearyml@curf.edu • NI • SHS/C • Northern Illinois Hillside IL • (IV 1988 MS PHD)

**O MEARA ELIZABETH EMILY** (810)263-3565
46188 Peach Grove St Macomb MI 48044-3494 • MI • Tchr • Immanuel Macomb MI • (810)286-7076 • (CQ 1997 MAT)

**O NEAL LORRE MARIE** (541)895-3482
34388 Christmas Tree Ln Creswell OR 97426-9430 • NOW • Tchr • Bethany Springfield OR • (541)726-7365 • (S 1968)

**OBERDIECK BRIAN**
1508 Saint Johns Church Rd NE Lanesville IN 47136-8538 • IN • Tchr • St John Lanesville IN • (812)952-2737 • (RF 1992)

**OBERKROM HOLLY ANN** (314)893-6307
4211 Pinehurst Ct Jefferson City MO 65109 • MO • 07/1990 07/2000 • (AU 1988)

**OBERLIES KATRINA ANN**
C/O Immanuel Luth Church PO Box 290 Rosebud MO 63091-0290 • MO • St John Lanesville IN • (CQ 1999 MED)

**OBERMANN DONNA S** (309)691-6475
7500 N Radnor Rd Peoria IL 61615-9437 • CI • Tchr • Good Shepherd Pekin IL • (309)347-2020 • (S 1975)

**OBERMUELLER ELIZABETH ANN** (402)643-3977
1348 Rainbow Ave Seward NE 68434-1326 • eao0906@seward.cune.edu • NEB • Tchr • St John Seward NE • (402)643-4535 • (S 1967)

**OBERMUELLER RUDOLPH W** (713)255-2238
402 N Pecan St Tomball TX 77375-4466 • TX • EM • (S 1931)

**OBERMUELLER STANLEY DR** (402)643-3977
1348 Rainbow Ave Seward NE 68434-1326 • sobermueller@seward.ccsn.edu • NEB • SHS/C • Nebraska Seward NE • (S 1968 MED PHD)

**OBERSAAT BUSMAN RUTH CHERYL** (651)779-6180
2260 Ariel St N North Saint Paul MN 55109-2852 • ruthstan@iname.com • MNS • SHS/C • Minnesota South Burnsville MN • (S 1981 MPH DED)

**OBLINGER CAROLYN DENISE** (616)556-1009
1355 Timberlane Dr Saint Joseph MI 49085 • TX • 06/1998 06/2000 • (AA 1997)

**OBRZUT HEIDE L**
2242 Westwood Dr Hillside IL 60162 • NI • Tchr • Immanuel Hillside IL • (708)562-5580 • (RF 1997)

**OBSUSZT KAREN JEAN** (815)874-0027
5219 Linden Rd #3302 Rockford IL 61109 • NI • Tchr • Immanuel Belvidere IL • (815)544-8058 • (RF 1997)

**OCHS DAVID L** (316)744-9390
4119 N Edgemoor St Wichita KS 67220-2033 • KS • Tchr • Holy Cross Wichita KS • (316)684-4431 • (S 1980)

**ODEAN WALTER H** (630)851-1048
560 4th Ave Aurora IL 60505-4800 • NI • EM • (CQ 1954 MA)

**ODINGA ARDITH A** (517)791-3520
4337 Persimmon Dr Saginaw MI 48603-1149 • MI • Tchr • Holy Cross Saginaw MI • (517)793-9795 • (S 1970 MAT)

**ODINGA MICHAEL D** (517)791-3520
4337 Persimmon Dr Saginaw MI 48603-1149 • MI • Tchr • Peace Saginaw MI • (517)792-2581 • (S 1969 MA)

**ODLE SUSAN H** (949)551-9050
33 Westport Irvine CA 92620-2656 • susanodle@aol.com • PSW • Tchr • Lutheran HS/Orange C Orange CA • (714)998-5151 • (CQ 1985)

**OEHLERT GEORGE J** (314)961-0805
740 Catalpa Ave Saint Louis MO 63119-4206 • MO • S Ex/S • Missouri Saint Louis MO • (314)317-4550 • (S 1967 MBA)

**OERKFITZ JOYCE A** (216)398-9287
4524 Wichita Ave Cleveland OH 44144-3663 • EN • Tchr • West Park Cleveland OH • (216)941-2770 • (RF 1965)

**OERKFITZ KENNETH J** (216)398-9287
4524 Wichita Ave Cleveland OH 44144-3663 • EN • West Park Cleveland OH • (RF 1965 MA)

**OERMAN REBECCA L** (507)776-7870
310 N 1st Ave E Truman MN 56088 • rebeccaoerman@excite.com • MNS • Tchr • Martin Luther Northrop MN • (507)436-5249 • (S 1985)

**OESTERREICH ALLAN C** (708)425-7585
9535 S Trumbull Ave Evergreen Park IL 60805-3058 • aoesterr@luthersouth.com • NI • Tchr • Luther HS South Chicago IL • (773)737-1416 • (RF 1959 MS MSED)
**OESTERREICH DONNA G** (218)879-9147
31 Erickson Rd Esko MN 55733-9556 • MNN • 10/1985 09/1999 • (SP 1980)
**OESTERREICH KARIN**
10036 W Capitol Dr Apt 4 Milwaukee WI 53222-1333 • koesterreich@lhskc.com • MO • Tchr • Missouri Saint Louis MO • (314)317-4550 • (RF 1994)
**OESTMANN MARVIN P** (303)693-9880
17812 E Lehigh Pl Aurora CO 80013-3418 • marv.oestmann@pwclc.org • RM • P/Tchr • Peace Aurora CO • (303)766-7116 • (CQ 1968 MA)
**OESTREICH ROBERT C** (217)428-7767
136 S Dipper Ln Decatur IL 62522 • CI • EM • (RF 1930)
**OESTRIECHER DIANE JULIANN** (504)466-3011
162 Miami Pl Kenner LA 70065-4030 • SO • Tchr • Faith Harahan LA • (504)737-9554 • (CQ 1995)
**OETTING AARON PETER** (979)247-4294
2016 Camp Lone Star Rd La Grange NE 78945-6067 • atoetting@juno.com • AT • 11/1998 • (S 1998)
**OETTING DANIEL L** (219)482-9254
316 N 6th St Seward NE 68434 • NEB • 09/1998 • (S 1987)
**OETTING DENNIS D**
10B International Tower 23 South Bay Close Repulse Bay HONG KONG • MDS • S Miss • Mid-South Cordova TN • (S 1966 MA)
**OETTING EUGENE M** (402)643-4198
1609 N 2nd St Seward NE 68434-1021 • NEB • EM • (S 1954 MED DED)
**OETTING HARRIET M** (402)643-4198
1609 N Second Seward NE 68434-1021 • NEB • EM • (S 1964 MED)
**OETTING JONATHAN W**
CMA BP 438 Conakry Rebublic of Guinea WEST AFRICA • CNH • 04/1996 04/1998 • (S 1987)
**OFFERMANN DAVID KENYON** (612)467-4317
605 George St Hamburg MN 55339-9455 • MNS • Tchr • Emanuel Hamburg MN • (612)467-2780 • (RF 1991)
**OFFERMANN GLENN W** (651)631-2637
1371 Burke Ave W Saint Paul MN 55113-5803 • offermann@luther.csp.edu • MNS • SHS/C • Minnesota South Burnsville MN • (RF 1958 MLS PHD)
**OFFERMANN WENDY KAY** (913)273-6532
2718 SW Staffordshire Rd Topeka KS 66614-4361 • KS • EM • (S 1985)
**OHLMAN KATHLEEN R**
4900 NW 10th St Lincoln NE 68521 • NEB • Tchr • Lincoln Luth Jr/Sr H Lincoln NE • (402)467-5404 • (S 1985 MED)
**OHLMANN GLENN E** (402)643-2769
510 Hillcrest Dr Seward NE 68434-2826 • gohlmann@seward.cune.edu • NEB • SHS/C • Nebraska Seward NE • (S 1963 MA)
**OHLMANN MARGARET** (913)367-0486
1012 S 5th St Atchison KS 66002-3116 • KS • EM • (S 1951)
**OHMIE KARLA JOANNE** (316)943-3261
1913 N Kessler Wichita KS 67203-1037 • johnoqt@yahoo.com • KS • Tchr • Bethany Wichita KS • (316)265-7415 • (S 1993)
**OKA CHRISTINA JULIA** (425)348-4899
12510 Meridian Ave S #2 Everett WA 98208-5770 • okafamily@earthlink.net • NOW • Tchr • Concordia Seattle WA • (206)525-7407 • (PO 1995)
**OKONSKI JOHN S** (619)743-4448
2162 Darby St Escondido CA 92025-6464 • PSW • 12/1981 12/1999 • (S 1967)
**OKUN JACKIE M** (813)681-5789
4112 Robin Way Valrico FL 33594-5429 • run4hlth@aol.com • FG • Tchr • Immanuel Brandon FL • (813)685-1978 • (BR 1977 MA)
**OLDEHOEFT HAROLD W** (402)675-7915
PO Box 1 Battle Creek NE 68715-0001 • NEB • P/Tchr • St John Battle Creek NE • (402)675-3605 • (S 1964)
**OLDENBURG KATHRYN L** (414)369-9773
1009 Hilger Rd Hartland WI 53029 • SW • Tchr • Divine Redeemer Hartland WI • (414)367-8400 • (S 1980)
**OLDENBURG MARY K** (719)687-3560
PO Box 9042 Woodland Park CO 80866-9042 • lvr@lvr.org • RM • 11/1990 11/2000 • (RF 1983)
**OLDENBURG MICHAEL P** (262)369-9773
1009 Hilger Rd Hartland WI 53029-1215 • SW • Prin • Divine Redeemer Hartland WI • (414)367-8400 • (RF 1976 MED MED)
**OLESON CINDY ANNE** (847)891-2404
368 Ferndale Ct Unit C2 Schaumburg IL 60193-2275 • NI • Tchr • St Peter Schaumburg IL • (847)885-7636 • (RF 1987 MA)
**OLESON DAVID G** (714)823-0201
9326 Date St Fontana CA 92335-5676 • PSW • Tchr • Redeemer Ontario CA • (909)986-6510 • (S 1967 MED)
**OLESON PEGGY L** (715)423-1844
3030 Sampson St Wisconsin Rapids WI 54494-6287 • olepeg@wctc.net • NW • Tchr • Immanuel Wisconsin Rapids WI • (715)423-0272 • (MQ 1985)
**OLIVER CHARLES A**
C/O Concordia University 12800 N Lake Shore Dr Mequon WI 53097-2402 • SW • SHS/C • South Wisconsin Milwaukee WI • (414)464-8100 • (MQ 1990)
**OLIVER JOANN** (734)283-1984
15660 Cumberland Riverview MI 48192-8173 • MI • Tchr • Calvary Lincoln Park MI • (313)381-6715 • (RF 1974)
**OLIVER TIMOTHY DEAN** (402)643-3249
233 E Northern Heights Dr Seward NE 68434-1159 • NEB • 08/1996 08/2000 • (S 1979)
**OLLHOFF JEANNE A** (517)784-3591
5525 S Jackson Rd Jackson MI 49201-8311 • jeanne³ollhoff@yahoo.com • MI • Prin • Trinity Jackson MI • (517)750-2105 • (RF 1962 MA)
**OLOFF JAMES L** (208)522-1440
3625 S Koester Rd Idaho Falls ID 83402-4333 • NOW • Tchr • Hope Idaho Falls ID • (208)529-8080 • (SP 1973 MED)
**OLSEN ADRIENNE** (303)788-0680
C/O Shepherd of the Hills 7691 S University Blvd Littleton CO 80122-3144 • RM • Tchr • Shepherd Hills Littleton CO • (303)798-0711 • (RF 2000)
**OLSEN HEIDI KAY** (507)285-5771
418 14th Ave NE Rochester MN 55901-4563 • MNS • Tchr • Rochester Central Rochester MN • (507)289-3267 • (SP 1995)
**OLSEN JOANN I** (941)341-0651
1036 Marlin Lakes Cir Apt 1427 Sarasota FL 34232-5982 • FG • Mem C • Our Savior Plantation FL • (954)473-6888 • (RF 1992)
**OLSEN MATTHEW W** (810)772-7768
15731 Mok Ave Eastpointe MI 48021-2368 • MI • Tchr • St Peter Eastpointe MI • (810)771-2809 • (AA 1990)
**OLSEN ROY CHARLES III** (941)341-0651
1036 Marlin Lakes Cir Apt 1427 Sarasota FL 34232-5982 • lightkeeper@home.com • FG • 05/1999 • (RF 1994)
**OLSON CAROL L** (507)278-4862
PO Box 33 Good Thunder MN 56037-0033 • clolson@gotocrystal.net • MNS • Tchr • St Johns Good Thunder MN • (507)278-3635 • (S 1981)
**OLSON JEAN M** (901)398-8449
1375 N Faronia Sq Memphis TN 38116-6510 • MDS • Tchr • Cross Of Calvary Memphis TN • (901)396-5566 • (S 1958)
**OLSON JOHN R** (517)662-6635
3791 Carter Rd Auburn MI 48611-9526 • MI • Tchr • Zion Auburn MI • (517)662-4264 • (RF 1971)
**OLSON JUDITH C** (816)468-6161
5806 N Kensington Ave Kansas City MO 64119-2887 • gjkn@juno.com • MO • Tchr • Holy Cross Kansas City MO • (816)453-7211 • (RF 1980 MA)
**OLSON PETER THOMAS** (920)208-3237
1131 Union Ave Sheboygan WI 53081-5938 • olson@lutheranhigh.com • SW • Tchr • Lutheran HS Sheboygan WI • (920)452-3323 • (RF 1997)
**OLSON RUTH E** (208)829-4214
1002 S 1900 E Hazelton ID 83335-5451 • NOW • Tchr • Trinity Eden ID • (208)825-5277 • (S 1962)
**OLSON SUSAN KAY** (314)428-7499
10894 Verhaven Dr Apt D St Louis MO 63114 • MO • Tchr • St Paul Jackson MO • (573)243-5360 • (S 1999)
**OLSON TAMARA MELANI**
10841 Humboldt Ave S Bloomington MN 55431-4220 • MNS • Tchr • Mount Hope-Redemptio Bloomington MN • (612)881-0036 • (SP 1993)
**OPEL EDGAR L** (517)686-0418
1631 Amelith Rd Bay City MI 48706-9378 • amelith@concentric.com • MI • Prin • St John Bay City MI • (517)686-0176 • (S 1958 MA)
**OPEL R WARREN** (810)463-5337
437 Esplanade St Mount Clemens MI 48043-6528 • MI • Prin • Trinity Clinton Township MI • (810)463-2921 • (S 1962 MED EDS)
**OPPERMANN BARBARA ANN** (414)549-0401
W225N2622 Alderwood Ln Waukesha WI 53186-8819 • SW • Tchr • Immanuel Brookfield WI • (414)781-4135 • (RF 1973)
**ORE CHARLES W**
PO Box 52 Seward NE 68434-0052 • NEB • SHS/C • Nebraska Seward NE • (S 1958 MMU)
**ORE CONSTANCE**
2523 Bluff Rd Seward NE 68434-8028 • NEB • Mem C • St John Seward NE • (402)643-2983 • (S 1959)
**ORLOW-BRANDT VICKI L**
5844 NE 24th Ave Portland OR 97211-6126 • NOW • Tchr • St Michael Portland OR • (503)282-0000 • (MQ 1986)
**ORTEGO SUSAN KAY** (337)584-3134
902 Travis Ln Elton LA 70532 • NI • Tchr • Our Saviour Chicago IL • (773)736-1120 • (RF 1996)
**OSBORN JAMES M** (216)398-7286
3310 Ralph Ave Cleveland OH 44109-5511 • OH • Tchr • St Thomas Rocky River OH • (440)331-2680 • (S 1973)
**OSBORN-NICHOLAS SUSAN M** (630)894-8610
312 Hempstead Ln Bloomingdale IL 60108 • NI • 02/1998 02/2000 • (RF 1976)
**OSBORNE MICHAEL J** (517)448-8309
2651 Elm Rd Hudson MI 49247 • mosborn@tc3net.com • MI • Prin • St John Adrian MI • (517)265-6998 • (CQ 2000 MED)
**OSBOURN LAURA E**
405 Old Orchard Dr #13 Essexville MI 48732 • MI • Tchr • Immanuel Bay City MI • (517)893-8521 • (RF 1999)
**OSBOURN SCOTT C**
405 Old Orchard Dr #13 Essexville MI 48732 • MI • Tchr • Immanuel Bay City MI • (517)893-8521 • (RF 1999)
**OSBUN NANCY** (219)426-9439
1213 W Jefferson Blvd Fort Wayne IN 46802-4013 • sarahartburn@hotmail.com • IN • Tchr • Unity Fort Wayne IN • (219)744-0459 • (S 1966)
**OSTERMANN SUSAN M** (817)861-6309
1705 Homedale Dr Apt 1701 Fort Worth TX 76112-3651 • TX • Tchr • Grace Arlington TX • (817)274-1654 • (SP 1985)
**OSTROWSKI VICKI LYNN** (414)358-2164
8227 W Brentwood Ave Milwaukee WI 53223-5530 • rvwsjdbm@aol.com • SW • Tchr • St Peter Milwaukee WI • (414)353-6800 • (MQ 1989)
**OTHLING-CARMAN SHARON L** (256)828-8562
324 Delynn Dr Hazel Green AL 35750 • othcar324@gateway.net • SO • Mem C • Ascension Huntsville AL • (256)536-9987 • (S 1974 MED)
**OTT DONNA JEAN** (517)790-8608
5100 Kentford Dr N Saginaw MI 48603-5547 • MI • Tchr • Peace Saginaw MI • (517)792-2581 • (RF 1982)
**OTTE CAROLYN A** (303)922-8845
2972 S Zenobia St Denver CO 80236-2031 • lcotte@aol.com • RM • Tchr • St John Denver CO • (303)733-3777 • (S 1979)
**OTTE LOREN L** (303)922-8845
2972 S Zenobia St Denver CO 80236-2031 • lcotte@aol.com • RM • Tchr • Denver Lutheran High Denver CO • (303)934-2345 • (S 1977 MA)
**OTTEN CARL W** (636)673-3030
2596 S Strack Church Rd Wright City MO 63390-5804 • MO • 02/1998 02/2000 • (RF 1965 MA EDS)
**OTTEN ELISE**
257 N Wilmette Ave Westmont IL 60559-1732 • PSW • Tchr • Pacific Southwest Irvine CA • (949)854-3232 • (RF 1997)
**OTTEN HANS K** (920)803-9572
412 Bell Ave Sheboygan WI 53083 • SW • Tchr • Lutheran HS Sheboygan WI • (920)452-3323 • (RF 1989)
**OTTERSTEIN JAMES**
24 Arrow Point Dr Hillsboro MO 63050-4412 • MO • EM • (RF 1970 MA)
**OTTO BRENDA L** (517)667-4207
902 N Dean St Bay City MI 48706-3616 • MI • Tchr • St Paul Bay City MI • (517)684-4450 • (AA 1990 MAT)
**OTTO DEANNA L**
6823 S Ivy St # 5-208 Englewood CO 80112-6220 • RM • Tchr • Emmaus Denver CO • (303)433-3303 • (S 1993)
**OTTO JANE M** (810)783-5671
636 Crest St Mount Clemens MI 48043-6433 • MI • Tchr • St Peter Macomb MI • (810)781-9296 • (S 1982 MA)
**OTTO PHYLLIS F** (616)738-9164
5432 Sand Dune Ct SW Grandville MI 49418 • pfordo7@iserv.net • MI • EM • (SP 1965 MA)
**OTTO TERRY J** (262)593-5117
W1266 Concord Center Dr Oconomowoc WI 53066-9005 • terryo@execpc.com • SW • P/Tchr • St Paul Oconomowoc WI • (262)567-5001 • (S 1968 MA)
**OTZEN LAURIE J**
9A International Tower 23 S Bay Close Repulse Bay HONG KONG • PSW • S Miss • Pacific Southwest Irvine CA • (949)854-3232 • (RF 1970 MA)
**OVERGAARD KIM A** (810)233-7996
2207 Monteith St Flint MI 48504-4663 • MI • Tchr • St Paul Flint MI • (810)239-6733 • (SP 1974 MA)
**OWEN ANGELA J** (219)485-1418
8317 Roanoke Dr Fort Wayne IN 46835-4348 • aowen4@aol.com • IN • Tchr • Concordia Fort Wayne IN • (219)426-9922 • (RF 1986)
**OWEN CHRISTINE ANN**
804 Walnut Ave Norfolk NE 68701-3938 • NEB • Tchr • Christ Norfolk NE • (402)371-5536 • (S 1991)
**OWEN LISA A** (219)465-7254
907 Wood St Valparaiso IN 46383-5065 • EN • 09/1984 09/1999 • (RF 1980)
**OYLER BERTHA J** (414)457-6336
321 Ontario Ave Sheboygan WI 53081-4133 • SW • Tchr • Trinity Sheboygan WI • (920)458-8248 • (S 1965 MED)

## P

**PAAPE ADAM D**
4423 Primrose Ct - #110 Sheboygan WI 53081 • SW • Tchr • Lutheran HS Sheboygan WI • (920)452-3323 • (MQ 2000)
**PABST LEROY W** (562)920-3827
9641 Faywood St Bellflower CA 90706-3016 • PSW • Tchr • Good Shepherd Downey CA • (562)803-4918 • (S 1964 MMU)
**PABST MARY H** (562)920-3827
9641 Faywood St Bellflower CA 90706-3016 • PSW • Tchr • Good Shepherd Downey CA • (562)803-4918 • (S 1964 MED)
**PACIFICI JONI B**
1173 Dublin Cir Jerome MI 49249 • MI • Tchr • St John Adrian MI • (517)265-6998 • (AA 1987)
**PACKARD HEATHER L** (630)483-0544
5825 Charleston Ct Hanover Park IL 60103 • leightheatre@aol.com • NI • Northern Illinois Hillside IL • (RF 1997)
**PACKARD MARY MARTHA** (630)483-0544
5825 Charleston Ct Hanover Park IL 60103-5209 • mmcp46@aol.com • NI • Tchr • Messiah Chicago IL • (773)725-8903 • (CQ 1995 MA)
**PAGANO MARY ANN** (616)465-5472
3228 Snow Rd Bridgman MI 49106-9785 • jpagano@remcll.k12.mi.us • MI • Tchr • Trinity Sawyer MI • (616)426-3937 • (RF 1974)
**PAGE CATHERINE MARIE** (281)448-7655
7811 Streamside Dr Houston TX 77088-4413 • cpage@stmarkhouston.org • TX • Tchr • St Mark Houston TX • (713)468-2623 • (RF 1994)
**PAGELS DORIS E** (810)949-3505
26425 Birchcrest Dr Chesterfield MI 48051-3015 • MI • Tchr • St Thomas Eastpointe MI • (810)772-3372 • (RF 1980 MA)
**PAGELS JAMES D** (810)949-3505
26425 Birchcrest Dr Chesterfield MI 48051-3015 • jpagels@luthsped.org • MI • Tchr • Special Ed Ministrie Detroit MI • (313)368-1220 • (RF 1964 PHD)
**PAHLKOTTER HENRY GORDON II** (810)727-7338
70274 Canterbury Dr Richmond MI 48062 • hpahlkotter@hotmail.com • MI • Prin • St Peter Richmond MI • (810)727-9693 • (AA 1987 MA)

**PAJKOWSKI EILEEN M** (516)234-5132
82 Snowberry Ln Islandia NY 11749 • AT • Tchr • Trinity Hicksville NY • (516)931-2211 • (BR 1990)

**PAKKALA DEBORAH** (313)733-7295
1284 Springborrow Dr Flint MI 48532-2171 • MI • Tchr • St Paul Flint MI • (810)239-6733 • (RF 1971)

**PALISCH DANIEL E** (573)204-1284
1515 Kimbeland Jackson MO 63755 • ddpalisch@aol.com • MO • Tchr • St Paul Jackson MO • (573)243-2236 • (S 1967 MA)

**PALISCH THEODORE M** (314)544-1866
10117 Zenith Ct Saint Louis MO 63123-7420 • MO • Tchr • Green Park Lemay MO • (314)544-4248 • (RF 1972)

**PALKA SUSAN E**
2030 S Commerce Rd Walled Lake MI 48390-2412 • MI • P/Tchr • St Matthew Walled Lake MI • (248)624-7677 • (S 1984 MA)

**PALKEWICK NATHANIEL ALAN** (914)948-9754
101 Woodside Ave E West Harrison NY 10604-2144 • natek9@aol.com • AT • Tchr • Our Saviour Bronx NY • (718)792-5665 • (BR 1998)

**PALLAS JACK D** (612)448-6993
845 Livingston Ct Chaska MN 55318-1291 • MNS • Mem C • St John Chaska MN • (612)448-2433 • (S 1987)

**PALMER CONNIE L** (414)752-9216
5801 N Meadows Dr Racine WI 53402-5514 • tocojo@exec.pc • SW • Tchr • Trinity Racine WI • (414)632-1766 • (S 1973)

**PALMER MARK T** (512)341-0405
3713 Bratton Heights Dr Austin TX 78728 • TX • 09/1998 • (AU 1991 MED)

**PALMER RACHEL M DR** (708)452-8342
1733 N 74th Ct Elmwood Park IL 60707-4225 • crfpalmerrm@crf.cuis.edu • NI • SHS/C • Northern Illinois Hillside IL • (RF 1968 MS DED)

**PALMETER DONALD W** (810)731-5009
5346 Wiley Dr Utica MI 48317-1274 • MI • Tchr • Trinity Utica MI • (810)731-4490 • (RF 1964 MA)

**PALMREUTER DAVID WARD**
11086 S Evergreen Birch Run MI 48415 • MI • Tchr • St Lorenz Frankenmuth MI • (517)652-6141 • (RF 1991 MS)

**PALMREUTER JOEL KENNETH** (303)337-0294
18035 E Utah Pl Aurora CO 80017-5359 • jpalmreute@aol.com • RM • Tchr • Lutheran HS Rockies Parker CO • (303)841-5551 • (IV 1993)

**PALMREUTER KATHY RAE** (414)327-3426
2335 S 78th St West Allis WI 53219 • SW • Tchr • St Paul West Allis WI • (414)541-6251 • (RF 1996)

**PALMREUTER KENNETH R DR** (303)988-1802
2783 S Depew St Denver CO 80227-4106 • kpalmreute@aol.com • RM • Prin • North Lutheran Broomfield CO • (720)887-9031 • (RF 1962 MA LLD)

**PALMREUTER MARTHA M** (303)988-1802
2783 S Depew St Denver CO 80227-4106 • kpalmreute@aol.com • RM • EM • (RF 1961)

**PALMREUTER MICHAEL EUGENE** (210)946-0311
5530 Mountain Vista Dr San Antonio TX 78247-4653 • mikep@concordia-satx.com • TX • Mem C • Concordia San Antonio TX • (210)479-1477 • (RF 1993)

**PALUCH ALLAN E** (713)661-9759
6410 Ferris Dr Apt 21 Houston TX 77081-4609 • TX • Tchr • Pilgrim Houston TX • (713)666-3706 • (RF 1969)

**PALUCH BETH ANN** (231)744-3487
3053 Ewing Rd Twin Lake MI 49457-9224 • paluchfam@cs.com • MI • Tchr • West Shore Muskegon MI • (616)755-1048 • (RF 1981)

**PALUCH KAREN** (281)516-1633
15319 Hunters Bend Dr Tomball TX 77375-3902 • TX • Tchr • Salem Tomball TX • (281)351-8122 • (RF 1977)

**PALUCH MARTIN W** (281)516-1633
15319 Hunters Bend Dr Tomball TX 77375-3902 • mpaluch@salem4u.com • TX • Prin • Salem Tomball TX • (281)351-8122 • (RF 1977 MED)

**PANGBURN ALBERT** (716)731-5991
5917 Shawnee Rd Sanborn NY 14132-9222 • EA • Tchr • St Peter Lockport NY • (716)433-9014 • (RF 1966 MS MS)

**PANGBURN CHERYL** (518)355-0518
2070 Giffords Church Rd Schenectady NY 12306-5420 • AT • Tchr • Our Savior Albany NY • (518)459-2273 • (RF 1969 MA)

**PANKOW ERIC J** (414)466-2992
5405 N 106th St Milwaukee WI 53225-3207 • SW • Tchr • Milwaukee LHS Milwaukee WI • (414)461-6000 • (RF 1983 MEPD)

**PANKOW MARCUS G**
N996 Fox Run Ln Apt #1 Oconomowoc WI 53066 • NW • EM • (RF 1958 MSED)

**PANKOW SHIRLEY M** (517)642-8333
2750 N Raucholz Rd Hemlock MI 48626-9680 • MI • EM • (RF 1951)

**PAPE DONALD E** (219)484-6088
3327 Collegiate Ct Fort Wayne IN 46805-1601 • dep@msn.com • IN • EM • (S 1953 MAD)

**PAPE JILL A** (815)229-5425
409 N 2nd St #2 Rockford IL 61104-4004 • derusha1@hotmail.com • NI • Tchr • Luther Academy Rockford IL • (815)877-9551 • (MQ 1995)

**PAPENBERG WALTER L** (231)972-2650
10791 Peninsula Dr Stanwood MI 49346-9746 • MI • EM • (RF 1943 MED)

**PAPENDORF LISA ANN** (715)823-5962
N2931 Cty Rd D Clintonville WI 54929 • NW • Tchr • St James Shawano WI • (715)524-4815 • (MQ 1994)

**PAQUET BEVERLY JEAN** (314)894-8422
5728 Hidden Stone Dr Saint Louis MO 63129-2926 • bevpaquet@hotmail.com • MO • Tchr • Green Park Lemay MO • (314)544-4248 • (CQ 1992 MAT)

**PARGEE HELENE THERESA** (714)637-1438
16322 E Heim Ave Orange CA 92865-2810 • PSW • Tchr • St Paul Orange CA • (714)637-2640 • (CQ 1993)

**PARKER DAVID W**
9086 E 2100 North Rd Oakwood IL 61858-6249 • SI • Tchr • Trinity Hoffman IL • (618)495-2545 • (RF 1987)

**PARKER EVA M** (205)473-1555
1572 Colgin St Mobile AL 36605-4822 • SO • Tchr • Trinity Mobile AL • (334)456-7929 • (S 1970)

**PARKER MICAH G** (402)643-3107
1230 N 7th Seward NE 68434 • mparker@cune.edu • NEB • SHS/C • Nebraska Seward NE • (S 1991 MED PHD)

**PARKER PATRICIA JEAN**
20061 Dunstable Cir Germantown MD 20876-6350 • SE • 02/2000 • (AU 1995)

**PARRIS CIMBERLY** (770)321-9711
936 East Lake Dr Marietta GA 30062 • FG • Tchr • Faith Marietta GA • (770)973-8877 • (S 2000)

**PARRIS FRANKLIN O** (913)367-7044
17304 290th Rd Atchison KS 66002 • fpmp@ponyexpress.net • KS • Tchr • Trinity Atchison KS • (913)367-2837 • (S 1989 MEAD)

**PARROT SCOTT A** (219)744-7372
541 Pinegrove Ln Apt C Fort Wayne IN 46807 • scott³parrot@email.com • FG • 01/1999 • (RF 1997)

**PARROTT CRAIG H** (303)940-9626
C/O Colorado Lutheran High Sch 3201 W Arizona Ave Denver CO 80219-3941 • cparrott@usa.net • RM • Tchr • Denver Lutheran High Denver CO • (303)934-2345 • (S 1979 MA MS)

**PARRY STEPHEN EDWARD** (219)778-9853
3456 E Sand Ridge Rolling Prairie IN 46371 • sparry@teacher.com • IN • Tchr • St John La Porte IN • (219)362-6692 • (RF 1990 MA)

**PARSCALE BRENDA L** (501)227-8673
23 Westoak Cir Little Rock AR 72223 • MDS • Tchr • Christ Little Rock AR • (501)663-5212 • (CQ 1999 MS)

**PARTON LAURIE J** (303)344-9085
584 Ursula St Aurora CO 80011-8518 • RM • Tchr • Hope Aurora CO • (303)364-1828 • (S 1994)

**PARVEY LINDA L** (612)753-2441
19940 Xavis St NW Cedar MN 55011-9260 • mccspov@aol.com • MNS • Tchr • Mount Olive Anoka MN • (612)421-9048 • (S 1974)

**PASCHAL RUTH ANN** (314)221-5977
10228 Lemgri Pl Hannibal MO 63401 • EN • Tchr • St John Hannibal MO • (573)221-0215 • (RF 1967)

**PASCHE RAYMOND F** (219)485-4965
4014 Knightway Dr Fort Wayne IN 46815-5030 • IN • EM • (S 1959 MED)

**PASELK RENATE E** (810)795-3072
35462 Wellston Ave Sterling Hts MI 48312-3773 • ptp555@aol.com • MI • Tchr • St Peter Macomb MI • (810)781-3434 • (S 1973)

**PATA RONDA CHARLYN** (310)318-9606
1521 Ford Ave Redondo Beach CA 90278-2801 • krcpata@aol.com • PSW • Tchr • First Manhattan Beach CA • (310)545-5653 • (CQ 1995)

**PATTERSON JUDY ELLEN** (419)352-3616
831 Jefferson Dr Bowling Green OH 43402 • OH • Tchr • St Philip Toledo OH • (419)475-2835 • (SP 1994)

**PATTERSON LAURA J** (414)873-0226
3267 N 88th St Milwaukee WI 53222-3603 • patterson@gna.net • SW • Tchr • Our Redeemer Wauwatosa WI • (414)258-4558 • (RF 1983)

**PATTERSON MYRA** (808)488-3309
98-2065 Pahiolo St Aiea HI 96701 • CNH • Tchr • Our Savior Aiea HI • (808)488-0000 • (S 1966)

**PATTERSON THOMAS** (808)488-3309
98 185 Puaalii St Aiea HI 96701 • CNH • Tchr • Our Savior Aiea HI • (808)488-0000 • (S 1973)

**PATTON DEBRA R** (914)376-3640
41 Central Park Ave # 3 Yonkers NY 10705-4746 • AT • Tchr • St Mark Yonkers NY • (914)237-4944 • (BR 1987)

**PATTON LINDA R** (636)938-9693
242 Walden Ct Eureka MO 63025-1130 • MO • Tchr • St Mark Eureka MO • (636)938-4432 • (RF 1987 MED)

**PAUL GREGORY L** (248)585-3288
314 Aqua Ct Royal Oak MI 48073-4004 • glpaul3288@earthlink.net • MI • Tchr • St Paul Royal Oak MI • (248)546-6555 • (S 1984)

**PAUL JEN YI IRENE**
Estrada da Vitoria 24 Edificio Long Chu Ter B 8 Macau MACAU • paulm@macau.ctm.net • MO • Tchr • St John Saint Louis MO • (314)773-0126 • (S 1990 MED)

**PAUL ROBIN M** (920)338-0568
801 Manitowish Pl De Pere WI 54115 • NW • Tchr • St Paul Luxemburg WI • (920)845-5248 • (RF 1996)

**PAUL WALTER H** (319)391-7826
2702 N Fillmore St Davenport IA 52804-1833 • IE • EM • (S 1934 MS)

**PAUL WARREN F** (850)492-4888
1090 Chandelle Lake Dr Pensacola FL 32507 • tchpaul@pcola.gulf.net • SO • Prin • Redeemer Pensacola FL • (850)455-0330 • (S 1969 MSED)

**PAULI ELAINE E** (248)651-4081
436 Meadow Ln Rochester MI 48307-2218 • MI • EM • (RF 1970 MA)

**PAULING FREDERICK J** (703)549-8062
411 Summers Dr Alexandria VA 22301-2448 • SE • Tchr • Immanuel Alexandria VA • (703)549-7323 • (S 1961)

**PAULOS VICTOR** (262)544-4691
1940 Dixie Dr Waukesha WI 53189-7332 • SW • EM • (RF 1949 MA MA)

**PAULSEL BRENDA KAY** (605)332-8966
401 S Sycamore # 105 Sioux Falls SD 57103 • SD • 11/1995 11/1999 • (S 1991)

**PAULSON BRENT E** (507)387-8177
7470 W 22nd Ave Lakewood CO 80215-2016 • bremen5@aol.com • RM • Tchr • Bethlehem Lakewood CO • (303)233-0401 • (S 1990)

**PAUTLER VERA** (618)785-2303
7615 Ruby Ln Baldwin IL 62217-1063 • SI • Tchr • St John Red Bud IL • (618)282-3873 • (RF 1968)

**PAVEL HEIDI LYNN** (402)643-2805
221 James Ave North Platte NE 69101 • NEB • Tchr • Our Redeemer North Platte NE • (308)532-6421 • (S 1985)

**PAVELSKI SUZANNE RAE**
2225 E 14 Mile Rd Birmingham MI 48009 • MI • Tchr • Our Shepherd Birmingham MI • (248)646-6100 • (CQ 1994)

**PAVIA CLAIRE C**
C/O Saint John Lutheran Church 305 Circle Ave Forest Park IL 60130 • NI • Tchr • St John Forest Park IL • (708)366-3226 • (RF 1999)

**PAWELK FRED**
PO Box 605 Lester Prairie MN 55354-0605 • NI • SHS/C • Northern Illinois Hillside IL • (RF 1989)

**PAWLITZ GAIL E** (314)647-3765
2913 Ellendale Ave Saint Louis MO 63143-3413 • rpawlitz@stlnet.com • MO • S Ex/S • Missouri Saint Louis MO • (314)317-4550 • (S 1970)

**PAWLITZ GARY L DR** (810)948-5169
50629 Cameron Macomb MI 48044-1337 • gpawlitz@rust.net • MI • Mem C • Immanuel Macomb MI • (810)286-4231 • (S 1968 MS PHD)

**PAWLITZ RONALD H** (314)647-3765
2913 Ellendale Ave Saint Louis MO 63143-3413 • rpawlitz#stlnet.com • MO • Prin • Concordia Middle Saint Louis MO • (314)865-1144 • (S 1970 MAR)

**PAYNE ALEX R** (713)895-9388
6000 Hollister Ave Houston TX 77040 • TX • Tchr • LHS North Houston TX • (713)880-3131 • (SP 1998)

**PEARA KAREN E** (312)741-5580
400 Lovell St Elgin IL 60120-3859 • NI • Tchr • St John Elgin IL • (847)741-0814 • (RF 1984)

**PEARSON KATHRYN L** (810)767-2037
2534 Orchard Ln Flint MI 48504 • MI • Tchr • St Paul Flint MI • (810)239-6733 • (RF 1988)

**PEARSON MARTHA ANNE**
C/O Linn Lutheran School Assoc 112 Church St Linn KS 66953-9543 • KS • Tchr • Linn Association Linn KS • (785)348-5792 • (S 2000)

**PECK DAVID** (618)282-5346
130 Brookview Apt 1 Red Bud IL 62278 • SI • Tchr • Christ Our Savior Evansville IL • (618)853-7300 • (AA 1999)

**PECK RUSSELL SCOTT** (314)457-1515
6609 Idaho Saint Louis MO 63111 • MO • Tchr • St Lucas Saint Louis MO • (314)351-2628 • (MQ 1992 MED)

**PEDERSEN FRED R**
C/O St Peter Lutheran Church 17051 24 Mile Rd Macomb MI 48042-2902 • fredpeders@webbernet.net • MI • Tchr • St Peter Macomb MI • (810)781-9296 • (RF 1971 MA)

**PEDERSEN MELISSA A** (712)325-9186
829 5th Ave Council Bluffs IA 51501 • IW • 06/2000 • (S 1982)

**PEEK MARY LEE** (425)483-4025
12809 NE 184th Ct Bothell WA 98011-3128 • NOW • Tchr • Concordia Seattle WA • (206)525-7407 • (CQ 1991)

**PEFFER LYNN EUGENE** (612)361-6305
321 N Oak St Chaska MN 55318-2037 • MNS • Tchr • St Johns Chaska MN • (612)448-2526 • (S 1987)

**PEGUES AGNES L** (205)872-7102
1804 Green St Selma AL 36703-3323 • SO • SHS/C • Southern New Orleans LA • (S 1967 MA)

**PEHLKE TODD MICHAEL**
506 N Genesee St Merrill WI 54452-1947 • NW • Tchr • St John Merrill WI • (715)536-4722 • (SP 1997)

**PELLETIER LESTER L** (808)487-1194
99-788 Aumakiki Pl Aiea HI 96701-3208 • CNH • Tchr • LHS Of Hawaii Honolulu HI • (808)949-5302 • (RF 1972)

**PELLETIER LORINE L** (808)487-1194
99-788 Aumakiki Pl Aiea HI 96701-3208 • CNH • Tchr • Our Redeemer Honolulu HI • (808)945-7765 • (S 1974)

**PELLTIER CAROL ANN** (419)592-2037
75 Vincennes Dr Napoleon OH 43545-2205 • OH • Tchr • St Paul Napoleon OH • (419)592-5536 • (AA 1987)

**PENA JANICE** (816)453-3527
5721 NE Wilson Blvd Kansas City MO 64118-5246 • MO • Tchr • Holy Cross Kansas City MO • (816)453-7211 • (S 1964 MED)

**PENA JOHN D** (773)251-4619
7363 N Winchester Ave #1E Chicago IL 60626 • jdpena77@hotmail.com • MO • 08/1997 • (RF 1995)

**PENN BELINDA E**
857 W Stetson Ave Apt 303 Hemet CA 92543-7074 • PSW • Tchr • St John Hemet CA • (909)652-5909 • (IV 1992)

**PENNEKAMP JACOB ERIK** (319)391-6412
426 E 29th St Davenport IA 52803-1610 • IE • Tchr • Trinity Davenport IA • (319)322-5224 • (RF 1996)

**PENNEKAMP SARAH ANNE** (319)324-5966
426 E 29th St Davenport IA 52803 • spennekamp@hotmail.com • IE • Tchr • Trinity Davenport IA • (319)322-5224 • (RF 1996)

**PENNIMAN REBECCA LYNN** (414)740-1701
N 4550 County Trunk P Delavan WI 53115 • rpenniman@worldnet.att.net • SW • Tchr • Our Redeemer Delavan WI • (262)728-4266 • (RF 1996)

**PENOSKE SANDRA LYNN** (812)342-9459
14000 W Lakeview Ct Seymour IN 47274-8710 • IN • Tchr • Immanuel Seymour IN • (812)522-1301 • (CQ 1993)

**PEPER VICTOR C** (630)790-9759
403 Turner Ave Glen Ellyn IL 60137-5020 • NI • EM • (RF 1956 MA)

**PERDUE KATHLEEN E M** (713)944-6236
1664 Main St Minden City MI 48456-9786 • TX • 10/1998 • (RF 1990 MED)

**PEREGOY RHONDA J**
106 Waldens Oak Ct Ellisville MO 63011 • MO • 06/2000 • (S 1978)

**PEREGOY SPENCER R**
106 Waldens Oak Ct Ellisville MO 63011 • MO • Prin • St John Ellisville MO • (314)394-4100 • (S 1977 MED)

**PEREZ JUDITH MORIA** (956)519-8594
1611 E Gastel Cir Mission TX 78572-3053 • TX • EM • (S 1975)

**PERICH CHERYL S** (248)399-2046
3306 Edgeworth Ferndale MI 48220-3422 • MI • Tchr • Hosanna-Tabor Redford MI • (313)937-2424 • (CQ 2000)

**PERICH LISA M** (714)256-1569
250 W Central Ave Apt 1012 Brea CA 92821-3370 • lperich@aol.com • PSW • Tchr • Christ Fullerton CA • (714)870-7460 • (IV 1986 MA)

**PERKINS KATHERINE S** (619)660-6062
2218 Durasno Ln Spring Valley CA 91977-7127 • kperk@lutheranschool.org • PSW • Tchr • Christ La Mesa CA • (619)462-5211 • (S 1971)

**PERR ORVILLE R JR.**
520 N Farmington Jackson MO 63755 • MO • Tchr • St Paul Jackson MO • (573)243-2236 • (S 1984)

**PERRY JOHN D** (636)464-4961
1148 New Towne Rd Arnold MO 63010 • MO • Tchr • LHS South Saint Louis MO • (314)631-1400 • (S 1997)

**PERRY-CLARK JULIA** (602)493-5478
2110 E Behrend Dr Phoenix AZ 85028-1256 • EN • Tchr • Christ Phoenix AZ • (602)957-7010 • (CQ 1995)

**PERSCHBACHER GERALD** (314)849-5249
8868 Rock Forest Dr Saint Louis MO 63123-1116 • MO • Christ Phoenix AZ • (RF 1972 MA)

**PERSICH LAURELL LEE** (314)739-9241
4212 Gardenview Dr #2 Saint Ann MO 63074-1011 • MO • 09/1997 09/1999 • (S 1980 MS)

**PERTCHI LAUREN** (708)532-9395
Trinity Lutheran Church 6850 159th St Tinley Park IL 60477 • NI • Tchr • Trinity Tinley Park IL • (708)532-9395 • (RF 1976)

**PESTER BETH ELAINE** (402)643-9460
137 E Roberts St Seward NE 68434-1643 • bpester@yahoo.com • NEB • Tchr • Nebraska Seward NE • (S 1996)

**PETER CARROLL E DR** (651)484-4472
806 Rose Pl Roseville MN 55113-3417 • cpeter1230@aol.com • MNS • EM • (CQ 1953 MA PHD)

**PETER HERBERT E** (913)962-4707
13502 W 74th Ter Shawnee KS 66216-3720 • herbpeter@aol.com • KS • EM • (S 1953 MED)

**PETER TONYA ANN** (314)721-8324
21 Seminary Ter Clayton MO 63105-3013 • MO • Tchr • Messiah Saint Louis MO • (314)772-4474 • (RF 1991)

**PETER VICTOR K** (402)646-2033
539 Bader Ave Seward NE 68434-1127 • NEB • EM • (S 1956 MS MS)

**PETERING CAROL J** (314)821-2885
751 Club Ln Kirkwood MO 63122-2928 • MO • Tchr • St Paul Des Peres MO • (314)822-2771 • (RF 1960)

**PETERING DONALD T** (314)821-2885
751 Club Ln Kirkwood MO 63122-2928 • MO • CCRA • Missouri Saint Louis MO • (314)317-4550 • (RF 1960 MCMU)

**PETERMAN CHARLES E** (314)846-3349
7408 Summertime Dr Oakville MO 63129-5741 • chuckpeterman@hotmail.com • MO • Prin • Green Park Lemay MO • (314)544-4248 • (RF 1965 MA)

**PETERMAN DIANE ROSE** (314)846-3349
7408 Summertime Dr Saint Louis MO 63129-5741 • MO • Tchr • Green Park Lemay MO • (314)544-4248 • (RF 1966)

**PETERMAN KARL F** (507)523-3415
RR 2 Box 63A Lewiston MN 55952-9615 • silopete@lakes.com • MNS • P/Tchr • Immanuel Lewiston MN • (507)523-3143 • (S 1972)

**PETERMAN KYLE P** (952)898-0688
14745 Portland Ave - Apt #14 Burnsville MN 55306 • MNS • Tchr • Trinity Lone Oak Eagan MN • (651)454-1139 • (SP 2000)

**PETERS AMANDA M**
123 Fontainbleau Dr Rochester Hills MI 48307-2419 • OH • Tchr • Grace Cincinnati OH • (513)661-8467 • (RF 1999)

**PETERS DENIS A**
7980 Auburn Rd Fort Wayne IN 46825-3012 • IN • Prin • Woodburn Woodburn IN • (219)632-5493 • (S 1965 MED)

**PETERS JOYCE K** (920)467-8524
149 Shelly Dr Sheboygan Falls WI 53085-1727 • peters@excel.net • SW • Tchr • Bethlehem Sheboygan WI • (920)452-5071 • (S 1966)

**PETERS LINDA J** (402)365-7795
RR 1 Box 20 Deshler NE 68340-9714 • NEB • Tchr • Deshler Deshler NE • (402)365-7858 • (S 1976)

**PETERS PHIL L** (812)358-5155
3122 E County Road 400 S Brownstown IN 47220-9637 • IN • Tchr • Central Brownstown IN • (812)358-2512 • (RF 1970 MS)

**PETERS REBECCA R** (714)637-5202
2570 N Dunbar St Orange CA 92865-2805 • becky.peters@cui.edu • PSW • Pacific Southwest Irvine CA • (949)854-3232 • (RF 1973 MED)

**PETERS SHARON KAY** (712)263-8920
2946 Highway 30 Trlr 19 Denison IA 51442-7561 • IW • Tchr • Zion Denison IA • (712)263-4766 • (S 1979)

**PETERS TIMOTHY C DR** (714)637-5202
2570 N Dunbar St Orange CA 92865-2805 • tim.peters@cui.edu • PSW • SHS/C • Pacific Southwest Irvine CA • (949)854-3232 • (RF 1973 MS EDD)

**PETERS BONNETT LEANNE MARIE**
Immanuel Luth Church 8231 Tanner Bridge Rd Jefferson City MO 65101-9601 • MO • Tchr • Immanuel Jefferson City MO • (573)496-3451 • (AU 1996)

**PETERSDORF HEATHER** (630)627-0624
1049 S Westmore Ave Apt 210 Lombard IL 60148 • NI • Tchr • Jehovah-El Buen Past Chicago IL • (773)342-5854 • (RF 1998)

**PETERSEN CALISSE K** (480)607-1630
8311 E Via de Ventura #2145 Scottsdale AZ 85258-6623 • calisse@msn.com • TX • Tchr • St Mark Houston TX • (713)468-2623 • (RF 1977)

**PETERSEN CONNIE M**
510 Wheelock Pkwy W Saint Paul MN 55117-4212 • MNS • Tchr • Central Saint Paul MN • (651)645-8649 • (SP 1967 MS)

**PETERSEN DORIS JEAN** (630)627-7919
545 S Westmore Lombard IL 60148 • EN • Tchr • Trinity Villa Park IL • (630)834-3440 • (RF 1962)

**PETERSEN ENOCH A**
10192 Chesterfield Ave Parma Heights OH 44130-2019 • OH • Tchr • LHS West Rocky River OH • (440)333-1660 • (RF 1992)

**PETERSEN GAYLE L** (817)557-0965
5203 Villa Del Mar Ave Apt 313 Arlington TX 76017 • TX • Tchr • Grace Arlington TX • (817)274-1654 • (RF 1975 MED)

**PETERSEN KRISTA L** (201)313-2196
45 Lincoln Ave Cliffside Park NJ 07010-3010 • AT • Tchr • Our Saviour Bronx NY • (718)792-5665 • (BR 1992 MSED)

**PETERSEN KRISTIN K** (216)886-7097
10192 Chesterfield Dr Parma Heights OH 44130-2019 • epete62873@aol.com • OH • Tchr • St John Garfield Heights OH • (216)587-1752 • (RF 1993)

**PETERSEN MARILYN ANN** (281)443-6043
16707 Rock West Dr Houston TX 77073-6301 • TX • Tchr • Trinity Spring TX • (281)376-5810 • (S 1971)

**PETERSEN MICHELLE L** (502)765-4309
206 Mercer St Elizabethtown KY 42701-2732 • IN • Tchr • Lutheran C Elizabethtown KY • (502)769-5910 • (RF 1981)

**PETERSEN RAYMOND W** (713)468-2623
2316 Triway Ln Houston TX 77043-2107 • TX • EM • (S 1951 MED)

**PETERSON CHRISTINA DIANE** (414)642-9370
W2999 County ES Elkhorn WI 53121 • EN • Tchr • Hales Corners Hales Corners WI • (414)529-6701 • (MQ 1997)

**PETERSON HEIDI S** (817)468-8573
5505 Petalwood Dr Arlington TX 76017-6261 • jepete@ticnet.com • TX • Tchr • Grace Arlington TX • (817)274-1654 • (RF 1992 MED)

**PETERSON JANICE**
260 Alachua Dr Winter Haven FL 33884 • FG • Tchr • Lake Wales Lake Wales FL • (941)676-7300 • (RF 1985)

**PETERSON JANIS RUTH** (805)522-6877
3543 La Mesa Ave Simi Valley CA 93063-1221 • PSW • Tchr • Canoga Park Canoga Park CA • (818)348-5714 • (RF 1967)

**PETERSON JON J**
260 Alachua Dr Winter Haven FL 33884-9118 • FG • Prin • Grace Winter Haven FL • (941)293-9744 • (RF 1985 MS)

**PETERSON KEITH B** (847)985-7933
1290 Diane Ln Elk Grove IL 60007 • crfpeterskb@curf.edu • NI • SHS/C • Northern Illinois Hillside IL • (RF 1975 MS)

**PETERSON KELLY A** (541)757-7398
1935 SE Bethel St Corvallis OR 97333-1836 • kkpetel@juno.com • NOW • Tchr • Zion Corvallis OR • (541)757-0946 • (S 1993)

**PETERSON LAVONNE M** (308)234-1337
568 V Road Kearney NE 68845 • NEB • Tchr • Zion Kearney NE • (308)234-3410 • (S 1969)

**PETERSON LORI E**
570 Carlton Ct Apt 208 Grand Forks SD 58203-2772 • ND • 07/2000 • (SP 1994)

**PETERSON MICHELLE LYNNE** (248)693-7043
458 Shorewood Ct Lake Orion MI 48362 • michellfish@cs.com • MI • 09/2000 • (AA 1992 MAT)

**PETERSON RALPH O** (847)658-6743
320 Jefferson St Algonquin IL 60102-2633 • NI • Tchr • St John Algonquin IL • (847)658-9311 • (MW 1980 MSED)

**PETERSON SHARON LEE** (914)779-5392
1 Concordia Pl Bronxville NY 10708-1802 • AT • Tchr • Chapel Bronxville NY • (914)337-3202 • (RF 1973 MLS)

**PETHES LORI ANN** (713)263-7998
5005 Georgi Ln #97 Houston TX 77092-5521 • livingbyprayer@aol.com • TX • Tchr • Shepherd Of The Hill San Antonio TX • (210)614-3741 • (RF 1993)

**PETITT COLETTE MAUREEN** (414)875-8385
2620 N 63rd St Wauwatosa WI 53213-1550 • cmp1016@aol.com • SW • 07/1999 • (MQ 1994 MED)

**PETKEWICZ KAREN KAY** (630)754-0015
6109 Allan Dr Woodridge IL 60517 • NI • Tchr • Salem Blue Island IL • (708)388-6175 • (RF 1984)

**PETROFF GAIL C** (763)786-2470
8751 Tamarack St NW Coon Rapids MN 55433-5959 • roadrunner @stix.com • MNS • Tchr • Prince Of Peace Spring Lake Park MN • (612)786-1755

**PETZOLD JULIAN HOWARD** (248)693-8459
2684 Cole Orion MI 48362-2149 • julianp@attglobal.net • MI • Tchr • Living Word Rochester MI • (248)651-9474 • (RF 1993 MA)

**PETZOLDT LOWELL K**
15942 County Road U Napoleon OH 43545-9754 • OH • Tchr • St John Napoleon OH • (419)598-8702 • (S 1976 MED)

**PEUSTER BARBARA J** (618)377-5507
171 Heatherland Dr Bethalto IL 62010-1895 • SI • 07/2000 • (S 1982)

**PEVESTORF BONNIE LOU** (612)353-2161
PO Box 74 New Germany MN 55367-0074 • MNS • Tchr • St Mark New Germany MN • (612)353-2151 • (SP 1966)

**PFABE JERRALD** (402)643-3278
773 N Columbia Ave Seward NE 68434-1554 • jpfabe@seward.ccsn.edu • NEB • SHS/C • Nebraska Seward NE • (RF 1960 MA PHD)

**PFAFF KIMBERLEY J** (281)464-2447
10803 Kirkwell Dr Houston TX 77089 • txpfaff@flash.net • TX • Tchr • Lutheran South Acade Houston TX • (281)464-9320 • (SP 1979)

**PFALZGRAFF BEVERLY D** (972)272-4858
1834 Whiteoak Dr Garland TX 75040-5411 • TX • 10/1997 10/1999 • (RF 1975)

**PFANKU SYLVIA** (970)669-8804
2652 Glendevey Dr Loveland CO 80538-2923 • RM • EM • (CQ 1989)

**PFANNKUCH DARRELL L** (616)459-6190
1317 Emerald Ave NE Grand Rapids MI 49505-5226 • MI • Tchr • Immanuel Grand Rapids MI • (616)363-0505 • (RF 1964)

**PFANTZ LYNNE M** (515)483-2663
2026 Hart Ave State Center IA 50247-9522 • IE • Tchr • Clemons Clemons IA • (515)477-8263 • (S 1980)

**PFEFFERLE KATHIE M** (440)357-5639
111 E Jackson St Painesville OH 44077-4004 • OH • Tchr • Our Shepherd Painesville OH • (440)357-7776 • (S 1972 MED)

**PFEIFFER ANN M** (734)721-3942
161 Larchmont Dr Westland MI 48185-3482 • tanpfeiffe@aol.com • MI • Tchr • St Matthew Westland MI • (734)425-0261 • (S 1969)

**PFEIFFER BENITA LYNN**
8935 Nicollet Ave Apt 106 Bloomington MN 55420 • biobenita@hotmail.com • MNS • Tchr • Luth HS Of Greater M Bloomington MN • (612)854-0224 • (S 1995)

**PFEIFFER CLETUS RALPH**
C/O Rochester Central School 2619 9th Ave NW Rochester MN 55901-2398 • cpfeiff@esu7.org • MNS • Luth HS Of Greater M Bloomington MN • (S 1965 MS AMD)

**PFEIFFER SARA LYNN*** (319)359-8939
5133 Eagle Ct Davenport IA 52807 • pfeiffer@qconline.com • IE • 04/1998 04/2000 • (RF 1992)

**PFEIFFER THOMAS E** (734)721-3942
161 Larchmont Dr Westland MI 48185-3482 • MI • Tchr • St Matthew Westland MI • (734)425-0261 • (S 1969 MA)

**PFLIEGER R CHARLES JR.** (505)265-5476
908 19th St NW Albuquerque NM 87104 • RM • Tchr • Immanuel Albuquerque NM • (505)242-0616 • (S 1984 MMTH)

**PFLIEGER ROBERT W** (402)643-3257
1038 Eastridge Dr Seward NE 68434-1328 • NEB • EM • (RF 1956 MA)

**PFLUGHAUPT DORIS E** (219)432-5683
1206 Wood Moor Dr Fort Wayne IN 46804-1424 • IN • Tchr • Emmanuel-St Michael Fort Wayne IN • (219)422-6712 • (RF 1965 MA)

**PFUND JONATHAN D**
53333 Briar Shelby Township MI 48316-2223 • MI • Tchr • St John Rochester MI • (248)652-8830 • (RF 1987)

**PFUND ROY E** (314)845-2857
4123 Monte Vista Dr Saint Louis MO 63129-3446 • MO • Tchr • LHS South Saint Louis MO • (314)631-1400 • (RF 1959 MA)

**PHILIPPI-ADEN MELODY** (402)223-3177
1423 N 11th St Beatrice NE 68310-2014 • NEB • Tchr • St Paul Beatrice NE • (402)223-3414 • (S 1990)

**PHILLIPS BETH LEE** (410)647-9065
366 Volley Ct Arnold MD 21012-1136 • SE • Tchr • St Paul Glen Burnie MD • (410)766-5790 • (BR 1982 MED)

**PHILLIPS JULIE L** (402)588-2308
PO Box 6 Garland NE 68360 • NEB • Tchr • Our Redeemer Staplehurst NE • (402)535-2625 • (S 1999)

**PHILP SHARON D** (507)333-5436
2 Aspen Ct Faribault MN 55021 • sphilp@juno.com • MNS • Tchr • Cannon Valley LHS Morristown MN • (507)685-2636 • (S 1997)

**PICHAN DARYL E*** (716)787-0157
41 Westfield Commons Rochester NY 14625-2917 • EA • 03/1999 • (RF 1972 MA)

**PICHAN MELINDA C** (734)454-3788
192 Pinewood Dr Plymouth MI 48170 • tomelp@worldnet.att.net • MI • 07/1997 07/2000 • (AA 1989)

**PICHAN THOMAS A** (313)454-3788
192 Pinewood Cir Plymouth MI 48170-6103 • MI • Tchr • Hosanna-Tabor Redford MI • (313)937-2233 • (AA 1989)

**PICKEL MICHELE L*** (763)757-6842
13001 Harpers St NE Blaine MN 55449 • pickel@csp.edu • MNS • SHS/C • Minnesota South Burnsville MN • (SP 1977 MED)

**PICKELMAN MAUREEN R** (810)463-1421
138 Mark Dr Mount Clemens MI 48043-1427 • MI • Tchr • St Luke Clinton Township MI • (810)791-1151 • (RF 1967)

**PICKELMANN HENRY M** (517)662-7497
44 E Salzburg Rd Bay City MI 48706-9712 • pickel6@concentric.net • MI • P/Tchr • Trinity Bay City MI • (517)662-4891 • (RF 1970 MA)

**PICKERILL LORI A**
18910 Bothell Everett Hwy #B2 Bothell WA 98012-5211 • NOW • Tchr • Zion Everett WA • (425)334-5064 • (PO 1984)

**PIDSOSNY MARY L** (810)774-2579
16612 Waterman Dr Roseville MI 48066 • russpidsosny@juno.com • MI • Tchr • Bethany Detroit MI • (313)885-7721 • (S 1980)

**PIEL PAUL F** (847)428-4013
2331 Stewart Ln West Dundee IL 60118-3351 • ppiel@chicago.avenew.com • NI • Tchr • St Peter Arlington Heights IL • (847)253-6638 • (RF 1977 MA)

**PIEPENBRINK ALLEN** (262)251-9258
N90W17625 Saint Stevens Dr Menomonee Falls WI 53051-1926 • allen.piepenbrink@cuw.edu • SW • SHS/C • South Wisconsin Milwaukee WI • (414)464-8100 • (S 1972 MA)

**PIEPENBRINK SHIRLEY ANN** (262)251-9258
N90W17625 Saint Stevens Dr Menomonee Falls WI 53051-1926 • aspiepen@execpc.com • SW • Tchr • Grace Menomonee Falls WI • (414)251-7140 • (S 1972)

**PIEPER DARALD A** (708)895-0519
17948 Commercial Ave Lansing IL 60438-2206 • NI • Tchr • Trinity Lansing IL • (708)474-8539 • (S 1961)

**PIEPER DENNIS ROGER** (708)283-1903
322 Osage St Park Forest IL 60466-2111 • NI • Prin • Zion Matteson IL • (708)747-1116 • (RF 1978 MED)

**PIEPER EDNA** (402)643-3738
1216 N 8th St Seward NE 68434-1214 • NEB • EM • (S 1949 MED)

**PIEPER JAMES R**
2563 Pine Dr Plover WI 54467-2937 • SI • Tchr • St John Red Bud IL • (618)282-3873 • (S 1985)

**PIEPER KEVIN M** (281)251-7526
8302 Amurwood Dr Tomball TX 77375-2807 • TX • Mem C • Salem Tomball TX • (281)351-8223 • (S 1980)

**PIEPER NANCY ANN** (612)441-6236
18174 Hudson St NW Elk River MN 55330-1840 • MNS • Tchr • St John Elk River MN • (612)441-6616 • (SP 1974)

**PIEPER ROBERT W** (708)447-4936
2323 S 7th Ave North Riverside IL 60546-1230 • NI • EM • (RF 1949 MA)

**PIERCE DEBORAH ANN** (810)294-4296
34575 Mulvey #166 Fraser MI 48026 • dapierce@tir.com • MI • Tchr • Our Shepherd Birmingham MI • (248)646-6100 • (AA 1991)

**PIERING DONETTE M** (319)662-4070
PO Box 35 Conroy IA 52220-0035 • dpiering@hotmail.com • IE • Tchr • Lutheran Interparish Williamsburg IA • (319)668-1711 • (SP 1984 MAT)

**PIERING VERNON CHARLES** (319)662-4070
PO Box 35 Conroy IA 52220-0035 • IE • Tchr • Lutheran Interparish Williamsburg IA • (319)668-1711 • (RF 1969 MED)

**PIKALEK GARY E** (708)614-6281
8120 Cherokee Trl Tinley Park IL 60477-7850 • garypikalek@prodigy.net • NI • Tchr • St John Country Club Hills IL • (708)799-7491 • (RF 1972 MA)

**PIKALEK JANICE E** (708)614-6281
8120 Cherokee Trl Tinley Park IL 60477-7850 • NI • Tchr • St Paul Chicago Heights IL • (708)754-4492 • (RF 1975)

**PIKE KAMIE LEE** (517)823-9925
5175 Cottrell Rd Vassar MI 48768-9499 • MI • Tchr • Trinity Reese MI • (517)868-4501 • (AA 1992)

**PINGEL GEORGE H** (507)288-2719
2628 Viola Heights Dr NE Rochester MN 55906 • MNS • EM • (RF 1931)

**PINGEL JAMES A** (952)442-3910
1601 Fountain Ln Waconia MN 55387-9439 • japingel@aol.com • MNS • Tchr • Lutheran High Mayer MN • (612)657-2251 • (MQ 1992 MA)

**PINGEL KARA M** (314)741-3067
6082 Kingsfont Apt 1 Florissant MO 63033 • MO • Tchr • Salem Florissant MO • (314)741-8220 • (MQ 1999)

**PINGEL KATHY MARIE** (608)757-2037
730 Sutherland Ave Janesville WI 53545 • SW • Tchr • St Paul Janesville WI • (608)754-4471 • (SP 1990)

**PINGEL MILTON J** (909)688-0168
7753 Cassia Ave Riverside CA 92504-3604 • PSW • EM • (RF 1952 MED)

**PINGEL NANCY ANN** (828)267-2610
1041 Lenoir Rhyne Blvd SE Hickory NC 28602 • clcyouth@twave.net • SE • Mem C • Christ Hickory NC • (828)328-1483 • (RF 1972)

**PINICK GREGG A** (714)998-5151ext
1234 E Del Mar Ave Orange CA 92865-3906 • pinick@lhsoc.org • PSW • Prin • Lutheran HS/Orange C Orange CA • (714)998-5151 • (S 1980 MSED)

**PINKERTON JAN S** (714)554-1779
15162 Reeve St Garden Grove CA 92843-5229 • PSW • 07/1997 07/2000 • (IV 1989)

**PINNOW ARTHUR C** (219)485-4531
5017 Hemlock Ln Fort Wayne IN 46815-5003 • IN • EM • (RF 1951 MA MA)

**PINNOW BARBARA J** (815)695-5516
12007 Lisbon Rd Newark IL 60541-9490 • NI • Tchr • Cross Yorkville IL • (630)553-7861 • (RF 1984 MA)

**PINTSCH CHERIE ANNE** (941)638-1093
164 Grant St Lake Wales FL 33853-7928 • cpintsch@gate.net • FG • 09/1997 09/1999 • (SP 1970 MA)

**PIPHO DONALD M** (712)448-2268
313 S Maple St Paullina IA 51046-1013 • IW • P/Tchr • Zion-St John Paullina IA • (712)448-3915 • (S 1963 MA)

**PIPHO GERHARDT E** (713)537-1914
15019 Draper Rd Houston TX 77014-1401 • TX • Mem C • Trinity Klein TX • (281)376-5773 • (CQ 1971)

**PIRIE MARY S** (360)491-7463
412 Bulldog St SE Olympia WA 98503-1420 • NOW • 08/1997 08/2000 • (S 1977)

**PITSCH LELAND A** (314)723-1868
450 S Pam Ave Saint Charles MO 63301-1326 • MO • Tchr • Immanuel Saint Charles MO • (636)946-0051 • (S 1964 MED)

**PITSCH MARTA JO** (660)463-4020
310 College Dr PO Box 424 Concordia MO 64020-0424 • MO • Tchr • Immanuel Saint Charles MO • (636)946-2656 • (S 1993)

**PITSCH MONTE GRANT** (660)463-2238
310 College Dr PO Box 424 Concordia MO 64020-0424 • montepitsch@yahoo.com • MO • SHS/C • Missouri Saint Louis MO • (314)317-4550 • (S 1994 MA)

**PITTELKO BEVERLY M** (847)437-3008
85 Brantwood Ave Elk Grove Village IL 60007 • emep@juno.com • EN • EM • (RF 1957)

**PITTMAN ELLEN MARIE** (612)890-1746
13009 Welcome Ln Burnsville MN 55337-3843 • MNS • Tchr • Trinity Lone Oak Eagan MN • (651)454-1139 • (SP 1969)

**PITTMAN ERIC G** (248)680-8658
1182 Winthrop Dr Troy MI 48083-5434 • MI • P/Tchr • St Paul Royal Oak MI • (248)546-6555 • (RF 1973 MA)

**PITTMAN SARA LYNN** (309)452-7430
2005 Tracy Dr #4 Bloomington IL 61701 • CI • Tchr • Trinity Bloomington IL • (309)829-7513 • (MQ 1994)

**PLAMANN MARVIN H** (402)643-3566
366 E Bek Ave Seward NE 68434-1163 • NEB • SHS/C • Nebraska Seward NE • (S 1956 MA)

**PLATE LORI ANN** (715)536-5734
1206 W Main St #B Merrill WI 54452-2126 • NW • Tchr • St John Wausau WI • (715)842-5212 • (MQ 1986)

**PLATH ARTHUR M** (651)388-9297
2241 Langsdorf Ave Red Wing MN 55066 • MNS • EM • (RF 1963)

**PLATZ KERRI R** (810)392-7105
34687 Potter St PO IBox 292 Memphis MI 48041 • MI • 04/2000 • (RF 1996)

**PLIESEIS-CHILD EUNICE L** (414)329-7389
4021 S 91st Pl Greenfield WI 53228-2225 • SW • Tchr • Our Father Greenfield WI • (414)282-8220 • (CQ 1987 MS)

**PLOPPER LINDA MICHELLE** (414)375-2031
W57N510 Hilbert Ave Cedarburg WI 53012-2013 • SW • 08/1999 • (RF 1993)

**PLOSS MARK A** (317)346-7004
3847 E 250 S Franklin IN 46131-7575 • Frugalmap@aol.com • IN • Tchr • Indiana Fort Wayne IN • (RF 1979 MS)

**PLOZIZKA JEANETTE** (217)793-0178
1021 W Governor St Apt 3 Springfield IL 62704-1767 • CI • Tchr • Trinity Springfield IL • (217)787-2323 • (S 1969 MSED)

**PLUCKNETT CARENN R** (206)661-9879
3860 SW 339th St Federal Way WA 98023-2973 • NOW • 10/1992 10/2000 • (PO 1982)

**PLUMMER DEAN** (320)234-7020
810 Bluff St NE Hutchinson MN 55350-1313 • djjrsp@hutchtel.net • MNS • P/Tchr • Our Saviors Hutchinson MN • (320)587-3318 • (S 1975 MS)

**PLVAN PHILLIPS JOY M** (804)634-0532
8100 Purdy Rd Emporia VA 23847 • jobuab@3rddoor.com • S • Tchr • St John Baptist Emporia VA • (804)634-4515 • (S 1981)

**POBANZ KATHRYN L** (402)379-4419
1210 Greenlawn Dr Norfolk NE 68701-2639 • NEB • Tchr • Christ Norfolk NE • (402)371-5536 • (S 1971)

**PODOLL DEBORAH K** (920)361-1477
188 W Berlin St Berlin WI 54923-2042 • SW • Tchr • St John Berlin WI • (920)361-0555 • (S 1985)

**PODWILS CAROL MARIE** (541)382-8548
60856 Onyx St Bend OR 97702-9100 • podwils@transport.com • NOW • Mem C • Trinity Bend OR • (541)382-1832 • (S 1975)

**POELLET JUDITH K** (708)749-1762
7140 W 32nd St Apt 1 Berwyn IL 60402-2810 • jkpoellet@juno.com • NI • 01/1996 02/2000 • (AA 1984)

**POELLOT LINDA A** (262)376-3878
W59 N445 Hilgen Aven Cedarburg WI 53012 • SW • Tchr • St Paul Grafton WI • (262)377-4659 • (MQ 1993 MA)

**POENITSKE TRACY LYNN**
2533 Park Green Ln Old Hickory TN 37138-2839 • SI • Tchr • Zion Bethalto IL • (618)377-8314 • (RF 1992)

**POERTNER SARAH E** (210)699-4617
11500 Huebner #1702 San Antonio TX 78230 • s³poertner@yahoo.com • TX • Tchr • LHS Of San Antonio San Antonio TX • (210)733-7771 • (RF 1991 MED)

**POHL JANE ANNE** (210)651-6520
22307 Navasota Cir San Antonio TX 78259-2602 • janeannep@prodigy.net • TX • Tchr • Concordia San Antonio TX • (210)479-1477 • (S 1974 MED MLS)

**POHLMAN BETTY L** (847)437-4557
1145 S Arlington Heights Rd Arlington Hts IL 60005-3140 • NI • Tchr • St Peter Arlington Heights IL • (847)253-6638 • (RF 1967)

**POHLMANN LAWRENCE H** (618)377-0586
523 Vermont St Bethalto IL 62010-1755 • SI • EM • (RF 1937 MS)

**POLEY CAROL L** (216)333-4176
21185 Maplewood Ave Rocky River OH 44116-1241 • OH • Tchr • St Thomas Rocky River OH • (440)331-4426 • (CQ 1989)

**POLITTE PAULA J**
3839 N Kilpatrick Portland OR 97217 • ppolitte@cu.portland.edu • NOW • SHS/C • Northwest Portland OR • (PO 1984)

**POLLARD AVIS D**
1853 W 38th St Los Angeles CA 90062 • PSW • Tchr • Good Shepherd Inglewood CA • (310)671-0427 • (CQ 1992)

**POLLATZ BRIAN** (248)584-1813
29027 Milton Madison Heights MI 48071-2512 • bbpollatz@aol.com • MI • Tchr • LHS Northwest Rochester Hills MI • (810)852-6677 • (AA 1987 MS)

**POLLERT KAREN L** (812)523-8025
425 Lasher Dr Seymour IN 47274-2213 • IN • Tchr • Immanuel Seymour IN • (812)522-1301 • (CQ 1993 MS)

**POLLEY CONNIE J** (512)837-1454
1109 Quail Park Dr Austin TX 78758-6618 • TX • Tchr • St Paul Austin TX • (512)472-3313 • (S 1977)

**POLLOCK LAWRENCE R**
4475 N 99th St Wauwatosa WI 53225-4701 • SW • Tchr • Milwaukee LHS Milwaukee WI • (414)461-6000 • (RF 1973 MAR)

**POLLOM CHERI RAE** (307)632-8917
419 Lori Rd Cheyenne WY 82007 • WY • P/Tchr • Trinity Cheyenne WY • (307)635-2802 • (S 1993)

**POLLOM TIMOTHY A** (307)632-8917
419 Lori Rd Cheyenne WY 82007-3142 • WY • 06/1995 • (S 1980)

**POLSON JANICE L** (203)374-1434
3726 Madison Ave # 112N Bridgeport CT 06606-1662 • NE • Tchr • Zion Bridgeport CT • (203)367-7268 • (BR 1980)

**POLZIN DAVID MICHAEL** (612)681-9896
4080 Halite Ln Eagan MN 55122-2914 • jimmy150@aol.com • MNS • Prin • Mount Hope-Redemptio Bloomington MN • (612)881-0036 • (SP 1975 MED)

**POLZIN MURIEL J** (651)681-9896
4080 Halite Ln Eagan MN 55122-2914 • jeanie15@aol.com • MNS • 06/1998 06/2000 • (SP 1976)

**POLZIN RICHARD H** (203)775-2958
16 Twilight Ln Brookfield CT 06804-1426 • NE • EM • (RF 1951 MS)

**PONDER ELAINE J** (765)963-3057
3753 W 600 N Sharpsville IN 46068 • IN • Tchr • Redeemer Kokomo IN • (765)864-6466 • (CQ 1998 MA)

**POOLE MICHELLE RHAE** (972)305-3007
3737 Timberglen Rd Apt #712 Dallas TX 75287-3614 • cshell@popcs.net • TX • Tchr • Prince Of Peace Carrollton TX • (972)447-9887 • (S 1994)

**POPENHAGEN MARGIE JANET** (319)396-8381
924 Owen St NW Cedar Rapids IA 52405-2848 • IE • Tchr • Share & Care Cedar Rapids IA • (319)396-9148 • (S 1967)

**POPKE-SHEPPARD LOREN KAE** (248)7388-1225
1120 Erskine St Waterford MI 48328-4228 • MI • Tchr • Special Ed Ministrie Detroit MI • (313)368-1220 • (AA 1983 MAT)

**POPP JESSICA DONN** (402)564-1584
3413 19th St Columbus NE 68601 • IE • Special Ed Ministrie Detroit MI • (S 1999)

**POPP MICHAEL SCOTT** (402)564-1584
3413 19th St Columbus NE 68601 • mpopp@gilligan.esu7.k12.ne.us • IE • Special Ed Ministrie Detroit MI • (S 1998)

**POPP ROBERT G** (815)459-3751
9308 Butternut Dr Crystal Lake IL 60014-3911 • blpopp@mc.net • NI • EM • (RF 1960 MSED)

**POPPE RICHARD A** (606)689-4714
5296 Country Club Ln Burlington KY 41005-9128 • OH • Prin • Concordia Cincinnati OH • (513)861-9568 • (S 1961 MA)

**PORTWOOD VON E** (402)371-7784
406 Market Pl Norfolk NE 68701-6936 • NEB • Tchr • Christ Norfolk NE • (402)371-5536 • (S 1985)

**POSTEL DIANE M** (320)732-2779
410 4th St S Long Prairie MN 56347 • MNN • 09/1998 • (SP 1965)

**POSTMA CECELIA M** (307)856-3620
1007 N Broadway Ave Riverton WY 82501-2613 • WY • Tchr • Trinity Riverton WY • (307)857-5710 • (S 1985)

**POTRATZ KEVIN J** (402)643-0564
755 N Columbia Ave Seward NE 68434-1554 • kevin@seward.cune.edu • NEB • SHS/C • Nebraska Seward NE • (S 1993 MS)

**POTTER MARGARET ROSE** (410)435-1332
1612 Walterswood Rd Baltimore MD 21239-2421 • hnybear105@aol.com • SE • Prin • Immanuel Baltimore MD • (410)435-6961 • (CQ 1990)

**POTTER MARY L** (219)493-4872
15802 Slusher Rd New Haven IN 46774-9650 • IN • Tchr • St Paul Fort Wayne IN • (219)423-2496 • (RF 1985)

**POTTSCHMIDT ROBERT L** (812)358-2864
2887 E State Road 250 Brownstown IN 47220-9694 • IN • Tchr • Central Brownstown IN • (812)358-2512 • (RF 1973)

**POTYANDY JOSEPH W**
C/O Grace Lutheran School 3628 Boudinot Ave Cincinnati OH 45211 • OH • Tchr • Grace Cincinnati OH • (513)661-8467 • (SP 2000)

**POWELL LUELLA M** (573)769-0101
210 Dawn Ave Palmyra MO 63461-1959 • MO • Tchr • Zion Palmyra MO • (573)769-3739 • (S 1972 MA)

**POWELL TRICIA JENNY** (217)726-7540
304 N Park Apt G Springfield IL 62702 • CI • Tchr • Trinity Springfield IL • (217)787-2323 • (MQ 1994)

**POYNTER RACHEL LEA** (219)456-3463
511 Pine Grove Ln Apt H Fort Wayne IN 46807 • mrpoynter@juno.com • IN • Tchr • Emmanuel Fort Wayne IN • (219)447-3005 • (RF 1994)

**PRAHL BONNIE C** (414)242-5890
12521 N Granville Rd # 111W Mequon WI 53097-2513 • SW • Tchr • St Peter-Immanuel Milwaukee WI • (414)353-6800 • (SP 1974)

**PRAHL HENRY W**
3407 Wyatt Ln Texarkana TX 75503-1410 • IN • EM • (RF 1938)

**PRAHL JENNIFER RENEE** (765)448-4252
1918 Castellan Dr Lafayette IN 47905-7606 • jenn@stillwaiting.com • IN • Tchr • St James Lafayette IN • (765)742-6464 • (RF 1994)

**PRAHLOW AUGUST J** (219)462-0795
458 Grove Ave Valparaiso IN 46385 • IN • Tchr • Immanuel Valparaiso IN • (219)462-8207 • (RF 1957 MA)

**PRAHLOW DONALD A DR** (314)845-0699
259 Bridgeview Ln Saint Louis MO 63129-3403 • djprahlow@postnet.com • MO • Tchr • LHS South Saint Louis MO • (314)631-1400 • (RF 1952 MA PHD)

**PRAHLOW JAMES D** (314)355-2735
6919 Jamestown Way Dr Florissant MO 63033-5125 • MO • Tchr • Lutheran North Saint Louis MO • (314)389-3100 • (RF 1976 MA)

**PRALLE ERIC A** (501)649-8598
201 Amherst Cir Fort Smith AR 72903 • pralle@ipa.net • MDS • Tchr • First Fort Smith AR • (501)452-5330 • (S 1992 MED)

**PRALLE GERHARDT R** (785)286-4379
3237 NW Hickory Ridge Ln Topeka KS 66618-2725 • tlsprin@networksplus.net • KS • Prin • Topeka Topeka KS • (785)357-0382 • (S 1963 MED)

**PRALLE JENNIFER ANN** (507)282-9730
2817 Pinewood Rd SE Rochester MN 55904 • MNS • Tchr • Rochester Central Rochester MN • (507)289-3267 • (S 1991)

**PRALLE MARILYN A**
3237 NW Hickory Ridge Ln Topeka KS 66618-2725 • KS • Tchr • Topeka Topeka KS • (785)357-0382 • (S 1963 MED)

**PRALLE RUTH D** (847)255-1713
1220 Village Dr 345C Arlington Heights IL 60004 • NI • EM • (S 1940 MS)

**PRANGE DEBRA J** (314)846-5837
6915 Turnesa Ln Saint Louis MO 63129-5524 • MO • Tchr • Green Park Lemay MO • (314)544-4248 • (S 1975)

**PRANGE MICHAEL** (314)739-4297
12671 Lonsdale Dr Bridgeton MO 63044-1508 • prangemj@stlnet.com • MO • Tchr • Lutheran North Saint Louis MO • (314)389-3100 • (S 1965 MED)

**PRANGE SHERRY L** (618)282-4630
9 Julie St Ruma IL 62278 • prangesl@htc.net • SI • Prin • Christ Our Savior Evansville IL • (618)853-7300 • (RF 1969 MA)

**PRATER DIANN C** (708)978-0934
586 7th Ave Aurora IL 60505-5365 • NI • Tchr • St Paul Aurora IL • (630)820-3450 • (RF 1963)

**PRATT DIANA M** (217)443-2981
161 Mauck Ln Danville IL 61832-5370 • CI • Tchr • Danville Danville IL • (217)442-5036 • (RF 1976)

**PRATT ELLEN M** (562)633-7334
2503 Candlewood St Lakewood CA 90712-2103 • teacherel@hotmail.com • PSW • Tchr • Good Shepherd Downey CA • (562)803-4459 • (CQ 1999)

**PRATT WILLIAM S**
273 Euclid Ave Brooklyn NY 11208-2013 • AT • Tchr • Atlantic Bronxville NY • (914)337-5700 • (RF 1968 MST)

**PRATT-BEST LINDA L** (616)429-9417
4011 Niles Rd St Joseph MI 49085 • danny3linda@yahoo.com • FG • 09/1996 09/1999 • (RF 1982 MA)

**PRECHEL DENNIS O** (734)421-6512
18214 Middlebelt Rd Apt 102 Livonia MI 48152-3626 • MI • Tchr • LHS Westland Westland MI • (734)422-2090 • (S 1971 MA MSLS MMU MED)

**PRECHT KENNETH P** (810)765-0595
343 N Elizabeth St Marine City MI 48039 • EN • EM • (RF 1956 MA)

**PRELOGER RONALD W** (812)523-8801
2292 Locust Dr Seymour IN 47274-8668 • IN • Tchr • Immanuel Seymour IN • (812)522-1301 • (RF 1970 MMU)

**PRENTICE SARAH N**
1185 Mountain Creek Rd - #508 Chattanooga TN 37405 • MDS • Mem C • Cross Of Christ Chattanooga TN • (423)877-7447 • (S 2000)

**PRESCOD YVONNE**
33 Vernon Ave Mount Vernon NY 10553-1615 • AT • Tchr • St Matthew New York NY • (212)567-5948 • (BR 1977)

**PRESS SARAH J** (708)354-1448
1640 Barnsdale Rd Apt 106 La Grange Park IL 60526 • NI • Tchr • St John La Grange IL • (708)354-1690 • (MQ 2000)

**PRESTON SHARON K** (561)496-6388
5399 Inwood Dr Delray Beach FL 33484-1103 • dhpreston@aol.com • FG • Tchr • Trinity Delray Beach FL • (561)276-8458 • (S 1970)

**PREUS JANET EDITH**
4040 HWY 101 N Plymouth MN 55446-2306 • klemjan@msn.com • MNS • 01/1999 • (CQ 1995)

**PREUSS ARTHUR L** (262)637-5886
1817 Arcturus Ave Racine WI 53404-2203 • SW • Tchr • St John Racine WI • (262)637-7011 • (RF 1954 MMU)

**PREUSS ELVIRA A** (812)522-8937
1111 Gaiser Dr Seymour IN 47274-3641 • IN • EM • (RF 1959)

**PREUSS JUDITH C** (402)643-3115
1056 Plainview Ave Seward NE 68434-1343 • jpreuss@seward.cune.edu • NEB • SHS/C • Nebraska Seward NE • (S 1960 MED PHD)

**PREUSS MARY L** (618)667-6513
103 Sugarmill Rd Troy IL 62294-3149 • preusstm@juno.com • SI • Tchr • Good Shepherd Collinsville IL • (618)344-3153 • (S 1960)

**PREUSS TIMOTHY LOUIS** (402)643-6578
1118 Sunrise Dr Seward NE 68434 • NEB • SHS/C • Nebraska Seward NE • (S 1983 MS)

**PREUSS WILLIAM J** (402)643-3115
1056 Plainview Ave Seward NE 68434-1343 • NEB • SHS/C • Nebraska Seward NE* • (S 1960 MED DED)

**PRICE JOHN ALLEN** (904)934-5980
2940 Duke Dr Gulf Breeze FL 32561 • SO • Tchr • Redeemer Warrington FL • (850)455-0330 • (RF 1989)

**PRICE LORA** (618)655-0778
2 Saint Andrews Ave Edwardsville IL 62025-1884 • SI • Tchr • St Paul Troy IL • (618)667-6314 • (CQ 1997)

**PRIDE JOHN F** (317)862-5752
4920 5 Points Rd Indianapolis IN 46239-9554 • jfskpride@aol.com • IN • Tchr • Trinity Indianapolis IN • (317)897-0243 • (S 1972 MED)

**PRIDE SANDRA K** (317)862-5752
4920 5 Points Rd Indianapolis IN 46239-9554 • jfskpride@aol.com • IN • Tchr • St John Indianapolis IN • (317)352-9196 • (S 1973 MSED)

**PRIEBE BONNIE S** (301)341-2788
5600 Inwood St Cheverly MD 20785-1119 • jbpriebe@erols.com • SE • Tchr • Concordia Hyattsville MD • (301)927-0266 • (RF 1964 MA)

**PRIEHS WARREN W**
35656 Electra Sterling Heights MI 48312-3953 • MI • Tchr • Peace Shelby Twp MI • (810)739-2431 • (RF 1974)

**PRIES LONNIE F** (414)466-9065
10524 W Villard Ave Milwaukee WI 53225-3939 • SW • Tchr • Milwaukee LHS Milwaukee WI • (414)461-6000 • (RF 1993)

**PRIGGE BARBARA J** (612)854-3158
2451 Skyline Dr Bloomington MN 55425-2188 • MNS • Tchr • Mount Calvary Richfield MN • (612)869-9441 • (SP 1973)

**PRILL ANN ELIZABETH** (715)257-7216
713 Mueller St Athens WI 54411 • aejcp1@juno.com • NW • Tchr • Trinity Athens WI • (715)257-7559 • (S 1973)

**PRILL JAMES C** (715)257-7216
713 Mueller St Athens WI 54411 • aejcp1@juno.com • NW • P/Tchr • Trinity Athens WI • (715)257-7559 • (S 1973 MS)

**PRILL JANA M** (949)635-9477
11 Acorn Ridge Rcho Santa Margarita CA 92688 • janaprill@hotmail.com • PSW • Tchr • Abiding Savior Lake Forest CA • (949)830-1461 • (S 1999)

**PRIM JOHN W** (216)221-4367
1201 Ramona Ave Lakewood OH 44107-2631 • OH • Tchr • LHS West Rocky River OH • (440)333-1660 • (S 1965 MA)

**PRIMEAU DOUGLAS** (313)574-0369
11436 Newbern Dr Warren MI 48093-2613 • MI • Tchr • Peace Warren MI • (810)751-8011 • (S 1967 MED)

**PRINCE MATTHEW GENE** (314)505-7656
801 De Mun Ave Fritz 3 AW Saint Louis MO 63105 • MO • 03/2000 • (S 1996)

**PRISKORN GARY J** (248)399-3313
1422 Dorothea Berkley MI 48072 • garypam@flash.net • MI • Mem C • Redeemer Birmingham MI • (248)644-4010 • (RF 1968 MED)

**PRITCHARD EMILY M** (636)938-7097
26 Hillside Dr Pacific MO 63069 • embo91@aol.com • MO • Tchr • St Mark Eureka MO • (636)938-4432 • (RF 1989)

**PROA STACIA ANNE** (714)734-9439
14612 Danborough Rd Tustin CA 92780-6710 • PSW • Tchr • St John Orange CA • (714)288-4406 • (S 1980 MA)

**PROCHNOW ADRIAN H** (219)424-2723
509 W State Blvd Fort Wayne IN 46808-3138 • IN • EM • (RF 1934 MSED)

**PROCHNOW ANDREA JOY**
602 Main Ireton IA 51027 • aprochnow@hotmail.com • IW • 05/2000 • (S 1996)

**PROCHNOW JEAN** (402)643-2505
535 N 3rd St Seward NE 68434-1817 • NEB • Tchr • St John Seward NE • (402)643-4535 • (RF 1958)

**PROCHNOW JOHN R** (507)235-5926
221 W Anna St Fairmont MN 56031-1558 • MNS • Tchr • St Pauls Fairmont MN • (507)238-9492 • (SP 1968 MA)

**PROCHNOW RONALD A** (407)851-1926
3614 Sedgewick Pl Orlando FL 32806-7204 • ronprochnow@juno.com • FG • Tchr • Trinity Orlando FL • (407)843-4896 • (S 1963 MMU MED)

**PROFILET JANET L** (636)441-3056
2800 Diekamp Farm Trl Saint Charles MO 63303-5479 • jlprofilet@aol.com • MO • Prin • Zion Harvester MO • (314)441-7424 • (RF 1985 MAD)

**PROFT MARLENE KAY** (310)831-3229
1918 Amelia Ave San Pedro CA 90731-1109 • PSW • Tchr • Christ Rancho Palos Verdes CA • (310)831-0848 • (SP 1972 MA)

**PROKOPF RACHEL**
426 E Fitch Rd Huntertown IN 46748-9737 • rachel@birdie.ge.niigata-u.ac.jp • IN • S Miss • Indiana Fort Wayne IN • (RF 1997)

**PROKOPY PAUL E** (313)432-5920
36077 Grennada St Livonia MI 48154-5278 • MI • EM • (RF 1953)

**PRUSAK KATHLEEN ANN** (313)582-1238
4905 Middlesex St Dearborn MI 48126-3106 • MI • Tchr • Emmanuel Dearborn MI • (313)561-6265 • (S 1977)

**PSENCIK ROBERT EVERETTE** (281)990-9182
483 Buoy Rd Webster TX 77598-2504 • TX • Tchr • Texas Austin TX • (S 1998)

**PSENCIK SHEILA LEE** (281)990-9182
483 Buoy Rd Webster TX 77598-2504 • rp80805@navix.net • TX • Tchr • Lutheran South Acade Houston TX • (281)464-9320 • (S 1996)

**PUCKETT PAUL R** (952)442-2464
616 E 2nd St Waconia MN 55387-1607 • MNS • P/Tchr • Trinity Waconia MN • (952)442-4165 • (S 1963 MA MA)

**PUDWELL KRISTIN L** (901)373-5144
6515 Elmore Rd Memphis TN 38134-5939 • MDS • Prin • Immanuel Memphis TN • (901)388-0205 • (RF 1975 MS)

**PUFFE SHIELA ANN** (414)353-1481
6960 N Raintree Dr Unit C Milwaukee WI 53223-5272 • shiela.puffe@cuw.edu • SW • SHS/C • South Wisconsin Milwaukee WI • (414)464-8100 • (RF 1982 MS)

**PULLABHOTLA SARADA** (702)254-7023
7570 W Flamingo Rd Apt 252 Las Vegas NV 89147-4314 • saradar@hotmail.com • PSW • Tchr • Faith LHS Las Vegas NV • (702)804-4400 • (S 1994 MEDADM)

**PULLEN SUSAN D** (410)866-2930
8100 Sagramore Rd Baltimore MD 21237-1662 • pullenp@grc.nia.nih.gov • SE • EM • (RF 1972)

**PULLMANN PAUL M**
62052 Don St Bend OR 97701-6219 • NOW • Tchr • Trinity Bend OR • (541)382-1850 • (RF 1985)

**PULS DOUGLAS W** (516)289-7629
38 Rose Ave Patchogue NY 11772-2826 • dougp@fnol.net • AT • Tchr • Emanuel Patchogue NY • (516)758-2250 • (BR 1987)

**PULS MARYANN** (516)289-7629
38 Rose Ave Patchogue NY 11772-2826 • AT • 03/1996 03/2000 • (AA 1989)

**PUMMILL LOUISA ANNE** (309)694-7247
4816 N Main St East Peoria IL 61611-1310 • CI • 01/1994 01/2000 • (RF 1985)

**PUTNAM CYNTHIA A** (262)253-0385
W156 N7727 Cherry Ct Menomonee Falls WI 53051 • cputnam@sailingwi.com • SW • Tchr • Trinity Mequon WI • (262)242-2045 • (MQ 1995)

**PUTNAM STEPHANEE** (713)661-8108
6410 Ferris Dr Apt 22 Houston TX 77096 • TX • Tchr • Pilgrim Houston TX • (713)666-3706 • (SP 1971)

**PYGMAN MARY ELLEN**
508 S 2nd St PO Box 93 Grove City MN 56243-0093 • MNS • Tchr • St John Atwater MN • (320)974-8982 • (RF 1994)

## Q

**QUADE GENE W** (810)677-5954
11236 Concord Ln Washington MI 48094-3045 • MI • EM • (S 1961 MA)

**QUADE JAMES A*** (503)648-2126
1029 NE 5th Avenue Dr Hillsboro OR 97124-2340 • jaqor@aol.com • NOW • EM • (S 1958 MS)

**QUADE KAREN JANE** (313)665-0604
4403 Hunt Clb Apt 2C Ypsilanti MI 48197-9108 • MI • Tchr • St Paul Ann Arbor MI • (734)665-0604 • (S 1972 MS)

**QUAM KAREN**
3405 SW Willow Seattle WA 98126 • NOW • Tchr • Amazing Grace Seattle WA • (206)723-5526 • (PO 2000)

**QUANDT CAROLYN LOUISE** (210)696-7796
3206 Yorktown Dr San Antonio TX 78230-3461 • TX • Tchr • Concordia San Antonio TX • (210)479-1477 • (S 1970)

**QUANDT LAURA ANN** (210)696-7796
3206 Yorktown Dr San Antonio TX 78230-3461 • TX • Tchr • LHS Of San Antonio San Antonio TX • (210)733-7771 • (AU 1999)

**QUICK KERRY J** (810)795-8208
13338 Pomona Dr Sterling Heights MI 48312-1529 • MI • 08/1996 • (CQ 1996)

**QUICKEL DALE E** (501)664-7204
6907 Blue Bird Dr Little Rock AR 72205-5015 • MDS • Tchr • Christ Little Rock AR • (501)663-5212 • (CQ 1999)

**QUICKEL LISA L** (501)664-7204
6907 Bluebird Dr Little Rock AR 72205-5015 • MDS • Tchr • Christ Little Rock AR • (501)663-5212 • (AU 1988)

**QUIGG JULIANN M** (217)754-3855
1085 Merritt Blacktop Rd Bluffs IL 62621-9724 • CI • Tchr • Salem Jacksonville IL • (217)243-3419 • (S 1981)

## R

**RAABE DAVID L** (708)677-8976
7915 Kostner Ave Skokie IL 60076-3533 • NI • SHS/C • Northern Illinois Hillside IL • (RF 1978 MS)

**RABE ELLEN JEAN** (517)879-5142
113 E Mt Forest Pinconning MI 48650-8926 • cen18946@centuryinter.net • MI • Tchr • Grace Auburn MI • (517)662-6161 • (S 1978)

**RABE NEAL F*** (636)583-3131
107 Indian Prairie Ln Union MO 63084-4201 • MO • EM • (RF 1960 MA)

**RABEL DONNA LAURA** (281)866-9937
100 Hollow Tree Ln #2005 Houston TX 77090 • doc7652@aol.com • TX • Tchr • Trinity-Messiah Houston TX • (713)224-7265 • (AU 1999)

**RABEN SANDRA M** (715)355-6933
802 Paramount Dr Wausau WI 54401-6700 • braben@dwave.net • NW • Tchr • Trinity Wausau WI • (715)848-0166 • (SP 1986)

**RACH JOANNE M** (630)922-0703
2412 Joyce Ln Naperville IL 60564 • NI • Tchr • Bethany Naperville IL • (630)355-2198 • (RF 1984)

**RACHUY TERRY L** (615)672-4724
604 Highland Dr White House TN 37188 • pstr1999@aol.com • MO • Tchr • Christ Community Kirkwood MO • (314)822-7774 • (SP 1984)

**RADEMACHER JOANN A** (313)287-2619
18240 Raleigh Square Dr Southgate MI 48195-2858 • MI • Tchr • Calvary Lincoln Park MI • (313)381-6715 • (S 1974)

**RADEWAHN HAROLD J** (414)771-0496
1515 N 50th St Milwaukee WI 53208-2210 • SW • EM • (RF 1955 MA)

**RADKE KRISTEN NOELLE** (920)683-2236
2233 La Follette Ave Manitowoc WI 54220-2530 • radke@lsol.net • SW • 06/1998 06/2000 • (SP 1987)

**RADKE MERLE L DR** (708)456-5867
1918 N 74th Ave Elmwood Park IL 60707-3725 • crfradtkem@crf.cuis.edu • NI • EM • (S 1943 MA PHD LITTD)

**RADL CLARENCE G** (414)235-6272
1102 Otter Ave Oshkosh WI 54901-5449 • SW • EM • (RF 1963 MS)

**RADLOFF NANCY L** (414)479-0747
2570 N 90th St Wauwatosa WI 53226-1812 • SW • Tchr • St Peter Milwaukee WI • (414)353-6800 • (MW 1980 MED)

**RADUE MARTIN B** (414)377-6252
908 3rd Ave Grafton WI 53024-1308 • SW • Tchr • St Paul Grafton WI • (414)377-4659 • (MQ 1988)

**RAEDEKE HENRY W*** (636)939-3082
2486 Annapolis Way Saint Charles MO 63303-2905 • hraedeke@immanuelluth.org • MO • Prin • Immanuel Saint Charles MO • (636)946-0051 • (S 1968 MED)

**RAFFERTY BRIAN C** (509)586-4956
213 N Palouse St Kennewick WA 99336-3322 • theraffman@juno.com • NOW • Tchr • Bethlehem Kennewick WA • (509)582-5624 • (S 1986 MED)

**RAGAISIS DEE ANN V**
PO Box 2425 Sun City AZ 85372-2425 • deeann@ibm.net • PSW • 11/1997 11/1999 • (RF 1989 MS)

**RAGLAND JOHN** (702)641-0998
2174 Brassy Dr Las Vegas NV 89122-2031 • PSW • Tchr • Faith LHS Las Vegas NV • (702)804-4400 • (S 1992)

**RAGLAND RAMONA KAY** (702)641-0998
2174 Brassy Dr Las Vegas NV 89122-2031 • PSW • Tchr • Redeemer Las Vegas NV • (702)642-7744 • (SP 1989)

**RAHN GAIL K** (714)832-9477
1282 Veeh Dr Tustin CA 92780-5140 • PSW • Tchr • Shepherd Of Peace Irvine CA • (949)786-3997 • (RF 1962)

**RAHN JOEL D** (619)479-1747
3053 Plaza Leonardo Bonita CA 91902 • jrjr66@aol.com • PSW • Tchr • Pilgrim Chula Vista CA • (619)420-6233 • (IV 1989 MA)

**RAHN MARLENE D** (262)255-5927
W159N11436 Red Oak Cir Germantown WI 53022-6011 • SW • EM • (S 1950)

**RAINEY ANTHONY G** (312)925-6660
8059 S Talman Ave Chicago IL 60652-2847 • arainey@luthersouth.com • NI • Tchr • Luther HS South Chicago IL • (773)737-1416 • (RF 1986 MA)

**RAMBO MARGARET E** (636)394-3523
819 Auber Ln Ballwin MO 63011-4104 • MO • 01/1983 10/1999 • (S 1966 MAT)

**RAMMING LEONARD C** (219)471-0410
2209 Saint Joe Center Rd Fort Wayne IN 46825-5099 • IN • EM • (RF 1934 MA)

**RAMSEY DAVID ALLEN** (219)589-2421
659 Lehman St Berne IN 46711-2334 • IN • 07/1996 07/2000 • (CQ 1987)

**RAMSEY MCNAIR** (334)875-8972
602 Woodrow Ave Selma AL 36701-4741 • SO • SHS/C • Southern New Orleans LA • (S 1968 MA DED)

**RAMSEY SUZANNE K** (219)589-2421
659 Lehman St Berne IN 46711-2334 • IN • Tchr • St Peter Fort Wayne IN • (219)749-5811 • (CQ 1995)

**RAMTHUN DANIEL W** (313)730-1374
1719 N Mildred St Dearborn MI 48128-1238 • MI • Tchr • LHS Westland Westland MI • (734)422-2090 • (AA 1983 MA)

**RAND SUSAN J** (727)938-1502
561 Centerwood Dr Tarpon Spgs FL 34689-7218 • FG • 09/1998 • (RF 1970)

**RANDALL CLAUDIA G** (818)303-4698
493 Royal View St Duarte CA 91010-1378 • PSW • Tchr • Mount Calvary Diamond Bar CA • (909)861-2740 • (SP 1968 MA)

**RANDALL KIMBERLY ANN**
128 Via Vicini Rancho Santa Margari CA 92688-3880 • PSW • Tchr • Abiding Savior Lake Forest CA • (949)830-1461 • (IV 1990)

**RANDALL SALLY ANN** (248)673-9512
3277 Alco Waterford MI 48329 • MI • Tchr • Trinity Utica MI • (810)731-4490 • (RF 1969)

**RANDLE LISA M** (507)834-6559
63856 240th Gibbon MN 55335-9710 • lmsmanny@yahoo.com • MNS • Tchr • St Peter Gibbon MN • (507)834-6676 • (MQ 1992)

**RANDT MIRIAM C** (612)864-6315
1409 Elm St Glencoe MN 55336 • MNS • Tchr • Our Saviors Hutchinson MN • (320)587-3318 • (S 1974)

**RANKIN PATRICIA A** (517)777-4706
3605 Mack Rd Saginaw MI 48601-7118 • MI • Tchr • Holy Cross Saginaw MI • (517)793-9795 • (CQ 1997)

**RANKIN PEGGY** (813)654-6875
2913 S John Moore Rd Brandon FL 33510-2160 • FG • Tchr • Immanuel Brandon FL • (813)685-1978 • (RF 1978)

**RANNOW JOHN ROGER** (509)582-8628
503 W 13th Ave Kennewick WA 99337-4724 • NOW • Mem C • Bethlehem Kennewick WA • (509)586-1062 • (CQ 1988 MA MA)

**RAPP GERALD D** (314)843-3522
12848 Pointe Dr Saint Louis MO 63127-1742 • grapp57@stlnet.com • MO • EM • (S 1957 MA MLS)

**RAPP MAYLENE K** (217)877-2644
3270 Upton Ln Decatur IL 62521-8631 • mrlsa49@aol.com • CI • Tchr • Lutheran School Asso Decatur IL • (217)233-2001 • (CQ 1980)

**RAPPE ROGER W** (920)458-4911
2020 N 8th St Sheboygan WI 53081-2742 • SW • EM • (S 1958 MED)

**RAPSON ANDREA KAY** (517)479-3485
237 S Huron Ave Harbor Beach MI 48441-1240 • akrapson@hbch.com • MI • Tchr • Zion Harbor Beach MI • (517)479-3615 • (SP 1982 MA)

**RASCHKE LEONARD R** (941)646-8451
315 Faye Cir N Lakeland FL 33813-1512 • FG • Prin • St Paul Lakeland FL • (941)644-7710 • (S 1970 MA)

**RASHID JANET M** (810)254-9485
4100 Montgomery Dr Shelby Township MI 48316-3914 • MI • Tchr • St Paul Sterling Heights MI • (810)247-4427 • (CQ 1986)

**RASMUSSEN KIMBERLY ANN** (505)271-1260
12016 Prospect Ave NE Albuquerque NM 87112-3426 • RM • Tchr • Christ Albuquerque NM • (505)884-3876 • (IV 1988)

**RASMUSSEN SUZANNE C** (406)755-2493
1442 Lake Blaine Rd Kalispell MT 59901-7633 • jaks@ptinet.net • MT • Tchr • Trinity Kalispell MT • (406)257-6716 • (S 1975)

**RASSBACH SHARON J** (314)843-3714
5000 Fernhill Dr Saint Louis MO 63128-2929 • MO • Tchr • Our Savior Fenton MO • (314)343-7511 • (SP 1965)

**RATH RICHARD L** (352)369-6344
2409 NE 20th Cir Ocala FL 34471 • rleerath@yahoo.com • FG • EM • (S 1956 MSED)

**RATHE HAROLD H** (303)433-3422
3405 W 32nd Ave # 705 Denver CO 80211-3103 • RM • EM • (S 1934)

**RATHE WILLARD W** (313)463-0893
61 High St Mount Clemens MI 48043-1782 • MI • EM • (S 1937)

**RATHER LORIS W**
W349N9150 Norwegian Rd Oconomowoc WI 53066-9617 • SW • EM • (S 1958 MA)

**RATHJE JOHN ROY** (517)787-7876
1038 Crestwood Ln Jackson MI 49203-3615 • jrathje@juno.com • MI • Mem C • Redeemer Jackson MI • (517)750-3100 • (CQ 1988 MA)

**RATHJE LYNDA L** (313)982-5761
2643 10th St Port Huron MI 48060-6649 • MI • Tchr • Trinity Port Huron MI • (810)984-2501 • (S 1974 MA)

**RATHJE MICHAEL L** (713)947-0385
202 Empress Dr Houston TX 77034-1502 • TX • Tchr • Lutheran South Acade Houston TX • (281)464-8299 • (S 1976 MEAD)

**RATHKE BECKIE LYNN** (308)237-4662
2121 W 39th #19 Kearney NE 68847-1242 • NEB • Tchr • Zion Kearney NE • (308)234-3410 • (S 1989)

**RATHKE GREG D** (402)844-3118
2409 Clearfield Norfork NE 68702 • NEB • Tchr • Nebraska Seward NE • (S 1988)

**RATHMANN DAWN A**
12859 Tammy Kay Dr Saint Louis MO 63128-3261 • MO • Mem C • Christ Memorial Saint Louis MO • (314)631-0304 • (CQ 1992 MED)

**RATHMANN RODNEY L**
12859 Tammy Kay Dr Saint Louis MO 63128-3261 • MO • S Ex/S • Missouri Saint Louis MO • (314)317-4550 • (SP 1974 MA EDD)

**RATTELMULLER BARBARA J** (618)345-1799
613 A Keebler Rd Collinsville IL 62234 • brattelmuller@aol.com • SI • Tchr • Good Shepherd Collinsville IL • (618)344-3153 • (S 1988)

**RAU CHRISTIAN W** (727)522-0839
5800 Denver St NE Saint Petersburg FL 33703-1847 • cwr@msm.com • FG • Tchr • Grace Saint Petersburg FL • (727)527-6213 • (RF 1965 MED)

**RAU GAYLE ELIZABETH**
405 Rush St Roselle IL 60172-2228 • NI • Tchr • Trinity Roselle IL • (630)894-3263 • (S 1992)

**RAUCH JOAN KAY** (309)694-2254
116 Sara St East Peoria IL 61611-3565 • IN • 06/1999 • (S 1986)

**RAUSCH HENRY G** (602)931-9164
4826 W Purdue Ave Glendale AZ 85302-3639 • hsrausch@aol.com • PSW • Prin • Martin Luther Phoenix AZ • (602)248-0656 • (RF 1970)

**RAUSCH JOYCE C** (516)822-7456
14 Westmoreland Rd Hicksville NY 11801-1627 • AT • Tchr • Trinity Hicksville NY • (516)931-2211 • (RF 1963)

**RAUSCH RICHARD O** (516)822-7456
14 Westmoreland Rd Hicksville NY 11801-1627 • AT • 11/1991 11/1999 • (RF 1963 MS)

**RAUSCH SUSAN K** (602)931-9164
4826 W Purdue Ave Glendale AZ 85302-3639 • hsrausch@aol.com • PSW • Tchr • Martin Luther Phoenix AZ • (602)248-0656 • (RF 1970)

**RAVANELLI RENEE** (660)463-2513
507 SW 7th Terrace Concordia MO 64020-9692 • rravanelli@galaxyispc.com • MO • Tchr • St Paul Concordia MO • (660)463-7654 • (S 1974 MSED)

**RAWLINGS JAMES E** (501)223-9040
14 White Willow Ct Little Rock AR 72212-2031 • rawcoach@aol.com • MDS • Tchr • Mid-South Cordova TN • (RF 1972 MS)

**RAWLINS CHERYL L** (415)369-5332
3212 Spring St Redwood City CA 94063-3931 • CNH • Tchr • Prince Of Peace Fremont CA • (510)797-8186 • (RF 1968)

**RAWLINS GARY R** (650)369-5332
3212 Spring St Redwood City CA 94063-3931 • grawlins@hotmail.com • CNH • Tchr • Prince Of Peace Fremont CA • (510)797-8186 • (CQ 1984)

**RAWSON KATHLEEN N** (517)652-2745
1296 S Beyer Rd Saginaw MI 48601-9437 • MI • Tchr • St Lorenz Frankenmuth MI • (517)652-6141 • (RF 1966)

**RAY DEANNA LYNN** (203)270-9517
40 Great Quarter Rd Sandy Hook CT 06482-1541 • dpray@prodigy.net • NE • 06/1994 • (BR 1990)

**REABE LOUISE A** (219)223-8747
908 Arthur St Rochester IN 46975-2400 • jimlouise@rtcol.com • IN • 08/1999 • (RF 1979 MA)

**REAGAN THERESA A** (210)499-4333
15019 Digger Dr San Antonio TX 78247-3046 • TX • Tchr • Concordia San Antonio TX • (210)479-1477 • (S 1979)

**REAVIS LISA ANN** (301)805-4758
8306 Satinleaf Ct Bowie MD 20715-4575 • SE • Tchr • Concordia Hyattsville MD • (301)927-0266 • (BR 1989 MA)

**REBECK DOUGLAS CARL** (708)460-1918
15722 Old Orchard Ct Apt 2W Orland Park IL 60462-7902 • mrrebe@webtv.net • NI • Prin • Salem Blue Island IL • (708)388-6175 • (RF 1976 MA)

**REBER CARRIE R***
C/O Crown Of Life Luth Church 6605 Pleasant Run Rd Colleyville TX 76034 • reber@arlington.net • TX • Tchr • Crown of Life Colleyville TX • (817)421-5683 • (SP 1984)

**RECK LINDA K** (312)351-9186
6 Whispering Ct Streamwood IL 60107-2306 • NI • Tchr • Immanuel Glenview IL • (847)724-1034 • (RF 1981)

**RECK THOMAS PAUL** (314)962-9677
17 Turf Ct Saint Louis MO 63119-4619 • laurawehrenberg@netscape.net • MO • Tchr • LHS South Saint Louis MO • (314)631-1400 • (RF 1967 MA MAT)

**RECK-MEYER CARRIE** (314)849-4996
10115 Glenfield Ter Crestwood MO 63126 • creckmeyer@yahoo.com • MO • Tchr • Christ Community Kirkwood MO • (314)822-7774 • (CQ 1998 MA)

**RECKELBERG SALLY A** (414)845-2213
E3411 State Rd 163 Luxemburg WI 54217-7845 • NW • Tchr • St Paul Luxemburg WI • (920)845-5248 • (RF 1973)

**RECKSIEDLER RONALD E** (619)588-1863
1217 Peerless Dr El Cajon CA 92021-3421 • PSW • Tchr • Christ La Mesa CA • (619)462-5211 • (RF 1977)

**REDDEMANN RICHARD W** (219)493-4844
2624 Busche Dr Fort Wayne IN 46815-7740 • reddeman@fortwayne.infi.net • IN • Tchr • Concordia Fort Wayne IN • (219)426-9922 • (S 1965 MAT)

**REDEKER SALLY M** (847)895-5629
1435 Parker Pl Elk Grove Vlg IL 60007-3136 • NI • Tchr • St Luke Itasca IL • (630)773-0509 • (RF 1962 MA)

**REDER NATALIE R** (513)942-3718
7866 Mill Creek Cir West Chester OH 45069-5808 • nreder@cinci.rr.com • OH • 09/1996 09/1999 • (RF 1981)

**REDMOND JANA LYNN** (512)759-1430
221 Green Pasture Hutto TX 78634-4004 • jredmond1@prodigy.net • TX • Tchr • Redeemer Austin TX • (512)451-6478 • (AU 1991)

**REED LAURIE DEE** (559)535-3707
10328 Rd 256 Terra Bella CA 93270-9722 • mreed@cwia.com • CNH • Tchr • Zion Terra Bella CA • (559)535-4346 • (IV 1986)

**REED MARGARET A** (210)735-4094
411 Green Meadow Blvd San Antonio TX 78213 • TX • Tchr • Concordia San Antonio TX • (210)479-1477 • (CQ 1997)

**REEM KAREN L** (612)739-2080
9448 Redwell Ln Woodbury MN 55125-9005 • MNS • Tchr • East St Paul Saint Paul MN • (612)774-2030 • (SP 1970)

**REEVES CAROL A**
3270 Upton Ln Decatur IL 62521-9631 • CI • Tchr • Lutheran School Asso Decatur IL • (217)233-2001 • (RF 1964)

**REFENES JAMES L** (414)502-0026
N69W13766 Manor Hills Ct Menomonee Falls WI 53051-5241 • SW • Tchr • Milwaukee LHS Milwaukee WI • (414)461-6000 • (RF 1982 MED)

**REGINELLI MARCY JANIS** (808)839-4651
1259 Ala Kula Pl Apt 102 Honolulu HI 96819-1344 • mjreginelli@hotmail.com • CNH • Tchr • LHS Of Hawaii Honolulu HI • (808)949-5302 • (RF 1966)

**REHBERG GREGORY A**
11260 N 92nd St #2109 Scottsdale AZ 85260 • vlhs@azlutheran.org • EN • Prin • Valley LHS Associati Phoenix AZ • (602)230-1600 • (CQ 1987 MS)

**REHKOP JANET M** (618)667-4686
964 Weathervane Ln Troy IL 62294-3140 • SI • 08/1999 • (S 1978)

**REHKOP THOMAS V** (618)667-4686
964 Weathervane Ln Troy IL 62294-3140 • SI • Southern Illinois Belleville IL • (S 1977)

**REHMER EDGAR P** (715)823-2455
E10646 County Road C Clintonville WI 54929-9526 • erehmer@frontiernet.net • NW • Prin • St Martin Clintonville WI • (715)823-6538 • (RF 1967 MSED)

**REHMER LOREN W** (952)447-9954
17026 Pheasant Meadow Ln SW Prior Lake MN 55372-2759 • MNN • EM • (RF 1958 MSED)

**REHMER ROBERT C** (612)424-4674
11865 100th Pl N Maple Grove MN 55369-3211 • MNS • Tchr • St John Maple Grove MN • (612)420-2426 • (RF 1969)

**REICK MYRON H** (605)371-3835
4212 E 38th St Sioux Falls SD 57103 • mrsrco@aol.com • SD • Tchr • Sioux Falls Sioux Falls SD • (605)335-1923 • (S 1973 MED)

**REID JAMES A** (909)393-1501
2454 Sandstone Ct Chino Hills CA 91709-2116 • PSW • 07/1997 07/1999 • (RF 1969 MS)

**REID JULIE ANN** (952)997-7985
7322 158th St W Apple Valley MN 55124-6938 • dandjreid@juno.com • MO • Tchr • Cross View Edina MN • (952)941-1094 • (IV 1991)

**REIGLES JAMES D** (414)255-1833
W146N8677 Keith Cir Menomonee Falls WI 53051-3201 • reigles@execpc.com • SW • Tchr • Martin LHS Greendale WI • (414)421-4000 • (RF 1966 MA)

**REIGLES KAREN L** (414)255-1833
W146N8677 Keith Cir Menomonee Falls WI 53051-3201 • SW • Tchr • Elm Grove Elm Grove WI • (262)797-2970 • (RF 1966)

**REIMAN NANETTE M** (402)461-4468
303 E 4th St Hastings NE 68901-5323 • greifam@cccins.gi.cccneb.edu • NEB • Tchr • Christ Juniata NE • (402)744-4991 • (S 1995)

**REIMANN ANDREW K** (914)793-6575
41 Pasadena Rd Bronxville NY 10708-5111 • AT • SHS/C • Atlantic Bronxville NY • (914)337-5700 • (RF 1962 MA MA)

**REIMANN MARY JO** (614)876-8780
5526 Cara Ct Dublin OH 43016-8700 • maryjo³reimann@fclass.hilliard.k12.oh.us • OH • 08/1984 08/2000 • (RF 1979 MAT)

**REIMER MATTHEW THOMAS** (715)758-7920
PO Box 704 Bonduel WI 54107 • NW • Tchr • St Paul Bonduel WI • (715)758-8532 • (MQ 1994)

**REIMERS KARI L** (308)284-3115
446 Road East 120 Ogallala NE 69153-5906 • NEB • 09/1998 • (S 1988)

**REIMERS NANCY** (847)426-2431
18N640 Field Ct Dundee IL 60118-9269 • NI • Tchr • Immanuel Dundee IL • (847)428-1010 • (RF 1973)

**REIMERS SUSAN ANN*** 
RR 1 Box 47 Ceylon MN 56121-9719 • MNS • Tchr • Zion Fairmont MN • (507)235-5153 • (S 1989)

**REINBOLD TRICIA KAY** (734)289-4339
4372 Third St Newport MI 48166 • MI • Tchr • Holy Ghost Monroe MI • (734)242-0509 • (AA 1995)

**REINCKE J NEIL** (219)463-2449
1110 E 455 S La Grange IN 46761-9760 • IN • EM • (CQ 1960 MS)

**REINCKE JOHN M** (810)463-0264
362 Cambridge Mount Clemens MI 48043 • kjreincke@aol.com • MI • Tchr • Michigan Ann Arbor MI • (RF 1990 MA)

**REINECK MARILYN E DR** (612)481-6956
2631 Cohansey St Roseville MN 55113-3521 • reineck@csp.edu • MNS • SHS/C • Minnesota South Burnsville MN • (S 1973 MA PHD)

**REINEKE DANIEL J** (320)656-0963
1406 N 36th AVE St Cloud MN 56303 • MNN • 01/1999 • (SP 1988)

**REINEKE JANE A*** (715)627-7718
515 5th Ave Antigo WI 54409 • NW • Tchr • Eau Claire Eau Claire WI • (715)835-9314 • (SP 1990)

**REINER KENNETH LOYD** (636)256-9634
315 Statewood Dr Ballwin MO 63021-6351 • kdreiner@mymailstation.com • MO • S Ex/S • Missouri Saint Louis MO • (314)317-4550 • (S 1960 MA)

**REINERT CONNIE S**
1648 18th St NW Cedar Rapids IA 52405-1555 • MO • Tchr • St John Arnold MO • (636)464-7303 • (RF 1996)

**REINERT DANIEL M** (810)659-0863
9186 Potter Rd Flushing MI 48433 • reindan88@hotmail.com • MI • Tchr • St Paul Flint MI • (810)239-6733 • (AA 1995)

**REINERT JODI L**
9186 Potter Rd Flushing MI 48433-1913 • MI • 07/2000 • (AA 1994)

**REINERTSON JEROME A** (714)639-0554
5847 E Rocking Horse Way Apt 3 Orange CA 92669 • princjar.aol.com • PSW • Prin • Zion Anaheim CA • (714)535-3600 • (S 1968 MED)

**REINERTSON MICKIE B** (714)630-3228
2856 Alden Pl Anaheim CA 92807 • PSW • P/Tchr • Hephatha Anaheim CA • (714)637-4022 • (S 1963)

**REINHARDT GARY P**
Cambridge Square Apts 27415 Greenfield Rd Apt 2 Southfield MI 48076 • MI • Tchr • Greenfld Peace Detroit MI • (313)838-3366 • (SP 1970)

**REINHARDT KAREN SUE** (313)242-8170
2484 Heiss Rd Monroe MI 48162-9456 • MI • Tchr • St John New Boston MI • (734)654-6366 • (RF 1976 MA)

**REINHART JANET LEE** (309)637-1969
2211 W Clarke Ave Peoria IL 61604-5119 • CI • Tchr • Christ Peoria IL • (309)637-5309 • (SP 1973)

**REINHART JULIE ELIZABETH**
Zion Luth Church 625 Church Dr Bethalto IL 62010-1830 • SI • Tchr • Zion Bethalto IL • (618)377-8314 • (S 1999)

**REINISCH SHERYL JOY** (503)408-7607
16433 NE Fargo Cir Portland OR 97230-5513 • sreinisch@cu-portland.edu • NOW • SHS/C • Northwest Portland OR • (RF 1980 MED)

**REINITZ JOYCE A** (314)428-2405
33 Gocke Pl Overland MO 63114-1327 • MO • Tchr • Our Redeemer Overland MO • (314)427-3462 • (S 1976 MA)

**REINKE ALLEN R** (913)367-9281
1309 Walnut St Atchison KS 66002 • KS • Tchr • Trinity Atchison KS • (913)367-2837 • (S 1984)

**REINKE BETTY J** (907)243-2250
9300 Emerald St Anchorage AK 99515-1058 • bjreinke@aol.com • NOW • Tchr • Beautiful Savior Anchorage AK • (907)522-3899 • (S 1964)

**REINKE EDWARD G** (402)643-4516
318 N 1st St Seward NE 68434-1802 • NEB • SHS/C • Nebraska Seward NE • (S 1985 MS PHD)

**REINKE KEVIN THOMAS** (480)357-0806
9340 E Plana Ave Mesa AZ 85212-1483 • kevnamy@uswest.net • PSW • Tchr • Christ Greenfield Gilbert AZ • (480)892-8521 • (S 1998)

**REINKE KRISTINE R** (715)758-8628
PO Box 426 Bonduel WI 54107 • NW • Tchr • St Paul Bonduel WI • (715)758-8532 • (CQ 1999)

**REINKE MELANIE ANN**
1014 Longfellow Edwardsville IL 62025 • dceduo@juno.com • SI • Tchr • Trinity Edwardsville IL • (618)656-2918 • (S 1992)

**REINKE PAUL MICHAEL** (310)214-7200
3570 Del Amo Blvd #E Torrance CA 90503 • PSW • Tchr • South Bay LHS Inglewood CA • (310)672-1101 • (S 1998)

**REINKE RALPH L** (512)331-9420
11204 Taterwood Dr Austin TX 78750-2532 • rlreinke@aol.com • TX • EM • (RF 1949 MA LITTD)

**REINKING TIMOTHY J** (219)747-2961
2150 Owaissa Way Fort Wayne IN 46809-1443 • IN • Tchr • Concordia LHS Fort Wayne IN • (219)483-1102 • (RF 1983)

**REINS KARI LYNN**
1118 City Park Ave #331 Fort Collins CO 80521-4481 • aqua360@hotmail.com • TX • Tchr • LHS Of San Antonio San Antonio TX • (210)733-7771 • (S 1998)

**REINS KEVIN JOHN** (307)721-3884
1460 N 9th Laramie WY 98116 • kjreins@aol.com • WY • 08/1996 • (S 1994)

**REISENBICHLER AUDREY ANN** (812)952-3855
7655 Rolling Hills Ln NE Lanesville IN 47136-8117 • IN • Tchr • St John Lanesville IN • (812)952-2737 • (S 1976 MS)

**REISENBICHLER MELVIN R** (616)756-9758
111 Poplar St Three Oaks MI 49128-1045 • MI • EM • (RF 1944 MA)

**REISENBICHLER ROBERT D** (812)952-3855
7655 Rolling Hills Ln NE Lanesville IN 47136-8117 • IN • P/Tchr • St John Lanesville IN • (812)952-2737 • (S 1976 MA)

**REISIG RAY** (503)284-0870
5520 NE Killingsworth St Portland OR 97218-2416 • NOW • Tchr • Trinity Portland OR • (503)288-6403 • (S 1970 MED)

**REISLER LOUISE L**
120 S Elm St Bonduel WI 54107 • NW • 09/1998 • (MQ 1994)

**REISS DEBORAH**
21 Fairview Ave Apt 425 Tuckahoe NY 10707-4127 • AT • Tchr • The Village Bronxville NY • (914)337-0207 • (BR 1984 MMU)

**REISS RICHARD G** (314)631-7869
9872 Arv Ellen Dr Saint Louis MO 63123-5304 • MO • Tchr • LHS South Saint Louis MO • (314)631-1400 • (RF 1968 MA)

**REITMEYER ROYCE J** (517)686-2616
4067 Allen Ct Bay City MI 48706-2444 • MI • EM • (RF 1950 MA)

**REITSMA JOY LYNN** (954)474-4451
3001 W Rolling Hills Cir Bld 1 #108 Davie FL 33328-1948 • joyoosocasion@att.net • FG • Tchr • Gloria Dei Davie FL • (954)475-0683 • (RF 1986 MAT)

**REITZ EDWARD W**
517 Innsbrook Est Innsbrook MO 63390-5325 • MO • Tchr • Missouri Saint Louis MO • (314)317-4550 • (S 1960 MED)

**REMER DAVID C** (804)498-8674
1037 Sir Timothy Dr Virginia Beach VA 23452-4627 • SE • 09/1998 • (RF 1973)

**REMER ROSE A** (810)739-0616
6667 Little Turkey Run Utica MI 48317-3746 • MI • Tchr • Trinity Utica MI • (810)731-4490 • (S 1970 MAT)

**REMMERT CELESTE PATRICIA*** (510)276-3074
17361 Via Julia San Lorenzo CA 94580 • CNH • EM • (RF 1959)

**REMPEL TIMOTHY E** (636)861-2791
411 Xavier Ct Valley Park MO 63088-2323 • MO • Tchr • Christ Community Kirkwood MO • (314)822-7774 • (S 1983 MA)

**REMPFER CRYSTAL DAWN**
5460 Rowley Apt 1511 San Antonio TX 78240-4736 • TX • Tchr • Messiah Midlothian TX • (972)723-1069 • (RF 1999)

**REMPFER RONALD H**
230 11th St W Chuluota FL 32766-9456 • S • Tchr • St Luke Oviedo FL • (407)365-3228 • (RF 1964)

**RENKEN BETTY R**
1068 S Heaman St Nashville IL 62263-2039 • SI • Tchr • Trinity-St John Nashville IL • (618)327-8561 • (CQ 1996)

**RENKEN RANDOLPH GENE** (219)492-8411
6335 Mapledowns Dr Fort Wayne IN 46835-3932 • IN • Tchr • Holy Cross Fort Wayne IN • (219)483-3173 • (S 1985 MS)

**RENN PETER C** (702)636-8611
5237 Clinging Vine St North Las Vegas NV 89031-1102 • PSW • Tchr • Faith LHS Las Vegas NV • (702)804-4400 • (S 1992 MA)

**RENNER ELIZABETH L**
19679 State Route 161 Irwin OH 43029-9610 • OH • 07/1985 07/2000 • (S 1981)

**RENQUEST DAVID WAYNE** (303)410-8071
5678 117th Pl Broomfield CO 80020 • RM • Tchr • Denver Lutheran High Denver CO • (303)934-2345 • (IV 1988 MED)

**RENSNER CHERYL L** (217)245-5676
205 Springbay Rd Jacksonville IL 62650 • clrensner@hotmail.com • CI • Tchr • Salem Jacksonville IL • (217)243-3419 • (RF 1983)

**RENSNER STEPHEN E** (217)245-5676
205 Springbay Dr Jacksonville IL 62650 • serensner@hotmail.com • CI • P/Tchr • Salem Jacksonville IL • (217)243-3419 • (RF 1982 MA)

**RENZELMAN RHONDA** (970)669-7293
1221 E Broadmoor Dr Loveland CO 80537-4466 • RM • Tchr • Immanuel Loveland CO • (970)667-7606 • (S 1994)

**RENZELMAN WILLIAM N** (970)669-7293
1221 E Broadmoor Dr Loveland CO 80537-4466 • RM • Tchr • Immanuel Loveland CO • (970)667-7606 • (S 1982)

**REPPERT KARI JEAN**
581 22nd Rd West Point NE 68788 • CNH • Tchr • Calvary San Lorenzo CA • (510)278-2556 • (S 2000)

**RESEBURG JULIE** (414)452-3773
1717 N 19th St Sheboygan WI 53081-2324 • SW • Tchr • Lutheran HS Sheboygan WI • (920)452-3323 • (CQ 1981)

**RESNER STEVEN A** (573)893-5330
2316 Colonial Hills Rd Jefferson City MO 65109-5638 • MO • Tchr • Trinity Jefferson City MO • (573)636-7807 • (WN 1983 MS)

**RESSIE LA DONNA KAY** (320)587-6016
325 Jefferson St SE Apt 9 Hutchinson MN 55350-2553 • osl@hutchtel.net • MNS • Tchr • Our Saviors Hutchinson MN • (320)587-3318 • (SP 1996)

**RETTIG JAMES F** (219)639-6032
7317 Monroeville Rd Hoagland IN 46745-9529 • IN • EM • (RF 1956 MS)

**RETTIG MARY KAY** (419)264-4931
G100 Rd 14 Holgate OH 43527 • OH • Tchr • St John Napoleon OH • (419)598-8961 • (RF 1971)

**REUTER JOHN F** (630)435-5742
6319 Bradley Dr Woodridge IL 60517-1236 • EN • EM • (RF 1954 MA)

**REVARD STEPHANIE RACHEL** (517)793-9723
530 Saint Andrews Rd Unit 2 Saginaw MI 48603-5943 • stephwel@yahoo.com • MI • Mem C • Holy Cross Saginaw MI • (517)793-9723 • (BR 1996)

**REYNOLDS DOUGLAS RAY** (219)478-9923
9212 Ridgetree Dr Fort Wayne IN 46819-2349 • reynolds@mtcalvarylutheran.com • IN • Mem C • Mount Calvary Fort Wayne IN • (219)747-4121 • (S 1987)

**REYNOLDS EARL L*** (818)362-6103
14456 Foothill Blvd Unit 26 Sylmar CA 91342-1532 • PSW • Prin • First San Fernando CA • (818)361-1638 • (S 1985)

**REYNOLDS EILEEN E** (818)362-6103
14456 Foothill Blvd Unit 26 Sylmar CA 91342-1532 • PSW • Tchr • First San Fernando CA • (818)361-4800 • (S 1975 MED)

**REYNOLDS JEANNETTE M** (303)427-0701
7100 Xavier St Westminster CO 80030-5746 • RM • Tchr • Emmaus Denver CO • (303)433-3303 • (S 1966)

**REYNOLDS LAURA MARIE**
4765 253rd Ave NE Isanti MN 55040-4359 • MNS • Tchr • Trinity Saint Francis MN • (612)753-1234 • (SP 1993)

**REYNOLDS NATALIE JANE** (219)478-9923
9212 Ridgetree Dr Fort Wayne IN 46819-2349 • dnzjmarey@hotmail.com • IN • 10/1992 10/1999 • (S 1987)

**RHEA PEGGY M** (309)691-3252
1924 W Barker Ave Peoria IL 61604-5508 • CI • Tchr • Concordia Peoria IL • (309)691-8921 • (CQ 1982)

**RHEINHEIMER TRACY** (303)695-4233
4633 S Crystal Way Unit D Aurora CO 80015-3930 • RM • Tchr • St John Denver CO • (303)733-3777 • (S 1991)

**RHINEHART CHARLES M** (941)481-4558
1564 Whiskey Creek Dr Fort Myers FL 33919-2724 • mrhinehart@sml.org • FG • Mem C • St Michael Fort Myers FL • (941)939-4711 • (S 1972 MSED)

**RHOADES JEAN MARIE** (520)290-8085
8357 E Louise Dr Tucson AZ 85730-1215 • PSW • Tchr • Fountain Of Life Tucson AZ • (520)747-1213 • (CQ 1995)

**RICE BARBARA LYNN** (313)320-1655
1310 Empire Ave Lincoln Park MI 48146-2049 • teach44@aol.com • MI • Tchr • Trinity Wyandotte MI • (734)282-5896 • (CQ 1999 MED)

**RICE DENISE L** (636)207-8510
835 La Bonne Pkwy Manchester MO 63021-7056 • jdsr@stlnet.com • MO • Tchr • St Paul Des Peres MO • (314)822-2771 • (AU 1984)

**RICE TRACEY JO**
Trinity Lutheran Church 123 E Livingston St Orlando FL 32801-1598 • FG • Tchr • Trinity Orlando FL • (407)843-4896 • (S 1997)

**RICH KRISTEL LYN** (225)753-1781
18481 Lake Iris Ave Baton Rouge LA 70817-7581 • OK • Tchr • First Ponca City OK • (580)762-1111 • (S 1995)

**RICH MONICA K*** (303)766-8643
17336 E Rice Cir #D Aurora CO 80015 • cmktrich@hotmail.com • RM • Tchr • Hope Aurora CO • (303)364-7416 • (IV 1987)

**RICHARD HELEN R** (626)281-5271
1138 S Chapel Ave Alhambra CA 91801-4827 • PSW • Tchr • Emmaus Alhambra CA • (626)289-3664 • (RF 1964)

**RICHARD JILL M**
PCS 41 Box 2719 APO AE 09464-2401 • jrich9@myfamily.com • NOW • 12/1997 12/1999 • (S 1995)

**RICHARDS JAMES K**
22828 Markham Way Boca Raton FL 33428-3930 • FG • Prin • Holy Cross Saginaw MI • (517)793-9723 • (CQ 2000 MED)

**RICHARDS KATHERINE M**
41 W 57th St Westmont IL 60559-2307 • NI • Tchr • St John LA Grange IL • (708)354-1690 • (RF 1991)

**RICHARDSON DEBORAH V** (626)614-0572
5940 1/2 N Camellia Ave Temple City CA 91780 • PSW • Tchr • First Temple City CA • (626)287-0968 • (AA 1990)

**RICHARDSON JENNIFER ELLEN**
850 Foxworth Blvd #201 Lombard IL 60148 • NI • Tchr • St Paul Melrose Park IL • (708)343-5000 • (RF 1999)

**RICHARDT KAREN LEE** (310)421-6210
4160 N Heather Rd Long Beach CA 90808-1624 • PSW • Tchr • Bethany Long Beach CA • (562)420-7783 • (CQ 1995)

**RICHBERG CONNIE LYNN**
23510 Oak Prairie Cir Sorento FL 32776 • FG • Tchr • Faith Eustis FL • (352)589-5433 • (MQ 1994)

**RICHENBURG PETER W** (636)928-5956
744 Blairbeth Dr Saint Charles MO 63304-7580 • richenburg@hotmail.com • MO • Tchr • LHS South Saint Louis MO • (314)631-1400 • (S 1974 MED)

**RICHERT ALVIN M** (517)752-9510
9818 Wadsworth Rd Saginaw MI 48601-9476 • MI • EM • (RF 1949 MA)

**RICHERT CARY M** (248)334-1303
2612 Crofthill Dr Auburn Hills MI 48326-3519 • cmric47@attglobal.net • MI • Mem C • Redeemer Birmingham MI • (248)644-4010 • (S 1973 MAT)

**RICHERT FAY R** (219)749-5538
1502 N Park Dr New Haven IN 46774-1720 • frrichert@juno.com • IN • EM • (RF 1954 MSED)

**RICHERT JAMES A** (317)882-4470
7627 Ardwell Ct Indianapolis IN 46237-9667 • jarichert@hotmail.com • IN • Prin • Calvary Indianapolis IN • (317)783-2000 • (RF 1977 MED)

**RICHERT RAY D** (618)495-2631
PO Box 206 Hoffman IL 62250-0206 • SI • EM • (RF 1953 MED)

**RICHERT SUSAN M** (317)882-4470
7627 Ardwell Ct Indianapolis IN 46237-9667 • IN • Tchr • Calvary Indianapolis IN • (317)783-2305 • (RF 1970)

**RICHHART JULENE C** (714)639-2369
534 N Turnberry Dr Orange CA 92869-2574 • PSW • Tchr • St Paul Orange CA • (714)921-3188 • (IV 1988)

**RICHTER AGNES C** (618)344-5290
227 Windridge Dr Collinsville IL 62234-4739 • SI • EM • (WN 1952)

**RICHTER EDGAR R** (713)447-1322
9210 Glen Shadow Dr Houston TX 77088-1930 • TX • Tchr • LHS North Houston TX • (713)880-3131 • (S 1963 MED)

**RICHTER JOSEPH B** (602)864-1047
2941 W Northview Ave Phoenix AZ 85051-7542 • azrichter@juno.com • EN • Tchr • English Farmington MI • (S 1978 MS)

**RICHTER KAREN**
C/O Shepherd Of The Hills L Ch 6914 Wurzbach Rd San Antonio TX 78240-3832 • TX • Tchr • Shepherd Hills San Antonio TX • (210)614-3742 • (AU 2000)

**RICHTER KIMBERLY** (512)898-2758
Rt 1 Box 21AAA Thorndale TX 76577 • richterkimberly@hotmail.com • TX • Tchr • St Paul Thorndale TX • (512)898-2711 • (AU 1998)

**RICHTER NATHAN D** (210)525-8386
5359 Fredericksburg Rd #402 San Antonio TX 78229 • TX • Tchr • LHS Of San Antonio San Antonio TX • (210)733-7771 • (S 1999)

**RICHTER ORVILLE W**
723 S Laclede Station Rd # 145 Saint Louis MO 63119-4966 • MO • EM • (RF 1933 MED MED)

**RICHTER RICHARD** (541)318-1248
CUENET 345 Cyber Ave Bend OR 97702 • crfrichterg@crf.cuis.edu • NI • SHS/C • Northern Illinois Hillside IL • (RF 1972 MED)

**RICHTER RONALD R DR** (402)643-6957
519 N 3rd Seward NE 68434 • rrichter@seward.cune.edu • NEB • SHS/C • Nebraska Seward NE • (S 1964 MED EDD)

**RICHTER SHARON L** (713)447-1322
9210 Glen Shadow Dr Houston TX 77088-1930 • TX • Tchr • Immanuel Houston TX • (713)861-8787 • (S 1963)

**RICHTER WALTER G** (407)365-7879
1506 Chipmunk Ln Oviedo FL 32765-8666 • SE • EM • (RF 1931)

**RICKELS ROBERT E** (406)896-0737
925 Delphinium Dr Billings MT 59102-3411 • MT • EM • (BY 1943 MA)

**RICKMAN SUSAN JANE** (414)728-2247
205 Spring St Delavan WI 53115-1636 • SW • Tchr • Our Redeemer Delavan WI • (262)728-6589 • (SP 1977)

**RICKORDS JEFFERY BRIAN** (505)833-5156
11015 Hackamore Ave SW Albuquerque NM 87121-9510 • jrickords@aol.com • RM • Tchr • Immanuel Albuquerque NM • (505)243-2589 • (S 1996)

**RIDOLF HELENE** (516)822-9455
110 Bay Ave Hicksville NY 11801 • AT • Tchr • Trinity Hicksville NY • (516)931-2211 • (RF 1972)

**RIECK MARLENE K** (763)546-5205
1501 Quebec Ave N Golden Valley MN 55427-4019 • teachermar@aol.com • MNS • 07/1999 • (S 1988 MED)

**RIEDEL SUZANNE R** (402)371-1420
112 Hillside Dr Hadar NE 68701 • NEB • Tchr • Christ Norfolk NE • (402)371-5536 • (S 1969)

**RIEDL JAMES MICHAEL** (503)257-8696
16337 NE Fargo Ct Portland OR 97230-5519 • ajjr@teleport.com • NOW • Prin • Trinity Portland OR • (503)288-6403 • (S 1968 MA EDS)

**RIEMER DELBERT F** (410)788-4522
1008 Pleasant Valley Dr Baltimore MD 21228-2602 • SE • P/Tchr • Emmanuel Baltimore MD • (410)744-0015 • (RF 1973 MS)

**RIEMER JONATHAN C** (718)460-6970
14932 Beech Ave Flushing NY 11355-1254 • AT • Tchr • St John Flushing NY • (718)463-2959 • (BR 1992)

**RIEMER KEVIN** (414)512-0094
12160 N Wauwatosa Rd Mequon WI 53097-2704 • SW • Tchr • Northwest Milwaukee WI • (414)463-4040 • (MQ 1996)

**RIEMER LAVONNE** (402)732-6810
PO Box 65 Benedict NE 68316-0065 • NEB • EM • (S 1964 MSLS)

**RIEMER NORMAN E** (414)353-4903
6525 N 76th St Milwaukee WI 53223-6103 • nd@execpc.com • SW • EM • (RF 1948 MS)

**RIES CHRISTINE C** (612)452-6955
3082 Sibley Memorial Hwy Eagan MN 55121-1612 • christmark@juno.com • MNS • 07/1995 07/2000 • (S 1963)

**RIESE CHERILYNN B** (402)379-3304
2304 N Eastwood St Lot 7A Norfolk NE 68701-1905 • NEB • 08/1998 08/2000 • (S 1985)

**RIESE RODNEY J** (715)845-3821
1311 Greenhill Dr Wausau WI 54401-4241 • NW • Tchr • Trinity Wausau WI • (715)848-0166 • (S 1968 MCMU)

**RIETSCHEL WILLIAM C DR** (708)246-2866
1121 Birch Ln Western Springs IL 60558-2103 • crfrietscwc@curf.edu • NI • SHS/C • Northern Illinois Hillside IL • (RF 1965 MA DED)

**RIEWE CINDI M** (507)549-3336
49896 132nd St Vernon Center MN 56090-9722 • abcfamily4@juno.com • MNS • Tchr • St Johns Vernon Center MN • (507)549-3036 • (SP 1979)

**RIFFEL KATHLEEN M** (219)464-1898
1307 Peachtree Dr Valparaiso IN 46383-4027 • kriffel@hotmail.com • IN • Tchr • Immanuel Valparaiso IN • (219)462-8207 • (S 1969 MSED)

**RIFFEL PERRY W DR** (219)464-1898
1307 Peachtree Dr Valparaiso IN 46383-4027 • Perry.Riffel@valpo.edu • IN • END • Indiana Fort Wayne IN • (S 1969 MSED DED)

**RIGGERT MARY L** (660)882-7209
1026 Wingate Boonville MO 65233 • MO • Tchr • Grace Lexington MO • (660)259-2932 • (S 1986)

**RIGGS TIMOTHY J** (561)498-7820
4822 Lincoln Rd Delray Beach FL 33445-3817 • FG • Tchr • Trinity Delray Beach FL • (561)276-8458 • (RF 1969 MA)

**RIKKELS ROBERT G** (314)961-7981
111 Saint George Pl Webster Groves MO 63119-4745 • MO • EM • (S 1959)

**RIKLI RICHARD LEE**
6965 W Frontage Rd Worden IL 62097-2431 • SI • P/Tchr • Trinity Worden IL • (618)633-2202 • (WN 1983)

**RILEY BARBARA A** (440)358-0838
467 W Jackson St Painesville OH 44077 • 3jbriley@ameritech.net • OH • Ohio Olmsted Falls OH • (S 1997)

**RILEY LORI**
1407 Nelson Ter Arlington TX 76011 • TX • Tchr • Grace Arlington TX • (817)274-1654 • (AA 1993)

**RINCKER KEITH E** (618)345-5796
414 Chapel Dr Collinsville IL 62234-4341 • SI • Tchr • Good Shepherd Collinsville IL • (618)344-3153 • (S 1980 MS)

**RINCKER KENT F** (317)473-5149
125 N Main PO Box 57 Hoyleton IL 62803-0057 • SI • 07/2000 • (S 1976 MA)

**RINCKER LOANA M** (618)478-2056
18059 State Rt 177 Nashville IL 62263 • SI • 09/1990 09/1997 • (S 1973)

**RINCKER PEGGY J** (618)345-5796
414 Chapel Dr Collinsville IL 62234-4341 • SI • Tchr • Good Shepherd Collinsville IL • (618)344-3153 • (S 1980)

**RINGERS DIANA L*** (334)986-5782
12521 Chicago St Elberta AL 36530-2543 • kringers@gulftel.com • SO • 08/1984 08/2000 • (S 1980)

**RINGLER LOUISE M** (402)535-2535
PO Box 217 Staplehurst NE 68439-9801 • NEB • Tchr • St Paul Utica NE • (402)534-2121 • (S 1964)

**RINK DIANA LYNN** (704)256-6241
2304 22nd Ave NE Hickory NC 28601-7966 • SE • Tchr • St Stephen Hickory NC • (828)256-2166 • (S 1978)

**RIPKE JUDITH L** (303)750-3715
16004 E Exposition Dr Aurora CO 80017-2116 • jripke1@juno.com • RM • Tchr • Hope Aurora CO • (303)364-7416 • (S 1977)

**RISCH CARL A** (219)724-8588
706 N 2nd St Apt 5 Decatur IN 46733-1381 • IN • Tchr • Zion Decatur IN • (219)728-9995 • (S 1979)

**RISCH DAVID A**
7400 Augusta St #BX-13N River Forest IL 60305-1402 • NI • SHS/C • Northern Illinois Hillside IL • (RF 1987)

**RISCHE DAVID** (812)372-6233
1128 Sycamore St Apt 2 Columbus IN 47201-4126 • IN • EM • (S 1962 MSED MA)

**RISENHOOVER SARAH L** (775)885-2856
3416 N Roop St Apt 3 Carson City NV 89706-0955 • srcrcg@msn.com • CNH • Tchr • Bethlehem Carson City NV • (775)882-5252 • (S 1995)

**RISKE CURTIS H*** (972)462-0149
636 Raintree Cir Coppell TX 75019-5447 • curt@coslc5.org • TX • Prin • Christ Our Savior Coppell TX • (972)393-7074 • (RF 1964 MA)

**RISKE HEIDI** (713)588-4549
6102 Winsomo #125B Houston TX 77057 • TX • Tchr • Texas Austin TX • (AU 1999)

**RISKE RALPH H** (517)662-2538
C/O Zion Lutheran Church 1556 Seidler Rd Auburn MI 48611-9732 • MI • Tchr • Zion Auburn MI • (517)662-4264 • (S 1974 MED)

**RISTOW BETH ANN** (810)776-8428
22236 Virginia Ave Eastpointe MI 48021-2351 • MI • Tchr • St Peter Eastpointe MI • (810)771-2809 • (AA 1986 MED)

**RITSCH DEBORAH SUE** (402)558-7737
4709 Cuming St Omaha NE 68132-2323 • NEB • Tchr • Mount Calvary Omaha NE • (402)551-7020 • (S 1985)

**RITTENHOUSE BARBARA LYNN** (818)342-6418
19512 Bassett St Reseda CA 91335-3602 • PSW • 08/1992 • (S 1986 MS)

**RITTER DALE LOUIS** (262)534-9860
30800 Meadow Ln Waterford WI 53185-3916 • kritter210@yahoo.com • SW • P/Tchr • St Peter Waterford WI • (262)534-3639 • (RF 1978 MAT)

**RITTMAN JUDITH** (660)463-2461
405 SW 10th St PO Box 911 Concordia MO 64020-0911 • MO • Tchr • St Paul Concordia MO • (660)463-7654 • (CQ 1986)

**RITTMANN DAVID F** (314)481-1636
3887 Holly Hills Blvd St Louis MO 63116-3134 • rittm@msn.com • MO • Prin • Missouri Saint Louis MO • (314)317-4550 • (RF 1964 MA LITTD)

**RITTMUELLER WALTER H** (660)438-3585
RR 2 Box 94-03 Edwards MO 65326-9583 • MO • EM • (RF 1942 MA)

**RITZ WANDA L**
511 Plum Ct Romeo MI 48065-5291 • MI • Tchr • St Peter Macomb MI • (810)781-9296 • (RF 1977)

**RIVENESS GARRET PAUL** (713)681-6130
4931 Oak Shadows Dr Houston TX 77091 • TX • Tchr • Concordia LHS Tomball TX • (281)351-2547 • (PO 1992)

**RIVERS JOEL A**
1138 Oak Hollow Dr Imperial MO 63052 • jrivers602@aol.com • MO • Tchr • St John Ellisville MO • (314)394-4100 • (S 1989)

**RIVERS MARLENE M** (316)229-8309
1305 E 7th Ave Winfield KS 67156-3122 • KS • Tchr • Trinity Winfield KS • (316)221-1820 • (S 1959 MED)

**RIVERS RONNIE L DR** (316)229-8309
1305 E 7th Ave Winfield KS 67156-3122 • rivers@horizon.hit.net • KS • EM • (S 1963 MED PHD)

**ROACH MICHELLE S**
8100 Park Plaza #261 Stanton CA 90680 • PSW • Tchr • St Paul Garden Grove CA • (714)534-6320 • (IV 1997)

**ROAN WILLIAM T** (619)670-0479
3818 Avenida Johanna La Mesa CA 91941-7312 • PSW • Tchr • Christ La Mesa CA • (619)462-5211 • (S 1971 MA)

**ROBBINS DORIS E** (507)288-3791
735 29th St NW Rochester MN 55901-2384 • MNS • Tchr • Rochester Central Rochester MN • (507)289-3267 • (SP 1968)

**ROBBINS KENNETH** (281)481-9498
13915 Knighton Cir Houston TX 77034-5439 • krobbins@mailman.ghgcorp.com • TX • Tchr • Lutheran South Acade Houston TX • (281)464-8299 • (S 1969 MS)

**ROBBINS PENNY S** (901)756-9314
6715 Amersham Dr Memphis TN 38119-8300 • MDS • 05/1998 05/2000 • (RF 1987)

**ROBERTS AUDREY V** (708)681-1915
907 Helen Dr Melrose Park IL 60160-2239 • NI • EM • (RF 1951 MA MA MS)

**ROBERTS GERALD M** (616)895-6058
5962 Bauer Rd Hudsonville MI 49426-9536 • gmroberts@hotmail.com • MI • Tchr • Our Savior Grand Rapids MI • (616)949-0710 • (CQ 1997)

**ROBERTS JAMES O DR** (708)681-1915
907 Helen Dr Melrose Park IL 60160-2239 • NI • EM • (RF 1951 MA PHD)

**ROBERTS MARY E** (636)947-6435
605 Rebecca Dr Saint Charles MO 63301-1385 • MO • Tchr • Immanuel Saint Charles MO • (636)946-0051 • (RF 1969)

**ROBERTS SANDRA LEE**
1145 N Sterling Ave Apt 111 Palatine IL 60067-1946 • NI • Tchr • St Matthew Lake Zurich IL • (847)438-6103 • (CQ 1994)

**ROBERTS SARA BETH**
2740 Associated Rd #D66 Fullerton CA 92835 • PSW • Tchr • Zion Anaheim CA • (714)535-1169 • (SP 1997)

**ROBERTSON CHARLOTTE L** (417)782-0931
2117 Park Pl Joplin MO 64804-1149 • MO • Tchr • Martin Luther Joplin MO • (417)624-1403 • (S 1971)

**ROBINSON DAVID PRESTON** (501)663-4794
1123 Mellon St Little Rock AR 72207 • MDS • Tchr • Christ Little Rock AR • (501)663-5212 • (S 1995)

**ROBINSON DIANA RAYE** (501)663-4794
1123 Mellon St Little Rock AR 72207 • MDS • Tchr • Christ Little Rock AR • (501)663-5212 • (S 1998)

**ROBINSON JAMES H*** (303)421-8589
11602 W 71st Ave Arvada CO 80004-1232 • RM • EM • (S 1951)

**ROBINSON JAMES L** (217)442-0707
310 Moore St Tilton IL 61833-8217 • CI • Tchr • Danville Danville IL • (217)442-5036 • (RF 1984)

**ROBINSON JOEL D** (713)857-8518
10507 N Laureldale Dr Houston TX 77041-7871 • joeldrob@hotmail.com • TX • Tchr • Our Savior Houston TX • (713)290-9087 • (S 1972 MMU)

**ROBSON DAWN M** (480)839-0906
1035 E Guadalupe Rd Tempe AZ 85283 • RM • Tchr • Christ Murray UT • (801)266-8714 • (SP 1976)

**ROBSON WENDELL L** (480)839-0906
1035 E Guadalupe Rd Tempe AZ 85283 • PSW • Christ Murray UT • (SP 1976 MED)

**ROCANS ROBERTA L** (708)635-9156
40 N 5th Ave Des Plaines IL 60016-2302 • NI • Tchr • St Paul Skokie IL • (847)673-5030 • (RF 1992)

**ROCHLITZ DAVID W** (810)791-1837
36190 Paddock Dr Clinton Twp MI 48035-1220 • MI • Tchr • LHS North Macomb MI • (810)781-9151 • (RF 1981 MA)

**ROCK MELISSA KAYE** (309)962-2239
304 E Green St Le Roy IL 61752 • CI • Tchr • St John Champaign IL • (217)359-1714 • (S 1987 MS)

**ROCKENBACH NANCY C** (561)362-0371
St Paul Luth School 701 W Palmetto Park Rd Boca Raton FL 33486-3561 • FG • Tchr • St Paul Boca Raton FL • (561)395-8548 • (S 1996)

**ROCKEY MARTHA P**
1628 Celebration Way Nashville TN 37211-6826 • jrockey@juno.com • MDS • 09/1994 09/1998 • (AU 1986)

**ROCKEY STEPHEN J** (813)719-3125
4307 Barret Ave Plant City FL 33567-7016 • afn05416@afn.org • FG • Prin • Hope Plant City FL • (813)752-4622 • (AU 1983 MS)

**ROCKWELL CINDY LEE** (520)682-7149
PO Box 89786 Tucson AZ 85752-9786 • cinrock2000@cs.com • EN • Tchr • Ascension Tucson AZ • (520)742-6229 • (SP 1985)

**RODE KURT A** (314)376-4507
5011 Diamond Dr High Ridge MO 63049-2746 • NI • EM • (RF 1936)

**RODENBECK ALLEN G** (219)484-9708
1216 Somerset Ln Fort Wayne IN 46805-2140 • IN • Tchr • Concordia LHS Fort Wayne IN • (219)483-1102 • (S 1976 MS)

**RODENBECK EDITH F** (219)485-0717
4728 Ottawa Dr Fort Wayne IN 46835-3436 • IN • Tchr • Holy Cross Fort Wayne IN • (219)483-3173 • (RF 1961 MSED)

**RODENBECK JANICE L** (206)566-9525
427 Del Monte Fircrest WA 98466 • NOW • Tchr • Concordia Tacoma WA • (253)475-9513 • (PO 1985)

**RODENBECK RONALD P** (219)484-6074
1321 Somerset Ln Fort Wayne IN 46805-2141 • IN • EM • (RF 1953 MS)

**RODENCAL KORINNA D** (402)467-2160
5600 Abbey Ct #87 Lincoln NE 68505 • jr45020@navix.net • NEB • Tchr • Lincoln Luth Jr/Sr H Lincoln NE • (402)467-5404 • (S 1998)

**RODEWALD BENJAMIN P**
424 W 70th Ter Kansas City MO 64113-2053 • MO • Tchr • Calvary Kansas City MO • (816)444-6908 • (S 1989)

**RODGERS LEWIS EDWARD** (217)483-6461
6 Knollcrest Ln Chatham IL 62629-1056 • CI • Prin • Trinity Springfield IL • (217)787-2323 • (RF 1982 MS)

**RODGERS SUSAN** (217)787-2323
6 Knollcrest Ln Chatham IL 62629-1056 • CI • 03/1996 • (RF 1981)

**RODRIGUEZ VICTOR M** (714)651-0239
5 Peacock Irvine CA 92604-1931 • PSW • SHS/C • Pacific Southwest Irvine CA • (949)854-3232 • (CQ 1992)

**ROEBER JOHN K** (402)944-7782
28211 Church Rd # 115 Murdock NE 68407-2329 • NEB • Tchr • Lincoln Luth Jr/Sr H Lincoln NE • (402)467-5404 • (S 1966)

**ROEDEL MARTIN O** (920)485-4902
510 City View Blvd Horicon WI 53032 • roedel7@powerweb.net • SW • Tchr • St Stephen Horicon WI • (920)485-6687 • (S 1975)

**ROEDER JOANNE L** (714)974-8504
5374 E Willowick Dr Anaheim CA 92807-4637 • cjroeder@earthlink.net • PSW • 11/1995 11/1999 • (RF 1964 MA)

**ROEGLIN KARLA L**
3030 N Fairwood Ct Wauwatosa WI 53222 • mnkroeglin@worldnet.att.net • SW • 08/2000 • (MQ 1996)

**ROEKLE THOMAS H** (517)753-1313
2700 Benjamin St Saginaw MI 48602-5773 • MI • Tchr • Valley Saginaw MI • (517)790-1676 • (S 1985 MAT)

**ROEMKE CAROL A** (518)438-3232
39 Washington Ave Albany NY 12205-5259 • AT • Tchr • Our Savior Albany NY • (518)459-2273 • (RF 1965)

**ROEMKE THOMAS L** (518)438-3232
39 Washington Ave Albany NY 12205-5259 • troemke@pathfindermail.com • AT • P/Tchr • Our Savior Albany NY • (518)459-2273 • (RF 1965 MS)

**ROEPKE MARY J*** (818)885-8401
10125 Lasaine Ave Northridge CA 91325-1509 • PSW • Tchr • Our Savior First Granada Hills CA • (818)368-0892 • (CQ 1990)

**ROESKE KARL FREDERICK** (414)377-4011
1972 Granville Rd Cedarsburg WI 53012 • SW • Tchr • First Immanuel Cedarburg WI • (262)377-6610 • (MW 1983)

**ROESKE KIMBERLY S**
PO Box 154 9500 Gen Santos PHILIPPINES • EN • 11/1991 11/1999 • (AA 1985)

**ROESLER JOYCE E** (301)647-0673
204 Holland Rd Severna Park MD 21146-3622 • SE • Tchr • St Paul Glen Burnie MD • (410)766-5790 • (S 1968 MA)

**ROETTJER JENNIFER MARIE** (970)748-1409
PO Box 6655 Avon CO 81620-6655 • jroettjer@vchs.org • RM • Tchr • Denver Lutheran High Denver CO • (303)934-2345 • (S 1999)

**ROGERS EMILY R** (715)848-2654
717 Stark St Wausau WI 54403-3626 • NW • 03/1993 03/2000 • (SP 1988)

**ROGERS KAREN A** (520)578-8027
6461 W Missouri St Tucson AZ 85735 • elfquest13@aol.com • EN • Tchr • Faith Tucson AZ • (520)881-0670 • (CQ 1995 MSED)

**ROGERS PHILLIP L** (715)848-2654
717 Stark St Wausau WI 54403-3626 • NW • Tchr • Trinity Wausau WI • (715)842-0769 • (SP 1988)

**ROGERS RANDALL J** (314)544-2944
9855 Ione Ln Saint Louis MO 63123-6448 • coachroge@aol.com • MO • Tchr • Missouri Saint Louis MO • (314)317-4550 • (RF 1983 MED)

**ROGERS SUSAN J** (714)998-8148
2615 N Dunbar St Orange CA 92865-2806 • PSW • Tchr • Zion Anaheim CA • (714)535-1169 • (S 1982 MA)

**ROGGATZ GEORGE R** (810)781-3186
11228 Manchester Rd Washington MI 48094-3061 • MI • EM • (S 1951)

**ROGNER DAVID** (708)524-3364
1042 Washington Blvd # 2 Oak Park IL 60302-3758 • rognerdw@curf.edu • NI • SHS/C • Northern Illinois Hillside IL • (RF 1982 MA PHD)

**ROGNER KENNETH C** (248)608-6421
3143 Lake George Rd Oakland MI 48363-2903 • krogner@tir.com • MI • Mem C • St John Rochester MI • (248)652-8830 • (RF 1974)

**ROHDE AARON T** (248)969-8647
4177 Seymour Lake Rd Oxford MI 48371-4036 • rdmstr1000@aol.com • MI • Tchr • St John Rochester MI • (248)652-8830 • (RF 1993)

**ROHDE DONALD J** (414)365-1160
8109 N Celina St Milwaukee WI 53224-2905 • dsrohde@execpc.com • SW • Prin • Immanuel Brookfield WI • (414)781-4135 • (RF 1970 MA MAD)

**ROHDE REBECCA A**
Concordia Lutheran HS 1601 St Joe River Dr Fort Wayne IN 46805 • gobluesbr@aol.com • IN • Tchr • Concordia LHS Fort Wayne IN • (219)483-1102 • (AA 1997)

**ROHE LINDA L** (618)377-9910
301 Wyoming St Bethalto IL 62010-1620 • linr1231@aol.com • SI • Tchr • Zion Bethalto IL • (618)377-5507 • (RF 1968)

**ROHE WM JAMES** (618)377-9910
301 Wyoming St Bethalto IL 62010-1620 • jimteach5@aol.com • SI • Tchr • Zion Bethalto IL • (618)377-5507 • (RF 1969 MS)

**ROHLF EMILY LINN** (402)564-0892
1914 1st St Columbus NE 68601-7504 • erohlf@mail.esu7.org • NEB • Tchr • Christ Columbus NE • (402)564-3531 • (S 1998)

**ROHLFING ROXANNE** (314)949-3927
3 Lynworth Ct Saint Charles MO 63301-1258 • rrohlfing@lycosmail.com • MO • Tchr • Immanuel Saint Charles MO • (636)946-0051 • (CQ 1992 MED)

**ROHLFING TERRENCE H** (618)763-4464
106 W Jacob Rd Jacob IL 62950 • christ@egyptian.net • SI • P/Tchr • Christ Jacob IL • (618)763-4663 • (RF 1968 MED)

**ROHMALLER BETTY JEAN** (714)751-4226
1008 Presidio Drive Costa Mesa CA 92626-5612 • drohmaller@earthlink.net • PSW • Tchr • Christ Costa Mesa CA • (949)631-1611 • (S 1976)

**ROHMALLER DUANE J** (714)751-4226
1008 Presidio Dr Costa Mesa CA 92626-5612 • PSW • EM • (S 1958 MSED)

**ROHR SHARON K**
638 N 400 E Seymour IN 47274 • IN • Tchr • St John Seymour IN • (812)523-3131 • (RF 1970)

**ROHWER MARLETTA M** (651)490-9035
1022 Tiller Ln Shoreview MN 55126-8149 • MNS • Tchr • King Of Kings Roseville MN • (651)484-9206 • (SP 1972)

**ROLAND LYDIA M** (317)474-5409
3146 Eagles Way Dr Apt 1570 Lafayette IN 47909 • IN • Tchr • St James Lafayette IN • (765)742-6464 • (RF 1981)

**ROLF CHERYL J** (248)651-9068
223 Pine St Rochester MI 48307-1931 • rolf@michigannet.com • MI • Tchr • Living Word Rochester MI • (248)651-9474 • (S 1978)

**ROLF CHERYL L** (743)722-7965
38837 Laurenwood Wayne MI 48184-2807 • rolfjrcr4g@aol.com • MI • Tchr • St Michael Wayne MI • (734)728-3315 • (RF 1975)

**ROLF ELDA C** (517)792-4345
1954 Passolt St Saginaw MI 48602-3255 • eldarolf@concentric.net • MI • EM • (RF 1968 MA)

**ROLF ERIKA J** (907)696-4733
9630 Nulato Cir Eagle River AK 99577-8649 • rolfeg@gci.net • NOW • 08/1998 08/2000 • (S 1989 MS)

**ROLF JAMES E** (248)651-9068
223 Pine St Rochester MI 48307-1931 • rolf@michigannet.com • MI • Tchr • St Stephen Waterford MI • (248)673-6621 • (RF 1978 MCRT)

**ROLF JOEL A** (317)861-0783
5078 Raesner North Dr New Palestine IN 46163-9710 • IN • Tchr • Trinity Indianapolis IN • (317)897-0243 • (RF 1988)

**ROLF JOHN E** (734)722-7965
38837 Laurenwood Dr Wayne MI 48184-2807 • rolfjrcr4g@aol.com • MI • Tchr • St Michael Wayne MI • (734)728-3315 • (RF 1975 MA)

**ROLF KRISTIN KAY**
4633 S Crystal Way Unit D Aurora CO 80015-3930 • CI • Tchr • Central Illinois Springfield IL • (S 1991)

**ROLF SHERYL LYN** (317)861-0783
5078 Raesner North Dr New Palestine IN 46163-9710 • IN • Tchr • Trinity Indianapolis IN • (317)897-0243 • (RF 1989)

**ROLLINS GLENN KEITH**
8821 Medicine Wheel Ave Las Vegas NV 89117 • PSW • Trinity Indianapolis IN • (S 1979 MA)

**ROMP WILBERT F** (517)894-0038
706 Main St Essexville MI 48732-1335 • MI • EM • (S 1953)

**ROMSA JERAD** (213)881-5574
8132 Darby Pl Reseda CA 91335-1316 • PSW • P/Tchr • Trinity Reseda CA • (818)342-1633 • (S 1968 MA)

**RONSCHKE WILLIAM P*** (216)252-5504
11421 Fidelity Ave Cleveland OH 44111-3647 • OH • P/Tchr • Luther Memorial Cleveland OH • (216)631-3640 • (RF 1968)

**ROOT STARLINE MICHELLE**
2731 Ridgeline Dr #E207 Corona CA 91720 • PSW • Tchr • Zion Anaheim CA • (714)535-3600 • (IV 1999)

**ROSE ANGELINE M** (305)296-6289
2906 Flagler Ave Key West FL 33040-4004 • FG • P/Tchr • Grace Key West FL • (305)296-8262 • (SP 1955)

**ROSE CAROL ANN** (612)456-0871
2262 Field Stone Dr Mendota Heights MN 55120-1918 • MNS • Tchr • Trinity Lone Oak Eagan MN • (651)454-1139 • (SP 1979 MA)

**ROSE DWAYNE K** (262)255-3507
W170N8736 Edgewood Pl Menomonee Falls WI 53051-2715 • SW • Tchr • Zion Menomonee Falls WI • (414)781-7437 • (MQ 1984)

**ROSE PATRICIA DR** (708)449-1629
525 N Irving Ave Hillside IL 60162-1221 • rosepk@cuis.edu • NI • SHS/C • Northern Illinois Hillside IL • (S 1976 MA PHD)

**ROSE RICHARD R** (312)865-8652
914 N 3rd Ave Maywood IL 60153-1017 • NI • Tchr • Northern Illinois Hillside IL • (RF 1975)

**ROSENBERG DONALD A** (715)845-6571
2509 Midway Blvd Wausau WI 54403-7053 • NW • EM • (RF 1944 MED LITTD)

**ROSENBERG JILL L** (818)763-5434
11919 Oxnard St North Hollywood CA 91606-3320 • PSW • 06/1996 • (S 1995)

**ROSENBERG JOANNA N** (714)665-2732
2960 Champion Way #806 Tustin CA 92782 • PSW • Tchr • Christ Brea CA • (714)529-2984 • (IV 1997)

**ROSENDAHL DARLA M** (402)643-7209
800 N Columbia Ave Seward NE 68434-1556 • drosendahl@seward.cune.edu • NEB • SHS/C • Nebraska Seward NE • (S 1973 MED)

**ROSENTHAL DENNIS** (402)478-4707
8823 Co Rd 9 Arlington NE 68002 • NEB • P/Tchr • St Paul Arlington NE • (402)478-4278 • (S 1970 MED)

**ROSENTHAL SALLIE E** (402)478-4707
8951 County Rd 9 Arlington NE 68002 • NEB • Tchr • St Paul Arlington NE • (402)478-4278 • (S 1970)

**ROSENTRETER KATHY E** (517)652-4494
642 Gruber St Apt C7 Frankenmuth MI 48734-1034 • MI • Tchr • St Michael Richville MI • (517)868-4809 • (AA 1990 MAT)

**ROSIN DELORES M** (414)387-2659
W3365 Raaschs Hill Rd Horicon WI 53032-9748 • rosgo44@hotmail.com • SW • Tchr • St John Mayville WI • (920)387-4310 • (RF 1966)

**ROSIN MICHAEL PAUL**
19240 Brody Ave Allen Park MI 48101-3438 • MI • P/Tchr • Christ The King Southgate MI • (734)285-9697 • (RF 1985 MED)

**ROSKAVICH ELOISE M** (214)423-7447
8005 Lake Bend Dr Rowlett TX 75088-8910 • TX • EM • (S 1959)

**ROSS DONALD G** (931)649-2841
105 Flower Pt Estill Springs TN 37330-3113 • donross@cafes.net • MDS • EM • (CQ 1985 EDD)

**ROSS GAYLE C** (616)935-3670
6211 - 25 Mile Rd Apt #6 Shelby Twp MI 48316-1768 • MI • Tchr • Peace Shelby Township MI • (810)731-4120 • (RF 1980 MED)

**ROSS LESLIE ANN** (216)739-1386
4179 River Ridge Dr Cleveland OH 44109-3790 • EN • Calvary Oroville CA • (RF 1990)

**ROSSMAN REBECCA LYNN**
16601 FM 1325 Apt 1222 Austin TX 78728-1158 • TX • 07/1998 07/2000 • (AU 1996)

**ROSSOW MEREDITH DEANN** (319)355-0961
3411 Jersey Ridge Rd #1015 Davenport IA 52807 • mererossow@yahoo.com • IE • Tchr • Trinity Davenport IA • (319)322-5224 • (S 1999)

**ROSTE LUCY M** (320)762-2606
1804 Kari St Alexandria MN 56308-8543 • MNN • 02/2000 • (SP 1990)

**ROTERMUND DONALD O** (972)889-1117
605 Olympic Richardson TX 75081-5159 • dondor@freewwweb.com • TX • EM • (RF 1955 MMU LITTD)

**ROTERMUND MELVIN E**
62 S Walnut North Aurora IL 60542-1545 • roter@enteract.com • NI • EM • (RF 1950 MA)

**ROTH ALFRED R DR** (503)654-4968
14665 SE Raintree Ct Portland OR 97267-2926 • allormilor@aol.com • NOW • EM • (CQ 1961 MED DED)

**ROTH ALVIN L** (218)697-2845
342 Henrietta Ave S PO Box 359 Hill City MN 55748 • MNS • EM • (RF 1938 MS)

**ROTH CHRISTOPHER DAVID** (651)771-0338
1269 Mc Lean Ave Apt 205 Saint Paul MN 55106-6564 • chrisroth1@aol.com • MNS • Tchr • Luth HS Of Greater M Bloomington MN • (612)854-0224 • (SP 1992)

**ROTH DANIEL C** (618)277-3649
110 Foxbrush Dr Belleville IL 62221-4563 • drothsid@aol.com • SI • Southern Illinois Belleville IL* • (RF 1965 MEAD)

**ROTH DAVID M** (952)447-7261
14728 Cherry Ct NE Prior Lake MN 55372-1137 • dmrothtwin@aol.com • MNS • Minnesota South Burnsville MN* • (RF 1965 MAD)

**ROTH EDGAR N** (573)547-6399
48 Christine St Perryville MO 63775 • SI • EM • * • (RF 1952 MA)

**ROTH JAMES A** (810)978-9349
35552 Marina Dr Sterling Heights MI 48312-4139 • rothjc@c3net.net • MI • Tchr • East Bethlehem Detroit MI • (313)892-2671 • (S 1962)

**ROTH JEANINE S** (952)447-7261
14728 Cherry Ct NE Prior Lake MN 55372-1137 • MNS • Tchr • St Peter Edina MN • (612)927-8400 • (RF 1963 MED)

**ROTH LESLIE D** (517)652-2592
683 Eastgate Dr Frankenmuth MI 48734-1201 • MI • Prin • St Michael Richville MI • (517)868-4809 • (S 1965 MED)

**ROTH MARILYN J** (618)277-3649
110 Foxbrush Dr Belleville IL 62221-4563 • drothsid@aol.com • SI • Tchr • Zion Belleville IL • (618)234-0275 • (CQ 1988)

**ROTH RONALD J** (419)599-0340
1125 Westmont Napoleon OH 43545 • rjroth@henry.net • OH • Tchr • St Paul Napoleon OH • (419)592-5536 • (RF 1969 MA)

**ROTHAS CYNTHIA K** (707)579-4710
2515 Hardies Ln Santa Rosa CA 95403-9431 • CNH • Tchr • St Luke Santa Rosa CA • (707)545-0526 • (SP 1984)

**ROTHE PAT K** (254)776-5482
2225 Rosewood Dr Waco TX 76710-1531 • TX • Tchr • Trinity Waco TX • (254)772-7840 • (RF 1968)

**ROTTERMOND LINDA IRENE** (517)323-8322
16979 Driftwood Dr Macomb MI 48042 • aforlife@aol.com • MI • Tchr • Immanuel Macomb MI • (810)286-4231 • (RF 1971)

**ROTTMANN DINEEN S** (262)695-1858
600 Westfield Way Unit 7 Pewaukee WI 53072-6524 • SW • Tchr • Elm Grove Elm Grove WI • (262)797-2970 • (MQ 1995)

**ROTTMANN MICHAEL S** (262)695-1858
600 Westfield Way Unit 7 Pewaukee WI 53072-6524 • SW • Tchr • Elm Grove Elm Grove WI • (262)797-2970 • (MQ 1994 MS)

**ROUNDEY WILLIAM G JR.** (402)420-2584
3022 Browning St Lincoln NE 68516 • counselor@lnklutheran.org • NEB • Tchr • Lincoln Luth Jr/Sr H Lincoln NE • (402)467-5404 • (S 1983 MED)

**ROUSE CAROLYN J** (214)340-2914
9959 Adleta Blvd # 1302 Dallas TX 75243 • TX • Tchr • Our Redeemer Dallas TX • (214)368-1465 • (RF 1987)

**ROUSH DONALD L** (847)705-8269
4545 Olmstead Dr Hoffman Estates IL 60195-1181 • NI • Northern Illinois Hillside IL • (RF 1956 MA)

**ROWE CHRISTINE E** (203)744-6353
27 Whippoorwill Rd Bethel CT 06801 • NE • P/Tchr • Immanuel Danbury CT • (203)748-7823 • (CQ 1997 MS)

**ROWELL CAROLYNN W** (562)598-3540
5622 Trinette Ave Garden Grove CA 92845-2439 • xttquioa@prodigy.com • PSW • Tchr • Bethany Long Beach CA • (562)421-4711 • (CQ 1995)

**ROWELL MARY ANN DR** (219)897-3387
1526 E Albion St Avilla IN 46710-9642 • IN • Tchr • Holy Cross Fort Wayne IN • (219)483-3173 • (RF 1961 MA MLS PHD)

**ROWSELL DAVID H** (319)362-6856
300 18th St NW Cedar Rapids IA 52405-3710 • IE • Tchr • Trinity Cedar Rapids IA • (319)362-6952 • (RF 1967)

**ROYBAL LINDA A** (303)934-7375
5080 W Oregon Pl Denver CO 80219 • RM • Tchr • Bethlehem Lakewood CO • (303)238-7676 • (CQ 2000)

**ROYUK BARBARAKAY T** (402)478-4797
1285 W Dodge Ave Arlington NE 68002-3040 • NEB • Tchr • Trinity Fremont NE • (402)721-5959 • (S 1969)

**ROYUK BRAD RONALD** (410)663-4227
1325 Taylor Ave FL 2 Baltimore MD 21234-5920 • 74601.1107@compuserve.com • SE • Tchr • Baltimore LHS Baltimore MD • (410)825-2323 • (S 1993)

**ROYUK BRENT R**
230 Hillcrest Dr Seward NE 68434-2822 • broyuk@seward.ccsn.edu • NEB • SHS/C • Nebraska Seward NE • (S 1988 MS)

**ROYUK RONALD JOHN** (507)235-8046
956 Albion Ave Fairmont MN 56031-3007 • rj-royuk@hotmail.com • MNS • Prin • Martin Luther Northrop MN • (507)436-5249 • (S 1963 MA)

**ROZAK DAVID O** (863)285-8796
4580 US Highway 98 E Fort Meade FL 33841-9375 • s072493d@aol.com • FG • EM • (S 1964 MED)

**ROZELLE RANDALL LYN**
C/O Vail Christian High School PO Box 2023 Edwards CO 81632 • rrozelle@vchs.org • RM • Tchr • Vail Christian Edwards CO • (970)926-3015 • (AA 1998)

**RUBEL JOHN C** (715)341-2204
2030 Adams St Plover WI 54467-2812 • NW • Tchr • St Paul Stevens Point WI • (715)344-5660 • (RF 1968)

**RUDI BRUCE D** (210)492-0683
10 Spring Lake Dr San Antonio TX 78248-2434 • brucer@concordia-satx.com • TX • Prin • Concordia San Antonio TX • (210)479-1477 • (RF 1975 MA)

**RUDICK ANNETTE KAY** (517)263-0075
103 N Charles St Apt 322B Adrian MI 49221 • MI • Tchr • St John Adrian MI • (517)265-6998 • (SP 1989)

**RUDICK BARBARA A** (616)842-7417
19097 Gildner Creek Ct Spring Lake MI 49456 • MI • Tchr • Our Redeemer Muskegon MI • (231)773-2667 • (RF 1968)

**RUDICK PAMELA MARIE**
1711 Ridge Rd Homewood IL 60430-1832 • prudick@juno.com • NI • Tchr • Salem Homewood IL • (708)206-0350 • (RF 1993)

**RUDLAFF RICHARD A** (712)735-4036
6676 Frederick Ave Ocheyedan IA 51354-7942 • MI • 04/1999 • (S 1969)

**RUDLOFF DEAN H** (218)353-7424
5736 Lax Lake Rd Silver Bay MN 55614-9502 • jdrlax@lake.net • MNN • 08/1994 08/2000 • (S 1967)

**RUDNICK CARLENE**
5518 Lachman Ave NE Albertville MN 55301 • MNS • EM • (RF 1960)

**RUDOLPH BARBARA R** (612)441-3394
9370 Viking Blvd NW Elk River MN 55330-8021 • bdrudolph@juno.com • MNS • Tchr • St John Elk River MN • (612)441-6616 • (S 1978)

**RUDOLPH ELTON A** (517)356-0409
433 Victoria Dr Alpena MI 49707-1126 • MI • EM • (S 1953)

**RUDOLPH LORNA M** (612)441-4114
19915 Proctor Rd NW Elk River MN 55330-8211 • MNS • Tchr • St John Elk River MN • (612)441-6616 • (SP 1984)

**RUDSINSKI CAROL A** (314)894-0483
10800 Arnett Dr Affton MO 63123-7114 • carolrudsinski@slcas.com • MO • Tchr • Salem Affton MO • (314)353-9242 • (RF 1975)

**RUDY SALLY L** (219)372-2668
1905-A Sand Dollar Dr Warsaw IN 46582-9014 • IN • Tchr • Redeemer Warsaw IN • (219)267-5656 • (S 1971)

**RUDY WAYNE A**
385 Grand St Apt L1005 New York NY 10002-3968 • AT • Tchr • St Mark Brooklyn NY • (718)453-4040 • (RF 1970)

**RUDZINSKI KEVIN RUSSELL**
4903 Seibert Ave Saint Louis MO 63123-4714 • MO • Tchr • Word Of Life Saint Louis MO • (314)832-1244 • (RF 1996)

**RUDZINSKI LEROY F** (816)942-4125
9725 Winslow Pl Kansas City MO 64131-3268 • lrudzinski@lhskc.com • MO • Tchr • Missouri Saint Louis MO • (314)317-4550 • (RF 1971)

**RUEBER BRUCE E**
314 E S First PO Box 307 Stewardson IL 62463-0305 • gbjerseys@aol.com • CI • P/Tchr • Trinity Stewardson IL • (217)682-5722 • (RF 1968 MA)

**RUEBER GLORIA JANE** (605)339-7016
1620 E Dana Dr Sioux Falls SD 57105-2024 • gbjerseys@aol.com • CI • 07/2000 • (RF 1968)

**RUETER NANCY J** (562)925-4728
13732 Cornuta Ave Bellflower CA 90706-2510 • PSW • Tchr • Good Shepherd Downey CA • (562)803-4918 • (S 1968)

**RUETER ROGER H** (562)925-4728
13732 Cornuta Ave Bellflower CA 90706-2510 • PSW • Tchr • St Paul Orange CA • (714)921-3188 • (S 1966 MED)

**RUFF ELAINE KATHLEEN** (410)836-9168
1303 Cheshire Ln Bel Air MD 21014-2553 • rrooo8@juno.com • SE • Tchr • St Paul Kingsville MD • (410)592-8100 • (S 1963 MSED)

**RUHTER JAMES A**
Hong Kong Intn'l School 6 South Bay Close Repulse Bay HONG KONG • IN • S Miss • Indiana Fort Wayne IN • (S 1969 MA MS)

**RULL KARA LYNNE** (618)377-3353
405 Whispering Oaks Dr Bethalto IL 62010-1055 • SI • 06/1993 06/2000 • (RF 1984)

**RULLMAN ARLYS S** (828)256-5538
4641 Glen Hollow Ln NE Hickory NC 28601-8733 • SE • Tchr • St Stephen Hickory NC • (828)256-2166 • (S 1966)

**RULLMAN GLENN L** (336)722-6278
2430 Maplewood Ave Winston Salem NC 27103-3535 • SE • Tchr • St John Winston-Salem NC • (336)725-1651 • (RF 1964 MED)

**RULLMAN JACQUELINE S** (336)722-6278
2430 Maplewood Ave Winston Salem NC 27103-3535 • SE • Tchr • St John Winston-Salem NC • (336)725-1651 • (RF 1964)

**RUMBOLD PAULA CHRISTINE** (920)426-3342
1212 Wheatfield Way Oshkosh WI 54904-7400 • SW • Tchr • Trinity Oshkosh WI • (920)235-1730 • (RF 1975 MS)

**RUMBOLD SHARON K** (309)469-4531
533 County Rd 850 E Sparland IL 61565 • CI • Tchr • Bethel Morton IL • (309)266-6592 • (CQ 1990)

**RUMSEY KRISSA M** (734)677-6155
2840 Canterbury Rd Ann Arbor MI 48104 • carlsk@ccaa.edu • MI • SHS/C • Michigan Ann Arbor MI • (AA 1994)

**RUNGE DAVID KENT** (319)442-3459
206 3rd Ave Keystone IA 52249 • drunge@mailcity.com • IE • Tchr • Central Newhall IA • (319)223-5271 • (S 1996)

**RUNGE SUSAN C** (830)627-0906
310 Castelwood #5 New Braunfels TX 78130 • TX • Tchr • Cross New Braunfels TX • (830)625-3666 • (AU 1999)

**RUNNELLS LEE ANNE** (217)425-5778
225 W William St Apt 2 Decatur IL 62522-2340 • CI • Tchr • Lutheran School Asso Decatur IL • (217)233-2001 • (RF 1985 MA)

**RUOPP ANNA L** (203)790-9911
37 Spruce Mountain Rd Danbury CT 06810-8221 • NE • Tchr • Immanuel Danbury CT • (203)748-7823 • (AA 1987)

**RUPE DOROTHY EMILY**
2862 N Cottonwood # 9 Orange CA 92865 • PSW • Tchr • Zion Anaheim CA • (714)535-3600 • (RF 1970)

**RUPP DONNA C** (210)494-0594
4839 Legend Well Dr San Antonio TX 78247-5611 • TX • Tchr • Concordia San Antonio TX • (210)479-1477 • (AU 1987)

**RUPPEL GLORIA CELESTE** (713)856-8061
9343 Adagio Ln Houston TX 77040 • gruppel@stmarkhouston.org • TX • Mem C • St Mark Houston TX • (713)468-2623 • (CQ 1997 MS)

**RUPPEL SONJA TINA** (847)359-9310
464 S Burno Dr Palatine IL 60067-6710 • NI • Tchr • Immanuel Palatine IL • (847)359-1936 • (RF 1996)

**RUPPERT RUTH M** (309)691-3705
1804 W Baywood Ave Peoria IL 61614-5615 • CI • Tchr • Concordia Peoria IL • (309)691-8921 • (RF 1966)

**RUPPERT THOMAS W** (309)691-3705
1804 W Baywood Ave Peoria IL 61614-5615 • CI • Tchr • Concordia Peoria IL • (309)691-8921 • (RF 1967 MS)

**RUPPRECHT EDWARD P** (630)466-4047
176 Mc Cannon St Sugar Grove IL 60554 • edrupprecht@yahoo.com • NI • Tchr • Luther HS North Chicago IL • (773)286-3600 • (RF 1964 MA)

**RUSCH DAVID L** (310)204-0366
4146 Center St Culver City CA 90232-4005 • PSW • P/Tchr • First Venice CA • (310)823-9367 • (RF 1970 MS)

**RUSCH WILBERT H** (314)894-0877
5918 Pennbrooke Dr Saint Louis MO 63129-7229 • MO • Tchr • LHS South Saint Louis MO • (314)631-1400 • (S 1961 MNS)

**RUSCHMEYER SARA LOUISE** (262)639-3923
4210 N Main St #210 Racine WI 53402 • sruschmeyer@hotmail.com • SW • Tchr • Trinity Racine WI • (414)632-2900 • (S 1997)

**RUSERT DAVID GENE** (636)282-2449
616 Hickory Manor Arnold MO 63010 • mdjj@postnet.com • MO • Tchr • Green Park Lemay MO • (314)544-4248 • (RF 1982)

**RUSNAK ERIC DOUGLAS**
3021 Moon Flower Ct Florissant MO 63031-1038 • MO • P/Tchr • Salem Florissant MO • (314)741-8220 • (RF 1975 MA)

**RUSSELL ALLYSON ANN** (916)773-3417
1463 Whitstable Dr Roseville CA 95747-6460 • arussell@jps.net • CNH • 09/1998 • (IV 1985)

**RUSSELL JAMES R** (219)546-4277
1636 W Grant St Bremen IN 46506-1918 • spls@skyenet.net • IN • P/Tchr • St Paul Bremen IN • (219)546-2790 • (RF 1972 MA)

**RUSSERT DAVID J**
155 Lenox Ave New Milford NJ 07646 • AT • SHS/C • Atlantic Bronxville NY • (914)337-5700 • (S 1986)

**RUST ANNA M** (812)378-2056
7861 W Seymour Rd Seymour IN 47274-9014 • IN • Tchr • St Peter Columbus IN • (812)372-5266 • (CQ 1982 MA)

**RUTHERFORD WILLIAM D** (713)681-6259
1803 Ebony Ln Houston TX 77018-5020 • bruther@compassnet.com • TX • EM • (S 1961 MED)

**RUTTER SANDRA L** (715)834-1132
1808 Sherwin Ave Eau Claire WI 54701 • rutter@ecol.net • NW • Tchr • Eau Claire Eau Claire WI • (715)835-9314 • (S 1978 MED)

**RUTZ HAROLD A** (512)452-5996
1606 Glenvalley Dr Austin TX 78723-1116 • halrutz@swbell.net • TX • EM • (RF 1952 MMU)

**RUTZ LEANN E** (312)690-1467
1282 Diane Ln Elk Grove Vlg IL 60007-3077 • NI • Tchr • Northern Illinois Hillside IL • (RF 1979)

**RUWALD JOAN E** (618)473-2650
PO Box 57 Hecker IL 62248-0057 • mrhw@aol.com • MO • 06/1993 • (RF 1965)

**RUYGROK KIM A** (818)841-2477
221 S Kenneth Rd Burbank CA 91501-1444 • PSW • 09/1993 09/1999 • (S 1984)

**RYAN RICHARD D** (512)898-5249
PO Box 501 Thorndale TX 76577-0501 • rdryan6@juno.com • TX • P/Tchr • St Paul Thorndale TX • (512)898-2711 • (AU 1982 MEDADM)

**RYHERD BRIAN D**
2709 Bennington Dr Springfield IL 62704-4222 • CI • Prin • Our Savior's Springfield IL • (217)546-4531 • (CQ 1991 MED)

**RYSKOWSKI RAYMOND J** (203)583-5649
176 Seneca Rd Bristol CT 06010-7183 • NE • Tchr • Immanuel Bristol CT • (860)583-5631 • (RF 1974 MA)

**RYSKOWSKI ROSEMARY JANE** (203)583-5649
C/O Immanuel Lutheran Church 154 Meadow St Bristol CT 06010-5730 • NE • Tchr • Immanuel Bristol CT • (860)583-5631 • (RF 1982)

## S

**SAALFELD LARRY D** (281)351-2707
14159 Limerick Ln Tomball TX 77375-4022 • saalfeld@clearsail.net • TX • Tchr • Salem Tomball TX • (281)351-8122 • (S 1974 MED)

**SABAL BARBARA L** (216)331-7315
19786 Battersea Blvd Rocky River OH 44116-1654 • jsabal@ameritech.net • OH • Tchr • St Thomas Rocky River OH • (440)331-4426 • (RF 1968)

**SABANOSH RACHEL ANN** (740)439-0479
61246 Greenbriar Dr Cambridge OH 43725 • S • 06/1998 06/2000 • (MQ 1996)

**SABOTIN JANICE R** (812)378-9887
5596 E Homestead Dr Columbus IN 47201-5097 • jsabotin@iquest.net • IN • Tchr • St Peter Columbus IN • (812)372-5266 • (RF 1983 MA)

**SADENWASSER JAMIE L** (919)932-3806
506 N Greensboro St Apt 31 Carrboro NC 27510-1775 • saden@bellsouth.net • OH • 01/1999 • (RF 1991)

**SADLER PATRICIA CAROL** (313)427-5557
32116 Maplewood St Garden City MI 48135-1718 • MI • Tchr • LHS East Harper Woods MI • (313)371-8750 • (CQ 1994)

**SADOWL MATTHEW PHILIP** (805)642-5424
2481 Monmouth Ventura CA 93001 • PSW • Tchr • Grace Ventura CA • (805)642-5424 • (S 1992)

**SAEGER DAVID R** (402)364-2462
201 N Poplar Ave PO Box 207 Davenport NE 68335 • djsaeger@juno.com • NEB • P/Tchr • St Peter Davenport NE • (402)364-2182 • (RF 1965 MA)

**SAEGER LYLE W** (715)536-3375
N2655 E Shore Dr Merrill WI 54452-8609 • EN • EM • (RF 1943 MA)

**SAEGER ROBERT A** (402)765-3431
2404 E 26th Rd Polk NE 68654-1702 • saeger@alltel.net • NEB • P/Tchr • Immanuel Polk NE • (402)765-7253 • (S 1973 MED)

**SAFARIK ANDREW C** (402)455-9198
4917 Grand Ave Omaha NE 68104-2380 • andyjd@juno.com • NEB • O Sp Min • Nebraska Seward NE • (S 1981 MRE)

**SAGE JANICE J**
600 J-K Ave Mc Allen TX 78502 • TX • EM • (S 1985)

**SAGEHORN DONALD J** (954)972-9498
3170 NW 68th Ct Fort Lauderdale FL 33309-1233 • FG • EM • (RF 1949 MS)

**SAGEHORN MARILYN R** (954)972-9498
3170 NW 68th Ct Fort Lauderdale FL 33309-1233 • FG • EM • (RF 1966 MED)

**SALATHE MARIE ELAINE** (504)288-5322
1719 Pressburg St New Orleans LA 70122-2755 • SO • Tchr • St Paul New Orleans LA • (504)947-1773 • (CQ 1995)

**SALEFSKI JEFFREY F** (217)875-2901
1391 W Pershing Rd Decatur IL 62526 • CI • Tchr • Pilgrim Decatur IL • (217)877-2444 • (RF 1985)

**SALES DEBORAH ANN** (817)337-0399
690 Montana Ct N Keller TX 76248 • TX • Tchr • Messiah Keller TX • (817)431-6139 • (CQ 1999)

**SALESKA THOMAS J** (262)335-4252
1777 Valley Rd West Bend WI 53090-8929 • tom.saleska@cuw.edu • SW • SHS/C • South Wisconsin Milwaukee WI • (414)464-8100 • (RF 1979 MS)

**SALESKA VANESSA MARIE** (414)335-4252
1777 Valley Rd West Bend WI 53090-8929 • SW • Tchr • St John West Bend WI • (414)334-3077 • (RF 1977 MA)

**SAMSELL ALVA L** (810)364-8043
1454 Carolina St Marysville MI 48040-1616 • samsell@aol.com • MI • Mem C • Immanuel Saint Clair MI • (810)329-7174 • (S 1969 MS)

**SAMSELL CHRISTOPHER NEAL**
7810 Rosmar Holly MI 48442-9130 • EN • Tchr • Child Of Christ Hartland MI • (248)887-3836 • (MQ 1995)

**SANDAU WILLIAM H** (510)278-8166
1849 Keller Ave San Lorenzo CA 94580-2124 • CNH • Tchr • Calvary San Lorenzo CA • (510)278-2598 • (RF 1962)

**SANDCORK ROBERT R II** (512)926-6202
6904 Notre Dame Austin TX 78723 • rockysandcork@hotmail.com • TX • Tchr • Hope Austin TX • (512)926-0003 • (SP 1997)

**SANDER REED S** (708)307-8020
1290 Coventry Ct Roselle IL 60172-1625 • NI • Prin • Trinity Roselle IL • (630)894-3263 • (S 1970 MSED)

**SANDER SHAROLYN** (708)307-8020
1290 Coventry Ct Roselle IL 60172-1625 • NI • Tchr • Trinity Roselle IL • (630)894-3263 • (S 1971 MS)

**SANDERS CHERYL E** (708)456-5479
2334 N 77th Ave Elmwood Park IL 60707-3041 • EN • English Farmington MI • (RF 1973 MA)

**SANDERS KENNETH W** (717)600-8187
14 Willomette Ct York PA 17402-4513 • SE • Tchr • St John York PA • (717)755-4779 • (S 1971)

**SANDERS ROBERT W** (210)692-7166
5380 Medical Dr Apt 804 San Antonio TX 78240-1961 • TX • P/Tchr • Redeemer San Antonio TX • (210)735-9903 • (AU 1991 MA)

**SANDERSFELD KIP R**
416 3rd Ave Marengo IL 60152-2426 • NI • Tchr • Immanuel Belvidere IL • (815)547-5346 • (MQ 1995)

**SANDERSFELD LAVONNE** (319)668-9439
1042 Chatham Dr Williamsburg IA 52361-9419 • IE • Tchr • Lutheran Interparish Williamsburg IA • (319)668-1711 • (S 1963)

**SANDFORT MARY E** (941)939-0526
3900 Central Ave Apt 204 Fort Myers FL 33901-7621 • FG • Tchr • St Michael Fort Myers FL • (941)939-1218 • (S 1990 MAD)

**SANDFORT MELVIN THOMAS** (812)372-8040
2034 Chandler Ln Columbus IN 47203-4015 • IN • Prin • St Peter Columbus IN • (812)372-5266 • (RF 1965 MEAD MS)

**SANDFORT NEIL I DR** (402)643-2366
623 N 6th St Seward NE 68434-1405 • neils@ndlems.org • NEB • Nebraska Seward NE* • (RF 1961 MED EDS LLD)

**SANDFORT STEPHEN D** (414)467-0874
1417 Trade Winds Ct Nashville TN 37214 • MDS • Mem C • Emmanuel Hermitage TN • (615)883-7533 • (RF 1989)

**SANDMANN DANNY C** (517)642-2853
17411 Geddes Rd Hemlock MI 48626-9616 • MI • Tchr • Valley Saginaw MI • (517)790-1676 • (S 1970)

**SANDOR DONALD R** (517)892-0423
527 N Hampton St Bay City MI 48708-6705 • dksandor@juno.com • MI • Tchr • Immanuel Bay City MI • (517)893-8521 • (RF 1962 MAT)

**SANFORD JULIANNE L** (515)576-1248
2007 11th Ave S Fort Dodge IA 50501-5904 • IW • Tchr • St Paul Fort Dodge IA • (515)955-7208 • (S 1985)

**SANGER DAVID JOHN** (760)322-5911
2082 S Lagarto Way Palm Springs CA 92264-9022 • oscdavid@aol.com • PSW • Mem C • Our Savior Palm Springs CA • (760)327-5611 • (IV 1985 MDIV)

**SANGER STACIE** (760)738-0718
1235 Ridgegrove Ln Escondido CA 92029-3227 • ksangerl@home.com • PSW • Tchr • Grace Escondido CA • (760)747-3029 • (CQ 1995 MA)

**SANKEY KENNETH T** (618)346-9132
14 Kimberly Ct Collinsville IL 62234-5527 • klsankey@hotmail.com • SI • Tchr • Zion Bethalto IL • (618)377-8314 • (S 1980 MED)

**SANKEY LORINDA L**
14 Kimberly Ct Collinsville IL 62234-5527 • SI • Tchr • Zion Bethalto IL • (618)377-8314 • (S 1980 MS)

**SANTEL DORENE J** (618)667-0716
542 Berkshire Dr Troy IL 62294 • SI • Tchr • Holy Cross Collinsville IL • (618)344-3145 • (S 1967 MS)

**SANTEL LYNETTE ALISE** (618)667-0716
542 Berkshire Dr Troy IL 62294 • slimzsister@yahoo.com • SI • Tchr • Good Shepherd Collinsville IL • (618)344-3151 • (S 1996)

**SARKKINEN AMY A** (616)651-6171
1101 E Congress St Sturgis MI 49091-1929 • MI • Tchr • Trinity Sturgis MI • (616)651-4245 • (AA 1995)

**SARR LISA L**
1587 Eldorado Dr Superior CO 80027-8201 • RM • Tchr • Mount Zion Boulder CO • (303)443-4151 • (IV 1985)

**SASSE DONALD G** (920)756-2292
203 Schley St Brillion WI 54110-1020 • SW • EM • (S 1961 MSED MSED)

**SASSE LINDA K** (810)826-3694
11788 Falcon Dr Sterling Heights MI 48313-5138 • MI • Tchr • Peace Shelby Twp MI • (810)739-2431 • (RF 1977)

**SATEK PAMELA A** (630)443-9708
6N655 Promontory Ct Saint Charles IL 60175-5448 • NI • Prin • Immanuel Crystal Lake IL • (815)459-1444 • (CQ 1997 MA)

**SATO STACY K** (702)341-0044
2413 Sterling Heights Dr Las Vegas NV 89134 • PSW • Tchr • Ascension Torrance CA • (310)793-0071 • (PO 1981 MA)

**SATTERLEE CASSIE ELAINE** (618)635-3269
18336 Windy Hill Rd Staunton IL 62088 • SI • Tchr • Zion Staunton IL • (618)635-3060 • (CQ 1998)

**SATTLER EUGENE A** (920)987-5979
W2228 Badger Ave Pine River WI 54965-9752 • sattlere1@juno.com • SW • EM • (RF 1952 MA)

**SATTLER KARL E** (414)642-5805
2006 Division St East Troy WI 53120 • ksattler@netwurx.net • SW • P/Tchr • Good Shepherd East Troy WI • (414)642-3310 • (S 1978)

**SAUER LAURA L** (818)982-7758
6906 Bluebell Ave North Hollywood CA 91605-5129 • sauerpowr3@aol.com • PSW • Tchr • Pacific Southwest Irvine CA • (949)854-3232 • (RF 1976 MA MS)

**SAUER THOMAS D** (810)658-2731
209 N Lapeer St Davison MI 48423-1421 • MI • Mem C • Trinity Davison MI • (810)658-3000 • (RF 1978)

**SAUNDERS DAVID R** (708)771-5804
7637 Adams St #2 Forest Park IL 60130-1713 • VBDRS6@aol.com • NI • Tchr • St John Forest Park IL • (708)366-2764 • (CQ 1980 MA)

**SAUNDERS JILL MARIE** (
14161 E Jewell Ave - #204 Denver CO 60010 • RM • Tchr • St John Saint Johns MI • (517)224-6796 • (S 2000)

**SAUSAMAN PAMELA ANN** (217)787-4773
3790 Tozer Rd Springfield IL 62707 • CI • Tchr • Trinity Springfield IL • (217)787-2323 • (RF 1987)

**SAVARD SHARON J** (612)488-9899
1053 California Ave W Saint Paul MN 55117-3372 • MNS • Tchr • Central Saint Paul MN • (651)645-8649 • (SP 1982)

**SAWHILL JULIA N** (713)475-1547
2224 Walnut Ln Pasadena TX 77502-4045 • dsawhill@ghgcorp.com • TX • Tchr • Zion Pasadena TX • (713)473-1789 • (S 1977)

**SAWYER CYNTHIA R** (810)953-9260
1105 Townline Ct Grand Blanc MI 48439-1627 • MI • Tchr • St Mark Flint MI • (810)736-6910 • (S 1981 MED)

**SAYLES PRISCILLA MARY** (605)341-0505
11375 Sheridan Lake Rd Rapid City SD 57702-6508 • zion@rapidnet.com • SD • P/Tchr • Zion Rapid City SD • (605)342-5749 • (RF 1971 MED)

**SCHAAF ROBERT R** (813)936-4521
6756 Fairview St Fort Myers FL 33912-1131 • FG • Tchr • St Michael Fort Myers FL • (941)939-1218 • (BR 1979)

**SCHAAR DENNIS RAYMOND** (909)592-7113
1802 Grasscreek Dr San Dimas CA 91773-1320 • PSW • Prin • First Temple City CA • (626)287-0968 • (RF 1967 MA)

**SCHAAR JULIE LYNN** (714)288-9702
1201 E Fairhaven #24K Santa Ana CA 92705 • PSW • Tchr • St John Orange CA • (714)288-4400 • (IV 1992 MA)

**SCHAAR RONALD G** (303)778-6406
166 S Logan St Apt 107 Denver CO 80209-1828 • RM • 06/1999 • (RF 1970)

**SCHACHTSIEK MARCIA** (341)735-4159
6938 County Road 249 Palmyra MO 63461-3421 • MO • Tchr • Zion Palmyra MO • (573)769-3739 • (S 1966)

**SCHADT DAREN E** (360)337-7786
8645 Sungate Pl NE Bremerton WA 98311-9300 • NOW • Tchr • Peace Bremerton WA • (360)373-2116 • (S 1976 MED)

**SCHAEDIG KELLI R** (812)423-3591
3140 Cascade Dr Evansville IN 47725 • kellihar22@aol.com • IN • Tchr • Trinity Evansville IN • (812)867-5279 • (AA 1998)

**SCHAEFER CAROL M** (717)741-5454
2790 Chestnut Run Rd York PA 17402-8858 • sjls-prin@blazenet.net • SE • Prin • St John York PA • (717)755-4779 • (S 1964 MED)

**SCHAEFER DANIEL V** (512)253-0047
Rt 1 Box 263 Giddings TX 78942 • schfr5@bluebon.net • TX • P/Tchr • Immanuel Giddings TX • (409)542-3319 • (S 1982 MA)

**SCHAEFER GARY JAMES** (314)293-0175
2664 Deloak Apt A Saint Louis MO 63129-4254 • gjspez@yahoo.com • MO • Tchr • Washington Saint Louis County MO • (314)892-4408 • (S 1986)

**SCHAEFER JEFFREY M** (815)547-6682
639 W 9th St Belvidere IL 61008-5541 • NI • Tchr • Immanuel Belvidere IL • (815)547-5346 • (S 1983 MED)

**SCHAEFER KATHRYN A** (773)794-9847
4037 N Mango Chicago IL 60634 • NI • Tchr • St John Chicago IL • (773)736-1196 • (MQ 1993 MA)

**SCHAEFER LES E**
C/O Lutheran HS 3960 Fruit St La Verne CA 91750-2951 • PSW • Tchr • Lutheran High School La Verne CA • (909)593-4494 • (MQ 1989)

**SCHAEFER MARGARET F** (913)354-8934
346 SW Jewell Ave Topeka KS 66606-1334 • KS • Tchr • Topeka Topeka KS • (785)357-0382 • (S 1968)

**SCHAEFER MICHELLE**
810 Loma Vista St El Segundo CA 90245-2109 • PSW • Tchr • Pilgrim Santa Monica CA • (310)829-2239 • (PO 1998)

**SCHAEFER ROBYN R** (319)662-4141
C/O Luth Interparish School PO Box 750 Williamsburg IA 52361 • IE • Tchr • Lutheran Interparish Williamsburg IA • (319)668-1711 • (S 1979)

**SCHAEFER RONALD ANDREW** (847)673-3219
5207 Galitz St Skokie IL 60077-2737 • NI • Tchr • St Paul Skokie IL • (847)673-5030 • (MQ 1984)

**SCHAEFER SARAH MARIE** (281)538-1001
3045 Marina Bay Dr #11110 League City TX 77573 • princess³sms@juno.com • TX • Tchr • Texas Austin TX • (AU 1999)

**SCHAEFER SUSAN G** (512)253-0047
Rt 1 Box 263 Giddings TX 78942 • schfr5@bluebon.net • TX • 02/2000 • (S 1982)

**SCHAEFER WENDI LYNN** (402)462-2289
2509 West 6th Hastings NE 68901-3101 • NEB • Tchr • Zion Hastings NE • (402)462-5012 • (S 1991)

**SCHAEFFER ORVILLE G*** (262)521-1891
W236N998 Archery Dr Waukesha WI 53188-1716 • helenorv@aol.com • SW • EM • (RF 1954 MA)

**SCHAEKEL BERT D**
C/O Salem Lutheran School 22607 Lutheran Church Rd Tomball TX 77375-3716 • TX • Zion Hastings NE • (RF 1975)

**SCHAEKEL NORBERT** (219)547-4463
9122 N 450 W Decatur IN 46733-7847 • IN • EM • (RF 1956 MA)

**SCHAFER BEVERLY A** (616)657-3069
407 E Michigan Ave # 2 Paw Paw MI 49079-1417 • MI • Tchr • Trinity Paw Paw MI • (616)657-4840 • (CQ 1987)

**SCHAFER JOYCE LORRAINE** (517)423-4222
10590 Macon Hwy Tecumseh MI 49286-9624 • schafer@lni.net • MI • Tchr • St Paul Ann Arbor MI • (734)665-0604 • (S 1972)

**SCHAFER ROBERT D** (810)781-9399
53282 Luann Dr Shelby Twp MI 48316-2604 • rschafere@stjohnrochester.org • MI • Mem C • St John Rochester MI • (248)652-8830 • (S 1985 MAT)

**SCHAFF JOHN M** (217)324-0354
10 Danday Ln Litchfield IL 62056-4241 • SI • Tchr • Zion Litchfield IL • (217)324-3166 • (IV 1991)

**SCHAFFER JENNIFER MARIE**
4419 Marquette Dr Fort Wayne IN 46806 • joelandjennifer@sprintmail • IN • Tchr • Emmaus Fort Wayne IN • (219)456-4573 • (RF 1994 MA)

**SCHAFFER JOEL PAUL**
4419 Marquette Dr Fort Wayne IN 46806 • joelandjennifer@sprintmail.com • IN • Tchr • Emmaus Fort Wayne IN • (219)456-4573 • (RF 1997)

**SCHAFSTALL MICHAEL D*** (317)578-4415
9277 Sea Pine Ln Indianapolis IN 46250 • IN • 07/1998 07/2000 • (RF 1989)

**SCHALK CARL F DR** (708)344-7167
1208 Park Dr Melrose Park IL 60160-2233 • tchschalk@cuis.edu • NI • EM • (RF 1952 MMU MAR LLD LHD)

**SCHALK LINDA SUE** (517)766-8073
8138 S Rogers Rd Hawks MI 49743-9714 • schalks@voyager.net • MI • Tchr • St John Rogers City MI • (517)734-3580 • (S 1973)

**SCHALL WALTER O**
8949 N 97th St Apt B 20 Milwaukee WI 53224-1666 • SW • EM • (RF 1926)

**SCHALLER BRUCE H** (713)880-3131
16418 Jersey Dr Houston TX 77040-2022 • TX • Prin • LHS North Houston TX • (713)880-3131 • (RF 1968 MA)

**SCHALLER LISA**
261 Harbor Dr Gun Barrel City TX 75147-3546 • MO • Tchr • Immanuel Saint Louis MO • (314)993-2394 • (AU 1996)

**SCHALLER RITA M** (713)937-9144
16418 Jersey Dr Houston TX 77040-2022 • TX • Tchr • St Mark Houston TX • (713)468-2623 • (RF 1968)

**SCHALLHORN KRISTIN JOYE**
205/20 Soi Chaiyakiat 1 Ngam Wang Wan Rd Bangkok 10210 THAILAND • kikbug@hotmail.com • FG • O Miss • Florida-Georgia Orlando FL • (AA 1996)

**SCHALLHORN MARK B**
4301 Underhill Dr Flint MI 48506 • MI • P/Tchr • St Mark Flint MI • (810)736-6680 • (RF 1978 MED)

**SCHALLHORN RANDY BRUCE** (608)524-4066
32 Barbara Ann Dr Reedsburg WI 53959 • ranschall@juno.com • SW • P/Tchr • St Peter Reedsburg WI • (608)524-4512 • (SP 1971 MA)

**SCHALLHORN VALJEAN ANN** (608)524-4066
32 Barbara Ann Dr Reedsburg WI 53959 • ranschall@juno.com • SW • Tchr • St Peter Reedsburg WI • (608)524-4512 • (S 1971)

**SCHALOW KATHLEEN SUE** (319)328-1591
2235 N Gaines St Davenport IA 52804-1906 • IE • St Peter Reedsburg WI • (RF 1985)

**SCHAMBER BONNIE L** (517)883-2518
5 Auch St Sebewaing MI 48759-1603 • kids@avci.net • MI • Tchr • St Paul Unionville MI • (517)674-8681 • (RF 1971 MED)

**SCHAMBER GORDON E** (225)272-5767
1505 Turret Dr Baton Rouge LA 70816-1397 • gschamber@bitworx.com • SO • P/Tchr • Baton Rouge Baton Rouge LA • (504)272-1288 • (S 1973 MED)

**SCHAMBER JEREMY K**
2509 1/2 Pennsylvania Ave Joplin MO 64804-2764 • MO • Tchr • Martin Luther Joplin MO • (417)624-1403 • (S 1998)

**SCHAMBER JOHN G** (219)485-9104
6804 Briarcliff Dr Fort Wayne IN 46835-4072 • IN • EM • (S 1960 MED)

**SCHAMBER KATHLEEN A** (225)272-5767
1505 Turret Dr Baton Rouge LA 70816-1397 • kschamber@bitworx.com • SO • Tchr • Baton Rouge Baton Rouge LA • (504)272-1288 • (S 1973 MED)

**SCHAMBER MARTHA ANN** (605)343-7408
3300 Bennett Rd Rapid City SD 57701-8591 • SD • 06/1999 • (S 1966)

**SCHAMBER MARY JO** (507)433-7637
200 21st St NW Austin MN 55912-4656 • MNS • Tchr • Holy Cross Austin MN • (507)433-7844 • (S 1965)

**SCHAMP BARBARA A** (303)431-8221
6176 W 75th Pl Arvada CO 80003-2806 • RM • Tchr • Bethlehem Lakewood CO • (303)233-0401 • (RF 1982 MED)

**SCHANBACHER JANET K** (319)386-9404
1517 W 46th Pl Davenport IA 52806-3614 • jkschan@aol.com • IE • Tchr • Trinity Davenport IA • (319)322-5224 • (S 1973 MAD)

**SCHATTE PAUL D** (405)762-9278
217 N Sunset St Ponca City OK 74601-3828 • OK • P/Tchr • First Ponca City OK • (580)762-4243 • (S 1979 MAD)

**SCHATTE ROCHELLE K** (405)762-9278
217 N Sunset St Ponca City OK 74601-3828 • OK • Tchr • First Ponca City OK • (580)762-4243 • (S 1979)

**SCHATTE WILLIAM A**
508 E Howard Ln Lot #233 Austin TX 78753 • TX • Tchr • Redeemer Austin TX • (512)451-6478 • (AU 1997)

**SCHATTSCHNEIDER ALLAN** (847)518-0927
516 N Home Ave Park Ridge IL 60068-3036 • NI • Prin • St Andrew Park Ridge IL • (847)823-9308 • (RF 1967 MA)

**SCHAU LINDA** (312)859-2720
801 Whitlock Ave Aurora IL 60506-5631 • NI • Tchr • Emmanuel Aurora IL • (630)851-2200 • (RF 1973)

**SCHAUBS CRAIG H** (262)376-9128
W59N770 Highwood Dr Cedarburg WI 53012-1459 • SW • Tchr • First Immanuel Cedarburg WI • (262)377-6610 • (MW 1983)

**SCHAUBS KRISTINE J** (414)668-8724
W59N770 Highwood Dr Cedarburg WI 53012-1459 • SW • Tchr • First Immanuel Cedarburg WI • (262)377-6610 • (MW 1983)

**SCHAUER BARBARA JEAN** (402)362-3159
1604 E 13th St York NE 68467-2116 • as43218@navix.net • NEB • Tchr • Emmanuel York NE • (402)362-6575 • (S 1967)

**SCHAULAND AMBER** (517)652-4053
211 Hubinger Frankenmuth MI 48734 • MI • Tchr • St Lorenz Frankenmuth MI • (517)652-6141 • (MQ 1999)

**SCHAULAND ERNEST P** (651)388-2343
4606 Valley View Dr Red Wing MN 55066-9429 • MNS • EM • (S 1944)

**SCHAUS MARVIN W**
12612 Woodruff Ave Bellflower CA 90706-2633 • PSW • O Sp Min • Pacific Southwest Irvine CA • (949)854-3232 • (S 1956)

**SCHAUS SARA MARIE** (630)773-3899
510 N Arlington Heights Rd Itasca IL 60143 • NI • Tchr • St Peter Arlington Heights IL • (847)253-6638 • (RF 1999)

**SCHECK BENJAMIN IAN**
4211 Angela St Simi Valley CA 93063 • abscheck@msn.com • PSW • Tchr • Trinity Simi Valley CA • (805)526-2429 • (S 1994)

**SCHEEL LINDA K** (913)233-1012
624 SW Roosevelt St Topeka KS 66606-1705 • KS • Tchr • Topeka Topeka KS • (785)357-0382 • (S 1976)

**SCHEELE DEAN M** (319)668-1922
2983 225th St Williamsburg IA 52361-8609 • dsscheele@hotmail.com • IE • Tchr • Lutheran Interparish Williamsburg IA • (319)668-1711 • (S 1985)

**SCHEETZ ELIZABETH ANN**
305 S Phillippi #212 Boise ID 83705-1937 • NOW • Tchr • Good Shepherd Boise ID • (208)343-4690 • (S 1997)

**SCHEFFT WALTER R** (618)345-4712
904 Lillian St Collinsville IL 62234-2046 • pscheff t@aol.com • SI • 08/2000 • (RF 1965 MSED)

**SCHEIBER VERNIE W** (219)347-1634
117 S Morton St Kendallville IN 46755-1634 • stjohn@noble.cioe.com • IN • P/Tchr • St John Kendallville IN • (219)347-2444 • (S 1974 MED)

**SCHEID SHERRY A** (414)342-7750
2903 W State St Milwaukee WI 53208-3422 • SW • Tchr • Mount Olive Milwaukee WI • (414)771-3580 • (S 1976)

**SCHEIMANN ROBERT E** (219)484-2821
3415 Kirkwood Dr Fort Wayne IN 46805-1521 • rscheimann@aol.com • IN • EM • (RF 1954 MA)

**SCHEIWE JEAN R** (517)684-4989
994 Amelith Rd Bay City MI 48706-9335 • warrens9@concentric.com • MI • Tchr • St John Bay City MI • (517)686-0176 • (RF 1965 MA)

**SCHEIWE ROBERT NEAL** (630)289-7279
549 Harbor Ter Bartlett IL 60103-4845 • scheiwer@trinityroselle.com • NI • Tchr • Trinity Roselle IL • (630)894-3263 • (RF 1978)

**SCHEIWE SHERRY LYNN** (414)442-5773
3076 N 72nd Apt 1 Milwaukee WI 53210 • sscheiwe@concentric.net • SW • Tchr • Mount Calvary Milwaukee WI • (414)873-3466 • (RF 1991)

**SCHEIWE WARREN A** (517)684-4989
994 Amelith Rd Bay City MI 48706-9335 • warrens9@concentric.net • MI • Tchr • St John Bay City MI • (517)686-0176 • (RF 1964 MMU)

**SCHEIWE WENDY ANN** (248)926-1323
31000 Westgate Blvd Apt 61 Novi MI 48377 • WScheiwe@concentric.net • MI • Tchr • St Matthew Walled Lake MI • (248)624-7677 • (RF 1990)

**SCHELEN DONNA JOAN** (817)788-8663
5617 Jamaica Cir N Richlnd Hls TX 76180-6575 • TX • 10/1999 • (RF 1986)

**SCHELK SHELBY JEAN** (715)758-6879
PO Box 171 Bonduel WI 54107 • NW • Tchr • St Paul Bonduel WI • (715)745-2299 • (MQ 1994)

**SCHELK SUE-LYNN** (414)376-9149
N89W6846 Evergreen Ct # 202 Cedarburg WI 53012-1182 • SW • Tchr • St Paul Grafton WI • (414)377-4659 • (MQ 1997)

**SCHELP KEITH A** (618)888-2404
7186 Renken Rd Dorsey IL 62021-1802 • kschelp@madisontelco.com • SI • Tchr • St Peter Dorsey IL • (618)888-2252 • (S 1974)

**SCHEMPF RICHARD H** (248)623-9593
5490 Frankwill Ave Clarkston MI 48346-3726 • schempfrichard@yahoo.com • MI • EM • (S 1955 MED)

**SCHEMPP ROBERTA ANN** (913)441-4548
8417 Lewis Dr Lenexa KS 66227 • rhenning@juno.com • KS • Tchr • Hope Shawnee KS • (913)631-6940 • (RF 1994 MA)

**SCHENCK SANDRA K** (308)384-8608
1030 Martin Ave Grand Island NE 68801-9026 • NEB • Tchr • Trinity Grand Island NE • (308)382-5274 • (S 1971)

**SCHENDEL JOHN E** (219)749-7560
9511 Pawnee Way New Haven IN 46774-2902 • lisjohn@aol.com • IN • Prin • Central New Haven IN • (219)493-2502 • (RF 1966 MED)

**SCHENDEL SARAH K**
1112 Jefferson St #J Jefferson City MO 65101-5207 • MO • Central New Haven IN • (RF 1995)

**SCHEPMANN DARRELL W** (713)726-1354
11611 Dunlap St Houston TX 77035-2321 • dorothyms@sprintmail.com • TX • Prin • Pilgrim Houston TX • (713)666-3706 • (RF 1962 MMTH)

**SCHEPMANN GILBERT F SR.** 754-2293
7874 Golden Meadow Dr Mason OH 45040 • gschep4258@aol.com • OH • Tchr • St Paul Cincinnati OH • (513)271-4147 • (S 1969 MED)

**SCHEPMANN HEATHER NOEL** (219)934-0170
2220 Teakwood Cir Apt G Highland IN 46322 • schepgrrl@aol.com • NI • Tchr • St John Lansing IL • (708)895-9280 • (AA 1999)

**SCHEPMANN JUDITH** 754-2293
7874 Golden Meadow Dr Mason OH 45040 • jds42179@aol.com • OH • Tchr • St Paul Cincinnati OH • (513)271-4147 • (S 1969)

**SCHERER GLENN D** (410)343-2124
16916 Flickerwood Rd Parkton MD 21120-9766 • SE • Southeastern Alexandria VA • (RF 1979 MA)

**SCHERER RONALD D** (313)777-6913
28925 Beste St St Clair Shrs MI 48081-1006 • MI • Tchr • St Peter Eastpointe MI • (810)771-2809 • (RF 1956 MA)

**SCHERMBECK ROBIN L** (402)335-2686
RR 1 Box 159 Elk Creek NE 68348-9501 • NEB • 12/1995 12/1999 • (S 1991 MS)

**SCHERMBECK TIMOTHY ROBERT** (815)224-0249
5121 E State St Apt 306 B Rockford IL 61108 • schermbeck@netzero.net • NI • SHS/C • Northern Illinois Hillside IL • (S 1998)

**SCHERPING ELIZABETH HILDA**
C/O Saint Paul Lutheran Church 1635 Chester St Tracy CA 95376-2927 • lisascherping@compuserve.com • CNH • Mem C • St Paul Tracy CA • (209)835-7438 • (S 1979)

**SCHETTENHELM KARLA J** (734)462-8438
14326 Knolson St Livonia MI 48154-4759 • jknschett@aol.com • MI • Tchr • Christ Our Savior Livonia MI • (313)513-8413 • (AA 1989 MA)

**SCHEUERMANN JOHN H JR.** (775)857-2279
2190 Sequoia Ln Reno NV 89502 • jshoyer@aol.com • CNH • Mem C • St Luke Reno NV • (775)825-0588 • (S 1983)

**SCHEURMAN LINDA LOU** (847)352-2180
819 S Salem Dr Schaumburg IL 60193-3806 • sonshine52@aol.com • NI • Mem C • St Peter Schaumburg IL • (847)885-3350 • (SP 1970)

**SCHEWE SHARYN J** (815)624-7262
877 Liddle Rd Rockton IL 61072-9441 • NI • Tchr • Concordia Machesney Park IL • (815)633-6450 • (RF 1972)

**SCHIEBEL MARTHA CLARA**
1671 Madison St NW Washington DC 20011-6812 • SE • Tchr • Concordia Hyattsville MD • (301)927-0266 • (BR 1996)

**SCHIEFER CARL L** (561)393-7405
2036 S Conference Dr Boca Raton FL 33486-3127 • FG • Tchr • St Paul Boca Raton FL • (561)395-8548 • (RF 1963 MA)

**SCHIEFER MARK T** (517)868-3259
3619 Tressla Rd Richville MI 48758 • MI • Tchr • St Michael Richville MI • (517)868-4809 • (RF 1974)

**SCHIELD BETTY E** (618)282-6836
1017 Randolph St Red Bud IL 62278-2619 • SI • Tchr • St John Red Bud IL • (618)282-3873 • (CQ 1983)

**SCHIEMANN JENNIFER LYNN** (440)352-2275
504 Maple Brook Dr Painesville OH 44077 • OH • Tchr • Our Shepherd Painesville OH • (440)357-7776 • (RF 1992)

**SCHIEMANN KATHLEEN RUTH** (517)642-8923
260 Doyle Rd Hemlock MI 48626-9439 • richkaths@juno.com • MI • Tchr • St Peter Hemlock MI • (517)642-5659 • (RF 1972)

**SCHILDWACHTER PAUL JOHN** (410)817-4297
12021 Belair Rd Kingsville MD 21087 • pjsjjs@juno.com • SE • Tchr • Baltimore LHS Baltimore MD • (410)825-2323 • (BR 1976 MA)

**SCHILF KRISTEN AMY** (219)934-0170
2220 Teakwood Cir Apt G Highland IN 46322 • kristenschilf@hotmail.com • NI • Tchr • St John Lansing IL • (708)895-9280 • (RF 1998)

**SCHILF PAUL RAYMOND DR** (651)768-8757
7838 77th St S Cottage Grove MN 55016-2086 • MNS • Tchr • Minnesota South Burnsville MN • (RF 1983 MMU)

**SCHILKE NADINE LOUISE** (414)425-4513
6109 S 116th St Hales Corners WI 53130-2462 • EN • Tchr • Hales Corners Hales Corners WI • (414)529-6700 • (RF 1983)

**SCHILLER CHARLES A** (504)845-0206
510 Markie Dr Mandeville LA 70471-6736 • SO • Tchr • St Paul New Orleans LA • (504)947-1773 • (S 1973)

**SCHILLER SUSANN M** (504)845-0206
510 Markie Dr Mandeville LA 70471-6736 • SO • P/Tchr • St Paul New Orleans LA • (504)947-1773 • (S 1973 MED)

**SCHILLING RAYMOND L** (810)293-7277
15462 Lincolnshire Ln Fraser MI 48026-2353 • raylucy3@juno.com • MI • EM • (RF 1955 MLS MA)

**SCHILLING SCOTT D** (219)864-1602
91 Chateau Dr Dyer IN 46311-2152 • NI • Tchr • Gloria Dei Chicago IL • (773)581-5259 • (RF 1980)

**SCHILLING TIMOTHY R** (810)771-6663
29880 Ruthdale St Roseville MI 48066-2120 • MI • Tchr • St Peter Eastpointe MI • (810)771-2809 • (RF 1984)

**SCHIMKE PAMELA LOUISE** (602)569-0065
19212 N 40th St Phoenix AZ 85050-2607 • PSW • 08/1993 08/2000 • (S 1977)

**SCHIMM THOMAS W*** (517)684-7477
5253 3 Mile Rd Bay City MI 48706-9029 • MI • Tchr • Holy Cross Saginaw MI • (517)793-9795 • (S 1973 MA)

**SCHINDELDECKER ARLENE MAE**
7721 Ivystone Ave S Cottage Grove MN 55016-2140 • MNS • Tchr • King Of Kings Roseville MN • (651)484-9206 • (SP 1971)

**SCHINDLER BELVA J**
119 N Marquette Ave Sioux Falls SD 57110-1290 • SD • 09/1998 • (S 1962)

**SCHINNERER MARILYN** (925)256-4648
417 Westcliffe Pl Walnut Creek CA 94596-3267 • marischin@aol.com • CNH • EM • (S 1955 MMU)

**SCHINNERER MARY** (408)441-6216
1709 Parkview Green Cir San Jose CA 95131-3222 • mschinnerer@msn.com • CNH • 07/1998 07/2000 • (S 1968 MED)

**SCHIPPER STUART P**
22007 Virginia Ave Eastpointe MI 48021-2342 • MI • Prin • St Thomas Eastpointe MI • (810)772-3372 • (SP 1977 MA MSF)

**SCHIPPOREIT JEANETTE E** (402)379-2286
825 S 9th Norfolk NE 68701-5830 • NEB • Tchr • Christ Norfolk NE • (402)371-5536 • (S 1973)

**SCHIPULL DOUGLAS W DR** (708)338-2162
655 Winston Dr Melrose Park IL 60160-2350 • dschipull@aol.com • NI • Prin • St Paul Chicago IL • (708)867-5044 • (S 1969 MED PHD EDS)

**SCHIRRMACHER MARY LOUISE** (949)654-0622
1042 Hayes Irvine CA 92720 • tandms@msn.com • PSW • Tchr • Zion Anaheim CA • (714)535-3600 • (IV 1994)

**SCHIWART MELVIN E** (281)351-4234
30619 Quinn Rd Tomball TX 77375-2902 • TX • Tchr • Trinity Klein TX • (281)376-5773 • (S 1967 MMU)

**SCHKADE JONATHAN WALTER** (507)523-2521
PO Box 194 Lewiston MN 55952-0194 • MNS • Tchr • Immanuel Lewiston MN • (507)523-3143 • (S 1999)

**SCHKADE KRISTI JO** (507)523-2521
65 N Fremont St PO Box 194 Lewiston MN 55952-0194 • jwaltscott@juno.com • MNS • Tchr • Immanuel Lewiston MN • (507)523-3143 • (S 1998)

**SCHKADE REBECCA RUTH** (970)330-7471
1707 N Cheyenne #4 Loveland CO 80538 • RM • Tchr • Gloria Christi Greeley CO • (970)353-2554 • (S 1995)

**SCHLACHT BRENDA LYNN** (541)312-3808
709 NE Savannah Ste #2 Bend OR 97701-4865 • lyndielou@earthlink.net • NOW • Tchr • Trinity Bend OR • (541)382-1832 • (S 1987)

**SCHLEGEL EDLYN R** (626)334-6251
850 S Vincent Ave Apt 81-G Azusa CA 91702 • PSW • 11/1995 11/1997 • (RF 1981)

**SCHLEGEL ORVIN L** (219)267-6530
3234 S Oak St Warsaw IN 46580-8199 • redeemer@compuserve.com • IN • Tchr • Redeemer Warsaw IN • (219)267-5656 • (RF 1961 MSED)

**SCHLEGL FRANK L** (716)693-7133
1289 Ruie Rd North Tonawanda NY 14120 • EA • EM • (S 1959 MSED)

**SCHLEHLEIN JOAN K** (414)895-7588
26614 Waubeesee Lake Dr Wind Lake WI 53185-2043 • EN • Tchr • Hales Corners Hales Corners WI • (414)529-6701 • (SP 1972)

**SCHLENSKER ERIN**
1801 Oak Ave Davis CA 95616-1005 • schleneb@hotmail.com • NI • Tchr • Northern Illinois Hillside IL • (RF 1997)

**SCHLESSELMAN DAVID A** (636)240-7612
3 Molloy Ct O Fallon MO 63366-3167 • dschlesselman@lhssc.org • MO • Prin • LHS St Charles Saint Peters MO • (636)928-5100 • (S 1970 MA MA)

**SCHLESSELMAN ROBERT H** (630)834-1419
599 Van Auken St Elmhurst IL 60126-1946 • NI • EM • (RF 1944 MA)

**SCHLESSELMAN ROBERTA W** (608)687-8730
S 3104 N Shore Dr Fountain City WI 54629 • rschless@tvsw.org • MNS • Tchr • St Martins Winona MN • (507)452-6056 • (RF 1975)

**SCHLEY MARGARET J** (810)468-5611
32955 North River Rd Harrison Twp MI 48045-1493 • cscheyatbignet.net • MI • Tchr • LHS North Macomb MI • (810)781-9151 • (CQ 1996 MA)

**SCHLICHTEMEIER KENT A** (949)552-7389
18 Greenleaf Irvine CA 92604-4554 • PSW • SHS/C • Pacific Southwest Irvine CA • (949)854-3232 • (S 1978 MA EDD)

**SCHLICHTING ALBERT C** (303)680-7420
17966 Aprils Way Parker CO 80134-3983 • RM • EM • (S 1950)

**SCHLICHTING KEVIN R** (281)259-9595
31956 S Wiggins St Magnolia TX 77355-3813 • schlichkev@selec.net • TX • Tchr • Salem Tomball TX • (281)351-8122 • (S 1979)

**SCHLICHTMANN DIAN M** (715)355-4205
5002 Crestwood Dr Apt 1 Schofield WI 54476-6206 • dians@dwave.net • NW • Mem C • Christ Wausau WI • (715)848-2040 • (S 1990)

**SCHLICKER DAVID J** (952)466-2232
14715 County Road 153 Cologne MN 55322-9143 • 0999zion@informns.k12.mn.us • MNS • P/Tchr • Zion Cologne MN • (612)466-3379 • (S 1968 MS)

**SCHLICKER ESTHER ANNA** (952)466-2232
14715 County Road 153 Cologne MN 55322-9143 • easchlick12@hotmail.com • MNS • Tchr • Zion Cologne MN • (612)466-3379 • (S 1969)

**SCHLIE ABIGAIL LOUISE** (713)644-3177
C/O Lutheran High School Assn 12555 Ryewater Dr Houston TX 77089-6625 • TX • Tchr • Lutheran South Acade Houston TX • (281)464-8299 • (AA 1995)

**SCHLIE ANGELA**
20240 E Quarry Rd Esmand IL 60129 • NI • Tchr • St Paul Rochelle IL • (815)562-6323 • (RF 1999)

**SCHLIE CHARLES S**
3997 Providence Dr Saint Charles MO 63304 • SI • 06/1998 06/2000 • (RF 1989 MA MA)

**SCHLIE DAVID J** (713)880-3131
C/O Lutheran HS North 1130 W 34th St Houston TX 77018 • TX • Tchr • LHS North Houston TX • (713)880-3131 • (S 1993)

**SCHLIE MARY BETH** (636)441-4221
3997 Providence Dr Saint Charles MO 63304 • SI • 07/1999 • (RF 1988)

**SCHLIE ORLYN A** (407)359-2766
2120 Sunbird Ct Oviedo FL 32765-5208 • FG • EM • (RF 1943 MSED)

**SCHLIE PENNY L** (816)453-0525
5553 N Woodland Ave Kansas City MO 64118-5652 • MO • Tchr • Holy Cross Kansas City MO • (816)453-7211 • (S 1974)

**SCHLIEBE CHARLES A** (805)238-1567
609 Palomino Cir Paso Robles CA 93446-2965 • CNH • Mem C • Trinity Paso Robles CA • (805)238-3702 • (S 1950 MA)

**SCHLIMPERT CHARLES E** (503)658-8282
PO Box 1689 Clackamas OR 97015-1689 • NOW • SHS/C • Northwest Portland OR • (RF 1968 MED PHD)

**SCHLIMPERT EDGAR T** (660)463-2860
310 Bismark St Concordia MO 64020 • MO • EM • (RF 1944 MED)

**SCHLOBOHM DANIEL W*** (507)334-4999
23595 Dahle Ave Faribault MN 55021-8175 • NEB • EM • (SP 1983)

**SCHLOTTERBECK KATHERINE L** (941)543-5060
17040 Carolyn Ln North Fort Myers FL 33917-3864 • kschlotterbeck@sml.org • FG • Tchr • St Michael Fort Myers FL • (941)939-1218 • (RF 1982)

**SCHLUCKBIER ROBERT ALAN** (517)823-9315
3611 S Vassar Rd Vassar MI 48768-9706 • MI • Tchr • Trinity Reese MI • (517)868-4501 • (S 1983 MAT)

**SCHLUCKEBIER LEE E DR** (402)643-6441
306 Bradford St Seward NE 68434-1836 • ls64534@alltell.net • NEB • SHS/C • Nebraska Seward NE • (S 1968 MED DED)

**SCHLUETER KENNETH E** (714)998-8864
234 E Woodvale Ave Orange CA 92865-2737 • PSW • EM • (S 1957 MAT)

**SCHLUETER WALTER H E** (708)627-2073
1137 S Church Ave Lombard IL 60148-4122 • NI • EM • (RF 1927)

**SCHMALTZ NORMAN J DR** (505)896-4871
699 Lakeview Cir SE Rio Rancho NM 87124-2277 • nschmaltz@aol.com • MI • EM • (RF 1954 MA PHD)

**SCHMALZ PAUL WILLIAM** (913)381-8593
6414 W 89th St Apt 35 Overland Park KS 66212-6066 • MO • 12/1996 12/1999 • (SP 1974 MA)

**SCHMAND MARY ANN** (901)382-4741
6056 Barrentine Dr Bartlett TN 38134-5934 • schmand@juno.com • MDS • EM • (RF 1966 MA)

**SCHMECKPEPER CATHY A** (708)478-0495
20011 Scott St Mokena IL 60448 • NI • Tchr • Zion Naperville IL • (630)904-1124 • (RF 1997)

**SCHMELZLE LUKE F** (713)869-1296
8715 Wind Side Dr Houston TX 77040-3455 • TX • Prin • Immanuel Houston TX • (713)864-2651 • (S 1987 MEAD)

**SCHMICH DEBORAH KAY** (314)296-3962
1554 Roy Dr Arnold MO 63010-1135 • MO • Tchr • St John Arnold MO • (636)464-7303 • (CQ 1994 MAT)

**SCHMID JOHN E** (815)963-0061
1736 Cumberland St Rockford IL 61103 • aikeas@freewwweb.com • NI • Tchr • Luther Academy Rockford IL • (815)877-9551 • (S 1993 MMU)

**SCHMID JONATHAN PAUL P** (618)532-5434
315 Anderson Centralia IL 62801 • SI • Tchr • Trinity Centralia IL • (618)532-5434 • (S 1998)

**SCHMID STEVEN PAUL** (414)427-2498
4537 S Oakwood Ter New Berlin WI 53151-6830 • spschmid@execpc.com • SW • Tchr • Martin LHS Greendale WI • (414)421-4000 • (MQ 1993)

**SCHMIDT ALLAN H**
Concordia Intern Schl Shanghai Plot S2 Huang Yang Rd Pudong Shanghai 201206 CHINA • allans@ciss.com.cn • NEB • S Miss • Nebraska Seward NE • (RF 1960 MA DED)

**SCHMIDT ANN E** (414)464-4269
11036 W Courtland Ave Wauwatosa WI 53225 • SW • Tchr • Our Redeemer Wauwatosa WI • (414)258-4558 • (CQ 1999)

**SCHMIDT ARNOLD E** (636)583-5970
2055 Denmark Rd Union MO 63084-4432 • MO • EM • (S 1956 MA MED PHD)

**SCHMIDT DAVID R*** (602)548-9009
15445 N 23rd Ln Phoenix AZ 85023-4211 • PSW • 10/1997 10/1999 • (CQ 1986)

**SCHMIDT DENNIS M** (517)662-2477
4854 S II Mile Rd Auburn MI 48611-9536 • zionlutu@cris.com • MI • P/Tchr • Zion Auburn MI • (517)662-4264 • (S 1971 MSED)

**SCHMIDT EDWARD E** (314)832-8889
72 Montague Ct Saint Louis MO 63123-3459 • ejschmidt@wanlab.com • MO • EM • (S 1958 MED)

**SCHMIDT ELIZABETH A**
St John Lutheran Church 1915 SE Lake Weir Rd Ocala FL 34471-5424 • FG • Tchr • St John Ocala FL • (352)629-1794 • (ME 1999)

**SCHMIDT EVELYN** (913)765-3788
PO Box 126 Mc Farland KS 66501-0126 • KS • Tchr • St John Alma KS • (785)765-3632 • (S 1957)

**SCHMIDT GAIL ANN**
3590 E Remington Dr Higley AZ 85236-7748 • wgschmidt@uswest.net • PSW • Tchr • Christ Greenfield Gilbert AZ • (480)892-8521 • (RF 1975)

**SCHMIDT GERALD R** (715)758-7282
W3592 Old Dump Rd Bonduel WI 54107-9166 • ger@mail.tds.net • NW • Tchr • St Paul Bonduel WI • (715)758-8559 • (MW 1982 MA)

**SCHMIDT GRANT L** (402)643-2591
1962 N 1st St Seward NE 68434-1095 • NEB • SHS/C • Nebraska Seward NE • (S 1983 MED)

**SCHMIDT HAROLD J** (763)792-1757
3926 88th Ave NE Circle Pines MN 55014 • schmidthc@juno.com • MNS • Tchr • Minnesota South Burnsville MN • (S 1978)

**SCHMIDT JAMES ARMIN** (870)673-7047
207 West 7th Stuttgart AR 72160 • MDS • P/Tchr • St John Stuttgart AR • (870)673-2858 • (S 1965)

**SCHMIDT JOEL H** (708)540-6513
325 Foxfire Dr Lake Zurich IL 60047-7963 • pevely@aol.com • NI • Tchr • St Peter Arlington Heights IL • (847)253-6638 • (RF 1960 MS)

**SCHMIDT JOHN C** (718)863-3239
1656 Williamsbridge Rd Bronx NY 10461-6202 • AT • Prin • Our Saviour Luth Hig Bronx NY • (718)792-5665 • (SP 1975 MA MS PHD)

**SCHMIDT JOYCE** (314)832-8889
72 Montague Ct Saint Louis MO 63123-3459 • ejschmidt@wanlab.com • MO • EM • (S 1975)

**SCHMIDT KARL G** (602)867-2289
17025 N 44th Pl Phoenix AZ 85032-9311 • EN • EM • (RF 1964 MA)

**SCHMIDT KARL W** (612)866-0777
1536 E 66th Richfield MN 55423 • kwfaschmidt@earthlink.net • MNS • Prin • Mount Calvary Richfield MN • (612)866-5405 • (S 1973 MA)

**SCHMIDT KENNETH E DR** (402)643-4805
2040 Parkview Dr Seward NE 68434 • kschmidt@seward.cune.edu • NEB • SHS/C • Nebraska Seward NE • (S 1967 MA MFA PHD)

**SCHMIDT KRISTEN A** (949)854-4873
13 Evening Breeze Irvine CA 92612-3731 • schmidt@cui.edu • PSW • SHS/C • Pacific Southwest Irvine CA • (949)854-3232 • (RF 1980 MA)

**SCHMIDT KURT E** (810)463-56292
51 Moross Ave Mount Clemens MI 48043 • mr.schmidt@school.tc • MI • Tchr • St John Fraser MI • (810)294-8740 • (S 1983)

**SCHMIDT KURT G** (304)496-8227
PO Box 118 Slanesville WV 25444-0118 • NE • EM • (RF 1959 MS)

**SCHMIDT LISA A**
4110 Paxton Lincoln NE 68521 • CI • 11/1999 • (S 1989)

**SCHMIDT MABEL** (319)393-5658
2540 Amber Dr NE Cedar Rapids IA 52402-3318 • IE • EM • (RF 1959)

**SCHMIDT MARA R** (708)366-6157
554 Forest Ave River Forest IL 60305-1708 • crfschmidmr@cuis.edu • NI • SHS/C • Northern Illinois Hillside IL • (RF 1979 MS)

**SCHMIDT MARTHA CORRINE** (815)873-9076
C/O Saint Paul Lutheran Church 600 N Horsman St Rockford IL 61101-6612 • NI • Tchr • St Paul Rockford IL • (815)965-3335 • (RF 1995)

**SCHMIDT MARTIN E**
1 Red Hill Rd 3 A Scenic View Tai Tam HONG KONG • mschmidt@hkis.edu.hk • NEB • S Miss • Nebraska Seward NE • (S 1990 MA)

**SCHMIDT MARY E** (847)540-6513
325 Foxfire Dr Lake Zurich IL 60047-7963 • pevely@aol.com • NI • Tchr • Immanuel Palatine IL • (847)359-1936 • (RF 1960 MED)

**SCHMIDT MICHELLE R** (619)421-2812
744 Cholla Rd Chula Vista CA 91910-6614 • PSW • 10/1991 10/1999 • (IV 1985)

**SCHMIDT MILTON A** (616)983-4214
814 Church St Saint Joseph MI 49085-1402 • MI • EM • (S 1945 MA)

**SCHMIDT PAUL M**
Saint John Lutheran Church 4950 Oakman Blvd Detroit MI 48204-2684 • MI • Tchr • St John Detroit MI • (313)933-8928 • (S 1964 MA)

**SCHMIDT PHYLLIS L** (847)692-9197
PO Box 241 Park Ridge IL 60068-0241 • EN • Tchr • Bethesda Chicago IL • (312)743-0800 • (RF 1962 MA)

**SCHMIDT RALPH R** (847)394-0526
1203 N Belmont Ave Arlington Hts IL 60004-4704 • lhnspc@aol.com • NI • EM • (RF 1954 MA MAT)

**SCHMIDT REBECCA S** (501)663-5212
Christ Luth Church and School 315 S Hughes St Little Rock AR 72205-5128 • schmidtrs@aol.com • MDS • Prin • Christ Little Rock AR • (501)663-5232 • (CQ 1993 MA)

**SCHMIDT TERRY L** (414)464-4269
11036 W Courtland Ave Milwaukee WI 53225-4421 • redeemer@execpc.com • SW • P/Tchr • Our Redeemer Wauwatosa WI • (414)258-4558 • (RF 1972 MED MA)

**SCHMIDT THOMAS** (212)796-9451
C/O Concordia College 171 White Plains Rd Bronxville NY 10708-1923 • AT • SHS/C • Atlantic Bronxville NY • (914)337-5700 • (CQ 1970)

**SCHMIDT WALTER R** (623)937-8835
5821 W Purdue Ave Glendale AZ 85302-3116 • PSW • Mem C • Mount Calvary Phoenix AZ • (602)263-0402 • (RF 1959)

**SCHMIDT WARREN M** (507)685-2310
10416 215th St Morristown MN 55052 • wschmidt@means.net • MNS • P/Tchr • Trinity Morristown MN • (507)685-2200 • (S 1972)

**SCHMIDT WAYNE A** (602)692-9153
3590 E Remington Dr Higley AZ 85236-7748 • wgschmidt@uswest.net • PSW • Prin • Christ Greenfld Gilbert AZ • (480)892-8314 • (RF 1972 MA)

**SCHMIDT WILLIAM G** (219)745-5728
5621 S Wayne Ave Fort Wayne IN 46807-3152 • williamgschmidt@juno.com • IN • Tchr • Emmaus Fort Wayne IN • (219)456-4573 • (SP 1967 MSED)

**SCHMIDTGOESSLING KAREN** (513)451-2013
2280 Townhill Dr Cincinnati OH 45238-3221 • schmidtgoess@hcca.ohio.gov • OH • Tchr • Grace Cincinnati OH • (513)661-8467 • (RF 1974)

**SCHMIEDING SUZANNE KAY** (618)277-3741
512 Lafayette Blvd Belleville IL 62220-3664 • schmieding@prodigy.net • SI • 01/2000 • (S 1967)

**SCHMIEGE ANN L**
1516 S 35th St Temple TX 76504-6777 • TX • Tchr • Grace Killeen TX • (254)634-4424 • (CQ 1998)

**SCHMIEGE LIZA L**
5750 N Sheridan Apt 306 Chicago IL 60660 • NI • Tchr • St Philip Chicago IL • (773)561-9830 • (AA 1997)

**SCHMIESING VALERIE LINDA**
308 Oak Manor Dr Glen Burnie MD 21061 • SE • Tchr • St Paul Glen Burnie MD • (410)766-2283 • (RF 1974)

**SCHMIT HARVEY M**
2553 River Woods Dr N Canton MI 48188-3286 • MI • P/Tchr • St Michael Wayne MI • (734)728-3315 • (RF 1975 MA DED)

**SCHMITT KRISTINE E** (810)724-6304
6753 Weyer Rd Imlay City MI 48444-9790 • MI • Tchr • St Paul Lapeer MI • (810)664-0046 • (S 1973)

**SCHMITT MARY B**
14205 Ida St Omaha NE 68142-1667 • samdur89@aol.com • NEB • 12/1997 12/1999 • (MQ 1988)

**SCHMITZ WALTER K** (630)628-6751
77 S Evergreen Ave Addison IL 60101-3447 • NI • Tchr • St Paul Addison IL • (630)543-6909 • (RF 1961 MSED)

**SCHMITZER MATTHEW T** (319)332-3414
3063 Willowwood Dr Bettendorf IA 52722-7229 • mtsdigger@aol.com • IE • 06/1998 • (RF 1994)

**SCHNABEL KIRSTEN L** (630)924-7617
250 Chatham Ln Roselle IL 60172 • NI • Tchr • St Paul Melrose Park IL • (708)343-5000 • (RF 1997)

**SCHNABEL ROBERT V DR** (219)465-7622
1076 Millpond Rd Unit G Valparaiso IN 46385-6287 • IN • EM • (CQ 1946 MS PHD LLD)

**SCHNACK DEBORAH G** (217)875-2769
54 Green Oak Dr Decatur IL 62526 • CI • Tchr • Lutheran School Asso Decatur IL • (217)233-2001 • (RF 1975)

**SCHNACK JOHN C** (618)826-4756
54 Green Oak Dr Decatur IL 62526 • CI • Tchr • Lutheran School Asso Decatur IL • (217)233-2001 • (RF 1975)

**SCHNACKENBERG MELVIN P** (301)593-9460
10011 Kinross Ave Silver Spring MD 20901-2216 • SE • EM • (RF 1956)

**SCHNAKE NORMAN P** (715)823-4362
E10074 County Road I Clintonville WI 54929-9578 • NW • EM • (RF 1974 MA)

**SCHNAKE RICHARD KARL DR** (262)241-9647
121 W Highview Dr Mequon WI 53092-5856 • rksdbs@execpc.com • SW • Tchr • St Peter Milwaukee WI • (414)353-6800 • (S 1972 MA PHD)

**SCHNARE DIANE J** (308)762-7745
1015 Box Butte Ave Alliance NE 69301-2519 • dianescn@aps.k12.ne.us • WY • 01/1996 01/2000 • (S 1976)

**SCHNEGELBERGER CHRISTINE L** (303)776-0640
1351 Francis St Longmont CO 80501-2511 • RM • Tchr • Immanuel Loveland CO • (970)667-7606 • (S 1971)

**SCHNEIDER AMY EMILY** (708)980-2470
455 Vermont Dr Elk Grove Vlg IL 60007-2750 • NI • Tchr • Immanuel Palatine IL • (847)359-1549 • (RF 1994)

**SCHNEIDER BETTY J** (217)443-4222
106 George Fox Dr Danville IL 61832-1152 • CI • Tchr • Danville Danville IL • (217)442-5036 • (RF 1969 MS)

**SCHNEIDER CAROL S** (913)599-4067
17528 W 116th St Olathe KS 66061-6501 • MO • Tchr • Messiah Independence MO • (816)254-9405 • (S 1979 MA MA)

**SCHNEIDER DEBRA ANN** (414)781-6543
4455 N 143rd St Brookfield WI 53005-1639 • jdschn@execpc.com • SW • Tchr • Immanuel Brookfield WI • (414)781-4135 • (RF 1976)

**SCHNEIDER DEITT C** (618)824-6335
8549 Primrose Rd Venedy IL 62214-1627 • SI • Tchr • St John Baldwin IL • (618)785-2344 • (RF 1976)

**SCHNEIDER DOROTHY ANN**
25 N Greeley St Palatine IL 60067 • NI • Tchr • Immanuel Palatine IL • (847)359-1936 • (RF 1993)

**SCHNEIDER JANET A**
17220 Garden Valley Rd Woodstock IL 60098-9155 • NI • 07/1995 07/1999 • (RF 1993)

**SCHNEIDER JANIS E** (313)928-1094
9322 Niver Ave Allen Park MI 48101-1542 • MI • Tchr • Special Ed Ministrie Detroit MI • (313)368-1220 • (RF 1975 MA)

**SCHNEIDER JESSICA LYN**
1451 Ramada Blvd Apt 3 Collinsville IL 62234 • SI • Tchr • Good Shepherd Collinsville IL • (618)344-3151 • (RF 1999)

**SCHNEIDER KARL F**
3248 Watson Rd Saint Louis MO 63139-2446 • MO • 03/1996 • (CQ 1984)

**SCHNEIDER KATHLEEN L**
7539 Shadow Bay Dr Panama City FL 32404 • SO • Tchr • Good Shepherd Panama City FL • (850)871-6311 • (S 1987)

**SCHNEIDER KRISTINE M*** (303)663-9533
3275 Blue Grass Circle Castle Rock CO 80104-7542 • tokandk@juno.com • RM • Tchr • Trinity Franktown CO • (303)841-8620 • (S 1991)

**SCHNEIDER KRISTOPHER E**
8809 Alder Grove PL Elk Grove CA 95624-1254 • kris:teacher@ulink.net • CNH • Tchr • Sacramento Lutheran Sacramento CA • (916)978-2720 • (IV 1995)

**SCHNEIDER REBEKAH J** (618)282-7714
311 N Main St #A Red Bud IL 62278 • SI • Tchr • St John Red Bud IL • (618)282-3873 • (RF 1993)

**SCHNEIDER RICHARD W** (920)458-8248
519 S 26th St Sheboygan WI 53081 • schneider@trinitysheboygan.org • SW • Prin • Trinity Sheboygan WI • (920)458-8246 • (RF 1989 MS)

**SCHNEIDER SARA LYNN** (660)826-4639
512 1/2 E 4th St Sedalia MO 65301-4604 • MO • Tchr • St Paul Sedalia MO • (816)826-1925 • (AU 1995)

**SCHNEIDER STEVEN J** (901)309-3034
2042 Bohemia Cove Cordova IN 38018 • scuber1@juno.com • MDS • Mem C • Grace Celebration Cordova TN • (901)737-6010 • (RF 1979)

**SCHNETZER THOMAS F** (718)224-2001
213-54 36th Ave Bayside NY 11361-1547 • AT • Tchr • Redeemer Bayside NY • (718)229-5770 • (CQ 1986)

**SCHOCKMAN COLETTE**
17600 14th Ave N - Apt #325 Plymouth MN 55447 • MNS • Tchr • Redeemer Wayzata MN • (612)473-5356 • (RF 2000)

**SCHOECH LOIS** (314)647-1882
6731 Plainview Ave Saint Louis MO 63109-2536 • MO • EM • (S 1950 MA)

**SCHOEDEL DAVID W** (573)477-8233
14 Rippling Water Ct St Charles MO 63303-2950 • hoops³001@msn.com • MO • Tchr • Immanuel Saint Charles MO • (636)946-0051 • (S 1980 MS)

**SCHOEN VALERIE ANN** (815)725-4459
325 Wheeler Ave Joliet IL 60436-2069 • NI • Tchr • St Peter Joliet IL • (815)722-3567 • (RF 1987)

**SCHOENBACK CHERYL LYNN** (616)827-9198
2122 Gettysburg Dr SE Kentwood MI 49508-6513 • MI • Tchr • St Mark Kentwood MI • (616)281-7892 • (SP 1986 MA)

**SCHOENBECK BARBARA F DR** (612)484-4386
3528 Cohansey Cir Shoreview MN 55126-3905 • bschoenbeck@csp.edu • MNS • SHS/C • Minnesota South Burnsville MN • (RF 1965 MA PHD)

**SCHOENBECK CARL J DR** (612)484-4386
3528 Cohansey Cir Shoreview MN 55126-3905 • cschoenbeck@csp.edu • MNS • SHS/C • Minnesota South Burnsville MN • (RF 1965 MA PHD)

**SCHOENBORN MARLYS J** (605)342-4296
5425 Meadowlark Dr Rapid City SD 57702-9017 • cmark@rapidnet.com • SD • 04/1998 04/2000 • (SP 1969)

**SCHOENFELD GRIGG PAULINE E**
494 W Munger Rd Munger MI 48747-9791 • MI • EM • (RF 1958)

**SCHOENHALS TAMMY ANN** (303)758-8677
3390 S Ash St Denver CO 80222 • RM • Tchr • Peace W Christ Aurora CO • (303)693-5618 • (CQ 1999)

**SCHOENKNECHT PAUL R** (517)871-2280
3825 Swaffer Rd Millington MI 48746-9142 • MI • Tchr • St Paul Millington MI • (517)871-4581 • (RF 1976 MA)

**SCHOENLEBER EDWARD F** (314)741-9640
1722 Martin Ln Apt 210 Saint Louis MO 63138-1748 • SI • EM • (CQ 1933)

**SCHOENNAUER ARTHUR H** (241)488-8659
1031 Park St Ashland OR 97520-3530 • NOW • EM • (S 1941 MED)

**SCHOEPP LEONARD H** (312)345-7730
618 N 2nd Ave Maywood IL 60153-1112 • NI • EM • (RF 1955 MA PHD)

**SCHOER RENEE K*** (508)650-9848
72 Main St Apt 72B Wayland MA 01778-4908 • NE • 05/1992 05/2000 • (S 1979 MRE)

**SCHOESSOW EUGENE E** (414)632-2251
1660 Village Dr Racine WI 53406-4731 • SW • P/Tchr • St Martini Milwaukee WI • (414)645-4094 • (RF 1957)

**SCHOLLMEYER ROBERT C** (517)652-8616
151 Beyerlein St Frankenmuth MI 48734-1501 • bscholl@concentric.net • MI • EM • (RF 1959 MA MA)

**SCHOLZ ARNOLD E** (952)466-3378
11025 134th St Cologne MN 55322-9153 • MNS • EM • (RF 1953)

**SCHOLZ CHRISTINA LYNN** (541)317-2913
696 NE Providence Dr Bend OR 97701 • NOW • Tchr • Trinity Bend OR • (541)382-1850 • (S 1997)

**SCHOLZ RICHARD S** (602)264-4827
1100 E Osborn #163 Phoenix AZ 85014 • EN • SHS/C • English Farmington MI • (IV 1999)

**SCHONHARDT WALTER A** (310)644-3848
12144 Grevillea Ave Apt 4 Hawthorne CA 90250-3777 • waschonhardt@webtv.net • PSW • Tchr • South Bay LHS Inglewood CA • (310)672-1101 • (RF 1981)

**SCHOONOVER DIANE L** (219)347-1856
1105 Richard Rd Kendallville IN 46755-2618 • IN • Tchr • St John Kendallville IN • (219)347-2444 • (RF 1976 MS)

**SCHOTT JULIE ANN** (410)224-6783
1904 Beeches Glory Path Annapolis MD 21401 • julie@funmark.com • SE • Tchr • St Paul Glen Burnie MD • (410)766-5790 • (RF 1989)

**SCHOTTE MARK L** (316)221-7178
1425 E 4th Ave Winfield KS 67156-2439 • trinity@horizon.hit.net • KS • Prin • Trinity Winfield KS • (316)221-1820 • (WN 1982 MS)

**SCHRADER AARON J** (801)671-7831
4850 S Bitteroot Dr Taylorsville UT 84116 • RM • Tchr • Salt Lake LHS Salt Lake City UT • (801)266-6676 • (S 1999)

**SCHRADER DIANA L**
678 Warburton Ave Yonkers NY 10701 • AT • Tchr • St Matthew New York NY • (212)567-2699 • (RF 1968)

**SCHRADER DIANE L** (618)635-3899
703 W 6th St Staunton IL 62088-1726 • schrader@midwest.net • SI • Tchr • St James Glen Carbon IL • (618)288-6120 • (RF 1984)

**SCHRADER JANICE LYNN** (651)603-0882
1392 Almond Ave Saint Paul MN 55108-2536 • sps44@aol.com • MNS • Tchr • Central Saint Paul MN • (651)645-8649 • (S 1977)

**SCHRADER SARAH M**
1392 Almond Ave St Paul MN 55108 • CNH • Tchr • Calvary San Lorenzo CA • (510)278-2556 • (S 2000)

**SCHRADER STEPHEN PAUL** (651)603-0882
1392 Almond Ave Saint Paul MN 55108-2536 • sps44@aol.com • MNS • Prin • Central Saint Paul MN • (651)645-8649 • (S 1972 MED)

**SCHRAGE PATRICIA** (319)285-4886
358 Country Club Ct Eldridge IA 52748-1228 • IE • EM • (S 1964)

**SCHRAMM CONNI LYNN** (714)643-2567
20 Tierra Vista Laguna Hills CA 92653 • PSW • Tchr • St John Orange CA • (714)288-4406 • (CQ 1981 MA)

**SCHRAMM WALTER H*** (713)320-9941
14614 Cedar Point Dr Houston TX 77070-2331 • TX • EM • (RF 1956 MED)

**SCHRANZ WILLIAM A** (402)643-4668
1134 Kolterman Seward NE 68434 • NEB • SHS/C • Nebraska Seward NE • (S 1981 MAT)

**SCHREIBER TRAYNOR C JR. DR** (909)592-5997
826 Avenida Bernardo San Dimas CA 91773-3937 • tschreiber@access1.net • PSW • 08/1999 • (RF 1967 MA EDD)

**SCHRIEBER JENNIFER L**
1229 S Dayton Ct Apt 318 Denver CO 80231-6333 • RM • Tchr • Denver Lutheran High Denver CO • (303)934-2345 • (CQ 1999)

**SCHRIEBER JONATHAN**
C/O Salt Lake Lutheran HS 4020 S 900 E Salt Lake City UT 84124-1169 • RM • Tchr • Salt Lake LHS Salt Lake City UT • (801)266-6676 • (MQ 1999)

**SCHRIEFER WILLIAM H** (808)946-8987
4176 Round Top Dr A Honolulu HI 96822 • whschrief@aol.com • CNH • Tchr • LHS Of Hawaii Honolulu HI • (808)949-5302 • (AU 1995)

**SCHROEDER AMY IRENE** (515)433-0409
530 6th St # D Boone IA 50036 • IW • Tchr • Trinity Boone IA • (515)432-6912 • (S 1997)

**SCHROEDER ANDREW M** (660)463-2704
205 Main St PO Box 719 Concordia MO 64020-9670 • amschelosheba@yahoo.com • MO • SHS/C • Missouri Saint Louis MO • (314)317-4550 • (S 1990 MED)

**SCHROEDER ARNOLD R** (219)947-2294
700 E 9th St Hobart IN 46342-5222 • IN • P/Tchr • Trinity Hobart IN • (219)942-3147 • (S 1960 MED)

**SCHROEDER BEVERLY A** (319)363-8725
1365 1st Ave SW Cedar Rapids IA 52405-4807 • IE • Tchr • Trinity Cedar Rapids IA • (319)362-6952 • (S 1965)

**SCHROEDER BEVERLY D** (618)288-2297
2 Shingle Oaks Dr Glen Carbon IL 62034 • bschroeder56@hotmail.com • SI • Tchr • Trinity Edwardsville IL • (618)656-7002 • (S 1978)

**SCHROEDER BOBBY L** (314)230-6314
822 Forest Village Dr Ballwin MO 63021-6118 • blswwjd@aol.com • MO • Mem C • St John Ellisville MO • (314)394-4100 • (AU 1990)

**SCHROEDER BRET A** (501)221-1327
13200 Chenal Pkwy #252 Little Rock AR 72211 • MDS • Tchr • Christ Little Rock AR • (501)663-5232 • (S 1998)

**SCHROEDER DEBORAH A**
2253 Nowack Rd Rosebud MO 63091-1503 • MO • 08/1999 • (S 1975 MED)

**SCHROEDER DENISE**
Immanuel Lutheran School 832 Lee St Des Plaines IL 60016-6408 • NI • Tchr • Immanuel Des Plaines IL • (847)390-0990 • (S 1989)

**SCHROEDER DIANE J** (605)745-4447
RR 1 Box 192A Hot Springs SD 57747 • SD • Tchr • Bethesda Hot Springs SD • (605)745-4834 • (S 1980)

**SCHROEDER DONALD A** (219)636-7101
C/O Camp Lutherhaven 1596 S 150 W Albion IN 46701-9695 • camplh@noble.cioe.com • IN • O Sp Min • Indiana Fort Wayne IN • (AA 1989)

**SCHROEDER DOROTHY J** (517)652-4829
831 W Ardussi St Frankenmuth MI 48734-1410 • MI • EM • (RF 1961 MA MLS EDS)

**SCHROEDER DOUGLAS R** (414)464-9553
9014 W Palmetto Ave Milwaukee WI 53225-5014 • SW • Tchr • Our Redeemer Wauwatosa WI • (414)258-4558 • (SP 1971)

**SCHROEDER ELLEN E** (847)517-7603
1345 E Thacker St Schaumburg IL 60173-6566 • NI • Tchr • St Luke Itasca IL • (630)773-0509 • (SP 1975 MED)

**SCHROEDER ERLEN O** (612)657-2475
112 5th St NE Mayer MN 55360-9607 • MNS • EM • (S 1957 MA)

**SCHROEDER GEORGE W**
26823 Summer Sunshine Dr Sun City CA 92585-9176 • PSW • EM • (RF 1949 MED MA)

**SCHROEDER JAMES E** (513)598-4640
6502 Hayes Rd Cincinnati OH 45248-1404 • schroeder³j@hccanet.org • OH • P/Tchr • Grace Cincinnati OH • (513)661-8467 • (S 1968 MED)

**SCHROEDER JARENE ELIZABETH** (281)252-0414
22619 Rainfern Dr Magnolia TX 77355-6957 • jes101269@yahoo.com • TX • 07/1999 • (AU 1992)

**SCHROEDER JULIE** (314)230-6314
822 Forest Village Dr Ballwin MO 63021-6118 • MO • Tchr • St John Ellisville MO • (314)394-4100 • (AU 1990)

**SCHROEDER KAREN L** (562)529-5328
5157 Verdura Ave Lakewood CA 90712-2225 • PSW • Tchr • Ascension Torrance CA • (310)371-3531 • (IV 1989)

**SCHROEDER KENNETH W** (517)734-4924
157 Hoeft Rd Rogers City MI 49779-2028 • MI • P/Tchr • St John Rogers City MI • (517)734-3580 • (S 1982 MA)

**SCHROEDER KEVIN P** (219)486-3132
4405 North Dr Fort Wayne IN 46815-4931 • IN • Tchr • Holy Cross Fort Wayne IN • (219)483-3173 • (RF 1984 MA)

**SCHROEDER KRISTINE L** (713)462-3542
5915 Flintlock #1412 Houston TX 77040 • TX • Tchr • Immanuel Houston TX • (713)861-8787 • (RF 1985 MS)

**SCHROEDER LELAND P**
20825 Timberlane Dr Elkhorn NE 68022-2120 • NEB • EM • (S 1954)

**SCHROEDER LINDA J** (706)937-4348
757 Haggard Rd Ringgold GA 30736-9808 • MDS • Tchr • Lutheran Chattanooga TN • (423)622-3755 • (S 1965 MED)

**SCHROEDER LORI A** (612)955-1006
PO Box 173 Watertown MN 55388-0173 • MNS • Tchr • Trinity Waconia MN • (952)442-4165 • (SP 1990)

**SCHROEDER LYDIA E** (707)255-9585
2831 Laurel St Napa CA 94558-5728 • CNH • Tchr • St John Napa CA • (707)226-7970 • (S 1965)

**SCHROEDER MARILYN A** (507)238-1066
610 E 1st St Fairmont MN 56031-3930 • MNS • EM • (S 1952)

**SCHROEDER MELVIN H** (708)423-3223
4137 W 100th St Oak Lawn IL 60453-3569 • tchschroem@crf.cuis.edu • NI • EM • (S 1961 MED EDS)

**SCHROEDER NANCY E** (801)265-8036
1051 E 3740 S Salt Lake City UT 84106-1916 • nesspark@aol.com • RM • Tchr • Redeemer Salt Lake City UT • (801)487-6283 • (RF 1968 MA)

**SCHROEDER NANCY L** (219)679-4309
58270 Ash Rd Osceola IN 46561-9635 • IN • Tchr • Trinity Elkhart IN • (219)522-1491 • (S 1968 MS)

**SCHROEDER NOEL J** (701)258-4938
1217 Prospect Pl Bismarck ND 58501-2434 • ND • EM • (RF 1956 MS)

**SCHROEDER PHYLLIS A** (701)258-4938
1217 Prospect Pl Bismarck ND 58501 • pschroed@btigate.com • ND • 11/1997 • (RF 1970 MA)

**SCHROEDER RALPH EDWARD** (414)529-5258
6985 Heathmeadow Ct Greendale WI 53129-2704 • ed.schroeder@cuw.edu • SW • SHS/C • South Wisconsin Milwaukee WI • (414)464-8100 • (S 1965 MA)

**SCHROEDER RUTH J** (219)639-3491
16629 Minnich Rd Hoagland IN 46745-9709 • IN • Tchr • Woodburn Woodburn IN • (219)632-5493 • (RF 1977)

**SCHROEDER STEPHANIE MARIE**
3528 N Claremont Chicago IL 60618 • NI • Tchr • St Philip Chicago IL • (773)561-9830 • (RF 1998)

**SCHROEDER STEPHEN P*** (636)405-7094
1628 Hwy 109 Wildwood MO 63038 • spssjls@hotmail.com • MO • Tchr • St John Ellisville MO • (314)394-4100 • (RF 1982)

**SCHROEDER TAMMY S** (402)693-2919
223 4th Rd Howells NE 68641-4024 • ltschro@gpcom.net • NEB • Tchr • St Paul West Point NE • (402)372-2111 • (S 1988)

**SCHROEDER TRACIE LYNN** (480)288-6623
1191 W 6th Ave Apache Junction AZ 85220 • bandt.schroeder@cwix.com • PSW • Tchr • Christ Greenfield Gilbert AZ • (480)892-8521 • (MQ 1995)

**SCHROLL NORMA R** (314)843-8638
8300 S Laclede Station Rd Saint Louis MO 63123-2140 • MO • Tchr • Christ Community Kirkwood MO • (314)822-7774 • (S 1970 MED)

**SCHROPPEL KRISTY R** (808)262-6993
420 Oneawa St #C Kailua HI 96734-2421 • schroppe@hawaii.edu • CNH • Tchr • Our Redeemer Honolulu HI • (808)945-7765 • (S 1985)

**SCHRUPP STEPHANIE ANN** (612)474-5541
5950 Glencoe Rd Excelsior MN 55331-3134 • MNS • Tchr • St Peter Edina MN • (612)927-8400 • (SP 1993)

**SCHUELER ANN M**
4518 Meadowbend Dr Richmond TX 77469-9072 • TX • 07/1997 07/2000 • (RF 1973)

**SCHUEMER LISA S** (708)261-1851
251 E Madison St Lombard IL 60148-3468 • NI • Tchr • Immanuel Elmhurst IL • (630)832-9302 • (RF 1990 MA)

**SCHUERMANN MICHELLE C** (573)332-0621
542 S Spring St - Apt E Cape Girardeau MO 63703 • MO • Tchr • Trinity Cape Girardeau MO • (573)334-1068 • (RF 2000)

**SCHUESSLER JOEL N** (651)578-8642
9210 Andrea Dr Saint Paul MN 55125-3406 • nozo@csp.edu • MNS • SHS/C • Minnesota South Burnsville MN • (SP 1983 MS)

**SCHUESSLER NORMA H** (314)773-8290
3441 Missouri Ave # A Saint Louis MO 63118-3236 • MO • Tchr • Holy Cross Saint Louis MO • (314)771-9521 • (RF 1966)

**SCHUETTE YVONNE V** (612)864-3237
1412 Fir Ave N Glencoe MN 55336-1105 • MNS • Tchr • First Glencoe MN • (320)864-3317 • (SP 1983)

**SCHUETZ GLORY JEAN** (303)904-0301
7942 S Depew St Apt B Littleton CO 80128-8404 • RM • Tchr • Redeemer Denver CO • (303)934-0422 • (S 1974)

**SCHUETZ LOIS M** (303)455-8246
3405 W 32nd Ave # 806 Denver CO 80211-3103 • RM • EM • (S 1948)

**SCHUKNECHT JEROLD C** (303)934-1003
3099 S Zurich Ct Denver CO 80236-2042 • jschuknecht@compuserv.com • RM • P/Tchr • Redeemer Denver CO • (303)934-0422 • (RF 1961 MED)

**SCHULDHEISZ DANIEL L** (509)586-1533
2329 W 15th Pl Kennewick WA 99337-2802 • dlsjrs@gte.net • NOW • Prin • Bethlehem Kennewick WA • (509)582-5624 • (S 1967 MAD)

**SCHULDHEISZ JAN R** (509)586-1533
2329 W 15th Pl Kennewick WA 99337-2802 • dlsjrs@gte.net • NOW • Tchr • Bethlehem Kennewick WA • (509)582-5624 • (S 1967)

**SCHULDHEISZ JOEL M DR** (503)282-4640
3207 NE Ainsworth St Portland OR 97211-6723 • jschuldheisz@cu-portland.edu • NOW • SHS/C • Northwest Portland OR • (SP 1978 MED PHD)

**SCHULENBERG LEONARD G** (507)334-3065
1050 Westwood Dr Faribault MN 55021-6656 • MNS • EM • (S 1932)

**SCHULENBURG CARL L** (317)861-6389
5665 W High Acres West Ct New Palestine IN 46163-9731 • IN • Tchr • LHS Of Indianapolis Indianapolis IN • (317)787-5474 • (RF 1970 MS)

**SCHULENBURG LINDA S** (317)861-6389
5665 W High Acres West Ct New Palestine IN 46163-9731 • IN • Tchr • Zion New Palestine IN • (317)861-4210 • (RF 1971 MA)

**SCHULER JEFFREY G**
1015 Tony Pl Longmont CO 80501-1804 • RM • 05/1999 • (S 1984)

**SCHULER NANCY A** (303)444-7413
1885 Upland Boulder CO 80304 • RM • Tchr • Mount Zion Boulder CO • (303)443-4151 • (S 1984)

**SCHULER VICTOR E** (812)424-0608
616 Thornberry Dr Evansville IN 47710-4250 • IN • EM • (RF 1950 MS)

**SCHULT DANIEL L** (219)485-0076
3329 Sudbury Pl Fort Wayne IN 46815-6245 • IN • EM • (RF 1956 MSED)

**SCHULT PHILIP D**
C/O Bethlehem Lutheran Church 2100 Wadsworth Blvd Lakewood CO 80215 • RM • Tchr • Bethlehem Lakewood CO • (303)238-7676 • (RF 1987)

**SCHULT SHERRY ANN** (812)858-9541
4944 Jamestown Rd Newburgh IN 47630 • Saschult@aol.com • IN • 08/1997 08/2000 • (RF 1991)

**SCHULTEIS DONALD H** (909)392-9554
2506 Hayes Dr La Verne CA 91750-3706 • PSW • 06/2000 • (RF 1965 MSCT MA)

**SCHULTEIS MELINDA S** (714)508-7881
2960 Champion Way #802 Tustin CA 92782-1234 • schulteis@cui.edu • PSW • SHS/C • Pacific Southwest Irvine CA • (949)854-3232 • (IV 1995 MS)

**SCHULTEIS MICHAEL WILLIAM** (714)508-7881
2960 Champion Way #802 Tustin CA 92782 • mschulteis@earthlink.net • PSW • Tchr • Lutheran HS/Orange C Orange CA • (714)998-5151 • (IV 1996 MA)

**SCHULTEIS MICHELE LYNN** (937)879-1042
634 Hidden Valley Ct Fairborn OH 45324-3977 • tmschulteis@earthlink.net • OH • Tchr • Bethlehem Fairborn OH • (937)878-0651 • (RF 1992 MA)

**SCHULTZ AMY E** (636)390-0439
4508 Scarecrow Ln Washington MO 63090 • jaschultz@juno.com • MO • Tchr • Salem Florissant MO • (314)741-6781 • (RF 1990 MA)

**SCHULTZ ANDREW J** (734)482-3319
6072 S Mohawk Ave Ypsilanti MI 48197-9709 • schula@ccaa.edu • MI • SHS/C • Michigan Ann Arbor MI • (S 1989 MMU)

**SCHULTZ CHERYL L** (970)663-7863
1669 Carol Dr Loveland CO 80537-6819 • RM • Tchr • Trinity Greeley CO • (970)330-2485 • (S 1971)

**SCHULTZ DAVID L** (352)799-4372
7007 Windmere Rd Brooksville FL 34602-7515 • FG • EM • (RF 1962 MA)

**SCHULTZ DAVID P**
753 Quincy St NE Minneapolis MN 55413-2317 • MNS • 07/1999 • (S 1985)

**SCHULTZ DAWN MARIE** (317)346-0684
766 Hannah Pl Franklin IN 46131 • IN • Tchr • Calvary Indianapolis IN • (317)783-2305 • (RF 1990)

**SCHULTZ DENNIS N** (847)426-5372
127 Aberdeen Dr East Dundee IL 60118-1615 • EN • 08/1990 08/2000 • (CQ 1964 MS)

**SCHULTZ DOROTHY R** (518)458-7231
24 Whitestone Way Slingerlands NY 12159 • AT • Tchr • The Village Bronxville NY • (914)337-0207 • (BR 1975 MSED)

**SCHULTZ ELIZABETH A** (402)467-2027
7130 Eagle Dr Lincoln NE 68507-2148 • NEB • Tchr • Faith Lincoln NE • (402)466-6861 • (S 1984)

**SCHULTZ ERIC M** (414)456-0268
11819 W Cherry St Wauwatosa WI 53226 • SW • Tchr • Our Redeemer Wauwatosa WI • (414)258-4555 • (S 1974)

**SCHULTZ FORREST E** (909)482-0343
729 Windham Dr Claremont CA 91711 • PSW • Tchr • First Monrovia CA • (626)357-3596 • (CQ 1989)

**SCHULTZ GILBERT P** (812)376-6039
3845 Cove Rd Columbus IN 47203-3605 • IN • EM • (RF 1954 MS)

**SCHULTZ HARRIET ANNE**
103 Upper Ridge St Reinbeck IA 50669-1450 • IE • 09/1997 09/1999 • (S 1971)

**SCHULTZ JACK M DR*** (949)766-6869
25 Paseo Brezo Rancho Santa Margari CA 92688 • schultz@cui.edu • PSW • SHS/C • Pacific Southwest Irvine CA • (949)854-3232 • (RF 1980 MA PHD)

**SCHULTZ JOHN E** (812)867-9633
740 Lancaster Crt Evansville IN 47711-7210 • jeschult@evansville.net • IN • Prin • Evansville Evansville IN • (812)424-7252 • (SP 1977 MEPD)

**SCHULTZ JOLENE** (636)239-4296
1416 E 5th St Apt 9 Washington MO 63090-3460 • MO • Tchr • Immanuel Washington MO • (314)239-1636 • (S 1965)

**SCHULTZ JONATHAN P** (520)663-3964
9579 E Ashford Dr Tucson AZ 85747-9205 • azschultz@earthlink.net • PSW • Tchr • Fountain Of Life Tucson AZ • (520)747-1213 • (S 1982 MSED)

**SCHULTZ JUDY K** (414)456-0268
11819 W Cherry St Wauwatosa WI 53226 • SW • Mem C • South Wisconsin Milwaukee WI • (414)464-8100 • (S 1974)

**SCHULTZ LAURIE MARIE**
109 S State St Merrill WI 54452 • laurieschultz@hotmail.com • NW • Tchr • Trinity Merrill WI • (715)536-5482 • (MQ 1996)

**SCHULTZ LLOYD N** (313)273-3758
18058 Greenfield Rd Detroit MI 48235-3119 • teacherschultz@gateway.net • MI • EM • (RF 1958 MED)

**SCHULTZ LOWELL E** (715)536-2174
N 736 Lake Rd Merrill WI 54452-1257 • NW • Tchr • St John Merrill WI • (715)536-7264 • (S 1966 MA)

**SCHULTZ MARGARETE L** (706)663-4588
1046 Robert Williams Rd Pine Mountain GA 31822-5410 • FG • EM • (RF 1954 MED)

**SCHULTZ MARK A** (734)457-3976
517 E 5th St Monroe MI 48161-2092 • mschultz@tlsmonroe.org • MI • Mem C • Trinity Monroe MI • (313)242-2308 • (SP 1980 MEPD)

**SCHULTZ MARK O** (502)254-5801
10314 Whipps Mill Rd Louisville KY 40223-1218 • IN • Tchr • Our Savior Louisville KY • (502)426-0864 • (SP 1978 MED)

**SCHULTZ PATRICIA A** (313)273-3758
18058 Greenfield Rd Detroit MI 48235-3119 • n2kidz2@gateway.net • MI • Prin • Greenfld Peace Detroit MI • (313)838-3366 • (S 1960 MED)

**SCHULTZ RALPH C DR** (518)458-7231
24 Whitestone Way Slingerlands NY 12159 • ccnyrcs@aol.com • AT • SHS/C • Atlantic Bronxville NY • (914)337-5700 • (RF 1954 MMU DMU)

**SCHULTZ RAMONA SUE** (734)457-3976
517 E 5th St Monroe MI 48161-2092 • maschultz@foxberry.net • MI • Tchr • Trinity Monroe MI • (734)241-1160 • (SP 1980 MAS)

**SCHULTZ ROBERT L** (616)929-3382
9980 Terra W Traverse City MI 49684-9637 • MI • EM • (S 1958 MA)

**SCHULTZ RONALD P** (314)527-9887
606 Rustic Valley Dr Ballwin MO 63021-6210 • ron.schultz@lcms.org • MO • S Ex/S • Missouri Saint Louis MO • (314)317-4550 • (RF 1983 MBA)

**SCHULTZ RUTH A** (618)259-4332
1301 Vaughn Rd Wood River IL 62095-1851 • mschultz@ezl.com • SI • Tchr • Trinity Edwardsville IL • (618)656-7002 • (RF 1982 MA)

**SCHULTZ RUTH ANN** (608)755-0362
1318 E Van Buren St Janesville WI 53545-4279 • rschultz@spsflames.k12.wi.us • SW • Tchr • St Paul Janesville WI • (608)754-4471 • (RF 1985 MSED)

**SCHULTZ RUTH ELLEN** (812)867-9633
740 Lancaster Crt Evansville IN 47711-7210 • jeschult@evansville.net • IN • Tchr • Evansville Evansville IN • (812)424-7252 • (SP 1977)

**SCHULTZ SHIRLEY A** (407)365-8064
1150 W Sugar Mill Rd Oviedo FL 32765 • SI • 08/1987 08/2000 • (SP 1981)

**SCHULTZ THOMAS WESLEY** (208)233-1752
830 Jones Dr Pocatello ID 83201-5561 • tschultz@gracepocid.org • NOW • Tchr • Grace Pocatello ID • (208)237-4142 • (IV 1990)

**SCHULTZ TIMOTHY P**
14 Goodhill Rd Bethel CT 06801-2437 • AT • SHS/C • Atlantic Bronxville NY • (914)337-5700 • (BR 1980 MMU DMU)

**SCHULTZ VALERIE D** (317)891-1568
1016 Copiah Ct Indianapolis IN 46239 • IN • Tchr • Emmaus Indianapolis IN • (317)632-1486 • (RF 1979)

**SCHULTZ WYATT A**
C/O Lutheran South Academy 12555 Ryewater Dr Houston TX 77089 • wschultz5@aol.com • TX • Tchr • Lutheran South Acade Houston TX • (281)464-9320 • (SP 1978 MS)

**SCHULTZE STACIE L** (413)594-0445
22 Henshaw St 2nd Floor Chicopee MA 01020-1806 • stacie123@hotmail.com • NE • Tchr • First Holyoke MA • (413)532-4272 • (S 1998)

**SCHULTZE THOMAS E** (618)826-4969
246 Young Ave Chester IL 62233 • schultze@midwest.net • SI • Tchr • St John Chester IL • (618)826-4345 • (RF 1977 MED)

**SCHULZ DELPHIN L** (314)389-2468
8042 Audrain Dr Saint Louis MO 63121-4602 • EN • EM • (CQ 1951 MA PHD)

**SCHULZ JANICE M**
6942 Payne Dearborn MI 48126 • MI • Tchr • Atonement Dearborn MI • (313)581-2525 • (S 1964 MED MCMU)

**SCHULZ JENNIFER** (708)410-1724
1122 N 32nd Ave #18 Melrose Park IL 60160 • NI • Tchr • Bethlehem River Grove IL • (708)453-1113 • (MQ 1998)

**SCHULZ KATHLEEN M**
Our Savior Lutheran Church 1500 San Simeon Way Fenton MO 63026-3443 • MO • Tchr • Our Savior Fenton MO • (314)343-7511 • (S 1975)

**SCHULZ LAWRENCE R** (818)353-3363
8423 Cora St Sunland CA 91040-3230 • PSW • EM • (RF 1956)

**SCHULZ LEROY E** (909)592-8409
1807 Via Palomares San Dimas CA 91773-4236 • PSW • EM • (S 1954 MA)

**SCHULZ MARLIN W DR** (949)951-1959
23542 Saint Elena Mission Viejo CA 92691-2239 • >marlinanddonna@home.comı • PSW • SHS/C • Pacific Southwest Irvine CA • (949)854-3232 • (CQ 1960 MS PHD)

**SCHULZ NANCY J** (847)234-8906
688 W Deerpath Rd Lake Forest IL 60045-1611 • njschulzll@aol.com • NI • 11/1998 • (SP 1982)

**SCHULZ NATHAN E** (206)361-1278
11719 Meridian Ave N Seattle WA 98133-8547 • nschulz@earthlink.net • NOW • Prin • Concordia Seattle WA • (206)525-7407 • (S 1964 MED MA MFA)

**SCHULZ PAUL A** (914)771-8560
224 Midland Ave Tuckahoe NY 10707 • pasccny@aol.com • AT • Prin • Emanuel Patchogue NY • (516)758-2250 • (BR 1981)

**SCHULZ ROBERT C** (414)764-9038
850 E Elm Rd Oak Creek WI 53154-6471 • SW • P/Tchr • Zion Menomonee Falls WI • (262)781-8133 • (S 1971)

**SCHULZ ROBERT L**
3010 Carmel Dr Flossmoor IL 60422-2265 • NI • Tchr • Northern Illinois Hillside IL • (S 1964 MA)

**SCHULZE BETTY J** (512)251-5129
504 Oak Ridge Dr Pflugerville TX 78660-2819 • TX • Tchr • St Paul Austin TX • (512)472-3313 • (S 1968)

**SCHULZE JACALYN A** (763)536-8538
4556 Lake Dr Apt 211 Robbinsdale MN 55422-1843 • MNS • Mem C • Peace Robbinsdale MN • (763)533-0570 • (SP 1974 MA)

**SCHULZE ROBERT JOHN SR.** (407)678-4421
10130 Cheshunt Dr Orlando FL 32817-3702 • rsch10130@aol.com • FG • Tchr • Florida-Georgia Orlando FL • (S 1964 MA)

**SCHUMACHER CYNTHIA** (860)589-1971
136 Fleetwood Rd Bristol CT 06010-2535 • NE • 03/1996 03/2000 • (S 1976)

**SCHUMACHER DEBORAH FAITH** (262)523-1344
N21W24248 Cumberland Rd Unit H Pewaukee WI 53072-5820 • debi@splcwa.org • SW • Tchr • St Paul West Allis WI • (414)541-6251 • (CQ 1989 MED)

**SCHUMACHER GORDON L**
6740 S State Road 39 North Judson IN 46366-8409 • IN • 06/1999 • (RF 1970)

**SCHUMACHER JAMES LEE** (517)671-2213
3464 Clover Ln Bay City MI 48706 • MI • Prin • Faith Bay City MI • (517)684-3448 • (RF 1966 MA)

**SCHUMACHER JOANN MARIE** (319)393-9135
3930 Georgia Ave NE Cedar Rapids IA 52411-6721 • IE • Tchr • Trinity Cedar Rapids IA • (319)362-6952 • (CQ 1996)

**SCHUMACHER RICHARD WESLEY JR.** (734)513-4126
29893 Dover St Garden City MI 48135-3427 • rjschumach@aol.com • MI • Mem C • St Matthew Westland MI • (734)425-0260 • (AA 1994)

**SCHUMACHER SCOTT ALLEN** (812)523-2035
929 Evergreen Dr Seymour IN 47274-3005 • IN • Tchr • Immanuel Seymour IN • (812)522-1301 • (RF 1993)

**SCHUMACHER STEVEN R** (217)732-7101
7 Forest Hills Dr Lincoln IL 62656-5311 • schu@abelink.com • CI • Tchr • Zion Lincoln IL • (217)732-3977 • (S 1976)

**SCHUMACHER TIMOTHY J** (303)655-1648
2456 Cherry Cir Brighton CO 80601 • tschu@aol.com • RM • Tchr • Zion Brighton CO • (303)659-3443 • (RF 1987)

**SCHUMACHER VIKKI L** (713)572-0943
3742 Chevy Chase Houston TX 77019 • TX • 04/1999 • (SP 1992)

**SCHUMANN DIANE E** (262)284-2541
639 N Montgomery St Port Washington WI 53074-1519 • studio-s@execpc.com • SW • Tchr • St Paul Grafton WI • (414)377-4659 • (MQ 1984)

**SCHUMANN LOIS J** (515)223-6517
209 Jordan Dr W Des Moines IA 50265-4027 • dschum209@aol.com • IW • Tchr • MT Olive Des Moines IA • (515)277-0247 • (CQ 1989 MS)

**SCHUMANN WILBER G** (817)485-6080
841 Ridge Dr Bedford TX 76021-4232 • TX • EM • (RF 1941 MA)

**SCHUMM DEBORAH A** (215)269-7451
508 Lancaster Ct Downingtown PA 19335-4210 • EA • Tchr • Christ Memorial Malvern PA • (610)644-4508 • (RF 1979)

**SCHUMM KAREN R** (708)553-7821
410 W Van Emmon St Yorkville IL 60560-1454 • krschumm@aol.com • NI • Tchr • Cross Yorkville IL • (630)553-7861 • (RF 1981 MSED)

**SCHUMM LAURA RUTH** (412)825-4557
2508 Hyer Ave Apt 55A North Versailles PA 15137-1149 • lrschumm@aol.com • EA • Tchr • Christ Pittsburgh PA • (412)271-7173 • (AA 1986)

**SCHUMPE JAMES E** (812)523-3064
788 S 1100 E Seymour IN 47274 • IN • P/Tchr • St John Seymour IN • (812)523-3131 • (S 1969)

**SCHUPPAN MARJORIE C** (314)843-5037
9301 Lawndale Dr Crestwood MO 63126-2619 • MO • EM • (RF 1964)

**SCHURIG KATHY A** (810)795-5697
14558 Maisano Dr Sterling Heights MI 48312-6722 • jschurig@flash.net • MI • 11/1998 • (RF 1977 MAT)

**SCHUSTER MICHELLE S** (308)384-5969
1709 N Taylor Grand Island NE 68803 • NEB • Tchr • Peace Grand Island NE • (308)384-5673 • (S 1997)

**SCHUTH DANIEL**
Luth HS Association 3411 N Alpine Rd Rockford IL 61114 • NI • Tchr • Northern Illinois Hillside IL • (RF 1996)

**SCHUTT KATHLEEN S** (515)285-0699
3824 Wakonda Dr Des Moines IA 50321-2137 • rcschutt@aol.com • IW • Tchr • MT Olive Des Moines IA • (515)277-0247 • (CQ 1975)

**SCHUTTE AMY CATHERINE** (651)983-8169
3107 ArcadeSt Little Canada MN 55109 • famousamos12@hotmail.com • MNS • Mem C • Old Emanuel Inver Grove Heights MN • (651)457-3929 • (SP 1999)

**SCHUTTE SUSAN E** (612)420-2673
19125 Schutte Rd Corcoran MN 55340-9587 • MNS • Tchr • St John Maple Grove MN • (612)420-2426 • (SP 1971)

**SCHUTZLER SHARON LEIGH** (517)673-3598
C/O Trinity Lutheran Church 9858 North St Reese MI 48757-9544 • MI • Tchr • Trinity Reese MI • (517)868-9901 • (CQ 1994)

**SCHWAB JEROME T** (573)374-9807
HC 69 Box 514 Sunrise Beach MO 65079-9418 • MO • EM • (RF 1953 MMU)

**SCHWAEGERLE JUDY LYNN** (313)525-2261
6545 Henry Ruff Garden City MI 48135-2010 • schwaggs@aol.com • MI • Tchr • St Matthew Westland MI • (734)425-0261 • (AA 1994)

**SCHWALENBERG MARLENE G** (330)644-9914
470 Bobwhite Trl Akron OH 44319 • OH • Tchr • Zion Akron OH • (330)253-3136 • (RF 1972)

**SCHWALGE ALICE M** (219)322-3060
2336 Peach Tree Ln Dyer IN 46311-1855 • NI • Tchr • St Paul Chicago Heights IL • (708)754-4492 • (RF 1968)

**SCHWAN JOANN E** (414)738-7958
3401 N Mariah Ln Appleton WI 54911-1238 • tijoschwan@aol.com • NW • 01/1996 01/2000 • (S 1973)

**SCHWAN PAUL ALLEN*** (863)385-5084
921 11th Ave Sebring FL 33875 • n4ftd@aol.com • FG • Tchr • Faith Sebring FL • (941)385-0406 • (RF 1977 MS)

**SCHWANKE WAYNE L** (407)895-8263
2233 Cypress Trace Cir Orlando FL 32825-8554 • waynelouis@aol.com • FG • Tchr • Trinity Orlando FL • (407)843-4896 • (RF 1964 MA MA)

**SCHWANTZ RICHARD G JR.** (219)493-1454
1931 S Tyland Blvd New Haven IN 46774-1551 • wishwewerekids@juno.com • IN • Tchr • Wyneken Memorial Decatur IN • (219)639-6177 • (CQ 1993)

**SCHWARK AUGUST C** (317)786-0735
6119 Shelby St Indianapolis IN 46227-4879 • IN • EM • (RF 1939)

**SCHWARTZ GRETCHEN C** (816)246-6797
601 NE Adams Dr Lees Summit MO 64086-6260 • EN • 06/1987 06/2000 • (S 1986 MA)

**SCHWARTZ HEIDI REBECCA** (406)257-9628
306 5th Ave E Apt A Kalispell MT 59901 • MT • Tchr • Trinity Kalispell MT • (406)257-6716 • (SP 1999)

**SCHWARTZ JUSTIN C** (313)565-9688
504 N Gulley Rd Dearborn MI 48128-1502 • MI • EM • (RF 1951 MA)

**SCHWARTZ PAULA GALE** (303)429-8128
3717 W 73rd Ave Westminster CO 80030-5217 • GPRBEARS@aol.com • RM • Tchr • Bethlehem Lakewood CO • (303)233-0401 • (S 1976)

**SCHWARTZ SUE LYNN** (314)487-2993
510 Bellsworth Saint Louis MO 63125-3601 • tipea@stlnet.com • MO • 06/2000 • (S 1989 MEAD)

**SCHWARTZKOPF MELISSA M**
4517 North F St San Bernardino CA 92407 • CNH • Tchr • Trinity Fairfield CA • (707)425-2944 • (S 2000)

**SCHWARZ MYRNA LOU** (847)438-9241
570 Ramblewood Ct Lake Zurich IL 60047-2556 • NI • Tchr • Immanuel Glenview IL • (847)724-1034 • (CQ 1991)

**SCHWARZ SUSAN E** (618)659-1877
416 Cherry St Edwardsville IL 62025-2451 • jennasue@juno.com • SI • Tchr • St John Chester IL • (618)826-3545 • (RF 1983 MS)

**SCHWARZ SUSAN L** (618)357-2556
2165 State Rd 154 Pinckneyville IL 62274-9509 • SI • Tchr • St Mark Steeleville IL • (618)965-3838 • (S 1977)

**SCHWARZ XAVRIA** (619)734-1344
5700 Baltimore Dr #174 La Mesa CA 91942 • xaschwarz@cs.com • PSW • St Mark Steeleville IL • (IV 1996 MED)

**SCHWAUSCH OTTO E** (816)461-5868
3901 N Osage St Independence MO 64050-1028 • MO • EM • (RF 1954 MA)

**SCHWECKE STEVEN A** (313)563-7614
23156 Cromwell St Dearborn MI 48128-1855 • MI • Prin • LHS Westland Westland MI • (734)422-2090 • (S 1980 MA)

**SCHWEINLER LOIS MARIE** (413)538-6951
705 Homestead Ave Holyoke MA 01040-1517 • locious333@hotmail.com • NE • Tchr • First Holyoke MA • (413)532-4272 • (S 1975)

**SCHWEIZER BARBARA** (704)252-1795
C/O Emmanuel Lutheran Church 51 Wilburn Pl Asheville NC 28806-2752 • SE • Tchr • Emmanuel Asheville NC • (828)252-1795 • (S 1989)

**SCHWENKHOFF MARY ANITA**
S4916 Golf Course Rd Rocksprings WI 53961-9735 • SW • Tchr • St Peter Reedsburg WI • (608)524-4066 • (SP 1965)

**SCHWERIN DANIEL P**
6010 Serene Run Lake Worth FL 33467-6559 • sschw525@aol.com • FG • 07/2000 • (RF 1982)

**SCOTT DEBORA HELEN V** (714)998-2023
2996 N Woods St Apt 10 Orange CA 92865-1249 • PSW • Tchr • St John Orange CA • (714)288-4400 • (IV 1988)

**SCOTT MABLELEAN D** (334)457-0947
3619 Owens St Mobile AL 36612-1137 • SO • P/Tchr • Trinity Mobile AL • (334)456-7929 • (S 1971 MED)

**SCOTT TINA M**
2049 Porte De Leau Ct Apt 202 Highland IN 46322-3724 • NI • Tchr • Northern Illinois Hillside IL • (S 1993)

**SCRIVEN JAMES ANTHONY** (209)334-2280
1800 W Pine St Lodi CA 95242-3147 • scrivster@aol.com • CNH • Tchr • St Peter Lodi CA • (209)333-2223 • (SP 1990)

**SEABORN JACQUELIN K** (410)592-6749
3909 Longmoor Cir Phoenix MD 21131-2108 • SE • Tchr • Baltimore LHS Baltimore MD • (410)825-2323 • (CQ 1990)

**SEACHMAN RUTH** (717)854-9040
1625 Old Farm Ln York PA 17403-4047 • SE • EM • (S 1976)

**SEARS CHRISTINE A**
119 Rice St #1 Little Rock AR 72205 • MDS • Tchr • Christ Little Rock AR • (501)663-5232 • (S 1994)

**SEBAN WENDY SUE**
358 Point Return Dr Apt # Ballwin MO 63021-4170 • MO • Tchr • St Paul Saint Louis MO • (314)822-0447 • (MQ 1996)

**SEBOLD MARCIA L** (313)462-9621
15561 Westbrook St Livonia MI 48154-2358 • MI • Tchr • Guardian Dearborn MI • (313)274-3665 • (S 1977)

**SEBOLDT EVERETT G** (562)692-6817
5456 Cadbury Rd Whittier CA 90601-2638 • seboldt@jps.net • PSW • EM • (RF 1951)

**SEBOLDT FRANKLIN O** (216)871-1609
26912 Osborn Rd Bay Village OH 44140-2346 • fseboldt@mail.n2net.net • OH • EM • (RF 1954 MA)

**SEEFELD MARILYN R** (414)358-2311
9828 W Green Tree Rd Milwaukee WI 53224-4669 • SW • Mem C • Our Redeemer Wauwatosa WI • (414)258-4555 • (S 1974)

**SEEHAFER MARY MARGARET**
608 Farwell Ave Antigo WI 54409-2321 • NW • Tchr • Peace Antigo WI • (715)623-2209 • (MQ 1987)

**SEELMAN CAROL A** (770)973-0876
1373 Merrifield Ln Marietta GA 30062-2068 • FG • Tchr • Faith Marietta GA • (770)973-8921 • (S 1970)

**SEEVERS GERALD A** (847)392-3193
1219 W Watling St Arlington Hts IL 60004-4557 • NI • EM • (S 1950 MA)

**SEEVERS JOHN J** (402)643-4703
1131 280th Seward NE 68434-7551 • NEB • EM • (S 1952 MPE DED)

**SEEVERS KENNETH F** (314)351-9317
4437 Taft Ave Saint Louis MO 63116-1535 • MO • EM • (S 1949 MEAD)

**SEEVERS SCOTT M** (330)864-8016
1842 Stabler Rd Akron OH 44313-6122 • seev44@neo.rr.com • OH • Tchr • Ohio Olmsted Falls OH • (S 1989 MSED)

**SEGERT RICHARD R** (708)757-4339
2255 207th Pl Lynwood IL 60411-1538 • NI • Tchr • St Paul Chicago Heights IL • (708)754-4492 • (RF 1975)

**SEGRIST LAISA** (909)685-9141
3134 Cabana St Mira Loma CA 91752-1395 • segrists@ccinet.com • PSW • Tchr • Loving Savior Chino Hills CA • (909)597-4668 • (IV 1994)

**SEIBEL DIANE L** (810)238-9516
642 Barrie Ave Flint MI 48507-1655 • MI • Tchr • St Michael Richville MI • (517)868-4809 • (S 1972)

**SEIBEL WALTER O** (573)651-8319
3120 Independence St Cape Girardeau MO 63703-5043 • MO • EM • (RF 1931 MED)

**SEIBERT MICHELLE ANN** (708)456-4651
9735 Sumac Rd Apt 417 Des Plaines IL 60016 • NI • Tchr • St Paul Chicago IL • (708)867-5044 • (RF 1993)

**SEIBERT RONALD J** (319)668-9238
1000 W Welsh St Williamsburg IA 52361-9514 • IE • Prin • Lutheran Interparish Williamsburg IA • (319)668-1711 • (S 1967 MS)

**SEIDER CANDYCE KAYE** (414)789-9124
2175 S Woodshire Dr New Berlin WI 53151-2302 • SW • SHS/C • South Wisconsin Milwaukee WI • (414)464-8100 • (S 1972 MSED)

**SEILER CHRISTINE R** (312)784-6359
4925 N Fairfield Ave Chicago IL 60625-2719 • wseilerjr@aol.com • EN • Tchr • Our Savior Chicago IL • (773)631-1606 • (RF 1978)

**SEILS ARDIS C** (773)238-1824
10331 S Christiana Ave Chicago IL 60655-2418 • NI • Tchr • St Paul Oak Lawn IL • (708)423-1040 • (RF 1990 MA)

**SEILS CYNTHIA E** (262)639-8603
1430 Melvin Ave Racine WI 53402-4152 • SW • Tchr • St Martini Milwaukee WI • (414)645-4094 • (RF 1988)

**SEIM DANIEL N** (503)693-6471
33495 SW Riedweg Rd Cornelius OR 97113-9651 • sandeim@aol.com • NOW • Prin • Forest Hills Cornelius OR • (503)359-4853 • (S 1965 MED)

**SEIM JOHN ROBERT** (402)362-5409
934 Valley View Ct York NE 68467-4512 • NEB • P/Tchr • Emmanuel York NE • (402)362-6575 • (S 1974 MED)

**SEITZ CONNIE S** (314)353-0157
7819 Benmore St Saint Louis MO 63123-3815 • MO • Tchr • Holy Cross Saint Louis MO • (314)771-9521 • (S 1977)

**SEITZ WAYNE A** (314)353-0157
7819 Benmore St Saint Louis MO 63123-3815 • seitzwas@stlnet.com • MO • 08/1999 • (S 1978)

**SELESKI DONALD E** (503)249-8162
4545 NE 125th Pl Apt 106 Portland OR 97230-1245 • NOW • Tchr • Trinity Portland OR • (503)288-6403 • (PO 1981)

**SELF LORI L** (970)663-5581
1312 Carlene Dr Loveland CO 80537-3707 • RM • Tchr • Immanuel Loveland CO • (970)667-7606 • (PO 1989)

**SELKING BARBARA J** (817)924-7034
2238 Mistletoe Blvd Fort Worth TX 76110-1130 • amselking@aol.com • TX • Tchr • St Paul Fort Worth TX • (817)332-4563 • (S 1978)

**SELLE JEAN E** (480)391-8474
11011 N 92nd St #1086 Scottsdale AZ 85260 • jeanselle@yahoo.com • NW • Tchr • St Paul Bonduel WI • (715)758-8559 • (S 1972)

**SELLE NATHAN P** (218)583-2267
RR 2 Box 291C Henning MN 56551 • npselle@hotmail.com • MNN • O Sp Min • Minnesota North Brainerd MN • (S 1996)

**SELLERS TAMMY LYNN** (248)435-5961
2445A Torquay Dr Apt 201 Royal Oak MI 48073 • MI • Tchr • Our Shepherd Birmingham MI • (248)646-6100 • (AA 1988)

**SELLKE CAROLYN R** (503)671-9926
550 NW 114th Ave Portland OR 97229-6134 • csellke@teleport.com • NOW • Tchr • Forest Hills Cornelius OR • (503)359-4853 • (RF 1961)

**SELLKE DAVID E** (440)843-2349
4410 Coral Gables Dr Parma OH 44134-6318 • dsellke.bls@iol13.com • OH • 09/1990 09/1999 • (RF 1979)

**SELLKE DONALD H** (612)490-0876
987 Tiller Ln Shoreview MN 55126-8151 • sellke@luther.csp.edu • MNS • SHS/C • Minnesota South Burnsville MN • (RF 1966 MSED DED)

**SELLMEYER DAVID P** (608)254-2258
732 Washington Ave Wisconsin Dells WI 53965-1545 • dsellmeyer@dellsnet.com • SW • P/Tchr • Trinity Wisconsin Dells WI • (608)253-3241 • (RF 1971 MA)

**SELLMEYER VIVIAN A** (608)254-2258
732 Washington Ave Wisconsin Dells WI 53965-1545 • dsellmeyer@dellsnet.com • SW • Tchr • Trinity Wisconsin Dells WI • (608)253-3241 • (RF 1971)

**SELMEYER DAVID A** (715)623-2074
230 Fairland St Antigo WI 54409-1037 • dselemey@antigoschools.k12.wi.us • NW • P/Tchr • Peace Antigo WI • (715)623-2209 • (RF 1969 MA)

**SELTZ ANNAMARY** (507)454-3576
517 E 4th St Winona MN 55987-4235 • MNS • Tchr • St Martins Winona MN • (507)452-6056 • (SP 1977 MS)

**SELTZ EMILY S**
7126 Indian Wells Dr Ypsilanti MI 48197-9559 • pseltz@aol.com • MI • Tchr • St Paul Flint MI • (810)239-6733 • (AA 1996)

**SEMLER ERIC JASON** (618)345-5947
143 Sky Line View Dr Collinsville IL 62234 • semler@worldspy.net • SI • Tchr • Good Shepherd Collinsville IL • (618)344-3153 • (S 1994)

**SENECHAL GEORGE D*** (507)932-5582
7 Lawrence Ln Saint Charles MN 55972-9300 • kgsenechal@juno.com • MNS • 10/1994 10/1999 • (S 1990 MA MS)

**SENECHAL JOHN W** (512)301-4108
6500 Clay Allison Pass Austin TX 78749 • senfrank@aol.com • TX • Prin • St Paul Austin TX • (512)472-3313 • (S 1966 MS)

**SENECHAL MARK D** (281)360-2710
3103 Silver Falls Dr Kingwood TX 77339-1938 • marks@christ-the-king.com • TX • Mem C • Christ King Kingwood TX • (281)360-7936 • (BR 1984 MMU)

**SENG REBEKAH JOY**
32 N Center Apt 1 Sebewaing MI 48759-1642 • bekahs@avci.net • MI • Tchr • Immanuel Sebewaing MI • (517)883-3050 • (AA 1994)

**SENGELE JOHN M** (913)334-9417
8305 Corona Ave Kansas City KS 66112-1701 • KS • EM • (RF 1957 MA)

**SENGELE MARK S** (618)345-5809
PO Box 13 Maryville IL 62062-0013 • mark.sengele@cph.org • MO • CCRA • Missouri Saint Louis MO • (314)317-4550 • (AA 1983 MAT)

**SENGELE MARY ANN** (913)334-9417
8305 Corona Ave Kansas City KS 66112-1701 • KS • EM • (RF 1957)

**SENGELE RICHARD C** (414)875-0923
3359 N 77th St Milwaukee WI 53222-3911 • SW • Tchr • Mount Olive Milwaukee WI • (414)774-2113 • (RF 1966 MA)

**SENKBEIL PETER LUCAS** (714)633-7971
1402 E Oakmont Ave Orange CA 92867 • senkbeil@cui.edu • PSW • SHS/C • Pacific Southwest Irvine CA • (949)854-3232 • (CQ 1997 MA PHD)

**SENNE ROGER P**
2329 N Glennwood St Orange CA 92865-3509 • PSW • Tchr • St John Orange CA • (714)288-4406 • (S 1963)

**SENSKE AL H DR** (314)822-7156
8738 Kathy Ct Saint Louis MO 63126-1813 • senske@stlnet.com • MO • EM • (S 1951 MA DED)
**SENSKE KURT MARTIN DR** (512)329-5557
1601 Shannon Oaks Trl Austin TX 78746-7348 • kurts@lsss.org • TX • Texas Austin TX • (CQ 1994 JD PHD)
**SENTESI MARY LOU** (281)376-1024
11206 Champion Wood Dr Tomball TX 77375-8341 • TX • Tchr • Trinity-Messiah Houston TX • (713)224-7265 • (RF 1969)
**SEPPA-GORWOOD SONJA L** (954)492-9656
5403 NE 22nd Ter Fort Lauderdale FL 33308-3228 • FG • Tchr • Peace Fort Lauderdale FL • (954)772-8010 • (RF 1980)
**SEPTEOWSKI DALE J DR** (708)953-1175
282 W 18th St Lombard IL 60148-6144 • crfsepteodj@crf.cuis.edu • NI • SHS/C • Northern Illinois Hillside IL • (RF 1973 MA DED)
**SEPTEOWSKI DAWN** (630)953-1175
282 W 18th St Lombard IL 60148-6144 • disept@mediaone.net • NI • Tchr • St John Lombard IL • (630)629-2515 • (RF 1973 MA)
**SERCK LEAH** (402)643-4851
158 E Hillcrest Dr Seward NE 68434-1336 • NEB • SHS/C • Nebraska Seward NE • (S 1958 MA DED)
**SERNETT GILBERT DR** (734)485-2976
2832 N Harris Rd Ypsilanti MI 48198-9608 • serneg@ccaa.edu • MI • SHS/C • Michigan Ann Arbor MI • (S 1967 MS SPA DED)
**SERRA DEBORAH LYNN** (630)372-9380
#6 - Glendale Ct Streamwood IL 60107 • NI • SHS/C • Northern Illinois Hillside IL • (RF 1986)
**SEVERSON BRENDA J** (217)258-6777
1001 S 15th St Mattoon IL 61938-5607 • CI • Tchr • St John Mattoon IL • (217)234-4911 • (RF 1978)
**SEVERSON DIANE L**
8100 Cypresswood Dr Apt 826 Spring TX 77379 • dlse@juno.net • TX • Tchr • Concordia LHS Tomball TX • (281)351-2547 • (SP 1981)
**SEVON MAIDA ROSE** (330)922-0001
1860 4th St Apt 3 Cuyahoga Falls OH 44221 • OH • Tchr • Redeemer Cuyahoga Falls OH • (330)923-1280 • (RF 1998)
**SEWING NANCY L** (712)263-8469
514 N 20th Denison IA 51442 • dsewing@frontiernet.net • IW • 10/1993 10/1999 • (SP 1976)
**SEYBOLD SHERYL A** (713)983-8321
7727 Woodland West Dr Houston TX 77040-2663 • TX • Tchr • Memorial Houston TX • (713)782-4022 • (S 1988)
**SHAFFER JENNIFER LYNN** (281)516-0922
30803 Mc Kinney Rd Tomball TX 77375-3006 • shaffer4th@hotmail.com • TX • Tchr • Salem Tomball TX • (281)351-8122 • (MQ 1993)
**SHAFFER JOHN O** (313)656-2935
971 Runyon Rd Rochester Hills MI 48306-4521 • MI • Tchr • St John Rochester MI • (248)652-8830 • (S 1974 MED)
**SHALTANIS PHAEDRA**
C/O Luth HS of Orange County 2222 N Santiago Blvd Orange CA 92867-2552 • PSW • St John Rochester MI • (MQ 1997)
**SHANE JULIE**
10707 Lake Crk Pkwy #115 Austin TX 78759-7444 • TX • Tchr • Redeemer Austin TX • (512)451-6478 • (S 1993)
**SHANE TONI L** (314)822-9447
653 Lewiston Dr Kirkwood MO 63122-3013 • MO • Tchr • Christ Community Kirkwood MO • (314)822-7774 • (CQ 1998 MAT)
**SHANKS ANETTE ANN** (615)885-4137
840 Chandler Grove Dr Hermitage TN 37076 • jashanks@home.com • MDS • 08/1990 08/2000 • (AA 1982 MA)
**SHARADIN DOLORES E** (503)288-3298
2635 NE Liberty St Portland OR 97211-5944 • NOW • EM • (RF 1969)
**SHARMAN LYLE D** (402)563-2247
2620 21st St Columbus NE 68601-3228 • NEB • Tchr • Immanuel Columbus NE • (402)564-8423 • (S 1970)
**SHARP DAVID F**
210 Pleasant St #3 Ionia MI 48846-1622 • MI • P/Tchr • Zion Hemlock MI • (517)642-2147 • (AA 1985)
**SHARP MARY K** (913)833-4115
5929 Greeley Rd Effingham KS 66023-5081 • KS • Tchr • Trinity Atchison KS • (913)367-4763 • (S 1962)
**SHARP RUTH ELIZABETH** (402)564-0892
1914 1st St Columbus NE 68601-7504 • rsharp@esu7.org • NEB • Tchr • Immanuel Columbus NE • (402)564-8423 • (S 1998)
**SHARPE WILLIAM L** (701)239-4218
2201 24th Ave S Fargo ND 58103-5119 • ndexec@aol.com • ND • North Dakota Fargo ND* • (S 1978 MED)
**SHAVER CAROLYN A** (956)781-2646
100 W Moore Rd Lot 57 Pharr TX 78577-6704 • shaverco@sprynet.com • TX • Tchr • St Paul Mc Allen TX • (956)682-2201 • (SP 1967)
**SHAW CAROL J** (847)543-8907
189 E Brittany Ln Grayslake IL 60030-1083 • NI • Tchr • St Matthew Lake Zurich IL • (847)438-6103 • (SP 1965)
**SHAW JULEE A** (517)780-7796
1901 Cortland Blvd Jackson MI 49203-1431 • MI • Tchr • Trinity Jackson MI • (517)750-2105 • (S 1980)
**SHEEHAN SANDRA A** (708)547-1355
152 S Orchard Ave Hillside IL 60162 • sheehansl@aol.com • NI • Tchr • Trinity Burr Ridge IL • (708)839-1200 • (RF 1996)
**SHEELY PAMELA** (618)826-2720
417 Riverview Blvd Chester IL 62233 • SI • Tchr • St John Chester IL • (618)826-4345 • (RF 1971)
**SHELBY KARLA L** (619)945-4342
843 Busch Dr Vista CA 92083-4528 • karla³shelby@hotmail.com • PSW • Tchr • Grace Escondido CA • (760)747-3029 • (PO 1989)
**SHELDON DAVID A** (810)954-0193
42994 Nebel Trl Clinton Township MI 48038-2456 • sheldondav@hotmail.com • MI • Mem C • Trinity Utica MI • (810)731-4490 • (S 1972 MA)
**SHELDON ERNEST L** (810)392-2301
34793 Sabin St # 596 Memphis MI 48041 • sheldon@klondyke.net • MI • EM • (RF 1949 MED)
**SHENTON KELLY SUE** (614)793-8170
5852 Rushwood Dr Dublin OH 43017-2252 • rshenton@hotmail.com • OH • 03/1999 • (AA 1989)
**SHEPPARD DUANE H** (520)343-2612
4211 W 13th St Yuma AZ 85364-4057 • PSW • Prin • Yuma Yuma AZ • (520)726-8410 • (IV 1985 MA)
**SHERIDAN DARINA LOUISE** (216)291-2793
1384 Plainfield Rd South Euclid OH 44121-2512 • OH • Tchr • St John Garfield Heights OH • (216)587-1752 • (RF 1972)
**SHERMAN RODNEY D** (562)941-6624
5722 E Stillwater #113 Orange CA 92869 • PSW • Tchr • Lutheran HS/Orange C Orange CA • (714)998-5151 • (IV 1997)
**SHERRILL SHARON L** (573)756-6886
20477 Straughn Rd Farmington MO 63640-7470 • msherril@fxnet.missouri.org • MO • Tchr • St Paul Farmington MO • (573)756-5147 • (S 1971)
**SHIDELER EILEEN K** (626)964-6636
2448 Flora St West Covina CA 91792-2162 • PSW • Tchr • Immanuel West Covina CA • (626)919-1072 • (S 1981)
**SHIELDS MARK J** (412)461-0584
1612 Greensprings Ave West Mifflin PA 15122-1560 • shields@genesis.cc.duq.edu • EA • Tchr • St Matthew Pittsburgh PA • (412)321-6662 • (RF 1986)
**SHIFFER WALTER C*** (630)960-0423
9 Wake Robin Ct Woodridge IL 60517 • NI • SHS/C • Northern Illinois Hillside IL • (CQ 1985 MED MA)
**SHILEY JONATHAN P** (219)485-1507
4792 Parkerdale Dr Fort Wayne IN 46835-1904 • shifive@prodigy.com • IN • Tchr • St Paul Fort Wayne IN • (219)424-0049 • (RF 1983)
**SHIMEK JILL MARIE** (216)476-3362
4637 W 146th St Cleveland OH 44135-4501 • OH • Tchr • LHS West Rocky River OH • (440)333-1660 • (RF 1984)
**SHINNO SHARI LYNN** (801)467-7441
860 Fairmont Cir #4 Salt Lake City UT 84106-1701 • RM • Tchr • Redeemer Salt Lake City UT • (801)487-6283 • (PO 1995)
**SHIPLER KIRK ALLAN** (612)657-1417
209 2nd St NW Mayer MN 55360 • shipler@hutchtel.net • MNS • 09/1999 • (SP 1997)
**SHIPLER TRACY MARIE** (952)657-1417
209 2nd St NW Mayer MN 55360 • shipler@tcinternet.net • MNS • Tchr • Zion Mayer MN • (612)657-2339 • (SP 1996)
**SHIPLEY KIMBERLY K** (559)592-5490
420 Prospect Ave Exeter CA 93221-2115 • tkshipley@mindinfo.com • PSW • 09/1993 09/1999 • (RF 1988 MA)
**SHIRLEY ANGELA K** (931)520-4018
4136 Woodview Dr Cookeville TN 38501-0711 • tanman@multipro.com • MDS • Tchr • Heavenly Host Cookeville TN • (931)520-3766 • (RF 1996)
**SHIRLEY KAREN S** (419)382-5043
1559 Glenbrook Dr Toledo OH 43614-4012 • OH • Tchr • Trinity Toledo OH • (419)385-2301 • (RF 1975)
**SHOAF CHESTER W** (303)985-1852
659 S Swadley St Lakewood CO 80228-3341 • chetshoaf@home.com • RM • Tchr • Bethlehem Lakewood CO • (303)233-0401 • (S 1971 MEAD)
**SHOAF SUSAN E** (303)985-1852
659 S Swadley St Lakewood CO 80228-3341 • shoafc@power-online.net • RM • Tchr • Shepherd Of The Hill Littleton CO • (303)798-0711 • (S 1973 MS)
**SHOCKEY JOANN M** (952)944-5606
10510 Buckingham Dr Eden Prairie MN 55347-2942 • joannshockey@mn.rr.com • EA • 10/1987 10/1997 • (RF 1985)
**SHOEMAKER KAY E** (314)842-5775
12006 Southwick Dr Saint Louis MO 63128-1725 • MO • Tchr • Hope Saint Louis MO • (314)832-1850 • (RF 1978 MAT)
**SHOEMAKER MARY** (618)533-1019
617 Meadowbrook Ln Centralia IL 62801-4420 • gmshoe@juno.com • SI • EM • (RF 1953)
**SHOLLENBERGER SUSAN**
4465 W Orland Rd Angola IN 46703-8101 • IN • Tchr • Concordia Fort Wayne IN • (219)422-2429 • (RF 1985)
**SHORE VICKIE LYNN** (810)264-1655
36638 Clifford Dr Sterling Heights MI 48312-3119 • MI • 08/1999 • (AA 1995)
**SHORT JOY** (720)962-6924
3324 Field St #132 Lakewood CO 80227 • RM • Tchr • Trinity Denver CO • (303)934-6160 • (IV 1999)
**SHOUMAKER LISA K** (309)693-0270
6811 N Hunters Trce Peoria IL 61614-3013 • CI • Tchr • Concordia Peoria IL • (309)691-8921 • (S 1981)
**SHREVE JENNIE L** (502)633-3472
32 Cherokee Dr Shelbyville KY 40065-1912 • IN • Tchr • Our Savior Louisville KY • (502)426-0864 • (SP 1969 MA)
**SHULL TONY EUGENE** (931)528-6501
695 N Mc Broom Chapel Rd Cookeville TN 38501 • tcshull@usit.net • MDS • Tchr • Heavenly Host Cookeville TN • (931)526-3423 • (WN 1984)
**SICKLES DIANE L**
28345 S Streamwood Dr Beecher IL 60401-3408 • NI • Tchr • Zion Beecher IL • (708)946-2272 • (S 1974 MS)
**SIEBARTH MONICA LYNN** (414)535-1043
11015 W Hampton Ave Apt 1 Milwaukee WI 53225-3847 • moe15@milwpc.com • SW • Tchr • Milwaukee LHS Milwaukee WI • (414)461-6000 • (RF 1996)
**SIEFERT MICHAEL A** (904)288-0394
C/O St John Lutheran Church 1915 SE Lake Weir Rd Ocala FL 34471-5424 • FG • Tchr • St John Ocala FL • (352)629-1794 • (S 1974 MA JD)
**SIEFKER DOROTHY I** (313)538-7749
19443 Lancashire St Detroit MI 48223-1209 • MI • Tchr • Greenfld Peace Detroit MI • (313)838-3366 • (RF 1966)
**SIEFKER ROY D** (313)538-7749
19443 Lancashire St Detroit MI 48223-1209 • siefkerdulhs@msn.com • MI • Prin • Detroit Urban Detroit MI • (313)582-9900 • (RF 1966 MED)
**SIEGER BARBARA JEAN** (440)516-1872
29922 Enid Rd Wickliffe OH 44092 • OH • Tchr • St John Cleveland OH • (216)531-8204 • (RF 1982)
**SIEGER BRUCE W** (630)933-8063
614 Red Hill Trl Apt 2D Carol Stream IL 60188-1741 • NI • 08/1999 • (RF 1983 MA)
**SIEGER MARK W**
29922 Enid Rd Wickliffe OH 44092 • OH • Tchr • St John Cleveland OH • (216)531-8204 • (RF 1983)
**SIEGERT LAURA ANNE** (714)516-9054
160-G N Mine Canyon Rd Orange CA 92869-5850 • siegerts@earthlink.com • PSW • Tchr • St Paul Garden Grove CA • (714)534-6320 • (IV 1992)
**SIEGERT MARK WALTER** (714)662-1035
160 N Mine Canyon Rd Apt G Orange CA 92869-5850 • siegert@cui.edu • PSW • SHS/C • Pacific Southwest Irvine CA • (949)854-3232 • (CQ 1989 MED)
**SIEGMEIER SCOTT** (715)524-4032
1255 S Waukechon Apt 4 Shawano WI 54166 • siggy@ezwebtech.com • NW • Tchr • St James Shawano WI • (715)524-4213 • (MQ 1998)
**SIEKMANN LORI C** (630)653-6586
420 Arrowhead Trl Carol Stream IL 60188-1577 • crfsiekmalc@curf.edu • NI • SHS/C • Northern Illinois Hillside IL • (RF 1989 MA)
**SIEKMANN STEPHEN V** (920)465-0422
547 Edelweiss Dr Green Bay WI 54302-5115 • NW • Prin • LHS Assoc Of NE Wisc Green Bay WI • (920)469-6810 • (RF 1974 MA)
**SIEKMANN TIMOTHY C** (810)254-4132
8730 Cologne Dr Sterling Hts MI 48314-1636 • MI • Tchr • Trinity Utica MI • (810)731-4490 • (RF 1985 MSED)
**SIELAFF SARA J** (217)732-6839
1841 1235th Ave Lincoln IL 62656-5058 • CI • Tchr • Good Shepherd Pekin IL • (309)347-2020 • (RF 1985)
**SIEMERS ILENE V** (314)867-2818
624 Gleason Dr Saint Louis MO 63137-3314 • MO • Tchr • Grace Chapel Bellefontaine Nbrs MO • (314)867-6564 • (SP 1968)
**SIEMERS JOHN W** (916)388-1826
3126 Maryknoll Ct Sacramento CA 95826-3502 • PSW • EM • (S 1941)
**SIEVERS DAVID A** (708)894-3263
313 Catalpa Ave Roselle IL 60172-2403 • NI • Tchr • Trinity Roselle IL • (630)894-3263 • (RF 1992)
**SIEVERS RUTH MARIE** (773)925-4250
2949 W 86th St Chicago IL 60652-3825 • wsievers@aol.com • NI • Tchr • St Paul Oak Lawn IL • (847)423-1058 • (RF 1961 MA)
**SIEVERT AMY LYNN** (810)784-9492
73475 Floral St Armada MI 48005 • MI • Tchr • St John Rochester MI • (248)652-8830 • (S 1995)
**SIEVERT DANIEL MARK** (810)784-9492
73475 Floral St Armada MI 48005-3361 • dsievert@lhsa.com • MI • Tchr • LHS North Macomb MI • (810)781-9151 • (S 1994 MED)
**SIEVERT DAVID R**
5633 Frank Rd Frankenmuth MI 48734-1260 • MI • Tchr • St Lorenz Frankenmuth MI • (517)652-6141 • (S 1987 MMU)
**SIEVERT RAYMOND RICHARD** (253)874-1373
32616 8th Ave SW Federal Way WA 98023-4904 • church@stlukesfedway.com • NOW • Mem C • St Luke Federal Way WA • (253)941-3000 • (S 1959 MA MED)
**SIEVING CORNELIUS B** (618)327-3456
651 W Center St Nashville IL 62263-1559 • foxxc2@midwest.net • SI • EM • (RF 1949 MSED)
**SIEWERT DEAN K** (818)504-6407
10022 Roscoe Blvd Sun Valley CA 91352-3633 • PSW • Tchr • Zion Glendale CA • (818)243-3119 • (S 1985)
**SIMMER EHREN WILLIAM** (317)421-0968
1701 Morningside Dr - Apt C Shelbyville IN 46176 • IN • Tchr • Zion New Palestine IN • (317)861-5544 • (S 1997)
**SIMMONS BETH ANN**
3789 Savannah Rd Fremont CA 94538-6132 • CNH • Mem C • Mount Olive Milpitas CA • (408)262-0506 • (S 1988)
**SIMMONS JERRY L** (714)785-1623
3184 Racine Dr Riverside CA 92503-5338 • jerrys@lutheranhigh.orange.ca.us • PSW • Tchr • Lutheran HS/Orange C Orange CA • (714)998-5151 • (S 1960 MED)
**SIMMONS LAURA D**
USAMC Mannheim Unit 29920 Box TBA APO AE 09086-9920 • SE • 01/1995 • (BR 1987)
**SIMMONS LYNNETTE DAWN** (317)297-0304
6111 Hickorywood Dr Indianapolis IN 46224-3203 • rlsimm@prodigy.net • IN • Tchr • Our Shepherd Indianapolis IN • (317)271-9103 • (SP 1969 MS)
**SIMON JULIE A** (949)651-8395
72 Echo Run Irvine CA 92614 • PSW • Tchr • St Paul Garden Grove CA • (714)534-6320 • (IV 1996 MA)
**SIMON LAURA L** (210)684-8048
5335 Glen Ridge Dr Apt 2203 San Antonio TX 78229-5407 • TX • EM • (S 1958)

**SIMON LOIS E**
8425 S Harvest Ln Highlands Ranch CO 80126-3223 • RM • Tchr • Shepherd Of The Hill Littleton CO • (303)798-0711 • (S 1973)

**SIMONEAUX TRISHA LEE** (504)639-1525
936 Asheville Slidell LA 70458 • SO • Tchr • Prince Of Peace New Orleans LA • (504)242-4348 • (AU 2000)

**SIMPSON CAROLYN DERA** (310)370-8447
3724 Spencer St Apt 227 Torrance CA 90503-3251 • miscpooh@aol.com • PSW • Tchr • First Manhattan Beach CA • (310)545-5653 • (PO 1998)

**SIMPSON DONALD L** (626)335-3658
1157 Steffen St Glendora CA 91741-3736 • PSW • EM • (RF 1951 MA)

**SIMPSON PAMELA SUE** (402)488-7011
PO Box 33 Bee NE 68314-0033 • NEB • Tchr • St John Seward NE • (402)643-4535 • (S 1990)

**SIMS CAROLYN C** (949)837-3203
27042 Pinjara Cir Mission Viejo CA 92691-4444 • carolynsims@hotmail.com • PSW • Tchr • Abiding Savior Lake Forest CA • (949)830-1461 • (S 1966 MA)

**SIMS SUE E** (812)342-4840
5620 W 700 S Columbus IN 47201-4605 • IN • Tchr • Immanuel Seymour IN • (812)522-1301 • (RF 1984)

**SINGER CONNIE L** (517)871-2544
7475 Barkley Rd Vassar MI 48768-9633 • MI • Tchr • St Paul Millington MI • (517)871-4581 • (RF 1989)

**SINKOSKE SHARON LYNNE** (301)572-3923
13016 Bellevue St Beltsville MD 20705-3234 • chuckandsharon@erols.com • SE • Tchr • Concordia Hyattsville MD • (301)927-0266 • (RF 1969 MED)

**SIPE D ELAINE** (708)681-9820
209 Augusta St Maywood IL 60153-1028 • crfsipede@curf.edu • NI • SHS/C • Northern Illinois Hillside IL • (RF 1964 MA DED)

**SIREK KATHRYN J** (402)488-4390
5625 La Salle Lincoln NE 68516 • ksirek@lps.org • NEB • Tchr • Trinity Lincoln NE • (402)466-1800 • (S 1973)

**SITAS REBECCA LYNNE**
1596 Beechwood Monroe MI 48162 • MI • Tchr • Holy Ghost Monroe MI • (734)242-0509 • (RF 1997)

**SITAS WILLIAM JAY JR.** (734)384-1706
1596 Beechwood Monroe MI 48162 • MI • Tchr • Holy Ghost Monroe MI • (734)242-0509 • (RF 1997)

**SITZE CASEY C** (619)497-6945
1010 Lillian Ln El Cajon CA 92020 • jehn@hotmail.com • PSW • Tchr • Christ La Mesa CA • (619)462-5211 • (IV 1997)

**SIUDAK PAMELA S**
220 Elm St Antigo WI 54409 • NW • Tchr • Peace Antigo WI • (715)623-2209 • (MQ 1992 MS)

**SKIBBE ANNETTE K** (219)896-2471
3415 W 625 S North Judson IN 46366-8396 • IN • Tchr • St Peter North Judson IN • (219)896-5933 • (AA 1991 MBA)

**SKILTON JON C** (254)773-7676
203 Timberline Rd Temple TX 76502-3532 • ajskilton@aol.com • TX • Prin • Immanuel Temple TX • (254)773-9485 • (S 1985 MED)

**SKINNER ELIZABETH MARIE** (708)462-1825
2027 Richton Dr Wheaton IL 60187-8057 • NI • Prin • St John Wheaton IL • (630)668-0701 • (CQ 1992)

**SKINNER KIM M** (516)579-8677
2393 Cooper Dr East Meadow NY 11554-2601 • kimskinner@aol.com • AT • Tchr • Trinity Hicksville NY • (516)931-2211 • (BR 1987 MS)

**SKINNER SANDRA** (818)367-6611
13972 Sayre St Sylmar CA 91342-4262 • PSW • Tchr • First San Fernando CA • (818)361-4800 • (S 1976)

**SKOOG KAREN L** (970)242-2986
1130 Hill Ave Grand Junction CO 81501-3237 • RM • Tchr • Messiah Grand Junction CO • (970)245-2838 • (CQ 1984 MA)

**SKOV FREDRICA A** (805)569-1132
1043 Portesuello Ave Santa Barbara CA 93105-4616 • freddya274@aol.com • PSW • Mem C • Emanuel Santa Barbara CA • (805)687-3734 • (S 1964)

**SKOV NEIL M DR** (734)971-7763
2728 Cranbrook Rd Ann Arbor MI 48104-6516 • skovn@ccaa.edu • MI • SHS/C • Michigan Ann Arbor MI • (S 1969 MSCT MS EDD)

**SKRABANEK JANEL SUE** (719)579-6753
7220 B Manila Rd Fort Carson CO 80913-2224 • jskrabanek@aol.com • RM • Tchr • Immanuel Colorado Springs CO • (719)636-5011 • (AU 1994)

**SKRASTINS IGOR**
1153 10th St W Winona MN 55987 • skrastns@ncfcomm.com • MNS • Immanuel Colorado Springs CO • (RF 1978)

**SKROCKE JACQUELINE** (801)571-5156
12785 S 1300 E Draper UT 84020-9607 • RM • Tchr • Christ Murray UT • (801)266-8714 • (CQ 1996)

**SKUDA DEANNA** (954)943-9114
430 SW 18th Ct Pompano Beach FL 33060-9036 • dskuda@email.msn.com • FG • Tchr • Hope Pompano Beach FL • (954)942-2570 • (RF 1968)

**SKVARENINA JOSEPH L** (317)467-4835
523 N Swope St Greenfield IN 46140-1640 • IN • Tchr • LHS Of Indianapolis Indianapolis IN • (317)787-5474 • (CQ 1997 MED)

**SKYRM DONNA LEE** (216)581-8273
5211 E 98th St Garfield Heights OH 44125 • OH • Prin • St Mark Cleveland OH • (216)749-3545 • (CQ 1997 MEDADM)

**SLETTVEDT CAROL E** (415)681-0085
150 Everglade Dr San Francisco CA 94132-1208 • EN • Tchr • West Portal San Francisco CA • (415)665-6330 • (CQ 1987)

**SLOAN JO ANNE E** (714)993-4129
2866 Devonshire Ave Fullerton CA 92835-3008 • PSW • Tchr • Christ Brea CA • (714)529-2984 • (RF 1967)

**SLOTHOWER ELIZABETH** (402)895-1544
15668 Orchard Ave Omaha NE 68135-1042 • NEB • Tchr • Abundant Life Omaha NE • (402)592-8005 • (SP 1970)

**SLUPIK KATHY ELLEN** (773)792-2917
4848 N Merrimac Ave Chicago IL 60630-2914 • kslupik@juno.com • EN • Tchr • Bethesda Chicago IL • (312)743-0800 • (RF 1977)

**SMALL CHRISTINE R** (619)282-4561
2204 Felton St San Diego CA 92104-5614 • csmall@lutheranschool.org • PSW • Tchr • Christ La Mesa CA • (619)462-5211 • (S 1978)

**SMALLBECK ANN CAROLIN** (206)822-4669
13020 NE 113th St Kirkland WA 98033-4105 • NOW • EM • (S 1967)

**SMALLWOOD CAROL J** (714)638-9314
9126 Carl Ln Garden Grove CA 92844-2217 • cjsmallwood@hotmail.com • PSW • Tchr • St Paul Garden Grove CA • (714)534-6320 • (S 1970)

**SMIDT DONALD J** (714)971-8067
11842 Kathy Ln Garden Grove CA 92840-2530 • PSW • EM • (CQ 1977)

**SMITH ALICE E** 011-822-3142-1422
C/O Seoul Foreign School 55 Yonhi Dong Seoul 120-113 KOREA • aesmith@crusader.sfs-h.ac.kr • MI • O Miss • Michigan Ann Arbor MI • (RF 1964)

**SMITH BEVERLY J** (954)981-6288
3701 Jackson St Apt 405 Hollywood FL 33021-7442 • FG • EM • (RF 1960)

**SMITH BURGE C** (954)981-6288
3701 Jackson St Apt 405 Hollywood FL 33021-7442 • FG • EM • (RF 1958)

**SMITH CARLENE N** (714)635-2726
837 S Lemon St Anaheim CA 92805-4608 • PSW • Tchr • Zion Anaheim CA • (714)535-3600 • (S 1979 MA)

**SMITH CHARLES E** (812)524-0531
1285 Jackson Park Dr - Apt A Seymour IN 47274 • IN • Tchr • Immanuel Seymour IN • (812)522-1301 • (AA 1999)

**SMITH DAVID WAYNE** (412)829-9293
2049 McKinney Dr Monroeville PA 15146-3922 • EN • Tchr • Redeemer Oakmont PA • (412)828-9323 • (S 1997)

**SMITH DONNA ANN** (317)884-0278
1140B Paradise Ct Greenwood IN 46143-2106 • IN • Tchr • Calvary Indianapolis IN • (317)783-2305 • (AA 1988)

**SMITH ERIK EDWIN**
940 Troost Forest Park IL 60130 • NI • Tchr • Grace Chicago IL • (773)762-1234 • (RF 1995)

**SMITH GARTH J** (708)423-8437
8948 S Mozart Evergreen Park IL 60805 • NI • 06/1999 • (SP 1987)

**SMITH GENE T** (414)242-9520
4829 W Hiawatha Dr Mequon WI 53092-4744 • gene3smith@cuw.edu • SW • SHS/C • South Wisconsin Milwaukee WI • (414)464-8100 • (RF 1966 MA MLS)

**SMITH JAMES F** (219)422-9791
1316 Kensington Blvd Fort Wayne IN 46805-5320 • IN • Prin • Bethlehem Fort Wayne IN • (219)456-3587 • (RF 1968 MA)

**SMITH JOANIE LYNN** (847)566-7297
6777 Creekside Long Grove IL 60047 • jebsmith@aol.com • NI • 07/1998 07/2000 • (RF 1989)

**SMITH KEVIN G** (714)635-2726
837 S Lemon St Anaheim CA 92805-4608 • smith@lhsoc.org • PSW • Tchr • Lutheran HS/Orange C Orange CA • (714)998-5151 • (S 1979 MSED)

**SMITH LISA M**
866 Tamarac Blvd Addison IL 60101-1697 • NI • Tchr • St Paul Melrose Park IL • (708)343-5000 • (RF 1992)

**SMITH LISA R**
5241 Regency Dr Columbus IN 47203-4135 • IN • Tchr • St Peter Columbus IN • (812)372-5266 • (AA 1993)

**SMITH LORI ELIZABETH** (513)573-0515
C/O Zion Lutheran Church 7401 Winkler Rd Fort Meyers FL 33919-7155 • OH • Tchr • King Of Kings Mason OH • (513)398-6089 • (RF 1985)

**SMITH MARGARET E** (308)237-7280
4306 Linden Dr Kearney NE 68847-2510 • NEB • Tchr • Zion Kearney NE • (308)234-3410 • (S 1964)

**SMITH MARY BETHANY** (517)892-1997
1900 S Warner St Bay City MI 48706-5268 • MI • Tchr • Zion Bay City MI • (517)893-5793 • (AA 1989)

**SMITH MARY C** (910)794-1348
3300 Greyleaf Wilmington NC 28409 • NE • Tchr • First Holyoke MA • (413)534-7071 • (SP 1984)

**SMITH MARY E** (219)749-2548
1915 Forest Valley Dr Fort Wayne IN 46815 • IN • Tchr • Woodburn Woodburn IN • (219)632-5493 • (RF 1991)

**SMITH MARYGENE E**
4545 N 92nd St #2222 Milwaukee WI 53225-4807 • marygenesmith@yahoo.com • AT • 11/1999 • (MQ 1987)

**SMITH MICHELLE ANN** (313)281-3032
15552 Clovernook Apt C Grand Haven MI 49417 • MI • Tchr • St John Grand Haven MI • (616)842-4510 • (RF 1994)

**SMITH MICHELLE ELIZABETH**
37741 S 59th Rd Blue Springs NE 68318 • NEB • 02/1999 • (S 1991)

**SMITH REBECCA**
900 NW 37th St Blue Springs MO 64015-2504 • MO • Tchr • Messiah Independence MO • (816)254-9405 • (S 1999)

**SMITH RICHARD L** (402)562-5402
3805 27th St #1 Columbus NE 68601 • rs63408@alltel.net • NEB • 08/2000 • (S 1978 MED)

**SMITH ROY W**
15776 W Amelia Dr Goodyear AZ 85338-8756 • NI • EM • (S 1961)

**SMITH SANDRA LEE** (630)773-1022
455 George St Itasca IL 60143-2178 • NI • Tchr • St John Lombard IL • (630)629-2515 • (RF 1969 MA)

**SMITH SUSAN MARIE** (217)352-5468
1522 W Clark St Champaign IL 61821-3152 • CI • Tchr • St John Champaign IL • (217)359-1123 • (RF 1995)

**SMUKOWSKI THERESA**
303 Cottage St Merrill WI 54452-1843 • NW • Tchr • St John Merrill WI • (715)536-7264 • (MQ 1993)

**SNELL WENDY L** (307)634-5242
Trinity Luth Church 1111 E 22nd St Cheyenne WY 82001-3932 • snellwendy@aol.com • WY • Tchr • Trinity Cheyenne WY • (307)635-2802 • (S 1981)

**SNIDER CHARLES A** (319)223-5451
17 C Ave Newhall IA 52315 • IE • Tchr • Central Newhall IA • (319)223-5271 • (S 1974 MSED)

**SNOW CURTIS D** (920)361-3794
152 E Marquette St Berlin WI 54923-1225 • cjsnow@vbe • SW • P/Tchr • St John Berlin WI • (920)361-0555 • (SP 1981 MS)

**SNOW MICHELE RENEE** (281)350-5688
22719 Bay Leaf Spring TX 77373-6401 • mmsnow@freewwweb.com • TX • Tchr • Salem Tomball TX • (281)351-8122 • (CQ 1994)

**SNURKA NANCY C** (303)471-9794
9848 S Bathurst Way Highlands Ranch CO 80126-7183 • sothpri@aol.com • RM • Tchr • Shepherd Of The Hill Littleton CO • (303)798-0711 • (RF 1965 MA)

**SNYDER FREDERICK E** (219)436-3283
318 Nordale Dr Fort Wayne IN 46804-1030 • IN • Tchr • St John Monroeville IN • (219)639-6404 • (RF 1968)

**SNYDER GEORGE H** (920)361-1187
396 SW Ceresco St Berlin WI 54923-1745 • racecar@vbe.com • SW • Tchr • St John Berlin WI • (920)361-0555 • (RF 1971 MA)

**SNYDER JOSEPH M** (314)477-0703
13 Rippling Water Ct Saint Charles MO 63303-2950 • joesnyder@cphnet.org • MO • CCRA • Missouri Saint Louis MO • (314)317-4550 • (RF 1981 MA)

**SNYDER LINDA J** (314)842-2436
9078 Crest Oak Ln Crestwood MO 63126-2444 • MO • Tchr • Christ Community Kirkwood MO • (314)822-7774 • (RF 1964 MA)

**SNYDER RONALD A** (618)282-2855
10250 Elm Shade Rd Red Bud IL 62278-4624 • SI • EM • (RF 1955 MAR)

**SOAT MARY P** (414)650-1134
300 W North St Apt 91 Waukesha WI 53188-5162 • SW • Tchr • Beautiful Savior Waukesha WI • (414)542-6558 • (MW 1980)

**SOCHOWSKI MARK D*** (910)725-1651
2166 New Castle Dr Winston Salem NC 27103-5763 • SE • Tchr • St John Winston-Salem NC • (336)725-1651 • (RF 1983)

**SODEMANN BETTY J** (414)786-4840
14100 W Glendale Dr New Berlin WI 53151-3012 • EN • Tchr • Hales Corners Hales Corners WI • (414)529-6701 • (MW 1982)

**SODEMANN PATRICIA A** (414)425-6599
13495 W Edgewood Ave New Berlin WI 53151 • EN • Tchr • Hales Corners Hales Corners WI • (414)529-6701 • (S 1976)

**SOEKEN VERNON E** (309)786-3667
2119 29th St Rock Island IL 61201-5023 • vksoek@qconline.com. • CI • P/Tchr • Immanuel Rock Island IL • (309)788-8242 • (S 1962 MED)

**SOENKSEN STEPHANIE SUE** (763)574-9436
159 63 1/2 Lane NE Fridley MN 55432 • claudia@maf.org • MNS • Tchr • Trinity Lone Oak Eagan MN • (651)454-1139 • (S 1992)

**SOHL JAMES R** (608)742-3678
431 E Albert St Portage WI 53901-1413 • jsohl@jvlnet.com • SW • Prin • St John Portage WI • (608)742-4222 • (S 1970 MED)

**SOHN DAVID L**
C/O LHS Of Orange County 2222 N Santiago Blvd Orange CA 92867-2552 • PSW • St John Portage WI • (S 1981 MA)

**SOHN LAWRENCE E** (414)873-6813
3063 N 53rd St Milwaukee WI 53210-1618 • lawrence.sohn@cuw.edu • SW • SHS/C • South Wisconsin Milwaukee WI • (414)464-8100 • (RF 1959 MED DED)

**SOHN MIRIAM LOUISE** (517)694-3248
2145 Aspenwood Dr Holt MI 48842-8725 • msohn@oursaviorchurch.org • MI • Tchr • Our Savior Lansing MI • (517)882-3550 • (S 1973 MA)

**SOHNS JULIA ANN** (254)420-4300
312 Hedrick Dr Hewitt TX 76643 • TX • Tchr • Trinity Waco TX • (817)772-4225 • (CQ 1999)

**SOKOLOWSKI JANET** (909)278-9697
1241 New England Dr Corona CA 91719-8308 • PSW • 06/1999 • (IV 1986)

**SOLHEIM CHRISTINE R** (707)838-8434
7088 Hastings Pl Windsor CA 95492-8760 • christychi@msn.com • CNH • Tchr • St Luke Santa Rosa CA • (707)545-0526 • (CQ 1984)

**SOLLENBERGER JAMES W** (812)376-9034
3285 Forsythia Dr Columbus IN 47203-2931 • IN • Tchr • St Luke Santa Rosa CA • (S 1976 MSED)

**SOLLENBERGER RETA M** (561)488-5513
10056 Country Brook Rd Boca Raton FL 33428-4216 • FG • Tchr • St Paul Boca Raton FL • (561)395-8548 • (CQ 1980)

**SOLLENERGER KAREN A**
3285 Forsythia Dr Columbus IN 47203-2931 • IN • Tchr • St Peter Columbus IN • (812)372-5266 • (RF 1977 MED MSED)

**SOMBKE DELORIS** (317)375-1956
1654 Justin Ct Indianapolis IN 46219-8505 • IN • Tchr • Trinity Indianapolis IN • (317)897-0243 • (S 1964 MS)
**SOMBKE KRISTIE L** (317)774-1557
10572 Talisman Dr Noblesville IN 46060-7623 • bksombke@iquest.net • IN • Mem C • Family Of Christ Fishers IN • (317)594-9157 • (S 1989)
**SOMMER BETH ALISON** (530)672-2040
3600 Santos Cir Cameron Park CA 95682-8210 • absommer@jps.net • CNH • Tchr • Trinity Fairfield CA • (707)425-2944 • (IV 1988 MA)
**SOMMER THOMAS C** (219)422-4200
823 Archer Ave Fort Wayne IN 46808-2320 • IN • P/Tchr • Bethlehem Ossian IN • (219)597-7366 • (RF 1970)
**SOMMERER SAMUEL ERIC** (314)724-1487
2003 Sibley St Saint Charles MO 63301-1659 • sommerer@stlnet.com • MO • Tchr • Immanuel Saint Charles MO • (636)946-0051 • (S 1992 MA)
**SOMMERFELD GENE W** (701)239-9327
1738 10th St S Fargo ND 58103-4912 • gracesch@farg.uswest.net • ND • P/Tchr • Grace Fargo ND • (701)232-7747 • (S 1970 MED)
**SOMMERMEYER DAVID A** (713)827-7564
2102 Southwick St Houston TX 77080-6306 • dsommermeyer@msn.com • TX • Tchr • Texas Austin TX • (S 1966 MA)
**SONLITNER GLENN R** (630)983-9198
449 Kensington Ct Naperville IL 60563-2445 • NI • Tchr • Bethany Naperville IL • (630)355-6607 • (RF 1969 MA)
**SONNENBERG E STEVEN** (949)443-1151
PO Box 4657 San Clemente CA 92674-4657 • essonn@flash.net • PSW • 09/1980 09/1997 • (S 1964 MS MS)
**SONNTAG ANNETTE M** (402)738-8519
8113 S 40th St Bellevue NE 68147-1836 • NEB • P/Tchr • Zion Omaha NE • (402)731-1418 • (S 1974)
**SONNTAG JUDITH RAE** (507)283-9865
1020 N Jackson St Luverne MN 56156-1104 • stjohn.2@rconnect.com • MNS • Tchr • Little Lambs Luverne MN • (507)283-2316 • (S 1968)
**SONSTROEM GWENDOLYN K** (414)425-4645
5205 S Menard Dr New Berlin WI 53151-8169 • EN • Tchr • Hales Corners Hales Corners WI • (414)529-6701 • (RF 1974)
**SONSTROEM ROLLAND R** (414)425-4645
5205 S Menard Dr New Berlin WI 53151-8169 • EN • EM • (RF 1957)
**SOPKO DARLENE K** (605)332-8904
217 E 41st St Sioux Falls SD 57105-5833 • msopko@msn.com • SD • Tchr • Sioux Falls Sioux Falls SD • (605)335-1923 • (S 1969)
**SOPKO MARVIN L** (605)332-8904
217 E 41st St Sioux Falls SD 57105-5833 • msopko@msn.com • SD • Tchr • Sioux Falls Sioux Falls SD • (605)335-1923 • (S 1968)
**SOPPE REBECA S** (402)933-1517
3936 R St Omaha NE 68107-3119 • beckyandallyn@earthlink.net • NEB • Tchr • Zion Omaha NE • (402)731-1418 • (S 1998)
**SORENSEN DEBRA ALICE** (503)492-0298
1092 SE 21st Ct Gresham OR 97080-7256 • NOW • Tchr • Portland Portland OR • (503)667-3199 • (PO 1992)
**SORENSON KARL E** (708)771-5031
7225 Thomas #1-E River Forest IL 60305-1515 • NI • EM • (RF 1960 MA)
**SORGATZ JAMES F** (901)737-4850
1589 Tern Rest Cv Cordova TN 38018-8730 • mdsjsorg@aol.com • MDS • Mid-South Cordova TN • (RF 1967 MA)
**SOSNOWSKI JENNIFER JOY** (630)907-1058
1581 Hawksley Ln North Aurora IL 60542 • NI • Tchr • Our Savior Carol Stream IL • (630)830-4851 • (RF 1996)
**SOUCEK AMBER** (402)332-5207
321 Bryan St Gretna NE 68028 • NEB • 08/1998 • (S 1998)
**SOUZA CONNIE R** (417)623-7088
1811 S Saint Louis Ave Joplin MO 64804-0962 • souzanna59@hotmail.com • MO • Tchr • Martin Luther Joplin MO • (417)624-1403 • (SP 1973)
**SOUZA WILLIAM F JR.** (417)623-7088
1811 S Saint Louis Ave Joplin MO 64804-0962 • billsouza@hotmail.com • MO • P/Tchr • Martin Luther Joplin MO • (417)624-1403 • (SP 1973 MS)
**SPANGLER JOHN L** (516)626-1197
131 Brookville Rd Brookville NY 11545 • jlswed@cs.com • AT • Tchr • Long Island Brookville NY • (516)626-1700 • (MQ 1996)
**SPANGLER KIMBERLY A** (314)397-6670
36 Glenwood Ln Saint Peters MO 63376-2049 • MO • Tchr • Our Savior Saint Charles MO • (636)947-8010 • (RF 1983)
**SPATZ CAROL J**
700 N 10th St Apt 4 Oostburg WI 53070 • SW • Tchr • St John Port Washington WI • (414)284-2131 • (RF 1982)
**SPAULDING KIMBERLY N**
612 Boxwood - Apt 22 Cape Girardeau MO 63701 • MO • Tchr • Trinity Cape Girardeau MO • (573)334-1068 • (S 2000)
**SPEAR ABIGAIL L** (310)541-7545
6600 Beachview Dr Apt 204 Rancho Palos Verdes CA 90275-5840 • aspear@clschool.org • PSW • Tchr • Good Shepherd Downey CA • (562)803-4459 • (S 1991 MA)
**SPECKHARD JOHN W** (314)894-0757
4655 Concord Oaks Dr Saint Louis MO 63128-1424 • 70176.1140@compuserve.com • EN • English Farmington MI • (RF 1959 MA)
**SPENCER MARGARET A** (517)784-4634
844 Lincoln St Jackson MI 49202-3281 • MI • 06/1999 • (RF 1974 MA)
**SPENNER CYNTHIA H** (618)493-6153
12163 Northprairie Rd Nashville IL 62263-3009 • cspenner@isbe.accessus.net • SI • Tchr • Trinity Hoffman IL • (618)495-2246 • (CQ 1998)
**SPIEGEL RHEA ANN** (512)990-1769
605 Cornell Dr Pflugerville TX 78660-4756 • TX • Tchr • St Paul Austin TX • (512)472-8301 • (CQ 1999)
**SPIELER CATHY M**
336 Todd Ln Belleville IL 62221 • SI • Tchr • Zion Belleville IL • (618)234-0275 • (S 1971)
**SPIELER GARY A**
336 Todd Ln Belleville IL 62221 • SI • Prin • Zion Belleville IL • (618)234-0275 • (S 1971)
**SPIESS KRISTINE ALICE** (651)772-1925
394 Kennard St Saint Paul MN 55106-6110 • krisspiess@aol.com • MNS • Tchr • Hand In Hand Saint Paul MN • (651)641-8491 • (SP 1985 MMFC)
**SPIETH RENEE ELAINE** (219)639-3111
15424 Minnich Rd Hoagland IN 46745-9707 • reneew@rexnet.net • IN • Tchr • Concordia Fort Wayne IN • (219)426-9922 • (RF 1994)
**SPILKER RUTH ANN** (618)483-3414
6339 N 475th St Altamont IL 62411 • CI • Tchr • Altamont Altamont IL • (618)483-6428 • (CQ 1995)
**SPILKER VERNON R** (618)483-3414
6339 N 475th St Altamont IL 62411-9720 • CI • Mem C • Immanuel Altamont IL • (618)483-6395 • (RF 1969)
**SPINNER DONNA L** (217)877-5956
1584 E Barrington Ave Decatur IL 62526-2702 • spindad1@aol.com • CI • Tchr • Lutheran School Asso Decatur IL • (217)233-2001 • (RF 1964)
**SPITZACK JAMES R** (612)866-1787
6245 3rd Ave S Richfield MN 55423-1626 • jrsbrs@juno.com • MNS • Tchr • Mount Calvary Richfield MN • (612)869-9441 • (S 1965 MA)
**SPITZER BETH ELLEN** (605)745-4876
RR 1 Box 100-AA Hot Springs SD 57747-9402 • spitfire@gwtc.net • SD • Tchr • Bethesda Hot Springs SD • (605)745-6676 • (CQ 1996)
**SPITZER JAMES R** (414)543-2733
2400 S 80th St West Allis WI 53219-1722 • spitz22@mixcom.com • SW • Tchr • Oklahoma Avenue Milwaukee WI • (414)543-3580 • (RF 1971)
**SPIVA DANIEL F** (805)239-4189
1959 Tulipwood Dr Paso Robles CA 93446-4469 • schooloffice@tcsu.net • CNH • P/Tchr • Trinity Paso Robles CA • (805)238-0335 • (S 1985)
**SPLETZER EDGAR R** (507)964-2954
33605 Jessenland Rd Henderson MN 56044 • MNS • EM • (RF 1941 MA)
**SPLITTGERBER ANTHONY BRIAN** (970)330-2485
3000 35th Ave Greeley CO 80634 • RM • Tchr • Trinity Greeley CO • (970)330-1203 • (S 2000)
**SPLITTGERBER LISA ROSE** (970)330-2485
3000 35th Ave Greeley CO 80634 • RM • Tchr • Trinity Greeley CO • (970)330-1203 • (S 2000)
**SPOHN CHRISTINE A** (419)385-4382
4057 Autumn View Ct Toledo OH 43614-3330 • espohn@buckeye-express.com • OH • Tchr • Trinity Toledo OH • (419)385-2301 • (RF 1972 MED)
**SPOHRER MICHELLE M** (713)784-8044
2301 Lazy Hollow #485A Houston TX 77063 • TX • Tchr • Memorial Houston TX • (713)782-6079 • (AA 1999)
**SPRECHER CHRISTINE H** (319)688-9787
910 W Benton St #D105 Iowa City IA 52246 • NEB • 12/1999 • (S 1998)
**SPRECHER SHEILA ANN** (414)466-8459
4021 N 91st St Milwaukee WI 53222 • SW • Tchr • Divine Redeemer Hartland WI • (414)367-8400 • (MQ 2000)
**SPREHE RAYMOND H** (217)394-2218
PO Box 75 Buckley IL 60918-0075 • CI • EM • (RF 1946 MED MS)
**SPREHE RONDA S** (618)243-6335
PO Box 217 Okawville IL 62271 • SI • Tchr • Immanuel Okawville IL • (618)243-6142 • (RF 2000)
**SPRENGEL CHARISE LYNN** (713)991-7157
11126 Bradford Way Houston TX 77075 • TX • Tchr • Lutheran South Acade Houston TX • (281)464-9320 • (S 1995)
**SPRENGEL NATHAN S** (281)464-7452
11126 Bradford Way St Houston TX 77075-2423 • TX • Tchr • Lutheran South Acade Houston TX • (281)464-9320 • (S 1997)
**SPRENGEL ROGER A** (309)691-8921
6505 N Talisman Ter Peoria IL 61615 • CI • Lutheran South Acade Houston TX • (S 1973 MS)
**SPRENGELER CATHY S** (515)432-9511
1424 1st St Boone IA 50036-4323 • IW • Tchr • Trinity Boone IA • (515)432-6912 • (RF 1982)
**SPRENGELER ELTON F** (515)573-4892
1224 4th Ave S Fort Dodge IA 50501-4823 • IW • EM • (RF 1952 MED)
**SPRING JOHN E** (516)794-3757
1935 Bly Rd East Meadow NY 11554-1112 • brinclhof@excite.com • AT • Tchr • Trinity Hicksville NY • (516)931-2211 • (RF 1974 MA)
**SPRINGER AMY MARIE** (920)485-0936
703B Horicon St #11 Horicon WI 53032 • springer@internetwis.com • SW • Tchr • St Stephen Horicon WI • (920)485-6687 • (SP 1997)
**SPRINGER HANS G** (636)861-7229
1115 Oakleaf Cove Ct Fenton MO 63026-7000 • hgs007@aol.com • MO • S Ex/S • Missouri Saint Louis MO • (314)317-4550 • (BR 1977 MPS)
**SPRINGER JAMES A** (219)489-4016
4815 Foxgrove Ave Fort Wayne IN 46818-2029 • IN • Tchr • St Peter Fort Wayne IN • (219)749-5811 • (RF 1966 MSED MA)
**SPRINGER JANICE R** (618)826-3830
303 Ben St Chester IL 62233-2235 • SI • Tchr • Zion Belleville IL • (618)234-0275 • (S 1973 MED)
**SPRINGER JOEL WILLIAM*** (319)359-8492
2613 E High St Davenport IA 52803-3440 • IE • Tchr • Trinity Davenport IA • (319)322-5224 • (RF 1993)
**SPRINGER MARIE E** (636)861-7229
1115 Oakleaf Cove Ct Fenton MO 63026-7000 • MO • Tchr • Hope High Ridge MO • (636)677-8788 • (RF 1965)
**SPRINGER MATTHEW J** (314)966-0532
741 W Lockwood Glendale MO 63122-4611 • mmspringer@stlnet.com • MO • Tchr • Word Of Life Saint Louis MO • (314)832-1244 • (RF 1987 MA)
**SPRINGER SHERYL LYNN** (319)359-8492
2613 E High St Davenport IA 52803-3440 • IE • Tchr • Trinity Davenport IA • (319)323-8001 • (RF 1991)
**SPROW KEITH ROBERT** (810)725-9024
33602 Bayview Dr New Baltimore MI 48047-2087 • MI • Tchr • LHS East Harper Woods MI • (313)371-8750 • (S 1971)
**SPURGAT FRED** (708)386-8129
1123 Miller Ave Oak Park IL 60302-1633 • spurgat@curf.edu • NI • EM • (RF 1952 MBA PHD)
**SQUIER NIKI L** (702)731-3820
5370 E Craig Rd Apt 2349 Las Vegas NV 89115-2530 • squiern@juno.com • PSW • Tchr • Redeemer Las Vegas NV • (702)642-6144 • (SP 1997)
**ST CLAIR GARY LYNN** (414)457-2118
1826 Lily Ct Sheboygan WI 53081-8465 • stclair@lutheranhigh.com • SW • Tchr • Lutheran HS Sheboygan WI • (920)452-3323 • (RF 1976 MED)
**ST MARTIN RUBY A**
35 Blackwell Jacksonville AR 72076 • MDS • P/Tchr • Hope Jacksonville AR • (501)982-1333 • (SP 1965 MA)
**ST PETERS CYNTHIA M** (618)467-8822
4912 Paris Dr Godfrey IL 62035-1616 • SI • Tchr • Faith Godfrey IL • (618)466-9153 • (RF 1989)
**STAAKE LINDA SUE** (714)974-0994
7310 Calle Granada Anaheim CA 92808 • hillsres@aol.com • PSW • Tchr • Hephatha Anaheim CA • (714)637-4022 • (RF 1970 MS)
**STACKHOUSE MELYNDA E**
235 Lincolnshire Dr Crystal Lake IL 60014 • NI • Tchr • St Matthew Lake Zurich IL • (847)438-6103 • (RF 1995)
**STADE LISA A** (909)428-5969
5387 Wagon Way Fontana CA 92336 • PSW • Tchr • St John Covina CA • (626)915-2122 • (IV 1987)
**STADLER RICHARD L**
3301 SE 56th Ter Ocala FL 34471 • FG • Tchr • St John Ocala FL • (352)629-1794 • (RF 1968 MED)
**STAEHR BRIAN TODD** (417)235-8818
222 N Main Freistatt MO 65654 • MO • Tchr • Trinity Freistatt MO • (417)235-5931 • (S 1994)
**STAFFORD JILL RENEE** (407)737-8678
3236 Arden Villas Blvd #18 Orlando FL 32817 • FG • 08/1997 08/1999 • (RF 1992)
**STAHL KATHRYN**
5400 Williams Blvd #4302 Tucson AZ 85711 • EN • Tchr • Faith Tucson AZ • (520)881-0670 • (AA 1999)
**STALLMAN RONALD H** (219)266-7116
1638E Cobblestone Blvd Elkhart IN 46514 • ron@trinityl.org • IN • Mem C • Trinity Elkhart IN • (219)522-1491 • (RF 1962 MA)
**STALLWORTH WILLIE P** (314)261-7750
6160 Lucille Ave Saint Louis MO 63136-4839 • MO • S Ex/S • Missouri Saint Louis MO • (314)317-4550 • (S 1983 MA)
**STAM CONNIE JEAN** (507)775-2867
942 1st Ave NW Byron MN 55920-1410 • MNS • Tchr • Rochester Central Rochester MN • (507)289-3267 • (SP 1968)
**STAMM JOANNE R** (217)796-3386
409 N Logan PO Box 107 Chestnut IL 62518-0107 • CI • Tchr • Zion Lincoln IL • (217)732-3977 • (RF 1963)
**STAMP ELLEN J** (972)394-6322
3715 Remington Dr Carrollton TX 75007-2840 • TX • Tchr • Holy Cross Dallas TX • (214)358-4396 • (S 1982 MED)
**STANDIFORD NANCY LORRAINE** (517)792-1133
6306 Dewhirst Dr Saginaw MI 48603-7369 • MI • Tchr • Peace Saginaw MI • (517)792-2581 • (RF 1960)
**STANGE KATHLEEN SUSAN** (515)222-6963
1362 NW 90th St Clive IA 50325-6240 • kathys5050@aol.com • IW • Tchr • MT Olive Des Moines IA • (515)277-0247 • (S 1970)
**STANHOPE DEBRA G** (707)966-4126
314 Carlson Way Napa CA 94558-9636 • dstanhop@napanet.net • CNH • Tchr • St John Napa CA • (707)226-7970 • (S 1976)
**STANLEY LISA SUE**
211 N Chilson Bay City MI 48706 • MI • Tchr • St Paul Bay City MI • (517)686-7140 • (AA 1986)
**STANLEY SHARON J** (760)746-2161
1411 Archwood Pl Escondido CA 92026-2749 • PSW • Tchr • Grace Escondido CA • (760)747-3029 • (S 1977)
**STARK KIMBERLY LEIGH** (281)485-5647
2902 Whispering Winds #310 Pearland TX 77581 • TX • 07/1999 • (S 1995)
**STARK MURIEL L** (952)447-8949
7140 Casey Pkwy Prior Lake MN 55372-2608 • mgstark1@juno.ocm • MNS • Tchr • Our Savior Excelsior MN • (612)474-9710 • (SP 1972)
**STARK PAUL ANDREW** (281)485-5647
2902 Whispering Winds #310 Pearland TX 77581 • TX • Tchr • Texas Austin TX • (S 1996)
**STAUB ARLYS R** (219)632-5567
5318 N State Rd 101 Woodburn IN 46797-9746 • IN • Tchr • Woodburn Woodburn IN • (219)632-5493 • (S 1973)

**STAUB SCOTT M** (219)632-5567
5318 State Rd 101 Woodburn IN 46797-9746 • IN • Tchr • Woodburn Woodburn IN • (219)632-5493 • (S 1972 MED)

**STAUDE EDMUND D** (636)925-1712
2809 Norwich Dr Saint Charles MO 63301-1345 • cstaude@postnet.com • MO • Tchr • LHS St Charles Saint Peters MO • (636)928-5100 • (S 1976 MED)

**STEARNS CHRIS A** (414)475-7088
2837 N 72nd St Milwaukee WI 53210-1106 • SW • P/Tchr • Emmaus Milwaukee WI • (414)444-6090 • (RF 1979 MS)

**STEC STEVEN J** (708)429-1776
16311 Cherry Hill Ave Tinley Park IL 60477-1136 • NI • Prin • Trinity Tinley Park IL • (708)532-3529 • (RF 1971 MA)

**STECH KELLY ANNE** (708)969-1705
8S430 Boundary Hill Rd Naperville IL 60565-9242 • NI • Tchr • St Paul Chicago IL • (773)378-6644 • (RF 1987)

**STECHHOLZ JANET LOU** (650)615-0255
335 Valverde Dr S San Francisco CA 94080-5624 • stecholz@infinex.com • CNH • Tchr • Hope Daly City CA • (650)991-4673 • (RF 1975)

**STECHMESSER KEITH H** (303)233-1675
150 Estes St Lakewood CO 80226-1256 • RM • Tchr • Bethlehem Lakewood CO • (303)238-7676 • (S 1977 MBA)

**STECKER HEIDI M** (517)642-6091
2558 N Orr Rd Hemlock MI 48626 • stecker4@juno.com • MI • Tchr • St Peter Hemlock MI • (517)642-8188 • (AA 1982)

**STEELE KENNETH MICHAEL** (517)752-1328
2205 N Clinton St Saginaw MI 48602-5013 • MI • Tchr • Bethlehem Saginaw MI • (517)755-1146 • (RF 1991)

**STEELE LISA DANIELLE**
1416 N Springfield Ave Chicago IL 60651 • piccolo375@hotmail.com • NI • Tchr • Bethel Chicago IL • (773)252-1104 • (RF 1998)

**STEENSMA RICHARD D JR.** (313)277-0867
24600 Union Dearborn MI 48124 • icsteenr@ccaa.edu • MI • Prin • Guardian Dearborn MI • (313)274-1414 • (AA 1990 MA)

**STEFAN MATTHEW JASON** (402)844-5874
208 Michigan Ave Norfolk NE 68701 • NEB • Tchr • Lutheran High Northe Norfolk NE • (402)379-3040 • (S 1997)

**STEFFE SARAH RUTH** (219)486-8579
5708 Thornbriar Ln Fort Wayne IN 46835 • srsteffe@juno.com • IN • Tchr • Woodburn Woodburn IN • (219)632-5493 • (RF 1997)

**STEFFEN LEE H** (920)452-8551
2216 S 11th St Sheboygan WI 53081-5909 • lsteffen@excel.net • SW • Tchr • Bethlehem Sheboygan WI • (920)452-5071 • (RF 1961 MA)

**STEFFENS ALLYN G** (573)547-1225
614 Bruce St Perryville MO 63775-1645 • immanuelluthsch@ldd.net • MO • Prin • Immanuel Perryville MO • (573)547-6161 • (S 1969 MA)

**STEFFENS CHRISTIE R** (573)547-1225
614 Bruce St Perryville MO 63775-1645 • immanuelluthsch@ldd.net • MO • Tchr • Immanuel Perryville MO • (573)547-6161 • (S 1969 MA)

**STEFFENS MARK C** (616)429-5487
6033 Bonanza Dr Stevensville MI 49127-9432 • MI • Tchr • Christ Stevensville MI • (616)429-7111 • (S 1967 MCMU)

**STEFFENS PAMELA A** (314)922-0841
5 Barkwood Trails Dr Saint Peters MO 63376-6675 • MO • Tchr • Zion Harvester MO • (314)441-7424 • (RF 1976 MAT)

**STEFFENS STEPHEN F DR** (503)661-2772
1675 NW 13th St Gresham OR 97030-4929 • ssteffens@cu3portland.edu • NOW • SHS/C • Northwest Portland OR • (S 1962 MA MPHIL PHD)

**STEFFENS WANDA B** (314)335-2758
806 Pheasant Cove Dr Cape Girardeau MO 63701-3448 • duscrub@showme.net • MO • Tchr • Trinity Cape Girardeau MO • (573)334-1068 • (S 1969)

**STEGALL BOBETTE LOIS**
9639 Springmont Dr Houston TX 77080-1238 • TX • Tchr • St Mark Houston TX • (713)468-2623 • (CQ 1996)

**STEGEMANN DELBERT V** (708)599-4956
6118 W 81st Pl Burbank IL 60459-1828 • NI • EM • (RF 1946 MED)

**STEHLE REBECCA SUZANNE**
3301 SW 13th St Apt L210 Gainesville FL 32608-3055 • OH • 01/1999 • (S 1997)

**STEIDER JANNESE M**
5730 L St Lincoln NE 68510-2115 • jmsteider@yahoo.com • KS • Tchr • Good Shepherd Marysville KS • (785)562-3181 • (S 1993 MED)

**STEIGERWALT SHERRI**
1885 Porter Rd White Lake MI 48383 • EN • Tchr • Child Of Christ Hartland MI • (248)887-3836 • (AA 1988)

**STEINACKER-ZUEST ROZALYN**
Open Arms Christian Early Chld 201 E 104th St Bloomington MN 55420 • S • Tchr • Open Arms Bloomington MN • (612)888-5116 • (SP 1999)

**STEINBACH ARLON J** (608)742-2256
505 W Slifer St Portage WI 53901-1134 • SW • Tchr • St John Portage WI • (608)742-4222 • (RF 1967 MCMU)

**STEINBACH CAROL L** (608)742-2256
505 W Slifer St Portage WI 53901-1134 • SW • Tchr • St John Portage WI • (608)742-4222 • (RF 1967)

**STEINBACH DONALD E** (301)864-8299
4114 33rd St Mount Rainier MD 20712-1946 • SE • Tchr • Concordia Hyattsville MD • (301)927-0266 • (RF 1961 MA)

**STEINBACHER DAVID A** (636)441-5395
152 Carriage House Ln Saint Peters MO 63376-6801 • steinbache@stlnet.com • MO • Tchr • LHS St Charles Saint Peters MO • (636)928-5100 • (S 1983)

**STEINBAUER SARA** (504)367-1129
1534 De Battista Pl New Orleans LA 70131-7904 • sssteinbauer@hotmail.com • SO • 08/1998 08/2000 • (RF 1974 MA)

**STEINBORN JULIE L** (612)955-3346
808 Hutchinson Rd Watertown MN 55388 • MNS • Tchr • St Paul-St Peter Watertown MN • (612)955-1419 • (AA 1988)

**STEINBRENNER GLENN ALAN** (303)840-1194
11323 Latigo Ln Parker CO 80134-7343 • gsteinbrenner@juno.com • RM • P/Tchr • Trinity Franktown CO • (303)841-4660 • (RF 1973 MA)

**STEINBRUECK JUDITH ANN** (813)684-7520
1109 Lakemont Dr Valrico FL 33594-6621 • steinbr1@ix.netcom.com • FG • Tchr • Immanuel Brandon FL • (813)685-1978 • (RF 1966)

**STEINBRUECK KATHRYN F** (314)843-0618
8237 Marvale Ln Affton MO 63123-2303 • ksteinbrueck@earthlink.net • MO • 10/1987 10/1999 • (SP 1981)

**STEINBRUECK KENNETH P** (314)843-0618
8237 Marvale Ln Affton MO 63123-2303 • itsteinbrueck@earthlink.net • MO • Tchr • LHS South Saint Louis MO • (314)631-1400 • (RF 1978 MAT)

**STEINBRUECK RICHARD G*** (813)684-7520
1109 Lakemont Dr Valrico FL 33594-6621 • steinbr1@ix.netcom.com • FG • 11/1988 11/1999 • (S 1966 MSED)

**STEINBURG SUSAN J**
3829 S 2940 E Salt Lake City UT 84109-3631 • RM • Tchr • Redeemer Salt Lake City UT • (801)487-6283 • (S 1970)

**STEINER PAMELA SUE**
351 La Setta Dr Lodi CA 95242-3319 • CNH • Tchr • St Peter Lodi CA • (209)333-2225 • (S 1971)

**STEINHAUS PAUL R** (920)465-6833
2488 Eileen St Green Bay WI 54311 • plstein@tcccom.net • NW • Tchr • LHS Assoc Of NE Wisc Green Bay WI • (920)469-6810 • (MQ 1996)

**STEINKE CHERYL** (440)777-1462
22441 Fairlawn Cir Fairview Park OH 44126 • cherylsteinke@hotmail.com • EN • Tchr • West Park Cleveland OH • (216)941-2770 • (AA 1997)

**STEINMANN JUDITH** (618)656-7503
PO Box 235 Hamel IL 62046-0235 • SI • Tchr • St Paul Hamel IL • (618)633-2209 • (S 1966)

**STEINMILLER GARY R** (402)643-3256
709 N 4th St Seward NE 68434-1515 • NEB • EM • (S 1960 MPE DED)

**STEINWEG HENRY W** (310)670-7279
7436 W 88th Pl Los Angeles CA 90045-3413 • PSW • EM • (RF 1935)

**STELLING DWIGHT D DR** (515)255-7639
662 34th St Des Moines IA 50312-3819 • MO • 08/1992 08/2000 • (CQ 1980 MS MA PHD)

**STELLING G EDMUND** (714)960-7087
20701 Beach Blvd Spc 10 Huntington Beach CA 92648-4973 • PSW • P/Tchr • Immanuel Orange CA • (714)538-2374 • (RF 1958 MA)

**STELLING TROY ALLEN** (904)629-5328
2470 S Naples Way Aurora CO 80013-1465 • stelling@digital.net • RM • Tchr • Denver Lutheran High Denver CO • (303)934-2345 • (S 1990)

**STELLWAGEN DAVID ROBERT** (414)639-8333
4211 Monterey Dr Racine WI 53402-2939 • SW • Tchr • St John Racine WI • (414)633-2758 • (RF 1985)

**STELMACHOWICZ CARY L DR** (262)692-2007
903 Martin Ave Fredonia WI 53021-9430 • cary.stelmachowicz@cuw.edu • SW • SHS/C • South Wisconsin Milwaukee WI • (414)464-8100 • (RF 1978 MA DED)

**STELTENPOHL GAYLE F** (815)547-9998
521 East 8th ST Belvidere IL 61008 • mearl4@aol.com • NI • Tchr • Immanuel Belvidere IL • (815)547-5346 • (RF 1975)

**STELTENPOHL WILLIAM M** (815)547-9998
521 E 8th St Belvidere IL 61008 • mearl4@aol.com • NI • Prin • Zion Marengo IL • (815)568-5156 • (RF 1975 MSED)

**STELTER JULIE ANN** (616)926-2758
1384 Pipestone Rd Benton Harbor MI 49022-2147 • sjls@juno.com • IN • Tchr • St John La Porte IN • (219)362-3726 • (AA 1986)

**STELZER KENNETH R** (219)744-0660
4607 S Calhoun St Fort Wayne IN 46807-2809 • IN • Tchr • Unity Fort Wayne IN • (219)744-0459 • (S 1980 MED)

**STENBECK SUSAN K** (314)849-6497
7224 Marlton Ln Saint Louis MO 63123-2302 • MO • Tchr • St Luke Saint Louis MO • (314)832-0118 • (SP 1973)

**STENKLYFT TERRY N** (414)353-6971
8425 W Helena Ave Milwaukee WI 53224-4851 • SW • Tchr • St John Glendale WI • (414)352-4150 • (MQ 1984)

**STENNETT LYN MICHELLE** (801)523-9214
10937 Mill Canyon Dr Sandy UT 84094-5907 • RM • Tchr • Rocky Mountain Aurora CO • (RF 1992)

**STEPHENS JUDITH L** (618)277-0922
1719 Page Ave Belleville IL 62221-4967 • SI • Tchr • Zion Belleville IL • (618)234-0275 • (CQ 1995)

**STEPHENS MARCELLA MARLENE** (312)625-0704
3450 N Panama Ave Chicago IL 60634-2923 • EN • Tchr • Our Saviour Chicago IL • (773)736-1120 • (RF 1966 MA)

**STEPHENSON ROZANNE M** (415)387-1836
682 23rd Ave San Francisco CA 94121-3709 • EN • Tchr • West Portal San Francisco CA • (415)661-0242 • (RF 1964)

**STERENBERG SARAH** (815)544-8121
722 Caswell St Belvidere IL 61008 • NI • Tchr • Immanuel Belvidere IL • (815)544-8058 • (MQ 2000)

**STERLING DANIEL T** (314)869-6681
1821 San Luis Rey Pkwy Fenton MO 63026-3235 • MO • Tchr • St Paul Des Peres MO • (314)822-2771 • (RF 1986)

**STERNBERG BONNIE J** (847)882-7305
308 E Schaumburg Rd Schaumburg IL 60194-3515 • NI • Tchr • St Peter Schaumburg IL • (847)885-7636 • (RF 1977)

**STETLER LOUANN** (717)741-0485
1904 Ebony Dr York PA 17402-4709 • SE • Tchr • St John York PA • (717)755-4779 • (RF 1971)

**STEVENS JASON R** (708)532-2121
15725 New England Ave Tinley Park IL 60477 • NI • Tchr • Luther HS South Chicago IL • (773)737-1416 • (RF 2000)

**STEVENS JILL ROCHELLE**
17 Sylvan Oak Way Perry Hall MD 21236 • SE • Tchr • Immanuel Baltimore MD • (410)435-6961 • (S 1997)

**STEVENS JOANNE M** (517)684-7331
2567 E Hotchkiss Rd Bay City MI 48706-9008 • MI • Tchr • St Paul Bay City MI • (517)684-4450 • (SP 1967)

**STEVENS JUDITH ANN** (713)944-2760
5331 Laurel Creek Way Houston TX 77017-6250 • bljstevens@aol.com • TX • Tchr • Trinity-Messiah Houston TX • (713)224-7265 • (CQ 1996)

**STEVENS-VERDI KATHRYN H**
2001 E Spring Creek Pkwy #9106 Plano TX 75074 • OK • 09/1999 • (BR 1976)

**STEVENSON BETTY JEAN** (313)624-6105
1188 Sigma Rd Walled Lake MI 48390-3753 • MI • Tchr • St Matthew Walled Lake MI • (248)624-7677 • (CQ 1984)

**STEVENSON JAMES** (512)834-2307
1002 Weeping Willow Dr Austin TX 78753-5847 • jims@austin.concordia.edu • TX • SHS/C • Texas Austin TX • (S 1964 MS PHD)

**STEWART SHANNA RUTH**
4247 Harvey Ave Western Springs IL 60558-1247 • shanna.stewart@juno.com • NI • 09/1998 • (S 1994)

**STIER JANEL LOUISE**
1449 Braidwood Rd Memphis MI 48041 • MI • Tchr • St Peter Richmond MI • (810)727-9693 • (AA 1992)

**STIGGE GERTRUDE** (405)765-7360
1205 E Bradley Ave Ponca City OK 74601-1706 • OK • 08/1985 08/2000 • (S 1966)

**STIGGE JUDITH E** (316)221-2868
517 E 34th Ave Winfield KS 67156-8716 • ajstigge@kcisp.net • KS • Tchr • Trinity Winfield KS • (316)221-1820 • (S 1969 MED)

**STIGGE MARY ANN** (316)687-5187
8321 E Orme St Wichita KS 67207-2361 • KS • EM • (S 1970)

**STINE MADELINE I** (309)527-6449
257 S Elm St El Paso IL 61738-1548 • NI • 09/1983 09/1999 • (RF 1978 MA)

**STINSON EDWARD L**
1095 Clovo Ave Menlo Park CA 94025 • CNH • Mem C • Bethany Menlo Park CA • (650)854-5897 • (SP 1971)

**STIRN TODD ERIC** (630)859-2093
741 Palace St Aurora IL 60506-3019 • NI • Tchr • Bethany Naperville IL • (630)355-6607 • (AA 1986 MA)

**STOCK KAREN JANE** (636)225-1110
1606 Hanna Rd Valley Park MO 63088-2303 • k2j6s@aol.com • MO • Tchr • Our Savior Fenton MO • (314)343-7511 • (RF 1982)

**STOCK MICHAEL R** (920)494-5797
1271 Ridgedale Ct Green Bay WI 54304-2322 • stockmike@hotmail.com • NW • Tchr • LHS Assoc Of NE Wisc Green Bay WI • (920)469-6810 • (RF 1972)

**STOCKHAUS ELAINE A** (216)226-4561
1611 Belle Ave Lakewood OH 44107-4314 • OH • Tchr • Bethany Parma OH • (440)884-1010 • (RF 1968)

**STOCKMAN JAN N**
10929 Sumter Ave S Bloomington MN 55438-2368 • MNS • Tchr • Cross View Edina MN • (612)941-0009 • (SP 1978)

**STOCKMAN ROZANNA M** (203)583-8325
36 South St Ext Bristol CT 06010-6523 • NE • Tchr • Immanuel Bristol CT • (860)583-5631 • (SP 1972)

**STOCKMAN WADE ANDREW** (828)324-7512
1230 18th Ave NE Hickory NC 28601-2036 • SE • Tchr • Concordia Conover NC • (828)464-3011 • (SP 1985)

**STOCKTON MARY NEBEL** (281)528-9298
3407 Arromanches Ln Spring TX 77388-4139 • TX • Tchr • Concordia LHS Tomball TX • (281)351-2547 • (AU 1995)

**STOECKEL LINDA M** (810)293-9563
22536 Corteville St Clair Shrs MI 48081-2558 • MI • Tchr • St Thomas Eastpointe MI • (810)772-3372 • (S 1969)

**STOECKMAN BONITA MAE** (612)657-2541
13880 County Road 30 Mayer MN 55360-9514 • MNS • Tchr • Trinity Waconia MN • (952)442-4165 • (SP 1971)

**STOELTING DANIEL D** (716)832-0668
190 Woodridge Ave Cheektowaga NY 14225-1533 • sdd65@aol.com • EA • Tchr • St Mark North Tonawanda NY • (716)693-3715 • (AA 1987)

**STOELTING LUCAS E** (660)463-7561
205 S Main St PO Box 719 Concordia MO 64020 • lstoelting@yahoo.com • MO • Tchr • St Paul Concordia MO • (660)463-2238 • (S 1999)

**STOELTING LUCILLE A*** (319)642-5263
1274 FF Ave Marengo IA 52301 • IE • Tchr • Central Newhall IA • (319)223-5271 • (S 1970 MA)

**STOELTING MELINDA L** (319)279-3496
240 1/2 Main St Box 156 Readlyn IA 50668 • mellou@netins.net • IE • Tchr • Community Readlyn IA • (319)279-3968 • (S 1996)

**STOEPPELWERTH BARBARA A** (770)973-3265
2614 Club Valley Dr NE Marietta GA 30068-3518 • stoppy@bellsouth.net • FG • Tchr • Faith Marietta GA • (770)973-8921 • (S 1971 MED)

**STOFFEL ELIZABETH ANN** (520)579-0987
4466 W Rose Mist Way Tucson AZ 85741 • jheastoffel@gateway.net • EN • Tchr • Open Arms Tucson AZ • (520)744-8505 • (SP 1967)

**STOHS DELTON G** (218)346-3265
246 6th Ave SW Perham MN 56573-1113 • bdstohs@eot.com • MNN • 08/1994 08/2000 • (S 1968)

**STOHS REUBEN V DR** (440)838-0749
5584 E Wallings Rd Broadview Hts OH 44147-1528 • rvs17@aol.com • NEB • EM • (RF 1947 MA PHD)

**STOLL KATHERINE JANELLE**
27 Glade Ave Baltimore MD 21236-4111 • NI • 07/2000 • (RF 1999)

**STOLL PAULA L** (314)832-9901
5452 Nagel Ave St Louis MO 63109 • pstoll@juno.com • MO • Tchr • St Mark Eureka MO • (636)938-4432 • (S 1998)

**STOLLENWERK MICHAEL P**
8 Winter Hill Ct O Fallon MO 63366-3961 • MO • Tchr • LHS North Houston TX • (713)880-3131 • (MQ 1995)

**STOLTENOW CURTIS J** (507)362-4318
1010 Southridge Ln Waterville MN 56096-9576 • djstolte@frontiernet.net • MNS • Tchr • Faribault Faribault MN • (507)334-7982 • (SP 1966)

**STOLTMANN CINDY J** (262)695-7409
N33W23215 Greenbriar Rd Pewaukee WI 53072-5760 • SW • Tchr • Immanuel Brookfield WI • (414)781-4135 • (S 1984)

**STONE LOREEN A** (708)394-2366
707 E Hackberry Ln Mount Prospect IL 60056-1309 • NI • Tchr • Immanuel Dundee IL • (847)428-4477 • (CQ 1989)

**STONEBURNER GORDON FORREST*** 
1112 Heritage Lane Milford OH 45150-9615 • gstoneburn@aol.com • OH • Prin • St Paul Cincinnati OH • (513)271-8266 • (RF 1984 MA)

**STONG JANET S**
6399 St Vrian Ranch Blvd Longmont CO 80504 • RM • Tchr • Beautiful Savior Broomfield CO • (303)469-2049 • (S 1977)

**STOPPEL CINDY ANN** (712)263-3248
2502 290th St Denison IA 51442-7712 • IW • Tchr • Zion Denison IA • (712)263-4766 • (S 1995)

**STOPPENHAGEN ARNOLD C** (219)447-7662
C/O Concord Village Apt E224 6723 S Anthony Blvd Fort Wayne IN 46816-2045 • IN • EM • (RF 1935)

**STORCK CHARLES L** (810)791-1104
23337 King Dr Clinton Twp MI 48035-2981 • MI • EM • (RF 1955 MS)

**STORCK ELLEN R** (217)423-7906
100 Bay Shore Dr Decatur IL 62521-5531 • CI • Tchr • Lutheran School Asso Decatur IL • (217)233-2001 • (RF 1972)

**STORCK RHODA T** (425)828-0743
12831 NE 83rd St Kirkland WA 98033-8013 • twstorck@gte.net • NOW • Tchr • Shepherd Of The Hill Snohomish WA • (425)485-8171 • (S 1970 MED)

**STORDAHL JEAN A** (847)895-7558
520 Samoset Ct Schaumburg IL 60193-1449 • NI • Tchr • St Peter Schaumburg IL • (847)885-7636 • (RF 1973)

**STORK ANNETTA L** (219)484-8382
460 Dalgren Ave Fort Wayne IN 46805-1922 • IN • Tchr • Holy Cross Fort Wayne IN • (219)483-3173 • (S 1969 MED)

**STORK MARTIN L** (402)643-4139
2808 Adams Rd Seward NE 68434-7553 • NEB • EM • (S 1942 MA DED)

**STORM DANIEL** (815)562-4926
1033 N 7th St Rochelle IL 61068 • NI • Tchr • St Paul Rochelle IL • (815)562-2744 • (RF 2000)

**STORM ROBERT W** (314)447-7647
2745 Sunny Meadows Dr Saint Charles MO 63303-4434 • MO • EM • (RF 1955 MED)

**STORTZ STEVEN B** (402)371-6335
102 Maple Hadar NE 68701 • NEB • Tchr • Christ Norfolk NE • (402)371-5536 • (S 1986 MED)

**STOTTS NANCY K**
913 S 3rd St Saint Charles MO 63301-2401 • MO • Tchr • Immanuel Saint Charles MO • (636)946-0051 • (RF 1976 MS)

**STOVER MARK P** (216)251-5272
3494 W 145th St Cleveland OH 44111-2205 • OH • Tchr • LHS West Rocky River OH • (440)333-1660 • (RF 1986)

**STRAHLE WILLIAM F** (847)259-9392
113 S School St Mount Prospect IL 60056-3316 • bestrahle@aol.com • NI • P/Tchr • Messiah Chicago IL • (773)736-6600 • (RF 1963 MED)

**STRAKIS RANDALL O** (765)497-1676
10 Wake Robin Ct W Lafayette IN 47906-5031 • IN • Tchr • St James Lafayette IN • (765)742-6464 • (S 1974 MSED)

**STRAND DIANA FLORY** (503)465-6727
4849 SW 11th St Apt G222 Gresham OR 97080-7301 • gregndianastrand@worldnet.att.net • MO • Tchr • Lutheran North Saint Louis MO • (314)389-3100 • (S 1995)

**STRAND SANDRA JANE** (414)607-9276
2657 N 68th St Wauwatosa WI 53213 • SW • Tchr • Pilgrim Wauwatosa WI • (414)476-0735 • (MQ 1999)

**STRANDT MARLENE ELLEN** (972)423-6208
2925 Monarch Dr Plano TX 75074 • TX • Tchr • Faith Plano TX • (972)423-7448 • (CQ 1997)

**STRANG DONNA** (734)595-4086
6705 Redman St Westland MI 48185-2740 • dstrang@lhsa.com • MI • Tchr • LHS Westland Westland MI • (734)422-2090 • (RF 1972 MED)

**STRANG WILLIAM J** (734)595-4086
6705 Redman St Westland MI 48185-2740 • MI • Tchr • St Matthew Walled Lake MI • (248)624-7677 • (RF 1972 MED)

**STRAUB CARL G** (517)871-4730
8961 Fulmer Rd Millington MI 48746-8708 • MI • EM • (RF 1951 MS MS)

**STRAUB MATTHEW A**
1011 Village Sq #634 Tomball TX 77375-6721 • TX • Tchr • Concordia LHS Tomball TX • (281)351-2547 • (S 1999)

**STRAUB VINCENT J** (541)738-8728
1710 NW Woodland Dr Corvallis OR 97330 • vstraub@proaxis.com • NOW • Tchr • Zion Corvallis OR • (541)753-7503 • (S 1974)

**STRAVERS KENNETH W** (414)639-4526
1105 Layard Ave Racine WI 53402-4326 • SW • Tchr • Trinity Racine WI • (414)632-1766 • (SP 1986)

**STREETER KIM E** (810)949-6204
48602 Wheatfield St Chesterfield MI 48051-2959 • kstreet@rust.net • MI • Tchr • St Peter Macomb MI • (810)781-9296 • (RF 1978 MED MA)

**STREETER LYLE DREW** (480)491-1385
3409 South Rural #224 Tempe AZ 85282 • OH • 09/1999 • (S 1985)

**STREFLING JESSICA L**
15839 Pardee Rd Galien MI 49113 • MI • Tchr • St John Midland MI • (517)835-5861 • (RF 2000)

**STREHLKE JAMES L**
17050 Utah Rd Mayer MN 55360 • MNS • Tchr • Lutheran High Mayer MN • (612)657-2251 • (S 1990)

**STREHLOW GLORIA JEAN** (262)641-0793
935 S 124th St Brookfield WI 53005-7302 • SW • Tchr • Grace Menomonee Falls WI • (414)251-7140 • (RF 1981)

**STREI MADELINE R** (612)472-5741
2056 Bellaire Ln Mound MN 55364-1004 • MNS • Tchr • St Paul-St Peter Watertown MN • (612)955-1419 • (SP 1976)

**STREIT RICHARD F** (312)238-3456
1661 W 102nd St Chicago IL 60643-2144 • NI • EM • (CQ 1959)

**STRESMAN KENNETH C**
1665 Appleblossom Ln Saginaw MI 48609-8808 • MI • EM • (RF 1963)

**STRESMAN KEVIN D**
9455 W Saginaw Box 114 Richville MI 48758-0114 • stresman@gateway.net • MI • Tchr • St Michael Richville MI • (517)868-4809 • (S 1981)

**STRESON RUTH E** (415)824-0628
1065 S Van Ness Ave Apt 308 San Francisco CA 94110-2646 • EN • Tchr • West Portal San Francisco CA • (415)665-6330 • (RF 1961 MA)

**STREUFERT EUNICE C** (651)429-4095
4150 Thornhill Ln Vadnais Heights MN 55127-3610 • MNS • SHS/C • Minnesota South Burnsville MN • (S 1970 MED PHD)

**STREUFERT FRANK C** (615)855-4703
506 Las Lomas Dr Chattanooga TN 37421-3923 • MDS • Tchr • Lutheran Chattanooga TN • (615)622-3755 • (RF 1976 MA)

**STREUTER MARTHA S** (618)345-1168
429 Chapel Dr Collinsville IL 62234-4342 • weeteachr@aol.com • SI • Tchr • Good Shepherd Collinsville IL • (618)344-3153 • (RF 1973)

**STRICKLAND ANDREW**
14651 Chicago Ave S #2 Burnsville MN 55306 • MNS • Tchr • East St Paul Saint Paul MN • (612)774-2030 • (SP 2000)

**STRIETELMEIER I DELORES** (812)372-7350
2314 Franklin St Columbus IN 47201-4161 • IN • EM • (RF 1958 MS)

**STROBEL BARBARA A** (414)338-9328
2021 Sylvan Way Apt 5 West Bend WI 53095-5258 • SW • Tchr • St John West Bend WI • (414)334-3077 • (SP 1972)

**STROH DEBORAH** (314)821-5912
431 Longview Blvd Kirkwood MO 63122-4469 • MO • Tchr • Mount Calvary Brentwood MO • (314)968-2360 • (S 1971)

**STROH LESTER*** (314)821-5912
431 Longview Blvd Kirkwood MO 63122-4469 • MO • 03/1991 03/2000 • (S 1971)

**STROH MYRNA L** (310)425-7852
4634 Pimenta Ave Lakewood CA 90712-3866 • PSW • EM • (RF 1962)

**STROHACKER CHARLES J** (616)429-0964
2888 Trail Ln Saint Joseph MI 49085-3231 • MI • Prin • Christ Stevensville MI • (616)429-7111 • (RF 1974 MA)

**STROHSCHEIN ROBIN J** (218)729-6256
PO Box 224 Annandale MN 55302 • MNN • 04/1996 04/2000 • (SP 1978)

**STROHSCHEIN TIMOTHY JOHN** (651)487-9061
49 Larpenteur Ave E Saint Paul MN 55117-2334 • tstrohschein@mail.concordia-academy.pvt.k12.mn.us • MNS • Tchr • Prince Of Peace Spring Lake Park MN • (763)786-1706 • (SP 1994)

**STROM JULIE M** (651)774-2030
14802 Co Rd 5 #9 Burnsville MN 55306 • bstrom@simeks.com • MNS • Tchr • East St Paul Saint Paul MN • (612)774-2030 • (CQ 1998)

**STROMING LINDA L** (612)427-5018
528 Western St Anoka MN 55303-2005 • MNS • Tchr • Mount Olive Anoka MN • (612)421-9048 • (SP 1981)

**STRONG ALYCE L** (402)987-3922
1806 H Ave Dakota City NE 68731-3060 • IW • Tchr • St Paul Sioux City IA • (712)258-6325 • (S 1981)

**STRONG BARBARA** (773)776-9057
2700 W 83rd St Chicago IL 60652-3902 • NI • Tchr • Timothy Chicago IL • (773)874-7333 • (S 1966)

**STRONG CONNIE** (541)929-5235
2679 Newton St Philomath OR 97370-9214 • NOW • Tchr • Zion Corvallis OR • (541)753-7503 • (CQ 1993)

**STROUP DARLA E*** (312)931-7671
1622 Mark Ave Apt 6 Elgin IL 60123-1964 • NI • Tchr • Good Shepherd Elgin IL • (847)741-7795 • (RF 1981 MA)

**STROUP DONALD R** (309)385-1642
212 N Ostrom Ave Princeville IL 61559-9535 • CI • Tchr • Concordia Peoria IL • (309)691-8921 • (RF 1969 MA)

**STRUCK CHRISTOPHER** (618)467-9598
1202 Surrey Ct #3 Godfrey IL 62035 • SI • Tchr • Faith Godfrey IL • (618)466-3833 • (MQ 1996)

**STRUCK MICHELE M** (507)234-5521
701 N Market St Janesville MN 56048-9556 • MNS • Tchr • Trinity Janesville MN • (507)231-6646 • (SP 1988)

**STRUCKMANN CYNTHIA K** (718)894-4310
60-19 59th Dr Fl 1 Maspeth NY 11378-3415 • AT • Tchr • Atlantic Bronxville NY • (914)337-5700 • (S 1986 MSCT)

**STRUDTHOFF HOLLY B** (402)721-6535
1340 Missouri Ave Fremont NE 68025-2026 • NEB • Tchr • Trinity Fremont NE • (402)721-5959 • (CQ 1989)

**STRUSSENBERG SARAH**
1201 Fairhaven Ave Apt 20G Santa Ana CA 92705-6788 • PSW • Tchr • St John Orange CA • (714)288-4406 • (MQ 1998)

**STRZEMIECZNY SYLVIA** (708)479-6069
11953 Brookshire Dr Orland Park IL 60467-7598 • NI • Tchr • St Paul Chicago Heights IL • (708)754-4493 • (RF 1975)

**STUART PAULA L** (801)621-6566
370 N Harrison Blvd Ogden UT 84404-4155 • RM • Tchr • St Paul Ogden UT • (801)392-2912 • (S 1975)

**STUBBE AMY K** (262)512-0437
223 Green Bay Rd Apt B Thiensville WI 53092 • SW • Tchr • Beautiful Savior Waukesha WI • (414)542-6558 • (MQ 1995 MA)

**STUBBLEFIELD LINDA K** (217)422-5217
210 S Woodale Ave Decatur IL 62522-2549 • CI • Tchr • Lutheran School Asso Decatur IL • (217)233-2001 • (CQ 1989)

**STUCKERT GORDON S** (770)631-8154
459 Plantain Ter Peachtree City GA 30269-4026 • gstuckprin@aol.com • FG • Prin • St Paul Peachtree City GA • (770)486-3545 • (RF 1969 MA)

**STUCKWISCH SHEILA KAY** (775)853-0198
8455 Offenhauser Dr #426 Reno NV 89511 • skstuckwisch@yahoo.com • CNH • Tchr • Bethlehem Carson City NV • (702)882-5252 • (RF 1997)

**STUCKY RHONDA L** (920)926-0597
1183 Carriage Cir Fond Du Lac WI 54935-6549 • rstucky@moraine.tec.wi.us • FG • 06/1999 • (S 1988)

**STUEBE DAVID F** (419)592-8946
35 Bordeaux Dr Napoleon OH 43545-2209 • dstuebe@bright.net • OH • Tchr • St Paul Napoleon OH • (419)592-5536 • (S 1968)

**STUEBE MICHAEL D**
20515 Sterncroft Ct Montgomery Village MD 20886-4002 • michael.stuebe@csst.com • RM • Tchr • Peace W Christ Aurora CO • (303)693-5618 • (RF 1997)

**STUEBER ALICIA JOY** (636)394-0638
181 Keystone Farm Dr Ballwin MO 63021-7912 • alicia.stueber@mindspring.co • MO • Tchr • St Paul Saint Louis MO • (314)822-0447 • (MQ 1999)

**STUEBER DARLENE L** (636)394-0638
181 Keystone Farm Dr Ellisville MO 63021-7912 • MO • Tchr • St John Ellisville MO • (314)394-4100 • (S 1968)

**STUEBER DAVID J** (651)487-3612
811 Como Ave Apt 2 Saint Paul MN 55103-1462 • stueber@csp.edu • MNS • SHS/C • Minnesota South Burnsville MN • (S 1968 MA)

**STUEBER LISA** (713)896-0669
7503 Split Oak Ct Houston TX 77040 • lstueber@hotmail.com • TX • Tchr • St Mark Houston TX • (713)468-2623 • (MQ 1996)

**STUEBER MATTHEW P** (713)896-0669
7503 Split Oak Ct Houston TX 77040 • mstueber@stmarkhouston.org • TX • Tchr • St Mark Houston TX • (713)468-2623 • (MQ 1995)

**STUEBER ROSS E DR** (636)394-0368
181 Keystone Farm Dr Ballwin MO 63021-7912 • clyman@mindspring.com • MO • S Ex/S • Missouri Saint Louis MO • (314)317-4550 • (S 1968 MSED EDD)

**STUEMKE APRIL L** (618)483-5162
27 Fairlane Cir Altamont IL 62411-1712 • CI • Tchr • Altamont Altamont IL • (618)483-6428 • (RF 1996)

**STUEMKE NORMAN C** (512)453-4508
2210 Kenbridge Dr Austin TX 78757-7735 • TX • EM • (RF 1955 MED)

**STUENKEL PAUL R** (713)466-8182
9611 Kindletree Dr Houston TX 77040-3909 • paulstuenkel@lea-hou.org • TX • Tchr • LHS North Houston TX • (713)880-3131 • (S 1974 MMU)

**STUENKEL RUTH A**
39 Shady Valley Chesterfield MO 63017 • PSW • 06/1998 06/2000 • (RF 1974)

**STUENKEL SHEILA KAY**
1941 1st Rd Greenleaf KS 66943-9413 • sstuenkel@hotmail.com • KS • 05/1999 • (S 1990)

**STUEVE HEATHER ANNE** (503)236-1078
3442 NE Flanders St Portland OR 97232-3301 • hstueve@cu-portland.edu • NOW • SHS/C • Northwest Portland OR • (CQ 1990 MA)

**STUEVEN MARJORIE A** (320)543-3027
2626 County Road 6 SW Howard Lake MN 55349-4913 • MNS • Tchr • St James Howard Lake MN • (320)543-2630 • (SP 1968)

**STUEWE DAVID R C**
1833 E 19th St Santa Ana CA 92705-7601 • ydstuewe@prodigy.net • PSW • Tchr • St John Orange CA • (714)288-4400 • (IV 1990)

**STUEWE ISABEL J** (714)557-3110
1734 New Hampshire Dr Costa Mesa CA 92626-2026 • PSW • Tchr • St John Orange CA • (714)288-4406 • (S 1962)

**STUEWE SHELLI RENAY** (512)252-0441
1104 Hatteras Dr Austin TX 78753-2062 • TX • Tchr • Hope Austin TX • (512)926-8574 • (CQ 1994)

**STUHR GARRY A** (281)353-2782
3632 Blue Lake Dr Spring TX 77388-5105 • TX • Mem C • Trinity Klein TX • (281)376-5773 • (S 1968)

**STUHR LONNIE JAMES** (712)276-6628
5519 Stone Ave Sioux City IA 51106-2039 • IW • P/Tchr • St Paul Sioux City IA • (712)258-6325 • (S 1965 MA)

**STULTS JEFFREY ALAN**
10555 W Jewell Ave Apt 17-102 Lakewood CO 30232-6217 • RM • Tchr • Denver Lutheran High Denver CO • (303)934-2345 • (S 1990)

**STULTS SUSAN ANNE** (520)229-1880
11 E Orange Grove Rd Apt 2121 Tucson AZ 85704-5544 • stults1Wjuno.com • EN • Tchr • Ascension Tucson AZ • (520)742-6229 • (RF 1964)

**STUMPF LINDA D** (219)934-9067
10348 Marlou Dr Munster IN 46321-4342 • ecstumpf@jorsm.com • NI • Tchr • Trinity Burr Ridge IL • (708)839-1200 • (RF 1970 MA)

**STURGESS JACQUELINE MARIE** (810)757-5549
23805 Lorraine Warren MI 48089-1736 • MI • Tchr • St Thomas Eastpointe MI • (810)772-3372 • (CQ 1994)

**STURM JOAN M** (630)904-1803
4811 Daggets Ct Naperville IL 60564-4318 • NI • Tchr • Zion Naperville IL • (630)904-1124 • (RF 1963 MA)

**STURM LOWEEN R** (763)856-4097
25490 102nd St PO Box 204 Zimmerman MN 55398-0204 • stjohnlutheranelkriver.org • MNS • Tchr • St John Elk River MN • (612)441-6616 • (S 1970)

**STURM THERESA IRENE** (217)386-2909
455 N 100 E Rd Buckley IL 60918 • CI • Tchr • St John Buckley IL • (217)394-2422 • (CQ 1994 MED)

**STURMFELS JOHN H** (734)434-5481
3643 Helen Ave Ypsilanti MI 48197-3760 • MI • EM • (RF 1955 MA SPA)

**STUTZMAN KATHRYN** (414)764-0265
2250 E Birch Dr Oak Creek WI 53154-1206 • SW • Tchr • Grace Oak Creek WI • (414)762-3655 • (S 1979)

**SUCHMAN LYNETTE K**
752 Lipscomb Republic MO 65738-2282 • MO • Tchr • Springfield Springfield MO • (417)883-5717 • (S 1991 MSED)

**SUDOL DONNA S** (918)274-7328
7804 N 154th East Ave Owasso OK 74055-7050 • OK • Tchr • Tulsa Tulsa OK • (918)834-3813 • (S 1982)

**SUHR HOWARD R** (312)343-4374
126 N 14th Ave Melrose Park IL 60160-3908 • NI • EM • (RF 1952 MA)

**SUHR JOHN D** (402)535-2865
RR 1 Box 133 Staplehurst NE 68439-9748 • NEB • SHS/C • Nebraska Seward NE • (S 1960 MS PHD)

**SUHR KIRSTEN J**
801 S 212th St Elkhorn NE 68022-2040 • NEB • Tchr • Bread Of Life Omaha NE • (402)391-3505 • (S 1990)

**SUHR MELANIE L** (402)643-3205
310 E Hillcrest Dr Seward NE 68434-1338 • NEB • Tchr • St John Seward NE • (402)643-2983 • (S 1989)

**SUHR MICHELLE K** (573)824-5157
1444 Perry Ave Cape Girardeau MO 63701 • michelleksuhr@yahoo.com • MO • 06/1999 • (S 1995)

**SULLIVAN JUDITH A** (608)754-4267
815 Sussex Dr Janesville WI 53546-1815 • SW • Tchr • St Paul Janesville WI • (608)754-4471 • (CQ 1999)

**SULLIVAN LOIS** (504)893-4301
312 Westwood Dr Mandeville LA 70471-8904 • SO • Tchr • St Paul New Orleans LA • (504)947-1773 • (S 1974)

**SUMMERSET CATHERINE ANN** (520)573-5925
1351 E Pewit Dr Tucson AZ 85706-1476 • PSW • Tchr • Fountain Life Tucson AZ • (520)747-1213 • (IV 1986 MA)

**SUMP MERRILEE A** (712)542-3058
701 N 12th St Clarinda IA 51632-1244 • merrileesump@clarinda.heartland.net • IW • P/Tchr • Clarinda Clarinda IA • (712)542-3657 • (S 1978 MSED MSED)

**SUNDERMANN DIANNE SUE** (810)731-3468
45465 Deshon St Apt 14 Utica MI 48317-5654 • MI • Tchr • Trinity Utica MI • (810)731-4490 • (RF 1968 MA)

**SUNSTROM MELISSA** (410)747-1924
C/O St Paul Lutheran Church 2001 Old Frederick Rd Baltimore MD 21228-4119 • SE • Tchr • St Paul Catonsville MD • (410)747-1897 • (BR 1990)

**SURPRENANT FAITH E** (714)879-4959
219 N Wanda Dr Fullerton CA 92833-2645 • PSW • Tchr • Hephatha Anaheim CA • (714)637-4022 • (RF 1971 MED)

**SURRIDGE SHELLY** (714)288-9452
1286 N Jamestown Way Orange CA 92869-1413 • PSW • Tchr • Salem Orange CA • (714)639-1946 • (PO 1982)

**SUTTER IRENE NORRIS** (810)474-4291
31770 Lamar Dr Farmington MI 48336-2524 • esutter@wwnet.net • MI • Tchr • St Paul Farmington Hills MI • (248)474-2488 • (CQ 1995)

**SUTTON DAVID CHARLES** (909)989-6906
7040 Archibald Ave #50 Alta Loma CA 91701-6418 • dkcrouton@juno.com • PSW • Tchr • Pacific Southwest Irvine CA • (949)854-3232 • (IV 1996)

**SUTTON KARIE ELIZABETH** (812)952-0048
925 St Peters Church Rd NE Corydon IN 47112-8351 • karies@otherside.com • IN • Tchr • St John Lanesville IN • (812)952-2737 • (RF 1997)

**SUYDAM PENELOPE LYNN** (847)884-0925
1962 Liberty Pl Hoffman Estates IL 60195-2830 • psuydam72@hotmail.com • NI • Tchr • St John Forest Park IL • (708)366-3226 • (RF 1994 MA)

**SVARC RENEE C** (949)768-4865
21862 Balcon Mission Viejo CA 92691-1323 • winne@home.com • PSW • Tchr • Abiding Savior Lake Forest CA • (949)830-1461 • (CQ 1997)

**SWAN SHEILA RENAE** (763)786-3939
8006 Terrace Rd NE Spring Lake Park MN 55432-1940 • MNS • Tchr • St John Elk River MN • (612)441-6616 • (SP 1987)

**SWANLUND NANCY E** (909)781-1071
375 Central Ave # 13 Riverside CA 92507-6501 • neswan@juno.com • PSW • Tchr • Immanuel Riverside CA • (909)682-7613 • (S 1977 MED)

**SWANSON CRAIG W** (801)545-8544
9631 South 1700 East Sandy UT 84092 • craigswanson52@hotmail.com • RM • Prin • Salt Lake LHS Salt Lake City UT • (801)266-6676 • (CQ 1987 MED)

**SWANSON DAVID W** (312)474-5668
18122 Wentworth Ave Lansing IL 60438-3900 • NI • Tchr • St John Lansing IL • (708)895-9280 • (RF 1970)

**SWANSON HOLLY A** (715)845-9114
609 N 9th Ave Wausau WI 54401-2922 • NW • Tchr • Trinity Wausau WI • (715)848-0166 • (MQ 1988)

**SWANSON JOAN E**
15022 W Maybob Rd Nine Mile Falls WA 99026-8639 • NOW • Prin • Spokane Spokane WA • (509)327-4441 • (WN 1986)

**SWANSON MARY B** (303)450-9460
2560 E 165th Ave Brighton CO 80601-7606 • RM • Tchr • Zion Brighton CO • (303)659-2339 • (CQ 1999)

**SWANSTROM VERNA M** (206)246-0436
620 SW 139th St Seattle WA 98166-1362 • swanie@wa.freei.net • NOW • Tchr • King Of Kings Renton WA • (206)255-8520 • (S 1962 MED)

**SWARTZ DIANE L** (520)574-1794
9895 E Paseo Juan Tabo Tucson AZ 85747-9131 • jdlswartz@worldnet.att.net • PSW • Tchr • Fountain Of Life Tucson AZ • (520)747-1213 • (SP 1988)

**SWEARINGEN MARTHA** (417)891-9903
2475 S Suprema Ave Springfield MO 65807 • MO • Tchr • Redeemer Springfield MO • (417)886-7069 • (S 1994)

**SWEM KATHERINE**
225 3rd Ave NE Osseo MN 55369 • MNS • Tchr • St John Maple Grove MN • (763)420-2426 • (RF 2000)

**SWENEY RICHARD E** (216)252-0151
3498 W 145th St Cleveland OH 44111-2205 • rsweney@sprynet.com • OH • Tchr • St Thomas Rocky River OH • (440)331-4426 • (RF 1984)

**SWENSON LEAH** (409)542-9083
755 E Bellville St Giddings TX 78942-4235 • TX • Tchr • Immanuel Giddings TX • (409)542-3319 • (AU 1991)

**SWETT ARTHUR** (352)372-6452
3959 NW 62nd Ln Gainesville FL 32653 • art@flcgainesville.org • FG • Mem C • First Gainesville FL • (352)376-2062 • (RF 1970 MED)

**SWORTS SANDRA JOY** (716)735-9237
9500 Graham Rd Middleport NY 14105-9610 • EA • Tchr • St Matthew North Tonawanda NY • (716)692-6862 • (BR 1986)

**SYLWESTER DONALD** (402)643-3335
1060 Fairlane Ave Seward NE 68434-1310 • NEB • SHS/C • Nebraska Seward NE • (S 1971 MS)

**SYLWESTER KURT L** (541)382-6402
1801 NE Lotus Dr Apt 305 Bend OR 97701-6189 • NOW • EM • (RF 1933)

**SYLWESTER SUZANNE** (402)643-3335
1060 Fairlane Ave Seward NE 68434-1310 • scs9575@seward.cune.edu • NEB • Tchr • St John Seward NE • (402)643-4535 • (RF 1969 MED)

**SYMMANK CELESTE RENE** (208)232-6506
921 E Lander St Pocatello ID 83201-5729 • NOW • Tchr • Grace Pocatello ID • (208)237-4142 • (PO 1984)

**SYMMANK RACHEL M** (913)764-1984
804 N Stevenson St Olathe KS 66061-2830 • KS • 08/1995 08/1999 • (S 1990)

**SZETO JENNY** (415)469-9340
12 Sala Ter San Francisco CA 94112 • EN • Tchr • West Portal San Francisco CA • (415)665-6330 • (IV 1996 MA)

**SZYMANSKI LAURA A** (630)279-3936
315 Pine St Villa Park IL 60181-2236 • szymanski@home.com • NI • Tchr • Zion Hinsdale IL • (630)323-0384 • (RF 1990)

## T

**TAEGE TERRENCE L** (402)339-7472
8221 Walnut Ln Ralston NE 68127-4242 • NEB • Mem C • Beaut Savior Omaha NE • (402)331-7376 • (S 1971 MA)

**TAGGART LINDA J** (810)775-6915
21736 Downing St St Clair Shrs MI 48080-3909 • MI • Tchr • St Thomas Eastpointe MI • (810)772-3372 • (RF 1976 MA)

**TAGGE BRUCE C** (309)686-0777
309 E Mc Clure Ave Peoria IL 61603-1705 • CI • Tchr • Concordia Peoria IL • (309)691-8921 • (RF 1971 MCMU)

**TAGGE NANCY J** (206)444-5047
11115 34th Pl SW Seattle WA 98146 • NOW • Tchr • Hope Seattle WA • (206)935-8500 • (S 1977)

**TAMBURELLO PAMELA** (281)820-9914
8102 Edgebrook Forest Ct Houston TX 77088-2823 • frauobo@aol.com • TX • Tchr • Immanuel Houston TX • (713)861-8787 • (RF 1984)

**TANGEN RENAE J** (218)346-2421
RR 1 Box 87 Perham MN 56573 • MNN • Tchr • St Paul Perham MN • (218)346-7725 • (SP 1988)

**TAPPENDORF CYNTHIA L** (602)485-5084
2840 E Gelding Dr Phoenix AZ 85032 • PSW • 12/1992 12/1999 • (RF 1983 MED)

**TARR JOHN M** (715)341-5840
3541 Patti Dr #2 Plover WI 54467 • NW • Tchr • Immanuel Wisconsin Rapids WI • (715)423-0272 • (MQ 1999)

**TARR SUE ANN**
2691 W 1st Ave Denver CO 80219-2124 • RM • Tchr • Redeemer Denver CO • (303)934-0422 • (S 1993)

**TASLER CHARLES ROBERT** (352)624-0800
11 Almond Trail Pl Ocala FL 34472-9418 • FG • Tchr • St John Ocala FL • (352)622-7275 • (S 1996)

**TASLER DEBORAH ANN** (352)624-0800
11 Almond Trail Pl Ocala FL 34472-9418 • FG • Tchr • St John Ocala FL • (352)622-7275 • (S 1996)

**TATE GARY R** (847)882-5052
695 Perry Ln Hoffman Est IL 60194-3128 • NI • Tchr • Trinity Roselle IL • (630)894-3263 • (RF 1969 MA)

**TATUM LINDA** (503)666-8145
3217 SW 28th Ct Gresham OR 97080-5473 • NOW • Tchr • Trinity Portland OR • (503)288-6403 • (CQ 1993)

**TAUBE TIMOTHY WALTER** (219)484-1088
11225 Pine Bank Ct Fort Wayne IN 46845-1841 • IN • Tchr • Concordia LHS Fort Wayne IN • (219)483-1102 • (S 1973 MA)

**TAUBENHEIM KAREN F** (414)251-3173
W166N8532 Theodore Ave Menomonee Falls WI 53051-2840 • tktauben@ameritech.net • SW • Tchr • Elm Grove Elm Grove WI • (262)797-2970 • (MQ 1997)

**TAYLOR BRET A** (949)462-3757
8 Chatri Cir Foothill Ranch CA 92610-2604 • bret.taylor@cui.edu • PSW • SHS/C • Pacific Southwest Irvine CA • (949)854-3232 • (S 1987 MA)

**TAYLOR JAMES F** (716)865-2681
24 Sparling Dr Rochester NY 14616-3102 • EA • Tchr • St Paul Hilton NY • (716)392-4000 • (RF 1969 MA)

**TAYLOR JENNIFER LEIGH** (612)224-6630
212 Congress St W Saint Paul MN 55107-2152 • sprout00@frontiernet.net • MNS • Tchr • Central Saint Paul MN • (651)645-8649 • (SP 1989)

**TAYLOR LAVONA MAE** (952)445-6955
1064 Merritt St Shakopee MN 55379-2922 • vonietaylor@aol.com • MNS • Tchr • Holy Cross Prior Lake MN • (612)445-1779 • (S 1989)

**TAYLOR MARCIA D** (517)652-8486
593 Churchgrove Rd Frankenmuth MI 48734-9791 • MI • EM • (CQ 1989 MA)

**TAYLOR PATRICIA A** (920)437-9339
704 Emilie St Green Bay WI 54301-3219 • NW • Tchr • Redeemer Green Bay WI • (920)499-1033 • (S 1964)

**TAYLOR SUSAN JANE** (414)691-8619
N32W23360 Fieldhouse Rd Pewaukee WI 53072-5724 • SW • Tchr • Our Redeemer Wauwatosa WI • (414)258-4558 • (RF 1978)

**TAYLOR T% DONALD** (507)238-4763
603 Albion Ave Apt 2 Fairmont MN 56031-2181 • tomdonaldtaylor@hotmail.com • MNS • Tchr • Martin Luther Northrop MN • (507)436-5249 • (S 1992)

**TAYON DAWN E** (314)429-5517
10479 Canter Way Overland MO 63114-1510 • tayon@primary.net • MO • Prin • Our Redeemer Overland MO • (314)427-3462 • (S 1983 LITTD)

**TEAGUE JUDY L** (219)482-9015
3916 Marigold Dr Fort Wayne IN 46815-5926 • IN • Tchr • Concordia LHS Fort Wayne IN • (219)483-1102 • (RF 1979 MS)

**TEAL KAREN ANNE** (901)757-0130
2898 Belgrave Dr Germantown TN 38138-7038 • MDS • Tchr • Christ King Memphis TN • (901)682-8404 • (RF 1975)

**TEETZEN CURTIS A** (414)462-3352
4942 N 105th St Milwaukee WI 53225-3919 • SW • EM • (RF 1952 MNS)

**TEGELER SHARON D** (708)771-1827
7742 Monroe 2nd Fl rear Forest Park IL 60130 • sharon5@stjohn.pvt.k12.il.us • NI • Tchr • St John Forest Park IL • (708)366-2764 • (RF 1987)

**TEGTMEIER LYNETTE J** (309)820-0131
819 E Monroe Bloomington IL 61701 • CI • Tchr • Trinity Bloomington IL • (309)829-7513 • (S 1989 MSED)

**TEINERT BONNIE J** (414)853-3990
246 N 10th St Hilbert WI 54129-9531 • SW • Tchr • St Peter Hilbert WI • (920)853-3851 • (RF 1975)

**TEINERT LAURIE F** (512)990-2955
14301 Anita Marie Ln Austin TX 78728-6813 • TX • Tchr • St Paul Austin TX • (512)472-3313 • (RF 1974)

**TELLE LADONNA CATHERINE** (573)449-2531
1302 Look Out Ct Columbia MO 65202 • MO • Tchr • Trinity Columbia MO • (573)445-1014 • (CQ 1996)

**TELLMAN CHERYL M** (219)772-5326
254 E New York St Knox IN 46534-1537 • IN • 04/1989 04/2000 • (AA 1985 MS)

**TELSCHOW ANNE D** (417)235-3872
414 N Main Freistatt MO 65654-9999 • MO • Tchr • Trinity Freistatt MO • (417)235-5931 • (S 1961)

**TELSCHOW EARL T** (417)235-3872
414 N Main Freistatt MO 65654 • MO • EM • (S 1964)

**TELSCHOW JONATHAN P** (409)542-3852
RR 2 Box 241 Giddings TX 78942-9796 • TX • Tchr • St Paul Giddings TX • (409)366-2218 • (S 1998)

**TEMME EDWIN G** (813)787-2281
3243 Roxmere Dr Palm Harbor FL 34685-1735 • FG • EM • (RF 1955)

**TEMPLE ELIZABETH** (815)874-5133
5065 Linden Rd Apt 4201 Rockford IL 61103 • NI • SHS/C • Northern Illinois Hillside IL • (MQ 1999)

**TEMPLIN LYNETTE** (507)334-2785
717 Winter Dr Faribault MN 55021 • MNS • Tchr • Faribault Faribault MN • (507)334-7982 • (SP 1966)

**TEN PAS SONIA MARIE** (414)467-3183
1024 Broadway Sheboygan Falls WI 53085-2746 • SW • 06/2000 • (MQ 1992)

**TENNANT SARAH** (616)365-0791
3910 Mayfield Ave Apt 1L NE Grand Rapids MI 49525 • MI • Tchr • Immanuel Grand Rapids MI • (616)454-3655 • (AA 1999)

**TENNIS DONNA MARIE** (708)489-2797
2542 New St Blue Island IL 60406-2322 • NI • Tchr • St Philip Chicago IL • (773)493-3865 • (RF 1988)

**TEPKER PAUL E** (661)589-2192
404 Sinaloa Ave Bakersfield CA 93312-9334 • ptepker@ev1.net • CNH • Mem C • St John Bakersfield CA • (661)834-1412 • (S 1975 MMU)

**TERESZKIEWICZ MARY F** (413)536-7583
409 S Elm St Holyoke MA 01040-3054 • mftereszkiewicz@hotmail.com • NE • Tchr • First Holyoke MA • (413)532-4272 • (RF 1984 MED)

**TERRASS BARRY S** (314)968-8871
1701 Blue Jay Cv Brentwood MO 63144-1604 • MO • Tchr • Missouri Saint Louis MO • (314)317-4550 • (S 1977 MED MCOUN)

**TERRELL VIRGINIA I** (847)783-0188
6714 Pine Ln Carpentersville IL 60110 • NI • Prin • Immanuel Dundee IL • (847)428-1010 • (S 1968 MA)

**TESCH DEBRA L** (414)353-0544
8259 W Acacia St Milwaukee WI 53223-5525 • SW • Tchr • Pilgrim Wauwatosa WI • (414)476-0736 • (S 1978)

**TESCH ROSANNE M** (507)248-3278
32633 Fort Rd Henderson MN 56044 • rctesch@prairie.lakes.com • MNS • Tchr • Immanuel Courtland MN • (507)359-2534 • (SP 1994)

**TESCH RUTH A** (651)695-1692
132 Wheeler St S St Paul MN 55105-1925 • ruthtesch@excite.com • MNS • Mem C • Trinity White Bear Lake MN • (651)429-4293 • (SP 1974)

**TESKE AMY KAY** (517)264-2506
3642 Hunt Rd Adrian MI 49221 • MI • Tchr • St John Adrian MI • (517)265-6998 • (AA 1998)

**TESKE INGEBORG L** (773)477-3862
2245 N Fremont St Chicago IL 60614-3613 • iteske@stjames³lutheranorg. • NI • SHS/C • Northern Illinois Hillside IL • (CQ 1987 MA)

**TESKE KATHRYN A** (708)946-6222
PO Box 397 Beecher IL 60401-0397 • NI • Tchr • Zion Beecher IL • (708)946-2272 • (RF 1962 MSED)

**TESKE RALPH WILLIAM** (309)697-8828
5724 W Colt Dr Peoria IL 61607-1134 • rteske@worldnet.att.net • CI • Tchr • Christ Peoria IL • (309)637-1512 • (RF 1989 MA)

**TESSENDORF KAREN KAY** (865)922-8432
6606 Trinity Dr Knoxville TN 37918-6230 • MDS • Tchr • First Knoxville TN • (423)524-0308 • (RF 1978)

**TESSENDORF ROGER W** (865)922-8432
6606 Trinity Dr Knoxville TN 37918-6230 • MDS • P/Tchr • First Knoxville TN • (423)524-0308 • (RF 1978 MS)

**TEWES TAMMY S** (217)824-7810
1448 N 1600 E Rd Taylorville IL 62568 • ptewes@ctitech.com • MO • Tchr • Zion Palmyra MO • (573)769-2739 • (S 1990)

**TEWES WILBUR G** (402)794-5001
17701 Basswood Dr Martell NE 68404-5019 • NEB • EM • (S 1956 MA)

**TEWS LARRY N** (812)376-9537
2835 Sassafrass Ln Columbus IN 47203-2926 • IN • Tchr • St Peter Columbus IN • (812)372-5266 • (RF 1974 MED)

**THACKER JESS MICHAEL** (913)651-4429
624 Kickapoo St Leavenworth KS 66048-1439 • KS • Tchr • St Paul Leavenworth KS • (913)682-5553 • (S 1992)

**THAEMERT FEROL S** (314)921-3277
2860 Sussex Dr Florissant MO 63033-1306 • fmthaement@aol.com • MO • Tchr • Salem Florissant MO • (314)741-8220 • (S 1961 MED)

**THAEMERT MELISSA J W**
5475 County Rd 23 #135 Mayer MN 55360-8518 • MNS • Tchr • Trinity First Minneapolis MN • (612)871-2353 • (SP 1997)

**THATE DAVID P** (301)277-2509
3708 Longfellow St Hyattsville MD 20782-3851 • dpthate@aol.com • SE • EM • (S 1954 MED)

**THAULAND DARLENE ANN** (541)269-0130
895 Oakway Dr Coos Bay OR 97420-1921 • NOW • Tchr • Christ Coos Bay OR • (541)267-3851 • (RF 1975)

**THEILGAARD DIANA LYNN** (708)597-7165
12850 Francisco Ave Blue Island IL 60406-1852 • dianatheilgaard@juno.com • NI • Prin • St Paul Dolton IL • (708)849-3225 • (RF 1984)

**THEMER HUGO D** (812)342-6707
14000 W Lake Rd Lot 71 Seymour IN 47274-8706 • IN • EM • (RF 1951)

**THEMER SUSAN R** (812)967-3810
11715 S Priddy Rd Pekin IN 47165-8694 • IN • 06/1996 • (RF 1979 MED)

**THEURER JOAN L** (562)425-6757
4246 Marwick Ave Lakewood CA 90713-3034 • jtheurer@u.arizona.edu • PSW • 07/1996 07/2000 • (S 1975 MA PHD)

**THEWS MELINDA LU** (618)346-4543
192 Skyline View Dr Collinsville IL 62234 • SI • Tchr • Trinity Edwardsville IL • (618)656-7002 • (MQ 1993)

**THIEDE DONNA KAY** (414)377-1568
756 6th Ave Grafton WI 53024-1414 • thiede@milwpc.com • SW • Tchr • St Paul Grafton WI • (414)377-4659 • (S 1977)

**THIEDE LORI ANNE** (616)423-8229
74821 40th St Paw Paw MI 49079 • MI • Tchr • Trinity Paw Paw MI • (616)657-4840 • (MQ 1998)

**THIEDE MARY A** (817)496-5549
6117 Lantana Ln Fort Worth TX 76112-118 • marythiede@yahoo.com • TX • 09/1999 • (SP 1969)

**THIES CARL N** (219)489-6629
8134 Medallion Pl Fort Wayne IN 46825-6456 • IN • Tchr • Christ Child Fort Wayne IN • (219)452-2240 • (RF 1964 MA)

**THIES EVERETT I** (402)564-3309
3991 SE 16th Columbus NE 68601-9009 • NEB • Tchr • Immanuel Columbus NE • (402)564-8423 • (S 1969 MED)

**THIES RONAL L** (715)341-5091
941 Ramble Ln Plover WI 54467-2135 • jthies@coredcs.com • NW • P/Tchr • St Paul Stevens Point WI • (715)344-5660 • (RF 1962 MED)

**THIES RUTH E** (334)986-5857
26575 US Highway 98 Elberta AL 36530-2711 • SO • EM • (RF 1952)

**THOELKE KATE ELIZABETH** (636)327-4416
317 W Pearce Blvd Wentzville MO 63385 • jtket@earthlink.com • MO • St Paul Stevens Point WI • (RF 1996)

**THOELKE MARK** (636)922-1043
14 Amanda Ct Saint Peters MO 63376-5535 • mtbrdthoelke@juno.com • MO • Mem C • Zion Saint Charles MO • (636)441-7425 • (RF 1989 MCMU)

**THOMAS GWEN D** (316)687-3278
3154 Cranberry St Wichita KS 67226-1222 • KS • Tchr • Holy Cross Wichita KS • (316)684-4431 • (S 1986)

**THOMAS JEAN G** (517)642-2992
14824 Boswell Rd Hemlock MI 48626-9709 • jeangt@juno.com • MI • Tchr • St Peter Hemlock MI • (517)642-5659 • (SP 1972 MA)

**THOMAS RICHARD M** (406)652-6512
3328 Tahoe Dr Billings MT 59102-6935 • MT • P/Tchr • Trinity Billings MT • (406)656-1021 • (S 1982 MA)

**THOMASON LINNETTE D** (909)620-9968
5 Hidden Hills Cir Phillips Ranch CA 91766 • LinDThom@aol.com • PSW • Tchr • Mount Calvary Diamond Bar CA • (909)861-2740 • (SP 1973)

**THOMASON ROBBIN K** (817)549-9611
218 E Bridge #14 Granbury TX 76048 • TX • Tchr • Cross Christ De Soto TX • (972)223-9340 • (S 1997)

**THOMASON VICTORIA R** (561)220-4970
814 E Madison Ave Stuart FL 34996-3263 • FG • Tchr • Redeemer Stuart FL • (561)286-0932 • (BR 1980)

**THOMPSON DOLORES** (205)264-7539
3603 Goode St Montgomery AL 36105-2122 • SO • EM • (S 1970)

**THOMPSON MELINDA MICHELLE** (501)664-6055
6806 Bluebird Dr Little Rock AR 72205 • my3kittens@hotmail.com • MDS • Tchr • Christ Little Rock AR • (501)663-5232 • (CQ 1999)

**THOMPSON MICHELLE R** (636)273-5971
C/O St John Lutheran Church 15808 Manchester Rd Ellisville MO 63011 • mthompson@stjohnsellisville.org • MO • Mem C • St John Ellisville MO • (314)394-4100 • (RF 1993)

**THOMPSON PAUL A**
3 Shaderest Ct Glen Carbon IL 62034-1488 • pthomp7939@aol.com • SI • Tchr • Southern Illinois Belleville IL • (SP 1991)

**THOMPSON RUTH ANN** (515)432-2813
1245 Knap Pl Boone IA 50036-7177 • IW • Tchr • Trinity Boone IA • (515)432-5140 • (S 1987)

**THOMPSON SHARON**
7818 W Cressett Dr Elmwood Park IL 60707-1344 • NI • Tchr • Bethlehem River Grove IL • (708)456-8786 • (RF 1973)

**THOMPSON STEVEN LEE**
C/O Faith Lutheran School 3033 Wilder Rd Bay City MI 48706-2398 • MI • Bethlehem River Grove IL • (AA 1987)

**THOMPSON WILLIAM J** (847)891-5009
1751 Heron Ave Unit C Schaumburg IL 60193 • NI • Tchr • Trinity Roselle IL • (630)894-3263 • (RF 1969 MA)

**THOMPSON WILLIAM WAYNE** (805)239-3734
3025 Adelaida Rd Paso Robles CA 93446-9779 • CNH • 08/1987 08/2000 • (S 1973 MED)

**THOMSON BARBARA KATE** (972)231-9018
3939 Crestpark Dallas TX 75244 • TX • Tchr • Holy Cross Dallas TX • (214)358-4396 • (AU 1995)

**THOMSON HEATHER S**
2742 Granada Dr Apt 3D Jackson MI 49202-5347 • MI • Tchr • Trinity Jackson MI • (517)750-2105 • (RF 1996)

**THOMSON KATHLEEN A** (314)723-5439
416 Longbow Trail Saint Charles MO 63301-1212 • MO • Tchr • Immanuel Saint Charles MO • (636)946-2656 • (RF 1986)

**THOMSON PAULA KAY** (972)231-9018
1310 Rusk Richardson TX 75081 • TX • Tchr • Our Redeemer Dallas TX • (214)368-1371 • (AU 1998)

**THORESEN JULI A** (512)929-5370
3622 Quiette Dr Austin TX 78754-4827 • jujufrog@hotmail.com • TX • Tchr • Hope Austin TX • (512)926-0003 • (AA 1999)

**THORNBURG TAMARA K** (559)732-1968
1225 S Atwood Ct Visalia CA 93277-3493 • dthorny4@aol.com • CNH • Tchr • Grace Visalia CA • (559)734-7694 • (S 1988)

**THORNE MARLENE** (417)623-6015
1015 S Saint Louis Ave Apt 1 Joplin MO 64801-8127 • mthorne@janics.com • MO • Tchr • Martin Luther Joplin MO • (417)624-1403 • (SP 1985)

**THORNSBROUGH KURT A** (217)427-5610
PO Box 175 Catlin IL 61817-0175 • CI • Tchr • Immanuel Danville IL • (217)442-5675 • (RF 1983)

**THORP GLADYS E**
3016 S Deerfield Lansing MI 48911 • MI • Tchr • Our Savior Lansing MI • (517)882-8665 • (S 2000)

**THORSEN MARK F** (561)219-4745
5338 SE Celestial Cir Stuart FL 34997 • FG • Tchr • Redeemer Stuart FL • (561)286-0911 • (S 1974)

**THUNDER-HAAB KETURAH A** (313)971-1744
2200 Glencoe Hills Dr Ann Arbor MI 48108-1019 • MI • EM • (RF 1959 MA)

**THURAU RACHEL ELLEN** (815)748-4713
3 Lee Ct De Kalb IL 60115-2630 • NI • 02/1995 • (AA 1983)

**THURBER DANIEL C** (402)643-6487
1340 Plainview Ave Seward NE 68434-1349 • NEB • SHS/C • Nebraska Seward NE • (S 1968 MA DART)

**THURBER REBECCA CAROL** (507)238-4621
650 Summit Dr - Apt 12 Fairmont MN 56031 • rthurber@lps.org • MNS • Tchr • St Pauls Fairmont MN • (507)238-9492 • (S 1996)

**THURMAN RICHARD SCOTT** (360)254-6061
9501 NE 19th St Vancouver WA 98664-2982 • NOW • SHS/C • Northwest Portland OR • (PO 1987 MED)

**THURMOND PATRICIA**
5675 S Lamar St Littleton CO 80123-0833 • RM • Tchr • St John Denver CO • (303)733-3777 • (S 1964)

**THURN DAVID G** (708)474-7455
2507 184th St Lansing IL 60438-2723 • NI • Tchr • Trinity Lansing IL • (708)474-8539 • (RF 1969 MA)

**THURN KATHLEEN C** (708)474-7455
2507 184th St Lansing IL 60438-2723 • NI • Tchr • Trinity Lansing IL • (708)474-8539 • (CQ 1988)

**THYPARAMBIL NANCY J** (402)484-7030
720 Smoky Hill Rd Lincoln NE 68520-1175 • nthypar@lps.org • NEB • Tchr • Faith Lincoln NE • (402)466-6861 • (S 1976 MED)

**TIDWELL HARVEY E**
12083 Hayes Cir Overland Park KS 66213 • KS • Tchr • Hope Shawnee KS • (913)631-6940 • (CQ 1999)

**TIEDJE NORMAN** (810)781-6731
55845 Jewell Rd Shelby Twp MI 48315-1048 • ntiedje@compserv.net • MI • Tchr • Trinity Utica MI • (810)731-4490 • (RF 1962 MMU)

**TIEFEL AMY D** (253)838-2001
7050 35th Ave NE Seattle WA 98115 • NOW • Tchr • Concordia Seattle WA • (206)525-7407 • (S 1999)

**TIEFEL TED LOUIS** (402)643-3145
1538 Eastridge Dr Seward NE 68434 • NEB • SHS/C • Nebraska Seward NE • (S 1999)

**TIEMAN EDSEL W** (217)423-4918
1125 Veech Ln Decatur IL 62521-4258 • etct@juno.com • CI • Prin • Lutheran School Asso Decatur IL • (217)233-2001 • (S 1960 MSED)

**TIEMANN ERNEST F**
1109 S Lyman Ave Oak Park IL 60304-2227 • NI • SHS/C • Northern Illinois Hillside IL • (RF 1965 MA MBA)

**TIEMANN LARRY G** (314)349-5354
304 Arlington Glen Ct Fenton MO 63026-3973 • MO • Tchr • Word Of Life Saint Louis MO • (314)832-1244 • (S 1968 MA)

**TIETJEN LEROY H** (219)947-2080
2531 Crowsnest Dr Hobart IN 46342-3821 • IN • Tchr • Trinity Hobart IN • (219)942-3147 • (S 1965)

**TIETMEYER LARRY** (209)525-3945
3805 Tumbleweed Ct Modesto CA 95355-5606 • ltietmeyer@aol.com • CNH • P/Tchr • Grace Modesto CA • (209)529-1800 • (S 1970)

**TIETZ CHERI L** (402)477-4676
4827 Bunker Hill Rd Lincoln NE 68521-1137 • ctietz@lps.org • NEB • Tchr • Faith Lincoln NE • (402)466-6861 • (S 1970)

**TIETZ JOAN MARIE** (217)586-7686
1604 S River Bluff Dr Mahomet IL 61853 • jmpt222@aol.com • CI • Tchr • St John Champaign IL • (217)359-1714 • (S 1975)

**TIETZ STUART D** (402)477-4676
4827 Bunker Hill Rd Lincoln NE 68521-1137 • stietz@lps.org • NEB • P/Tchr • Faith Lincoln NE • (402)466-6861 • (S 1970 MED)

**TIGHE CHRISTINE M**
306 E Schaumburg Rd Schaumburg IL 60194-3515 • NI • Tchr • St Peter Schaumburg IL • (847)885-3350 • (RF 1998)

**TILLMAN CYNTHIA YVONNE** (901)332-3529
1362 South Faronia Sq Memphis TN 38116 • MDS • Tchr • Cross/Calvary Memphis TN • (901)396-5566 • (RF 1983)

**TIMKEN GAYLE L**
8B Scenic View #1 Red Hill Rd Tai Tam HONG KONG • PSW • S Miss • Pacific Southwest Irvine CA • (949)854-3232 • (S 1963)

**TIMLER KAREN L**
107 Barranca Ln Moss Beach CA 94038-9773 • CNH • Tchr • Grace San Mateo CA • (650)345-9082 • (RF 1985)

**TIMM CONNIE L** (320)328-4331
PO Box 411 Brownton MN 55312-0411 • MNS • 09/1998 • (SP 1990)

**TIMM DIANE M** (414)463-6582
4330 N 83rd St Milwaukee WI 53222-1810 • dtimm@execpc.com • SW • Tchr • Northwest Milwaukee WI • (414)463-4040 • (RF 1965 MA)

**TIMM DONALD C** (313)379-5460
32710 Elm St Rockwood MI 48173-1108 • MI • EM • (RF 1957)

**TIMM EUNICE M** (615)624-2588
4010 Belvoir Dr Chattanooga TN 37412-2516 • MDS • Tchr • Lutheran Chattanooga TN • (423)622-3755 • (S 1968 MSED)

**TIMM JODY R** (816)454-7831
2015 NE Englewood Rd Kansas City MO 64118-5627 • MO • Tchr • Holy Cross Kansas City MO • (816)453-7211 • (CQ 1996)

**TIMM KAREN KAY** (708)257-8311
57 Stone Creek Dr Lemont IL 60439-8744 • NI • EM • (RF 1963)

**TIMM LOWELL H** (815)683-2422
1299 N 1450 East Rd Onarga IL 60955 • NI • P/Tchr • St Paul Milford IL • (815)889-4209 • (RF 1974 MA)

**TIMM MARCIA L** (402)553-7845
5813 Charles St Omaha NE 68132-1320 • NEB • Tchr • Mount Calvary Omaha NE • (402)551-7020 • (S 1965)

**TIMM NATALIE R** (507)282-4881
807 12th Ave SE Rochester MN 55904-7245 • MNS • Tchr • Rochester Central Rochester MN • (507)289-3267 • (S 1972)

**TIMM PAUL MICHAEL**
230 S 6th St Cedar Grove WI 53013-1603 • RM • 06/1998 06/2000 • (MQ 1992 MED)

**TIMM RICHARD P** (612)432-7981
5856 139th St W Apple Valley MN 55124-1520 • MNS • Prin • Trinity Lone Oak Eagan MN • (651)454-1139 • (S 1966 MA)

**TIMM SHARON RUTH** (815)697-2185
130 Mansfield Ct Chebanse IL 60922 • NI • Tchr • Zion Chebanse IL • (815)697-2212 • (RF 1970)

**TIMM SHERYL K** (636)447-6483
3253 Hyatt Ct Saint Charles MO 63303-5827 • stimm@lhssc.org • MO • Tchr • LHS St Charles Saint Peters MO • (636)928-5100 • (SP 1985 MBA)

**TIMM SUZANNE MARIE** (630)896-8036
500 W Oak St North Aurora IL 60542-1055 • chipskimom@aol.com • NI • Tchr • St Paul Aurora IL • (630)820-3457 • (RF 1967)

**TIMM TIMOTHY N** (619)728-9360
2640 Buenos Tiempos Fallbrook CA 92028-4547 • PSW • Tchr • Zion Fallbrook CA • (760)723-3500 • (S 1965 MA)

**TIMMERMAN BERNICE** (303)659-7082
757 S 11th Ave Brighton CO 80601-3240 • RM • EM • (S 1981)

**TIMMERMAN FLOY A**
C/O Faith Lutheran School 7075 Pacific Ave SE Lacey WA 98503 • floykent@hotmail.com • NOW • Tchr • Faith Lacey WA • (360)491-1733 • (CQ 1988 MA)

**TIMMERMAN KARLA K** (314)351-2740
5416 Sunshine Dr Saint Louis MO 63109-4008 • MO • Tchr • St John Saint Louis MO • (314)773-0126 • (S 1977)

**TIMMONS WILLIAM V**
413/10 Sukhumvit 55 Bangkok 10110 THAILAND • NEB • S Miss • Nebraska Seward NE • (S 1969)

**TINNIN HOPE K**
2242 Pinta Dr Warrenton MO 63383-3262 • CI • Tchr • Concordia Peoria IL • (309)691-8921 • (RF 1992)

**TIRMENSTEIN STEPHEN W** (314)741-2633
1923 Lakemont Ln Saint Louis MO 63138-1226 • MO • Tchr • Missouri Saint Louis MO • (314)317-4550 • (RF 1969 MA MMU)

**TITUS LEON G** (612)645-8046
206 Lexington Pkwy N Saint Paul MN 55104-6431 • MNS • EM • (CQ 1968 MA)

**TOBABEN KARA LYNN** (972)599-7811
2525 Alexa Ct S Plano TX 75075-3015 • ktobaben@popcs.net • TX • Tchr • Prince Of Peace Carrollton TX • (972)447-9887 • (S 1996)

**TODD AUDREY J** (303)797-6811
5111 S Meade St Littleton CO 80123-1707 • audnjim@ecentral.com • RM • Tchr • Bethlehem Lakewood CO • (303)233-0401 • (S 1978 MA)

**TODT JOHN H** (810)392-7051
79851 Main Memphis MI 48041-4639 • MI • Tchr • St Thomas Eastpointe MI • (810)772-3372 • (RF 1962)

**TOENSING DAVID W**
C/O Christ Luth Church 2555 S Engler Ave Yuma AZ 85365-3216 • PSW • P/Tchr • Yuma Yuma AZ • (520)726-8410 • (S 1965)

**TOENSING HERBERT F** (314)429-5509
8211 Jackson St Saint Louis MO 63114-6219 • MO • EM • (S 1933)

**TOEPKE ANITA** (309)682-3691
3704 N Melcosta Dr Peoria IL 61615-3929 • CI • EM • (RF 1960 MS)

**TOEPPER MARILYN A** (708)447-8218
7240 Ogden Ave Riverside IL 60546-2207 • NI • Tchr • St John LA Grange IL • (708)354-1690 • (RF 1962)

**TOEPPER ROBERT M** (708)447-8218
7240 Ogden Ave Riverside IL 60546-2207 • crftoepperm@crf.cuis.edu • NI • SHS/C • Northern Illinois Hillside IL • (RF 1962 MA PHD)

**TOLBERT SAMMIE L** (313)837-5177
18235 Midland St Detroit MI 48223-1328 • MI • P/Tchr • St Timothy Detroit MI • (313)535-1971 • (RF 1974 MA)

**TOMAN LAURA**
1441 Dover Hill N Walled Lake MI 48390-3118 • MI • Tchr • St Matthew Walled Lake MI • (248)624-7677 • (AA 1989)

**TOMASHEWSKY ANDREW C** (219)295-3195
22424-2B Stillwater Ct Elkhart IN 46516 • andrewt@trinityl.org • IN • Tchr • Trinity Elkhart IN • (219)522-1491 • (MQ 1999)

**TOMASHEWSKY SUZANNE BETH** (219)295-3195
22424 2B Stillwater Ct Elkhart IN 46516 • suzannet@trinityl.org • IN • Tchr • Trinity Elkhart IN • (219)522-1491 • (MQ 1999)

**TOMICH NANCY LYNN** (352)694-1166
4519 SE 6th Pl Ocala FL 34471-3270 • tomich@atlantic.net • FG • Tchr • St John Ocala FL • (352)622-7275 • (CQ 1996)

**TOMKO LINDA K** (216)884-3343
7704 Spring Garden Rd Parma OH 44129-3630 • OH • Tchr • Bethany Parma OH • (440)884-1010 • (S 1968)

**TONJES BERNARD J** (314)723-8080
3310 Principia Ave Saint Charles MO 63301-5724 • btonjes@lhssc.org • MO • Tchr • LHS St Charles Saint Peters MO • (636)928-5100 • (S 1974 MED)

**TONKINSON KATHRYN M**
2632 W Winona St Chicago IL 60625 • NI • Tchr • Immanuel Glenview IL • (847)724-1034 • (RF 1994)

**TONN DAVID W** (507)674-3930
RR 1 Box 13 Amboy MN 56010-9704 • amboydna@compuserv.com • MNS • Tchr • St James Northrop MN • (507)436-5289 • (SP 1975)

**TONN GLORIA J** (262)677-3366
N132W17380 Rockfield Rd Germantown WI 53022-1156 • gtonn@execpc.com • SW • Tchr • St Peter Milwaukee WI • (414)353-6800 • (RF 1968)

**TONNIGES MARVA R** (402)466-3400
531 N 57th St Lincoln NE 68505-2301 • RTonniges@aol.com • NEB • Tchr • Messiah Lincoln NE • (402)489-3024 • (S 1965)

**TOOLEY KATHERINE ANN*** (502)782-1021
160 Betsey Anne Ct Bowling Green KY 42103-8424 • mktooley@hotmail.com • MDS • 08/1999 • (RF 1990)

**TOOMAN MATTHEW MARVIN** (956)618-5943
1212 E Dallas Ave Apt B 3 Mc Allen TX 78501-8801 • TX • Tchr • St Paul Mc Allen TX • (956)682-2201 • (CQ 1997)

**TOPEL STANLEY R DR** (810)777-9599
24511 Rosalind Ave Eastpointe MI 48021-1311 • MI • EM • (S 1957 MA DED)

**TOPEL TIMOTHY** (810)446-6705
2463 Camel Dr Sterling Hts MI 48310-5222 • ttopel@lanw.lhsa.com • MI • Tchr • LHS Northwest Rochester Hills MI • (810)852-6677 • (S 1982 MAT)

**TOPP DAVID**
1450 Western Dr Kalispell MT 59901 • MT • Tchr • Trinity Kalispell MT • (406)257-6716 • (CQ 1998)

**TOPPE SHARON M** (812)523-6672
2477 N 400 E Seymour IN 47274 • IN • Tchr • Central Brownstown IN • (812)358-2512 • (RF 1969 MA)

**TORBECK LARRY P** (314)846-8480
2563 Black Water Ct Saint Louis MO 63129-4962 • MO • Tchr • LHS South Saint Louis MO • (314)631-1400 • (RF 1971 MA)

**TORBECK STEPHANIE LYNN** (314)416-7956
4029 Morningview Ct Saint Louis MO 63129-2055 • MO • Tchr • Green Park Lemay MO • (314)544-4248 • (RF 1998)

**TORRESON RODNEY T** (616)791-0073
1052 Dick Ave NW Grand Rapids MI 49504-3914 • MI • Tchr • Immanuel Grand Rapids MI • (616)363-0505 • (SP 1976 MFA)

**TOSO JUDITH ANN** (712)239-2206
4001 Teton Trce Sioux City IA 51104-4329 • IW • Tchr • St Paul Sioux City IA • (712)258-6325 • (CQ 1995)

**TOTH JASON M** (262)255-5078
N81 W18117 Tours Dr Menomonee Falls WI 53051 • SW • St Paul Sioux City IA • (MQ 1997)

**TOTSKY ADELE M** (608)586-4848
PO Box 141 Oxford WI 53952-0141 • SW • 08/1995 08/2000 • (MQ 1986)

**TOVEN DAVID O**
PO Box 207 Mc Gregor MN 55760-0207 • AT • 09/1985 09/1999 • (RF 1959 MA)

**TOWNSEND LAURENA MARIE** (818)956-0821
1101 N Maryland Apt N Glendale CA 91207 • laurenat@yahoo.com • PSW • Tchr • Pacific Southwest Irvine CA • (949)854-3232 • (IV 1991 MA)

**TRACEY JULIE A** (812)522-7957
840 Evergreen Dr Seymour IN 47274-3085 • IN • Tchr • Immanuel Seymour IN • (812)522-1301 • (CQ 1993)

**TRACY MARJORIE K** (314)946-2342
1678 Deergrass Dr Saint Charles MO 63303-4616 • MO • Tchr • Zion Harvester MO • (314)441-7424 • (S 1969)

**TRAH RICHARD HEINZ** (314)846-1583
2705 Chalet Hill Dr Saint Louis MO 63129-4203 • MO • Tchr • LHS South Saint Louis MO • (314)631-1400 • (RF 1973 MA)

**TRAH SHEILA E** (815)568-7481
975 Keppler DR Marengo IL 60152-9363 • NI • Tchr • Zion Marengo IL • (815)568-5156 • (RF 1975)

**TRAMPE LOIS J**
320 W Linden Edwardsville IL 62025 • SI • EM • (WN 1956)

**TRAMPE RONALD C** (636)936-1816
4529 Briargate Dr Saint Charles MO 63304-8745 • rtrampe@mail.win.org • MO • EM • (RF 1955 MMU)

**TRANUM CARLA J**
204 N Westridge Ave Covina CA 91724-2919 • PSW • 06/1999 • (RF 1971 MA)

**TRAPP DALE MARTIN DR** (651)776-7479
1286 Etna St Saint Paul MN 55106-2120 • dtrapp@csp.edu • MNS • SHS/C • Minnesota South Burnsville MN • (CQ 1968 MS PHD)

**TRASKA MARIE L** (715)359-4010
1899 Seville Rd Mosinee WI 54455-8166 • traska5@execpc.com • NW • Tchr • St John Wausau WI • (715)845-7031 • (SP 1973 MSCT)

**TRAUB GAIL ANN** (217)895-2583
970 Co Rd 500 E Toledo IL 62468 • CI • P/Tchr • St John Mattoon IL • (217)234-4911 • (CQ 1993 MS)

**TRAUTMANN LAURA E***
N2705 Forest View Ln Clintonville WI 54929 • NW • 04/1996 04/2000 • (S 1986)

**TRAUTMANN MARTHA JEAN** (765)420-9992
1918 Castellan Dr Lafayette IN 47905-7606 • marthat@stjameslaf.org • IN • Tchr • St James Lafayette IN • (765)423-1616 • (RF 1975)

**TRAUTMANN RUTH C** (219)484-5406
2114 Kenwood Ave Fort Wayne IN 46805-2769 • IN • EM • (RF 1966 MA)

**TRAUTNER DONN W** (956)682-2201
212 W Gardenia Ave Mc Allen TX 78501-1817 • donnwalter@aol.com • TX • Prin • St Paul Mc Allen TX • (956)682-2201 • (RF 1973 MED)

**TRAUTSCH HAROLD H** (561)286-5647
1030 E Dolphin Dr Stuart FL 34996-5823 • FG • EM • (RF 1950)

**TRAUTSCH MONICA E** (561)286-5647
1030 E Dolphin Dr Stuart FL 34996-5823 • FG • EM • (RF 1950)

**TRAVERS BARBARA NOSKE** (410)893-8755
124 Drexel Dr Bel Air MD 21014 • btravers85@hotmail.com • SE • Mem C • St James of Overlea Baltimore MD • (410)668-0158 • (BR 1985)

**TRAVIS JON D** (314)447-7181
349 Lemonwood Dr Saint Peters MO 63376-7063 • MO • Tchr • Zion Saint Charles MO • (636)441-7425 • (RF 1980)

**TRAVIS KRISTIN SHARON** (952)995-0068
303 S Mill Elmore MN 56027 • MNS • Tchr • Cross View Edina MN • (952)941-1094 • (SP 1984)

**TREDRAY CHRISTINA** (847)279-3975
200 Portwine Rd Northbrook IL 60062 • NI • Tchr • St John Mount Prospect IL • (847)593-7670 • (RF 2000)

**TRES MARLENE J** (708)670-0665
1111 N Pine Ct Arlington Hts IL 60004-4721 • NI • Tchr • Immanuel Palatine IL • (847)359-1936 • (RF 1983 MA)

**TRETTIN PAUL K** (847)526-0984
820 Osage Ter Wauconda IL 60084-1141 • NI • P/Tchr • Immanuel Glenview IL • (847)724-1034 • (RF 1973 MA)

**TRICKEL DONALD R** (309)828-8046
906 S Madison St Bloomington IL 61701-6647 • CI • 07/1988 07/2000 • (S 1960 MS)

**TRIMBERGER ELAINE L** (920)759-0528
4 Mc Farland Pl Kaukauna WI 54130-2682 • SW • EM • (RF 1964)

**TRINKLEIN DIANE M** (573)496-3769
7409 Tanner Bridge Rd Jefferson City MO 65101-8520 • MO • Tchr • Immanuel Jefferson City MO • (573)496-3451 • (S 1990)

**TRINKLEIN ERIN R** (636)926-0835
3355 Ridgeway Saint Charles MO 63303 • trinkler@webtv.net • MO • Tchr • Zion Saint Charles MO • (636)441-7425 • (RF 1997)

**TRINKLEIN FREDERICK E DR** (631)744-6509
36 Briarcliff Rd Shoreham NY 11786-1428 • AT • EM • (RF 1945 MA LITTD)

**TRINKLEIN JOAN** (770)973-2855
798 Forest Ridge Dr SE Marietta GA 30067-7154 • FG • EM • (RF 1955)

**TRINKLEIN KATHRYN B** (219)745-3172
1136 W Packard Ave Fort Wayne IN 46807-1550 • dtrink1@aol.com • IN • Tchr • Unity Fort Wayne IN • (219)744-0459 • (S 1973 MS)

**TRINKLEIN ROLAND G** (770)973-2855
798 Forest Ridge Dr SE Marietta GA 30067-7154 • FG • EM • (RF 1950)

**TRITTIN SANDRA JEANNE** (218)281-1399
111 Loring St #4 Crookston MN 56716 • MNN • Tchr • Our Savior Crookston MN • (218)281-5191 • (SP 1993)

**TROFKA MICHELE E** (414)434-1091
3900 Lark Rd Green Bay WI 54313-8400 • NW • Tchr • Pilgrim Green Bay WI • (920)494-6530 • (RF 1979)

**TROMBLEY KRISTIN JO** (651)714-4191
7990 Forest Blvd Apt G Woodbury MN 55125-4375 • MNS • Tchr • East St Paul Saint Paul MN • (612)774-2030 • (SP 1997)

**TRONDSON TERRI LYNN** (320)763-3611
308 7th Ave E Alexandria MN 56308-1828 • tntsales@rea-alp.com • MNS • 04/1999 • (SP 1991)

**TROST REBECCA J***
527 E Center #265 Anaheim CA 92805 • AT • 03/1999 • (S 1997)

**TROUTMAN ANN MARIE** (972)462-7496
104 Meadowglen Cir Coppell TX 75019-3009 • annm47@aol.com • TX • Tchr • Christ Our Savior Coppell TX • (972)393-7074 • (CQ 1985)

**TROUTMAN JOHN R** (972)462-7496
104 Meadowglen Cir Coppell TX 75019-3009 • john32roy@aol.com • TX • EM • (CQ 1985 MA DED)

**TRUNKHILL BRENDA EILEEN** (314)647-2945
1606 Kraft St Saint Louis MO 63139 • btrunkhill@immanuelluth.org • MO • Tchr • Immanuel Saint Charles MO • (636)946-2656 • (SP 1998)

**TRUOG DAVID J** (616)796-6651
20615 Okemos Rd Big Rapids MI 49307-9744 • dtruog@net-port.com • MI • P/Tchr • St Peter Big Rapids MI • (231)796-8782 • (S 1970 MA)

**TRUOG SUSAN L** (616)796-6651
20615 Okemos Rd Big Rapids MI 49307-9744 • dtruog@net-port.com • MI • Tchr • St Peter Big Rapids MI • (231)796-8782 • (S 1970 MA)

**TRUSHEIM ROBERT H** (630)553-9811
1594 Walsh Dr Yorkville IL 60560 • NI • EM • (RF 1953 MED)

**TSCHATSCHULA M LEROY DR** (281)345-9258
17126 Copper Shore Dr Houston TX 77095-4330 • TX • EM • (RF 1951 MED PHD)

**TUCKER KATHERINE L** (317)455-2749
5406 Buckskin Dr Kokomo IN 46902-5484 • IN • Tchr • Redeemer Kokomo IN • (765)864-6466 • (RF 1969 MED)

**TUCKER LORI D** (517)792-4466
1727 Passolt Saginaw MI 48603-4791 • MI • Tchr • Bethlehem Saginaw MI • (517)755-1144 • (CQ 1997 MAT)

**TUECKE ELIZABETH K** (319)659-1509
2604 244th St DeWitt IA 52742 • IE • 06/1998 06/2000 • (RF 1991)

**TULL BETTY L** (402)572-8118
9348 Jaynes St Omaha NE 68134-1719 • NEB • P/Tchr • St Paul Omaha NE • (402)451-2865 • (S 1977)

**TULL VIRGINIA** (847)669-1184
4 Camden Ct Lake In The Hills IL 60156-5624 • NI • Tchr • St John Algonquin IL • (847)658-9311 • (SP 1975)

**TUOMI BRUCE G**
C/O Walther Lutheran High Sch 900 Chicago Ave Melrose Park IL 60160-4120 • NI • Tchr • Walther LHS Melrose Park IL • (708)344-0404 • (RF 1976 MS)

**TURANSKI ELIZABETH ANN** (907)243-1899
8035 Lloyd Dr Anchorage AK 99502 • MI • 12/1999 • (AA 1995)

**TURCKES DENISE A** (414)790-0252
4730 N 135th St Brookfield WI 53005-7504 • SW • Tchr • Nazareth Milwaukee WI • (414)354-6601 • (RF 1983)

**TURKE CAROLYN D** (414)336-2735
408 Custer Ct Green Bay WI 54301-1247 • NW • Tchr • Pilgrim Green Bay WI • (920)494-6530 • (RF 1966)

**TURNBULL EVAN LEE**
1113 Lake Forest Dr - Apt 3 Fort Wayne IN 46815 • IN • Tchr • Zion Fort Wayne IN • (219)744-1389 • (S 1998)

**TURNBULL LEIGH M**
1113 Lake Forest Dr - Apt 3 Fort Wayne IN 46815-7985 • MI • Tchr • St John Adrian MI • (517)265-6998 • (S 1999)

**TURNER JENNIFER L** (303)682-2757
2337 Spindrift Dr Twin Peaks P & DC CO 80503-9183 • nturner@csn.net • RM • Tchr • Mount Zion Boulder CO • (303)443-4151 • (CQ 1994)

**TURPIN JANICE M** (757)484-8805
4301 Galston Ct Chesapeake VA 23321-4384 • CI • Tchr • Immanuel Rock Island IL • (309)786-3391 • (S 1981)

**TWORK CLARA J** (517)327-5459
4841 Sandstone Pass Apt 2B Ypsilanti MI 48197 • cjtwork@yahoo.com • MI • Tchr • St Paul Ann Arbor MI • (734)665-9117 • (S 1976 MA)

**TYSON MADELYN M**
33340 Wesley Rd Eustis FL 32736 • jand3m@aol.com • FG • Tchr • Faith Eustis FL • (352)589-5433 • (S 1976 MSED)

## U

**UDEN CYNTHIA L** (402)752-3367
600 N Brooks Ave Kenesaw NE 68956-1530 • NEB • Tchr • Christ Juniata NE • (402)744-4991 • (S 1979 MED)

**UDEN LORI D** (402)463-0403
1527 W 7th St Hastings NE 68901-4337 • logosfromldu@hotmail.com • NEB • Tchr • Zion Hastings NE • (402)462-5012 • (S 1985)

**UDEN MICHAEL D** (920)467-0624
228 Second St Sheboygan Falls WI 53085-1305 • michael³uden@cuw.edu • SW • SHS/C • South Wisconsin Milwaukee WI • (414)464-8100 • (MQ 1989 MS)

**UDY KRISTIN DENISE** (208)235-9778
1507 Eastridge #20 Pocatello ID 83201 • kudy@gracepocid.org • NOW • Tchr • Grace Pocatello ID • (208)237-4142 • (S 1999)

**UECKER BARRY D** (612)657-2347
15980 62nd St Mayer MN 55360-9683 • MNS • 08/1990 08/2000 • (SP 1980)

**UECKER CAROL S**
904 NE 5th St Madison SD 57042 • SD • Tchr • Peace Brookings SD • (605)692-5272 • (SP 1975)

**UELTZEN LARRY** (954)426-1607
1319 SE 14th Ter Deerfield Beach FL 33441-7145 • lueltzen@prodigy.net • NI • Tchr • Luther HS North Chicago IL • (773)286-3600 • (RF 1970 MS MA)

**UELTZEN VANESSA L** (773)481-5879
5501 W Newport Chicago IL 60641 • ueltzen@prodigy.net • NI • Tchr • Messiah Chicago IL • (773)767-2727 • (RF 1997)

**UETRECHT DONALD G** (314)353-3099
5859 Nottingham Ave Saint Louis MO 63109-2741 • MO • Tchr • Christ Community Kirkwood MO • (314)822-7774 • (S 1986 MA)

**UFFELMAN JANELL MARIE** (402)728-5424
1217 Road V Waco NE 68460 • juffelman@seward.cune.edu • NEB • SHS/C • Nebraska Seward NE • (S 1975 MED)

**UFFMANN LYNNE ANN** (808)247-5589
706 N Kainalu Dr Kailua HI 96734-1959 • CNH • Tchr • St Mark Kaneohe HI • (808)247-5589 • (RF 1969)

**UHLIG JUNE FRANCES** (702)396-3494
3701 Daisy Field Dr North Las Vegas NV 89032 • jfuvegas@aol.com • PSW • Tchr • Faith LHS Las Vegas NV • (702)804-4400 • (S 1977)

**ULMER LAURIE LYNN** (616)428-5013
1834 Sherwood Dr Stevensville MI 49127 • MI • Tchr • Christ Stevensville MI • (616)429-7111 • (AA 1985)

**ULMER MARIAN** (402)571-6351
8017 Manderson St Omaha NE 68134-4231 • NEB • EM • (RF 1968)

**ULMER ORVILLE K** (219)324-8071
205 Harrison St La Porte IN 46350-3629 • IN • Tchr • St John La Porte IN • (219)362-6692 • (RF 1959 MALS)

**ULMER RICHARD B** (402)571-6351
8017 Manderson St Omaha NE 68134-4231 • NEB • EM • (RF 1953 MS EDS)

**ULRICH DEAN R*** (815)654-9703
2612 Lorado Ln Rockford IL 61101-1844 • NI • Tchr • St Paul Rockford IL • (815)965-3335 • (RF 1975 MSED)

**UMLAND JEAN MARIE** (715)524-4815
324 S Andrews St Shawano WI 54166 • NW • Mem C • St James Shawano WI • (715)524-4815 • (S 1979)

**UMPHENOUR TERRY ALLEN** (314)894-9024
642 Reavis Barracks Rd Saint Louis MO 63125-3241 • MO • Tchr • Concordia Middle Saint Louis MO • (314)865-1144 • (CQ 1993)

**UNGER AMY** (716)964-9489
9694 Ridge Rd W Brockport NY 14420-9470 • EA • Tchr • St John Hamlin NY • (716)964-2550 • (BR 1994)

**UNGER GARRY D** (714)633-4805
C/O Saint Paul Lutheran Church 1250 E Heim Ave Orange CA 92865-2920 • PSW • Tchr • St Paul Orange CA • (714)921-3188 • (S 1985)

**UNGER MICHAEL** (313)581-5992
6401 Reuter St Dearborn MI 48126-2220 • munger@lhsa.com • MI • Tchr • LHS Westland Westland MI • (734)422-2090 • (S 1972 MED)

**UNGER ROBERT E** (920)749-1336
1800 N Winesap Ln Appleton WI 54914-1903 • NW • Mem C • Faith Appleton WI • (920)739-9191 • (RF 1979 MCMU)

**UNRATH EMANUEL** (636)227-0412
406 Brass Lamp Dr Ballwin MO 63011-3404 • MO • EM • (RF 1924)

**UNVERFEHRT KATHLEEN E** (828)464-6648
1506 Brentwood Cir Newton NC 28658 • bunver@aol.com • SE • Tchr • Concordia Conover NC • (828)464-3011 • (S 1977)

**UNVERFEHRT WILLIAM E** (828)464-6488
1506 Brentwood Cir Newton NC 28658 • bunver@aol.com • SE • P/Tchr • Concordia Conover NC • (828)464-3011 • (S 1978 MA)

**UNZICKER WILLIAM L III**
2102 Timothy Cir Cape Girardeau MO 63701-1838 • MO • Prin • Trinity Cape Girardeau MO • (573)334-1068 • (CQ 1985 MED)

**URBAN DOUGLAS J**
221 S Pleasant St Apt B Independence MO 64050-3668 • MO • Tchr • Messiah Independence MO • (816)254-9409 • (S 1984)

**URBAN DOUGLAS R** (830)895-2436
1690 Mountain Laurel Kerrville TX 78028-3861 • durban@shlutheran.org • TX • Tchr • Shepherd Of The Hill San Antonio TX • (210)614-3741 • (RF 1981)

**URBAN LAWRENCE W** (618)349-8735
C/O St Peter Lutheran School RR 1 Box 70 Saint Peter IL 62880-9721 • urbansix@csuol.com • CI • P/Tchr • St Peter Saint Peter IL • (618)349-8888 • (SP 1967)

**URBAN MARIANN** (708)366-6033
512 Thomas Forest Park IL 60130 • NI • Tchr • Bethlehem River Grove IL • (708)453-1113 • (RF 1983)

**URBAN MATTHEW TYSON**
8814 N Grace Ave Niles IL 60714-1409 • NI • Tchr • St Philip Chicago IL • (773)493-3865 • (RF 1998)

**URBAN MICHELLE** (773)472-1373
3528 N Claremont Chicago IL 60618 • NI • Tchr • St Philip Chicago IL • (773)493-3865 • (RF 2000)

**URQUHART CHRISTOPHER M** (618)826-2098
1212 Opdyke St Chester IL 62233-2005 • bumper@midwest.net • SI • Tchr • St John Chester IL • (618)826-4345 • (RF 1970)

**UTECH NORMAN C** (815)463-1847
881 Winter Park Dr New Lenox IL 60451 • ginnynormutech@juno.com • NI • EM • (RF 1943 MA MED)

**UTECH RALPH ARTHUR** (561)392-9739
4940 NW 5th Ter Boca Raton FL 33431-4634 • ralphutech@yahoo.com • FG • Tchr • St Paul Boca Raton FL • (561)395-8548 • (S 1972)

**UTECH RICHARD W** (719)395-2038
PO Box 807 Buena Vista CO 81211-0807 • RM • 07/1993 07/2000 • (RF 1969 MA)

**UTECH STEPHANIE ANNE**
200 E 5th St - Apt 5D York NE 68467-3671 • NI • Tchr • Luther Academy Rockford IL • (815)877-9551 • (RF 1997)

**UTECHT JOANNA PRISCILLA** (305)756-9978
5255 N Clinton Fort Wayne IN 46825-5741 • IN • Tchr • St Paul Fort Wayne IN • (219)423-2496 • (S 1996)

## V

**VAHRENHORST CHRISTOPHER**
PSC 79 Box 115 APO AE 09714 • internet.100757.2260@compuserve.com • SI • Tchr • Southern Illinois Belleville IL • (S 1990 MA)

**VALENTE ELIZABETH A**
1115 Park Rd Jackson MI 49203 • MI • Tchr • Trinity Jackson MI • (517)750-2105 • (AA 1998)

**VALENTINE DEBRA LYNN** (541)447-6226
843 NE Court St Prineville OR 97754-1643 • jimdebval@aol.com • NOW • Tchr • Trinity Bend OR • (541)382-1850 • (PO 1994)

**VALLESKEY ROMAN C** (219)583-4823
5749 E Indian Creek Rd Monticello IN 47960-2756 • MO • EM • (RF 1948 MA)

**VALLIN KURT R** (314)278-5519
13 Danson Dr Saint Peters MO 63376-4019 • kvallin@mail.win.org • MO • Tchr • Zion Harvester MO • (314)441-7424 • (S 1990 MED)

**VALLIN STEPHANIE** (314)278-5519
13 Danson Dr Saint Peters MO 63376-4019 • MO • Tchr • Zion Saint Charles MO • (636)441-7425 • (S 1992)

**VAN ANDEL JUDITH ELAINE** (512)837-6949
4209 Dauphine Dr Austin TX 78727 • vanandel@texas.net • TX • Tchr • Zion Georgetown TX • (512)863-5345 • (S 1971 MA)

**VAN ANDEL ROGER J** (512)837-6949
4209 Dauphine Dr Austin TX 78727 • r.vanandel@computer.org • TX • SHS/C • Texas Austin TX • (S 1971 MS MED)

**VAN ARSDALE LESLIE JANE** (281)440-3110
5110 Azalea Trace Dr Apt 1301 Houston TX 77066-4352 • padre95@juno.com • RM • S Miss • Rocky Mountain Aurora CO • (S 1973)

**VAN BLARCOM STEPHANIE L** (714)639-6988
204 N California St Orange CA 92866-1706 • PSW • Tchr • St John Orange CA • (714)288-4406 • (IV 1983)

**VAN DE VEIRE JO ANN**
551 28th Ave Moline IL 61265-5162 • jvndeveir@aol.com • CI • Tchr • Immanuel Rock Island IL • (309)786-3391 • (S 1963 MS)

**VAN DELLEN CAROL ANN** (248)391-1233
3378 Blasser Dr Orion MI 48359 • carjer@ameritech.net • MI • Tchr • St Stephen Waterford MI • (248)673-5906 • (CQ 1994 MAT)

**VAN DELLEN JAMES R**
7184 Glacier Pointe Dr Ypsilanti MI 48197-6113 • MI • Tchr • St Paul Ann Arbor MI • (734)665-0604 • (AA 1991)

**VAN DERMAY CORALYN J** (618)345-6010
110 Lexington Collinsville IL 62234-4347 • MO • Prin • Messiah Saint Louis MO • (314)771-7716 • (RF 1977 MA)

**VAN DYKE ELLEN L** (414)383-6218
1612 S 30th St Milwaukee WI 53215-1943 • SW • Tchr • Mount Zion Greenfield WI • (414)282-4900 • (S 1982)

**VAN LUCHENE DARRELL GENE**
2500 Bulevar Palem Raya Lippo Karawaci Tangerang 15811 INDONESIA • dvan@indo.net.id • MNS • S Miss • Minnesota South Burnsville MN • (S 1968 MED EDS)

**VAN LUCHENE SUE ZANN**
2500 Bulevar Palem Raya Lippo Karawaci Tangerang 15811 INDONESIA • dvan@indo.net.id • MNS • S Miss • Minnesota South Burnsville MN • (S 1969)

**VAN PELT CARLA N** (317)862-5184
4302 Wanamaker Dr Indianapolis IN 46239-1636 • IN • Tchr • St John Indianapolis IN • (317)352-9196 • (S 1971 MS)

**VAN RIXEL REBECCA CAROLINE** (715)257-7592
605 Alfred St Athens WI 54411-8200 • NW • Tchr • Trinity Athens WI • (715)257-7559 • (MQ 1995)

**VAN TOL REBECCA SUZANNE** (517)674-2947
2814 Cass St Unionville MI 48767 • reedr@avci.net • MI • Tchr • St Paul Unionville MI • (517)674-8681 • (AA 1998)

**VAN VOLKENBURGH CANDACE ANN** (816)363-5470
436 E 72nd Ter Kansas City MO 64131-1618 • MO • Tchr • Calvary Kansas City MO • (816)444-6908 • (CQ 1985)

**VANCE MARGUERITE R** (952)884-5252
10508 Upton Cir S Bloomington MN 55431-3730 • MNS • Tchr • St Peter Edina MN • (952)927-8408 • (SP 1972)

**VANDER MEER KATHERINE**
408 Belt Line Rd Apt 16 Collinsville IL 62234-4477 • SI • Tchr • Good Shepherd Collinsville IL • (618)344-3153 • (RF 1996)

**VANDERCOOK ARDITH J** (972)442-9598
612 Burchshire Wylie TX 75098 • TX • Tchr • Faith Plano TX • (972)423-7448 • (S 1971)

**VANDERCOOK JAMES L** (972)442-9598
612 Burchshire Wylie TX 75098 • jlvdc@usa.net • TX • Tchr • Faith Plano TX • (972)423-7448 • (S 1971)

**VANDREY WANDA J** (818)994-0873
7951 Lloyd Ave North Hollywood CA 91605-1704 • wjvandrey@juno.com • PSW • P/Tchr • First Van Nuys CA • (818)786-3002 • (CQ 1995)

**VANIC PATRICK** (210)684-9205
5011 Glen Ridge Dr U 34 San Antonio TX 78229 • pvanic@yahoo.com • TX • Tchr • LHS Of San Antonio San Antonio TX • (210)733-7771 • (MQ 1997)

**VANICK EDWARD W** (810)778-3729
18269 Glendale St Roseville MI 48066-3405 • MI • Tchr • St Thomas Eastpointe MI • (810)772-3372 • (RF 1969 MA)

**VANNESS MELINDA ANN** (515)579-6167
1644 Finch Ave Latimer IA 50452-7503 • IE • Tchr • St Paul Latimer IA • (515)579-6046 • (S 1985)

**VANNOY LISA KRISTINA** (402)435-6131
1401 SW 36th St Lincoln NE 68522-9136 • NEB • Tchr • Messiah Lincoln NE • (402)489-3024 • (S 1995)

**VARNER JANE M** (218)828-8623
2381 Woida Rd N Baxter MN 56425-8645 • MNN • Tchr • Family Of Christ Baxter MN • (218)829-9020 • (S 1975)

**VARNER ROGER V** (218)828-8623
2381 Woida Rd N Baxter MN 56425-8645 • MNN • 06/1997 06/2000 • (S 1958 MA)

**VARNES LINDA L** (208)463-0798
2600 San Marco Way Nampa ID 83686 • NOW • Tchr • Zion Nampa ID • (208)466-6746 • (S 1970 MED)

**VASQUEZ ROMAN S** (949)855-9908
24523 Los Alisos Apt 250 Laguna Hills CA 92653-4243 • PSW • Tchr • Abiding Savior Lake Forest CA • (949)830-1461 • (IV 1996 MA)

**VAUPEL CHRISTINA** (505)994-8878
700 Gral Trevino Dr Rio Rancho NM 87124 • savby3@yahoo.com • RM • Abiding Savior Lake Forest CA • (RF 1997)

**VAZQUEZ JEAN M** (305)267-4874
5720 SW 14th St West Miami FL 33144 • FG • Tchr • Faith Hialeah FL • (305)888-6706 • (AA 1987)

**VEAL ELIZABETH MARIE** (402)563-2246
3471 Pershing Rd #3 Columbus NE 68601 • NEB • Tchr • Christ Columbus NE • (402)564-3531 • (S 2000)

**VEDDER DAVID O**
815 Teal Point Rd Mountain Home AR 72653-7152 • PSW • Tchr • Lutheran HS Of San D San Diego CA • (619)262-4444 • (RF 1973 MCS)

**VEGVARY SHARON T** (707)935-9203
19432 Lovall Valley Ct Sonoma CA 95476-4872 • EN • 09/1996 09/1998 • (PO 1984)

**VEHMEIER KATHLEEN ANN** (815)235-4239
707 W American St Freeport IL 61032 • kamteach@juno.com • NI • Tchr • Immanuel Freeport IL • (815)232-3511 • (RF 1987)

**VEITH GENE E** (414)375-0782
W60N413 Hilgen Ave Cedarburg WI 53012-2413 • Edward-Veith@cuw.edu • SW • SHS/C • South Wisconsin Milwaukee WI • (414)464-8100 • (CQ 1987 MA PHD)

**VENDETTI DINA C**
352 West Wind Dr Dover DE 19901-6688 • dinacv@aol.com • SE • Prin • St John Dover DE • (302)734-1211 • (BR 1985 MED)

**VENZKE JEANETTE**
1318 City View Dr Denison IA 51442 • IW • Tchr • Zion Denison IA • (712)263-4766 • (RF 1960)

**VENZKE RANDELL C** (708)366-4247
1123 Bonnie Brae Pl River Forest IL 60305-1515 • NI • SHS/C • Northern Illinois Hillside IL • (RF 1977 MA)

**VERSEMAN DENNIS H DR** (734)844-3153
252 Brittany Dr Canton MI 48187-3203 • dverseman@stpaul.pvt.k12.mi.us • MI • Prin • St Paul Ann Arbor MI • (734)665-0604 • (RF 1962 MS EDD)

**VERSEMANN CALVIN E** (314)741-5002
6260 Pennyrich Ct Florissant MO 63033-7929 • MO • P/Tchr • River Roads Saint Louis MO • (314)388-0300 • (RF 1962 MSED)

**VEZNER HEATHER LEE**
10318 Milford St Westchester IL 60154-3528 • NI • SHS/C • Northern Illinois Hillside IL • (RF 1993 MA)

**VICK MICHAEL S** (949)858-9414
2 Flor De Mar Rcho Sta Marg CA 92688-1404 • PSW • Tchr • Abiding Savior Lake Forest CA • (949)830-1461 • (S 1983 MCI)

**VICKERS EILEEN H** (308)238-1584
4015 Avenue F Kearney NE 68847-2645 • NEB • Tchr • Zion Kearney NE • (308)234-3410 • (S 1970)

**VIEREGGE KEITH L** (262)253-0989
N90 W17657 W St Francis Dr Menomonee Falls WI 53051 • viereggek@cs.com • SW • Tchr • Peace Sussex WI • (262)246-3200 • (S 1981 MCMU)

**VIERK DENNIS L** (608)752-2495
1017 Laramie Ln Janesville WI 53546-1860 • dvierk@spsflames.k12.wi.us • SW • P/Tchr • St Paul Janesville WI • (608)754-4471 • (RF 1966 MA)

**VIETS CATHERINE L**
32719 Whiteman Rd Mora MO 65345-9522 • MO • Tchr • Lutheran School Asso Cole Camp MO • (660)668-4614 • (CQ 1996)

**VIETS DEBORAH ROSE** (206)524-0853
4318 NE 87th St Seattle WA 98115-3825 • vietsj.@gte.net • NOW • Tchr • Concordia Seattle WA • (206)525-7407 • (S 1971)

**VIETS NORMA J** (815)459-4851
1375 Knollwood Cir Crystal Lake IL 60014-1824 • oat@mc.met • NI • Tchr • Immanuel Crystal Lake IL • (815)459-1444 • (RF 1974 MA)

**VIGARS JEFFREY M** (209)551-1530
1829 Cashmere Dr Modesto CA 95355-9267 • CNH • Tchr • Grace Modesto CA • (209)529-1800 • (PO 1987)

**VILLARREAL BRITT ALAN** (512)457-0762
1917 David St Apt C Austin TX 78705 • TX • Tchr • Redeemer Austin TX • (512)451-6478 • (AU 1998)

**VINCENT ERIC TODD** (317)791-6168
4616C Mimi Dr Indianapolis IN 46237 • etv9876@aol.com • IN • Tchr • LHS Of Indianapolis Indianapolis IN • (317)787-5474 • (S 1999)

**VIOLETTE JAMES R** (714)289-2390
2837 Oakmont Ave Orange CA 92867 • violet4@jps.net • PSW • Tchr • Salem Orange CA • (714)639-1946 • (IV 1986)

**VIOTTO SHELLIE L**
1303 Lawrence St New London WI 54961 • NW • 11/1999 • (SP 1987)

**VISSER JEAN V** (916)726-7219
7066 Lynnetree Way Citrus Heights CA 95610-3932 • jvis15@yahoo.com • CNH • 08/1999 • (PO 1980)

**VOELKER CAROL SUE**
948 170th St Latimer IA 50452 • voelker@fiai.net • IE • P/Tchr • St Paul Latimer IA • (515)579-6046 • (S 1984)

**VOELKER CAROLYN R** (618)667-6169
439 Meadow Dr Troy IL 62294-1014 • SI • Tchr • Holy Cross Collinsville IL • (618)344-3145 • (RF 1961 MA)

**VOELKER DONALD F** (219)749-2120
3001 N Webster Rd New Haven IN 46774-9652 • IN • EM • (RF 1946 MSED)

**VOELKER FRANKLIN A** (618)667-6169
439 Meadow Dr Troy IL 62294-1014 • SI • EM • (RF 1962 MA)

**VOELKER HOWARD E** (402)372-2757
311 E Grove St Apt 1 West Point NE 68788 • sp75748@navix.net • NEB • P/Tchr • St Paul West Point NE • (402)372-2111 • (S 1969 MEAD MS)

**VOELKER MARY E** (402)372-2757
311 E Grove St Apt 1 West Point NE 68788 • sp75748@navix.net • NEB • 08/2000 • (S 1970 MS MS)

**VOELKER RODNEY W** (402)329-6359
RR 1 Box 133 Pierce NE 68767-9417 • NEB • Tchr • Zion Pierce NE • (402)329-4658 • (S 1968)

**VOELKER SHAWNA LYNAE** (308)687-6134
160 K Rd St Libory NE 68872 • NEB • Tchr • Zion Saint Libory NE • (308)687-6486 • (S 1997)

**VOELKER TED C** (715)435-3816
6444 2nd Ave Rudolph WI 54475-9556 • NW • Tchr • Immanuel Wisconsin Rapids WI • (715)423-0272 • (S 1973)

**VOELKER TIMOTHY K** (785)747-2427
2265 10th Rd Greenleaf KS 66943-9436 • KS • 09/1998 • (S 1982)

**VOELTZ BRUCE L**
700 Tai Tam Reservoir Rd 3D Tai Tam Gardens Tai Tam HONG KONG • fvoeltz@hkis.edu.hk • EN • S Miss • English Farmington MI • (SP 1970 MA)

**VOELTZ LOIS JEAN**
700 Tai Tam Reservoir Rd 3D Tai Tam Gardens Taitam HONG KONG • lvoeltz@hkis.edu.hk • EN • 11/1999 • (S 1969)

**VOELZ JUDY** (314)863-8704
14 S Seminary Ter Saint Louis MO 63105-3013 • MO • 05/1987 05/2000 • (RF 1968 MA)

**VOELZ ROBERT T** (313)386-6381
19342 Coachwood Riverview MI 48195 • MI • Tchr • Christ The King Southgate MI • (734)285-9697 • (S 1973 MS)

**VOGE JEAN L** (317)786-3955
3108 Asbury St Indianapolis IN 46237-1003 • IN • Tchr • Emmaus Indianapolis IN • (317)632-1486 • (RF 1965 MSED)

**VOGEL AARON C** (651)793-0422
1136 Kennard St Saint Paul MN 55106-2925 • MNS • Tchr • Concordia Academy Roseville MN • (612)484-8429 • (S 1996)

**VOGEL CRAIG A** (262)633-2835
3753 Saint Andrews Blvd Racine WI 53405-1725 • SW • Tchr • Lutheran High School Racine WI • (414)637-6538 • (S 1969 MS)

**VOGEL LOIS L** (913)236-5862
5920 Reeds Rd Apt 201 Mission KS 66202-3445 • lois@unicom.net • KS • EM • (RF 1951 MSED)

**VOGEL SUSAN G** (715)524-3093
1365 Dallman Ln Shawano WI 54166 • vogeljs@ezwebtech.com • NW • Tchr • St James Shawano WI • (715)524-4213 • (RF 1976)

**VOGELI MITCHELL R** (810)724-2863
1351 N Youngs Rd Attica MI 48412-9396 • MI • Mem C • St Peter Macomb MI • (810)781-3434 • (S 1977)

**VOGT DON A** (734)451-0488
9087 Woodgrove Dr Plymouth MI 48170-5747 • vogtd@ccaa.edu • MI • SHS/C • Michigan Ann Arbor MI • (S 1968 MS)

**VOGT JANIS JO** (504)888-5869
5808 Parkaire Dr Metairie LA 70003-2324 • sj071683@aol.com • SO • 08/1994 08/2000 • (SP 1982)

**VOGTMANN JANET L** (517)686-0356
3298 Parkway Dr Bay City MI 48706-3338 • MI • Tchr • Zion Bay City MI • (517)893-5793 • (RF 1962 MA)

**VOIGHT SHARON J**
144 Congress St Villa Park IL 60181-3232 • NI • Tchr • Gloria Dei Chicago IL • (773)581-5259 • (RF 1966 MCMU)

**VOIGT PEGGY SUE** (414)251-0840
N78W15364 Haymeadow Rd Menomonee Falls WI 53051-4265 • SW • Tchr • Our Redeemer Wauwatosa WI • (414)258-4558 • (S 1979)

**VOISINE JANET M** (860)589-2620
156 Harmony Rd Bristol CT 06010-7916 • NE • Tchr • Immanuel Bristol CT • (860)583-5631 • (RF 1965)

**VOLBERDING GARY L** (612)504-9947
3809 Colorado Ave N Crystal MN 55422-1926 • MNS • P/Tchr • St John Maple Grove MN • (612)420-2426 • (S 1981 MS)

**VOLKERT BRUCE R** (773)725-3391
3937 N Nottingham Ave Chicago IL 60634-2235 • NI • Tchr • Luther HS North Chicago IL • (773)286-3600 • (RF 1988)

**VOLKMAN HEATHER DAWN** (314)664-5382
3820 Wyoming St Saint Louis MO 63116-4841 • MO • Tchr • Messiah Saint Louis MO • (314)771-7716 • (AA 1998)

**VOLLMAN WILLIAM H** (727)461-1431
1101 Oakview Ave Clearwater FL 33756-4313 • wvollma1@tampabay.rr.com • FG • Tchr • First Clearwater FL • (727)461-3444 • (AA 1985)

**VOLLMER CORINE ALYCE** (309)346-6200
1614 Parkway Dr Apt 11 Pekin IL 61554 • cvollmer@gallatinriver.net • CI • Prin • Good Shepherd Pekin IL • (309)347-2020 • (RF 1999)

**VOLLMER JUDITH ALYCE** (309)346-6200
1614 Parkway Dr Apt 11 Pekin IL 61554 • jvollmer@gallatinriver.net • CI • Prin • Good Shepherd Pekin IL • (309)347-2020 • (RF 1999)

**VOLZ KAREN R** (517)652-9533
5110 Churchgrove Rd Frankenmuth MI 48734-9793 • MI • Tchr • St Lorenz Frankenmuth MI • (517)652-6141 • (RF 1974 MA)

**VOLZKE BETTY C** (402)466-1990
3900 N 42nd St Lincoln NE 68504-1214 • NEB • Tchr • Trinity Lincoln NE • (402)466-1800 • (CQ 1995)

**VON AHSEN KENNETH H** (314)724-1752
901 Penrose Ln Saint Charles MO 63301-4754 • MO • Tchr • Immanuel Saint Charles MO • (636)946-0051 • (S 1976 MA)

**VON BEHREN ERICH W** (517)652-8446
147 Frank Rd Frankenmuth MI 48734-1207 • MI • EM • (RF 1953 MMU)

**VON BEHREN JENNIFER L** (314)631-7613
4267 Heidelberg Ave Saint Louis MO 63123-7601 • kutya2@juno.com • MO • Tchr • St John Arnold MO • (636)464-7303 • (MQ 1996)

**VON BEHREN LINDA ROBERTA** (309)697-8386
4106 S Wheatfield Rd Mapleton IL 61547 • CI • Tchr • Christ Peoria IL • (309)637-1512 • (CQ 1999)

**VON DIELINGEN DAVID P** (314)278-8653
19 Strafford Dr Saint Peters MO 63376-4036 • dvondiel@mail.win.org • MO • Tchr • Zion Harvester MO • (314)441-7424 • (S 1970 MA)

**VON DIELINGEN JEAN L** (812)358-2871
2508 E 700S Brownstown IN 47220 • IN • Tchr • Immanuel Seymour IN • (812)522-3118 • (S 1979 MS)

**VON DIELINGEN JOYCE LEE** (314)278-8653
19 Strafford Dr Saint Peters MO 63376-4036 • MO • Tchr • Zion Harvester MO • (314)441-7424 • (CQ 1985 MMU)

**VON FANGE ERICH A DR** (517)263-8315
808 Savannah River Dr Adrian MI 49221-3704 • fangmer@lni.net • MI • EM • (S 1945 MA PHD)

**VON KAMPEN KURT E** (402)646-2243
515 S Evergreen Dr Seward NE 68434 • NEB • SHS/C • Nebraska Seward NE • (S 1983 MMU)

**VON KAMPEN PAULA** (480)483-9360
8180 Shea Blvd #1096 Scottsdale AZ 85260 • wvonkmpen@az.rmci.net • EN • EM • (RF 1976 MA)

**VON RENTZELL PAUL D** (303)458-0081
5465 W 86th Ave Arvada CO 80003-1423 • RM • Tchr • Denver Lutheran High Denver CO • (303)934-2345 • (S 1984)

**VON SOOSTEN MARK A**
1919 Butterfly Maiden Trl NE Albuquerque NM 87112 • RM • P/Tchr • Christ Albuquerque NM • (505)884-3876 • (S 1979 MED)

**VON STROHE PATRICIA J** (317)244-8928
6570 Rainer Dr Apt B Indianapolis IN 46214-3779 • IN • Tchr • Our Shepherd Indianapolis IN • (317)271-9103 • (AA 1986)

**VON DER LAGE DEBORAH** (818)989-4558
13401 Rangoon St Arleta CA 91331-6323 • PSW • Tchr • Grace Lancaster CA • (805)948-1018 • (RF 1974)

**VON DER LAGE MARK F** (818)989-4558
13401 Rangoon St Arleta CA 91331-6323 • PSW • Tchr • Grace Lancaster CA • (661)948-1018 • (S 1973)

**VONADA SHARON** (954)452-0331
8402 SW 26th St Davie FL 33324-5708 • sgvonada@aol.com • FG • Prin • Gloria Dei Davie FL • (954)475-8584 • (S 1973 MED)

**VONDERFECHT KELLI SUZANNE** (402)463-0319
816 N Kansas Ave Hastings NE 68901 • sv10638@alltel.net • MO • Tchr • Zion Palmyra MO • (573)769-2739 • (S 1995)

**VONDRAN KIMBERLY ANN** (415)876-2629
726 18th Ave Apt 2 San Francisco CA 94121 • kav24@aol.com • NI • 08/2000 • (RF 1995)

**VORWERK DALE H** (313)635-3709
9414 Seymour Rd Swartz Creek MI 48473-9129 • vorwerk@tir.com • MI • Prin • St Paul Flint MI • (810)239-6733 • (RF 1966 MA)

**VOS DONALD L** (402)643-6663
921 N 3rd St Seward NE 68434-1511 • dvos@seward.cune.edu • NEB • SHS/C • Nebraska Seward NE • (S 1983)

**VOSE GINGER** (515)573-2129
202 N 25th St Fort Dodge IA 67156 • IW • Tchr • St Paul Fort Dodge IA • (515)955-7285 • (CQ 1998)

**VOSS AMY RENEE** (402)643-9519
1150 Kolterman Seward NE 68434 • runatvbball@hotmail.com • NEB • 08/1992 • (S 1992)

**VOSS CYNTHIA C** (618)345-9103
95 Wendler Dr Collinsville IL 62234-1488 • macvoss@hotmail.com • SI • 07/1999 • (SP 1978 MS)

**VOSS MICHAEL E** (618)345-9103
95 Wendler Dr Collinsville IL 62234-1488 • macvoss@hotmail.com • SI • Tchr • Good Shepherd Collinsville IL • (618)344-3153 • (RF 1984 MS)

**VOSS SHARON L DR** (503)288-9371
2811 NE Holman St Portland OR 97211-6067 • svoss@cu-portland.edu • NOW • SHS/C • Northwest Portland OR • (RF 1973 MAT DED)

**VOSS TODD M** (402)643-9519
1150 Kolterman Ave Seward NE 68434 • NEB • SHS/C • Nebraska Seward NE • (S 1993)

**VOUGHT GARY L** (715)546-8254
1893 Koubenic Rd Three Lakes WI 54562-9206 • woody@campluther.com • NW • O Sp Min • North Wisconsin Wausau WI • (RF 1988)

**VRADENBURGH SHIRLEY A** (206)932-7466
3818 49th Ave SW Seattle WA 98116-3607 • NOW • Tchr • Seattle LHS Seattle WA • (206)937-7722 • (RF 1966 MA)

**VROOM NOLA J** (949)458-3911
27522 Halcon Mission Viejo CA 92691 • fornola@hotmail.com • PSW • Tchr • Prince Of Peace Anaheim CA • (714)774-0993 • (S 1973)

**VYHANEK CAROL B** (312)693-5728
548 W Lance Dr Des Plaines IL 60016 • NI • Tchr • Immanuel Des Plaines IL • (847)390-0990 • (RF 1978)

## W

**WAAK LE MOYNE D** (810)776-3889
22734 Liscomb Ave Eastpointe MI 48021-1730 • MI • EM • (S 1950)

**WACHHOLZ AARON A** (510)352-4509
1144 Hyde St #306 San Leandro CA 94577 • CNH • Tchr • Calvary San Lorenzo CA • (510)278-2556 • (RF 1998)

**WACHHOLZ DONALD FRED** (815)634-2912
Burt Estates 10 Churchhill Dr Coal City IL 60416 • EN • EM • (RF 1964 MA MED)

**WACHHOLZ EUGENE H** (815)939-4891
343 S Winfield Ave Kankakee IL 60901-3457 • NI • Tchr • St Paul Kankakee IL • (815)932-3241 • (RF 1965)

**WACHHOLZ JUDITH E** (402)643-2352
657 Bader Ave Seward NE 68434-1149 • jew8251@seward.ccsn.edu • NEB • Tchr • St John Seward NE • (402)643-4535 • (RF 1969 MED)

**WACHHOLZ KAREN L** (763)577-9419
5865 B Teakwood Lane N Plymouth MN 55442 • klwachholz@uswest.net • MNS • Tchr • Pacific Southwest Irvine CA • (949)854-3232 • (SP 1995)

**WACHMANN JOHN F** (907)789-5101
8678 Dudley St Juneau AK 99801-9050 • jwachmann@aol.com • NOW • 07/1992 07/2000 • (RF 1980 MA)

**WACHS CYNTHIA L** (262)532-0797
W164N10977 Grey Fox Ct Germantown WI 53022-5588 • swachs@aol.com • SW • Tchr • Northwest Milwaukee WI • (414)463-4040 • (S 1976 MED)

**WACHTMANN KATHLEEN** (419)267-3801
U 587 Rd 21 Archbold OH 43502 • OH • 01/1996 01/2000 • (S 1975)

**WACKER DANIEL R** (616)887-1423
1007 Coolidge Rd Conklin MI 49403-9514 • drwacker@aalweb.net • MI • Prin • Trinity Conklin MI • (616)899-2152 • (RF 1973)

**WACKER LINDA** (314)894-2405
5276 Camelot Estates Dr Oakville MO 63129-1540 • MO • 05/1986 05/2000 • (S 1984)

**WACKER SARA J** (616)887-1423
1007 Coolidge Rd Conklin MI 49403-9514 • EN • 06/1989 06/2000 • (SP 1984)

**WADE CHERYL LYNN**
PO Box 30 Westminster MA 01473-0030 • AT • 07/1998 • (S 1991)

**WAGENER CASSANDRA R** (612)442-2865
208 E 2nd St Waconia MN 55387-1507 • MNS • Tchr • Trinity Waconia MN • (952)442-4165 • (S 1972)

**WAGIE RICHARD C** (216)581-1767
11703 Granger Rd Garfield Heights OH 44125-2859 • OH • P/Tchr • St John Garfield Heights OH • (216)587-1752 • (RF 1973)

**WAGNER DAWN RENAE** (402)329-4313
832 E Main St Pierce NE 68767 • NEB • Tchr • Zion Pierce NE • (402)329-4658 • (S 1988)

**WAGNER DOUGLAS J** (314)723-7028
2941 Westerland Dr Saint Charles MO 63301-4212 • MO • Tchr • Immanuel Saint Charles MO • (636)946-0051 • (S 1974 MA)

**WAGNER JAMES A** (281)351-1634
13815 Boudreaux Rd Tomball TX 77375-7516 • jwagner@salem4u.com • TX • Mem C • Salem Tomball TX • (281)351-8223 • (MQ 1999)

**WAGNER MICHELLE LYNN**
31272 Springlake Blvd Novi MI 48377-1125 • mlwagner$^3$nozomi@hotmail.com • MI • Tchr • St Matthew Walled Lake MI • (248)624-7676 • (S 1996)

**WAGNER MONICA L**
8077 Mc Farland Ct Indianapolis IN 46227-6910 • IN • Tchr • LHS Of Indianapolis Indianapolis IN • (317)787-5474 • (RF 1993)

**WAGNER ROBIN R** (319)366-4330
2002 K St SW Cedar Rapids IA 52404-3622 • IE • Tchr • Trinity Cedar Rapids IA • (319)362-6952 • (S 1976)

**WAGONER MARY LOU** (712)542-5768
2716 200th St Clarinda IA 51632-9780 • IW • Tchr • Clarinda Clarinda IA • (712)542-3657 • (S 1965)

**WAHL RHODA M**
PO Box 20051 Wickenburg AZ 85358 • PSW • 08/2000 • (S 1976)

**WAHLERS JOEL D** (360)337-2687
2321 Eton Ln Bremerton WA 98311 • jwahlers.aol.com • NOW • Prin • Peace Bremerton WA • (360)373-2116 • (S 1986 MED)

**WAHLERS MARK E** (503)281-9549
3554 NE Ainsworth St Portland OR 97211-7353 • markw@cu-portland.edu • NOW • SHS/C • Northwest Portland OR • (S 1978 MS PHD)

**WAHNEFRIED CAROL H**
5709 Tipperary Trl Waterford MI 48329 • MI • Tchr • St Stephen Waterford MI • (248)673-6621 • (S 1969)

**WAHRLE LOIS L** (608)754-1563
3718 Goldenrod Pl Janesville WI 53546-1178 • SW • Tchr • St Paul Janesville WI • (608)754-4471 • (SP 1978)

**WAIBEL KENNETH J** (954)463-2471
740 NW 37 St Fort Lauderdale FL 33309 • kwaibel@trinitylcms.org • FG • P/Tchr • Trinity Fort Lauderdale FL • (954)463-2450 • (RF 1968)

**WAKELAND CATHIE JEAN**
APDO 5-714 Guadalajara 5 Jalisco MEXICO • SI • 11/1998 • (S 1978)

**WALCHESKI JEFFREY** (561)750-8215
289 SW 13th St Boca Raton FL 33432-7108 • jwalcheski@falcongate.com • FG • Tchr • St Paul Boca Raton FL • (561)395-8548 • (SP 1984)

**WALCHESKI MICHAEL J DR*** (612)603-6184
583 Sextant Ave W Roseville MN 55113-3400 • walcheski@luther.csp.edu • MNS • SHS/C • Minnesota South Burnsville MN • (SP 1983 MA PHD)

**WALD CAROL B** (312)577-6105
3265 Kirchoff Rd #320 Rolling Mdws IL 60008-2864 • NI • Tchr • St Peter Arlington Heights IL • (847)253-6638 • (CQ 1986 MED)

**WALDMANN TOVE E** (314)405-1148
16960 Kingstowne Place Dr Wildwood MO 63011-1885 • MO • Tchr • Immanuel Olivette MO • (314)993-5004 • (S 1972)

**WALDRON MARK A** (708)366-3810
7651 Monroe St Forest Park IL 60130-1722 • crfwaldroma@curf.edu • NI • SHS/C • Northern Illinois Hillside IL • (RF 1980 MA)

**WALGENBACH LINDA** (920)921-7481
8 Sumac Ct Fond Du Lac WI 54936-8836 • SW • 09/1997 09/1999 • (RF 1964)

**WALKER DAWN MARIE** (785)628-4603
Wiest Hall Hays KS 67601 • dwalker@fhsu.edu • KS • 08/1998 • (MQ 1991 MS)

**WALKER ELLEN LOUISE**
1361 S Greenfield Rd #1044 Mesa AZ 85206-3390 • EN • Tchr • Christ Phoenix AZ • (602)957-7010 • (RF 1997)

**WALKER JULIE ANN**
3 93rd Ave W Duluth MN 55808-1104 • SI • Tchr • St Paul Nokomis IL • (217)563-2487 • (S 1987)

**WALKER LOUISE A** (205)881-5515
2306 Britain Ave SW Huntsville AL 35803-2041 • SO • Tchr • Grace Huntsville AL • (256)881-0553 • (RF 1976)

**WALKER ROGER L** (863)297-9118
21 Lake Link Dr SE Winter Haven FL 33884-4120 • FG • Prin • Grace Winter Haven FL • (941)293-9744 • (RF 1965 MA)

**WALKER SANDRA LYNN** (616)695-1610
502 Days Ave Buchanan MI 49107-1618 • MI • Tchr • Trinity Berrien Springs MI • (616)473-1811 • (AA 1986)

**WALKMASTER VELMA L**
8671 Old Towne Dr Saint Louis MO 63132-3907 • MO • Tchr • Holy Cross Saint Louis MO • (314)772-8633 • (S 1964)

**WALL WILLIAM MICHAEL** (516)867-2405
110 Cornelius St Freeport NY 11520-5612 • AT • Tchr • Trinity Hicksville NY • (516)931-2211 • (CQ 1998)

**WALLACE DIANA L** (507)685-4346
10500 215th St W Morristown MN 55052-5083 • wallacmd@means.net • MNS • Tchr • Trinity Morristown MN • (507)685-2200 • (RF 1988)

**WALLACE JEFFERY L** (616)982-0525
2860 Cleveland Ave Apt 4-334 St Joseph MI 49085 • wallace$^3$jeff@hotmail.com • MI • Tchr • Christ Stevensville MI • (616)429-7111 • (RF 1998)

**WALLACE SHARON L**
27325 Bassett Rd Cleveland OH 44145-3004 • swallace@bellatlantic.net • OH • 05/1995 05/1997 • (AA 1992)

**WALLACE SHIRLEY MARIE** (313)676-0144
2769 Pinetree Dr Trenton MI 48183-2233 • dashwall@aol.com • MI • P/Tchr • St John Taylor MI • (734)287-3866 • (RF 1957 MA)

**WALLING JOAN M** (402)646-2163
193 E Lincoln St Seward NE 68434-1619 • jwalling@alltel.net • NEB • P/Tchr • Our Redeemer Staplehurst NE • (402)535-2251 • (S 1969 MED)

**WALLIS AILEEN C** (314)965-7314
13210 Dunroyal Dr Des Peres MO 63131-1919 • MO • Tchr • St John Ellisville MO • (314)394-4100 • (RF 1954)

**WALLIS DARRELL H** (314)965-7314
13210 Dunroyal Dr Des Peres MO 63131-1919 • MO • EM • (RF 1953 MA)

**WALLIS DIANE D** (512)694-4254
8703 Green Thread St San Antonio TX 78240-3703 • TX • Tchr • Shepherd Of The Hill San Antonio TX • (210)614-3741 • (RF 1970 MA)

**WALLMAN JOANN K** (402)477-5532
1002 B St Lincoln NE 68502-1239 • NEB • Tchr • Messiah Lincoln NE • (402)489-3024 • (S 1973 MA)

**WALLNER HEIDI ANN** (773)399-9880
5306 N Cumberland # 423 Chicago IL 60656 • hiidee@sprynet.com • NI • Tchr • St Paul Chicago IL • (708)867-5044 • (MQ 1998)

**WALLSCHLAEGER MARTHA L** (402)486-0334
845 Dale Dr Lincoln NE 68510-4002 • NEB • Tchr • Trinity Lincoln NE • (402)466-1800 • (S 1983)

**WALMSLEY MARLENE L** (401)433-3301
176 Becker Ave Riverside RI 02915-2006 • pmksandb@worldnet.att.net • NE • 10/1994 10/1999 • (BR 1988)

**WALTER BRET LARRY** (702)869-5427
10545 Beachwalk Pl Las Vegas NV 89134-1393 • PSW • Tchr • Faith LHS Las Vegas NV • (702)804-4400 • (S 1997)

**WALTER JONATHAN SCOT** (281)355-8580
3630 Lost Oak Dr Spring TX 77388 • scotwalt@swbell.net • TX • Tchr • Texas Austin TX • (S 1994)

**WALTER SANDRA KAY** (513)829-4346
5808 Leslie Dr Fairfield OH 45014-4715 • rnwalter@3z.net • OH • Tchr • Immanuel Hamilton OH • (513)895-9212 • (RF 1962)

**WALTER TERESA I** (517)871-9366
5427 Millington Rd Millington MI 48746-8700 • MI • Tchr • St Paul Millington MI • (517)871-4581 • (S 1982)

**WALTER TIMOTHY P** (517)871-9366
5427 Millington Rd Millington MI 48746-8700 • MI • Tchr • St Paul Millington MI • (517)871-4581 • (S 1982)

**WALTERS MARY BETH** (863)638-1190
2496 Lake Easy Rd Babson Park FL 33827-9556 • awalters-babsonpark@worldnet.att.net • FG • Tchr • Grace Winter Haven FL • (941)293-9744 • (RF 1977)

**WALTERS PAULETTE E** (616)651-4995
69516 Plumb School Rd Sturgis MI 49091-8415 • MI • Tchr • Trinity Sturgis MI • (616)651-4245 • (RF 1982)

**WALTERS TARAYCA**
C/O Faith Lutheran School 1190 N 6th East Mountain Home ID 83647 • NOW • Tchr • Faith Mountain Home ID • (208)587-4127 • (S 2000)

**WALTERSDORF JUDITH C** (602)893-6843
3825 E Tano St Phoenix AZ 85044-3842 • waltersdorf@juno.com • PSW • Tchr • Gethsemane Tempe AZ • (480)839-0906 • (RF 1968 MA)

**WALTHER DANIEL H** (708)832-1840
220 E Wilson St Elmhurst IL 60126-4514 • crfwalthed@curf.edu • NI • SHS/C • Northern Illinois Hillside IL • (S 1961 MED)

**WALTHER JOHN F** (414)462-7399
4555 N 109th St Wauwatosa WI 53225-4403 • jwalther@bach.cuw.edu • SW • SHS/C • South Wisconsin Milwaukee WI • (414)464-8100 • (S 1958 MA DED)

**WALTHER JULIE L** (956)412-2263
708 E Whitehouse Cir Harlingen TX 78550-2714 • TX • Tchr • St Paul Harlingen TX • (956)423-3926 • (S 1985)

**WALTHER MARY L** (573)243-2109
5481 State Highway 72 Jackson MO 63755-7492 • MO • Tchr • Trinity Cape Girardeau MO • (573)334-1068 • (S 1975)

**WALTON BARBARA O** (580)572-9409
PO Box 831 Perry OK 73077 • OK • Tchr • Trinity Guymon OK • (580)338-3820 • (WN 1982)

**WALTZ DAVID E*** (810)226-3962
17327 Knollwood Dr Clinton Twp MI 48038-2836 • mi$^3$10@hotmail.com • MI • Prin • St John Fraser MI • (810)293-0333 • (S 1978 MED)

**WALWICK PAUL A*** (423)928-0672
7 Beechwood Cir Johnson City TN 37604-6302 • MDS • EM • (CQ 1964 MS DED)

**WALZ CHRISTINE JO** (313)727-6005
9702 Crawford Rd Columbus MI 48063-2308 • MI • Tchr • St Peter Richmond MI • (810)727-9080 • (S 1977)

**WALZ JEFFREY S** (262)376-9132
W52 N851 Derby Ln Cedarburg WI 53012-1556 • SW • SHS/C • South Wisconsin Milwaukee WI • (414)464-8100 • (CQ 2000)

**WALZ ROBERT ALLEN**
1829 N Wright Dr Spokane WA 99224 • NOW • Tchr • Spokane Spokane WA • (509)327-4441 • (S 1992)

**WALZ TIMOTHY A** (248)334-0085
749 Jamestown Rd Auburn Hills MI 48326-3418 • timwalz@aol.com • MI • Tchr • St John Rochester MI • (248)652-8830 • (CQ 1992 MED)

**WANAGAT JAMES M** (618)346-2465
16B Holloway Ct Collinsville IL 62234 • SI • Tchr • Holy Cross Collinsville IL • (618)344-3145 • (S 1967)

**WANDRIE JULIE ELIZABETH** (440)427-1933
29581 Wellington Dr North Olmsted OH 44070-5059 • OH • Tchr • St Paul Westlake OH • (440)835-3051 • (RF 1994)

**WANGERIN KRISTIN ANNE**
1416 E Central Park Ave Davenport IA 52803-1929 • IE • Tchr • Trinity Davenport IA • (319)322-5224 • (RF 1996)

**WANISH STEPHANIE J** (715)842-5022
6104 N State Highway 52 Wausau WI 54403-9638 • NW • 12/1995 12/1999 • (S 1976 MGC)

**WANNER KARI**
4154 W Gardenia Battlefield MO 65619 • kjwanner1299@hotmail.com • MO • Tchr • Springfield Springfield MO • (417)883-5717 • (RF 1998)

**WAPPELHORST ALEXANDRA E** (630)351-9436
320 Brighton Bay Roselle IL 60172 • awappelhorst@kiwi.dep.anl.gov • NI • Tchr • Trinity Roselle IL • (630)894-3263 • (CQ 1995 MA)

**WARD DONNA JEAN** (517)479-6439
PO Box 222 Harbor Beach MI 48441-0222 • MI • EM • (CQ 1984 MAT)

**WARD JENNIFER ANNE** (281)412-2554
2900 Pearland Pkwy #7207 Pearland TX 77581 • buehring1@aol.com • TX • Tchr • Lutheran South Acade Houston TX • (281)464-9320 • (S 1996)

**WAREHAM JON G** (770)917-8992
1950 Roswell Rd Apt 5B5 Marietta GA 30065 • flswareh@juno.com • FG • Prin • Faith Marietta GA • (770)973-8921 • (RF 1982 MED)

**WARGO ANDREW A** (810)463-6827
113 High St Mount Clemens MI 48043 • MI • Tchr • St Luke Clinton Township MI • (810)791-1150 • (RF 2000)

**WARGO NICOLE N** (513)233-2929
2535 Spindlehill Dr #4 Cincinnati OH 45230 • nickiwargo@juno.com • OH • Tchr • St Paul Cincinnati OH • (513)271-8266 • (RF 1998)

**WARGO WILLIAM WALTER**
2127 N 74th Ct Apt 3W Elmwood Park IL 60707 • NI • Tchr • St John Wheaton IL • (630)668-0701 • (RF 1996)

**WARMBIER DAVID RUSSELL**
3053 Plaza Leonardo Bonita CA 91902-1610 • walfromp@wans.net • PSW • Tchr • Pilgrim Chula Vista CA • (619)420-6233 • (IV 1997)

**WARMBIER GERALD J** (313)255-1737
9026 Appleton Redford MI 48239-1236 • EN • EM • (RF 1959 MA)

**WARNEKE ALLARD D** (402)751-2402
PO Box 241 Juniata NE 68955-0241 • NEB • P/Tchr • Zion Hastings NE • (402)462-5012 • (S 1961 MA)

**WARNEKE ARLAN G** (402)329-6686
423 N 1st St Pierce NE 68767-1001 • awarneke@ptcnet.net • NEB • EM • (S 1958)

**WARNEKE JULIE RENE** (972)527-5612
7401 Alma Dr #1022 Plano TX 75025 • TX • Tchr • Faith Plano TX • (972)423-7447 • (S 1992)

**WARNEKE KIMBERLY KAY**
1411 Sunrise Ln Sachse TX 75048-2865 • kwarn61313@aol.com • TX • Tchr • Faith Plano TX • (972)423-7448 • (S 1993)

**WARNEKE SUSAN A** (402)371-1334
2100 Skyline Dr Norfolk NE 68701-2583 • NEB • Mem C • Christ Norfolk NE • (402)371-1210 • (SP 1981)

**WARNEKE TIMOTHY** (310)547-4753
1616 W 7th St San Pedro CA 90732-3422 • PSW • Tchr • South Bay HS-Torranc Torrance CA • (310)530-1231 • (S 1977 MED)

**WARNER DIANNE M** (319)279-3272
PO Box 58 Readlyn IA 50668-0058 • chester@netins.net • IE • Tchr • Community Readlyn IA • (319)279-3968 • (SP 1967)

**WARNICK HARRIET H** (517)624-5113
10520 Dehmel Rd Birch Run MI 48415-9706 • warnickh@svol.org • MI • EM • (RF 1960 MA)

**WARNICK HOWARD J** (517)624-5113
10520 S Dehmel Rd Birch Run MI 48415-9706 • warnickh@svol.org • MI • EM • (RF 1960 MA)

**WARNKEN MELINDA B** (914)779-8024
16 Hobart St Bronxville NY 10708-1805 • AT • Tchr • Chapel Bronxville NY • (914)337-3202 • (BR 1985)

**WARREN DE ANN J** (303)627-7445
16671 E Rice Circle Aurora CO 80015 • RM • Tchr • Trinity Franktown CO • (303)841-4660 • (S 1990)

**WARREN JANICE C** (518)439-9629
113 Brockley Dr Delmar NY 12054-2328 • gwarren@capital.net • AT • Tchr • Our Savior Albany NY • (518)459-2248 • (CQ 1976 MSED)

**WASCHER CHARRIDAN A**
307 Olbrich Rd Harvard IL 60033 • NI • Tchr • Zion Marengo IL • (815)568-5156 • (RF 1999)

**WASHBURN DEBRA S** (810)731-9390
13098 Concord Sterling Heights MI 48313 • MI • Tchr • St Peter Macomb MI • (810)781-9296 • (AA 1984 MA)

**WASMUND GARY W** (352)357-6814
1600 Lakeview Rd Eustis FL 32726-7110 • FG • Tchr • Faith Eustis FL • (352)589-5683 • (RF 1968)

**WATERMAN DAVID M** (314)845-2321
4220 Meadowgreen Trails Dr Saint Louis MO 63129-2178 • waterman@stlnet.com • MO • Missouri Saint Louis MO • (314)317-4550 • (S 1974 MA)

**WATERMAN ROBERT C** (708)668-7793
848 Casa Solana Dr Wheaton IL 60187-8208 • NI • Mem C • St John Wheaton IL • (630)668-0701 • (S 1966 MA)

**WATERMAN SHERYL L** (314)845-2321
4220 Meadowgreen Trails Dr Saint Louis MO 63129-2178 • sherryw@cphnet.org • MO • Tchr • Washington Saint Louis County MO • (314)892-4408 • (S 1974)

**WATERMAN WAYNE LARRY**
1151 Walnut Ave Apt 44 Tustin CA 92780-5652 • PSW • Tchr • Faith Whittier CA • (562)941-0245 • (IV 1996)

**WATSON DAWN L**
13765 Olive Blvd Chesterfield MO 63017-2601 • MO • 07/1997 07/2000 • (RF 1993)

**WATSON HEIDI M**
7755 Longs Peak Dr Riverside CA 92509-5444 • PSW • 06/1998 06/2000 • (S 1980 MSPED MS)

**WATSON MARIE C** (616)429-6034
5527 E Hiawatha Ln Stevensville MI 49127-9641 • MI • Tchr • Immanuel Bridgman MI • (616)465-3351 • (RF 1975)

**WATSON THERESA B** (512)833-7565
10013 Derringer Trl Austin TX 78753-3734 • twatson@del-valle.k12.tx.us • TX • 02/2000 • (AU 1991)

**WATSON THOMAS W**
C/O St John Luth Church 1915 SE Lake Weir Rd Ocala FL 34471 • FG • Tchr • St John Ocala FL • (352)629-1794 • (S 1979 MAD)

**WATT LOIS J** (308)894-6825
198 P Rd Palmer NE 68864-1147 • eandlwatt@juno.com • NEB • EM • (S 1974)

**WAY DANA LYNN**
47095 207th St Brookings SD 57006-5826 • PSW • Tchr • St Paul Garden Grove CA • (714)537-4243 • (IV 1994)

**WEAVER DEBRA S** (309)454-6741
325 S Bone Dr Normal IL 61761-4327 • CI • 02/2000 • (RF 1987 MA)

**WEAVER KASSIE E**
110533 Windmill Ct haska MN 55318-1347 • kkteacher@juno.com • TX • 12/1998 • (AU 1997)

**WEBB ANGELA D**
11156 Summer Squash Ln Las Vegas NV 89144-1609 • PSW • Tchr • Faith LHS Las Vegas NV • (702)804-4400 • (S 1998)

**WEBB JANET** (216)381-8146
2077 Campus Rd South Euclid OH 44121-4255 • jwebb@apk.net • OH • 07/1987 07/2000 • (S 1976 MA)

**WEBB NEIL F**
11156 Summer Squash Ln Las Vegas NV 89144-1609 • PSW • Tchr • Faith LHS Las Vegas NV • (702)804-4400 • (S 1998)

**WEBER ANN M** (952)831-7670
7201 Oaklawn Ave Edina MN 55435-4142 • MNS • Tchr • St Peter Edina MN • (612)927-8400 • (RF 1963)

**WEBER CAROL ANN** (517)871-9975
6316 Barnes Rd Millington MI 48746-9553 • MI • Tchr • St Paul Millington MI • (517)871-4581 • (AA 1986)

**WEBER CHRISTIE B** (419)592-5671
1005 Lynne Ave Napoleon OH 43545-1219 • OH • 07/1985 07/2000 • (S 1979)

**WEBER DIANE L*** (865)692-3335
516 Echo Valley Rd Knoxville TN 37923-6031 • tnwebers@aol.com • MDS • 06/1999 • (S 1996 MA)

**WEBER DONALD CLARENCE** (402)379-9954
608 Opal Ln Norfolk NE 68701-5480 • NEB • Prin • Christ Norfolk NE • (402)371-5536 • (S 1969 MED MAD)

**WEBER GARY G** (402)371-2865
1705 Skyline Dr Norfolk NE 68701-2652 • NEB • Tchr • Christ Norfolk NE • (402)371-5536 • (S 1974 MED)

**WEBER HEATHER JOY** (618)833-4765
402 Walton St Anna IL 62906-0592 • SI • 08/1995 08/2000 • (RF 1992 MS)

**WEBER JENNIFER JILL** (602)667-9689
3931 E Piccadilly #4 Phoenix AZ 85018 • EN • Tchr • Christ Phoenix AZ • (602)955-4830 • (S 1997)

**WEBER KARLTON R** (248)852-0265
2822 Walsh Dr Rochester Hills MI 48309-4325 • kweber@lhnw.lhsa.com • MI • Tchr • LHS Northwest Rochester Hills MI • (810)852-6677 • (CQ 1997 MED EDS EDS)

**WEBER LAURA J**
C/O Saint Luke Lutheran Church 3415 Taft Ave St Louis MO 63111-1431 • MO • LHS Northwest Rochester Hills MI • (MQ 1986)

**WEBER LOUISE S**
Concordia Intern Sch Shanghai Jinqiao Plot S2 Huang Yang Rd Pudong Shanghai 201206 CHINA • lweber@admin.lkis.edu.hk • NOW • S Miss • Northwest Portland OR • (RF 1969 MS)

**WEBER MICHAEL J**
Concordia Intern Sch Shanghai Plot S2 Huang Yang Rd JinQiao Pudong Shaghai 201206 CHINA • mweber@es.hkir.edu.hk • NOW • S Miss • Northwest Portland OR • (RF 1969 MAR MA)

**WEBER NANCY L** (402)371-2865
1705 Skyline Dr Norfolk NE 68701-2652 • NEB • Tchr • Christ Norfolk NE • (402)371-5536 • (S 1974)

**WEBER STEPHEN P** (405)222-1419
3408 S 25th St Chickasha OK 73018-7640 • facwebers@mercur.usao.edu • OK • 04/1994 04/1998 • (RF 1982 MMU PHD)

**WEBER THOMAS E**
7194 N Seneca Ave Glendale WI 53217 • SW • SHS/C • South Wisconsin Milwaukee WI • (414)464-8100 • (S 1980)

**WEBER TIMOTHY R** (956)682-6687
3511 N 29th Ln Mc Allen TX 78501 • TX • Mem C • St Paul Mc Allen TX • (956)682-2345 • (RF 1979)

**WEBER VICTORIA BEHLING**
10318 Rhode Island Cir S Bloomington MN 55438-2140 • MNS • 06/1999 • (SP 1991)

**WEBERN MARILYN** (314)428-5478
3012 Georgetown Farm Ct Saint Ann MO 63074-3730 • mar.webern@worldnet.att.net • MO • Tchr • St John Saint Louis MO • (314)773-0126 • (RF 1967 MED)

**WEDDE DEBORAH D** (616)473-6697
205 S Mechanic St Berrien Springs MI 49103-1138 • MI • Tchr • Trinity Berrien Springs MI • (616)473-1811 • (S 1978)

**WEDDICK KRISTIN ALISA** (303)410-8071
5678 117th Pl Broomfeld CO 80020 • RM • Tchr • Denver Lutheran High Denver CO • (303)934-2345 • (IV 1998)

**WEEMS STEPHEN BOYD** (858)578-7644
10957 Welsh Rd San Diego CA 92126-2449 • PSW • Tchr • Grace Escondido CA • (760)747-3029 • (IV 1988)

**WEERTS EDWARD R** (715)839-0571
3326 Midway St Eau Claire WI 54703-1167 • NW • EM • (S 1942 MA)

**WEERTS GRETCHEN J*** (219)749-7007
1727 Duart Ct New Haven IN 46774-2214 • IN • Tchr • St John Monroeville IN • (219)639-6404 • (S 1979 MA)

**WEERTS LUKE A** (334)875-9285
1000 Medical Center Pkwy #33 Selma AL 36701 • SO • 04/2000 • (S 1978)

**WEERTS MARGARET J** (715)839-0571
3326 Midway St Eau Claire WI 54703-1167 • NW • EM • (S 1942)

**WEESNER GRETCHEN ANNE**
Minami 13 Nifhi 1 Chome 1 41 Chuo Kuo Saporoshi Hokkaido 064 0913 JAPAN • IN • S Miss • Indiana Fort Wayne IN • (RF 1996)

**WEGENER BARBARA L** (954)946-5389
2930 NE 8th Ter Pompano Beach FL 33064-5335 • daveandbarb@falcongate.com • FG • Tchr • St Paul Boca Raton FL • (561)395-8548 • (S 1970)

**WEGENER KENNETH L** (504)246-2324
10212 Plainfield Dr Apt 306 New Orleans LA 70127-2364 • SO • Tchr • St Paul New Orleans LA • (504)947-1773 • (RF 1969)

**WEGENER LUANNE S** (517)662-6645
4526 Franklin St Auburn MI 48611-9202 • MI • Tchr • Zion Auburn MI • (517)662-4264 • (RF 1977 MA)

**WEGENER THOMAS L** (517)631-5877
2303 Cleveland Ave Midland MI 48640-5581 • tweg@tm.net • MI • Tchr • St John Midland MI • (517)835-7041 • (RF 1964 MS)

**WEGENER WILFIED W** (956)782-1566
101 E Sioux Rd Unit 1158 Pharr TX 78577-1735 • billandlill@acnet.net • NEB • EM • (S 1937 MA)

**WEGNER FRANK L** (715)526-2932
N6110 Wolf River Rd Shawano WI 54166-6006 • NW • P/Tchr • St Paul Bonduel WI • (715)758-8532 • (S 1968 MED)

**WEGNER JAMES TIMOTHY** (262)626-1447
262 Timblin Dr Apt 2 Kewaskum WI 53040 • james.wegner@gte.net • SW • Tchr • St John West Bend WI • (262)334-4901 • (MQ 1995)

**WEGNER JEFFREY PAUL**
262 Timblin Dr #2 Kewaskum WI 53040 • SW • Tchr • St John West Bend WI • (414)334-3077 • (MQ 1997)

**WEGNER JEFFREY S** (407)841-7484
116 1/2 E Amelia St Orlando FL 32801-1506 • FG • Tchr • Trinity Orlando FL • (407)843-4896 • (SP 1983)

**WEGNER RICHARD T** (920)994-9707
W5388 County Road SS Random Lake WI 53075-1236 • dwegner@y2kids.com • SW • P/Tchr • St John Random Lake WI • (920)994-9190 • (RF 1969)

**WEGNER RICHARD DR** (410)292-1957
924 Breezewick Cir Towson MD 21286-3301 • SE • Tchr • Immanuel Baltimore MD • (410)435-6861 • (RF 1946 MMU LLD)

**WEHLING CHRISTA J** (303)534-6166
1532 Perry St #1 Denver CO 80204-1441 • RM • Tchr • Emmaus Denver CO • (303)433-3303 • (S 1997)

**WEHLING MIRIAM KATHERINE*** (316)626-9742
912 N Calhoun Liberal KS 67901 • mimiam2@juno.com • FG • 06/1994 06/2000 • (S 1988)

**WEHLING PAULA M** (308)284-2944
1145 E 11th St Ogallala NE 69153-1623 • NEB • Tchr • St Paul Ogallala NE • (308)284-2944 • (S 1963)

**WEHLING STANLEY HENRY** (308)284-4873
1145 E 11th St Ogallala NE 69153-1623 • teacherstan@yahoo.com • NEB • P/Tchr • St Paul Ogallala NE • (308)284-2944 • (S 1964 MS)

**WEHMEIER SANDRA J** (414)377-5496
1005 6th Ave Grafton WI 53024-1805 • SW • Tchr • St Paul Grafton WI • (414)377-4659 • (CQ 1992 MSED)

**WEHMEYER BARBARA ANN** (314)947-4742
2315 Park Ave Saint Charles MO 63301-4752 • MO • Tchr • Our Savior Saint Charles MO • (636)947-8010 • (S 1972)

**WEHMEYER KENNETH G** (314)355-4449
11601 Doris Dr Saint Louis MO 63138-2446 • kenlow@stlnet.com • MO • Tchr • Grace Chapel Bellefontaine Nbrs MO • (314)867-6564 • (S 1968)

**WEHMEYER LOIS M** (314)355-4449
11601 Doris Dr Saint Louis MO 63138-2446 • kenlow@stlnet.com • MO • Tchr • Grace Chapel Bellefontaine Nbrs MO • (314)867-6564 • (S 1968)

**WEHMILLER MARY**
700 Tai Tam Revervoir Rd Tai Tam HONG KONG • mwehmiller@aol.com • CNH • Prin • Our Savior Aiea HI • (808)488-0000 • (S 1974 MS)

**WEHRMEISTER KRISTA RENEE** (810)791-6459
36788 Harper Ave Apt 104 Clinton Township MI 48035-5917 • krisworm@netzero.net • MI • Tchr • St Thomas Eastpointe MI • (810)772-3372 • (RF 1998)

**WEIDER MICHAEL J** (410)825-2323
1145 Concordia Dr Towson MD 21286 • mweider@worldnet.att.net • SE • Tchr • Baltimore LHS Baltimore MD • (410)825-2323 • (S 1998)

**WEIDLER JEAN G** (630)761-8830
1073 Ponca Dr Batavia IL 60510-1145 • NI • Tchr • Immanuel Batavia IL • (630)406-0157 • (RF 1972 MA)

**WEIDLER PEGGY L** (501)927-3589
3906 Philcrest Pl Springdale AR 72762-5981 • pweidler@hotmail.com • MDS • Tchr • Salem Springdale AR • (501)751-9359 • (S 1978 MA)

**WEIDNER DONALD R** (618)495-9037
7914 Bassen Rd PO Box 181 Hoffman IL 62250 • SI • P/Tchr • Trinity Hoffman IL • (618)495-2246 • (RF 1970 MA)

**WEIER KENT G** (734)422-2090
33300 Cowan Rd Westland MI 48185 • MI • Tchr • LHS Westland Westland MI • (734)422-2090 • (RF 1970 MED MA)

**WEIKUM LOIS J** (216)459-1615
4805 Broadview Rd Cleveland OH 44109-5706 • ljwteacher@hotmail.com • OH • Tchr • Luther Memorial Cleveland OH • (216)631-3640 • (SP 1972)

**WEINHOLD DEBORAH A** (816)279-2292
6002 Palomino Saint Joseph MO 64505-9802 • debtwein@ponyexpress.net • MO • Tchr • St Paul Saint Joseph MO • (816)279-1115 • (RF 1976)

**WEINHOLD J D DR** (402)643-4924
702 N 5th St Seward NE 68434-1520 • jweinhold@seward.ccsn.edu • NEB • SHS/C • Nebraska Seward NE • (S 1957 MA DED)

**WEINLAEDER KENNETH C** (507)534-3678
355 7th St SW Plainview MN 55964-1172 • MNS • Tchr • Rochester Central Rochester MN • (507)289-3267 • (S 1971 MED)

**WEINRICH CHRISTOPHER ALAN**
9 Bearclaw Apt 10C Irvine CA 92604 • PSW • Tchr • Salem Orange CA • (714)639-1946 • (IV 1995)

**WEINRICH K MARK** (314)256-6684
507 Hatteras Dr Ballwin MO 63011-2506 • lllweinrimk@lhm.org • MO • Holy Cross Los Gatos CA • (S 1975 MA)

**WEINRICH TIMOTHY P** (402)753-0617
1506 Jones Fremont NE 68025 • theweinrichs@ilovejesus.com • NEB • Tchr • Trinity Fremont NE • (402)721-5959 • (S 1979)

**WEINZ VICTORIA J**
16450 Juanita Dr NE Kenmore WA 98028 • NOW • 01/1999 • (S 1972)

**WEISENBACH JANICE L** (517)793-4291
1299 Allendale Dr Saginaw MI 48603-5411 • weisjan@aol.com • MI • Tchr • Zion Bay City MI • (517)894-2611 • (CQ 1993 MA)

**WEISER CARMEN M**
1615 Marie Rd Cordova TN 38018-4934 • MDS • Tchr • Christ The King Memphis TN • (901)682-8405 • (S 1992)

**WEISER ROSE MARIE** (210)349-7306
11800 Braesview Apt 2905 San Antonio TX 78213-4871 • TX • Tchr • Concordia San Antonio TX • (210)479-1477 • (AU 1989)

**WEISHEIT CAROLYN** (602)325-5359
5183 E Timrod St Tucson AZ 85711-7417 • PSW • EM • (RF 1978)

**WEISS CHARLES L** (715)421-3477
6420 Lenox Ave Wisconsin Rapids WI 54494-7191 • cwbw@tznet.com • NW • P/Tchr • Immanuel Wisconsin Rapids WI • (715)423-0272 • (RF 1962 MA)

**WEISS FREDERICK J** (219)489-6712
1214 Ludwig Park Dr Fort Wayne IN 46825-4026 • tchweissfj@crf.cuis.edu • IN • EM • (RF 1959 MS MA)

**WEISS JARED L** (810)791-2217
20866 Fleetwood St Clinton Twp MI 48035-1605 • jweiss@stlukemi.org • MI • Tchr • St Luke Clinton Township MI • (810)791-1151 • (S 1977 MED)

**WEISS LORI A** (218)825-8259
123 Kenwood Dr N Apt 206 Baxter MN 56425-9676 • MNN • Tchr • Family Of Christ Baxter MN • (218)829-9020 • (RF 1979)

**WEISS MARJORIE** (248)651-0806
1151 Pine Ridge Ct Rochester Hills MI 48306 • tweiss@tir.com • MI • Tchr • St John Rochester MI • (248)652-8830 • (RF 1965)

**WEISS MURIEL J** (517)755-1818
6680 E Holland Rd Saginaw MI 48601-9406 • bobweiss@juno.com • MI • Tchr • Immanuel Saginaw MI • (517)754-4285 • (SP 1975)

**WEISS ROBERT P** (773)721-5567
10637 Ave E Chicago IL 60617 • NI • Tchr • Trinity Tinley Park IL • (708)532-3529 • (S 1971)

**WEISS THOMAS H** (248)651-0806
1151 Pine Ridge Ct Rochester Hills MI 48306 • tweiss@stjohnrochester.org • MI • Prin • St John Rochester MI • (248)652-8830 • (RF 1965 MA)

**WEISZBROD MICHAEL W** (248)569-2522
30250 Woodgate Dr Southfield MI 48076-5380 • MI • 09/1999 • (S 1974)

**WELCH DONNA M** (319)322-2510
1003 W Central Park Ave Davenport IA 52804-1803 • welch1003@juno.net • IE • Tchr • Trinity Davenport IA • (319)322-5224 • (S 1970 MED)

**WELCH JENNIFER JOANN** (708)788-1876
1822 Oak Park Ave Grdn Apt Berwyn IL 60402 • NI • Tchr • St John Forest Park IL • (708)366-2764 • (RF 1994)
**WELLANDER RONALD E** (501)925-3131
14626 Arrowhead Dr Rogers AR 72756 • wellandr@ipa.net • MI • EM • (RF 1955 MMU)
**WELLEN JOHN B** (708)848-2362
1044 N Lombard Ave Oak Park IL 60302-1435 • NI • Tchr • St Philip Chicago IL • (773)561-9830 • (RF 1967 MCMU)
**WELLEN LAUREN A** (708)848-2362
1044 N Lombard Oak Park IL 60302-1435 • crfwellenla@curf.edu • NI • SHS/C • Northern Illinois Hillside IL • (RF 1969 MA)
**WELLENS LACEY ANN** (612)866-3270
6324 Irving Ave S Richfield MN 55423-1220 • MNS • SHS/C • Minnesota South Burnsville MN • (SP 1984)
**WELLS DAVID D** (770)969-2064
6970 Hobgood Rd Fairburn GA 30213-2692 • wellshome@aol.com • FG • 02/1996 02/2000 • (S 1990)
**WELLS RODGER D** (727)524-1145
1919 Northfork Cir Clearwater FL 34620-1744 • sputt2@juno.com • FG • Tchr • Grace Saint Petersburg FL • (727)527-6213 • (SP 1972 MED)
**WELTE YVONNE M** (817)428-6742
7221 Mesa Verde Trl Fort Worth TX 76137-4416 • TX • 04/1997 04/2000 • (S 1988)
**WELTON MICHAEL G** (815)369-5598
119 E Main St Lena IL 61048-8817 • NI • P/Tchr • Immanuel Freeport IL • (815)232-3511 • (CQ 1992 MA)
**WENDLING JANICE M** (815)942-4759
113 Glenwood Ln Morris IL 60450-1625 • janmarkw@uti.com • NI • 06/2000 • (RF 1985 MA)
**WENDT ELENITA A** (816)436-7170
6967 N Woodland Ave Gladstone MO 64118-2875 • MO • Tchr • Holy Cross Kansas City MO • (816)453-7211 • (S 1968)
**WENDT FRED N** (313)386-5620
6810 Osage Ave Allen Park MI 48101-2374 • MI • EM • (RF 1945 MA)
**WENDT RICHARD LEE** (414)543-9543
3212 S 76th St Milwaukee WI 53219-3703 • SW • Tchr • Mount Calvary Milwaukee WI • (414)873-3466 • (MQ 1997)
**WENDT RYAN DAVID**
1510 Sycamore Dr Fort Wayne IN 46825-4733 • RSWendt@rworld.com • NI • 06/2000 • (S 1998)
**WENDT SHANNON**
C/O Luth Church of St Philip 6232 S Eberhart Ave Chicago IL 60637 • NI • Tchr • St Philip Chicago IL • (773)493-3865 • (MQ 2000)
**WENDTE SUSAN K** (501)783-5468
2511 S L St Fort Smith AR 72901-5313 • MDS • Tchr • First Fort Smith AR • (501)452-5330 • (S 1972)
**WENGER CARRIE BERNADINE**
1003 W Harris St Appleton WI 54914-3857 • NW • 07/1997 07/2000 • (SP 1993)
**WENGER DANIEL PAUL**
2444A N 115th St Wauwatosa WI 53226 • SW • Tchr • Our Redeemer Wauwatosa WI • (414)258-4558 • (BR 1998)
**WENGER JOHN W**
545 Lake View Dr Woodbury MN 55129-9287 • wenger@csp.edu • MNS • SHS/C • Minnesota South Burnsville MN • (CQ 1973 MA)
**WENGER PATRICIA LEE** (816)690-5616
822 SE 15th St Oak Grove MO 64075-9556 • MO • Tchr • Messiah Independence MO • (816)254-9409 • (S 1973 MA)
**WENGERT DEAN D** (219)625-4590
6833 Leesburg Rd Fort Wayne IN 46818-9673 • IN • Tchr • St Peter Huntington IN • (219)356-6528 • (S 1956 MA)
**WENIGER CRISTY ALANE**
2905 N Bristol St #K Santa Ana CA 92706-1073 • PSW • Tchr • Zion Anaheim CA • (714)535-1169 • (IV 1995)
**WENIGER MICHAEL RICHARD**
10101 N 91st Ave #162 Peoria AZ 85345 • PSW • Tchr • Christian Phoenix AZ • (602)934-5896 • (PO 1999)
**WENIGER RICHARD L** (503)760-5650
11651 SE Flavel St Portland OR 97266-5981 • dickw@nowlcms.org • NOW • Northwest Portland OR • (S 1969 MED)
**WENKE CAROLYN ANN** (402)365-7899
RR 2 Box 100 Hebron NE 68370-9536 • rwenke@gpcom.net • NEB • Tchr • Deshler Lutheran Sch Deshler NE • (402)365-7858 • (S 1980)
**WENNINGER BARBARA ANN** (507)647-2469
29770 State Hwy 15 Winthrop MN 55396-9702 • MNS • 06/1997 06/2000 • (S 1984)
**WENTE STEVEN F** (708)681-4224
709 N 5th Ave Maywood IL 60153-1033 • crfwentesf@crf.cuis.edu • NI • SHS/C • Northern Illinois Hillside IL • (RF 1975 MCMU DMU)
**WENTHE WILLIAM D** (512)258-0489
12321 Double Tree Ln Austin TX 78750-1761 • TX • Tchr • St Paul Austin TX • (512)472-3313 • (S 1961)
**WENTHE WILLIAM D JR.** (210)490-0441
5610 Spring Fire San Antonio TX 78247 • williamw@concordia-satx.com • TX • Tchr • Concordia San Antonio TX • (210)479-1477 • (AU 1989)
**WENTLAND BETTY M** (312)860-2707
475 E Montrose Ave Wood Dale IL 60191-2163 • NI • Tchr • Northern Illinois Hillside IL • (RF 1983 MA)
**WENTLAND JAMES L** (812)522-6630
812 S Walnut St Seymour IN 47274 • IN • P/Tchr • Emmaus Indianapolis IN • (317)632-1486 • (RF 1967 MSED)
**WENTLAND KATHERINE MARIE** (219)489-8260
8118 Cha Ca Peta Pass Fort Wayne IN 46825 • IN • Tchr • Trinity Fort Wayne IN • (219)447-2411 • (RF 1970 MS)
**WENTLAND KENNETH HENRY** (219)489-8260
8118 Cha Ca Peta Pass Fort Wayne IN 46825 • IN • P/Tchr • Trinity Fort Wayne IN • (219)447-2411 • (RF 1969 MS)
**WENTZ MARK A** (402)866-2133
515 Washington PO Box 344 Sterling NE 68943-0344 • NEB • 05/1999 • (S 1989)
**WENTZ SHERI MARIE***
PO Box 344 Sterling NE 68443 • NEB • 05/1999 • (S 1992)
**WENTZEL HERMAN K DR** (651)484-1866
2582 Cohansey St Roseville MN 55113-3512 • hermankarl@aol.com • MNS • EM • (RF 1949 MA DED)
**WENTZEL STEVEN J** (419)598-8818
16840 Co Rd S Rt 4 Napoleon OH 43545-9444 • OH • Prin • St Paul Napoleon OH • (419)592-5536 • (RF 1973 MED)
**WENTZEL VICKI** (419)598-8818
16840 Co Rd S Napoleon OH 43545-9444 • swentzel@bright.net • OH • Tchr • St Paul Napoleon OH • (419)592-5536 • (RF 1973)
**WENZ RICHARD L** (319)386-1980
4205 Regency Ct Davenport IA 52806-4861 • IE • EM • (S 1956 MA)
**WENZEL ARTHUR P** (219)749-8298
1627 Lofton Way Fort Wayne IN 46815-7621 • IN • Mem C • St Peter Fort Wayne IN • (219)749-5816 • (RF 1974 MSED)
**WENZEL GARY E DR** (708)383-7409
647 N Cuyler Ave Oak Park IL 60302-1702 • crfwenzelg@curf.edu • NI • SHS/C • Northern Illinois Hillside IL • (RF 1970 MA MED PHD)
**WENZEL PAMELA B** (734)525-1365
8561 Liberty Blvd Westland MI 48185-1791 • MI • Tchr • Detroit Urban Detroit MI • (313)582-9900 • (AA 1983 MA)
**WENZEL RUTH ELLEN** (718)461-7579
124-07 11th Ave College Point NY 11356-1821 • AT • Tchr • St John College Point NY • (718)463-4790 • (BR 1976 MS)
**WENZELBURGER KURT R** (262)369-8349
526 Buckingham Way Hartland WI 53029-2507 • SW • Tchr • Divine Redeemer Hartland WI • (414)367-8400 • (RF 1988)
**WERDERMAN AMY L** (313)727-4123
68756 S Forest Ave Richmond MI 48062-1268 • MI • P/Tchr • St Peter Richmond MI • (810)727-9080 • (S 1970 MA)
**WERK ANN M** (716)344-0219
24 Park Ave Batavia NY 14020-2023 • werkasap@iinc.com • EA • Tchr • St Paul Batavia NY • (716)343-0488 • (RF 1979 MA)
**WERLING ARTHUR C** (219)749-5864
6931 Maysville Rd Fort Wayne IN 46815-8229 • IN • EM • (RF 1938 MS)
**WERLING CATHLEEN M** (219)672-9637
14818 Lafayette Center Rd Roanoke IN 46783-9601 • IN • Tchr • Central New Haven IN • (219)493-2502 • (S 1990)
**WERNER CHERYLANNE** (402)675-1265
PO Box 193 Battle Creek NE 68715-0193 • NEB • Tchr • St John Battle Creek NE • (402)675-3605 • (S 1991)
**WERNER DAUNA L** (414)675-6603
3459 Knollwood Rd West Bend WI 53095-9414 • SW • Tchr • St Paul Grafton WI • (414)377-4659 • (MQ 1987)
**WERNER DAVID J** (612)467-2287
311 Maria Ave Hamburg MN 55339-0004 • lhsmayer@skypoint.com • MNS • Tchr • Lutheran High Mayer MN • (612)657-2251 • (S 1973)
**WERNER DENNIS** (818)367-0681
13625 Henny Ave Sylmar CA 91342-2127 • PSW • Tchr • First Burbank CA • (818)848-3076 • (S 1973 MS)
**WERNER JOHN T** (612)467-2287
5005 Interstate 40 W Amarillo TX 79106 • TX • Tchr • Trinity Amarillo TX • (806)352-5629 • (S 2000)
**WERNER JOSEPH B**
936 Schilling Dr Dyer IN 46311 • IN • Tchr • St Paul Munster IN • (219)836-6270 • (S 1984 MAT)
**WERNER KAREN LYNN** (562)430-4364
8050 E Tarma St Long Beach CA 90808-3230 • educ8um@aol.com • PSW • Tchr • Bethany Long Beach CA • (562)420-7783 • (S 1973)
**WERNER MARK A** (636)527-5146
341 Hillcrest Blvd Ballwin MO 63021 • m3werner@juno.com • MI • Mem C • Peace Shelby Township MI • (810)731-4120 • (AA 1987)
**WERNER MICHAEL C** (303)940-0158
5031 Garrison St Wheat Ridge CO 80033-6790 • mcw56usa@yahoo.com • RM • Tchr • Shepherd Hills Littleton CO • (303)798-0711 • (S 1978 MED)
**WERNER PAMELA S**
3818 S Western Ave Sioux Falls SD 57105-6511 • awerner@gpcom.net • NEB • Tchr • St Peter Davenport NE • (402)364-2139 • (S 1984)
**WERNING E KATHY** (319)228-8489
7151 23rd Ave Van Horne IA 52346-9805 • IE • EM • (S 1971 MA)
**WERNSING DARREL G** (217)792-3961
508 N Lafayette St Mount Pulaski IL 62548-1039 • CI • P/Tchr • Zion Mount Pulaski IL • (217)792-5715 • (RF 1962 MSED)
**WERT MARY LOUISE** (630)859-8608
731 Lindsay Cir North Aurora IL 60542-9060 • NI • Tchr • Immanuel Batavia IL • (630)879-7163 • (RF 1988)
**WERTH DOROTHY J**
402 3rd Ave N Wahpeton ND 58075-4421 • ND • 08/1992 08/1998 • (SP 1970)
**WERTH GERALD J** (219)493-0858
10922 Trailwood Ln New Haven IN 46774-9571 • IN • Tchr • Central New Haven IN • (219)493-2502 • (S 1965 MED)
**WERTH JANICE M** (716)731-7183
2469 Stoelting Dr Niagara Falls NY 14304-2056 • EA • Tchr • St John North Tonawanda NY • (716)693-9677 • (RF 1985)
**WESCH GUSTAV W** (303)237-6296
3400 Estes St Wheat Ridge CO 80033-5931 • RM • EM • (S 1934 LLD)
**WESCHE DAVID P** (770)720-8618
355 Candy Ln Canton GA 30115 • davewoohoo@juno.com • FG • Mem C • Timothy Woodstock GA • (770)928-2812 • (S 1979 MS)
**WESCHE SARAH ANNE*** (770)720-8618
355 Candy Lane Canton GA 30115-8678 • davewoohoo@juno.com • FG • 09/1998 • (RF 1984)
**WESLOCK NAOMI Y** (630)980-8258
418 White Oak Dr Roselle IL 60172-2512 • weslockn@trinityroselle.com • NI • Tchr • Trinity Roselle IL • (630)894-3263 • (RF 1964)
**WESLOCK TERRY E** (630)980-8258
418 White Oak Dr Roselle IL 60172-2512 • weslockt@trinityroselle.com • NI • Tchr • Trinity Roselle IL • (630)894-3263 • (RF 1965 MA)
**WESSEL KATHY E** (612)494-8528
9139 Brockton Ln N Maple Grove MN 55311-1302 • MNS • 07/1998 • (RF 1981 MCMU DMIN)
**WEST AMY**
5234 Cliff Ct SE Olympia WA 98513-5376 • wildwest8@yahoo.com • NOW • Tchr • Faith Lacey WA • (360)491-1733 • (PO 1996)
**WEST KAREN**
10914 Versailles Blvd Clermont FL 34711-7344 • S • Tchr • St Luke Oviedo FL • (407)365-3408 • (BR 1990)
**WEST LINDA** (651)734-9904
1884 Stillwater Ave Saint Paul MN 55119 • linda-west@gateway.net • MNS • Tchr • East St Paul Saint Paul MN • (612)774-2030 • (SP 1997)
**WEST REBECCA L**
7022 Cottonwood Cir Sachse TX 75048-2115 • TX • Tchr • Messiah Lambs Richardson TX • (972)234-8948 • (AU 1992)
**WESTAD KAREN** (605)882-1171
1109 N Broadway Watertown SD 57201-1437 • SD • 08/1989 08/2000 • (SP 1980)
**WESTENDORF KAREN SUE** (810)254-6586
42141 Blairmoor Dr Sterling Hts MI 48313-2613 • MI • Tchr • Trinity Utica MI • (810)731-4490 • (CQ 1997)
**WESTERFELD JUDITH A** (920)499-2786
914 Neville Ave Green Bay WI 54303-4016 • NW • Tchr • Redeemer Green Bay WI • (920)499-1033 • (RF 1960)
**WESTFAHL SHARON K** (316)465-2441
7910 E Red Rock Rd Haven KS 67543-8085 • KS • EM • (S 1972)
**WESTIN BETHANY S** (517)789-7297
3310 W Franklin Jackson MI 49203 • ewestin@dmci.net • MI • Tchr • Trinity Jackson MI • (517)784-3135 • (AA 1985 MA)
**WESTOL JOHN L** (352)629-5769
2021 SE 38th St Ocala FL 34480-8836 • jrstol@cs.com • FG • Tchr • St John Ocala FL • (352)622-7275 • (RF 1969 MED)
**WESTOL RUTH D** (352)629-5769
2021 SE 38th St Ocala FL 34480-8836 • FG • Tchr • St John Ocala FL • (352)622-7275 • (RF 1977 MA)
**WESTPFAHL BARBARA J** (612)484-9674
2926 Woodbridge St Roseville MN 55113-2421 • MNS • Tchr • Central Saint Paul MN • (651)645-8649 • (SP 1971)
**WESTREM JOHN M** (219)485-3879
6024 Andro Run Fort Wayne IN 46815-8425 • IN • Tchr • St Peter Fort Wayne IN • (219)749-5811 • (S 1972 MS)
**WESTRICK EARL J**
PO Box 3276 Sunriver OR 97707 • IN • S Miss • Indiana Fort Wayne IN • (RF 1955)
**WETHERELL CARRI J** (904)671-6140
6 Fishermans Cir Apt 4 Ormond Beach FL 32174 • FG • Tchr • Trinity Holly Hill FL • (904)255-7580 • (RF 1982)
**WETJEN DENNIS D**
C5 South Bay Villa 4 South Bay Close Repulse Bay HONG KONG • PSW • S Miss • Pacific Southwest Irvine CA • (949)854-3232 • (S 1973 MA)
**WETJEN TAMARA J** (319)668-1626
1851 275th St Williamsburg IA 52361-8540 • IE • Tchr • Lutheran Interparish Williamsburg IA • (319)668-1711 • (S 1980)
**WETMORE MELBA L** (314)843-3112
10353 Roscommon Dr Saint Louis MO 63123-5072 • cmwetmore@postnet.com • MO • Tchr • Trinity Saint Louis MO • (314)621-0228 • (S 1973)
**WETZEL ANNE** (630)775-9491
460 S Ruth St Itasca IL 60143 • wetzel4@aol.com • FG • Tchr • Our Savior Plantation FL • (954)473-6888 • (MQ 1992)
**WETZEL MYRON E** (507)281-3282
2521 23rd Ave SE Rochester MN 55904-5811 • MNS • Tchr • Rochester Central Rochester MN • (507)289-3267 • (S 1972 MSED)
**WETZSTEIN SANDRA L**
6459 S Filbert Ln Littleton CO 80121 • RM • Rochester Central Rochester MN • (RF 1966 MED)
**WEYER EDITH C** (847)669-9223
2650 Melbourne Ln Lk In The Hls IL 60156 • NI • Tchr • Northern Illinois Hillside IL • (RF 1987)
**WEYHRICH RANDY J** (414)463-6481
5239 N 108th Ct Milwaukee WI 53225-3101 • SW • Tchr • Milwaukee LHS Milwaukee WI • (414)461-6000 • (CQ 1977 MA)

**WEYMIER AMY S**
3219 N 87th St Milwaukee WI 53222-3732 • SW • Tchr • Elm Grove Elm Grove WI • (262)797-2970 • (RF 1987)

**WHEELER JULIE A** (517)868-4360
C/O Zion Lutheran Church 17903 Dice Rd Hemlock MI 48626-9637 • MI • Tchr • Zion Hemlock MI • (517)642-5909 • (RF 1983)

**WHEELER LYNN A** (661)665-9451
7201 Sierra Rim Dr Bakersfield CA 93313-4512 • lawheelerl@aol.com • CNH • P/Tchr • St John Bakersfield CA • (661)398-5140 • (PO 1982)

**WHELPLY HAL H JR. DR** (949)857-6680
26 Firebird Irvine CA 92604-3323 • hal.whelply@cui.edu • PSW • SHS/C • Pacific Southwest Irvine CA • (949)854-3232 • (S 1965 MA DED)

**WHELPLY KAREN K** (949)857-6680
26 Firebird Irvine CA 92604-3323 • PSW • Tchr • Zion Anaheim CA • (714)535-3600 • (S 1965 MED)

**WHIGHTSIL PAMELA J** (504)832-8901
3704 W Bode Ct Metairie LA 70001-3904 • SO • Tchr • Atonement Metairie LA • (504)887-3980 • (S 1984)

**WHIPKEY ROBERT E JR.** (715)241-7156
PO Box 8064 Wausau WI 54402-8064 • bobw@nwdlcms.org • NW • North Wisconsin Wausau WI • (RF 1969 MSED)

**WHITAKER ANGELA YOUNGMAN** (760)665-2164
PO Box 254 Earp CA 92242-0254 • PSW • EM • (CQ 1986)

**WHITCOMB RHONDA J** (320)485-3323
PO Box 550 Winsted MN 55395-0550 • MNS • Tchr • St James Howard Lake MN • (320)543-2630 • (SP 1984)

**WHITE DIANE MICHELLE** (713)895-8147
5801 Hollister St Apt 905 Houston TX 77040-5706 • dbaker@oslschool.org • TX • Tchr • Our Savior Houston TX • (713)290-8277 • (RF 1996)

**WHITE ELLINOR BLACK DR** (404)766-8217
2408 Meadow Lark Dr East Point GA 30344 • clsprinebw@aol.com • FG • Prin • Christ East Point GA • (404)767-2892 • (CQ 1998 MSED PHD)

**WHITE LAURA A** (503)629-9856
15507 NW Andalusian Wy Portland OR 97229 • the3whiteshouse@cs.com • NOW • Tchr • Pilgrim Beaverton OR • (503)644-8697 • (PO 1988)

**WHITE PAMELA K** (517)356-2803
825 N 2nd Ave Alpena MI 49707-2231 • awhite@northland.lib.mi.us • MI • Tchr • Immanuel Alpena MI • (517)354-4805 • (S 1972)

**WHITE SIGNE GAIL**
32653 5 Points Rd Kingston IL 60145-8443 • NI • O Sp Min • Northern Illinois Hillside IL • (MQ 1994)

**WHITE TAMMY L**
60 Canvasback Ct Monticello GA 31064-8808 • hapeekampr@aol.com • FG • 06/1999 • (BR 1985)

**WHITNEY LARRY ALLEN** (303)351-8379
3806 5th St Greeley CO 80634-1629 • RM • Tchr • Trinity Greeley CO • (970)330-2485 • (S 1970)

**WHITNEY NANCY R** (407)365-2776
1105 Villa Ct Winter Springs FL 32708-4805 • nanrog@aol.com • S • Tchr • St Luke Oviedo FL • (407)365-3228 • (RF 1967)

**WHITNEY ROGER L** (407)365-2776
1105 Villa Ct Winter Springs FL 32708-4805 • nanrog@aol.com • S • Tchr • St Luke Oviedo FL • (407)365-3228 • (RF 1972 MED)

**WHITSON JANET SUSAN DR** (281)255-6278
28211 Camille Dr Tomball TX 77375 • TX • Tchr • Concordia LHS Tomball TX • (281)351-2547 • (RF 1971 DPH)

**WHITTOW HOLLY** (414)784-1652
3000 Huntington Cir Brookfield WI 53005 • EN • Tchr • Hales Corners Hales Corners WI • (414)529-6701 • (MQ 1998)

**WHYBREW DOREEN B** (217)682-5516
121 S Walnut St PO Box 307 Stewardson IL 62463-0307 • pkaw@stewstras.net • CI • 09/2000 • (AA 1985)

**WICHMAN CAMELA LEE** (828)428-4129
2382 Elbow Rd Newton NC 28658-9117 • SE • Tchr • Concordia Conover NC • (828)464-3324 • (AA 1986)

**WICHMAN DONALD LEE** (219)493-1364
2725 Kingsland Ct Fort Wayne IN 46815-8002 • IN • Tchr • Central New Haven IN • (219)493-2502 • (S 1975 MED)

**WICHMANN DIANNE L** (303)466-7612
10721 W 102nd Ave Broomfield CO 80021-5107 • RM • Tchr • Gethsemane Northglenn CO • (303)451-6908 • (S 1972)

**WICHMANN WERNER M**
5312 Cumberland Plain Dr Raleigh NC 27616-6367 • NI • EM • (RF 1938)

**WICKBOLDT CYNTHIA** (773)282-8211
6227 W Waveland Ave Chicago IL 60634-2533 • EN • Tchr • Our Savior Chicago IL • (773)631-1606 • (RF 1974)

**WICKBOLDT JOEL M**
821 Bode - Apt 9 Elgin IL 60120 • NI • Tchr • St John Elgin IL • (847)741-0814 • (RF 2000)

**WICKBOLDT MARK W** (773)282-8211
6227 W Waveland Ave Chicago IL 60634-2533 • NI • Tchr • Messiah Chicago IL • (773)736-6600 • (RF 1974 MA)

**WICKER JANET LEIGH** (618)965-9275
509 S Randall St Steeleville IL 62288-2004 • jwicker@egyptian.net • SI • 08/1999 • (RF 1981 MSED)

**WICKRE CAROL M** (612)866-1128
6412 14th Ave S Richfield MN 55423-1734 • MNS • Tchr • Mount Calvary Richfield MN • (612)869-9441 • (SP 1980)

**WICKRE PAUL N** (612)866-1128
6412 14th Ave S Richfield MN 55423-1734 • MNS • Tchr • Mount Calvary Richfield MN • (612)869-9441 • (SP 1977)

**WICKS JANICE L** (414)421-0416
4835 W College Ave Apt 130 Greendale WI 53129-2943 • SW • Tchr • Our Father Greenfield WI • (414)282-7500 • (SP 1968)

**WIDENHOFER DAVID**
5318 Litchfield Rd Fort Wayne IN 46835-8806 • IN • Prin • Concordia LHS Fort Wayne IN • (219)483-1102 • (RF 1967 MAR MS)

**WIEBOLD JUDITH**
1803 Willow Dr Hudson WI 54016-1457 • NI • Tchr • St Paul Dolton IL • (708)849-3225 • (RF 1965 MA)

**WIEBOLD LINDA J** (612)949-0447
6817 Lorena Lane Eden Prairie MN 55346-3549 • MNS • Tchr • Redeemer Wayzata MN • (612)473-5356 • (SP 1976)

**WIECHMAN JAMIE MARIE** (618)343-1181
398 Skyline View Dr Collinsville IL 62234 • SI • 07/2000 • (AU 1998)

**WIED ALWIN J** (616)972-7028
10280 Eagle Pass Stanwood MI 49346-9602 • MI • EM • (S 1938 MA)

**WIEDENKELLER HILBERT W** (414)529-4651
10180 Whitnall Edge Cir Unit I Franklin WI 53132-2836 • hwiedenkeller@hcl.org • EN • Tchr • Hales Corners Hales Corners WI • (414)529-6700 • (RF 1960 MMU)

**WIEDENMANN RUTH E** (407)677-4437
4924 Tangerine Ave Winter Park FL 32792-7150 • S • Tchr • St Luke Oviedo FL • (407)365-3228 • (RF 1976)

**WIEGAND JON MATTHEW**
1933 Woodbine St Apt 2R Ridgewood NY 11385 • AT • P/Tchr • Our Saviour Rego Park NY • (718)897-4343 • (BR 1995)

**WIEGERT JONATHAN REUBEN** (414)785-0117
1619 S Ranch Rd New Berlin WI 53151-1652 • jswiegs@aol.com • SW • Tchr • Martin LHS Greendale WI • (414)421-4000 • (RF 1995)

**WIEGERT SHANNON L** (414)785-0117
1619 S Ranch Rd New Berlin WI 53151-1652 • jswiegs@aol.com • SW • Tchr • St Paul West Allis WI • (414)541-6251 • (RF 1996)

**WIEGMANN MIRA DR** (402)643-2524
456 S Columbia Ave Seward NE 68434-2606 • mwiegmann@seward.cune.edu • NEB • SHS/C • Nebraska Seward NE • (S 1969 MA PHD)

**WIEGMANN RICHARD W** (402)643-2524
456 S Columbia Ave Seward NE 68434-2606 • rwiegmann@seward.cune.edu • NEB • SHS/C • Nebraska Seward NE • (S 1962 MFA)

**WIEMANN THOMAS E** (847)956-6323
440 W Kathleen Dr Des Plaines IL 60016-2620 • tomwie@yahoo.com • NI • Tchr • Luther HS North Chicago IL • (773)286-3600 • (S 1974 MA)

**WIEMER SCOTT H** (734)261-6676
33621 Tawas Trl Westland MI 48185-2315 • weemcoach@aol.com • MI • 02/1997 02/2000 • (S 1978 MS)

**WIEMERO MARY ELLEN** (909)877-3816
18883 13th St Bloomington CA 92316-3432 • mweimero@juno.com • PSW • Tchr • Lutheran High School La Verne CA • (909)593-4494 • (CQ 1997 MA)

**WIENEKE LORI**
2639 Ridgemoor SE Kentwood MI 49512 • MI • Tchr • Our Savior Lansing MI • (517)882-8665 • (AA 1998)

**WIENKE EMILIE C** (817)424-3748
2209 Spur Trl Grapevine TX 76051-4644 • eclairel@earthlink.net • TX • EM • (RF 1970)

**WIER BARRY L** (608)752-9330
2277 N Hawthorne Park Dr Janesville WI 53545-2033 • SW • Tchr • St Paul Janesville WI • (608)754-4471 • (RF 1976 MSED)

**WIER RUTH A** (608)752-9330
2277 Hawthorne Park Dr N Janesville WI 53545-2033 • SW • Tchr • St Paul Janesville WI • (608)754-4471 • (RF 1975 MED)

**WIERMAN JUDITH A** (414)529-5540
4955 S Brookdale Dr Greenfield WI 53228-3511 • SW • Tchr • Our Father Greenfield WI • (414)282-7500 • (MQ 1985)

**WIERSIG CHRISTINE C** (248)426-8370
29636 Trancrest Livonia MI 48152 • MI • Tchr • St Paul Farmington Hills MI • (248)474-2488 • (S 1969 MA)

**WIERSIG MELINDA A**
18491 Garfield Redford MI 48240-1717 • MI • Tchr • Detroit Urban Detroit MI • (313)582-9900 • (S 1997)

**WIERSIG W DAN** (248)426-8370
29636 Transcrest Livonia MI 48152-4530 • wdwiersig@aol.com • MI • Prin • St Paul Farmington Hills MI • (248)474-2488 • (S 1968 MED)

**WIESE ANITA E** (713)448-0632
6911 Northleaf Dr Houston TX 77086-1931 • TX • Tchr • Immanuel Houston TX • (713)861-8787 • (RF 1978)

**WIESE MARSHA**
C/O Concordia Luth High School 700 E Main St Tomball TX 77375-6721 • TX • Tchr • Concordia LHS Tomball TX • (281)351-2547 • (S 2000)

**WIEST KATHRYN S** (308)324-5574
801 E 11th St Lexington NE 68850-1704 • NEB • 06/1998 06/2000 • (S 1978)

**WIETFELDT CATHY L** (314)487-1045
5593 Baronridge Dr Apt 5 Saint Louis MO 63129-3034 • wiety@stlnet.com • MO • Tchr • LHS South Saint Louis MO • (314)631-1400 • (RF 1975 MS)

**WIETING BRUCE L** (970)356-2590
140 23rd Ave Lot 30 Greeley CO 80631-1721 • RM • Tchr • Faith Denver CO • (303)455-5878 • (S 1989)

**WIGGINS KATIE G** (205)264-1797
3365 Southmont Dr Montgomery AL 36105-1729 • SO • EM • (RF 1981)

**WIKOFF HALEY DIANNE** (319)391-3850
1639 W Hayes St Davenport IA 52804 • IE • Tchr • Trinity Davenport IA • (319)322-5224 • (S 1999)

**WILABY KEVIN L** (517)753-7110
2721 Benjamin St Saginaw MI 48602-5766 • wilabykl@hotmail.com • MI • Prin • Valley Saginaw MI • (517)790-1676 • (S 1987)

**WILABY STEPHANIE MARIE** (517)753-7110
2721 Benjamin St Saginaw MI 48602-5766 • wilabykl@svol.com • MI • 09/1995 • (S 1991)

**WILANT MICHELLE LYNN**
1954 N Main St Dubuque IA 52001-4410 • michelle@wilant.com • IN • Tchr • Bethlehem Fort Wayne IN • (219)744-3228 • (RF 1996)

**WILBERT WARREN N** (219)486-9501
5905 Bellingham Ln Fort Wayne IN 46835-1254 • olefox333@aol.com • MI • EM • (S 1950 MS MS DED)

**WILCOX SCOTT ROBERT** (402)646-2164
1889 N Columbia Seward NE 68434-9730 • scottandsusan@navix.net • NEB • Tchr • St John Seward NE • (402)643-4535 • (S 1993)

**WILDAUER BEVERLY JEAN** (308)384-0606
4310 Claussen Rd Grand Island NE 68803-1018 • plchurch@computer-concepts.com • NEB • Tchr • Peace Grand Island NE • (308)384-5673 • (S 1997 MED)

**WILDAUER CHARLES F** (972)359-0441
301 Droinwich Cir Allen TX 75002 • wildauer@ticnet.com • TX • Tchr • Faith Plano TX • (972)423-7448 • (S 1970 MS)

**WILDE ELYSE** (507)425-2356
701 N Saint Paul Ave Fulda MN 56131 • MNS • Tchr • St Paul Fulda MN • (507)425-2169 • (S 1994)

**WILHARM KEITH A** (847)776-8439
1533 King Edward Ct Palatine IL 60067 • crfwilharka@curf.edu • NI • SHS/C • Northern Illinois Hillside IL • (RF 1976 MA)

**WILHELM MARLENE E** (352)314-2248
21534 Prince Albert Ct Leesburg FL 34748 • granybelle@mplnet.net • FG • EM • (RF 1958)

**WILHORN BRIAN ROBERT**
6438 Ryland Ave Vesper WI 54489 • NW • Tchr • Immanuel Wisconsin Rapids WI • (715)423-3260 • (SP 1995)

**WILK MARK T** (210)681-0903
7263 Autumn Park San Antonio TX 78249-4285 • TX • Tchr • Redeemer San Antonio TX • (210)735-9903 • (RF 1975)

**WILKE CAROLYN M** (713)468-7295
1707 Bayram Dr Houston TX 77055-2312 • TX • Tchr • St Mark Houston TX • (713)468-2623 • (RF 1962 MED)

**WILKE JANE P** (314)965-2934
12951 Beaver Dam Rd Des Peres MO 63131 • jane.wilke@cph.org • MO • CCRA • Missouri Saint Louis MO • (314)317-4550 • (SP 1975 MS)

**WILKE KENNETH R** (206)937-2146
9603 California Ave SW Seattle WA 98136-2824 • NOW • Tchr • Hope Seattle WA • (206)935-8500 • (RF 1969)

**WILKE NANCY E** (517)823-2143
125 Timber Ridge Dr Vassar MI 48768-9009 • MI • Tchr • St Michael Richville MI • (517)868-4809 • (RF 1974)

**WILKE PAUL M** (512)339-1083
531 E Houston St Giddings TX 78942-2717 • TX • Tchr • Immanuel Giddings TX • (409)542-3319 • (MQ 1990)

**WILKE PHILLIP M** (713)941-1375
1707 Bayram Dr Houston TX 77055-2312 • TX • Tchr • Concordia LHS Tomball TX • (281)351-2547 • (MQ 1988)

**WILKEN MARIA C**
1437 Jamie Ln Waterloo IL 62298-5571 • SI • 12/1990 12/1999 • (S 1987)

**WILKIE ALICIA E**
C/O Cross Lutheran Church 8609 State Rt 47 Yorkville IL 60560 • NI • Tchr • Cross Yorkville IL • (630)553-7335 • (RF 2000)

**WILKIE MELBA J** (507)334-4225
1305 Highland Pl Faribault MN 55021-6603 • MNS • Tchr • Faribault Faribault MN • (507)334-7982 • (RF 1962)

**WILKS MYRIL A** (810)786-9795
6505 Northbrook Ct Washington MI 48094 • MI • Tchr • Peace Shelby Twp MI • (810)739-2431 • (S 1971)

**WILL DEBRA A** (708)532-4116
7459 Cashew Dr Orland Park IL 60462-5101 • kudohana928@hotmail.com • NI • Tchr • St Paul Oak Lawn IL • (847)423-1058 • (RF 1978)

**WILL MARLENE G** (219)362-8837
1710 Indiana Ave La Porte IN 46350-5204 • IN • Tchr • St John La Porte IN • (219)362-6692 • (S 1984 MED)

**WILLE KRISTA** (303)797-6511
1790 E Easter Ave Littleton CO 80122 • RM • Tchr • Shepherd Of The Hill Littleton CO • (303)798-0711 • (RF 2000)

**WILLE MARGARET L** (920)261-2570
215 Derby Ln Watertown WI 53094 • SW • Tchr • Good Shepherd Watertown WI • (920)261-2570 • (S 1969)

**WILLE MELVIN** (312)554-9093
30 Sedgwick Rd Oswego IL 60543 • NI • Tchr • St John La Grange IL • (708)354-1690 • (RF 1965 MA)

**WILLE RONALD G** (920)261-2570
1611 E Main St Watertown WI 53094-4109 • rgwdce@execpc.com • SW • Mem C • Good Shepherd Watertown WI • (920)261-2570 • (S 1970 MED)

**WILLER KIRSTEN M** (262)781-2534
15905 Brentwood Dr Brookfield WI 53005-1021 • mdwkmw@aol.com • SW • 08/1999 • (CQ 1999)

**WILLERT MARK E** (724)477-3114
148 Dusty Ln Butler PA 16001 • mkwillert@aol.com • EA • Tchr • St Luke Cabot PA • (724)352-2777 • (BR 1995)

**WILLIAMS ALLAN A*** (313)254-3304
8335 Canal Rd Utica MI 48317-5502 • MI • Tchr • Immanuel Macomb MI • (810)286-7076 • (S 1977)

**WILLIAMS BONNIE J** (773)202-0047
5544 W Leland Ave Apt 3D Chicago IL 60630-3529 • NI • Tchr • Immanuel Glenview IL • (847)724-1034 • (RF 1985 MA)
**WILLIAMS DEMETRICE** (773)278-6730
1633 N Harding Chicago IL 60647 • dee31@gateway.net • NI • Tchr • St Paul Melrose Park IL • (708)343-5000 • (RF 1991 MED)
**WILLIAMS DROXSAN J**
2010 15th St SW Loveland CO 80537-7722 • RM • Tchr • Immanuel Loveland CO • (970)667-7606 • (S 1999)
**WILLIAMS ELIZABETH V** (313)274-3945
7677 Beaverland Detroit MI 48239-1050 • MI • Tchr • Detroit Urban Detroit MI • (313)582-9900 • (RF 1972)
**WILLIAMS JANICE BARBARA** (408)296-2589
2299 Sunrise Dr San Jose CA 95124-2640 • CNH • Tchr • Our Savior Cupertino CA • (408)252-0345 • (S 1962)
**WILLIAMS JANICE** (718)931-6906
1805 Seminole Ave Bronx NY 10461-1830 • AT • Tchr • Our Saviour Bronx NY • (718)792-5665 • (RF 1965 MSED)
**WILLIAMS JUDY EVON** (810)954-4764
434 N Esplanade St Mt Clemens MI 48043-6502 • judyw@123.net • MI • Tchr • Trinity Clinton Township MI • (810)468-8511 • (CQ 1999)
**WILLIAMS LEWIS E** (718)931-6906
1805 Seminole Ave Bronx NY 10461-1830 • wmslew@aol.com • AT • Prin • Our Saviour Bronx NY • (718)792-5665 • (RF 1967 MA)
**WILLIAMS STACI ANN** (816)455-2030
2404 NE 63rd Pl Gladstone MO 64118-3715 • MO • Tchr • Holy Cross Kansas City MO • (816)453-7211 • (AU 1993 MED)
**WILLIAMSEN MICHAEL E** (517)894-8945
239 N Sherman Bay City MI 48708-6783 • MI • Tchr • Faith Bay City MI • (517)684-3448 • (RF 1983 MAT)
**WILLIAMSON PAMELA A** (847)690-9987
465 Florian Dr Des Plaines IL 60016 • IE • Tchr • Trinity Knoxville IA • (515)842-4724 • (RF 1979)
**WILLIG FREDRICK J** (317)356-3107
354 S Arlington Ave Indianapolis IN 46219-7304 • IN • Tchr • LHS Of Indianapolis Indianapolis IN • (317)787-5474 • (RF 1975 MS)
**WILLIS LINDA J** (517)356-2562
4605 M 32 Alpena MI 49707-8133 • MI • Tchr • Immanuel Alpena MI • (517)354-4805 • (CQ 1982)
**WILLIS LISA M** (812)882-1322
1266 S Oliphant Ave Vincennes IN 47591-4023 • IN • Tchr • St John Vincennes IN • (812)882-4662 • (RF 1985)
**WILLITS ELEANOR**
7106 Breighton Orange CA 92869 • PSW • Tchr • Salem Orange CA • (714)633-2366 • (CQ 1996)
**WILLMOTT SARAH LYNN** (651)681-1783
15768 Cicerone Ct Rosemount MN 55068 • MNS • Tchr • Trinity Lone Oak Eagan MN • (651)454-1139 • (SP 1993)
**WILLS CARLA MARIE** (727)343-3206
5876 4th Ave S Saint Petersburg FL 33707 • FG • Tchr • Our Savior Saint Petersburg FL • (727)344-1026 • (RF 1991)
**WILLS HERMAN C** (573)517-0975
400 Cinque Hommes Dr Perryville MO 63775 • IN • P/Tchr • Trinity Crown Point IN • (219)663-1586 • (RF 1959 MA)
**WILLS PAUL R** (717)382-9444
1208 Churchville Rd Suite 101 Bel Air MD 21014 • SE • S Ex/S • Southeastern Alexandria VA • (S 1971 MSED)
**WILLWEBER DAVID EDWARD** (808)235-5199
46-324 Haiku Rd #111 Kaneohe HI 96744 • willweber4@aol.com • CNH • Tchr • LHS Of Hawaii Honolulu HI • (808)949-5302 • (S 1992 MS)
**WILLWEBER MARIE ANNE** (808)235-5199
46 324 Haiku Rd #111 Kaneohe HI 96744 • willweber4@aol.com • CNH • Tchr • LHS Of Hawaii Honolulu HI • (808)949-5302 • (S 1993)
**WILLWEBER SHARON ALICE** (206)364-7613
1136 N 115th St Apt A102 Seattle WA 98133-8358 • lwillweber@aol.com • NOW • EM • (RF 1959)
**WILSHUSEN LOREN W** (402)721-3885
1331 Stanford Ave Fremont NE 68025-3731 • wilshusenl@yahoo.com • NEB • Tchr • Trinity Fremont NE • (402)721-5959 • (S 1972 MED)
**WILSON CRAIG G** (414)452-6636
206 Wahouly Rd Sheboygan WI 53081-8720 • clwilson@powercom.net • SW • Tchr • Lutheran HS Sheboygan WI • (920)452-3323 • (S 1979)
**WILSON GREGORY**
179 E Main St Patchogue NY 11772-3103 • AT • Tchr • Emanuel Patchogue NY • (516)758-2240 • (BR 1982)
**WILSON JAMES R** (713)251-2622
18802 Klein Church Rd Spring TX 77379-4938 • TX • Prin • Trinity Spring TX • (281)376-5810 • (SP 1979 MED)
**WILSON JODI S**
PO Box 44 Green Isle MN 55338-0044 • MNS • Tchr • Emanuel Hamburg MN • (612)467-2780 • (SP 1987)
**WILSON KATHERINE ANN** (712)362-2874
721 W 8th Ave N Estherville IA 51334-1245 • IW • 07/1998 07/2000 • (S 1986)
**WILSON MICHAEL EUGENE** (314)209-1924
717 Riderwood Dr Hazelwood MO 63042-3327 • MO • Tchr • Hope Saint Ann MO • (314)429-0988 • (S 1996)
**WILT JOHN THOMAS** (901)309-1165
8184 Planters Grove Memphis TN 38018 • jtwilt@aol.com • MDS • Prin • Christ King Memphis TN • (901)682-8404 • (CQ 1994 MED)
**WILT MARK B** (724)352-2747
736 Saxonburg Rd Butler PA 16002-0958 • EA • P/Tchr • St Luke Cabot PA • (412)352-2221 • (BR 1975)
**WING LINDA S** (716)876-6657
134 Parkwood Ave Kenmore NY 14217-2806 • EA • 08/1995 08/1997 • (RF 1972)
**WINGFIELD PHILLIP L** (414)421-7255
5623 Exeter St Greendale WI 53129-1617 • SW • Tchr • Martin LHS Greendale WI • (414)421-4000 • (RF 1982)
**WINKELMAN STEVEN R**
301 Castlewood Dr Apt 7D New Braunfels TX 78130 • TX • Prin • Cross New Braunfels TX • (830)625-3969 • (AU 1993 MED)
**WINKELMAN SUZAN H** (512)930-2354
400 Derby Ln Georgetown TX 78626-6322 • suzwinkelman@yahoo.com • TX • 08/1998 08/2000 • (AU 1988)
**WINKELMANN KRISTINE M** (608)742-5390
W7935 Laura Dr Pardeeville WI 53954 • SW • 04/2000 • (RF 1988)
**WINKLER CHRIS CHARLES** (512)990-0118
505 W Custers Creek Bnd Pflugerville TX 78660-4736 • TX • SHS/C • Texas Austin TX • (CQ 1991 MED)
**WINN TRACEY ANN** (651)429-6089
4203 Bellaire Ave White Bear Lake MN 55110-3947 • traceywinn@aol.com • MNS • Mem C • Trinity White Bear Lake MN • (651)429-4293 • (SP 1994)
**WINSOR SUE A**
10631 Dorothy Ave Garden Grove CA 92843 • PSW • 06/2000 • (S 1983)
**WINSTON VALERIE JOYCE** (313)538-6184
20538 W Warren #2 Detroit MI 48228-3243 • MI • Tchr • Detroit Urban Detroit MI • (313)582-9900 • (RF 1984)
**WINTER CATHERINE** (901)386-0389
6398 Trafalgar Rd Memphis TN 38134-6944 • cathwinter@hotmail.com • MDS • Tchr • Immanuel Memphis TN • (901)388-0205 • (RF 1971)
**WINTER ELLIS A** (901)386-0389
6398 Trafalgar Rd Memphis TN 38134-6944 • elliswinter@hotmail.com • MDS • Tchr • Immanuel Memphis TN • (901)388-0205 • (RF 1971 MA)
**WINTER ERNEST A** (616)983-3702
308 Winwood Dr Saint Joseph MI 49085-2342 • corbin1048@cybersol.com • MI • EM • (RF 1949 MED)
**WINTER JAMI D** (970)223-2770
3112 Colony Dr Fort Collins CO 80526-2749 • RM • 01/1993 01/2000 • (AU 1985)
**WINTER PAUL G** (616)465-3544
3170 Sunset Dr Bridgman MI 49106-9741 • MI • EM • (RF 1957)
**WINTERROTH PAMELA JEAN** (630)820-4807
3256 Anton Dr Aurora IL 60504 • iteachgrd6@aol.com • NI • Tchr • Bethany Naperville IL • (630)355-2198 • (RF 1996)
**WINTERSTEIN ALECIA M** (217)423-2401
2239 S Rainwater Dr Decatur IL 62521-4864 • CI • 07/1996 07/2000 • (RF 1987)
**WINTERSTEIN BARBARA R** (415)651-0950
4915 Everglades Park Dr Fremont CA 94538-3922 • CNH • EM • (RF 1965)
**WINTERSTEIN CHARLES** (217)423-2401
2239 S Rainwater Dr Decatur IL 62521-4864 • cawinter@midwest.net • CI • Tchr • Lutheran School Asso Decatur IL • (217)233-2001 • (RF 1971 MA)
**WINTERSTEIN JEROME A** (708)352-5795
329 Malden Ave La Grange Pk IL 60526-1709 • NI • Tchr • Zion Hinsdale IL • (630)323-0045 • (RF 1968 MED)
**WINTERSTEIN LUCILLE M** (402)228-1023
1920 S 11th St Beatrice NE 68310-5203 • NEB • EM • (RF 1963)
**WINTERSTEIN WILLIAM W** (402)228-1023
1920 S 11th St Beatrice NE 68310-5203 • NEB • EM • (RF 1961)
**WIPPICH DAVID D** (219)362-9288
508 Ottoson St La Porte IN 46350-4151 • IN • Tchr • St John La Porte IN • (219)362-6692 • (SP 1980 MED)
**WIPPICH SARAH J** (651)426-4903
3848 Scheuneman Rd Saint Paul MN 55110-4142 • MNS • Prin • Trinity First Minneapolis MN • (612)871-2353 • (MQ 1987)
**WIRTH ARLEEN ELIZABETH** (281)288-3480
28915 Sedgefield St Spring TX 77386-5470 • TX • 07/1999 • (CQ 1994)
**WIRZ DONNA L** (815)398-4303
432 Bancroft Ct Apt 6 Rockford IL 61107-5125 • NI • Tchr • Luther Academy At Gl Rockford IL • (815)226-4947 • (SP 1984)
**WISCHMEIER HENRY A** (812)376-6899
5550 E 275 S Columbus IN 47201-9511 • IN • Tchr • St Peter Columbus IN • (812)372-5266 • (RF 1966 MA)
**WISCHMEYER DONALD H*** (630)691-2117
2077 Navarone Dr Naperville IL 60565-2103 • dwischmeyer@bethanylcs.org • NI • Prin • Bethany Naperville IL • (630)355-6607 • (RF 1963 MED EDS)
**WISCHMEYER SUSAN L** (636)922-3285
220 Cedar Grove Saint Charles MO 63304 • swischme@mail.win.org • MO • Tchr • Zion Harvester MO • (314)441-7424 • (RF 1994)
**WISMAR RICHARD W** (503)253-7885
16519 NE Fargo Cir Portland OR 97230-5515 • NOW • SHS/C • Northwest Portland OR • (RF 1963 MED MED PHD)
**WISNESKI JEAN MARIE** (515)964-4263
1018 NW Linden St Ankeny IA 50021-1127 • gnjwisneski@aol.com • IW • Tchr • Christ King Altoona IA • (515)967-3349 • (SP 1965)
**WISSNER LARRY O** (972)540-2083
3306 Naples Cir Mc Kinney TX 75070 • TX • 09/1999 • (S 1969)
**WITHEE ROXANNE J** (605)348-7594
3230 Dover St Rapid City SD 57702-3490 • SD • Tchr • Zion Rapid City SD • (605)342-5749 • (S 1977)
**WITKOP MYRTHA S** (717)374-4914
41 Salem Manor Ct Selinsgrove PA 17870-8622 • EA • EM • (RF 1972 MSED)
**WITT COREY WELDEN** (909)600-4591
24030 Morella Cir Murrieta CA 92562 • PSW • Tchr • Zion Anaheim CA • (714)535-3600 • (IV 1997)
**WITT JOEL J** (402)564-8001
3505 21st St Columbus NE 68601-3009 • NEB • Tchr • Immanuel Columbus NE • (402)564-8423 • (S 1993)
**WITT SHARON RENEE** (618)853-4501
931 Church St Evansville IL 62242 • SI • Tchr • Southern Illinois Belleville IL • (S 1996)
**WITT TAMARA LEA**
316 S 10th St Wymore NE 68466-2116 • MO • Tchr • Trinity Saint Louis MO • (314)231-4092 • (S 1996)
**WITTCOP ERNEST JEFFREY** (561)223-0692
4342 SE Satin Leaf Pl Stuart FL 34997-2286 • jwittcop@bellsouth.net • FG • Prin • Redeemer Stuart FL • (561)286-0932 • (RF 1976 MS)
**WITTCOP PATRICIA A** (561)223-0692
4342 SE Satinleaf Pl Stuart FL 34997 • FG • Tchr • Redeemer Stuart FL • (561)286-0932 • (RF 1977)
**WITTE DENNIS E DR** (630)629-3835
1833 S Elizabeth St Lombard IL 60148-4406 • witte@curf.edu • NI • SHS/C • Northern Illinois Hillside IL • (RF 1973 MS PHD)
**WITTE KENNETH L** (262)377-7362
2075 1st Ave Apt 107 Grafton WI 53024-2531 • kwitte@execpc.com • SW • SHS/C • South Wisconsin Milwaukee WI • (414)464-8100 • (RF 1977 MAT)
**WITTE LUCIE E** (810)775-4636
28211 Fountain St Roseville MI 48066-4761 • MI • Tchr • Mt Calvary Detroit MI • (313)527-3366 • (RF 1972)
**WITTIG DAVID L** (808)235-9488
46-488 Kuneki St Kaneohe HI 96744 • dwittig@lava.net • CNH • Tchr • Our Savior Aiea HI • (808)488-3654 • (S 1980)
**WITTIG EVELYN D** (517)781-9067
8440 Shields Dr Apt 204 Saginaw MI 48609-8516 • evwittig@worldnet.att.net • MI • EM • (RF 1967)
**WITTIG MARSHA J**
46-488 Kuneki St Kaneohe HI 96744 • CNH • Tchr • St Mark Kaneohe HI • (808)247-5589 • (S 1979)
**WITTIG RAMON L** (909)737-7370
2373 Mangular Ave Corona CA 91720-5789 • dotwittig@snis.net • PSW • EM • (S 1955 MED)
**WITTLER RONALD T** (314)721-1895
7944 Bloom Dr Saint Louis MO 63133-1110 • rwittler@postnet.com • MO • Tchr • Immanuel Olivette MO • (314)993-5004 • (S 1993 MEDADM)
**WITTMAN ANTHONY A** (630)892-2793
2468 W Downer Pl Aurora IL 60506-4220 • awittyl@dellnet.com • NI • 08/2000 • (RF 1983)
**WITTMANN ROGER A** (618)667-3302
13 Cedarbrooke St Troy IL 62294 • wittman@tcip.net • SI • Tchr • St Paul Troy IL • (618)667-6314 • (RF 1968)
**WITTO KATHERINE I** (317)882-9063
5546 Ashview Dr Apt H Indianapolis IN 46237-7357 • kiw22@inct.net • IN • Tchr • LHS Of Indianapolis Indianapolis IN • (317)787-5474 • (RF 1990)
**WITTROCK JOHN H** (248)647-7142
1599 Bowers St Birmingham MI 48009-6884 • jhwittrock@ameritech.net • MI • Tchr • Our Shepherd Birmingham MI • (248)645-0551 • (S 1965 MMU)
**WITZEL RACHEL ANN** (407)207-3792
2314 River Park Cir #2123 Orlando FL 32817-4828 • witzelred@aol.com • FG • Tchr • Orlando Lutheran Aca Orlando FL • (407)275-7750 • (S 1997)
**WOEBKE KIMBERLY SUE** (952)831-2498
10009 Goodrich Rd Bloomington MN 55437 • MNS • Tchr • Redeemer Wayzata MN • (612)473-5356 • (SP 1989)
**WOEHR DAVID F** (314)209-0184
5326 Ville Angela Ln Hazelwood MO 63042-1140 • MO • Tchr • Grace Chapel Bellefontaine Nbrs MO • (314)867-6564 • (RF 1974 MAT)
**WOEHR VALEDA K** (314)209-0184
5326 Ville Angela Ln Hazelwood MO 63042-1140 • MO • Tchr • Grace Chapel Bellefontaine Nbrs MO • (314)867-6564 • (S 1976)
**WOLBERT GREGORY J** (713)787-5308
PO Box 571578 Houston TX 77257-1578 • TX • Tchr • Memorial Houston TX • (713)782-4022 • (BR 1998)
**WOLBERT JANET ANNE** (407)671-3590
1003 Village Ln Winter Park FL 32792-3416 • TX • 01/1999 • (RF 1996)
**WOLBRECHT CHERYL** (501)217-9373
12810 Misty Creek Dr Little Rock AR 72211 • tcwolbrecht@aristotle.net • MDS • 07/1998 07/2000 • (RF 1966)
**WOLDT JOYCE A**
5874 N 73rd St Milwaukee WI 53218-1826 • SW • EM • (RF 1950)
**WOLF CHARLES H** (313)468-6344
135 S Christine Cir Mount Clemens MI 48043-1510 • cwolf@lhsa.com • MI • Tchr • LHS North Macomb MI • (810)781-9151 • (RF 1975 MS)
**WOLF DIANE W** (319)378-6329
4211 Carpenter Rd Cedar Rapids IA 52411-7996 • wolfdw@aol.com • IE • Tchr • Trinity Cedar Rapids IA • (319)362-6952 • (AA 1985 MA)
**WOLF HAROLD E** (317)831-6063
100 Sarah Ln Mooresville IN 46158-7609 • IN • EM • (RF 1981 MA)
**WOLF JENNIFER ROSE** (414)338-8942
1201 Pear Tree Ct West Bend WI 53090-1728 • SW • Tchr • St John West Bend WI • (414)334-3077 • (CQ 1988)

**WOLF LISA J** (414)255-6041
W144N7074 Terrace Dr Menomonee Falls WI 53051-0930 • SW • Tchr • Immanuel Brookfield WI • (414)781-4135 • (MQ 1985)

**WOLF MELISSA LYNNE** (816)598-6215
RR 1 Box 31 A Rockville MO 64780-9022 • MO • 01/1993 02/2000 • (RF 1986 MA)

**WOLF MICHELLE PHYLLIS**
1428 Whitefence Rd Bartlett IL 60103-1871 • NI • 08/1999 • (RF 1994)

**WOLF ROBERT JOHN** (517)755-5023
826 Piper Dr Saginaw MI 48604-1833 • MI • Tchr • Valley Saginaw MI • (517)790-1676 • (SP 1994)

**WOLFANGER MILDRED** (708)893-5383
6N534 Glendale Rd Medinah IL 60157-9700 • NI • EM • (S 1954 MA)

**WOLFE THOMAS M**
1825 28th St Columbus NE 68601-2619 • NEB • 08/1994 08/2000 • (S 1969 MA)

**WOLFF AMANDA JOY** (618)282-6738
320 N Taylor St Red Bud IL 62278 • SI • Tchr • St John Red Bud IL • (618)282-3873 • (RF 1995)

**WOLFF GARRY F** (618)483-5877
5108 N 600th St Mason IL 62443 • CI • Tchr • Altamont Altamont IL • (618)483-6428 • (RF 1963 MED)

**WOLFGRAM BARBARA R** (818)367-6516
13982 Olive Grove Ln Sylmar CA 91342-1666 • PSW • 07/1994 07/2000 • (SP 1983 MA)

**WOLFGRAM DALE A** (818)367-6516
13982 Olive Grove Ln Sylmar CA 91342-1666 • dwlalhs@worldnet.att.net • PSW • Prin • Los Angeles Junior/S Sylmar CA • (818)362-5861 • (S 1975 MSED)

**WOLFGRAM LAURIE MICHELLE** (701)232-9289
1420 E Gateway Cir #207 Fargo ND 58103 • lwolfgram@uswest.net • ND • Tchr • Grace Fargo ND • (701)232-1516 • (SP 1995)

**WOLFRAM CARLENE DENISE** (281)351-6616
C/O Lutheran High North 1130 W 34th St Houston TX 77018-6294 • wolfll-@hotmail.com • TX • Tchr • LHS North Houston TX • (713)880-3131 • (S 1979)

**WOLFRAM TIMOTHY J**
C/O First Lutheran School 1207 Broadway St NE Knoxville TN 37917 • MDS • Tchr • First Knoxville TN • (423)524-0366 • (SP 1971 MA MMTH)

**WOLFRAM WILLIAM R** (402)643-2535
1036 Sunrise Dr Seward NE 68434-1351 • wwolfram@seward.cune.edu • NEB • SHS/C • Nebraska Seward NE • (CQ 1959 MA MFA)

**WOLFROM WAYNE D** (313)566-8887
37656 Palmar St Clinton Twp MI 48036-3627 • MI • Prin • East Bethlehem Detroit MI • (313)892-2671 • (CQ 1963 MA)

**WOLLANGK PAUL** (715)524-3521
W5860 Cedar Ln Shawano WI 54166 • NW • Tchr • St James Shawano WI • (715)524-4213 • (S 1968)

**WOLLENBURG JERRY LEE** (931)707-5684
331 Laurel Cir Crossville TN 38555 • MDS • 02/1993 02/2000 • (RF 1979)

**WOLLMAN CYNTHIA K** (410)592-7962
12028 Jerusalem Rd Kingsville MD 21087-1146 • SE • Tchr • St Paul Kingsville MD • (410)592-8100 • (S 1976)

**WOLSKE CLEE K** (402)454-2291
28670 547 Ave Madison NE 68748-6141 • cwolske@esu8.org • NEB • P/Tchr • St John Madison NE • (402)454-2440 • (S 1973)

**WOLSKE MONIQUE A** (402)454-2291
82670 547 Ave Madison NE 68748-6141 • NEB • Tchr • St John Madison NE • (402)454-2440 • (S 1973)

**WOLTER ARTHUR L** (517)882-7993
3415 Schlee St Lansing MI 48910-4467 • MI • EM • (RF 1930)

**WOLTER CYNTHIA KATHRYN** (507)893-4523
1911 270th Ave Granada MN 56039 • MNS • Tchr • St James Northrop MN • (507)436-5289 • (S 1992)

**WOLTER DAVID T**
500 Christ School Rd Arden NC 28704-9570 • PSW • SHS/C • Pacific Southwest Irvine CA • (949)854-3232 • (S 1976 MA)

**WOLTER LA JUNE K** (319)622-3509
4327 V St PO Box 28 Homestead IA 52236-0028 • IE • Tchr • Lutheran Interparish Williamsburg IA • (319)668-1711 • (S 1970)

**WOLTER MARTIN T** (440)871-4132
1689 Bassett Rd Westlake OH 44145-1906 • OH • EM • (RF 1925)

**WOLTER ROBERT A** (209)334-9423
1760 Lake St Lodi CA 95242 • CNH • Tchr • Sacramento Lutheran Sacramento CA • (916)978-2720 • (S 1992)

**WOLTER ROGER W**
C/O Holy Cross Luth Church 610 Court St Saginaw MI 48602-4249 • MI • Tchr • Holy Cross Saginaw MI • (517)793-9723 • (S 2000)

**WOLTER TERESA M**
1760 Lake St Lodi CA 95242-2437 • CNH • Tchr • St Peter Lodi CA • (209)333-2225 • (S 1992)

**WOLTERS ANN E** (660)463-7382
504 Bismark St Concordia MO 64020-9677 • MO • Tchr • St Paul Concordia MO • (660)463-7654 • (S 1964 MS)

**WONDRASCH RUTH M** (517)781-3154
9030 Greenway Blvd Apt D57 Saginaw MI 48609-6773 • MI • EM • (RF 1962 MA)

**WONG MICHAL E** (714)539-4322
10322 Eclipse Ct Garden Grove CA 92840-6320 • PSW • Tchr • St Paul Garden Grove CA • (714)534-6320 • (PO 1990)

**WOO LISA Y** (650)757-1984
89 Shelbourne Ave Daly City CA 94015-3918 • CNH • Tchr • Hope Daly City CA • (650)991-4673 • (IV 1999)

**WOOCK DALE D** (847)468-9488
1133 Clover Hill Ln Elgin IL 60120-2395 • NI • Mem C • St John Elgin IL • (847)741-0814 • (SP 1980)

**WOOD CHRISTY** (520)326-2958
4815 E Lee St Tucson AZ 85712 • EN • Tchr • Messiah Tucson AZ • (520)744-6984 • (IV 1997)

**WOOD ELLEN LORRAINE** (714)348-3854
26301 Buscador Mission Viejo CA 92692-3242 • PSW • Tchr • Abiding Savior Lake Forest CA • (949)830-1461 • (CQ 1995)

**WOOD JANICE M** (815t)226-0198
6318 Garrett Ln Apt 3 Rockford IL 61107-6654 • jano430@aol.com • NI • Mem C • Christ The Rock Rockford IL • (815)332-7191 • (AA 1985 MED)

**WOOD PAULA K** (504)486-7721
817 Solomon Pl New Orleans LA 70119-3635 • paulawood@earthlink.net • SO • Tchr • St John New Orleans LA • (504)488-6641 • (S 1979)

**WOODCOCK ROXANNE S** (517)793-1884
4398 Jameson St Saginaw MI 48603-4763 • roxanne@concentric.net • MI • Tchr • Peace Saginaw MI • (517)792-2581 • (AA 1993)

**WOODLEY JACQUELINE F** (716)731-7187
PO Box 462 Sanborn NY 14132-0462 • EA • Tchr • Holy Ghost Niagara Falls NY • (716)731-5877 • (BR 1977)

**WOODS AMY BETH** (660)463-1996
1319 Orange St PO Box 628 Concordia MO 64020 • MO • Tchr • St Paul Concordia MO • (660)463-2291 • (S 1995)

**WOODS ELIZABETH J** (281)391-3516
5330 Linda Ln Katy TX 77493-1737 • woods³liz@hotmail.com • TX • Tchr • St Mark Houston TX • (713)468-2623 • (AU 1999)

**WOODWARD PETER C*** (209)368-3108
574 Yellowstone St Woodbridge CA 95258 • CNH • Prin • St Peter Lodi CA • (209)333-2225 • (S 1975 MED EDS)

**WOOSTER LARRY D** (661)946-6670
43727 Carefree Ct Lancaster CA 93535 • lwooster@earthlink.net • PSW • Tchr • Grace Lancaster CA • (805)948-1018 • (S 1982 MA)

**WORCHESIK MICHAEL B** (713)675-9117
527 Oldcastle St Houston TX 77013-5322 • TX • Tchr • Lutheran South Acade Houston TX • (281)464-9320 • (AU 1998)

**WORDELL PAUL K**
C/O Lutheran HS East 3565 Mayfield Rd Cleveland Heights OH 44118 • OH • Tchr • Lutheran High School Cleveland Heights OH • (216)382-6100 • (RF 1987)

**WORDEN SHELLY ANN** (916)726-4964
7863 Crestleigh Ct Antelope CA 95842 • CNH • Tchr • Town & Country Sacramento CA • (916)481-2542 • (S 1981)

**WORRAL CAROLYN R** (701)293-0905
2814 Hickory St NE Fargo ND 58102 • ND • Tchr • Grace Fargo ND • (701)232-1516 • (SP 1986)

**WOTTRICH SHARON LEE*** (601)693-1879
4538 17th St Meridian MS 39307-5430 • swottrich@aol.com • SO • 05/1993 05/2000 • (CQ 1986 MA MSW)

**WRASE WILLIAM R** (734)374-1053
15519 Plaza South Dr Bldg 5 Taylor MI 48180 • MI • Tchr • Calvary Lincoln Park MI • (313)381-6715 • (S 1969)

**WREGE THOMAS W**
2625 Vista View Dr Evansville IN 47711 • twwrege@sprynet.com • IN • Prin • Trinity Evansville IN • (812)867-5279 • (S 1985 MSED)

**WREN LOIS G**
814 S 9th St De Kalb IL 60115-5012 • NI • EM • (RF 1977)

**WRIGHT DENISE M** (717)757-6707
650 S Hampton at Waterford York PA 17402 • SE • Tchr • St John York PA • (717)840-0382 • (BR 1979)

**WRIGHT JANICE MAY** (303)791-8614
9184 Sugarstone Cir Highlands Ranch CO 80130-4429 • RM • Tchr • Shepherd Hills Littleton CO • (303)798-0711 • (S 1968 MA)

**WRIGHT JOANN MARIE** (313)982-9923
PO Box 784 Dearborn Heights MI 48127-0784 • joannwri@concentric.net • MI • Tchr • Bethany Detroit MI • (313)885-0180 • (AA 1993 MA)

**WRIGHT JONATHAN K** (313)350-9032
28675 Franklin Rd Apt 502 Southfield MI 48034-1605 • MI • Tchr • Detroit Urban Detroit MI • (313)582-9900 • (AA 1988)

**WRIGHT KAREN M** (334)298-2048
171 Lee Road 2014 Salem AL 36874-4169 • FG • Mem C • Redeemer Columbus GA • (706)322-5026 • (RF 1984 MA)

**WRIGHT KENNETH** (619)421-5140
991 Rutgers Ave Chula Vista CA 91913-3026 • PSW • Tchr • Pilgrim Chula Vista CA • (619)420-6233 • (S 1970 MED)

**WRIGHT LUCINDA MAE*** (715)357-3411
PO Box 8 Almena WI 54805-0008 • bcwright@chibardun.net • NW • 06/1999 • (SP 1976)

**WRIGHT RIDELL M** (909)861-6776
21584 Running Branch Rd Diamond Bar CA 91765-3752 • ridellwright@hotmail.com • PSW • Tchr • Mount Calvary Diamond Bar CA • (909)861-2740 • (CQ 1995 MA)

**WRIGHT STACY RENA** (812)523-8645
1035 S 460 E Seymour IN 47274 • IN • Tchr • St John Seymour IN • (812)523-3131 • (RF 1994)

**WRIGHT STEVEN A** (414)695-2092
608 Pewaukee Rd Unit E Pewaukee WI 53072-6557 • swright@execpc.com • SW • Tchr • Martin LHS Greendale WI • (414)421-4000 • (S 1979 MS)

**WRIGHT WILLIAM R*** (715)357-3411
PO Box 8 Almena WI 54805-0008 • bcwright@chibardun.net • MNS • EM • (RF 1952 MED)

**WROBEL BARBARA LEE** (810)778-7857
23730 Marine Eastpointe MI 48021-3422 • MI • Tchr • Mt Calvary Detroit MI • (313)527-3366 • (S 1969 MA)

**WROBLESKI RICHARD E** (517)883-2818
87 Anton St Sebewaing MI 48759-1130 • rvwrob@avci.net • MI • EM • (RF 1961 MA)

**WRUCKE WESLEY JOHN** (920)261-5616
1325 Windsor Cir Watertown WI 53098-3400 • wpcc@globaldialog.com • SW • P/Tchr • Lebanon Watertown WI • (920)925-3791 • (RF 1980 MS)

**WRYE KAREN A** (503)284-4991
6306 NE 26th Ave Portland OR 97211-6049 • rkwrye@teleport.com • NOW • Tchr • Trinity Portland OR • (503)288-6403 • (RF 1966 MED)

**WRYE RICHARD F** (503)284-4991
6306 NE 26th Ave Portland OR 97211-6049 • rkwrye@teleport.com • NOW • EM • (RF 1967 MA MMU)

**WUDTKE CURTIS L** (407)677-7405
3638 Daventry Ct Orlando FL 32817 • FG • Prin • Orlando Lutheran Aca Orlando FL • (407)275-7750 • (MQ 1993)

**WUDTKE DEBORAH ANNE** (618)346-6842
124 Teckla Ave Collinsville IL 62234-2108 • debwudtke@hotmail.com • NW • Tchr • North Wisconsin Wausau WI • (MQ 1991)

**WUDTKE JENNIFER LYNN** (407)677-7405
3638 Daventry Ct Orlando FL 32817 • S • Tchr • St Luke Oviedo FL • (407)365-3408 • (MQ 1994 MA)

**WUDTKE KEVIN RAY** (618)346-6842
124 Teckla Ave Collinsville IL 62234-2108 • wudtke@lcms.org • MO • Tchr • Missouri Saint Louis MO • (314)317-4550 • (MQ 1991)

**WUDTKE MARIE EMMA** (618)345-0338
9 Chapel Ct Collinsville IL 62234-4330 • SI • Tchr • Good Shepherd Collinsville IL • (618)344-3153 • (CQ 1992)

**WUDY JAMES** (219)432-7085
1407 Edenton Dr Fort Wayne IN 46804-5815 • IN • Tchr • Emmanuel-St Michael Fort Wayne IN • (219)422-6712 • (SP 1971 MED)

**WUDY LAUREEN ALICE** (208)735-9735
665 Heyburn Ave Twin Falls ID 83301 • NOW • Tchr • Immanuel Twin Falls ID • (208)733-7820 • (S 1972)

**WUENSCHE ELMER LEE** (708)843-7927
2070 Greens Ct Hoffman Est IL 60194-1038 • eleew@mediaone.net • NI • Prin • St Matthew Lake Zurich IL • (847)438-7709 • (RF 1964 MA MA)

**WUERDEMAN LILY** (808)623-5140
94-346 Hokuala St Apt 124 Mililani HI 96789-2329 • CNH • EM • (RF 1965)

**WUERTZ DUANE W**
3665 Little Island Dr National City MI 48748-9540 • MI • EM • (S 1957)

**WUESTENBERG DANNA NICOLE** (360)493-2215
7627 3rd Way SE Apt 28 Olympia WA 98503-1509 • gdwuestenberg@msn.com • NOW • Tchr • Faith Lacey WA • (360)491-1733 • (MQ 1997)

**WUGGAZER DOROTHY E** (303)243-5712
125 Franklin Ave Apt 309 Grand Junction CO 81505-7157 • RM • EM • (S 1970 MA)

**WUNDERLICH ALAN W** (314)239-9062
2487 Highway A Washington MO 63090-4359 • MO • Mem C • Immanuel Washington MO • (314)239-4705 • (RF 1980)

**WUNDERLICH ERNEST O** (828)698-3807
108 Azalea Way Hendersonville NC 28792-2407 • SE • EM • (RF 1938 MA)

**WUNDERLICH KENNETH M** (314)353-0967
5715 Langley Ave Saint Louis MO 63123 • kenmwsr@stlnet.com • MO • EM • (RF 1949 MSED)

**WUNDERLICH KIMBERLY ANN** (314)239-9062
2487 Highway A Washington MO 63090-4359 • MO • 02/1995 02/2000 • (BR 1982)

**WUNSCH LORA A***
9604 Winston Ave Urbandale IA 50322-1319 • IW • Tchr • St Paul Fort Dodge IA • (515)955-7285 • (S 1982)

**WUTKE THOMAS A** (417)881-3890
1442 S Pickwick Ave Springfield MO 65804-1217 • MO • Tchr • Calvary Kansas City MO • (816)444-6908 • (S 1974 MA)

**WYKERT THOMAS ALBERT** (708)442-1149
4630 Hawthorne Ave Lyons IL 60534-1756 • NI • Tchr • St John LA Grange IL • (708)354-1690 • (RF 1991)

**WYLY JEANEEN T** (216)291-3262
3969 E Antisdale Rd Cleveland OH 44118-2331 • OH • Tchr • St John South Euclid OH • (216)381-8595 • (RF 1992)

**WYZARD DEBRA J** (309)263-8312
312 E Greenwood St Morton IL 61550-2556 • CI • Tchr • Bethel Morton IL • (309)266-6592 • (RF 1980)

## Y

**YAEGER MARGARET A** (630)852-0971
749 Chicago Ave Downers Grove IL 60515-3748 • NI • Tchr • Trinity Lombard IL • (630)627-5601 • (RF 1959)

**YAEGER ROBERT W** (630)852-0971
749 Chicago Ave Downers Grove IL 60515-3748 • NI • EM • (RF 1960)

**YAGOW DANIEL PAUL** (217)398-5851
1812 Oak Park Dr Champaign IL 61822 • drkc1@juno.com • CI • Tchr • St John Champaign IL • (217)359-1714 • (S 1981 MSED)

**YAGOW JAMES S** (920)687-0825
N3494 Hooyman Ct Appleton WI 54913-9218 • james³yagow@aal.org • NW • 07/1996 07/2000 • (S 1975 MSED)

**YAGOW LISA M** (630)539-6559
309 S Rush St Roselle IL 60172-2294 • NI • Tchr • Trinity Roselle IL • (630)894-3263 • (RF 1999)

**YAMABE KEVIN TADASHI** (415)759-8020
2101 31st Ave San Francisco CA 94116 • CNH • Tchr • Zion San Francisco CA • (415)221-7500 • (SP 2000)

**YANEZ ADRIANA** (713)956-9761
15818 Whipple Tree Dr Houston TX 77070-1637 • TX • Tchr • Bethany Houston TX • (713)695-0236 • (AU 1996)

**YARDLEY HEATHER L**
10443 W Lyndale Ave Melrose Park IL 60164-1818 • NI • Tchr • Grace Chicago IL • (773)762-1234 • (RF 1998)

**YARROLL CHRISTINE** (708)469-9284
586 Elm St Glen Ellyn IL 60137-3929 • cyarroll@stjohnwheaton.pvt.k12.il.us • NI • Tchr • St John Wheaton IL • (630)668-0701 • (RF 1961)

**YELDEN SUSAN I** (517)224-7327
3257 W Price Rd Saint Johns MI 48879-9268 • MI • Tchr • St Peter Saint Johns MI • (517)224-3113 • (S 1973 MA)

**YERGLER KELLY** (410)877-9374
2800 Jerusalem Rd Apt 2 Kingsville MD 21087 • kyergler@hotmail.com • SE • Tchr • St Paul Kingsville MD • (410)592-8100 • (RF 1999)

**YOAKUM MARILYN J**
RR 1 Box 169 Russell IA 50238 • IW • Tchr • Mount Olive Des Moines IA • (515)277-8349 • (S 1961)

**YODER MARIAN R** (419)599-3176
2170 Hawthorne Dr Defiance OH 43512-9670 • OH • Tchr • St Paul Napoleon OH • (419)592-5536 • (SP 1969 MA)

**YORK JOANN M** (712)582-3373
2344 255th Clarinda IA 51632 • IW • Tchr • St John Clarinda IA • (712)542-3708 • (S 1966)

**YOST JUDITH A** (517)894-7183
405 Old Orchard Dr Apt 17 Essexville MI 48732 • MI • 07/2000 • (RF 1978 MA)

**YOUMANS CHRISTY ANN** (808)484-4011
98-1038 Moanalua Rd Apt 2001 Aiea HI 96701-4614 • CNH • Tchr • Our Savior Aiea HI • (808)488-0000 • (IV 1998)

**YOUMANS KIM D*** (702)363-5603
7624 Oyster Cove Dr Las Vegas NV 89128-7252 • sky@lvdi.net • PSW • 02/1996 • (S 1973 MA)

**YOUMANS SANDRA B** (702)363-5603
7624 Oyster Cove Dr Las Vegas NV 89128-7252 • sky@lvdi.net • PSW • Tchr • Faith LHS Las Vegas NV • (702)804-4400 • (S 1973 MMU)

**YOUNG ANGELICA MARIE** (828)695-9879
433 Rock Barn Rd #B4 Conover NC 28613 • SE • Tchr • Concordia Conover NC • (828)464-3011 • (AA 2000)

**YOUNG ANN CAROL** (952)467-3792
606 Robert Ave Hamburg MN 55339-9452 • MNS • Tchr • St Johns Young America MN • (612)467-3461 • (SP 1978)

**YOUNG BRIAN A** (517)893-2486
1460 Calmac Ct Bay City MI 48708-9139 • bayoung@bay.k12.mi.us • MI • Prin • Immanuel Bay City MI • (517)893-8521 • (RF 1967 MA)

**YOUNG BRIAN KEITH** (402)744-4981
13235 W 70th St Juniata NE 68955-2139 • creation1@juno.com • NEB • P/Tchr • Christ Juniata NE • (402)744-4971 • (S 1993)

**YOUNG DANIEL B** (612)467-3792
606 Robert Ave Hamburg MN 55339-9452 • MNS • Tchr • St Johns Young America MN • (612)467-3461 • (SP 1981)

**YOUNG ERIC ANDREW** (847)788-0459
6 S School St Mount Prospect IL 60056-3315 • eayoung5@aol.com • NI • Tchr • St Paul Mount Prospect IL • (847)255-6733 • (RF 1997)

**YOUNG JEFFREY S**
Trinity Lutheran Church 721 Pine St Paw Paw MI 49079-1248 • MI • Tchr • Trinity Paw Paw MI • (616)657-4840 • (AA 1994)

**YOUNG KATHRYN JEAN** (810)736-8154
5181 Berneda Dr Flint MI 48506 • MI • Tchr • St Mark Flint MI • (810)736-6910 • (AA 1986)

**YOUNG NORMAN E** (708)771-6824
45 Franklin Ave River Forest IL 60305-2111 • NI • SHS/C • Northern Illinois Hillside IL • (RF 1956 MS DED)

**YOUNG PATRICIA JEAN** (714)974-8014
3145 N Hearthside St Orange CA 92865-1217 • goldenbear@telis.org • PSW • Tchr • Lutheran HS/Orange C Orange CA • (714)998-5151 • (S 1976 MED)

**YOUNG STEVEN JOHN** (402)466-9797
3305 N 63rd St Lincoln NE 68507-1801 • TX • 04/1999 • (S 1994)

**YOUNT SANDRA J** (316)221-4509
108 Red Bud Dr Winfield KS 67156-5320 • KS • Tchr • Trinity Winfield KS • (316)221-9460 • (WN 1982 MA)

**YOUNT SUSAN D** (925)754-5744
2912 Almondridge Dr Antioch CA 94509-7351 • CNH • Tchr • Our Savior Livermore CA • (925)447-2082 • (S 1971 MA)

**YUNG JANICE J** (281)992-2334
1201 Lake Shore Dr Pearland TX 77581 • TX • Prin • Lutheran South Acade Houston TX • (281)464-9320 • (CQ 1990 MSED)

**YURK MICHAEL JOHN** (773)274-7231
6719 N Campbell Chicago IL 60645 • michael.yurk@gte.net • NI • Tchr • Luther HS North Chicago IL • (773)286-3600 • (MQ 1992)

## Z

**ZABEL MARTIN W** (561)276-8458
30 Hastings Ln Boynton Beach FL 33426 • FG • Tchr • Trinity Delray Beach FL • (561)276-8458 • (SP 1972)

**ZABEL MARY** (407)641-4274
30 Hastings Ln Lake Worth FL 33462-7118 • FG • Tchr • Our Savior Lake Worth FL • (561)582-8624 • (SP 1972)

**ZABEL WILLIAM** (352)343-0460
9 Douglas Dr # C Tavares FL 32778-5227 • biodaddi@cybergate.com • FG • EM • (RF 1949)

**ZABINSKY LEE ANNE** (619)749-8043
14931 Cool Valley Rd Valley Center CA 92082-5223 • PSW • Tchr • Grace Escondido CA • (760)747-3029 • (RF 1979 MA)

**ZACHEK KAREN A** (920)725-0302
833 W Cecil St Neenah WI 54956-3744 • kazachek@juno.com • SW • Tchr • Trinity Menasha WI • (920)725-1715 • (RF 1964 MSED)

**ZACHO JOHN E** (915)944-4336
3305 Sierra Ct San Angelo TX 76904-6937 • fnjzacho@airmail.net • TX • Mem C • Trinity San Angelo TX • (915)944-8660 • (S 1968)

**ZACHOW DONNA JEAN** (507)237-5163
910 10th St Gaylord MN 55334 • MNS • Tchr • Immanuel Gaylord MN • (507)237-2804 • (S 1963)

**ZACHRICH ANN EUNICE** (330)633-5350
149 Parker Ln Tallmadge OH 44278-2522 • OH • Tchr • Redeemer Cuyahoga Falls OH • (330)923-1280 • (RF 1971 MA)

**ZAFFKE DEBORAH LEE** (414)353-4028
8801 W Petersik St Milwaukee WI 53224-4736 • EN • Tchr • Hales Corners Hales Corners WI • (414)529-6700 • (CQ 1996)

**ZAGEL JAMES R** (303)252-1485
16180 Dallas St Brighton CO 80601 • RM • Tchr • Zion Brighton CO • (303)659-3443 • (S 1979)

**ZAHN O THOMAS** (940)691-2364
4904 Bayberry Dr Wichita Falls TX 76310 • TX • 06/1990 06/2000 • (RF 1964 MA)

**ZANTA PATRICIA A** (602)571-9250
4665 S Primrose St Tucson AZ 85730-4123 • PSW • Tchr • Fountain Of Life Tucson AZ • (520)747-1213 • (S 1984 MLS)

**ZAPPITELL KATHLEEN MARY** (810)997-1781
43761 Via Antonio Dr Sterling Heights MI 48314-1807 • jkzapp@home • MI • Tchr • Trinity Utica MI • (810)731-4490 • (CQ 1992 MA)

**ZASTROW HAROLD G** (920)452-4959
2007 N 24th St Sheboygan WI 53081-2126 • SW • EM • (RF 1960)

**ZASTROW MARGARET B** (573)459-6432
9100 Highway YY Leslie MO 63056-1101 • MO • Tchr • Immanuel Washington MO • (314)239-1636 • (S 1972 MED)

**ZASTROW TIMOTHY E** (920)564-6510
1173 Center Ave Oostburg WI 53070 • SW • Tchr • St John Academy Port Washington WI • (414)284-2131 • (RF 1979)

**ZAVALIS ELIZABETH A** (610)647-0858
7 Pickwick Ln Malvern PA 19355-2833 • EA • Tchr • Christ Memorial Malvern PA • (610)644-4508 • (RF 1966)

**ZEDDIES MICHAEL F** (517)652-9425
378 Frank Rd Frankenmuth MI 48734 • mzeddies@juno.com • MI • Tchr • St Lorenz Frankenmuth MI • (517)652-6141 • (RF 1981 MA)

**ZEHENDNER CHARLES MICHAEL**
1651 Worms Rd Saint Libory NE 68872-2906 • NEB • Tchr • Zion Saint Libory NE • (308)687-6486 • (S 1996)

**ZEHENDNER CHERIE**
2208 San Carlos Ct Saint George UT 84790 • RM • Tchr • Trinity St George UT • (435)628-1850 • (S 1996)

**ZEHENDNER JACQULYN J** (308)687-6783
1651 Worms Rd St Libory NE 68872-2906 • zeh72@hotmail.com • NEB • Tchr • Heartland Luth HS Grand Island NE • (308)381-7415 • (S 1995)

**ZEHNDER DOLORES J**
15515 Curwood Dr Colorado Springs CO 80921-3542 • RM • EM • (WN 1949)

**ZEHNDER GEORGE F** (972)291-1692
1008 Tower Dr Cedar Hill TX 75104-3016 • TX • EM • (RF 1953 MED)

**ZEHNDER JAMES W** (517)646-6894
8884 Rossman Rd Dimondale MI 48821-9631 • MI • Tchr • Our Savior Lansing MI • (517)882-3550 • (RF 1965 MED)

**ZEHNDER JONATHAN J**
314 State St Albany NY 12210-2035 • AT • 09/1999 • (RF 1996)

**ZEHNDER KATHLEEN S** (712)239-3682
2426 Mohawk Dr Sioux City IA 51104-1544 • IW • Tchr • St Paul Sioux City IA • (712)258-6325 • (CQ 1977)

**ZEIGLER TIMOTHY R**
Zion Luth Church 303 S 10th St Independence KS 67301 • trzeigler@pcis.net • KS • Prin • Zion Independence KS • (316)332-3300 • (S 1994 MS MBA)

**ZEITZ ALLAN A** (402)371-3603
83652 559th 1/2 Ave Norfolk NE 68701 • NEB • Tchr • Christ Norfolk NE • (402)371-5536 • (S 1968)

**ZELINKA KOTY**
1532 NE 21st St #406 Portland OR 97232 • NOW • P/Tchr • Portland LHS Portland OR • (503)667-3199 • (PO 1998)

**ZELLAR CHRISTA MARIE** (360)666-7190
404 SW 11th St Battle Ground WA 98604-2844 • NOW • 07/1999 • (PO 1996)

**ZELLAR DOYLE M** (507)662-6436
309 Funk Ave Lakefield MN 56150-0357 • dzellar@hotmail.com • MNS • P/Tchr • Immanuel Lakefield MN • (507)662-5860 • (SP 1989)

**ZEMKE FRIEDA J** (708)343-4453
812 N 6th Ave Maywood IL 60153-1047 • NI • Tchr • St Paul Melrose Park IL • (708)343-5000 • (RF 1975)

**ZEMKE HERMAN J** (708)668-5561
216 N Dorchester Ave Wheaton IL 60187-4708 • NI • EM • (RF 1950 MA)

**ZERBY BETHANY**
C/O Concordia Luth Church&Sch 16801 Huebner Rd San Antonio TX 78258 • TX • Tchr • Concordia San Antonio TX • (210)479-1477 • (AU 2000)

**ZERSEN ROLF**
4918 N 106th St Milwaukee WI 53225-3926 • SW • Tchr • South Wisconsin Milwaukee WI • (414)464-8100 • (MQ 1997)

**ZESSIN CATHERINE E** (248)852-0349
140 Whippoorwill Ln Rochester Hills MI 48309-3486 • MI • EM • (RF 1951 MA)

**ZEUNER BRENDA M L** (414)728-1261
1220 E Wisconsin St Delavan WI 53115-1441 • SW • Tchr • Our Redeemer Delavan WI • (262)728-4266 • (SP 1980)

**ZEUNER CHRISTINA L** (920)208-1827
2350 N 13th St Sheboygan WI 53083-4725 • zeuners@bytehead.com • SW • 05/1998 05/2000 • (RF 1985)

**ZEUNER JOHN H** (414)728-1261
1220 E Wisconsin St Delavan WI 53115-1441 • SW • Tchr • Our Redeemer Delavan WI • (262)728-6589 • (SP 1980)

**ZEUNER RICHARD P** (920)208-1827
2350 N 13th St Sheboygan WI 53083-4725 • zeuners@bytehead.com • SW • Tchr • Lutheran HS Sheboygan WI • (920)452-3323 • (RF 1985)

**ZICKLER ANELA KRISTALIK** (314)849-0209
10538 Mimosa Ln Saint Louis MO 63126-3523 • MO • Tchr • Hope Saint Louis MO • (314)832-1850 • (RF 1973)

**ZICKUHR JARIANNE LILLIAN** (301)864-5869
5026 37th Ave Hyattsville MD 20782-3910 • jzickuhr@gateway.net • SE • Tchr • Concordia Hyattsville MD • (301)927-0266 • (RF 1963 MA)

**ZIEBA LORI ANN** (314)334-7524
1415 Rose St Cape Girardeau MO 63701-4621 • MO • Tchr • Trinity Cape Girardeau MO • (573)334-1068 • (S 1989 MED)

**ZIEBART THOMAS A** (407)391-7544
1060 Holland Dr Ste 3L Boca Raton FL 33487-2758 • FG • Tchr • Florida-Georgia Orlando FL • (RF 1979 MA)

**ZIEGLER CONSTANCE J** (941)278-4854
5091 Westminster Dr Fort Myers FL 33919 • cziegler@sml.org • CI • Tchr • Concordia Peoria IL • (309)691-8921 • (S 1980)

**ZIEGLER ROBERT J** (941)278-4854
5091 Westminster Dr Fort Myers FL 33919 • bziegler@sml.org • FG • Prin • St Michael Fort Myers FL • (941)939-4711 • (S 1981 MS)

**ZIEHR RICHARD MARK*** (512)282-9652
612 Kingfisher Creek Dr Austin TX 78748-2425 • TX • 10/1999 • (RF 1982)

**ZIELINSKI CAROLYN K** (715)359-6138
1811 Foothill Ave Schofield WI 54476-4849 • NW • Tchr • St Mark Wausau WI • (715)848-5511 • (RF 1971 MA)

**ZIELINSKI JASON R** (920)803-5723
2118 Meadowland Dr #101 Sheboygan WI 53081 • SW • Tchr • Lutheran HS Sheboygan WI • (920)452-3323 • (MQ 1996)

**ZIELINSKI SANDRA NOEL** (760)839-9229
1748 Firestone Dr Escondido CA 92026 • sanlee@home.com • PSW • Tchr • Grace Escondido CA • (760)747-3029 • (CQ 1990)

**ZIELINSKI SARA**
302 Northeast Dr Fort Wayne IN 46825 • IN • Tchr • Central New Haven IN • (219)493-2502 • (RF 2000)

**ZIELKE DONALD HENRY DR** (512)345-0716
3909 Silverspring Dr Austin TX 78759-7444 • zielke@concordia.edu • TX • SHS/C • Texas Austin TX • (CQ 1967 MA PHD)

**ZIELKE STEPHEN P** (630)832-1102
255 Elmhurst Ave Elmhurst IL 60126-2960 • steve³zielke@walther.com • NI • Tchr • Walther LHS Melrose Park IL • (708)344-0404 • (RF 1978 MED)

**ZIELSKE EDWIN E** (703)949-7454
415 Cherry Ave Waynesboro VA 22980-4401 • SE • EM • (RF 1949)

**ZIELSKE SCOTT DAVID**
C/O St Paul Luth Church 701 W Palmetto Park Rd Boca Raton FL 33486 • FG • Tchr • St Paul Boca Raton FL • (561)395-0433 • (BR 1986 MSED)

**ZIEMANN KURT R** (219)338-0557
911 Hathaway Rd Fort Wayne IN 46845 • SW • 06/2000 • (MQ 1986 MA)

**ZIEMS LYLE L** (402)464-2957
820 N 58th St Lincoln NE 68505-2805 • lziems@yahoo.com • NEB • Tchr • Lincoln Luth Jr/Sr H Lincoln NE • (402)467-5404 • (S 1989)

**ZIEMS SHEILA A** (402)464-2957
820 N 58th St Lincoln NE 68505-2805 • NEB • 10/1998 • (S 1989)

**ZIEROLD KARIN MICHELLE** (508)481-1837
760 Farm Rd #30 Marlboro MA 01752-2730 • NE • Tchr • Mount Calvary Acton MA • (978)263-5156 • (BR 1998)

**ZIESEMER WILLIAM** (319)247-1279
2018 Franklin Ave NE Cedar Rapids IA 52402-4306 • IE • EM • (RF 1951 MS)

**ZILL STEVEN E** (517)642-5697
17375 Dice Rd Hemlock MI 48626-9637 • MI • Tchr • Valley Saginaw MI • (517)790-1676 • (RF 1976 MS)

**ZILLINGER SARA J**
2095 Highway 31 Hannover ND 58563-9173 • weinerz@aol.com • MO • Tchr • Luth Association Saint Louis MO • (314)268-1234 • (S 1997)

**ZILLMAN LYNNE**
C/O St Paul School 1000 W Lake St Melrose Park IL 60160-4147 • NI • Tchr • St Paul Melrose Park IL • (708)343-1000 • (RF 1976)

**ZILLMAN O JOHN** (708)343-5817
818 N 5th Ave Maywood IL 60153-1036 • crfzillmaoj@crf.cuis.edu • NI • SHS/C • Northern Illinois Hillside IL • (RF 1976 MED PHD)

**ZIMBRICK CHARLES R** (510)651-5836
4764 Stratford Ave Fremont CA 94538-3337 • CNH • Tchr • Prince Of Peace Fremont CA • (510)797-8186 • (RF 1975)

**ZIMBRICK EMILIE A** (510)651-5836
4764 Stratford Ave Fremont CA 94538-3337 • CNH • Tchr • Prince Of Peace Fremont CA • (510)797-8186 • (RF 1977)

**ZIMDAHL BERNARD W** (847)695-8988
674 Algona Ave Elgin IL 60120-3999 • NI • Tchr • St John Elgin IL • (847)741-7633 • (RF 1969)

**ZIMDAHL JANET RUTH** (708)695-8988
674 Algona Ave Elgin IL 60120-3999 • zimdahl@postoffice.worldnet.att.net • NI • Tchr • Fox Valley Academy Elgin IL • (847)468-8207 • (RF 1968)

**ZIMMER CAROL** (708)343-4866
909 Helen Dr Melrose Park IL 60160-2239 • zimmerra2@aol.com • NI • EM • (RF 1966 MA)

**ZIMMER DENNIS W** (708)547-1005
5521 Bohlander Ave Berkeley IL 60163-1404 • roommusic@aol.com • NI • Tchr • St John Forest Park IL • (708)366-3226 • (RF 1985 MMU)

**ZIMMER JENIFER ROSE** (612)472-7035
2992 Highview Ln Mound MN 55364-9420 • MNS • Tchr • Redeemer Wayzata MN • (612)473-5356 • (RF 1990)

**ZIMMER MARK A** (317)783-0949
4602 Fairhope Dr Indianapolis IN 46237-2953 • pasqua720@aol.com • IN • Tchr • St John Indianapolis IN • (317)352-9196 • (RF 1977 MS)

**ZIMMER MARTIN K** (219)322-8584
513 Sycamore Dr Dyer IN 46311-1840 • IN • Tchr • St Paul Munster IN • (219)836-6270 • (RF 1979 MS)

**ZIMMER MICHAEL J** (952)472-7035
2992 Highview Ln Mound MN 55364-9420 • pasqualake@aol.com • MNS • Tchr • Lutheran High Mayer MN • (612)657-2251 • (RF 1982 MA)

**ZIMMER R ALLAN** (708)343-4866
909 Helen Dr Melrose Park IL 60160-2239 • zimmerra2@aol.com • NI • EM • (RF 1954 MA DED)

**ZIMMERMAN GLORIA N** (206)226-4089
7003 S 132nd St Seattle WA 98178-5028 • NOW • P/Tchr • Amazing Grace Seattle WA • (206)723-5526 • (RF 1971)

**ZIMMERMAN JONATHAN E** (714)639-8081
546 N Maplewood St Orange CA 92867 • PSW • Tchr • Lutheran HS/Orange C Orange CA • (714)998-5151 • (S 1981 MED)

**ZIMMERMAN KAREN LEE** (720)283-0991
1805 E Panama Dr Littleton CO 80121-2621 • klzheart@juno.com • RM • Tchr • Shepherd Of The Hill Littleton CO • (303)798-0711 • (S 1968)

**ZIMMERMAN LESTER H**
2823 Poteet Dr Mesquite TX 75150 • leslillzim@aol.com • TX • EM • (S 1954 MED)

**ZIMMERMAN MARGARET ELAINE** (415)665-4043
2353 Funston Ave San Francisco CA 94116-1948 • revtbz@aol.com • CNH • Tchr • Zion San Francisco CA • (415)221-7500 • (RF 1964)

**ZIMMERMAN MICHAEL PAUL** (972)686-0525
1931 Robert Jones Dr Mesquite TX 75150 • zmpdalas@iamerica.net • TX • Tchr • Lutheran HS of Dalla Dallas TX • (214)349-8912 • (CQ 1995)

**ZIMMERMANN BARBARA L** (414)628-9559
1516 Pine Dr Hubertus WI 53033-9632 • sb61@webtv.net • SW • Tchr • Immanuel Mayville WI • (920)387-2158 • (S 1984 MA)

**ZIMMERMANN DONNA D** (920)733-0635
1043 East Moorpark Appleton WI 54911 • NW • Tchr • Celebration Appleton WI • (920)734-8218 • (RF 1981)

**ZIMMERMANN JONATHAN C** (630)876-8244
221 Ainsley West Chicago IL 60185 • jzimm@juno.com • NI • Tchr • St John Wheaton IL • (630)668-0701 • (RF 1994)

**ZIMMERMANN LEA J**
C/O Memorial Lutheran Church 5800 Westheimer Rd Houston TX 77057-5617 • TX • Tchr • Memorial Houston TX • (713)782-6079 • (S 1987)

**ZINK JANET S** (309)788-3032
5 Blackhawk Hills Dr Rock Island IL 61201-6938 • CI • 09/1998 • (CQ 1981)

**ZINNEL JONATHAN PAUL**
1710 E Kammerer Rd Kendallville IN 46755-2962 • MNN • Tchr • St John Kendallville IN • (219)347-2444 • (S 1979 MS)

**ZINNEL NORA L** (510)443-9815
624 Shelley St Livermore CA 94550-8111 • drzinn@aol.com • CNH • Tchr • Our Savior Livermore CA • (925)447-2082 • (S 1974)

**ZINNEL RAYMOND E** (510)443-9815
624 Shelley St Livermore CA 94550-2370 • drzinn@aol.com • CNH • 08/1999 • (S 1974)

**ZIPAY RUTH KATHERINE** (314)544-3702
3930 Hoffmeister Ave Saint Louis MO 63125-1411 • MO • Tchr • St Luke Saint Louis MO • (314)832-0118 • (RF 1984)

**ZIRZOW CYNTHIA R**
27 S Grant St Westmont IL 60559-1803 • NI • Tchr • St Paul Brookfield IL • (708)485-0650 • (RF 1977)

**ZITZOW DONA MAE** (715)423-3738
1350 Monroe St Wisconsin Rapids WI 56573-1640 • NW • Tchr • Immanuel Wisconsin Rapids WI • (715)423-0272 • (SP 1984)

**ZOBEL BETH A** (630)553-9126
114 Poplar Dr Yorkville IL 60560-9523 • NI • EM • (RF 1973)

**ZOBEL CAROL L** (618)965-9585
602 Hillandale Steeleville IL 62288-1604 • cubs@egyptian.net • SI • Tchr • St Mark Steeleville IL • (618)965-3838 • (RF 1975)

**ZOBEL GLEN F** (813)535-6042
1913 Oakdale Ln S Clearwater FL 34624-6469 • FG • 03/1983 10/1999 • (S 1960 MA)

**ZOBEL JAMES R** (618)965-9585
602 Hillandale Steeleville IL 62288-1604 • cubs@egyptian.net • SI • Tchr • St Mark Steeleville IL • (618)965-3838 • (S 1981)

**ZOBEL MARLIN J** (630)553-9126
114 Poplar Dr Yorkville IL 60560-9523 • NI • 07/1995 • (S 1952 MED)

**ZOCH ANITA M** (409)366-2780
PO Box 462 Giddings TX 78942-0462 • TX • Tchr • St Paul Giddings TX • (409)366-2218 • (RF 1985 MA)

**ZOCH ELIZABETH** (512)926-5377
7205 Fred Morse Dr Austin TX 78723-1610 • TX • Tchr • Hope Austin TX • (512)926-0003 • (AU 1984)

**ZOCH EVA J** (713)466-7868
11122 Melba Ln Houston TX 77041-5425 • TX • Tchr • Trinity-Messiah Houston TX • (713)224-7265 • (RF 1964)

**ZOCH MELVIN C** (801)485-7261
2692 Preston St Apt A Salt Lake City UT 84106-4150 • RM • EM • (S 1958)

**ZOCH THEODORE F** (512)926-5377
7205 Fred Morse Dr Austin TX 78723-1610 • TX • SHS/C • Texas Austin TX • (S 1959 MPHE)

**ZOCH WENDY M** (972)889-0391
1603 Sara Ln Richardson TX 75081-2527 • TX • Tchr • Zion Dallas TX • (214)363-1630 • (AU 1993 MED)

**ZOOK RANDALL J** (407)282-2366
1324 Ravida Cir Orlando FL 32825-5589 • zookrj@aol.com • FG • Tchr • Orlando Lutheran Aca Orlando FL • (407)275-7750 • (PO 1982)

**ZORN GLEN R**
479 Eden St Kingsley Heights MI 49649 • MI • EM • (RF 1961 MA)

**ZORUMSKI SUSAN K** (314)725-2676
6408 Alamo Apt 1 East Saint Louis MO 63105 • szorumski@juno.com • MO • Tchr • Messiah Saint Louis MO • (314)771-7716 • (RF 1993)

**ZRUST DONA M**
2433 Clark St Stevens Point WI 54481 • NW • Tchr • St Paul Stevens Point WI • (715)344-5660 • (S 1988)

**ZUCH THOMAS A** (503)788-1412
10317 SE Rex St Portland OR 97266-6078 • NOW • Tchr • Portland Portland OR • (503)667-3199 • (RF 1961 MA)

**ZUEHLSDORF JAMES F** (414)355-7318
8279 N 46th St Brown Deer WI 53223 • jmzuehls@execpc.com • SW • Prin • Mount Olive Milwaukee WI • (414)771-3580 • (SP 1972 MA)

**ZUEHSOW ANGELA** (972)662-0676
6800 Columbine Way Plano TX 75093-6344 • TX • Tchr • Prince Of Peace Carrollton TX • (972)447-9887 • (S 1976)

**ZUELSDORF ANTHONY E** (518)459-5020
22 Laing St Albany NY 12205-3126 • AT • Tchr • Our Savior Albany NY • (518)459-2248 • (RF 1962)

**ZUELSDORF BETTY J** (518)459-5020
22 Laing St Albany NY 12205-3126 • AT • Tchr • Our Savior Albany NY • (518)459-2248 • (RF 1962)

**ZUELSDORFF BILLY J** (262)681-2913
4822 Wedgewood Dr Racine WI 53402 • bjzuels@execpc.com • SW • Tchr • Trinity Racine WI • (414)632-1766 • (SP 1991 MED)

**ZUM HOFE ALLEN W*** (763)784-5454
220 Aurora Ln Circle Pines MN 55014 • azumhofe@aol.com • MNS • Tchr • Redeemer Wayzata MN • (612)473-5356 • (SP 1969)

**ZUMHOFE JOAN M** (612)731-2566
1264 Cedarwood Dr Woodbury MN 55125 • MNS • Tchr • East St Paul Saint Paul MN • (612)774-2030 • (S 1976)

**ZUMHOFE LAURIE LYNNE**
4480 Parklawn Ave Apt 107 Minneapolis MN 55435-4611 • lauriezum@excite.com • MNS • Tchr • St Peter Edina MN • (612)927-8400 • (S 1996)

**ZUMWALT MARY E** (618)483-5519
2478 E 800th St PO Box 62 Altamont IL 62411-0062 • CI • Tchr • Altamont Altamont IL • (618)483-6428 • (RF 1977 MA)

**ZUTZ ELLEN SUE**
N4035 Riverview Heights Ct Chilton WI 53014-9303 • stel@tds.net • SW • Tchr • Trinity Hilbert WI • (920)853-3134 • (RF 1984)

**ZWERNEMANN BONNIE D** (914)337-8299
51 Edgewood Lane Bronxville NY 10708-1945 • AT • 02/2000 • (RF 1961 MAT)

**ZWICK RICHARD C DR** (402)643-2293
3006 Bluff Rd Seward NE 68434-7864 • NEB • EM • (S 1954 MA PHD)

# Section B Directors of Christian Education

During the 1983 synodical convention, delegates adopted a resolution that gave certified Directors of Christian Education membership status in the Synod under the classification of Ministers of Religion—Commissioned.

## A

**ACHONG ROBERT DREW** (580)336-5442
709 Maple St Perry OK 73077 • OK • Mem C • Christ Perry OK • (580)336-2347 • (IV 1999)

**AHLERS LAURA JANE** (402)329-4034
105 S Smith St Pierce NE 68767-1637 • NEB • Mem C • Zion Pierce NE • (402)329-4313 • (IV 1988)

**AHLES DAVID F**
1641 W Sunset Ave Decatur IL 62522-2620 • deldledave@aol.com • CI • Mem C • St Paul Decatur IL • (217)423-6955 • (RF 1994)

**ALTENBERND ERIC JOHN** (217)876-0568
4333 Lawson Dr Decatur IL 62526 • dcehomebuilder@yahoo.com • CI • Mem C • Missouri Saint Louis MO* • (314)317-4550 • (SP 1989 MED)

**ANAZAGASTY SERENA ALEXANDRIA** (417)338-4008
28 S Lantern Bay Rd Branson MO 65616 • serenazag@aol.com • MO • Bethlehem Fort Wayne IN • (S 1997 MPED)

**ANDERSON DEBORAH LEE** (507)439-6651
PO Box 235 Hanska MN 56041 • debdeb73@aol.com • MNS • Mem C • Redeemer New Ulm MN • (507)233-3470 • (SP 1998)

**ANDERSON ELLSWORTH** (509)928-3889
1015 S Little John Ct Spokane WA 99206-3549 • NOW • Mem C • Redeemer Spokane WA • (509)926-6363 • (RF 1966)

**ANDERSON JAMES C** (517)652-3119
8720 Gera Rd Birch Run MI 48415-9225 • MI • Mem C • St Lorenz Frankenmuth MI • (517)652-6141 • (RF 1980)

**ANDERSON JAMES W** (612)943-2447
7417 W 100th St Bloomington MN 55438-2101 • jander@pclink.com • MNS • Mem C • St Michael Bloomington MN • (952)831-5276 • (SP 1978 MED)

**ANDERSON MARK C** (785)267-3376
3616 SW Cambridge Ter Topeka KS 66610-1130 • mcadce@stjohnlcmstopeka.org • KS • Mem C • St John Topeka KS • (785)354-7132 • (PO 1989)

**ANGERMAN M RAY**
Good Shepherd Lutheran Church 1 Meigs Dr Shalimar FL 32579-1286 • SO • Mem C • Good Shepherd Shalimar FL • (850)651-1022 • (RF 1977)

**ARFSTEN DEBRA JOYCE** (970)663-1655
514 W 39th St Loveland CO 80538 • debja@mindspring.com • RM • Mem C • Immanuel Loveland CO • (970)667-4506 • (S 1990 MPED)

**ARLDT MICHAEL** (512)733-1083
2501 Louis Henna #813 Round Rock TX 78664 • texascws@aol.com • TX • 10/2000 • (AU 1996)

**ARMBRUST STEVEN D** (913)397-9884
14311 W 123rd St Olathe KS 66062-6027 • sa4903@aol.com • KS • Mem C • Bethany Shawnee Mission KS • (913)648-2228 • (S 1981)

**ARMSTRONG JEFFERY S** (713)688-4142
8147 Sweetgum Trce Houston TX 77040-2635 • TX • Mem C • Our Savior Houston TX • (713)290-9087 • (IV 1995)

**ARNETT GREGORY SCOTT** (517)672-4686
2319 S Fenner Rd Caro MI 48723-9689 • stpaul@centurytel.net • MI • Mem C • St Paul Caro MI • (517)673-4214 • (RF 1987)

## B

**BACH GARY D** (218)385-2686
320 N Broadway Ave New York Mills MN 56567 • trinity@wcta.net • MNN • Mem C • Trinity New York Mills MN • (218)385-2450 • (SP 1982)

**BACHMANN LORI L** (956)838-5160
4765 Elma St Brownsville TX 78521 • loribach@aol.com • TX • Mem C • El Calvario Brownsville TX • (956)546-2350 • (S 1981)

**BAHN CHARLES ALLEN** (309)829-6710
2808 Rutherford Dr Bloomington IL 61704-6516 • chuckab@fgi.net • CI • Mem C • Trinity Bloomington IL • (309)828-6265 • (IV 1993 MA)

**BAILEY-MC CRAY KELLY A** (541)388-3102
63415 Saddleback Pl Bend OR 97701-8567 • NOW • 08/1991 08/2000 • (IV 1983)

**BAKALYAR KENNETH W** (507)427-3360
407 9th St N PO Box 153 Mountain Lake MN 56159-0153 • krpacker@rconnect.com • MNS • Mem C • Trinity Mountain Lake MN • (507)427-2451 • (SP 1982)

**BAKER JODENE A** (704)566-0824
2601-12 Cross Point Cir Matthews NC 28105 • SE • Mem C • Messiah Charlotte NC • (704)541-1624 • (S 2000)

**BARG ESTHER M** (913)367-9194
1102 Price Blvd Atchison KS 66002 • ebargdce@journey.com • KS • Mem C • Trinity Atchison KS • (913)367-2837 • (SP 1997)

**BARGMANN JAMES FREDERICK** (651)917-8653
1351 Carling Dr #241 Saint Paul MN 55108 • dcejim@hotmail.com • MNS • Mem C • King Of Kings Roseville MN • (651)484-5142 • (SP 1999)

**BARKLAGE RICHARD C** (916)332-4001
C/O Zion Lutheran Church 3644 Bolivar Ave North Highlands CA 95660-4350 • i5dce@aol.com • CNH • Mem C • Zion North Highlands CA • (916)332-4001 • (S 1980)

**BARNES KATRINA L**
3304 W St Vancouver WA 98663-2629 • katrina@mlc.org • NOW • Mem C • Memorial Vancouver WA • (360)695-7501 • (SP 1988)

**BASS GEROD ROBERT**
Peace Lutheran Church 18615 SE 272nd St Kent WA 98042 • NOW • Mem C • Peace Kent WA • (253)631-3454 • (PO 1997)

**BATTERMAN STEVE DON**
2205 Blake Ave Glenwood Springs CO 81601-4232 • dce4him@aol.com • RM • 08/1997 • (IV 1995)

**BECK DANA J** (913)823-7151
815 E Wayne Ave Apt 4 Salina KS 67401-6759 • RDBeckdce@aol.com • KS • Mem C • Trinity Salina KS • (785)823-7151 • (S 1994)

**BECK JILL S** (972)315-3019
801 Hebron Pkwy Apt 5311 Lewisville TX 75057-5029 • TX • Mem C • Lamb Of God Flower Mound TX • (972)539-5200 • (S 1999)

**BECKER JEREMY MICHAEL** (314)729-1332
8618 Villa Crest Dr Saint Louis MO 63126 • dceskater@aol.com • MO • Mem C • Concordia Kirkwood MO • (314)822-7772 • (RF 1999)

**BEETHE IRENE E** (810)323-0383
51231 Sunny Hill Dr Shelby Twp MI 48316 • MI • 04/2000 • (S 1976)

**BELMAS LEE A**
1833 Plantation Ln Mosinee WI 54455-8842 • NW • North Wisconsin Wausau WI* • (SP 1985)

**BENDER KENDIS DIANE** (440)967-1792
4215 Telegraph Ln Vermilion OH 44089 • dkbender@apk.net • OH • Mem C • St Paul Amherst OH • (440)988-4157 • (RF 1991)

**BERG PAUL A** (320)587-9811
445 Glen St SW Hutchinson MN 55350-2431 • paulberg@cphnet.org • MNS • Mem C • Peace Hutchinson MN • (320)587-3031 • (SP 1975)

**BERGERON JANINE MARIE** (920)457-0516
1534 Georgia Ave Sheboygan WI 53081-5120 • janinebergeron@hotmail.com • SW • Mem C • Good Shepherd Sheboygan WI • (920)452-8759 • (S 1993)

**BICKEL KURT R** (407)281-0604
446 Bonifay Ave Orlando FL 32825-8002 • FG • Florida-Georgia Orlando FL • (S 1973 MA)

**BIEL LARRY ROBERT** (402)334-3853
2515 S 152nd Ave Cir Omaha NE 68144 • dcelarry@aol.com • NEB • Mem C • Pacific Hills Omaha NE • (402)391-9625 • (S 1975)

**BIERBAUM DARYL PAUL** (972)267-7620
4200 Horizon No Pkwy #1115 Dallas TX 75287 • dbierbaum@kearney.net • TX • St Paul Fort Worth TX • (S 1994)

**BIERLEIN HEIDI LYNN** (904)928-9136
Grace Lutheran Church 12200 Mc Cormick Rd Jacksonville FL 32225-4556 • heidibierlein@hotmail.com • FG • Mem C • Grace Jacksonville FL • (904)928-9136 • (SP 1999)

**BIMLER RICHARD W DR** (630)924-1522
336 W Hampshire Dr Bloomingdale IL 60108-2504 • wrmbimlerrw@wheatridge.org • NI • CCRA • Northern Illinois Hillside IL • (CQ 1976 MA LITTD LHD)

**BJORNSTAD CARSTEN OLAF** (612)235-9233
515 14th St SE Willmar MN 56201-4415 • MNN • EM • (SP 1978 MA)

**BLACK DENA MARIE** (734)455-9318
37920 Westwood Cir Westland MI 48185 • michigandena@hotmail.com • MI • Mem C • Christ Our Savior Livonia MI • (734)522-6830 • (IV 1999)

**BLAIR JANINE R** (954)894-4898
5141 Hollywood Blvd - #208 Hollywood FL 33020 • FG • Mem C • St Mark Hollywood FL • (954)922-7568 • (S 2000)

**BLICKHAHN HENRY ADAM** (316)665-9843
306 Crescent Blvd Hutchinson KS 67502-5512 • blick@ourtownusa.com • KS • Mem C • Our Redeemer Hutchinson KS • (316)662-5642 • (IV 1989)

**BOERSMA MELODY LYNN** (214)349-8104
12662 Jupiter Rd Apt 1412 Dallas TX 75238-3940 • meldoy1967@aol.com • TX • Mem C • Bethel Dallas TX • (214)348-0420 • (RF 1990)

**BOETCHER JASON D** (402)475-7103
710 W Belmont Ave Lincoln NE 68521-3400 • NEB • 08/2000 • (S 1993)

**BOMBALL ROBIN ANN**
2021 Aspen Dr Woodstock IL 60098-6909 • poplchurchmfwpreschool@juno.com • NI • 03/1999 • (RF 1990)

**BORCHERDING MARK C** (317)844-4919
505 Concord Ln Carmel IN 46032-2281 • mborcherding@clearcall.net • IN • Mem C • Carmel Carmel IN • (317)814-4252 • (S 1977)

**BORCHERS KEVIN L** (847)797-8629
114 W Olive St Arlington Hts IL 60004-4730 • NI • Mem C • St Peter Arlington Heights IL • (847)259-4114 • (RF 1981)

**BRADFIELD BECKY LYNN** (615)849-8197
1126 Gardendale Dr Murfreesboro TN 37130 • beckbrad@aol.com • MDS • Mem C • Grace Murfreesboro TN • (615)893-0338 • (S 1994)

**BRADSHAW JAMES P** (785)273-5175
1940 SW Stone Ave Topeka KS 66604-3353 • faithluth@networksplus.net • KS • Mem C • Faith Topeka KS • (785)272-4214 • (S 1982)

**BRAKHAGE CARLA JO** (918)255-6270
RR 1 Box 42 S Coffeyville OK 74072-9707 • KS • Mem C • St Paul Coffeyville KS • (316)251-2927 • (S 1980)

**BRANDON T KEVIN** (205)880-3110
3412 Marks Dr SW Huntsville AL 35805-5330 • SO • Mem C • Grace Huntsville AL • (256)881-0552 • (RF 1980)

**BRANDT LARRY L** (217)342-2738
904 N Oakwood St Effingham IL 62401-3242 • tlb@effmgham.net • CI • Mem C • St John Effingham IL • (217)342-4334 • (RF 1962 MA)

**BRANTSCH ROBERT JOHN** (716)649-6369
4389 Clark St Hamburg NY 14075-3826 • dcebobb@aol.com • EA • Mem C • Grace Hamburg NY • (716)649-6581 • (RF 1995 MPED)

**BREI ERIC KENNETH**
398 Springwell Ln Howell MI 48843-7479 • MI • Mem C • Shep Lakes Brighton MI • (810)227-5099 • (RF 1996)

**BREWER ZACHERY CHAD** (808)877-3037
520 W One St Kahului HI 96732 • brewdce@aol.com • CNH • Mem C • Emmanuel Kahului HI • (808)877-3037 • (IV 1999)

**BRIDGES MICHAEL R** (517)882-2405
3640 Dell Rd Holt MI 48842-9405 • MI • Mem C • Messiah Holt MI • (517)694-1280 • (S 1992)

**BRINK HEIDI ELIZABETH** (402)496-2240
10812 Jaynes Plaza Apt 1234 Omaha NE 68164 • NEB • 06/2000 • (IV 1992)

**BROCKHOFF BONNIE L** (914)667-1807
15 Locust Ln Mount Vernon NY 10552 • AT • 04/2000 • (S 1979)

**BROCKMAN REBECCA LYNN** (316)636-9456
7409 E 31st Street Ct N Wichita KS 67226-2213 • KS • Mem C • Holy Cross Wichita KS • (316)684-5201 • (IV 1986 MA)

**BROEKEMEIER ROBERT A** (402)293-1219
3216 Joann Ave Bellevue NE 68123-3176 • bob@kingofkingsomaha.org • NEB • Mem C • King Of Kings Omaha NE • (402)333-6464 • (S 1988 MS)

**BROSE GREGORY L**
1429 Via Salerno Escondido CA 92026-2252 • PSW • 05/2000 • (IV 1987)

**BROTEN DEREK JOHN** (316)722-4694
C/O Ascension Luth Church 842 N Tyler Rd Wichita KS 67212 • brotendce@msn.com • KS • Mem C • Ascension Wichita KS • (316)722-4694 • (SP 1998)

**BROVICK MARIA P** (970)225-9020
PO Box 273111 Fort Collins CO 80527-3111 • RM • Mem C • Redeemer Fort Collins CO • (970)225-9020 • (IV 1997)

**BROWN DAVID E** (810)463-5963
973 Crest St Mount Clemens MI 48043-6400 • dbrown@123.net • MI • Mem C • Trinity Clinton Township MI • (810)463-2921 • (RF 1975 MSED)

**BROWN JENNIFER ANN** (732)323-0042
270 Lindbergh Sq Lakehurst NJ 08733 • S • Mem C • Redeemer Lakehurst NJ • (732)657-2828 • (RF 1999)

**BROWN SCOTT DOUGLAS** (763)263-5901
570 Park Ave E Big Lake MN 55309 • MNN • Mem C • Lord Of Glory Elk River MN • (763)263-3090 • (SP 1993)

**BRUICK GEORGE ARTHUR II** (734)433-9134
761 Flanders St Chelsea MI 48118 • gbruick@pastors.com • MI • Mem C • Our Savior Chelsea MI • (734)475-1404 • (SP 1997)

**BRUNNER MELANIE TRAVIS** (828)304-4421
104 20th Ave SW Hickory NC 28602 • SE • Mem C • St John Conover NC • (828)464-4071 • (S 1998)

**BUCHHOLZ GORDON A**
7108 Horner Ave Apt A3 Richmond Heights MO 63117-2347 • CI • Mem C • St John Pekin IL • (309)347-2136 • (S 1991)

**BUCHHOLZ MARK DIETRICH**
2800 Keller Dr #308 Tustin CA 92782-1013 • PSW • Mem C • Bethlehem Santa Clarita CA • (661)252-0622 • (IV 1992)

**BUCHHOLZ ROBERT W** (253)850-5797
23808 112th Ave SE Kent WA 98031-3545 • lutheran³cross@hotmail.com • NOW • Mem C • Of The Cross Kent WA • (253)854-3240 • (S 1975 MA)

**BUELTMANN KEVIN J** (402)352-5989
1048 Rd 4 Schuyler NE 68661-7145 • bueltmann@alltel.net • NEB • Nebraska Seward NE • (S 1988)

**BURNHAM R JOSEPH** (707)836-7462
423 Woodbine Way Windsor CA 95492 • dcejb@vof.org • CNH • Mem C • Vineyard of Faith Windsor CA • (707)837-8712 • (S 1998)

**BUSS JAMES STEVEN**
7864 N Chadwick Rd Milwaukee WI 53217-3159 • NW • 11/1999 • (SP 1988)

**BUSSE DONALD R** (734)676-6568
3432 Anna Ave Trenton MI 48183 • dcedon@juno.com • MI • Mem C • St Paul Trenton MI • (734)676-1565 • (SP 1985)

## C

**CADWISING GARY** (503)674-9305
18200 NE Couch St Apt 232 Portland OR 97230-7272 • gtiggerc@usa.net • NOW • 08/2000 • (PO 1995)

**CARTWRIGHT MARLYS K** (509)747-6806
4320 S Conklin St Spokane WA 99203-6237 • cartright775344@juno.com • NOW • Mem C • Beautiful Savior Spokane WA • (509)747-6806 • (S 1979)

**CHAPMAN JOHN JAMES** (714)662-7624
219 E Flora St Santa Ana CA 92707-3215 • PSW • Mem C • Trinity Santa Ana CA • (714)542-0784 • (IV 1992)

**CHEATHAM DAVID ALAN**
St Peter Luth Church 208 E Schaumburg Rd Schaumburg IL 60194 • tx32@hotmail.com • NI • Mem C • St Peter Schaumburg IL • (847)885-3350 • (S 1997)

**CHRIST JASON ALEXANDER** (281)396-1896
22022 Cimarron Pkwy #2111 Katy TX 77450 • TX • Mem C • Memorial Katy TX • (281)391-0171 • (RF 2000)

**CHRISTIAN DAVID** (314)771-7372
1307 Sidney St Saint Louis MO 63104-4314 • MO • Mem C • Concordia Kirkwood MO • (314)822-7772 • (RF 1970 MMU)

**CHRISTOPHER STEVEN L** (925)447-1246
1385 S Livermore Ave Livermore CA 94550 • dceduo@aol.com • CNH • Mem C • Our Savior Livermore CA • (925)447-1246 • (S 1979 MA)

**CLARK TODD MATTHEW** (502)896-6260
425 S Hubbards Ln #186 Louisville KY 40207 • IN • Mem C • Our Savior Louisville KY • (502)426-1130 • (RF 1998)

**CLEVELAND JONATHAN DALE** (503)258-9605
11360 NE Davis Portland OR 97220 • NOW • Mem C • Trinity Portland OR • (503)288-6403 • (PO 1987)

**COLWELL CLINTON C** (806)798-8907
5917 72nd St Lubbock TX 79424 • clintccolwell@juno.com • TX • Mem C • Hope Lubbock TX • (806)798-2747 • (S 1992)

**CORUM SCOTT ANDREW** (310)370-9463
20714 Osage Ave #7 Torrance CA 90503 • PSW • Mem C • First Manhattan Beach CA • (310)545-5653 • (IV 1999)

**CRAGO ANDREA** (651)735-3397
2000 East 3rd St Saint Paul MN 55119 • andrea@chlc.org • MNS • Mem C • Eastern Hghts Saint Paul MN • (651)735-4202 • (SP 1999)

**CREUTZ MICHAEL S** (330)492-2583
1405 37th St NW Canton OH 44709-2641 • OH • Mem C • Holy Cross Canton OH • (330)499-3307 • (S 1985)

**CRISI DAVID ALLEN** (503)642-7722
859 SE 58th Ave Hillsboro OR 97123-6323 • dcedave@aol.com • NOW • Mem C • Trinity Hillsboro OR • (503)640-1693 • (PO 1988)

**CROSS HEIDI A** (661)949-9320
44535 Loneoak Ave Lancaster CA 93534-2909 • PSW • Mem C • Grace Lancaster CA • (661)948-1018 • (S 1982)

**CULLEN WILLIAM G**
C/O Concordia University 7400 Augusta St River Forest IL 60305-1402 • NI • SHS/C • Northern Illinois Hillside IL • (PO 1985 MED PHD)

## D

**D AMBROSIO ROBERT JAMES** (210)497-1780
1215 Cadley Ct San Antonio TX 78258-3134 • BobD@concordia-satx.com • TX • Mem C • Concordia San Antonio TX • (210)479-1477 • (RF 1977 MA)

**DAHLIA MARY ELIZABETH** (714)998-4082
2525 N Bourbon Unit H4 Orange CA 92865 • punluvndce@aol.com • PSW • Mem C • Peace Santa Ana CA • (714)731-2226 • (IV 1993)

**DAMMANN JAMES LEE**
C/O Camp Luther 1050 Rd 4 Schuyler NE 68661 • jddce@computerland.net • NEB • Nebraska Seward NE • (S 1990)

**DASH RUSSELL W**
6607 Yale Dr Apt 228 Westland MI 48185 • MI • Tchr • St Matthew Westland MI • (734)425-0260 • (BR 1977)

**DAVIS SUE ANN** (817)236-5698
7613 Skylake Dr Fort Worth TX 76179-2815 • TX • Mem C • St Paul Fort Worth TX • (817)332-2281 • (SP 1982)

**DAY LISA ANN** (612)473-5349
410 Niagara Ln N Plymouth MN 55447 • daydce@yahoo.com • MNS • 06/2000 • (SP 1988)

**DE CUIR LUTHER A** (314)938-4735
143 Shaw Dr Eureka MO 63025-1122 • ludecuir@afo.net • MO • Mem C • Our Redeemer Saint Louis MO • (314)772-7169 • (S 1985 MA SPA)

**DE MUTH GREGORY A**
9585 W Powers Cir Littlton CO 80123-2304 • RM • 03/1999 • (S 1988 MA)

**DE LA MOTTE TROY ANDREW** (954)522-5772
1209 NE 18th Ave Fort Lauderdale FL 33304-2411 • FG • Mem C • Trinity Fort Lauderdale FL* • (954)463-2450 • (IV 1999)

**DEHNING MELANIE L** (956)687-4879
413 W Hibiscus Ave Mc Allen TX 78501-1820 • stpaulmca@juno.com • TX • Mem C • St Paul Mc Allen TX • (956)682-2345 • (S 1981)

**DEKNATEL CHRIS DARRYL**
2407 Conway Dr Escondido CA 92026-1469 • PSW • Mem C • Community Escondido CA • (760)739-1650 • (SP 1990)

**DENHOLM GEORGE** (812)378-3198
4554 Hackberry Dr Columbus IN 47201-9501 • geoden3@juno.com • IN • Mem C • St Peter Columbus IN • (812)372-1571 • (RF 1983 MA)

**DETTLING MARIE A** (516)326-1285
361 Garden City Rd Franklin Square NY 11010-3949 • elmsdettling@worldnet.att.net • AT • Mem C • Trinity Hicksville NY • (516)931-2225 • (BR 1975 MA)

**DIEKHOFF PHILIP C** (907)455-8150
2136 Mc Cullam Ave Fairbanks AK 99701-5714 • 72732.3372@compuserve • NOW • 09/1998 • (SP 1987)

**DIERKER STEPHEN TIMOTHY** (707)254-2040
550 River Glen Dr Apt 22 Napa CA 94558-3566 • steve@stjohnslutheran.net • CNH • Mem C • St John Napa CA • (707)255-0119 • (IV 1995)

**DIETRICH JOEL MARK**
C/O Saint Paul Lutheran Church 1250 E Heim Ave Orange CA 92865-2920 • dcedietrich@gbonline.com • PSW • St Michael Richville MI • (IV 1998)

**DRAGER CHRISTOPHER SCOTT** (616)323-9300
1711 Birchton Ave Portage MI 49024 • cdrager@yahoo.com • MI • Mem C • Zion Kalamazoo MI • (616)382-2360 • (SP 1990)

**DU PREE RONALD STEVEN JR.** (909)794-5747
31694 Ave E Yucaipa CA 92399-1611 • dceronbo@cs.com • PSW • Mem C • Good Shepherd Yucaipa CA • (909)790-1863 • (IV 1996)

**DUENSING AUDREY MAE**
5100 W 84th St Apt 2 Bloomington MN 55437-1367 • MNS • Mem C • Cross View Edina MN • (952)941-1094 • (SP 1993)

**DUKLES DUANE MICHAEL** (440)543-6119
8890 Tanglewood Trl Chagrin Falls OH 44023-5641 • OH • Mem C • Valley Chagrin Falls OH • (440)247-0390 • (S 1986)

**DUNAVAN DEAN ALLEN** (651)633-8803
1440 Primrose Curve Roseville MN 55113 • MNS • Tchr • Minnesota South Burnsville MN • (SP 1991)

**DURHEIM STEVEN WAYNE** (405)263-4736
308 S 4th Okarche OK 73762 • EA • Mem C • St Paul Eden NY • (716)992-9112 • (S 1997)

## E

**EADS LANCE R**
4725 W Powell Blvd Apt 102 Gresham OR 97030-5016 • NOW • Mem C • Ascension Portland OR • (503)665-8821 • (PO 1998)

**EATON CHARLES EDWIN** (918)592-2999
PO Box 50921 Tulsa OK 74150-0921 • ceaton1@swbell.net • OK • Mem C • Grace Tulsa OK • (918)592-2999 • (SP 1975)

**EBERLE LISA** (603)352-8089
34 Woodburn St Apt 3 Keene NH 03431-2505 • NE • Mem C • Trinity Keene NH • (603)352-4446 • (CQ 1997)

**EDELEN THOMAS G**
12600 Braddock Dr #105 Los Angeles CA 90066 • tomedelen@aol.com • PSW • Mem C • First Venice CA • (310)821-2740 • (SP 1996)

**EID CHRISTINE R**
2760 Medicine Ridge Rd Plymouth MN 55441-3280 • christineeid@juno.com • MNS • Mem C • St Matthew Columbia Heights MN • (763)788-9427 • (CQ 1986)

**EITEL SANDRA FAUNE**
1334 S Conyer St Visalia CA 93277-4604 • CNH • Mem C • Grace Visalia CA • (559)734-7694 • (SP 1995)

**EITREIM TIMOTHY RANDALL** (509)328-3210
1207 W Cleveland Ave Spokane WA 99205-3429 • eitreim@hotmail.com • NOW • Mem C • Pilgrim Spokane WA • (509)325-5738 • (IV 1994)

**EIZENARMS-BLOM CHRYSTAL**
835 Parliament Dr Ravenna OH 44266 • OH • 12/1999 • (SP 1991)

**ELIASON CARL ALWIN** (763)263-2121
1119 Kilbirnie Rd Big Lake MN 55309-8837 • carlathome@juno.com • MNS • Mem C • St John Elk River MN • (763)441-3646 • (S 1995 MS MA MMU)

**ELMSHAUSER JOHN** (303)690-8401
3111 S Joplin Ct Aurora CO 80013-1745 • RM • Mem C • Peace W Christ Aurora CO • (303)693-5618 • (S 1972)

**EMAN KIMBERLY ANN** (303)439-2575
10259 Garrison St Westminster CO 80021-3883 • RM • 11/1999 • (S 1976)

**ENDICOTT JOEL** (949)581-6330
21472 D Lake Forest Dr Lake Forest CA 92630 • endicott@cui.edu • PSW • SHS/C • Pacific Southwest Irvine CA • (949)854-3232 • (IV 1995)

**ENDICOTT STEVEN K** (425)485-2309
17512 29th Dr SE Bothell WA 98012-6640 • steveendicott@juno.com • NOW • Mem C • Shepherd Hills Snohomish WA • (360)668-7881 • (SP 1968)

**ENGELHARDT MARK J** (952)997-3742
13420 Heather Hills Dr Burnsville MN 55337 • lcadce@excite.com • MNS • Mem C • Ascension Burnsville MN • (952)890-3412 • (S 1998 MPED)

**ERLANDSON KENNETH W** (816)505-3025
6666 NW 72nd St Kansas City MO 64151-1676 • MO • Mem C • Christ Platte Woods MO • (816)741-0483 • (SP 1985)

**EVERSON DAVID GLEN** (352)243-5595
14508 Pointe E Trl Clermont FL 34711-8122 • songster@juno.com • FG • Mem C • Woodlands Montverde FL • (407)469-2525 • (S 1993)

**EWELL ROBERT** (402)489-6373
4341 S 45th St Lincoln NE 68516-1116 • rewell@christlutheranchurch.org • NEB • Mem C • Christ Lincoln NE • (402)483-7774 • (RF 1969 MA)

## F

**FAIRCHILD NOEL MANSKE** (949)551-4484
14782 Elm Ave Irvine CA 92606 • noelfairchild@hotmail.com • PSW • Mem C • Mount Calvary Diamond Bar CA • (909)861-2740 • (IV 1996)

**FALK T SCOTT** (310)979-9034
823 S Bundy Dr Los Angeles CA 90049-5216 • tscottfalk@msn.com • PSW • 07/1995 • (RF 1991)

**FEHL STEPHEN G** (719)570-7951
5617 Old Farm Cir E Colorado Springs CO 80917-1142 • sgfehl"@aol.com • RM • Mem C • Holy Cross Colorado Springs CO • (719)596-0661 • (S 1977)

**FINGERLIN HEIDI N** (303)781-4941
3855 S Delaware St Englewood CO 80110-3513 • hfingerlin@bethluth.net • RM • Mem C • Bethlehem Lakewood CO • (303)238-7676 • (S 1991)

**FINKE LARRY L** (952)446-9643
9125 Oakwood Rd Saint Bonifacius MN 55375 • finkefamily@yahoo.com • MNS • Mem C • Redeemer Wayzata MN • (612)473-1281 • (S 1976 MMU)

**FISCHER JONATHAN M** (972)247-4724
3449 Pebble Beach Dr Dallas TX 75234-2218 • TX • Mem C • Holy Cross Dallas TX • (214)358-4396 • (S 1959 MED)

**FISCHER RANDALL DAVID** (715)355-0142
812 Maryland Ave Schofield WI 54476-1132 • NW • Mem C • Mount Olive Weston WI • (715)359-5546 • (SP 1986)

**FISHER VICKI L** (402)744-4771
8650 N Showboat Blvd Hastings NE 68901 • farrier@tcgcs.com • NEB • Mem C • Faith Hastings NE • (402)462-5044 • (S 1991)

**FOLEY KEVIN MARK**
C/O Trinity Lutheran Church 1428 N Pueblo Dr Casa Grande AZ 85222-2914 • PSW • Mem C • Trinity Casa Grande AZ • (520)836-2451 • (SP 1998)

**FORKE DAVID LYNN** (715)833-9067
2022 E Lexington Blvd Eau Claire WI 54701-6734 • NW • Mem C • Peace Eau Claire WI • (715)834-2486 • (S 1985)

**FORTMEYER BERNARD PAUL** (816)364-4781
4225 Oakland Saint Joseph MO 64506-2432 • MO • Mem C • St Paul Saint Joseph MO • (816)279-1110 • (S 1992)

**FOSSUM ROBERT B** (503)356-1512
3950 SW 191st Aloha OR 97006 • NOW • Mem C • Bethlehem Aloha OR • (503)649-3380 • (S 1975 MMFC)

**FOUND JAMES A** (651)645-7914
1761 Fernwood Ave Roseville MN 55113 • found@luther.csp.edu • MNS • Trinity Sheboygan WI • (CQ 1980 MA)

**FRANK HEIDI BORG** (503)253-3117
11102 NE Mason St Portland OR 97220-2628 • hborg@transport.com • NOW • Mem C • Living Savior Tualatin OR • (503)692-3490 • (PO 1981)

**FRANZEN KAREN J** (303)750-5496
17712 E Kansas Pl Aurora CO 80017 • RM • Tchr • Peace W Christ Aurora CO • (303)693-5618 • (S 1977)

**FREED R MICHAEL** (316)684-1630
3058 Euclid St Wichita KS 67217-1931 • freegrace@juno.com • KS • Mem C • Grace Wichita KS • (316)685-6781 • (RF 1979)

**FREITAG JAMES A** (503)492-3109
518 NW 23rd Ave Gresham OR 97030-2500 • jimlindakristadanielkayla@compuserve.com • NOW • 06/1998 06/2000 • (PO 1981 MAR)

**FRERICH HAROLD A** (419)592-3535
1140 E Riverview Ave Apt 6G Napoleon OH 43545 • OH • Mem C • St Paul Napoleon OH • (419)592-3535 • (SP 1999)

**FREUDENBURG BENJAMIN F** (314)821-4180
1201 Capri Dr Saint Louis MO 63126-1419 • MO • Mem C • Concordia Kirkwood MO • (314)822-7772 • (S 1972)

**FRICK ROGER P** (714)535-1169
C/O Zion Lutheran Church 222 N East St Anaheim CA 92805-3317 • rfrick@zionanaheim.org • PSW • Mem C • Zion Anaheim CA • (714)535-1169 • (IV 1987)

**FULBRIGHT MICHAEL ALLEN** (931)540-0928
1216 Hampshire Pike Apt B19 Columbia TN 38401-4622 • mfulbri@galis.com • MDS • Mem C • Trinity Columbia TN • (931)388-0790 • (SP 1997)

**FUNKE DAVID M** (314)355-2568
6787 Lesli Mari Ct Florissant MO 63033-4819 • EN • Mem C • Chapel Cross Saint Louis MO • (314)741-3737 • (SP 1981 MED)

## G

**GABBERT MARK K** (970)568-9220
PO Box 768 Wellington CO 80549-0768 • markdce@msn.com • RM • Mem C • St John Fort Collins CO • (970)482-5316 • (S 1982 MA)

**GABRIEL KAREN LOU** (307)745-9488
257 N 6th St Laramie WY 82072 • wyogabe@aol.com • WY • Mem C • Zion Laramie WY • (307)745-9262 • (S 1998)

**GAYLOR PHILLIP C** (909)599-5721
732 Payson St La Verne CA 91750-4151 • cadce@earthlink.net • PSW • Mem C • Trinity Whittier CA • (562)699-7431 • (IV 1991)

**GEHRING SUSANN MARIE** (256)873-0610
102 Crown Oak Ln NW Huntsville AL 35806 • serdman@hotmail.com • SO • Mem C • Ascension Huntsville AL • (256)536-9987 • (S 1996)

**GEHRKE ANDREA** (503)296-0863
8705 SW White Pine Ln Portland OR 97225-2445 • NOW • Mem C • Pilgrim Beaverton OR • (503)644-4656 • (IV 1999)

**GERKEN CHARLES ERWIN** (480)661-1585
9340 E Wood Dr Scottsdale AZ 85260-7407 • PSW • Mem C • Shepherd Desert Scottsdale AZ • (480)860-1188 • (S 1974 MA)

**GERKEN ERIC**
PO Box 121 Wild Rose WI 54984-0121 • SW • South Wisconsin Milwaukee WI • (414)464-8100 • (S 1998)

**GERMER JAMES T** (785)856-9979
321 W Skylark St Gardner KS 66030-1751 • KS • M Chap • Kansas Topeka KS • (S 1983)

**GIESEKING DAVID EUGENE** (954)316-7333
6251 Palm Trace Landings Dr Apt 303 Davie FL 33314-1884 • degieseking@gateway.net • FG • Mem C • St Paul Weston FL • (954)384-9096 • (RF 1982 MED)

**GILES JACK L DR** (630)271-0169
801 Kimberly Way Lisle IL 60532-3148 • jgiles427@aol.com • NI • Northern Illinois Hillside IL • (RF 1973 MED DED)

**GILLUM HEIDI K** (580)762-0887
312 N 11th St Ponca City OK 74601 • OK • Mem C • First Ponca City OK • (580)762-1111 • (IV 1998)

**GINKEL MARY E**
110 Craven Dr Apt 11 Paola KS 66071 • dcdmary@juno.com • KS • Mem C • First Paola KS • (913)294-3476 • (SP 1998)

**GLASKEY T JASON** (660)826-3347
621 W 7th St Sedalia MO 65301-4117 • MO • Mem C • Our Savior Sedalia MO • (660)827-0226 • (S 1998)

**GLITTENBERG DONALD H** (970)352-4966
2315 Apple Ave Greeley CO 80631-9029 • RM • 09/1996 09/1999 • (S 1990 MS MDIV DED)

**GLOTZHOBER LISA MARIE** (248)601-0777
1153 Ironwood Ct Apt 102 Rochester MI 49307-1271 • MI • Mem C • Living Word Rochester MI • (248)651-5316 • (RF 1998)

**GOLDGRABE ARTHUR D** (509)586-7193
605 W 13th Ave Kennewick WA 99337-4726 • NOW • EM • (S 1957 MED)

**GOMEZ WILLIAM LLOYD** (404)478-0822
C/O Christ Luth Church 2719 Delowe LDr East Point GA 30344 • FG • Mem C • Christ East Point GA • (404)767-2892 • (SP 1992)

**GOOD CYNTHIA M** (217)364-4227
PO Box 344 Dawson IL 62520 • CI • Mem C • Good Shepherd Sherman IL • (217)496-3149 • (RF 1999)

**GRADY ROBERT L** (512)259-3667
1514 Country Squire Dr Cedar Park TX 78613 • robgrady@aol.com • TX • Mem C • King Of Kings Round Rock TX • (512)255-0829 • (RF 1988)

**GRAME CLINT WILLIAM**
787 5th St W Kalispell MT 59901-4739 • KS • 09/1995 09/1999 • (S 1991 MA)

**GRAVES CHRISTOPHER TIMOTHY** (513)231-1031
1262 Meadowbright Ln Cincinnati OH 45230-1353 • cgraves@zionlc.org • OH • Mem C • Zion Cincinnati OH • (513)231-2253 • (RF 1994)

**GREEN CURTIS R** (402)786-3405
13910 Jamestown St Waverly NE 68462-1235 • greenandgrowing@hotmail.com • NEB • 12/1999 • (SP 1984)

**GROHN CAROLYN M**
C/O St John Luth Church 290 7th St Idaho Falls ID 83401-4757 • grohncar@brainerd.net • NOW • Mem C • St John Idaho Falls ID • (208)522-5650 • (SP 1988 MA)

**GUNDERMAN ALAN D** (913)273-7410
400 SW Yorkshire Rd Topeka KS 66606-2262 • agunderman@kslcms.org • KS • Kansas Topeka KS • (S 1966)

**GURGANIOUS BRADY DEL** (707)433-7380
760 Pordon Ln Healdsburg CA 95448 • CNH • Mem C • Good Shepherd Healdsburg CA • (707)433-3835 • (S 2000)

**GUSE TRAVIS BRYAN**
6447 Clayton Rd Apt 1E Saint Louis MO 63117-1867 • stguse@juno.com • EN • 01/2000 • (PO 1992)

**GUTEKUNST RICHARD K** (504)893-6865
1215 W Magnolia St Covington LA 70433-1838 • SO • Mem C • Holy Trinity Covington LA • (504)892-6146 • (SP 1986)

## H

**HAACK JAMES R** (402)593-7936
5712 S 91st St Omaha NE 68127 • kjhaack@earthlink.net • NEB • Mem C • Beaut Savior Omaha NE • (402)331-7376 • (RF 1980 MED)

**HACKER HOLLY J** (414)645-9598
1533 W Orchard St #A Milwaukee WI 53204-2776 • SW • Tchr • St Martini Milwaukee WI • (414)645-4094 • (RF 1975)

**HACKMANN STEVEN M** (513)825-1949
42 Drummond St Cincinnati OH 45218-1021 • dceshack@yahoo.com • OH • Mem C • Messiah Cincinnati OH • (513)825-4768 • (IV 1987)

**HAGGE JOHN B** (314)849-2738
5204 B Salinas Valley Dr Saint Louis MO 63128-4244 • MO • Mem C • Salem Affton MO • (314)352-4454 • (S 1975 MRE)

**HAHN JAMES G**
6241 Thousand Oaks Dr Lakeland FL 33813 • cajhahn@gte.net • FG • Mem C • St Paul Lakeland FL • (863)644-7710 • (S 1966 MED)

**HALL JENNIFER RENEE** (952)884-7560
9101 Blaisdell Ave S Bloomington MN 55420-3619 • gvlc@aol.com • MNS • Mem C • Golden Valley Golden Valley MN • (763)544-2810 • (SP 1992)

**HALL KEVIN J** (507)685-4551
22750 Lind Ave Waterville MN 56096 • omega@means.net • MNS • O Sp Min • Minnesota South Burnsville MN • (SP 1983 MBA)

**HALTOM PAMELA J** (402)721-1093
2434 N Nye Ave #111 Fremont NE 68025-2269 • dcepam@aol.com • NEB • Mem C • Good Shepherd Fremont NE • (402)721-8412 • (SP 1985)

**HAMMONTREE PAUL D** (661)664-7679
3719 Leyburn Bakersfield CA 93311 • IH8S8N@aol.com • CNH • Mem C • St John Bakersfield CA • (661)834-1412 • (IV 1990)

**HANESWORTH TIMOTHY A** (517)787-6178
1115 Union St Jackson MI 49203 • dce4god@juno.com • MI • Tchr • Trinity Jackson MI • (517)784-3135 • (RF 1995)

**HANKE JOHN L** (310)540-4435
706 Knob Hill Redondo Beach CA 90277 • PSW • Mem C • Immanuel Redondo Beach CA • (310)540-4435 • (S 1976 MED)

**HANSEN KENNETH J** (602)993-9424
Christ The Redeemer Luth Ch 8801 N 43rd Ave Phoenix AZ 85051 • hansendce@hotmail.com • PSW • Mem C • Christ Redeemer Phoenix AZ • (623)934-3286 • (IV 1989)

**HANSEN SHERYL MARIE** (817)795-0882
2616 Furrs St # 134 Arlington TX 76006 • TX • Mem C • Grace Arlington TX • (817)274-1626 • (S 1983)

**HARDY KRISTIN ELAYNE** (810)465-4790
44488 Bayview Ave Clinton Township MI 48038 • hirtke24@yahoo.com • MI • Mem C • Trinity Clinton Township MI • (810)463-2921 • (RF 1998)

**HARMS MYRON D** (405)728-1858
10605 Basswood Canyon Rd Oklahoma City OK 73162-6709 • OK • Oklahoma Tulsa OK* • (S 1984)

**HART PATRICK E** (425)821-2793
12429 NE 141st Pl Kirkland WA 98034 • NOW • 09/1997 09/1999 • (IV 1989)

**HART SUSAN A** (303)659-4954
287 S 13th Ave Brighton CO 80601-2228 • schart1@aol.com • RM • Mem C • Zion Brighton CO • (303)659-2339 • (S 1985)

**HARTJEN TRAVIS MICHAEL** (713)224-0684
C/O Redeemer Lutheran Church 1500 W Anderson Ln Austin TX 78757 • TX • Mem C • Redeemer Austin TX • (512)459-1500 • (S 1997)

**HARTMAN JILL DIANNE**
21403 Bentgrass Ct Katy TX 77450-8528 • hartmanjilld@cs.com • S • Mem C • Holy Emmanuel Bloomington MN • (952)888-2345 • (SP 1986)

**HARTMANN DARI R** (847)956-7785
810 E Shady Way Apt 310 Arlington Hts IL 60005-4365 • darihart@aol.com • NI • Mem C • St Paul Mount Prospect IL • (847)255-0332 • (SP 1983)

**HARVAN JAMIE** (708)460-6956
15802 Orlan Brook Apt 2B Orland Park IL 60467 • S • Mem C • Living Word Orland Park IL • (708)403-9673 • (RF 2000)

**HASSTEDT JILL A** (618)277-3236
348 Roanoke Dr Belleville IL 62221-5724 • jillhassle@aol.com • SI • Mem C • Zion Belleville IL • (618)233-2299 • (S 1977 MA)

**HASZ MARTIN ANDREW**
6821 12th St Indianapolis IN 46214 • IN • Mem C • Our Shepherd Indianapolis IN • (317)271-9103 • (RF 1992)

**HAUSCH MICHAEL F** (810)231-3385
7661 E M36 Whitmore Lake MI 48189 • MI • Mem C • St Paul Hamburg MI • (810)231-1033 • (S 1979)

**HAUSER DANIEL L** (281)599-8480
2007 Highland Bay Ct Katy TX 77450-6674 • dahausers@msn.com • TX • Mem C • Crosspoint Katy TX • (281)398-6464 • (RF 1996)

**HAYES MICHAEL EDWARD** (714)974-8955
4945 E Hillside Ave Orange CA 92867 • michaelhayes@juno.com • CNH • 03/2000 • (S 1997)

**HAYNES SHELLI** (714)671-4181
3214 Stonewood Ct Fullerton CA 92835-2330 • tshaynes@earthlink.net • PSW • Mem C • Hope Glendora CA • (626)335-5315 • (IV 1996 MS)

**HAYS JERRY DON** (817)563-7680
257 Country Meadow Dr Mansfield TX 76063-5911 • jhays@luther95.net • TX • Mem C • St John Mansfield TX • (817)473-4889 • (SP 1995)

**HEFLIN ROY WILLIAM** (806)785-1293
4601 52nd St Apt 5B Lubbock TX 79414-3847 • TX • O Sp Min • Texas Austin TX • (SP 1995)

**HEGGEMEIER LYLE M** (952)844-0128
8932 Kell Ave Bloomington MN 55437-1414 • lyle@crossview.com • MNS • Mem C • Cross View Edina MN • (952)941-1094 • (S 1978 MRE)

**HEINZ MICHAEL JOHN** (630)894-9524
300 Crestwood Dr Roselle IL 60172-3019 • mikenfran.@juno.com • NI • Mem C • Trinity Roselle IL • (630)894-3263 • (S 1972)

**HELLYER LISA MARIE**
C/O Lord of Life Lutheran 3105 W 135th St Leawood KS 66224-9540 • dcesjlc@aol.com • KS • Mem C • Lord Of Life Leawood KS • (913)681-5167 • (RF 1987)

**HELM KELLY LYNN** (712)662-4948
113 N 16th St Sac City IA 50583-1517 • sacluth@pionet.net • IW • Mem C • St Paul Sac City IA • (712)662-7029 • (S 1996)

**HENRY ROBERT STEPHEN** (630)665-0929
1000 S Lorraine #215 Wheaton IL 60187 • rshenry1@juno.com • NI • 03/1999 • (RF 1996 MA)

**HENZE CHRISTOPHER LEE**
205 Farlow Dr Knoxville TN 37922 • MDS • Mem C • Grace Knoxville TN • (865)691-2823 • (IV 1998)

**HERBOLD GLENN** (503)233-1488
2255 SE 35th Pl Portland OR 97214-5864 • NOW • Northwest Portland OR* • (RF 1953)

**HEREN THOMAS L** (815)568-5474
403 E Jackson St Marengo IL 60152 • theren@mc.net • NI • Mem C • Zion Marengo IL • (815)568-6564 • (RF 1998)

**HERTLING BARBARA J** (320)251-7195
2718 Serenity Dr Saint Cloud MN 56301-9192 • lsf@stcloudstate.edu • MNN • O Sp Min • Minnesota North Brainerd MN • (SP 1979)

**HETZNER TIMOTHY J** (847)991-6625
123 S Brockway St Palatine IL 60067-6125 • timhetzner@ilcp.org • NI • Mem C • Immanuel Palatine IL • (847)359-1549 • (SP 1978)

**HICKS BONNIE** (805)497-7110
603 Hampshire #453 Westlake Village CA 91361 • PSW • Mem C • Christ King Newbury Park CA • (805)498-2217 • (IV 1999)

**HILDEBRANDT MARY E** (972)315-7345
C/O Christ Our Savior 140 Heartz Rd Coppell TX 75019 • mary@coslcs.org • TX • Mem C • Christ Our Savior Coppell TX • (972)462-0225 • (SP 1994)

**HILLER PETER E** (763)576-0839
15430 Argon St NW Ramsey MN 55303-4259 • hillerpm@prodigy.net • MNS • Mem C • Family Christ Andover MN • (612)434-7337 • (SP 1991)

**HINCHEY MARGARET R** (303)773-9857
10906 E Berry Ave Englewood CO 80111-3904 • mhinchey@aol.com • RM • Mem C • Our Father Littleton CO • (303)779-1332 • (SP 1975 MED)

**HINCKFOOT MICHAEL S** (281)251-1423
5218 Nodaway Ln Spring TX 77379-8048 • readezra710@aol.com • TX • Mem C • Trinity Klein TX • (281)376-5773 • (CQ 1992)

**HINKEL SARAH BETH** (913)393-2050
525 N Somerset Ter #17 Olathe KS 66062 • dcesarah@juno.com • KS • Mem C • Beautiful Sav Olathe KS • (913)780-6023 • (S 1994)

**HINMAN STEVEN R**
C/O First Lutheran Church 1323 S Magnolia Ave Monrovia CA 91016-4021 • PSW • Mem C • First Monrovia CA • (626)357-3543 • (IV 1997)

**HINTZ DENNIS L** (785)235-9684
816 SW Buchanan St Topeka KS 66606-1428 • hintzdl@cjnetworks.com • KS • Mem C • St John Topeka KS • (785)354-7132 • (S 1971 MED)

**HINZ DAVID WALTER** (320)679-0645
C/O Zion Lutheran Church 401 Highway 65 S Mora MN 55051-1800 • zionlc@ncis.com • MNN • Mem C • Zion Mora MN • (320)679-1094 • (RF 1996)

**HINZ DIANNE M**
Moeller Hall 205 S Main St Concordia MO 64020-0719 • MO • Tchr • St Paul Concordia MO • (660)463-2238 • (S 1994)

**HISCHKE KEVIN** (303)255-0860
10638 Varese Ln Northglenn CO 80234 • khischke@aol.com • RM • Mem C • Risen Savior Broomfield CO • (303)469-3521 • (S 1983)

**HOEWISCH DARYL DANIEL** (507)764-2040
875 110th St Sherburn MN 56171 • MNS • Mem C • St John Sherburn MN • (507)764-5312 • (S 1997)

**HOLLMANN JOHN E** (480)832-2300
4215 E Aspen Ave Mesa AZ 85206-1128 • PSW • Mem C • St Luke Mesa AZ • (480)969-4414 • (S 1974)

**HOOK ALTA M** (901)861-1574
351 Cascade Falls Collierville TN 38017 • altah@juno.com • MDS • Mem C • Faith Collierville TN • (901)853-4673 • (S 1999)

**HOOVER ANDREA NICOLE** (219)482-1812
3816 Newport Ave Apt 4 Fort Wayne IN 46805-1374 • anhdce@hotmail.com • CI • 08/2000 • (RF 1999)

**HOOVER DAVID C** (503)643-9160
6755 SW Wilson Ave Beaverton OR 97008-5504 • david³c³hoover@msn.com • NOW • Mem C • Good Shepherd Portland OR • (503)244-4558 • (CQ 1995)

**HOPPENRATH MARY CHRISTINE** (970)224-0156
1225 W Prospect Rd # W 91 Fort Collins CO 80526-5631 • dcegirl@juno.com • RM • Mem C • Peace W Christ Fort Collins CO • (970)226-4721 • (IV 1994)

**HOPPER DEANN LYNN** (507)388-1766
115 Marion Ln Mankato MN 56001 • mdhopper@prairie.lakes.com • MNS • Mem C • Hosanna Mankato MN • (507)388-1766 • (S 1995)

**HOWARD BRENT ALAN** (720)870-9774
17912 E Brunswick Pl Aurora CO 80013 • bhoward@idcomm.com • RM • Mem C • Mount Olive Aurora CO • (303)755-9123 • (S 1996)

**HOWARD ROGER ALAN**
1946 Heatherlawn Dr Toledo OH 43614 • rhoward@trinity.pvt.k12.oh.us • OH • Mem C • Trinity Toledo OH • (419)385-2651 • (PO 1986)

**HUBBARD KARNA RENEE** (410)628-6032
1011 Misty Lynn Cir Apt F Cockeysville MD 21030-4653 • SE • Mem C • St John Blenheim Long Green MD • (410)592-8018 • (SP 1994)

**HUEBNER JASON WILLIAM** (847)429-1920
1023 Bellevue Elgin IL 60120 • NI • Mem C • St John Elgin IL • (847)741-0814 • (RF 1996)

## I

**IHSSEN TIM** (831)335-3739
PO Box 706 Mount Hermon CA 95041 • beeflips@juno.com • CNH • O Sp Min • Calif/Nevada/Hawaii San Francisco CA • (415)468-2336 • (PO 1992)

**INOUYE BRIAN CHRISTOPHER** (714)637-5824
1203 E Darby Ave Orange CA 92865-2909 • elroy@deltanet.com • PSW • Mem C • St Paul Orange CA • (714)637-2640 • (IV 1996)

**INSELMANN CYNTHIA LYNN** (616)894-4846
4612 Lasley St Montague MI 49437 • dcestjames@aol.com • MI • Mem C • St James Montague MI • (231)894-8471 • (SP 1998)

## J

**JACKSON LELAND P** (316)275-9712
1001 Fleming St Garden City KS 67846-6226 • tlcqck@odsgc.com • KS • Mem C • Trinity Garden City KS • (316)276-3110 • (S 1980)

**JACOB KAREN LYNN** (415)587-6849
95 Moneta Way San Francisco CA 94112 • EN • Mem C • West Portal San Francisco CA • (415)661-0242 • (PO 1997)

**JAMESON LEON CLIVE** (414)479-0368
1103 S 73rd St Milwaukee WI 53214-3130 • dcejameson@splcwa.org • SW • Mem C • St Paul West Allis WI • (414)541-6250 • (S 1999)

**JANDER COREEN TRACEE** (708)209-3735
7400 Augusta St #58W River Forest IL 60305-1402 • coreen³jander@hotmail.com • IN • 01/1999 • (RF 1996)

**JANDER LOUIS C** (281)970-4149
10810 Glenora Dr Houston TX 77065-4253 • ljander@aol.com • TX • Texas Austin TX • (S 1966 MED)

**JANETZKE GARY A** (248)624-5708
2055 Meadow Ridge Dr Walled Lake MI 48390-2658 • janetzke9@juno.com • MI • Mem C • St Matthew Walled Lake MI • (248)624-7676 • (RF 1974)

**JANK TIMOTHY A** (219)636-7101
1596 S 150 W Albion IN 46701-9695 • camp@lutherhaven.org • IN • O Sp Min • Indiana Fort Wayne IN • (S 1991)

**JENSEN BRIAN LESLIE** (815)695-5190
12019 Lisbon Rd Newark IL 60541-9574 • bljensen@juno.com • NI • Mem C • Cross Yorkville IL • (630)553-7335 • (RF 1982)

**JOHNSON LEANN JEAN** (920)832-4085
1509 W Franklin St Appleton WI 54914-3459 • lejohn@athenet.net • NW • Mem C • Good Shepherd Appleton WI • (920)734-9643 • (SP 1992 MED)

**JOHNSON META JEAN** (914)776-0392
1376 Midland Ave Apt 306 Bronxville NY 10708 • metavlc@vlc-ny.org • AT • Mem C • The Village Bronxville NY • (914)337-0207 • (S 1992)

**JOHNSON RICHARD DELAINE** (206)840-6947
2617 20th St SE Puyallup WA 98374-1492 • gslct@juno.com • NOW • Mem C • Good Shepherd Tacoma WA • (253)473-4848 • (PO 1982)

**JOHNSON RODNEY HAROLD**
8338 W Corrine Dr Peoria AZ 85381-5171 • MT • Mem C • Grace Hamilton MT • (406)363-1924 • (S 1978)

**JOHNSON STEVEM M**
PO Box 9042 Woodland Park CO 80866 • RM • Mem C • Faith Woodland Park CO • (719)687-2303 • (RF 2000)

**JOHNSON WADE** (330)733-2187
2860 Robindale Ave Akron OH 44312 • dcewade@yahoo.com • OH • Mem C • Faith Kent OH • (330)673-6633 • (SP 1999)

**JOHNSON WILLIAM R** (763)315-5408
7095 Deerwood Ln Maple Grove MN 55369 • bjohnson@beautifulsaviorlc.org • MNS • Mem C • Beautiful Savior Plymouth MN • (612)550-1000 • (SP 1980)

**JOHNSTON JULIE** (314)752-2377
C/O Luth Church Missouri Synod 1333 S Kirkwood Rd Saint Louis MO 63122-7226 • ic³johnstj@lcms.org • MO • S Ex/S • Missouri Saint Louis MO • (314)317-4550 • (S 1982)

**JONAS SCOTT ERIC** (619)627-0785
4134 Mt Alifan Pl #G San Diego CA 92111 • PSW • Mem C • St Paul San Diego CA • (619)272-6363 • (CQ 1996)

**JORDENING JONATHAN DAVID**
14531 Oak Chase Dr Houston TX 77062-2286 • jjordening@gdlc.org • TX • Mem C • Gloria Dei Houston TX • (281)333-4535 • (S 1987)

**JORGENSEN STEVE ANDREW** (816)228-4048
705 NW 12th St Blue Springs MO 64015 • sjorgensen@aol.com • MO • Mem C • Timothy Blue Springs MO • (816)228-5300 • (CQ 1991)

**JULIANO JANET** (330)920-8464
C/O Redeemer Lutheran Church 2141 5th St Cuyahoga Falls OH 44221-3213 • rlcdce@aol.com • OH • Mem C • Redeemer Cuyahoga Falls OH • (330)923-1445 • (S 1990 MPED)

**JUNG SCOTT L** (814)368-5939
525 E Main St Bradford PA 16701 • scottdce@penn.com • EA • Mem C • Grace Bradford PA • (814)362-3244 • (S 1998)

**JUST JANET L** (818)704-8102
7946 Rudnick Ave Canoga Park CA 91304-4709 • PSW • Mem C • Canoga Park Canoga Park CA • (818)348-5714 • (SP 1977)

## K

**KADING DOUGLAS R** (712)262-5963
523 E 13th St Spencer IA 51301-4831 • IW • O Sp Min • Iowa West Fort Dodge IA • (S 1971)

**KAMIS LISA ANN** (630)858-3756
416 Gregory Ave Apt 1A Glendale Heights IL 60139-2394 • NI • Mem C • Family In Faith Glendale Heights IL • (630)653-5030 • (RF 1998)

**KARLEN FRED W** (707)538-7410
5743 Los Alamos Ct Santa Rosa CA 95409-4470 • karlen@stluke-lcms.org • CNH • Mem C • St Luke Santa Rosa CA • (707)545-6772 • (S 1983 MED)

**KARPENKO WILLIAM O II DR** (219)477-5422
1402 Boca Lago Dr Valparaiso IN 46383-4420 • Bill.Karpenko@valpo.edu • IN • END • Indiana Fort Wayne IN • (CQ 1977 MA PHD)

**KAUFMANN JOY CELENA** (281)361-0814
3738 Clear Falls Dr Kingwood TX 77339-1959 • pxmedia@kingwoodcable.com • TX • Mem C • Lamb Of God Humble TX • (281)446-8427 • (RF 1994)

**KAUFMANN TIMOTHY PHILIP** (281)361-0814
3738 Clear Falls Dr Kingwood TX 77339-1959 • pxmedia@kingwoodcable.com • TX • Mem C • Lamb Of God Humble TX • (281)446-8427 • (RF 1992)

**KEANE CYNTHIA M** (702)880-9123
7575 Hauck Cr Las Vegas NV 89139 • sumo4me@aol.com • PSW • 12/1996 12/1999 • (IV 1992)

**KEHE MICHAEL** (314)653-6019
14439 Ocean Side Dr Florissant MO 63034-3040 • mikehe01@earthlink.net • MO • Mem C • Grace Chapel Saint Louis MO • (314)868-3232 • (RF 1983)

**KEITHLEY THOMAS W** (281)353-4413
C/O Resurrection Luth Church 1612 Meadow Edge Ln Spring TX 77388-6227 • tkeit20507@aol.com • TX • Mem C • Resurrection Spring TX • (281)353-4413 • (RF 1980 MA)

**KELLER CHRISTINA ARLENE** (760)333-1842
73 373 Country Club #3403 Palm Desert CA 92260 • christina@oursaviors.org • PSW • Mem C • Our Savior Palm Springs CA • (760)327-5611 • (IV 1999)

**KELLER CONNIE J** (248)332-1038
321 Douglas Dr Bloomfield Hills MI 48304 • MI • Tchr • LHS Northwest Rochester Hills MI • (810)852-6677 • (RF 1976)

**KERKMAN RANDALL J** (512)835-6755
11716 Barchetta Dr Austin TX 78758-3733 • rkerkman@redeemer.net • TX • Mem C • Redeemer Austin TX • (512)459-1500 • (RF 1975)

**KERSTEN KEVIN R**
225 W El Norte Pkwy #221 Escondido CA 92026 • PSW • Mem C • Community Escondido CA • (760)739-1650 • (S 1996)

**KIGHTLINGER TIMOTHY PAUL** (402)895-8780
17018 Orchard Ave Omaha NE 68135-1452 • timkightlinger@divineshepherd.org • NEB • Mem C • Divine Shepher Omaha NE • (402)895-1500 • (S 1993)

**KING WAYNE A**
04885 Boyne City Rd Boyne City MI 49712-9217 • MI • Mem C • Christ Boyne City MI • (231)582-9301 • (SP 1982)

**KLEINEDLER SHARLENE A** (313)732-0586
5385 Lamp Lighter Ln Flushing MI 48433-2457 • MI • Mem C • Holy Cross Flushing MI • (810)659-5926 • (S 1976 MA)

**KLEINERT BRUCE** (209)832-7315
1411 Maple Ct Tracy CA 95376-4321 • CNH • Mem C • St Paul Tracy CA • (209)835-7438 • (PO 1981)

**KOEHLER KENNETH W** (701)282-5098
307 10 1/2 Ave E West Fargo ND 58078-3031 • kkoehler@juno.com • ND • Mem C • St Andrew West Fargo ND • (701)282-4195 • (SP 1975)

**KOHLS TRACI LEIGH** (952)353-2328
7880 Co Rd 33 New Germany MN 55367 • tracik@xtratyme.com • MNS • Mem C • Good Shepherd Glencoe MN • (320)864-6157 • (SP 1997)

**KONRAD KARLA KAY** (806)788-0458
6195 34th St Lubbock TX 79407-3119 • TX • O Sp Min • University Lubbock TX • (806)763-3644 • (SP 1985)

**KOPPENHAUER INGER**
1645 W Friess Dr Phoenix AZ 85023-6171 • PSW • Mem C • St Mark Phoenix AZ • (602)992-1980 • (IV 1997)

**KORTMEYER LEAH R** (402)336-3108
114 N Madison St Oneill NE 68763-1204 • clc@inebraska.com • NEB • Mem C • Christ O Neill NE • (402)336-1884 • (S 1993)

**KOSBAB STEPHANIE JANE**
1437C Skyridge Dr Crystal Lake IL 60014 • NI • Mem C • Fellowship Of Faith Mc Henry IL • (815)759-0739 • (S 2000)

**KRANICH JEFFREY D** (206)762-1739
2431 SW Myrtle St Seattle WA 98106-1683 • hopeseatle@aol.com • NOW • Mem C • Hope Seattle WA • (206)937-9330 • (PO 1980)

**KRENTZ PAUL ARNO** (512)819-7575
103 Parque Vista Dr Georgetown TX 78626-4533 • Krentztx@txdistlcms.org • TX • Texas Austin TX • (S 1971)

**KRUEGER ROD MATTHEW**
2210 Brown Ct Naperville IL 60565 • NI • Mem C • St Paul Chicago IL • (708)867-5044 • (RF 1998)

**KRUSE LAVERN R** (248)624-3525
2270 Cedar Crest Blvd Walled Lake MI 48390-3952 • Lavern.Kruse@st-matthew.org • MI • Mem C • St Matthew Walled Lake MI • (248)624-7676 • (S 1966 MED)

**KUERSCHNER NICHOLE J M**
2658 Scotland Ct #209 Mounds View MN 55112 • MNS • Tchr • Prince Of Peace Spring Lake Park MN • (612)786-1755 • (RF 1999)

**KUNZE ELLEN L** (520)790-8802
6648 E 39th St Tucson AZ 85730-1612 • PSW • Mem C • Fountain Life Tucson AZ • (520)747-1213 • (S 1983)

**KURTH ROBIN RENEA** (612)552-5981
430 Mendota Rd W Apt 206 Saint Paul MN 55118 • MNS • Mem C • Old Emanuel Inver Grove Heights MN • (651)457-3929 • (SP 1998)

**KUSCHEL MATTHEW WAYNE** (763)784-8417
19148 Carson St NW Elk River MN 55330-2689 • mattwk@juno.com • MNS • Mem C • Good Shepherd Circle Pines MN • (763)784-8417 • (SP 1988 MA)

## L

**LA CROIX JENNIFER A** (319)848-7632
Lutheran Camp Perkins HC 64 Box 9384 Ketchum ID 83340 • bjlacroix@juno.com • NOW • Bethlehem Fort Wayne IN • (SP 1997)

**LA CROIX ROBERT A** (208)774-3372
Lutheran Camp Perkins HC 64 Box 9384 Ketchum ID 83340 • bjlacroix@juno.com • NOW • Bethlehem Fort Wayne IN • (SP 1995)

**LAMBETH ROBERT A** (915)581-9067
7225 Golden Hawk Dr El Paso TX 79912-7665 • RM • Mem C • Ascension El Paso TX • (915)833-1009 • (IV 1989 MA)

**LANE KATHLEEN R** (920)735-0282
1741 N Eugene St Appleton WI 54914-2426 • kjrlane@aol.com • NW • Mem C • Faith Appleton WI • (920)739-9191 • (SP 1978)

**LANGDON ARTHUR R** (206)531-4981
1116 116th St S Tacoma WA 98444-4028 • artsdg@msn.com • NOW • Mem C • Our Savior Tacoma WA • (253)531-2112 • (S 1968)

**LANGE PETER ARNO** (913)242-8049
1113 S College St Ottawa KS 66067-3617 • faithpal@yahoo.com • KS • Mem C • Faith Ottawa KS • (785)242-1906 • (IV 1991)

**LANGEFELD RHONDA KAY** (813)535-5344
118 Peace Blvd O Fallon IL 62269 • SI • 09/1996 • (S 1979)

**LANNING LORI ANN** (941)939-5429
2855 Winkler Ave #119 Fort Myers FL 33916 • llanning@sml.org • FG • Mem C • St Michael Fort Myers FL • (941)939-4711 • (SP 1999)

**LAUFER JOHN E**
261 Misty Isle #C Las Vegas NV 89107 • johnlaufer@hotmail.com • PSW • St Paul Flint MI • (S 1981)

**LAVRENZ CYNTHIA JEAN** (316)271-9080
2313 C St Garden City KS 67846-2818 • KS • Mem C • Trinity Garden City KS • (316)276-3110 • (S 1999)

**LE BORIOUS PETER J** (330)869-8819
1042 Emma Ave Akron OH 44302-1114 • dcepete@juno.com • EN • Mem C • Fairlawn Akron OH • (330)836-7286 • (SP 1991 MED)

**LE CAKES DEREK G**
17 Founders Way #8 Saint Louis MO 63105-3076 • dermyfam@aol.com • AT • O Sp Min • Atlantic Bronxville NY • (914)337-5700 • (SP 1995)

**LE FEVERE VERLYN E** (319)396-9745
3611 F Ave NW Cedar Rapids IA 52405-1958 • IE • Mem C • Concordia Cedar Rapids IA • (319)396-9035 • (RF 1966)

**LEE JANICE L** (209)238-9728
1120 Cedar Creek Ct #227 Modesto CA 95355 • CNH • Mem C • Grace Modesto CA • (209)522-8890 • (S 1999)

**LEESE WILLIAM CHARLES** (314)909-7286
1021 Danworth Ct Saint Louis MO 63122-7139 • wcleese@aolcom • MO • Mem C • Concordia Kirkwood MO • (314)822-7772 • (CQ 1986 MDIV)

**LESLIE RICHARD A**
C/O St Timothy Luth Church 14225 Hargrave Houston TX 77070 • TX • Mem C • St Timothy Houston TX • (281)469-2457 • (CQ 1988)

**LIBROJO PETER JUDE** (805)452-7482
Our Savior Lutheran Church 4725 S Bradley Rd Santa Maria CA 93455-5051 • calimyce@hotmail.com • CNH • 06/2000 • (IV 1995)

**LIGHTBODY MARY E** (815)385-5523
1205 Clover Ln Mc Henry IL 60050-4605 • dcemel@yahoo.com • NI • Mem C • Immanuel Crystal Lake IL • (815)459-1441 • (RF 1991)

**LILLEY JOAN E** (714)588-0057
25585 Mont Pointe Lake Forest CA 92630-5961 • lilley@cui.edu • PSW • SHS/C • Pacific Southwest Irvine CA • (949)854-3232 • (CQ 1992)

**LINDEMAN LISA B** (810)714-4245
200 Trealout Dr #12 Fenton MI 48430 • bogielind2@cs.com • MI • Mem C • Trinity Fenton MI • (810)629-7861 • (SP 1999)

**LINDEMAN TIMOTHY J** (303)425-0403
6424 W 82nd Dr Arvada CO 80003-1720 • RM • Mem C • Peace Arvada CO • (303)424-4454 • (S 1982 MA)

**LOESCH JONATHAN** (909)899-8219
11535 Claridge Dr Rancho Cucamonga CA 91730-7246 • PSW • Mem C • Shepherd Hills Alta Loma CA • (909)989-6500 • (S 1983)

**LOHMAN JAMES H** (314)821-7268
1289 Oakshire Ln Saint Louis MO 63122-7119 • james.lohman@cph.org • MO • S Ex/S • Missouri Saint Louis MO • (314)317-4550 • (CQ 1983 MA)

**LUEDERS KENNETH D** (913)271-0808
C/O Prince Of Peace Luth Ch 3625 SW Wanamaker Rd Topeka KS 66614-4566 • kenldce@aol.com • KS • Mem C • Prince Of Peace Topeka KS • (785)271-0808 • (S 1985)

**LUTTRELL RICHARD D** (916)663-3501
6407 Brodie Dr Newcastle CA 95658 • rdl@inreach.com • CNH • P/Tchr • Town & Country Sacramento CA • (916)481-2542 • (S 1968 MA)

**LYTLE AARON L** (520)615-2683
1220 W Magee Rd Tucson AZ 85704-3325 • mclytle@netzero.net • EN • Mem C • Ascension Tucson AZ • (520)297-3095 • (S 1998)

## M

**MAILAND ROGER LEE** (314)845-8568
4808 Towne South Rd Saint Louis MO 63128-2818 • rmailand@stlnet.com • MO • Missouri Saint Louis MO* • (314)317-4550 • (S 1963 MED)

**MALLEOS NICK**
1043 Churchill Boling Brook IL 60440 • NI • Mem C • Bethany Naperville IL • (630)355-2198 • (RF 1989)

**MARKIN JEROLD D** (852)2899-0947
C3 Tai Tam Gardens 700 Tai Tam Reservior Rd Tai Tam HONG KONG • jdmarkin@att.net.hk • PSW • S Miss • Pacific Southwest Irvine CA • (949)854-3232 • (S 1970 MED)

**MARTING PAUL** (661)664-8189
3504 Camino Minorca Bakersfield CA 93311-2731 • paulmarting@hotmail.com • CNH • Mem C • Grace Santa Maria CA • (805)925-3818 • (IV 1994)

**MATHEY MICHAEL J**
2004 Bellevue Apt A Maplewood MO 63143-2404 • mjmathee@aol.com • MI • Mem C • St Mark West Bloomfield MI • (248)363-0741 • (RF 1996)

**MATTOON STEVEN HOWARD** (714)589-3532
327 E Jacaranda Ave Orange CA 92867 • PSW • Mem C • Zion Fallbrook CA • (760)728-8288 • (IV 1994)

**MAY CAITLIN LEE**
40 Borica St San Francisco CA 94127 • katywood@aol.com • NOW • 03/1998 03/2000 • (PO 1997)

**MC CASLIN GREGG ALAN** (303)763-9104
12752 W Asbury Pl Lakewood CO 80228-4324 • RM • Mem C • Concordia Lakewood CO • (303)989-5260 • (IV 1989)

**MC CLELLAN RHONDA LEE** (402)423-8663
7201 S 33rd St Lincoln NE 68516-5767 • NEB • Mem C • Christ Lincoln NE • (402)483-7774 • (S 1995)

**MC CONNELL JAMES H**
1127 Thackeray Ln Pflugerville TX 78660 • mcconnellj@concordia.edu • TX • Tchr • Texas Austin TX • (S 1977 MA)

**MC COURT SHIRLEY J** (952)442-2833
868 Cross Point Rd Waconia MN 55387-9781 • mnmccourt@mail.com • MNS • 02/1994 02/2000 • (SP 1984)

**MC KINNEY ROBERT**
1008 Hillview Cir Simi Valley CA 93065-4307 • PSW • Mem C • Trinity Simi Valley CA • (805)526-2429 • (V 1969)

**MEINZ JEFFREY EDWARD** (815)784-2756
C/O Walcamp Outdoor Ministries 32653 5 Points Rd Kingston IL 60145-8443 • fozziemeinz@tbcnet.com • NI • O Sp Min • Northern Illinois Hillside IL • (S 1996)

**MELCHER HEATHER KATHERINE** (509)982-2819
1658 N Kulm Rd Ritzville WA 99169 • NOW • 04/2000 • (S 1999)

**MENZEL EUGENE W** (504)461-8658
4210 Saint Elizabeth Dr Kenner LA 70065-1645 • gwmenz@aol.com • SO • Southern New Orleans LA • (S 1969 MS)

**MERRICK BRANDON**
1209 NE 18th Ave Fort Lauderdale FL 33304-2411 • NOW • 08/1999 • (IV 1998)

**MERRICK SHARON**
356 Hull Ave San Jose CA 95125-1645 • sharonm123@aol.copm • CNH • 04/1999 • (IV 1994)

**MERTES JOHN H** (818)709-2195
10601 Owensmouth Ave Chatsworth CA 91311-2152 • frog61535@aol.com • PSW • Mem C • Our Savior First Granada Hills CA • (818)363-9505 • (CQ 1992 MBA)

**MEWS KURT F** (419)599-7914
0-899 Road 11-C Rt #5 Napoleon OH 43545 • OH • Mem C • St Paul Napoleon OH • (419)592-3535 • (RF 1984 MA)

**MEYER CHRISTINA M** (660)886-5166
418 Slater St Marshall MO 65340-1244 • MO • Mem C • Our Redeemer Marshall MO • (660)886-2270 • (SP 2000)

**MEYER DIANE MARY** (218)327-1321
21466 County Road 483 Grand Rapids MN 55744 • djmeyer@uslink • MNN • Mem C • First Grand Rapids MN • (218)326-5453 • (SP 1982 MA)

**MEYER JAMES T**
1907 Birchwood Dr Barnhart MO 63012-2610 • jimjenm@aol.com • MO • Mem C • Concordia Kirkwood MO • (314)822-7772 • (IV 1995)

**MEYER PHILIP J** (208)522-5650
3856 E 300 N Rigby ID 83442 • pjmeyer@srv.net • NOW • 04/1999 • (SP 1989)

**MEYER ROBERT E** (208)733-3294
3563 N 2700 E Twin Falls ID 83301 • MO • EM • (RF 1953 MA)

**MEYER RYAN WILLIAM** (972)396-9496
638 Mountain Side Dr Allen TX 75002-4736 • TX • Mem C • Lord of Life Plano TX • (972)867-5588 • (S 1997)

**MEYERS DENNIS J** (973)383-1066
37 Newton Sparta Rd Newton NJ 07860-2745 • NJ • Our Savior Grand Rapids MI • (S 1983)

**MIEGER PAUL A**
7620 N El Dorado #288 Stockton CA 95207 • skylark63@aol.com • CNH • Mem C • Trinity Stockton CA • (209)464-1936 • (IV 1987)

**MIELKE HEIDI PATRICIA** (317)596-9981
7898 Beanblossom Cir Indianapolis IN 46256 • hpm@hclc.in.lcms.org • IN • Mem C • Holy Cross Indianapolis IN • (317)823-5801 • (RF 1997)

**MILBRATH BRUCE** (361)572-8150
4405 N Navarro #208 Victoria TX 77904 • TX • Mem C • Grace Victoria TX • (361)573-2232 • (S 1998)

**MILLER JAYLENE M** (281)257-2721
8227 Amurwood Dr Tomball TX 77375-2809 • gsus1st@hotmail.com • TX • Mem C • St Timothy Houston TX • (281)469-2457 • (IV 1990)

**MILLER LAURIE J**
PO Box 153 Maineville OH 45039-0153 • mnmiller@earthlink.net • OH • 08/1998 • (S 1996)

**MILLER TODD ANTHONY** (419)462-1230
7712 W Hampton Ave Apt 2 Milwaukee WI 53218 • dcetodd@excite.com • SW • Mem C • Elm Grove Elm Grove WI • (262)797-2970 • (RF 1997)

**MOELLER JEFFERY R** (314)653-1604
12880 High Crest Black Jack MO 63033-4549 • EN • Mem C • Chapel Cross Saint Louis MO • (314)741-3737 • (S 1987)

**MOELLER STEVEN W** (630)351-5322
520 Dover Dr Roselle IL 60172-2611 • moellers@trinityroselle.com • NI • Mem C • Trinity Roselle IL • (630)894-3263 • (RF 1978 MA)

**MOEN RICHARD R** (507)685-2185
PO Box 382 Morristown MN 55052-0382 • MNS • Mem C • Trinity Faribault MN • (507)334-6579 • (SP 1992)

**MOERBE RANDALL R** (409)776-4089
5015 Whispering Oaks Dr College Station TX 77845-7672 • bryrandy@mail.myriad.net • TX • Mem C • Bethel Bryan TX • (979)822-2742 • (S 1973)

**MOORE DEBORAH SUE** (913)677-5350
6917 Lamar Ave Overland Park KS 66204-1428 • deb@tlcms.org • KS • Mem C • Trinity Mission KS • (913)432-5441 • (RF 1987)

**MOORHEAD MICHELLE ORA**
2012 215th St Grand Mound IA 52751-9650 • IE • Mem C • Grace De Witt IA • (319)659-9153 • (SP 1991)

**MORRIS EDWARD WILLIAM** (702)423-3808
1160 Harrigan Rd Fallon NV 89406 • dceewm@oasisol.com • CNH • Mem C • St John Fallon NV • (702)423-4146 • (S 1996)

**MORTENSON PHYLLIS J** (262)886-2370
3112 91st St Sturtevant WI 53177 • jpamortenson@juno.com • SW • Tchr • Concordia Racine WI • (262)554-1659 • (RF 1977)

**MOSES TIMOTHY JAMES**
C/O Redeemer Lutheran Church 2215 N Wahsatch Ave Colorado Springs CO 80907-6939 • RM • Mem C • Redeemer Colorado Springs CO • (719)633-7661 • (IV 1992)

**MOYER JILL A** (512)447-6284
9016 Marsh Dr Austin TX 78748-5145 • dingerj@aol.com • TX • Mem C • Christ Austin TX • (512)442-5844 • (S 1991)

**MUCK ALAN D** (314)991-3619
10416 Gold Dust Ave Saint Louis MO 63131-2821 • amuck726@aol.com • MO • Mem C • Village Saint Louis MO • (314)993-1834 • (CQ 1983)

**MUELLER GREGORY G** (309)795-9812
14328 161st St W Taylor Ridge IL 61284-9359 • dcehog@revealed.net • CI • Mem C • St Matthew Milan IL • (309)787-4295 • (RF 1979)

**MULL JOHN DAVID** (972)274-2118
119 Craddock Dr Glenn Heights TX 75154-2049 • jmull@crossofchrist.org • TX • Mem C • Cross Christ De Soto TX • (972)223-9340 • (SP 1997)

**MURAKAMI GREGORY** (708)345-5910
1001 N 12th Ave Melrose Park IL 60160-3525 • NI • 04/1994 04/2000 • (RF 1973 MA)

**MURDOCK LISA FRANCES**
2439 Andreo Ave Torance CA 90501-4405 • seadog49@hotmail.com • PSW • Mem C • Ascension Torrance CA • (310)793-0071 • (IV 1998)

**MURPHY MAX JOHN** (714)289-8288
382 N Shaffer St Orange CA 92866 • dcemax2@aol.com • PSW • Mem C • St John Orange CA • (714)288-4400 • (IV 1992)

**MUSSELMAN HILARY** (916)351-5789
C/O Mt Olive Luth Church 320 Montrose Dr Folsom CA 95630 • hmusselman@ttns.net • CNH • Mem C • Mount Olive Folsom CA • (916)985-2984 • (IV 1996)

## N

**NAGY SCOTT P**
2728 Delgar St Pittsburgh PA 15214-2804 • EA • Mem C • St Matthew Pittsburgh PA • (412)321-7720 • (RF 1989)

**NAMANNY CYNTHIA ANN** (601)591-0098
67 Springview Dr Brandon MS 39042 • orlcms@bellsouth.net • SO • Mem C • Our Redeemer Jackson MS • (601)372-7256 • (SP 1978)

**NELSEN CYNTHIA KAY** (630)893-8114
893 Mensching Rd Roselle IL 60172-1827 • NI • Mem C • St Luke Itasca IL • (630)773-0396 • (SP 1987)

**NELSON ANITA**
319 Regal Oaks Cir White Hall AR 71602-3053 • RM • 04/1997 04/2000 • (S 1989)

**NELSON GEORGE W**
6308 Quivira Shawnee KS 66216 • gwnone@aol.com • KS • Mem C • Hope Shawnee KS • (913)631-6940 • (S 1971)

**NELSON THOMAS E** (907)789-5101
8678 Dudley St Juneau AK 99801-9050 • mustangsru@aol.com • MNS • 04/1999 • (SP 1991)

**NERGER AMY E**
Christ Lutheran Church 315 N Shipley St Seaford DE 19973-2315 • SE • Mem C • Christ Seaford DE • (302)629-9755 • (RF 1999)

**NEUMILLER CRAIG C** (360)574-8293
102 NE 147th St Vancouver WA 98685-5749 • compuserve102634.3673 • NOW • Mem C • St John Vancouver WA • (360)573-1461 • (PO 1987)

**NIEBUHR KURT WILLIAM** (281)648-9926
1820 Barretts Glen Dr Pearland TX 77581 • kniebuhr@bayou.uh.edu • TX • Mem C • Pacific Southwest Irvine CA • (SP 1979)

**NITZ ANGELA M** (214)341-6352
8600 Coppertowne #1002 Dallas TX 75243 • teamnitz@concentric.net • TX • Mem C • Holy Cross Dallas TX • (214)358-4396 • (RF 1997)

**NOBLE NADINE J** (651)322-2803
15784 Cicerone Ct Rosemount MN 55068-2565 • MNS • Mem C • Christ Eagan MN • (651)454-4091 • (SP 1985)

**NOLL DAVID C** (509)926-9950
12509 E 26th Ave Spokane WA 99216-0369 • NOW • Mem C • Redeemer Spokane WA • (509)926-6363 • (S 1983)

**NORRIS SUSAN CAROL** (863)699-0768
114 Mc Kinley Ave NE Lake Placid FL 33852-5874 • s³norris123@yahoo.com • FG • Mem C • Trinity Lake Placid FL • (863)465-5253 • (BR 1980)

**NORTON TIMOTHY PAUL** (209)369-4373
2401 Aladdin Way Lodi CA 95242-2806 • meca@africaonline.co.ci • NOW • S Miss • Northwest Portland OR • (PO 1995)

**NUMMELA PAMELA RUTH** (913)652-0182
9320 Outlook Dr Overland Park KS 66207-2428 • nummelapr@aol.com • KS • Mem C • Bethany Shawnee Mission KS • (913)648-2228 • (S 1974)

**NUMMELA THOMAS A** (913)652-0182
9320 Outlook Overland Park KS 66207 • tom.nummela@cph.org • MO • S Ex/S • Missouri Saint Louis MO • (314)317-4550 • (S 1975 MA MCMU)

## O

**OESCH JOEL CALEB** (808)239-6893
47-531 Waipaipai St Kaneohe HI 96744-5448 • CNH • Mem C • St Mark Kaneohe HI • (808)247-4565 • (IV 1998)

**OLDENBURG CRAIG S** (719)687-3560
PO Box 9042 Woodland Park CO 80866-9042 • lvr@lvr.org • RM • Rocky Mountain Aurora CO • (RF 1981)

**OLLHOFF JAMES D** (952)431-0866
6707 Foliage Ct W Rosemount MN 55068-1279 • ollhoff@charter.net • MNS • SHS/C • Minnesota South Burnsville MN • (SP 1983 MA)

**OLSEN LINDA L** (303)973-9527
4902 S Robb Way Littleton CO 80127-1210 • olsenll@aol.com • RM • Mem C • Our Father Littleton CO • (303)779-1332 • (S 1982 MED)

**OLSON SHERYL B** (763)595-9576
3431 Yukon Ave N New Hope MN 55427-1837 • solson@beautifulsaviorlc.org • MNS • Mem C • Beautiful Savior Plymouth MN • (612)550-1000 • (CQ 1985 MED)

**ORTSTADT BETH A** (316)721-2673
1934 N Cardington St Wichita KS 67212-6465 • ortstadt@dtc.net • KS • 04/1997 04/1999 • (S 1989 MA)

**OTRHALIK KEVIN D**
622 Marcelletti Ave Paw Paw MI 49079-1219 • MI • Mem C • Trinity Paw Paw MI • (616)657-4840 • (CQ 1994 MRE)

**OTTE PAUL R** (320)587-5215
105 10th Ave NE Hutchinson MN 55350-1283 • MNS • Mem C • Peace Hutchinson MN • (320)587-3031 • (SP 1969 MSMU)

**OTTO ARLO E** (314)638-1786
9922 Canterleigh Dr Saint Louis MO 63123-5310 • MO • Mem C • Ascension Saint Louis MO • (314)832-5600 • (S 1970)

**OWENS ANNA MARIE**
901 Shady Brook Cir Birmingham AL 35226-1829 • SO • Mem C • Vestavia Hills Birmingham AL • (205)823-1883 • (IV 1989)

## P

**PARRIS MARTHA A** (715)423-5348
2231 Wickham Ave #201 Wisconsin Rapids WI 54495-5603 • dceparris@tcnet.com • NW • Mem C • St Luke Wisconsin Rapids WI • (715)423-5990 • (S 1988 MS)

**PARRON RICHARD KENNETH** (248)478-4059
30271 Timberidge Cir #103 Farmington Hills MI 48336 • MI • Mem C • Christ Our Savior Livonia MI • (734)522-6830 • (CQ 2000)

**PATTON MICHAEL A** (314)938-9693
242 Walden Ct Eureka MO 63025-1130 • mikep@stmarkseureka.org • MO • Mem C • St Mark Eureka MO • (636)938-4432 • (RF 1987)

**PAULUS JOHN** (303)750-5818
15997 E Kepner Dr Aurora CO 80017-3005 • john.paulus@pwclc.org • RM • Mem C • Peace W Christ Aurora CO • (303)693-5618 • (S 1978)

**PERA JEREMY J** (913)632-6456
616 Franklin St Clay Center KS 67432-1556 • KS • Mem C • St Paul Clay Center KS • (785)632-5301 • (S 1972)

**PETERS ELIZABETH ANN** (605)665-7337
1008 West 8th Apt 1 Yankton SD 57078-3336 • dceliz@willinet.net • SD • Mem C • St John Yankton SD • (605)665-7337 • (SP 1999)

**PETERSEN RALPH L** (503)655-1547
11568 S Finnegans Way Oregon City OR 97045-9770 • NOW • Mem C • Hope Woodburn OR • (503)981-0400 • (S 1963)

**PFOTENHAUER PATRA SUE** (949)854-8002
Concordia University 1530 Concordia W Irvine CA 92612-3203 • patra.pfotenhauer@cui.edu • PSW • SHS/C • Pacific Southwest Irvine CA • (949)854-3232 • (SP 1990 MS)

**PICKEL STEVEN L**
Concordia University 275 N Syndicate St Saint Paul MN 55104-5494 • MNS • 07/1998 07/2000 • (SP 1976)

**PIERCE AARON V** (850)934-2919
3241B College Ct Gulf Breeze FL 32561 • SO • Mem C • Good Shepherd Gulf Breeze FL • (850)932-3263 • (S 2000)

**POOL JEFFREY M** (920)324-2775
716 Sunrise Ave Waupun WI 53963 • SW • Mem C • Pella Waupun WI • (920)324-3321 • (RF 1973 MED)

**POPP MARY BETH**
980 Chestnut Oak Dr Saint Charles MO 63303-4193 • mbtpopp@msn.com • MO • 08/1999 • (SP 1988 MA)

**PORISCH BYRON D** (734)528-3854
3984 Palisades Blvd Ypsilanti MI 48197 • bporisch@stlukepa.org • MI • Mem C • St Luke Ann Arbor MI • (734)971-0550 • (SP 1977)

**POTRATZ LORI R**
1331 S Maple St Apt B18 Sioux City IA 51106 • dcelori@aol.com • IW • Mem C • Redeemer Sioux City IA • (712)276-1125 • (SP 1982)

**POTTS MICHELLE D**
6303 Alderson St Weston WI 54476 • michellebreeder@excite.com • NW • Mem C • Mount Olive Weston WI • (715)359-5546 • (SP 1998)

**POTTS RANDY LEE** (770)813-9017
5835 Haterleigh Dr Alpharetta GA 30005 • rpottsga@aol.com • EN • Mem C • Christ Shepherd Alpharetta GA • (770)475-0640 • (S 1979)

**PRESSEL TRACY LYNNE** (254)754-1090
2736 Lake Shore Dr #2510 Waco TX 76708 • TX • Mem C • St Paul Waco TX • (254)799-3211 • (S 2000)

**PRIME CAROLE ANN** (405)527-5440
PO Box 1534 Purcell OK 73080-1534 • caroleprime@juno.com • OK • Mem C • Trinity Norman OK • (405)321-3443 • (CQ 1997 EDS)

**PROBST DAVID A** (765)446-8767
102 Cochise Trl #115 Lafayette IN 47901 • dprobst@stjameslaf.org • FG • Mem C • Oak Road Lilburn GA • (770)979-6391 • (S 1998)

**PUCHBAUER ERIC B** (314)268-1180
2468 Wesford Dr Maryland Heights MO 63043-4146 • sentry1@email.com • MO • 09/1994 • (RF 1991)

## R

**RAHBERG DAVID E** (972)234-6972
3301 Lynbrook Dr Plano TX 75075-7728 • daver@messiahlutheran.com • TX • Mem C • Messiah Richardson TX • (972)234-6972 • (S 1978 MS)

**RAHBERG SAM**
1226 Hazelwood Apt 106 Saint Paul MN 55106 • MNS • Mem C • Our Saviour Saint Paul MN • (651)774-2396 • (SP 2000)

**RATH DANIEL D** (718)358-0703
2211 123rd St College Point NY 11356-2638 • danrath@aol.com • AT • Mem C • St John College Point NY • (718)463-4790 • (S 1966 MSED MA)

**RAUCH SCOTT M** (309)694-2254
116 Sara St East Peoria IL 61611-3565 • sjmrauch@bitwisesystems.com • CI • Mem C • Trinity Peoria IL • (309)676-4609 • (S 1986 MS)

**RAUSENBERGER REBECCA J**
11880 Lakefield Rd Saint Charles MI 48655 • brausenberger@sbbsnet.net • MI • 09/2000 • (SP 1994)

**REED JAMES W** (978)266-1366
133 Arlington Acton MA 01720-0986 • reedzf@juno.com • NE • Mem C • Mount Calvary Acton MA • (978)263-5156 • (IV 1986)

**REED ROBERT WARREN** (813)264-0812
5219 Lowell Rd Tampa FL 33624-4119 • rwr@aalweb.net • FG • O Miss • Florida-Georgia Orlando FL • (RF 1967 MA)

**REINEKE DAVID C** (715)627-7718
515 5th Ave Antigo WI 54409 • NW • Mem C • Peace Antigo WI • (715)623-2200 • (SP 1988)

**REINKE JANETTE MARIE** (785)840-9599
5200 Congressional Pl Lawrence KS 66049 • jr9412@aol.com • KS • 07/1998 • (S 1995)

**RENNISON CHRISTOPHER EDWARD** (440)248-4066
22 B First Ave Bedford OH 44146 • dcechris@earthlink.net • OH • Mem C • Our Redeemer Solon OH • (440)248-4066 • (RF 1997)

**RHOADS MARK RANDALL** (512)252-7528
808 Smoke Signal Pass Pflugerville TX 78660 • TX • Mem C • St Paul Austin TX • (512)472-8301 • (CQ 1984 MPAD)

**RICHARD KEITH RENE** (630)653-2039
606 Willow Wood Dr #201 Carol Stream IL 60188 • krichard@stjohnwheaton.org • NI • Mem C • St John Wheaton IL • (630)668-0701 • (RF 1999)

**RICKE DAVID W** (402)932-0955
831 S Harrison St Papillion NE 68046-2521 • dricke@home.com • NEB • Mem C • Divine Shepher Omaha NE • (402)895-1500 • (S 1977)

**RILEY JIMMY K** (440)358-0838
467 W Jackson St Painesville OH 44077-3147 • dcejim@ameritech.net • OH • Ohio Olmsted Falls OH • (S 1991)

**RIPPSTEIN TIMOTHY A** (708)771-8300
Concordia University 7400 Augusta St River Forest IL 66305-1499 • crfrippstta@curf.edu • NI • SHS/C • Northern Illinois Hillside IL • (PO 1984 MA)

**RITTER JAMES DANIEL** (801)392-6368
1487 Canyon Cove #15 Ogden UT 84401 • jritter@stpaullcms.org • RM • Mem C • St Paul Ogden UT • (801)392-6368 • (S 1998)

**ROGGOW TIMOTHY CARL**
C/O Immanuel Lutheran Church 1258 Broadway Fargo ND 58102-2637 • troggow@fidmail.com • ND • Zion Anaheim CA • (S 1990)

**ROMMEL GREGORY R** (573)335-3396
1149 Cypress St Cape Girardeau MO 63701-1709 • MO • Mem C • Good Shepherd Cape Girardeau MO • (573)335-3974 • (SP 1975)

**RONNING RANDALL L** (804)421-4922
1615 Swinton Ln Richmond VA 23233 • rronning@erols.com • SE • Trinity Reseda CA • (S 1983)

**ROSE JON C** (520)795-4344
10858 E Walking Stick Dr Tucson AZ 85748-7068 • jonrose@azstarnet.com • EN • 10/1997 • (PO 1980)

**ROSEL PHILIP J** (765)384-5107
PO Box 324 Sweetser IN 46987-0324 • IN • Mem C • St James Marion IN • (765)662-3092 • (S 1968)

**RUDAT SHEILA KAY** (847)695-9548
938 Congdon Ave #18 Elgin IL 60120-3102 • shesher13@netscape.net • NI • Mem C • Good Shepherd Elgin IL • (847)741-7788 • (RF 1996)

**RUEHS JONATHAN BRIAN** (818)557-6709
1157 Alameda Ave #14 Glendale CA 91201 • jbruehs@yahoo.com • PSW • Mem C • First Burbank CA • (818)848-7432 • (IV 1995)

**RUEHS TARA LYNN** (602)439-1364
3720 W Sierra St Phoenix AZ 85029 • PSW • 08/1996 • (SP 1996)

**RUELLE DAWN MICHELE** (714)776-0312
303 E Center St #309 Anaheim CA 92805 • PSW • Mem C • Zion Anaheim CA • (714)535-1169 • (RF 1998)

**RUETER DAVID L**
17260 Euclid St Apt H Fountain Valley CA 92708-4920 • PSW • Mem C • Faith Huntington Beach CA • (714)962-5571 • (IV 1996)

## S

**SANTAMARINA DANIEL**
2 Blackbird Ln Pomona CA 91766-4722 • PSW • Mem C • Mount Calvary Diamond Bar CA • (909)861-2740 • (IV 1998)

**SAUER DAVID P** (608)837-5621
206 Concord Dr Sun Prairie WI 53590-1702 • dcldps@hotmail.com • SW • Mem C • Bethlehem Sun Prairie WI • (608)837-7446 • (CQ 1980)

**SAVING DAVID W** (913)451-8447
11058 Rene St Lenexa KS 66215-2040 • KS • Mem C • Lord Of Life Leawood KS • (913)681-5167 • (SP 1978)

**SCHAUS JONATHAN F** (562)925-0132
13612 Woodruff Bellflower CA 90706 • EN • 10/1999 • (IV 1997)

**SCHECK DENNIS R** (719)272-0181
1950 Milliken Ct Colorado Springs CO 80918-3664 • RM • M Chap • Rocky Mountain Aurora CO • (RF 1973 MRE DED)

**SCHEDLER STEVEN P** (858)279-7581
8890 Armorss Ave San Diego CA 92123 • dce4bolts@access1.net • PSW • Mem C • St Paul San Diego CA • (619)272-6363 • (IV 1985)

**SCHEER STEVEN A** (616)846-8556
18288 Woodland Ridge Dr #19 Spring Lake MI 49456 • scheer@novagate.com • MI • Mem C • Lakeshore Fellowship Spring Lake MI • (616)846-8556 • (SP 1999 MME)

**SCHELER JASON J** (248)681-5869
5520 Millpointe Dr Waterford MI 48327-3086 • jjscheler@cphnet.org • MI • O Sp Min • Michigan Ann Arbor MI • (S 1993)

**SCHERCH RONALD C** (512)833-5242
1509 Braided Rope Dr Austin TX 78727-4625 • scherch@txdistlcms.org • TX • Texas Austin TX • (RF 1973 MED)

**SCHERMBECK CASSANDRA JO** (815)229-0249
5121 E State St Apt 306 B Rockford IL 61108 • cassie_schermbeck@hotmail.com • NI • SHS/C • Northern Illinois Hillside IL • (S 1999)

**SCHILF HARRY N** (608)362-7921
1974 Cleora Dr #4 Beloit WI 53511 • hs1959@webtv.net • SW • Mem C • St John Beloit WI • (608)362-8595 • (RF 1989)

**SCHILF KENNETH M** (219)485-1384
5005 Blum Dr Fort Wayne IN 46835-3421 • kschilf@holycrossfw.org • IN • Mem C • Holy Cross Fort Wayne IN • (219)483-3173 • (RF 1966 MA)

**SCHIPPOREIT DARCY ANN** (303)233-1552
7040 W 20th Ave #304 Lakewood CO 80215 • schipporeit@hotmail.com • RM • Mem C • St John Denver CO • (303)733-3777 • (IV 1999)

**SCHLECHT MARY TANIA** (309)828-8510
601 Fox Hill Apt G Bloomington IL 61701 • mts1@trinluth.org • CI • Tchr • Trinity Bloomington IL • (309)828-6265 • (RF 1998)

**SCHLECHTE SHEILA ANN** (651)489-8589
1025 Churchill St #2 Saint Paul MN 55103 • MNS • Mem C • Trinity Arden Hills MN • (651)633-2402 • (SP 1993)

**SCHLUCKEBIER MELINDA D**
2727 Nelson Rd Apt T210 Twin Peaks P&DC CO 80503-9358 • mschluckebier@juno.com • RM • Mem C • Messiah Longmont CO • (303)776-2573 • (RF 1994 MAR)

**SCHMECKPEPER TERRY D** (612)824-1882
5040 Oakland Ave S Minneapolis MN 55417 • tschmeck@aol.com • MNS • Mem C • Mount Zion Minneapolis MN • (612)824-1882 • (SP 1981)

**SCHMIDT KRISTINA MARIE**
29305 N Scottsdale Rd Scottsdale AZ 85262 • CNH • 09/1999 • (IV 1993)

**SCHMIDT LESTER** (636)256-6877
1571 Buckhurst Ct Ballwin MO 63021-8395 • ic_schmidlo@lcms.org • MO • S Ex/S • Missouri Saint Louis MO • (314)317-4550 • (RF 1962)

**SCHNEEWIND JENNIFER L**
6058 Webster Rd Orchard Park NY 14127-1814 • stjohns@buffnet.net • EA • Mem C • St John Orchard Park NY • (716)662-4747 • (S 1998)

**SCHOBER RONDA LYN** (407)382-5058
5216 Kempston Dr Orlando FL 32812-2430 • rsmime@aol.com • FG • 10/2000 • (S 1997)

**SCHOEPP MARK L** (517)426-8078
C/O Faith Lutheran Church 171 Eastmont Ave E East Wenatchee WA 98802-5303 • father@fitzfamily.com • NOW • Mem C • Faith East Wenatchee WA • (509)884-7623 • (S 1980 MA)

**SCHOEPP PAUL WALTER** (402)643-0580
587 Northern Heights Dr Seward NE 68434 • pschoepp@seward.cune.edu • NEB • SHS/C • Nebraska Seward NE • (SP 1985 MED)

**SCHOLZ ROBERT W** (909)336-2029
PO Box 217 Crest Park CA 92326-0217 • bobscholz@aol.com • PSW • Mem C • Mount Calvary Lake Arrowhead CA • (909)337-1412 • (IV 1995)

**SCHROEDER BYRON J (BARNEY)** (920)749-1744
519 S Schaefer St Appleton WI 54915-3575 • barnsch@juno.com • NW • Mem C • Good Shepherd Appleton WI • (920)734-9643 • (RF 1974)

**SCHUBERT JOY E** (480)730-6966
800 W Ray Rd Chandler AZ 85225 • dce1@telesouth1.com • PSW • Mem C • Epiphany Chandler AZ • (480)963-6105 • (RF 1995)

**SCHULTZ DAVID MAYNARD** (517)671-0617
6116 W S Saginaw Rd Bay City MI 48706 • dhschultz@juno.com • MI • Mem C • St Paul Bay City MI • (517)686-7140 • (RF 1993)

**SCHULTZ JONATHAN D** (918)331-2765
C/O Redeemer Luth Church 3700 SE Woodland Rd Bartlesville OK 74006-4531 • jdsmlbnusa@netscape.net • OK • Mem C • Redeemer Bartlesville OK • (918)333-6022 • (S 1976)

**SCHUMACHER BENJAMIN C** (314)741-9305
18 Nordell Ct Florissant MO 63033-4216 • MO • Mem C • Salem Florissant MO • (314)741-6781 • (S 1965 MMU)

**SCHUTT KIM DURAND** (734)675-6001
2672 Lenox St Trenton MI 48183-2511 • kim.schutt@stpaul-trenton.org • MI • Mem C • St Paul Trenton MI • (734)676-1565 • (SP 1980)

**SCHWARTZ TAMMY JO** (715)389-9281
1005 S Severns Ave Marshfield WI 54449 • dcetammy@commplusis.net • NW • Mem C • Christ Marshfield WI • (715)384-3535 • (S 1993)

**SCHWENNEKER CHRISTOPHER** (405)947-4406
4924 NW 36th St Oklahoma City OK 73122-2326 • dcenxp@aol.com • OK • Mem C • Our Savior Bethany OK • (405)495-1605 • (SP 1995)

**SELANDER CHERI LYNN** (619)589-0176
8110 Stadler St La Mesa CA 91942 • cheridce@aol.com • PSW • Mem C • Christ La Mesa CA • (619)462-5211 • (S 1984)

**SEMLER KARIN LYNNE** (618)345-5947
143 Skylineview Dr Collinsville IL 62234 • karin.semler@lcms.org • SI • S Ex/S • Southern Illinois Belleville IL • (SP 1993)

**SEYBERT MELISSA CHRISTIAN** (317)585-1688
8556 Laurell Valley Dr Indianapolis IN 46250 • dcemel@cs.com • IN • Mem C • Carmel Carmel IN • (317)814-4252 • (RF 1999)

**SHOUMAKER JEFFRY T** (309)693-0270
C/O Redeemer Lutheran Church 6801 N Allen Rd Peoria IL 61614-2480 • CI • Mem C • Redeemer Peoria IL • (309)691-2333 • (S 1981)

**SIEBARTH JOLENE RENEE** (314)966-7650
1984 Greenglen Dr Apt 301 Kirkwood MO 63122 • sloppyjo16@hotmail.com • MO • Mem C • Glendale Saint Louis MO • (314)966-3220 • (RF 1998)

**SIEGRIST WILLIAM C** (512)459-0343
3107 Skylark Dr Austin TX 78757-2036 • TX • Texas Austin TX • (S 1981)

**SIKORSKI LOIS ROSEMARIE** (480)945-6976
5314 N Woodmere Fairway Scottsdale AZ 85250-6458 • roygpski08@aol.com • EN • Inst C • English Farmington MI • (SP 1992 MMU)

**SILVA TIFFANY ANNE** (860)739-7254
253 Flanders Rd Unit 5 Niantic CT 06357-1225 • twiescamp@juno.com • NE • Mem C • Christ Niantic CT • (860)739-6849 • (S 1998)

**SIMON CHRISTINA LYNN** (616)844-4282
709 Clinton Ave #1 Grand Haven MI 49417-0613 • MI • Mem C • Lakeshore Fellowship Spring Lake MI • (616)846-8556 • (SP 1995)

**SIMPSON COLLEEN D** (309)243-9025
10213 N Radnor Rd Peoria IL 61615-9642 • simpson@bitwisesystems.com • CI • Mem C • Epiphany Dunlap IL • (309)243-5957 • (S 1987 MED)

**SMIDT STANLEY G** (623)536-1395
2613 N 127th Ave Avondale AZ 85323-7060 • PSW • Mem C • Mount Calvary Phoenix AZ • (602)263-0402 • (S 1967)

**SMITH CORY**
900 NW 37th St Blue Springs MO 64015-2504 • MO • Mem C • St Paul Independence MO • (816)373-5290 • (S 1999)

**SMITH ERIC RYAN** (217)352-5468
1522 W Clark St Champaign IL 61821-3152 • RM • Mem C • Immanuel Loveland CO • (970)667-4506 • (RF 1996 MS)

**SMITH MAVIS J**
PO Box 62 Brownton MN 55312-0062 • MNS • Mem C • Immanuel Brownton MN • (320)328-5522 • (S 1983)

**SMITH RANDALL** (727)577-4711
1566-86th Ave N Saint Petersburg FL 33702-2832 • FG • Mem C • Grace Saint Petersburg FL • (727)527-1168 • (S 1969 MA)

**SNYDER DIANE RENE** (219)369-9225
608 Center St Walkerton IN 46574 • IN • Mem C • Our Redeemer Knox IN • (219)772-4186 • (RF 1998)

**SOEKEN RICHARD W** (812)473-9956
3305 Sweetser Ave Evansville IN 47714-5448 • richorrita@juno.com • IN • Mem C • Our Redeemer Evansville IN • (812)476-7991 • (V 1967 MS)

**SOELDNER JEFFREY MARK** (262)369-0544
714 Sunnyslope Dr # 2 Hartland WI 53029-1423 • soelman@lightdog.com • SW • Mem C • Bethlehem Wales WI • (262)968-2194 • (SP 1995)

**SOULIGNY CLINTON J**
HC 61 Box 5241 Barnes WI 54873-9509 • soulcj@aol.com • PSW • S Miss • Pacific Southwest Irvine CA • (949)854-3232 • (S 1980)

**SPERRY MARK J** (281)493-3548
792 Bateswood #28 Houston TX 77079 • mjsperry@juno.com • TX • Mem C • Christ Memorial Houston TX • (281)497-0250 • (S 1995)

**SPRECHER ARLYN** (913)894-0576
9812 W 101st St Overland Park KS 66212-5343 • asprecher1@aol.com • KS • Mem C • Christ Overland Park KS • (913)345-9700 • (S 1970 MED)

**SPRENGELER DENISE E** (270)442-8343
C/O St Paul Lutheran Church 211 S 21st St Paducah KY 42003-3204 • MDS • Mem C • St Paul Paducah KY • (270)442-8343 • (SP 1981)

**STAPLETON MICHAEL RAY**
C/O Gloria Dei Lutheran Church 7601 SW 39th St Davie FL 33328-2716 • mstaple@abts.net • FG • Mem C • Gloria Dei Davie FL • (954)475-0683 • (S 1983)

**STARFELDT CHAD JOSEPH** (651)772-0656
1118 Kennard Saint Paul MN 55106 • cstarfeldt@juno.com • MNS • Mem C • Woodbury Woodbury MN • (651)739-5144 • (RF 1996)

**STAUDT SHONDA M** (561)691-2059
1132 Rainwood Cir Palm Beach Gardens FL 33410 • FG • 06/1999 • (CQ 1992)

**STEEGE SUSAN M** (716)834-2184
213 Glenhurst Rd Tonawanda NY 14150-8423 • sweetsoup@aol.com • EA • Mem C • First Trinity Tonawanda NY • (716)835-2220 • (S 1984)

**STERNBERG ALLISON JAYNE** (314)862-8518
1448 Lyndale Saint Louis MO 63130 • phil2two@juno.com • MO • Mem C • Peace Saint Louis MO • (314)892-5610 • (S 1997)

**STEVENS TODD COREY** (314)731-2435
6560 Villa Ave Saint Louis MO 63139-3464 • tstevens@nothnbut.net • MO • Mem C • Our Redeemer Overland MO • (314)427-3444 • (S 1997)

**STEWART BRENT D** (708)387-0889
3117 Maple Ave Brookfield IL 60513 • brentstewart@netzero.net • NI • Mem C • St John La Grange IL • (708)354-1690 • (S 1996)

**STEWART NICOLE DEANN** (281)554-3266
2323 W Bay Area Blvd #410 Webster TX 77598-3247 • nstewart@gdlc.org • TX • Mem C • Gloria Dei Houston TX • (281)333-4535 • (S 1994)

**STOCKER STEPHANIE R** (808)550-0443
2428 Wilder Ave Honolulu HI 96822 • CNH • Mem C • Our Redeemer Honolulu HI • (808)946-4223 • (IV 2000)

**STORM CINDY LOU** (712)274-1342
2205 S Patterson St Sioux City IA 51106-2924 • IW • Mem C • Calvary Sioux City IA • (712)239-1575 • (SP 1998)

**STROMING CARL R** (612)427-5018
528 Western St Anoka MN 55303-2005 • MNS • Mem C • Mount Olive Anoka MN • (763)421-3223 • (SP 1978)

**STROMING THEODORE G** (320)587-4019
315 E Pishney Ln SW Hutchinson MN 55350-2330 • MNS • Mem C • Peace Hutchinson MN • (320)587-3031 • (SP 1990)

**STROMING TIMOTHY J** (952)442-8273
109 Mill Rd Waconia MN 55387 • MNS • Mem C • Zion Albert Lea MN • (507)373-8609 • (SP 1985)

**STUHR LLOYD R** (734)482-2238
1530 Collegewood St Ypsilanti MI 48197-2023 • lstuhr@stlukeaa.org • MI • Mem C • St Luke Ann Arbor MI • (734)971-0550 • (S 1975 MS)

**STYSKAL AMBER LYNN** (330)798-5437
1771 Congo St Akron OH 44305-3614 • rev94@aol.com • OH • Mem C • Tallmadge Tallmadge OH • (330)633-4775 • (S 1996)

**SYMMANK JOEL ETHAN** (913)764-1984
804 N Stevenson St Olathe KS 66061-2830 • rlcjoel@planetkc.com • KS • Mem C • Redeemer Olathe KS • (913)764-2359 • (S 1992)

**SYVERSON SARAH JO** (509)464-1568
1110 E Cozza Dr #301 Spokane WA 99208 • NOW • Mem C • Holy Cross Spokane WA • (509)483-4218 • (PO 1999)

## T

**TANNEY MICHAEL H** (319)445-0184
722 Westerfield Davenport IA 52806 • m_tanney@hotmail.com • IE • Mem C • Trinity Davenport IA • (319)323-8001 • (S 1975)

**TASLER STACEY LEE** (719)638-5625
Holy Cross Luth Church 4125 Constitution Ave Colorado Springs CO 80909-1662 • kalmuck@aol.com • RM • Mem C • Holy Cross Colorado Springs CO • (719)596-0661 • (SP 1995 MS)

**TAYLOR JASON WARREN**
C/O Grace Lutheran Church 12200 Mc Cormick Rd Jacksonville FL 32225-5563 • jtaylor168@aol.com • FG • Mem C • Grace Jacksonville FL • (904)928-9136 • (S 1994)

**THEIS CHERIE ANN** (920)497-8218
1011 Gray St Green Bay WI 54303 • cherie@pilgrimluth.com • NW • Mem C • Pilgrim Green Bay WI • (920)494-1979 • (SP 1993)

**THOMA CHRISTOPHER IAN** (248)886-0173
1038 N Oakland Blvd Apt 1 Waterford MI 48327 • cthoma@flash.net • EN • Mem C • Our Savior Hartland MI • (248)887-4300 • (RF 1995)

**THOMACK ERIK PAUL** (517)547-4284
15327 Rome Rd Manitou Beach MI 49253 • youthguy@dmci.net • MI • Mem C • Of The Lakes Addison MI • (517)547-4261 • (S 1995)

**THOMACK JO ANN A** (931)552-0899
301 Castle Hts Clarksville TN 37040-2917 • thomackd@ten_nash.ten.k12.tn.us • MDS • Mem C • Grace Clarksville TN • (931)647-6750 • (S 1990)

**THOMACK SHEILA MARIE** (517)547-4284
15327 Rome Rd Manitou Beach MI 49253 • dceduo@juno.com • MI • Mem C • Of The Lakes Addison MI • (517)547-4261 • (S 1992 MS)

**THOMPSON ANN MARIE** (410)673-1930
PO Box 614 Preston MD 216555 • SE • Mem C • Immanuel Easton MD • (410)822-5665 • (S 1999)

**THOMPSON CAROLYN M** (573)445-3190
5901 N Oneal Rd Columbia MO 65202-7277 • cthomp1377@aol.com • MO • Mem C • Campus Columbia MO • (573)442-5942 • (RF 1992)

**THUER MARK** (308)962-7413
RR 2 Box 137 Arapahoe NE 68922 • NEB • Mem C • Trinity Arapahoe NE • (308)962-7667 • (S 2000)

**TONG ALLAN K L** (415)750-9610
894 46th Ave San Francisco CA 94121 • atong113@aol.com • CNH • Mem C • Holy Spirit San Francisco CA • (415)771-6658 • (IV 1997)

**TRENCH KAREN M** (231)845-6654
501 E Tinkham Ave Ludington MI 49431-1463 • ktrench@t-one.net • MI • Mem C • Our Savior Scottville MI • (231)757-2271 • (SP 1980)

**TROMBLY BARBARA J** (734)482-5330
6584 Stoney Creek Rd Ypsilanti MI 48197-6615 • stlukehas@aol.com • MI • 04/2000 • (SP 1993)

**TRUWE GARY M** (317)898-1725
1834 Zinnia Dr Indianapolis IN 46219-2845 • gary.truwe@trinityindy.org • IN • Mem C • Trinity Indianapolis IN • (317)897-0243 • (S 1969)

**TWEETEN DUANE** (262)938-2466
21945 Mayrose Blvd Brookfield WI 53045-3943 • dtweeten@cphnet.org • SW • O Sp Min • South Wisconsin Milwaukee WI • (414)464-8100 • (CQ 1984)

**TWILLMAN CYNTHIA LOUISE** (918)451-4742
5280 S Elm Pl Broken Arrow OK 74011-4849 • cindce@aol.com • OK • Mem C • Trinity Broken Arrow OK • (918)455-5750 • (SP 1996)

U

**ULICKY-WEERTS LAURA S** (316)342-8181
C/O Messiah Lutheran Church 1101 Neosho St Emporia KS 66801-2747 • KS • Mem C • Messiah Emporia KS • (316)342-8181 • (S 1986)

**ULRICH HEATHER C** (206)366-8814
4641 NE 201st Pl Lake Forest Park WA 98155 • ulrich@bigfoot.com • NOW • Mem C • Epiphany Kenmore WA • (425)488-9606 • (S 1992 MA)

**UPCHURCH AMY** (208)664-9231
8520 W Cloverleaf Dr Hayden ID 83835 • amy@ctkcda.org • NOW • Mem C • Christ King Coeur D Alene ID • (208)664-9231 • (S 1999 MPED)

V

**VANDE VOORT-SCHWEIM AMY L** (253)848-7496
1920 E Pioneer Ave Puyallup WA 98372 • alschweim@aol.com • NOW • Mem C • Immanuel Puyallup WA • (253)848-4548 • (SP 1994)

**VIEHL WARREN A** (402)483-0533
5555 S 78th St Lincoln NE 68516 • NEB • Mem C • Messiah Lincoln NE • (402)489-3024 • (S 2000)

**VON FANGE SUSAN D** (303)755-8992
2627 S Halifax St Aurora CO 80013 • sue³vonfange@pwclc.org • RM • Mem C • Peace W Christ Aurora CO • (303)693-5618 • (S 1980 MA)

W

**WACHTER JEROME A** (501)880-0298
403 E Fir St Russelville AR 72802 • MDS • Mem C • St John Russellville AR • (501)968-1309 • (S 2000)

**WACKER DAVID JOHN** (314)894-2405
5276 Camelot Estates Dr Oakville MO 63129-1540 • faithdce@aol.com • MO • Mem C • Faith Saint Louis MO • (314)846-8612 • (SP 1985)

**WALLINGER DENNIS E** (414)462-4105
8518 W Lawrence Ave Milwaukee WI 53225-5123 • walldpat@execpc.com • SW • Mem C • Covenant Milwaukee WI • (414)464-2410 • (RF 1972 MS)

**WARREN THADDEUS P**
16671 E Rice Cir Aurora CO 80015-1634 • RM • Mem C • Trinity Franktown CO • (303)841-8620 • (S 1991 MMFC)

**WEBB RICHARD E** (248)666-4398
6038 Barker Ave Waterford MI 48329-3100 • rickewebb@netscape.net • MI • Mem C • St John Rochester MI • (248)652-8830 • (S 1975)

**WEGNER PAULETTE E** (303)427-3177
6708 W 97th Ct Broomfield CO 80021-5458 • wegnerclan.juno.com • RM • Mem C • Peace Arvada CO • (303)424-4454 • (SP 1987)

**WEIDNER DAVID L** (636)230-5714
743 Trago Creek Dr Ballwin MO 63021-4405 • ic³weidned@lcms.org • MO • S Ex/S • Missouri Saint Louis MO • (314)317-4550 • (CQ 1989)

**WEINMEISTER MARK A** (253)661-7972
C/O St Luke Lutheran Church 515 S 312th St Federal Way WA 98003-4033 • stlukelc@tcmnet.com • NOW • Mem C • St Luke Federal Way WA • (253)941-3000 • (S 1991)

**WEINRICH DOUGLAS**
2431 Appley Way San Jose CA 95124-5347 • doug@holycrosslosgatos.org • CNH • Mem C • Holy Cross Los Gatos CA • (408)356-3525 • (S 1995)

**WEISS PAULA C** (501)316-1722
1326 Kimwood Dr Benton AR 72015-9590 • wsinark@juno.com • MDS • Mem C • Zion Alexander AR • (501)316-1100 • (SP 1982)

**WELTE JOHN ANDREW**
Peace Lutheran Church 941 W Bedford Euless Rd Hurst TX 76053-3808 • TX • Mem C • Peace Hurst TX • (817)284-1677 • (S 1990)

**WENDELIN SANDRA M** (303)237-1698
12429 W 17th Ave Lakewood CO 80215-2510 • swendelin@bethluth.net • RM • Mem C • Bethlehem Lakewood CO • (303)238-7676 • (SP 1990)

**WENDT PAUL R** (219)662-9317
931 E Joliet St Crown Point IN 46307-4605 • prwendt@mail.icongrp.com • IN • Mem C • Trinity Crown Point IN • (219)663-1578 • (SP 1991)

**WENGEL JOHN RUSSELL** (281)528-0624
46 N Deerfoot Cir The Woodlands TX 77380-3982 • jwengel@main.com • TX • Mem C • Living Word The Woodlands TX • (281)363-4860 • (IV 1988)

**WERNER HEIDI** (913)362-2814
4117 Adams #106 Kansas City KS 66103 • KS • Mem C • Our Saviour Kansas City KS • (913)236-6228 • (IV 1998)

**WESTRUP SUSAN J** (916)674-7284
536 Brown Ave Yuba City CA 95991-4834 • CNH • Mem C • First Yuba City CA • (530)673-8894 • (SP 1985)

**WETHERELL MARK E** (904)671-6140
6 Fishermans Cir Apt 4 Ormond Beach FL 32174 • FG • Mem C • Trinity Holly Hill FL • (904)255-7580 • (RF 1984)

**WEYHRICH RICHARD L** (931)707-1548
484 Sycamore Dr Crossville TN 38555 • rweyhrich@tnaccess.com • MDS • Mem C • Shepherd Hills Crossville TN • (931)484-3461 • (CQ 1984)

**WHEELER CYNTHIA A** (314)268-1009
2172 Santa Fe Cir Arnold MO 63010-5227 • cindy.wheeler@cph.org • MO • CCRA • Missouri Saint Louis MO • (314)317-4550 • (S 1979)

**WHITENECK ELAINE** (316)342-8181
1717 W Wilman Ct Emporia KS 66801 • ekwhite@kansas.net • KS • Mem C • Messiah Emporia KS • (316)342-8181 • (S 1982)

**WIDGER DOUGLAS D** (817)922-0015
2735 5th Ave Fort Worth TX 76110-3004 • dock1@flash.net • TX • Mem C • St Paul Fort Worth TX • (817)332-2281 • (S 1984 MA)

**WIEDERKEHR STEPHEN E** (405)237-3406
1701 Mimosa St Enid OK 73701-1751 • wiederkehr@enid.com • OK • Mem C • St Paul Enid OK • (580)234-6646 • (SP 1977)

**WIEGERT DAVID PAUL** (912)953-7272
226 Autumn Woods Dr Warner Robins GA 31088-6715 • FG • 03/2000 • (SP 1994)

**WIESNER CARLA DENISE**
C/O First Lutheran Church 15 E Sawyer St Rice Lake WI 54868 • NW • Mem C • First Rice Lake WI • (715)234-7505 • (SP 2000)

**WIEST ROBERT D** (308)324-5574
801 E 11th St Lexington NE 68850-1704 • NEB • Mem C • Trinity Lexington NE • (308)324-4341 • (S 1994 MS)

**WILKE LEROY R DR** (314)965-2934
12951 Beaver Dam Rd Des Peres MO 63131-2107 • leroy.wilke@lcms.org • MO • S Ex/S • Missouri Saint Louis MO • (314)317-4550 • (SP 1972 MS LITTD)

**WILLIAMS JOHN HERBERT** (281)359-2886
3911 Forest Village Dr Kingwood TX 77339-1817 • TX • Mem C • Christ King Kingwood TX • (281)360-7936 • (SP 1985)

**WILSCHETZ SUSAN MAUREEN** (805)527-6567
3131 Melody Ln Simi Valley CA 93063-1558 • PSW • Mem C • Trinity Simi Valley CA • (805)526-2429 • (RF 1994 MA)

**WINEGARDEN ALAN D DR** (651)490-0524
572 Sextant Ave W Roseville MN 55113-3505 • winegarden@csp.edu • MNS • SHS/C • Minnesota South Burnsville MN • (S 1979 MA PHD)

**WINKLER LESTER L** (512)486-1196
17228 Sandwick Pflugerville TX 78660 • TX • SHS/C • Texas Austin TX • (SP 1993)

**WINTER STACY ANN** (612)714-3835
1464 Parkwood Dr Woodbury MN 55125-2042 • MNS • Mem C • St Peter Afton MN • (651)436-3357 • (SP 1987)

**WIRTS JUDY ANN** (602)936-9780
11824 W Windsor Ave Avondale AZ 85323 • PSW • 07/1999 • (SP 1996)

**WITEK KRISTY LYNN** (409)722-1609
2711 Helena Ave Nederland TX 77627 • TX • Mem C • Holy Cross Nederland TX • (409)722-1609 • (SP 2000)

**WITHEE JANE M** (970)625-4978
1118 Firethorn Ct Rifle CO 81650 • SD • 11/1999 • (S 1978)

**WRIGHT BRIAN LYNN**
C/O Bethany Lutheran Ch 621 S Orchard Ave Vacaville CA 95688-4335 • CNH • Mem C • Bethany Vacaville CA • (707)451-6675 • (IV 1992)

**WUGGAZER DAVID** (708)995-8167
717 Miller St Holdrege NE 68949 • NEB • Mem C • Mount Calvary Holdrege NE • (308)995-2208 • (S 1998)

**WURDEMAN BRUCE E** (314)938-4525
119 W North St Eureka MO 63025-1119 • lllwurdembe@crf.cuis.edu • MO • St Paul Fort Dodge IA • (RF 1971 MA)

**WYCHERLEY SCOTT P** (715)276-3920
PO Box 38 Townsend WI 54175-0038 • NW • Mem C • St John Townsend WI • (715)276-7214 • (BR 1978)

Y

**YOUMANS JACOB** (808)484-4011
98-1038 Moanalua Rd Apt 2001 Aiea HI 96701 • islanddce@aol.com • CNH • Mem C • Our Savior Aiea HI • (808)488-3654 • (IV 1997)

**YOUNG KRISTA LYNN**
601 N Church St Union MO 63084-1503 • socratees@primary.net • MO • Missouri Saint Louis MO • (314)317-4550 • (SP 1993)

Z

**ZANDER JOEL R** (218)327-3043
710 NW 20th Ave Grand Rapids MN 55744 • MNN • Mem C • Our Redeemer Cohasset MN • (218)328-5165 • (SP 2000)

**ZELLAR DAVID MYRON**
201 Blace Ave Eagle Lake MN 56024-9604 • MNS • Mem C • Hosanna Mankato MN • (507)388-1766 • (CQ 1988)

**ZESCH BRENDA L** (501)224-6874
1812 Reservoir Rd Apt 109 Little Rock AR 72227-4923 • MDS • Mem C • Christ Little Rock AR • (501)663-5232 • (S 1982)

**ZIELKE ADOLPH E** (734)994-3718
914 Westwood Ave Ann Arbor MI 48103-3563 • azielke@stpaul.pvt.k12.mi.us • MI • Mem C • St Paul Ann Arbor MI • (734)665-9117 • (RF 1971 MED)

**ZIEMNICK TINA MARIE** (440)209-0956
5980 Marine Pkwy Apt B 116 Mentor on the Lake OH 44060 • tmziemnick@ameritech.net • OH • Mem C • Faith Mentor OH • (440)255-2229 • (SP 1996)

**ZIMMERMANN HANNAH L**
C/O Our Redeemer Lutheran 2301 E Court St Iowa City IA 52245-5217 • hannahz@bigfoot.com • IE • Celebration Appleton WI • (SP 1998)

**ZITZOW JANINE ALISON** (612)432-1378
14725 Chicago Ave S # 8 Burnsville MN 55306 • MNS • Mem C • Redemption Bloomington MN • (952)881-0035 • (SP 1994)

**ZOBEL SUZANNE E** (630)897-0660
C/O Lutheran Bible Translators PO Box 2050 Aurora IL 60507-2050 • suzanne³zobel@lbt.org • PSW • Pacific Southwest Irvine CA • (949)854-3232 • (S 1983 MED)

**ZOBEL TANYA RENEE** (316)689-8435
3141 George Washington Blvd Apt 202 Wichita KS 67210-1552 • KS • 07/1998 • (S 1996)

**ZUCKER DENYS MICHELLE** (608)985-7412
PO Box 140 La Valle WI 53941-0140 • tdzuke@jvlnet.com • SW • 07/1997 07/2000 • (SP 1993 MA)

# Section C
# Deaconesses

**During the 1989 synodical convention, delegates adopted a resolution that gave certified Deaconesses membership status in the Synod under the classification of Ministers of Religion—Commissioned.**

B

**BACKS PEGGY A** (440)205-9206
C/O Saint Paul Lutheran Church 250 Bowhall Rd Painesville OH 44077-5219 • deaconess@oh.verio.com • OH • Mem C • St Paul Painesville OH • (440)354-3000 • (RF 1990)

**BONFIELD DIANNA E** (630)653-7282
1038 Loughborough Ct Wheaton IL 60187-7613 • debonfied@juno.com • NI • 04/2000 • (V 1972)

**BORMUTH SARA B** (360)724-6302
1568 Barrel Springs Rd Bellingham WA 98226-9288 • NOW • Mem C • Trinity Bellingham WA • (206)734-2770 • (V 1971)

**BOWER CRYSTAL C** (219)936-9814
124 E Klinger Plymouth IN 46563 • cbower@blhs.org • IN • Indiana Fort Wayne IN • (RF 1990 MA)

**BRAEGER GRACE L** (314)961-4835
2320 Hill Ave Brentwood MO 63144-1729 • MO • EM • (V 1950)

**BROWN KATHLEEN**
7408 NW 116 Oklahoma City OK 73162 • OK • Inst C • Oklahoma Tulsa OK • (V 1977)

**BRUESKE MERTICE ADELLE** (320)834-2805
8100 County Rd 8 NW Alexandria MN 56308 • merabrue@juno.com • MNN • 09/1994 09/1999 • (V 1958)

**BUDZYNSKI LAURA**
9775 Highstone Dr Roscoe IL 67073-7112 • NI • Northern Illinois Hillside IL • (RF 1985)

C

**CAMPBELL IRENE C** (530)533-7504
2105 Park Ave Apt 27 Oroville CA 95966-5383 • CNH • EM • (RF 1983)

**CLARK KATHLEEN A** (815)772-8463
410 W Lincolnway Morrison IL 61270-2206 • heisrisen1@juno.com • IE • O Sp Min • Iowa East Marion IA • (RF 1994 MACED)

**CRAIG BEVERLY J** (716)433-8477
4824 Cottage Rd Lockport NY 14094-1604 • EA • Mem C • St Peter Lockport NY • (716)433-9014 • (V 1962)

D

**DICKE JEANNE M** (651)704-9464
2343 Larpenteur Ave E Apt 219 Maplewood MN 55109-4927 • >jdicke@blhs.orgı • MNS • Minnesota South Burnsville MN • (V 1979)

**DIEBEL LOIS ELAINE** (407)724-8338
1315 Kayford St NW Palm Bay FL 32907-8060 • FG • 07/1990 07/2000 • (V 1982)

**DOLLBERG SUZANNE F** (321)799-1928
318 W Osceola Ln Cocoa Beach FL 32931-3816 • dollberg@gateway.net • FG • 07/1990 07/2000 • (V 1977 MSW)

**DOST NANETTE HELEN**
1103 Gilmore Ave Wirona MN 55987 • tpdost@msn.com • NOW • Mem C • Northwest Portland OR • (V 1983)

**DREWS JANICE E** (416)588-1671
848 Shaw St Toronto ON M6G 3M2 CANADA • drewsfamily@attcanada.net • EN • 07/1990 06/2000 • (V 1972)

**DRUM RUTH KATHERYN** (701)271-8645
3446 19th St S Fargo ND 58104-6551 • ND • Mem C • Grace Fargo ND • (701)232-1516 • (RF 1997 MA)

E

**EVANGELISTA JUDY**
C/O Holy Spirit Lutheran Ch 150 Lions Dr Elk Grove Village IL 60007-4200 • deacje@aol.com • EN • Immanuel Colorado Springs CO • (RF 1997)

F

**FINGERLE SUZANNE KATHERINE** (815)338-4853
617 Silver Creek Woodstock IL 60098 • sfingrle@megsinet.net • NI • 11/1999 • (RF 1985 MA)

**FISHER RUTH ANN** (602)878-3054
14321 N 78th Ave Peoria AZ 85381-8528 • PSW • 11/1991 • (V 1978)

**FOOTE EUNICE L** (716)692-2445
10 Ellicott Ct Tonawanda NY 14150-4718 • EA • Eastern Williamsville NY • (716)634-5111 • (V 1955 MS)

**FOOTH RITA CORRINE** (701)453-3291
PO Box 224 Berthold ND 58718 • deacones@ndak.net • ND • Mem C • St Paul Minot ND • (701)852-2821 • (CQ 1998 MAR)

**FREDERKING DOLORES VALARIA** (618)327-8744
390 S Friendship Dr Nashville IL 62263-1315 • SI • 06/1990 06/1996 • (V 1961)

G

**GAFFNEY SARAH ELIZABETH** (815)774-9087
1907 Hosmer Ln Crest Hill IL 60435 • NI • 01/1998 02/2000 • (RF 1993)

**GAGE DONNA ANNE** (816)923-5542
4608 Wallace Ave Apt 10 Kansas City MO 64129-2189 • MO • 01/1997 02/2000 • (RF 1987 MA)

**GALLMEIER MICHELLE MARIA** (636)795-2308
140 Marine Ln Maryland Heights MO 63043 • TX • 08/1997 08/2000 • (RF 1993 MCMU)
**GOLDFISH CAROL M** (319)378-0826
4460 Westchester Dr NE #C Cedar Rapids IA 52402-7020 • carol-goldfish@uiowa.edu • IE • Mem C • Trinity Cedar Rapids IA • (319)366-1569 • (RF 1987 MAR)
**GOSSWEIN KATHRYN R** (919)783-8792
3200 A6 Quiet Mill Rd Raleigh NC 27612 • ktgoss@aol.com • SE • Mem C • Our Savior Raleigh NC • (919)832-8822 • (V 1981)
**GREPKE JOANN E** (219)347-9029
3189 E Kammerer Rd Kendallville IN 46755-3084 • fjgrepke@noble.cioe.com • IN • Mem C • St John Kendallville IN • (219)347-2158 • (V 1970)
**GROTH LORRAINE ELIZABETH** (618)692-0314
1925 Vassar Dr Edwardsville IL 62025-2664 • SI • Trinity Hoffman IL • (V 1976 MAR)
**GRUENHAGEN JUDITH K** (612)436-7324
832 Neal Ave N Stillwater MN 55082-1929 • MNS • EM • (V 1964)
**GRUENWALD CHERYL ANN** (616)363-4005
2438 College Ave NE Grand Rapids MI 49505-3639 • EN • 06/1990 06/2000 • (RF 1984)

## H

**HALTER CAROL LEE**
Flat A # 12 Wiltshire Rd Kowloon Tong Kowloon HONG KONG • CNH • S Miss • Calif/Nevada/Hawaii San Francisco CA • (415)468-2336 • (V 1965 MMIN)
**HARRIS MAGGIE D** (716)338-2420
942 Joseph Ave Rochester NY 14621-3444 • EA • O Sp Min • Eastern Williamsville NY • (716)634-5111 • (V 1979)
**HAUG-SCHULZ JACQUELINE J** (415)333-6743
421 Gennessee St San Francisco CA 94127-2328 • CNH • EM • (V 1961 MED)
**HECK JULIE ANN** (219)852-0479
4207 Dearborn Ave Apt 2A Hammond IN 46327 • jheck@mail.icongrp.com • IN • Mem C • St Paul Munster IN • (219)836-6270 • (RF 1998)
**HERZBERG KATHLEEN L** (816)474-9049
803 Quail Creek Dr Independence MO 64055-5233 • lmgskcmo@aol.com • MO • Missouri Saint Louis MO • (314)317-4550 • (V 1979 MA)
**HIBBARD MARY ANNE** (734)844-1268
C/O Risen Christ Lutheran Chur 46250 Ann Arbor Rd W Plymouth MI 48170 • EN • Mem C • Risen Christ Plymouth MI • (734)453-5252 • (CQ 1987 MMIN)
**HILL LORNA R V** (512)352-6686
101 Private Road 930 Taylor TX 76574-2092 • specialtyknits@juno.com • TX • EM • (V 1985)
**HILLER SALLY JANE** (703)971-9371
PO Box 10415 Alexandria VA 22310-0415 • sjhiller@aol.com • SE • Southeastern Alexandria VA • (V 1976)
**HILLHOUSE ROBERTA S** (301)774-7640
3920 Mount Olney Ln Olney MD 20832-1124 • srobie@ibm.net • SE • Mem C • Good Shepherd Olney MD • (301)774-9125 • (V 1980)
**HOFFMAN CHERRYLL IRENE** (712)276-7503
5620 Windsor Ave Sioux City IA 51106-3933 • cherrycook@aol.com • IW • Iowa West Fort Dodge IA • (V 1960 MA)

## J

**JANS LYDIA R**
General Delivery 7338 7th St Hill AFB UT 84056-5305 • gnljans@juno.com • SI • 06/1990 06/2000 • (RF 1984)
**JOHNSON CONNIE LOU** (715)834-6338
3253 Fern Ct Eau Claire WI 54703-1190 • lcjohnso@execpc.com • NW • Mem C • Our Redeemer Eau Claire WI • (715)835-5239 • (V 1962)

## K

**KAN SUNNY** 011-886-2-2254-0559
#18 - 5th Floor Lane 403 Hsin Hai Rd - Pan Chiao Taipei TAIWAN • EN • 06/2000 • (RF 1999)
**KING CAROLE R** (219)374-6885
13701 Lauerman #89 Cedar Lake IN 46303 • RM • 11/1999 • (RF 1986)
**KINZER ANITA M** (219)925-1190
3841 County Road 46A Auburn IN 46706-9712 • IN • EM • (V 1952 MSED)
**KNAPP BETTY J** (906)228-5180
230 W Ohio St Marquette MI 49855-3426 • rlutheranc@aol.com • NW • Mem C • Redeemer Marquette MI • (906)228-9883 • (V 1979 MED)
**KNIPPENBERG SHARON L** (219)482-1996
4625 Golfview Dr Fort Wayne IN 46818-9344 • sknip@prodigy.net • IN • Mem C • Sub Bethlehem Fort Wayne IN • (219)484-7873 • (V 1961)
**KOSBERG KAREN M** (219)749-0081
6963 Lake Forest Village Cir Fort Wayne IN 46815 • kkosberg@aol.com • IN • O Sp Min • Indiana Fort Wayne IN • (RF 1984)
**KRANS DOROTHY L**
Redeemer Lutheran Church 920 W 6th St Ontario CA 91762 • PSW • Mem C • Redeemer Ontario CA • (909)986-2615 • (V 1975)
**KRIEGER EDITH E** (231)932-8497
611 Hawthorne Ln Traverse City MI 49686 • MI • EM • (V 1976)
**KRUEGER GRETCHEN** (708)452-7515
7830 North Ave - # 609 Elmwood Park IL 60707 • NI • Mem C • Saint Paul Chicago IL • (773)378-6644 • (RF 2000)

## L

**LINGENFELTER NANCY L** (814)345-5779
RR 2 Box 326 Morrisdale PA 16858-9103 • f-nlingenfelter@juno.com • EA • Mem C • St John Morrisdale PA • (814)345-5741 • (V 1965)
**LIPSCOMB BEVERLY** (415)586-4977
2557 Alemany Blvd San Francisco CA 94112-3610 • bethelcenter@juno.com • CNH • Mem C • Bethel San Francisco CA • (415)587-2525 • (V 1979 MPAD)
**LIST THERESA JO** (314)725-2518
6447 Clayton Rd #1W Clayton MO 63117 • lutheranrose@juno.com • MO • 04/1997 04/2000 • (RF 1994 MA)
**LOCK KATHLEEN ANN**
9089 N 75th St Apt 104 Milwaukee WI 53223-2041 • tekalock@worldnet.att.net • EN • 08/1998 08/2000 • (RF 1993)
**LOZA JANE E** (913)262-7239
10210 W 56th St Merriam KS 66203-2358 • MO • Mem C • Good Shepherd Kansas City MO • (816)474-9049 • (RF 1988)
**LUCERO DARLA G**
585 Illinois Blvd Hoffman Estates IL 60194 • lightlove@mediaone.net • NI • 10/1997 10/1999 • (RF 1985)
**LUSTER-BARTZ LINDYSUE** (219)294-3191
56661 Wedgewood N Elkhart IN 46516-5810 • IN • EM • (V 1976)

## M

**MANSKE BARBARA M** (949)551-4484
14782 Elm Ave Irvine CA 92606-2658 • uscluther@aol.com • PSW • Mem C • Shepherd Peace Irvine CA • (949)786-3326 • (V 1961)
**MAPPES DORIS M** (812)944-6835
5369 State Road 62 Georgetown IN 47122-9227 • IN • EM • (V 1958)
**MARBURGER FAITH ALAYNE** (540)972-2405
508 Constitution Blvd HC 76 Box 20 Locust Grove VA 22508-9501 • FaithAllen@web.tv.com • SE • 04/2000 • (V 1977)
**MC COY KATHLEEN S** (561)844-4692
425 Marlin Rd North Palm Beach FL 33408-4321 • deackmc@aol.com • FG • Mem C • Faith North Palm Beach FL • (561)848-4737 • (V 1977)
**MEYER CATHY MARIE** (210)495-4343
43 Champions Run San Antonio TX 78258 • TX • Mem C • Crown Of Life San Antonio TX • (210)490-6886 • (RF 2000)
**MEYER LINDA A** (708)672-1754
27102 S Fountainview Dr Crete IL 60417-6309 • dcsmeyer@worldnet.att.net • NI • Mem C • Zion Beecher IL • (708)946-2271 • (RF 1990)
**MEYERS HELEN DEANNE** (513)923-9051
3317 Wheatcroft Dr Cincinnati OH 45239 • meyershd@healthall.com • OH • Inst C • Ohio Olmsted Falls OH • (V 1969)
**MOE JEANA A** (219)447-7298
6422 Winter St Fort Wayne IN 46816-3618 • IN • O Sp Min • Indiana Fort Wayne IN • (RF 1984)
**MORTIMER DARLENE E** (219)462-8459
352 Green Acres Dr Valparaiso IN 46383-1714 • IN • Mem C • Immanuel Valparaiso IN • (219)462-8207 • (V 1981 MA)
**MULHOLLAND BETTY R** (219)836-8832
8327 Howard Ave Munster IN 46321-1838 • IN • EM • (V 1955)

## N

**NEAGLEY CLAIRE ELLEN**
12 Maple St Terryville CT 06786-5220 • NE • Prince Of Peace New Orleans LA • (V 1975)
**NELSON CHRISTIE A**
205/20 Chaiyakiat 1 Ngam Wong Wan Rd Bangkok 10210 THAILAND • christie@mozart.inet.co.th • IN • S Miss • Indiana Fort Wayne IN • (RF 1990 MA)
**NIELSEN PAMELA J** (219)490-2342
2807 Longwood Ct Fort Wayne IN 46845 • pamjniel@aol • IN • St Lorenz Frankenmuth MI • (RF 1985 MA)
**NIERMANN ELIZABETH MARIE**
Pioneer Camp 9324 Lake Shore Dr Angola NY 14006-9416 • deac@juno.com • EA • Eastern Williamsville NY • (716)634-5111 • (RF 1990)
**NORDLING SARA A**
5305 Lake Charles Waco TX 76710 • TX • 07/1999 • (RF 1985)

## O

**O DELL PATRICIA M** (414)681-0219
2830 Crestview Park Dr Racine WI 53402 • deactrish@hotmail.com • SW • 08/1999 • (RF 1995)
**OLBETER CARLA LYNN** (513)481-7703
4032 Homelawn Ave Apt 4 Cincinnati OH 45211-3432 • OH • Inst C • Ohio Olmsted Falls OH • (RF 1991)
**OLDAY CAROL J** (619)356-2157
9182 Lantern Dr Lake Worth FL 33467-4746 • FG • 09/1997 09/1999 • (RF 1988)
**OLSEN BRENDA G** (515)225-7984
C/O Saint Mark Lutheran Church 27 Saint Marks Pl Yonkers NY 10704-4011 • AT • 09/1992 09/1999 • (V 1977)
**OLSEN LAUREN K** (815)568-9414
706 E Prairie St Apt B Marengo IL 60152-3416 • stjohnslutheranchurch@avenew.com • NI • Mem C • St John Union IL • (815)923-2733 • (RF 1987 MA)
**OSTERMANN JOYCE ANN** (219)489-1163
7934 Stonegate Pl Fort Wayne IN 46825-3048 • jao.51@aol.com • IN • Unity Fort Wayne IN • (V 1974)

## P

**PEREZ JESSIE** (305)227-1282
10301 SW 45th St Miami FL 33165-5611 • bperez6950@aol.com • FG • Mem C • Concordia Miami FL • (305)235-6123 • (CQ 1994)
**PFOTENHAUER JUDITH ANN** (605)352-3180
1065 Ashwood Ln Huron SD 57350 • SD • 03/1999 • (CQ 1995 MA)
**PHILIPP DIANE P**
C/O Faith Lutheran Church 680 W Deerpath Rd Lake Forest IL 60045-1611 • NI • Mem C • Faith Lake Forest IL • (847)234-1868 • (CQ 1996)
**POSEY ELIZABETH A**
1450 30th Ave East Moline IL 61244 • bposeyjr@yahoo.com • CI • Mem C • St John East Moline IL • (309)792-0755 • (S 1986 MA)
**PRYBYLSKI DOROTHY** (314)842-4761
10560 Hackberry Dr Apt 7 Saint Louis MO 63128-1347 • chapdorthy@aol.com • MO • S Ex/S • Missouri Saint Louis MO • (314)317-4550 • (V 1971 MMIN)

## R

**RAO GRACE V** (320)274-6378
340 E Chestnut St - Apt #2 Annandale MN 55302 • MNS • Mem C • Zion Annandale MN • (320)274-5226 • (RF 2000)
**REHBEIN ANN MARIE** (209)474-7828
C/O St Andrew Lutheran Church 4910 Claremont Ave Stockton CA 95207-5708 • CNH • Mem C • St Andrew Stockton CA • (209)957-8750 • (V 1981)
**REIN CAROLYN J** (507)685-4317
PO Box 449 Morristown MN 55052-0449 • cjrein@clear.lakes.com • MNS • 11/1999 • (V 1976)
**REITMEIER ANGELINE R** (417)833-2194
1861 E Arlington Dr Springfield MO 65803-4875 • MO • Mem C • Faith Springfield MO • (417)833-3749 • (RF 1994)
**REMMELE KARLA RUTH**
2401 W Broadway Apt 811 Columbia MO 65203 • MO • Trinity Utica MI • (RF 1996)
**ROCKROHR DEBORAH L** (314)727-5197
801 De Mun Ave Saint Louis MO 63105 • MO • 06/1990 06/2000 • (RF 1984 MAR)
**RODRIGUEZ MARIE T**
7725 W Vernon Hwy Detroit MI 48209-1515 • MI • Michigan Ann Arbor MI • (CQ 1994)
**ROGGOW GLORIA ANN** (708)488-4500
C/O Concordia University 7400 Augusta St River Forest IL 60305-1402 • NI • Zion Anaheim CA • (S 1992)
**ROJAS IRMA S** (407)207-0559
214 N Dean Rd Orlando FL 32825-3706 • amigorojas@aol.com • FG • O Miss • Florida-Georgia Orlando FL • (CQ 1995)
**ROSNAU LINDA J** (602)788-6013
5959 E Phelps Rd Scottsdale AZ 85254-9224 • PSW • 04/1990 04/2000 • (V 1981)

## S

**SALSIEDER CAROLYN D** (920)749-2913
914 W 3rd St Appleton WI 54914-5435 • NW • 03/1990 03/2000 • (RF 1983)
**SCHAEFER LINDA** (217)648-2824
Box 429 Atlanta IL 61723-0429 • CI • O Sp Min • Central Illinois Springfield IL • (V 1970 MS)
**SCHAUM MARTHA JOY** (219)938-0448
7516 Oak Ave Gary IN 46403 • IN • 03/1999 • (RF 1995)
**SCHMID ERNA I**
PO Box 45 Glenn MI 49416-0045 • MI • Mem C • Zion Holland MI • (616)392-7151 • (RF 1992 MA)
**SCHULER RHODA GREVER** (651)641-0264
1288 Marshall Ave Saint Paul MN 55104-6448 • rschuler@csp.edu • MNS • 05/1990 05/2000 • (V 1977 MA)
**SCHWARZ LORINDA LEE** (503)276-9762
73275 SE 54th St Pendleton OR 97801 • l³schwarz@hotmail.com • NOW • O Sp Min • Northwest Portland OR • (V 1977)
**SECKER KARNA ANN** (203)429-6739
76 Willowbrook Rd Storrs Mansfield CT 06268-2205 • NE • 06/1990 06/2000 • (V 1962)
**SHIMOI RUTH ANN** (206)772-9504
6905 S 120th Pl Seattle WA 98178-4138 • NOW • O Sp Min • Northwest Portland OR • (V 1976)
**SMITH LINDA ARLENE** (317)859-8351
1475 Millridge Dr Greenwood IN 46143-9745 • fbaggins1@hotmail.com • IN • Mem C • Emmaus Indianapolis IN • (317)632-1486 • (RF 1989)
**SMITH SUSANNE**
8405 N Kilbuck Rd Monroe Center IL 61052-9720 • suesmithl@juno.com • NI • O Sp Min • Northern Illinois Hillside IL • (RF 1986)
**SNYDER DOROTHY E** (716)218-0289
14 Hidden Springs Dr Pittsford NY 14534-2897 • EA • EM • (V 1952)
**SOKOFSKI CAROL** (203)372-3071
686 Westfield Ave Bridgeport CT 06606-4008 • NE • 05/1990 05/2000 • (V 1968)
**STALLMANN RUTH S** (314)48l-9195
4134 Judith Ct Saint Louis MO 63118-4741 • MO • EM • (V 1955)

## T

**TEAGUE SHARON LOU** (210)645-1400
9811 Sugarloaf San Antonio TX 78245 • OH • Concordia LHS Fort Wayne IN • (CQ 1998)
**THOMPSON CORINNE R** (414)459-8351
817 Oakland Ave Sheboygan WI 53081-6037 • SW • 08/1993 08/2000 • (V 1969)

**THURNER JANICE** (608)752-6808
2105 S Chatham St Janesville WI 53546-6114 • SW • Mem C • Mount Calvary Janesville WI • (608)754-4145 • (V 1967)

**TIMMER DORIS IRENE** (920)261-2027
N7976 High Rd Watertown WI 53094-9407 • SW • Mem C • South Wisconsin Milwaukee WI • (414)464-8100 • (RF 1992 MA)

**TINDALL JANET C**
N64 W14463 Poplar Dr Menomonee Falls WI 53051-5176 • pjtindall@juno.com • SW • 08/1993 08/2000 • (V 1968)

V

**VANDERBLES AUDREY E** (314)558-0369
1042 Julia St Saint Louis MO 63104-3708 • MO • Missouri Saint Louis MO • (314)317-4550 • (V 1963)

W

**WACKER-ROEPKE SUSAN DARLENE** (540)885-7740
555 Hilltop Dr Staunton VA 24401 • SE • 08/1999 • (V 1978)

**WASSILAK KRISTIN R** (708)366-8813
1038 Hannah Ave Forest Park IL 60130-2312 • CRFWASSILKR@curf.edu • NI • Faith Eustis FL • (RF 1986 MAR)

**WATERS JENNIE J**
55249 County Rd 38 Buffalo Lake MN 55314-2071 • NE • 06/1998 06/2000 • (RF 1993 MS)

**WATT NATALIE J** (219)452-3273
C/O Concordia Library 6600 N Clinton ST Fort Wayne IN 46825 • wattnj@mail.ctsfw.edu • IN • 06/1998 • (RF 1998 MAR)

**WESTBROOKS KAREN L** (314)231-6760
3511 N 25th St Saint Louis MO 63107-3540 • MO • Mem C • Christ Saint Louis MO • (314)776-0248 • (V 1983 MA PHD)

**WILBERT LORI A** (815)254-2352
2302 Buttercup Ln Crest Hill IL 60435 • lanngrace@aol.com • NI • Northern Illinois Hillside IL • (RF 1984)

**WILLIAMS ROSEMARY ANN** (217)942-3692
633 Maple St Carrollton IL 62016-1232 • SI • Southern Illinois Belleville IL • (RF 1991)

**WURSTER CATHERINE A** (715)477-2434
PO Box 2374 Eagle River WI 54521-2374 • thedeac@newnorth.net • NW • Mem C • Our Savior Eagle River WI • (715)479-6226 • (RF 1988)

Z

**ZABEL PATRICIA K** (773)763-0683
6458 N Oketo Ave Chicago IL 60631-1542 • NI • 06/1990 06/2000 • (V 1972)

**ZIEMKE ROSE B** (314)961-2961
8717 Watson Rd Apt 25 Saint Louis MO 63119-5131 • MO • EM • (FW 1942)

**ZUPFER GLORIA J** (510)791-1522
3623 Sutton Loop Fremont CA 94536-5139 • CNH • Mem C • Prince Peace Fremont CA • (510)793-3366 • (V 1956)

# Section D Directors of Christian Outreach

**During the 1992 synodical convention, delegates adopted a resolution that gave certified Directors of Christian Outreach membership status in the Synod under the classification of Ministers of Religion—Commissioned.**

B

**BEER LEROY F** (615)781-2275
4924 Alexis Dr Antioch TN 37013-4222 • LBeer@bellsouth.net • MDS • S Ex/S • Mid-South Cordova TN • (SP 1982)

**BODE TIMOTHY A** (734)394-1845
259 Coronation Ct Canton MI 48188-1570 • timbode@juno.com • MI • Mem C • Christ Our Savior Livonia MI • (734)522-6830 • (SP 1984)

**BUSH JAMES D** (209)832-8787
2159 Walsingham Ct Tracy CA 95376-2482 • CNH • Mem C • St Paul Tracy CA • (209)835-7438 • (IV 1990)

C

**CARLOS JACK**
3100 Aurther St Roseville MN 55113 • MNS • Mem C • St Stephanus Saint Paul MN • (651)228-1486 • (SP 1998)

**COOPER CRAIG LAURANCE** (320)229-8802
321 2nd Ave N Sauk Rapids MN 56379 • MNN • Mem C • Trinity Sauk Rapids MN • (320)252-3670 • (SP 1990)

D

**DRAKE DEBORAH K** (308)384-0850
627 E Mac Arthur Ave Grand Island NE 68801 • dd-victory@msn.com • NEB • Mem C • Trinity Grand Island NE • (308)382-0753 • (SP 1992)

F

**FREUDENBURG ERNEST F** (507)282-4162
2512 9th Ave NW Rochester MN 55901-2309 • efreud@holycross-church.org • MNS • Mem C • Holy Cross Rochester MN • (507)289-1354 • (S 1969)

**FRITZ-HALSTED JIMMY W** (417)581-7358
606 N 39th St Nixa MO 65714-7531 • dcojim@pastors.com • MO • O Sp Min • Missouri Saint Louis MO • (314)317-4550 • (SP 1989 MED)

G

**GALVIN DEAN RICHARD** (775)783-1586
1340 Chichester Dr Gardnerville NV 89410 • 5galvins@prodigy.net • CNH • Luther Academy Rockford IL • (SP 1991)

**GEISLER RALPH L** (314)391-9994
734 Memoir Ln Manchester MO 63021-7038 • ralph.geisler@lcms.org • MO • S Ex/S • Missouri Saint Louis MO • (314)317-4550 • (S 1960 MS)

**GLIMPSE EDWARD A** (320)203-1464
1620 14th Ave S Saint Cloud MN 56301-5606 • edgdco@aol.com • MNN • 12/1999 • (SP 1996)

H

**HELLBUSCH VERN D** (402)564-9920
1564 40th Ave Columbus NE 68601-4639 • NEB • EM • (S 1957 MS)

J

**JACQUES KENNETH LEO** (262)827-0369
3040 Princeton Rd Brookfield WI 53005-3854 • Ken.Jacques@juno • SW • Mem C • Brookfield Brookfield WI • (262)783-4270 • (SP 1983)

**JOHNSON PHILLIP L** (303)456-2030
6246 Ingalls Ct Arvada CO 80003-5037 • dcophil@juno.com • RM • Mem C • Peace Arvada CO • (303)424-4454 • (SP 1982 MNM)

K

**KIRCHNER LINDA** (517)777-7993
4052 S Towerline Bridgeport MI 48722 • lkirchner55@hotmail.com • MI • Mem C • Faith Bridgeport MI • (517)777-2600 • (S 1983 MS)

**KLOTZ LANCE W** (810)673-6575
2500 Mann Rd Lot 287 Clarkston MI 48346-4288 • MI • Mem C • St Trinity Clarkston MI • (248)625-4644 • (SP 1991)

**KUNDA NICOLE L**
225 W 12th St - #6 Kaukauna WI 54130 • NW • Mem C • Bethany Kaukauna WI • (414)766-1452 • (MQ 2000)

L

**LOVICK RICHARD NORMAN** (314)645-1431
2208 Alameda Ave Maplewood MO 63143-1306 • rlovick@juno.com • NOW • 08/1999 • (SP 1985)

**LOZANO SUZANNE MICHELLE** (414)647-9871
310 W Scott St Milwaukee WI 53204-2453 • 73562.1162@compuserve.com • EN • 03/1997 • (SP 1996)

M

**MC CLURE DANIEL K**
920 San Juan Rd Sacramento CA 95834-2211 • dmccl@tomatoweb.com • CNH • Mem C • Peace Sacramento CA • (916)927-5934 • (SP 1989)

**MONTANEZ RAMON E**
210 W Park Row Dr Arlington TX 76010-4318 • TX • O Miss • Texas Austin TX • (SP 1998)

**MUELLER DIANE L** (630)271-9871
4015 Liberty Blvd Westmont IL 60559-1331 • dmueller@blhs.org • NI • Northern Illinois Hillside IL • (SP 1995)

N

**NELSON NICOLE** (314)645-6364
7232 Wise Ave Richmond Hts MO 63117 • MO • Memorial Houston TX • (SP 1998)

O

**OLDENBURG BRENDA MARIE** (850)269-3927
955 Airport Rd No 1724 Destin FL 32541 • SO • Mem C • Grace Destin FL • (904)654-1679 • (SP 1997)

P

**PATTERSON CHRISTOPHER JOHN** (419)352-3616
831 Jefferson Dr Bowling Green OH 43402-1237 • pilgrimpost@msn.com • OH • Mem C • Community Of Christ Bowling Green OH • (419)352-5101 • (SP 1994)

**PETERSON SHEILA K** (218)878-0442
214 Ave D Cloquet MN 55720-1138 • mamasheila@aol.com • MNN • Mem C • Our Redeemer Cloquet MN • (218)879-3380 • (SP 1996)

**PREUSS THEODORE** (618)667-6513
103 Sugarmill Rd Troy IL 62294-3149 • preusstm@juno.com • SI • EM • (S 1960 MA)

R

**RISHER JOY LYNN** (612)323-9604
12961 Kerry St NW Coon Rapids MN 55448 • familyofch@aol.com • MNS • Mem C • Family Christ Andover MN • (612)434-7337 • (IV 1993 MA)

**ROSAMOND JERRY D** (612)443-4631
1117 77th St Victoria MN 55386 • MNS • Mem C • Our Savior Excelsior MN • (952)474-5181 • (SP 1987)

S

**SCHROEDER ROBERT H** (760)788-9415
1212 H St Spc 113 Ramona CA 92065-2877 • bobmyrts@flash.net • EN • EM • (IV 1983)

**SCOLES BRIAN R** (651)488-1705
674 Wheelock Pkwy W Saint Paul MN 55117-4150 • brian@bethel.bchub.com • MNS • Mem C • Bethel Saint Paul MN • (651)488-6681 • (SP 1996)

**STEPHENS KENT WILLIAM** (316)684-5201
Holy Cross Luth Church 600 N Greenwich Rd Wichita KS 67206-2633 • KentStephens@holycrosslutheran.net • KS • Mem C • Holy Cross Wichita KS • (316)684-5201 • (IV 1981)

# Section E Lay Ministers

**During the 1995 synodical convention, delegates adopted a resolution that gave certified Lay Ministers membership status in the Synod under the classification of Ministers of Religion—Commissioned.**

A

**AKELEY JOY** (516)475-9670
200 La Bonne Vie Dr Apt 47D East Patchogue NY 11772-4326 • emanluth@aol.com • AT • Mem C • Emanuel Patchogue NY • (516)758-2240 • (MQ 1992 MS)

**ALBERS EARL** (816)343-5602
Rt 1 Box 1226 A4 Otterville MO 65348-9801 • MO • EM • (MW 1981)

**ALBERS RICHARD E** (775)377-2174
PO Box 1727 Round Mountain NV 89045-1727 • CNH • Mem C • Grace Round Mountain NV • (775)377-1445 • (MQ 1987)

**ALLEN CHRIS B E**
3013 Chain Dr Apt 16 Menasha WI 54952-1176 • NW • North Wisconsin Wausau WI • (MQ 1980 MSW)

**APPEL VERNON LEE** (806)435-7642
609 S Grinnell Perryton TX 79070 • TX • Mem C • Bethlehem Perryton TX • (806)435-3522 • (MQ 1997)

**AUGHE KENT J** (248)398-3327
420 S Stephenson Hwy Royal Oak MI 48067-3956 • kjaughe@aol.com • MI • Michigan Ann Arbor MI • (MQ 1986)

B

**BAUER JOHN** (828)697-7021
126 Wynnbrook Dr Hendersonville NC 28792-9265 • SO • EM • (MW 1976)

**BILICH ANDREW J** (517)835-5165
3301 Haker St Midland MI 48642-4095 • ajbilich@mindnet.org • MI • EM • (MW 1984 MA MA)

**BINTZLER REUBEN** (414)377-9262
366 Homestead Trl Grafton WI 53024-1158 • SW • EM • (MW 1977)

**BOELTE RONALD E** (580)846-5794
Rt # 2 Box 27 Lone Wolf OK 73655-9615 • OK • Mem C • St John Lone Wolf OK • (580)846-5459 • (CQ 1999)

**BREHMER DAVID ERIC** (920)924-8237
N6366 Tower Rd Fond Du Lac WI 54935-9321 • SW • 07/1995 07/2000 • (MQ 1991)

**BREHMER TAMMY LYNN** (920)924-8237
N6366 Tower Rd Fond Du Lac WI 54935-9321 • hope@vbe.com • SW • Mem C • Hope Fond Du Lac WI • (920)922-5130 • (MQ 1992)

**BROWN AUGUST DON** (561)393-3125
870 NW 6th Dr Boca Raton FL 33486 • aug³sylv@bellsouth.net • FG • Mem C • St Paul Boca Raton FL • (561)395-0433 • (MQ 1994 MBA)

C

**CANTELE JOHN A** (912)920-2359
100 Red Fox Dr Savannah GA 31419-9584 • jac31419@bellsouth.net • FG • 11/1999 • (MQ 1997)

**CASTILLO CARLOS**
C/O Redeemer Lutheran Church 5247 W 23rd St Cicero IL 60804-2843 • NI • Mem C • Good Shepherd Berwyn IL • (708)788-9054 • (CHSRF 1990)

**CLAUDE WILBUR** (417)236-0139
11786 Lawrence 2190 Verona MO 65769 • MO • EM • (MW 1981)

**CLAUSS JULIAN H** (417)869-4913
1568 N Pearson Dr Springfield MO 65802 • MO • EM • (MQ 1987)

**COLLET BRUCE GORDON**
1537 Mija Ln Seabrook TX 77586-2408 • bcollet@gdlc.org • TX • Mem C • Gloria Dei Houston TX • (281)333-4535 • (MQ 1990)

**CONSOER PAUL** (605)338-6159
300 E Timber Cir Payson AZ 85541-4049 • SD • EM • (MW 1969)

**CORDES JERILYN** (909)672-4260
29374 Murrieta Rd Sun City CA 92586 • PSW • 05/1996 05/2000 • (MQ 1989)

**CORNETT CLARENCE** (402)529-6196
712 16th St Wisner NE 68791-2217 • NEB • EM • (MW 1969)

**COULSON RALPH** (503)669-7252
3117 SE Ankeny St Apt 9 Portland OR 92714-1901 • ralphingresham@webtv.net • NOW • EM • (CQ 1981)

D

**DELL MONTY A** (605)229-3878
13986 379th Ave Aberdeen SD 57401-8734 • SD • Mem C • St Paul Aberdeen SD* • (605)225-1847 • (MW 1978)

**DENOW LOLA** (414)377-3207
1807 Cedar Sauk Rd Saukville WI 53080-2405 • PSW • Mem C • Trinity Whittier CA • (562)699-7431 • (MW 1976)

**DITTMAN JAMES L** (307)638-2332
1915 Rayor Ave Cheyenne WY 82001-4148 • jlditt@msn.com • WY • EM • (MW 1963)

**DRAMSTAD HARRY** (701)769-2146
PO Box 14 Sutton ND 58484-0014 • dramstad@lctc.com • ND • EM • (MW 1973)

## E

**EGGEN ELMER N** (515)576-4993
1713 2nd Ave S Fort Dodge IA 50501-5022 • IW • EM • (MW 1963)

**EICHINGER KURT W** (517)892-4277
1703 Raymond St Bay City MI 48706-5255 • kurdiku@aol.com • MI • 09/1998 • (CQ 1983)

**ENSMINGER C T (TED) IV** (703)670-8775
4507 Eastlawn Ave Dale City VA 22193-2654 • SE • 07/1989 07/2000 • (MQ 1986)

**ENTERS DAVID THOMAS** (414)243-4211
Concordia University 12800 N Lake Shore Dr Mequon WI 53097-2402 • david.enters@cuw.edu • SW • Immanuel Lewiston MN • (MW 1980 MS)

**EVANS RICHARD ALLEN**
Grace Lutheran Church 360 W 400 N Moab UT 84532-2354 • gracelc@timp.net • RM • Mem C • Grace Moab UT • (435)259-5017 • (MQ 1989)

## F

**FAIRMAN DONALD** (352)799-8016
4125 Mayo St Brooksville FL 34601-8353 • SO • EM • (MW 1968)

**FARRELLY JAMES J** (414)452-9383
2120 N 25th St Sheboygan WI 53081-2139 • SW • EM • (MW 1963)

**FREDEL JOHN R** (414)648-8975
W6321 Highway A Johnson Creek WI 53038-9755 • EN • English Farmington MI • (MW 1964)

## G

**GALLERT ROGER D** (810)750-9428
1040 Granger Rd Fenton MI 48430 • MI • Mem C • Gethsemane Holly MI • (248)634-9452 • (MQ 1991)

**GARRISON THOMAS B** (314)505-7712
10D Founders Way Saint Louis MO 63105 • bibleprof@aol.com • CNH • 08/1991 08/2000 • (MQ 1985)

**GATCHELL MATTHEW W** (414)367-9402
735 Canterbury Cir Hartland WI 53029-2606 • deacon@peacesussex.org • SW • Mem C • Peace Sussex WI • (262)246-3200 • (MQ 1991)

**GIBBONS THOMAS ALLEN** (630)351-7378
529 S Park St Roselle IL 60172 • tomg@trinityroselle.com • NI • Mem C • Trinity Roselle IL • (630)894-3263 • (MQ 1999)

**GLEITZ MONTY** (270)234-1703
150 Ridgeway Dr East Elizabethtown KY 42701-9739 • gleitzmd@juno.com • IN • Mem C • Holy Trinity Leitchfield KY • (270)259-9241 • (MQ 1997)

**GOLBERG MICHAEL CARL** (414)871-6657
2856 N 54th St Milwaukee WI 53210-1629 • SW • Mem C • Nazareth Milwaukee WI • (414)354-2650 • (MQ 1991)

**GREPKE FRANKLIN LEROY** (219)347-9029
3189 E Kammerer Rd Kendallville IN 46755-3084 • fjgrepke@noble.cioe.com • IN • 08/1988 08/2000 • (MW 1977)

**GREVE KENNETH** (414)464-7447
4172 N 98th St Milwaukee WI 53222-1461 • EN • O Sp Min • English Farmington MI • (MW 1966)

**GROLEAU SANDRA JEAN** (414)695-1249
1348 Sunnyridge Rd Apt 6 Pewaukee WI 53072 • sgroleau@tcbi.com • SW • 09/1999 • (MQ 1997)

**GRUBER FRANK F SR.** (610)691-6975
1709A Briarwood Dr Bethlehem PA 18020-7588 • jyarfggru@aol.com • S • Mem C • Concordia Bethlehem PA • (610)691-7625 • (CQ 1979)

## H

**HAMMEL VINCENT STEVEN SR.** (410)242-7062
1226 Leeds Ter Baltimore MD 21227-1309 • SE • Mem C • Resurrection Baltimore MD • (410)789-0415 • (MQ 1992)

**HANSEN J B** (512)364-2511
HC 1 Box 95A Odem TX 78370-9715 • TX • EM • (CQ 1977)

**HANSEN JOHN** 011-225-34-72-46-13
B P 125 Grand Bereby Cote d IVOIRE WEST AFRICA • hansenjj@aviso.ci • SW • 07/1994 • (MQ 1992)

**HARLOW ARCHIE** (915)597-2498
HC 70 Box 77 Brady TX 76825-9730 • TX • Mem C • Mount Calvary Brady TX • (915)597-2498 • (MQ 1986)

**HAYES STEVEN** (949)548-5107
2063 Meadow View Costa Mesa CA 92627 • steve³hayes@msn • PSW • Mem C • Christ Costa Mesa CA • (949)631-1611 • (MQ 1985)

**HERING KURT MATHEW** (801)546-0613
385 W Golden Ave Layton UT 84041 • khering@sisna.com • RM • Mem C • Trinity Layton UT • (801)544-5770 • (MQ 1991)

**HEUER WALDEMAR** (414)425-4849
10464 Whitnall Edge Dr Apt 201 Franklin WI 53132-1269 • wcheuer@aol.com • EN • EM • (MW 1968)

**HEWITT FRANK E** (847)428-4211
223 Spring Point Dr Carpentersvle IL 60110-2828 • NI • Mem C • Bethlehem Dundee IL • (847)426-7311 • (MQ 1992 MA)

**HOLDER ROLAND E** (248)375-2098
2311 Walton Blvd Apt 27 Rochester Hills MI 48309 • EN • Mem C • Shepherd Hills Rochester Hills MI • (248)652-8420 • (CQ 1985)

**HOLMSTROM EARL A**
1225 Darwin Dr Grand Forks ND 58203-2030 • SW • 07/1998 07/2000 • (MQ 1989)

**HOLTHUS ELDON** (308)623-1567
1409 16th St Mitchell NE 69357-1525 • WY • 01/1991 • (MW 1982)

## J

**JACOBSEN GARY W** (616)794-4019
9945 Bricker Rd Belding MI 48809-9446 • MI • Mem C • Holy Cross Belding MI • (616)794-1310 • (MQ 1989)

**JAECKEL WALTER E** (414)258-5326
724 N 115th St Wauwatosa WI 53226-3605 • SW • EM • (MW 1977)

**JAHNKE RONALD H DR** (810)226-2178
18449 Greenmeadow Dr Clinton Township MI 48038 • ronjahnke@juno.com • MI • Mem C • Immanuel Macomb MI • (810)286-4231 • (MQ 1984 MBA DMIN)

## K

**KAEDING LEO** (916)991-9559
1108 Arrowhead Ave Rio Linda CA 95673-4308 • CNH • EM • (MW 1967)

**KASTER JOHN H** (210)543-7444
8730 White Quail San Antonio TX 78250 • TX • Mem C • Holy Cross San Antonio TX • (210)532-1300 • (MQ 1984)

**KEMP MARGARET**
2034 Inner Circle Dr Oviedo FL 32765-8707 • FG • EM • (MQ 1982)

**KORTH DALE W** (414)543-4291
2559 S 94th St Milwaukee WI 53227-2333 • SW • EM • (MW 1963)

**KORTHALS RICHARD G** (719)574-7774
2880 Inspiration Dr Colorado Springs CO 80917-3303 • RM • EM • (CQ 1981 MS LLD)

**KREYLING ARTHUR R** (908)754-0156
140 Sandford Ave North Plainfield NJ 07060-4348 • NJ • Mem C • Our Redeemer Fords NJ • (732)738-7470 • (CQ 1978)

**KRUEGER CARL L** (715)787-3653
W10947 Upper Red Lake Rd Gresham WI 54128-8994 • NW • Mem C • Immanuel Gresham WI* • (715)787-3653 • (MQ 1984)

## L

**LASKA GREGORY R** (920)773-2384
9208 Pigeon Lake Rd Valders WI 54245-9527 • SW • Mem C • Emmanuel Adell WI • (920)994-9005 • (MQ 1994)

**LEAL WILLIAM** (916)283-0384
PO Box 1214 Quincy CA 95971-1214 • CNH • 09/1988 09/1999 • (MW 1967)

**LEE CHANDARA ARONN** (562)595-0108
2599 Walnut Ave Unit 120 Signal Hill CA 90806-3665 • PSW • O Sp Min • First Cambodian Long Beach CA • (562)437-8532 • (IV 1989 MA)

**LEHENBAUER THEODORE** (314)248-0558
3600 Navajo St Hannibal MO 63401-2349 • EN • EM • (MW 1971)

**LEHR ROBERT W** (314)832-6640
4924 Neosho St Saint Louis MO 63109-2953 • MO • Mem C • Holy Cross Saint Louis MO • (314)772-8633 • (MQ 1988)

**LIST ROBERT** (636)938-9139
305 Wallach Dr Eureka MO 63025-2111 • Robert.List@wbb.org • MO • S Ex/S • Missouri Saint Louis MO • (314)317-4550 • (MW 1977)

**LLOYD PAUL F**
C/O Minnesota North District PO Box 604 Brainerd MN 56401-0604 • MNN • 06/1991 06/2000 • (MW 1978 MS)

**LOFMARK GEORGE E** (201)768-7720
166 Somerset Rd Norwood NJ 07648-1927 • NJ • Mem C • St Paul Closter NJ • (201)768-6310 • (MQ 1992 MA)

**LUCHT ELDA**
2656 Baltusrol Dr Saint Louis MO 63129-5438 • MO • EM • (CQ 1975 MRE)

## M

**MAHLER WILLIAM ARTHUR** (734)769-1142
3136 Dunwoodie Rd Ann Arbor MI 48105-4113 • mahlerw@ccaa.edu • MI • St Paul Royal Oak MI • (CQ 1983 MA PHD)

**MARTINEZ JESUS** (562)948-5388
11314 Flossmoor Rd Santa Fe Springs CA 90670-3144 • PSW • Mem C • La Santa Cruz Los Angeles CA • (323)269-7989 • (HIT 1991)

**MATHER JAY DEAN** (708)534-8171
26424 S 88th Ave Monee IL 60449-9512 • NI • Mem C • Good Shepherd Frankfort IL • (815)469-1028 • (MQ 1986)

**MATHER PAULA J** (414)376-0737
1739 11th Ave Grafton WI 53024-2405 • SW • Good Shepherd Frankfort IL • (MQ 1986)

**MAYNARD JOHN E**
C/O Faith Luth Church PO Box 1448 Buena Vista CO 81211-1448 • RM • Mem C • Faith Buena Vista CO • (719)395-2039 • (MQ 1987)

**MC COURT CRAIG T** (952)442-2833
868 Crosspoint Rd Waconia MN 55387 • mnmccourt@mail.com • MNS • Mem C • Trinity Waconia MN • (952)442-4165 • (MQ 1986)

**MC MARTIN HUGH H** (313)591-0251
9828 Eckles Rd Livonia MI 48150-4549 • EN • Mem C • Risen Christ Plymouth MI • (734)453-5252 • (MQ 1992)

**MEIER BRUCE K**
Peace Luth Church 407 Jackson Ave W Oxford MS 38655 • SO • Mem C • Peace Oxford MS • (662)234-6568 • (MQ 1997)

**MEINERT ROBERT W** (810)247-3510
49546 Bishop Ct Shelby Township MI 48315-3805 • MI • 09/1998 • (MW 1980)

**MEYER JUDITH E** (941)318-1213
416 Smiley Ct Winter Haven FL 33884 • FG • Mem C • Grace Winter Haven FL • (863)293-8447 • (MQ 1999 MS)

**MILZ G DAVID** (248)442-9584
31606 Merriwood Park Dr Livonia MI 48152-1397 • MI • Mem C • Hosanna-Tabor Redford MI • (313)937-2424 • (CQ 1984)

**MITTWEDE RICHARD A** (517)887-6379
6063 Rolfe Rd Lansing MI 48911-4944 • yuthweed@juno.com • EN • Mem C • Christ Lansing MI • (517)482-2252 • (MQ 1990)

**MONTGOMERY ALLEN O** (715)362-7605
W473 County Road D Gleason WI 54435-9648 • albea@newnorth.net • NW • Mem C • Our Savior Gleason WI • (715)362-2323 • (MQ 1990)

**MOOG MARK A** (812)867-2631
4220 Norwich Pl Evansville IN 47725 • mmooglm@aol.com • IN • Mem C • Trinity Evansville IN • (812)867-5279 • (MQ 1999)

**MORK DONNA M** (714)544-4869
12901A Newport Ave Tustin CA 92780-3532 • morkdm@cui.edu • PSW • Northern Illinois Hillside IL • (MQ 1986 MA)

## N

**NATZKE FLORENCE** (920)864-2360
8212 County Road W Greenleaf WI 54126 • NW • 05/1996 05/2000 • (MW 1980)

**NATZKE ROBERT A** (920)864-2360
8212 Hwy W Greenleaf WI 54126 • NW • 05/1996 05/2000 • (MQ 1986)

**NEIDHOLD FRED W** (509)328-9521
6602 N Jefferson St Spokane WA 99208-4236 • fneidhold@earthlink.net • NOW • EM • (MQ 1987)

**NORBERG KENNETH** (805)733-1109
273 Oakwood Cir Lompoc CA 93436-1352 • PSW • EM • (MW 1982)

## O

**ONASCH WILLIS**
1106 W 3rd St Weiser ID 83672 • NOW • EM • (MW 1979)

**ONNEN TIMOTHY G**
220 Mayden Ln Branson MO 65616 • MO • Mem C • Faith Branson MO • (888)777-3059 • (MQ 1983)

**OTT EDWIN** (313)937-9322
11324 Marion Redford MI 48239-2017 • MI • Mem C • St Michael Wayne MI • (734)728-1950 • (CQ 1984)

**OTT-HAGER DIANE LYNN** (612)728-0581
5042 29th Ave S Minneapolis MN 55417-1329 • diane.ott-hager@lutheranhighschool.com • EN • St Michael Wayne MI • (MW 1978)

## P

**PARRALES BOANERGES** (213)588-0934
C/O Redeemer Lutheran Church 2626 Liberty Blvd South Gate CA 90280-2004 • PSW • Mem C • Redeemer South Gate CA • (323)588-0934 • (HIT 1991)

**PASK WAYNE MARSHALL** (765)448-4138
7 Lockwood Ct Lafayette IN 47905-9699 • sotharvest@aol.com • IN • Mem C • Grace Lafayette IN • (765)474-1887 • (MQ 1997)

**PEREZ-ARCHE MARIO** (305)559-8859
12259 SW 17th Ln Apt 108 Miami FL 33175-1536 • FG • 06/1999 • (HIT 1991)

**PEREZ-ARCHE SARA** (309)559-8859
12259 SW 17th Ln Apt 108 Miami FL 33175-1536 • FG • 06/1999 • (HIT 1994)

**PLOPPER GARY A** (262)646-8006
2215C Circle Ridge Dr Delafield WI 53018-2047 • bslc@execpc.com • SW • Mem C • Blessed Savior New Berlin WI • (262)786-6465 • (MW 1967)

**PRIEHS WARREN F** (810)329-3957
925 Thornapple St Clair MI 48079-5440 • MI • EM • (CQ 1986)

**PRUITT THOMAS H** (402)484-8115
3101 Prescott Ave Lincoln NE 68502-5947 • tomp1949@prodigy.net • NEB • Mem C • Trinity Lincoln NE • (402)474-0606 • (MQ 1991)

## Q

**QUILLEN ERNEST** (580)362-3983
209 S Plum Newkirk OK 74647 • OK • Mem C • St John Ponca City OK* • (405)363-4603 • (CQ 1980)

## R

**RADES SANDRA J** (262)538-4119
W256N5660 N Hill Dr Sussex WI 53089-4123 • SW • Mem C • Bethlehem Wales WI • (262)968-2194 • (MQ 1987)

**RAINS W R** (405)728-8330
1190B Sundance Mtn Rd Oklahoma City OK 73162-1521 • OK • Mem C • Faith Oklahoma City OK • (405)632-5744 • (MQ 1999)

**RANDALL SCOTT M** (507)333-2996
C/O Messiah Lutheran Church 16725 Highview Ave Lakeville MN 55044 • smr@means.net • MNS • Mem C • Messiah Lakeville MN • (612)431-5959 • (MQ 1993 MSED)

**RAU DONALD RICHARD** (860)742-3166
146 Antrim Rd Coventry CT 06238-1301 • rau.d@worldnet.att.net • NE • Mem C • Our Savior South Windsor CT • (860)644-3350 • (MQ 1994)

**REINAP ENDEL ANDY**
1373 118th Ave Indianola IA 50125-9166 • CNH • EM • (MW 1966)

**RIDDLE FRANCES KAY**
10107 W Good Hope Rd Milwaukee WI 53224-3817 • SW • South Wisconsin Milwaukee WI • (414)464-8100 • (MW 1978)

**RITTER DONALD A** (810)254-9599
49575 Deer Run Dr Shelby Twp MI 48315-3329 • MI • Mem C • St John Rochester MI • (248)652-8830 • (CQ 1984)

**RITTER LARRY** (619)420-0636
1478 Platano Ct Chula Vista CA 91911-5129 • PSW • 01/1992 • (MQ 1984 MA)

**ROSENAU TERRY** (810)984-2452
1929 Lakewood Ave Port Huron MI 48060 • MI • Mem C • Trinity Port Huron MI • (810)984-2993 • (MW 1974)

**ROSENKOTTER ARTHUR H** (501)425-8648
1605 Gregg Rd Mountain Home AR 72653-5888 • MDS • EM • (MW 1964)

**ROSS JOAN M** (530)589-4916
42 Peak View Dr Oroville CA 95966-8937 • shalomfriends@onemain.com • CNH • Mem C • Calvary Oroville CA • (530)533-5017 • (MQ 1988)

**ROUSSEAU DONALD L** (314)878-6779
12824 Fishel Ct St Louis MO 63141 • MO • Mem C • Immanuel Saint Louis MO • (314)993-2394 • (MQ 1998)

**RUPPRECHT MARTHA L** (941)413-1026
814 Osceola St Apt 6 Lakeland FL 33801-5500 • FG • Mem C • St Mark Hollywood FL • (954)922-7568 • (MW 1969)

**RUPPRECHT PAUL** (812)476-9991
3201 Roselawn Cir Evansville IN 47711 • IN • Mem C • Our Redeemer Evansville IN • (812)476-9991 • (MQ 1996)

**RUSH RAYMOND E** (507)278-4293
RR 2 Box 4 Good Thunder MN 56037-9601 • MNS • 01/1991 01/2000 • (MW 1977)

S

**SANSBURY RICHARD W** (419)537-1015
2115 Mt Vernon Toledo OH 43607-1547 • OH • Mem C • St Philip Toledo OH • (419)475-2835 • (MQ 1998)

**SCHACHEL ERVIN D** (734)283-8625
930 Lindbergh St Wyandotte MI 48192-2853 • seschach@ili.net • MI • Mem C • Trinity Wyandotte MI • (734)282-5877 • (MQ 1987)

**SCHAFF RUDOLPH H** (402)425-3305
PO Box 47 Crookston NE 69212-0047 • NEB • Mem C • Zion Crookston NE • (402)425-3357 • (MQ 1986)

**SCHAUER DARWIN F** (218)335-2208
C/O Immanuel Lutheran Church PO Box 506 Cass Lake MN 56633-0506 • MNN • Mem C • Immanuel Cass Lake MN* • (218)335-6134 • (MQ 1989)

**SCHLICHTING J RICHARD**
2525 E 32nd Joplin MO 64804-3179 • MO • 06/1998 06/2000 • (MQ 1986 MBA PHD)

**SCHOEVERTH GAYLE DORIS** (440)327-3388
35278 Greenwich Ave North Ridgeville OH 44039-1394 • OH • 09/1994 09/1999 • (MQ 1993)

**SCHRECK JERRY D** (406)857-3388
248 Mission View Dr Lakeside MT 59922-9708 • MT • Mem C • Trinity Kalispell MT • (406)257-5683 • (MQ 1991)

**SCHROEDER LEO G** (918)676-5186
PO Box 219 Fairland OK 74343 • OK • Mem C • St Paul Fairland OK • (918)676-3059 • (MQ 1999)

**SCHULTZ JOHN W** (630)483-3148
495 Cheyenne Tr Carol Stream IL 60188 • NI • Mem C • Our Savior Carol Stream IL • (630)830-4833 • (MQ 1999)

**SCHWAUSCH DAVID A** (561)852-4735
18696 Cape Sable Dr Boca Raton FL 33498-6374 • schwaud1@gate.net • FG • 10/1990 10/1999 • (MW 1973)

**SEMONIOUS CLARENCE LEROY** (760)379-1828
124 Lake Dr PO Box 398 Bodfish CA 93205-0398 • CNH • 02/1999 • (MQ 1964)

**SENTER JACK** (209)586-5393
PO Box 204 Mi Wuk Village CA 95346-0204 • CNH • EM • (MW 1972)

**SHIVELY GARY L** (217)826-6166
613 N 6th St Marshall IL 62441-1221 • CI • Mem C • Concordia Marshall IL • (217)826-6130 • (MQ 1993 MS)

**SIEGEL GERALDINE**
5869 Berry Lake Rd Gillett WI 54124-9772 • SW • South Wisconsin Milwaukee WI • (414)464-8100 • (MQ 1987)

**SOK PETER ROS**
C/O Trinity Lutheran Church 444 N American St Stockton CA 95202-2129 • CNH • Mem C • Trinity Stockton CA • (209)464-1936 • (CQ 1982)

T

**THAYER ROY ELMOR** (360)928-9561
31 Daniel Pond Way Port Angeles WA 98363-7120 • PSW • Mem C • Christ Yuma AZ • (520)726-0773 • (MW 1981)

**TRAMPE ALVIN H** (618)656-1484
320 W Linden Edwardsville IL 62025 • SI • EM • (MQ 1990)

U

**UDEN DAVID A** (815)394-1342
7297 Montmorency Dr Rockford IL 61108-4434 • NI • Mem C • Concordia Machesney Park IL • (815)633-4983 • (MW 1967 MS)

W

**WATERS ROBERT O**
6430 Franke Rd Fort Wayne IN 46816-9722 • bobwaters@juno.com • TX • Mem C • Immanuel Mercedes TX • (956)565-1518 • (MQ 1998 MA)

**WATSON MILLARD** (210)659-1298
495 Emelia St Universal City TX 78148-4607 • TX • Mem C • Mount Calvary San Antonio TX • (210)824-8748 • (MQ 1996)

**WEGNER WILHELM R** (406)452-7543
2329 4th Ave SW Great Falls MT 59404-2615 • MT • EM • (MW 1971)

**WICKE ROY ALBERT** (717)692-1996
330 Moore St Millersburg PA 17061-1152 • EA • Mem C • Faith Herndon PA • (717)758-4970 • (MQ 1984)

**WOOD DALE F**
7801 W Acacia St Milwaukee WI 53223-5621 • SW • EM • (MQ 1985)

**WURL DORIS ANN**
2040 Yakima Valley Hwy Wapato WA 98951-9670 • NOW • 05/1995 05/2000 • (MQ 1989)

**WYATT FLOYD N** (504)872-6027
PO Box 5 Houma LA 70360-0005 • SO • EM • (CQ 1984)

Z

**ZOELLICK JEFFREY LEE** (630)690-9232
606 Topeka Ct Carol Stream IL 60188-2909 • NI • Mem C • Our Savior Carol Stream IL • (630)830-4833 • (MQ 1995)

# Section F
# Parish Assistants

During the 1998 synodical convention delegates adopted a resolution that gave Certified Parish Assistants membership status in the Synod under the classification of Ministers of Religion—Commissioned.

B

**BARBEY JAMES ALFRED**
Hope Lutheran Church 4635 26th St W Bradenton FL 34207-1702 • barbeyja@hotmail.com • EN • 03/1999 • (AA 1984 MSW)

C

**CHESTER THOMAS BRIAN** (616)538-1897
320 43rd St SE Kentwood MI 49548-3358 • MI • Mem C • St Mark Kentwood MI • (616)455-5320 • (AA 1987)

G

**GARRETT CAROL A** (316)722-0418
10613 Ponderosa Cir Wichita KS 67212-6812 • cgarrett@kscable.com • KS • 03/1999 • (AA 1986)

**GUSE STEPHANIE**
6447 Clayton Rd Apt 1E Saint Louis MO 63117-1867 • stguse@juno.com • CNH • 03/1999 • (PO 1991)

H

**HEINS RONALD O** (810)778-4160
19145 Victor Roseville MI 48066-3041 • MI • 06/1999 • (AA 1991)

J

**JURCHEN ESTHER EILEEN** (313)480-3841
1419 Gregory St Apt 12 Ypsilanti MI 48197-1673 • MI • Mem C • St Paul Ann Arbor MI • (734)665-9117 • (AA 1983 MSW)

K

**KOENIG HERMAN E** (520)579-3809
7714 W Summer Scene Dr Tucson AZ 85743-5187 • MO • 03/1999 • (AA 1984)

**KRUEGER RICHARD CARL** (616)361-8626
1659 Diamond Ct NE Grand Rapids MI 49505-4869 • messiahgr@juno.com • MI • Mem C • Messiah Grand Rapids MI • (616)363-2553 • (AA 1989 MMU)

L

**LEITER SAMUEL K** (317)858-3733
6465 Apollo Way Indianapolis IN 46278-1970 • cuinhvn@messiah-indy.org • IN • Mem C • Messiah Indianapolis IN • (317)858-3733 • (AA 1991)

M

**MOL JAMES M**
5160 Berneda Dr Flint MI 48506 • jimmol@aol.com • MI • Mem C • St Mark Flint MI • (810)736-6680 • (AA 1982)

R

**ROCKENSUESS LARRY H SR.** (734)692-2054
2972 Saint Paul St Trenton MI 48183-3603 • lrockensuess@yahoo.com • MI • Mem C • Grace Monroe MI • (734)242-1401 • (AA 1984)

S

**SCHUCK KATHLEEN A** (810)629-6722
11598 Farmhill Dr Fenton MI 48430-2532 • mschuckjr@aol.com • MI • Mem C • St Paul Flint MI • (810)239-6200 • (AA 1980 MA)

**STOJKOVIC JILL**
130 Mount Ridge Cir Rochester NY 14616-4830 • EA • 03/1999 • (AA 1984)

T

**TEDESCO KIMBERLY J** (810)793-1548
1184 Lake Shore Dr Columbiaville MI 48421-9770 • MI • Mem C • St Paul Lapeer MI • (810)664-6653 • (AA 1988)

W

**WITTO GREGORY PAUL** (217)345-1082
2227 University Dr Charleston IL 61920-3855 • csgpw@eiu.edu • CI • Mem C • Immanuel Charleston IL • (217)345-3008 • (AA 1994)

# CERTIFIED CHURCH WORKERS, LAY

Corrected to October 18, 2000

During the 1983 Synodical Convertion, delegates adopted a resolution for the listing of certified professional church workers, lay, in *The Lutheran Annual.*

Bylaw7.41: The Consecrated lay worker shall be under the ecclesiastical supervision of the President of the District in which he/she is serving (1992 Synodical Convention).

The listing that follows is divided into six sections. Lay Ministers: Lay Teachers: Parish Music: Parish Nurse: Parish Workers: Social Workers.

Certified records are formatted in the following order:

Name, previous name, mailing address, phone number, e-mail, district, position held, where serving, an asterisk (*) indicates that he/she is serving in more positions, or status EM or CAND, office phone number

In parenthesis: (Certifying Entity, Year of graduation or colloquy, and graduate degrees).

## KEY TO ABBREVIATIONS

### Certifying Entity

AA=Ann Arbor
AU=Austin
BR=Bronxville
IV=Irvine
MQ=Mequon
MW=Milwaukee
PO=Portland
RF=River Forest
S=Seward
SP=St. Paul
WN=Winfield
CQ=Colloquized

### Missouri Synod Districts

AT=Atlantic
CNH=Calif.-Nev.-Hawaii
CI=Central Illinois
EA=Eastern
EN=English
FG=Florida-Georgia
IN=Indiana
IE=Iowa East
IW=Iowa West
KS=Kansas
MI=Michigan
MDS=Mid-South
MNN=Minnesota North
MNS=Minnesota South
MO=Missouri
MT=Montana
NE=New England
NEB=Nebraska
ND=North Dakota
NJ=New Jersey
NW=North Wisconsin
NI=Northern Illinois
NOW=Northwest
OH=Ohio
OK=Oklahoma
RM=Rocky Mountain
S=SELC District
SD=South Dakota
SE=Southeastern
SI=Southern Illinois
SO=Southern
SW=South Wisconsin
TX=Texas
WY=Wyoming

### Position Titles

Aux=Auxiliary Ministry
CCRA=Cooperative Church Related Agency
D Ex/S=District Executive or Staff
Df Min=Deaf Missionary
END=Endorsed by Synod
HS/C=Synod HS/College/Univ/Seminary
Inst C=Institutional Chaplain
LHS=Lutheran HS Faculty or Staff
M Chap=Military Chaplain/Dir of Rel Ed
Mem C=Serving a Member Congregation
NMem C=Serving a Non-Member Congregation
O Miss=Other Missionary
O Sp Min=Other Special Ministry
P O EL=Principal Only Elementary
PO HS=Principal Only High School
RSO=Recognized Service Organization
S Ex/S=Synodical Executive or Staff
S HS/C=Synodical HS/College/Univ/Seminary
S Miss=Synodical Missionary
Sp S=Special School or Spec Lutheran Classes
T PS O=Teacher in a Pre-School Only
T EL=Teacher Elementary Only
T P EL=Teacher/Principal Elementary

## Lay Ministers

**(Eligible for membership but have not joined)**

### H

**HEFFERNAN JOYCE** (941)596-1558
4700 St Croix Ln #321 Naples FL 34109 • FG • Mem C • Grace Naples FL • (941)261-7421 • (MQ 1999)

### M

**MARLOWE REBECCA S**
239 1/2 N Main Adrian MI 49221 • MI • Mem C • Hope Adrian MI • (517)263-4317 • (MQ 2000)

### O

**OETTEL ROBERT**
Nitrianska 6 953 01 Zlate Moravce SLOVAKIA • NEB • 06/1988 • (MW 1965)

## Lay Teachers

**(Eligible for membership but have not joined)**

### A

**ABLEIDINGER LOLA M**
18540 W 60th Ave Golden CO 80403-1047 • RM • EM • (SP 1967)

**ACKMANN ELIZABETH** (219)486-1828
4008 Willshire Estates Dr Fort Wayne IN 46815-5335 • IN • EM • (RF 1967 MS)

**ACUNA SUSAN V**
31250 8th Ave S Federal Way WA 39566 • NOW • Tchr • Concordia Tacoma WA • (253)475-9513 • (S 1982)

**ALBERS BARBARA JEAN** (262)786-5272
620 Hi View Ct Elm Grove WI 53122 • albersrw@aol.com • SW • EM • (RF 1959)

**ALLEN JANET** (734)668-7593
475 Pine Brae St Ann Arbor MI 48105-2743 • divsheppre@aol.com • MI • Tchr • The Shepherds Ann Arbor MI • (734)761-7275 • (RF 1971 MA MA)

**ALLISON SUSAN P** (765)457-0346
1201 Arundel Dr Kokomo IN 46901-3920 • susiea2@yahoo.com • IN • Tchr • Redeemer Kokomo IN • (765)864-6466 • (S 1977)

**ANDERSON SARAH J** (414)578-0722
8631 W Lawrence Ave Milwaukee WI 53225-5124 • anderclan4@juno.com • SW • Tchr • Christ Memorial Milwaukee WI • (414)461-3371 • (RF 1979)

**ARLDT MEREDITH L** (512)733-1083
2501 Louis Henna Blvd #813 Round Rock TX 78664 • arldtteacher@hotmail.com • TX • Tchr • Redeemer Austin TX • (512)451-6478 • (IV 1997)

**ARNOLD ELLEN A** (517)662-6397
4812 Monica St Auburn MI 48611-9430 • MI • Tchr • Trinity Bay City MI • (517)662-4891 • (S 1971)

**ARNOLD KAREN L**
6804 Casselberry Ct Saint Louis MO 63123-3241 • MO • 10/1999 • (S 1968)

**ASHBY JENNIFER LYNN** (727)527-6213
PO Box 7132 St Petersburg FL 33734 • jashby1@juno.com • FG • Tchr • Grace Saint Petersburg FL • (727)527-6213 • (S 1994)

**AUFDEMBERGE JULANA L** (618)656-4354
991 Berkshire Dr Edwardsville IL 62025-3811 • SI • EM • (S 1972 MSED)

**AUFDEMBERGE LENORE C** (303)471-4123
1275 W Braewood Ave Highlands Ranch CO 80126-5674 • RM • Tchr • Bethlehem Lakewood CO • (303)238-7676 • (S 1958)

**AUMANN F EVELYN** (219)724-4431
9960 N US Highway 27 Decatur IN 46733-8773 • IN • 11/1995 • (RF 1956)

### B

**BAERWOLF CATHERINE E** (407)679-9687
225 Washington Ave Chuluota FL 32766-8602 • S • Tchr • St Luke Oviedo FL • (407)365-3228 • (AA 1985)

**BARKHAU PATRICIA** (708)823-3092
1711 Norman Blvd Park Ridge IL 60068-3850 • NI • EM • (RF 1958)

**BARRETO LOIS IRENE** (313)291-1253
9255 Pickwick Cir E Bldg 22 Taylor MI 48180-3822 • ggblib@gateway.net • MI • Tchr • Peace Detroit MI • (313)882-3030 • (RF 1977 MEC)

**BARTELS KATHI KAE** (715)467-2686
1143 Glacier Ridge Rd Stevens Point WI 54481 • NW • Tchr • St Paul Stevens Point WI • (715)344-5664 • (MQ 1995)

**BARTENS ELAINE A** (618)783-8739
903 Shup St Newton IL 62448-1814 • CI • Tchr • Good Shepherd Newton IL • (618)783-4105 • (S 1986)

**BARTS PHYLLIS J** (414)452-2628
1333 N 28th St Sheboygan WI 53081-3165 • SW • Tchr • St Paul Sheboygan WI • (920)452-6882 • (RF 1964)

**BASEL ANGELA MARIE** (708)534-8096
703 Burnham Dr Apt 18 University Park IL 60466 • NI • Tchr • St Paul Chicago Heights IL • (708)754-4492 • (RF 1990)

**BAUER LINDA** (303)985-9424
4225 W Yale Ave Denver CO 80219-5710 • LindaannBauer@juno.com • RM • 12/1989 • (S 1972)

**BAUMANN GEORGANN** (608)524-8503
1350 N Dewey Ave Reedsburg WI 53959-1029 • kbaumann@mwt.net • SW • Tchr • St Peter Reedsburg WI • (608)524-4066 • (SP 1969)

**BECCUE LESTER O** (760)735-9319
1912 Bear Valley Oaks Rd Escondido CA 92025-6300 • lester@beccue.com • PSW • EM • (RF 1957 MED)

**BECKA KAREN M** (216)398-5942
4755 Deborah Lynn Dr Brooklyn OH 44144 • OH • Tchr • St James Cleveland OH • (216)351-7194 • (RF 1978 MA)

**BEHMLANDER CHRISTINE E**
St Peter Lutheran Church 23000 Gratiot Ave Eastpointe MI 48021-1663 • MI • Tchr • St Peter Eastpointe MI • (810)776-1663 • (AA 1984)

**BEHRENS CYNTHIA ANN** (503)357-5790
PO Box 6740 Portland OR 97228 • behrenscy@aol.com • NOW • Tchr • Little Lambs Portland OR • (503)244-4558 • (RF 1964)

**BEHRENS JANET E** (863)325-8707
152 Chaucer Ln SE Winter Haven FL 33884-2303 • FG • Tchr • Grace Winter Haven FL • (863)293-8447 • (S 1963 MA)

**BEIER EUNICE L** (913)348-5820
RR 1 Clifton KS 66937-9801 • KS • Tchr • Linn Association Linn KS • (785)348-5792 • (S 1964 MS)

**BERG CAROLE J** (815)877-2897
4865 Burningtree Dr Rockford IL 61114-5311 • NI • Tchr • Immanuel Belvidere IL • (815)544-8058 • (RF 1976)

**BERG JUDY A** (214)271-1714
2409 Country Club Pkwy Garland TX 75041-2117 • TX • Tchr • Cross Of Christ De Soto TX • (972)223-9586 • (S 1967 MS)

**BERG KATHLEEN A** (414)652-4494
6233 64 St Kenosha WI 53142-2913 • SW • 06/1993 • (MQ 1988)

**BERGDOLT REBECCA J** (308)389-4402
118 E 10th St Grand Island NE 68801-3918 • NEB • 09/1993 • (S 1989)

**BERGER JUDITH** (314)997-6911
800 Berry Hill Dr Olivette MO 63132-3502 • dandj@juno.com • MO • Tchr • Village Ladue MO • (314)993-6743 • (RF 1962)

**BERNDT DIANN** (716)663-1726
191 Armstrong Rd Rochester NY 14612-4262 • EA • Tchr • Hope Rochester NY • (716)723-4673 • (RF 1953)

**BETKER BEVERLY J** (734)421-0073
7369 Manor Cir Apt 204 Westland MI 48185-2032 • glsgr1@aol.com • MI • Tchr • Guardian Dearborn MI • (313)274-3665 • (RF 1963)

**BEVER PEGGY S**
24765 Ridgecroft Ave Eastpointe MI 48021-1439 • PSW • 06/2000 • (RF 1972)

**BEYER JANET K** (714)589-6809
1 Paulownia Rancho Sta Margarita CA 92688-1328 • PSW • Tchr • Abiding Savior Lake Forest CA • (949)830-1461 • (RF 1978)

**BHATTI AVIS E** (414)444-1296
3146 N 49th St Milwaukee WI 53216-3202 • SW • Tchr • Christ Memorial Milwaukee WI • (414)461-3371 • (RF 1974)

**BICKEL JENNIFER LYNN** (810)997-9924
47780 Pinecrest Shelby Township MI 48317 • MI • Tchr • St Paul Sterling Heights MI • (810)247-4427 • (S 1997)

**BIERBAUM DONNA R** (785)692-4542
1509 3rd Rd Palmer KS 66962-8905 • debier@bluevalley.net • KS • 07/1994 • (S 1966 MED)

**BILGO DIANE K** (414)893-4561
403 Mulberry Ln Plymouth WI 53073-2556 • SW • Tchr • St John Plymouth WI • (920)893-5114 • (SP 1975)

**BIRKHOLZ KAREN** (810)791-1232
23147 Whitley Dr Clinton Twp MI 48035 • MI • Tchr • Trinity Clinton Township MI • (810)468-8511 • (S 1969)

**BLEEKE AUDREY** (414)637-4533
1410 Spring Valley Dr Racine WI 53405-1635 • SW • EM • (RF 1952)

**BOADWAY PAMELA J** (810)625-9384
9971 Misty Ridge Cir Clarkston MI 48348-1632 • MI • Tchr • East Bethlehem Detroit MI • (313)892-2671 • (S 1971)

**BOBB DONNA L** (314)631-1517
9806 Tiffany Sqare Pkwy Saint Louis MO 63123-6264 • MO • Tchr • Christ Community Kirkwood MO • (314)822-7774 • (RF 1973)

**BOCKELMAN SUZANNE** (515)255-8387
6220 Dawson Dr Des Moines IA 50322-5015 • IW • Tchr • Mount Olive Des Moines IA • (515)277-8349 • (S 1985)

**BOCKMEIER JOYCE L** (801)572-3793
860 Chariot Dr Sandy UT 84094 • RM • Tchr • Grace Sandy UT • (801)572-6375 • (S 1978)

**BOESCHEN MARILYN R** (660)584-2409
1206 Olive St Higginsville MO 64037-1233 • MO • Tchr • Immanuel Higginsville MO • (660)584-2854 • (RF 1964 MS)

**BOETTCHER CHRISTINE S** (208)326-3260
C/O Trinity Lutheran School 3558 N 1825 E Buhl ID 83316-6357 • pjboettc@cyberhighway.net • SW • 06/2000 • (MQ 1987)

**BOLDT JILL M**
7 Joy Springs Senoia GA 30276-3234 • FG • Tchr • St Paul Peachtree City GA • (770)486-3545 • (RF 1994)

**BONGARD REBECCA L** (219)462-8690
4203 Onyx Ct Valparaiso IN 46385 • rbongard@imail.valpo.k12.in.us • IN • 04/1994 • (RF 1984 MA)

**BONK CAROLYN A**
C/O Grace Lutheran Church 643 W 13th Ave Escondido CA 92025-5620 • PSW • Mem C • Grace Escondido CA • (760)745-0831 • (IV 1982)

**BORCHERDING WENDY S**
Messiah 613 S Main St Independence MO 64050-4499 • borcherding96@yahoo.com • MO • Grace Escondido CA • (RF 1993)

**BORTZ KIMBERLY J** (407)384-6741
12716 Woodbury Glen Dr Orlando FL 32828-5921 • S • Tchr • St Luke Oviedo FL • (407)365-3228 • (RF 1992)

**BOWDER FERN M** (573)636-3346
1018 Carol St Jefferson City MO 65101-3604 • rfbowder@midamerica.net • MO • Tchr • Trinity Jefferson City MO • (573)636-6750 • (S 1975 MED)

**BOYER LINDA R** (217)446-7443
1407 Woodridge Dr Danville IL 61832-1669 • CI • Tchr • Danville Danville IL • (217)442-5036 • (RF 1973)

**BRACKENSICK ALICE C** (630)325-1867
5519 Barclay Ct Clarendon Hills IL 60514-3607 • NI • EM • (S 1962)

**BRAMLEY SANDRA** (712)678-3807
454 S 4th Charter Oak IA 51439-0092 • IW • Tchr • St John Charter Oak IA • (712)678-3630 • (S 1969)

**BRAND ANITA M** (908)686-4269
2222 Vauxhall Rd Union NJ 07083-5825 • NJ • Tchr • Grace Union NJ • (908)686-3965 • (RF 1974)

**BRANDT PAMELA JANE** (816)826-6608
31695 Highway 65 Sedalia MO 65301-0736 • MO • Tchr • St Paul Sedalia MO • (816)826-1925 • (S 1982 MSPED)

**BRAUN SUZANNE L**
3710 Cheyenne Round Rock TX 78664 • braunsuzan@aol.com • MI • Tchr • Trinity Clinton Township MI • (810)468-8511 • (RF 1977 MSED)

**BREIDERT KATHLEEN G** (303)233-9418
7080 W 34th Pl Wheat Ridge CO 80033-6310 • RM • Tchr • Bethlehem Lakewood CO • (303)233-0401 • (S 1971)

**BREMER MELINDA K** (219)465-7746
1602 Sanibel Ct Valparaiso IN 46383-3882 • IN • Prin • St John La Porte IN • (219)362-6692 • (RF 1977)

**BROCKMEIER JOYCE L** (801)352-9846
860 Chariot Dr Sandy UT 84094 • RM • Tchr • Grace Sandy UT • (801)572-3793 • (S 1978)

**BROETZMANN MARLENE** (920)994-4210
W5489 County Road SS Random Lake WI 53075-1237 • SW • EM • (RF 1959)

**BROOKE MARY** (815)885-3950
13 Heather Ct Caledonia IL 61011 • NI • EM • (RF 1962 MA)

**BROSCH JOYCE ELAINE** (954)432-9083
8301 NW 17th Ct Pembroke Pines FL 33024-3401 • FG • Tchr • Holy Cross North Miami FL • (305)893-0851 • (S 1963)

**BROSCHEIT MARTHA ELAINE** (303)424-0343
4440 Cody St Wheat Ridge CO 80033-3248 • RM • Tchr • Bethlehem Lakewood CO • (303)233-0401 • (SP 1960)

**BROSZ NELDA F** (907)344-9903
7337 Foxridge Cir # 2 Anchorage AK 99518-2710 • kbanchor@aol.com • NOW • Tchr • Anchor Anchorage AK • (907)522-3636 • (S 1963 MS)

**BROWN SANDRA SUE** (904)271-9546
3209 Country Club Dr Lynn Haven FL 32444-5117 • shanker2@home.com • SO • Tchr • Good Shepherd Panama City FL • (850)871-6311 • (RF 1969)

**BRUEGGEMANN BEVERLY** (414)377-8108
1863 Shady Ln Grafton WI 53024-9526 • SW • Tchr • St Paul Grafton WI • (414)377-4659 • (AA 1969)

**BRUNS ELIZABETH A** (208)825-5802
1474 E 1100 S Eden ID 83325-5212 • jbbruns@magiclink.com • NOW • 06/1989 • (S 1975)

**BUBLITZ JOANNE** (715)526-5315
811 Oak St Shawano WI 54166-2031 • NW • EM • (RF 1958)

**BUCHHOLZ KELLY SUE** (414)353-2019
6835 N 58th St Milwaukee WI 53223-5201 • SW • 07/1999 • (MQ 1995)

**BUCHINGER SUSAN J** (815)547-5291
1120 Luther Ave Belvidere IL 61008-4593 • dbuchinger@aol.com • NI • Tchr • Immanuel Belvidere IL • (815)547-5346 • (S 1975)

**BULTEMEIER CHRISTINE L** (219)639-6332
9510 Hoagland Rd Hoagland IN 46745-9776 • IN • 07/1989 • (S 1971 MA)

**BUSACKER SUSAN L** (262)375-3607
132 W Juniper Dr Grafton WI 53024-2234 • wsbusacker@milwpc.com • SW • Tchr • St Paul Grafton WI • (414)377-4659 • (S 1975 MA)

**BUSSE LAURA M** (309)663-5745
1218 Bancroft Dr Bloomington IL 61704-3680 • lmbl@trinluth.org • CI • Tchr • Trinity Bloomington IL • (309)829-7513 • (S 1984)

**BUUCK LOIS C** (219)923-8365
3127 Maple Dr Highland IN 46322-1248 • IN • Tchr • St Paul Munster IN • (219)836-6270 • (RF 1965)

## C

**CARNEY NELDA** (573)364-0350
12199 Country Road 8030 Rolla MO 65401-7990 • MO • EM • (S 1974)

**CHENEY REBECCA J** (702)256-9158
3357 Kylemore St #103 Las Vegas NV 89129 • rcheneylasvegas@hotmail.com • PSW • Tchr • Faith LHS Las Vegas NV • (702)804-4400 • (S 1998)

**CLAUS DONNA MAE** (812)471-8619
1730 Dianne Ave Evansville IN 47714-5423 • kfcdmoc@juno.com • IN • Tchr • Evansville Evansville IN • (812)424-7252 • (RF 1962 MAT)

**CLEMENTS CHARLENE J** (636)239-6376
4 Eleanor Dr Washington MO 63090-3904 • clements@midwestis.net • MO • Tchr • Immanuel Washington MO • (314)239-4705 • (S 1965)

**CLINARD MARY JANE** (414)783-5820
4420 N 144th St Brookfield WI 53005-1604 • SW • Tchr • Immanuel Brookfield WI • (262)781-7140 • (RF 1969)

**CLOETER JANET R** (909)484-0130
6621 Canary Pine Ave Alta Loma CA 91737-4249 • jancloeter@aol.com • PSW • Tchr • Redeemer Ontario CA • (909)986-6510 • (S 1976 MA)

**COBURN PEGGY L** (612)757-3720
14440 Quinn Dr NW Anoka MN 55304-3327 • MNS • Tchr • Prince Of Peace Spring Lake Park MN • (612)786-1755 • (SP 1972)

**CONSTIEN SHARON L** (920)452-9144
5403 Pine Crest Cir Sheboygan WI 53081-8122 • SW • Tchr • Bethlehem Sheboygan WI • (920)452-5071 • (RF 1961)

**CROSMER BECKY JO** (727)344-2500
5896 27th Ave N Saint Petersburg FL 33710-3367 • crosjbjm@aol.com • FG • Tchr • Grace Saint Petersburg FL • (727)527-6213 • (RF 1980 MA)

**CRUISE GAIL S** (352)589-2732
507 Firewood Ave Eustis FL 32726-5631 • jrcruise@aol.com • FG • Tchr • Faith Eustis FL • (352)589-5683 • (RF 1973)

**CUNNINGHAM SARA**
2655 Calaveras Dr Valparaiso IN 46385-5380 • IN • Tchr • Immanuel Valparaiso IN • (219)462-8207 • (S 1977)

## D

**DAL FERRO CAROLYN K**
2518 Wilbur St Oakland CA 94602-3029 • CNH • Tchr • Zion Piedmont CA • (510)530-7909 • (RF 1968)

**DANCY HEIDI L** (810)677-9665
54817 Pimenta Macomb MI 48042-2219 • pdancy@lhsa.net • MI • Tchr • Our Saviour Armada MI • (810)784-9088 • (RF 1976)

**DANKENBRING NADINE** (216)227-0807
2200 Concord Dr Cleveland OH 44107-5375 • ddank5@flash.net • OH • 07/1997 • (S 1974)

**DEAN JOAN S** (414)783-5069
W176N5074 Evelyn Ter Menomonee Falls WI 53051-6558 • SW • EM • (RF 1967)

**DEHNKE CHRISTINE R** (314)481-6271
4060 Toenges Ave Saint Louis MO 63116-2840 • cdehnke@aol.com • MO • 08/1994 • (RF 1971 MA)

**DETTMERING ARLISS M** (217)394-2542
410 W Main St Buckley IL 60918-7001 • NI • EM • (RF 1957)

**DEXHEIMER RUTH ANN** (352)351-8539
2152 SE 7th Ter Ocala FL 34471-5368 • ldex@aol.com • FG • Tchr • Florida-Georgia Orlando FL • (RF 1968)

**DIBOS CAROLYN E** (702)648-3261
6521 Starcrest Dr Las Vegas NV 89108-2713 • PSW • Tchr • First Good Shepherd Las Vegas NV • (702)382-8610 • (S 1979)

**DICK SANDRA G** (313)781-3713
54450 Romeo Plank Rd Macomb MI 48042-2313 • MI • Tchr • St Peter Macomb MI • (810)781-9296 • (S 1973)

**DIETZ BEVERLY**
3100 E James Dr Oak Creek WI 53154-6536 • SW • Tchr • Grace Oak Creek WI • (414)762-3655 • (S 1973)

**DIRKS LYNN E** (209)836-0313
650 Petrig St Tracy CA 95376 • CNH • Tchr • Our Savior Livermore CA • (925)447-1246 • (SP 1971)

**DITTMER CHERYL**
1723 Mc Cready Ave Richmond Heights MO 63117-2105 • MO • Tchr • Christ Community Kirkwood MO • (314)822-7774 • (CQ 1998)

**DOBBERFUHL MARGARET** (414)258-8053
2516 N 66th St Wauwatosa WI 53213-1435 • SW • EM • (RF 1974)

**DOMMER DEBORAH**
2737 Morgan Dr San Ramon CA 94583-2461 • NI • 08/1993 • (S 1972)

**DUENSING BARBARA** (360)642-8196
PO Box 1171 Long Beach WA 98631-1171 • NOW • 07/1989 • (S 1971)

**DUERR MARGARET A** (714)288-8813
2537 E Collins Ave Orange CA 92867-6209 • duerr5@msn.com • PSW • Tchr • Lutheran HS/Orange C Orange CA • (714)998-5151 • (IV 1990 MA)

**DUNNING MARY F** (702)363-5889
2236 Juniper Berry Dr Las Vegas NV 89134 • mfd5889@aol.com • PSW • Tchr • Faith LHS Las Vegas NV • (702)804-4400 • (RF 1979)

**DUNSMORE SHARON K** (248)682-1792
28 Camley St Waterford MI 48328-3200 • MI • Tchr • St Stephen Waterford MI • (248)673-5906 • (AA 1982)

**DUTCHER ANNE** (612)492-3554
504 1st Ave NW New Prague MN 56071-1405 • MNS • Tchr • St John Chaska MN • (612)448-2433 • (S 1985)

## E

**EBERT ELAINE** (414)458-5067
934 Swift Ave Sheboygan WI 53081-6046 • SW • Tchr • Bethlehem Sheboygan WI • (920)452-5071 • (SP 1966 MS)

**EGGERSTEDT GAYLE L** (715)524-3999
410 S Sawyer St Shawano WI 54166-2928 • NW • Tchr • St Paul Bonduel WI • (715)758-8532 • (S 1966)

**EGGOLD MICHELLE A** (314)282-2924
1212 Walnut Dr Arnold MO 63010-1321 • michelleeggold@hotmail.com • MO • Tchr • Green Park Lemay MO • (314)544-4248 • (S 1984)

**EHLKE GERALDINE S** (619)670-3322
10804 Buggywhip Dr Spring Valley CA 91978-1906 • jgehlke@aol.com • PSW • Tchr • Pilgrim Chula Vista CA • (619)420-6233 • (RF 1969)

**EICKSTEAD DEBBIE** (210)695-9006
10235 Whip-O-Will Way Helotes TX 78023 • debeickste@aol.com • TX • Tchr • Shepherd Of The Hill San Antonio TX • (210)614-3741 • (RF 1980 MA)

**EINEM KAREN L** (713)224-0684
Trinity Lutheran Church 800 Houston Ave Houston TX 77007-7710 • TX • 06/1999 • (S 1976 MS)

**EINSPAHR KAREN L** (816)455-9210
1901 NE 55th Ter Kansas City MO 64118-5609 • MO • Tchr • Holy Cross Kansas City MO • (816)453-7211 • (S 1979)

**EMERY VICKIE A**
420 120th Lane NW Coon Rapids MN 55448-2266 • MNS • Tchr • Prince Of Peace Spring Lake Park MN • (612)786-1755 • (S 1981)

**ERNST SHARON L** (219)672-2015
11600 N 400 E Roanoke IN 46783-9437 • IN • Tchr • Bethlehem Ossian IN • (219)597-7366 • (RF 1961 MA)

**ERNSTMEYER TAMMY J** (402)466-6910
5331 Aylesworth Ave Lincoln NE 68507 • NEB • 06/2000 • (S 1995)

**ESCHMANN PAMELA K**
213 N Carolina Saginaw MI 48602 • MI • Tchr • Valley Saginaw MI • (517)790-1676 • (S 1995)

**EYERLY KATHLEEN M** (507)238-1802
443 Lake Park Blvd Fairmont MN 56031-2137 • MNS • Tchr • St Pauls Fairmont MN • (507)238-9492 • (SP 1973)

## F

**FAGA JULIE**
1001 S State Fair Blvd #25 Sedalia MO 65301-5161 • MO • Tchr • St Paul Sedalia MO • (660)826-1164 • (S 1996)

**FAIR CHRISTINE R**
5706 Inland Trl Fort Wayne IN 46825-5909 • IN • 09/1996 • (RF 1978)

**FELTEN DOROTHY J** (216)226-7516
2178 Concord Dr Lakewood OH 44107-5374 • OH • Tchr • Lakewood Lakewood OH • (216)221-6941 • (RF 1966)

**FENTON NANCY E** (909)887-2548
5536 N Dahlia St San Bernardino CA 92407-2425 • PSW • Tchr • Immanuel Riverside CA • (909)682-7613 • (RF 1959)

**FERGUSON JUDITH L** (214)867-0081
4109 Nightfall Dr Plano TX 75093-3833 • TX • Tchr • Our Redeemer Dallas TX • (214)368-1465 • (RF 1969)

**FINK MILDRED R**
3254 Land HBR Newland NC 28657-7945 • FG • Tchr • Trinity Orlando FL • (407)843-4896 • (RF 1960)

**FISCERI DARLENE N** (313)561-9179
705 N Vernon St Dearborn MI 48128-2512 • MI • Tchr • Guardian Dearborn MI • (313)274-3665 • (RF 1962 MS)

**FISCHER ANDREA T** (352)687-1592
9 Silver Ter Ocala FL 34472-2305 • FG • Tchr • St John Ocala FL • (352)622-7275 • (S 1973)

**FISCHER CATHERINE E** (801)272-1420
5138 Gurene Dr Salt Lake City UT 84117-6904 • RM • Tchr • Redeemer Salt Lake City UT • (801)467-4352 • (S 1969)

**FISCHER KAREN H** (480)706-5119
3712 E Summerhaven Dr Phoenix AZ 85044-4532 • PSW • Tchr • Zion Anaheim CA • (714)535-1169 • (S 1975 MED)

**FISCHER PEARL A** (920)892-4759
131 N Pleasant St Plymouth WI 53073-1621 • pfischer@excel.net • SW • Tchr • St John Plymouth WI • (920)893-5114 • (RF 1963 MA)

**FLANDERMEYER CLEONE E**
4211 W 183rd St Country Club Hills IL 60478 • wflander@intelnet.net.gt • IN • S Miss • Indiana Fort Wayne IN • (S 1966)

**FLEISCHFRESSER SHERI LYNN** (217)234-4582
708 N 1st Division Mattoon IL 61938 • packiskewl@aol.com • CI • Tchr • St John Mattoon IL • (217)234-4911 • (MQ 1985)

**FLORY KRISTA JOAN** (517)667-0181
5566 Michael Dr Bay City MI 48706-3113 • MI • 08/1993 • (S 1976 MED)

**FOGO VALERIE C**
2073 Seahurst Las Vegas NV 89142-2670 • PSW • Tchr • First Good Shepherd Las Vegas NV • (702)382-8610 • (IV 1993)

**FONT CASEY M** (219)264-9847
27350 Bittersweet Ln Elkhart IN 46514-8203 • caseyfont1@aol.com • IN • Tchr • Trinity Elkhart IN • (219)522-1491 • (RF 1994)

**FORNEY DAVID**
471 Glenview Dr Winona MN 55987-4153 • MNS • 05/1990 • (S 1983)

**FOUNTAIN JACQUELINE J** (320)864-3763
102 Desoto Ave N Glencoe MN 55336-3003 • MNS • Tchr • First Glencoe MN • (320)864-3317 • (SP 1968)

**FRANK KATHLEEN M** (219)749-9817
3220 Marias Dr Fort Wayne IN 46815-6324 • IN • Tchr • Bethlehem Fort Wayne IN • (219)744-3228 • (RF 1969 MA)

**FRANK LEANNE J** (517)792-4726
2416 N Woodbridge St Saginaw MI 48602-5256 • MI • Tchr • Bethlehem Saginaw MI • (517)755-1146 • (RF 1964)

**FREUDENBURG SUE** (517)893-1062
1903 S Kiesel St Bay City MI 48706-5243 • MI • Tchr • Immanuel Bay City MI • (517)893-4088 • (S 1960)

**FRIEDRICH KAREN L**
3024 W Valanna Ct Glendale WI 53209-2507 • kfriedrich@egl.org • SW • Tchr • Elm Grove Elm Grove WI • (262)797-2970 • (S 1975 MA)

**FRIELING MARILYN**
146 Narrows Loop #2176 Waleska GA 30183-4449 • FG • Tchr • St Paul Lakeland FL • (863)644-7710 • (S 1969 MS)

**FRINCKE SUSAN J** (219)486-7486
3231 Solitude Pl Fort Wayne IN 46815-6225 • suziejoy@aol.com • IN • Tchr • Concordia Fort Wayne IN • (219)426-9922 • (SP 1971)

**FRISCHMANN LOIS A** (972)480-9447
9915 Candlebrook Dr Dallas TX 75243-5062 • ffrischmann@prodigy.net • TX • Tchr • Our Redeemer Dallas TX • (214)368-1465 • (S 1979 MS)

**FRITSCH CHARLOTTE** (920)748-2242
526 Mayparty Dr Ripon WI 54971-1030 • SW • Tchr • St John Berlin WI • (920)361-0555 • (MW 1983)

**FUCHS LORI J** (440)333-8975
562 Humiston Dr Bay Village OH 44140-3018 • OH • Tchr • St Paul Westlake OH • (440)835-3051 • (RF 1983)

**FUITEN PAMELA R** (217)732-2782
445 Mayfair Dr Lincoln IL 62656-1338 • CI • 10/1990 • (CQ 1979)

## G

**GABLE KATHLEEN A** (425)277-1303
1108 Tacoma Ave NE Renton WA 98056-3539 • NOW • Tchr • Pilgrim Bellevue WA • (425)454-4790 • (RF 1963)

**GAKSTATTER KARI S** (517)659-2578
397 Brown Rd Munger MI 48747 • MI • Tchr • Trinity Bay City MI • (517)662-4891 • (CQ 1997)

**GALCHUTT ADELINE M** (612)784-9316
1351 78th Cir Spring Lake Park MN 55432-2849 • MNS • Tchr • Prince Of Peace Spring Lake Park MN • (612)786-1755 • (SP 1967 MED)

**GATLIN CONNIE E** (972)494-4875
1845 Westcreek Dr Garland TX 75042-4755 • TX • Tchr • Our Redeemer Dallas TX • (214)368-1465 • (S 1979)

**GAYER TRACY ANNE** (219)482-9815
1126 Clara Ave Fort Wayne IN 46805 • teach52301@aol.com • IN • Tchr • Concordia Fort Wayne IN • (219)422-2429 • (RF 1995)

**GERIKE DARLENE DORIS** (573)445-1200
12 Dundee Dr Columbia MO 65203-1213 • MO • Tchr • Trinity Columbia MO • (573)445-1014 • (RF 1972)

**GERLACH EILEEN K** (734)542-0480
17939 Woodside Livonia MI 48152-2760 • MI • Tchr • Guardian Dearborn MI • (313)274-3665 • (S 1968)

**GERLACH LINDA M** (716)692-8974
821 Ohio St N Tonawanda NY 14120-1972 • pgerlach@buffnet.net • EA • Tchr • St Paul North Tonawanda NY • (716)692-3255 • (S 1971 MED)

**GERMANN HELEN C** (972)509-8008
2209 Covered Wagon Dr Plano TX 75074-2757 • cageycougar@juno.com • TX • 06/1999 • (RF 1963)

**GERZEVSKE MARIE** (281)379-5132
8522 Sugar Pine Pl Tomball TX 77375 • TX • Tchr • Bethany Houston TX • (713)695-2933 • (RF 1967)

**GESCH HEIDI ANN** (612)472-5508
2459 Chateau Ln Mound MN 55364-1752 • MNS • Tchr • Redeemer Wayzata MN • (612)473-5356 • (S 1986)

**GESCH JUDY M** (216)934-5180
2560 Barkwood Dr Sheffield Village OH 44054-2461 • OH • Tchr • LHS West Rocky River OH • (440)333-1660 • (S 1977 MED)

**GEYER CHERYL M** (219)266-6564
160 Lakeview Aledo TX 76008 • IN • Tchr • Trinity Elkhart IN • (219)522-1491 • (RF 1982 MA)

**GIERTZ LOUISE N**
510 E Union St Edwardsville IL 62025-1252 • SI • Tchr • Trinity Edwardsville IL • (618)656-7002 • (RF 1977 MA)

**GIESCHEN LEANN G** (219)484-4652
3605 Walden Run Fort Wayne IN 46815 • IN • Tchr • Concordia Fort Wayne IN • (219)426-9922 • (RF 1978 MRD MA)

**GIGUERE IRENE M** (410)747-1619
6003 Keithmont Ct Baltimore MD 21228-2724 • SE • Tchr • Baltimore LHS Baltimore MD • (410)825-2323 • (RF 1966 MSED)

**GLANZER ANITA J** (801)566-5464
9180 Scirlein Dr Sandy UT 84094-3013 • RM • Tchr • Grace Sandy UT • (801)572-3793 • (S 1991)

**GLASSETT TRUDY A** (360)659-1082
5515 74th Ave NE Marysville WA 98270-8922 • glassettgang@juno.com • NOW • Tchr • Zion Everett WA • (425)334-5064 • (SP 1970)

**GLICK VIVIAN L** (208)524-4327
210 Donna Dr Idaho Falls ID 83402-5591 • NOW • Tchr • Hope Idaho Falls ID • (208)529-8080 • (RF 1968)

**GLIENKE SANDRA I** (512)832-8873
9712 Halifax Dr Austin TX 78753-4621 • TX • Tchr • Hope Austin TX • (512)926-0003 • (S 1975)

**GOETZKE JANIS M** (920)206-9650
608 Carriage Hill Dr Watertown WI 53098-1210 • stuff44@execpc.com • SW • Tchr • Mount Olive Milwaukee WI • (414)774-2113 • (RF 1970)

**GOLCHERT CHRISTINA A** (314)842-5934
10177 Hwy C Frohna MO 63748-9701 • ktgolch@showmenet.com • MO • Tchr • Concordia Frohna MO • (573)824-5435 • (S 1974 MA)

**GOLCHERT ELIZABETH A** (916)487-2533
2430 Verna Way Sacramento CA 95864-0759 • CNH • 06/1994 • (MW 1981)

**GORLINE LYNDA** (716)662-6105
6129 Armor Duells Rd Orchard Park NY 14127-3228 • EA • Tchr • Trinity West Seneca NY • (716)674-9188 • (RF 1968 MS)

**GOTTSCHALK NANCY J** (414)543-9714
2461 S 73rd St West Allis WI 53219-1807 • SW • Tchr • St Paul West Allis WI • (414)541-6251 • (RF 1965)

**GRAB MARGARET A** (708)957-2967
1349 Jeffery Dr Homewood IL 60430-4041 • grabd@flash.net • NI • Tchr • Salem Homewood IL • (708)206-0350 • (S 1969)

**GRADY LESLIE D** (512)259-3667
1514 Country Squire Dr Cedar Park TX 78613 • TX • Tchr • Zion Georgetown TX • (512)863-5345 • (RF 1991)

**GRASS GRACE L** (816)463-7686
PO Box 139 Emma MO 65327-0139 • MO • Tchr • Immanuel Higginsville MO • (660)584-2854 • (S 1974)

**GRAUDIN VALERIE LOU**
22 Trilane Dr Young America MN 55397-9603 • MNS • Tchr • Trinity Waconia MN • (952)442-4165 • (SP 1980)

**GREEN LESLIE C** (310)547-4297
1360 W Capitol Dr Apt 141 San Pedro CA 90732-5032 • PSW • Tchr • Christ Rancho Palos Verdes CA • (310)831-0848 • (RF 1988)

**GREEN PEGGY ANN** (561)734-7101
6313 Bengal Cir Boynton Beach FL 33437-3209 • blessed1@gate.net • FG • Tchr • Trinity Delray Beach FL • (561)276-8458 • (AA 1990)

**GRESENS JOAN R** (708)335-0193
3604 Wellington Ct Hazel Crest IL 60429-1528 • NI • Tchr • St Paul Dolton IL • (708)849-6929 • (RF 1974 MA)

**GREUNKE MARY E** (314)846-2113
2909 Coram Dr Saint Louis MO 63129-5613 • MO • Tchr • Good Shepherd Arnold MO • (636)296-1292 • (S 1969)

**GREVE WENDY F** (517)394-7259
1436 Lockbridge Dr Lansing MI 48911-6009 • MI • Tchr • Our Savior Lansing MI • (517)882-3550 • (S 1971)

**GREWE SHIRLEY JEAN** (217)222-1937
1507 Quail Creek Dr Quincy IL 62301 • CI • 08/1999 • (RF 1982)

**GRIFFIN HEATHER A**
417 E 98th St Apt 209 Bloomington MN 55420 • MNS • Tchr • Mount Calvary Richfield MN • (612)866-5405 • (SP 1999)

**GROTH DEBORAH LYNNE** (916)483-4645
3236 Chenu Ave Sacramento CA 95821-6114 • PSW • Tchr • Faith Whittier CA • (562)941-0245 • (IV 1992)

**GRUENHAGEN ELOIS J** (206)935-0743
4067 SW College St Seattle WA 98116-2034 • eloisgruenhaagen@hotmail.com • NOW • Tchr • Hope Seattle WA • (206)935-8500 • (SP 1973)

**GUNDELL EILEEN**
1404 University Ave Honolulu HI 96822-2414 • SE • Tchr • Bethlehem Baltimore MD • (410)488-4445 • (S 1968)

**GUSE' JANE C** (734)729-4959
38529 Cherry Hill Rd Westland MI 48186 • MI • Tchr • St Matthew Westland MI • (734)425-0260 • (AA 1987)

**GUSTAFSON GEORGIA D** (952)467-2962
115 Muirfield Cir Young America MN 55397 • MNS • Tchr • St Johns Young America MN • (612)467-3461 • (RF 1993)

**GUTZLER DONNA J** (262)598-0997
3027 Meyer Ct #4 Racine WI 53406 • SW • Tchr • Concordia Racine WI • (262)554-1659 • (RF 1970)

## H

**HAGEN STEPHANIE R** (253)848-5017
2606 38th Ave SE Puyallup WA 98374-1941 • athagen@aol.com • NOW • Tchr • Concordia Tacoma WA • (253)475-9513 • (S 1977 MED)

**HALFMANN NORMA J** (517)793-7489
5950 Willowbrook Dr Saginaw MI 48603-5487 • MI • Tchr • Holy Cross Saginaw MI • (517)793-9795 • (S 1976 MA)

**HALL STACY LYNN** (913)680-1121
1624 Shawnee St Leavenworth KS 66048 • dshall@birch.net • KS • 07/1998 • (S 1994)

**HALLET JAMIE K** (310)547-4297
1223 W Amar St San Pedro CA 90732-2605 • PSW • Tchr • Christ Rancho Palos Verdes CA • (310)831-0848 • (CQ 1986)

**HALVORSON CAROL JEAN** (619)656-0135
1738 Elmhurst St Chula Vista CA 91913-2613 • cvhalvorson@juno.com • PSW • Tchr • Pilgrim Chula Vista CA • (619)420-6233 • (RF 1971)

**HAMIT WANETA** (972)355-3773
3520 Spring Meadow Ln Flower Mound TX 75028-7419 • AT • 06/1994 • (AA 1984)

**HANEBUTT KATHLEEN L** (765)864-0736
1705 John D Dr Kokomo IN 46902 • IN • Tchr • Redeemer Kokomo IN • (765)864-6466 • (RF 1974 MS)

**HANFF DIANE E**
5049 Wingfoot Ln #B Corpus Christi TX 78413-2238 • TX • 01/1999 • (AU 1991)

**HANSELL KRISTA YVONNE** (412)486-0644
403 Laurel Hill Rd Allison Park PA 15101-3830 • kyh522@aol.com • EN • 08/1999 • (RF 1978 MS)

**HARDT CAROLE J** (216)877-2544
30 Chippewa Dr Thornton IL 60476-1129 • NI • Tchr • St John Country Club Hills IL • (708)798-4131 • (RF 1967)

**HARRE RUTH A** (217)438-6826
1211 W Jackson St Auburn IL 62615-9372 • CI • 05/1997 • (RF 1962)

**HART JUDY E** (219)749-9647
8601 Minnich Rd Fort Wayne IN 46816-9792 • IN • Tchr • Concordia Fort Wayne IN • (219)426-9922 • (RF 1968 MS)

**HARTKE SHERRY RUTH** (309)527-3585
260 E 8th St El Paso IL 61738-1279 • srh3old@yahoo.com • CI • Tchr • Trinity Bloomington IL • (309)829-7513 • (CQ 1993 MS)

**HARTMAN SALLY M** (573)635-5104
1729 Greenridge Ct Jefferson City MO 65101 • MO • Tchr • Trinity Jefferson City MO • (573)636-7807 • (RF 1973 MED)

**HARTMANN KRISTA R** (313)532-8252
17220 Gaylord Redford MI 48240-2312 • MI • 09/1998 • (AA 1993 MA)

**HASS SUSAN KAYE** (440)892-8735
24209 Russell Rd Bay Village OH 44140-2848 • chass@statos.net • OH • Tchr • Lakewood Lakewood OH • (216)221-6941 • (SP 1975)

**HAUSER ARLENE J** (517)893-2702
1172 N Pine St Essexville MI 48732-1930 • MI • EM • (RF 1967 MED)

**HAUSER DEBORAH ELISE** (517)497-9607
2254 Mayfield Rd Saginaw MI 48602 • MI • Tchr • Zion Hemlock MI • (517)642-5909 • (BR 1981)

**HAWKINS ALISON E** (630)906-0046
343 Wildwood Dr North Aurora IL 60542 • NI • Tchr • St Paul Aurora IL • (630)820-3457 • (RF 1999)

**HAYMAN EDNA M**
St Paul Lutheran School 2624 Burgundy New Orleans LA 70117-7304 • SO • Tchr • St Paul New Orleans LA • (504)947-1773 • (S 1971)

**HECKMAN SHIRLEY M** (626)286-3049
5212 N Burton Ave San Gabriel CA 91776-2014 • PSW • Tchr • First Temple City CA • (626)287-0968 • (S 1958)

**HEINS DAWN RENAE** (313)593-4887
6814 Heyden St Detroit MI 48228-4934 • MI • Tchr • Emmanuel Dearborn MI • (313)561-6265 • (S 1977)

**HELMER MARILYN M** (507)237-5331
314 Court Ave Gaylord MN 55334-0054 • MNS • Tchr • Immanuel Gaylord MN • (507)237-2804 • (S 1974)

**HELMREICH RUTH E** (616)983-2356
2860 Cleveland Ave Apt 150 Saint Joseph MI 49085-2238 • MI • Tchr • Christ Stevensville MI • (616)429-7111 • (RF 1965)

**HEMLER JANET MARIE** (847)429-1854
1042 Polly Ct Elgin IL 60120-3105 • ahemler@aol.com • NI • Tchr • St John Elgin IL • (847)741-0814 • (RF 1965)

**HENNIG POLLY** (219)456-4748
3702 Bobolink Crossover Fort Wayne IN 46815-6466 • IN • EM • (RF 1943)

**HENNING MARY JO** (314)477-8493
605 River Bend Est. Dr St Charles MO 63303 • mhenning@immanuelluth.org • MO • Tchr • Child Of God Saint Peters MO • (S 1969 MRD)

**HERBST JUDITH M**
1701 Western Pines Ct O Fallon MO 63366-6769 • RM • 10/1987 • (RF 1959)

**HERRMANN IONA K** (920)892-2271
315 N Stafford St Plymouth WI 53073-1242 • iherrman@excel.net • SW • Tchr • St John Plymouth WI • (920)893-5114 • (RF 1958)

**HERZOG MARLENE** (313)777-2652
15764 S Park Ave Eastpointe MI 48021-1635 • jahmherzog@cs.com • MI • Tchr • Special Ed Ministrie Detroit MI • (313)368-1220 • (S 1968 MS)

**HIEGEL LINDA G** (219)447-5697
826 Kensington Blvd Fort Wayne IN 46805-5310 • IN • Tchr • Bethlehem Fort Wayne IN • (219)744-3228 • (S 1978 MS)

**HILKEN LEVONNE L** (734)243-2015
1020 Donnalee Monroe MI 48162-5118 • jchilken@foxberry.net • MI • Tchr • Holy Ghost Monroe MI • (734)241-0525 • (S 1975 MA)

**HILL CAROL SUE** (850)769-1731
5214 Teri Ln Panama City FL 32404-6735 • SO • Tchr • Good Shepherd Panama City FL • (850)871-6311 • (S 1973)

**HILLER JUNE J** (703)569-7974
6220 Kentland St Springfield VA 22150-4117 • jjhiller@aol.com • SE • Tchr • Prince Of Peace Springfield VA • (703)451-5855 • (RF 1970 MS)

**HILLMAN CHARLOTTE M** (608)524-8103
1133 14th St Reedsburg WI 53959-1008 • SW • Tchr • St Peter Reedsburg WI • (608)524-4066 • (RF 1976)

**HINCK BARBARA A**
41950 Trent Ct Canton MI 48188-5208 • MI • Tchr • St Matthew Westland MI • (734)425-0261 • (S 1981)

**HODGSON JEAN** (602)956-8507
3301 E Turney Ave Phoenix AZ 85018-3925 • EN • 08/1999 • (RF 1966 MA)

**HOFFMAN LYNN** (712)678-3760
869 5th St Charter Oak IA 51439-7433 • clh1968oak@msn.com • IW • Tchr • St John Charter Oak IA • (712)678-3630 • (S 1967)

**HOFMAN RACHEL** (314)832-1476
8530 Elgin Ave Saint Louis MO 63123-3629 • MO • Tchr • Word Of Life Saint Louis MO • (314)832-1244 • (S 1993)

**HOHL LAURA M** (608)356-8640
W11941 State Road 33 Portage WI 53901-9696 • SW • Tchr • St John Portage WI • (608)742-4222 • (RF 1974)

**HOLLMANN DOROTHEA A** (219)432-1622
3715 Andover Pl Fort Wayne IN 46804-2671 • dholl27@aol.com • IN • Tchr • Bethlehem Fort Wayne IN • (219)744-3228 • (RF 1974 MA)

**HOLLOWAY AMY A** (517)639-9315
18905 Northway St Roseville MI 48066-1069 • MI • Tchr • Peace Shelby Twp MI • (810)739-2431 • (AA 1987)

**HOUSE AUDREY M** (972)279-9296
C/O Our Redeemer Luth School 7611 Park Ln Dallas TX 75225-2028 • audhouse@juno.com • TX • Tchr • Our Redeemer Dallas TX • (214)368-1465 • (S 1989)

**HOUSE KAREN E** (254)939-3412
1503 N Beal Belton TX 76513 • TX • Tchr • Grace Killeen TX • (254)634-4424 • (AU 1987)

**HOYER CONNIE A** (319)390-4111
4630 Pearl Ave NW 1583 13th St Cedar Rapids IA 52405 • OH • Tchr • Redeemer Cuyahoga Falls OH • (330)923-1280 • (S 1969 MS)

**HUBBARD DEBORAH S** (920)893-3123
106 Evergreen Rd Plymouth WI 53073-4137 • tdthub@aol.com • SW • Tchr • St John Plymouth WI • (920)893-3071 • (SP 1971)

**HUEBNER AMY KRISTEN**
1023 Bellevue Ave Elgin IL 60120 • NI • Tchr • St John Elgin IL • (847)741-7633 • (RF 1996)

**HUEBNER BARBARA P** (402)477-6170
5330 NW 4th St Lincoln NE 68521 • NEB • Tchr • Trinity Lincoln NE • (402)466-1800 • (S 1970)

**HUEBSCHMAN DOROTHEA**
520 Bader Ave Seward NE 68434 • NEB • Tchr • St John Seward NE • (402)643-4535 • (S 1962 MS)

**HUGHES KAREN L** (757)825-0107
125 Tide Mill Ln Apt 34C Hampton VA 23666-5214 • SE • Tchr • Emmanuel Hampton VA • (757)723-8782 • (RF 1961)

**HUNT JENNIFER LEE**
5234 Neosho St Saint Louis MO 63109-2967 • MO • 07/1997 • (RF 1993)

**HUSBERG MARY LINDA** (612)864-4479
711 9th St E Glencoe MN 55336-2914 • mbsm711@hutchtel.net • MNS • Tchr • First Glencoe MN • (320)864-3317 • (SP 1969)

### I

**ITZEL MARJORIE** (412)831-3737
5900 Dublin Rd Bethel Park PA 15102-1328 • mitzelz@juno.com • EA • Tchr • Christ Pittsburgh PA • (412)271-7173 • (RF 1968)

### J

**JAHNKE LISA K** (512)733-1413
1431 Thibodeaux Dr Round Rock TX 78664-7222 • ljahnke@aol.com • TX • Tchr • Redeemer Austin TX • (512)451-6478 • (AU 1995)

**JAMESON GRETCHEN**
1103 S 73rd St Milwaukee WI 53214-3130 • SW • Tchr • South Wisconsin Milwaukee WI • (414)464-8100 • (S 1997)

**JANDER MARTHA S** (281)970-4149
10810 Glenora Dr Houston TX 77065-4253 • TX • Tchr • St Timothy Houston TX • (281)469-2913 • (RF 1966 MA)

**JANSEN JOAN** (715)623-3079
300 Edison St Antigo WI 54409-1843 • NW • Tchr • Peace Antigo WI • (715)623-2200 • (S 1973)

**JEFFERS MARISA J** (708)209-3900
7400 Augusta St River Forest IL 60305-1499 • crfhouse@crf.cuis.edu • NI • SHS/C • Northern Illinois Hillside IL • (RF 1981 MA)

**JOBST ANN ELAINE** (262)781-3683
N53 W14345 Aberdeen Dr Menomonee Falls WI 53051 • EN • Tchr • Hales Corners Hales Corners WI • (414)529-6700 • (SP 1977)

**JOHNSON ADELINE MARIE** (330)733-2187
2860 Robindale Ave Akron OH 44312 • revelations210@juno.com • OH • Tchr • Redeemer Cuyahoga Falls OH • (330)923-1280 • (S 1994)

**JOHNSON MARY ANN J**
14273 Briarfield Ln Grand Haven MI 49417-9791 • MI • Tchr • St John Grand Haven MI • (616)842-4510 • (SP 1970)

**JONES BERNIECE M DR** (402)484-7032
4157 S 40th St Lincoln NE 68506-4902 • bmj@nebrwesleyan.edu • MO • 08/1999 • (S 1974 MED PHD)

**JONES MARK S** (330)374-1676
694 Ralph St Akron OH 44310 • OH • Tchr • Redeemer Cuyahoga Falls OH • (330)923-1280 • (RF 1977 MA)

**JONES ROZANNE K**
C/O St Paul Luth Pre School 17190 SW Scholls Sherwood Rd Sherwood OR 97140-8725 • NOW • Tchr • St Paul Sherwood OR • (SP 1967)

### K

**KAFER DOLORES** (414)685-5377
3169 N County Road K Omro WI 54963-9746 • SW • EM • (RF 1957)

**KAISER COLENE M** (712)263-6896
1989 N Ave Denison IA 51442-7451 • IW • Tchr • Zion Denison IA • (712)263-4766 • (S 1972)

**KALBFLEISCH EDITH A** (314)894-6803
4343 Colony Gardens Dr Saint Louis MO 63125-3989 • MO • Tchr • Salem Affton MO • (314)352-4454 • (RF 1968 MA)

**KARPINSKY KATHLEEN C** (414)634-6370
1703 Chatham St Racine WI 53402-4906 • SW • Tchr • St John Racine WI • (414)633-2758 • (RF 1967)

**KASCHINSKE JUNE ELIZABETH** (517)793-3607
4850 Hanover Dr Saginaw MI 48603-2921 • MI • Tchr • Peace Saginaw MI • (517)792-2581 • (RF 1967)

**KASSULKE CAROLYN ANN** (660)388-5935
201 E 4th St Salisbury MO 65281-1340 • wkass@cvalley.net • MO • Tchr • Immanuel Salisbury MO • (660)388-5192 • (S 1963)

**KASTEN JOYCELYN P** (314)243-4150
1203 Shady Ln Jackson MO 63755-2600 • MO • Tchr • St Paul Jackson MO • (573)243-2236 • (S 1968)

**KELL PAMELA** (810)340-9697
1600 Taylor Rd Auburn Hills MI 48326 • MI • Tchr • St Paul Sterling Heights MI • (810)247-4427 • (S 1972)

**KENNELL LINDA J** (414)354-6810
6336 W Donges Ln Brown Deer WI 53223-1237 • kennellc@execpc.com • SW • Tchr • St John Glendale WI • (414)352-4150 • (RF 1970)

**KERN MARCIA G** (419)267-5180
23120 US Highway 6 Stryker OH 43557 • OH • Tchr • St Paul Napoleon OH • (419)592-5536 • (RF 1967)

**KESKE CYNTHIA L**
4247 Honeysuckle Ct #F204 Sheboygan WI 53081 • SW • Tchr • Bethlehem Sheboygan WI • (920)452-4331 • (MQ 1999)

**KIESCHNICK LAUREN E** (314)849-6354
9938 Heatherton Dr Saint Louis MO 63123-4923 • n2lgik@aol.com • MO • Tchr • Salem Florissant MO • (314)741-6781 • (AU 1987 MA)

**KIMBLE MARILYNN J** (612)467-3581
303 4th Ave SW Young America MN 55397-9263 • MNS • Tchr • St Johns Young America MN • (612)467-3461 • (RF 1973)

**KLAUER SUSAN E** (810)752-3954
78625 Romeo Plank Rd Armada MI 48005-1620 • MI • Tchr • St Peter Richmond MI • (810)727-9693 • (CQ 1999 MA)

**KLEIN KIM MARIE** (618)545-0150
11 Edgewood Ln North Centralia IL 62801 • SI • 06/1994 • (S 1984)

**KLEMSZ SUSAN MARIE** (219)471-8110
8 Wycliffe Pl Fort Wayne IN 46825-4937 • klemszfamily@msn.com • IN • 02/1997 • (RF 1989)

**KLUG ALICIA**
5834 Nottingham Ave St Louis MO 63109-2733 • MO • Tchr • Our Savior Fenton MO • (636)343-2192 • (RF 1999)

**KNOTTS PAMELA D**
3135 Hawks Ann Arbor MI 48108 • MI • Tchr • St Paul Ann Arbor MI • (734)665-9117 • (AA 1984)

**KNUDTEN JACQUELINE E** (219)485-2120
6205 Graysford Pl Fort Wayne IN 46835-4721 • mytss@juno.com • IN • Tchr • Holy Cross Fort Wayne IN • (219)483-3173 • (S 1977 MS)

**KOEHLINGER MICHELLE E** (219)484-6352
5225 Stonecreek Trl Fort Wayne IN 46825-5962 • mkoehlinger@aol.com • IN • Tchr • Mount Calvary Fort Wayne IN • (219)747-4121 • (S 1982)

**KOEN LAUREEN** (636)942-3760
4090 State Rd M Imperial MO 63052-2940 • koenl@prodigy.net • MO • Tchr • Green Park Lemay MO • (314)544-4248 • (RF 1981)

**KOENIG DAWN MARIE**
1915 Cole Dr Jefferson City MO 65109-1201 • MO • Tchr • Trinity Jefferson City MO • (573)636-6750 • (SP 1992)

**KOHL COLLEEN M** (414)994-4772
N7120 School Dr Adell WI 53001-1362 • SW • Tchr • St John Plymouth WI • (920)893-5114 • (RF 1963)

**KOHRS CAROLE J** (262)790-1398
3360 Bermuda Blvd Brookfield WI 53045-2661 • SW • EM • (RF 1958)

**KOSMATKA JUDITH M** (810)731-4942
7211 Yorktown Ln Shelby Township MI 48317-4272 • MI • Tchr • St Peter Macomb MI • (810)781-9296 • (RF 1964 MA)

**KOTH LOIS J** (414)457-0807
4230 N 50th St Sheboygan WI 53083-1733 • SW • EM • (RF 1970)

**KOTTMEYER LORNA**
6055A Potomac St Saint Louis MO 63139-1928 • MO • Tchr • Word Of Life Saint Louis MO • (314)832-1244 • (RF 1973)

**KRAFFT ALBERTA G** (262)253-0726
N82W14115 Lilly Ct Menomonee Falls WI 53051-3937 • SW • EM • (RF 1947)

**KRAFFT JOANNE M** (702)656-5097
6525 Deadwood Rd Las Vegas NV 89108-4427 • jojotmg@aol.com • PSW • Tchr • Faith LHS Las Vegas NV • (702)804-4400 • (IV 1987)

**KRAFFT ORA MAY** (702)641-9599
2746 Wentworth Cir Las Vegas NV 89122-2712 • PSW • EM • (RF 1959)

**KRAFT BARBARA A** (708)849-8391
13821 S Edbrooke Ave Riverdale IL 60627-1702 • NI • Tchr • Bethlehem Chicago IL • (773)768-0441 • (RF 1974)

**KRAMER NORMA J** (281)464-2441
2114 Birdie Ct Pearland TX 77581 • TX • Tchr • Texas Austin TX • (S 1972)

**KRAUSE ELIZABETH A**
305 Shady Timbers Ln Murphy TX 75094-3535 • txkrause@aol.com • TX • Tchr • Lutheran HS of Dalla Dallas TX • (214)349-8912 • (S 1986 MED)

**KREIMEYER EVELYN ROSE** (915)653-1872
401 Rio Concho Dr Apt 402 San Angelo TX 76903-5500 • TX • EM • (S 1964)

**KREISSLER TONI R** (417)537-4798
RR 2 Box 10 Golden City MO 64748-9603 • MO • Tchr • Immanuel Lockwood MO • (417)232-4530 • (S 1976)

**KRENGEL AMY A**
1996 Armensko Ln Jackson MI 49201-8948 • MI • Tchr • St Paul Lapeer MI • (810)664-0046 • (RF 1986)

**KROHSE MARY ANN** (217)488-6135
729 E Gibson St New Berlin IL 62670-4511 • CI • Tchr • St John New Berlin IL • (217)488-3190 • (RF 1967)

**KRUEGER ROSEMARY Y**
3500 Lawndale Ln N Plymouth MN 55447-1171 • MNS • Tchr • Messiah Mounds View MN • (612)784-1786 • (S 1979)

**KRUMLAND LYNN MARIE**
6 Frost Dr Rolla MO 65401-3906 • MO • 07/1998 • (RF 1971)

**KRUSE PATRICIA G** (815)562-7746
1213 Pickwick Rochelle IL 61068-1094 • dpkruse@tbcnet.com • NI • Tchr • St Paul Rochelle IL • (815)562-6323 • (RF 1979)

**KUCHTA KATHY L** (814)725-9918
31 S Washington North East PA 16428-1516 • fivek@velocity.net • OK • Tchr • Central Illinois Springfield IL • (S 1979 MS)

**KUEHNER ELINOR R** (402)746-3703
840 N Franklin Red Cloud NE 68970-2008 • revron@gpoom.net • IE • Tchr • Community Readlyn IA • (319)279-3968 • (S 1967)

**KUSESKE CHERICE L** (612)774-7045
652 Mc Lean Ave Saint Paul MN 55106-6311 • MNS • Tchr • Trinity Lone Oak Eagan MN • (651)454-1139 • (SP 1968)

**KUTZ CATHY A** (810)792-3524
35737 Lucerne St Clinton Township MI 48035-2746 • MI • Tchr • St Luke Clinton Township MI • (810)791-1151 • (S 1970)

### L

**LA ROCQUE JANET E** (517)895-5436
1308 S Wenona St Bay City MI 48706-5178 • MI • Tchr • Zion Bay City MI • (517)894-2611 • (S 1978 MED)

**LAMBRIGHT MICHELLE R** (714)969-2934
20831 Glencairn Ln Huntington Beach CA 92646-6407 • PSW • 06/1999 • (IV 1988)

**LANGE BETH LYNNE** (248)476-7475
20916 Birchwood St Farmington MI 48336 • MI • 11/1999 • (RF 1994)

**LAPPE TRUDI** (314)781-8157
1014 Sanford Ave Apt 1 S Saint Louis MO 63139 • dtlappe@stlnet.com • MO • 09/1998 • (S 1996)

**LATZKE KATHIE M** (952)368-9571
855 Walnut Pl Chaska MN 55318 • MNS • Zion Bay City MI • (RF 1982)

**LAUBSCH DOROTHY H** (517)652-6885
9440 Junction Rd Frankenmuth MI 48734-9577 • MI • Tchr • Trinity Munger MI • (517)659-2506 • (S 1966)

**LAVIGNE NINA ROSE M** (314)429-2552
10742 Saint Cosmas Ln Saint Ann MO 63074-2524 • nina-lavigne@hope--lutheran.org • MO • 04/1998 • (RF 1974)

**LE PERE MARILYN J** (217)442-1739
1605 Skyline Dr Danville IL 61832-2034 • CI • Tchr • Danville Danville IL • (217)442-5036 • (RF 1973 MED)

**LEBRECHT PHYLLIS T** (714)529-5746
1981 Chevy Chase Brea CA 92821 • llebrecht@aol.com • PSW • Tchr • Christ Fullerton CA • (714)870-7460 • (RF 1969 MA)

**LEDER REBEKAH** (716)772-2429
3222 Quaker Rd Gasport NY 14067-9448 • EA • Tchr • Immanuel Lockport NY • (716)434-0521 • (RF 1966 MA)

**LEHMANN JEAN S** (214)239-6900
14919 Hillcrest Rd Dallas TX 75248-5535 • jlehmann@gte.net • TX • Tchr • Our Redeemer Dallas TX • (214)368-1465 • (S 1963)

**LINEBRINK CHERYL**
607 Institute Valparaiso IN 46383 • IN • 07/1999 • (RF 1971)

**LIPKE SALLY L**
630 Strawberry Ln Jackson MO 63755 • MO • Tchr • St Paul Jackson MO • (573)243-5360 • (RF 1964)

**LIST MARTHA L** (248)349-4092
21875 Novi Rd Northville MI 48167 • MI • Tchr • St Paul Northville MI • (248)349-3146 • (S 1969 MA)

**LIVELY JEANNE C** (440)269-1394
33450 Vine St #109C Eastlake OH 44095-3449 • OH • Tchr • St John Cleveland OH • (216)531-8204 • (AA 1985)

**LIVO REBECCA A** (702)812-1053
1830 N Buffalo Dr Unit 2032 Las Vegas NV 89128-2782 • rebecky-89128@yahoo.com • PSW • Tchr • Faith LHS Las Vegas NV • (702)804-4400 • (S 1995)

**LOCKE ELISE V** (734)913-5335
491 Pine Brae St Ann Arbor MI 48105-2743 • elocke@tri-church.com • MI • 08/1997 • (S 1961)

**LOESEL PAMELA LYNN** (636)946-8366
2824 Birch Tree Dr Saint Charles MO 63301-1235 • MO • Tchr • Immanuel Saint Charles MO • (636)946-0051 • (RF 1978)

**LOOMANS EUNICE P** (608)524-2735
S2504A Horkan Rd Reedsburg WI 53959-9708 • SW • Tchr • St Peter Reedsburg WI • (608)524-4066 • (RF 1963 MA)

**LUCAS DONNA M** (323)735-1083
2535 9th Ave Los Angeles CA 90018-1708 • PSW • Tchr • Zion Glendale CA • (818)243-3119 • (S 1983)

**LUINSTRA DONNA R** (541)383-3497
1920 SE Fairwood Dr Bend OR 97702-2481 • NOW • Tchr • Spokane Spokane WA • (509)327-4441 • (S 1967)

**LUKE JANET** (219)447-5119
2905 Hoevelwood Dr Fort Wayne IN 46806-5312 • IN • EM • (RF 1964 MED)

**LUSTILA GERALD JOHN**
4225 Sunnyview Dr Lakeland FL 33813 • FG • Tchr • St Paul Lakeland FL • (941)644-7710 • (AA 1986)

**LUTZ ELIZABETH J** (810)739-3568
8665 Elizabeth Ave Utica MI 48317 • MI • Tchr • Immanuel Macomb MI • (810)286-7076 • (S 1967)

### M

**MAC KAIN SANDRA K**
St John Luth Church 2654 CC Ave Victor IA 52347-8534 • IE • 01/1996 • (AA 1988)

**MACHEMER SUSAN M** (810)774-3419
24502 Grove Ave Eastpointe MI 48021-1031 • mmachemere@lhsa.net • MI • Tchr • St John Fraser MI • (810)294-8740 • (RF 1981)

**MADDOCK KRISTI J**
8164 Kingsbridge Dr Sacremento CA 95829-6010 • kristimaddock@hotmail.com • CNH • Tchr • Town & Country Sacramento CA • (916)481-2542 • (IV 1998)

**MALTER DOROTHY A** (504)461-0684
672 Ronson Dr Kenner LA 70065-2632 • dmalter@bellsouth.net • SO • Tchr • Atonement Metairie LA • (504)887-0225 • (RF 1964)

**MANGELS CAROLYN M** (714)998-2603
1219 E Ensign Cir Orange CA 92865-2911 • cmangels@stpaulsorg.org • PSW • Tchr • St Paul Orange CA • (714)921-3188 • (S 1968)

**MANSSEN DEBORAH A**
817 Washington St Grafton WI 53024-1844 • SW • Tchr • St Paul Grafton WI • (414)377-4659 • (RF 1984)

**MANTEUFFEL VIRGINIA** (810)268-8457
10934 Chicago Rd Warren MI 48093-5559 • KS • 07/1998 • (RF 1960 MA)

**MARA JULIE A** (209)472-9163
4516 Romano Dr Stockton CA 95207-6639 • CNH • Tchr • Trinity Stockton CA • (209)464-0895 • (S 1979)

**MARSH ALMA GAIL** (561)219-8139
323 Ridge Ln Stuart FL 34994-7127 • The3Marshes@hotmail.com • FG • Tchr • Redeemer Stuart FL • (561)286-0911 • (S 1974)

**MARSHALL VICKI L**
28 Riverside Dr Mount Clemens MI 48043-2534 • MI • Tchr • Peace Warren MI • (810)751-8011 • (RF 1976)

**MAY JUDY A** (765)474-6897
1905 Beck Ln Lafayette IN 47909-3109 • danmay587@cs.com • IN • Tchr • St James Lafayette IN • (765)742-6464 • (RF 1966 MED)

**MC CHRYSTAL KARYN D** (561)283-3598
282 SE Harbor Point Dr Stuart FL 34996-1350 • FG • Tchr • Redeemer Stuart FL • (561)286-0932 • (RF 1984)

**MC CLENDON GRETA A** (303)238-2818
8202 W 10th Ave Apt 2A Lakewood CO 80215-4986 • RM • Tchr • Bethlehem Lakewood CO • (303)233-0401 • (S 1991)

**MC DONALD KATHRYN B**
2118 Treeridge Dr SE Grand Rapids MI 49508-3719 • Kathrynm@gvi.net • MO • S Ex/S • Missouri Saint Louis MO • (314)317-4550 • (RF 1979 MA)

**MC LAIN KATHERINE C** (972)470-3361
1503 Reston Dr Richardson TX 75081-2653 • TX • Tchr • Zion Dallas TX • (214)363-1630 • (AU 1997)

**MEIER CAROLYN** (847)788-0097
2905 Thrush Ln Rolling Meadows IL 60008 • c3mmeier@aol.com • NI • 08/1999 • (RF 1987)

**MEIER HELEN L** (262)251-9017
W141N8314 Merrimac Dr Menomonee Falls WI 53051-3947 • SW • EM • (RF 1950)

**MEIER KATHY L** (612)657-2182
218 2nd St NW Mayer MN 55360-9692 • pkmeier@prodigy.net • MNS • Tchr • Lutheran High Mayer MN • (612)657-2251 • (RF 1978)

**MEIER PAULINE S** (312)767-0120
5540 S Menard Ave Chicago IL 60638-2836 • NI • EM • (RF 1950)

**MEINEKE TONI ANNE** (719)475-7379
1313 Wilbur Cir Colorado Springs CO 80909-3133 • RM • Tchr • Redeemer Colorado Springs CO • (719)633-7600 • (RF 1977)

**MEISINGER JUDITH J** (336)765-2942
3110 Shanno Dr Winston-Salem NC 27106-3648 • ardle4949@aol.com • NI • Tchr • St John Forest Park IL • (708)366-3226 • (S 1971)

**MELENDEZ KRISTIN M** (612)861-5745
7134 James Ave S Richfield MN 55423 • melendba@spacestar.net • MNS • 06/1993 • (RF 1990)

**MENK MARY ELIZABETH** (507)662-5868
511 Chicago St Lakefield MN 56150-1168 • MNS • Tchr • Immanuel Lakefield MN • (507)662-5860 • (SP 1974)

**MERRILL KENLYN SUE** (810)773-5798
19610 Rock St Roseville MI 48066-2629 • MI • Tchr • St John Fraser MI • (810)294-8740 • (S 1968 MCRT)

**MESEKE SHARON L** (810)468-0453
37228 Ingleside St Clinton Twp MI 48036-2615 • MI • Tchr • Trinity Clinton Township MI • (810)468-8511 • (RF 1974)

**MEYER ANN L** (414)327-2391
3130 S 53rd St Milwaukee WI 53219-4520 • ameyer@execpc.com • SW • 08/1994 • (RF 1963 MEPD)

**MEYER JEANINNE** (314)343-4519
1803 Rutger St Saint Louis MO 63104-2943 • meyerji@ibm.net • MO • Tchr • LHS South Saint Louis MO • (314)631-1400 • (S 1971 MA)

**MEYER JEANNE LEE** (414)761-1277
9470 S 27th St Oak Creek WI 53154-4314 • meyorch@msn.com • SW • Tchr • Grace Oak Creek WI • (414)762-3655 • (CQ 1989 MA)

**MEYER LAURIE A**
105 S Normandy Ct Anaheim CA 92806-3625 • PSW • Tchr • Christ Brea CA • (714)529-2984 • (RF 1968)

**MIEROW MARY ANN** (612)447-8928
15221 Fairlawn Shores Trl SE Prior Lake MN 55372-1932 • MNS • Tchr • St Johns Chaska MN • (612)448-2526 • (SP 1972)

**MILES MARY MARGARET** (517)892-6635
705 Park Ave Bay City MI 48708-6861 • MI • Tchr • Immanuel Bay City MI • (517)893-8521 • (RF 1964 MAT)

**MILLER CAROL L** (217)323-4490
1302 North St Beardstown IL 62618 • CI • Tchr • St John Beardstown IL • (217)323-1288 • (RF 1969)

**MILLER ENID S**
1515 N 18th St Grand Jct CO 81501-6601 • RM • Tchr • Messiah Grand Junction CO • (970)245-2838 • (S 1975)

**MILLER ROSEMARY LYDIA** (414)461-0639
4243 N 63rd St Milwaukee WI 53216-1242 • millers6@execpc.com • SW • Tchr • Emmaus Milwaukee WI • (414)444-6090 • (S 1970)

**MILLS ELLEN K** (810)477-6628
33549 8 Mile Rd Livonia MI 48152-1200 • MI • Tchr • Hosanna-Tabor Redford MI • (313)937-2233 • (RF 1972)

**MILLS KAREN L** (206)839-0473
28209 29th Ave S Federal Way WA 98003-3342 • NOW • Tchr • St Luke Federal Way WA • (253)941-3000 • (RF 1963)

**MINDA KATHLEEN M** (517)799-3308
2606 Blackmore St Saginaw MI 48602-3552 • MI • Tchr • Peace Saginaw MI • (517)792-2581 • (S 1976)

**MOERBE DOROTHY A** (409)242-5736
3121 Old Plum Hwy La Grange TX 78945-5013 • TX • Tchr • Mount Calvary La Grange TX • (979)968-3938 • (RF 1971 MA)

**MOONEY LESLIE A** (309)694-7061
11 Stahl Pl Bartonville IL 61607-1868 • CI • Tchr • Christ Peoria IL • (309)637-1512 • (S 1978)

**MORGAN ELLEN L** (513)697-0283
1884 Stockton Dr Loveland OH 45140-2028 • OH • Tchr • Concordia Cincinnati OH • (513)861-9568 • (S 1973)

**MORRIS RHODA J** (651)777-8634
4862 Granada Ave N Oakdale MN 55128-1923 • MNS • Tchr • East St Paul Saint Paul MN • (612)774-2030 • (SP 1988)

**MOSER BETTY L** (314)946-9866
3601 Runnymede Dr Saint Charles MO 63301-4509 • MO • EM • (RF 1979 MA)

**MUEHL DANA L** (812)523-1181
2175 N Lakeview Dr Seymour IN 47274-9288 • IN • Tchr • Immanuel Seymour IN • (812)522-1301 • (RF 1983)

**MUELLER SHARON K** (512)684-7826
7711 Susan Elaine St San Antonio TX 78240-3626 • TX • 12/1997 • (RF 1972)

**MUNDT JANIS M** (219)436-9557
3720 Winterfield Run Fort Wayne IN 46804-2661 • IN • Tchr • Emmaus Fort Wayne IN • (219)456-4573 • (RF 1969 MS)

**MURPHY ELIZABETH R** (714)289-8288
382 N Shaffer St Orange CA 92866 • PSW • Tchr • Lutheran HS/Orange C Orange CA • (714)998-5151 • (IV 1992)

**MUSSELL ANN E** (507)534-2551
RR 1 Box 186 Plainview MN 55964-9662 • MNS • Tchr • Immanuel Plainview MN • (507)534-2108 • (SP 1971)

**MYERS ANN J**
24120 NE 8th St Redmond WA 98053-3607 • NOW • 06/1986 • (PO 1982)

## N

**NELESEN TERESA R** (805)583-4271
6648 Bernal St Simi Valley CA 93063-3920 • jtnelesen@dellnet.com • PSW • Tchr • Canoga Park Canoga Park CA • (818)348-5714 • (RF 1959)

**NELSON ELIZABETH DAWN** (734)671-5170
3237 John R St Trenton MI 48183-3627 • grnelson@metroshores.net • MI • Tchr • St John New Boston MI • (734)654-6366 • (AA 1988 MA)

**NEUENDORF KAREN** (517)752-6413
1220 S Mueller Rd Saginaw MI 48601-9479 • MI • Tchr • Immanuel Saginaw MI • (517)754-4285 • (S 1979)

**NIEMEIER CARLA ANN** (810)294-4423
32133 Beacon Ln Fraser MI 48026-2108 • cniemeier@hotmail.com • MI • Tchr • Trinity Clinton Township MI • (810)468-8511 • (S 1965 MAT)

**NORRIS ARLENE** (816)353-5386
11924 E 56th Ter Kansas City MO 64133-3504 • MO • 09/1990 • (S 1987)

**NORTHROP NAOMI M** (818)967-2225
1621 E Ruddock St Covina CA 91724-2843 • PSW • Tchr • Emmaus Alhambra CA • (626)289-3664 • (RF 1983 MCMU)

## O

**O NEILL JULIE K** (716)693-5250
864 Deerfield Dr N Tonawanda NY 14120-1959 • EA • Tchr • St Mark North Tonawanda NY • (716)693-3715 • (RF 1984)

**OCHSANKEHL KATHRYN F** (313)394-1204
805 Red Pine Ct Prairie Du Sac WI 53578-1056 • SW • 06/1992 • (RF 1977)

**OLDENETTEL DAWN D** (316)331-7919
RR 1 Box 22A Independence KS 67301-9711 • roldenettel@terraworld.net • KS • 05/1992 • (S 1982)

**OPEL SUSAN REBECCA** (219)483-7053
6510 Azalea Dr Fort Wayne IN 46825-4737 • IN • Tchr • Woodburn Woodburn IN • (219)632-5493 • (AA 1991)

**OTT KAREN M** (810)296-2859
34371 Sycamore Dr Fraser MI 48026-3556 • MI • Tchr • St John Fraser MI • (810)294-8740 • (RF 1966 MA)

**OTT LOIS C** (906)485-4012
1765 S Rose St Ishpeming MI 49849-2740 • cohotim@aol.com • NW • Tchr • Christ The King Ishpeming MI • (906)485-4432 • (RF 1972)

## P

**PAAPE BARBARA A** (414)781-6654
N51W17197 Maple Crest Ln Menomonee Falls WI 53051-7522 • tchrpaa@aol.com • SW • Tchr • Zion Menomonee Falls WI • (414)781-7437 • (MQ 1989)

**PALISCH DORIS V** (573)204-1284
1515 Kimbeland Dr Jackson MO 63755-2017 • ddpalisch@aol.com • MO • Tchr • St Paul Jackson MO • (573)243-2236 • (RF 1971)

**PALMETER NANCY L** (810)731-5009
5346 Wiley Dr Utica MI 48317-1274 • MI • EM • (RF 1964)

**PANGBURN JANET K** (716)731-5991
5917 Shawnee Rd Sanborn NY 14132-9222 • EA • Tchr • St Matthew North Tonawanda NY • (716)692-6862 • (RF 1966)

**PARISEAU STEPHANIE R** (253)529-4661
2225 S 291st Federal Way WA 98003 • NOW • Tchr • Concordia Tacoma WA • (253)475-9513 • (PO 1989)

**PAWLITZ CAROL J** (810)247-3153
50629 Cameron Dr Macomb MI 48044-1337 • MI • Tchr • Immanuel Macomb MI • (810)286-7076 • (RF 1969)

**PAYNE DIANNE** (815)932-6212
465 Durham St Bradley IL 60915-1719 • NI • Tchr • St Paul Kankakee IL • (815)932-3241 • (RF 1969)

**PEDERSEN BRENDA L** (810)598-7544
C/O Saint Peter Lutheran Churc 17051 24 Mile Rd Macomb MI 48042-2902 • fredpeders@webbernet.net • MI • Tchr • St Peter Macomb MI • (810)781-3434 • (SP 1981)

**PEPERKORN KATHRYN M**
3425 Crescent Ave Fort Wayne IN 46805-1505 • SW • Tchr • Indiana Fort Wayne IN • (S 1993)

**PERA NORMA REBECCA**
9908 Nicollet Ave Apt 10 Bloomington MN 55420-4843 • MNS • EM • (RF 1963)

**PESCH JANET M**
1431 Arthur Ave Racine WI 53405-3325 • SW • Tchr • St John Racine WI • (414)633-2758 • (SP 1991 MA)

**PETER MARILYNN J** (913)962-4707
13502 W 74th Ter Shawnee KS 66216-3720 • herbpeter@aol.com • PSW • EM • (S 1953 MED)

**PETROS LINDA S** (248)735-4420
20830 E Glen Haven Cir Northville MI 48167 • lspetros@aol.com • MI • Tchr • St John Rochester MI • (248)652-8830 • (RF 1975 MED)

**PETT MARY E** (309)787-2531
509 Bruce Ave Milan IL 61264-3358 • branchpett@aol.com • CI • 11/1995 • (MQ 1989)

**PICKELMANN JANET M** (517)662-7497
44 E Salzburg Rd Bay City MI 48706-9712 • pickel6@concentric.net • MI • Tchr • Trinity Bay City MI • (517)662-4891 • (RF 1972 MAT)

**POLLATZ BETH A** (248)584-1813
29017 Milton Madison Heights MI 48071 • bbpollatz@aol.com • MI • Tchr • St John Rochester MI • (248)652-8830 • (AA 1987 MS)

**POPPE JEANNE** (606)689-4714
5296 Country Club Ln Burlington KY 41055 • OH • Tchr • Concordia Cincinnati OH • (513)861-9568 • (S 1962)

**PORTWOOD CAREY L** (402)371-7784
406 Market Pl Norfolk NE 68701-6936 • NEB • Tchr • Christ Norfolk NE • (402)371-5536 • (S 1985)

**POWELL ILENE EDITH** (303)756-1415
1515 S Elm St Denver CO 80222-3819 • RM • Tchr • Hope Aurora CO • (303)364-7416 • (S 1960)

**PRAHL NORMA G** (262)375-2049
535 Greenfield Dr Grafton WI 53024-1118 • njp1730@aol.com • SW • Tchr • St Paul Grafton WI • (414)377-4659 • (RF 1968)

**PRECHT RUTH W** (810)765-0595
343 N Elizabeth St Marine City MI 48039 • EN • EM • (RF 1956 MA)

**PRELOGER JOAN K** (812)523-8801
2292 Locust Dr Seymour IN 47274-8668 • IN • Tchr • Immanuel Seymour IN • (812)522-1301 • (RF 1969 MS)

**PRENTICE LINDSEY**
1185 Mountain Creek Rd Chattanooga TN 37405 • MDS • Tchr • Cross Of Christ Chattanooga TN • (423)877-7447 • (S 2000)

**PROCHNOW TERRI ANN** (507)235-5926
221 W Anna St Fairmont MN 56031-1558 • MNS • Tchr • St Pauls Fairmont MN • (507)238-9492 • (SP 1971)

## R

**RAABE PAULA**
7915 N Kostner Skokie IL 60076 • NI • Tchr • St Paul Skokie IL • (847)673-5030 • (RF 1979 MED)

**RADEWAHN LORRAINE D** (414)771-0496
1515 N 50th St Milwaukee WI 53208-2210 • SW • EM • (RF 1967)

**RADUE LINDA J** (414)377-6252
908 3rd Ave Grafton WI 53024-1308 • SW • Tchr • St Paul Grafton WI • (414)377-4659 • (RF 1977)

**RAEDEKE SUSAN M** (636)939-3082
2486 Annapolis Way St Charles MO 63303-2905 • sraedeke@immanuelluth.org • MO • Tchr • Immanuel Saint Charles MO • (636)946-0051 • (RF 1968)

**RANK KATHLEEN MARIE** (810)463-1421
138 Mark Dr Mount Clemens MI 48043-1427 • MI • Tchr • St Peter Macomb MI • (810)781-3434 • (AA 1992)

**RAUH MARY** (314)243-5067
2422 Litz Blvd Jackson MO 63755-3311 • MO • Tchr • St Paul Jackson MO • (573)243-5360 • (S 1963)

**REICK SANDRA L** (605)371-3835
4212 E 38th St Sioux Falls SD 57105 • SD • 09/1999 • (S 1973)

**REIMERS RHONDA KAY** (219)896-3275
108 N Hancock Ave North Judson IN 46366-1122 • IN • P/Tchr • St Peter North Judson IN • (219)896-5933 • (S 1980 MA)

**REINITZ DANIEL CHRISTIAN** (314)894-7880
33 Gocke Pl Overland MO 63114-1327 • MO • Tchr • Our Redeemer Overland MO • (314)427-3462 • (RF 1992)

**REINKE KATHERINE D** (414)789-7954
15646 W Ridge Rd New Berlin WI 53151-1578 • SW • Tchr • Grace Menomonee Falls WI • (414)251-7140 • (RF 1974)

**REISS KATHERINE L** (716)343-8126
8 Manhattan Ave Batavia NY 14020-2410 • EA • Tchr • St Paul Batavia NY • (716)343-0488 • (BR 1960)

**REITH JO ANN** (309)637-8207
2913 W Starr St Peoria IL 61605-1332 • CI • Tchr • Christ Peoria IL • (309)637-5309 • (RF 1967 MA MA)

**REMPFER JANET H** (407)359-8385
230 W 11th St Chuluota FL 32766-9456 • S • 07/1996 • (RF 1969)

**REUSCH ELIZABETH J** (313)978-7605
4435 Westover Dr West Bloomfield MI 48323-2875 • bettyjr47@aol.com • MI • 06/1993 • (RF 1969 MED)

**REZEK ROBIN R** )708)614-1588
16501 Patricia Ave Tinley Park IL 60477-1923 • NI • Tchr • Trinity Tinley Park IL • (708)532-3529 • (RF 1984 MA)

**RICHARDS SHERI L** (952)322-5650
4529 152nd St W Apple Valley MN 55124 • kurtandsheri@juno.com • EA • Tchr • St John Hamlin NY • (716)964-2550 • (AA 1990)

**RICKORDS ANNA**
11015 Hackamore Ave SW Albuquerque NM 87121-9510 • RM • Tchr • Immanuel Albuquerque NM • (505)243-2589 • (S 1996)

**RIEMER LORRIE** (262)512-0094
12160 N Wauwatosa Rd Mequon WI 53097-2704 • SW • Tchr • Trinity Mequon WI • (262)242-2045 • (MQ 1993)

**RIPPY KAROLYN K** (509)837-3122
115 Hemlock Ave Sunnyside WA 98944-2014 • grippy@bentonrea.com • NOW • Tchr • Calvary Sunnyside WA • (509)837-6771 • (PO 1968 MA)

**RISKE DONNA RUTH** (972)462-0149
636 Raintree Cir Coppell TX 75019-5447 • TX • Tchr • Christ Our Savior Coppell TX • (972)393-7074 • (RF 1963)

**RITTER SHANNON N** (801)334-9920
1487 Canyon Cove Ln #15 Ogden UT 84401 • loco4him@enerdz.net • CNH • 10/2000 • (S 1997)

**RIVERS LISA M**
1138 Oak Hollow Dr Imperial MO 63052 • jrivers602@aol.com • MO • Tchr • St John Ellisville MO • (314)394-4100 • (S 1987 MED)

**ROBBINS SUSAN L** (218)481-9498
13915 Knighton Cir Houston TX 77034-5439 • TX • Tchr • Lutheran South Acade Houston TX • (281)464-9320 • (S 1969)

**ROBINSON DIANE SHERRY** (713)856-8518
10507 N Laureldale Dr Houston TX 77041-7871 • drobins@oslschool.org • TX • Tchr • Our Savior Houston TX • (713)290-8277 • (S 1972 MCMU)

**ROBINSON JOANNA M** (217)442-0707
310 Moore St Tilton IL 61833-8217 • SE • 02/1996 • (S 1986)

**ROCKENBACH DARLENE MARIE** (402)228-2342
11666 W Hiwy 4 Beatrice NE 68310 • revrock@alltel.net • NEB • Tchr • Lambs Of Christ Crete NE • (402)826-4359 • (S 1994)

**ROEGGE JUDY A** (217)997-5960
774 Arenzville Rd Arenzville IL 62611 • CI • 09/1992 • (SP 1970)

**ROGERS CHRISTINE L** (714)472-6109
24411 Corta Cresta Dr Lake Forest CA 92630-3914 • PSW • Tchr • Abiding Savior Lake Forest CA • (949)830-1461 • (SP 1975)

**ROPER CAROL MARIE**
1963 Elmhurst Ln Jackson MI 49201-8937 • MI • 06/1997 • (RF 1970)

**ROTERMUND DORIS A** (972)889-1117
605 Olympic Richardson TX 75081 • dondor@freewwweb.com • TX • EM • (RF 1956)

**ROTH CARLYN J**
35552 Marina Dr Sterling Hts MI 48312-4139 • rothjc@c3net.net • MI • Tchr • East Bethlehem Detroit MI • (313)892-2671 • (S 1963)

**ROWOLD KATHLEEN M** (414)893-4441
105 Dewey Ln Apt 3 Plymouth WI 53073-2547 • SW • Tchr • St John Plymouth WI • (920)893-5114 • (RF 1973)

**ROYUK ELAINE A** (507)235-8046
956 Albion Ave Fairmont MN 56031-3007 • rj³royuk@hotmail.com • MNS • Tchr • St Pauls Fairmont MN • (507)238-9492 • (S 1962)

**RUDLAFF BONNIE L**
6676 Frederick Ave Ocheyedan IA 51354-7942 • IW • 07/1999 • (S 1969)

**RUDSINSKI CALVIN H** (314)894-0483
10800 Arnett Dr Saint Louis MO 63123-7114 • crudsinski20@aol.com • MO • Tchr • Green Park Lemay MO • (314)544-4248 • (RF 1973)

**RUSCH JEANNE** (262)695-0209
207 Westfield Way Pewaukee WI 53072 • jmrusch@execpc.com • SW • Tchr • Milwaukee LHS Milwaukee WI • (414)461-6000 • (RF 1966 MED)

**RUSNAK CAROLYN A** (636)397-6687
1225 Golden Harvest Dr Saint Peters MO 63376-5209 • MO • Tchr • Immanuel Saint Charles MO • (636)946-2656 • (RF 1982 MA)

**RUSNAK JANICE L** (314)839-2954
3021 Moon Flower Ct Florissant MO 63031-1038 • MO • Tchr • Salem Florissant MO • (314)741-8220 • (RF 1977)

## S

**SACHTLEBEN JOYCE L** (314)838-5491
1345 Nashua Dr Florissant MO 63033-2232 • rogjoy@juno.com • MO • Tchr • Salem Florissant MO • (314)741-8220 • (RF 1967)

**SAEGER RUTH** (715)536-3375
N2655 E Shore Dr Merrill WI 54452-8609 • EN • EM • (RF 1942)

**SAILER SARAH M** (605)330-0849
2105 S Lincoln Ave Sioux Falls SD 57105 • ssailer2@aol.com • SD • 06/1998 • (SP 1982)

**SANDCORK DEANNA L** (512)926-6202
6904 Notre Dame Austin TX 78723 • TX • 07/1999 • (SP 1997)

**SANDFORT IRMA MARIE** (812)372-8040
2034 Chandler Ln Columbus IN 47203-4015 • IN • Tchr • St Peter Columbus IN • (812)372-5266 • (RF 1963)

**SAWYER CAROLYN K** (601)992-9741
117 Christy Ln Brandon MS 39047 • seelsorge@aol.com • SO • Tchr • Good Shepherd Brandon MS • (601)992-4752 • (AU 1984)

**SCHADE DIANE J** (636)946-3546
821 Laurel Ln Saint Charles MO 63301-0716 • DSchade@Immanuelluth.org • MO • Tchr • Immanuel Saint Charles MO • (636)946-0051 • (S 1969 MED)

**SCHAEFER JILL** (847)673-3219
5207 Galitz St 1st Fl Skokie IL 60077-2737 • NI • Tchr • St Paul Skokie IL • (847)673-5030 • (RF 1991)

**SCHAEFER JUDY L** (815)547-6682
639 W 9th St Belvidere IL 61008-5407 • trincjs@gte.net • NI • Prin • Immanuel Belvidere IL • (815)547-5346 • (S 1981 MED)

**SCHAEKEL JOAN E**
C/O Salem Lutheran Church 22601 Luth Church Rd Tomball TX 77375-3716 • TX • Immanuel Belvidere IL • (RF 1976)

**SCHALLHORN VICKI L** (810)250-0265
4301 Underhill Dr Flint MI 48506 • mschall@seidata.com • MI • Tchr • St Mark Flint MI • (810)736-6680 • (RF 1977)

**SCHELER KRISTIE F** (248)681-5869
5520 Millpointe Dr Waterford MI 48327 • jjskfs@aol.com • MI • Tchr • St Matthew Walled Lake MI • (248)624-7677 • (S 1989)

**SCHENDEL ELISA R** (219)749-7560
9511 Pawnee Way New Haven IN 46774-2902 • lisjohn@aol.com • IN • Tchr • Central New Haven IN • (219)493-2502 • (S 1966 MED)

**SCHIEFERSTEIN DONNA J** (219)724-3280
10420 N 200 W Decatur IN 46733-8759 • IN • Tchr • Wyneken Memorial Decatur IN • (219)639-6177 • (RF 1961)

**SCHLECHTE ALAINE R** (281)255-6233
30726 Martens Rd Tomball TX 77375-2909 • schlechtek@hotmail.com • TX • Tchr • Salem Tomball TX • (281)351-8122 • (S 1973)

**SCHLEGL ELEANOR RUTH** (217)223-7845
2824 Sonata Dr Quincy IL 62301-6323 • schlegl@rnet.com • MO • EM • (RF 1962)

**SCHLUETER MARY K** (714)998-8864
234 E Woodvale Ave Orange CA 92865-2737 • PSW • EM • (S 1978)

**SCHMELZLE TANYA L**
1427 Arlington St Houston TX 77008 • TX • Tchr • Immanuel Houston TX • (713)861-8787 • (S 1987 MRD)

**SCHMIDT ELIZABETH R** (248)528-0107
C/O Faith Luther Co-Op PS 37635 Dequindre Rd Troy MI 48083-5709 • MI • Tchr • Faith Troy MI • (248)689-4664 • (RF 1970 MA)

**SCHMIDT HELEN R** (636)256-6877
1571 Buckhurst Ct Ballwin MO 63021-8395 • lsch1571@aol.com • MO • Tchr • Christ Community Kirkwood MO • (314)822-7774 • (CQ 1998)

**SCHMIDT MARGENE G** (402)643-4805
2040 Parkview Dr Seward NE 68434 • NEB • 06/1999 • (S 1967 MA)

**SCHMIDT SANDRA J** (517)662-2477
4854 S 11 Mile Rd Auburn MI 48611 • MI • Tchr • St John Midland MI • (517)835-7041 • (RF 1976 MA)

**SCHMIDTKE BEVERLY D** (507)685-4192
PO Box 154 Morristown MN 55052-0154 • ehschmidt@means.net • MNS • Tchr • Trinity Janesville MN • (507)231-6646 • (S 1975)

**SCHNEIDER CHRISTINE G** (309)697-9475
4916 West Linda Ct Peoria IL 61607-1548 • CI • Tchr • Christ Peoria IL • (309)637-1512 • (CQ 1992)

**SCHNEIDER EUGENE C** (414)421-4734
5402 Meadow Dr Greendale WI 53129-1420 • carolgene@webtv.net • SW • EM • (RF 1961 MS)

**SCHOENHEIT CAROL E** (313)562-0528
26658 Sunningdale Dr Inkster MI 48141-1843 • MI • EM • (RF 1958)

**SCHOENHERR KATHLINE A** (573)824-5429
983 PCR 432 Frohna MO 63748 • MO • Tchr • St Paul Jackson MO • (573)243-5360 • (S 1965)

**SCHOEPP CARLA**
618 N 2nd Ave Maywood IL 60153-1112 • NI • EM • (RF 1955 MA)

**SCHRAM CANDICE** (414)361-0507
N8066 Forest Ridge Rd Berlin WI 54923-9478 • SW • Tchr • St John Berlin WI • (920)361-0555 • (S 1980)

**SCHROEDER PAMELA LYNNE** (734)439-7050
13099 Petersburg Rd Milan MI 48160 • MI • Tchr • St Paul Ann Arbor MI • (734)665-0604 • (RF 1972 MA)

**SCHROEDER PEGGY S** (715)526-9390
911 S Main St Shawano WI 54166-3261 • NW • Tchr • St James Shawano WI • (715)524-4213 • (RF 1975)

**SCHROEDER REBECCA A** (219)486-3132
4405 North Dr Fort Wayne IN 46815-4931 • IN • Tchr • Holy Cross Fort Wayne IN • (219)483-3173 • (RF 1984 MS)

**SCHUBERT DOTTIE L**
1318 Flour Bluff Dr Corpus Christi TX 78418-5104 • adase@worldnet.att.net • FG • 06/1995 • (S 1986)

**SCHULT JANICE M** (219)485-0076
3329 Sudbury Pl Fort Wayne IN 46815-6245 • IN • EM • (RF 1958)

**SCHUMACHER ANNETTE LOUISE** (262)679-0500
S75W17721 Harbor Cir Muskego WI 53150-9187 • gschum@execpc.com • SW • EM • (RF 1961)

**SCHUMACHER CAROL E**
3718 Brenan Dr Nampa ID 83686-8678 • NOW • Tchr • Zion Nampa ID • (208)466-9141 • (RF 1980)

**SCHWAN SUSAN KAY** (863)385-5084
921 11th Ave Sebring FL 33875 • n4ftd@aol.com • FG • Tchr • Faith Sebring FL • (941)385-0406 • (RF 1976)

**SCHWANTZ YVONNE MARIE** (219)493-1454
1931 S Tyland Blvd New Haven IN 46774 • wishwewerekids@juno.com • IN • Tchr • Wyneken Memorial Decatur IN • (219)639-6177 • (RF 1989)

**SCHWEITZER ROBERT W** (414)674-2544
W4240 US Highway 18 Jefferson WI 53549-9774 • SW • Tchr • Bethesda Home Watertown WI • (414)261-3050 • (PO 1965 MED)

**SEGEBART PHYLISS J** (712)263-5814
2244 Highway 59 Denison IA 51442-7416 • IW • Tchr • Zion Denison IA • (712)263-4766 • (S 1969)

**SENECHAL CAROL ANN** (512)301-4108
6500 Clay Allison Pass Austin TX 78749 • senfrank@aol.com • TX • Tchr • St Paul Austin TX • (512)472-3313 • (S 1966)

**SENNHENN BARBARA L** (440)324-4442
42870 Woodhill Dr Elyria OH 44035-2078 • OH • 06/1993 • (S 1969)

**SESSION ETHEL M**
8224 Schaefer Hwy Detroit MI 48228-2747 • MI • Tchr • Detroit Urban Detroit MI • (313)582-9900 • (S 1971)

**SHELDON SUSAN L** (810)288-0538
42994 Nebel Trl Clinton Township MI 48038-2456 • MI • Tchr • Trinity Utica MI • (810)731-4490 • (S 1972)

**SHERIDAN GERTRUDE E**
E957 Hickory Ridge Rd Genoa WI 54632-8871 • SW • 08/1993 • (RF 1943 MMU)

**SHEROUSE BEVERLY J** (517)753-1575
4205 Lorraine Saginaw MI 48604 • MI • Tchr • Trinity Bay City MI • (517)662-6093 • (AA 1988)

**SHERRY BETH ELLEN** (517)662-7640
5545 S 8 Mile Rd Bay City MI 48706-9711 • orco23@tir.com • MI • Tchr • Grace Auburn MI • (517)662-6161 • (RF 1980)

**SIEVERS PHYLLIS K** (314)892-5246
155 Bridgeview Ln Saint Louis MO 63129-3401 • MO • Tchr • Green Park Lemay MO • (314)544-4248 • (RF 1968)

**SIEVERT BRENDA J** (517)652-2655
5633 Frank Rd Frankenmuth MI 48734-1260 • PSW • 07/1996 • (S 1988)

**SITZE JACOB C** (619)497-6945
1010 Lillian Ln El Cajon CA 92020 • PSW • Tchr • Christ La Mesa CA • (619)462-5211 • (IV 1998)

**SMITH ANNE K** (219)422-9791
1316 Kensington Blvd Fort Wayne IN 46805-5320 • IN • Tchr • Christ Child Fort Wayne IN • (219)452-2240 • (RF 1968)

**SMITH JOANNE E** (314)256-0325
601 Huntley Heights Ballwin MO 63021-5876 • MO • 11/1993 • (RF 1974)

**SORENSEN DELORES M** (303)685-9368
229 1/2 Santa Fe Pl Manitou Springs CO 80829-2536 • RM • Tchr • Immanuel Colorado Springs CO • (719)636-5011 • (S 1976)

**SORGATZ MARIAN A** (901)737-4850
1589 Tern Rest Cv Cordova TN 38018 • jmsorgatz@aol.com • MDS • Tchr • Immanuel Memphis TN • (901)388-0205 • (RF 1968)

**SPAHN LOUISE** (717)581-5836
243 Kingsbridge Dr Lititz PA 17543-9282 • EN • 07/1985 • (RF 1961)

**SPIVA CYNTHIA L** (805)239-4189
1959 Tulipwood Dr Paso Robles CA 93446-3002 • dcspiva@juno.com • CNH • Tchr • Trinity Paso Robles CA • (805)238-0335 • (PO 1988)

**STADLER CELESTE M** (352)291-1852
2901 SW 41st ST #2810 Ocala FL 34474 • rcstad@juno.com • FG • 08/1995 • (RF 1968)

**STARK LINDA J** (314)388-0624
801 De Mun Ave # 637 Saint Louis MO 63105-3168 • PSW • 04/1992 • (RF 1989)

**STAUDE CLAUDIA A** (636)925-1712
2809 Norwich Dr Saint Charles MO 63301-1345 • cstaude@postnet.com • MO • Tchr • LHS St Charles Saint Peters MO • (636)928-5100 • (S 1977 MED)

**STECKER PAULETTE F** (414)358-2593
2841 S 44th St Milwaukee WI 53219-3405 • SW • Tchr • Mount Olive Milwaukee WI • (414)774-2113 • (RF 1971)

**STEFFEN BEVERLY M** (920)452-8551
2216 S 11th St Sheboygan WI 53081-5909 • SW • Tchr • Bethlehem Sheboygan WI • (920)452-5071 • (RF 1963)

**STEIL MAXINE MAE** (715)362-2282
4372 S Shore Dr Rhinelander WI 54501-8259 • NW • Mem C • St Mark Rhinelander WI • (715)362-2470 • (S 1962)

**STEINBACH CONNIE M** (920)387-2342
W2302 Gill Rd Mayville WI 53050-2320 • steinbach@internetwis.com • SW • EM • (S 1966)

**STEINKE KATHERINE** (636)272-7566
5 Chambers Ct O Fallon MO 63366 • aksteink@gte.net • MO • Tchr • LHS St Charles Saint Peters MO • (636)928-5100 • (S 1994)

**STEINKE LAURIE J** (616)468-5935
492 Park St Coloma MI 49038-9485 • lsteinke@remcll.k12.mi.us • MI • Tchr • Trinity Berrien Springs MI • (616)473-1811 • (RF 1982 MA)

**STELLING KRISTEN L** (904)629-5328
2470 S Naples Way Aurora CO 80013-1465 • RM • Tchr • Florida-Georgia Orlando FL • (S 1990)

**STELTENPOHL ALICE** (812)966-2171
3982 S County Rd 1200 W Medora IN 47260-9777 • IN • 10/1994 • (RF 1970)

**STENBECK JON L**
Green Park Lutheran School 4249 Green Park Rd Saint Louis MO 63125-3021 • MO • Tchr • Green Park Lemay MO • (314)544-4248 • (SP 1973)

**STICKLEY BONNIE** (507)685-2662
24350 Holland Morristown MN 55052-5012 • MNS • Tchr • Trinity Morristown MN • (507)685-2307 • (SP 1987)

**STOLL JANET L** (920)336-9582
715 S Superior St De Pere WI 54115-3277 • arsnal@yahoo.com • NW • Tchr • Zion Greenleaf WI • (920)864-2463 • (RF 1967)

**STOLLENWERK JENNIFER L**
8 Winter Hill Ct O Fallon MO 63366-3961 • MO • Tchr • Luth Association Saint Louis MO • (314)268-1234 • (MQ 1997)

**STOLTENOW JODIE G**
2501 E Boulevard Ave Bismarck ND 58501-3045 • ND • Tchr • Martin Luther Bismarck ND • (701)224-9070 • (SP 1984)

**STORK MARTHA DEBORAH** (303)683-7869
9833 S Aftonwood St Highlands Ranch CO 80126 • RM • Tchr • Shepherd Hills Littleton CO • (303)798-0711 • (S 1984 MED)

**STREICH KIMBERLY J** (313)882-3914
4175 Yorkshire Rd Detroit MI 48224-2327 • MI • 09/1994 • (AA 1990)

**STRESMAN SHIRLEY M** (517)642-3074
1665 Appleblossom Ln Saginaw MI 48609-8808 • MI • EM • (CQ 1984)

**STREUFERT REBECCA DOLORES** (509)922-1385
4910 S Gillis Way Ct Spokane WA 99206-9440 • NOW • Tchr • Spokane Spokane WA • (509)327-4441 • (SP 1972)

**STROHACKER DIANE C** (616)429-0964
2888 Trail Ln Saint Joseph MI 49085-3231 • MI • Tchr • Trinity Berrien Springs MI • (616)473-1811 • (RF 1974 MA)

**STRUVE MARJORIE L** (414)771-8909
3030 N Fairwood Ct Wauwatosa WI 53222-4020 • SW • Tchr • Milwaukee LHS Milwaukee WI • (414)461-6000 • (RF 1969)

**STUEMKE DOROTHY H** (512)453-4508
2210 Kenbridge Dr Austin TX 78757-7735 • TX • EM • (RF 1955)

**STUENKEL NONA L** (217)496-2771
2659 Windfall Dr Sherman IL 62684-9548 • CI • Tchr • Good Shepherd Sherman IL • (217)496-3149 • (S 1973)

**SUEHS AUDREY** (414)596-2205
PO Box 208 Manawa WI 54949-0208 • NW • EM • (RF 1974)

**SWANSON CARIN L**
9631 S 1700 E Sandy UT 84092-3063 • RM • 06/1999 • (CQ 1989)

**SYMMANK JOAN E** (503)779-6256
181 Shaniko CT Medford OR 97504 • NOW • 09/1984 • (RF 1958)

## T

**TESINSKY MARLENE E** (407)365-5458
2136 Church St Oviedo FL 32765-7627 • S • Tchr • St Luke Oviedo FL • (407)365-3228 • (S 1965)

**TESKE MICHELE ANN** (309)697-8828
5724 W Colt Dr Peoria IL 61607-1134 • CI • Tchr • Christ Peoria IL • (309)637-1512 • (CQ 1996)

**TEWS SUSAN M**
9921 Wayne Trace Fort Wayne IN 46816-9742 • jrtfw@aol.com • IN • Tchr • St John Monroeville IN • (219)639-6404 • (S 1974 MA)

**THAEMERT KAREN SUE** (314)947-4860
9 Lee Ct Saint Charles MO 63301-0566 • kathaemert@aol.com • MO • Tchr • Salem Florissant MO • (314)741-6781 • (AA 1994)

**THAEMERT MARILYN R** (314)921-3277
2860 Sussex Dr Florissant MO 63033-1306 • fmthaemert@aol.com • MO • Tchr • Salem Florissant MO • (314)741-8220 • (RF 1962)

**THALHAMMER LESLIE A**
3816 Yorkland Dr NW #8 Comstock Park MI 49321-8874 • MI • Tchr • St Mark Kentwood MI • (616)281-7892 • (AA 1996)

**THOMPSON AMY BETH** (219)484-0328
3822 Newport Ave Apt 8 Fort Wayne IN 46805-1376 • IN • Tchr • Concordia Fort Wayne IN • (219)426-9922 • (RF 1996)

**THOMPSON JUDY C** (810)714-0638
5075 Island View Dr Linden MI 48451 • EN • 12/1998 • (RF 1981)

**THOMSON ELISABETH R**
3203 Dry Branch Rd White Falls MD 21161-9623 • EN • Tchr • Martin Luther Pennsauken NJ • (856)665-0231 • (BR 1990)

**TIEMANN LOUISE** (314)349-5354
304 Arlington Glen Ct Fenton MO 63026-3973 • MO • Tchr • Word Of Life Saint Louis MO • (314)832-1244 • (S 1968)

**TIETJEN BETTY B** (219)947-2080
2531 Crowsnest Dr Hobart IN 46342-3821 • IN • Tchr • Trinity Hobart IN • (219)942-3147 • (S 1965)

**TIMM WYANETA A** (619)921-6489
721 E Chanslor Way Blythe CA 92225-1250 • PSW • Tchr • Zion Blythe CA • (760)922-7355 • (S 1964)

**TOENJES JOYCE L** (847)888-1102
335 Pleasant Dr South Elgin IL 60177-2141 • hjtoenjes@hotmail.com • NI • Northern Illinois Hillside IL • (RF 1989 MSED)

**TOPEL WENDY S** (810)446-6705
2463 Camel Dr Sterling Heights MI 48310-5222 • MI • Tchr • St John Fraser MI • (810)294-8740 • (S 1982 MAT)

**TORMOEHLEN LOIS E**
3122 Country Bluff Dr Saint Charles MO 63301-3741 • MO • EM • (RF 1955)

**TRACY RALPH**
1678 Deergrass Dr Saint Charles MO 63303-4616 • MO • 06/1994 • (S 1970 MA)

**TRAUTNER PHYLLIS G** (956)630-5295
212 W Gardenia Ave Mc Allen TX 78501-1817 • donnwalter@aol.com • TX • Tchr • St Paul Mc Allen TX • (956)682-2201 • (S 1972)

**TRIMPE CAROL M**
22110 W 51st St Shawnee KS 66226-3862 • IN • 08/1995 • (S 1966 MA)

**TRINKLEIN REBECCA M** (517)893-4796
1117 Michigan Ave Bay City MI 48708-8766 • MI • Tchr • Immanuel Bay City MI • (517)893-8521 • (RF 1984 MA)

**TRUWE FAYE L** (317)898-1725
1834 N Zinnia Dr Indianapolis IN 46219 • o4truwes@aol.com • IN • 07/1997 • (S 1969)

## U

**UNGER ANDREA LYNN** (313)581-5992
6401 Reuter St Dearborn MI 48126-2220 • MI • Tchr • St Matthew Westland MI • (734)425-0260 • (S 1974)

**URBEN RUTH** (808)623-5140
94-346 Hokuala St Apt 124 Mililani HI 96789-2329 • CNH • EM • (S 1962 MED)

**UTECH SHARON L** (561)392-9739
4940 NW 5th Ter Boca Raton FL 33431-4634 • sharonutech@visto.com • FG • Tchr • St Paul Boca Raton FL • (561)395-8548 • (S 1973)

## V

**VALLESKEY AUDREY** (219)583-4823
5749 E Indian Creek Rd Monticello IN 47960-2756 • MO • EM • (RF 1948)

**VICK KATHY L** (714)858-9414
C/O Shepherd of Peace Luth Ch 18182 Culver Dr Irvine CA 92612-2702 • PSW • Tchr • Shepherd Of Peace Irvine CA • (949)786-3997 • (S 1983)

**VOIGT SHERRY** (414)461-5820
4251 N 86th St Milwaukee WI 53222-1703 • SW • Tchr • Northwest Milwaukee WI • (414)463-4040 • (MQ 1987)

**VOLKERT MARIANNE E** (773)725-3391
3937 N Nottingham Ave Chicago IL 60634-2235 • NI • Tchr • Luther HS North Chicago IL • (773)286-3600 • (RF 1989)

**VOLLMAN NATALEE J** (727)461-1431
1101 Oakview Ave Clearwater FL 33756 • FG • Tchr • First Clearwater FL • (727)461-3444 • (AA 1985)

**VON AHSEN SUSAN A** (314)724-1752
901 Penrose Ln Saint Charles MO 63301-4754 • MO • Tchr • Immanuel Saint Charles MO • (636)946-0051 • (S 1976 MED)

## W

**WAAK VERA C** (810)776-3889
22734 Liscomb Ave Eastpointe MI 48021-1730 • MI • EM • (S 1977 MED)

**WAGNER JOY LORRAINE** (608)362-8755
2491 Dewey Ave Beloit WI 53511-2462 • SW • Tchr • St John Beloit WI • (608)365-7838 • (S 1964)

**WAGNER LEE ANN** (314)723-7028
2941 Westerland Dr Saint Charles MO 63301-4212 • MO • Tchr • Immanuel Saint Charles MO • (636)946-2656 • (S 1978 MA)

**WAGNER SUSAN L** (509)328-7601
2933 W Sanson Ave Spokane WA 99205-5868 • NOW • Tchr • Immanuel Saint Charles MO • (S 1974 MS)

**WAGONER TRACY LEE**
511 S 15th St Clarinda IA 51632-2604 • FG • Tchr • Grace Saint Petersburg FL • (727)527-1168 • (S 1994)

**WAHLERS DAWN N** (360)337-2687
2321 NE Eton Ln Bremerton WA 98311-9591 • PSW • 07/1998 • (IV 1991 MA)

**WALDIE CHARLENE ANN** (517)684-9535
4453 Darla Dr Bay City MI 48706-2520 • MI • Tchr • Immanuel Bay City MI • (517)893-8521 • (S 1972)

**WALES KATHLEEN M**
4108 N 93rd St Milwaukee WI 53222-1507 • SW • Tchr • Northwest Milwaukee WI • (414)463-4040 • (SP 1972)

**WALKER LOIS J** (863)297-9118
21 Lake Link Dr SE Winter Haven FL 33884-4120 • FG • Tchr • Grace Winter Haven FL • (941)293-9744 • (S 1967)

**WARNEKE LINDA J** (310)547-4753
1616 W 7th St San Pedro CA 90732-3422 • PSW • Tchr • Christ Rancho Palos Verdes CA • (310)831-0848 • (S 1977)

**WARNKE LOIS M** (847)297-8132
1287 Webster Ln Des Plaines IL 60018-1419 • NI • 07/1988 • (RF 1965 MA)

**WARTICK RUTH V** (219)766-2724
PO Box 547 Kouts IN 46347-0547 • IN • Tchr • Trinity Crown Point IN • (219)663-1586 • (S 1982)

**WEGENER RUTH A** (517)631-5877
2303 Cleveland Ave Midland MI 48640-5581 • tweg@tm.net • MI • Tchr • Faith Bay City MI • (517)684-3448 • (RF 1964)

**WEINLAEDER CYNTHIA K** (507)534-3678
355 7th St SW Plainview MN 55964-1172 • MNS • Tchr • Immanuel Plainview MN • (507)534-2108 • (S 1971)

**WEINRICH CHERYL L** (402)753-0617
1506 Jones Dr Fremont NE 68025-2062 • theweinrichs@ilovejesus.com • NEB • Tchr • Trinity Fremont NE • (402)721-5959 • (S 1980)

**WENTHE HELEN R** (512)258-0489
12321 Double Tree Ln Austin TX 78750-1751 • TX • Tchr • St Paul Austin TX • (512)472-3313 • (RF 1961)

**WENZEL BARBARA F** (810)477-6076
18222 Fremont St Livonia MI 48152-3438 • MI • Tchr • St Timothy Detroit MI • (313)535-1971 • (RF 1958)

**WERNSING KAREN L** (217)792-3961
508 N Lafayette St Mount Pulaski IL 62548-1039 • CI • Tchr • Zion Mount Pulaski IL • (217)792-5715 • (RF 1965)

**WESSLER KATHLEEN V** (630)629-1436
342 N Martha St Lombard IL 60148-2017 • NI • 07/1996 • (RF 1968)

**WHEELER DAWN** (303)238-0178
11003 W Mexico Dr Lakewood CO 80232-6100 • RM • 07/1995 • (PO 1991)

**WIDENHOFER MARY E**
5318 Litchfield Rd Fort Wayne IN 46835-8806 • IN • Tchr • Holy Cross Fort Wayne IN • (219)483-3173 • (RF 1968 MS)

**WIEGERT KAREN E** (612)442-4908
640 E 2nd St Waconia MN 55387-1607 • MNS • Tchr • Trinity Waconia MN • (952)442-4165 • (SP 1985)

**WILDAUER CHERYL A** (972)359-0441
301 Droinwich Cir Allen TX 75002 • wildauer@ticnet.com • TX • Tchr • Faith Plano TX • (972)423-7448 • (S 1969 MS)

**WILSON DIANE V** (808)572-8224
175 Awakea Loop Makawao HI 96768-8879 • CNH • Tchr • Emmanuel Kahului HI • (808)877-3037 • (SP 1985)

**WINKELHAKE SHIRLEY**
116 N Peartree Ln Arlington Heights IL 60004-6628 • NI • EM • (RF 1955)

**WIRSING JANICE JOANN** (309)454-2015
1402 Henry St Normal IL 61761-4857 • jjwirsi@ilstu.edu • CI • Tchr • Trinity Bloomington IL • (309)829-7513 • (RF 1976 MED)

**WISCHMEIER WANDA L** (812)358-2205
2407 E Cty Rd 700 S Brownstown IN 47220-9633 • IN • Tchr • Central Brownstown IN • (812)358-2512 • (S 1975)

**WITTE LYNNE E** (810)783-5654
58 Union St Mount Clemens MI 48043-5507 • MI • Tchr • St Peter Macomb MI • (810)781-9296 • (RF 1976)

**WOELMER CAROLYN E**
1112 Chaseway Ct Bloomington IN 47401-8173 • IN • 10/1994 • (S 1981)

**WOHLERS JANET J** (309)963-3903
13 Briarwood Dr Danvers IL 61732-9198 • CI • Tchr • Trinity Bloomington IL • (309)829-7513 • (S 1973)

**WOLF LOIS L** (512)252-2584
17920 Holderness Ln Pflugerville TX 78660 • TX • Tchr • Texas Austin TX • (RF 2000)

**WRASE DIANNE L** (734)374-1053
15519 Plaza S Dr Bldg 5 Taylor MI 48180 • wrased@hom.com • MI • Tchr • Calvary Lincoln Park MI • (313)381-6715 • (S 1969 MS)

**WRIGHT SANDRA H** (619)421-5140
991 Rutgers Ave Chula Vista CA 91913-3026 • PSW • Tchr • Pilgrim Chula Vista CA • (619)420-6233 • (RF 1965)

**WURM JANICE K** (920)467-8612
N6771 Charter Rd Sheboygan WI 53083 • SW • Tchr • Zion Glenbeulah WI • (414)893-8888 • (S 1964 MSED)

## Y

**YOUNG ANGELA M** (847)788-0459
6 S School St Mount Prospect IL 60056-3315 • amyoung6@juno.com • NI • Tchr • Redeemer Highland Park IL • (847)831-2225 • (RF 1996)

**YOUNG BONITA B** (517)893-2486
1460 Calmac Ct Bay City MI 48708-9139 • MI • Tchr • St John Midland MI • (517)835-7041 • (RF 1969)

**YOUNG TARA LYNN**
13235 W 70th St Juniata NE 68955-2139 • creation1@juno.com • NOW • Tchr • Trinity Bend OR • (541)382-1832 • (S 1995)

**YURK JOY M** (773)274-7231
6719 N Campbell Ave #2 Chicago IL 60645-4615 • michael.yurk@gte.net • NI • Tchr • St Philip Chicago IL • (773)561-9830 • (MQ 1990 MA)

## Z

**ZABEL BARBARA KAYE** (515)332-3064
105 4th St S Humboldt IA 50548-2022 • IW • Tchr • Zion Humboldt IA • (515)332-3279 • (S 1974)

**ZAHRT BEVERLY**
2411 N 13th St Wausau WI 54403-9108 • NW • Tchr • St John Merrill WI • (715)536-4722 • (RF 1967)

**ZASTROW EARLENE M** (414)452-4959
2007 N 24th St Sheboygan WI 53081-2126 • SW • Tchr • St Paul Sheboygan WI • (920)452-6882 • (S 1965)

**ZECKZER DEBORAH L** (219)493-2143
8726 Greenmeadow Dr New Haven IN 46774-1825 • sazeck@aol.com • IN • Tchr • Central New Haven IN • (219)493-2502 • (S 1989)

**ZEHNDER MARIE** (414)463-5926
7506 W Marion St Apt 3 Milwaukee WI 53216-1020 • SW • EM • (RF 1959)

**ZEHNDER WILMA SHERRILL** (517)694-6785
8884 Rossman Rd Dimondale MI 48821-9631 • MI • Tchr • Our Savior Lansing MI • (517)882-8665 • (RF 1965)

**ZIELKE ALICE L** (517)238-2188
4051 Wayne Beach Rd Cold Water MI 49036-8509 • MI • EM • (RF 1960 MA)

**ZIMMER LOIS M** (219)322-8584
513 Sycamore Dr Dyer IN 46311-1840 • zimmer@megsinet.net • IN • Tchr • St Paul Munster IN • (219)836-6270 • (RF 1980 MS)

**ZUCH CAROL A** (503)788-1412
10317 SE Rex St Portland OR 97266-6078 • NOW • Tchr • Northwest Portland OR • (RF 1962)

**ZUEHLSDORF MARY A** (414)355-7318
8279 N 46th St Brown Deer WI 53223 • jmzuehls@execpc.com • SW • Tchr • Emmaus Milwaukee WI • (414)444-6090 • (SP 1972 MA)

**ZULKOSKY RUTH MARIE** (320)252-5516
8 6th Ave S Sauk Rapids MN 56379 • MNN • 07/1986 • (SP 1967)

**ZWERNEMANN BONNIE M** (914)337-8299
51 Edgewood Ln Bronxville NY 10708-1945 • pastaz1@aol.com • AT • SHS/C • Atlantic Bronxville NY • (914)337-5700 • (RF 1961 MAT)

# Parish Music

A

**ANKERBERG JENNIFER L** (313)724-8096
21514 Francis St Dearborn MI 48124-2905 • eankerberg@voyager.net • MI • Tchr • Emmanuel Dearborn MI • (313)565-4002 • (RF 1992 MCMU)

B

**BENDER SALLY ANN** (612)487-0331
989 Lafond Ave Saint Paul MN 55104-2111 • MNS • Mem C • St Stephanus Saint Paul MN • (651)228-1486 • (SP 1988)

H

**HAMMOND ANN** (440)247-3190
39 Lyndale Dr Chagrin Falls OH 44022-2716 • OH • 06/1996 • (SP 1995)

**HORST TIMOTHY LEE** (812)423-0605
1411 Olive St Evansville IN 47714 • IN • Mem C • St Paul Evansville IN • (812)422-5414 • (S 1999)

K

**KLEMP PHILIP ANDREW** (507)454-1713
1560 Willow Run Winona MN 55987 • PAKlemp@hotmail.com • MNS • Mem C • St Martin Winona MN • (507)452-8879 • (SP 1990 MMU)

L

**LOHMEYER MARK ALAN**
1724A Forest Lakes Cir West Palm Beach FL 33406 • malbach1@aol.com • FG • 03/2000 • (S 1987)

R

**ROSSOW CRYSTAL A DR** (402)438-2208
C/O Christ Lutheran Church 315 S Hughes Little Rock AR 72205 • NEB • 01/1992 • (S 1986 MMU DMA)

S

**SCHLECHT KATHERINE RENEE** (970)663-7929
3306 Franklin Ave Loveland CO 80538-7612 • RM • Mem C • Immanuel Loveland CO • (970)667-4506 • (SP 1984)

# Parish Nurse

S

**SCHNORR MARCIA ANNETTE DR** (815)562-6823
1225 Springdale Dr Rochelle IL 61068-1151 • NI • Mem C • St Paul Rochelle IL • (815)562-2744 • (MQ 1996 MS DED)

# Parish Workers

A

**ALBER RUTH ANN DORA** (316)683-8571
2111 S Cooper Ct Wichita KS 67207-5834 • nalbert@kscable.com • KS • 05/1995 • (WN 1976)

B

**BARNUM LYNNE ELLEN** (218)233-8041
1605 4th St S Moorhead MN 56560-4122 • MNN • Mem C • Our Redeemer Moorhead MN • (218)233-7569 • (WN 1966)

**BLASE CAROL** (612)788-9427
12061 Oak Park Blvd NE Minneapolis MN 55434-3077 • carolblase@juno.com • MNS • Mem C • St Matthew Columbia Heights MN • (763)788-9427 • (WN 1977)

**BOECK VALERIE L** (515)285-3769
C/O Peace Lutheran Church 5615 SW 14th St Des Moines IA 50315-4814 • IW • Mem C • Peace Des Moines IA • (515)285-3769 • (MQ 1987)

**BRANDT HARRIET**
C/O Immanuel Lutheran Church 630 Adams St Wausau WI 54403-3508 • NW • 07/1984 • (WN 1966)

C

**CLONKEY JEANETTE** (715)248-3838
84 206th St New Richmond WI 54017-5700 • MNS • SHS/C • Minnesota South Burnsville MN • (WN 1963 MA)

D

**DAVIDSON ALICE** (402)628-3333
PO Box 8 207 S 2nd St Cedar Bluffs NE 68015-0008 • kidavidson@navix.net • NEB • 11/1991 • (MQ 1986)

**DENNEY CONSTANCE L** (913)682-5144
27625 Tonganoxie Rd Leavenworth KS 66048-7579 • jcdenney@lvnworth.com • KS • Mem C • St Paul Leavenworth KS • (913)682-0387 • (WN 1967)

F

**FALKENHEIM-MONKE ANN** (303)449-6058
PO Box 3512 Boulder CO 80307-3512 • RM • 07/1985 • (WN 1967)

**FREITAG BETTY JEAN** (408)260-9472
100 Ash Ct Los Gatos CA 95032 • betsemail@juno.com • PSW • O Sp Min • Pacific Southwest Irvine CA • (949)854-3232 • (WN 1966)

H

**HAIGHT DIANE E** (253)529-1821
26467 8th Ave S Des Moines WA 98198 • diahai@stlukesfedway.org • NOW • Mem C • St Luke Federal Way WA • (253)941-3000 • (WN 1982)

**HARMON ARLEATA** (316)744-2978
4217 Country Ln Wichita KS 67220-1747 • risnsavior@aol.com • KS • Mem C • Risen Savior Wichita KS • (316)683-5538 • (WN 1979)

**HELLWEG CHRISTIE**
15935 E Radcliff Pl #A Aurora CO 80015-1552 • RM • 08/1990 • (WN 1979)

**HERBRICH JEANETTE**
21815 Stewart Rd Queens Village NY 11427-1107 • AT • S Ex/S • Atlantic Bronxville NY • (914)337-5700 • (WN 1964)

**HOFFMAN PAULA DIANE** (316)873-2728
PO Box 846 Meade KS 67864-0846 • KS • 08/1988 • (WN 1985)

J

**JANNE MAXINE** (316)267-7649
1755 Exchange St Wichita KS 67213-5101 • KS • EM • (WN 1939)

**JOHNSON JANE** (573)769-4022
210 S Spring St Palmyra MO 63461-1484 • pastorj@nemonet.com • IN • 08/1987 • (WN 1984)

**JOURDAN EILEEN** (402)731-6476
4133 T St Omaha NE 68107 • eileenjourdan@hotmail.com • NEB • 05/2000 • (WN 1982)

K

**KNOEPFEL LORI LEE** (918)446-1437
3214 W 69th Ct Tulsa OK 74132-1713 • llknoep@hotmail.com • OK • Mem C • Christ The Redeemer Tulsa OK • (918)492-6451 • (WN 1981)

**KUEHN JUDY** (520)883-7870
3663 S Heifner Pl Tucson AZ 85735 • PSW • 08/1987 • (WN 1985)

L

**LORENZEN ELIZABETH ELINOR** (507)348-3346
RR 3 Box 81 Pipestone MN 56164 • MNS • Mem C • St Paul Pipestone MN • (507)825-5271 • (WN 1979)

M

**MALONE VIVIAN**
419 S 78th St Apt 1 Omaha NE 68114 • AT • Mem C • Atlantic Bronxville NY • (914)337-5700 • (WN 1976)

**MENKE MARTHA A** (309)386-1154
3526 Fair Ave Davenport IA 52806-6009 • CI • Mem C • Immanuel Rock Island IL • (309)786-3391 • (WN 1970)

**MEYERHOFF SUE** (785)348-5578
606 S Elm St Linn KS 66953-9508 • lsmeyerhoff@bluevalley.net • KS • Mem C • Zion Linn KS • (785)348-5332 • (WN 1960)

**MILLER SHARON** (406)227-5207
3827 Chokecherry St East Helena MT 59635-3404 • OK • 09/1984 • (WN 1978)

O

**OLSEN BEVERLY** (218)828-0279
3241 Donald St N Baxter MN 56425-9612 • olefam@brainerd.net • MNN • Minnesota North Brainerd MN • (WN 1973)

**OLSON JOAN** (402)371-7959
2314 Belmont Dr Norfolk NE 68701-2337 • NEB • 08/1986 • (WN 1965)

**ORR NORMA NIE ANNE** (201)244-0561
71 W Madison Ave Apt A Dumont NJ 07628 • nieanne@aol.com • KS • 05/1995 • (O 1963 MHSA)

**OSCHWALD JILL**
Ta Hsueh Rd # 82 19-4 Hsinchu 300 TAIWAN • oschwald@gcn.net.tw • IN • S Miss • Indiana Fort Wayne IN • (WN 1977)

P

**PAEPER JOLAIN E** (513)851-1824
797 Hargrove Way Cincinnati OH 45240-1968 • messiahgnh@aol.com • OH • Mem C • Messiah Cincinnati OH • (513)825-4768 • (WN 1979)

**PUCCIARELLI CYNTHIA** (562)863-7524
14118 Clarkdale Ave Norwalk CA 90650-4104 • PSW • Mem C • St Paul Norwalk CA • (562)864-5654 • (WN 1977)

R

**ROSSOW CONSTANCE MARTHA** (507)662-6513
RR 2 Box 13A Lakefield MN 56150-9706 • MNS • Mem C • Immanuel Lakefield MN • (507)662-5718 • (WN 1968)

**ROTH VICKI MARIE** (419)599-0340
1125 Westmont Napoleon OH 43545 • rjroth@henry.net • OH • Mem C • St Paul Napoleon OH • (419)592-3535 • (WN 1977)

S

**SAATHOFF LYNNE JANINE** (402)331-8415
5613 S 91st Ave Omaha NE 68127-3508 • NEB • Mem C • Beaut Savior Omaha NE • (402)331-7376 • (WN 1971)

**SADLER DEBBIE J** (361)992-0270
229 Country Club Dr Corpus Christi TX 78412 • TX • Mem C • Lord Of Life Corpus Christi TX • (361)937-8158 • (UNKNWN 1967)

**SCHELLIN MARTHA A** (636)671-0127
5640 Saeger Ln House Springs MO 63051-2293 • maschell@stlnet.com • MO • 07/1991 • (WN 1978)

**SHACKLETON KATHRYN** (205)836-1867
218 90th St N Birmingham AL 35206-1314 • SO • 11/1993 • (WN 1978)

**STEINBRENNER SUSAN** (417)889-3171
1938 S Jefferson Ave Springfield MO 65807-2622 • ssteinb485@aol.com • MO • 06/1994 • (WN 1982)

**STELMACHOWICZ CARLA S** (262)692-2007
903 Martin Ave Fredonia WI 53021 • SW • 09/1998 • (WN 1977)

**STINNETT ESTHER** (406)452-5620
725 3rd Ave SW Great Falls MT 59404-2921 • MT • EM • (WN 1961 MA)

# Social Workers

S

**SHERMAN JO ANNE E** (208)664-6888
1126 E Montana Ave Coeur D Alene ID 83814-4327 • sherfish@msn.com • NOW • Mem C • Christ King Coeur D Alene ID • (208)664-9231 • (PO 1993 MS)

## PLEASE NOTE:

The information that follows is provided for the convenience of readers of the Annual.

# AUXILIARIES

Auxiliaries are organizations described in, and subject to the conditions set forth in, Bylaw 14.01 of the Synod Bylaws. As indicated in Bylaw 14.01 (b) (1), The Lutheran Church—Missouri Synod makes no representations or guarantees about the fiscal solvency or financial responsibility of any auxiliary organization or for any services expressly or implicitly offered by it.

## International Lutheran Laymen's League

**(Incorporated under the laws of Missouri, 1929)**

## Lutheran Hour Ministries International Headquarters

**U S Office: 660 Mason Ridge Center Dr**
**St Louis MO 63141**
**314/317-4100 FAX 314/317-4297**
**Canada Office: 270 Lawrence Ave**
**Kitchener Ontario Can N2M 1Y4**
**519/578-7420 FAX 519/742-8091**

### Officers

*President* Alvin Waldron
*Vice-President* Robert Beer
*Secretary* Robert A Andersen
*Financial Secretary* Loren Podell
*Treasurer* David Muck

### Board of Governors

Region 1 Richard Gruenhagen
Region 2 Richard Driessnack
Region 3 Dr Werner Essig
Region 4 Loren Volkman
Region 5 Weldon Schwiebert
Region 6 Alvin Krenke
Region 7 Scott Sommers
Region 8 Raymond Stuckemeyer
Region 9 Mick Onnen
Region 10 David Lichtenegger
Region 11 Harry Hall
Region 12 Ken Boettcher
Region 13 Robert Kratzke
Region 14 Wilmar (Bill) Buss
Region 15 Robert Hallman

### Staff Members

*Executive Director*, Rodger Hebermehl
*Lutheran Hour Speaker*, Dr Dale A Meyer
*Associate Lutheran Hour Speaker*, Dr Wallace Schulz
*Director of Finance & Administration*, Larry Pritchett
*Director of Marketing & Communication*, Jim Telle
*Director of International Ministries*, Rev Walt Winters
*Director of North American Ministries*, Jane Schmotzer
*Director of Volunteer Opportunities*, Joseph Collet
*Director of Lutheran Laymen's League of Canada*, Stephen Klinck
Development, Al Koepke

### District Presidents

*Alberta-British Columbia* Bob Felstend
*California-Nevada-Hawaii* John Foottit
*Capital* Alvin Etzler
*Carolinas* James Bradshaw
*Central Illinois* David Sturm
*East* Gary Zakel
*Eastern* Christian Klafehn
*Florida-Georgia* William Reister
*Grand Canyon* Edwin Hundt
*Gulf* Ron Morris
*Indiana* Paul Doenges
*Iowa East* Virgil Mauer
*Iowa West* John Tews
*Kansas* Wilbur Tegtmeier
*Lone Star* Carl Schroeder
*Central* Wayne Timm
*Michigan* Paul Pillsbury
*Michigan Southeast* Philip Krauss
*Mid-Atlantic* Gerhard Reinert
*Mid-South* David Kaucher
*Minnesota North* Arnold Beske
*Minnesota South* Donald Preston
*Missouri* Earl Eno
*Montana* Emil Neumann
*Nebraska* Marvin Swan
*New England* Paul Martin
*North Dakota* Donald Brandenburg
*North Wisconsin* Miles Zimmerman
*Northern Illinois* Charles Schild
*Ohio* Lee Goodeman
*Oklahoma* Ronald Schaulat
*Oregon* Vernon Keiper
*Rocky Mountain* V Dale Stoner
*South Dakota* Harvard Schulz
*South Wisconsin* Ronald Kabitzke
*Southern California* Clifton Shout
*Southern Illinois* Paul Walther
*Tennessee* John Hall
*Utah-Idaho* Lewis Eilers
*Washington/Alaska* Joel Ross
*Wyoming* David Schreibeis

### Periodical

*The Lutheran Layman.* Newspaper mailed 7 times a year to LLL members and sponsors and to all pastors of the Missouri Synod. Contains general news, columns, and feature stories about the League and the Synod.

## International Lutheran Women's Missionary League

**General Office**
**PO Box 411993**
**St Louis MO 63141-9998**
**314/268-1530 FAX 314/268-1532**
**TOLL FREE 800/252-LWML (5965)**
**E-Mail lwml@lwml.org**

### Officers

Virginia Von Seggern *President*, 87127 512th Ave Orchard NE 68764-6403 402/655-2204 FAX 402/655-2213 E-mail Virginiavs@aol.com
Helen Bice *Vice-President for Human Care*
Ida Luebke *Vice-President Christian Life*
Jan Rueter *Vice-President Gospel Outreach*
Linda Reiser *Vice-President Servant Resources*
Karol Selle *Vice-President Communications*
Barbara Volk *Recording Secretary*
Janet Miller *Treasurer*
Rev David P Buuck *Sr Pastoral Counselor*
Rev David Bernthal *Jr Pastoral Counselor*
Carol Zemke *PR Director*

### District Presidents

*Atlantic* Nancy Graf Peters
*California-Nevada-Hawaii* Louise Rickey
*Carolinas* Janis McDaniels
*Central Illinois* Betty Dietrich
*Chesapeake* Connie Kruelle
*Eastern* Dorothy Koschmann
*English* Connie Johnson
*Florida-Georgia* Margie Smith
*Gulf States* Linda Bailey
*Indiana* Bonnie Hazen
*Iowa East* Judy Westergren
*Iowa West* Luana Kading
*Kansas* Lois Llewllyn
*Louisiana-Mississippi* Anita Mallard
*Michigan* Barbara Hoffmeier
*Mid-South* Ladell McWhirter
*Minnesota North* Lucille Phillips
*Minnesota South* Joyce Swedean
*Missouri* Joyce Bischoff
*Montana* Jo Young
*Nebraska North* Gwen Lindberg
*Nebraska South* Edna Moll
*New England* Donna Gruel
*New Jersey* Eleanor Hoffman
*North Dakota* Kay Krekian
*North Wisconsin* Leah Lehman
*Northern Illinois* Carli Zygowicz
*Ohio* Ida Luebke
*Oklahoma* Carol Diekelman
*Oregon* Julia Riess
*Pacific SW* Barb Virus
*Rocky Mountain* Sue Anderson
*SELC* Millicent Kwaitkowski
*South Dakota* Janell McKinstry
*South Wisconsin* Joyce Kaestner
*Southern Illinois* Faith Richardson
*Texas* Eloise Kuhlmann
*Utah-Idaho* Jane Kaestner
*Washington-Alaska* Charlie Hamaker
*Wyoming* Eunice Boehlke

### Periodical

*Lutheran Woman's Quarterly.* Official quarterly publication of the Lutheran Women's Missionary League. Includes articles of a general missionary nature in the interest of missionary education, also study topics. Edited by the Editorial Staff of the LWML. Donna Streufert, Editor in Chief, 3121 Chelsea Ct, South Bend, IN 46614-2207. For Subscriptions write LWML Office, PO Box 411993, St. Louis, MO 63141-9998.

# RECOGNIZED SERVICES ORGANIZATIONS

Recognized Services Organizations are organizations described in and subject to the conditions set forth in Bylaw 14.03 of the Synod Bylaws. The Lutheran Church—Missouri Synod makes no representations or guarantees about the fiscal solvency or financial responsibility of any recognized organization or for any services expressly or implicitly offered by it.

## Social Ministry Organizations

*Dr. Carl Toelke, Jr., Director*
1333 S. Kirkwood Rd., St. Louis, MO 63122

Social Ministry Organizations are granted "Church Recognition" status by the Board for Human Care Ministries when they are in a responsible relationship with The Lutheran Church—Missouri Synod and the appropriate District(s) and comply with established criteria.

Social Ministry Organizations minister, in the name of Jesus Christ, to the needs of people with a variety of services. In the parenthesis following each listing, the services of each social ministry organization are identified according to the following key:

1. Information and Referral
2. Individual, Marital, Family Counseling
3. Foster Family Care
4. Adoption Services
5. Residential Treatment for Children
6. Problem Pregnancy Counseling
7. Day Care, Children and/or Adults
8. Emergency Aid and/or Shelter
9. Refugee Resettlement
10. Residential Care and/or Housekeeping for the Elderly
11. Residential Care and/or Service for the Developmentally Disabled
12. Residential Care and/or Service for the Deaf
13. Chaplaincy Services
14. Clinic Services
15. Special Education
16. Life Enrichment Program
17. Peer Counseling, Volunteer Service Programs
18. Welfare Planning, Coordinating
19. Community Concerns-Action, Advocacy
20. Consultation, Program Development for Pastors, Social Ministry Committees, Congregations and Community Groups.
21. Ombudsman Services
22. Alcohol and Substance Abuse Services
23. Development/Foundation
24. Abuse Prevention/Treatment

### ALABAMA

**Lutheran Ministries of Alabama**
200 Longwood Drive SE Huntsville AL 35801
Rev Mark Cerniglia *Exec Dir*
(334) 832-9006 FAX (334) 832-9006
(15-16-18-19-20)

**Lutheran Ministries of Central Alabama**
PO Box 3587
Montgomery, AL 36109-0587
Mike Twiss
(334) 279-1214 (Phone/FAX)

## ALASKA

**Lutheran Social Services of Alaska**
2606 "C" St Suite 2B Anchorage AK 99503
Carol Warren
(907) 272-0643 (1-8-19)

## ARIZONA/SOUTHERN NEVADA

**Lutheran Social Ministry of the Southwest**
1124 N 3rd Street #1 Phoenix AZ 85004
Lynn Baker
(602) 271-0828
(1-2-4-7-8-9-11-15-19-20)

*Program Offices:*
Adoption Center
919 N First St Phoenix AZ 85004
(602) 258-7201
Life Counseling
919 N First St Phoenix AZ 85004
(602) 258-7201
Steve Stenson
Westside Pantry & Referral Service
7310 W Camelback Glendale AZ 85303
(602) 848-8278
Rosemary Leiendecker
Phoenix Service Center
919 N First St Phoenix AZ 85004
(602) 258-7201
Rosemary Leiendecker
East Valley Adult Day Care Ctr
1125 N Power Rd Mesa AZ 85205
(602) 981-6260
Tom Perkovich
East Valley Services Center
424 W Broadway Mesa AZ 85204
(602) 964-4543
Rosemary Leiendecker
Tucson Service Center
1222 N Campbell Tucson AZ 85719
(520) 327-2800
Lynn Baker

## CALIFORNIA

**California Lutheran Homes & Community Services**
2835 N Naomi St Suite 300
Burbank CA 91803-4317
Rev Gary Wheeler
(818) 729-8104 FAX
(818) 729-8200
(1-10-12-13-14-19-20)

*Retirement:*
The Alhambra
2400 S Fremont Ave Alhambra CA 91803
Ray Mattes
Walnut Manor
891 S Walnut St Anaheim CA 92802
(714) 776-7150
Kate Whitehouse
Carlsbad by the Sea
2855 Carlsbad Blvd Carlsbad CA 92008
(760) 729-2377
Gary Stork
Southland Lutheran Home
11701 Studebaker Rd Norwalk CA 90650
(562) 868-9761
Robert Moses

*Health Facilities (Skilled Nursing):*
Lutheran Health Facility of Alhambra
2021 Carlos Street Alhambra CA 91803
(626) 570-5603
Nancy Spring
Walnut Manor Care Center
1401 W Ball Road Anaheim CA 92802
(714) 776-7150
Kate Whitehouse
Lutheran Health Facility of Carlsbad
201 Grand Ave Carlsbad CA 92008
(760) 729-4983
Gary Stork

*Housing:*
Altadena Vista Apts
815 E Calavaras Altadena CA 91001
(626) 794-6080
South Bay Retirement Residence
1001 W Cressey Compton CA 90222
(310) 609-0110
Henry Charles
Seaview Lutheran Plaza
2800 Pacific View Drive
Corona del Mar CA 92625
(714) 720-0888
Loretta Von Schriltz

**Good Shepherd Home of the West**
18350 Mount Langley St Suite 205
Fountain Valley CA 92708
Pamela McCrea
1-(888) 298-1588
(1-11-13-19-20-23)
Pilgrim Tower
1207 S Vermont Ave Los Angeles CA 90006
(213) 387-6541
Barbara Schwerdt

*Regional Offices:*
Arizona
3003 W Northern Ave #3 Phoenix AZ 86051
(602) 995-4722
Central California
64 W Putnam St Porterville CA 93270
(559) 783-6308
Northern California
1335 Mowry Ave Fremont CA 94538
(510) 791-6849
Northwest
4221 SW Golf Course Road Cornelius OR 97113
(503) 357-4790
Rocky Mountain
5630 S Curtice St Littleton CO 80120
(303) 795-2061

**Lutheran Care for the Aging**
1031 Franklin St San Francisco CA 94109
(415) 441-7777
Sharyn Womer
(10)
Rohlffs Memorial Manor
2400 Fair Dr Napa CA 94558
Edwina Hawbecker
(707) 255-9555
Concordia Manor
2435 Sutherland Dr Napa CA 94558
Edwina Hawbecker
(707) 255-7330

*Area Offices:*

**Lutheran Social Service of N CA**
433 Hegenberger Rd Suite 103
Oakland CA 94621
(510) 729-7246 FAX
(510) 729-7244
Mr Richard D Stahlke
(1-2-8-18-19-20)

*Area Offices:*
780 Ashbury Ave #2 El Cerrito CA 94530
(510) 559-7111
Deborah Elliott
16548 Ferris Ave Los Gatos CA 95032
(408) 356-0999
Diana Vogel

**Lutheran Social Services of S CA**
2424 S Fremont Ave Alhambra CA 91803
(626) 570-5200
Richard Stahlke CEO
(1-2-7-8-9-11-17-18-19-20-23-24)

*Area Offices:*
Avanti Adult Services
60 N Daisy Pasadena CA 91107
(626) 564-0191
Karen Ingram
1611 Pine Ave Long Beach CA 90813
(562) 599-1321
Ruth Foelber
704 N Glassell Orange CA 92667
(714) 771-2969
Ellen Yin
Hill House
529 N Hill Ave Pasadena CA 91106
Genesis
3772 Taft St Riverside CA 92503
(909) 689-7847
Dale Evola
3101 Fourth Ave San Diego CA 92103
(619) 291-8722
6425 Tyrone Ave Van Nuys CA 91401
(818) 901-9480

**Pleasant Ridge Home**
2030 23rd Street Sacramento CA 95818
(916) 455-1734
Ms Ruth Patkowski
(1-10)

## COLORADO

**Lutheran Family Services of Colorado**
363 S Harlan Suite 200 Denver CO 80226
(303) 922-3433
Beth Walker Acting Administrator
(1-3-4-6-9-17-20)
LFS/Colorado Northern Services
503 Reminston Ft Collins CO 80524
(970) 484-5955
Sharon Thomas

## CONNECTICUT

**See Massachusetts**

## DELAWARE

**Lutheran Community Services Inc.**
1304 N Rodney St Wilmington DE 19806-4242
(302) 654-8886
Donna deBussy
(1-8-16-17-18-19-20-23)

## DISTRICT OF COLUMBIA

**Lutheran Social Services of the National Capital Area**
4406 Georgia Ave NW Washington DC 20011
(202) 723-3000
Rev Mark Cooper
(1-2-3-4-8-9-17-18-19-20)

## FLORIDA

**Lutheran Haven Inc**
2041 State Rd 426 Oviedo FL 32765
(407) 365-5676
Donald Kovac
(7-10)

**Lutheran Services Florida**
2700 W Dr Martin Luther King Jr Blvd, Ste 308
Tampa FL 33607
(813) 875-1408
James Wells
(1-2-6-7-8-9-17-19-20)

*Children's Services*
P.E.P.P.I. Head Start Program
200 SE 9th St Belle Glade, FL 33450
Shirley Walker
(561)996-1718 FAX (561) 996-0287
Child Care Food Program
2700 W Dr Martin Luther King Jr Blvd Ste 200
Tampa FL 33607
(813) 877-9303
Rubis Castro

*Youth and Family Services*
*Southeast Service Area*
Broward Family Center
4980 N E 11th Ave Ft Lauderdale FL 33334
(954) 491-4133
Deborah Bowen
Lippman Youth Shelter
221 NW 43rd Ct Oakland Park FL 33309
(954) 568-2801

*Southwest Service Area*
Lutheran Ministries of Florida Inc
3634 Central Ave Ft Myers, FL 33901
(941) 278-5400
Oasis—A Safe Place for Teens
3642 Central Ave Ft Myers FL 33901
(941) 278-1032
Naples Program Office
281 S Airport Rd Naples FL 34104
(941) 649-4643

*Northeast Service Area*
Program Administration Office
4610 W Fairfield Dr Pensacola FL 32506
(850) 453-2772
Currie House Youth Shelter
4610 W Fairfield Dr Pensacola FL 32506
(850) 457-1090
Hope House Youth Shelter & Program Office
5127 Eastland St Crestview FL 32539
(850) 682-2374
Safe Haven
7008 N Palafox St Pensacola FL 32503
(850) 682-2374

*Resettlement Services*
Program Administration Office
4343 W Flagler St Suite 200 Miami FL 33134
(305) 567-2511
Elizabeth Van Werne
Legal Services Program
4343 W Flagler St Suite 200 Miami FL 33134
(305) 567-2511

Jacqueline Roman
*Employment Programs*
Employment for Refugees & Entrants
9750 Cons Way Miami FL 33165
(305) 559-1177
Mary Jane Gonzalez-Cruz
Refugee Employment Program
2539 N Dixie Hwy Lake Worth, FL 33460
(561) 582-4020
Ruth Pierre-Louis
Manpower for Refugees & Entrants
2700 W Dr MLK Blvd Suite 200
Tampa FL 33607
(813) 877-9303
Marie Hernandez
Manpower Employment Program
7901 4th St N Suite 308
St Petersburg, FL 33703
(813) 563-9400
Marie Hernandez
*Housing Programs*
Housing Programs
16201 SE 95th Ave Perrine FL 33157
(305) 256-6780
*Refugee/Immigration Programs*
Refugee Resettlement
4343 W Fagler St Suite 200 Miami FL 33134
(305) 567-2511
Ada Quarz
Refugee and Immigration Program
2700 W Dr MLK Blvd Suite 200
Tampa FL 33607
(813) 877-9303
Danielle Kearney
Refugee Resettlement
2140 Hwy 434 Longwood FL 32779
(407) 869-0988
Ann Kuyawa
*Church and Community Relations Services*
Inter-Lutheran Disaster Response Program
16201 SW 95th Ave
Perrine FL 33157
(305) 256-7728
Judith Bunker
*Guardianship Services*
Sarasota Guardianship Services
2033 Wood St Suite 210 Sarasota FL 34237
(941) 365-0045
Anne Ridings
Office of the Public Guardian-13th Judicial Circuit
2700 W Dr MLK Blvd Suite 200
Tampa FL 33607
(813) 877-9303
Margaret Suarez
Hillsborough Private Guardianship Services
2700 W Dr MLK Blvd Suite 200
Tampa FL 33607
(813) 877-9303
Margaret Suarez
Gulf Coast Guardianship Services
4600 Mobile Highway Suite 9-343
Pensacola FL 32506
(850) 453-7557
Marcia Thompson
Manatee Guardianship Services
1101 6th Ave W Suite 207 Bradenton FL 34205
(941) 741-8850
JoLynne Wigginton
**Lutheran Counseling Services, Inc.**
1600 S Orlando Ave Winter Park FL 32789
(407) 644-4692
Rev Melvin R Jacob
(2-20)

## GEORGIA

**Lutheran Ministries of Georgia Inc**
756 W Peachtree St NW
Atlanta GA 30308-1138
(404) 875-0201
Gary Danielsen
(1-3-4-5-6-9-17-20-23)

## ILLINOIS

**Lutheran Care Center**
702 W Cumberland Altamont IL 62411-0331
(618) 483-6136
Karen Hille
(1-2-13-17)
**Lutheran Child and Family Services of Illinois**
Administrative Office
7620 Madison St River Forest IL 60305
(708) 771-7180
Gene Svebakken
(1-2-3-4-5-6-8-13-19-20)
*Service Centers:*
Belleville
2408 Lebanon Ave Belleville IL 62221
(618) 234-8904
Nice Twice Resale Shop
116 & 118 E Main St
Belleville IL 62220
(618) 233-9895
Belvidere
1225 E Second St Belvidere IL 61008
(800) 845-6350
Bloomington
801 South Madison Bloomington IL 61701
(800) 845-6350
Carlyle
16996 Old State Rd Carlyle IL 62231
(618) 594-4322
Chester
302 W Holmes Chester IL 62233
(800) 845-6350
Chicago
6127 S University Dr Chicago IL 60637
(773) 753-0600
(773) 451-2190 FAX (773) 451-2191
5259 S Major Ave Chicago IL 60638
(800) 845-6350
Hispanic Outreach
3859 W 26th St Chicago IL 60623
(773) 278-7330
322 S. Green St Chicago IL 60607
(312) 243-6400
82485 Paulina Chicago IL 60620
(773) 723-2126
LSS Outpatient Services
4840 W Byron Chicago IL 60641
(773) 282-7347 x 245
Kathlen Dayer
Older Adult Services
6650 N Northwest Hwy #302 Chicago IL 60631
(773) 774-6959
Barbara Meyer
Collinsville
409 Beltline #140 Collinsville, IL 62234
(618) 345-7351 or (800) 845-6350
Decatur
109 S Edward Decatur IL 62522
(217) 428-8380
Downers Grove
1501 87th St Downers Grove IL 60516
(630) 985-2420
East Dundee
304 Main St E Dundee IL 60111
(800) 845-6350
East St Louis
4700 State St Suite #3 E St Louis IL 62205
(618) 874-1701
Effingham
1310 N Keller Dr #10 Effingham IL 62401
(800) 845-6350
Forest Park
Nice Twice Resale Shop
7628 W Madison St
Forest Park IL 60130
(708) 366-2229
Freeport
LCFS Family Counseling
1320 S Blackhawk
Freeport IL 61032-6302
(800) 845-6350
Gillespie
LCFS Family Counseling
309 W Spruce Gillespie IL 62033
(800) 845-6350
Glen Carbon
LCFS of Illinois
Near Meridian Rd & Hwy 157
(618) 656-3000
Hardin
PO Box 636
Hardin IL 62047
(618) 576-9023 or (800) 845-6350
Harvey
15411 S Broadway Ave
Harvey IL 60426
(708) 596-7464
Kankakee
LCFS Family Counseling
1580 Butterfield Trail
Kankakee, IL 60901
(800) 845-6350
LaFox
LCFS Family Counseling
LaFox IL 60147
(800) 845-6350
Marion
LSS Behavioral Health Services
1616 W Main Marion IL 62959
(618) 997-9196
Larry Hepburn
LSS Foster Care & Adoption
1616 W Main Marion IL 62959
(618) 997-9196
Laura Bennett
Mt Vernon
Mt Vernon Area Office
800 S 45th St Wells Bypass
Mt Vernon IL 62864
(618) 242-3284
Nice Twice Resale Shop
800 S 45th St Wells Bypass
Mt Vernon IL 62864
(618) 242-9306
Southern Thirty Adolescent Center
PO Box 964
Mt Vernon IL 62864
(618) 242-2238
New Minden
18047 State Route 177
New Minden IL 62263
(618) 478-5580
Olney
202 E Main #209 Olney IL 62450
(618) 395-1206
Peoria
LCFS
6801 N Allen Road
Peoria IL 61614-2480
(800) 845-6350
Quincy
431 Hampshire St Quincy IL 62301-2927
(217) 222-0106
Salem
LCFS
2400 S Broadway #12 Salem IL 62881
(618) 548-3771
South Elgin
182 Melrose Suite 1 South Elgin IL 60177
(800) 845-6350
Sparta
PO Box 439 Sparta IL 62286-0439
(800) 845-6350
Springfield
431 S Grand Ave West Springfield IL 62704
(217) 544-4631
Vandalia
726 W Fillmore Vandalia IL 62471
(618) 283-0616
Nice Twice Resale Shop
418 W Gallatin Vandalia IL 62471
(618) 283-4120
Waterloo
Camp Wartburg
5705 LRC Rd
Waterloo IL 62298
(618) 939-7715
LCFS Family Counseling
608 S Church St Waterloo IL 62298
(618) 939-8660
Waukegan
LCFS
824 N Lewis Ave Waukegan IL 60085
(800) 845-6350
Yorkville
LCFS
8609 Route 47 Yorkville IL 60560-9751
(800) 845-6350
**Lutheran Church Charities Fund**
333 W Lake St Addison IL 60101
(630) 628-6442
Carl Kahlfeldt *Pres*
**Lutheran Congregations for Career Development**
1500 N Mason Chicago IL 60651
(773) 745-9190
Yvonne Crumpton
**Lutheran Home and Services for the Aged**
800 W Oakton St Arlington Hgts IL 60004
(847) 253-3710 FAX (847) 368-7302

Roger W Paulsberg *Pres*
(1-2-7-10-13-14-17-20-23)
**Lutheran Senior Ministries, Inc.**
7019 N Galena Rd Peoria IL 61614-2294
(309) 692-4494
Ronald H Jaeger
(1-10-13)
**Lutheran Home for the Aged Development Corp**
PO Box 4 Danforth IL 60930
(815) 269-2970
Carol Peters
(10)
Luther Place
PO Box 4 Danforth IL 60930
(815) 269-2970
Carol Peters
Prairie Haven
PO Box 4 Danforth IL 60930
(815) 269-2970
Carol Peters *Admin*
Prairieview Foundation
PO Box 4 Danforth IL 60930
(815) 269-2970
Carol Peters
Judy Goldenstein
Prairieview Lutheran Home
PO Box 4 Danforth IL 60930
(815) 269-2970 FAX (815) 269-2930
**Silent Word Media Resources**
7400 W Augusta Blvd #24-S
River Forest IL 60305
(708) 209-3341
Mr Philip Hyssong
**Wheat Ridge Ministries**
One Pierce Place Suite 250E
Itasca IL 60143-2634
(630) 766-9066
Dr Richard Bimler *Pres*
(1-23)

## INDIANA

**Lutheran Child and Family Services of IN/KY**
1525 N Ritter Ave Indianapolis IN 46219
(317) 359-5467
Sven Schumacher
(1-2-3-4-5-6-8-13-19-20)
*Area Offices:*
Pilgrimage Center (an affiliate of LCFS)
10210 N Meridian St Indianapolis IN 46290
(317) 575-9855
Rev Max C Blankenburg
Lutherwood Residential Treatment Ctr
1525 N Ritter Ave Indianapolis IN 46219
(317) 353-8211
Jim Dalton
Columbus Counseling Center
918 Fifth St Columbus IN 47201
(812) 372-1571
Alan Reeves
LCFS of IN/KY
117 E Michigan St Evansville IN 47711
(812) 424-5620
Joyce Donaldson
LCFS
610 W 2nd St Seymour IN 47274
(812) 522-9549
Rev Edgar Keinath
Lutheran Family Services of Kentucky
Counseling Center
417 E Broadway Louisville KY 40206
(502) 899-5991
Rev Jeffrey Romer
Material Assistance
Sharing Place East
6024 E 21st St Indianapolis IN 46219
(317) 353-6566
Shelly Marqua
Sharing Place West
3976 Georgetown Rd Indianapolis IN 46254
(317) 298-3180
Elaine Adams
**Lutheran Homes Inc**
6701 S Anthony Blvd
Ft Wayne IN 46816-2035
(219) 447-1591
Rev Dwight Anderson
(1-10-13-17-23)
Lutheran Home
6701 S Anthony Blvd
Ft Wayne IN 46816-2035
(219) 447-1591
Kelly Borror
Concord Village
6723 S Anthony Blvd
Ft Wayne IN 46816-2045
(219) 447-1591
Susan Wolpert
Shepherd of the Hill
351 N Allen Chapel Rd PO Box 429
Kendallville IN 46755-0429
(219) 347-2256 or (219) 422-8150
William Langschied
**Lutheran Home of Northwest Indiana**
1200 E Luther Dr Crown Point IN 46307
(219) 663-3860
V Lloyd White
(10)
**Lutheran Social Services of Indiana**
330 Madison St PO Box 11329
Ft Wayne IN 46857-1329
(219) 426-3347
Stan Veit
(1-2-4-6-7-8-10-15-16-21-22)
*Regional Office:*
1400 N Broad St Griffith IN 46319
(219) 838-0996
**Mulberry Lutheran Home Inc**
502 W Jackson St Mulberry IN 46058-9538
(765) 296-2911
Gary E Neeley
(1-10-13)
Mulberry Lutheran Village
502 W Jackson Mulberry IN 46058-9538
(765) 296-2911
David M Hajduch
Lutheran Community Services
112 E Jackson St Mulberry IN 46058-9538
(765) 296-4520
Beverly Brewer

## IOWA

**Bethany Lutheran Home**
7 Elliott St Council Bluffs IA 51503-0297
(712) 328-9500
Sue Mortensen
(2-10-13-23)
*Senior Housing:*
Bethany Heights
11 Elliott St Council Bluffs IA 51503
(712) 328-8228
Laura Barker
**Luther Care Services**
2824 E 16th St Des Moines IA 50316
(515) 262-1153
Denny Garland
(10-13)
*Area Offices:*
Luther Park Health Center
1555 Hull Ave Des Moines IA 50316
Luther Park Apartments
2824 E 16th St Des Moines IA 50316
(515) 262-1153
Sue Garland
Valborg Lutheran Home
1101 Grandview Ave Des Moines IA 50316
(515) 265-1629
Candy Plew
**Lutheran Family Service**
230 Ninth Ave N Fort Dodge IA 50501
Rev Eric L Schillo *Exec Dir*
(515) 573-3138
(2-3-4-6-11-16-17-20-23-24)
*Counseling Offices:*
Executive Plaza Suite 304
4403 First Ave SE Cedar Rapids IA 52403
(319) 393-1000 FAX (319) 393-4969
5400 Morningside Ave Sioux City IA 51106
(712) 276-9000 FAX (712) 276-4917
1600 S Highway 275 Suite 170
Council Bluffs IA 51503
(712) 366-5272 FAX (712) 366-5472
7177 Hickman Road Suite 2 Des Moines, IA 50322
(515) 251-4900
FAX (515) 251-7311
230 9th Ave North Fort Dodge IA 50501
(515) 573-3138
FAX (515) 573-3130
1316 N Erie Storm Lake IA 50588
(712) 732-7955
FAX (712) 732-4479
1515 Rainbow Dr Belle Plaine IA 52208
(319) 444-3211
2307 S Olive Atlantic IA 50022
(712) 243-6440
**The Vinton Lutheran Home**
1301 Second Ave Vinton IA 52349
(319) 472-4751
Kim Emrich
The Perry Lutheran Home
2323 E Willis Ave Perry IA 50220
(515) 465-5342
LoDeen Glawe, Doug Wood
The Davenport Lutheran Home
1130 W 53rd St Davenport IA 52806
(319) 391-5342
Karen Wilson
**Lutheran Home for the Aged**
315 A Ave Vinton IA 52349
(319) 472-4211
Donald Pohlers and Diane Gleode
**St Luke Lutheran Home Inc**
1301 St Luke Dr Spencer IA 51301
(712) 262-5931
Terry Dandy
(1-10-13)

## KANSAS

**Lutheran Social Services of KS/OK**
1833 W 21st St Wichita KS 67203
(316) 838-5252
Bernice Karstensen
(1-2-3-4-6-9-16-17-18-19-20)
*Area Offices:*
2002 Main Hays KS 67601
(913) 625-4673
Rev Richard Kaczor
3000 United Founders Blvd Suite 141
Oklahoma City OK 73112
(405) 848-1733
Ruth Tatyrek
708 Boston Ave
Tulsa OK 74119
(918) 587-9439
Patricia Kopenhagen
2942 B Wanamaker Dr #1C Topeka KS 66614
(913) 272-7883
Peggy Henry
1855 N Hillside Wichita KS 67214-2399
(316) 686-6645
Bernice Karstensen
*Counseling Centers:*
1716 Gage Blvd Topeka KS 66604
(913) 272-0703
1010 Fleming Garden City KS 67846
(316) 276-3110
816 9th Clay Center KS 67432
(913) 632-5301
Country Club & E Fifth Colby KS
(913) 462-3497
24th & Adams Great Bend KS 67530
(316) 793-5734
Rev Richard Kaczor
**Shiloh Manor of Canton Inc**
601 S Kansas Box 67 Canton KS 67428
(316) 628-4403
Kaye Lynn Hoemie
(7-10-13-19)

## KENTUCKY

**Cedar Lake Inc**
7984 New LaGrange Rd Louisville KY 40222
(502) 425-5323
H James Richardson Jr
(1-11-13-23)
Cedar Lake Lodge Inc
3301 Jericho Rd PO Box 289
LaGrange KY 40031
(502) 222-7157
Clyde D Lang
Cedar Lake Residences Inc
4118 Browns Ln Louisville KY 40222
(502) 459-7706
Jennifer Frommeyer
Cedar Lake Foundation Inc
7984 New LaGrange Rd Louisville KY 40222
(502) 222-5013
Mr Tom Livers
Lutheran Children Family Services of Indiana & Kentucky
417 E Broadway Louisville KY 40202
(502) 589-5991
Rev Jeffrey Romer

## LOUISIANA

**See Texas**

## MARYLAND

**Augsburg Lutheran Home of MD Inc**
6811 Campfield Rd Baltimore MD 21207
(410) 486-4573
Glenn Scherer
(7-10)
Augsburg Lutheran Village
6825 Campfield Rd Baltimore MD 21207
(410) 484-3099
St Michael Adult Day Services
9534 Belair Rd Perry Hall MD 21236
(410) 256-2980
Margaret Burke
**Lutheran Mission Society of Maryland**
1201 S Charles St Baltimore MD 21230
(410) 539-7322
Richard L Alms PhD *Exec Dir*
(1-2-5-6-7-8-13-14-15-16-17-18-19-20-22)
*Regional Centers:*
Annapolis
230 West St Annapolis MD 21401
(410) 269-5016
Baltimore
1706 Eastern Ave Baltimore MD 21231
(410) 327-2220
Cambridge
415 Race St Cambridge MD 21613
(410) 228-8437
Essex
438 Eastern Blvd Essex MD 21221
(410) 391-6877
Havre de Grace
531 Legion Drive Havre de Grace MD 21078
(410) 939-0879

## MASSACHUSETTS

**Lutheran Social Services of New England**
One Apple Hill 600 Worchester Rd
Natick MA 01760
(508) 650-4400
Edith M Lohr
(1-4-5-7-9-11-17-20)
*Area Offices in Massachusetts:*
Emmanuel House Residence
Assisted Living and Group Adult Foster Care
25 East Nilsson St Brockton MA 02401
(508) 588-5334
Karen Walsh
Lutheran Home of Worcester and Adult Day Health Center
26 Harvard St Worcester MA 01609
(508) 754-8877
Ann Nadreau
Elderly with Development Disabilities
(508) 752-1090
Emmanuel Village and Group Adult Foster Care
59 Evelyn St Worcester MA 01607
(508) 753-7474
Ann Duncan
*Group Adult Foster Care*
The Ruth House-Teen Living
553 N Main St Brockton MA 02401
(508) 740-5773
Michael Walsh
Therapeutic Foster Care
1156 Main St
Brockton MA 02401
(508) 580-6716
Michael Walsh
Refugee Minor Services
1310 Center St Newton MA 02159
(617) 964-7220
Greentree Girls Program
659 Summer St Brockton MA 02401
(508) 588-2978
Michael Walsh
Greentree Boys Program
494 Copeland St Brockton MA 02401
(508) 584-7991
Michael Walsh
Refugee Services
425 Union St
West Springfield MA 01089
(413) 739-4428
Michael Walsh
Refugee Services
86 Murray Ave
Worcester MA 01610 (508) 754-1121
Transition to Independent Living for Boys
6 Dean St Worcester MA 01609
(508) 756-2511
Michael Walsh
David Forsberg Independent Living
416 Belmont Worcester MA 01609
(508) 849-2152
Michael Walsh
The Florence House
12 George St Worcester MA 01609
(508) 799-2499
Michael Walsh
Teen Living
414 Cambridge St Worcester MA 01609
(508)798-5248
Adoption Services
416 Belmont St Worcester MA 01609
(508) 791-4488
Michael Walsh
*Facilities in Connecticut:*
Luther Manor-Congregate Care
624 Congdon St W Middletown CT 06457
(860) 347-7144
Francis Mozea
Lutheran Home of Middletown
628 Congdon St W Middletown CT 06457
(860) 347-7479
Francis Mozea
Adoption Services
2139 Silas Deane Highway Suite 201
Rocky Hill CT 06067
(860) 257-9899
Vivian Backhaus
Lutheran Home of Southbury
990 Main St N Southbury CT 06488
(860) 264-9135
Linda Garcia
*Facilities in New Hampshire:*
Administration/Adoption/Therapeutic Foster Care/Community Services
85 Manchester St Concord NH 03301
(603) 224-8111
Robert Kay
Girls Shelter
55 Main St Antrim NH 03440
(603) 588-3124
Robert Kay
Day Developmental Services
117 Manchester St Concord NH 03301
(603) 225-2616
Robert Kay
Day Developmental Services
325 Merrill St Manchester NH 03103
(603) 647-5656
Robert Kay
Day Developmental Service
708 Union Ave
Laconia NH 03246
(603) 528-3350
Robert Kay
*Facilities in Maine:*
Developmental Services
495 Park St Lewiston ME 04240
(207) 783-3446
Jim DeCamillis
*Facilities in Rhode Island:*
Adoption Services
116 Rolfe St Cranston RI 02919
(401) 941-1070
Michael Walsh
*Facilities in Vermont:*
Good News Garage
23 King St Burlington VT 05401
(802) 864-3667
Robert Kay

## MICHIGAN

**Lutheran Child and Family Service of MI**
6019 W Side Saginaw Rd
PO Box 48 Bay City MI 48707-0048
(517) 686-7650
Robert G Miles *President/CEO*
(1-2-3-4-5-6-11-16-18-20-22)
*North Area:*
Regional Office
6019 W Side Saginaw Rd PO Box 48
Bay City MI 48707
(517) 686-7650
Robert Miles
860B N Mitchell Suite A Cadillac MI 49601
(231) 779-8607
104 E Seventh St Clare MI 48617
(517) 386-2101
3210A Pacquet Club Dr Traverse City MI 49684
(231) 935-4575
2210 N Franklin Flint MI 48506
(810) 238-5370
123 W Irwin St Bad Axe MI 48413
(517) 269-3841
The Lutheran Home
304 Tuscola Rd Bay City MI 48708
(517) 892-8564
Lutheran Adoption Service
PO Box 48 Bay City MI 48707
(517) 686-7650
*Southeast Area:*
Regional Office
10811 Puritan Ave Detroit MI 48283
(313) 341-1121
New Directions
665 E Grand Blvd Detroit MI 48207
(313) 921-3740
Marlowe House
20830 Rutland Dr Oak Park MI 48075
(248) 552-1050
15160 W Eight Mile Rd Oak Park MI 48327
(248) 968-0100
438 E Lake St Peroskey MI 49970
(231) 439-0821
Lutheran Adoption Service
21700 Northwestern Hwy Suite 1490
Southfield MI 48075
(248) 423-2770
James Lewis
*West Area:*
Regional Office
2130 Enterprise St Grand Rapids MI 49508
(616) 281-4601
Allegan Office
2041 30th St Allegan MI 49010
(616) 673-3869
Lutheran Adoption Service
801 S Waverly Suite 103 Lansing MI 48917
(517) 886-1380
Lutheran Adoption Service
2976 Ivanrest SW Suite 140
Grandville MI 49418-1140
(616) 532-8286
**The Lutheran Homes of Michigan Inc**
PO Box 329 Frankenmuth MI 48734
(517) 652-3470
David M Gehm
(10)
*Area Homes:*
The Lutheran Home—Monroe
1236 S Monroe St Monroe MI 48161
(734) 241-9533
Brenda Lawrence
The Lutheran Home—Frankenmuth
PO Box 268 Frankenmuth MI 48734
(517) 652-9951
Mark A Eubank
Lutheran Home Care Agency
9710 Junction Rd Frankenmuth MI 48734
(517) 652-4663
Marcia Stoddard
Lutheran Home—Livonia
28910 Plymouth Rd Livonia MI 48150
(734) 425-4814
Michael Bell

## MINNESOTA

**Crest View Corporation**
4444 Reservoir Blvd NE
Columbia Heights MN 55421
(763) 782-1615
Shirley E H Barnes
(7-10)
*Area Offices:*
Crest View Lutheran Home
4444 Reservoir Blvd NE
Columbia Hts MN 55421 (763) 788-2020
The Boulevard Apts
4458 Reservoir Blvd NE
Columbia Hts MN 55421 (763) 788-7105
Royce Place
1515 44th Ave NE Columbia Hts MN 55421
(763) 788-2020
Crest View Home Care
4444 Reservoir Blvd NE
Columbia Hts MN 55421 (763) 788-2020

**Good Shepherd Lutheran Home**
1115 4th Ave North Sauk Rapids MN 56379
Bruce Glanzer *CEO/Admin*
(320) 252-6525 FAX (320) 259-3463
(10-13-23)
Good Shepherd Lutheran Home
1115 4th Avenue N Sauk Rapids MN 56379
(320) 259-3470
Jane Bagley
Good Shepherd Lutheran Foundation
1115 4th Ave N Sauk Rapids MN 56379
(320) 252-6525
**Lutheran Counseling and Family Services**
1505 E Hwy 13 Burnsville MN 55337
(612) 894-4828
Dr Gene Betterman
(1-2)

## MISSISSIPPI

**Lutheran Social Ministries of MS**
PO Box 12246 Jackson MS 32936
(601) 977-9948
(1-4-14)

## MISSOURI

**Council of Lutheran Churches of Greater St Louis**
3558 S Jefferson Ave St Louis MO 63118
(314) 268-1200
Stephen Phelps
(1-19-20)
**Heisenger Lutheran Home**
1002 W Main St Jefferson City MO 65109
(573) 636-6288
Janice Sonnenberg
(1-7-10-12-21-23)
**Lutherans in Medical Missions**
812 Soulard St St. Louis MO 63104-4036
(314) 241-1138
John Speckhard
**Lutheran Senior Services**
709 S Laclede Station Rd St Louis MO 63119-4911
(314) 968-9313
Carl A Rausch
(1-2-10-13-17-19-20)
Laclede Groves Retirement Community (CCRC)
723 S Laclede Station Rd
Webster Groves MO 63119-4911
(314) 968-5570
Patricia Woodward
Laclede Commons
727 S Laclede Station Rd
Webster Groves MO 63119
(314) 968-5570
Sharon Rullkoetter
Laclede Oaks Manor
703 S Laclede Station Rd
Webster Groves MO 63119
(314) 968-5570
Dave Piehl
The Gables at Hidden Lake Retirement Community
11728 Hidden Lake Dr St Louis MO 63138
(314) 355-8833
Christy Adams
The Gables at Breeze Park Retirement Community
600 Breeze Park Dr St Charles MO 63304
(314) 939-5223
Terry Etling
*Affordable Housing*
Halls Ferry Manor
8725 Halls Ferry Road St Louis MO 63147
(314) 388-1944
Stevie Salas
Rose Hill House
255 W Rosehill
St Louis MO 63122
(314) 966-0747
Irma Reid
*In-Home Services*
Senior Support Services
723 S Laclede Station Rd
St Louis MO 63119
(314) 963-3430
Marcia Eckrich
Private Duty/Medicare Home Health
723 S Laclede Station Rd
St Louis MO 63119-4911
(314) 963-3430
Lutheran Good Neighbor Program
723 S Laclede Station Rd St Louis MO 63119
(314) 961-3468
Marge Warmann
Outreach Social Service Program
723 S Laclede Station Rd
St Louis MO 63119
(314) 961-3468
Cindy Sevin BSW
Volunteer Money Management Program
723 S Laclede Station Rd
St Louis MO 63119-4911
(314) 961-3468
Denise Hellwege
**Lutheran Charities Foundation St Louis**
211 N Broadway #1290
St Louis MO 63102-2733
(314) 231-2244
Fred Bleeke
**Family Connection**
3558 S Jefferson Ave PO Box 19214 St Louis MO 63118
(314) 268-1180 or (800) 351-1001
Spanish (800) 351-9903
(1-16-20)
Association of Family Life Professionals
3724 Executive Center Dr Suite #155
Austin TX 78731
(512) 343-8604 or (800) 393-8915
**Lutheran Family and Children's Services of MO**
4201 Lindell Blvd Suite 400
St Louis MO 63108
(314) 534-1515
Rev Alan M Erdman
(1-2-3-4-6-7-8-16-18-19-20)
*Area Offices:*
Mid-Missouri Office
3201 S Providence Road Suite 101
Columbia MO 65203
Southwest Office
PO Box 50544 Springfield MO 65805-0554
Southeast Missouri Area Office
2911 Breckenridge Dr
Cape Girardeau MO 63701 (636) 334-5866
Clarkson Executive Park
#116 Clarkson Rd Ballwin MO 63011
(636) 391-8778
Southeast County
4355 Butler Hill Rd
Mehlville, MO 63218
St. Charles
2800 W Elm St
St. Charles MO 63301
Chesterfield MO 63017 (314) 878-0160
South St Louis City
5218 Neosho
St Louis MO 63109
South County
2030 Union Road
St Louis MO 63125
North County Office
Hwy 367 at Hwy 70
St Louis MO 60136
Kirkwood Office
505 S Kirkwood St Louis MO 63122
Eureka Office
500 Meramec Blvd Eureka MO 63025
(636) 361-2121
**Lutheran Ministries Association**
3558 S Jefferson Ave St Louis MO 63118-3968
(314) 268-1166
Rev Richard D Tetzloff
(1-13-19-21)
Long Term Care Ombudsman Program
3028 N Lindbergh #A
St Ann MO 63074
(314) 918-8222
Dorothy Erickson

## MONTANA

**Lutheran Social Services of Montana**
725 W Alder #2
Missoula MT 59802
(406) 549-0147
Sharon Erickson
(2-3-4-6-16-20)
**Sapphire Lutheran Homes Inc**
501 North 10th St Hamilton MT 59840
(406) 363-2800
Lyn McKee
(1-2-10-16)

## NEBRASKA

**Lutheran Family Services of Nebraska Inc**
Central Adminstration
124 S 24th St Suite 230
Omaha NE 68102-1246
(402) 342-7038
Ruth A Henrichs
(1-2-3-4-6-17-19-20-22-23-24)
120 S 24th St Suite 100
Omaha NE 68102
(402) 342-7007
116 E Mission Ave
Bellevue NE 68005
(402) 291-6065
Robert Campbell
1318 Federal Square Dr
Bellevue NE 68005 (402) 292-9105
Dennis Crain
403 S 16th St Suite C Blair NE 68008
(402) 426-5454
Marti Wilson
1420 E Military Ave
Fremont NE 68025
(402) 721-1774
Robert Campbell
Nebraska AIDS Projects
139 South 40th St
Omaha NE 68131 (402) 342-4233
2612 S 158th Plz
Omaha NE 68130 (402) 333-5430
Robert Campbell
120 W Second St
Papillion NE 68048 (402) 592-0639
Marti Wilson
542 Main Street
Plattsmouth NE 68048 (402) 296-3315
Marti Wilson
North Central Regional Office
1109 S 13th St Suite 302
Norfolk NE 68701 (402) 371-7535
Betty King
1761 26th Ave PO Box 573
Columbus NE 68602 (402) 564-1616
Betty King
Panhandle Regional Office
1414 E 20th St #8
Scottsbluff NE 69361 (308) 635-2535
Karen Weston
PO Box 538
Alliance NE 69301 (308) 762-5435
Karen Weston
502 S Webster
Kimball NE 69145 (308) 235-4097
Karen Weston
PO Box 252
Sidney NE 69162 (308) 254-6283
Karen Weston
South Central Regional Office
2121 N Webb Road Suite 206
Grand Island NE 68801
(308) 382-0476
Wayne Littrell
Satellite Office
PO Box 282
Broken Bow NE 68822 (308) 872-6373
David Lund
422 N Hastings Ave Suite 106 Hastings NE 68901
(402) 461-3047
Wayne Littrell
4009 South 6th Avenue
Kearney NE 68845 (308) 236-8226
Wayne Littrell
118 North 19th
Ord NE 68862 (308) 532-0487
Wayne Kittrell
Southeast Regional Office
4620 Randolph
Lincoln NE 68510 (402) 489-7744
David Muench
Satellite Office
Trinity Lutheran Church
634 Alden Drive
Auburn NE 68305 (402) 274-4122
110 S 6th St Suite 221
Beatrice NE 68310 (402) 223-6039
David Muench
Southwest Regional Office
1300 E 4th St
North Platte NE 69101
(308) 532-0587

Dave Lund
Satellite Office
207 E 6th St
Lexington NE 68850 (308) 324-6223
Dave Lund
322 1/2 Norris Ave PO Box 443
McCook NE 69001 (308) 345-7914
Dave Lund
112 W 1st St #1
Ogallala NE 69153 (308) 284-6517
Dave Lund

**The Lutheran Home**
530 S 26th St Omaha NE 68124
(402) 346-3344
Cindy Soilien
(10-13)

**Martin Luther Home Society Inc**
Mill Towne Bldg Suite 305
650 J Street Lincoln NE 68508
(402) 434-3250
The Rev George M Meslow
(1-5-7-10-11-12-13-15-17-19-20-23-24)
Martin Luther Home Resource Center
(800) 443-4899
Martin Luther Home of Beatrice Inc
722 South 12th St
Beatrice NE 68310 (402) 223-4066
Ken Wellensiek
Martin Luther Homes of Nebraska Inc
220 W South 21st St York NE 68467
(402) 362-2180
Gerald Rus
Martin Luther Homes of Nebraska Inc
4437 S 102nd St Omaha NE 68127
(402) 592-2325
Dorothy Greene
Martin Luther Homes of Nebraska Inc
9989 J Street Omaha NE 68127
(402) 537-1040
Dorothy Greene
Martin Luther Homes of Nebraska Inc
235 N St Joseph Ave Hastings NE 68901
(402) 463-0518
Ben Robinson
Martin Luther Homes of Nebraska Inc
5050 Old Cheney Road
Lincoln NE 68516 (402) 420-5266
Rachel Mulcahy
Martin Luther Homes of Nebraska Inc
623 Grant St Beatrice NE 68310
(402) 228-4446
Tim Summers
Martin Luther Homes of Nebraska Inc
1645 N Cotner Lincoln NE 68505
(402) 464-2067
Deb Witfoth
Martin Luther Homes of Colorado Inc
3707 Parkmoor Village Drive Suite 101
Colorado Springs CO 80917
(719) 380-0451
Michael Paoli
Martin Luther Homes of Colorado Inc
109 Cameron Way Unit A
Fort Collins CO 80525 (970) 223-1751
Sally Montgomery
Martin Luther Homes of Colorado Inc
2480 W 26th Ave B-140 Denver CO 80211
(303) 455-8006
Dennis Busse
Martin Luther Homes of Illinois Inc
314 North Mill St Pontiac IL 61764
(815) 842-4166
Lori Frantz
Martin Luther Homes of Illinois Inc
5620 W Plank Road
Peoria IL 61604 (309) 697-3724
Lori Frantz
Martin Luther Homes of Iowa Inc
22 Second St NW PO Box 15
Waukon IA 52172 (319) 568-3992
Mary Lynn Revoir
Martin Luther Homes of Iowa Inc
217 E 7th St Box 153 Logan IA 51546
(712) 644-2378
Jim Poehlman
Martin Luther Homes of Iowa Inc
1904 NW 92nd Ct Clive IA 50325
(515) 222-1402
Tom Hoff
Evergreen
925 Heritage Dr Osage IA 50461
(515) 732-3284
Kathy Shaw
MLH, Inc
Martin Luther Homes of Texas Inc
302 Post Office St Bryan TX 77801
(409) 823-7622
Philip Haas
Martin Luther Homes of Texas Inc
324 S Loop 123 B Seguin TX 78155
(830) 372-3075
Barbara Hokom
Martin Luther Homes of Texas Inc
242 S Gordon St Suite 201 Alvin TX 77511
(281) 388-2292
Barbara Munyak
Martin Luther Homes of Texas Inc
1441 Oaklawn Corsicana TX 75110
(903) 874-3364
Debbie Fraysier
Martin Luther Homes of Texas Inc
16302 Puma Pass San Antonio TX 78247
(210) 967-0566
Cynthia Flores
Martin Luther Homes of Delaware Inc
260 Chapman Road Suite 104 A
Newark DE 19702 (302) 456-5995
Terry Olson
Martin Luther Homes of Kansas Inc
2120 E 9th Ave Winfield KS 67156
(316) 229-8702
Kelly Snyder

## NEW HAMPSHIRE

**See Massachusetts**

## NEW JERSEY

**Lutheran Social Ministries of NJ**
120 Route 156 Yardville NJ 08620-2202
(609) 585-0400
Roger Arnholt
(1-3-4-5-6-8-9-10-11-13-20-23)
Adoption Services
120 Rt 156 Yardville NJ 08620-2202
(609) 583-0303
Andrea Handel
Crane's Mill Lifecare
459 Passail Ave West Caldwell NJ 07006
(973) 575-0038 or (800) 500-5433
The Lutheran Home
255 E Main St Moorestown NJ 08057
(609) 235-1214
Tamara Moreland
The Lutheran Home
2721 Rt 9 Ocean View NJ 08230
(609) 624-3881
Susan Handron
Luther Towers
489 W State St Trenton NJ 08618
(609) 695-7755
John Newell
Luther Arms
323 S Broad St Trenton NJ 08618
(609) 392-5628
John Newell
Luther Acres
560 Sarah Pl Vineland NJ 08360
(609) 696-0896
Jeanne C Barber
Mt Olive Manor
49 Bartley-Flanders Rd Flanders NJ 07836
(201) 252-1403
Muhlenberg Gardens
1065 Summit Ave Jersey City NJ 07307
(201) 792-4475
Chris Wahl
Wittenburg Manor
66 Bleecker St Jersey City NJ 07307
(201) 792-4475
Chris Wahl
Runsen House
825 E Clements Bridge Rd
Runnemede NJ 08078
(609) 939-6564
Mott Center Street Apts
660 Centre St Trenton NJ 08611
(609) 585-5357
Elwood Driver Town Homes
Fountain & Sweets Ave
Trenton NJ 08618
(609) 585-5357
Irving St Apts
Irving & Summit Ave Jersey City NJ 07307
(609) 585-0400
Pleasant Grove Community Residence
229 Pleasant Grove Rd Long Valley NJ 07853
(908) 852-6062
Sayreville Community Residence
1079 Bordentown Ave Parlin NJ 08859
Deena Nagy *Mgr*
(732) 525-1800
Golden Nugget Thrift Shop
1142 Summit Ave Jersey City NJ 07307
(201) 656-2425 or (609) 585-0400
Lutheran Home for Children
440 Hoboken Ave Jersey City NJ 07307
(201) 420-6106
Michelle Peavy
Project Home
657 Bergen Ave Jersey City NJ 07304
Brauninger Community Service Center
PO Box 30 Trenton NJ 08601
(609) 393-4900
Dennis Mulligan

## NEW YORK

**Good Samaritan Group**
125 Rockefeller Rd Delmar NY 12054
(518) 439-8116
Leon Borman
(10)
Good Samaritan Lutheran Home
141 Rockefeller Road
Delmar NY 12054
(518) 439-8899
Kirsten Andersen

**Lutheran Association for Developmentally Disabled Inc (LADD)**
62 St Mary's Place Hamburg NY 14075
(716) 649-2662
Robert C Meissner Jr
(1-11)

**Lutheran Service Society of NY**
PO Box 1963
Williamsville NY 14231-1963
(716) 631-9212
Rev Hans Irmer
(1-2-3-4-6-11-13-17-20-23)

**Lutheran Social Services of Metropolitan NY**
27 Park Place New York NY 10007-2502
Rev Dr Russell Norris Jr
(212) 406-9110 FAX (212) 406-9130
(1-2-3-4-6-11-13-19-20-23)
Lutheran Family & Community Center
35 Fulton Ave Hempstead NY 11550
(516) 483-3240
Rev Theodore Grant
Lutheran Family & Community Services
523 Clinton Ave Brooklyn NY 11238
(718) 783-0232
Sr Cecelia Wilson
Lutheran Family & Community Services
430 North St White Plains NY 10605
(914) 761-8233
Janet Bouman

**Niagara Lutheran Heath Systems**
64 Hager St Buffalo NY 14208
(716) 886-4377
Jurgen Arndt
(1-10-21-23)
Niagara Lutheran Home and Rehabilitation Center Inc
64 Hager St Buffalo NY 14208-1298
(716) 886-4377
Maureen Caruana
Niagara Lutheran Health Foundation
64 Hager St Buffalo NY 14208-1298
(716) 886-4377
Jeffrey L Yates
Greenfield Health & Rehabilitation Center
5949 Boardway Lancaster NY 14086
(716) 684-3000
David Eaton

**Wartburg Adult Care Community**
Wartburg Place Mt Vernon NY 10552-3840
(914) 699-0800
Rev Dale G Gatz
(1-7-10-13-14-20-21-23)

**Wartburg Lutheran Services Inc**
50 Sheffield Ave Brooklyn NY 11207-9997
(718) 345-2273
Ronald J Rademacher

(7-10-13)
*Area Offices:*
Wartburg Lutheran Home for the Aging
50 Sheffield Ave Brooklyn NY 11207-9997
(718) 345-2273
Debora Lipsen
Wartburg Nursing Home Inc
50 Sheffield Ave Brooklyn NY 11207-9997
(718) 345-2273
Debora Lipsen
Lutheran Center for the Aging
7 Route 25A Smithtown NY 11787
(516) 724-2200
Gary Kleinberg
North Brooklyn Mobile Meals
50 Sheffield Ave Brooklyn NY 11207-9997
(718) 345-2002
Lisette Sosa
Lutheran Housing Development Fund Corp of LI
Martin Luther Terrace Apts
Wartburg Ct Kings Park NY 11754
(516) 544-0869
Sharon Mason
Martin Luther Court
380 Belmont Ave Brooklyn NY 11207-9997
(718) 345-3140
Sharon Mason
The King's Apartments
20 Pine Drive Pawling NY 12564
(914) 855-7230
Sharon Mason
Lutheran Care Center at Concord Village
411 Dutchess Turnpike
Poughkeepsie NY 12603
(914) 486-9494
Lynn Montanaro

## NORTH DAKOTA

**Dakota Boys Ranch Assn**
**Dakota Boys Ranch**
PO Box 5007 Minot ND 58702-5007
(701) 852-3628
Gene D Kaseman
(2-5-15)
Dakota Boys Ranch-Voelkerding Village
PO Box 90 Dutzow MO 63342
(636) 433-5677
John McCastle
Dakota Boys Ranch-Fargo Youth Home
1641 31st Ave S Fargo ND 58103
(701) 237-3123
Ronald Heit
**Lutheran Social Services of North Dakota**
Administrative Office
1325 11th St PO Box 389 Fargo ND 58107
(701) 235-7341
Keith Ingle
(1-2-3-4-5-6-9-11-22-23-24)
*Regional Offices:*
1616 Capital Way Bismarck ND 58504
(701) 223-1510
Lorelie Rinas-Britain
1325 S 11th St Fargo ND 58107
(701) 233-8905
412 Demers Ave Grand Forks ND 58201
(701) 772-7577
Jodi Dietz
615 S Broadway Minot ND 58701
(701) 838-7800
Judy Slorby
511½ W 2nd St Williston ND 58801
(701) 774-0749
Peggy Bearce
*Facilities:*
Luther Hall 1505 Fifth Ave S Fargo ND 58103
(701) 233-8905
Mary Weiler
Svee Rehabilitation Home
1101 13th Ave S Fargo ND 58103
(701) 232-6234
Kermit Bratholt
Great Plains Food Bank
1104 N P Ave Fargo ND 58102
(701) 232-6219
Steven Sellent
Native American Outreach
324 7th St N Fargo ND 58102
(701) 235-3124
Beverly Olson

## OHIO

**The Filling Memorial Home of Mercy**
N 160 S R 108 Napoleon OH 43545-9363
(419) 592-6451
Paul E Oehrtman
(1-3-4)
**Lutheran Chaplaincy Service**
4100 Franklin Blvd Cleveland OH 44113-4009
(216) 631-4444
Rev Richard D Warger
(1-13)
Alliance Community Hospital
Alliance OH 44601
(330) 829-4228
Chaplain Xiaoling Zhu
Children's Hospital Medical Center of Akron
Akron OH 44308-1062
(220) 279-8457
Rev Daniel Grossoehme
Community Hospice Fairview &
Lutheran Hospitals
Cleveland OH 44113
(216) 363-2397
Chaplain Kendall Lancaster
Cuyahoga County Juvenile Detention Center
Cleveland OH 44115
(216) 443-3333
Health Hill Hospital
Cleveland OH 44104
(216) 721-5400
Chaplain Diane Walker
Hospice of the Valley, Youngstown
Youngstown OH 44512
(330) 788-1992
Chaplain James Melick
Lutheran Hospital
(216) 368-2158
Chaplain James Kulma
Chaplain Ion Gherman
Lutheran Village at Wolf Creek
Holland OH 43528
(419) 861-2233
Median General Hospital
Medina OH 44258-0427
(330) 725-1000
MetroHealth Medical Center
Cleveland OH 44109-1998
(216) 778-4663
Rev Daniel Rossbach
Rev Raymond Holland
Diane Walker
Chaplain Bobbie Davis-Newhouse
Rev Luis A Torres
St Luke Lutheran Home
220 Applegrove St NE
North Canton OH 44720
(330) 499-8341
Shepherd of the Valley Lutheran Home
OH 44446
(330) 544-0771
Chaplain Donald Wilke
Stow-Glen Retirement Community
Stow OH 44224
(330) 686-4321
Chaplain Alvin Boehlke
UHHS Geauga Regional Hospital
Chardon OH 44024-0249
(216) 269-6270
Chaplain James Brandis
**Lutheran Children's Aid & Family Services**
4100 Franklin Blvd Cleveland OH 44113
(216) 281-2500
Rev Robert L Claine
(1-2-3-4-6-16-20)
**Luther Home of Mercy**
5810 N Main St Williston OH 43468-0187
(419) 836-7741
Rev Donald L Wukotich
(1-7-11-13-14-23)
**Lutheran Home**
2116 Dover Center Rd
Westlake OH 44145-3194
(440) 871-0090
Richard E Stilgenbauer
Mary J Zukie
(10)
Luther House
1221 Drury Ct Mayfield Heights OH 44124
(216) 461-3154
Robert Buettner

**Lutheran Metropolitan Ministry**
1468 W 25th St Cleveland OH 44113
(216) 696-2715
Rev Richard E Sering
(1-2-8-11-17-19-20-21-22-23)
**Lutheran Homes Society NW Ohio & SE Michigan**
1905 Perrysburg-Holland Holland, OH 43528
(419) 861-5500
David I Roberts
(1-2-3-4-6-10-16-17-20-23)
Lutheran Home at Toledo
131 Wheeling St Toledo OH 43605-1599
(419) 693-0751
Chris Cremean
Lutheran Home at Napoleon
1036 S Perry St Napoleon OH 43545
(419) 592-1688
Linda Dyer
Lutheran Village at Wolf Creek
2001 Perryburg-Holland
Holland OH 43528
(419) 861-2233
Mel Zehnder
Family & Youth Services
2411 Seaman St Toledo OH 43605-1599
(419) 693-1520
Harry Blackmon
*Elderly Independent Living Facilities:*
LHS Housing Services
2411 Seaman St Toledo OH 43605-1599
(419) 693-0751 x288
David Schellhase
Luther Crest
2519-21 N Holland Sylvania Rd
Toledo OH 43615
(419) 841-5689
Linda Jackson
Luther Pines
805 Mumaugh Rd Lima OH 45804
(419) 225-9045
Kay Morrissey
Luther Grove
2502-10 Seaman St Toledo OH 43605
(419) 698-1919
Lorraine Vas
Luther Oaks
36 Executive Dr Norwalk OH 44857
(419) 663-3529
Margaret Heckelman
Luther Meadows Apartments
100 Meadow Lane Gibsonburg OH 43431
(419) 637-2811
Sue Smith
Luther Hills
2472 Luther Hills Cir Oregon OH 43616
(419) 697-9397
Jill Schumacher
Luther Haus
800 Smith Rd Temperance MI 48182
Ruth Nagle
Luther Woods
2500 Royce Rd Toledo OH 43615
(419) 841-5689
Linda Jackson
Bavarian Village
1040 S Perry St Napoleon OH 43545
(419) 592-1688
Peggy Snyder
**Lutheran Social Services of Central Ohio**
750 E Broad St Columbus OH 43205-1000
(614) 228-5209
Rev Nelson C Meyer
(2-3-4-6-8-10-12-13-16-19-20-24)
*Individual and Family Services*
Supportive Housing Services & Homeless Prevention
(Individual/Families)
989 N High Columbus OH 43201
(614) 421-5860
Louise Alluis
*Community Service Centers:*
Fairfield County Homeless Services
PO Box 2266
Lancaster OH 43130
(740) 653-2012
Becky Edwards
Thrift Store/Food Pantry
2288 Sullivant Ave Columbus OH 43223
(614) 274-4000
Mitch Henderson

Food Pantry & Thrift Store
1460 S Champion Ave Columbus OH 43206
(614) 443-5130
Barbara Peters
Greenbriar Food Pantry
335 Virginia Lee Ct Columbus OH 43209
(614) 239-1030
Beth Rice
Food Pantry
704 E Main St Lancaster OH 43130
(740) 687-3510
Barbara Peters
*Facilities:*
Lutheran Village of Columbus
935 N Cassady Ave Columbus OH 43219
(614) 252-4987
Alex Bettinger
*Federal Subsidized Housing for Low-Income Elderly & Handicapped*
Greenfield Place
283 Green Ave Groveport OH 43125
(614) 836-5867
Shirley Baker
Grovewood Place
4301 Stoner Dr Grove City OH 43123
(614) 539-1022
Sara Monroe
Mount Pleasant Place
963 Prestige Blvd Lancaster OH 43130
(740) 681-9659
Janis Crist
Oakhurst Place
2178 Bruce Rd Delaware OH 43015
(740) 369-5267
Sister Gloria
Stone House Place
54385 National Rd Lansing OH 43934
(740) 633-9929
Sherry Renshaw
Woodridge Place
3565 Clime Road Columbia OH 43228
(614) 272-8960
Chris Karr

**Lutheran Social Services of the Miami Valley**
Executive Office
6430 Inner Mission Way
(937) 433-2140
Dayton OH 45459-7400
Willis O Serr II
(1-2-3-4-6-8-10-11-12-13-16-17-20)
*Area Offices:*
*Consumer Credit Counseling Service*
*Financial Advice Debt Management:*
3131 S Dixie Drive Suite 300 PO Box 292680
Dayton OH 45439 (937) 543-7906
Robert Frazer
121E North St Sidney OH 45365
(937) 492-1953
PO Box 1084 Springfield OH 45502
(937) 325-2898
*Family Services*
*LSS Adoptions Services*
3131 S Dixie Drive Suite 300
Dayton OH 45429
(937) 534-7903
Cynthia Bremer
Adoptions & Pregancy Counseling
11370 Springfield Pike Cincinnati OH 45242
(513) 612-6500
Cynthia Bremer
*Thrift Shops:*
Once Around Thrift Shops
142 Salem Ave Dayton OH 45406-5803
(937) 222-5231
113 S Cherry St Eaton OH 45320-2313
(937) 456-6560
1141 W Ohio Pike Amelia OH 45103
(937) 752-2221
*Services to the Aging:*
*Skilled Nursing Care Residential and Independent Living for the Aged:*
Bethany Lutheran Village
6451 Far Hills Ave Dayton OH 45459-2792
(937) 433-2110
Joseph Belanich
*Federal Subsidized Housing for Low-Income Elderly and Handicapped:*
Manors of the Valley
6430 Inner Mission Way Dayton OH 45459
(937) 436-6890
Charles Rush
*Group Homes and Supported Living Services for Adult Mentally Retarded & Developmentally Disabled:*
We Care Homes
11370 Springfield Pike Cincinnati OH 45242
(513) 612-6500
Michael Rench
*Transportation Services for Handicapped and Elderly:*
Handi Van/Tipp City
PO Box 97
Tipp City OH 45371-0097 (937) 667-3500
*Volunteer Service Programs*
Care Team Ministry
6430 Inner Mission Way
Dayton OH 45459 (937) 436-6894

**Lutheran Social Services of Northwestern OH**
2149 Collingwood Blvd Toledo OH 43620
(419) 243-9178
Norman J Merkel
(1-2-3-4-6-10-16-17-19-20-23)
*Regional Offices:*
Fremont Office
512 E State St Fremont OH 43420
(419) 334-3431
Nancy A Phillips
Lima Southside Center
1801 S Central Lima OH 45804
(419) 222-5011
Brenda Johnson
Bucyrus Office
PO Box 868 Bucyrus OH 44820
(419) 562-6070
Judith Streng
Findlay Office
115 E Lima St Findlay OH 45840
(419) 422-7917
Robert Thacker
Kenton Office
725 E Eliza St Kenton OH 43326
(419) 673-9264
Western Region Office
T-793 St Rt 66 Archbold OH 43502
(419) 267-5528 or (800) 577-8629
Paul R ZumFelde
Wood County Office
1011 Sandusky St Suite #1
Perrysburg OH 43551
(419) 872-9111
Nancy Yunker
Open Door Family Resource Center
1205 King Rd Toledo OH 43617
(419) 867-5733

**St Luke Lutheran Community**
220 Applegrove St NE
North Canton OH 44720
(330) 499-8341
Rev Luther Lautenschlager
(10)
The Waterford at St. Luke
201 Holl Rd NE North Canton OH 44720
(330) 490-2300
Joan Shaff

**Shepherd of the Valley Lutheran Home and Retirement Center–Niles**
1500 McKinley Ave Niles OH 44446
(330) 554-0771
Donald Kacmar
(1-7-10-13-17-23)
Shepherd of the Valley; Lutheran Retirement Services–Boardman
7148 West Blvd Boardman OH 44512
(330) 726-8061
Richard Limongi
Shepherd of the Valley Retirement Service Inc–Poland
301 W Western Reserve Rd
Poland OH 44514
(330) 726-7110
Richard Lomongi
Manor Home Care
301 W Western Reserve Rd Poland OH 44514
(330) 726-7110
Richard Limongi

## OKLAHOMA

**See Kansas**

## OREGON

**Fairlawn Good Samaritan Health Ctr**
3457 NE Division Gresham OR 97030
(503) 667-1965
Jacci Nickell
(1-10-13)

**Lutheran Family Service of Oregon and SW Washington**
605 SE 39th Ave Portland OR 97214
(503) 231-7480
Bruce Strade
(1-2-3-4-9-11-12-15-16-17-19-20-22-23-24)
*Metro Region:*
Community Services
605 SE 39th Ave Portland OR 97214-3298
(503) 233-0042
Salah Ansary
Family Works
4110 NE 122nd Suite 130 Portland OR 97230
(514) 256-2330
Khadim Chishti
Healthy Communities
605 SE 39th Ave Portland OR 97214
(503) 231-7480
Chris Bekomeier
*Central Oregon:*
Crook County Office
203 N Court Prineville OR 97754
(541) 447-7441
Klamath Falls Office
2545 N Eldorado Klamath Falls OR 97601
(541) 883-3471
Bob Pickel
Lake County Office
100 N D St Suite 123 Lakeview OR 97630
(541) 947-6021
Bob Pickel
*Oregon & Southwest Washington:*
819 N Hwy 99W Suite B
McMinnville OR 97128
(503) 472-4020
Kathleen Horgan
(503) 472-4020 FAX (503) 472-8630
Clatsop County Office
3749 Leif Erickson Dr Astoria OR 97103
(503) 325-6754
Angeln Ray
Forest Grove Office
2004 Main Suite 316 Forest Grove OR 97116
(503) 357-8423
Nedra Hathaway
Beaverton Office
8925 SW Beaverton-Hillsdale Hwy Suite B
Portland OR 97225
(503) 297-6263
Nedra Hathaway

## PENNSYLVANIA

**Concordia Lutheran Ministries**
615 N Pike Rd
Cabot PA 16023
(724) 352-1571
Keith Frndak

**Lutheran Services Northeast**
901 Stacie Dr Topton PA 19562
(717) 454-5300
Dr Daun McKee
(1-2-10-16)
Amity Village
901 Stacie Dr Hazleton PA 18201-0310
(717) 454-5300
Lutherwood
1 Lake Scranton Rd Scranton PA 18505
(717) 346-3009
Richard MacGregor
St Luke Manor
1711 E Broad St Hazleton PA 18291
(717) 455-8571
Cheryl Lehman
St Luke Pavilion
1000 Stacie Dr Hazleton PA 18201
(717) 455-7578
Ann Quinnan
Life Enrichment Counseling Centers
Fountain Court Hwy 611 Bartonsville PA 18321
(800) 468-9136
Douglas Trook
908 Main St Towanda PA 18848
3rd and Iron Sts Lehighton PA 18235

Volunteer Home Card
PO Box 466 Lehighton PA 18235
(717) 645-4262
Edith Thrash

## SOUTH DAKOTA

**The Evangelical Lutheran Good Samaritan Society**
PO Box 5038 Sioux Falls SD 57117-5038
(605) 362-3100
Judith A Ryan
(10)

## TENNESSEE

**Lutheran Services in Tennessee, Inc**
3508 Maryville Pike Knoxville TN 37920
(423) 577-8925
Herman A Fischer III
(3-4)
LFS-Williams-Henson Lutheran Home for Children
3508 Maryville Pike Knoxville TN 37920
(423) 577-8925
Lynne Marshall
LFS-Wilson County Youth Ranch
PO Box 551 Lebanon TN 37087
(615) 758-7390
W Mark Akers
LFS-William-Henson Lutheran Home for Children
PO Box 15864 Chattanooga TX 37415
(423) 870-4764
John Sims and Shula Yelliott

## TEXAS

**Lutheran Social Services of the South Inc**
PO Box 49589
Austin TX 78765-9589
(512) 459-1000
Dr Kurt Senske
(2-3-4-5-6-7-9-10-11-13-18-20-24)
314 Highland Mall Blvd Suite 200
Austin TX 78752
(512) 454-4611
5866 S Staples Corpus Christi TX 78413
3001 LBJ Freeway Suite 107 Dallas TX 75234
(972) 620-0581
3101 Richmond Suite 150 Houston TX 77098
(713) 521-0110
1931 Pecan McAllen TX 78501
(956) 687-8333
1201 SE 25th St Mineral Wells TX 76067
110 McCullough San Antonio TX 78215
(210) 223-4099
(817) 325-3275
*Services to the Poor:*
Ruth's House
10260 North Freeway Houston TX 77469
(281) 999-1122
Neighborhood House
1318 Broadway Lubbock TX 79401
(806) 741-0459
*Residential Treatment Center:*
New Life Children's Treatment Ctr
HC4 Box 406 Canyon Lake TX 78130
(830) 964-4390
Bokenkamp Children's Treatment Center
5517 S Alameda Corpus Christi TX 78412
(361) 994-1214
Nelson Children's Treatment Center
4601 I35 North Denton TX 76207
(940) 484-8232
Krause Children's Treatment Center
5638 Medical Center Dr Katy TX 77494
(281) 392-7505
*Services for the Elderly:*
Kruse Memorial Lutheran Village
1700 E Stone St Brenham TX 77833
(409) 830-1996
Lutheran Home of West Texas
5502 Fourth St Lubbock TX 79416
(806) 793-1111
Lutheran Home
6400 Hayne Blvd New Orleans LA 70126
(504) 246-7900
The Altenheim
100 North College Round Rock TX 78664
(512) 244-1967
Trinity Lutheran Home
1000 E Main St Round Rock TX 78664
(512) 255-2421
Giraud Lutheran Towers
10100 110 Service Road
New Orleans LA 70127
(514) 243-0900
Trinity Lutheran Home
Rt 3 Box 19 Shiner TX 77984
(512) 594-3353
Trinity Village
Rt 3 Box 19 Shiner TX 77984
(512) 594-3353
Copperfield Village
501 E Larkspur Victoria TX 77094
(361) 575-3978

## VIRGINIA

**Fellowship Square Foundation Inc**
560 Herndon Pkwy Suite 340
Herndon VA 20170-5477
(703) 471-5370
(1-10-13)
Hunters Woods Fellowship House
2231 Colts Neck Rd Reston VA 22091
(703) 620-4450
Rev Alfred M Ambrose
Lake Anne Fellowship House
11450 North Shore Dr Reston VA 22190
(703) 471-6474
Donna L Mayer
Lake Ridge Fellowship House
12800 Harbor Dr Woodbridge VA 22192
(703) 690-3366
Sharon Farmer
Largo Landing Fellowship House
1077 Largo Rd Upper Marlboro MD 20772
(301) 249-2100
Charlene Eley
**Lutheran Council of Tidewater**
1301 Colley Ave Norfolk VA 23517-1700
(757) 623-0155
Samuel Ross
(1-2-13-18-19-20-21-24)

## WASHINGTON

**The Hearthstone**
6720 E Green Lake Way N
Seattle WA 98103-5439
(206) 525-9666
Richard J Milsow
(10-13)
**Compass Health**
4526 Federal Ave Everett WA 98203
(425) 349-8415
Jess C Jamieson, Ph D
(2-3-8-23-24)
*Area Offices:*
College Hill Consolidation
PO Box 2097 Everett WA 98203-0097
(425) 349-6200
Ronald Jacobson
Lifenet Foundation
PO Box 2097 Everett WA 98203-0097
(425) 349-8498
Holly Jensen
**Lutheran Social Services of WA & ID**
4040 S 188th Seattle WA 98188
(206) 901-1685
Roberta Nestaas
(2-3-4-6-7-9-10-16-17-19-20-24)
*Area Offices:*
Southeast
3321 W Kennewick Ave Suite 150
Kennewick WA 99336
(509) 735-6446
Joanne Chapman
Northwest
433 Miner Ave North Seattle WA 98109-5439
(206) 694-5700
Dianne Shiner
Southwest
223 N Yakima Tacoma WA 98403
(253) 272-8433
Ken Villani
Inland Northwest
7 S Howard St Spokane WA 99204
(509) 747-8224
Dennis McGaughy
Olympic
830 Pacific Ave #101 Bremerton WA 98312
(360) 377-5511
S Idaho
420 W Bannock Boise ID 83707
(208) 344-0094
David Ernat
**Martha and Mary Lutheran Services**
Martha and Mary Health Services
PO Box 127
Poulsbo WA 98370-0127
(360) 779-7500
Karen Carter
(7-10-13)
Ebenezer Services
PO Box 127
Poulsbo WA 98370-0127
(360) 779-8405
Richard Huddy
**Riverview Retirement Community**
1801 E Upriver Dr Spokane WA 99207-5181
(509) 483-6483
Wm Patrick O' Neill
(10)
**Tacoma Lutheran Home and Retirement Community**
1301 N Highlands Parkway Tacoma WA 98406
(253) 752-7112
Paul Opgrande
(1-10-13-17-20)
**Lutheran Ministries Seattle**
4130 University Way NE
Seattle WA 98105-6214
(206) 634-3370
Rev Ronald Gocken

## WISCONSIN

**Bethesda Lutheran Homes & Services Inc**
700 Hoffmann Dr Watertown WI 53094
(920) 261-3050
Dr F David Geske
(1-5-7-11-13-15-17-19-20-23)
National Christian Resource Center
(800) 369-INFO (4636)
*Residential Facilities:*
Florida:
2608 Thornhill Rd Auburndale FL 33823
15425 County Rd 455 Montverde FL 34756
Illinois:
Supported Service Program
1138 S Spring Apt B Springfield IL 62704
400 W Allen Apt 2 Springfield IL 62704
Intermediate Care Facilities (ICF/MR)
1480 Reckinger Rd Aurora IL 60505
1205 S Spencer St Montgomery IL 60505
1761 Woodgate Dr Sycamore IL 60178
1100 S Pasfield Springfield IL 62704
Community Integrated Living Arrangement (CILA)
1037 Howell PL Apt 902 Aurora IL 60505
705 Short Tenth Lincoln IL 62658
709 Fifteenth Lincoln IL 62656
711 S Main St Apt B119 Sycamore IL 60178
2264 Jericho Rd Apt 3A Montgomery IL 60178
Support Living Arrangement
1112 S Pasfield Springfield IL 62704
Indiana:
110 N Nichols St Lowell IN 46356
1601 Sturdy Rd Valparaiso IN 46383
Kansas:
Community Assisted Living Program
16920 W 127th St
Olathe KS 66062
Faith Village
14150 W 113th St
Shawnee Mission KS 66215
(Regional Office and Residential Facility)
121 Colleen Gardner KS 66030
741 N Nelson Olathe KS 66061
Community Assisted Living Program
Olathe Apartment (CALP)
12210 Strang Line Ct Olathe KS 66062
Maryland:
201 W Second St Frederick MD 21701
Michigan:
3371 Mistywood Southeast
Caledonia MI 49316
210 Mayer St Frankenmuth MI 48734
Missouri:
1019 S Geyer Rd Kirkwood MO 63122
604 Buchanan St Maryville MO 64468

2310 W Elm St St Charles MO 63301
Ohio:
3951 Rocky River Dr Cleveland OH 44111
Texas:
Good Samaritan Main Campus
18937 K-Z Rd PO Box 429
Cypress TX 77429
(Regional Office, Respite Care Day Services and Chapel)
*Residential Facilities:*
18211 K-Z Road Cypress TX 77429
18937 K-Z Road Cypress TX 77429
17626 Kings Court Cypress TX 77429
16422 Cypress-Rosehill Rd Cypress TX 77429
1040 Heights Blvd Houston TX 77008
2315 Creekleaf Dr Houston TX 77068
17403 Deer Creek Spring TX 77379
*Apartments*
10730 Glenora Dr Houston TX 77065
16334 Maplemont Houston TX 77084
7434 Boysenberry Houston TX 77095
Wisconsin:
*Main Campus Day Services*
Camp Matz and Corporate Headquarters
700 Hoffmann Dr Watertown WI 53094
200 Jefferson St Ft Atkinson WI 53538
6515 W Holmes Ave Milwaukee WI 53220
10107 W Good Hope Rd Milwaukee WI 53224
100 Eickstaedt Lane Watertown WI 53094
8535 W North Ave Wauwatosa WI 53226
8529 W N Ave Wauwatosa WI 53226
2577 S 118th St West Allis WI 53227

**Lutheran Counseling & Family Services**
3800 N Mayfair Rd
Wauwatosa WI 53222-2200
(414) 536-8333
Dr Charles Meseck
(1-2-4-6-14-16-20-22-24)
*Area Offices:*
517 Superior Ave Sheboygan WI 53081
(888) 257-4011
501 E Fillmore Eau Claire WI 54701-7623
(800) 822-5744
324 S Andrews Shawano WI 54166
(888) 867-4840
503 ½ Jefferson St Suite D Wausau WI 54403
(888) 262-8022
260 Vincent St Fond du Lac WI 54935
(800) 868-8711
600 2nd Ave N Park Falls WI 54552-1327
(800) 538-5660

**Lutheran Home**
7500 W North Ave
Wauwatosa WI 53213-1797
(414) 258-6170
Robert Pieters
(1-10)

**Oakwood Foundation Inc**
**Oakwood Lutheran Homes Assoc Inc**
**Oakwood Tabor Oaks Assisted Living Facility**
**Oakwood Village Apartments Inc**
6201-09 Mineral Point Rd Madison WI 53705
(608) 231-3453
Mr John Noreika
(1-10-13-14-17-18-20-23)

## OTHER RECOGNIZED SERVICE ORGANIZATIONS

**Brazil Mission Society, Inc**
16801 Huebner Rd.
San Antonio, Texas 78258
(210) 479-1477 FAX (210) 479-9348
www.concordia-satx.com/brazil%20Missions.htm
Dr. William G. Thompson, President
Todd Reineck, Executive Director

**Camp ALOMA**
PO Box 3
Prescott AZ 86302
(520) 778-1690

**Camp Arcadia**
PO Box 229
Arcadia MI 49613
(231) 778-4361 FAX (231) 889-4140

**Camp CILCA**
4124 Camp Cilca Road
Cantrall, IL 62625
(217) 487-7497

**Camp Lakeview**
13500 W Lake Road
Seymour, IN 47274
(812) 342-4815

**Camp Luther**
1050 Road 4
Schuyler NE 68661
(402) 352-5655

**Camp Okojobi**
1531 Edgewood Drive
Milford IA 51351
(712) 337-3325

**Camp Woodmen**
1700 Farnam Street
Omaha NE 68102
(402) 271-7258 FAX (402) 449-7733

**Children's Christian Concern Society**
1000 SW 10th Topeka KS 66604
FAX (785) 539-2230
E-Mail: cccs@cccs-us.org
Website: www.cccs-us.org
*President:* Marlene Ernsting
173 SE 100 Ave Ellinwood KS 67526
(316) 564-2422
*Vice President:* Alfred Aufdemberge
Rt 2 Box 54 Lincoln KS 67455
(785) 524-3981
*Secretary* Edith Jorns
3031 Conrow Dr Manhattan KS 66503
(785) 539-6052
*Treasurer:* Kennard Kopp
3445 Treesmill Dr Manhattan KS 66503
(785) 539-1540
*Fin-Sec:* Norbert Zander
3952 SW Canterbury Ln Topeka KS 66610
(785) 478-3306
*President Emeritus:* Nathan Schepmann
228 Edgeford Dr Pratt KS 67124
*Board of Directors:* Marcia Blumberg, Rev A C Burroughs, Richard Hahn, Barbara Lammert, Dennis Martin, Eric Schieber, Rev Eugene Schmidt, Gaylord Shields, Marilyn Stewart, Marj Stuckert, Nannette Zander

**Council for Lutheran American Indian Ministry (CLAIM)**
Shepherd of the Hills Lutheran Church
7691 S University Blvd, Littleton CO 80122
(303) 798-0711 FAX: (303) 798-0718
*Executive Director:* Dr Bill Heinicke

**Lift High the Cross**
**Hot Air Balloon Ministry**
7601 SW 39th St Davie Fl 33328
(302) 521-2734 or (302) 521-2771
E-mail: LHTC@AOL.com
Rev Jay Mason

**Lutheran Association of Missionaries and Pilots (LAMP)**
3525 N 124th St., Brookfield, WI 53005-2498; (262) 783-5267, FAX (262) 783-5290. Rev Don Johnson, *Executive Director,* Al Kahlfeldt, *Director of Development;* Rev Landon Schkade, *Director of Ministry and Discipleship;* Ed Reger, *Chief Financial Officier,* Don Vahlsing, *President;* Daphne Gustafson, *Vice President,* Marilyn Egland, *Secretary;* Bill Ruthford, *Treasurer.*

**Lutheran Bible Institute in California**
5321 University Dr Suite H
Irvine CA 92715-2938
(949) 262-9222
Ben Johnson *Executive Director*

**Lutheran Bible Translators Inc**
USA 303 N Lake Street Box 2050
Aurora IL 60507-2050
(630) 897-0660 (800) 532-4253
FAX (630) 897-3567
E-Mail: lbt@xc.org WEB SITE: http://www.lbt.org
CANADA Box 934 Kitchener, Ontario N2G 4E3
(519) 742-3361 FAX (519) 742-5969
Marshall Gillam, *Executive Director*
Robert Schmitt, *Executive Director—Canada*
Walter De Moss, *Interim Director of Program Ministries*
James Pindras, *Interim Director of Support Ministries*
Board of Directors USA: R Fritsche, Chair; J Kennedy, Vice Chairman; W Schumacher, Secretary; J Sorensen, Treasurer; J Anderson, W Braun, B Bunkowske, J Hanson, C Kramer, R Roegner, E Stelling, J Vehling
Board of Directors CANADA: W Mundt, Chair; G Martens, Secretary; R Klages, Treasurer; A Feth, R Jacobsen, R Schallhorn, J Williams
Publications *The Messenger* published quarterly
Monthly letter to financial supporters
Monthly Prayer Calendar
Annual Report

**Lutheran Braille Workers Inc**
13471 California St PO Box 5000
Yucaipa CA 92399-1450
(909) 795-8977 E-mail - LBWBraille@aol.com
Mr Loyd Coppenger *Executive Director*
PO Box 5000 Yucaipa CA 92399-1450
(909) 795-8977 Office FAX (909) 795-8970
(909) 790-2592 Home
Biblical and Devotional BRAILLE and LARGE PRINT Materials are FREE to certified Blind and Visually Handicapped.
Available upon request:
English Braille Catalog
International Braille Catalog
Large Print Catalog
Quarterly Newsletter

**Lutheran City Ministries, Inc.**
15700 East Warren
Detroit MI 48224
(313) 884-7644 FAX: (313) 884-7821
E-Mail: MSmith@aol.cm
*Developers:* Jim Fleming, Ken Schmidt
*Central Office:* Mary E. Smith, Administrator/Secretary
*Park Side Sites (in Nazareth and Charity Lutheran Churches):* Vicar Steve Essenburg, Leader
*Southwest Hispanic Ministry:* Deaconess Teresita Rodriguez, Leader
*Rebert Center Annex and Cell Groups:* Sue Hatcher, Leader
*Operation Rebound:* Raymond Lewis, Leader
*Parish Lay Specialist Program Site:* Rev. Arnold Brammeier, Leader
*LCM Boys Choir of Detroit:* Rev David Rutter, Leader
*Board of Directors:* Sandy Seltz *President,* Jim Miller, Lisa Loesel, Rev. Arnold H Brammeier *Interim Director,* David Tirsell *Treasurer,* Rev Terry Rebert *Vice President*

**Lutheran Heritage Foundation**
PO Box 46
Sterling Heights MI 48311
(800) 554-0723 FAX (810) 791-9986
Website: www.LHFMissions.org
Rev Robert L Rahn *Executive Director*
Jeffrey R Rahn *Director of Operations*
Rev John Fehrmann *Director of Mission Advancement*
Prof Kurt Marquardt, *Chairman*
Richard Hallgren, *President*
Rev Richard Bolling *First Vice-President*
Lloyd Wittenmyer, *Second Vice-President*
Hank Haudas *Third Vice-President*
Gerald Radtke, *Secretary*
Philip Fluegge *Treasurer*
Brad Flaaen *Member at large*
John Wittenmyer *Legal Counsel*

**Lutherans in Jewish Evangelism**
Lutheran Ministries Center
7207 Monetary Dr
Orlando FL 32809
(407) 857-5556 FAX (407) 857-5665
E-mail: Blieske7@cs.com
Website www.ourfrontporch.Com/OSI/Messiah
Rev Bruce J Lieske *Executive Director*
Dr Erwin Kolb *Chairman of Board of Directors*
Dorothy Holtz *Treasurer*
Robin Greenspan *Prayer Coordinator*
Publications: *The Burning Bush* published monthly; monthly prayer letter.

**Mill Neck Foundation Inc**
Frost Mill Road PO Box 100 Mill Neck NY 11765
(516) 922-3880 (VOICE/TDD) 1-800-264-0662
FAX (516) 922-3759

President: Rev Thomas Armour
Executive Director: Dr Mark R Prowatzke
Representing the Mill Neck Family of Organizations: Lutheran Friends of the Deaf; Mill Neck Manor School for Deaf Children and Early Childhood Center; Mill Neck Services for Deaf Adults; Mill Neck Foundation for Deaf Ministry

**Ongoing Ambassadors for Christ Inc**
PO Box 41 Athens IL 62613-0041
(217) 636-7729 (217) Men-Pray
E-Mail: info@oafc.org
Rev Thomas Moyer, *Exec Dir* 3002 S Lincoln St Springfield IL 62704 (217) 726-7714
Board of Directors: Revs David Baumgarn, Daniel Smith, Tom Moyer; Erwin Ruhlig (treasurer) Lay: Ed Allen (chairman), Trey Fisk, Pam Rudick (secretary), Ellen Griffin; Youth: Adam Gless, David Kamin, Lisa Holmes, Donine Fink
Publication: *The OAFC Crier* published three times annually.

**Partners in Mission**
1115 East 19th Street
Minneapolis, MN 55404
(612) 870-9487
Richard Latterner, *Executive Director* (651) 603-6179
Art Bartels, *Chairman of Board of Directors* (612) 373-4640
Tom Bystryzcki, *Chairman,* Mission Committee (651) 459-7494
Tom Grundermann, *Deacon* (612) 870-9487

**Chicagoland Lutheran Educational Foundation**
234 N Plum Grove Suite 200 Palatine IL 60067
(847) 221-2623
E-mail: Chrisirelan@medial.net
www.goodnewsfund.org
Rev Christopher J Irelan *Executive Director*

**Family Shield Ministries, Inc.**
P.O. Box 230015 St Louis, MO 63123
(314) 352-2253 FAX (314) 752-4360
www.familyshieldministries.com
Kay L Meyer *President* 7045 Parkwood St
St Louis MO 63116
Dr John Oberdeck, *Chairman*
Vacant, *Vice-Chairman*
Ruth Houser, *Secretary*
Curt Wittbracht, *Treasurer*
Rev Gary Dahnke, *Pastoral Advisor*

**Lutheran Education Association**
7400 Augusta St River Forest IL 60305-1499
(708) 209-3343 FAX (708) 209-3458
lea@crf.cuis.edu WWW.LEA.ORG
Dr Jonathan Laabs, *Executive Director*
Marvin Oestmann, *President*
Peace With Christ Christian School 3290 S Tower Rd Aurora CO 80013-2367
Ken Kaschinske *President-Elect*
Peace Lutheran School
Saginaw MI
Charles Winterstein, *Vice President for Membership & Public Relations*
Lutheran School Assn 2001 E Mound Rd Decatur IL 62526–9305
Donna Tennis, *Secretary*
St Philip Lutheran School 2500 W Bryn Mawr Chicago IL 60659
Barbara Goodwin, *Office Manager*

**Lutheran Family Association/Family Connection**
3558 S Jefferson Avenue, St Louis MO 63118
(314) 268-1180 or (800) 351-1001
Vacant, *Executive Director*
Vivian Hauser

**Luther North School Association**
5700 W Berteau Ave Chicago IL 60634-1717
(773) 286-3600
Nathaniel Grunst MA CAS *Superintendent*

**Lutheran Special Education Ministries**
Headquarters
6861 E Nevada Ave Detroit MI 48234-2983
(313) 368-1220
*President/CEO:* Roger DeMeyere
Resource Center: James Krone
*Development Director:* Gregg Braun
*Great Lakes Region (MI, IN, OH) Director:* Kathy Krause
*Northeast Region (NY, PA, MD), Director:* Paula Rosen
(914) 395-4710
*Midwest Region (IL, WI) Director:* Susan Lewis
(708) 209-3344
*North Central Region (MN, SD, ND), Director:* Dennis Senne
(651) 603-6235
*Southwest Region (CA, AZ, NV), Director:* Laura Sauer
(818) 988-7667

**St John's College Alumni Assn**
PO Box 376 Winfield KS 67156
(316) 221-1572
Rev Dr Wallace Behrhorst *Executive Director*

**St Paul Lutheran High School**
Box 719 Concordia MO 64020
(660) 463-2238 FAX (660) 463-7621
E-mail: rggove@almanet.net
Richard Gove, *Headmaster/Principal*

**Wheat Ridge Ministries**
One Pierce Pl Suite 250E Itasca IL 60143-2634
(630) 766-9066 FAX (630) 766-9622
(800) 762-6748
E-mail: wrmin@aol.com
Dr Richard Bimler *President*

## HEADQUARTERS OF OTHER ASSOCIATIONS

Headquarters of other associations are merely listed for convience and purposes of information. The Lutheran Church—Missouri Synod makes no representations or guarantees about the fiscal solvency or financial responsibility of any recognized organization, or for any services expressly or implicitly offered by it.

*The Apple of His "Eye" Mission Society* P.O. Box 6977, St. Louis, MO 63123 888-51APPLE, e-mail scinfl@aol.com; website: www.appleofhiseye.org, Mr. Steve Cohen, Founder; Rev. Kevin Parviz, Congregation Chai V' Shalom (Life and Peace); Ivan Peterson, Office Manager, Gary Timm, Missionary to New York City, e-mail aplmission@aol.com.

*Association of Lutheran Older Adults (ALOA).* Valparaiso University, Valparaiso, IN 46383 (219) 464-6743 or 1-800-930-ALOA (2562) FAX (219) 464-6824. Dale Trimberger, *President;* Connie Miller, *Vice President;* Lee Vogel Kingdon, *Secretary;* John Miller, *Treasurer;* Arthur Constien, *Executive Director; Karl Lutze, Executive Director Emeritus.* Quarterly Publication *ENCORE TIMES.*

*Association of Lutheran Secondary Schools.* David Widenhofer, *President,* 1601 St. Joe River Drive, Fort Wayne, IN 46805. Dr Thomas Buck, *President-elect,* 5201 South 76th Street, Greendale, WI 53129, Randy Lowe, *Secretary/Treasurer,* 2400 North Dale Street, Roseville, MN 55113. Dwayne Jobst, Conference Coordinator, 9700 W Grantosa Drive, Milwaukee, WI 53222. Patricia Klekamp, *Member-at-large,* 8494 Stults Road. Dallas, TX 75243. Teresa Davis, *Administrative Assistant,* 1601 St Joe River Drive, Fort Wayne, IN 46805

*Concordia Deaconess Conference.* %Deaconess Joyce A Ostermann, 7934 Stonegate Place, Fort Wayne, IN Telephone: (219) 489-1163 *President:* Dcs. Joyce Ostermann; *Vice President:* Dcs. Faith Marburger, HC 76 Lake of the Woods, Locust Grove, VA 22508; *Secretary:* Dcs. Jeanne A Moe, 6422 Winter Street, Fort Wayne, IN 46806; Treasurer: Dcs. Laura Budzynski, 810 15th Street, Rockford, IL 61104; Board Member: Dcs. Pamela J Nielsen, 2807 Longwood Court, Fort Wayne, IN 46845; Board Member: Dcs. Beth Niermann, 9324 Lake Shore Road, Angola, NY 14006; Deaconess Kristin Wassilak, Director of the Deaconess Training Program at Concordia University, 7400 Augusta Street, River Forest, IL 60305 Phone (708) 209-3136.

*Concordia Gospel Outreach.* Box 201, St. Louis, MO 63166-0201. Telephone: (314) 268-1363 FAX (314) 268-1202. Annette Frank, *Mgr.,*
E-Mail: annette.frank@cphnet.org
Web: www.cgo-online.org

*Lutheran Institute on Aging and Family.* Concordia University, 800 N Columbia, Seward, NE 68434; Telephone: (402) 643-7432. FAX (402) 643-4073. Dr Shirley Bergman, *Director;* E-Mail: sbergman@seward.cune.edu

*International Lutheran Deaf Association.* 1333 S Kirkwood Rd., St. Louis, MO 63122-7295. Richard Norton, *President;* James Swalley, *President-elect;* Tim Johnston, *Secretary;* Karen Beiter, *Treasurer;* Rev Mark Anderson, *Pastoral Advisor;* Publication: *The Deaf Lutheran,* issued bimonthly. David Brown, *Editor* (see Publications of Synod for further information).

*Lutheran Church—Canada.* Rev Ralph E Mayan, *President,* 3074 Portage Ave, Winnipeg, MB, R3K OY2, *Vice Presidents:* Rev Dennis Putzman, 400 Glenridge Avenue, St Catharines, ON L2T 3L2; Rev Daniel Rinderknecht, R.R. #4, Site 1, Box 17, Stony Plain, Alberta, T7Z 1X4; Rev James Fritsche, 1541 St. Marys Road, Winnipeg, Manitoba, R2M 3V8; *Secretary:* Rev William Ney, 5021-52 Ave., Stony Plain, Alberta T7Z 1C1 *Treasurer:* Mr Allan Webster, 3074 Portage Avenue, Winnipeg, Manitoba R3K 0Y2:

*Lutheran Deaconess Association.* Center for Diaconal Ministry, 1304 LaPorte Avenue, Valparaiso, IN 46383. Telephone: (219) 464-6925. Louise Williams, *Executive Director;* Michael Cobbler *Director of Development and Public Relations;* Olivia Hartung, *Director of Formation/Laity Services;* Paul Thielo, *President;* Sheryl Andreasen, *Vice-President;* Karl Reichardt, *Treasurer;* Martha Rohlfing, *Secretary.*

*Lutheran Deaconess Conference.* 1304 LaPorte Ave., Valparaiso, IN 46383. Jeanette Rebeck, *President;* Lisa Scherzer, *Vice President;* Brenda Bass, *Secretary;* Mary Hackbarth, *Treasurer;* Virginia Brondos and April Boyden, *Board Members at Large.*

*Lutheran Evangelism Association.* PO Box 10021, Phoenix, AZ 85064. Telephone: (480) 949-5325, FAX (480) 994-9146, E-mail levapfi@futureone.com. Rev Ervin Rasmussen, *Executive Director;* Publications: *Prayer Concern Letter; The Net; Waiting Time Digest*, *Prayer And Witness Network* (the PAWN of God); Lay school of Witness *Workshop For Shy and Timid Christians.*

*Lutherans For Life.* 1120 S G Ave, Nevada, IA 50201-2774 Telephone (888) 364-LIFE: (515) 382-2077 FAX (515) 382-3020. Dr James Lamb, *Executive Director.*

*Lutheran Human Relations Association of America.* 5233 N 51st Blvd, Milwaukee, WI 53218-3302,. Voice: (414) 536-0585 FAX (414) 536-0690.E-mail: LHRA@ecunet.org. www.lhra.org Publication: *The Vanguard;* Annual Institute last weekend in June. Joyce Caldwell, *Director.*

*Lutheran Lay Ministry Association, Inc.* 2703 N Sherman Blvd, Milwaukee, WI 53210-2495. Telephone: (414) 445-5185 E-mail: LuthLMA@aol.com. Hugh McMartin, *President,* 9829 Eckles Livonia, MI 48152; Jeff Zoellick, *Vice President,* 1422 W Army Trail Road Carol Stream, IL 60188; Tom Gibbons, *Secretary,* 529 S Park St. Roselle, IL 60172; Mike Guymon, *Treasurer,* 2703 N Sherman Blvd Milwaukee, WI 53210-2495.

*Lutheran Music Program.* 122 W Franklin Ave, Suite 522, Minneapolis, MN 55404. Telephone: (612) 879-9555. FAX (612) 879-9547.
E-Mail: lmp@lutheranmusicprogram.org web site: www.lutheranmusicprogram.org
Dr. Victor Gebauer, *Executive Director,* Kristen Gasau, *Assistant for Public Relations,* Philip Mennicke, *Registrar,* Fredrick Moors, *Director of Advancement;* Melissa Olson, *Director of Admissions and Financial Aid,* Catherine Schauer, *Director of Management.*

*Lutheran Tape Ministry, Inc.* 203 E Broad St PO Box 218 Blue Springs NE 68318-0218 Telephone: 1-(800) 937-2591, E-Mail: ltmtape@juno.com website: TalkingScriptures.com, Fred Naumann III, *CEO;* Karen Knapp, *Administrative Assistant;* Nancy Schroeder, *Distribution.*

*People of the Book Lutheran Outreach (POBLO),* 35004 Michigan Ave Suite B, Wayne, MI 48184. Telephone (734) 467-6256, FAX (734) 467-8669. E-mail: pobloffice@aol.com.
Khurram Khan, *Missionary and Executive Director;* Dennis Tino, *Chairman Bd of Directors;* Debbie Rauner, *Office Manager.*

God's mission for POBLO is to evangelize Muslims, to raise up spiritual leaders among them and to establish Christ worshipping communities with them.

## LUTHERAN COOPERATIVE AGENCIES

**Lutheran Immigration and Refugee Service**
700 Light Street, Baltimore MD 21230
(410) 230-2700 FAX (410) 230-2890
E-Mail: lirs@lirs.org
Website: http://www.lirs.org

Ralston H. Deffenbaugh Jr, *President*
Pam Meyer, *Assistant to the President*

**Resettlement**

Barbara J Day, *Vice-President for Resettlement*

*Case Processing*
Florentina Chiu, *Director for Case Processing*
Lanai Michelle Byg, *Assistant Director for Case Processing Resettlement*
Chris Melendez, *Director for Resettlement*
Diane Landino and Terry Abeles, *Assistant Directors for Resettlement*

*RefugeeWorks*
Jane Bloom, *Director for RefugeeWorks*

**Programs**

Anne P Wilson, *Vice-President for Programs*

*Asylum and Immigration*
Matthew J Wilch, *Director for Asylum and Immigration*

*Grants and Management*
Joyce Hoebing *Director for Grants and Management*

*Legal Services*
Bindu Wolerson *Director for Legal Services*

*Children's Services*
Susan Schmidt, *Director for Children's Services*

*International Social Service/American Branch, Inc.*
Joanne Selinske, *Director for ISS/AB*
Beth Sadofsky, *Senior Intercountry Caseworker*
Marla J Dirks, *Senior Repatriation Caseworker*

**Agency Advancement**

Timatha S Pierce, *Vice-President for Agency Advancement*

*Communications*
Susan Baukhages, *Director for Communications*
Valerie Bost, *Communications Associate*

*Resource Development*
William C Tremitiere, *Director for Resource Development*
Denise Laugtug, *Director for Volunteer Development*

**Finance and Administration**

George N Letsa, *Vice-President for Finance and Administration*
Carol Bohatila, *Controller*
Raquel M De Leon, *Assistant Controller*
Darin Wood, *Loan Collection Manager*

**Washington Office:** 122 C St NW, Suite 125, Washington, DC 20001-2172
(202) 783-7509 FAX (202) 783-7502
E-Mail: lirswdc@aol.com
Merrill Smith, *Washington Representative*

**Lutheran Educational Conference of North America**
1001 Connecticut Ave NW Suite 504 Washington DC 20036 (202) 463-6486
Rev Donald Stoike ThD *Executive Director* (Washington)
E-Mail: stoiked@lutherancolleges.org
www.lutherancolleges.org

**Lutheran Film Associates**
Inter Church Center, 475 Riverside Dr 16th Floor, New York, NY 10015-0253,
www.lutheranfilm.org
Administrator: Walter A Jensen *Treasurer* (New York)

**Lutheran World Relief Headquarters**
700 Light Street, Baltimore MD 21230
(410) 230-2700 FAX (410) 230-2882
E-Mail: lwr@lwr.org, website: http://www.lwr.org/
Kathryn F Wolford, *President*
Cherri Waters, *Vice President for Programs and Planning*
Susanne Riveles, *Program Director for Africa*
Daniel Chelliah, *Program Director for Asia & the Middle East*
Kim Krasevac-Szekely, *Program Director for Latin America*
Kenlynn K Schroeder, *Director for Grants, Emergencies and Material Resources*

*Deputy Director for Grants, Emergencies and Material Resources*
Karen Smith Geon, Lutheran World Relief Material Resources Office, 605 S E 39th Avenue, Portland OR 97214-3298 (503) 731-9599 FAX (503) 731-9597
Jonathan C Frerichs, *Director for Communication*
Terri D Speirs, *Parish Communication Associate*
Michael S Malewicki, *Vice President for Finance & Administration*
Lisa A Negstad, *Comptroller*
Ann K Fries, *Manager for Human Resources*
Thomas VandenBosch, *Director for Mission Advancement*

**LCMS World Relief**
Financial support for Lutheran World Relief and other disaster response and self-help programs should be sent to this address: LCMS World Relief 1333 S Kirkwood Rd St Louis, MO 63122-7295.
Elaine Richter Bryant, *Director*
1-800-248-1930, Ext 1376
Credit Card gift line is 1-888-930-4438
E-Mail: lcms.worldrelief@lcms.org
Website: http://worldrelief.lcms.org

## OVERSEAS CHURCHES AND MISSIONS

### ANGOLA

**Evangelica Lutherana do Brasil (IELB)**
**Igreja Luterana Confessional em Angola**
B.P. 390 Cabinda (Angola) (Africa)
Rev. Jeremias Mavungu Vangu

### ARGENTINA

**Evangelical Lutheran Church of Argentina (Iglesia Evangelica Lutherana Argentina) IELA**
Ing L Silveyra 1639, 1607 Villa Adelina, Buenos Aires, Argentina, SA, Phone and FAX 011-54-11-4766-7948,

Officers
Rev Waldomiro Maili *President,* Silveyra 1655, 1607 Villa Adelina, Buenos Aires, Argentina, Phone and Fax 011-54-11-4766-7948
Rev Carlos Nagel *First Vice President,* Phone 011-54-03754-421195
Rev Jose Antonio Pfaffenzeller *Second Vice President*—Phone 011-54-11-4651-7475
Rev Eldor Rautenberg *Secretary*—Phone 011-54-11-4303-0778
Rev Juan Adolfo Beckmann *Treasurer*—Phone 011-54-11-4766-7948
Prof Dr Jorge Groh *Literature Editor*—Phone 011-54-11-4729-7991

SEMINARIO CONCORDIA
Casilla Correo 5 (Libertad 1650) 1655 José L Suarez, Buenos Aires, Argentina, Phone 011-54-11-4720-7797, FAX 011-54-11-4729-0345
Rev Antonio Schimpf *Director,* Phone 011-54-11-4729-0877

LIGA MISIONAL DE DAMAS LUTERANAS
Sra Nilda V De Muriano *President,* Concordia 426, 3360 OBERA, Misiones, Argentina, Phone 011-54-03755-422797

### AUSTRALIA

**Lutheran Church of Australia (LCA)**
Lutheran Church National Office 197 Archer St. North Adelaide South Australia 5006 Phone 011-61-8-8267-7300, FAX 011-61-8-8267-7310
E-Mail president@lca.org.au
Rev Lance G Steicke DD *President*
Rev Lionel Otto *First Vice President,* Concord House 15-17 Blaxland Rd Rhodes NSW 2138
Rev Wayne T Zweck Second Vice President 130 Eugaree Street Southport Queensland 4215
Mr Kevin J Kempin *Administrator*
Mr Gordon D Samuel FASA CPA ACIS *Missions Treasurer*
Dr Ulf Metzner *Dir of Church Cooperation in World Mission*
Rev Richard J Mau *Manager Lutheran Media Ministry*
Mr Adrienne Jericho *National Director Lutheran Schools*

LUTHER SEMINARY
104 Jeffcott St North Adelaide South Australia 5006 Phone Adelaide 011-61-8-8267-7400 FAX 011-61-8-8267-7350 E-Mail: luthersem@luthersem.edu.au
Principal Rev Dr John B Koch

OPEN BOOK PUBLISHERS
205 Halifax St Adelaide South Australia 5000, GPO Box 1368 Adelaide SA 5001, (Phone 011-61-8-8223-5468), FAX 011-61-8-8223-4552, Mr Warren A Schirmer *General Manager* E-Mail: enquiries@openbook.com.au

LUTHERAN LAYPEOPLE'S LEAGUE
175 Archer Street North Adelaide South Australia 5006 Phone 011-61-8-83607200 FAX 011-61-8-8267-1722 E-Mail: lll@lll.org.au

LUTHERAN ARCHIVES
101 Archer Street North Adelaide South Australia 5006 Phone Adelaide 011-61-8-8267-1737

***District Presidents***
New South Wales Rev Lionel Otto, Concord House, 15-17 Blaxland Rd, Rhodes NSW 2138, Phone 011-61-2-9736-2366, FAX 011-61-2-9736-1155 E-Mail: president@nsw.lca.org.au
Victoria Rev David G Stolz, 755 Station St, Box Hill Victoria 3128, Phone 011-61-3-9890-0566 FAX 011-61-3-9890-6771 E-Mail: stolz.david@vic.lca.org.au
Queensland Rev Tim R Jaensch, 24 McDougall St, Milton Queensland 4064, Phone 011-61-7-3511-4000 FAX 011-61-7-3511-4011 E-Mail: president@qld.lca.org.au
South Australia Rev Michael P Semmler, 137 Archer St, North Adelaide SA 5006, Phone Adelaide 011-61-8-8267-5790 or 011-61-8-8267-5211 E-Mail: president@sa.lca.org.au
Western Australia Rev G Burger 16 Aberdeen St. Perth WA 6000, Phone 61-8-9227-8072, FAX 61-8-9328-9481 E-mail: gburger@webace.com.au
New Zealand Rev Steen A. Olsen, 38 Somerset Crescent, Palmerston North New Zealand, Phone 011-64-6-355-3720 FAX 011-64-6-357-3897 E-Mail: president.lcnz@clear.net.nz

### BELGIUM

**The Evangelical Lutheran Church**
**Synod of France and Belgium**
Tabakvest 59 2000 Antwerpen Belgium
Phone 011-32-32-33-6250

### BENIN

**c/o Mr. Francois Zankou**
**Eglise Evangélique Luthérienne du Benin**
07 BP 570 Cotonou
Benin, West Africa
Phone 229-350001-303149

### Botswana

See Southern Africa

### BRAZIL

**Evangelical Lutheran Church of Brazil**
**(Igreja Evangelica Luterana do Brasil) IELB**
**Caixa Postal 1076**
90001-970 Porto Alegre RS Brazil, South America, Phone 011-55-51-332-2111, FAX 011-55-51-332-8145
Rev Carlos Walter Winterle *President*
Rev Vilson Regina *First Vice President*
Rev Arnildo Schneider *Second Vice President*
Mr Astomiro Romais *Secretary*
Mr Moacir Guenter *Treasurer*

**Concordia Seminary**
Concordia Institute, Av Getulio Vargas 4388
Caixa Postal 202, 93001-970, Sao Leopoldo RS, Brazil Phone/Fax 011-55-51-592-9035
Prof. Paulo M Nerbas, President

*Higher School of Theology*
Concordia Institute, Rua Raul dos Santos Machado 25, Caixa Postal 60754, 05786-990 Sao Paulo SP, Brazil, Phone 011-55-11-5841-7652, FAX 011-55-11-5841-7529, Prof Ari Lange *President*

## CHILE

**Corporación Iglesia Evangélica Luterana de la República de Chile (IELCHI)**

Church Address: Los Pellines 71, Playa Ancha–Valparaiso, República de Chile, P.O. Address: Casilla de Correo 10101, Correo 4
President: Rev Carlos Oscar Schumann
Phone: 00-56-32-689021 (office)
Fax: 00-56-32-699686
E-Mail: concordi@ctcinternet.cl

## CHINA

*(See Hong Kong LCMS China Ministry Team)*

## CONGO

**Eglise Evangélique Luthérienne du Congo (ELCCO)**

B.P. 1456 Brazzaville, Congo (Africa)
Rev. Albert Poungui

**Eglise Luthérienne Confessionnelle au Congo (ELCCO)**

(Formerly: ZAIRE): BP 18367 Kinshasa 13, Democratic Republic of Congo (Africa)
Rev. Mayala Mwana

## CÔTE D'IVOIRE

Mission Evangélique Luthérienne en Afrique, BP 129, Toulepleu Côte d'Ivoire, Rev Dan Ramsey, Phone and FAX 011-225-224-123-70,
E-Mail: MELA@AfricaOnline.co.ci
Rev Ronald Mudge
John Hansen
Dr. William Foster, MD
Mr Gary Schulte, *Business Manager* Emergency phone 874-0761-228-450 or 0730-0745 & 2100-2115 GMT
Rev Thomas Brinkley *Area Director*
Delano Meyer *Area Director*

## CUBA

**Iglesia Evangelica de Confesion Luterana De Cuba**

Rev Ramon E Ebanks, President
Calle 53 No 2608 A/26A Y 28, Nueva Gerona, A CP 25100, Isla De La Juventud, Cuba

## CZECH REPUBLIC

**Silesian Evangelical Church of the Augsburg Confession in the Czech Republic**

Na Nivach 7, 73701 Cesky Tesin, Czech Republic
Phone: 011-420-659-73-18-04
Fax: 011-420-659-73-18-15
Rev Vladislav Volny
E-mail: sceav@silesnet.cz
website: http://www.sceav.silesnet.cz

## CZECHOSLOVAKIA

(*See Slovakia*)

## DENMARK

**The Evangelical Lutheran Free Church of Denmark**

Rev Leif G Jensen *President*, Ewaldsvej 9, DK-8723 Losning Denmark, Phone 011-45-7565-1660 FAX 011-45-7565-1662
E-Mail: Lutheran@vivit.dk, website: www.vivit.dk
Ulrik Bay Jensen *Treasurer*, Roglevangen 17 Svogerslev, DK-4000 Roskilde Denmark, Phone 011-45-4638-5848

## EL SALVADOR

**The Lutheran Synod of El Salvador**

CALLE 5 de NOVIEMBRE No 242 APARTADO (02) 9 Barrio San Miguelito, San Salvador El Salvador CA
Dr Medardo E Gomez Soto *Bishop*, Phone 011-503-225-2942 (Church) 011-503-242-1282 (Home) FAX 011-503-225-1078 (Office)

## ENGLAND

**Evangelical Lutheran Church of England (ELCE)**

c/o Rev Karl Fry, 1 Cherry Tree Ave., Fareham, Hampshire PO14 1PY England
Phone and Fax: 011-441-329-239-319
Rev Karl Fry, *Chairman*, Phone: 011-441-329-284-172 (Home)
Rev Hans Leed, *Vice Chairman*, 49 Eastern Green Road, Coventry CV5 7LG England
Mr. Steve Smith *Treasurer*, c/o 28 Huntingdon Rd Cambridge CB3 OHH Phone: 011-441-223-355-265

**Theologian Training Program**

Westfield House, 30 Huntington Road, Cambridge CB3 OHH
Phone: 011-441-223-354331
Rev R Quirk, *Preceptor*

**Polish-Evangelical Church of the Augsburg Confession Abroad**

*Consistory*, 2 Leinster Rd, London N10 3AN England, Phone 0181-883-0396
P Sliwka *Secretary*
P Kurowski *Treasurer*

## ESTONIA

**Estonian Evangelical Lutheran Church**

Kiriku plats 3, 10130 Tallinn, Estonia, Phone: 011-372-627-7350, Fax: 011-372-627-7352, E-Mail: eelk@eelk.ee; home page: http://www.zzz.ee/eelk/ Archbishop: Jaan Kiivit

## FINLAND

**The Confessional Lutheran Church of Finland (CLCF)**

Rev Markku Sarela DD *President*, Kaukapellonk 9, 33710 Tampere Finland, Phone and FAX 011-358-31-3176565
Mr Kimmo Pälikkö *Vice President*, KP-ART OY, Väärämäentie 6 M, 00700 Helsinki Finland, Phone and FAX: 011-358-9-345-3719 E-Mail: kimmo.palikko@p-art.fi
Mr Jorma Nieminen *Treasurer*, Hurtinkatu 12 C 13, 20610 Turku Finland

## FRANCE

**The Evangelical Lutheran Church Synod of France and Belgium**

Rev Dr Wilbert Kreiss *President*, 16 Allee Maximillien Robespierre, 92290 Chatenay Malabry France, Phone 011-33-01-4631-1882, FAX 011-33-01-4630-3495
Rev Jean Haessig *Vice President*, BP 22, 67290 La Petite Pierre France, Phone 011-33-03-88-70-40-41, FAX 011-33-03-188-70-4084
Rev Claude Ludwig *Secretary*, 9 Rue Jules Barbier, 92290 Chatenay Malabry France, Phone 011-331-01-4094-9557
Mr Martin Kreiss *Treasurer*, 109A Rue de la Moder, 67330 Obermodern France, Phone 011-33-03-88-90-83-03

***Lutheran Study Center***

Rev Dr W Kreiss (see above)

*LUTHERAN HOUR*

Rev Jean Haessig (see above)

## GERMANY

**Independent Evangelical Lutheran Church**

Headquarters, Schopenhauerstr 7, D-30625 Hannover, Phone 011-49-511-557808, FAX 011-49-511-551588, E-Mail: selk@selk.de
*Bishop* Dr Diethardt Roth, Muenchhausenstr 11, D-30625 Hannover, Phone 011-49-511-557826 (Office), 011-49-511-553374 (Home)
E-Mail: selk@selk.de
Rev Michael Schaetzel *General Executive Secretary*, Schopenhauerstr 7, D-30625 Hannover, Phone 011-49-511-557808 (Office), 011-49-511-555669 (Home) E-Mail: schaetzel@selk.de

THEOLOGICAL SEMINARY

Lutherische Theologische Hochschule, Altkoenigstr 150, D-61440 Oberursel. Phone: 011-49-6171-24340, FAX 011-49-6171-926178. E-mail: LThH@selk.de (Rector: Prof Dr. Werner Klaen)

MISSION SOCIETY

Lutherische Kirchenmission (Bleckmarer Mission) Bleckmar 33, D-29303 Bergen, Phone 011-49-5051-98690, FAX 011-49-5051-986945, E-Mail: Lkm@selk.de (Rev Gerhard Heidenreich, *Director*)
Rev. James E Behnke, am Schwalbenschwanz 37, 60431 Frankfurt am Main, Germany, Phone: 011-49-69-95-63-1066, Fax: 011-49-69-95-63-1067, E-Mail: 100045.3106.@Compuserve.com

YOUTH MINISTRY

Hauptjugendpfarramt, Bergstr 17, D-34576 Homberg/Efze, Phone: 011-49-5681-1479, Fax 011-49-5681-60506, E-Mail jugendwerk@selk.de (Rev. Christian Utpatel)

## GHANA

**The Evangelical Lutheran Church of Ghana (ELCG)**

PO Box 197 Kaneshie Accra, Ghana West Africa, Phone 011-233-21-223487, FAX 011-233-21-233155 or 011-233-21-220947
Rt Rev Dr Paul Kofi Fynn *President*, Phone 011-233-21-775550 (Home), 011-233-21-232250 (Private Office)

**Missionary Support Committee**

Mr Larry Grooms *Business Manager*, PO Box C839 Cantonment Accra, Ghana West Africa
Mr Dalton Noack, *TEE Director*, ELCG, PO Box 3536 Kumasi, Ghana West Africa, Phone 011-233-51-27402
Ghana Mission Office (Grooms Residence), Phone 011-233-21-400782, FAX 011-233-21 507884

## GUATEMALA

**The Lutheran Church of Guatemala**

Rev Byron Rene Paz *President*, Apartado Postal 1111, Guatemala (01001) Guatemala CA, Phone and FAX 011-502-2541196
Rev Salamon Gudiel *Vice President*
Carlos Raul Sosa Aldana *Secretary*
Carlos Figueroa Acevedo *Treasurer*

***LCMS Missionary Team***

Thomas McWilliams *Business Manager*, Business office location: Apartment #2 Av Simeon Cañas 7-38, Zona Z Guatemala Guided Apartado Postal 1111, Guatemala (01001) Guatemala Central America.
Phones 011-502-2541205 and 011-502-2541031. Phone & Fax 011-502-2541196
Lutheran Center Antigua
Phone/Fax 011-502-8320225 For more urgent correspondence Federal Express, UPS, etc.

## GUINEA

**Mission Evangélique Luthérienne**

B. P. 438, Conakry , REPUBLIC OF GUINEA, West Africa
Missionary: Rev Tim Heiney, Lutheran Mission BP 438, Conakry, REPUBLIC OF GUINEA
Missionary: Mr Jon Oetting (same address)
Mr Thomas Norton (same address)

## HAITI

**Evangelical Lutheran Church of Haiti (ELCH)**
**Eglise Evangélique Luthérienne d'Haiti**

Rue Capitale #144, Les Cayes, Haiti (W.I.), President: Rev. Israel Izidor, Rue Chateaudin # 7, P.O. Box 15, LeCayes, Haiti, West Indies, Phone: 011-509-86-0860

## HONDURAS

**Lutheran Christian Church of Honduras**

Apartado Postal 2861, Tegucigalpa Honduras, Phone and FAX 011-504-254893, Rev Guillermo Flores *President*
18 Ave 7-8 Calle #724, Colonia Aurora, San Pedro Sula Honduras, Phone 011-504-56-7087

## HONG KONG

**The Lutheran Church—Hong Kong Synod**

68 Begonia Road Yau Yat Chuen, Kowloon Hong Kong, Phone 011-852-2-3973721, FAX 011-852-2-3974826
Rev Allan Yung *President*
Rev Daniel Li *First Vice President*
Rev Paul YS Chan *Second Vice President*
Rev Tony Lau *Treasurer*
Rev Daniel Cheung *General Executive Secretary*

CONCORDIA SEMINARY

68 Begonia Road Yau Yat Chuen, Kowloon Hong Kong, Phone 011-852-2397-3721, FAX 011-852-2397-5616, Rev Craig Molitoris *President*

**Martha Boss Community Centre**

89 Chung Hau Street, Homantin Kowloon Hong Kong, Phone 011-852-2711-9131, FAX 011-852-2761-9751, Mr Paul S K Chan *Executive Director*

**LCMS China Ministry Team**

Flat A G/F #12 Wiltshire Rd, Kowloon Tong,

Kowloon Hong Kong, Phone 011-852-2375-8987 Office, 011-852-2711-9267 Home, FAX 011-852-2375-9177, Rev Craig Molitoris *Director*

HONG KONG INTERNATIONAL SCHOOL

#1 Red Hill Rd, Tai Tam Hong Kong, Phone 011-852-28-139211, FAX 011-852-2813-4293, Mr Charles W Dull, *Head of School*

**Church of All Nations**

8 South Bay Close, Repulse Bay Hong Kong, Phone 011-852-2812-0375, FAX 011-852-2812-9508, Rev Dale Koehneke *Pastor*

## MACAU

Concordia English Centre Edf. Centro Com. Kong Fat 6B Rua Pequim 174 Macau, South Asia Phone (853) 531-404 & 702-612 FAX (853) 531-416
Rev Michael J Paul *Team-Leader*

## HUNGARY

**Lutheran Church in Hungary**

Presiding Bishop Dr. Bela Harmati, H-1088 Budapest, Puskin U. 12, H-1447 Budapest, POB 500. Phone 011-36-1-338-2302 or 011-36-1-338-4744, FAX 011-36-1-338-2302 *Sec. for Foreign Relations* Mrs. Margit Szirmai Phone/Fax: 011-36-1-266-5532 E-mail:south.district@lutheran.hu

## INDIA

**India Evangelical Lutheran Church**

Rev Isaac Moon, No 2 Fifteenth East Cross, Gandi Nager Vellore 632 006, Tamil Nadu India, Phone 011-91-416-43602 Office, 011-91-416-53654 Home, IELC Central Business Office, Lutheran Mission Compound, Nagercoil 629001, Tamil Nadu, India

CONCORDIA SEMINARY

Rev T Joy *Principal*, Nagercoil 629001, Tamil Nadu India , Phone 011-91-4652-22380

**The Lutheran Centre**

Rev S Alfred, Marve Road Malad, Bombay 400 064, India, Phone 011-91-22-882-3301

**Lutheran Hospital Compound**

Miss Alice Brauer RN *Missionary Nurse*, Vellore 635 802 Tamil Nadu, India, Phone 011-91-4174-43777, FAX 011-91-4176-43265

**IELC-Trivandrum Synod Office**

Lutheran Centre, Concordia Lutheran Church Compound, Perurkada, Trivandrum-695005, Kerala State, India

**IELC-Nagercoil Synod Office**

Lutheran Mission Compound, Nagercoil-6290001, K.K. Dist., Tamil Nadu State, India

**IELC-Ambur Synod Office**

Mission Compound, Ambur-635802 N.A.A. Dist., Tamil Nadu State, India

## JAMAICA

**Lutheran Ministries in Jamaica**

1 Morecambe Ave #1, PO Box 1085 Kingston 8 Jamaica West Indies, Phone 1-876-969-7651, FAX 1-876-925-3179.
E-Mail: Kirbypn@cwjamaica.com
Rev Peter Kirby *Missionary Counselor*
Rev James Weist *Evangelistic Missionary*
Mrs Carla Kirby, *Business Manager*
Mr Lumembo Tshiswaka, *Council Chairman*

## JAPAN

**Japan Lutheran Church**

2-32 Fujimi, 1-Chome, Chiyoda-ku, Tokyo 102-0071 Japan, Phone 011-81-3-3261-5266, FAX 011-813-3262-7759
Rev Kimio Takano *President*
Rev Chuzo Kitazawa *Vice President*
Rev Yutaka Kumei *Treasurer*
Mr Takashi Yuguchi *Secretary*
Rev Yutaka Kumei *General Secretary, Adm*
Rev Masahiro Ando *General Secretary Missions*, 2-32 Fujimi, 1-Chome, Chiyoda-ku, Tokyo 102-0071 Japan
Rev Richard E Nelson *Missionary Counselor*
Ms Jenny Koenig *OVYM Contact*

***Theological Training Program***

3-10-20 Osawa Mitaki-shi, Tokyo 181-0015 Japan
Dr Masao Shimodate ThD *President*

*JAPAN LUTHERAN HOUR*

Mr Takashi Yuguchi, 3-2 Higashi-Ikebukuro 5-Chome, Toshima-ku, Tokyo 170-0013 Japan, Phone 011-81-3-5954-7879, FAX 011-81-3-5954-7889

ST PAUL INTERNATIONAL LUTHERAN CHURCH

Rev Thomas Going, *Interim Pastor* 1-2-32 Fujimi Chiyoda Ku, Tokyo 102-0071 Japan
Jane Webb, *Treasurer*

**Okinawa Lutheran Church**

Rev Michael Nearhood, 362 Aza-Shimabuku, Kitanakagusuku-Son, Nakagami-gun, 901-2301, Okinawa Japan Phone and FAX 011-81-98-933-5535

## KAZAKSTAN

**RORC-LCMS in KAZ**

**Evangelical Lutheran Ministry**

Republic of Kazakstan, 480091 Almaty, Kazibek Bl 78 Admin office Phone 011-7-3272-32-17-08 or 32-18-85, FAX 011-7-3272-32-02-82
*Missionaries:* Mrs Amy & Marat Kashenov, Rev Roland Meyle, Mr Darren and Irina Schieman, Rev Larry and Mary Steckling

**Evangelical Lutheran Center/Synod**

President: Mikhail Eliseev
Phone: same as above

## KOREA

**Lutheran Church in Korea**

Mailing Address: CPO Box 1239 Seoul 100-612 Korea, Phone 011-822-414-7430, FAX 011-822-418-7457

***Lutheran Church Center***

7-20 Sinchun-Dong, Songpa-Gu, Seoul 138-240 Korea E-mail lck0001@chollian.net
Rev Song Huh, *President*
Rev In-Bong IM, *Vice-president*
Rev Hong-Yul Lee, Korean *Secretary*
Rev Young-Bok Han, English *Secretary*
Rev Evn-Seob Kim *Treasurer*
Rev Dr Hilbert Riemer *International Correspondent*

**Luther Theological University**

17 Sanggalli, Kiheungeub Yonginkun, Kyunggido 449-900 Korea, Phone 011-82-331-283-3593, FAX 011-82-331-283-1505
Rev Dr Hilbert Riemer *President*, Phone 011-82-331-283-3593 (office) (home tel. & fax) 011-82-331-283-6197

## LATVIA

**Evangelical Lutheran Church of Latvia**

M Pills iela, 4, 1050 Riga, Latvia, Phone: 011-371-722-6057, 011-371-722-9484 FAX: 011-371-782-0041, E-Mail: konsistorija@parks.lv
Archbishop: Most Rev Janis Vanags, DD, E-Mail: vanags@lanet.lv
ILLL office: Fax: 011-371-9-342-436
Latvia Bible Society: FAX: 011-371-786-0041

## LEBANON

**Middle East Lutheran Ministry**

PO Box 60-307, Jal El-Dib, Beirut Lebanon,
Phone 011-961-4-716-272,
FAX 011-961-4-724-312
Mobile Phone: 011-961-3-387797
E-Mail: melm@dm.net.lb
Web Site: http://www.melm.org.lb
Mr Moris A Jahshan *Director*

## LIBERIA

**Evangelical Lutheran Mission (ELM)**

Rev David Londenberg, Mission Evangélique Luthérienne en Afrique B.P. 216 Tabou, Côte d' Ivoire, West Africa

## LITHUANIA

**Lithuanian Evangelical Lutheran Church**

Vaizganto 50, LT-5900 Taurage, Lithuania, Office Phone 370-46-61406 and Fax: 011-370-46-61406
Bishop: The Rt Reverend Jonas Kalvanas

## MEXICO

**Lutheran Synod of Mexico**

Playa Manzanillo No 530, Mexico DF Mexico, Phone 011-525-633-82-56 or 547-70-27
Rev Samuel Perez Gaona *President*, Calle Rio San Juan y 16 No 53, Colonia San Francisco, Matamoros, Tamaulipas, Mexico, Phone 011-5288123613
Rev Federico Resendiz *Treasurer*
Rev Abiut Fajardo Ruiz *Secretary*,
Rev Jaziel E Lopez *Vice President*

**Lutheran Center of Mexico City**

Apdo Postal 20-416, 54 Calle de la Otra Banda, Colonia San Angel, Mexico City DF 01000, Phone 011-525-616-1121, FAX 011-525-616-1246
Rev David Brondos *Missionary Counselor*, Apartado Postal 135-021, Mexico DF 07969-Mexico, Phone/FAX 011-525-551-3651

## NIGERIA

**The Lutheran Church of Nigeria**

PO Box 49, Obot Idim Ibesikpo Uyo, Akwa Ibom State, Nigeria West Africa
Rev Samuel Udofia *President*
Phone 011-234-85-200505 (Office)
011-234-85-203809 or 011-234-85-204525 (Res)
Rev J E Utin *Vice President*
Mr Nkeveuwem *Secretary*
Mrs Ibiatke J Asuk *Treasurer*

***Jonathan Ekong Memorial Lutheran Seminary***

PO Box 33, Obot Idim Ibesikpo Uyo Akwa Ibom State, Nigeria West Africa, Dr Nelson Unwene, *Principal*

**Missionary Support Committee**

Mr Brent Fredericks *Business Manager*—PO Box 495, Jos Nigeria West Africa 011-234-73-53460
Hillcrest School, PO Box 652 13 Old Bukuru Road, Jos Plateau State Nigeria West Africa, Phone and FAX 011-234-73-55410
Rev Charles Tessaro, Missionary Support Committee, PO Box 1782, Uyo Akwa Ibom State, Nigeria West Africa

## PANAMA

**Panama Mission Team**

(AMLPA), Apartado Postal 2070, Balboa/Ancon Panama, Republic of Panama, Phone 011-507-228-4564, FAX 011-507-228-5742
Jerona de Preston *Office Manager*
Rev Michael Nemec, *Evangelist Missionary*
Rev Marcos Sonntag (IELB), *Evangelist Missionary*

## PAPUA NEW GUINEA

**Gutnius Lutheran Church**

PO Box 111, Wabag Enga Province Papua New Guinea, Phone 011-675-547-1002, FAX 011-675-547-1002
*Bishop* Rev David Piso

***Timothy Lutheran Seminary***

PO Box 381 Wabag Enga Province Papua New Guinea, Rev Dani Kopa *Principal*, Phone/FAX 011-675-547-1059

MARTIN LUTHER SEMINARY

PO Box 80 Lae Papua New Guinea, Rev Dr Z Kemung Phone 011-675-472-2699

HIGHLANDS LUTHERAN SCHOOL

PO Box 363 Wabag Enga Province Papua New Guinea, Phone 011-675-547-1235, FAX 011-675-547-1235

CONCORDIA LUTHERAN PROFESSIONAL MISSION SERVICES

Dr Stephen Lutz, acting *Missionary Counselor*, PO Box 363 Wabag Enga Province Papua New Guinea, Phone/FAX 011-675-547-1059

IMMANUEL LUTHERAN HOSPITAL

Dr Stephen Lutz, PO Box 363 Wabag, Enga Province Papua New Guinea, Phone 011-675-547-4098

## PARAGUAY

**The Evangelical Lutheran Church of Paraguay Iglesia Evangelica Luterana de Paraguay (IELPA)**

*President*, Rev Eugenio Wagner, Honehau II, Itapua 011-595-676-20082
*First Vice President*, Rev Alceu/Figur
*Second Vice President*, Rev Eugenio Wentzel
*Secretary*, Rev Luis Ruschel
*Vice Secretary*, Mr Werner Brandt

*Treasurer,* Mr. Airton Schmidt
*Vice Treasurer,* Mr Paulo Tomm

## PHILIPPINES

**The Lutheran Church in the Philippines**

Headquarters: Lutheran Building, 4461 Old Santa Mesa, Sampaloc Manila Philippines, Mailing Address: PO Box 507, 1099 Manila Philippines, Phone 011-632-715-70-84, FAX 011-632-714-2395

Rev Eduardo Ladlad *President,* Phone 011-63-63-517-525

Mr Excelso Hipe LCP *Business Manager/Treasurer*

LUTHERAN SEMINARY

8 South Drive, PO Box 16, Baguio City 2600 Philippines, Phone 011-6374-442-4127

Dr Jose B Fuliga *Dean,* Phone 011-63-74-442-3995

**Missionary Support Office**

Manilla Office Davao Office Corner Oak & Mars St, GSIS, Matina Heights, 8000 Davao FAX 011-632-921-5163

Mailing Address: PO Box 2258-1162, QCCPO 1100 Quezon City Philippines

Rev Donald Treglown *Missionary Counselor,* Mailing Address PO Box 81039, 8000 Davao City Philippines

## POLAND

**Evangelical Lutheran Church of The Augsburg Confession in Poland**

ul. Miodowa 21, 00-246 Warsaw, Poland, Phone: 011-48-22-831-51-87, Phone: 011-48-22-831-94-58, FAX: 011-48-22-831-23-48

Bishop: Rev Jan Szarek
E-Mail: konsystorz@luteranie.pl

## PUERTO RICO

**La Mission Luterana de Puerto Rico**

PO Box 3085, Mayaguez PR 00681, Phone (787) 833-5979, FAX (787) 831-2677 E-Mail: luterano@caribe.net

Rev Angel Perez *Missionary Counselor*

**Puerto Rico - Mayaguez**

Príncipe de Paz Lutheran Church

Calle Jose de Diego #115 E Mayaguez PR 00680 Phone (787) 833-5979 FAX (787) 831-2677 E-Mail: luterano@caribe.net

**Puerto Rico - Ponce**

Alientu de Vida PO Box 690, Mercedita, PR 00715, E-Mail: dcwoolsey@centennialpr.net

Rev David C Woolsey *Missionary,* (787) 844-7053, (787) 841-8378

## RUSSIA

**Evangelical Lutheran Ministries—St Petersburg**

18 Sredniy Prospect VO, St Petersburg 199004 Russia

Mailing Address: RELM (Missionary's Name) PO Box 729 St. Petersburg 1999397 RUSSIA

Phone 011-7-812-218-0477, FAX 011-7-812-850-1426, E-Mail: lcmsspb@neva.spb.ru

*Regional Team Leader:* Rev Douglas Reinders

**Evangelical Lutheran Ministries—Moscow**

(Missionary's Name) PO Box 76 International Post Office; 37 Varshavskoye Shosse 131000 Moscow RUSSIA

Phone 011-7-812-218-0417 FAX 0117-512-850-1426

E-Mail: lcmsmos@glasnet.ru

Rev John Mehl *Missionary*

**Evangelical Lutheran Ministries—Novosibirsk**

Kolivanskaya 8 KV24 Novosibirsk 63007, Russia

Mailing address: c/o Mr. Ken Reiner, LCMS World Mission, 1333 South Kirkwood Road, St. Louis MO 63122

Phone/FAX 011-3832-465-461
E-mail: lutheran@cdland.nsk.ru
*Regional Team Leader:* Rev Jeff Thormodson

**Evangelical Lutheran Ministries—Nizhniy Novgorod**

ul Gorkogo 149a KV44, Nizhniy Novgorod 603006, Russia

Mailing Address: c/o Mr Ken Reiner, LCMS World Mission, 1333 South Kirkwood Road, St. Louis MO 63122

Phone/Fax: 011-7-831-235-4607
E-Mail: nnrelm@relm.nnov.ru

## SIERRA LEONE

**Evangelical Lutheran Mission**

Direct all communication to Rev Ken Greinke, LCMS—BFMS, 1333 South Kirkwood Road, St Louis, MO 63122-7295, Phone 314-965-9000, FAX 314-965-0959

## SLOVAKIA

**The Evangelical Church of the Augsburg Confession in Slovakia**

OFFICE OF THE GENERAL BISHOP (GBU)

Palisády 46, 811-06 Bratislava Slovakia, Phone 011-4217-5330-827 and 011-4217-5332-842, FAX 011-4217-5330-500, Mail PO Box 289, 810 00 Bratislava

E-mail: evangelical@evangelical.sk
Website: http://www.evangelical.sk/

Dr Július Filo ThD *General Bishop*
Jan Holcik *General Inspector*
Ivan Osusky *Bishop*-Western District
Jan Midriak *Bishop*-Eastern District
Dr Daniela Zemlová *Foreign Secretary*

EVANGELICAL THEOLOGICAL FACULTY

Svoradova 1, 811 03 Bratislava Solvakia, Phone/FAX 011-4217-531-1140, E-mail: sd@fevth.uniba.sk, Igor Kiss *Dean*

LUTHERAN HOUR OFFICE

PO Box 104, 814 99 Bratislava Slovakia, Phone/FAX 011-4217-5332-861, Viola Fronková *Director*

AGAPÉ-CENTER OF EVANGELICAL DIAKONIA

Prostredná 37, 900 21 Svaty Jur Slovakia, Phone 011-4217-4497-1475 and 011-4217-4497-1338, Anna Filová *Director*

TRANOSCIUS PUBLISHING HOUSE

Tranovského 1, 031 01 Liptovsky Mikulas Slovakia, Phone/FAX 011-421-849-230-70, L'ubomir Michna *Director*

EVANGELICAL GYMNASIUM

Zvolenská cesta 14, 974 01 Banská Bystrica Slovakia, Phone 011-421-88-601-490, Emilia Remiarová *Director*

EVANGELICAL LYCEUM

Vranovská 2, 851 02 Bratislava Slovakia, Phone 011-4217-838-488, Dr L'udovit Kuruc *Director*

J A COMENIUS GYMNASIUM

Galaktická 9, 040 01 Kosice Slovakia, Phone 011-421-95-746-240, Ján Kunc *Director*

EVANGELICAL GRAMMAR SCHOOL

Janoskova 5, 031 01 Liptovski Mikulás Slovakia, Phone 011-421-849-514 073, Eva Raducká *Director*

EVANGELICAL GYMNASIUM

Nám. Legionárov 3, 080 01 Presov Slovakia, Phone 011-421-91-721-401, Dr Anna Pribulová *Director*

EVANGELICAL GYMNASIUM

Jesenského 836, 980 61 Tisovec Slovakia, Phone 011-421-865-932-00, Dr Helena Pasiaková *Director*

## SOUTHERN AFRICA

**(South Africa/Botswana/Swaziland)**
**REPUBLIC OF SOUTH AFRICA**

**Lutheran Church in Southern Africa**

PO Box 1424, 8 Henry St, 1459 Parkdene Republic of South Africa, Phone and FAX 011-27-11-917-4165 E-Mail: LCSA@hixnet.co.za

Rev David Tswaedi *Bishop,* Phone 011-27-11-917-4139, other phone 011-27-11-973-1853, FAX 011-27-11-917-6108
E-Mail: LCSAB@netactive.co.za

Deputy Bishop: Rev A M Lemkwe PO Box 14 2710 Ventersdorp Republic of South Africa Phone 011-27-18-26-42425

ENHLANHLENI Lutheran Seminary

PO Box 11, 3020 Pomeroy, Republic of South Africa

Rev R P Ntsimane *Principal,* Phone 011-27-34-642-1637 (Home)

Dr Edward W Weber Box 11 Romeroy 3020 Republic of South Africa Phone 011-27-34-642-1836

**Mission of Lutheran Churches**

#89 Sophia Street PO Box 73377, Fairland 2030, Republic of South Africa, Phone 011-27-11-678-0522, FAX 011-27-11-678-0522

Rev Edmund Hohls *LKM* Representative, Phone 011-27-11-678-3455 (Home)

**Free Evangelical Lutheran Synod in South Africa (FELSISA)**

331 Eastwood Str, Arcadia, 0083 Pretoria, Republic of South Africa, Phone and Fax: 011-27-12-3441202

President: Rev Peter Ahlers
E-Mail:felsisa@pixie.co.za
Business phone: 011-27-12-344-2918
Fax: 011-27-12-344-1202
Home phone: 011-27-12-344-2889
Vice President: Rev Siegfried Kohne

**Durban, South Africa**
**St. Thomas Lutheran Church**

139 Spoorlyn Rd Westcliff/Chatsworth

Sunday worship: 9:00 a.m.
Missionary Allen Konrad
Parsonage Phone/FAX 27-31-705-9718
E-Mail: onamission@eastcoast.co.za

## BOTSWANA

**Lutheran Church in Southern Africa**
**Botswana Diocese**

PO Box 1424, Boksburg 1460, Republic of South Africa

Rev David Tswaedi *Bishop*
*Dean* (Vacant)

## SWAZILAND

## SRI LANKA

**Sri Lanka Lutheran Mission**

Vacant *Missionary Counselor,* Colombo Center, 410/18 Bullers Rd, Colombo 7 Sri Lanka,
Phone 011-94-1-691023, FAX 011-94-1-691023

**Lanka Lutheran Church Center**

Rev M Sathiyanathan *President,* 53 Mt Mary Rd, Nuwara Eliya Sri Lanka, Phone 011-94-052-2975, FAX 011-94-52-3093 call 2975

**Colombo Lutheran Center/Immanuel Lutheran Church**

116A Layards Broadway, Colombo 14, Sri Lanka, Phone 011-94-1-439856

**Concordia Welfare and Education Society (CWES)**

Vacant, *Director,* 410/18 Bullers Rd, Colombo 7 Sri Lanka, Phone FAX 011-94-1-691023

## TAIWAN

**China Evangelical Lutheran Church**

4th Floor, #127 Sec 1 Fu Hsing S Rd, Taipei 10639, Taiwan ROC, Phone 011-8862-772-4673 or 2-772-8435, FAX 011-886-2-7724673

Executive Committee

Yi Jen-Yang *Chairman*
Wu Ming-hui *Treasurer*
Wang Mau-hsiung *Secretary*

The Legal Corporation

Lin Ah-Lien *Chairman*
Lin Chau-dzung *Secretary*
Wang Mau-hsiung *Treasurer*
Yangli-ju (Lisa) *Secretary/Headquarters*

TAIWAN OVERSEAS VOLUNTEER YOUTH MINISTRY

Kenneth James Boudreau *Director,* #32 Hang Chou, 2nd Street, Chia Yi 60035, Taiwan ROC, Phone 011-8-865-236-6081, FAX 011-8-865-236-6082

CONCORDIA MIDDLE SCHOOL

Mr Kenneth Chen *Principal,* Chien Kuo Rd, Sec 2 #31 Min-Hsiung Chia-Yi 621, Taiwan ROC, Phone 011-886-5-226-8047, FAX 011-886-5-220-0551

Kurt Buchholz, Chien Kuo Road, Sec. 2 #31 Min Hsiung Chi Yi 621, Phone 011-886-5-220-2875, FAX 011-886-5-221-0523

CHINA LUTHERAN SEMINARY

Dr Thomas Yu *Principal,* #11 Lane 51 Ta Hsueh Road, Hsin Chu 300, Taiwan ROC, Phone 011-886-3-571-0023

Rev Jeffrey A Oschwald, Ta Hsueh Road, Number 82 19-4, Hsinchu 300 Taiwan ROC

## THAILAND

**Concordia Gospel Ministry**

205/20 Chaiyakiat 1, Ngam Wong Wan Road Bangkok 10210 Thailand, Phone 011-66-2-589-6715, FAX 011-66-2-589-7821
E-mail: oratai@mozart.inet.co.th

MISSIONARY TEAM

Mr Tim Miller *Missionary,* Phone/ FAX 011-66-2-503-6644, E-mail: tmiller@ksc.th.com
DCS Christie Nelson
E-mail: christie@mozart.inet.co.th
Rev Mark Schultz E-mail:
schultzs@cscoms.com
Vicar Jeff Pautz

## TOGO

**Eglise Mission Luthérienne au Togo**

BP 38 Dapaong Togo West Africa
Missionary Advisory Committee
Rev John Palka *Senior Missionary*
Phone and FAX 011-228-708071

## UGANDA

**Evangelical Lutheran Mission in Uganda**

PO Box 290, Jinja, Uganda East Africa
President Mr Joshua J. L. Kalamawo
Evangelist: Mr John Shadrack Donkoh
Phone: 011-256-043-22186, Fax: 011-256-43-22186
Second office

**Evangelical Lutheran Mission in Uganda**

P.O. Box 21645, Kampala, Uganda, East Africa

## URUGUAY

Montevideo Congregación Evangélica Luterana San Pablo, Pastores: Christian Hoffmann y Mauro Ricardo Roll, Venancio Benavidez 3616, Código Postal 11.700. *Director General:* ULBRA-Colegio y Liceo San Pablo, Rev Mauro Ricardo Roll. Teléfonos: Casa Pastoral-Phone: 011-598-2-336-3669. Colegio y Liceo San Pablo-Phone and Fax: 011-598-2-336-4914

## VENEZUELA

**Lutheran Church of Venezuela**

Rev Alcides Franco *President,* Urbanizacion Colinas de Bello Monte, 1041 Avenida Caurimare Quinta Lutero, Caracas, Venezuela, Phone FAX 011-58-2-89-20-67 Phone 011-58-2-753-6031; 753-4683, FAX 011-58-2-753-4683

**Sociedad Luterana de Evangelizacion en Venezuela (SLEV)**

Headquarters, Avenida Caurimare Quinta Lutero Colinas de Bello Monte Caracas 1041 Venezuela, Phone 011-58-2-753-6031, Phone/FAX 011-58-2-753-4683

Mailing Address Books Apdo Postal 60387 Chacao, Caracas 1060-A Venezuela

Letters (Missionary Name) C-555 1408 NW 82nd Ave Miami, FL 33126-1508

**Missionary Council in Venezuela**

Sociedad Luterana Evangelizacion en Venezuela
Mr Mark Kempff *Missionary Counselor*
E-mail: kempffmr@telcel.net.ve
*Business Manager* Donald Ellcey
E-mail: slevvenz@telcel.net.ve

# CAMPUS MINISTRIES

**Rev. Richard Manus, Counselor for Campus Ministry**

The following list identifies by state, city, and school those campuses served by pastors or other professional workers of the Synod. In the margin, full-time campus ministries are identified by a bullet (•), part-time by a bar (–), and contact pastors by a dagger (†). Addresses and telephone numbers for campus workers are included in the respective Annual listings.

## United States

### Alabama

• *Auburn* U Edward Hornig 205/887-3901
† *Birmingham* Miles C Samford U Michael Johnson 205/251-3451
† U of Ala Birmingham Kurtis Schulz 205/933-0380
† Howard U Thomas Noon
† *Florence* U St JC Gary Faith 205/546-1712
† *Huntsville* U of Ala Bernard Ansorge 205/536-9987
– Alabama A & M Vacant
† *Jacksonville* St U Gary Faith 205/546-1712
† *Livingston* U Phillip Wottrich 601/483-5457
† *Mobile* U of S Ala Vacant
† *Montgomery* Auburn U C Paul Elam 205/272-6214
† Ala St U James Wiggins 205/262-4326
– *Selma* Concordia College David DeRamus 205/874-5700
† Selma U Steven Washington 205/875-9108
– *Tuscaloosa* U of Ala Vacant 205/752-8784
† *Tuskegee* Institute Edward Hornig 205/887-3901
† *Troy* Troy State U Kirk Miller 205/774-6758

### Alaska

*Anchorage* U of AK Rev Richard Rist, *Fairbanks,* U of AK 907/338-3838
Phil Kuehnert 907/456-7660

### Arizona

† *Bisbee* Cochise CC Emil Dinkel 520/432-5504
† *Bullhead City* Mohave CC Vacant 520/758-2301
† *Clarkdale* Yavapai C (Satellite) Michael Vahle 520/634-7876
† *Flagstaff* No Arizona U Warren Ueckert 520/526-9578
† *Glendale* Glendale CC Loel Haak 623/934-3286
† *Kingman* Mohave CC John Jaster 520/757-3625
† *Mesa* Mesa CC John Hollmann, DCE 602/969-4414
† *Phoenix* Glendale CC DeVry Inst of Tech Loel Haak 623/934-8286
† *Prescott* Embry-Riddle Aero U Prescott C Yavapai CC
• *Tempe* Ariz St U Lee Meyer 480/894-2610

### Arkansas

† *Batesville* Arkansas College Paul Mehl 870/793-3073
† *Clarksville* C of Ozarks
† *Conway* U of Cent Ark Carl Groh 501/329-3854
† *El Dorado* JC Rev Wayne Pick 870/862-1443
• *Fayetteville* U of Ark Roger Schoolcraft 501/443-3609
† *Fort Smith* West Ark CC
† *Jonesboro* Ark St U Russell Shewmaker 870/935-2001
† *Little Rock* U of Ark Med School James Walter 501/663-3631
† *Russellville* Ark Tech Darrell Kobs 501/968-1309

### California

† *Aptos* Cabrillo C Stan Abraham 408/475-6962
• *Arcata* Humboldt St C Carl Stenzel 707/822-5117
† *Blythe* Palo Verde C Gerald Hoemann 760/922-7321
† *Calexico* San Diego U Allen Deinert 619/344-1635
† *Claremont* Claremont McKenna C Harvey Mudd C Pomona C Scripps C Joel Shaltamis 909/623-6368
† *Chula Vista* Southwestern C Michael Beyer 619/482-1214
† *Cuyamaca* Cuyamaca CC John Ehlke 619/670-7174
† *Davis* U of CA Daniel A Schlensker 503/758-4546
† *El Centro* Imperial Valley CC UCSD Partnership Allen Deinert 760/356-4315
† *Glendale* JC John Hodde 818/243-3119
† *Hayward* Cal St C Gary Mohr 510/782-0872
† *Imperial* Valley Allen Deinert 760/356-4315
† *Irvine* U of Cal Irvine vacant 949/786-3326
– Concordia U Steve Borst & Dennis Denow 714/854-8002
† Irvine Valley JC Jerrold Nichols 714/786-3326
† *Kentfield* C of Marin Vacant
† *Long Beach* Cal St C Long Beach City C Brandon Jones 562/596-4409
† *Los Angeles* U of Cal (UCLA) Tim Seals 213/740-2669
• U of S Cal Tim Seals 213/740-2669
† Occident C Chris Schaar 626/793-1139
† Montebello Cal St U at LA E LA CC Doug Jones 310/692-6100
† *Mission Viejo* Saddleback JC Tom Rogers 714/830-1460
† *Moorpark* JC Jim Nelesen 805/532-1049
† *Oceanside* Mira Costa C Duane Behnken 619/433-2770
† *Orange* Chapman C Tim Klingenberg 714/288-4400
† *Palm Desert* C of the Desert Robert Smith 619/317-3971
† *Palo Alto* Stanford U Pastor Steward Crown 605/853-1295
† *Pasadena* CC Cal Tech Fuller Seminary Barry Foerster 626/793-1139
† *Ridgecrest* Cerro Coso CC Robert Hoffman 619/375-7921
† *Riverside* Riverside CC U of CA Paul Stark 909/684-6446
† U of CA at Riverside Paul Stark 909/684-6446
† *Sacramento* CC American River C Vacant 916/725-4550
† *San Bernardino* CA St U at SB Eugene Fenton 909/882-2989 Rev Mark McKenzie 909/825-5952
† *San Diego* Balboa Naval Train Hosp Tom Bunnett 619/299-2890
† Mesa JC 619/743-2478
† Miramar C Stewart Reimnitz 619/583-1436
† National U SD St U Paul Willweber 619/583-1436
† Point Loma C
† SD CC George Gunter 619/576-0006
• San Diego St US Int'l U Brian Hooper 619/453-0561
† San Marcos USD/San Marcos Beryl Droege-mueller
† *San Francisco* San Francisco State Daniel Woo 650/991-4673
– *San Jose* St U Cal St U Timothy Gerdes 408/292-5404
– *San Luis Obispo* Cal Poly St U Chris Molnar 805/543-8327
– *Santa Cruz* U of Cal Tim Jhessen 831/423-8330
† *Santa Monica* Santa Monica CC Ardon Albrecht 310/498-4813
† *Stockton* U of Pacific John Glover 209/957-8750
† *Thousand Oaks* Luther C Elroi Reimnitz 805/498-4813
† *Turlock* Stanislaus St C Ron Youngdale 209/667-7712
† *Ventura* Ventura C Benedict Yaspelkis 805/642-2267
† *Whittier* Whittier C Robert Schroeder 562/699-7431
† *Yucaipa* Crafton Hills C Phil Pledger 909/947-9313

### Colorado

† *Alamosa* Adams State C Karl Wright 719/589-4611
† *Boulder* U of Colo Robert Stuenkel 303/443-8720
† *Colorado Springs* Colo C DuWayne Kirkeide & Timothy Moses 719/633-7661
† CU the Springs Michael Flannery 719/632-9394
† Pikes Peak CC Ronald Baker 719/632-9394
† USAF Acad Robert Schaibley 719/548-7446
† *Denver* CC of Denver/Metro State Coll Roger Schlechte 303/433-3303
† U of CO-Denver Henry Corcoran 303/733-3777
† Loretto Heights James Bauer 303/934-2103
† Metro Roger Schlechte 303/433-3303
† U of Denver William Kohlmeier 303/722-1424
† U of Co Health Sciences ICU Med Vacant 303/388-9347
† Regis University Norbert Miles 303/455-5878
† *Durango* Ft Lewis C Tim Evers 970/247-0357
† *Ft Collins* Colo St U Eugene Brueggemann & Mark Gabbert DCE 970/482-5316
– *Ft Morgan* Fort Morgan CC Vacant 970/867-5721
† *Glenwood Springs* Colo MT Allen Anderson 970/945-6871
† *Golden* Colo Sch of Mines Dwight Hellmers 303/233-5658
† *Grand Junction* Mesa C Gary Buss & Bruce Skelton 970/245-2838
† *Greeley* U of No Colo Craig Bertram & Darrin Kohrt 970/353-2554
† Alms CC William Keller 970/330-1203
† *Gunnison* W St C C Craig Petersen 970/943-2135
† *La Junta* Otera JC Robert Kunz 719/384-6555
† *Lamar* Lamar David Rutter 719/336-5500
† *Littleton* Arapaho CC Arnold Voigt 303/794-4636

† *Pueblo* U of So Colo Christopher Kellogg 719/544-5269
† *Rangely* Colo NW CC Roger Sterle 970/675-8138
† *Sterling* Northeastern Colo JC Michael Paulison 970/522-5942

## Connecticut

† *Bridgeport* Sacred Heart U 203/268-7555
† *Danbury* W Conn St C Daniel Wehmeier 203/748-3320
† *Fairfield* U Emil Witschy 203/268-7555
† *Farmington* U of Conn Med Sch Carl Anton 860/521-5076
† *Manchester* CC Rev Henry Lubben 860/649-4243
† *Middletown* Wesleyan U Vacant 860/346-2641
† *New Haven* Yale S Conn St U of New Haven John Schettenhelm 203/795-3916
† *New London* Conn C USCG Acad Mitchell C Craig Donofrio 860/444-6529
– *Storrs* U of Conn Philip Secker 860/429-5409
† *Tunxis* CC H Lane Bridges 860/583-5649
† *Willimantic* Eastern Conn St U Scott Schuett 860/423-4320

## Delaware

† *Dover* Del St C Wesley C Arthur Kringel 302/734-7078
† *Newark* U of Del Carl Kruelle 302/787-6176

## District of Columbia

† *Washington* American U Georgetown U
– Gallaudet U for Deaf George Natonick 202/651-5102

## Florida

† *Babson Park* Webber C John V Glamann 941/676-4715
† *Boca Raton* Fla Atlantic U Dennis Glick 561/395-0433
† *Daytona Beach* Aero Inst Embry-Riddle Rev Fredrick Schultz 904/255-7589
† *Ft Myers* Fla Gulf Coast U Steve Graebner 941/394-0332
• *Gainesville* U of Fla Timothy Hinz 904/376-2062
† *Jacksonville* Fla CC Richard Engel 904/928-9136
† Jacksonville U John Bucheimer 904-249-5418
† *Lake Worth* Palm Beach CC Clarence Reinke Jr 561/582-4430
† *Ocala* Cent Fla CC Richard Lineberger 352/629-1794
– *Orlando* U of Central Fla Paul W von Werder 407/657-4556
† *Pensacola* Pensacola JC U of W FL Craig Bickel 904/476-5667
† *St Petersburg* CC Eckerd C Mark Couch 727/344-2684
• *Tallahassee* Fla A&M Fla State Tallahassee CC Thomas Dohrman 850/224-6059
† *Tampa* U of T/U of S Fla Lee Stisser 813/839-6847

## Georgia

† *Atlanta* Ga Tech Mark Schudde 404/255-0224
• *Athens* U of Ga Edward M Ralph 706/543-3801
† *Rome* Berry C Shorter C John Karch 706/232-7257
– *Statesboro* Ga Southern U Mark Louderback 912/681-2481
† *Valdosta* St U Richard Pieplow 912/244-0143

## Hawaii

† *Hilo* Hi CC Eugene Davidenas 808/935-8612
• *Honolulu* U of Hi Manoa Janelle Dryden 808/941-4040

## Idaho

† *Boise* St U Vacant 208/336-3616
† *Coeur d'Alene* N Idaho JC Dennis Lorenz 208/664-9231
*Lewiston* Lewis & Clark SC
– *Moscow* U of Idaho Dudley Nolting 208/466-6746
† *Nampa* NW Nazarene C Michael Schumacher 208/466-6746

## Illinois

† *Aurora* C Jock Ficken 630/820-3450
† *Bloomington* Ill Wesleyan U Dymann Jirovec 309/452-5971
† Mennonite Sch of Nursing Thomas Wersing 309/828-0831
† *Canton* Spoon River C Kirk Clayton 309/647-5123
• *Carbondale* S Ill U Robert Gray 618/549-1694
† *Carlinville* Blackburn C Christopher Sheets 217/854-8514
† *Carthage* Robert Morris C Karl Bollhagen 217/256-3215
• *Champaign* U of Ill Rick Milas 217/344-1558
• *Charleston* E Ill U Greg Wittos Rev Doug Fleisch 217/345-3008
† *Chicago* U of Chi Paul Hoemann 312/733-6886
† *Chicago* De Paul Steven Hummel 312/525-4990
† U of Ill Med Ctr Jason Carrier 312/733-6886
† *Chicago Heights* Prairie St CC David Steuernagel 708/754-4493
† *Crystal Lake* McHenry CC Ed Bergen 815/459-1441
† *Decatur* Millikin U William Abbott 217/877-2444
• *De Kalb* N Ill U Michael Thurau 815/756-6669
† *Dixon* Sauk Valley Robert Martinek 815/284-4554
† *East Peoria* Ill Cent C Vernon Bettermann 309/699-5411
– *Edwardsville* SIU Edward Wolfe 618/288-6120
† *Elmhurst* C Mark Bussert 708/832-1649
† *Eureka* C Joseph Murphy 309/467-5477
– *Evanston* Northwest U Victor Van Kanegan 847/328-9454
† *Freeport* Highland CC Willis Schwichtenberg 815/235-1993
† *Galesburg* Carl Sandburg C Knox C Joseph Cassidy III 309/342-7083
† *Greenville* C Jeffrey Nehrt 618/644-0223
† *Jacksonville* Ill C MacMurray C Peter Brechbuhl 217/243-3419
† *Joliet* Lewis C Joliet JC George Klima 815/741-2428
† *Kankakee* CC Martin Haeger 815/932-0312
† *Kewanee* Black Hawk C East Burnell Eckhardt 309/852-2461
† *Lake Forest* Barat C Lake Forest C Richard Schliepsiek 847/234-1868
† *Lebanon* McKendree C Garry McCraken 618/537-2300
† *Lincoln* C Mark Carnahan 217/732-3946
† *Lisle* Ill Benedictine C Art Beyer 708/964-1272
† *Lombard* Devry Inst of Tech Nat'l C of Chiro David Adams 708/629-2515
– *Macomb* W Ill U Michael Burdick 309/833-5483
† *McHenry* CC Tom Acton 815/385-0859
† *Moline* Black Hawk C Rev Kent Umbarger 309/792-0755
† *Monmouth* C Joseph Cassidy III 309/342-7083
† *Naperville* N Cent C Terry McReynolds 708/355-2198
• *Normal* Ill S U Dymann Jirovec 309/452-5971
† *Peoria* Bradley U Midstate C St Francis Nursing Schl Rev Ronold Moritz & Michelle Moorhead 309/676-4609
† *Quincy* U Gem City C Blessing College of Nursing Harold Bender 217/222-8579
• *River Forest* Concordia U Steven Smith 708/771-8300
† *River Grove* Triton C Roger Gallup 708/453-1113
† *Rockford* Rock Valley C Robert Rub 815/397-2227
† *Rock Island* Augustona C Rev Kevin Cramon 309/786-6296
† *Springfield* Lincoln Land CC Springfield C In Ill St John's C Ted Gall 217/528-5232
† Sangamon State Charles Olander 217/529-3307
† *Wheaton* C Scott Bruzek 630/668-0701

## Indiana

† *Anderson* C Mark Whitsett 765/642-2154
• *Bloomington* Indiana U Rich Woelmer 812/336-5387
† *Crawfordsville* Wabash C Al Hellert 765/362-5599
† *Culver* Culver Mil Ac Robert Bartz 219/842-3175
† *Evansville* U of Evansville Ind St U Thomas Wenig 812/476-9991
† *Franklin* C Roger Hubbard 317/736-7849
† *Gary* Indiana U NW Campus James Wetzstein 219/887-5031
– *Greencastle* De Pauw U Alan J Barber 317/653-6995
† *Hammond* Purdue U Paul Speebrecker 219/844-5616
† *Indianapolis* Butler U Indiana Cent C Indiana U Ron May 317/271-9103
† Indiana U/Purdue U Eugene Lauterbach 317/632-1486
† U of Indianapolis William Yates 317/783-2000
† *Marion* Indiana Wesleyan U Mark Carlson 765/662-3092
† *Mishawaka* Bethel C Kenneth Mangelsdorf 219/255-5585
• *Muncie* Ball St U Peter Cage 765/282-2537
† *New Albany* IN U SE Bruce Kischnick 812/944-1267
† *Oakland* OCC Kirk Horstmeyer 812/867-5088
† *Rensselear* St Joseph C Garry Wickert 219-866-7681
† *Richmond* Earlham C Vacant 765/825-4061
† *South Bend* Ind U Campus Daniel Streufert 219/288-8288
† U of Notre Dame Greg Fiechtner 219/271-1050
† *Terre Haute* Ind St Rose Poly Inst St Mary of the Woods C Philip Meyer 812/232-4972
† *Upland* Taylor U Mark E Carlson 765/662-3092
• *Valparaiso* U Daniel Brockopp & David Kehret 219/464-5093
† *Vincennes* U John Duke 812/882-4662
• *West Lafayette* Purdue U James Barton 765/743-2472
† *Zionsville* Marion C John Fiene 317/873-6318

## Iowa

• *Ames* Iowa St U Richard Osslund & Mark Heilman 515/292-5005
† *Ankeny* Des Moines Area CC Ed Grimm 515/964-1250
† *Boone* Des Moines Area CC Lindsay Watkins 515/432-5140
† *Buena Vista* Indian Hill CC Matthew Andersen 515/684-7279
† *Burlington* Southeastern CC Chris Roepke 319/754-4246
– *Cedar Falls* U of N Iowa Tom Ogilvie 319/266-1274
† *Cedar Rapids* Coe C Vacant 319/364-6026
† Kirkwood CC Wayne Schroeder 319/366-1569
† *Clarinda* Iowa Western CC Gary Jaeckle 712/542-3708
† *Clinton* CC Michael Holm 319/242-5328
† *Decorah* Luther C Victor Young 319/442-3393
– *Des Moines* Drake U Steven Olsen & Max Phillips Deacon 515/279-3609
† *Emmetsburg* Iowa Lake CC Dennis Angland 712/852-2367
† *Estherville* JC N Iowa Area CC Iowa Lakes CC Glenn Bohmer 712/362-3237
– *Fayette* Upper IA U Carl Richardson 319/425-3544
† *Fort Dodge* Iowa Cent CC Lyle Hansen 515/573-3174
† *Grinnell* C David Brandt 515/236-6691
† *Indianola* Simpson C Vacant 515/961-4321
• *Iowa City* U of Iowa Wilfred Eckhardt 319/337-3652
† *LeMars* Westmar Teikeo C Larry Fett 712/546-5516
† *Mason City* N Iowa Area CC Frederick Wood 515/423-0438
† *Mount Pleasant* Iowa Wesleyan C Keith Haerer 319/385-8427
† *Oskaloosa* William Penn C Steve Lane 515/573-6546
† *Storm Lake* Buena Vista C Steven Schulz 712/732-5005
– *Waterloo* Hawkeye CC Tom Ogilvie 319/266-1274
† *Waverly* Wartburg C Larry Sipe 319/352-2314
– *Webster City* Iowa Center CC Rev Travis Schmidt 515/832-3043

## Kansas

† *Arkansas City* Cowley Co CC Mark Boxman 316/442-5240
† *Chanute* Neosho Co JC Vacant 316/431-1341
† *Coffeyville* JC Richard Peckman 316/251-2927
*Colby* Colby CC Jack Ferguson 785/462-3497
† *Dodge City* CC Randy Jahnke 316/227-6204
† *El Dorado* Butler Co JC Brian Kohl 316/321-2423
– *Emporia* St U Clarence Marquardt 316/342-3590
† *Fort Scott* JC Larry Block 316/223-3596

- † *Garden City* Garden City CC Leland Jackson 316/276-3110
- † *Great Bend* Barton Co CC Vacant 316/792-6901
- – *Hays* Fort Hays St C Kenton Rohrberg 785/625-2057
- † *Highland* Highland CC Lawrence Boye 785/742-3995
- † *Hutchinson* JC Tom Mendenhall 316/662-5642
- † *Independence* JC Ron Oldenettel 316/332-3300
- † *Iola* Allen Co JC Bruce Kristalyn 316/365-6468
- † *Kansas City* Johnson Co JC Ken Sype 913/345-9700
- † KC JC Jim Cooley Ray Schiefelbein 913/299-6478
- • *Lawrence* U of Kansas Alan Estby 785/843-0620
- • Haskell Light House U Angela Jeppesen 785/841-4809
- † *Liberal* Seward Co JC Rev Andrew Wehling 316/624-5900
- † *McPherson* C Jeff Williams 316/241-1627
- • *Manhattan* Kans St U Rev Eric Wood 785/539-2604
- † *North Newton* Bethel C Ron Gloe 316/283-1441
- † *Ottawa* C John Duran 785/242-1906
- † *Parsons* Labette CC Vacant 316/421-6479
- † *Pittsburg* St U Steve Anderson 316/231-4267
- † *Pratt* PC JC Vacant 316/672-6203
- † *Salina* Kans Wesleyan U Robert Schaedel 785/823-7151
- † *Topeka* Washburn U of Topeka Rev Pete Tremain 785/272-4214
- – *Wichita* St U Susan Crane 316/684-5224
- † *Winfield* Southw C Rick Hathaway 316/221-9460

## Kentucky

- † *Berea* C Roland Bentrup 606/297-1604
- † *Bowling Green* W Ky St U James Betterman & Katherine Tooley 502/843-9595
- † *Danville* Centre C of Ky David Witten 606/236-2970
- † *Hopkinsville* CC James Redmann 502/885-3969
- – *Lexington* Transylvania C U of Ky John Johnson 606/269-6517
- † *Louisville* Catherine Spalding C U of Louisville Donald Garvue 502/458-4451
- – *Middlesboro* Southeast CC Arthur Avery 423/869-4359
- – *Murray* St U Vacant 502/753-6712
- † *Morehead* St U Roland Bentrup 606/297-1604
- † *Owensboro* Brescia C Tim Henning 502/685-0249
- † *Paducah* JC Paul Donner 502/442-8343

## Louisiana

- † *Alexandria* LA C LA St U Walter Schmidt 318/442-4325
- • *Baton Rouge* LA St U Gary Peterson 504/383-2962
- – *Hammond* Southeastern LA U Vacant 504/345-6008
- † *Lafayette* U of SW LA Vacant 318/235-3607
- † *Monroe* Northeast LA St C Eugene Kappeler 318/322-3507
- † *Natchitoches* NW LA U John Karle 318/352-8708
- – *New Orleans* U of New Orleans Southern U of New Orleans Rev Mark Buetow 604/822-6192
- – Tulane U
- † *Shreveport* Centenary C LA St U Wes Toncre 318/636-2310

## Maine

- † *North Windham* St Joseph C Edward Balfour 207/799-5941
- † *Orono* U of Maine Paul Nielsen 207/872-5208
- † *Portland* Law School of Maine U of Southern Maine Westbrook C Edward Balfour 207/799-5941
- † *Waterville* Colby C Paul Nielsen 207/872-5208

## Maryland

- † *Annapolis* St John's C Chesapeake CC US Naval Acad Vacant 410/268-2400
  *Arnold* Anne Arundel CC Vacant 410/268-2400
- † *Baltimore* Essex CC Donald Bendewald 410/488-4445
- † Morgan State Towson St C Vacant 410/825-8770
- † U of Md (Baltimore Co) James Bredeson 410/242-9441
- † *Bowie* St C Allen Behnke 301/262-5475
- † *Chestertown* Washington C Mike Hagebusch 410/778-2744
- † *College Park* U of Md Rudy Kampia 301/277-2302
- † *Rockville* Montgomery Co JC Lester D Stano 301/762-7565
- † *Salisbury* St C Kevin Wackett 410/742-1737
- † *Towson* Goucher C Vacant 410/825-8770
- † *Wye Mills* Chesapeake C Charles Braband 301/643-6545

## Massachusetts

- † *Beverly* Northshore CC Scott Calloway 508/887-5701
- – *Boston* Chamerlayne JC Emerson C Fisher JC Franklin Inst Harvard U Boston U MIT Garland JC Suffolk C Bryant-Stratton Sch Ingo Dutzmann 617/536-8851
  *Bridgewater* St C at Bridgewater
- † *Fitchburg* St C Phillip Alexander 508/343-7397
- † *Gardner* Mount Wachusett CC R M Hintze 617/874-2479
- † *Haverhill* Northern Essex CC Scott Calloway 508/887-5701
- † *Milton* Curry C Benjamin Ball 617/326-1346
- † *North Andover* Merrimack C Scott Calloway 508/887-5701
- † *Wellesley* Babson C Benjamin Ball 617/326-1346
- † *Westfield* SC Michael Gruel 413/567-1417

## Michigan

- † *Adrian* C Siena Heights C Paul Herter 517/263-4317
- † *Allendale* Grand Valley St C Richard Heller 616/895-4826
- † *Alpena* CC David Nickel 517/354-3443
- • *Ann Arbor* Concordia U Randy Shields 313/434-5221
- • *Ann Arbor* U of Mich Washtenaw CC David Winningham 313/663-5560
- – *Auburn Hts* Oakland CC Fred Traugott 810/528-9340
- † *Battle Creek* Kellogg CC Paul Naumann 616/327-7832
- • *Big Rapids* Ferris C Vacant 616/796-5593
- † *Centreville* Glen Oaks CC Kurt Kuhlmann 616/489-5539
- – *Dearborn* U of Mich Fred Traugott 810/528-9340
- – *Detroit* U of Detroit Wayne St U Fred Traugott 810/528-9340
- • *East Lansing* Mich St U David Dressel 517/332-0778
- – *Farmington* Oakland CC-Orchard Ridge Campus Fred Traugott 810/528-9350
- † *Grand Rapids* Aquinas C Dave Davis 616/454-3655
- † Calvin C Vacant 616/455-5320
- – *Hancock* Suomi C David Weber 906/482-4750
- † *Harrison* Mid-Mich CC Warren W Graff 517/539-6312
- † *Hillsdale* C L Daniel Johnson 517/437-2762
- † *Holland* Hope C John Westra 616/392-7151
- – *Houghton* Mich Tech David Weber 906/482-4750
- † *Interlochen* Arts Acad Timothy Mowry 616/276-6372
- † *Ironwood* Gogebic CC Todd Frusti 906/932-3022
- † *Jackson* CC Doug Krengel 517/784-3135
- † *Kalamazoo* C Nazareth C Vacant 616/349-1100 Jane Sumec 616/387-5350
- • W Mich U Vacant 616/345-8090
- † *Lansing* CC Richard Laeder 517/372-1631
- † *Livonia* Schoolcraft CC Luther Werth 810/522-6830
- – *Marquette* N Mich U Paul Weber & Betty Knapp; Wes Baumeister 906/288-9883
- † *Midland* Northwood Inst Thomas Fischer 517/832-3667
- † *Monroe* CC Ronald Schultz 810/242-1401
- – *Mt Clemens* Macomb Co CC Center Campus Fred Traugott 810/528-9340
- – *Mt Pleasant* Cent Mich U Samuel Reith, James Krach 517/773-5050
- † *Muskegon* Bus C Co CC Dennis Lassanske 616/755-1292
- † *Olivet* C Tim Olson 517/543-4360
- † *Petoskey* N Cent Mich C Walter Teske 616/347-3438
- † *Port Huron* St Clair CC Robert Mann 810/984-2993
- • *Rochester* Oakland St U Fred Traugott 810/528-9340
- † *Roscommon* Kirtland CC Vacant 517/348-5921
- † *Saginaw* Valley C Delta C David Reed 517/662-6161
- † *Sault Ste Marie* LSSU Charles Burhop 616/757-2271
- † *Scottville* W Shore CC James E Schroeder 616/757-2271
- – *Southfield* Lawrence IT Fred Traugott 810/528-9340
- † *Traverse City* Northw Mich C Don Engebretson 810/528-9340
- – *Union Lake* Oakland CC Highland Lakes Fred Traugott 810/528-9340
- – *Warren* Macomb Co CC South Campus Fred Traugott 810/528-9340

## Minnesota

- † *Alexandria* AVTI Terry Finnern 612/834-2547
- † *Arden Hills* Bethel C Northwestern C Byron Northwick 612/633-2402
- † *Bemidji* St U Karen Krueger 218/751-4271
- † *Bloomington* Normandale CC Jim Anderson 612/831-5276
- † *Brainerd* Central Lakes C Vacant 218/829-4317
- † *Crookston* U of MN Steven Bohler 218/281-1239
- – *Duluth* U of Minn C of St Scholastica Robert Frank 218/724-2500
- † *Fergus Falls* CC David Knuth 218/736-4869
- † *Grand Rapids* Itasca CC William Zeige 218/326-9560
- † *Hibbing* CC Mark Palmer 218/263-3955
- † *International Falls* Rainy River St JC Vacant 218/283-2642
- † *Inver Grove Heights* Inver Hills St JC Deane Schuessler & Dan Matasovsky 612/457-3929
- • *Mankato* St C Rev Monte Meyer 507/387-6587
- † *Marshall* Southw Minn St C Keith Bicknase DCO Lyn Adams 507/532-4857
- • *Minneapolis* U of Minn Augsburg C Vacant 612/331-2747
- – *Moorhead* St U Guy Roberts 218/233-7569
- – *Morris* U of Minn Rob Jarvis 320/589-2744
- † *Northfield* St Olaf C Carleton C Vacant 507/645-4438
- † *Pine City* AVTI Glen Kleppe 612/629-3683
- • *St Cloud* St U David Emmrich & Barb Hertling DCE 612/259-1577
- • *St Paul* Concordia U Rev Robert Beinke 612/641-8278
- † *St Peter* Gustavus Adolphus Rev Monte Meyer 507/387-6587
- † *Staples* AVTI Robin Collins 218/894-2372
- † *Wadena* AVTI Vacant 218/631-3000
- † *Worthington* St JC Vacant 507/376-6168
- – *Winona* St U Vacant 507/452-8879

## Mississippi

- † *Cleveland* Delta St U Weldon Brinkley 601/846-0233
- † *Columbus* Miss U for Women Leonard Poppe 601/328-1757
- – *Hattiesburg* U of S Miss Vacant 601/583-4898
- † *Ittabena* Miss Valley St U Vacant 601/453-8323
- † *Jackson* St U Mark Griffin 601/353-0504
- † *Meridian* JC Philip Wottrich 601/483-5457
- – *Oxford* U of Miss 601/234-6568
- † *Raymond* Hinds JC Vacant
- – *Starkville* Miss St U Marlo Lemke 601/323-3050

## Missouri

- † *Boonville* Kemper Sch Rev Jerry Riggert 660/882-2208
- – *Cape Girardeau* Southeast Mo St U Rev David Dissen 573/334-5375
- • *Columbia* Christian C Stephens C U of Mo David Benson & Carol Thompson 573/442-5942
- † *Fayette* Cent Methodist C Vacant 660/248-3486
- † *Jefferson City* Lincoln U Robert King 573/635-6538
- † *Joplin* Mo Southern C Lowell Rossow 417/624-0333

- † *Kirksville* C of Osteop Med Mark Appold 660/665-6122
- – *Truman* Mo St U Mark Appold 660/665-6122
- † *Maryville* NW Mo St U Theo Mayes 660/582-3262
- † *Parkville* Park C R R Krueger 816/741-0483
- † *Point Lookout* Sch of Ozarks Michael Wanner 888/777-3059
- • *Rolla* U of Mo at Rolla Douglas Ochner 573/364-4525
- † *Sedalia* State Fair CC Ronald Hoehne 660/827-0226
- † *St Charles* Lindenwood C Ed Arle 314/724-1658
- † *St Joseph* Mo West St Terry Weinhold 816/279-1110
- – *St Louis* St Louis U Med Washington U Jonathan Lange 314/776-4993
- † *Springfield* Drury C Burge School of Nursing Missionary Ron Merritt 417/866-5543
- • SW Mo St St John's School of Nursing Ron Merritt
- • *Warrensburg* Cent Mo St U Ron Merritt 660/747-7603

## Montana

- † *Billings* Rocky Mtn C Mont St U-Billings Rev Mark Grunst 406/245-3984
- – *Bozeman* Mont St U Rev Bruce Linderman 406/586-5374
- † *Butte* U of Mont Chris Wareham 406/782-5935
- † *Glendive* Dawson Co JC Jim Hageman 406/365-3890
- † *Great Falls* Mont St U-Tech C Fred Grundmann 406/452-2121
- † *Havre* Mont St U-Northern Rev Al Ebel 406/265-7637
- † *Kalispell* Flathead Valley CC Darold Reiner 406/257-5683
- † *Miles City* CC James Mavis 406/232-4983
- – *Missoula* U of Mont Rev Dave Renfro 406/546-3311

## Nebraska

- † *Blair* Dana C John Emslie 213/671-7644
- † *Chadron* St C Peter Bertram 308/432-5698
- † *Crete* Doane C Nathan Ristvedt 402/826-4359
- † *Curtis* Nebraska College of Technical Agriculture Rev Paul Warneke 308/367-4238
- † *Fremont* Midland Lutheran C Tim Gierke 402/721-8412
- † *Hastings* C Donald Boeschen 402/462-9023
- • *Kearney Univ of Nebr* Daniel Heuer 308/236-8253
- • *Lincoln* U of Nebr William Steinbauer 402/477-3997
- † *McCook* C Carl Pullmann 308/345-2595
- – *Norfolk* Northeast CC Vacant
- † *North Platte* N C Fredrick A Simon 308/532-4753
- • *Omaha* Creighton U St Mary C U of Nebr U of Nebr C of Med Bellevue C Metropolitan CC Clarkson Sch of Nursing Methodist Sch of Nursing James Cavener 402/558-0874
- – *Peru* State C Vacant 402/274-4210
- † *Scottsbluff* Nebr Western C Mervyn Bauer 308/635-1722
- • *Seward* Concordia U Gregory Mech 402/643-3651
- – *Wayne* St C Jeff Anderson 402/375-1905
- † *York* C Arthur Schauer 402/362-3000

## Nevada

- † *Boulder City* U of Nev at Las Vegas Steve Cluver 702/293-4332
- † *Las Vegas* U of Nev at Las Vegas Wally Quandt 702/384-6106
- † *Reno* U of Nev Vacant

## New Hampshire

- † *Durham* U of New Hampshire Steven Bartell 603/772-8803
- † *Keene* St C Rev James Berry 603/352-4446
- † *Rindge* Franklin Pierce C Vacant 603/924-4019

## New Jersey

- † *Belleville* Clara Maass Nurs Sch Evan Haener 973/483-4938
- † *Bloomfield* C David B Hill 973/429-8654
- † *Cranford* Union JC Paul Kritsch 908/232-1517
- † *Edison* Middlesex CC David Yarrington 908/738-7470
- † *Hackettstown* Centenary C for Women Thomas P Armour 908/852-2156
- † *Lincroft* Brookdale CC Paul Huneke 732/542-2727
- † *Mahwah* Ramapo C Dennis Kruger 201/529-2117
- – *Princeton* U John Goerss 609/924-3642

## New Mexico

- † *Alamogordo* N Mex St U David Bergman 505/437-1482
- † *Albuquerque* U of N Mex T-VI Vacant
- † *Carlsbad* New Mexico St U Paul Neuberger 505/885-5780
- † *Clovis* Clovis CC Scott Blazek 505/763-4526
- † *Farmington* San Juan JC Gary Thur 505/325-3420
- † *Hobbs* Hobbs C of Southw / N Mex JC Michael Erickson 505/393-4911
- – *Las Cruces* N Mex St U Ralph Patrick 505/522-0465
- † *Las Vegas* N Mex Highlands U Earnest Hengst 505/425-6833
- † *Portales* East N Mex U Rob Sandley & John Kenney 505/366-4712
- † *Roswell* N Mex Mil Inst/ EN Mex U Warren Ruland 505/622-2853
- † *Santa Fe* C of Sante Fe / Sante Fe CC Doug Escue 505/983-7568
- † *Silver City* W N Mex U 505/538-9446
- † *Socorro* N Mex Inst of Mining & Tech Douglas May 505/835-3736
- – *Taos* U of New Mexico Taos Charles Keogh 505/758-5944

## New York

- – *Albany* SUNY Dennis Meyer (ELCA) 518/489-8573
- † *Auburn* CC Vacant 716/384-5667
- – *Brockport* SUNY C Carl Klug 716/637-5930 and Mary Ellen Larson (ELCA)
- • *Bronxville* Concordia U Deric Taylor 914/337-9300
- • *Buffalo* SUNY C Gail Riina 716/688-4064
- – *Ithaca* Cornell U Ithaca C Bob Foote 607/273-9017 E-Mail trnity@baka.com
- † *Jamestown* CC Vacant
- – *Manhattan* New York U Manfred Bahmann (ELCA) 212/998-4711
- • Columbia U Luther Kriefall 212/854-8797
- • *Rochester* RIT U of Rochester Jeffrey Hering 716/475-2135
- – NTID Jeffrey Hering
- † *Saratoga Springs* Skidmore C James Jaekel 518/584-5501
- † *Stony Brook* SUNY Charles Bell
- † *Syracuse* U Ray Kirk 315/437-8203
- † *Utica* Mohawk Valley CC Utica C Herb Grieves 315/732-7869
- • *West Point* US Mil Acad Norman Brinkman 201/664-6807

## North Carolina

- † *Asheville* U of NC Mark Nieting 704/252-1795
- † *Burlington* Elon C Vacant 910/227-7092
- † *Charlotte* Cent Piedmont CC Richard Runge 704/372-7317
- † Johnson C Smith U Vacant 704/392-6098
- † U of NC Richard Runge 704/372-7317
- † *Durham* Duke U Joseph Dzugan 919/682-6030
- – *Duke* U NC Cent U
- † *Greensboro* U of NC Daniel Koenig 919/272-5321
- – NC A&T U Jim McDaniels 910/272-1174
- † *Hickory* Lenoir-Rhyne C Richard Schwandt 704/328-1483
- † *High Point* C Charles Baldwin 910/886-4947
- † *Raleigh* St Mary's JC Meredith C NC St U Peace C Vacant 919/832-8822
- † *Salisbury* Catawba C Livingston C Vacant 704/392-6098
- † *Statesville* Mitchell C Peter Varvaris 704/873-3591
- † *Wilson* Atlantic Christian C Vacant 919/243-6706
- † *Winston-Salem* Salem C Wake Forest U Philip McLain 910/725-1651
- † Winston-Salem St William Parson 910/724-0035

## North Dakota

- † *Bismarck* JC U of Mary Rev Timothy Jenks 701/255-1433
- † *Bottineau* Minot St U Bottineau Dean Rothchild 701/228-3021
- † *Devils Lake* Lake Region JC Roger Leonhardt 701/662-2245
- † *Dickinson* St C Todd Smelser 701/225-2180
- – *Fargo* N Dak St U Bernard Worral 701/293-7979
- • *Grand Forks* U of N Dak Mark Buchhop 701/772-3992
- † *Minot* St U Carlyle Roth 701/839-4663
- † *Wahpeton* N Dak St C of Science Rev Al Werth 701/642-6910

## Ohio

- † *Akron* U of Akron John G Eiwen 216/253-3136
- † *Ashland* C Wayne Giesler 216/262-2456
- † *Berea* Baldwin-Wallace C Daniel Wegrzyn 216/884-1230
- • *Bowling Green* St U Todd Jenks & Chris Patterson DCO 419/352-5101
- † *Defiance* C Donald Luhring 419/782-5766
- † *Findlay* C Garry Mohr 614/587-0345
- † *Granville* Denison U Daniel Ruff 614/587-0345
- † *Hiram* C Rev Douglas Riley 216/274-2849
- • *Kent* St Rev Kent Pierce Thomas Mroch 216/673-6633
- – *Oberlin* C Richard Docekal 216/775-3271
- † *Painesville* Lake Erie C Kenton Wendorf 216/357-5174
- † *Tiffen* U Jan Kucera 419/447-7794
- † *Toledo* U of Toledo Douglas Meilander 419/382-0410
- † *Wooster* C of Wooster Wayne Giesler 216/262-2456

## Oklahoma

- † *Ada* E Cent St C Gary Brandt 405/332-3433
- † *Altus* Western OK St C William Geis 405/482-2222
- † *Alva* Northwestern Okla St C Joel Picard 405/327-0510
- † *Chickasha* U of Sc & Arts of OK David Thompson 405/224-1552
- † *Claremore* Rogers St C Bruce Cottrell 918/341-1429
- † *Durant* SE St Robert Heckmann 405/993-2510
- † *Edmond* U of Cent OK Peter Heckmann 405/340-0192
- † *Enid* Philips U Kenneth Wade 405/234-6646
- † *Goodwell* Panhandle St U Vacant 405/423-7224
- † *Langston* U Merlyn Lohrke 405/282-3914
- † *Lawton* Cameron St C Don Howard DCE 405/357-7684
- † *Miami* NE U Donald Kirchhoff 918/542-4681
- – *Norman* U of Okla David Nehrenz 405/321-3443
- † *Oklahoma City* U Clinton McMullin 405/525-5793
- – *Stillwater* Okla St U Carlton Riemer 405/372-3703
- † *Tahlequah* Northeastern St C Cecil Nixon 918/456-5070
- † *Tonkawa* Northern OK U Thomas Ramsey 405/762-1111
- † *Tulsa* Oral Roberts U John Raddatz 918/492-6451
- † U of Tulsa James Haner 918/592-2999
- † *Weatherford* Southwestern St Matthew Larson 405/623-5099

## Oregon

- † *Ashland* S Oregon C Anthony Schultz 503/482-1661
- • *Corvallis* Oreg St U Donna King (Deaconess) 503/753-5213
- † *Eugene* U of Oreg Phil Schoenherr 503/342-4844
- † *Forest Grove* Pacific U Dan Bohlken 503/357-2511
- † *Gresham* Mount Hood CC Eric Lange
- † *Klamath Falls* Oreg Tech Inst Paul Frerichs 503/884-6793
- † *McMinnville* Linfield C Vacant 503/472-6677
- † *Monmouth* Western Oreg Vacant 503/838-3459
- † *Ontario* Treasure Valley CC Fred Schuett 503/889-5758
- – *Portland* Concordia C Orlie Trier 503/282-0000
- † Lewis & Clark C Portland CC Glen Zander 503/244-4558
- † Reed C Sidney Johnson 503/236-7823

## Pennsylvania

- – *Pittsburgh* Carnegie-Mellon U U of Pittsburgh Douglas Spittel 412/683-4121
- • *Slippery Rock* St C Augusta Mennell 412/794-4334
- – *State College* Penn St David Sailer 814/234-8177
- † *Wilkes-Barre* Kings C Wilkes C Vacant 717/823-7332

## Rhode Island

- † *Providence* Brown U Pembroke C Providence C RI C RI JC RI School of Design Roger Williams C Leon Schultz 401/941-5100

## South Carolina

- † *Charleston* C of Charleston Med U of SC Citadel Robert Duddleston 803/766-3113
- † *Columbia* Allen U Benedict C Columbia C Columbia Bible C Midlands Tech Ed Ctr U of SC Carl Voges 803/799-7224
- † *Florence* Francis Marion C Vacant 803/662-9639
- † *Greenville* Bob Jones U Furman U Greenville Tech Vacant 864/244-5825
- † *Spartanburg* Converse C Spartanburg JC Wofford C U of SC John Rockert 864/579-2062

## South Dakota

- – *Aberdeen* Northern St U Presentation C Monty Dell Deacon 605/225-1847
- † *Brookings* S Dak St U Richard Townes 605/692-2678 E-Mail lsfjacks@brooking.net
- † *Huron* U Dale Sattgast 605/352-7121
- – *Madison* Dakota St U Warren Uecker 605/256-4483
- † *Mitchell* Dakota Wesleyan U Victor Dorn 605/996-7530
- † *Rapid City* S Dak Sch of Mines and Tech National C Duane Duley & Robert Bailey 605/342-5749 & 605/342-8943
- † *Sioux Falls* Augustana U of Sioux Falls Dean Ducan 605/332-2326
- † *Spearfish* Black Hills St U Gene Bauman 605/642-2929
- – *Vermillion* U of S Dak Michael Boykin 605/624-3459
- † *Watertown* Lake Area Vo Tech Bob Westad 605/886-5671
- † *Yankton* Mt Marty C David Gunderson & Paul Wenz 605/665-7337

## Tennessee

- † *Harrogate* Lincoln Memorial U Arthur Avery 423/869-4359
- † *Jackson* Lambuth C Lane C Union C Luther Hasz 901/668-0757
- † *Johnson City* E Tenn St U Steve Harmon 423/926-5261
- • *Knoxville* U of Tenn Bill Couch 865/524-0612
- † *Memphis* Christian Brothers C U of Memphis Vacant 901/327-3234
- † Rhodes C U of Tenn Ronald Wiese 901/525-1056
- † *Murfreesboro* Middle Tenn St U Becky Bradfield 615/893-0337
- † *Nashville* Belmont C Richard Jones 615/292-0982
- † George Peabody C for Teachers Dan Otto 615/833-1500
- † Meharry Med Ctr Vanderbilt U Richard Jones 615/292-0982

## Texas

- † *Abilene* Hardin-Simmons U Laverne Janssen 915/692-6163
- • *Arlington* U of Tex at Arlington Vera Sweet 817/274-9201
- • *Austin* U of Tex Norbert Firnhaber 512/472-5461
- • Concordia U Carl Trovall 512/452-7661
- † *Baytown* Lee JC Richard Turner 713/422-2207
- † *Belton* Mary Hardin-Baylor C Robert Budewig 817/939-0824
- † *Big Spring* Howard Co JC Steve Stutz 915/267-7163
- † *Borger* Frank Phillips C Vacant 806/273-7546
- † *Brownsville* Tex Southmost C Steve Morfitt 512/546-2350
- † *Brownwood* Howard Payne C Philip Graf 915/646-2045
- • *Bryan* Allen Acad Larry Krueger & Beth Kroeger 409/846-6687
- † *Canyon* West Texas St U Vacant 806/655-4086
- † *Cisco* JC Martin Kaufman 817/442-2090
- • *College Station* Tex A&M U Larry Krueger & Beth Kroeger 409/846-6687
- – *Commerce* E Tex St U Fred Rogers 214/886-6810
- † *Corpus Christi* Del Mar C Al Schubert III 512/937-8158
- † *Corsicana* Navarro JC Vacant 903/874-8795
- † *Dallas* Baylor U El Centro JC Southw Med C Robert Preece 214/363-1639
- † *Denison* Grayson Co JC Mike Mattil 903/465-1016
- † *Deer Park* San Jacinto JC Vacant 713/479-2201
- – *Denton* N Tex St U Tex Women's U Russell Tieken 817/387-1575
- † *El Paso* El Paso CC Charles Canada 915/566-4667
- † U of Texas at El Paso Robert Lambet DCE 915/833-1009
- † *Fort Worth* Tex Christian U Tarrant Co JC John Messmann 817/332-2281
- † *Hillsboro* JC Russell Nebhut 817/582-5782
- • *Houston* U of Houston Kurt Niebuhr; DCE 713/741-6171
- † *Huntsville* Sam Houston St C Dick Wuensche 409/295-5298
- † *Kerrville* Schreiner Inst Joseph Watson 512/257/6767
- † *Killeen* Cent Tex JC Michael Ramming 817/634-5858
- † *Laredo* JC John Diaz 210/722-2601
- † *Longview* Le Tourneau C Adrian Bacarisse 903/758-2019
- • *Lubbock* Christian C Tex Tech U Roy Heflin 806/763-3644
- † *Lufkin* Angelina C Frank Starr 409/634-7468
- – *Nacogdoches* Stephen F Austin St C James Otte 409/564-6729
- † *Nederland* Lamar U Francis Schroeder 409/722-1609
- † *Odessa* C Dean Kelm 915/337-5451
- † *Paris* JC Jerry Conley 903/784-3753
- † *Port Arthur* JC Tim Dinger 409/983-1130
- † *San Angelo* Angelo St U Howard CC Kenneth Holdorf 915/944-8660
- † *San Antonio* St Philip's C Vacant 210/648-0081
- – Concordia Steve Farmer
- – *Stephenville* Tarleton St C Tomas Konz 817/968-2710
- † *Temple* JC Rev Alan Strackmeyer 903/593-1528
- † *Texarkana* C Richard Cody 903/792-5253
- † *Uvalde* Southw Tex JC Art Hill 210/278-9474
- † *Weatherford* C Ken Watson 817/594-5143
- † *Wharton* Co JC Barry Sharp 409/532-2336
- † *Wichita Falls* Midwestern U Tom Handrick 817/322-6112

## Utah

- † *Cedar City* So Utah State C 801/586-7103
- – *Logan* Utah St U Vacant 801/752-1453
- † *Ogden* Weber St U Gary Trickey & Ralph Wendt DCE 801/392-6368
- † *Provo* Brigham Young U / Utah Valley State C Ronald Saatkamp 801/225-5777
- † *St George* Dixie C Rev John Manweiler 801/628-1850
- † *Salt Lake City* U of Utah / Westminster C David Fischer
- † Salt Lake CC Bryan Lindemood 801/364-2873

## Vermont

- † *Burlington* Champlain C Trinity C U of Vermont Rev Jefrey Jensen 802/864-5537
- † *Middlebury* C Rev Jefrey Jensen 802/864-5537
- † *Winooski* St Michael C Rev Jefrey Jensen 802/864-5537

## Virginia

- † *Charlotteville* U of Virginia Vacant 804/295-4038
- † *Chester* John Tyler CC Hilbert Dorn 804/748-6058
- † *Danville* Averett C Danville CC Stratford C James Kleinfelter 804/836-2132 or 836-6888
- † *Farmville* Longwood C Donald R Ortner 804/392-6767
- † *Hampton* Sidney C Donald R Ortner 804/836-2132
- † *Norfolk* Old Dominion C Vacant 757/853-5655
- † *Richmond* Virginia Commonwealth U U of Richmond Gary Olson 804/353-4413
- † *Roanoke* VA Western CC Vacant 703/774-8746
- † *Salem* Roanoke C Vacant 703/774-8746
- † *Staunton* Mary Baldwin C Vacant 540/942-5574

## Washington

- † *Auburn* Green River CC Terry Dill 206/833-5940
- † *Centralia* C Vacant 206/748-4108
- † *Mount Vernon* Skagit Valley C Robert Bendick 206/428-0290
- † *Oak Harbor* Skagit Valley CC Raymond Hagen 360/675-2548
- † *Olympia* S Puget Sound CC Centralia C Ted Kriefall 360/357-6574
- † *Pasco* Columbia Basin C Art Werfelmann 509/547-3466
- • *Pullman* Wash St U Dudley Nolting 509/332-2830
- • *Seattle* U of Wash Ted Wuerffel 206/528-9340
- † *Spokane* Whitworth C Wilton Hille 509/747-9984
- † Luth Student Fellowship Tim Cartwright 509/747-6806
- † *Tacoma* Pacific Luth U John Schmidt 206/584-2565
- † U of Puget Sound David Schmidt 206/752-1264
- † *Vancouver* Clark C Ted Will 206/695-7501
- † *Yakima* Valley JC Arden Walz 509/457-5822

## West Virginia

- † *Huntington* Marshall U Jeffery Henry 304/529-7365
- † *Institute* W Virginia St C Kirk Duecker 304/744-6251

## Wisconsin

- † *Appleton* Lawrence U Tom Part 920/734-9643
- † *Ashland* Northland C Martin Kaarre 715/682-6075
- † *Beloit* Blackhawk C Robert Frank 608/362-3607
- † *Eau Claire* U of Wis Brent Parrish 715/835-9155
- † *Fond Du Lac* Vocal Sch David Jensen 414/922-5130
- † *Green Bay* U of Wis U Center David Boettcher 920/468-4246
- † *Kenosha* Tech U of Wis Parkside Vacant 414/551-8182
- – *La Crosse* U of Wis Western Wis Tech Viterbo C 608/782-3696
- † *LadySmith* Mount Senario C Brent Berkesch 715/532-5780
- • *Madison* U of Wis Vacant 608/255-7214
- † *Manitowoc* U of Wis Richard Miller 414/684-3989
- † *Marinette* U of Wis Martin Frusti 715/735-6506
- † *Marshfield* U of Wis Mark Krueger 715/384-3535
- † *Menomonee* U of Wis-Stout Vacant 715/235-1653
- • *Mequon* Concordia U Vacant 414/243-4389
- • *Milwaukee* U of Wis-Milwaukee Greg Fairow 414/962-2470
- † *Oshkosh* U of Wis Thomas Bye 414/231-0530
- • *Platteville* U of Wis Platteville Frank Kinast 608/348-9901
- † *Rhinelander* Nicolet C & Tech In Jeff Shearier 715/362-2470
- † *Rice Lake* Barron Co Br Gerald Benecker 715/234-7505
- † *Ripon* C Bryan Fritsch 414/748-3882
- – *River Falls* U of Wis Vacant 715/425-2699
- † *Sheboygan* U of Wis Sheboygan Co Ctr Vacant 414/458-8246
- – *Stevens Point* U of Wis Rev Carl Selle & Lynne Johnson lay 715/345-6510
- † *Waukesha* Carroll C Tim Bruss 414/542-2496
- † U of Wis-Waukesha Cent John Kelling 414/547-1817
- † *Wausau* U of Wis Ext Keith Haldeman 715/842-0769
- † N Cent Tch Inst Bruce Lamont 715/848-5511
- † *Wautoma* Waushara Co Teachers C Frank Frye 920/787-2891
- † *West Bend* U of Wis Wash Co Campus Dan Kelm 414/334-4901
- • *Whitewater* U of Wis Don Stein 414/473-5274

### Wyoming

- † *Casper* C David Boehnke 307/234-0558
- † *Cheyenne* Laramie Co CC Richard Boche 307/632-2580
- • *Laramie* U of WY Daniel Decker 307/745-5892
- † *Powell* Northw CC Ainslie Wagner 307/754-3168
- † *Riverton* Cent WY CC Marlin Rempfer 307/856-9340
- † *Rock Springs* W Wyoming CC James Hennig 307/362-5088
- † *Torrington* Eastern WY C Marvin Temme 307/532-5801

## MINISTRY TO THE DEAF

**Rev Ronald Friedrich Interim Counselor for Deaf Mission**
**1333 S Kirkwood Rd St Louis MO 63122**
(For complete addresses see main roster)

### Pastors

Altenberger Roger Cedar Rapids IA
Anderson Mark Chicago IL
Bassett Carl Chicago IL
Bauer Robert Edmonton AB Can
Bergstresser Edwin Columbus OH
Blesi, Roger, Seattle WA
Bush David Ft Wayne IN
Carstens David L Portland OR
Christudoss A Amjur India
Dahmann Roy Fremont CA
Deterding Paul Jackson MS
Dorr Paul Jacksonville IL
Drummond Henry Great Falls MT
Eckert Tim Quad Cities IA
Eckstrom Cory Omaha NE
Fritz John Aurora IL
Gehlbach Daryl W Minneapolis MN
Gehrs Gerhard A Jr Riverside CA
Hewitt Martin A Spokane WA
Hoopman John Australia
Knaack William N WI
Larsen Larry Largo FL
Lawson Gary Cleveland OH
Leber Donald Los Angeles CA
Leonhardt Roger L Devils Lake ND
Lieder Larry Houston TX
MacDonald Philip Charlotte NC
Marsh Prentice Chicago IL
Moody Richard St Louis MO
Munz Jerold Indianapolis IN
Nielsen, David, AB Canada
Nix Matthew Sioux Falls SD
Palmer William Milwaukee WI
Petzoldt Shirrel Toledo OH
Reinke John Omaha NE
Rowland Robert Sacramento CA
Seeger Mark Austin TX
Smith Brian Los Angeles CA
Tessaro Paul Memphis TN
Wrede William New York NY
Wurst Robert Evansville IN
Ziegler Erick Clifton NJ

### Lay Ministers, Assistants, Deaconesses, and Directors of Christian Education

Budzynski Laura Prospect Heights IL
Gorecki Heather St Augustine FL
Knaack Jennifer St Augustine FL
Manning Denise, Fremont CA
Monroe Pat Omaha NE
Noack Dalton Ghana
Oettel Robert Tokyo Japan
Windisch Richard Clark NJ

### Lutheran Schools for the Deaf

DeMeyer Roger Executive Director Lutheran Special Education Ministries Detroit MI
Mark Prowatzke Headmaster Mill Neck School for Deaf Children Mill Neck NY

## MILITARY CHAPLAINS

**Chaplain Rodger R Venzke USA Ret**
**Director**
**Ministry to the Armed Forces**
**Board for Mission Services**
**1333 S Kirkwood Rd St Louis MO 63122-7295**
**(314)965-9917 ext 1337**
**FAX (314)965-0959**

### UNITED STATES CHAPLAINS

### U.S. Air Force Regular
**ON ACTIVE DUTY**

Bomberger Gary D
Brooks Gary D
Harris Marlin L
Maack David R
Piepkorn Gary A
Savage Leon E
Sherouse Paul L
Wilshek David E

### U.S. Air Force Reserve
**ON ACTIVE DUTY**

Boarts Matthew A
Elbert Thomas J
Franke Matthew P
Jans Gregory D
Rosenthal Timothy S

### U.S. Air Force Reserve
**NOT ON ACTIVE DUTY**

Alexander Robert D
Bowditch Mark A
Davis Warren H
Hagan Raymond L
Houser Philip
Larsen Steven M
McFarland Michael R
McHone Randolph W
Myers Larry W
Nutter Martin S
Obersat Thomas F
Rowe Daniel
Schaarschmidt Mark F
Stringer Gregory S
Taylor Kurt S
Wolter Derek M

### U.S. Air National Guard
**NOT ON ACTIVE DUTY**

Allshouse William N
Bettermann Vernon L
Beyer Michael R
Bok Vern L
Bush David S
Cooper Donald E
Gottschalk Kenton A
Irmer Douglas D
Jennings Lance R
Kemp Calvin
Knuth James A
Krueger Carl N
Lingsch Keith A
Otten Christopher L
Smith Charles A
Weinrich William C
Yates William T

### U.S. Army Regular
**ON ACTIVE DUTY**

Bauer John A
Decker Thomas R
Erkkinen Eric J
Graves Richard P
Heller David R
Hokana Steven C
Howe Paul F
Isler Albert C
Larson Raymond E
Mueller Peter L
Nagler Stephen L
Pederson Joe Ed
Pingel Gilbert H
Rau Carl R
Robinson James W
Rogers Richard S
Schneider Eugene W
Shaw Jonathan E
Sowers Timothy E
Watson James C
Waynick Thomas C
Williamson Gregory K

### U.S. Army Reserve
**ON ACTIVE DUTY**

Block Larry H
Eliason Gilbert M
Jacob David K
Keller William L
Moss Mark E
Mueller Peter L
Sager William A
Von Seggern Arleigh F
Vesey Matthew W
Wollberg Jeffrey

### U.S. Army Reserve
**NOT ON ACTIVE DUTY**

Bacon Arthur D
Beyer William D
Brunold William L
Buckman James D
Burmeister Robert J
Byers Gary W
Cochrane Robert S
Cramm Kevin J
Danielsen Gary L
Ettner Dann J
Hermann John V
Hill Gary E
Hoke James L
Jones Ronald W
Krienke Howard A
Mau Jon C
Meyer John A
Mitkos Leslie J
Nuckols Mark S
Palkewick Robert J
Pflughoeft Darren M
Raddatz John F
Ratcliffe Kermit H
Rebert Terry J
Roberts Kenneth
Schumm Herbert L
Shimkus William E
Simpson Scott E
Sorenson David E
Thompson Mark A
Uttech Gary R
Vanderbilt Thomas
Williams Gary C

### U.S. Army National Guard
**NOT ON ACTIVE DUTY**

Anderson David L
Armon Rodney A
Artigas Cristiano
Bookshaw John A
Burns James D
Butt James C
Cage Peter C
Cimpa Frank G
Cotter James R
Dineen Russell H
Ebb Eric L
Everson Gale R
Flath Richard E
Fleischfresser Douglas H
Geaschel Robert E
Gunderson David E
Henke Gene G
Hess Steven J
Hoogland Kevin J
Jones Daniel G
Koehler Robert A
Lucas James A
Molnar Stephen C
Morehouse Michael A
Morris Bruce B
Norton James E
Oberdieck David L
Olson Gary C
Palke Thomas J
Rengstorf Dwight E
Shaffer George W
Tews David E
Wenger Timothy E

### U.S. Navy Regular
**ON ACTIVE DUTY**

Crossan Robert D
Frusti Jonathan
Gunderlach David P
Hermann Rory M
Jack Edward E
Kalsow Larry D
Kirk John E
Krans Glen A
Logid Mark J
Muehler Craig G
Precup J Lee
Puttler James D
Stahl Martin R
Steiner Mark G
Todd Gregory N
Warnke Matthew L
Wohlrabe John C

### U.S. Navy Reserve
**ON ACTIVE DUTY**

Carlson Andrew J
Christensen Lynn W
Conroe Jon W
Cox Ronald L
Crandall Ted L
Glaspie James J
Gordish Timothy R
Kearney Channing L
Klein Brent A
Manila John K
Moreno Michael P
Otten David L
Reckling Michael J
Reschke Mark C
Russell Randall H
Schilling David D
Schreiber Mark J
Smith Andrew D
Smith Jonathan M
Steele Walter R
Szczesny Jonathan D
Tews Mark W

### U.S. Navy Reserve
**NOT ON ACTIVE DUTY**

Bartell Stephen D
Berteau Daniel C
Bodley Christopher R
Boeck Richard J
Burtzlaff Paul S
Busch Lewis M
Coop Gregory S
Drevlow Marcus O
Eaton Steven A
Foster Edwin M
Gard Daniel L
Leeland David A
Liersemann F Paul
Lochner Daniel E
Lytle Jeffrey S
Magruder David B
May Ronald P
Nelson Dewayne R
Riley Patrick J
Rumsch Bruce A
Rupe Ryan R
Schinkel John A
Schoessow Daniel
Sliger Dwain E
Sneath Michael W
Thomson John M
Varga Ernest L
Varsogea Charles E
Williams S T Jr
Wilson Robert H
Winters Raymond F
Wolfram Michael C
Wolfram Richard J

### Civil Air Patrol

Anderson Hyle R
Bier Louis H G
Boldt Gerald E
Budke Clarence E
Bush David S
Eckelman Robert
House Thomas W
Krogen Richard A
Panning John F
Pittelko Roger D
Schweitzer Keith W
Steenbock Elmer J
Thomas Steven E
Vernava Michael N
Williams Jeffrey B
Wuensche Reinhard

### Directors of Religious Education

Scheck Dennis R

### Canadian Active Duty

Klein Kevin

### Canadian Armed Forces Reserve

Buck Rod
Cooley Charles S
Estes Jon R
Lewis Allan
Schiemann Arthur W
Sprung Arvid Peter

## VETERANS AFFAIRS CHAPLAINS

### Full-Time

Bier Louis—Veterans Affairs Medical Center Boston MA
Diekroger Walter—Veterans Affairs Medical Center Chillicothe OH
Kerr Joseph R—U S Soldier's & Airmen's Home Washington DC
Matelski Harry—Veterans Affairs Medical Center Long Beach CA
Meritt Kelly-Ray—Veterans Affairs Medical Center The Bronx NY
Olson Wayne—Veterans Affairs Medical Center Indianapolis IN
Reddel Eugene—Veterans Affairs Medical Center Pittsburgh PA
Smith Charles—Veterans Affairs Medical Center Hampton VA
Steinke Richard—Veterans Affairs Medical Center Des Moines IA
Stier Larry—Veterans Affairs Medical Center Shreveport LA

### Part-Time

Bassett Carl W—Wood Dale IL
Fosse Kenneth—Manalapan NJ
Kohl Carroll—Big Spring TX
Schaarschmidt Mark—Newington, CT
Wyneken Karl—Fresno CA

### Intermittent/Contract

Bauch Gary—Canandaigua NY
Brooks Dana A—Hot Springs, SD
Konz J Louis—Houston TX
Nixon Cecil Jr—Muskogee OK
Popp Milton N—Prescott AZ
Schnepp Kenneth—Baltimore MD
Stauffer W Roger—Madison WI
Voges Ethan C—Seattle/Tacoma WA

## INSTITUTIONAL CHAPLAINS

**Deaconess Dorothy Prybylski**
**Board for Human Care Ministries**
**1333 S Kirkwood Rd**
**St Louis MO 63122**
**314/965-9917 Ext 1384**

**FOR VETERAN AFFAIRS CHAPLAINS**
**Reverend Rodger R Venzke**
**Ministry to the Armed Forces**
**1333 S Kirkwood Rd**
**St Louis MO 63122**
**314/965-9917 Ext 1346**

* Indicates District Executive Chaplain
** Indicates Clinical Pastoral Education Supervisor
(List includes all who serve in specialized ministries (Bylaw 2.15h) and who may be designated as chaplain by the institution which they serve.)

### Alabama

*Birmingham*—Charles F Pieplow** *(SO)

### Arizona

*Green Valley*—John Stieve
*Lake Havasu City*—Harold Kallio—EM
*Lakeside*—Robert J Weinhold—EM
*Scottsdale*—Lois Sikorski
*Sierra Vista*—Oliver E Kolberg—EM
*West Bullhead*—Robert Wudy (Police)

### Arkansas

*Benton*—Andrew Toopes (Police)

### California

*Bakersfield*— James Tyler
*Buena Park*—Ralph Juengel (Police)
*Hayward*—Neal Ostruske
*Hemet*—Willard Niederbrach (Police)
*Long Beach*—Harry Matelski (VA)
*Oakland*—Paul Holt
*Riverside*—Frederick Huscher (Police)
*Sacramento*—Paul Janke*
*San Diego*—Mike Mitschke (Police)
Warren Naegele
*San Francisco*—Beverly Lipscomb
Fred H Stennfeld *(CNH)
*San Pablo*—Donald Jordan (Police)
*San Pedro*—William C Scar
*Terra Bella*—John Baumgartner (Police)
*Van Nuys*—Ronald Rehrer *(PSW)

### Colorado

*Colorado Springs—Steven Lee* (Police)
*Denver*—Arthur F Schroeder
*Florence*—Jon Mau
*Golden*—Bruce Rippe
*Littleton*—Donald Hinchey (Police)
*Loveland*—David Feeder *(RM)

### Connecticut

*Greenwich*—Ronald Erbe (Police)
*Lebanon*—Scott Schuett (Fire)
*Newington*—Mark Schaarschmidt (VA, PT)
*Southbury*—Robert Schipul *(NE)

### District of Columbia

*Washington DC*—Wesley A Toepper

### Florida

*Bay Pines*—Adrian R Kelly—EM
*Hudson*—Daryl Larson
Edgar Trinklein
*Miami*—Jesse Perez
*Pensacola*—Neil Pape—EM

### Georgia

*Atlanta*—Gary Danielson
Martin M Platzer
*Tifton*—Earl Steffens *(FG)

### Hawaii

*Maui*— Milton Fricke (Police)

### Idaho

*Coeur d'Alene*—Luther Gutz
*Jerome*—Baldwin Camin (Police)

### Illinois

*Aurora*—Phil Gruenbaum
*Arlington Heights*—William J Hughes
*Carbondale*—Robert Gray (Police)
*Chester*—David Kollmeyer
*Chicago*—Kevin Dean (Police)
*Clayton*—Donald Busboom
*E. Peoria*—Vernon Bettermann (Police)
*E. St. Louis*—Chuck Sampson
*Fairview Heights*—Doug Nicely (Police)
*Ferrin*—Mitchel Schuessler
*Golconda*—Gary Harroun
*Greenville*—Jeffrey Nehrt
*Hillsboro*—Maurice Alms *(SI)
*Hillside*—Donald Kretzschmar
*Hines*—Carl Bassett
*Hines*—Bernard Danner—EM
*Joliet*—George Klima
Lori Wilbert
*Kankakee*—Lori Wilbert
*Lincoln*—Linda Schaeffer
Charles Olander
*Marion*—Edward J Rivett
William Schmidt
*Mt. Prospect*—John Golisch
*Mt Sterling*—Stephen Southward
*Murphysboro*—Jonathan Cholcher
*Oak Forest*—Ruth Drum
*Oak Park*—Bernard Danner (VA) EM
*Olympia Fields*—Paul Haberstock
*Park Ridge*—Richard Heller
LeRoy Joesten**
*Pinckneyville*—Russell Helbig
*Rend Lake*—Greg Hyatt
*Rockford*—Milford Brelje
*Roselle*—Dianna Bonfield
*Sheridan*—Lori Wilbert
*Springfield*—Joel Cluver *(CI)
*Tams*—Carl Miller
*Taylorville*—Rodney Bloomquist
*Vandalia*—Lawrence W Saeger
*Vienna*—Paul Weber
*Waukegan*—John C Philipp
*Wheaton*—Donald C Kretzschmar
*Wood Dale*—Carl Bassett (Police)

### Indiana

*Crown Point*—Dwight Rengstorf
*Fort Wayne*—Karen Kosberg
Keith J Knippenberg
Roger F Olson
Ralph Wetzel
*Greensburg*—Jan Kiel
*Indianapolis*—
Michael Bristol
Alfred Hellert (VA, PT)
Dale H Knuteson EM
Raymond H Main
Ron Welsh
*Mulberry*—Karl Bliese
*Valparaiso*—Michael Porter

### Iowa

*Belle Plaine*—Kathleen Clark
*Des Moines*—Mark Baldwin
*Fort Dodge*—Eric Schillo *(IW)
*Fort Madison*—Steven Rasmussen
*Iowa City*—John C McKiness—EM
Carol Goldfish
Harold A. Scheer *(IE)
*Sioux City*—Dennis Grohn
Leland Schmidt
*Spencer*—Paul Bussert
*West Union*—Victor Young

### Kansas

*Kansas City*—George W Mundinger—EM
Stephen Streufert
*Shawnee Mission*—Ervin A Daugherty Jr
*Topeka*—George J Bruening—EM
*Wichita*—Rocky Mease
John Pool EM

### Kentucky

### Louisiana

*Shreveport*—Larry Stier (VA)

### Maine

*Portland*—Norman A Bumby

### Maryland

*Baltimore*—John W Freed
Stephen Funck
*Forest Height*—Wesley Toepper (Police)
*Temple Hills*—Kenneth Schnepp (VA)

### Massachusetts

*Canton*—David Mahn (state police)
*Westwood*—Louis Bier

### Michigan

*Adrian*—Wayne Zirzow
*Allen Park*—Joel Holls (Police)
*Ann Arbor*—Julie Nielsen-Schmidt
*Arcadia*—James Moehring—EM
*Brighton*—Donald R Neiswender—EM
*Cedar*—Dwain Gade—EM
*Dearborn*—Kenton Gottschalk (Police)
*Detroit*—Edward H Einem—EM
Thomas Oie
*Farmington*—John Angle—EM
*Frankenmuth*—Joel Kaiser
*Grand Rapids*—Walter Bunkowske
Robert Cordes—EM
*Jackson*—Warren L Paulson—EM *(MC)
Michael Martin
*Lansing*—David L Voorhees—EM
*Midland*—Roger Stauffer
*Milan*—Dale Kleimola
*Waterford*—Earle Beck—EM

### Minnesota

*Brainerd*—Marvin A Berkeland—EM
Orville E Aho—EM*(MNN)
*Edina*—Clyde J Burmeister** *(MNS)
*Fergus Falls*—Norm E Nissen
*Garrison*—Curtis Foreman
*Lomita*—Steve Leinhos (Police)
*Minneapolis*—Don Becker—EM
Kenneth J Siess**—EM
*Montrose*—Jeffrey Harter
*Northfield*—Jerry Markel
*Rochester*—Donald E Knick—EM
Martin E Mueller
Bruce Stam
*St Paul*—Jeanne Dicke
Gerald B Wunrow—EM
*Stillwater*—J Nevin Crowther (Police)
*Walker*—Tom E Palomaki—EM
*White Bear Lake*—John Christensen (Police)

### Missouri

*Cape Girardeau*—David V Dissen (Police)
Karl Leeman
William A Matzat
*Columbia*—George A Rattelmuller
*Jefferson City*—Allen F Mack
Alvin H Lange
*O'Fallon*—Donald Christiansen (Police)
*St James*—Paul Goddard (Police)
*St Louis*—Darryl Anderson
Paul A Beins—EM
Simon Bodley—EM
Martin W Brauer—EM
Michael Carter
Robert Demchuk
Joel R Hempel**
Ronald P Hilmer
Dorothy Prybylski
Al Schenk
King Schoenfeld
Vincent Stanley
Milton E Stohs—EM
Richard Tetzloff *(MO)
Audrey Vanderbles
Ed Watson
Karen Westbrooks
Jimmie Wilson

### Montana

*Boulder*—Gale R Everson *(MT)

### Nebraska

*Gering*—Ralph Morris
*Norfolk*—John A Fale
Jack H Thiesen
*Omaha*—Vern Albrecht

### Nevada

*Pahrump*—Ronald Mayer (Police)
*Reno*—William J Faust—EM

### New Hampshire

*Exeter*—Steve Bartell (Police)

### New Jersey

*New Milford*—Jack D Wangerin (Fire)
*Norwood*—George Lofmark *(NJ)
*Old Bridge*—Norman L Johnson (Fire)
*Union*—Donald Brand (Police)

### New Mexico

*Las Vegas*—Earnest Hengst (Police)

### New York

*Albany*—William Hempel III
Joel Janzow
*Binghamton*—Carl Roemer
*Bronx*—Kelly-Ray Meritt (VA)
*Brooklyn*—Anita Crooks
*Concordia*—Viji George
*Delmar*—William Hempel III
*E Moriches*—John Fleischmann
*Ellicottville*—William Kay (Police Chaplain)
*Flushing*—David Elseroad
*Islip*—Walter J Baepler**
*Latham*—Gordon Rakow
*Lockport*—Beverly Craig
*Mendon*—Erwin H Stechholz—EM
*New York*—Paul Steinke**(AT)
*Niskayuna*—Gordan Johnston
*N Tonawanda*—Adolph Moldenhauer (Police)

*Rochester*—Maggie Harris
*Rome*—John A O Conno—EM
*St Albans*—Wayne F Olson (VA)
*Sayville*—Ralph Scofield—EM
*Schenectady*—Ernest Varga Jr
*Tonawanda*—David Brammer *(EA)—EM
*West Henriette*—Gary Bauch (VA)
*Williamsville*—Eunice Foote
Robert C Spilman**

**North Carolina**
*Asheville*—Frederick A Stiemke—EM
*Raleigh*—John M Costello—EM**

**North Dakota**
*Devils Lake*—Roger Leonhardt
*Fargo*—William Sharpe *(ND)
Alfred Thiem
*Grafton*—Bernhard M Seter
*Minot*—Ronald W Mahnke**
Terry Merrill

**Ohio**
*Canton*—Mark Luecke (OH)
*Chillicothe*—Walter E Diekroger (VA)
*Cincinnati*—Carl DeMerritt Jr
Carla Olbetor
William A Ross—EM
*Cleveland*—Walther Marcis (Police)
James Jasper
Luis A Torres
*Columbus*—Steve Rice
*Fairborn*—Manfred Rembold (Police)
*Ravenna*—Everett W Schleef *(OH)
*Stow*—Alvin Boehlke
*West Lake*—Wayne Decker

**Oklahoma**
*Oklahoma City*—Kathleen Brown

**Oregon**
*Ashland*—David Campbell—EM
*Cornelius*—Kasimir Kachmarek
*Eagle Point*—Ron Norris (Police)
*Portland*—Harold Iben—EM
Max Metcalf—EM
Harry G Scholz—EM
*Roseburg*—Ken Kausch (VA)
*Salem*—Kenneth L Ollek—EM
Edwin L Schultze—EM
Dell Schomburg
*Umatilla*—Lorinda Schwarz

**Pennsylvania**
*Cabot*—Richard Grammes
Jack Hartman
*Gibsonia*—Eugene Reddel** (VA)

**Rhode Island**

**South Dakota**
*Brookings*—Marvin A Berkeland—EM
*Hot Springs*—Lowell Boettcher—EM
*Sioux Falls*—Orlett D Brack—EM *(SD)

**Tennessee**
*Chattanooga*—Roger P Frobe
*Memphis*—Philip Schmidt *(MDS)

**Texas**
*Austin*—Bert Klein
*Baytown*—Richard Turner (Police)
*Big Spring*—Carroll C Kohl (VA, PT)
*Bryan*—K Lynn Stroud
*College Station*—George Gibson Jr—EM
*Dallas*—Geri Smith
*Denton*—Dennis D Schurter
*Galveston*—Robert B Wedergren—EM
*Gatesville*—Robert F Kamrath—EM
*Houston*—J. Louis Konz (VA, PT)
John Lindner (Police)
Ed J Mahnke—EM**
John F Stelling (TX)
*Huntsville*—Donald Kaspar
*McAllen*—Ernie L Garcia
*Navasota*—Gerald R Discher—EM
*Rosharon*—Robert Cardaro
*Temple*—Victor M Kilian—EM
*Tennessee Colony*—J W Ristvedt

**Virginia**
*Hampton*—James Lauer MDIV—EM (VA)
*Portsmouth—Richard Hill MDIV*

**Washington**
*Bothell*—Mark Lieske (Fire Department)
Ed Johnson
*Lacey*—David Williams (Police)
*Seattle*—Clarence Born
William Clements
Ron E Gocken
John Nelson Sr
Ruth Ann Shimoi
Ethan Voges
*Spokane*—Virginia Brondos
Ward Robak
David C Stunkel
Richard C Zagel—EM
*Tacoma*—John Bauer (Army hospital)
Raynold H Eckhoff
Daniel Gerken (VA)
*Vancouver*—Robert E Kunz—EM *(NOW)

**Wisconsin**
*Beloit*—Bill Wagner (Police)
*Green Bay*—Paul W Emmel **(NW)—EM*
*Greenwood*—Melvin Gohdes
*Irma*—Gary Uttech
*Luxemburg*—A E Batiansila
*Madison*—James M Ehlers—EM
Stephen Wenk *(SW)
*Marshfield*—Steven Sutterer
*Mequon*—Richard Eyer
*Milwaukee*—Robert Alsleben
Martin Bangert—EM
Earl Bleke
Paul H Eggold *(EN)
Thomas Hinz—EM
David E Sorensen**
Charles Weinrich**
*New Berlin*—Ed F Eggert—EM
*Oshkosh*—Thomas Bye (Police)
David Habermas—EM
*Sheboygan*—Thomas Fleischmann
Richard J Matthies—EM
*Watertown*—Michael Schempf
Victor D Tegtmeier—EM
*Waupaca*—Edward F Kletzien
*Waupun*—Steven Thomas
*Wauwatosa—James Greear IV*

**Wyoming**
*Casper*—Ron Garwood *(WY)

**Canada-Ontario**
Sarnia—Roger Ellis (Police)

## PASTORAL COUNSELORS

**Board for Human Care Ministries**
**1333 S Kirkwood Rd**
**St Louis MO 63122**

(Qualified by various professional organizations such as the American Association of Pastoral Counselors and others)

**Alabama**
*Birmingham*—Charles F Pieplow MDiv
*Fairbanks*—David Hinz MDiv

**Alaska**
*Fairbanks*—Phil Kuehnert MDiv ThD
Fred Schramm DMin

**Arkansas**
*Fort Smith*—Fred W Hagemeier MDiv

**California**
*Carmichael*—Vernon R Kettner DMin—EM
*Chester*—Vernon R Kettner DMin—EM
*Danville*—Ihno Janssen MDiv PhD—EM
*Orange*—John Kuntz MDiv
*Redwood City*—Harold S Draeger MS DMin
*San Diego*—Lawrence P Rudolph MA—EM
*San Pedro*—William Scar DMin
*Van Nuys*—Ronald L Rehrer MA

**Colorado**
*Denver*—Robert Weston MDiv
*Golden*—Bruce W Rippe MDiv
*Littleton*—Werner K Boos STM

**Connecticut**
*Enfield*—Paul C Dorn STM
*Southbury*—William A Scar—EM

**Florida**
*Key Marathon*—David A Mueller MDiv
*Lake Worth*—Douglas Fountain MDiv PhD
*Pensacola*—Niel Pape MDiv
*St Petersburg*—Richard Armstrong MDiv
*Venice*—Randy Winkel

**Georgia**
*Decatur*—Walter J Bartling PhD—EM
Lance A Netland ThM
*Duluth*—Martin M Platzer ThM
*Rome*—R Rex Hussmann ThM
*Savannah*—Walter J Warneck PhD

**Idaho**
*Buhl*—Mark Latham
*Coeur d' Alene*—Luther Gutz
*Idaho Falls*—Richard Collin (police)

**Illinois**
*Belleville*—Mark Wiesner MDiv MS
*Chicago*—John E Golisch PhD
Ray A Fontaine DMin MA
James P Stephens MDiv
*Crystal Lake*—Thomas H Tews MDiv

**Indiana**
*Dyer*—John C Kolb STM
*Ft Wayne*—Randall Schroeder MDiv PhD
Ken Wesemann PhD
*Seymour*—Edgar M Keinath DMin
*Valparaiso*—Thomas A Droege PhD

**Iowa**
*Cedar Rapids*—Ann McDonald LISW
Randy Nord MDiv
*Council Bluffs*—Paul Haugen MDiv
*Fort Dodge*—Eric L Schillo MDiv MS
James Wonnacott MDiv
Cherryll Hoffman Deaconess MA
*Sioux City*—Dennis Grohn MDiv

**Kansas**
*Hays*—Richard J Kaczor MDiv
*Kansas City*—George W Mundinger MA
*Topeka*—Carroll Ohlde MDiv
*Wichita*—Richard Zabel MDiv MS

**Kentucky**
*Louisville*—Jeff Romer

**Maryland**
*Baltimore*—Richard L Alms PhD
Roger Fink PhD
Robert J Kretzschmar MDiv
*Fort Washington*—W Toepper MDiv

**Massachusetts**
*Framingham*—Charles R Mueller MA

**Michigan**
*Beverly Hills*—Ronald Farah MDiv MA
*Bullock Creek/Midland*—John Langewisch MDiv
*Clinton Township*—Mark H Gaertner MDiv
*Oak Park*—Luke Stephan MDiv MSW

**Minnesota**
*Burnsville*—Gene Bettermann PhD
*Chisholm*—Steven E Breitbarth MDiv
*Minneapolis*—Don Beiswenger MDiv
Roger Ernst MDiv
Roger A Holland STM
Willard E Kehrberg PhD

**Missouri**
*St Charles*—Edward Arle DMin
*St Louis*—Gary H Behm STM
Alan Erdman STM
Bruce Hartung PhD
Joel R Hempel MDiv
Dale R Kuhn STM
David Muench MDiv MS
Bryan Salminen MDiv MED PhD
Allen E Schenk STM
Karen Westbrooks PhD

**Nebraska**
*Norfolk*—John Fale MDiv
Jack H Thiesen MDiv
*Omaha*—Roger Kruger MDiv
*Seward*—Paul Vasconcellos MED MDiv MS PhD

**New Jersey**
*Dover*—Raymond D Schmidt MRE

**New York**
*Lockport*—David F C Wurster STM PhD
*New York*—Paul D Steinke MDiv
*Niagara Falls*—Erwin A Brese DMin
*Schenectady*—Marlow Olson
Gordon E Johnston BA
*Williston Park*—Allen Kebschull

**North Carolina**
*Hickory*—David Ludwig PhD
*Jacksonville*—Joel Kettner MDiv

**North Dakota**
*Bismarck*—Irvin H Bruenjes MDiv
*Jamestown*—Robert Leiste
*Mandan*—Ralph La Fontaine MDiv
*Minot*—Ronald Mahnke MDiv
Terry Merrill

**Ohio**
*Cleveland*—Walter Marcis MDiv MA DMin
*Hudson*—Ron Duer MDiv MA STM DMin
*Tiffin*—Jan Kucera MDiv MA

**Oregon**
*Portland*—Bruce B Strade STM

**Texas**
*Amarillo*—Robert T Kuhlmann STM
*Austin*—William B Knippa PhD MA
Peter Steinke DRel Med MA
*Commerce*—Charles F Rogers MDiv
*Grand Prairie*—Raymond F Kahle MA MDiv—EM
*Nacogdoches*—James Otte MDiv
*San Angelo*—Chester McCown
*San Antonio*—Mark W Steege MDiv
*Spring*—Alvin Franzmeier MDiv

**Virginia**
*Virginia Beach*—Arne P Kristo MDiv

**Washington**
*Federal Way*—David Kruger DMin
*Mercer Island*—William K Clements DMin

**Wisconsin**
*Eau Claire*—Gerald DeLove PhD MA
*New Berlin*—Martin W Bangert MDiv—EM
*Oshkosh*—David Habermus MSEd EM
*Wausau*—Gary D Yeast MSMFT
*West Bend*—Cal Seban MA

## HIGHER EDUCATION

### VALPARAISO UNIVERSITY

Valparaiso IN 46383
*Alan F Harre* PhD President
219/464-5000

Staff members who are synodical seminary or teacher graduates:
Albers James ThD (StL)
Austensen Roy PhD (RF)
Cunningham Joseph (FW)
Daley Jeffrey PhD (RF)
Fevig David MS (Milw)

Harre Alan F PhD (StL)
Karpenko William O II PhD (Sew)
Koetke Donald PhD (RF)
Linebrink Michael (RF)
Ludwig Theodore ThD PhD (StL)
Maddox Richard JD (StL)
Meilander Gilbert PhD (StL)
Miller John A DBA (FW)
Morgan David PhD (Sew)
Niedner Frederick ThD (StL)
Noffke James MDiv (StL)
Rast Walter E PhD (StL)
Reiser Ann PhD (RF)
Riffel Perry EdD (Sew)
Truemper David STD (StL)
Weber David (FW)

VU Professors Emeritus who are synodical seminary or teacher graduates:

Baepler Richard P PhD (StL)
Brockopp Daniel STM (Spr)
Droege Thomas PhD (StL)
Keller Walter E PhD (StL)
Koepke Luther STD (StL)
Krekeler Carl PhD (StL)
Lasky Dale PhD (StL)
Lutze Karl BA (StL)
Rubel Warren PhD (StL)
Schaefer Martin MA (StL)
Senne Edgar MA (StL)
Speckhard Gerald EdD (Sew)
Westermann Ted PhD (StL)

## BOARDING/ RESIDENTIAL HIGH SCHOOL

### ST PAUL RESIDENTIAL LUTHERAN HIGH SCHOOL

Box 719 Concordia MO 64020
660/463-2238 FAX 660-463-7621
E-mail RGGOVE@ALMANET.NET
Year Founded 1883
Gove Richard G MAEd, Headmaster/Principal

**Professors Emeriti**

Fuhrmann Earl EdD
Helge Erich EdD
Mehl Lambert EdD

**Faculty/Staff**

Beerman John MSEd
Bobzin John C MS Coordinator of Communications
Burden Bambi Director Learning Resource Center
Burrow Gloria BA Director of Recruitment
Christiansen Keith MDiv Director of Development
Dahlke James E MSEd
Einspahr Kirk D MSEd
Engelbrecht John MA Assistant Principal
Fiene Rita Yearbook Sponsor
Gasau Linda BSEd
Gasau William L MSEd Director of Music
Gerdts Terry Missouri District Planned Giving Counselor
Gove Dorothy Coach NHS & Student Gov't Sponsor
Hinz Dianne MS Residence Hall Counselor
Krause Valerie G MSEd
Laubenstein Larry P MSEd
Larimore Richard Technology Dir
Miille Pam Drama Coach
MacLean Arthur Coach
Pfannkuch Alyssa BSEd
Pollard Ian MSEd
Pitsch Monte MSEd Athletic Dir
Schnakenberg Don Missouri District Planned Giving Counselor
Stoelting, Lucas BSEd Residence Hall Counselor
Schroeder Andrew M MSEd
Wenberg Marie BSEd Busines Mgr

## HIGH SCHOOLS AND JUNIOR HIGH SCHOOLS

Dagger (†) behind school name indicates accredited by National Lutheran School Accreditation

Pound (#) behind school name indicates a Recognized Service Organization

*No Report Received

### ARIZONA

#### *VALLEY LUTHERAN HIGH SCHOOL ASSOCIATION#*

525 W Colter St Phoenix AZ 85013
602/230-1600 FAX 602/230-1602
E-mail valleyl@goodnet.com
Rehberg Gregory A MSEA Principal
Ellefsen Kathryn
Harman Lisa BA
Hodgson Jean
Hubeler John
Klusman Carole MA
Krieger Randy MED
Moriarity Daniel Rev MDiv
Richter Joseph MA
Scholz Richard BA
Wellman Heather
Zimmerman Dorothea BA

### ARKANSAS

#### *LUTHERAN HIGH SCHOOL ASSOCIATION#*

6711 West Markham
Little Rock AR 72205
501/663-5117 FAX 501/663-1017
Wolbrecht Thomas MDiv EdD Principal
Marks Krista MSW School Counselor
Biesel Matt
Browning Kristen BS
Cheeks Ron
Luckey Sara MA
Pierce Holly
Rawlings James MS
SanRoman Lee MSEd
Sullivan Sarita
Thomas Missy
Toopes Andy Rev MDiv
Williams Paul

### CALIFORNIA

#### *LUTHERAN HIGH SCHOOL ASSOCIATION OF SOUTHERN CALIFORNIA*

3570 Eldridge Ave Sylmar CA 91342

#### LOS ANGELES LUTHERAN JR/SR HIGH SCHOOL#

13570 Eldridge Ave
Sylmar CA 91342
818/362-5861 Fax 818/367-0043
E-mail lalhsoffice@yahoo.com
Wolfgram Dale MS Principal
Gummelt Mike BSEd Vice-Principal
Alley Kim
Bauer Kenneth MA Fine Arts Director
Campuzano Lila MA
Chapman John
Dobler Lori MA
Dobler Stan BSEd
Foster A Christine MA
Imme John MDiv (PT)
Janzen Chad BA
Jardim Susan BS
Ludtke Alvin MAEd
Murillo Pat
Peterson Ruth BA
Senechal Christin
Senechal Martin
Sullivan James BA

#### SOUTH BAY LUTHERAN HIGH SCHOOL#*

3600 W Imperial Hwy
Inglewood CA 90303
310/672-1101 FAX 310/672-1115
E-mail Huskrmg@aol.com
Second Location-See Torrance
Grasz Michael J MA Principal
Warneke Timothy MA Principal
Barker Scott BA
Bender Betty BA
Brennan Tami W BA
Buckner Cleveland MA
Cotton Marion BA
Doyle Erin BA
Fernz John M BA
Flett Mary BS
Gonzalez JoAnne
Grasz Tanya M BA
Mc Auley Paul PHD
Min Carol BA
Moorman Seth BA
Norris Sharon BA
Reinke Paul BA
Rich Nanci BA
Schonhardt Walter BA
William Kelly BA

#### LUTHERAN HIGH SCHOOL#*

3960 Fruit St La Verne CA 91750-2951
909/593-4494 FAX 909/596-3744
E-mail lhlv@juno.com
Haynal John MEd Executive Director/Principal
Spano Cynthia BS Development Officer
Clausen Juls MA Vice Principal
Geach James MA Vice Principal
Chang Janet BA
Doyle Lori BA Student Activities
Hartman Sarah BA
Matthew Lisa BA
McPeters Robin MS BA
Miller Michael BA Athletic Director
Nicolopoulos John BA
Pobanz Teri BA
Schaefer Les MA
Smith Charemon BA
Sorensen Eric BA BS
Sutton David BA
Wiemero Mary MA

#### LUTHERAN HIGH SCHOOL ASSOCIATION OF ORANGE COUNTY*

2222 North Santiago Blvd
Orange CA 92867
714/998-5163
Internet http:/www.lutheranhigh.orange.ca.us
E-mail webmaster@lutheranhigh.orange.ca.us
Dr Kenneth Ellwein LLD Executive Director
Richard Kahler MA Operations Manager
Karle Blanke MA Development Director
Rev Norm Laesch MDiv Planned Giving

#### LUTHERAN HIGH SCHOOL OF ORANGE COUNTY†#*

2222 North Santiago Blvd
Orange CA 92867-2552
714/998-5151 FAX 714/998-1371
E-mail greggp@lutheranhigh.orange.ca.us
Pinick Gregg MSEd Principal
Glandorf Steven BS Assistant Principal
Swanson Craig BA Assistant Principal
Blackwell Angela AA Activities Director
Chaplain Vacant
Bergman Jim BA Network Coordinator
Bosch John MA Registrar
Ellwein Kenneth L LLD
Huston Lynn MA
Kahler Richard MA
Laesch Norman Rev MDiv
Smith Kevin MS Student Activities
Beavers Jeffrey MA
Blanke Karl BA
Cassidy Shawn C BA
Duerr Margaret MA
Eastman Dennis BA
Elfman David H MEd
Ermeling Lyndsay R BA
Gihring Diane BA
Hansen Matthew BA
Heinicke Miriam MA
Held Jeff BA
Howard Tom BA
Kempf Anna BA
Kempf Mark MA
Kempton Alana BA
Knoedler Walter BA
Kramer Michael MA
Kromminga Kevin BA
Kromminga Rebecca MA
Kunau James MA
LaPointe Robert BA
Lothian Joan MA
Lukes Gina MA
Maietta Mark BA
Malmquist John BA
Murphy Beth BA
Neben Julie MA
Odle Susan MA
Paul Nancy BA
Pearsall Esther MS
Pipho Amy BA
Raymond Michelle BA
Sanchez Jeff MA
Schachter Cynthia BS
Schulteis Michael MA
Sherman Rodney BA
Simmons Jerry MA
Smith Kevin MS
Spors Robert MA
Varnes Linda MA
Varnes Walt BA
Vieselmyer Brent BA
Walck Robert BA
Whelply Krista BA
Young Patricia MA
Zimmerman Jonathan MA

#### TRINITY LUTHERAN JR/SR HIGH SCHOOL*

18425 Kittridge St
Reseda CA 91335
818/342-7855 FAX 818/342-4491
Romsa Jerad R MA Principal
Anderson Stephen L BA
Clakley-Jonas Karen E MA Assistant Principal
Alexander William AA
Clakley Matthew M BA
Fredericks Kristin K
Gomez Patricia AA
Kuegele Amy BS
Zelinka Koty BA

#### SACRAMENTO LUTHERAN HIGH SCHOOL†#

2331 Saint Marks Way
Sacramento CA 95864-0626
916/978-2720
Kretzmann David C BA Executive Director
Brauer Norman P MA Principal
Anido Jamie
Bobo Shannon BS
Juelg Mark
Mildred Erika BA
Payne Clare MA
Reufs Ron
Rowland Robert Rev MDiv
Schlensker Erin
Schneider Kristopher E BA
Tiedemann Esther
Weber Eric BA
Wolter Robert A BS

#### CENTER FOR LUTHERAN EDUCATION#

2755 55th St
San Diego CA 92105-5043 619/262-4444

#### LUTHERAN HIGH SCHOOL OF SAN DIEGO*

2755 55th St
San Diego CA 92105-5043 619/262-4444
Principal—Vacant
Bendixen Catherine BA
Glaeser Todd BA
Jonas Scott BA

Lawyer Casey MA Guidance Counselor
Lucas Marsha MA
Meyer Neil H F Jr MA
Suchland John BS
Vedder David MS
Weston Martha MA

**FIRST LUTHERAN HIGH SCHOOL***
13361 Glenoaks Blvd
Sylmar CA 91342
818/362-9223 FAX 818/362-9713
Stark William BS Principal
Altman Gary D MA
Garcia Brenda BS
Hansen Darren BS Athletic Director
Hansen Lori BS
Klein Frederick BS Vice Principal
Knapp Patricia PT
Kocis Greg BS
Newman Marcia
Nuoffer Marcelle BS 8
Stark Susan BS

**SOUTH BAY *LUTHERAN HIGH SCHOOL****
2930 Eldorado PO Box 3295
Torrance CA 90510
310/530-1231
First Location-See Inglewood
Warneke Timothy MEd Principal
Brennan Tammy BS
Fitzgerald Lucas BS
Moorman Seth BS
McAuley Paul PhD
Doyle Erin BS
Ferris Mark BA

## COLORADO

***THE COLORADO LUTHERAN HIGH SCHOOL ASSOCIATION†***
3201 W Arizona Ave
Denver CO 80219-3999
303/934-2345 FAX 303/934-0455
Palmreuter Kenneth Superintendent
Hoener Janet L Development Director

**NORTH LUTHERAN HIGH SCHOOL**
3031 West 144th Ave
Broomfield CO 80020
Palmreuter Kenneth
Braun Douglas
Mountjoy Kathrena
Oeltjen Robert Rev
Paschen Dean
Pontasch Conny

***DENVER LUTHERAN HIGH SCHOOL†#***
3201 W Arizonia Ave
Denver CO 80219-3999
303/934-2345 FAX 303/934-0455
E-mail office@denverlhs.org
Palmreuter Kenneth MA LLD Executive Director
Otte Loren L MA Principal
Bauer Steve Rev MDiv
Block Jason BA
Brandhorst Ronald MA
Duensing Paul S BS
Elliott David
Eman Michael MS
Gehrke Daniel BA
Gertner Susan
Hagen Mary MA
Hauekost Marilyn
Hoener Janet MA
Hollenbeck K Mark BS
Kettner Warren BA
Knapp Andrew BS
Larrabee Loren MSEd
Mountjoy Kathrena BS
Noffze Denise
O'Brien Karen BS
Otte Carolyn Recruitment
Parrott Craig MA
Pyle Karen MA Counselor
Renquest David BA
Roettjer Jennifer
Sloan Keith R MA
Stelling Troy BS
Van Der Werf Leonarda BA
Von Rentzell Paul BA
Weddick Kristin

**SHEPHERD OF THE SPRINGS LUTHERAN HIGH SCHOOL**
9550 Otero Avenue
Colorado Springs CO 80920
719/598-7446 FAX 719/598-8920
E-mail lutheran@ix.netcom.com
Aron Barbara BS
Dorris Joseph MA
Hein Steven Rev Phd
Schaibley Robert Rev MDiv
Scott Frances MA
Stratton Richard D MEd
Tregarthen Suzanne MA
Vaughan Daniel MA

**VAIL CHRISTIAN HIGH SCHOOL**
33520 Highway 6 PO Box 2023
Edwards CO 81632
970-926-3015 FAX 970/926-5682
E-mail Sgilen@vchs.org
Glandorf Steven P MA Executive Director/Principal
Isbell Robert Principal
Baden Corey BA
Chambers Kim BA
Dalzell Kristen BS
Glandorf Todd MCSE
Isbell Linda MA
Sharpe David BS
Sparhawk Molly MEd

**LUTHERAN HIGH SCHOOL OF THE ROCKIES**
10461 S Parker Rd Parker CO 80134
303/841-5551 FAX 720/842-1015
Aufdemberge Richard
Cramer Joan
Grice Richard MA
Hipenbecker Timothy
Palmreuter Joel BA
Prince Susan

**NORTHERN COLORADO LUTHERAN HIGH SCHOOL**
PO Box 2708 Loveland CO 80539
970-962-5304
New

## FLORIDA

**ST JOHN LUTHERAN HIGH SCHOOL**
1915 S E Lake Weir Rd
Ocala FL 32671-5498
352/622-7275 FAX 352/622-5564
Burtzlaff Paul Rev MDiv Principal
Theus Katherine BS Assistant Principal
Craven James MAEd Guidance
Dexheimer Larry BS
Eggold Joshua MA
Grelecki Carolyn BS
Heath Deborah MS
Holliday Cynthia R BA
Lark Peter BA
Mennicke Steve BA Dean of Students
Rath Richard MA
Roy Anna-Barbara MS
Schmidt Elizabeth BA
Schmidt Timothy K BA
Tasler Charles BA

***Lutheran Education Association of Central Florida#***
***550 N Econlockhatchee Trl***
Orlando FL 32825
407/275-7750 FAX 407-277-1288
E-mail orluther@aol.com

**ORLANDO LUTHERAN ACADEMY†#**
550 N Econlockhatchee Trl
Orlando FL 32825
407/275-7750 FAX 407-277-1288
E-mail orluther@aol.com
Wudtke Curtis BS Principal
Bailey David C BA
Bailey Pamela L
Bortz Todd BA
Henderson Cynthia
Jurchen James BS
Jurchen Sarah
Justice Chris
Kallina Carol MA
Mobley Pamela G BA
Shaw Mary Lee MEd
Stafford Jill
Strawn Raymond
Wallis Matthew Rev MDiv
Witzel Rachel A BS
Zook Randall BA

## HAWAII

**LUTHERAN HIGH SCHOOL *ASSOCIATION HONOLULU***

**LUTHERAN HIGH SCHOOL OF HAWAII#**
1404 University Ave
Honolulu HI 96822
808/949-5302 FAX 808/947-3701
E-mail lhsl@pixi.com
Gundell Arthur I MS Principal
Facchini Aljendra
Awaya Clarence BS
Crockett Ruth MEd
Gaudi Robert MEd
Lutz Frank E PhD
Pelletier Lester BA
Rappeline Peter MS
Reginelli Marcy BA
Schriefer William BA
Stocker Stephanie
Utsumi Daryl MA
Utsumi Deems BEd
Villaverde Nancy MA
Willweber David MS
Willweber Marie BA

## ILLINOIS

**LUTHERAN HIGH SCHOOL ASSOCIATION OF GREATER CHICAGO LUTHERAN EDUCATIONAL SERVICE CENTER#**
333 W Lake St Addison IL 60101
630/628-6289 FAX 630/628-8796
Paul Trettin President

**CHRIST LUTHERAN HIGH SCHOOL#**
201 West Lincoln PO Box 8
Buckley IL 60918
217/394-2547 FAX 217/394-2097
E-mail Miski@n2.com
Brauer Jennifer BSEd
Hecht Debra BA
Keup Joel BSEd
Miskimen David M Athletic Director
Meyer Elizabeth BA
Prather Natalie BA Guidance Director

**LUTHER HIGH SCHOOL NORTH#**
5700 W Berteau Ave
Chicago IL 60634-1717
773/286-3600 FAX 773/286-0304
Grunst Nathaniel CAS Superintendent
Kurek Stephen MA Principal
Aufdenkumpe Charles
Bach Carol MA
Bartels Ruth MA
Braker Daniel BA BME
Calvin Matthew
Galek Linda MA
Gauger Andrea MAT Registrar
Grim David BS
Kachka Arlene MS
Kinzie Benjamin MMus
Lorenz Timothy
Lutevi Donna
Markworth Douglas MA
Miller Richard MS Athletic Director
Rueger Floyd
Rundio Ann MA (PT)
Samarrai Vanessa
Schaefer Ronald
Schmidt Katherine BA
Taylor Janet MEd
Tetzler Danielle
Ueltzen Larry MS MA
Volkert Bruce BA
Volkert Marianne BA (PT)
Wiemann Thomas MA CAS
Yurk Michael BA

**LUTHER HIGH SCHOOL SOUTH†#**
3130 W 87th St
Chicago IL 60652
312/737-1416
Oesterreich Allan MS Executive Director/Principal
Bode Jessica BA
Bosch Jerome MS
Enderle Paul MA
Fode Ronald MMus Junior High Principal
Gierke Julie MLS Librarian
Griffin Wm Rev PhD (PT)
Harrison John BS
Hoth Cheryl MEd Guidance Director
Iyassu Zerezghi BS
Janosek Nancy BS
Kieschnick Oscar BS
Kikos James BA
Kube Brian BA
Kube Lisa BA
Lamar Christine MA Registrar
Malone Robert Rev MDiv
Mason Sharon MMus
Moravec Alan MA
Oesterreich Gertrude MS (PT)
Rainey Anthony MEd Assistant Principal
Schulz Robert L MA Assistant Financial
Sohn David MA
Witt Donald E BS

**LUTHERAN SCHOOL ASSOCIATION#**
2001 E Mound Rd
Decatur, IL 62526-9305
217/233-2001 FAX 217/233-2002
E-mail lsa@midwest.net
Winterstein Charles A Superintendent
Heibel Matthew Principal
Bruer Robert
Bryant Janice Lou
Damery Dorothy A
Droll Linda Gifted Program Director
Harper Janet Counselor
Jenson Thomas E Jr High Principal
Mitchell Cathy Jo
Runnells Lee Anne
Sablotny Gayle D
Salefski Jeffrey
Schank John C

**METRO-EAST LUTHERAN HIGH SCHOOL#**
6305 Center Grove Rd
Edwardsville IL 62025
618/656-0043 FAX 618/656-3315
Bohnet Sigmund EdS Principal
Alwardt Michael
Anderson Kathleen BA
Eden Ellen BA Dean of Students
Fossieck Charles
Frey Hope MA (PT)
Gillespie Vicki BA
Giordano Jonathon BA
Heinz Suzanne BA
Henschen Ronald MS Registrar/Counselor
Hipple Eric BA
Hoft Bethany BA
Hutchinson Rebecca
Lauber Lynn MSW (PT) Counselor
Liebman Laura BS
Lindsey Dean Jay BA
Mattson Yvonne (PT)
Nuttmann Quentin BS
Tilashalski Jo Ann
Thompson Paul BA

**FOX VALLEY LUTHERAN ACADEMY#***
220 Division Street Elgin IL 60120
847/468-8207
Libka Robert J MA Exec Dir
McDonald Ian K MA Principal
Kruse Dale BA Development Dir

Zimdahl Janet BA Middle School Director
Butler Judy BA
Frederichs Clifford Rev MDiv
Knutson Luz Maria Acosta MA (PT)
Miller Nikelle BA
O Connor Kathy Eds
Pullabhotla Sarada BA
Weyer Edith BA

**CHRIST OUR SAVIOR LUTHERAN HIGH SCHOOL**
901 Church St Evansville IL 62242
618/853-7300 FAX 618/853-7361
E-mail prange@isbe.accessus.net
Eckert Leroy Rev MDiv
Hormann Rhonda
Janneke Alan Rev MDiv
Meacham Matt
Peck David
Witt Sharon

**LUTHER EAST HIGH SCHOOL#**
2750 Glenwood-Lansing Rd
PO Box 404 Lansing IL 60438-0404
708/895-8441 FAX 708/895-5220
E-mail lehs@aol.com
Brudi Daniel BA
Daake Jennifer BSEd
Erke Alan MA Counselor
Flores Joseph MA
Johnson Jill
Knea Heather BSEd
Lehmann Charles
Malak Paula BS (PT)
Stephens Margurete
Stoner Sara BA
Terlep Matthew

**WALTHER LUTHERAN HIGH SCHOOL†#***
900 Chicago Ave
Melrose Park IL 60160
708/344-0404 FAX 708/344-0525
Gillingham Donald BS Executive Director
Zielke Steven MA Principal
Koehne Robert BA Dean of Students
Bartels Ruth MA
Biancofiore Gabriella BA
Block Melvin W MA
Brown Christine MA
Carpentier Kevin BA
Ehretsman Lucia MA
Finnegan Peter BME
Fisher Todd BA
Graves Matthew BM
Greco Vicky BS
Hoger Warren BA Director of Athletics
Howard Connie BA
Hoy Heather BA
Katzenberger Stephanie BA
Kiger Brent MA
Koehne William BA
Korff Lynn MA
Korntheuer Barbara MLA
Korntheuer Mark MA
Miller Nikelle BA
Mueller Andrew BA
Niziolek Alice BA
Rose Richard BA
Schult Philip BA
Sheys Kathy BA
Sievert Araceli BS
Wentland Betty MA

**LUTHERAN CHRIST ACADEMY#**
23756 W 127th St
Plainfield IL 60544-6706
815/254-8770 FAX 815/254-8770
E-mail dblock@christlutheran academy.org
Block Richard

**LUTHER ACADEMY AND HIGH SCHOOL†#**
3411 N Alpine Rd
Rockford IL 61114-4801
815/877-9551 FAX 815/877-4024
E-mail rlhs@rockfordlutheran.com
Erickson Don Superintendent
Kortze Donald MA Principal
Davis Patricia MA Principal
Stanicek William Athletic Director
Alpers Norman Guidance Counselor
Austen Jane
Bates Jessie
Bertram Neal BS
Bier Rick BA
Boyer Karen (PT)
Bryne Maxine MA
Driscoll Michael MA
Federwitz David BA
Freudenberg Howard T BA
Freudenberg Karen J BA
Gallup Kathleen MA
Gerrond Marjorie BS
Hartz Doreen BS
Hausknecht Nancy MA
Heffner Dennis MA
Hess Katherine (PT)
Horvath Tony R
Jarrett Ehren
Johnson Kimberly BA
Kern Theresa BA
Koselke Cathie BA
Lebryk Ann BA
Lindwall Betty
Lynn Gloria BA
Martin Douglas MA
McCabe Sue MA
McConnell Amy
McLaughlin Bill BA 7
Meggers David L
Mertz Darryl H
Muther Timothy MA
Odegard Gordon A
Pape Jill A
Rogers Dana (PT)
Saltzgiver Jennie
Schermbeck Cassandra Jo
Schermbeck Timothy BA
Schmid John MA
Stanicek William
Temple Elizabeth BA
Vandaele Michael (PT)
Wilson Carol
Williams Judy BA
Wolfgram Steven BA

**LUTHERAN HIGH SCHOOL†#**
3500 West Washington
Springfield IL 62707-7922
217/546-6363 FAX 217/546-6489
E-mail lhs@family-net.net
Nitz Ralph MA Principal
Burch Mary MA Guidance Director
Cuttriss Rachel MA
Devine Rita BA
Duensing Don BA-Counselor
Filter Mike MA Assistant Principal
Fisk Harold T III BA
Gillette Diane L BME
Harris Linda BA
Harris Rena BS
Kammerlohr William BA
Klug James
Koehler Elizabeth
Sperry Robert BS PT
Strong Cynda BS
Tinsley Amy BA
Wilson Lynn MA
Workman Michael

**FAITH LUTHERAN HIGH SCHOOL**
PO Box 173 Union IL 60180
815/338-5159 FAX 815/338-9377
New

## INDIANA

**CONCORDIA LUTHERAN HIGH SCHOOL†#**
1601 St Joe River Dr
Fort Wayne IN 46805
219/483-1102 FAX 219/471-0180
Widenhofer David MAR MS Executive Director
Marks John MA Principal
Anderson Jon K Rev M MDiv
Bahr David BA
Bierbaum Maj Tibor MS
Borchers Dennis Rev MDiv Student Activities
Burgan Diana MA
Conrad Alan
Converset Michelle BS
Doerffler Dean
Dolde Mark BS
Eastman Pamela MS
Fiebig Ronald MAT Coordinator of Educ Technology
Fluegge Paul MA
Friedrich Sandra MA
Gehring Teresa MS
Gerken Eve BS
Gieschen Christopher MS
Grossman Joan MS
Gudel Joseph P Rev MDiv Chaplain
Hoffman Lance BA
Holtslander Amy BA
Kaschinske Eric BS
Koehlinger Mervin MS
Koenig David MA Recruitment Director/Guidance Counselor
Kusch David BA
LaCroix Timothy MMu
LeBeau Edward MS
Lewis Diane MS
Luepke Donald MS
Mannigel Timothy BS
Marks Stephanie BA
Moellering Dianne MS
Nash Kimberly BS
Neumeyer William MS Media Specialist
Ober Vicki MA Director of Guidance
Panning Wayne MA
Peterson Bradley BA
Petroff Barbara MS
Reinking Timothy BS
Rodenbeck Allen MS
Rohde Rebecca BA
Samra Todd MMu
Sassmannshausen Walter MS
Sherrod Lisa BS
Taube Sandra MS IMC Director
Taube Timothy MA
Teague Judy MS
Tucker Sandra MA
Warner Michael BS
Wells Amy BS
Wesley Lisa MS
Widenhofer David
Wiehe Cheryl MS

**LUTHERAN HIGH SCHOOL OF INDIANAPOLIS†#**
5555 S Arlington Ave
Indianapolis IN 46237-2366
317/787-5474 FAX 317/787-2794
E-mail lhsi@inct.net
Willig Fredrick J MA Asst Principal
Benning Evelyn M MA Administrative Assistant
Beringer David C
Baughman Terry A BA
Behrens Calvin M MA Guidance Dir
Brandt Michael B MA
Coneybeer Kristine A MA
Finchum Thomas J MA
Fritz Donald D MS
Groteluesschen David P BA
Guerrettaz Donald E MA
Haw Steven R BS
Johnson Paul W MMus
Lewer Steven F MA
Miller L Kathryn BA
Minnick Brent A MA
Schulenburg Carl L MA
Skvarenina Joseph L MA Development Director
Vincent Eric T BS
Wagner Monica L BA
Wilkes Judith K MA
Witto Katherine I BA

**DUNELAND LUTHERAN HIGH SCHOOL**
1237 E Coolspring
Michigan City, IN 46360
219/872-4419
E-mail mrd@ads.net
Albertin David Rev MDiv
Albertin Jonathan
Harvey Alan
Harvey Brenda
Kilkenny Diane
Klewer Patricia
McDonnell Andrea
Schooley Madeline
Trowbridge William

**TRINITY LUTHERAN HIGH SCHOOL**
101 S Broadway St
Seymour IN 47274
812/524-8547 FAX 812/524-8523
E-mail trinitylutheranhs@hotmail.com
LandsKroener Joel P MA School Adm/Principal

## IOWA

**QUAD CITIES LUTHERAN HIGH SCHOOL ASSOCIATION#**
6509 Northwest Blvd
Bettendorf IA 52722-0903
319/355-6556 FAX 319/355-6403

**CHRIST LUTHERAN HIGH SCHOOL**
PO Box 903
Bettendorf IA 52722-0903
319/355-6556 FAX 319/391-1401
Boye Janet K MAEd
Anderson David C
Gibson Joyce L
Logue Rebecca
McMurray Nathan A
Pett Mary E
Rutledge Joel G
Stuhr Jo Ann M
VanAcker Gloria J
Weber Elizabeth

**LUTHERAN HIGH SCHOOL ASSOCIATION OF CENTRAL IOWA#**
2501 Grand Avenue Suite C West
Des Moines IA 50312

**EASTERN IOWA LUTHERAN HIGH SCHOOL ASSOCIATION**
1024 W 8th St
Waterloo IA 50702
c/o Rev Bruce Boyce
207 Randall St
Reinbeck IA 50669-1250
319/345-2766
New

## LOUISIANA

**LUTHERAN HIGH SCHOOL#**
3864 17th St Metairie LA 70002-4440
504/455-4062 FAX 504/455-4453
Rost Lois A MEd Principal
Augustin Antoinette BA
Barrios Janie
Book Marjorie
Chatelain Joycelyn
Dantin Kerri
Drew Brad Rev MDiv
Hernandez Mercedes
James Denise BA
Lofthus David Rev MDiv
Mancuso Paul J MEd Director of Guidance
Minto Angela
Mull Kenneth BA
Roark Dan
Schaff Janice BA
Simmons Elena BS
Smith Shannon
Tramonte Ryan BA
Turpie George
Wilson Leslie

## MARYLAND

**BALTIMORE LUTHERAN HIGH SCHOOL#**
1145 Concordia Dr Towson MD 21286
410/825-2323 FAX 410/825-2506
Bainbridge Martha E BA
Barth Gary R BA
Bell Melody A BS
Bickel Martha R BA
Bickel Paul V Rev MDiv
Callaway William MA
Chrysam Cynthia S BA
Chuhran Cheryl
Chuhran Kyle
Ciola Marcell BS

Coons Kevin
Doellinger Douglas D MA
Eastin Noel BA
Foelber Thomas
Freeman Alan L BS
Freeman Kristin MA
Frey Carol
Funck Lynne
Gast Randal
Giguere Irene M MSEd
Gregory Stephen Phd
Haar Stephen BA Business Manager
Henn Theodore L BA
Keck Robert MEd
King Michelle BA
Lentsch Thomas B Jr BA Athletic Dir
Luedemann Bart
Luedemann Sheri
Millhoff Donna L MSEd
Morse Edward H BA
Natarajan Lois Development Dir
Osbourn William E MA
Porembski Susan MA Guidance Dir
Royuk Brad R BS
Schildwachter Paul J BA
Seaborn Jacquelin K BA
Walbert Rosemary MA
Weider Michael BS
Weinreich Linda S BA

## MICHIGAN

### *LUTHERAN HIGH SCHOOL ASSOCIATION#(Detroit)*

20150 Kelly Harper Woods MI 48225
313/372-1600 FAX 313/372-3056
Herzog John A PhD Supt
jherzog@lhsa.com
Meseke Steven D Asst Supt
smeseke@lhsa.com
Hoegeman Julie CPA Controller
jhoegeman@lhsa.com

### DETROIT URBAN LUTHERAN HIGH SCHOOL*

8181 Greenfield Rd
Detroit MI 48228-2220
313/582-9900 FAX 313/582-0817

### LUTHERAN HIGH SCHOOL EAST

20100 Kelly Rd Harper Woods MI 48225
313/371-8750 FAX 313/371-7600
E-mail smeseke@lhsa.com
Bell David E
Dolan Rachel BS (PT)
Doebler David BS
Gottula Holly A
Gutenkunst Gary A
Justice Donald BS Athletic Director
Koss Sarah L
Lempke George MA Administrative Asst
Machemer Melvin MMus
Meske Steven D
Olson Christine Phd
Ruml Donna G
Sadler Patricia BS Administrative Asst
Schilling Raymond MLS
Sienkiewicz Melissa MSW MA Counselor
Smith Susan MA
Sprow Keith MA
Teitler Robert F
Todd Suzanne MLS

### LUTHERAN HIGH SCHOOL NORTH†

16825 24 Mile Rd Macomb MI 48042
810/781-9151 FAX 810/781-8673
Buuck Steven PhD Principal
Karsten Kyle MEd Asst Principal
Brandt John MAT
Dallmann LaVerne BS
Dumar John MS
Dunklau Edward MA
Ebel Will BA
Fabbro Ruth MS
Faszholz Gary MA
Felten Mark BA
Freitag Gene MA
Garrabrant Steve
Gierach Raymond MEd
Grobelny Cheryl MS
Hardy Timothy BA
Harris Rachel M
Hoch Christine
Hoft Anne BA
Johnson Penny BA
Karsten Kyle L
Kearney Robin
Kleine Racheal
Kratz Dean MM
Kuschmann Margie MAT
Leinberger David MA
Neidigk Matthew BA
Nieman Lenore BA
Reincke John MEd
Rochlitz David MA
Schley Margaret MA
Sievert Daniel BA
Slagel Steven
Verschaeve Carrie BA
Wargo Paul MEd
Welch Daniel MS
Wolf Charles MS

### LUTHERAN HIGH SOUTH

8260 N Telegraph Rd
Newport MI 48166
734/586-8832
Diroff Jayne
Lucas Bruce Rev MDiv
Lucas Krista
McMillan Herb
Ramthun Dan
Schilke Sharon
Van Washenova Tamara

### LUTHERAN HIGH SCHOOL NORTHWEST†

1000 Bagley Rochester Hills MI 48309
810/852-6677 FAX 810/852-2667
E-mail plooker@lhsa.com
Looker Paul MA Principal
McLoughlin Mark MA Assistant Principal
Chrissman Debbie
Davis Jeffrey BA
Gerds Fred A
Guenther Scott MA
Keller Connie BA
Klerm Christina
MacKenzie Elizabeth BA
McDonald Gilbert Rev
McDonald Ian MA
Pollatz Brian MA
Teitler Robert J
Topel Timothy MA
Verner Denise BS
Weber Karlton MA
Zielinski Jason BA

### SAGINAW VALLEY LUTHERAN HIGH SCHOOL ASSOCIATION

### VALLEY LUTHERAN HIGH SCHOOL†#

3560 McCarty Saginaw MI 48603
517/790-1676 FAX 517/790-1680
Brandt John M MAT Principal
Baker Adrienne
Baldwin Beverly MS
Boehm Jerry MA Counselor
Doyle Barbara BA
Eschmann Pam BA
Eschmann Paul BA Music Director
Feldkamp Beverly BA
Flora Kris MAT
Frank Jon BA
Grueber David BA
Guenther Douglas MAT
Hofmeister Kurt
Kaelberer Jay BA
Major Cyndi BA
Meyers Lisa MAT
Mueller John BA MDiv
Roekle Thomas MAT
Sandmann Danny MA
Westendorf Jeannine BA
Wilaby Kevin BA Asst Principal/Athletic Director
Wittig Barry BA
Wolf Robert BA
Zill Steven MA

### LUTHERAN HIGH SCHOOL WESTLAND†

33300 Cowan Road Westland MI 48185
734/422-2090 FAX 734/422-8566
E-mail sschwecke@lhsa
Schwecke Steven MA Principal
Berndt Norlean BA
Born Lois MA
Brenner Renee C BA
Brown David MA
Eickmann Amy MA
Gentz Ronald BA
Gerlach John MA
Gieschen Timothy J MA
Guse´ Paul BA
Knorp Brendan BA
Lienau Jane MA
Ollinger John
Prechel Dennis MA Media Specialist
Ruth David MA
Strang Donna MA
Twietmeyer Julie H
Unger Michael MEd Athletic Director
Weier Kent MA

## MINNESOTA

### LUTHERAN HIGH SCHOOL OF GREATER MINNEAPOLIS#*

8201 Park Avenue South
Bloomington MN 55420
612/854-0224
Ash Randall MEd Administrator
Adams Walter MA Academic Dean
Bentz Todd BA
Duitzman Jennifer BA
Franzen Roger Rev MDiv Pastoral Care
Jensen Mitchell MA
Kelzer Grace MSE Registrar & Guidance
Kuhlman Robert BA Director of Development
Martchenke Bill BA Dean of Students
Meier Kerry MA
Melde Robert MEd
Melendez Brian BA
Moore Tanja MA (PT)
Mueller Phyllis BA Librarian (PT)
Ohnstad Susan BSEd (PT)
Ott-Hager Diane BA
Pfeiffer Benita BS
Roth Christopher BA Director of Recruitment/Public Relations
Schilf Paul PhD MusEd

### LUTHERAN HIGH SCHOOL#

305 Fifth St NE PO Box 143
Mayer MN 55360-0143
952/657-2251 FAX 952/657-2344
E-mail lhsmayer@aol.com
Aurich Dean R BA
Beck Sally MA
Berg Andrew J BS
Bierbaum Pamela K BS
Bierbaum Timothy M BS
Bisping Diane
Boozikee Kevin T MA
Dorn Richard MA
Dulas James BA
Goetz John BA
Guse Kristen
Grimsley Joelle BA
Hilk Ronald BA
Hoback Barbara BA
Lane David BA
LeClere Bruce BA
Luecke Robert MA
Meier Kathy
Pingel James MA
Strehlke James BA
Thomas Gerald BA
Werner David BA
Zimner Kim BS

### CANNON VALLEY LUTHERAN HIGH SCHOOL

406 W Franklin
Morristown MN 55052-0346
507/685-2636
New

### MARTIN LUTHER HIGH SCHOOL†#

Country Highway 38 PO Box 228
Northrop MN 56075-0228
507/436-5249 FAX 507/436-5240
E-mail rj_royuk@hotmail.com
Royuk Ronald J MA Administrator
Berndt Bruce Rev MDiv Worship Director
Bishop Maryanne
Bittenbinder Dianne BA (PT)
Daul Wade
Diepenbrock Ina (PT)
Ellis Phyllis BA Guidance Director
Geistfield Jodi BA
Holthus James Rev (PT)
Larson Michelle
Oerman Rebecca BS
Patrick Robert MMus Music Director
Patrick Sharon
Taylor Tom BS Athletic Director

### CONCORDIA ACADEMY# 2400

Dale St N
Roseville MN 55113-4598
651/484-8429 FAX 651/484-0594
E-mail rlowe@concordia-academy.pvt.k12.mn.us
Lowe Randy D MA Chief Administrative Officer
Henry Lynn MEd Principal
Aurich Michael MA Athletic Director
Berner Rebekah BS Director of Development
Berner Rev Timothy MDiv Chaplain
Boll David BS
Braun Jo Anna
Chilman John BA
Dickhudt Steve BA
Dunavan Dean BA
Esala Keith MMus
Fritz Gary BA
Fritz Rebecca
Henry Lynn E
Kuseske Thomas MAT
Lark DeVon MAT Counselor
Lowe Randy D
Novotny Shelley BS
Nystuen Sara BA
Schmidt Harold BS
Sohn Martha BA
Strohschein Timothy
Urban Bruce MST
Urban Cindy BS
Vogel Aaron BS
Vomhof Molly BA

## MISSOURI

### SAXONY LUTHERAN HIGH SCHOOL

804 N Cape Rock Dr
Cape Girardeau MO 63701-3605
573/335-6635 FAX 573/335-6765
ORGANIZING

### SAINT PAUL RESIDENTIAL LUTHERAN HIGH SCHOOL†*

Box 719 Concordia MO 64020
660/463-2238 FAX 660/463-7621
E-mail RGGOVE@ALMANET.net
Year Founded 1883

***Headmaster/Principal:***
Gove Richard G MAEd

***Professors Emeriti***
Fuhrmann Earl EdD
Helge Erich EdD
Mehl Lambert EdD

***Faculty/Staff***
Beerman John MSEd
Bobzin John C MS Coordinator of Communications
Burden Bambi Director Learning Resource Center
Burrow Gloria BA Director of Recruitment

Christiansen Keith MDiv Director of Development
Dahlke James E MDiv
Einspahr Kirk D MSEd
Engelbrecht John M MA Assistant Principal
Fabry Timothy MSEd Director of Athletics, Counselor
Fiene Rita Yearbook Sponsor
Gasau Linda BSEd
Gasau William L MSEd Director of Music
Gerdts Terry Missouri District Planned Giving Counselor
Gove Dorothy Coach
Heins Karen International Student Advisor
Krause Valerie G MSEd
Larimore Richard Technology Director
Laubenstein Larry P MSEd
MacLean Arthur Coach
Miile Pam Drama Coach
Payne Alex BSEd Residence Hall Counselor
Pfannkuch Alyssa BSEd
Pitsch Monte BSEd
Pollard Ian MSEd
Remmele Karla BA Deaconess Diploma Residence Hall Counselor
Schroeder Andrew M MSEd
Wienberg Marie BSEd Business Manager

**KANSAS CITY LUTHERAN HIGH SCHOOL#**
414 Wallace Ave
Kansas City MO 64125-1132
816/241-5478 FAX 816/241-4216
E-mail info@lhskc.com
Rudzinsky LeRoy BA Acting Principal
Boettcher Joel W MALS Librarian
Conner Deborah A
Domsch Christopher BA Athletic Director
Einspahr Kelvin W BS
Fritts Douglas
Jeeninga Emil C MA
Liebmann Martin W III BSEd
Meier Paula
Murphy Kimberly BA (PT)
Potter Dan
Rudzinski Lee
Schiefelbein Rona F MA
Smith Cory

***LUTHERAN HIGH SCHOOL ASSOCIATION OF ST LOUIS#***
5401 Lucas & Hunt
St Louis MO 63121-1599
314/382-6650
David F Rittmann President

**LUTHERAN HIGH SCHOOL NORTH**
5401 Lucas & Hunt Rd
St Louis MO 63121-1599
314/389-3100 FAX 314/389-3103
E-mail crislerp@slu.edu
Crisler Paul G MEd Principal
Mueller Kirk H MEd Director of Recruitment
Bergdolt Kurt P BS
Brackman Timothy J BS
Bullard Cedric
Dart Jason
Dart Jeanette
Durst Christine M MEd
Fei Amy PhD
Grupe Michael J MA
Hemminghaus Shirley J MEd
Hillemann Jeanine
Hobbs Kelly L BA
Holschen Carl C MS
Hope John BA
Hunt Elaine F BS
Kersten John V MS
Klingsick Barbara L MS
Kratzer Michael J MEd
Kunkel Sara
Langefeld Richard A BA
Manion Jim
McCollister David P MA
Meschke Mark W Rev MDiv
Prahlow James D MA
Prange Michael MEd Counselor
Rueter Brent
Russell Michael D MEd Director of Athletics
Terrell Sally A BA
Thomas Elizabeth L MA
Thomas John E BA
Tirmenstein Stephen W MA
Williams Ramona

**LUTHERAN HIGH SCHOOL SOUTH**
9515 Tesson Ferry Rd
St Louis MO 63123-4317
314/631-1400 FAX 314/631-7762
Buetow Paul E MA Principal
Albers Michael R MS
Arnold Richard J MA Director of Guidance
Baker Vesta BSEd
Bauer Kenneth MEd Assistant Principal
Beaver Bruce MEd
Becker Kristin BA
Behling Mark T BA
Berendzen Jana S
Bertani Sandra MA
Brown DeAnne MBA
Collins Suzanne MAT
Connors Adam S BSEd
Eggold Stephen F MA Athletic Director
Eischer Deborah BS
Goris Susan J MM (PT)
Griffard Sandra M MEd (PT) Guidance
Harms Daniel B MEd Assistant Principal
High Susan G BS
Hill Arthur MEd
Hill June M MAT
Hintze Gretchen
Hochbrege William
Holliday D Robert MA
Iezzi Jean MA (PT)
Jerry Elfriede MA
Kalbeleisch Edith
Klug Zachary
Krieser Aaron
LaBore Richard D Rev STM PhD
Lackey Larry MEd (PT)
Lind Brian BSEd
McMillan Ike MAT (PT)
Meyer Jeaninne MA Librarian
Miller Ellen K BA
Miller John W MM
Olkander Remkea
Omura Ann
Perry John BSEd
Pfund Roy E MA
Pickett Allen
Prahlow Donald A PhD (PT)
Rauh Shirley P MEd
Reck Thomas P MA
Redman William
Reinitz Carol BSEd (PT)
Reiss Richard G MA
Richenburg Peter W MAT
Rogers Randall J BA Guidance
Roma Ron T Rev MDiv Guidance
Rusch Wilbert H MA
Sanders Jeff BSEd
Smith Alan J BSEd
Spencer Elizabeth A MAT
Stark Nicholas BA
Steinbrueck Kenneth P BA
Torbeck Larry P MA
Trah Richard H MA
Wietfeldt Cathy L MS
Zoernig Deborah M BSEd

***LUTHERAN HIGH SCHOOL ASSOCIATION OF ST CHARLES COUNTY INC#***

**ST CHARLES LUTHERAN HIGH SCHOOL†**
5100 Mexico Rd St Peters MO 63376
636/928-5100 FAX 636/928-8451
Schlesselman David A MEd Executive Director
Marty Larry D MEd Principal
Bernhardt Jonathan BA
Bredow Gordon J MEd
Christian Erica L BS
Cox Joe Rev MDiv
Flandermeyer Michael D MA
Fruend Elizabeth L BS (PT)
Gaertner Christi
Gibbs Renee MA (PT)
Haak Armand L MS
Hendricks Jr Steven L BS
Holtmeier Michael G MAR
Lail Christopher J MS
Lewis Jennifer MS (PT)
Limback Kelley
Michaelson Paul R MA
North Marcy Allen MA (PT)
Staude Claudia A MA
Staude Edmund D MEd
Steinbacher David A BS
Steinke Katherine BS
Stollenerk Michael P MAR
Timm Sheryl K MBA
Tonjes Bernard J MEd Guidance
Walkenhorst Bonnie

## NEBRASKA

**LUTHERAN HIGH SCHOOL ASSOCIATION OF CENTRAL NEBRASKA#**
PO Box 2277
Grand Island NE 68802-2277

**HEARTLAND LUTHERAN HIGH SCHOOL**
3900 Husker Hwy PO Box 2277
Grand Island NE 68802-2277
308/385-3900
E-mail fischerone@msn.com
Fischer Curt Executive Director
Zehendner Jackie

**LINCOLN LUTHERAN JR/SR HIGH SCHOOL#**
1100 N 56th Lincoln NE 68504-3296
402/467-5404 FAX 402/467-5405
E-mail info@lnklutheran.org
Rabe Robert EDS Principal/ Chief Administrator
Sirek Steve B MEd Chaplain
Roundey William G MA Counselor
Duitsman Donald L MEd Activities Director
Bartels Nylene BA
Bassett Nathan C MA
Bockelmann Katie BA
Carlson Susan J MA
Ernstmeyer Craig
Ernstmeyer Scott J BSEd
Guilford Thomas K BSEd
Kuhlman Douglas J BA
Lebo Renae L BSEd
Leeper Susan BS
Loontjer Gary L MA
Loontjer Susan BS
Metzgar Michelle R BSEd
Ohlman Kathleen R MA
Petersen Dianne E MS
Pester Beth BSEd
Rodencal Korinna D BA
Roeber John K BS
Schodel Mary
Willet Donna S BS
Ziegler Susan M BA
Ziems Lyle L BA

**LUTHERAN HIGH SCHOOL ASSOCIATION#**

**LUTHERAN HIGH SCHOOL NORTHEAST**
2010 N 37th St PO Box 2454 Norfolk NE 68702-2454
402/379-3040 FAX 402/379-8340
E-mail luthhigh@ncfcomm.com
Leckband Paul R MS Executive Director
Beam Hope A BS
Christman John T BS
Gebhardt Charles E MS
Leavitt Deanne MA
Lockard Tria
Pape Stephanie
Rathke Greg BS
Riege Cheryl
Shively Sally K BS
Sorensen Juli
Stefan Matt
Sweigard Maria
Urwiler Daryle
Volkman Susan MA

**CONCORDIA LUTHERAN JR/SR HIGH SCHOOL**
15656 Fort St c/o 9020 Q St
Omaha NE 68127
402/592-8005 FAX 402/331-1123
ORGANIZING

**CROSS LUTHERAN HIGH SCHOOL**
2902 S 20th Street
Omaha NE 68108-1301
402/341-2603 FAX 402/342-6511
E-mail cross@mitec.net
Yaksich Pam BS Administrator
Clanton Shauna BS
Kane Karen BS
Lehman Janine RN
Loewen Cynthia
Pruitt Lacey
Rodriguez Wanda
Ruff Katherine BS
Schlesiger Chris
Struble Karla
Tynan Mary Jane

## NEVADA

***LUTHERAN SECONDARY SCHOOL ASSOCIATION***

**FAITH JUNIOR/SENIOR HIGH SCHOOL#**
2015 Hualapai Way
Las Vegas NV 89117
702/804-4400 FAX 702/804-4488
E-mail kmd2236@aol.com
Dunning Kevin M MS Principal
Desruisseaux Margaret BS Director of Management Services
Ball Emily
Barrett Rebecca Secretary
Beery Brenda
Bever David
Bever Peggy
Bieber Douglas MA
Bowline Melanie BA
Boyd Alecia
Boyd Jason BA
Buikema Daniel BA
Cheney Mark BA
Cheney Rebecca BA
Collins Rosemarie BA
Crawley Patricia
Day Bonnie BA
Diaz Jose J BA
Dunning Mary F BA
Fogo R Scott BS
Gentry Susan AS Administrative Assistant
Giannosa Linda
Greene Hilary BA
Heimlich Carrie M BA
Honea Elizabeth
Karpinsky Kristen S BA
Kasting Melanie S BA
Kothe Jacob BA
Krafft Joanne M BA Curriculum Director
Laufer John
Livo Rebecca A BS
Mathers Richard
McAllister Lisa BA
Mueller Randall H BA
Nagel Matthew C MEd
Nordstrom Laura BA
Ongman Cathy BS
Pomeroy Todd
Pullabhotla Sarada BS
Ragland John
Rasco Susan A
Renn Peter MEd Dean of Students
Rollings Glenn
Russo Ruth BS
Sato Stacy
Schulze Diana MRE

Scobell Jessica BA
Severino Suzanne
Simon Christin
Swissman Megan BA
Uhlig June BS
Underhill Nadine BA
Vergina Veronica MEd
Walter Bret L MS
Washington Elayanne BA
Webb Angela D BS
Webb Neil F BA
Youmans Sandra B MA

## NEW YORK

**OUR SAVIOUR LUTHERAN HIGH SCHOOL**
1734 Williamsbridge Rd
Bronx NY 10461
718/792-5665
Schmidt John C PhD Principal
Bailey Larry MA
Ervin John MM
Horgan Charles
Johnson Larry MA
Kendall Brian
Lewis Carlson
Mesiano Linda
Ramspott Paul MA
Warner F Richard MA
Wheeler Anthony

**LONG ISLAND LUTHERAN MIDDLE & HIGH SCHOOL#**
131 Brookville Rd
Brookville NY 11545-3329
516/626-1700 FAX 516/626-1773
E-mail info@luhi.org
Hahn David PhD Executive Director
Wenger Paul MS Principal
Alberda John MA
Anderson Margaret
Andreoli Lisa
Beers Charles MEd
Brancaccio Bobbee
Callahan Laura BA
Colangelo Anthony BA
Corrigan Ann MA
Cunningham Louise BA
Dragos Christine BA
Gallagher Jennifer
Gonzalez Tama
Gothberg Ronald Rev MDiv Chaplain
Grenz Greyson
Hahn David
Hahn Janet
Hall Katherine MA
Hebling Audrey PhD
Hess Karen BS
Hinsch John MA
Huebner Todd BS
Isakson Vivian MS
Karsch Marilyn MA Guidance Counselor
Kast JoAnn MA
Krahn Lisa MSW Guidance Counselor
Lauricella Jane MS
Lescault Jonathan
Lievano Rafael BA
Malusa Robert MA
Margiasso Kathleen MS
O Brien JoAnn MST
O'Hanlon Laurie MA
Rand Michael
Reno Chris
Rodis John BA
Sanders Julie
Sommermeyer Joshua BA
Spangler John BA
Tuthill Richard
Vila Donna
Voegler Carolyn MA Librarian
Vogel Nancy MEd
Weaver Jacqueline MEd
Wenger Margaret MS
White Jacqueline MA
Wilner Nicole MA
Zanzi Monica BS
Zimardo Alexandra MA
Zuclich Joanne MA

**MARTIN LUTHER HIGH SCHOOL#**
60-02 Maspeth Ave PO Box 780017
Maspeth NY 11378-0017
718/894-4000 FAX 718/894-1469
E-mail mlutherhs@aol.com
Herbrich Ben T MA Executive Director
Crowe Elizabeth MA Principal
Adams Nichole
Ahamad Ilene BS
Alizadeh Changiz
Andersen Lane BA
Bennett Cheryl BA
Borchert Joan MA Dean of Students
Boyle Ann MSEd
Bullock Beatrice MA
Coger Osia
Daniels Lisa BS
Fanara Annette BA
Finkelman Phyllis BA
Fredericksen Gary BA Operations Director
Freudenburg David MA
Gamez Delilah BA
Greco Felicia
Halloran Julia
Hicks Steven BA
Howlett Anne MA
Johnson Kenneth BS
Jordan-Jones Elizabeth
Kay Eric
Lizotte Richard BA
McCann Elizabeth MA
Regan James MA
Savage Susan BA
Shapiro Susan BA Finance Dir
Stohlman John Rev MDiv
Struckmann Cynthia
Vedder David
Westfal Kelli MA Communications Dir
Woodroffe Stella EdM
Zinkowski Dawn BA

## NORTH CAROLINA

***RESURRECTION CHRISTIAN HIGH SCHOOL***
2825 Shenandoah Ave
Charlotte NC 28205-6938
704/334-9898 FAX 704/377-6578
Miller William R BA
Lockman Barbara BA
Robinson Linnea
Croft Ronda
Sprang Joy
Sweatt Patricia

## OHIO

***LUTHERAN HIGH SCHOOL ASSOCIATION# (CLEVELAND)***
14805 Detroit Ave #250
Lakewood, OH 44107
216/227-2190 FAX 216/227-2194
E-mail jlatra@aol.com
Ahlersmeyer Thomas R Rev PhD Exec/Development Dir
Smolik John W MBA Business Mgr
Forni Peggy BS Development/Alumni

**LUTHERAN HIGH SCHOOL EAST***
3565 Mayfield Rd
Cleveland Heights OH 44118-1401
216/382-6100 FAX 216/382-6119
Bruhn Paul R PhD Principal
Bullard Cedric BA
Bruhn Deborah BA (PT)
Clark Nancy MEd
DeWitt David BA
Fitzpatrick Timothy BA
Geer Wesley BA
Harris Jeanette MA
Kelly Janet MLS
Krug Lisa BA
Laufer John BS
Martello Heather MS
Mims O Dennis MDiv (PT)
Murphy Margo BA
Patton Georgia MS
Souza Ann BME (PT)
Riley Barbara BA
Williams Walter BA (PT)
Wordell Deborah BA
Wordell Paul BA
Wyly Jeaneen BA

**LUTHERAN HIGH SCHOOL WEST***
3850 Linden Rd
Rocky River OH 44116-4099
440/333-1660 FAX 440/333-1729
Linn Richard W MEd Asst Principal
Ahlersmeyer Thomas Rev PHd
Becker Michael R BS
Brazel Gregory BS
Brinkmann Paula M MEd
Dus Ramona BA
Fehrs Troy BS
Felten John C MS
Fenske James L MED
Fuchs Steven M MED
Gesch Joel T MEd Athletic Dir
Gesch Judy M MEd
Haberhern Jean MLS
Haberhern Dennis MS Guidance
King Joseph C MA
Maechner Kurt BA
Matthews Darlene BA
Mc Keen (Smith) Tina BA
Merriman Lynn T BS
Miller Christopher J BA
Miller Donna BA
Miller Heidi MA
Moses Debra Lynn BA
Pegels Nancy J BA
Petersen Enoch BME
Prim John W MA
Ressler David BA
Robbins Nathan BA
Rolik Judith A MEd Guidance
Schanz Eleanor MA
Shimek Jill M MA
Stover Mark BA
Vavroch John Rev MDiv
Wittrock Karen D MEd

## OREGON

**PORTLAND LUTHERAN HIGH SCHOOL#**
740 SE 182nd Portland OR 97233-4960
503/667-3199 FAX 503/667-4520
E-mail pls@teleport.com
Maier Donald BAE Principal
Birnstein Karl MEd Executive Director
Bloom Maggie BS
Licht Robert MST
Petke Michael
Petke Thomas MST
Rush Chad BA Athletic Dir
Speer Deborah
Strand Diana
Strand Gregory Rev MDiv
Wong Leslie S MA
Zelinka Katy

## TEXAS

**ST TIMOTHY LUTHERAN MIDDLE/HIGH SCHOOL**
5901 New York Ave
Arlington TX 76018-2409
817-557-9411 FAX 817-557-9412
E-Mail robertmalzahn@aol.com
Malzahn Robert W EdD Headmaster
Bahn Nicole M
Bremer Valerie A

**LUTHERAN HIGH SCHOOL ASSOCIATION OF GREATER SOUTH DALLAS AND FORT WORTH AREA #**
PO Box 541776
Grand Prairie TX 75054-1776
972/264-8681 FAX 972/264-2512

**LUTHERAN HIGH SCHOOL OF DALLAS†#**
8494 Stults Road
Dallas TX 752431-4006
214/349-8912 FAX 214/340-3095
E-mail sgreimann@usa.net
Brunworth Gerald C EdD Headmaster
Klekamp Patricia A MA Principal
Abbott Phillip G BM
Allmon Steven A MEd
Burow Peter J
Cain Camille BS
Couser Thomas D MEd
DeStefano Nancy M
Flickinger Chris W
Fluegel Doyle W BS
Frieling Kurt BS (PT)
Fry Timothy K MS
Greimann Steve P MA
Heislen Sarah C BS
Krause Bradley R MEd
Krause Elizabeth A MEd
Lindsay Kay BS
Lund Steven P MA
McLain Michael BSEd
Meyer Kay MEd
Morris Christine M BSEd
Nitz Todd E BSEd
Noack Kristin M BS (PT)
Roldan Lisa G BSEd
Thompson David L
Warneke Kevin BA
Zimmerman Michael P BS

***Lutheran Education Association of Houston#***
12555 Ryewater Drive
Houston, TX 77089
281/464-6155 FAX 281/464-6119
E-mail dsommermeyer@msn.com
Sommermeyer David A MA Executive Director
Christian Donald A MA Associate Director

**LUTHERAN HIGH NORTH*†**
1130 W 34th St Houston TX 77018
713/880-3131
Schaller Bruce MA Principal
Benkendorf Rod BA
Bowden Cindy BA
Buchheimer Peggy BA
Burroughs Dorothy MA Elem Music
Carpenter Aaron BA
Cooper Jeff BM
Culli Ben BME
Eickemeyer Lynn MA Counselor
Gerard Dana MA
Hall Charles BA
Heath Mary BS
Hynous Terry MA
Irlanda Tamariz BA
Kemnitz Detlef MA
Larsen Melissa BS
Morgan Daniel BS
Mulder Tara BA
Richter Ed MEd Athletic Director
Riveness Garret BA
Schlie David BS
Stueber Matt BS
Stuenkel Paul MEd Asst Principal
Wolfram Carlene BS

**LUTHERAN SOUTH ACADEMY†**
12555 Ryewater Drive
Houston TX 77089-6625
281/464-8299 FAX 281/464-6119
Kramer Wayne EdD Headmaster
Rathje Michael Principal
Annweiler Frank
Baacke Bruce MEd Registrar
Baacke Mark MS
Ballard Diana
Benson Gene MA
Britton Jim
Buchman Archie
Hergenrades Christina
Himmler Gary W MS
Inglis Kathi
Isbell Ann BS
Myers Marjorie MA
Psencik Rob
Robbins Kenneth MS Athletic Director
Schlie Abigail BA
Schultz Wyatt
Stark Paul BS
Tedeschi Anthony BS
Ward Jennifer
Whitfield Linda MEd, LPC(tl)

Worchesik Michael BS

***LUTHERAN HIGH SCHOOL ASSOCIATION# (SAN ANTONIO)***
1826 Basse Road
San Antonio TX 78213
210/733-7771 FAX 210/735-3644
Quandt Gary P Chairman Board of Directors

**LUTHERAN HIGH SCHOOL OF SAN ANTONIO†**
1826 Basse Road
San Antonio TX 78213-4606
210/733-7771 FAX 210/735-3644
E-mail LHSSA@yahoo.com
Miller Michael A MA Principal
Becker Michael D BA
Biedinger Bruce R MA
Claridge Anita L BA
Fuchs Judith M MA
Halder Guido MEd
Lindau Rebecca E
Lopez Valeria A
Merkord Lanny D BS
Poertner Sarah E MEd
Quandt Laura A BS
Richter Nathan D
Vanic Patrick R BA

**CONCORDIA LUTHERAN HIGH SCHOOL OF NORTH HARRIS COUNTY#†**
700 E Main Street
Tomball TX 77375-6721
281/351-2547 281/255-8806
E-mail info@concordiacrusaders.org
Cooper Dale MEd Principal
Blakney Marla BBA Admissions Dir
Bode Joel MA Assistant Principal
Brewer Lynn M
Carpenter Sandra L
Cluiss Hahnah
Dunagin Marilyn BS
Hall Freddie BS
Helmer Rebecca BS
Henderson Don
Ilten Steven BA Ath Dir
Ironside Carolyn BS
Johnson James J BA
Kasper Ann
King Tracy
MacDonald Neil BA (PT)
Malm Erik
McClain Randy R BS
McQueen Babette
Navarrete Ana S
Nordling Philip J BS
Parker Christine
Payne Nancy L BA
Pender Anna
Petrosky Jeffrey
Riveness Garret P BA
Scheyder Paul Rev MDiv
Schulz Juergen BS
Schwab Lawrence P BS
Severson Diane
Steele Sandra B MA
Stender Debbie Counselor/Librarian
Straub Matthew
Timmins George
Walter J Scot BS
Weaver Nevilee A
Whitson Jan PhD
Wiese Marsha D
Wilke Harold
Wilke Phillip MA

## UTAH

**SALT LAKE LUTHERAN HIGH SCHOOL#**
4020 South 900 East
Salt Lake City UT 84124-1169
801/266-6676 FAX 801/266-1953
Asche Nancy D BS
Davis Shelly BA
Eick Petra M MA
Going Glenn W BSEd
Kimball Michel
Mousley Erinn BA
Payne John BM
Schrader Aaron J BS
Schrieber Jonathan
Thornton Joshua

## WASHINGTON

**SEATTLE LUTHERAN HIGH SCHOOL#***
4141 41st Ave SW
Seattle WA 98116
206/937-7722 FAX 206/937-6781
E-mail
dcoursey@seattlelutheran.org
Coursey Donna MA Principal
Biesenthal Bruce Rev MDiv Development Director
Black Dana BA
Boyd Marla Ann BA
DeCou Robert MA (PT) Music Director
Dowding Robert MA Athletic Director
Dufour Joanne MS
Hamry Carl MFA
Hemme Mathilda BA Business Manager
Herzel-Harding Ute MA
Klein John BA
Koosmann Kenneth BS
Matthews Robert MA
Norton Jeff BA
Norton Kenneth MA
Pedersen Nora MA
Pena Lois BS Librarian
Vradenburgh Shirley MA (PT)

**LUTHERAN HIGH SCHOOL ASSOCIATION OF SOUTH PUGET SOUND#**
c/o Concordia Lutheran School
202 E 56th St Tacoma WA 98404
253/475-9513

**MOUNT RAINIER LUTHERAN HIGH SCHOOL**
c/o Concordia Lutheran School
202 E 56th St Tacoma WA 98404
253/475-9513
ORGANIZING
Christian Robert Interim Executive Director

## WISCONSIN

***LUTHERAN HIGH SCHOOL ASSOCIATION OF NORTH-EASTERN WISCONSIN#***
1311 South Robinson Ave
Green Bay WI 54311
920/469-6810 FAX 920/469-2200
E-mail newlhs@gbonline.com
Siekmann Stephen MS Principal
Blocker Holly B MS
Doell Jean M
Fosheim Cynthia M BA
Heller Ruth A
Lange Leanne A BA
McClellan James R BA
Meerstein Mark W BA
Schumacher Krystal K BA
Sommerfeldt Nancy BA
Steinhaus Paul R BA
Stock Michael R BA

**LUTHERAN HIGH SCHOOL ASSOCIATION OF GREATER MILWAUKEE#**
5201 S 76th St
Greendale WI 53129-1197
414/421-9100 FAX 414/421-9120
Buck Thomas M MS Supt
Bartelt Stephen R MDiv MPA MM Director of Finances and Association Services
Batterman-Smith Mary B MA Development Associate
Greenfield James G BA Director of Development

**MARTIN LUTHER HIGH SCHOOL**
5201 S 76th St
Greendale WI 53129-1197
414/421-4000 FAX 414/421-4071
Eisman Carl S MA MSEd Principal
Au Laura BA
Aumann James C BA
Bangert David MA Director of Student Services
Barwa William H BS
Burgess David MA Admission Director, Assistant Principal
Dietz James MAE
Doerr Paul A MA
Franz Timothy MCM
Gabler Frank MSEd
Garlock Rebecca
Greenfield James G
Hackbarth Michael R
Handy Rebecca MEd
Heffelfinger Jana M
Herzog Phillip MA
Jung Jeanie MS
Kahlscheuer Sarah L MS
Kindschi Paul S MEd
Klotz Joy C MA
Kollmorgen Paul G BA
Land Lori
Leeland Nicole MA
Limmer Andrew MS
Loveless Michael P MEd
Mellendorf Craig MS
Menzel Marianne BS
Miller James MS
Nelson Frederick MS
Nickel Scott BA
Reigles James D MA
Schmid Julie BA
Schmid Steven P BA
Wiegert Jonathan BME
Wingfield Jeanne BS
Wingfield Phillip BA Athletic Director
Wright Steven MS

**LAKE COUNTRY LUTHERAN HIGH SCHOOL**
31385 W Hill Rd Hartland WI 53029
262/369-4935 FAX 262/369-4936
Bahr Mark M MA Principal
Dahm-Tegtmeier Janel (PT)
Denkert Sally (PT)
Eckels Mary Beth (PT)
Garlock Rebecca (PT)
Hoffman Henry II BS
Miller Christy (PT)
Newman Mark

**LIVING WORD LUTHERAN HIGH SCHOOL#**
N 167 W20900 Main St
Jackson WI 53037
262/376-2222
New

**MILWAUKEE LUTHERAN HIGH SCHOOL#**
9700 W Grantosa Dr
Milwaukee WI 53222-1497
414/461-6000 FAX 414/461-2733
Bahr Paul M MA Principal
Adams Lonnie MA
Alles Brad A MS
Anderson Ellen BA
Bahr Paul M
Birmingham Carol BA
Bolz Sarah MS
Bull Bernard D
Clinard Randall MLS Director of Media Services
Darien Thomas L
Forke Brian BA
Gnan Paul BA
Goetzinger Joanne MEPD
Guilford John BS
Hafemann Craig A MBA
Harrmann Bruce MDiv
Hauser Anne BA
Heinkel Robert MS
Hobus Steven R BS
Irish David MS
Irvine Todd
Jameson Gretchen BS
Jensen Wayne E MEPD
Jobst Dwayne MA Assistant Principal
Jurgensen James D MA Dean of Students
Jurss Jason BS
Kalous Keith MA
King Thomas
Koebert Jay BS
Koebert Linda BS
Kohrs Stephen MEPD
Krause Steven MS
Krubsack, Kathryn
Krueger Nancy MST
Lamping Laurene Ann
Little Tasha N
Miller Christy S
Moeller Joan MA
Moesch Jason BS
Nelson Nancy MEPD
Pankow Eric BS
Pankow Matthew BS Athletic Director
Pollock Larry MAR
Pretzel Judy MA
Pries Lonnie F
Refenes James MEPD
Riofrio Jan MA
Roeglin Carol MEd
Rohde Mark MS
Rusch Jeanne MEd
Saugstad Maynard MA
Schmidt Delevan MS
Schwarz Rozanne MA
Siebarth Monica BA
Struve Marjorie MA
Wangerin Kathryne BS
Weyhrich R Jay MA
Widener Anne BA
Young Sharon MEPD
Zerzen Rolf BS

**EAST CENTRAL WISCONSIN LUTHERAN HIGH SCHOOL ASSOCIATION***
420 E Green Bay St STE 205
Shawano WI 54166
715/526-4336
NEW

**LUTHERAN HIGH SCHOOL#**
251 Luedtke Ave Racine WI 53405
414/637-6538 FAX 414/637-6601
E-mail rlhs@execps.com
Baganz Randal MA Principal
Banning Benjamin
Bickel Nathan BA Dean of Students
Bruening John BA
Bunderman Julie
Eickhorst Willard MS
Flanagan Patricia EDd Guidance Dir
Frederickson Lynette BSN
Guethling Cory BA
Jensen Daniel MS
Jensen Linda BA
Krug Lisa
Kruschke Sally BS
Luchterhand Karl Rev MDiv
Masengarlo David
Porter Julie BS
Rognsvog Diane BA
Tertel Robert MS
Thieme Janet MSS
Vogel Craig MS
Ware Janet BA Librarian

**SHEBOYGAN AREA LUTHERAN HIGH SCHOOL#**
3323 University Dr
Sheboygan WI 53081-4761
920/452-3323 FAX 920/452-1310
E-mail
administration@lutheranhigh.com
Adameak Ryan
Arnholt Laura BA
Dudek Lori BA
Heffelfinger Mark MS
Holt Jeffrey BA
Johnson Donald MDiv
Jurss Jeff BA
Lastusky Myrna BA
Muth Tim MA
Olson Peter BME
Otten Hans BS
Paape Adam
Reseburg Julie BS
St Clair Gary BA
Voitek Diana BA (PT)
Wilson Craig BS
Zajkowski Kelly
Zeuner Richard BS
Zielinski Jason

# DIRECTORY OF EARLY CHILDHOOD SCHOOLS, AND ELEMENTARY SCHOOLS

Updated to October 27, 2000

Schools are listed according to the state and physical town, village, or city in which the school building is located.

School records are formatted in the following order: Physical City, Name, low-high grade, Recognized Service Organization designation, National Lutheran School Accreditation designation, year established, address, phone number, fax number, e-mail address, principal (in bold), teachers.

Address: If the school has both a physical address and a mailing address, then the physical address lines and zip code are printed first, followed by the mailing address, city and zip code.

NO REPORT = Information to update the school records were not received by the due date.

**KEY TO ABBREVIATIONS**

NLSA = School is accredited by National Lutheran School Accreditation

RSO = School is a Recognized Service Organization

**SCHOOL GRADE CODES**

K = Kindergarten PS = Preschool (this would include Day Care, Nursery etc.)

## United States

### ALABAMA

**ARLINGTON-**EPIPHANY PS-3
• 1964
Highway 5 PO Box 309
36722-0309
(334)385-2435
Walker Sandra R PS-3

**BESSEMER-**ZION 1-3
• 1951
1201 24th St N 35020-3339
(205)425-2091
NO REPORT

**BIRMINGHAM-**PILGRIM
• 1924
447 1st St N 35204-4323
(205)251-3451
NO REPORT

PRINCE OF PEACE PS
4413 10th Ave N 35212
(205)592-2207 •
FAX(205)836-6657
NO REPORT

VESTAVIA HILLS PS
• 1987
201 Montgomery Hwy 35216-1801
(205)823-1883
Barberini Cindy PS
Deyo Lisa PS
Lide Barbara PS
Michael Cindy PS
Piasky Virginia MA

**CULLMAN-**ST PAUL PS-6
• 1954
510 3rd Ave SE 35055-4315
(205)734-6580 •
FAX(205)734-3540
Blanton Martha MA 2
Ewald Gene K BA
Falter Becky 6
Grissom Linda K 6
Heinze Frederick C BS 4
Heinze Hazel B BS 3
Ivey Pamela K BS PS
Jester Carla L BSED 3-6
Jester Sheila A BA K-5
Lanier Cecilia 5
Mc Graw Nella K
Scott Joyce 1
Tucker Kathy PS

**DECATUR-**ST PAUL PS
• 1995
1700 Carridale St SW 35601-4638
(256)353-8759 •
FAX(256)353-7496
stpaulsdec@aol.com
NO REPORT

**DOTHAN-**TRINITY PS-K
• 1959
1440 S Park Ave 36301-3438
(334)793-6381
NO REPORT

**FOLEY-**SAINT PAULS PS
400 N Alston St 36535 PO Box
759 36536
(334)970-3769
stpaul@gulftel.com
**Taylor Susan L PS**

**GADSDEN-**TRINITY PS
• 1995
1885 Rainbow Dr 35901
(256)546-1712 •
FAX(256)546-7516
tlc@cybrtyme.com
Anders Jan PS
Wilbourn Stacy PS

**HUNTSVILLE-**ASCENSION PS
• 1978
3803 Oakwood Ave NW
35810-4061
(256)536-5245 •
FAX(256)536-8104
NO REPORT

GRACE PS-8
• NLSA • 1963
3321 S Memorial Pkwy
35801-5342
(256)881-0553 •
FAX(256)881-0563
gls@hiwaay.net
**Hauer Raymond P MA**
Behnken Donna D MED 2
Cypher Alan J MS 7
Doelling Michelle L BA 1
Forrester Kathryn PS-8
Halbritter Dorothea W BA 8
Hayes Sandra 6-8
Kissinger Doris A PS-8
Ladd Lynda L MA PS-8
Mc Clure Joyce A BS 5
Naatz Monica A BSED 4
Naatz Thomas J BS 8
Sims Terri 6-8
Stephens Joyce H MED K
Tosado Nancy PS
Walker Louise A BA 3
Wank Sabina B BA PS
Young Karen 6-8

**LILLIAN-**SHEPHERDS LAMBS PS
12851 Perdido St 36549
(334)962-7682
Cowart Diedre PS
Meszaros Jill PS

**MOBILE-**FAITH PS-5
• 1924
1703 Dr Martin L King Jr Ave
36617-3905
(334)471-1629
Kirksey Daisy B BS K-6
Scott Mablelean D MED
Washington Danita J BS K

MOUNT CALVARY PS-7
• 1947
1660 Dominick St 36605-4858
(205)471-4200
NO REPORT

OUR SAVIOR LUTHERAN PS
5101 Government Blvd 36693
(334)661-4524 •
FAX(334)661-3369
Cleveland Suzy
Erdman Mary

TRINITY PS-5
• 1955
2668 Berkley Ave 36617-1704
(334)456-7960 •
FAX(334)456-7909
**Brown Bettye D**
Casher Zephneah BS PS
Jones Juanita K
King Tammy S 3-5
Lindsey Stephanie 1-2

**TUSCALOOSA-**MARTIN LUTHER-CHRIST PS
• 1961
2913 18th St 35401-4215
(205)752-0108
NO REPORT

### ALASKA

**ANCHORAGE-**ANCHOR K-8
• 1979
8100 Arctic Blvd 99518-3003
(907)522-3636 •
FAX(907)522-3359
kbanchor@aol.com
NO REPORT

BEAUTIFUL SAVIOR PS
• NLSA • 1985
8100 Arctic Blvd 99518-3003
(907)522-3899 •
FAX(907)522-3359
bjreinke@aol.com
NO REPORT

ZION PS
• 1985
2100 Boniface Pkwy 99504-3002
(907)222-3838 •
FAX(907)333-4014
Driskell Lynn PS
Dunbar Anna PS
Fijalka Audrey PS

**DELTA JUNCTION-**DENALI PS
• 1992
Richardson Hwy PO Box 1284
99737
(907)895-1910 •
FAX(907)869-3079
anbrg@uaa.alaska.edu
NO REPORT

**FAIRBANKS-**OPEN ARMS-ZION PS-K
2980 Davis Rd 99709
(907)455-9466 •
FAX(907)455-7208
**Rogers Bonnie PS-K**
Bennett Elizabeth PS
Boddy Bettina PS
Boormann Kiana PS
Bruckner Susan PS
Campbell Travis PS
Clark Patricia PS
Cotten Carrie PS
Crandall Heather PS
Crismore Shari PS-K
Duvlea Mackenzie K
Eady Carl PS-K
Garcia Theresa PS
Gilkey Ingrid PS-K
Grant Wyan PS
Gross Amber PS-K
Harmon Laura M PS
Kennedy Kathleen PS
King Rebecca PS
Koch Heather PS
Loftus Eileen PS-K
Lopez Nadine PS
Navarro Lisa PS
Polyakova Anna PS
Roger Mark PS-K
Sarapa Joy PS
Schroeder Jillian PS
Scoles Windy PS
Shirk Jonie PS
Smith Kelly PS
Spontak Katrina PS
Yates Kristina PS

**HOMER-**FAITH PS
• 1996
3634 Soundview Ave 99603-8332
(907)235-7600 •
FAX(907)235-7660
www.xyz.net/~faithlut/
Neels Marian S PS

**JUNEAU-**FAITH PS-7
• 1982
2500 Sunset Dr 99801-9371
(907)789-7568 •
FAX(907)789-7568
faithjno@alaska.net
NO REPORT

### ARIZONA

**APACHE JUNCTION-**MOUNTAIN VIEW LUTHER PS
2122 S Goldfield Rd 85217-0868
(480)288-8534 •
FAX(480)982-3374
NO REPORT

**CASA GRANDE-**TLC-TRINITY PS
1428 N Pueblo Dr 85222
(520)836-2451
trinity_lutheran_church@yahoo.com
**Urand Rebecca**
Chavez Elena PS
Krukow Jessica PS
Tate Natalie PS

**CHANDLER**-EPIPHANY PS-K
• 1979
800 W Ray Rd 85224-3120
(602)899-5889 •
FAX(602)963-6170
child1@telesouth1.com
Austalu Chris PS
Mohrman Judy MS K
O Dell Donita
Styx Kristy PS
**COTTONWOOD**-HILLTOP-FAITH PS
• 1975
2021 E Fir St 86326-4558
(602)639-0793
NO REPORT
**FLAGSTAFF**-PEACE PS-K
• 1972
3430 N 4th St 86004-1793
(520)526-9256 •
FAX(520)526-9578
NO REPORT
**GILBERT**-CHRIST GREENFIELD PS-6
• 1986
425 N Greenfield Rd 85234-5053
(480)892-8521 •
FAX(480)503-0437
wgschmidt@mindspring.com
**Schmidt Wayne A MA**
Cox Janell D BA PS
Dilzer Rhonda PS
Hudnall Gail A BA 1
Lappe Trudi 4
Mayes Pamela
Myers Nina PS
Reinke Kevin T BS 5-6
Roberts Rena PS
Schabacker Lee AA PS
Schmidt Gail A 3-4
Schroeder Tracie L BA 2
Stapleton Rebecca PS
Stark Cindy PS
Toma Barbara PS
Wornick Jane K
Wyssmann Laurie BA PS
**GLENDALE**-ATONEMENT PS
• 1987
4001 W Beardsley Rd 85308-4713
(602)582-8785
NO REPORT
**LITCHFIELD PARK**-TRINITY PS-1
• 1986
830 Plaza Circle 85340-4915
(623)935-4690 •
FAX(623)935-5540
dlpmcgarry@aol.com
De Poe Anita PS
Gurnsey Jody 1
Hansen Cindy AA PS
Healey Darla PS
Mc Garry Deborah
Mosley Anita BSED K
Mossi Erin PS
Northrup Mona PS
Thompson Julie PS
TRINITY
830 Plaza Cir 85340
(623)935-5517 •
FAX(623)935-5540
NO REPORT
**MESA**-ST LUKE PS
• 1979
807 N Stapley Dr 85203-5698
(480)969-3848 •
FAX(480)969-4801
stlukeslutheranecc@juno.com
Gerken Kathryn A BS PS
Kosberg Amanda L BS PS
**PAGE**-SHEPHERD OF THE DESE PS
• 1984
331 S Lk Powell Blvd 86040 PO Box 668 86040-0668
(602)645-9398
**Schubert Sonya PS**
Corn Linda PS
Lucero Stacy PS
White Kim PS
Yniguez Niki PS
**PEORIA**-APOSTLES PS
• 1995
7020 W Cactus Rd 85381-5318
(623)979-3497 •
FAX(623)979-5778
Jones Nancy BAED
Maddox Barbara PS
**PHOENIX**-CHRIST PS-8
• 1955
3901 E Indian School Rd 85018-5236
(602)957-7010 •
FAX(602)955-8073
**Harman Gregory E MED 5-8**
Atwatter Catherine PS
Biar Cynthia L BSED K
Bischoff Beverly BA 4
Brittain Thomas W 6-8
Broermann Lori K-2
Burke Susan BED K
Cleland Marlene M MED 1
Ehlers Cheryl 2
Gehring Mary MS K
Greder Gary L BED 6
Hirschi Vicky K-8
Hodgson William E Jr. MED 5-7
Hubeler Patricia PS
Krieger Susan L BS 3
Laubenstein Joan L MA 4
Merritt Bonnie A MED 6
Merritt Robert A MED 8
Nobis Sharon BA 2
Perry-Clark Julia BMU 3-8
Petty Joyce PS
Porter Ellen L BA 7-8
Sawyer Lorna BS 1
Schultz Carol 5
Wahl Cynthia AAS PS
Wood Carol MDIV 3
CHRISTIAN PS-4
• 1992
8801 N 43Rd Ave 85051-3641
(623)934-5896 •
FAX(623)934-3298
ctrlutheran@ctrlutheran.com
**Kiehl Karen K BSED**
Bartzsch Daina M K
Bonner Susan K BA K
Deise Constance PS
Gnam Janet S BA 1
Gough Caryl PS-4
Hecker Corinne E PS
Heim Jennifer PS
Jones Helen J 3-4
Mertins Stacy M BSED 2
Northrop Adell PS
Rodgers Linda PS
Ruiz Roberta K-4
Turner Rodney E 1-4
Umbaugh Hazel PS
FAMILY OF CHRIST PS-K
• 1993
3501 E Chandler Blvd 85048-5801
(480)759-9004 •
FAX(480)759-9004
Director@Family-of-Christ.com
Canino Cabrina PS
Cardin Kathy PS
Caron Madelyn PS
Christiansen Nancy
Connell Lynora PS
Gauby Lola PS
Leonard Kathy K
Reed Linda PS
MARTIN LUTHER K-8
• RSO • 1972
1806 W Glenrosa Ave 85015-4738
(602)248-0656 •
FAX(602)604-8257
James Jim K
Just Darrel D 4-5
Lutz Sharon MED 2
Mau Aaron J BS 7
Mc Dowell Marsha BS 3
Piepenbrink Karen BSED 8
Plumb Donna 1
Rausch Hank 6
Simon Sandra A BSED K
MOUNT CALVARY PS
• 1990
5199 N 7Th Ave 85013-2286
(602)266-9717 •
FAX(602)263-0403
**Smidt Stanley G BSED**
Greer Mary PS
Mc Gee Traci PS
Vaughn Kristen G PS
ST MARK PS
• 1977
3030 E Thunderbird Rd 85032-5685
(602)992-1160
Blanchard Rachelle PS
Collier Breanna PS
Gerlach Becky PS
ST PAUL PS-1
• 1980
6301 W Indian School Rd 85033-3338
(623)846-2235 •
FAX(623)846-1851
Hexum Susan PS
Love Tammi 1
Mathieson Jean PS
Quinones Leann L
Ransom Dawn K
THE MASTERS PS
• 1981
2340 W Cactus Rd 85029-2799
(602)997-7439
**Schimke Pamela L BS PS**
Detlaff Christine PS
Graham Laura PS
**PRESCOTT VALLEY**-GODS WORLD-TRINITY PS-K
• 1989
3950 N Valorie Dr 86314-8234
(602)772-0460
NO REPORT
**SCOTTSDALE**-DESERT FOOTHILLS PS-K
• 1998
29305 N Scottsdale Rd 85262
(480)585-8007 •
FAX(480)502-9427
**Holliday Karen A MA K**
Betcher Martha A PS
Larkin Cindy PS
Mc Neill Nancy PS
Rising Robin PS
SHEPHERD OF THE DESE PS-K
• NLSA • 1983
9590 E Shea Blvd 85260-6724
(480)860-1677 •
FAX(480)860-4152
**Brandt Paul M MA**
Brandt Susan M BA PS-4
Clemens Christine PS
Eliason Connie 1
Fleming Barbara 1-4
Gomm Debbie PS
Gregory Julia PS
Hendrickson Deborah K
Lenich Sherry 1-4
Petersen Calisse K BA 3-4
Philipp Nancy 1-4
Rainer Carol PS
Roberts Jeanne K-4
Selle Jean E BSED 2
Tinker Diane F
Visser Lucy K
**TEMPE**-GETHSEMANE PS-8
• 1978
1035 E Guadalupe Rd 85283-3091
(480)839-0906 •
FAX(480)839-8876
**Robson Wendell L MED**
Crosby Elaine E K
Krueger Nancy L BSED 2
Nelson Marcia L PS-K
Nunnally Wilma J 4
Obermann Melissa 5-6
Robson Dawn M BA 3
Rogers Cheryl PS
Waltersdorf Judith C MA 1
**TUCSON**-ASCENSION PS-K
• 1983
1220 W Magee Rd 85704-3325
(520)742-6229 •
FAX(520)742-4781
Rockwell Cindy L BA
Stults Susan A BS K
CATALINA PS
• 1984
15855 N Twin Lakes Dr 85739-8895
(520)825-4057
NO REPORT
FAITH PS-8
• 1952
3925 E 5th St 85711-1953
(520)881-0670 • FAX(520) 325-5625
Beck Mary 6
Cline Lisa J BA PS
Cline Thomas L BSED 5
Gaub Susan 3
Giles Seth 7
Lewis Mildred C 6
Nehls Rosemary BA 4
Nehls William A MA 8
Rogers Karen A MSED 2
Stahl Kathryn BA 1
Tyboroski Jennifer K
Unruh Marian C BSED
Warren B C
FOUNTAIN OF LIFE PS-8
• NLSA • 1962
710 S Kolb Rd 85710-4998
(520)747-1213 •
FAX(520)747-9444
NO REPORT
OPEN ARMS-MESSIAH PS-K
• 1992
9095 N Bald Eagle Ave 85742-9517
(520)744-8505 •
FAX(520)579-8947
oabaldeagle@uswest.net
Alfred Kristen PS
Barry Carolyn PS-K
Blomn Sharon PS
Calhoun Shannon PS
Clayton Beverly PS
Esala Kate PS
Ewert Betty AA PS
Johnson Dorothy PS
Kellam Mary PS
Le Vario Tammy PS
Mendoza Tammy 1
Mire Michelle PS
Nelson April PS
Schmanke Carolyn PS
Shafer Sarah PS
Simpson Connie PS
Solem Joyce H
Steninger Teresa PS
Welch Cassandra PS
Wood Christy K
**YUMA**-YUMA-CHRIST PS-8
• 1957
2555 S Engler Ave 85365-3298
(520)726-8410 •
FAX(520)726-6674
christyuma@aol.com
NO REPORT

## ARKANSAS

**ALEXANDER**-ZION PS
• 1990
300 Avilla E 72002-9602
(501)316-1100 •
FAX(501)316-1101
Fluger Penny M MS
Gilbert Dana PS
Mc Daniel Laura H PS
Page Kim PS
Rapier Jewel M PS

**BATESVILLE**-HOPE PS-8
• 1997
2417 E Main 72501-9409
(870)793-3078 •
FAX(870)793-3078
**Mehl Paul M MDIV 6-8**
Cox Heidi 6-8
Cupp Michelle PS-K
Lawrenz Denise L BS 3-5
Mead Jana K-2
**CHEROKEE VILLAGE**-PEACE PS
• 1996
12 Chotaw Center 72529 PO Box
960 72525-0960
(870)257-4298
Harris Shannon M PS
Pummill Karen PS
**FAYETTEVILLE**-ST JOHN PS
2730 E Township Rd 72703-4362
(501)443-3620 •
FAX(501)443-3609
NO REPORT
**FORT SMITH**-BETHEL PS
• 1998
5400 Euper Ln 72903-3232
(501)452-1521
**Herring Barbara**
Esobar Juanita
Goobey Elizabeth
Lamproe Jennifer
Mersiovsky Sally
Pender Kelly
Pitsch Seanna
Raymond Kathy
Vela Carol
Young Jana
FIRST PS-9
• NLSA • 1853
2407 Massard Rd 72903-5201
(501)452-5330 •
FAX(501)452-3553
fls@ipa.net
**Kosinsky John P MS 8**
Borges Bridget 3
Godfrey Charlotte 2
Graves Candace A BA PS
Griesse Marge BSED PS
Hopkins Nikki 4
Humphreville Thomas 6-9
Knight Ashley 5-9
Kolterman Jeanette BA PS
McCluney Kathleen 3-9
McKinney Elaine C 1
Netherton Dana J BA K
Nieting Kathryn A BSED 5
Potts Brenda
Pralle Eric A MED 6
Wendte Susan K BS 7-9
OUR REDEEMER PS
• 1971
2100 Cavanaugh Rd 72908-7844
(501)646-7611
Fitch Janet PS
**GILLETT**-ST PAUL PS
• 1979
2nd & Rose Sts PO Box 419
72055-0419
(501)548-2861
NO REPORT
**HOT SPRINGS**-LITTLE LAMBS PS
• 1996
105 Village Rd 71913-6715
(501)525-0322
NO REPORT
**JACKSONVILLE**-HOPE PS-2
• 1994
1904 Mc Arthur Dr 72076
(501) 982-8678 •
FAX(501)982-1333
**St Martin Ruby A MA 2**
Barrington Cathi PS
Ford Laura T BS K
Heimsoth Heather BA 1
Lombardi Skotti PS
**JONESBORO**-CONCORDIA
ACADEMY PS-8
1812 South Rains St 72401
(870)935-2273 •
FAX(870)935-4717
concordia@bscn.com
Krohe Lois A BA PS-K
**LITTLE ROCK**-CHRIST PS-8
• NLSA • 1870
315 S Hughes St 72205-5128
(501)663-5212 •
FAX(501)663-9542
rschmidt@clutheran.org
**Schmidt Rebecca S MA**
Becker Connie S BS 4
Boyd Pam 2-8
Breashears Tracey 7-8
Breite Mary M MA 2
Browning Scott D BS 6
Colen Harlene 3
Doering Rachel J MED 5
Gruber Miriam BA 2
Hartmann Deidre J BSED 3
Hartmann Dennis R BA 7-8
Koss Virginia MSLS
Lieb Trina K MED K-8
Matthews Melanie K
Mc Nabb Sally A BS K
Olsen Shawn R PS
Osborn Barbara R 5
Parscale Brenda L MS 1
Quickel Dale E BSED K
Quickel Lisa L BA 4
Rawlings Emily K BA 6
Robinson David P BS 7-8
Robinson Diana R BA 3
Rossow Dana S
Schroeder Bret A BS 7-8
Sears Christine A BS K-8
Shimp Charla 2-6
Tenison Mary Jo MMU K
Thompson Michelle M PS
Walter Brenda BA 1
Weed Linnea K-6
GRACE CHLDHD DEVLP C PS
• 1990
5124 Hillcrest Ave 72205 PO Box
250769 72225-0769
(501)663-0755 •
FAX(501)663-0625
**Moorman Colleen BS**
Babb Rachel PS
Browne Betsy PS
Dent Ashley PS
Duckworth Tameka PS
Fastenau Carrie PS
Ferguson Jennifer PS
Galbraith Aimee PS
Harrison Ellen PS
Hurley Ruth PS
Johnson Taylor PS
Scotter Michelle PS
Smith Dianne PS
Speer Janet PS
Wakelyn Alexandra PS
LORD OF LIFE PS
• 1993
800 Kirby Rd 72211-3018
(501)223-3001 •
FAX(501)223-3606
NO REPORT
**N LITTLE ROCK**-TRINITY PS
• 1981
119 W H St 72116-8733
(501)753-6831 •
FAX(501)753-6833
trinity@aristotle.net
NO REPORT
**SPRINGDALE**-SALEM PS-5
• 1979
1800 W Emma Ave 72762-3905
(501)751-9359 •
FAX(501)750-2028
**Busch Kris PS**
**Knapp Ronald F MED K-5**
Bragg Cheryl PS
Collins Rhonda PS
Gordley Linda PS
Gordley Shannon PS
Grayson Trisha L BSED 1-5
High Holly PS
Hudgens Barbara PS
Rush Melody PS
Suttle Theresa PS
Teeters Kathy L PS
Weidler Peggy L MA K
**STUTTGART**-ST JOHN PS-7
• 1885
2019 S Buerkle St 72160-6507
(870)673-7096
**Schmidt James A BS 6-7**
Frizzell Mickey A BA K
Henson Kimberly A 6-7
Hildebrand Susi PS
Lammers Cheri PS
Leibig Rebecca A BA 3
Mc Pherson Debi BS 1
Prislovsky Gertrude PS
Senko Janie BSED 4
Smith Marlyn 2
Stewart Brenda S BA 5

## CALIFORNIA

**ALHAMBRA**-EMMAUS PS-8
• NLSA • 1941
840 S Almansor St 91801-4599
(626)289-3664 •
FAX(626)576-0476
**Nielsen Allan C BA 5**
**Schaar Dennis R MA**
Boyd Heidi A BA 1
Hart Regina A MA 3
Hittinger Kit A BA 7
Howard Judy BA 8
Jow Esther MA PS
Krach Mary L MA K
Lestina Emma L BA 4
Lewis Ellen K BS 6
Malucky Maralyn B MA 1-8
Richard Helen R BS 2
**ANAHEIM**-HEPHATHA PS-8
• 1983
5900 E Santa Ana Canyon Rd
92807-3280
(714)637-4022 •
FAX(714)637-0872
**Reinertson Mickie B BS 8**
**Surprenant Faith E MED 8**
Arana Susana PS
Baudot Terry L
Beiter Ruth M BS 1
Couch Teri PS
Devin-Christelman Deleen L BA
PS
Divine Rebecca 5-8
Juliano Jill PS
Juliano Suzanne R
Kahler Nancy K
Lopez Sherry PS
Martin Maripat K
Mc Clary Richard W BSED 7
Miquelon Ellie PS
Murphy Teri PS
Redfox Dale 4
Rogers Darla R
Root Stephanie L
Sanchez Sylvia PS
Sharp Erin 5-8
Staake Linda S MS 2
Strack Candice PS
Van Ry Jamie PS
Weber Bonnie PS
PRINCE OF PEACE PS-8
• NLSA • 1962
1421 W Ball Rd 92802-1799
(714)774-0993 •
FAX(714)774-0183
princeofpeacelutheran@yahoo.com
**Humphrey Roxane M MA**
Alduenda Ernestina PS
Anderson Mary J BSED K
Boardman Debra PS
Brehm Paul A MS 6
Corl Brenda PS
Dunham Keri PS
Haack Loren F MA 7-8
Haack Verna M BA 7
Hemmings Jenny R BS 3
Howard Nancy J BS 5
Kaudy Betty J PS
Kercher Elaine B BS 2
Livingston Pamela A PS
Mc Lellan Yvonne K
Morner Leah M BA 4
Newton Dawn PS
Sardo June 8
Thompson Sylvia A AA PS
Vroom Nola J BSED 1
ST MARKS LUTH PRESCH PS
10418 Katella Ave 92804
(714)535-1947 •
FAX(714)535-7077
NO REPORT
ZION PS
• 1972
222 N East St 92805-3317
(714)535-1172 •
FAX(714)254-7013
NO REPORT
ZION PS-8
• 1972
1244 E Cypress St 92805-3317
(714)535-3600 •
FAX(714)254-7013
**Reinertson Jerome A MED**
Bakalyar Judith A BA 5
Barone Kathleen J BSED 3
Drevlow Henry J MED 6
Farley Jennifer J K
Haynes Travis M MED 7-8
Heinecke Norma F BA 2
Kangas Sean 4
Kincebach Lynette BA 7-8
Lindquist Julie A MSED 7-8
Roberts Sara 5
Root Starline M BA 1
Rupe Dorothy E BA K
Schirrmacher Mary L BA 2
Stewart Amanda L 3
Taylor Tracy 6
Trost Rebecca J BSED 1
Wasson Dollyeanna K
Whelply Karen K MED 3
**ARROYO GRANDE**-PEACE PS
• 1981
244 N Oak Park Blvd 93420-2436
(805)489-9644 •
FAX(805)474-1823
**Clark Roseanna M PS**
Day Beth Ann A AA PS
Farrar Janet PS
Marrufo Kathy PS
Morales Alicia PS
**BAKERSFIELD**-ST JOHN PS-8
• 1977
4500 Buena Vista Rd 93311
(661)398-5140 •
FAX(661)398-5143
**Appold Patrice M BA 2**
**Wheeler Lynn A BA**
Adams Stacey K-8
Altergott Midge PS
Arroaga Nellie PS
Barber Kenna PS
Bloner Jennifer PS
Brown Sharon PS
Bumerts Lynn 1
Garcia Albert 5-8
Gaunt Joni PS
Giego Ruth PS
Hammontree Amy K
Hobbs Janice PS
Hobbs Rhonda PS
Holian Patricia Y BS 5
Lwin Katy PS
Marting Paul BA 1-8
Marting Sandi PS
Meeks Jeff PS
Michaels Linda K
Mitchell Anastasia 7

Moore Toni PS
Omdahl Leslie PS
Pahler Sheryl PS
Riese-O Rourke Janice MA
Shelton Mary PS
Sorensen Terri PS
Swenson Debi A BS K
Tepker Carol 4
Terry Carol PS
Thomas Jodi PS
Tingle Jana PS
Turpin Carol BA 8
Wheeler Barbara BA 6
Williams LaDonna PS
Williams Vickie PS
Zimmerman Barbara PS
WONDER WINDOW-PRAYER PS-K
• 1973
8001 Panorama Dr 93306-7302
(661)871-7051
Hender Charla PS
Huggard Bernice PS
Merchant Sharon PS
Pennington Dons
Radford Sharon PS
Smith Carmeleta PS
**BARSTOW-**CONCORDIA PS
• 1985
420 Avenue E 92311-2613
(760)256-8979 •
FAX(760)256-5455
Ahles Francine PS
Brunner Carley PS
Gomez Patricia AA PS
Navarette Cristina PS
Rawlinson Jackie
Rawson Shelly PS
Reveles Ramona PS
Wilhelm Denise PS
**BENICIA-**NOAHS ARK PS
• 1993
201 Raymond Dr 94510-2747
(707)746-1868 •
FAX(707)751-0873
janisdk@cs.com
Coffelt Helena PS
De Seve Rhonda PS
Gascoigne Lorraine AAS PS
Hodel Sabrina PS
King Janis D MED
Magallanes Susana PS
Saltz Dawn PS
Walker Jeanne PS
**BISHOP-**GRACE PS-K
• 1980
711 N Fowler St 93514-2617
(619)873-8818
NO REPORT
**BLYTHE-**ZION PS-8
• 1981
721 E Chanslor Way 92225-1250
(760)922-7355
NO REPORT
**BURBANK-**FIRST K-5
• 1950
1001 S Glenoaks Blvd 91502-1594
(818)848-3076 •
FAX(818)848-3801
flschool@pacificnet.net
Burk Shelly 1
Chrzan Beth E BED 3-4
Kruse Laura M BA 5
O Dea Judy BA 2
Simmons Monique K
Todd Katie M BA 4
**CAMARILLO-**FIRST
380 Arneill Rd 93010
(805)482-3411 •
FAX(805)484-0427
NO REPORT
PEACE PS
• NLSA • 1979
71 Loma Dr 93010-2315
(805)987-1613 •
FAX(805)482-6044
preschool@peacelcms.org
Fitch Nancy J BA

Linaweaver Carol PS
Thompson Sharon PS
**CANOGA PARK-**CANOGA PARK K-8
• NLSA • 1957
7357 Jordan Ave 91303-1277
(818)348-5714 •
FAX(818)348-1516
Anderson Janet 5
Boyle Lolita A
Clark Steve 6-8
Day Brady 6-8
Gratz Janice K
Guetschoff Karen 1
Lua Andrea L BSED 4
Nelesen Teresa R BS 3
Peterson Janis R BS 2
Rooney Mary A 6-8
OUR REDEEMER PS-2
• 1984
8520 Winnetka Ave 91306-1124
(818)700-0390 •
FAX(818)772-2788
NO REPORT
**CERRITOS-**CONCORDIA PS-6
• 1980
13633 183Rd St 90703-8940
(562)926-2491 •
FAX(562)407-0610
**Gagan Patrick S BS 4-6**
**Seaman Nola BA PS**
Barton Margaret J PS
Canning Jennifer A BA 4-6
Dominguez Carol PS
Gorter Marsha PS
Hegedus Diana BA 3
Jennings Susan M BA K
Mateik Shirley PS
Mc Combs Mary Anne BA 5-6
Peterson Scott MA 2
Ponce Terri PS
Voelker Kim J AA 1
**CHICO-**REDEEMER PS-6
• 1984
746 Moss Ave 95926-2971
(530)893-2512 •
FAX(530)893-2512
redeemerlutheranschool@juno.com
Bliss Elizabeth K
Espinoza Margarita PS
Renne Lisa
Smith Linda 3-5
Tankersley Karen S PS
Whittaker Shelley 1-2
**CHINO HILLS-**LOVING SAVIOR PS-6
• 1993
14816 Peyton Dr 91709-2073
(909)597-2948
Bredehoft Susan L BA 1-3
Clark Belinda PS
Contreras Isidra PS
Fisher Marilyn
Hottinger Stacy L BA 3-5
Johnson Karen M BS K-8
Maes Erica V K
Segrist Laisa BA 2-5
Wirtz Nicholas D MDIV 5-6
**CHULA VISTA-**PILGRIM PS-8
• 1963
497 E St 91910-2498
(619)420-6233 •
FAX(619)422-2740
NO REPORT
**COLTON-**ST JOHN PS
• 1989
820 N LA Cadena Dr 92324-2774
(909)825-6434 •
FAX(760)240-6456
NO REPORT

**CONCORD-**FIRST PS-8
• 1990
4002 Concord Blvd 94519-1515
(925)671-9717 •
FAX(925)671-9943
gradeschool@firstlutheranconcord.org
**Minner Bobby B MEAD K-8**
Cantrell Laura PS
Dube Tammy PS
Grimshaw Debbie BA PS
Harper Adel K-8
Minner Renee E BA PS-8
Neely Karen PS
Newton Janelle M PS-8
Roy Kim K-8
Sherwood Nancy 3-5
Stein Georgia K-8
Stone Susan 2-6
Sutherland Corinne 2
Von Dollen Sharon 1-8
Wiltrout Lisa 6-8
**CORONA-**GRACE K-8
• 1979
1811 S Lincoln Ave 92882
(909)737-2187 •
FAX(909)731-1750
Bucka Barbara MA 1
Fontanilla Jacqueline
Goodman Marylou 3-4
Maddock Joyce K
Meade Christopher 6
Mohr Lynn C BS
Stade Lisa A BED 1
Stevens Margaret K
**CORONADO-**RESURRECTION PS
• 1983
1111 5Th St 92118-1898
(619)435-0286
NO REPORT
**COSTA MESA-**CHRIST PS-8
• NLSA • 1958
760 Victoria St 92627-2999
(949)548-6866 •
FAX(949)631-6224
**Meyer Gerhardt M DED**
Anderson Quinton 6-8
Bouffard Peter BSED 6-8
Courvoisier Elinor L MA 2
Courvoisier Wesley A BA 5
Dueck Daniel BA 6-8
Dueck Erin L BED 3-4
Ebel Karen J MA 4
Force Sharon K PS
Gardiner Linda L MED 1
Hayes Lois 1
Hemenway Susan BA 6-8
Jordan Jenny L MED 6-8
Meyer Lo Anne 2
Rivard Sally L AA PS
Rohmaller Betty J BSED K
Tornow Leah K MED 3
Willson Connie E 5
**COVINA-**ST JOHN PS
• 1954
304 E Covina Blvd 91722-2826
(626)915-2122 •
FAX(626)332-1783
Head Ellen M AA PS
TRINITY PS
• 1982
16050 E San Bernardino Rd 91722-3941
(626)337-9888
NO REPORT
**CRESCENT CITY-**GRACE PS
• 1987
190 E Cooper Ave 95531-2741
(707)464-7604 •
FAX(707)464-4070
Personal-Karl628@webtv.net
Goss Jane E
Quick Pennye PS

**CUPERTINO-**SCHOOL OF OUR SAVIOR PS-8
• 1958
5825 Bollinger Rd 95014-3536
(408)252-0250 •
FAX(408)252-0558
principal@lcos.org
Bestul Barbara BS 7-8
Frese Jeanette BSED 1-2
Frese Leland G BSED 3-4
Moody Carl A BSED
Phillips Tammy 3-4
Small Carol K
Small Victor MA 7-8
**CYPRESS-**HOLY CROSS PS-8
• 1983
4321 Cerritos Ave 90630-4216
(714)527-7928 •
FAX(714)527-8472
**Miller La Mar Jr. MA**
Anderson Charlotte A PS
Barr Michelle E 3
Burk Carol A BSED 1
Culley Kathleen A K
Fox George G BA 5-6
Fox Starlayne G BA 4
Lerch Kathleen P BA 7-8
Renken Jo Ann M BLA 2
Weiss Melinda S
**DALY CITY-**HOPE PS-2
• 1987
55 San Fernando Way 94015-2065
(650)991-4673 •
FAX(650)991-9723
Alfonso Celedonia PS
Batongbakal Priscilla PS
Brown Christine 2
Castaneda Blanca PS
Castillo Maria PS
Frias Agripina PS
Garcia Dora PS
Mangabat Magdelena L
Petersen Perlita A PS
Phoupraseut Alisa S PS
Stechholz Janet L BA K
Woo Lisa Y BA 1
**DIAMOND BAR-**MOUNT CALVARY PS-8
• 1983
23300 E Golden Springs Rd 91765-2001
(909)861-2740 •
FAX(909)861-5481
pmarquardt@hotmail.com
**Marquardt Paul J MEAD**
Bowling Pam PS
Courvoisier Jeff MA 4
Cox Brenda K BA 6-8
Cox John E BA 6-8
Doyle Jonathan T BS 6-8
Gadbury Andrea M MA K
Garton Terry PS
Hardin Sandra M MA 1
Hobbs Nancy J BA 2
Holdeman Jean A MA 4
Kotovich Barbara PS
Lobosky Pam 2
Marquardt Meg 3
Musella Miriam L BA K
Padilla Adryann PS
Pugliese Michael 3
Randall Claudia G MA 5
Smith Teresa K-8
Thomason Linnette D BA 1
Tingesdahl Sheri PS
Waldhanz Linda
Wright Ridell M MA 2
**DOWNEY-**GOOD SHEPHERD K-8
• NLSA • 1956
13200 S Clark Ave 90242-4723
(562)803-4918 •
FAX(562)803-4450
Bunce Karen L BA 2
Flinn Dian E 7-8
Pabst Leroy W MMU 5-6
Pabst Mary H MED K
Pratt Ellen M BS 3

Rueter Nancy J BS 1
Senglaub Jennifer L 4
**DUBLIN-**ST PHILIP PS-8
• 1984
8850 Davona Dr 94568-1132
(925)829-3857
NO REPORT
**EL CAJON-**CHRIST THE KING PS
• 1979
750 Medford St 92020-2048
(619)469-3531
NO REPORT
FIRST PS-K
• 1986
867 S Lincoln Ave 92020-6424
(619)444-0559 •
FAX(619)444-9892
Knudsen Karen
Meier Darci PS
Perez Kathy PS
Rische Lori K
Robinson Betty PS
Spain Sanshree
VanDeweghe Mona
Young Lani K
**EL CENTRO-**GRACE K-8
• 1984
768 W Holt Ave 92243-3228
(760)352-4204 •
FAX(760)352-5389
Brown Lisa K BS 3-4
Creiglow Brenda 7-8
Lira Brenda 1-2
Nava Maritza K
Weller Patricia 5-6
**EL MONTE-**FIRST PS-K
• 1998
4900 Kings Row 91731-1483
(626)448-0767
**Rameriz Cyndi PS**
Deus Tara PS-K
Lambrecht Donna PS
Seck Lisabet K
Taylor Karelon PS
**EL SEGUNDO-**ST JOHN PS
• 1960
1611 E Sycamore Ave 90245-3331
(310)615-1072
NO REPORT
**ESCONDIDO-**COMMUNITY PS
• 1993
3575 E Valley Pkwy 92027-5227
(760)739-8649 •
FAX(760)739-8655
NO REPORT
GRACE PS-8
• NLSA • 1957
643 W 13Th Ave 92025-5696
(760)747-3029 •
FAX(760)745-1612
jwlohmeyer@aol.com
NO REPORT
JOYFUL NOISES-GLORIA DEI PS-K
• 1993
1087 W Country Club Ln
92026-1101
(760)743-5472 •
FAX(760)746-4463
Acebedo Jennifer PS
Carrillo Anita PS
Castillo Ann Marie PS
Iverson Cheryl L BA
Johnson Adonica PS
Myers Jennie K
Pool Josie PS
Soto Manuela PS
Vancil Yolanda PS
Zakavian Karen PS
**EXETER-**LITTLE LAMBS PS
• 1991
420 Sequoia Dr 93221-1232
(209)592-1935
NO REPORT
**FAIR OAKS-**FAITH PS-8
• NLSA • 1955
4000 San Juan Ave 95628-6829
(916)961-4253 •
FAX(916)961-2604
gevensen@juno.com
Barklage Carol E BSED 1
Beltran Alice A BSED 5-6
Dexter Tonja PS
Evensen George H MED 7-8
Finn Lisa M K
Fischl Mary Jo BA 3-4
Maddock James 7-8
Moyer Justine L BED
Powers Irene D BA 2
**FAIRFIELD-**TRINITY PS-4
• 1989
2075 Dover Ave 94533-2346
(707)435-1123 •
FAX(707)435-1122
mrcee42@hotmail.com
**Camberg Terry N BSED 5**
Bargenquast Bridget 2
Camberg Christina L BA 4
Campbell Mary BA 1
Cantrell Gloria D MA K-5
Cramer Jennifer PS
Escobedo Laura PS
Escobedo Maribel PS
Henrich Heidi PS
Matlock Victoria PS
Middlestead Sally PS
Padilla Tina PS
Patton Yolonda C
Sanchez Mary PS
Schwartzkopf Melissa M BSED 3
Smith Debra PS
Wiley Karen PS
**FALLBROOK-**ZION PS
• 1985
203 Laurine Ln 92028-4109
(760)723-2118
NO REPORT
ZION PS-8
• 1984
1405 E Fallbrook St 92028-2427
(760)723-3500 •
FAX(760)723-3951
**Timm Timothy N MA 6-8**
Arnett Beverly L MSED 5
Cleveland Leta 4
Culver Lorrie 1-8
Douglas 1 E PS
Dufresne Scott 6-8
Ellis Susan D 1
Gordenier Karen L BA 2
Greenwald Celia J 3
Hahn Dodie 6-8
Hullum Maxine N PS
Kressin Deborah K BS 4
Majewski Michael M BA 6-8
O Berg Michelle 5
Oslund Darlene 2
Roberts Gail 6-8
Salampessy Cathy L PS
Schmad Becky 1-8
Schmidt Deborah A PS
Smith Cynthia A BS 1-8
Soon Charlene BS 3
Sternberg Deanne K K
Summers Sarah PS
Taylor Dana 1-8
Tudor Minamaree E MS 6-8
Valencia Katherine 1-8
Wilemon Kathey 1-8
Woods Donna M BS 1-8
Zielinski Lee MS 6-8
**FOLSOM-**MOUNT OLIVE PS
• 1993
320 Montrose Dr 95630-2720
(916)985-3016 •
FAX(916)985-2998
NO REPORT
**FONTANA-**FIRST K-8
• 1965
9315 Citrus Ave 92335-5596
(909)823-3457 •
FAX(909)823-3499
**Haynes Victor**
Adran Deirdre BA 5-8
Arizmendi Nilian PS
Castanon Gail 5-8
Dirner Paula
Gerber Christine L 1-3
Pabon Mary A K
Schueman LaVerne 1-3
**FREMONT-**OUR SAVIOR PS-K
• 1979
858 Washington Blvd 94539-5222
(510)657-9269 •
FAX(510)657-3174
NO REPORT
PRINCE OF PEACE K-8
• 1957
38451 Fremont Blvd 94536-6030
(510)797-8186 •
FAX(510)793-6993
princepeace@home.com
**Meyer Judith A BA**
Garcia Susan Kay K
Glock Stephen L BS 8
Hall Melissa 2
Houseworth Marcia G MED 5
Rawlins Cheryl L BA 4
Rawlins Gary R BA 6
Synovec Michele L BA 1
Zimbrick Charles R BA 7
Zimbrick Emilie A BA 3
**FULLERTON-**CHRIST PS-8
• NLSA • 1978
3401 N Harbor Blvd 92835
(714)870-7460
maxdr@msn.com
NO REPORT
ST STEPHEN PS
• 1971
2311 E Chapman Ave 92631-4290
(714)871-6641
NO REPORT
**GARDEN GROVE-**ST PAUL PS-8
• 1961
13082 Bowen St 92843-1092
(714)534-6320 •
FAX(714)741-8353
**Smallwood Carol J BS**
Elliott Marie H PS
King Judith I MCOUN 6-8
King Robert A MSED
Martinez Susan 6-8
Nguyen Brenda BA 4
Pham Hong D PS
Preston Karen 2
Roach Michelle S BA 5
Siegert Laura A BA PS
Simon Julie A MA 3
Valek Carolyn R PS
Wong Michal E BED K
**GILROY-**THE VINEYARD-GOOD SHEPHERD PS
• 1975
1735 Hecker Pass Rd 95020-9401
(408)847-8463
Fortino Renee PS
Green Monica PS
Grove Kimberly A BA PS
Kirkpatrick Diane L AA
Penkethman Lenore BA PS
Wilcher Denise PS
**GLENDALE-**ZION PS-6
• 1954
301 N Isabel St 91206-3699
(818)243-3119 •
FAX(818)243-9640
Chow Terry S 3
Finerty Kimberly PS
Garbe Carole J BA 1
Johnston Diane M 2
Lehman John 4
Lucas Donna M BS
Mc Coy Gaye 5
Parker Alletta S PS
Parker Lorraine G PS
Pino Dottiann K
Siewert Dean K BSED 6
Silva Susan A K
**GLENDORA-**HOPE PS-8
• NLSA • 1960
1041 E Foothill Blvd 91741-3699
(626)335-5315 •
FAX(626)852-0836
**Gugel Robert A MA**
Bristol Nancy E BA 6
DeChenne Carol A AAS PS
Ebel Lance E AA 7
Grantham Janice PS
Hall Rennae L PS
Hill Bonnie K
Hooper Deborah L MS 8
Kendel Marylee BA K
Ludke Alison BA 5
Marshall Jennifer L BA 2
Molina Barbara PS
Peterson Chris PS
Schaar Karen A BA 1
Terhune Lynn D MA 4
Tranum Carla J MA 3
**GOLETA-**GOOD SHEPHERD PS
• 1986
380 N Fairview Ave 93117-2299
(805)967-6101
Alexander Margaret BA PS
Huthsing Susan L
Knopke Katie PS
Richardson Laurie L BA PS
Thompson Cindy A PS
**GRANADA HILLS-**OUR SAVIOR FIRST PS-6
• 1954
16603 San Fernando Mission Blv
91344-4288
(818)368-0892 •
FAX(818)831-9222
NO REPORT
**HACIENDA HEIGHTS-**HOLY TRINITY PS-K
• 1985
15710 Newton St 91745-4143
(626)961-2070 •
FAX(626)333-6468
Flores Mayra PS
Garcia Sylvia PS
Grieco Jenny PS
Lucht Darleen J BA
Lynne Rose PS
Ortiz Gayle PS
**HANFORD-**FIRST PS
• 1980
9075 12Th Ave 93230-2407
(209)582-1135
NO REPORT
**HEMET-**ST JOHN PS-6
• 1983
26410 Columbia St 92544-6299
(909)652-5909 •
FAX(909)925-6136
NO REPORT
**HOLLYWOOD-**BETHANY K-8
• 1948
1518 N Alexandria Ave
90027-5204
(323)662-5769 • FAX(323)
665-5769
**Williams Aleta E K-5**
Bell Helen K
Marquez Linda K-2
Oguna Sophie 6-8
**HUNTINGTON BEACH-**CHILD/ FAITH EARLY LE PS
• 1986
8200 Ellis Ave 92646-1839
(714)962-1864
NO REPORT

REDEEMER PS-K
• 1987
16351 Springdale St 92649-2773
(714)840-7117 •
FAX(714)840-2679
missio@earthlink.net
Heinsma Sara PS
Hile Jan PS
Jalili Nicola E
Kinnie Elaine M PS
Kolarinski Sue PS
Martinez Rowana PS
Mc Geein Christie PS
Pfifer Tammy K
Wotjlewicz Nili K

**IMPERIAL BEACH**-ST JAMES PS-K
• 1979
866 Imperial Beach Blvd
91932-2799
(619)423-8648 •
FAX(619)424-5129
lyyk70a@prodigy.com
NO REPORT

**INDIO**-TRINITY PS-K
• 1981
81-500 Miles Ave PO Box W
92201-2923
(760)347-3838 •
FAX(760)347-3971
NO REPORT

**INGLEWOOD**-GOOD SHEPHERD K-8
• 1941
901 S Maple St 90301-3892
(310)671-0427
NO REPORT

**IRVINE**-SHEPHERD OF PEACE PS
• 1980
18182 Culver Dr 92612-2702
(949)786-3997 •
FAX(949)786-7186
**Manske Barbara M BA**
**Preus Sherry**
Brighton Michelle L PS
Grobelch Sheryl PS
Rahn Gail K BSED PS
Vick Kathy L BSED PS
Walmsley Jill PS

**LA MESA**-CHRIST PS-8
• NLSA • 1957
7929 La Mesa Blvd 91941-5029
(619)462-5211 •
FAX(619)462-5275
**Small Christine R BED 3**
Barkett Alexandra PS
Glaeser Kristy L MA 1
Haar Sharon PS
Mathiowetz Barbara E BA 5-7
Moeller Marcy J MA K
Payne Margaret
Perkins Kathie 7
Recksiedler Cynthia BA 2
Recksiedler Ronald E BS 8
Roan William T MA 4
Sitze Casey C BA 5
Sitze Jacob C BA 6
Wutke Mari BS K

**LAKE ARROWHEAD**-MOUNT CALVARY PS
• RSO • 1989
27415 School Rd 92326 PO Box 332 92326-0332
(909)337-7750 •
FAX(909)357-1412
NO REPORT

**LAKE FOREST**-ABIDING SAVIOR PS-8
• NLSA • 1976
23262 El Toro Rd 92630-4898
(949)830-1461 •
FAX(949)830-7921
abidingsavior@hotmail
**Hebel Harry G MS PS-8**
**Howland Beth M AA PS**
**Sims Carolyn C MA K-8**
Ahles Pamela S MED 2
Beyer Janet K BA PS
Block E C BA 5
Bradley Lorena V BS 3
Cain Leslye PS
Chittick Cari A BS
Christman Kimberlie D BA 5
Christman Nathaniel BA 4
Doyle Debra PS
Fitzsimons Sandra K BA K
Geisler Ruth E MA 1
Hantula Brenda M BA K
Hebel Suzanne MED 1
Howard Pamela J PS
Kaufman Roxanne K
Macare Jennifer M PS
Martin Anne BA 4
Morton Cristina 6
Prill Jana M BA 6
Randall John BA K-8
Randall Kimberly A BA 3
Rogers Christine L PS-8
Svarc Renee C BA 2
Vasquez Roman S MA 7
Vick Michael S MCI 8
Wood Ellen L BA K

**LANCASTER**-GRACE PS-8
• NLSA • 1958
856 W Newgrove St 93534-3092
(661)948-1018 •
FAX(661)948-2731
graceluth@qnet.com
**Hansen Darren D BSED 1-8**
Barckholtz Margaret L BS 4
Boyer Esther L 1
Cross Heidi A BSED 2
Escamilla Marta 5-8
Gater Linda F PS
Hansen Lori V BED 7
Jones Deborah A PS
Rottman Kathryn A MA 6
Szalai Mary K BSED 3
Ward Rachelle C K
Wooster Larry D MA 1-8
Wooster Lynette M 5

**LIVERMORE**-OUR SAVIOR K-8
• 1975
1385 S Livermore Ave 94550-9532
(925)447-2082 •
FAX(925)606-9947
**Dirks Dennis J MS**
**Miller Lawren L MS 5**
**Yount Susan D MA 2**
Claassen Martha 7-8
Clobes Carol MED K
Dirks Lynn E BA 6
Dobbs Tonina K
Greenhagen Linda MA 5
Handrock Sarah 7
Hartman Martha S 3
Hill Darren 1
Jalanivich Deborah MED 4
Johnson Delores K
Kramer Harriet
Managan Jayne W MS 7
Meek Nancie 3
Poppe Karen MED 2
Streufert Melanie 4
Zinnel Nora L BSED 1

OUR SAVIOR PS
• 1965
1135 Bluebell Ave 94550 1385 S Livermore Ave 94550-4829
(925)443-0124
NO REPORT

**LODI**-ST PETER K-8
• NLSA • 1904
2400 Oxford Way 95242-2854
(209)333-2225 •
FAX(209)334-4633
therock@softcom.net
**Woodward Peter C EDS**
Goetz Bruce G BA 6-8
Knoedler Robert H MA 4
Kuchenbecker Randall D BS 6-8
Milz Charlene K BS 6-8
Mundinger Barbara K MED 5
Nishimoto Jacqueline M K
O Keefe Ruth E BS 1
Scriven James A BA K-8
Steiner Pamela S BSED 2
Wolter Teresa M BSED 3

**LONG BEACH**-BETHANY K-8
• 1947
5100 E Arbor Rd 90808-1105
(562)420-7783 •
FAX(562)429-1693
**Hensley Douglas D BS**
Choate Phyllis A 6
Dahlin Jeanette A BS K
Fink Mary E MED 1-8
Fink Nadine BSED 1
Fink Robert J BSED 8
Grothaus Peter D BSED 7
Hazlewood Betty Ann J 3
Imes Kim R 5
Kehr Sarah M BA 7
Krieger Lynette A 3
Lofton Bobbette M 1
Moorman Jill L BSED 8
Nelson Janice S 2
Niermann Kathleen M
Nissen Amy J BA 4
Richardt Karen L BA 4
Sandlin Leigh A K
Shidner Erin K 2
Sulimoff Jean A 6
Werner Karen L BS 5

BETHANY PS
• 1974
4644 Clark Ave 90808-1298
(562)429-7335 •
FAX(562)429-1693
dedabursu@aol.com
Burdett Marilyn A AA
Graham Vicki S PS
Krueger Verlys PS
Lagana Alicia PS
Padias Belinda PS
Santos Dorothy PS
Stejskal Shirley PS
Stroh Myrna L BS PS
Sutherlin Karen BS PS
Swensen Lisa PS
Teague Betty PS

FIRST PS-K
• 1910
946 Linden Ave 90813-4582
(562)437-0777 •
FAX(562)437-5194
firstlutheran@juno.com
Flexor Adelia 6 PS
Hay Phyrun PS
Jones Victoria PS
Kim Kristine
Latrice Alexander PS
Saleem Karimah PS
Smith Carolyn A BA K

GRACE PS
• 1989
245 W Wardlow Rd 90807-4496
(213)424-7668
NO REPORT

ST PAULS PS
2283 Palo Verde 90815
(562)598-4729 •
FAX(562)598-5629
NO REPORT

**LOS ANGELES**-ST PAUL PS
• 1998
3911 W Adams Blvd 90018-1756
(323)733-9677
NO REPORT

**LOS GATOS**-HOLY CROSS CHILDRENS PS
• 1990
15885 Los Gatos Almaden Rd
95032-3803
(408)356-6828 •
FAX(408)356-0349
NO REPORT

**MAMMOTH LAKES**--MAMMOTH LAKES CHRIST PS
• 1980
379 Old Mammoth PO Box 3543
93546-3543
(619)934-2056
NO REPORT

**MANHATTAN BEACH**-CIRCLE OF LOVE-FIRST PS-2
• 1986
1100 N Poinsettia Ave 90266-4918
(310)545-5653 ext 19 •
FAX(310)546-2318
**Lubs Christine M BA**
Allen Nancy PS
Bero Diana PS
Cannon Dana 1-2
Doyle Marjorie L PS
Lang Ingrid K
Mejla Denise PS
Mollgaard Julie PS
Pata Ronda C BA PS
Simpson Carolyn D BA K
Theveny Cindi PS
Tierney Peggy PS

**MANTECA**-UNITED PS
• 1973
649 Northgate Dr 95336-3144
(209)823-1971 •
FAX(209)823-9335
NO REPORT

**MAYWOOD**-A GARDEN OF CHILDREN-PALABRA DE DIOS PS
• 1999
4411 E 61st St 90270
(323)560-0089 •
FAX(323)560-5936
NO REPORT

**MENIFEE**-GOOD SHEPHERD PS
• 1994
26800 Newport Rd 92584-9218
(909)672-6679
NO REPORT

**MENLO PARK**-LITTLEST ANGELS BETH PS
• 1996
1075 Cloud Ave 94025-6203
(415)854-4973 •
FAX(415)854-5910
preschol@flash.net
NO REPORT

**MERCED**-ST PAUL PS-5
• 1988
2916 Mckee Rd 95340-2721
(209)383-3302 •
FAX(209)383-3642
sklipfez@cyberlynk.com
**Klipfel Sanna L MA**
Alvarado Monica PS
Berg Margaret PS
Blank Stephen M BA 4
Bush Ally 4
Ehlers Heidi S BA 2
Faulkner Angelique PS
George Kathy PS
Kelly Melissa 2
Leistico Laurene E BA 5
Mejia Marci PS
Meyer Tammie BA
Mognis Brenda A 1
Murakami Apryl PS
Silveira Anna PS

**MISSION HILLS**-CHAPEL OF THE CROSS PS-K
• 1992
10000 Sepulveda Blvd 91345-2918
(818)830-5496
NO REPORT

**MODESTO**-GRACE PS-8
• 1984
617 W Orangeburg Ave
95350-4246
(209)529-1800 •
FAX(209)529-7721
ltietmeyer@aol.com
Boswell Stacey L K

Brown Cassandra L 4
Cogzill Debbie PS
Connick Sharon J BSED 7-8
Mc Cormack Pamela G 2
Pinto Cindy PS
Schmelzer Daniel 5-6
Sluder Nancy PS
Stelle Cindy PS
Tietmeyer Karen BA 3
Tietmeyer Larry BSED
Toepfer Deborah PS
Trevino Lupe PS
Vigars Jeffrey M BA 1
**MONROVIA-**FIRST PS-8
• 1949
1323 S Magnolia Ave 91016-4021
(626)357-3596 •
FAX(626)357-8296
Lahn Tracy L BA 4
Maas Terry P
**MONTEBELLO-**ST JOHN PS-8
• 1913
433 N 18Th St 90640-3940
(213)721-3910 •
FAX(213)721-3910
NO REPORT
**MORENO VALLEY-**SHEP OF THE VALLEY PS-K
• 1987
11650 Perris Blvd 92557-6536
(909)924-3422 •
FAX(909)243-1834
svls@juno.com
**Williams Jacqueline PS-K**
Decker Linda PS
Florez Martha PS
Jordan Catherine K
Menchaca Tracey PS
Patterson Laurie BS PS
Wheel Lora PS
Wirtz Patricia PS
**MOUNTAIN VIEW-**ST PAUL PS-K
• 1988
1075 El Monte Ave 94040-2320
(415)969-2696 •
FAX(415)967-0667
NO REPORT
**NAPA-**ST JOHN PS-8
• 1938
3521 Linda Vista Ave 94558-2703
(707)226-7970 •
FAX(707)226-7974
hlawson@napanet.net
**Lawson Herman E MED**
Burmester Ellen J BA 1
Gewirz Betsy A BS 3
Hagberg Sandra L BA K
Hauch Robert BA 7
Klein Doris J BA 4
Kusel Mark 8
Lawson Sandra M BS K-8
Newton David M 5
Pace Carolynn L PS
Schroeder Lydia E BS 2
Stanhope Debra G BS 6
**NEWBURY PARK-**CHRIST THE KING PS
• 1982
3947 W Kimber Dr 91320-4829
(805)499-7022 •
FAX(805)498-9798
NO REPORT
**NORWALK-**ST PAUL PS
• 1982
11943 Rosecrans Ave 90650-3132
(562)929-6325
Anqulo Christina PS
Haislip Lynne PS
Lopez-Garfias Mayra PS
Munden Dannie PS
Murphy Joyce AA
**OAKLAND-**PILGRIM PS
• 1988
3900 35Th Ave 94619-1435
(510)531-3715
NO REPORT
**OCEANSIDE-**IMMANUEL PS
• 1985
1900 S Nevada St 92054-6418
(760)433-2784
Adkison Jeannie PS
Diaz Pedro PS
Dohrman Anna PS
Healy Patricia
Quiroz Mary PS
SHEP OF CHILDREN-SHEP OF VALLEY
• 1988
4510 N River Rd 92057-5199
(619)433-8840
NO REPORT
**ONTARIO-**REDEEMER PS-8
• 1952
920 W 6Th St 91762-1299
(909)986-6510 •
FAX(909)986-0757
Ahlschwede Gordon E MA
Alba Pattie PS
Arterburn Sherri K
Baughman Marlene K BS 5
Benham Janice M BA 2
Cloeter Janet R MA 4
Herrmann Jonathan BSED 7
Keenan Sara E BA 6
Krans Dorothy L BA 3
Loeper Leslie BS PS
Loesch Tonya L 1
Mc Leod Sandy 1-8
Oleson David G MED 8
Seckrater Donna K-8
**ORANGE-**IMMANUEL PS-8
• NLSA • 1922
147 S Pine St 92866-1600
(714)538-2374 •
FAX(714)538-5275
Immanuel.school@juno.com
Benne B J BSED 7-8
Caithamer Betty K
Davis Katherine 5-8
Guebert Susan J BA 1
Guerra Jennifer 2
Newcom Beverly PS
Powell Leslie PS
Stelling G E MA 3-4
Waterman Wayne L 3-6
SALEM PS-8
• NLSA • 1983
6411 E Frank Ln 92869-1539
(714)639-1946 •
FAX(714)639-6484
**Meyer Charlotte H MCOUN**
Blair Katherine PS
Burnett Jennifer J BA PS
Davis Dixie 1
Duerr Philip G MEAD 7
Flores de Apodaca Lucille H BA 3
Gala Laura PS
Gallmann Grace M 2
Howard Terry PS
Kelso Danielle C MED K
Kelso Darren L BA 8
Morgan Sara K-8
Norquist Alison PS
Prizio Amy PS
Raymond Mariann 5
Rock Rose E BS K-8
Rosenberg Joanna N BA 1
Senefsky Lisa PS
Surridge Shelly BS 3
Violette James R BA 4
Weinrich Christopher A BA 4
Weinrich Kasey 2
Willits Susie BA 6
ST JOHN PS-8
• NLSA • 1882
154 S Shaffer St 92866-1610
(714)288-4406 •
FAX(714)288-4411
gbeyer@sjls.org
**Beyer Gary A MS**
Behnken Mil 1
Bode Corinne A BS K
Cariker Gretchen D BA K
Collett Chris 5-8
Durkovic Heidi 5-8
Ellwein Lisa J MSED 6-8
Hafer Marsha J MS 2
Heide William J MMU
Hopkirk Pamela J MA 3
Hoyt Adele M BS
Jaeger Lori A MA 4
Koehnke Phillip C 5
Meier Cathy 2
Meier Lester T 6-8
Neben Jason BA
Odle Timothy 6-8
Pauge Mary Lou MA 4
Proa Stacia A MA 3
Schramm Conni L MA 6-8
Senne Roger P BS 6-8
Strussenberg Sarah BA K
Stuewe David R BA 6-8
Stuewe Isabel J BS 5
Stuewe Yvette K EDS 5
Thobe Carolyn BA 4
Van Blarcom Stephanie L BA 6-8
Webster Marilyn G BS 1
ST JOHN LAMBS LOT PS
• 1986
151 S Center St 154 S Shaffer St 92866-1609
(714)288-4409 •
FAX(714)288-4411
**Rohm Kristine PS**
Amling Carol PS
Kant Debbie A PS
Moore Cheryl PS
Tidball Jamie PS
Wayland Kathy PS
ST PAUL PS-8
• 1908
901 E Heim Ave 92865-2817
(714)921-3188 •
FAX(714)921-0131
**Beaudoin James M MA**
**Unger Garry D BS**
Bredehoft Thomas A BED 3-8
Busseau Craig R BSED 6-8
Cattau Ruth A BS 4
De Mello Olga PS
De Montmorency Kim K
Dielmann Marilyn K BA 2
Erickson Jon 3-8
Gross Lisabeth K BA K
Hight Steven R BS 6-8
Juranek Patricia BA 6-8
Lahn Tracy L BA 3
Lebrecht Diane AA PS
Lebrecht Richard MA 6-8
Lofink Karen L BS 2
Lofink Mark C BA 5
Loll Kari L 6
Lutz Alan O MA
Malone Veta B BS 3
Mangels Carolyn M BS 1
Marlow Margaret BA 1
Mattoon Janette D MA K
Mc Cann Timothy E BS 4
Mercier Nathan 5
Miller Julie PS
Richhart Julene C BED PS
Rueter Roger H MED 8
Schulte Vicki 6-8
Smith Susan PS
Surridge Timothy L BS
ST PAUL E CHLD CTR PS
• 1985
1250 E Heim Ave 92865-2920
(714)637-2416 •
FAX(714)637-1963
NO REPORT
**OROVILLE-**CALVARY CHILDRENS CE PS
10 Concordia St 95966-6300
(916)534-7082
NO REPORT
**OXNARD-**ST JOHN K-8
• NLSA • 1950
1500 N C St 93030-3599
(805)983-0330 •
FAX(805)983-2171
Hoffschneider Bonnie J BA 2
Hoffschneider Joel T BA 6
**PACIFIC PALISADES-**PALISADES PS
• 1980
15905 W Sunset Blvd 90272-3499
(213)459-3425
NO REPORT
**PARADISE-**OUR SAVIOR PS
• 1983
6404 Pentz Rd 95969-3626
(916)877-7321 •
FAX(916)877-4447
NO REPORT
**PASADENA-**FAITH CHILD CARE CTR PS
• 1982
835 Hastings Ranch Dr 91107-2245
(818)351-0610 •
FAX(626)351-5414
Daffron Christina PS
Gillette Shirley PS
Summers Erika PS
Woolsey Oleta K BA PS
**PASO ROBLES-**TRINITY PS-8
• 1962
940 Creston Rd 93446-3002
(805)238-0335 •
FAX(805)238-7501
schooloffice@tcsn.net
**Fairbank Jane BA PS**
**Spiva Daniel F BS**
Ernst Jo Ann PS
Gehrke Amy C BA 5
Hafner Janice K 1
Henry Doralyn 2
James Nikki PS
Loper Jacqueline 7-8
Mockler Gaye L BSED K
Norman Kim PS
Reynolds Ila K
Ruiz Virginia 3
Spiva Cynthia L BA 4
Weygandt Mandi PS
Wilson Kelly 6
**PERRIS-**REDEEMER PS-K
• 1986
555 N Perris Blvd 92571-2811
(909)943-4928 •
FAX(909)940-4668
**Zamora Luz**
Henderson Rita
Nava Diana PS-K
**PICO RIVERA-**PEACE PS
• 1988
9412 Shade Ln 90660-5340
(213)949-3210
Camancho Marcella PS
Frometa Maria PS
Pulido Marie PS
Wright Claudia AA
**PIEDMONT-**ZION K-8
• NLSA • 1883
5201 Park Blvd 94611-3328
(510)530-7909 •
FAX(510)530-2635
Alle Bonnie J BS PS-2
Andresen Cynthia I MED 7
Dal Ferro Carolyn K BA K
Hackerd Ellen BA 6
Heinitz John R MS
Heinitz Lindsey BAED 2
Heinitz Ruth A BS 5
Lyon Gina BA 5
Packard Trudy G MAT 3
Strelow Alberta M MA

**PLACERVILLE**--FIRST PS
• 1987
1200 Pinecrest CT 95667-4728
(530)626-8503 •
FAX(530)622-1326
NO REPORT

**POWAY**-MT OLIVE PS
• 1983
14280 Poway Rd 92064-4929
(619)679-8169
**Andrews Patrice PS**
Breen Leslie PS
Cannon Michelle PS
Dass Mary Anne PS
Esposito Stacy PS
Higley Tina PS
Knox Kathy PS
Perkins Esther PS

**RAMONA**-RAMONA PS-8
• 1976
520 16th St 92065-2622
(760)789-4804 •
FAX(760)789-7372
rls@connectnet.com
Boehne Bruce K MA

**RANCHO PALOS VERDES**-MOUNT OLIVE PS
• 1991
5975 Armaga Spring Rd 90275-4801
(310)377-8821 •
FAX(310)377-9903
NO REPORT

**REDDING**-TRINITY PS
• 1990
2440 Hilltop Dr 96002-0506
(530)222-5868 •
FAX(530)221-6695
trinityps@juno.com
**Killgore Denise A BA**
Anderson Karin PS
Baker Becky PS
Garland Shannon PS
Kraft Gwen PS
Mannion Stacy PS
Shirley Barbara PS
Stark Patsy V AA PS

**REDLANDS**-CHRIST THE KING PS-K
• 1981
1505 E Ford St 92373-7128
(909)793-8722
Beveridge Heather PS
Brents Christine K
Brook Darlene PS
Carlson Martha PS
Coe Sheri PS
Eason Jane PS
Edleson Carole
Hoekstra Erin PS
Lascheider Tara PS
Lockwood Norma PS
Lumabao Tania PS
Manuel Nora PS
McIntyre Judy PS
Mulder Becky PS
Pittmun Tami PS
Standley Cathy
Tellyer Yolanda
Thibodo Pam PS
Trujillo Terry PS

**REDONDO BEACH**-IMMANUEL PS
• 1998
706 Knob Hill Ave 90277-4398
(310)316-6040 •
FAX(310)316-7732
noahark@worldnet.att.net
**Mc Donald Margaret G**
De Benedictis Gina M PS
Mc Donald Meghan L PS
Stephens Suzan L PS

**REDWOOD CITY**-REDEEMER K-8
• NLSA • 1957
468 Grand St 94062-2062
(650)366-3466 •
FAX(650)366-5897
gbehrens@ricochet.net
**Behrens Gary E MA 6-8**
Greene Janine 7
Kuefner Marla R MA 4
Lenahan Denise BS 3
Maier Denise 2
Mancini Mike 8
Meyer Sue K
Montallo Jennifer 6
Schneider Kathy 1
Wolf Jennifer 5

**RIDGECREST**-RIDGECREST-OUR SAVIOR K-6
• 1971
725 N Fairview St 93555-3576
(760)375-9121 •
FAX(760)375-7921
**Hoffman Mary A BS**
Benson Marianne 3
Gallagher JoEllen 4
Napper Traci 1
Sloan Corlette 2
Zimmerman Caroline 5-6

**RIVERSIDE**-IMMANUEL PS-6
• 1957
5545 Alessandro Blvd 92506-3596
(909)682-7613 •
FAX(909)682-9403
NO REPORT

**RUNNING SPRINGS**-MT CALVARY LUTHERAN PS
32054 Hunsaker Way PO Box 3558 92382
(909)867-7228 •
FAX(909)337-2003
NO REPORT

**SACRAMENTO**-PEACE PS-K
• NLSA • 1982
924 San Juan Rd 95834-2211
(916)927-4060 •
FAX(916)927-5418
Alsante Julie PS
Bertsch Bernadette PS
Farnsworth Rebecca PS
Growney Deborah PS
Haas Dee A BA K
Haas Greg PS
Hey Sheng PS
Kruithoff Ruth L BED PS
Mc Clure Elizabeth A BA K
Michehl Katie PS
Michehl Shana PS
Nixon Pennie PS
Perkins Gale PS
Wilt Kathleen PS

TOWN & COUNTRY K-8
• 1958
4049 Marconi Ave 95821-3940
(916)481-2542 •
FAX(916)481-0648
Einspahr Donna M BA

**SALINAS**-OUR SAVIORS ECC PS
• 1999
1230 Luther Way 93901-1725
(831)422-4614 •
FAX(831)422-5320
**Conley Gloria PS**
Brickman Julie PS
Salcedo Lupe PS

**SAN DIEGO**-CHRIST THE CORNERSTO PS-6
• 1978
9028 Westmore Rd 92126-2406
(619)566-1741 •
FAX(619)566-1965
**Smith Judy E BSED**
Ambereen Sadaf PS
Belt Roxanne K
Davis Beth 1
Dishong Nancy PS
Dusi Karen 2
Martin Carol L 4
Mc Geachy Robert 3
Roberts Katie 5
Share Ellwood MA 6
Sinha Paramita PS

GRACE PS-6
• NLSA • 1947
3993 Park Blvd 92103-3598
(619)299-2890 •
FAX(619)295-4472
grace@lanz.com
NO REPORT

ST PAUL PS-8
• NLSA • 1947
1376 Felspar St 92109-3099
(858)272-6282 •
FAX(858)272-4397
Andersen Ruth BED 5
Cook Shelley BA 1
Denke Muriel A K
Friedrichs Fred R 7
Irmer Christine C BSED 2
Muller Amanda 6
Pollock Michelle 8
Pribnow Philayne 4
Ross Kim PS
Seal Catherine R 3

TRINITY PS-3
• 1981
7210 Lisbon St 92114-3098
(619)263-7020 •
FAX(619)262-8971
NO REPORT

**SAN FERNANDO**-FIRST K-6
• 1950
777 N Maclay Ave 91340-2138
(818)361-4800 •
FAX(818)361-9725
Courtney Peggy A 4
Durham Sharon A 2-6
Johnson Mary M 2
Leonhardt Carolyn P 1
Meier Margaret M K
Reynolds Eileen E MED 5
Skinner Sandra BS 3

**SAN FRANCISCO**-WEST PORTAL K-8
• NLSA • 1950
200 Sloat Blvd 94132-1621
(415)665-6330 •
FAX(415)661-8402
**Merrill Shirley J MA**
Boyer Michele F K
Campbell Christine 6
Chan Jason BA K-6
Finley Margaret A MA
Frese Arthur E MA 8
George Patricia S 4
Holt Daniel V MED 7-8
Howard Teresa L BA 4-8
Huang Cynthia BA K
Jacob Frederick R MA 7-8
Jew Irene BA 2
Keiser Pamela M BA 4
Kolsanoff Eugenia F BA 6
Kvale Edith BA 3
Lucchesi Josephine M 1
Martin Peter 7-8
Mills Elaine E 5
Morris Leslie R MTH 7-8
O Connor Kari A BA 6
Praeger Dorothy F BA
Pulesevich Christine 4-8
Sandvik Irene 5
Slettvedt Carol E BA 7-8
Stephehnson Rozanne 3
Stresow Ruth E MA 1
Szeto Jenny MA 2
Toloski Diane K-6
Wurschmidt Randall 8

ZION K-8
• 1947
495 9Th Ave 94118-2912
(415)221-7500 •
FAX(415)221-7141
cgrundt@zionlutheranchurch.org
**Grundt Carolyn J MAD K-8**
Agee Helen K
Jacobsen JoAn R MS 1
Jacobsen John C MSED K-8
Klein Charles 4
Lew Viola 5
Lueck John W MA 6-8
Mueller Ron 6-8
Mueller Susan 6-8
Shinbori Wendy MA K-8
Sway Tom 7-8
Torrey Kristy K-8
Varney Andrea 6-8
Yamabe Kevin T BA 2
Zimmerman Margaret E BA 3

**SAN JOSE**-SHEP OF THE VALLEY PS
• 1981
1281 Redmond Ave 95120-2747
(408)997-4846 •
FAX(408)997-4841
svalleylut@aol.com
**Mosier Erna M BA**
Adams Amy PS
Burnham Maureen PS
Eckert Nancy PS
Kennedy Tania PS
Leatherman Sandy PS
Seip Deborah PS
Von Pinnon Teresa PS

**SAN LORENZO**-CALVARY PS-8
• NLSA • 1950
17200 Via Magdalena 94580-2928
(510)278-2598 •
FAX(510)278-2557
**Adams Forrest E MED**
Blank Norma L BA K
Hertenstein Margo L 3
Luehrs Marjorie L BS 2
Marr Rhoda S 6-8
Penrose Joan C BSED 4
Reppert Kari J BA 5
Sandau William H BSED 6-8
Schrader Sarah M BA 1
Vincent Chrystle PS
Wacholz Aaron A 6-8

**SAN MATEO**-GRACE K-8
• 1984
2825 Alameda DE Las Pulgas 94403-3262
(650)345-9082 •
FAX(650)377-4831
**Meier Robert P BA 3-4**
Bethke Susan BA 5-6
Bethke William R BA 7-8
Enge Heidi A BA 2
Grams Susan E BA K
Meier Elisabeth E BA 3-4
Timler Karen L BA 1

**SAN PEDRO**-CHRIST PS-8
• NLSA • 1955
28850 S Western Ave 90275-0835
(310)831-0848 •
FAX(310)831-0090
NO REPORT

**SAN RAFAEL**-TRINITY PS-K
• 1987
333 Woodland Ave 94901-5007
(415)453-4526 •
FAX(415)454-6230
trinityforkids@aol.com
Allen Kathleen PS
Barthel Kris PS
Bauer Tina BS PS
Bauer Vivian BA
Brohm Ann BSED K
Dahl Valerie A BED PS
Eaglin Jill PS
Erikson Mary PS
Franz Lynne PS
Isaacs Mindy PS
Ista Tammy PS
Moestretti Michelle PS
Romo Mikelle BA PS
Streckfus Barbara PS

**SANTA ANA**-TRINITY K-8
• 1944
906 S Broadway 92701-5647
(714)543-0341 •
FAX(714)543-0388
morner@juno.com
**Morner Timothy S MED 7-8**
Blau Deborah D MA 3-4
Burke Kimberly K BS 5-6
Durkovic Nancy BA 1-2
Jones Abeatrice K-8
Morton Linda J BS 3-4
**SANTA CLARITA**-BETHLEHEM PS-K
• 1985
27303 Luther Dr 91351-3711
(805)251-6027
NO REPORT
**SANTA CRUZ**-MESSIAH PS
• 1982
801 High St 95060-2528
(831)458-1498
NO REPORT
**SANTA MARIA**-GRACE PS
• 1966
420 E Fesler St 93454-4510
(805)922-5419
**Teague Judy**
Adami Mary PS
Anderson Cynthia PS
Gumm Mary PS
**SANTA MONICA**-PILGRIM PS-8
• 1930
1730 Wilshire Blvd 90403-5598
(310)829-2239 •
FAX(310)453-5345
smpilgrim@hotmail.com
**Falk Suzanne R BA**
Anderson Britt S BA PS
Epperson Linda-Marie MMU 2
Gsell Kara L BA 7-8
Hoffer Angie N BA 3
Maas Terry P 4
Nagel Judy 1
Schaefer Michelle BA K
Schneider Lindy 6-8
Urbach Allison 5
**SANTA ROSA**-ST LUKE PS-8
• 1975
905 Mendocino Ave 95401-4812
(707)545-0526 •
FAX(707)544-2112
Baldaramos Debra PS
Claasen Laurie E BS 4
Hagenlocher Aenne E BA 5
Hvasta Mary 6
Karlen Fred W MED 1-8
Knight Rose BA PS
Martin Ronald 5-8
Martin Suzanne M BA K
Rose Tammi E BA 7-8
Rothas Cynthia K BA 2
Solheim Christine R BED 1
Stohlmann Joyce A BA 3
**SANTA YNEZ**-SHEPERD OF THE VALLE PS
• 1995
3550 Baseline Ave 93460-9744
(805)686-9979
NO REPORT
**SEBASTOPOL**-MOUNT OLIVE PS
• 1986
460 Murphy Ave 95472-3611
(707)823-4093
NO REPORT
**SHERMAN OAKS**-SHERMAN OAKS PS
• 1994
14847 Dickens St 91403-3627
(818)784-9480 •
FAX(818)784-5736
Amobi Hazel PS
Amstutz Tammy PS
Amundson-Mingin Audrey PS
Carnavaciol Theresa PS
Chavez Anita PS
Golby Judy
Lapnow Linda PS
Mursalim Maria
Nixon Diane
O Byrne Leslie
Pascual Cecilia
Santiago Deborah PS
Syed April PS
Trmrian Lucia
Utterback Cristina
**SIMI VALLEY**-GOOD SHEPHERD K-8
• RSO • NLSA • 1979
2949 Alamo St 93063-2185
(805)526-2482 •
FAX(805)526-4857
NO REPORT
TRINITY PS
• 1978
2949 Alamo St 93063-2185
(805)526-5975 •
FAX(805)526-4857
NO REPORT
**SONOMA**-FAITH PS
• 1991
19355 Arnold Dr 95476-6301
(707)938-9464 •
FAX(707)996-7365
piller@vom.com
Crocker Drew A PS
Dunhum Mary C PS
Piller Debbie K PS
**SOUTH GATE**-REDEEMER K-8
• 1949
2626 Liberty Blvd 90280-2096
(323)588-0934 •
FAX(323)588-0701
NO REPORT
**STOCKTON**-IMMANUEL PS
• 1994
2343 Country Club Blvd 95204-4704
(209)465-3725
NO REPORT
NEWDAY-ST ANDREW PS
• 1975
4910 Claremont Ave 95207-5708
(209)957-4089 •
FAX(209)957-1887
**Wagner Norma A**
Budesa Kim PS
Laird Elizabeth PS
Pilkington Marilyn PS
Rivas Marla PS
Urbano Pat PS
TRINITY PS-8
• 1910
444 N American St 95202-2129
(209)464-0895 •
FAX(209)464-1287
Colyer Kenneth R BA 5-8
Conti Rhonda 1
Lee Linda M BA 3-4
Mara Julie A BA K
Mara Rodney J MED
Martin Nancy J BA 1-2
Spohn Rita 3-5
**TEHACHAPI**-GOOD SHEPHERD PS
• 1994
329 S Mill St 93561-1623
(805)823-7740 •
FAX(805)823-1554
NO REPORT
**TEMECULA**-NEW COMMUNITY PS-K
• 1997
30470 Pauba Rd 92592-6214
(909)693-5524 •
FAX(909)695-1520
Bradshaw Mary P PS
Harnetiaux Jennifer PS
Jones Ingrid PS
Ornelas Isabel PS
Williams Elizabeth PS
**TEMPLE CITY**-FIRST PS-8
• 1945
9123 Broadway 91780-2399
(626)287-0968 •
FAX(626)285-8648
**Fellwock Geraldine R BA 5-6**
Allen Bernadette K
Berni Kathy A BA 1
Blume Kathy 3
Pica Sandi 2
Richardson Deborah V BA 4
Swickard Tricia 7-8
**TERRA BELLA**-ZION K-8
• 1909
10368 Road 256 93270-9722
(559)535-4346 •
FAX(559)535-2719
zionschool@jps.net
**Brauer Frederick E MEDADM 7-8**
Anderson Eloise M BS 2-4
Kunz Marshall 5-6
Reed Laurie D BA K-1
**TORRANCE**-ASCENSION PS-8
• 1960
17910 S Prairie Ave 90504-3713
(310)371-3531 •
FAX(310)214-8713
**Dickerson Joe B EDD**
**Geisler Carol A MAD**
Bryan Cheryl 5
Cabral Jennifer PS
Caithamer Joe
De Santiago Rocio PS
Hettig Teri AA
Hopkins Steve 7
James Cheryl
Joseph Lisa PS
Miller Helen 1
Morrow Vicki MA 2
Schroeder Karen L BA 4
Schubarth Joanne L BSED 3
Shepherd Cynthia A PS
Smith Nancy PS
Wiley Susan MA K
Woods Carol BA K
**TRACY**-ST PAUL PS
• 1987
1635 Chester Dr 95376-2927
(209)835-8803
NO REPORT
**TUJUNGA**-FOOTHILLS-FAITH K-6
• RSO • 1975
3561 Foothill Blvd 91214-1850
(818)248-4141
Bobzin Kathy K
Galbo Angelina 4
Hollis Thoms
Hughes Cynthia 1-2
Pfeiffer Amanda 5
Stradiotto Tammy 2-3
**VACAVILLE**-BETHANY PS-3
• 1974
621 S Orchard Ave 95688-4335
(707)451-6678 •
FAX(707)451-1740
**Ignatieff Claudia R BA**
Bartz Jan K
Baste Karen K PS
Brown Kristin N PS
Crabtree Nicole M PS-K
Doss Christine E PS
Dougherty Lisa J PS
Holbrook Lynn A MS PS
Kaminski Nancy L PS
Kanagaki Leta G PS
Mollenbernd Deborah S PS
Plitt Brenda J PS
Sanderson Margaret J PS
Schrader Deborah J 2
Skarshaug Irma K
Van Buskirk Sarah M 3
Whitfield Julie BA PS
Wright Lisa A K
**VAN NUYS**--FIRST PS
• 1994
6903 Tyrone Ave 91405-4011
(818)988-1982 •
FAX(818)989-0337
NO REPORT
FIRST K-6
• 1944
6952 Van Nuys Blvd 91405-3984
(818)786-3002 •
FAX(818)786-0894
principal@flvn.org
**Vandrey Wanda J BS**
Baker Candice K
Dickerson Joylyne B MAR 2
Draeger Linda M MA 1
Friedrich Ronald P BA 6
Geer Julie 4
Moody Elizabeth 3
Romsa Kathleen BED 5
**VENICE**-FIRST K-8
• 1948
815 Venice Blvd 90291-4998
(310)823-9367 •
FAX(310)823-4822
Embretson Angela R BA 1-2
Jacobson Dennis M BS 5-8
Jacobson Sharon L BA 3-4
Parks Danette 2
Rusch David L MS 7-8
Rusch Laura N 5-6
**VENTURA**-GRACE K-5
• 1985
6190 Telephone Rd 93003-5381
(805)642-5424
**Evans Clifford H MED**
Evans Susan K BS 3
Forehand Ruth K
Henke Jeanine 2
Janssen Jean A MA 1
Johnston Ronda 4-5
**VICTORVILLE**-ZION PS-6
• 1982
15342 Jeraldo Dr 92394-5527
(760)243-3074 •
FAX(760)245-5945
NO REPORT
**VISALIA**-GRACE K-6
• 1977
1111 S Conyer St 93277-2537
(559)734-7694 •
FAX(559)734-0146
**Gaffney Susanne MA**
Andreas Sherri L BA K
Cook Joanne M BA 1-2
Moos Elizabeth PS
Riesner Nancy BA 3
Thornburg Tamara K BS 5-6
Walters Andrea 4
**VISTA**-FAITH K-8
• 1979
700 E Bobier Dr 92084-3804
(760)724-7700 •
FAX(760)724-6151
**Henkell Joe D MA 8**
Bade Barbara L BS 2
Bade William L MMU 6
Fadel Haroldine BS 3
Fick Patricia A MPED 5
Gaudi Karen 1
Griffith Judith A BA K
Helmick Judith A BA K
Polacek Barbara 1
Rehberger Louis 7-8
Rutan Jill BA 7-8
Wygant Christina 4
LAMBS OF FAITH PS
• 1976
700 E Bobier Dr 92084-3804
(760)724-7700 •
FAX(760)724-6151
Cardwell Annie PS
Droegemueller Carolyn R AA
Freeman Karen B MA PS
Gallup Deborah PS
Helmick Jaime PS
Holden Chanda PS

Larson Jane PS
Youngdale Ginger L BA PS
**WALNUT CREEK**-HIS TOO-TRINITY PS-K
• 1969
2317 Buena Vista Ave 94596-3017
(925)935-3362 •
FAX(925)935-7902
NO REPORT
**WATSONVILLE**-TRINITY PS-5
• 1980
175 Lawrence Ave 95076-2916
(408)724-0176
NO REPORT
**WEST COVINA**-IMMANUEL PS-8
• 1957
512 S Valinda Ave 91790-3007
(626)919-1072 •
FAX(626)919-5979
NO REPORT
**WESTMINSTER**-ST LUKE NEW LIFE
• 1974
13552 Goldenwest St 92683-3119
(714)897-3074 •
FAX(714)897-1569
NO REPORT
**WHITTIER**-FAITH PS-8
• NLSA • 1961
9920 S Mills Ave 90604-1097
(562)941-0245 •
FAX(562)941-4451
faithwildcat@earthlink.net
**Lockhart John W BSED**
Adickes Mark W BSED 4
Buehring Cyra M 5-8
Hambarian Carol A 2
Koenemann Julie A MED K
Lockhart Carol E BSED 3
Mc Colister Eunice 1
Reiland Chris 5-8
Sadowl Matthew P BS 5-8
Vincent Joanne C PS
Wood Rhonda L K
HOPE PS
10327 Valley Home Ave 90603-2657
(562)943-3888 •
FAX(562)943-5308
NO REPORT
TRINITY PS-8
• 1943
11716 Floral Dr 90601-2898
(562)699-7431 •
FAX(562)699-1821
andrich5@prodigy.net
**Andrich Janie L MA**
Bonawitz Debbie
Butts Jennifer M AA
Dewberry Carolyn 1
Dupler Patricia BA 4
Felten Joanna L BA 5
Gutierrez Peter BS 8
Knox Marlo 6-8
Lambert Timothy BA 6
Mc Cray Cheryl AA K
Mericle Angie K-5
Mericle Heather 7
Rivera Sharon 2
Schroeder Susan BA 3
**WOODLAND**-ST PAUL PS
• 1983
625 W Gibson Rd 95695-5143
(916)662-1935 •
FAX(916)662-1999
Borchers Charlise
Gould Karly
Jacques Pat
Moore Jessica
Morales Isabel
Morawec Marianne BS
Rauhauser Elizabeth A

**YUBA CITY**-FIRST PS-8
• 1954
850 Cooper Ave 95991-3849
(530)673-9426 •
FAX(530)673-3454
**Oliva Kimberly**
Akin Carol 2-3
Elrod Linda K
Hannaford Jaynee 1-2
Taylor Sandra A BA 7-8
Trinklein Steve MS 4-6

## COLORADO

**ALAMOSA**-TRINITY PS-3
• 1982
52 El Rio Dr PO Box 787 81101-0787
(719)589-3271
Conner Mary L PS
Lucero Abby K
Lucero Joy E K
Mc Avoy Linda 1
Ryker Jan PS-3
Sanchez Theresa PS-K
Schofield Lisa 2-3
**AURORA**-HOPE PS-8
• 1966
1345 Macon St 80010-3516
(303)364-1828 •
FAX(303)364-5320
hopelcms@juno.com
**Le Doux Kathy**
Boye Jane A MA 3-5
Flores Rosina PS
Kniss Stefani PS
Kraft Melissa 1-2
Parton Laurie J BED 6-8
MOUNT OLIVE PS-K
• 1972
11500 E Iliff Ave 80014-1177
(303)750-9856 •
FAX(303)745-5912
Albers Jo Anne PS
Carlson Patricia PS
Knight Rebecca PS
Ripke Judith L BS PS-K
Stibrich Jo Ann
Zierk Dorene PS
PEACE PS
• NLSA • 1987
3290 S Tower Rd 80013-2367
(303)693-8687 •
FAX(303)699-2777
Davis Sharon PS
Frawley Patricia PS
Greiner Janice PS
Mc Arthur Jo Ann PS
Smith Joan E
Stork Brenda PS
PEACE K-8
• NLSA • 1994
3290 S Tower Rd 80013-2367
(303)766-7116 •
FAX(303)699-2777
marv.oestmann@pwclc.org
**Oestmann Marvin P MA 5-8**
Baumgartel Jonathan 6-8
Benecke Emily E BA 5
Franzen Karen J 4
Grages Cynthia R BS K
Hettick Rosemarie 6-8
Hueske Suzie BA K-8
Johnson Eileen K BA 1
Johnson P J 6-8
Paulus Linda C MA 2
Ritchen Mary K K-8
Schoenhals Tammy A 3
**BOULDER**-MOUNT HOPE PS
• 1994
1345 S Broadway St 80305-6722
(303)499-9800
Binger Kimberley K PS
Jenson Kristin M BS PS

MOUNT ZION PS-8
• 1986
1680 Balsam Ave 80304-3539
(303)443-8477 •
FAX(303)448-9547
mtzion@indra.com
**Crabbs Cheryl L MA**
Beagle Lynette PS
Heppler Debbie L PS
Leimer Ann E BS 1
Leimer David J 5-6
Lindsey Christy
Renken Nancy 7-8
Sarr Lisa L 2
Schuler Nancy A BA 3-4
Traughber Elsie F BAED PS-K
Turner Jennifer L BA K
**BRIGHTON**-ZION PS-8
• NLSA • 1899
1400 Skeel St 80601-2336
(303)659-3443 •
FAX(303)659-2342
zionbrighton@juno.com
**Friedrich Ronald H MA**
Bell Mary C BA
Coffman Brooke L K-5
Dollase Tina M BA 2
Frick Dean D BA 6-8
Frick Deborah S BA PS
Gedde Suzanna BA 1-2
Grein Linda L BSED 1
Hart Charles M BS 3
Heitschmidt Katherine S BS K
Hubach Timothy P BS 3-4
Janetzke Bruce D BA 5
Mumby Robert J MA 4
Schumacher Timothy J BA 5
Swanson Mary B BED 6-8
Zagel James R 6-8
**BROOMFIELD**-BEAUTIFUL SAVIOR PS-8
• 1980
6995 W 120Th Ave 80020-2365
PO Box 8 80038-0008
(303)469-2049 •
FAX(303)469-6999
**Thomas Craig B MDIV**
Bourland F M BSED PS
Bower Kristine E BA PS
Dyslin Elaine C 3-4
Eman Kimberly A K
Meyer Seth 5-6
Shelley Judy 1
Stong Janet S BS 7-8
Toliver Twila M BA 2
**COLORADO SPRINGS**-HOLY CROSS PS
• 1999
4125 Constitution Ave 80909
(719)596-0661 •
FAX(719)596-0699
BDKrause@aol.com
NO REPORT
IMMANUEL PS-8
• NLSA • 1951
828 E Pikes Peak Ave 80903-3636
(719)636-3681 •
FAX(719)636-3995
Allison Kristine K
Driller Cathy A MA 4
Esa Willene K BA 5
Euken Philip L BA 6
Gerhardt Kristine BA PS
Gohl Mary M MA
Grasz Duane F MSED 3
Longstaff Heather 3-4
Schumaker Michelle K
Skrabanek Janel S BA 6-8
Stanley Cheryl R BA 6-8
Thomas Brian MPE K
Waldron Deanna J BA 1-2
Woerner Angeline F 1
Wright Sandra B BSED K

REDEEMER PS-8
• 1956
2215 N Wahsatch Ave 80907-6939
(719)633-7600 •
FAX(719)633-2127
NO REPORT
ROCK OF AGES PS
• 1983
120 N 31St St 80904 PO Box 6941 80934-6941
(719)632-9491 •
FAX(719)632-0772
NO REPORT
**CORTEZ**-TRINITY PS
• 1983
208 N Dolores Rd 81321-4210 PO Box 989 81321-0989
(303)565-3166 •
FAX(303)565-9346
**Snow Jackie**
Bloedel Gabrielle PS
Chance Nicole PS
Crawford Julie PS
Miller Judy PS
Norris Donna PS
Peck Mary PS
Phelps Evelyn PS
Reed LeEtta PS
Reiners Tonya PS
Smith Linda PS
Wittwer Dona R AA PS
**DENVER**-CHRIST PS-K
• 1984
2695 S Franklin St 80210-5924
(303)722-1424 •
FAX(303)722-0933
**Adam Betty L BS PS**
Kats Jennifer L K
Sees Kay H PS
EMMAUS PS-8
• 1992
3120 Irving St 80211-3632
(303)433-3303 • FAX(313) 433-2280
Bonnette Kristal PS
Cordova Connie L BA 3-4
Couillard Chris 7-8
Gerlach Michelle R BA K
Lopez Jay PS
Medina Denise PS
Meyer Heather N BS 2
Reynolds Jeannette M BSED 1
Romero Viola PS
Schlechte Roger E MDIV
Smith Cathleen H 5-6
Vigil Rena PS
MOUNT ZION PRESCHOOL PS
• 1972
500 Drake St 80221-4128
(303)428-8630
**Hathaway Janice E AAS**
Brueggemann Susan PS
REDEEMER K-8
• 1944
3400 W Nevada Pl 80219-2787
(303)934-0422 •
FAX(303)935-9256
luthschoold@aol.com
Martin Kerry J BA 5-6
Schuetz Glory J BSED 2-4
Schuknecht Jerold C MED
Tarr Sue A BSED K-1
ST ANDREW PS-3
• 1970
Andrews Dr & Peoria 12150 E Andrews Dr 80239-4441
(303)371-7014 •
FAX(303)371-1099
**Foglesong Lucille A BS K**
Brekke Helen L MA 1
Durr Ginger J BS PS
Heldt Amy L BSED 2-3
Wall Kristi BA PS

ST JOHN PS-8
• NLSA • 1899
700 S Franklin St 80209-4505
(303)733-3777 •
FAX(303)778-6070
st_johns@junoc.com
**Helmkamp Robert K EDD PS-8**
**Jefferies Dorothy R MA**
Beach Luann 2
Bertram Stephanie EDS 5
Crook Laurie MA 5-8
Findell Susan PS-8
Kaelberer Mary L BA K
Macht Kim PS-8
Rheinheimer Tracy BA 4
Saunders Jill M BA 6-8
Swartz Elizabeth PS
Terranova William 6-8
Thurmond Patricia BS 3
Vermeer Rebeccah 1
TRINITY PS-K
• 1993
4225 W Yale Ave 80219-5710
(303)934-6160 •
FAX(303)934-6672
trinitylutheran@uswest.net
**Marshall Gwen E MA PS**
Hall Jennifer PS
Short Joy BA K
UNIVERSITY HILLS PS-8
• NLSA • 1952
4949 E Eastman Ave 80222-7309
(303)759-5363 •
FAX(303)757-7110
school.uhills@qadas.com
Connell Debra L
Crawford Cathy A PS
Delimont Brian T 3-4
Gallo Amy J BSED 1-2
Hazel Ann E BA K
Kawcak Donna L PS
Kleinsasser Vickie L BA
Luetzen Gail PS
Newton Shelly R PS
Rich Monica K BA 5-6
Tripplett Tracy PS
**DURANGO**-ST PAUL PS PS
2611 Junction St 81301-4168 PO Box 2282 81301
(970)247-0357
NO REPORT
**FORT COLLINS**-OPEN ARMS-ST JOHN PS
• 1996
305 E Elizabeth St 80524-3705
(970)482-5316
Belleau Joan PS
Lange Pam PS
Moddelmog Sharon PS
PEACE WITH CHRIST PS
• 1985
1412 W Swallow Rd 80526-2413
(970)226-4721 •
FAX(970)226-1857
pwclc@info2000.net
NO REPORT
REDEEMER PS
• 1994
6630 Brittany Dr 80525-5823
(970)225-9020 •
FAX(970)225-9870
gbergmann@netzero.net
Bergmann Gabriele H BSED PS
Conover Nancy J PS
**FORT MORGAN**-TRINITY PS-7
• 1979
1215 W 7th Ave 80701-2842
(970)867-4931 •
FAX(970)867-9384
trinitys@twol.com
**Kogelmann Gerald F 4**
Arneson Crystal 2
Freidenberger Karen L BS 1
Ishmael Lynn A BMU 3
Kembel Sharon A MA 6-7
Nelson Judy PS
Steege April 5
Walek Sonja J BA K
**FRANKTOWN**-TRINITY PS-8
• 1993
4740 N Highway 83 80116-9661
(303)841-4660 •
FAX(303)841-2761
trinityfranktown@juno.com
Ewen Patricia BA 3
Foos Susan C AAS PS
Hall Ellen 6-8
Halloran Susan PS
Keith Jenny 5-8
Kerrins Melia R BA 4
Koppenhafer Debra A BSED 1
Linwood Lorelei PS
Lund Nancy A BS PS
Mc Master Susan 1
Plaza Fay K-8
Steinbrenner Corinne K BA PS
Steinbrenner Glenn A MA 6-8
Warren De Ann J BSED 2
Willis Karen 5
Zwinck Mary 6-8
**GLENWOOD SPRINGS**-HOLY CROSS PS
• 1993
62 County Road 135 81601-2715
(970)945-6871
aanderson5@juno.com
NO REPORT
**GRAND JUNCTION**-MESSIAH K-8
• 1979
840 N 11th St 81501-3218
(970)245-2838 •
FAX(970)245-8145
messiahgj@juno.com
**Miller Enid S BS 2**
De Berard Mary I BS 4-5
Gruner Sharon R BA 3
Hollatz Kathy G 1
Joseph Linda L MA 6
Miller Corwin L MED 7-8
Skoog Karen L MA K
**GREELEY**-GLORIA CHRISTI PS
• 1973
1322 31st Ave 80634-6328
(970)353-2554
gchristi@netzero.net
Grush Mary PS
Lamb Judy PS
Lengel Erin
Peter Karen PS
Wakeman Cindy
TRINITY K-8
• NLSA • 1946
3000 35th Ave 80634-9418
(970)330-2485 •
FAX(970)330-2844
tlsgreeley@ctos.com
**Whitney Larry A BSED**
Arnusch Lucile 7
Boxum Pat A 1-8
Jaynes Brenda 2
Keller Karen BS 1
Schultz Cheryl L BSED K
Splittgerber Anthony B BSED 7-8
Splittgerber Lisa R BSED 5-6
Wieting Bruce L 3
**HIGHLANDS RANCH**-HOLY CROSS PS
• 1997
9770 S Foothills Canyon Blvd 80126
(303)683-1311 •
FAX(303)470-0165
Carter Joni PS
Holle Beth PS
Mason Mary A BA
Rossi Karen PS
Spotts Dorey PS
**LAKEWOOD**-BETHLEHEM PS-8
• NLSA • 1940
2100 Wadsworth Blvd 80215
(303)233-0401 •
FAX(303)238-7691
**Landon Beth D MA**
Adam David J 7-8
Bauer Linda BS 3
Borer Rita BA PS
Breidert Dennis D MA 8
Breidert Kathleen G BS 2
Fingerlin Heidi N BSED PS-8
Fowler Ellie 3
Gerlach Lucas J BS 4
Gnagy Susan C BS 1
Havekost Jeffrey BS 6
Hischke Martha BSED 4
Hock Kristine L MA 5
Hurst Carrie L 7-8
Kitashima Robbin R 2
Lindeman Lisa A 5-8
Mc Clendon Greta A BS 7-8
Mc Dowell Kathy MA K-8
Roybal Linda A 8
Schamp Barbara A MED 1
Schult Philip D BMU 4-8
Schwartz Paula G BS K
Seamon Carol S PS-8
Shoaf Chester W MEAD 6
Todd Audrey J MA 5
CONCORDIA PS-K
• 1985
13371 W Alameda Pkwy 80228-3431
(303)989-5260 •
FAX(303)989-3746
Barton Pamela PS
Carroll Beth PS
Hanson Leslie M BS PS
Rahe Laura J K
**LITTLETON**-HOSANNA PS-K
• 1982
10304 W Belleview Ave 80127-1732
(303)973-6485
NO REPORT
OUR FATHER PS
• 1999
6335 S Holly St 80121
(303)779-1332 •
FAX(303)779-1668
Anderson Marjorie PS
Bergstrom Terry PS
Cochran Jeanne A PS
D Agosta Billie J PS
De Bartolomeis Jamie PS
Gemmill Karen PS
Hamilton Marianne PS
Mc Donald Karen R
Mendiola Kandice PS
Oppenheim Diane PS
Riggs Terry PS
Roberts Marlene PS
Scarpa Diane PS
Wetstein Kathy PS
SHEPHERD OF THE HILL K-8
• 1985
7691 S University Blvd 80122-3144
(303)798-0711 •
FAX(303)798-0718
NO REPORT
**LONGMONT**-MESSIAH PS-2
• 1990
1335 Francis St 80501-2511
(303)776-2573 •
FAX(303)776-2599
**Mertens Barbara J BS**
Thomson Audrey K
**LOVELAND**-IMMANUEL PS-8
• NLSA • 1977
1101 Hilltop Dr 80537-4446
(970)667-7606 •
FAX(970)667-0120
immloveland@juno.com
**Geidel David O MS**
Aho Timothy J BA 5
Arfsten Debra J MPED PS-8
Brown Lynn 6-8
Ellzey Sheila R 4
Gilbert Cheryl E BSED PS
Grimm Elizabeth A BSED 4
Hanneman Darlene H 1
Hein Gail E BS 1
Heldt Sandra L K-8
Hemmen Rosella K BS 3
Howard Duncan R 6-8
Mead Karen M BS 6-8
Metcalfe Leona K BA 2
Meyer Juliet L BSED 2
Renzelman Rhonda BS 5
Renzelman William N BS 6-8
Schnegelberger Christine L K
Self Lori L BA 6-8
Voth Blaine 6-8
Williams Droxsan J BA 3
**MONTE VISTA**-ST PETER PS-6
• 1993
330 Faraday St 81144
(719)852-5449
stpeters@amigo.net
Archuleta Emerlinda PS
Barnes Paul M MA K
Bryant Arleen PS
Davis Cindy PS
Navo Linda F BA
**MONUMENT**-FAMILY OF CHRIST PS
• 1998
PO Box 1010 80132
(719)481-0796
NO REPORT
**NORTHGLENN**-GETHSEMANE PS-8
• 1962
10675 Washington St 80233-4101
(303)451-6908 •
FAX(303)451-1067
Daniell Sheri L BA 2
**PAGOSA SPRINGS**-OUR SAVIOR K-8
• NLSA • 1992
56 Meadows Dr 81147-7662
(970)731-4668
rockies@frontier.net
NO REPORT
**PUEBLO**-TRINITY PS
• 1999
701 W Evans 81004
(719)562-9235
trinityecc1@juno.com
**Lawrenz Deann**
Ayalla Melissa
Krupka Cassandra
Larson Tiffany
Olthoff Barbara
Thorade Theresa
Walker Joy PS
TRINITY PS-8
• 1893
701 W. Evans Ave 81004-1523
(719)542-1864 •
FAX(719)542-1864
trinityp1@juno.com
**Daberkow Randolph K 8**
Arguto Rocco F IV BS 7
Bolt Jeanine L BA 2
Clostner Paula 6
Cooley Cyrisse 3
Daberkow Debby 1-8
Daberkow Evelyn M BS 5
Fetty Carrie 1
Kite Tracy K-8
Losey Virgil L 4
Miller Ellen 8
Samec Frances BA K
Tristaro Denise 3
**RIFLE**-EMMANUEL PS
• 1999
652 E 5th St 81650
(970)625-2369
NO REPORT
**STERLING**-TRINITY PS
• 1998
732 Clark St 80751
(970)522-5942
Davis Beverly J
Smith Leila PS

**WHEAT RIDGE**-WHEAT RIDGE PS
• 1997
8600 W 38th Ave 80033
(303)424-4341 •
FAX(303)424-4378
dcekotk@yahoo.com
**Mann Daria E BS PS**
Hessner Terri PS
Wehling Christa J BA PS
**WOODLAND PARK**-FAITH PS
1310 Evergreen Hgts Dr
80863-3304
(719)687-2303 •
FAX(719)687-4576
Iorio Kathy PS
Steinke Suzan PS

## CONNECTICUT

**BRIDGEPORT**-ZION PS-8
• 1903
612 Grand St 06604-3218
(203)367-7268 •
FAX(203)335-6143
ZionSchool@aol.com
Brown Margaret PS
Conner Nancy E 2
Cote Ann K
Lupa Theresa K MA 3
Muller Eileen 1
Polson Janice L BA 7-8
Poremba Michelina M 5-6
Schmidt Dorothy L BS
Van Camp John W 4
**BRISTOL**-IMMANUEL PS-8
• NLSA • 1898
154 Meadow St 06010-5730
(860)583-5631 •
FAX(860)585-4785
il.church@snet.net
**Koch Vernon C MS 5-8**
**Neagley Claire E BA**
Aszklar Mary K MA 7-8
Blase Marie L BSED 3
Hartford Kathy K
Licki Shannon K-8
Mack Mary B 7-8
Moll Marion C MS 7-8
Moll Patricia J BS 5
Ryskowski Raymond J MA 6
Ryskowski Rosemary J BA 4
Sasani Donna K-8
Schafer Jennifer 1-8
Stockman Rozanna M BA 1
Tonn Holly PS
Voisine Janet M BA 2
**CHESHIRE**-LITTLE CHERUBS-CHESHIRE PS
• 1997
660 W Main St 06410
(203)272-5106 •
FAX(203)272-3523
NO REPORT
**COVENTRY**-PRINCE OF PEACE PS
• 1970
10 N River Rd 06238-1633
(203)742-7548
NO REPORT
**DANBURY**-IMMANUEL PS-8
• NLSA • 1881
35 Foster St 06810-7836
(203)748-7823 •
FAX(203)744-3446
Baker Victoria 5
Connolly P V 6-8
Dittmar Barbara BA 2
Gladstone Melissa K-8
Harper Walter J MDIV
Lutz David D BSED 6-8
Lutz Nancy A BSED 6-8
Mc Grath Jane 1
Mc Manemin Betty 3
Person Sylvia C MED PS
Press David 1
Puglisi Suzanne 4
Rolfes Janelle K
Ruopp Anna L BA 6-8
Thomson Elizabeth A MA 1
**ENFIELD**-OUR REDEEMER PS
• 1986
20 North St PO Box 887
06082-0887
(860)749-3167
NO REPORT
**GREENWICH**-ST PAUL PS
• 1978
286 Delavan Ave 06830-5946
(203)531-5905
Cassano Sue PS
Kondo Mikiko PS
Vojtzboray Jeannette MSED PS
**GROTON**-FAITH PS
• 1990
625 Poquonnock Rd 06340-4567
(860)448-9500 •
FAX(860)445-0483
Kreisler Tina PS
Wagner Tammy PS
**MADISON**-MADISON PS
• 1986
9 Britton Ln 06443-2921 PO Box
210 06443-0210
(203)245-8784 •
FAX(203)245-4145
NO REPORT
**MERIDEN**-ST JOHN PS
• 1971
520 Paddock Ave 06450-6946
(203)630-3997 •
FAX(203)237-9540
NO REPORT
**MIDDLETOWN**-GRACE PS
• 1988
1055 Randolph Rd 06457-5190
(860)346-2641 •
FAX(860)344-0611
grace.evan.lutheran@snet.net
**Mentlick Lisa A BSED PS**
Asante Lydia PS
Duval Debbie PS
Hayn Janet L PS
Nettis Lisa PS
Nordstrom Donna PS
Spitzmacher Debbie PS
**NEW BRITAIN**-ST MATTHEW PS-5
• 1896
87 Franklin Sq 06051-2606
(860)223-7829
**Boettner Martin R BA 3**
Butler Sandra MA 4-5
Gouveia Theresa K
Landrie Marcia 2
Modifica Edith PS
Rosshirt Nancy BSED 1
Webb-Mower Amy PS-5
**NEW HARTFORD**-ST PAUL COMMUNITY PS
• 1968
30 Prospect St 06057-2221
(860)379-3172 •
FAX(860)379-3172
Yeadon Ruth BS PS
**NIANTIC**-CHRIST PS
• 1994
24 Society Rd 06357
(860)739-9575
clcms@uconect.net
**Raffa Linda BSED PS**
Murphy Sharon PS
Shirey Christine PS
**SOUTH WINDSOR**-OUR SAVIOR PS
• 1985
239 Graham Rd 06074-1422
(860)644-6458
jaerni@compuserve.com
NO REPORT
**TRUMBULL**-HOLY CROSS PS
• 1987
5995 Main St 06611
(203)268-6471 •
FAX(203)268-5499
**Janssen Michele**
Barker Cynthia PS
Coles Linda PS
Deigel Cynthia PS
**W HARTFORD**-BETHANY PS
• 1959
1655 Boulevard 06107-2502
(860)521-5976 •
FAX(860)521-7066
blcwhtfd@aol.com
**Mikulastik Mari PS**
La Cava Julie PS
Provenzano Jessie PS
**WALLINGFORD**-LITTLE ZION PS
• 1986
235 Pond Hill Rd 06492-5205
(203)269-0401
**Rufleth Ursula A BA PS**
Boisvert Sandy PS
Cody Carol PS
Fernicola Angela PS
Maiocco Beverly PS
Platenyk Wendy
Verna Marilyn PS
**WESTPORT**-ST PAUL PS-K
• 1976
41 Easton Rd 06880-2213
(203)227-7920 •
FAX(203)222-9205
NO REPORT

## DELAWARE

**BEAR**-FAITH PS
• 1997
2265 Red Lion Rd 19701-1849
(302)834-1214
faithl1@juno.com
NO REPORT
**DOVER**-ST JOHN PS-K
• 1989
113 Lotus St 19901
(302)734-1211 •
FAX(302)734-1211
artk770@aol.com
NO REPORT
**NEWARK**-OUR REDEEMER PS
• 1968
Chestnut Hills Est 10 Johnson Rd
19713-1808
(302)737-6176
**Morris Margaret PS**
Holt Marsha L PS
**WILMINGTON**-CONCORDIA PRESCHOOL PS
• 1982
3003 Silverside Rd 19810-3441
(302)478-3004 •
FAX(302)478-7403
NO REPORT

## FLORIDA

**BARTOW**-REDEEMER PS
• 1993
390 E Parker 33830-4721
(941)519-0096
NO REPORT
**BOCA RATON**-ST PAUL PS-8
• 1962
701 W Palmetto Park Rd
33486-3561
(561)395-8548 •
FAX(561)395-2902
**Kernkamp Lynn M MA PS**
**Krempler Jeffrey E PHD**
**Richards James K MED**
**Zielske Scott D MSED 7-8**
Barbieri Michele PS
Budd Barbara 7
De Rojas Regina H 2
Dorlac Barbara BA 1
Fick Marsha L BA 4
Glasnapp Susan M K
Gulisano Leala 5
Hovan Cheryl BS 3
Hurley Linda PS
Kamprath Fredric W MAT
Krempler Lisa 6
Lee Nancy 6
Mc Carthy Kate 5
Rockenbach Nancy C BSED 7
Schiefer Carl L MA
Schiefer Virgina BS 2
Schwausch Glorianne BA PS
Slinker Cynthia PS
Sollenberger Reta M BA 3
Stoeckel Melissa 4
Tumminello Janet BSED 6
Utech Ralph A BS 7
Utech Sharon L BS 1
Walcheski Jeffrey BS
Walcheski Monika BS PS
Wegener Barbara L BSED 8
Weider Jennifer
**BRADENTON**-HOPE PS
• 1983
4635 26th St W 34207-1702
(941)753-1128
NO REPORT
**BRANDON**-IMMANUEL K-8
• NLSA • 1980
2913 John Moore Rd 33511-7139
(813)685-1978 •
FAX(813)681-6852
1ead1221@prodigy.net
**Mischnick Walter T MA**
Albers Deborah M BA K-7
Dodd Kathleen 5-8
Hamer Jennifer L BA 4-8
Johnson Rebecca M BED 3
Moenning Glenn A MA 6-8
Okun Jackie M MA K
Rankin Peggy BA K-8
Reikowski Ellen J 5
Richards Nancy A BSED 6-8
Smith-Stephens Georgianna BA 1
Steenis Susan D 4
Steinbrueck Judith A BA 2
**CALLAWAY**-GOOD SHEPHERD PS-8
• 1973
929 S Tyndall Pkwy 32404-7242
(850)871-6311 •
FAX(850)871-3077
**Miessler Mark L BA**
Brannon Tonya PS
Brown Sandra S BS K
Frey Karen BSED 2
Haires Mary E PS
Hill Carol S BS 1
Moore Leanne M PS
O'Mera Lynn A PS
Paoli Renee PS
Pelletier Jean M PS
Schmidt Rita M 3-4
Schneider Kathleen L BS 5-6
Stelljes Nancy E MA
**CAPE CORAL**-TRINITY PS-5
• 1995
706 SW 6Th Ave 33991-2490
(941)772-1549 •
FAX(941)573-6336
kmtrinity@aol.com
**Mecsics Karen E BA**
Davis Paula K-1
Dow Kathleen PS
Goza Diana PS
Guenther Karen 2-3
Lakers Kathleen PS
Materio Sandra PS
Moore Natalya 4-5
**CARROLWOOD**-MESSIAH PS
• 1987
14920 Hutchison Rd 33625
(813)961-2182
**Fedele Carol J BA PS**
Klaitz Jodie PS
Schweichler Jo Ellen MA PS
**CASSELBERRY**-ASCENSION PS
• 1991
351 Ascension Dr 32707-3801
(407)831-7788 •
FAX(407)831-2350
**Neubauer Janet M BA PS**
Berhow Patrica PS

Hawkinson Mary E PS
Hewitt Crystal PS
Howell Susan PS
Silva Christina PS
**CLEARWATER**-FIRST PS-8
• NLSA • 1975
1644 Nursery Rd 33756-2437
(727)461-3444 •
FAX(727)442-7473
Mende Kelly S 5
**CRAWFORDVILLE**-TRINITY PS
• 1985
3254 Coastal Hwy 32327-4200
(850)926-5557
cld2020@aol.com
Broadway Patricia PS
Burton Carla PS
Dance Cheryl BS
Franklin Zora PS
Hope Laura PS
Mispel Glyndal PS
Waggamon Michelle PS
**DAVIE**-GLORIA DEI PS-8
• NLSA • 1979
7601 SW 39th St 33328-2716
(954)475-8584 •
FAX(954)474-2313
**Vonada Sharon MED 2**
Almeda Aixa 2
Carl Kathy J BA PS
Case Robin PS
Donahue Jason 6
Drucker Kristine PS
Gonzalez Jean BSED 2-4
Hammonds Theria 5
Harbar Marie
Herron Barbara BFA
Macartney Rose PS
Maisa Tami PS
Manfready Barbara PS
Ramlow Harold 3
Rivers Lisa 8
Rossano Carla PS
Sanger Jane L BSED K
Sanger Robert
Sethman Barbara PS
Snow Portia
Stapleton Barbara 2
Talbott Deborah PS
Turner Sunny
Turpin Wendy PS
Van Landingham Sarah C K
Van Scott Cecilia BSED 4
Zapata Beatrice PS
**DELRAY BEACH**-TRINITY PS-8
• NLSA • 1948
400 N Swinton Ave 33444-3954
(561)276-8458 •
FAX(561)272-3215
trinitydelray.org
**Novy Andrew J MED**
Borg Steven E BA 8
Buerk Jodie
Calabretta Susan 4
Green Peggy A BA 2
Guelzow Timothy MED
Johnson Nancy K
Klemm Karri L BA 7
Knight Sara PS
Knutson Francesca L BA
Knutson Jeffrey R BA 6
Lang Emma J BA PS
Mooney Joan B BFA K
O Malley Nancy K
Preston Sharon K BS 3
Riggs Norma L PS
Riggs Timothy J MA 5
Rullman Joan K K
Selva Marilyn MED PS
Wilsher Kathy BED 1
Yeckering Polly K
Zabel Martin W BA

**ENGLEWOOD**-REDEEMER PS
• 1998
6970 Mineola Rd 34224-8035
(941)475-2631 •
FAX(941)475-9726
Byrne Shirley J PS
Pelletier Brenda PS
Richard Shawn J
**EUSTIS**-FAITH PS-8
• 1965
2727 S Grove St 32726-7302
(352)589-5683 •
FAX(352)589-1328
faithmail@aol.com
**Heinemann Charles E MED**
Bierlein Kimberly K BA 2
Blythe Heather M 4
Cruise Gail S BA 8
Cruise James R MA 5
Ford Lois J BA 1
Heilman Deborah E BSED 7
Hood Nancy MA PS
Neas Michael PS-8
Peteson Gail A 3
Richards Diana J BS K
Richberg Connie L BA PS
Tyson Madelyn M MSED 3
Wasmund Gary W BA 8
**FORT LAUDERDALE**-FAITH PS-8
• NLSA • 1955
1161 SW 30th Ave 33312-2856
(954)581-2918 •
FAX(954)581-2918
Johnson Karen M BS 1-2
GRACE LEARNING CENTE PS
1801 NE 13Th St 33304-1819
NO REPORT
PEACE PS-8
• NLSA • 1974
1901 E Commercial Blvd
33308-3726
(954)772-8010 •
FAX(954)772-8010
beachpew@aol.com
**Zielske Scott D MSED**
ST PAUL PS
• 1996
580 Indian Trce 33326-3366
(954)384-1261 •
FAX(954)384-1037
NO REPORT
TRINITY PS
• 1985
11 SW 11th St 33315-1225
(954)463-2456 •
FAX(954)463-3928
NO REPORT
TRINITY K-8
• 1933
110 SW 11Th St 33315-1227
(954)463-7471 •
FAX(954)463-3928
kwaibel@trinitylcms.org
**Waibel Kenneth J BA 7-8**
Burnett Barbara H BAED K
Church Candace L 1
Fulop Susan M 5-6
Maxwell Lisa 3
Meeks Carol A BA 4
Waibel Joyce E BA 2
**FORT MYERS**-ST MICHAEL PS-8
• NLSA • 1956
3595 Broadway 33901-8021
(941)939-1218 •
FAX(941)939-1839
rziegler@sml.org
NO REPORT
**GAINESVILLE**-ABIDING SAVIOR PS
• 1995
9700 W Newberry Rd 32606-5545
(352)331-7770 •
FAX(352)331-7777
abidingsavior@juno.com
NO REPORT

**GULF BREEZE**--LITTLE LAMBS-GOOD SHEPHERD PS
• 1998
4257 Gulf Breeze Pkwy 32561
(850)932-3263 •
FAX(850)934-6372
goodshepherd@freent.com
NO REPORT
**HIALEAH**-FAITH PS-8
• 1975
293 Hialeah Dr 33010-5218
(305)885-2845 •
FAX(305)885-2845
0
**Wessling Ruth L BS K**
Baez Rose 1-2
Callava Esther PS
Kouri Mayda 7-8
Miguel Monica 3-4
Vasquez Jean M 5-6
**HOBE SOUND**-BETHEL PS
• 1986
7905 SE Federal Hwy 33455-7012
(561)546-7506
**Mannion Maureen A BS**
Coughlin Pat PS
Grubbs Kimberly J PS
Hemp Tanya PS
Lerette Lisa PS
Perez Katy PS
Raymer Deborah G PS
**HOLLY HILL**-TRINITY PS-6
• 1981
1205 Ridgewood Ave 32117-2721
(904)255-7580 •
FAX(904)255-7589
NO REPORT
**HOLLYWOOD**-ST MARK PS-8
• NLSA • 1956
502 N 28th Ave 33020-3811
(954)922-7572 •
FAX(954)925-5388
jimessig@mindspring.com
**Essig James P MED 7-8**
Champlin Nadine 5-8
Drumm Deborah K BA 2
Fleming Evangelina A PS-8
Garman Gloria PS
Harrison Sara L MMU 1-8
Hofman Sue E BSED PS
Kiesel Elaine D 4
Kiesel Richard C BA 8
Klein Lois J MS 5-8
Lee Joan K
Lehl Ella L BS 3
Pazos Joanne S PS
Santana Norma N PS
Sica Joseph D 5-8
Ullmann Lois A MA 1
**HUDSON**-HOPE PS
• 1985
12321 Canton Ave 34669-1929
(727)863-6446 •
FAX(727)861-1820
Elkins Merrill PS
Hines Linda PS
Mangold Mary PS
Rule Hanna PS
Timony Marie
**JACKSONVILLE**-GRACE PS-K
• 1998
12200 Mc Cormick Rd 32225-4556
(904)928-9136 •
FAX(904)928-0181
grace5@bellsouth.net
**Jaranowsk Elizabeth B MED**
Bierlein Heidi L BA
Dillard Cheryl D K
Grimm Anita L PS
Mayher Marnie L PS
Navarro Tracy R K-1
O Dell Shelly J PS-1
HOLY CROSS PS
• 1961
6620 Arlington Expy 32211-7233
(904)725-5140
NO REPORT

OUR REDEEMER PS
• 1992
5401 Dunn Ave 32218-4329
(904)766-4728 •
FAX(904)766-4728
NO REPORT
**JACKSONVILLE BEACH**-BETHLEHEM PS
• 1987
1423 8th Ave N 32250-3555
(904)249-5418 •
FAX(904)249-7572
NO REPORT
**KENDALL**-CONCORDIA PS
• 1961
8701 SW 124Th St 33176-5215
(305)235-0160 •
FAX(305)235-6525
clsmiami@bellsouth.net
Adams Kimberley PS
Almodovar Robyn PS
Brathwaite Donna PS
Creelman Pauline
Douglas Lydia PS
Duperrouzel Christine PS
Flowers Dianne G PS
Green Maria E PS
Hewes-Starnes PS
Hill Betty PS
Johnson Patricia
Mc Namara Teresa PS
Prieto Cleo PS
Riley Lula PS
Santos Alicia PS
Streeter Melvena PS
Varela Tula PS
**KEY WEST**-GRACE PS-2
• 1951
2713 Flagler Ave 33040-3981
(305)296-8262
NO REPORT
**LAKE MARY**-HOLY CROSS ACADEMY 1-2
• 1999
760 N Sun Dr 32746-2507
(407)333-0797 •
FAX(407)333-9977
Guelzow Erin R BA 1
Jennison Christine 1-2
**LAKE PLACID**-TRINITY TOTS PS
• 1989
25 Lakeview Ave 33852-9687 PO Box 1082 33862-1082
(863)465-6313 •
FAX(863)465-1074
s_norris123@yahoo.com
**Norris Susan C BS PS**
Armstead Betty Jo PS
Kane Ann PS
Parker Carol L PS
**LAKE WALES**-LAKE WALES PS-9
• NLSA • 1981
640 S Scenic Hwy 33853-4832
(941)676-7300 •
FAX(941)676-5578
**Bush Kathy R**
Allen Jeffery A 8-9
Barker Mary PS
Doederlien-Wyant Karen 3-4
Fackender Barbara S BS K
Flowers Mary S PS
Mason Kimberly S PS
Peterson Janice BA 1-2
Rickman Sally PS
Seyfert Carol M PS
Thiele Barbara L PS
Tolson Deborah A 5-7
**LAKE WORTH**-EPIPHANY PS
• NLSA • 1988
4460 Lyons Rd 33467-3614
(561)968-1257 •
FAX(561)968-3627
Blanchard Sarah PS
Boos Elizabeth PS
Griffin Jessica PS
Rice Nicole BA PS

OUR SAVIOR PS-5
• 1954
1615 Lake Ave 33460-3670
(561)582-8624 •
FAX(561)582-1074
Cordahl Deanna D K
Di Edwardo Alona PS
Gaspard Diane C 5-6
Hanna Thomas W BA PS-6
Mook Lynn 3-4
Parlontieri Pamela 1-2
Weller Rachel leigh PS
**LAKELAND-**CHRIST PS
• 1999
2715 Lakeland Hills Blvd
33805-2219
(941)682-7802 •
FAX(941)616-1040
NO REPORT
ST PAUL PS-8
• 1964
4450 Harden Blvd 33813-1433
(863)644-7710 •
FAX(863)644-7491
**Floetke Karl D MED**
**Raschke Leonard R MA**
Ackerly Ann MA PS
Brayton Sandra K PS
Brekke Janice M BED 1
Bruce Nancy W BA PS-5
Buckner Sherrie PS-5
Dodgson Jayne PS
Eschmann Johanna F BS 4
Evans Jill 6-8
Gage Jonathan K-8
Gosch Denise A BS 3
Hahn Carol A BS K
Hall Nancy P BA 3
Harthun Kim R MS 6-8
Koerner Julia V MA 6-8
Lingard Helen M PS
Lingard Sandra
Lustila Gerald J BA 6-8
Mc Mahan Kristen 5-8
Meyer Jennifer M BA 6-8
Miller Martha S PS-8
Poole Melody 1
Rogala Ronald BSED 2
Ryals Candie 6-8
Shackelford Carolyn 2
Shaver Phillip 6-8
Syfrett Joan K
Tanner Norman 6-8
Vangor Maryann 5
Wagner Debra MA 4
Walker Sandra BA 5
**LAND O LAKES-**LITTLE LAMBS-HOLY TRINITY PS
• 1997
20735 Leonard Rd 33549-9324
(813)949-3611 •
FAX(813)949-7173
Hutchinson Kim PS
Putman Melissa PS
**LARGO-**ROGATE LEARNING CTR PS
• 1979
4825 E Bay Dr 33764
(727)539-6309 •
FAX(727)539-6309
barron55@msn.com
**Ferguson Kathy PS**
Reidy Virginia M
Welch Laurie PS
**MARATHON-**MARATHON LS-MARTIN LUTHER K-6
• 1985
325 122nd St 33050-3503
(305)289-0700 •
FAX(305)289-0700
sflet16888@aol.com
**Fletcher Sandra 1-6**
Roberts Paula S AA K

**MERRITT ISLAND-**FAITH PS
• 1966
280 E Merritt Ave 32953-3415
(321)452-4143 •
FAX(321)452-9147
Cupac Constance PS
Lugo S K PS
Mays Teresa PS
Parker Kelly PS
Pritchard Wendy M BS
Starnes Deborah E PS
Turla Julie
**MIAMI-**ST MATTHEW PS-8
• 1970
621 Beacom Blvd 33135-2931
(305)642-4177
**Kloss Sandra BA 7-8**
Diaz Liana W 1-2
Garcia Ana PS
Gonzalez Ulises 5-6
Heonart Maria 3-4
Rosales Graciela K
ST PAUL PS-6
• NLSA • 1968
10700 SW 56Th St 33165-7044
(305)271-3109 •
FAX(305)271-5315
NO REPORT
**MIRAMAR-**MIRAMAR PS
• 1963
7790 Lasalle Blvd 33023-4612
(954)987-1234 •
FAX(954)987-2532
**Brothers Janice PS**
de Armas Carmen PS
**MONTVERDE-**WOODLANDS PS
• NLSA • 1993
15333 County Road 455
34756-3776
(407)469-3355 •
FAX(407)469-3199
www.woodlands.com
Olsen Heather H
Perry Brenda J PS
Speckman Geraldine PS
**NAPLES-**CHRIST COMMUNITY K-3
• RSO • 1998
777 Mooring Line Dr 34102
(941)430-2655 •
FAX(941)430-2672
JKuers2811@aol.com
**Kuerschner John P MA**
Birner Sandra J BA 2-3
Kuerschner Shirley A BA K
Owens Linda R BS 1
GRACE PS
• 1994
860 Banyan Blvd 34102-5112
(941)261-7700 •
FAX(941)261-9337
NO REPORT
LAMBS OF FAITH PS PS
• 1991
4150 Goodlette Rd N 34103-3363
(941)434-9277 •
FAX(941)434-5410
NO REPORT
**NORTH FORT MYERS-**GOOD SHEPHERD PS-8
• 1973
4770 Orange Grove Blvd
33903-4556
(941)995-7711 •
FAX(941)995-0473
NO REPORT
**NORTH MIAMI-**HOLY CROSS PS-8
• 1951
650 NE 135Th St 33161-7519
(305)893-0851 •
FAX(305)893-1845
EllenM@holycrossministries.com
**Miessler Mark L BA 6-8**
Auger Edmund III 1-8

**NORTH PALM BEACH--**FAITH PS
• NLSA • 1962
555 US Highway 1 33408-4901
(561)848-4737 •
FAX(561)881-1613
FAITHNPB@aol.com
NO REPORT
**OCALA-**ST JOHN PS-8
• 1964
1915 SE Lake Weir Rd
34471-5424
(352)622-7275 •
FAX(352)622-5564
**Rath Richard L MSED**
Bartelt Heather R BA
Bennett Richard L BS
Bier Helena
Boothe Melissa PS
Craven James A MA
Craven Kathryn E BA 2
Daugherty Tamara S BS
Dexheimer Larry J BS
Dzelzkalns Stacy BA 4
Eggold Joshua M BA
Fischer Andrea T BS 1
Fischer Robert BS 5
Grelecki Carolyn BSED
Guynn Ceci
Havener Pamela A BA PS
Heath Deborah MA
Holliday Cynthia R BA
Hudson Ruth 5
Janousky Katherine BS 8
Keenan Carolyn A MA 3
Lark Peter J
Leinberger Timothy BA
Lineberger Carla BS 4
Lineberger Laura PS
Mennicke Sally J BS 6
Peake Patricia S AA K
Roberson Barbara G PS-K
Roy Anna-Barbara BA
Schmidt Elizabeth A 8
Schmidt Timothy K BA
**OKEECHOBEE-**PEACE PS
• 1982
750 NW 23Rd Ln 34972-4315
(941)763-5042
NO REPORT
**ORLANDO-**CHRIST THE KING PS
• 1997
4962 Apopka Vineland Rd
32819-3104
(407)876-8155
NO REPORT
HOPE PS
• 1994
2600 N Dean Rd 32817-2735
(407)657-7750
NO REPORT
PRINCE OF PEACE PS-K
• NLSA • 1959
1515 S Semoran Blvd 32807-2919
(407)275-6703 •
FAX(407)380-1802
pschro4016@aol.com
NO REPORT
TRINITY PS-8
• NLSA • 1953
123 E Livingston St 32801-1506
(407)843-4896 •
FAX(407)423-2085
tlschool@trinitydowntown.org
**Kuck William E**
**Schwanke Wayne L MA 6-8**
Ackermann Eleanor K-8
Araya Sharmilla 6-8
Blackwood Debra BSED 5
Blackwood Jennifer M BA 3
Connor Myrtle PS
Dingle Karen 4
Eggert Janet G MS 6-8
Fink Carolyn K-8
Foust Gladys A PS
Guy Diana PS
Kunze Sandra PS
Mc Connell Shelley BSED

Mc Fadden Debbie PS
Prochnow Jean MS K
Prochnow Ronald A MED 4-8
Retzlaff Catherine L BSED 2
Sabin Darlene R BS 1
Shatzer Natasha
Smith Deborah A BA PS
Wegner Jeffrey S BA 6-8
Wells Julie PS
**OVIEDO-**LUTHERAN HAVEN PS
• 1970
2035 W SR #426 32765
(407)365-3108 •
FAX(407)366-0128
lhaven@sundial.net
NO REPORT
ST LUKE K-8
• 1947
2025 W State Road 426
32765-8524
(407)365-3228 •
FAX(407)366-9346
**Hanas Susan D BSED 6**
**Wudtke Jennifer L MA 6-8**
Baerwolf Catherine E BA 4
Baerwolf Paul R BA 4
Baumer Charmane C BA 2
Baumer Scott L BA K-8
Bortz Kimberly J BA 6-8
Clark Wendy K
Clarke Gina K-8
DeLemos Beverly L BA K
Deckman Chuck 6-8
Gaudette Julie A BA 3
Hardin Laura K-6
Jakubcin Caroline M BA 1
La Rocca Tracey BSN
Lehenbauer Becky A BS 5
Lehenbauer Steven L BS K-8
Love Kathy MSS
Naruta Gloria J BED 1
Nowicki Sarah E BS 3
Owens Barbara A 2
Patton Pam K-3
Rempfer Ronald H BS 6-8
Roby Dina K-8
Smith Janet K EDD 6-8
Stutts Laura 6-8
Tesinsky Marlene E BS 2
Weisenbarger Mary A AAS K-6
Whitney Nancy R BA 1-3
Whitney Roger L MED K-8
Wiedenmann Ruth E BA 6-8
**PALM COAST-**OPEN ARMS-SHEPHERD COAST PS
• 1993
101 Pine Lakes Pkwy N 32164
(904)446-1782
Allam Barbara PS
Clark Amy S PS
De Mayo Shari J
Haney Kimberly A PS
Macher Sarina L PS
Whitaker Tracie A PS
**PENSACOLA-**AMAZING GRACE CHRIST PS
6601 N 9th Ave 32504
(850)505-7735 •
FAX(850)476-1772
NO REPORT
JEHOVAH PS
• 1924
2801 N 9th Ave 32503-3603
(850)433-2091 •
FAX(850)433-9767
Grier Terretta PS
Steen Geraldine
Walker Carlos M PS
RESURRECTION PS
• 1980
4524 W Fairfield Dr 32506 PO Box 3099 32516
(904)453-4570
NO REPORT

**PLANT CITY-**HOPE PS-8
• 1977
2001 N Park Rd 33566-2038
(813)752-4621 •
FAX(813)707-1244
hopelutheran@geocities.com
**Rockey Stephen J MS**
Baldwin Lana M BA K
Griffin Brenda S PS
Howell Sandra H 1-2
Huntington Jeffrey D BA 5-8
Laatsch Joel M MA 5-8
Moeller Leslie A BA 3-4
Warren Margaret E PS
**PLANTATION-**OUR SAVIOR PS-6
• 1963
8001 NW 5th St 33324-1914
(954)473-6947 •
FAX(954)473-0395
OSLS@gate.net
**Matthews Ellen 3**
Battani Melinda J 3
Beck Debra A PS
Buffington Jo Ann PS
Cruz Aurea R 4
Farmer Catherine J PS
Fischer Barbara
Hogge Diane K
Jeselsohn Laurie PS-6
Leslie Warren K-6
Long Becky L PS
Lopez Ilia I K
Root Linda B 2
Sacco Lisa R PS
Santos Yamina PS
Sisley Katheryn J 1
Strubbe Megan E PS
Swift Donna M PS
Vazquez Rita 5-6
Volz Nancy K-6
Wagner Maraly C PS
**POMPANO BEACH-**HOPE PS-8
• NLSA • 1959
1840 NE 41St St 33064-6071
(954)942-2570 •
FAX(954)782-4673
NO REPORT
**PORT SAINT LUCIE-**GRACE PS
• 1998
710 SW Port Saint Lucie Blvd
34953-2617
(561)871-6786 •
FAX(561)871-7991
gracepsl@juno.com
Schlamp Karen L PS
**ROCKLEDGE-**TRINITY PS-6
• 1959
1330 Fiske Blvd S 32955-2318
(321)636-9146 •
FAX(321)638-4498
tlcsschool@iol15.com
**Frick Joanne R BA K**
**Meyr Pamela 2-3**
Ball Karen PS
Chase Rita 1-6
Duda Lynn K-6
Fournier Sheila K-6
Hartney Karen F PS-K
Losada Lavonia 4
Marquardt Nancy 1
Millhouse Donna PS
Milliman Andrea PS-6
Penna Mary F PS
Posey Nina E AA PS
Rousseau Jeanne PS
Scobie Dorothy 5-6
Wallace Carla L PS
**SAINT PETERSBURG-**GRACE PS-8
• NLSA • 1956
4301 16Th St N 33703-4425
(727)527-6213 •
FAX(727)522-4535
Einspahr Byron B BSED 3
Eissfeldt Anna E MA
Kehr Sara M BA
OUR SAVIOR PS-6
• NLSA • 1982
5843 4th Ave S 33707-1714
(727)344-1026 •
FAX(727)381-3980
JECROSMER@AOL.COM
**Crosmer Jesse MED**
Buren Lidia
Clark Ann BA 1
Eissfeldt Anna E MA PS-6
Elsesser Judith PS
Kragel Mary F 2
Kroll Renee L BA PS-1
Linder Diane L 6
Mende Kelly S PS
Peterson Christina L PS
Pisieczko Janice 5
Skaggs Beverly BS 3
Slone Michelle PS
Walker Kristen BS K
Wills Carla M BA 4
**SARASOTA-**CONCORDIA PS-8
• 1979
5651 Honore Ave 34233-3248
(941)922-8164 •
FAX(941)923-6512
**Olsen Roy C III BA**
**Weingart Patricia A**
Basinger Christina M BSED 4-5
Bothast Janet
Connell Rachel
Downing Faye M BS 1
Helton Joyce PS
Ireland Becky PS
Krieg Michelle PS
Lynch Cathy 6-8
Maxham Janet PS
Olach Jeanie 2-3
Olsen Joann I BA K
Owens Jonna PS
Peters Sharon PS
Santiago Brandy PS
Sinkfield Sandy PS
Thomas Michelle PS
Wilson Charnetta PS
Wismar Tiffany
Wolf Jennifer PS
**SEBRING-**FAITH PS-6
• NLSA • 1975
2230 NE Lakeview Dr 33870-2300
(863)385-0406 •
FAX(863)385-9439
fls@strato.net
Bartusch Ann BED 2
Batz Maria
Buth Kenneth M BSED 5-6
Buth Linda BS PS
Caldwell Stacy D PS
Gose Betty A PS
Kruichak Lu Wayne K BA 1
Mendoza Maria MED
Rupprecht Terry L BS 3-4
Schwan Paul A MS
Schwan Susan K BA K
**SOUTH DAYTONA-**HOLY CROSS PS
• 1983
724 Big Tree Rd 32119-1821
(904)788-8370 •
FAX(904)788-3754
NO REPORT
**ST CLOUD-**GRACE PS
• 1998
1123 Louisiana Ave 34769
(407)892-9814 •
FAX(407)892-9814
NO REPORT
**STUART-**REDEEMER PS-8
• NLSA • 1978
2450 SE Ocean Blvd 34996-3312
(561)286-0932 •
FAX(561)287-0434
**Wittcop Ernest J MS**
Braley Debra PS-8
Chorley Carol A 4
Essenburg Sheryl A BED PS
Grubb Crislyn R BS 8
Hascup Donna PS-8
Loveday Lisa PS
Marsh Gail K
Marsh Keith A BS 6
Mc Chrystal Karyn D BA 3
Thomason Victoria R BED 5
Thorsen Mark F BSED 7
Wittcop Patricia A BA 2
Wolfe Jane BA 1
Woodruff Rhonda K-8
**TALLAHASSEE-**EPIPHANY PS-6
• NLSA • 1981
8300 Deerlake Rd West 32312
(904)385-9822 •
FAX(904)422-0984
epipstar@aol.com
**Ulrich Jean A MA**
Dolly Sharon 2
Mc Knight Susan BS K
Poppell Sandy 1
Rykard Dewey 3-4
Scaff Donna PS
Sima Willetta 6
Vestal Sandy 4-5
Weiss Margie PS
**TAMPA-**CONCORDIA 6-8
• 1997
5601 Hanley RD 33634-4905
(813)806-9199 •
FAX(813)806-9199
concordiatampa@juno.com
Gabbert Tim 6-8
Gatlin Carlee BA 6-8
Wallinger Miariam 6-8
FAMILY OF CHRIST CHI PS
16190 Bruce B Downs Blvd 33647
(813)558-9343
NO REPORT
HOLY TRINITY PS-5
• NLSA • 1958
3712 W El Prado Blvd 33629-8722
(813)839-0665 •
FAX(813)839-2706
holytrinity5@juno.com
NO REPORT
**TITUSVILLE-**GOOD SHEPHERD PS
• 1987
2073 Garden St 32796-3243
(321)264-1069
Childears Nancy
Flake Patricia
**VENICE-**LAKESIDE PS
• 1986
2401 Tamiami Trl S 34293-5000
(941)497-5858 •
FAX(941)493-8606
lakesdluth@aol.com
Atwell Lisa PS
Errera Stephanie PS
Gjedrem Elizabeth PS
Gjedrem Sharon PS
Grosse Candice PS
Litano Dawnee PS
Rhines Jennifer PS
Sutton Lindsay PS
**VERO BEACH-**REDEEMER PS-K
• 1996
900 27th Ave 32960-4011
(561)770-0021 •
FAX(561)567-8109
**Moss Amy K**
Bell Ingrid PS
Birks Lorna PS
Castillo Natalie
Cruce Ellen PS
Nunziata Mona PS
**WARRINGTON-**REDEEMER PS-8
• 1955
333 Commerce St 32507-3422
(850)455-0330 •
FAX(850)455-3083
rlschool@bellsouth.net
Baker Wendy 2
Byrant Elizabeth W 6-8
Cornwell Kathryn M 1
Duncan Pamela S BA PS
Felix Jayne A 4
Kamprath Susan J BS 6-8
Leonard Tami L 6-8
Preston Denise L K
Price John A BA 4-5
Wanek Laura A 3
Warren Paul
**WINTER HAVEN-**GRACE PS-8
• NLSA • 1969
320 Bates Ave SE 33880-3268
(863)293-9744 •
FAX(863)291-0935
glsroglw@gte.net
**Peterson Jon J MS**
**Ray Kim L PS**
**Walker Roger L MA**
Aceto Fred A 7-8
Aceto Linda M BA 1
Arbeiter Arlin A MA 3-8
Arbeiter Bonnie M BS 7-8
Beacham Patricia A PS
Beasley Vicki PS
Bridwell Julie D 3
Carter Rebecca L MA PS
Dolde Donovan J BA 6
Goldsboro Lana J 2
Hendrick Irmgard BA 7-8
Holm Claudia PS
Hostler Ruth B BA K
Kirin Wendy J BA 5
Lamas Maria 3-8
Maffin Daniel F BSED PS-8
Martinez Martha K
Neitsch Howard W BA 5
Seckel Bonnie A BA 4
Straughn Tammi J 6
Templeton Janice 1-8
Thompson Heidi L 2
Tremblay Laurie E BA 7-8
Ulch Rebecca A AA 7-8
Van Devender Dorene K BS 1
Walker Lois J BS 4
Walters Mary B BA 3

## GEORGIA

**ALPHARETTA-**OPEN ARMS CHILD DEVE PS
• 1990
4655 Webb Bridge Rd 30005
(770)475-6570 •
FAX(770)475-2219
openarms@mindspring.com
Elseroad Bonnie J
Slaton Stacy
**ATHENS-**TRINITY PS
• 1987
2535 Jefferson Rd 30607-5121
(706)546-8081 •
FAX(706)546-0150
**Malueg Brenda MA PS**
Paulishen Marianne BA PS
**ATLANTA-**OPEN ARMS CH DEV CTR-RIVERCLIFF PS
• 1993
8750 Roswell Rd 30350-1828
(770)640-8611 •
FAX(770)640-1219
NO REPORT
OPEN ARMS CHILD DVPL-ASCENSION PS
• 1989
4000 Roswell Rd NE 30342-4195
(404)256-1330 •
FAX(404)256-0037
NO REPORT
**AUGUSTA-**OUR REDEEMER PS
• 1985
402 Aumond Rd 30909-3597
(706)733-6076
NO REPORT
**COLUMBUS-**REDEEMER PS-6
• 1979
4700 Armour Rd 31904-5229
(706)322-5026 •
FAX(706)322-4408
lap4408@aol.com
Knight Alisa L PS

Latham Kristine PS
Lewis Roxanne PS
Loucks Krista Z K-2
Peterson Lois Anne MA 3-6
**EAST POINT**-CHRIST PS-5
• NLSA • 1982
2719 DeLowe Dr 30344-2303
(404)767-2892 •
FAX(404)767-0516
**White Ellinor B PHD**
Doremus Camilla PS
Gilmore Cheryl K
Grantham Darlene
Grantham Nicole PS-5
Johnson Betty K BA 1-5
Knighton Mildred PS
Larson Katherine BA 2-5
Mdluli Samuel BSED 3-5
Morris Wendy E MA
Poling Kathy PS-5
Ragland Jane PS
Ramey Janice PS
Sims Marcella PS
Williams Deniece PS
**GAINESVILLE**-GOOD SHEPHERD PS
• 1995
600 S Enota Dr NE 30501-2470
(770)532-3883
NO REPORT
**MARIETTA**-FAITH PS-8
• NLSA • 1958
2111 Lower Roswell Rd 30068-3355
(770)973-8921 •
FAX(770)971-7796
faithls@bellsouth.net
**Wareham Jon G MED**
Arndt Karen 1
De Boer Kristine K BSED 3
Freudenstein Julie PS
Grienke Ann 6-8
Griffith David K-8
Hickman Gina PS
Lane Michelle K-8
Moore Sandra
Nodar Jane S 5
Parris Cimberly BA K
Sasser Merideth 2
Seelman Carol A BS 6-8
Stoeppelwerth Barbara A MED 6-8
Trinklein Valerie
Whitlow Joanne MS
OPEN ARMS-LIVING HOPE PS
• 1996
3450 Stilesboro Rd NW 30152-3208
(770)428-2767 •
FAX(770)425-1142
openarmswc@aol.com
NO REPORT
**PEACHTREE CITY**-ST PAUL PS-8
• 1997
700 Ardenlee Pkwy 30269
(770)486-3545 •
FAX(770)486-3545
gstuckprin@aol.com
**Stuckert Gordon S MA**
Abresch Mark T BS 6-8
Anderson Linda L MA K
Barr Kathleen E MED 6-8
Boldt Harold D BA 6-8
Dobler Brenda PS
Flegler Brenda K MED 2
Haupt Sarah E BA K
Kuhl Linda L MA 3
Land Julie A BA 4
Lee Teresa PS
Neill Marie 6-8
Schilling Brenda 5
Stuckert Mary B MA PS-8
Worthington Tamara S BA 1
**TIFTON**--PEACE PS
• 1973
604 Tennessee Dr 31794-4223 PO Box 812 31793-0812
(912)382-7344
peace@csunet.net
NO REPORT
**WOODSTOCK**-TIMOTHY PS
• 1986
556 Arnold Mill Rd 30188-2905
(770)924-7995 •
FAX(678)445-7151
Bailey Vicki PS
Blake Julia PS
Bulger Nancy T BSED
Burns Mary Ann PS
Donovan Kolette M PS
Howard Michelle PS
Jameson Marguerite PS
Painter Kerri PS
Robbins Denise PS

## HAWAII

**AIEA**-OUR SAVIOR PS-8
• NLSA • 1970
98-1098 Moanalua Rd 96701-4617
(808)488-0000 •
FAX(808)488-4515
osls@hawaii.rr.com
NO REPORT
**EWA BEACH**-MESSIAH K-8
• 1961
91-679 Fort Weaver Rd 96706-2533
(808)689-6649 •
FAX(808)689-3337
NO REPORT
**HONOLULU**-GOOD SHEPHERD PS
• 1970
638 N Kuakini St 96817-2204
(808)533-3088 •
FAX(808)536-1923
gspreschool@cs.com
Bowditch Barbara H BA PS
Gima Carolyn
Gross Angela PS
Louie Karen S BA
Tam Rita PS
Villanueva Alma PS
Wolf Jenny PS
OUR REDEEMER K-8
• NLSA • 1948
2428 Wilder Ave 96822-2418
(808)945-7765 •
FAX(808)944-1414
orls4@inix.com
Alle Bonnie J BS 1
**KAHULUI**-EMMANUEL PS-5
• 1978
520 W One St 96732-1352
(808)877-3037 •
FAX(808)877-6819
elgs@mauigateway.com
Fricke Judy BA PS
Kaio Andrea BSED K
Kottwitz Maxine R BSED 1
Kottwitz Roger L BS 3
Okumura Irene PS
Orde Gail A BS 4
Proctor Naomi BA PS
Reppun Mary Joan BA 5-6
Spangler Penny PS
Wilson Diane V BA 2
Yamashige Iris PS
**KANEOHE**-ST MARK K-8
• NLSA • 1956
45-725 Kamehameha Hwy 96744-2955
(808)247-5589 •
FAX(808)235-6155
smls@lava.net
NO REPORT
**WAHIAWA**-TRINITY PS-8
• NLSA • 1953
1611 California Ave 96786-2511
(808)621-6033 •
FAX(808)621-6029
Benson Mary 5-8
Brough Jennifer K
Broyles Bobby D MSED
Gustine Kathleen BA 2
Klemp Kyle BA K
Lutz Mindi 5
Nicholson Allyson 4
Pflughoeft Carolyn 6-8
Spradlin Torrey 5-8
Weinberg Annie 3
Wilson Paula 1
Zornick Pam BS PS

## IDAHO

**ASHTON**-ZION PS
• 1985
901 Main 83420 PO Box 387 83420-0387
(208)652-7438 •
FAX(208)652-7438
zionashton@juno.com
NO REPORT
**BOISE**-BEAUTIFUL SAVIOR-BEAU SAVIOR PS
• 1985
2981 E Boise Ave 83706-5717
(208)385-0300 •
FAX(208)385-0137
Eden Christine M PS
BEGINNING YEARS-BEAU SAVIOR
• 1985
2981 E Boise Ave 83706
(208)385-0300
**Edmondson Sandy PS**
GOOD SHEPHERD PS-5
• 1965
5009 Cassia St 83705-1950
(208)343-4690
**Pauls Timothy J MDIV**
Brune Justin D 3-5
Hawkins Randy M BA 1-2
Jensen Lori PS
Pasewalk Mary PS
Scheetz Elizabeth A BS K
**BUHL**-CLOVER TRINITY PS-8
• 1915
3552 N 1825 E 83316-6357
(208)326-5198 •
FAX(208)326-5105
clovertls@filertel.com
**Reinke Yvonne S**
Crismor Diane M 3-4
Frey Jacqueline PS
Hadley Shirley K K
Heinz Shar R MED 5-6
Keseman Brent A BSED 7-8
Milam Sheila 1-2
**BURLEY**-ZION PS-K
• 1964
2410 Miller Ave 83318-2919
(208)678-9621 •
FAX(208)678-9621
zion@cyberhighway.net
Bettis Barbara A PS
McFarland Jennifer L PS
Veneman Marie E K
**CALDWELL**-GRACE PS
• 1976
2700 S Kimball Ave 83605-5622
(208)459-4191
rainey@rmci.net
Alldredge Karen BED PS
Bohlken Kathleen M BA PS
Rainey Emily MA
Sievers Colleen J BA PS
Stadick Connie PS
**COEUR D ALENE**-KINGS KIDS-CHRIST KING PS
• 1992
1700 Pennsylvania Ave 83814-5563
(208)765-2536 •
FAX(208)664-9233
cdcenter@ctkcda.org
Franks Laura PS
Hackney Contessa PS
Harms Linda PS
Hoven Tiffinay PS
Murphy Loretta PS
Scott Tami PS
Stilkey Jennifer PS
**EDEN**-TRINITY PS-K
• 1982
1602 E 1100 S 83325-5216
(208)825-5277
Olson Ruth E BS
**EMMETT**-NOAHS ARK PS
• 1987
407 S Hayes Ave 83617-2971
(208)365-5214
NO REPORT
**IDAHO FALLS**-HOPE PS-6
• NLSA • 1958
2071 12th St 83404-5728
(208)529-8080 •
FAX(208)529-8880
mrash@srv.net
Meyer Paula S BA K
**MERIDIAN**-FRIENDSHIP CELEBRATI PS
• 1998
765 E Chinden Blvd 83642-5243
(208)288-2404 •
FAX(208)288-2402
NO REPORT
**MOUNTAIN HOME**-FAITH PS-6
• 1985
1190 N 6th E 83647-2032
(208)587-4127 •
FAX(208)587-6712
**Kohtz Alice J BA 5-6**
Clapp Kimberl;y A 1-2
Lord Linda D 3-4
Walters Tarayca BA PS-K
Wohlfeil Ruth A K-6
**NAMPA**-ZION PS-7
• 1961
1012 12th Ave Rd 83686-5737
(208)466-9141 •
FAX(208)466-8826
jschmidt20@juno.com
Irwin Kay M BA 2
Schmidt James A BS
**POCATELLO**-FAITH PS
• 1983
856 W Eldredge Rd 83201-5525
(208)237-2391
Phelps Diane R BA
GRACE PS-8
• 1959
1350 Baldy Ave 83201-7104
(208)237-4142 •
FAX(208)237-0931
gflicker@gracepocid.org
**Austin Marie**
**Flicker Gaylord E MAD**
Atkinson Joanne PS
Besel Dana E BS K-3
Besel Ross E BA 3
Bopp Anne E MED 4
Camin Jan PS-8
Coast Christenia 2
Cummings Tami 1
Del Bosque Sonia 1-8
Eberle Amanda B BS 1
Edel Christina PS
Faure Caroline 8
Flicker Karen M MA PS
Ford Nancy J BS 6
Grayson Ronee 2
Griffin Peter W BA 3-8
Heiden Teresa L BA 5
Lossee Linda PS

Mc Ateer Lisa 4
Mercogliano Melissa 5-8
Montgomery Marna K
Pitcher Loretta PS
Stokes Susan BA
Symmank Celeste R BA K
Tatham Chris
Udy Kristin D BSED 7
Weerheim Sherrie PS
Williams Diane 5
Williams Marie PS
**RATHDRUM**-SHEPHERD OF THE HILL PS
• 1990
7255 W Hwy 53 83858
(208)687-1809
NO REPORT
**SANDPOINT**-LITTLE LAMBS-CHRIST OUR REDE PS-K
• 1990
1900 N Pine St 83864-9328
(208)263-7516 •
FAX(208)263-7516
corlc@micron.net
**Van Natta Kirk D BAED**
Buckmaster Betty G PS
Davis Verna M PS
Houidobre Anita PS
Rogler Claudia A PS
**TWIN FALLS**-IMMANUEL PS-8
• 1946
2055 Filer Ave E 83301-4342
(208)733-7820 •
FAX(208)735-9970
immanuel@magiclink.com
**Mumm Marvin 7-8**
Bruns Beth K
Champlin Cindy M BA 5
Henson Curtis 1
Jund Michelle PS
Kramer Marilyn M BS 3
Moulson Amy 4
Sherrets Verna L PS
Shirley Carol M BAED 6
Wudy Laureen A BS 2

## ILLINOIS

**ADDISON**-CONCORD PS-8
• NLSA • 1989
105 W Army Trail Blvd 60101-3502
(630)543-6404 •
FAX(630)543-7363
**Falcone Garry K MA**
Dellar Frances A BS 4
Green Daniel 6
Grube Renee L BA 1
Haase Judy A BSED PS
Hartwig Sandra L BA 2
Nicholas Susan 3
Niehaus Ruth BA 7
Pearce Roberta J BA 5
Schmitz Walter K MSED 8
Schubert Barbara R BA K
**ALGONQUIN**-ST JOHN PS-8
• NLSA • 1876
300 Jefferson St 60102-2633
(847)658-9311 •
FAX(847)658-9331
**Peterson Ralph O MSED 5**
Gates Jill BED 3-4
Guigli Dawn M PS
Killian Lisa M BA 1-2
Mueller Susan PS
Porstner Faye A MA 5-6
Tull Virginia BA K-8
Vucic Lynn BA 7-8
**ALTAMONT**-ALTAMONT K-8
• RSO • 1973
7 S Edwards St 62411-1203
(618)483-6428 •
FAX(618)483-6296
**Kassel Robert G MA 2-8**
Benning Carl D MS 1-8
Deadmond Jana S BA K
Kopplin Elaine A MA 3
Mathias Connie J BSED 1
Milleville Judy A BA 5-8
Spilker Ruth A BA 2
Stuemke April L BA 5
Wolff Garry F MED 6-8
Zumwalt Mary E MA 4
**ARENZVILLE**-TRINITY PS-6
• 1872
Frederick St PO Box 118
62611-0118
(217)997-5535
**Roegge Judy A BA 1-2**
Bishop Deanna K-6
Huppe Carole K
Rhodes Jenny BS 3-4
Schone Lynne PS
Werries Amanda 5-6
**ARLINGTON HEIGHTS**-SHEPHERDS FLOCK PS
• 1997
800 W Oakton 60004
(847)253-3710
NO REPORT
ST PETER PS-8
• 1864
111 W Olive St 60004-4766
(847)253-6638 •
FAX(847)259-4185
gehrkede@concentric.net
**Gehrke Dennis E MA**
**Piel Paul F MA 6-8**
Capouch Judith R MED 4
Carnehl Janet E MA 5
De Mars Lorraine MA
Drake Kristin R BPSY PS
Fritz Andrew S BA 5-8
Gehrke Dorothy J MA 2
Golemo Carol K
Henderson Diane 6-8
Herzog Janet S MA 4
Keller Stephanie L MA K
Kelm George G BA K
Klopke Julie S BA PS
Knea Mariana E BA 1
Kramer Sybil J MPD 2
Kueker Linda C BA 3
Meehan Kimberley PS
Mielke Karen J MA 6-8
Noble Sandra J MA K
Pohlman Betty L BA 3
Schaus Sara M BA PS
Schmidt Joel H MS 6-8
Shuger Judith H K
Siok Sandy K
Smith Susan M 6-8
Von Boeckman Jill C BS 5
Wald Carol B MED 1
**AURORA**-ST PAUL PS-8
• NLSA • 1865
550 2ND Ave 60505-4416
(630)820-3457 •
FAX(630)820-4520
Bright Doris M BA
Elkins John D 8
Granholm Kathleen E BA K
Granholm Peter E 6
Griesmann Roxane AAS PS
Hartman Pamela D BSED
Hawkins Alison E BA 3
Heimsoth Beth PS
Katz Diane L MA 5
Kirshtner Diann C
Lutze Karen A AAS
Michelson Lorraine
Miller Jane A BSED 4
Palacios Laura S 1
Peara Karen E BA 2
Ruschmeyer Sara L BA
Schmidt Marguerite
Timm Suzanne M BA 7
Wurtz Joan M K
Yocom Michelle PS
**BARTLETT**-IMMANUEL PS
• 1994
1116 E Devon Ave 60103-4760
NO REPORT
**BATAVIA**-IMMANUEL PS-5
• 1989
950 Hart Rd 60510-9346
(630)406-0157 •
FAX(630)879-7614
ilseagle@megsinet.net
Brewner Linda S MA
Cleghorn Cathryn PS
Cook Kelly
Dalpini Sharon N BS K-5
Dickenson Lisa PS-K
Gutwein Susan M BSED 3
Holmes Terri PS
Iteen Barbara BAED 4-5
Nelson Wendy M BA 2
Schmidt Nancy
Weidler Jean G MA 1
**BEARDSTOWN**-ST JOHN PS-8
• 1848
220 E 6th St 62618-1868
(217)323-1288
Bremer Sharon BS 2-4
Folks Catherine 3-4
Miller Carol L BA K-1
Miller Phyllis J BA 5-8
**BEECHER**-ZION PS-8
• NLSA • 1904
540 Oak Park Ave PO Box 369
60401-0369
(708)946-2272 •
FAX(708)946-2611
Arndt Maria A BA 2
Arndt Richard E BA 6-8
Bachert Zina M BA 3
Bruns Loralee L BS 1
Crolius Michelle 4
Ge Rue Valerie F BAED 6-8
Hinze Donald BA 6-8
Luecke Audrey L PS
Ostermeyer Deborah L BS K
Sickles Diane L MS PS
Termuende Edwin BS
Teske Kathryn A MSED 1
Toensing Shelley 5
**BELLEVILLE**-ZION PS-8
• 1861
1810 Mcclintock Ave 62221-6460
(618)234-0275 •
FAX(618)233-2324
principalgas@aol.com
**Ledebuhr James A MPE 8**
**Spieler Gary A BS**
Baker Rachel P BSED 1-8
Call Krista J PS
Hasstedt Frederick O BA 2
Klein Paula C K
Klitzing Gayle L BSED 5
Lotz Beth PS
Mahoney Michelle L BA 3-6
Meyer Margret F 6
Mueller Lynn R BSED 4-8
Navarskis Miriam 3
Neuhaus Jill 1-8
Roth Marilyn J BS 4-8
Spieler Cathy M BS K-8
Springer Janice R MED 1-3
Stephens Judith L BSED 1
**BELVIDERE**-IMMANUEL PS-8
• NLSA • 1953
1225 E 2ND St 61008-4523
(815)547-5346 •
FAX(815)544-8059
trincjs@gte.net
**Schaefer Judy L MED**
Albrecht Daniel R MCMU 1-8
Buchinger Daniel C MA 6-8
Buchinger Susan J BS PS
Clausing Karen A MA K
Goltermann Vicky L BA 3
Gritzmacher Katrina E BA 1
Hauch James E MED 4
Kelsey Nancy 6-8
Leonard Charles 3
Marks June M MSED 2
O Dea Pamela L BS 6-8
Obsuszt Martin S BS 4
Rasmussen Nancy J 1
Sandersfeld Kip R BA 6-8
Schaefer Jeffrey M MED 6-8
Steltenpohl Gayle F BA 5
Sterenberg Sarah BA 2
**BERWYN**-CONCORDIA LITTLE LAM PS
• 1992
3144 Home Ave 60402-2910
(708)795-7563 •
FAX(708)484-9832
lambsteacher@hotmail.com
Matthews Kay L BA PS
**BETHALTO**-ZION PS-8
• NLSA • 1962
625 Church Dr 62010-1830
(618)377-5507 •
FAX(618)377-3630
zionschooloffice@ezl.com
**Hinkle David BS**
Bailey Norma J
Balsters Sandra M MSED
Buckley Sara L
Engelage Elizabeth K BA
Graser Faith
Helmkamp Barbara BS
Helmkamp Trella S
Hipple Eric C BMED
Keiser Janice
Lane Violet A
Mathias Gloria J
Morris Debbie
Reinhart Julie E BS
Rohe Linda L BA
Rohe Wm J MS
Sankey Kenneth T MED
Sankey Lorinda L MS
**BLOOMINGTON**-TRINITY PS-8
• NLSA • 1858
701 S Madison St 61701-6462
(309)829-7513 •
FAX(309)828-0831
phl1@trinluth.org
**Leupold Patrick H MA**
Blair Lana PS
Brockett Linda M 3
Busse Kurt A MA 5-8
Busse Laura M BSED K
Evelsizer Melanie 3-8
Fuemmeler Nancy K-8
Gordon Mary K-8
Griffin Rebecca L BED PS
Hartke Sherry R MS 3
Heidloff Linda S BS 4
Hoffmann Shawn M BA 6-8
Hoffmann Susan M BA 1
Huppe Karla 1
Kinnaman Karen 1-4
Mikesell Donna L BED PS
Niemann Crystal I BA 2
Pittman Sara L BA 2
Tegtmeier Lynette J MSED 4
Thomsen Amy
Vasel Judy 5-8
Weaver Debra 5-6
Wirsing Janice J MED 6-8
Wohlers Janet J BSED K
**BLUE ISLAND**-SALEM K-8
• NLSA • 1910
12951 Maple Ave 60406-2054
(708)388-6175 •
FAX(708)388-5176
mrrebe@webtv.net
**Rebeck Douglas C MA**
Block Gregory E MA 7-8
Bottorff Ruth E 3-4
Davis Lynette C 5-6
Gresens Joan R MA 1-3
Groth Barbara BSED K
Petkewicz Karen K BA 1-2
**BOLINGBROOK**-DIVINE SHEPHERD PS
• 1992
985 Lily Cache Ln 60440-3131
(630)759-3995
**Kuhnert Susan E PS**

**BRISTOL**--LOVING ARMS CHILD CA PS
7481 Mill Rd 60512
(630)553-5957 •
FAX(630)553-5946
NO REPORT
**BROOKFIELD**-ST PAUL K-8
• 1902
9035 Grant Ave 60513-1625
(708)485-0650 •
FAX(708)485-7448
Kruse Deborah 5-6
Kutschke Diane 4
Lams E T MMU 7-8
Marciniak Trudy BA 1-2
Otten Ruth A BSED K
Zirzow Cynthia R 2-3
**BUCKLEY**-ST JOHN PS-8
• NLSA • 1870
206 E Main St 60918-0006 PO Box 148 60918-0148
(217)394-2422 •
FAX(217)394-2422
StJohns@illicom.net
**Dippel Lisa K MSED 3-8**
Bahler Karen 5-6
Cowan Mary T BS 3-4
Miskimen Bethany A BA 2
Morrison Barbara J PS
Pacey Denise 1
Sturm Theresa I MED K
Teske Carolyn BSED 7-8
Timm Katherine J MED 5-6
**BUNKER HILL**-LITTLE BLESSINGS-ZION PS
• 1988
609 E Warren St 62014-0366
(618)585-3606
NO REPORT
**BURR RIDGE**-TRINITY PS-8
• NLSA • 1865
11503 German Church Rd 60521-0831
(708)839-1444 •
FAX(708)839-8503
nhammes@kiwi.dep.anl.gov
NO REPORT
**CARLINVILLE**-ZION PS
• 1981
501 S Broad St 62626-4373
(217)854-2419
NO REPORT
**CAROL STREAM**-OUR SAVIOR PS
• 1987
1244 W Army Trail Rd 60188-9000
(630)830-4851 •
FAX(630)483-3140
NO REPORT
**CARY**-HOLY CROSS PS-K
• 1989
27 W Three Oaks Rd 60013-1626
(847)639-6533 •
FAX(847)639-6702
NO REPORT
**CENTRALIA**-TRINITY PS-8
• 1897
203 S Pleasant Ave 62801-3657
(618)532-5434 •
FAX(618)532-4277
**Klein Dave R MSED**
Biagi Cheryl L PS
Caldwell Rose Marie 2
Crouse Karen S MS 4
De Board Christina K BA 3
Gullen Linda S BSED 8
Harm Fred W 7
Harm Mary 5
Prosise Mona G BS 1
Schmid Jonathan P BA 6
Weidner Ellen D BAED K
**CHAMPAIGN**-ST JOHN PS-8
• NLSA • 1983
509 S Mattis Ave 61821-3630
(217)359-1714 •
FAX(217)359-7972
clowell@stjohn-lcms.org
**Lowell Chuck**
Bailey Thomas 7-8
Barbee Marilyn K PS
Carr Heath D 7-8
Haase Pamela S BS 1
Hill Shirley M 7-8
Hoffmann Julie M BA 7-8
Howard Kim 2
Jenkins Laura 1
Louden Crystal 3-8
Mihm Susan V BA K
Milas Martha J BED 6-7
Niemann Carol S BA PS
Niemann Randy L MS 6-8
Rock Melissa K MS 3
Tappendorf Julie B K
Tietz Joan M BSED 2
Valbert Faye K-6
Welch Marlene E BSED 4
Yagow Daniel P MSED 5
**CHARLESTON**-IMMANUEL PS
• 1973
902 S Cleveland 61920-3441
(217) 345-3042
Andra Sherry
Biggs Jeana
Coffey Christina
Fidler Courtney
Griffin Barbara
Jackson Dina M BA
Mc Elwee Molly
Metzler Tema
Miller Susan
Webster Laura
Wrye Kathy
**CHATHAM**-ST JOHN PS
• 1969
N Main St PO Box 377 62629-0377
(217)483-2612
NO REPORT
**CHEBANSE**-ZION PS-8
• 1926
160 Concordia Dr 60922-9761
(815)697-2212 •
FAX(815)697-2212
zionschool@dlogue.net
**Whybrew Doreen B BA**
Burgess Crystal D BS 1-2
Chapman Betty PS
Cotter Jennifer A BA 3-4
Johnson Teresa 5-7
Wilken Libby K
**CHESTER**-ST JOHN PS-8
• 1849
302 W Holmes St 62233-1398
(618)826-4345 •
FAX(618)826-4804
bumper@midwest.net
**Schultze Thomas E MED 7**
Belcher Kathy 4
Ebers Judith BS 6
Knop Margaret E BS 3
Lochhead Wendy L MS K
Mattingly Connie 1
Mullholland Lari PS
Parrish Malinee 4
Schwarting April 3
Sheely Pamela BA 2
Stallman Mary BA 5
Urquhart Christopher M BA
**CHICAGO**-BETHEL PS-8
• 1891
1410 N Springfield Ave 60651-2042
(773)252-1104 •
FAX(773)252-4852
**Kurth Elizabeth F MED**
Fichtner Ann 3-4
Fichtner L J BS 7-8
Hernandez Madeline PS
Jerez Evelia PS-K
Kehl Allison 1-2
Koenig Karen 1-8
Steele Lisa D BA 5-6
Wente Sue MCMU 1-8
BETHESDA PS-8
• 1952
6803 N Campbell Ave 60645-4607
(312)743-0800 •
FAX(312)743-4415
ksupik@juno.com
NO REPORT
BETHLEHEM K-8
• 1875
3715 E 103Rd St 60617-6040
(773)768-0441 •
FAX(773)768-0390
**Gehrs Pauline A BA 7-8**
Banks Lenora 1-2
Benne Carlene W AA 5-6
Brudi Eileen H BED 3-4
Weiss Shirley A K
CHRIST ENGLISH K-6
• 1954
5335 W Le Moyne St 60651-1331
(773)622-4563 •
FAX(773)622-4563
NO REPORT
CHRIST THE KING PS-8
• 1973
3701 S Lake Park Ave 60653-2012
(773)536-1984 •
FAX(773)536-2387
mrsgb@earthlink.net
**Brazeal Geraldine BA 4-8**
Bailey Rachel 3
Brown Tanya 1-3
Lloyd Ta Agua 4-5
Vaughn Jeanne PS-K
GLORIA DEI PS-8
• 1960
5259 S Major Ave 60638-1503
(773)581-5259 •
FAX(773)767-4670
GloriaDeiluth@webtv.net
Dundek Hilary J BSED 1-2
Enderle Janette W BA PS
Kimminau Elizabeth K BA 5-6
Rosas Elaine 7-8
Schilling Scott D BA
Voight Sharon J MCMU 3-4
GOOD SHEPHERD PS-K
• 1983
4200 W 62ND St 60629-5042
(773)581-0096
**Loven Sandra A AAS PS-K**
Clarkson Victoria L PS
GRACE PS-8
• RSO • 1896
4106 W 28th St 60623-4358
(773)762-1234 •
FAX(773)762-4476
**Carrier Lori J BS**
GRACE ENGLISH K-8
• 1920
2725 N Laramie Ave 60639-1615
(773)637-2250 •
FAX(773)637-1188
Hoppe Carl E BA 1-2
Jones Michelle A 5-6
Novak Charles J Jr. MA
Novak Gayle 3-4
Rowland Margaret K K
HOPE LUTHERAN SOUTH PS-4
• 1961
6416 S Washtenaw Ave 60639
(312)776-9849
NO REPORT
JEHOVAH PS-8
• 1904
3740 W Belden Ave 60647-2348
(312)342-5854 •
FAX(312)342-6048
Jehovah@megsinet.net
Bierlein Beth N BED 3-4
MESSIAH PS-8
• NLSA • 1926
6200 W Patterson Ave 60634-2528
(773)736-6600 •
FAX(773)736-6611
**Carrier Lori J BS 7-8**
Appleton Beth 1
Grim Caryn M BS 3
Packard Mary M MA PS
Shirley Valerie K BA 4
Ueltzen Vanessa L BA 7-8
Wickboldt Mark W MA 5-6
Zyrkowski Nancy J MSLS 2
OUR SAVIOUR PS-8
• 1937
7151 W Cornelia Ave 60634-3628
(773)736-1157 •
FAX(773)736-4851
**Hoffman LaDonna R BA**
Battaglia Beverly MSED
Howard Susan 5-6
Moeller Sarah BS K
Perry Doris PS-K
Schaeffer Linda 1-2
Smith Margaret 7-8
RESURRECTION PS-6
• 1952
9349 S Wentworth Ave 60620-1428
(312)928-6311
NO REPORT
ST JAMES PS-8
• NLSA • 1857
850 W Dickens Ave 60614-4326
(773)525-4990 •
FAX(773)525-0518
iteske@stjames-lutheran.org
Haak Carol L BSED 5-6
ST JOHN PS-8
• NLSA • 1876
4939 W Montrose Ave 60641-1525
(773)736-1196 •
FAX(773)736-3614
stjohnslutheran@juno.com
**Berg Alan M MA**
Bowman Nancy BA 6-8
Glasbrenner Sandra K-8
Johnson Leslee L BS K
Klein Sharon L BA 1
Mackie Debra J BA 2
Morse Hilary I BA 5
Papanek James 3
Schaefer Kathryn A MA PS
Struve Amy L 4
Valentin Christal D 6-8
Williams Mark L 6-8
ST PAUL K-8
• NLSA • 1886
846 N Menard Ave 60651-2663
(773)378-6644 •
FAX(773)378-7442
stpaul@ameritech.net
Bersie Mark B 5-8
Garrett Denine 5-6
Kuck Glen MA 5-8
Mitchell LaTanya K
Moss Donna 1-2
Owens Katherine 3-4
ST PAUL PS-8
• 1889
7621 S Dorchester Ave 60619-3425
(773)721-1438
NO REPORT
ST PHILIP PS-8
• NLSA • 1937
2500 W Bryn Mawr Ave 60659-5104
(773)561-9830 •
FAX(773)561-9831
**Blatt Richard H MED**
**Messerschmidt Edna MA**
**Tennis Donna M BA PS-K**
Blatt Janice M BS 2
Carlson Janette M BED 1-7
Haase Dorothy K 3
Hanna Laura PS
Hopfensperger Emily A BA 1
Hopfensperger Nick A BA 6-8
Malone Rachel 4
Massmann Ruth E 5-7
Miller Jason T BED 1-8
Miller Stephanie M BA PS-1
Mowery Kathleen A MA 1-8

Oestreicher Joan G PS
Schmiege Liza L BA K
Urban Matthew T BA 6-8
Urban Michelle BA 5-8
Wellen John B MCMU PS-8
Wendt Shannon BA K
Yurk Joy M MA 5-7
TIMOTHY PS-8
• 1935
1700 W 83rd St 60620-4621
(773)874-7333 •
FAX(773)874-7032
Brown Latoya 1
Dixon Teresa D BA PS
Fitzpatrick Karen 7
Hawkins Stacy 2
Lewis Brenda 5
Manuel Lorrain E 6
Smith Marilyn 4
Smith William T
Sonii Janet K
Strong Barbara BS 8
Taylor Gloria 3
ZION
• 1950
10858 S Dr Martin L King Jr Dr
60628-3720
(773)928-3530 •
FAX(773)928-3465
NO REPORT
**CHICAGO HEIGHTS**-ST PAUL PS-8
• NLSA • 1893
330 W Highland Dr 60411-2043
(708)754-4492 •
FAX(708)754-9807
**Loewe Gilbert C Jr. BA**
Basel Angela M BA 4
Benne Robert A 7
Bimm Connie S
Bunte Maria L MA 6
Couch Robert L BS
Engel Cathy J PS
Hoy Lynn C MA 5
Kranz Leslie J BA 1
Pieper Valerie J BA 1
Pikalek Janice E BA 3
Schwalge Alice M BA K
Segert Richard R BA 8
Strzemieczny Sylvia BA 2
**CLINTON**-CHRIST PS
• 1997
701 South Mulberry 61727-2480
(217)935-4675
Conner Melinda M BS PS
Miller Julie Ann BSED PS
**COLLINSVILLE**-GOOD SHEPHERD PS-8
• NLSA • 1984
1300 Belt Line Rd 62234-4373
(618)344-3153 •
FAX(618)344-3156
gslsl@hotmail.com
Bergelin Dianna 6-7
Bohnet Kathleen K MSED 4
Bostian Shirley K-8
Chabot Angela R BA K
Dahn Julie A BA 5
Daniels Denise 5-8
Gimbel Jill PS
Henderson Diana K-8
Hudson Anneke O BA 1
Krueger Michael D BSED 5-7
Marti Joann M K-8
Mayhew John R MS
Mc Kinnon Peggy 5-8
Petersen Sue K-8
Preuss Mary L BS 3
Rattelmuller Barbara J BS 2
Rincker Keith E MS 7-8
Rincker Peggy J BS 2
Santel Lynette A BA 4
Schneider Jessica L BA PS
Semler Eric J BMU 6
Streuter Martha S BA PS
Vander Meer Katherine BA 3
Voss Michael E MS 7-8
Winters Phil K-8
Wudtke Marie E BS 1
HOLY CROSS PS-8
• NLSA • 1848
413 S Seminary St 62234-2643
(618)344-3145 •
FAX(618)344-1222
Sankey Kenneth T MED 8
Sankey Lorinda L MS 7
**COLUMBIA**-ST PAUL PS
• 1992
227 N Goodhaven Dr 62236
(618)281-4190 •
FAX(618)281-3821
Dohrman Sandra PS
Gross Wanda M PS
Schmaltz Barbara A PS
**COUNTRY CLUB HILLS**-ST JOHN PS-8
• 1849
4231 183Rd St 60478-5337
(708)799-7491 •
FAX(708)798-4193
Cook June M BA 3
Strzemieczny Sylvia BA
**CRYSTAL LAKE**-IMMANUEL PS-8
• NLSA • 1875
178 Mchenry Ave 60014-6007
(815)459-1444 •
FAX(815)459-1462
ils@mc.net
**Satek Pamela A MA**
Becker Kevin J BA 4
Cleland Diane D BS
Dahn Jennifer M BA K
De Reus Laura BA 3
Dubberke Robert D BS
Dubberke Sheri J BS 3
Johnson Robert D MA 7
Koenig Brenda 2
Kuerschner Tracey 2
Lapp Fe 3
Lawin Tanya 1
Mans Lisa A BA 3
Marsh Linda BSED 8
Schnulle Valerie C BSED 2
Schultz Alma
Schultz Bonnie J BED 6
Smith Judy L 1
Tripoli Gail BS PS
Viets Norma J MA 5
MY FATHERS WORLD-PRINCE PEACE PS
• 1993
932 Mchenry Ave 60014-7449
(815)455-3200 •
FAX(815)455-6323
poplchurchmfwpreschool@juno.com
NO REPORT
**DANVILLE**-DANVILLE PS-8
• NLSA • 1983
1930 N Bowman Avenue Rd
61834-2008
(217)442-5036
**Muehl Paul H MED**
Boyer Linda R BA 1
Ceader Trish PS
Frank Warren G MSED
Hubner Patricia J MSED 4
Huff Cathy K
Le Pere Marilyn J MED
Meyer Susan PS
Parker David W 6
Pratt Diana M BED 3
Robinson James L BA 5
Schneider Betty J MS 2
Schroeder Dave
Thornsbrough Kurt A BA 8
**DARIEN**-ST JOHN PS-K
• 1966
7S214 Cass Ave 60561-3219
(630)969-7987 •
FAX(630)969-8204
Blandi Katherine PS
Cloninger Nancy PS
Dorsey Lynn PS
Hardy Janet PS
Hayduck Sally PS
Januska Victoria PS
Kowalski Cynthia PS
Lagori Gloria PS
Mc Ilwee Shannon PS
Smith Sherrie PS
Weinberger Joan MED
**DE KALB**-LITTLE LAMBS-IMMANUEL PS
• 1996
511 Russell Rd 60115-2221
(815)756-6669 •
FAX(815)756-9585
Howells Sherri PS
Thurau Rachel E BA PS
**DECATUR**-LUTHERAN SCHOOL ASSO K-12
• RSO • NLSA • 1959
2001 E Mound Rd 62526-9305
(217)233-2001 •
FAX(217)233-2002
office@lsadecatur.net
**Heibel Matthew S MED 9-12**
**Jensen Thomas K-8**
**Winterstein Charles A MA K-12**
Altenbernd Sharon 5
Bardeleben Alan MS 5
Bishop Rita L MS 2
Bruer Robert L MDIV 9
Bryant Janice L MA 6-8
Damery Dorothy A BABIO 6-8
Droll Linda 2-8
Guldenstein Paul MA 4
Harper Janet K-9
Hinz Kenneth E MED 1
Hinz Lois BS K
Mitchell Cathy J BMED 5-9
Murphy Deanna M BSED 2
Ornberg Sarah 1
Piper Nicole BSED
Rapp Maylene K BSED 3
Reeves Carol A 6-8
Runnells Lee A MA 6-9
Sablotny Gayle D 6-8
Salefski Jeffrey F BA 6-8
Schnack Deborah G BA K
Schnack John C 6-8
Spinner Donna L BS 4
Standerwick Julie A K-8
Storck Ellen R BS 3
Strong Donna
Stubblefield Linda K BS 1
Tomkinson Mary 2
Voelker Julie C K
MT CALVARY PS
• 1971
2055 S Franklin Street Rd
62521-5269
(217)428-0641 •
FAX(217)428-0641
Harting Barb A AA PS
Perkes Laurel D AAS PS
ST JOHN RAINBOW PS
• 1986
2727 N Union St 62526-3247
(217)875-3656
NO REPORT
ST PAUL PS
• 1998
340 W Wood St 62522-3108
(217)424-9183 •
FAX(217)424-9189
NO REPORT
ST PAUL PS
• 1975
352 W Wood St 62522-3108
(217)423-6955 •
FAX(217)423-6959
NO REPORT
**DES PLAINES**-IMMANUEL PS-8
• NLSA • 1871
832 Lee St 60016-6408
(847)390-0990 •
FAX(847)294-9640
**Klemm Lowell E MA 7-8**
Allor Cindy A MA 1
Eigenfeld Janice R BA 2-8
Kraatz Kathy J BSED K-4
Kraatz Ronald A BSED 1-8
Schroeder Denise BSED 3-4
Swanson Debra L 5-8
Vyhanek Carol B BA PS
**DOLTON**-ST PAUL PS-8
• NLSA • 1864
233 E 138Th St 60419-1060
(708)849-3225 •
FAX(708)849-2276
NO REPORT
**DOWNERS GROVE**-IMMANUEL PS
• 1996
5211 Carpenter St 60515-4519
(630)968-3448 •
FAX(630)968-3183
NO REPORT
**DU QUOIN**-BETHEL PS
• 1979
699 W Main St 62832-9301
(618)542-3418
Roethe Betty BA PS
**EAST DUNDEE**-IMMANUEL PS-8
• 1863
407 Johnson St 60118-2305
(847)428-1010 •
FAX(847)836-6217
**Terrell Virginia I MA**
Bartelt Kristine S BA K-8
Becker Cena C BA 5-8
Becker Kenneth J MA 6
Dougherty Courtney A BSED 3
Faga Barry MS 5
Geye Cynthia A BA PS
Koehlert Marilyn E BA K
Meyer David J BS 5-8
Navarro Christina BSED 2
Niss Muriel D BA 1
Pieper Shelly S BSED 4
Reimers Nancy BA PS
Simonsen Holly L MA 6
**EAST MOLINE**-LITTLE LAMBS-ZION PS
• 1994
17628 Hubbard Rd 61244-9782
(309)496-3512
NO REPORT
ST JOHN PS-K
• 1979
1450 30th Ave 61244-3831
(309)792-0755 •
FAX(309)792-0776
Engstrom Heather E BS K
Mac Donald Wendy PS
Orey Sherry
Sims Pam PS
Turek Judy PS
**EDWARDSVILLE**-TRINITY PS-8
• NLSA • 1901
600 Water St 62025-1799
(618)656-7002 •
FAX(618)656-5941
sprengel@plantnet.com
Hemler Heather A BA 3
Hipple Eric C BMED 5-8
**EFFINGHAM**-ST JOHN PS
• 1997
901 West Jefferson Ave 62401
(217)342-4334 •
FAX(217)342-6599
Becker Jane PS
Gratz Rachel PS
Holtz Carla M BSED PS
**ELBURN**-LORD OF LIFE PS
• 1994
40W605 Rt 38 60119 PO Box 70
60147-0070
(630)513-7346 •
FAX(630)513-7692
lolps@megsinet.net
**Laughridge Marliss R PS**
Haidle Kathy PS
Hebden Bonnie
O Brien Carol PS
Stenzel Joyce PS
Tomaschek Erin PS

**ELGIN**-GOOD SHEPHERD PS-8
• NLSA • 1961
1111 Van St 60123-6016
(847)741-7795 •
FAX(847)741-6904
**Bierlein Leon C MA 8**
Cummings Deborah A PS
Handrock Carole J BS PS
Holtz Carole J 2
Jungkuntz Curt L 6-8
Klein Karen K BA 4
Knosher Bruce A MA 6-8
Kolzow Janet L BS 3
Kovari Kristine L MS PS
Monkemeyer Joy J 6-8
Phillips Peggy A K
Robar Debra J 1
Stroup Darla E MA 5
ST JOHN PS-8
• NLSA • 1866
109 N Spring St 60120-5578
(847)741-7633 •
FAX(847)741-0859
**Hemler Arthur G MED**
Bimler Kimberly A BA 3
Childers Linda A BAED PS
Hemler Janet BAED 1
Huske Pamela 1-8
Jacobson Kay MED 4
Ladwig Barbara 7-8
Mac Farlane Amy 2
Sherly Margarita 6-8
Wickboldt Joel M BA 5
Woock Dale D BS
Woock Donna K BS K
Zimdahl Bernard W BA 6
**ELK GROVE VILLAGE**-HOLY SPIRIT PS-K
• 1968
150 Lions Dr 60007-4200
(847)437-5898 •
FAX(847)437-5899
Baumann Laura PS
Gorecki Susan P PS
Heath Joyce S AA PS-K
Meyer Wendy PS
Ozyurt Kathryn PS
Rodriguez Gladys BS PS
Snyder Sharon PS
Stein David T PHD
Walz Jean PS
**ELMHURST**-IMMANUEL PS-8
• NLSA • 1879
148 E 3Rd St 60126-2465
(630)832-9302 •
FAX(630)832-5761
**Kuerschner Vernon C MA**
Baerenklau James BA 5-8
Bredehoft David P BSED 6-8
Craven Stephanie S BA 5-8
Daugird Virginia MA 1
Frederiksen Diana L BA PS-8
Hepburn Joyce A BA 2
Koehler Henry E MA 6-8
Marten Caryn L 4
Nottingham Kim L BA 5-8
Schuemer Lisa S MA PS
Zielke Karen L BA 3
**FERRIN**-BETHLEHEM PS
• 1995
12903 Clara St 62231-3837
(618)226-3550
NO REPORT
**FOREST PARK**-ST JOHN PS-8
• NLSA • 1870
305 Circle Ave 60130-1609
(708)366-2764 •
FAX(708)771-6666
sjfpl25@aol.com
Abbe Linda M MA PS
Brod Charles W MA 8
Bunsold Laura MA PS
Gillingham Pamela K
Gnewuch Minnie M EDD 1
Johnson Linda E MA 3
Kirchenberg Christine MA 2
Luetje Anita M BA 7
Miranda Tracy O BA PS
Pavia Claire C BA PS
Saunders David R MA 6
Shone George H MA
Suydam Penelope L MA 4
Tegeler Sharon D BA 5
Welch Jennifer J BED K
**FREEPORT**-IMMANUEL PS-8
• NLSA • 1877
1964 W Pearl City Rd 61032-9332
(815)232-3511 •
FAX(815)233-9158
immanuelfrpt@mwci.net
**Welton Michael G MA 6-8**
Barton Beth 8
Dietmeier Diane L K-8
Gieseke Karen A BED 1
Glandorf Brenda K BA 3
Janis Sharon Y BA 6-8
Julius Penny K-8
Larson Bonnie PS-K
Luepke Nancy 8
Mysliwiec Kimberly K-8
Schwichtenberg Alice BS
Truckenmiller Christine MSED 2
Vehmeier Kathleen A BA 4
Voreis Linda 6-8
White Naomi R BS 5
**GALESBURG**-MT CALVARY PS
• 1977
1372 W Fremont St 61401-2437
(309)342-7083
Hensen Chanda R BS PS
Sperry Jennifer PS
**GENESCO**-CONCORDIA LUTHERAN P PS
316 S Oakwood Ave 61254-1445
(309)949-3993 •
FAX(309)945-4400
lcms@genesco.net
NO REPORT
**GENEVA**-FAITH PS-2
• 1979
1745 Kaneville Rd 60134-1828
(630)232-8533 •
FAX(630)232-7344
Anast Sherry BSED
Arnold Charlea PS
Dusenberry Maria 1-2
Haboush Lisa PS
Hall Cindy PS
Jugenitz Helen K-2
Kloese Judy PS
Kroning Diana PS
Linkimer Lori 1-2
Stearns Kim PS
**GENOA**-TRINITY PS
• 1995
33930 N State Rd 60135-8420
(815)784-2522 •
FAX(815)784-5208
trinity@tbcnet.com
NO REPORT
**GLEN CARBON**-ST JAMES PS
• 1989
146 N Main St 62034-1611
(618)288-6120
Schrader Diane L BA PS
**GLENVIEW**-IMMANUEL PS-8
• 1876
1850 Chestnut Ave 60625-1688
(847)724-1034 •
FAX(847)724-1038
ilgadmin@family-safe.net
Berkson Dori PS
Hilger Ronald O BA 3-4
Holder Melissa I BS 5-8
Mau Rita J BS K
Pearson Beth 5-8
Trettin Paul K MA
Williams Bonnie J MA 1-2
**GODFREY**-FAITH PS-8
• 1983
6809 Godfrey Rd 62035-2222
(618)466-9153 •
FAX(618)466-3839
Ebke Harold D BS
Mattsfield Michelle L BS 1-2
Meyer Mardelle M BA K
Ponivas Nancy F BS PS
St Peters Cynthia M BA 3-4
Struck Christopher BED 7-8
Zilm Sharon 5-6
**GRANITE CITY**-LITTLE LAMB-HOPE PS
• 1972
3715 Wabash Ave 62040-3977
(618)876-4132
NO REPORT
**GRAYSLAKE**-GLORYLAND PS
• 2000
607 W Belvidere Rd 60030
(847)548-0112 • FAX(847) 548-6796
Zehner Julie PS
**GURNEE**-BETHEL PS
• 1986
5110 Grand Ave 60031-1813
(847)244-9672
Allie Roberta PS
Deaton Joanne PS
Kozlik Karen MA
Strakusek Eleanor B BA PS
**HAMEL**-TRINITY-ST PAUL K-8
• 1989
6961 W Frontage Rd 62097-2431
(618)633-2202
tsp@madisontelco.com
**Rikli Richard L BS**
Hemann Dennis 5-8
Reimche Carrie A BSED 5-6
Rethwisch Jennifer BED 1-2
Sander Lois MS 3-4
Steinmeyer Cindy BS
**HERRIN**-TRINITY LEARNING CTR PS
• 1995
1000 N Park Ave 62948-2720
(618)942-4750
Caplinger Phyllis PS
Duff Ruth PS
Kenner Patricia PS
Mc Neill Jeanette
**HIGHLAND PARK**-THE ARK-REDEEMER PS-K
• 1987
1731 Deerfield Rd 60035-3704
(847)831-2224 •
FAX(847)831-2226
Hildebrandt Megan PS
Huelsman Stephanie K BA
Ludvigsen Susanne PS
Rauchleitner Michelle PS
**HILLSIDE**-IMMANUEL K-8
• NLSA • 1852
2329 S Wolf Rd 60162-2211
(708)562-5580 •
FAX(708)562-6085
general@immanuel-hillside.org
**King Linda L 2-8**
Boettcher Elaine A 1-2
Hempel Donn F BA 3-4
Hudgins Barbara A 7-8
Hurt Gayle S BAED 1-4
Koehler Karen L K
Obrzut Heide L BA 5-6
**HINSDALE**-ZION PS-8
• NLSA • 1890
125 S Vine St 60521-4039
(630)323-0045 •
FAX(630)323-1425
jellef@zionhinsdale.org
Berg Deborah G BA K
Cappa Susan D BA PS
Celentano Carrie PS
Ellefson James E MA 5-8
Kroll Mary Lou 2
Niehaus Susan 3-4
Smith Marian 5-8
Winterstein Jerome A MED 5-8
**HOFFMAN**-TRINITY PS-8
• 1874
8701 Huey Rd PO Box 200 62250-0200
(618)495-2246 •
FAX(618)495-2692
Boehne Erna PS
Boehne Ruth E BS K
Eggerman Kimberly A BA 3-4
Grotelueschen Timothy L BA
Hasz Denese BA 1-2
Spenner Cynthia H BSED 5-6
Weidner Donald R MA
**HOMEWOOD**-SALEM PS-K
• 1993
18328 Ashland Ave 60430-3403
(708)206-0350 •
FAX(708)798-1590
NO REPORT
**HOOPESTON**-HIS LITTLE LAMBS-GOOD SHEPHERD PS
• 1992
302 N Market St 60942-1320
(217)283-7966
NO REPORT
**HOYLETON**-TRINITY PS-8
• 1867
155 N Main St 62803-2003 PO Box 57 62803-0057
(618)493-7754 •
FAX(618)493-7754
tlcshoyl@accessus.net
**Gifford Charles J Sr. BA 7-8**
Bachmann Charlene K BS 3-4
Bourgeois Janis K BA 1-2
Guebert Janel S BSED 5-6
Martin Sandra R MSED PS
**HUNTLEY**-TLC-TRINITY PS-K
• 1993
11008 N Church St PO Box 186 60142-0186
(847)669-5781 •
FAX(847)669-5978
NO REPORT
**ITASCA**-ST LUKE PS-8
• NLSA • 1885
410 S Rush St 60143-2130
(630)773-0509 •
FAX(630)773-0786
Aumann Richard 4-8
Hoffman Tara L PS
Hogan Kimberly 4
Lorenz David E MA 6-8
Peters Karen 2
Redeker Sally M MA 1
Schopen Tamara J MED 5-8
Schroeder Ellen E MED K
Wille Melvin MA
**JACKSONVILLE**-OUR REDEEMER PS
• 1988
405 Massey Ln 62650-2615
(217)245-0474 •
FAX(217)243-2746
NO REPORT
SALEM PS-8
• NLSA • 1859
222 E Beecher PO Box 1057 62651-1057
(217)243-3419 •
FAX(217)245-0289
salemlutheran@netscape.net
**Rensner Stephen E MA 7-8**
Aring Elizabeth R BED PS
Hester Julie A 7-8
Jud Carolyn R MLS 5-6
Quigg Juliann M BSED 3-4
Rensner Cheryl L BA K
Steinacher Deborah M 2
Sweatman Sandra D BA 1
**JACOB**-CHRIST K-8
• 1876
146 W Jacob Rd 62950-9629
(618)763-4664 •
FAX(618)763-4363
christ@egyptian.net
**Rohlfing Terrence H MED 6-8**

Bierman Barbara 1-2
Davis Denise R K
Korando Melissa M 3-5
**JOLIET**-OUR SAVIOR PS
• 1992
1910 Black Rd 60435-3423
(815)725-1688 •
FAX(815)725-1689
NO REPORT
ST PETER PS-8
• 1869
310 N Broadway St 60435-7169
(815)722-3567 •
FAX(815)722-6544
Antonides Jodie 3-4
Pautz Claudia 7-8
Pehlke Julie 1-2
Peters Polly K
Schoen Valerie A BA 5-6
Sheppard Andrea J BA PS
**KANKAKEE**-ST PAUL PS-8
• NLSA • 1864
1580 Butterfield Trl 60901-2933
(815)932-3241 •
FAX(815)932-7588
**Nordmeyer Richard C MED**
Duchene Sherri 2
Eyster Carol M BSED 3
Eyster Timothy K BA 4
Ferrebee Duane R BED 7-8
Freeman Lesley PS
Heil John O MS 6-8
Hess Mark BSED 5-8
Hinze Adele L BA 1
Payne Dianne BA K
Ross Laurie
Shamblin Linda M BSED PS
Wachholz Eugene H BA 6-8
**LA GRANGE**-ST JOHN PS-8
• NLSA • 1886
505 S Park Rd 60525-6198
(708)354-1690 •
FAX(708)354-4910
Beck Luke 6-8
Behnke Fred H MA 7
Clark Susan BA 6-8
Cordes Nancy A BS 2
Erke Lisa K 3
Gottschalk Ann C MA PS
Hackelberg Holly R MED 1
Janowski Shelley A 5-8
Kahl Lynn M MA 5
Kuker Gerald W MCMU 5-6
Kunz Susan M BA 6-8
Niccolai Cynthia PS
Press Sarah J BS PS-7
Toepper Marilyn A BS K
Willig Elizabeth K-8
Wykert Thomas A BA 4
**LAKE FOREST**-FAITH PS
• 1998
680 W Deerpath Rd 60045
(847)234-2753 •
FAX(847)234-1929
NO REPORT
**LAKE VILLA**-GOOD SHEPHERD PS
• 1992
25100 W Grand Ave 60046-9704
(847)356-1776
mmchale549@aol.com
Mc Hale Susan K MED
Smith Virginia BS PS
**LAKE ZURICH**-ST MATTHEW PS-8
• NLSA • 1863
24480 N Old McHenry Rd
60047-8400
(847)438-6103 •
FAX(847)438-0376
stmatts@dls.net
Durheim Cheryl 5-8
Hacias Nancy PS
Koch Paige 5-8
Lazarus Phyllene D BA 6
Moza Paulette J BA 2
Norwell Christine J BA 3
Rayner Darlene K

Rescho Valerie 5
Roberts Sandra L BSED K
Schulz Gerrie PS
Shaw Carol J BA 1
Smith Joanie L BA 1-8
Stackhouse Melynda E BA 4
Struble Susan PS
Wulbert Cindy 5-8
**LANSING**-ST JOHN PS-8
• 1893
18100 Wentworth Ave 60438-3900
(708)895-9280 •
FAX(708)895-9303
**Swanson David W BA**
Anderson Mary A PS
Cannata Christine BED 5-8
Costenaro Lorilee BA 3
Helming Lynne K BA 1
Joza Carol PS
Schepmann Heather N BA 5-8
Schif Kristen A BA 3-4
Wrona Jan PS-2
TRINITY PS-8
• NLSA • 1866
18144 Glen Terrace 60438-2152
(708)474-8539 •
FAX(708)474-0820
sbhelming@aol.com
Brackmann Diane BA K
Buffano Kristin 4
Garrett Sheri L BA 1
Graves Myra 3
Helming Scott B MSED
Hoard Cheryl S 6-8
Luetgert Lynn L 5
Mihich Nancy MED PS
Pieper Darald A BSED 5-8
Thurn David G MA 7
Thurn Kathleen C BS 2
**LEBANON**-ME-MESSIAH PS
• 1998
801 N Madison 62254
(618)537-2300 •
FAX(618)537-4230
Meyer Orra Lee BSED
**LEXINGTON**-ST PAUL PS
• 1997
107 East Chatham 61753 107 E Chatham 61753-1018
(309)365-5100 •
FAX(309)365-8251
stpaul@davesworld.net
Hall Kathleen R PS
Silver Ruth A PS
**LINCOLN**-ZION PS-8
• NLSA • 1975
1600 Woodlawn Rd 62656-9787
(217)732-3977 •
FAX(217)732-3398
zlslinc@abelink.com
**Krueger Frederic R MA 6-8**
Baker Patricia 6-8
Fuiten Pamela R BS 3
Mc Cormick Sara A 2
Miller Peggy A BMU K
Sauer Donna E BSED 4
Schumacher Steven R BSED 6-8
Sielaff Sara J BA PS-K
Stamm Joanne R BS 1
Thomas Kyra 5
**LISLE**-TRINITY PS
• 1974
1101 Kimberly Way 60532-3175
(630)964-1276 •
FAX(630)241-9826
NO REPORT
**LITCHFIELD**-ZION PS-8
• 1888
1301 N State St 62056-1199
(217)324-3166 •
FAX(217)324-3166
**Schaff John M BA 4**
Bayer Roxanne M MED 7-8
Cordani Sharon D BA 3
Fraser Barb 4
Gehner Norma J BS 1
Langhoff Susan BED 5

Pryor Jami L BS 6
Taylor Lisa PS-K
**LOCKPORT**-ST PAUL PS
• 1996
1500 S Briggs St 60441-4546
(815)838-1390
NO REPORT
**LOMBARD**-PEACE COMMUNITY PS
• 1980
21W500 Butterfield Rd 60148-5134
(630)627-1135 •
FAX(630)627-1103
Hensel Linda PS
Herlein Anya BSW PS
Herlein Lynn PS
Marks Ruth PS
Scheiwe Vyonne BED
Smith Connie BS PS
Stephenson Barb PS
ST JOHN PS-8
• NLSA • 1888
215 S Lincoln St 60148-2510
(630)629-2515 •
FAX(630)629-2515
stjohnslombard@mediaone.net
Anderson Janet A BSED 2
Carlsen Christina BA 1
Corrigan Robin 3
Hall Steven L BSED 7-8
Heuser Adele MA
Hinz Ann M MCMU PS-8
Holler Nora F BA PS
Hyssong Angie MA K
Kalal Thomas C BA 5-6
Koehler Debra G MA 7-8
Roete Elaine C BA 1-8
Septeowski Dawn MA PS-8
Smith Sandra L MA 4
Walton Tricia D BSED 5-6
TRINITY PS-8
• NLSA • 1860
1008 E Roosevelt Rd 60148-4143
(630)627-5601 •
FAX(630)627-5676
**Krohse Kenneth C MA 5-6**
Graves Jean E BA 1
Gutwein Manfred MA 7-8
Krohse Marlene K MED PS-K
Perez Patricia A BA 3-4
Schmidt Karen 2
Solyom Arlene M AAS PS
Yaeger Margaret A BS 3
**LYONS**-ZION PS
• 1983
7930 W Ogden Ave 60534-1333
(708)447-4499
Paulsen Barbara J MA PS
Renn Carolyn J PS
**MACHESNEY PARK**-CONCORDIA PS-8
• NLSA • 1961
7424 N 2ND St 61115-2814
(815)633-6450 •
FAX(815)633-1345
Detrick Jeanette A PS
Ferguson Jennifer J BA 7-8
Fowler Suzanne B BSED 3
Hahn Rick E BA
Johnson Faye E 1
Klein Donald E BA 6
Loch Danielle E 4
Pape Sheri PS-8
Schewe Sharyn J BA 2
Stahl Jane L BA 5
Willard Joyce B K
**MARENGO**-ZION PS-8
• NLSA • 1888
408 Jackson St 60152-3204
(815)568-5156 •
FAX(815)568-0547
zion@mc.net
**Steltenpohl William M MSED**
Bassuener Jennifer A BA K
Benecke Vera L BSED 3
Dahn Michael R BA 7
Dunker Sandee S MA PS

Emerson Nancy 2
Ettner Susan K BA 5
Hagenmueller Ernest H MA 5-8
Hinck Diane E MA 6
Jones Mary A BS 1
Koplin Joyce E BA 4
Mahnke Glenn R MMU 5-8
Mahnke Marie A BA K-8
Trah Sheila E BA 2
Wascher Charridan A BA 8
Wascher Erin M BED 1
**MARKHAM**-MARKHAM PS-K
• 1947
160th & Clifton Park Ave 60426
(708)331-4885
NO REPORT
**MARYVILLE**-ST JOHN LITTLE LAMBS PS
• 1987
7201 W Main St 62062 Po Box 517 62062-0517
(618)344-8989
dteach5@juno.com
Decker Rebecca PS
Mc Mahan Diana L PS
**MASCOUTAH**-ZION PS
• 1982
101 S Railway 62258-0131
(618)566-7345 •
FAX(618)566-9519
zionlcms@accessus.net
NO REPORT
**MASON CITY**-LITTLE LAMB OF CHRIS PS
• 1991
114 E Walnut St 62664-1164
(217)482-3761
NO REPORT
**MATTESON**-ZION PS-8
• NLSA • 1868
3840 216Th St 60443-2717
(708)747-7490 •
FAX(708)747-1194
**Wunderlich Diane**
Engel Nadine L K
Griffin Shirley A 2
Kasper Jill 1
Lisius Charlotte M BED 5
Nelis Brooke 7
Nieminsk Bruce 8
Sammons Lu Anne 3
Stevens Lynne M BS PS
Thomas Rebecca 4
Weiss Kathleen J 6
**MATTOON**-ST JOHN PS-7
• 1956
200 Charleston Ave 61938-4428
(217)234-4911 •
FAX(217)234-4925
**Nack Delton L MS**
Curry Nina PS
Diepholz Christi L AA PS
Fleischfresser Sheri L BA 5-6
Hilchen Anne F MA 2
Nack Judith A 1
Phelps Erin 3
Severson Brenda J BA K
Traub Gail A MS K
Webster Laura K
**MC HENRY**-ZION PS
• 1983
4206 W Elm St 60050-4001
NO REPORT
**MELROSE PARK**-APOSTLES PS
• 1993
10429 W Fullerton Ave 60164-1860
(847)455-8189
NO REPORT
ST PAUL PS-8
• 1889
1025 W Lake St 60160-4150
(708)343-5000 •
FAX(708)343-8635
dggrebasch@aol.com
**Grebasch Douglas H MA**
Beierwaltes Ruth E MA K

Bierlein Beth N BED 7
Boos Sharon A MSLS
Erickson Megan L BA 1
Haak Charles E MA 8
Hemmann Oliver R MA 5
Johnson Melissa L MA 2
Richardson Jennifer E BA 6
Schnabel Kirsten L BA PS
Williams Demetrice MED 4
Zemke Frieda J BA 3
**MOKENA**-IMMANUEL PS
• 1975
10731 W LA Porte Rd 60448-9284
(708)479-5600 •
FAX(708)479-9492
loisrmayer@yahoo.com
Beugger Tina PS
Mayer Lois R MA
Mc Clafferly Debbie PS
Mc Garry Barbara J BA PS
Poplawski Beth PS
Smith Maetha AA PS
Starwvich Carol PS
Vogler Judy AAS PS
**MONTGOMERY**-ST LUKES PS-3
• 1971
11 Pembrooke Rd 60538-2016
(630)892-0310 •
FAX(630)892-0166
Hoffman Janyce E MED 1
Kersten Jayne E BA 3
Lutze Sonya S BA 2
Mc Neilly Nancy AA PS
Nelson Kathryn PS
Paydon Kathleen PS
Theis Laura PS
Voss Ruth M K
**MORTON**-BETHEL PS-8
• 1982
425 N Missouri (PS) 325 E
Queenwood Rd 61550-9715
(309)266-6592 •
FAX(309)266-8510
alexanderjames@hotmail.com
**Alexander James L MA 6-8**
Dierker Lisa K PS
Dobrinsky Vicki L PS
Elsas Sandra L BS K
Ewald Paula J BA PS
Hamer Patricia J BSED PS
Hansen Celeste PS
Harris Jan L BA PS
Lehnert Katie PS
Marks Kimberly 5-8
Moore Linda M BSED 3
Olson Katherine PS
Patton Jackie A PS
Rumbold Sharon K BED 1
Stetzler Carol L BSED 2
Stidman Linda 5
Wyzard Debra J BA 4-8
Ziemniak Jennifer D PS
**MOUNT PROSPECT**-ST JOHN PS-5
• 1848
1101 S Linneman Rd 60056-4167
(847)593-7670 •
FAX(847)593-2601
elizabeth300@home.com
Kratz Donald L MA
Myers Elizabeth D MA
Neumann Martha BSED
Nulton JoAn
Roach Sandra
Tredray Christina BAED
Vondran Kimberly A BA
ST PAUL PS-8
• NLSA • 1913
18 S School St 60056-3315
(847)255-6733 •
FAX(847)255-6834
splsmp@aol.com
**Meier Matthew C MS**
Bechtel Ann 4-8
Crawford Patricia C MED K
De Cant Crystine K-8
Ferdinand Sharon 5-8
Franck Donna J MED 1

Garin Paulette K-8
Gunia Matthew 6-8
Gutzler Matthew M BA 4
Jacobsen Carol K-8
Klingelhofer Carol MED 2
Krebs Nang 4
Lachmann Susan 5-8
Morris Jo Ann PS
Rittle Deborah BS 3
Troemner Nancy BA PS
Young Angela M BA PS
Young Eric A BA 5
**MOUNT PULASKI**-ZION PS-8
• 1851
203 S Vine St 62548-1256
(217)792-5715 • FAX(217)
792-5965
Cooper Julie A K
Davis Jean E 4-5
Droegemueller Wilma A BS PS
Maske Kathy M BSED K-1
Wernsing Darrel G MSED
Wernsing Karen L BA 2-3
**MURPHYSBORO**-IMMANUEL PS-8
• 1897
1915 Pine St 62966-1935
(618)687-3917 •
FAX(618)684-5115
immanuellutheran@globaleyes.net
**Fark Terry G MA 7-8**
Clough Jean BS K
Graeff Jennifer PS
Merz Charles W BS 5-6
Merz Kathy M BS 1-2
Van Winkle Julie 3-4
**NAPERVILLE**-BETHANY PS-8
• NLSA • 1930
1550 Modaff Rd 60565-6191
(630)355-6607 •
FAX(630)355-2216
dwischmeyer@bethanylcs.org
**Wischmeyer Donald H EDS**
Armbrecht Carole 6-8
Bolt Louise R BA PS
Bolt R K MA 3
Di Giovanni Jane MA 6
Fiene Charlene BS 2
Hahn Lana J BED 5
Jahnke Nancy BS K
Lenich Sharon S BS K-5
Mueller Pam MA 1
Noffke Christine A BA K-8
Rach Joanne M BA 4
Rasmussen-Sislow JoAnn BA K-8
Sonlitner Glenn R MA 6-8
Staunch Carole K-8
Stirn Todd E MA 6-8
Yonker Nancy PS
WORD OF LIFE PS
• 1989
879 Tudor Rd 60563-2100
(630)355-7648 •
FAX(630)355-2220
randil0391@aol.com
Baker Irene BS PS
Cook Mary PS
Dietrich Jo Anne PS
Ferrari Maureen PS
Kunnemann Randi L BA
Mickens Joyce PS
Richards Darlene S PS
Taylor Marsha B PS
ZION PS
• 1995
11007 Book Rd 60564
(630)904-1124 •
FAX(630)904-4149
zionlutheran@core.com
Block Marajean A BA PS
Drive Debra PS
Mitchell Rose PS
Rost Ruth BS PS
Schmeckpeper Cathy A BA PS
Sturm Joan M MA

**NASHVILLE**-TRINITY-ST JOHN
PS-8
• NLSA • 1974
680 W Walnut St 62263-1158
(618)327-8561 •
FAX(618)327-4540
tsjohn@isbe.accessus.net
**McClintock Laurie J 1**
Backs Diane K BA 3
Cameron Nelda
Ford Amber 5-8
Lange Debra K BS 4
Lange Janice A BA 2
Mittendorf Kristie BS PS
Renken Betty R 5-8
Rincker Loana M BS 5-8
Wesseln Tabatha A K
**NEW BERLIN**-ST JOHN 1-8
• 1870
304 E Gibson St 62670-0197
(217)488-3190
**Krohse Ronald D BA 5-8**
Krohse Mary A 1-4
**NEW LENOX**-TRINITY PS
• 1983
508 N Cedar Rd 60451-1408
(815)485-6973 •
FAX(815)485-6384
emb825@aol.com
Bacon Annette L BED PS
Schlak Janet BBA PS
Welsh Jeanine PS
**NEWTON**-GOOD SHEPHERD PS
• 1985
110 Edwards St 62448-1736
(618)783-4105
NO REPORT
**NOKOMIS**-ST PAUL K-8
• NLSA • 1870
18379 N 22nd Ave 62075-3708
(217)563-8670 •
FAX(217)563-8670
kritter210@yahoo.com
Ritter Dale L Jr. MAT 6-8
**NORMAL**-GOOD SHEPHERD PS
• 1995
201 S Main St 61761-2945
(309)862-0101
Davis Michelle L PS
Stuckey Gerilyn J AA PS
SHINING LIGHTS-CHRIST PS
• 1998
311 N Hershey Rd 61761
(309)452-5609 •
FAX(309)888-9085
NO REPORT
**NORTH PLATO**-ST PETER LITTLE
SAIN PS
• 1996
43W301 Plank Rd 60140-7901
(847)464-5721 •
FAX(847)464-4204
NO REPORT
**NORTHBROOK**-THE MUSTARD
SEED-GRACE PS
• 1983
2245 Walters Ave 60062-4529
(847)498-3060 •
FAX(847)498-3061
Hanusin Sharon J MA
Kohrs Jennifer D PS
Waldeck Judy A BS PS
**NORWOOD PARK**-OUR SAVIOR
PS-8
• 1924
6035 N Northcott Ave 60631-2413
(773)631-1606 •
FAX(773)775-9265
**Seiler Christine R BA**
Brazelton William T Jr. BED 5-6
Fritsche Mark 7-8
Hand Genese PS
Schug Michelle 3-4
Stephens Marcella M MA 1-2
Wickboldt Cynthia BA K

**NORWOOD PARK TWP**-ST PAUL
PS-8
• NLSA • 1903
5650 N Canfield Ave 60631-3318
(708)867-5044 •
FAX(708)867-0083
**Schipull Douglas W PHD**
Graf Jennifer S MED 2
Gyllstrom Betty W 7
Heinze Michael E MA 8
Ilten Karla N 1
Johnson Deborah L BA 4
Johnston Christopher J BA 6
Seibert Michelle A BS PS-K
Turner Amy L 3
Wallner Heidi A BA 5
**O FALLON**-BETHANY PS
• 1996
5600 Old Collinsville Rd
62208-3741
(618)632-1985
bethany@icss.ney
NO REPORT
**OAK LAWN**-ST PAUL PS-8
• NLSA • 1959
4660 W 94th St 60453-2513
(847)423-1058 •
FAX(847)423-1588
ilcpalatine@juno.com
**Landgrave Aaron M MED**
Behnke Elaine BA 3
Kastellorizios Donna MA 5-8
Larson Mary E PS
Lysen Kim PS
Mc Farlin Jerry A MA 5-8
Mc Farlin Vickie BS 2
Moller Martha 1-6
Moravec Kathy M BA
Puder Barbara PS
Seils Ardis C MA 1-8
Sievers Ruth M MA PS-K
Steinmetz Pamela 4
Thomas Lisa 5-8
Volk Susan 1
Will Debra A BA 5-8
**OAK PARK**-CHRIST PS
• 1989
607 Harvard St 60304-2015
(708)386-3306
Dame Christine M BA PS
**OKAWVILLE**-IMMANUEL PS-8
• 1908
606 S Hanover St 62271-2208
(618)243-6142 •
FAX(618)243-6142
**Kleckner Eric M BA 3-8**
Fox Joy L BS 1-2
Green Sara PS
Kleckner Pamela S BA K
Mason Terry E BA 7-8
Sprehe Ronda S BA 3-6
**ORLAND PARK**-CHRIST PS
• 1983
14700 S 94Th Ave 60462-2656
(708)349-0431 •
FAX(708)349-0668
Bareither Patricia MED PS
Higgins Sara PS
Lindemulder Deb PS
Mc Partlin Marjorie PS
LIVING WORD PS
• 1996
16301 S Wolf Rd 60467
(708)226-1160 •
FAX(708)403-5869
lwlc@aol.com
NO REPORT
**OTTAWA**-ZION PS
• 1986
622 W Jefferson St 61350-2737
(815)433-1408
**Sommer Ann M BA PS**
Mc Cullough Teresa PS
Werth Karen S PS

**PALATINE**-IMMANUEL PS-8
• NLSA • 1870
200 N Plum Grove Rd 60067-5233
(847)359-1936 •
FAX(847)359-1583
immanuel@ilcp.org
**Bauder Karen F MA**
Buhrke Lynn D MA 3
Coakley Joan BA 7-8
Corliss Kathleen MED 6-8
Crimmins Ruth E BED
Dahlinghaus Gloria MSW 7-8
De Witt Richard MS 6-8
Fast Carol MA 4
Fowler Katrina M BED 1
Grau Cheryl BSED 7-8
Hertel Delores L MA 2
Hetzner Jacquelyn L MED PS
Kinsella Linda PS
Kirchhoff John BA 6-8
Kist Susannah 1-8
Klose Scott 2-8
Laabs Jenny 2-8
Lorenz Nancy D MA 5
Lorenz Thomas 6-8
Lovell Jacqueline MA 5
Mac Lean Karen BED PS
Meyer Jean MS 3
Ruppel Sonja T 5
Schmidt Mary E MED 1
Schneider Dorothy A BA 3
Schneider Kimberly 1-8
Sinibaldo Janine BA K
Sobel Jennifer A BS 2
Tres Marlene J MA

**PARIS**-GRACE PS
• 1998
712 S Central Ave PO Box 493
61944-0493
(217)466-1234 •
FAX(217)466-5085
1234@comwares.net
Barrett Jamy D PS
Bell Trudy L AECE PS
Comstock Heather C PS
Fiene Sheryl A BA
Flori Amy L PS
Hancock Melissa A PS
Hinesley Debbie J PS
Kirby Anne C PS
Ludington Jenny R PS
Tolen Brandy S PS

**PARK FOREST**-LITTLE ANGELS PS
• 1998
424 Indianwood Blvd 60466
(708)747-5751 •
FAX(708)748-1940
NO REPORT

**PARK RIDGE**-ST ANDREW PS-8
• NLSA • 1911
260 N Northwest Hwy 60068-3353
(847)823-9308 •
FAX(847)823-1846
NO REPORT

**PEKIN**-GOOD SHEPHERD PS-8
• RSO • 1980
333 State St 61554-3244
(309)347-2020
**Vollmer Corine A BA 4**
**Vollmer Judith A BA 2**
Barth Stephanie PS
Brush Nancy D BA 5-8
Dennis Tina 5-8
Fleming Ruth A BA 1
Lutz Sheila BSED K-8
Mickley Ralph E MA 4-8
Nehls Robin PS
Richmond Judith BS K
Robinson Cynthia 5-6
Timiam Patti PS

**PEORIA**-CHRIST PS-8
• 1894
1311 S Faraday Ave 61605-3315
(309)637-1512 •
FAX(309)637-7829
**Mooney Terry M MSED**
Burch Julie A PS
Kelly Kirsten E BA 3
Lelm Kathleen 2
Magnusson Dawn BS 6
Martin Angie PS
Miller Jackye R PS
Mooney Leslie A BS 8
Reith JoAnn MA 2
Schneider Christine G BA K
Teske Michele A BS 1
Teske Ralph W MA 4
Von Behren Linda R BMU 5

CONCORDIA K-8
• RSO • NLSA • 1959
2000 W Glen Ave 61614-4643
(309)691-8921 •
FAX(309)691-2913
concordiap@home.com
NO REPORT

HOLY CROSS PS
• 1990
618 S Maxwell Rd 61607-1039
(309)697-8450
NO REPORT

REDEEMER PS
• 1953
6801 N Allen Rd 61614-2480
(309)691-2333 •
FAX(309)691-4388
**Dunham Doris E BSED**
Andreasen Cynthia J PS
Beringer Elizabeth S PS
Burdick Laura C MA PS
Crosson Vickie L PS
Fernandez Cathy J PS
Foulk Carol A BS PS
Ista Linda BMU PS
Jensen Debra L BA PS
Kane Barbara A BSED PS
Schlatter Donna J BS PS
Streitmatter Pamela PS

**PRAIRIETOWN**-ST PETER K-8
• 1857
7182 Renken Rd 62021-1802
(618)888-2252 •
FAX(618)888-2353
splcasop@madisontelco.com
**Schelp Keith A BS 6-8**
Frankford Sandra A BS K-2
Schelp Kathleen J BSED 3-5

**PROSPECT HEIGHTS**-
SONSHINE-OUR REDEEMER PS
• 1982
304 W Palatine Rd 60070-1135
(708)520-1116
NO REPORT

**QUINCY**-ST JAMES PS-8
• NLSA • 1851
900 S 17th St 62301-5542
(217)222-8447 •
FAX(217)222-3415
grewe5@dstream.net
**Grewe Mark J MA**
Adams Donald W MA 7-8
Adams Sue Anne R 5
Bunch Cynthia 6
Floyd Debra L MA
Grewe Shirley J BA 2
Mohr Renita A BA 3
Scott Kristina PS
Strackeljahn Sherry BS 1
Walt Rita 6
Yelton Sherry BSED 4

**RED BUD**-ST JOHN PS-8
• 1868
104 E South 6Th St 62278-1746
(618)282-3873 •
FAX(618)282-4087
St Johns62278@juno.com
Becker William F BA 3
Devall Ryan L 1-8
Kaaz Raymond E MED 5
Kastens Alice C MS 4
Miller Rachel E BED 1
Schield Betty E BS K
Schneider Deitt C BA 8
Schneider Rebekah J BA 2
Steele Cindy S PS
Wolff Amanda J BA 7

TRINITY PS-8
• 1842
10247 S Prairie Rd 62278-4611
(618)282-2881 •
FAX(618)282-2881
trinity1@htc.net
**Knight Valerie R BSED 7-8**
Bottcher Karen S PS-K
Bottcher Ronald R BS
Eckert Lois C MA 1-2
Marotzke Judy L BS 3-4

**RIVER FOREST**-CONCORDIA PS
• NLSA • 1976
7400 Augusta St 60305-1402
(708)209-3099 •
FAX(708)209-3176
crfknuthde@curf.edu
Bartell Judith E MA K
Christian Beth PS
Keller Jennifer M MA PS
Knuth Doris E
Neumann Amy L MA PS
Trieu Thanh N PS
Vezner Heather L MA PS

SPECIAL EDUC MINISTR K-12
• 1984
7400 Augusta St # 1N 60305-1402
(708)209-3344 •
FAX(708)209-3176
lsem@curf.edu
**Lewis Susan L MA**
Adams Elease BA 9-12
Bauer Michelle C MED K-12
Bower Jennifer O BA K-8
Bunker Stacy L K-8
Calabrese Deborah L MA K-8
Ellenstein Margaret M MS K-8
Gilbert Camille K-8
Gutow Theresa K-8
House Patricia 9-12
Jones Joycelyn K-8
Kinninger Julie K-8
Lapsansky Arlene K-8
Mahal Carolyn MS K-8
Mankiewicz Deborah V MED K-8
Musa Gretchen J MSED K-8
Piper Nicole BSED K-8
Q Donnell Sue K-8
Sadek Nancy L MA K-8
Saiki Cheryl K MSED K-8
Salemi-Kim Christine K-8
Seldera Joselito K-8
Stanley Jacalyn MS K-12
Stevenson Susanne L MA K-8
Stewart Shawn BED K-8

**RIVER GROVE**-BETHLEHEM PS-8
• 1901
2624 Oak Street 60171-1696
(708)456-8786
NO REPORT

**ROCHELLE**-ST PAUL PS-8
• NLSA • 1961
1415 10Th Ave 61068-1233
(815)562-6323 •
FAX(815)561-8074
stpaul@rochelle.net
**Kruse Daryl M MEDADM**
Blumenberg Sherry K
Chaplin Gene 7-8
Cole Julie A MAT 4
Cole Sheri 3
Crystal Theresa PS
Dayton Timothy
Gleissner Nancy
Kruse Patricia G BA 2
Mallory Cindy 1
Reineck Jane PS
Rissman Lora MA 5
Schlie Angela BA 6
Storm Daniel BA 5-8

**ROCHESTER**-GOOD SHEPHERD PS
• 1974
1 Camelot Dr 62563-9203
(217)498-7991
Ayers Wendy
Bane Deborah
Cooper Janette
Thompson Janie

**ROCK ISLAND**-IMMANUEL PS-6
• 1856
3300 24th St 61201-6212
(309)788-8242 •
FAX(309)786-3392
ilcsgm@aol.com
Dolk Vickie BA K
Hedrick Franklin J MA 5-6
Hedrick Julia BA 2
Mosher Ryan 1
Soeken Vernon E MED 3-4
Witmer Susan PS-4

**ROCKFORD**-CHRIST THE ROCK PS
• 1996
8330 Newburg Rd 61108-6935
(815)332-7191
NO REPORT

LUTHER ACADEMY AT GL K-6
4700 Augustana Dr 61107
(815)226-4947 •
FAX(815)226-4886
NO REPORT

MOUNT OLIVE PS
• 1991
2001 N Alpine Rd 61107-1417
(815)399-3171 •
FAX(815)399-3174
Montgomery Mary PS

REDEEMER PS
• 1988
827 16Th St 61104-3322
(815)397-2227
NO REPORT

ST PAUL PS-8
• NLSA • 1887
811 Locust St 61101-6699
(815)965-3335 •
FAX(815)965-3335
Bauschke Stefanie 6
Berg Carole J BA 1
Brackett Susan
Fritz Debra 1-8
Hendryx Sheryl D BA 3
Horvath Tera D BA 5-6
Keske Richard P MA
Schmidt Martha C BA 2
Simonson Janice PS
Snow Debra S BS
Ulrich Dean R MSED 4
Webb James W 7-8

**ROSELLE**-TRINITY PS-8
• NLSA • 1899
405 Rush St 60172-2228
(630)894-3263 •
FAX(630)894-1430
office@trinityroselle.com
**Knitter Susan K BA 6-8**
**Sander Reed S MSED**
Berdis Juanita M BA 1
Boenker Mary J BS K
Catapano Kristin MA PS
De Witt Gretchen A PS
Deibel Peggy
Dohse JoAnne BSED PS-5
Epting Kim BSED 2
Gallagher Karen MA K-8
Heinz Francie A BSED 3
Helmke Phyllis MA K-8
Klemme Stephine 2
Lovitsch Lisa MED 4
March Kim BA 5-8
Milnikel Amy B BA 6-8
Moeller Amy L MA 6-8
Moeller Steven W MA 6-8
Ostrander Karen M BA 5-8
Pudell Lisa MA PS
Saeger Jon 6-8

Sander Sharolyn MS 2
Scheiwe Robert N BA 6-8
Studt Nancy J MA PS
Tate Gary R MA 4
Weslock Naomi Y BS 5
Weslock Terry E MA 5
Winter Kathryn L PS
Wolfanger Mildred MA 3
Yagow Lisa M BMED K-8

**SADORUS**-NOAHS ARK-ST PAUL PS
• 1992
101 E Church St PO Box 230 61872-0230
(217)598-2259 •
FAX(217)598-2259
NO REPORT

ST PAUL K-1
• 1999
101 Church St 61872 PO Box 230 61872-0230
(217)598-2259 •
FAX(217)598-2259
stpaul96@juno.com
NO REPORT

**SAINT CHARLES**-ST MARK PS
• 1980
101 S 6Th Ave 60174-2107
(630)584-4850 •
FAX(630)584-8646
stmarksstc@aol.com
Cudworth Linda PS
Culley Linda L BA PS
Hutton Patti
Kingsley Patte PS
Silber Kathleen W PS
Strub Sue PS

**SAINT PETER**-ST PETER K-8
• 1872
RR 1 Box 70 62880-9721
(618)349-8888 •
FAX(618)349-8888
spsaints@csuol.com
Benning Karen L BS 3-4
Crain Lori M K
Gallo Gretchen L 5-6
Rinkel Angela M 1-2
Urban Lawrence W BA

**SCHAUMBURG**-ST JOHN PS
• 1998
1800 S Rodenburg Rd 60193
(847)524-5328 •
FAX(847)524-6376
Graham Julie A BED PS

ST PETER PS-8
• 1848
208 E Schaumburg Rd 60194-3517
(847)885-7636 •
FAX(847)885-9157
Barrick Sharon R MA 5
Bauer Karen M 6
Blinn Kristen K BA K
Bohlman Derek 8
Carlton Joann M 7
Flett Douglas A BA K
Johnson Pamela A MA PS
Jonke Jain A BS 1
Jungkuntz Sandra S MA 3
Kirsch Roger A MA
Kruel Kathy 4
Monroe Amy BA 5
Noble Kristen L BA K
Oleson Cindy A MA 2
Reck Linda K PS
Schiestel Delaine S BA
Schneider Amy E BA 3
Sternberg Bonnie J BA PS
Stordahl Jean A BA 1
Tighe Christine M BA 4
Voth Joann M BA 2

**SECOR**--ST JOHN PS
• 1996
208 N Second 61771 PO Box 229 61771-0229
(309)744-2256 •
FAX(309)744-2255
NO REPORT

**SHERMAN**-GOOD SHEPHERD PS
• 1983
6086 Bus 55 PO Box 237 62684-0237
(217)496-3149
Agrall Annette PS
Jensen Cindy PS

**SKOKIE**-ST PAUL K-8
• NLSA • 1881
5201 Galitz St 60077-2737
(847)673-5030 •
FAX(847)673-9828
**Luksha Dale W MED 7-8**
Croon Rosalie J K-3
Hebble Paula A K-4
Heidlauf Joanne V BA 1
Malone Ronald 5-8
Raabe Paula MED 6-8
Rocans Roberta L BA 4-5
Sammartino Maria MA 2
Schaefer Jill BA 3
Schuman John K-8
Struck Barbara K
Wehrle Michael 6-8

**SPARTA**-ST JOHN PS
• 1980
PO Box 334 62286-0334
(618)443-2010 •
FAX(618)443-5695
Luedders Ann L AAS

**SPRINGFIELD**-CONCORDIA PS-8
• 1931
2300 E Wilshire Rd 62703-4949
(217)529-3307 •
FAX(217)529-3096
Bandelow Denise E BA 5-6
Billotte Pamela A BS 1-2
Dart Anne L MSED 7-8
Henschen Daniel R MS 7-8
Ritz Jennifer K
Smith Kathy L BA 3-4
Steffen Patricia BS PS
Stuenkel Nona L BS PS

IMMANUEL PS-6
• 1916
2750 E Sangamon Ave 62702-1419
(217)528-5232 •
FAX(217)528-5232
**Eckert Linn W MA 5-6**
Castelletti Judith A BS K
Eckert Michele K BS PS
Moldenhauer Donna L BA 3-4
Nobbe Sherry L PS
Oschwald Jeni 1-2

OUR SAVIOR'S PS-8
• NLSA • 1962
2645 Old Jacksonville Rd 62704-3199
(217)546-4531
osl@fgi.net
**Ryherd Brian D MED**
Alexander Kathy L BS 6-8
Benning Cathleen M BA 4
Bergt Richard D BED 5-8
Bernhardt Edythe E MSED 3
Boehme Joyce A MED K
Claus Lori V BA 1
Du Bois Nancy J 1-5
Farmer Vickie L BSED 2
Franzen Arlyn D MA 6-8
Garvue Kimberly L BA PS
Harkins La Jean M 1-8
Heppe Rebecca L 5-8
Morgan Amy C BA PS
Ryherd Ann C 6-8

TRINITY PS-8
• NLSA • 1860
515 S MacArthur Blvd 62704-1744
(217)787-2323 •
FAX(217)787-1145
tls@fginet
**Rodgers Lewis E MS**
Benning Russell D MMED 5-8
Bottrell Sandra B BA 3
Filter Laura 1
Fliege Judith B MA 5-8
Fliege Laura L MCMU 5
Hill Linda K
Kochman Elizabeth BS 4
McMahon Barbara MA 2
Powell Tricia J BA 2
Rodgers Susan 4
Sausaman Pamela A BA 5-8
Sochowski Mark D BA 5-8
Voigtmann Brenda 5-8

**STAUNTON**-ZION PS-8
• NLSA • 1858
220 W Henry St 62088-1819
(618)635-3060 •
FAX(618)635-3994
zionstau@midwest.net
Brackman Barbara J K
Inserra Carolyn M BA 1
Miller Paul M MA
Moehle Sharilyn R MA 2
Ott Dale C MSED 5-8
Satterlee Cassie E BS 5-8
Seelbach Rachel A BS PS
Steinmann Judy 3-4

**STEELEVILLE**-ST MARK PS-8
• NLSA • 1874
504 N James St 62288-1433
(618)965-3838 •
FAX(618)965-3060
stmarks@egyptian.net
**Baginski John C BED**
Gramenz Carolyn S BSED PS
Gramenz Karen M BA 1
Gremmels Donna S BS 6-8
Luedders Larry A BSED 4
Mayer Carol BA 2
Mayer Helen 5
Salger Erna M PS
Schwarz Debra BA 3
Schwarz Susan L BSED K
Zobel Carol L BA 6-8
Zobel James R BSED 6-8

**STERLING**-CHRIST PS-8
• 1983
2000 18Th Ave 61081-1600
(815)625-3800 •
FAX(815)625-3585
**Cluver Daniel D MA**
Behmlander Debra 3-4
Block Helen O K
Cluver Ellen S MA 5-6
Miatke Linda 7-8
Peterson Cherie K
Ringler Janice PS
Schave Karin L 1
Vallier Patricia 3
kregar Debra 2-3

**STEWARDSON**-TRINITY PS-8
• 1868
318 E S First PO Box 307 62463-0307
(217)682-3881 •
FAX(217)682-3881
Jack Diane BS PS
Jesgarz Sherri L BSED K
Kirby Kathryn J BSED 1-3
Rueber Bruce E MA 4-8

**STREAMWOOD**-GRACE PS-K
• NLSA • 1989
780 S Bartlett Rd 60107-1312
(630)289-9658 •
FAX(630)289-7104
Beilich Suzanne PS
Kuhnlohe Charlene AA PS
Schroeder Linda L BSED K

**STREATOR**-HOLY TRINITY PS
• 1982
101 Trinity Dr 61364-3119
(815)672-2393
Cassady Mary I BA PS
Sass Gloria J PS

**TAYLORVILLE**-TRINITY PS
• 1974
1010 N Webster St 62568-1277
(217)824-8148
Norris Cindy PS
Sams Anna M PS

**TINLEY PARK**-TRINITY PS-8
• NLSA • 1859
6850 159Th St 60477-1629
(708)532-3529 •
FAX(708)532-0799
trinityschool@psn.net
**Stec Steven J MA**
Anderson Barbara A BS 4
Boor John M K
Claus Richard J MA 6-8
Cook June M BA 4-5
Elder Gloria A 6-8
Gurgel Tiffany BA 6-8
Hull Renee N K-8
Leverenz Joyce M BS 2
Lisius Carl H MA 4-8
Matyus Carol J 6-8
Moses Nancy PS
Najewski Amy N 5
Niemeier Gay L BS 1
Pertchi Laurie B 1
Richards Donna L BSED K
Schellhorn Lisa 2-3
Schmeckpeper Stacey E BA 6-8

**TROY**-ST PAUL PS-8
• 1864
112 N Border St 62294-1147
(618)667-6314
**Irwin David W MA 7-8**
Aebel Carol A 1-8
Doyle Ida R BED 5-6
Klueter Ada M MA PS
Price Lora 1-2
Reed Karen 1-8
Schultz Norbert 1-8
Wittmann Roger A BA 3-4

**URBANA**-WEE DISCIPLES-TRINITY PS
• 1997
701 East Florida Ave 61801-5950
(217)356-8317 •
FAX(217)367-8928
weedisciples@prairienet.org
Isaac-Rossow Kerry A
Rodriguez Jo A AAS

**VILLA PARK**-TRINITY PS
• 1968
300 S Ardmore Ave 60181-2603
(630)833-1080 •
FAX(630)834-5232
Strock Mary PS
Thon Mary L MA PS

**WASHINGTON**-OUR SAVIOR PS
• 1988
1209 Kingsbury Rd 61571-1212
(309)444-4030
Iverson Jody PS

**WATERLOO**-IMMANUEL PS
• 1979
110 Hoener Ave 62298-1429
(618)939-7010
Troup Cindy BA

**WATSEKA**-CALVARY PS
• 1984
120 E Hickory St 60970-1339
(815)432-4137
Harwood Denise V PS
Koester Diane BS PS

**WAUKEGAN**-REDEEMER PS
• 1994
620 W Grove Ave 60085-1847
(847)336-4892 •
FAX(847)336-4892
NO REPORT

**WEST CHICAGO**--TRINITY PS-1
• 1982
331 George St 60185-3118
(708)231-5849 •
FAX(708)231-6926
NO REPORT
**WHEATON**-ST JOHN PS-8
• NLSA • 1956
125 E Seminary Ave 60187-5308
(630)668-0701 •
FAX(630)871-9931
webservant@stjohnwheaton.org
NO REPORT
**WOOD DALE**-CALVARYS LAMBS PS
107 N Wood Dale PO Box 862
60191
(630)766-3092 •
FAX(630)766-8125
**Dailey Judith PS**
Mc Cauley Linda PS
**WOOD RIVER**-ST PAUL PS
• 1974
1327 Vaughn Rd 62095-1890
(618)259-0055
Plummer Tammy L AA
Searles Peggy Ann PS
**WOODSTOCK**-ST JOHN PS
• 1982
401 Saint Johns Rd 60098-2726
(815)338-5185 •
FAX(815)338-9377
stjohnws@stans.net
Fuchs Karen PS
Hansen Deborah PS
Huff Renee PS
Learman Chris PS
Morris Tina PS
**WOODWORTH**-ST PAUL PS-8
• NLSA • 1872
108 W Woodworth 60953
(815)889-4209 •
FAX(815)889-4364
stpauls@colint.com
Borgers Karen J BA 3-4
Lebeck Sandra I BS K
Ristow Samuel D 7-8
Schleef Shirley A BS 5-6
Schuldt Lisa M PS
Stuckwisch Sandra L BA 1-2
Timm Lowell H MA
**WORDEN**-TRINITY PS
• 1983
219 W Mcgaughey St PO Box 296
62097-0296
(618)459-3621
NO REPORT
**YORKVILLE**-CROSS PS-8
• NLSA • 1881
8535 State Route 47 60560-9751
(630)553-7861 •
FAX(630)553-2580
lopezsw@juno.com
Chandler Tami L 1
Floetke Kamela S BA 5-8
Hahn Jeffrey S BA 5-8
Lee Nancy A BA 1
Lopez Susan W BA 1-2
Miller Karen L K
Morkert Christopher A BA 5-8
Pinnow Barbara J MA 3
Raavel Kay PS
Randall Myrla 2
Schumm Karen R MSED 5-8
Wilkie Alicia E BA 4

## INDIANA

**AURORA**-ST JOHN PS-8
• 1864
222 Mechanic St 47001-1322
(812)926-2656
Schallhorn Mark B MED
Schallhorn Vicki L BA 1-2
**BEDFORD**--CALVARY PS
• 1979
3705 Austin Dr 47421-9291
(812)275-5488
NO REPORT
**BLOOMINGTON**-FAITH PS
• 1995
2200 S High St 47401-4313
(812)334-2209 •
FAX(812)332-2206
JMBertermann@compuserve.com
Bertermann Joan G PS
Erwin Mendy PS
Gleason Jenny PS
Hanek Linda PS
Hildreth Sherry PS
Nolting Dawn PS
Papke Emily PS
Waggoner Mary BS PS
**BREMEN**-ST PAUL PS-8
• NLSA • 1846
605 S Center St 46506-1701
(219)546-2790 •
FAX(219)546-3242
spls@skyenet.net
**Russell James R MA 6-8**
Blakley Sylvia A PS
Bradley Donnell S BA 2-8
Eichinger Kenneth R MS 4-8
Hudkins Kristine A PS
Leeper Karmen K BA 1-8
Middaugh Barbara A MS K-8
Ryan Paula MS PS-5
Thornton Kelly PS
**BROWNSBURG**-CHRIST PS
• 1989
701 E Tilden Dr 46112-1718
(317)852-3343
NO REPORT
**BROWNSTOWN**- CENTRAL 1-8
• RSO • 1966
415 N Elm St 47220-1309
(812)358-2512 •
FAX(812)358-9905
lcs@hsonline.net
**Pottschmidt Robert L BA 5-8**
Blackwell Carol A MA 1
Jones Carolyn 1
Lucas Julia 4
Mundt Sarah L BSED 5-8
Peters Phil L MS 3
Thompson Adrienne 5-8
Warren Julie 5-8
Wischmeier Wanda L BS 2
ST PETER PS
• 1985
403 W Bridge St 47220-1303
(812)358-2539 •
FAX(812)358-2524
lcs@hsonline.net
Osterman Sharon L MED PS
**CARMEL**-KIDS OF THE KINGDOM-CARMEL PS-K
• 1985
4850 E 131st St 46033-9311
(317)814-4262 •
FAX(317)814-4260
skeller@clearcall.net
**Keller Sandra L BED PS**
Davis Mary R BSED K
Estrada Mary PS
Hodges Sandra PS
Jacobson Nancy PS
Knollman Diane PS
Moore Brenda PS
Ralls Karla PS
Stephens Debra PS
Tremblay Donna PS-K
**COLUMBUS**-FAITH PS
• 1981
6000 W State Road 46
47201-4691
(812)342-3587 •
FAX(812)342-7267
faithlc@hsonline.net
Clark Karen PS
Foust Melinda PS
Shaw Patricia PS
GRACE PS
• 1994
3201 Central Ave 47203-2253
(812)372-4859 •
FAX(812)372-4862
NO REPORT
ST PAUL PS
• 1981
2555 S 300 E 47201
(812)376-6504
Kruger Karen M BS PS
Shaffer May E BSN
ST PETER K-8
• NLSA • 1863
719 5th St 47201-6306
(812)372-5266 •
FAX(812)372-7556
dflorine@stpeters-columbus.org
**Florine David A MSED**
**Sandfort Melvin T MEAD 3**
Arnold Robin K-8
Baack Joleen G MS 1
Baack Larry D MPE 4
Banks Laura L BA 3
Bodart Michael
Burr Cathy B MMU K-5
Buss Mark A MA 4-5
Carothers Cheryl L BA 4
Davidsmeyer Diann R MS 3
Dietrich Julie L BA 2
Eisenbraun Kathryn A BS 2
Flohr Shirley A MED 7-8
Florine Sharon BA 1-3
Howard Kay H BA 1
Kruger Richard J BS 5
Malinsky Teresa 2
Morton Rebecca BA 1
Rust Anna M MA 7-8
Sabotin Janice R MA K
Sollenberger James W MSED 6
Sollenerger Karen A MSED 7-8
Tews Larry N MED 5
Wischmeier Henry A MA 7-8
Witte Lisa R BA 6
WHITE CREEK-ST JOHN K-8
• 1840
16270 S 300 W 47201
(812)342-6832 •
FAX(812)342-6832
**Buss Janice L MED 7-8**
Barnett Michelle D K
Clow Kay J MS 1-2
Enzinger Kimberly J BS 3-4
Tower Cathy 5-6
**CROWN POINT**-TRINITY PS-8
• 1868
250 S Indiana Ave 46307-4174
(219)663-1586 •
FAX(219)663-9606
trinluth@mail.icongrp.com
**Hubacek Carol L MS**
Bramstadt Lois A MA 5-8
Chelap Terry L BSED K
Dean Brenda K BED 3
Esala Carole K
Grotelueschen Krista K-8
Ickstadt Kathleen L MMU 4
Ketcher Karol R 2
Lehman Arron L BS 6-8
Miller Christine E BA 6-8
Pavlovick Laura PS
Rosenwinkel Sandra L MALS PS
Sauerman Laura J BS 6-8
Wartick Ruth V BSED 1
**DARMSTADT**-TRINITY PS-8
• 1853
1403 W Boonville New Harmony R
47725-9511
(812)867-5279 •
FAX(812)867-5333
tls@dynasty.net
**Wrege Thomas W MSED 7-8**
Beermann Sandra 1
Brown Chelsea 7-8
Dardeen Phyllis J MS K
Mearling Marilynn BA 3-4
Mearling Stephen R MED
Rothrock Debbie PS
Schaedig Kelli R BA 2
Swallow Donna 3
Williams Sara
**DEMOTTE**-FAITH PS
• 1994
1700 S Halleck PO Box 396
46310-0396
(219)987-3430
NO REPORT
**DECATUR**-ST PETER-IMMANUEL K-8
• 1969
3845 E 1100 N 46733
(219)623-6115 •
FAX(219)623-3865
sleepingzeke@decaturnet.com
**Martin Keith D MA 7-8**
Bauermeister Lori A BS 5-6
Blomenberg Saundra 1-2
Jeffrey Connie S MA 3-4
Niemeyer Debra L K
WYNEKEN MEMORIAL PS-8
• RSO • 1969
11565 N US Highway 27
46733-9799
(219)639-6177 •
FAX(219)639-3050
wynekenlutheran@juno.com
**Wass Dean W MS 6**
Drier Marvin D BA 7
Fuhrmann Rae L MA PS
Hess Anne L MS PS
Klenke Rebecca A BA 1-2
Martin Michelle M BSED 3
May Sarah E BS
Nichols Mary L BS 5
Norder Emily 2
Schieferstein Donna J BS 1
Schwantz Richard G Jr. BA 5
Schwantz Yvonne M 8
Werling Heidi R 4
ZION PS-8
• 1955
1022 W Monroe St 46733-1529
(219)728-9995
**Dierks David J MA**
Aumann Evelyn K
Bittner Carol S MS 1-2
Burman Jason 7-8
Cobb Suzette 5-6
Creek Rebecca E MSED PS
Risch Carl A BSED 3-4
**DILLSBORO**-ST JOHN PS
• 1983
7301 State Route 62 47018-9139
(812)667-6975 •
FAX(812)432-5053
johlmans@seidata.com
Olhmansiek Jane
**EAST CHICAGO**-ST PAUL PS
• 1985
2001 Franklin St 46312-3124
(219)397-8933
NO REPORT
**EDWARDSVILLE**-SHEPHERD HILLS PS
• 1999
5231 SR 62 47122-9277
(812)923-2101 •
FAX(812)923-8812
Jenkins@iglou.com
NO REPORT
**ELKHART**-TRINITY PS-6
• NLSA • 1874
425 Massachusetts Ave
46514-2037
(219)522-1491 •
FAX(219)389-3021
school@trinityl.org
**Font Michael A MEAD PS-6**
**Price Sandra M BSED 3**
Burnham Suzanne K
Emmack Sue
Freshour Jodi L MA 1
Schroeder Nancy L MS PS

Tomashewsky Andrew C BA 2
Tomashewsky Suzanne B BA 4
Veen Rebecca R BSED 2
**EVANSVILLE**-EVANSVILLE K-8
• RSO • NLSA • 1971
1000 W Illinois St 47710-1114
(812)424-7252 •
FAX(812)424-7340
jeschult@evansville.net
**Claus Kenneth F MA 8**
**Schultz John E MEPD**
Benford Blair A MED 7
Claus Donna M MAT K
De Hart William C BA 6
Esterline Wendy K BA 3
Grimm Carol L MS 1
Hosmon Michele M BA 4-8
Jipp Alicia M BA 5
Johann Kristin L BA 2
Raymond Teresa BMED
Schultz Ruth E BA 4
MESSIAH PS
• 1981
7700 Middle Mount Vernon Rd
47712-3025
(812)985-2278
Gatewood Judy A AAS
Mans Yvonne PS
Mewes Jill PS
Randall Toni L PS
REDEEMER PS
• 1978
1811 Lincoln Ave 47714-1505
(812)476-9991 •
FAX(812)476-4561
NO REPORT
ST PAUL PS
• 1982
100 E Michigan St 47711-5428
(812)424-4367 •
FAX(812)422-5363
Blocker Amy BS PS
Cochran Hope
Serr Alice B MA PS
Smith Lisa PS
**FISHERS**-FAMILY OF CHRIST PS-4
• 1998
11965 Allisonville Rd 46038-2315
(317)594-9157 •
FAX(317)594-9155
focl@oaktree.net
**Sombke Kristie L BS PS**
Huske Michele L BA 1
Morrison Judy E BA 2-4
Wheeler Lynda J BS PS-K
**FORT WAYNE**-ASCENSION PS-8
8811 Saint Joe Rd 46835-1037
(219)486-2226
church@fwi.com
Franke Tommy L MS 7-8
Hartley Yolonde MS PS-K
Niemoeller Marilyn MS 1-2
Vernick Linda 5-6
Wiseman Charlotte M BA 3-4
BETHLEHEM PS-8
• 1925
3705 S Anthony Blvd 46806-4329
(219)456-3587 •
FAX(219)744-3229
NO REPORT
CHRIST CHILD PS
• 1996
6600 N Clinton St 46825
(219)452-2240 •
FAX(219)452-2121
NO REPORT
CONCORDIA PS-8
• 1900
4245 Lake Ave 46815-7219
(219)426-9922 •
FAX(219)422-3415
bboyd@concordiachurch.org
**Boyd Robert C MA**
Frincke Susan J BS K
Fuhrmann Amy B BS 1
Gayer Tracy A BA 4
Gieschen Leann G MA 2
Grim Stephen M 5
Hardy Dana K-8
Hart Judy E MS 2
Henneman Nancy S MA K
Hoffschneider Joel T BA 6-7
Howard Jean M BA 3
Jordan Jodi M PS
Koschmann Mark E MED 7-8
Meraz Barbara J PS
Meyers Heidi MA 5
Miller Deborah L BED 6-8
Neuman Lorraine A MSED PS-K
Niehus Christina PS-8
Nixon Joann M 3
Owen Angela J BA PS-8
Reddemann Richard W MAT 4
Sipes Susan K MS PS-8
Williamson Christine A BA 1
EMMANUEL PS
• 1977
917 W Jefferson Blvd 46802-4007
(219)423-1369 •
FAX(219)426-6147
NO REPORT
EMMANUEL-ST MICHAEL K-8
• 1867
1123 Union St 46802-4049
(219)422-6712 •
FAX(219)422-3553
**Daenzer Charles G MS 8**
Ackmann Jennifer E BS 1
Birkey Sally BSED K-6
Brumbaugh Michelle M 5-6
Cole Carolyn M MS 7-8
Daenzer Mary E MS K
Doenges Jane M 5
Etzler Bruce A 6
Hobby Jennifer L MS 2
Hockemeyer Phyllis A MS 3
Jung Charlene E MS 4
Labrash Jewell 1-2
Launer Pamela BED 2
Murphy Christopher L MS 8
Pflughaupt Doris E MA K
Sassmannshausen Lynn J MA 7
Wudy Jim R MA 1-8
EMMAUS PS-8
• 1901
2320 Broadway 46807-1104
(219)456-4573 •
FAX(219)745-0104
inreking@aol.com
**King Ross E MA**
Carney Kelly J BA K-8
Coffey Jessica M BA 4-8
Mundt Allen F MS 7-8
Mundt Janis M MS K
Schaffer Jennifer M MA 1-2
Schaffer Joel P BA 2-6
Schmidt William G MSED 3-4
Snyder Susan J BA PS
HOLY CROSS K-8
• NLSA • 1946
3425 Crescent Ave 46805-1505
(219)483-3173 •
FAX(219)471-6141
holycross@fwi.org
**Mc Nally Norman E**
Albertin Daniel A MS 6
Albertin Karen E MS 4
Bauman Michelle A BS 6-8
Bolinger Adrienne S MA 6-8
Bottomley Peter R 4-8
Diehm Carole J MS 3
Fair Diana K MA 4
Fluegge Kathleen M MA 7
Hitzeman Jacqueline A BA 3
Huebner-Rowell Mary K-8
Knudten Jacqueline E MS 1
Koehlinger Mark R BS K-8
Koehlinger Michelle E BED K-2
La Croix Susan M BA K-5
Luepke James E MED 5
Mueller Barbara M MA K
Norris Barbara J 6-8
Renken Randolph G MS 5
Rodenbeck Edith F MSED 1
Schroeder Kevin P MA K-8
Schroeder Rebecca A MS 2
Stork Annetta L MED 7-8
Swartz Jacob J 6-8
Widenhofer Mary E MS 2
LUTH ASSOC ELEM ED
• 1968
1145 Barr St 46802-3135
(219)422-9662 •
FAX(219)423-1514
Dietrich Clifford A EDS
Kurtz Diane A
Orban Ervin MMU
Phillips Todd
MOUNT CALVARY PS
• 1990
1819 Reservation Dr 46819
(219)747-4121 •
FAX(219)747-2564
Conrad Lori L PS
Doepner Sue Ann E BA
Koening Lynn R BAED PS
PEACE PS
4900 Fairfield Ave 46807-3215
(219)744-3869
NO REPORT
ST MICHAEL PS
• 1970
2131 Getz Rd 46804-1625
(219)432-2033
Brumbaugh Michelle M PS
ST PAUL K-8
• NLSA • 1837
1125 Barr St 46802-3107
(219)424-0049 •
FAX(219)969-2052
bearpaw1@gte.net
**Marinko Paul B MED**
Fritz Ann R BA 6
German Sue 4
Hathaway Mary BSED 1
Higgins Jenny BA 3
Koelper Lawrence R MA 7
Marth Laura A BA 2
Shiley Jonathan P BA 5
Utecht Joanna P BS 8
Weiss Ernestine K
ST PETER K-8
• 1855
7810 Maysville Rd 46815-6682
(219)749-5811 •
FAX(219)749-9967
wildcats@stpetersfw.org
**Bultemeyer Daniel P BA**
Frick Karl G MED 5
Gaff Connie J MS 3
Gevers Margery D MA 1
Henkes Patricia 8
Hieber Janice M MS 7
Ramsey Suzanne K BA K
Rodenbeck Jill B MED 6
Springer James A MA 4
Westrem John M MS 2
Westrem Joyce E MA
SUBURBAN BETHLEHEM PS-8
• 1882
6318 W California Rd 46818-9737
(219)483-9371 •
FAX(219)483-9371
sbls-joyce@juno.com
**Grewe Ralph A MED**
Dittmer Adele BS 3
Easterday Joyce E BSED 8
Enterline Kathy K K
Fox Sharon MED 1
Geller Amy S BA 5-8
Gottschalk Dan 5-8
Hemingway Jolene PS-8
Kaeding Shirley PS
Loppnow Amy S 2
Mews Gary R BA PS-8
Moran Kelli 4
Zelt Mary PS
TRINITY PS
• 1993
7819 Decatur Rd 46816-2604
(219)447-2411 •
FAX(219)447-0962
trinity1853@juno.com
Venderley Cindy A PS
TRINITY PS-6
• 1893
1636 Saint Marys Ave 46808-3271
(219)426-4292 •
FAX(219)969-4005
**Wentland Kenneth H MS 2**
Grannis Glenna G MSED 3-4
Hines Mary M MED K
Meyer Sandy PS
Thomas Jeff 5-6
Wentland Katherine M MS 1
UNITY K-8
• 1973
5401 S Calhoun St 46807-3316
(219)744-0459 •
FAX(219)745-1800
brune1254@aol.com
Brewer Pamela A BA K
Brune Pamela J BA K
Brune Richard F MA
Doepner Mark D MS 8
Koch Gene E MA 7
Mittelstaedt Susan A MED 4
Nehrenz Sheila K BA 1
Osbun Nancy 6
Pixley Joyce M MSED 3
Stelzer Kenneth R MED 5
Trinklein Kathryn B MS 2
ZION ACADEMY PS-8
• 1882
2313 Hanna St 46803-2477
(219)745-2979
NO REPORT
**FREMONT**-PEACE PS
• 1992
355 E State Road 120 46737-9743
(219)495-6162 •
FAX(219)495-5076
Conklin Denille J PS
Everly Cindy A PS
Simons Aimee D
**GARRETT**-ZION PS
• 1979
1349 S Randolph St 46738-1970
(219)357-4658
zelc@juno.com
Faulkner Julie K PS
**GREENCASTLE**-PEACE PS-K
• 1984
218 S Bloomington St 46135-1733
(765)653-6995 •
FAX(765)653-6995
NO REPORT
**GREENFIELD**-FAITH PS
• 1992
200 W Mckenzie Rd 46140-1018
(317)462-4609 •
FAX(317)467-1716
Haeck Victoria L MA PS
**GREENWOOD**-CONCORDIA PS
• 1979
305 N Howard Rd 46142-3836
(317)881-4477 •
FAX(317)881-4498
concordia@concordia-lcms.org
Boesenberg Cynthia MA PS
Riemer Jo A PS
**HAMMOND**-TRINITY PS
• 1967
7227 Hohman Ave 46324-1817
(219)932-4660
NO REPORT
**HOBART**-TRINITY PS-8
• 1880
891 S Linda St 46342-5239
(219)942-3147 •
FAX(219)942-6637
**Schroeder Arnold R MED 1-2**
Arndt Sharon L BA PS
Jelneck Ruth A MMU 4

Tietjen Betty B BS 3
Tietjen Leroy H BS 5-6
Toth Cynthia L BA 4
**HUNTERTOWN-**OUR HOPE PS
• 1998
1826 Trinity Dr 46748
(219)637-4673 •
FAX(219)637-4673
**Boyd Rebecca PS**
Houser Karen PS
**HUNTINGTON-**ST PETER PS-5
• 1849
605 Polk St 46750-1932
(219)356-6528
**Eddie Phyllis J 2-3**
Carroll Beverley J 1
Kanning Gwen H BA K
Riggs Jennifer L 4-5
Stockman Cathy PS
**INDIANAPOLIS-**CALVARY PS-8
• 1950
6111 Shelby St 46227-4879
(317)783-2305 •
FAX(317)783-7096
jarichert@hotmail.com
**Richert James A MED**
Beringer Christine A BA 6-8
Blazek Rosalyn J MS 1
Bock Patricia L MA 6-8
Brandt Gilbert H MA 4
Dillard Gretchen K
Galyean Darlene PS-8
Graves Angela 3
Haak Carol L BSED 6-8
Hinchmann Ann 2
Kuhlmann Trisha PS
Moore Kimberly A BSED K
Nennig Melissa 3
Prange Sarah MA 4
Richert Susan M BA 1
Schultz Dawn M BED 6-8
Smith Donna A BA 6-8
Wilson Christine 5
EMMAUS PS-8
• 1904
1224 Laurel St 46203-1908
(317)632-1486 •
FAX(317)632-2620
emmaus@inct.net
Andrews Melinda 1-8
Broughton Kristi K-8
Brutcher June E MS 1
Duncan Sandra J BA 2
Fritz Beverly A BED 5-8
Groth Robert W MA 3-8
Smith Jennifer PS-3
Thoele Carla 1-8
Voge Jean L MSED 4
Wentland James L MSED 5-8
HOLY CROSS PS-K
• 1991
8115 Oaklandon Rd 46236-8578
(317)826-1234 •
FAX(317)826-0622
Block Marajean A BA PS
Edsall Kelly J PS
MESSIAH PS
• 1988
6100 N Raceway Rd 46234
(317)858-3733 • FAX(317)
858-3735
Amato Michelle PS
Williams Lisa PS
OUR SAVIOR 6
• 1999
261 W 25th St 46208
(317)925-1721 •
FAX(317)925-3734
darrylfrancine@worldnet.aft.net
NO REPORT
OUR SHEPHERD PS-8
• NLSA • 1982
9101 W 10th St 46234-2006
(317)271-9100 •
FAX(317)271-3084
jimandellen@hotmail.com
**Kluender Selma BS 2**
**Landskroener James A MED 4**
Brauer Sheila K BSED 3
Cronauer Shirley J BS K
Landskroener Ellen A MA 4
Martin Margo M BA 7-8
Simmons Lynnette D MS 1
Von Stohe Patricia 5-6
Woolsey Judith A PS
ST JOHN PS-8
• NLSA • 1852
6630 Southeastern Ave
46203-5834
(317)352-9196 •
FAX(317)352-9196
stjohnindy@iquest.net
**Kerr Homer U MED**
Burger Ronald G MSED 6
Groteluesschen Lesley A MS 3
Herre Norma E MS 8
Johnson Pamela D MA 4
Lehenbauer Pauline E BSED PS
McCartney Kristen R BS 5
Pride Sandra K MSED 1
Van Pelt Carla N MS 2
Willig Cheryl L BA K
Zimmer Mark A MS 7
ST PAUL SCHOOL PS-K
• 1990
3932 Mi Casa Ave 46237-3213
(317)787-4464 •
FAX(317)787-4464
**Larimore Beth A BA PS**
Johnson Carol A K
Nowlin Michele PS
Shadday Sherry PS
TRINITY PS-8
• 1872
8540 E 16th St 46219-2503
(317)897-0243 •
FAX(317)897-5277
principal@trinityindy.org
NO REPORT
**KENDALLVILLE-**ST JOHN PS-8
• 1981
301 S Oak St 46755-1758
(219)347-2444 •
FAX(219)347-1770
stjohn@noble.cioe.com
Albertin Paul L MA 6
Atz Linda S BS 1
Buuck Darlene L BA K
Buuck Paul A BA 3
Christian Barbara A BSED 2
Hunter Janet M MED PS
Leaman Wanda MED 7
Scheiber Vernie W MED
Schoonover Diane L MS 4
Schroeder Margaret A BS 5
Zinnel Jonathan P MS 8
**KNOX-**LITTLE LAMBS PS
• 1985
1600 S Heaton St 46534-2318
(219)772-4186
NO REPORT
**KOKOMO-**REDEEMER PS-6
• NLSA • 1984
705 E Southway Blvd 46902-4384
(765)864-6466 •
FAX(765)864-6468
rlschool@netusa1.net
**Hanebutt Richard C EDS**
Allison Susan P BS 5
Beale Naomi J BED PS
Dunkin Suzanne M BED 3
Gonzalez Jane A MA 1
Grecu Debra Kay BSED 2
Hanebutt Kathleen L MS 2-3
Johnson Susan D BSED K
Ponder Elaine J MA 4
Tucker Katherine L MED 6
Wessel Beth M PS
**LA PORTE-**ST JOHN PS-8
• NLSA • 1857
111 Kingsbury Ave 46350-5299
(219)362-6692 •
FAX(219)362-2237
sjls@juno.com
**Bremer Melinda K BA**
Brinckman Lori PS
Eigenmann Karla S 2
Foglesong Sally L 2
Jones Candace L PS
Krider Lois 3
Light Rio E PS
Martinsen Janis K 4
Olse Sally A PS
Parry Stephen E MA 7
Radke Ruth A MA 6
Stelter Julie A BA 8
Will Marlene G MED 1
Wippich David D MED 5
**LAFAYETTE-**ST JAMES PS-8
• 1850
615 N 8th St 47901-1008
(765)742-6464 •
FAX(765)742-4642
billk@stjameslaf.org
**Knea William E MA**
Dietel Joann H BA 2
Dombkowski Amy M BS 5
Groth Paul W BA 6-8
Holladay Melody 2
Huth Carol A
Knea Katherine E BA 3
Krause Brenda K BS PS
May Judy A MED 4
Roberts Melissa 1
Roland Lydia M BA 1
Strakis Randall O MSED 6-8
Trautmann Martha 3-8
Truelsen Jeanie M BA K
Wells Lyndsi 1-6
Wiens Ivy 3-8
**LANESVILLE-**ST JOHN PS-8
• 1861
1507 Saint Johns Church Rd NE
47136-8568
(812)952-2737
rreisenb@venus.net
**Reisenbichler Robert D MA**
Erber Phyllis 2
Mc Kim Shirley 5-8
Oberdieck Brian BA 3-4
Reisenbichler Audrey A MS 1
Robinson Teresa A MA PS-K
Sutton Karie E BA 5-6
**LAWRENCEBURG-**BETHLEHEM PS
• 1990
495 Ludlow St 47025-1532
(812)537-5243
Oelker Tonja PS
Robin Lewis A
Sullivan Shirley PS
**LOWELL-**TRINITY PS
PO Box 236 46356
(219)696-9338 •
FAX(219)696-0447
NO REPORT
**MARION-**GOOD SHEPHERD-ST
JAMES PS
• 1982
1206 N Miller Ave 46952-1535
(765)662-3092 •
FAX(765)662-9197
NO REPORT
**MARTINSVILLE-**PRINCE OF
PEACE PS-2
• 1995
3496 E Morgan St 46151-1540
(317)342-2004
NO REPORT
**MICHIGAN CITY-**LITTLE
LAMBS-IMMANUEL PS
• 1997
1237 E Coolspring Ave 46360
(219)879-9508 •
FAX(219)872-4419
NO REPORT
**MONROEVILLE-**ST JOHN PS-8
• NLSA • 1849
12912 Franke Rd 46773-9559
(219)639-0123 •
FAX(219)639-7383
flatrockls@juno.com
**Meyer Peter J MED**
Davis Christine S BA 1
Embree Karen MS PS
Lafrentz Laverne BS 2
Lafrentz Randall BSED 7
Roy Cindy M BSED 4
Snyder Frederick E BS 8
Tews Susan M MA 5
Weerts Gretchen J MA 6
**MUNSTER-**ST PAUL PS-8
• NLSA • 1886
8601 Harrison Ave 46321-2398
(219)836-6270 •
FAX(219)836-3724
stpaulls@mail.icongrp.com
**Lessner Marlene BSED PS**
**Mau John MED**
Brandt David R BS 6-8
Burkman Mary 2
Buuck Lois C BA 4
Dykman Patricia 2
Eitzen Fred K
Eschbach June MED 1
Grant Ann BS K-8
Hansen Cathi D BA 1
Hopkins Jeannette K-8
Hopkins Tammy A BA K-8
Innes Renee PS
Lang Angela BSED 3
Lewandowski Heather J BA PS
O Donnell Sue MED K-8
Schmidt Deborah L BSED K
Schriner Carol A BA 3
Witt Nina L MS 6-8
Zimmer Lois M MS 5-8
Zimmer Martin K MS 6-8
**NEW ALBANY-**GRACE PS-K
• 1982
1787 Klerner Ln 47150-1986
(812)941-1912
graceluthschool@juno.com
**Weathers Georgianne V PS**
Hinz Carol L PS
Knudtson Jean R BSED K
Libs Tara N PS
Lyon Melissa A PS
**NEW HAVEN-**CENTRAL K-8
• RSO • 1952
1400 Elm St 46774-1740
(219)493-2502 •
FAX(219)493-2503
**Schendel John E MED K-8**
Aumick James T MS 3
Best Helen M BS 1-8
Castens Christine M BA 1
Hackett Darlene 6-7
Hayward Janet K BSED 4
Herman Carol S MS 2
Herman Sandra K MA 6-8
James Patricia R MS K
Jones Nancy M MS 5
Koehlinger Suzanne R 1-8
Kremer James G MA 6-8
Moellering Thomas P BSED 6-8
O Dea Elaine J BA 3
Schendel Elisa R MED 1
Schmidt Deborah J BA 6-8
Werth Gerald J MED 4
Wichman Donald L MED 6-8
Zielinski Sara 5
**NEW PALESTINE-**ZION PS-8
• 1863
6513 W 300 S 46163
(317)861-4210 •
FAX(317)861-8153
zionluth@inct.net
**Krupski James F MSED**
Baughman Kristina L BA 4-6
Boerger Karen M BS 1
Dickmander Julie M PS
Edsall Kelly J PS

Gatzke Laura A BA 4
Grotelueschen Daniel R BS 5-8
Knippenberg Kimberly M BA K
Sass Susan C 3
Schulenburg Linda S MA 2-6
Simmer Ehren W BS 5-8
**NEW SALISBURY**-JESUS LITTLE LAMBS-EPIPHANY PS
• 1993
8600 Highway 135 NE 47161-8601
(812)347-2534
NO REPORT
**NOBLESVILLE**-CHRIST PS
• 1980
10055 E 186th St 46060-1659
(317)773-3669 •
FAX(317)773-7773
Gendron Janice BS PS
Ginebaugh Amy PS
Lasley Marie MA PS
Misko Darlene PS
**NORTH JUDSON**-ST PETER PS-8
• NLSA • 1880
810 W Talmer Ave 46366-1348
(219)896-5933 •
FAX(219)896-2082
rreimers@njsp.k12.in.us
Boisvert Paula R 5-6
Frusti Cassandra K
Frusti Philip J BA 7-8
Ransom Rochelle PS
Reimers Rhonda K MA 1
Skibbe Annette K MBA 1-2
Sutton Shirley A MS 3-4
Torsell Mary K
**OSSIAN**-NEW HOPE PS
• 1981
8824 N State Rd 1 PO Box 341
46777-0341
(219)622-7954
NO REPORT
**PERU**-ST JOHN PS-8
• 1860
181 W Main St 46970-2049
(765)473-6659 •
FAX(765)473-6659
Esterline Wendy K BA 2
**PLYMOUTH**-CALVARY PS
• 1988
1314 N Michigan St 46563-1118
(219)936-2903
Flick Melinda K PS
Tanner M J PS
**RENSSELAER**-ST LUKE PS
• 1978
704 E Grace St 47978-3299
(219)866-7681
**Feagans Monica PS**
**REYNOLDS**-ST JAMES PS
• 1996
Hwy 24 & 421 PO Box 327 47980
(219)984-5994
NO REPORT
**SCHERERVILLE**-PEACE PS
• 1975
144 W Parkway Dr 46375-2100
(219)322-5490
NO REPORT
**SEYMOUR**-IMMANUEL 1-8
• 1874
520 S Chestnut St 47274-3044
(812)522-1301 •
FAX(812)523-2186
Perr Orville R Jr. BA 4
ST JOHN K-8
• 1840
1058 S County Road 460 E
47274-9572
(812)523-3131 •
FAX(812)523-3131
Kern Edward A MA 3-4
Rohr Sharon K 1-2
Schumpe James E BS 6-8
Wright Stacy R BA K
ZION PS-K
• 1974
1501 Gaiser Dr 47274-3627
(812)522-5911 •
FAX(812)523-7526
Hill Lori PS
Keinath Janeen K
Lipka Nancy J BS K
Schneider Maggie PS
Southerland Ruth PS
**SOUTH BEND**-RESURRECTION ACADEMY PS-K
• RSO • 1998
St Paul Lutheran Church 51490
Laurel Rd 46637 PO Box 2318
46680
(219)257-0506
luthschool@aol.com
**Fussell Jill**
Lehmann Marcia PS
Moore Mary Ann PS
Polizzotto Michele K
**TERRE HAUTE**-IMMANUEL PS
• 1975
645 Poplar St 47807-4203
(812)232-4972 •
FAX(812)234-3935
Seger Doris J PS
**TIPTON**-EMANUEL PS
• 1976
1385 S Main St PO Box F
46072-8460
(765)675-4090 •
FAX(765)675-4200
emanuel@tiptontel.com
Calvin Julie PS
Gremel Kurt H MED
Hayes Penelope S PS
**TOCSIN**-BETHLEHEM K-8
• 1897
7545 N 650 E 46777-9632
(219)597-7366
NO REPORT
**VALPARAISO**-IMMANUEL PS-8
• 1950
1700 Monticello Park Dr
46383-3847
(219)462-8207 •
FAX(219)531-2238
alb@immanuel.pvt.k12.in.us
**Bremer Alvin L MSED 6-8**
**Hord Sue A MA PS**
Becker Timothy J BA 5-8
Bickel Karen E MED 1
Boetel Robert C MA 1-8
Bowker Joanne M BS PS
Cunningham Sara A BSED 4
Daiber Dorothy A MA 3
Eagan Delores J 5-8
George Connie M MMU 2
Hill Mary S K-8
Ickstadt William M MBA 1-8
Jankowske Lynn R BA 5
Lundgren Linda J MSED K
Miller Eunice A MED 5-8
Miller Judith L MA 3-4
Mues Candy-Lu B BAED PS
Rahmel Melanie S 1
Riffel Kathleen M MSED 2
Stritof Deanna M BA 6-7
**VINCENNES**-LUTHERAN COMMUNITY K-8
• 1997
707 N 8th St 47591
(812)882-4188 •
FAX(812)882-4188
coomerdl@fld.aal.org
Booher Susan K 1
Holzmeyer Julie E K
Jones Cindy J 2-3
Madison Michelle 6-7
Taylor Cheryl A BA 4-5
**WARSAW**-REDEEMER PS-6
• NLSA • 1983
1692 West Lake St 46580-3602
(219)267-2056 •
FAX(219)267-5242
redeemer@compuserve.com
Coxey Wendy C BA 5-6
Doyle Faith J BA 3-4
Frush Shawn M BA PS
Rudy Sally L BSED 1-2
Schlegel Orvin L MSED
Tjernagel Ellen M K
**WOODBURN**-WOODBURN PS-8
• RSO • 1954
4502 N State Rd 101 PO Box 159
46797-0159
(219)632-5493 •
FAX(219)632-0005
wls@mail.fwi.com
**Peters Denis A MED**
Brown Helen J MS 1
Hoeppner Karen L 4
Hoffschneider Bonnie J BA 2
Maxson Andrew T 6-8
Opel Susan R BA 6-8
Schroeder Ruth J BA 5
Staub Arlys R BSED PS-K
Staub Scott M MED 6-8
Steffe Sarah R BA 3
**ZIONSVILLE**-ADVENT PS
• 2000
11250 N Michigan Rd 46077
(317)873-6318 •
FAX(317)873-6369
advent@inquest.net
**Trewartha Debalyn E**
Dooms Lois J PS
Hunter Patricia L PS

## IOWA

**ADAIR**-LITTLE CHERUBS PS
• 1983
709 Adair St 50002-1121
(515)742-3737
Brahms Donna PS
Scarlett Connie R PS
**ADEL**-FAITH PS
• 1981
602 S 14Th St 50003-1947
(515)993-3848
NO REPORT
**ALGONA**-TRINITY LITTLE LAMBS PS
• 1977
520 N Garfield St 50511-1615
(515)295-3518
Coleman Marlene
**ALTA**-ST JOHN PS
• 1977
169 630Th St 51002-7447
(712)284-2542
NO REPORT
**ALTOONA**-CHILDREN OF CHRIST-CHRIST KING PS
• 1978
600 1St Ave N 50009-0537
(515)967-3349
Blanchard Colleen
Hinrichs Kelly
Mueller Greta D BA
**ANITA**-NURSERY EXPRESS PS
• 1971
401 Maple St 50020-9107 1319
Brown Ave 50020
(712)762-4106
Brahms Donna PS
Scarlett Connie R PS
**ANKENY**-ST PAUL PS
• 1979
1100 SE Sharon Dr 50021-3738
(515)964-1250
pastorofstpaul@juno.com
**Suominen Susan K BS PS**
**ARCADIA**--NOAHS ARK-ZION PS
118 Tracy Street 51430
(712)689-2441
NO REPORT
**ATLANTIC**-LITTLE LAMBS-ZION PS
• 1978
811 Oak St 50022-1740
(712)243-4421
zionluth@netins.net
Claussen Kathy PS
Mc Connell Lori PS
Williams Dianna PS
**AUDUBON**-ST JOHN PS
• 1978
815 E Division St 50025-1318
(712)563-3333
NO REPORT
**BETTENDORF**-OUR SAVIOR PS
• 1998
3775 Middle Rd 52722-2215
(319)332-5141 •
FAX(319)332-2117
oursavior@qconline.com
Bullock Jennifer R BA
**BOONE**-TRINITY PS-8
• 1872
712 12Th St 50036-2240
(515)432-6912 •
FAX(515)432-1059
**Fick Jeffrey A BA 7-8**
Koenen Genelle L BS PS-K
Moeller Janet K 3-4
Schroeder Amy I BSED 5-6
Sprengeler Cathy S BA 1-2
Trowbridge Marisa J PS-8
**BURLINGTON**-GOOD SHEPHERD-CONCORDIA PS
2901 Cliff Rd 52601-2410
(319)754-4246
Henry Mary PS
Willeford Kelly PS
**BURT**-KIDS OF THE KINGDOM -ST JOHN PS
• 1989
109 Maple St 50522 PO Box 98
50522-0098
(515)924-3344
NO REPORT
**CARROLL**-LITTLE LAMBS-ST PAUL PS
• 1992
1844 Highland Dr 51401-3573
(712)792-1221
schmidt5@pionet.net
NO REPORT
**CEDAR FALLS**-OUR REDEEMER PS
• 1992
904 Bluff St 50613-3326
(319)266-2509
NO REPORT
**CEDAR RAPIDS**-BETHANY PS
• 1982
2202 Forest Dr SE 52403-1654
(319)366-4897
Duggan Susan J PS
Thomas Diane PS
SHARE & CARE-CONCORDIA PS
• 1980
4210 Johnson Ave NW
52405-4218
(319)396-9148
Popenhagen Margie J BS PS
Zadow Linda K PS
TRINITY PS-8
• 1884
1361 7th Ave SW 52404-1831
(319)362-6952 •
FAX(319)366-1569
**Hoyer Dexter C MS**
Becker Mary BS K
Bills Debbie J PS
Boyles Kristine A BS 4
Chaplin Liesl 2
Frahm Barbara BA 6
Heinsen Barbara S BS 3
Hoyer Connie A MS 4

Kroemer Karen J BED 2
Lavrenz Ruth H BS 5
Marner Lisa M BMU K-8
Mueller Mark S BSED 8
Murken Matthew P BA 7
Nord Lois A MA K-8
Reinkoester Victoria M 1
Rowsell David H BA 5
Schroeder Judith 1-8
Schumacher JoAnn M BS 1
Wagner Robin R BS 3
Wolf Diane W MA 6
**CHARTER OAK**-NOAHS ARK PS-ST JOHN PS
• 1981
104 Birch Ave Box 73 51439 258 S First St 51439-0154
(712)678-3421
NO REPORT
**CLARINDA**-CLARINDA K-8
• RSO • NLSA • 1988
707 W Scidmore St 51632-1055
(712)542-3657 •
FAX(712)542-3657
Anderson John A 5-8
Clement Laveta M BED 3-4
Neumeyer Rosalie A BSED 1-2
Stoops Linda 5-8
Sump Merrilee A MSED
Wagoner Mary Lou 5-8
York JoAnn M BSED K
ST JOHN PS-K
• 1982
301 N 13Th St 51632-1755
(712)542-3708
stjohnluth@clarinda.hearland.net
Brown Heather D PS
Wittmuss Shirley J BS PS
York Joann M K
**CLEMONS**-CLEMONS PS-8
• 1980
302 Bevin St PO Box 120 50051-0120
(641)477-8263 •
FAX(641)477-8262
CLSchool@netins.net
Berrey Bonnie L K-1
Condon Connie C BS 5-6
Hennis Merikay J BA 2-8
Maddick Melanie K BA 2-4
Pfantz Lynne M BS PS
Riese Lisa C BAED 7-8
**CLINTON**-ST JOHN PS
• 1971
416 Main Ave 52732-1938
(319)242-5588
Martinez Joyce L BA PS
**COUNCIL BLUFFS**-TIMOTHY PS
• 1973
3112 W Broadway 51501-3310
(712)323-0693 •
FAX(712)323-7582
timothylc@juno.com
Mc Connell Nancy E BSED PS
TRINITY INTERPARISH K-5
• RSO • 1996
1500 N 16th St 51501
(712)322-3294 •
FAX(712)328-3338
**Heinemann Doreen L MED**
Hanusa Lois M MED K-2
Kurtz Amy L 3-5
**CRESTON**-TRINITY PS
• 1986
800 N Sumner Ave 50801-1349
(515)782-5095
dmcknig@creston.heartland.net
NO REPORT
**DAVENPORT**-IMMANUEL PS
• 1995
3834 Rockingham Rd 52802-2503
(319)324-6431
Yaudas Kathy K PS
NOAHS ARK-HOLY CROSS PS
• 1997
1705 E Locust St 52803-3205
(319)322-2654
NO REPORT
RISEN CHRIST PS
• 1997
6021 Northwest Blvd 52806-1848
(319)386-1738 •
FAX(319)386-8969
lamcf8@aol.com
NO REPORT
TRINITY PS-8
• NLSA • 1870
1122 W Central Park Ave 52804-1805
(319)322-5224 •
FAX(319)324-1153
Krenz Stacie L BA 3
Lehenbauer Becky A BS 6
**DENISON**-OUR SAVIOR PS
• 1997
500 N 24th St 51442
(712)263-4405
NO REPORT
ZION PS-8
• 1884
1004 1St Ave S 51442-2615
(712)263-4766 •
FAX(712)263-6010
zionls@frontiernet.net
Fink Debra K AA PS
Flikkema Andra 3-8
Johnson Andrea C BA 1
Kaiser Colene M BS K
Mohr Rhonda J BSED 5-8
Niblock Karen K-8
Peters Sharon K BS 4-5
Segebart Phyliss J BS 2
Stoppel Cindy A BSED K-8
Uhl Martha K
Venzke Jeanette BS 3
**DES MOINES**-HOPE PS
• 1977
3857 E 42nd St 50317-8105
(515)265-2057 •
FAX(515)265-8775
NO REPORT
MT OLIVE PS-8
• 1960
5625 Franklin Ave 50310-1031
(515)277-0247 •
FAX(515)274-2723
mustangs@aalweb.net
**Buescher Barbara A MED K-8**
Beikmann David R BS 6-8
Eckhardt Marcus 6-8
Geurink Brenda R BA 2
Hayes Aubrey 6
Light Linda AA PS
Miller Christa K BMED K-8
Schumann Lois J MS 1
Schutt Kathleen S BSED 5
Stange Kathleen S BS K
Steinke Terry 3
Wulff Karen MA 4
**DUBUQUE**-OUR REDEEMER PS
• 1971
2145 John F Kennedy Rd 52002-3817
(319)588-1247
NO REPORT
**ELDORA**-GOOD SHEPHERD-ST PAUL PS
• 1974
1105 Washington St 50627-1627
(641)858-5928 •
FAX(641)858-2464
**Ritter Karen L BA PS**
Struck Kathleen PS
**ELDRIDGE**-SHARE & CARE-PARK VIEW PS
• 1977
14 Grove Rd 52748-9632
(319)285-7111
Lockhart Betty J BA PS
Weiss Denise A PS
**EMMETSBURG**--ST PAUL PS
• 1986
805 Harrison St 50536-1522
(712)852-2367
NO REPORT
**FAIRBANK**-SUNSHINE-ST JOHN PS
• 1977
208 N 4th St 50629-8550 PO Box 465 50629-0465
(319)635-2181
Helmuth Marilyn A BA
**FAIRFIELD**-IMMANUEL PS
• 1983
1601 S Main St 52556-2090
(515)472-5333
NO REPORT
**FENTON**-ST JOHN PS
• 1981
205 2ND Ave 50539-5004 PO Box 169 50539-0169
(515)889-2839
NO REPORT
**FORT DODGE**-PRINCE OF PEACE PS
• 1982
1023 S 27th St 50501-6310
(515)573-8618
NO REPORT
ST PAUL PS-8
• 1863
1217 4Th Ave S 50501-4822
(515)955-7208 •
FAX(515)573-7839
stpaulschool@dodgenet.com
Dreyer Debra J BA PS
Fendrick Dawn L BS 6-8
Galles Kimberly 5
Haake Jean M BSED 1
Kraayenbrink Sally J MED
Kratz Robyn M BA 6-8
Malo Kane J BA 4
Motzkus Kyle BA 6-8
Sanford Julianne L 2
Sieveking Sue 1-8
Vose Ginger 3
Vought Dawn PS
**FREDERICKSBURG**-FUN IN THE SON-ST PAUL PS
• 1993
109 E Railroad 50630 PO Box 336 50630-0336
(319)237-6117
Cahoy Karen L PS
Deterding Amy PS
Kueker Janiece A BA PS
Langreck Kathleen PS
Larson Michelle PS
Skoda Sarah PS
**GARNER**-LITTLE LAMBS-ST PAUL PS
• 1976
870 State St 50438-1631
(515)923-2261
NO REPORT
**GREENFIELD**-IMMANUEL LITTLE LAMB PS
• 1981
505 NE Dodge St 50849-1106
(515)743-2116
NO REPORT
**HAMPTON**-CARE & SHARE-TRINITY PS
• 1984
16 12th Ave NE 50441-1113
(515)456-4816
NO REPORT
**HIAWATHA**-LITTLE LAMBS PS
• 1981
201 1St Ave 52233-1601
(319)393-8507
Lensch Inez PS
Seeber Peggy PS
**HUMBOLDT**-ZION PS
• 1981
1005 11Th Ave N 50548-1223
(515)332-3279
zion@trvnet.net
Zabel Barbara K BS PS
**INDIANOLA**-MOUNT CALVARY PS
• 1996
Indianola 805 N 1St St 50125
(515)961-4321
NO REPORT
**IOWA CITY**-OUR REDEEMER PS
• 1981
2301 E Court St 52245-5218
(319)338-3949 •
FAX(319)338-9171
Moran Pamela G BS
**KNOXVILLE**-TRINITY PS
• 1991
814 W Pleasant St 50138-2740
(515)842-4724
NO REPORT
**LATIMER**-ST PAUL K-8
• 1925
404 W Main PO Box 609 50452-0609
(515)579-6046 •
FAX(515)579-6046
Fahrmann Marilyn BA 1-8
Grummer Joyce 5-6
Marshall Lawrence E 6-8
Tripp Karen K-8
Tyrrell Pam BED K-2
Vanness Melinda A BA 3-5
**MALLARD**-TRINITY LITTLE LAMB PS
• 1990
311 N Hwy 4 PO Box 216 50562-0216
(712)425-3432
NO REPORT
**MANNING**-ZION PS
• 1985
1204 Center St 51455-1531
(712)653-2352
NO REPORT
**MAPLETON**-LITTLE LAMB-ST MATTHEW PS
• 1983
506 Walnut St 51034-1123
(712)882-2243
Witzel Lavone PS
**MARENGO**-ST JOHN PS
• 1977
780 Court Ave 52301-1433
(319)642-5452 •
FAX(319)642-5452
Jensen Dayle PS
Loffer Michelle
**MASON CITY**-SUNBEAM-BETHLEHEM PS
• 1979
419 N Delaware Ave 50401-7009
(515)423-0438
NO REPORT
**MISSOURI VALLEY**-ONE WAY PS
• 1979
724 N 8Th St 51555-1134
(712)642-4219
Mc Williams Denise PS
**MONTICELLO**-ST JOHN PS
• 1988
18927 Highway 38 52310-7764
(319)465-5369
NO REPORT
**MOUNT PLEASANT**-SON SHINE ACADEMY-FAITH PS
910 Mapleleaf Dr 52641
(319)385-8427
NO REPORT
**MUSCATINE**-OUR SAVIOR PS
• 1984
2611 Lucas St 52761-2109
(319)263-2662
Egger Bonnie L BA PS
Saunders Karen PS

**NEWHALL**-CENTRAL PS-8
• RSO • 1965
310 3rd St W Newhall PO Box 190
52315-0190
(319)223-5271 •
FAX(319)223-5257
mlheureux@cent-luth.pvt.k12.ia.us
**L Heureux Mark J BSED**
Block Denise R BSED 5
Jorgenson Cheryl 3-4
Krueger Ross L BS 1
L Heureux Kathyrine R BSED 2
Mac Kain Sandra K BA PS
Rempfer Deborah BS K
Runge David K BA 6-7
Snider Charles A MSED 8
**OCHEYEDAN**-OCHEYEDAN PS
• 1996
874 Main St PO Box 56
51354-0056
(712)758-3425
Vogel Muriel PS
**OELWEIN**-PEACE LUTHERAN PRESC PS
1308 E Charles St 50662-1962
(319)283-5778
nswendel@sbtek.net
NO REPORT
**OGDEN**-EDUCATING LITTLE MIR PS
319 W Elm St PO Box L 50212
(515)275-2234
NO REPORT
**OSCEOLA**-OVER THE RAINBOW-IMMANUEL PS
• 1983
101 E View Pl 50213-1300
(515)342-3121
Crandall Kathie S BA
Hitz Kathy
Stuva Belinda
**PAULLINA**-ZION-ST JOHN PS-8
• RSO • 1976
103 W Bertha St PO Box 249
51046-0249
(712)448-3915 •
FAX(712)448-3657
zsschool@pionet.net
**Boehne Bruce K MA 7-8**
Heeren Susan A BA 1-2
Hetlevedt Joyce R PS
Laue Dolores L K
Massmann Linda C BA 3-4
Sweeney Charlene F 5-6
**PERRY**-NOAHS ARK-TRINITY PS
• 1985
2715 Iowa St 50220-2414
(515)465-5574
Appenzeller Shirley A PS
Hammer Lori L PS
**POLK CITY**-BEAUTIFUL SAVIOR PS
• 1999
1701 W Jester Park Dr 50226
(515)784-6146
bslccdc@aol.com
NO REPORT
**READLYN**-COMMUNITY PS-8
• RSO • 1977
2681 Quail Ave 50668-9798
(319)279-3968
cls@netins.net
NO REPORT
**SAC CITY**-ST PAUL HELPING HAND PS
• 1984
1112 Bailey St 50583-2003
(712)662-3298
NO REPORT
**SCHLESWIG**-IMMANUEL PS
• 1984
5Th & Glad St 51461
(712)676-2235
Fink Debra K AA

**SIOUX CITY**-KINDERCOTTAGE-REDEEMER PS
• 1976
3204 S Lakeport St 51106-4505
(712)276-1125 •
FAX(712)276-1146
redeemer_church@yahoo.com
Johnson Robin PS
Mace Valery PS
ST PAUL PS-6
• 1880
614 Jennings St 51105-1918
(712)258-6325 •
FAX(712)252-1141
**Stuhr Lonnie J MA 5-6**
Brown Gail L BA K
Eggers Carol J BA 2
Fett April A BS 5
Godwin Sharon L BS PS
Shook Marcia M BA
Strong Alyce L BS 1
Toso Judith A BS 3
Zehnder Kathleen S BED 4
**SPENCER**-FIRST ENGLISH PS
• 1979
23 E 10Th St 51301-4317
(712)262-3699 •
FAX(712)262-8396
NO REPORT
IOWA GREAT LAKES K-5
• RSO • 1999
500 4th Ave SW 51301
(712)262-1187 •
FAX(712)262-1189
**Pipho Donald M MA**
Bohl Noreen F BSED K
Metz Debra L 1-5
**STORM LAKE**-CONCORDIA K-2
1723 W Milwaukee PO Box 1383
52588
(712)732-8356 •
FAX(712)732-8357
**Pipho Donald M MA**
Elston Kathy A K
Larson Barbara 1-2
GRACE PS
• 1982
1407 W 5th St 50588-1225
(712)732-5005 •
FAX(712)732-5005
Huseman Roxanne K PS
Stern Annette L PS
KIDS N CHRIST-ST JOHN PS
• 1981
402 Lake Ave 50588-2445
(712)732-8143 •
FAX(712)732-2401
NO REPORT
**SWEA CITY**-OUR SAVIOR LITTLE LA PS
• 1994
301 3rd Ave 50590 710 5Th St N
50590-1025
(515)272-4696
NO REPORT
**VENTURA**-REDEEMER PS
• 1985
301 S Main 50482-0138
(515)829-3615 •
FAX(515)829-3612
korth@netins.net
NO REPORT
**VINTON**-TLC-TRINITY PS
• 1984
1002 E 13th St 52349-2385
(319)472-5571 •
FAX(319)472-5571
Fleming Debra J PS
**WATERLOO**-IMMANUEL PS-8
• 1879
207 Franklin St 50703-3515
(319)233-3967 •
FAX(319)232-6184
immanuelluth@home.com
**Gomez Carlos A MED**
Gomez Linda J BA 8

Holste Richard W 6
Holtzman Chad 4
Kelderman Laverne I BA 2
Knea Sara 3
Limback Sharon K BS PS
Ruethler Holly 1
Schaefer Sara 5
Sexe Jeanne 7
**WEBSTER CITY**-ST PAUL PS
• 1969
1005 Beach St 50595-1951
(515)832-3043 •
FAX(515)832-3069
stpaulwc@ncn.net
Mingus Cynthia J BA
Muessigmann Mary PS
Ribbey Patricia PS
Schmidt Jennifer PS
Seiser Lorilee PS
**WEST DES MOINES**-SHEPHERDS FLOCK-SHEP/VALLEY PS-K
• 1992
3900 Ashworth Rd 50265-3048
(515)225-1623 •
FAX(515)225-0871
NO REPORT
**WEST UNION**-OPEN ARMS-GOOD SHEPHERD PS
• 1998
311 Highway 150 S 52175-1506
(319)422-3393
Dedor Rhonda L MCMU
**WESTGATE**-LOVE & JOY PS
• NLSA • 1981
Main & Eastline St 50681-0067 PO Box 220 50681-0220
(319)578-8664
NO REPORT
**WILLIAMSBURG**-LUTHERAN INTERPARISH PS-8
• RSO • 1967
804 Court PO Box 750
52361-0750
(319)668-1711 •
FAX(319)668-9054
liswmsbg@avalon.net
**Seibert Ronald J MS**
Armbrecht Andy P BSED 6-8
Durr Marna A BA 7-8
Frese Rosetta K-8
Grimm Peggy L BS 1-3
Meyer Carol J BS PS
Piering Vernon C MED 5
Roberts Cara PS
Sandersfeld Lavonne BS K-8
Schaefer Robyn R BS 4
Scheele Dean M BS 8
Scheele Sheila J BSED K
Wille Linda K-7
Wolter La June K BS 1
**WILTON**-ZION PS-6
• 1929
117 W Prairie St PO Box 429
52778-0008
(319)732-2912 •
FAX(319)732-2106
Feuerbach Tona BS K
Fredericksen Heather J BA 2-3
Freie Sheila K PS
Hammes Cynthia A PS
Levins Lori J PS
Souhrada Karie A K-1
Waech Elaine BA 4-6
Willis Connie M PS

## KANSAS

**ALMA**-ST JOHN 1-8
• NLSA • 1873
209 W 2nd PO Box 368
66401-0368
(785)765-3914 •
FAX(785)765-7777
sjls@kansas.net
Altevogt Orville C MEAD 5-8
Eckelberry Joyce 5-8
Frank Rebecca J BS 1-2

Miller Christa R 3-4
**ATCHISON**-TRINITY PS-8
• NLSA • 1869
609 N 8th St 66002-1703
(913)367-4763 •
FAX(913)367-4763
**Parris Franklin O MEAD 6**
Aversman Tohnya R 5
Dougherty Stacie J K
Duitsman Joyce E BS 4
Estes Lori K BSED 3
Goodpasture Linda A PS
Lowe Jill M PS
Parris Melissa A BSED 1
Sharp Mary K BSED 2
Watkins Charles Jr. 7-8
**ATWOOD**-GODS LITTLE SAINTS-REDEEMER PS
• 1999
808 S 1st St 67730-2108
(785)626-3178 •
FAX(785)626-3183
redluth@juno.com
NO REPORT
**BURLINGTON**-TRINITY PS
• 1988
902 Kennedy St 66839-1130
(316)364-2857
Berkenmeier Wendy PS
Dunlop Tina PS
**CHANUTE**-SON SHINE-ZION PS
• 1988
1202 W Main St 66720-1414
(316)431-1935
NO REPORT
**CHENEY**-ST PAUL PS-8
• 1894
612 Lincoln St PO Box 278
67025-0278
(316)542-3584
kjopp@hit.net
Adolph Lisa J PS
Hillman Becky R BS 1-8
Jopp Keith R MED
Osler Kris 5-8
Williams Arlene R BS 1-4
**COFFEYVILLE**-ST PAUL PS
• 1978
506 W 9th St 67337-5002 PO Box 263 67337-0263
(316)251-2927 •
FAX(316)251-3276
stpaul@terraworld.net
Brakhage Carla J BS PS
**DERBY**-FAITH PS
• 1988
214 S Derby Ave 67037-1443
(316)788-1715
flcschool@aol.com
Dahlke Cynthia PS
Hamer Connie S PS
Herman Judy A PS
Jarvis Kathy BSED PS
Judd Cheryl L PS
Ronnfeldt Gwen M PS
**ELLINWOOD**-ST JOHN PS
• 1994
615 N Main 67526
(316)564-2885
NO REPORT
**EMPORIA**-THE LORDS LAMB-FAITH PS
• 1982
1348 Trailridge Rd 66801-6142
(316)342-4669
Davis Barbee A MED PS
Heese Lu PS
Lyon Teresa A PS
**FAIRVIEW**-ST PAUL PS
• 1985
110 East Maple PO Box 158
66425-0158
(785)467-8810
NO REPORT

**FORT SCOTT**--PRECIOUS LAMBS-TRINITY PS
• 1989
2824 Horton St 66701-3100
(316)223-3596
NO REPORT
**GARDEN CITY**-TRINITY PS
• 1984
1010 Fleming St 67846-6225
(316)276-3110
Hewes Suzanne M BSED PS
Lampe Tammy J PS
**GARDNER**-KING OF KINGS LUTHER PS
Box 264 66030
(913)884-5437 •
FAX(913)856-2500
NO REPORT
**HAVEN**-ST PAUL PS-6
• 1885
8403 E Arlington Rd 67543-8014
(316)465-3425
**Huster Brenda K BSED 3-6**
Lowden Michelle L BA 1-2
Peshek Michelle D K
Wiese Angeline K BSED PS
**HERINGTON**-OUR REDEEMER PS
• 1995
802 East Trapp Street 67449-2850
(785) 258-2615
Dehning Terri PS
**INDEPENDENCE**-ZION PS-8
• 1884
301 S 11th St 67301-3625
(316)332-3331 •
FAX(316)332-3330
lions@terraworld.net
**Zeigler Timothy R MS 5-8**
Bosse Marcia A BSED 1
Heath Karen
Marten Dennis L BS
O Brien Stella K-6
Oldenettel Dawn D BSED 5-8
Sullivan Kathy PS
**IOLA**-GRACE PS
• 1978
401 S Walnut St 66749-3248
(316)365-3755
NO REPORT
**JUNCTION CITY**-IMMANUEL PS-K
• 1954
630 S Eisenhower Dr 66441-3321
(785)238-5921 •
FAX(785)238-6473
immanuel@oz-online.net
Chyba Tara L PS
Gardels Ann M MED K
Howard Sue E PS
Smith Christine A K
**KANSAS CITY**-GRACE PS-7
• 1932
3333 Wood Ave 66102-2137
(913)371-7851 •
FAX(913)281-2587
NO REPORT
IMMANUEL PS
• 1969
3232 Metropolitan Ave 66106-2802
(913)831-4535
NO REPORT
OUR SAVIOUR PS
• 1931
4153 Rainbow Blvd 66103-3110
(913)236-6228 •
FAX(913)236-8522
Lionsden@Shy.Net
Bottemuller Donna M
**KENSINGTON**-FIRST ST JOHN PS
• 1984
Hwy 36 PO Box 57 66951-0057
(913)476-2246
Cole Stacy PS
**LAWRENCE**-IMMANUEL PS
• 1994
2104 W 15th St 66049-2722
(913)842-8131
Bachman Rachel PS
Belzer Carol
La Fluer Camille PS
Morris Gloria PS
**LEAVENWORTH**-ST PAUL PS-8
• 1863
320 N 7th St 66048-1933
(913)682-5553 •
FAX(913)682-5553
**Floetke Jay W MED**
Burton Paula PS
Coffey Deborah S BA 1
Daniels Vera 5-8
Denney Constance L
Denney Rebecca R BA 5-8
Floetke Pamela B BS K
Genter Helen L BA 3
Kirkendoll Cheryl R BSED 2
Thacker Jess M BED 4
Wells Susan G PS
Williams Carolyn 5-8
TRINITY PS-K
• 1990
2101 10Th Ave 66048-4210
(913)682-4747 •
FAX(913)682-7767
NO REPORT
**LEAWOOD**-LORD OF LIFE PS
• 1994
3105 W 135th St 66224-9540
(913)681-5146 •
FAX(913)681-9143
lolskj@aol.com
Helmer Debby K
**LINN**-LINN ASSOCIATION 1-8
• RSO • 1967
112 Church St 66953-9543
(785)348-5792
Bierbaum Edward W MED
Bruenger Marilyn J BS 1-2
Pearson Martha A 3-5
**LYONS**-GRACE LITTLE LAMBS PS
1111 W Lincoln 67554
(316)257-2204
Libhart Rebecca A BS PS-8
**MANHATTAN**-ST LUKE PS
• 1981
330 Sunset Ave 66502-3757
(913)539-2604
presch@flinthills.com
Meyer Kathleen A BS PS
Newkirk Mary J BS PS
**MARYSVILLE**-GOOD SHEPHERD PS-8
• RSO • 1995
206 S 17th St 66508-1750
(785)562-3181 •
FAX(785)562-3679
gsls@bluevalley.net
**Macy John A MED 7-8**
Barber Ellen L 5-6
Harries Terry L PS-K
Hofman Amy R BA 3-4
Kruse Sheryl M BSED 1-2
**MISSION**-TRINITY PS
• 1955
5601 W 62nd St 66202-3532
(913)432-5441 •
FAX(913)432-3530
NO REPORT
**NEWTON**-ZION PS
• 1988
225 S Poplar St PO Box 885 67114-3637
(316)283-1441
NO REPORT
**OLATHE**-REDEEMER PS
• 1985
920 S Alta Ln 66061-4105
(913)780-9912
NO REPORT
**OTTAWA**-FAITH PS
• 1980
316 E 12Th St 66067-3605
(785)242-7366
Circle Stephanie E BA
Seegar Teresa L PS
**OVERLAND PARK**-BETHANY K-2
• 1999
9101 La Mar 66207
(913)648-2228 •
FAX(913)648-2283
**Niedner Norma L**
Cezus Sharon M 1
Horrigan Karen J BS K
BETHANY PS
• 1966
9101 Lamar Ave 66207-2452
(913)648-2228 •
FAX(913)648-2283
Belshe Sue Z BSED
Purcell Denise F BS PS
Spong Jennifer C BS PS
Swezy Carol A BSED PS
Wadsworth Rebecca J PS
CHRIST PS
• 1988
11720 Nieman 66210
(913)345-9700 •
FAX(913)345-9707
leta.sprecher@together-in-christ.org
**Sprecher Leta L BSED PS**
Brinkmeyer Jan K PS
Cardwell Mary PS
Helmer Debby K PS
Leighnor Debbie K PS
**PAOLA**-TRINITY 1-8
• NLSA • 1868
34944 Block Rd 66071-6241
(913)849-3343
**Barnes Audrey J MA 6-8**
Brown Jody R BSED
Kettler Lucinda C
**PRATT**-OUR SAVIOR PS
• 1982
2nd & Thompson PO Box 192 67124-0192
(316)672-6203
NO REPORT
**SABETHA**-FIRST PS
• 1989
204 Ohio St 66534-2424 PO Box 65 66534-0065
(789)284-3570
Moser Wilma J
**SALINA**-LITTLE LAMBS-CHRIST KING PS
• 1987
111 W Magnolia Rd 67401-7546
(913)827-7492
NO REPORT
**SHAWNEE**-HOPE PS-8
• NLSA • 1983
6308 Quivira Rd 66216-2744
(913)631-6940 •
FAX(913)268-9525
schooloffice@hopelutheran.org
**Brueggemann Milton R MAT**
Alsin Kristine BA K
Edge Aleen D BS 2
Eichholz Diane M BS
Fitzgerald Theresa PS
James Frank 7-8
Klepacki Nina L BS 5
Krzesinski Marjorie 1
Limback Jane L MED 6
Mansour Joan 1-8
Meinzen Faith 4
Musgrove Jane 7-8
Nelson Sandra J BA 7-8
Nettling Kathy M MED 3
Schoettlin Diane BS PS
Tidwell Harvey E 8
**TOPEKA**-FAITH PS
• 1995
1716 SW Gage Blvd 66604-3334
(913)272-1070 •
FAX(913)272-1046
Altevogt Carmen S BA PS
Baker Tisha R PS
Burget Judith A
Gowin Kristin K PS
HOPE PS
• 1982
2636 SE Minnesota Ave 66605-1642
(913)266-5206
NO REPORT
PRINCE OF PEACE PS
• 1990
3625 SW Wanamaker Rd 66614-4566
(785)271-0913 •
FAX(785)271-5324
NO REPORT
TOPEKA PS-8
• RSO • NLSA • 1951
701 SW Roosevelt St 66606-1745
(785)357-0382 •
FAX(785)357-7338
tls@networkplus.net
**Pralle Gerhardt R MED**
Bartels Kathy L MED
Bitter Denise A MA 4
Blair Jovanna 1-8
Blankenship Jennifer R PS
Bradshaw Joanna D BSED 2
Dain Sandy S PS
Eakins Donna MMU 1-8
Fitzgerald Corrie A PS
Geske Laura R BS 1-2
Glinka Cara D PS
Hamilton Cindy 1-8
Hass Donna M BS 3
Helmke Beth D BSED K
Jones Jane L PS
Kamprath Thomas E BA 4
Malone Kendra L PS
Malone Walter D BS 5-8
Mc Comas Barbara L BA 5-6
Moege Kim K
Offerman Wendy 3-8
Pralle Marilyn A MED K
Schaefer Margaret F BS 6-8
Scheel Linda K BS 1
Schmidt Lori B BSED PS
Smith Heather D BS 5-6
Spaulding Carolyn L PS
Trump Crystal J PS
Zimmerman Brenda J PS
**WATHENA**-CHRIST PS
• 1990
E Hwy 36 PO Box 427 66090-0427
(913)989-3348
NO REPORT
**WHEATON**-ST LUKE LUTHERAN CHI-ST LUKE PS
304 Highway 16 66551
(785)396-4404
NO REPORT
**WICHITA**-ASCENSION PS
• 1965
842 N Tyler Rd 67212-3239
(316)722-4694 •
FAX(316)729-7027
Lungwitz Karen M PS
Milleville Deanna D BS PS
Nelson Diane S PS
Shook Vicki L PS
BETHANY PS-5
• 1958
1000 W 26th St S 67217-2922
(316)265-7415 •
FAX(316)265-0887
**Kleber Susan K MED K-5**
Broten Kristin L PS
Freed Linda M BA 1-2
Wagner Ruth BAED 3-5
HOLY CROSS PS-8
• NLSA • 1959
600 N Greenwich 67206-2633
(316)684-4431 •
FAX(316)684-2847
office@holycrosslutheran.net
**Dieckhoff Bill D MA**
Aberle Jan C K
Amey Betty MSED 6-8
Boss Kathryn BS PS

Castens Neal C BA 6-8
Dieckhoff Brent W BS K-5
Dobler Janet R BS 1
Goering Glen 5-6
Helmer Theodore N MA 5
Longhauser Donna BA 2
Mc Ginness Linda K-8
Newlin Janet B MSED PS
Ochs David L BSED 6-8
Reida Tracie BED 3
Thomas Gwen D BSED 4
Vanwey Teresa L MLS 6-8
Weikal Jane BED K
Wilgers Karen A MED
**WINFIELD-**TRINITY PS-6
• 1888
910 Mound St 67156-3929
(316)221-1820 •
FAX(316)221-3779
trinity@hit.net
**Schotte Mark L MS**
Glasgow Diane M MED PS
Haist Amy M BS K
Helmer Luther MA 5-6
Schnoor Vanessa
Stigge Judith E MED 3-4

## KENTUCKY

**BOWLING GREEN-**HOLY TRINITY PS-6
• 1967
553 Ashmoore Ave 42101-3799
(270)843-1001 •
FAX(270)843-7466
kjmitchellhtls@yahoo.com
**Mitchell Karen J BSED**
Bitterling Heather L PS
Callaham Betty MS K
Collins Lynita 6
Markel Elizabeth 5
Sanborn Melinda G BED 4
Struss Donna K MS 3
Talley Susanne MA 1
Wilson Linda V 2
**ELIZABETH-**GLORIA DEI K-3
1701 Ring Rd E 42701
(270)769-5910 •
FAX(270)769-5703
glordei@ne.infi.net
NO REPORT
**ELIZABETHTOWN-**LUTHERAN C-GLORIA DEI PS-K
• 1991
1701 Ring Rd E 42701-9497
(502)769-5910
NO REPORT
**ERLANGER-**BETHANY PS
• 1975
3501 Turkeyfoot Rd 41018-2670
(606)586-9570
NO REPORT
**LA GRANGE-**HOLY TRINITY PS
• 2000
2416 S Hwy 53 40031
(502)222-5827
pastordale@unidial.com
Harp Shalleen PS
Huffman Rebecca PS
**LEXINGTON-**GOOD SHEPHERD PS
• 1986
425 Patchen Dr 40517-4312
(606)266-3433
NO REPORT
ST JOHN PS
• 1986
516 Pasadena Dr 40503-2217
(606)275-1907
NO REPORT
**LOUISVILLE-**OUR SAVIOR PS-8
• NLSA • 1990
8307 Nottingham Pkwy 40222-5539
(502)426-0864 •
FAX(502)394-0648
oslcmeyer@aol.com
**Meyer Mary L MED**
Blazek Krista J BA 6-8
Brockhoff Marian F MAD 1
Brown Linda 2
Exner Carol A BA 4
Exner Jeffrey L MA 6-8
Francis Jeanette K MA PS
Hiegel Jack L MED 5
Kahre Lillian R BA PS-8
Kamman Scott R MMU PS
Nickel Linda K
Schultz Mark O MED 6-8
Shreve Jennie L MA 3
**OWENSBORO-**PEACE PS
• NLSA • 1976
2200 Carter Rd 42301-4131
(270)685-2211
Beane Barbara PS
Gleim Karen
Horsman Rebecca L PS
Mattingly Kathy PS
Morgan Dianne H PS
Ulber Sherri PS
**SHEPHERDSVILLE-**DIVINE SAVIOR PS
• 1998
1025 N Buckman St 40165-7926
(502)543-2905 •
FAX(502)543-2905
pastor@dslc.org
Houtler Carol M
**WINCHESTER-**GRACE PS
• 1994
108 Hemlock Rd 40391-2342
(859)745-0587
Adams Kimberly PS
Bankes Jean F
Dobbs Mary E PS
Kincaid Tammy PS
Massaro Kathryn PS
Moore Jennifer PS
Nickels Louise PS
Varner Deborah PS

## LOUISIANA

**BATON ROUGE-**BATON ROUGE-TRINITY PS-8
• 1957
10925 Florida Blvd 70815-2009
(225)272-1288 •
FAX(225)272-8504
brlutheran@bitworx.com
**Schamber Gordon E MED**
Adams Sonya K 3
Bean Jana K 6-8
Bratton Beverly R 5
Breaux Kristin 2
Buvens Barbara 4
Foil Diane H PS
Greene Leigh M 6-8
McGehee Marinea 6-8
Rich Kristel L BS K
Schamber Kathleen A MED 1
Schmieding Susan D MA 6-8
Scott Susan P PS
**BOSSIER CITY-**IMMANUEL PS
• NLSA • 1968
2565 Airline Dr 71111-5812
(318)746-2215 •
FAX(318)742-2220
NO REPORT
**COVINGTON-**HOLY TRINITY KIDS DA PS
• 1994
1 N Marigold Dr 70433-9160
(504)892-6146 •
FAX(504)892-3012
HTLC@neosoft.com
**Blackbird Pamela PS**
Anderson Noel PS
Billiot Ada PS
Fouquet Carmen PS
Johansen Kenda PS
Nelson Deborah A PS
Williams Renee G PS
**GRETNA-**SALEM PS-8
• 1892
418 4th St 70053-5317
(504)367-5144 •
FAX(504)367-5128
althag@salemlutheranschool.com
**Althage Richard A MED K-8**
Althage Joseph 6
Benedum Kate 5
Bovy Sharon
Brda Ellen J MMU K-8
Brown Dianne L BED 2
Congemi Pamela BA 8
Enos Judy C BA PS
Gieseler Donna
Le Blanc Christopher J BA 7
Le Blanc Jaime
Mc Sherry Sharon PS
Meyer Merle J BS PS
Royer Kristen
Schexnayder Bonnie V K
Trombatore Melanie 3
Walther Joleen N BA
**HAMMOND-**ST PAUL PS
• 1989
707 W Dakota St 70401-2413
(504)542-5304 •
FAX(504)345-6027
stpaulschool@i-55.com
Deokaran Terry J PS
Taylor Sharon S BED
Varisco Sandy M PS
**HARAHAN-**FAITH PS-8
• 1958
300 Colonial Club Dr 70123-4428
(504)737-9554 •
FAX(504)739-9470
**Leissinger Marilyn J MED PS**
Feindel Lisa L MA 3
Flake Michelle W PS
Honoree Cheryl C 4-5
Leonard Carolon M BSED 1
Mandry Alexis V BA 6-8
Miller Wilene S 4-8
Oestriecher Diane J BA 2
Plauche Judith M 6-8
Pool Jane E K
**LAKE CHARLES-**ST JOHNS LITTLE LAMB PS
• 1980
600 University Dr 70605-5634
(337)478-2659 •
FAX(337)478-8196
Falcon Deborah PS
Jacobson Maureen MA PS
Koppenhagen Cindy PS
Lanier Lorna PS
Mancil Kathy PS
Nichols Paulette PS
Reynolds Diane PS
Shandersky Susan PS
Ward Djuana BA
self Elizabeth PS
**MARRERO-**CONCORDIA PS-8
• 1965
6700 Westbank Expy 70072-2699
(504)347-4155 •
FAX(504)348-9345
TJSRICH@bellsouth.com
NO REPORT
**METAIRIE-**ATONEMENT K-8
• 1960
6205 Veterans Memorial Blvd 70003-3998
(504)887-3980 •
FAX(504)887-7876
schooloffice@alcs.org
**Molin Douglas C MA**
Haerer Connie B BS 3-8
Harney Rachel L BA 5
Hellmers Tina M BS 1
Jackson Rhonda L BS 2
Lacey Michael W MS 3-8
Lefave Susan M 3-8
Malter Dorothy A BA K
Menzel Lorna R MED 4
Orlando Charlotte D 6-8
Reagan Sibyl 6-8
Whightsil Pamela J BA 6-8
MT OLIVE PS
• 1976
315 Ridgelake Dr 70001-5315
(504)835-3891
NO REPORT
**NEW ORLEANS-**PRINCE OF PEACE PS-8
• 1982
9301 Chef Menteur Hwy 70127-4137
(504)242-4348 •
FAX(504)246-9131
poplschool@aol.com
**Kehr Mark A MED**
Bollinger Kelli M BA 2
Bradford Julie 8
Glapion Kevin 6
Gremillion Gaynell 4
Jones Raina PS
Rainey Angela 5
Rosch Debra 1
Rosch Thomas 7
Simela Phyllis BA K
Simoneaux Trisha L BA 3
ST JOHN PS-8
• 1854
3937 Canal St 70119-6002
(504)488-6641 •
FAX(504)482-5869
stjluth@cs.com
**Falkner David A PHD**
Chisum John 5
Daly Michelle BA 8
Falkner Margaret MA 2
Griffin Stephanie
Koenig Pamela W 4
Platt Heather PS
Prins Gloria 3
Schrenk Kathleen T BS 6
Sharbel Melanie 1
Tingstrom Jodi 7
Wood Paula K BS K
ST PAUL PS-8
• NLSA • 1840
2624 Burgundy St 70117-7304
(504)947-1773 •
FAX(504)945-3743
sptigers@beesouth.net
NO REPORT
**SHREVEPORT-**ST PAUL PS
• 1976
4175 Lakeshore Dr 71109-1936
(318)635-7732
Brobst Katrina
Foster Shenika
Griffith Sandy PS
Johnson Monica
Moreno Debra R PS
Primus Carla
Stone Roxanne
Strong Sonja
Washington Christina
Washington Katrina
Watson La Tonya
**SLIDELL-**AMAZING GRACE-BETHANY PS
• 1999
627 Gause Blvd 70461
(504)643-1589 •
FAX(504)643-1698
NO REPORT

## MARYLAND

**ACCIDENT-**ZION PS
• 1973
209 N Main PO Box 171 21520-0171
(301)746-8170 •
FAX(301)746-7375
zion@gcnet.net
NO REPORT

**ANNAPOLIS**-ST PAUL PS
• 1986
31 Roscoe Rowe Blvd 21401-1517
(410)267-9543 •
FAX(410)268-2884
**Broderick Debra C AA PS**
Galloway Evelyn A PS
**ARBUTUS**-HOLY NATIVITY PS
• 1954
1200 Linden Ave 21227-2423
(410)247-5972 •
FAX(410)242-0295
**May Eileen R AECE PS**
Bredeson Sue PS
Farrier Virginia L PS
Mc Alexander Denise A PS
Rey Dawn PS
**BALTIMORE**-BETHLEHEM PS-8
• NLSA • 1972
4815 Hamilton Ave 21206-3827
(410)488-8963 •
FAX(410)488-2689
bethlemsch@aol.com
NO REPORT
CALVARY PS-6
• 1949
2625 E Northern Pkwy 21214-1118
(410)426-4302 •
FAX(410)426-7590
NO REPORT
IMMANUEL PS-6
• NLSA • 1864
5701 Loch Raven Blvd
21239-2936
(410)435-6961 •
FAX(410)433-3646
mpotter@immanuellutheran.org
**Potter Margaret R**
Balog Joan E BS 1
Bowersox Ellen D K
Charles Joyce C PS
Fuller Michael
Hasselbarth Sandra I 4
Hawley Cynthia A BS 6
Hiske Beverly G BS 3
James Marguorite PS
Mauser Jane A 2
Moore Karen K
Stevens Jill R BA PS
Weider Sara E 5
NAZARETH PS
• 1988
3405 Bank St 21224
(410)732-6554 •
FAX(410)732-3125
NO REPORT
OUR SAVIOR PS
3301 The Alameda 21218
(410)235-9553 •
FAX(410)235-1913
NO REPORT
REDEEMER PS
• 1967
4211 Vermont Ave 21229-3517
(410)644-6780
NO REPORT
**BEL AIR**-ADVENT PS
• 1998
2230 Rock Spring Rd 21050
(410)638-9445 •
FAX(410)638-6016
NO REPORT
ST MATTHEW PS
• 1972
1200 E Churchville Rd 21014-3412
(410)838-3178
Hill Jean PS
Mead Jane PS
**CATONSVILLE**-EMMANUEL PS-8
• 1956
929 Ingleside Ave 21228
(410)744-0015 •
FAX(410)744-1199
NO REPORT
ST PAUL PS-8
• 1957
2001 Old Frederick Rd
21228-4119
(410)747-1924 •
FAX(410)747-7248
NO REPORT
**EASTON**-IMMANUEL PS
• 1994
7215 Ocean Gtwy 21601-4605
(410)822-5665
NO REPORT
**ELDERSBURG**-FAITH PS
1700 Saint Andrews Way 21784
(410)781-6826 •
FAX(410)781-6826
NO REPORT
**GLEN BURNIE**-ST PAUL PS-8
• 1950
308 Oak Manor Dr 21061-5509
(410)766-5790 •
FAX(410)766-8758
rcolr@stpauls-lutheran.org
NO REPORT
**HYATTSVILLE**-CONCORDIA PS-8
• RSO • NLSA • 1944
3799 E West Hwy 20782-2007
(301)927-0266 •
FAX(301)699-0071
NO REPORT
**KENSINGTON**-CALVARY PS
• 1995
3101 University Blvd W 20895
(301)942-3815 •
FAX(301)589-0931
NO REPORT
**KINGSVILLE**-ST PAUL PS-8
• 1956
12022 Jerusalem Rd 21087-1146
(410)592-8100 •
FAX(410)592-3282
**Kolb Thomas W BA**
Dager Janice E BED 5
Foelber Debbie 6-8
Goehner Janice E BA 1
Hogan Diane S 2
Novak Thelma A BS 4
Ruff Elaine K MSED PS
Sanders Carol J BA K
Wollman Cynthia K BA 7-8
Wright Denise M BED 6
Yergler Kelly BA 3
**LA PLATA**-GRACE PS-5
• 1974
1200 Charles St PO Box 446
20646-0446
(301)932-0963 •
FAX(301)934-1459
gracelutheran@cccomp.com
**Blackwell Ruth BA**
Anderson Theresa PS
Bailey Tonya BS 3
Bankston Sheron MA K
Farmer Virginia
Jones Kate 5
Knauer Ruth PS
Kunz Rebekah M MS 2
Mora Kathi 4-5
Ritter Pat 1
Thompson Sharon PS
Weimert Carolyn PS
**LANDOVER HILLS**-ASCENSION K-8
• NLSA • 1952
7415 Buchanan St 20784-2323
(301)577-0500 •
FAX(301)577-9558
ascenluth@aol.com
NO REPORT
**LAUREL**-OUR SAVIOR PS
• 1995
13611 Laurel Bowie Rd
20708-1563
(301)497-9720 •
FAX(301)776-2872
oslc@erols.com
Bodden Cheryl PS
Dryden Theresa PS
**LEXINGTON PARK**-LITTLE SONBEAMS-TRINITY PS
• 1989
46707 S Shangri La Dr 20653
(301)863-9512 •
FAX(301)863-8185
Buttrick Carol PS
Diaduk Tina PS
**LONG GREEN**-ST JOHN PS
• 1955
13300 Manor Rd 21092-9999
(410)592-8019 •
FAX(410)592-5185
nursery@stjohnslcms.org
Philipp Pam L PS
Rider Nancy J PS
Roth Lynne M PS
Stark Nancy BA PS
Zabora Nancy C BS
**MECHANICSVILLE**-ST PAUL PS
• 1984
37707 New Market Turner Rd
20659
(301)884-5184
NO REPORT
**MILFORD**-PILGRIM CHRISTIAN DA
• 1948
7200 Liberty Rd 21207-3801
(410)484-9240 •
FAX(410)484-9962
NO REPORT
**ODENTON**-FIRST PS
• 1959
1306 Odenton Rd 21113-1302 PO Box 3 21113-0003
(410)551-9189 •
FAX(410)551-9189 *51
Erwin Viia
Jenkins Cecelia D PS
**OLNEY**-SHEPHERDS CARE PS
• 1997
4200 Olney-Laytonsville Rd 20830
PO Box 280 20830-0280
(301)570-7566
shepherds_care@juno.com
NO REPORT
**OVERLEA**-ST JAMES PS-5
• 1956
8 W Overlea Ave 21206-1026
(410)668-0158 •
FAX(410)668-0158
NO REPORT
**PASADENA**-GALILEE PS
• 1973
4652 Mountain Rd 21122-5463
(410)255-3504 •
FAX(410)360-4303
Gallagher Joyce PS
Gallo Janet L
Richter Kristy L PS
Smith Valerie L PS
Spilman Christy PS
**PRESTON**-IMMANUEL PS
Main St PO Box 39 21655-0039
(410)673-7107
Cannon Darlene PS
Patchett Diana PS
**ROCKVILLE**-CROSS PS
• 1966
12801 Falls Rd 20854-6155
(301)762-7566
NO REPORT
**SILVER SPRING**-CALVARY K-7
• NLSA • 1951
9545 Georgia Ave 20910-1438
(301)589-4001 •
FAX(301)589-0931
NO REPORT
ST ANDREW PS
• 1964
12247 Georgia Ave 20902-5523
(301)942-3732 •
FAX(301)942-0170
ockendrick@aol.com
Esparraguera Nancy PS
Kendrick Carol
Mazzeo Kelly PS
Rhoads Lynn W MS PS
Rosenvold Susan P PS
**SUNDERLAND**-LITTLE LAMBS-FIRST PS
6300 Southern Maryland Blvd
20689-0129
(410)257-3030 •
FAX(410)257-4337
NO REPORT
**TOWSON**-HOLY CROSS PS
• 1976
8516 Loch Raven Blvd
21286-2303
(410)825-7905
NO REPORT
**UPPER MARLBORO**-CONCORDIA PS-K
• 1991
10201 Old Indian Head Rd
20772-7936
(301)372-6763 •
FAX(301)372-1954
NO REPORT

## MASSACHUSETTS

**ACTON**-MT CALVARY CHRISTIAN PS-K
• 1987
472 Massachusetts 01720-2937
PO Box 986 01720-0013
(978)263-0337 •
FAX(978)264-0167
mcalvary@wtranet.com
Baldrate Janice PS
Brown Elaine K
Gonor Patricia A BS
Lombard Taralee PS
Rudenauer Sandy PS
Saaristo Karen PS
Sauta Sandra PS
Smutok Wendy
Tobia Jill PS
Welch Jerrlyn PS
Zierold Karin M BA K
**BEDFORD**-OPEN ARMS-OF THE SAVIOR PS
• 1996
426 Davis Rd 01730
(781)271-1148 •
FAX(781)275-1308
Bruha Geralline PS
Bumann Brenda PS
Cyphers Michelle PS
Giannotti Lori L PS
Grose-Richards Kim PS
Nappi Janet PS
Naughton Nancy W AAS
Veilleux Rachel PS
**CANTON**-YORKBROOK-ST JAMES PS
• 1969
214 York St 02021-2466
(781)828-0620 •
FAX(781)821-4752
prho@tiac.net
Bradford Joan PS
Brousseau Joanne AAS PS
Buckman Jane PS
Di Pirro Elaine PS
Dockray Diane PS
Dostie Lee PS
**DEDHAM**-ST LUKE PS
• 1963
950 East St 02026-6335
(781)326-1346 •
FAX(781)326-4094
NO REPORT
**FITCHBURG**-MESSIAH PS
• 1988
750 Rindge Rd 01420-1312
(508)343-7397
NO REPORT

**HANOVER**--THE LUTHERAN-OF THE CROSS PS
• 1968
77 Rockland St 02339-2220 PO Box 103 02339-0103
(617)826-6107
NO REPORT
**HOLYOKE**-FIRST PS-8
• 1981
1810 Northampton St 01040-1923
(413)532-4272 •
FAX(413)534-7071
lfrerking@hotmail.com
**Frerking Lois A MA**
Beaulieu Laurel A MA 3
Brown Martha A 7
Costley Dorothy C BSED 5
Elias Kathryn J BS 8
Heeren Lynelle M BA K
Knapp Gayle L BA PS
Mosher William W BSED 6
Schultze Stacie L BSED 2
Schweinler Lois M BS 1
Tereszkiewicz Mary F MED 4
**LYNNFIELD**-MESSIAH PS
• 1995
708 Lowell St 01940
(781)334-6591
NO REPORT
**RAYNHAM**-JOYFUL NOISE-OF THE WAY PS
• 1998
110 Robinson St 02767
(508)822-5900
NO REPORT
**SOUTHWICK**-RAINBOW IMAGES PS
• 1988
568 College Hwy 01077-9774 PO Box 1107 01077-1107
(413)569-5151
NO REPORT

## MICHIGAN

**ADRIAN**-ST JOHN PS-8
• 1847
430 E Church St 49221-2938
(517)265-6998 •
FAX(517)264-2512
mosborn@tc3net.com
NO REPORT
**ALBION**-LITTLE LAMBS JESUS-ST PAUL PS
• 1984
100 Luther Blvd 49224-2056
(517)629-8379 •
FAX(517)629-8802
spelc@voyager.net
Weaver Kathleen A PS
**ALLEN PARK**-MT HOPE K-8
• 1940
5323 Southfield Rd 48101-2896
(313)565-9140 •
FAX(313)565-2426
mthopeluthschool@hotmail.com
**Tuomi Mary A 5-6**
Blackwell Judith BA 7-8
Hansen Barbara 5-6
Hempel Ruth R BA 3-4
Reinke Pamela 1-2
Timm Nancy K
**ALPENA**-IMMANUEL PS-8
• 1874
355 Wilson St 49707-1493
(517)354-4805 •
FAX(517)358-1102
ils@amaesd-net.com
**Mikkelson Elizabeth A**
Barrie Pamela PS
Hoch Arthur G BA 3-4
Hoch Judith L BA 7-8
Karsten Beverly M 1
Nelson Geraldine BS K
White Pamela K BS 5-6
Willis Linda J BSED 2

**ANN ARBOR**-ST PAUL PS
420 W Liberty St 48103-4397
(313)668-0887 •
FAX(313)665-9449
Bastian Joan PS
Kalmes Patricia A MA
Myer Sandra PS
Rosenzweig Nancy PS
ST PAUL PS-8
• NLSA • 1964
495 Earhart Rd 48105-2799
(734)665-0604 •
FAX(734)665-7809
**Verseman Dennis H EDD**
Cloeter Amy M BA K
Draves Thomas MSSED 7
Fairclough Suzanne 7-8
Grese Susan J MA 3
Hile Claudia 7-8
Knotts Pamela D BA 2
Massey Alaine
Massey Bradley R MS 5
Novak Julie M BA K
Quade Karen J MS 1
Schafer Joyce L BS 4
Schroeder Pamela L MA 1
Schulz Stephanie
Shields Sharon K
Twork Clara J MA 6-8
Van Dellen James R 8
THE SHEPHERDS-DIVINE SHEPHERD PS
• NLSA • 1967
2600 Nixon Rd 48105-1497
(734)761-7275 •
FAX(734)761-7257
DivShepPre@aol.com
NO REPORT
**ARMADA**-OUR SAVIOUR K-8
• 1995
22511 W Main St 48005-0497
(810)784-9088 • FAX(810) 784-9771
OSLSchool@teleweb.net
**Manthei Gayle E MED 7-8**
Dancy Heidi L BED 3-4
Diesing Sharla K
Nieman Dale W MA 1-2
Spens Eileen L BS 5-6
**AUBURN**-GRACE 1-8
• 1959
303 W Ruth St 48611-9463
(517)662-4791 •
FAX(517)662-0091
revdavidreed@aol.com
**Fredrich Peter D BS 7-8**
Gengler Constance C BA 5-6
Rabe Ellen J BA 1-2
Sherry Beth E BA 3-4
ZION PS-8
• 1887
1557 W Seidler Rd 48611-9758
(517)662-4264 •
FAX(517)662-7052
dszion@hotmail.com
Horning Diane 7-8
Jammer Bonnie M BS 1-2
Olson John R BA 3-4
Riske Ralph H MED 5-6
Schmidt Dennis M MSED
Schoenherr Barbara I BS PS-3
Wegener Luanne S MA K-1
**BAD AXE**-OUR SAVIOR PS
• 1983
123 W Irwin St 48413-1014
(517)269-7642
Rochefort Donna
**BAY CITY**-FAITH PS-8
• NLSA • 1961
3033 Wilder Rd 48706-2398
(517)684-3448 •
FAX(517)684-3545
**Schumacher James L MA**
Eckstorm Kay E BA 2
Evans Evelyn L 1
Grimpo Ronald D MA 6-8
Grueber Catherine M 4

Hofmeister Kaye L 3
Houghteling Elizabeth 6-8
Knight Carole BMU 1-8
Sonntag Connie K
Thompson Steven 6-8
Wegener Ruth A BSED PS
Williamsen Michael E MAT 5
IMMANUEL PS-8
• NLSA • 1863
247 N Lincoln St 48708-6406
(517)893-8521 •
FAX(517)893-4172
ils@immanuelbaycity.com
**Young Brian A MA**
Carey Kristie L 1-8
Freudenburg Daris S 1
Fulkersin Patsy A PS
Gakstatter Kari S K-8
Hauser Arlene J MED 1-8
Hauser Ronald L MCMU 6-8
Mc Alpine Deborah M PS
Miles Mary M MAT 4
Osbourn Laura E BA 2
Osbourn Scott C BA 7
Pett Ellen 6-8
Sandor Donald R MAT 5
Trinklein Rebecca M MA K
Waldie Charlene A BS 3
ST JOHN PS-8
• NLSA • 1852
1664 Amelith Rd 48706-9378
(517)686-0176 •
FAX(517)686-2169
office@stjohn-amelith.org
Bauer Nancy K BS 1-2
Hall Karen B 5-6
Kraenzlein Judy A BA K
Rauschert Cynthia BA 7-8
Scheiwe Jean R MA 3-4
Scheiwe Warren A MMU 5-6
ST PAUL PS-8
• 1848
6094 Westside Saginaw Rd 48706-9357
(517)684-4450 •
FAX(517)684-0882
684-0199stpaul@isd.bay.k12.mi.us
Gibson Lisette L MA 3-4
Hopp Jerry L MA
Otto Brenda L MAT 5-6
Stanley Lisa S BA PS-K
Stevens Joanne M BA 1-2
TRINITY PS-8
• NLSA • 1880
20 E Salzburg Rd 48706-9763
(517)662-4891 •
FAX(517)662-6173
Arnold Ellen A BA K
Feinauer Joy K BAED 5-6
Pickelmann Henry M MA
Pickelmann Janet M MAT 1-2
Rohde Mary Ann PS
Sherouse Beverly J BA 3-4
ZION PS-8
• NLSA • 1901
1707 S Kiesel St 48706-5295
(517)893-5793 •
FAX(517)893-4633
**Klemm Pam 4**
Eichinger Diane J MA 1
Freudenburg Curtis C MED 6
Glumm Julie K BA 5
La Rocque Janet E MA 7-8
Martin Kathy A BSED 3
Nobis Judy A K
Smith Mary B BA PS
Vogtmann Janet L MA 2
Weisenbach Janice L MA
**BERRIEN SPRINGS**-TRINITY PS-8
• NLSA • 1925
9123 George Ave 49103-1622
(616)473-1811 •
FAX(616)473-2322
**Bagby Timothy D BA 4-8**
Hildebrand Laura A BA 5-6
Krieger Ruth A MA 2
Lueders Kim 6-8

Michael Patricia M BA 1
Steinke Laurie J MA PS-K
Strohacker Diane C MA 3
Walker Sandra L BA PS
Wedde Deborah D BS K-8
Wiskow Ingrid E BS K-8
**BIG RAPIDS**-ST PETER PS-8
• 1871
408 W Bellevue St 49307-1399
(231)796-8782 •
FAX(231)796-1186
dtruog@net-port.com
Bailey Karen BS 5
Griffith Susan MAT 7-8
Heck Zonna L MA K
Miller Joanne M MED 6
Sims Karen PS
Truog David J MA
Truog Susan L MA 3
Wortz Julie 1-2
**BIRMINGHAM**-OUR SHEPHERD PS-8
• 1956
1658 E Lincoln St 48009-7112
(248)645-0551 •
FAX(248)645-2427
psalm23@ameritech.net
**Brockberg Kevin H MA**
Austin Lori PS
Brockberg Susan M 3-8
Garrabrant Rachel A BA 1
Giese Esther M BA 6-8
Haddon Amy A BA 4
Kern Kimberly L MA 3
Klausmeier Caroline L MED 5
Kowitz Susan A BA 1-8
Lanthier Elizabeth 3
Lemke Terry J BSED 6-8
Mazur Tammy E BA 2
Mc Auliffe Cyndi PS
Mc Loughlin Janet M BA PS-K
Needham Brenda R BA 5
O Boyle Sharilyn M BA 2
Pavelski Gregg 6-8
Pavelski Suzanne R BS 1-8
Pierce Deborah A BA 1
Sellers Tammy L BA 4
Wernecke Ann M BS PS
Wittrock John H MMU 4-8
Woitha Deborah PS
WESTMAPLE PS
• 1954
1800 W Maple Rd 48009-1596
(810)646-5155
Grove Cynthia PS
Schlak Andrea
Schweibold Erin PS
Sweitzer Katherine PS
**BRIDGEPORT**-FAITH PS
• 1970
4241 Williamson Rd 48722
(517)777-2600 •
FAX(517)777-5069
FaithLC@concentric.net
Braeutigam Lucinda A BSED
**BRIDGMAN**-IMMANUEL PS-8
• 1896
9650 N Church St PO Box 26 49106
(616)465-3351 •
FAX(616)465-6409
immanuel.1896@juno.com
Ackerman Barbara PS
Bagby Kathryn L BA 3-4
Catania Janice PS
Peterson Patricia A 1-2
Schaekel Lynn C 7-8
Sukupchak Lori A K
Watson Marie C BA 5-6
**BRIGHTON**-SHEPHERD OF THE LAKE PS-K
• 1982
2101 S Hacker Rd 48114-8764
(810)227-6473 •
FAX(810)227-3566
**Niska Heidi A BA K**
Hawker Diane BS PS

Tatterson Marilyn PS
**BULLOCK CRK**-MESSIAH PS
• 1977
0 48640 1550 S Poseyville Rd
48640-9599
(517)835-7143 •
FAX(517)835-5325
**Gledhill Kristin A BA PS**
Behmlander Hope PS
Crook Ellie PS
Fauver Linda PS
Howard Eileen PS
Langewisch Phyllis PS
**BURTON**-PILGRIM PS
3222 S Genesee Rd 48519-1424
(810)744-1188 •
FAX(810)744-0452
NO REPORT
**CANTON**-CHRIST THE GOOD
SHEP PS
• 1991
42690 Cherry Hill Rd 48187-3402
(734)981-0286 •
FAX(734)981-2474
ctgslc@juno.com
Schwecke Shirley D BSED
**CARROLLTON**-MESSIAH PS
• 1997
4640 N Michigan Ave 48604-1013
(517)753-7281 •
FAX(517)753-7905
Hauser Deborah E BA PS
**CASSOPOLIS**-OPEN ARMS-ST
PAUL PS
• 1997
305 West State Street PO Box 382
49031
(616)445-3950 •
FAX(616)445-3350
stpaul@beanstalk.net
Stolpe Jennifer PS
**CHARLOTTE**-FIRST PS
• 1986
550 E Shepherd St 48813-0368
(517)543-4360 •
FAX(517)543-4360
flclcms@inter-view.net
NO REPORT
**CHELSEA**-LAMBS OF OUR
SAVIOR PS
• 1994
1515 S Main St 48118-1433
(734)475-7338 •
FAX(734)475-9197
**Murphy Laura J AA PS**
Ballagh Dianne C PS
**CLARKSTON**-ST TRINITY PS
• 1983
7925 Sashabaw Rd 48348-2905
(810)620-6154
NO REPORT
**CLINTON TOWNSHIP**-ST LUKE
PS-8
• NLSA • 1957
21400 S Nunneley Rd 48035-1632
(810)791-1151 •
FAX(810)791-1591
stluke@stlukemi.org
**Kutz John C MED**
Dahn Mary L MAT 4
Fielitz Jane L BA 1-8
Goetz Lois A BA PS
Hildebrand Kevin J MMU 6
Hilsabeck Janet E BA 2
Kutz Cathy A BS 6
Mills Paulette V BS K
Neumeyer Joel K BA 5-8
Pickelman Maureen R BA 5
Polehna Barbara BS 1
Wargo Andrew A BA 3-6
Weiss Jared L MED 7-8
**COLDWATER**-ST PAUL SONSHINE
KID PS-K
• 1995
95 W State St 49036-1000
(517)278-8061 •
FAX(517)279-6232
stpaullccw@cbpu.com
Blansit Cheryl K
Kaepp Kay PS
**COLOMA**-SALEM PS
• 1972
275 Marvin St PO Box 729
49038-0729
(616)468-6569
Hub Sandra M AA
**CONKLIN**-TRINITY K-5
• 1869
1401 Harding St 49403-9519
(616)899-2152 •
FAX(616)899-2930
drwacker@aalweb.net
NO REPORT
**DE WITT**-HOPE CHILD DEV CENTE
PS
• 1982
1180 W Herbison Rd 48820-9580
(517)669-3930 •
FAX(517)669-1580
NO REPORT
**DEARBORN**-ATONEMENT K-8
• 1926
6961 Mead St 48126-1784
(313)581-2525 •
FAX(313)581-1156
atone6961@aol.com
**Becker Shirley E**
Gottschalk Kenton R MDIV 6-8
Hochthanner Kelly A BA 6-8
Iseler Janet A BA K-2
Schulz Janice M MCMU 3-5
EMMANUEL PS-8
• NLSA • 1944
22425 Morley Ave 48124-2103
(313)561-6265 •
FAX(313)565-4195
Ankerberg Jennifer L MCMU 5-8
Brandon Katherine J MA 5-8
Daniell Sheri L BA 2-3
Fenton Julie 5-8
Foreman Janise M 3
Glotzhober Alyce K MA
Heins Dawn R BS 4
Mac Kenzie Amy 5-8
Martin Anita C 5-8
Prusak Kathleen A BED PS-K
Walsh Judy PS
GUARDIAN PS-8
• NLSA • 1959
24544 Cherry Hill St 48124-1398
(313)274-3665 •
FAX(313)274-2076
lcsteenr@ccaa.edu
**Steensma Richard D Jr. MA**
Betker Beverly J BA 1
Braun Jayne L BA 4
Ebendick Colleen S K
Eisenman Barbara M MA 5-8
Fisceri Darlene N MS 3
Gerlach Eileen K BS 2
Gieschen Denise MA
Heins Eric J BS 5-8
Matthias John W MCMU 4-8
Sebold Marcia L BS PS
Steffke Angela BA 5-8
Turgeon Karen BA 5-8
OUR REDEEMER PS
• 1962
24931 Union St 48124-1398
(313)562-9246 •
FAX(313)562-9247
Ramthun Linda L BA
**DEARBORN HEIGHTS**-HAND N
HAND-IMMANUEL PS
• 1997
26969 Ann Arbor Trl 48127-1061
(313)278-6779
Bohn Carol
Bohn Taleese
Olson Carol L
**DECKERVILLE**-ST JOHNS PS-K
• 1995
3451 Main St 48427-9701 6600 N
Ruth Rd 48465-9706
(810)376-8639 •
FAX(517)864-3411
peerhank1@aol.com
**Malone Henry B MDIV PS-K**
Bungart Tina PS-K
Malone Dianne PS-K
**DETROIT**-BETHANY PS-8
• 1889
11475 E Outer Dr 48224-3291
(313)885-0180 •
FAX(313)885-0180
bethanyls@juno.com
**Johnson Mary L MED 1**
Ambs Cheryl 7
Dale Greg K-8
Davenport Stephani 6-8
Deyo Dan 6-8
Keita La Tanya 4
Klein Debbie K-8
Kunze Beverly A BS K
Mayer Wanda PS
Nyquist Ina R 3
Pidsosny Mary L BSED 5
Wright Johann C 2
DETROIT URBAN K-8
• NLSA • 1972
8181 Greenfield Rd 48228-2286
(313)582-9900 •
FAX(313)582-0817
siefkerdulhs@msn.com
NO REPORT
EAST BETHLEHEM K-8
• 1944
3510 E Outer Dr 48234-2658
(313)892-2671 •
FAX(313)892-1754
Difatta David C BS 6
GREENFIELD PEACE K-8
• 1952
7000 W Outer Dr 48235-3193
(313)838-6588
**Schultz Patricia A MED**
**Wiersig Dan**
Fischer John
Fisher Jessica
Lewis Concetta
Mitchell Cecilee
Nelson Jennifer
Reinhardt Gary P
Siefker Dorothy I BA
Williams Tressa
MT CALVARY PS-8
• 1923
17100 Chalmers St 48205-2899
(313)527-3366 •
FAX(313)527-7535
mtcal@voyager.net
Krone Shirley M MA 1
Krone Walter K MA
Lewis Christopher A 7-8
McNally Brian M 5-6
Wallace Sylvia A BA 2
Witte Lucie E BA K
Wrobel Barbara L MA 3-4
NEW MOUNT OLIVE PS
• 1986
8590 Esper Blvd 48204-3183
(313)834-4396
venice.douglas@gte.net
NO REPORT
PEACE K-8
• 1929
15760 E Warren Ave 48224-3297
(313)882-3030 •
FAX(313)882-5680
**Lewis Patricia T BS**
Berry Gerald 5-6
Jackson Dominique 4
Nickel Janice 3
Small Sheila K
Wenskay Carolyn 1
Wills Kristine A 2
RESURRECTION PS
• 1998
20531 Kelly Rd 48225
(313)372-7912
Meyer Judith A 4
SPECIAL ED MINISTRIE
• RSO • 1873
6861 E Nevada St 48234-2983
(313)368-1220 •
FAX(313)368-0159
Lubbers Jill D BA
Sheppard Loren K
ST JOHN PS-8
• 1879
4950 Oakman Blvd 48204-2684
(313)933-8928 •
FAX(313)933-5842
NO REPORT
ST TIMOTHY PS-8
• 1958
19400 Evergreen Rd 48219-2025
(313)535-1971 •
FAX(313)535-9732
stlsoet@aol.com
NO REPORT
**DRYDEN**-HOLY REDEEMER PS
• 1996
4538 Dryden Rd 48428
(810)796-3951
NO REPORT
**EASTPOINTE**-ST PETER PS-8
• 1850
23000 Gratiot Ave 48021-0396
(810)777-6300 •
FAX(810)777-0347
tbehml@aol.com
**Behmlander Todd G MA**
Attenberger David F MA 4
Behmlander Christine E BS PS
Brown Melissa 2
Gugel Ruth 3
Johnson Christine A BS 6
Jurczak Joyce K
Leidecker Karla J BA 2
McNeeley Mark
Olsen Matthew W BA 7
Rich Mary B K
Ristow Beth A MED 1
Scherer Ronald D MA 8
Schilling Timothy R BA 5
Ziegler Dawn 1
ST THOMAS PS-8
• 1908
23801 Kelly Rd 48021-3499
(810)772-3372 •
FAX(810)772-6265
ttiot@ameritech.net
**Andrzjcwski Kristen**
**Schipper Stuart P MSF**
**Todt John H BSED 5**
Alter Tracey 6
Conger Julie 1
Hendrickson Lisa BA 2-3
Leidich Roy E BA 3
Pagels Doris E MA K
Stoeckel Linda M BS 4
Sturgess Jacqueline M 7
Taggart Linda J MA 2
Vanick Edward W MA 8
Wehrmeister Krista R BA 1-2
Ziegler Sharon PS
**ESCANABA**-OUR SAVIOR PS
• 1999
2401 N Lincoln Rd PO Box 1232
49829
(906)789-9350
NO REPORT
**ESSEXVILLE**-PILGRIM PS
• 1981
1705 Nebobish Ave 48732-1698
(517)893-7224
Seymour Lori

**FARMINGTON HILLS**-ST PAUL PS-8
• 1892
20815 Middlebelt Rd 48336-5545
(248)474-2488 •
FAX(248)474-1945
Donal Karyn M BA 3
Fisher Sue 7-8
Hoelter Stephen W MMU 4
Jones Michelle 6
Luckey Caroline BS 2
Maurer Stacy
Mc Donald Deborah M BA PS
Sutter Irene N BS K
Wiersig Christine C MA 5
**FLINT**-REDEEMER PS-8
• 1942
460 W Atherton Rd 48507-2666
(810)249-1381 •
FAX(810)249-1384
NO REPORT
ST MARK PS-8
• NLSA • 1966
5073 Daly Blvd 48506-1599
(810)736-6910 •
FAX(810)736-6960
stmarkfl@gfn.org
**Schallhorn Mark B MED 5-8**
Arends Carol E MAT 7-8
Kirchhoff David W BA 5-6
Kirchhoff Susan K BA 3-4
Posluszny Jo 1-8
Sawyer Cynthia R MED K
Schallhorn Vicki L BA 1-2
Young Kathryn J BA PS
ST PAUL PS-8
• NLSA • 1928
402 S Ballenger Hwy 48532-3600
(810)239-6733 •
FAX(810)239-5466
vorwerk@tir.com
**Vorwerk Dale H MA**
Abresch Vera K BSED 6-8
Fahlsing Gloria D MA PS
Heublein Metta F MA 5
Heublein Robert R MA 8
Jaremba Marcia BA 2
Kah Beth PS
Lanning Chantal M BA 1
Lauckner Edie H MAT
Overgaard Kim A MA 6
Pakkala Deborah BA 3
Pearson Kathryn L BA K
Reinert Daniel M BA 4
**FRANKENMUTH**-ST LORENZ PS-8
• NLSA • 1846
140 Churchgrove Rd 48734-1097
(517)652-6141 •
FAX(517)652-9071
pab@stlorenz.org
**Bresemann Perry MA**
Ahlschwede Joanne I BA
Anderson Lisa M 4
Baarck Stephanie L BA 7
Bender Michael H BS
Brandt Karen PS
Bresemann Linda G MED 8
Buchinger Steven L MA 1
Curtis Amber 3
Dahlke Dorothy H MED 2
Danz Shirley M MED
Dietrich Mary K-8
Felten Daniel L BA 6
Fortkamp Lisa 2
Gehrs Kathleen A BA 3
Gioe Christopher M MA 5
Gioe Louise E BA 1
Hyslop Dora J BA PS-K
Kern Aaron F BA 7-8
Kern Heidi S BA 6
Kramer Sarah J BS
Laubsch Terry J 8
Liddle Candace BA
List Kay K
List Vicky L BA 4
Nielsen Michelle R 3
Nightlinger Cathy J BA 2
Nobis Lloyd B BA
Palmnueter Dave 7-8
Rawson Kathleen N BA 4
Schlaegel Megan PS
Sievert David R MMU
Volz Karen R MA 5
Zeddies Lynn K-3
Zeddies Michael F MA 6
**FRASER**-ST JOHN PS-8
• 1864
16339 E 14 Mile Rd 48026-2098
(810)294-8740 •
FAX(810)294-9565
**Waltz David E MED**
Auten Glen 6-8
Barone Robin C BS PS
Green Sheila M MA 2
Havrilscak Laura BA K
Hoerauf Karen F MED 1
Korbely Marie A 6-8
Leidecker Rory 6-7
Machemer Susan M BA 3
Merrill Kenlyn S MCRT PS
Muehl Marian PS
Ott Karen M MA 4
Schmidt Kurt E BSED 5
Topel Wendy S MAT PS
**GAYLORD**-TRINITY PS
• 1979
1354 S Otsego Rd 49735 PO Box 542 49734-0542
(517)732-4816
Kersten Kristie A PS
**GRAND BLANC**-FAITH PS
• 1996
12534 Holly Rd 48439-1815
(810)694-9351 •
FAX(810)694-3949
NO REPORT
**GRAND HAVEN**-ST JOHN PS-8
• 1946
525 Taylor Ave 49417-2125
(616)842-0260 •
FAX(616)842-0934
NO REPORT
THIS LITTLE LIGHT-UNITED PS
• 1998
11790 120th Ave 49417
(616)847-4005 •
FAX(616)846-8707
**Kolka Sandy**
Beehr Angela PS
Garza Kathleen PS
Honeysett Amie PS
Marston Cindy PS
Palmquist Sara PS
Semmens Linda PS
Stimson Joella PS
Tenbrink Melissa PS
Varso-Suits Jody PS
**GRAND RAPIDS**-IMMANUEL PS-8
• 1973
2066 Oakwood NE 49505-4195
(616)363-0505 •
FAX(616)363-0505
NO REPORT
MESSIAH PS
• 1987
2727 5 Mile Rd NE 49525-1709
(616)363-2553 •
FAX(616)363-7843
messiahgr@juno.com
Anderson Marlene AAS
Florip Eunice E MA PS
Oppenneer Diane J PS
OUR SAVIOR PS-8
• 1955
1916 Ridgewood Ave SE 49506-5031
(616)949-0710 •
FAX(616)975-7840
bblom@maindex.com
Blomquist Barry E MA 3-4
De Bruin Judy E BA PS
Derrick Wendy L BS PS
Dunn Karen BA PS
Fleming Jo M PS
Gallert Frederick D MED 5-6
Kutch Pam BA 1
McGladdery Christine A MED K
Meyers Anita G MA 2
Roberts Gerald M BA 7-8
REDEEMER PS
• 1993
1905 Madison Ave SE 49507-2539
(616)452-1520 •
FAX(616)452-1450
NO REPORT
**GREENVILLE**-MT CALVARY PS
• 1980
908 W Oak St 48838-2149
(616)754-4886
NO REPORT
**GROSSE POINTE WOODS**-CHRIST THE KING PS
• 1986
20338 Mack Ave 48236-1718
(313)884-5598 •
FAX(313)889-5927
NO REPORT
**HARBOR BEACH**-ZION PS-8
• NLSA • 1882
299 Garden 48441-1100
(517)479-3615 •
FAX(517)479-6551
hbbrown1@yahoo.com
**Brown Cynthia A BA 7-8**
Grim Rebecca R BA 3-4
Koehn Shirley 7-8
Meyer Susan E BA 5-6
Rapson Andrea K MA 1-2
Wood Paula R BS K
**HARTLAND**-CHILD OF CHRIST-OUR SAVIOR PS-8
• 1979
3375 Fenton Rd 48353-2207
(248)887-3836 •
FAX(248)889-8279
cocls20@tir.com
**Burger Stephen F MSED 8**
Annas Michelle L BA 1
Arnold Larry J BA 5-8
Falconer Barbara 5-6
Gramzow William K IV MCMU 5
Hay Donna D BS 4
Helmreich Emily L MS 5-8
Johnson Andrea L MA 3
Korte Sara J MA 2
Samsell Christopher N BA 5-8
Steigerwalt Sherri BA K
Thompson Judy C BA 1-8
Weston Amy PS-8
**HASLETT**-ST LUKE LITTLE LAMBS PS
• 1993
5589 Van Atta Rd 48840-9726
(517)339-2333 •
FAX(517)339-5430
st.lukehas@aol.com
Fishel Rhonda D BED
**HEMLOCK**-ST PETER PS-8
• NLSA • 1881
2440 N Raucholz Rd 48626-9461
(517)642-5659 •
FAX(517)642-9052
**Altevogt Lester L EDS**
Earley Karen L BA PS
Eisman Kathleen S BA 4
Fehn Kelley J BA 4
Fehn Lynn A BA 2
Hagenow Eric M BA 7
Hagenow Margaret A BA 6
Harvey Amy L 3
McQueen Carla J 1
Neumeyer Scott R BA 5
Schiemann Kathleen R BA 2
Thomas Jean G MA 8
ZION PS-5
• 1895
17903 Dice Rd 48626-9637
(517)642-2147 •
FAX(517)642-2147
Hauser Deborah E BA K-2
Wheeler Julie A BA 3-5
**HOLLAND**-ZION PS
• 1982
77 W 32nd St 49423-5034
(616)392-6611 •
FAX(616)392-7180
Ledbetter Jacquelynn PS
Teslaa Mary BA PS
Zorn Molly PS
**HOWARD CITY**-PRECIOUS GIFTS-BETHEL PS
• 1991
18669 Howard Cty Edmore - M46 49329-9312
(231)937-4921 •
FAX(231)937-4921
bethelhc@pathwaynet.com
NO REPORT
**HUNTINGTON WOODS**-HUNTINGTON WOODS PS
• 1975
12935 W 11 Mile Rd 48070-1099
(248)542-3031
Carter Victoria
Fishman Barbara
Gerfen Lynne
Gustafson Mary
Levin Barbara
Sleeman Julie B
**IONIA**-ST JOHN K-8
• NLSA • 1880
617 N Jefferson St 48846-1299
(616)527-1250
stjohns@ionia.mi.net
Edwards Lynn A 7-8
Nagel Charles E BA 1-2
Pretzel Kathy L 3-4
Sharp David F BA 5-6
Yanke Terry L K
**IRON RIVER**-ST PAUL PS
• 1999
4221 W US 2 49935
(906)265-4750 •
FAX(906)265-4750
NO REPORT
**IRONWOOD**-TRINITY PS
• 1984
E5104 E Margaret St 49938-1536
(906)932-3080
skusz@portup.com
Kusz Sally M
Richter Sharon
**ISHPEMING**-CHRIST THE KING PS
• 1996
440 Stoneville Rd 49849-0548
(906)485-4432
NO REPORT
**JACKSON**-TRINITY PS-8
• 1961
4900 Mc Cain Rd 49201-8959
(517)750-2105 •
FAX(517)750-9945
tls@trinitylutheranjackson.com
**Ollhoff Jeanne A MA**
Dopp Sherry E MA 4
Erfourth Lee E 2
Frusti Kathleen H MED K
Gruenhagen Heather S 7
Kusserow Mary L BA 3
Kusserow Thomas E MA 4
Mohlenhoff William H MS 6
Moilanen Karen K BS 8
Shaw Julee A BA PS
Valente Elizabeth A BA
Way Jennifer
Westin Beth K
**JENISON**-DAILY SHEPHERD-HOLY CROSS PS
• 1978
1481 Baldwin St 49428-8910
(616)457-1780
Dykstra Esther PS-K
Howell Tara PS-K
Meyer Jennifer PS-K
Meyne Lois A BA PS-K
Thoms Erica PS-K
Vanderslik Julie PS-K
Vrederoogd Peggy PS-K

Wolff Barb PS-K
**KALAMAZOO**-ZION FRIENDS OF JESU PS
• 1976
2122 Bronson Blvd 49008-1993
(616)382-2360 •
FAX(616)382-2367
Klug Deborah BS PS
Sward Pamela PS
**KENTWOOD**-ST MARK PS-5
• 1967
1934 52ND St SE 49508-4915
(616)281-7892 •
FAX(616)455-8487
0
Aldrich Patricia PS
Brouwer Rachel PS-5
Byle Crystal
Crawford-Poyner Debi MA K
Dunbar Pam K-5
Kersting Connie PS
Oster Amy 1
Peless Gretchen K-5
Ringel David 4-5
Sanders Julie K-5
Shanstrom Deborah L MA
Sheeran Kimberley K
Sorg Stacie AA PS
Van Eerden Rebecca 2-3
**LAKE ORION**-GOOD SHEPHERD PS
• 1996
1950 S Baldwin Rd 48360-1016
(248)391-7244 •
FAX(248)391-1680
Bemis Susan PS
Donnelly Kimberly A BA PS
**LAMBERTVILLE**-CHRIST THE KING PS
• 1997
2843 Sterns Rd 48144
(313)856-1461
Corron Amy PS
Evans Tami K AAS PS
**LANSING**-OUR SAVIOR PS-8
• NLSA • 1957
1601 W Holmes Rd 48910-4394
(517)882-3550 •
FAX(517)882-3477
alank@oursaviorchurch.org
**Krause Alan MS**
Arthurton Melissa BA 6-8
Glenn Michael 5-8
Goetsch Debra 6-8
Greve Wendy F BS 6
Jackinchuk Elaine BS PS
Krause Beth E BS 1
Sohn Miriam L MA K
Thorp Gladys E BA 3
Walker Sharon 4
Wieneke Lori BA K-8
Zehnder James W MED 5
Zehnder Sherrill 2
TRINITY PS
• 1994
501 W Saginaw St 48933-1091
(517)372-3003
Arends Jon PS
Headley Nelia PS
Kocab Sandra K BA
**LAPEER**-ST PAUL PS-8
• 1987
90 Millville Rd 48446-1696
(810)664-0046 •
FAX(810)245-4082
**Ingwersen David J MS 6-8**
Arsenault Jennifer L K
Choroba Katherine J BA 3
Dube Patricia A PS
Kenny Marie 6-8
King David M BA 6-8
Korpalski Kari A 5
Koyl Valerie S BA 1
Schmitt Kristine E BS 4
Stricker Ida L BS 2
Sturm Laurie M BS PS
Sturm Raymond T MAT 6-8
**LESLIE**--GRACE DAY CARE CENTE PS
212 S Sherman St 49251 PO Box 511 49251-0511
(517)589-0250
NO REPORT
**LINCOLN PARK**-CALVARY PS-8
• 1924
3320 Electric Ave 48146-3103
(313)381-6716 •
FAX(313)381-3584
calvary@webbernet.net
**Schnuell-Ruth Karen D MEDADM 1-2**
Faith Nancy A K-2
Hartsough Tracey PS
Meija Jessica PS
Rademacher JoAnn A BS 3-8
Wrase Dianne L MS
Wrase William R BSED 5-8
**LIVONIA**-CHRIST OUR SAVIOR PS-K
• 1982
14175 Farmington Rd 48154-5491
(313)513-8413 •
FAX(313)522-5949
NO REPORT
**MACOMB**-IMMANUEL PS-8
• 1853
47120 Romeo Plank Rd 48044-2809
(810)286-7076 •
FAX(810)286-8645
ils@immanuelluth.pvt.k12.mi.us
NO REPORT
ST PETER PS-8
• 1877
17051 24 Mile Rd 48042-2902
(810)781-9296 •
FAX(810)781-9726
rgolm@rust.net
**Davis Terry M MA**
**Hoch Robert M MAT**
Barodte Mary PS
Bennett Susan E MAT 3
Daenzer Katherine L MA 6
Davis Jasmine PS
Dembeck David E MA 8
Dembeck Valorie J MA PS
Dick Sandra G BS 1
Dunklau Linda J MA 7
Fischer Karen E BA 5
Gluski Karen BS PS
Golm Ruth A BS K-8
Hohnstadt Charlene PS
Kasper Deborah L BA PS
Kosmatka Judith M MA 4
Miller Debra A PS
Otto Jane M MA 5
Paselk Renate E BS 4
Pedersen Fred R MA 8
Rank Kathy M 7
Ritz Wanda L BA 1
Schuessler Jennifer K 3
Stange Janet K BS 2
Streeter Kim E MA 6
Washburn Debra S MA K
Witte Lynne E BA 2
**MANISTEE**-TRINITY PS-8
• 1870
420 Oak St 49660-1697
(616)723-8700 •
FAX(616)723-9755
trinityk8@voyager.net
Jesgarz Fred K 3-4
Masengarb Virginia R BA K
**MARLETTE**-OUR SAVIOR PS-K
• 1998
6770 W Marlette Rd 48453-9203
(517)735-7994 •
FAX(517)635-8306
osl@centurytel.net
Kilmer Kristyne L PS-K
**MARQUETTE**-REDEEMER PS
• 1984
1700 W Fair Ave 49855-2569
(906)228-9884 •
FAX(906)228-8192
Albert Carmen K
Pond Ruth MA PS
Tatzmann Karen K PS
**MARSHALL**-CHRIST PS
• 1980
440 West Dr N 49068-9619
(616)781-5842
NO REPORT
**MESICK**-FAITH PS
• 1998
320 N Clark St PO Box 603 49668-9215
(616)885-1072
NO REPORT
**MIDLAND**-ST JOHN PS-8
• NLSA • 1946
505 E Carpenter St 48640-5495
(517)835-7041 •
FAX(517)835-2443
**Eisman Jerry M BA 6-8**
Ceplecha Paula MED K
Eldridge Barbara J PS
Hitzeman Anne 8
Kell Mary L MA 2
Schmidt Sandra J MA 1
Strefling Jessica L BA 4
Wegener Thomas L MS 4-5
Woods Mary Ann MCOUN 3
Young Bonita B BA 1
**MILFORD**-CHRIST PS
• 1999
620 General Motors Rd 48381
(248)684-0895 •
FAX(248)684-0895
Carlton Ruth PS
Read Jacquie PS
**MILLINGTON**-ST PAUL PS-8
• 1905
4941 Center St 48746-9676
(517)871-4581 •
FAX(517)871-5573
stpaul@tds.net
Bickel Elaine C MA
Buchinger Lori A MA 1
Erdman Jonathan A BA 7
Kaiser David A 8
Kaiser Erika J 4
Keinath Kay A BA K
Keinath Terri J PS
Knudsen Kristie J BSED 4
Schoenknecht Paul R MA 5
Singer Connie L BA 3
Walter Teresa I BS 1
Walter Timothy P BS 3
Weber Carol A BA 2
**MONROE**-HOLY GHOST PS-8
• 1844
3563 Heiss Rd 48162-9432
(734)242-0509 •
FAX(734)242-2701
hgls@hglcms.org
Hall Barbara E BA K
Hall Carl G MED 7-8
Heusman Helen BA PS
Hilkin Levonne 1
Reinbold Tricia K BA 3-4
Sitas Rebecca L BA 2-3
Sitas William J Jr. BA 5-6
TRINITY PS-8
• 1844
315 Scott St 48161-2191
(734)241-1160 •
FAX(734)241-6293
jhilken@tlsmonroe.org
**Hilken John C MA**
Atkinson Patty 5
Au Buchon Barbara A BA 2
Berns Nancy E 3
Boldt John P BS 4
Bunkelman James O 7
Hackbarth Tracey J 1
Hand Marsha J BA 8
Holtzen Mary K MA 6
Holtzen Richard O BS 2
Lemke Jane E BA 1
Lucas Cindy L MA K
Schultz Mark A MEPD 5-8
Schultz Ramona S MAS PS
**MONTAGUE**-GOOD SHEPHERD-ST JAMES PS
• 1983
8945 Stebbins St 49437-1263
(616)894-8471
NO REPORT
**MOUNT CLEMENS**-TRINITY PS-8
• NLSA • 1885
38900 Harper Ave 48036-3222
(810)468-8511 •
FAX(810)463-2389
tlct@123.net
Alwardt Karen BA PS
Anders Brian L BSED 6
Bickmeier Stephanie C BA 1-8
Birkholz Karen BS PS
Brown Joanne BA 3
Buss Sally O 8
Hollrah Deanna S MED 5
Meier Roger E BA 7
Meseke Sharon L BA 4
Niemeier Carla A MAT 1
Opel Warren
Pitters Karen PS
Schwark Janice B MED K
Smith Kelly L 2
Williams Judy E BS
**MOUNT PLEASANT**-ZION PS
• 1972
701 E Maple St 48858-2757
(517)772-1516
Ellis Nancy E BSED
Milan Sharon L BS PS
Tohm Mae PS
**MUNGER**-TRINITY-ST JAMES PS
• 1986
119 E Munger Rd 48747 PO Box 156 48747-0156
(517)659-2506
Laubsch Dorothy H BS PS
**MUSKEGON**-ST MARK PS
• 1980
4475 Henry St 49441-4927
(231)798-2197 •
FAX(231)798-7448
stmark2000@yahoo.com
Mc Kenzie Maxine PS
WEST SHORE PS-8
• 1995
3225 Roosevelt Rd 49441-3898
(616)755-1048 •
FAX(616)755-6942
Buhl Maren PS
Cowan Beth A MA 5-6
Gallagher John BS 1-2
Hutton William P 7-8
Klug David H
Lassanske Lynn D BA K-8
Leatzow Edward A MA 7-8
Mazurek Christin PS
Paluch Beth A BA 3-4
Rudick Barbara A BA PS-K
Stefanich Janet PS
Vanderkooi Jeffrey 5-8
**NEW HAVEN**-ST JOHN PS-8
• 1947
59900 Haven Ridge Rd 48048-1915
(810)749-3121 •
FAX(810)749-7778
Diesing Sharla PS
Schulz Janice M MCMU 3-4
Spens Eileen L BS 5-8
**NORTHVILLE**-ST PAUL PS-8
• 1959
201 Elm St 48167-1293
(248)349-3146 •
FAX(248)349-7493
0
**Ritt Carol J 7-8**
**Schultz Lloyd N MED 7-8**

Decheim Sandra BS 1
List Martha L MED PS
Peedle Jean M 4-5
Schmidt Jill M BA 6-8
Stephan Carole A MA PS-K
Walsh Tanya M 2-3
**ONEKAMA**-TRINITY PS
• 1980
5471 Fairview St 49675 PO Box 119 49675-0119
(616)889-4429
NO REPORT
**OXFORD**-HOLY CROSS PS
• 1965
136 S Washington St 48371-4975
(248)628-0116 •
FAX(248)628-9966
holycrossps@juno.com
Mundy Susan K PS
Salerno Vicci MA
Winkler Debra S BSED PS
**PAW PAW**-TRINITY PS-8
• 1985
725 Pine St 49079-1248
(616)657-5921 • FAX(616) 657-3359
trinityschool@trinitylutheran.com
**Hindenach Deanna J BA PS-8**
Fechik Carol A BA K
Gooding Sandy PS
Hershberger Peggy PS
Larsen Margaret 1
Morse Karen PS
Potter Carol 4-8
Schafer Beverly A BS 2-3
Thiede Lori A BA 4-8
Vandoonik Leah K 4-8
Weatherwax Olivia 4-8
Young Jeffrey S BA 4-8
**PETERSBURG**-KINGS KIDS-ST PETER PS
• 1997
343 East Center St 49270
(734)279-1108
lam@cass.net
Cress Becky PS
Wagner Leslie H BA PS
**PETOSKEY**-ZION PS
500 W Mitchell 49770-2231
(231)347-2757 •
FAX(231)348-7606
NO REPORT
**PINCONNING**-ST JOHN PS
• 1987
1633 E Pinconning Rd 48650-9302
PO Box 56 48650-0056
(517)879-5006
NO REPORT
**PORT HOPE**-ST JOHN PS-8
• 1883
7885 State Rd 48468-9783 PO Box 206 48468-0206
(517)428-4811 •
FAX(517)428-4811
st_john@teacher.com
**Wolf Peter 5-8**
Bender Andrea PS
Emerick Suellen M K-4
Gust Clara F 3-5
**PORT HURON**-TRINITY PS-8
• 1865
1517 10th St 48060-5814
(810)984-2501 •
FAX(810)982-3906
**Bacon Harold L MA 5-8**
Blake Sharon E BS 1
Clark Dennis W 3
Eichberger Kathy L MAT 2
Helmreich Christine A MA 7-8
Mann Joan 4-5
Myers Paula M BA 6-8
Rathje Lynda L MA PS-K
Seidler Jack MMU
**PORTAGE**--CHRIST FOR KIDS-ST MICHAEL PS
• 1999
7211 Oakland Dr 49024
(616)327-7832 •
FAX(616)327-3148
NO REPORT
**PORTLAND**-WEE GROW PS
• 1993
8867 Kent St 48875-1986
(517)647-4473 •
FAX(517)647-5153
**Peabody Sandy**
Sandborn Mary
**REDFORD**-HOSANNA-TABOR K-8
• 1955
9600 Leverne 48239-2293
(313)937-2233 •
FAX(313)937-2173
scfaith2@juno.com
**Faith Scott BSED 3-5**
Ebendick Tim J 5
Garfield Andrea 2
Hoeft James M BA 7-8
Hoeft Rebekah J BA 3-4
Hoeft Stacy J BA 5-8
Mills Ellen K BA 1
Perich Cheryl S K
**REED CITY**-TRINITY PS-8
• 1880
139 W Church Ave 49677-1381
(231)832-5186 •
FAX(231)832-5186
trinitylutheran@hotmail.com
**Bailey Andrew D MA K-5**
Danzeisen Bonnie 1-2
Giese Marjorie A AA PS
Pontz Angelin 6-8
Shaltry Sue A BS 3-5
**REESE**-TRINITY PS-8
• 1921
1935 Rhodes St 48757-9958
(517)868-4501 •
FAX(517)868-3702
tlcsreese@juno.com
Wheeler Julie A BA PS
**RICHMOND**-ST PETER PS-8
• 1872
37601 31 Mile Rd 48062-1907
(810)727-9080 •
FAX(810)727-3370
stpeters@massnet1.net
**Pahlkotter Henry G II MA PS-8**
Contreras Andrew J MAT 4
Dunker Dorcas M MS K
Hass Esther E BS PS
Hass Kenneth E MA 5-8
Klauer Susan E MA 5-8
Kuznia Edward I MA 5-8
Powers Deanna K 5-8
Schade Marilyn J BA 1
Steinbrink Kathryn 3
Walz Christine J BSED 2
Werderman Amy L MA 5-8
**RICHVILLE**-ST MICHAEL PS-8
• NLSA • 1851
9444 W Saginaw Rd 48758
(517)868-4809 •
FAX(517)868-4288
NO REPORT
**ROCHESTER**-LIVING WORD PS
• 1997
3838 N Rochester Rd 48306
(248)651-9474 •
FAX(248)608-9285
livword@attglobal.net
Macks Cynthia S PS
Petzold Julian H MA
Rolf Cheryl J BS PS
ST JOHN PS-8
• NLSA • 1943
1011 W University Dr 48307-1862
(248)652-8830 •
FAX(248)652-9916
**Boldt H J MS**
**Petros Linda S MED PS**
**Weiss Thomas H MA**
Bauer Todd D BA 8
Brautnick Janice M MAT 2
Cardella Mary Kay BS 2
Faerber David 5
Frobel David P BA 7
Glanville Kristina BSED K
Grothaus Timothy A BS 8
Herald Sue
Horstman Candace J BS
Jones Leah M BA 1
Klein Patricia K MLS
Koch Beverly J MA
Leitzke Heidi L K
Leucht Ruth J MED PS
Miller Roger PS
Milz Amy E BA 7
Moerer Lucille P MA
Nelson Kristen 4
Pfund Jonathan D BA 6
Pfund Susan E 1
Pollatz Beth A MS 6
Rebeck Christine J BS 3
Rogers Mary
Rogner Kenneth C BA
Rohde Aaron T BA 2
Schafer Robert D MAT
Shaffer Barb M 3
Shaffer John O MED 5
Sheppard Loren K
Sievert Amy L BS 3
Singleton Lisa 4
Standfest Lynn M BA
Stathakis Carol MA 1
Walz Timothy A MED 6
Weiss Marjorie BA 4
**ROCKFORD**-ST PETER PS
• 1986
310 E Division St 49341-1358
(616)866-3700 •
FAX(616)866-1258
NO REPORT
**ROGERS CITY**-ST JOHN PS-8
• 1916
145 N 5Th St 49779-1622
(517)734-3580 •
FAX(517)734-2120
stjohns@george.lhi.net
Mc Clelland Karen K MA 7-8
Mc Fall Kathleen A BA 1-2
Purol Stacy L BSED 5-6
Schalk Linda S BA K
Schroeder Kenneth W MA 3-4
ST MICHAEL K-8
• 1940
5932 M 451 Rd 49779-9771
(517)734-4178
Besler William MED
Karsten Jeanette BA K
Myers Michael J BSED 5-8
**ROSEVILLE**-BETHLEHEM PS-8
• 1957
29675 Gratiot Ave 48066-4195
(810)777-9130 •
FAX(810)777-9131
Hoeft Rebekah J BA 7-8
**ROYAL OAK**-ST PAUL PS-8
• 1916
508 Williams St 48067-2696
(248)546-6555 •
FAX(248)546-8096
stpaullutheran@home.com
**Pittman Eric G MA 4-8**
Bergman Mary B BS 7-8
Chapman Lisa A MA 2
Costakes Barbara J PS-K
Eising Tina 4
Klotz Debra A 3
Lochner Judy A MS 1
Mc Clatchey Rita I BA 6
Paul Gregory L BSED 5
Zink Charlene J 4
**SAGINAW**-BETHLEHEM PS-8
• NLSA • 1914
2777 Hermansau Rd 48604-2495
(517)755-1146 •
FAX(517)755-3969
**Dressler Ronald L MA**
Bergant David F BA 6
Bergant Virginia A BA 5
Brandt Susan R MLS 3
Fjerstad Susan K K
Frank George C MCMU 4
Frank Leanne J BS K
Millerick Patricia W 2
Sowatsky Janice M AA PS
Steele Kenneth M BA 8
Tucker Lori D MAT 1
Weiss Jane E BMU 7
GOOD SHEPHERD PS-K
• 1957
5335 Brockway Rd 48603-4423
(517)793-8252 •
FAX(517)793-9525
**Arundel Dawn E**
Krenz Angela M PS
Lindner Loree A K
HOLY CROSS PS-8
• 1850
610 Court St 48602-4249
(517)793-9795 •
FAX(517)793-7441
**Halfmann Walter K MED 6-8**
Halfmann Norma J MA K
Hurd James BS 7-8
Hurd Loraine K BS 1
Jahnke Lisa 4-5
Odinga Ardith A MAT 2
Rankin Patricia A BA PS
Schimm Naomi BA 4-5
Schimm Thomas W MA 5-8
Wolter Roger W BA 3
IMMANUEL PS-8
• 1847
8220 E Holland Rd 48601-9479
(517)754-4285 •
FAX(517)754-0454
school@frankentrost.org
**Neumeyer Dennis K MED**
Grueber Susan E MA PS
Kern Stuart C BA 7-8
Neuendorf Karen BSED 5-6
Neumeyer Marsha J MED 1-2
Weiss Muriel J BA 3-4
PEACE PS-8
• NLSA • 1940
3427 Adams Ave 48602-2999
(517)792-2581 •
FAX(517)792-8266
peacelu1@svol.org
**Kaschinske Kenneth A MED**
Campbell Gary H MA 6-8
Drinan Lori J 2
Gulliver Holly A 1
Kaschinske June E BA K
Klages Kenneth J BA 1-8
Koboldt Mary E BS 4
Krause Sandra L BS 5
Mayer Henry P 1-8
Minda Kathleen M BS 3
Minda Keith A MED 8
Mueller Robert K BA 7
Odinga Michael D MA 3
Ott Donna J BA 5
Standiford Nancy L BS PS
Witchger Ann G 1-8
Woodcock Roxanne S BA 1
ST MARK PS
• 1999
2565 N Miller Rd 48609
(517)781-3205
NO REPORT
**SAINT CLAIR**-IMMANUEL PS
• 1998
415 N 9th St 48079-3251
(810)329-7174 •
FAX(810)329-4104
immanuelsc@firststep.net
Kling Dawn PS

**SAINT JOHNS**--ST PETER K-8
• 1941
8982 Church Rd 48879-9230
(517)224-3113 •
FAX(517)224-8962
lcmsplc@abraham.ccaa.edu
NO REPORT

**SAINT JOSEPH**-TRINITY PS-8
• NLSA • 1867
613 Court St 49085-1395
(616)983-3056 •
FAX(616)983-0037
rhackbar@remc11.k12.mi.us
**Hackbarth Richard O MA**
**Ursprung Cynthia PS**
Ashmead Darcy
Baker Susan G MA 4
De Forest Thaddeus PS-K
De Lapa Linda R MA PS
Ernst Cynthia S MA 5-8
Ernst Timothy L MS 5-8
Hamilton Beth 7-8
Hartfield Kathryn J BA PS
Hinterlong Angela K-8
Koch Shirlene L MA 1
Koehneke Karen L MED 2
Krokker Le Ann 6-8
Lubbers Jill D BA 1-8
Matzke Sally L MA K
Milnikel Jenifer J MA 5
Rhew Amy PS
Stein Lovena 3

**SAND LAKE**-RESURRECTION PS
• 1989
180 Northland Dr 49343-9701
(616)636-5502
NO REPORT

**SANDUSKY**-PEACE PS
• 1984
58 Flynn St 48471-1011
(810)648-2485
NO REPORT

**SAWYER**-TRINITY PS-8
• NLSA • 1913
5791 Sawyer Rd PO Box 247
49125
(616)426-3151 •
FAX(616)426-3151
kbeckman@remc11.k12.mi.us
**Beckman Katherine S BS 1**
Bender Susan 6-7
Gnodtke Sandra BSED PS-K
Kacmar Dawn 6
Kugler Colleen BSED 2-3
Pagano Mary Ann 4-5
Roose Abby 8
Stauffer Evelyn M MSED 1

**SCOTTVILLE**-OUR SAVIOR PS-K
• 1997
765 W US Hwy 10 49454 PO Box
132 49454-0132
(616)757-0226 •
FAX(616)757-4320
Trench Karen M BA PS-K

**SEBEWAING**-CHRIST THE KING
PS-8
• 1999
612 E Bay St 48759-1655
(517)883-3730 •
FAX(517)883-9171
mwarrrior@avci.net
**Marxhausen Gary P MS**
Beringer Daniel W MA 5-8
Beringer Gloria L BA 1
Bunke Connie L MA PS
Bunke James E MA 5-8
Engelhard Cynthia M MA 2
Schamber Bonnie L MED 4
Seng Rebekah J BA 3
Vantol Rebecca 5-6
Werschky Sharon L BA K-8

**SHELBY TWP**-PEACE PS-8
• NLSA • 1969
6580 24 Mile Rd 48316-3306
(810)739-2431 •
FAX(810)731-8935
Sheppard Loren K

**SOUTH LYON**-CROSS OF CHRIST
PS
• 1990
24155 Griswold Rd 48178-9707
(248)437-0871 •
FAX(248)437-7708
crosslut@bignet.net
Schultz Beverly MS PS

**SOUTHGATE**-CHRIST THE KING
PS-8
• 1953
15600 Trenton Rd 48195-2096
(734)285-9697 •
FAX(734)285-5275
miker@ctk-church.org
Cashmer Carol L MA 6-7
De Lage Deborah L BA 4
Difatta Rebecca L BA 1
Edenfield Marilyn J MAT 5
Frazier Alma K BS 6-7
Hermann Randi S BS K
Hubmeier Linda E BED PS
Jordan Sharon B BA 3
Konkel Lynnette S MA 6-8
Rosin Michael P MED
Voelz Mary B 2
Voelz Robert T MS 6-7

**ST CLAIR SHRS**-REDEEMER PS-K
• 1991
30003 Jefferson Ave 48082-1737
(313)294-0640
NO REPORT

**STERLING HEIGHTS**-ST PAUL
PS-8
• 1885
42681 Hayes Rd 48313-2914
(810)247-4427 •
FAX(810)247-1476
0
**Kell Luther P BA 5-8**
Bickel Eric J BA 5-8
Bickel Jennifer L BA 2
Chaplin Heidi 5-8
Dodt Cherie PS
Kell Pamela BS 5-8
Kokuba Ann M PS
Labadie Melissa E BA K
Parmann Heather L BAED 1
Rashid Janet M BSED 3-4

**STEVENSVILLE**-CHRIST PS-8
• 1956
4333 Cleveland Ave 49127-9509
(616)429-7111 •
FAX(616)429-3788
**Strohacker Charles J MA**
Farrand Thomas J MA 4
Gerken Terri 6
Helmreich Ruth E BA 2
Kern Dennis L MRD 5
Kern Joan M BS PS-K
Knuth Fred F MA 8
Steffens Mark C MCMU 3
Ulmer Laurie L BA 1
Wallace Jeffery L BA 7

**STURGIS**-TRINITY PS-8
• NLSA • 1978
406 S Lakeview Ave 49091-1953
(616)651-4245 •
FAX(616)659-2909
trinityl@Trinity.pvt.kl2.mi.us
Anders Kathy E BA PS
Balzer Jo A BA K
Colberg Jennifer 7-8
Kosman Paul K BA
Kyle Jean A BS 3-4
Sarkkinen Amy A BA 1-2
Walters Paulette E BA 5-6

**TAYLOR**-ST JOHN PS-8
• 1931
13115 Telegraph Rd 48180-4693
(734)287-3866 •
FAX(734)287-0532
**Wallace Shirley M MA K**
Avery Wayne F 5-6
Burns Veronica L BA 1
Grage Glenn G MA 2
Holls Susan C MA 3-4
Koenemann Darin D BA 7-8
Parsons Linda M PS

**TRAVERSE CITY**-ST MICHAEL PS
• 1998
912 S Garfield 49686-3403
(616)947-5393
stmichluth@aol.com
NO REPORT

TRINITY K-8
• NLSA • 1950
1003 S Maple St 49684-4025
(231)946-2720 •
FAX(231)946-4796
www.schoolnotes.com/49684/
trinity.wtml
Anderson Jana 7
Brand Susan L BA 4
Christie Linda MA K
Corad Bruce 3
Covell Mary A BSED 1
Dickinson Melinda S BS 2
Dockery Daniel L MSW 5
Helmreich Harry J MA 6
Klemp Ann 8
Schmucker Calvin F

**TRENTON**-ST PAUL PS
• 1993
2550 Edsel Dr 48183-2487
(313)676-1565
NO REPORT

**TROY**-FAITH PS
• 1975
37635 Dequindre Rd 48083-5709
(248)689-4664 •
FAX(248)689-1554
**Schmidt Elizabeth R MA PS**
Giannotta Karen K MA
Hall Diane PS
Kennedy Rosemary PS
Laman Nola A PS
Mahrle Elaine PS
Meyerand Sue PS
Mitchell Susan PS
Parker Diane MA PS
Tosch Casey PS

ST AUGUSTINE PS
• 1998
5475 Livernois 48098
(248)879-2893
Baumgras Jeanette PS
Goshgarian Charlene BA
St Cyr Debbie L BA PS

**UNION CITY**-OUR SAVIOR LITTLE
LI PS
• 1994
405 South St 49094-1221
(517)741-8405
NO REPORT

**UTICA**-TRINITY PS-8
• 1882
45160 Van Dyke Ave 48317-5578
(810)731-4490 •
FAX(810)731-1071
trinityschool@ameritech.net
**Kosmatka Bruce J MSED**
Angott Donna L MA K
Brunk Donna J MA 1
Burgess Robert M BA K-8
Carlson Sandra 2
Delmotte Karen M BA 4
Felten Jolyn R BA 3
Gast Carolyn R MA PS
Grupe Elizabeth F BSED 1-8
Harris Valerie J MAT 1
Havers Brenda E MA 7-8
Henwood Jane D MA 4
Horak John B MMU 5-8
Horak Susan 1-8
Jacobs M E AAS PS
Kowalke Julie A BA 5
Kuschmann Helmut P MAT 7-8
Meyer Barbara K BSED K
Palmeter Donald W MA 7-8
Randall Sally A BA K
Remer Rose A MAT 7-8
Sheldon Susan L 5
Siekmann Timothy C MSED 6
Sundermann Dianne S MA 3
Tiedje Norman MMU K-8
Westendorf Karen S BS 2
Zappitell Kathleen M MA 6

**WALLED LAKE**-ST MATTHEW
PS-8
• NLSA • 1957
2040 S Commerce Rd 48390-2412
(248)624-7677 •
FAX(248)624-0685
Susan.Palka@st-matthew.org
Brei Traci A 1
Engelhardt Janet 7
Hartmann Royce R MA 8
Kitzman Laura A BA 2
Lenghart Susan M BS K
Moldenhauer Corleen 7
Palka Susan E MA
Scheiwe Wendy A BA 3
Scheler Kristie F BS PS
Schonsheck Joyce L AAS PS
Stevenson Betty J BA 4
Strang William J MED 6
Toman Laura 5

**WALTZ**-ST JOHN PS-8
• 1870
28320 Waltz Rd 48164-9607
(734)654-6366 •
FAX(734)654-3675
**Grassley Shirley M BSED K**
Bacic Frances M BA 4
Davis Kathryn R BA 2
Heyniger Kristen M BA 6
Manthei Gregory W BA 5
Morris Cheryl J BA PS
Nelson Elizabeth D MA 3
Nelson Gary R MA 7-8
Reinhardt Karen S MA 1

**WARREN**-PEACE PS-8
• 1962
11701 E 12 Mile Rd 48093-3492
(810)751-8011 •
FAX(810)751-8558
peacewarrn@cs.com
Difatta David C BS 5-6
Gerds Roslyn L BA K
Marshall Vicki L BA 1-2
Primeau Douglas MED 7-8
Primeau Lynette BA 3-4
Schilling Rebecca A MED PS

**WASHINGTON**-LITTLE LAMBS-OUR
REDEEMER PS
• 1983
8600 27 Mile Rd 48094-2303
(810)781-5567 •
FAX(810)781-0672
orlc@glis.net
Bigelow Joanne PS
Falker Robin PS
Friedli Robin PS
Funk Marge PS
Geraci Deidre PS
Giancarli Annette M PS
Harbach Barbara PS
Verellen Ellen PS
Wegner Kathleen G PS

**WATERFORD**-PEACE PS
• 1996
7390 Elizabeth Lake Rd 48327
(810)681-9379
NO REPORT

ST STEPHEN PS-8
• NLSA • 1980
4860 Midland Dr 48329-1743
(248)673-5906 •
FAX(248)673-4826
Bergkoetter Molly A BSED 2
Devine Amy J
Dunsmore David M BA 5
Dunsmore Sharon K BA 3
Fischer Karen K BA 6-8
Geyer Stephen H BS 4
Heinert Karla S BA 6-8
Kiehler Elaine A PS
Klemm Christine M 7-8
Miller Tammy L BA
Rolf James E MCRT 6-8

Van Dellen Carol A MAT 1
**WAYNE**-ST MICHAEL PS-8
• 1982
3003 Hannan Rd 48184-1009
(734)728-3315 •
FAX(734)728-9569
Bevins Nancy D BA 5-6
Dent Kelli L BA 2
Greer Theresa MA 4
Hinck John T MED 1
Hoeft Karen R BA 5-8
Hughes Judith D BA PS
Moro Martin L III MSED 6-8
Rolf Cheryl L BA 3
Rolf John E MA 2
Schmit Harvey M DED
**WEST BLOOMFIELD**-SHEPHERD KING PS
• 1992
5300 W Maple Rd 48322-3801
(248)626-2121 •
FAX(248)626-0324
Eldridge Kathleen BA
**WESTLAND**-ST MATTHEW PS-8
• NLSA • 1949
5885 N Venoy Rd 48185-2899
(734)425-0261 •
FAX(734)425-7932
ministry@stmatthewwestland.com
**Burkee Jeffrey R BA**
Dash Russell W BA 7-8
Guse Jane 3
Hinck Barbara A 2
Pfeiffer Ann M BS PS
Pfeiffer Thomas E MA 5-6
Schwaegerle Judy L BA 4
Unger Andrea L BSED 1
**WHITE CLOUD**-CHRIST PS
• 1993
701 S Evergreen Dr 49349 PO Box 625 49349-0625
(231)689-1704
Warner Jody A PS
**WIXOM**-HEARTS AND HANDS PS
48340 Pontiac Trl 48393
(248)624-9525
NO REPORT
**WYANDOTTE**-TRINITY K-8
• 1863
465 Oak St 48192-5898
(734)282-5896 •
FAX(734)282-2707
Cox Lori L BA
Hartley Tammy M BS 1-2
Lindenfelser Lynn M 3-4
Rice Barbara L MED 5-8
Scheitz Kathleen E 5-8
Zanley Joyce D K
**WYOMING**-GRACE PS
• 1996
150 50Th St SW 49548-5636
(616)534-0805 •
FAX(616)534-0808
Doss Cheryl B BSED PS
Oppenneer Diane J PS

## MINNESOTA

**AFTON**-ST PETER PS
• 1972
880 Neal Ave S 55001-9760
(651)436-3357
stpeterafton@juno.com
Ayers Amy PS
Law Linda PS
**ALEXANDRIA**-ZION PS-8
• NLSA • 1890
300 Lake St 56308-1531
(320)763-4842 •
FAX(320)763-3676
zionschl@rea-alp.com
**Bowden Sue A MA 4-8**
Bauer Peter W MSEDADM 4-8
Brogaard Jo Nette L BA K
Bumgarner Maureen H BA 2
Harbig Rachel A BED 1
Kutz Doris M BSED 3
Roste Lucy M PS
Sabolik Marisa A 4-8
Sellin Amber L 4-8
**ANOKA**-MOUNT OLIVE PS-K
• 1981
700 Western St 55303-2001
(763)421-9048 •
FAX(763)576-9626
linda@mtolive-anoka.org
**Stroming Linda L BA**
Heiden Sheila M PS
Neuenfeldt Jane PS
Parvey Linda L BSED PS-K
**ATWATER**-ST JOHN K-6
• 1873
19911 56Th Ave NE 56209-9356
(320)974-8982 •
FAX(320)974-8982
**Pygman Mary E BA K-2**
Ellson Jessica M 3-6
**AUSTIN**-HOLY CROSS PS-5
• 1945
300 16Th St NE 55912-4524
(507)433-7844
HCAustin@smig.net
Anderley Mary J PS
Luehmann Lloyd L MA
Luehmann Miriam 3-5
Olson Kristen K
Schamber Mary J BSED 1-2
Wollenburg Susan R PS
**BAXTER**-FAMILY OF CHRIST PS-6
• RSO • 1992
2711 Woida Rd N 56425-8646
(218)829-9020 •
FAX(218)829-9020
focls@uslink.net
**Andersen Larry A MED 5-6**
Andersen Rhonda J BA 3
Koehler Patricia M AA 3-5
Varner Jane M BS PS
Weiss Lori A BA 1-2
**BLACKDUCK**-HOLY TRINITY PS
• 1992
1St & Margaret St PO Box 219 56630-0219
(218)835-4355
Depew Tammi PS
**BLOOMINGTON**-MOUNT HOPE-REDEMPTIO PS-8
• 1956
927 E Old Shakopee Rd 55420-4599
(612)881-0036 •
FAX(612)881-0036
mhreast@mail.com
**Polzin David M MED**
Ahlman Lillian A BA K
Bratsch Cheryl Y BA 1-4
Forseth Eric 8
Hale Angela M BS 7
Johnson Amy B MA PS
Jones Kathryn L MED 6
Mac Donald Kimberly 4
Maycroft Leslie K
Mueller Nancy PS
Olson Tamara M BA 5
Peterson Diane PS
Sherren Judy L BA 2
Walz Carol BA 3
Warnke Sandra 1-6
OPEN ARMS-HOLY EMMANUEL PS
• 1994
201 E 104th St 55420-5305
(952)888-5116 •
FAX(952)888-2349
Adams Katie
Bergstrom Kim
Brewer Shayne
Brokke Linda
Carmona Ignacio
Davis June
Frank Anna M BA
Grant Joel BS
Kettlewell Anne E
Martonik Carrie
Nelson Kelly
Nicholas Larua
Peter Jennifer
Squires Pat
Vinge Becky
ST MICHAEL PS
• 1966
9201 Normandale Blvd 55437-1997
(952)831-5276 •
FAX(612)831-5225
stoerz@pclink.com
Crown Mary J BA PS
Gadbury Anika PS
Stoerzinger Kara M MED
**BROWNSDALE**-OUR SAVIOR PS
• 1998
411 Main St West 55918 PO Box 216 55918-0216
(507)567-2329
jfrichter@smig.net
NO REPORT
**BROWNTON**-NOAHS ARK-IMMANUEL PS
• 1990
700 Division St PO Box 147 55312-0147
(612)328-5325
**Jahr Marsha K BS PS**
**BUFFALO**-NOAH'S ARK-ST JOHN PS
• 1988
302 NE 2nd St 55313-1609 PO Box 238 55313-0238
(612)682-1883
Haskins Nicolette J
**CAMBRIDGE**-JOYFUL KIDS-JOY PS
• 1995
1155 Joy Cir 55008-2637
(612)689-4355
NO REPORT
**CHANHASSEN**-LIVING CHRIST PS
820 Lake Dr 55317 PO Box 340 55317-0340
(952)906-0514
NO REPORT
**CHASKA**-ST JOHNS PS-8
• NLSA • 1886
314 N Oak St 55318-2096
(612)448-2526 •
FAX(612)448-9500
NO REPORT
**CLOQUET**-HOPE
• NLSA • 1985
4093 Munger Shaw Rd 55720-9255
(218)729-6380
NO REPORT
OUR REDEEMER PS
• 1990
515 Skyline Blvd 55720-1138
(218)879-3380
Kuhlman Jennifer J
**COLOGNE**-ZION PS-8
• 1873
14735 County Road 153 55322-9143
(612)466-3379
**Schlicker David J MS 7-8**
Latzke Kathie M BA 3-4
Lindquist Jean E BED PS-K
Marcsisak Thomas A BA 5-6
Schlicker Esther A BS 1-2
**COON RAPIDS**-OLIVE BRANCH PS
• 1988
2135 Northdale Blvd NW 55433-3006
(612)755-2707
Fischer Terry L
Guenther Marla L BA PS
Lenz Paulette J BS PS
Owens Barbara L PS
**COTTAGE GROVE**--ROSE OF SHARON PS
• 1992
7241 80th St S 55016-3004
(651)459-4526
NO REPORT
**COURTLAND**-IMMANUEL PS-8
• 1864
RR 1 Box 40 56021-9701
(507)359-2534
NO REPORT
**CROOKSTON**-OUR SAVIOR PS-6
• NLSA • 1983
217 S Broadway 56716-1953 PO Box 477 56716-0477
(218)281-5191
**Kietzman Janna K BED PS-K**
Janssen Lisa M BA 1-2
Lutz Robert K BA 5-6
Trittin Sandra J BS 3-4
**CROWN**-ZION PS-8
• 1883
7515 269Th Ave NW 55070-9345
(763)856-2099
Borkenhagen Jennifer 3-4
Carlson Gary BS 5-8
Carlson Janice M BS PS-K
Noennig Rachel M BED 1-2
**DODGE CENTER**-GRACE PS-1
• 1973
0 404 Central Ave N 55927
(507)374-2253 •
FAX(507)374-2783
Marquardt Patricia K BS PS
Marquardt Susan J K-1
**DULUTH**-LAKE SUPERIOR-CHRIST KING PS-K
• 1991
4219 Grand Ave 55807-2748
(218)624-0641 •
FAX(218)624-3696
rhberg@qwest.net
**Ahlberg Michelle A PS**
Witherspoon Pattie L PS
**EAGAN**-CHRIST PS
• 1995
1930 Diffley Rd 55122-2203
(612)454-4091 •
FAX(651)405-6881
Endorf Ann F BS
Jopp Jill M BA PS
TRINITY LONE OAK PS-8
• NLSA • 1883
2950 Highway 55 55121-1520
(651)454-1139 •
FAX(651)454-0109
**Timm Richard P MA 7-8**
Bahn Sherlyn J BA 3
Block Sandra K MED 1
Hollatz Jacob D BA 4
Kuseske Cherice L BA K
Maser Gail R BA PS
Miller Stephanie 6
Peterman Kyle P BA 5
Pittman Ellen M BA 2
Rose Carol A MA 1-8
**EAST GRAND FORKS**-FIRST PS
• 1986
203 5Th St NW 56721-1857
(218)773-3207
**Klawitter Mary**
Perez Mary PS
**EDINA**-CROSS VIEW PS
• 1987
6645 Mc Cauley Trl W 55439-1076
(952)941-0009 •
FAX(952)941-5513
jan@crossview.com
**Finney Tamara B**
**Stockman Jan N**
Bolter Heidi L BA PS
Campion Susan R PS
Cloutier Tia K PS
Gillard Rebekah M PS
Hart Kimberly R PS
Jopp Tracy M BA PS
Marks Tia L PS

Radder Jan A PS
Reid Julie A BA PS
Travis Kristin S BA PS
Wachholz Karen L BA PS
Warpeha Sherie L PS
ST PETER PS-8
• NLSA • 1945
5421 France Ave S 55410-2357
(952) 927-8400 • FAX(952) 926-6545
stpeters@visi.com
**Aurich John B MA**
Gaudineer Elizabeth M BA 2
Griswold Rene A BA PS
Hofer Deanne M 3
Kirchner Cheryl N BA 4
Kirchner John A BS 6-8
Matousek Matthew M 6-8
Roth Jeanine S MED 1
Schrupp Stephanie A BA 5-6
Vance Marquerite R 5-6
Von Der Ahe Jeanne M BSED 1-8
Weber Ann M BA K
Zumhofe Laurie L BS 7-8
**ELK RIVER**-EMMANUEL GUIDING HAN PS
• 1998
1506 Main St 55330-1827
(612)441-2555 •
FAX(612)241-0731
emmanuel_luth@worldnet.att.net
NO REPORT
ST JOHN PS-8
• 1888
9243 Viking Blvd NW 55330-8019
(612)441-6616 •
FAX(612)441-9858
Brisbin Rae L BSED 5-8
Ford Deana 1
Kick Jennifer L BSED 4
King Judith H BA 2
Krinke Arlen D MA
Pieper Nancy A BA PS
Rudolph Barbara R BSED K
Rudolph Lorna M BA 1
Sandeno Laura K-8
Sturm Loween R BS 3
Swan Sheila R BA 4-5
**EXCELSIOR**-OUR SAVIOR PS-8
• NLSA • 1984
23290 Highway 7 55331-3139
(952)474-9710 •
FAX(952)470-1985
Anderson Dorothy I BS 1-2
Beck Connie PS
Bergan Linda J BS 2
Biatek Jill PS
Klatt Marian PS
Lano Janeen BS 3-4
Limmel Fred B BS
Limmel Tamara J BS K
Oelfke Joyce PS
Stark Muriel L BA 7-8
Zittergruen David BA 5-6
**FAIRMONT**-ST PAULS PS-8
• 1895
201 Oxford St 56031-2998
(507)238-9492 •
FAX(507)238-9492
splfm2@hotmail.com
**Bergt Gerald A MS 8**
Abel Joan K BA 6
Beckendorf Sandra K BA
Bergt Pauline C BS PS-8
Closs Kara 1
Engelby Paul J BA 4
Eyerly Kathleen M BA 3
Eyerly Richard A MA 5
Gratz Kathryn M BSED PS
Matthees Barbara J BA 2
Prochnow John R MA 7
Prochnow Terri A BA 1
Royuk Elaine A BS K
Thurber Rebecca C BSED K
**FARIBAULT**--FARIBAULT K-8
• 1996
526 4Th St NW 55021-5033
(507)334-7982 •
FAX(507)334-1726
NO REPORT
PEACE PS
• 1974
213 SW 6th Ave 55021-5836
(507)334-5999
Cross Shermayne L PS
Korte Judith E PS
TRINITY PS
• 1990
526 NW 4Th St 55021-5069
(507)334-7982
Velzke Betty A AA PS
**FERGUS FALLS**-TRINITY PS-6
• 1983
1150 W Cavour 56537-1051
(218)736-5847 •
FAX(218)739-3667
trlschff@prairietech.net
Rohlfing Terrence H MED
**FRAZEE**-BETHLEHEM PS
• 1992
210 Maple Ave E 56544-4417 PO Box 335 56544-0335
(218)334-2866
bethlech@means.net
Christensen Kay PS
Stohs Delton G BS
**FULDA**-ST PAUL PS-8
• 1893
208 Third St NE PO Box 394 56131-0394
(507)425-2169 •
FAX(507)425-3310
Buschena Wendy L BS 1-2
Heintz Janis E MA PS-K
Krenz Stacie L BA 3-4
Wilde Dennis 7-8
Wilde Elyse BED 5-6
**GAYLORD**-IMMANUEL PS-8
• NLSA • 1882
417 High Ave PO Box 448 55334-0448
(507)237-2804
Helmer Marilyn M BS PS-K
Kuphal Myrna M 1-2
Monson Kathryn P BS 6-8
Zachow Donna J BS 3-5
**GIBBON**-ST PETER K-8
• 1890
63872 240 St 55335-2001
(507)834-6676
spls@means.net
Monson Kathryn P BS
**GLENCOE**-FIRST PS-8
• 1884
1015 14th St E 55336-1595
(320)864-3317 •
FAX(320)864-6813
firstev.lcms@juno.com
Bargmann Debra BS 4
Dierks Markham W BA 3
Donnay Linda J MS PS
Ehlers Kathryn M BA 5-8
Fountain Jacqueline J BA 2
Fountain Joseph C BA 5-8
Husberg Mary L BA 5-8
Husberg William A BA 5-8
Kohls Craig V BS
Schuette Yvonne V BA 1
Wolter Dawn BS K
**GOLDEN VALLEY**-GOLDEN VALLEY PS
• 1989
5501 Glenwood Ave 55422-5070
(763)544-0590 •
FAX(763)542-7824
Anderson Holly K PS
Breth Wendy PS
Dahlberg Mae PS
Gieseke Angela L AA PS
Lammlein Marcia J PS
Lovhaug Brenda A BA PS
Marek Jan PS
Mc Goff Heidi A PS
Meyer Lynda PS
Mieloch Natalie PS
Scherschligt Kristie PS
Sorensen Deanne M PS
Williams Stephanie PS
**GOOD THUNDER**-ST JOHNS PS-8
• NLSA • 1875
Sherman & Hubbell St PO Box 37 56037-0037
(507)278-3635 •
FAX(507)278-3966
sjlschgt@hickorytech.net
Brase Alice A BA PS-K
Garman Carolyn A BS 1-2
Olson Carol L BS 6-8
Rose Shirley A PS
Shoemaker Brandee A 3-5
**GRAND RAPIDS**-FIRST PS
• 1987
735 NE 1St Ave 55744-2613
(218)326-5453 •
FAX(218)326-9729
mleckert@uslink.net
Eckert Michael L MDIV
Venditto Leslie S BS PS
**HAMBURG**-EMANUEL K-8
• 1860
18155 County Road 50 55339-9406
(612)467-2780 •
FAX(612)467-2473
Mackenthun Katherine M 5-6
Oelfke Brend K PS
Offermann David K BA 3-4
Vollbrecht Marilyn G BAED K-2
Werner Betsy 7-8
Wilson Jodi S BA K-2
**HASTINGS**-SHEPHERDS FLOCK-SHEP VALLEY PS
• 1993
1450 4th St W 55033-1509
(651)480-2273
Kitt Deb
Spitzack Jil
**HINCKLEY**-ST PAUL LITTLE LAMBS PS
• 1999
PO Box 99 55037-0099
(320)384-6267
NO REPORT
**HOWARD LAKE**-ST JAMES PS-8
• 1918
1000 Sixth Ave 55349 PO Box 680 55349-0680
(320)543-2630
**Baumann Gregory J BA 7**
Boehlke Michele R BA 4
Chaney Carin K BA 1
Dahl Luke A BA 3
Glessing Marlene K BA 2
Hirsch Lisa L BA 5
Schmidt Jennifer A 6
Stueven Marjorie A BA PS-K
Whitcomb Rhonda J BA 8
**HUGO**-LITTLE LAMBS-SHEPHERD FIELDS PS
• 1977
6000 N 148th St 55038-9309 PO Box 78 55038-0078
(651)429-6848
Johnson Michelle D BS PS
Kupfer Mary M PS
Lindahl Noomie PS
**HUTCHINSON**-LITTLE LAMBS-PEACE PS
• 1983
400 Franklin St S 55350-2493
(320)587-3031 •
FAX(320)587-1162
peace@hutchtel.net
NO REPORT
OUR SAVIORS PS-6
• NLSA • 1961
800 Bluff St 55350-1313
(320)587-3318 •
FAX(320)234-7861
osl@hutchtel.net
NO REPORT
ST JOHNS K-8
• 1892
60987 110th St 55350-8210
(320)587-4851
Kruse Robin F BS 1-4
Schroeder Dawn 5-7
Wegner Doris BS K
**JANESVILLE**-TRINITY PS-8
• 1890
501 N Main St 56048-9794
(507)231-6646 •
FAX(507)231-6191
trinity2@frontiernet.net
**Kleimola David A BSED**
Dimmel-Schultz Marcia K BS 2
Fury Norma J BA 5
Huelsnitz Ingrid M BSED 1
Kleimola Linda R BSED 3
Kroenke Carrie 5
Lund Louise E 4
Mertens Bruce A BSED 6-8
Schmidtke Beverly D BS K
Schreader Amy 3
Trahms Cindi J BA 6-8
Williams Sheryl 6-8
Youngerberg Kimberly PS
**LAKE CITY**-ARK OF BETHANY PS
• 1999
517 S 6th St 55041-0188
(651)345-0188
**Hoffman Sylvia PS**
Lutjen Bobbi PS
Rodewald Marin PS
**LAKEFIELD**-IMMANUEL PS-8
• 1899
620 Bush St 56150 PO Box 750 56150-0750
(507)662-5860 •
FAX(507)662-5820
immanuel@rconnect.com
**Zellar Doyle M BA 7-8**
Ackermann Kelly J 3-4
Baumann Donna L BSED 1-2
Berglund LaVonne J MA 4
Menk Mary E BA 5-6
Place Susan L PS-2
Rossow Doris J 3-8
Swanson Rhonda J BSED K
**LAKEVILLE**-HEART N HAND-MESSIAH PS
• 1989
16725 Highview Ave 55044-9294
(612)432-9451 •
FAX(612)431-5980
NO REPORT
**LEWISTON**-IMMANUEL PS-8
• 1862
RR 2 Box 63A 55952-9615
(507)523-3143 •
FAX(507)523-1049
silopete@lakes.com
Engelhardt Sandra K BS 1-2
Harstad Susan K BA 5-6
Mueller Julia E BA PS-K
Peterman Karl F BS 7-8
Schkade Kristi J BSED 3-4
**LONG PRAIRIE**-TRINITY PS-8
• 1896
610 2nd Ave SE 56347-1706
(320)732-2238 •
FAX(320)732-3435
**Larson Tammy L BA 3-5**
Collins Mary L BA 1-2
Golnitz Robert M MAR 6-8
Henry Lana PS-K

**LUVERNE-**LITTLE LAMBS-ST JOHN PS
• 1982
803 N Cedar St 56156-1398
(507)283-2316
stjohn2@rconnect.com
Schneekloth Sheila D BA PS
Sonntag Judith R BS PS
Suhr Kristin L PS
**MAHNOMEN-**BETHLEHEM PS
• 1994
5th & Monroe W PO Box 202
56557-0202
(218)935-2456
Salvhus Lorain C MA
**MAPLE GROVE-**SHEPHERDS CARE-SHEPHERD GROVE PS-2
• 1989
11875 W Eagle Lake Dr
55369-5598
(763)493-3623 •
FAX(763)425-0622
**Rosenberg Jayne**
Bullen Sue PS
Christianson Valerie PS
Gamache Barbara PS
Herrlin Susanne M MA PS
Tyson Jane PS
ST JOHN PS-8
• NLSA • 1864
9141 County Road 101 N
55311-1304
(763)420-2426 •
FAX(763)420-7198
**Volberding Gary L MS PS-8**
Cummins LeAnn J MA 2
Droogsma Ruth E BA 3
Johnson Stephen P BA 6-8
Kliche Gretchen I BS 6-8
Rehmer Robert C BA 5
Schutte Susan E BA PS-K
Swem Jeremy M 6-8
Swem Katherine E BA 4
Volberding Deborah L BS 1
**MAYER-**ZION PS-8
• 1912
209 Bluejay Ave PO Box 109
55360-0109
(612)657-2339 •
FAX(612)657-2337
zionmayer@mcg.net
Evans Lee A BA PS-K
Henkelman Timothy A BA 7-8
Kelzer Debra S MA
Ketcher Ronald L BA 5-6
Shipler Tracy M BA 1-2
**MINNEAPOLIS-**MOUNT ZION PS
• 1971
5645 Chicago Ave 55417-2429
(612)824-1882 •
FAX(612)824-4612
Gartland Susan PS
TRINITY FIRST PS-8
• 1859
1115 E 19th St 55404-2099
(612)871-2353
NO REPORT
**MINNETONKA-**BETHLEHEM PS
• 1997
5701 Eden Prairie Road
55345-5807
(612)934-5959 •
FAX(612)934-5959
**Grimm Tosca M BA PS**
Barbeau Tina M PS
Giardini Carole PS
Jenks Amy D BA PS
Kelsey Lisa PS
Lunderby Joan PS
Makela Michelle L BA PS
Sash Carey A PS
Sauter Justin PS
Solom Tammy L PS

LOVING SHEPHERD-FAIRVIEW PS
• 1998
4215 Fairview Ave N 55343-8698
(612)352-9940
NO REPORT
**MOORHEAD-**OUR REDEEMER PS
• 1985
1000 14Th St S 56560-3798
(218)233-8270
Biby Cheryl
Heiraas Jennifer
Johnson Kathy
Loewen Theresa
Maas Kristi
Miller Stacey
Oslowski Angela
Williams Shelley
**MORA-**ZION PS
• NLSA • 1993
401 Highway 65 S 55051-1800
(320)679-1094 •
FAX(320)679-1096
zionlc@ncis.com
**Halbert Audra J PS**
**MORRISTOWN-**TRINITY K-8
• 1892
10500 215th St W 55052-5083
(507)685-2200
tls@means.net
Liffengren Brenda 1-4
Schmidt Sandra K-8
Schmidt Warren M 5-8
Wallace Diana L BA K-8
**MOUNDS VIEW-**MESSIAH PS
• 1973
2848 County Road H2 55112-3810
(763)784-1786 •
FAX(763)784-1927
messiah@citilink.com
Beyer Shirley A
Edelen Marian K BA PS
Masso Kristine M BA PS
Schultz Melissa PS
**NEW GERMANY-**ST MARK-ST JOHN PS-8
• RSO • 1968
211 Adams Ave S PO Box 129
55367-0129
(952)353-2464 •
FAX(952)353-2464
**Giesselmann Darryl L BS 7-8**
Aurich Becky R 1-2
Edmison Gordon D MS 5-6
Edmison Linda K BS 1-2
Pevestorf Bonnie L BA 3-4
Stahlke Connie C BS PS-K
**NEW YORK MILLS-**TRINITY PS
• 1988
424 E Gilman St PO Box J
56567-0370
(218)385-2450 •
FAX(218)385-4533
trinity@wcta.net
Bach Gary D BA
Peters Tammy PS
**NORTH BRANCH-**GENTLE SHEPHERD-ST JOHN PS
• 1990
28168 Jodrell St NE 55056-6310
(612)444-5988
NO REPORT
**NORTHROP-**ST JAMES PS-8
• NLSA • 1892
108 James St PO Box 315
56075-0315
(507)436-5289 •
FAX(507)436-5547
**Dierks Eugene D MSED 3-5**
Brummond Heather BS PS
Koeritz Heidi S BSED K
Tonn David 6-8
Wolter Cynthia K BSED 1-2

**OWATONNA-**-GOOD SHEPHERD PS
• 1996
2500 7th Ave NE 55060-1488
(507)451-6821
NO REPORT
**PARK RAPIDS-**ST JOHN ABC PS
• 1987
803 W 1st St 56470-9802
(218)732-9783
jimneu@unitelc.com
Branham Margaret L PS
Neubauer Kimberly F PS
**PERHAM-**ST PAUL PS-6
• NLSA • 1910
560 2nd St SW 56573-1439
(218)346-2300 •
FAX(218)346-2300
stpauls@eot.com
Bauck Diane K BS PS
Borchardt MaryLynn B BSED 5-6
Gleason Nichole 1-2
Riemer Debra J K
Stohs Bonnie S BA
Tangen Re Nae J 3-4
**PIPESTONE-**ST PAUL PS
• 1989
621 W Main St 56164-1299
(507)825-2142
stpaulpipestone@rconnect.com
NO REPORT
**PLAINVIEW-**IMMANUEL PS-8
• 1921
30 S Wabasha 55964-1399
(507)534-2108
**Lutringer Alvin E MA 7-8**
Frederickson Sharon K BA 5-6
Koehler Paul E BA 3-4
Lindeman Marilyn BA K
Lutringer Barbara A BS PS-8
Mussell Ann E BS PS
Weinlaeder Cynthia K BS 1-2
**PLYMOUTH-**PRECIOUS CORNER-BEAUTIFUL SAVIOR PS
• 1999
5005 Northwest Blvd 55542-3504
(612)694-9449
NO REPORT
**PRIOR LAKE-**HOLY CROSS PS
• 1987
14085 Pike Lake Trl NE
55372-9024
(612)445-1779
Taylor LaVona M BS
ST PAUL PS-6
• 1982
5634 Luther Dr SE 55372-2030
(612)447-2117 •
FAX(612)447-2119
NO REPORT
**RED WING-**CONCORDIA-IMMANUEL K-8
• 1969
1805 Bush St 55066-3629
(612)388-3839
cils@win.bright.net
**Lieder Charles H MED**
Burns Kim 1-2
Kietzman Cynthia B BA PS
Lieder Elaine T MED 3-4
Stone Jane 5-6
HIS KIDS-CONCORDIA PS
• 1999
1811 Bush St 55066-3629
(651)388-8719
**Savage Gladys**
**Stam Connie J BA PS**
Bergan Katherine A PS
Lieder Katherine M PS
Nauer Christine j PS
Taylor Sharon M PS
Trost Janice M PS
Trost Lisa M PS

**RICHFIELD-**MOUNT CALVARY PS-8
• NLSA • 1944
6541 16th Ave S 55423-1799
(612)869-9441 •
FAX(612)866-6005
kwfaschmidt@earthlink.net
**Schmidt Karl W MA**
Gottschalk Ardelle D 3
Gottschalk John R MA 8
Griffin Heather A BA 2
Kovach Jill M BA 4
Manthe-Hogan Karen PS-8
Prigge Barbara J BA 1
Schmidt Frances A BSED 6
Spitzack James R MA 5
Wickre Carol M BA K
Wickre Paul N BA 7
**ROBBINSDALE-**CHILDREN OF PEACE PS
• 1985
4512 France Ave N 55422-1306
(763)533-5517 •
FAX(612)533-0026
Raykovich Barbara R
Schepker Dawn A PS
Sweazey Sharon K PS
REDEEMER PS
• 1979
4201 Regent Ave N 55422-1257
(763)533-2564
Barrera Helinda PS
Bonin LeeAnn PS
Tushar Lisa F PS
Witt Verna J PS
**ROCHESTER-**ROCHESTER CENTRAL PS-8
• RSO • NLSA • 1959
2619 9th Ave NW 55901-2398
(507)289-3267 •
FAX(507)287-6588
**Pfeiffer Cletus R AMD**
Aschlimann Eric W 6
Clark Stanley H BA 5
Freudenburg Kathryn A BA 1
Haas Phyllis L 1-8
Jurgensen Jennifer A BA 5
Klemp Peter S BA K-8
Lehman Michelle A BS 6-8
Mack Martin M 6-8
Nelson Brenda J MED 2
Nelson Corey A MA 2
Olsen Heidi K BA 3
Peter Ann E BS K-8
Pfingsten Karen C 3
Pralle Jennifer A BSED 6-8
Prentice Julie A 3
Robbins Doris E BA 4
Schoppers Lynn M
Timm Natalie R BS K
Weinlaeder Kenneth C MED 6-8
Wetzel Linda K PS
Wetzel Myron E MSED 6-8
**ROSEMOUNT-**OUR SAVIOR PS
• 1987
14980 Diamond Path W
55068-4505
(651)423-2580 •
FAX(651)423-2581
**Ristow Tamara**
Astle Kim PS
Christianson Jane A PS
**ROSEVILLE-**KING OF KINGS K-8
• 1964
2330 Dale St N 55113-4510
(651)484-9206 •
FAX(651)484-9206
**Kuball Daniel C MED 7-8**
Boll Dolores A BS 7-8
Cook David A MS 3-4
Fringer Eileen E BA 5-6
Gadow Doris
Rohwer Marletta M 1-2
Schindeldecker Arlene M BA K

**SAINT FRANCIS**-TRINITY PS-8
• 1980
3812 229Th Ave NW PO Box 700
55070-0700
(763)753-1234 •
FAX(763)753-1774
trinitysf@juno.com
**Dunk William F MED 7-8**
Bergmann Maureen J BA 1
Bergmann Peter A BA 5
Dunk Deloris E MED 4
Koch Karen L BS 2
Koch Kenneth C BS 6
Moritz Diane PS
Porisch Dorleen K
Reynolds Laura M BA 3
**SAINT JAMES**-ST JOHN 1-8
• 1888
RR 1 Box 89 56081-9735
(507)375-3433
**Kaelberer Jerome T BS 6-8**
Kaelberer Betty A 4-6
Zinke Edith F AA 1-3
**SAINT PAUL**-CENTRAL PS-8
• RSO • NLSA • 1942
775 Lexington Pkwy N 55104-1497
(651)645-8649 •
FAX(651)645-8640
**Schrader Stephen P MED**
Brubak Janet BED PS
Heuton Eugene W BA 8
Jahr Rachel R BSED 6
Johnson William C 5
Maas Matthew 7
Petersen Connie M MS 1
Savard Sharon J K
Schrader Janice L BSED 2
Souther Debra A PS
Taylor Jennifer L BA 3
Westpfahl Barbara J BA 4
Yernberg Jackie
EAST ST PAUL K-8
• RSO • NLSA • 1957
674 Johnson Pkwy 55106-4731
(612)774-2030 •
FAX(612)774-6759
esplsaints4@juno.com
**Fallert Barbara G BA K-4**
Block Richard W MED 8
Claugherty Darlene J BA 2
Guse Anne M BA 2
Hagen Phyllis C K
Reem Karen L BS 3
Strickland Andrew BA 7
Strom Julie M BED 4
Trombley Kristin J BA 1
West Linda BA K
Zellmer Sue 5
Zumhofe Joan M BS 6
HAND IN HAND PS
• 1982
1250 Concordia Ave 55104 275
Syndicate St N 55104-5495
(651)641-8491 •
FAX(651)659-0207
spless@csp.edu
**Spiess Kristine A MMFC**
Garland Bonnie PS
Hafner Marlene PS
Lobin Tracy PS
Schoer Tammy PS
Wellens Lacey A BA PS
Williams Dina PS
JOY-BETHLEHEM PS
• 1971
655 Forest St 55106-4508
(651)771-6982
bethstpaullcms@juno.com
Ewald Wendy M BA PS
**SAUK RAPIDS**-CENTRAL
MINNESOTA
219 4th St N 56379
(320)251-1477
NO REPORT

TRINITY PS-6
• NLSA • 1888
219 4th St N 56379-1634
(320)251-1477 •
FAX(320)251-8996
Trinity@cloudnet.com
**Rehmer Loren W MSED**
Clitty Cynthia S BSED 5-6
Copeland Carol L BA PS
Krohe Kathryn L BS 4
Lentz Lori BS K
Mehrhoff Sheryl
Morford Kimberly A
Peterson Mary K
Strohschein Karen BA K
Stueve Kathleen K BS 1
**SLAYTON**-TRINITY PS
• 1984
2105 King Ave 56172-1024
(507)836-8129
Harms Judy BS PS
**SPRING LAKE PARK**-PRINCE OF
PEACE PS-8
• 1961
7700 Monroe St NE 55432-2741
(612)786-1755 •
FAX(612)786-2473
popeace@uswest.net
**Emery Glen A BA 5-8**
Coburn Peggy L BA 1
Coburn Wayne E 2-8
Emery Vickie A BS 2-8
Galchutt Adeline M MED 5-8
Kietzman Carol D BS 5-8
Petroff Gail C BA 3
Tikkanen Beverly PS
**STEWARTVILLE**-ST JOHNS WEE
CARE PS
• 1983
111 2nd Ave NE 55976-1299
(507)533-6260
Dux Kathy PS
Howes Barbara L BS
Torgerson Lori PS
**TRUMAN**-ST PAUL PS-8
• 1900
114 E 4th St N 56088-1132
(507)776-6541 •
FAX(507)776-3060
Burmeister Sylvia A BA K
Diepenbrock Ray L MA
Fitzner Cynthia E BA 1-2
Geistfeld Christine K BS 3-5
Geistfeld Yolanda M BS PS
Johnson Heidi BS PS
**TWIN VALLEY**-TRINITY TOTS PS
• 1996
Highway 32 South Box 248
56584-0248
(218)584-8440
Salvhus Lorain C MA PS
**VERNON CENTER**-ST JOHNS 1-8
• 1869
49894 132nd St 56090-9722
(507)549-3036
Cummins Celeste G PS
Reinke Barbara A BA 5-8
Riewe Cindi M BA 1-4
**WACONIA**-TRINITY PS-8
• NLSA • 1865
601 E 2nd St 55387-1608
(952)442-4165 •
FAX(952)442-4644
school@trinitywaconia.org
**Puckett Paul R MA 8**
Anenson Ronald D 4
Beise Melissa BA K
Berg Nicholle MA 6-8
Burandt Shelah J BA PS
Dierks Julie A BA 6-8
Graudin Peter J BS 5-8
Graudin Valerie L BA 5-8
Hilk Miriam R BA 3
Mahlum Jacqueline BED PS
Paine Amy 1-8
Radde Kathy 1
Schroeder Lori A BA 6-8

Schwalbe Rachel 5-8
Stoeckman Bonita M BA 1
Thompson Beth BA 1-8
Wagener Cassandra R BS 2
Wegner James BA
Wiegert Karen E BA 4-5
**WADENA**-ST JOHN PS
• 1991
710 Franklin Ave SW 56482-1755
(218)631-3000
Walz Tammi PS
**WALKER**-IMMANUEL PS-K
• 1998
4656 State 200 NW PO Box 307
56484-0307
(218)547-4139 •
FAX(218)547-1330
NO REPORT
**WARREN**-ZION-IMMANUEL PS
• 1986
Hwy 1 E PO Box 102 56762-0102
(218)745-4766
Gornowicz Linda J BSED PS
**WASECA**-ST PAUL LITTLE LAMBS
PS
314 Fourth Ave NE 56093-2925
(507)835-2647
NO REPORT
**WATERTOWN**-CHRIST
COMMUNITY PS-8
• RSO • NLSA • 1949
0 512 County Rd 10 55388
(952)955-1419 •
FAX(952)955-1424
Binstock Kelli Jo 5-8
Boehlke Jeffrey K BA 5-8
Cox Brenda R 3-4
Laabs Barbara R BA 5-8
Schwichtenberg Phyllis J BS
Steinborn Julie L BA 1-2
Strei Madeline R BA PS
**WAYZATA**-REDEEMER PS-8
• 1978
115 Wayzata Blvd W 55391-1541
(952)473-5356 •
FAX(952)473-3295
rlutheran@uswest.net
**Brofford Eric M MA 6-8**
Bates Janice A BA 2
Bruenger Adam J BSED 3
Bruenger Jennifer E K-8
Finke Larry L MMU K-8
Gesch David S BS 5
Gesch Heidi A BS 6-8
Klahsen Jane A BA K
Schockman Colette BA PS
Schrader Kristen
Wiebold Linda J BED 1
Woebke Kimberly S BA 6-8
Zimmer Jenifer R BA PS-4
Zum Hofe Allen W BS 6-8
**WHITE BEAR LAKE**-OPEN ARMS
PS
• 1999
2464 South Shore Blvd
55110-3898
(651)429-4147
NO REPORT
S SHORE TRINITY PS
• 1948
2480 S Shore Blvd 55110-3898
(612)429-4293 •
FAX(612)663-3634
sstcnbl@juno.comm
Miller Lisa M BA PS
**WINDOM**-SONSHINE-OUR SAVIOR
PS
• 1987
1157 3Rd Ave 56101-1452
(507)831-3522
NO REPORT
**WINONA**-REDEEMER PS
• 1978
1664 Kraemer Dr 55987-2064
(507)452-3869
Flesch Sharon BSED
Norton Rhonda PS

ST MARTINS PS-8
• 1866
253 Liberty St 55987-3799
(507)452-6056 •
FAX(507)457-0884
smlschool@tvsw.org
**Skrastins Igor BA 5-6**
Brand Gregory D BS 5-6
Cichoski Bette J BS K
Dost Nanette H BA 7-8
Krueger Jolene D BSED PS
Schlesselman Roberta W BA 3-4
Seltz Annamary MS 1-2
**WOODBURY**-WOODBURY PS-K
• 1968
7380 Afton Rd 55125-1502
(651)739-5146 •
FAX(651)739-3536
NO REPORT
**WYKOFF**-ST JOHN K-8
• 1876
245 S Line St 55990 PO Box 189
55990-0189
(507)352-4671 •
FAX(507)352-7671
stjhnsch@hmtel.com
**Boll John V MED 6-8**
Boll Caroline A BSED K
Eberle Gladys 2-8
Eickhoff Darlene BA 3-5
Kaun Charles R BS
**YOUNG AMERICA**-ST JOHNS PS-8
• NLSA • 1875
27 1st St NW 55397-9494
(952)467-3461 •
FAX(952)467-2937
stjohnsnya@yahoo.com
**Kuerschner Edwin F BA 6**
Balzum Mary J BA 4
Bartels Renee L BA 1
Gustafson Georgia D BA 5-7
Kimble Daniel F BA 5-8
Kimble Marilynn J BA 2
Knea Linda A BA 5-8
Luecke Rita V BA 3
Winter Peggy PS
Young Ann C BA K
Young Daniel B BA 5-8

## MISSISSIPPI

**BILOXI**-GOOD SHEPHERD PS
• 1956
2004 Pass Rd 39531-3126
(228)388-4720 •
FAX(228)388-8300
NO REPORT
**BRANDON**-GOOD SHEPHERD
• 1995
Highway 25 PO Box 5013
39047-5013
(601)992-4752
NO REPORT

## MISSOURI

**AFFTON**-CHRIST MEMORIAL PS-K
• 1979
9712 Tesson Ferry Rd 63123-5322
(314)631-0992 •
FAX(314)631-8583
NO REPORT
SALEM PS-8
• NLSA • 1909
5025 Lakewood Ave 63123-3799
(314)353-9242 •
FAX(314)353-9328
edbower@slcas.com
**Bower Edward R MA**
Akerson Brian S 6-8
Biesendorfer Lynette K BS 6-8
Burford Sandra L BA PS
Burford Susan 1
Groerich Deborah J BS 2
Grossheider Nelson L BA 4
Johnson Wanda
Kipp Anita E 1

Mc Ferran Peggy J BS 6-8
Mehl Kathryn L MA 5
Rivers Lisa M MED PS-8
Rudsinski Carol A BA 3
Schuermann Glenda L K
Sullivan Barbara K-8

**ALMA**-TRINITY PS-8
• NLSA • 1878
304 N Waverly PO Box 257
64001-0257
(660)674-2444 •
FAX(660)674-2747
trinity@almanet.net
**Bauer Arlin J MS**
Boehmer Judy L BS 3-4
Bredehoeft Kathy D BSED PS-K
Buchholz David A MED 7-8
Mac Lean Joyce L BA 1-2
Martens Lisa M BED 5-6
Sims Connie BSED K-7

**ARNOLD**-GOOD SHEPHERD PS
• 1980
2211 Tenbrook Rd 63010-1516
(636)296-1292
goodsheparnold@juno.com
Greunke Mary E BS PS
Hilkerbaumer Wendy L BSED PS

ST JOHN PS-8
• 1848
3511 Jeffco Blvd 63010-3996
(636)464-7303 •
FAX(636)464-8424
stjohnluth@stlnet.com
Behling Gail A MA 7
Berndt Rosalie S BSED 6
Crangle John 8
Frank Ann M MS K
Huxol Kathy PS
Kelm Dianne F BA
Kersten Lois M BS 2
Krieser Elizabeth 3
Mathany Karen PS
Mc Daniel Joyce A BA 4
Miller Pamela S BA 1
Schmich Deborah K MAT PS
Von Behren Jennifer L BA 5

**BELLEFONTAINE NBRS**-GRACE CHAPEL PS-8
• 1955
10015 Lance Dr 63137-1564
(314)867-6564 •
FAX(314)868-2485
Buerck Bradley J BS 5
Garvey Barbara A MED K-8
Gruenwald Beverly A MA PS
Irwin Deborah A 3
Jost Sylvia M BS 1
Nierman Brenda K-8
Siemers Ilene V BA 7
Skeen Jessica K
Trinklein Lynda M 8
Wehmeyer Kenneth G BS 4
Wehmeyer Lois M BS 2
Woehr David F MAT 6
Woehr Valeda K BA K

**BLACK JACK**-SALEM PS-8
• 1861
5190 Parker Rd 63033-4653
(314)741-8220 •
FAX(314)741-1797
**Rusnak Eric D MA 5-8**
Brinker Sharon H 2
Heard Cindy PS
Joersz Ann BA K
Mansfield Cheri PS-8
Martz Rosanna BS 5-8
Nebel Ingrid A BAED 3
Nebel Mark C MAT 5-8
Pingel Kara M BA 1
Rusnak Janice L 4
Sachtleben Joyce L BA 5-8
Thaemert Ferol S MED 5-8
Thaemert Marilyn R BS K

**BLUE SPRINGS**-TIMOTHY TREASURES PS
• 1975
425 NW R D Mize Rd 64014-2420
(816)228-5300 •
FAX(816)228-5323
**Koehnlein Lorna K**
**Warren Lois**
Bartolotta Robin PS
Bowman Lauren PS
Daub Anna PS
Goetsch Laurie PS
Heusted Sandy PS
Koogler Patty PS
Mansell Betsy PS
Mc Danel Nicole PS
Micheletti Christine PS
Myers Karen PS
Robinson Kathi PS
Smith Heather PS
Thompson Mary F PS
Vogt Laura PS
Volkers June PS

**BOONVILLE**-IMMANUEL PS
• 1977
1001 Immanuel Dr 65233-1895
(660)882-2208
Toellner Sharron K BSED

**BRANSON**-OUR SHEPHERDS PS
• 1998
221 Malone St 65616-2011
(417)332-1922
oslc@tri-lakes.net
NO REPORT

**BRENTWOOD**-MOUNT CALVARY PS
• 1974
9321 Litzsinger Rd 63144-2127
(314)968-2360 •
FAX(314)968-4943
Stutz Brenda BSED PS

**BRIDGETON**-TRINITY K-8
• 1991
3765 Mc Kelvey Rd 63044-2002
(314)739-8330
Ellerbrock Dawn K
Hofius Nancy E MA 2-8

**CAPE GIRARDEAU**-TRINITY PS-8
• NLSA • 1854
55 N Pacific St 63701-5413
(573)334-1068 •
FAX(573)334-1068
tlscape@mvp.net
**Unzicker William L III MED**
Babchak Elizabeth A MA 2
Bartley Marsha 3-8
Bruening Fayleen M BS 7
Callin Diane
Dynneson Lane A BS
Martens Melanie M BED 8
Meyr Delvin G MED 5
Meyr Dorothy R BSED 4
Meyr Teresa 6
Schuermann Michelle C BA 1
Short Jeanne M BS PS
Spaulding Kimberly N 3
Walther Mary L BS K

**CARROLLTON**-IMMANUEL PS
• 1980
402 S Folger St 64633-1223
(816)542-2064
NO REPORT

**CHESTERFIELD**-KING OF KINGS PS
• 1980
13765 Olive Blvd 63017-2601
(314)469-2224 •
FAX(314)469-0601
Dyson Pamela M BS PS
Krentz-Wippold Carol A BA PS
Masterson Christine PS
Miller Anita PS
Ratliff Kathleen PS
Weinrich Judith A

LORD OF LIFE PS
• 1993
15750 Baxter Rd 63017-4983
(636)230-4024 •
FAX(636)536-2322
Dailey Cathy A PS
Ehrmann Linda E PS
Frank Teresa F PS
Houston Wendy M PS
Kammeyer Janet L PHD PS
Kuntz Anna R PS
Okimi Laura M PS
Palmer Helen E PS
Robertson Elaine A BSED
Rose Mary Ann PS
Stutz Brenda BSED PS
Suchland Patricia A BA PS
Tilton Diane PS

**COLE CAMP**-LUTH SCHOOL ASSOC 1-8
• RSO • 1961
204 E Butterfield 65325-1122
(660)668-4614 •
FAX(660)668-2456
lsaccmo@iland.net
Brinkman Annette D BSED 5-6
Glaskey Lyla J BSED 3-8
Lutz David D BSED 1-2
Schnakenberg Barbara L BSED 1-8
Viets Catherine L BA 3-4

**COLUMBIA**-TRINITY PS-K
• 1980
2201 W Rollins Rd 65203-1433
(573)445-1014 •
FAX(573)445-4078
**Easterhaus Carol J BSED**
Boenisch Donna BS PS
Enfield Mary L PS
Faulkner-Neds Catherine PS
Frisch Patsy A PS
Gerike Darlene D BA PS
Golay Krista PS
Neubauer Kimberly S PS
Peterson Linda C PS
Pfeiffer Donna PS
Telle LaDonna C BA K

**CONCORDIA**-ST PAUL PS-8
• 1840
407 Main St 64020 PO Box 29
64020-0029
(660)463-7654 •
FAX(660)463-7173
oaheimsoth@galaxyispc.com
**Heimsoth Orlyn A MSED**
Ebers Jim L BS 7
Freund Joyce E BS PS
Grass Larry E BS K
Hinck Sandra S BA 6
Kammeyer Laurel E MS 8
Muinch Linda C 4
Ravanelli Renee MSED 1
Rittman Judith BSED
Umbach Betty PS
Virus Christopher A 2
Wolters Ann E MS 3
Woods Amy B BSED 5

**CRYSTAL CITY**-IMMANUEL CHRISTIAN P PS
• 1993
19 N 3rd St 63028-1967
(636)937-0043
NO REPORT

**DES PERES**-ST PAUL PS-8
• NLSA • 1849
1300 N Ballas Rd 63131-3601
(314)822-2771 •
FAX(314)822-6574
**Koopman David L MED**
Bender Mark L MCMU 5-8
Cox Denise K-4
Ernst Thomas J MED 5-8
Fish Carolyn A BA 3-4
Hemler Heather A BA 3
Hesse Bonnie J BA 5-6
Hohenstein Rebecca A BA K
Hollrah Joyce E BA 1
Kremmel Mary Beth A BED 2
Olderman Pamela 1-8
Pesselato Rebecca 4-8
Petering Carol J BS PS
Rhodes Sandra 1-4
Rice Denise L BA 6-8
Seban Wendy S BA 4-8
Smith Joanne E BA K
Springer Mara L BA K-8
Sterling Daniel T 5-8
Wehmeyer Allison M BSED 1

ST PAULS PS
• 1992
823 N Ballas Rd 63131-3704
(314)822-9219 •
FAX(314)822-6574
Petering Carol J BS PS

**ELLISVILLE**-ST JOHN PS-8
• NLSA • 1851
15808 Manchester Rd 63011-2208
(314)394-4100 •
FAX(314)394-6274
Arico Karen L MED
Behling Gail A MA 3
Rivers Lisa M MED

**EMMA**-HOLY CROSS PS-8
• 1864
500 N Elm PO Box 121
65327-0121
(660)463-2553 •
FAX(660)463-2853
Brandt Deborah L BS 6-8
Lehmann Judith E BS 1-2
Long Patricia K BSED PS-K
Martens Gina R BS 3-5
Pitsch Marta J BSED 6-8

**EUREKA**-ST MARK PS-8
• NLSA • 1982
500 Meramec Blvd 63025-1147
(636)938-4432 •
FAX(636)938-9858
jhouse@stmarkseureka.org
**House James L MS**
Armbruster Deborah A MED 5-8
Beckman Loretta E MED 1
Brinkman Liane K BA 4
House Rhoda A BSED PS
Jackson Jill K
Kesel Delores 2
Patton Linda R MED 5-8
Pritchard Emily M BED 3
Stoll Paula L BS 5-8

**FARMINGTON**-ST PAUL PS-8
• NLSA • 1873
608 E Columbia St 63640-1310
(573)756-5147 •
FAX(573)756-8669
stpaul@knights.farmington.k12.mo.us
**Duncan Les**
Bishop Paulette MED 2
Braxton Karin 6-8
Easley Debbie M K
Eaves Amy L 3
Giesselmann Duane L MA 6-8
Johnson Leanna 6-8
Judge Diane 4
Keown Mary R PS
Pacilli Denise MA PS
Rains Suzanne K-5
Revior Rosemary BSED 5
Sherrill Sharon L BS 1
Towler Barbara E 1-8

**FARRAR**-SALEM K-8
• NLSA • 1867
287 PCR 328 63746-9999
(573)824-5472 •
FAX(573)824-5389
Goodson Laura N BS 2-3
Koenig Robyn J BS 6-8
Lorenz Linda BA K-1
Suhr Michelle K BED 4-5

**FENTON**-OUR SAVIOR PS-8
• 1964
1500 San Simeon Way
63026-3423
(314)343-7511 •
FAX(314)343-4921
**Moeller Randall J**
Bueckman Blair K BS 6-8
Clark Gail A BA PS
Fiala R J BSED 6-8
Klug Alicia BA 6-8
Langford Sherry 2
Miller Sheryl J BSED K
Rassbach Sharon J BA 4
Schiller Angela L BS 5
Schulz Kathleen M BA 3
Stock Karen J BA 1
Winfrey Patricia A PS
**FREISTATT**-TRINITY PS-8
• 1875
218 N Main 65654-9999
(417)235-5931 •
FAX(417)235-5931
tls@mo-net.com
**Kleiboeker Carole A BSED 5-6**
Doss Jane V 1
Enlow Summer 2
Hansen Fawn L PS-K
Meehan Diane 5-6
Prater Nick L MA 4
Schnelle Aaron 5-8
Staehr Brian T BSED 5-8
Staehr Jerrita K-8
Telschow Anne D BS 3
**FROHNA**-CONCORDIA 1-8
• NLSA • 1839
10158 Hwy C 63748-9744
(573)824-5218
**Golchert Kent R MA 7-8**
Golchert Christina A MA 5-6
Koeberl Nelda E BSED 1-2
Seabaug Bette 3-4
**GLENDALE**-EARLY LEARNING-GLENDALE PS
• 1991
1365 N Sappington Rd
63122-1823
(314)966-3220 •
FAX(314)966-3243
glendale@freewwweb.com
Gieselmann Tracy PS
Himebaugh Mary PS
Lohman Andrea K MED PS
Steele Pat A BA PS
**GRANDVIEW**-HOLY TRINITY PS
• 1995
5901 E 135th St 64030-3744
(816)763-3211
holytrinityl@juno.com
Crawford Carol
Stork Kristine R
**HANNIBAL**-ST JOHN PS-6
• 1860
1317 Lyon St 63401-4117
(573)221-0215 •
FAX(573)221-8384
Begley Janet L BS 4
Cruse Laura 5-6
Curtis Jenny PS
Dann Kristie BS 1
Eagan Carla 2-3
Jackson Donald
Paschal Ruth A BA K
**HARVESTER**-ZION PS-8
• NLSA • 1851
3866 Harvester Rd 63304-2825
(314)441-7424 •
FAX(314)441-7424
**Debrick Marc W MS 5-6**
**Profilet Janet L MAD**
Andermann Rosemary S BA PS
Anderson Ruth A BA 3
Beaty Karen A MED 7-8
Eisold Sandi 1
Eriksen Laurie B BSED K
Felten Daniel K MED 5
Fridley Sandra K MED 2
Gerler Susan M
Glover Martha MA 4
Hendrichs Janelle 2
Koenig Carol J MA 1
Lail Cheryl L BA K
Schubbe Angela
Steffens Pamela A MAT 7-8
Steinbacher Melinda BS 1-4
Tracy Marjorie K BSED 5
Trinklein Erin R BA 3
Vallin Kurt R MED 7-8
Von Dielingen David P MA 6
Von Dielingen Joyce L MMU 4
Wischmeyer Susan L BA 6
**HIGGINSVILLE**-IMMANUEL PS-8
• RSO • 1951
1500 Lipper Ave 64037-1335 PO Box 267 64037-0267
(660)584-2854 •
FAX(660)584-5914
immzi@ctcis.net
**Gesch Ronald D BS 5-6**
**Marth Marlin J MA 7-8**
Boeschen Marilyn R MS 1-2
Buchholz Mary B BSED K
Grass Grace L BSED 3-4
Houston Tammie PS
Wood Mary MSED 7-8
**HIGH RIDGE**-HOPE PS
• 1999
2308 Gravois Rd 63049-2505
(314)677-8688 •
FAX(636)677-3188
hopelutheran3@juno.com
Harper Stefanie PS
Young Darlene PS
**INDEPENDENCE**-MESSIAH PS-8
• NLSA • 1943
613 S Main St 64050-4411
(816)254-9409 •
FAX(816)254-9407
messiah@oz.sunflower.org
**Arndt Ann L BSED**
Arndt John E 3
Borcherding David F MBA 7-8
Borcherding Wendy S BA K
Haesemeier Carol A BSED
Harries Cynthia L BSED 4
Holst Larry R MA 6
Holst Sharon L BSED 2
Kempfe Lora M AA PS
Mc Intyre Trudy PS
Mourey Debra J BS 7
Myers Kimberly A BA 1-2
Smith Becke 7
Urban Douglas J BSED 5-6
Wenger Patricia L MA 1
PRECIOUS LAMBS PS
• 1996
17200 E 39th St 64055-3832
(816)373-3582 •
FAX(816)373-5863
shpllc@aol.com
NO REPORT
**JACKSON**-ST PAUL K-8
• NLSA • 1894
216 S. Russell Street 63755-2040
(573)243-5360 • FAX(573)
243-4527
**Palisch Daniel E MA 8**
Bockelman Rebecca M BS 7
Crader Renee 2
Floyd Martha MA 1
Franke Judith G BSED 1
Graefe Joseph A BA 4
Koenig Helenmarie BSED 3
Lipke Alan K MA
Lipke Lisa K
Lipke Sally L BS 2
Mirly Timothy S BA 8
Mueller Tamera 4
Palisch Doris V BA K
Perr Orville R Jr. BA 6
Rauh Mary 5
Shaw Leah 5
Wachter Lavern 6
**JEFFERSON CITY**-IMMANUEL-HONEY CREEK PS-8
• NLSA • 1868
8231 Tanner Bridge Rd
65101-9601
(573)496-3766 •
FAX(573)496-3451
Bonnett Le Anne 5-6
Duenckel Virginia L AA K-10
Koffarnns Dallas L 2-4
Morris Beverly 5-6
Rogers Jon L 7-8
Rogers Stephanie E PS
TRINITY PS
• 1993
803 Swifts Highway 65109-2547
**Steffens Shelly PS**
Jennings Kathy PS
Mears Teresa PS
Ousley Cheri PS
Rhodes Amber PS
Sommerer Marilyn PS
TRINITY K-8
• NLSA • 1870
812 Stadium Blvd 65109-2404
(573)636-7807 •
FAX(573)636-7348
trinityk8@home.com
**Hartman Kenneth W MED**
Bowder Fern M MED 1
Cowan Nancy E BED 6
Gonzales Rachael 1
Gonzales Stephan P 7
Hartman Sally M MED 3
Hopkins Sofia K MA 6
Koenig Matthew L BA 5
Martin Wanda 2
Mooney Jeanelle BSED 4
Resner Debbie AA K
Resner Steven A MS 8
Robinett Candace K BS 3
Rudsinski Amy 2
Schendel Sarah K BA 4
Steffens Karen L 5
**JENNINGS**-ST JACOBI PS
• 1992
8646 Jennings Station Rd
63136-6306
(314)388-0591
Davidson Jennie
**JOPLIN**-MARTIN LUTHER-IMMANUEL PS-8
• NLSA • 1953
2616 Connecticut Ave 64804-3027
(417)624-1403 •
FAX(417)624-2774
gracealone@joplin.com
**Souza William F Jr. MS 5-8**
Berndt Betty E BSED 5-8
Bosworth Gwen L BS 1-4
Doner Joan BS 5-8
Edman Elaina M 6-8
Kralik Chuck W BS 5-8
Lamp Cathy 5-6
Moreland Jonathan 1-8
Randles Susan K PS
Robertson Charlotte L BSED 2
Rossow Cynthia L EDS 3-4
Schamber Jeremy K BA 3-4
Souza Connie R BA 1
Thorne Marlene BA PS-K
**KANSAS CITY**-CALVARY PS-8
• 1948
7500 Oak 64114-1945
(816)444-5517 •
FAX(816)444-5696
0
**Goeglein Eric W EDS**
**Kletke Dale B MED 6**
Curtis Susan MED PS
Goeglein Donna BS 8
Hodgson Carol I MA 2
Jamision Beverly S MA 1-2
Kaldahl Susan 1-8
King Jo Anna K
Kunkel Ruth Marie E BSED 4
Latham Janet K
Leimer Coralee BA PS
Leimer John F MSED 7
Loontjer Jacqueline L BSED 3
Murphy Wendi PS
Parker Susie PS
Pham Hong PS
Potter Dan
Spaeth Carol BA 5
Van Volkenburgh Candance
Wenzl Melissa 1
GROW IN PEACE PS
• 1996
8240A Blue Ridge Blvd
64138-1565
(816)353-3910 •
FAX(816)353-3886
peace@safe4kids.net
Alexander Anne PS
Allen Emily PS
Becraft Christy PS
Bonner Ruby PS
Brown Allison PS
Burkholder Elizabeth PS
Cantrell Debbie PS
Farquharson Michelle PS
Farris Jessica PS
Forbey-Jones Deborah PS
Forman Desiree PS
Gilbert Lilly PS
Griffie Laura PS
Hamilton Carla M PS
Harris Evelyn PS
Henry Jonie PS
Johnson Rachael PS
Masoner Kim PS
Masoner Linda PS
Mayfield Patricia PS
Mc Bee Sandra PS
Phillips Jeanette PS
Simon Jacki PS
Wahl Nancy PS
Waltree Sharon PS
Washington Michelle PS
Wheeler Natasha PS
Wiggins La Kisha PS
HOLY CROSS PS-8
• NLSA • 1964
2003 NE Englewood Rd
64118-5698
(816)453-7211 •
FAX(816)452-5573
hclskcmo@aol.com
**Bork Ronald D DED**
Bork Marilyn J BS 4
Einspahr Karen L BA 5
Honig Khristy D PS
Kastman Lisa 1-4
Maas John H BS 8
Maas Nancy L BS 1
Meier Paula K BSED K-8
Olson Judith C MA 3
Pena Janice MED 6
Schenk Holly MED 6-8
Schlie Penny L BS K
Timm Jody R BSED 7
Wendt Elenita A BSED 2
Williams Staci A MED 4
Wollberg Barbara L BSED 2
KING OF KINGS PS
• 1996
1701 NE 96th St 64155-2167
(816)436-7680
O Donnell Kathy E BA
**KIRKSVILLE**-FAITH PS-2
• 1976
1820 S Baltimore St 63501-4504
(660)665-8166 •
FAX(660)665-6122
Fouch Janie BS K
Hoshaw Deborah L BS PS
Thompson Jane 1-2

**KIRKWOOD**-CHRIST COMMUNITY PS-8
• RSO • NLSA • 1973
110 W Woodbine Ave 63122-5890
(314)822-7774 •
FAX(314)822-5472
cochraned@aol.com
**Cochran William D MSED**
**Eggers Mark F MA**
**Leet Janet B MED 2**
Bickel Connie MAT PS
Blackford Bryan 6-8
Blaile Jane E BS 5
Bobb Donna L BA K
Brannan Carol A MAT 6-8
Brown De Anne 7-8
Charpiot Larry 5-8
Dehn Linda M BED 6-8
Dittmer Cherie L K
Dittmer Emily BA 6-8
Dreessen Charles R MS 6-8
Dreessen Jean A MA 2
Duesenberg Jan 2
Ebest Jo C MA 1-5
Gerber Judith L MAT 4
Haun Cheryl A MA PS
Heerboth Christine R PS
Krenning Carrie 6-8
Ladd Marcia A MA 2
Loduca Sandra G BA
Mangels Jessica 1
Meinhart Michelle
Miller Ellen K BED 6-8
Miller John W MMU 5-8
Olson Susan K BED 5
Reck-Meyer Carrie MA 1-8
Schmidt Helen R BS K-8
Schroll Norma R MED 3
Shane Toni L MAT 4
Snyder Linda J MA 1
Uetrecht Donald G MA
Volsey Kelly
Zoernig Deborah M BS 7-8
**LA GRANGE**-ST PETER PS
• 1978
300 N 7th St 63448-1100
(314)655-4416
NO REPORT
**LADUE**-VILLAGE PS
• 1979
9237 Clayton Rd 63124-1509
(314)993-6743 •
FAX(314)993-8920
vlcpre@aol.com
Berger Judith BS
Cowlen Rosemary O
Gilligan Maria B
Hawes Nancy
Hippler Susan D
Mc Gowan Wendy B
Robinson Gayle S
Striker Viola D
Wesolich Sarah H
**LEES SUMMIT**-ST MATTHEW PS
• 1999
700 NE Chipman Rd 64063-2571
(816)524-4354 •
FAX(816)524-9012
st.matt-lcms@worldnet.att.net
NO REPORT
**LEMAY**-PEACE PS
• 1977
737 Barracksview Rd 63125-5409
(314)892-8844 •
FAX(314)892-7345
NO REPORT
**LEXINGTON**-GRACE PS
• 1986
806 Hwy 13 PO Box 69
64067-0069
(816)259-2932
NO REPORT
**LIBERTY**-ST STEPHEN PS
• 1988
205 N Forest Ave 64068-1007
(816)781-3377
Reagan Sue D BA PS
Snider Karrie A BSED PS
**LOCKWOOD**-IMMANUEL K-8
• 1882
212 W 4th St 65682 PO Box H
65682-0363
(417)232-4530 •
FAX(417)232-4476
ilslock@ipa.net
**Meyer Wilfred G MA 6-8**
Julian Teresa K 2-3
Kirby Patti K
Kreissler Toni R BS K-1
Meyer Diane J K-8
Shadle Carolyn A BED 4-5
**LONE ELM**-ZION 1-8
• 1896
17291 Lone Elm Rd 65237-2116
(816)838-6307
NO REPORT
**MARSHFIELD**-ST PAUL PS
• 1999
611 N Locust 65706-1212
(417)468-5683
**Conrad Jennifer PS**
Alexander Ina PS
Brake Theresa PS
Rush Sally PS
Scheer Beverly PS
**MOBERLY**-ZION PS
• 1979
1075 E Urbandale Dr 65270-1963
(660)263-3256
NO REPORT
**MONETT**-ST JOHN PS
• 1999
23237 Highway H 65708-8416
(417)235-2085 •
FAX(417)235-8442
stjohn@mo-net.com
NO REPORT
**O FALLON**-CHILD OF GOD K
• 2000
8945 Veterans Memorial Pkwy
63366 PO Box 2355 63376-2355
(636)379-4871 •
FAX(636)379-4918
childofgodlutheran@juno.com
**Arico Karen L MED**
Henning Mary J MRD K
**OAK GROVE**-LITTLE LAMBS-SHEP OF VALLEY PS
• 1998
600 SE 12th St 64075-9540
(816)690-4020
NO REPORT
**OAKVILLE**-FAITH PS
• 1976
6101 Telegraph Rd 63129-4715
(314)846-8612 •
FAX(314)846-7157
Austin Melinda MA
Beining Laurie PS
Kuhlenberg Dolores PS
Smith Marge PS
Weltmer Debra PS
**OLIVETTE**-IMMANUEL PS-8
• NLSA • 1894
9733 Olive Blvd 63132-3003
(314)993-5004 •
FAX(314)993-0311
**Koosman Howard E MED**
Eckert Kenneth L MA 5
Hartmann Melissa A BA PS
Hente Brenda J BA
Jackson Linda J BS 4
Krenning Marguerite M BS 3
Lessing Lisa G 7
Mertz Paula M MED 6
Meyr Christine A MED 2
Niewald Pamela J BA 1
Waldmann Tove E BSED K
Wittler Ronald T MEDADM 8
**OSAGE BEACH**--HOPE CHAPEL MOTHERS PS
1027 Industrial Dr 65065-3006
(573)348-2108 •
FAX(573)348-2108
NO REPORT
**OVERLAND**-OUR REDEEMER PS-8
• 1914
9135 Shelley Ave 63114-4812
(314)427-3462 •
FAX(314)427-8273
redeemer@postnet.com
**Tayon Dawn E**
Benton Karen S MA 7
Diehl Millie PS
Froeschner Alma BSED 8
Hoelting Lori PS
Kuntz Cynthia G BS 6
Mueller Mary M BA 1
Pearson Phyllis BS 3
Reinitz Daniel C BA 5
Reinitz Joyce A MA 2
Sansone Donna BS K
Titus Denise BS 4
**PALMYRA**-ZION PS-8
• 1866
120 S Spring St 63461-1468
(573)769-3739 •
FAX(573)769-4014
zionluth@nemonet.com
Ahland Margaret E
Lovercheck Nancy L BSED 1-2
Meade Karen
Powell Luella M MA
Schachtsiek Marcia BSED 3-5
Whitaker Cindy 6-8
**PERRYVILLE**-IMMANUEL PS-8
• NLSA • 1866
225 W South St 63775-2542
(573)547-6161 •
FAX(573)547-8205
IMMANUELLUTHSCH@ldd.net
Keller Jennifer M MA PS
Pavelski Suzanne R BS 7
**PLATTE WOODS**-CHRIST PS
• 1972
6700 NW 72nd St 64151-1678
(816)741-8031
NO REPORT
**POPLAR BLUFF**-ZION PS-4
• 1952
450 N Main St 63901-5150
(573)785-6112 • FAX(573)
785-7273
zion@pbmo.net
Carter Cheryl K
De Witt Cindy 3-4
Schulz Kristi J BSED 1-2
Wells Annette PS
**PRAIRIE CITY**-ZION 1-8
• 1868
RR 1 Box 31 64780-9022
(660)598-6213
**Bennett Robert E BSED 4-8**
Rapp R Paulette 1-3
**RAYMORE**-GUIDING STAR-BETHLEHEM PS
• 1993
PO Box 1155 64083-1155
(816)322-3606
NO REPORT
**ROLLA**-ROLLA-IMMANUEL PS-6
• NLSA • 1996
807 W 11th St 65401-2103
(573)364-3915
Wehmeyer Allison M BSED PS
**ROSEBUD**-IMMANUEL K-8
• 1904
Hwy 50 300 N 1st St 63091
(573)764-3495
Boetcher Audrey 2-4
Oberlies Katrina A MED 5-8
Trost Janet K-1
Wehmeyer Sara K-1
**SAINT ANN**-HOPE PS-8
• 1943
3721 Saint Bridget Ln 63074-2505
(314)429-0988 •
FAX(314)429-3809
gil-livo@hope--lutheran.org
**Livo Gilbert R MED**
Harris Phyllis W MS K
Klein Candace PS
Lavigne Nina Rose M BA 5-6
Osiek Karen F BSED 1-2
Wilson Michael E BED 7-8
**SAINT CHARLES**-IMMANUEL PS-8
• 1848
115 S 6th St 63301-2712
(636)946-0051 •
FAX(636)946-0166
hraedeke@immanuelluth.org
**Bader Joanne E MA PS-8**
**Raedeke Henry W MED PS-8**
Bargen Christine A MS 1-8
Bayer Lynn C MAT 6-8
Beaver Elissa M PS
Boyer Deborah K BSED 4
Brandt Nadine M BS 5
Carlson James A BS 5
Cluppert Elizabeth A BA 6-8
Ferber Denise M MA 1
Hartke Laura M 7
King Dorothy L BA 8
King Tom 7
Loesel Allen H MCMU 5-8
Loesel Pamela L BS 1-5
Mahnken Carol A BSED 3
Marty Sherrie B MA K
Maurer Diane B MA 2
Meers Diana D 5
Pitsch Leland A MED 6
Raedeke Susan M BA 4
Roberts Mary E BA 2
Rohlfing Roxanne MED 3
Schade Diane J MED 1
Schoedel David W MS 1-8
Sommerer Samuel E MA 6
Stotts Nancy K MS 8
Trunkhill Brenda E BA 2
Vesper Jennifer K
Von Ahsen Kenneth H MA 4
Von Ahsen Susan A MED 3
Wagner Douglas J MA 7-8
Wagner Lee Ann MA 1
OUR SAVIOR PS
• 1976
2800 W Elm St 63301-4618
(314)947-8010 •
FAX(314)947-1925
NO REPORT
TRINITY 1-8
• 1862
4689 N Highway 94 63301-6405
(636)250-3654 •
FAX(636)250-3654
**Chapin Kathryne A 1-8**
Loeffler Esther M BS 1-8
**SAINT CLAIR**-HOLY TRINITY PS
• 1988
1351 Parkway Dr 63077-2438
(314)629-6337
NO REPORT
**SAINT JOSEPH**-ST PAUL PS-8
• 1996
4715 Frederick Ave 64506-3241
(816)279-1118 •
FAX(816)279-1114
**James Ronnie 6-8**
Buford Melanie S K
Fortmeyer Amelia PS
Peckman Aaron 1-8
Peckman Janet A BS 4-5
Shade Helen K-8
Stagner Hope 2-3
Weinhold Deborah A BSED 1

**SAINT LOUIS**--CONCORDIA MIDDLE 6-8
• RSO • 1999
3630 Ohio Ave 63118-3916
(314)865-1144 •
FAX(314)772-4210
NO REPORT

HOLY CROSS PS-5
• 1850
3630 Ohio Ave 63118-3916
(314)771-9521 •
FAX(314)772-0071
hcstlou@inlink.com
Boehlke Keith W MED 4-5
Haffer Barbara D PS
Kurka Gerald E 1
Schuessler Norma H BA 2-3
Seitz Connie S K

HOPE PS-8
• NLSA • 1923
5320 Brannon Ave 63109-3230
(314)832-1850 •
FAX(314)832-0184
hholschen@hopelutheranstl.org
**Holschen Howard H MAT**
Consolino Jeanine E MA 4
Holschen Judith A MAT 8
Hunt G Warren BA 6
Mangels Anne MED PS
Nerger Martina N BA
Nutt Elizabeth A BA 5
O Neill Cheryl R MAT K
Shoemaker Kay E MAT 1
Williams Amy K BS 7
Winston Barbara J BA 2
Zickler Anela K BA 3

IMMANUEL CHAPEL PS
• 1984
11100 Old Halls Ferry Rd 63136-4632
(314)741-7236 •
FAX(314)741-4700
NO REPORT

LUTH ASSOC/SPEC ED
• RSO • 1956
3558 S Jefferson Ave PO Box 19222 63118-3968
(314)268-1234 •
FAX(314)268-1232
luthsped@cs.com
**Speckhard Norma J PHD**
Alms Natasha A BS
Beckerman Lisa J MED
Christiansen Lori B MA
Curran Julie M
Davis Deborah K
Fienup Judith B
Gerler Susan M
Grandison April
Hagge Betty J BS
Lewis Diane H MA
Lima Carol
Loduca Sandra G BA
Luedde Kim
Manus Alice L
Menner Janey A MED
Moore Sandra
Oberdeck Virginia A BA
Paquette Kimberly A BS
Potts Cynthia
Pries Judith C
Riordan Jeanine M
Schultze Betty
Shaw Joy R
Stollenwerk Jennifer L BA
Tomlinson Christine J
Traffton Treresa
Treis Audrey F
Uetrecht Donald G MA
Voisey Kelly T

MESSIAH K-5
• 1948
2900 S Grand Blvd 63118-1033
(314)771-7716 •
FAX(314)771-7716
ls111@aol.com
**Van Dermay Coralyn J MA**
Janis Donna J BS 4-5
Jeske Joanne R BS 3
Peter Tonya A BA 2
Volkman Heather D BA 1
Zorumski Susan K BA K

RIVER ROADS PS-8
• 1970
8623 Church Rd 63147-1997
(314)388-0300 •
FAX(314)388-4903
**Versemann Calvin E MSED**
Bahr Donald G MSED 5-6
Campbell Rosalee E 7-8
Eggers David E BS K-8
Lampe Diann V K
Lobaugh Shane PS
Mackey-Boyd Yvonne 4
Mohl Andrea 3
Olson Theresa 2
Schmidt Cristy 1

ST JOHN K-8
• 1865
3716 Morganford Rd 63116-1615
(314)773-0784 •
FAX(314)773-0126
dkarnerstj@postnet.com
NO REPORT

ST LUCAS PS-K
• 1980
7100 Morganford Rd 63116-2110
(314)351-7298
NO REPORT

ST LUKE PS-8
• 1893
3415 Taft Ave 63111-1431
(314)832-0118 •
FAX(314)832-7074
NO REPORT

ST MATTHEW PS-8
• 1901
5403 Wren Ave 63120-2441
(314)261-7708 •
FAX(314)261-7707
stmath@swbell.net
Banks Fonya T BA 4
Blackwell Clester 5
Boyd Larry 6
Johnson Toya 2-3
Lewis Johnathan 7-8
Livingston Romenetha K
Stallworth Claudia PS
White Louise 1

TRINITY K-8
• 1839
1809 S 8th St 63104-4007
(314)621-0228 •
FAX(314)231-5430
Grunden Kristine A PS
Mangels Alan G BA
Risner Deborah L 1
Rozelle Angie J 4-5
Wetmore Melba L BS 3-4
Winter Erin R K

WORD OF LIFE PS-8
• RSO • NLSA • 1974
6535 Eichelberger St 63109-2624
(314)832-1244 •
FAX(314)832-1540
**Conover Charles W MCRT**
Benninghoff Carol R MMED 1-8
Brackman Jana M BS PS
Bude Catherine MED 1
Colloton Connie BA K
Dehnke Christine R MA 1
Dehnke Nathan G 4-8
Duke Deborah L 1
Hammer Judith M 3
Headrick Claire 5
Hetz Ellen M BS 2
Hofman Rachel BS 4
Kottmeyer Lorna BA 4
Mackay Jena R 7
Maxfield Melissa A 6
Morrison Laura J BA 2
Rudzinski Kevin R BA 4-8
Springer Matthew J MA 8
Thomas Anne L BA K
Tiemann Larry G MA 5
Tiemann Louise BS 8

**SAINT LOUIS COUNTY**-ABIDING SAVIOR PS
• 1984
4355 Butler Hill Rd 63128-3717
(314)894-9703 •
FAX(314)894-0212
asic@primary.net
Bordeaux Betty J MA PS
Cooper Joan PS

CHAPEL CROSS PS
• 1990
11645 Benham Rd 63136-6112
(314)741-3737 •
FAX(314)741-3746
Mueller Kathleen K BSED PS
Timm Diane L BS PS
Truetken Doris PS

WASHINGTON K-8
• RSO • NLSA • 1984
4474 Butler Hill Rd 63128-3635
(314)892-4408 •
FAX(314)892-4469
washls@stlnet.com
**Bordeaux Joseph A PHD**
Carney Diane K-5
Clements Kimberly 2
Farnhum Jennifer 1
Frank Warren G MSED 6-8
Fuchs Carol M K-5
Haake Jean C BS K
Halter Lois A BA 3
Horvath Gail BS K
Johnson Lynda P BA 6-8
Mezinis Ellen L MA 5-8
Montgomery Laura BS 4
Mueller Dawn M BS 6-8
Schaefer Gary J BSED 5
Schmidt Bethany K-7
Wiesehan Marilyn K K-8

**SALISBURY**-IMMANUEL PS
• 1983
124 W 3rd St 65281-1445
(660)388-5192
wkass@cvalley.net
Kassulke Carolyn A BED PS

**SAPPINGTON**-RESURRECTION PS
• 1977
9907 Sappington Rd 63128-1644
(314)843-4980 •
FAX(314)843-5154
sholzborn@aol.com
Bohler Jean PS
Carman Linda PS
Carobeth Kelly PS
Feigenbutz Judith G PS
Haverstick Le Anne PS
Hesse Roberta M PS
Hillmann Judith N PS
Holdegraver Tina E PS
Holzborn Susan P
Huffman Marsha G PS
Kesselring Karen S PS
Krueger Lisa PS
Lower Karen A PS
Luechtefeld Kathleen L BSED PS
Mackay Shirley PS
Mc Clanahan Donna PS
Perniciaro Mary V PS
Reichley Karen L PS
Shafer Karen L AA PS
Signorelli MaryAnn R PS
Sutkowski Mary L PS
Wilsman Elizabeth A PS

**SEDALIA**-ST PAUL PS-8
• 1957
701 S Massachusetts Ave 65301-4599
(816)826-1925 •
FAX(816)826-1925
stpauls@iland.net
**Nail John BSED 7-8**
Anderson Kimberly K BA 3-4
Ficken Jenna Lee BSED 1
Kamprath Christopher M BSED 5-6
Nichols Darla PS
Schneider Sara L BA 2
Tatkenhorst Gloria K-3

**SPRINGFIELD**-FAITH PS
• 1994
1517 E Valley Water Mill Rd 65803-3743
(417)833-3749
NO REPORT

REDEEMER PS
• NLSA • 1979
2852 S Dayton Ave 65807-3644
(417)886-7069 •
FAX(417)881-5470
Stouder Jane M BS

SPRINGFIELD K-8
• RSO • 1984
2852 S Dayton Ave 65807-3644
(417)883-5717 •
FAX(417)875-9227
pbaker@pcis.net
**Baker Paul MS**
Becker Alvina BSED K
Beckman Gary L MS 1
Brockman Mary L BSED 5
Gerdes Drew D BA K
Heilman Jon 3
Kohls Jeffrey J MS 8
Lynn Karen L BA 2
Magnus Mary K MSED 6
Petrich Connie 4
Stouder Jane M BS 1
Wanner Joshua BA 5
Wanner Kari BA 3
Youngsteadt Jean K-8

**ST. LOUIS**-GREEN PARK K-8
• RSO • NLSA • 1961
4248 Green Park Rd 63125-3021
(314)544-4248 •
FAX(314)544-0237
GPLS4248@hotmail.com
**Peterman Charles E MA**
Cibulka Janine E MA
Eggold Michelle A BS 6
Gieseke Ruthann L MMU 3
Hesse Wayne MAT
Horvath Kenneth E MAT 5-8
Knox Wendy A BA 4
Koen Laureen BA
Koopman Janice E MSED 1
Lind Charles E MAT 7
Nelson Paula B MEAD
Palisch Theodore M BA
Paquet Beverly J MAT
Peterman Diane R BA 3
Rudsinski Calvin H BA 5
Rusert David 7
Sievers Phyllis K BA 5
Simmons Melissa 5-6
Torbeck Stephanie L BA K

**STOVER**-ST PAUL PS-8
• 1865
310 N Forest PO Box 9 65078-0009
(573)377-2690
NO REPORT

**SULLIVAN**-ST MATTHEW PS
• 1994
528 N Church St 63080-1532
(573)860-3212
NO REPORT

**UNION**-ST PAUL PS
• 1987
208 W Springfield Ave 63084-1757
(636)683-2209
Berger Kris L BS PS
Randolph Penny PS

**UNIONTOWN**-GRACE PS
• 1981
84 Grace Ln PO Box 105 63783-0105
(573)788-2226
NO REPORT

**WARRENTON**-LITTLE LAMBS-ST JOHN PS
• 1987
950 S Highway 47 63383-2600
(314)456-2888
Cunningham Sharon
Feldkamp Dianne M BSED

**WASHINGTON**-IMMANUEL PS-8
• 1863
214 W 5th St 63090-2304
(314)239-1636 •
FAX(314)239-0589
waynec@midwestis.net
**Clements Wayne E MA 7-8**
Bangert Lisa BS PS
Beckerman Lisa J MED K-8
Clements Charlene J BSED 5-8
Dempsey Debra 5-6
Fuhr Phyllis BED 2
Grellner Angela M PS
Hallien Aaron M BA 5-8
Harles Katherine J BS PS
Marschel Mary R BED 4
Murray Monica L BS K
Nafzger Janis BSED 5-8
Potts Cynthia K-8
Schultz Jolene BSED 1
Wunderlich Alan W BA 7-8
Zastrow Margaret B MED 3

**WAYNESVILLE**-FAITH PS
• 1992
981 Hwy Z 65583
(573)336-4464
NO REPORT

**WELDON SPRINGS**-MESSIAH PS-K
• 1997
5911 S Hwy 94 63304-5611
(314)926-9773 •
FAX(314)926-9924
Wehmeyer Barbara A BSED K

**WENTZVILLE**-IMMANUEL PS-8
• 1880
317 W Pearce Blvd 63385-1421
(636)327-4416 •
FAX(636)327-5054
rbohning@immanuelwentzville.org
**Bohning Roy W MA 8**
**Kratzer Sandy**
**Lovelace Joann PS**
Brune Sherry 4
Daugherty Laura J BA 6-8
Dorow Susan E K
Haake Samatha BS 1-8
Hackbarth Iris MA 1
Heppermann Lori BS 2
Jacklin Robert M BA 3
Kirk Jill BA 1-6
Palmer Jill
Peters Donna 5-7
Thoelke Kate E BA K-8

**WRIGHT CITY**-GOOD SHEPHERD PS
• 1992
101 S Elm Ave 63390-1217 PO Box 44 63390-0044
(636)745-8000
NO REPORT

## MONTANA

**BILLINGS**-MOUNT OLIVE PS
• 1993
2336 Saint Johns Ave 59102-4710
(406)656-2635
Evanson Norma L PS
Smith Barbara PS
Zier Darla D BSED PS

TRINITY K-8
• 1954
2802 Belvedere Dr 59102-3715
(406)656-1021 •
FAX(406)656-1936
**Thomas Richard M MA**
Erger Lynne M BS 1
Gourley Debra BS
Gray Marcia 2
Jackson Starla 8
Johnson Ardith BA 3
Kesler Susan BS 7
Loomans Ted P BA 5
Speed Cynthia 6
Thomas Patricia S K
Thompson Janis 4

**BOZEMAN**-FIRST PS
• 1997
225 S Black 59715 102 N Weaver 59714
(406)756-8754
NO REPORT

**COLSTRIP**-LITTLE LAMBS-MOUNT CALVARY PS
• 1990
Olive & Poplar PO Box 218 59323-0218
(406)748-2516
Simonich Pamela

**GREAT FALLS**-WEE DISCIPLES-TRINITY PS
• 1991
1226 1St Ave N 59401-3201
(406)452-2121
Lee Debra PS

**HAMILTON**-GRACE PS
• 1994
275 Hattie Ln 59840-0927
(406)363-7563 •
FAX(406)363-1925
glc@cybernet1.com
Campbell Tina
Scott Kathleen MA
Smith Nora PS
Snodgrass Carolyn
Snodgrass Joan PS
Wiediger Debra R PS

**HELENA**-GOOD SHEPHERD-FIRST PS
• 1979
2231 E Broadway St 59601-4807
(406)442-5367 •
FAX(406)442-5285
Glueckert Ann PS
Locke Martha BS
Sparks Doris BS PS

**KALISPELL**-TRINITY PS-8
• 1958
495 5th Ave WN 59901
(406)257-6716 •
FAX(406)257-6717
**Hobus David A MED**
Bennett Judy K
Braaten Rebecca L BA 6
Holste Kenneth E MED 8
Johnson Melody A BS PS
Junk Susan K
Kern Becky S BS 3
Ondov Carol A BA K-7
Pollock Terri 1-8
Rasmussen Suzanne C BS 1
Schwartz Heidi R BA 2
Shepherd Jill 5-8
St Pierre Colleen BA 7
Topp David BA 4
Werk Karla 5

**LAUREL**-ST JOHN PS
• 1997
417 West 9th St PO Box 185 59044-0185
(406)628-4775 •
FAX(406)628-1591
stjohnlaurelmt@juno.com
Sanderson Cathy S PS

**LIBBY**-ST JOHN PS
• 1956
1024 Montana Ave 59923-2016
(406)293-4248 •
FAX(406)293-4248
Anderson Alyce PS
Gehrke Sharon PS
Hooper Rhonda PS
Howard Freda MED PS
Kenedy Stephanie
Laffoon Sunny PS
Larson Janeen
Lucas Jason PS
Marquez Diana PS
Miner Melisa PS
Neils Joanne PS
Schaumberg Hyland PS
Williams Karen PS
Wilson Sheila PS

**MILES CITY**-TRINITY PS
• 1988
221 S Center Ave 59301-4401
(406)232-4983
NO REPORT

**MISSOULA**-FIRST PS
• 1955
1104 S Higgins Ave 59801-4143
(406)549-3311
NO REPORT

MESSIAH PS
• 1967
3718 Rattlesnake Dr 59802-3028
(406)543-4750
NO REPORT

**PARK CITY**-ST PAUL PS
• 1994
301 1St Ave SW PO Box 188 59063-0188
(406)633-2356
NO REPORT

**POLSON**-MOUNT CALVARY PS
• 1992
1608 2ND St W 59860-4005
(406)883-4041
NO REPORT

**RONAN**-LITTLE LAMBS-ST PAUL PS
• 1982
429 Terrace Lake Rd E 59864-2408
(406)676-8280
NO REPORT

**STEVENSVILLE**-OUR SAVIOR PS
• 1994
184 Pine Hollow Rd 59870-6621
(406)777-5625 •
FAX(406)777-5583
KIMBER1949@aol.com
NO REPORT

**THREE FORKS**-GRACE PS
• 1987
305 S 5Th Ave PO Box 857 59752-0857
(406)285-6865
NO REPORT

## NEBRASKA

**ARLINGTON**-ST PAUL PS-8
• 1876
8951 Co Rd 9 68002-5030
(402)478-4278 •
FAX(402)478-5378
stpaul@genesisnet.net
Dunklau Joyce E BS K
Ferguson Shelli K 5-6
Kremke Charlene 1-8
Luebbe Ranelle J BS PS-8
Rosenthal Dennis L MED 7-8
Rosenthal Sallie E BSED 2
Schmidt Dana L 3-4
Shanahan Missy J 1

**AUBURN**-TRINITY PS
• 1981
634 Alden Dr 68305-3013
(402)274-4210
**Fritz Julie PS**
Tanderup Michele PS

**BANCROFT**-ZION K-8
• 1880
1710 20th Rd 68004-4027
(402)648-7534
zionluth@gpcom.net
Brockmann Colleen D K-5
Wobken Constance S BS K-5

**BATTLE CREEK**-ST JOHN PS-8
• 1882
301 S 2ND PO Box 67 68715-0067
(402)675-3605
holde@conpoint.com
Awe Susan E BA 4
Cornett Ronald C BS 4-5
Long Marcheta BS 3
Masters Sarah R BS 2
Masters William L Jr. BS 6-7
Oldehoeft Harold W BSED 8
Schurman Gail L BAED 1
Werner CherylAnne BS PS-K

**BEATRICE**-ST PAUL PS-5
• 1916
930 Prairie Ln 68310-2647
(402)223-3414 •
FAX(402)223-3418
**Duensing Lonnie G MED 5**
Brott Carolyn M BSED 5
Carnes Brenda H PS
Duensing Beverly A BS K
Genrich LeeAnn E BSED 4
Grandstaff Melinda K BS 2
Hagemeier Jonetta E BA 1
Philippi-Aden Melody BSED 3

**BELLEVUE**-PILGRIM PS
• 1994
2311 Fairview Rd 68123-5318
(402)293-2813 •
FAX(402)292-7836
**kEMP Jane**
Brown Mary PS
Cohen Sandra PS
Davitt Ashley PS
Griffin Paula PS
Kemp Melissa PS
Krueger Kerri PS
Lukins Ardis PS
Robinson Kristin PS
Rodgers Michelle PS
Thares Jill PS
Trumpjonas Rosiha PS
Williams Jodie PS

**BLAIR**-JOY PS
• 1982
141 S 20th St 68008-1884
(402)426-8538
**Hendrickson Laura PS**
Bouwman Jane PS

**BURWELL**-NOAHS ARK-ST JOHN PS
• 1996
350 N 8th St 68823 PO Box 595 68823-0595
(308)346-5060
Christensen Joyce PS
Masin Valerie L
Perrott Nancy PS

**COLUMBUS**-CHRIST PS-8
• 1871
32312 - 122nd Ave 68601-8727
(402)564-3531 •
FAX(402)564-6637
Johannes Nancy 7-8
Korte Kathy L K
Muhle Sandy PS
Rohlf Emily L BS 5-6
Veal Betsy 1-2
Wurdeman Kathleen M 3-4

FIRST STEPS-PEACE PS
• 1998
2720 28th St 68001-2418
(402)562-8437 •
FAX(402)564-8643
Brestel Lisa A PS

IMMANUEL PS-8
• NLSA • 1893
2520 28th St 68601-2548
(402)564-8423 •
FAX(402)564-1162
jwitt@esu7.org
**Godemann Dennis P**
Boyle Kimberly K MA 4
Franzen Kimberly D K
Garber Darla R MA 3

Godemann Dawn R BA 2
Graf Lynne M BS 8
Kimmel Joyce M AA PS
Kuhn Kathleen R BA 5
Sharman Lyle D 1
Sharp Ruth E BSED 1
Smith Richard L MED 6
Thies Everett I MED 7
Vollbracht Lynn M AA PS
Witt Joel J BS 2
Witte Lisa R BA PS
ST JOHN K-8
• 1888
39209 205th Ave 68601-9687
(402)285-0335 •
FAX(402)285-0335
sjlschl@megavision.com
Brandt Eunice F BS K-2
Gronau Jane M BA 6-8
Howe Vanessa E 3-5
**CRETE**-LAMBS OF CHRIST-BETHLEHEM PS
• 1991
837 Hawthorne Ave 68333-2956
PO Box 249 68333-0249
(402)826-4375
Henning Elizabeth A
Rockenbach Darlene M BS PS
**DAVENPORT**-ST PETER PS-8
• 1913
208 W 10th St 68335 PO Box 207 68335-0207
(402)364-2139
Cotton Lauren M AA PS
Fahr Julie K BSED K-1
Hesman Stacey R 5-8
Saeger David R MA 5-8
Werner Pamela S BSED 1-4
**DESHLER**-DESHLER-ST PETER K-8
• 1889
509 E Hebron PO Box 340 68340-0340
(402)365-7858
ghasseld@esu6.org
**Hasseldahl Gregory C MS 7-8**
Dankenbring Elizabeth A BA 3-4
Hasseldahl Cynthia L BS 5-6
Peters Linda J BS K
Vonderfecht Sheryl 5-6
Wenke Carolyn A BSED 1-2
**DONIPHAN**-ST PAUL PS
• 1993
207 N 4th St 68832 PO Box 462 68832-0462
(308)845-2390
Gartner Sonja K BSED
**FALLS CITY**-ST PAUL PS
• 1984
RR 3 Box 102 68355-9634
(402)245-4010 •
FAX(402)245-4643
Von Behren Glenda J
**FRANKLIN**-GRACE PS
• 1992
1206 N St 68939-1343
(308)425-3774
Saathoff Cindy J PS
Tank Lynn PS
**FREMONT**-TRINITY PS-8
• NLSA • 1884
1546 N Luther Rd 68025-3784
(402)721-5959 •
FAX(402)721-5537
bmeyer@esu2.esu2.k12.ne.us
**Meyer William C MED**
Aronson Devie S BS 2
Bowman Patricia PS
Cook Barbara L BSED 6
Dahlhauser Mary L BS 1
Dunklau Carol S BSED K
Meyer Stacey L BA 5
Patchen Julie
Royuk Barbarakay T BS 4
Schwarting Amy 5
Strudthoff Holly B BA 3
Weinrich Cheryl L BSED PS
Weinrich Timothy P BSED 7
Wilshusen Loren W MED 8
**GORDON**-LITTLE LAMBS-GRACE PS
• 1987
801 N Elm St 69343-1138 PO Box 239 69343-0239
(308)282-0584
Evans Debra K
**GRAND ISLAND**-GRACE PS
• 1980
545 Memorial Dr 68801-7854
(308)381-0777
graccare@kdsi.net
NO REPORT
PEACE PS
• 1982
4018 Zola Ln 68803-1520
(308)384-5673 •
FAX(308)384-2001
plchurch@computer-concepts.com
Dobbins Janet A BA PS
Jorn Nancy J PS
Shultz Janice L PS
Splattstoesser Julie A PS
Voelker Judith I BSED PS
Wildauer Beverly J MED PS
TRINITY PS-8
• NLSA • 1882
208 W 13th St 68801-3881
(308)382-5274 •
FAX(308)389-2418
**Chandler F W MNS**
Armstrong Sandra A BA 6-8
Beckler Judith K BSED K
Bergdolt Karl J BS 6-8
Brandt Lillian C MED 3-4
Eickmeier Hans W BA 5-8
Heider Wendy E BA 3
Helland Rachel E BA PS
Herring Jamie E 2
Hesterman Phillip K MAT K-8
Hiegel Connie J BSED 4
Kitten Aline R BS 2
Mann Randa R 1
Mc Carty Eunice J BS PS
Roscoe Barbara J
Schenck Sandra K BS 1
Schuster Michelle S BA 5
**HAMPTON**-HAMPTON PS-6
• 1969
732 N 3rd St 68843-9243
(402)725-3347
kgloyste@esu9.esu9.k-12.ne.us
**Gloystein Kathy M BA PS-K**
Bankson Nadine M 2-3
Carnoali Jean C BS 4-6
Regier Mary A 1
**HASTINGS**-ZION PS-8
• 1900
465 S Marian Rd 68901-7401
(402)462-5012 •
FAX(402)462-5375
Ahrens Linda A BS PS
Anderson Ann M BS K
Ernest Iola M BS 4
Koepke Beth A 6-8
Meyer Donna 5-6
Schaefer Wendi L 1
Starla Berry K-8
Uden Lori D BS 3
Warneke Allard D MA 6-8
Warneke Janice H BS 2
**HOOPER**-IMMANUEL K-8
• 1880
27053 Co Rd 12 68031-9608
(402)654-3663 •
FAX(402)654-2814
ilbluejay@htcnet.com
Manwarren Joey L 1-8
Riedemann Sarah R 1-8
**JUNIATA**-CHRIST K-8
• 1890
13175 W 70th St 68955-2138
(402)744-4991
**Young Brian K BSED 6-8**
Reiman Nanette M BA 3-5
Uden Cynthia L MED K
**KEARNEY**-HOLY CROSS PS
• 1981
3315 11th Ave 68847-8002
(308)237-2944 •
FAX(308)237-2695
Kitzelman Deanna D BS
ZION PS-8
• 1930
2421 Avenue C 68847-4541 PO Box 778 68848-0778
(308)234-3410 •
FAX(308)236-8100
jknoepfe@genie.esu10.k12.ne.us
**Knoepfel James B MAD 7-8**
Fattig Ann K 3
Gentry Verleen F BSED PS
Heiden Lorraine L K
Knoepfel Lisa C BS 7-8
Peterson Lavonne M BA 1
Rathke Beckie L BS 5-6
Smith Margaret E BSED 2
Vickers Eileen H 4
**LEIGH**-ZION COMMUNITY PS
• 1987
PO Box 215 68643-0215
(402)487-2502
NO REPORT
**LEXINGTON**-TRINITY PS
• 1979
205 E 7Th St P O Box L 68850-2101
(308)324-4341
Suhr Debra S PS
Wiest Robert D MS
**LINCOLN**-CHRIST PS
• 1979
4325 Sumner St 68506-1165
(402)483-7774 •
FAX(402)483-7776
clcl@inebraska.com
Lambrecht Jo A MA
FAITH PS-6
• NLSA • 1980
6345 Madison Ave 68507-2564
(402)466-6861 •
FAX(402)466-3857
faith@inetnebr.com
Barnhouse Krista K BS 5
Kamprath Holly C MA 6
Licht Karen BSED 3
Marxhausen Kim D MA K
Mc Mahan Cassandra BMU
Niemeyer Catherine A
Schultz Elizabeth A BS 1
Thurber Rebecca C BSED
Thyparambil Nancy J MED 4
Tietz Cheri L BS 2
Tietz Stuart D MED
HELPING HANDS PS
• 1996
3825 Wildbriar Ln 68516-4502
(402)423-7639
Anderson Kristy K IV BSED
Bock Kimberly K PS
Hanson Susan R PS
Nyhof Judith K BSED PS
IMMANUEL PS
• 1980
2001 S 11Th St 68502-2215
(402)474-6275 •
FAX(402)474-6275
immanuellutheran@juno.com
Snoozy Karla K
MESSIAH PS-6
• 1930
1800 S 84Th St 68506-1870
(402)489-3024 •
FAX(402)489-3093
messiah@navix.net
**Fehlhafer Stanley O MED**
Beck Dawn E BA 3
Brummer Rochelle M BSED 5
Cram Beverly J MSED 4
Fehlhafer Virginia BSED 2
Grothuis Sharon K-6
Hein Martin A MSED 3
Thimijan Sherry A AA PS
Tonniges Marva R BS K
Vannoy Lisa K BA 1-2
Wallman JoAnn K MA 1
Wilkening Roger K-6
TRINITY PS-6
• 1882
1200 N 56Th St 68504-3253
(402)466-1800 •
FAX(402)466-1820
lhuebner@lps.org
**Huebner Leland D MED**
Bamesberger JoAnn BA K
Bartels Judith MED PS
Darrohn Amber M BSED PS-6
Dirks Keith R MA 4
Huebner Barbara P BSED 5-6
Leimbach Stacy C BA
Lorenzen Jeanne MA 3
Naber Bonnie 1
Sirek Kathryn J BS 6
Volzke Betty C 5
Wallschlaeger Martha L BS 2
**MADISON**-ST JOHN K-8
• 1877
28670 547 Ave 68748-6141
(402)454-2440 •
FAX(402)454-2440 *51
cwolske@pluggers.esu8.k12.ne.us
Wolske Clee K BSED
Wolske Monique A BS K
TRINITY PS-8
• 1906
6Th & Grove PO Box 969 68748-0969
(402)454-2651 •
FAX(402)454-3408
tls@ncfcomm.com
**Clarkson Julene M**
**Eggers Lucinda L MA 7-8**
Jones Linda 1-3
Rumsey Annie PS
Steger Joyce 4-6
**MC COOK**-CREATIVE-PEACE PS
• 1979
411 E 6th St 69001-3815 PO Box 240 69001-0240
(308)345-2595
NO REPORT
**MILFORD**-GOOD SHEPHERD PS
• 1982
620 Second PO Box 90 68405-0090
(402)761-3146
Schluckebier Julianna
**NORFOLK**-CHRIST PS-8
• 1871
511 S 5Th St 68701-5278
(402)371-5536 •
FAX(402)371-1288
postmaster@christlutherannorfolk.org
**Weber Donald C MAD**
Bass Janice L BS 8
Cook Kathy M BS 1
Davis Darlene B BS 4
Drefke Gary L MA 6
Gansebom Kenneth
Gebhardt Deborah E BSED 5
Leckband Lois E BED 1
Owen Christine A BS 2
Pobanz Kathryn L BS 2
Portwood Carey L 3
Portwood Von E BS 5
Riedel Suzanne R BA PS
Schipporeit Jeanette E BSED 7
Stortz Steven B MED PS
Sunderman Brenda K
Uher Lynda MED 6
Warneke Susan A BA 4
Wasson Patricia 4
Weber Gary G MED 8
Weber Nancy L BED 3
Zeitz Allan A BS 7

OUR SAVIOR KINGS KID-OUR SAVIOR PS
• 1977
2500 W Norfolk Ave 68701-4427
(402)371-9005 •
FAX(402)371-1378
Hoffman Margaret E BS PS
Swan Barbara PS
**NORTH PLATTE**-BEAUTIFUL SAVIOR PS
• 1984
402 S Baytree Ave 69101-4823
(308)534-7004 •
FAX(308)534-3177
pastkey@kdsi.net
Melonne Kelsey L
Morales Molly
OUR REDEEMER PS-8
• 1927
1400 E D St 69101-5770
(308)532-6421
Groves Linda 7-8
Jensen Gail L BS PS
Leech William A MA 3-4
Leisy Jodi 3-4
Livingston Janet L BED 1
McCall Gaylene K PS
Montgomery Deann K
Pavel Heidi L 5-6
Sabin Caroline BS 2
**OGALLALA**-ST PAUL PS-8
• 1943
312 W 3rd St 69153-2522
(308)284-2944
stpauls@megavision.com
Crick Cynthia PS
Dobbertien Glenda L BSED PS-8
Medbery Christina A BS 3-8
Wehling Paula M BSED 1-2
Wehling Stanley H MS 3-8
**OMAHA**-ABUNDANT LIFE K-6
• 1998
9020 Q St 68127-3549
(402)592-8005 •
FAX(402)331-1123
abundantlifelutheran@yahoo.com
**Mueller Carol R BA 4**
Bowman Jo Ann BS 5-6
Chinberg Kathleen L K-6
Dartmann Shelley K BS K
Gedwillo Lori K-6
Neilsen Jenifer L 3
Slothower Elizabeth 1
Trinklein Susan M 2
BEAUTIFUL SAVIOR PS
• 1974
9012 Q St 68127-3549
(402)331-7376 •
FAX(402)331-1123
bslc@radiks.net
Chaillie Linda PS
Cupich Connie PS
Haack James R MED
Spencer Kelly PS
BETHANY PS
• 1974
5151 NW Radial Hwy 68104-4361
(402)558-6212 •
FAX(402)561-6928
BethanyOffice@aol.com
NO REPORT
BREAD OF LIFE K-1
• 1999
1821 N 90th St 68114-1314
(402)391-3505 •
FAX(402)399-1682
dwmueller@yahoo.com
**Mueller David W MED**
Gnatzig Linda M BA 1
Suhr Kirsten J BS K
CROSS PS-8
• 1917
2902 S 20th St 68108-1301
(402)341-2603 •
FAX(402)342-6511
Clanton Shauna 1-8
Crow Coleen K
Dahlbeck Grace E PS
Endorf Tracy M BS 1-2
Holland Joy PS
Long Cheryl 7-8
Swartz Amy J BSED 5-6
West Diane B 3-4
West Jay W 6-8
KING OF KINGS PS
• 1981
11615 I St 68137-1211
(402)333-6464 •
FAX(402)333-0644
kingofkingsomaha@radiks.net
Albers Danae BS PS
Harper Patti J BS PS
Sherman Lisa K PS
Stirtz Lisa R PS
Weber Anita H PS
Yount Bonnie PS
LAMB OF GOD-PACIFIC HILLS PS
• 1996
1110 S 90th St 68124-1202
(402)391-2288 •
FAX(402)399-8929
glidewell1@aol.com
Brummond Daphne PS
Glidewell Pamela C BED PS
Irwin Carleen PS
Wohlers Mary PS
LITTLE LAMB-DIVINE SHEPHER PS
• 1984
15005 Q St 68137-2525
(402)895-1500 •
FAX(402)895-5377
NO REPORT
MOUNT CALVARY K-8
• 1929
5529 Leavenworth St 68106-1349
(402)551-7020 •
FAX(402)551-9299
mtcalvary@home.com
Coufal Lori L BSED K
Kohtz Terri MA 5-6
Lange Robert E MS 7-8
Ritsch Deborah S BED 3-4
Timm Marcia L BS 1-2
MOUNT OLIVE PS
• 1980
7301 N 28th Ave 68112-2816
(402)455-8700
mountolv@aol.com
NO REPORT
ST MARK PS
• 1985
1821 N 90th St 68114-1314
(402)391-6148 •
FAX(402)399-1682
preschool@st-marklcms.org
**Greve Deje K MA PS**
ST PAUL PS-8
• 1887
5020 Grand Ave 68104-2367
(402)451-2865 •
FAX(402)451-6816
Schroeder Bret A BS 8
Simmer Ehren W BS 7
ZION PS-8
• 1887
4001 Q St 68107-2462
(402)731-1418 •
FAX(402)731-3121
zionstrs@ne.uswest.net
Davis Laurel K
Deardoff Laura R MS 7-8
Meseck Julie A BS 3-4
Skiles Karla BED 1-2
Sonntag Annette M BSED 5-6
Soppe Rebeca S BA PS-6
**ORD**-ST JOHNS PS
• 1994
725 S 14th St 68862-1962
(308)728-3253
NO REPORT
**OSMOND**-IMMANUEL PS-K
• 1906
806 Main St 68765 PO Box 10
68765-0010
(402)748-3303 • FAX(402)
748-3301
**Williams Dawn BS PS-K**
**PAPILLION**-FIRST PS
• 1990
332 N Washington St 68046-2232
(402)339-1178 •
FAX(402)339-3693
Beethe Rhonda J BSED
Peck Jana R PS
**PIERCE**-ZION PS-8
• 1903
520 E Main St 68767-1668
(402)329-4658 •
FAX(402)329-6406
nkurtz@ptcnet.net
Kurtz Neal I MS
Maas Julie A MA 4
Test Kathryn J BED 3
Voelker Rodney W BS 7-8
Wagner Dawn R BA 1-2
Weber Carey A BSED PS
**PLAINVIEW**-ZION PS-8
• 1895
102 N 6Th St PO Box 159
68769-0159
(402)582-3312
zionplvw@plvwtelco.net
Gutz Emmelyn M BED K
Lederer Bonnie B 6-8
Masat Krista L BS K
Mauch Jeannine A MED 3-5
Mc Coy Margaret M BS 1-2
**POLK**-IMMANUEL K-8
• 1886
2406 E 26Th Rd 68654-1702
(402)765-7253 •
FAX(402)765-7253
immanuel@navix.net
**Saeger Robert A MED K-8**
Lenz Lisa A K-3
**SAINT LIBORY**-ZION K-8
• 1884
1655 Worms Rd 68872-2906
(308)687-6486 •
FAX(308)687-6486
ZLSworms@kdsi.net
Meinert Jill M BSED 3-5
Voelker Shawna L BSED K
Zehendner Charles M BS 6-8
**SEWARD**-ST JOHN PS-8
• NLSA • 1884
877 N Columbia Ave 68434-1598
(402)643-4535 •
FAX(402)643-4536
drm3465@seward.cune.edu
Asplin Laura D BS 3
Brettmann Linda BS 3
Buck Karen MED 4
Fiala Maxine MA K
Forke Donna J MED 2
Giesselman Cindy 7-8
Holthus Terry W MED
Huebschman Dorothea MS 2
Hughes Donita G MA 5
Kohlmeier Jonathan W BS 5
Kohtz Virginia MA 1
Lemke Cynthia M MED 6
Mannigel David R MED
Martens Sean P BSED 6-8
Meyer Arlen L MED 6-8
Obermueller Elizabeth A BS 7-8
Oliver Annette BA PS
Prochnow Jean BS 7-8
Simpson Pamela S BS
Sylwester Suzanne MED 6-7
Wachholz Judith E MED 4
Wilcox Scott R BSED 3
**SHELTON**-ST PAUL PS
• 1989
705 S A St 68876 PO Box 326
68876-9669
(308)647-6733
Bierbaum Deanna J BA
**STAPLEHURST**-OUR REDEEMER PS-8
• 1966
425 South St PO Box 187
68439-0187
(402)535-2251
redeemwalling@clarks.net
Jurchen Tamra BA PS
Mc Coy Laura
Phillips Julie L 1-4
Walling JoAn M MED
**TECUMSEH**-ST JOHN PS
• 1997
Hwy 50 & Webster 68450 PO Box
867 68450-0867
(402)335-3816
st62912@navix.net
Hein Renee D BA PS
**TILDEN**-LITTLE LAMBS-IMMANUEL PS
• 1985
500 S Center PO Box 266
68781-0266
(402)368-5690 •
FAX(402)368-2158
imnlluth@ncfcomm.com
Bossard Cindy S PS
Johnson Yvonne PS
**TOBIAS**-ZION PS-8
• 1879
RR 1 Box 85 68453-9759
(402)243-2354
Bartels Judy K MED 5-8
Endorf Janice BSED PS-K
Myers Cindy L BA 1-4
**UTICA**-ST PAUL K-8
• 1900
1100 D St 68456-6043
(402)534-2121 •
FAX(402)534-2318
sp34117@navix.net
**Brauer Robert D MA 7-8**
Fehlhafer Betty J 3-4
Koch Patricia A BS K
Luce Ronald E MED 5-6
Ringler Louise M BED 1-2
**WACO**-ST JOHN 1-8
• 1882
1011 B Road U 68460-9767
(402)728-5244 •
FAX(402)728-5446
st41810@navix.net
NO REPORT
**WEST POINT**-ST PAUL PS-8
• 1883
244 E Walnut St 68788-1426
(402)372-2355 •
FAX(402)372-2742
sp75748@navix.net
**Voelker Howard E MEAD 6-8**
Erickson Margie A BS 1-3
Koehlmoos Lynn M BS K
Reppert Nancy J PS
Schroeder Tammy S BSED 4-5
**WINNEBAGO**-JESUS OUR SAVIOR PS
• 1998
531 Mercer 68071- PO Box 401
68071-0401
(402)878-2522
RezRevRJ@huntel.net
Inglehart Jana M BA PS
**WISNER**-ZION ST JOHN PS-8
• 1960
998 6th Rd 68791-3021
(402)529-3348
NO REPORT

**YORK-**EMMANUEL PS-8
• 1957
806 Beaver Ave 68467-2432
(402)362-6575 •
FAX(402)362-5485
em31235@navix.net
**Seim John R MED 7-8**
Beversdorf Andrea J BS K
Beversdorf Richard A MED 4
Cradick Rachel 7-8
Fritz Alice 1
Gray Janniece MA 3
Hankel Kathy PS
Kern Kathy BSED 5
Naber Lynette I BS 2
Schauer Barbara J BSED 6

## NEVADA

**BOULDER CITY-**LITTLE LAMBS CHRIST-CHRIST PS
• 1999
1401 5th St 89005
(702)293-4332 •
FAX(702)293-3221
NO REPORT
**CARSON CITY-**BETHLEHEM PS-8
• 1988
1837 N Mountain St 89703-2439
(775)882-5252 •
FAX(775)882-9278
bethlehemschool@inetmail.att.net
**Laurente Marvin L MA 5-8**
Archibald Linda BS 4
Bolton Sheila 5
Callahan Kristi PS
Douglas Cathy PS
Haug Marion BA 1
Jones Kimberly D BA K
Karges Lonnie R MED 5-8
Medel Natalee G 2
Paul Clare BA 8
Risenhoover Sarah L BSED 3
Sitze Linda BS 6-8
Winkleman Debbie PS
**ELKO-**ST MARK PS
• 1988
277 Willow St 89801-2851
(702)738-4750 •
FAX(702)738-5456
smlps@cyberhighway.net
**Johnston Caroline B PS**
Barris Kim PS
Collen Carmen R PS
Hansche Rhea A PS
Kennison Karla K PS
**FALLON-**ST JOHN PS
• 1993
1170 S Taylor St 89406-8837
(702)423-6325 •
FAX(702)423-6235
NO REPORT
**GARDNERVILLE-**TRINITY PS
• 1984
1480 Douglas Ave 89410-5103
(702)782-5437 •
FAX(702)782-8154
NO REPORT
**LAS VEGAS-**ABC DAY PS
• 1973
1730 N Pecos Rd 89115-0608
(702)642-5176 •
FAX(702)642-7744
lutheran1730@aol.com
**Davis Patricia C PS**
Davis Daniel PS
Harris April PS
Hurley Belinda L PS
Rhodes Willa PS
FIRST GOOD SHEPHERD K-6
• 1958
301 S Maryland Pkwy 89101-5320
(702)382-8610 •
FAX(702)384-2080
fgslschool@aol.com
**Krafft James E BS 6**
Dey Marilynn L BS 3
Dibos Carolyn E BS 6
Dibos Wayne W BS 4
Fogo Valerie C BA 2
Henshaw Barbara 1
Landskroener Nathan L MA 5
Mac Donald Dallas M 1
Sprouse Michelle L K
LITTLE LAMBS OF GOD PS
• 1995
6220 N Jones Blvd 89130-1501
(702)645-4941 •
FAX(702)645-7605
loglc@vegas.net
Summey Teresa PS
MOUNTAIN VIEW K-1
• 1990
9550 W Cheyenne Ave 89129
(702)233-9323 •
FAX(702)360-2099
NO REPORT
REDEEMER K-6
• 1981
1730 N Pecos Rd 89115-0608
(702)642-6144 •
FAX(702)642-2434
**Cooper Annie PS-K**
Dendy Latrica 1-2
Fukey Victoria 5-6
Jackson Da Shawna 3-4
Turville Victor W 5-8
**WINNEMUCCA-**ZION PS
• 1972
3205 N Highland Dr 89445-3905
(775)623-3796 •
FAX(775)623-3796
zion@the-onramp.net
Bultema Jean BA PS
Montgomery Anita PS
Sorenson Patricia PS
Stone Debbie PS
Wilson Linda

## NEW HAMPSHIRE

**KEENE-**TRINITY PS-3
• 1955
28 Arch St 03431-2236
(603)352-9403 •
FAX(603)357-9096
fellendorf@webryders.com
Acosta Debbie BSED 2-3
Bunn Cynthia A CAS 1-2
Donnelly Diane PS
Dostilio Karen 2-3
Fellendorf George W
Malloy Esther L MA
Williams Karen S BA
**MANCHESTER-**IMMANUEL PS
• 1984
673 Weston Rd 03103-3197
(603)622-1514 •
FAX(603)622-5203
secretary@immanuel-mnh.org
Brulet Laura H BSED PS
Kearns Cristina R PS
**NEW IPSWICH-**NOAHS ARK-OUR REDEEMER K
• 1987
200 Ashby Rd 03071-3707 PO Box 387 03071-0387
(603)878-1837 •
FAX(603)878-0891
our_redeemer@netzero.net
La Ronde Bonnie K
**TROY-**TENDER SHEPHERD-CHRIST PS-K
• 1985
4 Fitzwilliam Rd 03465-2309 PO Box 189 03465-0189
(603)242-7283
NO REPORT

## NEW JERSEY

**BASKING RIDGE-**GENTLE SHEPHERD-SOMERSET HILLS PS
• 1993
350 Lake Rd 07920
(908)766-1430 •
FAX(908)766-6546
Albanese Beth PS
Chapman Wendy PS
Gilmore Martha PS
Graber Trish PS
Haines Sonia PS
Harvey Margaret PS
Hughes Kathy PS
Kuppler Lois PS
Lombardi Barbara PS
Maragni Mary PS
Rizzo Arlene PS
Thomas Gretchen PS
**BLAIRSTOWN-**GOOD SHEPHERD PS
• 1988
168 Rt 94 07825-2115
(908)362-5819 •
FAX(908)362-9405
NO REPORT
**BORDENTOWN-**HOLY CROSS PS-6
• 1977
280 Crosswicks Rd 08505-2608
(609)298-2880 •
FAX(609)298-1411
ruth44@webtv.net
NO REPORT
**CLARK-**ZION PS
• 1996
559 Raritan Rd 07066
(732)382-7663
Schulz Rebecca Y PS
**CREAMRIDGE-**ROSE OF SHARON PS
• 1990
13 Arnytown-Hornestown Rd 08514 PO Box 72 08533-0072
(609)758-3680
NO REPORT
**EAST BRUNSWICK-**CROSSROADS COUNTRY P-CHRIST MEMORIAL PS-K
• 1981
114 Old Stage Rd 08816-4818
(908)251-3221 •
FAX(908)723-9026
NO REPORT
**FAIR LAWN-**OUR SAVIOR PS
• 1954
1-22 Hartley Pl 07410-3048
(201)797-1585 •
FAX(201)796-7949
Herzberg Suzanne M BA PS
Latyak Virginia L PS
**FLEMINGTON-**ST PAUL PS-5
• 1962
201 Highway 31 08822-5737
(908)782-3979 •
FAX(908)782-1633
st.paul.luth@worldnet.att.net
**Archambault Jill PS**
**Bertrand Brenda L BA 3-4**
Dwyer Janice K
Harris Janet PS
Maslott Eileen 1-2
Meyer Pamela PS
Pieper Suzanne BS PS
**FORDS-**OUR REDEEMER PS-8
• 1962
28 S 4th St 08863-1647
(732)738-7470 •
FAX(732)738-6547
ourredeemer@home.com
**Sadlo Christopher BMU**
Behr Sharon 2
Farrelly Mary E 1
Fisher Kathleen 5-8
Johnson Carol R BED K
Kreyling Rebekah 3
Peterson Linda BSED 3-4
Pignone Debbie PS
Zurawski Kerlyn 5-8
**HACKETTSTOWN-**GETHSEMANE PS
• 1973
409 E Baldwin St 07840-1422
(908)852-2285 •
FAX(908)852-8556
Holz Janice Q PS
Padden Sara E BA PS
**HAMBURG-**PRINCE OF PEACE PS-K
• 1975
3320 Rt 94 07419 PO Box 5 07419-0005
(973)827-5080 •
FAX(973)827-5249
popchurch@juno.com
Andrews Roberta M BA K
Gleason Catherine PS
Kuehm Joan
Maute Marilyn PS
**LAKEHURST-**REDEEMER PS
• 1995
2309 Route 70 08733-3641
(732)657-0333 •
FAX(732)657-7462
NO REPORT
**LAMBERTVILLE-**ST PETER PS
• 1997
1608 Harbourton Rocktown Rd 08530
(609)466-6511 •
FAX(609)466-0939
dubbins@voicenet.com
NO REPORT
**MAHWAH-**HOLY CROSS PS
• 1958
125 Glasgow Ter 07430-1635
(201)529-2117 •
FAX(201)529-5538
**Rupert Shirley**
Ayre Lesley BED PS
Downton Jane R MA PS
Morris Ellen MS PS
Mosher Sue A PS
Rainsford Lynn PS
Steffen Susan BSED PS
Vaughan Amy M PS
**MAYWOOD-**NOAHS ARK-ZION PS
• 1997
120 E Pleasant Ave 07607
(201)843-6636 •
FAX(201)843-4109
NO REPORT
**MEDFORD-**LITTLE CHRISTIANS-CALVARY PS
• 1979
3 Eayrestown Rd 08055-3940
(609)714-2489
NO REPORT
**MOUNTAIN LAKES-**KING OF KINGS PS
• 1972
Route 46 07046-9806
(201)334-4085
NO REPORT
**NEWTON-**REDEEMER PS
• 1974
37 Newton Sparta Rd 07860-2745
(973)383-0217 •
FAX(973)383-3954
Bessemer Denise PS
Brunovsky Diane J BS PS
Chaney Dianne L PS
Kappelmeier A BSED
Vitz Shirley J BA PS
**OAK RIDGE-**PARADISE-HOLY FAITH PS
• 1997
104 Paradise Rd 07438
(973)697-2118 •
FAX(973)697-6060
Bennett Dolores PS
Burgstahler Cathilynn PS

Gonter Bonnie PS
Kleindienst Elizabeth E PS
Lapszynski Mary B PS
Mendel Catherine PS
Reynolds Valarie Jean Z PS
**OLD BRIDGE-**GOOD SHEPHERD PS-K
• 1968
3139 County Road 516 08857
(732)679-8887 •
FAX(732)679-8996
gscc@lc-goodshepherd.org
Burke Laurie BA PS
Carusi Leslie K
Chan Susan
Samolewicz Susan PS
Troutman Helen PS
**PENNSAUKEN-**MARTIN LUTHER PS-6
• 1950
4106 Terrace Ave 08109-1626
(856)665-0231 •
FAX(856)665-0130
**Kehr Mark A MED**
**PLAINFIELD-**MESSIAH DAY CARE PS
• 1975
630 E Front St 07060-1414
(908)755-4525
NO REPORT
**RINGWOOD-**CHRIST THE KING PS
• 1972
50 Erskine Rd 07456-2150
(973)962-6767
christtheking3@juno.com
Foreman Jan PS
Gati Donna PS
Gretina Georgette L MA
Williams Linda J PS
**STANHOPE-**OUR SAVIOR PS
• 1971
143 Brooklyn Rd 07874-2869
(201)347-1818 •
FAX(201)347-1818
Crowell Jennifer M PS
Doring Lois R BS
Gargano Elizabeth PS
Kanter Gail E PS
Squier Kathleen M PS
**UNION-**GRACE PS
• 1990
2222 Vauxhall Rd 07083-5825
(908)686-3965
NO REPORT
**WEST NEW YORK-**SAN PABLO PS-K
• 1991
5106 Palisade Ave 07093-1919
(201)348-0713 •
FAX(201)348-0713
0
**Lopez Mercedes**
Bermudez Paula A PS
Gibney Lorraine
Lopez Katlyn
Marquez Doris PS
Maruri Lynne
Ruiz Mirna E
Satterfield Erica
**WESTFIELD-**REDEEMER PS-6
• 1953
229 Cowperthwaite Pl 07090-4015
(908)232-1592 •
FAX(908)317-9301
**Borchin Roger G MA**
Borchin Jane BA PS-K
Fantini Beverly K
Ferraro Roberta PS
Frusco Diane I 2
Marks Susan E BA 3
Nusse Janice 5-6
Rogers Karen PS
Sabanosh Marlene A 1
Stofa Janet
Stofa Stefeny
Vellucci Natalie Jo 4
Wilson Janet K
**WESTWOOD-**ZION PS-8
• 1961
64 1st Ave 07675-2130
(201)664-8060 •
FAX(201)664-7092
zlsic@bellatlantic.net
**Meisten Michele BS**
Dawson Andrea 4-8
Grotto Douglas BS 4-8
Heinz Betty Jane J BS PS
Hofmann Sandra E BA 2
Hoglund Ann E BA 1
Krause Dorene A 4-8
Moyer Eileen C BSED PS
Munsch Donna J BS 4-8
Quillio Merianne BA 7-8
Snyder Katherine 4-8
Sprague Eileen MS 3
Walz Karen K

## NEW MEXICO

**ALBUQUERQUE-**CHRIST PS-5
• 1989
7701 Candelaria Rd NE 87110-2752
(505)884-3876 •
FAX(505)888-0655
clc@lobo.net
**Von Soosten Mark A MED 4-5**
Beetstra Joan W 4-5
Dillon Wendy J BS 2-3
Haas Deon 1
Hemphill Lishelle L BS K
Rasmussen Kimberly A BA PS-2
IMMANUEL K-8
• 1924
300 Gold Ave SE 87102-3537
(505)243-2589 •
FAX(505)242-0616
immanuel@integrity.com
**Pflieger R C K-8**
Bartels Connie M MA 3
Beene Patricia 6-8
Edgel Lisa 5
Geuder Helen J BSED 2
Johnson Jennie 4
Lomas Monica 6-8
Montano Darla 1
Rickords Anna BA 6-8
Rickords Jeffery B BSED 6-8
Vaupel Christina BA 6-8
Walquist Elaine E BSED K
OUR SAVIOR PS
• 1996
4301 Atrisco Dr NW 87120-1662
(505)836-7007
NO REPORT
**CEDAR CREST-**PRINCE OF PEACE PS-4
• 1995
0 12121 North Hwy 14 87008
(505)281-6833 •
FAX(505)281-2430
popschool@juno.com
**Geuder Alan B EDS**
Christian Kari J K
Englund Holly A 1-2
Ford Mary Ann PS-K
Gibbs Rosalie
Glover George 5-6
Hance Rachel M BS 3-4
Schein Kari PS
Tills Halli S BS PS
Wenrich Beth-Ann
**CLOVIS-**IMMANUEL PS
• 1992
1021 N Prince St 88101-6152
(505)763-1952
immanuel@pdrpip.com
Bean A S BS PS
Huffaker Jodie PS
**LAS CRUCES-**MISSION PS
• 1997
2752 Roadrunner Parkway 88011
(505)532-5489 •
FAX(505)532-5489
mlpreschool@zianet.com
Jakesy Ruth E PS
Martin Mary C PS
**LOS LUNAS-**CHRIST THE KING
• 1997
700 Camelot Blvd SW 87031
(505)865-9226
NO REPORT
**RIO RANCHO-**LITTLE LAMBS-CALVARY PS
• 1998
305 Unser PO Box 15595 87174
(505)892-9407 •
FAX(505)891-2080
donald_neidigk@juno.com
NO REPORT
**SANTA FE-**GENTLE SHEPHERD-IMMANUEL PS
• 1989
207 E Barcelona Rd 87501-4609
(505)983-9383
NO REPORT

## NEW YORK

**ALBANY-**SMALL STEPS-CHRIST PS
• 1973
1500 Western Ave 12203-3525
(518)456-1530 •
FAX(518)456-3526
Fike Carol PS
ST MATTHEW PS-K
• 1971
75 Whitehall Rd 12209-1436
(518)463-6495 •
FAX(518)463-9417
NO REPORT
ST PAUL PS
• 1973
475 State St 12203-1004
(518)463-0649 •
FAX(518)463-0571
**Duncan Joanne**
Childs Leasha 1
Galea Christine PS
Grieve Erica PS
Moore Megan PS
**ARCADE-**HOPE PS
• 1979
2 E Main St 14009
(716)492-2529 •
FAX(716)492-2530
NO REPORT
**BATAVIA-**ST PAUL PS-5
• 1966
31 Washington Ave 14020
(716)343-0488 •
FAX(716)344-0470
werkasap@iinc.com
Hoverstock Amy K
Porter Deborah PS
Shetler Janice 3-5
Werk Ann M MA 1-2
**BAYSIDE-**BAYSIDE-IMMANUEL KOREAN PS-2
• 1980
164-05 35th Ave 11358-1715
(718)961-6062 •
FAX(718)321-0367
NO REPORT
**BERGHOLZ-**HOLY GHOST PS-8
• 1843
6630 Luther St 14304-2011
(716)731-3030 •
FAX(716)731-3030
lcmshg@aol.com
NO REPORT
**BRONX-**GRACE
2930 Valentine Ave 10458-2608
NO REPORT
OUR SAVIOUR PS-8
• 1942
1734 Williamsbridge Rd 10461-6204
(718)792-5665 •
FAX(718)409-3877
Krass Robert J MS 2
TRINITY PS-8
• 1945
2125 Watson Ave 10472-5401
(718)828-1234 •
FAX(718)828-3474
Browne Pataricia
Collado Judelca
Ellis Marleen
Foster Gloria
Foster Veronica B
Lopez Barbara
Michaux Lanetta
Rodriquez Lisa
Vargas Marisol
**BRONXVILLE-**CHAPEL-THE VILLAGE PS-8
• NLSA • 1947
172 White Plains Rd 10708-1954
(914)337-3202 •
FAX(914)771-9711
jdhyne@vlc-ny.org
**Dhyne James T MA PS-8**
**Schultz Michael MSCT PS-8**
Booker Joan 6-8
Brockhoff Bonnie K
Castro Linda M PS
Hartwell Susan PS
Johnson Meta J 1-8
Keating Virginia A BA 3
Kollmann Marcia E MMU PS
Macdonald Catherine 2
Maschke Samuel R BA 5-8
Morejon Christiane E 1-8
Nagel Molly PS
Peterson Sharon L MLS PS-8
Rende Jennifer 1
Romano Vera PS
Toub Michelle 4
Tween Michelle K
Walton Roberta PS
Warnken Melinda B BED 5-8
**BROOKLYN-** OF THE RISEN CHRIST PS-5
• 1970
250 Blake Ave 11212-5502
(718)498-3651 •
FAX(718)498-7786
NO REPORT
ST JOHN K-8
• 1965
195 Maujer St 11206-1332
(718)963-3074
NO REPORT
ST MARK PS-8
• 1868
626 Bushwick Ave 11206-6024
(718)455-5743
NO REPORT
ST PETER PS
105 Highland Pl 11208-1222
(718)647-1014
NO REPORT
**BUFFALO-**MARTIN LUTHER PS-8
• RSO • NLSA • 1948
1085 Eggert Rd 14226-4196
(716)836-3554 •
FAX(716)803-1274
mlcs1948@aol.com
**Duncan Patricia MED**
Beutel Kathleen M MSED 4-7
Foerster Judy E MA 1
Huber Jennifer 6-8
Kopper Patricia E MA 5
Liss Candace PS
Mumm Heidi S BS 3
Parks Amy 4-8
Rice Sandra J K
Warner Debra L 2
Zimberg Paul M K-8

NAZARETH PS-8
• 1967
269 Skillen St 14207-1633
(716)876-7709
NO REPORT
**CAIRO**-JOYFUL-RESURRECTION PS
• 1983
Route 23B & 32 12413 PO Box 563 12413-0563
(518)622-3286 •
FAX(518)622-2083
resurrectionluch@cs.com
NO REPORT
**CANANDAIGUA**-LITTLE LAMBS-GOOD SHEPHERD PS
• 1993
320 S Pearl St 14424-1748 PO Box 690 14424-0690
(716)394-2760 •
FAX(716)394-2760
NO REPORT
**CENTEREACH**-OUR SAVIOR NEW AMERI PS-8
• 1967
140 Mark Tree Rd 11720-2220
(516)588-2757 •
FAX(516)588-2617
NO REPORT
**CENTRAL ISLIP**-LITTLE LAMBS-GRACE PS
• 1994
75 Calebs Path 11722-1805
(516)232-3272 •
FAX(516)435-8724
lambs75@aol.com
Ceramello Joan PS
Smith Debra A AAS
Sonera Sarita PS
Stublick Dianne L PS
**COHOCTON**-ST PAUL PS
• 1995
97 Maple Ave PO Box 316 14826-0316
(716)384-5667 •
FAX(716)384-5667
stpaulcohocton@juno.com
Bernard Ruth M BA PS
Sick Jane PS
**COLLEGE POINT**-ST JOHN
123-07 22nd Ave 11356-2644
NO REPORT
**COLONIE**-OUR SAVIOR PS-6
• NLSA • 1956
63 Mountain View Ave 12205
(518)459-2273 •
FAX(518)459-1330
**Roemke Thomas L MS**
Bantz Jo A 1
Barker Anthony W K-6
Bruso Barbara BS 5
Cobb Patricia PS-6
Kocsis Betsy MRE 2
March John D BA 6
Mendoza Divina P 5-6
Niemann Claudia MA 4
Pangburn Cheryl MA 3
Roemke Carol A BS PS
**CORTLAND**-ST PAUL PS
• 1989
49 Hamlin St 13045-1706
(607)753-7101
Johnston Diane PS
Walter Deborah PS
**DEPEW**-ST JOHN PS
• 1991
67 Litchfield Ave 14043-3207
(716)683-3947
NO REPORT
**DIX HILLS**-ST LUKE PS
• 1966
20 Candlewood Path 11746-5304
(516)462-5216 •
FAX(516)462-6496
Backmeier Elaine
Boronow Trisha PS
Borracci Connie PS
Cavalcante Joan PS
Davidson Joyce PS
Fyfe Elizabeth PS
Hohn Sue MS PS
Kahn Janet MS PS
Leo Charlene PS
Masi Lorraine PS
Pavlica Barbara MS PS
Rogener Amy MA PS
Velez Lois PS
Weissmann Debbie PS
**EAST MEADOW**-CALVARY PS
• 1981
36 Taylor Ave 11554-2126
(516)520-4067 •
FAX(516)735-1804
**Gottschalk Janet C MA PS**
Waters Janice PS
**EAST SETAUKET**-MESSIAH PS
• 1998
465 Pond Path PO Box 519 11733-0519
(516)751-1775 •
FAX(516)751-1775
messiah_lutheran_churchl@juno.com
NO REPORT
**ELMA**-FAITH PS
• 1995
1230 Bowen Rd 14059-8906
(716)652-2221
NO REPORT
**FARMINGTON**-ST JOHN PS
• 1969
153 Church Ave 14425
(315)986-3045
NO REPORT
**FISHKILL**-LITTLE LAMBS-OUR SAVIOR PS
• 1995
1167 Route 52 Ste 204 12524-1616
(914)897-4423 •
FAX(914)897-4429
oslcfish@aol.com
NO REPORT
**FLUSHING**-CHAPEL OF THE REDEEM PS-6
• 1945
220-16 Union Tpke 11364-3543
(718)465-4236 •
FAX(718)465-2808
**Krass Robert J MS**
Campbell Karen
Entis Jennfier PS
Entis Pamela K
Forte Christine 3
Gonzalez Christine R BA 4
Hippeli Kimberly 2
Pedro Fernanda 1
Stevens Judith 5
Toth Max
FLUSHING & BAYSIDE PS-8
• RSO • NLSA • 1991
36-01 Bell Blvd 11361
(718)229-5262 •
FAX(718)225-7446
NO REPORT
**GARDEN CITY**-RESURRECTION PS
• 1962
420 Stewart Ave 11530-4620
(516)741-6447
NO REPORT
**GLEN COVE**-TRINITY LUTHERAN EAR PS
78 Forest Ave 11542
(516)656-0386 •
FAX(516)674-4297
NO REPORT
**GLENDALE**-REDEEMER PS-8
• 1955
69-26 Cooper Ave 11385-7103
(718)821-6670 •
FAX(718)366-0338
**Williams Michael**
Callahan Cheryl M BA PS
Colon Janet M MA 6
Gadson Daisy 5
Galdo Carolyn 3
Kwak Susan PS
Morse Annette K
Mulhall Glenna 2
Nieves Gina 1-8
Prevou Darnel 4
Rudy Wayne A 7-8
Salas Brenda 1
Stahl Diane BSED 7-8
ST JOHN PS-8
• 1848
88-24 Myrtle Ave 11385-7821
(718)441-2120 •
FAX(718)805-4735
Folwaczny Katherine 3
**GOWANDA**-IMMANUEL PS-6
• 1989
40 S Chapel St 14070-1304
(716)532-4342
fishthenet@gnn.com
NO REPORT
**HAMLIN**-ST JOHN PS-6
• 1874
1107 Lake Road West Frk 14464-9601
(716)964-2550 •
FAX(716)964-5859
kfmyr@frontiernet.net
Kruger Donna BS K
Maher M V MED PS
Meyer Karl F MED
Nettnin Kathleen L BA 1
Peters Katherine 3-4
Presutti Donna
Reese Heidi 2
**HASTINGS-ON-HUDSON**-HILLTOP PS
• 1993
7 Farragut Ave 10706
(914)478-1065
NO REPORT
**HAWTHORNE**-TRINITY PS
• 1995
292 Elwood Ave 10532
(914)773-1108 •
FAX(914)769-5326
NO REPORT
**HENRIETTA**-PINNACLE PS-K
• 1962
250 Pinnacle Rd 14623-1842
(716)334-6500 •
FAX(716)334-6022
NO REPORT
**HICKSVILLE**-TRINITY PS-8
• NLSA • 1954
40 W Nicholai St 11801-3806
(516)931-2211 •
FAX(516)931-6345
**Kuck William E**
Hahn Janet BA 2
**HILTON**-ST PAUL PS-8
• 1957
158 East Ave 14468-1318
(716)392-4000 •
FAX(716)392-4001
NO REPORT
**HOLBROOK**-ST JOHN PS
• 1976
1675 Coates Ave 11741-2413
(516)588-4347 •
FAX(631)588-8159
**Breslau Patricia BS PS**
Callihan Linda PS
Cilluffo Marie PS
De Marie Roberta PS
Di Napoli Theresa PS
Hayden Donna PS
Jennings Margaret PS
Kelly Maureen
Kirschenheiter Kim PS
Kletecka Margaret PS
Kuehl Gladys PS
Mac Connie Marilyn PS
Maler Carole A PS
Mazeski Marilyn BA PS
Muller Diane PS
Onorato Elizabeth MA PS
Ritchie Angela PS
**ISLIP**-TRINITY PS
• 1985
111 Nassau Ave 11751-3626
(631)277-5855 •
FAX(631)277-3134
Angermaier Jean PS
Antonelli Rosemarie PS
Barron Ellen BSED
Brown Peggy PS
Connor Virginia PS
Fagerland Jo Anne PS
Iannone Aixa PS
Jeanes Phyllis PS
Vikingstad Susan PS
**ITHACA**-TRINITY PS
• 1979
149 Honness Ln 14850-6253
(607)273-9017 •
FAX(607)273-9438
trinity@baka.com
NO REPORT
**LOCKPORT**-MOUNT OLIVE PS
• 1969
6965 Chestnut Ridge Rd 14094-3429
(716)434-9550
Annalora Carol A PS
Bernardi Veronica PS
ST PETER K-8
• 1948
4169 Church Rd 14094-9724
(716)433-9013 •
FAX(716)433-9014
stpeternr@adelphia.net
**Noone Eleanor**
Craig Beverly J 2-3
Gildersleeve Margaret 1
Harless Anita 3-8
Muck Bonita M K-8
Muck Ruth E MA 6
Musall David J 5-8
Peck Brian K-8
Peck Katherine 7-8
Petty Trisha 7-8
Sallach Marilyn 4-5
Zastrow Patti PS
**LONG ISLAND CITY**-QUEENS PS-8
• 1952
31-20 37th St 11103-3933
(718)721-4313 •
FAX(718)721-7662
Karatzias Louiza 3
Smith Diane PS-8
Stravopoulos Jenny 6
**MANHATTAN**-ST MATTHEW PS-8
• 1752
200 Sherman Ave 10034-3301
(212)567-2699 •
FAX(212)567-5604
NO REPORT
**MILL NECK**-MILL NECK MANOR DEAF
Frost Mill Road PO Box 12 11765-0012
NO REPORT
**MONROE**-ST PAUL PS-1
• 1975
21 Still Rd 10950
(845)783-1068 •
FAX(845)783-7593
school@stpaulmonroeny.org
Adams Ramona BA PS
Brennan Kathi J PS
Conklin Erin PS
Forrest Janis R MSED
Keff Karin A PS
Macal Susan M PS
Motyka Linda PS
Muller Linda 1
Siegriest Sally PS
Sklenarik Angela K

**MOUNT VERNON**-IMMANUEL PS-K
• 1992
17 E Grand St 10552-2209
(914)668-4569 •
FAX(914)668-3431
immanuel-kid@yahoo.com
**Wynn Karen**
Hetzer Susan PS
Mossinghoff Christen K
Urebb Sheba PS
**NEW HYDE PARK**-TRINITY PS
• 1968
5 Durham Rd 11040-2018
(516)354-9050
NO REPORT
**NEW YORK**-OPEN ARMS-ALL NATIONS PS
• 1998
417 W 57th St 10019
(212)333-5583 •
FAX(212)333-5864
cfanlcms.netzero.net
NO REPORT
**NORTH TONAWANDA**-GREAT BEGINNINGS-REDEEMER PS
• 1992
Falconer & Thompson St 14120
(716)692-5734
NO REPORT
ST JOHN PS-8
• NLSA • 1853
6950 Ward Rd 14120-1413
(716)693-9677 •
FAX(716)693-2686
jn6950@wzrd.com
NO REPORT
ST MARK PS-8
• 1891
1135 Oliver St 14120-2637
(716)693-3715 •
FAX(716)693-3932
NO REPORT
ST MATTHEW PS-8
• NLSA • 1956
875 Eggert Dr 14120-3330
(716)692-6862 •
FAX(716)692-0242
stmattnt@aol.com
**Hummel Clifford W MS**
Bars Deborah A PS
Cudney Denise 5-8
Donop Christine M BED 2
Felbinger Darlene M BA K
Gibson Kathy J PS-8
Haseley Susan M 1
Kelly Jacqueline 5-8
Meyerhofer Nancy L BA 3
Pangburn Janet K BA 4
Schulz Jane 5-8
Sims Dale 5-8
Spear Bill 4-8
Williams Jill 7-8
ST PAUL PS-8
• 1861
453 Old Falls Blvd 14120-3107
(716)692-3255 •
FAX(716)692-3643
stpaulnt@buffnet.net
NO REPORT
**OLD WESTBURY**-REDEEMER PS
• 1991
1 Old Westbury Rd 11568-1603
(516)333-3355 •
FAX(516)333-7046
redeemerli@yahoo.com
Dennelly Lisa PS
Rousso Jill PS
Tommaso Deborah C MA PS
Winter Joanne PS
**OLEAN**-IMMANUEL PS
• 1984
419 Laurens St 14760-2515
(716)372-8533
Hedlund Victoria M PS
Shorter Alison M PS

**ORCHARD PARK**-ST JOHN PS
• 1976
4536 S Buffalo St 14127-2915
(716)662-4747 •
FAX(716)667-3580
stjohns@buffnet.net
Felong Mary K PS
Mc Cumber M Louise BSED PS
**OWEGO**-ZION PS-6
• 1981
3917 Waverly Rd 13827-2841
(607)687-6376 • FAX0
zionluthrn@stny.rr.com
Folwaczny Katherine 5-6
Pawlak Janet A 3-4
Rothrock Heather K
Sorensen Karen BS PS
Wilkinson Bonnie 1-2
**PATCHOGUE**-EMANUEL PS-6
• 1956
179 E Main St 11772-3103
(516)758-2250 •
FAX(516)758-2418
Emanluth.aol.com
**Joerz Lori L MA**
Begy Carol K
Bianca Paula MA PS
Dragone Cathy 2
Emeritz Edith
Farraro Jo Anne 1
Froelich Honora PS
Galli Denise A BA PS
Hannigan Joan 1
Harper Karen K
Haufe Mary MA 5
Laudicina Janine 6
Maertz Bettyann MS 3
Mihalik Doreen K
Milton Maren MA
Munz Elizabeth
Norman Denise L MS
Pallas Jamie
Perry Cheryl PS
Puls Douglas W BA 2
Reoch Angela PS
Shaddix Mary Deene MA 4
Stahl Joyce
Strychalsky Keith
Trapasso Janet K
Wiebelt Janet PS
**PENFIELD**-FAITH PS
• 1986
2576 Browncroft Blvd 14625-1530
(716)385-2360 •
FAX(716)381-6407
FCCNS1@EZNET.NET
Alongi Robin MA PS
Cirilla Patricia PS
Costello Karen MS
Fink Susan PS
Flammann Christine M BA PS
Fornari Betty A BS PS
Giese Debra PS
Gosiewski Barbara PS
Hinds Ellen M PS
Martin Carrie PS
Ozimek Janice PS
Piraino Christine PS
Pucci Patricia PS
Richards Karen PS
Salmon Kathleen PS
Schmitt Valerie PS
Szklany Nancy PS
**PUTNAM VALLEY**-ST LUKE PS
• 1982
Oscawana Lk Rd PO Box 533
10579-0533
(914)526-3560
NO REPORT
**QUEENS VILLAGE**-GRACE K-8
• 1956
100-05 Springfield Blvd
11429-1619
(718)465-1010 •
FAX(718)465-9069
graceluth@aol.com
**Di Stephan Corinne E MSED**

Balducci Adriane L MS K-8
Beaver Thomas S K-8
Bertolotti Monique 4
Brown Kathleen K-8
Flynn Bernadette 5
Hundt Janet K
Losee Shannon 1-8
Moses Lizzie
Oblander Michelle M BME 6
Power Catherine
Stanczuk Deborah 1
Suber Verna 7-8
Ward Carolyn 2
Wolfanger Lisa MSED 7-8
Wright Eileen F MS 3
**REGO PARK**-OUR SAVIOUR PS-6
• 1945
64-33 Woodhaven Blvd
11374-5051
(718)897-4343 •
FAX(718)830-9275
NO REPORT
**RIDGEWOOD**-IMMANUEL PS
• 1980
7147 Ridge Rd 14094-9457
(716)434-0521
Wrdslewski Francine PS
LITTLE LAMBS PS
• 1991
60-10 67Th Ave 11385
(718)821-5252
NO REPORT
**RIVERHEAD**-OUR REDEEMER PS-1
• 1985
11931 269 Main Road PO Box 960
11931-0960
(516)722-8446
Byer Carol E BS 1-2
Drower Jennifer K
Keating Beth 1-2
Roehrig Mary B
Van Scoy Barbara PS-2
**ROCHESTER**-HOPE PS
• 1962
1301 Vintage Ln 14626-1760
(716)723-4673 •
FAX(716)723-8549
Harrington Nancy M BA PS
Lambrecht Barbara C
Mc Donald Carol A PS
RISEN CHRIST PS
• 1982
1000 Moseley Rd 14450-3852
(716)223-9653
Barkau Ilene PS
Keys Kaye PS
**ROME**-ST JOHN PS
• 1983
502 W Chestnut St 13440-2620
(315)336-8090
Roth Cheryl PS
Suits Jean PS
Tuthill Judith A BA
**SAINT JAMES**-ST JAMES PS
• 1969
Woodlawn & 2nd Avenues 11780
PO Box 2036 11780-0602
(516)862-8934 •
FAX(516)862-7809
NO REPORT
**SARATOGA SPRINGS**-ST PAUL PS
• 1996
149 Lake Ave 12866
(518)584-0904 •
FAX(518)584-2180
office@
stpaullutheranchurchsaratoga.com
Collins Terri PS
Creviston Ann PS
O Brien Laura PS
Varga Joan I BS
**SAYVILLE**-ST JOHN PS
• 1966
48 Greene Ave 11782-2723
(516)589-3202
NO REPORT

**SCHENECTADY**--ZION PS
• 1974
153 Nott Ter 12308-3130
(518)374-1811 •
FAX(518)374-4438
NO REPORT
**SPENCERPORT**-TRINITY PS
191 Nichols St 14559-2160
(716)352-3143 •
FAX(716)352-3143
De Sormeau Laurie J PS
Kelley Elizabeth PS
**SPRINGVILLE**-SALEM LUTH PRESCHOOL PS
91 W Main St 14141-1057
(716)592-4893 •
FAX(716)592-0800
NO REPORT
**STATEN ISLAND**-ST JOHN PS-8
• 1952
663 Manor Rd 10314-4523
(718)761-1858 •
FAX(718)761-4962
st.johnscho@aol.com
**Liescheidt Richard H BSED**
Di Martino Carolyn N MS K
Diamond Sheila A 3
Erkman Mary M MED
Gay Carolyn E MS 1
Hernandez Gail M 6-8
Long Patricia BSED
Murphy Rosanne 6-8
Palisay Rosemary M MS 2
Penna Alison D BSED 5
Rubinate Delores B BS 7
Schwenker Carol P MA PS
**TONAWANDA**-FIRST TRINITY PS
• NLSA • 1961
1570 Niagara Falls Blvd
14150-8433
(716)835-2220 •
FAX(716)833-6998
SWEETSOUP@AOL.COM
Boccolucci Sharon PS
Cuomo Susan M PS
Fennell Christine PS
Kolber Margaret M MED PS
Vance Beth A BA PS
**UTICA**-TRINITY PS
• 1974
2620 Genesee St 13502-6003
(315)732-7869 •
FAX(315)732-7869
trin1@juno.com
Hagan Carmen PS
Johnson Ann M AAS
Zimbler Mary PS
**VESTAL**-GRACE PS
• 1969
701 Main St 13850-3157
(607)748-0840
NO REPORT
**WALDEN**-TRINITY PS
• 1983
2520 State Route 208 12586-2816
(914)778-7057
NO REPORT
**WARWICK**-GOOD SHEPHERD PS PS
• 1965
95 Kings Highway PO Box 218
10990-1919
(914)986-8393 •
FAX(914)986-3050
NO REPORT
**WATERLOO**-CALVARY PS
• 1980
2414 Rt 414N 13165
(315)539-8053 •
FAX(315)539-6225
NO REPORT
**WELLSVILLE**-TRINITY PS
• 1985
470 N Main St 14895-1043
(716)593-3311 •
FAX(716)593-1194
Link Nancy

Tipton Sherri
**WEST HENRIETTA**-ST MARK PS
• 1969
779 Erie Station Rd 14586 PO Box 287 14586-0287
(716)334-4130 •
FAX(716)334-4795
Bauchle Allen PS
Bauchle Nancy P
Tirabassi Karen W PS
**WEST SENECA**-TRINITY PS-8
• NLSA • 1851
146 Reserve Rd 14224-4016
(716)674-5353 •
FAX(716)674-4910
Rice Sandra J K-1
**WHITESTONE**-IMMANUEL PS-8
• 1949
12-10 150th ST 11357-1748
(718)767-5656 •
FAX(718)747-1124
NO REPORT
**WOLCOTTSVILLE**-ST MICHAEL PS
• 1995
6379 Wolcottsville Rd 14001-9002
(716)542-2886
Baehr Phyllis PS
Maier Marlene BSED PS
Rehwaldt Dawn PS
**YONKERS**-ST MARK PS-8
• 1962
Kimball Ave & St Marks Pl 10704
27 Saint Marks Pl 10704-4011
(914)237-4944 •
FAX(914)237-1346
stmarkslu.@earthlink.com
NO REPORT

## NORTH CAROLINA

**ASHEVILLE**-EMMANUEL PS-6
• 1958
51 Wilburn Pl 28806-2752
(828)252-1795 •
FAX(828)285-0064
**Janisko David A MA**
Carpenter Tracey PS
Fitzsimmons Dana PS
Giese Lillian P PS
Keller Marta 2
Leyva Colleen A MED K
Roupp Elesha PS
Schallhorn Elaine MA 4
Schmitz Barbara 1
Winkler Sandra 3
**CARY**-RESURRECTION PS
• 1984
100 Lochmere Dr W 27511-9129
(919)851-7270 •
FAX(919)851-6411
Bigelow Kim PS
Cotten Amelia PS
Doster Melissa PS
Ehlerit Lori PS
Johanson Chris A PS
Johnston Marsha PS
Jones Sue PS
Kapadoa Wendy PS
Laubscher Linda PS
Miller Gina PS
Owy Michelle PS
Park Elaine BSN PS
Prawdzik Kristy PS
Spitz Cheri M
Taylor Suzanne PS
Velaskei Wendy PS
Visentin Susan J PS
Williamson Mary A BA PS
Wright Nancy R PS
Wurst Beth PS
**CHAPEL HILL**-ADVENT MONTESSORI PS PS
• 1998
230 Erwin Rd 27514
(919)968-7690 •
FAX(919)933-9233
Robertson Laura PS
Schnell Jeannene PS
**CHARLOTTE**-CHARLOTTE PS-5
• 1942
1225 E Morehead St 28204-2816
(704)372-7738 •
FAX(704)372-7318
fguy@charlottelutheran.org
**Guy Frederick**
Blessing Tamara J BS 3
Ferner Shelley V 2
Greene Marilyn L PS
Hunt Kathryn A MA K
Morice Sharon 1
Shropshire Cassandra O AA PS
Stohlmann Janice H 5
Watkins Salliejean MED 4
MESSIAH PS
• 1987
8300 Providence Rd 28277-9752
(704)541-1624
NO REPORT
RESURRECTION PS-8
• 1978
2825 Shenandoah Ave 28205-6938
(704)334-9898 •
FAX(704)377-6578
rcs.saints@juno.com
Atwell Janet 6
Cosner Candace 3
Di Donato Allan MA 7-8
Edwards Wanda 1-6
Emmrich Ann 7-8
Hailey Roxann BA 1
Hasty Rebecca PS
Hershelman Laura 4
Miller William R
Ridge Michael
Smrcina Paula K
Sparrow Matt 7-8
Sprang Joy 7-8
Tice Kim 1-6
Wentz Charlotte MA 5
White Sharon 2
**CONOVER**-CONCORDIA PS-8
• NLSA • 1878
215 5Th Ave SE 28613-1916
(828)464-3011 •
FAX(828)464-9899
**Unverfehrt William E MA**
Banwart Randolph J BA 5
Banwart Sindy S PS
Carter Kimberly 4
Couch Kathy MA 6-8
Isenhour Elizabeth BA K
Lehman Harriet BS 3
Lineberger Rebecca K-8
Reed Leslie M 4
Stockman Wade A BA K-8
Triplett Rebecca J BA PS-8
Unverfehrt Kathleen E BS 2
Urtel Diane K-8
Young Angelica M BA 6-8
SAINT JOHN PS
2126 Saint John's Church Rd PO Box 575 28613
(828)464-4071 •
FAX(828)464-6590
stjohnlc@wave.net
Drum Dana PS
Frye Bill PS
Huffman Ashley PS
Johnson Denise PS
Sinclair Elayne PS
Smith Sara PS
ST PETER PS
• 1952
6175 Saint Peters Church Rd 28613-8752
(828)256-2970 •
FAX(828)256-6633
sblazer@w3link.com
NO REPORT
**FRANKLIN**--GREAT BEGINNINGS-RESURRECTION PS
• 1990
38 Wayah St 28734-3329
(704)369-2411
roberts@dnet.net
NO REPORT
**HICKORY**-ST STEPHEN PS-8
• NLSA • 1943
2304 Springs Rd NE 28601-3066
(828)256-2166 •
FAX(828)256-7994
ssls@twave.net
**Guelzow Jonathan P MS**
Anderson Debra PS
Boldt Stephen BA 5-8
Bradtmueller Debra A BA PS
Eckard Rebecca F 1-8
Eliasson Cynthia K 3
Guelzow Jane E MA 4
Illig Dorothy O BED 1
Jones Jennifer R BA 5
Jones Sharon PS
Le Noir Beverlee B BA 7-8
Matthews Sandra H BS 2
Rink Diana L BS 5-8
Rullman Arlys S BS 1-4
Stephens Jason 4-8
Sundbom Beth K
Whitely Jennifer 1-8
Wray Jo Anne PS-4
**JACKSONVILLE**-CALVARY PS
• 1988
206 Pine Valley Rd 28546-8237
(910)353-4016
calvluth@onslowonline.net
Mc Kay Julie PS
**KERNERSVILLE**-FOUNTAIN OF LIFE PS-K
• 1991
323 Hopkins Rd 27284-9374
(336)993-9628 •
FAX(336)993-0941
Ambrose Rosette PS
Angel Lynn PS
Baker Lisa PS
Beeson Marilyn PS
Brinker Mary A PS
Creed Kim PS
Fisher Donna PS
Griffin Melissa PS
Hodges Debbie PS
Hoover Angela K
Kepner Renee PS
Kernitski Diane PS
Lundberg Mary PS
Okey Linda F
Parrish Jackie PS
Reavis Dawn PS
Rorie Carrie
Thompson Tammy K
Travis Deborah PS
Vegas Carolyn PS
Wilson Jeana PS
**NAGS HEAD**-GRACE-GRACE BY SEA PS
• 1996
PO Box 1356 27959
(919)441-1530
gracelu@juno.com
NO REPORT
**RALEIGH**-FAITH K-8
• 1994
1809 Capital Blvd 27604
(919)829-5899 •
FAX(919)829-5858
NO REPORT
**WAKE FOREST**-HOPE PS
• 1997
701 S Main St 27587
(919)554-8109 •
FAX(919)554-0412
Brown Julie PS
Burman Veronica PS
Edens Jennifer PS
Fisher Regina MA
Franklin Charity PS
Furr Sherri PS
Howle Gina PS
Mannette Denise PS
Moss Wendi PS
Ogle Deanie PS
Thornton Kathie PS
**WINSTON-SALEM**-ST JOHN PS-8
• 1951
2415 Silas Creek Pkwy 27103-4820
(336)725-1651 •
FAX(336)725-1603
stjohnsws@aol.com
Becker Joel C BS 5-8
Bodling Linda M MED 1
Bodling Paul F III BA 1-8
Boyles Dave K-8
Bryant Sandra S K
Burroughs Susan E BA 6-8
Guelzow Stephanie J MED 2
Hardin Beth A 4
McLain Margaret B 5
Meisinger Ardel MAD 8
Meisinger Judith J BS 3
Rullman Glenn L MED 6-8
Rullman Jacqueline S BS PS
Verano Victoria N BA PS-8

## NORTH DAKOTA

**BISMARCK**-MARTIN LUTHER PS-8
• RSO • 1995
413 East Ave D 58502 PO Box 399 58502-0399
(701)224-9070 •
FAX(701)258-2146
mluther@btigate.com
Abeling Pam PS
Baneck Myrna BA 1
Carlson Rhea K
Drevlow Joanne K-8
Hansen Carol 7-8
Hartsoch Sara PS-8
Krueger Juanita L MED 3-4
Stoltenow Jodie G 5-8
Wolfgram Denise 5-8
Zittleman Shawna 2
SHEPHERD OF THE VALL PS
• 1996
801 E Denver Ave 58502 PO Box 2564 58502-2564
(701)258-4231
NO REPORT
ZION PS
413 E Avenue D 58501-3949
(701)223-8286
NO REPORT
**DICKINSON**-REDEEMER PS
• 1992
711 10Th Ave W 58601-3716
(701)483-4463
rlc4him@pop.ctctel.com
**Smelser Susan A BED PS**
Olin Kathy L PS
**FARGO**-GRACE PS-8
• NLSA • 1908
1025 14th Ave S 58103-4137
(701)232-7747 •
FAX(701)237-0618
gracesch@farg.uswest.net
Buteyn Brian P BSED 6-8
Cziok Kathleen M BA 3
Jahnke Susan R BED 7-8
Koppinger Janet L PS
Link Pat L 8
Roeszler Alpha H PS-8
Sande Lisa H 6
Scholten Beth A 4
Sommerfeld Gene W MED 8
Sommerfeld Linda M BA 2
Stevenson Aaron K-8
Syverson Jean M BA 5
Wolfgram Laurie M BA 1
Worral Carolyn R BA K

**GLENBURN**--LYNCH IMMANUEL PS-K
• 1949
18301 Hwy 83 North 58740-9507
(701)727-4994
NO REPORT

**GRAND FORKS**-IMMANUEL PS
• 1999
1710 Cherry St 58201
(701)775-7125 •
FAX(701)775-4356
immanuel@thequest.net
NO REPORT

## OHIO

**AKRON**-FAIRLAWN PS
• 1997
3415 W Market St 44333
(330)864-7724 •
FAX(330)864-8373
Becenti Jill
Evangelist Bonnie
Frantz Lori
Lange Mary Jane MA
Reed Denise
Scalera Danielle
Schnitzler Elizabeth
Zavodney Gayle

HOPE PS
• 1997
999 Portage Lakes Dr 44139-1538
(330)644-3522
jakozak@bright.net
NO REPORT

OPEN ARMS-CONCORDIA PS
• 1999
724 Sumner St 44311-1660
(330)535-1433
openarms@celc.org
NO REPORT

ZION K-8
• 1863
139 S High St 44308-1498
(330)253-3137 •
FAX(330)253-3615
np_zion@sceca.ohio.gov
**Meder Karen A BA**
Alspach Monica BSED 5-6
Cihlar Jennifer L BS K
Fox Dana 7-8
Hiles Jill S BA 3
Kidd Kristina 1
Kruger Robert F 4
Pierce Jeannette N BS 2

**AMHERST**-ST PAUL PS
• 1978
115 Central Dr 44001-1601
(440)988-5427
NO REPORT

**AURORA**-HOPE PS
• 1974
456 S Chillicothe Rd 44202-8824
(330)562-8260
NO REPORT

**AVON**-FAITH PS
• 1976
2265 Garden Dr 44011-2608
(440)934-4710 •
FAX(440)934-1917
Hille Laurel A BSED

**BRUNSWICK**-ST MARK PS-8
• NLSA • 1962
1330 N Carpenter Rd 44212-3113
(330)225-4395 •
FAX(330)225-4380
**Diener John H MDIV**
Bryant Phyllis J BSED 7
Courter Amy 7
Furfari Monica PS
Gresock Mary 2
Harris Walter 4
Heldman Sandra J BA 5
Lee Wendy
Leu Carolyn A MED PS
Lucarelli Cathie L MED K
Mitchem Sandra 8
Solgos Carrie 6
Tew Pamela J BS
Trausch Marianne MA 3

**CHAGRIN FALLS**-VALLEY PS
• 1995
87 E Orange St 44022-2732
(216)247-0390 •
FAX(216)247-0125
valleyluth@aol.com
**Forrester Connie PS**
Ferrone Ellen BS PS
Powers Jeri MA PS
Teagno Cheryl BSED PS
Yane Jeni PS

**CHARDON**-PEACE PS
• 1979
12686 Bass Lake Rd 44024-8316
(440)286-3310
Eismon Patricia R BA PS
Vought Carol M PS

**CHESTERLAND**-ST MARK PS
• 1976
11900 Chillicothe Rd 44026-1934
(440)729-1668 •
FAX(440)729-1669
Haberman Beverly L AA PS
Storer Mary A PS

**CHILLICOTHE**-OUR SAVIOR PS
• 1989
151 University Dr 45601-2117
(740)775-2470
Angus Jackie
Mc Leod Sandra A BS
Segelhorst Brenda
Wilkes Beverly

**CHUCKERY**-ST PAUL K-7
• NLSA • 1892
7960 State Route 38 43045-9722
(937)349-5939 •
FAX(937)349-5939
stpaul@bright.net
**Boerger Karen L MED 5-7**
Dellinger Carol C BED K
Mortimer Kay L 1-2
Vollrath Lois E BSED 3-4

**CINCINNATI**-CONCORDIA PS-8
• 1976
1133 Clifton Hills Ave 45220-1405
(513)861-9568 •
FAX(513)861-9552
Concordia@fuse.net
**Poppe Richard A MA**
De Meritt Elizabeth A K
Fickel Denise PS
Lau Anne 7-8
Lilley Becky 5-6
Mayo Catherine M BS 1
Mayo Michael A BS 4
Morgan Ellen L BS 2
Poppe Jeanne BS 3
Zoutis Julie PS

GRACE K-8
• NLSA • 1928
3628 Boudinot Ave 45211-4922
(513)661-8467 •
FAX(513)661-3728
schroeder_j@hccanet.org
**Schroeder James E MED 6-8**
Cope Lavell J BED 5-8
Dumke Jane L BA 2
Hesse Merlene J BA 1
Mandel April R 3
Potyondy Joseph W 6-8
Riggins James BS 4
Schmidtgoessling Karen BA K
Williams James D 6-8

PRESCHOOL-CHRIST PS
• 1998
3301 Compton Rd 45251-2595
(513)385-8404 •
FAX(513)385-8342
lschwan@eclink.com
Allen Wanda PS
Nadler Joan PS
Schwan Lynn PS

ST PAUL PS-8
• 1906
5427 Madison Rd 45227-1507
(513)271-8266 •
FAX(513)271-8558
gstoneburn@aol.com
**Stoneburner Gordon F MA**
Milam Marcia A BA K
Mueller Victoria L BA 5-6
Sant Jennifer R 7-8
Smith Mary 3-4
Stoneburner Audrey A BA PS
Wargo Nicole N BA 1-2

**CLEVELAND**-LUTHER MEMORIAL K-8
• RSO • 1948
4215 Robert Ave 44109-1255
(216)631-3640 •
FAX(216)631-4073
np_luther_01@lnoca4.lnoca.gov
**Stuenkel Margaret**
Cashin John T 7-8
Fawcett Carol J BS 3-4
Gersdorf Linda J K
Menz Diana E 2
Weikum Lois J BA 5-6
Woodburn Gretchen B 1

MT CALVARY PS
• 1973
12826 Lorain Ave 44111-2611
(216)671-2099
Ronschke Roberta L BS

ST JAMES PS
• 1981
4771 Broadview Rd 44109-4669
(216)351-7194
Becka Karen M MA
Haffner Linda J PS

ST JOHN K-8
• 1892
1027 E 176th St 44119-3109
(216)531-8204 •
FAX(216)531-8204
sophardt@aol.com
Dill Susan 2
Lively Jeanne C BA 3
Marcis Joy MSW 4
Maynard Vicki 6
Neugebauer Dorothy BS 5
Ophardt Susan M BS
Sieger Barbara J BA K
Sieger Mark W BED 8
Vernick Kristyn B 7-8
Vollman Laura BA 1

ST MARK K-8
• 1895
4464 Pearl Rd 44109-4224
(216)749-3545 •
FAX(216)749-4270
**Skyrm Donna L MEDADM**
Bowersox Lynn 3
Carmichael Patricia 1
Clum Peggy 5-8
Forster Christopher K-8
Hirsimaki Beverly K
Riccio Jennifer 2
Valenzisi Annette 5-8
Veinot Lee 4
Woodbridge John 5-8

TRINITY PS
• 1982
2038 W 29th St 44113-4006
(216)281-1912
Motko Renee S AAS PS
Oberberger Carol PS

WEST PARK K-8
• RSO • 1981
13712 Bellaire Rd 44135-2135
(216)941-2770 •
FAX(216)941-3035
wpls@oh.verjo.com
**Kloha Glenn E MA**
Chamot Susan A 5
Hurst Doreen L BED 1
Mc Dermott Michael S BSED 7-8
Oerkfitz Joyce A BA K
Oerkfitz Kenneth J MA 3
Ross Leslie A BA 4
Steinke Cheryl BA 2
Weseloh Harold 6

**COLUMBUS**-ATONEMENT PS
• 1989
1621 Francisco Rd 43220-2536
(614)451-5212 •
FAX(614)451-9825
Chafin Mariann PS
Gage Hope C BA PS
Gage Laura L MA PS

BETHANY PS
• 1985
1000 Noe Bixby Rd 43213-3526
(614)866-1211
Zoebl Veronika E MED

**CUYAHOGA FALLS**-REDEEMER PS-8
• NLSA • 1959
2141 5th St 44221-3213
(330)923-1280 •
FAX(330)923-4517
dchatrcs@juno.com
Auerbach D K 7
Boehlke Christine M BA 6
Burnside Lisa M 1
De Simpelare Susan M BA PS
Hach Mark W 4
Johnson Adeline M BSED 3
Jones Mark S MA 8
Kieffer-Takacs Sandra L K-8
Lietz Brenda L 5
Mueller Kathleen M MED 3
Remendowski Laurel M BA K
Sevon Maida R BA 2
Swansinger Ginger E 4
Zachrich Ann E MA 1

**DAYTON**-CONCORDIA PS
• 1992
250 Peach Orchard Ave 45419-2642
(937)299-1912 •
FAX(937)293-9790
**Aldrich Beth PS**
Jett Colleen PS

**DEFIANCE**-ST JOHN PS-8
• 1873
655 Wayne Ave 43512-2659
(419)782-1751 •
FAX(419)782-0954
brieschke-sjl@defnet.com
**Brieschke Martin A MED**
Boris Jennifer R BA 3
Boris Scott W BED PS
Gyurnek Sandra D BSED 2
Hartman Lorna J MSED K
March Marian 1
Marshall Patricia L BSED 8
Maxey Deborah S BS 4
Mc Ghee D M MA 7
Mc Ghee Janice L BS 5
Rogliatti Kelly J BS 6

**DUBLIN**-ST JOHN PS
• 1985
6135 Rings Rd 43016-6718
(614)889-5893 •
FAX(614)760-0412
**Stottlemyer Bonnie H MA**
Larson Linda PS
Mc Mullen Lisa A MA PS
Niemie Judy PS
Rudowicz Carole PS

**ELMORE**-TRINITY PS
• 1989
412 Fremont St PO Box 22 43416-0022
(419)862-3461
Engle Mary PS
Floro Lisa PS

**ELYRIA**-GRACE PS
• 1970
9685 E River Rd 44035-8147
(216)322-5497 •
FAX(216)322-5497
NO REPORT

ST JOHN PS
• 1990
1140 W River Rd N 44035-2814
(440)324-4070
King Margaret M PS
Lesniak Linda PS
Strickler Paula
Trunk Rose PS
**EUCLID-**SHORE HAVEN PS
• 1969
280 E 222nd St 44123-1719
(216)731-4100 •
FAX(216)731-6821
Jakubs-Schmidt Barbara PS
Pollack Sandra MA
**FLORIDA-**ST PETER PS
• 1988
CO Rd 17-D 107 E School St
43545-9802
(419)762-5075
Arnold JoAnne M
**GARFIELD HEIGHTS-**ST JOHN PS-8
• 1854
11333 Granger Rd 44125-2851
(216)587-1752 •
FAX(216)587-5615
Lewis Ingrid E BA 1-8
Naso Cari 5-6
Petersen Kristin K BA 2
Poskocil Janelle K BS PS
Ronschke William P BA 7-8
Schelien Ann L 1
Schelien Heidi 3-4
Sheridan Darina L BA K
Wagie Richard C BA
**GENEVA-**ST JOHN PS
• 1994
811 S Broadway 44041 PO Box
500 44041-0500
(440)466-2473
Gruber Diane S BA PS
Heinz Darlene PS
**GRAFTON-**TRINITY PS
• 1976
38307 Royalton Rd 44044-9184
(440)748-2154
NO REPORT
**HAMILTON-**IMMANUEL PS-6
• NLSA • 1953
1285 Main St 45013-1621
(513)895-9212 •
FAX(513)863-2502
imlutheran@aol.com
**Speicher Richard C MED PS-6**
Dingledine Opal K-6
Kuhn Betzy L BSED K
Protzman Rebecca J BA PS
Riley Barbara A BA 3
Shope Douglas G K-6
Stephens Diane M 2
Tedesco Steven K 1-6
Tilney Joanne M 4
Walter Sandra K BS 1
Zieber Barbara S 5-6
**HOLGATE-**ST JOHN PS
• 1979
501 S Wilhelm St 43527-9760 PO
Box 97 43527
(419)264-4641
Bostelman Judith
Gerken Nancy
**HUBER HEIGHTS-**ST TIMOTHY PS
• 1965
5040 Rye Dr 45424-4397
(937)233-2443 •
FAX(937)233-0028
sttim@juno.com
Liepold Carol
Simola Cindy
Wilmer Pam
Wright Mary

**HUDSON--**GLORIA DEI PS
• 1988
2113 Ravenna St 44236-3451
(330)650-6550 ex. 16 •
FAX(330)650-6685
NO REPORT
**KETTERING-**EMMANUEL PS-3
• 1995
4865 Wilmington Pike 45440-2022
(937)291-2236 •
FAX(937)434-2234
discoverus@emmanuellc.org
**Day Howard**
Culp Mary 1
Folck Elizabeth A 2-3
Johnson Maryanna R BSED K
Larson Irene PS
Paris Stephanie A BA PS-3
Rutledge Deborah J PS
Walters Carla O
Wickizer Angela A PS
Woodall Joyce PS-3
**LAKEWOOD-**LAKEWOOD PS-8
• RSO • NLSA • 1905
1419 Lakeland Ave 44107-3814
(216)221-6941 •
FAX(216)226-4082
**Dittmar Gary D MS**
Dankenbring David A BS 6-8
Dankenbring Nadine BSED 6-8
Felten Dorothy J BA 2
Folwaczny Monica K
Giese Mary A BA 1
Hass Susan K BA 5
Potantus Carolyn R BSED 4
Ristau Edward J 6-8
West Laura J 3
PENTECOST PS
• 1981
13303 Madison Ave 44107-4812
(216)221-6265 •
FAX(216)221-0927
NO REPORT
**LANCASTER-**REDEEMER PS-K
• 1959
1400 Concordia Dr 43130-2003
(740)653-9727 •
FAX(740)653-0801
redeemer@ameritech.com
**Daubenmire Rebecca PS**
Bradford Sharman PS
Geyer Rita M PS
Locke Mari-Beth J PS
Parrish Jane PS
Plescher Holly PS
Pohold Catherine E PS
Raddatz Angela K
Wickham Rebecca A PS
Wolfinger Ona PS
Young Joanna G PS
**LIBERTY CENTER-**ST PAUL PS
• 1969
8074 County Road T 43532-9735
(419)533-3041
Fetterman Patricia A BS
Glanz Deb BSED PS
**LIMA-**IMMANUEL K
2120 Lakewood Ave 45805
(419)222-2541 •
FAX(419)229-2416
immanuel@wcoil.com
Eberle Nancy M K
**LORAIN-**ZION PS
• 1995
5100 Ashland Ave 44053-3418
(440)282-8418
Ackerman Kathie PS
Mihalic Jacki PS
Saylor Wanda PS
Shiltz Debra K PS
Shiltz Patricia A BED
Strauser Amanda PS

**MARYSVILLE-**ST JOHN PS-8
• 1843
12809 State Route 736
43040-9056
(937)644-5540 •
FAX(937)644-1086
Crawford-Lowry Lois BS 2
Demlow Kristen S BA 7
Geiger Ruth A BS 5-8
Harms Martha J MS 4
Laux Linda L BA 1
Miller Susan 3
Mock Herbert J MA
Rudlaff Joanna L BA 6
Swartz Joshua D BA 8
Walker Cynthia K
**MASON-**KING OF KINGS PS-K
• 1995
3621 Socialville Foster Rd
45040-9335
(513)398-6089 •
FAX(513)459-9896
gschep4258@aol.com
Cook Elizabeth A PS
Hazel Diane L PS
Russell Debbie K
Schepmann Gilbert F Sr. MED PS
Wolery Kathleen A PS
**MASSILLON-**ST JOHN PS-2
• 1989
1900 Wales Rd NE 44646-4172
(330)837-4644 •
FAX(330)837-2918
Baker Holly PS-2
Clymer Mary B BA 1-2
Haines Debra J AA PS
Hess Mary K BSED PS
Highben Sherilyn S BSED
Myers Carla PS
Smer Jodi M BS K
Telloni John L MDIV
White Rachelle PS
**MIDDLETOWN-**MESSIAH PS
• 1971
4715 Holly Ave 45044-5314
(513)422-4991
Connor Lynn E
Niebur Tina M PS
**MILFORD-**ST MARK PS-K
• 1998
5849 Buckwheat Rd 45150-2459
(513)575-0292
Heidle Sue A MA
Smith A K
Vedder Jennifer A PS
**NAPOLEON-**ST JOHN K-8
• NLSA • 1869
16035 County Road U 43545-9753
(419)598-8702 •
FAX(419)598-8518
**Johnson Ross E MED 5-6**
Barton Faith M K-6
Damman Sandra K MED 1-2
Petzoldt Lowell K MED 3-4
Rettig Mary Kay 7-8
ST PAUL PS-8
• NLSA • 1933
1075 Glenwood Ave 43545-1250
(419)592-5536 •
FAX(419)592-0652
nap_npub_sw@nwoca.org
**Wentzel Steven J MED**
Aschemeier Susan K BA K
Creager Lisa PS
Doenges Joanne E BA 4
Eberle Donald 5
Eggebrecht Paul A BED 6
Eggebrecht Stephanie R BAED 1
Hammon John F BA 8
Kern Marcia G BA 2
Kramer Patricia A MED 7
Laubsch Jennifer M BA 3
Longmire Duane L BA 5
Longmire Kari L BA PS-8
Pelltier Carol A BED 1
Roth Ronald J MA 6
Stuebe David F BS 8

Sundermann Tamara K BA 4
Woelzlein Chrissy 7-8
Yoder Marian R MA 2
**NORTH CANTON-**HOLY CROSS PS-K
• 1994
7707 Market Ave N 44721-1642
(330)494-6478 •
FAX(330)499-2319
Buttrill Shawn K
Creutz Nancy J BSED PS
Hugo Brenda PS
James Marjorie A BSED
Menke Karen BSED PS
Samara Ginger E BS PS
**NORTH OLMSTED-**ASCENSION PS-K
• 1977
28081 Lorain Rd 44070-4026
(440)777-6365 •
FAX(440)777-1609
ascnprscl@aol.com
**Schneider Laurel**
Dunn Cheris PS
Eyman Brandy PS
Hoffman Dana PS
Neiswonger Jan PS
Roshetko Beth K
Sadlon Susan L PS
Soltis Maribeth PS
**NORTH RIDGEVILLE-**SHEPHERD OF RIDGE PS
• 1976
34555 Center Ridge Rd
44039-3155
(440)327-7321
Bridges Carol PS
Kilby Jane AA PS
Massatti Rebecca PS
Oberhaus Sharon PS
Wrona Marian BA PS
**NORTH ROYALTON-**ROYAL REDEEMER PS-1
• 1984
11680 Royalton Rd 44133-4461
(440)237-7988 •
FAX(440)237-6992
NO REPORT
**OREGON-**PRINCE OF PEACE PS
• 1989
4155 Pickle Rd 43616-4135
(419)691-9407 •
FAX(419)691-8406
Ashe Deanne PS
Beckman Kim M PS
Kelly Wendy PS
Turski Sue PS
**PAINESVILLE-**OUR SHEPHERD K-8
• RSO • NLSA • 1980
508 Mentor Ave 44077-2628
(440)357-7776 •
FAX(440)357-7158
jblelle@oh.verio.com
Beifuss Patricia J 6-8
Koscik Annette E BS 2
Koscik James R MS 5
Lelle John B MED
Lelle Wilberta J BSED 1
Miller Kristin A BA 3
Peck Martha E BSED 6-8
Pfefferle Kathie M MED 4
Schiemann Jennifer L BA 6-8
Wojkowski Leigh A BSED K
ST PAUL PS
• 1969
250 Bowhall Rd 44077-5219
(440)354-3000 •
FAX(440)354-7085
stpauls@oh.veriocom
NO REPORT

**PARMA**-BETHANY PS-8
• NLSA • 1935
6041 Ridge Rd 44129-4498
(440)884-1010 •
FAX(440)884-9834
kboerger.BLS@IOL13.com
**Boerger Kenneth M MA**
Apana Sandra L BSED PS
Arthur Joleen L BED 1-8
Boerger Susan J BS 2
Burke Suzanne C 3
Deutsch Danielle R 1
Dorn Joyce E 2
Georgi Mary Ellen BA 8
Gery Margit R BA 3
Liese Marc T BED 6
Morrison Janet L BED 7-8
Rasoletti Janis M 1-8
Schultz Wendy BSED 4
Sellke David E BA 5
Stockhaus Elaine A BA 1
Tomko Linda K BS K
BETHLEHEM PS
• NLSA • 1987
7500 State Rd 44134-6102
(440)884-0430 •
FAX(440)884-0095
NO REPORT
**ROCKY RIVER**-ST THOMAS PS-8
• 1959
21165 Detroit Rd 44116-2211
(440)331-4426 •
FAX(440)331-2681
stls@juno.com
Engel Betty PS-K
Felice Judy A BA 4
Liese Matthew P BA 7
Miller Stacey 5-8
Moehring David P MED 6-8
Noll Terry E MED 3
Poley Carol L BSED 2
Sabal Barbara L BA 1
Sweney Richard E BA 5
Wallace Sharon L BA 6-8
**SHEFFIELD VILLAGE**-HOPE PS
• 1986
4792 Oster Rd 44054-1446
(440)949-2537 •
FAX(440)949-5749
hope2000@bright.net
**Georgi Gary D MDIV**
Ambers Anita PS
Wondrak Frances PS
**SOLON**-OUR REDEEMER PS
• 1975
7196 SOM Center Rd 44139-4230
(440)248-4066 •
FAX(440)248-9413
Berger Patricia A PS
Licht June C PS
Stumph Paula-Jean K MA PS
**SOUTH EUCLID**-ST JOHN PS-8
• 1860
4386 Mayfield Rd 44121-3608
(216)381-8595 •
FAX(216)381-1564
np_stjlut_01@lnoca4.lnoca.ohio.gov
**Bahr Joel M BA**
Aukerman Laura BS 2
Bradach Gail L BS K
Clark Ruthmary BSED 5
Fox Patricia MA 3
Hassink Elise C BA PS
Knight Barbara BSED 8
Mossey Arlene 7
Panella Karen BA 4
Parsons Mark 6
Sanford Francheska
Souza Ann K-8
Trapp Joanne E 1
**SPRINGFIELD**-RISEN CHRIST PS
• 1993
41 E Possum Rd 45502-9477
(937)323-3688 •
FAX(937)323-3746
NO REPORT

**TALLMADGE**--TALLMADGE PS
• 1995
759 East Ave 44278-2566
(330)633-4775 •
FAX(330)633-4846
tallmadgeluthchurch@juno.com
NO REPORT
**TOLEDO**-CONCORDIA PS
• 1968
3636 S Detroit Ave 43614-4412
(419)382-0410 •
FAX(419)382-6383
NO REPORT
GOOD SHEPHERD K-4
• 1991
3934 W Laskey Rd 43623-3705
(419)474-0322 •
FAX(419)474-0520
goodshep5@juno.com
NO REPORT
IMMANUEL PS-K
• 1980
710 Buckeye St 43611-3805
(419)726-3991
Brierley Martha M PS
Herder Jane R BAED
ST PHILIP PS-K
• 1981
3002 Upton Ave 43606-3964
(419)475-2835 •
FAX(419)472-9032
Hayward Tiffany C PS
TRINITY PS-8
• NLSA • 1874
4560 Glendale Ave 43614-1907
(419)385-2301 •
FAX(419)385-2636
**Spohn Christine A MED**
Gordon Marianne M BS 3
Howard Roger A BA PS-8
Kollmorgen Rebecca J BS 5
Kollmorgen Timothy A BSED 6-8
Kranz Bonnie J BS 1
Mc Clintock Kirstin 6-8
Quackenbush Randa S BA PS
Schefft Sandra 2
Shirley Karen S K
Strieter Alice E BSED
Winterstein Teresa 6-8
Winterstein Timothy C BS 2-4
**WAUSEON**-EMMAUS PS
• 1971
841 N Shoop Ave 43567-1800
(419)337-8471 •
FAX(419)335-7446
Drummer Denise PS
Huner Katherine A
Prior Margie PS
**WESTLAKE**-ST PAUL PS-8
• 1858
27981 Detroit Rd 44145-2149
(440)835-3051 •
FAX(440)835-8216
Campsey-Clutter Lynn 7-8
Felten Pamela S BA 4
Felten Scott A BA 7-8
Ferrell Rebecca A MA 3
Fuchs Lori J BED 4
Gerken Beverly J MA 2
Gundiff Judy 1
Lawrence Gloria M BA 1
Lehrke Dale A MA
Lockwood Karin 3
Moehring Mary M MAT 2
Osborn James M 6
Pangrace Ruth A 5-8
Peeples Lauren 5
Retzloff Mardelle G K
Sennhenn Barbara L BS 7-8
Wandrie Julie E BA 5
**YOUNGSTOWN**-LITTLE LAMBS-ST MARK PS
• 1997
280 Mill Creek Dr 44512-1405
(330)788-8995
shonconn@aol.com
Harris Walter PS

## OKLAHOMA

**ALVA**--ZION PS
• 1993
902 2ND St 73717-2810
(405)327-1318
NO REPORT
**BARTLESVILLE**-REDEEMER PS
• 1988
3700 Woodland Rd 74006-4531
(918)333-6033
NO REPORT
**BLACKWELL**-TRINITY PS
• 1981
125 Vinnedge Ave PO Box 545
74631-0545
(405)363-4026
NO REPORT
**BROKEN ARROW**-IMMANUEL CHRIST PS-K
• 1977
216 Luther Dr 74012-1405
(918)258-7622 •
FAX(918)251-8365
rrush@immanuelba.org
Aussieker Phyllis A PS
Krahn Donna M PS
Rush Ranelle D BS
**CLAREMORE**-CLAREMORE-REDEEMER PS
220 N Seminole Ave 74017-8425
(918)341-3125
Beckford Ruby PS
Karst Sharon
Meisinger Darla
Nuttle Nila PS
**EDMOND**-HOLY TRINITY PS
• 1987
308 NW 164Th St 73013-2006
(405)348-3292
NO REPORT
ST MARK PS
1501 N Bryant 73034
(405)340-0192 •
FAX(405)340-0290
stmarkluth@ionet.net
NO REPORT
**ENID**-ST PAUL PS-6
• 1926
1810 E Broadway Ave 1626 E Broadway Ave 73701-4539
(580)234-6646 •
FAX(580)234-6692
stpaulsenid@juno.com
Eldridge Kathleen BA 4
Grantz Amy K
Ingels Ginger PS
Lamle Rhonda E BS PS
Lemoins Anna PS
Loesch Johnna K 5-6
Lohse Lisa K BED 1
Mueller Sharyn L MA
Parks Patricia A 2
Stevens Sally A MED 3
**FAIRLAND**-ST PAUL PS
Washington & Pine PO Box 219
74343-0219
(918)676-3059
NO REPORT
**FAIRMONT**-ZION PS
• 1985
RR 1 Box 16 73736-9701
(580)358-2291
Dorsch Ruth PS
**GUYMON**-TRINITY PS
• 1962
1212 N Crumley St 73942-3643
(580)338-6000
Bohlmann Deborah A BA PS
Johnson Myrene K BSED PS
**LAHOMA**-ZION PS
• 1985
5Th & Oklahoma St PO Box 128
73754-0128
(580)796-2243 •
FAX(580)796-2243
NO REPORT

**LAWTON**--HOLY CROSS PS
• 1984
2105 NW 38Th St 73505-1809
(405)357-9005 •
FAX(405)357-7684
NO REPORT
ST JOHN PS
• 1997
102 SW 7th St 73501-3922
(580)353-0556
Lorrett Deena PS
Martinez Rhonda PS
Peterson Peggy PS
Putnam Diana PS
Saravey Donna PS
White Chris PS
**MIAMI**-MT OLIVE PS-2
2337 N Main St 74354-1621
(918)542-4681 •
FAX(918)542-4681
NO REPORT
**MIDWEST CITY**-GOOD SHEPHERD PS-8
• 1982
700 N Air Depot Blvd 73110-3763
(405)732-0070 •
FAX(405)732-3977
Boarts Alicia 7-8
Christman Thomas P MSED
Cunningham Lynn M BA 1-2
Junghanns Marla BA 3-4
Kuschnereit Gary 5-6
Litzer Nancy K
Lohrke Loetta 5-6
Mc Nair Lynne A PS
Ogle Carolyn S PS
**MOORE**-ST JOHN PS
• 1997
1032 NW 12th 73160
(405)794-8686 •
FAX(405)794-5690
SJLSchool@aol.com
NO REPORT
**MUSTANG**-CHRIST PS-5
• 1986
501 N Clear Springs Rd
73064-1518 PO Box 92
73064-0092
(405)376-4235 •
FAX(405)376-3118
NO REPORT
**NORMAN**-TRINITY PS-5
• 1989
603 Classen Blvd 73071-5048
(405)329-1503
Moydell Anita PS
Schmidt Sharon
Storm Cathy PS
Wheeler Jill BSED K
Williams Jamie 1-2
**OKARCHE**-ST JOHN PS-8
• 1893
202 S Fifth 73762
(405)263-4488 •
FAX(405)263-4488
Bartelt Jenise J BA 1-2
Bomhoff Diane PS
Klade Jeffrey H BS
Klade Kathy L BSED K
Schroeder Barbara BS 3-5
**OKLAHOMA CITY**-MESSIAH PS-K
• 1989
3600 NW Expressway 73112-4410
(405)946-0681 •
FAX(405)946-0682
NO REPORT
**OKMULGEE**-TRINITY LUTHERAN SCH PS
1314 E 6th St 74447
(918)756-6046 •
FAX(918)756-6046
tlcokmulgee@aol.com
NO REPORT

**OWASSO**--SONSHINE-FAITH PS
• 1989
9222 N Garnett Rd 74055-4424
(918)272-8534
NO REPORT

**PONCA CITY**-FIRST PS-8
• 1953
1104 N 4Th St 74601-2731
(580)762-4243 •
FAX(580)762-4243
lutheran@poncacity.net
Belzer Pam J 6-8
Freeman Jeanne M PS
Goll Janet L BSED 6-8
Hunt Edith J MS 3
Jones Denise 6-8
Kelle Josette 5-8
Klein Cheryl M BSED 4
Kurtz Christy A BA 1
Lawrence Jernda K
Mc Gregor Dan L MS 8
Miller Elaine PS-4
Powell Carol 2
Schatte Rochelle K BSED 5
Turney Darla
Watson Elizabeth

**TAHLEQUAH**-JESUS LAMBS-FIRST PS
• 1994
2111 Mahaney Ave 74464-5761
(918)456-5070
NO REPORT

**TULSA**-CHRIST THE REDEEMER PS-K
• 1980
2550 E 71St St 74136-5531
(918)492-1416 •
FAX(918)492-3524
CTRECC@hotmail.com
Ackerman Michele F BA
Aussiker Jodi PS
Boos Angie
Brown Virginia PS
Caruthers Veronica
Coakley Marion PS
Diley Sharon PS
Flasch Micky PS
Hansen Carole PS
Houseman Susan PS
Kahle Ernestine PS
Kernoske Shirley BED K
Kygar Shirley PS
Newman Linda PS
Osman Patricia PS
Reeves Sharri PS
Sen Bharati
Sen Debjani PS
Shisler Cathy PS
Taylor Tara
Thresher Angie

TULSA PS-8
• RSO • 1983
146 S Sheridan Rd 74112-1719
(918)834-3813 •
FAX(918)834-3814
tls@geotec.net
NO REPORT

## OREGON

**ALOHA**-BETHLEHEM PS
• 1962
18865 SW Johnson St 97006-3164
(503)649-3380 •
FAX(503)649-1530
bthlhm@teleport.com
NO REPORT

**ASHLAND**-GRACE PS-3
• 1988
660 Frances Ln 97520-3410
(541)482-1661 •
FAX(541)482-2860
grace75552@aol.com
NO REPORT

**BEAVERTON**-PILGRIM PS-8
• NLSA • 1981
5650 SW Hall Blvd 97005-3918
(503)644-8697 •
FAX(503)644-8182
pilgrimlutheran.net
**Leapaldt Reuben L BSED**
Bredehoft George W MED 3
Davitt Jill M BA 2
Howard Kathleen A K
Loseke Mary A MED 4
Reitmeier N J PS
Visser Diana J BA 6
White Laura A BA 1
Wichner Sharon 5

**BEND**-TRINITY PS-8
• 1959
2550 NE Butler Market Rd
97701-9523
(541)382-1850 •
FAX(541)382-1850
saints@bendcable.com
**Fowls Robert W MA**
Brisk Donna M BS 3
Carnahan Suzanne 1-8
Clift Greg L 4
Clift Tonja J 3
Davis Jane R K
Fitz Henry Wendy 5-8
Hamilton Susan M PS
Kenniston Rita F BS
Leitz Catherine J PS
Linn Darla J BS 8
Maurer Mary D BS 2
Meyer Stephanie A BSED PS
Mockaitis James K-6
Newman Susan L BSED 4
Podwils Carol M BS PS-8
Pullmann Paul M BA 6
Scholz Christina L BA 1
Valentine Debra L BA 1
Weber Dina PS

**CLACKAMAS**-CHRIST THE VINE PS-K
• 1985
18677 SE Highway 212
97015-6703
(503)658-5650 •
FAX(503)658-3081
cthevine@aol.com
**Waetzig Lori BA K**
Balke Barbara PS
Cooley Velvet PS

**COOS BAY**-CHRIST PS-4
• 1993
1835 N 15Th St 97420-2159
(541)267-3851
De Andrea Kristen 1-2
Geddes Ashleigh BA 3-4
Miller Laura PS-K
Neal Lugene PS
Porter La Donna K BS 1-2
Socia Sarah PS
Thauland Darlene A BA K

**CORNELIUS**-FOREST HILLS K-8
• 1994
4221 SW Golf Course Rd
97113-6017
(503)359-4853 •
FAX(503)357-2213
foresthills@integrityonline.com
**Seim Daniel N MED**
Bolton Richard D MAT 6-8
Hoffman Sandra E BSED K
Hoffman Sarah R BA 2
Jones Lorne E BSED 4
Nelson Scott D BS 6-8
Nistad Phyllis J BSED 6-8
Rickman Julie A BA 5
Sellke Carolyn R BS 3
Spidal Elaine A 1

**CORVALLIS**-ZION PS-8
• 1907
2800 NW Tyler Ave 97330-5220
(541)753-7503 •
FAX(541)754-8254
zionschool@proaxis.com
**Musfeldt Jay N BSED**
Brown Elizabeth L MS 1
Demarest Ellen C MS PS
Gutierrez Sherry L MA PS
Mc Namar Terria BA 3
Messer La Vaun M BA K
Munster Mervin D BS 6-8
Reed William A 6-8
Schwartz Elaine R BED 5
Straub Pam 2
Straub Vincent J BS 6-8
Strong Connie 4

**COTTAGE GROVE**-TRINITY PS
• 1982
675 S 7th St 97424-2502
(541)942-2373 •
FAX(541)942-5321
tlclcms@efn.org
Fordyce Patricia A PS

**EAGLE POINT**-ST JOHN PS-K
• 1987
42 Alta Vista Rd 97524 PO Box
1049 97524-1049
(541)826-4334
stjohnEP@juno.com
NO REPORT

**EUGENE**-LIFE PS-8
• RSO • 1978
710 E 17Th Ave 97401-4438
(541)342-5433 •
FAX(541)342-2241
**Allen Jeffrey A MSED**
Bedard Julie K-8
Blair Claudia PS
Jackson Corenne PS-K
Johnson Elizabeth 5
Lewis LaBrenda C 1-2
Rabe Jane BA 3-4
Susuico Dawn 6-8

**GRANTS PASS**-ST PAUL PS
• NLSA • 1984
865 NW 5th St 97526-1530
(541)476-2565
**Goth Mae BS PS**
Crews Claudia PS
Miller Tina PS

**HERMISTON**-BETHLEHEM PS
• 1978
515 SW 7th St 97838-2203
(541)567-6811 •
FAX(541)567-6811
mntadams@ucinet.com
Adams Teresa
Holthus Ginny
Mallon Tammy PS
Royer Debbie PS

**HILLSBORO**-ZION PS
• 1993
30900 NW Evergreen Rd
97124-1806
(503)640-8914
jaqor@aol.com
Quade Doris J AA PS

**KLAMATH FALLS**-LITTLE LAMBS-ZION PS-K
• 1994
1025 High St 97601-2831
(541)882-9552 •
FAX(541)884-6793
zionlutchl@juno.com
Collins Lori K
Hay Bonnie L BA PS

**LAKE OSWEGO**-TRIUMPHANT KING PS
• 1994
4700 SW Lamont Way 97035-5426
(503)636-3436
NO REPORT

**MC MINNVILLE**-ST JOHN PS-4
• 1979
2142 NE Mc Donald Ln
97128-3231
(503)472-9189
stjlsch@vielink.com
**Kroemer Char MAT PS-4**
Helgerson Lisa PS
Hoggard Karin K
Johnson Bonnie M BSED 1-2
Kindred Tracy A 3-4
Myers Joanne L BA PS
Thurston Lynne PS

**MEDFORD**-ST PETER PS
• 1990
1020 E Main St 97504-7449
(541)772-4395
NO REPORT

**MONMOUTH**-FAITH PS
• 1987
200 Monmouth Independence Hwy
PO Box 327 97361-0327
(503)838-2884
faithlc@open.org
Dockery Ellen BSED PS
Gustafson May PS

**OREGON CITY**-TRINITY PS
• 1994
1201 JQ Adams St 97045-1457
(503)656-4504 • FAX(503)
656-2438
Walters Susan A BS PS

**PLEASANT HILL**-PLEASANT HILL PS
• 1989
84421 Gaupp Ln 97455-9610
(541)747-8913 •
FAX(541)747-8164
NO REPORT

**PORTLAND**-ASCENSION PS-K
• 1962
1440 SE 182nd Ave 97233-5009
(503)667-6750 •
FAX(503)618-0810
**Colbert Lenetta J BS PS-K**
Endresen Noreen PS
Kinnear Sheri PS
Lane Barbara L PS
Montambo Sarah K
Shay Jan PS
Wentela Susan BA PS
Wolfe Sabrina PS

BEAUTIFUL SAVIOR PS-K
• 1981
9800 SE 92nd Ave 97266-7088
(503)788-7000 •
FAX(503)788-8468
Merritt Ingrid R PS

IMMANUEL PS
• 1984
7810 SE 15Th Ave 97202-6014
(503)236-7823 •
FAX(503)236-5867
NO REPORT

LITTLE LAMBS-GOOD SHEPHERD PS
• 1984
3405 SW Alice St 97219-5334
(503)244-4558 •
FAX(503)244-1396
**Behrens Cynthia A BS PS**
Stupak Inge PS

PORTLAND PS-12
• 1986
740 SE 182nd Ave 97233-4960
(503)667-3199 •
FAX(503)667-4520
pls@teleport.com
**Kunert Patricia L BS**
**Maier Donald BED**
Aufderheide Ruth PS
Bergmann Dawn K
Bishop Natalie MED 7
Bloom Maggie BPSY K-6
Brooks Sharilyn L BA 1
Chism De Ann C BA 1
Driessner Kimberly BSED PS

Holler Jean 5-8
Jones Donald 8
Krueger Walter E DMU 5-8
Kunert Nancy A MA 2
Maier Karin 4
Mannion Ruth BED 5
Pritchard Mary D 3-4
Sorensen Debra A BA K
Stelling Gretchen BSED 3
Von Behren Marie
Windust Sandra 5-8
Zuch Thomas A MA 6
PRINCE OF PEACE PS-K
• 1983
14175 NW Cornell Rd 97229-5406
(503)645-1211 •
FAX(503)531-2534
NO REPORT
ST MICHAEL PS
• 1998
6700 NE 29th Ave 97211
(503)282-0000 •
FAX(503)282-1336
NO REPORT
TRINITY PS-8
• NLSA • 1890
5520 NE Killingsworth St
97218-2416
(503)288-6403 •
FAX(503)288-1095
office@trinityportland.org
**Riedl James M EDS**
Dooley Suzette MA 4
Estrada Heather BA 3
Gray Ruth PS-4
Green Diane 1-8
Grunow Karin B BA PS-8
Holman Frank MED 5-8
Kuhlmann Linda J MAT 8
Mann Nancy L BS 1
Miles Sharon R BA 5
Reisig Raymond MA 7
Ruecker Lisa 5-8
Seleski Donald E 6
Standley Melissa 7-8
Tatum Linda BA K
Wrye Karen A MED 2
**REEDSPORT**-BEAUTIFUL SAVIOR PS
• 1968
2160 Elm Ave 97467-1135
(503)271-3936
Hasel Ruth PS
Mac Rae Pamela K PS
**ROSEBURG**-ST PAUL PS-6
• 1969
750 W Keady CT 97470-2749
(541)673-7212 •
FAX(541)677-9561
stpaul@rosenet.net
NO REPORT
**SAINT HELENS**-SONSHINE-CALVARY PS
• 1986
58251 S Division Rd 97051-3240
(503)397-1739
calvary.lutheran.church.lcms@juno.com
NO REPORT
**SALEM**-CONCORDIA K-6
• RSO • 1996
4663 Lancaster Dr NE 97305 PO Box 21778 97307-1778
(503)393-7188 •
FAX(503)463-5336
concordiasalem@juno.com
**Alley Vale BA 2-3**
Haynes Coleen R BS 4-6
Maas Judy K
Mertes Judy 1-2
REDEEMER PS
• 1962
4663 Lancaster Dr NE PO Box 17128 97305-7128
(503)393-7121
redeemer@open.org
NO REPORT
ST JOHN PS-K
• 1961
1350 Court St NE 97301-4127
(503)588-0171 •
FAX(503)585-2801
Crabtree Kelly BSED PS
Farnsworth Dawn PS
Moorehead Diane K
**SANDY**-IMMANUEL PS
39901 Pleasant St PO Box 686
97055-0686
(503)668-6232
NO REPORT
**SANTA CLARA**-MESSIAH PS
• 1978
3280 River Rd 97404-1766
(541)688-0735
NO REPORT
**SCAPPOOSE**-GRACE PS
• 1993
51737 S Columbia River Hwy
97056-4409
(503)543-3153
gracelutheran@columbia-center.org
NO REPORT
**SEASIDE**-FAITH PS
• 1994
1115 Broadway St 97138-7817
(503)738-3929
Teas Cindy PS
Williams Jane PS
**SHERWOOD**-ST PAUL PS
17190 SW Scholls Sherwood Rd
97140-8725
NO REPORT
**SPRINGFIELD**-BETHANY PS
• 1994
3360 Game Farm Rd 97477-7521
(541)726-7365
Atchison Kimiko D PS
Baker Jessica N PS
O Neal Lorre M BS
**STAYTON**-LEARNING TREE-CALVARY PS
• 1993
198 Fern Ridge Rd 97383-1257
NO REPORT
**TUALATIN**-LIVING SAVIOR PS
• 1980
8740 SW Sagert St 97062-9114
(503)692-3303
NO REPORT
**WOODBURN**-HOPE PS
• 1998
211 Parr 97071 PO Box 355
97071-0355
(503)981-0400 •
FAX(503)981-0400
hope-lcms@juno.com
Cardenas Veronica
Ramirez Martha

## PENNSYLVANIA

**ALBION**-HOLY TRINITY PS
• RSO • 1981
80 3rd Ave 16401-1366
(814)756-3426 •
FAX(814)756-3426
English Jean L BSED PS
**ALLENTOWN**-THE LUTHERAN ACADEMY
• 1998
802 N 19th St 18104
NO REPORT
**BEAVER FALLS**-MOUNT OLIVE PS
• 1991
2679 Darlington Rd 15010-1239
(412)843-0952
Clark Paula
Greiner Cheryl
Kaszer Brenda
**BETHLEHEM**--CONCORDIA PS-K
• 1993
1240 E 4th St 18015-2010
(610)691-7625
NO REPORT
**BRADDOCK**-IMMANUEL PS
• 1989
420 5th St 15104-1530
(412)271-1995 •
FAX(412)271-1984
**Glasser Peggy E BA**
Mc Cants Johnnie PS
**BRIDGEVILLE**-ZION PS-6
• 1980
3197 Washington Pike 15017-1423
(412)221-4776 •
FAX(412)220-9741
NO REPORT
**BRUSHTON**-UNITY MISSION PS
• 1995
7825 Hamilton Ave PO Box 56913
15208-0913
(412)731-2811
NO REPORT
**CABOT**-ST LUKE PS-8
• 1866
330 Hannahstown Rd 16023-2204
(412)352-2221 •
FAX(412)352-2355
NO REPORT
**CROYDON**-LITTLE LAMB CHILDREN PS
• 1979
1305 State Rd 19021-6126
(215)788-6416
NO REPORT
**EASTON**-FAITH PS
• 1995
2012 Sullivan Trl 18042
(610)253-1625
NO REPORT
**FOREST HILLS**-CHRIST PS-8
• 1981
400 Barclay Ave 15221-4036
(412)271-7173 •
FAX(412)271-4921
principal@christlutheranfh.org
**Carpenter Shirley A BSED**
Archer Maria I PS-5
Dorman Joyce K-8
Forschner Deborah BS K
Gastler Susan BSED 3
Honoree Cheryl L BS 7-8
Itzel Marjorie BA PS
Kunst Cathy BS 6
Laux Lori MA 2
Messick Miriam K
Mikula Christopher K-8
Patton Kristen 7-8
Pavlik Beverly PS
Schorr Charlene 4
Schumm Laura R BA 5
Stern Gloria MA 1-6
Townsend Angela 1
Walker Brenda K-8
**FREEDOM**-PRINCE OF PEACE PS
• 1976
60 Rochester Rd 15042-9364
(724)728-3881 •
FAX(724)728-6708
popluth@bellatlantic.net
Stiger Christine A AA PS
**GIRARD**-FAITH PS
• 1986
824 E Main St 16417-1722 PO Box 56 16417-0056
(814)774-2040 •
FAX(814)774-2040
NO REPORT
**GLENSHAW**-BETHEL PS
• 1986
301 Scott Ave 15116-1625
(412)486-5777
Barricella Henrietta G AA PS
Lindbloom Marcia PS
**HAVERTOWN**-LAMBS OF THE SHEPHER PS
PO Box 1032 19083
(610)789-1287 •
FAX(610)924-0706
**Ingram Sophia PS**
Black Janet PS
Brady Kimberly PS
Di Bello Rosemary K
Evans Deanna PS
Ferrez Cynthia PS
Kane Lisa PS
Lidstone Amy PS
Mac Anally Elizabeth PS
Masciarelli Dana PS
Richardson Jennifer PS
Spera Elieth PS
Thomas Linda PS
**HAZELTON**-ALL GODS CHILDREN-ST JOHN PS
• 1996
621 N Vine St 18201-4233
(570)459-6423
stjohns@ccomm.com
Mandak Gertrude A BSED PS
**HOP BOTTOM**-GRACE PS
• 1985
PO Box 435 18824-0435
(717)289-4921
NO REPORT
**LANCASTER**-OPEN ARMS PS
• 1985
140 E Orange St 17602-2844
(717)394-1471 •
FAX(717)207-0731
openarmsdt@juno.com
Bernoske Melissa PS
Boxleitner Joy PS
Breen Cherie
Condict Holly PS
D Orozio Lisa PS
Dudel Nicole PS
Hall Lorrie BS
Hershey Brandy PS
Smith Jennifer PS
Spedden Rebekah PS
Spurrier Virginia
Wallace Rachel PS
Weist Susan PS
**LEVITTOWN**-HOPE PS-8
• 1953
2600 Haines Rd 19055-1808
(215)946-3467 •
FAX(215)946-5926
**Bollmann Bret MA**
Clarke Ruth PS
Harvey Kimberly S MEDSC 2
Housel Norman 8
Kampschnieder Yvette AA 4
Kunst Richard O BS 5
Lissy Natalie BS 1
Lorentz Deborah A BA 3
Marks Elizabeth BA K
Mc Aleer Bridgette 7
Moser Kristi 6
Puchino Donna M BS PS
**MACUNGIE**-CONCORDIA PS
• 1991
2623 Brookside Rd 18062-9045
(610)965-3265
NO REPORT
**MALVERN**-CHRIST MEMORIAL PS-K
• 1974
89 Line Rd 19355-2879
(610)296-0650 •
FAX(610)644-4677
cmlcs@chesco.com
Allen Claudia PS
Gavin Claire A PS
Grauch Elaine PS
Horan Karen K
Lucash Dana J PS
Proto Barbara T
Thompson Elaine M PS

**MANDATA**-FAITH PS
• 1981
RR 1 Box 818 17830-9766
(570)758-4970 •
FAX(570)758-4970
Rissinger Janet PS
**MECHANICSBURG**-CALVARY PS
• 1989
208 Woods Dr PO Box 374
17055-0374
(717)796-1369
**Miller Michaelena K BA PS**
Clouser Kelli BS PS
**MILLVALE**-ST JOHN PS
• 1976
501 North Ave 15209
(412)821-6367 •
FAX(412)821-0179
Beran Kim PS
Stipetich Deena PS
**MONROEVILLE**-TRINITY PS
• 1995
2555 Haymaker Rd 15146-3507
(412)372-9046 •
FAX(412)372-9046
Hoener Kathleen PS-2
Sourbeer Kathleen L MED
**MORRISDALE**-ST JOHN PS
• 1980
RR 2 Box 322 16858-9103
(814)345-5741
NO REPORT
**MOUNT POCONO**-OUR SAVIOR PS
• 1995
675 Belmont Ave 18344-1014
(570)839-9868 •
FAX(570)839-9868
mtpoursavior@enter.net
NO REPORT
**MURRYSVILLE**-CALVARY PS-K
• 1996
4725 Old William Penn Hwy
15668-2012
(724)327-2898 •
FAX(724)327-2878
calvarylut@aol.com
NO REPORT
**NEW KENSINGTON**-ST PAUL PS
• 1986
1001 Knollwood Rd 15068-5315
(724)339-1910 •
FAX(724)339-8905
NO REPORT
**OAKMONT**-REDEEMER PS-6
• 1983
1261 Pennsylvania Ave
15139-1140
(412)828-9323 •
FAX(412)828-1860
gholzer@redeemer-oakmont.org
**Holzer Gail J BA K**
Abernathy Judye A BA 1-2
Henkelmann Priscilla PS
Smith David W BA 5-6
Stubenbort Stephanie L BA PS
Walker Brenda 1-6
Weldon Sharen 3-4
**OIL CITY**-CHRIST PS
• 1995
1029 Grandview Rd 16301-1226
(814)677-4484 •
FAX(814)677-4484
Schreiber Karen L MED
**PHILADELPHIA**-NAZARETH PS
• 1983
1357 E Luzerne St 19124-5358
(215)743-6475
NO REPORT
ST LUKE PS
• RSO • 1992
7206 Castor Ave 19149-1106
(215)745-7651
De Nicuolo Linda 1 PS
Edwards Kim PS
Evans Lisa R BA
Newton Lynda
Wagner Betty PS
Wojtowicz Jennifer PS
Zink Tracey A PS
ST LUKE PS
• 1988
7200 Castor Ave 19149-1106
(215)745-8922
NO REPORT
**PITTSBURGH**-FIRST PS-8
• 1866
610 Clay St 15215-2204
(412)782-2772 • FAX(412)
782-3093
**Kenny Donna M BA K**
Cline Catherine MS 7-8
Cochenour Melody 5-6
Conroy Marcella 3-4
Cooper Mary A PS
Haberman Cheryl J 1-2
Sheets Jean MAT 7-8
GOOD SHEPHERD PS
• 1993
418 Maxwell Dr 15236-2040
(412)884-3232 •
FAX(412)884-3233
NO REPORT
ST MATTHEW PS-8
• 1862
600 E North Ave 15212-4845
(412)321-6662 •
FAX(412)321-3515
knagy@stmattpitt.org
**Shields Mark J BA K-8**
Baling Lori 5-6
Basinski Susan PS-K
Martin Maria M 2
Mc Coullum Sonya L 7-8
Nagy Scott P BA 5-8
Takos Regina 3-4
Vioral Sandra K MED 1
**RIDLEY PARK**-ST MARK PS-K
• 1951
628 E Chester Pike 19078-1701
PO Box 285 19078-0285
(610)532-4322
Eichinger Deborah PS
Gandy Mary Ann PS
Murphy Martha AAS PS
Stauffer Barbara PS
**SHARON**-ST PETER & PAUL PS-K
• 1999
699 Stambaugh Ave 16146
(724)347-5655
NO REPORT
**STATE COLLEGE**-GOOD SHEPHERD PS
• 1993
851 N Science Park Rd
16803-2225
(814)234-1388 •
FAX(814)234-0877
goodsheppreschool@netzero.net
NO REPORT
**UPPER ST CLAIR**-LITTLE LAMBS-HOPE PS
• 1995
2799 Old Washington Rd
15241-1999
(724)941-9441 •
FAX(724)941-9442
Kline Bonnie L BSED PS
Sharp Denise F PS
Spencer Gwen G BA PS
Streiner Diane M PS
**WARMINSTER**-GRACE PS
• 1970
1169 W Street Rd 18974-3104 PO
Box 196 18974-0520
(215)672-0212
NO REPORT
**WELLSBORO**-TRINITY PS-6
• 1981
West Ave & Luther Lane 53 West
Ave 16901-1336
(717)724-7723 •
FAX(717)723-1053
trinity@ptdprolog.net
**Miller Lisa BED 1**
Baker Cindy 1-2
Brought Ellen 3
Clark Candy K
Hughes Janice 4-6
Kichline Linda
Kohler Brenda PS-6
Laczi Marilyn MSED PS
Smethers Patty 4-6
**YORK**-ST JOHN PS-8
• NLSA • 1874
2580 Mount Rose Ave 17402-7854
(717)755-4779 •
FAX(717)840-4817
sjls.prin@blazenet.net
**Schaefer Carol M MED**
Dell Kathy PS
Hennig Sharon F BSED 5-6
Hood Wendy PS
Hubicz Michelle 4
Macken Mary Ann 3
Reed Connie L MAEQ 1
Ropp Rosemary 7-8
Sanders Kenneth W BSED 3
Stetler Louann BA 2

## RHODE ISLAND

**ASHAWAY**-TRINITY PS
• 1984
110 High St 02804-1504
(401)377-4340
**Calcagni Lori BS PS**
Antach Lori PS
Hammond Valerie J PS
James Delia M PS
Wnuk Sue PS

## SOUTH CAROLINA

**COLUMBIA**-HOLY SPIRIT PS-1
• 1967
2015 Lorick Ave 29203-7247
(803)786-1577 •
FAX(803)735-0580
NO REPORT
**HILTON HEAD ISLAND**-ISLAND PS
• 1998
4400 Main ST 29926 PO Box
22297 29925
(843)342-2500 •
FAX(843)342-5200
llittlefriend@aol.com
Perdue Karen PS
Torin Deiha PS
**MYRTLE BEACH**-HOLY LAMB PS
• 1999
2541 Forestbrook Rd 29588
**Smith Diane PS**
Jepson Cheryl PS
RISEN CHRIST PS-8
• 1976
10595 Highway 17 N 29572-5712
(843)272-8163 •
FAX(843)272-4039
**Gnewuch Cynthia A MA**
Baldwin Mary A MSED 4
Baxter Emily
Cuffe Anne E 5-6
Lapham Joy F 7-8
Palmer Nancy E K
Rowe Bonnie 2-3
Todd Susan M PS
Vereen Michelle 1
**SIMPSONVILLE**-IMMANUEL PS
• 1994
2820 Woodruff Rd 29681-9347
(864)297-5815 •
FAX(864)297-1771
NO REPORT

## SOUTH DAKOTA

**BRANDON**--BLESSED REDEEMER PS
• 1995
705 S Sioux Blvd 57005-1731
(605)582-2396
NO REPORT
**BROOKINGS**-PEACE PS-K
• 1997
1910 10th St S 57006
(605)692-5272
peaceluth@choicetech.net
Hartmann Sarita PS
Uecker Carol S BA K
**CANISTOTA**-ZION PS
• 1997
350 W Elm 57012
(605)296-3166
adalthof@unitelsd.com
Althoff Diane M BS PS
**DAKOTA DUNES**-HOLY CROSS PS
• 1995
149 Bison Trl 57049 PO Box 1902
57049-1731
(605)235-1688 •
FAX(605)235-1688
Krause Diane D BA
**HOT SPRINGS**-BETHESDA K-6
• NLSA • 1980
1537 Baltimore Ave 57747-2205
(605)745-6676 •
FAX(605)745-5374
bethesda@gwtc.net
**Spitzer Beth E BA K-1**
Peterson Susan R 4-6
Schroeder Diane J BS 2-3
**HURON**-MOUNT CALVARY PS
• 1994
688 Dakota Ave S 57350-2857
(605)352-7121
mtcalvhuronsd@santel.net
Danley Elthea A PS
**MILBANK**-EMANUEL PS
• 1979
701 S 1St St 57252-2803
(605)432-9555
Tillma Karen K PS
**PHILIP**-JESUS LOVES ME-OUR REDEEMER PS
• 1994
PO Box 964 57567-0964
(605)859-2721
Backman Dawn PS
**PIERRE**-FAITH PS
• 1978
714 N Grand Ave 57501-1723
(605)224-2216 •
FAX(605)224-2226
faith@dtgnet.com
Hobart Sandra L BSED PS
Larson Janet K BS PS
**RAPID CITY**-PEACE PS
• 1989
219 E Saint Anne St 57701-5665
(605)342-8943
Bailey Robert G MDIV
Hillman Cindy PS
Holen Luciene
Jacobson Jolene PS
Potter Lyn AA PS
Vedder Karen PS
ZION PS-6
• NLSA • 1957
4550 S Highway 16 57701-8913
(605)342-5749 •
FAX(605)342-4469
zion@rapidnet.com
**Sayles Priscilla M MED 3**
Christian Brenda S BA 1
Hennies Hope M BA PS
Hofer Sherry 4
Kirschenmann Jane A BS 2
Leivestad Claire 6
Lemery Shellene 3
Oltmanns Ann 5
Windjue Theresa K-6

Withee Roxanne J BSED K
**SIOUX FALLS**-SIOUX FALLS PS-8
• RSO • NLSA • 1977
308 W 37Th St 57105-5706
(605)335-1923 •
FAX(605)335-1930
principal@midco.net
**Cooksey Robert L MA 6-8**
Asmus Lisa 1-8
Bittner Kristen H BS PS
Carda Patricia 5-8
Dooley Karen K-8
Doremus Penelope R BS 1
Groninger Pamela 1-8
Herther Ann P 4
Hollenbeck Sherri L K
Krause Sandra K BA PS
Lafrentz Louise J BSED 3
Larsen Jackie PS
Reick Myron H MED 5-8
Reick Sandra L BSED 5-8
Sailer Sarah M BA K
Sopko Darlene K BSED 2
Sopko Marvin L BSED K-8
Tams Sandra K BA PS
Yde Julie MA 6
ZION PS
• 1997
1400 South Duluth Avenue 57105
(605)338-5226 •
FAX(605)338-8936
Phelps Tracie A PS
Schindler Belva J BS PS
**TRIPP**-LITTLE LAMBS PS
• 1997
PO Box M 57376
(605)935-6725
NO REPORT
**WOLSEY**-ST JOHN - CONCORDIA PS
• 1992
PO Box 445 57384-0445
(605)883-4972
NO REPORT
**YANKTON**-ST JOHN PS
• 1992
1009 Jackson St 57078-3336
(605)665-7337 •
FAX(605)665-7293
stjohns@willinet.net
Buxcel Susan BA PS

## TENNESSEE

**ATHENS**-ATHENS PS
710 Forrest Ave 37371-0841
(615)334-5411
**Rymer Joy**
Clendenen Debra PS
De Witt Linda PS
Eaton Stefanie PS
**CHATTANOOGA**-FIRST CHILD DEVELOPM PS
• 1990
2800 Mccallie Ave 37404-3902
(423)698-6443 •
FAX(423)629-1508
NO REPORT
LUTHERAN PS-8
• NLSA • 1887
800 Belvoir Ave 37412-2508
(423)622-3755 •
FAX(423)622-0177
wel@lutheranschool.net
**Luedtke William E MSED**
Allen Deborah L BSED K
Amstutz Jane BS 2-4
Beam Amber PS
Colbert Karen S BSED 1
Duderstadt Lorna MED 2
Fisher Katherine J MED 8
Generazio Jill BS K
Ingram Becky J BS 1-8
Jackson Janet 1
Mc Daniel Theresa BA PS-8
Morkert David L BS PS
Naylor Audrey PS
Patterson Todd PS
Pinkerton Irma MA PS
Prentice Lindsey E BS 5-8
Schroeder Linda J MED 5
Sparks Deborah BS PS
Streufert Frank C MA PS
Streufert Randi 5
Timm Eunice M MSED 3
Townsend Carlinda
**CLARKSVILLE**-GRACE PS PS
2041 Madison St 37043-5058
(931)645-3497 •
FAX(931)645-3374
gracelutheranch@juno.com
NO REPORT
**COLLIERVILLE**-FAITH PS
• 1994
507 N Byhalia Rd 38017-1301
(901)853-0050 •
FAX(901)853-5015
Abplanalp Marilyn PS
Arthur Diane PS
Babin Pamela PS
Baker Rika PS
Bizzell Pam PS
Chiavario Annie PS
Craig Caroline PS
Hahn Pamela PS
Krenik Susan PS
Mills Cindy PS
Musser Kathy
Ott Debbie PS
Sanders J J PS
Sarrio Michelle PS
Shuman Sue PS
**COLUMBIA**-TRINITY PS
• 1997
5001 Trotwood Ave 38401-5048
(931)381-8207
Senefeld Jane E PS
Smith Judy E PS
**COOKEVILLE**-HEAVENLY HOST PS-6
• 1993
777 S Willow Ave 38501
(931)520-3766 •
FAX(931)520-3766
hhls@multipro.com
Bennett Adele PS
Copeland Kari 4-6
Dever Jennie 1
Glasgow Diane BA K-6
Mc Broom Pam 4-6
Methvin Tina 2
Olson Linda 1
Parr-Beaty Kathryn K
Rubright Cara K-6
Soard Jo Ann 3
Stringer Kaye PS
Vickers Brenda J
**CORDOVA**-OPEN ARMS CHILD-CARE-GRACE CELEBRATION PS
Ecs 7600 Macon Rd Cordora 8601 Trinity Rd 38018
(901)737-6091 •
FAX(901)683-2021
gracecelel@aol.com
NO REPORT
**CROSSVILLE**-SHEP LITTLE FLOCK-SHEP OF THE HILLS PS
PO Box 1134 38557 1461 Sparta Hwy 38555
(931)484-3461
shepherdofhills@tnaccess.com
NO REPORT
**FRANKLIN**-FAITH PS
• 1995
415 Franklin Rd 37069-8207
(615)791-1880 •
FAX(615)790-8746
Faith_Franklin@juno.com
NO REPORT
**GALLATIN**-TRINITY PS
• 1995
720 Lock 4 Rd 37066-3466
(615)452-9009 •
FAX(615)452-3358
NO REPORT
**JACKSON**-CONCORDIA PS
• 1967
637 Wallace Rd 38305-4229
(901)668-0757 •
FAX(901)668-7820
conluth@usit.net
Antee Shirley J PS
August Kathryn D PS
Curry Tracy L PS
Eddings Charlotte D PS
Gilbert Evelyn M PS
Hasz Barbara J BS
Lynch Vicki S PS
Mc Garity Shelly L PS
Nelson Elise PS
Rosser Deborah A PS
Taylor Gwendolyn F PS
**KNOXVILLE**-FIRST PS-8
• 1869
1207 Broadway St NE 37917-6530
(865)524-0308 •
FAX(865)524-5636
FirstKnox@aol.com
Boatman Christina PS
Bushur Ann J BA K
Cooper Jennifer L MS 5
Hartman Julie PS
Hinds Harriett A BS 2
Holste Cynthia K BS 3
Holste Timothy J BSED 4
Irwin Kay M BA K
Lane Jennifer PS
Lowe Pamela PS
Mattice Kaile L BA 6-7
Ratcliffe Joyce PS
Samuel Marion PS
Tauscher Darla K BSED 1
Tessendorf Karen K BA 7-8
Tessendorf Roger W MS
Treece Carol PS
Wolfram Timothy J MMTH 6-8
**MADISON**-ASCENSION K-6
• 1997
610 W Old Hickory Blvd 37115-3514
(615)868-7980 •
FAX(615)868-7674
Dail Christine M BA 2-3
Iwanowski Jana B 4-6
Miller Donna M BAED K-1
**MEMPHIS**-BEAUTIFUL SAVIOR PS
• 1998
5740 Winchester Rd 38115-4711
(901)547-0407 •
FAX(901)362-6040
rev.elkins@vantek.net
**Elkins Jana PS**
Cooper Lue E PS
Cox Felica PS
Davis Annie PS
Ivy Sheronda PS
Justice Sharon PS
Larry Mary PS
Mc Clore Denise PS
Paez Yaira PS
Person La Juana PS
Register Keysha PS
Waterman Andrea PS
CHRIST THE KING PS-8
• NLSA • 1960
5296 Park Ave 38119-3506
(901)682-8405 •
FAX(901)682-7687
**Calhoun Felicia S 1-8**
**Wilt John T MED**
**Wright Cynthia T BSED PS**
Bartlett Susan D PS
Buchanan Gisele K-8
Cheshier Natalie 5
Coerber Teckla R BSED PS
Gable Donna J BSED 3
Johnson Matthew K-8
Keath Janette PS
Kohlhof Sarah L K
Legge Jean L MED 4
Mc Leary Mary Beth 1
Moore Norma R
Neugebauer Diane PS
Novy James R BS 5-8
Parker Lorraine C MA K
Rogalski Susan B 1-6
Schmidt Lorna W MA 1-8
Shepard Deborah 7
Summey Teresa PS
Swan Genie B MA K-8
Teal Karen A BA 2
Weiser Carmen M 5
Welch Cissy 6
Williams Barbara 1-8
CROSS OF CALVARY PS-7
• 1993
4327 Elvis Presley Blvd 38116-6405
(901)396-5566 •
FAX(901)396-5567
NO REPORT
IMMANUEL PS-8
• NLSA • 1947
6319 Raleigh Lagrange Rd 38134-6907
(901)388-0205 •
FAX(901)377-7371
school@ilcmemphis.org
**Pudwell Kristin L MS**
Andreasen Dennis C MA 5-8
Barden Judith A BSED K
Barnes Richard M 7
Booze Brenda G PS
Collins Marianne B 1
Ernest Erica K
Fryman Sharon M PS
Hammons Cynthia J MA PS-8
Herron Judith PS-8
Maclin Judy 1-2
Maples Karlene PS
Mell Lori D MED 5-8
Pollan Rebecca S 2
Sorgatz Marian A BA 3-4
Tieman Rebecca BSED 6-8
Winter Catherine BA 4
Winter Ellis A MA 3
THE REDEEMER PS
• 1985
294 S Highland St 38111-4558
(901)327-0015 •
FAX(901)327-3234
NO REPORT
**NASHVILLE**-CARE FOR KIDS-OUR SAVIOR PS
• 1996
5110 Franklin Rd 37220-1814
(615)833-3779 •
FAX(615)331-1123
Boaz Kris PS
Hall Angela PS
Jetter Melissa PS
Rockey Martha P BA PS
Wray Angela PS
**TULLAHOMA**-FAITH PS
101 Bragg Cir 37388-2975
(931)393-2869
Childers Auasa PS
Clark Kelly PS
Kleinfeld Sharon L PS
Rice Theresa PS
Thomason Juanita E PS
**WARTBURG**-ST PAUL PS
• 1981
222 Church St PO Box 67 37887-0067
(423)346-3554
NO REPORT

## TEXAS

**0**-KING OF KINGS PS
• 1985
0 0 17000 Smyers Ln 78681
(512)255-0446 •
FAX(512)255-4582
Appelt Marian
Coronado Cathy
Dearman Katie
Franke Lisa
Jones Nicole
Lehmann Katy
Ray Shirley
Remeny Cindy
Reski Barb
Salter Jennifer
Stevenson Nancy
Troester Cathy J
**AMARILLO**-TRINITY PS-5
• 1948
5005 I-40 W 79106-4756
(806)352-5620 •
FAX(806)353-7785
tls@arn.net
**Cattau Rollin C MA**
Braunersreuther Rachel 4-5
Fluegel Janice L AA PS
Hauter Donna R BA K
Hurst Nancy L BSED 1
Kuhlmann Eloise S MED 5
Mc Connell Sharon L 5
Morrow Diane 1
Werner John T BSED 3
**ARLINGTON**-GRACE PS-6
• NLSA • 1982
308 W Park Row 76010-4302
(817)274-1654 •
FAX(817)277-9353
gracelutheransch@home.com
**Hohnbaum James M MA**
**Stacy Dawn E PS**
Baumann Cassandra PS
Brown Erika PS
Duppstadt Uvonne PS
Finke Julie A BA 2
Foster Carol PS
Fuller Patricia PS
Hintze Charlotte PS-2
Hoy Gretchen PS
Hutchins Karin PS
Inayat Angelina PS
Joeckel Kristy PS
Lauer Kerry PS
Mc Intosh Terry M BBA PS
Mickelson Nancy PS
Newman Rachel PS
Ostermann Susan M BA 5-6
Ott Elizabeth PS
Peterson Heidi S MED K
Riley Lori BA K
Salas Christine PS
Schrimsher Rhonda K-6
Taylor Catherine L BA 1
HOLY CROSS LUTHERAN PS
4400 W Arkansas Ln 76016
(817)451-7561 •
FAX(817)429-6944
holycrlc@arlington.net
NO REPORT
**AUSTIN**-BETHANY PS-K
• NLSA • 1969
6215 Manchaca Rd 78745-4998
(512)444-0412 •
FAX(512)444-2811
blccc@freewwweb.com
Ashness Linda
Bohrer Doreen
Bost Patty A BA K
Garrett B J PS
Howe Tambrea PS
Lankford Amy PS
Lara Maria PS
Lopez Denise PS
Luna Rose PS
Medina Theresa PS
Mitchell Mattie PS
Mullen Tessa PS
Reyes Doris PS
Richards Jewel
Richards Megan PS
Shirley Jennifer PS
Shirley Linda K PS
HOPE PS-8
• NLSA • 1964
6414 N Hampton Dr 78723-2043
(512)926-0003 •
FAX(512)926-0708
dsglienke@swbell.net
**Glienke David H MED 5-8**
**Zoch Elizabeth BA**
Brady Tia M BA 6-8
Brewster James 6-8
Buchta Amanda W BS K
Glienke Sandra I BA PS
Henry Deborah BS 4
Herrerra Connie PS
Kluth Carol M MED 1
Kokel Sylvia J BSED 2
Lantion Alice PS
Matthys Jennifer N BA 3
Miller Matthew 6-8
Sandcork Robert R II BA 5
Thoresen Juli A BA 6-8
MOUNT OLIVE PS
• 1991
7416 W Highway 71 78735-8202
(512)288-2330 •
FAX(512)288-2375
**Maroney Amber M BA**
Arnett Susan PS
Brown Sunshine PS
Ellisor Melinda PS
Haas Kelli PS
Kikta Regilean PS
Nelson Doris PS
Peterson Julie PS
Reardon Audrey PS
Votaw Cherenae PS
OUR SAVIOR PS-5
• NLSA • 1974
1513 E Yager Ln 78753-7117
(512)836-9600 •
FAX(512)836-4660
oslc@io.com
**Leitner George W MS**
Bockelmann Liesl PS
Drees Emily A BA PS
Dube Beverly J BS PS
Frank Margaret A BS 1
Helms Carol M BS K
Leitner Linda D BS 2-3
Menke Tom O 4-5
Svihla Ericka PS
REDEEMER PS-8
• NLSA • 1955
1500 W Anderson Ln 78757-1497
(512)451-6478 •
FAX(512)459-6779
gkieschnick@redeemer.net
**Kieschnick Glen MED**
Adams-Borneman Roberta PS
Childress Joan 6
Dinda Laura J BA PS
Dodic Erin L BA 3
Dodson Alicia K
Ford Kathy BS
Fromme Melinda G BA 4
Hinz Carol
Holle Linda 1
Horn Lesley A BA PS
Jahnke Lisa K BA 3
Jahnke Steven M BA 7
Keyburn Danna BA PS
King Jennifer A BA K
Krause Kristine A BS K
Landfried Elizabeth A BS 1
Lyons Eileen S BA 2
Miles Catherine BS 5
Nun Sandra J BA 2
Redmond Jana L BA
Ricks Catherine 8
Schaffer Nancy PS
Schatte Karin E BMU
Schatte William A BA 8
Shane Julie BS 5
Suchan Carol PS
Turner Ann K
Unnasch Loretta PS
Vacchio de Capra Rene
Villarreal Britt A BA 1
Zielke Dorothy 4
ST PAUL PS-8
• NLSA • 1893
3407 Red River St 78705-2631
(512)472-3313 •
FAX(512)469-0785
stpaul@prismnet.com
**Senechal John W MS 6-8**
Achterberg Kathleen R MCMU 5-8
Alcocer Marlene T 1-4
Arldt Meredith L BA 5-8
Belt Kelli L BA PS-4
Dagar Fred A 5-8
Freshour Teresa A PS
Grissett Rose A MED K
Johnson Elaine A PS-K
Le Tulle Mary F 1-8
Meyer Christine A BA 5-8
Polley Connie J BS PS-4
Schulze Betty J BS 2
Senechal Carol A BS 3
Wenthe Helen R BA 1
Wenthe William D BS 6
Zieschang Cynthia D 1-4
**BAYTOWN**-REDEEMER PS
• 1996
1200 E Lobit St 77520-5348
(281)422-2252 •
FAX(281)427-3517
Mc Dowell Scottie
**BEAUMONT**-REDEEMER PS
• 1990
4330 Crow Rd 77706-6911
(409)892-2518 •
FAX(409)924-8300
NO REPORT
**BISHOP**-ST PAUL PS-4
• 1912
801 E Main St 78343-2720
(512)584-2778
st_paul_bishop@juno.com
Bade Cheree PS
Eckert Caroline BA 4-5
Eulenfeld Teri PS
Felder Kathie PS
Forrester Raelene PS
Meerscheidt Rebecca PS
Moerbe Susan L MED K-1
Sanchez Delia PS
Sedory Adline PS
Soliz Maria PS
Yaklin Lynette BS 2-3
**BRENHAM**-GRACE PS-8
• NLSA • 1947
1212 W Jefferson St 77833-2943
(979)836-2030 •
FAX(979)836-0510
grace@phoenix.com
**Fritsche Ronald W MED 7-8**
Bredehoft Dorothy R BS 1
Campbell Pat BA K
Clausen Sandy 3
Faske Kathy PS
Fritsche Cathy PS
Haevischer Judy A BSED 2
Mc Arthur Linda 5-8
Miessler Merwyn L MMU 4
Moerbe Anita 5-8
**BROWNSVILLE**-TRINITY PS
• 1986
901 Boca Chica Blvd 78520-8304
(956)542-0027 •
FAX(956)546-3237
NO REPORT
**BURLESON**--CHARITY PS
• 1991
1101 SW Wilshire Blvd
76028-5718
(817)295-8059 •
FAX(817)295-1985
NO REPORT
**CARROLLTON**-PRINCE OF PEACE PS-8
• NLSA • 1980
4000 N Midway Rd 75007-1903
(972)447-9887 •
FAX(972)447-0877
pop1@popcs.net
**Baker Kevin C MED**
**Hahn Christopher J BED**
**Liersemann Kathryn S MA**
Anderson Cathy S 7-8
Anthony Jean PS-5
Aufdemberge Carol MSED 1
Bailey Gloria K-4
Bertocci Sandi PS-5
Bierbaum Deanna J BA 1
Blackwell Karen MA PS-5
Boriack Betty BED 2
Byroad Allene MA 6-8
Canto Beatriz 1-4
Caruthers Elizabeth 6-8
Cleland Laura BSED 6
Crone Karen BED 6-8
De Satterlee Lois BS K
Dolliver La Vonne 5
Dover Raelynn BS 3
Frizzell Pam PS
Geyer William MMED 5-8
Hardy MaryAnn 1
Hoffschneider Steven L MED 6-8
Hurt Patti K
Jacobson Jennifer 6-8
James Karen L MED 5
Jeffries Kate 2
Lawson Tammy PS
Maloney Laura 6-8
Manssen Rebecca 4
Meyer Eunice A BA K
Newfang Melissa 6-8
Noack Dorothy 3
Peterson Diane MED PS
Poole Michelle R BS 4
Porter Brenda PS
Saxon Carolyn MSPED 2
Schwab Dorothy C BED 3
Stelzl Barbara K-4
Taylor Nancy PS
Thorman Jeff BBA 6-8
Tobaben Kara L BS 5
Van Dine Kathy 6-8
Williams Linda K
Zuehsow Angela BSED 4
**CEDAR PARK**-GOOD SHEPHERD PS-K
• 1979
FM 1431 At Royal Ln 78630-0340
700 W Whitestone Blvd
78613-2119
(512)258-7602 •
FAX(512)258-2335
goodslc@aol.com
NO REPORT
**CISCO**-REDEEMER PS
• 1998
1711 Conrad Hilton Ave 76437
(254)442-2090 •
FAX(254)442-2090
heisrisn@flash.net
NO REPORT
**COLLEYVILLE**-CROWN OF LIFE K-6
• 1996
6605 Pleasant Run Rd
76034-6609
(817)421-5683 •
FAX(817)421-9263
www.crownoflife.org
**Malzahn Ellen M MED**
Gillam Jennifer L MA 5-6
Greer Rebecca BS 1

Jung Ann M MA 2
Kamrath Angela S BA K
Reber Carrie R BA 4
Vandercook-Black Sarah L 3
**CONROE**-ST MARK PS-K
• 1992
2100 Tickner St 77301-1341
(409)756-6335
NO REPORT
**COPPELL**-CHRIST OUR SAVIOR PS-6
• NLSA • 1986
140 S Heartz Rd 75019-3330
(972)393-7074 •
FAX(972)462-0881
**Riske Curtis H MA**
Apse Amy L BA 4
Brede Kathy PS
Brookman Ginger PS
Collier Natasha PS
Crosby Darleen MA 1
Davis Lucy MA PS
Fischer Debra PS
Forrester Suanne 3
Harris Rachel A BA PS
Junod Monica L BA K
Linnell Lindsey A BA 1
Long JoAnn PS
Perrin LeAnn T BA 2
Riske Donna R BA 3
Scott Diane PS
Sutterfield Carol D PS
Troutman Ann M BSED PS
Wallace Carolyn S BS PS
Wenzel James E 5-6
**CORPUS CHRISTI**-LORD OF LIFE PS
• 1991
1317 Flour Bluff Dr 78418-5104
(361)937-6414 •
FAX(361)937-1796
Armijo Tammy PS
Boyd Devon PS
Demaret Tonja PS
Matlock Ann PS
Mc Manus Karon PS
Puckett Julia PS
Roe Margie PS
Sadler Debbie J
Schmidt Laurel PS
MT OLIVE PS-K
• 1977
5101 Saratoga Blvd 78413-2812
(361)991-9289 •
FAX(361)991-8851
mtolivelutheran@juno.com
Bogs Gayle PS
Charo Claudette PS
Contreras Adelita PS
Figueroa Crystal PS
Foy Sarah G K
Hanelt Mary PS
Johnson Jane PS
Long Amalie PS
Peddicord Michelle
Sielk Norma E AA PS
**CYPRESS**-ST JOHN PS-K
• 1982
15235 Spring-Cypress Rd 77429
PO Box 898 77410-0898
(281)373-5241 •
FAX(281)373-5102
CJNemer@aol.com
Englert Elizabeth G PS
Hedgepeth Jill PS
Hughes Kim PS
Jackson Kirsten PS
Johnson Lynette PS
Juergen Lisa M PS
May Celeste A PS
Moreno Leticia O PS
Odom Diane G PS
Reagan Brandi PS
Schmidt Beth PS
Schulze Sarah N PS
Smith Landa A PS
Snapp Kerri PS
Williams Claudia PS
Young Yvonne R PS
**DALLAS**-BETHEL PS
• 1959
11211 E Northwest Hwy
75238-3826
(214)348-8375 •
FAX(214)348-7756
Bethel@airmail.net
Burden Janis AAS PS
Burgess Cathey L BSED
Gaskill Lisa PS
Neguse Elsa PS
Stonecipher Charlee PS
Varela Naiomi PS
HOLY CROSS PS-6
• 1962
11425 Marsh Ln 75229-2637
(214)358-4396 •
FAX(214)358-4393
**Hoffschneider Larry E MED**
Frayre Liz PS
Fritsch Kregg C MA 5
Held Lisa M BSED 4
Hinkel Barbara K BA 6
Hoffschneider Nancy M MED PS
Hoyum Jerry L BSED K-6
Hoyum Lynette M BSED K
Hubing Rosemary
Huse Helen L PS
Ladendorf Janice F MS 2
Olivo Carlos K-6
Stamp Ellen J MED 1
Zetsche Carol B BS 3
OUR REDEEMER PS-8
• NLSA • 1960
7611 Park Ln 75225-2028
(214)368-1465 •
FAX(214)368-1473
gwl@ourredeemer-dallas.org
**Ladendorf Gene W MSED**
Berg Judy A MS K
Eick Tammara A PS
Ferguson Judith L BA 2
Frieling Gary M BS 6-8
Frischmann Lois A MS K
Gatlin Connie E BSED PS
Gibson David B PS-8
Greimann Elaine C BSED 1
House Audrey M BS 6-8
Janak Cynthia M PS
Lehmann Jean S BS 3
Rouse Carolyn J BA 4
Schwarze Sarah S K
Sosinski Rachel L PS
Thomson Paula K 5
Wharton Jacqueline BA PS
ZION PS-8
• NLSA • 1948
6121 E Lovers Ln 75214-2088
(214)363-1630 •
FAX(214)361-2049
zionlcms@ziondallas.org
**Chandler Carol A MED**
Bandy Angela R 5-6
Behrend Elisabeth A MS 6-8
Bohmfalk Sue 1-4
Dierks Kevin G MA 6-8
Hanssen Carol 2
Jones Laureen H 6-8
Kraft Alison PS-2
Krause Barbara J BS PS
Mayerhoff Marilynn 4
Mc Lain Katherine C BA K
Morrison Faith A BA 5
Speaks Paula BA 1
Symmank Barbara 3
Tesauro June M BS PS-8
Zoch Wendy M MED 3
**DE SOTO**-CROSS OF CHRIST PS-6
• NLSA • 1988
512 N Cockrell Hill Rd 75115-3602
(972)223-9586 •
FAX(972)223-0660
dboldt@crossofchrist.org
**Birnbaum David C MAD 2-6**
**Boldt Dennis H MS**
Aldana Rita BA 5
Boldt Jean L BA 1
Cook Kris PS
Hahn Melissa V BSED 2
Henry Deborah S BS 4
Hill Tammy BS
Hinckley Linda G PS
Lain Christine L PS-K
Nimtz Faith D BA 3
Stodola Eugenia PS
Thomason Robbin 1
**DENTON**-ST PAUL DAY CARE PS
703 N Elm St 76201-6903
(817)387-6651
NO REPORT
**EL PASO**-ASCENSION PS-K
• 1987
6520 Loma De Cristo Dr
79912-7301
(915)833-4849 •
FAX(915)581-3216
NO REPORT
OUR SAVIOR DAY CARE PS
• 1987
10200 Album Ave 79925-5439
(915)591-9371 •
FAX(915)590-0851
NO REPORT
ST MATTHEW PS
• 1996
11995 Montwood Dr 79936-0708
(915)857-7492 •
FAX(915)857-2692
stmattelpaso@juno.com
NO REPORT
ZION PS
• 1995
2800 Pershing Dr 79903
(915)565-7999
NO REPORT
**FARWELL**-LIFE IN CHRIST ACADE PS
• 1999
RR 1 Box 146 79325
(806)825-2409
NO REPORT
**FLOWER MOUND**-LAMB OF GOD PS
• 1989
1401 Cross Timbers Rd
75028-1276
(972)539-0055 •
FAX(972)539-8194
NO REPORT
**FORT WORTH**-REDEEMER PS-6
• 1956
4513 Williams Rd 76116-8809
(817)560-0032 •
FAX(817)560-0031
wenzelje@flash.net
Wenzel James E
ST PAUL PS-8
• NLSA • 1969
1800 West Fwy 76102-5977
(817) 332-2281 •
FAX(817)332-2640
stpaul@flash.net
**Geyer Thomas W MA**
Auger Edmund III PS-8
Bernet Jennifer 5-8
Bielefeldt Teresa K MED K
Dobbins Katherine BS K
Geyer Cheryl M MA 4
Graham Michael A BS 5
Henning Gail 5-7
Lange Rebecca A BA 1-9
Marut Janice B BSED 7-9
Mc Camant Diane BSED 3
Menzel Kathleen B MED K
Miesner Susan B BS 4
Moorehouse Chris 3-8
Noto Donna J BS PS
Rusert Brett 2
Selking Barbara J BS 6-8
Tauscher Jane BS PS-7
Thiede Mary A 1
West Tracye PS-8
**FREDERICKSBURG**--RESURRECTION
• 1999
2215 N Llano St 78624
(830)997-9408
NO REPORT
**FRIENDSWOOD**-HOPE MOTHERS DAY OUT PS
• 1990
1804 S Friendwood Dr PO Box 1076 77549-1076
(281)482-7943
NO REPORT
**GARLAND**-CONCORDIA PS
• 1991
5702 N Jupiter Rd 75044-3601
(972)495-7839 •
FAX(972)496-1133
cncordialc@aol.com
NO REPORT
**GEORGETOWN**-FAITH PS
• 1996
4010 Williams Dr 78628
(512)863-7332
NO REPORT
**GIDDINGS**-IMMANUEL PS-8
• NLSA • 1899
382 N Grimes St 78942-2630
(979)542-3319 •
FAX(979)542-9084
ilschool@bluebon.net
**Schaefer Daniel V MA 7-8**
Beisert Betty PS
Berry Jerome G MED K-8
Biar Kristine R BA 6-8
Durrenberger Claudia PS
Frusch Jennifer 1
Hendrickson Eunice M BS K
Iselt Pamela G BA K-4
Koslan Carolyn S BS 4
Larsen Sara N BSED 2
Martin Jennifer K
Mc Clain Leann E BSED 1-8
Oetting Tara PS
Placke Jennifer BS 6-8
Schaefer Susan G BED 5
Swenson Leah BA 3
Walther Susan PS
Wilke Paul M 7
**GROVES**-ST PAUL PS
• 1981
5801 W Jefferson St 77619-3724
(409)963-0834 •
FAX(409)962-2007
NO REPORT
**HAMILTON**-ST JOHN PS
• 1999
122 Cheyenne Mesa Rd 76531
(254)386-3158 •
FAX(254)386-3159
cteamcarr@htcomp.net
Carr Catherine G BA PS
**HARLINGEN**-ST PAUL PS-8
• NLSA • 1948
1920 E Washington 78550-5142
(956)423-3926 •
FAX(956)423-3942
**Althage Richard A MED**
Rudy Sally L BSED 1
**HOUSTON**-BEAUTIFUL SAVIOR PS-K
• 1972
161 West Rd 77037-1144
(281)445-2965 •
FAX(281)445-2966
NO REPORT
BETHANY PS-8
• NLSA • 1927
522 Lindale St 77022-5599
(713)695-0236 •
FAX(713)695-2726
Bodin Kathy D BA 6-8
Cook Janet L PS
Counts Karen I PS
De La Cerda Garrett PS-8
Elias Victoria PS-8
Gillespie Stacie 3

Hawkins Gregg 5-8
Hawkins Joy 1
Hughes Janis 5-8
Mueller Martin B MED
Pilato Barbara 5-8
Ritcher Valenda PS
Sauceda Michelle I PS
Small Diane 5-8
Yanez Adriana BA 4
CALVARY PS-3
• RSO • 1971
10635 Homestead Rd 77016-2703
(713)633-1146 •
FAX(713)633-3896
NO REPORT
CHRIST PS-K
• 1967
6603 Uvalde Rd 77049-4501
(281) 458-3231 • FAX(281)
458-4625
Anderson Laurie PS
Hudson Karen K
Johnson Pamela PS
Scott Rhonda
Warner Janie PS
CHRIST MEMORIAL PS-K
• NLSA • 1969
14200 Memorial Dr 77079-6702
(281)497-2055 •
FAX(281)497-1424
cmleclc@juno.com
NO REPORT
EPIPHANY PS
• 1986
8101 Senate St 77040-1277
(713)896-1316 •
FAX(713)896-7568
NO REPORT
GETHSEMANE PS
• 1992
4040 Watonga Blvd 77092-5321
(713)688-8346 •
FAX(713)688-5235
Conley Linda PS
Ehrhardt Monica MED
Flores Carol PS
Gentempo Denise PS
Knoll Dona PS
Logan Vicki PS
Mellott Gwen PS
Schneider Kay PS
GLORIA DEI PS
• 1980
18220 Upper Bay Rd 77058-4108
(281)333-3323 •
FAX(281)335-0574
kwalker@gdlc.org
NO REPORT
IMMANUEL PS-8
• NLSA • 1927
306 E 15th St 77008-4291
(713)861-8787 •
FAX(713)861-8787
ils@swbell.net
**Schmelzle Luke F MEAD**
Floyd Betty R AA PS
Gumtow Elaine BS K
Gumtow William A BS
Lamascus Rick 5
Mau Delmer J MA 8
Mau Jacqueline J BA 2
Richter Sharon L BS 6
Schmelzle Tanya L MRD 4
Schroeder Kristine L MS 5-8
Tamburello Pamela BA K
Taylor Charis 1
Wiese Anita E 3
LUTHERAN SOUTH ACADE 1-8
• 1998
12555 Ryewater Dr 77089-6625
(281)464-9320 •
FAX(281)464-6119
**Goecker Lowell R MSED 6-8**
**Kramer Wayne C EDD 6-8**
Ballard Diana 6-8
Dabney Beth 3
Deist Carrie S BA 6-8
Dicke Mark L BA 4
Einspahr Karla M BS 6-8
Fink Dawn 1
Harrison Rayann 6-8
Hergenrader Christina L BS 6-8
Himmler Kelly BA 4
Inglis Katherine E BA 6-8
Isbell Ann 6-8
Karcher Troy A BSED 6-8
Kramer Norma J BS 5
Lunz Georgette V 5
Martin Olga 6-8
Mc Allister Donna 2
Palmquist Sandra K BA 6-8
Psencik Robert E BA 6-8
Psencik Sheila L BS 6-8
Reynolds Charla
Sprengel Nathan S BA 6-8
Stark Kimberly L BSED 6-8
Tedeschi Anthony 6-8
MEMORIAL PS-8
• 1980
5800 Westheimer Rd 77057-5617
(713)782-4022 •
FAX(713)782-1749
jwlohmeyer@mlchouston.org
**Lohmeyer Jan W MED**
Alexander Ann
Barnes Holly M BA 1
Becker Mary BS PS
Bohot Kim L BA 6-8
Burroughs Dorothy P MMU
Delmonte Cindy C PS
Duran Diana D PS
Fredenburg Martha A BS 3
Hall Belinda J BA PS
Kitchell Sharon MED 5
Kunz Hilda PS
Muth Janet J BA
Nelson Michael T 6-8
Ramos Nyree PS
Razzook Moayyad DSC
Razzook Shatha P
Seybold Sheryl A BS K
Spomrer Michelle 4
Ssekyanzi Anna K AA PS
Wagner Pat
Wolbert Gregory J BA 6-8
Zimmerman Lea BSED 2
MESSIAH PS
• 1982
5103 Rose St 77007-5240
(713)864-5394 •
FAX(713)861-7952
Brown Kim
Cook Stacey PS
Silva-lea Elena PS
MOUNT CALVARY PS
• 1994
1055 W Tidwell Rd 77091-4633
(713)680-1419 •
FAX(713)680-1449
NO REPORT
MOUNT OLIVE PS-K
• 1994
10310 Scarsdale Blvd 77089-5665
(713)922-5673 •
FAX(281)922-5914
0
**Garcia Christi**
Brown Janet PS
Cook Cherie PS
Dixon Connie PS
Griffith Paula PS
Hardcastle La Nan PS
Hollen Barbara PS
Kelly Jennifer PS
OUR REDEEMER PS-8
• NLSA • 1954
215 Rittenhouse St 77076-2007
(713)694-0332 •
FAX(713)699-1032
d.dieters@worldnet.att.net
Birdsong John L BA 3-4
Schoppe Malynda F
OUR SAVIOR PS-8
• NLSA • 1945
500 W Tidwell Rd 77091 PO Box
925188 77292-5188
(713)290-8277 •
FAX(713)290-0850
school@oslschool.org
**Henke Stephen M MED**
**Mc Donald Alice PS**
Armstrong Jeffery S 1-8
Christ Jaime 1
Crow Casey
Crow Trista
Eifert Jimmy 6-8
Gerard Lance D BSED 5
Hoffert Corinne MS 4
Jeseritz Laura BA 2
Kemnitz Dirk MSED 6-8
Leger Sandra K BA K
Lunsford Jeanene BS PS-8
Morrissey Erik S BS 4-8
Mueller JoCaroll BS K
Rankin Grant
Robinson Diane S MCMU 1
Robinson Joel D MMU 3
Sanchez Gloria PS
Smithson Patricia A MED PS
Stephens Diana J BS 2
White Diane M BED K-8
PILGRIM PS-8
• NLSA • 1954
8601 Chimney Rock Rd
77096-1399
(713)666-3706 •
FAX(713)666-6585
plschool@pilgrimhouston.co
**Schepmann Darrell W MMTH**
Bertrand Elizabeth K
Casavant Darcy D 6-8
Comotto Marilyn BS 2
Fritz Sharlyn S MS PS
Hall Karen M MMU PS
Henke Chad R BA 8
Hermes Molly 1
Kressin Heidi C BA PS
Lunsford Amy J 3
Maas Ruth E BA 2-8
Marotzke Cindy PS-8
Mitchell Joel D BA 5-8
Paluch Allan E BA 7-8
Putnam Stephanee BED 5
Sheppard Kaye K
Smith Patricia BSED 4
Smolen Kim R BA 1
Streger Sue BS
Strickland James K-8
SAN PABLO PS
602 Majestic St 77020-5139
(713)673-4339
NO REPORT
SAN PEDRO PS
• 1973
1501 Houston Ave 77007-4135
(713)228-2866
**Puente Maria R PS**
Acevedo Diana PS
ST ANDREW PS-K
• 1992
1353-A Witte Rd 77055-4003
(713)468-0026 •
FAX(713)468-9566
office@standrew-lcms.org
NO REPORT
ST MARK PS-8
• NLSA • 1949
1515 Hillendahl Blvd 77055-3411
(713)468-2623 •
FAX(713)468-6735
paulbuch@stmarkhouston.org
**Buchheimer Paul D MS**
Almquist Jane
Arbizu Victoria 3-8
Bacarisse Charlie PS
Baer Penny 4
Birdsong John L BA
Brandenburger Corey J BA K
Brandenburger Melissa J BA 6
Buchheimer Peggy A BA 5
Buie Jane K
Chopp Sylvia BS 2
Cohrs Christine L PS
Cooper Jeffrey N
Davis Betsy
Denkler Elisa BS 1
Eberts Rosanne BSED 1
Ellis Janette PS
Fischer Trina M BSED
Fonville Sandy
Gresham Kathleen
Handrick Heidi Y BA 3
Hudson Jennifer E PS
Kleinert Karl R BA 8
Larsen Melissa E MED 8
Loveless Michelle 1
Mc Glynn Liz PS
Mc Manners Wendy PS
Mierschin Gwen
Mountford Mary J BS
Mueller Eva
Netherton Karen A MSED 6
Neumann Rebecca PS
Page Catherine M BA 2
Schaller Rita M BA K
Schoppe Malynda F 6
Smith Kathleen PS
Stegall Bobette L BED PS
Stueber Lisa BA 3
Stueber Matthew P BARCH 7
Thompson Janice 5
Washburn Linda 5
Weyer Jeff
Whitson Clay 4
Wilke Carolyn M MED 7
Woods Elizabeth J BA 2
ST PHILIP PS-K
• 1978
9745 Bissonnet St 77036-8007
(713)771-4601 •
FAX(713)771-8922
NO REPORT
ST TIMOTHY PS
• 1978
14225 Hargrave Rd 77070-3843
(281)469-2913 •
FAX(281)469-2921
**Jander Martha S MA**
Di Luca Christina L PS
Franks Judy PS
Kelley Karen S
Maldonado Sandra PS
Requenez Christina L PS
TRINITY-MESSIAH PS-8
• 1879
800 Houston Ave 77007-7710
(713)224-7265 •
FAX(713)224-1163
jmay@tmls.org
**Einem Randy H MS**
Boatman Amy G BS 6
Calvin Renee Y PS
Carroll Dana L PS
Chaisson Kimberly A BA
Cook Ethelynn D K
Einem Karen L MS K
Evans Darlene
Inman Willie Mae PS
Lockwood Desha R PS
Mangels Cheryl 8
Palacios Brenda PS
Rabel Donna L BA 5
Schuller Richard L BD
Sentesi Mary L BA 7
Sprengel Charise L BA 1
Stevens Judith A BS 3
Swindler E J
Witt Fredrick W 4
Zoch Eva J BA 2

**HUMBLE**-LITTLE LAMB-LAMB OF GOD PS-K
• 1981
1400 Bypass 1960 E 77338
(281)446-5262 •
FAX(281)446-0289
lllc@lambofgod.net
Baker Denise M BS PS
Berry Peggy D BS
Bowling Jane PS
Callahan Kimberly
Everett Lisa PS
George Belinda PS
Kohler Kerri PS
Lee Cynthia PS
Mitchell Jo Ann BS K
Small Kaye PS
Wright Anita PS

**HUNTSVILLE**-FAITH PS-4
• 1987
111 Sumac Rd 77340-8943
(409)291-1706 •
FAX(409)295-8266
school@lcc.net
Blystone Teresa L 2
Connell Marilyn PS
Conroy Karen M BS K
Freeman Carolyn 1
Hale Augusta L 3-4
Heaton Pam A 2
Johnson Shirley PS
Monteau Karma PS
Register Betty A BS
Vestal Bonnie S K
Winfield Leah PS
Zender Dalene PS

**HURST**-RED APPLE PS-K
• 1966
941 W Bedford Euless Rd 76053-3808
(817)284-7833 •
FAX(817)284-3950
NO REPORT

**KATY**-CROSSPOINT PS
• 2000
700 Westgreen Blvd 77450
(281)398-6464 •
FAX(281)398-6464
ccsir@crosspt.org
NO REPORT

MEMORIAL PS-K
• 1993
1015 Avenue C 5810 3rd St 77493-2425
(281)391-0172 •
FAX(281)391-7579
preschool@mlc.com
Alger Gaye L PS
Bishop Lori R PS
Michalk Cindy K BS PS
Nash Charlotte PS
Newman Karen L BS
Plautz Debra P BSE PS
Plomer Linda F PS
Poese Cheryl AA PS
Walsh Maribeth PS
Woolf Rita K MA K

**KELLER**-MESSIAH PS-K
• 1996
1308 Whitley Rd 76248-0399 PO Box 797 76244
(817)431-6139 •
FAX(817)431-6640
NO REPORT

**KERRVILLE**-HOLY CROSS PS-1
• 1946
210 Spence St 78028-5131
(512)257-6750
NO REPORT

**KILLEEN**-GRACE PS-4
• NLSA • 1979
1007 Bacon Ranch Rd 76542-2799
(254)634-4424 •
FAX(254)634-5474
gracelcmskilleentx@juno.com
**House David A BA**
Burgess Sandra L PS
Clark Dorcas PS
House Karen E BA 1
Hyde Peggy S 4
Matthys Naomi R BSED K
Michalk Terri S BA 3
Schmiege Ann L PS

**KINGWOOD**-KIDS OF THE KINGDOM-CHRIST KING PS
• 1992
3803 W Lake Houston Pkwy 77339-5209
(281)360-7936 •
FAX(281)360-2965
suzannep@christ-the-king
Hughes Sherry M
Mc Euen Paula PS
Palmer Suzanne M
Swallows Carolyn
Tews Camie
Woerner Linda BA PS

**LA GRANGE**-MOUNT CALVARY PS
• 1981
800 N Franklin St 78945-1620
(409)968-5913 •
FAX(409)242-5588
Bragdon Georgette PS
Conway Debbie PS
Dunk Shery L PS
Leer Becky PS
Mersiovsky Carolyn PS
Moerbe Dorothy A MA
Templin Linda PS

**LAKE JACKSON**-ST MARK PS
• 1983
501 Willow Dr 77566-4700 PO Box 858 77566-0858
(409)297-9082
justjac@sat.net
NO REPORT

**LINCOLN**-ST JOHN PS-8
• 1886
RR 1 Box 279 78942-0279
(512)253-6358 •
FAX(512)253-6350
**Mc Clain Mark A MED K**
Beisert Deborah K BA 5-8
Bohm Lisa PS
Bradshaw Maxine A BA 1-4

**LIVINGSTON**-TRINITY PS
• 1978
221 Pan American Dr PO Box 1163 77351-1163
(936)327-8783
Winkelman Sandra PS

**LUBBOCK**-HOPE PS-K
• 1988
5700 98th St 79424-4458
(806)798-3824 •
FAX(806)798-3019
Hope@llano.net
NO REPORT

REDEEMER C A R E PS
• 1999
2221 Avenue W 79411-1023
(806)744-6178 •
FAX(806)744-3889
pdo@rlcms.org
**Loveless Traci**
Lamb Carolyn L BA PS

**MANSFIELD**-ST JOHN PS-K
• 1991
1218 E Debbie Ln 76063-3378
(814)473-0303 •
FAX(814)473-3661
ledmondson@luther95.net
**Edmondson Laura PS**
Acuff Sheila PS
Anderson Kathleen PS
Beltz Pam K
Cole Wendi PS
Fodder Michelle PS
Joyce Jeri PS
Kenney Rhonda PS
Lenz Nannette PS
Maddux Amy PS
Mainer Karen PS
Pride Lori PS-K
Rogers Mary PS
Travis Lisa PS

**MARLIN**-GRACE PS
• 1982
432 Houghton Ave 76661-4399
(254)883-2145
marlinrev@hotl.net
**Drews JoAnn**
Blansit Julie A PS
Feldman Margaret A PS
Lehmann Kathy L PS

**MC ALLEN**-ST PAUL PS-8
• NLSA • 1943
300 W Pecan Blvd 78501-2397
(956)682-2201 •
FAX(956)682-7148
stpaulmca@juno.com
**Trautner Donn W MED**
Arredondo Adelina
Bravo Sandra PS
Cardenas Nora PS
Compoverde Joy K
Corrado Caroline K PS
Davey Carolyn K BS 7
Dehning Mervin W BSED 5
Gallegos Becky PS
Grimsted Ann
Guzman Patty PS
Karle Shirley M PS
Kirchner Peggy J MA 4
Leija Gloria PS
Leveck-Nelia Elva
Lucas Priscilla E MED 2
Malone Amy PS
Moreno Cindy PS
Roberson Laurie 1
Sage Gary
Sage Janice J BA K
Seale Jennifer
Shaver Carolyn A BS 6
Stotler Rebecca D 3
Tooman Matthew M BA 8
Trautner Phyllis G BS
Vega Elizabeth

**MC KINNEY**-OUR SAVIOR PS
• 1992
2708 W Virginia Pkwy 75070-4916
(972)542-4860 •
FAX(972)548-9673
NO REPORT

**MERCEDES**-IMMANUEL PS-K
• 1996
703 W 3Rd St 78570
(956)565-1518
Guzman Virginia PS

**MIDLAND**-GRACE PS
• 1982
3000 W Golf Course Rd 79701-2998
(915)694-3063 •
FAX(915)697-3536
**Nelson Amy**
Bragg Karrie PS
Brewer Nickey PS
Dains Sandy PS
Holder Becky PS
Jones Carissa PS
Kendall Janet PS
Lary Kelly PS
Lindquist Judi
Miranda Anissa PS
Parsley Sandra PS
Pittinger Karen PS
Stark Diane PS
Walsh Patty PS
White Pat PS

**MIDLOTHIAN**-MESSIAH PS-K
• 1996
111 Roundabout Dr 76065-0635
(972)723-1069 •
FAX(972)775-4007
mlcinmid@flash.net
Rempfer Crystal D BA K

**NAVASOTA**-TRINITY PS
• 1997
1530 East Washington 77868
(936)825-9244 •
FAX(936)825-6851
betty@rvctexas.com
Castillo Jessica N PS
Discher Betty J
Duncan Joan BS PS
Harris Patricia K PS
Mc Walters Lisa L PS
Mock Mary G PS

**NEDERLAND**-HOLY CROSS PS
• 1982
2711 Helena Ave 77627-6901
(409)722-2177 •
FAX(409)722-1194
NO REPORT

**NEW BRAUNFELS**-CROSS PS-5
• 1973
169 S Hickory Ave 78130-5821
(830)625-3969 •
FAX(830)625-5019
lutheran@sat.net
**Winkelman Steven R MED 4-5**
Brinkkoeter Dorothy PS
Ergang Marta PS
Fraker Sharon 4-5
Fredrick Marcia PS
Goebel Linda PS
Mc Dowell Carol BA K
Murken Joan 1
Runge Susan C BA 2-3

**PASADENA**-ZION PS-8
• NLSA • 1955
4116 W Pasadena Blvd 77503 PO Box 5665 77508-5665
(281)478-5849 •
FAX(281)478-5843
**Wolf Bernice**
Bradley Albert M BSED 5-6
Bradley Carol J BSED K
Brunig Ruth A BS 3-4
Linkugel Gary L BA 8
Parnell Kevin 7
Sawhill Julia N BS 1-2
Shaffer Jenny PS

**PEARLAND**-EPIPHANY MOTHERS DAY PS
• 1994
5515 W Broadway St 77581-3739
(713)485-7833
NO REPORT

**PLANO**-FAITH PS-8
• NLSA • 1972
1701 E Park Blvd 75074-5123
(972)423-7448 •
FAX(972)423-9618
school@faith.plano.tx.us
**Kieser Stephen W MA**
Audley Nancy L BS PS
Brackney Martha M BS 1
Cumming Brenda L BA 5-6
Germann Kenneth R EDS 4
Geyser Paige W BA 7
Johnson Cathy PS-8
Kirby Jean C 5
Kueck Janice M BSED 1
Marks Connie L BA 6
Merritt Timothy T BA 3
Michel Gloria J PS
Orea Blanca
Reaves Janie PS
Stevens-Verdi Kathryn H 2
Strandt Marlene E BS 2
Vandercook Ardith J BSED K
Vandercook James L BSED 6
Warneke Julie R BA 4
Warneke Kimberly K BS K-8
Wildauer Charles F MS 8
Wildauer Cheryl A MS 3

ST PAUL PS
• 1995
6565 Independence Pkwy
75023-3402
(972)491-5443 •
FAX(972)618-4266
NO REPORT
**RICHARDSON**-MESSIAH LAMBS PS-K
• 1961
1245 W Belt Line Rd 75080-5851
(972)234-8948 •
FAX(972)234-6975
**Nilmeier Joan L BA**
Buchwald Brenda PS
Cole Brooke PS
Davis Amber PS
Germann Helen C BSED PS
Haedge Cathy PS-K
Hanko Pam PS
Huechteman Kimberly PS
Huston Kim PS
La Monte Traci PS
Lisot Lisa PS
Ma Grace PS
Mergent Lianne PS
Myers Amy PS
Potter Becky PS
Rowan Carmen PS
West Rebecca L BA PS
Winningham Gail L MA K
Wolkenstein Barbara PS
**RIESEL**-TRINITY PS
• NLSA • 1996
264 CR 143 76682
(254)896-7105 •
FAX(254)896-7105
0
Dunbar Brenda 4
Gallmeier Kathy E BS 4
Moeller Brenda 4
Rosas Kristi 4
**ROWLETT**-CROWN OF LIFE PS
• 1994
4301 Miller Rd 75088-5811
(972)475-1348 •
FAX(972)412-6686
cindyh@crownoflife-lcms.org
**Hadley Cynthia D BS**
Mac Cormack Margaret
Neidenbach Barbara
Walthall Tonya
**SAN ANGELO**-TRINITY PS-6
• NLSA • 1951
3516 Ymca Dr 76904-7154
(915)947-1275 •
FAX(915)947-1377
**Dunk Carl C MED**
Anderson Bonnie PS
Baden Thomas W MED 5-6
Beal Sharon PS
Black Glinda PS
Chavez Jennifer
Fuessel Susan BA 1
Granning Melissa PS
Jones Christine M BA 4
Keilman Amy R BA K
Keilman Tamara S BA 2
Kelm Lydia BS 3
Kimball Karen PS
King Staci ~ PS
Martin Candace PS
Martinez Genevieve PS
Mc Cullough Tracey L K
Oates Cindy
Philipp Perry K
Rabb Tracy PS
Salazar Hallie PS
Sheridan Lisa PS-6
**SAN ANTONIO**-CONCORDIA PS-8
• NLSA • 1952
16801 Huebner Rd 78258-4456
(210)479-1477 •
FAX(210)479-9416
**Reagan Theresa A BSED 6**
**Rudi Bruce D MA**
Austin Laura 7
Benge Matthew 8
Buffington Linda G BA 7
Burghard Grace L 1
Cahill Cheryl L BA 4
Cahill Robert A Sr. BA
Christian Suzanne M BA 8
Davis Shirley A 6-8
Dykes Joyce L BA K
Entzenberger Kathryn S BED
Firgens Cy 6-8
Gremmer Elizabeth PS
Koops Willis T BS 6-8
Lautner Vickie 1
Moody Wanda E BA 4
Pohl Jane A MLS 2
Quandt Carolyn L BS 5
Reed Margaret A BA PS
Rodgers Clint
Rudi Carol BA 6-8
Rupp Donna C BA
Sachse Mary 3
Sigoloff Deborah 5
Toth Sheri 2
Weiser Rose M BA 3
Wenthe William D Jr. BA 6
Zerby Bethany BA 1
CROWN OF LIFE PS
• 1984
19291 Stone Oak Pkwy
78258-3216
(210)490-9860 •
FAX(210)490-1552
NO REPORT
KING OF KINGS PS
• 1975
13888 Dreamwood Dr 78233-4913
(210)656-6509 •
FAX(210)656-7012
KingLuthECDC@earthlink.net
Baldwin Margaret PS
Beutnagel Shannon M PS
Blakeman Jillian PS
Broadbeck Jennifer PS
Flack Amy PS
Gabrysch Theresa PS
Garcia Irma PS
Giehsler Amanda PS
Jimenez Conception PS
Jimenez Lisa PS
Johnson Sara PS
Kuehn Penny PS
Miller Helen PS
Peterson Debra AA
Strickler Helen PS
Taylor Belinda PS
Wise Linda L
Woefel Mary PS
LITTLE ANGELS PS
• 1998
1826 Basse Rd 78213-4606
(210)773-9444 •
FAX(210)735-3644
mamiller98@yahoo.com
NO REPORT
REDEEMER PS-8
• 1944
2507 Fredericksburg Rd
78201-3711
(210)735-9903 •
FAX(210)735-2868
NO REPORT
SHEPHERD OF THE HILL PS-8
• NLSA • 1979
6914 Wurzbach Rd 78240-3832
(210)614-3741 •
FAX(210)692-7554
school@shlutheran.org
**Eickstead F T MA**
Axtell Virginia D BA 4
Becker Kathryn L BA 5
Bledsoe Linda 3
Diaz Linda K BA K
Eickstead Debbie MA 5
Foley Audrey 2
Forseth Ole J BSED PS-6
Frahm Timothy R BA 7-8
Gary Susan D BA 7-8
Hinojosa Margie PS
Hoyt Shelly D BA 4
Johnson Cindy R 7-8
Larssen Susan S BS 3
Miller Linda E BA K
Mull Lisa R MSED 1
Mycock Carol L BS 1
Olson Kay BA PS-5
Rempfer Crystal D BA 2
Richter Kari B K
Salinas Debbie PS-8
Templeton Ann 7-8
Urban Douglas R BA 7-8
Wallis Diane D MA PS
ST PAUL PS
• 1913
2302 S Presa St 78210-2840
(210)534-8577 •
FAX(210)534-2998
Allen Michelle PS
Alvarez-Llamas Maricela PS
Ambros Camilla PS
Barrera Tina
Barrientos Carol PS
Betancourt Frances PS
Cardenas Lydia PS
Casas Raquel PS
Cazares Linda PS
Contreras Dora PS
Cortez Maria PS
Erfurth Christina PS
Escobedo Elizabeth PS
Escobedo Richard PS
Foster Linda PS
Gonzales Jeannette PS
Herrera Stella PS
Hidalgo Betty J PS
Idrogo Victoria PS
Jimenez Mary J PS
Leonard Sheila PS
Longley Jody PS
Lutzenberger Elsie PS
Ramos Mary A PS
Reyes Mary L PS
Sanchez Yvonne PS
Stephenson Deborah
Torres Elena PS
**SEALY**-TRINITY PS
• 1992
402 Atchison St 77474-2702
(409)885-2211
NO REPORT
**SEGUIN**-GRACE PS
• 1979
935 E Mountain St 78155-5010
(830)372-0641 •
FAX(830)379-1690
lamsfussfk@ev1.com
**Lamsfuss Kristen MED PS**
Alverez Celia PS
Armstrong Stacy PS
Braune Elaine PS
Druckammer Rachel PS
Flores Audra PS
Hall Judy PS
Hanna Ruth PS
Harrison Patricia PS
Johnson Shannon PS
Leos Monica PS
Linebarger Clara PS
Mc Whorter Juanita PS
Parker Wanda PS
Rucker Geraldine PS
Salyer Camille PS
Sands Diana PS
Toellner Fayette PS
**SERBIN**-ST PAUL PS-8
• NLSA • 1854
RR 2 Box 154 78942-9769
(409)366-2218 •
FAX(409)366-2200
bachmus@cvtv.net
**Hohle Raymond L MED**
Droegemueller Kim M BA 7-8
Krause Pamela S BS K
Mertink Rachel A 1-4
Telschow Jonathan P BSED 5-6
Zoch Anita M MA 1-2
**SMITHVILLE**-GRACE PS
• 1992
309 Wilkes 78957-1617
(512)237-4700 •
FAX(512)242-5588
Moerbe Dorothy A MA
Oetting Tara PS
**SPRING**-RESURRECTION PS
• 1975
1612 Meadow Edge Ln
77388-6227
(281)353-4413 •
FAX(281)353-1642
Hallowell Robin L PS
Keltner Mona G PS
Paulson Deborah L BS
TRINITY PS-8
• NLSA • 1874
18926 Klein Church Rd
77379-4999
(281)376-5810 •
FAX(281)251-7021
tlseagle@flash.net
**Wilson James R MED**
Alyea-Brooks Elizabeth F
Barbee Elaine BA 1
Bielefeldt Angie K BSED 3
Brandenburg Jeanne E MA K
Brennan Stephen M BS 1-8
Brugman Janet L 5
Burdick Brenda R BA
Canez Joan M MED 4
Church Susan K
Cooper Carolyn M MA 2
Deutsch Cathlyn M BS 2
Eisenbraun Joel A BS 5
Frerking Nathan D BS 7-8
Fritsche Sharon PS
Goedecke Keith D BA
Goedecke Stephanie K
Griedl Mary S MA PS
Hampton Sandra E BA 6-8
Huwyler Sue 1
Kelley Linda S PS
Kunkel Gail BSED 5-7
Miller Susan PS
Mueller David J 1-8
Mueller Donna K 3
Petersen Marilyn A BA 4
Poore Kelly BS 6-7
Roach Dawn BA PS
Teichmiller Kathy BS K
**SUGAR LAND**-FAITH PS-8
• 1975
800 Brooks St 77478-3816
(281)242-4453 •
FAX(281)242-8749
Bill@flcsl.org
**Kulow William S MED K-8**
Aikins Tamara 2
Bass Elwyn S MA 6-8
Benckenstein Sandra BA 6-8
Cheeseborough Gladys PS-8
Dye Kimberly G 1
Evert Catherine L BED 5
Findlay Cathy 1
Fowler Cheryl K-3
Franks Karen PS
Gardner Rachelle BS 4
Gehrke Rhonda PS
Goodier Ronda 4
Henkel Maria BS 6-8
Karavellas Ioanna PS
Kulow Mary AA PS
Lacy Kim K
Mc Dowell Delamion 1-8
Mortel Yanick PS
Neal Bonnie PS
Nowland Patricia 2
Pilcher Elizabeth M BS
Sokol Jan PS
Sokol Karen PS
Suliman Mona PS
Terwilliger Diane BS K-7
Thames Frances E 3
Thanos Nia BA K

Thomas Elizabeth S BA
Weesner Helen PS
Wells Jennifer BS K
Wendler Carol 3
Winters Bert K-8
FISHERS OF MEN PS
• 1996
2011 Austin Pkwy 77479-1254
(281)265-5656 •
FAX(281)242-2164
terry@fishersofmen.org
Albrecht Mary L PS
Brindley Patricia PS
Jones Elaine PS
Lambert Lisa L PS
Lynch Lydia PS
Picard Linda L PS
Reeley Toni L
Snider Leslie R PS
Till Terry A
**TAYLOR-**TRINITY PS
PO Box 72 76574
(512)352-6728
Boi749@aol.com
NO REPORT
**TEMPLE-**IMMANUEL PS-8
• NLSA • 1978
2109 W Avenue H 76504-5216
(254)773-9485 •
FAX(254)773-2844
**Skilton Jon C MED**
Buchhorn Robin 1-3
Buser Shirley BSED 1-3
Dake-Mendez Andrea PS
Lewis Heather PS
Lewis Mona PS
Loa Jodi 3-4
Michalk Susan 5-6
Raabe Tammy PS
Salinas Barbara PS
Self Vance K
**THE WOODLANDS-**LITTLE GOSPEL LIGHT- PS
• 1998
9500 N Panther Creek Dr 77381
(281)363-4860 •
FAX(281)363-3447
gina@lwlc.org
Chesnutt Mickey J PS
Ritze Sharon R BSED PS
Wengel John R BA
**THORNDALE-**ST PAUL PS-8
• 1890
101 N 3rd St 76577 PO Box 369 76577-0369
(512)898-2711 •
FAX(512)898-5298
splcthorndale@hotmail.com
Brymer Kelly A PS
Buchhorn Alice L BA 5-8
Fischer Kristi L 1-2
Mann Evelyn R K
Melcher Cynthia A BS 5-6
Morton Catherine G 3-4
Ryan Richard D MEDADM 7-8
Schneider Eileen C
**TOMBALL-**SALEM PS-8
• NLSA • 1870
22607 Lutheran Church Rd 77375-3716
(281)351-8122 •
FAX(281)351-8190
salemschool@salem4u.com
**Gaertner Mary Beth MED**
Albe Cheryl PS
Bennett Chris 6
Berger Yvonne F AA PS
Berry Linda PS
Callihan Juanita L BA 3
De Wulf Marilyn
Fehrle Adeline PS
Guggenmous Leanna
Hall Tammy PS
Helmich Sheri
Karisch Kristin 7-8
Kokel Joyce L MED 1
Kretzmann Jennifer PS
Love Carolyn PS
Miller Pauline R MRE 4
Miller Perry M BA 8
Mueller Tawana PS
Nisayas Elly 5
Paluch Karen BA
Pieper Mary 2
Rodriguez Carrie PS
Saalfeld Larry D MED 8
Saalfeld Vicki BS
Schaekel Bert D BS 6
Schaekel Joan E BA
Schlechte Alaine R BSED K
Schlichting Betsy
Schlichting Kevin R BS 3
Schneider Margaret BSED 2
Schultz Viola PS
Shaffer Jennifer L BA 4
Snow Michele R BA K
Stalinsky Laura 6
Warman Debra PS
Wasmund Connie PS
Willeford Joyce PS
ZION PS-2
• 1991
907 Hicks St 77375-4125
(713)255-6203 •
FAX(713)255-8696
NO REPORT
**TYLER-**TRINITY PS-K
• 1951
2001 Hunter St 75701-4828
(903)593-7465 •
FAX(903)593-7664
NO REPORT
**UVALDE-**TRINITY PS
768 N Getty St 78801-4302
(512)278-5341
Jett Patricia PS
**VERNON-**ST PAUL PS-K
• 1912
4405 Hospital Dr 76384-4022
(940)552-6651 •
FAX(940)552-6651
**Schur Cristi**
Carr Patti K
Gfeller Melissa PS
Kieschnick Debbie PS
Koch Sherri PS
Walker Pam PS
**WACO-**TRINITY PS-8
• NLSA • 1953
6125 Bosque Blvd 76710-4170
(254)772-7840 •
FAX(254)772-2576
dbliss@prodigy.net
Bliss David A MA 5-8
Bliss Marcia E 3
Netherland Linda 5-6
Reeves Jennifer PS
Smith Diane 7-8
Sohns Julia A BA K
Webster Lois 4
**WALBURG-**ZION PS-8
• NLSA • 1882
6101 FM 1105 78626-9792
(512)863-5345 •
FAX(512)869-5659
zion@texasnet.com
**Braun Suzanne L MSED**
Capdeville Roy M MED 4
Faris Paula BSED K
Fischer Sheri L BS 1
Grady Leslie D BA PS
Hamre Scott H BA 6
Hight Pamela J BS 1
Menke Steven A MA 8
Mersiovsky Jean M BA 3
Meyer Janet C BS 2
Pitts Katheryn L MA K
Van Andel Judith E MA 5
**WICHITA FALLS-**SONSHINE STATION-OUR REDEEMER PS
• 1991
4605 Cypress Ave 76310-2540
(940)692-3690 •
FAX(940)692-0382
orlc@wf.net
Baldys Lisa K-6
Davis Jolene PS
Fuhrman Gretchen C
Garrett Brenda K
Lindsey Tommie J PS
Peterson Beth A PS
Roy Janice PS
Spence Phyllis PS
Wirmel Beckie PS
Yates Connie L

## UTAH

**BOUNTIFUL-**CROSS OF CHRIST PS
• 1997
1840 S 75 E 84010
(801)397-0765
Call Janelle PS
Hansen Sue PS
Larm Candice PS
Long Claudia PS
Nisbet Liz PS
Weiss Alyssa PS
**LAYTON-**TLC-TRINITY PS-K
• 1979
385 W Golden Ave 84041-2312
(801)544-5770
Mc Donough Diane L MA PS-K
Schafer Cynthia BA PS
**MURRAY-**CHRIST PS-8
• 1955
240 E 5600 S 84107-6113
(801)266-8714 •
FAX(801)266-8799
cls@inconnect.com
**Robson Wendell L MED**
Losser Lori K BSED 2
Robson Dawn M BA K
Topp David BA 3
**OGDEN-**ST PAUL PS-8
• 1945
3329 Harrison Blvd 84403-4228
(801)392-2912 •
FAX(801)392-7562
**Eggert Christine**
Coleman Ralph
Lechman Peggy 4
Luther Nikki BS 6
Miller Julia A BA K
Miller Terry W 5
Ritter Shannon N BA 1
Rizvi Pat A PS
Stuart Paula L BA 3
Trickey Sharon K BSED 2
Xavier Cheri 7-8
**SALT LAKE CITY-**REDEEMER K-8
• NLSA • 1961
1955 Stratford Ave 84106-4151
(801)487-6283 •
FAX(801)463-7904
admin@redeemer-slc.org
**Brockmeier Russel L BSED 6**
Angell Paul M MSED
Cochran Krystal R 5
Einspahr Donna M BA 1-3
Fischer Cathy S BS K
Henkes Michael MA 7
Knapp Jeffery W 8
Losser Lori K BSED 2
Patterson Robin
Robinson Jean BLA
Schroeder Nancy E MA 4
Shinno Shari L BA 1
Steinburg Susan J BA 2
ST JOHN PS
• 1997
475 Herbert Ave 84111
(801)364-4874
lisaobrien@juno.com
NO REPORT
**SANDY-**GRACE PS-8
• 1984
1815 E 9800 S 84092-3856
(801)572-3793 •
FAX(801)553-2403
school@glcs-lcms.org
**Fangmann Dennis D MSED**
Bellini Angela K PS
Brockmeier Joyce L BSED 3
Dueck-Stueber Denise A 4
Eick Petra M 7-8
Fjeldsted Kristeen K 1
Ganchero Roselle 7
Glanzer Anita J BS 2
Glanzer John H BS 8
Glanzer Stephanie E BSED 5
Johnson Phil 4-8
Marlatt Kristine M MA 1-8
Neward Donna R BA 6
Wolff Patricia K BSED K
**ST GEORGE-**TRINITY K-6
• 1993
2260 Red Cliff 84790-8153
(435)628-6115
trinityl@infowest.com
**Nyen Duane M BS 5-6**
Meyer Paula S BA K
Schubert Laura 3-4
Zehendner Cherie BA 1-2

## VERMONT

**SOUTH BURLINGTON-**COMMUNITY PS
1560 Williston Rd 05403-6425
NO REPORT

## VIRGINIA

**ALEXANDRIA-**BETHANY PS
• 1959
2501 Beacon Hill Rd 22306-1699
(703)765-8687
preschool@bethany-lcms.org
NO REPORT
IMMANUEL K-8
• 1945
109 Bellaire Rd 22301-1931
(703)549-7323 •
FAX(703)549-7323
Ashby Vicki L K-8
Claxton Celinda M MA 4-8
Garrett Amy D 2
Graham Leslie J 4-8
Hiener Terry 4-8
Humphreys Deborah K-8
Kerrigan Jocelyne K-8
Pauling Frederick J BSED 3
Plinski Tonya K-8
Rudder Alaise K
Seret James 4-8
Walker Adrianne K-8
Zensinger Margaret W 1
**ARLINGTON-**OUR SAVIOR K-8
• 1953
825 S Taylor St 22204-1461
(703)892-4846 •
FAX(703)892-4847
Battaglia S J BA 2
Bolt Rachel K BA 1
Donlon Lynee M BA 6
Drews Natalie L BA K
Fischer Catherine J 8
Fischer Charles E MA
Hambridge Deborah R MA 2
Hambridge Les BA 5
Klug Joshua A BA 7
Klug Sarah L BA 3
Moody Jennifer C BA 4

**ASHBURN**-OPEN ARMS-OUR SAVIORS WAY PS
• 1999
43115 Waxpool Rd 20147-2317
(703)729-9144 •
FAX(703)729-9149
oswlc@aol.com
**Schneider Lori A BA PS**
Bailey Christina PS
Basir Mandana PS
Benteler Monica PS
Boisot-Ebert Aimee PS
Clair Anne PS
Harris Stacey PS
Harrison Charles A PS
Lauffer Mary PS
Le Favour Sheryl A PS
Stewardson Amy PS

**BON AIR**-REDEEMER PS
• NLSA • 1971
9400 Redbridge Rd 23236-3598
(804)272-7824 •
FAX(804)272-6310
Bailey Kathyrn PS
Bakken Kathleen PS
Hughes Kathleen BA PS
Jones Linda BA
Mc Lamb Kristeen PS
Oglesby Rixie Z BS PS
Stiles Gale PS

**DANVILLE**-CHRIST THE KING PS-K
• 1978
1172 Franklin Tpke 24540-1328
(804)836-6888
NO REPORT

**EMPORIA**-ST JOHN PS
• 1998
1351 W Atlantic St 23847
(804)634-0532 •
FAX(804)634-4515
**Phillips Joy P PS**

**FAIRFAX STATION**-LIVING SAVIOR PS-K
• 1991
5500 Ox Rd 22039-1020
(703)352-4208 •
FAX(703)352-1421
preschooldirector@livsavluthch
Baird Carolann K
Deibert Debbie PS
Frommelt Geri PS
Gross Kathy PS
Huss Chelly PS
Luukkonen Cindy PS
Mc Nally Gwen PS
Peterson Marcie
Trieber Julia
Williams Micki PS

**FALLS CHURCH**-ST PAUL PS
• 1994
7426 Idylwood Rd 22043-2915
(703)573-0494 •
FAX(703)573-3273
NO REPORT

**FRANCONIA**-ST JOHN PS
• 1983
5952 Franconia Rd 22310-1736
(703)971-3581
Aubuchon Gina PS
Bocchicchio Judith PS
Galarza Patricia PS
Guerra Maritza
Minner Patricia PS
Salguero Francia PS

**FREDERICKSBURG**-REDEEMER PS
• 1994
5120 Harrison Rd 22408-1803
(540)898-4748 •
FAX(540)891-9106
rlclcms@erols.com
NO REPORT

**HALLWOOD**--ST PAUL ON THE SHORE PS
• 1984
28281 Main St 23359-2624
(804)824-3500
stpauls@intercom.net
NO REPORT

**HAMPTON**-EMMANUEL PS-8
• 1947
23 Semple Farm Rd 23666-1456
(757)865-7800 •
FAX(757)865-2853
elc-school@mindspring.com
**Matern John H MSED 7-8**
**Napier Dawn L MED**
Baugham Carol E BA 1-2
Busher Mary A 3-4
Euker Wendy PS
Fisher Kathryn A BED K
Hughes Karen L BSED PS
Matern Carol 7-8
Sharp Margaret PS
Weinaug Mary PS
Yarrington Sheri 5-6

**KING GEORGE**-PEACE PS
• 1975
10365 Luther Lane PO Box 298
22485-0298
(540)775-7529 •
FAX(540)775-9131
peacekgva@luther95.net
Giorgis Karen L PS
Harder Jayne A PS

**NORFOLK**-TRINITY PS-5
• 1945
6001 Granby St 23505-4816
(757)489-2732 •
FAX(757)489-8413
tlsnorfolk@aol.com
Bradley Johanna M BS 4
Cordner Edith K
Dinini Ivana BSED 2
Gillooly Bobbie
Goldman Traci
Hales Melissa PS
Hughes Jo Ann PS
Miller Jane 1
Morgan Martha
Myers Pam 3
O Connor Karen
Pendry Brenda
Shoemaker Etta 5
Sykes Judy BA PS

**RESTON**-GOOD SHEPHERD PS
• 1981
1516 Moorings Dr 20190-4299
(703)437-4511 •
FAX(703)689-4803
NO REPORT

**RICHMOND**-LUTHER MEMORIAL PS-8
• NLSA • 1856
1301 Robin Hood Rd 23227-4742
(804)321-6420 •
FAX(804)321-2884
**Hubbard Christa M MA**
Barnes Beale Shelly 1
Berlin Dave M 6-8
Cannon Michael
Enright Betty MLS
Gray Mary PS
Hamlin Ann K
Hildebrand Carolyn BS 6-7
Kelly Eric
Lancaster Lisa BSED 2
Link Debbie 2
Miller Cida D MA PS
Muller Kathy 4
Oliver David W MA 7
Olson Karen 3
Patterson Sylvia PS
Peay Evan 5-8
Perdue Vanessa PS
Ronning Kay K
Scott Pat MA
Skeen Sylvia PS
Swift Marie PS

TRINITY PS
• 1995
2315 N Parham Rd 23229-3163
(804)270-5042
Carter Sherry PS
Dessart Patricia PS
Dowdy Cheryl PS
Flowe Nancy PS
Smith Lorraine PS

**ROANOKE**-GOOD SHEPHERD PS
• 1986
1887 Electric Rd 24018-1618
(703)774-8746
Andrews Michelle
Cooper Joy 1
Hamilton Carsonette 1
Hartness Connie 6
Peterson Katey 2
Secrist Diana 8
Snider Libby 4
Thomas Kathy 11

**SPRINGFIELD**-PRINCE OF PEACE PS-K
• NLSA • 1969
8304 Old Keene Mill Rd
22152-1640
(703)451-6177 •
FAX(703)569-0978
cina.deaton@poplc.org
NO REPORT

**VIRGINIA BEACH**-HOPE PS-K
• 1987
5350 Providence Rd 23464-4100
(757) 424-4894 •
FAX757-424-7626
**Powell Carolyn W**
Gusewelle Wanda S PS
Monacelli Barbara W K
Smith Penny T PS
Stein Carol K PS

PRINCE OF PEACE PS
• 1970
424 Kings Grant Rd 23452-6921
(757)340-3033 •
FAX(757)340-8421
noisygiant@juno.com
NO REPORT

**WAYNESBORO**-BETHANY PS
• 1878
100 Maple Ave 22980-4607
(540)941-8853
**Teachey Beth D**
Almarode Sue PS
Cooke Joyce PS
Kelley Karen Sue PS
Mowen Karen B PS
Phillips Donna PS
Upton Linda L PS

**WILLIAMSBURG**-KING OF GLORY PS
• 1999
4897 Longhill Rd 23188-1572
(757)258-1070 •
FAX(757)564-9810
klutheran@aol.com
**Wheatall Jane PS**
Olver Judy PS

## WASHINGTON

**ABERDEEN**-CALVARY PS
• 1983
2515 Sumner Ave 98520-4316 PO Box 1957 98520-0324
(360)532-3980 •
FAX(360)532-2596
calvary@techline.com
NO REPORT

**AUBURN**-ZION PS
• 1995
1305 17th St SE 98002-6934
(253)833-5940
NO REPORT

**BATTLE GROUND**-PRINCE OF PEACE PS
• 1990
14208 NE 249th St 98604-9772
(360)687-7455
**Tuchardt Caroline PS**
Gomulkiewicz Sheri PS

**BELLEVUE**-PILGRIM PS
• 1992
10420 SE 11th St 98004-6852
(425)454-4790 •
FAX(425)637-7016
Beroakas Chris PS
Brumberg Lois PS
De Chant Paula PS
Fleming Cindy A MA PS
Gable Kathleen A BS
Hoffman Debbie PS
Jaech Renata A BA PS
Mc Taggart Nancy PS
Neel Maxine PS
Smallbeck Rachel PS
Uchikara Ritsuko PS
Wyneken Margaret PS

**BELLINGHAM**-REDEEMER PS
• 1978
858 W Smith Rd 98226-9613
(360)384-5923 •
FAX(360)380-3378
NO REPORT

TRINITY PS
• 1970
119 Texas St 98225-3725
(206)734-2770
White Lorna J BED PS

**BONNEY LAKE**-OUR REDEEMER PS
• 1990
12407 214th Ave E 98390-7630
PO Box 7127 98390-0903
(253)862-0715 •
FAX(253)862-0715
Morris Cynthia A AAS

**BREMERTON**-MEMORIAL PS
• 1988
916 Veneta Ave 98337-1341
(360)377-0161 •
FAX(360)373-5249
Rolfe Lois E MA
Stockwell Deborah L PS

PEACE PS-8
• 1980
1234 NE Riddell Rd 98310-3637
(360)373-2116 •
FAX(360)377-0686
**Wahlers Joel D MED**
Board Beth PS
Flewell Pam PS
Gierke Terri 1-2
Gihring Barbara J MEAD 3
Joslin Francey
Juszczak Sherilyn D BED
Kruzan Drienne K
Kubert Julie PS
Mc Auley Virginia M MED 7-8
Schadt Daren E MED K
Sparling Kathy 1
Wahlers Dawn N MA
Wayne Marie 4

**CHEHALIS**-PEACE PS
• 1995
2071 Bishop Rd 98532
(360)748-4108
NO REPORT

**CROSS**-SUNBEAMS-OF THE CROSS PS-K
• 1978
23810 112th Ave SE 98031-3545
(253)854-3240 •
FAX(253)854-2721
lutheran_cross@hotmail.com
NO REPORT

**DEER PARK**--FAITH PS-K
• 1986
214 S Weber Rd PO Box 1428
99006-1428
(509)276-5268
NO REPORT
**EDMONDS**-ST TIMOTHY PS
• 1981
5124 164th St SW 98026-4833
(425)741-8723 •
FAX(425)745-4744
ruthannd@GTE.net
Danielson Ruth A BA
Kellogg Paula AAS PS
Olson Carol
**EPHRATA**-OUR SAVIOR PS
• 1995
500 D St SE 98823-2242
(509)754-3468
NO REPORT
**EVERETT**-ZION PS-8
• 1901
0 98205 3923 103rd Ave SE
98205-3103
(425)334-5064 •
FAX(425)334-4106
jrlzls@juno.com
**Lynch James R BS**
Castens Jennifer D BA 6
Glassett Trudy A BS 2
Hereth Lynne A MED 7-8
Konkel Ronda 1-2
Laskey Debbie BED 1
Lucas Mark C MS 3
Lynch Joyce M PS
May Sharon L BA 5
Novak Jan A BA 7-8
Novak Mari-Jane G BA 4
Pickerill Lori A BA K
Soukup Ellen PS-8
Yocum Laurie L 3-4
**FEDERAL WAY**-LIGHT OF CHRIST PS
• 1992
2400 SW 344th St 98023-3032
(206)874-2517
NO REPORT
ST LUKE PS-K
• 1968
515 S 312th St 98003-4033
(253)839-0172 •
FAX(253)941-3994
Conklin Dodie PS
Cook Karen K-2
Esslinger Carin K
Grothe Janice BA PS
Harrison Suzanne PS
Martinez Joy
Morley Jennifer PS
Ollila Mitzie J BA
Stam Jennifer PS
Wilson Teresa PS
**GEORGE**-CHRIST THE SAVIOR PS
• 1983
214 Deacon PO Box 5325
98824-0325
(509)785-4350
NO REPORT
**KENMORE**-ARROWHEAD INGLEMOOR-EPIPHANY PS
• 1986
16450 Juanita Dr NE 98028
(425)488-9800
epiphany@tement.com
NO REPORT
**KENNEWICK**-BETHLEHEM K-8
• 1911
1409 S Garfield St 99337-4766
(509)582-5624 •
FAX(509)586-6702
bls-office@worldnet.att.net
**Schuldheisz Daniel L MAD**
**Schuldheisz Jan R BSED K**
Anfinson Beth J BS K-8
Blank Jonathan H MED 5
Bobiles Pamela 3
Courtney Angela N MA 6
Rafferty Brian C MED 7
Schuldheisz Brooke L 1
Schwisow Deborah BA PS
Spahr Nancy 8
Stiles Pamela J 4
Stout Jone K BED 2
**KENT**-PEACE PS
• 1992
18615 SE 272nd St 98042-5484
(206)631-5876
Gehr Brenda PS
Poppie Tracy
Thom Diane PS
**LACEY**-FAITH PS-6
• 1971
7075 Pacific Ave SE 98503-1473
(360)491-1733 •
FAX(360)459-3784
eaglesoffaith@yahoo.com
**Timmerman Floy A MA**
Avery Sharon PS
Costi Sandra PS
Holmquist Erin R BA K
Klumb Deborah L MED 2
Koehler Marie BED PS
Kolumban Robin L MED 1
Suelzle Amy BA 3-5
**MALTBY**-SHEPHERD OF THE HILL PS
• 1986
9225 212th St SE 98296-7164
(360)668-7881 •
FAX(425)485-8171
shephill@wwdb.org
Storck Rhoda T MED PS
**MARYSVILLE**-MESSIAH PS
• 1979
9209 State Ave 98270-2214
(360)659-4112 •
FAX(360)659-4112
NO REPORT
**MILTON**-BEAUTIFUL SAVIOR PS
• 1980
2306 Milton Way 98354-9311 PO Box 1326 98354-1326
(253)922-6977
Frost Angel D
Hohnstein Vivian J PS
Larsen Sheila A PS
Pelissier Jennifer
Shula Michelle K BA
Wells Mary R
**MONROE**-LITTLE DOVES-PEACE PS-K
• 1986
202 Dickinson St 98272-2127
(360)794-7230
Bowen Carol L BA PS-K
Frieson Cheryl PS
Griswold Jennie PS
Herman Linda MA PS
Mc Grath Kay PS
Wirt Jennifer PS
**MOUNTLAKE TERRACE**-MT ZION PS
• 1976
21428 44th Ave W 98043-3509
(425)778-3577
NO REPORT
**OAK HARBOR**-LITTLE LAMBS-CONCORDIA PS
• 1979
590 N Oak Harbor St 98277-2104
(360)679-1697
NO REPORT
**PORT ANGELES**-ST MATTHEW PS
• 1983
132 E 13th St 98362-7818
(360)457-4122 •
FAX(360)457-2836
**Meier Maureen E BA PS**
**PROSSER**-MESSIAH PS
• 1993
801 Luther Ln PO Box 1168
99350-1549
(509)786-5922
messiah@bentonrea.com
Parker Vicky PS
**PURDY**-KING OF GLORY PS
• 1979
6411 154th St NW 98332-9016
(253)857-4574
Peterson Sandra PS
**PUYALLUP**-IMMANUEL PS
• 1995
720 W Main Ave 98371-5320
(253)848-4548 •
FAX(253)848-3147
NO REPORT
**RENTON**-BETHLEHEM PS
• 1978
1024 Monroe Ave NE 98056-3424
(206)255-9772
NO REPORT
KING OF KINGS PS-K
• 1986
18207 108th Ave SE 98055-6440
(206)255-8520 •
FAX(206)226-4119
NO REPORT
**SEABECK**-EVERGREEN PS
• 1995
PO Box 740 98380-0740
(360)830-4180
NO REPORT
**SEATTLE**-AMAZING GRACE PS-4
• 1999
10056 Renton Ave S 98178-2255
(206)723-5526 •
FAX(425)226-4089
davpauzim@msn.com
Alston Norman 4
Cacabelos Beverly PS
Gould Corey 2-4
Munson Amy PS
Nobis Pam PS-4
Quam Karen BA 1
Zimmerman David-Paul DMIN
Zimmerman Gloria N BA
Zimmerman Michelle K
BEAUTIFUL SAVIOR PS
• 1993
16919 33rd Ave S 98188-3134
(206)246-9533 •
FAX(206)246-9534
NO REPORT
CONCORDIA PS-8
• RSO • 1905
7040 36th Ave NE 98115-5966
(206)525-7407 •
FAX(206)525-2062
email@concordia.seattle.wa.us
**Norton Kenneth J MED**
Baricevic Julie I BA PS
De Pano Lydia PS
Deaver Sarah G BSED K
Hughes Julie PS
Hylton Holly L 3
Jennings Jennifer L BA 4
Jennings Matthew H BA 6
Johnson Helga MAT K-8
Newton Roselyn 6-8
Oka Christina J BA 6-8
Peek Mary L BED 5
Schatz Lois M BARCH 1
Stoddard Sylvia PS
Tiefel Amy D BS PS
Viets Deborah R BS 2
Voss Karen L BS 6-8
HOPE PS-8
• 1959
4446 42nd Ave SW 98116-4223
(206)935-8500 •
FAX(206)937-9332
Ludke Alison BA 6
OUR SAVIOR PS
• 1985
12509 27th Ave NE 98125-4309
(206)486-4653
NO REPORT
**SEQUIM**-FAITH PS
• 1994
354 W Cedar St PO Box 925
98382-0925
(206)683-4803
NO REPORT
**SHELTON**-MOUNT OLIVE PS
• 1996
206 E Wyandotte Ave 98584
(360)427-3165
**Dohring Margarete MED PS-K**
Drake Anita PS
Drake Tanya M PS
Fish Eve M BED PS-K
Jones Nichole PS
Kasperski Lisa PS
Macero Dotty PS-K
Price Jeanette PS-6
Rex Tammy PS
Robinson Brian 1-6
Weeth Sherry L PS-K
**SPOKANE**-BEAUTIFUL SAVIOR PS
• 1970
43205 S Conklin St 99203-6237
(509)747-6806 •
FAX(509)747-7342
NO REPORT
REDEEMER PS
• 1965
3606 S Schafer Rd 99206-9518
(509)926-6363 •
FAX(509)926-4573
NO REPORT
SON SHINE-HOLY CROSS PS
• 1991
7307 N Nevada St 99208-5516
(509)483-4218
Kunkel Janette PS
SPOKANE PS-8
• RSO • NLSA • 1902
1888 N Wright Dr 99224-5273
(509)327-4441 •
FAX(509)327-4441
**Swanson Joan E BS 7-8**
Erickson Mary E 4
Johnson Michelle M BAED K
Mahan Cynthia L BS 2-3
Nielson Vivian
Person Kathleen A 5-6
Vedder La Wynna PS
Walz Robert A BSED 1
**SUNNYSIDE**-CALVARY PS-K
• 1979
804 S 11th St PO Box 507
98944-0507
(509)837-6771 •
FAX(509)837-6771
Gant Rebecca A PS
Rippy Karolyn K MA
**TACOMA**-CONCORDIA PS-8
• RSO • NLSA • 1939
202 E 56th St 98404-1236
(253)475-9513 •
FAX(253)475-5445
mpb453@integrityol.com
**Bethke Paul H MAT**
**Dybwad David B MED 8**
Acuna Sue BA 6
Bethke Karen E MED 1
Brown Marcus V 4
Buettner Richard E MA 5
Dressler Ardyce M 1
Dressler Derwin J 3
Dybwad Linda E BS PS
Ehli Randi M K
Gibelyou Sherrie L MA K-8
Hagen M A MED 8
Hagen Stephanie R MED 3
Harman Anthony C MED 7
Koch Margene A MA 5
Kuhlmann Jean L BA 2
Mindemann Nancy K BSED 2

Nelson Kristine BED K
Pariseau Stephanie R BA 3
Qunell Jeanne A
Reis Kimberly L BA 7
Schlatter Tracy S
Schmidt Connie R
Sievert Kathleen R 4
Winters Robert M
OUR SAVIOR PS
• 1972
4519 112th St E 98446-5229
(206)531-2112 •
FAX(206)531-2997
info@oslc.com
**Mc Dowell Peggy PS**
Anderson Judy PS
**VANCOUVER**-GRACE PS
• 1984
9900 E Mill Plain Blvd 98664-3966
(360)254-0663 •
FAX(360)256-1326
gracech@pacifier.com
NO REPORT
MEMORIAL PS
• 1972
2700 E 28th St 98661-4528
(360)693-6054 •
FAX(360)993-2797
Cook Debra J PS
Donald Trina PS
Epperson Vicky L
Lawson Anna Marie PS
Minor Nancy PS
ST JOHN PS
• 1979
11005 NE Highway 99 98686-5620
(360)574-4900
NO REPORT
**WALLA WALLA**-TRINITY PS
• 1982
109 S Roosevelt St 99362-2432
(509)527-0846
**Hamilton Ruth PS**
Farnsworth Rhonda PS
Pickett Kara PS
**WENATCHEE**-ST PAUL PS-5
• 1978
312 Palouse 98801-2641 PO Box 2219 98807-2219
(509)662-3659 •
FAX(509)662-5274
**Bergman Paul R BA**
Adair Carla PS-5
Bergman Ann M MED PS
Bertermann Rena BA 1
Black Patricia A 3
Borrelli Therese 1-5
Brown Karen A PS
Colpitts Phyllis K
DeLozier Jackie L PS
Krumdieck Gary A BA 2-3
Leslie Judith E 2
Matheson Carol J BSED 5
North Susan L MA K
Scharr Kathy BSED K
Shrable Janet L AA PS
Yeager Susan M 4
**YAKIMA**-MOUNT OLIVE PS
• 1992
7809 Tieton Dr 98908-1543
(509)966-2190
Losek Janet PS
Waits Marilyn K PS

## WEST VIRGINIA

**HUNTINGTON**-OUR REDEEMER PS
• 1984
3043 Washington Blvd 25705-1632
(304)529-7365
Barthel Cathy L BA PS
**PARKERSBURG**-ST PAUL PS
• 1971
3500 Broad St 26104-2118
(304)428-5826
NO REPORT

## WISCONSIN

**ABBOTSFORD**-CLC-CHRIST PS
• 1997
308 W Linden St 54405-0489 PO Box 489 54405
(715)223-1445 •
FAX(715)223-8183
Chenier Heather J PS
Firnstahl Mary M PS
Graham Colleen M PS
Kalepp Katie L PS
**ADELL**-EMMANUEL PS
• 1999
320 Center Ave #88 53001
(920)994-4609
**Anger Ellen M BA PS**
Laganowski Susan PS
Schallock Barbara BS PS-6
Timm De Ann PS
**ALTOONA**-LITTLE STAR-BETHLEHEM PS
• 1993
2245 Hayden Ave 54720-1548
(715)832-9953 •
FAX(715)832-6761
bethch@execpc.com
NO REPORT
**AMHERST**-ST PAUL PS
• 1993
203 Grant St 54406-9042
(715)824-3314
stpauls@wi-net.com
Frizzell Ioa
Jensen Barb PS
Kropidlowski Sarah A
**ANTIGO**-PEACE PS-8
• NLSA • 1888
300 Lincoln St 54409-1346
(715)623-2209 •
FAX(715)627-4117
Breutzmann Paula J BA 1
Brown Aimee C BA 7
Harger Steven K BA 6
Kohler Delores M 1-8
Kramer Janet BA 3
Luerssen Holly A BA 4
Marsh Mary Jo BS 3
Meador Jill M BA 6-8
Schultz Linda 5
Seehafer Mary M BA 2
Selmeyer David A MA
Siudak Pamela S MS K
**APPLETON**-CELEBRATION PS-3
• 1998
3100 E Evergreen Dr 54913-9206
(920)734-8218 •
FAX(920)734-7890
celebration.lutheran@juno.com
Klaas Joan E BA 1
Laatsch Sarah A BA 2-3
Rugotska Karen PS
Zimmermann Donna D BA K
FAITH PS
• 1989
601 E Glendale Ave Alice St Entrance 54911-2944
(920)739-7772
Amundson Sandra BSED
Baumann Jennifer PS
Brown Cheryl R PS
Clark Janice PS
Dain Dawn PS
De Groot Joan A PS
Decker Linda PS
Dreyer Karen PS
Gutierrez M J PS
Heil Mary PS
Hull Mary PS
Jenks Lori PS
Kempen Cynthia PS
Krueger Cindy A PS
Mc Hugh Kay PS
Petit Leslie PS
Rickert Linda PS
Schmidt Karen PS
Simmons Marilyn A
Vander Heiden Sarah PS
GOOD SHEPHERD PS
• 1978
2220 E College Ave 54915-3146
(920)734-9643 •
FAX(920)734-3544
goodshep@athnet.net
**Johnson Leann J MED**
Cousins Jane PS
Fisher Kris PS
Weller Peggy PS
**ARLINGTON**-ST PETER PS
• 1994
303 Park PO Box 45 53911-0045
(608)635-4825
Ellis Mary Ellen PS
Hendrickson Connie M AA
Ryce Jan PS
Schulz Carol PS
**ASHLAND**-LITTLE FRIENDS JESUS PS
• 1991
1114 12th Ave West 54806 PO Box 31 54806-0031
(715)682-6075
**Draeger Peggy A PS**
Lunda Amy K BAED PS
ZION K-8
• 1994
1111 11Th Ave W 54806-2846 PO Box 31 54806-0031
(715)682-6075
zlcs@ncis.net
NO REPORT
**ATHENS**-ST JOHN PS
• 1994
486 County Rd F 54411
(715)536-1810
NO REPORT
TRINITY PS-8
• 1901
301 Elm St PO Box 100 54411-0100
(715)257-7559
**Prill James C MS 7-8**
Gilles Rachel B BA 3-4
Peter Julie PS-K
Prill Ann E BS 1-2
Van Rixel Rebecca C BA 5-6
**AUGUSTA**-GRACE PS
• 1986
814 Hudson St 54722-9015
(715)286-2116
Jacobs Barbara A
**BARABOO**-OUR SAVIOR PS
1120 Draper St 53913-1229
(608)356-9792 •
FAX(608)356-5848
oslcb@chorus.net
NO REPORT
**BARRON**-SALEM PS
• 1982
1360 E Lasalle Ave 54812-1636
(715)537-3011
Schuettpelz Kathleen BA PS
**BELOIT**-ST JOHN PS-8
• 1949
1000 Bluff St 53511-5167
(608)365-7838
NO REPORT
**BERLIN**-ST JOHN PS-8
• 1867
146 Mound St 54923-1729
(920)361-0555
Fritsch Charlotte BA 1-2
Mueller Robin BA 5-6
Podoll Deborah K BA PS
Schram Candice BS 3-4
Snow Curtis D MS
Snyder George H MA 7-8
**BIRNAMWOOD**-ST PAUL PS
• 1993
N9035 Highway 45 S PO Box 208 54414-0208
(715)449-2101
NO REPORT
**BONDUEL**-ST PAUL PS-8
• NLSA • 1863
240 E Green Bay St PO Box 577 54107-9250
(715)758-8532 •
FAX(715)758-6352
Buchholz Margaret L BS 4
Doell Lorraine K BA
Eggerstedt Gayle L BS 5-7
Muther Cindy B BS
Otte Deanna BA 1
Reep Robin C BSN K
Reimer Matthew T BA 5-8
Reinke Kristine R 3
Schelk Shelby J BA 6-7
Schmidt Gerald R MA
Tinlin Debbie PS
Wegner Frank L MED
**BROOKFIELD**-IMMANUEL PS-8
• 1950
13445 Hampton Rd 53005-7513
(262) 781-4135 • FAX(262) 781-5460
immanuel@execpc.com
**Rohde Donald J MAD**
Bunnow Mary Beth K
Clinard Mary Jane BA 3
Gohde Paul F BA 5
Kaelberer Kent J BA 7
Miskimen Harvey D BSED 8
Oppermann Barbara A BA 1
Schneider Debra A BA 6
Schneider Jeri L BA 4
Stoltmann Cindy J BA 2
Wolf Lisa J BS PS
Zehnder Marie BS
**BURLINGTON**-IN HIS ARMS-OUR SAVIOR PS
• 1995
417 S Kane St 53105-2111
(414)763-3883 •
FAX(414)763-5716
**Joslyn Traci A BS PS**
Jarosz Jane E PS
Kaufmann Catherine M BS PS
Mc Murry Gail A PS
Weis Traci L BA PS
**CASCADE**-ST PAUL PS
• 1990
509 Milwaukee Ave PO Box 167 53011-0167
(920)528-8094
NO REPORT
**CEDARBURG**-FIRST IMMANUEL PS-8
• NLSA • 1853
W67N622 Evergreen Blvd 53012-1848
(262)377-6610 •
FAX(262)377-9606
0
**Mielke Jon A MA**
Becker Julianne 3
Eberhart Robert Jr. MA 8
Everts Eric 6-8
Giordano Tom MA 5
Grabenhofer Kaethe K BA 5
Halter Mary BS K
Hamann Janine A BA 3
Jackson Teri L BA 1
Kison Connie L BA 1
Kohn Courtney J BA 7
Kolander Kevin MS 6
Kowalewsky Angela BS PS
Kramer Kourtney P BA 6
Meyer Barbara MA K
Mielke Judy M BA 2
Neuman Denise L BS PS-6
Pergande Tammie
Pinnow Ruth BSED 6-8
Rank Carrie PS
Roeske Karl F BA 8
Schaubs Craig H 4
Schaubs Kristine J PS
Sievers Steven R BA 2
Tolzman Ellen K
Valdez Nicole BSED 4

**CHIPPEWA FALLS**-FAITH PS
• 1978
733 Woodward Ave 54729-3283
Juedes Tresa J PS
ZION PS
• 1978
110 E Grand Ave 54729-2525
(715)723-6380
NO REPORT
**CLINTONVILLE**-ST MARTIN PS-8
• NLSA • 1886
100 S Clinton Ave 54929-1610
(715)823-6538 •
FAX(715)823-1464
stml@frontiernet.net
**Rehmer Edgar P MSED**
Cloeter Christine A BSED 7
Federwitz Virginia C BS 1
Flaherty Barbara A 4
Hopp LeAnn BSED 5
Justman Bonnie J BA 2
Krake Carrie A 3
Lipanot Rebecca BA K
Rohan Rebecca D 8
Shingler James L 6
Westphal Sharyl D PS
**COLBY**-ZION PS
• 1989
PO Box 438 54421-0438
(715)223-2166
Boss Karen PS
Brandt Alice PS
Dolle Eloise G PS
Good Linda L PS
Jecevieus Stacey PS
Yessa Pamm PS
ZION PS
• 1981
PO Box 438 54421-9653
(715)223-2166
**Guthman Delores J BA PS**
**CRANDON**-LITTLE LAMBS-GOOD SHEPHERD PS
• 1997
1507 N Lake Ave PO Box 146
54520
(715)478-3555
dbahn@newnorth.net
Chaney Mary PS
Maison Edna J PS
**CUDAHY**-ST JOHN PS
• 1970
4850 S Lake Dr 53110-1743
(414)482-0554 •
FAX(414)481-0736
**Erickson Karen S AA**
Antonia Sa Donna PS
Bartlett Debbie PS
Bisci Kim PS
Damitz Lynn R PS
Galaska Gail PS
Morgan Linda PS
Naqellari Silvana PS
Owen Velma PS
Palasz Laura PS
Perry Michelle PS
Stuessi Holly PS
**DELAVAN**-OUR REDEEMER PS-8
• 1983
416 W Geneva St 53115-1698
(262)728-6589 •
FAX(262)728-5581
**Breytung James S MED**
Becker Judith L MA K
Breytung Barbara A MSED 1
Grabow Kathryn L MA PS
Kramer Kirsten J BA 4
Leuner Brenda M 2
Penniman Rebecca L BA 3
Renk Linda M MS
Rickman Susan J BA 7-8
Zeuner John H BA 5-6

**EAST TROY**-GOOD SHEPHERD PS-4
• 1980
1936 Emery St 53120-1131
(262)642-3310 •
FAX(262)642-3310
gsl@netwurx.net
Clonkey Elizabeth M BA 2-3
Flogel Sue M PS
Johnson Mary K
Rachul Janice L PS
Sattler Carol K BS 1-2
Sattler Karl E BA
**EAU CLAIRE**-EAU CLAIRE K-8
• NLSA • 1958
3031 Epiphany Ln 54703
(715)835-9314 •
FAX(715)835-9166
eclsa@aol.com
**Hudson Jo BA 4**
Bickel Reenie
Bystol Orvin 7-8
Heren Andrew S BA 5-8
Jaenke Jane E BA 7-8
Kleinke Alice 1
Koopman Karleen J BA 2
Laskowski Carolyn
Lemke Linda M BS 3
Rutter Sandra L MED K
Sabelko Laurie K-1
Yocca Christine
REDEEMER PS
• 1976
601 Fall St 54703-3157
(715)835-5239 •
FAX(800)231-4098
NO REPORT
ZION PS
• 1981
Hwy 93 at HH 54702 PO Box 3033
54702-3033
(715)878-4512
NO REPORT
**ELM GROVE**-ELM GROVE PS-8
• NLSA • 1957
945 Terrace Dr 53122-2099
(262)797-2970 •
FAX(262)797-2977
ggoeres@egl.org
**Goeres Glenn W MA**
Anderson Terri 1-8
Bailey Emmain 1
Bessert Karla M BS 1-8
Braun Carole J BS 1
Daley Sheila R MED 6-8
Friedrich Karen L MA 5
Ganswindt Pamela K BSED 2
Grelk Margaret C BA 4
Gruetzmacher Paul M MS 7-8
Hoffmann Linda L BSED K
Kohlmeier Sara J BA PS
Kuehl Mary L BA 5
Langelin Peggy BS 4-8
Mareno Carrie BA 3
Margrett Deborah A BA PS
Marose David BED 6-8
Reigles Karen L BA 6-8
Rottman Dineen 4
Rottmann Michael S MS 6-8
Schroeder Mary E BA
Taubenheim Karen F BA 2
Weymier Amy S BA 8
**FALL CREEK**-ST PAUL PS
• 1991
721 S State St 54742-9794
(715) 877-3501 • FAX(715)
877-3256
Orr PS
**FOND DU LAC**-HOPE PS
• 1982
260 Vincent St 54935-5331
(920)922-5130 •
FAX(920)922-9832
Mumper Dawn PS
Wickman Carol J BS PS

**FRANKLIN**--RISEN SAVIOR PS
• NLSA • 1989
9501 W Drexel Ave 53132-9627
(414)529-5647 •
FAX(414)529-5673
NO REPORT
**FREDONIA**-ST JOHN PS
• 1991
824 Fredonia Ave 53021-9412
(414)692-2734
Gnan Michele PS
Liermann Beverly PS
**FREISTADT**-TRINITY PS-8
• NLSA • 1839
10729 W Freistadt Rd 53097-2503
(262)242-2045 •
FAX(262)242-4407
trinluth@execpc.com
**Becker Herbert H MED**
Adams Kathleen A BA 2
Anderson Robert C MSED 5-8
Durkin Mary 4
Ernst Karen BS 4-8
Ernst Susan J BSED 1
Hohnstadt Rebecca S BA K-8
Hovey Daniel R BA 6-8
Klemp Gary 5
Klemp Joyce BA 6-8
Lewis Lori J MA 3
Michel Mary BA PS
Putman Cindy K
Riemer Lorrie BA 1-8
**FREMONT**-ST PAUL PS
• 1998
107 Tustin Rd 54940-9412
(920)446-3633
NO REPORT
**GERMANTOWN**-FAITH PS
• 1993
W172N11187 Division Rd
53022-4066
(262)251-5003
Anderson Lisa A PS
Cummins Michele A PS
**GLENDALE**-ST JOHN PS-8
• NLSA • 1951
7877 N Port Washington Rd
53217-3132
(414)352-4150 •
FAX(414)352-4221
sj1@execpc.com
Schneider Jeri L BA 3
**GRAFTON**-ST PAUL PS-8
• NLSA • 1851
701 Washington St 53024-1898
(262)377-4659 •
FAX(262)377-7808
splgrafton@aol.com
**Busacker William P BS**
Adler Clinton J BA 6-8
Boeckeler Elizabeth MSED
Brueggemann Beverly BS 6-8
Brueggemann Karen B BA PS
Busacker Susan L MA 3
Denow Lola 6-8
Gallun Jennifer PS-8
Groppe Eva E BA 1
Kapelke Patricia A BA 6-8
Kell Jeremy J BA 6-8
Manssen Deborah A BA 2
Maschke Sharon L MS K
Meier Rosalie A BA 5
Mercier Gary L MA 5
Monson Dorothy E BS
Poellot Linda A MA 2
Prahl Norma G BA 2
Radue Linda J BA 3
Radue Martin B BA 1
Schelk Sue-Lynn BA K
Schumann Diane E BA 4
Sisley Dawn
Thiede Donna K BS 4
Werner Dauna L BSED PS

**GREEN BAY**-FAITH PS
• 1993
2335 S Webster Ave 54301-2123
(414)435-2282 •
FAX(414)435-2282
Jones Kathleen F
Kuske Janice M PS
Smith Rebecca MSPED PS
OUR SAVIOUR PS-K
• 1977
120 S Henry St 54302-3405
(414)468-4065 •
FAX(414)468-5757
NO REPORT
PILGRIM PS-8
• NLSA • 1981
1731 Saint Agnes Dr 54304-3059
(920)494-6530 •
FAX(920)494-2079
ken@pilgrimluth.com
**Longmire Kenny L MS 5-8**
Bordeleau Eileen BS K
DeRoach Sharon M BS PS
Eichstaedt Pauline E BA 2
Giovanetti Patricia J BS 5-8
Jones David W BA 7
Lehman Linda J BA 1
Nesbitt Nancy J BS 4
Schuettpelz Karen 8
Stock Judith A BA 6
Trofka Michele E BA 5
Turke Carolyn D BA 3
Zinkel Stephanie J BA 5-8
REDEEMER PS-8
• NLSA • 1960
205 Hudson St 54303-1947
(920)499-1033 •
FAX(920)496-0795
**Kuske Kevin E MED 7-8**
Jones Kathleen F 2-6
Kramer Llewellyn J BA 5-8
Kuske Janice M PS
Murphy Nancy A BA 3-4
Taylor Patricia A BS 1-2
Westerfeld Judith A BSED K
**GREENFIELD**-MOUNT ZION PS
• 1995
3820 W Layton Ave 53221-2038
(414)282-4900
Van Dyke Ellen L BSED PS
Wickert Patricia L BS PS
OUR FATHER PS-8
• 1964
6023 S 27th St 53221-4804
(414)282-7500 •
FAX(414)282-9737
NO REPORT
**GREENVILLE**-HILLSIDE-SHEPHERD HILLS PS
• 1976
N 1615 Meadowview Ln
54942-9625
(414)757-5722
NO REPORT
**HALES CORNERS**-HALES CORNERS PS-8
• NLSA • 1960
5425 S 111th St 53130-1247
(414)529-6701 •
FAX(414)529-6712
aamling@hcl.org
**Batterman-Smith Mary B MS PS**
**Fronk Eva M MS K-8**
**Sodemann Betty J**
Amling Albert J III MS
Bangert Jean M BA K
Bartholomew Diana L BA 1
Cozatt Kathleen R 1-8
Eisman Lynne C 2
Gabriel Lynn PS
Granley Brenda S BSED 2
Hammer Margaret 2-3
Herz Karen L MA 6-8
Jobst Ann E BED 3
Kogutkiewicz Chad A BA 8
Krolikowski Mary J K
Kutz Amy J BMU PS-8

Leiber Rebecca MA K-8
Lemerande Cynthia A BSED 3
Lillquist Judy 5
Lindeman Lois E BS 4
Masengarb Virginia R BA PS-1
Mason Nancy PS
Mathe Evangeline 1
Mc Cabe Holly BA K
Meyer Denise PS
Miskimen Grace V BA PS
Monfre Susan E BS PS
Nelson Christopher C BA K-8
Peterson Christina D BA 7
Pospyhalla Jeralyn 5-6
Sauer Clare 7-8
Schlehlein Joan K BA 1-8
Scortino Johanna PS
Sonstroem Gwendolyn K BA 6
Wagenecht Katie 7-8
Wallman Katherine 5-7
Wood Gloria A 1-8
Zaffke Deborah L 4
Zellmer Judi 6-8

**HARTLAND**-DIVINE REDEEMER PS-8
• 1980
31385 W Hill Rd 53029-8501
(262)367-3664 •
FAX(262)367-9410
mike@drlc.org
**Oldenburg Michael P MED**
Adams Joyce A BS 3
Bahr Kristan J MA PS
Bretzmann Nancy L BS K
Brueser Diane PS
Buelo Lynne 1-8
Conlon Neva 1-8
Crank Mary PS
Dahm Janet A BS K
Depenbrok Karen 1
Gruetzmacher Heidi BA 1
Kangas Leah J BA 3
King Tami L BED 4
Kleba Dale J MA 5-8
Lippert Karen BS K-8
Mahaney Janette BED PS
Oldenburg Kathryn L 2
Pordon Jean BA 1-8
Rohde Rebecca BS 5-8
Saydel Nettie BA 1-8
Sprecher Sheila A BA 2
Wenzelburger Kurt R BED 5-8
Wolfe Shaunna 5-8

**HILBERT**-ST PETER K-8
• 1878
42 N 3rd St PO Box 190
54129-0190
(920)853-3851 •
FAX(920)853-3851
NO REPORT

**HORICON**-ST STEPHEN PS-8
• 1864
505 N Palmatory St 53032-1099
(920)485-6687 •
FAX(920)485-2545
jbraun@ststephen-lcms.org
**Braun James R BA 8**
Ehlert Lorna M MA 3
Glawe Joel M BA 4
Klomberg Stacey A BSED PS-8
Lindemann Sharon BA 5
Meyer Kevin E BA 7
Roedel Karen R BA 1
Roedel Martin O BS 6
Springer Amy M BA 2
Wrucke Janice E BS K

**HOWARDS GROVE**-TRINITY PS
• 1990
W2776 Hwy 32 53083-5236
(920)565-3349 •
FAX(920)565-4592
Bergelin Deede PS
Kuhlow Kathy PS
Scharinger Roberta PS

**HUDSON**-TRINITY PS-5
• 1977
1205 6Th St 54016-1341
(715)386-9349 •
FAX(715)386-9707
lbecken@tlshudson.org
Becken Linda M MA
Buelow Cheri MA 1
Coulter Maren M BS 3
Dobberstein Christina M BSED 5
Feia Brigitte J BA 2-5
Huber Kathy BS 2
Kremer Paul 4
Leonard Cindy R BA K-1
Malick Linda PS
Mc Andrew Carrie K
Mc Donald Beth BA PS
Mc Ginnis Christine 2-5
Mc Lain Laurie PS-5
Meissen Jan BS PS
Mork Debra PS
Paulus Dawn PS
Sommers Carol PS
Urbik Joanne PS
Wolf Caroline PS
Yannarelly Carol PS

**JANESVILLE**-LOVING ARMS-MOUNT CALVARY PS
• 1994
2940 Mineral Point Ave
53545-3297
(608)754-4145 •
FAX(608)754-0781
rtomcole@juno.com
Seeman Joan PS
Swaim Shirley PS

ST PAUL PS-8
• 1865
210 S Ringold St 53545-4199
(608)754-4471 •
FAX(608)754-4050
dvierk@spsflames.k12.wi.us
**Vierk Dennis L MA 8**
Benedict Susan M BS K
Brooks Kimberly 1-8
Cook Carla J BA 1-6
Ebeling Patricia A BA 2
Ebeling Timothy J MEPD 5-8
Fenrick Mark O BA 6-8
Garchow Christine L MED PS
Gestrich Kristen M BED 2
Hays Karen A BA 6-8
Jacobsen Lynne M MSED 6-8
Kroll James W BA 3
Natz Debra J BS 5-8
Newkirk Jennifer E BA 5
Pingel Kathy M BA 3-8
Redmann Karen L 7-8
Schultz Ruth A MSED 1
Sullivan Judith A BS 4
Wahrle Lois L BA 4
Wier Barry L MSED 5-8
Wier Ruth A MED K-8

**KENOSHA**-LITTLE LAMBS-MESSIAH PS
• 1995
2026 22nd Ave 53140-4601
(414)551-8167
NO REPORT

**LADYSMITH**-ST JOHN PS
• 1987
515 College Ave W 54848-2107
(715)532-5780
NO REPORT

**LEBANON**-LEBANON PS-8
• NLSA • 1985
N 534 County Rd 53047 N 534
County Rd R 53098-4805
(920)925-3791 •
FAX(920)925-3799
lebluth@globaldialog.com
**Wrucke Wesley J MS 7-8**
Gudenkauf Cindy 3-4
Melcher Greta PS
Messmann Dennis K-8
Obert Angela M BSED 5-6
Steinfeldt Joy 1-2
Wolgast Lisa K-8

**LUXEMBURG**-ST PAUL K-8
• 1884
N4107 County Rd AB 54217-7926
(920)845-2095 •
FAX(920)845-9075
stpauls@netnet.net
**Zeitler Kristen S 3-4**
Dahlke Lois 1-5
Kriescher Kelly L 6-8
Paul Robin M BA 1-2
Shin Sarah L BA 3-6
Zeitler Sedonie O PS

**MADISON**-CHRIST PS
• 1968
2833 Raritan Rd 53711-5232
(608)271-2811 •
FAX(608)271-2849
cmlcdc@chorus.net
Chellew Deborah S BA
Hart Lisa A PS
Vollmer Janet M MSED PS

LIVING CHRIST PS
• 1990
110 N Gammon Rd 53717-1301
(608)829-2136 •
FAX(608)827-3513
Becker Debra PS
Bolitho Betty A MA

MOUNT OLIVE PS
• 1987
4018 Mineral Point Rd 53705-5198
(608)238-5656 •
FAX(608)238-5714
molc@execpe.com
**Tonsager Janelle J BA PS**
Frei Jan PS
Richter Trisa PS

**MANAWA**-ST PAUL PS-8
• NLSA • 1891
750 Depot St 54949-9564
(920)596-2815 •
FAX(920)596-2851
NO REPORT

**MANITOWOC**-REDEEMER PS
• 1988
1712 Menasha Ave 54220-1839
(920)684-3989 •
FAX(920)684-3277
redeemer@manty.com
Andrastek Kim PS
Hamann Beverly PS
Orth Mary PS
Rathjen Jerri PS
Schneider Penny PS

**MARINETTE**-FAITH PS
• 1984
4009 Irving St 54143-1001
(715)735-6506
NO REPORT

**MARSHFIELD**-CHRIST PS
• 1995
1208 W 14th St 54449-0237
(715)384-3535 •
FAX(715)384-6945
christlu@tznet.com
Boson Marlane K MA PS
Retz Patricia BS PS
Schultz Janet M PS

IMMANUEL PS-8
• NLSA • 1886
604 S Chestnut Ave 54449-3606
(715)384-5121 •
FAX(715)389-9113
imanuel@tznet.com
Albert Gary M MAR 5-6
Albert Jolene K BA 3
Bahn Karen E MS 4-6
Helgerson Jill R BS 2
Henning Donna J BS 1
Henning James C MED 7-8
Huber Phyllis K-8
Johnson Laura 5-8
Lindow Marcia K-8
Majerus Kim PS-K
Schmidt Pam PS
Schultz Maxine PS

**MAYVILLE**-IMMANUEL PS-8
• 1854
N8076 County Ay 53050-2510
(920)387-2158 •
FAX(920)387-1360
imluth@interwisc.com
**Elmhorst Brian D BA 6-8**
Elmhorst Lori L 3-5
Koenitzer V Kay PS-K
Zimmermann Barbara L MA 1-2

ST JOHN PS-8
• NLSA • 1892
520 Bridge St 53050-1552
(920)387-4310 •
FAX(920)387-2321
stjls@internetwis.com
**Bell Scott W MA**
Bell Jill R BA 7
Brockhaus Elaine R BSED K
Bushke Tammy J 6
Conrad John A Sr. MS 4
Gassner Nanette K MA 8
Hazelberg Faye M BS 3
Hessler Edward A MA 5
Lehman Janet R BA 2
Rosin Delores M BA 1
Zuelsdorf Leslie A PS

**MENASHA**-TRINITY PS-6
• NLSA • 1945
300 Broad St 54952-3077
(920)725-1715 •
FAX(920)722-7692
jord@athenet.net
**Jording David C MA**
Bedroske Camala K
Boettcher Paul J BA 5-6
Johnston Janice M BA 4
Kamprath Elizabeth I BA PS
Lehman Rebekah BS 2-3
Zachek Karen A MSED 1-2

**MENOMONEE FALLS**-GRACE PS-8
• NLSA • 1963
N87W16173 Kenwood Blvd
53051-2996
(262)251-7140 •
FAX(262)251-3460
**Anderson Steven M MAD**
Brauer Brian BA 6
Bull Joyanna 7
Fritsch Jane SPRD
Gruber Kurt 8
Heckler Sandra L MSED 1
Hinze Neal T MA 8
Jobe Delores BS K
Krafft Arthur E MS 8
Laabs Sharon MA 4
Mueller Joann MEPD 5
Piepenbrink Shirley A BA 2
Reinke Katherine D BA 3
Strehlow Gloria J BA PS

PRINCE OF PEACE PS
• 1996
W156 N7149 Pilgrim Rd
53051-5029
(414)251-3360
Janus Lisa A BA

ZION PS-8
• 1883
W188N4868 Emerald Hills Dr
53051-6416
(414)781-7437 •
FAX(414)781-4656
**Schulz Robert C BS 7-8**
Ensweiler Lee A
Kalchbrenner Susan K BSED 3
Maske JoAnn K BS PS-K
Maske Richard J BS 5
Miller Barbara L BA 4
Paape Barbara A BA 1-2
Rose Dwayne K BA 6
Schroeder Ronald 7-8

**MERRILL-**ST JOHN PS-8
• 1883
1104 E 3rd St 54452-2530
(715)536-7264 •
FAX(715)539-3381
eagle@dwave.net
Breitwisch John A BA 7
Breitwisch Ruthann L BA 1
Duginski Peggy BS 1-7
Fritz Karen D BS 2
Hahn Kathleen M BS 4
Klug Kay E BA 3
Mueller Robert P MS 8
Pehlke Todd M BA 5
Savaske Wendy PS
Schultz Lowell E MA 6
Smukowski Theresa BA K
TRINITY K-8
• 1886
611 W Main St 54452-2235
(715)536-7501 •
FAX(715)539-8531
**Labbus Paul MEPD 7-8**
Frank Glenn W MA 6
Johnson Scott R BA 4
Kamps Sallie J BA 3
Marnholtz Laura M MED 1
Miller Amy 6-8
Schult Diane 5
Schultz Laurie M BA 2
Smallman Linda L BA K-8
Zomchek Patricia A K
**MILWAUKEE-**CHRIST MEMORIAL K-8
• 1945
5719 N Teutonia Ave 53209-4198
(414)461-3371 •
FAX(414)461-3374
**Marton Kenneth R BA 7-8**
Ander Cynthia 2
Bhatti Avis E 6
Foxe Katherine L BA
Krafft Alberta G 8
Kubiak Kathy 3-4
Lindgren Joanne L BSED 1
Taylor Jennifer K
Toth Jason 5
CHRIST MEMORIAL PS
3105 W Thurston Ave 53209-4137
(414)461-3737
NO REPORT
COVENANT PS
• 1995
8121 W Hope Ave 53222-1980
(414)464-2410 •
FAX(414)464-1942
Douyette Joely A PS
Rosynek Marcia PS
Wallinger Dennis E MS
EMMAUS PS-8
• 1890
2818 N 23rd St 53206-1645
(414)444-6090 •
FAX(414)444-3336
**Simms Marilyn PS**
**Stearns Chris A MS**
Bartel Shauna 2
Clark-Bosman Jane
Kurkiewicz Ann 2
Liebenow Herbert W MED
Miller Rosemary L BS 7-8
Niedfeldt Carol S 3-4
Puechner Amy L MA K
Shelly 371872 K
Wolff Sara 1
GOSPEL K-8
• 1919
3965 N 15th St 53206-2916
(414)372-5159 •
FAX(414)372-5179
gospelutheranschool@juno.com
**Markworth Alfred E BSED 7-8**
Boeck Susan A BA 3-4
Eckert Judith A MA 1-2
Lundgren Frederick C 1-8
Rohde Sharon A BA K
Tally Marlene 5-6

LUTHERAN 1-8
• RSO • NLSA • 1986
9700 W Grantosa Dr 53222-1497
(414)461-8500 •
FAX(414)461-4930
lutheranspecialschool@juno.com
**Schultz Judy K**
Acton Carol L MA
Clemens Jennifer K BA
Gruber Kim M
Jones Kristin R
Lowe Maryellen
Spitzack Nancy A
MOUNT CALVARY PS-8
• 1925
2862 N 53rd St 53210-1692
(414)873-3466 •
FAX(414)873-0567
demiller@execpc.com
Eggebrecht Tamara BS PS
Greear Michelle PS
Hinze Janice M 2
Klenz Tammy BS 5-8
Lindauer Dawn 1
Miller Carrie L BA 4
Miller Duane E MA
Scheiwe Sherry L BA 3
Sohn Ellen H BSED K
Wendt Richard L BA 5-8
Woehrmann Judith S MA 5-8
MOUNT OLIVE PS-8
• NLSA • 1950
5301 W Washington Blvd
53208-1798
(414)774-2113 •
FAX(414)771-3855
**Zuehlsdorf James F MA 2-8**
Berndt Holly R BS 1-8
Bohmann Kari S BA 1
Byal Karen PS
Corozza Robin PS
Dean Kathryn 1-3
Goetzke Janis M BS K
Harks Linda D BA PS
Knox Tyrie A PS
Kohrs Ralph L BS 7-8
Lange Ruth BA 3
Lerret Brian W BA 6
Librizzi Kathryn A BA 2
Martin Lyn BS 5-8
Sengele Richard C MA 5-8
Stecker Paulette F BA 4
NAZARETH PS-7
• 1992
8242 N Granville Rd 53224-2754
(414)354-6601
Eubank Beth PS
Harms Hillard H BS 5-7
Herka Catherine M BS 1-2
Kroll Sharon J BS K
Turckes Denise A BA 3-4
NORTHWEST PS-8
• RSO • 1957
4119 N 81st St 53222-1979
(414)463-4040 •
FAX(414)463-0524
nwls@execpc.com
**Kellerman David M BA**
Atkinson Janice BA 6
Bartz Jonathan 8
Buck Jane E BSED K
Cucinello Georgia M BA
Garrow Lynn C BED PS
Gruetzmacher Gene E BS 2
Henning David W MS 3
Jipp Kimberly A BS
Milbrath Judith L BA 1-2
Schroeder Marilyn MAS
Timm Diane M MA 5
Voigt Sherry BA 6
Wachs Cynthia L MED 1
Wales Kathleen M BA 4
Wilds Joy BS

OKLAHOMA AVENUE PS-8
• 1989
5335 W Oklahoma Ave
53219-4416
(414)543-3580 •
FAX(414)543-3610
oalcs@execpc.com
**Gottschalk Richard E MA 7-8**
Fromm Clay M BED 1-2
Fromm La Rae L BA PS
Kilimann Andrew D
Spitzer James R BA 5-6
Wallis Carol A 3-4
SHERMAN PARK PS-K
• 1970
2703 N Sherman Blvd 53210-2426
(414)447-0266 •
FAX(414)445-6556
NO REPORT
ST MARTINI PS-8
• 1883
1557 W Orchard St 53204-4066
PO Box 04066 35204-4066
(414)383-7058 •
FAX(414)383-0637
**Schoessow Eugene E BA 7-8**
Granley Russell J BED 5-6
Hacker Holly J BA 3-4
Hedemann Carolyn P BSED K-5
Page Julie
Proeber Linda
Seils Cynthia E BA
Zwicke Donna 1
ST PETER-IMMANUEL PS-8
• 1866
7801 W Acacia St 53223-5698
(414)353-6800 •
FAX(414)353-5510
Dapelo Matthew C 6-8
Goeres Rhonda J BA 3
Heiden Deborah
Johnson Karin K BA 2
Kolb Kathy S BS K
Kostrewa Kathleen 4
Kurth Barbara T MA
Lambrecht Cheryl K-8
Michels Gerald L MA 6-8
Ostrowski Vicki L BA 5
Prahl Bonnie C BA 1
Radloff Nancy L MED K
Schnake Richard K PHD 6-8
Tonn Gloria J BA 1
**NEENAH-**NEW HOPE
• 1991
1368 Cold Spring Rd 54956-1108
(920)725-8797 •
FAX(920)725-4058
newhope@vbe.com
NO REPORT
**NEW BERLIN-**BLESSED SAVIOR PS
• 1990
15250 W Cleveland Ave
53151-3728
(414)786-6465 •
FAX(414)786-6799
bslc@execpc.com
Dagenhardt Ann M PS
Gihring Diane C BS PS
Heller Kathryn T PS
Hojnacki Joan D BA PS
Murack Susan PS
LITTLE LAMBS OF PEAC PS
• 1989
17651 W Small Rd 53146-5530
(414)679-1441 •
FAX(414)679-8550
peacenet@peacelutheran.org
Krauss Cindy M PS
Kuchler Doris K BA PS
Schoner Linda L BSED PS
**NEW RICHMOND-**NOAH'S ARK-ST LUKE PS
• 1985
365 W River Dr 54017-1435
(715)246-4861
NO REPORT

**NORTH FOND DU LAC--**DIVINE SAVIOR PS
• 1979
1081 Van Dyne Rd 54937-9777
(414)923-1532
NO REPORT
**NORTH PRAIRIE-**ST JOHN PS-K
• 1990
312 N Main St 53153-9728
(414)392-9649
NO REPORT
**OAK CREEK-**GRACE PS-8
• NLSA • 1980
8537 S Pennsylvania Ave
53154-3333
(414)762-3655 •
FAX(414)762-8869
graceoc@execpc.com
**Haas Walter D MED**
Dietz Beverly 5-6
Jipp Andrew W BSED 7-8
Meyer Jeanne L MA 1-2
Nickel Kirsten L BA 2-8
Sarenac Lisa PS-8
Spaeth Margie BSED PS-K
Stroik Marilyn MED 3-4
Stutzman Kathryn BSED K
**OCONOMOWOC-**ST PAUL K-8
• 1877
210 E Pleasant St 53066-3050
(262)567-5001 •
FAX(262)567-1207
NO REPORT
**OMRO-**GRACE PS
• 1988
720 Jackson Ave 54963-1718
(920)685-2621 •
FAX(920)685-6786
Kester Brenda A BA PS
**ONALASKA-**SHEPHERDS FLOCK-SHEPHERD HILLS PS
• 1982
1215 Redwood St 54650 PO Box 416 54650-0416
(608)783-0330 •
FAX(608)783-1876
Clark Stephanie PS
Fuss Kathy BSED PS
Mueller Heide PS
Ruesch Judy BS PS
**OSHKOSH-**TRINITY PS-8
• NLSA • 1856
819 School Ave 54901-5398
(920)235-1730 •
FAX(920)235-1738
**Reinl Joe 6-8**
Dillman Sue 4
Hilgendorf Roberta BSED PS-8
Hilgendorf William A MA 3
Hoppe Patti PS-8
Hunter Karen 7-8
Kolb Vicki L BSE 2
Koplitz Jane 5-6
Menchaca Tracy PS
Nevers Ruth A BS K
Retzlaff Cathy PS-8
Rumbold Paula C MS 1
**PARK FALLS-**PEACE PS
• 1989
600 2nd Ave N 54552-1327
(715)762-4492
pldcare@win.bright.net
**Page Michelle M PS-6**
Hanish Berta PS-5
Heizler Jennifer S PS
Hinkley Faye PS-6
Oswald Jeremy PS
Seidl Nancy PS
**PLEASANT PRAIRIE-**GOOD SHEPHERD PS
• 1983
4311 104th St 53158-3723
(262)694-4405 •
FAX(262)694-0964
Hackbarth Donald L DMIN
Kolesar Tanya BED PS

**PLYMOUTH**-ST JOHN PS-8
• NLSA • 1864
222 N Stafford St 53073-1839
(920)893-5114 •
FAX(920)892-2845
stjohns5@hotmail.com
**Hubbard Terry L MS**
Bain Patricia 6-8
Bilgo Diane K BA 4
Christensen Jessica 6-8
Fischer Pearl A MA 5
Herrmann Iona K BSED PS-4
Hubbard Deborah S BA 1
Huebschman Timothy P BSED PS-8
Kohl Colleen M BS 3
Kohlman Todd A 4-7
Krall Jayson S BS 6-8
Rowold Kathleen M BA 2
Schuh Geoffrey 5-8
Steinhardt Vicki L BS K-4
Steltenpohl Linda A BS PS
Zickert Marilyn PS
**PORT EDWARDS**-TENDER LOVING CARE PS
• 1994
990 3Rd St 54469-1250 PO Box 75 54469-0075
(715)887-3795
**Elsen Heidi**
Davis Connie PS
Davis Leslie PS
Haas Tami PS
Morz Sandi PS
Schla Lori PS
Vallin Willa PS
**PORT WASHINGTON**-ST JOHN ACADEMY PS-6
• 1996
403 W Foster St 53074-2111
(262)284-2131 •
FAX(262)284-3935
**Klieve John E MDIV**
Jones Nondee K-6
Kittelson Tanya L 4-6
Spatz Carol J BA PS-K
Van Pietersom Annette M PS
Yokes Diane M AA PS
Zastrow Timothy E BA 1-3
**PORTAGE**-ST JOHN PS-8
• NLSA • 1865
430 W Emmett St 53901-1642
(608)742-4222 •
FAX(608)742-4222
**Sohl James R MED 6-8**
Baars Marilyn J BA 1
Detert Vickie 4-8
Hohl Laura M BA 5
Jakeman Sara BA K-8
Knuth Sara A BA 4
Leeland Carlene L BA K
Norland Sharon L BED 1-2
Schroeder Nina R BS K
Steinbach Arlon J MCMU 7-8
Steinbach Carol L BA 3
Winkelmann Kristine BA 7
**POTTER**-TRINITY PS-8
• NLSA • 1867
N6081 W River Rd 54129-9428
(920)853-3134
trinity@tds.net
**Zutz Ellen S BA 3-5**
Holze Kimberly 6-8
Jandrey Rebecca PS
Lemke Jayne S BS 1-2
Lemke Kathleen L BA K
**QUINCY**-ST JOHN
2823 County Hwy Z 53910-9768
(608)339-7869 •
FAX(608)339-0257
NO REPORT
**RACINE**-CONCORDIA PS-8
• RSO • 1970
3350 Lathrop Ave 53405-4711
(262)554-1659 •
FAX(262)554-0047
**Bellin Willard H MS 6-8**
Bellin Sharon L BS 7-8
Fuerstenau Jeannine L BED 2
Giles Donna L BA 1
Gutzler Donna J BA 3
Gutzler Mark D BA 5
Kosmala Diane L BSED 4
Mierow Theresa PS
Miller Caroline L BA 6
Mortenson Phyllis J BED K
PRINCE OF PEACE PS
• 1978
4340 6 Mile Rd 53402-9621
(414)639-1277
NO REPORT
ST JOHN PS-8
• 1863
510 Kewaunee St 53402-5095
(414)633-2758 •
FAX(414)637-7089
kougarss@execpc.com
**Albright Janice M BA 3**
Baganz Chad D BA 3-7
Jennings Janet J BS 2
Karpinsky Kathleen C BA 1
Karpinsky Roy D BA 7
Meyer Rebekah A BA 5-8
Pesch Janet M MA 4
Stellwagen David R 8
Witek Cheryl A BS PS-K
Zuelsdorff Carmen BA 6-7
TRINITY PS-8
• 1905
2035-65 Geneva St 53402-4627
(262)632-1766 •
FAX(262)632-1766
**Baganz Mark J MA 8**
Dziekan Miriam M BSED 3
Fick Kenneth W BS 6
Fick Rebecca S MA 4
Jacob Connie L 2-8
Koepke Joel L MAT 5-8
Koepke Marlene E BS K-3
Namowicz Susan
Palmer Connie L BS 2
Ruschmeyer Sara L BA
Stravers Kenneth W BS 7
Zuelsdorff Billy J MED 8
**RANDOM LAKE**-ST JOHN K-8
• NLSA • 1855
W5407 Hwy Ss 53075-1236
(920)994-9190 •
FAX(920)994-9721
Braun Linda S BA 1-2
Forshee Marlene J BA K
Kohler Greg 5-6
Wegner Janette K 3-4
Wegner Richard T BA 7-8
**REEDSBURG**-ST PETER PS-8
• NLSA • 1867
346 N Locust St 53959-1643
(608)524-4066 •
FAX(608)524-8821
Baumann Georgann BS 1
Baumann Kenneth E MED
Blake Deborah 6-8
Blake Kenneth W III BA K-8
Brandt Joanne BS 5
Fry Lori S 2
Hendrikson Kevin J BA 6-8
Hillman Charlotte M BA K
Loomans Eunice P MA 4
Schallhorn Randy B MA
Schallhorn Valjean A BS 3
Schwenkhoff Mary A BA K
Zimmerman Sharon J PS
**RHINELANDER**-ST MARK PS
• 1998
21 S Baird Ave 17 S Baird Ave 54501-3502
(715)362-0390 •
FAX(715)362-2037
Schneider Marcia PS
Steil Maxine M BA
**RICE LAKE**-FIRST PS
• 1995
15 E Sawyer St 54868-2560
(715)234-7505
Degerman Jane M PS
Nielsen Christine M PS
Schultz Mary E PS
**SCHOFIELD**-MT OLIVE PS
• 1976
6205 Alderson St 54476-3905
(715)359-9392 •
FAX(715)359-9245
Balk Kari PS
Du Chateau Penny PS
Goetsch Sandra-Lee N BS PS
Pegorsch Grace M BS PS
Rinehart Gina PS
**SHARON**-TRIUNE PS
• 1982
N1584 County Road K 53585-9723
(414)736-4712
Pasche Vienna R PS
**SHAWANO**-ST JAMES PS-8
• NLSA • 1889
324 S Andrews St 54166-2406
(715)524-4213 •
FAX(715)524-4876
mre_sjs@hotmail.com
**Eggerstedt Kim L MA**
Barnes Karen BSED K
Beversdorf Jan BA 4
Dobberstein Mary E BA 7-8
Grover Karen 7-8
Grunwald Karen W BA 2
Koenig Stephen 6
Lundt Wendy 3
Mueller Ralph P BS 5
Piehl Kerry 7-8
Schroeder Peggy S BA 2
Siegmeier Scott BS 6-8
Stroming Judy BMU K-8
Urban Joan A PS
Vogel Susan G BA 6-8
Wollangk Paul BSED 5
Wollenzien Kathy BA 1
ST JAMES DAY CARE PS
• 1995
324 S Andrews St 54166-2406
(715)524-5422 •
FAX(715)526-4876
Dobberstein Leah
Downs Debbie
Heling Carmen
Johnson Christine
Knope Katrina
Olsen Debra
Peterman Melody
Staniak Susan
Urban Joan A
Waldvogel Vicki
**SHEBOYGAN**-BETHLEHEM PS-8
• NLSA • 1890
1121 Georgia Ave 53081-5398
(920)452-5071 •
FAX(920)452-0209
bethlehemsheb@juno.com
**Gundlach Kenneth L MED**
Bajus Kay BED 3
Bajus Luther J II BA 7
Constien Sharon L BS 8
Ebert Elaine MS 1
Eifert Mary M BA 5-8
Feile Annette M MA 1-8
Kasten Sandra L BA 5
Keske Cynthia L BA PS-K
Peters Joyce K BSED 4
Steffen Beverly M BS 2
Steffen Lee H MA 6
IMMANUEL K-8
• 1878
1626 Illinois Ave 53081-4896
(920)452-9681 •
FAX(920)452-0102
Buss Joely A BA 1-2
Fibiger Mary A
Genszler Amy BA 5-6
Holzheimer Allen J II BA 7-8
Kamprath Carol A BSED PS
Landgraf Jana 1-2
Stelter Ellen BS
ST PAUL PS-8
• 1889
1819 N 13th St 53081-2526
(920)452-6882 •
FAX(920)452-7893
spls@execpc.com
Barts Phyllis J BSED 2
Cecil Jo Anne M 4
Gundlach Jerilynn M BS 5-8
Hartman Grace A MS 1
Jentsch Bradley 7
Kamprath Ronald P MA 5-8
Kretschmar Wendy M BED 5-8
Lasher Todd 5-8
Mueller Roxanna P MSED
Powers Linda 5-8
Veldboom Tracy L BSED 3
Zastrow Earlene M BS PS
SUNSHINE CORNER-ST MARK PS
• 1994
1019 N 7th St 53081-4019
(920)458-4343 •
FAX(920)458-3484
stmark@excel.net
**Rose Linda S**
Lyon Julie B PS
Staggs Danielle PS
TRINITY PS-8
• NLSA • 1853
824 Wisconsin Ave 53081-4062
(920)458-8248 •
FAX(920)458-8267
principal@trinitysheboygan.org
**Schneider Richard W MS**
Becker Gregory N MS 5-7
Dalla Valle Lucille 5-8
Eifert Jonathan D MMU 1-8
Fenske Sandra L BS 4
Foster Jeanette M BED PS-K
Hering Ruth A BA 1
Howard Karen J BA 3
Howard Kenneth D MA 8
Kirst Kathleen L BA 2
Krueger Paul H MED 7
Miske Christel H 1-8
Oyler Bertha J MED 6
**SHEBOYGAN FALLS**-ST PAUL PS
• 1986
730 County Rd PPP 53085 PO Box 185 53085-0185
(920)467-6733 •
FAX(920)467-4239
stpaul@execpc.com
Davis Deborah PS
Hartman Marianna BA PS
Zeuner Christina L BA
**SPOONER**-FAITH PS
• 1984
W7148 Luther Rd 54801-9781
(715)635-2261
**Gozdzialski Cheryl R PS**
Walker Joy D PS
**STEVENS POINT**-ST PAUL PS-8
• NLSA • 1955
1919 Wyatt Ave 54481-3650
(715)344-5660 •
FAX(715)344-5240
Lamb Curt K
Lazarski Debra L PS
Lilienthal Sue A MA 2
Pieper Lisa BS 4-8
Rubel Elaine M BS K
Rubel John C BA 5-6
Schield Beth 2-8
Selle Carol
Thies Ronal L MED
West Rae K 1
Zrust Dona M BSED 3
**SURING**-ST JOHN PS-8
• 1926
8945 Saint John Rd 54174-9706
(920)842-4443 • FAX(920) 842-4443
Buhrandt Tammy L BA PS

Hischke Nancy J BSED K-2
Rakow Ruben MS
Vorphal Penny 3-5
**SUSSEX-**PEACE PS-8
• 1995
W240 N6145 Maple Ave PO Box 123 53089-0123
(262)246-3200 •
FAX(262)246-8455
academy@peacesussex.org
**Bender Peter C MDIV**
**Gatchell Matthew W BA**
Bliese-Darling Elisabeth J 1-3
Krohn Linda 4-6
Laubenstein Susan PS
Schumacher Anne L 4-6
Simon Cindy PS
Vieregge Keith L MCMU 7-8
**TWO RIVERS-**GOOD SHEPHERD PS
• 1987
3234 Mishicot Rd 54241-1556
(920)793-1716
NO REPORT
**UNION GROVE-**ST PAUL PS
• 1970
1610 Main St 53182-1721
(414)878-2600
NO REPORT
**WALES-**BETHLEHEM PS
• 1989
470 N Oak Crest Dr 53183-9711
(414)968-2194 •
FAX(414)968-5355
Bialozynski Deborah L PS
Goodman Karol L PS
Rades Sandra J AA PS
Spoerke Laurie J PS
**WATERFORD-**ST PETERS-RAINBOW PS-2
• 1991
145 S 6th St 53185-4441
(262)534-6066 •
FAX(262)534-2571
stpeters@setnet.net
Birkholz Joan M PS
Blawat Dawn PS
Czuta Sandra A PS
Kintop Dolores L
Laux Becky PS
Ritter Dale L Jr. MAT 1-2
Rutkoski Marian PS
Stone Mary M BA PS
Zirbel Jeannette K-1
**WATERTOWN-**BETHESDA HOME
• 1904
700 Hoffman Dr 53094-6294
(414)261-3050
NO REPORT
FAITH PS-8
• 1988
626 Milford St 53094-6020
(920)261-8060
Schempf Karen PS
GOOD SHEPHERD PS-4
• 1983
1611 E Main St 53094-4109
(920)261-2570 •
FAX(920)261-2769
rgwdce@execpc.com
**Wille Margaret L BS 3-4**
Schempf Karen 1-2
Schroeder Mary E BA K
Wille Ronald G MED
Zillmer Judy BED PS
**WAUKESHA-**BEAUTIFUL SAVIOR PS-2
• 1986
1205 S East Ave 53186-6666
(414)542-6558 •
FAX(414)542-8574
bslc@ticon.net
**Schmidt Peter A STM**
Marose Sherry PS-2
Soat Mary P BA 1-2
Stubbe Amy K MA PS-K

CHRIST THE LIFE PS-4
• 1997
3031 Summit Ave 53188-2660
(262)547-1817 •
FAX(262)547-7394
**Kelling John T MSED**
Caldwell Rozann 1
Elvers Theresa A BA K
Marriott Catherine C MED 2-4
Martin Joelle L PS
**WAUPUN-**IN HIS HANDS-PELLA PS
• 1997
315 S Madison St 53963-2002
(920)324-3321 •
FAX(920)324-9734
dcejeff@go.com
**Pool Jeffrey M MED**
Kind Laurie A PS
Pool Karen S BSED
Preston Kathleen L PS
**WAUSAU-**RIB MOUNTAIN PS
• 1974
3010 Eagle Ave 54401-7345
(715)845-2313
Hagedorn Judith PS
Utegaard Lisa PS
Whitkey Marilyn PS
Wolf Sandra BS PS
SHINING STAR-ZION PS
• 1996
E7195 Star Rd 54408-9622
(715)845-2014
NO REPORT
ST JOHN PS-8
• 1920
E10723 County Road Z 54403-8915
(715)845-7031
Plate Lori A BA 6-8
Sazama Ruth A BA
Traska Marie L MSCT 1-2
Weber Susan K
Wipperman Kristin BA K
ST MARK PS
• RSO • 1973
600 Stevens Dr 54401-2977
(715)848-5511 •
FAX(715)849-3523
Cornelius Debra PS
Hartman Marlys A BSED PS
Haworth Carol A PS
Zielinski Carolyn K MA PS
TRINITY K-8
• NLSA • 1908
501 Stewart Ave 54401-4562
(715)848-0166 •
FAX(715)843-7278
trinity@trinitynet.org
**Hartman David A MA**
Bluhm Don G MA 6
Bristol Kelly J 2-8
Grass John P MS 8
Hartman Elisa J BA 2
Hoelter Mary C 3
Hoffman Nancy L BA K
Kufahl Judy A BA 3
Larson Darlene M 1-6
Mansk Daniel J MAT 7
Maroszek Gina M MA 2
Raben Sandra M BA 1
Riese Pamela BA 4
Riese Rodney J MCMU 4
Rogers Emily R BA 4-5
Rogers Phillip L BA 5
Schult Donald Jr. 7
Schultz Nancy J BS 5
Swanson Holly A BA 1
**WAUWATOSA-**OUR REDEEMER PS-8
• NLSA • 1931
10025 W North Ave 53226-2501
(414)258-4558 •
FAX(414)258-5775
redeemer@execpc.com
Augustine Lisa R BS
Berg James N BS 7-8
Berg Ruth BA PS

Boehme Carolyn K MA PS
Burger Nancy C 5
Burger Robert L MED 4
Dobberfuhl Marjorie L MA 3
Gerth Yvonne M MA 1-6
Gobeli Jane 6
Hans Sara R BSED 4
Irish Mary E MEDSD 7-8
Kaddatz Jill A MA 6
Kegley Denise R MS 1
Kohlmeier James N BA 5
Patterson Laura J BA 1
Schmidt Ann E BA 2
Schmidt Terry L MA
Schroeder Douglas R BA 1-8
Taylor Susan J BA PS
Voigt Peggy S BS 3
Wenger Daniel P BA 6-8
Willer Kirsten M BSED 2
PILGRIM PS-8
• NLSA • 1928
6717 W Center St 53210-1298
(414)476-0736 •
FAX(414)476-2820
pilgls@execpc.com
**Atkinson Keith MED**
Brown Mary K BS 4
Dopke Robert A 6-8
Herbst Kathryn A BS K
Komp Jennifer L BA 2
Krause Hope M BS 3
Krause Jerald A BS 5
Nelson Constance BA PS
Strand Sandra J BED 6-8
Tesch Debra L BS 1
Weerts Lynn 6-8
**WAYSIDE-**ZION OF WAYSIDE PS-8
• NLSA • 1873
8374 County Rd W 54126-9468
(414)864-2468 •
FAX(414)864-2684
waysidezion@yahoo.com
Burns Esther L 7-8
Cheslock Beth A BAED PS-K
Derricks Linda S 5-6
Hagenow Ruth
Hansen Karen R BA 3-4
Martin Joy BA 2
Moran Mark A BA
Stoll Janet L BA 1
**WEST ALLIS-**ST PAUL PS-8
• 1926
7821 W Lincoln Ave 53219-1797
(414)541-6251 •
FAX(414)541-2205
**Graf Duane S MA**
Brook Nichole F BA 2
Burkee John G MA 8
Dittman James B BA 6
Eckelman Rebecca S BS 1
Gottschalk Nancy J BS PS
Gottschalk Roger A MAT 5
Graf Patricia S BS 5-6
Graf Susan R MA 1
Heimsoth Barbara R BS 2
Jahnke Jane A BS 4
Marsh Cheryl L 3
Palmreuter Kathy R BA 6
Schumacher Deborah F MED 3-4
Shemanske JoAnne BA K
Wiegert Shannon L BMU
Woller Robert W 7
TRINITY PS-K
• 1986
2500 S 68th St 53219-2613
(414)321-6470 •
FAX(414)321-6470
Barth Monica J PS
Krueger JoAnn BS K
**WEST BEND-**ST ANDREW PS
• 1997
7750 N Hwy 144 53090-9004
(262)335-4200 •
FAX(262)335-4175
Ruback Sandra K PS

ST JOHN PS-8
• NLSA • 1872
899 S 6th Ave 53095-4697
(414)334-3077 •
FAX(414)334-3591
Beineke Esther B K-8
Bremser Carol BA 3
Buntrock Judith E 2
Gerhardt Elsie A SPRD
Graf Debra S BSED 6
Guse Earl W MED
Hardt James W BSED 7
Knoll Lois E BA 4
Knoll Martin A BA 6
Kohler Ruth PS
Kraase Peggy A BS 5
Muther Pamela J BS 3-4
O Connor Dawn K BA 1-2
Saleska Vanessa M MA 1
Wegner James T BA 5-8
Wegner Jeffrey P BA 5-6
Wolf Jennifer R BSED K
**WEST BLOOMFIELD-**CHRIST PS-8
• 1874
N6412 State Rd 49 54983-5618
(920)867-3263
Robbert Ila M BA
Schliepp Carol M BS PS
Schneckloth Stephanie 6-8
**WHITEWATER-**LITTLE ANGELS PS
• 1988
885 S Janesville St 53190-2508
(414)473-8686
NO REPORT
**WISCONSIN DELLS-**TRINITY PS-6
• NLSA • 1958
728 Church St 53965-1517
(608)253-3241 •
FAX(608)254-7585
tls@chorus.net
**Sellmeyer David P MA 5-6**
Bailey Enith C BA 3-4
Baird Barbara K MS 1-2
Jonas Laurel M BA PS
Schuette Darlene K K
Sellmeyer Vivian A BA 1-6
**WISCONSIN RAPIDS-**IMMANUEL K-8
• NLSA • 1884
111 11th St N 54494-4549
(715)423-0272 •
FAX(715)423-2853
imluthsc@wctc.net
**Weiss Charles L MA 7-8**
Altis Chriss M BSED K
Altis Marvin R MCMU
Betts Brian J BA 6-8
Betts Wendy S BS 6-8
Buchwald Gretchen A BED 5
Dykstra Sharon L BA 3
Henke Nona A BS 3
Krueger Barbara L BS 1
Mc Collor Rebekah L BA 5
Oleson Peggy L BA 4
Rucks Lois E 2
Schultz Joyce E K
Tarr John M BA 6-7
Voelker Ted C BS 7-8
Vollert Linda M 3
Weiss Bonnie J BED 2
Wilhorn Brian R BA 4
Wilhorn Jennifer L 1
Zitzow Dona M BA 6-7
ST LUKE PS
• 1972
2011 10th St S 54494-6302
(715)423-5990 •
FAX(715)423-5936
Jansen Amy PS
Tommet Deberah K PS

## WYOMING

**CASPER-**MOUNT HOPE PS-3
• 1984
2300 S Hickory St 82604-3430
(307)234-6865
Christiansen Leesha K-2
Garwood Betty L 2-3
Karst Deanna PS
Raugutt Jane L PS
Snyder Linda K-1

**CHEYENNE-**OUR SAVIOR PS
• 1963
5101 Dell Range Blvd 82009-5653
(307)632-2580
NO REPORT

TRINITY PS-6
• NLSA • 1891
1111 E 22nd St 82001-3932
(307)635-2802 •
FAX(307)778-0799
**Snell Wendy L BSED 4-6**
Caspersen Carol A BSED PS
Funk Stanna 2-3
Mc Daniel Pat K
Pollom Cheri R BS 1-2

**CODY-**CHRIST THE KING PS
• 1987
1207 W Stampede PO Box 355
82414-0355
(307)587-5680
NO REPORT

**GILLETTE-**TRINITY PS
• 1980
PO Box 485 82717-0485
(307)682-4886
NO REPORT

**POWELL-**IMMANUEL PS
• 1992
223 E 5th St 82435-3112
(307)754-9670
immanuel@wavecom.net
NO REPORT

**RIVERTON-**TRINITY PS-8
• 1991
419 E Park Ave 82501-3650
(307)857-5710 •
FAX(307)856-9454
Coniglio Steven L BA 6-8
Conilogue Susan AA PS
Postma Cecelia M BS 1-2
Praeuner Roxanne BAED 3-5
Tucker Susan K BA

**ROCK SPRINGS-**TRINITY PS
• 1996
1007 9th St 82901-5414
(307)362-5088
NO REPORT

**TORRINGTON-**FIRST STEPS-OUR SAVIOR PS
• 1988
2973 E B St 82240-2039
(307)532-5801
NO REPORT

## ONTARIO CANADA

**MISSISSAUGA-**ST MARK PS
• 1988
130 Mineola Rd E L5G 2E5
(905)510-1141 •
FAX(905)278-6751
NO REPORT

# RETREAT CENTERS AND SUMMER CAMPS

For information regarding seasons, workshops, seminars, and evaluations of camps and programs—

Write to National Lutheran Outdoors Ministry Association (NLOMA)
Mr Garland Midgett, President
P.O. Box 457
LaGrange, TX 78945
979-247-4978
Website- http://www.nloma.org
E-Mail lomt@cvtv.net

Furthermore, arrangements have not been completed so that camps can become "recognized service organizations," so the names and addresses of the following camps are provided as a convenience for congregations that are members of The Lutheran Church—Missouri Synod and for the individual members of those congregations. While some of them may be operated by or affiliated with Districts of the Synod, the inclusion of the names and addresses in the *Annual* does not constitute an endorsement of the camps by the Synod, and the Synod makes no representations or guarantees about the fiscal solvency or financial responsibility of any such camp or with respect to any services implied or expressly offered by any camp. It is the sole responsibility of any organization or individual that might want to use the service of such a camp, to otherwise contract with such a camp, or to make contributions to such a camp, to make appropriate inquiries about the camp and its relationship, if any, to any District of the Synod.

## Alabama

Camp Dixie
Chris Walsh
29711 Josephine Dr
Elberta AL 36530
334-987-1201 FAX-same
E-Mail louchris@USA.net
Website http://www.gulftel.com/campdixi

## Arizona

Camp Aloma
Robert Urie
PO Box 3
Prescott AZ 86302
520-778-1690 FAX-same

## Arkansas

Lutheran Camp on Petit Jean Mountain
Phil Hill
110 Montgomery Trace
Morrilton AR 72110
501-727-5656

## California

Camp Arrowhead
PO Box 11
Crest Park CA 92326
909-336-2076
FAX 909-337-9883
E-Mail camparrowh@aol.com

Lutheran Outdoor Ministries of Northern California
Paul Christ
Mount Cross
PO Box 387
Felton CA 95018
408-336-5179
FAX 408-336-2548
E Mail paul@mtcross.org
Website http://www.mtcross.org

## Colorado

Lutheran Valley Retreat Inc
Craig Oldenburg
PO Box 9042
Woodland Park CO 80866-9042
719-687-3560
FAX 719-687-3560
E-Mail lutheranvalleyretreat@lvr.org
Website http://www.lvr.org

## Florida

Woodlands Lutheran Camp
Rev Milan Weerts
15749 CR 455
Montverde FL 34756
407-469-2792
FAX 407-469-4742
E-Mail woodlands@woodlandscamp.com
Website http://www.woodlandscamp.com

## Idaho

Camp Perkins
Lutheran Outdoor Ministry Inc
Bob LaCroix
Box 1965
Hailey ID 83333
208-774-3372

Lutherhaven
Inland Northwest Lutheran Outdoors Ministry
Bob Baker *Director*
3000 W Lutherhaven Rd
Coeur d'Alene ID 83814
208-667-3459 FAX 208-765-1713
E-Mail onmicabay@juno.com

## Illinois

Camp CILCA
Rich Harkins
4124 Camp CILCA Rd
Cantrall IL 62625
217-487-7497
E-Mail camp@cilka.org
Website http://www.cika.org

Camp Wartburg
Lutheran Retreat Center Inc
Bob Polansky
5705 LRC Rd
Waterloo IL 62298
618-939-7715
E-Mail wartburg@frontiernet.net
Website http://www.wartburg.com

Walcamp Outdoor Ministries
Jeff Meinz
32653 Five Points Rd
Kingston IL 60145
815-784-5141 FAX 815-784-4085
E-Mail fozziemeinz@tbcnet.com

## Indiana

Camp Lakeview
Tom Franke
13500 W Lake Rd
Seymour IN 47274
812-342-4815
E-Mail lakeview@hsonline.net
Website http://www.camplakeview.com

Camp Lutherhaven
Tim Jank
1596 S 150 W
Albion IN 46701
219-636-7101 FAX 219-636-3032
E-Mail tim@lutherhaven.org
Website http://www.lutherhaven.org

## Iowa

Camp IO-DIS-E-CA
Paul Golke
3271 Sandy Beach Rd NE
Solon IA 52333
319-848-4187
FAX 319-848-4165
E-Mail iodiseca@juno.com
Website http://www.campiodiseca.org

Camp Okoboji
Douglas R Kading
1531 Edgewood Dr
Milford IA 51351
712-337-3325 FAX 712-337-3318
E-Mail cokoboji@rconnect.com
Website
http://www.homepage.rcorrect.com/cokoboji

## Kansas

Camp Tomah Shinga
Angela Agan
6605 W. Lyon Creek Rd.
Junction City KS 66441
785-238-3654
FAX 785-238-6168
E-Mail aagan@oz-online.net

## Maryland

Raven Rock Lutheran Camp
Mark Yates
PO Box 136
Sabillasville MD 21780-0136
800-321-5824 FAX 717-794-5883
E-Mail ravenrock@innernet.net
Website http://www.ravenrock.org

## Michigan

Camp Arcadia Lutheran Camp Association
Chip May
PO Box 229
Arcadia MI 49613-0229
231-889-4361 FAX 231-889-4140
E-Mail kjass@aol.com

Camp Lu Lay Lea
Jamie Schluckbier
Henderson Lake
Lupton, MI 48635
517-345-1635

Camp Concordia
Sue Hatfield
13400 Pinewood Rd
Gowen MI 49326
616-754-3785 FAX 616-754-3856
E-Mail mordecai@iserv.net
Website http://www.iserv.net/~mordecai

Mahn-Go-Tah-See
Outdoor Education Center
LeRoy Paul
PO Box 126
Hale MI 48739
517-728-2495 FAX 517-728-5161

## Minnesota

Camp Omega
Kevin Hall
22750 Lind Ave
Waterville MN 56096
507-685-4266 FAX 507-685-4401
E-Mail info@campomega.org
Website http://www.campomega.org

Lutheran Island Camp
Rt 2 Box 291 C
Henning MN 56551
218-583-2905 FAX 218-583-2906
E-Mail islandcamp@hotmail.com
Website http://www.mns.lcms.org/islandcamp

## Missouri

Camp Trinity
Ruth Otten
3277 Boeuf Lutheran Rd
New Haven MO 63068-2213
573-237-2072 FAX 573-237-3858
E-Mail otten@aol.com

Heit's Point Lutheran Camp
The Dr Paul Spitz Center
Rt 2 Box 110A
Lincoln MO 65338
660-668-2363 FAX 660-668-2422
E-Mail heitspoint@iland.net

SEMO Camp Wappapello
922 Hawthorn
Sikeston, MO 63801
573-471-7422

## Montana

Camp Trinity
William Ludwig
594 4th Ave West North
Kalispell MT 59901
406-257-2477 FAX 406-756-8994

### Nebraska

Camp Luther of Nebraska
Kevin Bueltmann
1050 Rd 4
Schuyler NE 68661-7145
402-352-5655 FAX-same
E-Mail campluther@juno.com
Website http://www.campluter.org

### New York

SonRise Lutheran Outdoor Ministry
Larry McReynolds
Rt 9 PO Box 51
Pottersville NY 12860
518-494-2620
FAX 518-494-0121
E-Mail sonrise@netheaven.com
Website http://www.sonriseministries.com

Pioneer Retreat & Conference Center
Linda Gage
9324 Lake Shore Dr
Angola NY 14006
716-549-1420 FAX 716-549-6018
E-Mail pioneercamp@webt.com
Website http://www.pioneercamp.org

### North Carolina

Camp Linn Haven
Lewis Hollar
PO Box 385
Linville, NC 28646
704-733-2135 or 828-464-4085

### North Dakota

Shepherds Hill Retreats
Rev Joel L Brandvold *Director*
10451 County Road 49
Bottineau ND 58318-7024
701-263-4831 FAX 701-263-4068
E-Mail shr@ndak.net
Website http://www.shr-lcms.org

### Oklahoma

Camp Lutherhoma
John Busch
PO Box 1672
Tahlequah OK 74465
918-458-0704 FAX 918-456-2919
E-Mail lutherhoma@lutherhoma.com
Website http://www.lutherhoma.com

### Oregon

Camp Lutherwood
22960 Hwy 36
Cheshire, OR 97419
541-998-6444 FAX 541-998-7164
E-Mail lutherwood@aol.com
Website http://www.lutherwood.org

Lutheran Retreat—Camp Serene
Dan Ley
91707 Poodle Creek Rd
Noti OR 97461
503-998-2593

### Tennessee

First Lutheran Church Camp
Doug Roberts
2800 McCallie Ave
Chattanooga TN 37404
615-629-5990

### Texas

Lutheran Outdoors Ministry of Texas Inc
877-397-2401 E-Mail lomt@texoma.net
877-452-0099 E-Mail lomt@cutv.net
Website http://www.lomt.com

Camp Lone Star
Jim Holmlund
2016 Camp Lone Star Rd
LaGrange TX 78945
409-247-4128 FAX 409-247-4120
E-Mail lonestar@cvtv.net
Website http://www.lomt.com

Texoma Lutheran Camp
Cheryl Wilkie
418 Lutheran Drive
Pottsboro TX 75076-6183
903-786-3121 FAX 903-786-8883
E-Mail lomtexoma@texoma.net
Website http://www.lomt.com

### Washington

Loma Center for Renewal
Patrick Brady
3607 228th Ave SE
Issaguah, WA 98029
209-392-1871

VaLLLey Camp
Thom Proehl
49515 SE Middle Fork Rd
North Bend WA 98045
425-888-1852
E-Mail vallleycamp@lutherans.net
Website http://www.lutherans.net/vallleycamp

Camp Ortoha
Leonard Kuhlmann
9 W Lost Lake Rd
Tonasket WA 98855
Website
http://www.televar.com/~immanuel/ortoha.html

### Wisconsin

Camp Luther
Gary Vought
1889 Koubenic Rd
Three Lakes WI 54562
715-546-3647 FAX 715-546-2396
E-Mail luther@campluther.com
Website http://www.campluther.com

Camp LuWiSoMo
Kurtis Bueltmann
W5421 Aspen Rd
Wild Rose WI 54984
920-622-3350 FAX 920-622-4960
E-Mail luwisomo@vbe.com

## LUTHERAN CHURCH BODIES IN NORTH AMERICA

Directory of Executives

### American Association of Lutheran Churches

Rev Thomas V Aadland
801 W 106th St Suite 203
Minneapolis MN 55420-5603
(952) 884-7784 FAX (952) 884-7894
E-Mail: aadland@ aol.com

### Apostolic Lutheran Church of America

*President:* Rev Richard C Juuti
RR 1
Bentley AB TOC OJO Canada
*Secretary:* Rev Ivan Seppala
332 Mt Washington Way
Clayton CA 94517

### Association of Free Lutheran Congregations

*President:* Rev Robert L Lee
3110 E Medicine Lake Blvd
Minneapolis MN 55441
*Secretary:* Rev Brian Davidson
3110 E Medicine Lake Blvd
Minneapolis MN 55441

### Church of the Lutheran Brethren of America

*President:* Rev Robert M Overgaard
PO Box 655
Fergus Falls MN 56538-0655
*Secretary:* Rev Richard Vettrus
707 Crestview Drive
West Union IA 52175

### Church of the Lutheran Confession

*President:* Rev Daniel Fleischer
201 Princess Drive
Corpus Christi TX 74810-1615
*Secretary:* James A Albrecht
102 W Market St
Okabena MN 56161

### Eielsen Synod (Evangelical Lutheran Church in America)

*President:* Truman L Larson
Jackson MN 56143
*Vice President:* Marion Birkland
Somers IA 50586
*Secretary:* Daryl Schauer
Annandale MN 55302
*Treasurer:* Melvin Bjur
Howard Lake MN 55349

### Evangelical Lutheran Church in America

*Bishop:* Rev Dr H George Anderson
8765 W Higgins Rd
Chicago IL 60631-4197
Phone (773) 380-2600
*Vice President:* Dr Addie J Butler
5417 Laurens Street
Philadelphia PA 19144-4519
*Secretary:* Rev Dr Lowell G Almen
8765 W Higgins Rd
Chicago IL 60631-4198
Phone (773) 380-2801
*Treasurer:* Mr Richard L McAuliffe
8765 W Higgins Rd
Chicago IL 60631-4184
Phone (773) 380-2901

### Evangelical Lutheran Church in Canada

Rev Telmor Sartison
302-393 Portage Avenue
Winnipeg MB R3B 3H6
Phone (204) 984-9150
FAX (204) 984-9185
E-Mail sartison@elcic.ca
*Secretary:* Robert H Granke
302-393 Portage Avenue
Winnipeg MB R3B 3H6
Phone (204) 984-9150
FAX (204) 984-9185
E-Mail rhgranke@elcic.ca
*Treasurer:* Doreen Lecuyer
302-393 Portage Avenue
Winnipeg MB R3H 3H6
Phone (204) 984-9150
FAX (204) 984-9185
E-Mail dlecuyer@elcic.ca

### Evangelical Lutheran Synod

*President:* Rev George M Orvick
6 Browns Ct
Mankato, MN 56001
*Secretary:* Rev Craig Ferkenstad
Route 3 Box 40
St Peter MN 56082
*Treasurer:* Leroy Meyer
1038 S Lewis Ave
Lombard IL 60148
*Missions Counselor:* Rev Steven Petersen
6 Browns Ct
Mankato, MN 56001
*Business Administrator:* Keith Wiederhoeft
6 Browns Ct
Mankato, MN 56001
*Deferred Giving:* Rev Richard Wiechmann
6 Browns Court
Mankato, MN 56001

### The Fellowship of Lutheran Congregations

*President:* Robert J Lietz

320 Erie St
Oak Park IL 60302
Phone (708) 386-6773

### Lutheran Church—Canada

*President:* Rev Ralph Mayan
3074 Portage Ave
Winnipeg Manitoba R3K 0Y2
*Secretary:* Rev William Ney
5021–52 Avenue
Stony Plain Alberta T7Z ICI
*Treasurer:* Mr Allan Webster
3074 Portage Avenue
Winnipeg Manitoba R3K 0Y2

### The Lutheran Church—Missouri Synod

*President:* Dr Alvin L Barry
1333 S Kirkwood Rd St Louis MO 63122-7295
*Secretary:* Dr Raymond Hartwig
1333 S Kirkwood Rd St Louis MO 63122-7295
*Treasurer:* Mr Paul W Middeke
1333 S Kirkwood Rd St Louis MO 63122-7295

### Lutheran Churches of the Reformation

Administrator: Rev Kenneth K Miller
4014 Wenonah Ln
Ft Wayne IN 46809
*Secretary:* Dennis W Rieken
PO Box 126
Morrisonville IL 62546

### Wisconsin Evangelical Lutheran Synod

*President:* Rev Karl R Gurgel
2929 North Mayfair Rd
Milwaukee WI 53222
*Secretary:* Rev Douglas L Bode
1005 E Broadway Rd
Prairie du Chien WI 53821

# PRINCIPAL STATIONS IN WORLD AREAS

This list includes only strategically located stations in the countries named for the convenience of travelers and military personnel.

## ARGENTINA

*Bahia Blanca.* Rev. Martin Völz, Santa Fe 859, 8000 Bahia Blanca, Buenos Aires (Tel 011-54-0291-4539094)

*Buenos Aires.* Rev. Oscar Dirr. R.S. Naón 1988, 1430 (Belgrano) Cap.Federal.Bs.Aires. (Tel 011-54-11-4552560)

*Buenos Aires.* Rev. Eldor Rautenberg, Isabel la Católica 830 1269.Cap.Federal.Bs.Aires. (Tel 011-54-11-4303-0778)

*Córdoba.* Rev. Digno Rosin, Sol de Mayo 837, 5000 CORDOBA, Córdoba (Tel 011-54-0351-4893883)

*Rio Cuarto.* Rev. Gabriel González, Ayacucho 2233, 5800 Rio Cuarto, Córdoba (Tel 011-54-03586-428532

*Mar del Plata.* Rev. Rodolfo Sexauer, Funes 3178, 7600 Mar del Plata, Buenos Aires (Tel 011-54-0223-4723734)

*Oberá.* Rev. Arturo Eisner, Rivadavia 807, 3360, Misiones (Tel 011-54-03755-422844)

*Puerto Madryn.* Rev. Carlos Heidel, Gob.Maíz 429 9120 Puerto Madryn Chubut (Tel 011-54-02965-471149)

*Rosario.* Rev. Eldor Hamann, Ameghino 1078, 2000 Rosario Santa Fe (Tel 011-54-0341-4636688)

*Tucumán.* Rev. Claudio Herber Avda. Belgrano 4182, S.M. de Tucuman, Tucumán (Tel 011-54-0381-4351477

## AUSTRALIA*

*Adelaide.* Bethlehem, 170 Flinders St., S.P. Shultz (Tel 011-61-8-8332-1786) D J Christian (Tel 011-61-8-8331-2858) Services 9 a.m., 11 a.m. and 7 p.m.; Immanuel, 139 Archer St., North Adelaide, P. M. Smith (Tel 8/8344-1717) Services 9:30 a.m.; St. Stephen's, 152 Wakefield St., R.J. Kempe (Tel 011-61-8/8272-2319) T. I. Muller (Tel 8/8431-4078) Services 9:30 a.m., 11:00 a.m. and 7 p.m.

*Alice Springs.* Lutheran, 49 Gap Rd., R. Borgas (Tel 8/8952-1408) Service 9:00 a.m.

*Brisbane.* St. Andrew, 1 Wickham Terr. (Tel 7-3870-9128) S. G. Nuske; Services 10 a.m. and 7 p.m.

*Brisbane South.* Nazareth, 12 Hawthorne St., Woolloongabba, W. R. Kerber (Tel 011-61-7-3391-2854) Service 8:30 a.m.

*Canberra.* St. Peter, 6 Boolee St., Reid, (Tel 011-61-2/6248-0064) Vacant; Service 10:30 a.m.

*Darwin.* St. Andrew, 14 Trower Rd., Nightcliff, J. Vitale (Tel 011-61-8/8948-1613) Service 8:30 a.m.

*Hobart.* St. Peter, 207 Davey St., J. H. S. Heidenreich (Tel 011-61-3/6228-2919) Service 10:00 a.m.

*Melbourne.* St. John Southgate, 20 City Road, South Bank T.E. Peitsch (Tel 3/9682-4995) Services 8:30 a.m. and 10:30 a.m.

*Perth.* St. John, 16 Aberdeen St., G. J. Burger (Tel 011-61-8/9444-9484) Service 8:30 a.m. and 10:00 a.m.

*Southport.* (Gold Coast) Trinity, Queen St., W. T. Zweck (Tel 011-61-7/5532-7366) Services 8:30 a.m. and 7 p.m.

*Sydney.* St. Paul, 3 Stanley St., (off Hyde Park), F. Veerhuis (Tel 011-61-2/9419-6586) Services 10:30 a.m.; Trinity, 17-19 Valentine St. 10:30 a.m.

## BELGIUM

*Antwerp.* Evangelical Lutheran Church. Pastor Gijsbertus van Hattem, Tabakvest 59, 2000 Antwerpen (Tel 011-32-3/233-6250) Services Antwerp Sundays 10 a.m. (Flemish/Dutch)

*Brussels.* All Lutheran Church, Av Salome 7, St. Pieters-Woluwe; Services 2nd and 4th Sundays 4:30 p.m. (English); Information: Pastor Gijsbertus van Hattem (Tel 011-32-32-33-6250) Fam. Kollacks Tel. 011-32-23-54-25-49

## BRAZIL

*Aracaju, SE.* Rev. Edson Nimbu. Rua Neopolis, 30 49075-400 Aracaju, SE. Tel (079) 236-1558

*Belem, PA.* Rev Ari Schulz, Trav. Barão de Mamore, 451 Bairro Guama, Caixa Postal 505, 66073-070 Belém, PA, Phone 091-229-5869

*Belo Horizonte, MG.* Rev Arnaldo Hoffmann Fiho, Caixa Postal 329, Rua Piaui 138, Bairro Santa Efigenia, 30161-970 Belo Horizonte, MG, Phone 031-241-1540

*Blumenau, SC.* Rev Adilson Schunke, Rua Roseli Schoenau, 173, Itoupava Norte, Caixa Postal 4562, 89052-970 Blumenau, SC Phone 047-323-8104

*Boa Vista, PR.* Rev Denilson Flegler, Caixa Postal 385, 69301-970 Boa Vista, RR, Phone 095-224-4896

*Brasilia, DF.* Rev Urbana Lehrer SHCGN 709 Bloco L - Casa 21. Caixa Postal 02374, 70849-970 Brasilia, DF. Phone (61) 274-9214

*Campo Grande MS.* Rev. Carlos Wilhelms Rua Luiz Braile, 423 Bairro N Sia de Fátima 79010-080 Campo Grande MS Phone 67-751-7204

*Cuiabá MT,* Rev Horst Musskopf, Rua Profa Zulmira Canavarros, 375, Centro Norte, 78005-340 Cuiabá, MT, Phone (65) 322-6398

*Curitiba, PR.* Rev Flavio Horlle, Ruâ Alcino Guanabara, 2374, Bairro Vila Hauer, 81630-190 Curitiba, PR, Phone 41-278-5024

*Florianopolis SC.* Rev. Daltro Tomm, Ruâ Sao Pedro, 368, Estreito Balneário, 88075-520 Florianopolis, SC. Phone (48) 244-8522

*Fortaleza, CE.* Rev Paulo R Verdin, Rua Carlos Camara, 1638 Jardim America, Caixa Postal 12141, 60021-970 Fortaleza, CE Phone (085) 494-2709

*Foz do Iguacu, PR.* (National Park, Iguaçu Falls) Rev. Celso Wottrich, Rua Marechal Deodoro, 1258. Caixa Postal 305, 85851-970 Foz do Iguaçu, PR. Phone (45) 574-3049

*Goiania, GO.* Rev. Ivo Wille. Alameda das Rosas 2023, Setor Oeste, 74125-010 Goiânia, GO, Phone (62) 233-5554

*Gramado, RS.* Rev. Arno Elicker, Rua Borges de Medeiros, 3200, Caixa Postal 14, 95670-000 Gramado, RS, Phone (54) 286-1958

*João Pessoa, PB* Rev Arno Eller, Rua Maria Eliete C Fabricio, 240, Bancarios, Caixa Postal 1150, 58051-600 João Pessoa, PB, Phone 83-235-1324

*Maceio, AL.* Rev. Waldyr Hoffmann, Rua Gazeta de Alagoas, 4 P.dos Martirios, B Cambona, 57080-130 Maceio, AL Phone 82- 221 7925

*Manaus, AM.* Rev. Paulo Kuck, Av Codajas, 239, Bairro Cachoeirinha, 69065-130 Manaus, AM Phone 92-663-5577

*Natal, RN.* Rev Airton Schroeder, Rua Piquia, 7830, Cidade Satelite III Etapa, 59067-580 Natal, RN Phone 84-218-2655

*Palmas, TO* Rev Laudir Franca da Rosa, ARNE 13, Q II, Alam 12 Lte 41, 77065-440 Palmas, TO, Phone 63-213-3080

*Ponta Grossa PR.* (National Park), Rev Sergio Flor, Rua Cel. Dulcidio, 1501. Caixa Postal 521, 84001-970 Ponta Grossa, PR. Phone (42) 224-2193

*Porto Alegre, RS.* Rev. Horst Kuchenbecker. Av. Pátria, 631/203, Bairro Sao Geraldo. 90230-971 Porto Alegre, RS, Phone (51) 342-6013

*Porto Velho, RO* Rev Derio Krause, Rua João Pedro da Rocha, 882, Bairro Nova Porto Velho, 78906-200 Porto Velho, RO Phone 69-222-2745

*Recife, PE.* Rev. Fernando H Huf, Rua Des. Motta Jr., 45, Casa Amarela, 52051-360, Recife, PE, Phone (81) 268-4735

*Rio Grande.* Rev Adelar Munieweg, AV. Presidente Vargas, 729 Cx. Postal 113, 96.500-970 Rio Grande, RS Phone (532) 32-8926

*Rio de Janeiro, RJ.* Rev. Egon Starosky Rua Gonçalves Crespo, 341, 20270-320 Rio de Janeiro, RJ Phone 21-268-4398

*Salvador BA.* Rev. Fredolino Seiboth Filho, Rua Pará s/n Bairro Paripe 40800-500 Salvador, BA Phone: (71) 521-3903

*São Luis, MA.* Rev. Milton Proschold, Caixa Postal 624, Rua Manoel Coelho Alencar, 1120 Planalto Pingáro, 65001-970 São Luis, MA. Phone 98-225-2303

*São Paulo SP.* Rev. Mario Rost. Rua Januario Zingaro, 67. Campo Limpo Caixa Postal 60826, 05799-970 São Paulo, SP. Phone (11) 5841-4254

*Teresina, PI.* Rev Renato Hannisch, Rodovia BR 316, 7200 Parque Piaui, 64025-970 Teresina, PI, Phone 086-227-3252

*Vitória, ES.* Rev. Eiter Schneider, Rua Osvaldo Cruz, 468 Maruipe 29043-740 Vitória ES Phone 27-323-2129 Velha, ES Phone 27-326-5080

## CHILE

*Valparaiso.* Rev. Cristian Rautenberg, Los Pellines 71-Playa Ancha-Valparaiso Tel 00-56-32-281157 FAX 00-56-32-288923
E-mail: luterano@tutopia.com

*Viña del Mar.* Rev. Carlos Schumann, Calle 4 N° 2035, Santa Inés—Viña del Mar Tel 00-56-32-689021 FAX 00-56-32-699686
E-Mail: concordi@ctcinternet.cl

*El Belloto,* Rev. Cristian Rautenberg, Puelches 220—Villa El Belloto 2000 Phone: 00-56-32-943709
E-mail: luterano@tutopia.com

*Instituto Biblico Luterano* Rev Sergio Fritzler, Los Pellines 71—Playa Ancha—Valparaiso Casilla de Correo 45—Correo Central
E-Mail: ibl-ielchi@starmedia.com

## CHINA

(See Hong Kong) LCMS China Ministry Team

## DENMARK

*Aarhus.* Gratiakirken, Bissensgade 14C, 8000 Aarhus C. Rev. Leif G. Jensen, Ewaldsvej 9, DK8723 Losning Tel 011-45-7565-1660 FAX 011-45-7565-1662. E-Mail Lutheran@vivit.dk

*Copenhagen.* Martinskirken, Martinsvej 4, DK-1926 Frederiksberg Rev. Vagn Lyrstrand, Aalekistevej 157, DK-2720 Vanlose Tel 011-45-3874-6661 E-Mail Lyrstrand@vivit.dk

*Lohals, Langeland, Lohals Kirke.* Ostergade 34, DK-5953 Tranekaer, Rev. Vagn Lystrand, Aalekistevej 157, DK-2720 Vanlose. Tel 011-45-3874-6661 E-Mail Lyrstrand@vivit.dk

*Losning, Jytland, The Lutheran Freechurch,* Vinkelvej, DK-8723 Losning, Rev. Leif G. Jensen, Ewaldsvej 9 DK-8723 Losning. Tel 011-45-7565-1660. FAX 011-45-7565-1662. E-Mail Lutheran@vivit.dk

*Haderslev, Jytland, Treenighedskirken,* Buegade, DK 6100 Haderslev, Rev. Leif G. Jensen Ewaldsvej 9, DK 8723 Losning. Tel 011-45-7565-1660. FAX 011-45-7565-1662. E-Mail Lutheran@vivit.dk

## EL SALVADOR

*Ahuachapan.* Rev. Antonio Lorenzana

*Pasaquina.* La Santa Trinidad, Rev. Mauro Recinos

*San Miguel.* El Divino Redentor, Colonia Hirlemann,

Rev. Jose Amador Torres, Tel 011-661-3641

*San Salvador.* Resurrection, Calle 5 Noviembre 242, Dr. Medardo Gomez

*Santa Ana.* Cristo Rey, 9 Ave. Norte 59 Barrio Sta. Barbara, Rev. Carlos Najera, Tel 011-503-41-1847

*Usulutan.* Rev. Crisanto Castaneda

## ENGLAND

*Borehamwood.* St. Paul (Service 11 a.m.), Cranes Way, Borehamwood, Hertfordshire WD6 2EU (Tel 011-44-953-3308); Vacant Parsonage same address

*Cambridge.* Resurrection (Service 11 a.m.), 25 Westfield Lane, Cambridge CB4 3QS (Tel 011-44-223-461465), Pastor: Vacant

*Coventry.* Good Shepherd, (Service 11 a.m.) 49 Eastern Green Rd., Coventry CV5 7LG (Tel 011-44-203 470780), Pastor H. J. M. Leed

*Fareham.* Our Saviour, (Service 10:30 a.m.) Mendips Rd., Fareham, Hants P014-1QD; Pastor Karl Fry, 1 Cherry Tree Ave., Fareham, Hants PO14 1PY (Tel 011-44-1329 284172)

*Harlow.* Redeemer, (Service 6:00 p.m.) Bush Fair Harlow Essex CM18 6PN (Tel 011-44-1279 423870); Pastor Paul Fry

*Kentish Town.* Luther Tyndale, (Service 10 a.m.) Leighton Crescent London NW5 (Tel 011-44-170 267-3994) Pastor G. Jenks, 6 Dunollie Place, London NW5 2XR (Tel 011-44-171 485 9638)

*Liverpool.* Immanuel (Service 11 a m), Rockbourne Ave., Liverpool L25 4NT, (Tel 011-44-151 428-9300); Pastor A. E. Smith, 4, Holdings Road, Norfolk Park, Sheffield. S2 2RE Tel 011-427 87232

*Petts Wood.* Christ (Service 11 a.m.), Poverest Road, Petts Wood, Kent, BR5 1RD (Tel 011-44-1689-822340); Pastor John Ehlers

*Plymouth.* St. Peter (Services 11 a.m. and 6 p.m.), Larkham Lane, Plympton, Plymouth, Devon PL7 4EG, (Tel 011-44-1752-336240). Pastor E Brockwell, 1 The Dell, Plympton, Plymouth, Devon PL7 4PS, (Tel 011-44-1752-335698)

*Ruislip.* St. Andrew (Service 11 a.m.), Whitby Rd. & Queens Walk, Ruislip, Middlesex HA4 9DY (Tel 011-44-181-866-2703); Pastor J. Naumann, Parsonage 394, Victoria Rd., South Ruislip, Middlesex HA4 OEH (Tel 011-44-181-845-4242)

*Sheffield (Pennine Parish).* Holy Cross (Service 11:15 a.m.), 4 Holdings Rd., Norfolk Park, Sheffield S2 2RE Preaching Station contact Liverpool for service times; Pastor Alan Smith (Tel 011-44-1742-787232)

*Sunbury-on-Thames.* All Hallows, (Service 11:00 a.m.) 139 Groveley Rd., Sunbury-on-Thames, Middlesex TW16 7JT (Tel 011-44-181-890-1770) Pastor: Larry Labatt

*Sunderland.* St. Timothy, (Service 6:30 p.m.) Queen Alexandra Rd., Sunderland SR2 9AA (Tel 011-44-191-5284424); Pastor R. Englund

*Tottenham.* Holy Trinity (Service 11 a.m.), 53 Antill Rd., N15 4AR (Tel 011-44-181-801-0527) Pastor D Van der Linde

## FINLAND

*Helsinki.* Chapel, Fabianink. 13 A 1 00130 Helsinki.

*Lahti.* Church, Rajak 7, 15100 Lahti

## FRANCE

*Mulhouse.* Frederic Bohy, 21 Chemin des Ardennes 68100 Mulhouse (Tel 011-33-03-89-44-27-00)

*Paris.* St. Sauveur, Francois Poillet 105 Rue de Abbe Groult 75015, Paris (Tel 011-33-01-48-42-58-09)

*Paris.* Eastern Suburbs St. Jean (St. Maur), Gilles Aoustin, 109 Ave. Beaurepaire, 94100 Saint-Maur (Tel 011-33-01-48-89-30-91)

*Paris.* Northern Suburbs St. Etienne, Vacant, 16 rue des Cas Rouges 95100 Argenteuil (Tel 011-33-01-34-10-34-25)

*Paris.* Southern Suburbs St. Pierre, Claude Ludwig 9 rue Jules Barbier, 92290 Chatenay-Malabry (Tel 011-33-01-40-94-95-57)

*Prailles.* (Poitou) St. Paul, Marc Amilhat, Maupertuis de la Couarde, 79800 La Mothe St. Heray (Tel 011-33-05-49-79-87-63)

*Schillersdorf & Obersoultzbach.* Martin Jautzy, Schillersdorf 67340, Ingwiller (Tel 011-33-03-88-89-48-21)

*Strasbourg & Heiligenstein.* Jean-Louis Schaeffer, 6a Place d'Austerlitz, 67000 Strasbourg (Tel 011-33-03-88-36-27-34)

*Woerth & Lembach.* Philippe Volff, 12 Route de Haguenau, 67360 Woerth S. Sauer (Tel 011-33-03-88-09-30-99)

## GERMANY

*Berlin-Mitte.* Lutherische Kirche, Annenstr. 53, D-10719 Berlin; Pastor Wilhelm Torgerson, (Tel 011-49-30-2785102, FAX 011-49-30-27560719)

*Berlin-Spandau.* Heilig-Geist, Schönwalder Allee 57, 13587 Berlin, (Tel 011-43-30-37595530, FAX 011-49-30-37595531)
E-Mail HeiligGeist.Spandau@selk.de

*Berlin-Wilmersdorf.* Zum Heilige Kreuz, Nassauische Str. 17, D-10717 Berlin, Pastor Markus Fischer, (Tel and FAX 011-49-30-8731805)

*Berlin-Zehlendorf.* St Marien, Riemeisterstr. 10-12, D-14169 Berlin, Pastor Dr. Gottfried Martens (Tel 011-49-30-8027034, FAX 011-49-30-80903013; E-Mail StMarien.Berlin@selk.de)

*Braunschweig,* Paul-Gerhardt, Dresdenstr 8, D-38124 Braunschweig, Pastor Helmut Neddens (Tel 011-49-531-64165, E-Mail Helmut.Neddens@t-online.de)

*Bremen.* Bethlehem, Ludwig-Roselius-Allee 95, D-28329 Bremen, Pastor Eggert Klaer (Tel 011-49-421-471082, FAX 011-421-4799911)

*Dresden.* Dreieinigkeit, Bautzener Str. 88. D-01099 Dresden, Pastor Andreas Rehr, Rabenauer Str. 7, 01159 Dresden (Tel and FAX 011-49-351-4126238)

*Duesseldorf.* Erloeser, Eichendorffstr. 7, D-40474 Duesseldorf, Supt. Detlef Budniok (Tel 011-49-211-433032, FAX 011-49-211-4542323)

*Erfurt.* Christus Tettaustr 3–4, D-99094 Erfurt, Supt. Norbert Rudzinski (Tel 011-49-361-2251911, FAX 011-49-361-2253045, E-Mail Rudzinski.Norbert@t-online.de)

*Essen.* Lutherische Kirche, Moltkeplatz 19, D-45138 Essen, Propst Hartmut Hauschild (Tel 011-49-201-263394, FAX 011-49-201-252070)

*Frankfurt,* Trinitatis, Theobald-Christ-Str 23–25, D-60316 Frankfurt/Main, Pastor Eberhard Ramme (Tel 011-49-69-448617, FAX 011-49-69-94415158)

*Goettingen.* Martin Luther, Walkemüehlenweg 28b, D-37083 Goettingen, Pastor Stefan Foerster (Tel 011-49-551-77981) FAX 011-49-511-7707784, E-Mail ste.foerster@t-online.de

*Gotha,* Kreuz, Schelihastr 12, D-99867 Gotha, Pastor Joerg Kallensee (Tel 011-49-3621-850785)

*Halle/Saale.* Maria-Magdalena auf der Moritzburg, Pastor Dr. Klaus Engelbrecht, Advokatenweg 48, D-06114 Halle/Saale (Tel and FAX 011-49-345-5233764)

*Hamburg.* Dreieinigkeit, Burgstr. 10, D-20535 Hamburg, Pastor Wolfgang Schmidt (Tel 011-49-40-255622, FAX 011-49-40-25178101) or, Zion, Wandsbeker Stieg 29c, D-22087 Hamburg Pastor Frank Eisel (Tel 011-49-40-255316, FAX 011-49-40-25497218)

*Hannover.* Bethlehem, Große Barlinge 35/37, D-30171 Hannover, Pastor: Gert Kelter (Tel 011-49-511-815830, FAX 011-49-511-2880913, E-Mail luth.beth@t-online.de or St Petri, Weinstr 5, D-30171 Hannover, Pastor Konrad Uecker (Tel 011-49-511-855989, FAX 011-49-511-855959)

*Heidelberg.* St. Thomas, Freiburger Straße, D-69126 Heidelberg-Rohrbach; Pastor Ekkehard Heicke Friedrich-Ebert-Allee 53b, D-69117 (Tel 011-49-6221-22186, FAX 011-49-601487)

*Kaiserslautern.* St. Michaelis, Karpfenstr. 7, D-67655 Kaiserslautern (Tel and FAX 011-49-631-64327, E-Mail Kaiserslautern@selk.de)

*Kassel.* St. Michaelis, Tischbeinstr 73, D-34121 Kassel Pastor Juergen Schmidt (Tel 011-49-561-23674, FAX 011-49-561-2889559)

*Koeln.* St. Johannis Waisenhausgasse 67, D-50676 Koeln, Pastor Hans-Ulrich Otto (Tel 011-49-221-316590)

*Leipzig.* St. Trinitatis, Kleiststr 56, D-04157 Leipzig, Pastor Fritz-Adolf Haefner (Tel 011-49-341-9126503, FAX 011-49-341-9126543)

*Limburg,* St Johannes, In der Erbach, D-65549 Limburg, Pastor Joerg Ruecker, Diezer Str 67, D-65549 Limburg (Tel 011-49-6431-3381, FAX 011-49-6431-932807)

*Marburg.* Auferstehung (Kirche am Barfuessertor), D-35037 Pastor Manfred Brockmann, Savignystr 11a, D-35037 Marburg (Tel and FAX 011-49-6421-21777)

*Muenchen.* Trinitatis, Lustheimst. 20, D-81247 Muenchen, Pastor Dr Hans Horsch (Tel and FAX 011-49-89-8114347, E-Mail hans.horsch@t-online.de)

*Muenster.* St Thomas, Flandernstr 40, D-48147 Muenster, Pastor Volker George, Masurenweg 10, 48147 Muenster (Tel 011-49-251-271683)

*Oberursel,* St. Johannes, Altkönigstr. 154, D-61440 Oberursel, Pastor Richard Tepper (Tel 011-49-6171-24977, FAX 011-49-6171-268320)

*Potsdam.* Christus, Hebbelstr 14, D-14469 Potsdam, Pastor Christoph Schulze (Tel 011-49-331-295820)

*Stuttgart.* Immanuel, Schwarenbergstr 150, D-70184 Stuttgart, Pastor Lienhard Krueger, Metzlerweg 3, D-70186 Stuttgart (Tel 011-49-711-461523, FAX 011-49-711-485507, E-Mail Stuttgart@selk.de)

*Wiesbaden.* Christus, Daimlerstr, 38, D-65197 Wiesbaden, Supt Wolfgang Schillhahn (Tel 011-49-611-424868, FAX 011-49-611-9410478, E-Mail Wiesbaden@selk.de)

*Wuppertal.* St. Petri, Paradestr. 41, D-42107 Wuppertal, Pastor Michael Bracht (Tel 011-49-202-4468160, FAX 011-49-202-4468162, E-Mail StPetri.Wuppertal@selk.de)

## GHANA

*Accra.* St. Paul, PO Box 197, Kaneshie, Accra, Ghana, W Africa (Tel 011-233-21-232250 and 011-233-21-223487, FAX 011-233-21-233155) FAX 011-233-21-220947 (Physical Address: Ring Road, Kanda, near Broadcasting House and Kanda Estate Boys Junior Secondary School) President's Home Phone: 011-233-21-775550

*Kumasi.* Trinity. PO Box 3536 Kumasi, Ghana West Africa

*Bunkpurugu.* St. Andrews Lutheran Church, PO Box 43, Gambaga, N.R., Ghana, W Africa

*Sekondi.* All Saints, Old A.M.E. Chapel, Hosanna Hills, Box 474, Takoradi, Ghana, W Africa

*Sofokrom.* Via Takoradi. Bethel Lutheran Congregation

*Takoradi.* Tonokrom. St. John, PO Box 474, Takoradi, Ghana, W Africa

*Tema.* Trinity, Community 2, Aggrey Rd., PO Box 143, Tema, Ghana, W Africa

*Kintampo.* (for stations in BA Region) All Nations Lutheran Church, PO Box 26, Kintampo, BA, Ghana, W Africa

*Tamale.* Evangelical Lutheran Church of Ghana, c/o GILLBT, PO Box 378, Tamale, NR, Ghana, W Africa

*Gbintiri.* Lutheran Training Centre, Gbintiri, PO Box 43, Gambaga, NR, Ghana, W Africa

*Bawku.* (for stations in UER) Lutheran Mission, PO Box 136, Bawku, UER, Ghana, W Africa.

## GUAM

*Agana.* Lutheran Church of Guam, 787 W. Marine Dr., Anigua (Agana), Guam 96910 (Tel 011-671-477-8595) Rev. Randall L. Weinkauf, Field Service Pastor, Sunday 10:30 a.m.

## GUATEMALA

*Antigua.* La Resurrection, 1 Ave. Norte. No. 35; Deacon Carlos Garcia, Centro Luterano (Tel and FAX 011-502-8320225) Mail Apdo. Postal 234 Antigua Guatemala

*Chajabal.* San Andres Xecul, Totonicapan, Nueva Jerusalem, Pastor Martin Chan

*Chiquimula.* Conlut mission site, Pastor Tiburcio Girõn Mejia.

*Gualan.* Apdo. Postal 8, Gualan, Zacapa, Guatemala. Pastor Luis Jacinto, La Resurreccion.

*Guatemala City.* Christo Rey, 4 Calle 2-55. Zone 9; Pastor David Rodriguez, Adolfo Borges, Assistant (Tel 011-502-3327270, 011-502-3603356 and 011-502-3604289) Mail Apdo. Postal 234 Guatemala City (01001), Guatemala

*Las Pacayas.* Uspantan, El Quiche; Mission Church, *"Cristo El Camino"* Mail Apdo. Postal 1111 Guatemala City (01001) Guatemala

*Puerto Barrios.* Izabal, Cristo El Salvador, 5 Ave. 12 y 13 Calles, Apartado Postal 416 (18001) Tel/FAX 011-502-9480751; Pastor Byron Paz

*Quetzaltenango.* La Ascension, Diagonal 8 11-10 Zone 1; (Tel 011-502-7618519) Deacon Ignacio Chan Cux; Mail Apdo. Postal 383, Quetzaltenango, Guatemala

*San Marcos.* El Buen Samaritano, Mail Apartado Postal 8 San Marcos, San Marcos, Guatemala, C.A. Rev. Salomõn Gudiel (Tel 011-502-766-3481)

*Santiago Zamora.* Redeemer of the World, Mail Santiago Zamora, San Antonio, Aguas Calientes, Depto. Sacatepequèz,Guatemala, C.A. Deacon: Nicolas Hernàndez and Gerardo Lòpez.

*Zacapa.* El Divino Salvador, Barrio San Marcos (Tel 011-502-9410-063 or 011-502-9410-254) Pastor Gerardo Vasquez, Deacon Ared Rodriguez

## HONDURAS

*Tegucigalpa.* Iglesia Cristiana Luterana de Honduras, Barrio Villa Adela, 20 Calle Entre 6 Y 7 Ave. Casa #624 Comayaguela. (Tel/FAX #37-4893) Apdo. Postal #2861 Tegucigalpa

*San Pedro.* Iglesia Cristiana Luterana de Honduras, Pasaje Juventud, Bloque #15, Colonia La Union. Tel/FAX 52-3087, Apartado Postal #1176, San Pedro Sula, Honduras

## HONG KONG

*Hong Kong Island.* Church of All Nations, Lutheran 8 South Bay Close-Repulse Bay, Hong Kong. Phone: 011-852-2812-0375, FAX 011-852-2812-9508, E-Mail <can@admin.hkis.edu.hk> Rev Dale Koehneke Home Phone: 011-852-2873-3585 Hong Kong International School 6 & 23 South Bay Close, Repulse Bay, Hong Kong Phone: 011-852-2812-2305 FAX 011-852-2812-9590 Dr Charles Dull, Head of School Home Phone: 011-852-2813-1269

*Kowloon.* LCMS China Ministry Team, Flat A No. 12 Wiltshire Road, Kowloon Tong, Kowloon, Hong Kong Phone: 011-852-2375-8987 FAX 011-852-2375-9177. The Lutheran Church—Hong Kong Synod and Concordia Seminary, 68 Begonia Rd, Yau Yat Chuen, Kowloon, Hong Kong. Phone: 011-852-2397-3721, FAX 011-852-2397-5616

## INDIA

*Bombay.* Lutheran Centre, Marve Rd., Malad, Rev. S. Alfred, Marve Rd, Malad, Bombay 400064 India (Tel 011-91-22683-301)

*Kodaikanal.* Zion (Tel 286) Loch End, Kodaikanal 624101 Tamil Nadu

*Trivandrum.* Perurkada Lutheran Centre, Trivandrum 695005, Kerala

*Madras.* Christian Media Centre-India, Dr. S. Suviseshamuthu, Executive Director 21 Eldams Rd, Teynampet Madras 600018, India Phone: 011-91-44-458556 (office), 429208 (residence) FAX 044-499-1360

*Nagercoil* Concordia Seminary, Nagercoil 629001, Tamil Nadu, India Phone and FAX 011-91-4652-23445

*Cochin.* Rev. Herbert Marshall 39/3459 Lutheran Center Ravipuram, M.S. Road Ernakulam, Cochin 632 016, Kerala

## JAMAICA

*Kingston.* St. Andrew Lutheran, at Jamaica Theological Seminary, 14 West Avenue, Kingston 8 Jamaica; Montego Bay. Rev. James Weist. Contact Kingston for information, Rev. Peter Kirby. Sunday 9:15 a.m. Tel 876-969-7651 FAX 925-3179. Office 1 Morecambe Ave #1, PO Box 1085 Kingston 8

## JAPAN

*Sapporo.* Sapporo Lutheran Center, Nishi, 6-3-1, Nishi, Odori Chuo-Ku Sapporo-Shi, 060-0042 Hokkaido; (Tel 001-81-11-251-1311). FAX 001-81-11-251-4805

*Tokyo.* Japan Lutheran Church, 2-32 Fujimi 1-Chome, Chiyoda-ku, Tokyo 102-0071; Rev. Yutaka Kumei, Tel 011-81-3-3261-5266) St. Paul International Lutheran Church, 2-32 Fujimi, 1-Chome, Chiyoda-ku 102-0071, (Tel 011-813-3261-3740)

*Okinawa.* Rev. Michael Nearhood, 362 Aza-Shimabukuro, Kitanakagusuku-Son, Nakagami-Gun, Okinawa 901-2301; Home Tel 011-81-98-932-6560, Church Tel and FAX 011-81-98-933-5535

## KOREA

*Seoul.* Lutheran Church Center, 7-20 Sinchun-Dong. Songpa-Gu, Seoul, Korea. E-Mail LCK0001@Chollian.net. Hilbert W. Riemer (Office: 011-82-2-752-6040 Home: 011-82-331-283-6197)

*Seoul.* International Lutheran Church, 726-39 Hannam-Dong Yonsan-ku 140-210, Rev. Dwayne Hoyer, Field Service Pastor. Sunday 9:30 a.m. (Tel 011-82-2-794-6274)

*Pusan.* Pusan Jeil Lutheran Church, 1036-3 Kwangandong, Namku, Pusan 613-103. Tel 011-82-51-753-0378

Pusan Shin-Il Lutheran Church, 540-87 Kaekeum 1-dong, Jun-Gu, Pusan 614-111, Korea Tel 011-82-51-893-5950

## LEBANON

*Beirut.* Middle East Lutheran Ministry, Georges Abou, Jaoudeh Bldg., lst Floor, Kanj Quarter-Jal-El-Dib, Beirut, Lebanon (Tel 011-961-4-716272) Tel and Fax 011-961-4-724312 Director: Moris A Jahshan

## LIBERIA

*Monrovia.* The Evangelical Lutheran Mission (ELM) Rev David Londenberg

## MACAU

*Macau.* St Paul, Rua Da Silva Mendes Eddificio Jade Garden Block L-M Macau Tel: 011-853-593-314

## MEXICO

*Cd. Juarez:* Cristo Rey, Calle Hospital 2830 Pte., Federico Resendiz Ortega, Rvdo. Tel 14-77-98, 32160 Cd. Juarez, Chih.

*Chihuahua.* Gloria Dei, Ave. 20 de Noviembre 806, Tel 10-27-59, 31030 Chihuahua, Chih.

*Guadalajara.* All Saints Lutheran Church, 1084 Prado de los Pinos, Vacant, Tel 21-67-41, Apdo. Postal 5-714, Guadalajara 5

*Guasave.* Divino Emanuel, Av. Vicente Guerrero 63 Sur, Rvdo. Rosalio Hernandez Osuna, Apdo. Postal 258, 81000 Guasave, Sin.

*Matamoros.* La Santisima Trinidad, Ave. Rio San Juan 53 Col. San Francisco, Samuel Perez Gaona Tel 2-36-13 87350 Matamoros, Tamps.

*Mexicali.* San Juan, Ave. Chihuahua 1101 y Calle Uxmal, Col. Guajardo, Rev. Juan Rosas Aguilar, Tel 55-22-88, 21030 Mexicali, B. C.

*Mexico City.* El Buen Pastor (Good Shepherd), Paseo de las Palmas 1910 Lomas de Chapultepec, Rev Todd Roberts, Tel 596-10-34, 11000 Mexico, D. F.

*Mexico City.* San Pablo Dr. Atl. 187, Col. Sta. Ma. la Ribera., Rev. Jaziel E. Lopez Fajardo, Tel 547-70-27, 06400 México, D. F.

*Mexico City.* San Pedro, Playa Manzanillo 534, Col. Marte, Rvdo. Abiut Farjardo Ruiz, Tel 633-82-56, 08830 Mexico, D. F.

*Monterrey.* El Sembrador, Vidrios y Cristales 823, Col. Vidriera, Rev Pablo Gamaliel Dominquez, Tel 43-23-40 64000 Monterrey, N. L.

*Sonora Mission.* San Marcos, Callejon Felix Contreras 400 y Calle Cuarta, Rev Filiberto Jimenez J., 843400 San Luis, Rio Colorado, Son

*Tijuana.* El Mesias. Camino Viejo a Tecate Km 23, Rvdo Daniel Saavedra Teran, Tel 89-07-32, 22660 La Mesa Tijuana, B. C.

*Torreon.* La Transfiguracion, Paseo do las Jacarandas 245 Pte, Jose Angel Hernandez Marquez (Vicario), 27110 Torreon, Coah.

## NEW ZEALAND

*Auckland.* St. John, 32 Akiraho St., Mt. Eden, M. R. Schultz (Tel 011-9/579-4490) Service 10:00 a.m..

*Christchurch.* St. Paul, Burwood and Travis Rds., Burwood, T. J. Klein (Tel 011-3-383-3450) Service 9:30 a.m.

*Wellington.* St. Paul, King St. Newtown, R. P. Bartholomaeus (Tel 011-4/235-7331) Services 9:00 a.m. and 11:00 a.m..

## NIGERIA

*Aba.* LCN, No. 264 Ehi Rd., Imo State

*Abak.* LCN, Abak (Temporary Site) Opposite AKBC, Abak, Via Hospital Rd., Abak

*Abuja*.* LCN c/o Church Village, Abuja

*Abuja*.* LCN Bwari, Abuja (Behind Government Primary School) Market Road Bwari, PO Box 3031, Abuja, F.C.T.

*Calabar*.* LCN, 90 Nelson Mandela Rd., Calabar, Box 187

*Calabar*.* LCN, Primary School, Ediba Qua

*Eket.* LCN, Eket Town, Oron Rd., Eket

*Enugu*.* 70 Port Harcourt St., Uwani, Enugu

*Etinan*.* LCN, Etinan (off Uyo Road)

*Ibadan.* Former Aresa Modern Secondary School, Okiado, Ibadan, Box 27382

*Ikom*.* LCN, 5 Uyo St., Ikom

*Ikot Ekpene.* Ibong Rd (Off Umuahia Rd.) Ikot Ekpene

*Jos*.* ELM House, Bukuru Rd., Box 495 Tel 011-234-73-54243

*Lagos*.* PO Box 294, Suru-Lere, Lagos, 36 Ladipo Labingo Crescent (off Eric Moore) Tel MR. A.O. Udo 011-234-1-526257

*Ogoja*.* LCN, Ogoja Town (opposite General Hospital)

*Okigwe.* LCN, Okigwe (off Umuezegem Road)

*Oron.* No. 12 Akwa Edung St., Oron

*Owerri*.* Uzii Primary School, Owerri

*Port Harcourt.* 9 Dim St (Off Azikiwe Rd), Mile 2 Diobu, PO Box 1716, Diobu, Port Harcourt.

*Sapele.* Sapele State

*Uyo*.* 37 Enwe St., Uyo

*Lutheran Church of Nigeria (urban congregations)

## PANAMA

*Balboa/Ancon.* (Panama City); Tel Office: (011-507-228-9628) Redeemer Lutheran Church Avda Arnulfo Arias Madrid, 830 Balboa Road Worship (English Sundays 9:00 a.m.), (Spanish, Domingo, Sunday 11:00 a.m.)

Asociacíon Misionera Luterana de Panama (AMILPA) & Lutheran Bible Institute Apartado Postal 2070, Balboa/Ancon, Republic of Panama Tel 011-507-228-4564 & 011-507-211-0886, FAX 011-507-228-5742

## PAPUA NEW GUINEA

*Amapyak.* Highlands Lutheran School, PO Box 363 Wabag Enga Province Papua New Guinea, Tel 011-675-547-1235, FAX 011-675-547-1235

*Goroka.* St John, English service 9:00 a.m.

*Lae.* Martin Luther Seminary, English Sunday Vesper Service 7:30 p.m.

*Lae.* St. Paul, Markham Road, English service 7:30 p.m. 7th Street Church, English service 9:00 a.m.

*Madang.* Memorial, English service 10:30 a.m. (December and January 9:30 a.m.)

*Mount Hagen.* Calvary, English service 8:00 a.m.

*Port Moresby.* Good Shepherd-Koki, English services 9:00 a.m. and 7:30 p.m.

*Wapenamanda.* St. Paul's High School Pausa, Schaus Memorial Chapel, English service 9:00 a.m.

## PARAGUAY

*Asunción.* Vacant, Departamento Central, Casilla de Correo 896 (Tel 021-504-135)

*Casilla Dos.* Vacant. Departamento de Caaguazú, Casilla de Correo 10018, Tres Palmas, Caaguazú, Paraguay

*Edelira.* 21. Rev. Norberto Meyer, Departamento de Itapúa, Post of Hohenau II

*Hernandarias.* Rev. Alceu Alton Figur, Caixa Postal 315, CEP 85851-970, Fóz do Iguaçú, Paraná, Brazil (Tel: 063-122-585)

*Hohenau II.* Rev.Osmar Ickert, San Roque Gonzales, Esq Guillermo Closs (6290) Hohenau II, Departamento de Itapúa, Paraguay (Tel 075.398)

*Iruna.* Rev Eugenio Wagner; Coop. Yacuy Ltda. Casilla de Correo 118, Ciudad Del Este, Paraná, Caixa Postal 747, CEP 85851-970, Fóz do Iguaçú, Paraná, Brazil

*Katueté.* Rev. Luis Krachinski, Departamento de Canindiyú, Caixa Postal 315, CEP 85851-970, Fóz do Iguaçú, Paraná, Brazil

*Marangatú.* Rev Nei Poerner, Departamento de Canindiyú, Caixa Postal 315, CEP 85851-970, Fóz do Iguaçú, Paraná, Brazil

*Naranjal.* Rev. Eugenio Wentzel, Caixa Postal 747, CEP 85851-970, Fóz do Iguaçú, Paraná, Brazil (Tel 0676-20082)

*Santa Rita.* Rev. Aldino Borth, Departamento Alto Paraná, Caixa Postal 1207, CEP 85851-970 Fóz do Iguaçú, Paraná, Brazil

*Santa Rita.* Sinuelo. Rev. Miguel Lavrovic, Departamento Alto Paraná, Paraguay. Caixa Postal 747, CEP 85851-970 Fóz do Iguaçú, Paraná, Brazil

*Tuparenndá* Rev. Gerardo Wagner, Departamento de Caazapá, Caixa Postal 747, CEP 85851-970, Fóz do Iguaçú, Paraná, Brazil

## THE PHILIPPINES

*Baguio City* St Stephen Lutheran Church Corner Gen. Luna and Zamora Baguio City Service 10:00 a.m. (Tel 074-442-2285)

*Cagayan De Oro City* Christ Lutheran Church 113 Corrales Avenue 9000 Cagayan de Oro City Service 10:00 a.m. (Tel 088-8561807)

*Davao City.* Christ Our Savior, Matina Aplaya, 8000 Davao City, Pastor Rev Fidel Quintana Service 10:00 a.m.

*Manila* Gloria Dei Lutheran Church 4461 Old Sta. Mesa Sampaloc, Metro Manila, Phil Service 10:00 a.m. (Tel 715-7084)

*Quezon City.* Trinity Lutheran Church 835 EDSA Kamuning, Quezon City Service 10:00 a.m. (Tel 0632-9387647)

## PORTUGAL

*Lisboa.* Lutheran Hour, Apartado 50166, 1704 Lisboa Codex, Rua da Conceicao da Gloria 46 1o Dto., 1200 Lisboa. Tel. 01-3430559 FAX 01-3430561. Director Rev. Clovis V Gedrat, Rua Andre de Gouveia, Lote B, 50 Dto., 1700 LISBOA, (Tel 01-7587550)

*Vila Nova De Gaia* Igreja Evangelica Luterana Portuguesa, Rua Cinco de Outubro, 1095, Gueifaes, 4470, Maia. Rev Adalberto Hiller Rua do Anel, 143, 1o Esq. Oliveira do Douro, 4400 Vila Nova de Gaia. Tel 02-7824729 FAX.

## SCOTLAND

*Glasgow.* St. Columba (Service 11 a.m.), 151 Westwood Hill, East Kilbride, Glasgow G75 8QA (Tel 011-44-3552-39608); Rev. J.D. Fraser, 22 New Plymouth Westwood, East Kilbride, Glasgow G75 8QB Tel (011-44-3552-23950)

*Glasgow—Edinburgh.* Polish Evangelical-Lutheran Congregation Glasgow, Edinburgh, served by Pastor from Birmingham, England. Chairman: Mr. P. Sliwka

## SIERRA LEONE

*Freetown.* c/o Rev. Ken Greinke, World Services, The Lutheran Church—Missouri Synod, Board for Mission Services, 1333 South Kirkwood Road, St. Louis, MO 63122-7295

## SOUTH AFRICA

*Durban.* St. Thomas Lutheran Church (Chatsworth) Rev. Allen Konrad, PO Box 2544, New Germany 3620, South Africa (Tel and FAX 011-27-31-705-9718, E-Mail onamission@eastcoast.co.sa)

## SRI LANKA

*Colombo.* Immanuel Lutheran Church 116A Layards Broadway, Colombo 14, Sri Lanka (Tel 011-94-1-439856)

*Colombo.* Lutheran Mission, 410/18 Bullers Road, Colombo 7, Tel/FAX 011-94-691023

*Nuwara Eliya.* Lanka Lutheran Church, Rev. M. Sathiyanathan, President, 53 Mt. Mary Road, Nuwara Eliya Tel 011-94-052-2975

## TAIWAN

*Chia Yi Concordia Middle School* 31 Sec. 2 Chien Kuo Rd., Min-Hsiung, Chia-Yi 621, Taiwan, R.O.C. Tel 886-5-221-3045, English 886-5-221-8047. *Concordia Youth Center and Volunteer Office* #32 Hang Chou 2nd Street, Chia Yi, Taiwan Tel 886-5-236-6081, FAX 886-5-236-6082. Missionary Counselor, Kurt Buchholz (home at Concordia Middle School) Tel 886-5-220-2875, FAX 886-5-221-0523

*Taipei.* China Evangelical Lutheran Church, 4th Floor, #127, Fu Hsing South Road, Section 1, Taipei 10639, Taiwan ROC., Tel 886-2-7724673 or 7728435, FAX 886-2-7724673.

## THAILAND

*Concordia Gospel Ministry.* 205/20 Chaiyakiat 1 Ngam Wong Wan Road Bangkok 10210, Thailand Tel 011-66-2-589-6715, FAX 011-66-2-589-7821 E-Mail<oratai@mozart.inet.co.th>

## TOGO

*Bagre.* Lutherienne (E.L.T.), B.P. 38, Dapaon, Vacant

*Dapaong.* B.P. 53, Rev John Palka

*Dapaong.* Mission Lutherienne, BP 38-Rev Glenn Fluegge

*Lokpano.* B.P. 53, Dapaon

*Lome.* B.P. 20493 Lomé, Vacant

*Mogou.* B.P. 59, Mango, Mr James A Turner

*Nano.* B.P. 53, Dapaon, Vacant

*Ponio.* B.P. 164, Dapaon, Vacant

## URUGUAY

*Montevideo.* Congregación Evangélica Luterana San Pablo, Pastor Christian Hoffmann, Venancio Benavidez 3612, código postal 11.700. Director General, ULBRA/Colegio y Liceo San Pablo, Pastor Mauro Roll. Teléfonos: casa pastoral Phone: 011-598-2-203-95-64. Colegio y Liceo San Pablo Phone and FAX: 011-598-2-336-49-14

## VENEZUELA

*Caracas.* El Salvador Lutheran Church, and Colegio La Concordia, Avenida Tocuyo, Colinas de Bello Monte, Caracas. Tel: (02) 751-1468; 753-3482. Iglesia Luterana La Santa Trinidad: Calle Mexico, No 16, Catia, D.F. Apartado Postal 30.012, Caracas 1031-A Tel (02-89-20-67). Rev. Alcides Franco, Iglesia Luterana El Mesias: Abanico a Maturin, Altagracia, Caracas 1010 Tel (02)-564.2317). Iglesia Lutherana La Paz: Entrada Principal Barrio El Esfuerzo, No 272 Petare. Tel (02) 243-5628

*Mission Office.* Quinta Lutero, Avenida Caurimare, Colinas de Bello Monte, Caracas (Tel (02) 753.46 83; 753.6031) (FAX 753-4683)

*Lutheran Hour Office.* Cristo Para Todas Las Naciones, Ave. Caurimare y Ave. Motatan, Colinas de Bello Monte, Caracas. (Tel 752.25.02 & 751.21.11)

*Estado Monagas.* Maturin. Iglesia Cristo Rey, Maturin. Apartado Postal No. 187, Maturin Tel: (091) 51.29.34. Pastor Adrian Ventura.

Lutheran congregations in Rural Monagas, Apartado Postal No. 187 *Maturin,* Estado Monagas: El Calvario-La Pica; El Redentor-San Antonio de Maturin; Roca De La Eternidad-Quebrada Seca; Betel-Rio Chiquito; El Buen Pasto-La Morrocoya.

*Estado Bolivar-Puerto Ordaz.* Iglesia Luterana Fuente de Vida: Urbanizacion Rio Caura, Unare II. Apartado Postal No. 216, Puerto Ordaz, 8015-A Tel: (086)51-5910; 51-5821 Pastor Luis Coronado

*Estado Bolivar San Felix* Iglesia Luterana La Ascension: Calle Simon Planas No. 23, Urbanizacion Moreno Mendoza, San Felix, Tel: (086) 31-5151 Pastor Elias Lozano

*Estado Carabobo:* Valencia: Iglesia Luterana La Fe, Valencia. Pastor Gerardo Hands,

*Estado Lara-Barquisimeto.* Iglesia Luterana Cristo es Amor: Calle 41, entre Carrera 15 y 16 No. 15-55, Quinta Rena, Barquisimeto, (Tel 051-45.74.41. (FAX:(051)-45.42.87. Rev. Jim Tino

*Estado Anzoategui Barcelona.* Iglesia Luterana de Barcelona: Multicenteo Cristiano Concordia. Barrio El Espejo de Barcelone, Av. Intercomunal, calle Progreso, Edificio El Progreso, #24-42, Mezzanina, Barcelona, (Tel: (081)-76-90-73; FAX 081-76-90-55. Rev. Arturo Boone, Rev. Henry Witte

*Estado Sucre* Iglesia Emanuel, Aricagua, Edo Sucre. Apartado Postal No. 187, Maturin, Edo. Monagas

*Estado Barinas* Iglesia Luterana, "Corpus Christi" Calle 7, No 6-112, Barrio El Cambio, Barinas

*Estado Aragua* Mission Luterana, Av. 5 de Julio, entre Av. Bolivar y Santos Michelena, edf. Seis - 1, local B, Maracay

*Estado Bolivar* Iglesia Luterana Principe de Paz. Pastor Adrian Rivero

## WALES

*Cardiff.* St. David (Services 11 a.m. & 6:30 p.m.). St. Fagans Rd. & Doyle Ave., Fairwater, Cardiff (Tel 011-44-1222-561911); Vacant 67 Doyle Ave., Fairwater, Cardiff CF5 3HT

*Penrhos.* Polish Evangelical-Lutheran Congregations, Penrhos, Wrexham. Chairman: Mr. Z. Kaniewski, Pastor: Rev. T. Bogucki

*Retired Pastor:* Rev. M. R. Brammeier, 10 Woldcroft Road, Coventry, CV5 8AW

*Retired Pastor:* Rev. A. Rakow, 1 Turnberry Way Petts Wood

## SUMMARY OF CHANGES IN SYNOD'S MINISTRIES IN 1999—ORDAINED MINISTERS

| Districts—LCMS | A. Entered Synodical Service in 1999 Graduates Assigned to: | | | | | | | | | | B. Left Synodical Service in 1999 | | | | | C. Other Changes during 1999 | | | | | |
|---|---|---|---|---|---|---|---|---|---|---|---|---|---|---|---|---|---|---|---|---|---|
| | Parish Ministry and District Missionary | Assoc. or Assist. | World Missions | Synodical Colleges or Seminaries | Other Specialized Ministries | Other Educational Institutions | Total Graduates Assigned | Reinstated on Clergy Roster | Colloquized | Total Entered | Died in Office | Retired | CANDIDATE | Permanently Resigned from the Ministry | Total | Changes within the District | Transferred to Other Dist. | Transferred from Other Dist. | Died (While EM or CAND) | Total | GRAND TOTAL |
| **United States** | | | | | | | | | | | | | | | | | | | | | |
| 03 Atlantic | 1 | 2 | — | — | — | 1 | 4 | — | — | 4 | 1 | 3 | — | 1 | 5 | 3 | 3 | 3 | 2 | 11 | 20 |
| 05 California-Nevada-Hawaii | 7 | 1 | — | — | — | — | 8 | — | 2 | 10 | — | 4 | 5 | 2 | 11 | 14 | 12 | 8 | 6 | 40 | 61 |
| 07 Pacific Southwest | 2 | 1 | — | — | — | — | 3 | — | 5 | 8 | — | 16 | 5 | 2 | 23 | 19 | 18 | 25 | 5 | 67 | 98 |
| 12 Eastern | 2 | — | 1 | — | — | — | 3 | — | 1 | 4 | 1 | 4 | 2 | 3 | 10 | 6 | 5 | 8 | 2 | 21 | 35 |
| 14 English | 1 | 1 | — | — | — | — | 2 | — | — | 2 | 1 | 9 | 4 | 5 | 19 | 13 | 12 | 12 | 2 | 39 | 60 |
| 16 Florida-Georgia | 3 | 3 | — | — | — | — | 6 | 1 | — | 7 | 1 | 7 | 3 | 2 | 13 | 21 | 16 | 15 | 4 | 56 | 76 |
| 20 Illinois, Central | 2 | 1 | — | — | — | — | 3 | — | — | 3 | — | — | 1 | — | 1 | 4 | 11 | 12 | 1 | 28 | 32 |
| 22 Illinois, Northern | 4 | 3 | 1 | — | — | — | 8 | 1 | — | 9 | — | 3 | 2 | — | 5 | 16 | 20 | 13 | 4 | 53 | 67 |
| 24 Illinois, Southern | — | 2 | — | — | — | — | 2 | — | — | 2 | — | 2 | 2 | 2 | 6 | 5 | 7 | 9 | 3 | 24 | 32 |
| 26 Indiana | 2 | 1 | — | — | — | — | 3 | — | 1 | 4 | 1 | 7 | 7 | 2 | 17 | 19 | 13 | 18 | 5 | 55 | 76 |
| 28 Iowa East | 2 | — | — | — | — | — | 2 | — | — | 2 | — | 1 | 3 | 1 | 5 | 1 | 10 | 9 | 2 | 22 | 29 |
| 30 Iowa West | 2 | 2 | — | — | — | — | 4 | — | — | 4 | — | 4 | 4 | 1 | 9 | 9 | 19 | 18 | 3 | 49 | 62 |
| 32 Kansas | 3 | 1 | — | — | — | — | 4 | — | 2 | 6 | 1 | 8 | 4 | 1 | 14 | 11 | 10 | 10 | 1 | 32 | 52 |
| 37 Michigan | 5 | — | — | — | — | — | 5 | — | 1 | 6 | 1 | 9 | 6 | 6 | 22 | 29 | 11 | 19 | 3 | 62 | 90 |
| 38 Mid-South | 2 | — | — | — | — | — | 2 | — | 1 | 3 | 1 | 5 | 3 | 3 | 12 | 7 | 3 | 7 | 2 | 19 | 34 |
| 39 Minnesota North | 2 | — | — | — | — | — | 2 | — | — | 2 | — | 1 | 6 | 2 | 9 | 10 | 22 | 7 | 2 | 41 | 52 |
| 41 Minnesota South | 4 | 3 | — | — | — | — | 7 | — | — | 7 | — | 7 | 4 | 5 | 16 | 16 | 14 | 14 | 3 | 47 | 70 |
| 43 Missouri | 7 | 3 | — | — | — | — | 10 | — | 2 | 12 | 2 | 10 | 3 | 6 | 21 | 22 | 30 | 22 | 7 | 81 | 114 |
| 44 Montana | 3 | 1 | — | — | — | — | 4 | — | — | 4 | — | 2 | — | 1 | 3 | 3 | 6 | 5 | — | 14 | 21 |
| 47 Nebraska | 4 | 1 | 1 | — | — | — | 6 | — | 2 | 8 | — | 1 | 3 | 2 | 6 | 15 | 20 | 13 | 4 | 52 | 66 |
| 49 New England | 3 | 1 | — | — | — | — | 4 | — | — | 4 | — | 2 | 1 | — | 3 | 3 | 4 | 2 | — | 9 | 16 |
| 51 New Jersey | 2 | 1 | — | — | — | — | 3 | — | — | 3 | — | 1 | 2 | 2 | 5 | 2 | — | 5 | — | 7 | 15 |
| 53 North Dakota | 2 | — | — | — | — | — | 2 | — | — | 2 | — | 2 | 1 | 1 | 4 | 3 | 8 | 1 | — | 12 | 18 |
| 55 Northwest | 4 | 1 | — | — | — | — | 5 | — | — | 5 | 4 | 20 | 2 | 4 | 30 | 26 | 11 | 19 | 7 | 63 | 98 |
| 56 Ohio | 5 | — | — | — | 1 | — | 6 | — | — | 6 | 1 | 6 | 2 | 2 | 11 | 11 | 9 | 13 | 2 | 35 | 52 |
| 58 Oklahoma | 5 | — | — | — | — | — | 5 | — | — | 5 | — | — | 1 | 1 | 2 | — | 7 | 6 | 2 | 15 | 22 |
| 60 Rocky Mountain | 1 | — | — | — | — | — | 1 | — | — | 1 | — | 2 | 4 | 2 | 8 | 9 | 16 | 12 | 3 | 40 | 49 |
| 61 South Dakota | 2 | — | — | — | — | — | 2 | — | — | 2 | — | 2 | 1 | 1 | 4 | 4 | 4 | 7 | 1 | 16 | 22 |
| 63 Southeastern | 1 | 3 | 1 | — | — | — | 5 | — | 2 | 7 | — | 11 | 7 | 4 | 22 | 19 | 7 | 7 | — | 33 | 62 |
| 65 Southern | 2 | — | — | — | — | — | 2 | — | — | 2 | 2 | 1 | 2 | 1 | 6 | 11 | 16 | 7 | 4 | 38 | 46 |
| 97 SELC | 1 | — | — | — | — | — | 1 | — | 1 | 2 | 2 | 1 | 2 | — | 5 | 4 | 3 | — | 1 | 8 | 15 |
| 67 Texas | 5 | 3 | — | — | 1 | 1 | 10 | — | — | 10 | — | 7 | 7 | 6 | 20 | 45 | 16 | 17 | 7 | 85 | 115 |
| 76 Wisconsin, North | 4 | 1 | — | — | — | — | 5 | — | 1 | 6 | 1 | 5 | 5 | 2 | 13 | 14 | 9 | 20 | 2 | 45 | 64 |
| 78 Wisconsin, South | 2 | 2 | — | — | — | — | 4 | — | — | 4 | 1 | 10 | 2 | 2 | 15 | 16 | 12 | 23 | 6 | 57 | 76 |
| 79 Wyoming | 1 | — | — | — | — | — | 1 | — | — | 1 | — | — | 1 | — | 1 | 5 | 5 | 7 | — | 17 | 19 |
| *Totals* | 98 | 38 | 4 | — | 2 | 2 | 144 | 2 | 21 | 167 | 21 | 173 | 107 | 75 | 376 | 415 | 389 | 393 | 96 | 1,293 | 1,836 |
| *1998 Totals* | 95 | 40 | 6 | 1 | 4 | 1 | 147 | 10 | 31 | 189 | 14 | 167 | 87 | 48 | 316 | 337 | 371 | 372 | 73 | 1,152 | 1,633 |

## SUMMARY OF CHANGES IN SYNOD'S MINISTRIES IN 1999—COMMISSIONED MINISTERS

| Districts—LCMS | A. Entered Synodical Service in 1999 Graduates Assigned to: | | | | | | | | | | B. Left Synodical Service in 1999 | | | | | C. Other Changes during 1999 | | | | | | |
|---|---|---|---|---|---|---|---|---|---|---|---|---|---|---|---|---|---|---|---|---|---|---|
| | EC-Elementary Schools | High Schools | Synodical Colleges or Seminaries | World Missions | To Other Church Positions | Total Graduates Assigned | Reinstated on Teacher Roster | Colloquized | Other Roster Additions*** | Total Entered | Died in Office | Retired | CAND Resigned Temporarily | Permanently Resigned | Total | Changes within the District | Transferred to Other Dist. | Transferred from Other Dist. | Died (exclusive of Active Teachers) | Total | GRAND TOTAL | Women Eligible for Roster** |
| **United States** | | | | | | | | | | | | | | | | | | | | | | |
| 03 Atlantic | 3 | 1 | — | — | 1 | 5 | 1 | — | — | 6 | — | 1 | 5 | 1 | 7 | 3 | 12 | 4 | — | 19 | 32 | 2 |
| 05 California-Nevada-Hawaii | 8 | 2 | — | — | 5 | 15 | — | — | — | 15 | — | — | 8 | 6 | 14 | 12 | 16 | 11 | — | 39 | 68 | 8 |
| 07 Pacific Southwest | 19 | 17 | — | — | 1 | 37 | 4 | 1 | — | 42 | 1 | 2 | 11 | 11 | 25 | 26 | 31 | 25 | 2 | 84 | 151 | 24 |
| 12 Eastern | 1 | — | — | — | — | 1 | — | 2 | — | 3 | — | — | 2 | — | 2 | 6 | 7 | 3 | — | 16 | 21 | 3 |
| 14 English | 6 | 3 | — | — | 3 | 12 | — | — | — | 12 | 1 | 3 | 4 | 9 | 17 | — | 15 | 15 | 1 | 31 | 60 | 7 |
| 16 Florida-Georgia | 9 | — | — | — | 4 | 13 | 1 | 1 | — | 15 | — | 3 | 12 | 9 | 24 | 3 | 26 | 29 | — | 58 | 97 | 10 |
| 20 Illinois, Central | 3 | — | — | — | 2 | 5 | — | 2 | — | 7 | 1 | 1 | 2 | 3 | 7 | 2 | 16 | 11 | 2 | 31 | 45 | 7 |
| 22 Illinois, Northern | 29 | 8 | — | — | 4 | 41 | 9 | — | — | 50 | 2 | 23 | 22 | 29 | 76 | 29 | 29 | 50 | 4 | 112 | 238 | 29 |
| 24 Illinois, Southern | 7 | — | — | 1 | 1 | 9 | — | 3 | — | 12 | 1 | 1 | 9 | 6 | 17 | 9 | 23 | 21 | 1 | 54 | 83 | 11 |
| 26 Indiana | 4 | 2 | — | — | 2 | 8 | — | 3 | — | 11 | — | 3 | 12 | 12 | 27 | 11 | 25 | 22 | 3 | 61 | 99 | 4 |
| 28 Iowa East | 4 | — | — | — | — | 4 | — | — | — | 4 | — | — | — | 2 | 2 | 3 | 5 | 3 | — | 11 | 17 | 3 |
| 30 Iowa West | 1 | — | — | — | — | 1 | — | 1 | — | 2 | — | — | 1 | 2 | 3 | 3 | 1 | 7 | — | 11 | 16 | 1 |
| 32 Kansas | 1 | — | — | — | 2 | 3 | — | — | — | 3 | 1 | — | — | 1 | 2 | 4 | 6 | 7 | — | 17 | 22 | 3 |
| 37 Michigan | 20 | 5 | — | — | 5 | 30 | 12 | 6 | — | 48 | — | 18 | 21 | 39 | 78 | 41 | 38 | 34 | 3 | 116 | 242 | 26 |
| 38 Mid-South | 2 | — | — | — | 3 | 5 | — | 3 | — | 8 | — | 2 | 5 | — | 7 | 5 | 8 | 8 | — | 21 | 36 | 6 |
| 39 Minnesota North | 1 | — | — | — | — | 1 | — | — | — | 1 | — | — | 4 | 5 | 9 | 3 | 3 | 2 | 1 | 9 | 19 | 1 |
| 41 Minnesota South | 12 | 2 | 2 | — | 4 | 20 | 4 | — | — | 24 | — | 2 | 13 | 16 | 31 | 12 | 14 | 29 | — | 55 | 110 | 14 |
| 43 Missouri | 11 | 2 | — | — | 6 | 19 | — | 12 | — | 31 | — | 7 | 12 | 21 | 40 | 20 | 30 | 40 | 1 | 91 | 162 | 25 |
| 44 Montana | 1 | — | — | — | — | 1 | — | — | — | 1 | — | — | — | — | — | — | 1 | 1 | — | 2 | 3 | 1 |
| 47 Nebraska | 6 | 1 | 2 | — | 2 | 11 | 2 | — | — | 13 | — | 17 | 8 | 18 | 43 | 10 | 11 | 27 | 3 | 51 | 107 | 5 |
| 49 New England | 1 | — | — | — | — | 1 | — | — | — | 1 | — | — | — | — | — | 3 | 5 | 1 | — | 9 | 10 | 1 |
| 51 New Jersey | — | — | — | — | — | — | — | — | — | — | — | 1 | — | 1 | 2 | 1 | 1 | — | — | 2 | 4 | — |
| 53 North Dakota | — | — | — | — | — | — | — | 1 | — | 1 | — | — | — | — | — | — | 1 | — | — | 1 | 2 | 1 |
| 55 Northwest | 5 | — | — | 1 | 3 | 9 | — | — | — | 9 | — | 6 | 5 | 13 | 24 | 19 | 13 | 19 | — | 51 | 84 | 9 |
| 56 Ohio | 6 | — | — | — | 4 | 10 | 1 | — | — | 11 | — | 3 | 12 | 7 | 22 | 3 | 15 | 11 | — | 29 | 62 | 6 |
| 58 Oklahoma | — | — | — | — | — | — | 1 | — | — | 1 | — | — | — | — | — | — | 4 | — | — | 4 | 5 | — |
| 60 Rocky Mountain | 4 | 2 | — | — | 1 | 7 | — | 2 | — | 9 | 1 | 7 | 25 | 10 | 43 | 6 | 26 | 15 | 1 | 48 | 100 | 7 |
| 61 South Dakota | — | — | — | — | 1 | 1 | 2 | — | — | 3 | — | — | 3 | — | 3 | — | — | 2 | — | 2 | 8 | 1 |
| 63 Southeastern | 4 | 1 | — | — | 3 | 8 | 3 | 1 | — | 12 | — | — | 5 | 9 | 14 | 6 | 11 | 7 | — | 24 | 50 | 8 |
| 65 Southern | 1 | — | — | — | — | 1 | 2 | — | — | 3 | — | 3 | 6 | 4 | 13 | 2 | 10 | 3 | — | 15 | 31 | 1 |
| 97 SELC | 3 | — | — | — | 1 | 4 | — | — | — | 4 | — | 1 | 2 | — | 3 | — | 2 | 2 | — | 4 | 11 | 4 |
| 67 Texas | 23 | 8 | — | — | 4 | 35 | 9 | 6 | 1 | 51 | 1 | 11 | 12 | 31 | 55 | 33 | 26 | 42 | 1 | 102 | 208 | 32 |
| 76 Wisconsin, North | 4 | — | — | — | — | 4 | — | 1 | — | 5 | — | 1 | 1 | 7 | 9 | 4 | 10 | 16 | — | 30 | 44 | 2 |
| 78 Wisconsin, South | 10 | 3 | — | 1 | 2 | 16 | 4 | 6 | — | 26 | 1 | 5 | 6 | 16 | 28 | 29 | 21 | 34 | 2 | 86 | 140 | 16 |
| 79 Wyoming | — | — | — | — | — | — | — | — | — | — | — | — | — | — | — | 1 | 3 | 1 | 1 | 6 | 6 | — |
| *Totals* | 209 | 57 | 4 | 3 | 64 | 337 | 55 | 51 | 1 | 444 | 10 | 121 | 228 | 288 | 647 | 309 | 465 | 502 | 26 | 1,302 | 2,393 | 278 |
| *1998 Totals* | 214 | 40 | 2 | — | 55 | 311 | 85 | 37 | 2 | 435 | 10 | 78 | 206 | 305 | 600 | 290 | 453 | 455 | 28 | 1,226 | 2,237 | 300 |

** Women not previously enrolled on roster. This column not used in grand totals.
*** All Teachers/DCEs/Deaconesses having roster status for the first time.

## 1999 SUMMARIZED TOTALS OF PAROCHIAL REPORTS

| DISTRICTS | Parish Pastors | % of Total in U.S. | Congregations: Members of Synod | Congregations: Total Stations | % of Total in U.S. | Preaching Stations | Vacant Parishes | Baptized Members | % of Total in U.S. | Compared with 1998 | Percentage of Gain | Confirmed Members | % of Total in U.S. | Compared with 1998 | Percentage of Gain | Rank in % of Gain |
|---|---|---|---|---|---|---|---|---|---|---|---|---|---|---|---|---|
| 03 Atlantic | 77 | 1.49 | 99 | 104 | 1.67 | 2 | 24 | 41,998 | 1.63 | + 1,182 | + 2.81 | 28,078 | 1.44 | + 354 | + 1.26 | 3 |
| 05 California-Nevada-Hawaii | 161 | 3.11 | 185 | 194 | 3.12 | 9 | 31 | 57,508 | 2.23 | - 1,320 | - 2.30 | 42,443 | 2.18 | - 638 | - 1.50 | 31 |
| 07 Pacific Southwest | 231 | 4.47 | 254 | 283 | 4.55 | 27 | 48 | 103,100 | 3.99 | - 192 | - .19 | 76,662 | 3.94 | - 568 | - .74 | 23 |
| 12 Eastern | 118 | 2.28 | 149 | 151 | 2.43 | 1 | 30 | 55,452 | 2.15 | - 1,555 | - 2.80 | 40,151 | 2.06 | - 1,077 | - 2.68 | 34 |
| 14 English | 144 | 2.79 | 164 | 167 | 2.68 | 2 | 35 | 63,141 | 2.45 | - 788 | - 1.25 | 48,512 | 2.49 | - 39 | - .08 | 15 |
| 16 Florida-Georgia | 159 | 3.08 | 175 | 178 | 2.86 | 1 | 32 | 71,149 | 2.76 | + 105 | + .15 | 55,259 | 2.84 | + 102 | + .18 | 10 |
| 20 Illinois, Central | 150 | 2.90 | 155 | 162 | 2.60 | 1 | 14 | 75,885 | 2.94 | - 1,069 | - 1.41 | 57,226 | 2.94 | - 727 | - 1.27 | 30 |
| 22 Illinois, Northern | 235 | 4.55 | 236 | 242 | 3.89 | 4 | 41 | 153,093 | 5.93 | + 94 | + .06 | 113,392 | 5.83 | + 95 | + .08 | 12 |
| 24 Illinois, Southern | 95 | 1.84 | 98 | 100 | 1.61 | — | 7 | 44,173 | 1.71 | - 542 | - 1.23 | 34,220 | 1.76 | - 272 | - .79 | 24 |
| 26 Indiana | 223 | 4.31 | 236 | 247 | 3.97 | 1 | 38 | 115,279 | 4.46 | + 737 | + .64 | 85,294 | 4.38 | - 262 | - .31 | 19 |
| 28 Iowa East | 100 | 1.93 | 119 | 122 | 1.96 | — | 17 | 49,633 | 1.92 | - 351 | - .71 | 37,907 | 1.95 | - 302 | - .80 | 25 |
| 30 Iowa West | 139 | 2.69 | 175 | 180 | 2.89 | — | 28 | 71,571 | 2.77 | + 262 | + .37 | 54,127 | 2.78 | - 626 | - 1.16 | 29 |
| 32 Kansas | 137 | 2.65 | 165 | 169 | 2.72 | — | 31 | 64,156 | 2.48 | + 65 | + .10 | 48,332 | 2.48 | + 362 | + .75 | 4 |
| 37 Michigan | 363 | 7.02 | 369 | 377 | 6.06 | 1 | 62 | 233,735 | 9.05 | + 813 | + .35 | 174,181 | 8.95 | + 803 | + .46 | 5 |
| 38 Mid-South | 92 | 1.78 | 115 | 120 | 1.93 | 5 | 19 | 33,318 | 1.29 | + 534 | + 1.60 | 25,919 | 1.33 | + 499 | + 1.93 | 1 |
| 39 Minnesota North | 127 | 2.46 | 207 | 214 | 3.44 | 6 | 54 | 68,921 | 2.67 | - 157 | - .23 | 53,202 | 2.73 | - 54 | - .10 | 16 |
| 41 Minnesota South | 220 | 4.26 | 244 | 255 | 4.10 | 2 | 30 | 141,336 | 5.47 | - 792 | - .56 | 107,614 | 5.53 | - 960 | - .89 | 27 |
| 43 Missouri | 254 | 4.91 | 301 | 313 | 5.03 | 3 | 53 | 145,168 | 5.62 | + 1,149 | + .79 | 109,417 | 5.62 | + 405 | + .37 | 6 |
| 44 Montana | 39 | .75 | 62 | 64 | 1.03 | 2 | 8 | 16,005 | .62 | - 103 | - .64 | 11,837 | .61 | - 81 | - .68 | 22 |
| 47 Nebraska | 196 | 3.79 | 244 | 250 | 4.02 | 2 | 48 | 111,589 | 4.32 | - 244 | - .22 | 85,218 | 4.38 | + 39 | + .05 | 13 |
| 49 New England | 58 | 1.12 | 70 | 70 | 1.13 | — | 17 | 24,394 | .94 | - 90 | - .37 | 18,080 | .93 | + 33 | + .18 | 9 |
| 51 New Jersey | 52 | 1.01 | 61 | 61 | .98 | — | 9 | 19,378 | .75 | + 5 | + .03 | 14,238 | .73 | + 215 | + 1.51 | 2 |
| 53 North Dakota | 47 | .91 | 94 | 96 | 1.54 | — | 27 | 24,398 | .94 | - 619 | - 2.54 | 19,216 | .99 | - 300 | - 1.56 | 32 |
| 55 Northwest | 222 | 4.29 | 261 | 272 | 4.37 | 3 | 48 | 81,784 | 3.17 | - 1,782 | - 2.18 | 59,784 | 3.07 | - 361 | - .60 | 21 |
| 56 Ohio | 174 | 3.37 | 167 | 177 | 2.85 | 6 | 20 | 73,227 | 2.84 | + 147 | + .20 | 54,491 | 2.80 | - 150 | - .28 | 18 |
| 58 Oklahoma | 63 | 1.22 | 77 | 79 | 1.27 | 1 | 13 | 24,530 | .95 | - 45 | - .18 | 18,746 | .96 | + 19 | + .10 | 11 |
| 60 Rocky Mountain | 159 | 3.08 | 182 | 182 | 2.93 | — | 22 | 60,205 | 2.33 | - 866 | - 1.44 | 45,134 | 2.32 | - 391 | - .87 | 26 |
| 61 South Dakota | 70 | 1.35 | 115 | 116 | 1.86 | — | 20 | 32,630 | 1.26 | - 450 | - 1.38 | 25,168 | 1.29 | - 227 | - .90 | 28 |
| 63 Southeastern | 172 | 3.33 | 196 | 205 | 3.30 | 7 | 47 | 75,643 | 2.93 | + 336 | + .44 | 56,420 | 2.90 | + 135 | + .24 | 7 |
| 65 Southern | 114 | 2.21 | 166 | 168 | 2.70 | 1 | 50 | 37,238 | 1.44 | - 2,849 | - 7.65 | 29,095 | 1.50 | - 1,593 | - 5.48 | 35 |
| 97 SELC | 43 | .83 | 53 | 54 | .87 | 1 | 9 | 17,632 | .68 | + 276 | + 1.57 | 13,659 | .70 | - 218 | - 1.60 | 33 |
| 67 Texas | 307 | 5.94 | 333 | 343 | 5.51 | 6 | 70 | 141,583 | 5.48 | - 956 | - .68 | 107,279 | 5.51 | + 222 | + .21 | 8 |
| 76 Wisconsin, North | 174 | 3.37 | 222 | 223 | 3.59 | — | 31 | 106,996 | 4.14 | - 1,669 | - 1.56 | 83,669 | 4.30 | - 4 | + .00 | 14 |
| 78 Wisconsin, South | 208 | 4.02 | 212 | 216 | 3.47 | — | 28 | 130,260 | 5.04 | - 943 | - .72 | 99,509 | 5.11 | - 328 | - .33 | 20 |
| 79 Wyoming | 47 | .91 | 64 | 66 | 1.06 | 2 | 14 | 16,332 | .63 | + 31 | + .19 | 12,367 | .64 | - 33 | - .27 | 17 |
| *Grand Totals* | 5,170 | 100 | 6,025 | 6,220 | 100 | 96 | 1,075 | 2,582,440 | 100 | -11,646 | - .45 | 1,945,846 | 100 | - 5,928 | - .30 | — |

## 1999 SUMMARIZED TOTALS OF PAROCHIAL REPORTS (Continued)

| DISTRICTS | Children Baptized | Compared with 1998 | Juniors Confirmed | Compared with 1998 | Adults Conf. or Baptized | Compared with 1998 | Total Gained from Outside | Elementary Schools: Number of Luth. Day Schools | Elementary Schools: Pupils | Elementary Schools: Compared with 1998 | Elementary Schools: Male Teachers | Elementary Schools: Women Teachers |
|---|---|---|---|---|---|---|---|---|---|---|---|---|
| 03 Atlantic | 990 | + 25 | 571 | + 7 | 426 | + 8 | 973 | 44 | 5,374 | + 0 | 34 | 296 |
| 05 California-Nevada-Hawaii | 1,443 | + 7 | 704 | - 37 | 938 | + 9 | 1,689 | 73 | 7,995 | + 155 | 70 | 511 |
| 07 Pacific Southwest | 2,639 | + 85 | 1,437 | + 22 | 2,470 | +231 | 4,333 | 135 | 19,578 | + 945 | 178 | 1,047 |
| 12 Eastern | 1,025 | - 15 | 633 | - 50 | 529 | - 46 | 845 | 69 | 4,061 | + 92 | 22 | 264 |
| 14 English | 1,143 | - 104 | 639 | - 114 | 623 | -134 | 1,452 | 60 | 4,952 | + 326 | 42 | 289 |
| 16 Florida-Georgia | 1,544 | - 21 | 813 | + 21 | 1,167 | - 62 | 2,538 | 82 | 10,750 | + 77 | 95 | 632 |
| 20 Illinois, Central | 1,100 | + 44 | 864 | + 32 | 761 | + 22 | 1,163 | 56 | 5,747 | + 293 | 53 | 313 |
| 22 Illinois, Northern | 2,875 | - 162 | 2,070 | + 154 | 1,640 | + 4 | 2,986 | 122 | 18,095 | + 796 | 167 | 817 |
| 24 Illinois, Southern | 641 | + 10 | 568 | + 7 | 369 | + 3 | 538 | 39 | 4,585 | + 40 | 50 | 202 |
| 26 Indiana | 2,062 | - 16 | 1,259 | - 147 | 1,373 | -139 | 2,077 | 104 | 11,998 | + 356 | 142 | 578 |
| 28 Iowa East | 733 | + 29 | 620 | + 8 | 378 | + 30 | 681 | 38 | 2,765 | - 14 | 19 | 139 |
| 30 Iowa West | 1,040 | - 41 | 859 | - 30 | 554 | - 13 | 949 | 50 | 2,551 | + 124 | 16 | 136 |
| 32 Kansas | 1,003 | - 11 | 784 | - 16 | 632 | - 37 | 1,114 | 54 | 3,825 | + 106 | 25 | 211 |
| 37 Michigan | 4,298 | - 139 | 2,898 | - 15 | 2,875 | - 31 | 4,587 | 162 | 21,067 | + 763 | 265 | 851 |
| 38 Mid-South | 543 | - 18 | 437 | + 68 | 530 | + 29 | 943 | 36 | 3,145 | + 217 | 20 | 242 |
| 39 Minnesota North | 1078 | + 105 | 938 | + 68 | 418 | + 63 | 952 | 26 | 1,057 | + 62 | 9 | 52 |
| 41 Minnesota South | 2,143 | + 21 | 1,842 | + 47 | 877 | + 46 | 2,254 | 88 | 8,578 | + 256 | 96 | 415 |
| 43 Missouri | 2,215 | - 309 | 1,616 | - 106 | 1,456 | -343 | 2,414 | 105 | 13,264 | + 290 | 135 | 676 |
| 44 Montana | 280 | + 8 | 221 | + 47 | 217 | + 71 | 311 | 20 | 889 | + 101 | 5 | 58 |
| 47 Nebraska | 1,783 | + 58 | 1,543 | + 38 | 908 | + 12 | 1,635 | 75 | 6,648 | + 16 | 60 | 305 |
| 49 New England | 449 | + 36 | 291 | - 4 | 302 | + 10 | 557 | 31 | 1,449 | + 26 | 10 | 117 |
| 51 New Jersey | 422 | - 25 | 264 | + 39 | 213 | + 59 | 484 | 23 | 1,614 | - 219 | 3 | 77 |
| 53 North Dakota | 325 | - 1 | 298 | - 49 | 118 | + 9 | 305 | 6 | 204 | + 0 | 1 | 15 |
| 55 Northwest | 1,584 | - 144 | 940 | - 32 | 1,091 | + 7 | 2,172 | 123 | 9,020 | + 228 | 73 | 492 |
| 56 Ohio | 1,313 | + 12 | 878 | - 52 | 955 | + 53 | 1,657 | 72 | 7,255 | + 128 | 56 | 344 |
| 58 Oklahoma | 412 | + 1 | 312 | + 44 | 351 | - 8 | 542 | 26 | 1,306 | + 377 | 5 | 93 |
| 60 Rocky Mountain | 1,235 | - 15 | 816 | - 50 | 819 | + 85 | 1,669 | 67 | 6,959 | + 233 | 73 | 360 |
| 61 South Dakota | 436 | - 56 | 398 | - 94 | 237 | - 4 | 527 | 13 | 829 | - 2 | 3 | 35 |
| 63 Southeastern | 1,300 | - 217 | 757 | - 78 | 908 | + 89 | 2,018 | 87 | 8,049 | + 1,241 | 53 | 545 |
| 65 Southern | 758 | - 31 | 450 | - 80 | 558 | - 81 | 1,003 | 38 | 3,101 | - 16 | 21 | 220 |
| 97 SELC | 325 | + 8 | 192 | + 18 | 311 | + 30 | 519 | 17 | 1,193 | + 64 | 6 | 91 |
| 67 Texas | 2,729 | - 121 | 1,776 | - 67 | 2,536 | - 52 | 4,097 | 123 | 15,545 | + 363 | 147 | 1,093 |
| 76 Wisconsin, North | 1,618 | - 14 | 1,495 | + 8 | 662 | - 27 | 1,716 | 55 | 4,852 | + 149 | 54 | 234 |
| 78 Wisconsin, South | 2,184 | + 134 | 1,801 | + 120 | 1,138 | + 83 | 2,666 | 94 | 11,082 | + 72 | 152 | 532 |
| 79 Wyoming | 233 | - 30 | 211 | - 13 | 139 | - 46 | 247 | 13 | 569 | + 23 | 3 | 28 |
| *Grand Total* | 45,901 | - 907 | 32,195 | - 286 | 29,479 | - 70 | 54,613 | 2,226 | 229,951 | + 7,668 | 2,163 | 12,310 |

## 1999 SUMMARIZED TOTALS OF PAROCHIAL REPORTS (Continued)

| DISTRICTS | Sunday Schools | | | | | Enrollment for Sunday and Weekday Bible Classes | Vacation Bible Schools | | | | Weekday Religion Classes | | | |
|---|---|---|---|---|---|---|---|---|---|---|---|---|---|---|
| | Number | Pupils | Compared with 1998 | Teachers and Officers | Total Pupils and Teachers | | Number | Pupils | Children of Nonmembers | Teachers | Number | Enrollment | Children of Nonmembers | Staff |
| 03 Atlantic | 90 | 7,427 | - 158 | 1,014 | 8,441 | 3,836 | 50 | 5,075 | 2,269 | 1,378 | 75 | 1,826 | 139 | 131 |
| 05 California-Nevada-Hawaii | 176 | 11,629 | - 1,220 | 1,798 | 13,427 | 12,160 | 104 | 8,032 | 4,083 | 1,961 | 139 | 3,453 | 222 | 345 |
| 07 Pacific Southwest | 245 | 18,017 | - 601 | 2,618 | 20,635 | 16,734 | 157 | 13,485 | 6,459 | 3,021 | 178 | 5,467 | 456 | 544 |
| 12 Eastern | 133 | 9,491 | - 1,455 | 1,472 | 10,963 | 5,195 | 92 | 8,143 | 4,947 | 2,191 | 101 | 1,882 | 68 | 148 |
| 14 English | 146 | 11,172 | - 1,039 | 1,740 | 12,912 | 7,614 | 91 | 6,107 | 2,953 | 1,538 | 117 | 3,177 | 394 | 214 |
| 16 Florida-Georgia | 166 | 14,697 | + 27 | 1,906 | 16,603 | 11,824 | 104 | 7,991 | 3,820 | 2,109 | 123 | 3,721 | 193 | 212 |
| 20 Illinois, Central | 144 | 14,760 | - 182 | 1,837 | 16,597 | 9,796 | 121 | 8,067 | 2,597 | 2,340 | 119 | 2,297 | 125 | 190 |
| 22 Illinois, Northern | 226 | 24,846 | - 211 | 3,281 | 28,127 | 15,549 | 176 | 15,754 | 6,497 | 3,865 | 181 | 5,944 | 329 | 429 |
| 24 Illinois, Southern | 88 | 7,064 | - 111 | 908 | 7,972 | 3,997 | 67 | 4,422 | 1,734 | 1,290 | 76 | 1,732 | 128 | 142 |
| 26 Indiana | 223 | 20,402 | - 657 | 2,931 | 23,333 | 14,212 | 154 | 10,359 | 3,617 | 2,933 | 172 | 4,158 | 294 | 299 |
| 28 Iowa East | 116 | 9,876 | + 223 | 1,387 | 11,263 | 6,043 | 95 | 5,695 | 2,016 | 1,329 | 100 | 2,998 | 149 | 378 |
| 30 Iowa West | 166 | 14,566 | + 3 | 2,073 | 16,639 | 8,090 | 135 | 9,122 | 2,909 | 2,300 | 138 | 4,056 | 122 | 493 |
| 32 Kansas | 159 | 14,588 | - 223 | 2,088 | 16,676 | 10,069 | 125 | 8,171 | 2,841 | 2,502 | 142 | 4,856 | 197 | 646 |
| 37 Michigan | 349 | 38,538 | + 1,294 | 4,928 | 43,466 | 27,558 | 279 | 28,624 | 11,916 | 7,476 | 292 | 11,737 | 884 | 991 |
| 38 Mid-South | 112 | 8,889 | - 378 | 1,204 | 10,093 | 6,933 | 75 | 4,024 | 1,313 | 1,127 | 83 | 1,628 | 86 | 154 |
| 39 Minnesota North | 194 | 11,146 | - 289 | 1,928 | 13,074 | 6,470 | 161 | 8,016 | 2,604 | 2,003 | 165 | 4,530 | 302 | 421 |
| 41 Minnesota South | 239 | 26,998 | - 453 | 3,723 | 30,721 | 16,193 | 193 | 13,575 | 3,868 | 3,864 | 208 | 6,714 | 295 | 744 |
| 43 Missouri | 244 | 24,387 | - 2,825 | 3,199 | 27,586 | 15,503 | 174 | 13,287 | 5,104 | 3,727 | 204 | 6,963 | 154 | 586 |
| 44 Montana | 54 | 3,376 | - 46 | 475 | 3,851 | 2,560 | 35 | 2,159 | 1,016 | 574 | 47 | 854 | 12 | 87 |
| 47 Nebraska | 240 | 23,861 | + 321 | 3,293 | 27,154 | 15,572 | 193 | 12,874 | 3,431 | 3,672 | 217 | 7,592 | 423 | 795 |
| 49 New England | 67 | 5,088 | - 178 | 814 | 5,902 | 2,673 | 45 | 2,961 | 1,442 | 690 | 57 | 990 | 97 | 56 |
| 51 New Jersey | 52 | 3,945 | - 43 | 679 | 4,624 | 1,821 | 32 | 1,550 | 821 | 657 | 41 | 810 | 38 | 70 |
| 53 North Dakota | 90 | 4,651 | - 381 | 761 | 5,412 | 2,719 | 69 | 2,546 | 629 | 609 | 66 | 1,091 | 24 | 152 |
| 55 Northwest | 240 | 18,091 | - 556 | 2,731 | 20,822 | 16,189 | 174 | 13,744 | 6,462 | 3,567 | 178 | 4,869 | 407 | 352 |
| 56 Ohio | 164 | 14,343 | + 162 | 2,106 | 16,449 | 10,616 | 132 | 8,885 | 3,480 | 2,533 | 140 | 3,352 | 387 | 341 |
| 58 Oklahoma | 74 | 6,261 | - 713 | 712 | 6,973 | 5,611 | 53 | 3,774 | 1,599 | 1,106 | 55 | 1,664 | 61 | 222 |
| 60 Rocky Mountain | 171 | 13,809 | + 5 | 2,014 | 15,823 | 10,974 | 118 | 7,152 | 3,064 | 1,982 | 143 | 4,058 | 257 | 388 |
| 61 South Dakota | 103 | 6,144 | + 251 | 933 | 7,077 | 3,772 | 85 | 3,468 | 760 | 861 | 89 | 1,705 | 27 | 175 |
| 63 Southeastern | 188 | 15,768 | + 38 | 2,428 | 18,196 | 11,432 | 136 | 8,727 | 3,490 | 2,581 | 148 | 3,499 | 115 | 301 |
| 65 Southern | 148 | 9,117 | + 193 | 1,264 | 10,381 | 7,278 | 96 | 5,394 | 2,091 | 1,303 | 108 | 1,819 | 260 | 119 |
| 97 SELC | 48 | 3,262 | + 19 | 506 | 3,768 | 2,332 | 35 | 2,493 | 1,054 | 503 | 44 | 857 | 14 | 83 |
| 67 Texas | 319 | 38,600 | - 111 | 4,708 | 43,308 | 28,043 | 233 | 19,704 | 7,767 | 5,132 | 253 | 7,396 | 824 | 668 |
| 76 Wisconsin, North | 202 | 15,272 | - 756 | 2,409 | 17,681 | 7,759 | 162 | 10,318 | 2,904 | 2,327 | 177 | 4,668 | 218 | 442 |
| 78 Wisconsin, South | 204 | 18,891 | - 358 | 2,708 | 21,599 | 11,456 | 150 | 9,127 | 2,715 | 2,327 | 166 | 4,018 | 184 | 416 |
| 79 Wyoming | 65 | 3,033 | - 394 | 464 | 3,497 | 2,656 | 44 | 1,982 | 792 | 480 | 59 | 1,127 | 14 | 104 |
| *Grand Total—U.S.* | 5,645 | 492,005 | - 10,802 | 69,040 | 561,045 | 341,239 | 4,145 | 294,807 | 115,064 | 77,858 | 4,601 | 127,508 | 7,899 | 11,838 |

## 1999 GAINS AND LOSSES IN CONFIRMED MEMBERSHIP

| DISTRICTS | MEMBERSHIP INCREASE | | | | | | | MEMBERSHIP DECREASE | | | | | NET GAIN + NET LOSS − |
|---|---|---|---|---|---|---|---|---|---|---|---|---|---|
| | Juniors Confirmed | | Adults Conf. or Baptized | Reinstated by Prof. of Faith | Received from: | | TOTAL INCREASE | By Death of Confirmed Members | Defections, Removals from Roster | Released to: | | TOTAL DECREASE | |
| | Member Children | Non-Member Children | | | Sister Congre-gations | Other Lutheran Bodies | | | | Other Lutheran Bodies | Sister Congre-gations | | |
| 03 Atlantic | 479 | 92 | 426 | 341 | 171 | 114 | 1,623 | 274 | 700 | 114 | 223 | 1,311 | + 312 |
| 05 California-Nevada-Hawaii | 655 | 49 | 938 | 522 | 975 | 180 | 3,319 | 526 | 1,437 | 190 | 897 | 3,050 | + 269 |
| 07 Pacific Southwest | 1,249 | 188 | 2,470 | 1,188 | 2,227 | 487 | 7,809 | 941 | 2,933 | 400 | 1,778 | 6,052 | + 1,757 |
| 12 Eastern | 578 | 55 | 529 | 165 | 446 | 96 | 1,869 | 519 | 1,118 | 166 | 447 | 2,250 | - 381 |
| 14 English | 614 | 25 | 623 | 534 | 996 | 270 | 3,062 | 601 | 1,353 | 318 | 889 | 3,161 | - 99 |
| 16 Florida-Georgia | 757 | 56 | 1,167 | 765 | 1,853 | 550 | 5,148 | 754 | 2,543 | 382 | 1,239 | 4,918 | + 230 |
| 20 Illinois, Central | 837 | 27 | 761 | 277 | 990 | 98 | 2,990 | 676 | 911 | 149 | 1,029 | 2,765 | + 225 |
| 22 Illinois, Northern | 1,932 | 138 | 1,640 | 816 | 2,374 | 392 | 7,292 | 1,348 | 2,512 | 577 | 2,454 | 6,891 | + 401 |
| 24 Illinois, Southern | 554 | 14 | 369 | 116 | 576 | 39 | 1,668 | 446 | 753 | 49 | 548 | 1,796 | - 128 |
| 26 Indiana | 1,228 | 31 | 1,373 | 464 | 2,076 | 209 | 5,381 | 993 | 1,529 | 235 | 1,904 | 4,661 | + 720 |
| 28 Iowa East | 595 | 25 | 378 | 176 | 762 | 102 | 2,038 | 485 | 834 | 251 | 708 | 2,278 | - 240 |
| 30 Iowa West | 824 | 35 | 554 | 196 | 1,055 | 164 | 2,828 | 702 | 1,205 | 278 | 1,000 | 3,185 | - 357 |
| 32 Kansas | 747 | 37 | 632 | 289 | 1,118 | 156 | 2,979 | 522 | 923 | 167 | 926 | 2,540 | + 439 |
| 37 Michigan | 2,762 | 136 | 2,875 | 1,253 | 3,847 | 323 | 11,196 | 1,811 | 3,576 | 496 | 3,274 | 9,157 | + 2,039 |
| 38 Mid-South | 416 | 21 | 530 | 262 | 1,048 | 130 | 2,407 | 301 | 702 | 105 | 676 | 1,784 | + 623 |
| 39 Minnesota North | 870 | 68 | 418 | 281 | 956 | 185 | 2,778 | 732 | 488 | 460 | 886 | 2,566 | + 212 |
| 41 Minnesota South | 1,750 | 92 | 877 | 624 | 1,987 | 661 | 5,991 | 1,212 | 1,431 | 1,072 | 1,701 | 5,416 | + 575 |
| 43 Missouri | 1,536 | 80 | 1,456 | 580 | 2,850 | 298 | 6,800 | 1,228 | 1,906 | 150 | 2,617 | 5,901 | + 889 |
| 44 Montana | 212 | 9 | 217 | 55 | 224 | 30 | 747 | 132 | 214 | 86 | 227 | 659 | + 88 |
| 47 Nebraska | 1,492 | 51 | 908 | 452 | 2,078 | 224 | 5,205 | 960 | 1,395 | 447 | 1,930 | 4,732 | + 473 |
| 49 New England | 270 | 21 | 302 | 161 | 279 | 73 | 1,106 | 244 | 520 | 95 | 220 | 1,079 | + 27 |
| 51 New Jersey | 240 | 24 | 213 | 132 | 129 | 115 | 853 | 170 | 350 | 113 | 143 | 776 | + 77 |
| 53 North Dakota | 279 | 19 | 118 | 74 | 272 | 94 | 856 | 258 | 183 | 159 | 290 | 890 | - 34 |
| 55 Northwest | 854 | 86 | 1,091 | 627 | 1,350 | 368 | 4,376 | 752 | 2,020 | 344 | 1,098 | 4,214 | + 162 |
| 56 Ohio | 823 | 55 | 955 | 337 | 877 | 310 | 3,357 | 659 | 948 | 258 | 821 | 2,686 | + 671 |
| 58 Oklahoma | 299 | 13 | 351 | 101 | 468 | 77 | 1,309 | 231 | 451 | 40 | 379 | 1,101 | + 208 |
| 60 Rocky Mountain | 757 | 59 | 819 | 593 | 1,624 | 198 | 4,050 | 468 | 1,733 | 240 | 1,364 | 3,805 | + 245 |
| 61 South Dakota | 376 | 22 | 237 | 115 | 585 | 153 | 1,488 | 330 | 378 | 233 | 594 | 1,535 | - 47 |
| 63 Southeastern | 705 | 52 | 908 | 673 | 1,235 | 385 | 3,958 | 540 | 1,331 | 411 | 875 | 3,157 | + 801 |
| 65 Southern | 402 | 48 | 558 | 293 | 705 | 104 | 2,110 | 369 | 690 | 110 | 613 | 1,782 | + 328 |
| 97 SELC | 179 | 13 | 311 | 144 | 313 | 51 | 1,011 | 236 | 125 | 138 | 183 | 682 | + 329 |
| 67 Texas | 1,681 | 95 | 2,536 | 896 | 3,615 | 570 | 9,393 | 961 | 2,901 | 476 | 2,962 | 7,300 | + 2,093 |
| 76 Wisconsin, North | 1,432 | 63 | 662 | 518 | 1,307 | 473 | 4,455 | 994 | 1,610 | 469 | 1,186 | 4,259 | + 196 |
| 78 Wisconsin, South | 1,727 | 74 | 1,138 | 965 | 2,078 | 489 | 6,471 | 1,200 | 2,101 | 676 | 2,052 | 6,029 | + 442 |
| 79 Wyoming | 206 | 5 | 139 | 97 | 311 | 6 | 764 | 133 | 235 | 81 | 316 | 765 | - 1 |
| *Grand Total—U.S.* | 30,317 | 1,878 | 29,479 | 15,082 | 43,757 | 8,174 | 128,687 | 22,708 | 44,039 | 9,935 | 38,451 | 115,133 | + 13,554 |

## SUMMARIZED STATISTICS—1969 to 1999
## (North American Districts Only)

| Year | Parish Pastors | Congregations | | Members | | Com-muned Average Times | Membership Gains | | | | Early Childhood & Elementary Schools | | | |
|---|---|---|---|---|---|---|---|---|---|---|---|---|---|---|
| | | Members of Synod | Total Stations | Baptized | Confirmed | | Children Baptized | Juniors Confirmed | Adults Confirmed or Baptized | Total Gain from Without | Number | Pupils | Men Teachers | Women Teachers |
| 1969 | 4,893 | 5,765 | 6,013 | 2,875,187 | 1,958,384 | 5.78 | 67,990 | 61,573 | 27,866 | 59,785 | 1,236 | 154,235 | 2,605 | 3,984 |
| 1970 | 4,949 | 5,817 | 6,015 | 2,877,291 | 1,980,925 | 5.91 | 68,289 | 58,490 | 26,074 | 56,747 | 1,215 | 150,980 | 2,682 | 3,934 |
| 1971 | 5,060 | 5,846 | 6,094 | 2,886,207 | 2,011,348 | 5.91 | 65,734 | 59,734 | 26,775 | 56,515 | 1,177 | 146,214 | 2,718 | 3,854 |
| 1972 | 5,103 | 5,886 | 6,102 | 2,878,406 | 2,028,728 | 6.09 | 62,066 | 57,477 | 25,276 | 54,873 | 1,243 | 151,668 | 2,735 | 4,243 |
| 1973 | 5,170 | 5,882 | 6,144 | 2,873,814 | 2,049,799 | 6.26 | 57,701 | 58,568 | 25,920 | 57,164 | 1,239 | 151,590 | 2,709 | 4,373 |
| 1974 | 5,120 | 5,968 | 6,179 | 2,866,481 | 2,077,393 | 6.32 | 57,862 | 57,834 | 27,278 | 57,387 | 1,229 | 151,954 | 2,724 | 4,502 |
| 1975 | 5,114 | 5,942 | 6,160 | 2,859,153 | 2,085,821 | 6.68 | 57,708 | 56,878 | 27,758 | 57,647 | 1,218 | 151,179 | 2,724 | 4,527 |
| 1976 | 5,033 | 5,985 | 6,114 | 2,853,574 | 2,094,448 | 6.75 | 55,961 | 54,383 | 27,207 | 57,126 | 1,361 | 155,054 | 2,677 | 4,857 |
| 1977 | 4,825 | 5,878 | 6,051 | 2,766,958 | 2,052,180 | 6.86 | 55,948 | 50,819 | 26,329 | 55,562 | 1,337 | 154,822 | 2,645 | 4,736 |
| 1978 | 4,785 | 5,872 | 6,023 | 2,724,313 | 2,036,011 | 6.88 | 55,815 | 47,161 | 25,864 | 54,569 | 1,360 | 154,397 | 2,582 | 5,009 |
| 1979 | 4,864 | 5,883 | 6,043 | 2,717,996 | 2,034,248 | 7.19 | 57,506 | 43,715 | 26,454 | 55,812 | 1,327 | 160,020 | 2,904 | 5,362 |
| 1980 | 4,958 | 5,937 | 6,048 | 2,719,319 | 2,042,644 | 7.45 | 59,733 | 40,926 | 30,306 | 60,326 | 1,453 | 165,352 | 2,544 | 5,750 |
| 1981 | 5,072 | 5,936 | 6,063 | 2,721,883 | 2,051,708 | 7.65 | 60,816 | 39,508 | 30,838 | 60,819 | 1,479 | 171,966 | 2,540 | 6,435 |
| 1982 | 5,185 | 6,006 | 6,105 | 2,725,623 | 2,051,168 | 7.90 | 60,682 | 36,106 | 30,953 | 59,605 | 1,584 | 177,171 | 2,580 | 6,740 |
| 1983 | 5,252 | 6,034 | 6,147 | 2,725,540 | 2,054,336 | 7.96 | 59,930 | 36,398 | 30,435 | 58,266 | 1,629 | 178,323 | 2,507 | 6,834 |
| 1984 | 5,372 | 6,029 | 6,173 | 2,723,019 | 2,056,915 | 7.24 | 58,387 | 40,045 | 29,575 | 57,418 | 1,698 | 183,591 | 2,538 | 7,242 |
| 1985 | 5,461 | 6,137 | 6,236 | 2,732,791 | 2,052,723 | 8.35 | 58,220 | 38,296 | 29,048 | 56,600 | 1,747 | 185,959 | 2,536 | 7,517 |
| 1986 | 5,483 | 6,150 | 6,256 | 2,723,756 | 2,043,753 | 8.66 | 62,557 | 35,198 | 28,597 | 55,688 | 1,825 | 185,837 | 2,454 | 7,852 |
| 1987 | 5,544 | 6,164 | 6,269 | 2,707,134 | 2,041,567 | 8.37 | 55,768 | 32,627 | 28,640 | 55,268 | 1,839 | 183,159 | 2,452 | 7,985 |
| 1988 | 5,551 | 6,200 | 6,294 | 2,695,222 | 2,030,250 | 8.43 | 55,520 | 32,025 | 27,986 | 54,915 | 1,883 | 180,524 | 2,284 | 7,522 |
| 1989 | 5,574 | 6,218 | 6,315 | 2,691,639 | 2,022,262 | 8.26 | 54,278 | 31,863 | 26,401 | 59,536 | 1,844 | 181,799 | 2,274 | 8,178 |
| 1990 | 5,550 | 6,245 | 6,471 | 2,692,607 | 2,020,850 | 8.45 | 54,483 | 30,699 | 26,684 | 54,946 | 1,832 | 185,904 | 2,259 | 8,500 |
| 1991 | 5,383 | 5,956 | 6,218 | 2,615,567 | 1,958,839 | 8.59 | 52,278 | 30,806 | 27,339 | 54,254 | 1,786 | 182,129 | 2,025 | 7,926 |
| 1992 | 5,389 | 5,969 | 6,150 | 2,617,272 | 1,958,747 | 8.65 | 50,241 | 30,898 | 26,699 | 53,344 | 1,892 | 188,199 | 2,087 | 8,617 |
| 1993 | 5,344 | 5,974 | 6,156 | 2,606,370 | 1,950,648 | 8.63 | 39,319 | 26,299 | 21,226 | 41,818 | 1,946 | 196,278 | 2,110 | 9,087 |
| 1994 | 5,304 | 5,991 | 6,168 | 2,604,037 | 1,950,305 | 8.80 | 47,763 | 32,280 | 26,265 | 52,138 | 1,990 | 203,413 | 2,086 | 9,567 |
| 1995 | 5,263 | 5,995 | 6,175 | 2,601,753 | 1,948,700 | — | 49,728 | 33,051 | 29,018 | 54,927 | 2,031 | 210,270 | 2,188 | 10,140 |
| 1996 | 5,290 | 6,004 | 6,191 | 2,601,144 | 1,951,730 | — | 47,971 | 32,648 | 28,934 | 55,554 | 2,076 | 201,980 | 2,120 | 9,285 |
| 1997 | 5,230 | 6,022 | 6,215 | 2,603,036 | 1,951,391 | — | 46,984 | 32,399 | 29,508 | 55,504 | 2,149 | 214,079 | 2,178 | 11,099 |
| 1998 | 5,187 | 6,022 | 6,218 | 2,594,404 | 1,952,020 | — | 46,808 | 32,481 | 29,549 | 53,218 | 2,200 | 222,308 | 2,227 | 11,810 |
| 1999 | 5,170 | 6,121 | 6,220 | 2,582,440 | 1,945,846 | — | 45,901 | 32,195 | 29,479 | 51,931 | 2,226 | 229,951 | 2,163 | 12,310 |

| Year | Weekday Rel. Classes | | Sunday Religion Classes | | | Enroll-ment in All Bible Study Groups | Vacation Classes | | Contributions | | | | | |
|---|---|---|---|---|---|---|---|---|---|---|---|---|---|---|
| | Number | People | Number | Pupils | Teachers and Officers | | Number | Pupils | Work at Home | Average per Conf. Mem. | Work at Large | Average per Conf. Mem. | Synods Budget | Average per Conf. Mem. |
| 1969 | 4,182 | 123,863 | 5,916 | 813,719 | 100,670 | 312,750 | 4,100 | 379,057 | 188,947,586 | 96.48 | 50,411,077 | 25.74 | 24,059,781 | 12.29 |
| 1970 | 4,148 | 135,381 | 5,899 | 786,374 | 98,754 | 306,533 | 4,162 | 376,299 | 196,534,555 | 99.21 | 48,846,524 | 24.66 | 24,360,384 | 12.25 |
| 1971 | 4,868 | 141,706 | 5,889 | 750,482 | 94,077 | 295,100 | 4,174 | 363,018 | 207,473,101 | 103.15 | 50,044,260 | 24.88 | 24,040,724 | 11.95 |
| 1972 | 5,096 | 146,393 | 5,890 | 719,661 | 91,859 | 301,422 | 4,202 | 354,248 | 220,961,115 | 108.92 | 52,061,231 | 25.66 | 24,322,419 | 11.99 |
| 1973 | 5,271 | 148,021 | 5,920 | 694,333 | 87,180 | 309,158 | 4,170 | 345,392 | 234,957,520 | 114.62 | 55,771,023 | 27.21 | 24,309,799 | 11.86 |
| 1974 | 5,297 | 142,390 | 5,925 | 660,974 | 87,494 | 317,906 | 4,237 | 337,135 | 253,719,257 | 122.13 | 56,456,836 | 27.18 | 24,136,072 | 11.62 |
| 1975 | 5,308 | 136,509 | 5,855 | 640,583 | 84,677 | 324,812 | 4,228 | 328,649 | 271,768,089 | 130.29 | 57,419,976 | 27.53 | 21,734,697 | 10.42 |
| 1976 | 5,302 | 130,195 | 5,843 | 620,256 | 82,718 | 338,419 | 4,208 | 317,704 | 293,077,266 | 139.93 | 58,542,200 | 27.95 | 21,556,309 | 10.29 |
| 1977 | 5,167 | 118,966 | 5,728 | 594,309 | 80,250 | 347,431 | 4,145 | 299,892 | 307,611,052 | 149.89 | 59,027,994 | 28.76 | 21,737,983 | 10.59 |
| 1978 | 5,119 | 110,255 | 5,702 | 578,952 | 78,705 | 356,348 | 4,156 | 292,040 | 336,412,733 | 165.23 | 61,208,534 | 30.06 | 23,204,300 | 11.40 |
| 1979 | 5,117 | 104,123 | 5,766 | 579,218 | 77,468 | 363,538 | 4,228 | 229,070 | 369,244,520 | 181.51 | 65,954,068 | 32.42 | 24,758,854 | 12.17 |
| 1980 | 5,138 | 103,847 | 5,793 | 579,801 | 79,132 | 378,230 | 4,289 | 306,429 | 399,898,631 | 195.29 | 69,274,271 | 33.91 | 25,939,478 | 12.70 |
| 1981 | 5,179 | 104,151 | 5,838 | 583,467 | 79,168 | 389,332 | 4,428 | 316,948 | 440,400,512 | 215.28 | 90,229,552 | 44.11 | 25,798,059 | 12.61 |
| 1982 | 5,305 | 104,389 | 5,848 | 582,258 | 79,698 | 394,690 | 4,486 | 318,895 | 480,583,914 | 234.30 | 78,811,379 | 38.42 | 26,418,083 | 12.88 |
| 1983 | 5,385 | 103,447 | 5,911 | 584,161 | 80,907 | 399,846 | 4,565 | 318,967 | 511,842,461 | 249.15 | 80,732,382 | 39.30 | 27,222,679 | 13.25 |
| 1984 | 5,370 | 96,608 | 5,951 | 591,511 | 81,135 | 411,494 | 4,623 | 321,063 | 539,346,935 | 270.51 | 81,742,006 | 41.00 | 26,952,707 | 13.52 |
| 1985 | 5,354 | 91,484 | 5,967 | 590,078 | 82,712 | 419,837 | 4,634 | 333,719 | 581,078,582 | 283.08 | 87,102,107 | 42.43 | 28,553,792 | 13.91 |
| 1986 | 5,361 | 88,618 | 6,006 | 593,457 | 83,527 | 422,212 | 4,677 | 329,068 | 623,219,584 | 304.94 | 91,971,638 | 45.00 | 28,997,212 | 12.33 |
| 1987 | 5,436 | 88,552 | 6,022 | 677,216 | 84,739 | 422,658 | 4,696 | 327,556 | 636,201,793 | 311.62 | 91,081,794 | 44.61 | 29,698,359 | 11.63 |
| 1988 | 5,413 | 87,809 | 6,033 | 587,253 | 83,553 | 413,802 | 4,692 | 329,404 | 676,355,005 | 333.13 | 92,842,299 | 45.72 | 29,941,620 | 14.75 |
| 1989 | 4,963 | 109,214 | 6,016 | 600,556 | 78,325 | 383,262 | 4,698 | 339,190 | 798,887,072 | 395.00 | 104,335,721 | 51.59 | 30,285,448 | 14.98 |
| 1990 | 4,992 | 122,956 | 6,042 | 613,400 | 78,325 | 395,398 | 4,733 | 348,860 | 729,824,336 | 361.15 | 101,757,161 | 49.11 | 30,109,858 | 15.36 |
| 1991 | 4,729 | 134,319 | 5,783 | 590,439 | 77,804 | 383,739 | 4,524 | 341,211 | 741,823,412 | 378.71 | 94,094,637 | 48.04 | 29,049,183 | 14.83 |
| 1992 | 4,862 | 143,836 | 5,778 | 581,260 | 77,218 | 379,358 | 4,422 | 324,575 | 777,467,488 | 396.92 | 97,275,934 | 49.66 | 27,844,253 | 14.21 |
| 1993 | 4,808 | 134,872 | 5,763 | 568,634 | 76,441 | 374,497 | 4,385 | 315,881 | 789,821,559 | 313.17 | 96,355,945 | 49.40 | 26,731,671 | 13.70 |
| 1994 | 4,872 | 135,919 | 5,754 | 565,213 | 76,708 | 377,230 | 4,322 | 311,113 | 817,412,113 | 419.12 | 96,048,560 | 49.25 | 26,369,155 | 13.52 |
| 1995 | 4,921 | 143,941 | 5,735 | 547,550 | 74,858 | 332,179 | 4,281 | 304,622 | 832,701,255 | 427.31 | 98,139,835 | 50.36 | 26,295,995 | 13.49 |
| 1996 | 4,954 | 141,580 | 5,742 | 540,902 | 74,525 | 345,881 | 4,245 | 305,226 | 855,461,015 | 438.31 | 104,076,876 | 53.33 | 25,748,616 | 13.19 |
| 1997 | 4,813 | 141,926 | 5,739 | 533,573 | 72,835 | 350,998 | 4,134 | 296,460 | 887,928,255 | 455.02 | 110,520,917 | 56.64 | 24,919,551 | 12.77 |
| 1998 | 4,702 | 130,422 | 5,688 | 502,807 | 70,061 | 339,691 | 4,157 | 295,931 | 933,949,566 | 478.54 | 121,536,226 | 66.26 | 24,925,239 | 12.76 |
| 1999 | 4,601 | 127,508 | 5,645 | 492,005 | 69,040 | 341,239 | 5,645 | 294,807 | 986,295,136 | 506.87 | 123,632,549 | 27.17 | 25,233,082 | 12.93 |

## SIZE OF STATIONS ANALYZED BY DISTRICTS 1999

| DISTRICTS | Av. Size Membership | | Classified According to Confirmed Membership | | | | | | | | | | | | | | | | | | | | |
|---|---|---|---|---|---|---|---|---|---|---|---|---|---|---|---|---|---|---|---|---|---|---|---|
| | Baptized | Confirmed | Total Stations | 0 | 1–49 | 50–99 | 100–199 | 200–299 | 300–399 | 400–499 | 500–599 | 600–699 | 700–799 | 800–899 | 900–999 | 1000–1099 | 1100–1199 | 1200–1299 | 1300–1399 | 1400–1499 | 1500–1999 | 2000 and Over |
| 03 Atlantic | 404 | 270 | 104 | 4 | 11 | 19 | 27 | 11 | 11 | 5 | 5 | 3 | 1 | 1 | 1 | — | 1 | 2 | 1 | 1 | — | — |
| 05 California-Nevada-Hawaii | 296 | 219 | 194 | 2 | 26 | 37 | 54 | 24 | 22 | 11 | 3 | 8 | 4 | 2 | — | — | — | 1 | — | — | — | — |
| 07 Pacific Southwest | 364 | 271 | 283 | 11 | 32 | 45 | 72 | 48 | 22 | 10 | 16 | 4 | 4 | 5 | 3 | 2 | 2 | — | 4 | 1 | — | 2 |
| 12 Eastern | 367 | 266 | 151 | 1 | 13 | 21 | 46 | 32 | 7 | 9 | 8 | 3 | 4 | 3 | — | 1 | 2 | — | — | 1 | — | — |
| 14 English | 378 | 290 | 167 | 2 | 14 | 34 | 45 | 24 | 11 | 15 | 3 | 7 | 2 | 4 | 1 | 1 | — | 1 | — | — | 1 | 2 |
| 16 Florida-Georgia | 400 | 310 | 178 | 2 | 15 | 24 | 48 | 24 | 21 | 7 | 8 | 10 | 7 | 3 | 2 | 3 | 2 | 1 | — | — | 1 | — |
| 20 Central Illinois | 468 | 353 | 162 | 6 | 8 | 13 | 37 | 30 | 19 | 10 | 9 | 8 | 11 | 1 | 1 | 3 | 2 | — | — | 1 | 3 | — |
| 22 Northern Illinois | 633 | 469 | 242 | 3 | 11 | 27 | 41 | 36 | 19 | 25 | 15 | 15 | 7 | 8 | 8 | 5 | 4 | 2 | 4 | 3 | 5 | 4 |
| 24 Southern Illinois | 442 | 342 | 100 | 2 | 9 | 7 | 28 | 15 | 14 | 4 | 7 | 1 | 2 | 1 | 1 | 1 | 4 | 1 | 1 | 1 | — | 1 |
| 26 Indiana | 467 | 345 | 247 | 11 | 18 | 30 | 54 | 39 | 29 | 23 | 10 | 3 | 7 | 3 | 4 | 2 | 3 | 2 | — | 3 | 3 | 3 |
| 28 Iowa East | 407 | 311 | 122 | 3 | 4 | 14 | 27 | 28 | 14 | 10 | 11 | 4 | 1 | 1 | 1 | — | 2 | — | — | 1 | 1 | — |
| 30 Iowa West | 398 | 301 | 180 | 5 | 8 | 22 | 44 | 33 | 28 | 11 | 5 | 11 | 5 | 4 | — | 1 | 1 | — | 1 | — | — | 1 |
| 32 Kansas | 380 | 286 | 169 | 5 | 8 | 23 | 49 | 34 | 13 | 12 | 9 | 2 | 3 | 2 | 2 | 4 | 1 | 1 | — | — | — | 1 |
| 37 Michigan | 620 | 462 | 377 | 6 | 25 | 25 | 61 | 70 | 42 | 37 | 25 | 12 | 11 | 9 | 9 | 10 | 6 | 6 | 6 | 4 | 7 | 6 |
| 38 Mid-South | 278 | 216 | 120 | 1 | 12 | 29 | 26 | 20 | 16 | 7 | 2 | 2 | 4 | — | — | — | 1 | — | — | — | — | — |
| 39 Minnesota North | 322 | 249 | 214 | 3 | 15 | 28 | 75 | 32 | 26 | 13 | 6 | 1 | 7 | 2 | 3 | — | 2 | — | 1 | — | — | — |
| 41 Minnesota South | 554 | 422 | 255 | 9 | 4 | 17 | 49 | 43 | 32 | 26 | 17 | 16 | 11 | 5 | 7 | 5 | 1 | 4 | 1 | 2 | 4 | 2 |
| 43 Missouri | 464 | 350 | 313 | 12 | 27 | 41 | 63 | 60 | 30 | 16 | 17 | 8 | 10 | 6 | 2 | 2 | 3 | 2 | 4 | — | 5 | 5 |
| 44 Montana | 250 | 185 | 64 | 1 | 10 | 20 | 15 | 5 | 4 | 3 | 3 | — | 1 | 1 | — | 1 | — | — | — | — | — | — |
| 47 Nebraska | 446 | 341 | 250 | 4 | 12 | 36 | 69 | 41 | 26 | 18 | 10 | 6 | 5 | 1 | 6 | 2 | 3 | 1 | 2 | 1 | 3 | 4 |
| 49 New England | 348 | 258 | 70 | — | 4 | 7 | 21 | 15 | 12 | 7 | 1 | 1 | — | — | — | 1 | 1 | — | — | — | — | — |
| 51 New Jersey | 318 | 233 | 61 | 1 | 6 | 9 | 14 | 13 | 9 | 4 | 2 | — | 2 | 1 | — | — | — | — | — | — | — | — |
| 53 North Dakota | 254 | 200 | 96 | 2 | 14 | 20 | 27 | 15 | 6 | 3 | 3 | 2 | 2 | 1 | — | 1 | — | — | — | — | — | — |
| 55 Northwest | 301 | 220 | 272 | 11 | 32 | 47 | 65 | 50 | 30 | 16 | 10 | 4 | 2 | — | 1 | — | 1 | — | 2 | — | 1 | — |
| 56 Ohio | 414 | 308 | 177 | 3 | 12 | 21 | 46 | 27 | 30 | 10 | 14 | 1 | 2 | 2 | 1 | 3 | — | — | — | 1 | 3 | 1 |
| 58 Oklahoma | 311 | 237 | 79 | 1 | 10 | 13 | 20 | 13 | 7 | 6 | 3 | 2 | 2 | 2 | — | — | — | — | — | — | — | — |
| 60 Rocky Mountain | 331 | 248 | 182 | 2 | 26 | 39 | 38 | 27 | 20 | 8 | 6 | 3 | 1 | 4 | 2 | 1 | 2 | 1 | — | — | 2 | — |
| 61 South Dakota | 281 | 217 | 116 | 1 | 13 | 23 | 42 | 12 | 12 | 2 | 2 | 2 | — | 3 | — | 3 | 1 | — | — | — | — | — |
| 63 Southeastern | 369 | 275 | 205 | 6 | 13 | 28 | 63 | 28 | 20 | 17 | 12 | 3 | 5 | 4 | 2 | 1 | 1 | — | — | 1 | 1 | — |
| 65 Southern | 222 | 173 | 168 | 2 | 31 | 40 | 44 | 24 | 11 | 7 | 3 | 2 | 2 | 1 | 1 | — | — | — | — | — | — | — |
| 97 SELC | 327 | 253 | 54 | — | 1 | 7 | 21 | 12 | 5 | 3 | 2 | 1 | 1 | — | — | — | — | — | — | — | 1 | — |
| 67 Texas | 413 | 313 | 343 | 3 | 35 | 55 | 83 | 54 | 26 | 31 | 13 | 7 | 11 | 4 | 5 | 2 | 1 | 4 | 1 | 2 | 3 | 3 |
| 76 North Wisconsin | 480 | 375 | 223 | 1 | 9 | 22 | 58 | 41 | 28 | 22 | 9 | 4 | 6 | 2 | 2 | 1 | 3 | 4 | 3 | 3 | 2 | 3 |
| 78 South Wisconsin | 603 | 461 | 216 | 3 | 10 | 17 | 42 | 32 | 28 | 25 | 10 | 7 | 7 | 6 | 5 | 2 | — | 4 | 1 | 7 | 7 | 3 |
| 79 Wyoming | 247 | 187 | 66 | — | 6 | 17 | 22 | 10 | 5 | 1 | 2 | 2 | — | 1 | — | — | — | — | — | — | — | — |
| *Average & Totals—U.S.* | 415 | 313 | 6,220 | 129 | 504 | 877 | 1,536 | 1,022 | 655 | 434 | 281 | 165 | 150 | 93 | 70 | 58 | 50 | 37 | 32 | 33 | 53 | 41 |
| Percentages of Total Stations | | | 100% | 49% | | | | 34% | | | 12% | | | | | 5% | | | | | | |

## 1999 WEEKDAY RELIGION CLASSES

| District | Number of Schools | Enrollment by Grades | | | | | | Total Enrollment | Nonmember Children | Staff | | | | Staff Total |
|---|---|---|---|---|---|---|---|---|---|---|---|---|---|---|
| | | Preschool | Grades 1 & 2 | Grades 3 & 4 | Grades 5 & 6 | Grades 7 & 8 | High School | | | Pastors | Professional Teachers | Volunteer Teachers | Non Teaching Staff | |
| 03 Atlantic | 72 | 37 | 6 | 62 | 319 | 891 | 105 | 1,420 | 139 | 58 | 9 | 47 | 1 | 115 |
| 05 California-Nevada-Hawaii | 129 | 206 | 230 | 262 | 352 | 1,168 | 150 | 2,368 | 222 | 107 | 24 | 167 | 26 | 324 |
| 07 Pacific Southwest | 166 | 367 | 85 | 167 | 450 | 1,885 | 312 | 3,266 | 456 | 146 | 48 | 255 | 52 | 501 |
| 12 Eastern | 95 | 110 | 44 | 37 | 231 | 892 | 74 | 1,388 | 68 | 68 | 16 | 46 | 9 | 139 |
| 14 English | 107 | 362 | 177 | 165 | 294 | 1,182 | 128 | 2,308 | 394 | 92 | 25 | 81 | 13 | 211 |
| 16 Florida-Georgia | 111 | 29 | 36 | 51 | 306 | 1,226 | 189 | 1,837 | 193 | 95 | 10 | 92 | 9 | 206 |
| 20 Illinois, Central | 116 | 41 | 57 | 119 | 368 | 1,156 | 61 | 1,802 | 125 | 104 | 18 | 52 | 2 | 176 |
| 22 Illnois, Northern | 177 | 258 | 146 | 309 | 660 | 2,699 | 219 | 4,291 | 329 | 151 | 28 | 145 | 76 | 400 |
| 24 Illinois, Southern | 73 | 100 | 57 | 94 | 317 | 766 | 27 | 1,361 | 128 | 64 | 2 | 65 | 5 | 136 |
| 26 Indiana | 164 | 176 | 76 | 203 | 608 | 1,692 | 86 | 2,841 | 294 | 132 | 23 | 92 | 32 | 279 |
| 28 Iowa East | 97 | 282 | 108 | 248 | 585 | 1,142 | 110 | 2,475 | 149 | 86 | 12 | 154 | 99 | 351 |
| 30 Iowa West | 137 | 159 | 341 | 668 | 1,091 | 1,466 | 63 | 3,788 | 122 | 141 | 16 | 278 | 41 | 476 |
| 32 Kansas | 141 | 300 | 383 | 597 | 853 | 1,521 | 209 | 3,863 | 197 | 131 | 30 | 341 | 98 | 600 |
| 37 Michigan | 284 | 789 | 417 | 664 | 1,675 | 4,330 | 325 | 8,200 | 884 | 240 | 100 | 471 | 151 | 962 |
| 38 Mid-South | 81 | 81 | 51 | 62 | 121 | 624 | 92 | 1,031 | 86 | 68 | 7 | 70 | 4 | 149 |
| 39 Minnesota North | 163 | 75 | 324 | 644 | 856 | 1,709 | 204 | 3,812 | 302 | 140 | 12 | 218 | 30 | 400 |
| 41 Minnesota South | 204 | 118 | 191 | 501 | 1,207 | 3,167 | 344 | 5,528 | 295 | 195 | 47 | 394 | 56 | 692 |
| 43 Missouri | 199 | 1,036 | 316 | 532 | 952 | 2,650 | 116 | 5,602 | 154 | 177 | 40 | 287 | 48 | 552 |
| 44 Montana | 46 | 5 | 33 | 64 | 157 | 319 | 23 | 601 | 12 | 42 | — | 35 | 3 | 80 |
| 47 Nebraska | 214 | 234 | 298 | 771 | 1,697 | 2,494 | 151 | 5,645 | 423 | 199 | 41 | 468 | 52 | 760 |
| 49 New England | 54 | 79 | 4 | 8 | 67 | 506 | 17 | 681 | 97 | 42 | 4 | 10 | — | 56 |
| 51 New Jersey | 39 | 11 | 10 | 30 | 99 | 391 | 40 | 581 | 38 | 32 | 11 | 21 | 4 | 68 |
| 53 North Dakota | 62 | 7 | 11 | 25 | 198 | 587 | 58 | 886 | 24 | 55 | 1 | 90 | 4 | 150 |
| 55 Northwest | 169 | 353 | 152 | 185 | 457 | 1,635 | 335 | 3,117 | 407 | 134 | 31 | 133 | 37 | 335 |
| 56 Ohio | 134 | 121 | 62 | 145 | 395 | 1,376 | 70 | 2,169 | 387 | 112 | 26 | 121 | 50 | 309 |
| 58 Oklahoma | 54 | 126 | 114 | 246 | 238 | 461 | 152 | 1,337 | 61 | 44 | 9 | 106 | 58 | 217 |
| 60 Rocky Mountain | 137 | 216 | 87 | 274 | 372 | 1,484 | 107 | 2,540 | 257 | 121 | 30 | 192 | 30 | 373 |
| 61 South Dakota | 86 | 15 | 29 | 149 | 374 | 754 | 31 | 1,352 | 27 | 79 | 2 | 89 | 2 | 172 |
| 63 Southeastern | 143 | 275 | 196 | 191 | 427 | 1,572 | 79 | 2,740 | 115 | 105 | 7 | 140 | 28 | 280 |
| 65 Southern | 102 | 165 | 22 | 36 | 200 | 558 | 50 | 1,031 | 260 | 66 | 17 | 30 | 2 | 115 |
| 97 SELC | 39 | — | 3 | 44 | 115 | 341 | 34 | 537 | 14 | 31 | 8 | 22 | 2 | 63 |
| 67 Texas | 244 | 306 | 305 | 362 | 954 | 2,584 | 451 | 4,962 | 824 | 190 | 41 | 233 | 156 | 620 |
| 76 Wisconsin, North | 174 | 176 | 162 | 222 | 733 | 2,342 | 121 | 3,756 | 218 | 163 | 31 | 177 | 30 | 401 |
| 78 Wisconsin, South | 162 | 133 | 59 | 80 | 754 | 2,262 | 105 | 3,393 | 184 | 149 | 20 | 132 | 86 | 387 |
| 79 Wyoming | 58 | 61 | 114 | 98 | 178 | 399 | 28 | 878 | 14 | 56 | 2 | 42 | 3 | 103 |
| *Totals—U.S.* | 4,433 | 6,809 | 4,706 | 8,315 | 18,660 | 50,231 | 4,666 | 93,387 | 7,899 | 3,815 | 748 | 5,296 | 1,299 | 11,158 |

## SUNDAY CLASSES AND BIBLE STUDY GROUP REPORTS—1999

| DISTRICTS | Number of Sunday Schools Tabulated | Preconfirmation Classes: Nursery Ages 2 & 3 | Kindergarten Ages 4 & 5 | Primary Grades 1 & 2 | Junior Grades 3 & 4 | Preteen Grades 5 & 6 | Junior High Grades 7 & 8 | Physical or Developmental Disabilities | Postconfirmation Classes: High School Bible Class Grades 9–12 | Combined Youth—Adult* All Ages | Total Pupils Enrolled | Nursery Roll: Number | Nursery Roll: Enrollment |
|---|---|---|---|---|---|---|---|---|---|---|---|---|---|
| 03 Atlantic | 90 | 625 | 889 | 1,161 | 1,287 | 1,053 | 624 | 26 | 463 | 1,293 | 7,427 | 44 | 1,032 |
| 05 California-Nevada-Hawaii | 176 | 767 | 966 | 1,229 | 1,178 | 1,027 | 971 | 165 | 1,018 | 4,308 | 11,629 | 81 | 811 |
| 07 Pacific Southwest | 245 | 1,447 | 1,498 | 2,027 | 2,070 | 1,758 | 1,554 | 95 | 1,584 | 5,984 | 18,017 | 100 | 1,508 |
| 12 Eastern | 133 | 810 | 838 | 1,053 | 1,172 | 1,116 | 984 | 14 | 849 | 2,642 | 9,491 | 71 | 1,140 |
| 14 English | 146 | 782 | 1,087 | 1,312 | 1,314 | 1,144 | 1,203 | 38 | 918 | 3,369 | 11,172 | 75 | 1,712 |
| 16 Florida-Georgia | 166 | 999 | 1,078 | 1,393 | 1,414 | 1,328 | 1,242 | 87 | 1,427 | 5,729 | 14,697 | 90 | 1,302 |
| 20 Illinois, Central | 144 | 1,136 | 1,154 | 1,471 | 1,520 | 1,464 | 1,325 | 158 | 1,547 | 4,985 | 14,760 | 80 | 1,196 |
| 22 Illinois, Northern | 226 | 1,999 | 2,540 | 3,231 | 3,189 | 2,770 | 2,230 | 118 | 1,819 | 6,950 | 24,846 | 128 | 3,812 |
| 24 Illinois, Southern | 88 | 565 | 599 | 826 | 812 | 757 | 701 | 6 | 692 | 2,106 | 7,064 | 44 | 691 |
| 26 Indiana | 223 | 1,786 | 1,842 | 2,180 | 2,082 | 1,807 | 1,631 | 34 | 1,816 | 7,224 | 20,402 | 114 | 1,799 |
| 28 Iowa East | 116 | 879 | 819 | 1,010 | 1,118 | 1,027 | 1,165 | 12 | 957 | 2,889 | 9,876 | 73 | 988 |
| 30 Iowa West | 166 | 1,202 | 1,244 | 1,530 | 1,680 | 1,648 | 1,590 | 39 | 1,786 | 3,847 | 14,566 | 96 | 1,283 |
| 32 Kansas | 159 | 1,088 | 1,322 | 1,311 | 1,412 | 1,366 | 1,461 | 45 | 1,805 | 4,778 | 14,588 | 82 | 1,318 |
| 37 Michigan | 349 | 2,744 | 4,361 | 4,228 | 4,152 | 3,799 | 3,164 | 232 | 3,184 | 12,673 | 38,538 | 181 | 4,497 |
| 38 Mid-South | 112 | 628 | 547 | 705 | 725 | 702 | 670 | 78 | 903 | 3,931 | 8,889 | 55 | 472 |
| 39 Minnesota North | 194 | 804 | 1,095 | 1,523 | 1,546 | 1,506 | 1,508 | 29 | 790 | 2,343 | 11,146 | 97 | 1,207 |
| 41 Minnesota South | 239 | 2,214 | 2,709 | 3,108 | 3,369 | 3,091 | 2,827 | 58 | 2,587 | 7,031 | 26,998 | 143 | 3,268 |
| 43 Missouri | 244 | 2,146 | 2,152 | 2,569 | 2,618 | 2,385 | 2,330 | 107 | 2,221 | 7,859 | 24,387 | 119 | 2,353 |
| 44 Montana | 54 | 238 | 303 | 354 | 388 | 319 | 304 | 59 | 273 | 1,138 | 3,376 | 24 | 217 |
| 47 Nebraska | 240 | 2,056 | 1,950 | 2,651 | 2,833 | 2,697 | 2,609 | 38 | 2,448 | 6,579 | 23,861 | 145 | 2,508 |
| 49 New England | 67 | 502 | 437 | 601 | 654 | 601 | 546 | 7 | 384 | 1,356 | 5,088 | 40 | 596 |
| 51 New Jersey | 52 | 355 | 420 | 595 | 595 | 463 | 459 | 10 | 292 | 756 | 3,945 | 33 | 602 |
| 53 North Dakota | 90 | 317 | 400 | 584 | 593 | 591 | 584 | 28 | 435 | 1,119 | 4,651 | 47 | 477 |
| 55 Northwest | 240 | 1,272 | 1,515 | 1,771 | 1,805 | 1,623 | 1,595 | 74 | 2,035 | 6,399 | 18,091 | 115 | 1,168 |
| 56 Ohio | 164 | 1,193 | 1,289 | 1,515 | 1,585 | 1,291 | 1,189 | 10 | 1,370 | 4,901 | 14,343 | 96 | 1,442 |
| 58 Oklahoma | 74 | 343 | 358 | 413 | 473 | 430 | 434 | 6 | 666 | 3,138 | 6,261 | 29 | 292 |
| 60 Rocky Mountain | 171 | 884 | 1,147 | 1,472 | 1,470 | 1,258 | 1,305 | 47 | 1,449 | 4,777 | 13,809 | 84 | 1,170 |
| 61 South Dakota | 103 | 478 | 520 | 709 | 741 | 727 | 727 | 19 | 689 | 1,534 | 6,144 | 55 | 647 |
| 63 Southeastern | 188 | 1,319 | 1,299 | 1,698 | 1,678 | 1,436 | 1,365 | 153 | 1,569 | 5,251 | 15,768 | 89 | 1,082 |
| 65 Southern | 148 | 648 | 641 | 662 | 756 | 710 | 679 | 75 | 1,026 | 3,920 | 9,117 | 48 | 402 |
| 97 SELC | 48 | 250 | 376 | 363 | 369 | 344 | 289 | 25 | 274 | 966 | 3,262 | 28 | 427 |
| 67 Texas | 319 | 3,079 | 2,864 | 3,335 | 3,294 | 3,232 | 3,239 | 133 | 4,396 | 15,028 | 38,600 | 159 | 2,351 |
| 76 Wisconsin, North | 202 | 1,230 | 1,842 | 2,293 | 2,364 | 2,281 | 1,894 | 111 | 816 | 2,441 | 15,272 | 109 | 2,368 |
| 78 Wisconsin, South | 204 | 1,402 | 1,988 | 2,376 | 2,509 | 2,284 | 2,098 | 202 | 1,068 | 4,964 | 18,891 | 121 | 3,049 |
| 79 Wyoming | 65 | 188 | 216 | 279 | 283 | 284 | 251 | 11 | 415 | 1,106 | 3,033 | 31 | 280 |
| *Totals—U.S.* | 5,645 | 38,375 | 44,305 | 53,538 | 55,048 | 50,319 | 46,747 | 2,349 | 45,971 | 155,314 | 492,005 | 2,926 | 49,467 |

* In previous years these totals were reported separately as Adult Bible Classes Ages 18-24, Adult Bible Classes Ages 25 & Older, Combined Youth Adult All Ages.

## SUNDAY CLASSES AND BIBLE STUDY GROUP REPORTS 1999 (Continued)

| DISTRICTS | Preconfirmation Teachers: Lay Teachers | Pastors | Commissioned | Other | Postconfirmation Teachers: Lay Teachers | Pastors | Commissioned | Other | Nonteaching S.S. Officers | Total S.S. Staff Tabulated | Weekday Bible Classes: Held Weekly: Number | Held Weekly: Enrollment | Less than Weekly Number |
|---|---|---|---|---|---|---|---|---|---|---|---|---|---|
| 03 Atlantic | 661 | 18 | 7 | 45 | 91 | 47 | 7 | 1 | 137 | 1,014 | 171 | 1,965 | 135 |
| 05 California-Nevada-Hawaii | 1,054 | 40 | 15 | 56 | 300 | 132 | 29 | 15 | 157 | 1,798 | 535 | 3,675 | 188 |
| 07 Pacific Southwest | 1,526 | 50 | 28 | 104 | 360 | 192 | 44 | 60 | 254 | 2,618 | 764 | 5,923 | 263 |
| 12 Eastern | 876 | 23 | 7 | 49 | 197 | 93 | 6 | 13 | 208 | 1,472 | 155 | 1,950 | 178 |
| 14 English | 1,064 | 34 | 10 | 44 | 232 | 106 | 15 | 28 | 207 | 1,740 | 342 | 3,571 | 185 |
| 16 Florida-Georgia | 1,055 | 41 | 10 | 87 | 301 | 148 | 28 | 35 | 201 | 1,906 | 351 | 3,914 | 258 |
| 20 Illnois, Central | 1,155 | 19 | 12 | 63 | 247 | 136 | 22 | 17 | 166 | 1,837 | 258 | 2,422 | 233 |
| 22 Illinois, Northern | 1,898 | 51 | 25 | 192 | 334 | 186 | 58 | 62 | 475 | 3,281 | 537 | 6,273 | 354 |
| 24 Illinois, Southern | 556 | 13 | 3 | 23 | 114 | 78 | 5 | 13 | 103 | 908 | 113 | 1,793 | 91 |
| 26 Indiana | 1,799 | 31 | 35 | 85 | 384 | 207 | 37 | 49 | 304 | 2,931 | 431 | 4,452 | 367 |
| 28 Iowa East | 841 | 15 | 5 | 101 | 143 | 91 | 3 | 20 | 168 | 1,387 | 194 | 3,147 | 231 |
| 30 Iowa West | 1,437 | 31 | 1 | 51 | 220 | 96 | 6 | 11 | 220 | 2,073 | 253 | 4,178 | 318 |
| 32 Kansas | 1,246 | 22 | 8 | 84 | 379 | 120 | 27 | 19 | 183 | 2,088 | 328 | 5,053 | 280 |
| 37 Michigan | 2,832 | 81 | 52 | 224 | 556 | 296 | 112 | 93 | 682 | 4,928 | 1,022 | 12,621 | 635 |
| 38 Mid-South | 638 | 22 | 5 | 58 | 233 | 95 | 11 | 26 | 116 | 1,204 | 192 | 1,714 | 174 |
| 39 Minnesota North | 1,371 | 26 | 5 | 82 | 119 | 98 | 10 | 8 | 209 | 1,928 | 309 | 4,832 | 315 |
| 41 Minnesota South | 2,501 | 45 | 28 | 174 | 286 | 187 | 39 | 49 | 414 | 3,723 | 684 | 7,009 | 422 |
| 43 Missouri | 1,913 | 46 | 21 | 125 | 458 | 198 | 51 | 64 | 323 | 3,199 | 454 | 7,117 | 418 |
| 44 Montana | 289 | 12 | 1 | 19 | 55 | 32 | — | 11 | 56 | 475 | 123 | 866 | 81 |
| 47 Nebraska | 2,178 | 48 | 27 | 114 | 380 | 162 | 33 | 27 | 324 | 3,293 | 626 | 8,015 | 620 |
| 49 New England | 554 | 10 | 7 | 21 | 91 | 49 | 5 | 3 | 74 | 814 | 101 | 1,087 | 94 |
| 51 New Jersey | 450 | 12 | 2 | 22 | 70 | 33 | 2 | 1 | 87 | 679 | 73 | 848 | 43 |
| 53 North Dakota | 552 | 17 | — | 29 | 50 | 41 | 2 | 1 | 69 | 761 | 111 | 1,115 | 111 |
| 55 Northwest | 1,553 | 47 | 20 | 90 | 451 | 204 | 44 | 47 | 275 | 2,731 | 669 | 5,272 | 281 |
| 56 Ohio | 1,231 | 28 | 9 | 49 | 291 | 138 | 27 | 34 | 299 | 2,106 | 416 | 3,739 | 258 |
| 58 Oklahoma | 407 | 16 | 1 | 17 | 121 | 57 | 8 | 16 | 69 | 712 | 142 | 1,725 | 81 |
| 60 Rocky Mountain | 1,171 | 25 | 16 | 114 | 258 | 156 | 22 | 35 | 217 | 2,014 | 477 | 4,315 | 366 |
| 61 South Dakota | 669 | 19 | 2 | 34 | 74 | 53 | — | 7 | 75 | 933 | 135 | 1,732 | 152 |
| 63 Southeastern | 1,415 | 40 | 7 | 115 | 401 | 171 | 8 | 52 | 219 | 2,428 | 418 | 3,593 | 230 |
| 65 Southern | 681 | 22 | 10 | 29 | 267 | 106 | 15 | 20 | 114 | 1,264 | 203 | 2,079 | 139 |
| 97 SELC | 326 | 19 | 2 | 16 | 49 | 30 | 6 | 8 | 50 | 506 | 85 | 871 | 31 |
| 67 Texas | 2,568 | 88 | 73 | 162 | 794 | 294 | 51 | 103 | 575 | 4,708 | 705 | 8,220 | 697 |
| 76 Wisconsin, North | 1,588 | 37 | 11 | 193 | 122 | 84 | 13 | 22 | 339 | 2,409 | 363 | 4,886 | 351 |
| 78 Wisconsin, South | 1,631 | 45 | 15 | 183 | 204 | 165 | 33 | 36 | 396 | 2,708 | 505 | 4,202 | 293 |
| 79 Wyoming | 300 | 9 | 1 | 4 | 53 | 44 | 1 | 5 | 47 | 464 | 111 | 1,141 | 83 |
| *Totals—U.S.* | 41,986 | 1,102 | 481 | 2,858 | 8,685 | 4,325 | 780 | 1,011 | 7,812 | 69,040 | 12,356 | 135,315 | 8,956 |

## TWO DECADES OF CHANGE

| Fields of Activity | 1979 | 1989 | 1999 |
|---|---|---|---|
| Number of Districts (North America) | 40 | 38 | 35 |
| Number of Circuits (North America) | 610 | 647 | 627 |
| Number of countries served | 30 | 30 | 64 |
| **Pastors** (North America) | | | |
| Total number on clergy roster | 7,874 | 8,616 | 8,722 |
| Pastors, missionaries, and teachers | 5,541 | 6,253 | 5,790 |
| Serving Synod, Districts, and others | 230 | 274 | 270 |
| Entered the ministry (graduates) | 188 | 215 | 144 |
| **Congregations** (North America) | | | |
| Number of stations | 6,043 | 6,315 | 6,220 |
| Average size in baptized members | 449 | 423 | 415 |
| Average size in confirmed members | 336 | 320 | 313 |
| Number of vacant parishes | 705 | 753 | 1,075 |
| **Membership** (North America) | | | |
| Baptized members | 2,717,996 | 2,691,639 | 2,582,440 |
| Change over previous decade | –5.48% | –.970% | –4.06% |
| Confirmed members | 2,034,248 | 2,022,262 | 1,945,846 |
| Change over previous decade | +3.87% | –.589% | –3.78% |
| **Christian Education** (North America) | | | |
| *Elementary Schools:* Number | 1,400 | 1,844 | 1,010 |
| Pupils enrolled | 158,373 | 181,799 | 182,087 |
| Teachers—Men | 2,904 | 2,274 | 1,538 |
| Teachers—Women | 5,362 | 8,178 | 8,074 |
| *Community High Schools:* Number | 58 | 63 | 71 |
| Pupils enrolled | 15,663 | 15,861 | 18,300 |
| Teaching staff | 1,007 | 1,118 | 1,239 |
| *Colleges and Seminaries:* Number | 14 | 16 | 12 |
| Students enrolled | 7,178 | 9,625 | 14,961 |
| Teaching staff | 634 | 583 | 1,355 |
| *Sunday Schools:* Number | 5,766 | 6,016 | 5,645 |
| Pupils and teachers enrolled | 656,686 | 600,556 | 492,005 |
| Teachers and officers | 77,468 | 13,303 | 69,040 |
| *Weekday Religion Schools:* Number | 5,117 | 4,963 | 4,601 |
| Pupils enrolled | 104,123 | 109,214 | 135,407 |
| Children of nonmembers | 12,113 | 9,109 | 7,899 |
| *Vacation Bible Schools:* Number | 4,228 | 4,698 | 4,145 |
| **Sacred Acts** (North America) | | | |
| Children baptized | 57,506 | 54,278 | 45,901 |
| Juniors confirmed | 43,715 | 31,863 | 32,195 |
| Adults confirmed or baptized | 26,454 | 26,401 | 29,479 |
| Total gained from outside | 55,812 | 59,536 | 54,627 |
| Communed, average times per confirmed member | 7.19 | 8.26 | — |
| **Contributions** (North America) | | | |
| For work at home | $369,244,520 | $718,752,757 | $986,295,136 |
| Average per confirmed member | 181.51 | 355.42 | 506.87 |
| For work at large | 65,954,068 | 96,432,514 | 123,632,549 |
| Average per confirmed member | 32.42 | 47.69 | 63.54 |
| Total for all purposes | 435,198,588 | 815,185,271 | 1,109,927,685 |
| Average per confirmed member | 213.94 | 403.11 | 570.41 |
| Remitted for Synod's budget | 24,758,584 | 30,285,448 | 25,233,082 |
| Average per confirmed member | 12.17 | 14.98 | 12.93 |

* Remitted for Synod's budget figures for 1997 and 1998 were reported in error.
1997 reported figure of $67,690,817 should have been $24,919,551.
1998 reported figure of $70,932,312 should have been $24, 925,239.

## MISSOURI SYNOD ACCORDING TO STATES AND COUNTRIES—1999

| | States and Countries | Number of Pastors | Number of Stations | Baptized Members | Confirmed Members | Sunday School Pupils | 1999 Total Contributions | Av. per Confirmed |
|---|---|---|---|---|---|---|---|---|
| 01 | Alabama | 41 | 62 | 12,118 | 9,495 | 3,408 | $ 5,390,185 | $567.69 |
| 02 | Alaska | 11 | 13 | 4,119 | 2,847 | 1,167 | 2,055,031 | 721.82 |
| 03 | Arizona | 58 | 65 | 24,862 | 19,324 | 4,146 | 14,238,823 | 736.85 |
| 04 | Arkansas | 45 | 62 | 14,910 | 11,921 | 3,898 | 9,483,672 | 795.54 |
| 05 | California | 337 | 413 | 135,458 | 99,943 | 25,304 | 70,379,300 | 704.19 |
| 06 | Colorado | 111 | 124 | 48,228 | 36,215 | 10,508 | 24,224,996 | 668.92 |
| 07 | Connecticut | 32 | 37 | 13,893 | 10,609 | 2,733 | 5,724,191 | 539.56 |
| 08 | Delaware | 7 | 7 | 2,074 | 1,613 | 322 | 990,115 | 613.83 |
| 09 | District of Columbia | 1 | 4 | 935 | 751 | 204 | 735,214 | 978.98 |
| 10 | Florida | 152 | 170 | 72,486 | 56,525 | 14,439 | 39,198,665 | 693.47 |
| 11 | Georgia | 32 | 38 | 10,049 | 7,534 | 3,108 | 6,236,531 | 827.78 |
| 12 | Hawaii | 9 | 10 | 1,853 | 1,366 | 498 | 1,077,834 | 789.04 |
| 13 | Idaho | 33 | 44 | 13,973 | 9,952 | 2,323 | 4,198 480 | 421.87 |
| 14 | Illinois | 505 | 531 | 282,155 | 211,960 | 48,298 | 115,779,383 | 546.23 |
| 15 | Indiana | 217 | 235 | 114,267 | 84,543 | 19,895 | 53,052,854 | 627.53 |
| 16 | Iowa | 239 | 302 | 121,204 | 92,034 | 24,442 | 38,505,147 | 418.38 |
| 17 | Kansas | 137 | 170 | 64,254 | 48,405 | 14,599 | 31,852,526 | 658.04 |
| 18 | Kentucky | 20 | 29 | 6,438 | 4,802 | 1,765 | 3,553,475 | 740.00 |
| 19 | Louisiana | 40 | 62 | 15,842 | 12,342 | 3,301 | 6,085,334 | 493.06 |
| 20 | Maine | 2 | 2 | 434 | 283 | 79 | 265,327 | 937.55 |
| 21 | Maryland | 62 | 72 | 28,469 | 20,630 | 5,563 | 13,705,981 | 664.37 |
| 22 | Massachusetts | 18 | 21 | 7,165 | 5,140 | 1,601 | 3,221,596 | 626.77 |
| 23 | Michigan | 396 | 415 | 248,259 | 185,112 | 41,063 | 118,155,321 | 638.29 |
| 24 | Minnesota | 346 | 466 | 208,179 | 159,460 | 37,745 | 67,636,917 | 424.16 |
| 25 | Mississippi | 17 | 26 | 3,379 | 2,602 | 1,034 | 1,770,668 | 680.50 |
| 26 | Missouri | 259 | 319 | 151,504 | 114,165 | 25,076 | 61,122,658 | 535.39 |
| 27 | Montana | 38 | 63 | 15,795 | 11,693 | 3,293 | 5,248,096 | 448.82 |
| 28 | Nebraska | 209 | 271 | 117,658 | 89,961 | 24,951 | 42,723,699 | 474.91 |
| 29 | Nevada | 15 | 23 | 7,563 | 5,649 | 1,427 | 3,810,310 | 674.51 |
| 30 | New Hampshire | 5 | 7 | 1,982 | 1,375 | 576 | 978,413 | 711.57 |
| 31 | New Jersey | 58 | 72 | 22,698 | 16,708 | 4,635 | 9,575,455 | 573.11 |
| 32 | New Mexico | 28 | 34 | 5,659 | 4,462 | 1,755 | 3,495,566 | 783.41 |
| 33 | New York | 153 | 201 | 83,549 | 57,664 | 14,380 | 25,349,933 | 439.61 |
| 34 | North Carolina | 53 | 57 | 21,487 | 16,382 | 5,113 | 10,645,294 | 649.82 |
| 35 | North Dakota | 47 | 95 | 24,269 | 19,104 | 4,636 | 6,072,547 | 317.87 |
| 36 | Ohio | 194 | 197 | 80,879 | 60,119 | 15,635 | 35,398,814 | 588.81 |
| 37 | Oklahoma | 63 | 79 | 24,530 | 18,746 | 6,261 | 12,248,511 | 653.39 |
| 38 | Oregon | 77 | 92 | 22,862 | 17,663 | 5,782 | 11,397,910 | 645.30 |
| 39 | Pennsylvania | 71 | 89 | 21,521 | 16,374 | 3,920 | 9,131,455 | 557.68 |
| 40 | Rhode Island | 2 | 3 | 1,083 | 846 | 134 | 474,458 | 560.83 |
| 41 | South Carolina | 11 | 16 | 3,226 | 2,502 | 536 | 2,148,506 | 858.72 |
| 42 | South Dakota | 70 | 117 | 32,759 | 25,280 | 6,159 | 8,942,773 | 353.75 |
| 43 | Tennessee | 44 | 54 | 16,868 | 12,850 | 4,513 | 9,473,770 | 737.26 |
| 44 | Texas | 314 | 349 | 143,288 | 108,466 | 39,011 | 90,103,592 | 830.71 |
| 45 | Utah | 12 | 18 | 4,566 | 3,246 | 1,152 | 3,120,154 | 961.23 |
| 46 | Vermont | 2 | 3 | 785 | 586 | 133 | 253,641 | 432.83 |
| 47 | Virginia | 37 | 49 | 18,545 | 13,843 | 3,982 | 11,011,535 | 795.46 |
| 48 | Washington | 101 | 122 | 40,776 | 29,294 | 8,797 | 18,289,473 | 624.34 |
| 49 | West Virginia | 2 | 3 | 579 | 447 | 232 | 377,643 | 844.84 |
| 50 | Wisconsin | 387 | 441 | 245,451 | 189,805 | 35,361 | 85,314,028 | 449.48 |
| 51 | Wyoming | 36 | 44 | 11,219 | 8,418 | 2,120 | 3,577,323 | 424.96 |
| 52 | Bahamas | — | 1 | 191 | 134 | 49 | 53,362 | 398.22 |
| 53 | Hong Kong | 1 | 1 | 225 | 150 | 105 | 220,000 | 466.67 |
| | *Totals* | **5,157** | **6,200** | **2,576,520** | **1,941,340** | **491,167** | **108,076,485** | **570.78** |

## SUMMARY OF CONTRIBUTIONS DURING 1999

| DISTRICTS | TOTAL CONTRIBUTIONS (Work at Home & Work at Large) | | | | | | TOTAL FOR WORK AT HOME | | | | | |
|---|---|---|---|---|---|---|---|---|---|---|---|---|
| | Totals 1999 | Compared with 1998 | Per Confirmed Member Avgs. | | | | Totals 1999 | Compared with 1998 | Per Confirmed Member Avgs. | | | |
| | | | 1993 | 1998 | 1999 | District Rank | | | 1993 | 1998 | 1999 | District Rank |
| 03 Atlantic | $ 12,504,855 | $ - 40,640 | $400.41 | $ 452.51 | $455.36 | 28 | $ 11,268,430 | $ - 4,672 | $357.86 | $406.62 | $401.33 | 27 |
| 05 California-Nevada-Hawaii | 31,707,232 | + 2,122,585 | 599.44 | 686.72 | 747.05 | 3 | 28,470,518 | + 2,841,454 | 530.71 | 594.90 | 670.79 | 2 |
| 07 Pacific Southwest | 52,021,649 | + 2,301,601 | 560.95 | 643.79 | 678.58 | 7 | 45,074,136 | + 2,450,492 | 502.67 | 551.91 | 587.96 | 9 |
| 12 Eastern | 18,756,477 | + 626,648 | 385.09 | 439.75 | 467.15 | 25 | 16,755,403 | + 307,121 | 346.78 | 398.96 | 417.31 | 26 |
| 14 English | 28,698,557 | + 1,572,857 | 492.31 | 558.71 | 591.58 | 16 | 24,701,982 | + 812,282 | 436.17 | 492.05 | 509.19 | 18 |
| 16 Florida-Georgia | 38,044,237 | + 4,372,020 | 537.83 | 610.48 | 688.47 | 6 | 33,973,841 | + 4,271,385 | 487.43 | 538.51 | 614.81 | 6 |
| 20 Illinois, Central | 27,886,185 | + 851,213 | 449.35 | 466.50 | 487.30 | 22 | 25,203,379 | + 989,372 | 395.30 | 417.82 | 440.42 | 22 |
| 22 Illinois, Northern | 68,251,798 | + 2,225,163 | 473.86 | 582.77 | 601.91 | 14 | 62,755,005 | + 2,216,281 | 423.34 | 534.34 | 553.43 | 13 |
| 24 Illinois, Southern | 15,606,424 | + 167,505 | 363.81 | 447.61 | 456.06 | 26 | 14,337,698 | + 1,382,203 | 326.32 | 375.61 | 418.99 | 24 |
| 26 Indiana | 53,947,885 | + 3,791,258 | 499.55 | 586.24 | 632.49 | 11 | 49,335,427 | + 3,800,587 | 446.74 | 532.22 | 578.42 | 11 |
| 28 Iowa East | 16,050,155 | + 114,208 | 349.18 | 417.07 | 423.41 | 29 | 13,838,656 | + 89,759 | 306.74 | 359.83 | 365.07 | 29 |
| 30 Iowa West | 22,454,992 | + 1,741,185 | 327.37 | 378.31 | 414.86 | 30 | 19,019,876 | + 1,440,152 | 272.93 | 321.07 | 351.39 | 30 |
| 32 Kansas | 31,816,460 | + 2,877,022 | 448.39 | 603.28 | 658.29 | 8 | 28,953,599 | + 3,320,325 | 397.26 | 534.36 | 599.06 | 7 |
| 37 Michigan | 112,433,528 | + 5,902,086 | 514.98 | 614.45 | 645.50 | 10 | 102,501,729 | + 6,498,844 | 461.45 | 553.72 | 588.48 | 8 |
| 38 Mid-South | 19,888,619 | + 1,306,870 | 591.85 | 730.99 | 767.34 | 2 | 16,056,226 | + 92,016 | 514.58 | 628.02 | 619.48 | 5 |
| 39 Minnesota North | 16,020,640 | + 667,292 | 263.39 | 288.29 | 301.13 | 35 | 13,979,207 | + 554,513 | 233.26 | 252.08 | 262.76 | 35 |
| 41 Minnesota South | 52,032,649 | + 3,554,017 | 390.37 | 446.50 | 483.51 | 23 | 45,460,911 | + 3,310,759 | 344.76 | 388.22 | 422.44 | 23 |
| 43 Missouri | 59,035,550 | - 2,863,629 | 453.71 | 567.82 | 539.55 | 20 | 52,977,499 | - 2,364,700 | 392.13 | 507.67 | 484.18 | 20 |
| 44 Montana | 5,319,390 | + 433,179 | 370.85 | 409.99 | 449.39 | 27 | 4,631,715 | + 328,885 | 314.52 | 361.04 | 391.29 | 28 |
| 47 Nebraska | 40,874,381 | + 2,580,020 | 362.57 | 449.58 | 479.64 | 24 | 35,624,787 | + 4,278,346 | 314.08 | 368.01 | 418.04 | 25 |
| 49 New England | 10,237,123 | + 553,084 | 465.47 | 536.60 | 566.21 | 18 | 9,332,745 | + 454,321 | 424.08 | 491.96 | 516.19 | 17 |
| 51 New Jersey | 8,252,165 | + 88,787 | 414.77 | 582.14 | 579.59 | 17 | 7,500,986 | + 36,712 | 369.76 | 532.29 | 526.83 | 15 |
| 53 North Dakota | 6,072,547 | - 283,274 | 277.35 | 325.67 | 316.02 | 34 | 5,185,400 | - 324,721 | 232.07 | 282.34 | 269.85 | 34 |
| 55 Northwest | 36,096,703 | + 1,987,771 | 463.61 | 567.11 | 603.79 | 13 | 31,141,080 | + 866,068 | 409.18 | 503.37 | 520.89 | 16 |
| 56 Ohio | 32,236,324 | + 1,621,759 | 460.32 | 560.29 | 591.59 | 15 | 28,789,317 | + 1,381,873 | 403.75 | 501.59 | 528.33 | 14 |
| 58 Oklahoma | 12,248,511 | + 730,964 | 457.80 | 615.02 | 653.39 | 9 | 10,878,321 | + 756,110 | 397.50 | 540.51 | 580.30 | 10 |
| 60 Rocky Mountain | 31,878,458 | + 2,388,303 | 527.28 | 647.78 | 706.31 | 4 | 28,764,776 | + 1,598,039 | 475.97 | 596.74 | 637.32 | 3 |
| 61 South Dakota | 8,942,773 | + 619,181 | 293.70 | 327.76 | 355.32 | 33 | 7,475,284 | + 247,528 | 252.24 | 284.61 | 297.02 | 33 |
| 63 Southeastern | 39,375,922 | + 3,115,756 | 535.95 | 644.22 | 697.91 | 5 | 35,041,926 | + 3,260,045 | 477.76 | 564.66 | 621.09 | 4 |
| 65 Southern | 16,031,695 | + 350,498 | 447.80 | 510.99 | 551.01 | 19 | 14,681,490 | + 252,819 | 409.80 | 470.17 | 504.61 | 19 |
| 97 SELC | 8,528,607 | + 1,336,544 | 513.04 | 518.27 | 624.39 | 12 | 7,657,598 | + 1,557,702 | 468.59 | 439.57 | 560.63 | 12 |
| 67 Texas | 89,086,653 | + 5,595,177 | 627.52 | 779.88 | 830.42 | 1 | 78,760,999 | + 4,830,849 | 554.73 | 690.57 | 734.17 | 1 |
| 76 Wisconsin, North | 31,198,084 | + 1,931,047 | 322.90 | 349.78 | 372.88 | 32 | 27,598,232 | + 1,670,983 | 286.02 | 309.86 | 329.85 | 32 |
| 78 Wisconsin, South | 51,463,266 | + 242,813 | 426.43 | 513.04 | 517.17 | 21 | 44,338,057 | - 718,836 | 377.02 | 451.30 | 445.57 | 21 |
| 79 Wyoming | 4,927,191 | - 138,977 | 365.76 | 408.56 | 398.41 | 31 | 4,228,901 | - 139,326 | 307.74 | 352.28 | 341.95 | 31 |
| *Grand Total* | $1,109,927,685 | $ + 54,441,893 | $454.36 | $540.78 | $570.41 | — | $ 986,295,136 | $+ 52,345,570 | $402.46 | $478.51 | $506.87 | — |

## SUMMARY OF CONTRIBUTIONS DURING 1999 (Continued)

| DISTRICTS | TOTALS FOR WORK AT LARGE (Including District, Synod, and Other at-large Purposes) | | | | | | | | | |
|---|---|---|---|---|---|---|---|---|---|---|
| | Totals 1999 | Compared with 1998 | Av. per Con-firmed Member | District Rank | Synod's Budget | Av. per Con-firmed Member | District Rank | Nonbudget Purposes | Av. per Con-firmed Member | District Rank |
| 03 Atlantic | $ 1,236,425 | $ - 35,968 | $ 44.04 | 32 | $ 65,619 | $ 2.37 | 34 | $ 552,971 | $ 19.69 | 27 |
| 05 California-Nevada-Hawaii | 3,236,714 | - 718,869 | 76.26 | 7 | 340,387 | 7.90 | 23 | 1,142,782 | 26.93 | 11 |
| 07 Pacific Southwest | 6,947,513 | - 148,891 | 90.63 | 3 | 180,000 | 2.33 | 35 | 3,890,465 | 50.75 | 2 |
| 12 Eastern | 2,001,074 | + 319,527 | 49.84 | 27 | 110,000 | 2.67 | 33 | 962,838 | 23.98 | 17 |
| 14 English | 3,996,575 | + 760,575 | 82.38 | 5 | 205,940 | 4.24 | 30 | 2,352,140 | 48.49 | 3 |
| 16 Florida-Georgia | 4,070,396 | + 100,635 | 73.66 | 8 | 402,124 | 7.29 | 24 | 1,952,499 | 35.33 | 6 |
| 20 Illinois, Central | 2,682,806 | - 138,159 | 46.88 | 29 | 1,050,000 | 18.12 | 6 | 604,503 | 10.56 | 32 |
| 22 Illinois, Northern | 5,496,793 | + 8,882 | 48.48 | 28 | 900,000 | 7.94 | 22 | 2,261,600 | 19.94 | 25 |
| 24 Illinois, Southern | 1,268,726 | - 1,214,698 | 37.08 | 35 | 484,935 | 14.06 | 14 | 300,957 | 8.79 | 33 |
| 26 Indiana | 4,612,458 | - 9,329 | 54.08 | 24 | 1,469,687 | 17.18 | 9 | 1,841,810 | 21.59 | 21 |
| 28 Iowa East | 2,211,499 | + 24,449 | 58.34 | 18 | 551,881 | 14.44 | 12 | 773,579 | 20.41 | 24 |
| 30 Iowa West | 3,435,116 | + 301,033 | 63.46 | 13 | 1,223,900 | 22.35 | 2 | 1,221,248 | 22.56 | 19 |
| 32 Kansas | 2,862,861 | - 443,303 | 59.23 | 17 | 803,598 | 16.75 | 10 | 1,023,358 | 21.17 | 23 |
| 37 Michigan | 9,931,799 | - 596,758 | 57.02 | 21 | 3,001,979 | 17.31 | 8 | 3,785,690 | 21.73 | 20 |
| 38 Mid-South | 3,832,393 | + 1,214,854 | 147.86 | 1 | 518,000 | 20.38 | 3 | 2,295,182 | 88.55 | 1 |
| 39 Minnesota North | 2,041,433 | + 112,779 | 38.37 | 34 | 644,856 | 12.11 | 18 | 663,819 | 12.48 | 31 |
| 41 Minnesota South | 6,571,738 | + 243,258 | 61.07 | 16 | 2,185,951 | 20.16 | 5 | 3,257,974 | 30.27 | 10 |
| 43 Missouri | 6,058,051 | - 498,929 | 55.37 | 23 | 1,360,628 | 12.45 | 17 | 2,771,600 | 25.33 | 13 |
| 44 Montana | 687,675 | + 104,294 | 58.10 | 20 | 86,663 | 7.27 | 25 | 251,547 | 21.25 | 22 |
| 47 Nebraska | 5,249,594 | - 1,698,326 | 61.60 | 15 | 1,907,897 | 22.40 | 1 | 2,106,837 | 24.72 | 14 |
| 49 New England | 904,378 | + 98,763 | 50.02 | 26 | 106,514 | 5.90 | 29 | 356,954 | 19.74 | 26 |
| 51 New Jersey | 751,179 | + 52,075 | 52.76 | 25 | 87,550 | 6.24 | 27 | 229,333 | 16.11 | 28 |
| 53 North Dakota | 887,147 | + 41,447 | 46.17 | 31 | 347,568 | 17.81 | 7 | 156,992 | 8.17 | 34 |
| 55 Northwest | 4,955,623 | + 1,121,703 | 82.89 | 4 | 249,383 | 4.15 | 31 | 2,841,323 | 47.53 | 4 |
| 56 Ohio | 3,447,007 | + 239,886 | 63.26 | 14 | 500,000 | 9.15 | 21 | 1,380,499 | 25.33 | 12 |
| 58 Oklahoma | 1,370,190 | - 25,146 | 73.09 | 9 | 265,000 | 14.15 | 13 | 462,399 | 24.67 | 15 |
| 60 Rocky Mountain | 3,113,682 | + 790,264 | 68.99 | 11 | 275,000 | 6.04 | 28 | 1,485,763 | 32.92 | 8 |
| 61 South Dakota | 1,467,489 | + 371,653 | 58.31 | 19 | 283,225 | 11.15 | 20 | 595,435 | 23.66 | 18 |
| 63 Southeastern | 4,333,996 | - 144,289 | 76.82 | 6 | 407,037 | 7.23 | 26 | 2,396,866 | 42.48 | 5 |
| 65 Southern | 1,350,205 | + 97,679 | 46.41 | 30 | 106,383 | 3.47 | 32 | 431,458 | 14.83 | 30 |
| 97 SELC | 871,009 | - 221,158 | 63.77 | 12 | 184,000 | 13.14 | 16 | 330,582 | 24.20 | 16 |
| 67 Texas | 10,325,654 | + 764,328 | 96.25 | 2 | 2,160,000 | 20.18 | 4 | 3,358,069 | 31.30 | 9 |
| 76 Wisconsin, North | 3,599,852 | + 260,064 | 43.02 | 33 | 1,169,729 | 13.98 | 15 | 1,313,974 | 15.70 | 29 |
| 78 Wisconsin, South | 7,125,209 | + 961,649 | 71.60 | 10 | 1,447,754 | 14.50 | 11 | 3,471,090 | 34.88 | 7 |
| 79 Wyoming | 698,290 | + 349 | 56.46 | 22 | 149,894 | 12.09 | 19 | 52,753 | 4.27 | 35 |
| Grand Total | $ 123,632,549 | $ + 2,096,323 | $ 63.54 | — | $ 25,233,082 | $ 12.93 | — | $ 52,876,889 | $ 27.17 | — |

Synod's Budget
* District fiscal year ends December 31.
** District fiscal year ends March 31.
NOTE: This report is prepared on the district fiscal year basis, February 1, 1999–January 31, 2000.

# LUTHERAN CHURCH BODIES IN THE UNITED STATES AND CANADA
## Statistics for 1998

| Church Bodies | Ordained Ministers | Ministers Serving Parishes | Congre-gations | Baptized Membership | Confirmed Membership | Sunday Schools | | |
|---|---|---|---|---|---|---|---|---|
| | | | | | | Number | Teachers | Pupils |
| **UNITED STATES** | | | | | | | | |
| 1. Evangelical Lutheran Church in America | 17,589 | 9,646 | 10,862 | 5,178,225 | 3,840,136 | 8,913 | 134,280 | 814,455 |
| 2. American Association of Lutheran Churches | 141 | 95 | 103 | 19,128 | 14,682 | 83 | 484 | 3,229 |
| 3. Apostolic Lutheran Church of America* (1995 data) | 35 | 35 | 61 | 7,700 | NA | 40 | 340 | 2,000 |
| 4. Association of Free Lutheran Congregations | 212 | 141 | 246 | 32,659* | 24,488* | 213* | NA | 6,345* |
| 5. Church of the Lutheran Brethren | 238 | 139 | 127 | 14,253 | NA | 110 | 1,240 | 7,873 |
| 6. Church of the Lutheran Confession | 76 | 59 | 72 | 8,628 | 6,462 | 57 | NA | 1,031 |
| 7. Concordia Lutheran Conference* (1989 data) | 5 | 5 | 5 | 358 | 208 | 5 | 25 | 103 |
| 8. Conservative Lutheran Association | 24 | 7 | 5 | 1,313 | 841 | 4 | 15 | 150 |
| 9. Estonian Evangelical Lutheran Church† | 28 | 18 | 31 | 7,981 | NA | 2 | 8 | 148 |
| 10. Evangelical Lutheran Synod | 178 | 112 | 139 | 22,264 | 16,829 | 126 | 595 | 3,015 |
| 11. Fellowship of Lutheran Congregations* (1997) | 3 | 2 | 5 | 446 | 373 | 4 | NA | NA |
| 12. International Lutheran Fellowship, Inc. | 15 | 10 | 8 | 1,204 | 800 | 8 | 32 | NA |
| 13. Latvian Evangelical Lutheran Church in America† | 62 | 51 | 71 | 15,019 | 13,473 | 35 | NA | NA |
| 14. Lithuanian Evangelical Lutheran Church in Diaspora†* (1997 data) | 7 | 6 | 20 | 4,000 | NA | NA | NA | NA |
| 15. Lutheran Churches of the Reformation* (1993 data) | 12 | 10 | 13 | 500 | 300 | 10 | 15 | 60 |
| 16. The Lutheran Church—Missouri Synod | 8,713 | 5,187 | 6,126 | 2,594,404 | 1,952,020 | 5,688 | 70,061 | 502,807 |
| 17. The Lutheran Ministerium and Synod—USA* | 16 | 8 | 6 | NA | NA | NA | NA | NA |
| 18. The Protestant Conference | 9 | 7 | 6 | 760 | 500 | 6 | 18 | 125 |
| 19. Wisconsin Evangelical Lutheran Synod | 1,668 | 1,224 | 1,239 | 410,164 | 315,581 | 1,201 | 5,733 | 39,669 |
| **TOTAL in United States** | **29,031** | **16,762** | **19,145** | **8,319,006** | **6,186,693** | **16,505** | **212,846** | **1,381,010** |
| 1. Evangelical Lutheran Church in Canada | 862 | 450 | 640 | 196,165 | 140,616 | 394 | 3,384 | 17,117 |
| 2. Lutheran Church—Canada | 366 | 228 | 324 | 80,526 | 59,229 | 290 | 2,367 | 9,442 |
| **TOTAL in Canada** | **1,228** | **678** | **964** | **276,691** | **199,845** | **684** | **5,751** | **26,559** |
| **GRAND TOTAL United States and Canada** | **30,259** | **17,440** | **20,109** | **8,595,697** | **6,386,538** | **17,189** | **218,597** | **1,407,569** |

Statistics as of December 31, 1998 *Indicates other than 1998 data † Statistics include Congregations in Canada NA = Not Available
Compiled by office of the Secretary, Rosters and Statistics, Evangelical Lutheran Church in America

| Church Bodies | Congregational Finances | | | | |
|---|---|---|---|---|---|
| | Property Evaluation | Indebtedness | Local Expenditures | Work at Large | Total Expenditures |
| **UNITED STATES** | | | | | |
| 1. Evangelical Lutheran Church in America | $12,626,272,302 | $1,073,874,543 | $1,822,915,831 | $208,853,359 | $2,031,769,190 |
| 2. American Association of Lutheran Churches* | NA | NA | NA | NA | NA |
| 3. Apostolic Lutheran Church of America* (1995 data) | 8,028,000 | 514,121 | 1,129,170 | 87,356 | 1,216,526 |
| 4. Association of Free Lutheran Congregations | NA | NA | NA | 1,570,770 | 1,570,770 |
| 5. Church of the Lutheran Brethren | 65,591,894 | NA | 11,244,546 | 1,931,707 | 13,176,253 |
| 6. Church of the Lutheran Confession | NA | NA | 4,036,699 | 660,269 | 4,696,968 |
| 7. Concordia Lutheran Conference* (1989 data) | 1,075,000 | 0 | NA | 15,500 | 15,500 |
| 8. Conservative Lutheran Association | NA | NA | NA | NA | NA |
| 9. Estonian Evangelical Lutheran Church† | NA | NA | NA | NA | NA |
| 10. Evangelical Lutheran Synod | 58,150,677 | 5,625,011 | 9,363,126 | 1,120,386 | 10,483,512 |
| 11. Fellowship of Lutheran Congregations* (1997) | NA | NA | NA | NA | NA |
| 12. International Lutheran Fellowship, Inc. | NA | 0 | NA | 1,000 | 1,000 |
| 13. Latvian Evangelical Lutheran Church in America† | 27,393,216 | NA | 3,134,229 | 485,619 | 3,619,848 |
| 14. Lithuanian Evangelical Lutheran Church in Diaspora†* (1997 data) | NA | NA | NA | NA | NA |
| 15. Lutheran Churches of the Reformation* (1993 data) | NA | NA | NA | 30,000 | 30,000 |
| 16. The Lutheran Church—Missouri Synod | 5,896,485,062 | 814,993,327 | 933,949,566 | 121,536,226 | 1,055,485,792 |
| 17. The Lutheran Ministerium and Synod—USA* | NA | NA | NA | NA | NA |
| 18. The Protestant Conference | NA | NA | NA | NA | NA |
| 19. Wisconsin Evangelical Lutheran Synod | NA | 127,753,058 | 178,509,021 | $ 44,674,782 | 223,183,803 |
| **TOTAL in United States** | **$18,682,996,151** | **$2,022,760,060** | **$2,964,282,188** | **$380,966,974** | **$3,345,249,162** |
| 1. Evangelical Lutheran Church in Canada | $ 360,287,535 | $ 21,651,335 | $ 49,345,813 | $ 6,921,066 | $ 56,266,879 |
| 2. Lutheran Church—Canada | 131,428,000 | 12,043,000 | 31,908,000 | 5,569,000 | 37,477,000 |
| **TOTAL in Canada** | **$ 491,715,535** | **$ 33,694,335** | **$ 81,253,813** | **$ 12,490,066** | **$ 93,743,879** |
| **GRAND TOTAL—United States and Canada** | **$19,174,711,686** | **$2,056,454,395** | **$3,045,536,001** | **$393,457,040** | **$3,438,993,041** |

Statistics as of December 31, 1998 *Indicates other than 1998 data † Statistics include Congregations in Canada NA = Not Available
Compiled by office of the Secretary, Rosters and Statistics, Evangelical Lutheran Church in America

# FEDERAL INCOME TAX EXEMPTION
# THE LUTHERAN CHURCH—MISSOURI SYNOD

The Internal Revenue Service has issued rulings under Internal Revenue Code Section 501 (c) (3), which recognize the exempt status of the Synod and its component parts, and which grant a blanket federal income tax exemption to member corporations, their unincorporated elementary schools, and to those incorporated elementary schools and high schools that consent in writing to their inclusion in the group ruling. These rulings are dated June 3, 1992, and any reference to the Synod's exempt status or to the group ruling should refer to that date. Also, the Synod's group ruling is identified by the number 1709. The exisiting rulings are applicable to all of the following:

1. All of the Synod's boards, commissions, and councils, including:

Board for Congregational Services
- Child Ministry
- Evangelism Ministry
- Family Ministry
- School Ministry
- Youth Ministry including Lutheran Youth Fellowship

Board for Mission Services, including Lutheran Student Fellowship
Board for Higher Education Services
Board for Communication Services
Board for Human Care Ministries
- Districts/Congregations
- LCMS Health Ministries
- LCMS World Relief
- Social Ministry Organizations
- Specialized Pastoral Care and Clinical Education

Board for Church Extension
Board of Managers—Worker Benefit Plans
Board for Black Ministry Services
Commission on Constitutional Matters
Commission on Ministerial Growth and Support
Commission on Organizations
Commission on Theology and Church Relations
Commission on Worship
Council of Presidents
Council of Administrators
Council on Human Resources

2. Concordia Historical Institute
3. Lutheran Church Extension Fund—Missouri Synod
4. The Lutheran Church—Missouri Synod Foundation
5. Radio Station KFUO
6. Concordia University System
7. Concordia Asia Educational Foundation
8. Synodical Districts operating in the United States, to wit:

Atlantic
California-Nevada-Hawaii
Central Illinois
Eastern
English
Florida-Georgia
Indiana
Iowa East
Iowa West
Kansas
Michigan
Mid-South
Minnesota North
Minnesota South
Missouri
Montana
Nebraska
New England
New Jersey
North Dakota
North Wisconsin
Northern Illinois
Northwest
Ohio
Oklahoma
Pacific Southwest
Rocky Mountain
SELC
South Dakota
South Wisconsin
Southeastern
Southern
Southern Illinois
Texas
Wyoming

9. Incorporated church extension funds of districts, to wit:
   California-Nevada-Hawaii District Lutheran Church Extension Fund, Inc.
   Central Illinois District Lutheran Church Extension Fund, Inc.
   Ohio District Lutheran Church Extension Fund, Inc.
   Church Extension Fund of the Michigan District of The Lutheran Church—Missouri Synod
   Southeastern District Lutheran Church—Missouri Synod Church Extension Fund, Inc.
10. The education institutions of the Synod, to wit:
   Concordia Seminary (the legal name of which is Concordia College), St. Louis, MO
   Concordia Theological Seminary, Fort Wayne, IN
   Concordia University, River Forest, IL
   Concordia University, Seward, NE
   Concordia College, Ann Arbor, MI
   Concordia University at Austin, Austin, TX
   Concordia College, Bronxville, NY
   Concordia University Wisconsin, Mequon, WI
   Concordia University, Portland, OR
   Concordia University, St. Paul, MN
   Concordia College, Selma, AL
   Concordia University, Irvine, CA

11. The congregations of The Lutheran Church—Missouri Synod located in the United States and including those listed, by states, in the Directory of Congregations set forth on prior pages of this *Annual,* as well as those in the formative stages of membership, as established by records that exist in the offices of the Synod's districts listed above.

12. The elementary schools, middle schools and junior high schools, and high schools (a) that are operated by member congregations of the Synod and are not separately incorporated, as well as those (b) that are either separately incorporated or are otherwise identified as entities separate from congregations and which have consented in writing to be included in the Synod's group ruling.

The separately incorporated preschools and day care centers that are controlled by member congregations of the Synod and that have consented to inclusion in the group exemption ruling of the Synod, while not expressly included within the scope of the rulings listed above, like separately incorporated elementary schools, middle schools, junior high schools, and high schools that are operated by member congregations of the Synod, are listed among the organizations covered by the federal income tax exemption of the Synod, because they are controlled by congregations of the Synod and are teaching ministries of those congregations.

# TOPICAL INDEX

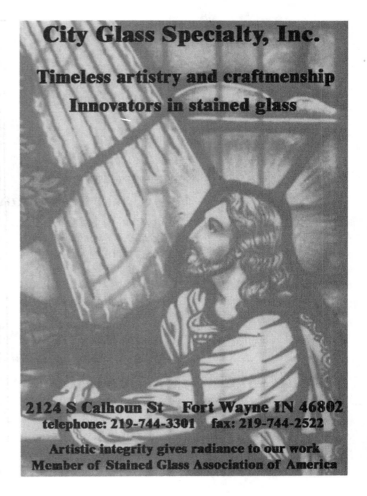

# Your Christian Education Specialists
## *From Concordia Publishing House*

***Director***

**Mr. James Lohman**
Concordia Publishing House
3558 South Jefferson Avenue
St. Louis, MO 63118
Phone: Toll-free 800/325-3040, ext. 1147
FAX: 314/268-1277
E-mail: james.lohman@cph.org

*Minnesota*

**Mr. Paul Berg**
445 Glen South West
Hutchinson, MN 55350
Phone and FAX:
Toll-free 877/515-0892
E-mail: paul.berg@cph.org

***All regions not listed***

**Dr. Dave Ebeling**
CPH facilitator to the church-at-large
1724 Windsor Drive
Bloomington, IN 47401
Phone and FAX:
Toll-free 800/468-5548
E-mail: david.ebeling@cph.org

*Michigan/Ohio*

**Mr. Jason J. Scheler**
5520 Millpointe Drive
Waterford, MI 48327
Phone and FAX:
Toll-free 800/487-6563
E-mail: jason.scheler@cph.org

*Iowa/Kansas/Nebraska/ Western Missouri*

**Ms. Gloria Lessmann**
P.O. Box 61
303 Patterson Avenue
Winside, NE 68790
Phone and FAX:
Toll-free 888/277-0338
E-mail: gloria.lessmann@cph.org

**Part-time** *Florida*

**Rev. Ronald W. and Betty L. Brusius**
1204 Buena Vista Drive
North Fort Myers, FL 33903
Phone: 941/731-1247
FAX: 941/731-1273
E-mail: rbrusius@aol.com

*Wisconsin/Northern Illinois*

**Mr. Duane Tweeten**
21945 Mayrose Boulevard
Brookfield, WI 53045
Phone and FAX:
Toll-free 800/485-8949
E-mail: duane.tweeten@cph.org

**Part-time** *North Dakota/ South Dakota*

**Ms. Sarah Sailer**
2105 South Lincoln Avenue
Sioux Falls, SD 57105
Phone: 605/330-0849
E-mail: ssailer2@aol.com

CONVINCING YOUTH THEY ARE VALUABLE AND CAN CHOOSE TO LIVE LIFE TO THE FULLEST!
CONVINCING YOUTH THEY ARE VALUABLE AND CAN CHOOSE TO LIVE LIFE TO THE FULLEST!
CONVINCING YOUTH THEY ARE VALUABLE AND CAN CHOOSE TO LIVE LIFE TO THE FULLEST!

# BUSINESS RESOURCE DIRECTORY

**AAL Capital Management Corporation**
222 W. College Ave.
Appleton, WI 54919-0007
920-734-5721
Please see our ad on page 16.

**The A. I. Root Company**
P.O. Box 706
Medina, OH 44258
330-725-6677
800-289-7668
The A. I. Root Company produces candles of uncompromising quality—longer burning, bend resistant, beeswax/liquid and paraffin—as well as ecclesiastical supplies and services.
Please see our ad on page 18.

**Board of Higher Education/Concordia University System LCMS**
1333 S. Kirkwood Rd.
St. Louis, MO 63122
314-996-1254
Please see our ad on the inside front cover.

**Cathedral Candle Company**
Please call 800-325-3040 to order. Provides candles for various church uses.
Please see our ad on page 8.

**Christian Healthcare Network**
P.O. Box 2057
Cathedral City, CA 92235
800-871-7056
Health Insurance Provider
Please see our ad on page 16.

**Church Information Center**
LCMS International Center
1333 S. Kirkwood Rd.
St. Louis, MO 63122
314-996-1086
Information/LCMS resources
Please see our ad on page 19.

**Chime Master Systems**
P.O. Box 936
Lancaster, OH 43130
740-746-9221
800-344-7464
Complete line of Carillons and affordable up-dates to existing bell systems. Bell automation, chimes, and architectural products. Please see our ad on page 449.

**City Glass Specialty, Inc.**
2124 S. Calhoun St.
Fort Wayne, IN 46802
219-744-3301
Innovators in stained glass.
Please see our ad on page 449.

**Journeys Unlimited**
500 8th Ave
New York, NY 10018-6504
800-486-8359
www.journeys-unlimited.com
Specializing in high-quality church-group travel experiences to major historic Christian sites around the world.
Please see our ad on page 453.

**The Kerry Collection**
6070 Corte del Cedro
Oceanside, CA 92009
760-931-0191
Religious articles and candles
Please see our ad on page 452.

**LCMS Foundation**
1333 S. Kirkwood Rd.
St. Louis, MO 63122
314-996-1653
Please see our ad on page 7.

**Life Promotions**
213 E. College Ave.
Appleton, WI 54911
920-738-5588
Life Promotions and National Youth Communicator Bob Lenz
Please see our ad on page 453.

# BUSINESS RESOURCE DIRECTORY

**Lutheran Church Extension Fund**
P.O. Box 229009
St. Louis, MO 63122-9009
314-965-1222
Please see our ad on the back cover.

**Lutheran Fraternities of America, a division of GBU**
37060 Garfield, Ste. T5
Clinton Township, MI 48036
810-286-4753
Please see our ad on page 454.

**Lutheran Women's Missionary League**
3558 S. Jefferson
St. Louis, MO 63118
314-268-1533
800-252-LWML (5965)
Provide materials for Lutheran women in mission; multicultural resources; videocassettes and discussion guides; LWML handbook.
Please see our ad on page 451.

**Martin Luther Home Society, Inc**
650 J Street, Ste 305
Lincoln, NE 68508-2924
402-434-3250
800-727-8317
www.mlhs.com
A social ministry providing our Lord's touch of love to people with developmental disabilities and other special needs. Please see our ad on page 17.

**Nawas International Travel**
777 Post Rd.
Darien, CT 06820
800-221-4984
203-656-3033
fax 203-655-1577
International travel specializing in Holy Land tours.
Please see ad on page 4.

**Stevens Van Lines**
527 Morley Dr.
Saginaw, MI 48601
517-755-3000
Moving services
Please see our ad on page 451.

**The Studios of Potente, Inc.**
914 Sixtieth St.
Kenosha, WI 53140
800-776-3585
Since 1923 Potente designers have worked with clergy and church councils on space planning, remodeling, restoring, and renovating religious buildings across the country.
Please see our ad on page 31 for more details.

**TTI-Travel, Inc.**
Marcus, Inc.
401 S. Milwaukee Ave.
Wheeling, IL 60090
847-459-6600
info@marcusinc.com
www.marcusinc.com
Specializing in trips to the Holy Land.
Please see ad on page 2.

**Valparaiso University**
Office of Church Relations
Kretzmann Hall
Valparaiso, IN 46383
1-800-GO-VALPO
Office of Admissions: www.valpo.edu.
e-mail: undergrad_admissions@valpo.edu
A Lutheran university ranked one of the top comprehensive universities in the Midwest. A "best buy" in price to quality ratio.
Please see our ad on the inside back cover.

**Worker Benefit Plans**
1333 S. Kirkwood Rd.
St. Louis, MO 63122-7295
314-965-9917
Health, retirement, disability, and survivor benefits for church workers of the LCMS.
Please see our ad on page 3.

# CPH supplies all your church needs

CPH banners are rugged and durable for use indoors and outdoors at churches and schools. Constructed from strong 12 mm polyethylene, these are tough enough for outdoors and look fantastic indoors, too. They come with rod pockets or grommets that make them easy to hang anywhere. White background. Weather resistent. 3' x 5'. $90 each. Must specify rod pockets or grommets.

**Predesigned banners**

90-2960

90-2961

90-2962

**90-2963** (comes with your church name and designated anniversary)

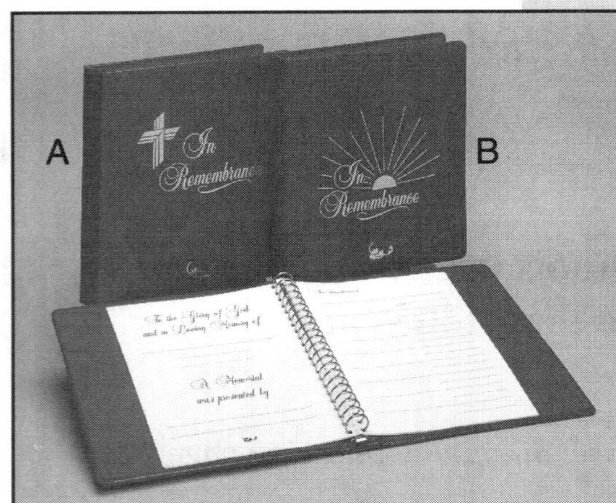


## In Remembrance

Excellent quality leather books for recording gifts, bequests, and memorials in your choice of two styles. Pages are masterfully lettered in red. Includes one each of seven sample pages.

**A. LCMS Cross (9-1/2" x 11-3/4")**
**81-1430 $60**

**B. Sun Ray (9-1/2" x 11-3/4")**
**81-1435 $60**

## Multi-Ring Guest Books

Excellent quality, bonded leather guest books feature padded covers and rounded corners. Includes a title page and 25 sheets with space for 500 names, addresses, home congregation. 9-1/2" x 11-3/4".

**C. LCMS Cross Design**
**81-1499 $60**

**D. Star Cross Design**
**81-1497 $60**

C

D

**Interior sheets for Multi-Ring Guest Book available in packages of 25.**
**81-1498 $10**

**Concordia Publishing House**
3558 South Jefferson Avenue
Saint Louis, MO 63118-3968

Call our toll-free line to order:
**1-800-325-3040**
www.cphmall.com

# Great ways to use

Enhance the worship life of your church or school and encourage growth through new expressions of timeless truths. Hymnal Supplement 98's balance of historic and new materials can help prepare your congregation for future resources.

**☑ Bridge to New Expressions of Faith**
- Chorales
- Songs of African, Hispanic, and Caribbean origins
- Psalm settings with refrains
- Taizé settings
- The Divine Service and Evening Prayer with hymn-based settings
- Guitar chords for many songs and hymns

**☑ Choral/Vocal Resource**
- Choir anthems
- Hymn alternations
- Communion meditations
- Psalm settings
- Descants
  (use the Vocal descant/melody edition)
- Solos

**☑ Instrumental Resource**
- Band/ Orchestra
  (use the Instrumental descant edition)
- Solos
- Small ensembles
- Handbell and chime choirs
  (use the Handbell descant edition)
- Accompany the congregation or choir

**☑ Cross-Curricular Learning Resource**
- Music (theory, part singing, musical styles)
- Religion (Scripture, theology, catechesis)
- Literature (poetry, form, structure, meter)
- Social Studies (world cultures, world music, history)

**☑ Devotional/Study Resource**
- School chapel
- Classroom devotions
- Sunday school
  (opening devotions, church-year studies)
- Bible classes
  (*The Word Behind the Text* study series)
- Committee/Auxiliary meetings

## *Reproducible* Descant Editions

## Handbell Descants

John A. Behnke, composer

46 harmonic settings plus descants. Most for two or three octaves. Soft cover, spiral-bound.

0-78777-01064-5 97-6720 $40.00

## Instrumental Descants

Donald Busarow, composer

Two independent descants for instruments in B-flat/C for each hymn in *Hymnal Supplement 98*. Plus, the melody is scored for instruments in C (treble, alto, and bass clef), F, and B-flat. Soft cover, spiral-bound.

0-78777-01063-8 97-6719 $50.00

## Vocal Descants

Carl Schalk, editor

82 descants/melodies. Includes final stanza of text. Soft cover, spiral-bound.

0-78777-01062-1 97-6718 $40.00

CPH
3558 South Jefferson Avenue
Saint Louis, MO 63118-3968

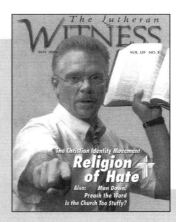

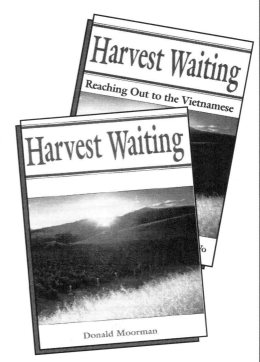

# Reach beyond Sunday Morning

## and touch the rest of their lives.

You know he can be a challenge (his reputation preceeds him). It's all the more reason you want him to feel welcome in your class and to know that Jesus loves him. And that's why you teach Sunday school.

*Our Life in Christ*® is *your* Sunday school curriculum. It's faithful to Scripture, our Lutheran heritage, and the needs of children. Christ-centered lessons and creative materials make the connection between God's Word and everyday life.

**Isn't it great to know that Sunday school really does make a difference?**

For a free catalog, call **1-800-325-3040** or visit our website for more information, **www.cph.org**. Also available through your local participating Christian bookstore.

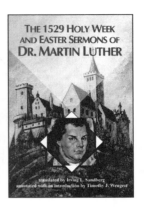

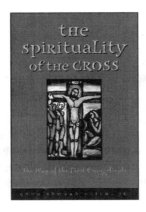

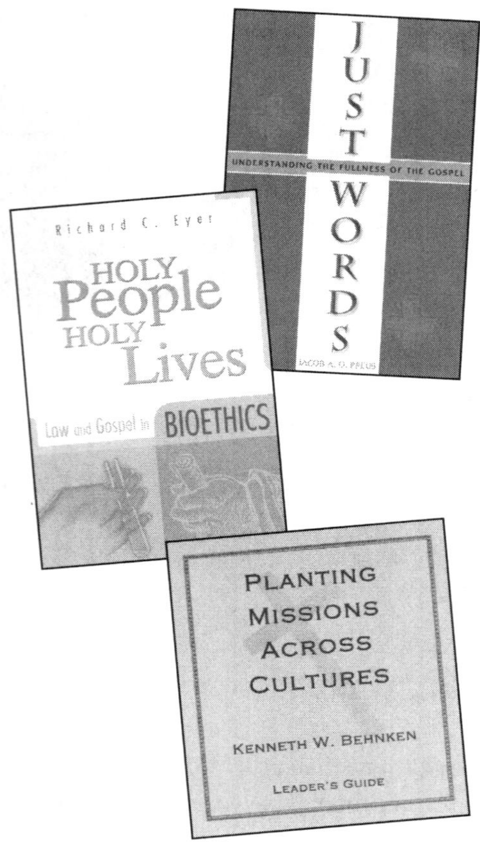


## NEW! Just Words

***Understanding the Fullness of the Gospel***

*By J. A. O. Preus*

*Just Words* explores the language used by the Bible's writers to describe and convey what it is that God has done for us in Christ. It helps the reader see the wonderful variety, rich texture, and clear doctrine with which God communicates His Good News. Through six metaphors, Preus interprets and applies the Gospel to virtually all of life's contexts: creation, commerce, legal, personal, sacrifice, and deliverance. 235 pp. Paperback. 0-570-05378-1.
**12-3429 $12.99**

## NEW! Holy People Holy Lives

***Law and Gospel in Bioethics***

*By Richard Eyer*

Enables church professionals and lay people to understand the issues involved in bioethical decisions, especially relating to medical technology. A guide for making God-pleasing decisions. 208 pp. 6 x 9. Paperback. 0-570-05255-6 **12-4065 $16.99**

## Planting Missions Across Cultures

*By Kenneth W. Behnken*

A combination leader's and study guide, here is a practical discussion of how God uses us to share His means of grace as we reach out to those around us. Fully reproducible binder includes materials for Bible studies, worship services, and more. 220 pp. Three-ring binder. 0-570-05251-3 **12-4061 $39.95**

CPH books can help you

# live by God's Word

Concordia Publishing House
3558 South Jefferson Avenue
Saint Louis, MO 63118-3968

**To order** call CPH at **1-800-325-3040**

## NEW! Servant of the Word

*By August Suelflow*

This is a complete biography of C.F.W. Walther, the first president of The Lutheran Church—Missouri Synod. Suelflow, an LCMS pastor, wrote a detailed account of the life of the man who first led the LCMS. Church workers, students, and interested laity will enjoy the descriptions of Walther from his early years to what brought him to the forefront of the Lutheran faith. 0-570-04271-2
**53-1030 $22.99**

## NEW! Sermon on the Mount

***The Church's First Gospel Statement***

*By David Scaer*

This book offers a fresh, exciting interpretation of this well-known and beloved portion of Scripture. By reading the Sermon through the lens of Christology and ecclesiology, Dr. Scaer demonstrates how St. Matthew's catechetical teaching prepares disciples—of every time and place—to experience the cross and resurrection as eschatological events and the sacraments as foundational for the Church's life. In this carefully written book, Scaer studies each unit of the sermon, presenting its rich Law and Gospel truths in Jesus' words. 320 pp. 0-570-05254-8 **12-4064 $18.99**

## NEW! Cherish the Word

***Reflections on Luther's Spirituality***

*By Thomas C. Peters*

Presents Luther's Christ-centered, Gospel-focused faith and life in a fresh, readable manner. Connects Luther's texts with questions people ask today about doubt, hope, guilt, and other important topics. 128 pp. Paperback. 0-570-05252-1 **12-4062 $13.99**

into LCMS, Bible stories

**To order** call CPH at **1-800-325-3040**

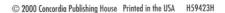

# RAISE THE BANNERS HIGH

## Celebrations of Faith

*By Carla Krazl*

The 60 colorful, creative banner designs form a striking visual message. Includes reproducible patterns for family life, praise, weddings, missions, school, prayer, and much more. Also includes detailed instructions and options for text and colors. 96 pp. Paperback. 0-570-05393-5
**12-4020 $10.99**

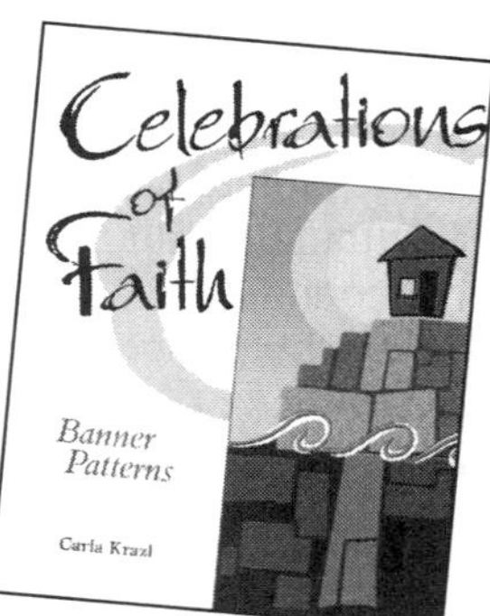


## Banner Patterns for Worship

*By Carol Jean Harms*

Inside this packet, you'll find full-size patterns and step-by-step instructions to make six elegant banners. In 9" x 12" envelope. 0-570-04491-X
**12-3114 $13.95**

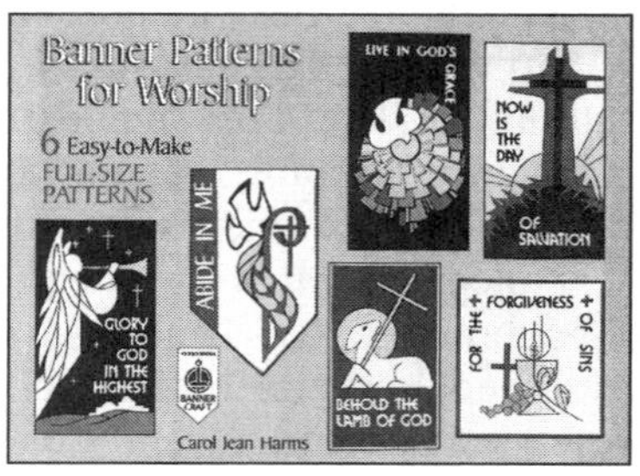


## Banners on Favorite Bible Verses

*By Sally Beck*

This collection of 58 original designs combines calligraphy and images that allow banner makers to artistically illustrate favorite Bible verses. Includes directions and suggestions for fabrics, colors, and construction techniques. These designs also work well for bulletin boards, worship folders, greeting cards, needlework, wall hangings, and more. 80 pp. Paperback. 0-570-04988-1
**12-3337 $9.99**

## Banners for Worship

*By Carol Jean Harms*

Explains all the basic information and techniques necessary for preparing banners from start to finish. 122 pp. 0-570-04492-8 **12-3113 $9.99**

**CPH can help with those, too!**

**To order** call CPH at **1-800-325-3040**

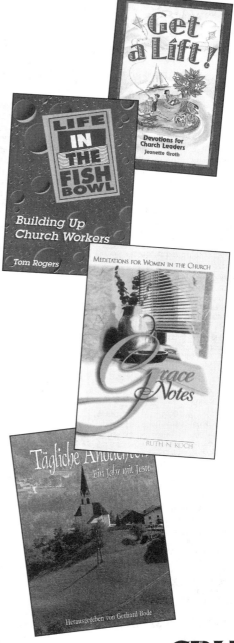

# Teaching Resources—*For Early Childhood*

***NEW!* Hallelujah! Hurray!**
By Judith Christian

Children ages 7 to 10 are ready to participate in worship, and can learn what all the parts mean. *Hallelujah! Hurray!* offers information and activities that explain the liturgy and give meaning and purpose to the worship service. Reproducible. For grades 2-4; ages 7-10.
64 pp. 8-3/8 x 10-7/8. Lay-flat paperback. (B)
0-570-05596-2
**12-4071 $8.99**

***NEW!* Celebration Puzzle Pieces**
By Judith Christian

The liturgical church year calendar is confusing enough for adults; how can you effectively teach children about it? With *Celebration Puzzle Pieces!* Through age-appropriate information and activities, this resource helps children understand the purpose and intent of the calendar and how it helps us celebrate in worship. Reproducible. For grades 2-4; ages 7-10.
64 pp. 8-3/8 x 10-7/8. Lay-flat paperback. (B)
0-570-07058-9
**12-4070 $8.99**

***NEW!* Toe Ticklers**
By Lori Miescke

30 fun foot-shaped Bible crafts teach children how to walk with Jesus. These simple crafts are designed to be completed in one sitting with minimal help. Each includes a Bible reference, lists of materials, instructions and ideas for sharing the project. For grades K-2; ages 4-7. 64 pp. 8-3/8 x 10-3/8. Paperback. (B)
0-570-05381-1
**12-4009 $8.99**

**Ready...Set...Tell!**
By Marti Beuschlein and Karen Wright

Formerly titled *I Love to Tell Bible Stories.* Includes pages of tips, props and visual ideas, plus active and interactive skills to capture children's attention and draw them into the learning process. For grades K-2; ages 4-7.
64 pp. 8-3/8 x 10-3/8. Paperback. (B)
0-570-05384-6
**12-4012 $8.99**

**CALL 1-800-325-3040**
**TO ORDER**

***NEW!* Bringing God's Seasons Inside**
***NEW!* More of God's Seasons Inside**
By Lisa Hahn and Wendy Nimtz

Help children link Christian concepts with the changing seasons for these versatile bulletin board designs. Book I includes designs for fall and winter; Book II has designs for spring and summer. For grades K-3; ages 4-9. 64 pp. each.
10-7/8 x 8-3/8. Paperback. (B) **$8.99 each**

**Bringing God's Seasons Inside**
0-570-05385-4 **12-4013**

**More of God's Seasons Inside**
0-570-05223-8 **12-4030**

***NEW!* Sing-Along Praise**
By Anita Reith Stohs

Use the familiar tunes in this book to help children with no knowledge of traditional songs or hymns join in immediately and sing Gospel-based songs. Choose from 150 songs. For grades PreK-2; ages 3-8. 64 pp.
8-3/8 x 10-3/8. Paperback. (B)
0-570-05245-9
**12-4054 $9.50**

**Bible Story Skitlets**
***NEW!* Bible Story Skitlets Too**
By Sandra Collier and Jean Bruns

Every student will learn and remember the Bible stories told through these mini-skits, or "skitlets." Completely rehearsal-free, the 10 skits in each book are led by a narrator who guides the entire class in simple actions and dialogue. For PreK-3; ages 3-9. 64 pp.
8-3/8 x 10-7/8. Paperback. (B) **$8.99 each**

**Bible Story Skitlets**
0-570-05317-X **12-3367**

**Bible Story Skitlets Too**
0-570-05374-9 **12-3425**

**Save It!**
By Anita Reith Stohs

These projects create environmental awareness while reinforcing Bible lessons. All 52 crafts are made with recyclable items. For grades PreK-4; ages 4-9. 64 pp. 8-3/8 x 10-3/8. Paperback. (B)
0-570-04602-5
**12-3188 $8.99**

**Little Hands Can Too**
These 37 projects teach Old and New Testament stories using simple directions and adjustable tasks for age and skill level. For grades PreK-2; ages 2-7.
48 pp. 8-3/8 x 10-3/8. Paperback. (B)
0-570-04647-5
**12-3229 $7.99**

CPH
Concordia Publishing House

# Teaching Resources—*Especially for Teachers*

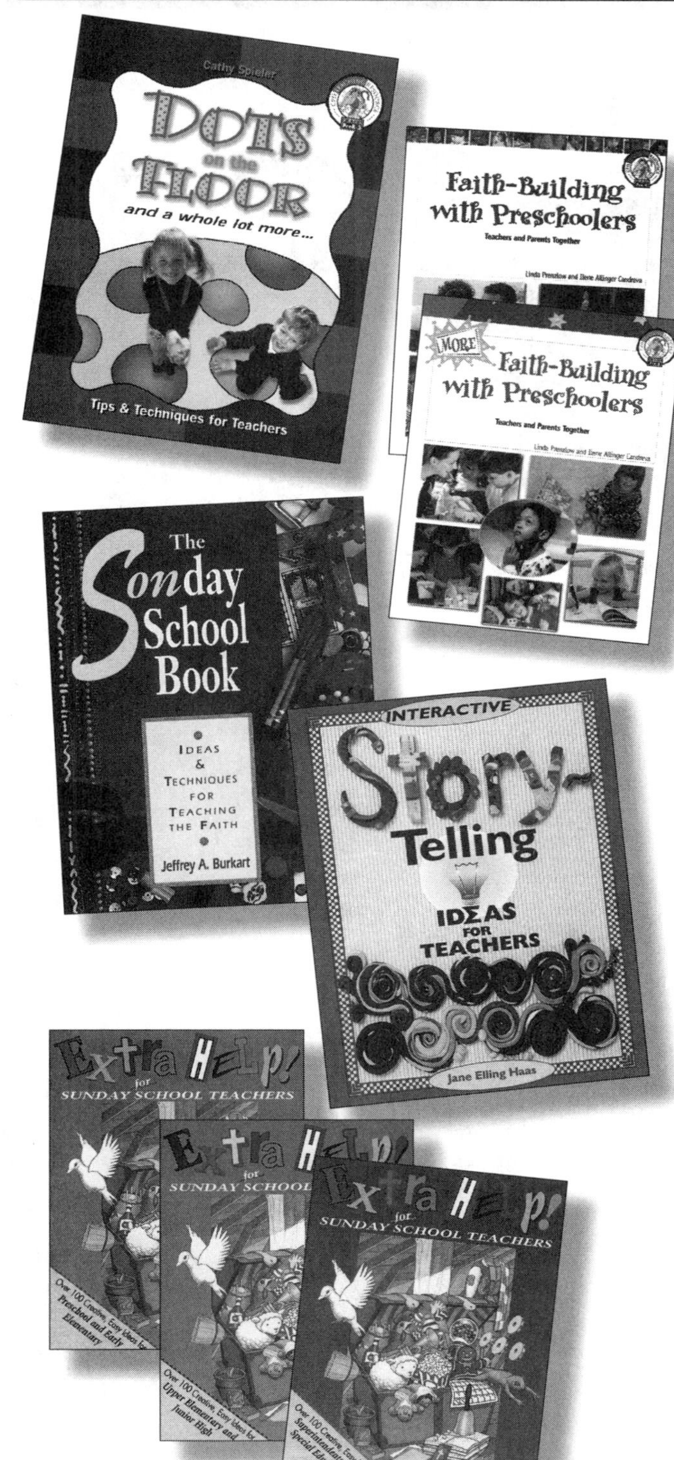


***NEW!* Dots on the Floor and a Whole Lot More...**
By Cathy Spieler

Create an effective and fun learning environment with practical tips and classroom-tested techniques. Learn how to teach concepts, maintain order and more with children in preschool through second grade. 64 pp. 8-3/8 x 10-3/8. Paperback. (B)
0-570-05365-X
**12-3416 $8.99**

**Faith-Building with Preschoolers**
***NEW!* More Faith-Building with Preschoolers**
By Linda Prenzlow and Ilene Allinger Candreva

The six thematic units in these books help teachers show young children how to share their faith through daily events like meals and playtime. Each unit focuses on one Bible story and suggests six types of activities. For PreK; ages 1-4. 112 pp. 8-3/8 x 10-7/8. Paperback. (B) **$12.99 each**

| | | |
|---|---|---|
| **Faith-Building...** | 0-570-05328-5 | **12-3376** |
| **More Faith-Building...** | 0-570-05366-8 | **12-3417** |

**The Sonday School Book**
By Jeffrey Burkart

These tried-and-true ideas used by professional teachers will work in your Sunday school and VBS classroom, too. You'll find techniques to encourage memorization, maintain discipline and make students eager to learn God's Word. Proven ideas are included for better lesson preparation, cultivating creativity, storytelling and use of multimedia.
176 pp. 8-3/8 x 10-7/8. Paperback. (B)
0-570-04694-7
**12-3253 $12.99**

**Interactive Storytelling Ideas for Teachers**
By Jane Haas

Draw kids into lessons with this collection of 52 storytelling ideas. Each one encourages children to learn about God's Word by role-playing, singing, discussion and more. Step-by-step instructions, tips and patterns. For grades PreK-3; ages 4-9. 64 pp. 8-3/8 x 10-3/8. Paperback. (B)
0-570-04821-4
**12-3263 $8.99**

**Extra Help! For Sunday School Teachers**
Edited by Martha Jander

Sunday school teachers of all denominations can appreciate these successful ideas for activities, lesson presentations, class worship time, crafts and more. Each book is a collection of the best age-appropriate ideas from *Teachers Interaction.* The superintendent's/special education volume features great ideas for special Sunday school leadership and meeting the challenges of special education. 48-64 pp. 8-1/2 x 11. Paperback. (B)

**Preschool/Early Elementary**
0-570-04649-1 **12-3231 $8.99**
**Elementary/Junior High**
0-570-04650-5 **12-3232 $8.99**
**Superintendent's/Special Education**
0-570-04651-3 **12-3233 $7.99**

**CALL 1-800-325-3040**
**TO ORDER**

# Teaching Resources—*For Early Childhood*

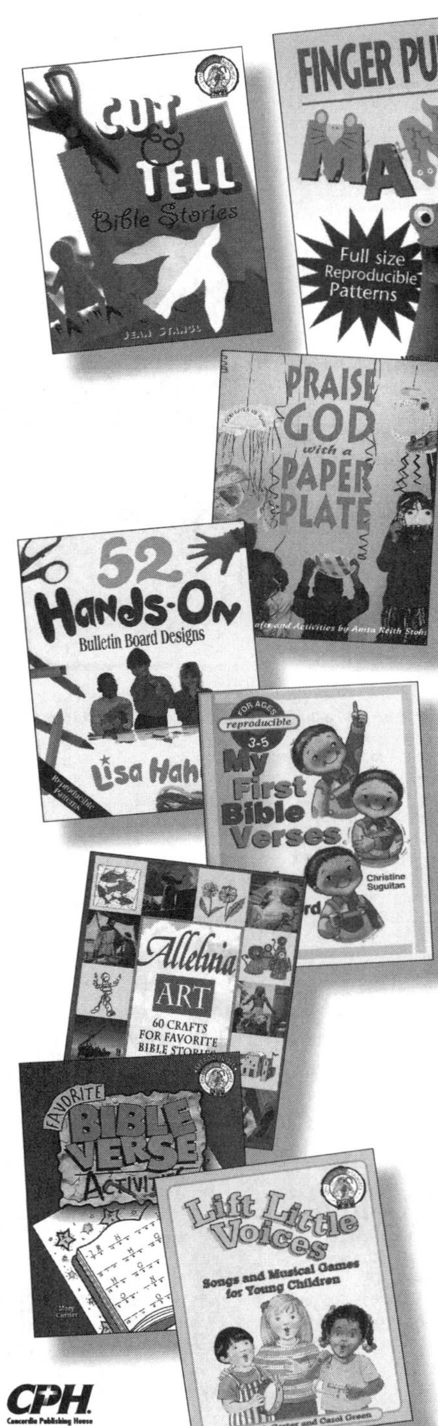


***NEW!* Finger Puppet Mania!**
By Karen Hartigan Whiting

This great resource includes full-size reproducible patterns to create 19 unique finger puppets, plus sample scripts and pantomimes, directions for building simple stages and even exercises for learning to manipulate the puppets. For grades PreK-2; ages 3-8. 64 pp. 8-3/8 x 10-3/8. Paperback. (B)
0-570-05373-0
**12-3424 $8.99**

***NEW!* One-Stop Thematic Units**
By Jane Jarrell and Deborah Saathoff

These imaginative classroom idea books coordinate with curriculum to actively reinforce lessons. Filled with Scripture, Bible stories, songs, play ideas, crafts and even math games, children will love to learn when you use these resources! For grades PreK-1; ages 3-6. 64 pp. each. 8-3/8 x 10-3/8. Paperback. (B)
**$9.50 each**

| | | |
|---|---|---|
| **On the Move!** | 0-570-05239-4 | **12-4046** |
| **Swing into Spring!** | 0-570-05241-6 | **12-4048** |
| **Easter!** | 0-570-05242-4 | **12-4049** |
| **Christmas!** | 0-570-05257-2 | **12-4067** |
| **My Five Senses** | 0-570-05258-0 | **12-4068** |

**Cut & Tell Bible Stories**
By Jean Stangl

While telling the Bible story, make quick cuts in a piece of paper. As the story unfolds, so does an impressive visual aid! Patterns and directions are provided for 10 Old and 10 New Testament stories. For PreK-3; ages 3-9. 64 pp. 8-3/8 x 10-7/8. Paperback. (B)
0-570-05310-2
**12-3361 $8.99**

**Praise God with a Paper Plate**
By Anita Reith Stohs

Over 50 great craft ideas for Sunday school, day school, vacation Bible school and home projects—all using a paper plate as foundation material. For grades PreK-2; ages 2-7. 64 pp. 8-3/8 x 10-3/8. Paperback. (B)
0-570-04567-3
**12-3167 $8.99**

**52 Hands-on Bulletin Board Designs**
By Lisa Hahn

Choose from general and seasonal interactive bulletin board designs with Christian themes. Includes objectives, directions, sketches and reproducible patterns. For grades PreK-2; ages 4-7. 64 pp. 8-3/8 x 10-3/8. Paperback. (B)
0-570-04627-0
**12-3208 $8.99**

**My First Bible Verses**
By Christine Suguitan

Actively involves young children in learning over 25 simple Bible verses using finger play actions and illustrations. No additional materials required! Reproducible for PreK-K; ages 3-5. 48 pp. 8-3/8 x 10-3/8. Paperback. (B)
0-570-04841-9
**12-3278 $7.99**

**Alleluia Art**
By Anita Reith Stohs

These craft and art projects reinforce 28 Old Testament and 32 New Testament stories. Each project includes Bible reference, materials list, directions and suggested variations. For grades 1-4; ages 6-10. 64 pp. 8-3/8 x 10-3/8. Paperback. (B)
0-570-04632-7
**12-3213 $8.99**

**Favorite Bible Verse Activities**
By Mary Currier

46 reproducible word puzzles, dot-to-dots, mazes and other activities that make memory work fun! For grades K-3; ages 5-8. 48 pp. 8-3/8 x 10-3/8. Paperback. (B)
0-570-04898-2
**12-3311 $7.99**

**Lift Little Voices**
By Carol Greene and Deborah Carter

A book collection of 60 original songs along with games and activities for a full year's worth of praise. Developed to help anyone who teaches music plan meaningful education experiences for young children. For grades PreK-2; ages 3-7. 96 pp. 8-3/8 x 10-3/8. Paperback. (B) 0-570-04981-4
**12-3331 $12.99**
*Also available:*
**Audiocassette**
(N) 0-570-00783-6 **22-2896 $10.99**
**Compact disc**
(N) 0-570-00784-4 **22-2897 $15.99**

CPH
Concordia Publishing House

# Drama Resources

People involved in church drama have the rare privilege of bridging the Word and life for God's people. That is no small task. But where the Word is, there the Spirit is as well. And where the Spirit is, there is always drama. The dramas in this section depict a truth that Jesus exhibited again and again—the Word of God is illustrated all around us. Use these dramas in your midweek classes, in school chapels, in Bible studies, with youth groups, or with congregations. Look for more dramas to come from Concordia in 2000 and 2001!

**15 Life-Related Dramas**
By Theodore W. Schroeder
Add a change of pace to the worship service and even small group Bible studies with this collection of short dramas. Each reproducible drama addresses spiritual issues families and individuals face in everyday life. Memorization is not required; the scripts are perfect for "reader's theater" drama. Includes short homily, questions and discussion activities, introductory guidelines and drama presentation options. 126 pp. 8-3/8 x 10-7/8. Paperback. (B) 0-570-04858-3
**12-3293 $14.99**

**NEW! Command Performances**
By Larry Vogel
Students learn and remember the Ten Commandments with these simple dramas. Each of the 11 scripts addresses one of the Commandments and uses a Bible story to illustrate it. Use these simple plays for class or chapel. For grades K-6. Ages 6-12. Reproducible. 80 pp. 8-3/8 x 10-7/8. Paperback. (B) 0-570-5370-6
**12-3421 $12.99**

**Cross Views**
**Story Dramas that Teach the Faith**
By Dean W. Nadasdy
A collection of 26 short dramas in parable form to use as chancel dramas, high school chapel services, youth meetings and Bible studies. Each drama ends with questions to use as discussion starters or sermon helps. Dramas can be memorized or performed as "readers' theater." 128 pp. 8-3/8 x 10 7/8. Paperback. (B) 0-570-04864-8
**12-3355 $15.99**

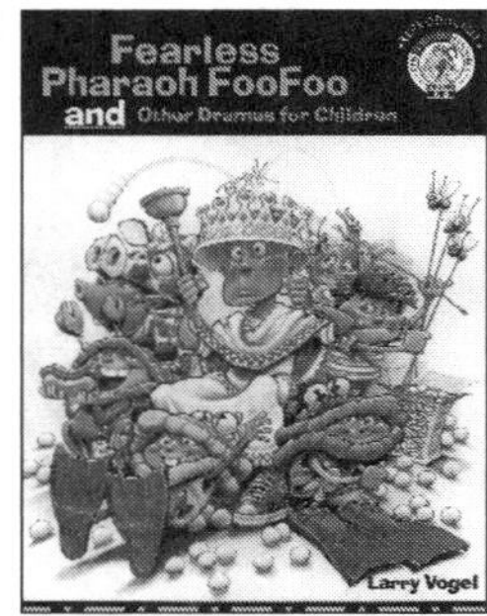


**Fearless Pharoah FooFoo and Other Dramas for Children**
By Larry Vogel
A school year's worth (38 dramas) of simple Bible-based plays for use by children in chapel, Sunday school, children's worship or lesson openings. Provides unique opportunities for learning and fun. For grades K-6. Ages 6-12. 160 pp. 8-3/8 x 10-7/8. Paperback. (B) 0-570-05332-3
**12-3380 $14.99**

**The Pilgrim Path**
**Five Discipleship Dramas**
By Theodore Schroeder
This collection of five reproducible plays helps youth and adults explore the radical call of discipleship and what it means for the Christian who is walking that narrow road. *The Pilgrim Path* also helps church workers introduce drama as a learning tool. Church members and audiences enjoy and learn during these unique presentations based on Scripture. Each play has accompanying homilies and questions/activities to encourage discussion. 64 pp. 8-3/4 x 10-7/8. Paperback. (B) 0-570-04978-4
**12-3328 $10.99**

**Sure Can Use a Little Good News**
**12 Gospel Plays in Rhyme**
By Jeffrey Burkhart
A collection of short, lively and humorous plays based on the events and parables of Jesus' ministry for ages 12 through adult. Use the plays for chancel dramas, Gospel readings in church, Sunday school and VBS, school openings, and discussion starters for youth and adult Bible study programs. Scripts are reproducible. 108 pp. 8-3/8 x 10-7/8. Paperback. (B) 0-570-04866-4
**12-3357 $13.99**
**Accompanying Video**
*Gospel Rhyme in Gospel Time Players*
Features live performances of five plays from the above book. 65 min. VHS (K)
**17-7064 $12.95**

**NEW! InterMission Scripts** are a great way to illustrate Gospel messages with impact. Each book includes four to seven dramas ranging from 3-4 minutes to 30-45 minutes. Use them for worship services, Sunday school programs, Bible studies and more. Each Christ-centered script includes a purpose, theme and Scripture reference. Quick reference information for time, cast, costumes, props, sound, lighting and set are on the first page of each script. A note to the leader and study questions are included. Reproducible. Royalty-free.

**Strong and Sturdy: Dramas for Children**
0-570-05389-7 **12-4016 $12.99**
**Wearing the Mask: Dramas for Youth**
0-570-05376-5 **12-3427 $14.99**
**Anticipation: Dramas for Advent**
0-570-05386-2 **12-4014 $12.99**
**Celebration: Dramas for Christmas**
0-570-05387-0 **12-4015 $12.99**
**Preparation: Dramas for Lent**
0-570-05391-9 **12-4018 $12.99**
**Jubilation: Dramas for Easter**
0-570-05390-0 **12-4017 $12.99**

**CALL 1-800-325-3040 TO ORDER**

# The New Learning About Sex

## The New Learning About Sex

Praised by teachers, parents, pastors and doctors, this series has stood as a leader in Bible-based sex education for more than 30 years. Each book in the series helps children see sex as a good gift from God to be used responsibly.

In a positive, Christ-centered manner, *The New Learning About Sex* series helps you cultivate open and honest communication about sex, present accurate, age-appropriate information and explain physiological and socio-psychological aspects of sex. The series includes a parent's handbook to help you deal sensitively with your children through all their stages of development.

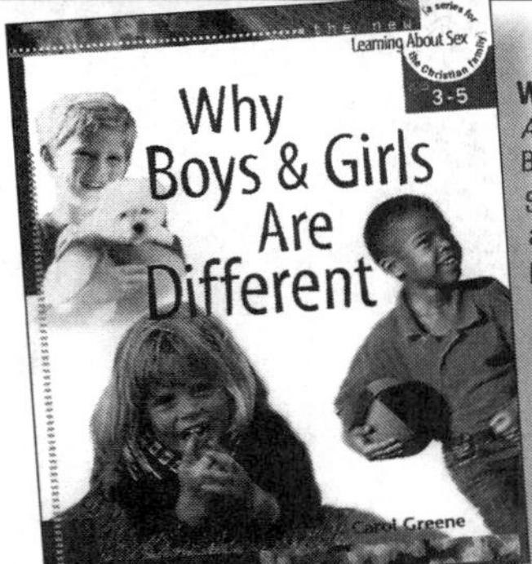


**Why Boys and Girls Are Different**
*Ages 3-5*
By Carol Greene
Simple and accurate terminology and age-appropriate pictures help preschoolers understand the similarities and differences between boys and girls. 32 pp. 8-1/2 x 10-1/4. Hardback. (B)
0-570-03562-7
**14-2113 $9.99**

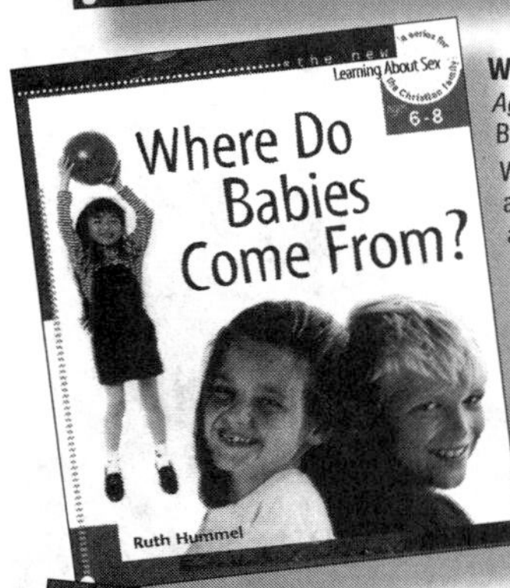


**Where Do Babies Come From?**
*Ages 6-8*
By Ruth Hummel
When this little question comes up, the answer must be direct, yet appropriate. Clear pictures and terminology explain birth and the physiological difference between boys and girls. 32 pp. 8-1/2 x 10-1/4. Hardback. (B)
0-570-03563-5
**14-2114 $9.99**

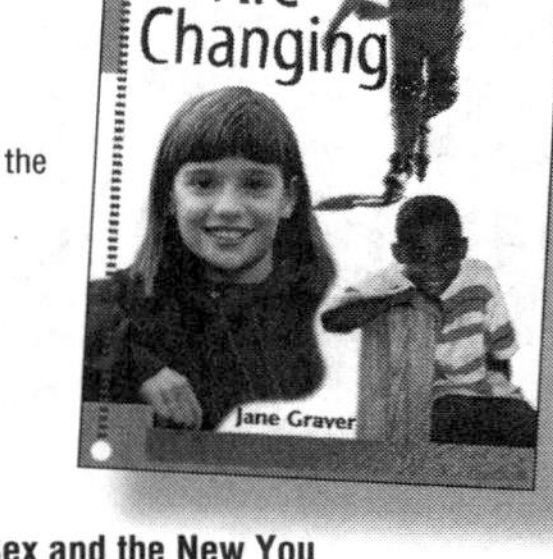


**How You Are Changing**
*Ages 8-11*
By Jane Graver
This book explains that the physical changes preteens experience are normal. Sexual intercourse is introduced as a way for husbands and wives to express love. 64 pp. 6 x 9. Paperback. (B)
0-570-03564-3
**14-2115 $9.99**

**Sex and the New You**
*Ages 11-14*
By Rich Bimler
Encourages young people to feel good about becoming men and women. Presents a matter-of-fact explanation of sexual maturation, intercourse, conception and birth. A discussion of premarital sex and sexually transmitted diseases is introduced. 64 pp. 6 x 9. Paperback. (B) 0-570-03565-1
**14-2116 $9.99**

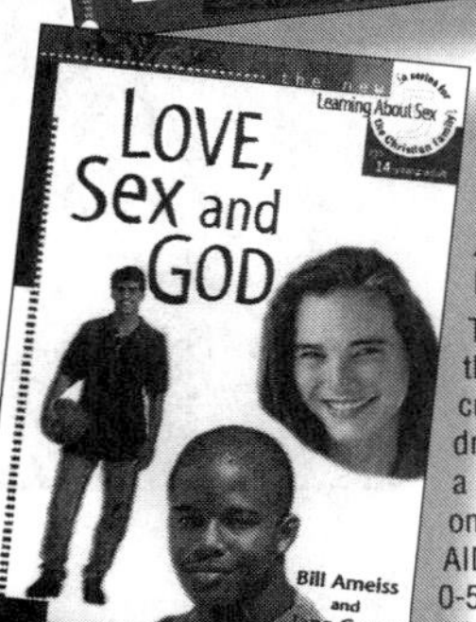


**Love, Sex and God**
*Ages 14 and up*
By Bill Ameiss and Jane Graver
Teens need encouragement to respect their bodies and the place that God has created for sex in their lives. This book addresses family roles and what to look for in a marriage partner. Presents straight facts on sexually transmitted diseases including AIDS. 128 pp. 6 x 9. Paperback. (B)
0-570-03566-X
**14-2117 $9.99**

**How to Talk Confidently with Your Child about Sex**
**Parent's Guide**
By Lenore Buth
This guide shows parents ways to naturally share parental views on sexuality with children of all ages and development. 160 pp. 6 x 9. Paperback. (B)
0-570-03567-8
**14-2118 $9.99**

**Human Sexuality**
**A Christian Perspective**
By Roger Sonnenberg
This book helps adults better understand their own sexuality and its place in their lives. Addresses important aspects of sexuality including the spiritual, emotional and physical. 224 pp. 6 x 9. Hardback.
(B) 0-570-03568-6
**14-2119 $16.99**

**CPH**
Concordia Publishing House

# Introducing
## *Science DiscoveryWorks—*
## Concordia Edition

Through the study of science, students learn more about God—the One who made the world, redeemed it, and supports and preserves all things. The distinctively Christian perspective in this curriculum is designed to help students unearth connections between science concepts and God's Word.

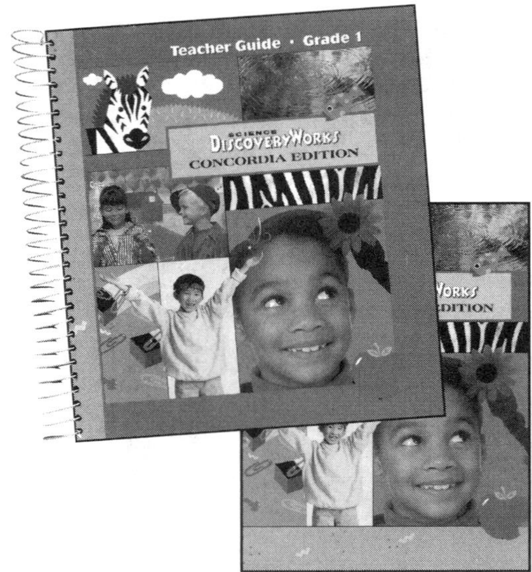


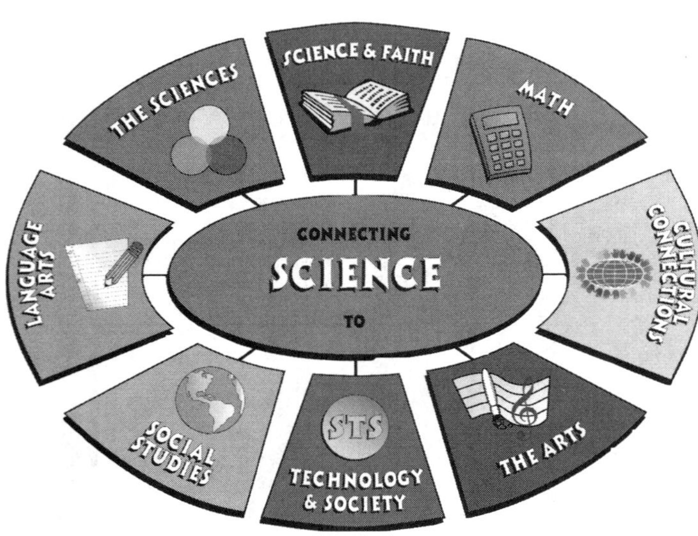

**By the power of the Holy Spirit, science instruction helps students develop:**

**Knowledge and Understanding To**

- Express the conviction that God is creator and ruler of the universe
- Use scientific methodology to investigate the phenomena of God's world
- Apply scientific laws as they describe God's creation

**Thoughtful Attitudes To**

- Appreciate God's power and majesty in establishing and governing the universe
- Recognize the constancy and order of the natural world God created
- Respond to God's grace by helping make the world a beautiful place for generations to come

**Practical and Analytical Skills To**

- Use scientific insights in a life of devotion to God
- Think critically and wisely, looking to God for guidance

### *Science Discovery Works—* Concordia Edition

| | | |
|---|---|---|
| **Grade 1** | | |
| Student Edition | 52-1001DCB | $21.94 |
| Teacher Guide | 52-2001DCB | $105.93 |
| **Grade 2** | | |
| Student Edition | 52-1002DCB | $23.00 |
| Teacher Guide | 52-2002DCB | $105.93 |
| **Grade 3** | | |
| Student Edition | 52-1003DCB | $33.42 |
| Teacher Guide | 52-2003DCB | $90.93 |
| **Grade 4** | | |
| Student Edition | 52-1004DCB | $35.25 |
| Teacher Guide | 52-2004DCB | $90.93 |
| **Grade 5** | | |
| Student Edition | 52-1005DCB | $37.98 |
| Teacher Guide | 52-2005DCB | $90.93 |
| **Grade 6** | | |
| Student Edition | 52-1006DCB | $37.98 |
| Teacher Guide | 52-2006DCB | $90.93 |

For a complete listing of this dynamic new curriculum or to place an order, call **1-800-325-3040** or e-mail to www.cphorder@cph.org

**Coming Spring 2001**

# The Blessing Place

## A Christ-centered Curriculum for Child-care Providers from CPH

"Jesus said, 'Let the little children come to me'." With *The Blessing Place,* you can create an environment where babies and toddlers experience Jesus' love and your nuturing care.

*The Blessing Place* is a complete manual for child-care programs, church nurseries, and any setting where very young children are cared for. This resource gives practical helps for making Jesus real to very young children through the environment and parental involvement. Activities are well-paced and designed to help children grow spiritually, physically, intellectually, emotionally, and socially.

This handbook provides suggestions for setting up an infant and toddler facility and includes a 12-month curriculum with monthly themes. Guidelines for directors include suggestions for worker qualifications, child development and behavior guidelines, tips for activities, how to engage parents as partners, and more.

***The Blessing Place* is ideal for**

- **Day-care facilities**
- **Home-care providers**
- **Church nurseries**
- **Mothers-day-out programs**
- **Baby-sitters**
- **Other child-care programs**

**Parents are often anxious about leaving their infants and toddlers for the day, or even for an hour. With *The Blessing Place,* you can assure them that their little ones are receiving the best care possible—and Jesus' love, too. It's the next best thing to being at home!**

**Chapters:**

- **Qualifications/Characteristics of Workers**
- **The Importance of Environment**
- **The Organization of the Classroom**
- **Parents and Partners**
- **How To Do Curriculum**
- **Administration**
- **Child Development**
- **Behavior Guidance**
- **Curriculum**
- **List of Additional Resources**
- **Reproducible Pages** (stories, songs, finger plays with growth activities, parent pages)

**_The Blessing Place_ will include an 8-1/2" x 11" loose-leaf, three-hole-punched manual as well as a Child-care Kit full of support materials that will help you share the love of Jesus with the very young.**

**Coming Spring 2001**

# Connect Kids and Christ with Children's Ministry Resources from CPH

Kid-friendly and easy-to-implement, ***CrossTown*** and ***Jesus Company*** encourage children in first through sixth grades to connect with one another and Christ in a friendly, fun environment. These materials motivate kids to dig deeper in Scripture by providing activities, songs, crafts, an age-appropriate Bible study, and more. Flexibility is built right in to help you use ***CrossTown*** and ***Jesus Company*** to fit your church's needs.

**Children's ministry resources are great for:**

- **After-school programs**
- **Extracurricular alternatives**
- **Meeting nights**
- **Family nights**
- **Camp or summer programs**

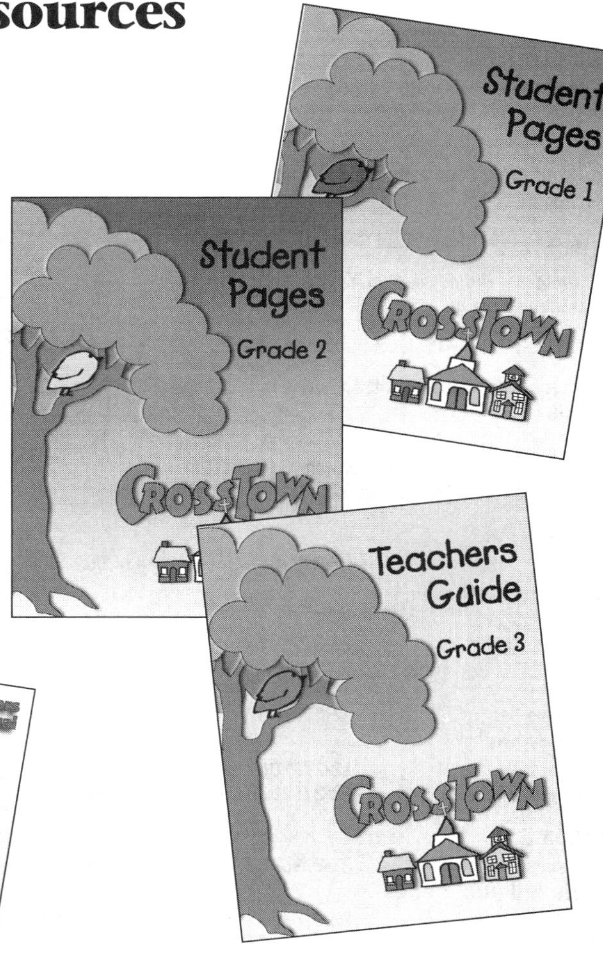


### Maximizing Midweek Possibilities

This convenient handbook is packed with basic tips for midweek ministry. Perfect for administrators who want to begin, expand, or reorganize a midweek program.

**22-2793DCB $15.00**

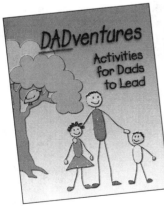

### DADventures

Don't leave Dad out of the picture! This fun resource is packed with great ideas for involving fathers or significant male figures in your children's ministry program. There are dozens of easy-to-do activities that can be used alone or with ***CrossTown***. Reproducible.

**22-2885DCB $8.99**

### Under Construction

Now on the drawing table—a new curriculum for children ages 3 to 5. Prekindergarten through kindergarten. Look for it in the spring of 2001.

## CrossTown Curriculum

### Grades 1–3

Encourage early elementary students to grow in their faith and in their Christian community. Each level has a wide variety of interactive experiences to help children learn that Jesus is part of all they do in life.

## CrossTown

| Item | Order No. | Price |
|---|---|---|
| **Grade 1** | | |
| Teachers Guide | **22-2879DCB** | **$15.99** |
| Student Materials | **22-2880DCB** | **$8.99** |
| **Grade 2** | | |
| Teachers Guide | **22-2881DCB** | **$15.99** |
| Student Materials | **22-2882DCB** | **$8.99** |
| **Grade 3** | | |
| Teachers Guide | **22-2883DCB** | **$15.99** |
| Student Materials | **22-2884DCB** | **$8.99** |
| **Accessories** | | |
| Logo Pencils | **22-2900DCB** | **$1.49/5** |
| Logo Poster | **22-2901DCB** | **$2.49** |
| Logo Buttons | **22-2902DCB** | **$2.49/5** |
| Logo Postcards | **22-2903DCB** | **$2.99/10** |
| Fisherman's Cap | **22-2904DCB** | **$4.99** |
| Logo Beachball | **22-2905DCB** | **$2.99** |

# Youth Confirmation Resources from Concordia Publishing House

## My Christian Faith

Help junior high students learn what God's love and forgiveness mean. *My Christian Faith* shows students how to apply basic doctrine to their everyday lives.

The *Teachers Book* includes lesson plans on the Six Chief Parts of the Catechism and provides ideas for cooperative learning, parental involvement, mentoring, games, activities, and devotions. Thirty reproducible blackline masters are included.

The *Student Response Book* is a keepsake-quality text with 4-color, magazine-style presentation of the Catechism and portions of God's Word. Students can personalize lessons with the included space for journal entries, article clippings, and pictures. 30 sessions.

**Teachers Guide** 176 pp.
**22-2484DCB** **$19.95**

**Student Response Book** 112 pp.
**22-2483DCB** **$14.95**

## My Journey in Faith

A companion to *My Christian Faith, My Journey in Faith* provides an overview of the entire Bible. This keepsake-quality workbook gives students engaging, active, and cooperative lessons that focus on applying the Gospel to their lives.

This course introduces students to Jesus Christ and helps them understand how the Bible is relevant to them today.

**Student Response Book** 112 pp.
**22-2481DCB** **$14.95**

**Teachers Guide** 160 pp.
**22-2482DCB** **$19.95**

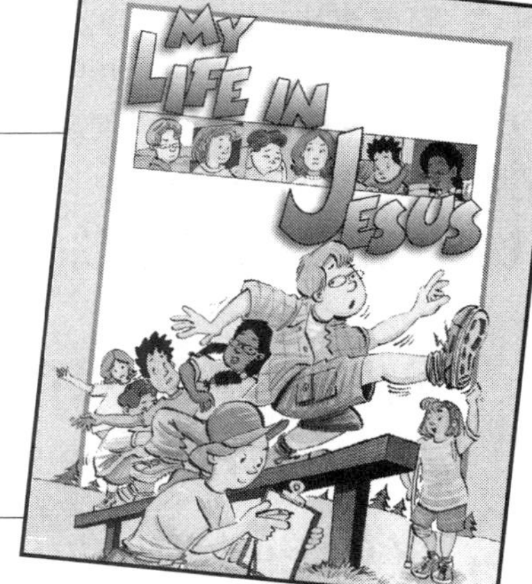


## My Life in Jesus

This hands-on Bible curriculum gives fifth- and sixth-grade students a clearer understanding of God's plan. Thirty sessions examine the Ten Commandments, the Apostles' Creed, the Lord's Prayer, and the Sacraments. The *Teachers Guide* takes an active approach in helping you present memorable lessons. Each session involves a skit that reinforces the Catechism lesson.

**Student Guide**
30 sheets. 3-hole punched for use in binders.
**22-2874DCB** **$7.99**

**Teachers Guide**
Spiral bound 3-hole punched. 80 pp.
**22-2873DCB** **$15.99**

Concordia Publishing House
3558 South Jefferson Ave.
Saint Louis, Missouri 63118

To receive a complete listing of our Catechism resources or to place an order, call **1-800-325-3040** or e-mail at cphorder@cph.org

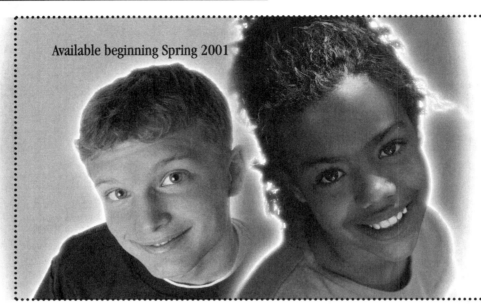

BX 8061 .M7 A1 2001
The Lutheran annual